2018 Higher Education Directory®

Published by
Higher Education Publications, Inc.

Edited by
Mary Pat Rodenhouse

Editor Emerita
Jeanne M. Burke

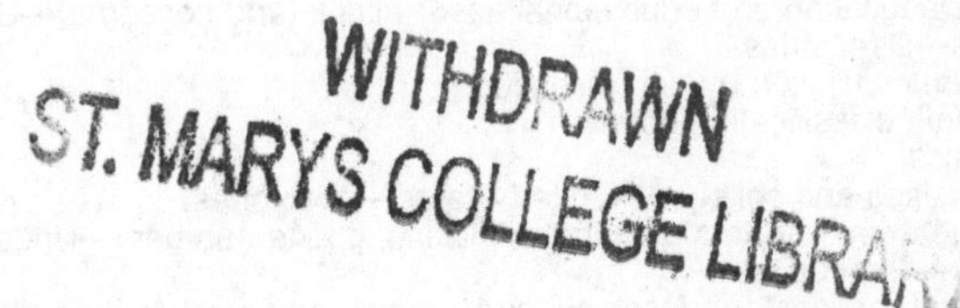

Reston, Virginia

2018

2018 Edition

Higher Education Publications, Inc.
1801 Robert Fulton Drive, Suite 350
Reston, VA 20191-5499
(888) 349-7715
(571) 313-0478
FAX (571) 313-0526
Email: info@hepinc.com
Internet address: www.hepinc.com

Carnegie classification codes with permission from
The Carnegie Foundation for the Advancement of Teaching.

Internet addresses (URL's) were originally drawn from lists maintained by Washington and Lee University and the University of North Carolina-Chapel Hill and through the annual survey sent out by Higher Education Publications, Inc.

Printed in the United States of America

ISBN-10: 0-914927-78-7; ISBN-13: 978-0-914927-78-5
ISSN 0736-0797
Library of Congress Catalogue Card Number: 83-641119
Library of Congress Cataloging-in Publication Data

HEP. . . Higher Education Directory®
Reston, VA; Higher Education Publications.
V.: 28cm
Annual
Began with issue for 1983.

A directory of accredited postsecondary, degree-granting institutions in the U.S., its possessions and territories accredited by regional, national, professional and specialized agencies recognized as accrediting bodies by the U.S. Secretary of Education and the Council for Higher Education Accreditation (CHEA) which honors recognition provided by the former Council on Postsecondary Accreditation (COPA)/Commission on Recognition of Postsecondary Accreditation (CORPA)
Description based on 2017.
Cover title: 2018 Higher Education Directory®
Spine title: 2018 Higher Education Directory® Thirty-sixth Edition

ISSN 0736-0797 = The Higher Education Directory®.

1. Education, Higher—United States—Directories.
2. Recognized accrediting agencies and associations—United States—Directories.
3. Acronyms, explanatory notes and symbols—United States—Directories.
4. Institution changes (additions, deletions, mergers and name changes)—United States—Directories.
5. Administrative officers, titles and title codes—United States—Directories.
6. United States Department of Education offices, statewide agencies for higher education and educational associations (and consortia)—United States—Directories.
7. Religious affiliation by denomination.
8. Carnegie classification codes.
9. Statistics.
10. Universities and colleges—United States—Directories.
11. College administrators alphabetical listing, phone numbers—United States—Directories.
12. Regional, national, professional and specialized accreditation alphabetical listing—United States—Directories.
13. Institutional FICE & Unit ID Number listing—United States—Directories.
14. Institutional alphabetical listing—United States—Directories.

I. Higher Education Publications, Inc.
II. Title: Higher Education Directory®.

L901.E34 378.73-dc19 83-641119 AACR 2 MARC-S

Table of Contents

Acknowledgments

Thirty-five years ago, Higher Education Publications, Inc. was formed to produce a directory to succeed the Department of Education's *Education Directory: Colleges and Universities*.

When we undertook the *Higher Education Directory* project, we worked toward three main goals: To publish accurate data, to make the directory more usable, and to have the directory ready for distribution much earlier in the academic year.

We continue to meet these objectives and more, while keeping the changing landscape of reference publishing in mind. In 2014, we modified our definition of branch campuses to conform to the definition used by the United States Department of Education (34 CFR §600.2). As a result, we added or reclassified over 1,400 institutional listings. Due to space limitations in the printed directory, we list limited information on these additional branch campuses, but more detailed information is available online with HED-Connect.

Our thanks to the thousands of people who have supplied us the necessary data contained in the directory. Over this past year we have had a response/update rate of 99.5% from main campuses—truly outstanding! We are most appreciative of the many subscribers who have supported us in our efforts to bring you the most accurate and current information available. And, a special thanks to all of you who suggest improvements to our directory.

We continue to work on a tight schedule starting in mid-June to distribution in November—especially when you consider the complexity and increase in the size of the database.

The accuracy and completeness of the contents of the 2018 edition was assured by a group of editors, updating and proofing specialists including Mary Pat Rodenhouse, Jodi Mondragon, Emmy Brown, Jackie Hafner, Doris Jean, Ebony Neal, Bryan Callow and Fred Hafner. Barbara Herrman handled our typesetting. Mark Schreiber managed the HED-Connect update system and the database.

You may be familiar with our new Website, but if you have not yet visited it, I encourage you to go to www.hepinc.com. The site features the latest news on higher education, accreditations and administrative changes along with many helpful resources. Also, please visit our new LinkedIn and Facebook pages. We feel that our increased Internet and social media presence will help us to continue to meet the goals we established for ourselves thirty-five years ago—to provide you with the most authoritative, timely and accurate information on the higher education community.

Frederick F. Hafner
Publisher

Reston, Virginia

Foreword

The 2018 edition of the *Higher Education Directory*® contains listings of accredited, degree-granting institutions of postsecondary education in the United States and its territories.

Criteria for Listing in this Directory

To be listed in this Directory, an institution must meet the following guidelines:

(1) They are degree-granting (legally authorized to offer and are offering a program of college-level studies leading toward a degree[1]);
(2) They have submitted the information required for listing; and
(3) They meet one of the following criteria for listing:
  A. The institution is accredited at the college level by an accrediting agency that is recognized by the U.S. Secretary of Education;
  B. The institution holds pre-accredited status with an accrediting agency recognized by the U.S. Secretary of Education whose recognition includes the pre-accreditation status;
  C. The institution is accredited at the college level by an accrediting agency recognized by the Council for Higher Education Accreditation (CHEA).

"College level" means a postsecondary associate, baccalaureate, post-baccalaureate, or rabbinical education program.

Verification of Accreditations

Verification of each accreditation for all institutions was done by comparing the accreditation against the current Directory (and updated lists) for each respective regional, national, professional and specialized association or agency, along with telephone calls to numerous accrediting associations whenever there was a question of accuracy. Over 22,500 accreditations were verified through September 2017.

The reader is reminded that many institutions have programs which may not be recognized by a professional or specialized association, but are considered fine programs. The institutions may or may not have sought such recognition.

General Organization of the Directory

Our approach to the organization of the material is to make the desired information readable and easy to find. There are four indexes which are cross-referenced to the main institutional listing.

A. Prologue
  1. Accrediting agencies with addresses. Regional accrediting commissions are listed alphabetically while national, professional and specialized bodies are listed alphabetically under headings showing their specialties.
  2. Acronyms used in the Directory for accrediting bodies are listed alphabetically.
  3. Explanatory notes and symbols.
  4. U.S. postal abbreviations of states.
  5. Institution changes.
  6. Administrative officers' description and job codes.
  7. U.S. Department of Education offices.
  8. Statewide agencies of higher education.
  9. Higher education associations.
  10. Consortia of institutions of higher education.
  11. Association name index.
  12. Religious affiliation by denomination.
  13. Carnegie classification codes.
  14. Statistical data.

B. College and university listings by state with institutional characteristics and administrative officers.
  1. Institution Name. If an * appears before the institution's name, it is a part of a system. A line between institutions separates two systems.
  2. Alpha Code. The first institution listed on a page is coded (A), the second (B), etc. The Administrators' index is also coded to enable the reader to locate the desired institution quickly.
  3. Address.
  4. County.
  5. FICE Identification. This was the Federal Interagency Commission on Education number originally assigned by the Department of Education. We continue to use the term FICE. However, the Department of Education in their Office of Student Financial Assistance uses OPEID, Office of Postsecondary Education Identification. OPEID consists of the first six digits of the FICE plus two more digits indicating branch campuses. Numbers beginning with 66 are for accredited institutions for which we cannot locate a FICE or OPEID number. These are identification numbers only.
  6. Telephone Number.
  7. Unit ID Number. A unique number developed by the National Center for Education Statistics (NCES) for the Education Department's IPEDS Reports.
  8. Carnegie Classification Code. (see page **xlix**)
  9. Main FAX Number.
  10. School Calendar.
  11. URL (Universal Resource Locator).
  12. Date Established.
  13. Annual Tuition & Fees for 2016-17 school year.
  14. Fall 2016 Enrollment. Head count (not FTE) in degree programs as reported on the latest IPEDS survey.
  15. Type of Student Body.
  16. Affiliation or Control.
  17. IRS Status.
  18. Highest Degree Offered.
  19. Accreditation (see page **vi**). **N.B. Institutional accreditation is in bold face.**
  20. Administrative and academic officers with job classification code (see page **xxvii** for descriptions).
  21. Non-system branch campuses. The names of these campuses are in italic type and their listings are shortened. Non-system branch campuses are listed if they are identified by the parent institutions' accrediting organization as a branch campus.

C. Index of administrators is an alphabetical listing of all the administrators with their most direct phone number and E-mail address. The page and reference letter indicate the page on which the administrator's institution listing begins.

D. Index of regional, national, professional and specialized accreditation alphabetically by state. This index standardizes and simplifies reviewing of the 140 accrediting classifications.

E. FICE number index. Numeric listing of FICE number and school.

F. Alphabetic index of institutions.

[1]The *Higher Education Directory*® lists degree-granting institutions approved by regional, national, professional or specialized accrediting agencies.

Accrediting Agencies

The following regional, national, professional and specialized accrediting agencies are recognized by the U.S. Secretary of Education or the Council for Higher Education Accreditation (CHEA). The U.S. Department of Education (USDE) dates specified are the date of initial listing as a U.S. Department of Education recognized agency, the date of the U.S. Secretary's most recent grant of renewed recognition based on the last full review of the agency by the National Advisory Committee on Institutional Quality and Integrity, and the date of the agency's next scheduled review for renewal of recognition.[1] The Council for Higher Education (CHEA) date reflects initial or continued recognition by CHEA.

Regional Accrediting Bodies

Delaware, District of Columbia, Maryland, New Jersey, New York, Pennsylvania, Puerto Rico, Virgin Islands

Middle States Commission on Higher Education M
USDE: 1952/2012/2017 CHEA: 2013
3624 Market Street, Second Floor West
Philadelphia, PA 19104
(267) 284-5000 Fax (215) 662-5501
Elizabeth H. Sibolski, President
E-mail: info@msche.org
URL: www.msche.org

Connecticut, Maine, Massachusetts, New Hampshire, Rhode Island, Vermont

Commission on Institutions of Higher Education
New England Association of Schools and Colleges EH
USDE: 1952/2015/2017 CHEA: 2013
3 Burlington Woods Drive, Suite 100
Burlington, MA 01803-4514
(781) 425-7785 Fax (781) 425-1001
Barbara E. Brittingham, President
E-mail: cihe@neasc.org
URL: http://cihe.neasc.org

Arizona, Arkansas, Colorado, Illinois, Indiana, Iowa, Kansas, Michigan, Minnesota, Missouri, Nebraska, New Mexico, North Dakota, Ohio, Oklahoma, South Dakota, West Virginia, Wisconsin, Wyoming

Higher Learning Commission NH
USDE: 1952/2015/2017 CHEA: 2015
230 South LaSalle Street, Suite 7-500
Chicago, IL 60604-1411
(800) 621-7440 Fax (312) 263-7462
Barbara Gellman-Danley, President
E-mail: info@hlcommission.org
URL: www.hlcommission.org

Alaska, Idaho, Montana, Nevada, Oregon, Utah, Washington

Northwest Commission on Colleges and Universities NW
USDE: 1952/2015/2018
8060 165th Avenue, NE, Suite 100
Redmond, WA 98052
(425) 558-4224 Fax (425) 376-0596
Sandra E. Elman, President
E-mail: selman@nwccu.org
URL: www.nwccu.org

Alabama, Florida, Georgia, Kentucky, Louisiana, Mississippi, North Carolina, South Carolina, Tennessee, Texas, Virginia

Commission on Colleges
Southern Association of Colleges and Schools SC
USDE: 1952/2014/2017 CHEA: 2015
1866 Southern Lane
Decatur, GA 30033-4097
(404) 679-4500 Fax (404) 679-4558
Belle S. Wheelan, President
E-mail: questions@sacscoc.org
URL: www.sacscoc.org

California, Hawaii, American Samoa, Guam, Commonwealth of the Northern Marianas, Federated States of Micronesia, Republic of the Marshall Islands, Republic of Palau

Senior College and University Commission
Western Association of Schools and Colleges WC
USDE: 1952/2012/2017 CHEA: 2014
985 Atlantic Avenue, Suite 100
Alameda, CA 94501
(510) 748-9001 Fax (510) 748-9797
Mary Ellen Petrisko, President
E-mail: wasc@wscuc.org
URL: www.wscuc.org

The Accrediting Commission for Community and Junior Colleges
Western Association of Schools and Colleges WJ
USDE: 1952/2015/2017 CHEA: 2016
10 Commercial Boulevard, Suite 204
Novato, CA 94949
(415) 506-0234 Fax (415) 506-0238
Richard Winn, President
E-mail: accjc@accjc.org
URL: www.accjc.org

[1]U.S. Department of Education, Nationally Recognized Accrediting Agencies, www2.ed.gov/admins/finaid/accred/accreditation.html.

National, Professional and Specialized Accrediting Bodies

Acupuncture

Accreditation Commission for Acupuncture and Oriental Medicine (ACAOM)
USDE: 1988/2016/2021
8941 Aztec Drive
Eden Praire, MN 55347
(952) 212-2434 Fax (952) 657-7068
Mark S. McKenzie, Executive Director
E-mail: info@acaom.org
URL: www.acaom.org

First-professional master's degree, professional master's level certificate and diploma programs and professional post-graduate doctoral programs in acupuncture and Oriental medicine, and free-standing institutions that offer such programs **ACUP**

Allied Health

Accrediting Bureau of Health Education Schools (ABHES)
USDE: 1969/2016/2021
7777 Leesburg Pike, Suite 314N
Falls Church, VA 22043
(703) 917-9503 Fax (703) 917-4109
Florence Tate, Executive Director
E-mail: info@abhes.org
URL: www.abhes.org

Institutions specializing in allied health education **ABHES**
Specialized programs for
- Medical assistant **MAAB**
- Medical laboratory technician **MLTAB**
- Surgical technologist **SURTEC**

Commission on Accreditation of Allied Health Education Programs (CAAHEP)
CHEA: 2014
25400 US Hwy 19 N., Suite 158
Clearwater, FL 33756
(727) 210-2350 Fax (727) 210-2354
Kathleen Megivern, Executive Director
E-mail: mail@caahep.org
URL: www.caahep.org

The Commission on Accreditation of Allied Health Education Programs (CAAHEP) is recognized as an accrediting agency for accreditation of education for the allied health occupations. In carrying out its accreditation activities, CAAHEP cooperates with the Committees on Accreditation sponsored by various allied health and medical specialty organizations. CAAHEP is the coordinating agency for accreditation of education for the following allied health occupations:
- Anesthesiologist assistant **AA**
- Blood bank technology **BBT**
- Cardiovascular technologist **CVT**
- Cytotechnologist **CYTO**
- Diagnostic medical sonographer **DMS**
- Emergency medical technician-paramedic **EMT**
- Exercise science **EXSC**
- Kinesiotherapy **KIN**
- Medical assistant **MAC**
- Medical illustrator **MIL**
- Neurodiagnostic technologist **NDT**
- Orthotist/prosthetist **OPE**
- Perfusionist **PERF**
- Polysomnographic technologist **POLYT**
- Recreation therapist **CARTE**
- Surgical assistant **SURGA**
- Surgical technologist **SURGT**

Anesthesiologist Assistant

Commission on Accreditation of Allied Health Education Programs (see listing under Allied Health)
Accreditation Review Committee for the Anesthesiologist Assistant
N84 W33137 Becker Lane
Merton, WI 53066
(612) 836-3311
Jennifer Anderson Warwick, Executive Director
E-mail: arc-aa@arc-aa.org
URL: www.caahep.org/arc-aa

Post-baccalaureate programs for anesthesiologist assistant **AA**

Art

Commission on Accreditation
National Association of Schools of Art and Design (NASAD)
USDE: 1966/2014/2017
11250 Roger Bacon Drive, Suite 21
Reston, VA 20190
(703) 437-0700 Fax (703) 437-6312
Karen P. Moynahan, Executive Director
E-mail: info@arts-accredit.org
URL: nasad.arts-accredit.org

Institutions and departments within institutions offering degree and non-degree granting programs in art/design and art/design-related programs **ART**

Athletic Training

Commission on Accreditation of Athletic Training Education (CAATE)
CHEA: 2014
6850 Austin Center Boulevard, Suite 100
Austin, TX 78731-3184
(512) 733-9700
Micki Cuppett, Executive Director
E-mail: micki@caate.net
URL: www.caate.net

Programs for athletic training **CAATE**

Audiology

Accreditation Commission for Audiology Education
CHEA: 2012
11480 Commerce Park Drive, Suite 220
Reston, VA 20191
(202) 986-9500 Fax (202) 986-9550
Doris Gordon, Executive Director
E-mail: info@acaeaccred.org
URL: www.acaeaccred.org

Programs leading to the Doctor of Audiology degree **ACAE**

Council on Academic Accreditation in Audiology and Speech Language Pathology
American Speech-Language-Hearing Association (ASHA)
USDE: 1967/2015/2020 CHEA: 2014
2200 Research Boulevard
Rockville, MD 20850-3289
(301) 296-5700 Fax (301) 296-8580
Patrima L. Tice, Director of Accreditation
E-mail: accreditation@asha.org
URL: www.asha.org

Doctoral degree programs in audiology **AUD**

Aviation

Aviation Accreditation Board International
CHEA: 2016
3410 Skyway Drive
Auburn, AL 36830
(334) 844-2431 Fax (334) 844-2432
Gary J. Northam, President
E-mail: bayenva@auburn.edu
URL: www.aabi.aero

Non-engineering programs for aviation **AAB**

Bible College Education

Commission on Accreditation
Association for Biblical Higher Education (ABHE)
USDE: 1952/2014/2017 CHEA: 2011
5850 T. G. Lee Boulevard, Suite 130
Orlando, FL 32822
(407) 207-0808 Fax (407) 207-0840
Ron Kroll, Director, Commission on Accreditation
E-mail: info@abhe.org
URL: www.abhe.org

Bible colleges and programs offering undergraduate and graduate programs **BI**

Blood Bank Technology

Commission on Accreditation of Allied Health Education Programs (see listing under Allied Health)
American Association of Blood Banks (AABB)
Committee on Accreditation of Specialists in Blood Bank Technology Schools
4550 Montgomery Avenue, Suite 700 North Tower
Bethesda, MD 20814
(301) 907-6977 Fax (301) 907-6895
Anne Chenoweth, Senior Deputy Director of Accreditation and Quality Department
E-mail: aabb@aabb.org
URL: www.aabb.org

Programs for blood bank technologist **BBT**

Business

Accrediting Council for Independent Colleges and Schools (ACICS)
CHEA: 2012
750 First Street NE, Suite 980
Washington, DC 20002-4223
(202) 336-6780 Fax (202) 842-2593
Michelle Edwards, President
E-mail: info@acics.org
URL: www.acics.org

Institutions offering certificates/diplomas, associate, baccalaureate and master's degree programs to educate students for professional, technical, or occupational careers **ACICS**

Accreditation Council for Business Schools and Programs (ACBSP)
CHEA: 2011
11520 West 119th Street
Overland Park, KS 66213
(913) 339-9356 Fax (913) 339-6226
Jeffrey Alderman, President/CEO
E-mail: info@acbsp.org
URL: www.acbsp.org

Business administration, management, accounting and related business fields **ACBSP**

International Accreditation Council for Business Education
CHEA: 2011
11374 Strang Line Rd
Lenexa, KS 66215
(913) 631-3009 Fax (913) 631-9154
Phyllis Okrepkie, Interim President
E-mail: iacbe@iacbe.org
URL: www.iacbe.org

Undergraduate and graduate level business programs in institutions that grant bachelor's and/or graduate degrees **IACBE**

Cardiovascular Technology

Commission on Accreditation of Allied Health Education Programs (see listing under Allied Health)
Joint Review Committee on Education in Cardiovascular Technology (JRC-CVT)

1449 Hill Street
Whitinsville, MA 01588-1032
(978) 456-5594
Jackie Long-Goding, Executive Director
E-mail: office@jrccvt.org
URL: www.jrccvt.org

Programs for cardiovascular technology **CVT**

Chiropractic

The Council on Chiropractic Education (CCE)
USDE: 1974/2016/2018 CHEA: 2015
8049 North 85th Way
Scottsdale, AZ 85258-4321
(480) 443-8877 Fax (480) 483-7333
Craig S. Little, President
E-mail: cce@cce-usa.org
URL: www.cce-usa.org

Programs leading to and institutions offering the Doctorate of Chiropractic (D.C.) degree **CHIRO**

Christian Studies Education

Accreditation Commission
Transnational Association of Christian Colleges and Schools (TRACS)
USDE: 1991/2013/2018 CHEA: 2011
15935 Forest Road
Forest, VA 24551
(434) 525-9539 Fax (434) 616-2638
Timothy Eaton, President
E-mail: info@tracs.org
URL: www.tracs.org

Christian liberal arts institutions which offer certificates/diplomas and associate, baccalaureate and graduate degrees **TRACS**

Clinical Laboratory Sciences

National Accrediting Agency for Clinical Laboratory Sciences (NAACLS)
CHEA: 2013
5600 North River Road, Suite 720
Rosemont, IL 60018
(773) 714-8880 Fax (773) 714-8886
Dianne M. Cearlock, Chief Executive Officer
E-mail: info@naacls.org
URL: www.naacls.org

Programs for:
- clinical assistant **CA**
- cytogenetic technologist **CGTECH**
- diagnostic molecular scientist **DMOLS**
- histologic technician/technologist **HT**
- medical laboratory technician **MLTAD**
- medical technologist/laboratory scientist **MT**
- pathologists' assistant **PA**
- phlebotomy **PHLEB**

Clinical Pastoral Education

Accreditation Commission
Association for Clinical Pastoral Education, Inc. (ACPEI)
USDE: 1969/2013/2017
One West Court Square, Suite 325
Decatur, GA 30030
(404) 320-1472 Fax (404) 320-0849
Trace Haythorn, Executive Director
E-mail: acpe@acpe.edu
URL: www.acpe.edu

Basic, advanced and supervisory clinical pastoral education programs **PAST**

Construction Education

American Council for Construction Education (ACCE)
CHEA: 2011
825 West Bitters Road, Suite 103
San Antonio, TX 78216
(210) 495-6161 Fax (210) 495-6168
Michael Holland, President
E-mail: mholland@acce-hq.org
URL: www.acce-hq.org

Associate and baccalaureate degree programs **CONST**

Continuing Education

Accrediting Council for Continuing Education and Training (ACCET)
USDE: 1978/2013/2018
1722 N Street NW
Washington, DC 20036
(202) 955-1113 Fax (202) 955-1118
William V. Larkin, Executive Director
E-mail: info@accet.org
URL: www.accet.org

Institutions offering noncollegiate continuing education and institutions offering occupational associate degree programs **CNCE**

Cosmetology

National Accrediting Commission of Career Arts and Sciences (NACCAS)
USDE: 1970/2015/2020
3015 Colvin Street
Alexandria, VA 22314
(703) 600-7600 Fax (703) 379-2200
Anthony Mirando, Executive Director
E-mail: info@naccas.org
URL: www.naccas.org

Postsecondary schools and departments of cosmetology arts and sciences and massage therapy **COSME**

Counseling and Related Educational Programs

Council for Accreditation of Counseling and Related Educational Programs (CACREP)
CHEA: 2015
1001 North Fairfax Street, Suite 510
Alexandria, VA 22314
(703) 535-5990 Fax (703) 739-6209
Charles F. Gressard, Interim President and CEO
E-mail: cacrep@cacrep.org
URL: www.cacrep.org

Programs in counseling and its specialties **CACREP**

Culinary Arts

Accrediting Commission
American Culinary Federation
CHEA: 2015
180 Center Place Way
St. Augustine, FL 32095
(904) 824-4468 Fax (904) 940-0741
Heidi Cramb, Executive Director
E-mail: acf@acfchefs.net
URL: www.acfchefs.org

Programs in culinary arts which award certificates, diplomas or associate degrees and bachelor degree programs in culinary management **ACFEI**

Cytotechnology

Commission on Accreditation of Allied Health Education Programs (see listing under Allied Health)
Cytotechnology Programs Review Committee
American Society of Cytopathology
100 West 10th Street, Suite 605
Wilmington, DE 19801
(302) 543-6583 Fax (302) 543-6597
Elizabeth Jenkins, Executive Director
E-mail: asc@cytopathology.org
URL: www.cytopathology.org

Programs for the cytotechnologist **CYTO**

Dance

Commission on Accreditation
National Association of Schools of Dance (NASD)
USDE: 1983/2015/2019
11250 Roger Bacon Drive, Suite 21
Reston, VA 20190
(703) 437-0700 Fax (703) 437-6312
Karen P. Moynahan, Executive Director
E-mail: info@arts-accredit.org
URL: nasd.arts-accredit.org

Institutions and departments within institutions offering degree and non-degree-granting programs in dance and dance-related disciplines **DANCE**

Dental and Dental Auxiliary Programs

Commission on Dental Accreditation
American Dental Association (ADA)
USDE: 1952/2013/2017
211 East Chicago Avenue, Suite 1900
Chicago, IL 60611
(800) 621-8099 Fax (312) 440-2915
Sherin Tooks, Director
E-mail: tooks@ada.org
URL: www.ada.org/coda

Programs leading to:
- D.D.S. or D.M.D. degree, advanced general dentistry and specialty programs **DENT**
- Dental hygiene **DH**
- Dental assisting **DA**
- Dental laboratory technology **DT**

Diagnostic Medical Sonography

Commission on Accreditation of Allied Health Education Programs (see listing under Allied Health)
Joint Review Committee on Education in Diagnostic Medical Sonography
6021 University Boulevard, Suite 500
Ellicot City, MD 21043-6090
(443) 973-3251 Fax (866) 738-3444
Gerry Magat, Executive Director
E-mail: mail@jrcdms.org
URL: www.jrcdms.org

Programs for the diagnostic medical sonographer **DMS**

Dietetics

Accreditation Council for Education in Nutrition and Dietetics
Academy of Nutrition and Dietetics
USDE: 1974/2012/2017
120 South Riverside Plaza, Suite 2190
Chicago, IL 60606-6995
(312) 899-0040 Fax (312) 899-4817
Mary B. Gregoire, Executive Director
E-mail: acend@eatright.org
URL: www.eatright.acend.org

Coordinated programs in dietetics **DIETC**
Didactic programs **DIETD**
Post-baccalaureate internships **DIETI**
Dietetic technician programs **DIETT**

Distance Education and Training

Distance Education Accrediting Commission
USDE: 1959/2012/2017 CHEA: 2013
1101 17th Street NW, Suite 808
Washington, DC 20036
(202) 234-5100 Fax (202) 332-1386
Leah K. Matthews, Executive Director

E-mail: info@deac.org
URL: www.deac.org

Distance education institutions including associate, baccalaureate, master's, and doctoral degree-granting programs primarily through the distance learning method **DEAC** (formerly DETC)

Emergency Medical Services

Commission on Accreditation for Allied Health Programs (see listing under Allied Health)
Committee on Accreditation of Educational Programs for the Emergency Medical Services Professions
8301 Lakeview Parkway, Suite 111-312
Rowlett, TX 75088
(214) 703-8445 Fax (214) 703-8992
George Hatch Jr., Executive Director
E-mail: george@coaemsp.org
URL: www.coaemsp.org

Programs for the emergency medical technician-paramedic **EMT**

Engineering

ABET, Inc.
CHEA: 2015
415 North Charles Street
Baltimore, MD 21201
(410) 347-7700 Fax (410) 625-2238
Michael Milligan, Executive Director
E-mail: accreditation@abet.org
URL: www.abet.org

Baccalaureate programs in computer science **CS**
Basic (baccalaureate) and advanced (master's) level programs in engineering **ENG**
Applied science programs at the associate, baccalaureate and master's level **ENGR**
Associate and baccalaureate degree programs in engineering technology **ENGT**

English Language

Commission on English Language Program Accreditation (CEA)
USDE: 2003/2016/2018
1001 North Fairfax Drive, Suite 630
Alexandria, VA 22314
(703) 665-3400 Fax (703) 519-2071
Mary Reeves, Executive Director
E-mail: info@cea-accredit.org
URL: www.cea-accredit.org

English language programs **CEA**

Exercise Sciences

Commission on Accreditation of Allied Health Education Programs (see listing under Allied Health)
Committee on Accreditation for the Exercise Sciences
401 West Michigan Street
Indianapolis, IN 46202
(317) 777-1135 Fax (317) 634-7817
William Coale, Director
E-mail: trush@acsm.org
URL: www.coaes.org

Programs for exercise science and related departments **EXSC**

Family and Consumer Sciences

Council for Accreditation
American Association of Family and Consumer Sciences (AAFCS)
CHEA: 2014
400 North Columbus Street, Suite 202
Alexandria, VA 22314
(703) 706-4600 Fax (703) 706-4663
Carolyn W. Jackson, Executive Director
E-mail: accreditation@aafcs.org
URL: www.aafcs.org

Baccalaureate programs in family and consumer sciences **AAFCS**

Fire and Emergency

International Fire Service Accreditation Congress
CHEA: 2011
1812 West Tyler Avenue
Oklahoma State University
Stillwater, OK 74078
(405) 744-8303 Fax (405) 744-8802
Clayton Moorman, Director IFSAC Administration
E-mail: admin@ifsac.org
URL: www.ifsac.org

Undergraduate fire and emergency related programs **IFSAC**

Forensic Science

Forensic Science Educational Program Accreditation Commission
American Academy of Forensic Sciences (AAFS)
CHEA: 2015
410 North 21st Street
Colorado Springs, CO 80904
(719) 636-1100 Fax (719) 636-1993
Nancy J. Jackson, Director of Development and Accreditation
Email: njackson@aafs.org
URL: www.aafs.org

Bachelor or master's degree programs in forensic science **FEPAC**

Funeral Service Education

Committee on Accreditation
American Board of Funeral Service Education (ABFSE)
USDE: 1972/2015/2017 CHEA: 2012
992 Mantua Pike, Suite 108
Woodbury Heights, NJ 08097
(816) 233-3747 Fax (856) 579-7354
Robert C. Smith III, Executive Director
E-mail: exdir@abfse.org
URL: www.abfse.org

Institutions and programs awarding diplomas, associate and bachelor's degrees in funeral service or mortuary science **FUSER**

Health Informatics and Information Management

Commission on Accreditation for Health Informatics and Information Management Education (CAHIIM)
CHEA: 2012
233 North Michigan Avenue, 21st Floor
Chicago, IL 60601-5800
(312) 233-1100 Fax (312) 233-1948
Claire Dixon-Lee, Executive Director
Email: info@cahiim.org
URL: www.cahiim.org

Associate and baccalaureate degree programs in health information management and master's degree programs in health informatics and health information management **CAHIIM**

Healthcare Management

Commission on Accreditation of Healthcare Management Education (CAHME)
CHEA: 2014
6110 Executive Boulevard, Suite 614
Rockville, MD 20852
(301) 298-1820 Fax (301) 298-1830
Anthony Stanowski, President and CEO
E-mail: info@cahme.org
URL: www.cahme.org

Graduate programs in healthcare management **HSA**

Human Services

Council for Standards in Human Services Education (CSHSE)
CHEA: 2014
3337 Duke Street
Alexandria, VA 22314
(571) 257-3959
Elaine Green, President
E-mail: info@cshse.org
URL: www.cshse.org

Human services educational programs **CSHSE**

Industrial Technology

The Association of Technology, Management, and Applied Engineering
CHEA: 2013
3801 Lake Boone Trail, Suite 190
Raleigh, NC 27607
(919) 635-8335 Fax (919) 779-5462
Caitlin Schwab-Falzone, Director of Accreditation
E-mail: accreditation@atmae.org
URL: www.atmae.org

Technology, applied technology, engineering technology and technology-related programs at the associate, baccalaureate and master's degree level **NAIT**

Interior Design

Council for Interior Design Accreditation (CIDA)
CHEA: 2013
206 Grandville Avenue, Suite 350
Grand Rapids, MI 49503
(616) 458-0400 Fax (616) 458-0460
Holly Mattson, Executive Director
E-mail: info@accredit-id.org
URL: www.accredit-id.org

Professional degree level programs (master's and baccalaureate degrees) **CIDA**

Jewish Studies

Association of Institutions of Jewish Studies (AIJS)
USDE: 2015/2020
500 West Kennedy Bouevard
Lakewood, NJ 08701
(732) 363-7330 Fax (732) 415-8198
Doniel Ginsberg, President
E-mail: info@theaijs.com
URL: theaijs.com

Postsecondary institutions of Jewish studies **AIJS**

Journalism and Mass Communications

Accrediting Committee
Accrediting Council on Education in Journalism and Mass Communications (ACEJMC)
CHEA: 2014
University of Kansas School of Journalism
Stauffer-Flint Hall
1435 Jayhawk Boulevard
Lawrence, KS 66045-7575
(785) 864-3973 Fax (785) 864-5225
Susanne Shaw, Executive Director
E-mail: sshaw@ku.edu
URL: www.acejmc.org

Units within institutions offering professional baccalaureate and master's degree programs in journalism and mass communications **JOUR**

Kinesiotherapy

Commission on Accreditation of Allied Health Education Programs (see listing under Allied Health)
Committee on Accreditation of Education Programs for Kinesiotherapy
118 College Drive #5142
Hattiesburg, MS 39406-0002
(601) 266-5371 Fax (601) 266-4445
Jerry W. Purvis, Coord COPSKT
E-mail: jerry.purvis@usm.edu
URL: www.akta.org

Kinesiotherapy programs **KIN**

Landscape Architecture

Landscape Architectural Accreditation Board
American Society of Landscape Architects (ASLA)
CHEA: 2015
636 Eye Street, NW
Washington, DC 20001-3736
(202) 898-2444 Fax (202) 898-1185
Kristopher Pritchard, Accreditation and Education Programs Manager
E-mail: info@asla.org
URL: www.asla.org

Baccalaureate and master's programs leading to the first professional degree **LSAR**

Law

Council of the Section of Legal Education and Admissions to the Bar
American Bar Association (ABA)
USDE: 1952/2013/2018
321 North Clark Street, 21st Fl
Chicago, IL 60654-7598
(312) 988-6738 Fax (312) 988-5681
Barry A. Currier, Managing Director of Accreditation and Legal Education
E-mail: legaled@americanbar.org
URL: www.americanbar.org/groups/legal_education.html

Programs in legal education; professional schools of law **LAW**

Librarianship

Committee on Accreditation
American Library Association (ALA)
CHEA: 2017
50 East Huron Street
Chicago, IL 60611-2795
(312) 280-2432 Fax (312) 280-2433
Karen O'Brien, Director of Accreditation
E-mail: accred@ala.org
URL: www.ala.org/accreditation

Master's programs in library and information studies **LIB**

Marriage and Family Therapy

Commission on Accreditation for Marriage and Family Therapy Education
American Association for Marriage and Family Therapy (AAMFT)
CHEA: 2014
112 South Alfred Street
Alexandria, VA 22314-3061
(703) 253-0473 Fax (703) 253-0508
Tanya A. Tamarkin, Director of Accreditation
E-mail: coa@aamft.org
URL: www.coamte.org

Clinical training programs at the master's, doctorate and post-graduate levels **MFCD**

Massage Therapy

Commission on Massage Therapy Accreditation
USDE: 2002/2015/2020
2101 Wilson Boulevard, Suite 302
Arlington, VA 22201
(202) 888-6790 Fax (202) 888-6787
Dawn Hogue, Acting Executive Director
E-mail: info@comta.org
URL: www.comta.org

Institutions that award postsecondary certificates, diplomas, and associate degrees in the practice of massage therapy, bodywork, aesthetics/esthetics and skin care **COMTA**

Medical Assistant Education

(see listing under Allied Health)
Accrediting Bureau of Health Education Schools (ABHES)

Medical assistant programs **MAAB**

Commission on Accreditation of Allied Health Education Programs (see listing under Allied Health)
Medical Assisting Education Review Board
20 North Wacker Drive, Suite 1575
Chicago, IL 60606-2963
(800) 228-2262 Fax (312) 899-1259
Sarah R. Marino, Executive Director
E-mail: maerb@maerb.org
URL: www.maerb.org

One and two year medical assistant programs **MAC**

Medical Illustrator Education

Commission on Accreditation of Allied Health Education Programs (see listing under Allied Health)
Accreditation Review Committee for the Medical Illustrator
Saint Luke's Hospital Instructional Resources
32531 Meadowlark Way
Pepper Pike, OH 44124
(216) 595-9363
Kathy Jung, Chair, ARC-MI
E-mail: kijung@aol.com
URL: www.ami.org

Programs for medical illustrator **MIL**

Medical Laboratory Technician Education

(see listing under Allied Health)
Accrediting Bureau of Health Education Schools (ABHES)

Schools and programs for the medical laboratory technician **MLTAB**

(see listing under Clinical Laboratory Sciences)
National Accrediting Agency for Clinical Laboratory Sciences (NAACLS)

Programs for medical laboratory technician **MLTAD**

Medical Technology

(see listing under Clinical Laboratory Sciences)
National Accrediting Agency for Clinical Laboratory Sciences (NAACLS)

Programs for medical technologist/laboratory scientist **MT**

Medicine

Liaison Committee on Medical Education (LCME) of the Council on Medical Education of the American Medical Association and the Association of American Medical Colleges
USDE: 1952/2014/2018
The LCME is administered in odd-numbered years, beginning each July 1, by:
Council on Medical Education of the American Medical Association (AMA)
330 North Wabash Avenue
Chicago, IL 60611
(312) 464-4690 Fax (312) 464-5830
Barbara Barzansky, LCME Co-Secretary
E-mail: barbara.barzansky@ama-assn.org
URL: www.ama-assn.org

The LCME is administered in even-numbered years, beginning each July 1, by:
Association of American Medical Colleges (AAMC)
655 K Street NW, Suite 100
Washington, DC 20001-2399
(202) 828-0400 Fax (202) 828-1125
Veronica Catanese, LCME Co-Secretary
E-mail: vcatanese@aamc.org
URL: www.aamc.org

Programs leading to the M.D. degree **MED**

Midwifery Education

Midwifery Education Accreditation Council (MEAC)
USDE: 2001/2015/2017
850 Mt. Pleasant Avenue
Ann Arbor, MI 48103
(360) 466-2080 Fax (480) 907-2936
Timberly Robinson, Executive Director
E-mail: info@meacschools.org
URL: www.meacschools.org

Accreditation of direct-entry midwifery educational institutions and programs conferring degrees and certificates **MEAC**

Montessori Teacher Education

Montessori Accreditation Council for Teacher Education (MACTE)
USDE: 1995/2015/2017
420 Park Street
Charlottesville, VA 22902
(434) 202-7793 Fax (888) 525-8838
Rebecca Pelton, Executive Director
E-mail: info@macte.org
URL: www.macte.org

Montessori teacher-education programs and institutions **MACTE**

Music

Commission on Accreditation
National Association of Schools of Music (NASM)
USDE: 1952/2015/2019
11250 Roger Bacon Drive, Suite 21
Reston, VA 20190
(703) 437-0700 Fax (703) 437-6312
Karen P. Moynahan, Executive Director
E-mail: info@arts-accredit.org
URL: nasm.arts-accredit.org

Institutions and departments within institutions offering degree and non-degree-granting programs in music and music-related disciplines **MUS**

Naturopathic Medical Education

Council on Naturopathic Medical Education (CNME)
USDE: 2003/2015/2020

PO Box 178
Great Barrington, MA 01230
(413) 528-8877 Fax (413) 528-8880
Daniel Seitz, Executive Director
E-mail: council@cnme.org
URL: www.cnme.org

Graduate-level, four-year naturopathic medical education programs **NATUR**

Neurodiagnostic Technology

Commission on Accreditation of Allied Health Education Programs (see listing under Allied Health)
Committee on Accreditation for Education in Neurodiagnostic Technology
1449 Hill Street
Whitinsville, MA 01588
(978) 338-6300 Fax (978) 832-2638
Jackie Long-Goding, Executive Director
E-mail: office@coa-ndt.org
URL: http://coa-ndt.org

Programs for the electroneurodiagnostic technologist **NDT**

Nuclear Medicine Technology

Joint Review Committee on Educational Programs in Nuclear Medicine Technology
CHEA: 2013
2000 West Danforth Road, #B1
Edmund, OK 73003
(405) 285-0546 Fax (405) 285-0579
Jan M. Winn, Executive Director
E-mail: mail@jrcnmt.org
URL: www.jrcnmt.org

Programs for the nuclear medicine technologist **NMT**

Nurse Anesthetists

Council on Accreditation of Nurse Anesthesia Educational Programs
USDE: 1955/2015/2018 CHEA: 2014
222 South Prospect Avenue, Suite 304
Park Ridge, IL 60068-4001
(847) 655-1160 Fax (847) 692-7137
Francis Gerbasi, Executive Director
E-mail: accreditation@coa.us.com
URL: home.coa.us.com

Nurse anesthesia educational institutions and programs at the post-master's certificate, master's and doctoral degree levels **ANEST**

Nurse-Midwifery

Accreditation Commission for Midwifery Education
USDE: 1982/2014/2017
8403 Colesville Road, Suite 1550
Silver Spring, MD 20910
(240) 485-1800 Fax (240) 485-1818
Heather Maurer, Executive Director
E-mail: hmaurer@acnm.org
URL: www.midwife.org/accreditation

Pre-certification, basic certificate and master's degree nurse-midwifery educational programs **MIDWF**

Nursing

Commission on Collegiate Nursing Education (CCNE)
USDE: 2000/2014/2017
655 K Street NW, Suite 750
Washington, DC 20001
(202) 887-6791 Fax (202) 887-8476
Jennifer Butlin, Executive Director
E-mail: jbutlin@ccneaccreditation.org
URL: www.aacnnursing.org/ccne

Baccalaureate and higher degree nursing education **NURSE**

Accreditation Commission for Education in Nursing
USDE: 1952/2015/2017 CHEA: 2011
3343 Peachtree Road NE, Suite 850
Atlanta, GA 30326
(404) 975-5000 Fax (404) 975-5020
Marsal P. Stoll, CEO
E-mail: info@acenursing.org
URL: www.acenursing.org

Programs in:
Practical nursing (certificate) **PNUR**
Diploma nurse education **DNUR**
Associate degree **ADNUR**
Baccalaureate and higher degree nurse education **NUR**

Occupational Education

Council on Occupational Education (COE)
USDE: 1969/2016/2021
7840 Roswell Road, Bldg 300, Suite 325
Atlanta, GA 30350
(770) 396-3898 Fax (770) 396-3790
Gary Puckett, Executive Director
E-mail: info@council.org
URL: www.council.org

Occupational/vocational institutions that grant certificates or diplomas and the applied associate degree in specific career and technical education **COE**

Occupational Therapy

Accreditation Council for Occupational Therapy Education
American Occupational Therapy Association
USDE: 1952/2012/2017 CHEA: 2013
4720 Montgomery Lane, Suite 200
Bethesda, MD 20814-3449
(301) 652-6611
Heather Stagliano, Associate Chief Officer for Accreditation
E-mail: accred@aota.org
URL: www.aota.org

Occupational therapy programs **OT**
Occupational therapy assistant programs **OTA**

Opticianry

Commission on Opticianry Accreditation
CHEA: 2010
PO Box 592
Canton, NY 13617
(703) 468-0566
Debra White, Director of Accreditation
E-mail: director@COAccreditation.com
URL: www.coaccreditation.com

Two-year opticianry degree programs **OPD**
One year programs for opthalmic laboratory technician **OPLT**

Optometry

Accreditation Council on Optometric Education
American Optometric Association (AOA)
USDE: 1952/2015/2017 CHEA: 2012
243 North Lindbergh Boulevard
St. Louis, MO 63141
(314) 991-4100 Fax (314) 991-4101
Joyce L. Urbeck, Administrative Director
E-mail: accredit@aoa.org
URL: www.theacoe.org

Programs in:
First professional **OPT**
Optometric residency **OPTR**
Optometric technology **OPTT**

Orthotic and Prosthetic Education

Commission on Accreditation of Allied Health Education Programs (see listing under Allied Health)
National Commission on Orthotic and Prosthetic Education (NCOPE)
330 John Carlyle Street, Suite 200
Alexandria, VA 22314
(703) 836-7114 Fax (703) 836-0838
Robin C. Seabrook, Executive Director
E-mail: info@ncope.org
URL: www.ncope.org

Programs for orthotic and prosthetic education **OPE**

Osteopathic Medicine

Commission on Osteopathic College Accreditation
American Osteopathic Association
USDE: 1952/2011/2018
Department of Education
142 East Ontario Street
Chicago, IL 60611-2864
(312) 202-8048 Fax (312) 202-8200
Brian Kim, Interim Secretary, COCA
E-mail: predoc@osteopathic.org
URL: www.aoacoca.org

Programs leading to and institutions offering the D.O. (Doctor of Osteopathy/Osteopathic Medicine) degree **OSTEO**

Perfusion

Commission on Accreditation of Allied Health Education Programs (see listing under Allied Health)
Accreditation Committee - Perfusion Education (AC-PE)
6663 South Sycamore Street
Littleton, CO 80120
(303) 794-6283 Fax (206) 350-1651
Linda Cantu, Executive Director
E-mail: office@ac-pe.org
URL: www.ac-pe.org

Programs for the perfusionist **PERF**

Pharmacy

Accreditation Council for Pharmacy Education (ACPE)
USDE: 1952/2014/2017 CHEA: 2014
135 South LaSalle Street, Suite 4100
Chicago, IL 60603
(312) 664-3575 Fax (312) 664-4652
Peter H. Vlasses, Executive Director
E-mail: csinfo@acpe-accredit.org
URL: www.acpe-accredit.org

Professional degree programs in pharmacy **PHAR**

Physical Therapy

Commission on Accreditation in Physical Therapy Education
American Physical Therapy Association (APTA)
USDE: 1977/2014/2017 CHEA: 2012
Trans Potomac Plaza
1111 North Fairfax Street
Alexandria, VA 22314
(703) 706-3245 Fax (703) 684-7343
Sandra Wise, Senior Director
E-mail: accreditation@apta.org
URL: www.capteonline.org

Professional programs for the physical therapist **PTA**

Programs for the physical therapist assistant **PTAA**

Physician Assistant

Accreditation Review Commission on Education for the Physician Assistant (ARC-PA)
CHEA: 2015
12000 Findley Road, Suite 150
John's Creek, GA 30097
(770) 476-1224 Fax (770) 476-1738
Sharon Luke, Executive Director
E-mail: arc-pa@arc-pa.org
URL: www.arc-pa.org

Programs for the physician assistant **ARCPA**

Planning (City and Regional)

Planning Accreditation Board
CHEA: 2013
2334 West Lawrence Avenue, Suite 209
Chicago, IL 60625
(773) 334-7200
Shonagh Merits, Executive Director
E-mail: smerits@planningaccreditationboard.org
URL: www.planningaccreditationboard.org

Bachelor and master's level programs in planning **PLNG**

Podiatry

Council on Podiatric Medical Education
American Podiatric Medical Association (APMA)
USDE: 1952/2016/2021 CHEA: 2015
9312 Old Georgetown Road
Bethesda, MD 20814-1621
(301) 581-9200 Fax (301) 571-4903
Alan R. Tinkleman, Director
E-mail: artinkleman@apma.org
URL: www.cpme.org

Colleges and programs of podiatric medicine, including first professional and doctorate degree programs **POD**

Polysomnographic Technology

Commission on Accreditation of Allied Health Education Programs (see listing under Allied Health)
Committee on Accreditation for Polysomnographic Technologist Education
1711 Frank Avenue
New Bern, NC 28560
(252) 626-3238
Karen Monarchy Rowe, Executive Director
E-mail: office@coapsg.org
URL: www.coapsg.org

Programs for polysomnographic technology **POLYT**

Psychology

Psychological Clinical Science Accreditation System (PCSAS)
CHEA: 2012
1800 Massachusetts Avenue NW, Suite 402
Washington, DC 20036-1218
(301) 455-8046
Alan G. Kraut, Executive Director
Email: akraut@pcsas.org
URL: www.pcsas.org

Psychological clinical science doctoral training programs **PCSAS**

Commission on Accreditation
American Psychological Association (APA)
USDE: 1970/2013/2018 CHEA: 2016
750 First Street NE
Washington, DC 20002-4242
(202) 336-5979 Fax (202) 336-5978
Jacqueline Remondet Wall, Director Program Consultation and Accreditation
E-mail: apaaccred@apa.org
URL: www.apa.org

Doctoral programs in:
- Clinical psychology **CLPSY**
- Counseling psychology **COPSY**
- Combined professional-scientific psychology **PSPSY**
- School psychology **SCPSY**
- Doctoral internship program in health service psychology **IPSY**
- Post-doctoral residency in health service psychology **PDPSY**

Public Affairs and Administration

Commission on Peer Review and Accreditation
Network of Schools of Public Policy, Affairs and Administration (NASPAA)
CHEA: 2014
1029 Vermont Avenue, NW, Suite 1100
Washington, DC 20005
(202) 628-8965 Fax (202) 626-4978
Crystal Calarusse, Chief Accreditation Officer
E-mail: copra@naspaa.org
URL: www.naspaa.org

Master's degree programs in public affairs, public policy and administration **SPAA**

Public Health

Council on Education for Public Health (CEPH)
USDE: 1974/2013/2018
1010 Wayne Avenue, Suite 220
Silver Spring, MD 20910-5600
(202) 789-1050 Fax (202) 789-1895
Laura Rasar King, Executive Director
E-mail: lking@ceph.org
URL: www.ceph.org

Baccalaureate and graduate level programs in schools of public health and public health programs outside of schools of public health **PH**

Rabbinical and Talmudic Education

Accreditation Commission
Association of Advanced Rabbinical and Talmudic Schools (AARTS)
USDE: 1974/2015/2018 CHEA: 2011
11 Broadway, Suite 405
New York, NY 10004
(212) 363-1991 Fax (212) 533-5335
Bernard Fryshman, Interim Executive Director
E-mail: office@aarts-schools.org

Advanced rabbinical and Talmudic schools **RABN**

Radiologic Technology

Joint Review Committee on Education in Radiologic Technology
USDE: 1957/2016/2021 CHEA: 2014
20 North Wacker Drive, Suite 2850
Chicago, IL 60606-3182
(312) 704-5300 Fax (312) 704-5304
Leslie F. Winter, Chief Executive Officer
E-mail: mail@jrcert.org
URL: www.jrcert.org

Programs for:
- Magnetic resonance **RADMAG**
- Medical dosimetry **RADDOS**
- Radiographer **RAD**
- Radiation therapist technologist **RTT**

Recreation, Park and Leisure Studies

Council on Accreditation of Parks, Recreation, Tourism and Related Professions
National Recreation and Park Association
CHEA: 2014
22377 Belmont Ridge Road
Ashburn, VA 20148-4501
(703) 858-2155 Fax (703) 858-0794
Jennifer Stromberg, Awards and Accreditation Manager
E-mail: coaprt@nrpa.org
URL: www.nrpa.org

Baccalaureate degree programs in recreation, park resources and leisure studies **NRPA**

Recreation Therapy

Commission on Accreditation of Allied Health Education Programs (see listing under Allied Health)
Committee on Accreditation of Recreational Therapy Education (CARTE)
Grand Valley State University
Cook DeVos Center for Health Sciences
301 Michigan Street NE, Suite 113
Grand Rapids, MI 49503
(616) 331-2735
Teresa M. Beck, Chair
E-mail: beckt@gvsu.edu
URL: www.atra-online.com/education

Recreational therapy education programs **CARTE**

Rehabilitation Education

Commission on Standards and Accreditation
Council on Rehabilitation Education (CORE)
*On July 1, 2017, The Council of Rehabilitation Education (CORE) merged with Council for Accreditation of Counseling and Related Educational Programs **CACREP**

Respiratory Care

Commission on Accreditation for Respiratory Care (CoARC)
CHEA: 2015
1248 Harwood Road
Bedford, TX 76021-4244
(817) 283-2835 Fax (817) 354-8519
Thomas Smalling, Executive Director
Email: tom@coarc.com
URL: www.coarc.com

Degree programs in respiratory care **COARC**
Certificate programs in polysomnography **COARCP**

Social Work

Commission on Accreditation
Council on Social Work Education (CSWE)
CHEA: 2014
1701 Duke Street, Suite 200
Alexandria, VA 22314-3457
(703) 683-8080 Fax (703) 683-8099
Jo Ann Regan, Vice President of Education
E-mail: info@cswe.org
URL: www.cswe.org

Master's and baccalaureate degree programs **SW**

Speech-Language Pathology

Council on Academic Accreditation in Audiology and Speech Language Pathology
American Speech-Language-Hearing Association (ASHA)
USDE: 1967/2015/2020 CHEA: 2014
2200 Research Boulevard
Rockville, MD 20850-3289

(301) 296-5700 Fax (301) 296-8580
Patrima L. Tice, Director of Accreditation
E-mail: accreditation@asha.org
URL: www.asha.org

Master's in speech-language pathology **SP**

Surgical Assisting and Technology

(see listing under Allied Health)
Accrediting Bureau of Health Education Schools (ABHES)

Surgical technologist programs **SURTEC**

Commission on Accreditation of Allied Health Education Programs (see listing under Allied Health)
Accreditation Review Council on Education in Surgical Technology and Surgical Assisting
6 West Dry Creek Circle, Suite 110
Littleton, CO 80120
(303) 694-9262 Fax (303) 741-3655
Ron Kruzel, Executive Director
E-mail: info@arcstsa.org
URL: www.arcstsa.org

Programs for the surgical technologist **SURGT**
Programs for the surgical assistant **SURGA**

Teacher Education

Council for the Accreditation of Educator Preparation*
CHEA: 2016
1140 19th Street NW, Suite 400
Washington, DC 20036
(202) 223-0077 Fax (202) 296-6620
Christopher Koch, President
Email: caep@caepnet.org
URL: caepnet.org

Educator preparation programs **CAEP**
NCATE Educator preparation program **CAEPN**
TEAC Education preparation program **CAEPT**

Theatre

Commission on Accreditation
National Association of Schools of Theatre (NAST)
USDE: 1982/2015/2019
11250 Roger Bacon Drive, Suite 21
Reston, VA 20190
(703) 437-0700 Fax (703) 437-6312
Karen P. Moynahan, Executive Director
E-mail: info@arts-accredit.org
URL: nast.arts-accredit.org

Institutions and departments within institutions offering degree granting and non-degree-granting programs in theatre and theatre-related disciplines **THEA**

Theology

Commission on Accrediting of the Association of Theological Schools (ATS)
USDE: 1952/2013/2021 CHEA: 2012
10 Summit Park Drive
Pittsburgh, PA 15275-1110
(412) 788-6505 Fax (412) 788-6510
Frank Yamada, Executive Director
E-mail: ats@ats.edu
URL: www.ats.edu

Freestanding schools, as well as schools or programs affiliated with larger institutions, offering graduate professional education for ministry and graduate study of theology **THEOL**

Trade and Technical Education

Accrediting Commission of Career Schools and Colleges (ACCSC)
USDE: 1967/2016/2021
2101 Wilson Boulevard, Suite 302
Arlington, VA 22201
(703) 247-4212 Fax (703) 247-4533
Michale McComis, Executive Director
E-mail: info@accsc.org
URL: www.accsc.org

Private, postsecondary degree-granting and non-degree-granting institutions that are predominantly organized to educate students for trade, occupational or technical careers **ACCSC**

Veterinary Medicine

Council on Education
American Veterinary Medical Association (AVMA)
USDE: 1952/2016/2018 CHEA: 2015
1931 North Meacham Road, Suite 100
Schaumburg, IL 60173
(800) 248-2862 Fax (847) 285-5732
Karen Martens Brandt, Director Education and Research
E-mail: avmainfo@avma.org
URL: www.avma.org

Colleges of veterinary medicine offering programs leading to a D.V.M./D.M.V. professional degree **VET**

Other

New York State Board of Regents Commission of Education
USDE: 1952/2012/2017
State Education Department
The University of the State of New York
89 Washington Avenue, Room 1106B
Albany, NY 12234
(518) 474-5844 Fax (518) 473-4909
MaryEllen Elia, Commissioner of Education
E-mail: commissioner@nysed.edu
URL: www.nysed.gov

United States Department of Education

Degree-granting institutions of higher education in New York that designate the agency as their sole or primary nationally recognized accrediting agency for purposes of establishing eligibility to participate in Higher Education Act programs **NY**

On December 12, 2016, the Secretary withdrew recognition from the Accrediting Council for Independent Colleges and Schools (ACICS). By statute, as a result of ACICS's loss of recognition, all affected institutions will be placed on provisional certification until such time as they gain accreditation by another federally recognized accreditor, or the expiration of the 18-month period. During the period of provisional participation, the Secretary will deem institutions to hold recognized accreditation, which will allow institutions to avoid consequences in which are triggered in certain states when an institution is no longer accredited by a federally recognized accrediting agency.

Formerly ACICS accredited schools that are in a provisional program participation agreement with U.S. Department of Education **PPPA**

Accrediting Agencies Recognized for their Pre-accreditation Categories[1]

Under the terms of the Higher Education Act and other Federal legislation providing funding assistance to postsecondary education, an institution or program is eligible to apply for participation in certain Federal programs if, in addition to meeting other statutory requirements, it is accredited by a nationally recognized accrediting agency—or if it is an institution with respect to which the U.S. Secretary of Education has determined that there is satisfactory assurance the institution or program will meet the accreditation standards of such agency or association within a reasonable time. An institution or program may establish satisfactory assurance of accreditation by acquiring pre-accreditation status with a nationally recognized accrediting agency which has been recognized by the U.S. Secretary of Education for the award of such status. According to the Criteria for Nationally Recognized Accrediting Agencies, if an accrediting agency has developed a pre-accreditation status, it must demonstrate that it applies criteria and follows procedures that are appropriately related to those used to award accreditation status. The criteria for recognition also requires an agency's standards for pre-accreditation to permit an institution or program to hold pre-accreditation no more than five years.

The following is a list of accrediting agencies recognized by the U.S. Secretary of Education for their pre-accreditation categories and the categories which are recognized.

Regional Institution Accrediting Bodies

Middle States Commission on Higher Education:
Candidate for Accreditation

New England Association of Schools and Colleges:
Commission on Institutions of Higher Education: *Candidate for Accreditation*

Higher Learning Commission: *Candidate for Accreditation*

Northwest Commission on Colleges and Universities:
Candidate for Accreditation

Southern Association of Colleges and Schools
Commission on Colleges: *Candidate for Accreditation*

Western Association of Schools and Colleges
The Accrediting Commission for Community and Junior Colleges: *Candidate for Accreditation*

Western Association of Schools and Colleges
Senior College and University Commission: *Candidate for Accreditation*

National, Institutional and Specialized Accrediting Bodies

Academy of Nutrition and Dietetics
Accreditation Council for Education in Nutrition and Dietetics: *Pre-accreditation*

Accreditation Commission for Acupuncture and Oriental Medicine: *Pre-accreditation, Candidate for Accreditation*

Accreditation Commission for Midwifery Education: *Pre-accreditation*

Accreditation Council for Pharmacy Education: *Candidate, Pre-candidate*

American Optometric Association
Accreditation Council on Optometric Education: *Preliminary Approval* (for professional degree programs); *Candidacy Pending* (for optometric residency programs in Veterans Administration facilities)

American Osteopathic Association
Commission on Osteopathic College Accreditation: *Provisional Accreditation*

American Physical Therapy Association
Commission on Accreditation in Physical Therapy Education: *Candidate for Accreditation*

American Podiatric Medical Association
Council on Podiatric Medical Education: *Candidate for Accreditation*

American Speech-Language-Hearing Association
Council on Academic Accreditation: *Candidate for Accreditation*

American Veterinary Medical Association
Council on Education: *Reasonable Assurance of Accreditation*

Association for Biblical Higher Education
Commission on Accreditation: *Candidate for Accreditation*

Association of Advanced Rabbinical and Talmudic Schools
Accreditation Commission: *Correspondent, Candidate for Accreditation*

Commission on Accrediting of the Association of Theological Schools: *Candidate for Accredited Membership*

Council on Education for Public Health: *Pre-accreditation*

Council on Naturopathic Medical Education: *Pre-accreditation*

Council on Occupational Education: *Candidate for Accreditation*

Midwifery Education Accreditation Council: *Pre-accreditation*

Transnational Association of Christian Colleges and Schools
Accreditation Commission: *Candidate for Accreditation*

[1]U.S. Department of Education, Nationally Recognized Accrediting Agencies and Associations, www2.ed.gov/admins/finaid/accred/accreditation_pg8.html.

Abbreviations, Explanatory Notes and Symbols

Abbreviations

Listed below are the abbreviations used in this Directory for the recognized regional accrediting commissions and the recognized national, professional and specialized accrediting bodies. Addresses for these associations can be found under our listing of Accrediting Agencies beginning on page viii.

The recognized regional accrediting commissions are indicated throughout this Directory by the following abbreviations:

EH New England Association of Schools and Colleges, Commission on Institutions of Higher Education

M Middle States Commission on Higher Education

NH Higher Learning Commission, North Central Association

NW Northwest Commission on Colleges and Universities

SC Southern Association of Colleges and Schools, Commission on Colleges

WC Western Association of Schools and Colleges, Senior College and University Commission

WJ Western Association of Schools and Colleges, The Accrediting Commission for Community and Junior Colleges

National, professional and specialized accrediting agencies and associations are listed below. Wherever possible, degree levels are shown by the following symbols: (C) diploma/certificate; (A) associate; (B) baccalaureate; (M) master's; (S) beyond master's but less than doctorate; (FP) first professional; (D) doctorate.

AA Commission on Accreditation of Allied Health Education Programs: anesthesiologist assistant (M)

AAB Aviation Accreditation Board International: aviation (A,B,M,D)

AAFCS American Association of Family and Consumer Sciences: family and consumer sciences (B)

ABHES Accrediting Bureau of Health Education Schools: allied health (C,A,B,M)

ACAE Accreditation Commission for Audiology Education: audiology (D)

ACBSP Accreditation Council for Business Schools and Programs: business administration, management, accounting and related business fields (A,B,M,D)

ACCSC Accrediting Commission of Career Schools and Colleges: occupational, trade and technical education (C,A,B,M)

ACFEI American Culinary Federation, Inc.: culinary arts and culinary management (C,A,B)

ACICS Accrediting Council for Independent Colleges and Schools: business and business-related programs (C,A,B,M)

ACUP Accreditation Commission for Acupuncture and Oriental Medicine: acupuncture (C,M,D)

ADNUR Accreditation Commission for Education in Nursing: nursing (A)

AIJS Association of Institutions of Jewish Studies: Jewish studies (C, A,B)

ANEST Council on Accreditation of Nurse Anesthesia Educational Programs: nurse anesthesia (C,M,D)

ARCPA Accreditation Review Commission on Education for the Physician Assistant: physician assisting programs (C,A,B,M)

ART National Association of Schools of Art and Design: art and design (C,A,B,M,D)

AUD American Speech-Language-Hearing Association: audiology (D)

BBT Commission on Accreditation of Allied Health Education Programs: blood bank technology (C,M)

BI Association for Biblical Higher Education: bible college education (C,A,B,M,FP,D)

CA National Accrediting Agency for Clinical Laboratory Sciences: clinical assistant (C)

CAATE Commission on Accreditation of Athletic Training Education: athletic training (B,M)

CACREP Council for Accreditation of Counseling & Related Education programs: counseling and its specialties (M,D)

CAEP Council for the Accreditation of Educator Preparation: teacher education (B,M,D)

CAEPN Council for the Accreditation of Educator Preparation: teacher education (B,M,D)

CAEPT Council for the Accreditation of Educator Preparation: teacher education (B,M,D)

CAHIIM Commission on Accreditation for Health Informatics and Information Management Education: health information management and health informatics (A,B,M)

CARTE Commission on Accreditation of Recreational Therapy Education: recreational therapy (B,M)

CEA Commission on English Language Program Accreditation: english language (C)

CGTECH National Accrediting Agency for Clinical Laboratory Sciences: cytogenetic technologist (B)

CHIRO Council on Chiropractic Education: chiropractic education (FP,D)

CIDA Council for Interior Design Accreditation: interior design (B,M)

CLPSY American Psychological Association: clinical psychology (D)

CNCE Accrediting Council for Continuing Education and Training: continuing education (C,A)

COARC Commission on Accreditation for Respiratory Care: respiratory care (A,B,M)

COARCP Commission on Accreditation for Respiratory Care: polysomnography (C)

COE Council on Occupational Education: occupational, trade, and technical education (C,A)

COMTA Commission on Massage Therapy Accreditation: massage therapy, bodywork, aesthetics/esthetics and skin care (C,A)

CONST American Council for Construction Education: construction education (A,B)

COPSY American Psychological Association: counseling psychology (D)

COSME National Accrediting Commission of Career Arts and Sciences: cosmetology and massage therapy (C)

CS ABET, Inc.: computer science (B)

CSHSE Council for Standards in Human Services Education: human services (A,B,M)

CVT Commission on Accreditation of Allied Health Education Programs: cardiovascular technology (C,A,B)

CYTO Commission on Accreditation of Allied Health Education Programs: cytotechnology (C,B,M)

DA American Dental Association: dental assisting (C,A)

DANCE National Association of Schools of Dance: dance (C,A,B,M,D)

DEAC Distance Education and Accrediting Commission: home study schools (A,B,M,D)

DENT American Dental Association: dentistry (FP,D)

DH American Dental Association: dental hygiene (C,A,B,M)

DIETC Academy of Nutrition and Dietetics: coordinated dietetics programs (B,M)

DIETD Academy of Nutrition and Dietetics: didactic dietetics programs (B,M)

DIETI Academy of Nutrition and Dietetics: dietetic post-baccalaureate internships

DIETT Academy of Nutrition and Dietetics: dietetic technician (A)

DMOLS National Accrediting Agency for Clinical Laboratory Sciences: diagnostic molecular scientist (C,B,M)

DMS Commission on Accreditation of Allied Health Education Programs: diagnostic medical sonography (C,A,B,M)

DNUR Accreditation Commission for Education in Nursing: nursing (C)

DT American Dental Association: dental laboratory technology (C,A)

EMT Commission on Accreditation of Allied Health Education Programs: emergency medical technician-paramedic (C,A,B)

ENG ABET, Inc.: engineering (B,M)

ENGR ABET, Inc.: applied science (A,B,M)

ENGT ABET, Inc.: engineering technology (A,B)

EXSC Commission on Accreditation of Allied Health Education Programs: exercise science (C,B,M)

FEPAC American Academy of Forensic Sciences: forensic science (B,M)

FUSER American Board of Funeral Service Education: funeral service education (C,A,B)

HSA Commission on Accreditation of Healthcare Management Education: healthcare management (B,M)

HT National Accrediting Agency for Clinical Laboratory Sciences: histologic technology (C,A,B)

IACBE International Accreditation Council for Business Education: business programs in institutions that grant bachelor/graduate degrees (A,B,M,D)

IFSAC International Fire Service Accreditation Congress Degree Assembly: fire and emergency related degree (A,B)

IPSY American Psychological Association: doctoral internships in health service psychology

JOUR Accrediting Council on Education for Journalism and Mass Communications: journalism and mass communications (B,M)

KIN Commission on Accreditation of Allied Health Education Programs: kinesiotherapy (B)

LAW American Bar Association: law (FP,D)

LIB American Library Association: librarianship (M)

LSAR American Society for Landscape Architects: landscape architecture (B,M)

MAAB Accrediting Bureau of Health Education Schools: medical assisting (C,A)

MAC Commission on Accreditation of Allied Health Education Programs: medical assisting (C,A)

MACTE Montessori Accreditation Council for Teacher Education: Montessori teacher education (C)

MEAC Midwifery Education Accreditation Council: midwifery education (C,A,B,M,D)

MED Liaison Committee on Medical Education: medicine (FP,D)

MFCD American Association for Marriage and Family Therapy: marriage and family therapy (M,D)

MIDWF Accreditation Commission for Midwifery Education: nurse midwifery (C,M,D)

MIL Commission on Accreditation of Allied Health Education Programs: medical illustrator (M)

MLTAB Accrediting Bureau of Health Education Schools: medical laboratory technician (C,A)

MLTAD National Accrediting Agency for Clinical Laboratory Sciences: medical laboratory technician (C,A)

MT National Accrediting Agency for Clinical Laboratory Sciences: medical technology/laboratory scientist (C,B)

MUS National Association of Schools of Music: music (C,A,B,M,D)

NAIT The Association of Technology, Management, and Applied Engineering: technology, applied technology, engineering technology and technology-related programs (A,B,M)

NATUR Council on Naturopathic Medical Education: naturopathic medical education (FP,D)

NDT Commission on Accreditation of Allied Health Education Programs: neurodiagnostic technology (C,A)

NMT Joint Review Committee on Educational Programs in Nuclear Medicine Technology: nuclear medicine technology (C,A,B)

NRPA National Recreation and Park Association: recreation, park resources, and leisure studies (B)

NUR Accreditation Commission for Education in Nursing: nursing (B,M,D)

NURSE Commission on Collegiate Nursing Education: nursing (B,M,D)

NY New York State Board of Regents:
Degree-granting institutions of higher education in New York that designate the agency as their sole or primary nationally recognized accrediting agency for purposes of establishing elibility to participate in Higher Education Act programs

OPD Commission on Opticianry Accreditation: opticianry (A)

OPE Commission on Accreditation of Allied Health Education Programs: orthotics and prosthetics (C,B,M)

OPLT Commission on Opticianry Accreditation: opthalmic laboratory technician (C)

OPT American Optometric Association: optometry (FP,D)

OPTR American Optometric Association: optometric residency programs

OPTT American Optometric Association: optometric technician (C,A)

OSTEO American Osteopathic Association, Office of Osteopathic Education: osteopathic medicine (FP,D)

OT American Occupational Therapy Association: occupational therapy (M,D)

OTA American Occupational Therapy Association: occupational therapy assistant (C,A)

PA National Accrediting Agency for Clinical Laboratory Sciences: pathologist's assistant (C,M)

PAST Association for Clinical Pastoral Education: clinical pastoral education

PCSAS Psychological Clinical Science Accreditation System: psychological clinical science (D)

PDPSY American Psychological Association: post-doctorate residency in health service psychology

PERF Commission on Accreditation of Allied Health Education Programs: perfusionist (C,B,M)

PH Council on Education for Public Health: public health (B,M,D)

PHAR Accreditation Council for Pharmacy Education: pharmacy (FP,D)

PHLEB National Accrediting Agency for Clinical Laboratory Sciences: phlebotomist (C)

PLNG Planning Accreditation Board: certified planning (B,M)

PNUR Accreditation Commission for Education in Nursing: practical nursing (C)

POD American Podiatric Medical Association: podiatry (FP,D)

POLYT Commission on Accreditation of Allied Health Education Programs: polysomnographic technologist education (C,A)

PPPA Provisional Program Participation Agreement

PSPSY American Psychological Association: combined professional-scientific psychology (D)

PTA American Physical Therapy Association: physical therapy (M,D)

PTAA American Physical Therapy Association: physical therapy assistant (A)

RABN Association of Advanced Rabbinical and Talmudic Schools: rabbinical and Talmudic education (B,M,D)

RAD Joint Review Committee on Education in Radiologic Technology: radiography (C,A,B)

RADDOS Joint Review Committee on Education in Radiologic Technology: medical dosimetry (C,B,M)

RADMAG Joint Review Committee on Education in Radiologic Technology: magnetic resonance (C,B)

RTT Joint Review Committee on Education in Radiologic Technology: radiation therapist/technologist (C,A,B)

SCPSY American Psychological Association: school psychology (D)

SP American Speech-Language-Hearing Association: speech-language pathology (M)

SPAA Network of Schools of Public Policy, Affairs and Administration: public affairs and administration (M)

SURGA Commission on Accreditation of Allied Health Education Programs: surgical assistant (C,A)

SURGT Commission on Accreditation of Allied Health Education Programs: surgical technology (C,A)

SURTEC Accrediting Bureau of Health Education Schools: surgical technologist (C,A)

SW Council on Social Work Education: social work (B,M)

THEA National Association of Schools of Theatre: theatre (C,A,B,M,D)

THEOL Association of Theological Schools: theology (M,FP,D)

TRACS Transnational Association of Christian Colleges and Schools: christian studies education (C,A,B,M,D)

VET American Veterinary Medical Association: veterinary medicine (FP,D)

Explanatory Notes and Symbols

Associate degree: includes junior colleges, community colleges, technical institutes, and schools offering at least a two-year program of college-level studies, either leading to an associate degree wholly or principally creditable toward a baccalaureate degree.

Baccalaureate: includes those institutions offering programs of studies leading to the customary bachelor of arts or bachelor of science degrees.

First professional degree: includes those institutions that offer the academic requirements for selected professions based on programs that require at least two academic years of previous college work for entrance and a total of at least six years of college work for completion.

Master's: includes those institutions offering the customary first graduate degree, master of arts or master of science degree in the liberal arts and sciences, or the next degree in the same field after the first professional degree.

Beyond master's but less than doctorate: includes those institutions offering "postgraduate pre-doctoral degrees".

Graduate non-degree granting: includes institutions offering work beyond the bachelor's level but not conferring degrees. In some instances the degrees are conferred by cooperating institutions.

Doctorate: includes those institutions offering a Ph.D. or its equivalent in any field.

Postdoctoral research only: includes institutions operating solely for the purpose of research at the postdoctoral level.

First Talmudic degree: undergraduate degree granted by accredited Rabbinical schools. The schools in New York "using this designation do not imply that the 'First Talmudic Degree' is equivalent to any secular academic degree recognized by the Board of Regents".*

Second Talmudic degree: graduate degree granted by accredited Rabbinical schools. The schools in New York "using this designation do not imply that the 'Second Talmudic Degree' is equivalent to any secular academic degree recognized by the Board of Regents".*

---

*The University of the State of New York, The State Education Department, Albany, New York, letter August 17, 1983.

Symbols

* The institution is part of a system.

Used preceding any of the acronyms for the accrediting agencies the following symbols indicate that:

The accrediting agency has stated publicly that the institution or program is preliminary or provisionally accredited, accredited with some reservations, or approved on probation.

@ The institution or program has attained a pre-accredited status.

& The institution is covered under the regional accreditation of the parent institution.

U.S. Postal Abbreviation of States and Territories

Alabama	AL
Alaska	AK
American Samoa	AS
Arizona	AZ
Arkansas	AR
California	CA
Colorado	CO
Connecticut	CT
Delaware	DE
District of Columbia	DC
Florida	FL
Georgia	GA
Guam	GU
Hawaii	HI
Idaho	ID
Illinois	IL
Indiana	IN
Iowa	IA
Kansas	KS
Kentucky	KY
Louisiana	LA
Maine	ME
Maryland	MD
Marshall Islands	MH
Massachusetts	MA
Michigan	MI
Micronesia	FM
Minnesota	MN
Mississippi	MS
Missouri	MO
Montana	MT
Nebraska	NE
Nevada	NV
New Hampshire	NH
New Jersey	NJ
New Mexico	NM
New York	NY
North Carolina	NC
North Dakota	ND
Northern Marianas	MP
Ohio	OH
Oklahoma	OK
Oregon	OR
Palau	PW
Pennsylvania	PA
Puerto Rico	PR
Rhode Island	RI
South Carolina	SC
South Dakota	SD
Tennessee	TN
Texas	TX
Utah	UT
Vermont	VT
Virgin Islands	VI
Virginia	VA
Washington	WA
West Virginia	WV
Wisconsin	WI
Wyoming	WY

Institution Changes

Institutions and Offices Added

	FICE/ID Number
Alabama	
Alabama Community College System	667303
Arizona	
Indian Bible College	667317
Arkansas	
Arkansas College of Osteopathic Medicine	042568
Baptist Health College Little Rock	031052
California	
California Career College	039745
California Graduate School of Theology	667307
Eagle Rock College	041192
Ezra University	667316
Homestead Schools	041497
Institute for Business and Technology	021283
Institute of Buddhist Studies	667312
Kernel University	667308
Latin American Bible Institute	667319
Meridian University	667300
Reach Institute for School Leadership	667313
St. Luke University	667299
Trinity School of Health and Allied Sciences	041601
University of West Los Angeles	667301
Weimar Institute	667302
Colorado	
Auguste Escoffier School of Culinary Arts	037763
District of Columbia	
Daniel Morgan Academy	667304
Educatore School of Education	667305
Florida	
Emergency Educational Institute	667310
Universal Career School	038563
Georgia	
Athens College of Ministry	667306
Helms College	042064
Indiana	
American National University	770696
Caris College	667314
St. Vincent College of Health Professions	667315
Minnesota	
Red Lake Nation College	667311
New Jersey	
Yeshiva Gedolah of Cliffwood	667322
New York	
Bais Medrash Ateres Shlomo	667321
Mechon L'Hoyroa	042615
North Carolina	
Southeastern Free Will Baptist College	667309
Pennsylvania	
Institute of Medical and Business Careers	041551
South Dakota	
Institute of Lutheran Theology	667318
Texas	
Auguste Escoffier School of Culinary Arts	037276
Christ Mission College	667320
Virginia	
Stratford University Alexandria Campus	770856
Stratford University Virginia Beach Campus	770857

Institutions and Offices Dropped

	FICE/ID Number
Alabama	
Brown Mackie College - Birmingham *(Closed)*	770625
Fortis College *(No longer degree granting)*	023410
Fortis College-Montgomery (Eastdale Circle) *(Main campus no longer offers degree)*	770512
Legacy Christian University *(No longer accredited by ABHE)*	667251
Southeastern Bible College *(Closed)*	022704
University of Phoenix Birmingham Campus *(Closed)*	770187
Arizona	
Brown Mackie College-Phoenix *(Closed)*	666782
Coconino County Community College Page/Lake Powell Campus *(No longer listed as a branch with NH)*	770006
Le Cordon Bleu College of Culinary Arts in Scottsdale *(Closed)*	026167
Tohono O'odham Community College West Campus *(No longer listed as a branch with NH)*	770022
Arkansas	
University of Phoenix Little Rock Campus *(Closed)*	770188

Institution Changes

FICE/ID Number

California

Allied American University 041893
(Closed)

Bristol University 033083
(No longer ACICS accredited)

Casa Loma College-Anaheim 770519
(Closed)

Herguan University 667236
(No longer accredited by ACICS)

Institute of Technology 770555
(No longer degree granting)

International Professional School of Bodywork 041347
(Closed)

Le Cordon Bleu College of Culinary Arts 022202
(Closed)

Le Cordon Bleu College of Culinary Arts in Los Angeles 032103
(Closed)

Nine Star University of Health Sciences 667207
(No longer accredited by ACUP)

Sage College 030695
(Closed)

SBBCollege Santa Barbara 666099
(Closed)

South Baylo University 770911
(No longer listed as a branch with WC)

The Art Institute of California, A College of Argosy University - Los Angel 666045
(Closed)

The Art Institute of California, A College of Argosy University - Sunnyvale 666620
(Closed)

Colorado

Colorado Heights University 032893
(Closed)

Colorado School of Healing Arts 035844
(No longer degree granting)

Heritage College 026110
(Closed)

National American University-Denver 770392
(Closed)

William Loveland College 667234
(No longer accredited by DEAC)

Florida

Azure College 770981
(Closed)

Bay Medical Center 011127
(No longer accredited by ANEST)

Brown Mackie College-Miami 666110
(Closed)

Digital Media Arts College 041274
(Closed)

Everest University-Brandon Campus 666416
(Closed)

Everest University-Largo 025998
(Closed)

Everest University-Melbourne Campus 666417
(Closed)

Everest University-Orange Park 666590
(No longer degree granting)

Everest University-Pompano Beach Campus 008146
(Closed)

Everest University-South Orlando Campus 666418
(Closed)

Everest University-Tampa Campus 007735
(No longer degree granting)

FICE/ID Number

Florida Career College 770680
(No longer accredited by ACICS)

Fortis Institute-Pensacola 770513
(Main campus no longer offers degree)

Heritage Institute-Fort Myers 025971
(Closed)

Heritage Institute-Jacksonville 030358
(Closed)

Jones College 001497
(Closed)

Le Cordon Bleu College of Culinary Arts in Miami 666369
(Closed)

Le Cordon Bleu College of Culinary Arts in Orlando 666064
(Closed)

Sanford-Brown College Tampa 030314
(Closed)

Sanford-Brown Institute 026164
(Closed)

Touro College South 770147
(Closed)

Georgia

Brown Mackie College-Atlanta 026214
(Closed)

Le Cordon Bleu College of Culinary Arts in Atlanta 666298
(Closed)

University of Phoenix Savannah Campus 770201
(Closed)

Idaho

Brown Mackie College-Boise 666780
(Closed)

University of Phoenix Idaho Campus 770204
(Closed)

Illinois

Carl Sandburg College The Extension Center 770070
(No longer listed as a branch with NH)

Ellis University 041433
(Closed)

Illinois Institute of Technology Institute of Design 770076
(No longer listed as a branch with NH)

Knowledge Systems Institute 026227
(Resigned accreditation from NH)

Le Cordon Bleu College of Culinary Arts in Chicago 023522
(Closed)

Prince Institute - Southeast 022960
(Closed)

Roosevelt University Albert A. Robin Campus 770092
(No longer listed as a branch with NH)

Sanford-Brown College 021603
(Closed)

SOLEX College 045816
(No longer degree granting)

Southwestern Illinois College Red Bud Campus 770096
(No longer listed as a branch with NH)

Southwestern Illinois College Sam Wolf Granite City Campus 770095
(No longer listed as a branch with NH)

Indiana

American National University 010489
(Closed)

Brown Mackie College-Indianapolis 666394
(Closed)

Brown Mackie College-Merrillville 021032
(Closed)

	FICE/ID Number
Brown Mackie College-South Bend *(Closed)*	004583
Harrison College - Elkhart Campus *(Closed)*	666143
MJS College School of Nursing *(voluntary withdrawal from ACICS)*	667272
Ottawa University Jeffersonville *(Closed)*	666088
Saint Joseph's College *(Closed)*	001833
Trine University-Fort Wayne Regional Campus *(No longer listed as a branch with NH)*	770105
Trine University-South Bend Regional Campus *(No longer listed as a branch with NH)*	770106
University of Phoenix Indianapolis Campus *(Closed)*	770206

Iowa

Brown Mackie College-Quad Cities *(No longer accredited by ACICS/now Ross (ABHES) but main campus is non-degree)*	666792
Iowa Western Community College Clarinda Center *(No longer listed as a branch with NH)*	770057

Kansas

Barton County Community College Fort Riley Campus *(No longer listed as a branch with NH)*	770251
Brown Mackie College-Kansas City *(Closed)*	666091
Heritage College-Wichita *(Closed)*	770529
Pinnacle Career Institute *(Closed)*	026130
Southwestern College Wichita East *(No longer listed as a branch with NH)*	770260
University of Kansas Edwards Campus *(No longer listed as a branch with NH)*	770261

Kentucky

Brown Mackie College-Hopkinsville *(No longer accredited by ACICS/now Ross (ABHES) but main campus is non-degree)*	666516
Brown Mackie College-Northern Kentucky *(Closed)*	666446
Daymar College Online *(Closed)*	770615
Daymar College-Bellevue *(No longer accredited by ACICS)*	666390
Daymar College-Madisonville *(No longer accredited by ACICS)*	667079
Daymar College-Owensboro *(Closed)*	009313

Louisiana

Blue Cliff College *(No longer degree granting)*	032943
University of Phoenix Baton Rouge Campus *(Closed)*	770208

Massachusetts

Le Cordon Bleu College of Culinary Arts in Cambridge *(Closed)*	770576

Michigan

	FICE/ID Number
Grand Valley State University Meijer Campus *(No longer listed as a branch with NH)*	770275
Grand Valley State University Pew Campus *(No longer listed as a branch with NH)*	770274
Kalamazoo Valley Community College Arcadia Commons Campus *(No longer listed as a branch with NH)*	770276

Minnesota

Crossroads College *(Closed)*	002366
Globe University *(Closed)*	004642
Globe University *(Closed)*	770717
Globe University *(Closed)*	770734
Le Cordon Bleu College of Culinary Arts in Minneapolis/St Paul *(Closed)*	666370
Metropolitan State University *(No longer listed as a branch with NH)*	770301
Minnesota School of Business *(Closed)*	770715
Minnesota School of Business *(Closed)*	770716
Minnesota School of Business *(No longer accredited by ACICS)*	770718
Minnesota School of Business *(Closed)*	770719
Minnesota School of Business *(Closed)*	666453
Minnesota School of Business *(Closed)*	770713
Sanford-Brown College *(Closed)*	770733
Sanford-Brown College-Mendota Heights *(Closed)*	007351
University of Phoenix Minneapolis/St. Paul Campus *(Closed)*	770212

Mississippi

Miller-Motte Technical College *(Closed)*	770845
University of Phoenix Jackson Campus *(Closed)*	770215

Missouri

Brown Mackie College-St. Louis *(Closed)*	666793
Court Reporting Institute of St. Louis *(Closed)*	770617
Heritage College *(Closed)*	666155
Missouri College *(Closed)*	009795
University of Phoenix Kansas City Campus *(Closed)*	770213
Wentworth Military Academy and College *(Closed)*	002522

Nevada

Le Cordon Bleu College of Culinary Arts in Las Vegas *(Closed)*	666303

Institution Changes

	FICE/ID Number
Sanford-Brown College *(Closed)*	770744

New Hampshire

Daniel Webster College *(Closed)*	004731

New York

Bramson ORT College *(Closed)*	021068
LIU Hudson at Rockland *(Closed)*	666077
New York Career Institute *(Closed)*	021634
SBI Campus-An Affiliate of Sanford-Brown *(Closed)*	011647
Technical Career Institutes *(Closed)*	011031
The Art Institute of New York City *(Closed)*	025256
Yeshiva and Kollel Harbotzas Torah *(Voluntary withdrawal from AARTS)*	023506
Yeshiva Mikdash Melech *(Voluntary withdrawal from AARTS)*	025068

North Carolina

Charlotte School of Law *(Closed)*	041435

Ohio

American National University *(Closed)*	770699
American National University *(Closed)*	770703
American National University *(Closed)*	770702
American National University *(Closed)*	770698
American National University *(Closed)*	770700
Bexley Seabury *(Closed)*	037473
Brown Mackie College-Cincinnati *(Closed)*	005127
Brown Mackie College-Findlay *(Closed)*	026162
Brown Mackie College-North Canton *(No longer accredited by ACICS/now Ross (ABHES) but main campus is non-degree)*	030778
Miami-Jacobs Career College *(Closed)*	770757
Miami-Jacobs Career College *(Closed)*	770755
Ohio Business College *(Closed)*	030658
Ohio College of Massotherapy *(No longer accredited by ACCSC)*	031163
Trumbull Business College *(Closed)*	020543
University of Phoenix Cleveland Main Campus *(Closed)*	770238

Oklahoma

	FICE/ID Number
Brown Mackie College-Oklahoma City *(Closed)*	770252
Brown Mackie College-Tulsa *(Closed)*	666783
Career Point College *(Closed)*	770761
Comanche Nation College *(Closed)*	667123
Eastern Oklahoma State College McAlester Campus *(No longer listed as a branch with NH)*	770368
Heritage College *(Closed)*	031151
McCurtain County Higher Education Center *(No longer listed as a branch with NH)*	770369
Northern Oklahoma College *(No longer listed as a branch with NH)*	770375
Northern Oklahoma College *(No longer listed as a branch with NH)*	770374
Northwestern Oklahoma State University *(No longer listed as a branch with NH)*	770377
Northwestern Oklahoma State University *(No longer listed as a branch with NH)*	770376
Platt College *(No longer degree granting)*	770584
Platt College *(No longer degree granting)*	770971
Southwestern Oklahoma State University-Sayre *(No longer listed as a branch with NH)*	770382

Oregon

Le Cordon Bleu College of Culinary Arts in Portland *(Closed)*	030226

Pennsylvania

Allegany College of Maryland Somerset County Campus *(Closed)*	770123
Consolidated School of Business *(Closed)*	030299
Keystone Technical Institute *(Closed)*	022342
Orleans Technical College *(No longer degree granting)*	021830
The Art Institute of York - Pennsylvania *(Closed)*	025578

South Dakota

Globe University *(Closed)*	770780

Tennessee

American National University *(Closed)*	770786
National College *(Closed)*	770784

Texas

Brown Mackie College - Dallas/Ft. Worth *(Closed)*	770798
Career Point College *(Closed)*	025911
DeVry University - Houston Campus *(Closed)*	666219
Everest College *(No longer degree granting)*	770790
Le Cordon Bleu College of Culinary Arts in Austin *(Closed)*	025693

FICE/ID Number

Le Cordon Bleu College of Culinary Arts in Dallas 666728
(Closed)
Lutheran Seminary Program of the Southwest 770081
(No longer listed as a branch with NH)
National American University-South Austin 770412
(No longer listed as a branch with NH)
Sanford-Brown College 666733
(Closed)
The Art Institute of Fort Worth 770918
(Closed)
University of Phoenix Austin Campus 770226
(Closed)

Virginia

American College of Commerce and Technology 667273
(No longer accredited by ACICS)
American National University 666505
(Closed)
Everest College 667298
(Closed)
Everest College 009267
(Closed)
University of Phoenix Richmond-Virginia Beach Campus 770233
(Closed)

Washington

Sanford-Brown College 666265
(Closed)

West Virginia

Marshall University-South Charleston Campus 770467
(No longer listed as a branch with NH)
Potomac State College of West Virginia University 003829
(No longer listed as a branch with NH)
West Virginia Business College 666507
(Closed)
West Virginia Business College 010861
(Closed)
West Virginia University Institute of Technology 003825
(No longer listed as a branch with NH)

Wisconsin

Chippewa Valley Technical College-Chippewa Falls Campus 770419
(No longer listed as a branch with NH)
Fox Valley Technical College 770425
(No longer listed as a branch with NH)
Globe University-Appleton 770800
(Closed)
Globe University-Eau Claire 770801
(Closed)
Globe University-La Crosse 770803
(Closed)
Globe University-Madison East 770804
(Closed)
Globe University-Wausau 770806
(Closed)
University of Phoenix Milwaukee Main Campus 770235
(Closed)

Wyoming

CollegeAmerica Cheyenne 770609
(Closed)

FICE/ID Number

Merged Institutions

Alabama

Alabama Southern Community College *into* 001034
Coastal Alabama Community College 001060
Jefferson Davis Community College *into* 001021
Coastal Alabama Community College 001060

California

SBBCollege Online *into* 770628
SBBCollege Ventura 009989

Georgia

Darton State College *into* 001543
Albany State University 001544

Illinois

Shimer College *into* 001756
North Central College 001734

Massachusetts

Episcopal Divinity School *into* 002149
Union Theological Seminary 002890

Pennsylvania

Lutheran Theological Seminary at Philadelphia *into* 003292
United Lutheran Seminary 003291
Palmer Theological Seminary of Eastern University *into* 003260
Eastern University 003259
Philadelphia University *into* 003354
Thomas Jefferson University 012393

Washington

Pinchot University *into* 041612
Presidio Graduate School 667150

Wisconsin

Rasmussen College - Appleton *into* 667059
Rasmussen College - Green Bay 667063

Name Changes

Alabama

from: James H. Faulkner State Community College 001060
to: Coastal Alabama Community College

Arizona

from: Chamberlain College of Nursing-Phoenix Campus 770502
to: Chamberlain University-Phoenix

Institution Changes

FICE/ID Number

Arkansas

	FICE/ID Number
from: Pulaski Technical College *to:* University of Arkansas - Pulaski Technical College	020753
from: Rich Mountain Community College *to:* University of Arkansas Rich Mountain	021111

California

	FICE/ID Number
from: Academy of Couture Art *to:* Beverly Hills Design Institute	041855
from: American Evangelical University *to:* America Evangelical University	667090
from: California Northstate University College of Pharmacy *to:* California Northstate University	667020
from: Chamberlain College of Nursing-Sacramento *to:* Chamberlain University-Sacramento	770978
from: Dongguk University *to:* Dongguk University Los Angeles	031095
from: El Camino College Compton Center *to:* Compton College	001188
from: Ex'pression College *to:* SAE Expression College	039733
from: Ex'pression College - San Jose *to:* SAE Institute - San Jose	770552
from: Humphreys College *to:* Humphreys University	001212
from: META Business School *to:* California Institute of Management and Technology	667286
from: Palmer College of Chiropractic, San Jose Campus *to:* Palmer College of Chiropractic, West Campus	021849
from: Stanbridge College *to:* Stanbridge University	038893
from: The Master's College and Seminary *to:* The Master's University	001220

Colorado

	FICE/ID Number
from: Colorado Mountain College Summit Campus-Breckinridge Campus *to:* Colorado Mountain College Summit Campus-Breckinridge Center	770033
from: Colorado Mountain College Vail/Eagle Valley Campus *to:* Colorado Mountain College Vail Valley Campus at Edwards	770034
from: Everest College *to:* Altierus Career College	004503
from: Everest College *to:* Altierus Career College	004507
from: Redstone College *to:* Spartan College	007297

Florida

	FICE/ID Number
from: Advance Science Institute *to:* Advance Science College	037573
from: Chamberlain College of Nursing-Jacksonville Campus *to:* Chamberlain University-Jacksonville	770501
from: Chamberlain College of Nursing-Miramar *to:* Chamberlain University-Miramar	770498
from: Keiser University *to:* Keiser University-Jacksonville Campus	770902
from: Palmer College of Chiropractic, Port Orange Campus *to:* Palmer College of Chiropractic, Florida Campus	666330
from: Thomas M. Cooley Law School Tampa Bay Campus *to:* WMU - Cooley Law School Tampa Bay Campus	770290

Georgia

	FICE/ID Number
from: Chamberlain College of Nursing-Atlanta *to:* Chamberlain University-Atlanta	770504
from: Truett McConnell College *to:* Truett McConnell University	001597

Idaho

	FICE/ID Number
from: Eastern Idaho Technical College *to:* College of Eastern Idaho	011133

Illinois

	FICE/ID Number
from: Blessing-Rieman College of Nursing *to:* Blessing-Rieman College of Nursing & Health Sciences	006214
from: Chamberlain College of Nursing-Addison *to:* Chamberlain University-Addison	006385
from: Chamberlain College of Nursing-Administrative Office *to:* Chamberlain University-Administrative Office	667149
from: Chamberlain College of Nursing-Chicago *to:* Chamberlain University-Chicago	770495
from: Chamberlain College of Nursing-Tinley Park *to:* Chamberlain University-Tinley Park	770496
from: Greenville College *to:* Greenville University	001684
from: Illinois Institute of Technology Chicago-Kent College of Law *to:* Illinois Institute of Technology Downtown Campus	770075
from: Loyola University Water Town Campus *to:* Loyola University Water Tower Campus	770079

Indiana

	FICE/ID Number
from: Chamberlain College of Nursing-Indianapolis Campus *to:* Chamberlain University-Indianapolis Campus	770503
from: Ivy Tech Community College of Indiana-Central Office *to:* Ivy Tech Community College of Indiana-System Office	008546

Iowa

	FICE/ID Number
from: Waldorf College *to:* Waldorf University	001895

Louisiana

	FICE/ID Number
from: Career Technical College *to:* McCann School of Business and Technology	770723
from: Our Lady of the Lake College *to:* Franciscan Missionaries of Our Lady University	031062

Maine

	FICE/ID Number
from: University of Maine System Office *to:* University of Maine System	008012

Michigan

	FICE/ID Number
from: Chamberlain College of Nursing-Troy *to:* Chamberlain University-Troy	770851

FICE/ID Number

from: Wayne County Community College District Western Campus — 770294
to: Wayne County Community College District Ted Scott Campus

Minnesota

from: Minnesota State College-Southeast Technical — 002393
to: Minnesota State College Southeast

from: Northland Community and Technical College-East Grand Forks — 770311
to: Northland Community and Technical College East Grand Forks Campus

from: University of Minnesota-Rochester Campus — 770316
to: University of Minnesota Rochester

from: University of Minnesota-Twin Cities — 003969
to: University of Minnesota

Missouri

from: Chamberlain College of Nursing-St. Louis — 770494
to: Chamberlain University-St. Louis

from: Saint Louis Community College Center — 002471
to: Saint Louis Community College - Cosand Center

from: Three Rivers Community College — 004713
to: Three Rivers College

Montana

from: The University of Montana - Missoula College — 007561
to: Missoula College-University of Montana

from: University of Great Falls — 002527
to: University of Providence

Nebraska

from: Doane College — 770333
to: Doane University

from: Doane College — 770334
to: Doane University

Nevada

from: Chamberlain College of Nursing-Las Vegas — 770852
to: Chamberlain University-Las Vegas

from: Everest College — 022375
to: Altierus Career College

New Jersey

from: Centenary College — 002599
to: Centenary University

from: Chamberlain College of Nursing-North Brunswick — 770850
to: Chamberlain University-North Brunswick

from: Rutgers the State University of New Jersey Camden Campus — 004741
to: Rutgers University - Camden

from: Rutgers the State University of New Jersey New Brunswick Campus — 006964
to: Rutgers University - New Brunswick

from: Rutgers the State University of New Jersey Newark Campus — 002631
to: Rutgers University - Newark

New Mexico

from: Navajo Technical College — 023576
to: Navajo Technical University

FICE/ID Number

New York

from: Beth Benjamin Academy of Connecticut — 029120
to: Bais Binyomin Academy, Inc

from: Elim Bible Institute — 667245
to: Elim Bible Institute and College

from: Phillips Beth Israel School of Nursing — 006438
to: Phillips School of Nursing at Mount Sinai Beth Israel

from: Syracuse University Main Campus — 002882
to: Syracuse University

North Carolina

from: Chamberlain College of Nursing-Charlotte — 770979
to: Chamberlain University-Charlotte

Ohio

from: Chamberlain College of Nursing-Cleveland — 770505
to: Chamberlain University-Cleveland

from: Chamberlain College of Nursing-Columbus Campus — 770499
to: Chamberlain University-Columbus

from: Kent State University Main Campus — 003051
to: Kent State University Kent Campus

from: Ohio Business College, Lorain Branch — 021585
to: Ohio Business College

Oklahoma

from: Family of Faith College — 036763
to: Family of Faith Christian University

from: Oklahoma Wesleyan University — 770378
to: Oklahoma Wesleyan University Tulsa Campus

Pennsylvania

from: Clarion University Venango College — 003319
to: Clarion University, Venango

from: Dickinson Law — 003254
to: Penn State Dickinson Law

from: Harrisburg Area Community College — 003273
to: HACC, Central Pennsylvania's Community College

from: Hussian School of Art — 007469
to: Hussian College

from: Kaplan Career Institute — 770766
to: Brightwood Career Institute

from: Lutheran Theological Seminary at Gettysburg — 003291
to: United Lutheran Seminary

from: Pittsburgh Technical Institute — 007437
to: Pittsburgh Technical College

from: Rosedale Technical Institute — 012050
to: Rosedale Technical College

from: Summit University of Pennsylvania — 002670
to: Clarks Summit University

from: The Commonwealth Medical College — 041672
to: Geisinger Commonwealth School of Medicine

Puerto Rico

from: Centro de Estudios Multidisciplinarios — 021891
to: CEM College

from: Centro de Estudios Multidisciplinarios — 770591
to: CEM College

from: Centro de Estudios Multidisciplinarios — 770590
to: CEM College

from: Centro de Estudios Multidisciplinarios — 770589
to: CEM College

FICE/ID Number

Tennessee

from: Tennessee Wesleyan College 003525
to: Tennessee Wesleyan University

Texas

from: Arlington Baptist College 020814
to: Arlington Baptist University

from: Cardiotech Ultrasound School 041385
to: Houston International College-Cardiotech Ultrasound School

from: Chamberlain College of Nursing-Houston Campus 770500
to: Chamberlain University-Houston

from: Chamberlain College of Nursing-Irving 770853
to: Chamberlain University-Irving

from: Chamberlain College of Nursing-Pearland 770934
to: Chamberlain University-Pearland

from: Everest College 770788
to: Altierus Career College

from: Houston College of Law 004977
to: South Texas College of Law Houston

from: National American University Harold D. Buckingham Graduate School 770931
to: Roueche Graduate Center of National American University

from: Redeemer Theological Seminary 667055
to: Reformed Theological Seminary

Utah

from: Uintah Basin Applied Technology College 011165
to: Uintah Basin Technical College

Virginia

from: Chamberlain College of Nursing-Arlington Campus 770497
to: Chamberlain University-Arlington Campus

from: Institute for the Psychological Sciences 038724
to: Divine Mercy University

from: Mary Baldwin College 003723
to: Mary Baldwin University

from: Stratford University 770819
to: Stratford University Glen Allen Campus

from: Stratford University 770817
to: Stratford University Woodbridge Campus

from: Stratford University 770818
to: Stratford University Newport News Campus

from: Virginia Wesleyan College 003767
to: Virginia Wesleyan University

Washington

from: Faith Evangelical College & Seminary 036894
to: Faith International University

from: South Seattle Community College 009706
to: South Seattle College

West Virginia

from: Future Generations Graduate School 666714
to: Future Generations

from: New River Technical College Greenbrier Valley Campus 770468
to: New River Community and Technical College Greenbrier Valley Campus

FICE/ID Number

Wisconsin

from: Lakeland College 003854
to: Lakeland University

Wyoming

from: Institute of Business and Medical Careers 666738
to: IBMC College/Institute of Business and Medical Careers

Codes and Descriptions of Administrative Officers

We have modified the Manpower Codes used in the *Higher Education Directory* to better reflect the organizational structures of colleges and universities. Codes are now grouped by major organizational divisionäExecutive, Academic, External Affairs, Fiscal Affairs, Institutional Affairs, Information Technology, and Student Affairs. Some codes have been redefined and several have been added. New and modified codes are marked by an asterisk (*).

Executive

(01) **Chief Executive Officer (President/Chancellor)** - Directs all affairs and operations of a higher education institution.

(02) **Chief Executive Officer Within a System (President/ Chancellor)** - Directs all affairs and operations of a campus or an institution which is part of a university-wide system.

(03) **Executive Vice President** - Responsible for all or most functions and operations of an institution under the direction of the Chief Executive Officer.

(100) **Chief of Staff** - Senior non-secretarial staff assistant to the President/Chancellor. Manages administration and operations of The Office of the President.

(00)* **Chairman of the Board** - Directs the operations of the institutionÖs Board of Directors.

(101) **Secretary of the Institution/Board of Governors** - Responsible for liaison between the Board and the institution. Maintains governance and official Board records.

(125)* **President/Chancellor Emeritus** - A past chief executive currently holding an advisory or honorary position at the institution.

(17) **Chief of Health Care Professions** - Senior administrator of academic health care programs, hospitals, clinic or affiliated health-care programs.

(12) **Director of Branch Campus** - Official who is in charge of a branch campus.

(04) **Administrative Assistant to the President** - Senior administrative assistant to the Chief Executive Officer.

(41) **Athletic Director** - Manages intramural and intercollegiate programs including employment, scheduling, promotion, maintenance and related functions.

Academic Affairs

(05) **Chief Academic Officer** - Directs the academic program of the institution. Typically includes academic planning, teaching, research, extensions and coordination of interdepartmental affairs. May include Provost.

(20) **Associate Academic Officer** - Responsible for many of the functions and operations under the direction of the Chief Academic Officer.

(08) **Chief Library Officer** - Directs the activities of all institutional libraries.

Dean or Director. Serves as the principal administrator for the institutional program indicated:

(47) **Agriculture**
(76) **Allied Health Sciences**
(48) **Architecture**
(49) **Art and Sciences**
(50) **Business**
(77) **Computer Science**
(51) **Continuing Education**
(78) **Cooperative Education**
(52) **Dentistry**
(53) **Education**
(54) **Engineering**
(55) **Evening Division**
(56) **Extension**
(57) **Fine Arts**
(97) **General Studies**
(80) **Government/Public Affairs**
(58) **Graduate Programs**
(59) **Home Economics**
(92) **Honors Program**
(79) **Humanities**
(60) **Journalism/Communications**
(61) **Law**
(62) **Library Services**
(81) **Mathematics/Sciences**
(63) **Medicine**
(64) **Music**
(65) **Natural Resources**
(66) **Nursing**
(75) **Vocational/Occupational Education**
(106) **Online Education/E-learning**
(67) **Pharmacy**
(68) **Physical Education**
(82) **Political Science/International Affairs**
(107) **Professional Studies**
(69) **Public Health**
(83) **Social and Behavioral Sciences**
(70) **Social Work**
(87) **Summer School/Session**
(71) **Special Session**
(72) **Technology**
(73) **Theology**
(74) **Veterinary Medicine**
(94) **Women's Studies**

External Affairs

(111)* **Director of Institutional Advancement** - Responsible for the comprehensive plan to ensure ongoing growth in public awareness of an institution and its strategic goals.

(30) **Chief Development/Advancement Officer** - Organizes and directs programs connected with the fund raising activities of the institution. May include Advancement.

(110)* **Associate Advancement/Development Officer** - Assists and supports the Chief Development Officer.

(29) **Director of Alumni Relations** - Coordinates alumni activities between the institution and the alumni.

(44) **Director of Annual or Planned Giving** - Operates the annual giving from all supporters of the institutions.

(112)* **Director Planned Giving/Major Gifts** - Identifies, cultivates and solicits planned and major gifts for ongoing fi nancial support.

(102) **Director of Foundation/Corporate Relations** - Directs institution's efforts in the area of soliciting grants and gifts from foundations and corporations.

(26) **Chief Public Relations/Marketing/Communications Officer** - Directs public relations program. May include alumni relations, publication, marketing and development.

(27) **Associate Public Relations/Marketing/Communications Officer** - Assists and reports to the Chief Public Relations/Marketing/ Communications Officer.

(31) **Chief Community Relations Officer** - Directs the educational (usually non-credit), cultural and recreational services to the community.

(103) **Director of Workforce Development** - Directs the institution's efforts in course development and instruction for students and the community in skills necessary to gain employment.

Fiscal Affairs

(10) **Chief Financial/Business Officer** - Directs business and financial affairs including accounting, purchasing, investments, auxiliary enterprises and related business matters.

(21) **Associate Business Officer** - Assists and reports to the Chief Business Officer. May include Controller.

(45) **Chief Institutional Planning Officer** - Directs the long-range planning and the allocation of the institution's resources.

(115)* **Chief Investment Officer** - Responsible for the oversight of the endowment and other financial assets of the college.

(25) **Chief Contract and Grants Administrator** - Conducts administrative activities in connection with contracts and grants.

(109) **Chief Auxiliary Services Officer** - Responsible for management and operations of college support services including food service, bookstore, vending, student union, and printing.

(114)* **Chief Budget Administrator** - Responsible for preparation and management of institutional budgets.

(113)* **Bursar** - Responsible for the overall operations of student financial services including billing, receivables and cashiering functions.

(96) **Director of Purchasing** - Coordinates purchasing of goods and services.

(116)* **Audit Officer** - Responsible for independent assessment of the effectiveness of internal administrative accounting controls and helps ensure conformance with managerial policies.

(40) **Director of Bookstore** - Responsible for the operation of the bookstore including purchasing, advertising, sales, employment, inventory and related functions.

Institutional Affairs

(11) **Chief of Operations/Administration** - Responsible for administrative functions that are generally non-academic and non-financial.

(117)* **Chief Risk Management Officer** - Responsible for the oversight of the collegeÖs risk management programs including emergency and crisis response management, operational risk, technology and cyber risks, insurance and facility vulnerability, and threat assessment.

(15) **Chief Human Resources Officer** - Administers the institution's personnel policies and programs for staff or faculty and staff.

(16) **Associate Human Resources Officer** - Assists and reports to the Chief Human Resources Officer.

(118)* **Director Employee Benefits** - Manages the collegeÖs compensation and benefit programs, policies and procedures.

(09) **Director of Institutional Research** - Conducts research and studies on the institution including design of studies, data collection, analysis and reporting.

(46) **Chief Research Officer** - Initiates and directs research in using the facilities and personnel in new areas of academic and scientific exploration.

(108) **Director of Institutional Assessment** - Facilitates and directs institution-wide assessment activities for academic programs and non-academic departments.

(22) **Director of Affirmative Action/Equal Opportunity** - Responsible for the institution's program relating to affirmative action and equal opportunity.

(28) **Director of Diversity** - Responsible for the institution's diversity programs.

(43) **Director of Legal Services (General Counsel)** - Salaried staff person responsible for advising on legal rights, obligations and related matters.

(19) **Director of Security/Safety** - Manages campus police. Responsible for security programs, training, traffic and parking regulations.

(18) **Chief Facilities/Physical Plant Officer** - Responsible for the construction, rehabilitation and maintenance of buildings and grounds.

(86) **Director of Government Relations** - Coordinates institution's relations with local, state, and federal government.

Information Technology (IT)

(13) **Chief Information Technology Officer (CIO)** - Responsible for oversight of IT infrastructure and support, computation and communication infrastructure and services, and administrative information systems across the institution.

(14) **Associate Information Technology Officer** - Assists and reports to the Chief Information Officer.

(24) **Director of Educational Media** - Responsible for audio-visual services and multi-media learning devices.

(90) **Director of Academic Computing** - Responsible for operation and coordination of the institution's various academic computer facilities and labs.

(91) **Director of Administrative Computing** - Responsible for operation of the institution's administrative computing facility.

(105) **Director of Web Services** - Directs the development, operations and content of the institution's web sites.

(119)* **Director of IT Security** - Responsible for technology security in order to protect information and prevent unauthorized access.

(120)* **Director of Online/E-learning Platform** - Coordinates all aspects of institutionÖs online learning platforms.

Student Affairs

(32) **Chief Student Affairs/Student Life Officer** - Responsible for the direction of student life programs including counseling and testing, housing, placement, student union, relationships with student organizations and related functions.

(35) **Associate Student Affairs/Student Life Officer** - Assists Chief Student Life Officer in the non-academic student life activities.

(84) **Director of Enrollment Management** - Plans, develops, and implements strategies to sustain enrollment. Supervises administration of all admissions and financial aid operations.

(07) **Director of Admissions** - Responsible for the recruitment, selection and admission of students.

(123)* **Director of Graduate Admissions** - Responsible for the recruitment, selection and admission of graduate students.

(06) **Registrar** - Responsible for student registration, scheduling of classes, examinations and classroom facilities, student records and related matters.

(37) **Director of Student Financial Aid** - Directs the administration of all forms of student aid.

(39) **Director of Student Housing** - Manages student housing operations.

(36) **Director of Student Placement** - Directs the operation of the student placement office to provide career counseling and job placement services to undergraduates, graduates and alumni.

(38) **Director of Student Counseling** - Directs non-academic counseling and testing for students including referral to outside agencies.

(121)* **Director of Student Success/Academic Advising** - assists students in the development and ongoing achievement of their educational goals through academic support and planning.

(124)* **Director of Student Retention** - Develops and evaluates programs and initiatives to improve student retention, engagement and transition.

(89) **Director of First Year Experience** - Works with academic and students affairs to facilitate freshman engagement, learning, transition and integration into the college community.

(93) **Director of Minority Education/Students** - Develops and supports the overall success of students, particularly those from underrepresented minority groups.

(23) **Director of Health Services** - Directs the operation of clinics, medical staff and other programs which provide institutional health services.

(42) **Chaplain/Director Campus Ministry** - Plans, directs the pastoral ministry and religious activities.

(85) **Director of Foreign Students** - Directs student life activities solely concerned with foreign students.

(104) **Director of Study Abroad** - Coordinates and advises students and faculty on academic studies conducted internationally.

(33) **Dean of Men** - Directs student life activities solely concerned with male students.

(34) **Dean of Women** - Directs student life activities solely concerned with female students.

(122)* **Director of Greek Life** - Responsible for all aspects of fraternity and sorority life on campus.

Other

(88) Use this code for those titles that do not fit the above positions.

United States Department of Education Offices

Betsy DeVos (A)
Secretary of Education
United States Department of Education
400 Maryland Avenue, SW
Washington, DC 20202
(202) 401-3000
FAX: (202) 260-7867
URL: www.ed.gov

Mr. James Manning (B)
Acting Under Secretary of Education
United States Department of Education
400 Maryland Avenue, SW
Room 7E307
Washington, DC 20202
(202) 453-6236
URL: sites.ed.gov/ous/

Lynn Mahaffie (C)
Dpty Asst Secretary for Policy/Planning/Innovation
Office of Postsecondary Education
United States Department of Education
400 Maryland Avenue, SW
Room 6C107
Washington, DC 20202
(202) 453-7862
URL: www2.ed.gov/about/offices/list/ope/index.html

Jennifer Hong Ed.D. (D)
Executive Director
National Advisory Committee on Institutional Quality & Integrity
Office of Postsecondary Education
United States Department of Education
400 Maryland Avenue, SW
Room 6W250
Washington, DC 20202
(202) 453-7805
E-MAIL: jennifer.hong@ed.gov
URL: www.ed.gov/about/bdscomm/list/naciqi.html

Herman Bounds Jr., Ed.S. (E)
Director
Accreditation Group
U.S. Department of Education
400 Maryland Avenue, SW
Room 6W243
Washington, DC 20202
(202) 453-7615
E-MAIL: herman.bounds@ed.gov
URL: www2.ed.gov/admins/finaid/accred/index.html

Dr. Peggy G. Carr (F)
Acting Commissioner
National Center for Education Statistics
550 12th Street, SW
Room 4061
Washington, DC 20202
(202) 245-6788
URL: www.nces.ed.gov

Jennifer Hong Ed.D. (G)
Executive Director
National Committee on Foreign Medical Education
and Accreditation (NCFMEA)
Office of Postsecondary Education
United States Department of Education
400 Maryland Avenue, SW
Room 6W250
Washington, DC 20202
(202) 453-7805
E-MAIL: jennifer.hong@ed.gov
URL: www2.ed.gov/about/bdscomm/list/ncfmea.html

Statewide Agencies of Higher Education

ALABAMA

Alabama Commission on Higher Education (H)
PO Box 302000
Montgomery, AL 36130-2000
(334) 242-2123
FAX: (334) 242-0268
Dr. Jim Purcell
Executive Director
E-MAIL: jim.purcell@ache.alabama.gov
URL: www.ache.alabama.gov

Alabama Community College System (I)
PO Box 302130
Montgomery, AL 36130-2130
(334) 293-4524
FAX: (334) 293-4605
Jimmy H. Baker
Chancellor
E-MAIL: jimmy.baker@accs.edu
URL: www.accs.edu

ALASKA

Alaska Commission on Postsecondary Education (J)
PO Box 110505
Juneau, AK 99811-0505
(907) 465-6740
FAX: (907) 465-3293
Ms. Stephanie Butler
Executive Director
E-MAIL: ACPE.execdirector@alaska.gov
URL: www.acpe.alaska.gov

ARIZONA

Arizona Board of Regents (K)
2020 North Central Avenue
Suite 230
Phoenix, AZ 85004-4593
(602) 229-2500
FAX: (602) 229-2555
Eileen Klein
President
E-MAIL: eileen.klein@azregents.edu
URL: www.azregents.edu

Arizona Commission for Postsecondary Education (L)
2020 North Central Avenue
Suite 650
Phoenix, AZ 85004-4503
(602) 258-2435
FAX: (602) 258-2483
Dr. April L. Osborn
Executive Director
E-MAIL: acpe@azhighered.gov
URL: highered.az.gov

ARKANSAS

Arkansas Department of Higher Education (M)
423 Main Street
Suite 400
Little Rock, AR 72201
(501) 371-2030
FAX: (501) 371-2003
Dr. Maria Markham
Director of Higher Education
E-MAIL: maria.markham@adhe.edu
URL: www.adhe.edu

CALIFORNIA

California Community Colleges Chancellor's Office (N)
1102 Q Street
Suite 4400
Sacramento, CA 95811
(916) 322-4005
FAX: (916) 322-4783
Mr. Eloy Ortiz Oakley
Chancellor
E-MAIL: eoakley@cccco.edu
URL: www.cccco.edu

COLORADO

Colorado Department of Higher Education (O)
1560 Broadway
Suite 1600
Denver, CO 80202
(303) 862-3001
FAX: (303) 996-1329
Dr. Kim Hunter Reed
Executive Director
E-MAIL: executivedirector@dhe.state.co.us
URL: highered.colorado.gov

Colorado Community College System (P)
9101 East Lowry Boulevard
Denver, CO 80230-6011
(303) 595-1552
FAX: (303) 620-4043
Dr. Nancy J. McCallin
President
E-MAIL: president@cccs.edu
URL: www.cccs.edu

CONNECTICUT

Board of Regents for Higher Education (Q)
Connecticut State Colleges & Universities
61 Woodland Street
Hartford, CT 06105
(860) 723-0011
FAX: (860) 723-0009
Mark Ojakian
President
E-MAIL: ojakianm@ct.edu
URL: www.ct.edu/regents

Office of Higher Education (R)
North Building, 5th Floor
450 Capitol Avenue, Suite 510
Hartford, CT 06103-1841
(860) 947-1801
FAX: (860) 947-1309
Mr. Keith M. Norton
Executive Director
E-MAIL: knorton@ctohe.org
URL: www.ctohe.org

DELAWARE

Delaware Department of Education Higher Education Office (S)
Townsend Building
401 Federal Street
Suite 2
Dover, DE 19901
(302) 735-4120
FAX: (302) 739-5894
Shana Payne
Director
E-MAIL: dheo@doe.k12.de.us
URL: www.delawaregoestocollege.org

Delaware Technical Community College (T)
PO Box 897
Dover, DE 19903
(302) 857-1667
FAX: (302) 857-1647
Dr. Mark T. Brainard
President
E-MAIL: brainard@dtcc.edu
URL: www.dtcc.edu

DISTRICT OF COLUMBIA

Office of the State Superintendent of Education Government of the District of Columbia (U)
810 First Street, NE
3rd Floor
Washington, DC 20002
(202) 741-0471
FAX: (202) 727-2019
Antoinette S. Mitchell
Asst Superintendent, Postsecondary & Career Educ
E-MAIL: antoinette.mitchell@dc.gov
URL: www.osse.dc.gov

District of Columbia Higher Education Licensure Commission (V)
810 First Street, NE
2nd Floor
Washington, DC 20002
(202) 727-6436
FAX: (202) 741-0229
Ms. Angela Lee
Executive Director
E-MAIL: osse.elcmail@dc.gov
URL: helc.ossse.dc.gov

FLORIDA

Board of Governors State University System of Florida (W)
325 West Gaines Street
Suite 1614
Tallahassee, FL 32399-0400
(850) 245-0466
FAX: (850) 245-9685
Mr. Marshall M. Criser III
Chancellor
E-MAIL: chancellor@flbog.edu
URL: www.flbog.edu

Florida Department of Education Division of Florida Colleges (X)
325 West Gaines Street
Suite 1544 Turlington Building
Tallahassee, FL 32399
(850) 245-0407
FAX: (850) 245-9525
Ms. Madeline M. Pumariega
Chancellor
E-MAIL: chancellorfcs@fldoe.org
URL: www.fldoe.org/schools/higher-ed/fl-college-system/

GEORGIA

Board of Regents of the University System of Georgia (Y)
270 Washington Street, SW
Atlanta, GA 30334
(404) 962-3000
FAX: (404) 962-3013
Dr. Steve Wrigley
Chancellor
E-MAIL: chancellor@usg.edu
URL: www.usg.edu

University System of Georgia (Z)
270 Washington Street, SW
Atlanta, GA 30334
(404) 962-3000
FAX: (404) 962-3013
Dr. Steve Wrigley
Chancellor
E-MAIL: chancellor@usg.edu
URL: www.usg.edu

HAWAII

University of Hawaii Board of Regents (a)
2444 Dole Street
Bachman Hall, Room 209
Honolulu, HI 96822
(808) 956-8213
FAX: (808) 956-5156
Ms. Jan Sullivan
Chair
E-MAIL: bor@hawaii.edu
URL: www.hawaii.edu/offices/bor/

Statewide Agencies of Higher Education

IDAHO

Idaho State Board of Education (A)
PO Box 83720
Boise, ID 83720-0037
(208) 334-2270
FAX: (208) 334-2632
Mr. Matt Freeman
Executive Director
E-MAIL: matt.freeman@osbe.idaho.gov
URL: www.boardofed.idaho.gov

ILLINOIS

Illinois Board of Higher Education (B)
1 N. Old State Capitol Plaza
Suite 333
Springfield, IL 62701-1377
(217) 782-2551
FAX: (217) 782-8548
Executive Director
URL: www.ibhe.org

Illinois Community College Board (C)
401 East Capitol Avenue
Springfield, IL 62701-1874
(217) 785-0123
FAX: (217) 785-7495
Dr. Karen Hunter Anderson
Executive Director
E-MAIL: karen.h.anderson@illinois.gov
URL: www.iccb.org

INDIANA

Indiana Commission for Higher Education (D)
101 West Ohio Street
Suite 300
Indianapolis, IN 46204
(317) 464-4400
FAX: (317) 464-4410
Mrs. Teresa Lubbers
Commissioner for Higher Education
E-MAIL: tlubbers@che.in.gov
URL: www.che.in.gov

IOWA

Board of Regents, State of Iowa (E)
11260 Aurora Avenue
Urbandale, IA 50322-7905
(515) 281-3934
FAX: (515) 281-6420
Mr. Keith Saunders
Interim Executive Director
E-MAIL: keith.saunders@iowaregents.edu
URL: www.iowaregents.edu

Iowa College Student Aid Commission (F)
430 East Grand Avenue
3rd Floor
Des Moines, IA 50309
(515) 725-3410
FAX: (515) 725-3401
Ms. Karen Misjak
Executive Director
E-MAIL: karen.misjak@iowa.gov
URL: www.iowacollegeaid.gov

Iowa Department of Education Division of Community Colleges and Workforce Preparation (G)
400 East 14th Street
Grimes State Office Building
Des Moines, IA 50319-0146
(515) 281-8260
FAX: (515) 242-5988
Jeremy Varner
Administrator
E-MAIL: jeremy.varner@iowa.gov
URL: www.educateiowa.gov

KANSAS

Kansas Board of Regents (H)
1000 SW Jackson
Suite 520
Topeka, KS 66612-1368
(785) 430-4240
FAX: (785) 430-4233
Dr. Blake Flanders
President and CEO
E-MAIL: bflanders@ksbor.org
URL: www.kansasregents.org

Kansas Legislative Research Department (I)
Room 68 West, State Capitol Building
300 SW 10th Avenue
Topeka, KS 66612-1504
(785) 296-3181
FAX: (785) 296-3824
Mr. Raney L. Gilliland
Director
E-MAIL: kslegres@klrd.ks.gov
URL: www.kslegresearch.org

KENTUCKY

Kentucky Council on Postsecondary Education (J)
1024 Capital Center Drive
Suite 320
Frankfort, KY 40601
(502) 892-3000
FAX: (502) 573-1535
Mr. Robert L. King
President
E-MAIL: mary.allison@ky.gov
URL: cpe.ky.gov

Kentucky Community & Technical College System (K)
300 North Main Street
Versailles, KY 40383
(859) 256-3132
FAX: (859) 256-3116
Dr. Jay K. Box
President
E-MAIL: president@kctcs.edu
URL: www.kctcs.edu

LOUISIANA

Louisiana Board of Regents (L)
PO Box 3677
Baton Rouge, LA 70821-3677
(225) 342-4253
FAX: (225) 342-9318
Dr. Joseph C. Rallo
Commissioner of Higher Education
E-MAIL: joseph.rallo@la.gov
URL: www.regents.la.gov

Louisiana Department of Education (M)
PO Box 94064
Baton Rouge, LA 70804-9064
(225) 342-3607
FAX: (225) 342-7316
Mr. John White
State Superintendent of Education
E-MAIL: louisianabelieves@la.gov
URL: www.louisianabelieves.com

MAINE

Maine Department of Education Office of Higher Education (N)
23 State House Station
Augusta, ME 04333-0023
(207) 624-6600
FAX: (207) 624-6700
Mr. Robert G. Hasson Jr.
Commissioner of Education
E-MAIL: commish.doe@maine.gov
URL: www.maine.gov/doe/

MARYLAND

Maryland Higher Education Commission (O)
6 North Liberty Street, 10th Floor
Baltimore, MD 21201
(410) 767-3300
FAX: (410) 332-0270
Dr. James D. Fielder
Secretary of Higher Education
E-MAIL: james.fielder@maryland.gov
URL: www.mhec.maryland.gov

MASSACHUSETTS

Massachusetts Department of Higher Education (P)
One Ashburton Place
Room 1401
Boston, MA 02108
(617) 994-6901
FAX: (617) 727-6656
Mr. Carlos Santiago
Commissioner
E-MAIL: commissioner@dhe.mass.edu
URL: www.mass.edu

MICHIGAN

Department of Licensing and Regulatory Affairs Corporations, Securities & Commercial Licensing Bureau Licensing Division (Q)
PO Box 30018
Lansing, MI 48909-8214
(517) 241-9221
FAX: (517) 373-2162
Mr. Michael Beamish
Director
E-MAIL: beamishm@michigan.gov
URL: www.michigan.gov/pss

Michigan Workforce Development Agency Division of Education and Training (R)
201 North Washington Square
Victor Office Center, 3rd Floor
Lansing, MI 48913
(517) 335-5858
FAX: (517) 241-8217
URL: www.michigan.gov/wda

MINNESOTA

Minnesota Office of Higher Education (S)
1450 Energy Park Drive
Suite 350
St. Paul, MN 55108-5227
(651) 642-0567
FAX: (651) 642-0675
Mr. Larry Pogemiller
Commissioner
E-MAIL: info.ohe@state.mn.us
URL: www.ohe.state.mn.us

Minnesota State Colleges and Universities (T)
30 7th Street East
Suite 350
St. Paul, MN 55101-7804
(651) 201-1696
FAX: (651) 297-7465
Dr. Devinder Malhotra
Interim Chancellor
E-MAIL: devinder.malhotra@so.mnscu.edu
URL: www.mnscu.edu

MISSISSIPPI

Mississippi Board of Trustees of State Institutions of Higher Learning (U)
3825 Ridgewood Road
Jackson, MS 39211
(601) 432-6198
FAX: (601) 432-6972
Dr. Glenn F. Boyce
Commissioner of Higher Education
E-MAIL: gboyce@ihl.state.ms.us
URL: www.mississippi.edu

Mississippi Community College Board (V)
3825 Ridgewood Drive
Jackson, MS 39211
(601) 432-6684
FAX: (601) 432-6480
Dr. Andrea Mayfield Ph.D.
Executive Director
E-MAIL: info@mccb.edu
URL: www.mccb.edu

MISSOURI

Coordinating Board for Higher Education Missouri Department of Higher Education (W)
PO Box 1469
Jefferson City, MO 65102-1469
(573) 751-2361
FAX: (573) 751-6635
Commissioner of Higher Education
URL: www.dhe.mo.gov/cbhe/

MONTANA

Office of the Commissioner of Higher Education (X)
PO Box 203201
Helena, MT 59620-3201
(406) 444-0374
FAX: (406) 444-1469
Mr. Clayton Christian
Commissioner
E-MAIL: cchristian@montana.edu
URL: www.mus.edu/che

NEBRASKA

Nebraska's Coordinating Commission for Postsecondary Education (Y)
PO Box 95005
Lincoln, NE 68509-5005
(402) 471-2847
FAX: (402) 471-2886
Dr. Michael Baumgartner
Executive Director
E-MAIL: mike.baumgartner@nebraska.gov
URL: ccpe.nebraska.gov

NEVADA

Nevada System of Higher Education (Z)
4300 S. Maryland Parkway
Las Vegas, NV 89119
(702) 889-8426
FAX: (702) 889-8492
Mr. John White
Chancellor
E-MAIL: chancellor@nevada.edu
URL: www.nevada.edu

Nevada System of Higher Education (a)
4300 S. Maryland Parkway
Las Vegas, NV 89119
(702) 889-8426
FAX: (702) 889-8492
Mr. Thom Reilly
Chancellor
E-MAIL: chancellor@nevada.edu
URL: www.nevada.edu

NEW HAMPSHIRE

New Hampshire Department of Education Division of Higher Education Higher Education Commission (b)
101 Pleasant Street
Concord, NH 03301-3860
(603) 271-0256
FAX: (603) 271-1953
Director
E-MAIL: patricia.edes@doe.nh.gov
URL: www.education.nh.gov/highered

Community College System of New Hampshire (c)
26 College Drive
Concord, NH 03301
(603) 230-3501
FAX: (603) 271-2725
Dr. Ross Gittell
Chancellor
E-MAIL: rgittell@ccsnh.edu
URL: www.ccsnh.edu

NEW JERSEY

State of New Jersey Office of the Secretary of Higher Education (d)
20 West State Street, 4th Floor
PO Box 542
Trenton, NJ 08625-0542
(609) 292-4310
FAX: (609) 292-7225
Rochelle Hendricks
Secretary of Higher Education
E-MAIL: njhe@njhe.state.nj.us
URL: www.state.nj.us/highereducation

NEW MEXICO

New Mexico Higher Education Department (e)
2044 Galisteo Street
Santa Fe, NM 87505
(505) 476-8400
FAX: (505) 476-8454
Dr. Barbara Damron
Cabinet Secretary
E-MAIL: exec.admin@state.nm.us
URL: www.hed.state.nm.us

NEW YORK

New York State Education Department (f)
89 Washington Avenue
Education Building, Room 111
Albany, NY 12234
(518) 474-5844
FAX: (518) 473-4909
MaryEllen Elia
Commissioner
E-MAIL: commissioner@nysed.gov

Community Colleges and the Education Pipeline (A)
The State University of New York
SUNY Plaza, 353 Broadway, Room T7
Albany, NY 12246
(518) 320-1276
FAX: (518) 320-1570
Johanna Duncan-Poitier
Senior Vice Chancellor
E-MAIL: johanna.duncan-poitier@suny.edu
URL: www.suny.edu/powerofsuny/educationpipeline/

New York State Education Department Office of Higher Education (B)
Education Building Annex
Room 977
Albany, NY 12234
(518) 486-3633
FAX: (518) 486-2254
Mr. John D'Agati Ph.D.
Deputy Commissioner
E-MAIL: john.dagati@nysed.gov
URL: www.highered.nysed.gov

NORTH CAROLINA

The University of North Carolina (C)
910 Raleigh Road
Chapel Hill, NC 27514
(919) 962-9000
Margaret Spellings
President
E-MAIL: president@northcarolina.edu
URL: www.northcarolina.edu

North Carolina Community College System (D)
200 West Jones Street
Raleigh, NC 27603
(919) 807-6950
FAX: (919) 807-7166
Dr. James C. Williamson
President
E-MAIL: williamsonj@nccommunitycolleges.edu
URL: www.nccommunitycolleges.edu

NORTH DAKOTA

North Dakota State Board of Higher Education (E)
600 East Boulevard Avenue
State Capitol
10th Floor, Dept. 215
Bismarck, ND 58505-0230
(701) 328-2960
FAX: (701) 328-2961
Mr. Don Morton
Board Chair
E-MAIL: don.morton@ndus.edu
URL: www.ndus.edu/board

OHIO

Ohio Department of Higher Education (F)
25 South Front Street
Columbus, OH 43215
(614) 466-6000
FAX: (614) 466-5866
Mr. John Carey
Chancellor
E-MAIL: chancellor@highered.ohio.gov
URL: www.ohiohighered.org

OKLAHOMA

Oklahoma State Regents for Higher Education (G)
655 Research Parkway
Suite 200
Oklahoma City, OK 73104
(405) 225-9100
FAX: (405) 225-9235
Dr. Glen D. Johnson
Chancellor
E-MAIL: gjohnson@osrhe.edu
URL: www.okhighered.org

OREGON

Higher Education Coordinating Commission (H)
255 Capitol Street NE
Third Floor
Salem, OR 97310
(503) 378-5690
FAX: (503) 378-8434
Ben Cannon
Executive Director
E-MAIL: info.HECC@state.or.us
URL: www.oregon.gov/HigherEd

Oregon Office of Community Colleges and Workforce Development (I)
255 Capitol Street, NE
Salem, OR 97310
(503) 947-2414
Mr. Patrick Crane
Director
E-MAIL: patrick.crane@state.or.us
URL: www.oregon.gov/highered/institutions-programs/ccwd

PENNSYLVANIA

Pennsylvania Department of Education Postsecondary and Higher Education Institutions (J)
333 Market Street
12th Floor
Harrisburg, PA 17126-0333
(717) 772-3737
FAX: (717) 772-3622
Deputy Secretary, Postsecondary & Higher Education
URL: www.education.pa.gov

Pennsylvania Department of Education Liaison to Postsecondary and Higher Education Institutions (K)
333 Market Street
12th Floor
Harrisburg, PA 17126-0333
(717) 783-8228
FAX: (717) 772-3622
Ms. Patricia Landis
Division Chief - Higher and Career Education
E-MAIL: plandis@pa.gov
URL: www.education.pa.gov

RHODE ISLAND

Rhode Island Office of the Postsecondary Commissioner (L)
560 Jefferson Boulevard
Warwick, RI 02886
(401) 736-1100
Dr. Brenda Dann-Messier
Commissioner of Postsecondary Education
URL: www.riopc.edu

Community College of Rhode Island (M)
400 East Avenue
Warwick, RI 02886
(401) 825-2188
FAX: (401) 825-2166
Dr. Meghan Hughes
President
E-MAIL: president@ccri.edu
URL: www.ccri.edu

SOUTH CAROLINA

South Carolina Commission on Higher Education (N)
1122 Lady Street
Suite 300
Columbia, SC 29201
(803) 737-2275
FAX: (803) 737-2297
Mr. Jeff Schilz
Interim President and Executive Director
E-MAIL: jschilz@che.sc.gov
URL: www.che.sc.gov

South Carolina State Board for Technical and Comprehensive Education (O)
111 Executive Center Drive
Columbia, SC 29210
(803) 896-5280
Dr. Tim Hardee
System President
URL: www.sctechsystem.edu

SOUTH DAKOTA

South Dakota Board of Regents (P)
306 East Capitol Avenue
Suite 200
Pierre, SD 57501
(605) 773-3455
FAX: (605) 773-5320
Dr. Michael G. Rush
Executive Director and Chief Executive Officer
E-MAIL: mike.rush@sdbor.edu
URL: www.sdbor.edu

South Dakota Department of Education (Q)
Office of the Secretary
800 Governors Drive
Pierre, SD 57501-2291
(605) 773-5669
FAX: (605) 773-6139
Dr. Melody Schopp
Secretary
E-MAIL: melody.schopp@state.sd.us
URL: www.doe.sd.gov

TENNESSEE

Tennessee Higher Education Commission (R)
404 James Robertson Parkway
Suite 1900
Nashville, TN 37243
(615) 741-3605
Mr. Mike Krause
Executive Director
URL: www.tn.gov/thec/

Tennessee Board of Regents (S)
1 Bridgestone Park
Nashville, TN 37214
(615) 366-4448
FAX: (615) 366-3903
Dr. Randy Schulte
Interim Vice Chancellor for Academics
E-MAIL: randy.schulte@tbr.edu
URL: www.tbr.edu

University of Tennessee Board of Trustees (T)
719 Andy Holt Tower
Knoxville, TN 37996-0170
(865) 974-3245
FAX: (865) 974-0100
Ms. Catherine S. Mizell
Secretary to the Board of Trustees
E-MAIL: cmizell@tennessee.edu
URL: trustees.tennessee.edu

TEXAS

Texas Higher Education Coordinating Board (U)
PO Box 12788
Austin, TX 78711
(512) 427-6101
FAX: (512) 427-6127
Dr. Raymund A. Paredes
Commissioner of Higher Education
E-MAIL: raymund.paredes@thecb.state.tx.us
URL: www.thecb.state.tx.us

Texas Higher Education Coordinating Board Division of College Readiness and Success (V)
PO Box 12788
Austin, TX 78711-2788
(512) 427-6247
FAX: (512) 427-6444
Jerel Booker J.D.
Assistant Commissioner
E-MAIL: jerel.booker@thecb.state.tx.us
URL: www.thecb.state.tx.us

UTAH

Utah System of Higher Education State Board of Regents (W)
60 South 400 West
Salt Lake City, UT 84101-1284
(801) 321-7101
FAX: (801) 321-7156
David L. Buhler
Commissioner of Higher Education
E-MAIL: dbuhler@ushe.edu
URL: higheredutah.org

VERMONT

Vermont Agency of Education (X)
219 North Main Street
Suite 402
Barre, VT 05641
(802) 479-1043
Mr. Brad James
Education Finance Manager
E-MAIL: brad.james@vermont.gov
URL: www.education.vermont.gov

VIRGINIA

State Council of Higher Education for Virginia (Y)
101 North 14th Street
James Monroe Building, 10th Floor
Richmond, VA 23219
(804) 225-2600
FAX: (804) 225-2604
Mr. Peter Blake
Director
E-MAIL: peterblake@schev.edu
URL: www.schev.edu

Virginia's Community Colleges (Z)
300 Arboretum Place
Suite 200
Richmond, VA 23236
(804) 819-4903
FAX: (804) 819-4760
Dr. Glenn DuBois
Chancellor
E-MAIL: gdubois@vccs.edu
URL: www.vccs.edu

WASHINGTON

Washington Student Achievement Council (a)
917 Lakeridge Way, SW
PO Box 43430
Olympia, WA 98504-3430
(360) 753-7800
FAX: (360) 753-7808
Mr. Michael P. Meotti
Executive Director
E-MAIL: info@wsac.wa.gov
URL: www.wsac.wa.gov

Washington State Board for Community and Technical Colleges (b)
PO Box 42495
Olympia, WA 98504-2495
(360) 704-4355
FAX: (360) 704-4415
Jan Yoshiwara
Executive Director
E-MAIL: mbrown@sbctc.edu
URL: www.sbctc.edu

WEST VIRGINIA

West Virginia Higher Education Policy Commission (c)
1018 Kanawha Boulevard, East
Suite 700
Charleston, WV 25301-2800
(304) 558-0699
FAX: (304) 558-1011
Dr. Paul L. Hill
Chancellor
E-MAIL: paul.hill@hepc.wvnet.edu
URL: www.wvhepc.edu

WISCONSIN

State of Wisconsin Higher Educational Aids Board (d)
PO Box 7885
Madison, WI 53707-7885
(608) 267-2206
FAX: (608) 267-2808
Mr. John Reinemann
Executive Secretary
E-MAIL: heabmail@wi.gov
URL: heab.wi.gov

Wisconsin Technical College System (e)
PO Box 7874
Madison, WI 53707-7874
(608) 267-9066
FAX: (608) 266-1285
Dr. Morna K. Foy
President
E-MAIL: president@wtcsystem.edu
URL: www.wtcsystem.edu

WYOMING

Wyoming Community College Commission **(A)**
2300 Capitol Avenue
5th Floor, Suite B
Cheyenne, WY 82002
(307) 777-7763
FAX: (307) 777-6567
Dr. Jim Rose
Executive Director
E-MAIL: jim.rose@wyo.gov
URL: communitycolleges.wy.edu

AMERICAN SAMOA

Board of Higher Education (American Samoa) American Samoa Community College **(B)**
PO Box 2609
Pago Pago, AS 96799
(684) 699-9155
FAX: (684) 699-6259
E-MAIL: info@amsamoa.edu
URL: www.amsamoa.edu

FEDERATED STATES OF MICRONESIA

Board of Regents College of Micronesia-FSM **(C)**
PO Box 159
Kolonia Pohnpei, FM 96941
(691) 320-2480
FAX: (691) 320-2479
Dr. Tulensru Waguk
Chairman of the Board
E-MAIL: national@comfsm.fm
URL: www.comfsm.fm

PUERTO RICO

Puerto Rico Council on Education **(D)**
PO Box 19900
San Juan, PR 00910-1900
(787) 641-7100, ext. 2045
FAX: (787) 641-2573
Ms. Maria L. Varas Garcia
Interim Executive Director
E-MAIL: mvaras@ce.pr.gov
URL: www.ce.pr.gov

Higher Education Associations

AACSB International-The Association to Advance Collegiate Schools of Business (A)
777 South Harbour Island Boulevard
Suite 750
Tampa, FL 33602-5730
(813) 769-6500
FAX: (813) 769-6559
Mr. Thomas R. Robinson
President and Chief Executive Officer
E-MAIL: mediarelations@aacsb.edu
URL: www.aacsb.edu

AASA, The School Superintendents Association (B)
1615 Duke Street
Alexandria, VA 22314
(703) 528-0700
FAX: (703) 841-1543
Dr. Daniel A. Domenech
Executive Director
E-MAIL: ddomenech@aasa.org
URL: www.aasa.org

AAUW (C)
1310 L Street, NW
Suite 1000
Washington, DC 20005
(202) 785-7700
FAX: (202) 872-1425
Kimberly Churches
Chief Executive Officer
E-MAIL: connect@aauw.org
URL: www.aauw.org

ABET (D)
415 North Charles Street
Baltimore, MD 21201
(410) 347-7700
FAX: (443) 552-3644
Michael K. J. Milligan Ph.D., PE
Executive Director and CEO
E-MAIL: info@abet.org
URL: www.abet.org

Academy of Legal Studies in Business (E)
Miami University
3111-Farmer School of Business
Department of Finance
Oxford, OH 45056
(513) 529-1560
Mr. Daniel Herron
Executive Secretary
E-MAIL: herrondj@miamioh.edu
URL: www.alsb.org

Academy of Nutrition and Dietetics Accreditation Council for Education in Nutrition and Dietetics (ACEND) (F)
120 South Riverside Plaza
Suite 2190
Chicago, IL 60606-6995
(312) 899-0040, ext. 5400
FAX: (312) 899-4817
Dr. Mary B. Gregoire
Executive Director
E-MAIL: acend@eatright.org
URL: www.eatrightpro.org/acend

Accreditation Commission for Acupuncture and Oriental Medicine (ACAOM) (G)
8941 Aztec Drive
Eden Prairie, MN 55347
(952) 212-2434
FAX: (952) 657-7068
Mr. Mark McKenzie
Executive Director
E-MAIL: mark.mckenzie@acaom.org
URL: www.acaom.org

Accreditation Commission for Education in Nursing (ACEN) (H)
3343 Peachtree Road, NE
Suite 850
Atlanta, GA 30326
(404) 975-5000
FAX: (404) 975-5020
Dr. Marsal Stoll
CEO
E-MAIL: mstoll@acenursing.org
URL: www.acenursing.org

Accreditation Commission for Midwifery Education (ACME) (I)
8403 Colesville Road
Suite 1550
Silver Spring, MD 20910
(240) 485-1803
FAX: (240) 485-1818
Heather L. Maurer MA
Executive Director
E-MAIL: hmaurer@acnm.org
URL: www.midwife.org/Accreditation

Accreditation Committee - Perfusion Education (J)
6663 South Sycamore Street
Littleton, CO 80120
(303) 794-6283
Ms. Theresa Sisneros
Executive Director
E-MAIL: office@ac-pe.org
URL: www.ac-pe.org

Accreditation Council for Business Schools and Programs (K)
11520 West 119th Street
Overland Park, KS 66213
(913) 339-9356
FAX: (913) 339-6226
Mr. Jeffrey Alderman
President & CEO
E-MAIL: info@acbsp.org
URL: www.acbsp.org

Accreditation Council for Pharmacy Education (L)
135 South LaSalle Street
Suite 4100
Chicago, IL 60603
(312) 664-3575
FAX: (312) 664-4652
Peter H. Vlasses, PharmD BCPS
Executive Director
E-MAIL: pvlasses@acpe-accredit.org
URL: www.acpe-accredit.org

Accreditation Review Commission on Education for the Physician Assistant (ARC-PA) (M)
12000 Findley Road
Suite 275
Johns Creek, GA 30097
(770) 476-1224
FAX: (770) 476-1738
Ms. Sharon Luke
Executive Director
E-MAIL: executivedirector@arc-pa.org
URL: www.arc-pa.org

Accreditation Review Committee for the Anesthesiologist Assistant (N)
N84 W33137 Becker Lane
Oconomowoc, WI 53066
(612) 836-3311
Ms. Jennifer Anderson Warwick
Executive Director
E-MAIL: arc-aa@arc-aa.org
URL: www.caahep.org/arc-aa

Accreditation Review Committee for the Medical Illustrator (O)
32531 Meadowlark Way
Pepper Pike, OH 44124
(216) 595-9363
Kathleen Jung
ARC-MI Chair
E-MAIL: kijung@aol.com
URL: www.caahep.org/arc-mi

Accreditation Review Council on Education in Surgical Technology and Surgical Assisting (P)
6 West Dry Creek Circle
Suite 110
Littleton, CO 80120
(303) 694-9262
FAX: (303) 741-3655
Mr. Ron Kruzel
Executive Director
E-MAIL: info@arcstsa.org
URL: www.arcstsa.org

Accrediting Bureau of Health Education Schools (Q)
7777 Leesburg Pike
Suite 314 N
Falls Church, VA 22043
(703) 917-9503
FAX: (703) 917-4109
Florence Tate
Executive Director
E-MAIL: info@abhes.org
URL: www.abhes.org

Accrediting Commission for Community and Junior Colleges Western Association of Schools and Colleges (R)
10 Commercial Boulevard
Suite 204
Novato, CA 94949
(415) 506-0234
FAX: (415) 506-0238
Dr. Richard Winn
President
E-MAIL: accjc@accjc.org
URL: www.accjc.org

Accrediting Commission of Career Schools and Colleges (S)
2101 Wilson Boulevard
Suite 302
Arlington, VA 22201
(703) 247-4212
FAX: (703) 247-4533
Dr. Michale McComis
Executive Director
E-MAIL: mccomis@accsc.org
URL: www.accsc.org

Accrediting Council for Continuing Education & Training (ACCET) (T)
1722 N Street, NW
Washington, DC 20036
(202) 955-1113
FAX: (202) 955-1118
Mr. Bill Larkin
Executive Director
E-MAIL: info@accet.org
URL: www.accet.org

Accrediting Council for Independent Colleges and Schools (U)
750 First Street, NE
Suite 980
Washington, DC 20002-4223
(202) 336-6780
FAX: (202) 842-2593
Ms. Michelle Edwards
President
E-MAIL: medwards@acics.org
URL: www.acics.org

Accrediting Council on Education in Journalism and Mass Communications (V)
University of Kansas, School of Journalism
1435 Jayhawk Boulevard
Stauffer-Flint Hall
Lawrence, KS 66045-7515
(785) 864-3986
FAX: (785) 864-5225
Prof. Susanne Shaw
Executive Director
E-MAIL: sshaw@ku.edu
URL: www.acejmc.org

ACPE: The Standard in Spiritual Care & Education (W)
One West Court Square
Suite 325
Decatur, GA 30030
(404) 320-1472
FAX: (404) 320-0849
RevDr. Trace Haythorn
Executive Director/CEO
E-MAIL: acpe@acpe.edu
URL: www.acpe.edu

ACT, Inc. (X)
500 ACT Drive
Box 168
Iowa City, IA 52243-0168
(319) 337-1079
FAX: (319) 337-1059
Mr. Marten Roorda
CEO
E-MAIL: sandy.serbousek@act.org
URL: www.act.org

American Academy for Liberal Education (AALE) (Y)
1200 G Street NW
Suite 883
Washington, DC 20005
(202) 434-8971
Mary Ann Powers
Executive Director
E-MAIL: aaleinfo@aale.org
URL: www.aale.org

American Anthropological Association (Z)
2300 Clarendon Boulevard
Suite 1301
Arlington, VA 22201
(703) 528-1902
FAX: (703) 528-3546
Dr. Edward Liebow
Executive Director
E-MAIL: eliebow@americananthro.org
URL: www.americananthro.org

American Association for Adult and Continuing Education (AAACE) (a)
1827 Powers Ferry Road
Building 14, Suite 100
Atlanta, GA 30339
(678) 271-4319
FAX: (404) 393-9506
Steven B. Frye Ph.D.
President
E-MAIL: office@aaace.org
URL: www.aaace.org

American Association for Employment in Education (b)
PO Box 173
Slippery Rock, PA 16057
(614) 485-1111
FAX: (360) 244-7802
Ms. Deb Snyder
Executive Director
E-MAIL: execdir@aaee.org
URL: www.aaee.org

American Association for Marriage and Family Therapy Commission on Accreditation for Marriage and Family Therapy Education (c)
112 South Alfred Street
Alexandria, VA 22314-3061
(703) 253-0448
FAX: (703) 253-0508
Ms. Tanya A. Tamarkin
Director of Accreditation
E-MAIL: coa@aamft.org
URL: www.aamft.org

American Association for Vocational Instructional Materials (d)
220 Smithonia Road
Winterville, GA 30683
(706) 742-5355
FAX: (706) 742-7005
Mr. Gary Farmer
Manager
E-MAIL: sales@aavim.com
URL: www.aavim.com

American Association for Women in Community Colleges (AAWCC) (e)
PO Box 3098
Gaithersburg, MD 20855
Dr. DeRionne Pollard
President
E-MAIL: info@aawccnatl.org
URL: www.aawccnatl.org

American Association of Blood Banks Committee on Accreditation of Specialist in Blood Banking Technology Schools (f)
4550 Montgomery Avenue
Suite 700 North Tower
Bethesda, MD 20814-3304
(301) 215-6586
FAX: (301) 657-0957
Meredith Eller
Staff Liaison Accreditation and Quality
E-MAIL: accreditation@aabb.org
URL: www.aabb.org

American Association of Colleges for Teacher Education (g)
1307 New York Avenue, NW
Suite 300
Washington, DC 20005-4701
(202) 293-2450
FAX: (202) 457-8095
Dr. Lynn M. Gangone
President & Chief Executive Officer
URL: www.aacte.org

Higher Education Associations

American Association of Colleges of Nursing (A)
1 Dupont Circle, NW
Suite 530
Washington, DC 20036-1120
(202) 463-6930
Fax: (202) 785-8320
Dr. Deborah Trautman
President & Chief Executive Officer
E-mail: dtrautman@aacn.nche.edu
URL: www.aacn.nche.edu

American Association of Colleges of Osteopathic Medicine (B)
7700 Old Georgetown Road
Suite 250
Bethesda, MD 20814
(301) 968-4142
Fax: (301) 968-4101
Stephen C. Shannon DO, MPH
President and CEO
E-mail: president@aacom.org
URL: www.aacom.org

American Association of Collegiate Registrars and Admissions Officers (AACRAO) (C)
1 Dupont Circle, NW
Suite 520
Washington, DC 20036-1135
(202) 293-9161
Fax: (202) 872-8857
Mr. Michael Reilly
Executive Director
E-mail: reillym@aacrao.org
URL: www.aacrao.org

American Association of Community Colleges (D)
1 Dupont Circle, NW
Suite 410
Washington, DC 20036
(202) 728-0200, ext. 235
Fax: (202) 452-1461
Dr. Walter G. Bumphus
President/CEO
E-mail: wbumphus@aacc.nche.edu
URL: www.aacc.nche.edu

American Association of Family and Consumer Sciences (AAFCS) (E)
400 North Columbus Street
Suite 202
Alexandria, VA 22314
(703) 706-4602
Fax: (703) 636-7648
Lori A. Myers PhD, CFCS
Sr Director, Credentialing, Education & Research
E-mail: lmyers@aafcs.org
URL: www.aafcs.org

American Association of Medical Assistants (F)
20 North Wacker Drive
Suite 1575
Chicago, IL 60606
(312) 899-1500
Fax: (312) 899-1259
Mr. Donald A. Balasa J.D., MBA
Chief Executive Officer
E-mail: dbalasa@aama-ntl.org
URL: www.aama-ntl.org

American Association of Physics Teachers (G)
One Physics Ellipse
College Park, MD 20740-3845
(301) 209-3311
Fax: (301) 209-0845
Dr. Beth A. Cunningham
Executive Officer
E-mail: eo@aapt.org
URL: www.aapt.org

American Association of Presidents of Independent Colleges and Universities (H)
PO Box 7070
Provo, UT 84602-7070
(801) 422-2235
Mr. Steven M. Sandberg
Executive Director
E-mail: aapicu@byu.edu
URL: www.aapicu.org

American Association of State Colleges and Universities (I)
1307 New York Avenue, NW
5th Floor
Washington, DC 20005-4701
(202) 293-7070
Fax: (202) 296-5819
Dr. Muriel A. Howard
President
E-mail: howardm@aascu.org
URL: www.aascu.org

American Association of Teachers of Slavic and East European Languages (J)
University of Southern California
3501 Trousdale Parkway
THH 255L
Los Angeles, CA 90089-4353
(213) 740-2734
Fax: (213) 740-8550
Dr. Elizabeth Durst
Executive Director
E-mail: aatseel@usc.edu
URL: www.aatseel.org

American Association of University Professors (K)
1133 19th Street, NW
Suite 200
Washington, DC 20036
(202) 737-5900
Fax: (202) 737-5526
Dr. Julie Schmid
Executive Director
E-mail: aaup@aaup.org
URL: www.aaup.org

American Bar Association Section of Legal Education and Admissions to the Bar (L)
321 North Clark Street
21st Floor
Chicago, IL 60654
(312) 988-6746
Fax: (312) 988-5681
Mr. Barry A. Currier
Managing Director Accreditation & Legal Education
E-mail: legaled@americanbar.org
URL: www.americanbar.org/groups/legal_education

American Board of Funeral Service Education Committee on Accreditation (M)
992 Mantua Pike
Suite 108
Woodbury Heights, NJ 08097
(816) 233-3747
Fax: (856) 579-7354
Robert C. Smith III
Executive Director
E-mail: exdir@abfse.org
URL: www.abfse.org

American Catholic Philosophical Association (N)
University of St. Thomas
3800 Montrose Boulevard
Houston, TX 77006
(713) 942-5062
Fax: (713) 942-3464
Dr. Mirela Oliva
National Secretary
E-mail: acpa@stthom.edu
URL: www.acpaweb.org

American Chemical Society Committee on Professional Training (O)
1155 Sixteenth Street, NW
Washington, DC 20036
(202) 872-4589
Fax: (202) 872-6066
Ms. Cathy A. Nelson
Assistant Director
E-mail: cpt@acs.org
URL: www.acs.org/cpt

American College of Microbiology Committee on Postgraduate Educational Programs (P)
1752 N Street, NW
Washington, DC 20036-2804
(202) 942-9225
Fax: (202) 942-9353
Ms. Peggy McNult
Director
E-mail: clinmicro@asmusa.org
URL: www.asm.org/cpep

American College of Nurse-Midwives (Q)
8403 Colesville Road
Suite 1550
Silver Spring, MD 20910
(240) 485-1800
Fax: (240) 485-1818
Ms. Kate McHugh CNM
Interim Executive Director
E-mail: info@acnm.org
URL: www.midwife.org

American College Personnel Association (ACPA) (R)
1 Dupont Circle, NW
Suite 300
Washington, DC 20036-1188
(202) 835-2272
Fax: (202) 827-0601
Dr. Cindi Love
Executive Director
E-mail: info@acpa.nche.edu
URL: www.myacpa.org

American Collegiate Retailing Association (S)
Oklahoma State University
435 Human Sciences Building
Stillwater, OK 74078
(405) 744-5049
Ms. Jane Swinney
President
E-mail: jane.swinney@okstate.edu
URL: www.acraretail.org

American Conference of Academic Deans (ACAD) (T)
1818 R Street, NW
Washington, DC 20009
(202) 884-7419
Fax: (202) 265-9532
Ms. Laura A. Rzepka
Executive Director
E-mail: info@acad.org
URL: www.acad.org

American Council for Construction Education (U)
825 W. Bitters Road
Suite 103
San Antonio, TX 78216
(210) 495-6161
Fax: (210) 495-6168
Mr. Michael Holland
President
E-mail: acce@acce-hq.org
URL: www.acce-hq.org

American Council of Trustees and Alumni (V)
1730 M Street, NW
Suite 600
Washington, DC 20036-4511
(202) 467-6787
Fax: (202) 467-6784
Dr. Michael B. Poliakoff
President
E-mail: info@goacta.org
URL: www.goacta.org

American Council on Education (W)
1 Dupont Circle, NW
Washington, DC 20036
(202) 939-9300
Fax: (202) 833-4760
Ted Mitchell
President
E-mail: president@acenet.edu
URL: www.acenet.edu

American Council on Education Center for Education Attainment and Innovation (X)
1 Dupont Circle, NW
Suite 250
Washington, DC 20036
(202) 939-9300
Fax: (202) 833-3005
Chief Academic Innovation Officer
URL: www.acenet.edu

American Counseling Association (Y)
6101 Stevenson Avenue
Alexandria, VA 22304
(800) 347-6647, ext. 231
Fax: (800) 473-2329
Mr. Richard Yep CAE, FASAE
Chief Executive Officer
E-mail: ryep@counseling.org
URL: www.counseling.org

American Culinary Federation Education Foundation Accrediting Commission (Z)
180 Center Place Way
St. Augustine, FL 32095
(904) 484-0507
Fax: (904) 940-0741
Ms. Lori Weber
Director of Education & Programs
E-mail: lweber@acfchefs.net
URL: www.acfchefs.org

American Educational Research Association (a)
1430 K Street, NW
Suite 1200
Washington, DC 20005
(202) 238-3200
Fax: (202) 238-3250
Dr. Felice J. Levine
Executive Director
E-mail: flevine@aera.net
URL: www.aera.net

American Forensics Association (b)
3502 Watt Way, ASC-124
Los Angeles, CA 90089-0281
(323) 201-7147
Dr. Gordon Stables
President
E-mail: amerforenassoc@gmail.com
URL: www.americanforensics.org

American Institute of Architecture Students (c)
1735 New York Avenue, NW
Washington, DC 20006-5209
(202) 808-0068
Keshika De Saram
President
E-mail: president@aias.org
URL: www.aias.org

American Library Association Office for Accreditation (d)
50 East Huron Street
Chicago, IL 60611-2729
(312) 280-2432
Fax: (312) 280-2433
Karen O'Brien
Director, Office for Accreditation
E-mail: accred@ala.org
URL: www.ala.org/accreditation

American Mathematical Association of Two Year Colleges (e)
Southwest Tennessee Community College
5983 Macon Cove
Memphis, TN 38134
(901) 333-5643
Fax: (901) 333-5651
Cheryl Cleaves
Interim Executive Director
E-mail: amatyc@amatyc.org
URL: www.amatyc.org

American Occupational Therapy Association (f)
4720 Montgomery Lane
Suite 200
Bethesda, MD 20814-3449
(301) 652-6611 Ext. 2042
Fax: (240) 762-5140
Dr. Heather Stagliano
Associate Chief Officer for Accreditation
E-mail: accred@aota.org
URL: www.aota.org

American Optometric Association Accreditation Council on Optometric Education (g)
243 North Lindbergh Boulevard
Floor 1
St. Louis, MO 63141
(314) 991-4100
Fax: (314) 991-4101
Ms. Joyce L. Urbeck
Director
E-mail: jlurbeck@aoa.org
URL: www.theacoe.org

American Osteopathic Association (h)
Commission on Osteopathic College Accreditation
142 East Ontario Street
Chicago, IL 60611-2864
(312) 202-8039
Brian G. Kim JD
Interim Secretary
E-mail: predoc@osteopathic.org
URL: www.aoacoca.org

American Physical Therapy Association (A)
1111 North Fairfax Street
Alexandria, VA 22314
(703) 706-3253
Mr. Justin Moore
Chief Executive Officer
E-MAIL: dorisellmore@apta.org
URL: www.apta.org

American Political Science Association (B)
1527 New Hampshire Avenue, NW
Washington, DC 20036
(202) 483-2512
FAX: (202) 483-2657
Dr. Steven Rathgeb Smith
Executive Director
E-MAIL: apsa@apsanet.org
URL: www.apsanet.org

American Psychological Association Office of Program Consultation & Accreditation (C)
750 First Street, NE
Washington, DC 20002-4242
(202) 572-3037
FAX: (202) 336-5978
Dr. Jacqueline Remondet Wall
Director
E-MAIL: apaaccred@apa.org
URL: www.apa.org/ed/accreditation/

American Real Estate and Urban Economics Association (D)
404 BNA Drive
Suite 650
Nashville, TN 37217
(800) 242-0528
FAX: (615) 367-0012
Lindsay Buchanan CMP
Executive Director
E-MAIL: areuea@travelink.com
URL: www.areuea.org

American Society for Engineering Education (E)
1818 N Street, NW
Suite 600
Washington, DC 20036
(202) 331-3545
FAX: (202) 265-8504
Dr. Norman L. Fortenberry
Executive Director
E-MAIL: n.fortenberry@asee.org
URL: www.asee.org

American Society for Microbiology (F)
1752 N Street, NW
Washington, DC 20036
(202) 942-9264
FAX: (202) 942-9329
Ms. Amy L. Chang
Director, Education Department
E-MAIL: education@asmusa.org
URL: www.asm.org

American Society of Cytopathology Cytotechnology Programs Review Committee (CPRC) (G)
100 West 10th Street
Suite 605
Wilmington, DE 19801
(302) 543-6583
FAX: (302) 543-6597
Deborah M. Sheldon
Cytology Education Coordinator
E-MAIL: asc@cytopathology.org
URL: www.cytopathology.org

American Society of Landscape Architects Landscape Architectural Accreditation Board (H)
636 Eye Street, NW
Washington, DC 20001-3736
(202) 216-2359
FAX: (202) 898-1185
Mr. Kristopher Pritchard
Accred & Education Programs Manager
E-MAIL: kpritchard@asla.org
URL: www.asla.org

American Student Government Association (I)
412 NW 16th Avenue
Gainesville, FL 32601-4203
(352) 373-6907
FAX: (352) 373-8120
Mr. W. H. Oxendine Jr.
Executive Director
E-MAIL: info@asgaonline.com
URL: www.asgahome.com

American Veterinary Medical Association (J)
1931 North Meacham Road
Suite 100
Schaumburg, IL 60173
(800) 248-2862
FAX: (847) 285-5732
Dr. Karen Martens Brandt
Director Education and Research
E-MAIL: kbrandt@avma.org
URL: www.avma.org

APPA (K)
1643 Prince Street
Alexandria, VA 22314
(703) 684-1446
FAX: (703) 549-2772
E. Lander Medlin
Executive Vice President
E-MAIL: lander@appa.org
URL: www.appa.org

Association for Asian Studies (L)
825 Victors Way
Suite 310
Ann Arbor, MI 48108
(734) 665-2490
FAX: (734) 665-3801
Mr. Michael Paschal
Executive Director
E-MAIL: mpaschal@asian-studies.org
URL: www.asian-studies.org

Association for Biblical Higher Education Commission on Accreditation (M)
5850 T.G. Lee Boulevard
Suite 130
Orlando, FL 32822
(407) 207-0808
FAX: (407) 207-0840
Dr. Ronald C. Kroll
Director, Commission on Accreditation
E-MAIL: coa@abhe.org
URL: www.abhe.org

Association for Business Communication (N)
323 Shanks Hall (0112)
181 Turner Street, NW
Blacksburg, VA 24061
(540) 231-8460
FAX: (540) 231-1452
Dr. James Dubinsky
Executive Director
E-MAIL: exec_director@businesscommunication.org
URL: www.businesscommunication.org

Association for Business Simulation and Experiential Learning (O)
University of South Carolina Aiken
School of Business Administration
471 University Parkway
Aiken, SC 29801
(803) 641-3340
Dr. Mick Fekula
VP/Executive Director
E-MAIL: mickf@usca.edu
URL: www.absel.org

The Association for Canadian Studies in the United States (ACSUS) (P)
1004 Clemens Hall
University of Buffalo - SUNY
Buffalo, NY 14260
(716) 645-8440
FAX: (716) 645-5976
Mr. Munroe Eagles
President
E-MAIL: info@acsus.org
URL: www.acsus.org

Association for Collaborative Leadership (ACL) (Q)
c/o NELLCO
756 Madison Avenue
Suite 102
Albany, NY 12208
(518) 772-3921
FAX: (518) 694-3027
E-MAIL: admin@national-acl.org
URL: www.national-acl.org

Association for Continuing Higher Education (R)
University of Oklahoma
OCCE Administration Building, Room 129C
1700 Asp Avenue
Norman, OK 73072-6400
(800) 807-2243
FAX: (405) 325-7196
Nina Barbee Ph.D.
Operations Manager
E-MAIL: nbarbee@acheinc.org
URL: www.acheinc.org

Association for Education in Journalism and Mass Communication (S)
234 Outlet Pointe Boulevard
Suite A
Columbia, SC 29210-5667
(803) 798-0271
FAX: (803) 772-3509
Ms. Jennifer H. McGill
Executive Director
E-MAIL: aejmchq@aol.com
URL: www.aejmc.org

Association for General and Liberal Studies (T)
428 5th Street
Columbus, IN 47201
(812) 376-7468
Ms. Joyce Lucke
Executive Director
E-MAIL: execdir@agls.org
URL: www.agls.org

Association for Information Systems (U)
PO Box 2712
Atlanta, GA 30301-2712
(404) 413-7445
Mr. Jody McGinnis
Associate Executive Director
E-MAIL: ed@aisnet.org
URL: aisnet.org

Association for Institutional Research (V)
1983 Centre Pointe Boulevard #101
Tallahassee, FL 32308
(850) 385-4155
FAX: (850) 385-5180
Ms. Christine M. Keller
Executive Director & CFO
E-MAIL: ckeller@airweb.org
URL: www.airweb.org

Association for Library and Information Science Education (ALISE) (W)
2150 N. 107th Street
Suite 205
Seattle, WA 98133
(206) 209-5267
FAX: (206) 367-8777
Mr. Andrew Estep
Executive Director
E-MAIL: office@alise.org
URL: www.alise.org

Association for Prevention Teaching and Research (X)
1001 Connecticut Avenue, NW
Suite 610
Washington, DC 20036
(202) 463-0550
FAX: (202) 463-0555
Ms. Allison L. Lewis
Executive Director
E-MAIL: info@aptrweb.org
URL: www.aptrweb.org

Association for the Study of Higher Education (ASHE) (Y)
UNLV
4505 South Maryland Parkway
Box 453068
Las Vegas, NV 89154-3068
(702) 895-2737
Dr. Kimberly Nehls
Executive Director
E-MAIL: ASHE@unlv.edu
URL: www.ashe.ws

Association for Theatre in Higher Education (ATHE) (Z)
1000 Westgate Drive
Suite 252
St. Paul, MN 55114
(800) 918-9216
FAX: (800) 809-6374
Mr. Eric Ewald
Executive Director
E-MAIL: erice@athe.org
URL: www.athe.org

Association of Advanced Rabbinical and Talmudic Schools Accreditation Commission (a)
11 Broadway
Suite 405
New York, NY 10004
(212) 363-1991
FAX: (212) 533-5335
Dr. Bernard Fryshman
Interim Executive Director
E-MAIL: office@aarts-schools.org

Association of American Colleges & Universities (b)
1818 R Street, NW
Washington, DC 20009
(202) 387-3760
Dr. Lynn Pasquerella
President
E-MAIL: information@aacu.org
URL: www.aacu.org

Association of American Law Schools (c)
1614 20th Street, NW
Washington, DC 20009-1001
(202) 296-1526
FAX: (202) 296-8869
Ms. Judith Areen
Executive Director
E-MAIL: aals@aals.org
URL: www.aals.org

Association of American Medical Colleges (d)
655 K Street, NW
Suite 100
Washington, DC 20001-2399
(202) 828-0460
FAX: (202) 481-7801
Dr. Darrell G. Kirch
President/CEO
E-MAIL: aamcpresident@aamc.org
URL: www.aamc.org

Association of American Universities (e)
1200 New York Avenue, NW
Suite 550
Washington, DC 20005
(202) 408-7500
FAX: (202) 408-8184
Dr. Mary Sue Coleman
President
E-MAIL: leah.norton@aau.edu
URL: www.aau.edu

Association of American University Presses (f)
1412 Broadway
Suite 2135
New York, NY 10018
(212) 989-1010
Peter M. Berkery Jr.
Executive Director
E-MAIL: info@aaupnet.org
URL: www.aaupnet.org

Association of Catholic Colleges and Universities (g)
1 Dupont Circle, NW
Suite 650
Washington, DC 20036
(202) 457-0650
FAX: (202) 728-0977
Michael Galligan-Stierle Ph.D.
President/CEO
E-MAIL: accu@accunet.org
URL: www.accunet.org

Association of College and University Housing Officers-International (h)
1445 Summit Street
Columbus, OH 43201-2105
(614) 292-0099
FAX: (614) 292-3205
Ms. Mary DeNiro
Executive Director
E-MAIL: office@acuho-i.org
URL: www.acuho-i.org

Association of College and University Religious Affairs (i)
University of Puget Sound
1500 N. Warner
CMB #1082
Tacoma, WA 98416
(253) 879-2751
Mr. David P. Wright
President
E-MAIL: dwright@pugetsound.edu
URL: www.acura-online.org

Association of College Unions International (A)
One City Centre, Suite 200
120 West Seventh Street
Bloomington, IN 47404-3839
(812) 245-2284
FAX: (812) 245-6710
Dr. John Taylor
Chief Executive Officer
E-MAIL: acui@acui.org
URL: www.acui.org

Association of Collegiate Conference and Events Directors-International (B)
2900 South College Avenue
Suite 3B
Fort Collins, CO 80525
(970) 449-4960, ext. 4
FAX: (970) 449-4965
Ms. Karen Nedbal
Executive Director
E-MAIL: karen@acced-i.org
URL: www.acced-i.org

Association of Collegiate Schools of Architecture (C)
1735 New York Avenue, NW
3rd Floor
Washington, DC 20006
(202) 785-2324
FAX: (202) 628-0448
Michael Monti Ph.D.
Executive Director
E-MAIL: mmonti@acsa-arch.org
URL: www.acsa-arch.org

Association of Collegiate Schools of Planning (D)
c/o Donna Dodd, Executive Director
6311 Mallard Trace Drive
Tallahassee, FL 32312
(850) 385-2054
FAX: (850) 385-2084
Dr. Weiping Wu
President
E-MAIL: ddodd@acsp.org
URL: www.acsp.org

Association of Community College Trustees (E)
1101 17th Street NW
Suite 300
Washington, DC 20036
(202) 775-4667
FAX: (202) 223-1297
Mr. J. Noah Brown
President and CEO
E-MAIL: nbrown@acct.org
URL: www.acct.org

Association of Departments of English (F)
85 Broad Street
Suite 500
New York, NY 10004-2434
(646) 576-5137
Dr. Douglas Steward
Director
E-MAIL: dsteward@mla.org
URL: ade.mla.org

Association of Departments of Foreign Languages (G)
85 Broad Street
Suite 500
New York, NY 10004-2434
(646) 576-5140
FAX: (646) 458-0033
Dr. Dennis Looney
Director
E-MAIL: adfl@mla.org
URL: www.adfl.org

Association of Governing Boards of Universities and Colleges (H)
1133 20th Street, NW
Suite 300
Washington, DC 20036
(202) 296-8400
FAX: (202) 223-7053
Mr. Richard Legon
President
E-MAIL: rlegon@agb.org
URL: www.agb.org

Association of Graduate Liberal Studies Programs (I)
c/o University of Oklahoma
1700 Asp Avenue, Suite 126
Norman, OK 73072
(405) 325-1245
Ms. Martha Banz
President
E-MAIL: info@aglsp.org
URL: www.aglsp.org

Association of International Education Administrators (J)
Campus Box 90404
Duke University
Durham, NC 27708-0404
(919) 668-1928
FAX: (919) 684-8749
Dr. Darla K. Deardorff
Executive Director
E-MAIL: aiea@duke.edu
URL: www.aieaworld.org

Association of Jesuit Colleges and Universities (K)
1 Dupont Circle, NW
Suite 405
Washington, DC 20036
(202) 862-9893
FAX: (202) 862-8523
Rev. Michael J. Sheeran S.J.
President
E-MAIL: msheeran@ajcunet.edu
URL: www.ajcunet.edu

Association of Military Colleges and Schools of the United States (L)
Fairfax, VA 22033
(703) 272-8406
Ray Rottman
Executive Director
E-MAIL: amcsus1@gmail.com
URL: www.amcsus.org

Association of Performing Arts Professionals (M)
1211 Connecticut Avenue, NW
Suite 200
Washington, DC 20036
(202) 833-2787
FAX: (202) 833-1543
Ms. Margaret Stevens
Director, Executive Affairs
E-MAIL: info@artspresenters.org
URL: www.apap365.org

Association of Practical Theology (N)
Yale University Divinity School
409 Prospect Street
New Haven, CT 06517
(203) 432-5371
Prof. Joyce Ann Mercer
President
E-MAIL: joyce.mercer@yale.edu
URL: www.practicaltheology.org

Association of Presbyterian Colleges and Universities (O)
c/o Agnes Scott College
Box 1102
141 E. College Avenue
Decatur, GA 30030
(470) 443-1948
Mr. Jeff Arnold
Executive Director
E-MAIL: jeff.arnold@presbyteriancolleges.org
URL: www.presbyteriancolleges.org

Association of Public and Land-Grant Universities (P)
1307 New York Avenue, NW
Suite 400
Washington, DC 20005-4722
(202) 478-6040
FAX: (202) 478-6046
M. Peter McPherson
President
E-MAIL: pmcpherson@aplu.org
URL: www.aplu.org

Association of Research Libraries (Q)
21 Dupont Circle, NW
Suite 800
Washington, DC 20036
(202) 296-2296
FAX: (202) 872-0884
Dr. Elliott Shore
Executive Director
E-MAIL: elliott@arl.org
URL: www.arl.org

Association of Schools of Allied Health Professions (R)
122 C Street, NW
Suite 650
Washington, DC 20001-2151
(202) 237-6481
FAX: (202) 237-6485
Mr. John Colbert
Executive Director
E-MAIL: john@asahp.org
URL: www.asahp.org

Association of Specialized and Professional Accreditors (S)
3304 North Broadway Street
#214
Chicago, IL 60657
(773) 857-7900
Mr. Joseph Vibert
Executive Director
E-MAIL: aspa@aspa-usa.org
URL: www.aspa-usa.org

Association of Teacher Educators (T)
PO Box 793
Manassas, VA 20113
(703) 659-1708
FAX: (703) 595-4792
Dr. David Ritchey
Executive Director
E-MAIL: dritchey@ate1.org
URL: www.ate1.org

The Association of Technology, Management, and Applied Engineering (ATMAE) (U)
3801 Lake Boone Trail
Suite 190
Raleigh, NC 27607
(919) 635-8335
FAX: (919) 779-5642
Mr. Jim Thompson IOM, CAE
Executive Director
E-MAIL: executive@atmae.org
URL: www.atmae.org

Association of Theological Schools in the United States and Canada The Commission on Accrediting (V)
10 Summit Park Drive
Pittsburgh, PA 15275-1110
(412) 788-6505
FAX: (412) 788-6510
Dr. Frank M. Yamada
Executive Director
E-MAIL: ats@ats.edu
URL: www.ats.edu

Association of University Programs in Health Administration (W)
1730 M Street, NW
Suite 407
Washington, DC 20036
(202) 763-7283
Gerald L. Glandon Ph.D.
President & CEO
E-MAIL: gglandon@aupha.org
URL: www.aupha.org

Association of University Research Parks (X)
6262 North Swan Road
Suite 125
Tucson, AZ 85718
(520) 529-2521
FAX: (520) 529-2499
Ms. Carol Stewart
Chief Executive Officer
E-MAIL: info@aurp.net
URL: www.aurp.net

Aviation Accreditation Board International (Y)
3410 Skyway Drive
Auburn, AL 36830
(334) 844-2431
FAX: (334) 844-2432
Mr. Gary J. Northam
President
E-MAIL: bayenva@auburn.edu
URL: www.aabi.aero

Big Ten Academic Alliance (Z)
1819 South Neil Street
Suite D
Champaign, IL 61820-7271
(217) 333-8475
FAX: (217) 244-7127
Mr. Keith Marshall
Executive Director
E-MAIL: info@btaa.org
URL: www.btaa.org

Broadcast Education Association (a)
1771 N Street, NW
Washington, DC 20036-2891
(202) 602-0584
FAX: (202) 609-9940
Ms. Heather Birks
Executive Director
E-MAIL: heather@beaweb.org
URL: www.beaweb.org

Career Education Colleges & Universities (b)
1530 Wilson Boulevard
Suite 1050
Arlington, VA 22209
(571) 970-3941
FAX: (571) 970-6753
Mr. Steve Gunderson
President and CEO
E-MAIL: president@career.org
URL: www.career.org

Carnegie Foundation for the Advancement of Teaching (c)
51 Vista Lane
Stanford, CA 94305
(650) 566-5100
FAX: (650) 326-0278
Dr. Anthony S. Bryk
President
URL: www.carnegiefoundation.org

CETE (Center on Education and Training for Employment) (d)
The Ohio State University
1900 Kenny Road
Columbus, OH 43210-1016
(614) 292-9072
FAX: (614) 292-3742
Mr. Robert A. Mahlman
Director
E-MAIL: mahlman.1@osu.edu
URL: www.cete.org

College and University Professional Association for Human Resources (CUPA-HR) (e)
1811 Commons Point Drive
Knoxville, TN 37932-1989
(877) 287-2474
FAX: (865) 637-7674
Mr. Andy Brantley
President & Chief Executive Officer
E-MAIL: memberservice@cupahr.org
URL: www.cupahr.org

College Art Association (f)
50 Broadway
21st Floor
New York, NY 10004
(212) 691-1051
FAX: (212) 627-2381
Mr. Hunter O'Hanian
Executive Director
E-MAIL: nyoffice@collegeart.org
URL: www.collegeart.org

The College Board (g)
250 Vesey Street
New York, NY 10281
(212) 713-8000
David Coleman
President and CEO
URL: www.collegeboard.org

College English Association (h)
Borough of Manhattan Community College
Dept. of Academic Literacy and Linguistics
199 Chambers Street, N499L
New York, NY 10007
(212) 220-1406
Dr. Juliet Emanuel
Executive Director
E-MAIL: cea.english@gmail.com
URL: cea-web.org

College Media Association (i)
355 Lexington Avenue
15th Floor
New York, NY 10017
(212) 297-2195
Meredith Taylor
Executive Director
E-MAIL: mltaylor@kellencompany.com
URL: www.collegemedia.org

Columbia Scholastic Press Association (A)
Columbia University
90 Morningside Drive
Suite B01
New York, NY 10027
(212) 854-9400
FAX: (212) 854-9401
Mr. Edmund J. Sullivan
Executive Director
E-MAIL: cspa@columbia.edu
URL: www.columbia.edu/cu/cspa

Commission on Accreditation for Health Informatics and Information Management Education (CAHIIM) (B)
233 North Michigan Avenue
21st Floor
Chicago, IL 60601-5800
(312) 233-1100
FAX: (312) 233-1948
Dr. Claire Dixon-Lee
Executive Director
E-MAIL: info@cahiim.org
URL: www.cahiim.org

Commission on Accreditation of Allied Health Education Programs (C)
25400 US Hwy 19 N
Suite 158
Clearwater, FL 33763
(727) 210-2350
FAX: (727) 210-2354
Dr. Kathleen Megivern J.D.
Executive Director
E-MAIL: megivern@caahep.org
URL: www.caahep.org

Commission on Accreditation of Healthcare Management Education (CAHME) (D)
6110 Executive Boulevard
Suite 614
Rockville, MD 20852
(301) 298-1820
Mr. Anthony Stanowski
President & CEO
E-MAIL: astanowski@cahme.org
URL: www.cahme.org

Commission on Collegiate Nursing Education (CCNE) (E)
655 K Street NW
Suite 750
Washington, DC 20001
(202) 887-6791
FAX: (202) 887-8476
Dr. Jennifer Butlin
Executive Director
E-MAIL: jbutlin@ccneaccreditation.org
URL: www.ccneaccreditation.org

Commission on Dental Accreditation (F)
211 East Chicago Avenue
Suite 1900
Chicago, IL 60611
(312) 440-4653
FAX: (312) 587-5107
Dr. Sherin Tooks
Director
E-MAIL: tookss@ada.org
URL: www.ada.org/en/coda

Commission on English Language Program Accreditation (CEA) (G)
1001 North Fairfax Street
Suite 630
Alexandria, VA 22314
(703) 665-3400, x101
Dr. Mary Reeves
Executive Director
E-MAIL: mhreeves@cea-accredit.org
URL: www.cea-accredit.org

The Commission on Independent Colleges and Universities (CICU) in New York (H)
17 Elk Street
Albany, NY 12207
(518) 436-4781
FAX: (518) 436-0417
Mrs. Mary Beth Labate
President
E-MAIL: info@cicu.org
URL: www.cicu.org

Commission on Massage Therapy Accreditation (I)
2101 Wilson Boulevard
Suite 302
Arlington, VA 22201
(202) 888-6790
FAX: (202) 888-6787
Ms. Dawn Hogue
Acting Executive Director
E-MAIL: dhogue@comta.org
URL: www.comta.org

Commission on Opticianry Accreditation (J)
PO Box 592
Canton, NY 13617
(703) 468-0566
Mrs. Debra White
Director of Accreditation
E-MAIL: director@coaccreditation.com
URL: www.coaccreditation.com

Committee on Accreditation for Education in Neurodiagnostic Technology (K)
1449 Hill Street
Whitinsville, MA 01588
(978) 338-6300
FAX: (978) 832-2638
Dr. Jackie Long-Goding RRT-NPS
Executive Director
E-MAIL: office@coa-ndt.org
URL: www.coa-ndt.org

Committee on Accreditation for Education Programs for Kinesiotherapy (CoA-KT) (L)
University of Southern Mississippi
118 College Drive
#5142
Hattiesburg, MS 39406-0002
(601) 266-5371
FAX: (601) 266-4445
Jerry W. Purvis
E-MAIL: jerry.purvis@usm.edu
URL: www.coakt.org

Committee on Accreditation for the Exercise Sciences (M)
401 West Michigan Street
Indianapolis, IN 46202
(317) 637-9200
FAX: (317) 634-7817
Mr. William Coale
Director
E-MAIL: wcoale@coaes.org
URL: www.coaes.org

Committee on Accreditation for Polysomnographic Technologist Education (N)
1711 Frank Avenue
New Bern, NC 28560
(252) 626-3238
Ms. Karen Monarchy Rowe
Executive Director
E-MAIL: office@coapsg.org
URL: www.coapsg.org

Committee on Accreditation of Educational Programs for the Emergency Medical Services Professions (O)
8301 Lakeview Parkway
Suite 111-312
Rowlett, TX 75088
(214) 703-8445, ext. 112
FAX: (214) 703-8992
Dr. George W. Hatch Jr.
Executive Director
E-MAIL: george@coaemsp.org
URL: www.coaemsp.org

Conference on College Composition and Communication (P)
1111 West Kenyon Road
Urbana, IL 61801-1096
(877) 369-6283
FAX: (217) 328-0977
Dr. Jessie L. Moore
Secretary
E-MAIL: cccc@ncte.org
URL: www.ncte.org/cccc

Council for Accreditation of Counseling and Related Educational Programs (CACREP) (Q)
1001 North Fairfax Street
Suite 510
Alexandria, VA 22314
(703) 535-5990
FAX: (703) 739-6209
Mr. Rick Gressard
Interim President and CEO
E-MAIL: cacrep@cacrep.org
URL: www.cacrep.org

Council for Adult and Experiential Learning (R)
55 East Monroe Street
Suite 2710
Chicago, IL 60603
(312) 499-2600
FAX: (312) 499-2601
Ms. Pamela Tate
President & CEO
E-MAIL: ptate@cael.org
URL: www.cael.org

Council for Advancement and Support of Education (S)
1307 New York Avenue, NW
Suite 1000
Washington, DC 20005-4701
(202) 328-2273
FAX: (202) 387-4973
Ms. Sue Cunningham
President and CEO
E-MAIL: president@case.org
URL: www.case.org

Council for Agricultural Science and Technology (CAST) (T)
4420 West Lincoln Way
Ames, IA 50014-3447
(515) 292-2125
FAX: (515) 292-4512
Mr. Kent G. Schescke
Executive Vice President
E-MAIL: cast@cast-science.org
URL: www.cast-science.org

Council for Aid to Education (U)
215 Lexington Avenue
16th Floor
New York, NY 10016-6023
(212) 217-0808
FAX: (212) 661-9766
Dr. Roger Benjamin
President & CEO
E-MAIL: roger@cae.org
URL: www.cae.org

Council for Christian Colleges & Universities (V)
321 8th Street, NE
Washington, DC 20002-6107
(202) 546-8713
FAX: (202) 546-8913
Shirley V. Hoogstra J.D.
President
E-MAIL: council@cccu.org
URL: www.cccu.org

Council for Economic Education (W)
122 East 42nd Street
Suite 2600
New York, NY 10168
(212) 730-7007 or (800) 338-1192
FAX: (212) 730-1793
Ms. Nan Morrison
President and CEO
E-MAIL: njmorrison@councilforeconed.org
URL: www.councilforeconed.org

Council for Higher Education Accreditation (X)
1 Dupont Circle, NW
Suite 510
Washington, DC 20036-1135
(202) 955-6126
FAX: (202) 955-6129
Dr. Judith Eaton
President
E-MAIL: chea@chea.org
URL: www.chea.org

Council for Interior Design Accreditation (CIDA) (formerly FIDER) (Y)
206 Grandville Avenue
Suite 350
Grand Rapids, MI 49503
(616) 458-0400
FAX: (616) 458-0460
Ms. Holly Mattson
Executive Director
E-MAIL: info@accredit-id.org
URL: www.accredit-id.org

Council for Research in Music Education (Z)
University of Illinois Press
1325 South Oak Street
Champaign, IL 61820
(217) 244-6310
FAX: (217) 244-9910
Dr. Janet R. Barrett
Editor
E-MAIL: janetbar@illinois.edu
URL: bcrme.press.illinois.edu

Council for the Accreditation of Educator Preparation (a)
1140 19th Street, NW
Suite 400
Washington, DC 20036
(202) 223-0077
Mr. Christopher Koch
President
E-MAIL: caep@caepnet.org
URL: www.caepnet.org

Council for the Advancement of Standards in Higher Education (b)
PO Box 1369
Fort Collins, CO 80522
(202) 862-1400
FAX: (202) 296-3286
Dr. Marybeth Drechsler Sharp
Executive Director
E-MAIL: executive_director@cas.edu
URL: www.cas.edu

Council of Colleges of Acupuncture and Oriental Medicine (CCAOM) (c)
PO Box 65120
Baltimore, MD 21209
(410) 464-6041
FAX: (410) 464-6042
Mr. David M. Sale J.D., LL.M
Executive Director
E-MAIL: executivedirector@ccaom.comcastbiz.net
URL: www.ccaom.org

Council of Colleges of Arts & Sciences (d)
c/o The College of William and Mary
PO Box 8795
Williamsburg, VA 23187-8795
(757) 221-1784
FAX: (757) 221-1776
Amber Elaine Cox MSW
Executive Director
E-MAIL: ccas@wm.edu
URL: www.ccas.net

Council of Graduate Schools (e)
1 Dupont Circle, NW
Suite 230
Washington, DC 20036-1146
(202) 223-3791
FAX: (202) 461-3877
Dr. Suzanne Ortega
President
E-MAIL: sortega@cgs.nche.edu
URL: www.cgsnet.org

Council of Independent Colleges (f)
1 Dupont Circle, NW
Suite 320
Washington, DC 20036-1142
(202) 466-7230
FAX: (202) 466-7238
Dr. Richard Ekman
President
E-MAIL: cic@cic.nche.edu
URL: www.cic.edu

The Council of Writing Program Administrators (g)
University of Delaware
Department of English
212 Memorial Hall
Newark, DE 19716
(302) 831-2361
Mr. Michael McCamley
Secretary
E-MAIL: mccamley@udel.edu
URL: www.wpacouncil.org

Council on Academic Accreditation in Audiology and Speech-Language Pathology American Speech-Language-Hearing Association (A)
2200 Research Boulevard
Rockville, MD 20850
(301) 296-5700
Dr. Arlene A. Pietranton
Chief Executive Officer
E-MAIL: accreditation@asha.org
URL: caa.asha.org

Council on Accreditation of Nurse Anesthesia Educational Programs (COA) (B)
222 South Prospect Avenue
Park Ridge, IL 60068-4001
(847) 655-1154
FAX: (847) 692-7137
Francis Gerbasi CRNA,Ph.D.
Executive Director/Chief Executive Officer
E-MAIL: fgerbasi@coa.us.com
URL: www.home.coa.us.com

Council on Chiropractic Education (C)
8049 North 85th Way
Scottsdale, AZ 85258-4321
(480) 443-8877
FAX: (480) 483-7333
Craig S. Little D.C., M.Ed
President
E-MAIL: cce@cce-usa.org
URL: www.cce-usa.org

Council on Education for Public Health (D)
1010 Wayne Avenue
Suite 220
Silver Spring, MD 20910-5660
(202) 789-1050
FAX: (202) 789-1895
Ms. Laura Rasar King
Executive Director
E-MAIL: lking@ceph.org
URL: www.ceph.org

Council on Governmental Relations (E)
1200 New York Avenue, NW
Suite 460
Washington, DC 20005
(202) 289-6655
FAX: (202) 289-6698
Mr. Anthony DeCrappeo
President
E-MAIL: tdecrappeo@cogr.edu
URL: www.cogr.edu

Council on Higher Education Solutions for Adults (F)
104 Johnson Street
Marshall, TX 75670
(903) 472-2762
FAX: (903) 935-3890
Dr. Tracy Andrus
President/CEO
E-MAIL: tandrus@chesa1.com
URL: www.chesa1.com

Council on Law in Higher Education (G)
9386 Via Classico West
Wellington, FL 33411
(561) 795-5671
Mr. Daren Bakst
President
E-MAIL: info@clhe.org
URL: www.clhe.org

Council on Naturopathic Medical Education (H)
PO Box 178
244 Main Street
Great Barrington, MA 01230
(413) 528-8877
Dr. Daniel Seitz J.D., Ed.D
Executive Director
E-MAIL: danseitz@cnme.org
URL: www.cnme.org

Council on Occupational Education (I)
7840 Roswell Road
Building 300, Suite 325
Atlanta, GA 30350
(800) 917-2081
FAX: (770) 396-3790
Dr. Gary Puckett
Executive Director/President
E-MAIL: gary.puckett@council.org
URL: www.council.org

Council on Podiatric Medical Education (J)
9312 Old Georgetown Road
Bethesda, MD 20814
(301) 581-9200
FAX: (301) 571-4903
Mr. Alan R. Tinkleman
Director
E-MAIL: artinkleman@apma.org
URL: www.cpme.org

Council on Social Work Education (K)
1701 Duke Street
Suite 200
Alexandria, VA 22314-3457
(703) 519-2048
FAX: (703) 683-8099
Dr. Jo Ann Regan
VP of Education
E-MAIL: jregan@cswe.org
URL: www.cswe.org

Council on Undergraduate Research (L)
734 15th Street, NW
Suite 850
Washington, DC 20005
(202) 783-4810
FAX: (202) 783-4811
Dr. Elizabeth L. Ambos
Executive Officer
E-MAIL: eambos@cur.org
URL: www.cur.org

CSAB, Inc. (M)
417 Terrace Way
Towson, MD 21204-3725
(410) 339-5456
Ms. Liz Glazer
Executive Director
E-MAIL: lglazer@csab.org
URL: www.csab.org

Cultural Vistas (N)
440 Park Avenue South
2nd Floor
New York, NY 10016
(212) 497-3500
FAX: (212) 497-3535
Ms. Linda Boughton
Acting President & CEO
E-MAIL: info@culturalvistas.org
URL: www.culturalvistas.org

Data & Marketing Association (O)
1333 Broadway
Suite 301
New York, NY 10018
(212) 768-7277
FAX: (212) 790-1406
Mr. Thomas J. Benton
CEO
E-MAIL: jsestito@thedma.org
URL: www.thedma.org

Decision Sciences Institute (P)
University of Houston
C.T. Bauer College of Business
4750 Calhoun Road, Suite 325A
Houston, TX 77204-6021
(713) 743-4815
Ms. Vivian Landrum
Executive Director
E-MAIL: info@decisionsciences.org
URL: www.decisionsciences.org

Distance Education Accrediting Commission (Q)
1101 17th Street, NW
Suite 808
Washington, DC 20036
(202) 234-5100
FAX: (202) 332-1386
Dr. Leah K. Matthews
Executive Director
E-MAIL: info@deac.org
URL: www.deac.org

Education Commission of the States (R)
700 Broadway
Suite 810
Denver, CO 80203-3442
(303) 299-3600
FAX: (303) 296-8332
Mr. Jeremy Anderson
President
E-MAIL: janderson@ecs.org
URL: www.ecs.org

Education Development Center, Inc. (S)
43 Foundry Avenue
Waltham, MA 02453-8313
(617) 969-7100
FAX: (617) 969-5979
Mr. David Offensend
President and CEO
E-MAIL: contact@edc.org
URL: www.edc.org

EDUCAUSE (T)
1150 18th Street, NW
Suite 900
Washington, DC 20036-3816
(202) 872-4200
FAX: (202) 872-4318
John O'Brien Ph.D.
President and CEO
E-MAIL: info@educause.edu
URL: www.educause.edu

FHI 360 (U)
359 Blackwell Street
Suite 200
Durham, NC 27701
(919) 544-7040
FAX: (919) 544-7261
Mr. Patrick C. Fine
Chief Executive Officer
URL: www.fhi360.org

Financial Management Association International (V)
University of South Florida
Muma College of Business
4202 East Fowler Avenue, BSN 3416
Tampa, FL 33620-9951
(813) 974-2084
FAX: (813) 974-3318
Ms. Michelle Lui
Executive Director
E-MAIL: fma@coba.usf.edu
URL: www.fma.org

Friends Association for Higher Education (W)
1501 Cherry Street
Philadelphia, PA 19102
(215) 241-7116
FAX: (215) 241-7078
Ms. Kimberley Haas
Recording Clerk
E-MAIL: fahe@quaker.org
URL: www.quakerfahe.com

The George Washington University HEATH Resource Center at the National Youth Transitions Center Graduate School of Education & Human Development (X)
2134 G Street, NW
Suite 308
Washington, DC 20052-0001
E-MAIL: askheath@gwu.edu
URL: www.heath.gwu.edu

The Gerontological Society of America (Y)
1220 L Street, NW
Suite 901
Washington, DC 20005-4001
(202) 587-2821
FAX: (202) 587-5860
Mr. James Appleby
Executive Director and CEO
E-MAIL: geron@geron.org
URL: www.geron.org

Graduate Record Examinations Board (Z)
Educational Testing Service
Mail Stop 57L
660 Rosedale Road
Princeton, NJ 08541
(609) 683-2014
FAX: (609) 683-2040
Dr. David G. Payne
Vice President & COO of Global Education Division
E-MAIL: dpayne@ets.org
URL: www.ets.org/highered

H. Wiley Hitchcock Institute for Studies in American Music (a)
Brooklyn College, CUNY
2900 Bedford Avenue
Brooklyn, NY 11210-2889
(718) 951-5655
FAX: (718) 951-4502
Dr. Jeffrey J. Taylor
Director
E-MAIL: isam@brooklyn.cuny.edu
URL: www.hisam.org

Higher Education Resource Services (HERS) (b)
University of Denver
1901 East Asbury Avenue
Denver, CO 80208
(303) 871-6866
FAX: (303) 871-6766
Dr. Judith White
President/Executive Director
E-MAIL: judith.white@du.edu
URL: www.hersnet.org

Higher Learning Commission (c)
230 South LaSalle Street
Suite 7-500
Chicago, IL 60604-1411
(312) 263-0456 / (800) 621-7440
FAX: (312) 263-7462
Dr. Barbara Gellman-Danley
President
E-MAIL: info@hlcommission.org
URL: hlcommission.org

Hispanic Association of Colleges and Universities (d)
8415 Datapoint Drive
Suite 400
San Antonio, TX 78229
(210) 692-3805
FAX: (210) 692-0823
Dr. Antonio R. Flores
President and CEO
E-MAIL: hacu@hacu.net
URL: www.hacu.net

IACLEA (International Association of Campus Law Enforcement Administrators) (e)
1110 Bonifant Street
Suite 220
Silver Spring, MD 20910
(855) 442-2532
FAX: (202) 618-8841
Ms. Sue Riseling
Executive Director
E-MAIL: sriseling@iaclea.org
URL: www.iaclea.org

The Institute for Higher Education Policy (f)
1825 K Street, NW
Suite 720
Washington, DC 20006
(202) 861-8223
FAX: (202) 861-9307
Michelle A. Cooper Ph.D.
President
E-MAIL: institute@ihep.org
URL: www.ihep.org

Institute of International Education (g)
809 United Nations Plaza
New York, NY 10017-3580
(212) 883-8200
FAX: (212) 984-5496
E-MAIL: info@iie.org
URL: www.iie.org

Institute of International Education Council for International Exchange of Scholars (h)
1400 K Street, NW
Suite 700
Washington, DC 20005
(202) 686-4000
FAX: (202) 686-4029
Maria de los Angeles Crummet
Executive Director
E-MAIL: scholars@iie.org
URL: www.cies.org

Intercollegiate Broadcasting System, Inc. (i)
367 Windsor Highway
New Windsor, NY 12553-7900
(845) 565-0003
Mr. Fritz Kass
Director-Operations
E-MAIL: ibshq@aol.com
URL: www.collegeradio.tv

International Accreditation Council for Business Education (j)
11374 Strang Line Road
Lenexa, KS 66215
(913) 631-3009
FAX: (913) 631-9154
Dr. Phyllis Okrepkie
Interim President
E-MAIL: iacbe@iacbe.org
URL: www.iacbe.org

International Association of Baptist Colleges and Universities (A)
Samford University
800 Lakeshore Drive
Birmingham, AL 35229
(205) 726-2036
Mrs. Ashley Hill
Executive Secretary
E-MAIL: ashleyhill@baptistschools.org
URL: www.baptistschools.org

International Communication Association (B)
1500 21st Street, NW
Washington, DC 20036
(202) 955-1444
FAX: (202) 955-1448
Ms. Laura Sawyer
Executive Director
E-MAIL: lsawyer@icahdq.org
URL: www.icahdq.org

International Council on Education for Teaching (C)
5201 University Boulevard
Sue and Radcliffe Killam Library 429A
Laredo, TX 78041
(956) 326-2420
FAX: (956) 326-2419
James O'Meara
President
E-MAIL: president@icet4u.org
URL: www.icet4u.org

International Fire Service Accreditation Congress (D)
1812 W. Tyler Avenue
Stillwater, OK 74078
(405) 744-8303
FAX: (405) 744-8802
Mr. Clayton Moorman
Director
E-MAIL: admin@ifsac.org
URL: ifsac.org

Joint Review Committee on Education in Cardiovascular Technology (JRC-CVT) (E)
1449 Hill Street
Whitinsville, MA 01588-1032
(978) 456-5594
FAX: (727) 210-2354
Ms. Jackie Long-Goding
Executive Director
E-MAIL: office@jrccvt.org
URL: www.jrccvt.org

Joint Review Committee on Education in Diagnostic Medical Sonography (F)
6021 University Boulevard
Suite 500
Ellicott City, MD 21043-6090
(443) 973-3251
FAX: (866) 738-3444
Mr. Gerry Magat MS
Executive Director
E-MAIL: mail@jrcdms.org
URL: www.jrcdms.org

Joint Review Committee on Education in Radiologic Technology (G)
20 North Wacker Drive
Suite 2850
Chicago, IL 60606-3182
(312) 704-5300
FAX: (312) 704-5304
Leslie F. Winter
Chief Executive Officer
E-MAIL: lwinter@jrcert.org
URL: www.jrcert.org

Joint Review Committee on Educational Programs in Nuclear Medicine Technology (H)
820 West Danforth Road
Suite B1
Edmond, OK 73003
(405) 285-0546
FAX: (405) 285-0579
Ms. Jan M. Winn
Executive Director
E-MAIL: mail@jrcnmt.org
URL: www.jrcnmt.org

Journalism Association of Community Colleges (I)
c/o CNPA Services, Inc.
2701 K Street
Sacramento, CA 95816-5131
(916) 288-6021
FAX: (916) 288-6002
Mr. Joe Wirt
Administrator
E-MAIL: joe@cnpa.com
URL: jacconline.org

Laspau, Inc. (J)
25 Mount Auburn Street
Suite 203
Cambridge, MA 02138-6095
(617) 495-5255
FAX: (617) 495-8990
Ms. Angelica Natera
Executive Director
E-MAIL: angelica_natera@harvard.edu
URL: www.laspau.harvard.edu

Law School Admission Council (K)
662 Penn Street
Newtown, PA 18940
(215) 968-1001
FAX: (215) 968-1119
Ms. Kellye Testy
President and CEO
E-MAIL: lsacinfo@lsac.org
URL: www.lsac.org

Liaison Committee on Medical Education (LCME) American Medical Association (L)
330 North Wabash
Suite 39300
Chicago, IL 60611-5885
(312) 464-4933
Barbara Barzansky Ph.D.,MHPE
LCME Co-Secretary
E-MAIL: barbara.barzansky@ama-assn.org
URL: www.lcme.org

Linguistic Society of America (M)
522 21st Street, NW
Suite 120
Washington, DC 20006-5012
(202) 835-1714
FAX: (202) 835-1717
Ms. Alyson Reed
Executive Director
E-MAIL: lsa@lsadc.org
URL: www.linguisticsociety.org

Literacy Research Association, Inc. (N)
222 South Westmonte Drive
#101
Altamonte Springs, FL 32714
(407) 774-7880
FAX: (407) 774-6440
Lynn Hupp
Executive Director
E-MAIL: lhupp@kmgnet.com
URL: www.LiteracyResearchAssociation.org

Lutheran Educational Conference of North America (O)
PMB #377
2601 South Minnesota Avenue
Suite 105
Sioux Falls, SD 57105-4750
(605) 271-9894
FAX: (605) 271-9895
Ms. Wendy Hoyne
Director of Business Operations
E-MAIL: hoyne@lutherancolleges.org
URL: www.lutherancolleges.org

Marketing EDGE (P)
1333 Broadway
Suite 301
New York, NY 10018
(212) 790-1512
FAX: (212) 790-1561
Terri L. Bartlett
President
E-MAIL: admin@marketingedge.org
URL: www.marketingedge.org

Medical Assisting Education Review Board (Q)
20 N. Wacker Drive
Suite 1575
Chicago, IL 60606-2963
(800) 228-2262
FAX: (312) 899-1259
Mr. Jim Hardman
Assistant Director of Accreditation
E-MAIL: jhardman@maerb.org
URL: www.maerb.org

Middle States Commission on Higher Education (R)
3624 Market Street
Second Floor West
Philadelphia, PA 19104-2680
(267) 284-5025
FAX: (215) 662-5501
Dr. Elizabeth H. Sibolski
President
E-MAIL: info@msche.org
URL: www.msche.org

Midwest Association of Colleges and Employers (S)
3601 East Joppa Road
Baltimore, MD 21234
(410) 931-8100
FAX: (410) 931-8111
Ms. Renee Theragood
Executive Director
E-MAIL: admin@mwace.org
URL: www.mwace.org

Midwestern Higher Education Compact (MHEC) (T)
105 Fifth Avenue South
Suite 450
Minneapolis, MN 55401
(612) 677-2777
FAX: (612) 767-3353
Mr. Larry A. Isaak
President
E-MAIL: mhec@mhec.org
URL: www.mhec.org

Midwifery Education Accreditation Council (MEAC) (U)
850 Mt. Pleasant Avenue
Ann Arbor, MI 48103
(360) 466-2080, ext. 4
Dr. Timberly Robinson
Executive Director
E-MAIL: info@meacschools.org
URL: www.meacschools.org

Modern Language Association (V)
85 Broad Street
Suite 500
New York, NY 10004-2434
(646) 576-5000
FAX: (646) 458-0030
Dr. Paula M. Krebs
Executive Director
E-MAIL: execdirector@mla.org
URL: www.mla.org

Montessori Accreditation Council for Teacher Education (MACTE) (W)
420 Park Street
Charlottesville, VA 22902
(434) 202-7793
FAX: (888) 525-8838
Dr. Rebecca Pelton
President
E-MAIL: rebecca@macte.org
URL: www.macte.org

NACADA: The Global Community for Academic Advising (X)
2323 Anderson Avenue
Suite 225
Manhattan, KS 66502-2912
(785) 532-5717
FAX: (785) 532-7732
Dr. Charlie L. Nutt
Executive Director
E-MAIL: nacada@ksu.edu
URL: www.nacada.ksu.edu

NACAS (Y)
3 Boar's Head Lane
Suite B
Charlottesville, VA 22903-4610
(434) 245-8425
FAX: (434) 245-8453
Kelsey Finn
CEO
E-MAIL: info@nacas.org
URL: www.nacas.org

NASPA-Student Affairs Administrators in Higher Education (Z)
111 K Street, NE
10th Floor
Washington, DC 20002-4409
(202) 265-7500
FAX: (202) 898-5737
Dr. Kevin Kruger
President
E-MAIL: office@naspa.org
URL: www.naspa.org

The National Academy of Education (a)
500 5th Street, NW
Washington, DC 20001
(202) 334-2340
FAX: (202) 334-2350
Mr. Gregory White
Executive Director
E-MAIL: info@naeducation.org
URL: www.naeducation.org

National Academy of Kinesiology (b)
PO Box 5076
Champaign, IL 61825-5076
(217) 403-7545
FAX: (217) 351-1549
Ms. Kim Scott
Business Manager
E-MAIL: kims@hkusa.com
URL: www.nationalacademyofkinesiology.org

National Accreditation Council for Blind and Low Vision Services (c)
PO Box 40453
Cincinnati, OH 45240
(513) 505-6750
Mr. Michael Walsh
Executive Director
E-MAIL: mwalsh.llc2015@gmail.com
URL: www.nacblvs.org

National Accrediting Agency for Clinical Laboratory Sciences (d)
5600 North River Road
Suite 720
Rosemont, IL 60018
(773) 714-8880
FAX: (773) 714-8886
Dr. Dianne M. Cearlock Ph.D.
CEO
E-MAIL: dcearlock@naacls.org
URL: www.naacls.org

National Accrediting Commission of Career Arts & Sciences (e)
3015 Colvin Street
Alexandria, VA 22314
(703) 600-7600
FAX: (703) 379-2200
Tony Mirando M.S., D.C.
Executive Director
E-MAIL: amirando@naccas.org
URL: www.naccas.org

National Association for College Admission Counseling (f)
1050 North Highland Street
Suite 400
Arlington, VA 22201
(703) 836-2222
FAX: (703) 836-8015
Ms. Joyce E. Smith
Chief Executive Officer
E-MAIL: jsmith@nacacnet.org
URL: www.nacacnet.org

National Association for Equal Opportunity in Higher Education (g)
110 Maryland Avenue, NE
Suite 511
Washington, DC 20002
(202) 552-3300
FAX: (202) 552-3330
Lezli Baskerville Esquire
President & CEO
E-MAIL: lbaskerville@nafeo.org
URL: www.nafeonation.org

National Association for Ethnic Studies (h)
Virginia Commonwealth University
Founders Hall, Third Floor
827 W. Franklin Street
PO Box 842542
Richmond, VA 23284
(804) 828-8051
E-MAIL: naes@ethnicstudies.org
URL: www.ethnicstudies.org

National Association for the Legal Support of Alternative Schools (i)
18520 N.W. 67th Avenue #188
Miami, FL 33015
(800) 456-7784
FAX: (954) 538-8041
Mrs. Chau Trinh
Institutional Representative
E-MAIL: educate@nalsas.org
URL: www.nalsas.org

National Association for Practical Nurse Education and Service, Inc. (A)
2071 N. Bechtle Avenue
PMB 307
Springfield, OH 45504
(703) 933-1003
FAX: (703) 940-4089
Ann Bauer LPN
President
E-MAIL: president@napnes.org
URL: www.napnes.org

National Association of Agricultural Educators (B)
300 Garrigus Building
University of Kentucky
Lexington, KY 40546-0215
(859) 257-2224
FAX: (859) 323-3919
Dr. Wm. Jay Jackman
Executive Director
E-MAIL: jjackman.naae@uky.edu
URL: www.naae.org

National Association of College and University Attorneys (C)
1 Dupont Circle, NW
Suite 620
Washington, DC 20036
(202) 833-8390
FAX: (202) 296-8379
Ms. Kathleen Curry Santora Esq.
President & Chief Executive Officer
E-MAIL: ksantora@nacua.org
URL: www.nacua.org

National Association of College and University Business Officers (D)
1110 Vermont Avenue, NW
Suite 800
Washington, DC 20005
(202) 861-2500
FAX: (202) 861-2583
Mr. John D. Walda
President & Chief Executive Officer
E-MAIL: john.walda@nacubo.org
URL: www.nacubo.org

The National Association of College & University Food Services (E)
1515 Turf Lane
Suite 100
East Lansing, MI 48823
(517) 332-2494
FAX: (517) 332-8144
Gretchen M. Couraud CAE, CFRE
Executive Director
E-MAIL: gcouraud@nacufs.org
URL: www.nacufs.org

National Association of College Stores (F)
500 East Lorain Street
Oberlin, OH 44074-1294
(440) 775-7777
FAX: (440) 775-4769
Mr. Robert A. Walton
Chief Executive Officer
E-MAIL: info@nacs.org
URL: www.nacs.org

National Association of College Wind and Percussion Instructors (G)
Department of Music
University of Montevallo
Davis Hall, Station 6670
Montevallo, AL 35115
(205) 665-6672
FAX: (205) 665-6676
Dr. Lori Ardovino
President
E-MAIL: ardovinl@montevallo.edu
URL: www.nacwpi.org

National Association of Colleges and Employers (H)
62 Highland Avenue
Bethlehem, PA 18017-9481
(610) 868-1421
FAX: (610) 868-0208
Dr. Marilyn Mackes
Executive Director
E-MAIL: mmackes@naceweb.org
URL: www.naceweb.org

National Association of Educational Procurement (I)
8840 Stanford Boulevard
Suite 2000
Columbia, MD 21045
(443) 543-5540
FAX: (443) 219-9687
Mrs. Doreen Murner
CEO
E-MAIL: dmurner@naepnet.org
URL: www.naepnet.org

National Association of Independent Colleges and Universities (J)
1025 Connecticut Avenue, NW
Suite 700
Washington, DC 20036-5405
(202) 785-8866
FAX: (202) 835-0003
Dr. David L. Warren
President
E-MAIL: geninfo@naicu.edu
URL: www.naicu.edu

National Association of Schools of Art and Design (K)
11250 Roger Bacon Drive
Suite 21
Reston, VA 20190
(703) 437-0700
FAX: (703) 437-6312
Karen P. Moynahan
Executive Director
E-MAIL: info@arts-accredit.org
URL: www.arts-accredit.org

National Association of Schools of Dance (L)
11250 Roger Bacon Drive
Suite 21
Reston, VA 20190
(703) 437-0700
FAX: (703) 437-6312
Karen P. Moynahan
Executive Director
E-MAIL: info@arts-accredit.org
URL: www.arts-accredit.org

National Association of Schools of Music (M)
11250 Roger Bacon Drive
Suite 21
Reston, VA 20190
(703) 437-0700
FAX: (703) 437-6312
Karen P. Moynahan
Executive Director
E-MAIL: info@arts-accredit.org
URL: www.arts-accredit.org

National Association of Schools of Theatre (N)
11250 Roger Bacon Drive
Suite 21
Reston, VA 20190
(703) 437-0700
FAX: (703) 437-6312
Karen P. Moynahan
Executive Director
E-MAIL: info@arts-accredit.org
URL: www.arts-accredit.org

National Association of State Directors of Teacher Education and Certification (O)
1629 K Street, NW
Suite 300
Washington, DC 20006
(202) 204-2208
FAX: (202) 204-2210
Dr. Phillip S. Rogers
Executive Director
E-MAIL: philrogers@nasdtec.org
URL: www.nasdtec.net

National Association of Student Financial Aid Administrators (P)
1801 Pennsylvania Avenue, NW
Suite 850
Washington, DC 20006-3606
(202) 785-0453
FAX: (202) 785-1487
Mr. Justin Draeger
President
E-MAIL: info@nasfaa.org
URL: www.nasfaa.org

National Association of System Heads (Q)
3300 Metzerott Road
Adelphi, MD 20783
(301) 445-2780
Rebecca Martin
Executive Director
E-MAIL: rebecca@nash-dc.org
URL: www.nashonline.org

National Catholic Educational Association (R)
1005 North Glebe Road
Suite 525
Arlington, VA 22201-5792
(800) 711-6232
FAX: (703) 243-0025
Dr. Thomas W. Burnford
President/CEO
E-MAIL: president@ncea.org
URL: www.ncea.org

National Coalition for Campus Children's Centers (S)
188 Front Street
Suite 116-104
Franklin, TN 37064
(615) 614-3723
FAX: (615) 614-3723
Ms. Tonya Palla
Executive Director
E-MAIL: tonyap@campuschildren.org
URL: www.campuschildren.org

National Collegiate Athletic Association (T)
PO Box 6222
Indianapolis, IN 46206-6222
(317) 917-6222
Mr. Todd Petr
Managing Director of Research
E-MAIL: tpetr@ncaa.org
URL: www.ncaa.org

National Commission on Orthotic and Prosthetic Education (NCOPE) (U)
330 John Carlyle Street
Suite 200
Alexandria, VA 22314
(703) 836-7114 x 225
FAX: (703) 836-0838
Ms. Robin Seabrook
Executive Director
E-MAIL: rseabrook@ncope.org
URL: www.ncope.org

National Communication Association (V)
1765 N Street, NW
Washington, DC 20036
(202) 464-4622
FAX: (202) 464-4600
Paaige Turner
Executive Director
E-MAIL: pturner@natcom.org
URL: www.natcom.org

National Council for Continuing Education and Training (W)
PO Box 2916
Columbus, OH 43216-2916
(888) 771-0179
FAX: (877) 835-5798
Jennifer Starkey
Executive Director
E-MAIL: nccetdirector@nccet.org
URL: www.nccet.org

National Council of Instructional Administrators (NCIA) Dept of Educational Administration (X)
141 Teachers College Hall
PO Box 880360
University of Nebraska - Lincoln
Lincoln, NE 68588-0360
(402) 472-8958
FAX: (402) 472-4300
Katherine Wesley
Executive Director
E-MAIL: ncia@unl.edu
URL: ncia.unl.edu

National Council of University Research Administrators (Y)
1015 18th Street, NW
Suite 901
Washington, DC 20036
(202) 466-3894
FAX: (202) 223-5573
Kathleen M. Larmett
Executive Director
E-MAIL: info@ncura.edu
URL: www.ncura.edu

National Education Association (Z)
1201 16th Street, NW
Suite 810
Washington, DC 20036
(202) 833-4000
FAX: (202) 822-7974
Mr. John C. Stocks
Executive Director
E-MAIL: lmallard@nea.org
URL: www.nea.org/he

National Forensic Association (a)
Illinois State University
School of Communication
Campus Box 4480
Normal, IL 61790-4480
(309) 438-8447
FAX: (309) 438-3048
Prof. Megan Koch
National Secretary-Treasurer
E-MAIL: mkoch@ilstu.edu
URL: www.nationalforensics.org

National Institute for Learning Outcomes Assessment (b)
University of Illinois at Urbana-Champaign
360 Education Building
Champaign, IL 61820
(217) 244-2155
E-MAIL: niloa@education.illinois.edu
URL: www.learningoutcomeassessment.org

National League for Nursing (c)
The Watergate Building, 8th Floor
2600 Virginia Avenue, NW
Washington, DC 20037
(202) 909-2500
Dr. Beverly Malone
Chief Executive Officer
E-MAIL: oceo@nln.org
URL: www.nln.org

National Recreation and Park Association Council on Accreditation of Parks, Recreation, Tourism and Related Professions (COAPRT) (d)
22377 Belmont Ridge Road
Ashburn, VA 20148-4501
(703) 858-2155
FAX: (703) 858-0794
Ms. Jennifer Stromberg
Awards and Accreditation Manager
E-MAIL: jstromberg@nrpa.org
URL: www.nrpa.org/certification/accreditation/

National Rural Education Association (e)
615 McCallie Avenue
Hunter Hall 212
Chattanooga, TN 37421
(425) 425-4539
Dr. Allen Pratt
Executive Director
E-MAIL: allen-pratt@utc.edu
URL: www.nrea.net

National Society for Experiential Education (f)
c/o Talley Management Group, Inc.
19 Mantua Road
Mt. Royal, NJ 08061
(856) 423-3427
FAX: (856) 423-3420
Haley Brust
Executive Director
E-MAIL: nsee@talley.com
URL: www.nsee.org

National Writing Project (g)
2105 Bancroft Way
#1042
University of California
Berkeley, CA 94720-1042
(510) 642-0963
FAX: (510) 642-4545
Elyse Eidman-Aadahl
Executive Director
E-MAIL: nwp@nwp.org
URL: www.nwp.org

Network of Schools of Public Policy, Affairs, and Administration (h)
1029 Vermont Avenue, NW
Suite 1100
Washington, DC 20005
(202) 628-8965
FAX: (202) 626-4978
Laurel McFarland
Executive Director
E-MAIL: naspaa@naspaa.org
URL: www.naspaa.org

New England Association of Schools and Colleges, Inc. Commission on Institutions of Higher Education (A)
3 Burlington Woods Drive
Suite 100
Burlington, MA 01803-4514
(781) 425-7747
FAX: (781) 425-1001
Dr. Barbara E. Brittingham
President of the Commission
E-MAIL: cihe@neasc.org
URL: cihe.neasc.org

New England Board of Higher Education (B)
45 Temple Place
Boston, MA 02111
(617) 357-9620, ext. 119
FAX: (617) 338-1577
Dr. Michael K. Thomas
President and CEO
E-MAIL: mthomas@nebhe.org
URL: www.nebhe.org

North American Association of Summer Sessions (C)
342 N. Main Street
Suite 301
West Hartford, CT 06117
(860) 586-7530
Ms. April M. Duquette
Executive Director
E-MAIL: aduquette@naass.org
URL: www.naass.org

Northwest Commission on Colleges and Universities (D)
8060 165th Avenue, NE
Suite 100
Redmond, WA 98052
(425) 558-4224
FAX: (425) 376-0596
Dr. Sandra E. Elman
President
E-MAIL: selman@nwccu.org
URL: www.nwccu.org

Planning Accreditation Board (E)
2334 W. Lawrence Avenue
Suite 209
Chicago, IL 60625
(773) 334-7200
Ms. Shonagh Merits
Executive Director
E-MAIL: smerits@planningaccreditationboard.org
URL: www.planningaccreditationboard.org

Quality Education for Minorities (QEM) Network (F)
1818 N Street, NW
Suite 350
Washington, DC 20036
(202) 659-1818
FAX: (202) 659-5408
Ivory Toldson
President
E-MAIL: itoldson@qem.org
URL: www.qem.org

Society for College and University Planning (G)
1330 Eisenhower Place
Ann Arbor, MI 48108
(734) 669-3270
Mike Moss CAE
President
E-MAIL: info@scup.org
URL: www.scup.org

Society for Slovene Studies (H)
148 Russsell Street #3
Worcester, MA 01609
Ms. Kristina Helena Reardon
Secretary
E-MAIL: kristina.reardon@gmail.com
URL: www.slovenestudies.com

Society for Values in Higher Education (I)
c/o Western Kentucky University
1906 College Heights Boulevard
#8020
Bowling Green, KY 42101
(270) 745-2907
FAX: (270) 745-5347
Dr. Eric Bain-Selbo
Executive Director
E-MAIL: society@svhe.org
URL: www.svhe.org

Society of American Foresters (J)
10100 Laureate Way
Bethesda, MD 20814-2198
(866) 897-8720
FAX: (301) 897-3690
Mr. Matt Menashes
Chief Executive Officer
E-MAIL: membership@safnet.org
URL: www.eforester.org

Society of Professors of Education (K)
University of West Georgia
Department of ECSE
1600 Maple Street
Carrollton, GA 30118-5160
(678) 839-6132
FAX: (678) 839-6097
Dr. Robert C. Morris
Secretary-Treasurer
E-MAIL: rmorris@westga.edu

Southeastern Universities Research Association (L)
1201 New York Avenue, NW
Suite 430
Washington, DC 20005
(202) 408-7872
FAX: (202) 408-8250
Dr. Jerry Draayer
President & CEO
E-MAIL: draayer@sura.org
URL: www.sura.org

Southern Association for College Student Affairs (M)
Armstrong State University
11935 Abercorn Street
Savannah, GA 31419
(912) 344-2510
Dr. Joe Buck
Executive Director
E-MAIL: joe.buck@armstrong.edu
URL: www.sacsa.org

Southern Association of Colleges and Schools Commission on Colleges (N)
1866 Southern Lane
Decatur, GA 30033-4097
(404) 679-4500
FAX: (404) 994-6592
Dr. Belle S. Wheelan
President
E-MAIL: bwheelan@sacscoc.org
URL: www.sacscoc.org

Southern States Communication Association (O)
College of Charleston
Office of the Dean
School of Humanities and Social Sciences
2 Green Way
Charleston, SC 29424
(843) 953-0760
FAX: (843) 953-0758
Mr. Jerold L. Hale
Executive Director
E-MAIL: director@ssca.net
URL: www.ssca.net

State Higher Education Executive Officers (P)
3035 Center Green Drive
Suite 100
Boulder, CO 80301-2205
(303) 541-1600
FAX: (303) 541-1639
Dr. Robert Anderson
President
E-MAIL: randerson@sheeo.org
URL: www.sheeo.org

Tennessee Independent Colleges and Universities Association (Q)
1031 17th Avenue South
Nashville, TN 37212
(615) 242-6400
FAX: (615) 242-8033
Dr. Claude O. Pressnell Jr.
President
E-MAIL: pressnell@ticua.org
URL: www.ticua.org

Transnational Association of Christian Colleges and Schools (TRACS) (R)
15935 Forest Road
Forest, VA 24551
(434) 525-9539
Dr. Timothy W. Eaton
President
E-MAIL: info@tracs.org
URL: www.tracs.org

The Tuition Exchange, Inc. (S)
3 Bethesda Metro Center
Suite 700
Bethesda, MD 20814
(301) 941-1827
FAX: (301) 657-9776
Mr. Robert D. Shorb
Executive Director/CEO
E-MAIL: rshorb@tuitionexchange.org
URL: www.tuitionexchange.org

UNCF (T)
1805 7th Street NW
Washington, DC 20001
(202) 810-0200
FAX: (202) 234-0222
Dr. Michael Lomax
President & CEO
URL: www.uncf.org

University Aviation Association (U)
2787 N. 2nd Street
Second Floor
Memphis, TN 38127
(901) 563-0505
Ms. Dawn Vinson
Executive Director
E-MAIL: uaamail@uaa.aero
URL: www.uaa.aero

University Film and Video Association (V)
960 War Eagle Drive S
Colorado Springs, CO 80919
(646) 498-1182
Ms. Heather Addison
President
E-MAIL: ufvahome@gmail.com
URL: www.ufva.org

University Photographers' Association of America (W)
Moraine Valley Community College
9000 W. College Parkway
Palos Hills, IL 60465
(708) 974-5495
Mr. Glenn Carpenter
UPAA President
E-MAIL: carpenter@morainevalley.edu
URL: www.upaa.org

University Professional & Continuing Education Association (UPCEA) (X)
One Dupont Circle, NW
Suite 615
Washington, DC 20036
(202) 659-3130
FAX: (202) 785-0374
Dr. Robert Hansen
CEO
E-MAIL: rhansen@upcea.edu
URL: www.upcea.edu

University Risk Management and Insurance Association, Inc. (Y)
400 West 7th Street
Suite 301
Bloomington, IN 47404
(812) 727-7130
FAX: (812) 727-7129
Ms. Jennifer Whittington
Executive Director
E-MAIL: urmia@urmia.org
URL: www.urmia.org

Urban Affairs Association (Z)
c/o Urban Studies Program
University of Wisconsin-Milwaukee
PO Box 413
Milwaukee, WI 53201-0413
(414) 229-3025
Dr. Margaret Wilder
UAA Executive Director
E-MAIL: info@uaamail.org
URL: www.urbanaffairsassociation.org

WASC Senior College and University Commission (a)
985 Atlantic Avenue
Suite 100
Alameda, CA 94501
(510) 748-9001
FAX: (510) 748-9797
Mary Ellen Petrisko
President
URL: www.wascsenior.org

Western Interstate Commission for Higher Education (b)
3035 Center Green Drive
Suite 200
Boulder, CO 80301-2204
(303) 541-0201
FAX: (303) 541-0245
Mr. Joseph A. Garcia
President
E-MAIL: jgarcia@wiche.edu
URL: www.wiche.edu

Consortia of Institutions of Higher Education

Alabama Association of Independent Colleges and Universities (A)
5950 Carmichael Place
Suite 213
Montgomery, AL 36117
(334) 356-2220
FAX: (334) 356-2202
Paul M. Hankins
President
E-MAIL: hankinsp@knology.net
URL: www.aaicu.net

Arkansas' Independent Colleges and Universities (B)
One Riverfront Place
Suite 610
North Little Rock, AR 72114
(501) 378-0843
FAX: (501) 374-1523
Dr. Rex M. Horne
President
E-MAIL: rhorne@arkindcolleges.org
URL: www.arkindcolleges.org

Associated Colleges of Central Kansas (C)
210 South Main Street
McPherson, KS 67460
(620) 241-5150
FAX: (620) 241-5153
Ms. Beverly Schottler
Program Director
E-MAIL: bev@mail.acck.edu
URL: www.acck.edu

Associated Colleges of the Midwest (D)
11 East Adams Street
Suite 800
Chicago, IL 60603
(312) 263-5000
FAX: (312) 263-5879
Dr. Christopher Welna
President
E-MAIL: acm@acm.edu
URL: www.acm.edu

Association of Independent California Colleges and Universities (E)
1121 L Street
Suite 802
Sacramento, CA 95814
(916) 446-7626
FAX: (916) 446-7948
Ms. Kristen F. Soares
President
E-MAIL: aiccu@aiccu.edu
URL: www.aiccu.edu

Association of Independent Colleges and Universities in Massachusetts (F)
11 Beacon Street
Suite 1224
Boston, MA 02108-3093
(617) 742-5147
FAX: (617) 742-3089
Mr. Richard Doherty
President
E-MAIL: richard.doherty@aicum.org
URL: www.aicum.org

Association of Independent Colleges and Universities in New Jersey (G)
797 Springfield Avenue
Summit, NJ 07901-1107
(908) 277-3738
FAX: (908) 277-0851
Mr. John B. Wilson
President and CEO
E-MAIL: jbwilson@njcolleges.org
URL: www.njcolleges.org

Association of Independent Colleges and Universities of Ohio (H)
41 South High Street
Suite 1690
Columbus, OH 43215
(614) 228-2196
FAX: (614) 228-8406
Mr. C. Todd Jones
President & General Counsel
E-MAIL: tjones@aicuo.edu
URL: www.aicuo.edu

Association of Independent Colleges and Universities of Pennsylvania (I)
101 North Front Street
Harrisburg, PA 17101-1405
(717) 232-8649
FAX: (717) 233-8574
Dr. Don L. Francis
President
E-MAIL: francis@aicup.org
URL: www.aicup.org

Association of Independent Colleges and Universities of Rhode Island (J)
50 Park Row West
Suite 100
Providence, RI 02903
(401) 272-8270
Mr. Daniel Egan
President
E-MAIL: degan@aicuri.org
URL: www.aicuri.org

Association of Independent Colleges of Art & Design (K)
236 Hope Street
Providence, RI 02906
(401) 270-5991
FAX: (401) 270-5993
Ms. Deborah Obalil
President & Executive Director
E-MAIL: deborah@aicad.org
URL: www.aicad.org

Association of Independent Kentucky Colleges and Universities (L)
484 Chenault Road
Frankfort, KY 40601
(502) 695-5007
FAX: (502) 695-5057
Dr. Gary S. Cox
President
E-MAIL: gary.cox@aikcu.org
URL: www.aikcu.org

Association of Vermont Independent Colleges (M)
PO Box 254
Montpelier, VT 05601
(802) 828-8826
Susan Stitely
President
E-MAIL: sstitely@vermont-icolleges.org
URL: www.vermont-icolleges.org

Atlanta Regional Council for Higher Education (N)
141 E. College Avenue
Box 1084
Decatur, GA 30030
(404) 246-0659
Ms. Tracey Johnson
Sr. Program Coordinator
E-MAIL: tjohnson@atlantahighered.org
URL: www.atlantahighered.org

Boston Theological Institute (O)
PO Box 391395
Cambridge, MA 02139
(617) 527-4880
Dr. Ann McClenahan
Executive Director
E-MAIL: mcclenahan@bostontheological.org
URL: www.bostontheological.org

CCUMC (Consortium of College & University Media Centers) (P)
Indiana University
306 N. Union Street
Bloomington, IN 47405-3888
(812) 855-6049
Aileen Scales
Executive Director
E-MAIL: ccumc@ccumc.org
URL: www.ccumc.org

Central Pennsylvania Consortium (Q)
c/o Franklin & Marshall College
PO Box 3003
Lancaster, PA 17604-3003
(717) 358-4282
FAX: (717) 358-4455
Ms. Kathryn Missildine
Executive Assistant
E-MAIL: kathy.missildine@fandm.edu
URL: www.centralpennsylvaniaconsortium.org

CHESLA (R)
10 Columbus Boulevard
Hartford, CT 06106-1978
(860) 761-8453
Ms. Jeanette W. Weldon
Executive Director
E-MAIL: jweldon@chesla.org
URL: www.chesla.org

Christian College Consortium (S)
255 Grapevine Road
Wenham, MA 01984-1899
(978) 867-4802
FAX: (978) 867-4650
Dr. Stan D. Gaede
President
E-MAIL: stan.gaede@gordon.edu
URL: www.ccconsortium.org

Community College Futures Assembly (T)
University of Florida, College of Education
Box 117040
229 Norman Hall
Gainesville, FL 32611-7044
(352) 273-4293
Dr. Dale F. Campbell
Director
E-MAIL: futures@coe.ufl.edu
URL: www.education.ufl.edu/futures/

The Consortium for Graduate Study in Management (U)
229 Chesterfield Business Parkway
Chesterfield, MO 63005
(636) 681-5487
FAX: (636) 681-5497
Mr. Peter J. Aranda III
Executive Director and CEO
E-MAIL: recruiting@cgsm.org
URL: www.cgsm.org

Consortium of Universities of the Washington Metropolitan Area (V)
1100 H Street, NW
Suite 500
Washington, DC 20005
(202) 331-8080
FAX: (202) 331-7925
Dr. John Cavanaugh
President & CEO
E-MAIL: jcavanaugh@consortium.org
URL: www.consortium.org

Consortium on Financing Higher Education (W)
1 Main Street
Suite 1210
Cambridge, MA 02142
(617) 253-5030
FAX: (617) 258-8280
Dr. Kristine E. Dillon
President
E-MAIL: cofhe-info@mit.edu
URL: www.cofhe.org

Cooperating Raleigh Colleges (X)
Meredith College
Wainwright Hall 110
3800 Hillsborough Street
Raleigh, NC 27607-5298
(919) 760-8538
Ms. Jenny Spiker
Director
E-MAIL: crc@meredith.edu
URL: www.crcraleighcolleges.org

Council of Independent Colleges in Virginia (Y)
PO Box 1005
Bedford, VA 24523
(540) 586-0606
FAX: (540) 586-2630
Mr. Robert B. Lambeth Jr.
President
E-MAIL: lambeth@cicv.org
URL: www.cicv.org

Council of North Central Two Year Colleges (Z)
200 South 14th Street
Parsons, KS 67357
(620) 820-1223
FAX: (620) 421-0921
Dr. George Knox
Executive Director
E-MAIL: meganf@labette.edu
URL: www.labette.edu/cnctyc

Council of Presidents (a)
410 Eleventh Avenue, SE
Suite 101
Olympia, WA 98501
(360) 292-4100
FAX: (360) 292-4110
Mr. Paul Francis
Executive Director
E-MAIL: pfrancis@cop.wsu.edu
URL: www.councilofpresidents.org

Federation of Independent Illinois Colleges and Universities (b)
1123 South Second Street
Springfield, IL 62704
(217) 789-1400
FAX: (217) 789-6259
Mr. David W. Tretter
President
E-MAIL: davetretter@federationedu.org
URL: www.federationedu.org

Five Colleges, Incorporated (c)
97 Spring Street
Amherst, MA 01002
(413) 542-4009
FAX: (413) 542-4029
Dr. Neal B. Abraham
Executive Director
E-MAIL: nabraham@fivecolleges.edu
URL: www.fivecolleges.edu

Georgia Independent College Association (d)
600 West Peachtree Street, NW
Suite 1710
Atlanta, GA 30308
(404) 233-5433, Ext. 21
FAX: (404) 233-6309
Dr. Susanna Baxter
President
E-MAIL: sbaxter@georgiacolleges.org
URL: www.georgiacolleges.org

Graduate Theological Foundation Oxford/Rome/Indiana Consortia (e)
Dodge House
415 Lincoln Way East
Mishawaka, IN 46544-2213
(800) 423-5983
FAX: (574) 255-7520
Bethany Morgan MBA
Registrar
E-MAIL: information@gtfeducation.org
URL: www.gtfeducation.org

Great Lakes Colleges Association (f)
535 West William
Suite 301
Ann Arbor, MI 48103
(734) 661-2350
FAX: (734) 661-2349
Dr. Richard A. Detweiler
President
E-MAIL: detweiler@glca.org
URL: www.glca.org

Greater Cincinnati Collegiate Connection (g)
Northern Kentucky University
241 Campbell Hall
Highland Heights, KY 41099
(859) 392-2428
Ms. Janet Piccirillo
Executive Director
E-MAIL: gc3@nku.edu
URL: www.gccollegiateconnection.org

Hartford Consortium for Higher Education (h)
31 Pratt Street
5th Floor
Hartford, CT 06103
(860) 702-3800
FAX: (860) 241-1130
Dr. Martin Estey
Executive Director
E-MAIL: mestey@metrohartford.com
URL: www.hartfordconsortium.org

Higher Education Consortium for Urban Affairs, Inc. (HECUA) (i)
2233 University Avenue West
Suite 210
St. Paul, MN 55114
(651) 287-3300
FAX: (651) 659-9421
Mr. Andrew Williams
Executive Director
E-MAIL: hecua@hecua.org
URL: www.hecua.org

Higher Education Consortium of Metropolitan St. Louis (j)
8420 Delmar Boulevard
Suite 504
St. Louis, MO 63124-2180
(314) 991-2700
FAX: (314) 991-2874
Mr. Thomas George
Chair
E-MAIL: purchasing@heccstl.com
URL: www.heccstl.com

Higher Education Data Sharing (HEDS) Consortium (A)
Wabash College
410 West Wabash Avenue
Crawfordsville, IN 47933
(765) 361-6331
Charles Blaich
Director
E-MAIL: blaich.cila.heds@icloud.com
URL: www.hedsconsortium.org

Independent Colleges and Universities of Missouri (B)
PO Box 1865
Jefferson City, MO 65102-1865
(573) 635-9160
FAX: (573) 635-6258
Mr. William A. Gamble
Executive Director
E-MAIL: bill@molobby.com
URL: www.icum.org

Independent Colleges and Universities of Texas, Inc. (C)
1303 San Antonio
Suite 820
Austin, TX 78701
(512) 472-9522
FAX: (512) 472-2371
Ray Martinez III
President
E-MAIL: sam.rauschenfels@icut.org
URL: www.icut.org

Independent Colleges of Indiana (D)
30 S. Meridian Street
Suite 800
Indianapolis, IN 46204
(317) 236-6090
FAX: (317) 236-6086
David W. Wantz EdD
President and CEO
E-MAIL: smartchoice@icindiana.org
URL: www.icindiana.org

Independent Colleges of Washington (E)
600 Stewart Street
Suite 600
Seattle, WA 98101
(206) 623-4494
Ms. Violet A. Boyer
President & CEO
E-MAIL: info@icwashington.org
URL: www.icwashington.org

Inter-University Consortium for Political and Social Research (F)
The University of Michigan
Institute for Social Research
PO Box 1248
Ann Arbor, MI 48106-1248
(734) 615-8400
FAX: (734) 647-8200
Dr. Margaret Levenstein
Director
E-MAIL: maggiel@umich.edu
URL: www.icpsr.umich.edu

Inter-University Council of Ohio (IUC) (G)
10 West Broad Street
Suite 450
Columbus, OH 43215
(614) 464-1266
FAX: (614) 464-9281
Ms. Cindy McQuade
Vice President of Operations
E-MAIL: mcquade.2@osu.edu
URL: www.iuc-ohio.org

Iowa Association of Community College Trustees (H)
855 East Court Avenue
Des Moines, IA 50309
(515) 282-4692
FAX: (515) 282-3743
M. J. Dolan J.D.
Executive Director
E-MAIL: mjdolan@iacct.com
URL: www.iacct.com

Iowa Association of Independent Colleges and Universities (I)
505 Fifth Avenue
Suite 1030
Des Moines, IA 50309-2399
(515) 282-3175
FAX: (515) 282-8177
Mr. Gary W. Steinke
President
E-MAIL: president@iaicu.org
URL: www.iowaprivatecolleges.org

Kansas Independent College Association (J)
700 South Kansas Avenue
Suite 622
Topeka, KS 66603
(785) 235-9877
FAX: (785) 235-1437
Mr. Matthew E. Lindsey
President
E-MAIL: matt@kscolleges.org
URL: www.kscolleges.org

Lehigh Valley Association of Independent Colleges (K)
1309 Main Street
Bethlehem, PA 18018
(610) 625-7888
Diane Dimitroff
Executive Director
E-MAIL: dimitroffd@lvaic.org
URL: www.lvaic.org

Louisiana Association of Independent Colleges and Universities (L)
320 Third Street
Suite 104
Baton Rouge, LA 70801
(225) 389-9885
FAX: (225) 389-0149
Ms. Mary Ann Coleman
President
E-MAIL: maryann@laicu.org
URL: www.laicu.org

Maryland Independent College and University Association (M)
140 South Street
Annapolis, MD 21401
(410) 269-0306
FAX: (410) 269-5905
Ms. Tina M. Bjarekull
President
E-MAIL: tbjarekull@micua.org
URL: www.micua.org

Massachusetts Education & Career Opportunities Inc (N)
484 Main Street
Suite 500
Worcester, MA 01608
(508) 754-6829
FAX: (508) 797-0069
Ms. Pamela Boisvert
CEO
E-MAIL: pboisvert@massedco.org
URL: www.massedco.org

Michigan Independent Colleges & Universities (O)
One Michigan Avenue
Suite 950
Lansing, MI 48933
(517) 372-9160
FAX: (517) 372-9165
Robert LeFevre
E-MAIL: rlefevre@micolleges.org
URL: www.micolleges.org

Minnesota Private College Council, Inc. (P)
445 Minnesota Street
Suite 500
St. Paul, MN 55101-2903
(651) 228-9061
FAX: (651) 228-0379
E-MAIL: colleges@mnprivatecolleges.org
URL: www.mnprivatecolleges.org

Mississippi Association of Independent Colleges and Universities (Q)
PO Box 2933
Ridgeland, MS 39158-2933
(601) 206-5360
Dr. E. Harold Fisher
Executive Director
E-MAIL: ehfisher@bellsouth.net

National Student Exchange (R)
2613 Northridge Parkway
Suite 106
Ames, IA 50010
(515) 450-5529
Dr. Debra Sanborn
President
E-MAIL: info@nse.org
URL: www.nse.org

New England Faculty Development Consortium (S)
Mount Ida College
777 Dedham Street
Newton, MA 02459
(617) 928-7396
Dakin Burdick Ph.D.
President
E-MAIL: dburdick@mountida.edu
URL: www.nefdc.org

New Hampshire College & University Council (T)
3 Barrell Court
Suite 100
Concord, NH 03301-8543
(603) 225-4199
FAX: (603) 225-8108
Mike Vlacich
President and CEO
E-MAIL: vlacich@nhcuc.org
URL: www.nhcuc.org

New Jersey Association of State Colleges and Universities (U)
150 West State Street
Trenton, NJ 08608
(609) 989-1100
Dr. Michael W. Klein
CEO
E-MAIL: mwklein@njascu.org
URL: www.njascu.org

New Jersey Council of County Colleges (V)
330 West State Street
Trenton, NJ 08618
(609) 392-3434
FAX: (609) 392-8158
Dr. Lawrence A. Nespoli
President
E-MAIL: info@njccc.org
URL: www.njccc.org

New Orleans Educational Telecommunications Consortium, Inc. (W)
2045 Lakeshore Drive
Suite 401
New Orleans, LA 70122
(504) 524-0350
E-MAIL: noetc@noetc.org
URL: www.noetc.com

North Carolina Independent Colleges and Universities (X)
530 North Blount Street
Raleigh, NC 27604
(919) 832-5817
FAX: (919) 833-0794
Dr. A. Hope Williams
President
E-MAIL: williams@ncicu.org
URL: www.ncicu.org

North Dakota Independent College Fund (Y)
University of Mary
7500 University Drive
Bismarck, ND 58504
(701) 355-8222
FAX: (701) 255-7687
Mr. Jeff Beauchamp
Executive Director
E-MAIL: jrbeauchamo@umary.edu

Northeast Consortium of Colleges and Universities in Massachusetts (NECCUM) (Z)
c/o Office of the President
Salem State University
352 Lafayette Street
Salem, MA 01970
(978) 542-6134
FAX: (978) 542-6126
Katie Sadowski
E-MAIL: ksadowski@salemstate.edu

Northeast Ohio Council on Higher Education (a)
6000 Rockside Woods Boulevard
Suite 325
Independence, OH 44131
(216) 420-9200
Ms. Holly J. Harris Bane
President
E-MAIL: hharrisbane@noche.org
URL: www.noche.org

Oak Ridge Associated Universities (b)
MC-100-22
PO Box 117
Oak Ridge, TN 37831-0117
(865) 576-3300
FAX: (865) 576-3816
Mr. Harry A. Page
President and CEO
E-MAIL: andy.page@orau.org
URL: www.orau.org

Oklahoma Independent Colleges and Universities (c)
PO Box 57148
Oklahoma City, OK 73157-7148
(405) 371-1780
Lesa Smaligo
Executive Director
E-MAIL: lesa@oicu.org
URL: www.oicu.org

Oregon Alliance of Independent Colleges & Universities (d)
1211 SW Fifth Avenue
Suite 1900
Portland, OR 97204
(503) 796-2852
Ms. Kristen Grainger
President
E-MAIL: grainger@oaicu.org
URL: www.oaicu.org

Pennsylvania Association of Colleges and Universities (e)
950 Walnut Bottom Road
Suite 15-214
Carlisle, PA 17015
(800) 687-9010
FAX: (717) 240-0673
URL: www.pacu.org

Pennsylvania's State System of Higher Education Foundation, Inc. (f)
2986 North Second Street
Harrisburg, PA 17110
(717) 720-4056
FAX: (717) 720-7082
Ms. Jennifer S. Hartman
President/CEO
E-MAIL: jhartman@thepafoundation.org
URL: www.thepafoundation.org

Pittsburgh Council on Higher Education (g)
201 Wood Street
Pittsburgh, PA 15222
(412) 657-8105
Ms. Karina Chavez
Executive Director
E-MAIL: kchavez@pointpark.edu
URL: www.pchepa-pa.org

Quad-Cities Graduate Study Center (h)
WIU - QC Campus
3300 River Drive
Moline, IL 61265
(309) 762-9481
Shirley Moore
E-MAIL: qc@gradcenter.org
URL: www.gradcenter.org

South Carolina Independent Colleges & Universities, Inc. (i)
PO Box 12007
Columbia, SC 29211
(803) 799-7122
FAX: (803) 254-7504
Mr. Michael G. LeFever
President & CEO
E-MAIL: mike@scicu.org
URL: www.scicu.org

South Metropolitan Higher Education Consortium (j)
202 S. Halsted Street
ATOC-144
Chicago Heights, IL 60411
(708) 709-2942
Ms. Genevieve F. Boesen
Executive Director
E-MAIL: gboesen@prairiestate.edu
URL: www.southmetroed.org

Southern Regional Education Board (k)
592 Tenth Street, NW
Atlanta, GA 30318-5776
(404) 875-9211
FAX: (404) 872-1477
Dr. David S. Spence
President
E-MAIL: dave.spence@sreb.org
URL: www.sreb.org

Southwestern Ohio Council for Higher Education (SOCHE) (A)
3155 Research Boulevard
Suite 204
Dayton, OH 45420-4015
(937) 258-8890
FAX: (937) 258-8899
Dr. Sean Creighton
President
E-MAIL: soche@soche.org
URL: www.soche.org

Texas International Education Consortium (B)
1103 West 24th Street
Austin, TX 78705
(512) 477-9283, ext. 114
FAX: (512) 322-0592
Dr. Ronald Aqua
President & CEO
E-MAIL: ron.aqua@tiec.org
URL: www.tiec.org

Tuition Plan Consortium/Private College 529 Plan (C)
7425 Forsyth Boulevard
Suite 194
St. Louis, MO 63105
(314) 727-0900
FAX: (314) 727-0930
Ms. Kimberly Woolridge
Executive Assistant/Assistant Treasurer
E-MAIL: kimberly@pc529.com
URL: www.privatecollege529.com

University City Science Center (D)
3711 Market Street
Suite 800
Philadelphia, PA 19104
(215) 966-6000
FAX: (215) 966-6002
Dr. Stephen Tang
President & CEO
E-MAIL: info@sciencecenter.org
URL: www.sciencecenter.org

The Virginia College Fund (E)
4900 Augusta Avenue
Suite 101
Richmond, VA 23230
(804) 355-3271
FAX: (804) 359-5765
Mr. James K. Dill
President
E-MAIL: jkdill@thevcf.org
URL: www.thevcf.org

Virginia Tidewater Consortium for Higher Education (F)
4900 Powhatan Avenue
Norfolk, VA 23508-1836
(757) 683-3183
FAX: (757) 683-4515
Dr. Lawrence G. Dotolo
President
E-MAIL: lgdotolo@aol.com
URL: www.vtc.odu.edu

Washington Theological Consortium (G)
415 Michigan Avenue, NE
Suite 105
Washington, DC 20017
(202) 832-2675
Dr. Larry Golemon
Executive Director
E-MAIL: wtc@washtheocon.org
URL: washtheocon.org

West Virginia Independent Colleges & Universities, Inc. (H)
c/o Suttle & Stainaker
1411 Virginia Street East
Suite 100
Charleston, WV 25301
(304) 433-2604
FAX: (304) 345-5526
Becky Ceperley
Executive Director
E-MAIL: rebeccaceperley@wvicu.org
URL: www.wvicu.org

Wisconsin Association of Independent Colleges and Universities (I)
122 West Washington Avenue
Suite 700
Madison, WI 53703-2723
(608) 256-7761
FAX: (608) 256-7065
Dr. Rolf Wegenke
President
E-MAIL: mail@waicu.org
URL: www.waicu.org

The Work Colleges Consortium (J)
CPO 2163
Berea, KY 40404
(859) 985-3154
Ms. Robin Taffler
Executive Director
E-MAIL: robin@workcolleges.org
URL: www.workcolleges.org

NAME INDEX

US Department of Education Offices, Statewide Agencies of Higher Education, Higher Education Associations, Consortia of Institutions of Higher Education

Institutions By Religious Affiliation

African Methodist Episcopal
- Allen University ... SC
- Edward Waters College ... FL
- Paul Quinn College ... TX
- Payne Theological Seminary ... OH
- Shorter College ... AR
- Wilberforce University ... OH

African Methodist Episcopal Zion Church
- Clinton College ... SC
- Hood Theological Seminary ... NC
- Livingstone College ... NC

Alabama Baptist State Convention
- Judson College ... AL

American Baptist
- Alderson Broaddus University ... WV
- American Baptist Seminary of the West ... CA
- Bacone College ... OK
- Eastern University ... PA
- Franklin College of Indiana ... IN
- Judson University ... IL
- Linfield College ... OR
- Northern Seminary ... IL
- Ottawa University ... KS
- University of Sioux Falls ... SD

Assemblies Of God Church
- Assemblies of God Theological Seminary MO
- Bethel College ... VA
- Evangel University ... MO
- Global University ... MO
- Native American Bible College ... NC
- North Central University ... MN
- Northpoint Bible College ... MA
- Northwest University ... WA
- Southeastern University ... FL
- Southwestern Assemblies of God University ... TX
- Trinity Bible College & Graduate School ... ND
- University of Valley Forge ... PA
- Vanguard University of Southern California ... CA

Baptist
- American Baptist College ... TN
- Arkansas Baptist College ... AR
- Arlington Baptist University ... TX
- Baptist Bible College ... MO
- Baptist Missionary Association Theological Seminary ... TX
- Baptist University of the Americas ... TX
- Baylor University ... TX
- Bethel University ... MN
- Bluefield College ... VA
- Boston Baptist College ... MA
- Brewton-Parker College ... GA
- Campbell University ... NC
- Campbellsville University ... KY
- Cedarville University ... OH
- Central Baptist College ... AR
- Central Baptist Theological Seminary ... KS
- Central Baptist Theological Seminary of Minneapolis ... MN
- Chowan University ... NC
- Clarks Summit University ... PA
- Dallas Baptist University ... TX
- East Texas Baptist University ... TX
- Gardner-Webb University ... NC
- Georgetown College ... KY
- Hardin-Simmons University ... TX
- Howard Payne University ... TX
- Huntsville Bible College ... AL
- International Baptist College and Seminary ... AZ
- Jacksonville College ... TX
- Maple Springs Baptist Bible College & Seminary ... MD
- Missouri Baptist University ... MO
- Morris College ... SC
- Oakland City University ... IN
- Selma University ... AL
- Shaw University ... NC
- Shorter University ... GA
- Simmons College of Kentucky ... KY
- Southeastern Baptist College ... MS
- The Crown College of the Bible ... TN
- The John Leland Center for Theological Studies ... VA
- Trinity Baptist College ... FL
- Truett McConnell University ... GA
- University of the Cumberlands ... KY
- Virginia Baptist College ... VA
- Virginia Beach Theological Seminary ... VA
- Virginia Union University ... VA
- Washington University of Virginia ... VA
- West Coast Baptist College ... CA

Brethren Church
- Ashland University ... OH

Christian Church (Disciples Of Christ)
- Barton College ... NC
- Bethany College ... WV
- Chapman University ... CA
- Christian Theological Seminary ... IN
- Columbia College ... MO
- Culver-Stockton College ... MO
- Eureka College ... IL
- Jarvis Christian College ... TX
- Lexington Theological Seminary ... KY
- Lynchburg College ... VA
- Midway University ... KY
- Northwest Christian University ... OR
- Phillips Theological Seminary ... OK
- Texas Christian University ... TX
- Transylvania University ... KY
- William Woods University ... MO

Christian Churches And Churches of Christ
- Belmont University ... TN
- Boise Bible College ... ID
- Central Christian College of the Bible ... MO
- Cincinnati Christian University ... OH
- Dallas Christian College ... TX
- Great Lakes Christian College ... MI
- Johnson University ... TN
- Kentucky Christian University ... KY
- Lincoln Christian University ... IL
- Manhattan Christian College ... KS
- Point University ... GA

Christian Methodist Episcopal
- Lane College ... TN
- Miles College ... AL
- Texas College ... TX

Christian Reformed Church
- Calvin College ... MI
- Calvin Theological Seminary ... MI
- Dordt College ... IA

Church Of Christ
- Pepperdine University ... CA

Church Of God
- Anderson University ... IN
- Lee University ... TN
- Mid-America Christian University ... OK
- Pentecostal Theological Seminary ... TN
- The University of Findlay ... OH
- Universidad Teologica Del Caribe ... PR
- Warner Pacific College ... OR
- Warner University ... FL

Church of New Jerusalem
- Bryn Athyn College of the New Church ... PA

Church Of The Brethren
- Bethany Theological Seminary ... IN
- Bridgewater College ... VA
- Elizabethtown College ... PA
- Manchester University ... IN
- McPherson College ... KS

Church Of The Nazarene
- Eastern Nazarene College ... MA
- MidAmerica Nazarene University ... KS
- Mount Vernon Nazarene University ... OH
- Nazarene Bible College ... KS
- Nazarene Theological Seminary ... MO
- Northwest Nazarene University ... ID
- Olivet Nazarene University ... IL
- Point Loma Nazarene University ... CA
- Southern Nazarene University ... OK
- Trevecca Nazarene University ... TN

Churches Of Christ
- Abilene Christian University ... TX
- Amridge University ... AL
- Crowley's Ridge College ... AR
- Faulkner University ... AL
- Freed-Hardeman University ... TN
- Harding University Main Campus ... AR
- Heritage Christian University ... AL
- Lipscomb University ... TN
- Lubbock Christian University ... TX
- Mid-Atlantic Christian University ... NC
- Ohio Valley University ... WV
- Southwestern Christian College ... TX
- York College ... NE

Cumberland Presbyterian
- Bethel University ... TN
- Memphis Theological Seminary ... TN

Evangelical Congregational Church
- Evangelical Theological Seminary ... PA

Evangelical Covenant Church Of America
- North Park University ... IL

Evangelical Free Church Of America
- Trinity International University ... IL

Evangelical Lutheran Church In America
- Augsburg College ... MN
- Augustana College ... IL
- Augustana University ... SD
- Bethany College ... KS
- California Lutheran University ... CA
- Capital University ... OH
- Carthage College ... WI
- Concordia College ... MN
- Finlandia University ... MI
- Gettysburg College ... PA
- Grand View University ... IA
- Gustavus Adolphus College ... MN
- Lenoir-Rhyne University ... NC
- Luther College ... IA
- Luther Seminary ... MN
- Lutheran School of Theology at Chicago ... IL
- Midland University ... NE
- Muhlenberg College ... PA
- Newberry College ... SC
- Pacific Lutheran University ... WA
- Roanoke College ... VA
- St. Olaf College ... MN
- Susquehanna University ... PA
- Texas Lutheran University ... TX
- Thiel College ... PA
- Trinity Lutheran Seminary ... OH
- United Lutheran Seminary ... PA
- Wartburg College ... IA
- Wartburg Theological Seminary ... IA
- Wittenberg University ... OH

Evangelical Lutheran Synod
- Bethany Lutheran College ... MN

Fellowship Of Grace Brethren Churches
- Grace College and Seminary ... IN

Free Methodist
- Central Christian College of Kansas ... KS
- Greenville University ... IL
- Seattle Pacific University ... WA
- Spring Arbor University ... MI

Free Will Baptist
- California Christian College ... CA
- Randall University ... OK
- Southeastern Free Will Baptist College ... NC
- Welch College ... TN

Friends
- Earlham College and Earlham School of Religion ... IN
- George Fox University ... OR
- Guilford College ... NC
- Malone University ... OH
- William Penn University ... IA
- Wilmington College ... OH

Greek Orthodox
- Hellenic College-Holy Cross Greek Orthodox School of Theology ... MA

Interdenominational
- Athens College of Ministry ... GA
- Bethany Global University ... MN
- California Graduate School of Theology ... CA
- Christian Witness Theological Seminary ... CA
- Denver Seminary ... CO
- Evangelical Seminary of Puerto Rico ... PR
- Faith International University ... WA
- God's Bible School and College ... OH
- Inste Bible College ... IA
- Interdenominational Theological Center ... GA
- Kentucky Mountain Bible College ... KY
- Messiah College ... PA
- Oak Hills Christian College ... MN
- Palm Beach Atlantic University ... FL
- Phoenix Seminary ... AZ
- Rocky Mountain College ... MT
- South Florida Bible College ... FL
- Union Bible College ... IN
- Wesley Biblical Seminary ... MS

Jewish
- Academy for Jewish Religion ... CA
- Bais Medrash Ateres Shlomo ... NY
- Hebrew Union College-Jewish Institute of Religion ... NY
- Mechon L'Hoyroa ... NY
- New York Medical College ... NY
- Reconstructionist Rabbinical College ... PA
- Women's Institute of Torah Seminary ... MD

Latter-day Saints
- Brigham Young University ... UT
- Brigham Young University Hawaii ... HI
- Brigham Young University-Idaho ... ID
- LDS Business College ... UT

Lutheran
- Valparaiso University ... IN

Lutheran Church - Missouri Synod
- Concordia College ... NY
- Concordia College Alabama ... AL
- Concordia Seminary ... MO
- Concordia Theological Seminary ... IN
- Concordia University ... CA
- Concordia University ... NE
- Concordia University ... OR
- Concordia University Ann Arbor ... MI
- Concordia University Chicago ... IL
- Concordia University Texas ... TX
- Concordia University Wisconsin ... WI
- Concordia University, St. Paul ... MN

Mennonite Brethren Church
- Fresno Pacific University ... CA
- Tabor College ... KS

Mennonite Church
- Anabaptist Mennonite Biblical Seminary ... IN
- Bethel College ... KS
- Bluffton University ... OH
- Eastern Mennonite University ... VA
- Goshen College ... IN
- Hesston College ... KS
- Rosedale Bible College ... OH

Missionary Church
- Bethel College ... IN

Moravian Church
- Moravian College ... PA
- Salem College ... NC

Multiple Protestant Denominations
- Huston-Tillotson University ... TX
- LeMoyne-Owen College ... TN
- Paine College ... GA

Non-denominational
- Carolina College of Biblical Studies ... NC
- Cedar Crest College ... PA
- China Evangelical Seminary North America ... CA
- Faith Theological Seminary ... MD
- Grove City College ... PA
- Heartland Christian College ... MO
- Midwest University ... MO
- Montreat College ... NC
- North American University ... TX
- Pacific Bible College ... OR
- Providence Christian College ... CA
- University of Fort Lauderdale ... FL
- Williamson College ... TN

North American Baptist
- Sioux Falls Seminary ... SD

Original Free Will Baptist Church
- University of Mount Olive ... NC

Other Protestant
- Beulah Heights University ... GA
- Grace College of Divinity ... NC
- Ohio Christian University ... OH
- Saint Louis Christian College ... MO

Urshan Graduate School of Theology ..... MO

Pentecostal Church of God
Messenger College .... TX
Universidad Pentecostal Mizpa .... PR

Pentecostal Holiness Church
Emmanuel College .... GA
Southwestern Christian University .... OK

Pentecostal/Charismatic Non-Denominational
Christian Life College IL

Presbyterian
Sterling College .... KS
Whitworth University .... WA

Presbyterian Church (U.S.A.)
Agnes Scott College .... GA
Austin College .... TX
Austin Presbyterian Theological Seminary .... TX
Belhaven University .... MS
Blackburn College IL
Bloomfield College .... NJ
Buena Vista University .... IA
Carroll University .... WI
Columbia Theological Seminary .... GA
Davidson College .... NC
Davis & Elkins College .... WV
Eckerd College .... FL
Grace Mission University .... CA
Hampden-Sydney College .... VA
Hanover College .... IN
Hastings College .... NE
King University .... TN
Lees-McRae College .... NC
Louisville Presbyterian Theological Seminary .... KY
Lyon College .... AR
Macalester College .... MN
Mary Baldwin University .... VA
Maryville College .... TN
McCormick Theological Seminary IL
Millikin University IL
Missouri Valley College .... MO
Monmouth College IL
Muskingum University .... OH
Pittsburgh Theological Seminary .... PA
Presbyterian College .... SC
Princeton Theological Seminary .... NJ
Queens University of Charlotte .... NC
Rhodes College .... TN
San Francisco Theological Seminary ...... CA
Schreiner University .... TX
Stillman College .... AL
Tusculum College .... TN
Union Presbyterian Seminary .... VA
University of Dubuque .... IA
University of Jamestown .... ND
University of Pikeville .... KY
University of the Ozarks .... AR
Warren Wilson College .... NC
Waynesburg University .... PA
Westminster College .... PA
William Peace University .... NC
Wilson College .... PA

Presbyterian Church In America
Covenant College .... GA
Covenant Theological Seminary .... MO
Presbyterian Theological Seminary in America .... CA
Reformed University .... GA

Protestant Episcopal
Bexley Seabury IL
Church Divinity School of the Pacific .... CA
General Theological Seminary .... NY
Nashotah House .... WI
Protestant Episcopal Theological Seminary in Virginia .... VA
Saint Augustine's University .... NC
Seminary of the Southwest .... TX
Sewanee: The University of the South .... TN
Trinity Episcopal School for Ministry .... PA
Voorhees College .... SC

Reformed Church In America
Central College .... IA
Hope College .... MI
New Brunswick Theological Seminary ..... NJ
Northwestern College .... IA
Western Theological Seminary .... MI

Reformed Episcopal Church
Reformed Episcopal Seminary .... PA

Reformed Presbyterian Church
Evangelia University .... CA
Geneva College .... PA
Reformed Presbyterian Theological Seminary .... PA

Roman Catholic
Alvernia University .... PA
Ancilla College .... IN
Anna Maria College .... MA
Aquinas College .... MI
Aquinas College .... TN
Aquinas Institute of Theology .... MO
Assumption College .... MA
Assumption College for Sisters .... NJ
Athenaeum of Ohio .... OH
Augustine Institute .... CO
Ave Maria School of Law .... FL
Avila University .... MO
Barry University .... FL
Belmont Abbey College .... NC
Benedictine College .... KS
Benedictine University IL
Boston College .... MA
Brescia University .... KY
Briar Cliff University .... IA
Cabrini University .... PA
Caldwell University .... NJ
Calumet College of Saint Joseph .... IN
Canisius College .... NY
Cardinal Stritch University .... WI
Carlow University .... PA
Carroll College .... MT
Catholic Theological Union IL
Chestnut Hill College .... PA
Christ the King Seminary .... NY
Christendom College .... VA
Christian Brothers University .... TN
Clarke University .... IA
College of Our Lady of the Elms .... MA
College of Saint Benedict .... MN
College of Saint Elizabeth .... NJ
College of Saint Mary .... NE
College of St. Joseph .... VT
College of the Holy Cross .... MA
Conception Seminary College .... MO
Creighton University .... NE
DePaul University IL
DeSales University .... PA
Divine Word College .... IA
Dominican School of Philosophy and Theology .... CA
Dominican University IL
Donnelly College .... KS
Duquesne University .... PA
Edgewood College .... WI
Emmanuel College .... MA
Fairfield University .... CT
Felician University .... NJ
Fontbonne University .... MO
Franciscan Missionaries of Our Lady University .... LA
Franciscan University of Steubenville ...... OH
Gannon University .... PA
Georgetown University .... DC
Georgian Court University .... NJ
Gonzaga University .... WA
Gwynedd Mercy University .... PA
Holy Apostles College and Seminary ...... CT
Holy Cross College .... IN
Holy Family University .... PA
Immaculata University .... PA
John Carroll University .... OH
Kenrick-Glennon Seminary, Kenrick School of Theology .... MO
King's College .... PA
La Roche College .... PA
La Salle University .... PA
Laboure College .... MA
Lewis University IL
Loras College .... IA
Lourdes University .... OH
Loyola Marymount University .... CA
Loyola University Chicago IL
Loyola University Maryland .... MD
Loyola University New Orleans .... LA
Madonna University .... MI
Marian University .... IN
Marian University .... WI
Marquette University .... WI
Marygrove College .... MI
Marymount California University .... CA
Marymount University .... VA
Marywood University .... PA
Mercy College of Health Sciences .... IA
Mercy College of Ohio .... OH
Mercyhurst University .... PA
Merrimack College .... MA
Misericordia University .... PA
Mount Angel Seminary .... OR
Mount Carmel College of Nursing .... OH
Mount Marty College .... SD
Mount Mary University .... WI
Mount Mercy University .... IA
Mount Saint Mary's University .... CA
Mount St. Joseph University .... OH
Mount St. Mary's University .... MD
Neumann University .... PA
Newman University .... KS
Northeast Catholic College .... NH
Notre Dame College .... OH
Notre Dame of Maryland University .... MD
Notre Dame Seminary, Graduate School of Theology .... LA
Oblate School of Theology .... TX
Ohio Dominican University .... OH
Our Lady of the Lake University .... TX
Pontifical College Josephinum .... OH
Pontifical Faculty of the Immaculate Conception at the Dominican House of Studies .... DC
Pontifical John Paul II Institute for Studies on Marriage and Family .... DC
Pope St. John XXIII National Seminary ... MA
Presentation College .... SD
Providence College .... RI
Quincy University IL
Regis University .... CO
Rivier University .... NH
Rockhurst University .... MO
Rosemont College .... PA
Sacred Heart Major Seminary .... MI
Sacred Heart Seminary and School of Theology .... WI
Saint Anselm College .... NH
Saint Anthony College of Nursing IL
Saint Bernard's School of Theology & Ministry .... NY
Saint Charles Borromeo Seminary .... PA
Saint Francis Medical Center College of Nursing IL
Saint Francis University .... PA
Saint Gregory the Great Seminary .... NE
Saint John's Seminary .... CA
Saint John's Seminary .... MA
Saint John's University .... MN
Saint Joseph Seminary College .... LA
Saint Joseph's College of Maine .... ME
Saint Joseph's Seminary .... NY
Saint Joseph's University .... PA
Saint Leo University .... FL
Saint Louis University .... MO
Saint Martin's University .... WA
Saint Mary Seminary and Graduate School of Theology .... OH
Saint Mary's College .... IN
Saint Mary's College of California .... CA
Saint Mary's Seminary and University ..... MD
Saint Mary's University of Minnesota ...... MN
Saint Mary-of-the-Woods College .... IN
Saint Meinrad School of Theology .... IN
Saint Michael's College .... VT
Saint Norbert College .... WI
Saint Patrick's Seminary & University ..... CA
Saint Peter's University .... NJ
Saint Vincent College .... PA
Saint Vincent Seminary .... PA
Saint Xavier University IL
Salve Regina University .... RI
Seattle University .... WA
Seton Hall University .... NJ
Seton Hill University .... PA
Siena Heights University .... MI
Silver Lake College of the Holy Family .... WI
Spring Hill College .... AL
SS. Cyril and Methodius Seminary .... MI
St. Ambrose University .... IA
St. Bonaventure University .... NY
St. Catherine University .... MN
St. Gregory's University .... OK
St. John Vianney College Seminary .... FL
St. John Vianney Theological Seminary .. CO
St. John's University .... NY
St. Mary's University .... TX
St. Thomas University .... FL
St. Vincent De Paul Regional Seminary .. FL
Stonehill College .... MA
The Catholic University of America .... DC
The College of Saint Scholastica .... MN
The Pontifical Catholic University of Puerto Rico .... PR
The University of Scranton .... PA
Thomas More College .... KY
Trinity Washington University .... DC
Universidad Central de Bayamon .... PR
University of Dallas .... TX
University of Dayton .... OH
University of Detroit Mercy .... MI
University of Holy Cross .... LA
University of Mary .... ND
University of Notre Dame .... IN
University of Providence .... MT
University of Saint Francis .... IN
University of Saint Joseph .... CT
University of Saint Mary .... KS
University of Saint Mary of the Lake-Mundelein Seminary IL
University of Saint Thomas .... MN
University of San Diego .... CA
University of San Francisco .... CA
University of St. Francis IL
University of St. Thomas .... TX
University of the Incarnate Word .... TX
University of the Sacred Heart .... PR
Ursuline College .... OH
Villanova University .... PA
Viterbo University .... WI
Walsh University .... OH
Wheeling Jesuit University .... WV
Wyoming Catholic College .... WY
Xavier University .... OH
Xavier University of Louisiana .... LA

Russian Orthodox
Holy Trinity Orthodox Seminary .... NY

Seventh-day Adventist
Adventist University of Health Sciences .. FL
Andrews University .... MI
Kettering College .... OH
La Sierra University .... CA
Loma Linda University .... CA
Oakwood University .... AL
Pacific Union College .... CA
Southern Adventist University .... TN
Southwestern Adventist University .... TX
Union College .... NE
Universidad Adventista de las Antillas ..... PR
Walla Walla University .... WA
Washington Adventist University .... MD

Southern Baptist
B.H. Carroll Theological Institute .... TX
Blue Mountain College .... MS
California Baptist University .... CA
Carson-Newman University .... TN
Charleston Southern University .... SC
Clear Creek Baptist Bible College .... KY
Gateway Seminary .... CA
Hannibal-LaGrange University .... MO
Houston Baptist University .... TX
Louisiana College .... LA
Midwestern Baptist Theological Seminary MO
Mississippi College .... MS
New Orleans Baptist Theological Seminary .... LA
North Greenville University .... SC
Oklahoma Baptist University .... OK
Ouachita Baptist University .... AR
Samford University .... AL
Southeastern Baptist Theological Seminary .... NC
Southwest Baptist University .... MO
Southwestern Baptist Theological Seminary .... TX
The Baptist College of Florida .... FL
The Southern Baptist Theological Seminary .... KY
Union University .... TN
University of Mary Hardin-Baylor .... TX
University of Mobile .... AL
Wayland Baptist University .... TX
William Carey University .... MS
Williams Baptist College .... AR
Wingate University .... NC

The Christian And Missionary Alliance
Crown College .... MN
Nyack College .... NY
Simpson University .... CA
Toccoa Falls College .... GA

Unification Church
Unification Theological Seminary .... NY

Unitarian Universalist
Meadville Lombard Theological School IL
Starr King School for the Ministry .... CA

United Brethren Church
Huntington University .... IN

United Church Of Christ
Catawba College .... NC
Chicago Theological Seminary IL
Doane University .... NE
Eden Theological Seminary .... MO
Elmhurst College IL
Heidelberg University .... OH
Lakeland University .... WI
Lancaster Theological Seminary .... PA
Northland College .... WI

Piedmont College .... GA
The Defiance College .... OH
Tougaloo College .... MS
United Theological Seminary of the Twin Cities .... MN

United Methodist

Adrian College .... MI
Albion College .... MI
Albright College .... PA
Allegheny College .... PA
American University .... DC
Andrew College .... GA
Baker University .... KS
Baldwin Wallace University .... OH
Bennett College .... NC
Bethune Cookman University .... FL
Birmingham-Southern College .... AL
Brevard College .... NC
Centenary College of Louisiana .... LA
Central Methodist University .... MO
Claflin University .... SC
Claremont School of Theology .... CA
Clark Atlanta University .... GA
Columbia College .... SC
Cornell College .... IA
Dakota Wesleyan University .... SD
DePauw University .... IN
Dillard University .... LA
Emory & Henry College .... VA
Emory University .... GA
Ferrum College .... VA
Florida Southern College .... FL
Garrett-Evangelical Theological Seminary IL
Greensboro College .... NC
Hamline University .... MN
Hendrix College .... AR
High Point University .... NC
Hiwassee College .... TN
Huntingdon College .... AL
Iliff School of Theology .... CO
Iowa Wesleyan University .... IA
Kansas Wesleyan University .... KS
Kentucky Wesleyan College .... KY
LaGrange College .... GA
Lebanon Valley College .... PA
Lindsey Wilson College .... KY
Louisburg College .... NC
Lycoming College .... PA
MacMurray College IL
Martin Methodist College .... TN
McKendree University IL
McMurry University .... TX
Methodist Theological School in Ohio .... OH
Methodist University .... NC
Millsaps College .... MS
Morningside College .... IA
Nebraska Wesleyan University .... NE
North Carolina Wesleyan College .... NC
North Central College IL
Ohio Northern University .... OH
Ohio Wesleyan University .... OH
Oklahoma City University .... OK
Otterbein University .... OH
Pfeiffer University .... NC
Philander Smith College .... AR
Randolph College .... VA
Randolph-Macon College .... VA
Reinhardt University .... GA
Rust College .... MS
Saint Paul School of Theology .... KS
Shenandoah University .... VA
Simpson College .... IA
Southern Methodist University .... TX
Southwestern College .... KS
Southwestern University .... TX
Spartanburg Methodist College .... SC
Tennessee Wesleyan University .... TN
Texas Wesleyan University .... TX
Union College .... KY
United Theological Seminary .... OH
University of Evansville .... IN
University of Indianapolis .... IN
University of Mount Union .... OH
Virginia Wesleyan University .... VA
Wesley College .... DE
Wesley Theological Seminary .... DC
Wesleyan College .... GA
West Virginia Wesleyan College .... WV
Wiley College .... TX
Wofford College .... SC
Young Harris College .... GA

Wesleyan Church

Allegheny Wesleyan College .... OH
Houghton College .... NY
Indiana Wesleyan University .... IN
Oklahoma Wesleyan University .... OK
Southern Wesleyan University .... SC

Wisconsin Evangelical Lutheran Synod

Martin Luther College .... MN

Carnegie Classification Code Definitions*

The *Higher Education Directory®* lists the updated 2015 Carnegie Classifications. Due to space limitation, the *Higher Education Directory®* only lists the basic classification—which was substantially revised in 2015. These new codes are listed below:

Associate's Colleges: Institutions at which the highest level degree awarded is an associate's degree. The institutions are sorted into nine categories based on the intersection of two factors: disciplinary focus (transfer, career & technical or mixed) and dominant student type (traditional, nontraditional or mixed). Excludes Special Focus Institutions and Tribal Colleges.

Assoc/HT-High Trad: Associate's Colleges: High Transfer-High Traditional
Assoc/HT-Mix Trad/Non: Associate's Colleges: High Transfer-Mixed Traditional/Nontraditional
Assoc/HT-High Non: Associate's Colleges: High Transfer-High Nontraditional
Assoc/MT-VT-High Trad: Associate's Colleges: Mixed Transfer/ Vocational & Technical-High Traditional
Assoc/MT-VT-Mix Trad/Non: Associate's Colleges: Mixed Transfer/Vocational & Technical-Mixed Traditional/ Nontraditional
Assoc/MT-VT-High Non: Associate's Colleges: Mixed Transfer/ Vocational & Technical-High Nontraditional
Assoc/HVT-High Trad: Associate's Colleges: High Vocational & Technical-High Traditional
Assoc/HVT-Mix Trad/Non: Associate's Colleges: High Vocational & Technical-Mixed Traditional/Nontraditional
Assoc/HVT-High Non: Associate's Colleges: High Vocational & Technical-High Nontraditional

Baccalaureate/Associate's Colleges. Includes four-year colleges (by virtue of having at least one baccalaureate degree program) that conferred more than 50 percent of degrees at the associate's level. Excludes Special Focus Institutions, Tribal Colleges, and institutions that have sufficient masterÖs or doctoral degrees to fall into those categories.

Bac/Assoc-Assoc Dom: Baccalaureate/Associate's Colleges: Associate's Dominant
Bac/Assoc-Mixed: Baccalaureate/Associate's Colleges: Mixed Baccalaureate/Associate's

Baccalaureate Colleges. Includes institutions where baccalaureate or higher degrees represent at least 50 percent of all degrees but where fewer than 50 master's degrees or 20 doctoral degrees were awarded during the update year. (Some institutions above the master's degree threshold are also included; see Methodology) Excludes Special Focus Institutions and Tribal Colleges.

Bac-A&S: Baccalaureate Colleges: Arts & Sciences Focus
Bac-Diverse: Baccalaureate Colleges: Diverse Fields

Master's Colleges and Universities. Generally includes institutions that awarded at least 50 master's degrees and fewer than 20 doctoral degrees during the update year (with occasional exceptions; see Methodology). Excludes Special Focus Institutions and Tribal Colleges.

Masters/L: Master's Colleges & Universities: Larger Programs
Masters/M: Master's Colleges & Universities: Medium Programs
Masters/S: Master's Colleges & Universities: Small Programs

Doctoral Universities. Includes institutions that awarded at least 20 research/scholarship doctoral degrees during the update year (this does not include professional practice doctoral-level degrees, such as the JD, MD, PharmD, DPT, etc.). Excludes Special Focus Institutions and Tribal Colleges.

DU-Highest: Doctoral Universities: Highest Research Activity
DU-Higher: Doctoral Universities: Higher Research Activity
DU-Mod: Doctoral Universities: Moderate Research Activity

Special Focus Institutions, Two-year. Institutions where a high concentration of degrees is in a single field or set of related fields. Excludes Tribal Colleges.

Spec 2-yr-Health: Special Focus Two-Year: Health Professions
Spec 2-yr-Tech: Special Focus Two-Year: Technical Professions
Spec 2-yr-A&S: Special Focus Two-Year: Arts & Design
Spec 2-yr-Other: Special Focus Two-Year: Other Fields

Special Focus Institutions, Four-year. Institutions where a high concentration of degrees is in a single field or set of related fields. Excludes Tribal Colleges.

Spec-4-yr-Faith: Special Focus Four-Year: Faith-Related Institutions
Spec-4-yr-Med: Special Focus Four-Year: Medical Schools & Centers
Spec-4-yr-Other Health: Special Focus Four-Year: Other Health Professions Schools
Spec-4-yr-Eng: Special Focus Four-Year: Engineering Schools
Spec-4-yr-Other Tech: Special Focus Four-Year: Other Technology-Related Schools
Spec-4-yr-Bus: Special Focus Four-Year: Business & Management Schools
Spec-4-yr-Arts: Special Focus Four-Year: Arts, Music & Design Schools
Spec-4-yr-Law: Special Focus Four-Year: Law Schools
Spec-4-yr-Other: Special Focus Four-Year: Other Special Focus Institutions

Tribal Colleges. Colleges and universities that are members of the American Indian Higher Education Consortium, as identified in IPEDS Institutional Characteristics.

Tribal: Tribal Colleges

---

*All data provided by Carnegie Classification of Institutions of Higher Education by Indiana University Center for Postsecondary Research. For more detailed information on the revised Carnegie Codes, please visit http://carnegieclassifications.iu.edu/. Basic Classification methodology can be found at http://carnegieclassifications.iu.edu/methodology/basic.php.

Statistics

Institutions of Higher Education by Control, Level and State

STATE	TWO YEAR		FOUR YEAR		TOTAL		SYSTEM	GRAND
	PRIVATE	PUBLIC	PRIVATE	PUBLIC	PRIVATE	PUBLIC	OFFICE	TOTAL
AL	0	24	22	15	22	39	3	64
AK	2	0	3	3	5	3	1	9
AZ	9	19	25	4	34	23	1	58
AR	3	22	13	11	16	33	2	51
CA	50	105	249	48	299	153	28	480
CO	18	12	24	17	42	29	2	73
CT	0	12	20	7	20	19	1	40
DE	1	0	4	3	5	3	0	8
DC	0	0	16	3	16	3	0	19
FL	41	2	72	40	113	42	1	156
GA	9	24	40	28	49	52	1	102
HI	2	6	7	4	9	10	2	21
ID	0	4	5	4	5	8	0	13
IL	14	47	91	12	105	59	6	170
IN	8	1	44	14	52	15	2	69
IA	1	18	39	3	40	21	3	64
KS	2	25	26	9	28	34	0	62
KY	1	16	33	8	34	24	1	59
LA	7	18	14	16	21	34	4	59
ME	3	7	11	8	14	15	2	31
MD	4	16	22	16	26	32	1	59
MA	3	16	80	14	83	30	2	115
MI	4	23	43	21	47	44	1	92
MN	4	30	45	11	49	41	3	93
MS	0	15	10	9	10	24	0	34
MO	10	17	60	13	70	30	3	103
MT	6	5	7	6	13	11	1	25
NE	6	7	17	7	23	14	2	39
NV	4	1	3	6	7	7	1	15
NH	1	7	10	4	11	11	2	24
NJ	4	19	36	13	40	32	1	73
NM	0	13	9	8	9	21	0	30
NY	25	36	189	44	214	80	5	299
NC	2	59	51	16	53	75	2	130
ND	1	4	7	7	8	11	1	20
OH	22	23	71	17	93	40	1	134
OK	4	12	15	15	19	27	0	46
OR	4	16	27	8	31	24	0	55
PA	49	16	111	20	160	36	1	197
RI	0	1	8	3	8	4	0	12
SC	2	19	23	14	25	33	0	58
SD	0	5	11	6	11	11	1	23
TN	10	13	52	10	62	23	2	87
TX	25	62	75	47	100	109	8	217
UT	2	3	13	7	15	10	1	26
VT	0	1	16	5	16	6	1	23
VA	15	24	58	17	73	41	1	115
WA	2	16	22	23	24	39	2	65
WV	8	8	12	11	20	19	2	41
WI	2	16	32	14	34	30	2	66
WY	1	7	1	1	2	8	0	10
AS	0	0	0	1	0	1	0	1
GU	0	1	1	1	1	2	0	3
MH	0	1	0	0	0	1	0	1
MP	0	0	0	1	0	1	0	1
PR	8	0	41	14	49	14	3	66
FM	0	1	0	0	0	1	0	1
PW	0	1	0	0	0	1	0	1
VI	0	0	0	1	0	1	0	1
Total	**399**	**876**	**1936**	**688**	**2335**	**1564**	**110**	**4009**

Figures do not include 1,091 additional branch campuses.

50 Largest Universities by Fall 2015 Enrollment

Institution	Enrollment
1. Liberty University	80494
2. Western Governors University	70504
3. Grand Canyon University	69444
4. Texas A & M University	63813
5. University of Central Florida	62953
6. Southern New Hampshire University	61285
7. The Ohio State University Main Campus	58663
8. Walden University	52799
9. American Public University System	52361
10. Arizona State University	51984
11. University of Texas at Austin	50950
12. University of Minnesota	50678
13. University of Florida	50645
14. Michigan State University	50538
15. University of Maryland University College	50248
16. New York University	50027
17. Florida International University	49782
18. Rutgers University - New Brunswick	49428
19. Indiana University Bloomington	48514
20. Penn State University Park	47307
21. University of Illinois at Urbana-Champaign	45842
22. University of Washington	45408
23. Kaplan University	45355
24. Brigham Young University-Idaho	43803
25. University of Michigan-Ann Arbor	43651
26. University of Southern California	43401
27. University of Wisconsin-Madison	42716
28. University of Houston	42704
29. University of Arizona	42595
30. Ashford University	42452
31. University of South Florida	42067
32. The University of Texas at Arlington	41988
33. University of California-Los Angeles	41908
34. California State University-Northridge	41548
35. Florida State University	40830
36. Purdue University Main Campus	40472
37. Ohio University (all campuses)	39447
38. California State University-Fullerton	38948
39. University of California-Berkeley	38189
40. University of Maryland College Park	38140
41. Temple University	38007
42. Texas State University	37979
43. California State University-Long Beach	37446
44. University of North Texas	37299
45. The University of Alabama	37098
46. University of Georgia	36130
47. University of Cincinnati Main Campus	36042
48. Texas Tech University	35859
49. Iowa State University	35714
50. University of Missouri - Columbia	35424

Institutions by Control and Tuition Range

Tuition	Public*	Private	Total
0 - 1,000	75	717	792
1,001 - 2,000	159	0	159
2,001 - 4,000	442	24	466
4,001 - 6,000	378	58	436
6,001 - 8,000	229	65	294
8,001 - 10,000	130	71	201
Over 10,000	151	1400	1551
Total	**1564**	**2335**	**3899**

* Figures for Public Institutions are In-State Tuitions

Universities, Colleges and Schools

by State*

*Includes the District of Columbia and, separately, U.S. Service Schools, American Samoa, Federated States of Micronesia, Guam, Marshall Islands, Northern Marianas, Palau, Puerto Rico, and Virgin Islands.

ALABAMA

Alabama Agricultural and Mechanical University (A)

4900 Meridian Street, Normal AL 35762-1357
County: Madison FICE Identification: 001002
Unit ID: 100654
Telephone: (256) 372-5230 Carnegie Class: Masters/L
FAX Number: (256) 372-5244 Calendar System: Semester
URL: www.aamu.edu
Established: 1875 Annual Undergrad Tuition & Fees (In-State): $9,366
Enrollment: 5,628 Coed
Affiliation or Control: State IRS Status: 501(c)3
Highest Offering: Doctorate
Accreditation: SC, AAFCS, CACREP, CAEPN, CS, DIETD, ENG, ENGT, PLNG, SP, SW

01 President ..... Dr. Andrew HUGINE, JR.
03 Executive VP/COO ..... Dr. Kevin A. ROLLE
05 Provost/VP Academic Affairs ..... Dr. Daniel K. WIMS
10 Vice President Business & Finance ..... Mr. Clayton GIBSON
26 VP Mktg/Comm/Advancement ..... Mr. Archie TUCKER
32 Vice President Student Affairs ..... Dr. Gary CROSBY
46 Interim VP Inst Rsrch/Spons Pgms ..... Dr. James WALKE
88 Special Assistant to the President ..... Dr. Malinda GILMORE
21 AVP Budget & Planning ..... Mr. Gregory JACKSON
84 AVP of Enrollment Mgmt/Dir Admiss ..... Ms. Venita KING
13 Chief Information Officer ..... Dr. Kimberly MARSHALL
21 AVP Finance/Comptroller ..... Mr. Norman JONES
15 Director Human Resources ..... Ms. Cassandra TARVER-ROSS
18 Dir Facilities and Admin Services ..... Mr. Brian SHIPP
06 Registrar ..... Ms. Brenda K. WILLIAMS
30 Int Director of Development ..... Ms. Reba JASMIN
41 Director of Athletics ..... Mr. Bryan HICKS
35 Director of Student Activities ..... Ms. Diann ANDERSON
37 Director of Financial Aid ..... Mr. Darryl JACKSON
88 Director of Emergency Management ..... Vacant
23 Dir Student Health & Counseling ..... Dr. Michael JOHNSON
36 Dir Career Development Services ..... Ms. Yvette CLAYTON
09 Dir Institutional Research ..... Dr. James WALKE
88 Director Marketing & PR ..... Mr. Jerome SAINTJONES
39 Interim Dir of Residential Housing ..... Ms. Karla MILLER
19 Chief of Police ..... Mr. Nadis CARLISLE
08 Director Learning Resources Center ..... Dr. Annie PAYTON
96 Director of Purchasing ..... Mr. Timothy THORNTON
58 Dean Graduate School/AVP Acad Affs ..... Dr. Colmore CHRISTIAN
47 Dean Col Agricultural/Life/Nat Sci ..... Dr. Lloyd WALKER
53 Interim Dean College of Education ..... Dr. Rodney WHITTLE
54 Dean College of Engineering ..... Dr. Chance GLENN
50 Dean Col of Business/Pub Affs ..... Dr. Del SMITH
49 Interim Dean University College ..... Dr. Juarine STEWART
04 Administrative Asst to President ..... Ms. Michele WESSON
102 Dir Foundation/Corporate Relations ..... Mr. Allen VITAL
29 Director Alumni Relations ..... Mrs. Sandra STUBBS
43 Dir Legal Services/General Counsel ..... Mrs. Angela DEBRO
45 Chief Institutional Planning ..... Mr. Archie TUCKER

Alabama College of Osteopathic Medicine (B)

445 Health Sciences Boulevard, Dothan AL 36303
County: Houston Identification: 667138
Unit ID: 483975
Telephone: (334) 699-2266 Carnegie Class: Not Classified
FAX Number: N/A Calendar System: Semester
URL: www.acomedu.org
Established: 2011 Annual Graduate Tuition & Fees: N/A
Enrollment: 460 Coed
Affiliation or Control: Independent Non-Profit IRS Status: 501(c)3
Highest Offering: First Professional Degree; No Undergraduates
Accreditation: OSTEO

01 President ..... Rick SUTTON
05 Dean/Senior Vice President ..... Craig J. LENZ
32 Assoc Dean Student Services ..... Philip REYNOLDS
84 Exec Dir Enrollment Management ..... Bob WILLIS
06 Registrar ..... Saimara SOTO
07 Dir of Admissions & Enrollment ..... Linda GOODSON
26 Dir of Communications & Marketing ..... Sarah SENN

*Alabama Community College System (C)

135 South Union Street, Montgomery AL 36104-4340
County: Montgomery Identification: 667303
Telephone: (334) 293-4500 Carnegie Class: N/A
FAX Number: (334) 293-4504
URL: www.accs.cc

01 Chancellor ..... Jimmy H. BAKER

*Bevill State Community College (D)

1411 Indiana Avenue, Jasper AL 35501
County: Walker FICE Identification: 005733
Unit ID: 102429
Telephone: (205) 387-0511 Carnegie Class: Assoc/HVT-Mix Trad/Non
FAX Number: (205) 387-5192 Calendar System: Semester
URL: www.bscc.edu
Established: 1965 Annual Undergrad Tuition & Fees (In-State): $4,410
Enrollment: 3,619 Coed
Affiliation or Control: State IRS Status: 501(c)3
Highest Offering: Associate Degree
Accreditation: SC, ADNUR, EMT, PNUR, SURGT

02 Interim President ..... Dr. Kim ENNIS
05 Vice President/Dean of Instruction ..... Dr. Leslie CUMMINGS
26 Director of Public Relations ..... Ms. Tana COLLINS
10 Dean of Accounting & Finance ..... Ms. Carolyn MORGAN
32 Dean of Students ..... Ms. Melissa STOWE
15 Director of Human Resources ..... Ms. Mary KINARD
18 Director of Facilities & Security ..... Mr. Randy STULTS
121 Dean of Student Success ..... Mr. Max WEAVER
76 Dean for Health Sciences ..... Ms. Penne MOTT
75 Dean for Career Technical Education ..... Mr. Al MOORE
25 Director of Grants/Federal Programs ..... Wanda JACKSON

*Bishop State Community College (E)

351 N Broad Street, Mobile AL 36603-5898
County: Mobile FICE Identification: 001030
Unit ID: 102030
Telephone: (251) 405-7000 Carnegie Class: Assoc/HVT-Mix Trad/Non
FAX Number: N/A Calendar System: Semester
URL: www.bishop.edu
Established: 1965 Annual Undergrad Tuition & Fees (In-State): $4,380
Enrollment: 3,111 Coed
Affiliation or Control: State IRS Status: 501(c)3
Highest Offering: Associate Degree
Accreditation: SC, ACBSP, ADNUR, CAHIIM, FUSER, PNUR, PTAA

02 President ..... Dr. Reginald SYKES
11 Interim Vice President of Opers ..... Mrs. Ann CLANTON
05 Dean of Instructional Services ..... Dr. Latitia MCCANE
12 Director of Carver Campus ..... Mr. LaKeith MILLER
12 Dir Baker-Gaines Central Campus ..... Mrs. Madeline STOKES
72 Dean of Tech Educ/Workforce Dev ..... Mr. Karl HENRY
32 Dean of Students ..... Dr. Terry HAZZARD
10 Dean of Business/Finance ..... Vacant
06 Registrar ..... Mr. Philip URBANEK
15 Director of Human Resources ..... Ms. Marquita LYONS
18 Director of Physical Plant ..... Mr. Lorenzo GRAYSON
26 Director of Public Relations ..... Vacant
45 Director of Inst Effectiveness ..... Mr. Roderick MCSWAIN
37 Mgr Student Fin Aid/Veterans Svcs ..... Dr. Samuel CHUKS
13 Chief Info Technology Officer (CIO) ..... Mr. Marty FORSYTHE
19 Director Security/Safety ..... Chief Lloyd WASHINGTON
41 Athletic Director ..... Mr. Trenton EAGER

*Calhoun Community College (F)

PO Box 2216, Decatur AL 35609-2216
County: Limestone FICE Identification: 001013
Unit ID: 101514
Telephone: (256) 306-2500 Carnegie Class: Assoc/MT-VT-Mix Trad/Non
FAX Number: (256) 306-2877 Calendar System: Semester
URL: www.calhoun.edu
Established: 1963 Annual Undergrad Tuition & Fees (In-State): $4,460
Enrollment: 9,985 Coed
Affiliation or Control: State IRS Status: 501(c)3
Highest Offering: Associate Degree
Accreditation: SC, ADNUR, DA, EMT, MLTAD, PNUR, PTAA, SURGT

02 President ..... Dr. James S. KLAUBER
05 Acting VP Instruct/Student Success ..... Mr. Bret MCGILL
32 Dean of Student Affairs ..... Dr. Patricia WILSON
10 Director of Accounting & Acting CFO ..... Ms. Jenny SEWELL
07 Actg Dir Admiss/Records/Registrar ..... Mr. Cedric ARRINGTON
08 Director of Library Services ..... Mr. James LOYD
13 Director Information Systems ..... Mr. Nathan TYLER
30 Institutional Advancement ..... Ms. Janet KINCHERLOW-MARTIN
12 Dean Research Park Campus ..... Mr. Mark BRANNON
55 Coordinator of Evening Program ..... Dr. Vinetta WESLEY
26 Director of Public Relations ..... Ms. Janet KINCHERLOW-MARTIN
18 Director of Physical Plant ..... Mr. Bruce CAUSEY
09 Dean Planning/Research & Grants ..... Dr. Debra HENDERSHOT
103 Acting Director Workforce Solutions ..... Mr. Vincent VINCENT
84 Act Dir of Recruit/Retent & Success ..... Mrs. Kelli MORRIS
76 Dean Health Sciences ..... Mr. Bret MCGILL
81 Int Dean Math/Natural Sciences ..... Mr. Rodney ALFORD
79 Dean Humanities & Social Sciences ..... Dr. Donna ESTILL
15 Director Human Resources & Payroll ..... Mrs. Kim GAINES
19 Director Public Safety ..... Mr. Kevin DAVENPORT
36 Director of Career Services & Co-op ..... Mrs. Kelli MORRIS
37 Director Student Financial Aid ..... Mrs. Janett SPENCER
04 Secretary to President ..... Ms. Belinda NOE
41 Athletic Director ..... Dr. Nancy KEENUM

*Central Alabama Community College (G)

1675 Cherokee Road, Alexander City AL 35010
County: Tallapoosa FICE Identification: 001007
Unit ID: 100760
Telephone: (256) 234-6346 Carnegie Class: Assoc/HT-High Trad
FAX Number: (256) 234-0384 Calendar System: Semester
URL: www.cacc.edu
Established: 1963 Annual Undergrad Tuition & Fees (In-State): $4,380
Enrollment: 1,787 Coed
Affiliation or Control: State IRS Status: 501(c)3
Highest Offering: Associate Degree
Accreditation: #SC, ADNUR

02 President ..... Dr. Susan BURROW
10 Dean of Financial Services ..... Mr. Bobby MOYE
05 Dean of Instruction ..... Dr. Carry DEATLEY
32 Dean of Students ..... Dr. Sherri TAYLOR
35 Associate Dean of Student Services ..... Ms. Glenda BLAND
09 Assoc Dean of Inst Effect/Compl ..... Ms. Cindy ENTREKIN
76 Associate Dean of Health Science ..... Dr. Melanie BOLTON
08 Librarian ..... Ms. Denita OLIVER
06 Records Manager ..... Ms. Marian MARTIN
26 Public Relations Officer ..... Mr. Brett PRITCHARD
13 Chief Information Officer ..... Mr. Rickey CREEL
37 Director Student Financial Aid ..... Mr. Phillip NELSON
04 Executive Asst to President ..... Mr. Mark MCGHEE
88 Dean of Adult Education ..... Mr. Danny COLEMAN
15 Exec Director of Human Resources ..... Ms. Tina SHAW

*Chattahoochee Valley Community College (H)

2602 College Drive, Phenix City AL 36869-7960
County: Russell FICE Identification: 012182
Unit ID: 101028
Telephone: (334) 291-4900 Carnegie Class: Assoc/HT-High Trad
FAX Number: (334) 291-4944 Calendar System: Semester
URL: www.cv.edu
Established: 1973 Annual Undergrad Tuition & Fees (In-State): $4,254
Enrollment: 1,665 Coed
Affiliation or Control: State IRS Status: 501(c)3
Highest Offering: Associate Degree
Accreditation: SC, ADNUR, PNUR

02 Interim President ..... Mr. Mark ELLARD
05 Vice President/Dean of the College ..... Dr. David HODGE
103 Assoc Dean of Workforce Development . Dr. Shirley ARMSTRONG
50 Chair of Business & Social Sciences ..... Dr. Bob DANSBY
81 Chair of Science ..... Ms. Susan MCCOLLUM
79 Chair of Humanities ..... Ms. Samantha VANCE
76 Chair of Health Sciences ..... Ms. Resa LORD
81 Chair of Mathematics ..... Ms. Mary JOHNSON
88 Program Dir Public Safety Academy ..... Mr. Kenneth HARRISON
77 Chair Computer & Information Tech ..... Ms. Debra PLOTTS
08 Director Learning Resources Center ..... Vacant
37 Director of Financial Aid ..... Ms. Susan BRYANT
18 Director Facilities & Maintenance ..... Mr. Johann WELLS
111 Dean of Advancement/Inst Effect ..... Dr. Joree JONES
41 Director of Athletics ..... Mr. Adam THOMAS
38 Dir Counseling/Advising & Testing ..... Vacant
13 Director of Information Systems ..... Mr. Jody NOLES
32 Director of Student Development ..... Mrs. Vickie WILLIAMS
51 Director of Adult Education ..... Ms. Laodecea SEAY
15 Director of Human Resources ..... Ms. Debbie BOONE
30 Director of Development ..... Ms. Karen KELLY
10 Business Manager ..... Ms. Christer SANKS
55 Evening Coordinator ..... Mr. Reggie GORDY
07 Director of Admissions/Registrar ..... Ms. Sanquita ALEXANDER
04 Administrative Asst to President ..... Ms. Terrah LONG
19 Security/Safety ..... Mr. Keith MANUEL
26 Marketing & Media Coordinator . Ms. Kelly WILLIAMS-SOWERS

*Coastal Alabama Community College (I)

1900 Highway 31 S, Bay Minette AL 36507-2698
County: Baldwin FICE Identification: 001060
Unit ID: 101161
Telephone: (251) 580-2100 Carnegie Class: Assoc/HT-High Trad
FAX Number: (251) 580-2253 Calendar System: Semester
URL: www.faulknerstate.edu
Established: 1965 Annual Undergrad Tuition & Fees (In-State): $4,380
Enrollment: 4,580 Coed
Affiliation or Control: State IRS Status: 501(c)3
Highest Offering: Associate Degree
Accreditation: SC, ACFEI, ADNUR, DA, EMT, PNUR, SURGT

02 President ..... Dr. Gary L. BRANCH
32 VP of Inst Adv & Student Dev ..... Dr. Brenda J. KENNEDY
15 VP Human Resources/Employee Rels ..... Mrs. Laura BURKS
05 Dean of Instruction ..... Ms. Melinda BYRD-MURPHY
35 Director Student Support Services ..... Mr. Carl CUNNINGHAM
86 Dean of Federal Programs ..... Mrs. Lena DEXTER
11 Dean Administrative Services ..... Mr. Jim FITZ-GERALD
103 Dean of Workforce Development ..... Vacant
106 Director Distance Education ..... Ms. Ann STRICKLAND
06 Registrar ..... Ms. Beth BRYARS
08 Dir Learning Resource Center ..... Ms. Rheena ELMORE
37 Financial Aid Director ..... Dr. Jim THEEUWES
18 Director Maintenance/Facilities ..... Mr. Richard LYNN
19 Chief College Police ..... Mr. Chris JOHNSON
39 Residence Hall Director ..... Ms. Danielle BROWN
66 Director Nursing & Allied Health ..... Ms. Jean GRAHAM
36 Academic Career Advisor ..... Ms. Theresa MCCLELLAND

*Enterprise State Community College (J)

PO Box 1300, Enterprise AL 36331-1300
County: Coffee FICE Identification: 001015
Unit ID: 101143
Telephone: (334) 347-2623 Carnegie Class: Assoc/HVT-Mix Trad/Non
FAX Number: (334) 393-6223 Calendar System: Semester
URL: www.escc.edu
Established: 1963 Annual Undergrad Tuition & Fees (In-State): $4,380

Enrollment: 1,882 Coed
Affiliation or Control: State IRS Status: 501(c)3
Highest Offering: Associate Degree
Accreditation: SC

02 Interim President Dr. Vicky OHLSON
05 Dean of Instruction Ms. Leslie REEDER
32 Dean of Students Dr. Olivier CHARLES
10 Dean Administration & Finance Ms. Alonzetta LANDRUM-SIMS
35 Assoc Dean of Students/Athletic Dir Mr. Kevin AMMONS
26 Dir Marketing & Media Relations Mr. Stephen SCHMIDT
37 Director Student Financial Aid Dr. Henry L. QUISENBERRY, JR.
55 Director Evening Division Mr. Carl HOLBROOK
04 Administrative Asst to President Ms. Jennifer ADAMS
07 Director of Admissions Mr. Joey HOLLEY
08 Head Librarian Ms. Linda STEPHENS
102 Dir Foundation/Corporate Relations Ms. Chellye STUMP
103 Dir Workforce/Career Development Ms. Ann KELLEY
13 Chief Info Technology Officer (CIO) Mr. Jason TRULL
15 Director Personnel Services Ms. Jessica HERBSTER
18 Chief Facilities/Physical Plant Mr. Michael HELMS
38 Director Student Counseling Dr. Felicia FORD
105 Director Web Services Mr. Stephen SCHMIDT
106 Dir Online Education/E-learning Dr. Amy WISE
108 Director Inst Effectiveness & Plng Mr. Andrew DAVIS
19 Director Security/Safety Mr. Jeff SPENCE
50 Director of Business Mrs. Jennifer C. NELSON

*Gadsden State Community College (A)

1001 George Wallace Dr, PO Box 227,
Gadsden AL 35902-0227
County: Etowah FICE Identification: 001017
Unit ID: 101240
Telephone: (256) 549-8200 Carnegie Class: Assoc/HVT-Mix Trad/Non
FAX Number: (256) 549-8288 Calendar System: Semester
URL: www.gadsdenstate.edu
Established: 1925 Annual Undergrad Tuition & Fees (In-State): $3,264
Enrollment: 5,018 Coed
Affiliation or Control: State IRS Status: 501(c)3
Highest Offering: Associate Degree
Accreditation: SC, ADNUR, COMTA, EMT, MLTAD, PNUR, RAD

02 President Dr. Martha G. LAVENDER
10 Dean Financial/Administrative Svcs Dr. James R. PRUCNAL
84 Dean Enrollment & Retention Dr. Teresa C. RHEA
72 Dean Tech Educ/Workforce Develop Mr. Tim GREEN
76 Dean Health Sciences Dr. Deborah CURRY
05 Dean of Academic Programs/Services Dr. Leslie WORTHINGTON
111 Assoc Dean Inst Advance/Cmty Svcs Ms. Pam JOHNSON
51 Assoc Dean Instruct Svcs/Adult Educ Dr. Karen BLYTHE-SMITH
26 Director Public Relations/Marketing Ms. Jackie EDMONDSON
19 Director Physical Plant Mr. Stewart DAVIS
21 Director of Financial Services Ms. Jacqueline CLARK
43 Director of Legal Affairs/Title IX Ms. Michele BRADFORD
15 Director Human Resources Ms. Kim S. COBB
41 Athletic Director Mr. Mike CANCILLA
38 Assoc Dean Stdnt Svcs & Couns Svcs Dr. Cheryl C. VICKERS
37 Director of Financial Aid Ms. Kelly D'EATH
06 Registrar Ms. Cassie MORGAN
13 Chief Information Officer Mr. Tim SMITH

*George C. Wallace Community College - Dothan (B)

1141 Wallace Drive, Dothan AL 36303-9234
County: Dale FICE Identification: 001018
Unit ID: 101286
Telephone: (334) 983-3521 Carnegie Class: Assoc/HVT-High Trad
FAX Number: (334) 983-6066 Calendar System: Semester
URL: www.wallace.edu
Established: 1947 Annual Undergrad Tuition & Fees (In-State): $4,320
Enrollment: 4,769 Coed
Affiliation or Control: State IRS Status: 501(c)3
Highest Offering: Associate Degree
Accreditation: SC, ADNUR, COARC, EMT, MAC, PNUR, PTAA, RAD

02 President Dr. Linda C. YOUNG
32 Dean of Student Affs/Sparks Campus Ms. Jacqueline B. SCREWS
05 Dean of Instructional Affairs Mr. Tony HOLLAND
10 Dean of Business Affairs Mr. Lynn BELL
07 Director Enroll Svcs/Registrar Mr. Keith SAULSBERRY
08 Dir Learning Resources Ctrs System Mr. A. P. HOFFMAN
37 Director of Financial Aid Ms. Erma PERRY
13 AS-400 Program/System Admin Mr. Anthony HARDY
15 Director of Human Resources Ms. Brooke STRICKLAND
09 Dir Institutional Effectiveness Ms. Mandy LANIER
40 Bookstore Manager Mr. Jeremy JAMES
21 Director of Accounting & Finance Ms. Kay GAMBLE
26 Dir Public Relations & Marketing Mrs. Barbara THOMPSON
30 Dean Institutional Svcs/Com Dev Dr. Ashli WILKINS
41 Athletic Director Mr. Mackey SASSER

*George Corley Wallace State Community College - Selma (C)

PO Box 2530, 3000 Earl Goodwin Pkwy,
Selma AL 36702-2530
County: Dallas FICE Identification: 005699
Unit ID: 101301
Telephone: (334) 876-9227 Carnegie Class: Assoc/HVT-High Non
FAX Number: (334) 876-9250 Calendar System: Semester
URL: www.wccs.edu
Established: 1963 Annual Undergrad Tuition & Fees (In-State): $4,080
Enrollment: 1,591 Coed
Affiliation or Control: State IRS Status: 501(c)3
Highest Offering: Associate Degree
Accreditation: SC, ACBSP, ADNUR, PNUR

02 President Dr. James M. MITCHELL
05 Acting Dean of Instruction Dr. Donitha GRIFFIN
20 Instructional Administrator Mr. Raji GOURDINE
10 Dean of Business & Finance Mrs. Jacqueline SMITH
32 Dean of Students/Exec to President Dr. Donitha GRIFFIN
08 Librarian Ms. Minnie CARSTARPHEN
76 Director of Health Science Dr. Tracey SHANNON
37 Financial Aid Director Ms. Anessa KIDD
07 Director of Admissions/Counselor Mr. Lonzy CLIFTON
09 Asst Dean of Institutional Effect Mrs. Veronica BROWN
26 Director of Community Relations Mrs. Veronica CHESNUT
19 Public Safety Coordinator Mr. Charles DYSART
41 Athletic Director Mr. Marcus HANNAH
18 Director of Facilities & Safety Mr. Keith JACKSON
28 Director of Diversity Vacant
40 Bookstore Manager Ms. Marie JONES
15 Human Resource Director Mr. Nawanya STROUD

*J.F. Drake State Community and Technical College (D)

3421 Meridian Street N, Huntsville AL 35811-1584
County: Madison FICE Identification: 005260
Unit ID: 101462
Telephone: (256) 539-8161 Carnegie Class: Assoc/HVT-High Non
FAX Number: (256) 539-6439 Calendar System: Semester
URL: www.drakestate.edu
Established: 1961 Annual Undergrad Tuition & Fees (In-State): $4,350
Enrollment: 996 Coed
Affiliation or Control: State IRS Status: 501(c)3
Highest Offering: Associate Degree
Accreditation: SC

02 Interim President Mr. Chris LEWIS
05 Dean of Instruction Mrs. Nicole B. PREWITT
10 Director of Fiscal Affairs Mrs. UMeeka SMITH
103 Director of Grants/Workforce Dev Ms. Tomeka CROSS
45 Dean of Planning & Research Dev Vacant
15 Human Resource Specialist Mrs. Katie CHANCE
13 Director Computer Services Vacant
08 Director of Library Services Ms. Carla CLIFT
07 Director of Admissions/Registrar Dr. Pamela LITTLE
37 Director Student Financial Aid Ms. Jennifer O'LINGER
26 Director of Public Relations Mr. Kenya RUSSELL
36 College Counselor Ms. Denise GAYMON
108 Director of Institutional Effective Dr. Alice RAYMOND
32 Dean of Student Support Services Vacant
51 Director of Adult Education Dr. Stacey GILL
18 Director of Operations Mr. Bruce BULLUCK
84 Enrollment Services Manager Ms. Tiffany GREEN

*J.F. Ingram State Technical College (E)

PO Box 220350, Deatsville AL 36022-0350
County: Elmore FICE Identification: 030025
Unit ID: 101471
Telephone: (334) 285-5177 Carnegie Class: Assoc/HVT-Mix Trad/Non
FAX Number: (334) 285-5328 Calendar System: Semester
URL: www.istc.edu
Established: 1965 Annual Undergrad Tuition & Fees (In-State): $4,896
Enrollment: 422 Coed
Affiliation or Control: State IRS Status: 501(c)3
Highest Offering: Associate Degree
Accreditation: COE

02 Interim President Mrs. Annette FUNDERBURK
05 Dean of Instruction Mr. Bill GRISWOLD
11 Dean of Administration Dr. Brannon LENTZ
32 Dean Students/Support Services Mrs. Rosie EDWARDS
20 Associate Dean of Instruction Dr. Julliana PROBST
35 Student Services Director Mrs. Tawanna THORNTON
15 Human Resources Coordinator Ms. Erica PORTIS-TURNER
88 Re-Entry/Counseling Programs Coord Mr. Rick VEST
10 Business Office Director Mrs. Amelia FOX
04 Administrative Asst to President Mrs. Julie VARNER

*Jefferson State Community College (F)

2601 Carson Road, Birmingham AL 35215-3098
County: Jefferson FICE Identification: 001022
Unit ID: 101505
Telephone: (205) 853-1200 Carnegie Class: Assoc/MT-VT-Mix Trad/Non
FAX Number: (205) 853-8505 Calendar System: Semester
URL: www.jeffersonstate.edu
Established: 1963 Annual Undergrad Tuition & Fees (In-State): $4,440
Enrollment: 8,821 Coed
Affiliation or Control: State IRS Status: 501(c)3
Highest Offering: Associate Degree
Accreditation: SC, ACBSP, ACFEI, ADNUR, CONST, EMT, FUSER, MLTAD, PTAA, RAD

02 Interim President Mr. Keith A. BROWN
05 Dean of Instruction Ms. Danielle COBURN
75 Dean Career & Technical Education Ms. Norma G. BELL
30 Dean Campus Development/Campus Svcs Mr. Keith A. BROWN
10 Director Financial Services Ms. Mary WATSON
32 Director of Student Services Dr. Linda J. HOOTON
97 Assoc Dean Transf Gen Stds Shelby Ms. Liesl W. HARRIS
97 Assoc Dean Transf Gen Stds Jeffrsn Dr. Aliakbar R. YAZDI
106 Associate Dean Distance Education Mr. Alan B. DAVIS
51 Director College/Cmty/Corp Educ Ms. Kay C. POTTER
13 Chief Information Officer Mr. Stephen MOORE
37 Director Financial Aid Ms. Theresa MAYS
84 Dean of Enrollment Services Dr. Phillip M. HOBBS
18 Director Maintenance Mr. Perry HARRIS
08 Director of Learning Resources Ms. Barbara GOSS
36 Director Career/Job Resource Center Dr. Tamara PAYNE
07 Director Admissions and Retention Dr. Lillian OWENS
15 Director Human Resources Mr. Shain WILSON
26 Director Media Relations Mr. David BOBO
96 Purchasing Coordinator Ms. Ann CIMALORE
19 Director Safety & Security Mr. Mark BAILEY
09 Assoc Dean Inst Effectiveness Ms. Amanda E. KIN
04 Administrative Asst to President Ms. Janie STARNES
25 Director Resource Development Ms. Kelli CREAMER
86 Director Community Outreach Mr. Guin ROBINSON

*Lawson State Community College (G)

3060 Wilson Road, SW, Birmingham AL 35221-1798
County: Jefferson FICE Identification: 001059
Unit ID: 101569
Telephone: (205) 925-2515 Carnegie Class: Assoc/MT-VT-Mix Trad/Non
FAX Number: (205) 925-1390 Calendar System: Semester
URL: www.lawsonstate.edu
Established: 1949 Annual Undergrad Tuition & Fees (In-State): $4,380
Enrollment: 3,172 Coed
Affiliation or Control: State IRS Status: 501(c)3
Highest Offering: Associate Degree
Accreditation: SC, ACBSP, ADNUR, DA, PNUR

02 President Dr. Perry W. WARD
05 Vice Pres Instructional Services Dr. Bruce CRAWFORD
11 Vice President of Administration Mrs. Sharon CREWS
32 Acting Dean of Students Mr. Darren ALLEN
09 Coordinator of Data Management Mrs. Jamie GLASS
10 Dir Fin Services/Risk Assessment Dr. Craig D. LAWRENCE
20 Academic Dean Dr. Sherri DAVIS
21 Director of Accounting Ms. Monique SILAS
50 Assoc Dean Bus/Information Tech Dr. Alice MILTON
49 Assoc Dean Lib Arts/Coll Trans Pgms Dr. Karl PRUITT
76 Assoc Dean of Health Occupations Dr. Shelia MARABLE
75 Assoc Dean Career Tech Programs Mr. Donald SLEDGE
84 Asst Dean of Admissions/Records Mr. Darren ALLEN
07 Director of Admissions Dr. Jeff SHELLEY
08 Librarian Ms. Sandra HENDERSON
37 Director Student Financial Aid Ms. Cassandra HOLLINS
15 Director of Personnel Services Mrs. Janice MCGEE
26 Chief Public Relations Officer Mrs. Geri ALBRIGHT
18 Chief Facilities/Physical Plant Mr. Chad YANCY
19 Director Safety/Security Mr. James BLANTON
13 Dir Computing and Information Mgmt Mr. James MANKOWICH
41 Athletic Director Mr. Carlton RICE
06 Registrar Ms. Lori CHISEM
39 Director Student Housing Mr. Stanley TRIPLETT
38 Coordinator Student Counseling Dr. Renee HERNDON
106 Dir Online Education/E-learning Dr. Kesha JAMES
25 Chief Contracts/Grants Admin Dr. Myrtes D. GREEN
103 Asst Dean Workforce Development Mr. Tommy HOBBS

*Lurleen B. Wallace Community College (H)

PO Drawer 1418, 1000 Dannelly Blvd,
Andalusia AL 36420-1224
County: Covington FICE Identification: 008988
Unit ID: 101602
Telephone: (334) 222-6591 Carnegie Class: Assoc/HVT-High Trad
FAX Number: (334) 881-2300 Calendar System: Semester
URL: www.lbwcc.edu
Established: 1969 Annual Undergrad Tuition & Fees (In-State): $4,380
Enrollment: 1,732 Coed
Affiliation or Control: State IRS Status: 501(c)3
Highest Offering: Associate Degree
Accreditation: SC, ADNUR, DMS, EMT, SURGT

02 President Dr. Herbert H. RIEDEL
05 Dean of Instruction Ms. Peggy LINTON
32 Dean of Student Affairs Mr. Jason JESSIE
10 Director of Finance/Comptroller Ms. Lynne DAYTON
21 Director of Business Services Ms. Debra MOODY
103 Assoc Dean Adult Educ/Workforce Dev Mr. Jimmy HUTTO
13 Assoc Dean Instr/Info Technology Mr. Greg APLIN
15 Human Resources Coordinator Ms. Ashley BASS
09 Dir Inst Effectiveness & Quality Dr. Shannon LEVITZKE
18 Dir College Facilities/Maintenance Mr. Tim JONES
07 Director Admissions & Records Ms. Jan RILEY
41 Athletic Director Mr. Steve HELMS
08 Director of Learning Resources Mr. Hugh CARTER
121 Director Student Support Services Dr. Patricia POWELL
88 Dir Upward Bound/Andalusia Camp Dir Mr. Bridges ANDERSON
37 Director of Financial Aid Ms. Donna BASS
26 Public Info Officer/Dir Mktg & Dev Ms. Renee LEMAIRE

04 Administrative Asst to President ... Ms. Cindy GREEN
111 Assoc Dean of Institutional Advance ... Dr. Arlene DAVIS
11 Dean of Administrative Services ... Ms. Peige JOSEY

*Marion Military Institute (A)

1101 Washington Street, Marion AL 36756-3213
County: Perry FICE Identification: 001026
Unit ID: 101648
Telephone: (800) 664-1842 Carnegie Class: Assoc/HT-High Trad
FAX Number: (334) 683-2380 Calendar System: Semester
URL: www.marionmilitary.edu
Established: 1842 Annual Undergrad Tuition & Fees (In-State): $9,418
Enrollment: 457 Coed
Affiliation or Control: State IRS Status: 501(c)3
Highest Offering: Associate Degree
Accreditation: SC

02 President ... Col. David J. MOLLAHAN
03 Executive Vice President/CAO ... Dr. Susan G. STEVENSON
10 VP for Finance & Business Affs ... Mr. Brian HARRISON
05 Chief Instructional Officer ... LTC. Timothy ULLMANN
32 Actg VP Student Affairs/Commandant ... Col. Ed PASSMORE
30 VP for Institutional Advancement ... Mrs. Suzanne MCKEE
41 Director of Athletics ... Dr. Michelle IVEY
84 Director of Enrollment Management ... Mrs. Brittany CRAWFORD
29 Director of Alumni and Comm Affairs ... Mrs. O'Neal HOLMES
88 ROTC Professor of Military Science ... LTC. Cory ARMSTEAD
09 Director of Institutional Research ... Mrs. Donna LEEMON
06 Registrar ... 1Lt. Caleb LOGAN
15 Dir Human Resources/Compliance ... Ms. Carmon PAIGE
37 Director of Financial Aid ... Ms. Jacqueline WILSON
08 Director Service Academy Program ... LTC. Thomas BOWEN
18 Director of Facilities ... SCPO. Robert D. SUMLIN
17 Director of Health Services ... Mrs. Rene SUMLIN

*Northeast Alabama Community College (B)

PO Box 159, 138 Alabama Highway 35,
Rainsville AL 35986-0159
County: DeKalb/Jackson FICE Identification: 001031
Unit ID: 101897
Telephone: (256) 638-4418 Carnegie Class: Assoc/HVT-High Trad
FAX Number: (256) 638-3052 Calendar System: Semester
URL: www.nacc.edu
Established: 1963 Annual Undergrad Tuition & Fees (In-State): $4,380
Enrollment: 2,700 Coed
Affiliation or Control: State IRS Status: 501(c)3
Highest Offering: Associate Degree
Accreditation: SC, ADNUR, EMT, PNUR

02 President ... Dr. J. David CAMPBELL
05 Vice Pres/Dean of Instruction ... Dr. Joseph D. BURKE
56 Director Extended Day/Distance Educ ... Mr. Chad GORHAM
32 Dean of Student Services ... Ms. Sherie GRACE
11 Dean of Admin Services ... Mr. Larry D. GUFFEY
37 Director of Financial Aid ... Mr. Nixon WILLMON
103 Dir Workforce Devel/Skills Training ... Mr. Mike KENNAMER
26 Director of Promotions & Marketing ... Mrs. Debra A. BARRENTINE
45 Dir Inst Planning & Assessment ... Mr. Brad FRICKS
18 Chief Facilities/Physical Plant ... Mr. Kent JONES
06 Registrar/Chief Bus Ofcr/Dir Purchg ... Mr. Larry D. GUFFEY
30 Development Director ... Ms. Heather RICE
19 Director of Police/Security ... Mr. Norman SMITH
04 Administrative Asst to President ... Ms. Brenda STRINGER
08 Dir Learning Resource Ctr/Library ... Mrs. Julia EVERETT
15 Human Resources Director ... Mrs. Lynde MANN
29 Event Planning/Alumni Relations ... Ms. Chasley BELLOMY
72 Director of Educational Technology ... Ms. Patricia COMBS

*Northwest - Shoals Community College (C)

800 George Wallace Boulevard,
Muscle Shoals AL 35661-3205
County: Colbert FICE Identification: 005697
Unit ID: 101736
Telephone: (256) 331-5200 Carnegie Class: Assoc/HVT-High Trad
FAX Number: (256) 331-5222 Calendar System: Semester
URL: www.nwscc.edu
Established: 1963 Annual Undergrad Tuition & Fees (In-State): $4,351
Enrollment: 3,700 Coed
Affiliation or Control: State IRS Status: 501(c)3
Highest Offering: Associate Degree
Accreditation: SC, ADNUR, EMT, MAC

02 President ... Dr. Humphrey LEE
05 Vice President of Instruction ... Dr. Glenda COLAGROSS
09 Assoc Dean Inst Effect/Dist Ed/Dev ... Mr. John MCINTOSH
20 Assoc Dean Instructional Programs ... Dr. Timmy JAMES
37 Director of Financial Aid ... Ms. Sheron KEMP
07 Asst Dean Recruit/Adm/FA ... Mr. Tom CARTER
15 Human Resources Coordinator ... Ms. Tia STONE
88 Talent Search Director ... Ms. Cindy STEWART
13 Director of Management Info Systems ... Mr. Alan MITCHELL
06 Registrar/Coordinator of Admissions ... Ms. Tracy RABY
103 Assoc Dean of Workforce Develop ... Ms. Rose JONES
21 Comptroller ... Ms. Janet JONES

88 Director of Adult Educ and RTW ... Ms. Tara BRANSCOME
88 Dir College and Career Readiness ... Mr. Ed CARTER
88 Coordinator/Advisor RTW ... Ms. Tara BRANSCOME
04 Administrative Asst to President ... Ms. Teresa HARRISON
26 Public Information Officer ... Mr. Trent RANDOLPH
121 Coordinator of Advising & Graduate ... Ms. MaLea MILSTEAD
124 Director of Student Support Svcs ... Ms. Ann LYNDON
25 Grants Admin ... Ms. Leslie TOMLINSON

*Reid State Technical College (D)

PO Box 588, 100 Hwy 83, Evergreen AL 36401-0588
County: Conecuh FICE Identification: 005692
Unit ID: 101994
Telephone: (251) 578-1313 Carnegie Class: Assoc/HVT-Mix Trad/Non
FAX Number: (251) 578-5355 Calendar System: Semester
URL: www.rstc.edu
Established: 1966 Annual Undergrad Tuition & Fees (In-State): $4,440
Enrollment: 571 Coed
Affiliation or Control: State IRS Status: 501(c)3
Highest Offering: Associate Degree
Accreditation: COE

02 Acting President/Business Manager ... Mr. David J. RHODES
05 Dean Students/Instructional Svcs ... Dr. Tangela PURIFOY
103 Assoc Dean Workforce Development ... Dr. Alesia K. STUART
09 Asst Dean for Institutional Effect ... Ms. Coretta BOYKIN
37 Director Financial Aid ... Ms. Christy GOODWIN
15 Director of Human Resources ... Ms. Brenda JACKSON
07 Asst Dir Admissions & Records ... Ms. Mandy GODWIN
10 Office Administration ... Ms. Lois ROBINSON
06 Registrar ... Ms. Vickie NICHOLSON
38 Director of Counseling/ADA Coord ... Vacant

*Shelton State Community College (E)

9500 Old Greensboro Road, Tuscaloosa AL 35405-8522
County: Tuscaloosa FICE Identification: 005691
Unit ID: 102067
Telephone: (205) 391-2211 Carnegie Class: Assoc/HVT-Mix Trad/Non
FAX Number: (205) 391-2426 Calendar System: Semester
URL: www.sheltonstate.edu
Established: 1953 Annual Undergrad Tuition & Fees (In-State): $4,107
Enrollment: 4,834 Coed
Affiliation or Control: State IRS Status: 501(c)3
Highest Offering: Associate Degree
Accreditation: SC, ADNUR, COARC, PNUR

02 Interim President ... Dr. Jason HURST
05 Associate Dean of Academic Services ... Ms. Ginger GLASS
10 Comptroller Business Services ... Mrs. Ann BRACKNELL
32 Dean of Student Services ... Mrs. Amanda HARBISON
13 Assoc Dean Info Technology Services ... Mr. Claude LAKE
12 Dean Fredd Campus/Title III ... Mr. Ronald RANGE
88 Assoc Dean for Corporate Programs ... Mr. Jason MOORE
30 Assoc Dean of Advancement ... Mr. Byron ABSTON
38 Assoc Dean of Student Support ... Ms. Fran TURNER
76 Allied Health Assistant Dean ... Ms. Gladys HILL
37 Director of Financial Aid ... Ms. Rhonda SMITH
88 Executive Asst to the President ... Ms. Channing H. MARLOWE
07 Director of Admissions/Registrar ... Mrs. Fannie BATES-REESE
08 Director Library Services ... Mr. Glen JOHNSON
103 Dean of Instruction & Workforce Dev ... Ms. Joye JONES
88 Director Adult Education ... Mr. Phillip JOHNSON
15 Dean of Human Resources ... Vacant
88 Assoc Dean of Technical Services ... Mr. Grant COCKRELL
109 Dean of Auxiliary Services ... Dr. Thomas TAYLOR
04 Administrative Asst to President ... Mrs. Betty PRUITT
09 Dir Institutional Effective/Rsrch ... Mr. Louis SHEDD
106 Instructional Tech and eLearning ... Mr. John ALEXANDER
106 Instructional Tech and eLearning ... Ms. Molly BOOTH
18 Chief of Facilities ... Mr. Tim HINTON
26 Asst Dir of Media Communication ... Ms. Lisa WALDROP
105 Assoc Dean of Info/Tech Services ... Mr. Claude LAKE

*Snead State Community College (F)

PO Box 734, Boaz AL 35957-0734
County: Marshall FICE Identification: 001038
Unit ID: 102076
Telephone: (256) 593-5120 Carnegie Class: Assoc/HT-High Trad
FAX Number: (256) 593-7180 Calendar System: Semester
URL: www.snead.edu
Established: 1898 Annual Undergrad Tuition & Fees (In-State): $4,440
Enrollment: 2,456 Coed
Affiliation or Control: State IRS Status: Exempt
Highest Offering: Associate Degree
Accreditation: SC, ADNUR

02 President ... Dr. Robert EXLEY
32 Vice President for Student Services ... Mr. Jason CANNON
10 VP for Finance & Administration ... Mr. Joe WHITMORE
13 Chief IT Officer ... Mr. Randy MALTBIE
26 Director of Marketing/PR ... Ms. Shelley SMITH
88 Coordinator of Testing/Secondary Ed ... Ms. Tonya SHIELDS
05 Vice President for Academic Affairs ... Dr. Annette CEDERHOLM
106 Associate Dean of Online Learning ... Mr. Michael GIBSON
81 Science Division Director ... Ms. Deborah RHODEN
79 English/Languages Division Director ... Dr. Cynthia DENHAM
83 Soc Sci/Human Svcs/PS Div Director ... Dr. Karen WATTS
81 Mathematics Division Director ... Mr. Blake LEETH
50 Business/Tech/Computer Sc Div Dir ... Mr. Vann SCOTT

57 Art/Humanites/Commun/Design Div Dir ... Dr. Jonathan WATTS
103 Director Workforce Development ... Ms. Teresa WALKER
76 Director Health Sciences ... Ms. Amy LANGLEY
41 Athletic Dir/Dean Auxiliary Svcs ... Mr. Mark RICHARD
08 Head Librarian ... Mr. John MILLER
15 Director of Human Resources ... Ms. Amanda GUNNELS
18 Director of Physical Plant ... Mr. Steve WILLIAMS
07 Director of Admissions/Recruitment ... Ms. Tristin CALLAHAN
19 Director Security/Safety ... Mr. Paul GORE
29 Director Alumni Relations ... Ms. Shelley SMITH
30 Development Coordinator ... Ms. Kelli CONLEY
37 Financial Aid Coordinator ... Ms. Amanda CHILDRESS
04 Executive Asst to President ... Ms. Kelli CONLEY

*Southern Union State Community College (G)

PO Box 1000, Wadley AL 36276-1000
County: Randolph FICE Identification: 001040
Unit ID: 251260
Telephone: (256) 395-2211 Carnegie Class: Assoc/HT-High Trad
FAX Number: (256) 395-2215 Calendar System: Semester
URL: www.suscc.edu
Established: 1922 Annual Undergrad Tuition & Fees (In-State): $4,352
Enrollment: 4,716 Coed
Affiliation or Control: State IRS Status: 501(c)3
Highest Offering: Associate Degree
Accreditation: SC, ADNUR, EMT, RAD, SURGT

02 Interim President ... Dr. Glenda COLAGROSS
05 Dean of Academics ... Dr. Linda NORTH
32 Dean of Students ... Ms. Tiffany SANDERS
20 Assoc Dean of Instruction ... Mr. Steve SPRATLIN
72 Dean of Technical Educ/Wrkfce Dev ... Dr. Darin BALDWIN
35 Dean Student Development ... Mr. Gary BRANCH
41 Athletic Director ... Mr. Ron RADFORD
06 Registrar ... Ms. Catherine STRINGFELLOW
10 Business Manager ... Mr. Ben JORDAN

*Trenholm State Technical College (H)

PO Box 10048, Montgomery AL 36108
County: Montgomery FICE Identification: 005734
Unit ID: 102313
Telephone: (334) 420-4200 Carnegie Class: Assoc/HVT-Mix Trad/Non
FAX Number: (334) 420-4206 Calendar System: Semester
URL: www.trenholmstate.edu
Established: 1963 Annual Undergrad Tuition & Fees (In-State): $4,134
Enrollment: 1,401 Coed
Affiliation or Control: State IRS Status: 501(c)3
Highest Offering: Associate Degree
Accreditation: SC, ACFEI, DA, DMS, EMT, MAC, PNUR, #RAD

02 President ... Mr. Sam MUNNERLYN
10 Dean of Finance/Admin Svcs ... Ms. Cathy WRIGHT
05 VP of Instructional Services ... Dr. Kemba CHAMBERS
30 Dean of Development ... Dr. Suresh C. KAUSHIK
32 Dean of Students ... Dr. Greg HUDSON
103 Dean of Workforce Development ... Vacant
13 Assoc Dean of IT ... Mr. Charles HARRIS
09 Director of Institutional Research ... Dr. Mimi JOHNSON
18 Director Physical Plant ... Mr. Robert ALLEN
37 Director Student Financial Aid ... Ms. Betty EDWARDS
07 Director of Admissions/Registrar ... Mrs. Tennie S. MCBRYDE
26 Public Information Officer ... Ms. Angela HURST
15 Director of Human Resources ... Ms. Pam ROLLINS
51 Dir Title III/Marketing/Cont Educ ... Ms. Arlinda KNIGHT
36 Coordinator Job Placement ... Ms. Maria RICHARDSON
04 Administrative Asst to President ... Ms. Angela W. CONE
08 Head Librarian ... Mr. Paul BLACKMON

*Wallace State Community College - Hanceville (I)

PO Box 2000, 801 Main Street, NW,
Hanceville AL 35077-2000
County: Cullman FICE Identification: 007871
Unit ID: 101295
Telephone: (256) 352-8000 Carnegie Class: Assoc/HVT-High Trad
FAX Number: (256) 352-8228 Calendar System: Semester
URL: www.wallacestate.edu
Established: 1966 Annual Undergrad Tuition & Fees (In-State): $4,380
Enrollment: 5,418 Coed
Affiliation or Control: State IRS Status: 501(c)3
Highest Offering: Associate Degree
Accreditation: SC, ACBSP, ACFEI, ADNUR, CAHIIM, COARC, DA, DH, DMS, EMT, MAC, MLTAD, OTA, PNUR, POLYT, PTAA, RAD

02 President ... Dr. Vicki KAROLEWICS
03 Executive Vice President ... Dr. Tomesa SMITH
45 College Dean ... Dr. Johnny MCMOY
10 Dean of Finance & Admin Svcs ... Jason MORGAN
05 Dean of Academic Affairs ... Dr. Beth BOWNES-JOHNSON
20 Dean of Applied Technologies ... Jimmy HODGES
76 Dean of Health Sciences ... Lisa GERMAN
84 Asst Dean Enrollment Management ... Jennifer HILL
121 Director of Advising ... Dr. Matthew MCCRICKARD
109 Auxiliary Director ... Mark BOLIN
08 Head Librarian ... Lisa HULLETT
37 Director of Financial Aid ... Becky GRAVES
55 Extended Day Program Director ... Wayne MANORD

15 Director of Human Resources ....Alyce FLANIGAN
111 Director of Advancement ....Suzanne HARBIN
18 Director of Physical Plant ....Billy ROSE
13 Director of Technology ....Bruce TENISON
26 Director Communications/Marketing ....Kristen HOLMES
06 Registrar ....Jennifer TWITTY
36 Job Placement Coordinator ....Jamie BLACKMON
09 Coordinator of Inst Research ....Mattie HUDSON

Alabama State University (A)

915 S Jackson Street, Montgomery AL 36101-0271
County: Montgomery FICE Identification: 001005
Unit ID: 100724
Telephone: (334) 229-4200 Carnegie Class: Masters/M
FAX Number: (334) 834-6861 Calendar System: Semester
URL: www.alasu.edu
Established: 1867 Annual Undergrad Tuition & Fees (In-State): $9,220
Enrollment: 5,383 Coed
Affiliation or Control: State IRS Status: 501(c)3
Highest Offering: Doctorate
Accreditation: SC, ACBSP, ART, CACREP, CAEPN, CAHIIM, MUS, OPE, OT, PTA, SW, THEA

01 Interim President ....Dr. Leon C. WILSON
05 Provost/Vice Pres Academic Affs ....Dr. Leon C. WILSON
10 Asst President Bus & Finance ....Ms. Alondrea PRITCHETT
13 Director Technology Services ....Mr. Larry COBB
30 Vice Pres Institutional Advancement ....Ms. Zillah FLUKER
15 Director Human Resources ....Mrs. Willie DIXON
04 Assoc Prov/Vice Pres Academic Affs ....Vacant
32 Vice Pres Student Affairs ....Dr. Davida HAYWOOD
84 Assistant Vice Pres Enrollment Mgmt ....Dr. Courtney GRIFFIN
45 Assoc Prov Inst Effectiveness ....Vacant
35 Asst Vice Pres Student Affairs ....Vacant
21 Int Comt/Asst VP Business & Finance ....Mrs. Alondrea J. PRITCHETT
20 Assistant VP Academic Advisement ....Vacant
108 Dir Acad Planning & Evaluation ....Dr. Christine C. THOMAS
09 Director Institutional Research ....Dr. Yiyun JIE
88 Dir Quality Enhancement Plng ....Dr. Denise VAUGHN
08 Dean Libraries/Learning Resource ....Dr. Janice FRANKLIN
07 Director Admissions/Recruitment ....Dr. William SMITH
37 Interim Financial Aid Director ....Ms. Patricia COTTON
36 Dir Placement Svcs/Cooperative Educ ....Mr. Jeremy HODGE
50 Dean College Business Admin ....Dr. Kamal HINGORANI
89 Dean University College ....Dr. Evelyn HODGE
53 Dean College of Education ....Dr. Doris SCREWS
64 Dean Visual & Performing Arts ....Dr. Tommie T. STEWART
58 Dean Graduate Studies ....Dr. William PERSON
81 Dean College of Sci Math & Tech ....Dr. Kennedy WEKESA
49 Dean Liberal Arts/Social Sci ....Dr. Anthony T. ADAMS
76 Dean College Health Sciences ....Dr. Cheryl EASLEY
51 Director Continuing Education ....Mr. Olan L. WESLEY
29 Director Alumni Relations ....Mr. Cromwell HANDY
23 Director Student Health Services ....Ms. Gwendolyn MANN
19 Chief of Campus Police ....Mr. James GRAYBOYS
38 Dir Counseling & Development Svcs ....Mr. Chris JOHNS
39 Dir Housing/Residential Life ....Mr. Gourdine WADE
41 Director of Athletics ....Mr. Melvin HINES
25 Director Grants Sponsored Pgms ....Mrs. Tamara LEE
96 Director of Purchasing ....Ms. Arlene THOMPSON
101 Board Liaison ....Vacant
106 Dir Online Education/E-learning ....Dr. William PERSON
43 General Counsel ....Mr. Kenneth THOMAS
06 Registrar ....Ms. Marie MCNEAR
26 Chief Public Relations/Marketing ....Mr. Kenneth MULLINAX

Amridge University (B)

1200 Taylor Road, Montgomery AL 36117-3553
County: Montgomery FICE Identification: 025034
Unit ID: 100690
Telephone: (800) 351-4040 Carnegie Class: Masters/S
FAX Number: (334) 387-3878 Calendar System: Semester
URL: www.amridgeuniversity.edu
Established: 1967 Annual Undergrad Tuition & Fees: $7,180
Enrollment: 627 Coed
Affiliation or Control: Churches Of Christ IRS Status: 501(c)3
Highest Offering: Doctorate
Accreditation: SC

01 President ....Dr. Michael C. TURNER
05 Academic Vice President/Dean ....Dr. Lee TAYLOR
32 VP of Student Affairs ....Mrs. Laina T. COSTANZA
06 Registrar ....Mrs. Elaine P. TARENCE
08 Director of Library ....Ms. Kay S. NEWMAN
10 Chief Business Officer ....Mrs. B. P. TURNER
21 Chief Accountant ....Dr. Anita L. CROSBY
37 Financial Aid Director ....Ms. Starr FAIN
42 Director of Church Relations ....Mr. Curtis SAMPLEY
88 Director of World Missions ....Mr. Demar ELAM
29 Director of Alumni Relations ....Vacant
13 System Admin Network Operations ....Mr. Jack TEMPLE
18 Chief Facilities/Physical Plant ....Mr. Robert SHIRLEY
24 Coordinator of Network Opers ....Mr. Thomas PATTERSON
38 Director of Student Counseling ....Vacant
26 Chief Public Relations Officer ....Mrs. Laina COSTANZA
73 Dean of School of Theology ....Dr. Rodney CLOUD
50 Dean of Col of Business & Ldrshp ....Dr. Kenyetta MCCURTY
97 Dean of College of General Studies ....Dr. Roger SHEPHERD
88 Dean of Sch of Human Svcs ....Dr. Jerry MARTIN
15 Director Personnel Services ....Vacant
08 Head Librarian ....Mr. Terence SHERIDAN
84 Enrollment Management Coordinator ....Mr. Brooks HOUSLEY

Athens State University (C)

300 N Beaty Street, Athens AL 35611-1902
County: Limestone FICE Identification: 001008
Unit ID: 100812
Telephone: (256) 233-8100 Carnegie Class: Bac-Diverse
FAX Number: (256) 216-3324 Calendar System: Semester
URL: www.athens.edu
Established: 1822 Annual Undergrad Tuition & Fees (In-State): N/A
Enrollment: 3,041 Coed
Affiliation or Control: State IRS Status: 501(c)3
Highest Offering: Master's
Accreditation: SC, ACBSP, CAEPN, CS

01 President ....Dr. Robert K. GLENN
05 Provost & VP for Academic Affs ....Dr. Joseph DELAP
20 Associate VP for Academic Affairs ....Ms. Belinda KRIGEL
20 Asst VP for Academic Affairs ....Dr. Jackie SMITH
32 Vice Pres for Enroll & Student Supp ....Ms. Sarah MCABEE
35 Asst VP for Enrollment & Stdnt Svcs ....Ms. Crystal CREEKMORE
10 Vice President Financial Affairs ....Mr. Mike MCCOY
21 Business Manager ....Mr. Jonathan CRAFT
111 Vice Pres for University Advance ....Dr. Keith FERGUSON
08 Director of Libraries ....Dr. Katherine QUINNELL
50 Dean College of Business ....Dr. Kimberly LAFEVOR
53 Dean College of Education ....Dr. Patricia SIMS
49 Dean College of Arts & Sciences ....Dr. Ronald FRITZE
36 Dir of Career Services ....Ms. Saralyn MITCHELL
37 Dir of Student Financial Services ....Ms. Mary CHAMBLISS
06 Registrar ....Ms. Teresa SUIT
07 Director of Admissions & Records ....Ms. Necedah HENDERSON
35 Director of Student Activities ....Mr. Terry STEPP
29 Director of Alumni Affairs/Ann Giv ....Ms. Trish DI LULLO
30 Director of Institutional Develop ....Mr. David BROWN
88 Director of Printing & Public Rels ....Mr. Guy MCCLURE
09 Director of Institutional Research ....Ms. Sylvia CORREA
18 Director of Physical Plant ....Mr. Jerry BRADFORD
15 Director of Human Resources ....Ms. Suzanne SIMS
51 Director of Ctr for Lifelong Lrng ....Dr. Kimberly BELL
121 Director of Student Success Ctr ....Mr. Derrek SMITH
04 Administrative Asst to President ....Mrs. Carol E. RACHAL
101 Secretary of the Institution/Board ....Mrs. Jackie GOOCH
13 Chief Info Technology Officer (CIO) ....Ms. Belinda KRIGEL
19 Chief of Security/Safety ....Mr. Jerry CRABTREE

Auburn University (D)

Auburn AL 36849
County: Lee FICE Identification: 001009
Unit ID: 100858
Telephone: (334) 844-4000 Carnegie Class: DU-Higher
FAX Number: N/A Calendar System: Semester
URL: www.auburn.edu
Established: 1856 Annual Undergrad Tuition & Fees (In-State): $10,696
Enrollment: 27,287 Coed
Affiliation or Control: State IRS Status: 501(c)3
Highest Offering: Doctorate
Accreditation: SC, AAB, ART, AUD, CACREP, CAEPN, CIDA, CLPSY, CONST, COPSY, CS, DIETD, ENG, JOUR, LSAR, MFCD, MUS, NURSE, PHAR, SP, SPAA, SW, THEA, VET

01 President ....Dr. Steven LEATH
03 Executive Vice President ....Dr. Donald L. LARGE, JR.
05 Provost/VP Academic Affairs ....Dr. Timothy R. BOOSINGER
29 VP Alumni Affairs ....Ms. Gretchen R. VANVALKENBURG
10 VP Business & Finance & CFO ....Ms. Kelli D. SHOMAKER
30 VP Development ....Ms. Jane DIFOLCO PARKER
32 VP & Assoc Provost Student Affairs ....Dr. Bobby R. WOODARD
46 VP Research & Economic Development ....Dr. John M. MASON
101 Secretary to Board of Trustees ....Mr. C. Grant DAVIS, JR.
43 General Counsel ....Mr. Lee F. ARMSTRONG
13 Chief Information Officer ....Mr. James O'CONNOR
84 Interim Dean of Enrollment Services ....Ms. Velda ROOKER
56 Dir AL Cooperative Extension Syst ....Dr. Gary D. LEMME
41 Director of Athletics ....Mr. John O. JACOBS, JR.
86 Exec Director Governmental Affairs ....Mr. Charles J. HINCY
11 Director Public Affairs ....Mr. Brian C. KEETER
116 Assoc VP Int Audit/Compl & Privacy ....Mr. M. Kevin ROBINSON
117 Exec Director Risk Mgmt & Safety ....Ms. Christine L. EICK
26 Assistant VP Univ Comm & Mktg ....Mr. Mike CLARDY, JR.
88 Univ Ombudsperson ....Mr. Kevin COONROD
20 Associate Provost & Professor ....Dr. Emmett WINN
28 Assoc Prov/VP Inclus & Diversity . Dr. Taffye BENSON-CLAYTON
20 Assoc Provost Undergrad Studies ....Dr. Constance C. RELIHAN
25 Assistant VP Research ....Ms. Martha M. TAYLOR
35 Assistant VP Student Affairs ....Ms. Lady D. COX
56 VP University Outreach ....Dr. Royrickers COOK
85 Asst Provost Intl Programs ....Dr. Andrew R. GILLESPIE
109 Associate VP Auxiliary Services ....Mr. Jon G. WAGGONER
18 Associate VP Facilities ....Mr. Daniel P. KING
15 Associate VP Human Resources ....Ms. Karla S. MCCORMICK
21 Controller ....Ms. Amy K. DOUGLAS
96 Exec Dir Procurement/Payment Svcs ....Ms. Melissa M. MORRIS
37 Exec Dir Student Financial Svcs ....Mr. Michael C. REYNOLDS
22 Director Affirmative Action/EEO ....Ms. Kelley G. TAYLOR
108 Director Academic Assessment ....Dr. Megan R. GOOD
09 Director Institutional Research ....Dr. James A. CLARK
88 Director University Writing ....Dr. Margaret J. MARSHALL
88 Director Teaching & Learning Center ....Dr. Diane E. BOYD
88 Director JCS Museum of Art ....Dr. Marilyn LAUFER
39 Director Residence Life ....Dr. Virginia A. KOCH
36 Director Student Career Services ....Mrs. Nancy M. BERNARD
38 Director Student Counseling Svcs ....Dr. Doug HANKES
14 Exec Dir Office of Info Tech ....Mr. Bliss N. BAILEY
40 Director University Bookstore ....Ms. Catherine LEE
06 University Registrar ....Ms. Laura Ann FOREST
47 Dean Agriculture & Dir AAES ....Dr. Paul M. PATTERSON
48 Dean Architecture/Design/Construct ....Dr. Vini NATHAN
50 Dean Business ....Dr. Bill HARDGRAVE
53 Dean Education ....Dr. Betty Lou WHITFORD
54 Dean Engineering ....Dr. Christopher B. ROBERTS
65 Dean Forestry/Wildlife Sci ....Dr. Janaki R. ALAVALAPATI
59 Dean Human Sciences ....Dr. June M. HENTON
49 Dean Liberal Arts ....Dr. Joseph AISTRUP
66 Dean Nursing ....Dr. Gregg NEWSCHWANDER
67 Dean Pharmacy ....Dr. Richard A. HANSEN
81 Dean Sciences & Mathematics ....Dr. Nicholas J. GIORDANO
74 Dean Veterinary Medicine ....Dr. Calvin M. JOHNSON
58 Dean Graduate School ....Dr. George FLOWERS
08 Dean University Libraries ....Dr. Bonnie MACEWAN
04 Administrative Asst to President ....Ms. Tammy MAYO

Auburn University at Montgomery (E)

PO Box 244023, Montgomery AL 36124-4023
County: Montgomery FICE Identification: 008310
Unit ID: 100830
Telephone: (334) 244-3000 Carnegie Class: Masters/L
FAX Number: (334) 244-3762 Calendar System: Semester
URL: www.aum.edu
Established: 1967 Annual Undergrad Tuition & Fees (In-State): $9,640
Enrollment: 4,919 Coed
Affiliation or Control: State IRS Status: 501(c)3
Highest Offering: Doctorate
Accreditation: SC, CACREP, CAEPN, MT, NURSE, SPAA

01 Chancellor ....Dr. Carl A. STOCKTON
05 Provost ....Dr. Mrinal VARMA
111 Vice Chancellor Advancement ....Ms. Carolyn GOLDEN
88 Vice Chanc Outreach/Strat Init ....Dr. Katherine WEBB
32 Vice Chancellor of Student Affairs ....Ms. Janice LYN
10 Vice Chanc Financial & Admin Svcs ....Mr. Scott PARSONS
58 Assoc Provost Research/Grad Studies ....Dr. Matthew RAGLAND
20 Assoc Provost Undergraduate Studies ....Dr. Joy CLARK
09 Asst Provost IE & Accreditation ....Dr. Cara Mia BRASWELL
41 Athletic Director ....Ms. Jessie ROSA
85 Director of Global Initiatives ....Mr. Gokhan ALKANAT
15 Chief Human Resources Officer ....Ms. Jeanine BODDIE-LAVAN
18 Sodexo ....Mr. Ken CORNELIUS
08 Dean of Library ....Mr. Phil JOHNSON
07 Director of Admissions/Recruiting ....Mr. Rahmel COWEN
37 Sr Director of Financial Aid ....Mr. Anthony RICHEY
109 Chief Campus Services Officer ....Mr. Daryl MORRIS
39 Dir Housing & Residence Life ....Mr. Iyisha HAMPTON
13 Chief Information Officer ....Mr. Tobias MENSE
35 Associate Dean of Student Affairs ....Dr. Chaundra THOMPSON
19 Director of Police Operations ....Ms. Brenda MITCHELL
06 Registrar ....Ms. Holly BENSON
36 Director Career Development ....Mr. Bradley ROBBINS
26 Exec Dir Strategic Comm & Marketing ....Ms. Marla VICKERS
25 Director of Sponsored Programs ....Ms. Fariba S. DERAVI
85 Coord Intl Student Admissions ....Ms. Krystin BRYMER
49 Dean of College of Arts & Sciences ....Dr. Michael BURGER
50 Dean of College of Business ....Dr. Wanda Rhea INGRAM
53 Dean of College of Education ....Dr. Sheila AUSTIN
66 Dean of Nursing ....Dr. Jean LEUNER
51 Exec Dir of Continuing Education ....Ms. Kathy GUNTER
88 Associate Director of Clinical Svcs ....Ms. Greta CHAMBLESS
96 Dir of Procurement & Payment Svcs ....Ms. Lori NIELSEN
04 Executive Admin Assoc to Chancellor ....Ms. Robin FORESTER
106 Dir Online Education/E-learning ....Ms. Carolyn RAWL

Birmingham-Southern College (F)

900 Arkadelphia Road, Birmingham AL 35254-0001
County: Jefferson FICE Identification: 001012
Unit ID: 100937
Telephone: (205) 226-4600 Carnegie Class: Bac-A&S
FAX Number: (205) 226-4627 Calendar System: 4/1/4
URL: www.bsc.edu
Established: 1856 Annual Undergrad Tuition & Fees: $34,448
Enrollment: 1,346 Coed
Affiliation or Control: United Methodist IRS Status: 501(c)3
Highest Offering: Baccalaureate
Accreditation: SC, MUS

01 President ....Ms. Linda FLAHERTY-GOLDSMITH
05 VP Academic Affairs/Provost ....Dr. Brad CASKEY
10 VP Business and Finance/CFO ....Mr. Eli PHILLIPS
100 VP Cmty Relations/Chief of Staff ....Mr. Lane ESTES
111 VP Advancement ....Ms. Virginia G. LOFTIN
13 VP Information Technology ....Mr. Anthony HAMBEY
32 VP Student Development ....Dr. David EBERHARDT
07 VP Admission and Financial Planning ....Ms. Sara NEWHOUSE
88 Asst to the President Emeriti ....Mrs. Terri HICKS
20 VP Academic Affairs/Assoc Provost ....Dr. Tim SMITH
20 Assistant Provost ....Ms. Martha Ann STEVENSON
06 Registrar ....Mr. Keith KARRIKER
42 Chaplain ....Rev. Julie HOLLY
29 Director Alumni Affairs/Stewardship ....Vacant
23 Assoc Director of Health Services ....Ms. Yvette SPENCER

04 Asst to the President .... Mr. Chuck EVANS
26 Director of Communications .... Ms. Hannah WOLFSON
08 Director of the Library .... Ms. Nancy COLYAR
18 Director of Facilities & Events .... Ms. Anne CURRY
37 Director of Financial Planning .... Vacant
15 Assoc VP/Director Human Resources .... Ms. Susan KINNEY
27 Director of New Media .... Mr. Mike HAMILTON
38 Director of Counseling/Health Svcs .... Ms. Sara HOOVER
41 Athletic Director .... Ms. Kyndall WATERS
19 Chief of Campus Police .... Mr. Randy YOUNGBLOOD
36 Director of Career Services .... Mr. Michael LEBEAU
30 Director Advancement Services .... Vacant
28 Director of Multicultural Affairs .... Ms. Erica BROWN
68 Dir Physical Fitness & Recreation .... Mr. Mike ROBINSON
88 Director of Leadership Studies .... Mr. Kent ANDERSEN
88 Director of Service Learning .... Ms. Kristin HARPER
104 Assoc Dir of International Programs .... Ms. Anne LEDVINA
40 Bookstore Manager .... Mr. William ALEXANDER
96 Purchasing Manager .... Mr. Tim WILDING
44 Director Development/Annual Giving .... Mr. Bobby WATSON

Columbia Southern University (A)

21982 University Lane, Orange Beach AL 36561-3845
County: Baldwin — FICE Identification: 041215
Unit ID: 450933
Telephone: (251) 981-3771 — Carnegie Class: Masters/L
FAX Number: (251) 981-3815 — Calendar System: Other
URL: www.columbiasouthern.edu
Established: 1993 — Annual Undergrad Tuition & Fees: $5,175
Enrollment: 20,823 — Coed
Affiliation or Control: Proprietary — IRS Status: Proprietary
Highest Offering: Master's
Accreditation: DEAC

01 President .... Mr. Robert G. MAYES, JR.
03 Executive Vice President .... Ms. Chantell COOLEY
05 Provost/CAO .... Dr. Jeffrey BARKSDALE
100 Chief of Staff .... Mr. Ken STYRON
26 VP of Marketing/Outreach .... Mr. Eric MCHANEY
13 Vice Pres Information Technology .... Mr. Scott OSWALD
10 Vice Pres Business Affairs .... Mr. Pat TROUP
88 VP Business Development/Mil Init .... Mr. Rick COOPER
15 VP of Human Resources .... Ms. Sue BUTTS
49 Asst Provost Col Arts & Sciences .... Dr. John WEIDERT
32 Vice Provost Student Affairs .... Mr. Scott ROUNDS
20 Asst Provost College of Business .... Dr. Elwin JONES
108 Asst Prov Inst Effect/Accreditation .... Ms. Khalilah BURTON
07 Assoc VP Admissions .... Ms. Chelsea HOFFMAN
24 Director of Instructional Design .... Mr. Dayna FULLER
27 Director of Marketing .... Mr. Jacob HARRIS
29 Dir Student & Alumni Engagement .... Ms. Amanda MANJONE
40 Director of Bookstore Operations .... Mr. David BARNES
09 Dir of Inst Research/Assessment .... Ms. Cherea SCHELLHASE
06 Registrar .... Ms. Rachel FARRIS
37 Director of Financial Aid .... Ms. Tammy COMALANDER
88 Director of Quality Assurance .... Ms. Mona MCPHERSON
08 Dean of Library .... Ms. Jennifer STEINFORD
88 Director of State Authorization .... Ms. Alexis BANKS

Concordia College Alabama (B)

1712 Broad Street, Selma AL 36701
County: Dallas — FICE Identification: 010554
Unit ID: 101073
Telephone: (334) 874-5700 — Carnegie Class: Bac-Diverse
FAX Number: (334) 874-5755 — Calendar System: Semester
URL: www.ccal.edu
Established: 1922 — Annual Undergrad Tuition & Fees: $10,320
Enrollment: 487 — Coed
Affiliation or Control: Lutheran Church - Missouri Synod
IRS Status: 501(c)3
Highest Offering: Baccalaureate
Accreditation: SC

01 Int President/Chief Exec Officer .... Mr. Dexter JACKSON
05 Vice Pres Academic Affairs .... Dr. Cheryl WASHINGTON
10 Exec VP/Chief Fin Ofcr/Int COO .... Mr. Dexter JACKSON
32 VP of Student Services .... Dr. Donald JEFFERSON
30 VP Institutional Advancement .... Mr. Daniel JENKINS
84 Vice Pres Enrollment Management .... Ms. Meseret ALEMU
37 Director Financial Aid .... Mrs. Tharsteen BRIDGES
09 Dir Effectiveness/Research/Plng .... Ms. Betty HUBBARD
64 Band Director .... Mr. Steven JOHNSON
08 Library Director .... Mr. J. Scott WHITING
06 Registrar .... Mrs. Chinester GRAYSON
29 Director Alumni Affairs .... Mrs. Minnie MCMILLAN
26 Director Public Relations .... Ms. Abigail CAMPBELL
36 Dir Student Placement/Counseling .... Ms. Sadie JARETT
13 IT Director .... Mr. Wayne GREEN
41 Director of Athletics .... Mr. Frankie PEOPLES
35 Director Student Activities .... Mr. Coley C. CHESTNUT, SR.
42 College Chaplain .... Mr. LaVaughn WIGGINS
07 Director of Admissions .... Mr. Daniel HENKARO
15 Human Resources Coordinator .... Ms. Gail PICKNEY

*Education Corporation of America (C)

3660 Grandview Parkway Suite 300,
Birmingham AL 35243
County: Jefferson — Identification: 666006
Telephone: (205) 329-7900 — Carnegie Class: N/A
FAX Number: (205) 329-7906
URL: www.ecacolleges.com

01 President/Chief Executive Officer .... Mr. Stuart C. REED
43 Exec VP/Chf Compl Ofcr/Gen Counsel .... Mr. Roger L. SWARTZWELDER
26 Exec VP/Chief Marketing Officer .... Mr. Steve MCCLEARN
10 Exec VP/Chief Financial Officer .... Mr. Christopher BOEHM
15 EVP/Chief Human Resources Officer .... Ms. Paula FREY
05 Exec VP Chief Academic Officer .... Dr. John WOODS
13 Exec VP Chief Information Officer .... Mr. Tom MIKKELSON
21 SVP Finance .... Mr. Ryan BREWER
37 SVP Student Finance .... Vacant
27 SVP of Marketing .... Vacant
84 SVP of Student Enrollment .... Mr. Mike MILLER
20 SVP Academic Operations .... Ms. Rita CHUBICK
20 SVP Academic Compliance Curriculum .... Ms. Judy E. LIMA
88 SVP Associate General Counsel .... Mr. Benjamin J. DEGWECK
88 Group President .... Mr. John SCHUMAN
88 Group President Emerging Brands .... Ms. Megan BROADWIN
88 Group President .... Mr. Dominick FEDELE

*Virginia College (D)

488 Palisades Boulevard, Birmingham AL 35209
County: Jefferson — FICE Identification: 030106
Unit ID: 420307
Telephone: (205) 802-1200 — Carnegie Class: Bac/Assoc-Mixed
FAX Number: (205) 271-8225 — Calendar System: Quarter
URL: www.vc.edu
Established: 1993 — Annual Undergrad Tuition & Fees: $14,632
Enrollment: 2,138 — Coed
Affiliation or Control: Proprietary — IRS Status: Proprietary
Highest Offering: Master's
Accreditation: ACICS, ACFEI, COARC, DMS, SURGT

02 Campus President .... Mr. Dale TURNER
07 Vice President of Enrollment .... Vacant
05 Academic Dean .... Mr. Hiram HOLT

*Virginia College (E)

2021 Drake Avenue SW, Huntsville AL 35801
Telephone: (256) 533-7387 — Identification: 666400
Accreditation: ACICS

† Branch campus of Virginia College, Birmingham, AL.

*Virginia College (F)

3725 Airport Boulevard, Suite 165, Mobile AL 36608
Telephone: (251) 343-7227 — Identification: 666069
Accreditation: ACICS, ACFEI, SURGT

† Branch campus of Virginia College, Birmingham, AL.

*Virginia College (G)

6200 Atlanta Highway, Montgomery AL 36117-2802
Telephone: (334) 277-3390 — Identification: 666408
Accreditation: ACICS

† Branch campus of Virginia College, Birmingham, AL.

Edward Via College of Osteopathic Medicine-Auburn Campus (H)

910 S. Donahue Drive, Auburn AL 36832
Telephone: (334) 442-4000 — Identification: 770965
Accreditation: &OSTEO

† Branch campus of Edward Via College of Osteopathic Medicine, Blacksburg, VA

Faulkner University (I)

5345 Atlanta Highway, Montgomery AL 36109-3398
County: Montgomery — FICE Identification: 001003
Unit ID: 101189
Telephone: (334) 272-5820 — Carnegie Class: Masters/S
FAX Number: (334) 386-7107 — Calendar System: Semester
URL: www.faulkner.edu
Established: 1942 — Annual Undergrad Tuition & Fees: $20,130
Enrollment: 3,262 — Coed
Affiliation or Control: Churches Of Christ — IRS Status: 501(c)3
Highest Offering: Doctorate
Accreditation: SC, CAEPN, LAW, @THEOL

01 President .... Dr. Michael D. WILLIAMS
00 Chancellor .... Dr. Billy D. HILYER
05 Vice President Academic Affairs .... Dr. Dave RAMPERSAD
10 Vice President Financial Services .... Mrs. Wilma D. PHILLIPS
32 Vice President Student Services .... Dr. Jean-Noel THOMPSON
84 Vice President Enrollment Mgmt .... Dr. Keith MOCK
111 Vice President Advancement .... Dr. John TYSON
43 General Counsel .... Dr. Gerald JONES
61 Dean Jones School of Law .... Mr. Charles NELSON
49 Dean College Arts & Sciences .... Dr. Jeffrey ARRINGTON
50 Dean College Business/Exec Educ .... Dr. Dave KHADANGA
73 Dean College of Biblical Studies .... Dr. Scott GLEAVES
53 Dean College of Education .... Dr. Leslie COWELL
20 Associate VP Academic Affairs .... Dr. Jendia GRISSETT
21 Associate Vice President of Finance .... Mr. Jamie HORN
30 Assoc Vice President Development .... Mr. Billy CAMP
88 Assoc Vice Pres Exec & Prof Enroll .... Mr. Mark HUNT
15 Asst VP Human Resources/Diversity .... Ms. Renee DAVIS
61 Assoc Dean Academics Jones Law .... Mr. Charles CAMPBELL
06 Registrar .... Mr. Don REYNOLDS
37 Director Student Financial Aid .... Mr. Buddy JACKSON
12 Director Mobile Center .... Mrs. Diane NEWELL
12 Director Birmingham Center .... Mrs. Karen BRUCE
12 Director Huntsville Center .... Mr. Bryan COLLINS
41 Athletic Director .... Mr. Hal WYNN
08 Director of Libraries .... Mrs. Barbara KELLY
104 Director of Study Abroad .... Dr. Ed HICKS
26 Director of University Marketing .... Mr. Patrick GREGORY
07 Director of Admissions .... Mr. Neil SCOTT
121 Director Student Success .... Mrs. Michelle OTWELL
29 Director of Alumni Relations .... Mr. Adam DONALDSON
92 Director of Honors Program .... Dr. Andrew JACOBS
35 Dean of Students .... Ms. Candace CAIN
36 Director Career Services .... Mrs. Marie OTTINGER
38 Director Counseling Center .... Mrs. Michelle BOND
04 Exec Assistant to the President .... Mrs. Beverly TOLLIVER
19 Director Security/Safety .... Mr. Anthony DEAN
39 Director Student Housing .... Mrs. Keri ALFORD
42 Assistant Dean for Spiritual Life .... Mr. Jon PODEIN
106 Director Faulkner University Online .... Mrs. Tiffany CANTRELL

Fortis Institute (J)

100 London Parkway Suite 150, Birmingham AL 35211
Telephone: (205) 940-7800 — Identification: 666683
Accreditation: ACICS, DH, MLTAD

† Branch campus of Fortis Institute, Erie, PA.

Heritage Christian University (K)

PO Box HCU, Florence AL 35630-0050
County: Lauderdale — FICE Identification: 021997
Unit ID: 101453
Telephone: (256) 766-6610 — Carnegie Class: Spec-4-yr-Faith
FAX Number: N/A — Calendar System: Semester
URL: www.hcu.edu
Established: 1968 — Annual Undergrad Tuition & Fees: $9,792
Enrollment: 92 — Coed
Affiliation or Control: Churches Of Christ — IRS Status: 501(c)3
Highest Offering: Master's
Accreditation: BI

01 President .... Vacant
05 Vice President of Academic Affairs .... Dr. Bill BAGENTS
10 VP Business/Finance/Operations .... Mr. Freddie P. MOON
111 Vice President of Advancement .... Mr. Philip GOAD
32 Dean of Students .... Mr. Brad MCKINNON
33 Dean of Men .... Dr. Ed GALLAGHER
34 Dean of Women .... Dr. Rosemary SNODGRASS
58 Director of Graduate Studies .... Dr. Jeremy BARRIER
06 Registrar .... Mrs. Alana MARKS
08 Librarian .... Miss Jamie S. COX
42 Director of Christian Service .... Mr. Brad MCKINNON
84 Dir Enrollment Svcs/Stdnt Fin Aid .... Mr. Jim COLLINS
106 Dir Online Education/E-learning .... Mr. Travis HARMON
108 Dir of Institutional Effectiveness .... Mr. Michael JACKSON
13 Web Communications and Tech Manager .. Mr. Justin CONNOLLY

Herzing University (L)

280 W Valley Avenue, Birmingham AL 35209-4816
Telephone: (205) 916-2800 — FICE Identification: 010193
Accreditation: &NH, EMT

† Regional accreditation is carried under the parent institution in Madison, WI.

Huntingdon College (M)

1500 East Fairview Avenue, Montgomery AL 36106-2148
County: Montgomery — FICE Identification: 001019
Unit ID: 101435
Telephone: (334) 833-4497 — Carnegie Class: Bac-Diverse
FAX Number: (334) 833-4347 — Calendar System: Semester
URL: www.huntingdon.edu
Established: 1854 — Annual Undergrad Tuition & Fees: $25,800
Enrollment: 1,166 — Coed
Affiliation or Control: United Methodist — IRS Status: 501(c)3
Highest Offering: Baccalaureate
Accreditation: SC, MUS

01 President .... Rev. J. Cameron WEST
10 Treasurer & SVP for IE/Plng & Admin .... Mr. Jay A. DORMAN
30 SVP Inst Dev & Alumni Relations .... Mr. Anthony J. LEIGH
05 Provost & Dean of the College .... Dr. Anna MCEWAN
84 VP for Enrollment Management .... Ms. Laura H. DUNCAN
09 VP Accreditation/Acad Services/IR .... Dr. Sidney J. STUBBS
26 VP Communications & Marketing .... Ms. Suellen S. OFE
32 VP Stdnt Affairs/Dean of Students .... Mrs. Francis H. TAYLOR
20 Associate Provost .... Dr. Tom PERRIN
04 Exec Asst to President/Corp Secy .... Ms. Sandra B. KELSER
21 Comptroller .... Ms. Jo-Ann M. HOLSTON
19 Chief of Security .... Mr. Michael S. WARD
06 Registrar .... Ms. Adrienne S. GAINES
55 Director Evening Studies Program .... Mr. Vinson BRADLEY
88 Dir of Student Financial Services .... Ms. Belinda G. DUETT
41 Director of Athletics .... Mr. Michael W. TURK
08 Director Houghton Memorial Library .... Mr. Eric A. KIDWELL
88 Dir Staton Ctr for Lrng Enrichment .... Ms. Maryann M. BECK
13 Dir of Institutional Technology .... Mr. Frank O. GRIER

18 Director of Facilities and Grounds .... Mr. T. Michael DUNN
37 Dir of Student Financial Aid .... Ms. Brittany DAVIS
36 Dir of Center for Career & Vocation .... Ms. Sherry Leigh LACEY
23 Director of Student Health Services .... Vacant
38 Director of Counseling Services .... Ms. Kelley REHM
35 Director of Student Activities .... Ms. Kathleen PENNEY
88 Dir Huntingdon Leadership Academy ...... Mr. Macon ARMISTEAD
35 Assistant Dean of Students .... Mr. Craig SHORE
07 Assoc Dir of Admission .... Ms. Stephanie HICKS
42 Chaplain .... Rev. Rhett BUTLER
40 Manager Follett Bookstore .... Ms. Sharon HENDERSON

Huntsville Bible College (A)

906 Oakwood Avenue NW, Huntsville AL 35811-1632

County: Madison | FICE Identification: 038943 | Unit ID: 449348
Telephone: (256) 469-7536 | Carnegie Class: Spec-4-yr-Faith
FAX Number: (256) 469-7549 | Calendar System: Semester
URL: www.hbc1.edu
Established: 1986 | Annual Undergrad Tuition & Fees: $4,415
Enrollment: 161 | Coed
Affiliation or Control: Baptist | IRS Status: 501(c)3
Highest Offering: Master's
Accreditation: BI

01 President .... Dr. John L. CLAY
05 Dean of Academics/Instruction .... Rev. David L. FAYLOR
07 Admissions Officer .... Mrs. Shonda GREEN-FULLER
10 Chief Financial Officer .... Ms. Jacqueline ROBINSON
30 Advancement Officer .... Ms. Eloise MCNEALEY
58 Dean of Graduate Studies .... Dr. Mitchell WALKER
08 Director of Library Media .... Ms. Vernita CHANDLER

Jacksonville State University (B)

700 Pelham Road N, Jacksonville AL 36265-1602

County: Calhoun | FICE Identification: 001020 | Unit ID: 101480
Telephone: (256) 782-5781 | Carnegie Class: Masters/L
FAX Number: (256) 782-5291 | Calendar System: Semester
URL: www.jsu.edu
Established: 1883 | Annual Undergrad Tuition & Fees (In-State): $7,500
Enrollment: 8,314 | Coed
Affiliation or Control: State | IRS Status: 501(c)3
Highest Offering: Doctorate
Accreditation: SC, AAFCS, ART, CACREP, CAEPN, #COARC, CS, DIETD, JOUR, MUS, NAIT, NURSE, SPAA, SW, THEA

01 President .... Dr. John M. BEEHLER
05 Provost/VP Academic Affairs .... Dr. Rebecca O. TURNER
10 VP Finance & Administration .... Dr. Ashok ROY
111 VP University Advancement .... Dr. Charles R. LEWIS
32 VP Student Affairs .... Dr. Tim KING
11 Chief Opers/Strategy/Audit Officer .... Mr. Jim BRIGHAM
15 Chief Human Res/Diversity Officer .... Dr. Heidi LOUISY
13 Chief Information Officer .... Mr. Vinson HOUSTON
43 Legal Counsel .... Mr. Sam MONK
41 Director Athletics .... Mr. Greg SEITZ
86 Chief Govt Rels/Cmty Engagement ..... Dr. Don KILLINGSWORTH
20 Vice Provost .... Dr. Joe WALSH
57 Acting Dean School of Arts & Hum .... Dr. Lori J. OWENS
81 Dean School of Science .... Dr. Timothy LINDBLOM
76 Dean School Health Prof & Wellness .... Dr. Christie SHELTON
53 Acting Dean School of Education .... Dr. Tommy TURNER
50 Dean School of Business & Industry .... Dr. William FIELDING
83 Dean School Human Svc & Soc Science ... Dr. Maureen NEWTON
08 Dean Library Services .... Mr. John-Bauer GRAHAM
32 Dean Student Life .... Mr. Terry CASEY
88 Associate Vice Provost .... Ms. Lisa M. WILLIAMS
06 Registrar .... Ms. Emily WHITE
84 Director of Enrollment Management .... Mr. Andy GREEN
21 University Controller .... Mr. Kevin MCFRY
109 Director Auxiliary Svcs .... Vacant
30 Director University Development .... Mr. Earl WARREN
39 Director Residence Life .... Ms. Rochelle SMITH
39 Dir Univ Housing Operations .... Ms. Brooke LYON
88 Dir International Programs .... Ms. Chandni KHADKA
108 Dir Institutional Effectiveness .... Ms. Kim PRESSON
29 Director of Alumni Relations .... Ms. Kaci OGLE
37 Dir Student Financial Svcs .... Vacant
18 Dir Capital Planning/Facilities .... Mr. David THOMPSON
36 Director Career Placement Services .... Ms. Rebecca E. TURNER
38 Dir Counseling/Disability Sppt Svcs .... Ms. Julie NIX
96 Dir of Procurement/Fixed Assets .... Ms. Pamela L. FINDLEY
26 Chief Marketing/Comm Officer .... Mr. Tim GARNER
19 Director Security/Safety .... Mr. Shawn GIDDY
22 Coord Diversity/EEO/Title IX .... Mr. Jai INGRAHAM

Judson College (C)

302 Bibb Street, Marion AL 36756-2504

County: Perry | FICE Identification: 001023 | Unit ID: 101541
Telephone: (334) 683-5100 | Carnegie Class: Bac-A&S
FAX Number: (334) 683-5147 | Calendar System: Semester
URL: www.judson.edu
Established: 1838 | Annual Undergrad Tuition & Fees: $17,376
Enrollment: 374 | Female
Affiliation or Control: Alabama Baptist State Convention | IRS Status: 501(c)3
Highest Offering: Baccalaureate
Accreditation: SC, MUS, SW

01 President .... Dr. David E. POTTS
05 Sr Vice Pres & Academic Dean .... Dr. Scott W. BULLARD
32 Sr VP & Dean of Students .... Ms. Susan JONES
84 Exec Dir for Enrollment Services .... Mrs. Tyne OLKIE
111 VP Institutional Advancement .... Dr. Terry SMITH MORGAN
06 Registrar .... Ms. Susanna BARKLEY
106 Dir Online Education/E-learning .... Vacant
13 Director of Info Technology .... Mrs. Traci L. FOSTER
36 Director Student Placement .... Vacant
37 Interim Dir Student Financial Aid .... Ms. Melina VERITY
26 Dir of Marketing & Communications .... Ms. Mary A. TAYLOR

Miles College (D)

5500 Myron Massey Boulevard, Fairfield AL 35064-2621

County: Jefferson | FICE Identification: 001028 | Unit ID: 101675
Telephone: (205) 929-1000 | Carnegie Class: Bac-Diverse
FAX Number: (205) 929-1453 | Calendar System: Semester
URL: www.miles.edu
Established: 1898 | Annual Undergrad Tuition & Fees: $11,604
Enrollment: 1,873 | Coed
Affiliation or Control: Christian Methodist Episcopal | IRS Status: 501(c)3
Highest Offering: Baccalaureate
Accreditation: SC, ACBSP, CAEPN, SW

01 President .... Dr. George T. FRENCH, JR.
05 Dean & VP Academic Affairs .... Dr. Emmanuel CHEKWA
10 Sr VP Finance/Business Admin .... Ms. Diana KNIGHTON
42 VP/Dean Student Engagement/Chapel .... Rev. Larry BATIE
100 Special Asst/Chief of Staff .... Mr. Kenneth COACHMAN
07 Director Admissions & Recruitment .... Mr. Christopher ROBERTSON
08 Director Library .... Dr. Geraldine BELL
32 Director Student Activities .... Ms. Manisha MISHRA
20 Associate Dean .... Dr. Joyce DUGAN-WOOD
09 Director Strategic Initiatives .... Dr. Ba-Shen T. WELCH
37 Director Financial Aid .... Mr. Percy LANIER
18 Director Physical Plant .... Mr. Thomas BROWN
38 Dir Counseling/Advising/Testing .... Ms. Keisha LEWIS
15 Director Human Resources .... Mrs. Verlanda TATE

Oakwood University (E)

7000 Adventist Boulevard, NW, Huntsville AL 35896-0003

County: Madison | FICE Identification: 001033 | Unit ID: 101912
Telephone: (256) 726-7000 | Carnegie Class: Bac-Diverse
FAX Number: (256) 726-8334 | Calendar System: Semester
URL: www.oakwood.edu
Established: 1896 | Annual Undergrad Tuition & Fees: $16,750
Enrollment: 1,749 | Coed
Affiliation or Control: Seventh-day Adventist | IRS Status: 501(c)3
Highest Offering: Master's
Accreditation: SC, ACBSP, CAEPN, DIETD, DIETI, NUR, SW

01 President .... Dr. Leslie POLLARD
03 Provost & Sr Vice President .... Dr. Colwick WILSON
05 Vice Pres Academic Affairs .... Dr. Karen BENN-MARSHALL
10 Vice President Financial Affairs .... Ms. Sabrina COTTON
32 Vice President Student Services .... Mr. David KNIGHT
111 Executive Director Advancement/Dev .... Mrs. Cheri WILSON
20 Asst VP Academic Affairs .... Dr. Finbar BENJAMIN
21 Asst VP Financial Affs/Controller .... Mrs. Gail CALDWELL
35 Asst Vice Pres Student Services .... Ms. Adrienne MATTHEWS
15 Exec Dir of Employee Srvs/Human Res .... Dr. LaVerne BARNETT
25 Contracts .... Mrs. Evangeline RIVERS LANG
26 Director Public Relations .... Mr. Kenn DIXON
84 Director Enrollment Management .... Mr. Malcolm TAYLOR
37 Director Financial Aid .... Mrs. Lynda BARTHOLOMEW
06 Registrar .... Ms. Traci MOORE
39 Residence Life Coordinator-Men .... Mr. Woodrow VAUGHN
88 Resident Life Coordinator-Women .... Ms. Linda ANDERSON
08 Director Library Services .... Mrs. Paulette JOHNSON
18 Director Physical Plant .... Vacant
19 Director Security .... Mr. Melvin HARRIS
38 Dir Counseling & Health Services .... Ms. Wanda MISORI
51 Dir Adult & Continuing Education .... Mrs. Ellengold GOODRIDGE
42 Chaplain .... Mr. David RICHARDSON
46 Dir Research & Faculty Dev .... Dr. Prudence L. POLLARD
88 Dean for Student Success .... Vacant
50 Chair Business & Info Systems .... Dr. Hyacinth BURTON
53 Chair Education .... Dr. James MBYIRUKIRA
76 Chair Allied Health .... Dr. Earl HENRY
60 Chair English & Foreign Languages .... Dr. Benson PRIGG
64 Chair Music .... Dr. Jason FERDINAND
65 Chair Biological Sciences .... Dr. Juliett BAILEY PENROD
65 Chair Chemistry .... Dr. Kenneth LAI HING
66 Chair Nursing .... Dr. Arlene JOHNSON
68 Chair Health & Exercise Sciences .... Dr. Andrew YOUNG
70 Chair Social Work .... Dr. Octavio RAMIREZ
73 Chair Religion & Theology .... Dr. Dedrick BLUE
81 Chair Math & Computer Science .... Dr. Lisa JAMES
82 Chair History .... Dr. Samuel LONDON
83 Chair Psychology .... Dr. Martin HODNETT
60 Chair Communication .... Dr. Rennae ELLIOTT
13 Chief Info Technology Officer (CIO) .... Mr. Kirk NUGENT

Remington College, Mobile Campus (F)

828 Downtowner Loop W, Mobile AL 36609-5404

County: Mobile | FICE Identification: 026055 | Unit ID: 366535
Telephone: (251) 343-8200 | Carnegie Class: Spec 2-yr-Tech
FAX Number: (251) 343-0577 | Calendar System: Quarter
URL: www.remingtoncollege.edu
Established: 1986 | Annual Undergrad Tuition & Fees: $14,953
Enrollment: 436 | Coed
Affiliation or Control: Independent Non-Profit | IRS Status: 501(c)3
Highest Offering: Baccalaureate
Accreditation: ACCSC

01 President .... Mr. Michael SELTZER

Samford University (G)

800 Lakeshore Drive, Birmingham AL 35229-0001

County: Jefferson | FICE Identification: 001036 | Unit ID: 102049
Telephone: (205) 726-2011 | Carnegie Class: Masters/L
FAX Number: (205) 726-2171 | Calendar System: 4/1/4
URL: www.samford.edu
Established: 1841 | Annual Undergrad Tuition & Fees: $29,402
Enrollment: 5,206 | Coed
Affiliation or Control: Southern Baptist | IRS Status: 501(c)3
Highest Offering: Doctorate
Accreditation: SC, ANEST, CAATE, CAEPN, CIDA, #COARC, DIETD, @DIETI, LAW, MUS, NURSE, PHAR, @PTA, @SP, SW, THEA, THEOL

01 President .... Dr. T. Andrew WESTMORELAND
05 Provost .... Dr. Michael HARDIN
32 Vice President for Student Affairs .... Dr. Phil KIMREY
111 Vice President of Advancement .... Mr. W. Randall PITTMAN
10 Exec VP Business/Financial Affairs .... Mr. Harry B. BROCK, III
26 VP for Marketing and Communication ... Dr. Betsy B. HOLLOWAY
20 Senior Assoc Provost .... Dr. Tom WOOLLEY
45 Chief Strategy Officer .... Mr. Colin M. COYNE
04 Assistant to the President .... Dr. Michael D. MORGAN
21 Controller .... Mr. Mike DARWIN
27 Executive Dir Broadcast Media .... Mr. Brad RADICE
13 Chief Information Officer .... Mr. Doug RIGNEY
43 General Counsel .... Mr. W. Clark WATSON
11 Associate Provost Administration .... Dr. Nancy BIGGIO
108 Asst Provost Assess & Accreditation .... Dr. Katrina H. MINTZ
41 Athletic Director .... Mr. Martin NEWTON
88 Director of Mann Center .... Hon. Drayton NABERS, JR.
88 Director Parent Programs .... Ms. Susan DOYLE
88 Director of Business Services .... Mr. Mike MCCORMACK
88 Director of Capital Planning & Imp .... Mr. David T. WHITT
88 Dir Event Management .... Ms. Allison BRYMER
18 Director of Facilities Management .... Mr. Mark FULLER
37 Dir of Student Financial Services .... Mr. Lane M. SMITH
21 Assoc VP Business & Fin Affairs .... Ms. Lisa IMBRAGULIO
88 Assoc VP Operations & Campus Init .... Dr. Kimberly BROWN
08 Dean of University Library .... Dr. Kimmetha D. HERNDON
15 Asst VP & Dir of Human Resources .... Mr. Joel WINDHAM
30 Asst VP Univ Adv & Exec Dir Devel .... Mr. Douglas WILSON
19 Dir Public Safety & Emergency Mgmt .... Mr. Wayne PITTMAN
39 Asst VP Campus & Residential Life .... Ms. Lauren M. TAYLOR
117 Director of Risk Mmgt & Insurance .... Mr. James A. CLEMENT
114 Dir of Budget & Financial Planning .... Mr. Matt DEFORE
102 Dir Development & Legacy League .... Ms. Sharon SMITH
07 Dean of Admissions .... Mr. Jason BLACK
35 Asst VP for Student Development .... Dr. Matthew S. KERLIN
35 Asst VP Stdnt Affs/Title IX Coord .... Mr. Garry L. ATKINS
27 Exec Dir University Communication .... Mr. Philip POOLE
88 Director of University Fellows .... Mr. Bryan M. JOHNSON
53 Dean OB Beason School of Education .... Dr. Jean A. BOX
49 Dean Howard College Arts/Sciences .... Mr. Tim HALL
17 Vice Provost College Health Science .... Dr. Nena F. SANDERS
76 Dean of Health Professions .... Dr. Alan JUNG
69 Dean of Public Health .... Dr. Keith ELDER
67 Dean School of Pharmacy .... Dr. Michael A. CROUCH
73 Dean Beeson School of Divinity .... Dr. Timothy F. GEORGE
50 Dean Brock School of Business .... Dr. J. Howard FINCH
61 Dean Cumberland School of Law .... Mr. Henry C. STRICKLAND
57 Dean School of the Arts .... Dr. Joseph HOPKINS
06 Registrar .... Mr. Jay FLYNN
110 Director of Stewardship/Univ Advanc .... Ms. Kimberly CRIPPS
112 Director Gift and Estate Planning .... Mr. Gene HOWARD
28 Dir Diversity & Intercultural Init .... Dr. Denise GREGORY
104 Director Global Engagement .... Ms. Lauren DOSS
105 Exec Dir Web/Digital Marketing .... Mr. Todd COTTON
88 Dir of Congregational Resources .... Mr. Michael WILSON
88 Dir Strat & Appl Analysis .... Dr. Randolph HORN
88 Director QEP & CTLS .... Dr. Eric FOURNIER
88 Creative Dir Marketing & Comm .... Ms. Laine WILLIAMS

Selma University (H)

1501 Lapsley Street, Selma AL 36701-5232

County: Dallas | FICE Identification: 001037 | Unit ID: 102058
Telephone: (334) 872-2533 | Carnegie Class: Spec-4-yr-Faith
FAX Number: (334) 872-7746 | Calendar System: Semester
URL: www.selmauniversity.edu
Established: 1878 | Annual Undergrad Tuition & Fees: N/A
Enrollment: 333 | Coed
Affiliation or Control: Baptist | IRS Status: 501(c)3
Highest Offering: Master's

Accreditation: BI

01 President .... Dr. Alvin A. CLEVELAND, SR.
05 Vice President Academic Affairs .... Dr. Stanford ANGION
32 Vice Pres Student Affairs .... Rev. Frankie HUTCHINS
06 Registrar .... Mr. Terrence JACKSON
37 Director of Financial Aid .... Ms. Yolanda GORDON
07 Director of Admissions .... Mrs. Tammy MAUL
10 Chief Financial/Business Officer .... Mrs. Robin THOMAS

South University (A)

5355 Vaughn Road, Montgomery AL 36116-1120
Telephone: (334) 395-8800 FICE Identification: 004463
Accreditation: &SC, ACBSP, MAC, NURSE, PTAA

† Regional accreditation is carried under the parent institution in Savannah, GA.

Spring Hill College (B)

4000 Dauphin Street, Mobile AL 36608-1791
County: Mobile FICE Identification: 001041
Unit ID: 102234
Telephone: (251) 380-4000 Carnegie Class: Bac-A&S
FAX Number: (251) 460-2182 Calendar System: Semester
URL: www.shc.edu
Established: 1830 Annual Undergrad Tuition & Fees: $35,794
Enrollment: 1,479 Coed
Affiliation or Control: Roman Catholic IRS Status: 501(c)3
Highest Offering: Master's
Accreditation: #SC, NURSE

01 President .... Dr. Christopher PUTO
05 Provost/Vice Pres Academic Affairs .... Dr. George E. SIMS
10 Vice President Finance/Accounting .... Ms. Rhonda SHIRAZI
30 Vice Pres Alumni Relations/Devel .... Mrs. Mary MCDONALD
32 Vice Pres Student Affairs .... Ms. Rosalie CARPENTER
84 Vice Pres Enrollment Svcs .... Mr. Robert STEWART
13 Chief Information Officer .... Dr. Margaret MASSEY
20 Associate Provost .... Ms. Jennifer GOOD
35 Dean of Students .... Vacant
21 Controller .... Ms. Marianne WILKINS
37 Interim Director of Financial Aid .... Mrs. Melinda MCCALL
06 Registrar .... Ms. Linnea BATTLES
88 Director Student Advising Services .... Ms. Ashley DUNKLIN
29 Director of Alumni Programs .... Vacant
15 Director of Personnel .... Ms. Patricia A. DAVIS
07 Director of Admissions .... Mr. Kendrick DUNKLIN
19 Director of Public Safety/Security .... Mr. Todd WARREN
23 Director of Health Services .... Mrs. Melissa MELTON
42 Director of Campus Ministry .... Ms. Maureen BERGAN
41 Director Athletics & Recreation .... Mr. James HALL
31 Dir Foley Community Service Center .... Dr. Erik GOLDSCHMIDT
26 Dir Communications/Instl Mktng .... Mrs. Donna HEROUX
27 Communications Officer .... Ms. Natasha MOORE
36 Director of Career Services .... Mr. Jeremy MOORE
40 Bookstore Manager .... Mr. Blaike PATTERSON
38 Director of Counseling Services .... Dr. Chelsea GREER

Stillman College (C)

3601 Stillman Boulevard, Tuscaloosa AL 35401
County: Tuscaloosa FICE Identification: 001044
Unit ID: 102270
Telephone: (205) 349-4240 Carnegie Class: Bac-A&S
FAX Number: N/A Calendar System: Semester
URL: www.stillman.edu
Established: 1876 Annual Undergrad Tuition & Fees: $10,418
Enrollment: 895 Coed
Affiliation or Control: Presbyterian Church (U.S.A.) IRS Status: 501(c)3
Highest Offering: Baccalaureate
Accreditation: SC, CAEPN, IACBE, MUS

01 President .... Dr. Cynthia WARRICK
05 Provost/VP Academic Affairs .... Dr. Mark MCCORMICK
10 Vice President Fiscal Affairs .... Dr. Daarel BURNETTE
108 Dean Institutional Effectiveness .... Dr. Mary J. KROTZER
111 Director Institutional Advancement .... Ms. Luanne BAKER
32 Vice President for Students Affairs .... Dr. Joseph SCRIVNER
31 Director Community Relations .... Mr. Mason BONNER
84 Dean Enrollment Mgmt/Tech Integrat .... Ms. Tamara MARSHALL
26 Director Stategic Initiatives .... Dr. Lamin DRAMMEH
21 Business Manager .... Ms. Daphne HOOD
29 Director Alumni Affairs .... Ms. Jean WILSON-SYKES
18 Director Plant Operations .... Mr. Tremelle TURNER
53 Dean of Education .... Dr. Linda BRADFORD
49 Dean of Arts & Sciences .... Dr. Linda BEITO
08 Dean of Library .... Mr. Robert HEATH
09 Director Institutional Research/ IT .... Ms. Georanda JACKSON-RICHARDSON
06 Registrar .... Dr. Brittany HOSKIN
37 Director of Financial Aid .... Ms. Christy JACKSON
38 Dir Student Development/Health Svcs .... Ms. Jacqueline CURRIE
13 Director of Info Technology .... Vacant
07 Director of International Affairs .... Mr. Kyris BROWN
19 Chief of Campus Police .... Ms. Cassandra COOPER
41 Athletic Director .... Mr. Kenyon ALSTON
15 Director Human Resources .... Ms. LaKeya GOINS
42 College Chaplain .... Dr. Mark MCCORMICK
04 Asst to President/Board Liaison .... Ms. Cassandra BLACKBURN
50 Dean School of Business .... Dr. Carol WILLIAMS

Talladega College (D)

627 W. Battle Street, Talladega AL 35160-2354
County: Talladega FICE Identification: 001046
Unit ID: 102298
Telephone: (256) 761-6100 Carnegie Class: Bac-Diverse
FAX Number: (256) 761-9206 Calendar System: Semester
URL: www.talladega.edu
Established: 1867 Annual Undergrad Tuition & Fees: $12,340
Enrollment: 989 Coed
Affiliation or Control: Independent Non-Profit IRS Status: 501(c)3
Highest Offering: Baccalaureate
Accreditation: SC, SW

01 President .... Dr. Billy C. HAWKINS
05 Int Provost/VP for Academic Affairs .... Dr. Lisa LONG
10 Vice Pres Finance & Administration .... Mr. Sama MONDEH
32 President Student Affairs .... Dr. Sharon WHITTAKER-DAVIS
111 Int VP of Institutional Advancement .... Mr. Walvid KING
18 Director Facilities Management .... Mr. Geno MCGRUE
37 Director Financial Aid .... Dr. Maureen CRUMP-PHILLIPS
07 Int Director of Admissions .... Mrs. Victoria BOMAN
09 Int Director Institutional Research .... Dr. Syed RAZA
35 Dean/Director of Student Activities .... Mr. Tre M. FINKLEA
41 Athletic Director .... Mr. Kevin HEROD
08 Librarian .... Dr. Joseph MCDONALD
13 Director Information Technology .... Mrs. LaRita BREWSTER
36 Director of Career Placement .... Ms. Delores TRAYLOR
19 Chief Campus Police .... Mr. Ronald DYE
50 Dean Div Administration & Business .... Ms. Charmaine BALFOUR
79 Dean Div Humanities/Fine Arts .... Dr. Isaac BRUNSON
81 Dean Div of Natural Sci/Math .... Dr. Charlie STINSON
83 Dean Div EWJ Social Sciences/Educ .... Dr. Susan VICKERSTAFF
21 Controller .... Mr. Bruce SMITH
23 Health Services on Campus .... Mrs. Valarie ALFRED
25 Title III Coor/Grants Administrator .... Ms. Miliani SINCLAIR
29 Director Alumni Relations .... Mr. Walvid KING
06 Registrar .... Ms. Barbra SMITH
38 Director Student Counseling .... Ms. Delores TRAYLOR
04 Exec Admin Asst to President .... Mrs. Nicole GUYTON-MCCLENDON
104 Director Study Abroad .... Mr. John VERBURG
22 Dir Affirmative Action/EEO .... Mrs. Brenda RHODEN
15 Human Resources Manager .... Mrs. Brenda RHODEN
26 Director of Public Relations .... Mr. Walvid KING
39 Director Student Housing .... Mr. Marcus FLUKER

Troy University (E)

University Avenue, Troy AL 36082-0001
County: Pike FICE Identification: 001047
Unit ID: 102368
Telephone: (334) 670-3100 Carnegie Class: Masters/L
FAX Number: (334) 670-3774 Calendar System: Semester
URL: www.troy.edu
Established: 1887 Annual Undergrad Tuition & Fees (In-State): $8,260
Enrollment: 17,765 Coed
Affiliation or Control: State IRS Status: 501(c)3
Highest Offering: Doctorate
Accreditation: SC, ACBSP, ADNUR, CAATE, CACREP, CAEP, ENGR, MUS, NUR, SW

01 Chancellor .... Dr. Jack HAWKINS, JR.
05 Sr Vice Chanc for Academic Affairs .... Dr. Earl INGRAM
32 Sr Vice Chanc Student Svcs/Admin .... Dr. John R. DEW
111 Sr Vice Chanc Advance/External Affs .... Gen. Walter GIVHAN
10 Sr VC for Finance & Business Affs .... Dr. James BOOKOUT
15 Assoc VC for Human Resources .... MS. Ashley ENGLISH
12 Assoc VC for Troy Online .... Dr. Glynn CAVIN
12 Vice Chancellor Troy Dothan .... Dr. Don JEFFREY
12 Vice Chancellor Troy Phenix City .... Dr. David WHITE
35 Assoc Dean of Student Svcs Dothan .... Ms. Sandra HENRY
49 Asst Dean Col Arts/Sci Troy Dothan .... Dr. Robert SAUNDERS
20 Asst Dean of Academics .... Dr. Carmen LEWIS
53 Assoc Dean Col of Education .... Dr. Dionne ROSSER-MIMS
12 Vice Chanc Troy Montgomery .... Mr. Lance TATUM
11 Asst Dean of Administration .... Dr. Siegfried HARDEN
30 Assoc Vice Chanc for Development .... Ms. Rebecca WATSON
37 Director of Financial Aid .... Ms. Angela JOHNSON
20 Associate Provost for Academics .... Dr. Lee VARDAMAN
26 Assoc VC for Mktg/Communication .... Ms. Donna SCHUBERT
06 Registrar .... Ms. Vickie MILES
84 Assoc VC for Enrollment Management .... Mr. Buddy STARLING
08 Dean Library Services .... Dr. Chris SHAFFER
13 Chief Technology Officer .... Dr. Greg PRICE
27 Director University Relations .... Mr. Matthew CLOWER
29 Director Alumni Affairs .... Ms. Faith W. WARD
36 Coordinator Career Services .... Ms. Lauren COLE
18 Director Facilities/Physical Plant .... Mr. Mark SALMON
60 Director of Journalism .... Dr. Jefferson SPURLOCK
04 Exec Assistant to the Chancellor .... Mr. Tom DAVIS
38 Director Student Counseling .... Ms. Teresa P. RODGERS
123 Director of Graduate Admissions .... Ms. Jessica KIMBRO
88 Dir Not for Profit/Assoc Controller .... Ms. Lauri DORRILL
106 Senior Dir/Dean for TROY-Online .... Mr. Ronnie CREEL
86 Director of Governmental Relations .... Mr. Marcus PARAMORE
44 Director of Annual Giving .... Ms. Bronda DENISON
25 Director Sponsored Programs .... Ms. Judy FULMER
08 Dir of Library Svcs Troy Dothan .... Mr. Chris SHAFFER
08 Dir of Library Svcs Troy Montgomery .... Mr. Kent SNOWDEN
20 Dean Undergrad Pgms/Assoc Provost .... Dr. Hal FULMER
35 Dean of Student Svcs Troy Campus .... Mr. Herbert REEVES
49 Dean Arts & Sciences .... Dr. Steven TAYLOR
49 Assoc Dean Col Arts/Sci .... Dr. Bill GRANTHAM
50 Dean Business .... Dr. Judson EDWARDS
53 Dean Education .... Dr. Royce DASINGER
58 Assoc Provost/Dean Graduate Pgms .... Dr. Mary TEMPLETON
76 Dean Health/Human Services .... Dr. Denise GREEN
57 Dean Communication/Fine Arts .... Dr. Larry BLOCHER
35 Assoc Dean Student Svcs Troy Mont .... Dr. James SMITH
09 Director of Institutional Research .... Ms. Kimberly B. JONES
39 Director Student Housing .... Mr. Herbert REEVES
41 Athletic Director .... Mr. Jeremy MCCLAIN
85 Assoc Dean Intl Student Services .... Ms. Maria FRIGGE
105 Director Web Services .... Mr. John LESTER
108 Director Institutional Assessment .... Ms. Wendy BROYLES
19 Police Chief .... Mr. John MCCALL
104 Study Abroad Coordinator .... Ms. Sarah MCKENZIE
96 Coordinator Purchasing & Asset Mgt .... Ms. April JOHNSON

Tuskegee University (F)

1200 W. Montgomery Road, Tuskegee Inst. AL 36088
County: Macon FICE Identification: 001050
Unit ID: 102377
Telephone: (334) 727-8011 Carnegie Class: Masters/S
FAX Number: (334) 727-5276 Calendar System: Semester
URL: www.tuskegee.edu
Established: 1881 Annual Undergrad Tuition & Fees: $20,015
Enrollment: 2,996 Coed
Affiliation or Control: Independent Non-Profit IRS Status: 501(c)3
Highest Offering: Doctorate
Accreditation: SC, CAEPN, CONST, CS, DIETD, ENG, MT, NUR, OT, SW, #VET

01 Interim President .... Dr. Charlotte P. MORRIS
05 Provost/VP Academic Affairs .... Dr. Tejinder FARA
10 Vice President Finance/CFO .... Dr. Sharron T. BURNETT
30 Int Vice Pres Dev & Advancement .... Mr. Don WINSTON
46 Vice Pres Research/Sponsored Pgms .... Dr. Shaik JEELANI
18 Int VP Capital Proj/Facility Svcs .... Mr. Marcus DEAN
84 VP Student Affairs/Enrollment Mgmt .... Ms. Regina BURDEN
26 Sr Dir Comm/Public Rels/Mktg .... Mr. Michael TULLIER
101 Exec Asst to Pres/Secy to the Board .... Ms. Robin L. GRAY
88 Special Asst to President .... Ms. Barbara L. OWENS
13 Chief Information Officer .... Ms. Jenell SARGENT
45 Asst VP & Dir Budget & Planning .... Ms. Belinda HOGUE
20 Asst Provost .... Dr. Tamara FLOYD-SMITH
47 Vice Provost/Dean of CAENS .... Dr. Walter A. HILL
53 Dean School of Education .... Dr. Carlton E. MORRIS
50 Dean Col Business/Info Sci .... Dr. Kai KOONG
54 Dean College of Engineering .... Dr. Heshmat AGLAN
74 Int Dean Sch Nursing/Allied Health .... Dr. Doris HOLEMAN
32 Dean of Students .... Vacant
42 Dean of the Chapel .... Dr. Gregory S. GRAY
08 Director of Library Services .... Mrs. Juanita ROBERTS
29 Alumni Affairs Director .... Ms. Kimberly HOLLAND
86 Director Federal Relations .... Mrs. Willa HALL SMITH
51 Int Assoc Prov Cont Educ/Extension .... Dr. Ntam BAHARANYI
36 Assoc Dir Career Devel/Placement .... Ms. Sarah STRINGER
21 Bursar .... Ms. Barbara CHISHOLM
37 Director of Financial Aid .... Mr. Advergus D. JAMES, JR.
15 Director Human Resources .... Ms. Carleen THOMPSON
18 Project Mgr Sodexho/Physical Plant .... Mr. Tony WARD
91 Director of Applications Support .... Mr. James E. COOPER
06 Registrar .... Dr. Elaine BROMFIELD
38 Director Student Health .... Dr. June SAMUEL
09 Director Institutional Research .... Vacant
96 Int Director of Purchasing .... Ms. Cassandra PARKER

United States Sports Academy (G)

One Academy Drive, Daphne AL 36526-7055
County: Baldwin FICE Identification: 021706
Unit ID: 102395
Telephone: (251) 626-3303 Carnegie Class: Spec-4-yr-Other
FAX Number: (251) 621-2527 Calendar System: Semester
URL: www.ussa.edu
Established: 1972 Annual Undergrad Tuition & Fees: N/A
Enrollment: 319 Coed
Affiliation or Control: Independent Non-Profit IRS Status: 501(c)3
Highest Offering: Doctorate
Accreditation: SC

01 President & CEO .... Dr. Thomas J. ROSANDICH
05 Dean of Academic Affairs .... Dr. Stephen L. BUTLER
10 Dean of Admin & Finance .... Ms. Holly H. MCLELLAN
26 Director of Communications .... Mr. Keith AYERS
32 Dean of Student Services .... Dr. Vince NIX
88 Director of Sports Management .... Dr. Brandon SPRADLEY
58 Director of Doctoral Studies .... Dr. Fred CROMARTIE
88 Chair of Recreation Management .... Dr. Rodney BLACKMAN
88 Director of Sports Studies .... Dr. Sandra GERINGER
88 Chair of Exercise Science .... Dr. Vincent RAMSEY
88 Chair of Sports Coaching .... Dr. Bret SIMMERMACHER
06 Registrar .... Ms. Sara LEE
08 Director of Library/Archivist .... Ms. Marcie BOUTWELL
18 Building and Grounds .... Mr. Bill POTTS

*University of Alabama System Office (H)

500 University Boulevard East, Tuscaloosa AL 35401
County: Tuscaloosa FICE Identification: 008004
Unit ID: 100733
Telephone: (205) 348-5861 Carnegie Class: N/A
FAX Number: (205) 348-9788
URL: www.uasystem.ua.edu

01 Chancellor ... Mr. Ray HAYES
101 Sec Board & Exec Asst to Chanc ... Vacant
05 Vice Chanc Academic/Student Affairs ... Dr. Charles R. NASH
10 Vice Chanc Finance/Administration ... Dr. Dana KEITH
26 Vice Chanc Communications/Cmty Rels ... Mrs. Kellee C. REINHART
86 Vice Chanc/Economic Development ... Mr. Jo BONNER
21 General Auditor ... Ms. Sabrina B. HEARN

*The University of Alabama (A)

739 University Blvd, Tuscaloosa AL 35487-0100
County: Tuscaloosa FICE Identification: 001051
Unit ID: 100751
Telephone: (205) 348-6010 Carnegie Class: DU-Higher
FAX Number: (205) 348-9046 Calendar System: Semester
URL: www.ua.edu
Established: 1831 Annual Undergrad Tuition & Fees (In-State): $10,470
Enrollment: 37,098 Coed
Affiliation or Control: State IRS Status: 501(c)3
Highest Offering: Doctorate
Accreditation: SC, ART, CAATE, CACREP, CAEPN, CEA, CIDA, CLPSY, CS, DANCE, DIETC, DIETD, ENG, JOUR, LAW, LIB, MUS, NURSE, SP, SW, THEA

02 President ... Dr. Stuart R. BELL
05 Executive Vice President & Provost ... Dr. Kevin WHITAKER
28 VP for Diversity/Equity & Inclusio ... Dr. G. Christine TAYLOR
10 Vice Pres for Financial Affairs ... Dr. Lynda GILBERT
111 Vice Pres for Advancement ... Mr. Robert 'Bob' PIERCE
32 Vice Pres for Student Life ... Dr. David L. GRADY
88 Vice Pres for Community Affairs ... Dr. Samory T. PRUITT
26 Vice President Communications ... Ms. Linda BONNIN
46 Vice President for Research ... Dr. Carl PINKERT
13 Vice Provost/Chief Information Ofcr ... Dr. John MCGOWAN
18 Assistant VP University Facilities ... COL. Duane LAMB
18 Ast VP Univ Facilities/Construction ... Mr. Tim LEOPARD
19 Assoc VP Public Safety ... Mr. Ronnie ROBERTSON
20 Assoc Provost Academic Affairs ... Ms. Lisa RHINEY
20 Assoc Provost Academic Affairs ... Dr. Luoheng HAN
20 Assoc Provost Academic Affairs ... Dr. Patty SOBECKY
11 Assoc Provost for Administration ... Dr. Jennifer GREER
15 Assoc VP Human Resources ... Ms. Nancy H. WHITTAKER
21 Assoc Vice President for Finance ... Ms. Julie SHELTON
21 Asst Vice Pres Financial Affairs ... Ms. Cheryl MOWDY
27 Assoc VP Communications ... Ms. Monica WATTS
88 Assoc VP Marketing & Brand Strategy ... Mr. Ryan BRADLEY
29 Director of Alumni Affairs ... Mr. Calvin BROWN
85 Assoc Provost Internatl Educ ... Dr. Teresa WISE
06 University Registrar ... Dr. Kenneth H. FOSHEE
09 Director Inst Research/Assessment ... Dr. Lorne KUFFEL
36 Exec Director of Career Center ... Ms. Melinda KING
84 Assoc VP Enrollment Mgt ... Dr. Richard (Rick) BARTH
22 Dir & University Compliance Officer ... Ms. Gwendolyn D. HOOD
37 Director of Student Financial Aid ... Ms. Helen ALLEN
88 Director Enrollment Management ... Mr. Landon WAID
39 Director Dept of Housing/Res Cmty ... Mr. Matthew KERCH
40 Director of University Supply Store ... Ms. Teresa SHREVE
41 Athletic Director ... Mr. Greg BYRNE
43 Chief University Counsel ... Mr. Mike SPEARING
08 Dean of University Libraries ... Dr. Donald GILSTRAP
49 Dean of Arts & Sciences ... Dr. Robert F. OLIN
50 Dean College of C&BA ... Dr. Kay M. PALAN
51 Dean Col of Cont Studies ... Dr. Craig EDELBROCK
53 Dean College of Education ... Dr. Peter HLEBOWITSH
54 Dean College of Engineering ... Dr. Charles L. KARR
58 Dean Graduate School/Asst Acad VP ... Dr. Susan CARVALHO
59 Dean Human Environmental Sciences ... Dr. Milla BOSCHUNG
60 Dean Col of Communication/Info Sci ... Dr. Mark NELSON
61 Dean School of Law ... Dr. Mark E. BRANDON
62 Int Dir Sch of Library/Info Studies ... Dr. Ann E. PRENTICE
38 Manager Stdnt Support Svcs-Trio Pgm ... Ms. Wendy L. COGBURN
96 Assc Purchasing Mgr Gen Procurement ... Ms. Pollye HARDY
76 Dean Cmty Health Sciences ... Dr. Rick STREIFFER
66 Dean Capstone College of Nursing ... Dr. Suzanne S. PREVOST
70 Dean School of Social Work ... Dr. Vikki VANDIVER
92 Dean of Honors College ... Dr. Shane SHARPE
94 Dir Women & Gender Resource Ctr ... Ms. Lamea SHAABAN-MAGANA

*University of Alabama at Birmingham (B)

1720 2nd Avenue South, Birmingham AL 35294-0001
County: Jefferson FICE Identification: 001052
Unit ID: 100663
Telephone: (205) 934-4011 Carnegie Class: DU-Highest
FAX Number: N/A Calendar System: Semester
URL: www.uab.edu
Established: 1969 Annual Undergrad Tuition & Fees (In-State): $8,040
Enrollment: 18,333 Coed
Affiliation or Control: State IRS Status: 501(c)3
Highest Offering: Doctorate
Accreditation: SC, ANEST, ARCPA, ART, CACREP, CAEPN, CEA, CLPSY, CS, DENT, DIETI, ENG, FEPAC, HSA, IPSY, MED, MT, MUS, NMT, NURSE, OPT, OPTR, OT, PAST, PH, PTA, SPAA, SW, THEA

02 President ... Dr. Ray L. WATTS
05 Provost ... Dr. Pam BENOIT
10 Vice Pres Financial Affairs/Admin ... Mr. G. Allen BOLTON
17 CEO UAB Health System ... Dr. Will FERNIANY
30 VP Development ... Mr. Thomas I. BRANNAN
13 Vice Pres Info Technology/CIO ... Dr. Curtis A. CARVER, JR.
28 Vice Pres for Equity and Diversity ... Dr. Paulette P. DILWORTH
46 Vice Pres for Research ... Dr. Chris BROWN
63 Sr VP/Dean School of Medicine ... Dr. Selwyn M. VICKERS
20 Sr VP Student/Faculty Success ... Dr. Suzanne E. AUSTIN
32 Vice Pres Student Affairs ... Dr. John R. JONES, III
43 University Counsel ... Mr. W. John DANIEL
49 Dean College of Arts & Sciences ... Dr. Robert PALAZZO
50 Dean School of Business ... Dr. Eric JACK
52 Dean School of Dentistry ... Dr. Michael S. REDDY
53 Dean School of Education ... Dr. Deborah L. VOLTZ
54 Dean School of Engineering ... Dr. Iwan ALEXANDER
76 Dean School of Health Professions ... Dr. Harold P. JONES
66 Dean School of Nursing ... Dr. Doreen C. HARPER
88 Dean School of Optometry ... Dr. Kelly NICHOLS
69 Dean School of Public Health ... Dr. Max MICHAEL, III
58 Dean Graduate School ... Dr. Lori L. MCMAHON
18 Assoc Vice President Facilities ... Mr. Robert E. MCMAINS, III
109 Assoc VP Business/Auxiliary Svcs ... Mr. Christopher CLIFFORD
29 Int Assoc VP Alumni/Annual Giving ... Dr. Jennifer R. BRELAND
110 Asst Vice Pres Development ... Ms. Rebecca J. GORDON
26 Assoc VP Public Relations & Mktg ... Ms. Anne BUCKLEY
84 Assoc Provost Enrollment Management ... Dr. Bradley BARNES
21 Assoc VP Financial Affairs ... Ms. Stephanie B. MULLINS
08 Dean of Libraries ... Mr. John M. MEADOR
08 Director Lister Hill Library ... Mr. Scott PLUTCHAK
41 Director of Athletics ... Mr. Mark T. INGRAM
15 Chief Human Resources Officer ... Ms. Alesia M. JONES
09 Exec Dir Inst Effect & Analysis ... Mr. Jon CORLISS
19 Assistant VP & Chief of Police ... Mr. Anthony B. PURCELL
07 Director Undergraduate Admissions ... Mr. Tyler M. PETERSON
37 Director of Financial Aid ... Ms. Helen M. MCINTYRE
06 University Registrar ... Ms. Tina DENEEN
39 Director Student Housing ... Mr. Marc BOOKER
36 Interim Exec Dir Career Services ... Ms. Melissa L. WHATLEY
38 Asst VP Student Dev/Health & Well ... Mr. Jacob BAGGOTT
04 Executive Asst to President ... Ms. Jane K. LUCAS
106 Int Dir E-Learning & Prof Studies ... Dr. Elizabeth A. FISHER
96 Director of Purchasing ... Ms. Belinda MITCHELL
101 Board Liaison ... Ms. Kirsten N. BURDICK

*University of Alabama in Huntsville (C)

301 Sparkman Drive, Huntsville AL 35899-1911
County: Madison FICE Identification: 001055
Unit ID: 100706
Telephone: (256) 824-1000 Carnegie Class: DU-Higher
FAX Number: (256) 824-6073 Calendar System: Semester
URL: www.uah.edu
Established: 1950 Annual Undergrad Tuition & Fees (In-State): $9,842
Enrollment: 7,866 Coed
Affiliation or Control: State IRS Status: 501(c)3
Highest Offering: Doctorate
Accreditation: SC, ART, CAEPN, CS, ENG, MUS, NURSE

02 CEO/President ... Dr. Robert A. ALTENKIRCH
05 Provost & Exec VP Academic Affairs ... Dr. Christine CURTIS
10 VP Finance & Administration ... Vacant
41 Director Intercollegiate Athletics ... Dr. William E. BROPHY, JR.
43 University Counsel ... Mr. John CATES
46 VP Research & Econ Dev ... Dr. Ray VAUGHN
111 VP University Advancement ... Mr. Robert LYON
28 VP Diversity ... Ms. Delois SMITH
32 VP of Student Affairs ... Dr. Kristi MOTTER
100 Chief of Staff/Dir Community Rels ... Mr. Ray GARNER
35 Assoc VP for Student Affairs ... Mr. John MAXON
46 Assoc VP Research ... Dr. Thomas M. KOSHUT
46 Associate VP for Research ... Dr. Robert LINDQUIST
35 Interim Dean of Students ... Mr. TJ BRECCIAROLI
11 Assoc VP Finance & Business Svcs ... Mr. Robert LEONARD
13 Interim CIO ... Mr. Malcolm RICE
18 Assoc VP Facilities & Operations ... Mr. Mark COWHERD
20 Assoc Provost UG Studies/Inst Effec ... Dr. Brent M. WREN
114 Associate VP Budgets & Fin Planning ... Mr. Chih LOO
26 Assoc VP of Marketing and Comm ... Mr. Joel C. LONERGAN
15 Assoc VP Human Resources ... Ms. Laurel LONG
09 Director Institutional Research ... Dr. Suzanne SIMPSON
116 Director Internal Audit ... Ms. Tharanee M. RAVINDRAN
85 Dir International Engagement ... Dr. David BERKOWITZ
25 Director Sponsored Programs ... Ms. Gloria GREENE
88 Director Institute for Science Educ ... Dr. James A. MILLER
08 Director Library ... Dr. David P. MOORE
79 Dean Arts/Humanities/Soc Science ... Dr. Mitch BERBRIER
81 Dean College of Science ... Dr. Sundar CHRISTOPHER
50 Dean College Business Admin ... Dr. Jason GREENE
51 Dean Prof & Cont Studies ... Dr. Karen CLANTON
54 Dean College of Engineering ... Dr. Shankar MAHALINGAM
58 Dean Graduate Studies ... Dr. David BERKOWITZ
66 Dean College of Nursing ... Dr. Marsha ADAMS
53 Dean Education ... Dr. Beth QUICK
88 Dir of Cybersecurity Research & Edu ... Mr. Tommy MORRIS
40 Bookstore Manager ... Ms. Amber YOUNG
37 Director Financial Aid ... Mr. Patrick JAMES
38 Dir Counseling & Disability ... Ms. Rebecca MATTER
23 Dir Faculty & Staff Clinic ... Ms. Louise O'KEEFE
19 Director Public Safety ... Mr. Michael R. SNELLGROVE
06 Registrar ... Ms. Janet WALLER
07 Director Admissions ... Ms. Peggy MASTERS
29 Director Alumni Relations ... Ms. Mallie HALE
110 Director Advancement Services ... Ms. Marcie T. EPPLING
23 Director Student Health Services ... Ms. Kathleen S. RHODES
88 Director ITSC ... Dr. Sara J. GRAVES
88 Dir Small Business Develop Center ... Mr. Foster PERRY
102 Asst Dir Corp & Foundation Gifts ... Ms. Katie S. THURSTON
96 Director of Procurement ... Mr. Terence HALEY
88 Director Library Computer Systems ... Mr. Jack DROST
90 Manager Academic Technology ... Mr. John THYGERSON
88 Director Research Institute ... Dr. Steven MESSERVY
88 Director CMSA ... Dr. Sara GRAVES
88 Director SMAP Center ... Dr. Gary MADDUX
88 Director Rotocraft Center ... Mr. Dave ARTERBURN
88 Director Ctr for Applied Optics ... Dr. Robert LINDQUIST
88 Dir Ctr Mgmt & Econ Research ... Mr. Nic LOYD
88 Director Propulsion Research Center ... Dr. Robert FREDERICK
88 Dir Center Space Plsm & Aeron Res ... Dr. Gary ZANK
88 Director Earth Systems Science Ctr ... Dr. John R. CHRISTY
88 Dir University Ctr & Charger Union ... Mr. William M. HALL
91 Director Enterprise Apps & IAM ... Mr. Malcolm RICE
104 Director Global Studies Program ... Dr. David JOHNSON
92 Dean of the Honors College ... Dr. William WILKERSON

University of Mobile (D)

5735 College Parkway, Mobile AL 36613-2842
County: Mobile FICE Identification: 001029
Unit ID: 101693
Telephone: (251) 675-5990 Carnegie Class: Bac-Diverse
FAX Number: (517) 313-0526 Calendar System: Semester
URL: www.umobile.edu
Established: 1961 Annual Undergrad Tuition & Fees: $21,400
Enrollment: 1,566 Coed
Affiliation or Control: Southern Baptist IRS Status: 501(c)3
Highest Offering: Master's
Accreditation: SC, ACBSP, #CAATE, MUS, NURSE

01 President ... Dr. Timothy SMITH
05 Provost/VP for Academic Affairs ... Dr. Chris MCCAGHREN
10 Chief Financial Officer ... Mr. Scott HUVAL
30 VP for Business Development ... Mr. Kevin WILBURN
84 VP Enrollment Services ... Mrs. Charity WITTNER
26 VP for Marketing/Public Relations ... Mrs. Lesa MOORE
32 VP for Student Life ... Mr. Neal LEDBETTER
20 Vice Provost ... Dr. Lonnie BURNETT
21 Associate VP for Business Affairs ... Ms. Carol CAMP
37 Assoc VP Enroll/Dir Financial Aid ... Ms. Marie BATSON
110 Associate VP for Development ... Mrs. Tonya GOLLETTE
20 Asst VP for Accreditation for AA ... Mrs. Debra H. CHANCEY
20 Asst VP for Academic Affairs ... Mr. Bruce EARNEST
41 Athletic Director ... Mr. Joe NILAND
07 Director for Admissions/Enrollment ... Mrs. Hali GIVENS
09 Senior Dir for Inst Research ... Mrs. Kim LEOUSIS
08 Director for Library Services ... Mr. Jeffrey D. CALAMETTI
27 Director for Media Relations ... Mrs. Kathy L. DEAN
15 Director for Human Resources ... Mrs. Diane BLACK
50 Dean School of Business ... Dr. Todd GREER
49 Dean College of Arts & Sciences ... Dr. Lonnie BURNETT
53 Dean School of Education ... Dr. Carolyn CORLISS
66 Interim Dean School of Nursing ... Dr. Kathy SHEPPARD
57 Dean of AL School of the Arts ... Dr. Al MILLER
88 Dean Office for Global Engagement ... Dr. Doug WILSON
06 Registrar ... Mr. Stuart MOORE
29 Sr Dir for Alumni/Annual Giving ... Mrs. Lauren MCCAGHREN
120 Director for Faculty Support ... Dr. Pamela B. MILLER
121 Director for Student Success ... Mrs. Shirley SUTTERFIELD
14 Senior Support Specialist - IT ... Ms. Larkisha WINBUSH
56 Director for Academic Partnerships ... Mr. Danny CHANCEY
89 Asst Dir for 1st Year Experience ... Mrs. Brenda DAVIS

University of Montevallo (E)

Station 6001, Montevallo AL 35115-6001
County: Shelby FICE Identification: 001004
Unit ID: 101709
Telephone: (205) 665-6000 Carnegie Class: Masters/M
FAX Number: N/A Calendar System: Semester
URL: www.montevallo.edu
Established: 1896 Annual Undergrad Tuition & Fees (In-State): $12,040
Enrollment: 3,031 Coed
Affiliation or Control: State IRS Status: 501(c)3
Highest Offering: Beyond Master's But Less Than Doctorate
Accreditation: SC, AAFCS, ART, CACREP, CAEPN, DIETC, MUS, SP, SW

01 President ... Dr. John W. STEWART, III
05 Provost and VP Academic Affairs ... Dr. James MCDONALD
32 Dean of Students ... Dr. Tammi DAHLE
10 VP Business Affairs & Treasurer ... Ms. Mary Ellen HEUTON
18 Director Physical Plant ... Mr. Cody JONES
35 Director Student Life ... Ms. Jenny BELL
06 Registrar ... Ms. Amanda FOX
08 Director Libraries ... Dr. Charlotte FORD
07 Director Admissions ... Ms. Audrey CRAWFORD
13 Chief Information Officer ... Mr. Craig GRAY
37 Dir of Student Financial Services ... Mr. Robert WALKER
38 Director Counseling Services ... Mr. Joshua MILLER
19 Chief of Police ... Mr. Chadd ADAMS
39 Dir Housing & Residence Life ... Mr. John DENSON
41 Director Athletics ... Mr. Mark RICHARD
15 Director of HR and Risk Management ... Ms. Barbara FORREST
51 Dir of Regional Inservice Center ... Mr. Dwight JINRIGHT
49 Dean College Arts & Sciences ... Dr. Mary Beth ARMSTRONG
50 Dean College of Business ... Dr. Stephen CRAFT
53 Interim Dean College of Education ... Dr. Charlotte DAUGHHETEE
57 Dean College of Fine Arts ... Dr. Steven PETERS
09 Director of Institutional Research ... Ms. Kris MASCETTI

University of North Alabama (A)

One Harrison Plaza, Florence AL 35632-0001
County: Lauderdale FICE Identification: 001016
Unit ID: 101879
Telephone: (256) 765-4100 Carnegie Class: Masters/L
FAX Number: (256) 765-4644 Calendar System: Semester
URL: www.una.edu
Established: 1830 Annual Undergrad Tuition & Fees (In-State): $8,114
Enrollment: 7,078 Coed
Affiliation or Control: State IRS Status: 501(c)3
Highest Offering: Beyond Master's But Less Than Doctorate
Accreditation: **SC**, ACBSP, ART, CACREP, CAEPN, CIDA, CS, ENGR, JOUR, MUS, NURSE, SW

01 President ... Dr. Kenneth KITTS
05 Vice Pres Acad Affairs & Provost ... Dr. Ross ALEXANDER
88 Senior Vice Provost Intl Affairs ... Dr. Chunsheng ZHANG
10 VP Business/Financial Affs ... Mr. Evan THORNTON
32 Vice President Student Affairs ... Mr. David P. SHIELDS, JR.
111 Vice President Advancement ... Dr. Deborah L. SHAW
84 Assoc VP Enrollment Management ... Mr. Ron PATTERSON
110 Assoc VP Advancement Services ... Dr. Judy T. JACKSON
49 Dean College of Arts & Sciences ... Dr. Carmen L. BURKHALTER
50 Dean College of Business ... Dr. Gregory A. CARNES
53 Dean Col Education/Human Sciences ... Dr. Donna P. LEFORT
66 Dean College of Nursing ... Dr. Vicki G. PIERCE
31 Director University Events ... Mr. Bret JENNINGS
41 Director of Athletics ... Mr. Mark LINDER
43 University Attorney ... Ms. Amber FITE-MORGAN
21 Controller ... Vacant
37 Director Student Financial Svcs ... Ms. Shauna JAMES
15 Asst VP for Human Resources ... Ms. Catherine D. WHITE
26 Dir Univ Communications ... Mr. Bryan RACHAL
18 Asst VP for Facilities ... Mr. Michael B. GAUTNEY
19 Chief of University Police ... Mr. Kevin L. GILLLILAN
23 Director University Health Services ... Ms. Teresa U. DAWSON
07 Int Director of Admissions ... Ms. Julie Y. TAYLOR
09 Dir Inst Rsrch/Plng & Assessment ... Vacant
29 Director Alumni Relations ... Ms. Haley T. BRINK
96 Asst VP Business Services ... Ms. Cindy H. CONLON
28 Dir Diversity/Institutional Equity ... Ms. Joan J. WILLIAMS
36 Dir Career Planning & Development ... Ms. Melissa T. MEDLIN
06 Registrar ... Vacant
38 Director University Advising ... Dr. Amy CREWS
40 Manager University Bookstore ... Mr. Griffin HITE
08 Dean Library/Educ Tech Svcs ... Dr. Melvin D. DAVIS
13 Chief Info Technology Officer (CIO) ... Mr. Stephen PUTMAN
04 Administrative Asst to President ... Ms. Regina B. SHERRILL

University of South Alabama (B)

307 University Boulevard, N, Mobile AL 36688-0002
County: Mobile FICE Identification: 001057
Unit ID: 102094
Telephone: (251) 460-6101 Carnegie Class: DU-Higher
FAX Number: (251) 461-1537 Calendar System: Semester
URL: www.southalabama.edu
Established: 1963 Annual Undergrad Tuition & Fees (In-State): $7,548
Enrollment: 16,211 Coed
Affiliation or Control: State IRS Status: 501(c)3
Highest Offering: Doctorate
Accreditation: **SC**, ARCPA, AUD, CACREP, CAEPN, COARC, CS, EMT, ENG, MED, MUS, NURSE, OT, PSPSY, PTA, RAD, RTT, SP, SW

01 President ... Dr. Tony G. WALDROP
03 Executive Vice President ... Dr. John SMITH
05 Provost & Sr VP Academic Affairs ... Dr. G. David JOHNSON
23 Vice Pres Med Affairs/Dean COM ... Dr. John MARYMONT
10 VP Financial Affairs & Admin ... Mr. Scott WELDON
30 Vice Pres Developmental/Alumni Rels ... Ms. Margaret SULLIVAN
46 VP for Research & Economic Devel ... Dr. Lynne CHRONISTER
43 Sr University Attorney ... Ms. Jean TUCKER
58 Assc VP Acad Affs/Dean Grad Sch ... Dr. J. Harold PARDUE
20 Assc VP Acad Success/SVP Acad Affs ... Dr. Nicole T. CARR
84 Dir Enrollment Services ... Mr. Christopher LYNCH
13 Exec Director of Information Tech ... Mr. Chris CANNON
20 Assoc Vice Pres Academic Affairs ... Dr. Charles GUEST
15 Asst Vice President Human Resources . Ms. Pamela HENDERSON
17 Dean College of Medicine ... Dr. John MARYMONT
86 Exec Dir Government Relations ... Mr. William J. FULFORD
32 VP Stdnt Affairs/Dean of Stdnt ... Dr. Michael MITCHELL
88 Dir of Assessment/Sr VP Acad Affair ... Ms. Cecelia MARTIN
26 Exec Dir Marketing/Communication ... Mr. Michael HASKINS
41 Director of Athletics ... Dr. Joel ERDMANN
07 Director of Admissions ... Ms. Norma J. TANNER
85 Director Intl Student Services ... Ms. Regina GEORGE
07 Director New Student Recruitment ... Mr. Christopher LYNCH
09 Dir Inst Research/Plng & Analysis ... Dr. Gordon E. MILLS, JR.
06 Registrar ... Ms. Kelly OSTERBIND
29 Director Alumni Relations ... Ms. Karen EDWARDS
19 Chief of Police ... Mr. Zeke AULL, JR.
37 Director of Financial Aid ... Ms. Emily JOHNSTON
36 Director Career Services ... Ms. Bevley W. GREEN
12 Director USA Baldwin County ... Ms. Cynthia WILSON
18 Director Facilities Management ... Mr. Randy MOON
38 Interim Dir Student Counseling/Test ... Dr. Darlene DEMPSTER
28 Director Multicultural Student Affs ... Dr. Carl G. CUNNINGHAM
96 Purchasing Agent ... Mr. Robert M. BROWN
54 Dean College of Engineering ... Dr. John STEADMAN
51 Assc VP of Global USA ... Dr. Richard CARTER
49 Dean of Arts and Sciences ... Dr. Andrzej WIERZBICKI
08 Exec Dir of University Libraries ... Ms. Lorene FLANDERS
50 Dean Mitchell College of Business ... Dr. Bob C. WOOD
53 Dean College of Educ & Prof Studies ... Dr. Andrea KENT
66 Dean of College of Nursing ... Dr. Debra C. DAVIS
76 Dean of Allied Health Professions ... Dr. Gregory FRAZER
77 Dean Computer & Information Science ... Dr. Alec YASINSAC
39 Asst VP Auxiliary Svcs/Univ Housing ... Dr. Mary Christine VINET
04 Executive Asst to President ... Ms. Suzanne GOINS
101 Executive Asst Board Affairs ... Ms. Monica EZELL
104 Director Study Abroad ... Ms. Holly HUDSON

The University of West Alabama (C)

205 N Washington Street, Livingston AL 35470-2099
County: Sumter FICE Identification: 001024
Unit ID: 101587
Telephone: (205) 652-3400 Carnegie Class: Masters/L
FAX Number: (205) 652-3718 Calendar System: Semester
URL: www.uwa.edu
Established: 1835 Annual Undergrad Tuition & Fees (In-State): $8,876
Enrollment: 4,032 Coed
Affiliation or Control: State IRS Status: 501(c)3
Highest Offering: Beyond Master's But Less Than Doctorate
Accreditation: **SC**, ACBSP, ADNUR, #CAATE, CAEPN

01 President ... Dr. Ken TUCKER
05 Provost ... Dr. Tim EDWARDS
10 Interim Vice Pres Financial Affairs ... Mr. Lawson EDMONDS
111 Vice Pres Institutional Advancement ... Mr. Chris THOMASON
32 Vice President for Student Affairs ... Mr. Richard HESTER
49 Dean of Liberal Arts ... Dr. Mark DAVIS
50 Dean of Business & Technology ... Dr. Wayne BEDFORD
53 Dean College of Education ... Dr. Jan MILLER
81 Dean of Natural Science/Math ... Dr. John MCCALL
58 Dean of Graduate Studies ... Dr. B.J KIMBROUGH
51 Dean Continuing Education ... Dr. Tina N. JONES
106 Dean Online Programs ... Dr. Jan MILLER
66 Chairperson of Nursing ... Mrs. Lynn LASHLEY
08 Director of Library ... Dr. Neil SNIDER
09 Dir Institutional Effectiveness ... Mrs. Angel JOWERS
41 Athletic Director ... Mr. Stan WILLIAMSON
35 Director of Student Life ... Mr. Byron THETFORD
06 Registrar ... Mrs. Susan SPARKMAN
37 Director Student Financial Aid ... Mr. Don RAINER
13 Director Information Systems ... Mr. Michael PRATT
18 Director of Physical Plant ... Mr. Bobby TRUELOVE
109 Director of Auxiliary Services ... Mr. Lee WALKER
36 Director Career Services/Placement ... Ms. Tammy S. WHITE
29 Director Alumni Relations ... Ms. Danielle BUCKALEW
38 Director Student Success Center ... Dr. Vicki P. SPRUIELL
86 Director Government Relations ... Mr. Tom TARTT
07 Dir of Undergraduate Recruiting ... Dr. Blake BEDSOLE
96 Director of Purchasing ... Mr. Lawson C. EDMONDS
89 Director Freshmen Studies ... Dr. James GENTSCH
92 Director Honors Program ... Dr. Lesa SHAUL
15 Director Personnel Services ... Mrs. Brenda KILLOUGH
30 Director of Development ... Mr. Chris THOMASON
20 Associate Academic Officer ... Mrs. Angel JOWERS
26 Chief Public Relations Officer ... Ms. Betsy COMPTON
19 Director of Security/Safety ... Mr. Jeff MANUEL
103 Director Economic Development ... Mrs. Allison BRANTLEY
105 Director of Web Services ... Mrs. Christi GEORGE
101 Secretary Board of Trustees ... Mrs. Katie BEARD
28 Director of Diversity ... Dr. Tim EDWARDS
85 Int Director of Foreign Students ... Dr. Mark DAVIS

ALASKA

Alaska Bible College (D)

248 East Elmwood Avenue, Palmer AK 99645
County: Matanuska-Susitna FICE Identification: 008843
Unit ID: 102580
Telephone: (907) 745-3201 Carnegie Class: Spec-4-yr-Faith
FAX Number: (907) 745-3210 Calendar System: Semester
URL: www.akbible.edu
Established: 1966 Annual Undergrad Tuition & Fees: $9,300
Enrollment: 33 Coed
Affiliation or Control: Independent Non-Profit IRS Status: 501(c)3
Highest Offering: Baccalaureate
Accreditation: **BI**

01 President ... Mr. David LEY
05 Vice Pres Academic Affairs ... Mr. John FERCH
32 Vice Pres Student Development ... Mr. Jonathan GARLAND
11 Vice Pres Business Admin ... Mr. John MCKISSICK
06 Registrar ... Mr. Ben OLSON
08 Library Director ... Ms. Noel MAXWELL
07 Director of Admissions ... Mr. Justin ARCHULETTA
37 Director Financial Aid ... Ms. Sandy ANDERSON

Alaska Career College (E)

1415 E. Tudor Road, Anchorage AK 99507-1033
County: Anchorage FICE Identification: 025410
Unit ID: 103501
Telephone: (907) 563-7575 Carnegie Class: Spec 2-yr-Other
FAX Number: (907) 563-8330 Calendar System: Other
URL: www.alaskacareercollege.edu
Established: 1985 Annual Undergrad Tuition & Fees: N/A
Enrollment: 378 Coed
Affiliation or Control: Proprietary IRS Status: Proprietary
Highest Offering: Associate Degree
Accreditation: **ACCSC**

01 Director ... Ms. Linda STURE

Alaska Pacific University (F)

4101 University Drive, Anchorage AK 99508-4672
County: Anchorage FICE Identification: 001061
Unit ID: 102669
Telephone: (907) 561-1266 Carnegie Class: Masters/S
FAX Number: (907) 562-4276 Calendar System: Semester
URL: www.alaskapacific.edu
Established: 1957 Annual Undergrad Tuition & Fees: $20,310
Enrollment: 516 Coed
Affiliation or Control: Independent Non-Profit IRS Status: 501(c)3
Highest Offering: Doctorate
Accreditation: **NW**, CAEPN, IACBE

01 President ... Dr. Robert ONDERS
04 Executive Assistant to President ... Ms. Debbie ROLL
05 Provost ... Ms. Tracy STEWART
10 Chief Financial Officer ... Ms. Deborah JOHNSTON
32 Dean of Students ... Mr. Ben HAHN
06 Registrar ... Ms. Michelle WHEELER
07 Asst Director of Admissions ... Mr. Brian MCDERMOTT
37 Director of Financial Aid ... Mr. Scott GRAVES
18 Director Facilities Management ... Ms. Kathy MINCKS
13 Director Information Technology ... Mr. Dave WILGA
30 Chief Development Officer ... Vacant
42 Chaplain ... Vacant
15 Director Human Resources ... Ms. Kathleen WYRICK
40 Campus Store Manager ... Ms. Lydia HARVEY
29 Alumni Relations Coordinator ... Vacant
19 Director Security/Safety ... Mr. Tyler EGGEN
38 Dir of Career/Counseling & Disabil ... Vacant
39 Director Student Housing ... Ms. Manda HILL

Charter College (G)

2221 E Northern Lights Blvd, #120,
Anchorage AK 99508-4157
County: Anchorage FICE Identification: 025769
Unit ID: 102845
Telephone: (907) 277-1000 Carnegie Class: Bac/Assoc-Mixed
FAX Number: (907) 274-3342 Calendar System: Quarter
URL: www.chartercollege.edu
Established: 1985 Annual Undergrad Tuition & Fees: $21,887
Enrollment: 1,945 Coed
Affiliation or Control: Proprietary IRS Status: Proprietary
Highest Offering: Master's
Accreditation: **ACICS**, ADNUR

01 President ... Mr. Josh BICCHINELLA
07 Director of Admission ... Ms. Michelle MUELLER

Ilisagvik College (H)

PO Box 749, Barrow AK 99723
County: North Slope Borough FICE Identification: 034613
Unit ID: 434584
Telephone: (907) 852-3333 Carnegie Class: Tribal
FAX Number: (907) 852-3003 Calendar System: Semester
URL: www.ilisagvik.edu
Established: 1996 Annual Undergrad Tuition & Fees: $3,820
Enrollment: 193 Coed
Affiliation or Control: Independent Non-Profit IRS Status: 501(c)3
Highest Offering: Associate Degree
Accreditation: **NW**

01 President ... Mrs. Pearl K. BROWER
06 Registrar ... Mrs. Meghan GALLIGAN
05 Dean of Academic Affairs ... Mrs. Birgit MEANY
15 Director Human Resources ... Mrs. Linda STANFORD
18 Chief Facilities/Physical Plant ... Mr. Tom CARAWAY
26 Chief Public Relations Officer ... Mr. John BERGMAN
32 Dean of Students ... Ms. Amanda SIALOFI
37 Director Student Financial Aid ... Mrs. Nancy GRANT

† Granted candidacy at the Baccalaureate level.

*University of Alaska System (I)

910 Yukon Drive, Suite 202, Fairbanks AK 99775-5000
County: Fairbanks FICE Identification: 008005
Unit ID: 103529
Telephone: (907) 450-8000 Carnegie Class: N/A
FAX Number: (907) 450-8012
URL: www.alaska.edu

01 President ... Dr. James R. JOHNSEN
26 Vice President for Univ Relations ... Ms. Michelle RIZK
05 VP for Academic Affairs & Research ... Dr. Daniel M. WHITE
10 Chief Finance Officer/Controller ... Mr. Myron DOSCH
46 Chief Strategy/Planning/Budget Ofcr ... Ms. Michelle RIZK
09 AVP Institutional Rsrch & Analysis ... Ms. Gwendolyn GRUENIG
84 Assoc VP Student/Enrollment Strat ... Mr. Saichi T. OBA
86 Assoc VP Public Affairs ... Ms. Robbie GRAHAM
43 General Counsel ... Mr. Michael HOSTINA
15 Chief HR Officer ... Ms. Keli H. MCGEE
13 Chief Information Technology Ofcr ... Mr. Karl KOWALSKI
06 Registrar & Director of Admissions ... Mr. Mike EARNEST
16 Director Labor & Employee Relations ... Mr. Geoff BACON
117 Chief Risk Officer ... Mr. Timothy EDWARDS

*University of Alaska Anchorage (A)

3211 Providence Drive, Anchorage AK 99508-8000
County: Anchorage FICE Identification: 011462
Unit ID: 102553
Telephone: (907) 786-1800 Carnegie Class: Masters/L
FAX Number: (907) 786-4888 Calendar System: Semester
URL: www.uaa.alaska.edu
Established: 1954 Annual Undergrad Tuition & Fees (In-State): $5,784
Enrollment: 16,762 Coed
Affiliation or Control: State IRS Status: 501(c)3
Highest Offering: Doctorate
Accreditation: **NW**, ACFEI, ADNUR, ART, CAEPN, CLPSY, CONST, CS, CSHSE, DA, DH, DIETD, DIETI, EMT, ENG, ENGR, JOUR, MAC, MT, MUS, NUR, NURSE, PH, PTAA, SW

02 Interim Chancellor .... Samuel GINGERICH
05 Interim Provost .... Duane HRNCIR
10 Interim Vice Chanc Admin Services .... Pat SHIER
09 Sr Vice Provost Inst Effectiveness .... Renee CARTER-CHAPMAN
84 Int Assoc Vice Chanc Enroll Svcs .... Lora VOLDEN
30 Vice Chancellor Univ Advancement .... Megan OLSON
32 Vice Chancellor Student Affairs .... Bruce SCHULTZ
26 Asst Vice Chanc Univ Relations .... Kristin DESMITH
13 Int CIO/Assoc Vice Chanc ITS .... Adam PAULICK
09 Assoc Vice Provost Inst Research .... Erin HOLMES
18 Assoc VC Facilities & Campus Svcs .... Christopher TURLETES
96 Assoc Vice Chanc Admin Services .... Sandi CULVER
29 Asst Vice Chanc Alumni Relations .... Rachel MORSE
88 Exec Dir Acad & Multicul Success .... Theresa LYONS
35 Interim Dean of Students .... Dawn DOOLEY
37 Dir Student Financial Assistance .... Sonya STEIN
85 Director Multicultural Center .... E. Andre THORN
35 Director Student Life & Leadership .... Annie ROUTE
07 Director of Admissions .... Cathy EWING
41 Director Athletics .... Keith HACKETT
06 Interim University Registrar .... Lindsey CHADWELL
15 Director Human Resources .... Ron KAMAHELE
08 Dean Consortium Library .... Stephen ROLLINS
63 Director WWAMI Biomedical Program .... Jane SHELBY
88 Director Native Student Services .... William TEMPLETON
38 Director Student Health & Counsel .... Georgia DEKEYSER
50 Dean Col Business & Public Policy .... Rashmi PRASAD
51 Dean Community & Technical College .... Denise RUNGE
76 Dean College of Health .... William HOGAN
54 Dean College of Engineering .... Fred BARLOW
49 Dean College Arts & Sciences .... John STALVEY
53 Interim Dean College of Education .... Paul DEPUTY
92 Interim Dean Honors College .... John MOURACADE
106 Director Academic Innov E-learning .... Dave DANNENBERG
20 Vice Provost Undergrad Acad Affairs .... Susan KALINA
58 Vice Prov Research & Grad School .... Helena WISNIEWSKI
39 Director Univ Housing Dining & Conf .... David WEAVER
25 Director Grants & Contracts .... Heather PAULSEN
45 Dir Facility Planning & Construct .... John FAUNCE

*University of Alaska Fairbanks (B)

505 South Chandlar Drive, Fairbanks AK 99775
County: Fairbanks North Star Borough FICE Identification: 001063
Unit ID: 102614
Telephone: (907) 474-7500 Carnegie Class: DU-Higher
FAX Number: (907) 474-5379 Calendar System: Semester
URL: www.uaf.edu
Established: 1917 Annual Undergrad Tuition & Fees (In-State): $5,976
Enrollment: 8,638 Coed
Affiliation or Control: State IRS Status: 501(c)3
Highest Offering: Doctorate
Accreditation: **NW**, CAEPN, CLPSY, CS, DH, EMT, ENG, MAC, MUS, SW

02 Chancellor .... Mr. Daniel M. WHITE
05 Provost .... Dr. Susan M. HENRICHS
11 Vice Chancellor Administrative Svcs .... Ms. Kari BURRELL
18 Assoc Vice Chancellor Facilities .... Mr. Scott BELL
32 Int Vice Chancellor Student Svcs .... Dr. Gary GRAY
46 Vice Chancellor Research .... Mr. Larry HINZMAN
10 AVC for Financial Services .... Mrs. Julie QUEEN
30 Director of Development .... Ms. Emily DRYGAS
58 Interim Dean Graduate School .... Dr. Michael CASTELLINI
81 Dean Col of Natural Science/Math .... Dr. Paul LAYER
35 Assoc Vice Chanc for Student Life .... Mr. Alexis KNABE
31 VC Rural/Cmty & Native Educ .... Mr. Evon PETER
12 Dean UAF Comm & Tech College .... Ms. Michele STALDER
88 Dean Sch Fisheries & Ocean Sciences .... Mr. Bradley MORAN
50 Dean School of Management .... Dr. Mark HERRMANN
54 Dean Col of Engineering & Mines .... Dr. Doug GOERING
88 Dir Intl Arctic Research Center .... Dr. Hajo EICKEN
88 Dir Institute of Arctic Biology .... Dr. Brian M. BARNES
54 Int Dir Inst Northern Engineering .... Dr. William SCHNABEL
15 Director Human Resources .... Mr. Brad LOBLAND
19 Chief of Police .... Mr. Stephen GOETZ
37 Director Financial Aid .... Ms. Deanna L. DIERINGER
41 Director Athletics .... Dr. Gary GRAY
35 Dean of Students .... Ms. Laura L. MCCOLLOUGH
56 Vice Provost for Extension/Outreach .... Mr. Fred SCHLUTT
109 Director of Aux/Recharge/Cntrct Ops .... Vacant
85 Director International Programs .... Ms. Donna ANGER
88 Fire Chief .... Mr. Doug SCHRAGE
88 Dir Institute of Marine Science .... Dr. Terry WHITLEDGE
49 Dean College of Liberal Arts .... Mr. Todd SHERMAN
53 Dean School of Education .... Dr. Steve ATWATER
12 Director Bristol Bay Campus .... Ms. Cynthia ROGERS
12 Acting Dir Chukchi Campus .... Ms. Kristen DAU
12 Interim Dir Interior Alaska Campus .... Mr. Bryan YHER
12 Director Kuskokwim Campus .... Ms. Mary C. PETE
12 Director Northwest Campus .... Mr. Robert METCALF
28 Director of Diversity & EO .... Ms. Margo GRIFFITH
23 Director Health and Counseling .... Dr. B.J ALDRICH
29 Exec Director Alumni Association .... Ms. Kate RIPLEY
06 Registrar .... Mr. Mike EARNEST
88 Director Geophysical Institute .... Mr. Robert MCCOY
21 Director Business Operations .... Ms. Amanda WALL
36 Director Career Services .... Ms. Patti PICHA
121 Director Academic Advising Center .... Ms. Linda M. HAPSMITH
92 Director Honors Program .... Ms. Marsha SOUSA
94 Coordinator Women's Studies .... Dr. Sine ANAHITA
09 Dir Planning/Analysis/Inst Research .... Mr. Ian OLSON
26 Director University Relations .... Ms. Michelle RENFREW
08 Interim Dean of Libraries .... Ms. Suzan HAHN
88 Interim Dir UA Museum of the North .... Dr. Aldona JONAITIS
13 Chief Info Technology Officer .... Mr. Karl KOWALSKI
22 Director for Disability Services .... Ms. Mary MATTHEWS
96 Dir of Procurement & Contract Svcs .... Mr. John HEBARD
88 Director Wood Center Student Union .... Mr. Mark OLDMIXON
97 Vice Provost/Dean Gen Studies .... Dr. Alex FITTS
04 Executive Asst to Chancellor .... Ms. Deborah QUEEN
106 Executive Director for E-learning .... Ms. Carol GERING

*University of Alaska Southeast (C)

11120 Glacier Highway, Juneau AK 99801-8681
County: Juneau FICE Identification: 001065
Unit ID: 102632
Telephone: (907) 796-6000 Carnegie Class: Masters/M
FAX Number: N/A Calendar System: Semester
URL: www.uas.alaska.edu
Established: 1956 Annual Undergrad Tuition & Fees (In-State): $8,415
Enrollment: 2,800 Coed
Affiliation or Control: State IRS Status: 501(c)3
Highest Offering: Master's
Accreditation: **NW**, CAEPN, CAHIIM, MAC

02 Chancellor .... Dr. Richard CAULFIELD
05 Provost & Executive Dean SCE .... Dr. Karen CAREY
75 Exec Dean Sch of Career Educ .... Mr. Pete TRAXLER
46 Interim Vice Provost for Research .... Dr. Paula MARTIN
11 Vice Chanc Admin Services .... Mr. Michael CIRI
12 Sitka Campus Director .... Dr. Paula MARTIN
12 Ketchikan Campus Director .... Dr. Priscilla SCHULTE
49 Interim Dean of Arts & Sciences .... Dr. Paula MARTIN
53 Dean Education & Graduate Studies .... Dr. Deborah LO
37 Financial Aid Director .... Ms. Janelle COOK
26 Public Relations .... Ms. Keni CAMPBELL
06 Registrar .... Ms. Barbara HEGEL
84 VC Enrollment Mgmt & Stdnt Affs .... Mr. Joseph NELSON
09 Dir Institutional Effectiveness .... Mr. Brad EWING
10 Director Business Services .... Mr. Tom DIENST
15 Director Personnel Services .... Dr. Gail CHENEY
18 Director Facilities Services .... Mr. Nathan LEIGH
08 Director Library Services .... Ms. Elise TOMLINSON
13 Director Information/Technology .... Mr. Michael CIRI
30 Dir Development/Alumni Relations .... Ms. Lynne JOHNSON
29 Alumni Relations/Annual Fund Mgr .... Ms. Jessy POSTY
21 Chief Budget Officer .... Ms. Julie VIGIL
88 Director Learning Center .... Ms. Hildegard SELLNER
15 Title IX Coordinator/HR Training .... Ms. Lori KLEIN
39 Director of Campus Life .... Mr. Eric SCOTT
88 Director of PITAAS .... Ms. Ronalda CADIENTE-BROWN
88 Director of AK Coastal Rainforest .... Ms. Allison BIDLACK

*Prince William Sound Community College (D)

PO Box 97, Valdez AK 99686-0097
Telephone: (907) 834-1600 Identification: 666659
Accreditation: **&NW**

† Branch campus of University of Alaska Anchorage, Anchorage, AK

ARIZONA

Acacia University (E)

7665 South Research Drive, Tempe AZ 85284-1812
County: Maricopa Identification: 667017
Telephone: (480) 428-6034 Carnegie Class: Not Classified
FAX Number: (480) 428-6033 Calendar System: Other
URL: www.acacia.edu
Established: 2003 Annual Undergrad Tuition & Fees: N/A
Enrollment: N/A Coed
Affiliation or Control: Proprietary IRS Status: Proprietary
Highest Offering: Master's
Accreditation: **DEAC**

01 President .... Mr. Tim MOMAN
05 Provost/Executive Vice President .... Dr. Marilynn D. HENLEY
13 CIO .... Mr. Michael TURICO

Argosy University, Phoenix (F)

2233 W Dunlap Avenue, Phoenix AZ 85021
Telephone: (602) 216-2600 Identification: 666790
Accreditation: **&WC**, ACBSP, CACREP, CLPSY

† Regional accreditation is carried under the parent institution in Orange, CA.

Arizona Christian University (G)

2625 E Cactus Road, Phoenix AZ 85032-7042
County: Maricopa FICE Identification: 007113
Unit ID: 105899
Telephone: (602) 489-5300 Carnegie Class: Bac-Diverse
FAX Number: (602) 404-2159 Calendar System: Semester
URL: www.arizonachristian.edu
Established: 1960 Annual Undergrad Tuition & Fees: $23,896
Enrollment: 779 Coed
Affiliation or Control: Independent Non-Profit IRS Status: 501(c)3
Highest Offering: Baccalaureate
Accreditation: **NH**

01 President .... Mr. Len MUNSIL
05 Provost and Chief Operating Officer .... Dr. Steve ADAMSON
10 Chief Financial Officer .... Mr. Timothy FISCHER
84 VP for Enrollment .... Mr. Pete HAMSTRA
21 Controller .... Mr. Rick SHARPE
09 Director of Institutional Research .... Vacant
06 Registrar & Asst Dir of Enroll Mgmt .... Mr. Lambert CRUZ
37 Director Financial Aid .... Mrs. Courtney ROSE
13 Director of Information Technology .... Mr. Robert TERRY
08 Librarian .... Mr. Robert OLIVERIO
19 Director of Campus Security .... Mr. John HOEBEE
18 Director of Facilities .... Mr. David HOOK
41 Athletic Director .... Mr. Jeff RUTTER
39 Residence Director .... Mrs. Wendy CLYDE
15 Human Resources Coordinator .... Mrs. Nancy STOCKING
04 Assistant to President and Provosts .... Mrs. Julie ROSEN
32 Chief Student Affairs/Student Life .... Dr. Jared BLACK

Arizona College (H)

4425 W Olive Avenue, Suite 300,
Glendale AZ 85302-3851
County: Maricopa FICE Identification: 031150
Unit ID: 421708
Telephone: (602) 222-9300 Carnegie Class: Spec 2-yr-Health
FAX Number: (602) 200-8726 Calendar System: Other
URL: www.arizonacollege.edu
Established: 1991 Annual Undergrad Tuition & Fees: $15,524
Enrollment: 567 Coed
Affiliation or Control: Proprietary IRS Status: Proprietary
Highest Offering: Associate Degree
Accreditation: **ABHES**

01 President .... Mr. Nick MANSOUR

Arizona College-Mesa (I)

163 N. Dobson Road, Mesa AZ 85201
Telephone: (480) 265-3600 Identification: 770514
Accreditation: **ABHES**, NURSE

Arizona School of Acupuncture and Oriental Medicine (J)

2856 E Fort Lowell Rd., Tucson AZ 85716
County: Pima FICE Identification: 036955
Unit ID: 446039
Telephone: (520) 795-0787 Carnegie Class: Spec-4-yr-Other Health
FAX Number: (877) 222-4606 Calendar System: Quarter
URL: www.asaom.edu
Established: 1996 Annual Graduate Tuition & Fees: N/A
Enrollment: 32 Coed
Affiliation or Control: Proprietary IRS Status: Proprietary
Highest Offering: Master's; No Undergraduates
Accreditation: **ACUP**

00 Owner .... Mr. Jonathan HU
01 President .... Mr. Alex HOLLAND
05 Academic Dean .... Dr. Julian CHANG
37 Financial Aid Advisor .... Ms. Susan WAGNER
07 Admissions Director .... Mr. Tim DUNN

Arizona State University (K)

300 E. University Drive, Tempe AZ 85281
County: Maricopa FICE Identification: 001081
Unit ID: 104151
Telephone: (855) 278-5080 Carnegie Class: DU-Highest
FAX Number: N/A Calendar System: Semester
URL: www.asu.edu
Established: 1885 Annual Undergrad Tuition & Fees (In-State): $10,370
Enrollment: 51,984 Coed
Affiliation or Control: State IRS Status: 501(c)3
Highest Offering: Doctorate
Accreditation: **NH**, AAB, ART, AUD, CACREP, CIDA, CLPSY, CONST, COPSY, CS, DIETD, DIETI, ENG, ENGT, IPSY, JOUR, LAW, LSAR, MT, MUS, NRPA, NURSE, PCSAS, PLNG, SP, SPAA, SW

01 President .... Dr. Michael M. CROW
05 Exec VP & University Provost .... Dr. Mark S. SEARLE
10 Exec Vice President/Treasurer & CFO .... Dr. Morgan R. OLSEN
101 Sr Vice Pres/Sec of the University .... Dr. Christine K. WILKINSON
102 CEO ASU Foundation .... Mr. Rick SHANGRAW
43 Sr Vice President & General Counsel .... Mr. José A. CÁRDENAS
32 Sr VP Educ Outreach & Student Svcs .... Dr. James A. RUND
07 Vice President for Admissions .... Mr. Kent HOPKINS

41 Vice President for Athletics ... Mr. Ray ANDERSON
13 Chief Information Officer ... Mr. Gordon D. WISHON
15 VP & Chief Human Resources Ofc ... Mr. Kevin J. SALCIDO
100 Sr VP Univ Affairs/Chief of Staff ... Mr. Jim O'BRIEN
106 Exec Vice Provost/Dean EdPlus ... Dr. Philip R. REGIER
49 VP/Dean of Liberal Arts & Sciences ... Dr. Patrick KENNEY
84 Vice Provost Enrollment Management ... Mr. Kent HOPKINS
50 Dean WP Carey School of Business ... Dr. Amy HILLMAN
54 Dean Fulton School of Engineering ... Dr. Kyle SQUIRES
53 Dean Mary Lou Fulton Teachers Col ... Dr. Carole BASILE
92 Dean of Barrett Honors College ... Dr. Mark JACOBS
12 Dean New College of Int Arts & Sci ... Dr. Todd SANDRIN
57 Dean Herberger Inst for Design/Arts ... Dr. Steven J. TEPPER
60 Dean Cronkite Sch Journal/Mass Comm ... Mr. Christopher CALLAHAN
61 Dean College of Law ... Mr. Douglas SYLVESTER
66 Dean College of Nursing & Health In ... Dr. Teri PIPE
47 Dean School of Sustainability ... Dr. Christopher G. BOONE
20 Vice Provost Undergrad Education ... Dr. Frederick C. COREY
76 Dean Health Solutions ... Dr. Deborah HELITZER
88 Dean College of Public Svc & Comm ... Dr. Jonathan KOPPELL
08 University Librarian ... Dr. James O'DONNELL
107 CEO/DirGen Thunderbird Sch Glbl Mgt ... Dr. Allen MORRISON
97 Dean Col Letters & Sci/Univ College ... Mr. Duane ROEN

Arizona Summit Law School (A)

One North Central Avenue, 14th Flr, Phoenix AZ 85004
County: Maricopa — FICE Identification: 041314
Unit ID: 450942
Telephone: (602) 682-6800 — Carnegie Class: Spec-4-yr-Law
FAX Number: (602) 682-6999 — Calendar System: Semester
URL: www.azsummitlaw.edu
Established: 2005 — Annual Graduate Tuition & Fees: N/A
Enrollment: 580 — Coed
Affiliation or Control: Proprietary — IRS Status: Proprietary
Highest Offering: First Professional Degree; No Undergraduates
Accreditation: #LAW

01 President ... Mr. Donald LIVELY
05 Dean of Academic Programs ... Mr. Joe PEREZ
07 Assoc Dean of Admissions ... Mr. Rick JACKSON
08 Assoc Dean Law Library ... Ms. Christy RYAN
15 Director Human Resources ... Ms. Desiree COE
06 Academic Records Operations Manager ... Ms. Jacquelyn ELSER
37 Financial Aid Counselor ... Mr. Lawrence MUSHKIN

Arizona Western College (B)

2020 South Avenue 8E, Yuma AZ 85365
County: Yuma — FICE Identification: 001071
Unit ID: 104160
Telephone: (928) 317-6000 — Carnegie Class: Assoc/MT-VT-Mix Trad/Non
FAX Number: (928) 344-7730 — Calendar System: Semester
URL: www.azwestern.edu
Established: 1963 — Annual Undergrad Tuition & Fees (In-District): $2,600
Enrollment: 7,514 — Coed
Affiliation or Control: State/Local — IRS Status: Exempt
Highest Offering: Associate Degree
Accreditation: NH, ADNUR, EMT, RAD

01 President ... Dr. Daniel P. CORR
05 Vice President Learning Services ... Dr. Linda ELLIOTT-NELSON
10 Vice Pres Finance/Administration ... Mr. Shahrooz ROOHPARVAR
26 Dean Public Relations & Marketing ... Mrs. Lori STOFFT
09 Dean Instl Effect/Research/Grants ... Dr. Mary SCHAAL
51 Assoc Dean of Continuing Educ ... Mrs. Maria AGUIRRE
32 Vice President for Student Services ... Mr. Bryan E. DOAK
75 Dean of Career & Tech Educ ... Ms. Reetika DHAWAN
111 Director Institutional Advancement ... Mrs. Renee L. SMITH
07 Director of Admissions/Registrar ... Mrs. Nicole D. HARRAL
21 Dir Financial Services/Controller ... Mrs. Diana G. DOUCETTE
15 Chief Human Resources Officer ... Ms. Kari GARDNER
96 Dir Purchasing & Auxiliary Services ... Ms. Margaret HAYES
18 Director of District Operations ... Mr. Steve ECKERT
13 Director of Computer Info Services ... Vacant
14 Director of Tech Support Services ... Ms. Brenda WARNOCK
08 Director of Library Services ... Ms. Angie CREEL
41 Director of Athletics ... Mr. Jerry SMITH
19 Chief of Police ... Mr. John EDMUNDSON
32 Dean of Students ... Ms. Mary Kay HARTON
12 Associate Dean La Paz County Svcs ... Ms. Kathy OCAMPO
12 Assoc Dean for South Yuma County ... Ms. Susanna ZAMBRANO
37 Director of Financial Aid ... Ms. Ana ENGLISH
85 Director of International Program ... Vacant
106 Associate Dean for Distance Educ ... Mrs. Jana MOORE
88 Director of Testing Services ... Mrs. Leticia MARTINEZ
105 Webmaster II ... Mr. Damien BATES
04 Executive Assistant to President ... Ms. Grace PRATT
36 Director Career/Advisement Services ... Mr. James R. HUTCHISON

The Art Institute of Phoenix (C)

2233 W Dunlap Avenue, Phoenix AZ 85021-2859
County: Maricopa — FICE Identification: 040513
Unit ID: 428444
Telephone: (602) 331-7500 — Carnegie Class: Spec-4-yr-Arts
FAX Number: (602) 331-5301 — Calendar System: Quarter
URL: www.artinstitutes.edu/phoenix
Established: 1995 — Annual Undergrad Tuition & Fees: $17,412
Enrollment: 999 — Coed
Affiliation or Control: Proprietary — IRS Status: Proprietary
Highest Offering: Baccalaureate
Accreditation: #ACICS, ACFEI, CIDA

01 President ... Mr. Chad WILLIAMS
05 Dean of Academic Affairs ... Mr. Gil MEJIA
07 Senior Director of Admissions ... Ms. Shaunna DI MAIO
32 Director of Student Services ... Ms. Kristin FRANK
15 Human Resources Generalist ... Ms. Betty Ann FIELD
37 Director of Financial Services ... Ms. Abigail GARCIA
06 Registrar ... Ms. Misty SPICER

The Art Institute of Tucson (D)

5099 East Grant Road, Suite 100, Tucson AZ 85712-2733
Telephone: (520) 318-2700 — FICE Identification: 037405
Accreditation: #ACICS

† In teach-out mode.

Benedictine University at Mesa (E)

51 E Main Street, Suite 105, Mesa AZ 85201
Telephone: (602) 888-5000 — Identification: 770068
Accreditation: &NH

† Branch campus of Benedictine University, Lisle, IL

Brighton College (F)

8777 E. Via de Ventura, Scottsdale AZ 85258
County: Maricopa — Identification: 666710
Telephone: (602) 212-0501 — Carnegie Class: Not Classified
FAX Number: (602) 212-0502 — Calendar System: Other
URL: www.brightoncollege.edu
Established: 1961 — Annual Undergrad Tuition & Fees: N/A
Enrollment: N/A — Coed
Affiliation or Control: Proprietary — IRS Status: Proprietary
Highest Offering: Associate Degree
Accreditation: DEAC

01 President ... Paul ZAGNONI
03 Executive Vice President ... Sam FERNENDEZ
26 Vice President Marketing Operations ... Vacant
84 Vice Pres Enrollment Management ... Renee NASLUCHACZ
10 Director of Financial Operations ... Patricia MCCOY
32 Director of Student Management ... Sean DIXON

Brookline College (G)

2445 West Dunlap Avenue, Suite 100, Phoenix AZ 85021
County: Maricopa — FICE Identification: 022188
Unit ID: 104090
Telephone: (602) 242-6265 — Carnegie Class: Bac-Diverse
FAX Number: (602) 973-2572 — Calendar System: Other
URL: www.brooklinecollege.edu
Established: 1979 — Annual Undergrad Tuition & Fees: N/A
Enrollment: 1,379 — Coed
Affiliation or Control: Proprietary — IRS Status: Proprietary
Highest Offering: Baccalaureate
Accreditation: ACICS, MLTAD, NUR, NURSE, PTAA

01 Campus Director ... Mr. Jerry COLLINS

Brookline College (H)

1140 South Priest Drive, Tempe AZ 85281
Telephone: (480) 545-8755 — Identification: 666403
Accreditation: ACICS, SURTEC

† Branch campus of Brookline College, Phoenix, AZ.

Brookline College (I)

5441 E 22nd Street, Suite 125, Tucson AZ 85711-5444
Telephone: (520) 748-9799 — Identification: 666402
Accreditation: ACICS

† Branch campus of Brookline College, Phoeniz, AZ.

Brown Mackie College-Tucson (J)

4585 E Speedway Boulevard, Tucson AZ 85712-5300
Telephone: (520) 319-3300 — FICE Identification: 009451
Accreditation: ACICS, OTA, SURTEC

† In teach-out mode.

Bryan University (K)

350 West Washington Street, Ste 100, Tempe AZ 85281
Telephone: (602) 384-2555 — Identification: 770627
Accreditation: ACICS

† Branch campus of Bryan University, Springfield, MO.

Carrington College - Mesa (L)

1001 W Southern Avenue, Suite 130, Mesa AZ 85210
Telephone: (480) 212-1600 — FICE Identification: 023352
Accreditation: &WJ, DH, MAAB, PTAA

† Regional accreditation is carried under the parent institution in Sacramento, CA.

Carrington College - Phoenix East (M)

2149 W Dunlap Avenue, Phoenix AZ 85021-2982
Telephone: (602) 216-7700 — Identification: 666248
Accreditation: &WJ, COARC

† Regional accreditation is carried under the parent institution in Sacramento, CA.

Carrington College - Phoenix North (N)

8503 N 27th Avenue, Phoenix AZ 85051-4063
Telephone: (602) 393-5900 — FICE Identification: 021006
Accreditation: &WJ, ADNUR, MAAB

† Regional accreditation is carried under the parent institution in Sacramento, CA.

Carrington College - Tucson (O)

201 N. Bonita Ave., Ste. 101, Tucson AZ 85745
Telephone: (520) 888-5885 — FICE Identification: 030898
Accreditation: &WJ, MAAB

† Regional accreditation is carried under the parent institution in Sacramento, CA.

Central Arizona College (P)

8470 N Overfield Road, Coolidge AZ 85128-9779
County: Pinal — FICE Identification: 007283
Unit ID: 104346
Telephone: (520) 494-5444 — Carnegie Class: Assoc/MT-VT-High Non
FAX Number: (520) 494-5008 — Calendar System: Semester
URL: www.centralaz.edu
Established: 1961 — Annual Undergrad Tuition & Fees (In-District): $2,520
Enrollment: 5,849 — Coed
Affiliation or Control: Local — IRS Status: 501(c)3
Highest Offering: Associate Degree
Accreditation: NH, ADNUR, CAHIIM, DIETT, EMT, IFSAC, MAC, RAD

01 President ... Dr. Jacquelyn ELLIOTT
05 VP Academic Affairs ... Dr. Mary K. GILLILAND
32 Interim VP Student Services ... Ms. Jennifer CARDENAS
107 Academic Dean ... Dr. Janice PRATT
49 Academic Dean ... Ms. Terri ACKLAND
103 Academic Dean ... Ms. Jani ATTEBERY
81 Interim Academic Dean ... Mr. Jeff BUNKELMANN
10 Vice President Business Affairs ... Mr. Chris WODKA
15 Executive Director Human Resources ... Ms. Brandi CLARK
08 Director Library Services ... Ms. Adriana SAAVEDRA
37 Director of Financial Aid ... Ms. Elisa JUAREZ
41 Athletic Director ... Mr. Chuck SCHNOOR
39 Director of Residence Life ... Ms. Rosemary RAMIREZ
18 Exec Director of Facilities ... Mr. Ernesto VALENZUELA
96 Director of Purchasing ... Mr. Mark SALAZ
06 Registrar/Interim Dean of Students ... Ms. Veronica DURAN
07 Director of Admissions/Recruitment ... Mr. Luis SANCHEZ
21 Exec Dir Accounting Svc/Comptroller ... Ms. Luisa OTT
102 Director Foundation ... Ms. Margaret DOOLEY
35 Asst Dean Student Life ... Mr. Tramaine RAUSAW
04 Exec Asst to President & Gov Board . Ms. Mary Lou HERNANDEZ
13 Chief Info Technology Officer (CIO) ... Ms. Candice ROSS
19 Chief of Police ... Mr. James MATHENEY
26 Exec Dir PR & Marketing ... Ms. Angela ASKEY
45 Director Planning and Effectiveness ... Ms. Sylvia GIBSON
25 Director Resource Development ... Mr. Hugo STEINCAMP

Chamberlain University-Phoenix (Q)

2149 West Dunlap Avenue, Phoenix AZ 85021
Telephone: (602) 331-2720 — Identification: 770502
Accreditation: &NH, NURSE

† Branch campus of Chamberlain University-Addison, Addison, IL

Cochise College (R)

901 N Colombo Avenue, Sierra Vista AZ 85635-2317
County: Cochise — FICE Identification: 001072
Unit ID: 104425
Telephone: (800) 966-7943 — Carnegie Class: Assoc/HVT-High Non
FAX Number: (520) 417-4006 — Calendar System: Semester
URL: www.cochise.edu
Established: 1964 — Annual Undergrad Tuition & Fees (In-District): $1,896
Enrollment: 4,437 — Coed
Affiliation or Control: State/Local — IRS Status: 170(c)1
Highest Offering: Associate Degree
Accreditation: NH, #COARC

01 Chief Executive Officer (President) ... Dr. James D. ROTTWEILER
04 Administrative Asst to President ... Ms. Crystal WHEELER
05 VP for Instruction/Provost ... Dr. Verlyn FICK
10 VP Administration ... Mr. LaMont SCHIERS
15 VP Human Resources ... Dr. Wendy DAVIS
13 VP Information Technology ... Mr. Carlos CARTAGENA
102 Exec Dir Foundation & Ext Affairs ... Ms. Denise HOYOS
18 Exec Dir Fac Mgt Planning ... Mr. Frank DYKSTRA
07 Registrar/Director of Admissions ... Ms. Debra QUICK
06 Assistant Registrar ... Ms. Heather AUGENSTEIN
49 Dean Liberal Arts ... Mr. Chuck HOYACK
81 Dean Math and Science ... Dr. Beth KRUEGER
76 Dean Nursing/Allied Health ... Ms. Jennifer LAKOSIL

50 Dean Business and Technology .... Dr. Clyne NAMUO
56 Dean Extended Learning .... Mr. George SELF
32 Dean Student Services/Athl Director .... Dr. James HALL
09 Dean Institutional Effectiveness .... Vacant
35 Asst Dean Student Services .... Mr. Mark BOGGIE
08 Director Library Services .... Dr. John WALSH
96 Director of Procurement .... Mr. Scott ARLEDGE
39 Director Student Housing .... Ms. Marisol ARENIVAS
88 Director Occ Health Safety .... Mr. Randy DENNEY
37 Director Student Financial Aid .... Ms. Karen EMMER
38 Director Counseling and Advising .... Ms. Nanette ROMO
88 Dir TRIO Student Support Services .... Ms. Gabriela AMAVIZCA
22 Director Disability Support Service .... Ms. Carla BOYD
26 Director Marketing & Communication .... Ms. Robyn MARTIN
88 Director Continuous Improvement .... Ms. Karen DALE
66 Director Nursing .... Ms. Polly GOSA
88 Director Aviation Programs .... Mr. Kevin AUSTIN
88 Director Adult Education .... Ms. Susan MORSS
88 Director Small Business Dev Center .... Mr. Mark SCHMITT
51 Director Ctr for Lifelong Learning .... Ms. Sharon GILMAN
12 Director Fort Huachuca .... Mr. John SOMERS
12 Director Willcox Center .... Ms. Barbara RICHARDSON
12 Director Santa Cruz Center .... Mr. Gabriel GALINDO
12 Director Benson Center .... Ms. Barbara RICHARDSON
106 Director Virtual Campus .... Ms. Tasneem ASHRAF
88 Assistant Director Virtual Campus .... Mr. Adam WOODROW

Cochise College (A)

4190 W. Highway 80, Douglas AZ 85607-6190
Telephone: (800) 966-7943 Identification: 770004
Accreditation: &NH, ADNUR, EMT

Coconino Community College (B)

2800 S Lone Tree Road, Flagstaff AZ 86005
County: Coconino FICE Identification: 031004
Unit ID: 404426
Telephone: (928) 527-1222 Carnegie Class: Assoc/HT-High Non
FAX Number: (928) 226-4105 Calendar System: Semester
URL: www.coconino.edu
Established: 1991 Annual Undergrad Tuition & Fees (In-State): $3,060
Enrollment: 3,540 Coed
Affiliation or Control: State IRS Status: 501(c)3
Highest Offering: Associate Degree
Accreditation: NH

01 President .... Dr. Colleen A. SMITH
111 Exec Dir Institutional Advancement .... Mr. Scott TALBOOM
05 Interim Provost .... Dr. Dudley GARDNER
03 Executive Vice President .... Ms. Jami VAN ESS
32 Dean of Student Development .... Ms. Veronica HIPOLITO
12 Page Center Director .... Mr. Jim HUNTER
49 Dean of Learning Services CTE .... Mr. Jeff JONES
49 Dean of Learning Svcs Arts&Sciences .... Dr. Kimberly BATTY-HERBERT
49 Dean of Learning Svcs PT Faculty .... Dr. Monica BAKER
15 Exec Director for Human Resources .... Mr. Dietrich SAUER
09 Dir Institutional Research/Assess .... Mr. Michael MERICA
37 Director for Financial Aid/Veterans .... Mr. Robert VOYTEK
06 Registrar/Dir Enrollment Services .... Ms. Kimmi GRULKE
18 Executive Director Facilities .... Mr. Kurt STULL
13 Chief Innovation Officer .... Mr. Ron HURLE
96 Director Purchasing/Auxiliary Svcs .... Vacant
21 Dean of Finance .... Ms. Siri MULLANEY
04 Exec Assistant to the President .... Ms. April SANDOVAL

Coconino County Community College Flagstaff Fourth Street Campus (C)

3000 N Fourth Street, Flagstaff AZ 86004
Telephone: (928) 526-7600 Identification: 770005
Accreditation: &NH

CollegeAmerica-Flagstaff (D)

399 S. Malpais, 2nd Floor, Flagstaff AZ 86001
County: Coconino FICE Identification: 031203
Unit ID: 103945
Telephone: (928) 213-6060 Carnegie Class: Spec-4-yr-Other Health
FAX Number: (928) 526-3468 Calendar System: Other
URL: www.collegeamerica.edu
Established: 2001 Annual Undergrad Tuition & Fees: $16,968
Enrollment: 137 Coed
Affiliation or Control: Independent Non-Profit IRS Status: 501(c)3
Highest Offering: Baccalaureate
Accreditation: ACCSC

01 Campus Director/Dean of Education .... Mr. Tresban RIVERA
07 Director of Admissions .... Doreen EVANS

CollegeAmerica-Phoenix (E)

9801 N. Metro Parkway East, Phoenix AZ 85051
Telephone: (602) 589-9860 Identification: 666017
Accreditation: ACCSC

† Branch campus of CollegeAmerica-Flagstaff, Flagstaff, AZ

DeVry University - Phoenix Campus (F)

2149 W Dunlap Avenue, Phoenix AZ 85021-2995
Telephone: (602) 749-7301 FICE Identification: 008322
Accreditation: &NH, ENGT, MT

† Regional accreditation is carried under the parent institution in Downers Grove, IL.

Diné College (G)

One Circle Drive, Tsaile AZ 86556-9998
County: Apache FICE Identification: 008246
Unit ID: 105297
Telephone: (928) 724-6671 Carnegie Class: Tribal
FAX Number: (928) 724-3327 Calendar System: Semester
URL: www.dinecollege.edu
Established: 1968 Annual Undergrad Tuition & Fees (In-District): $725
Enrollment: 1,490 Coed
Affiliation or Control: Local IRS Status: 501(c)3
Highest Offering: Baccalaureate
Accreditation: NH

01 President .... Dr. Charles ROESSEL
10 Vice President for Finance .... Ms. Bo LEWIS
32 Vice Pres of Student Success .... Ms. Glennita HASKEY
05 Vice President of Academics .... Dr. Geraldine GARRITY
86 Vice Pres Government Affairs .... Ms. Marie R. NEZ
06 Registrar .... Ms. Louise LITZIN
37 Director Student Financial Aid .... Mr. Formon THOMPSON
15 Dir Department of Human Resources .... Mr. Meryl DAYZIE
18 Supt Maintenance Operations .... Mr. Delbert PAQUIN
21 Controller .... Ms. Raychelle LEONARD
46 Dir Inst Grants/Sponsored Projects .... Ms. Amanda MCNEIL

Dunlap-Stone University (H)

19820 North 7th Street, Suite 100, Phoenix AZ 85024
County: Maricopa Identification: 666315
Telephone: (602) 648-5750 Carnegie Class: Not Classified
FAX Number: (602) 648-5755 Calendar System: Other
URL: www.dunlap-stone.edu
Established: 1995 Annual Undergrad Tuition & Fees: N/A
Enrollment: N/A Coed
Affiliation or Control: Proprietary IRS Status: Proprietary
Highest Offering: Master's
Accreditation: DEAC

01 President .... Dr. Donald N. BURTON
05 Chief Academic Officer .... Mrs. Caulyne BARRON

Eastern Arizona College (I)

615 N Stadium Avenue, Thatcher AZ 85552-0769
County: Graham FICE Identification: 001073
Unit ID: 104577
Telephone: (928) 428-8233 Carnegie Class: Assoc/HVT-Mix Trad/Non
FAX Number: (928) 428-2578 Calendar System: Semester
URL: www.eac.edu
Established: 1888 Annual Undergrad Tuition & Fees (In-District): $2,400
Enrollment: 6,320 Coed
Affiliation or Control: State/Local IRS Status: 501(c)3
Highest Offering: Associate Degree
Accreditation: NH, ADNUR

01 President .... Mr. Mark BRYCE
03 Executive Vice President .... Mr. Brent MCEUEN
10 Chief Business Officer .... Mr. Timothy CURTIS
05 Provost .... Mrs. Jeanne BRYCE
20 Dean of Instruction .... Mr. Michael CROCKETT
20 Dean of Instruction .... Dr. Phil MCBRIDE
20 Dean of Curriculum and Instruction .... Dr. Janice LAWHORN
32 Dean of Students .... Dr. Gary SORENSEN
06 Associate Dean/Registrar .... Dr. Randall SKINNER
38 Assistant Dean of Counseling .... Ms. Sharon ALLEN
12 Director of Discovery Park Campus .... Mr. Paul ANGER
21 Director Fiscal Control/Controller .... Mr. Heston WELKER
37 Director of Financial Aid .... Mr. William OSBORN
13 Director of Information Resources .... Mr. Thomas THOMPSON
09 Director of Institutional Research .... Mr. Glen SNIDER
08 Director of Library Services .... Ms. Kristen BECKER
26 Dir of Marketing & Public Relations .... Mr. Todd HAYNIE
18 Director of Physical Resources .... Mr. Dan WELKER
102 Executive Director EAC Foundation .... Mr. David UDALL
35 Director of Student Life .... Mr. Danny BATTRAW
41 Athletic Director .... Mr. James BAGNALL
15 Assoc Director Admin Support EEO Co .... Ms. Lauri AVILA
04 Exec Asst to the President and DGB .... Mrs. Laurie PENNINGTON

Eastern Arizona College Gila Pueblo Campus (J)

8274 Six Shooter Canyon PO Box 2656, Globe AZ 85502
Telephone: (928) 425-8481 Identification: 770008
Accreditation: &NH

Eastern Arizona College Payson Campus (K)

201 N Mud Springs Rd., PO Box 359, Payson AZ 85547
Telephone: (928) 468-8039 Identification: 770009
Accreditation: &NH

Embry-Riddle Aeronautical University-Prescott (L)

3700 Willow Creek Road, Prescott AZ 86301-3270
Telephone: (800) 888-3728 FICE Identification: 021047
Accreditation: &SC, AAB, ENG

† Regional accreditation is carried under the parent institution in Daytona Beach, FL.

Fortis College, Phoenix (M)

555 N 18th Street, Suite 110, Phoenix AZ 85006
Telephone: (602) 254-3099 Identification: 666761
Accreditation: ACCSC, DH

† Branch campus of Fortis College, Centerville, OH. Tuition varies by degree program.

Frank Lloyd Wright School of Architecture (N)

12621 N Frank Lloyd Wright Blvd, Scottsdale AZ 85259
County: Maricopa FICE Identification: 025332
Unit ID: 104665
Telephone: (480) 627-5345 Carnegie Class: Spec-4-yr-Arts
FAX Number: (480) 860-8472 Calendar System: Other
URL: www.taliesin.edu
Established: 1932 Annual Undergrad Tuition & Fees: N/A
Enrollment: 17 Coed
Affiliation or Control: Independent Non-Profit IRS Status: 501(c)3
Highest Offering: Master's
Accreditation: NH

01 Head of School and Dean .... Mr. Aaron BETSKY
05 Director of Academic Affairs .... Dr. Chris LASCH
08 Director of Libraries .... Ms. Elizabeth AL-HAZZAM DAWASARI
07 Dir Admissions/Student Services .... Mr. Gerasimos (Jerry) KAVALIERATOS
10 Chief Financial Officer .... Ms. Lisa MURPHY
30 Director of Development .... Mr. Jason DONOFRIO

Golf Academy of America (O)

2031 N. Arizona Ave Suite 2, Chandler AZ 85225
Telephone: (800) 342-7342 Identification: 666023
Accreditation: ACICS

† Branch campus of Virginia College, Birmingham, AL.

Grand Canyon University (P)

3300 W Camelback Road, Phoenix AZ 85017-3030
County: Maricopa FICE Identification: 001074
Unit ID: 104717
Telephone: (602) 639-7500 Carnegie Class: DU-Mod
FAX Number: N/A Calendar System: Semester
URL: www.gcu.edu
Established: 1949 Annual Undergrad Tuition & Fees: $17,050
Enrollment: 69,444 Coed
Affiliation or Control: Proprietary IRS Status: Proprietary
Highest Offering: Doctorate
Accreditation: NH, ACBSP, CAATE, NURSE, @THEOL

01 President/Chief Executive Officer .... Mr. Brian MUELLER
10 Chief Financial Officer .... Mr. Dan BACHUS
11 Chief Operating Officer .... Dr. Stan MEYER
05 Provost .... Dr. Hank RADDA
20 Sr VP Academic Affs/Univ Registrar .... Dr. Jennifer LECH
108 Vice Pres Inst Effectiveness .... Dr. Antoinette FARMER-THOMPSON
41 Vice President of Athletics .... Mr. Mike VAUGHT
32 VP Student Svcs/Dean of Students .... Pastor Tim GRIFFIN
50 Dean Colangelo College Business .... Dr. Randy GIBB
53 Dean College of Education .... Dr. Kimberly LAPRADE
66 Dean College Nursing/Hlth Care Prof .... Dr. Lisa SMITH
49 Dean College Sci/Engineering/Tech .... Dr. K. Mark WOODEN
58 Dean College Doctoral Studies .... Dr. Michael BERGER
57 Dean of Fine Arts and Production .... Mr. Claude PENSIS
73 Dean College of Theology .... Dr. Jason HILES
79 Dean College Human/Social Science .... Dr. Sherman ELLIOTT

Han University of Traditional Medicine (Q)

2856 E. Fort Lowell Road, Tucson AZ 85716
County: Pima FICE Identification: 041193
Telephone: (520) 322-6330 Carnegie Class: Not Classified
FAX Number: (520) 322-5661 Calendar System: Quarter
URL: www.hanuniversity.edu
Established: 2000 Annual Undergrad Tuition & Fees: N/A
Enrollment: N/A Coed
Affiliation or Control: Proprietary IRS Status: Proprietary
Highest Offering: Master's
Accreditation: ACUP

01 President .... Mr. Alex HOLLAND
05 Academic Dean .... Mr. Chiu-An CHANG
07 Admissions Director .... Mr. Gary BONHARD
06 Registrar .... Mr. Alex HOLLAND

Harrison Middleton University (A)

1105 East Broadway Road, Tempe AZ 85282-1505

County: Maricopa | Identification: 666169
Telephone: (877) 248-6724 | Carnegie Class: Not Classified
FAX Number: (800) 762-1622 | Calendar System: Other
URL: www.hmu.edu
Established: 1998 | Annual Undergrad Tuition & Fees: N/A
Enrollment: N/A | Coed
Affiliation or Control: Proprietary | IRS Status: Proprietary
Highest Offering: Doctorate
Accreditation: DEAC

01 President ... Mr. David CURD
05 Vice Pres/Director of Education ... Mr. Michael CURD
51 VP/Dean Continuing Education ... Ms. Rebecca FISHER
06 Registrar/Director of Accreditation ... Ms. Lauren GUTHRIE

Indian Bible College (B)

2237 E. Cedar Avenue, Flagstaff AZ 86004

County: Coconino | Identification: 667317
Telephone: (928) 774-3890 | Carnegie Class: Not Classified
FAX Number: (928) 774-2655 | Calendar System: Semester
URL: www.indianbible.org
Established: 1958 | Annual Undergrad Tuition & Fees: N/A
Enrollment: N/A | Coed
Affiliation or Control: Independent Non-Profit | IRS Status: 501(c)3
Highest Offering: Baccalaureate
Accreditation: @BI

01 President ... Dr. Jason KOPPEN

International Baptist College and Seminary (C)

2211 W Germann Road, Chandler AZ 85286

County: Maricopa | FICE Identification: 033473
Unit ID: 436614
Telephone: (480) 245-7903 | Carnegie Class: Spec-4-yr-Faith
FAX Number: (480) 245-7909 | Calendar System: 4/1/4
URL: www.ibcs.edu
Established: 1980 | Annual Undergrad Tuition & Fees: $10,500
Enrollment: 70 | Coed
Affiliation or Control: Baptist | IRS Status: 501(c)3
Highest Offering: Doctorate
Accreditation: TRACS

00 Chancellor ... Dr. Jerry C. TETREAU
01 President ... Rev. Kenneth M. ENDEAN
32 Dean of Students ... Mr. Jeffrey G. CAUPP
05 Chief Academic Officer ... Dr. Wayne A. BLEY
10 Chief Financial Officer ... Mr. Matt EBERLE
20 Graduate Academic Officer ... Dr. David SHUMATE
30 Chief Development/Advancement ... Dr. Jerry C. TETREAU
07 Director of Admissions ... Pastor Dan OLSON
09 Director of Inst Effectiveness ... Mrs. Lauren BRADY
88 Teaching Site Liaison ... Dr. Keith HUHTA
08 Media Center Director ... Mr. Lee WILL
34 Dean of Women ... Mrs. Marcia L. GAMMON
06 Registrar ... Mrs. Rebecca M. STERTZBACH
37 Financial Aid Administrator ... Mrs. Jane L. BUSHEY
04 Exec Asst to President/Office Mgr ... Mrs. Rebecca M. STERTZBACH

*Maricopa County Community College District Office (D)

2411 W 14th Street, Tempe AZ 85281-6941

County: Maricopa | FICE Identification: 001075
Unit ID: 105136
Telephone: (480) 731-8000 | Carnegie Class: N/A
FAX Number: (480) 731-8850
URL: www.maricopa.edu

01 Chancellor ... Dr. Maria HARPER-MARINICK
05 Int Exec Vice Chancellor/Provost ... Dr. Paul DALE
102 President/CEO Foundation ... Ms. Christina SCHULTZ
10 Vice Chanc Business Services ... Ms. Gaye MURPHY
15 Vice Chancellor Human Resources ... Ms. LaCoya SHELTON-JOHNSON
13 Chief Information Officer ... Mr. Ed KELTY
103 Dir Center Workforce Development ... Dr. Randy KIMMENS
30 Exec Director Resource Development ... Ms. Mary O'CONNOR
09 Assoc VC Inst Strategy/Rsrch/Effect ... Vacant
18 Assoc Vice Chanc Cap Plng/Spec Proj ... Mr. Arlen SOLOCHEK

*Chandler-Gilbert Community College (E)

2626 E Pecos Road, Chandler AZ 85225-2499

County: Maricopa | FICE Identification: 030722
Unit ID: 364025
Telephone: (480) 732-7000 | Carnegie Class: Assoc/HT-Mix Trad/Non
FAX Number: (480) 732-7090 | Calendar System: Semester
URL: www.cgc.maricopa.edu
Established: 1992 | Annual Undergrad Tuition & Fees (In-District): $2,094
Enrollment: 14,654 | Coed
Affiliation or Control: State/Local | IRS Status: 501(c)3
Highest Offering: Associate Degree
Accreditation: NH, ADNUR, DIETT

02 Interim College President ... Dr. William GUERRIERO
04 Administrative Asst to President ... Ms. Susan D. AROZ
05 Vice President Academic Affairs ... Vacant
32 Vice President Student Affairs ... Dr. William H. CRAWFORD, III
11 Vice Pres Administrative Services ... Mr. Bradley S. KENDREX
49 Dean of Arts and Sciences ... Mr. Chris SCHNICK
20 Dean of Instruction ... Ms. Gabriela ROSU
31 Dean of Community Affairs ... Dr. Cindy BARNES
32 Dean of Student Affairs ... Mr. Daniel HERBST
10 Assoc Dean for Business Operations ... Ms. Bernadette LA MAZZA
07 Director Admissions ... Ms. Linda SHAW
13 Vice President of IT & Media Svcs ... Dr. Charles NWANKWO
09 Dir Research/Planning/Development ... Ms. Theresa WONG
36 Dir Career/Education Planning Svcs ... Vacant
85 Director International Educ Program ... Ms. Annie A. JIMENEZ
88 Dir Disability Resources & Svcs ... Ms. Dawn GRUICHICH
18 Director Col Facilities Plng & Dev ... Mr. Charles POURE
35 Director Student Life & Leadership ... Mr. Michael GREENE
41 Athletic Director ... Mr. Edward YEAGER
19 Public Safety Commander ... Mr. Donald KEANE, JR.
37 Director Financial Aid ... Mr. Timothy WOLSEY
88 Director Learning Center ... Ms. Eva R. FALLETTA
88 Director Early Outreach Programs ... Ms. Laura MATYAS
88 Director Instr Tech & Course Prod ... Ms. Juliane M. ROYBAL
66 Director Nursing & Health Sciences ... Ms. Karen FLANIGAN
14 Director Computer Labs/Instr Svcs ... Ms. Joni M. BRUMMER
21 Manager College Cashiers Office ... Ms. Julie WRIGHT
15 Senior Human Resource Manager ... Mr. Daniel ROSEN

*Estrella Mountain Community College (F)

3000 N Dysart Road, Avondale AZ 85392

County: Maricopa | FICE Identification: 031563
Unit ID: 384333
Telephone: (623) 935-8000 | Carnegie Class: Assoc/HT-Mix Trad/Non
FAX Number: (623) 935-8008 | Calendar System: Semester
URL: www.estrellamountain.edu
Established: 1990 | Annual Undergrad Tuition & Fees (In-District): $2,094
Enrollment: 9,303 | Coed
Affiliation or Control: State/Local | IRS Status: 501(c)3
Highest Offering: Associate Degree
Accreditation: NH, ADNUR

02 President ... Dr. Ernest LARA
11 Vice President Admin Services ... Dr. Heather WEBER
32 Vice President Student Affairs ... Dr. Patricia CARDENAS-ADAME
05 Vice President of Learning ... Dr. Rey RIVERA
20 Dean of Academic Affairs ... Dr. Kathleen IUDICELLO
20 Dean of Academic Affairs ... Dr. Sylvia ORR
35 Dean of Student Services ... Ms. Laura DULGAR
09 Dean Planning/Rsrch/Effectiveness ... Dr. Rene G. WILLEKENS
08 Division Chair Information Resource ... Mr. Terry MEYER
18 Director Facilities Planning/Devel ... Mr. Randy L. NAUGHTON
13 Director Information Technology ... Mr. Chad GALLIGAN
07 Director of Enrollment Services ... Mr. Frank AMPARO
10 Mgr College Fiscal/Budget Services ... Ms. Leda JOHNSON
102 Dir Corp Foundation Rels/Dev Ops ... Mr. Jonathan ROBLES
37 Director Student Financial Aid ... Ms. Rosanna SHORT
114 Manager College Budget ... Ms. Maggie CASTILLO

*Gateway Community College (G)

108 N 40th Street, Phoenix AZ 85034-1795

County: Maricopa | FICE Identification: 008303
Unit ID: 105145
Telephone: (602) 286-8000 | Carnegie Class: Assoc/HVT-High Non
FAX Number: (602) 286-8072 | Calendar System: Semester
URL: www.gatewaycc.edu/
Established: 1968 | Annual Undergrad Tuition & Fees (In-District): $2,094
Enrollment: 5,637 | Coed
Affiliation or Control: State/Local | IRS Status: 501(c)3
Highest Offering: Associate Degree
Accreditation: NH, ADNUR, COARC, DMS, NDT, NMT, POLYT, PTAA, SURGT

02 President ... Dr. Steven GONZALEZ
05 Vice President Academic Affairs ... Dr. Maria WISE
32 Vice President Student Affairs ... Dr. Maria WISE
11 Vice President Administrative Svcs ... Mr. Tony ASTI
07 Director Enrollment Services ... Ms. Kristie FOK
09 Dir Research Planning & Development ... Ms. Cathy HERNANDEZ
114 College Budget Analyst ... Ms. Janet BOSE
10 Manager College Fiscal Services ... Ms. Cecilia SOTO
18 Chief Facilities/Physical Plant ... Vacant
26 Director Marketing/Public Relations ... Ms. Christine LAMBRAKIS
30 Asst Director of Development ... Ms. Kristin GUBSER
37 Director Student Financial Aid ... Ms. Suzanne RINGLE
84 Coordinator Enrollment Services ... Ms. Kelly MCPHEE
15 Manager College Employee Services ... Ms. Shanel CARTER
06 Registrar ... Ms. Kristie FOK

*Glendale Community College (H)

6000 W Olive Avenue, Glendale AZ 85302-3006

County: Maricopa | FICE Identification: 001076
Unit ID: 104708
Telephone: (623) 845-3000 | Carnegie Class: Assoc/HT-Mix Trad/Non
FAX Number: (623) 845-3329 | Calendar System: Semester
URL: www.gccaz.edu
Established: 1965 | Annual Undergrad Tuition & Fees (In-District): $2,094
Enrollment: 19,871 | Coed
Affiliation or Control: State/Local | IRS Status: 170(c)1
Highest Offering: Associate Degree
Accreditation: NH, ADNUR, EMT

02 Interim President ... Dr. Teresa LEYBA RUIZ
05 Interim VP Academic Affairs ... Dr. Eric LESHINSKIE
11 Int VP Admin Services & CIO ... Ms. Augustine ERPELDING
20 Dean of Academic Affairs ... Dr. Fernando CAMOU
20 Dean of Academic Affairs ... Mr. Scott SCHULZ
20 Dean of Academic Affairs ... Mr. Charles JEFFERY
84 Dean Enrollment Services ... Ms. Yolanda ESPIZONA
32 Interim Dean Student Life ... Ms. Laura DODRILL
12 Dean GCC North ... Mr. Charles JEFFERY
37 Director Financial Aid ... Ms. Jennifer KESTER
18 Director Facilities ... Mr. Al GONZALES
10 Director College Business Services ... Ms. Kim GOLIS
26 Dir Sales Mktg & Public Rels ... Vacant
45 Dean of Strat/Plng & Accountability ... Dr. Alka ARORA SINGH
15 Manager College Employee Svcs ... Ms. June S. FESSENDEN
30 Director of Development ... Ms. Frances MATEO
38 Dept Chair Counseling ... Ms. Marjane MATON
08 Dept Chair Library ... Mr. Frank TORRES
19 Director College Safety ... Ms. Debra PALOK
04 Admin Assistant I to College Pres ... Ms. Esmeralda M. ACOSTA
41 Athletic Director ... Mr. Peter OLISZCZAK
79 Dept Chair Art & Humanities ... Ms. Pam HALL
81 Dept Chair Biology ... Ms. Karen CONZELMAN
50 Dept Chair Business & Info Tech ... Mr. Gary MARRER
81 Dept Chair Chemistry ... Ms. Debbie LEEDY
88 Dept Chair Comm & World Languages ... Dr. Jim REED
60 Dept Chair Eng/Reading/Journalism ... Mr. David MILLER
88 Dept Chair Fitness & Wellness ... Ms. Lisa LEWIS
77 Dept Chair Math/Computer Science ... Mr. Chris MILLER
66 Dept Chair Nursing ... Dr. Susan MAYER
88 Dept Chair Performing Arts ... Mr. Donald SMITH
88 Dept Chair Philosophy/Religious Std ... Mr. Peter LUPU
81 Dept Chair Physical Sciences ... Mr. David RAFFAELLE
88 Dept Chair Psychology ... Dr. Ilder BETANCOURT LOPEZ
88 Dept Chair Public Safety Sciences ... Mr. Jeff HYNES
83 Dept Chair Social Sciences ... Mr. Dean WHEELER
72 Dept Chair Tech & Consumer Sciences ... Ms. Laura AVILA

*Mesa Community College (I)

1833 W Southern Avenue, Mesa AZ 85202-4866

County: Maricopa | FICE Identification: 001077
Unit ID: 105154
Telephone: (480) 461-7000 | Carnegie Class: Assoc/HT-Mix Trad/Non
FAX Number: (480) 461-7805 | Calendar System: Semester
URL: www.mesacc.edu/
Established: 1965 | Annual Undergrad Tuition & Fees (In-District): $2,094
Enrollment: 21,491 | Coed
Affiliation or Control: State/Local | IRS Status: 501(c)3
Highest Offering: Associate Degree
Accreditation: NH, ADNUR, DH, EMT

02 Interim President ... Mr. Sasan POUREETEZADI
05 Interim Vice Pres Academic Affairs ... Dr. Rodney HOLMES
32 Vice Pres Student Affairs ... Dr. Sonya PEARSON
10 Vice Pres Admin Services ... Mr. Jeff DARBUT
13 Interim VP Information Technology ... Mr. Andrew GIDDINGS
09 Dean of Inst Planning & Analysis ... Mr. Matthew ASHCRAFT
20 Dean Academic Affairs ... Mr. Michael VOSS
20 Dean Instruction ... Dr. Jeffrey ANDELORA
20 Dean Instruction ... Ms. Carol ACHS
12 Vice Provost MCC Red Mountain ... Dr. Nora REYES
84 Dean Enrollment Services ... Dr. Carmen NEWLAND
111 Director of Institutional Advance ... Ms. Sonia FILAN
30 Director of Development ... Mr. Jared LANGKILDE
37 Dir Fin Aid/Scholarships ... Ms. Patricia PEPPIN
19 Director Security/Safety ... Mr. Steve LIEBER
25 Chief Contracts/Grants Admin ... Mr. Kenichi MARUYAMA
29 Director Alumni Relations ... Ms. Marcy SNITZER
41 Athletic Director ... Mr. John MULHERN
18 Interim Director Facilities ... Mr. Steve AZEVEDO
04 Administrative Asst to President ... Ms. Kacie TAKATA
07 Supv Admiss/Registration/Records ... Mr. Daniel ADAMS

*Paradise Valley Community College (J)

18401 N 32nd Street, Phoenix AZ 85032-1210

County: Maricopa | FICE Identification: 026236
Unit ID: 364016
Telephone: (602) 787-6500 | Carnegie Class: Assoc/HT-High Non
FAX Number: (602) 787-6625 | Calendar System: Semester
URL: www.paradisevalley.edu
Established: 1985 | Annual Undergrad Tuition & Fees (In-District): $2,094
Enrollment: 8,684 | Coed
Affiliation or Control: State/Local | IRS Status: 501(c)3
Highest Offering: Associate Degree
Accreditation: NH, ADNUR, DIETT, EMT

02 President ... Dr. Paul DALE
05 Vice President of Academic Affairs ... Dr. Denise DIGIANFILIPPO
11 VP Administrative Services ... Mr. Herman GONZALEZ
32 Vice President of Student Affairs ... Ms. Tanisha MAXWELL
20 Dean of Academic Affairs ... Vacant
35 Dean of Students ... Vacant
84 Dean Admin Affs/Enrollment Services ... Ms. Sandy MCDILL
15 Director Personnel Services ... Ms. Lori LINDSETH
18 Chief Facilities/Physical Plant ... Mr. Robert METEVIER
37 Director Student Financial Aid ... Ms. Katharine JOHNSON

38 Director Student Counseling .... Dr. James RUBIN
06 Registrar .... Ms. Angela ACUNA
36 Director Student Placement .... Ms. Norma CHANDLER
26 Dir of Marketing/Public Relations .... Vacant
09 Dir Institutional Research/Effect .... Mr. John SNELLING
19 Director Security/Safety .... Mr. Scott MEEK
41 Athletic Director .... Ms. Christina HUNDLEY

*Phoenix College (A)

1202 W Thomas Road, Phoenix AZ 85013-4234
County: Maricopa FICE Identification: 001078
Unit ID: 105428
Telephone: (602) 285-7800 Carnegie Class: Assoc/HT-Mix Trad/Non
FAX Number: (602) 285-7700 Calendar System: Semester
URL: www.pc.maricopa.edu
Established: 1920 Annual Undergrad Tuition & Fees (In-District): $2,094
Enrollment: 11,865 Coed
Affiliation or Control: State/Local IRS Status: 501(c)3
Highest Offering: Associate Degree
Accreditation: NH, ADNUR, CAHIIM, DA, DH, EMT, HT, MLTAD

02 Interim President .... Ms. Christina HAINES
05 VP of Academic Affairs .... Dr. Casandra KAKAR
11 VP Administrative Services .... Mr. Paul DEROSE
32 Vice Pres of Student Affairs .... Dr. Meredith WARNER
35 Dean of Student Affairs .... Dr. Heather KRUSE
20 Dean of Academic Affairs .... Mr. Wilbert NELSON
88 Dean of Industry & Public Service .... Vacant
13 Dean of Technology .... Dr. Mark KOAN
08 Department Chair Library .... Ms. Linda SOLAND
38 Department Chair Counseling .... Ms. Nancy NAVARRETE
06 Dir Admissions/Registration/Records .... Ms. Brenda STARCK
07 Director of Enrollment Services .... Vacant
41 Athletic Director .... Ms. Samantha EZELL
37 Director Financial Aid .... Ms. Cynthia RAMOS
88 Int Director Student Leadership .... Ms. Diana MARTINEZ
84 Director Advisement Enrollment .... Ms. Felicia RAMIREZ-PEREZ
09 Dir Instl Plng/Rsrch/Effectiveness .... Vacant
19 Director of College Safety .... Mr. Doug SPARKS
30 Director Institutional Advancement .... Ms. Michelle KLINGER
18 Director of Facilities .... Mr. Douglas MCCARTHY
10 Manager Business Services .... Ms. Angela GENNA
15 Supv College Employee Services .... Ms. Martha ANDERSON
29 Coord Alumni/Community Relations .... Ms. Deborah SPOTTS
04 Assistant to the President .... Ms. Renee MITCHELL

*Rio Salado College (B)

2323 W 14th Street, Tempe AZ 85281-6950
County: Maricopa FICE Identification: 021775
Unit ID: 105668
Telephone: (480) 517-8000 Carnegie Class: Assoc/HVT-High Non
FAX Number: (480) 377-4719 Calendar System: Semester
URL: www.riosalado.edu
Established: 1978 Annual Undergrad Tuition & Fees (In-District): $2,094
Enrollment: 20,533 Coed
Affiliation or Control: State/Local IRS Status: 501(c)3
Highest Offering: Associate Degree
Accreditation: NH, DA, DH

02 President .... Dr. Chris BUSTAMANTE
05 Vice President Academic Affairs .... Ms. Kate SMITH
10 Vice Pres Business & Employee Svcs .... Mr. Todd SIMMONS
32 Vice President Student Affairs .... Dr. LeRodrick TERRY
88 Vice President Maricopa Corp Col .... Mr. Corey PRUITT
13 Vice President Information Services .... Mr. David O'SHEA
20 Dean of Instruction .... Mr. Rick KEMP
15 Dean Administrative and Empl Svcs .... Ms. Maria BELLINO
20 Dean Instructional Tech & Support .... Ms. Dana REID
20 Dean of Instruction .... Ms. Janelle ELIAS
07 Dean of Enrollment Services .... Ms. Rachelle CLARKE
88 Assoc Dean Instruction and Support .... Ms. Earnestine HARRISON
88 Assoc Dean Instruction & Community .... Ms. Barbara KHALSA
88 Assoc Dean Adult Basic Education .... Mr. Blair LIDDICOAT
88 Interim Dean Instruction & Comm Dev .... Mr. Greg PEREIRA
88 Assoc Dean Judicial Affairs .... Ms. Ruby MILLER
21 Assoc Dean Business Service .... Mr. Anthony DISCALA
37 Associate Dean of Financial Aid .... Ms. Nanci REGEHR
09 Assoc Dean Institutional Research .... Mr. Dustin MARONEY
18 Director of Facilities .... Mr. Ernest ADKINS
19 Public Safety Commander .... Mr. John PORVAZNIK
16 Senior Manager Employee Services .... Ms. Anna FLORES
08 Library Faculty Chair .... Ms. Hazel DAVIS
04 Administrative Asst to President .... Ms. Cortney MESAROS

*Scottsdale Community College (C)

9000 E Chaparral, Scottsdale AZ 85256-2626
County: Maricopa FICE Identification: 008304
Unit ID: 105747
Telephone: (480) 423-6000 Carnegie Class: Assoc/HT-High Non
FAX Number: (480) 423-6200 Calendar System: Semester
URL: www.scottsdalecc.edu
Established: 1970 Annual Undergrad Tuition & Fees (In-District): $2,094
Enrollment: 10,083 Coed
Affiliation or Control: State/Local IRS Status: 501(c)3
Highest Offering: Associate Degree
Accreditation: NH, ACFEI, ADNUR

02 President .... Dr. Jan L. GEHLER
32 Vice Pres Student Affairs .... Dr. Donna YOUNG
05 Vice Pres Academic Affairs .... Dr. Stephanie FUJII
11 Vice Pres Administrative Services .... Ms. Colleen O'NEILL
13 Dir ITS/College CTO .... Mr. Vargha MOHEBBI
20 Dean of Instruction .... Ms. Susan PETERSON
32 Dean of Student Affairs .... Ms. Larissa TRAIN
84 Dean of Student Enrollment .... Ms. Gia TAYLOR
07 Director of Admissions .... Ms. Laura KRUEGER
09 Director of Institutional Research .... Dr. Laurie COHEN
111 Exec Dir Inst Advance/Cmty Eng .... Ms. Nancy NEFF
08 Director of Library Services .... Ms. Danielle CARLOCK
37 Director Financial Aid/Placement .... Ms. Stacie BECK
18 Director Buildings/Grounds .... Mr. Samuel J. VAN CLEAVE
19 Director of College Safety .... Mr. Les STRICKLAND
41 Athletic Director .... Mr. Michael MCNALLY
38 Director Student Advisement .... Mr. Michael CORNELIUS
04 Administrative Asst to President .... Ms. Donna COLE
10 Chief Business Officer .... Ms. Mirna ROSAS
15 Director Personnel Services .... Ms. Karen JOHNSON

*South Mountain Community College (D)

7050 S 24th Street, Phoenix AZ 85042-5806
County: Maricopa FICE Identification: 021466
Unit ID: 105792
Telephone: (602) 243-8000 Carnegie Class: Assoc/HT-Mix Trad/Non
FAX Number: (602) 243-8329 Calendar System: Semester
URL: www.southmountaincc.edu
Established: 1979 Annual Undergrad Tuition & Fees (In-District): $2,094
Enrollment: 4,083 Coed
Affiliation or Control: State/Local IRS Status: 501(c)3
Highest Offering: Associate Degree
Accreditation: NH, MACTE

02 President .... Dr. Shari L. OLSON
05 Interim Vice Pres of Learning .... Ms. Matilda CHAVEZ
11 Vice Pres Administrative Svcs .... Dr. Janet ORTEGA
32 Vice Pres Student Affairs .... Dr. Osaro IGHODARO
09 Dean Research/Plng & Development .... Ms. Damita KALOOSTIAN
20 Interim Dean Academic Affairs .... Mr. Stephen HUSTEDDE
84 Dean Enrollment Services .... Mr. Guy GOODMAN
37 Director Financial Aid .... Ms. Inez MORENO-WEINERT
07 Director of Admission & Records .... Ms. Jean WATERMOLEN
10 Director College Business Services .... Mr. John MOLL
18 Director of Facilities .... Mr. Robert HOLMES
21 Manager Fiscal Services .... Ms. Jeanette CERNETIC
15 Coordinator Human Resources .... Ms. Judy BELSHER
07 Coordinator Advisement/Recruitment .... Ms. Christine NEILL
36 Coordinator Job Placement .... Ms. Suzanne HIPPS

*Chandler-Gilbert Community College-Williams Campus (E)

7360 E Tahoe Avenue, Mesa AZ 85212-0908
Telephone: (480) 988-8000 Identification: 770178
Accreditation: &NH, FUSER

*Glendale Community College North (F)

5727 W Happy Valley Road, Phoenix AZ 85310
Telephone: (623) 845-4000 Identification: 770179
Accreditation: &NH

*Mesa Community College at Red Mountain (G)

7110 East McKellips Road, Mesa AZ 85207
Telephone: (480) 654-7200 Identification: 770180
Accreditation: &NH

Midwestern University (H)

19555 N 59th Avenue, Glendale AZ 85308
Telephone: (623) 572-3215 Identification: 666001
Accreditation: &NH, ANEST, ARCPA, CLPSY, DENT, OPT, OSTEO, OT, PERF, PHAR, POD, PTA, @SP, @VET

† Regional accreditation is carried under the parent institution in Downers Grove, IL.

Mohave Community College (I)

1971 E. Jagerson Avenue, Kingman AZ 86409-1238
County: Mohave FICE Identification: 011864
Unit ID: 105206
Telephone: (928) 757-0879 Carnegie Class: Assoc/MT-VT-High Non
FAX Number: (928) 757-0836 Calendar System: Semester
URL: www.mohave.edu
Established: 1971 Annual Undergrad Tuition & Fees (In-District): $2,112
Enrollment: 4,360 Coed
Affiliation or Control: State/Local IRS Status: 501(c)3
Highest Offering: Associate Degree
Accreditation: NH, ADNUR, DH, EMT, PTAA, RAD, SURGT

01 President .... Dr. Michael KEARNS
05 Dean of Instruction .... Mr. Stephen EATON
32 Dean of Student Services .... Ms. Ana MASTERSON
10 Dean of Business Services .... Ms. Sonni MARBURY
111 Director College Advancement .... Ms. Carrie KELLY
13 Chief Information Officer .... Mr. Mark VANPELT
26 Chief Public Relations Officer .... Mr. James JARMAN
12 Campus Dean Bullhead City .... Mr. Shawn BRISTLE
12 Campus Dean Lake Havasu .... Ms. Jann WOODS
12 Campus Dean Neal Kingman .... Dr. Fred GILBERT
12 Campus Dean North Mohave .... Ms. Carolyn HAMBLIN
113 Bursar .... Vacant
37 Financial Aid Director .... Ms. Heather PATENAUDE
09 Dir of Institutional Research .... Mr. Bob FAUBERT
15 Director Personnel Services .... Ms. Jenny DIXON
84 Enrollment Services Manager .... Ms. Sharon HANKS
06 Registrar .... Ms. Michelle BREHMEYER
04 Administrative Asst to President .... Ms. Amy CURLEY

National Paralegal College (J)

717 East Maryland Avenue, Phoenix AZ 85014-1561
County: Maricopa FICE Identification: 041574
Unit ID: 461023
Telephone: (800) 371-6105 Carnegie Class: Spec-4-yr-Other
FAX Number: (866) 347-2744 Calendar System: Other
URL: nationalparalegal.edu
Established: 2003 Annual Undergrad Tuition & Fees: $7,995
Enrollment: 1,038 Coed
Affiliation or Control: Proprietary IRS Status: Proprietary
Highest Offering: Master's
Accreditation: DEAC

01 President .... Avi KATZ
05 Dean/Director .... Stephen HAAS
88 Technical Director .... David COHEN
07 Director of Admissions .... Danielle BACKMAN
37 Director Student Financial Aid .... Lisa PIMBER

Northern Arizona University (K)

South San Francisco Street, Flagstaff AZ 86011-0001
County: Coconino FICE Identification: 001082
Unit ID: 105330
Telephone: (928) 523-9011 Carnegie Class: DU-Higher
FAX Number: (928) 523-1848 Calendar System: Semester
URL: www.nau.edu
Established: 1899 Annual Undergrad Tuition & Fees (In-State): $10,764
Enrollment: 29,021 Coed
Affiliation or Control: State IRS Status: 501(c)3
Highest Offering: Doctorate
Accreditation: NH, ACBSP, ARCPA, CAATE, CACREP, CAEPN, CIDA, CONST, CS, DH, ENG, EXSC, MUS, NRPA, NURSE, OT, PSPSY, PTA, SP, SW

01 President .... Dr. Rita CHENG
03 Executive VP and Chief of Staff .... Ms. Joanne KEENE
05 Provost .... Dr. Daniel KAIN
30 VP Development and Alumni Engmnt .... Dr. Betsy MENNELL
84 VP Enrollment Mgmt/Student Affs .... Ms. Sheila Jane KUHN
09 VP Finance Inst Plng & Analysis .... Mr. Bjorn FLUGSTAD
10 VP Capital Planning & Campus Ops .... Dr. Daniel OKOLI
46 Vice President Research .... Dr. William GRABE
86 VP Govt Affairs/Bus Partnerships .... Ms. Christy FARLEY
41 VP Intercollegiate Athletics .... Ms. Lisa CAMPOS
88 VP of Native American Initiatives .... Dr. Chad HAMILL
88 Ex Dir Inst for Tribal Env Prof .... Dr. Ann Marie CHISCHILLY
88 Exec Dir Native Amer Cultural Ctr .... Dr. Ora MAREK-MARTINEZ
43 General Counsel .... Ms. Michelle PARKER
88 Vice Provost Academic Personnel .... Dr. Roger BOUNDS
13 Chief Information Officer .... Dr. Steven BURRELL
32 Associate VP Student Affairs .... Ms. Erin GRISHAM
12 Assoc VP/Campus Exec Officer - Yuma .... Dr. Michael SABATH
15 Chief HR Officer .... Ms. Diane VERKEST
21 Associate VP Comptrollers Office .... Ms. Wendy SWARTZ
20 Vice Provost Academic Affairs .... Dr. Pauline ENTIN
85 Int Exec Dir International Educ .... Mr. Daniel PALM
108 Chief Institutional Data Officer .... Ms. Laura JONES
110 Assoc VP Devel & Alumni Engagement .... Ms. Bonnie BAKER
110 Assoc VP Devel & Alumni Engagement .... Ms. Meghan FROST
29 Director Alumni Engagement .... Ms. Stephanie SMITH
08 Dean/University Librarian .... Dr. Cynthia A. CHILDREY
53 Dean College of Education .... Dr. Ramona MELLOTT
54 Dean College Eng/Forestry/Nat Sci .... Dr. Paul JAGODZINSKI
50 Dean WA Franke College of Business .... Dr. Dan GOEBEL
49 Dean Col of Arts & Letters .... Dr. Valerio FERME
83 Dean Col Social/Behavioral Sciences .... Dr. Karen L. PUGLIESI
88 Dean Col of Health/Human Svcs .... Dr. Lynda RANSDELL
06 University Registrar .... Ms. Pamela L. ANASTASSIOU
19 Interim Chief of Police .... Ms. Melissa FRESHOUR
88 Dir Emergency Management .... Mr. Marc BURDISS
22 Assistant VP Equity and Access .... Ms. Priscilla L. MILLS
23 Exec Dir Campus Health Svcs .... Ms. Julie RYAN
39 Exec Dir Housing/Residence Life .... Mr. Rich PAYNE
36 Dir Gateway Student Success Center .... Ms. Monica BAI
07 Interim Director of Admissions .... Mr. Chad EICKHOFF
26 Chief Marekting Officer .... Vacant
35 Dean of Students .... Ms. Cynthia ANDERSON
38 Dir Counseling & Testing Center .... Ms. Carol O'SABEN
96 Executive Director of Purchasing .... Ms. Becky E. MCGAUGH
88 Assistant to the President ECMR .... Ms. Kim OTT
102 Chief Foundation Officer .... Ms. Cheryl HEITZ
104 Director Study Abroad .... Dr. Eric DESCHAMPS
37 Director Student Financial Aid .... Ms. Nydia NITTMANN
16 Director Human Resource Programs .... Ms. Cynthia A. CHILCOAT
64 Director School of Music .... Vacant
92 Dean Honors Program .... Dr. George GUMERMAN
94 Director Women and Gender Studies .... Ms. Sheila NAIR
58 Dean Graduate College .... Dr. Maribeth WATWOOD
106 Director E-Learning Center .... Mr. Don CARTER
14 Director of IT Services .... Mr. Ricky ROBERTS

121 Exec Dir Academic Advising ....Ms. Terri HAYES
88 VProvost Tchg/Lrng/Design & Assmt ....Dr. Laurie DICKSON
114 Dir University Budget Office ....Ms. Sadie HUTCHISON
88 Assoc VP of Off Campus Education ....Dr. Susan JOHNSTAD
88 Associate VP Research ....Dr. Diane STEARNS
88 Associate VP ....Mr. Rich BOWEN
88 Assoc VP NAU Online ....Ms. Gina VANCE
88 Assoc VP for Government Affairs ....Ms. Katy YANEZ
88 Assoc VP Educational Partnerships .... Ms. Kathrine YEAGER
88 Assoc VP Sponsored Projects .... Dr. Michael NICHOLS
88 Asst VP Regulatory Compliance .... Dr. David FAGUY

Northern Arizona University Yuma Branch Campus (A)

2020 S Avenue 8E, Yuma AZ 85365
Telephone: (928) 317-6400 Identification: 770011
Accreditation: &NH

Northland Pioneer College (B)

PO Box 610, Holbrook AZ 86025-0610
County: Navajo FICE Identification: 011862
Unit ID: 105349
Telephone: (928) 524-7311 Carnegie Class: Not Classified
FAX Number: (928) 524-7312 Calendar System: Semester
URL: www.npc.edu
Established: 1973 Annual Undergrad Tuition & Fees (In-State): $1,760
Enrollment: 3,354 Coed
Affiliation or Control: State IRS Status: 501(c)3
Highest Offering: Associate Degree
Accreditation: NH, ADNUR, EMT

01 President .... Dr. Jeanne SWARTHOUT
05 Vice Pres Learning/Student Services ....Mr. Mark H. VEST
10 Assoc VP/Chief Business Officer ....Ms. Maderia ELLISON
11 Assoc VP/Chief Operations Office ....Mr. Jason FOUTZ
13 Director of Information Services ....Mr. Phillip WAY
32 Director of Student Services ....Mr. Josh ROGERS
04 Assistant to the President ....Mr. John Paul HEMPSEY
21 Controller ....Ms. Amber HILL
15 Director of Human Resources ....Mr. William FEE
37 Director of Financial Aid ....Ms. Beaulah BOB-PENNYPACKER
88 Director of Developmental Services ....Ms. Gail CAMPBELL
103 Dean of Career/Technical Education .... Ms. Peggy BELKNAP
49 Dean of Arts & Sciences .... Mr. Rickey JACKSON
66 Dean of Nursing and Allied Health ....Ms. Debra MCGINTY
18 Director of Facilities and Vehicles ....Mr. David HUISH
26 Dir of Marketing/Public Relations .... Ms. Ann HESS
09 Director of Institutional Effective ....Vacant
14 Network and Systems Administrator ....Vacant
88 Director Small Business Development ....Ms. Tracy MANCUSO
08 Head Librarian ....Mr. Stan PIROG
19 Director of Public Safety .... Mr. Stuart BISHOP
84 Director of Enrollment Services .... Mr. Jeremy RAISOR

Northland Pioneer College Little Colorado Campus (C)

1400 E. Third Street, Winslow AZ 86047
Telephone: (928) 289-6511 Identification: 770015
Accreditation: &NH

Northland Pioneer College Painted Desert Campus (D)

2251 E Navajo Boulevard, Holbrook AZ 86025
Telephone: (928) 524-7311 Identification: 770012
Accreditation: &NH

Northland Pioneer College Silver Creek Campus (E)

1611 S Main Street, Snowflake AZ 85937
Telephone: (928) 536-6211 Identification: 770014
Accreditation: &NH

Northland Pioneer College White Mountain Campus (F)

1001 W Deuce of Clubs, Show Low AZ 85901
Telephone: (928) 532-6111 Identification: 770013
Accreditation: &NH

Ottawa University Arizona (G)

9414 North 25th Avenue, Phoenix AZ 85021
Telephone: (602) 371-1188 Identification: 666066
Accreditation: &NH

† Regional accreditation is carried under the parent institution in Ottawa, KS.

The Paralegal Institute at Brighton College (H)

8777 E. Via de Ventura, Suite 300, Scottsdale AZ 85258
County: Maricopa FICE Identification: 030737
Unit ID: 105385
Telephone: (602) 212-0501 Carnegie Class: Not Classified
FAX Number: (602) 212-0502 Calendar System: Other
URL: www.theparalegalinstitute.edu
Established: 1974 Annual Undergrad Tuition & Fees: N/A
Enrollment: N/A Coed
Affiliation or Control: Proprietary IRS Status: Proprietary
Highest Offering: Associate Degree
Accreditation: DEAC

01 President ....Paul ZAGNONI
03 Vice President ....Sam FERNANDEZ
05 Vice President Academic Affairs .... Rene NASLUCHAZ
32 Director of Student Services .... Sean DIXON

Penn Foster College (I)

14300 N Northsight Blvd, Suite 125,
Scottsdale AZ 85260-3673
County: Maricopa FICE Identification: 004049
Unit ID: 211486
Telephone: (480) 947-6644 Carnegie Class: Not Classified
FAX Number: (480) 951-6030 Calendar System: Other
URL: www.pennfostercollege.edu
Established: 1974 Annual Undergrad Tuition & Fees: N/A
Enrollment: N/A Coed
Affiliation or Control: Proprietary IRS Status: Proprietary
Highest Offering: Baccalaureate
Accreditation: DEAC

01 Chief Executive Officer .... Mr. Frank BRITT
05 Chief Certification/Licensing Ofcr ....Ms. Connie DEMPSEY
10 Chief Financial Officer ....Mr. Thomas BLESSO
26 Vice Pres Marketing ....Ms. Kate MOSTELLER
07 Vice Pres Admissions ....Mr. Pat GAFFEY
06 Registrar ....Ms. Stephanie SCHROEDER

Phoenix Institute of Herbal Medicine and Acupuncture (J)

301 E Bethany Home Road, Ste A-100,
Phoenix AZ 85012-1275
County: Maricopa FICE Identification: 036175
Unit ID: 447698
Telephone: (602) 274-1885 Carnegie Class: Spec-4-yr-Other Health
FAX Number: (602) 274-1895 Calendar System: Semester
URL: www.pihma.edu
Established: 1996 Annual Graduate Tuition & Fees: N/A
Enrollment: 125 Coed
Affiliation or Control: Proprietary IRS Status: Proprietary
Highest Offering: Master's; No Undergraduates
Accreditation: ACUP

01 President ....Ms. Catherine NIEMIEC
05 Dean for Academic Affairs ....Mr. David MYRICK
07 Admissions ....Ms. Lisa DUNN
06 Registrar ....Ms. Judy DRAYER

Phoenix Seminary (K)

7901 E. Shea Boulevard, Scottsdale AZ 85260-5510
County: Maricopa FICE Identification: 034784
Unit ID: 381459
Telephone: (602) 850-8000 Carnegie Class: Spec-4-yr-Faith
FAX Number: (602) 850-8080 Calendar System: Semester
URL: www.phoenixseminary.edu
Established: 1988 Annual Graduate Tuition & Fees: N/A
Enrollment: 206 Coed
Affiliation or Control: Interdenominational IRS Status: 501(c)3
Highest Offering: Doctorate; No Undergraduates
Accreditation: NH, THEOL

01 President .... Dr. Darryl L. DELHOUSAYE
05 Exec VP/Chief Academic Officer ....Dr. W. Bingham HUNTER
11 Exec VP for Strategic Advancement .... Mr. Steve JOHNSON
32 Vice President Student Development ....Dr. Chip MOODY
20 Asst Dean Academic Services ....Ms. Roma ROYER
06 Registrar .... Mrs. Merry STENSON
84 Director Enroll & Student Service .... Mr. Jonathan GRIFFIN
10 Comptroller ....Mr. Eric BELMAR
08 Director of Library Services ....Mr. Doug OLBERT

Pima Community College (L)

4905 East Broadway Boulevard, Tucson AZ 85709-1005
County: Pima FICE Identification: 007266
Unit ID: 105525
Telephone: (520) 206-4500 Carnegie Class: Assoc/HT-Mix Trad/Non
FAX Number: (520) 206-4535 Calendar System: Semester
URL: www.pima.edu
Established: 1966 Annual Undergrad Tuition & Fees (In-District): $2,046
Enrollment: 26,880 Coed
Affiliation or Control: State/Local IRS Status: 501(c)3
Highest Offering: Associate Degree
Accreditation: NH, ADNUR, COARC, DA, DH, DT, EMT, MAC, MLTAD, RAD

01 Chancellor ....Mr. Lee D. LAMBERT
05 Provost/Chief Academic Ofcr ....Dr. Dolores DURAN-CERDA
10 Exec Vice Chanc for Finance/Admin ....Dr. David BEA
15 Vice Chanc for Human Resources .... Mr. Daniel BERRYMAN
26 Vice Chancellor External Relations .... Ms. Lisa BROSKY
18 Vice Chancellor Facilities ....Mr. Bill WARD
12 President Northwest Campus ....Dr. David DORE
12 President East Campus .... Dr. Lorraine MORALES
12 President Downtown Campus ....Dr. David DORE
12 President Community Campus ....Dr. Lorraine MORALES
12 President West Campus ....Dr. Morgan PHILLIPS
12 President Desert Vista Campus ....Dr. Morgan PHILLIPS
43 College General Counsel ....Mr. Jeffrey SILVYN
13 Asst Vice Chanc Information Tech ....Dr. Raj MURTHY
88 Asst Vice Chanc Accreditation ....Dr. Bruce MOSES
09 AVC Planning & Inst Research ....Dr. Nicola RICHMOND
84 AVC Enrollment Mgmt/Stdnt Affairs .... Dr. Karrie MITCHELL
21 Asst Vice Chanc Finance ....Mr. Terry QUEST
86 Exec Dir Media & Govt Rels ....Ms. Elizabeth HOWELL
19 Exec Dir Dept of Public Safety ....Mr. Christopher ALBERS
37 Exec Director of Financial Aid .... Ms. Melissa MOSER
28 Actg Diversity & Inclusion Officer ....Dr. Sofia RAMOS
76 Dean of Allied Health Programs .... Mr. James CRAIG
96 Director of Purchasing .... Mr. Mark DWORSCHAK
07 Acting Director & Registrar ....Mr. Michael TULINO
103 VP Workforce Development ....Dr. Ian ROARK
41 Dean of Athletics ....Mr. Edgar SOTO

Pima Community College Community Campus (M)

401 North Bonita Avenue, Tucson AZ 85709
Telephone: (520) 206-3933 Identification: 770016
Accreditation: &NH

Pima Community College Desert Vista Campus (N)

5901 South Calle Santa Cruz, Tucson AZ 85709
Telephone: (520) 206-5000 Identification: 770017
Accreditation: &NH, SURGT

Pima Community College Downtown Campus (O)

1255 North Stone Avenue, Tucson AZ 85709-3000
Telephone: (520) 206-7171 Identification: 770018
Accreditation: &NH

Pima Community College East Campus (P)

8181 East Arrington Road, Tucson AZ 85709-4000
Telephone: (520) 206-7000 Identification: 770019
Accreditation: &NH

Pima Community College Northwest Campus (Q)

7600 North Shannon Road, Tucson AZ 85709-7200
Telephone: (520) 206-2200 Identification: 770020
Accreditation: &NH

Pima Community College West Campus (R)

2202 West Alklam Road, Tucson AZ 85709-0001
Telephone: (520) 206-6600 Identification: 770021
Accreditation: &NH

Pima Medical Institute-East Valley (S)

2160 S Power Road, Mesa AZ 85209
Telephone: (480) 898-9898 Identification: 770515
Accreditation: ABHES

Pima Medical Institute-Mesa (T)

957 S Dobson Road, Mesa AZ 85202-2903
Telephone: (480) 644-0267 FICE Identification: 011570
Accreditation: ABHES, COARC, EMT, OTA, PTAA, RAD

Pima Medical Institute-Tucson (U)

3350 E Grant Road, Suite 200, Tucson AZ 85716-2932
County: Pima FICE Identification: 022171
Unit ID: 105534
Telephone: (520) 326-1600 Carnegie Class: Spec-4-yr-Other Health
FAX Number: (520) 326-4125 Calendar System: Other
URL: www.pmi.edu
Established: 1972 Annual Undergrad Tuition & Fees: N/A
Enrollment: 2,023 Coed
Affiliation or Control: Proprietary IRS Status: Proprietary
Highest Offering: Baccalaureate
Accreditation: ABHES, COARC, NURSE, OTA, PTAA, RAD

01 Director ....Mr. Dale BERG

Prescott College (V)

220 Grove Avenue, Prescott AZ 86301-2912
County: Yavapai FICE Identification: 020653
Unit ID: 105589
Telephone: (928) 350-2100 Carnegie Class: Masters/S
FAX Number: (928) 776-5137 Calendar System: Semester
URL: www.prescott.edu
Established: 1966 Annual Undergrad Tuition & Fees: $28,943
Enrollment: 819 Coed
Affiliation or Control: Independent Non-Profit IRS Status: 501(c)3
Highest Offering: Doctorate

Accreditation: NH

01 President .... Mr. John FLICKER
05 Executive Vice President & Provost .... Dr. Paul BURKHARDT
10 Chief Financial Officer .... Ms. Andrea JAECKEL
84 Chief Enrollment Management .... Dr. Stephanie KRUSEMARK
30 Chief Advancement Officer .... Mrs. Ashley HUST
32 Chief Student Affairs Officer .... Ms. Kristine PREZIOSI
124 Director of Student Retention .... Ms. Jerri BROWN
06 Registrar .... Ms. Bobbie DAVIDSON
04 Executive Assistant .... Ms. Cathy CHURCH
07 Director of Admissions .... Mr. David WHITE
09 Director of Institutional Research .... Ms. Mary Frances CAUSEY
15 Chief Human Resources Officer .... Mr. James MINER
35 Associate Student Affairs Officer .... Ms. Megan LETCHWORTH
18 Director of Facilities .... Mr. Greg LAZZELL
08 Director of Library .... Mr. Richard LEWIS
13 Dir Information Technology Services .... Mr. Eric WARTHAN
29 Director of Alumni Relations .... Ms. Marie SMITH
20 Associate Academic Officer .... Ms. Erin LOTZ

The Refrigeration School (A)

4210 E Washington Street, Phoenix AZ 85034-1816
County: Maricopa FICE Identification: 011689
Unit ID: 105659
Telephone: (602) 275-7133 Carnegie Class: Spec 2-yr-Tech
FAX Number: (602) 267-4805 Calendar System: Other
URL: www.refrigerationschool.com
Established: 1965 Annual Undergrad Tuition & Fees: N/A
Enrollment: 688 Coed
Affiliation or Control: Proprietary IRS Status: Proprietary
Highest Offering: Associate Degree
Accreditation: ACCSC

01 Campus President .... Mr. Stephen M. MALUTICH
37 Director of Financial Aid .... Ms. Melanie ZUVERINK
07 Director of Admissions .... Mr. John PALUMBO
05 Director of Education .... Mr. Greg HARRIS
10 Director of Accounting .... Mr. David FULFORD
06 Registrar .... Ms. Tara BOURLOTOS

Sessions College for Professional Design (B)

51 W. Third Street, Suite E-301, Tempe AZ 85281
County: Maricopa FICE Identification: 042176
Unit ID: 475839
Telephone: (480) 212-1704 Carnegie Class: Spec 2-yr-A&S
FAX Number: (480) 212-1705 Calendar System: Semester
URL: www.sessions.edu
Established: 1997 Annual Undergrad Tuition & Fees: $8,100
Enrollment: 124 Coed
Affiliation or Control: Proprietary IRS Status: Proprietary
Highest Offering: Associate Degree
Accreditation: DEAC

00 CEO .... Ms. Doris GRANATOWSKI
01 President .... Mr. Gordon DRUMMOND
03 Executive Vice President .... Mr. Louis J. SCHILT
11 Chief Operating Officer .... Mr. Robert TIMM
10 Chief Financial Officer/Bursar .... Ms. Carole Anne BAILO
32 Dir Student Services/Acad Pgms .... Mr. Tyler DRAKE

Sonoran Desert Institute (C)

8767 E. Via de Ventura, Suite 126,
Scottsdale AZ 85258-3376
County: Maricopa Identification: 667057
Telephone: (480) 314-2102 Carnegie Class: Not Classified
FAX Number: (480) 314-2138 Calendar System: Semester
URL: www.sdi.edu
Established: 2000 Annual Undergrad Tuition & Fees: N/A
Enrollment: N/A Coed
Affiliation or Control: Proprietary IRS Status: Proprietary
Highest Offering: Associate Degree
Accreditation: DEAC

01 President .... Traci LEE

Southwest College of Naturopathic Medicine & Health Sciences (D)

2140 E Broadway Road, Tempe AZ 85282-1751
County: Maricopa FICE Identification: 031070
Unit ID: 420246
Telephone: (480) 858-9100 Carnegie Class: Spec-4-yr-Other Health
FAX Number: (480) 858-9116 Calendar System: Quarter
URL: www.scnm.edu
Established: 1993 Annual Graduate Tuition & Fees: N/A
Enrollment: 385 Coed
Affiliation or Control: Independent Non-Profit IRS Status: 501(c)3
Highest Offering: First Professional Degree; No Undergraduates
Accreditation: NH, NATUR

01 President/Chief Executive Officer .... Paul A. MITTMAN
05 Dean of Academic Affairs .... Garrett THOMPSON
10 Vice Pres Finance & Administration .... Dawn RECTOR
32 Vice President Student Affairs .... Melissa WINQUIST
13 Chief IT Officer .... Mark LIERLEY
04 Administrative Asst to President .... Tracy LINDBERGH
06 Registrar .... Nancy NORMAN
07 Director of Admissions .... Eve ADAMS
08 Head Librarian .... Sally HARVEY
103 Dir Workforce/Career Development .... Joanna HAGAN
108 Director Institutional Assessment .... Tammy ARAGON

Southwest Institute of Healing Arts (E)

1100 E Apache Boulevard, Tempe AZ 85281-5822
County: Maricopa FICE Identification: 035933
Unit ID: 442879
Telephone: (480) 994-9244 Carnegie Class: Spec 2-yr-Health
FAX Number: (480) 994-3228 Calendar System: Other
URL: www.swiha.edu
Established: 1992 Annual Undergrad Tuition & Fees: N/A
Enrollment: 690 Coed
Affiliation or Control: Proprietary IRS Status: Proprietary
Highest Offering: Associate Degree
Accreditation: CNCE

01 President/Owner .... Mrs. K. C. MILLER
05 Exec Director of Online Education .... Mr. David DYE
10 Dir Finance & Human Res/Controller .... Ms. Salisha TAMANDL
32 Director Online Student Services .... Ms. Bernadett BILACH
07 Sr Admissions Advisor .... Ms. Janell ERICKSON
37 Director of Financial Aid .... Ms. Amber IMES
06 Registrar .... Ms. Frannie WALSH
35 Student Services Support Manager .... Ms. Angelica VALENZUELA

Southwest University of Visual Arts (F)

2525 N Country Club Road, Tucson AZ 85716-2505
County: Pima FICE Identification: 024915
Unit ID: 104188
Telephone: (520) 325-0123 Carnegie Class: Spec-4-yr-Arts
FAX Number: (520) 325-5535 Calendar System: Semester
URL: www.suva.edu
Established: 1983 Annual Undergrad Tuition & Fees: $23,069
Enrollment: 139 Coed
Affiliation or Control: Proprietary IRS Status: Proprietary
Highest Offering: Master's
Accreditation: NH

01 President/CEO .... Mrs. Sharmon WOODS
05 Chief Academic Officer .... Marvin WOODS
84 Dir Enr Mngt/Admissions/Stdnt Servs .... Mr. Rob MAIRS
11 Dir Admin Resources/HR .... Ms. Julie MAIRS
07 Asst Director of Enrollment Mgmt .... Ms. Joanne PILS
06 Registrar .... Ms. Crystal ROCHE

Tohono O'odham Community College (G)

PO Box 3129, Sells AZ 85634-3129
County: Pima FICE Identification: 037844
Unit ID: 442781
Telephone: (520) 383-8401 Carnegie Class: Tribal
FAX Number: (520) 383-0029 Calendar System: Semester
URL: www.tocc.edu
Established: 1998 Annual Undergrad Tuition & Fees: $842
Enrollment: 212 Coed
Affiliation or Control: Tribal Control IRS Status: 501(c)3
Highest Offering: Associate Degree
Accreditation: NH

01 President .... Dr. Paul ROBERTSON
05 Vice President for Education .... Ms. Juana Clare JOSE
10 Vice Pres Admin Services/Finance .... Ms. Karla VOLPI
32 Vice Pres of Student Services .... Ms. Sylvia HENDRICKS
46 Vice Pres Inst Research/Development .... Ms. Jane LATANE
75 Acad Chair Occupational Pgms .... Mr. George MIGUEL
97 Acad Chair for General Education .... Dr. Mario MONTES-HELU
07 Director of Admissions/Records .... Mr. Leslie LUNA
08 College Librarian .... Ms. Elaine CUBBINS
37 Director of Financial Aid .... Ms. Novia JAMES
88 Director Project NATIVE .... Ms. Camille MARTINEZ-YADEN
88 Director Project NATIVE .... Dr. Sandra LUCAS
30 Director of Fundraising .... Ms. Andrea AHMED
15 Human Resources Director .... Ms. Stacy OWSLEY
09 Dir Institutional Effectiveness .... Ms. Annabah CONN

Universal Technical Institute (H)

10695 W Pierce Street, Avondale AZ 85323-7946
County: Maricopa FICE Identification: 008221
Unit ID: 106041
Telephone: (623) 245-4600 Carnegie Class: Spec 2-yr-Tech
FAX Number: (623) 245-4601 Calendar System: Other
URL: www.uti.edu
Established: 1965 Annual Undergrad Tuition & Fees: N/A
Enrollment: 2,100 Coed
Affiliation or Control: Proprietary IRS Status: Proprietary
Highest Offering: Associate Degree
Accreditation: ACCSC

01 Campus President .... Mr. Michael ROMANO
05 Director of Education .... Mr. Patrick BENNETT
32 Director of Student Services .... Ms. Lindsay KINGSLEY
10 Director of Campus Accounting .... Mrs. Gayle PARSONS
07 Admissions Director .... Mr. Adam HELLER
36 Director of Graduate Employment .... Ms. Cheryl RADKE
37 Director of Financial Aid .... Ms. Terri MEIXSEL-CORDERO
18 Maintenance Director .... Mr. George MICKENS

University of Advancing Technology (I)

2625 W Baseline Road, Tempe AZ 85283-1056
County: Maricopa FICE Identification: 025590
Unit ID: 363934
Telephone: (602) 383-8228 Carnegie Class: Spec-4-yr-Other Tech
FAX Number: (602) 383-8250 Calendar System: Other
URL: www.uat.edu
Established: 1983 Annual Undergrad Tuition & Fees: $21,064
Enrollment: 724 Coed
Affiliation or Control: Proprietary IRS Status: Proprietary
Highest Offering: Master's
Accreditation: NH

01 President .... Mr. Jason PISTILLO
05 Provost and Dean .... Mr. Dave BOLMAN
100 Chief of Staff .... Ms. Valerie CIMAROSSA
07 Director of Admissions .... Ms. Megan BENSON
10 Senior Controller .... Ms. Jodi ROBINSON

University of Arizona (J)

1401 E University Blvd, Tucson AZ 85721-0001
County: Pima FICE Identification: 001083
Unit ID: 104179
Telephone: (520) 621-2211 Carnegie Class: DU-Highest
FAX Number: (520) 621-9323 Calendar System: Semester
URL: www.arizona.edu
Established: 1885 Annual Undergrad Tuition & Fees (In-State): $11,769
Enrollment: 42,595 Coed
Affiliation or Control: State IRS Status: 501(c)3
Highest Offering: Doctorate
Accreditation: NH, ANEST, ART, AUD, CACREP, CEA, CLPSY, CS, DANCE, DIETD, ENG, ENGR, IPSY, JOUR, LAW, LIB, LSAR, MED, MUS, NURSE, PCSAS, PERF, PH, PHAR, PLNG, SCPSY, SP, SPAA, THEA

01 President .... Dr. Robert C. ROBBINS
05 Sr VP for Acad Affairs & Provost .... Dr. Andrew C. COMRIE
10 Sr VP and CFO/Business Affairs .... Mr. Gregg GOLDMAN
26 Sr VP University Relations .... Dr. Teresa THOMPSON
17 Sr VP Health Sciences .... Dr. Joe GARCIA
32 Sr VP Student Affairs & Enroll Mgmt .... Dr. Melissa VITO
46 Sr VP for Research .... Dr. Kimberly A. ESPY
41 VP and Director Athletics .... Mr. Gregory K. BYRNE
88 VP Strategic Planning & Analysis .... Dr. Barbara BRYSON
43 VP Legal Affs/General Counsel .... Dr. Laura T. JOHNSON
88 VP Global Initiatives .... Dr. Michael A. PROCTOR
49 VP Innovation & Strategy .... Dr. Joaquin RUIZ
21 VP Business Affairs .... Mr. Robert R. SMITH
29 VP Alumni Relations .... Ms. Melinda W. BURKE
15 VP Institutional Effectiveness & HR .... Dr. Allison M. VAILLANCOURT
88 VP Digital Learning/Student Engmnt .... Mr. Vincent J. DEL CASINO
88 VP Tech Launch AZ .... Dr. David N. ALLEN
27 VP Communications .... Mr. Chris W. SIGURDSON
07 VP/Std Aff/Enr Mgmt/Dean Adm .... Dr. Kasandra K. URQUIDEZ
88 Vice Provost Faculty Affairs .... Dr. Thomas P. MILLER
47 V Provost/Dean Agri/Life Sci .... Dr. Shane C. BURGESS
20 Sr Vice Provost Academic Affairs .... Dr. Gail D. BURD
86 Sr Assoc VP Legis & Comm Relations .... Mr. Timothy S. BEE
88 Sr Assoc VP Health Sciences .... Mr. Mike JONEN
88 Sr Assoc to the Pres/Secretary Univ .... Dr. Jon DUDAS
88 Assoc VP External Relations-Phoenix .... Ms. Judith A. BERNAS
88 Assoc VP Research .... Ms. Caroline M. GARCIA
88 Assoc VP for Research .... Dr. Jennifer K. BARTON
88 Assoc VP Health Sci-Interprof Educ .... Dr. Sally J. REEL
88 Assoc VP Precision Health Sciences .... Mr. Kenneth RAMOS
88 Assoc VP Clinical Affairs .... Mr. Steven GOLDSCHMID
88 Assoc VP Institutional Analysis .... Mr. James S. FLORIAN
88 Assoc VP Tech Parks Arizona .... Mr. Bruce A. WRIGHT
88 Assoc VP Marketing/Brand Mgmt .... Mr. Michael A. PROUDFOOT
88 Assoc VP & Chief Health Sci Develop .... Ms. Jennifer L. FLORES
108 Assoc Vice Provost Instruc/Assess .... Dr. Debra J. TOMANEK
88 Assoc VP Federal Relations .... Mr. Shay D. STAUTZ
88 Assoc VP Population Health Sciences .... Ms. Elizabeth CALHOUN
88 Assoc VP Research .... Mr. Neal R. ARMSTRONG
88 Interim Assoc VP Financial Services .... Mr. Duc D. MA
13 Int CIO/Exec Dir UITS/Dean of Lib .... Ms. Karen A. WILLIAMS
88 Sr Asst VP Finance Administration .... Ms. Marilyn TAYLOR
35 Asst VP Student Affs/Enroll Mgmt .... Mr. Joel S. HAUFF
09 Asst Provost Inst Research .... Dr. Angela Y. BALDASARE
18 Asst VP Plng/Design & Construction .... Mr. Peter DOURLEIN
88 Asst VP Tribal Relations .... Ms. Karen F. BEGAY
88 Asst VP Program Innovation .... Dr. Randy M. BURD
31 Asst VP Community Relations .... Ms. Tannya R. GAXIOLA GAXIOLA
88 Asst VP Health Sciences/Pub Affairs .... Mr. George D. HUMPHREY
88 Asst VP Budget .... Ms. Kathryn E. WHISMAN
88 Asst VP Admin Systems Integration .... Mr. Barry T. BRUMMUND
88 Asst VP Hemispheric Programs .... Mr. Francisco J. MARMOLEJO
18 Asst VP Facilities Management .... Mr. Christopher M. KOPACH
19 Asst VP Risk Management/Safety .... Mr. Steven C. HOLLAND
88 Asst VP Finance & Administration .... Ms. Karen L. TUMLINSON
88 Asst VP Divisional Initiatives .... Ms. Jennifer M. PICKARD
06 Asst VP Registrar/Enrollment Mgmt .... Dr. Elizabeth A. ACREE

88 Asst VP Govt Affairs ... Mr. Ethan R. ORR
83 Dean Social/Behav Science ... Dr. John P. JONES
88 Asst VP Dean of Students . Ms. Kendal H. WASHINGTON WHITE
92 Dean Honors College ... Dr. Patricia MACCORQUODALE
48 Dean Col Arch & Landscape Arch ... Dr. Janice A. CERVELLI
53 Dean Education ... Dr. Ronald W. MARX
58 Dean Graduate College ... Dr. Andrew H. CARNIE
61 Dean James E Rogers College of Law ... Dr. Marc L. MILLER
66 Dean College of Nursing ... Dr. Joan L. SHAVER
12 Dean UA South ... Dr. James W. SHOCKEY
79 Dean College of Humanities ... Dr. Mary E. WILDNER-BASSETT
57 Dean Fine Arts ... Dr. Jory L. HANCOCK
54 Dean College of Engineering ... Dr. Jeffrey B. GOLDBERG
50 Dean Eller College of Management .. Dr. Jeffrey W. SCHATZBERG
69 Dean Public Health ... Dr. Iman A. HAKIM
63 Interim Dean College of Medicine ... Dr. Charles B. CAIRNS
63 Dean College of Med-Phoenix Campus ... Dr. Stuart D. FLYNN
81 Dean College of Optical Sciences ... Dr. Thomas L. KOCH
67 Dean Pharmacy ... Dr. J. L. BOOTMAN
22 Dir Office of Institutional Equity ... Ms. Mary E. TUCKER
36 Exec Director Career Services ... Ms. Eileen M. MCGARRY
40 Exec Director Univ of AZ Bookstores ... Ms. Debby L. SHIVELY
88 Exec Director Campus Health ... Mr. Harry MCDERMOTT
88 Exec Dir Analytics & Inst Research ... Mr. Henry A. CHILDERS
96 Dir Procurement & Contract Services ... Mr. Edward D. NASSER
25 Director Sponsored Proj/Services ... Ms. Sherry L. ESHAM
85 Director International Admissions ... Dr. Rachel A. BEECH

University of Arizona Phoenix Biomedical Campus (A)

550 E Van Buren Street, Phoenix AZ 85004
Telephone: (602) 827-2001 Identification: 770023
Accreditation: &NH, MED, PHAR

University of Arizona South (B)

1140 N Colombo Avenue, Sierra Vista AZ 85635
Telephone: (520) 458-8278 Identification: 770024
Accreditation: &NH

University of Phoenix (C)

1625 W. Fountainhead Parkway, Tempe AZ 85282
County: Maricopa FICE Identification: 020988
Unit ID: 484613
Telephone: (480) 557-2000 Carnegie Class: Not Classified
FAX Number: N/A Calendar System: Other
URL: www.phoenix.edu
Established: 1976 Annual Undergrad Tuition & Fees: $9,690
Enrollment: 165,743 Coed
Affiliation or Control: Proprietary IRS Status: Proprietary
Highest Offering: Doctorate
Accreditation: NH, ACBSP, CACREP, NURSE

01 President University of Phoenix ... Mr. Peter COHEN
04 Assistant to the President ... Ms. Cindy WHIPPO
05 Provost ... Dr. Meredith CURLEY
03 Chief Operating Officer ... Mr. Raghu KRISHNAIAH
09 Vice Provost Inst Effectiveness ... Dr. Kathleen SCHNIER
100 Chief of Staff ... Dr. Sherri ONDRUS
10 Chief Financial Officer ... Mr. Byron JONES
15 Chief Human Resources ... Ms. Cheryl NAUMANN
26 Chief Marketing Officer ... Ms. Joan BLACKWOOD
13 Chief Information Officer ... Mr. Mike SAJOR
53 Exec Dean College of Education ... Dr. Andy DROTOS
50 Exec Dean School of Business ... Ms. Ruth VELORIA
88 Exec Dean Sch of Advanced Studies ... Dr. Hinrich EYLERS
76 Exec Dean Col of Health Prof ... Ms. Doris SAVRON
72 Exec Dean Info Systems/Technology ... Mr. Dennis BONILLA
79 Exec Dean Col of Humanities & Sci ... Dr. Constance ST. GERMAIN
83 Exec Dean Col of Social Sciences ... Dr. Constance ST. GERMAIN
88 SVP Academic Operations ... Dr. Russ PADEN
37 SVP Student Administrative Services ... Mr. Jeff SONNENBERG
88 SVP Campus Services ... Mr. Matt JOHNSTON
84 SVP Enrollment Services ... Mr. Ron KISHEN
21 VP Financial Services ... Mr. Bronson LEDBETTER
06 Registrar ... Ms. Audra MCQUARIE

University of Phoenix Southern Arizona Campus (D)

300 S Craycroft Road, Tucson AZ 85711-4574
Telephone: (520) 881-6512 Identification: 770236
Accreditation: &NH, ACBSP

West Coast Ultrasound Institute (E)

4250 E Camelback Road, #K158, Phoenix AZ 85018
Telephone: (602) 954-3834 Identification: 770550
Accreditation: ACCSC

† Branch campus of West Coast Ultrasound Institute, Beverly Hills, CA

Western International University (F)

1601 W. Fountainhead Parkway, Tempe AZ 85282
County: Maricopa FICE Identification: 021715
Unit ID: 106102
Telephone: (602) 943-2311 Carnegie Class: Spec-4-yr-Bus
FAX Number: (602) 371-8637 Calendar System: Other
URL: www.west.edu
Established: 1978 Annual Undergrad Tuition & Fees: $6,000
Enrollment: 1,301 Coed
Affiliation or Control: Proprietary IRS Status: Proprietary
Highest Offering: Master's
Accreditation: NH

01 President ... Ms. Tracy LORENZ
05 Provost ... Dr. Christopher DAVIS
10 CFO ... Ms. Heidi PHIPPS
32 Sr Dir Student Admin Svcs/Registrar ... Ms. Beth CARLISLE

† In teach-out mode.

Yavapai College (G)

1100 E Sheldon Street, Prescott AZ 86301-3297
County: Yavapai FICE Identification: 001079
Unit ID: 106148
Telephone: (928) 445-7300 Carnegie Class: Assoc/MT-VT-Mix Trad/Non
FAX Number: (928) 776-2109 Calendar System: Semester
URL: www.yc.edu
Established: 1966 Annual Undergrad Tuition & Fees (In-District): $2,280
Enrollment: 7,385 Coed
Affiliation or Control: Local IRS Status: 501(c)3
Highest Offering: Associate Degree
Accreditation: NH, ADNUR, EMT, IFSAC, RAD

01 President ... Dr. Penelope WILLS
05 VP Instruction/Stdnt Dev ... Dr. Ron LISS
10 Vice Pres Finance/Admin Svcs ... Dr. Clint EWELL
26 VP Community Relations ... Mr. Rodney JENKINS
20 Dean for Comp Tech & Instr Support ... Ms. Stacey HILTON
12 Exec Dean Verde Valley Campus ... Dr. James PEREY
75 Dean Career Technical Education ... Mr. John MORGAN
66 Dean Sci/Health/Public Safety ... Mr. Scott FARNSWORTH
79 Dir of Performing Arts Center ... Dr. Craig RALSTON
32 Assoc VP for Student Development ... Ms. Tania SHELDAHL
27 Director of Marketing/Public Info ... Mr. Kim KAPIN
37 Assoc Dean Stdnt Dev & Dir Fin Aid ... Ms. Diana DOWLING
09 Dir Inst Effectiveness & Research ... Mr. Tom HUGHES
15 Director for Human Resources ... Dr. Monica BELKNAP
19 Chief of Police ... Mr. Jerald MONAHAN
21 Dir of Business Svcs & Controller ... Mr. Frank D'ANGELO
07 Recruitment Officer ... Vacant
18 Director for Facilities ... Mr. David LAURENCE
13 Chief Information Officer ... Mr. Patrick BURNS
06 Registrar ... Ms. Sheila JARRELL
96 Director of Purchasing ... Mr. Ryan BOUWHUIS
04 Administrative Asst to President ... Ms. Karen JONES

Yavapai College Verde Valley Campus (H)

601 Black Hills Drive, Clarkdale AZ 86324
Telephone: (928) 634-7501 Identification: 770029
Accreditation: &NH

ARKANSAS

Arkansas Baptist College (I)

1621 Martin Luther King Drive, Little Rock AR 72202-6099
County: Pulaski FICE Identification: 001087
Unit ID: 106306
Telephone: (501) 370-4000 Carnegie Class: Bac/Assoc-Mixed
FAX Number: (501) 372-7992 Calendar System: Semester
URL: www.arkansasbaptist.edu
Established: 1884 Annual Undergrad Tuition & Fees: $8,760
Enrollment: 990 Coed
Affiliation or Control: Baptist IRS Status: 501(c)3
Highest Offering: Baccalaureate
Accreditation: NH

01 President ... Dr. Joseph JONES
05 Sr VP of Academic Affairs ... Dr. Sherlynn HALL
04 President's Executive Assistant ... Ms. Patsy BIGGS
10 Chief Finance Officer ... Ms. Shayla LOWE
11 Vice President Administration ... Dr. Mark PERRY
84 VP of Enrollment Management ... Dr. Tracey MOORE
100 Chief of Staff ... Mrs. LaCresha NEWTON
09 Director of Institutional Research ... Dr. Jerelyn L. DUNCAN
07 Director of Admissions/Recruitment ... Mr. Willie HICKS
88 Ombudsman ... Dr. Vicki WILLIAMS
37 Int Director of Financial Aid ... Ms. Charlotte COMER
08 Director of Library/Media Services ... Dr. Wille HARDIN
26 Dir College Relations/Marketing ... Mrs. Linda GILLAM WEIR
32 Dean of Students ... Ms. Tameka HARPER
19 Chief of Campus Safety ... Mr. Curtis JOHNSON
18 Director Facilities/Maintenance ... Mr. Larry THOMPSON
06 Registrar ... Dr. Jerelyn DUNCAN

Arkansas College of Osteopathic Medicine (J)

7000 Chad Colley Blvd, Fort Smith AR 72916
County: Sebastion FICE Identification: 042568
Unit ID: 488527
Telephone: (479) 308-2200 Carnegie Class: Not Classified
FAX Number: (479) 308-2766 Calendar System: Semester
URL: arcomed.org
Established: 2017 Annual Graduate Tuition & Fees: N/A
Enrollment: N/A Coed
Affiliation or Control: Independent Non-Profit IRS Status: 501(c)3
Highest Offering: Doctorate; No Undergraduates
Accreditation: @OSTEO

05 Dean/VP/Chief Academic Officer ... Kenneth A. HEILES

Arkansas Northeastern College (K)

2501 S Division Street, Blytheville AR 72315-5111
County: Mississippi FICE Identification: 012860
Unit ID: 107327
Telephone: (870) 762-1020 Carnegie Class: Assoc/HVT-Mix Trad/Non
FAX Number: (870) 763-3704 Calendar System: Semester
URL: www.anc.edu
Established: 1974 Annual Undergrad Tuition & Fees (In-District): $2,206
Enrollment: 1,361 Coed
Affiliation or Control: State/Local IRS Status: 501(c)3
Highest Offering: Associate Degree
Accreditation: NH, DA, EMT

01 President ... Dr. James SHEMWELL
05 Executive Vice President/CAO ... Mrs. June WALTERS
10 Vice President for Adminstration ... Mr. Don RAY
88 Vice Pres for College Readiness ... Mrs. Sherri BENNETT
13 Vice President Student Affairs/IT ... Mr. James W. MCCLAIN
26 Assoc VP for Dev/College Relations ... Ms. Rachel GIFFORD
09 Dean Efectiveness/Assess/Planning ... Mrs. Robin SINGLETON
20 Associate Vice Pres/Asst CAO ... Mrs. Deborah PARKER
88 Assoc VP for Economic Development ... Mr. Gene BENNETT
21 Assoc Vice President for Finance ... Ms. Pacey BOWENS
66 Dean Nursing/Allied Hlth/PE/Rec ... Mrs. Brenda HOLIFIELD
49 Dean for Arts and Sciences ... Mrs. Deanita HICKS
32 Director for Student Services ... Mrs. Courtney FISHER
31 Community Education Specialist ... Ms. Mary Ann GARREN
08 Director of College Library/AV ... Ms. Karen ELLIS
36 Director ACE Advising Center ... Dr. Bridget SHEMWELL
37 Director Financial Aid ... Mrs. Melinda WALKER
72 Associate Dean MITS ... Mrs. Ruby MEADOR
21 Controller ... Mrs. Melissa ANDREW
15 Human Resources & ADA Coordinator ... Mrs. Tabatha HAMPTON
90 Director Academic Tech Services ... Mr. James ODOM
18 Director Physical Plant and Grounds ... Mr. Scott CREECY
88 Director Talent Search/Educ Opp Ctr ... Mrs. Tonya HARRIS
35 Director Student Support Services ... Ms. Lisa MCGHEE
04 Assistant to Board/President ... Ms. Jody HIPWELL
06 Registrar ... Mrs. Rosemary LOWE

*Arkansas State University System (L)

501 Woodlane Drive, Suite 600, Little Rock AR 72201
County: Pulaski Identification: 666187
Telephone: (501) 660-1000 Carnegie Class: N/A
FAX Number: (501) 660-1010
URL: www.asusystem.edu

01 President ... Dr. Charles L. WELCH
04 Exec Assistant to the President ... Ms. Pam KAIL
10 Executive Vice President ... Ms. Julie BATES
86 Vice Pres Governmental Relations ... Mr. Shane BROADWAY
45 Vice Pres Strategic Comm/Econ Dev ... Mr. Jeff HANKINS
102 President ASU System Foundation ... Mr. Philip JACKSON
43 Legal Counsel ... Ms. Lucinda MCDANIEL
116 Internal Auditor ... Ms. Jo LUNBECK

*Arkansas State University-Beebe (M)

PO Box 1000, Beebe AR 72012-1000
County: White FICE Identification: 001091
Unit ID: 106449
Telephone: (501) 882-3600 Carnegie Class: Assoc/MT-VT-High Non
FAX Number: (501) 882-8970 Calendar System: Semester
URL: www.asub.edu
Established: 1927 Annual Undergrad Tuition & Fees (In-State): $3,480
Enrollment: 3,935 Coed
Affiliation or Control: State IRS Status: 501(c)3
Highest Offering: Associate Degree
Accreditation: NH, EMT, MLTAD, NAIT

02 Interim Chancellor ... Dr. Roger L. MOORE
100 Executive Assistant to Chancellor ... Ms. Pam JONES
12 Vice Chancellor ASU-Heber Springs ... Dr. James C. BOYETT
12 Vice Chancellor of ASU-Searcy ... Mr. Barry FARRIS
05 Vice Chancellor Academic Affairs ... Dr. Theodore J. KALTHOFF
32 Vice Chancellor Student Services ... Dr. Deborah A. GARRETT
10 Vice Chanc Finance/Administration ... Dr. Roger MOORE
13 VC Information Technology Services ... Mr. Chris LEE
30 Vice Chanc Advancement ... Ms. Rose Mary JACKSON
15 Assoc VC Human Resources ... Ms. Susan A. COLLIE
21 Assoc VP Business Operations ... Ms. Charlette MOORE
26 Exec Director of Marketing/PR ... Mr. Keith MOORE
06 University Registrar ... Ms. Amy J. MAHAN
08 Library Director ... Ms. Tracy D. SMITH
19 Chief of Police ... Mr. James J. MARTIN
18 Director of Physical Plant ... Mr. Jerry L. THOMPSON
37 Director Student Financial Aid ... Ms. Louise DRIVER
09 Director of Institutional Research ... Ms. Bonnie SMYTH-MCGAHA
21 Controller ... Ms. Sharon A. BEEN
35 Assoc VC/Dean Student Affairs ... Mr. David M. MAYES
72 Director Advanced Tech/Allied Hlth ... Mr. Michael TROOP
106 Director of Distance Learning ... Ms. Rhonda DURHAM
96 Executive Director Procurement ... Ms. Robin LANCASTER
12 Dir ASU-Beebe Degree Ctr at LRAFB . Ms. Nancy A. SHEFFLETTE
07 Director of Admissions ... Ms. Robin A. HAYES
35 Manager of Campus Relations ... Mr. Andy ISOM

105 Webmaster .... Mr. Rikky L. FREE
88 Coord Concurrent Enrollment .... Ms. Kristine PENIX
24 Learning Center Coordinator .... Ms. Kayla DEAN

*Arkansas State University-Jonesboro (A)

PO Box 600, State University AR 72467
County: Craighead FICE Identification: 001090
Unit ID: 106458
Telephone: (870) 972-2100 Carnegie Class: Masters/L
FAX Number: (870) 972-3465 Calendar System: Semester
URL: www.astate.edu
Established: 1909 Annual Undergrad Tuition & Fees (In-State): $8,200
Enrollment: 13,410 Coed
Affiliation or Control: State IRS Status: 501(c)3
Highest Offering: Doctorate
Accreditation: NH, ADNUR, ANEST, ART, #CAATE, CACREP, CAEPN, CEA, DIETC, DMS, ENG, JOUR, MLTAD, MT, MUS, NUR, OTA, PTA, PTAA, RAD, RADMAG, RTT, SP, SPAA, SW, THEA

02 Chancellor .... Dr. Kelly DAMPHOUSSE
05 Provost & VC Acad Affair & Research .... Dr. Lynita COOKSEY
10 VC Finance & Administration .... Dr. Len T. FREY
32 Vice Chancellor Student Affairs .... Dr. William R. STRIPLING
111 Vice Chancellor Univ Advancement .... Dr. Jason PENRY
28 Asst Vice Chancellor Diversity .... Dr. Maurice GIPSON
41 Director of Athletics .... Mr. Terry MOHAJIR
20 Sr Assoc Vice Chancellor AAR .... Dr. Karen WHEELER
21 Assoc Vice Chancellor Finance .... Dr. Russ HANNAH
114 Asst Vice Chanc Budget .... Ms. Donna MCMILLIN
15 Asst VC Human Resources .... Ms. Lori WINN
35 Assoc Vice Chanc Student Affairs .... Dr. Lonnie R. WILLIAMS
46 Assoc Vice Chancellor Research .... Dr. Andrew SUSTICH
35 Asst Vice Chanc Student Affairs .... Dr. Craig JOHNSON
13 Asst Vice Chanc/CIO .... Mr. Henry TORRES
18 Asst Vice Chancellor Facilities .... Mr. David HANDWORK
84 Asst Vice Chanc Enrollment Services .... Mr. Terry FINNEY
108 Asst VC Institutional Effectiveness .... Dr. Fnu MIHIR
06 Dir Admissions/Records/Registration .... Ms. Tracy FINCH
07 Admissions/Records/Registration .... Mr. Christopher BOOTHMAN
39 Director of Residence Life .... Mr. Patrick DIXON
88 Director of Leadership Center .... Ms. Martha SPACK
19 Chief University Police .... Mr. Randy MARTIN
22 Director of Disability Services .... Dr. Jenifer RICE-MASON
36 Director Career Services .... Vacant
38 Director Counseling Center .... Dr. Phil HESTAND
23 Director Student Health Center .... Ms. Victoria WILLIAMS
29 Exec Dir Alumni Relations .... Ms. Lindsay BURNETT
26 Assoc VC University Marketing/Comm .... Dr. Bill SMITH
27 Director of Media Relations/Comm .... Ms. Gina BOWMAN
88 Director Pub & Creative Services .... Mr. Mark REEVES
96 Dir Procurement & Travel Svcs .... Ms. Carol BARNHILL
04 Admin Assistant to the Chancellor .... Ms. Julie WYATT
08 Dir Library .... Mr. Jeff BAILEY
47 Dean College Agri/Engineering/Tech .... Dr. Timothy BURCHAM
81 Int Dean College Sciences & Math .... Dr. Anne GRIPPO
50 Interim Dean College of Business .... Dr. Kathy LOYD
53 Dean Col of Educ & Behavioral Sci .... Dr. Mary Jane BRADLEY
60 Dean Liberal Arts & Communication .... Dr. Carl CATES
66 Dean College of Nursing Health Prof .... Dr. Susan N. HANRAHAN
88 Assoc VC Undergraduate Studies .... Dr. Jill SIMONS
57 Dean Fine Arts .... Vacant
92 Director of The Honors College .... Ms. Rebecca OLIVER
54 Dean College of Engineering .... Vacant

*Arkansas State University-Mid-South (B)

2000 W Broadway, West Memphis AR 72301-3829
County: Crittenden FICE Identification: 023482
Unit ID: 107318
Telephone: (870) 733-6722 Carnegie Class: Assoc/HVT-High Non
FAX Number: (870) 733-6799 Calendar System: Semester
URL: www.asumidsouth.edu
Established: 1992 Annual Undergrad Tuition & Fees (In-District): $2,554
Enrollment: 1,896 Coed
Affiliation or Control: State/Local IRS Status: 501(c)3
Highest Offering: Associate Degree
Accreditation: NH, #COARC

02 Chancellor .... Dr. Debra WEST
05 Sr Vice Chanc Learning/Instruction .... Dr. Cliff JONES
10 Vice Chanc Finance & Administration .... Ms. JaNan ABERNATHY
111 Vice Chanc Inst Advancement .... Ms. Diane HAMPTON
32 Vice Chanc Student Affairs .... Mr. Jeremy REECE
103 AVC Workforce Education .... Mr. Pete SELDEN
21 AVC Finance .... Ms. Karyn WEAVER
20 AVC Learning/Instruction .... Ms. Roshell COLEMAN
37 Interim Director of Financial Aid .... Ms. Crystal BURGER
08 Director of Library/Media Center .... Ms. Rene JONES
06 Registrar .... Ms. Leslie ANDERSON
15 Director of Human Resources .... Ms. Jackie LEECH
18 Director Facilities/Physical Plant .... Vacant
84 AVC Enrollment Management .... Mr. John EASLEY
35 AVC Student Success .... Dr. Derek MOORE
13 AVC for Information Systems Tech .... Mr. Ernesto MUNIZ
45 AVC Strategic Initiatives .... Dr. Callie DUNAVIN
09 AVC Institutional Research .... Ms. Michelle MCMILLEN
121 Dir of Learning Success Center .... Mr. Brice JAMES-BATTELLE
04 Administrative Asst to Chancellor .... Ms. Emilee SIDES

19 Director Public Safety .... Mr. Ross PROCTOR
25 Chief Contracts/Grants Admin .... Ms. Sherri REID
41 Athletic Director .... Mr. Chris PARKER
30 Director of Development .... Ms. Debbie YEN
90 Instructional Tech Coordinator .... Ms. Melissa POWERS
96 Business Manager .... Ms. Wendy CRAWFORD

*Arkansas State University-Mountain Home (C)

1600 S College Street, Mountain Home AR 72653-5326
County: Baxter Identification: 666311
Unit ID: 420538
Telephone: (870) 508-6100 Carnegie Class: Assoc/MT-VT-High Non
FAX Number: (870) 508-6287 Calendar System: Semester
URL: www.asumh.edu
Established: 1995 Annual Undergrad Tuition & Fees (In-District): $2,784
Enrollment: 1,384 Coed
Affiliation or Control: State/Local IRS Status: 501(c)3
Highest Offering: Associate Degree
Accreditation: NH, EMT, FUSER

02 Chancellor .... Dr. Robin MYERS
05 Vice Chanc Academic Affairs .... Dr. Martin EGGENSPERGER
10 Vice Chanc Administrative Affairs .... Ms. Laura YARBROUGH
18 Chief Facilities/Physical Plant .... Mr. Nickey L. ROBBINS
26 Director Comm & Inst Advancement .... Mrs. Christy C. KEIRN
32 Director Student Affairs .... Mr. Mason CAMPBELL
37 Director Student Financial Aid .... Mr. Clay BERRY
08 Director of Library .... Ms. Tina BRADLEY
09 Dir of Inst Research/Effectiveness .... Mr. David CULLIPHER
07 Admissions Coordinator .... Mr. Christopher CONSTANTINE

*Arkansas State University-Newport (D)

7648 Victory Boulevard, Newport AR 72112-8912
County: Jackson Identification: 666153
Unit ID: 440402
Telephone: (870) 512-7800 Carnegie Class: Assoc/HVT-High Non
FAX Number: (870) 512-7807 Calendar System: Semester
URL: www.asun.edu
Established: 2001 Annual Undergrad Tuition & Fees (In-State): $2,689
Enrollment: 2,651 Coed
Affiliation or Control: State IRS Status: Exempt
Highest Offering: Associate Degree
Accreditation: NH, SURGT

02 Chancellor .... Dr. Sandra MASSEY
04 Assistant to the Chancellor .... Ms. Laura KING
05 Vice Chancellor Academic Affairs .... Dr. Holly AYERS
10 Vice Chancellor Finance & Admin .... Mr. Adam ADAIR
32 Vice Chancellor Student Affairs .... Dr. Ashley BUCHMAN
103 Vice Chancellor Econ/Workforce Dev .... Mr. Charley APPLEBY
45 Vice Chanc Strategic Initiatives .... Mr. Jeff BOOKOUT
30 Dean for Community Engagement .... Mr. Ike WHEELER
09 Dean of Institutional Effectiveness .... Dr. Allen MOONEYHAN
72 Dean for Applied Science .... Mr. Robert SUMMERS
97 Dean for General Education .... Mr. Joeseph CAMPBELL
84 Dean of Enrollment Services .... Ms. Candace GROSS
13 Director of IT Services .... Ms. Tamya STALLINGS
15 Director Human Resources .... Ms. Sara MOSS
06 Assistant Registrar .... Ms. Phyllis WORTHINGTON
18 Director of Physical Plant .... Mr. David WINSTON
21 Controller .... Ms. Monika PHILLIPS
37 Director Financial Aid .... Ms. Bonnie BURGOYNE
35 Dean of Students .... Ms. Kimberly LONG
08 Librarian .... Ms. Jennifer BALLARD
20 Director Academic Support Center .... Ms. Christy MANN
19 Chief of Police .... Mr. Johnathan TUBBS
96 Director of Procurement .... Ms. Lee WEBB
66 Dean of Nursing/Allied Health .... Ms. Crystal GILLIHAN
36 Director of Career Pathways .... Ms. Scott HINSON
75 Director of Adult Education .... Ms. Martha TAUSSIG
26 Director of Marketing/PR .... Mr. Jeremy SHIRLEY
88 Advancement Officer .... Ms. Teriann TURNER

*Arkansas State University-Heber Springs (E)

101 River Crest Drive, Heber Springs AR 72543
Telephone: (501) 362-1100 Identification: 770001
Accreditation: &NH

*Arkansas State University-Searcy (F)

1800 East Monroe Avenue, Searcy AR 72143
Telephone: (501) 207-6200 Identification: 770002
Accreditation: &NH

Arkansas Tech University (G)

1509 North Boulder Avenue, Russellville AR 72801-2222
County: Pope FICE Identification: 001089
Unit ID: 106467
Telephone: (479) 968-0389 Carnegie Class: Masters/L
FAX Number: (479) 964-0522 Calendar System: Semester
URL: www.atu.edu
Established: 1909 Annual Undergrad Tuition & Fees (In-State): $6,624
Enrollment: 12,054 Coed
Affiliation or Control: State IRS Status: 501(c)3
Highest Offering: Doctorate
Accreditation: NH, CAEPN, CAHIIM, CEA, CS, ENG, MAC, MUS, NRPA, NUR, PTAA

01 President .... Dr. Robin E. BOWEN
10 Vice Pres Administration/Finance .... Ms. Bernadette HINKLE
05 Vice Pres Academic Affairs .... Dr. Mohamed ABDELRAHMAN
32 VP Student Services .... Dr. Keegan NICHOLS
30 Vice President Advancement .... Mr. Michael V. HUTCHISON
12 Chancellor Ozark Campus .... Mr. Bruce SIKES
20 Assoc Vice Pres Academic Affairs .... Dr. David UNDERWOOD
43 Associate VP & Counsel to President .... Mr. Thomas PENNINGTON
88 Assoc VP University Initiatives .... Dr. Rick MASSENGALE
110 Associate VP for Development .... Mr. Bryan FISHER
20 Assistant VP for Student Success .... Dr. Jason WARNICK
84 Assistant VP Enrollment Management .... Ms. Shauna H. DONNELL
35 Dean of Students .... Ms. Amy PENNINGTON
35 Chief Student Officer Ozark Campus .... Mr. Richard HARRIS
05 Chief Academic Officer Ozark Campus .... Dr. Michael MURDERS
10 Chief Fiscal Officer Ozark Campus .... Ms. Sandra CHEFFER
100 Chief of Staff .... Dr. Jeff MOTT
06 Registrar .... Ms. Tammy WEAVER
88 Controller .... Ms. Donna RANKIN
08 Librarian .... Mr. Brent ETZEL
09 Director of Institutional Research .... Mr. Wyatt WATSON
13 Director Information Systems .... Mr. Ken WESTER
37 Director of Student Accounts .... Ms. Angela CROW
15 Director of Human Resources .... Mr. Robert FREEMAN
37 Director Student Financial Aid .... Ms. Niki SCHWARTZ
29 Director Alumni Relations .... Mr. Kelly DAVIS
85 Director of International Students .... Mr. Yasushi ONODERA
18 Director of Physical Plant Services .... Mr. Brian LASEY
96 Director of Purchasing .... Ms. Jessica HOLLOWAY
92 Director of Honors Program .... Dr. Jan JENKINS
22 Director of Affirmative Action .... Ms. Jennifer FLEMING
108 Dir Assessment/Inst Effectiveness .... Dr. Christine AUSTIN
105 Director Web Strategies/Operations .... Mr. Michael STOKER
19 Director Public Safety .... Mr. Josh MCMILLIAN
26 Director of University Relations .... Mr. Sam STRASNER
36 Director of Career Services .... Mr. Brandon WRIGHT
44 Director Annual Giving Programs .... Ms. Caroline VINING
41 Athletic Director .... Mr. Steve MULLINS
88 Director of Prospect Research .... Ms. Pam COOPER
112 Director of Gift Planning .... Ms. Peggy MITCHELL-FERRIS
53 Dean of College of Education .... Dr. Mary GUNTER
49 Dean College of Arts & Humanities .... Dr. Jeffrey WOODS
50 Dean of College of Business .... Dr. Lisa TOMS
77 Dn Col Engineering & Applied Sci .... Dr. Douglas BARLOW
81 Dean College of Natural & Health Sc .... Dr. Jeff ROBERTSON
106 Dean College of eTech .... Dr. Hanna NORTON
58 Dean of Graduate College .... Dr. Mary GUNTER
28 Assoc Dean Diversity & Inclusion .... Dr. MarTeze HAMMONDS
38 Assoc Dean Student Student Wellness .... Ms. Kristy DAVIS
39 Associate Dean Residence Life .... Mr. Aaron HOGAN

Arkansas Tech University-Ozark Campus (H)

1700 Helberg Lane, Ozark AR 72949
Telephone: (866) 225-2884 Identification: 770003
Accreditation: &NH, CAHIIM, CVT, EMT, OTA

Baptist Health College Little Rock (I)

11900 Colonel Glenn Rd, Ste 1000, Little Rock AR 72210
County: Pulaski FICE Identification: 031052
Unit ID: 106546
Telephone: (501) 202-6200 Carnegie Class: Not Classified
FAX Number: N/A Calendar System: Semester
URL: www.bhclr.edu
Established: 1921 Annual Undergrad Tuition & Fees: $9,194
Enrollment: 663 Coed
Affiliation or Control: Independent Non-Profit IRS Status: 501(c)3
Highest Offering: Associate Degree
Accreditation: ABHES, ADNUR, DNUR, HT, MT, NMT, OTA, PNUR, POLYT, RAD, SURGT, SURTEC

01 Chancellor .... Dr. Judy INGRAM PILE
11 Vice President & Administrator .... Vacant
06 Registrar .... Ana HUNT

Black River Technical College (J)

PO Box 468/1410 Hwy 304 East, Pocahontas AR 72455-0468
County: Randolph FICE Identification: 020522
Unit ID: 106625
Telephone: (870) 248-4000 Carnegie Class: Assoc/MT-VT-Mix Trad/Non
FAX Number: (870) 248-4100 Calendar System: Semester
URL: www.blackrivertech.org
Established: 1991 Annual Undergrad Tuition & Fees (In-State): $2,904
Enrollment: 1,739 Coed
Affiliation or Control: State IRS Status: 501(c)3
Highest Offering: Associate Degree
Accreditation: #NH, COARC, #DIETT, EMT

01 President .... Dr. Eric TURNER
05 Vice President for Academics .... Dr. Sheila TAYLOR
32 Vice President for Student Affairs .... Mrs. Martha NELSON
111 VP for Institutional Advancement .... Mrs. Karen LIEBHABER
10 Vice President for Finance .... Mrs. Rhonda STONE
37 Director of Financial Aid .... Mrs. Brandi CHESTER
06 Registrar .... Mrs. Kimberly BIGGER
04 Administrative Asst to President .... Mrs. Vickie FRENCH

106 Dir Online Education/E-learning ... Mrs. Regina MOORE
15 Director Personnel Services ... Mrs. Julie EDINGTON
19 Director Security/Safety ... Mr. Tony SAYLORS
26 Chief Public Relations/Marketing ... Ms. Ann SAVAGE
96 Director of Purchasing ... Mr. Michael SMITH
13 Chief Info Technology Officer (CIO) ... Mr. Michael GREENE
18 Chief Facilities/Physical Plant ... Mr. Trent INGRAM
09 Director of Institutional Research ... Mr. Daniel PARKER
07 Director of Admissions ... Mrs. Angie FRENCH
36 Director of Student Placement ... Mr. Neal HARWELL

Bryan University (A)

3704 West Walnut Street, Rogers AR 72756-1825
Telephone: (479) 899-6644 Identification: 666252
Accreditation: ACICS

† Branch campus of Bryan University, Springfield, MO.

Central Baptist College (B)

1501 College Avenue, Conway AR 72034-6470
County: Faulkner FICE Identification: 001093
Unit ID: 106713
Telephone: (501) 329-6872 Carnegie Class: Bac-Diverse
FAX Number: (501) 329-2941 Calendar System: Semester
URL: www.cbc.edu
Established: 1952 Annual Undergrad Tuition & Fees: $15,000
Enrollment: 881 Coed
Affiliation or Control: Baptist IRS Status: 501(c)3
Highest Offering: Baccalaureate
Accreditation: NH

01 President ... Mr. Terry KIMBROW
04 Admin Asst to President ... Mrs. Peggy PILLOW
05 VP for Academic Affairs ... Dr. Gary MCALLISTER
10 VP for Finance ... Mr. Paul CHERRY
111 VP for Advancement ... Mrs. Sancy FAULK
84 VP for Enrollment Mgmt ... Mr. Ryan JOHNSON
32 Assoc VP for Student Services ... Mrs. Rachel STEELE
06 Registrar ... Mrs. Stacy JORDAN
07 Director of Admissions ... Mr. Justin MOORE
19 Dean of Students/Campus Security ... Mr. Chris MITCHELL
08 Library Director ... Mrs. Rachel WHITTINGHAM
26 Director of Public Relations ... Mrs. Deanna OTT
37 Director of Financial Aid ... Mrs. Tonya HAMMONTREE
09 Dir of Institutional Effectiveness ... Mr. Steve ELDER
41 Athletic Director ... Mr. Lyle MIDDLETON
39 Director of Student Housing ... Mr. Michael MAYO
15 Director of Human Resources ... Mrs. Britni ELDER
29 Alumni & Communications Officer ... Ms. Meagan LOWRY
88 Director of Military Relations ... Mr. Steven HALL
108 Director Institutional Assessment ... Mr. Dwain EAST
18 Director of Physical Plant ... Mr. Jerry CLIFTON
106 Director of Online Studies ... Mr. Chad LINN

College of the Ouachitas (C)

One College Circle, Malvern AR 72104-0816
County: Hot Spring FICE Identification: 009976
Unit ID: 107521
Telephone: (501) 337-5000 Carnegie Class: Assoc/HVT-High Non
FAX Number: (501) 337-9382 Calendar System: Semester
URL: www.coto.edu
Established: 1991 Annual Undergrad Tuition & Fees (In-State): $3,620
Enrollment: 1,346 Coed
Affiliation or Control: State IRS Status: 501(c)3
Highest Offering: Associate Degree
Accreditation: NH

01 President ... Dr. Steve ROOK
04 Administrative Asst to President ... Mrs. Jill HOULIHAN
05 Vice President of Instruction ... Mr. Pat SIMMS
32 Vice President Student Affairs ... Dr. Kim ARMSTRONG
10 Vice Pres Admin & Operations ... Mr. David SEE
111 Exec Dir College Advancement ... Ms. Amber CHILDERS
108 Exec Dir Planning & Assessment ... Ms. Carla CRUTCHFIELD
20 Dean of Learning ... Ms. Tricia BAAR
76 Dean of Health Sciences ... Ms. Melinda SANDERS
51 Director Adult Education ... Mr. Randy MORRIS
08 Director Learning Resources ... Vacant
75 Director Career & Technical Studies ... Mr. Mike DINGLER
92 Director Honors College ... Mrs. Tricia BAAR
88 Director Concurrent Enrollment ... Mrs. Terri COLANANNI
37 Director of Financial Aid ... Ms. Vickie YOUNG
36 Director Career Pathways ... Ms. Johnnie MITCHELL
88 Dir TRIO Student Support Services ... Ms. Vergina SMITH
121 Director Student Success ... Ms. Janet HUNT
07 Director of Admissions/Registrar ... Ms. Keesha JOHNSON
21 Controller ... Ms. Anita MARTGIN
15 Human Resources ... Mrs. Kori CLAYTON
13 Director IT ... Mr. Carlos MILLER

Crowley's Ridge College (D)

100 College Drive, Paragould AR 72450-9775
County: Greene FICE Identification: 001095
Unit ID: 106810
Telephone: (870) 236-6901 Carnegie Class: Bac/Assoc-Mixed
FAX Number: (870) 236-7748 Calendar System: Semester
URL: www.crc.edu
Established: 1964 Annual Undergrad Tuition & Fees: $12,500
Enrollment: 226 Coed
Affiliation or Control: Churches Of Christ IRS Status: 501(c)3
Highest Offering: Baccalaureate
Accreditation: NH

01 President ... Mr. Ken HOPPE
05 Vice President for Academic Affairs ... Dr. Bruce BRYANT
32 Vice President for Student Affairs ... Mr. Art SMITH
111 Vice President for Advancement ... Mr. Richard JOHNSON
06 Registrar ... Mr. Paul MCFADDEN
37 Director Student Financial Services ... Mr. David W. GOFF
26 Director Public Information ... Mrs. Andrea JOHNSON
07 Director Admissions ... Mr. Chris HUGHES
41 Athletic Director/Campus Minister ... Mr. Paul MCFADDEN
08 Director Learning Center ... Mr. Mark WARNICK
10 Business Office Manager ... Mrs. Sonia JOHNSON
13 Director of Information Services ... Mr. Larry JOHNSON

East Arkansas Community College (E)

1700 Newcastle Road, Forrest City AR 72335-2204
County: Saint Francis FICE Identification: 012260
Unit ID: 106883
Telephone: (870) 633-4480 Carnegie Class: Assoc/HT-High Non
FAX Number: (870) 633-7222 Calendar System: Semester
URL: www.eacc.edu
Established: 1974 Annual Undergrad Tuition & Fees (In-District): $2,850
Enrollment: 1,200 Coed
Affiliation or Control: State/Local IRS Status: 501(c)3
Highest Offering: Associate Degree
Accreditation: NH, ADNUR, EMT

01 President ... Dr. Coy F. GRACE
05 Vice President Academic Affairs ... Dr. Janie BAILEY
10 Vice President Business Affairs ... Mr. Richard STIPE
32 Vice President Student Affairs ... Mrs. Catherine T. COLEMAN
37 Director Student Financial Aid ... Mr. Kevin JUMPER
88 Assoc VP for Applied Sciences ... Mrs. Joanne LAWSON
31 AVP for Community/Business Outreach ... Mrs. Tiffany BILLINGSLEY
97 Assoc VP for General Studies ... Dr. Cathie CLINE
08 Director Library Services ... Mrs. Paige LAWS
84 Director Enrollment Management ... Mrs. Sharon COLLIER
26 Director of Public Relations/Mktg ... Mrs. Lindsay MIDKIFF
15 Director of Human Resources ... Mrs. Yvonne RUCKER-FRANKLIN
18 Director Physical Plant ... Mr. Glenn FORD
35 Assoc VP for Student Affairs ... Mrs. Michelle WILSON
96 Purchasing Specialist ... Mrs. Susan GUEST
51 Director of Continuing Education ... Mrs. Logan BRASFIELD

Ecclesia College (F)

9653 Nations Drive, Springdale AR 72762-8159
County: Benton FICE Identification: 038553
Unit ID: 446233
Telephone: (479) 248-7236 Carnegie Class: Spec-4-yr-Faith
FAX Number: (479) 248-1455 Calendar System: Semester
URL: www.ecollege.edu
Established: 1975 Annual Undergrad Tuition & Fees: $15,140
Enrollment: 283 Coed
Affiliation or Control: Independent Non-Profit IRS Status: 501(c)3
Highest Offering: Master's
Accreditation: BI

01 President ... Mr. Oren PARIS, III
05 Academic Dean ... Dr. Robert HEADRICK
10 Business Office Manager ... Ms. Shannon NEWMAN
32 Dean of Students ... Mr. Jesse E. WADKINS
30 Director of Financial Development ... Mr. Mike NOVAK
26 Director of Communications ... Ms. Angie P. SNYDER
37 Director Student Financial Aid ... Mr. Tommy STRINGFELLOW
41 Athletic Director ... Mr. Dean SKINNER
06 Registrar ... Mrs. Donna BROWN
08 Head Librarian ... Mrs. Joanne CAMPBELL
103 Director Work/Learning/Service Pgms ... Mr. Jesse E. WADKINS
07 Director of Admissions ... Mr. Chad HOWARD
04 Administrative Asst to President ... Mrs. Elizabeth NEWLUN
18 Chief Facilities/Physical Plant ... Mr. Dennis HAGGARD
106 Director Distance Education ... Vacant
39 Director Student Housing ... Ms. Kathrynn FINK

Harding University Main Campus (G)

915 E. Market Avenue, Searcy AR 72149-5615
County: White FICE Identification: 001097
Unit ID: 107044
Telephone: (501) 279-4000 Carnegie Class: Masters/L
FAX Number: (501) 279-4600 Calendar System: Semester
URL: www.harding.edu
Established: 1924 Annual Undergrad Tuition & Fees: $18,635
Enrollment: 6,009 Coed
Affiliation or Control: Churches Of Christ IRS Status: 501(c)3
Highest Offering: Doctorate
Accreditation: NH, ACBSP, ARCPA, CAATE, CACREP, CAEP, CIDA, DIETD, ENG, MUS, NURSE, PHAR, PTA, SP, SW

01 President ... Dr. Bruce D. MCLARTY
03 Executive Vice President ... Dr. David COLLINS
05 Provost ... Dr. Marty SPEARS
88 Senior Vice President ... Dr. James W. CARR
10 Vice President Finance ... Dr. Mel SANSOM
30 Vice President Advancement ... Dr. Bryan BURKS
42 Vice President of Church Relations ... Dr. Dan WILLIAMS
13 VP Information Systems & Technology ... Mr. Keith CRONK
41 Athletic Director ... Mr. Greg HARNDEN
29 VP of Alumni Relations ... Mrs. Liz HOWELL
20 Assistant Provost for Accreditation .. Dr. Julie HIXSON-WALLACE
88 Dean College of Bible & Ministry ... Dr. Monte COX
92 Dean of Honors College ... Dr. Mike JAMES
50 Dean College of Business ... Dr. Al FRAZIER
53 Dean College of Education ... Dr. Donny LEE
66 Dean College of Nursing ... Dr. Susan KEHL
79 Dean College of Arts & Humanities ... Dr. Warren CASEY
81 Dean College of Sciences ... Dr. Travis THOMPSON
76 Dean College of Allied Health ... Dr. Beckie WEAVER
88 Dean of International Programs ... Dr. Jeffrey HOPPER
84 Asst VP Enrollment Management ... Mr. Glenn DILLARD
21 Asst VP Finance ... Mrs. Tammy HALL
32 Asst VP Student Life/Dean Students ... Mr. Zach NEAL
88 Asst VP of IS&T ... Mr. Mike CHALENBURG
06 Registrar ... Mr. Tod MARTIN
38 Director of Counseling ... Dr. Lew MOORE
19 Director Security/Safety ... Mr. Craig RUSSELL
26 VP of Communication ... Mrs. Jana RUCKER
37 Director Student Financial Aid ... Dr. Jonathan ROBERTS
58 Director of Graduate Studies ... Vacant
08 Librarian ... Mrs. Jean WALDROP
18 Chief Facilities/Physical Plant ... Mr. Danny DERAMUS
15 Director Personnel Services ... Mr. David ROSS
36 Director Student Placement ... Mr. Butch GARDNER
09 Director of Institutional Research ... Mr. Dustin HOWELL
96 Purchasing Coordinator ... Mrs. Shelly MATHEWS
35 Assistant Dean of Students ... Mr. Brandon TITTLE
35 Assistant Dean of Students ... Mrs. Kara ABSTON
35 Assistant Dean of Students ... Mrs. Ranan HESTER
35 Assistant Dean of Students ... Mr. Chad JOICE
28 Director of Diversity ... Mrs. Tiffany BYERS
39 Director Student Housing ... Mrs. Kathy ALLEN
07 Director of Admissions ... Mr. Glenn DILLARD

Henderson State University (H)

1100 Henderson Street, Arkadelphia AR 71999-0001
County: Clark FICE Identification: 001098
Unit ID: 107071
Telephone: (870) 230-5000 Carnegie Class: Masters/M
FAX Number: (870) 230-5144 Calendar System: Semester
URL: www.hsu.edu
Established: 1890 Annual Undergrad Tuition & Fees (In-State): $8,340
Enrollment: 3,527 Coed
Affiliation or Control: State IRS Status: 501(c)3
Highest Offering: Beyond Master's But Less Than Doctorate
Accreditation: NH, #CAATE, CAEPN, DIETD, MUS, NURSE

01 President ... Dr. Glendell JONES
05 Provost/VPAA ... Dr. Steve ADKISON
10 Vice Pres Finance & Administration ... Mr. Brett POWELL
32 VP Student Services/External Affair ... Dr. Lewis A. SHEPHERD, JR.
111 VP Advancement/Exec Dir Found ... Ms. Jennifer BOYETT
43 General Counsel ... Ms. Elaine KNEEBONE
35 Asst VP for Student Affairs ... Mr. Eric FLOWERS
39 Director of Residence Life ... Dr. Nicole LAIRD
13 AVP Computer/Comm Svcs & CIO ... Mr. Al VALBUENA
30 Director of Development & Alumni ... Ms. Carrie ROBERSON
41 Director Athletics ... Mr. Shawn JONES
26 Exec Director of Marketing/Comm ... Ms. Tonya OAKS SMITH
49 Dean Ellis Col Arts/Sciences ... Dr. John HARDEE
50 Dean of School of Business ... Dr. Marc MILLER
53 Dean Teachers College Henderson ... Dr. Celya TAYLOR
58 Dean of Graduate School ... Dr. Kenneth TAYLOR
06 Registrar ... Mr. Elwyn MARTIN
08 Director Huie Library ... Ms. Lea Ann ALEXANDER
15 Director of Human Resources ... Ms. Kathy TAYLOR
19 Director of University Police ... Mr. Jonathan CAMPBELL
38 Dir Student Health/Counseling Ctr ... Ms. Deborah COLLINS
07 Director Univ Relations/Admissions ... Ms. Brandie BENTON
37 Director of Financial Aid ... Ms. Alexandra TUBBS
92 Director of Honors College ... Dr. David T. THOMSON
88 Director of Student Research ... Dr. David BATEMAN
96 Director of Purchasing ... Mr. Tim JONES
24 Dir Multi Media Learning Center ... Ms. Jennifer HOLBROOK
85 Director International Students ... Dr. Drew SMITH

Hendrix College (I)

1600 Washington Avenue, Conway AR 72032-3080
County: Faulkner FICE Identification: 001099
Unit ID: 107080
Telephone: (501) 329-6811 Carnegie Class: Bac-A&S
FAX Number: (501) 450-1200 Calendar System: Semester
URL: www.hendrix.edu
Established: 1876 Annual Undergrad Tuition & Fees: $42,440
Enrollment: 1,338 Coed
Affiliation or Control: United Methodist IRS Status: 501(c)3
Highest Offering: Master's
Accreditation: NH, CAEPN, MUS

01 President ... Dr. William M. TSUTSUI
04 Executive Assistant to President ... Ms. Donna PLEMMONS
88 VP for Strategic Initiatives/Chief ... Ms. Courtney Lee CORWIN
111 Sr Exec Vice Pres/Dean Inst Advance ... Mr. W. Ellis ARNOLD, III
05 Provost ... Dr. Terri BONEBRIGHT
26 Vice Pres Marketing Communications ... Mr. Rob O'CONNOR
10 Executive Vice President and CFO ... Mr. Tom SIEBENMORGEN
84 Vice Pres for Enrollment ... Mr. Sam NICHOLS
15 Vice Pres for Human Resources ... Ms. Vicki LYNN

18 VP Operations/Facilities ..... Mr. Skip HARTSELL
32 Exec VP Student Affs/Dean of Stdnts ..... Mr. Jim WILTGEN, JR.
27 Assoc VP Marketing Communications ..... Ms. Amy FORBUS
06 Registrar ..... Ms. Brenda ADAMS
08 Director of Libraries ..... Ms. Britt Anne MURPHY
13 VP Technology/Chief Info Officer ..... Mr. Sam NICHOLS
29 Director Alumni Relations ..... Ms. Pamela OWEN
37 Director of Financial Aid ..... Ms. Kristina BURFORD
40 Bookstore Manager ..... Ms. Suzannne TOLLETT
79 Area Head/Humanities ..... Dr. Alex VERNON
81 Area Head/Natural Sciences ..... Dr. Matt MORAN
83 Area Head/Social Sciences ..... Dr. Leslie TEMPLETON
42 Chaplain ..... Rev. J.J WHITNEY
07 Director of Admission ..... Vacant
20 Associate Academic Officer ..... Dr. David SUTHERLAND
21 Associate Business Officer ..... Mr. Shawn MATHIS
36 Assistant Director Career Services ..... Ms. Jamie FOTIOO
38 Director Student Counseling ..... Ms. Mary Anne SIEBERT
09 Director of Institutional Research ..... Mr. Randy PETERSON
28 VP for Diversity & Inclusion ..... Dr. Dionne JACKSON

Jefferson Regional Medical Center School of Nursing (A)

1600 W. 40th Avenue, Pine Bluff AR 71603
County: Jefferson FICE Identification: 023308
Unit ID: 107123
Telephone: (870) 541-7850 Carnegie Class: Not Classified
FAX Number: (870) 541-7807 Calendar System: Semester
URL: www.jrmc.org
Established: 1981 Annual Undergrad Tuition & Fees: N/A
Enrollment: 67 Coed
Affiliation or Control: Independent Non-Profit IRS Status: 501(c)3
Highest Offering: Associate Degree
Accreditation: **ABHES**, PAST

01 Director ..... Ms. Kathy PIERCE
06 Registrar/School Secretary ..... Ms. Lucy MULLIKIN

John Brown University (B)

2000 W University Street, Siloam Springs AR 72761-2121
County: Benton FICE Identification: 001100
Unit ID: 107141
Telephone: (479) 524-9500 Carnegie Class: Masters/M
FAX Number: (479) 524-7278 Calendar System: Semester
URL: www.jbu.edu
Established: 1919 Annual Undergrad Tuition & Fees: $25,324
Enrollment: 2,781 Coed
Affiliation or Control: Independent Non-Profit IRS Status: 501(c)3
Highest Offering: Master's
Accreditation: **NH**, ACBSP, CAEPN, CONST, ENG

01 President ..... Dr. Charles POLLARD
10 Vice Pres Finance & Administration ..... Dr. Kim HADLEY
84 Vice Pres Enrollment Management ..... Mr. Donald W. CRANDALL
111 Vice Pres of University Advancement ..... Dr. Jim KRALL
32 Vice Pres for Student Development ..... Dr. Stephen T. BEERS
05 VP Academic Affairs/Dean of Faculty ..... Dr. Ed ERICSON, III
88 Dean Degree Completion Program ..... Dr. Stacey DUKE
42 Campus Pastor/Assoc Dean of Stdnts ..... Dr. Rod REED
06 Registrar ..... Dr. Rebecca LAMBERT
21 Controller ..... Mr. Tom PERRY
13 Chief Information Systems Ofcr ..... Mr. Paul NAST
18 Director of Facilities Services ..... Mr. Steve BRANKLE
44 Director of Planned Giving ..... Mr. Eric GREENHAW
08 Director of Library ..... Mr. Brent SWEARINGEN
85 Director International Programs ..... Mr. Bill STEVENSON
29 Director of Alumni/Parent Relations ..... Mr. Brad EDWARDS
37 Assoc Director of Financial Aid ..... Mr. David BURNEY
07 Senior Admission Couns Degree Compl ..... Mr. Kent SHAFFER
41 Athletic Director ..... Ms. Robyn DAUGHERTY
38 Director of Counseling ..... Dr. Tim DINGER
04 Administrative Asst to President ..... Ms. Kory J. DALE
09 Director of Institutional Research ..... Dr. Cal PISTON

Lyon College (C)

PO Box 2317, Batesville AR 72503-2317
County: Independence FICE Identification: 001088
Unit ID: 106342
Telephone: (870) 307-7000 Carnegie Class: Bac-A&S
FAX Number: (870) 307-7001 Calendar System: Semester
URL: https://www.lyon.edu/
Established: 1872 Annual Undergrad Tuition & Fees: $26,290
Enrollment: 715 Coed
Affiliation or Control: Presbyterian Church (U.S.A.) IRS Status: 501(c)3
Highest Offering: Baccalaureate
Accreditation: **NH**, CAEPN

01 President ..... Dr. W. Joseph KING
05 Provost ..... Vacant
10 Vice President Business & Finance ..... Mr. John D. JONES
32 Vice President Student Life ..... Dr. Patrick MULICK
07 VP Enrollment Services ..... Mr. Matthew CRISMAN
08 Director Library ..... Dr. Robert KRAPOHL
26 Assoc VP Marketing & Communication ..... Mr. Eric BORK
111 Executive Dir of Advancement ..... Mrs. Gina GARRETT
15 Director of Administration and HR ..... Mrs. Clarinda L. FOOTE
37 Director of Financial Assistance ..... Mr. Tommy TUCKER
36 Director Career Development ..... Mrs. Annettee CASTLEBERRY
13 Director Information Services ..... Mr. Josh KEMP
41 Director of Athletics ..... Mr. Kevin JENKINS
42 Chaplain ..... Rev. Margaret ALSUP
53 Int Director of Teacher Education ..... Ms. Kim CROSBY
38 Director Student Counseling ..... Ms. Diane ELLIS
18 Director Security ..... Mr. Donald HUTCHINS
40 Director Bookstore ..... Mrs. Donna GLASCOCK
08 Head Librarian ..... Ms. Kathy WHITTENTON
23 Director of Health Services ..... Mrs. LuAnn BAKER
18 Chief Facilities/Physical Plant ..... Vacant
20 Associate Academic Officer ..... Dr. Anthony GRAFTON
06 Registrar ..... Mrs. Tami HALL
44 Director Annual Giving ..... Mr. Daniel HANEY

National Park College (D)

101 College Drive,
Hot Springs National Park AR 71913-9174
County: Garland FICE Identification: 012105
Unit ID: 106980
Telephone: (501) 760-4222 Carnegie Class: Assoc/HT-Mix Trad/Non
FAX Number: (501) 760-4100 Calendar System: Semester
URL: www.np.edu
Established: 1973 Annual Undergrad Tuition & Fees (In-District): $3,200
Enrollment: 3,014 Coed
Affiliation or Control: State/Local IRS Status: 501(c)3
Highest Offering: Associate Degree
Accreditation: **NH**, ADNUR, CAHIIM, #COARC, EMT, MLTAD, RAD

01 President ..... Dr. John HOGAN
05 Vice Pres Academic Affairs ..... Dr. Wade DERDEN
10 Vice Pres Finance & Admin ..... Mr. Steve TRUSTY
32 Vice Pres Student Affairs ..... Dr. Jerry THOMAS
26 Vice Pres External Relations ..... Mr. Jeff WEAVER
45 Chief Planning/Development Officer ..... Ms. Kelli ALBRECHT
21 Assoc Vice Pres Business & Tech ..... Mr. David HUGHES
15 Assoc Vice Pres Human Resources ..... Ms. Janet BREWER
35 Dean of Students ..... Mr. John TUCKER
07 Dean of Enrollment Services ..... Mr. Jason HUDNELL
08 Director of Library Services ..... Ms. Sara SEAMAN
37 Director of Financial Aid ..... Ms. Lisa HOPPER
30 Director of Development ..... Ms. Sara BROWN
06 Registrar ..... Ms. Ana HUNT
100 Chief of Staff ..... Ms. Darla THURBER
13 Chief Info Technology Officer ..... Mr. Blake BUTLER

North Arkansas College (E)

1515 Pioneer Drive, Harrison AR 72601-5599
County: Boone FICE Identification: 012261
Unit ID: 107460
Telephone: (870) 743-3000 Carnegie Class: Assoc/MT-VT-High Trad
FAX Number: (870) 391-3250 Calendar System: Semester
URL: www.northark.edu
Established: 1974 Annual Undergrad Tuition & Fees (In-District): $2,088
Enrollment: 1,796 Coed
Affiliation or Control: State/Local IRS Status: 501(c)3
Highest Offering: Associate Degree
Accreditation: **NH**, ACBSP, ADNUR, EMT, MLTAD, RAD, SURGT

01 President ..... Dr. Randy ESTERS
05 Vice President of Academic Affairs ..... Dr. Donna WOOD
10 Vice Pres Finance & Administration ..... Mr. Donald SUGG
111 Vice Pres Institutional Advancement ..... Dr. Rodney ARNOLD
04 Executive Assistant to President ..... Mrs. Trish VILLINES
49 Dean Arts & Science/Business & IT ..... Dr. Laura BERRY
66 Dean Nursing/Allied Hlth/Tech Pgms ..... Mrs. Cindy MAYO
103 Dean of Outreach & Workforce Dev ..... Mrs. Nell BONDS
08 Interim Director of Libraries ..... Mrs. Michelle PALMER
108 Dir Institutional Effectiveness ..... Mrs. Katherine VAUGHN
121 Dean of Student Success ..... Mrs. Tavonda BROWN
41 Athletic Director ..... Mrs. Stacie KLOTT
15 Director Human Resources ..... Mrs. Kris GREENING
18 Chief Facilities/Physical Plant ..... Mr. Kevin SOMERS
96 Director of Purchasing ..... Mrs. Shari HOLT
37 Director Student Financial Aid ..... Mrs. Jennifer HADDOCK
06 Registrar ..... Mrs. Charla JENNINGS
07 Director of Admissions ..... Mrs. Charla JENNINGS
26 Director of Public Relations ..... Mrs. Micki SOMERS
13 Director of IT Services ..... Mr. Rick WILLIAMS
31 Asst Dir of Community Education ..... Ms. Sarah BING

NorthWest Arkansas Community College (F)

1 College Drive, Bentonville AR 72712-5091
County: Benton FICE Identification: 030633
Unit ID: 367459
Telephone: (479) 636-9222 Carnegie Class: Assoc/HT-Mix Trad/Non
FAX Number: (479) 619-4335 Calendar System: Semester
URL: www.nwacc.edu
Established: 1989 Annual Undergrad Tuition & Fees (In-District): $3,208
Enrollment: 7,744 Coed
Affiliation or Control: State/Local IRS Status: 501(c)3
Highest Offering: Associate Degree
Accreditation: **NH**, ACBSP, ACFEI, ADNUR, CAHIIM, COARC, EMT, IFSAC, PTAA

01 President ..... Dr. Evelyn E. JORGENSON
10 VP of Finance & Administration ..... Ms. Debi BUCKLEY
05 Vice Pres for Learning ..... Dr. Ricky TOMPKINS
32 VP of Student Services ..... Dr. Todd KITCHEN
36 VP of Career & Workforce Education ..... Mr. Tim CORNELIUS
103 Dean of Workforce Development ..... Mr. Keith PETERSON
13 AVP IT/Chief Information Officer ..... Mr. Jason DEGN
88 Dir Retail & Supplier Education ..... Ms. Teresa WARREN
11 Executive Director of Operations ..... Mr. Jack THOMPSON
51 Dean of Adult Education ..... Mr. Ben ALDAMA
35 Dean of Students ..... Mr. Dale MONTGOMERY
06 Dean of Learner Success & Registrar ..... Ms. Brooke HOLT
30 Executive Director of Development ..... Ms. Annetta TIREY
88 Exec Dir High School Relations ..... Dr. Diana JOHNSON
108 Exec Dir Effectiveness/Plng & PR ..... Dr. Lisa ANDERSON
26 Exec Dir Community/Government Rels ..... Mr. Jim HALL
21 Assistant Controller ..... Mr. John HIXSON
114 Exec Dir Budget/Fin Analysis/Report ..... Ms. Gulizar BAGGSON
15 Exec Director of Human Resources ..... Ms. Wendi CADLE
106 Director of Distance Learning ..... Dr. Kate BURKES
50 Exec Dir of Business Development ..... Ms. Teresa WHITMIRE
88 Coordinator of Building Sciences ..... Mr. Mike DEWBERRY
88 Director of Learning Resources ..... Ms. Gwen DOBBS
25 Director of Grants/Perkins CTE Pgms ..... Mr. Marcus WILLIAMS
121 Associate Dean Student Success ..... Ms. Tay Sha CARTER
07 Director of Admissions/Advising ..... Mr. Zach PHARR
37 Director Student Financial Aid ..... Ms. Michelle CORDELL
88 Director Academic Success Center ..... Mr. Eric VEST
28 Policy & Staff Enhancement Director ..... Ms. Brenda MEYER
109 Dir Food Services/Event Management ..... Ms. Diane BOSS
09 Institutional Research Manager ..... Ms. Kim PURDY
18 Director of Physical Plant ..... Mr. Jim NELSON
88 Coordinator Culinary & Hospitality ..... Vacant
77 Dean for Bus/Computer Information ..... Dr. Christine DAVIS
76 Dean of Health Professions ..... Vacant
04 Administrative Asst to President ..... Ms. Lindsey WHITE
22 Int Exec Dir Policy/Risk & Comp ..... Ms. Teresa TAYLOR
44 Annual Giving Officer ..... Ms. Karen O'DONOHOE
96 Purchasing Manager ..... Mr. Denton WEDDLE

Ouachita Baptist University (G)

410 Ouachita Street, Arkadelphia AR 71998-0001
County: Clark FICE Identification: 001102
Unit ID: 107512
Telephone: (870) 245-5000 Carnegie Class: Bac-A&S
FAX Number: (870) 245-5500 Calendar System: Semester
URL: www.obu.edu
Established: 1886 Annual Undergrad Tuition & Fees: $24,940
Enrollment: 1,538 Coed
Affiliation or Control: Southern Baptist IRS Status: 501(c)3
Highest Offering: Baccalaureate
Accreditation: **NH**, DIETD, MUS

01 President ..... Dr. Ben R. SELLS
111 Vice Pres Institutional Advancement ..... Dr. Keldon HENLEY
05 Vice President Academic Affairs ..... Dr. Stan POOLE
10 Chief Financial Officer ..... Mr. Jason TOLBERT
32 Vice Pres for Student Development ..... Dr. Wesley KLUCK
30 Vice President for Development ..... Mrs. Terry G. PEEPLES
26 Vice Pres for Communications ..... Mr. Trennis HENDERSON
04 Asst to President/Administration ..... Mr. Philip W. HARDIN
07 Director of Admissions Counseling ..... Mrs. Lori MOTL
09 Director of Institutional Research ..... Mr. Phil HARDIN
15 Director of Human Resources ..... Mrs. Sherri PHELPS
18 Chief Facilities/Physical Plant ..... Mr. John HARDMAN
29 Director of Alumni Relations ..... Mr. Jon MERRYMAN
35 Dean of Students ..... Mr. Rickey ROGERS
20 Assoc Vice Pres Academic Affairs ..... Dr. Doug REED
36 Director of Career Services ..... Mrs. Rachel JONES
38 University Counselor ..... Mr. Dan JARBOE
08 Librarian ..... Dr. Ray GRANADE
06 Registrar/Director of Admissions ..... Mrs. Susan ATKINSON
37 Assoc Vice Pres Student Fin Svcs ..... Mrs. Susan HURST
96 Director of Purchasing ..... Ms. Heather MOORE
92 Director Honors Program ..... Dr. Barbara PEMBERTON
13 Asst to Pres for Info Tech Svcs ..... Mr. Bill PHELPS
39 Director of Housing ..... Ms. Stacey PERRY
41 Athletic Director ..... Mr. David SHARP
43 General Counsel ..... Mr. Bryan MCKINNEY
21 Director of Financial Services ..... Mr. Jason TOLBERT
40 Bookstore Manager ..... Ms. Beverly DICKERSON
57 Dean of School of Fine Arts ..... Dr. Gary GERBER
50 Dean of the School of Business ..... Mr. Bryan MCKINNEY
53 Dean Sch of Interdisciplinary Stds ..... Dr. Stan POOLE
73 Dean School of Christian Studies ..... Dr. Danny HAYS
53 Interim Dean School of Education ..... Dr. Jeff ROOT
79 Dean School of Humanities ..... Dr. Jeff ROOT
81 Dean School of Natural Sciences ..... Dr. Tim KNIGHT
83 Dean School of Social Sciences ..... Dr. Randall WIGHT

Ozarka College (H)

PO Box 10, Melbourne AR 72556-0010
County: Izard FICE Identification: 020870
Unit ID: 107549
Telephone: (870) 368-7371 Carnegie Class: Assoc/MT-VT-Mix Trad/Non
FAX Number: (870) 368-2091 Calendar System: Semester
URL: www.ozarka.edu
Established: 1991 Annual Undergrad Tuition & Fees (In-State): $2,776
Enrollment: 1,108 Coed
Affiliation or Control: State IRS Status: 501(c)3
Highest Offering: Associate Degree
Accreditation: **NH**, ACFEI

01 President ..... Dr. Richard L. DAWE

05 Executive Vice Pres & Provost .... Dr. Keith MCCLANAHAN
10 Vice President of Finance ....Mrs. Tina WHEELIS
11 Vice President of Administration ....Mr. Jason LAWRENCE
32 Vice President of Student Services ....Dr. Josh WILSON
45 Assoc Vice President of Planning/IR ....Dr. Deltha SHARP
13 Chief Information Officer ....Mr. Scott PINKSTON
04 Executive Asst to the President ....Mrs. Fay MITCHELL
30 Director of College Advancement ....Mrs. Suellen DAVIDSON
29 Development Officer/Dir Alumni Rels ....Vacant
37 Director of Financial Aid ....Ms. Laura LAWRENCE
07 Director of Admissions ....Vacant
06 Registrar ....Mrs. Zeda WILKERSON
26 Dir Public Relations/Marketing ....Mrs. Manda JACKSON
21 Business Manager ....Mrs. Amber RUSH

Philander Smith College (A)

900 W. Daisy L. Gatson Bates Drive,
Little Rock AR 72202-3799

County: Pulaski   FICE Identification: 001103
Unit ID: 107600

Telephone: (501) 375-9845   Carnegie Class: Bac-A&S
FAX Number: (501) 370-5277   Calendar System: Semester
URL: www.philander.edu
Established: 1877   Annual Undergrad Tuition & Fees: $12,714
Enrollment: 584   Coed
Affiliation or Control: United Methodist   IRS Status: 501(c)3
Highest Offering: Baccalaureate
Accreditation: NH, ACBSP, CAEPN, SW

01 President ....Dr. Roderick L. SMOTHERS, SR.
04 Admin Assistant to the President .... Ms. Elmyra D. CAMPBELL
03 Executive Vice President ....Dr. Darnell WILLIAMS
05 Acting VP of Academic Affairs ....Dr. Zollie STEVENSON, JR.
10 Acting VP of Fiscal Affairs ....Mrs. LaTonya HAYES
32 VP of Student Affs/Enrollment Mgmt ....Dr. Dakota DOMAN
111 Acting VP Institutional Advancement ....Mrs. Sercia COLE
108 Assoc VP of Inst Effectiveness .... Dr. Annie WILLIAMS
20 Assoc VP Academic Affairs ....Vacant
06 Registrar ....Ms. Bertha OWENS
42 Chaplain/Dean of Religious Life ....Rev. Ronnie MILLER-YOW
35 Dean of Students ....Ms. Rhonda LOVELACE
15 Exec Director of Human Resources ....Mr. Christopher NEWTON
37 Director of Financial Aid ....Mr. Kelvin FRANCOIS
18 Director of Physical Plant ....Mr. Robert YOUNG
26 Director Marketing/Public Relations ....Mrs. Jenelle PRIMM
88 Executive Director of WISE -P3 .... Mr. Glenn SARGEANT
07 Director of Admissions ....Mr. Maurice OSBORNE
08 Director of the Library ....Ms. Teresa OJEZUA
84 VP of Enrollment Management ....Dr. Dakota DOMAN
29 Director of Alumni Relations ....Mrs. Brenda HATTON-FICKLIN
41 Athletic Director ....Mr. Nathan COCHRAN
13 Chief Information Officer ....Mr. Brian CLAY
09 Director of Institutional Research ....Vacant
19 Chief of Security ....Mr. Arthur WILLIAMS
51 Dir of Continuing Education (PSMI) .... Mr. Bruce JAMES
88 Kendall Mission Center Director .... Dr. Cynthia BURROUGHS
40 Bookstore Manager ....Mr. Alvin HARRIS
17 Campus Nurse ....Vacant
88 Dean of Campus Culture .... Mr. Ronnie MILLER-YOW
49 Div Chair Natural/Physical Sciences ....Dr. Samar SWAID
50 Div Chair of Business/Economics ....Dr. Kathryn DAVIS
53 Acting Division Chair of Education ....Dr. Lloyd HERVEY
70 Division Chair for Social Work ....Dr. Daniel EGBE
79 Div Chair Humanities ....Dr. Lia STEELE-MARCELL
83 Div Chair Social Sciences ....Dr. Daniel EGBE
38 Director of Counseling Services .... Mrs. LaTisha JACKSON
39 Director of Housing and Res Life ....Mr. Waylon METOYER

Remington College-Little Rock (B)

10600 Colonel Glenn Road, Suite 100,
Little Rock AR 72204

Telephone: (501) 312-0007   Identification: 666286
Accreditation: ACCSC

† Branch campus of Remington College, Dallas, TX.

Shorter College (C)

604 Locust Street, North Little Rock AR 72114

County: Pulaski   FICE Identification: 001105
Unit ID: 107840

Telephone: (501) 374-6305   Carnegie Class: Assoc/HT-Mix Trad/Non
FAX Number: (501) 374-9333   Calendar System: Semester
URL: www.shortercollege.edu
Established: 1886   Annual Undergrad Tuition & Fees: $4,904
Enrollment: 236   Coed
Affiliation or Control: African Methodist Episcopal   IRS Status: 501(c)3
Highest Offering: Associate Degree
Accreditation: TRACS

01 President ....Dr. O. Jerome GREEN
05 Dean of Academic Affairs ....Dr. Jean MANNING
32 Student Services Coordinator ....Rev. Mary WILLIAMS
10 Chief Financial Officer ....Mr. George MACKEY

South Arkansas Community College (D)

300 S West Avenue, PO Box 7010,
El Dorado AR 71731-7010

County: Union   FICE Identification: 020746
Unit ID: 107974

Telephone: (870) 862-8131   Carnegie Class: Assoc/HVT-Mix Trad/Non
FAX Number: (870) 864-7190   Calendar System: Semester
URL: www.southark.edu
Established: 1992   Annual Undergrad Tuition & Fees (In-State): $2,508
Enrollment: 1,558   Coed
Affiliation or Control: State   IRS Status: 501(c)3
Highest Offering: Associate Degree
Accreditation: NH, COARC, EMT, OTA, PHLEB, PTAA, RAD, SURGT

01 President ....Dr. Barbara JONES
05 Interim VP AA & SA/Provost ....Dr. Jim BULLOCK
32 Vice Pres for Student Services ....Dr. Jim BULLOCK
11 VP for Finance & Administration ....Mr. Carey TUCKER
13 Assoc VP Administration/CIO ....Dr. Tim KIRK
26 Public Information Officer ....Mr. Heath WALDROP
84 Dean of Enrollment Services ....Mr. Dean INMAN
08 Director Library Media Center .... Mr. Philip SHACKELFORD
31 Dean Workforce & Continuing Educ ....Ms. Sherry HOWARD
37 Director of Financial Aid ....Ms. Veronda TATUM
04 Executive Asst to the President ....Ms. Susan JORDAN
15 Human Resources Director ....Mr. Bill FOWLER
18 Director of Physical Plant ....Vacant
30 Dir of Foundation/External Funding ....Ms. Cynthia REYNA
09 CIEAO ....Dr. Stephanie TULLY-DARTEZ
96 Director of Purchasing ....Ms. Ann SOUTHALL
07 Student Recruitment ....Ms. Micah SANFORD
49 Dean of Liberal Arts ....Dr. James YATES
76 Dean Health Sciences ....Ms. Caroline HAMMOND

Southeast Arkansas College (E)

1900 Hazel Street, Pine Bluff AR 71603-3900

County: Jefferson   FICE Identification: 005707
Unit ID: 107637

Telephone: (870) 543-5900   Carnegie Class: Assoc/HVT-High Trad
FAX Number: (870) 850-8636   Calendar System: Semester
URL: www.seark.edu
Established: 1991   Annual Undergrad Tuition & Fees (In-State): $3,190
Enrollment: 1,548   Coed
Affiliation or Control: State   IRS Status: 501(c)3
Highest Offering: Associate Degree
Accreditation: NH, ADNUR, COARC, EMT, PHLEB, RAD, SURGT

01 President ....Dr. Stephen HILTERBRAN
05 Vice President Academic Affairs ....Dr. Kaleybra MOREHEAD
32 Vice President Student Affairs ....Mr. Scott KUTTENKULER
10 Vice President Financial Affairs .... Ms. Debbie WALLACE
21 Controller ....Mr. Steve BALLARD
13 Director of Technology Services ....Ms. JoAnn DUPRA
06 Registrar/Director of Admissions .... Ms. Lozanne CALHOUN
15 Director of Human Resources ....Ms. Kristi CAMPBELL
18 Chief Facilities/Physical Plant ....Mr. Joel BARBAREE
37 Director Student Financial Aid ....Ms. Donna COX
04 Administrative Asst to President ....Ms. Karen BOGARD
08 Head Librarian ....Ms. Kim WILLIAMS
103 Dir Workforce/Career Development ....Ms. Wanda LINDSAY
105 Webmaster ....Mr. Terry CLAUSEN
53 Dean or Director Education ....Dr. Mark SHANLEY
96 Director of Purchasing ....Ms. Alice WEATHERLY

Southern Arkansas University (F)

100 E University Street, Magnolia AR 71753-5000

County: Columbia   FICE Identification: 001107
Unit ID: 107983

Telephone: (870) 235-4000   Carnegie Class: Masters/M
FAX Number: (870) 235-5005   Calendar System: Semester
URL: www.saumag.edu
Established: 1909   Annual Undergrad Tuition & Fees (In-State): $8,196
Enrollment: 4,095   Coed
Affiliation or Control: State   IRS Status: 501(c)3
Highest Offering: Master's
Accreditation: NH, #CAATE, CAEPN, MUS, NUR, SW

01 President ....Dr. Trey BERRY
05 Provost/Vice Pres Academic Affairs .... Dr. David LANOUE
11 VP Administration/General Counsel ....Mr. Roger W. GILES
32 Vice President Student Affairs ....Dr. Donna Y. ALLEN
18 Director of Facilities ....Mr. Robert NASH
10 Vice President for Finance ....Ms. Shawana REED
30 Asst Vice President for Development ....Mr. Josh KEE
49 Dean Col Liberal/Perform Arts .... Dr. Helmut LANGERBEIN
50 Dean College of Business ....Dr. Robin SRONCE
53 Dean College of Education ....Dr. Zaidy MOHDZAIN
81 Int Dean College of Sci & Eng .... Dr. Abdel BACHRI
58 Dean School of Graduate Studies .... Dr. Kim K. BLOSS
06 Registrar ....Mrs. Sandra WALKER
84 Dean Enrollment Services ....Ms. Sarah E. JENNINGS
35 Associate Deans of Students .... Mr. Carey BAKER
08 Director of Library ....Mr. Del G. DUKE
13 Director Info Technology Services ....Mr. Mike A. ARGO
38 Director Counsel/Testing Center ....Ms. Paula WASHINGTON-WOODS
39 Dean of Housing ....Ms. Sandra E. MARTIN

29 Director of Alumni Affairs ....Ms. Ceil L. BRIDGES
110 Director of Development ....Ms. Jeanie BISMARK
37 Director of Financial Aid ....Ms. Marcela C. MCRAE-BRUNSON
51 Director of Continuing Education .... Ms. Caroline WALLER
41 Director of Athletics ....Mr. Steve BROWNING
121 Director Student Support Services ....Ms. Eunice E. WALKER
36 Director of Placement Services ....Vacant
26 Asst Dean Integrated Marketing .... Mr. Aaron J. STREET
28 Assoc Dean Multicultural Affairs ....Mr. Cledis D. STUART
27 Assoc Dir Communications Center ....Ms. Vicki BUTLER
04 Asst to President ....Ms. LaTricia DAVIS
09 Director of Institutional Research .... Ms. Christine PACHECO
86 Director Government Relations ....Mrs. Sheryl EDWARDS

Southern Arkansas University Tech (G)

Post Office Box 3499, Camden AR 71711

County: Calhoun   FICE Identification: 007738
Unit ID: 107992

Telephone: (870) 574-4500   Carnegie Class: Assoc/MT-VT-High Non
FAX Number: (870) 574-4520   Calendar System: Semester
URL: www.sautech.edu
Established: 1967   Annual Undergrad Tuition & Fees (In-State): $4,677
Enrollment: 1,650   Coed
Affiliation or Control: State   IRS Status: 501(c)3
Highest Offering: Associate Degree
Accreditation: NH

01 Chancellor ....Dr. Jason MORRISON
10 VC for Finance & Administration ....Mrs. Gaye MANNING
05 Vice Chancellor for Academics ....Dr. Valerie WILSON
32 VC for Student Services ....Mr. David MCLEANE
26 Director of Communications ....Mrs. Kim COKER
09 Director of Research ....Mr. Lee SANDERS
84 Dean of Enrollment Services ....Mrs. Jenny SANDERS
103 Director of Career Pathways ....Ms. LaTonya REED
88 Director of Career Academy ....Mrs. Juanita MITCHELL
88 Director of AETA & Workforce ....Mr. Randy HARPER
88 Director of AFTA ....Mrs. Rachel NIX
13 Director of ITS ....Mrs. Laura JOHNSON
37 Director of Financial Aid ....Ms. Jennifer WILLIAMS
18 Director of Physical Plant ....Mr. Mike LARKINS
35 Director of Student Life ....Mr. Courtney HAYGOOD
06 Registrar ....Mr. Wayne BANKS
08 Director of LRC ....Ms. Allison MALONE
04 Assistant to the Chancellor ....Mrs. Tammy LARKINS
15 Human Resources Director ....Mrs. Olivia CLACK
21 Controller ....Mr. Dale TOMMEY
96 Buyer ....Mrs. Angela FRY
51 Director of Adult Education ....Mrs. Barbara HAMILTON
19 Director Security/Safety ....Mr. Jud MITCHELL

*University of Arkansas System Office (H)

2404 N University Avenue, Little Rock AR 72207-3608

County: Pulaski   FICE Identification: 008008
Unit ID: 108056

Telephone: (501) 686-2500   Carnegie Class: N/A
FAX Number: (501) 686-2507
URL: www.uasys.edu

01 President ....Dr. Donald R. BOBBITT
04 Assistant to the President ....Ms. Angela HUDSON
05 Vice President Academic Affairs ....Dr. Michael K. MOORE
26 Vice President University Relations ....Ms. Melissa RUST
47 Vice President Agriculture ....Dr. Mark J. COCHRAN
10 Interim CFO/Dir Planning & Resource ....Ms. Chaundra HALL
43 General Counsel ....Mrs. JoAnn MAXEY
88 Director Internal Audit ....Mr. Jacob W. FLOURNOY
27 Director of Communications ....Mr. Nate HINKEL

*University of Arkansas Main Campus (I)

2105 East Aggie Road, Fayetteville AR 72701-1201

County: Washington   FICE Identification: 001108
Unit ID: 106397

Telephone: (479) 575-2000   Carnegie Class: DU-Highest
FAX Number: (479) 575-2361   Calendar System: Semester
URL: www.uark.edu
Established: 1871   Annual Undergrad Tuition & Fees (In-State): $8,820
Enrollment: 26,754   Coed
Affiliation or Control: State   IRS Status: 501(c)3
Highest Offering: Doctorate
Accreditation: NH, AAFCS, ART, CAATE, CACREP, CAEPN, CIDA, CLPSY, CS, DIETD, ENG, #JOUR, LAW, LSAR, MUS, NURSE, SP, SW

02 Chancellor ....Dr. Joseph E. STEINMETZ
04 Executive Asst to the Chancellor .... Ms. Sally Ann ADAMS
05 Provost & EVC Academic Affs .... Dr. James COLEMAN
10 Vice Chanc Finance & Admin .... Mr. Tim O'DONNELL
30 Vice Chanc for Advancement ....Mr. Mark POWER
86 Vice Chanc Governmental Relations ....Mr. Randy MASSANELLI
45 Vice Provost Planning ....Dr. Kathy M. VAN LANINGHAM
46 Vice Provost Research/Econ Dev ....Dr. James M. RANKIN
32 Vice Chanc Student Affairs ....Mr. Charles ROBINSON
84 Vice Prov Enrol Mgt/Dean Admissions .... Dr. Suzanne MCCRAY
26 Assoc Vice Chanc Univ Relations ....Ms. Laura JACOBS
25 AVP Research & Sponsored Pgms ....Ms. Jennifer TAYLOR

15 Assoc Vice Chanc Human Resources .... Ms. Debbie MCLOUD
18 Assoc Vice Chanc Facilities Mgmt .... Mr. Mike JOHNSON
21 Assoc Vice Chanc Business Affairs .... Ms. Colleen M. BRINEY
35 Sr Assoc VC & Dean of Students .... Ms. Melissa HARDWOOD-ROM
08 Dean of Libraries .... Ms. Carolyn H. ALLEN
49 Dean of Arts & Sciences .... Dr. Todd G. SHIELDS
50 Dean Sam Walton College of Business .... Dr. Eli JONES
47 Int Dean of Agriculture .... Dr. Lona ROBERTSON
53 Dean Education/Health Professions .... Dr. Michael T. MILLER
48 Dean of Architecture .... Mr. Peter MACKEITH
58 Dean of Graduate School .... Dr. Kim NEEDY
54 Dean of Engineering .... Dr. John ENGLISH
92 Dean Honors College .... Dr. Lynda COON
61 Dean of the Law School .... Ms. Stacy LEEDS
29 Assoc Vice Chanc for Alumni .... Ms. Brandy A. COX
22 Director of Equal Opportunity .... Ms. Danielle L. WOOD-WILLIAMS
37 Exec Director Financial Aid .... Ms. Wendy D. STOUFFER
38 Dir of Counseling/Psych Services .... Dr. Jonathan C. PERRY
19 Director University Police .... Mr. Steve GAHAGANS
36 Exec Dir of Career Develop Center .... Ms. Angela S. WILLIAMS
13 Assoc VC for Info Technology .... Dr. Chris MCCOY
06 Registrar .... Mr. Dave DAWSON
96 Director of Purchasing .... Ms. Linda FAST
58 Director Graduate & Intl Admissions .... Ms. Lynn MOSESSO

*University of Arkansas at Fort Smith (A)

PO Box 3649, Fort Smith AR 72913-3649

County: Sebastian — FICE Identification: 001110
Unit ID: 108092
Telephone: (479) 788-7000 — Carnegie Class: Bac-Diverse
FAX Number: (479) 788-7003 — Calendar System: Semester
URL: www.uafs.edu
Established: 1928 — Annual Undergrad Tuition & Fees (In-District): $5,390
Enrollment: 6,720 — Coed
Affiliation or Control: State/Local — IRS Status: 501(c)3
Highest Offering: Master's
Accreditation: NH, CAEPN, DH, DMS, MUS, NAIT, NUR, NURSE, RAD, SURGT

02 Chancellor .... Dr. Paul B. BERAN
05 Provost/Vice Chanc Academic Affairs .... Dr. Georgia HALE
111 Vice Chancellor Univ Advancement .... Dr. Mary LACKIE
10 Vice Chanc Finance & Administration .... Mr. Brad SHERIFF
32 Vice Chancellor Student Affairs .... Dr. Lee KREHBIEL
58 Assoc Provost/Dir of Grad Studies .... Dr. Margaret TANNER
31 Assoc VC Campus/Cmty Events .... Mr. Stacey JONES
86 Director Govt & Univ Relations .... Mr. Jordan HALE
20 Asst to Provost/Dir Dev Educ .... Ms. Diana ROWDEN
20 Asst to Provost .... Ms. Penny PENDLETON
100 Chief of Staff & Vice Chanc .... Mr. Edward SERNA
76 Dean College of Health Sciences .... Dr. Carolyn MOSLEY
50 Dean College of Business .... Dr. Ashok SUBRAMANIAN
72 Dean Col Applied Science/Tech .... Dr. Ken WARDEN
72 Dean Col Sci/Tech/Engineering/Math .... Dr. Ron DARBEAU
60 Dean Col of Comm/Lang/Arts & Soc .... Dr. Paul HANKINS
15 Dir Human Resources/EEO Officer .... Ms. Bev MCCLENDON
12 Dir Western Arkansas Tech Ctr .... Dr. Darrell C. RINK
88 Dir of Student Professional Dev Ctr .... Mr. Ron ORICK
45 Asst Provost Inst Effectiveness .... Dr. John JONES
88 Director of Instructional Support .... Dr. Tara MISHRA
08 Director of Library Services .... Ms. Anne LIEBST
39 Director of Student Housing .... Ms. Beth EPPINGER
37 Director of Financial Aid .... Mr. David SEWARD
07 Dean of Admissions .... Mr. Steve ERVIN
121 Director of Advisement .... Ms. Julie MOSLEY
06 Registrar .... Mr. Wayne WOMACK
88 Exec Dir of International Relations .... Mr. Nicolas PATTILLO
26 Dir Creative Mktg/Comm .... Ms. Laura WATTLES
41 Director of Athletics .... Mr. Curtis JANZ
96 Director of Procurement Services .... Ms. Rhonda CATON
27 Director of Public Information .... Mr. John POST
18 Director of Plant Operations .... Mr. Bill PIERCE
103 Dir CBPD/Family Enterprise Ctr .... Mr. Dave ROBERTSON
13 Director Technology Services .... Mr. Terry MEADOWS
19 Dir Chief of University Police .... Mr. Ray OTTMAN
29 Director of Alumni Affairs .... Mr. Rick GOINS
112 Director of Planned Giving .... Ms. Anne THOMAS
36 Asst Director Career Services .... Mr. Jeff ADAMS
53 Executive Director Education .... Vacant

*University of Arkansas at Little Rock (B)

2801 S University Avenue, Little Rock AR 72204-1099

County: Pulaski — FICE Identification: 001101
Unit ID: 106245
Telephone: (501) 569-3000 — Carnegie Class: DU-Mod
FAX Number: (501) 569-8915 — Calendar System: Semester
URL: www.ualr.edu
Established: 1927 — Annual Undergrad Tuition & Fees (In-State): $8,061
Enrollment: 11,891 — Coed
Affiliation or Control: State — IRS Status: 501(c)3
Highest Offering: Doctorate
Accreditation: NH, ADNUR, ART, CACREP, CAEPN, CONST, CS, DENT, ENG, ENGT, LAW, MUS, NUR, SPAA, SW, THEA

02 Chancellor .... Dr. Andrew ROGERSON
05 Executive Vice Chancellor & Provost .... Dr. Velmer S. BURTON
32 Vice Chancellor for Student Affairs .... Dr. Mark A. POISEL
10 Vice Chanc Finance & Administration .. Mr. Steve J. MCCLELLAN
111 Vice Chancellor Advancement .... Mr. Christian O'NEAL
41 Athletic Director .... Mr. Chasse S. CONQUE
86 Chief Govt Relations Officer .... Ms. Joni C. LEE
13 Associate Vice Chancellor & CIO .... Mr. John M. RATHJE
06 Registrar .... Ms. Malissa MATHIS
15 Director of Human Resources .... Dr. Ignatius C. AZEBEOKHAI
26 Associate VC of Communications Mktg ... Ms. Judy G. WILLIAMS
09 Director Inst Research .... Dr. William C. DECKER
37 Director Financial Aid .... Ms. Carlia G. SMITH
07 Director of Admissions .... Ms. Kathryn YOUNG
88 Assoc Prov for UALR Collect and Arc .... Dr. Deborah J. BALDWIN
19 Director of Public Safety .... Ms. Regina W. CARTER
25 Director Research & Sponsored Prog .... Ms. Tammie L. CASH

*University of Arkansas for Medical Sciences (C)

4301 W Markham, Little Rock AR 72205-7199

County: Pulaski — FICE Identification: 001109
Unit ID: 106263
Telephone: (501) 686-7000 — Carnegie Class: Spec-4-yr-Med
FAX Number: (501) 686-5905 — Calendar System: Semester
URL: www.uams.edu
Established: 1879 — Annual Undergrad Tuition & Fees (In-State): N/A
Enrollment: 3,021 — Coed
Affiliation or Control: State — IRS Status: 501(c)3
Highest Offering: Doctorate
Accreditation: NH, ARCPA, AUD, CAHIIM, COARC, CYTO, DH, DIETI, DMS, EMT, HSA, IPSY, MED, MT, NMT, NURSE, PH, PHAR, @PTA, RAD, SP, SURGT

02 Chancellor .... Dr. Daniel RAHN
05 Provost and CAO .... Dr. Stephanie F. GARDNER
10 Vice Chancellor Finance & CEO .... Mr. Bill BOWES
26 Vice Chancellor Communications .... Ms. Leslie W. TAYLOR
30 Vice Chancellor Development .... Mr. Lance E. BURCHETT
11 Vice Chancellor Campus Operations .... Mr. Mark A. KENNEDAY
28 Vice Chancellor for Diversity .... Dr. Billy R. THOMAS
08 Assoc Provost Library/Stdnt Svcs .... Dr. Jan HART
13 Chief Information Officer .... Ms. Rhonda JORDEN
15 Assoc Vice Chancellor for HR .... Mr. Jeff A. RISINGER
20 Assoc Provost Teaching Lrng Support .... Dr. Steve E. BOONE
07 Assoc Provost Enroll Svcs Admin .... Ms. Elizabeth BARD
37 Director Financial Services .... Ms. Gloria KEMP
63 Dean College of Medicine .... Dr. Pope H. MOSELEY
76 Dean College of Health Professions .... Dr. Douglas L. MURPHY
66 Dean College of Nursing .... Dr. Patricia COWAN
67 Dean College of Pharmacy .... Dr. Keith M. OLSEN
58 Dean of the Graduate School .... Dr. Robert E. MCGEHEE, JR.
88 Dean College of Public Health .... Dr. James M. RACZYNSKI
06 Dir Enrollment Svcs Chief Registrar ..... Mr. Clinton D. EVERHART
39 Dir Campus Life/Stdnt Support Svcs .... Ms. Cheri D. GOFORTH

† Tuition figure is for Medical School. Other school's tuitions vary widely.

*University of Arkansas at Monticello (D)

346 University Drive, Monticello AR 71656-3596

County: Drew — FICE Identification: 001085
Unit ID: 106485
Telephone: (870) 367-1020 — Carnegie Class: Bac/Assoc-Mixed
FAX Number: (870) 460-1321 — Calendar System: Semester
URL: www.uamont.edu
Established: 1909 — Annual Undergrad Tuition & Fees (In-State): $7,210
Enrollment: 3,643 — Coed
Affiliation or Control: State — IRS Status: 501(c)3
Highest Offering: Master's
Accreditation: NH, CAEPN, EMT, MUS, NUR, SW

02 Chancellor .... Dr. Karla HUGHES
100 Chief of Staff .... Ms. Lisa SHEMWELL
05 VC for Academic Affairs .... Dr. Peggy DOSS
11 VC for Univ Operations/Student Aff .... Mr. Jay HUGHES
12 VC for UAM College of Tech-Crossett .... Ms. Linda RUSHING
12 VC for UAM College of Tech-McGehee .... Mr. Bob WARE
04 Assistant to the Chancellor .... Ms. Christy PACE
10 Assoc VC for Finance and Admin .... Ms. Debbie GASAWAY
29 Assoc VC of Alum & Comm Strategy .... Mr. Mike OWENS
13 Chief Information Officer .... Ms. Anissa ROSS
111 Director of Advancement .... Dr. John DAVIS
86 Director of Government Relations .... Dr. John DAVIS
35 Dean of Students .... Ms. Renea MCCLENDON
84 Exec Dir of Admission/Enroll Mgmt .... Ms. Tawana GREENE
19 Director of University Police .... Mr. John KIDWELL
22 Dir Affirmative Action/EEO .... Ms. Sage LOYD
41 Director of Athletics .... Mr. John HARVEY
38 Director of Counseling/Testing .... Ms. Laura HUGHES
37 Interim Director of Financial Aid .... Ms. Becky HAMMETT
09 Director of Institutional Research .... Ms. Lisa CATER
08 Director of Library .... Mr. Daniel BOICE
26 Director of Media Services .... Mr. Jim BREWER
18 Director of Physical Plant .... Mr. Rusty RIPPEE
96 Director of Purchasing .... Ms. Gay PACE
06 Registrar .... Ms. Carol DOLBERRY

*University of Arkansas at Pine Bluff (E)

1200 N University Drive, Pine Bluff AR 71601-2799

County: Jefferson — FICE Identification: 001086
Unit ID: 106412
Telephone: (870) 575-8000 — Carnegie Class: Bac-Diverse
FAX Number: (870) 543-8009 — Calendar System: Semester
URL: www.uapb.edu
Established: 1873 — Annual Undergrad Tuition & Fees (In-State): $6,898
Enrollment: 2,658 — Coed
Affiliation or Control: State — IRS Status: 501(c)3
Highest Offering: Doctorate
Accreditation: NH, AAFCS, ACBSP, ART, CAEPN, MUS, NAIT, NURSE, SW

02 Chancellor .... Dr. Laurence B. ALEXANDER
05 Vice Chanc Academic Affairs .... Dr. Jacquelyn MCCRAY
10 Vice Chanc Finance & Admin .... Dr. Carla M. MARTIN
32 Vice Chancellor Student Affairs .... Mr. Elbert BENNETT
45 Vice Chanc Research/Innovation .... Vacant
84 Vice Chanc Enrollment Management .... Dr. Linda OKIROR
100 Chief of Staff .... Mrs. Janet BROILES
41 Athletics Director .... Mr. Lonza HARDY
15 Director of Human Resources .... Mrs. Gladys BENFORD
13 Director of Technical Services .... Mrs. Willette TOTTEN
09 Director of Institutional Research .... Mrs. Margaret TAYLOR
06 Registrar .... Mrs. Erica FULTON
29 Director of Alumni Affairs .... Mr. John KUYKENDALL
08 Head Librarian .... Mr. Edward FONTENETTE
103 Dir Workforce/Career Development .... Mrs. Shirley CHERRY
108 Director Institutional Assessment .... Dr. Steve LOCHMANN
37 Director Student Financial Aid .... Mrs. Janice KEARNEY
22 Dir Affirmative Action/EEO .... Mrs. Karen BAKER
88 Director of Recruitment .... Mr. Chris ROBINSON
07 Director of Admissions .... Ms. Philomena OWASOYO
18 Director Facilities/Physical Plant .... Mr. Robert WALL
19 Director Security/Safety .... Chief Maxcie THOMAS
30 Chief Development/Advancement .... Ms. Marla MAYBERRY
44 Director Annual or Planned Giving ... Dr. Margaret MARTIN-HALL
50 Dean Sch of Business & Management ... Mr. Lawrence AWOPETU
53 Dean School of Education .... Dr. George HERTS
96 Director of Purchasing .... Ms. Rose CELESTIN

*Cossatot Community College of the University of Arkansas (F)

183 College Drive, De Queen AR 71832

County: Sevier — FICE Identification: 022209
Unit ID: 106795
Telephone: (870) 584-4471 — Carnegie Class: Assoc/HVT-Mix Trad/Non
FAX Number: N/A — Calendar System: Semester
URL: www.cccua.edu
Established: 1991 — Annual Undergrad Tuition & Fees (In-District): $3,015
Enrollment: 1,642 — Coed
Affiliation or Control: State/Local — IRS Status: 501(c)3
Highest Offering: Associate Degree
Accreditation: NH, ACBSP, OTA

02 Chancellor .... Dr. Steve COLE
05 Vice Chancellor of Academics .... Mrs. Ashley AYLETT
45 VC of Planning and Facilities .... Mr. Mike KINKADE
10 Vice Chancellor Business/Finance .... Mrs. Charlotte JOHNSON
32 Director of Student Services .... Mr. Justin WHITE
37 Director Student Financial Aid .... Mrs. Denise HAMMOND
111 Director Institutional Advancement .... Ms. Emily NEWLIN
06 Registrar/Institutional Reporting .... Mrs. Brenda MORRIS
103 Dir of Public Svc/Workforce Dev .... Mrs. Tammy COLEMAN
12 Director of Ashdown Campus .... Mr. Barrett REED
15 Director of Human Resources .... Ms. Kelly PLUNK
13 Director of Technology .... Mr. Tony HARGROVE
30 Coordinator of Development .... Mr. Dustin ROBERTS
07 Coordinator of Admissions .... Ms. Olivia WEBB

*Phillips Community College of the University of Arkansas (G)

PO Box 785, Helena AR 72342-0785

County: Phillips — FICE Identification: 001104
Unit ID: 107619
Telephone: (870) 338-6474 — Carnegie Class: Assoc/MT-VT-High Non
FAX Number: (870) 338-7542 — Calendar System: Semester
URL: www.pccua.edu
Established: 1965 — Annual Undergrad Tuition & Fees (In-District): $2,720
Enrollment: 1,661 — Coed
Affiliation or Control: State/Local — IRS Status: 501(c)3
Highest Offering: Associate Degree
Accreditation: NH, ACBSP, ADNUR, MLTAD, PHLEB

02 Chancellor .... Dr. G. Keith PINCHBACK
05 Vice Chancellor for Instruction .... Dr. Deborah KING
10 Vice Chanc Finance & Administration .... Mr. Stan SULLIVANT
32 Vice Chanc Student Svcs/Registrar .... Mr. Scott POST
30 Vice Chanc Col Advancement/Res Dev .... Mrs. Rhonda ST. COLUMBIA
12 Vice Chancellor Stuttgart Campus .... Mrs. Kim KIRBY
12 Vice Chancellor DeWitt Campus .... Mrs. Carolyn TURNER

*University of Arkansas Community College at Batesville (H)

2005 White Drive, PO Box 3350,
Batesville AR 72503-3350

County: Independence — FICE Identification: 020735
Unit ID: 106999
Telephone: (870) 612-2000 — Carnegie Class: Assoc/MT-VT-High Trad
FAX Number: (870) 793-4988 — Calendar System: Semester
URL: www.uaccb.edu
Established: 1975 — Annual Undergrad Tuition & Fees (In-District): $2,262
Enrollment: 1,387 — Coed

Affiliation or Control: State/Local IRS Status: 501(c)3
Highest Offering: Associate Degree
Accreditation: NH, ADNUR, EMT

02 Chancellor .... Ms. Deborah J. FRAZIER
04 Assistant to the Chancellor .... Ms. Hannah KELLER FLANERY
05 Vice Chancellor for Academics .... Dr. Brian SHONK
32 Vice Chanc Student Affairs .... Mr. Greg THORNBURG
10 Vice Chancellor Finance and Admin .... Mr. Gayle COOPER
09 VC Research/Planning/Assessment .... Dr. Anne AUSTIN
49 Chair Div of Arts & Humanities .... Ms. Susan TRIPP
50 Chair Div Business/Tech/Public Svc .... Dr. Tamara GRIFFIN
76 Chair Div Nursing/Allied Health .... Ms. Marietta CANDLER
81 Chair Div of Math and Science .... Mr. Douglas MUSE
103 Dir of Workforce Development .... Mr. Zachery HARBER
09 Dir of Institutional Research .... Ms. Beth BRUCE
07 Director of Admissions .... Ms. Amy FOREE
13 Director Information Services .... Mr. Steve COLLINS
06 Dir Student Information/Registrar .... Ms. Shelly MOSER
37 Director of Financial Aid .... Ms. Kristen CROSS
30 Director of Development .... Ms. Tina PAUL
18 Director of Maintenance .... Mr. Heath WOOLDRIDGE
36 Director Student Development .... Ms. Louise HUGHES
38 Career/Disabilities Coordinator .... Ms. Becky WARREN
08 Director Library .... Mr. Jay STRICKLAND
21 Controller .... Ms. Waynna DOCKINS
15 Personnel Officer .... Ms. Alexa SMITH
96 Purchasing Agent .... Ms. Peggy JACKSON
40 Bookstore Manager .... Ms. Luanne BARBER

*University of Arkansas at Hope-Texarkana (A)

PO Box 140, 2500 S Main Street, Hope AR 71802-0140
County: Hempstead FICE Identification: 005732
Unit ID: 107725
Telephone: (870) 777-5722 Carnegie Class: Assoc/HVT-Mix Trad/Non
FAX Number: (870) 777-5957 Calendar System: Semester
URL: www.uacch.edu
Established: 1991 Annual Undergrad Tuition & Fees (In-State): $2,540
Enrollment: 1,406 Coed
Affiliation or Control: State IRS Status: 501(c)3
Highest Offering: Associate Degree
Accreditation: NH, EMT, FUSER

02 Chancellor .... Mr. Chris THOMASON
05 Vice Chancellor for Academics .... Ms. Laura CLARK
32 Vice Chancellor Student Services .... Mr. Brian BERRY
10 Vice Chancellor for Finance .... Dr. Belinda AARON
108 Dean of Institutional Effectiveness .... Mr. John HOLLIS
88 Directory of Hempstead Hall .... Ms. Dolly HENLEY
111 Dir of Institutional Advancement .... Ms. Jill BOBO
13 Chief Info Technology Officer (CIO) .... Mr. Chuck JORDAN

*University of Arkansas Community College at Morrilton (B)

1537 University Boulevard, Morrilton AR 72110-9601
County: Conway FICE Identification: 005245
Unit ID: 107585
Telephone: (501) 354-2465 Carnegie Class: Assoc/MT-VT-High Trad
FAX Number: (501) 977-2044 Calendar System: Semester
URL: www.uaccm.edu
Established: 1961 Annual Undergrad Tuition & Fees (In-State): $2,996
Enrollment: 2,042 Coed
Affiliation or Control: State IRS Status: 501(c)3
Highest Offering: Associate Degree
Accreditation: NH

02 Chancellor .... Dr. Larry D. DAVIS
05 Vice Chancellor Academic Services .... Ms. Diana ARN
10 Vice Chancellor for Finance .... Ms. Lisa WILLENBERG
11 Vice Chancellor for Administration .... Dr. Linda M. BIRKNER
32 Vice Chancellor Student Services .... Mr. Darren JONES
09 Director of Institutional Research .... Ms. Beth HAWKINS
08 Librarian .... Ms. Rebecka VIRDEN
06 Registrar .... Ms. Linda HOLLAND
37 Financial Aid Director .... Mrs. Teresa Y. CASH
26 Dir Marketing & Public Relations .... Ms. Mary CLARK
13 Chief Information Officer .... Mr. Richard O. GROWNS
18 Director of the Physical Plant .... Mr. C. Allen HOLLOWAY
07 Director of Admissions .... Ms. Rachel MULLINS
103 Coord Workforce Develop/Cmty Educ .... Ms. Vicki SHADELL
15 Director Personnel Services .... Ms. Judy SANDERS
30 Chief Development .... Ms. Morgan ZIMMERMAN
38 Director Student Counseling .... Ms. Staci DUVALL
96 Director of Purchasing .... Ms. Anna HALBROOK

*University of Arkansas - Pulaski Technical College (C)

3000 W Scenic Drive, North Little Rock AR 72118-3399
County: Pulaski FICE Identification: 020753
Unit ID: 107664
Telephone: (501) 812-2200 Carnegie Class: Assoc/MT-VT-High Trad
FAX Number: (501) 771-2844 Calendar System: Semester
URL: www.pulaskitech.edu
Established: 1991 Annual Undergrad Tuition & Fees (In-State): $5,011
Enrollment: 7,641 Coed
Affiliation or Control: State IRS Status: 501(c)3
Highest Offering: Associate Degree
Accreditation: NH, ACFEI, COARC, DA, OTA

02 President .... Dr. Margaret ELLIBEE
05 Interim Provost .... Mr. Mike MCMILLAN
32 Vice Chancellor for Student Service .... Ms. Kelly OWENS
10 Vice Chancellor for Finance .... Ms. Stacey HOGUE
30 VC for Economic Development .... Mr. Bentley WALLACE
20 Associate Vice President/Learning .... Vacant
111 Vice Chancellor for Advancement .... Ms. Shannon BOSHEARS
84 Dean Enrollment Svcs .... Mr. Zachary PERRINE
07 Director of Admissions .... Mr. Ronald HUDSON
08 Library Director .... Ms. Wendy DAVIS
18 Director of Physical Plant .... Mr. Bryan RUSHER
09 Assoc VC for Institutional Research .... Ms. Jasmine RAY
96 Director of Purchasing .... Ms. Carlas SMITH
13 Assoc VC for Information Services .... Mr. David GLOVER
15 Assoc VC of Human Resources .... Ms. Sherry YOUNG
04 Assistant to the President .... Ms. Tena CARRIGAN
37 Director of Financial Aid .... Ms. Lavonne JUHL
26 Assoc VC Public Relations/Marketing .... Mr. Tim JONES
72 Dean Technical Education Division .... Mr. Dick BURCHETT
81 Dean Mathematics/Nat Social Scis .... Mr. Ben RAINS
50 Interim Dean Business/IT Division .... Ms. Rebecca STERLING
57 Dean Fine Arts & Humanities .... Mr. Joey COLE
06 Registrar .... Ms. Catherine DIVITO
76 Dean Allied Health/Human Services .... Ms. Jeanne WILLIAMS

*University of Arkansas Rich Mountain (D)

1100 College Drive, Mena AR 71953-2500
County: Polk FICE Identification: 021111
Unit ID: 107743
Telephone: (479) 394-7622 Carnegie Class: Assoc/MT-VT-High Non
FAX Number: (479) 394-7295 Calendar System: Semester
URL: www.uarichmountain.edu
Established: 1983 Annual Undergrad Tuition & Fees (In-District): $2,568
Enrollment: 929 Coed
Affiliation or Control: State/Local IRS Status: 501(c)3
Highest Offering: Associate Degree
Accreditation: NH

02 Chancellor .... Dr. Phillip WILSON
05 Vice Chancellor Academic Affairs .... Dr. Krystal THRAILKILL
32 VC Student Affairs/Registrar .... Mr. Chad FIELDS
10 Vice Chancellor Administration/CFO .... Mr. Morris BOYDSTUN
13 Chief Information Officer .... Mr. Chris MASTERS
08 Director Library Services .... Ms. Brenda MINER
37 Financial Aid Director .... Ms. Mary STANDERFER
30 Director of Development .... Ms. Tammy YOUNG
18 Director of Physical Plant .... Mr. Dennis HILL
97 Coordinator Adult Basic Education .... Ms. Terry FRANCIS
15 Director of Human Resources .... Ms. Amy LUDWIG
07 Director of Admissions .... Ms. Wendy MCDANIEL
21 Controller .... Ms. Patricia HALL
26 Chief Public Relations Officer .... Ms. Tammy YOUNG
40 Bookstore Manager .... Mr. Jason WOOD
09 Coordinator Institutional Research .... Ms. Tammy ODOM
21 Fiscal Project Coordinator .... Ms. Amy LUDWIG
04 Executive Asst to Chancellor .... Joyce SANDEN

*Phillips Community College of the University of Arkansas-DeWitt (E)

1210 Rice Belt Avenue, DeWitt AR 72042
Telephone: (870) 946-3506 Identification: 770174
Accreditation: &NH

*Phillips Community College of the University of Arkansas-Stuttgart (F)

2807 Hwy 165 South, Stuttgart AR 72160-2408
Telephone: (870) 673-4201 Identification: 770175
Accreditation: &NH

*University of Arkansas at Monticello College of Technology-Crossett (G)

1326 Highway 52 W, Crossett AR 71635
Telephone: (870) 364-6414 Identification: 770176
Accreditation: &NH

*University of Arkansas at Monticello College of Technology-McGehee (H)

PO Box 747, McGehee AR 71654
Telephone: (870) 222-5360 Identification: 770177
Accreditation: &NH

University of Central Arkansas (I)

201 Donaghey Avenue, Conway AR 72035-0001
County: Faulkner FICE Identification: 001092
Unit ID: 106704
Telephone: (501) 450-5000 Carnegie Class: Masters/L
FAX Number: (501) 450-5003 Calendar System: Semester
URL: uca.edu
Established: 1907 Annual Undergrad Tuition & Fees (In-State): $8,224
Enrollment: 11,754 Coed
Affiliation or Control: State IRS Status: 501(c)3
Highest Offering: Doctorate
Accreditation: NH, ART, CAATE, CAEPN, CIDA, COPSY, CS, DIETD, DIETI, MUS, NURSE, OT, PTA, SCPSY, SP, THEA

01 President .... Dr. Houston D. DAVIS
05 Provost/Exec VP Academic Affairs .... Dr. Steven W. RUNGE
10 VP Finance/Administration .... Ms. Diane D. NEWTON
32 VP Student Services/Inst Diversity .... Mr. Ronnie D. WILLIAMS
43 General Counsel .... Mr. Warren READNOUR
111 VP for University Advancement .... Dr. T. Kale GOBER
41 Athletic Director .... Dr. Brad TEAGUE
15 Assoc Vice Pres for Human Resources .... Dr. Graham GILLIS
85 AVP International Engagement .... Dr. Phillip BAILEY
26 Assoc VP Comm/PR/Marketing .... Ms. Christina MADSEN
100 Chief of Staff .... Mr. Kelley ERSTINE
21 Controller .... Mr. Jeremy BRUNER
58 Dean of Graduate School .... Dr. Angela BARLOW
50 Dean of Col Business Admin .... Dr. Michael HARGIS
53 Dean of College of Education .... Dr. Victoria GROVES-SCOTT
76 Dean Col Health/Applied Science .... Dr. Jimmy ISHEE
49 Dean of Col of Liberal Arts .... Dr. Peter MEHL
81 Dean Col Natural Sci/Math .... Dr. Steve ADDISON
57 Dean Fine Arts & Communication .... Mr. Terry WRIGHT
35 Dean of Students .... Vacant
92 Dean of Honors College .... Dr. Patricia SMITH
07 Director of Admissions .... Ms. Courtney BRYANT
08 Library Director .... Mr. Robert D. COVINGTON
06 Registrar .... Ms. Becky D. RASNICK
09 Director Institutional Research .... Ms. Amber L. HALL
13 VP Information Systems & Technology .... Dr. Chris DAVIS
37 Director Student Financial Aid .... Ms. Cheryl C. LYONS
36 Dir Career Svcs/Cooperative Educ .... Dr. Kathy RICE-CLAYBORN
19 Chief University Police .... Mr. John MERGUIE
38 Director Counseling Center .... Dr. Susan SOBEL
39 Director Housing & Residence Life .... Dr. Stephanie H. MCBRAYER
29 Director of Alumni Services .... Mr. Jesse THILL
116 Director Internal Audits .... Ms. Pamela L. MASSEY
18 Director Physical Plant .... Mr. Larry D. LAWRENCE
96 Director of Purchasing .... Ms. Cassandra MCCUIEN-SMITH
113 Director Student Accounts .... Mr. Chad HEARNE
108 Director Institutional Assessment .... Dr. Brandon J. COMBS

University of the Ozarks (J)

415 College Avenue, Clarksville AR 72830-2880
County: Johnson FICE Identification: 001094
Unit ID: 107558
Telephone: (479) 979-1000 Carnegie Class: Bac-Diverse
FAX Number: (479) 979-1355 Calendar System: Semester
URL: www.ozarks.edu
Established: 1834 Annual Undergrad Tuition & Fees: $23,750
Enrollment: 651 Coed
Affiliation or Control: Presbyterian Church (U.S.A.) IRS Status: 501(c)3
Highest Offering: Baccalaureate
Accreditation: NH, CAEPN

01 President .... Mr. Richard L. DUNSWORTH
05 Provost .... Vacant
10 VP for Finance & Administration .... Mr. Jeff SCACCIA
07 Assistant Director of Admission .... Mr. Joseph HUGHES
42 Chaplain .... Rev. Jeremy WILHEMI
06 Registrar .... Ms. Wilma K. HARRIS
08 Librarian .... Mr. Stuart P. STELZER
36 Director of Career Services .... Ms. Ruth WALTON
29 Director Alumni Affairs .... Mr. Brett WOOD
41 Athletic Director .... Mr. Jimmy CLARK
26 Dir University/Public Relations .... Mr. Larry A. ISCH
30 VP of Advancement .... Ms. Lori A. MCBEE
88 Director Jones Learning Center .... Ms. Julia H. FROST
09 Director of Institutional Research .... Mr. Caleb KEITH
89 Director of Freshmen Studies .... Dr. Karen FRANK
13 Director of Information Technology .... Ms. Vickie ALSTON
32 Dean of Students .... Mr. Steven WEAVER
81 Dean Div of Mathematics & Sciences .... Mr. Stacy KEY
53 Dean Div Business/Comm/Education .... Dr. Brett STONE
79 Dean Div Fine Arts/Human/Soc Sci .... Dr. Steve OATIS
105 Director Web Services .... Ms. Cara FLINN
15 Human Resources Manager .... Ms. Karen SCHLUTERMAN
19 Director Security/Safety .... Mr. Cyrus SMITH
21 Controller .... Mr. Albert LEDING
18 Chief Facilities/Physical Plant .... Mr. Joey ETHERIDGE
37 Director Student Financial Aid .... Mr. Glendon JENKINS
39 Director Student Housing .... Mr. Brian HULL
44 Director Annual or Planned Giving .... Ms. Leslie CARTER
84 Director Enrollment Management .... Mr. Reggie HILL

Williams Baptist College (K)

60 W. Fulbright Avenue, Walnut Ridge AR 72476
County: Lawrence FICE Identification: 001106
Unit ID: 107877
Telephone: (870) 886-6741 Carnegie Class: Bac-Diverse
FAX Number: (870) 886-3924 Calendar System: Semester
URL: www.wbcoll.edu
Established: 1941 Annual Undergrad Tuition & Fees: $17,320
Enrollment: 541 Coed
Affiliation or Control: Southern Baptist IRS Status: 501(c)3
Highest Offering: Master's
Accreditation: NH, CAEPN

01 President .... Dr. Tom O. JONES
05 Vice Pres Academic Affairs .... Dr. Brad BAINE
10 Vice President for Business Affairs .... Dr. W. Dale LEATHERMAN
30 Vice Pres Institutional Advancement .... Dr. Brett COOPER

84 VP for Enrollment Mgmt/Student Svcs . Dr. Jeremy D. DUTSCHKE
32 Dean of Students ..... Ms. Amber N. GRADY
06 Registrar ..... Mrs. Tonya D. BOLTON
04 Administrative Asst to President ..... Mrs. Jo C. PHILLIPS
08 Director Library Services ..... Mrs. Pamela MERIDITH
37 Director Student Financial Aid ..... Mrs. Barbara J. TURNER
38 Director of Counseling ..... Ms. Aneita COOPER
42 Campus Minister ..... Mr. Hayes HOWELL
18 Director Physical Plant ..... Mr. Tony CONLEY
44 Dir of Annual Giving & Alumni Rels ..... Mr. Aaron ANDREWS
13 Director Information Technologies ..... Mr. Blake MCGINNIS
41 Athletic Director ..... Mr. Jeff RIDER
07 Director of Admissions ..... Mr. Andrew WATSON
58 Dean of Graduate & Online Programs ..... Dr. Rose Mary WEAVER

CALIFORNIA

Abraham Lincoln University (A)

3530 Wilshire Blvd, Ste 1430, Los Angeles CA 90010
County: Los Angeles Identification: 667049
Unit ID: 488031
Telephone: (213) 252-5100 Carnegie Class: Not Classified
FAX Number: (213) 788-3572 Calendar System: Other
URL: www.alu.edu
Established: 1996 Annual Undergrad Tuition & Fees: N/A
Enrollment: N/A Coed
Affiliation or Control: Proprietary IRS Status: Proprietary
Highest Offering: First Professional Degree
Accreditation: **DEAC**

01 President & CEO/Dean School of Law ..... Mr. Hyung PARK
13 CIO & Associate Dean School of Law ..... Ms. Jessica PARK
11 Director of Administration ..... Dr. Vivek SHARMA
121 Acad Succ Pgm/Acad Supp/Mktg Coord ..... Mr. Daniel JUNG
06 Registrar ..... Ms. Elizabeth GOMEZ
07 Director of Admissions ..... Mr. Richard LINGLE
10 Chief Financial Officer ..... Mr. Joshua SUNG
37 Director Student Financial Aid ..... Ms. Lisa INGOLDSBY
14 Director of Operations & Technology ..... Mr. Michael YAP

Academy for Jewish Religion (B)

574 Hilgard Avenue, Los Angeles CA 90024-3234
County: Los Angeles FICE Identification: 041555
Unit ID: 457271
Telephone: (213) 884-4133 Carnegie Class: Spec-4-yr-Faith
FAX Number: (213) 884-4136 Calendar System: Trimester
URL: www.ajrca.edu
Established: 2001 Annual Graduate Tuition & Fees: N/A
Enrollment: 64 Coed
Affiliation or Control: Jewish IRS Status: 501(c)3
Highest Offering: Master's; No Undergraduates
Accreditation: **WC**

01 Interim President ..... Rabbi Laura OWENS
73 VP/Dean of Chaplaincy School ..... Rabbi Rochelle ROBINS
05 Dean of Rabbinical School ..... Rabbi Liat YARDENI-FUNK
10 Chief Financial Officer ..... Dr. Alvin MARTIN
11 Director Administration ..... Ms. Lauren GOLDNER
06 Registrar/Operations Coordinator ..... Ms. Elea FRIEDMAN
07 Director of Admissions/Recruitment ..... Ms. Robin FEDERMAN
26 Chief Public Relations Officer ..... Vacant
36 Director of Internships/Placement ..... Rabbi Faith TESSLER
88 Dean of Cantorial School ..... Cantor Hazzan Nathan LAM
88 Associate Dean of Cantorial School ..... Cantor Perryne ANKER

Academy of Art University (C)

79 New Montgomery Street,
San Francisco CA 94105-3410
County: San Francisco FICE Identification: 007531
Unit ID: 108232
Telephone: (415) 274-2200 Carnegie Class: Spec-4-yr-Arts
FAX Number: (415) 274-8665 Calendar System: Semester
URL: www.academyart.edu
Established: 1929 Annual Undergrad Tuition & Fees: $21,252
Enrollment: 13,800 Coed
Affiliation or Control: Proprietary IRS Status: Proprietary
Highest Offering: Master's
Accreditation: **WC**, ART, CIDA

01 President ..... Dr. Elisa STEPHENS

Academy of Chinese Culture and Health Sciences (D)

1600 Broadway Street, Suite 200, Oakland CA 94612
County: Alameda FICE Identification: 032883
Unit ID: 108269
Telephone: (510) 763-7787 Carnegie Class: Spec-4-yr-Other Health
FAX Number: (510) 834-8646 Calendar System: Other
URL: www.acchs.edu
Established: 1982 Annual Undergrad Tuition & Fees: N/A
Enrollment: 136 Coed
Affiliation or Control: Independent Non-Profit IRS Status: 501(c)3
Highest Offering: Master's; No Lower Division
Accreditation: **ACUP**

01 President ..... Dr. Yenwei CHOONG
03 Exec Vice President ..... Mr. Andres BELLA
11 Vice President of Administration ..... Ms. Jane ZHANG

Acupuncture and Integrative Medicine College-Berkeley (E)

2550 Shattuck Avenue, Berkeley CA 94704-2724
County: Alameda FICE Identification: 033274
Unit ID: 384306
Telephone: (510) 666-8248 Carnegie Class: Spec-4-yr-Other Health
FAX Number: (510) 666-0111 Calendar System: Trimester
URL: www.aimc.edu
Established: 1990 Annual Undergrad Tuition & Fees: N/A
Enrollment: 105 Coed
Affiliation or Control: Independent Non-Profit IRS Status: 501(c)3
Highest Offering: Master's; No Lower Division
Accreditation: **ACUP**

01 President ..... Mr. Yasuo TANAKA
05 Academic Dean ..... Mr. Peter BLACKMAN
88 Clinic Dean ..... Mr. Mike MORGAN
07 Director of Admissions ..... Ms. Julie SCHEFF
06 Registrar ..... Mr. Brian LIESKE
20 Student Advisor ..... Mr. Peter BLACKMAN
08 Head Librarian ..... Ms. Patricia WARD
37 Director Student Financial Aid ..... Ms. Victoria LABRADOR

Advanced College (F)

13180 Paramount Boulevard, South Gate CA 90280-7956
County: Los Angeles FICE Identification: 037863
Unit ID: 444343
Telephone: (562) 408-6969 Carnegie Class: Spec 2-yr-Health
FAX Number: (562) 408-0471 Calendar System: Other
URL: www.advancedcollege.edu
Established: 1999 Annual Undergrad Tuition & Fees: N/A
Enrollment: 81 Coed
Affiliation or Control: Proprietary IRS Status: Proprietary
Highest Offering: Associate Degree
Accreditation: **COE**

01 President ..... Dr. Lida MANSOURIAN
66 Director Vocational Nursing ..... Dr. Minnie L. DOUGLAS
11 Director of Operations ..... Dr. Mehdi KARIMPOUR
37 Director Financial Aid ..... Mr. Roberto QUINONES

Advanced Computing Institute (G)

3470 Wilshire Blvd #1100, Los Angeles CA 90010
County: Los Angeles Identification: 667142
Unit ID: 481234
Telephone: (213) 383-8999 Carnegie Class: Spec 2-yr-Tech
FAX Number: (213) 383-5765 Calendar System: Semester
URL: www.advancedcomputinginstitute.com
Established: 1992 Annual Undergrad Tuition & Fees: N/A
Enrollment: 346 Coed
Affiliation or Control: Proprietary IRS Status: Proprietary
Highest Offering: Associate Degree
Accreditation: **COE**

01 School Director/CEO ..... Mr. Daniel MAINCA
05 Vice Pres Academic Affairs ..... Dr. Michael RAHNI

Advanced Training Associates (H)

1810 Gillespie Way, Suite 104, El Cajon CA 92020-1234
County: San Diego FICE Identification: 035324
Unit ID: 444361
Telephone: (619) 596-2766 Carnegie Class: Spec 2-yr-Tech
FAX Number: (619) 596-4526 Calendar System: Other
URL: www.advancedtraining.edu
Established: 2000 Annual Undergrad Tuition & Fees: N/A
Enrollment: 103 Coed
Affiliation or Control: Proprietary IRS Status: Proprietary
Highest Offering: Associate Degree
Accreditation: **COE**

01 President/CEO ..... Henry MARENTES
12 Vice President of Operations ..... Valerie PHILLIPS
88 Director of Compliance ..... Nick FLEETWOOD
07 Director of Admissions ..... Steven HOWARD
05 Director of Education ..... James R. KYLE
06 Registrar/Financial Aid Officer ..... Dionne SIMPSON

Alhambra Medical University (I)

55 S. Raymond Avenue, Alhambra CA 91801
County: Los Angeles Identification: 667052
Unit ID: 487995
Telephone: (626) 289-7719 Carnegie Class: Not Classified
FAX Number: (626) 289-8641 Calendar System: Quarter
URL: www.amuedu.com
Established: 2005 Annual Graduate Tuition & Fees: N/A
Enrollment: N/A Coed
Affiliation or Control: Proprietary IRS Status: Proprietary
Highest Offering: Master's; No Undergraduates
Accreditation: **ACUP**

01 President ..... Dr. Jonathan WU
05 Academic Dean ..... David LEE
23 Director of University Clinic ..... Elizabeth JIN
07 Director of Admissions ..... Qing MA
06 Registrar ..... Xiao Ting DING
08 Librarian ..... Dr. Luke CHEN

Allan Hancock College (J)

800 S College Drive, Santa Maria CA 93454-6399
County: Santa Barbara FICE Identification: 001111
Unit ID: 108807
Telephone: (805) 922-6966 Carnegie Class: Assoc/HT-Mix Trad/Non
FAX Number: (805) 347-9896 Calendar System: Semester
URL: www.hancockcollege.edu
Established: 1920 Annual Undergrad Tuition & Fees (In-District): $1,346
Enrollment: 10,949 Coed
Affiliation or Control: State/Local IRS Status: 501(c)3
Highest Offering: Associate Degree
Accreditation: **WJ**

01 Superintendent/President ..... Dr. Kevin G. WALTHERS
10 Assoc Supt/VP Finance/Admin ..... Dr. Michael R. BLACK
05 Assoc Supt/VP Academic Affairs ..... Dr. George A. RAILEY
32 VP Student Services ..... Ms. Nohemy ORNELAS
11 Vice Pres Operations ..... Mr. Felix HERNANDEZ
108 Vice Pres Inst Effectiveness ..... Dr. Paul MURPHY
15 Director Human Resources ..... Ms. Kelly UNDERWOOD
35 Dean Student Services ..... Mr. Rob PARISI
38 Dean Counseling & Matriculation ..... Ms. Yvonne TENIENTE
20 Dean Academic Affairs ..... Dr. Robert CURRY
20 Dean Academic Affairs ..... Dr. Sofia RAMIREZ-GELPI
20 Dean Academic Affairs ..... Ms. Margaret LAU
56 Dean The Extended Campus ..... Mr. Rick RANTZ
41 Assoc Dean Kines/Rec/Athletics ..... Ms. Kim ENSING
111 Exec Director College Advancement ..... Ms. Susan HOUGHTON
88 Artistic Director PCPA ..... Mr. Mark BOOHER
13 Director Information Technology ..... Ms. Carol MOORE
21 Director Business Services ..... Ms. Jessica BLAZER
07 Director Admissions & Records ..... Ms. Marian QUAID-MALTAGLIATI
37 Director Student Financial Aid ..... Mr. Robert PARISI
26 Dir Public Affairs/Publications ..... Mr. Andrew MASUDA
78 Dir Cooperative Work Experience ..... Ms. Emily SMITH
88 Director EOPS & Special Outreach ..... Mr. Will BRUCE
18 Director Plant Services ..... Mr. Rex VANDENBERG
19 Dir Public Safety/Chief of Police ..... Vacant
88 Director Cal-SOAP ..... Ms. Diana PEREZ
88 Director College Achievement Now ..... Ms. Petra GOMEZ
25 Director Institutional Grants ..... Vacant
88 Counselor/Coordinator MESA ..... Ms. Christine REED
88 Managing Director PCPA ..... Ms. Jennifer SCHWARTZ
04 Administrative Asst to President ..... Ms. Carmen S. CAMACHO

*Alliant International University President's Office (K)

One Beach Street, Suite 100,
San Francisco CA 94133-1221
County: San Francisco Identification: 666132
Unit ID: 110431
Telephone: (415) 955-2100 Carnegie Class: N/A
FAX Number: (414) 955-2062
URL: www.alliant.edu

01 President ..... Mr. Andy VAUGHN
05 Provost/Vice Pres Academic Affairs ..... Dr. Tracy HELLER
32 VP Student Affairs/Policy Assurance ..... Dr. Mary OLING-SISAY
07 Vice President for Admissions ..... Ms. Amy KWIATKOWSKI
10 Vice Pres Finance/Int CFO ..... Ms. Diane ERDEI
06 Registrar ..... Mr. Paul WELCH
15 Chief Human Resources Officer ..... Dr. Michael RUSSELL
13 Chief Information Officer ..... Ms. Sue WIERENGA
11 Director Campus Services ..... Ms. Angela DICKSON

*Alliant International University-San Diego (L)

10455 Pomerado Road, San Diego CA 92131-1799
County: San Diego FICE Identification: 011117
Unit ID: 110468
Telephone: (858) 635-4772 Carnegie Class: DU-Mod
FAX Number: (858) 693-8562 Calendar System: Semester
URL: www.alliant.edu
Established: 1952 Annual Undergrad Tuition & Fees: $17,312
Enrollment: 3,509 Coed
Affiliation or Control: Independent Non-Profit IRS Status: 501(c)3
Highest Offering: Doctorate
Accreditation: **WC**, CLPSY, MFCD

32 VP Student Services ..... Ms. Amber ECKERT
05 Provost/Vice Pres Academic Affairs ..... Dr. Tracy HELLER
12 Campus Director ..... Mr. Adam KASADA

**Alliant International University-Fresno* (M)

5130 E Clinton Way, Fresno CA 93727-2014
Telephone: (559) 456-2777 FICE Identification: 001158
Accreditation: **&WC**, CLPSY, MFCD

* Alliant International University-Irvine (A)

2855 Michelle Drive, Suite 300, Irvine CA 92606
Telephone: (949) 812-7440 Identification: 666157
Accreditation: &WC, MFCD

* Alliant International University-Los Angeles (B)

1000 S Fremont Avenue, Unit 5,
Alhambra CA 91803-1360
Telephone: (626) 284-2777 FICE Identification: 010013
Accreditation: &WC, CLPSY, MFCD

* Alliant International University-San Francisco (C)

One Beach Street, San Francisco CA 94133-1221
Telephone: (415) 955-2100 FICE Identification: 011881
Accreditation: &WC, CLPSY, IPSY, MFCD

AMDA College and Conservatory of the Performing Arts (D)

6305 Yucca Street, Los Angeles CA 90028
County: Los Angeles Identification: 666721
Telephone: (323) 469-3300 Carnegie Class: Not Classified
FAX Number: (323) 469-1448 Calendar System: Semester
URL: www.amda.edu
Established: 1964 Annual Undergrad Tuition & Fees: N/A
Enrollment: N/A Coed
Affiliation or Control: Independent Non-Profit IRS Status: 501(c)3
Highest Offering: Baccalaureate
Accreditation: THEA

01 President/Artistic Director ..... David MARTIN
05 Executive Director/Vice President ..... Jan RUGGAR MARTIN
07 Director Admissions ..... Joseph SIRIANO
37 Associate Director of Financial Aid ..... Jillian DOYLE
20 Director Education Services ..... Cynthia MOJ
32 Asst Director Student Affairs ..... Caroline HARRINGTON

American Academy of Dramatic Arts, Los Angeles Campus (E)

1336 N La Brea Avenue, Hollywood CA 90028-7504
Telephone: (323) 464-2777 FICE Identification: 021069
Accreditation: &M, THEA

† Regional accreditation is carried under the parent institution in New York, NY.

American Baptist Seminary of the West (F)

2606 Dwight Way, Berkeley CA 94704-3097
County: Alameda FICE Identification: 001120
Unit ID: 108861
Telephone: (510) 841-1905 Carnegie Class: Spec-4-yr-Faith
FAX Number: (510) 841-2446 Calendar System: Semester
URL: www.absw.edu
Established: 1871 Annual Graduate Tuition & Fees: N/A
Enrollment: 73 Coed
Affiliation or Control: American Baptist IRS Status: 501(c)3
Highest Offering: Doctorate; No Undergraduates
Accreditation: THEOL

01 Interim President ..... Dr. Nick CARTER
03 Vice President ..... Rev. Michelle M. HOLMES
05 Academic Dean ..... Dr. LeAnn SNOW FLESHER
10 Chief Financial Officer ..... Rev. Michelle M. HOLMES
06 Registrar ..... Anna E. SONG
07 Director of Admissions ..... Megan WOOD
32 Director of Student Services ..... Anna E. SONG
04 Administrative Asst to President ..... Rev. Carolyn E. MATTHEWS

American Career College-Los Angeles (G)

4021 Rosewood Avenue, Los Angeles CA 90004
County: Los Angeles FICE Identification: 022418
Unit ID: 109040
Telephone: (323) 668-7555 Carnegie Class: Spec 2-yr-Health
FAX Number: (322) 953-3654 Calendar System: Other
URL: www.americancareercollege.edu
Established: 1978 Annual Undergrad Tuition & Fees: N/A
Enrollment: 1,543 Coed
Affiliation or Control: Proprietary IRS Status: Proprietary
Highest Offering: Associate Degree
Accreditation: ABHES, SURTEC

01 Director ..... Mr. Chris TUREN

American Career College-Ontario (H)

3130 East Sedona Court, Ontario CA 91764
County: San Bernardino FICE Identification: 039713
Unit ID: 447768
Telephone: (909) 218-3253 Carnegie Class: Spec 2-yr-Health
FAX Number: (909) 218-3340 Calendar System: Other
URL: www.americancareercollege.edu
Established: 2006 Annual Undergrad Tuition & Fees: N/A
Enrollment: 1,521 Coed
Affiliation or Control: Proprietary IRS Status: Proprietary
Highest Offering: Associate Degree
Accreditation: ABHES, COARC, SURTEC

01 Campus President ..... Mr. Scott WARDALL

American Career College-Orange County (I)

1200 North Magnolia Avenue, Anaheim CA 92801-2607
Telephone: (714) 952-9066 Identification: 667073
Accreditation: ABHES, CAHIIM, COARC, OTA, PTAA, SURTEC

American Conservatory Theater (J)

30 Grant Avenue, 6th floor, San Francisco CA 94108-5800
County: San Francisco FICE Identification: 020992
Unit ID: 109086
Telephone: (415) 439-2350 Carnegie Class: Spec-4-yr-Arts
FAX Number: (415) 834-3210 Calendar System: Semester
URL: www.act-sf.org
Established: 1969 Annual Graduate Tuition & Fees: $27,801
Enrollment: 46 Coed
Affiliation or Control: Independent Non-Profit IRS Status: 501(c)3
Highest Offering: Master's; No Undergraduates
Accreditation: WC

01 Conservatory Director ..... Melissa SMITH
88 Artistic Director ..... Carey PERLOFF
05 Director of Academic Affairs ..... Jack SHARRAR
10 Finance Director ..... Laurence YUAN
30 Director Development ..... Caitlin QUINN
37 Director of Financial Aid ..... Jerry LOPEZ
26 Assoc Marketing Director ..... Christine MILLER

America Evangelical University (K)

1818 S. Western Avenue #409, Los Angeles CA 90006
County: Los Angeles Identification: 667090
Telephone: (323) 643-0301 Carnegie Class: Not Classified
FAX Number: (323) 643-0302 Calendar System: Semester
URL: www.aeu.edu
Established: 2001 Annual Undergrad Tuition & Fees: N/A
Enrollment: N/A Coed
Affiliation or Control: Independent Non-Profit IRS Status: 501(c)3
Highest Offering: Doctorate
Accreditation: BI

01 President ..... Dr. Jongkil RYU
05 Academic Dean ..... Dr. Mark YOON
32 Dean of Student Affairs ..... Rev. Samuel LEE
10 CFO ..... Rev. Sung CHO
30 Chief Development Officer ..... Dr. Yo Han PYEON
08 Director of Library ..... Dr. Duk YOUNG WON
06 Registrar ..... Mimi LEE
07 Director of Admissions ..... Jin LEE
37 Director Student Financial Aid ..... Cindy CHO

American Film Institute Conservatory (L)

2021 N Western Avenue, Los Angeles CA 90027-1657
County: Los Angeles FICE Identification: 022220
Unit ID: 108870
Telephone: (323) 856-7600 Carnegie Class: Spec-4-yr-Arts
FAX Number: (323) 467-4578 Calendar System: Semester
URL: www.afi.com
Established: 1969 Annual Graduate Tuition & Fees: N/A
Enrollment: 328 Coed
Affiliation or Control: Independent Non-Profit IRS Status: 501(c)3
Highest Offering: Master's; No Undergraduates
Accreditation: WC, ART

01 Director American Film Institute ..... Mr. Bob GAZZALE
11 Chief Operating Officer ..... Ms. Nancy HARRIS
30 Chief Advancement Officer ..... Mr. Tom WEST
05 Dean of Conservatory ..... Mr. Richard GLADSTEIN
20 Exec Vice Dean of Conservatory ..... Mr. Joe PETRICCA
88 Director Thesis Production ..... Ms. Patty WEST
88 Assoc Dean Dir Productions Svcs ..... Ms. Betsy POLLOCK
32 Director Fellow Affairs ..... Mr. Jonathan S. LEOS
57 Artistic Director ..... Mr. James L. BROOKS
06 Registrar ..... Ms. Carmela CHANEY
15 Director Human Resources ..... Ms. Roschoune FRANKLIN
37 Financial Aid Director ..... Ms. Trina RODLER
08 Librarian ..... Mr. Robert VAUGHN
13 Director Information Technology ..... Mr. Scott BLY
113 Bursar ..... Ms. Jasmin CARROLL

American Graduate University (M)

733 N Dodsworth Avenue, Covina CA 91724-2408
County: Los Angeles Identification: 666982
Unit ID: 109095
Telephone: (626) 966-4576 Carnegie Class: Not Classified
FAX Number: (626) 915-1709 Calendar System: Other
URL: www.agu.edu
Established: 1969 Annual Graduate Tuition & Fees: N/A
Enrollment: N/A Coed
Affiliation or Control: Proprietary IRS Status: Proprietary
Highest Offering: Master's; No Undergraduates
Accreditation: DEAC

01 President ..... Mr. Paul R. MCDONALD
05 Director Academic Affairs ..... Mr. Paul R. MCDONALD
11 Dir of Administration/Admissions ..... Ms. Laurie MEJIA
32 Director of Student Services ..... Ms. Rachel RUIZ
06 Registrar ..... Ms. Debbie MCDONALD
26 Director of Marketing ..... Ms. Barbara YOUNG

American Jewish University (N)

15600 Mulholland Drive, Los Angeles CA 90077-1599
County: Los Angeles FICE Identification: 002741
Unit ID: 116846
Telephone: (310) 476-9777 Carnegie Class: Bac-A&S
FAX Number: (310) 471-1278 Calendar System: Semester
URL: www.aju.edu
Established: 1947 Annual Undergrad Tuition & Fees: $30,338
Enrollment: 174 Coed
Affiliation or Control: Independent Non-Profit IRS Status: 501(c)3
Highest Offering: Master's
Accreditation: WC

01 President ..... Dr. Robert WEXLER
05 Vice Pres Academic Affairs ..... Dr. Daniel GRASSIAN

American Medical Sciences Center (O)

225 West Broadway, Ste 115, Glendale CA 91204
County: Los Angeles FICE Identification: 041597
Unit ID: 461263
Telephone: (818) 240-6900 Carnegie Class: Not Classified
FAX Number: (818) 240-6902 Calendar System: Semester
URL: www.amscedu.com
Established: Annual Undergrad Tuition & Fees: N/A
Enrollment: 73 Coed
Affiliation or Control: Proprietary IRS Status: Proprietary
Highest Offering: Associate Degree
Accreditation: ABHES

01 President ..... Mr. Vardan KARAGEZIAN

American University of Armenia (P)

1000 Broadway, Suite 280, Oakland CA 94607
County: Alameda Identification: 666013
Telephone: (510) 925-4282 Carnegie Class: Not Classified
FAX Number: (510) 925-4283 Calendar System: Semester
URL: www.aua.am
Established: 1991 Annual Undergrad Tuition & Fees: N/A
Enrollment: N/A Coed
Affiliation or Control: Independent Non-Profit IRS Status: 501(c)3
Highest Offering: Master's
Accreditation: WC

01 President ..... Dr. Armen DER KIUREGHIAN
05 Provost ..... Dr. Randall RHODES
11 Vice President Operations ..... Ashot GHAZARYAN
10 Vice President of Finance ..... Gevorg GOYUNYAN
30 VP Development/External Relations ..... Paul YEGHIAYAN
06 Associate Registrar ..... Chaghig ARZROUNI-CHAHINIAN
26 Public Relations Coordinator ..... Diana MANUKYAN
07 Dir Admissions/Recruit/Intl Stdnts ..... Arina ZOHRABIAN
09 Institutional Research Manager ..... Anush BEZHANYAN
08 Head Librarian ..... Satenik AVAKIAN
101 Secretary of the Institution/Board ..... Caren MEGHREBLIAN
15 Director Personnel Services ..... Arina BEKCHIAN
29 Director Alumni Relations ..... Narine PETROSYAN
50 Dean of Business and Economics ..... Eric VAN GENDEREN
69 Dean of Public Health ..... Varduhi PETROSYAN

American University of Health Sciences (Q)

1600 E Hill Street, Building #1, Signal Hill CA 90755
County: Los Angeles FICE Identification: 032253
Unit ID: 433004
Telephone: (562) 988-2278 Carnegie Class: Spec-4-yr-Other Health
FAX Number: (562) 988-1791 Calendar System: Quarter
URL: www.auhs.edu
Established: 1994 Annual Undergrad Tuition & Fees: $21,058
Enrollment: 257 Coed
Affiliation or Control: Proprietary IRS Status: Proprietary
Highest Offering: Master's
Accreditation: WC, NURSE

01 President ..... Dr. Caroll RYAN
11 Chief Operating Officer ..... Dr. Marilyn UVERO

Anaheim University (R)

1240 S State College Blvd, Ste 110,
Anaheim CA 92806-5152
County: Orange Identification: 666651
Telephone: (714) 772-3330 Carnegie Class: Not Classified
FAX Number: (714) 772-3331 Calendar System: Other
URL: www.anaheim.edu
Established: 1996 Annual Graduate Tuition & Fees: N/A
Enrollment: N/A Coed
Affiliation or Control: Proprietary IRS Status: Proprietary

Highest Offering: Doctorate; No Undergraduates
Accreditation: DEAC

01 President .... Dr. Andrew E. HONEYCUTT
11 Administrative Director .... Ms. Kate STRAUSS
30 Chief Development/Advancement .... Mr. David BRACEY

Angeles College (A)

3440 Wilshire Boulevard, Suite 310,
Los Angeles CA 90010
County: Los Angeles FICE Identification: 041604
Unit ID: 457299
Telephone: (213) 487-2211 Carnegie Class: Spec-4-yr-Other Health
FAX Number: (213) 487-2299 Calendar System: Semester
URL: www.angelescollege.edu
Established: 2004 Annual Undergrad Tuition & Fees: N/A
Enrollment: 183 Coed
Affiliation or Control: Proprietary IRS Status: Proprietary
Highest Offering: Baccalaureate
Accreditation: ABHES

01 CEO/School Director .... Ms. Teresa KRAUSE

Angeles College-City of Industry (B)

17595 Almahurst Street, Suite 101-3,
City of Industry CA 91748
Telephone: (626) 965-5566 Identification: 770518
Accreditation: ABHES

Antelope Valley College (C)

3041 W Avenue K, Lancaster CA 93536-5426
County: Los Angeles FICE Identification: 001113
Unit ID: 109350
Telephone: (661) 722-6300 Carnegie Class: Assoc/HT-High Trad
FAX Number: (661) 722-6333 Calendar System: Semester
URL: www.avc.edu
Established: 1929 Annual Undergrad Tuition & Fees (In-District): $1,104
Enrollment: 14,399 Coed
Affiliation or Control: State/Local IRS Status: 501(c)3
Highest Offering: Baccalaureate
Accreditation: WJ, COARC, RAD

01 President/Superintendent .... Mr. Edward T. KNUDSON
05 VP Academic Affairs .... Dr. Bonnie SUDERMAN
32 VP Student Services .... Dr. Erin E. VINES
15 Vice President Human Resources .... Mr. Mark BRYANT
84 Dean Enrollment Services .... Ms. LaDonna TRIMBLE
35 Dean of Student Services .... Dr. Jill ZIMMERMAN
22 Director Disabled Students .... Dr. Louis LUCERO
26 Exec Director Marketing/Public Info .... Ms. Elizabeth DIACHUN
18 Exec Dir Maintenance/Operations .... Mr. Doug JENSEN
13 Director Information Technology .... Mr. Rick SHAW
30 Dir Inst Advancement & Foundation .... Ms. Dianne KNIPPEL
09 Director Inst Research & Planning .... Dr. Meeta GOEL
37 Director Financial Aid .... Ms. Nichelle WILLIAMS
68 Dean PE/Athlet/Visual and Perf Arts .... Dr. Peter CHEGE
79 Dean Language Arts/Academic Dev .... Dr. Duane RUMSEY
83 Dean Soc & Beh Sci/Bus/Comp Stds .... Dr. Tom O'NEIL
38 Dean Counseling & Matriculation .... Mr. Gary ROGGENSTEIN
72 Dean Career Technical Education .... Dr. Laureano FLORES
81 Dean of Math/Science & Engineering .... Dr. Les UHAZY

Antioch University Los Angeles (D)

400 Corporate Pointe, Culver City CA 90230
Telephone: (310) 578-1080 Identification: 666236
Accreditation: &NH

† Regional accreditation is carried under the parent institution in Yellow Springs, OH.

Antioch University Santa Barbara (E)

602 Anacapa Street, Santa Barbara CA 93101
Telephone: (805) 962-8179 Identification: 666231
Accreditation: &NH

† Regional accreditation is carried under the parent institution in Yellow Springs, OH.

APT College (F)

1939 Palomar Oaks Way, Suite A,
Carlsbad CA 92011-1311
County: San Diego Identification: 666245
Telephone: (800) 431-8488 Carnegie Class: Not Classified
FAX Number: (888) 431-8588 Calendar System: Quarter
URL: www.aptc.edu
Established: 1993 Annual Undergrad Tuition & Fees: N/A
Enrollment: N/A Coed
Affiliation or Control: Proprietary IRS Status: Proprietary
Highest Offering: Associate Degree
Accreditation: DEAC

01 President/Chief Executive Officer .... Vacant
05 Director of Academics .... Dr. Gabriella MAIELLO
06 Registrar/Academic Comp Manager .... Ms. Julie B. LOVE
10 Dir of Accounting & Administration .... Ms. Cheryl DODDS

Argosy University, Inland Empire (G)

3401 Centre Lake Drive, Suite 200, Ontario CA 91761
Telephone: (909) 472-0800 Identification: 666007
Accreditation: &WC, ACBSP

† Regional accreditation is carried under the parent institution in Orange, CA.

Argosy University, Los Angeles (H)

5230 Pacific Concourse Drive, Los Angeles CA 90045
Telephone: (310) 531-9700 Identification: 666011
Accreditation: &WC, ACBSP

† Regional accreditation is carried under the parent institution in Orange, CA.

Argosy University, Orange County (I)

601 South Lewis Street, Orange CA 92868
County: Orange FICE Identification: 021799
Unit ID: 436438
Telephone: (714) 620-3700 Carnegie Class: DU-Mod
FAX Number: (714) 620-3802 Calendar System: Semester
URL: www.argosy.edu/orangecounty
Established: 1999 Annual Undergrad Tuition & Fees: $13,152
Enrollment: 536 Coed
Affiliation or Control: Proprietary IRS Status: Proprietary
Highest Offering: Doctorate
Accreditation: WC, ACBSP, CAEPN, CLPSY

01 University President .... Dr. Cynthia BAUM
12 Campus President .... Marilyn AL-HASSAN
05 Vice President of Academic Affairs .... Diana SIGANOFF
32 Director of Student Services .... Amy ROBINSON
06 Registrar .... Amanda OLMOS

† Main Campus and HQ moved from Chicago, IL to Orange, CA

Argosy University, San Diego (J)

1615 Murray Canyon Rd, Suite 100,
San Diego CA 92108-4423
Telephone: (619) 321-3000 Identification: 666034
Accreditation: &WC, ACBSP

† Regional accreditation is carried under the parent institution in Orange, CA.

Argosy University, San Francisco Bay Area (K)

1005 Atlantic Avenue, Alameda CA 94501-1148
Telephone: (510) 217-4700 Identification: 666081
Accreditation: &WC, ACBSP, CLPSY

† Regional accreditation is carried under the parent institution in Orange, CA.

Art Center College of Design (L)

1700 Lida Street, Pasadena CA 91103-1999
County: Los Angeles FICE Identification: 001116
Unit ID: 109651
Telephone: (626) 396-2200 Carnegie Class: Spec-4-yr-Arts
FAX Number: N/A Calendar System: Semester
URL: www.artcenter.edu
Established: 1930 Annual Undergrad Tuition & Fees: $40,596
Enrollment: 2,133 Coed
Affiliation or Control: Independent Non-Profit IRS Status: 501(c)3
Highest Offering: Master's
Accreditation: WC, ART

01 President .... Dr. Lorne M. BUCHMAN
10 Sr VP/Chief Financial Officer .... Mr. Rich HALUSCHAK
05 Provost .... Mr. Fred FEHLAU
30 Sr Vice Pres Development .... Ms. Emily LASKIN
07 VP Admissions/Enrollment Mgmt .... Mr. Tom STERN
88 VP Exhibitions .... Mr. Steve NOWLIN
13 VP Information Technology .... Ms. Theresa ZIX
26 VP Marketing & Communication .... Mr. Jered GOLD
15 Vice Pres Human Resources .... Ms. Lisa M. SANCHEZ
18 Assoc VP Facilities/Campus Planning .... Mr. Rollin HOMER
88 VP Professional Dev/Industry Engage .... Ms. Kristine BOWNE
32 Associate Provost Student Affairs .... Mr. Ray QUIROLGICO
08 College Librarian & Managing Dir .... Mr. Mario ASCENCIO
21 Controller .... Ms. Diane WITTENBERG
37 Managing Director Financial Aid .... Ms. Cheryl GILLIES
06 Director of Enrollment & Registrar .... Mr. William GARTRELL
09 Director of Institutional Research .... Ms. Esmeralda NAVA
20 Director Academic Affairs .... Ms. Leslie JOHNSON
102 Sr Dir Foundation/Govt Relations .... Mr. Darryl MORI
36 Director of Career Development .... Ms. Denise GIANOUSSOPOULOS
96 Director of Purchasing .... Ms. Monica MATSUO

The Art Institute of California, A College of Argosy University - Hollywood (M)

5250 Lankershim Boulevard, North Hollywood CA 91601
Telephone: (213) 251-3636 FICE Identification: 031254
Accreditation: &WC, ACFEI, CIDA

† Regional accreditation is carried under the parent institution, Argosy University in Orange, CA.

The Art Institute of California, A College of Argosy University - Inland Empire (N)

674 East Brier Drive, San Bernardino CA 92408-2800
Telephone: (909) 915-2100 FICE Identification: 016471
Accreditation: &WC, ACFEI

† Regional accreditation is carried under the parent institution, Argosy University in Orange, CA.

The Art Institute of California, A College of Argosy University - Orange County (O)

3601 W Sunflower Avenue, Santa Ana CA 92704-7931
Telephone: (714) 830-0200 Identification: 666182
Accreditation: &WC, ACFEI, CIDA

† Regional accreditation is carried under the parent institution, Argosy University in Orange, CA.

The Art Institute of California, A College of Argosy University - Sacramento (P)

2850 Gateway Oaks Drive, Suite 100,
Sacramento CA 95833-4348
Telephone: (916) 830-6320 Identification: 666619
Accreditation: &WC, ACFEI

† Regional accreditation is carried under the parent institution, Argosy University in Orange, CA.

The Art Institute of California, A College of Argosy University - San Diego (Q)

7650 Mission Valley Road, San Diego CA 92108-4423
Telephone: (858) 598-1200 FICE Identification: 023276
Accreditation: &WC, ACFEI, CIDA

† Regional accreditation is carried under the parent institution, Argosy University in Orange, CA.

The Art Institute of California - San Francisco, a campus of Argosy University (R)

10 United Nations Plaza, San Francisco CA 94102-4928
Telephone: (888) 493-3261 FICE Identification: 007236
Accreditation: &WC

† Regional accreditation is carried under the parent institution, Argosy University in Orange, CA.

Asher College (S)

1215 Howe Street, Suite 101, Sacramento CA 95825
County: Sacramento FICE Identification: 040573
Unit ID: 447777
Telephone: (916) 649-9600 Carnegie Class: Spec 2-yr-Tech
FAX Number: (916) 649-9700 Calendar System: Other
URL: www.asher.edu
Established: 1998 Annual Undergrad Tuition & Fees: N/A
Enrollment: 485 Coed
Affiliation or Control: Proprietary IRS Status: Proprietary
Highest Offering: Associate Degree
Accreditation: CNCE

01 President .... David VICE

Ashford University (T)

8620 Spectrum Center Blvd, San Diego CA 92123
County: San Diego FICE Identification: 001881
Unit ID: 154022
Telephone: (866) 711-1700 Carnegie Class: Masters/L
FAX Number: (866) 685-4091 Calendar System: Semester
URL: www.ashford.edu
Established: 1918 Annual Undergrad Tuition & Fees: $11,032
Enrollment: 42,452 Coed
Affiliation or Control: Proprietary IRS Status: Proprietary
Highest Offering: Master's
Accreditation: WC, IACBE

01 University President/CEO .... Dr. Craig SWENSON
05 SVP Academic Affairs/CAO .... Dr. Laura PALMER-NOONE
10 SVP Finance/Chief Finance Officer .... Mr. Jim SMITH
11 SVP University Svcs & Strat Plng .... Ms. Sheri JONES
88 VP University Services & Policy .... Mr. Mike ROBINSON
06 VP University Registrar .... Ms. Katie SCHEIE
32 VP Student Services .... Mr. Kirk MORRISON
35 AVP Student Affairs .... Ms. Poppy FITCH
37 Dir Financial Aid & Policy .... Ms. Stephanie STEWART
49 Dean Division of General Education .... Dr. Justin HARRISON
50 Dean Forbes School of Business .... Mr. Bob DAUGHERTY
53 Dean College of Education .... Dr. Tony FARRELL

Azusa Pacific University (U)

901 E Alosta Avenue, Azusa CA 91702-7000
County: Los Angeles FICE Identification: 001117
Unit ID: 109785
Telephone: (626) 969-3434 Carnegie Class: DU-Mod
FAX Number: (626) 969-7180 Calendar System: Semester
URL: www.apu.edu
Established: 1899 Annual Undergrad Tuition & Fees: $36,120

Enrollment: 9,975 Coed
Affiliation or Control: Independent Non-Profit IRS Status: 501(c)3
Highest Offering: Doctorate
Accreditation: WC, ART, CAATE, CAEPN, CLPSY, IACBE, MUS, NURSE, PTA, SW, THEOL

01 President Dr. Jon R. WALLACE
05 Provost Dr. Mark STANTON
26 Exec Vice Pres External Affairs Mr. David E. BIXBY
12 Chancellor University College Dr. John C. REYNOLDS
32 Senior Vice Pres for Student Life Dr. Terry FRANSON
10 Vice President Business Affairs/CFO Mr. Bob L. JOHANSEN
03 Senior Vice President/Gen Counsel Dr. Mark DICKERSON
43 General Counsel Mr. Chris JENNINGS
13 Vice President/CIO Dr. Don DAVIS
84 VP Grad/Nontrdtnl Enroll/Stdnt Svc Dr. Heather PETRIDIS
84 VP for Enrollment Management Mr. David DUFAULT-HUNTER
58 Vice Provost Graduate Programs Dr. Diane GUIDO
20 Vice Provost Undergraduate Programs Dr. Vicky BOWDEN
35 AVP Student Life/Chief Judicial Ofc Mr. Willie HAMLETT
88 Assoc VP University Services Mr. Roger HODSDON
27 VP University Relations Dr. David PECK
49 Dean College Liberal Arts/Sci Dr. Jennifer WALSH
83 Dean School Behav/Applied Sciences Dr. Robert WELSH
50 Dean School of Business Mgmt Dr. Robert ROLLER
53 Dean School of Education Dr. Anita HENCK
73 Dean Haggard School of Theology Dr. Robert DUKE
64 Dean College of Music and the Arts Dr. Stephen JOHNSON
66 Dean School of Nursing Dr. Aja LESH
92 Dean Honors College Dr. David WEEKS
35 Assoc Dean Students/Dir Student Act Mrs. Shino SIMONS
15 Exec Director Human Resources Mr. John BAUGUS
30 VP University Advancement Mr. Corbin HOORNBEEK
21 Executive Director Finance Ms. Cynthia SOUZA
42 Campus Pastor Dr. Woody MOORWOOD
37 Dir Graduate Student Financial Svcs Ms. Michelle JOHNSON
06 Registrar-Graduate Mrs. Michelle JOHNSON
06 Associate Registrar-Undergraduate Ms. Mona MIKHAIL
29 Director Alumni Relations Mr. Phil BRAZELL
09 Director Acad Info Mgmt Analysis Vacant
41 Director Athletics Mr. Gary PINE
38 Director Counseling Center Dr. Bill FIALA
37 AVP for UG Academic Financial Svcs Mr. Todd ROSS
18 Associate VP Facilities Management Mr. Thomas HUNT
07 Director Undergraduate Admissions Mr. Samuel KIM
36 Director Career Services Mr. Phil BRAZELL
28 Exec Dir Diversity Planning/Assess Mr. Richard MARTINEZ
96 Purchasing Manager Mrs. Jo Ann BENGEL

Barstow Community College District (A)

2700 Barstow Road, Barstow CA 92311-6699
County: San Bernardino FICE Identification: 001119
Unit ID: 109907
Telephone: (760) 252-2411 Carnegie Class: Assoc/HT-High Non
FAX Number: (760) 252-1875 Calendar System: Semester
URL: www.barstow.edu
Established: 1959 Annual Undergrad Tuition & Fees (In-District): $1,104
Enrollment: 3,108 Coed
Affiliation or Control: State/Local IRS Status: 170(c)1
Highest Offering: Associate Degree
Accreditation: WJ

01 Superintendent/President Dr. Eva BAGG
04 Exec Assistant to the President Ms. Michelle HENDERSON
10 Vice President Admin Services Dr. Brenda FINDLEY
05 Vice President Academic Affairs Dr. David MORSE
32 Vice President Student Services Dr. Khushnur Z. DADABHOY
15 Assoc Vice President of HR Mr. Lyle ENGELDINGER
49 Dean of Instruction Ms. Penny SHREVE
103 Dean Workforce & Econ Dev Ms. Sandi THOMAS
106 Dean DE & Learning Support Svc Mr. Richard BOTENGAN
22 Dean Student Success & Equity Dr. Tonia TERESH
41 Assoc Dean of Students & Athletics Mr. Bryan KING
09 Dir Research Dev & Planning Ms. Lisa HOLMES
26 Dir of Public Rels/Comm & Marketing Mr. Chris CLARKE
18 Director Maintenance & Operations Mr. Richard HERNANDEZ
21 Director Fiscal Services Ms. Shawna L. ROBBINS
91 Director of Information Technology Mr. Morgan BOHNSACK
84 Director Enrollment Services Ms. Heather MINEHART
35 Director Student Life & Dev Ms. Joann GARCIA
25 Director CTE Grants Mr. James LEE
88 Director Military Programs Mr. Jerry PETERS
71 Director Special Pgms & Svcs Ms. Christina CALDERON
108 Director Assessment Services Ms. Kim YOUNG
88 Civic Center & Event Manager Mr. Ed WILL
90 Program Manager College Promise Ms. Melissa MEADOWS
114 Budget Analyst Vacant

Bergin University of Canine Studies (B)

5860 Labath Avenue, Rohnert Park CA 94928
County: Sonoma FICE Identification: 041763
Unit ID: 461643
Telephone: (707) 545-3647 Carnegie Class: Bac/Assoc-Mixed
FAX Number: (707) 545-0800 Calendar System: Semester
URL: www.berginu.edu
Established: 1991 Annual Undergrad Tuition & Fees: N/A
Enrollment: 61 Coed
Affiliation or Control: Independent Non-Profit IRS Status: 501(c)3
Highest Offering: Master's
Accreditation: ACICS

01 President Dr. Bonita M. BERGIN
05 Chief Academic Officer Dr. Bonita M. BERGIN
06 Registrar Denise GREGERSEN
07 Director of Admissions Connie VAN GUILDER
30 Director of Development Anastasia PRYOR
88 Director of College Governance Rebecca RICHARDSON

Bethesda University of California (C)

730 N Euclid Street, Anaheim CA 92801-4115
County: Orange FICE Identification: 032663
Unit ID: 110060
Telephone: (714) 517-1945 Carnegie Class: Spec-4-yr-Faith
FAX Number: (714) 683-1440 Calendar System: Semester
URL: www.buc.edu
Established: 1976 Annual Undergrad Tuition & Fees: $7,370
Enrollment: 364 Coed
Affiliation or Control: Independent Non-Profit IRS Status: 501(c)3
Highest Offering: Doctorate
Accreditation: BI, TRACS

01 President Vacant
10 Vice President/Chief Financial Ofcr Dr. Esther CHO
05 Chief Academic Officer Dr. Sin Ho KIM
32 Dean of Student Affairs Dr. Song YIL
08 Librarian Ms. Ho Kyung WOO
07 Admissions Director Ms. Monica KIM
37 Financial Aid Officer Mr. Isaac KO

Beverly Hills Design Institute (D)

8484 Wilshire Boulevard, Suite 730,
Beverly Hills CA 90211-3235
County: Los Angeles FICE Identification: 041855
Unit ID: 475635
Telephone: (310) 360-8888 Carnegie Class: Spec-4-yr-Arts
FAX Number: (310) 857-6974 Calendar System: Quarter
URL: www.bhdi.edu
Established: 2005 Annual Undergrad Tuition & Fees: $23,220
Enrollment: 17 Coed
Affiliation or Control: Proprietary IRS Status: Proprietary
Highest Offering: Baccalaureate
Accreditation: ACICS

01 CEO Sonia ETE
05 Chief Academic Officer Douglas SPESERT
11 Chief Operating Officer Thierry ETE
07 Director of Admissions/Career Svcs Marylou VON HEYMAN

Biola University (E)

13800 Biola Avenue, La Mirada CA 90639-0001
County: Los Angeles FICE Identification: 001122
Unit ID: 110097
Telephone: (562) 903-6000 Carnegie Class: DU-Mod
FAX Number: (562) 903-4748 Calendar System: Semester
URL: www.biola.edu
Established: 1908 Annual Undergrad Tuition & Fees: $36,696
Enrollment: 6,227 Coed
Affiliation or Control: Independent Non-Profit IRS Status: 501(c)3
Highest Offering: Doctorate
Accreditation: WC, ACBSP, ART, CLPSY, IPSY, MUS, NURSE, @SP, THEOL

01 President Dr. Barry H. COREY
05 Provost/Sr Vice President Dr. Deborah TAYLOR
10 Vice Pres Univ Operations & Finance Mr. Michael PIERCE
111 Vice President Advancement Dr. Adam MORRIS
84 Vice Pres Enrollment Management Mr. Greg VAUGHAN
26 VP Univ Communications & Marketing Mr. Lee WILHITE
32 VP Student Development Mr. Andre STEPHENS
20 Vice Provost/Academic Admin Dr. Patricia PIKE
07 Assoc VP University Admissions Ms. Amanda SLAUGHTER
73 Dean Talbot School Theology Dr. Clinton E. ARNOLD
83 Dean Rosemead School Psychology Dr. Clark D. CAMPBELL
88 Dean Cook Sch Intercultural Studies Dr. Bulus GALADIMA
53 Dean School of Education Dr. June HETZEL
50 Dean Crowell School of Business Dr. Gary LINDBALD
81 Dean of Science/Tech & Health Dr. Paul FERGUSON
57 Interim Dean of Fine Arts & Comm Mr. Jonathan PULS
79 Interim Dean of Humanities/Soc Sci Ms. Jamie CAMPBELL
08 Dean of the Library Dr. Gregg GEARY
42 Dean of Spiritual Development Dr. Todd PICKETT
06 Dean Academic Records/Inst Research Mr. Ken GILSON
15 Sr Director Human Resources Ms. Lisa SZABO
109 Sr Dir Auxiliary Services Ms. Sandie WEAVER
110 Senior Director of Advancement Dr. Richard BEE
37 Sr Director Financial Aid Mr. Geoff MARSH
21 Sr Dir Financial Mgmt/Reporting Mr. David KOONTZ
19 Chief Campus Safety Mr. John O. OJEISEKHOBA
90 Sr Director Information Technology Mr. Steven R. EARLE
36 Interim Dir Career Dev & Success Ms. Tiffany LEE
41 Athletics Director Dr. Bethany MILLER
40 Manager Bookstore Ms. Melissa CASTELLANO
18 Sr Director Facilities Management Mr. Brian PHILLIPS
38 Director Counseling Center Dr. Melanie TAYLOR
96 Purchasing Manager Mrs. Breanna KLETT
13 Chief Education Technology Officer Mrs. Susan ISHII
108 Director of University Assessment Dr. Rebecca HONG
43 University Legal Counsel Mr. Jerry MACKEY

Brandman University (F)

16355 Laguna Canyon Road, Irvine CA 92618
County: Orange FICE Identification: 041618
Unit ID: 262086
Telephone: (949) 753-4774 Carnegie Class: Masters/L
FAX Number: (714) 753-7875 Calendar System: Other
URL: www.brandman.edu
Established: 1958 Annual Undergrad Tuition & Fees: $12,300
Enrollment: 8,004 Coed
Affiliation or Control: Independent Non-Profit IRS Status: 501(c)3
Highest Offering: Doctorate
Accreditation: WC, CAEPN, NURSE, SW

01 Chancellor Dr. Gary BRAHM
12 Campus Director Ms. Tara PULLEE
05 Associate Dean School of Education Ms. Patricia CLARK-WHITE

† A member of the Chapman University System.

Brightwood College (G)

1914 Wible Road, Bakersfield CA 93304
Telephone: (661) 836-6300 Identification: 666291
Accreditation: ACICS

† Branch campus of Brightwood College, Sacramento, CA.

Brightwood College (H)

555 Broadway, Suite 144, Chula Vista CA 91910-5342
Telephone: (619) 498-4100 Identification: 770560
Accreditation: ACICS

Brightwood College (I)

44 Shaw Avenue, Clovis CA 93612
Telephone: (559) 325-5100 Identification: 770559
Accreditation: ACICS

Brightwood College (J)

6180 Laurel Canyon Blvd, Ste 101,
North Hollywood CA 91606
County: Los Angeles FICE Identification: 025391
Unit ID: 118967
Telephone: (818) 763-2563 Carnegie Class: Not Classified
FAX Number: (818) 763-1623 Calendar System: Other
URL: www.brightwood.edu
Established: 1982 Annual Undergrad Tuition & Fees: N/A
Enrollment: 828 Coed
Affiliation or Control: Proprietary IRS Status: Proprietary
Highest Offering: Associate Degree
Accreditation: ACICS, RAD

01 Campus President Mr. Josh LEVENSON

Brightwood College (K)

2475 E Tahquitz Canyon Way, Palm Springs CA 92262
Telephone: (760) 778-3540 Identification: 770558
Accreditation: ACICS

Brightwood College (L)

4330 Watt Avenue, Suite 400,
Sacramento CA 95821-7000
County: Sacramento FICE Identification: 023519
Unit ID: 118259
Telephone: (916) 649-8168 Carnegie Class: Spec 2-yr-Other
FAX Number: (916) 649-8344 Calendar System: Quarter
URL: www.brightwood.edu
Established: 1982 Annual Undergrad Tuition & Fees: N/A
Enrollment: 473 Coed
Affiliation or Control: Proprietary IRS Status: Proprietary
Highest Offering: Associate Degree
Accreditation: ACICS

01 Executive Director Scott KING
05 Director of Education Vacant
37 Director of Student Financial Aid Ryan SMITH
07 Director of Admissions Zach FELDHEGE
36 Director of Career Services Julie MUIR

Brightwood College (M)

5172 Kiernan Court, Salida CA 95368
County: Stanislaus FICE Identification: 023063
Unit ID: 366960
Telephone: (209) 543-7000 Carnegie Class: Spec 2-yr-Health
FAX Number: (209) 543-1755 Calendar System: Other
URL: www.brightwood.edu
Established: 1986 Annual Undergrad Tuition & Fees: N/A
Enrollment: 429 Coed
Affiliation or Control: Proprietary IRS Status: Proprietary
Highest Offering: Associate Degree
Accreditation: ACICS, COARC

01 Campus President Mr. Bill JONES

Brightwood College (A)

9055 Balboa Avenue, San Diego CA 92123-1509
County: San Diego | FICE Identification: 020917 | Unit ID: 118277
Telephone: (858) 279-4500 | Carnegie Class: Spec 2-yr-Health
FAX Number: (858) 279-4885 | Calendar System: Other
URL: www.brightwood.edu
Established: 1976 | Annual Undergrad Tuition & Fees: N/A
Enrollment: 1,173 | Coed
Affiliation or Control: Proprietary | IRS Status: Proprietary
Highest Offering: Associate Degree
Accreditation: ACICS, CAHIIM

01 Campus President .... Mr. David MOVSESIAN
05 Director of Education .... Ms. Tammy ESQUIVEL
07 Director of Admissions .... Ms. Serica ERVIN

Brightwood College (B)

2022 University Drive, Vista CA 92083-7736
County: San Diego | FICE Identification: 025490 | Unit ID: 118286
Telephone: (760) 630-1555 | Carnegie Class: Spec 2-yr-Other
FAX Number: (760) 630-1656 | Calendar System: Other
URL: www.brightwood.edu
Established: 1976 | Annual Undergrad Tuition & Fees: N/A
Enrollment: 754 | Coed
Affiliation or Control: Proprietary | IRS Status: Proprietary
Highest Offering: Associate Degree
Accreditation: ACICS

01 Executive Director .... Ms. Laura PITTS
05 Director of Education .... Mr. Destry LIEVANOS
07 Director of Admissions .... Ms. Renee CODNER
36 Director of Career Services .... Ms. Sipel TAHA
37 Director of Financial Aid .... Ms. Peetee MALLORY
66 Dean of Nursing .... Ms. Beth BUNYI

The Broad Center for the Management of School Systems (C)

2121 Avenue of the Stars, Ste 3000,
Los Angeles CA 90067
County: Los Angeles | Identification: 667228
Telephone: (310) 954-5080 | Carnegie Class: Not Classified
FAX Number: N/A | Calendar System: Other
URL: www.broadcenter.org
Established: | Annual Graduate Tuition & Fees: N/A
Enrollment: N/A | Coed
Affiliation or Control: Independent Non-Profit | IRS Status: 501(c)3
Highest Offering: Master's; No Undergraduates
Accreditation: WC

01 Executive Director .... Becca BRACY KNIGHT
13 Asst Director Information Systems .... Eulogio GALLO
26 Senior Director Communications .... Stephanie GERMERAAD

Bryan University (D)

350 South Lake Avenue #260, Pasadena CA 91101
County: Los Angeles | FICE Identification: 007164 | Unit ID: 110219
Telephone: (213) 484-8850 | Carnegie Class: Bac/Assoc-Assoc Dom
FAX Number: (213) 483-3936 | Calendar System: Semester
URL: www.bryancollege.edu
Established: 1940 | Annual Undergrad Tuition & Fees: $13,975
Enrollment: 1,417 | Coed
Affiliation or Control: Proprietary | IRS Status: Proprietary
Highest Offering: Master's
Accreditation: ACICS

01 President .... Mr. John KOLACINSKI

Butte College (E)

3536 Butte Campus Drive, Oroville CA 95965-8399
County: Butte | FICE Identification: 008073 | Unit ID: 110246
Telephone: (530) 895-2511 | Carnegie Class: Assoc/MT-VT-High Trad
FAX Number: (530) 895-2345 | Calendar System: Semester
URL: www.butte.edu
Established: 1966 | Annual Undergrad Tuition & Fees (In-District): $1,368
Enrollment: 11,669 | Coed
Affiliation or Control: State/Local | IRS Status: 501(c)3
Highest Offering: Associate Degree
Accreditation: WJ, COARC, EMT

01 Superintendent/President .... Dr. Samia YAQUB
05 Vice Pres Student Learning .... Ms. Virginia GULEFF
10 VP Administrative Service/CBO .... Mr. Andrew SULESKI
45 Vice President Planning/Research .... Mr. Lester JAURON
32 Vice President Student Services .... Mr. Allen RENVILLE
20 Dean Student Learning .... Ms. Suzanne GRIPENSTRAW
20 Dean Student Learning .... Ms. Kam BULL
20 Dean Student Learning .... Ms. Donna WEAVER
20 Dean Student Learning .... Ms. Denise ADAMS
20 Int Dean Student Learning .... Dr. Cheryl BABLER
37 Director Financial Aid/Vet Svcs .... Ms. Tammera SHINAR
15 Director Human Resources .... Mr. Chris LITTLE
18 Dir Facilities Planning/Management .... Ms. Kim JONES
09 Director of Institutional Research .... Vacant
07 Director Admissions/Records .... Ms. Monica BOYES
103 Exec Dir Econ Workforce Development .... Ms. Linda ZORN
111 Director Institutional Advancement .... Ms. Lisa DELABY
41 Director Athletics/Kinesiology .... Mr. Craig RIGSBEE
13 Chief Technology Officer .... Mr. Tom ONWILER
08 Director of Library Services .... Dr. Cheryl BABLER
21 Director Business Services .... Mr. Jim NICHOLAS
38 Coordinator of Counseling .... Ms. Debbie REYNOLDS

Cabrillo College (F)

6500 Soquel Drive, Aptos CA 95003-3194
County: Santa Cruz | FICE Identification: 001124 | Unit ID: 110334
Telephone: (831) 479-6100 | Carnegie Class: Assoc/MT-VT-High Trad
FAX Number: (831) 479-6425 | Calendar System: Semester
URL: www.cabrillo.edu
Established: 1959 | Annual Undergrad Tuition & Fees (In-District): $1,456
Enrollment: 13,086 | Coed
Affiliation or Control: State/Local | IRS Status: 501(c)3
Highest Offering: Associate Degree
Accreditation: WJ, DH, MAC, RAD

01 Superintendent/President .... Dr. Laurel JONES
04 Executive Assistant to President .... Ms. Ronnette CHANDLER
05 Asst Supt/Vice Pres Instruction .... Dr. Kathleen WELCH
11 Asst Supt/VP Administrative Svcs .... Ms. Victoria LEWIS
32 Asst Supt/Vice Pres Student Svcs .... Ms. Suzanne GOCHIS
15 Director of HR and Labor Relations .... Ms. Angela HOYT
13 Director Information Technology .... Ms. Spring ANDREWS
07 Director of Admissions/Records .... Mr. Kip NEAD
96 Dir Purchasing/Contracts/Risk Mgmt .... Mr. Michael ROBINS
26 Director Marketing & Communications .... Ms. Kristin FABOS
21 Director Business Services .... Mr. Graciano MENDOZA
88 Dir Community and Contract Ed .... Mr. Scott JOHNSON
18 Dir Facilities Planning/Plant Ops .... Vacant
25 Dir Grants Development .... Ms. Carrie MULCAIRE
88 Dir Student Equity and Success .... Ms. Leticia MALDONADO
88 Dir Student Resource and Support .... Ms. Karen REYES
08 Director Library .... Mr. Georg ROMERO
88 Dir Small Business Development Ctr .... Ms. Teresa THOMAE
09 Dean Research/Planning/Inst Effect .... Mr. Terrence WILLETT
35 Dean Student Services .... Ms. Michelle DONOHUE
38 Dn Stdnt Counseling/Educ Spprt Svcs .... Ms. Margery REGALADO RODRIGUEZ
102 Exec Dir Cabrillo Col Foundation .... Ms. Eileen HILL
40 Bookstore Manager .... Ms. Linda CULLENS
37 Director Financial Aid .... Ms. Tootie TZIMBAL

California Baptist University (G)

8432 Magnolia Avenue, Riverside CA 92504-3297
County: Riverside | FICE Identification: 001125 | Unit ID: 110361
Telephone: (951) 689-5771 | Carnegie Class: Masters/L
FAX Number: (951) 351-1808 | Calendar System: Semester
URL: www.calbaptist.edu
Established: 1950 | Annual Undergrad Tuition & Fees: $31,372
Enrollment: 8,541 | Coed
Affiliation or Control: Southern Baptist | IRS Status: 501(c)3
Highest Offering: Doctorate
Accreditation: WC, ACBSP, #ARCPA, CAATE, CONST, ENG, MUS, NURSE, @SP, @SW

01 President .... Dr. Ronald L. ELLIS
04 Admin Asst to the President .... Ms. Julie MOULTON
10 VP for Finance & Administration .... Mr. Mark HOWE
15 Director of Human Resources .... Ms. Julie FRESQUEZ
18 Director Facilities/Planning Svcs .... Mr. Steve SMITH
21 Director of Financial Services .... Mr. Calvin SPARKMAN
21 Director of Accounting .... Ms. Jackie STILWELL
37 Director of Financial Aid .... Mr. Joshua MOREY
40 Director of University Campus Store .... Ms. Carol BRACEY
26 VP for Marketing & Communication .... Dr. Mark A. WYATT
88 Director of Conferences & Events .... Mr. Coreylon POLK
27 Director of Marketing .... Mr. Jacob M. ROBERTSON
27 Director of Communications .... Mr. Isaiah AGUIRRE
105 Sr Web Services Manager .... Mr. Waylon BAUMGARDNER
84 VP Enrollment & Student Services .... Mr. Kent DACUS
32 Dean of Students .... Mr. Anthony LAMMONS
07 Dean of Admissions .... Mr. Taylor NEECE
41 Director of Athletics .... Dr. Micah PARKER
42 Dean Spiritual Life/Campus Minister .... Mr. John MONTGOMERY
19 Director of Public Safety .... Mr. Jim WALTERS
39 Director of Residence Life .... Mr. Daron HUBBERT
36 Sr Director Career Services .... Mr. Mike BISHOP
111 Assoc VP University Advancement .... Mr. Dan WESTERMANN
44 Director Annual Giving/Stewardship .... Mr. Brian BUNNELL
102 Grants Administrator .... Mr. Sam LIVELY
29 Director Alumni & Parent Relations .... Mr. Joshua MOSS
88 VP for Global Initiatives .... Dr. Larry LINAMEN
88 Dir of International Admissions .... Ms. Marissa YOUNG
85 Dean of International Programs .... Mr. Bryan DAVIS
106 VP for Online & Prof Studies .... Dr. David POOLE
13 Assoc VP of Technology .... Dr. Tran HONG
106 Assoc VP Academics Online/Prof Stds .... Dr. Dirk DAVIS
43 VP and General Counsel .... Mr. Adam BURTON
05 VP of Academic Affairs/Provost .... Dr. Charles SANDS
88 Assoc Provost/Administration .... Dr. Tracy WARD
20 Assoc Provost/Faculty Dev .... Dr. Dawn Ellen JACOBS
108 Assoc Provost/Accred & Assessment .... Dr. Elizabeth MORRIS
06 University Registrar .... Ms. Shawnn KONING
08 Director of Library .... Dr. Steve EMERSON
90 Dir of Instructional Technology .... Mr. Keith CASTILLO
20 Dean of Academic Services .... Dr. Jeffrey BARNES
09 Director of Institutional Research .... Vacant
48 Dean College of Architecture .... Mr. Mark A. ROBERSON
49 Dean College of Arts & Sciences .... Dr. Gayne ANACKER
50 Dean School of Business .... Dr. Andrea SCOTT
53 Dean School of Education .... Dr. John SHOUP
54 Dean College of Engineering .... Dr. Anthony DONALDSON
64 Dean School of Music .... Dr. Joseph BOLIN
66 Dean College of Nursing .... Dr. Geneva OAKS
73 Dean School of Christian Ministries .... Dr. Chris MORGAN
83 Dean Sch Behavioral & Soc Sci .... Dr. Jacqueline GUSTAFSON
76 Dean College of Health Science .... Dr. David PEARSON
104 Director of Academic Engagements .... Ms. Aura DONALDSON

California Career College (H)

7003 Owensmouth Avenue, Canoga Park CA 91303
County: Los Angeles | FICE Identification: 039745 | Unit ID: 447713
Telephone: (818) 710-1310 | Carnegie Class: Not Classified
FAX Number: (818) 710-1329 | Calendar System: Semester
URL: www.californiacareercollege.edu
Established: 2001 | Annual Undergrad Tuition & Fees: N/A
Enrollment: 86 | Coed
Affiliation or Control: Proprietary | IRS Status: Proprietary
Highest Offering: Associate Degree
Accreditation: ABHES

01 President .... Susan NAIMI

California Christian College (I)

5364 E. Belmont Ave, Fresno CA 93727
County: Fresno | FICE Identification: 008844 | Unit ID: 110918
Telephone: (559) 251-4215 | Carnegie Class: Spec-4-yr-Faith
FAX Number: (559) 385-2329 | Calendar System: Semester
URL: www.calchristiancollege.edu
Established: 1955 | Annual Undergrad Tuition & Fees: $8,990
Enrollment: 18 | Coed
Affiliation or Control: Free Will Baptist | IRS Status: 501(c)3
Highest Offering: Baccalaureate
Accreditation: TRACS

01 President .... Dr. Timothy L. POWELL
05 Int Vice Pres of Academic Affairs .... Mr. Trent WALLEY
06 Registrar .... Mrs. Makenzie ZUERCHER
10 Chief Business Officer .... Mrs. Anna-Jean WALLEY
09 Dir Institutional Effectiveness .... Ms. Jennifer WALLEY
08 Head Librarian .... Mrs. Nancy SINGH
37 Coordinator Financial Aid .... Ms. Melinda SCROGGINS
07 Director of Admissions .... Mr. Billy PARRIS
39 Director Student Housing .... Ms. Jennifer WALLEY

California Coast University (J)

925 N. Spurgeon Street, Santa Ana CA 92701-3515
County: Orange | FICE Identification: 041276 | Unit ID: 110936
Telephone: (714) 547-9625 | Carnegie Class: Not Classified
FAX Number: (714) 547-5777 | Calendar System: Other
URL: www.calcoast.edu
Established: 1973 | Annual Undergrad Tuition & Fees: N/A
Enrollment: N/A | Coed
Affiliation or Control: Proprietary | IRS Status: Proprietary
Highest Offering: Doctorate
Accreditation: DEAC

01 President .... Dr. Thomas M. NEAL
03 Executive Vice President .... Ms. Shelly MARQUARDT
32 Vice Pres of Student Affairs/CAO .... Dr. Murl TUCKER
05 Director of Academic Affairs .... Mr. Douglas PETRIKAT
06 Registrar .... Ms. Angela CENINA

California College of the Arts (K)

1111 Eighth Street, San Francisco CA 94107-2247
County: San Francisco | FICE Identification: 001127 | Unit ID: 110370
Telephone: (415) 703-9500 | Carnegie Class: Spec-4-yr-Arts
FAX Number: (510) 655-3541 | Calendar System: Semester
URL: www.cca.edu
Established: 1907 | Annual Undergrad Tuition & Fees: $45,466
Enrollment: 1,975 | Coed
Affiliation or Control: Independent Non-Profit | IRS Status: 501(c)3
Highest Offering: Master's
Accreditation: WC, ART, #CIDA

01 President .... Mr. Stephen BEAL
05 Provost .... Ms. Tammy Rae CARLAND
10 Sr VP Finance & Administration .... Mrs. Laura HAZLETT
111 Sr Vice President of Advancement .... Ms. Susan AVILA
45 VP of Institutional Planning .... Ms. Jennifer STEIN
84 Vice Pres of Enrollment Svcs .... Mr. Scott CLINE
26 Vice Pres Marketing/Comm Strategy .... Ms. Becky RUDEN
32 Vice President Student Affairs .... Mr. George SEDANO
15 Assoc Vice Pres Human Resources .... Ms. Leslie GRAY

21 Assoc Vice Pres Financial Services ..... Mr. Ken TANZER
20 Associate Provost ..... Vacant
36 Director Career Development ..... Dr. Diana CHAVEZ
06 Registrar ..... Mr. Jerry ALLEN
37 Director Financial Aid ..... Mr. Dewayne BARNES
29 Dir of Alumni/Parent Engagement ..... Ms. Jessica AREVALO-HILLEN
13 CIO/VP Technology ..... Ms. Mara HANCOCK
07 Director Undergrad Admissions ..... Mr. Arnold ICASIANO
38 Director Student Counseling ..... Dr. Tara RECH
88 Director Campus Planning ..... Mr. David MECKEL
18 Operations & Planning Executive ..... Mr. Jason BLACKWELL
07 Director Graduate Admissions ..... Mr. Noel DAHL
09 Director of Institutional Research ..... Ms. Jennifer JURAS
96 Manager of Purchasing ..... Ms. Jackie CRADDOCK
04 Exec Assistant to the President ..... Ms. Gail DAVIES
08 Director of Libraries ..... Ms. Annemarie HAAR
104 Dir International Programs ..... Ms. Jessica MCMILLAN
19 Director Public Safety ..... Mr. Abe LEAL
28 Asst Dean of Students for Diversity ..... Ms. Nicole WHITNER
39 Director Residential Life ..... Ms. Monique BUTLER
44 Director of Annual Giving ..... Ms. Jennifer JANSEN

California College San Diego (A)

6602 Convoy Court, Suite 100, San Diego CA 92111
County: San Diego FICE Identification: 021108
Unit ID: 485263
Telephone: (619) 680-4430 Carnegie Class: Not Classified
FAX Number: (619) 295-5985 Calendar System: Other
URL: www.cc-sd.edu
Established: 1978 Annual Undergrad Tuition & Fees: $16,968
Enrollment: 931 Coed
Affiliation or Control: Independent Non-Profit IRS Status: 501(c)3
Highest Offering: Baccalaureate
Accreditation: ACCSC, COARC

01 Executive Director ..... Dr. Ken WEBB
03 Executive Vice President ..... Mr. Eric JUHLIN
05 Chief Academic Officer ..... Dr. Jason KART
06 Registrar ..... Ms. Lashanna BOYKIN
07 Director of Admissions ..... Mr. Baris YUCELT
08 Head Librarian ..... Ms. Patricia BERMEL
36 Director Student Placement ..... Mr. Bill KILBY

California College San Diego (B)

277 Rancheros Drive, Suite 200, San Marcos CA 92069
Telephone: (619) 680-4430 Identification: 770551
Accreditation: ACCSC, COARC

California Graduate School of Theology (C)

11277 Garden Grove Blvd, 2nd Floor,
Garden Grove CA 92843
County: Orange Identification: 667307
Telephone: (714) 636-1722 Carnegie Class: Not Classified
FAX Number: (714) 636-1725 Calendar System: Semester
URL: cgsot.edu
Established: 1969 Annual Undergrad Tuition & Fees: N/A
Enrollment: N/A Coed
Affiliation or Control: Interdenominational IRS Status: 501(c)3
Highest Offering: Doctorate
Accreditation: @TRACS

01 President ..... Mr. Kang WON LEE

California Health Sciences University (D)

120 N. Clovis Ave, Clovis CA 93612
County: Fresno Identification: 667218
Telephone: (559) 325-3600 Carnegie Class: Not Classified
FAX Number: (559) 473-1487 Calendar System: Semester
URL: www.chsu.org
Established: 2012 Annual Graduate Tuition & Fees: N/A
Enrollment: N/A Coed
Affiliation or Control: Proprietary IRS Status: Proprietary
Highest Offering: Doctorate; No Undergraduates
Accreditation: @PHAR

01 President ..... Florence DUNN
04 Administrative Asst to President ..... Kathleen HAEBERLE
05 Sr VP Academic Affairs/Provost ..... Wendy DUNCAN
100 Chief of Staff ..... McKenna WALKER
09 Dir Inst Effectiveness & Research ..... Julie MARTY-PEARSON
11 VP Operations ..... Jimmy DUNN
10 Controller ..... Aron FLORES
13 Exec Dir of Info Technology ..... John BRIAR
32 VP of Student Affairs ..... Carolyn HARRIS
06 Registrar ..... Kevin HOOVER
07 Director of Admissions ..... Leslie WILLIAMS
26 VP Marketing/Communications ..... Richele KLEISER
30 Dir of Development and Comm ..... Sherrie BAKKE
20 Asst Dean of Education ..... Will OFSTAD
88 Assoc Dean Professional Devel ..... Patty HAVARD
08 Librarian ..... Anna YANG
37 Director Student Financial Aid ..... Kevin HOOVER

California Institute of Advanced Management (E)

9550 Flair Dr, Ste #201, El Monte CA 91731
County: Los Angeles FICE Identification: 042506
Unit ID: 487649
Telephone: (626) 350-1500 Carnegie Class: Not Classified
FAX Number: (626) 350-1515 Calendar System: Other
URL: www.ciam.edu
Established: Annual Graduate Tuition & Fees: N/A
Enrollment: 9 Coed
Affiliation or Control: Independent Non-Profit IRS Status: 501(c)3
Highest Offering: Master's; No Undergraduates
Accreditation: @WC, ACICS

01 President ..... Ms. Jennie TA
125 President Emeritus ..... Dr. William A. COHEN
05 Vice Pres/Chief Academic Officer ..... Dr. Eric MCLAUGHLIN
20 Dean ..... Dr. Harish AMAR
07 Director Admissions/Registrar ..... Ms. Penny LI

California Institute of the Arts (F)

24700 McBean Parkway, Valencia CA 91355-2397
County: Los Angeles FICE Identification: 001132
Unit ID: 111081
Telephone: (661) 255-1050 Carnegie Class: Spec-4-yr-Arts
FAX Number: (661) 254-8352 Calendar System: Semester
URL: www.calarts.edu
Established: 1961 Annual Undergrad Tuition & Fees: $45,646
Enrollment: 1,448 Coed
Affiliation or Control: Independent Non-Profit IRS Status: 501(c)3
Highest Offering: Doctorate
Accreditation: WC, ART, DANCE

01 President ..... Ravi S. RAJAN
05 Provost ..... Dr. Jeannene PRZYBLYSKI
10 Vice Pres/Chief Financial Officer ..... Vacant
111 Vice Pres Advancement ..... Elizabeth ROBISON
21 Assoc Vice President and Controller ..... Karla TALAVERA
15 Assoc Vice Pres Human Resources ..... Charmagne SHEARRILL
11 Assoc VP/Chief Operating Officer ..... Jesse SMITH
88 Asst VP Special Projects ..... Patricia GONZALEZ
20 Assoc Provost Academic Affairs ..... Brian HARLAN
28 Institute Diversity Officer ..... Eva GRAHAM
20 Assistant Provost Academic Affairs ..... Bree HOWARD
08 Dean Div of Library & Info Resource ..... Vacant
32 Dean of Student Affairs ..... Travis GREENE
57 Dean School of Art ..... Thomas LAWSON
64 Dean Herb Alpert School of Music ..... David ROSENBOOM
88 Dean School of Critical Studies ..... Amanda BEECH
88 Dean Sharon D Lund School of Dance ..... Vacant
88 Dean School Film & Video ..... Leighton PIERCE
88 Dean School of Theater ..... Travis PRESTON
06 Registrar ..... Anna JABLONSKI
26 Executive Director Marketing ..... James WOLKEN
37 Director of Financial Aid ..... Robin BAILEY-CHEN
29 Director Alumni & Parent Engagement ..... Rageshwar GOLDBERG
88 Artistic Director Community Arts ..... Glenna AVILA
88 Director Community Arts Partnership ..... Nadine RAMBEAU
39 Asst Director of Residence Life ..... Vacant
87 Director of Summer Session ..... Hilary DARLING
19 Campus Safety Supervisor ..... Mark FARLEY
88 Director of Leadership Gifts ..... Sally BICKERTON
88 Director of Institute Partnerships ..... Claudia BLOOM
112 Director of Development/Major Gift ..... Aaron CAMPBELL
23 Director Health Services ..... Audrey HAMPTON
88 Director Advancement Services ..... Korey JANSE
88 Director Prospect Strategy ..... Natalie LARMON
13 Director Information Technology ..... Vacant
102 Director Corp/Foundation/Govt ..... Sarah NELSON
44 Director Development/Indiv Giving ..... Aiza KEESEY
88 Director Special Events ..... Lindsey SCHIFF-ABRAMS
36 Director Career Services ..... Rita SOLTANIAN
18 Director Facilities Management ..... John THOMAS
04 Sr Administrative Asst to President ..... Judy MCGINNIS
104 Asst Dir Intl Students & Programs ..... Anessa ESCOBAR
105 Director Web Communications ..... Christine ZIEMBA
88 Director of Creative Services ..... Stuart SMITH
88 Director of Project Development ..... Lisa BARR
114 Director Academic Contracts/Budget ..... Trish PATRYLA
84 Dean of Enrollment Management ..... Robert BORDEN

California Institute of Arts & Technology (G)

2820 Camino Del Rio South, Ste 100,
San Diego CA 92108
County: San Diego Identification: 667289
Telephone: (858) 225-4301 Carnegie Class: Not Classified
FAX Number: N/A Calendar System: Other
URL: www.calarttech.edu
Established: 2008 Annual Undergrad Tuition & Fees: N/A
Enrollment: N/A Coed
Affiliation or Control: Proprietary IRS Status: Proprietary
Highest Offering: Associate Degree
Accreditation: CNCE

01 President ..... Jamie DOYLE
11 Director of Operations ..... Claire PARK
06 Registrar ..... Ed BRANCHEAU
07 Director of Admissions ..... Frank GANAN
26 Director of Marketing ..... Tierra MURGUIA

California Institute of Integral Studies (H)

1453 Mission Street, 4th Floor,
San Francisco CA 94103-2557
County: San Francisco FICE Identification: 012154
Unit ID: 110316
Telephone: (415) 575-6100 Carnegie Class: DU-Mod
FAX Number: (415) 575-1264 Calendar System: Semester
URL: www.ciis.edu
Established: 1968 Annual Undergrad Tuition & Fees: N/A
Enrollment: 1,488 Coed
Affiliation or Control: Independent Non-Profit IRS Status: 501(c)3
Highest Offering: Doctorate
Accreditation: WC, ACUP

01 President ..... Dr. Judie G. WEXLER
05 Provost ..... Dr. Liz BEAVEN
10 Controller/VP of Finance ..... Mr. David BLOHM
30 Vice President of Development ..... Dr. Robert MCDERMOTT
88 VP China Projects/Exec Dir ACTCM ..... Ms. Lixin HUANG
32 Dean of Students ..... Ms. Yunny YIP
29 Dean of Alumni/Dir of Travel Pgms ..... Dr. Richard BUGGS
20 Associate Provost ..... Mr. Chip B. GOLDSTEIN
07 Director of Admissions ..... Ms. Ellen DURST
06 Registrar ..... Mr. Dan GURLER
26 Director of Communications ..... Ms. Lisa DENENMARK
37 Director of Financial Aid ..... Mr. Larry BLAIR
51 Dir Public Programs/ Performances ..... Ms. Britta CONROY-RANDALL
18 Director Facilities & Operations ..... Mr. Frank TALAMANTEZ
85 International Student Advisor ..... Ms. Jody O'CONNOR
04 Administrative Asst to President ..... Ms. Anne TEICH
09 Director of Institutional Research ..... Mr. Peter JONES
28 Director of Diversity ..... Ms. Denise BOSTON

California Institute of Technology (I)

1200 E California Boulevard, Pasadena CA 91125-0001
County: Los Angeles FICE Identification: 001131
Unit ID: 110404
Telephone: (626) 395-6811 Carnegie Class: DU-Highest
FAX Number: (626) 795-1547 Calendar System: Trimester
URL: www.caltech.edu
Established: 1891 Annual Undergrad Tuition & Fees: $47,577
Enrollment: 2,255 Coed
Affiliation or Control: Independent Non-Profit IRS Status: 501(c)3
Highest Offering: Doctorate
Accreditation: WC, ENG

01 President ..... Dr. Thomas F. ROSENBAUM
101 Secretary to the BOT ..... Ms. Mary L. WEBSTER
05 Provost ..... Dr. Edward M. STOLPER
88 Vice President/Director JPL ..... Dr. Michael WATKINS
10 VP of Admin/Chief Financial Officer ..... Ms. Margo STEURBAUT
21 AVP for Finance & Treasurer ..... Ms. Sharon E. PATTERSON
30 Vice Pres Devel/Institute Relations ..... Mr. Brian K. LEE
88 VP for Strategy Implementation ..... Dr. Diana JERGOVIC
32 Vice President Student Affairs ..... Dr. Joseph E. SHEPHERD
43 General Counsel ..... Ms. Victoria D. STRATMAN
04 Exec Asst to the Pres/Asst Sec BOT ..... Ms. Carol SCHUIL
20 Vice Provost ..... Dr. Cindy A. WEINSTEIN
20 Vice Provost ..... Dr. Kaushik BHATTACHARYA
15 Assoc Vice Pres Human Resources ..... Ms. Julia M. MCCALLIN
110 Assoc Vice President Development ..... Ms. Valerie A. OTTEN
112 AVP for Campaigns ..... Ms. Diane M. BINNEY
44 Asst VP Engagement & Annual Program ..... Ms. Theresa A. DAVIS
86 Director Government Relations ..... Mr. Hall P. DAILY
35 Senior Director Student Activities ..... Mr. Tom N. MANNION
26 Chief Strat Communications Officer ..... Ms. Farnaz KHADEM
81 Chair Biology & Biological Engr Div ..... Dr. Stephen L. MAYO
81 Chair Chemistry & Chemical Engr Div . Dr. Jacqueline K. BARTON
54 Chair Engr & Applied Science Div ..... Dr. Guruswami RAVICHANDRAN
65 Chair Geology/Planet Science Div ..... Dr. John P. GROTZINGER
79 Chair Humanities/Social Science Div ..... Dr. Jean-Laurent ROSENTHAL
81 Chair Physics/Math/Astro Division ..... Dr. Fiona HARRISON
06 Interim Registrar ..... Ms. Kim MAWHINNEY
07 Exec Director of Admissions ..... Mr. Jarrid WHITNEY
08 University Librarian ..... Ms. Kristin ANTELMAN
13 Chief Information Officer ..... Mr. Jin CHANG
18 Assoc Vice Pres for Facilities ..... Mr. James W. COWELL, JR.
18 Sr Director Facilities Management ..... Mr. William R. TAYLOR
19 Int Chief of Campus Sec & Parking ..... Mr. William HEIM
16 Exec Director of Human Resources ..... Ms. Tara KRUCKEBERG
23 Director Health Services ..... Dr. Stuart C. MILLER
25 Director Sponsored Research ..... Dr. Richard P. SELIGMAN
117 Exec Dir Audit Svcs & Inst Comp ..... Ms. Pamela KOYZIS
29 Executive Director Alumni Assoc ..... Ms. Alexandra C. TOBEK
37 Director Financial Aid ..... Mr. Don CREWELL
109 AVP for Student Affairs Operations ..... Mr. Dimitris SAKELLARIOU
36 Director Career Development ..... Ms. Lauren B. STOLPER
40 Manager Bookstore ..... Ms. Karyn SEIXAS
41 Dir Athletics & Physical Education ..... Ms. Betsy MITCHELL
58 Dean of Graduate Studies ..... Dr. Doug C. REES
35 Dean of Students ..... Dr. Kevin M. GILMARTIN
85 Assoc Dir International Student Pgm ..... Ms. Laura FLOWER KIM
96 Dir Purchasing & Payment Services ..... Ms. Tina LOWENTHAL

102 Director Foundation Relations .... Ms. Marjorie A. BEALE
104 Dir Fellowshp Advising/Study Abroad ..... Ms. Lauren B. STOLPER
38 Director Counseling Center .... Ms. Jennifer HOWES
09 Dir of Institutional Research .... Mr. Ken HARGREAVES
39 Director Student Housing .... Ms. Maria A. KATSAS

California Institute of Management and Technology (A)

2361 Campus Drive, Suite 180, Irvine CA 92612

County: Orange Identification: 667286
Telephone: (949) 872-2224 Carnegie Class: Not Classified
FAX Number: (949) 872-2229 Calendar System: Other
URL: www.metabusinessschool.edu
Established: 2010 Annual Graduate Tuition & Fees: N/A
Enrollment: N/A Coed
Affiliation or Control: Proprietary IRS Status: Proprietary
Highest Offering: Master's; No Undergraduates
Accreditation: **DEAC**

05 Provost .... Dr. H. Clarissa CHAIY

California Intercontinental University (B)

17310 Red Hill Ave, Ste 200, Irvine CA 92614

County: Orange Identification: 666670
Unit ID: 485546
Telephone: (866) 687-2258 Carnegie Class: Not Classified
FAX Number: (949) 861-9431 Calendar System: Semester
URL: www.caluniversity.edu
Established: 2003 Annual Undergrad Tuition & Fees: $8,385
Enrollment: 473 Coed
Affiliation or Control: Proprietary IRS Status: Proprietary
Highest Offering: Doctorate
Accreditation: **DEAC**

00 Executive Chairman .... Dr. Finian TAN
01 Chief Executive Officer .... Dr. Leslie GARGIULO
58 Dean of Graduate Studies .... Dr. Steve HESS
05 Chief Academic Officer .... Dr. Bonny NICKLE
10 Director of Finance .... Mr. Bryan KELLY
06 Registrar .... Mr. Mark WILLS
37 Director Student Financial Aid .... Mr. Richard MADRIGAL
07 Director of Enrollment Management .... Mr. Frederick THOMAS

California International Business University (C)

550 West B Street, San Diego CA 92101

County: San Diego Identification: 666711
Telephone: (619) 702-9400 Carnegie Class: Not Classified
FAX Number: (619) 702-9476 Calendar System: Quarter
URL: www.cibu.edu
Established: 1994 Annual Undergrad Tuition & Fees: N/A
Enrollment: N/A Coed
Affiliation or Control: Independent Non-Profit IRS Status: 501(c)3
Highest Offering: Master's
Accreditation: **ACICS**

01 President .... Dr. Anya ESKILDSEN
32 Dean Stdnt Affs/Special Pgms/MBA .... Mr. Brian HAWKINS
10 Chief Financial Officer/COO .... Ms. Anne HYRUP MADSEN
58 Doctoral Pgm Admin/Compliance Ofcr .. Dr. Marcus BENNIEFIELD
37 Financial Aid Director .... Mr. Mike MARTIN
07 Recruitment & Admission .... Ms. Nicole WITTENBORG
06 Registrar/Admin Ofcr .... Ms. Amy CULLEY

California Jazz Conservatory (D)

2087 Addison Street, Berkeley CA 94704

County: Alameda Identification: 667217
Unit ID: 486488
Telephone: (510) 845-5373 Carnegie Class: Not Classified
FAX Number: (510) 841-5373 Calendar System: Semester
URL: www.cjc.edu
Established: 2009 Annual Undergrad Tuition & Fees: $17,400
Enrollment: 55 Coed
Affiliation or Control: Independent Non-Profit IRS Status: 501(c)3
Highest Offering: Baccalaureate
Accreditation: **MUS**

01 President .... Susan MUSCARELLA
11 Director of Operations .... Max HODES

California Lutheran University (E)

60 W Olsen Road, Thousand Oaks CA 91360-2787

County: Ventura FICE Identification: 001133
Unit ID: 110413
Telephone: (805) 492-2411 Carnegie Class: Masters/L
FAX Number: (805) 493-3513 Calendar System: Semester
URL: www.callutheran.edu
Established: 1959 Annual Undergrad Tuition & Fees: $39,793
Enrollment: 4,126 Coed
Affiliation or Control: Evangelical Lutheran Church In America
IRS Status: 501(c)3
Highest Offering: Doctorate
Accreditation: **WC**, CLPSY, THEOL

01 President .... Dr. Christopher KIMBALL
05 Provost/Vice Pres Academic Affairs .... Dr. Leanne NEILSON
111 Vice Pres University Advancement .... Mr. Stephen WHEATLY
10 Vice Pres Admin/Finance/Treasurer .... Ms. Karen DAVIS
32 Vice Pres Stdnt Life/Dean of Stdnts .... Ms. Melinda ROPER
84 VP Enrollment Mgmt & Marketing .... Dr. Matthew WARD
13 Chief Information Officer .... Mr. Zareh MARSELIAN
18 Assoc Vice Pres Facilities .... Mr. Ryan VAN OMMEREN
26 Assoc VP University Relations .... Ms. Lynda FULFORD
49 Dean College Arts & Sciences .... Dr. Jessica LAVARIEGA MONFORTI
53 Dean of School of Education .... Dr. Michael HILLIS
50 Dean of School of Management .... Dr. Gerhard APFELTHALER
83 Dean Grad School of Psychology .... Dr. Rick HOLIGROCKI
15 Asst VP for Human Resources .... Ms. Patricia PARHAM
06 Assoc Prov Academic Svcs/Registrar .... Ms. Maria KOHNKE
42 University Pastor .... Rev. Scott MAXWELL-DOHERTY
42 Vice President Mission and Identity .... Rev. Melissa MAXWELL-DOHERTY
112 Director Major Planned Giving .... Mr. Richard HOLMES, IV
41 Director Athletics .... Mr. Daniel KUNTZ
107 Director Professionals .... Dr. Lisa BUONO
36 Director of Career Services .... Ms. Cindy LEWIS
85 Sr Dir Multicultural/Intl Std Svc .... Dr. Juanita HALL
114 Dir of Budget/Management Analysis .... Ms. Barbara REX
29 Dir Alumni and Family Relations .... Ms. Rachel RONNING LINDGREN
38 Director Counseling Services .... Dr. Virginia MARIL
19 Director Security/Safety .... Mr. David HILKE
07 Director of Undergrad Admissions .... Mr. Michael ELGARICO
09 Director of Institutional Research .... Dr. Rodney REYNOLDS
37 Director of Financial Aid .... Mr. Jerry MCKEEN
104 Director of Study Abroad .... Dr. Lisa LOBERG
39 Director of Residence Life .... Dr. Christine PAUL
23 Director of Health Services .... Ms. Kerri LAUCHNER
101 Secretary of the Institution/Board .... Ms. Rian CURLEY

California Miramar University (F)

3550 Camino Del Rio N. Suite 208, San Diego CA 92108

County: San Diego Identification: 666713
Unit ID: 480781
Telephone: (858) 653-3000 Carnegie Class: Spec-4-yr-Bus
FAX Number: (858) 653-6786 Calendar System: Other
URL: www.calmu.edu
Established: 2005 Annual Undergrad Tuition & Fees: $7,960
Enrollment: 319 Coed
Affiliation or Control: Proprietary IRS Status: Proprietary
Highest Offering: Doctorate
Accreditation: **ACICS**

01 Dean .... Kim LOBERA
07 International Admissions Director .... Carol KULIS
06 Registrar .... Brooke NELSON

California National University for Advanced Studies (G)

18520 Hawthorne Blvd 1st Floor, Torrance CA 90504

County: Los Angeles Identification: 666786
Telephone: (800) 782-2422 Carnegie Class: Not Classified
FAX Number: (310) 370-7072 Calendar System: Trimester
URL: www.cnuas.edu
Established: 1993 Annual Undergrad Tuition & Fees: N/A
Enrollment: N/A Coed
Affiliation or Control: Proprietary IRS Status: Proprietary
Highest Offering: Master's
Accreditation: **DEAC**

01 President .... Mr. Carlton G. BRYANT
32 Vice Pres Student Affs/Registrar .... Ms. Stephanie M. SMITH
07 Admissions .... Ms. Cynthia SPEED
05 Director of Instruction .... Dr. Carol BACKER
50 Assoc Dean Business Administration .... Dr. Philip CHONG
54 Associate CNU Col of Engineering .... Dr. Robert RYAN
13 MIS Director .... Mr. Charles NG
06 Registrar .... Ms. Stephanie M. SMITH

California Northstate University (H)

9700 West Taron Dr, Elk Grove CA 95757

County: Sacramento Identification: 667020
Telephone: (916) 686-7400 Carnegie Class: Not Classified
FAX Number: (916) 686-8143 Calendar System: Semester
URL: www.cnsu.edu
Established: 2008 Annual Undergrad Tuition & Fees: N/A
Enrollment: N/A Coed
Affiliation or Control: Independent Non-Profit IRS Status: 501(c)3
Highest Offering: Doctorate
Accreditation: **WC**, #MED, PHAR

01 President .... Dr. Alvin CHEUNG
11 Vice President of Operations .... Dr. Grant LACKEY
108 VP of Inst Effect/Assessment .... Dr. Karen MCCLENDON
32 VP for Admissions & Student Service .... Dr. Xiaodong FENG
43 Legal Counsel .... Mr. Paul WAGSTAFFE
67 Dean of Pharmacy .... Dr. Hieu TRAN
10 VP of Finance/CFO .... Ms. Shoua XIONG
08 Director of Library Resources .... Mr. Scott MINOR
06 Registrar .... Ms. Amanda WILDER
07 Asst Dean Admissions/Student Affs .... Dr. Tiffany-Jade KREYS
76 Dean of Health Sciences .... Dr. Heather BROWN

California Southern University (I)

3330 Harbor Boulevard, Costa Mesa CA 92626

County: Orange Identification: 666770
Telephone: (800) 477-2254 Carnegie Class: Not Classified
FAX Number: (714) 480-0834 Calendar System: Semester
URL: www.calsouthern.edu
Established: 1978 Annual Undergrad Tuition & Fees: N/A
Enrollment: N/A Coed
Affiliation or Control: Proprietary IRS Status: Proprietary
Highest Offering: Doctorate
Accreditation: **WC**

01 President/Founder .... Dr. Donald HECHT

*The California State University System Office (J)

401 Golden Shore, Long Beach CA 90802-4210

County: Los Angeles FICE Identification: 001136
Unit ID: 110501
Telephone: (562) 951-4000 Carnegie Class: N/A
FAX Number: (562) 951-4986
URL: www.calstate.edu

01 Chancellor .... Dr. Timothy P. WHITE
05 Exec Vice Chanc Acad/Stdnt Affairs ..... Dr. Loren J. BLANCHARD
10 Executive Vice Chancellor & CFO .... Mr. Steve RELYEA
15 Vice Chanc Human Resources .... Ms. Melissa BARD
30 Vice Chanc Univ Rels/Advancement .... Mr. Garrett P. ASHLEY
43 Exec Vice Chanc/General Counsel .... Mr. Framroze M. VIRJEE
21 Vice Chancellor/Chief Audit Officer .... Mr. Larry MANDEL
100 Chief of Staff .... Dr. Lars WALTON

*California Polytechnic State University-San Luis Obispo (K)

1 Grand Avenue, San Luis Obispo CA 93407-9000

County: San Luis Obispo FICE Identification: 001143
Unit ID: 110422
Telephone: (805) 756-1111 Carnegie Class: Masters/L
FAX Number: (805) 756-5400 Calendar System: Quarter
URL: www.calpoly.edu
Established: 1901 Annual Undergrad Tuition & Fees (In-State): $9,075
Enrollment: 20,944 Coed
Affiliation or Control: State IRS Status: 501(c)3
Highest Offering: Master's
Accreditation: **WC**, ART, CONST, CS, DIETD, DIETI, ENG, LSAR, MUS, NAIT, NRPA, PLNG

02 President .... Dr. Jeffrey D. ARMSTRONG
100 AVP & Chief of Staff .... Ms. Jessica DARIN
05 Provost .... Dr. Kathleen ENZ FINKEN
32 Vice President Student Affairs .... Dr. Keith HUMPHREY
30 COO University Development .... Mr. David DOBIS
10 Senior Vice Pres Admin & Finance .... Ms. Cynthia VILLA
20 Senior Vice Provost Academic Pgms .... Dr. Mary E. PEDERSEN
20 Vice Provost Intl/Grad & Ext Educ .... Dr. Brian TIETJE
41 Athletic Director .... Mr. Don OBERHELMAN
13 Int CIO/Cybrsec Ctr Dir .... Mr. Bill BRITTON
88 Exec Dir Cal Poly Corporation .... Ms. Lorlie LEETHAM
46 Int VP Research & Economic Dev .... Mr. Bradford ANDERSON
21 Associate Vice Pres Admin & Finance .... Mr. Victor BRANCART
111 Assoc Vice Pres Advancement Ops .... Mr. Grant TREXLER
26 Chief Communications Officer .... Mr. Chris MURPHY
18 Associate Vice Pres Facilities Mgmt .... Ms. Juanita HOLLER
39 Exec Dir Univ Housing & Assoc VP/SA .... Dr. Jo CAMPBELL
15 Assoc Vice Prov Academic Personnel .... Dr. Al LIDDICOAT
88 Assoc Vice Prov Systems & Resources .... Ms. Kimi M. IKEDA
84 Assoc Vice Prov Mktg & Enrollment .. Mr. James L. MARAVIGLIA
88 Dir Ctr Teaching/Learning & Tech .... Mr. Patrick O'SULLIVAN
29 Assoc VP Alumni Outreach .... Ms. Ellen COHUNE
19 University Police Department .... Chief George HUGHES
06 University Registrar .... Mr. Cem SUNATA
28 Assoc VP Diversity and Inclusion .... Dr. Jamie PATTON
22 Director Equal Opp/Title IX Coord .... Mr. Brian GNANDT
45 Dir Facil Planning/Capital Projects .... Mr. Joel NEEL
23 Exec Dir Health & Well Being .... Dr. David HARRIS
38 Director of Counseling Services .... Dr. Geneva ABIKO
35 ASI Executive Director .... Ms. Marcy MALONEY
14 Deputy Chief Information Officer .... Mr. Ryan MATTESON
40 Interim Dir University Bookstore .... Mr. Frank CAWLEY
35 Assoc VP Student Affairs & DOS .... Dr. Kathleen PERLMUTTER
88 Director Econ Dev & Tech Transfr .... Mr. Jim DUNNING
47 Dean Agriculture/Food & Env Sci .... Dr. Andrew THULIN
48 Dean Architect/Environmental Design .... Ms. Christine THEODOROPOULOS
50 Dean College of Business .... Mr. Scott DAWSON
54 Interim Dean College of Engineering .... Mr. Jim MEAGHER
49 Dean College of Liberal Arts .... Dr. Douglas EPPERSON
81 Dean Science & Mathematics .... Dr. Dean WENDT
53 Director School of Education .... Dr. J. Kevin TAYLOR
16 Assoc VP Human Resources .... Ms. Beth E. GALLAGHER
96 Asst VP Strat Business Sup Svcs .... Mr. Dru ZACHMEYER
37 Interim Director Financial Aid .... Ms. Gerrie HATTEN
36 Exec Director Career Services .... Ms. Eileen C. BUECHER
09 Exec Director Inst Research .... Mr. Mauricio SAAVEDRA
104 Director International Center .... Ms. Caroline MOORE
92 Director Honors Program .... Dr. Gregg FIEGEL
04 Administrative Asst to President .... Vacant
07 Director Admissions Operations .... Mr. Terrance HARRIS

08 Interim Dean of Library Services ....Ms. Adriana POPESCU
25 Director Grants Development ....Ms. Amy VELASCO
43 University Legal Counsel ....Ms. Dawn S. THEODORA
86 Dir Govt & Community Relations ....Mr. Justin WELLNER

*California State Polytechnic University-Pomona (A)

3801 W Temple Avenue, Pomona CA 91768-2557
County: Los Angeles FICE Identification: 001144
Unit ID: 110529
Telephone: (909) 869-7659 Carnegie Class: Masters/L
FAX Number: (909) 869-4535 Calendar System: Quarter
URL: www.cpp.edu
Established: 1938 Annual Undergrad Tuition & Fees (In-State): $7,067
Enrollment: 23,717 Coed
Affiliation or Control: State IRS Status: 501(c)3
Highest Offering: Master's
Accreditation: WC, ART, CEA, CIDA, CS, DIETD, DIETI, ENG, ENGT, LSAR, MUS, PLNG, SPAA

02 President ....Dr. Soraya M. COLEY
05 Provost/VP Academic Affairs ....Dr. Sylvia A. ALVA
32 Vice Pres Student Affairs ....Dr. Lea M. JARNAGIN
10 VP Administrative Affairs/CFO ....Ms. Danielle MANNING
111 VP University Advancement ....Mr. Daniel MONTPLAISIR
102 Interim Exec Dir CPP Found Inc ....Ms. Danielle MANNING
20 Assoc Provost Academic Affairs ....Vacant
18 Assoc VP Facilities Planning & Mgmt ....Dr. Walter MARQUEZ
35 Assoc VP & Dean of Students ....Dr. Thomas CRUZ-SOTO
84 Assoc VP Enroll Management & Svcs ....Ms. Kathleen A. STREET
88 Exec Asst to the Provost ....Ms. Marissa M. MARTINEZ
46 AVP Research/Innovation/Econ Dev ....Dr. Sadiq SHAH
20 AVP Acad Planning & Faculty Affairs ....Dr. Sepehr ESKANDARI
26 Assoc Vice Pres for Univ Relations ....Mr. Tim LYNCH
21 Assoc VP Finance/Admin Svcs ....Vacant
35 Assoc VP Student Services ....Dr. Kevin T. COLANER
35 AVP Student Affairs Administration ....Ms. Christi R. CHISLER
13 Vice President & CIO ....Mr. John W. MCGUTHRY
09 AVP Inst Rsrch/Planning & Analytics ....Dr. Heather BROWN
15 AVP for Human Resources ....Ms. Sharon L. REITER
100 Interim Chief of Staff ....Ms. Anita R. JESSUP
04 Exec Assistant to the President ....Ms. Paulette M. BLUMBERG
47 Interim Dean College of Agriculture ....Dr. Lisa KESSLER
49 Dean Col Letters/Arts/Soc Sci ....Dr. Sharon HILLES
50 Dean Col of Business Admin ....Dr. Erik ROLLAND
54 Int Dean College of Engineering ....Dr. Cordelia ONTIVEROS
48 Dean Col Environmental Design ....Mr. Michael WOO
88 Dean Collins College of Hosp Mgmt ....Dr. Lea R. DOPSON
81 Dean College of Science ....Dr. Alison BASKI
53 Dean Col Educ/Integrat Stds ....Dr. Jeff PASSE
30 Assoc VP for Development ....Vacant
08 Dean University Library ....Dr. Ray WANG
41 Director of Athletics ....Mr. Brian R. SWANSON
86 Dir of Government/External Affairs ....Vacant
19 Chief of Police ....Mr. Dario ROBINSON
88 Exec Dir Acad Rsrch & Acad Resource ......Ms. Lisa M. ROTUNNI
37 Dir Financial Aid & Scholarships ....Ms. Diana Y. MINOR
06 Registrar/Academic Records Svcs ....Dr. Maria L. MARTINEZ
96 Director of Procurement ....Ms. Kathleen A. PRUNTY
07 Exec Dir Admissions & Outreach ....Ms. Deborah L. BRANDON

*California State University-Bakersfield (B)

9001 Stockdale Highway, Bakersfield CA 93311-1022
County: Kern FICE Identification: 007993
Unit ID: 110486
Telephone: (661) 654-2011 Carnegie Class: Masters/L
FAX Number: (661) 654-3194 Calendar System: Semester
URL: www.csub.edu
Established: 1965 Annual Undergrad Tuition & Fees (In-State): $6,857
Enrollment: 9,228 Coed
Affiliation or Control: State IRS Status: 501(c)3
Highest Offering: Doctorate
Accreditation: WC, CAEPN, NURSE, SPAA, SW

02 President ....Dr. Horace MITCHELL
100 Chief of Staff to the President ....Dr. Evelyn YOUNG SPATH
04 Admin Asst to the President ....Vacant
05 Provost/Vice Pres Academic Affairs ....Dr. Jenny ZORN
10 Vice Pres Business/Admin Services ....Mr. Thom DAVIS
32 Vice President Student Affairs ....Dr. Thomas WALLACE
111 VP University Advancement ....Mr. Victor MARTIN
20 VP Academic Affairs ....Dr. David SCHECTER
84 Assoc VP for Enrollment Management ....Dr. Jacqueline MIMMS
20 Assoc VP for Academic Programs ....Dr. Vernon HARPER
85 Director of International Students ....Ms. Sonia SILVA
15 AVP Human Res/Administrative Svcs ....Ms. Kellie GARCIA
13 AVP Information Tech Services ....Mr. Faust GORHAM
88 Spec Asst to Provost Academic Aff ....Ms. Leslie WILLIAMS
21 Controller ....Ms. Queen KING
114 Univ Budget Director ....Ms. Michelle MILLS
18 Asst VP Facilities Management/Dev ....Mr. Pat JACOBS
09 Asst VP Inst Rsrch/Planning/Assess ....Dr. Kris KRISNAN
25 Assoc Vice Pres Grants/Resources ....Dr. Imeh EBONG
124 Assoc VP Student Success ....Dr. Vikash LAKHANI
12 Int Dean Antelope Valley Center ....Dr. Randy SCHULTZ
50 Dean Business/Public Admin ....Dr. Angappa GUNASEKARAN
53 Dean Social Sciences/Education ....Dr. Steve BACON
79 Dean Arts & Humanities ....Dr. Robert FRAKES
81 Dean Natural Sciences/Math/Eng ....Dr. Kathleen MADDEN
56 Dean Extended University ....Dr. Mark NOVAK
88 Dir of Academic Operation & Support ....Dr. John DIRKSE
08 Dean University Library ....Dr. Curt ASHER
06 Registrar ....Ms. Lisa ZUZARTE
91 Dir Admn Computing Svcs/CMS Pgm Dir ......Mr. Kallya SHENOY
07 Director Admissions & Records ....Mr. Ben PERLADO
29 Director Alumni Relations ....Ms. Sarah HENDRICK
41 Director Athletics ....Mr. Kenneth (Ziggy) SIEGFRIED
36 Dir for Cmty Engagement/Career Edu ....Dr. Markel QUARLES
88 Director Children's Center ....Ms. Gladys GARCIA
96 Dir Contract Services/Procurement ....Mr. Michael CHAVEZ
38 Admin Supervisor Counseling Center ....Dr. Janet MILLAR
106 Director E-Learning Services ....Vacant
37 Int Director Financial Aid ....Mr. Chad MORRIS
92 Int Director CSUB Honors Program ....Dr. Jacquelyn KEGLEY
39 Director Housing & Residential Life ....Ms. Crystal BECKS
117 Director Safety & Risk Management ....Mr. Tim RIDLEY
22 Dir Svcs Students w/Disabilities ....Ms. Janice CLAUSEN
17 Director Student Health Services ....Dr. Oscar RICO
30 Director of Development ....Ms. Melissa WATKINS
88 Director Outreach Services ....Mr. Darius RIGGINS
19 Chief University Police ....Chief Marty WILLIAMSON
109 Director of Food Services ....Mr. David HVEEM
18 Manager Facilities Operations ....Mr. Tom VELASQUEZ
40 Bookstore Manager ....Mr. Richard SALCEDO
26 Director of Public Affairs ....Mr. Michael LUKENS
28 Asst to the President for EIC ....Ms. Claudia CATOTA

*California State University Channel Islands (C)

One University Drive, Camarillo CA 93012-8599
County: Ventura FICE Identification: 039803
Unit ID: 441937
Telephone: (805) 437-8400 Carnegie Class: Masters/S
FAX Number: (805) 437-8414 Calendar System: Semester
URL: www.csuci.edu
Established: 2002 Annual Undergrad Tuition & Fees (In-District): $6,547
Enrollment: 6,167 Coed
Affiliation or Control: State/Local IRS Status: 501(c)3
Highest Offering: Master's
Accreditation: WC, ACBSP, NURSE

02 President ....Dr. Erika D. BECK
05 Provost ....Dr. Geoffrey CHASE
10 VP Business & Financial Affairs ....Ms. Ysabel TRINIDAD
32 VP Student Affairs ....Dr. Wm Gregory SAWYER
13 VP Technology & Innovation ....Dr. Michael BERMAN
111 VP University Advancement ....Ms. Nichole IPACH
100 Chief of Staff ....Dr. Genevieve EVANS TAYLOR
20 Assistant Provost ....Vacant
56 Associate VP & Dean Extended Univ ....Dr. Gary BERG
49 Dean of Arts & Sciences ....Dr. James H. MERIWETHER
50 Dean of MVS School of Bus & Econ ....Dr. William CORDEIRO
84 Associate VP Enrollment Management ....Mr. Hung D. DANG
53 Interim Dean of School of Education ....Dr. Merilyn BUCHANAN
25 Director Sponsored Programs ....Mr. Scott PEREZ
08 Dean of University Library ....Ms. Amy WALLACE
35 Associate VP & Dean of Students ....Ms. Toni DEBONI
88 Associate VP Wellness & Athletics ....Mr. Ed LEBIODA
21 Associate VP Financial Services ....Ms. Missy JARNAGIN
15 Senior Director Human Resources ....Ms. Laurie NICHOLS
09 Dir Instl Rsrch/Plng/Effectiveness ....Dr. Michael BOURGEOIS
86 Sr Dir Community & Govt Relations ....Ms. Celina ZACARIAS
22 Title IX & Inclusion Officer ....Ms. Brittany GRICE
30 Dir Advancement Operations ....Mr. Christopher ABE
88 Dir Major Gifts ....Mr. Carrick DEHART
29 Dir Development/Alumni Relations ....Ms. Tania GARCIA
112 Director Planned & Major Gifts ....Ms. Grace G. ROBINSON
44 Dir Annual Giving & Special Gifts ....Ms. Eva C. GOMEZ
19 Dir Public Safety & Chief of Police ....Mr. John REID
88 Dir Transportation & Pkg Svcs ....Mr. Ray PORRAS
39 AVP Housing/Residential Educ & ASI ....Ms. Cindy DERRICO
06 Assoc Dir Records & Registration ....Vacant
07 Dir of Admissions & Records ....Ms. Ginger REYES
108 Assoc VP for SA/ROISS ....Dr. Charles E. OSIRIS
104 Dir Intl Pgms/AD Ctr Intl Affairs ....Ms. Mayumi KOWTA
26 Dir Communication & Marketing ....Ms. Nancy GILL
37 Dir Financial Aid & Scholarships ....Ms. Sunshine GARCIA
88 Dir Special Projects for F&A ....Ms. Caroline DOLL
96 Dir Procurement & Contract Services ....Vacant
04 Presidential Aide ....Ms. Alanna TREJO

*California State University-Chico (D)

400 W First Street, Chico CA 95929-0001
County: Butte FICE Identification: 001146
Unit ID: 110538
Telephone: (530) 898-6116 Carnegie Class: Masters/L
FAX Number: (530) 898-6824 Calendar System: Semester
URL: www.csuchico.edu
Established: 1887 Annual Undergrad Tuition & Fees (In-State): $7,040
Enrollment: 17,220 Coed
Affiliation or Control: State IRS Status: 501(c)3
Highest Offering: Master's
Accreditation: WC, ART, CAEPN, CONST, CS, DIETD, DIETI, ENG, JOUR, MUS, NAIT, NRPA, NURSE, SP, SPAA, SW, THEA

02 President ....Dr. Gayle E. HUTCHINSON
100 Chief of Staff ....Ms. Brooke F. BANKS
05 Provost/Vice Pres Academic Affairs ....Dr. Debra LARSON
10 Vice Pres Business & Finance/CFO ....Mr. Robbi STIVERS
32 Vice President Student Affairs ....Mr. Pedro DOUGLAS
30 Vice Pres University Advancement ....Mr. Ahmad BOURA
45 Vice Prov Planning/Res Allocation ....Ms. Patricia WAID
46 Interim Assoc Vice Pres Research ....Dr. Kevin M. KELLEY
84 Assoc Vice Pres Enroll Management ....Ms. Barbara FORTIN
13 Vice Prov Information Resources/CIO ......Mr. Michael SCHILLING
21 Assoc VP Financial Svcs/Univ Budget ....Ms. Stacie CORONA
15 Asst Vice Pres Staff HR ....Ms. Sheryl WOODWARD
16 Int Assoc Vice Pres Fac Affairs ....Ms. Sarah BLAKESLEE
47 Dean College of Agriculture ....Dr. John A. UNRUH
51 Dean Continuing Education ....Ms. Debra E. BARGER
72 Dean Col Engr/Comp Sci/Const Mgmt ....Dr. Ricardo JACQUEZ
83 Dean Col Behavior & Social Sci ....Dr. Eddie VELA
50 Dean College of Business ....Dr. Judith HENNESSEY
79 Dean College Humanities/Fine Arts ....Dr. Robert M. KNIGHT
81 Dean College Natural Sciences ....Dr. David M. HASSENZAHL
60 Dean Coll Communication & Educ ....Dr. Angela TRETHEWEY
20 Dean Undergraduate Education ....Dr. William M. LOKER
58 Interim Dean Graduate Studies ....Dr. Sharon A. BARRIOS
08 Dean Library ....Dr. Patrick A. NEWELL
26 Director Public Affairs ....Vacant
29 Asst Vice Pres Alumni Relations ....Ms. Susan M. ANDERSON
09 Interim Chief Instit Research Off ....Dr. Ben JULIANO
06 Registrar ....Mr. Daniel A. PARKS
07 Director of Admissions ....Mr. Adam STOLTZ
36 Director Career Center ....Ms. Megan ODOM
37 Director Financial Aid/Scholarships ....Mr. Dan REED
18 Dir Facilities Management Svcs ....Mr. Michael A. GUZZI
96 Director of Procurement ....Ms. Sara RUMIANO
92 Director Univ Honors Program ....Mr. John MAHONEY
35 Director Student Judicial Affairs ......Ms. Sandy PARSONS-ELLIS
28 Director of Diversity and Inclusion ....Mr. Tray ROBINSON
04 Executive Asst to President ....Ms. Kathleen A. HASSIG
104 Int Assoc VP International Educ ....Dr. Frank LI
19 Chief of Police ....Mr. John J. FEENEY
25 Int Exec Dir Research Foundation ....Ms. Jessica BOURNE
109 Exec Director Associated Students ....Mr. David BUCKLEY
23 Medical Chief of Staff ....Dr. Deborah C. STEWART
38 Assoc Director Counseling ....Dr. Juni BANERJEE-STEVENS
39 Director University Housing ....Ms. Abeer A. MUSTAFA
41 Athletic Director ....Ms. Anita S. BARKER
53 Director School of Education ....Dr. Lynne BERCAW

*California State University-Dominguez Hills (E)

1000 E Victoria Street, Carson CA 90747-0005
County: Los Angeles FICE Identification: 001141
Unit ID: 110547
Telephone: (310) 243-3696 Carnegie Class: Masters/L
FAX Number: N/A Calendar System: Semester
URL: www.csudh.edu
Established: 1960 Annual Undergrad Tuition & Fees (In-State): $6,423
Enrollment: 14,635 Coed
Affiliation or Control: State IRS Status: 501(c)3
Highest Offering: Master's
Accreditation: WC, CAEPN, CS, MT, MUS, NURSE, OPE, OT, SPAA, SW, THEA

02 President ....Dr. Willie J. HAGAN
05 Provost/VP Academic Affairs ....Dr. Michael SPAGNA
10 Interim VP Administration/Finance ....Ms. Naomi GOODWIN
32 Vice President Student Affairs ....Dr. William FRANKLIN
111 VP Univ Advancement ....Ms. Carrie E. STEWART
11 Assoc VP Administration/Finance ....Mr. Stephen MASTRO
30 Assoc Vice President Development ....Mr. Jeff POLTORAK
13 VP/Chief Information Officer ....Mr. Chris MANRIQUEZ
35 AVP Student Life/Dean of Stdnts ....Dr. Marcelo VAZQUEZ
100 Interim Chief of Staff ....Dr. Rod HAY
07 Director of Admissions ....Ms. Michelle TAYLOR
84 Assoc VP Enrollment Mgmt ....Ms. Brandy MCLELLAND
09 Assoc Director Institutional Rsrch ...Mr. Pete VAN HAMERSVELD
37 Director of Financial Aid ....Ms. Delores LEE

*California State University-East Bay (F)

25800 Carlos Bee Boulevard, Hayward CA 94542-3001
County: Alameda FICE Identification: 001138
Unit ID: 110574
Telephone: (510) 885-3000 Carnegie Class: Masters/L
FAX Number: N/A Calendar System: Quarter
URL: www.csueastbay.edu
Established: 1957 Annual Undergrad Tuition & Fees (In-State): $6,564
Enrollment: 15,528 Coed
Affiliation or Control: State IRS Status: 501(c)3
Highest Offering: Doctorate
Accreditation: WC, ENG, MUS, NURSE, SP, SW

02 President ....Dr. Leroy M. MORISHITA
05 Provost/VP Academic Affairs ....Dr. Edward INCH
10 Vice Pres Admin & Finance ....Ms. Debbie CHAW
111 Vice President Univ Advancement ....Mr. William JOHNSON
32 Interim Vice Pres Student Affs ....Dr. Jo VOLKERT
28 University Diversity Officer ....Dr. Dianne RUSH WOODS
100 Chief of Staff ....Mr. Derek AITKEN
49 Dean Col of Ltrs/Arts/Soc Sci ....Dr. Kathleen ROUNTREE
50 Inter Dean Col of Bus/Econ ....Dr. Xinjian LU
53 Dean Col of Educ/Allied Studies ....Dr. Carolyn NELSON
81 Dean College of Science ....Dr. Jason SINGLEY
08 Dean of Libraries ....Dr. John WENZLER
13 CIO ....Dr. Jake HORNSBY
06 Registrar ....Ms. Angela SCHNEIDER
07 Assoc Dir Enrollment Planning ....Mr. Michael MCKEON

*California State University-Fresno (A)

5200 N. Barton Avenue, Fresno CA 93740-8027

County: Fresno FICE Identification: 001147
Unit ID: 110556
Telephone: (559) 278-4240 Carnegie Class: DU-Mod
FAX Number: (559) 278-4715 Calendar System: Semester
URL: www.csufresno.edu
Established: 1911 Annual Undergrad Tuition & Fees (In-State): $6,313
Enrollment: 24,136 Coed
Affiliation or Control: State IRS Status: 501(c)3
Highest Offering: Doctorate
Accreditation: WC, #CAATE, CACREP, CAEPN, CIDA, CONST, DIETD, DIETI, ENG, MUS, NAIT, NRPA, NURSE, PH, PTA, SP, SPAA, SW, THEA

02 President ... Dr. Joseph I. CASTRO
05 Provost/Vice Pres Academic Affs ... Dr. Lynnette ZELEZNY
10 VP Administration/Asc VP Auxiliary ... Dr. Deborah ADISHIAN-ASTONE
111 Vice Pres University Advancement ... Ms. Paula CASTADIO
32 Vice Pres Student Affs/Enroll Mgmt ... Dr. Frank LAMAS
100 Chief of Staff ... Ms. Diana RALLS
43 General Counsel ... Mr. Darryl HAMM
26 Assoc VP University Communications ... Ms. Shirley ARMBRUSTER
20 Vice Provost Academic Affairs ... Dr. Dennis L. NEF
09 AVP Inst Research/Assessment ... Dr. Angel SANCHEZ
30 Int Assoc VP University Development ... Ms. Caty PEREZ
21 Int Chief Fin Ofcr/Asc VP Fin Svcs ... Ms. Deborah ADISHIAN-ASTONE
18 Associate Vice President Facilities ... Mr. Robert BOYD
84 Assoc Vice Pres Enrollment Mgmt ... Ms. Malisa LEE
51 Dean/AVP Continuing/Global Educ ... Dr. Scott MOORE
47 Dean Agricultural Science/Tech ... Dr. Sandra WHITE
79 Dean of Arts & Humanities ... Dr. Saul JIMENEZ-SANDOVAL
50 Dean Craig School of Business ... Dr. Robert HARPER
53 Dean of Kremen School of Education ... Dr. Paul BEARE
54 Dean of Engineering ... Dr. Ramakrishna NUNNA
76 Dean of Health/Human Services ... Dr. Jody HIRONAKA-JUTEAU
83 Int Dean of Social Sciences ... Dr. Michelle DENBESTE
81 Int Dean of Science & Mathematics ... Dr. Robert G. DUNDAS
08 Dean of Library Services ... Mr. Peter MCDONALD
58 Dean Research/Graduate Studies ... Dr. James MARSHALL
86 Exec Dir Governmental Relations ... Mr. Larry SALINAS
23 Director Health Services ... Ms. Wendy OLIVER
19 Dir of Public Safety/Chief Police ... Mr. David HUERTA
41 Director of Athletics ... Mr. Jim BARTKO
15 Director of Human Resources ... Ms. Nicole LANE
13 Chief Information Officer ... Mr. Orlando LEON
37 Director of Financial Aid ... Ms. Kelly RUSSELL
27 Director of Publications ... Mr. Bruce WHITWORTH
29 Executive Director Alumni Relations ... Ms. Jacquelyn GLASENER
36 Dir of Career Development Center ... Ms. Debbie YOUNG
39 Director Univ Courtyard (Housing) ... Ms. Erin BOELE
96 Dir Procurement & Support Services ... Mr. Brian COTHAM
07 Director of Admissions & Records ... Ms. Tina BEDDALL
35 Assoc Dean Student Involvement ... Mr. Colin STEWART
40 Bookstore Director ... Mr. Curt PARKINSON

*California State University-Fullerton (B)

PO Box 34080, 800 N State Col Blvd, Fullerton CA 92831-3547

County: Orange FICE Identification: 001137
Unit ID: 110565
Telephone: (657) 278-2011 Carnegie Class: DU-Mod
FAX Number: (657) 278-2649 Calendar System: Semester
URL: www.fullerton.edu
Established: 1957 Annual Undergrad Tuition & Fees (In-State): $6,560
Enrollment: 38,948 Coed
Affiliation or Control: State IRS Status: 501(c)3
Highest Offering: Doctorate
Accreditation: WC, ANEST, ART, CAATE, CACREP, CAEPN, CS, CSHSE, DANCE, ENG, IPSY, JOUR, MIDWF, MUS, NURSE, PH, SP, SPAA, SW, THEA

02 President ... Dr. Mildred GARCIA
100 Deputy Chief of Staff ... Ms. Danielle GARCIA
05 Int Provost & VP Academic Affairs ... Dr. Anil PURI
10 VP Admin & Finance/CFO ... Mr. Danny C. KIM
32 Vice President of Student Affairs ... Dr. Berenecea J. EANES
111 VP University Advancement ... Mr. Greg SAKS
13 VP Info Tech/Chief Info Ofcr ... Mr. Amir DABIRIAN
15 VP of HR/Diversity & Inclusion ... Dr. David FORGUES
102 Executive Director/CFO Foundation ... Ms. Tara GARCIA
43 University Counsel ... Ms. Monique SHAY
30 Assoc VP University Advancement ... Mrs. Michele CESCA
35 AVP Student Affairs ... Dr. Tonantzin OSEGUERA
35 AVP Student Affairs ... Dr. Clint-Michael RENEAU
58 Int AVP Academic Programs ... Dr. Pamella OLIVER
26 AVP Strategic Communications ... Mr. Jeffrey COOK
20 AVP Academic Operations ... Dr. Karen SCISSUM GUNN
88 AVP Research and Sponsored Projects ... Dr. Chris LIU
88 Int AVP South County Ops & Init ... Dr. Steve WALK
21 AVP of Academic Opers & Finance ... Ms. Lisa KOPECKY
86 Assc VP Public Affs/Government Rels ... Mr. Tami BUI
88 Int AVP of Academic HR ... Dr. Emily BONNEY
45 Asst VP for Resource Planning ... Ms. Laleh GRAYLEE
35 Int AVP Student Affairs ... Mr. Darren BUSH
88 Int Chief of Operations Stdnt Affs ... Dr. Deanna LEONE
11 Chief of Operations Admin & Finance ... Ms. Mary CLARK
18 AVP Capital Planning/Fac Mgt ... Dr. Ali IZADIAN
84 Asst Vice Pres Enrollment Services ... Ms. Nancy DORITY
09 Dir Inst Res/Analytical Stds ... Dr. Sunny MOON
29 Exec Director Alumni Relations ... Ms. Dianna L. FISHER
109 Exec Dir/CEO Auxiliary Svcs Corp ... Mr. Frank MUMFORD
88 Director of Budget Student Affairs ... Mr. Robert SCIALDONE
08 Dean of the Library ... Dr. Clement GUTHRO
07 Director of Admissions ... Ms. Jessica WAGONER
36 Director Career Center ... Dr. Elizabeth ZAVALA-ACEVEZ
40 Director Titan Shops ... Ms. Kimberly BALL
23 Director Health Center ... Vacant
19 Chief University Police ... Mr. Dennis DEMAIO
28 Director Diversity/Equity Programs ... Vacant
37 Int Director Financial Aid ... Ms. Kelly ENGLAND
41 Director of Athletics ... Mr. James DONOVAN
96 Director of Contracts & Procurement ... Mr. Nelson NAGAI
35 Dean of Students ... Ms. Hallie HUNT
88 Dir Intl Admissions & Outreach ... Mr. Joseph SAÑOSA
85 Dir Intl Students & Scholars ... Ms. Christine PIRCHER-BARNES
88 Director Women's Center/Re-Entry ... Dr. Alisa FLOWERS
88 Dir Educational Partnerships ... Ms. Melba CASTRO
39 Director Housing ... Mr. Larry MARTIN
88 Int Dir Univ Outreach/New Stdnt Pgm ... Ms. Sharnette UNDERDUE
88 Dir Athletic Academic Services ... Ms. Meredith BASIL
88 Dir Center for Internship/Com Eng ... Ms. Dawn MACY
88 Dir Student Academic Services ... Dr. Rochelle WOODS
88 Dir Veteran Student Services ... Mr. Lui AMADOR
38 Dir Counseling/Psychological Svcs ... Dr. Leticia GUTIERREZ-LOPEZ
14 AVP IT/Infrastructure Services ... Mr. Berhanu TADESSE
90 Int AVP IT/Academic Technology Svcs ... Mr. Willie PENG
51 Dean Extend Educ/AVP Intl Pgm ... Dr. Kari KNUTSON-MILLER
79 Dean Humanities/Social Sciences ... Dr. Sheryl FONTAINE
81 Dean Natural Sciences & Math ... Dr. Marie JOHNSON
50 Int Dean Mihaylo Col Business/Econ ... Dr. Morteza RAHMATIAN
83 Dean Health/Human Development ... Dr. Laurie ROADES
57 Dean College of the Arts ... Mr. Dale MERRILL
53 Dean College of Education ... Dr. Lisa KIRTMAN
54 Int Dean Col Engineering & Comp Sci ... Dr. Susamma BARUA
60 Int Dean College of Communications ... Dr. Edward FINK
88 Title IX Coordinator ... Ms. Mary BECERRA
88 ASI Executive Director ... Dr. Dave EDWARDS

*California State University-Long Beach (C)

1250 Bellflower Boulevard, Long Beach CA 90840

County: Los Angeles FICE Identification: 001139
Unit ID: 110583
Telephone: (562) 985-4111 Carnegie Class: Masters/L
FAX Number: (562) 985-5419 Calendar System: Semester
URL: www.csulb.edu
Established: 1949 Annual Undergrad Tuition & Fees (In-State): $6,460
Enrollment: 37,446 Coed
Affiliation or Control: State IRS Status: 501(c)3
Highest Offering: Doctorate
Accreditation: WC, AAFCS, ART, CAATE, CAEPN, CEA, CONST, CS, DANCE, DIETD, DIETI, ENG, #HSA, IPSY, JOUR, MUS, NRPA, NURSE, PH, PTA, SP, SPAA, SW, THEA

02 President ... Dr. Jane C. CONOLEY
05 Provost/Sr Vice Pres Academic Affs ... Dr. Brian JERSKY
11 Vice Pres Administration/Finance ... Ms. Mary E. STEPHENS
13 VP/Chief Information Officer ... Dr. Min YAO
32 Vice President Student Affairs ... Dr. Carmen TILLERY TAYLOR
30 Vice Pres University Rels/Devel ... Ms. Andrea TAYLOR
100 Chief of Staff ... Dr. Karen NAKAI
10 Assoc VP Financial Management ... Ms. Sharon TAYLOR
20 Assoc VP Undergraduate Studies ... Dr. Kerry JOHNSON
35 Assoc Vice Pres Student Affairs ... Dr. Mary Ann TAKEMOTO
82 Assoc VP Intl Education ... Dr. Jeet JOSHEE
18 Assoc VP Phys Plng/Facilities Mgt ... Mr. David SALAZAR
20 Interim Vice Provost/Dean Grad Stds ... Dr. Jody CORMACK
20 Vice Provost Academic Planning ... Dr. Dhushy SATHIANATHAN
46 Assoc Vice Pres University Research ... Dr. Simon KIM
15 Assoc VP Human Resource Mgmt ... Mr. Scott APEL
91 Assoc VP Academic Technology ... Dr. Shawna DARK
29 Assoc VP Alumni and Univ Relations ... Ms. Janice HATANAKA
09 Director Institutional Research ... Dr. Mahmoud ALBAWANEH
84 Asst VP Enrollment Services ... Ms. Susan LEIGH
14 Assoc VP Information Technology ... Ms. Janet FOSTER
76 Dean College Health/Human Svcs ... Dr. Monica LOUNSBERY
50 Dean College of Business Admin ... Dr. Michael SOLT
53 Dean College of Education ... Dr. Shireen PAVRI
54 Dean College of Engineering ... Dr. Forouzan GOLSHANI
57 Dean College of the Arts ... Ms. Cyrus PARKER-JEANNETTE
81 Dean College Natural Sciences/Math ... Dr. Curtis BENNETT
49 Dean College of Liberal Arts ... Dr. David WALLACE
51 Dean Col Continuing & Profess Educ ... Dr. Jeet JOSHEE
08 Dean Library ... Mr. Roman KOCHAN
06 University Registrar ... Ms. Donna GREEN
39 Interim Dir Housing & Res Life ... Ms. Claudia PLAZA
16 Director Staff Human Resources ... Ms. Nancy TORRES
41 Director Athletics ... Mr. Andy FEE
07 Interim Director of Admissions ... Ms. Janice MILLER
36 Director Career Development Ctr ... Mr. Manuel PEREZ
23 Director Health Services ... Dr. Mary Ann TAKEMOTO
19 Chief University Police ... Mr. Fernando SOLORZANO
38 Director Counseling/Psych Services ... Dr. Brad COMPLIMENT
37 Director Financial Aid ... Mr. Nicolas VALDIVIA
25 Senior Director Sponsored Programs ... Ms. Maria REYES
102 Chief Op Ofcr/Rsrch Foundation ... Dr. Brian NOWLIN
28 Director of Equity & Diversity ... Ms. Larisa HAMADA
96 Director Procurement & Contracts ... Ms. Malia KINIMAKA
109 General Manager/49'er Shops ... Mr. Donald PENROD
104 Director Education Abroad ... Ms. Sharon OLSON
44 Director Leadership Giving ... Ms. Sireth TORRES
86 AVP Legislative & External Rels ... Ms. Terri CARBAUGH
88 Assoc VP Budget & Univ Svcs ... Mr. Ted KADOWAKI
88 Asst VP Administrative Services ... Ms. Mishelle LAWS
88 Assoc VP Faculty Affairs ... Dr. Mark WILEY
04 Deputy Chief of Staff ... Ms. Coleen FOLLOWELL
108 Director Program Review/Assessment ... Dr. Sharlene SAYEGH
22 Dir Affirmative Action/EEO ... Ms. Larisa HAMADA
26 Assoc VP Univ Rels & Communications ... Mr. Andy HOANG
21 Director Internal Audit ... Ms. Aysu SPRUILL

*California State University-Los Angeles (D)

5151 State University Drive, Los Angeles CA 90032-8530

County: Los Angeles FICE Identification: 001140
Unit ID: 110592
Telephone: (323) 343-3000 Carnegie Class: Masters/L
FAX Number: (323) 343-2670 Calendar System: Quarter
URL: www.calstatela.edu
Established: 1947 Annual Undergrad Tuition & Fees (In-State): $6,383
Enrollment: 27,680 Coed
Affiliation or Control: State IRS Status: 501(c)3
Highest Offering: Doctorate
Accreditation: WC, ART, CACREP, CAEPN, CS, DIETC, DIETD, ENG, MT, MUS, NAIT, NURSE, SP, SPAA, SW

02 President ... Dr. William A. COVINO
11 Exec VP and Chief Operating Officer ... Dr. Jose A. GOMEZ
05 Provost/Vice Pres Academic Affs ... Dr. Lynn P. MAHONEY
10 VP Administration & CFO ... Ms. Lisa M. CHAVEZ
32 Vice President Student Life ... Dr. Nancy WADA-MCKEE
13 AVP for Information Technology ... Ms. Tosha PHAM
44 Vice Pres University Advancement ... Dr. Janet S. DIAL
84 Vice Provost for Enrollment Svcs ... Mr. Tom ENDERS
88 Vice Prov Diversity/Engage Lrng ... Dr. Octavio VILLALPANDO
21 Assoc VP Admin & Finance/Budget ... Ms. Mae SANTOS
35 Dean of Students ... Dr. Jennifer MILLER
30 Assoc VP University Advancement ... Dr. Mario PEREZ
20 AVP Research ... Dr. Jeffrey UNDERWOOD
29 Exec Director Alumni Relations ... Ms. Maria UBAGO
26 Exec Dir Comm/Public Affairs ... Mr. Robert LOPEZ
41 Exec Dir Intercollegiate Athletics ... Dr. Daryl J. GROSS
83 Dean Natural & Social Sciences ... Dr. Pamela SCOTT-JOHNSON
83 Assoc Dean Natural/Social Sciences ... Dr. Nancy MCQUEEN
08 Dean of the University Library ... Mr. Carlos RODRIGUEZ
06 University Registrar ... Mr. Christopher COBB
58 Dean Graduate Studies ... Dr. Karin A. ELLIOT BROWN
09 Director Institutional Research ... Dr. Mark PAVELCHAK
36 Director Career Placement & Plng ... Dr. Christopher LENZ
37 Director Student Financial Services ... Ms. Tamie NGUYEN
23 Director Health Center ... Dr. Monica JAZZABI
39 Director Housing Svc/Residence Life ... Ms. Rebecca PALMER
22 Director Equal Opportunity Pgm ... Dr. Becky HOPKINS
18 AVP Fac/Plng/Design & Construct ... Mr. Warren JACOBS
19 Chief of Police ... Mr. Rick WALL
15 AVP Human Resources Management ... Ms. Susie VARELA
85 Director Intl Programs & Services ... Ms. Amy WANG
43 University Counsel ... Mr. Victor I. KING
07 Director Admissions & Recruitment ... Mr. Vince LOPEZ
96 Director Procurement & Contracts ... Mr. Thomas JOHNSON
09 Asst Dir Institutional Research ... Dr. Michelle DUNBAR
28 Dir Equity/Diversity/Inclusion ... Ms. Mariel MULET
40 General Manager Bookstore ... Ms. Elaine REED
88 Assoc Dean Undergrad Studies ... Dr. Margaret GARCIA
49 Int Dean Arts & Letters ... Dr. Rennie SCHOEPFLIN
88 Int Associate Dean Arts/Letters ... Dr. David CONNORS
54 Dean Engr/Computer Science/Tech ... Dr. Emily ALLEN
88 Int Assoc Dean Engr/Comp Sci/Tech ... Dr. Jianyu (June) DONG
107 Dean Col of Profess/Global Studies ... Dr. Eric A. BULLARD
76 Dean Health & Human Services ... Dr. Ronald VOGEL
88 Assoc Dean Health & Human Svcs ... Dr. Denise HERZ
53 Dean Charter Col of Education ... Dr. Cheryl L. NEY
50 Dean Business & Economics ... Dr. Rami MAYSAMI
88 Associate Dean Business & Economics ... Dr. Angela YOUNG
97 Dean Undergraduate Studies ... Dr. Michelle HAWLEY
92 Director Honors College ... Dr. Trinh PHAM

† Grants Joint Doctoral degree in cooperation with the University of California-Los Angeles.

*CSU Maritime Academy (E)

200 Maritime Academy Drive, Vallejo CA 94590-0644

County: Solano FICE Identification: 001134
Unit ID: 111188
Telephone: (707) 654-1000 Carnegie Class: Bac-Diverse
FAX Number: (707) 654-1001 Calendar System: Semester
URL: www.csum.edu
Established: 1929 Annual Undergrad Tuition & Fees (In-State): $6,808
Enrollment: 1,075 Coed
Affiliation or Control: State IRS Status: 501(c)3
Highest Offering: Master's
Accreditation: WC, ENG, ENGT, IACBE

02 President ... RADM. Thomas A. CROPPER, USMS
05 Provost/VP Academic Affairs ... Dr. Susan OPP
10 VP of Administration/Finance ... Mr. Franz LOZANO
32 VP of Student Affairs ... Mr. Steve KRETA
111 VP of University Advancement ... Mr. Robert ARP

15 Assistant VP of Human Resources .... Dr. Ingrid WILLIAMS
13 Chief Information Officer .... Mr. Daman GREWAL
100 Chief of Staff .... Mr. Brigham TIMPSON
88 Master of Training Ship .... Capt. Harry BOLTON
20 Associate Vice President .... Dr. Graham BENTON
112 Senior Development Officer .... Ms. Melissa COHEA
06 Registrar .... Ms. Peg SOLVESON
08 Dean of Library .... Ms. Michele VAN HOECK
07 Director of Admissions .... Mr. Marc MCGEE
37 Director of Financial Aid .... Ms. Priscilla MUHA
109 Associate Vice President .... Mr. Mark GOODRICH
88 Director of SEAS .... Ms. Vineeta DHILLON
35 Dean of Students .... Mr. James DALSKE
18 Director Facilities Planning .... Mr. Isidro FARIAS
19 Chief of Police Services .... Chief Donny GORDON
21 University Controller .... Ms. Ashley ANDERSEN
41 Director of Athletics .... Mr. Marv CHRISTOPHER
26 Director of Public Relations .... Mr. Robert KING
40 Bookstore Manager .... Mr. Andre JIMENEZ
96 Director of Purchasing .... Ms. Lorrie DINEEN-THACKERAY
09 Director of Institutional Research .... Mr. Gary MOSER
29 Director of Alumni Relations .... Mr. Eric COOPER
101 Asst Director University Affair .... Ms. Jennifer HEMBREE
114 Budget Director .... Mr. Andrew SOM
11 Associate Vice President .... Mr. Kevin BERTELSEN
117 Director of Risk Management .... Ms. Marianne SPOTORNO
39 Director Residential Life .... Ms. Kate KIMBLE-TUSZYNSKI
36 Director Career Services .... Ms. Wendy HIGGINS
23 Chief Medical Officer .... Mr. Bruce WILBUR

*California State University-Monterey Bay (A)

100 Campus Center, Seaside CA 93955-8000

County: Monterey | FICE Identification: 032603 | Unit ID: 409698

Telephone: (831) 582-3000 | Carnegie Class: Masters/M

FAX Number: (831) 582-3783 | Calendar System: Semester

URL: www.csumb.edu

Established: 1994 | Annual Undergrad Tuition & Fees (In-State): $6,379

Enrollment: 7,102 | Coed

Affiliation or Control: State | IRS Status: 501(c)3

Highest Offering: Master's

Accreditation: WC, NURSE, SW

02 President .... Dr. Eduardo M. OCHOA
05 Provost .... Dr. Bonnie IRWIN
10 Vice Pres Admin & Finance/CFO .... Mr. Kevin SAUNDERS
30 Vice Pres University Development .... Ms. Barbara ZAPPAS
32 VP Student Affairs & Enroll Service .... Dr. Ronnie HIGGS
26 Assoc VP for University Affairs .... Mr. Andre LEWIS
35 Dean of Student Life .... Vacant
21 Assoc Vice President for Finance .... Mr. John FITZGIBBON
28 Assoc VP Inclusive Excellence .... Dr. Patti HIRAMOTO
108 AVP Institutional Effect/Acad Plng .... Dr. Fran HORVATH
06 Registrar .... Ms. Sheila HERNANDEZ
13 Chief Information Officer .... Mr. Chip LENNO
22 Director Employee Rels/EEO & ADA .... Ms. Tamberly PETROVICH
37 Director Financial Aid .... Ms. Angeles FUENTES
15 Assoc VP for Human Resources .... Ms. Natalie KING
19 Chief of Police .... Chief Earl LAWSON
18 AVP Facilities Services & Operation .... Mr. Mario FORTE
07 Interim Director of Admissions .... Ms. Paula CARTER
29 Director Alumni Relations .... Ms. Annie WARR
41 Athletic Director .... Mr. Kirby GARRY
96 Director of Purchasing .... Mr. Art EVJEN

*California State University-Northridge (B)

18111 Nordhoff Street, Northridge CA 91330-0001

County: Los Angeles | FICE Identification: 001153 | Unit ID: 110608

Telephone: (818) 677-1200 | Carnegie Class: Masters/L

FAX Number: N/A | Calendar System: Semester

URL: www.csun.edu

Established: 1958 | Annual Undergrad Tuition & Fees (In-State): $6,587

Enrollment: 41,548 | Coed

Affiliation or Control: State | IRS Status: 501(c)3

Highest Offering: Doctorate

Accreditation: WC, AAFCS, ART, CAATE, CACREP, CIDA, CONST, CS, DIETD, DIETI, ENG, IPSY, JOUR, MFCD, MUS, NRPA, NURSE, PH, PTA, RAD, SP, SW, THEA

02 President .... Dr. Dianne F. HARRISON
05 Provost/Vice Pres Academic Affairs .... Dr. Yi LI
10 Vice President Admin Finance/CFO .... Mr. Colin DONAHUE
32 VP Student Affairs/Dean of Students .... Dr. William WATKINS
111 VP Univ Advan/Foundation President .... Dr. Robert GUNSALUS
13 Vice President IT/CIO .... Ms. Hilary BAKER
88 Exec Director University Corp .... Mr. Rick EVANS
20 Vice Provost Academic Affairs .... Dr. Stella THEODOULOU
100 Chief of Staff .... Ms. Jill SMITH
18 Assoc VP Facilities Dev/Operations .... Mr. Ken ROSENTHAL
58 Assoc VP Grad Studies/Intl Pgms .... Dr. Crist KHACHIKIAN
21 Associate VP Financial Services .... Ms. Deborah WALLACE
15 Assoc VP of Human Resources .... Ms. Kristina DE LA VEGA
29 Asst Vice Pres Alumni Relations .... Ms. Shellie HADVINA
26 Assoc VP of Mktg/Comm .... Mr. Jeffrey NOBLITT
20 Assoc VP for Student Success .... Dr. Elizabeth T. ADAMS
91 Assoc VP of Acad Resources/Planning .. Ms. Diane S. STEPHENS
07 Director of Admissions and Records .... Ms. Patty R. LORD
08 Dean University Library .... Dr. Mark STOVER
51 Dean College of Extended Learning .... Dr. Joyce A. FEUCHT-HAVIAR
79 Dean College of Humanities .... Dr. Elizabeth A. SAY
50 Int Dean College Business/Economics .... Dr. Deborah A. COURS
53 Interim Dean College of Education .... Dr. Shari A. TARVER-BEHRING
57 Dean College Arts/Media/Comm .... Mr. Dan HOSKEN
83 Dean Col Social/Behavioral Sci .... Vacant
76 Dean Col Health/Human Development .... Dr. Farrell WEBB
81 Dean College Science & Math .... Dr. Jerry STINNER
54 Dean College Engr/Computer Science .... Vacant
09 Dir Institutional Research .... Dr. Janet S. OH
37 Director Financial Aid/Scholarships .... Ms. Linda M. BRIGNONI
38 Director Univ Counseling Services .... Dr. Julie L. PEARCE
36 Director Career Center .... Ms. Ann N. MOREY
25 Dir Research/Graduate Studies .... Ms. Hedy L. CARPENTER
18 Senior Dir Physical Plant Mgmt .... Mr. Jason WANG
19 Director of Police Services .... Ms. Anne P. GLAVIN
28 Director of Equity/Diversity .... Vacant
86 Dir Government/Community Relations .... Ms. Francesca VEGA
23 Director Student Health Center .... Dr. Linda REID-CHASSIAKOS
39 Dir Student Housing/Conf Services .... Mr. Timothy J. TREVAN
40 Director Matador Bookstore .... Ms. Amy C. BERGER
41 Dir of Intercollegiate Athletics .... Dr. Brandon MARTIN
88 Director Student Involvement & Dev .... Mr. Patrick BAILEY
92 Dir General Education Honors Pgm .... Dr. Beth A. WIGHTMAN
96 Manager Purchasing .... Ms. Deborah FLUGUM
06 Registrar .... Mr. Todd WOLFE
28 Int CDO/Title IX Coordinator .... Ms. Susan HUA

*California State University-Sacramento (C)

6000 J Street, Sacramento CA 95819-2694

County: Sacramento | FICE Identification: 001150 | Unit ID: 110617

Telephone: (916) 278-6011 | Carnegie Class: Masters/L

FAX Number: (916) 278-6664 | Calendar System: Semester

URL: www.csus.edu

Established: 1947 | Annual Undergrad Tuition & Fees (In-State): $6,900

Enrollment: 30,284 | Coed

Affiliation or Control: State | IRS Status: 501(c)3

Highest Offering: Doctorate

Accreditation: WC, ART, CAATE, CACREP, CIDA, CONST, CS, DIETD, DIETI, EMT, ENG, MUS, NRPA, NURSE, PTA, SP, SW, THEA

02 President .... Dr. Robert S. NELSEN
05 Provost/VP Acad Affairs .... Dr. Ching-Hua WANG
11 VP of Administration & CFO .... Dr. Ming-Tung (Mike) LEE
111 Interim VP Univ Advancement .... Dr. Lisa CARDOZA
32 VP Student Affairs .... Dr. Edward MILLS
13 VP & Chief Information Officer .... Dr. Christine E. MILLER
15 Vice President for Human Resources .... Dr. Christine D. LOVELY
26 Vice Pres Public Affairs/Advocacy .... Dr. Phil GARCIA
46 Assoc VP Research Affairs .... Mr. David EARWICKER
20 Vice Provost .... Dr. Stephen PEREZ
18 Assoc Vice Pres Facilities Mgmt .... Dr. Justin REGINATO
27 Assoc VP University Communications .... Ms. Jeannie WONG
35 AVP Student Engagement & Support .... Dr. Beth LESEN
21 Assoc VP Financial Svcs .... Ms. Gina CURRY
43 University Counsel .... Ms. Jill PETERSON
09 Director Institutional Research .... Vacant
07 Interim Dir Outreach & Admissions .... Dr. Jeff WESTON
08 Library Dean .... Ms. Amy KAUTZMAN
29 Assoc VP Alumni Relations .... Ms. Jennifer BARBER
19 Chief of Police .... Mr. Mark IWASA
39 Dir Housing and Residential Life .... Mr. Michael SPEROS
41 Director of Athletics .... Dr. Mark ORR
37 Director Financial Aid .... Ms. Anita KERMES
22 Director of Equal Opportunity .... Mr. William BISHOP
40 Bookstore Director .... Ms. Pam PARSONS
100 Interim Chief of Staff .... Dr. Cely SMART
06 University Registrar .... Mr. Dennis GEYER
85 AVP Intl Pgm/Global Engagement .... Dr. Paul HOFMANN
23 Dir Student Health Ctr & Psych Svcs .Dr. Joy STEWART-JAMES
96 Mgr Procurement/Contract Services .... Mr. John GUION
49 Dean College of Arts & Letters .... Dr. Sheree MEYER
50 Dean Col of Business Admin .... Dr. Pierre BALTHAZARD
53 Dean College of Educ .... Dr. Alexander SIDORKIN
54 Dean College of Engr/Computer Sci .... Dr. Lorenzo SMITH
76 Dean College of Health/Human Svcs .... Dr. Fred BALDINI
81 Dean College of Natural Sci/Math .... Dr. Joanna MOTT
51 Dean College Continuing Education .... Dr. Helen WUSSOW
83 Dean College Soc Sci/Interdisc Stds .... Dr. Orn BODVARSSON
58 Dean Graduate Studies .... Dr. Chevelle NEWSOME
28 Director of Diversity .... Dr. Robin CARTER

*California State University-San Bernardino (D)

5500 University Parkway, San Bernardino CA 92407-2393

County: San Bernardino | FICE Identification: 001142 | Unit ID: 110510

Telephone: (909) 537-5000 | Carnegie Class: Masters/L

FAX Number: N/A | Calendar System: Quarter

URL: www.csusb.edu

Established: 1960 | Annual Undergrad Tuition & Fees (In-State): $6,610

Enrollment: 20,024 | Coed

Affiliation or Control: State | IRS Status: 501(c)3

Highest Offering: Doctorate

Accreditation: WC, ART, CACREP, CS, DIETD, ENG, MUS, NURSE, SPAA, SW, THEA

02 President .... Dr. Tomas MORALES
05 Provost/VP Academic Affairs .... Dr. Shari MCMAHAN
10 Vice Pres Administration/Finance .... Dr. Doug FREER
32 Vice Pres Student Affairs .... Dr. Brian L. HAYNES
111 Vice Pres University Advancement .... Dr. Ronald FREMONT
13 Vice Pres ITS/CIO .... Dr. Samuel SUDHAKAR
28 Co-Chief Diversity Officer .... Mr. Cesar PORTILLO
28 Co-Chief Diversity Officer .... Dr. Jacqueline HUGHES
88 Director Executive Affairs .... Ms. Pamela LANGFORD
20 Int Assoc Provost Acad Programs .... Dr. Rong CHEN
46 Interim Assoc Provost Research .... Dr. Cynthia CRAWFORD
20 Assoc VP & Dean Undergrad Studies .... Dr. Craig R. SEAL
21 Assoc VP Finance .... Mr. M. Monir AHMED
15 Assoc VP Human Resources .... Mr. Cesar PORTILLO
84 Assoc VP Enrollment Mgmt .... Ms. Olivia ROSAS
35 Assoc VP and Dean of Students .... Dr. Alysson M. SATTERLUND
14 Assoc VP ITS .... Mr. Gerard AU
26 Assoc VP Strategic Communications .... Mr. Bob TENCZAR
09 AVP Inst Effectiveness & Dir IR .... Dr. Muriel LOPEZ-WAGNER
88 Int Assoc Provost Acad Personnel .... Dr. J. Paul VICKNAIR
22 Director Title IX & Gender Equity .... Ms. Cristina MARTIN
36 Director Career Center .... Ms. Denise GIANOUSSOPOULOS
06 Int Director University Registrar .... Ms. Amy BRACEROS
07 Director Admissions .... Vacant
23 Director Health Center .... Dr. Grace CASTILLO JOHNSON
08 University Librarian .... Mr. Cesar CABALLERO
37 Director Financial Aid .... Ms. Roseanna RUIZ
39 Director Housing & Residential Life .... Dr. John YAUN
45 Director Plng Design/Construction .... Mr. Hamid U. AZHAND
18 Director Facilities Management .... Ms. Jennifer SORENSON
41 Director Athletics .... Mr. Shawn FARRELL
29 Director Alumni Affairs .... Ms. Doreen HATCHER
96 Director Purchasing .... Mr. David GEE
40 Director Bookstore .... Mr. David WATTS
94 Director Gender & Sexuality Studies .... Dr. Todd JENNINGS
92 Director University Honors Program .... Dr. David MARSHALL
56 Dean Col of Extended Learning .... Dr. Tatiana KARMANOVA
49 Dean College of Arts & Letters .... Dr. Terry BALLMAN
81 Dean Col Natural Sciences .... Dr. Kirsten FLEMING
83 Dean Col Social/Behavioral Sciences .... Dr. Rafik MOHAMED
53 Dean College of Education .... Dr. Jay FIENE
50 Dean College of Business .... Dr. Lawrence D. ROSE
58 Dean Graduate Studies .... Dr. Francisca BEER
12 Dean CSUSB Palm Desert .... Dr. Sharon BROWN-WELTY
100 Chief of Staff .... Ms. Julie M. LAPPIN
102 Sr Dir Foundation/Corp Rels .... Mr. Ron FREMONT
44 Operations Manager Annual Giving .... Ms. Carolina VAN ZEE
104 Co-Director Study Abroad .... Dr. Vipin GUPTA
104 Co-Director Study Abroad .... Mr. Frank LIN

*California State University-San Marcos (E)

333 S Twin Oaks Valley Road, San Marcos CA 92096-0001

County: San Diego | FICE Identification: 030113 | Unit ID: 366711

Telephone: (760) 750-4000 | Carnegie Class: Masters/M

FAX Number: (760) 750-4030 | Calendar System: Semester

URL: www.csusm.edu

Established: 1989 | Annual Undergrad Tuition & Fees (In-State): $7,383

Enrollment: 12,793 | Coed

Affiliation or Control: State | IRS Status: 501(c)3

Highest Offering: Doctorate

Accreditation: WC, NURSE, SP, SW

02 President .... Dr. Karen S. HAYNES
04 Presidential Aide .... Ms. Viviana GARCIA
10 Vice President Finance/Admin Svcs .... Mr. Neal HOSS
05 Vice President Academic Affairs .... Dr. Graham OBEREM
32 Vice President of Student Affairs .... Dr. Lorena CHECA
111 Vice Pres University Advancement .... Mrs. Cathy BAUR
20 Dean Academic Affairs .... Dr. Regina EISENBACH
45 Vice Provost Plan/Acad Resources .... Dr. Kamel HADDAD
84 Assoc Vice Pres Enrollment Mgmt .... Mr. Scott HAGG
15 Assoc VP Human Resource/Equal Oppty .... Mr. Travis GREGORY
49 Dean Col Hum Arts/Behav & Soc Sci .... Dr. Julia JOHNSON
50 Dean Col Business Administration .... Dr. Jim HAMERLY
53 Dean Col Educ/Health & Human Svcs .... Dr. Janet POWELL
08 Dean of Library Services .... Dr. Jennifer FABBI
81 Dean Col of Science & Mathematics .... Dr. Katherine KANTARDJIEFF
56 Dean of Extended Studies .... Mr. Michael SCHRODER
72 Dean Instructional/Info Technology .... Mr. Kevin MORNINGSTAR
06 Registrar .... Ms. Lisa MEDINA
07 Dir of Admissions & Recruitment .... Ms. Carol MCALLISTER
100 Chief of Staff/Dir Inst Plng & Anal .... Dr. Matthew CEPPI
21 Associate Business Officer .... Mrs. Mary HINCHMAN
29 Director Alumni/Parent Relations .... Ms. Lori BROCKETT
96 Director Procurement/Support Svcs .... Ms. Bella NEWBERG
121 Director Undergraduate Advising .... Mr. David MCMARTIN

† Grants Joint Doctoral degree in cooperation with the University of California-San Diego.

*California State University-Stanislaus (F)

1 University Circle, Turlock CA 95382-0299

County: Stanislaus | FICE Identification: 001157 | Unit ID: 110495

Telephone: (209) 667-3122 Carnegie Class: Masters/L
FAX Number: N/A Calendar System: Semester
URL: www.csustan.edu
Established: 1957 Annual Undergrad Tuition & Fees (In-State): $6,728
Enrollment: 9,282 Coed
Affiliation or Control: State IRS Status: 170(c)1
Highest Offering: Doctorate
Accreditation: WC, ART, MUS, NURSE, SPAA, SW, THEA

02 President ... Dr. Ellen JUNN
05 Provost/VP Academic Affairs ... Dr. Kimberly GREER
10 VP Business/Finance/CFO ... Mr. Darrell HAYDON
32 VP Student Affairs ... Dr. Suzanne M. ESPINOZA
111 VP University Advancement ... Dr. Michele LAHTI
84 VP Strategic Plng/Enroll Mgmt/Innov ... Dr. Gitanjali KAUL
15 Sr AVP HR/EO/Compliance ... Ms. Julie JOHNSON
35 AVP Student Services ... Dr. J. Martyn GUNN
100 Dir Presidential Initiatives ... Ms. Neisha RHODES
79 Dean College Arts/Humanities & SS ... Dr. James A. TUEDIO
50 Dean College of Business Admin ... Dr. Thomas GOMEZ-ARIAS
53 Dean College of Education ... Dr. Oddmund R. MYHRE
81 Dean College of Science ... Dr. David EVANS
08 Dean Library Services ... Mr. Ron RODRIGUEZ
106 Dean Stockton Center ... Dr. Faimous HARRISON
51 Dean Extended Education ... Dr. Helene CAUDILL
20 AVP Academic Affairs ... Dr. Shawna YOUNG
41 Director Athletics ... Mr. Michael MATOSO
07 Dir Admissions & Fin Aid ... Ms. Noelia GONZALEZ
35 AVP Student Affs/Dean of Students ... Mr. Matthew LOPEZ-PHILLIPS
21 Assoc VP Financial Services ... Ms. Regan LINDERMAN
13 Assoc VP Information Technology ... Mr. Stan TREVENA
18 Assoc VP Facilities Services ... Ms. Melody MAFFEI
26 Sr AVP Comm & Public Affairs ... Dr. Rosalee RUSH
19 Chief of Police ... Mr. Andy ROY
22 Campus Compliance Officer ... Ms. Julie A. JOHNSON
06 Registrar ... Ms. Lisa M. BERNARDO

*Humboldt State University (A)

1 Harpst Street, Arcata CA 95521-8222
County: Humboldt FICE Identification: 001149
Unit ID: 115755
Telephone: (707) 826-3011 Carnegie Class: Masters/M
FAX Number: (707) 826-5555 Calendar System: Semester
URL: www.humboldt.edu
Established: 1913 Annual Undergrad Tuition & Fees (In-State): $7,209
Enrollment: 8,790 Coed
Affiliation or Control: State IRS Status: 501(c)3
Highest Offering: Master's
Accreditation: WC, ART, ENG, IACBE, MUS, SW

02 President ... Dr. Lisa ROSSBACHER
100 Chief of Staff ... Vacant
05 Provost ... Dr. Alex ENYEDI
20 Vice Prov Acad Pgms/Undergrad Stds ... Dr. Mary GLENN
32 VP Student Affairs & Enroll Mgmt ... Dr. Peg BLAKE
10 Vice Pres Admin & Finance ... Ms. Joyce LOPES
30 Vice President of Advancement ... Mr. Craig WRUCK
15 Sr AVP Faculty Affairs and HR ... Dr. Colleen MULLERY
88 Executive Director Philanthropy ... Ms. Kimberley PITTMAN-SCHULZ
106 Assoc VP eLearning & Ext Educ ... Dr. Alex HWU
26 Assoc VP for Mktg & Communications ... Mr. Frank WHITLATCH
18 Assoc Vice President Facilities ... Ms. Traci FERDOLAGE
88 Assoc Vice President of Retention ... Ms. Radha WEBLEY
09 Assc VP Institutional Effectiveness ... Dr. Lisa CASTELLINO
114 Director University Budget Office ... Ms. Amber BLAKESLEE
88 Director of Academic Resources ... Mr. Volga KOVAL
06 Registrar ... Mr. Clint REBIK
07 Director of Admissions ... Mr. Steven LADWIG
08 Dean of Library ... Dr. Cyril OBERLANDER
44 Director of Annual Giving ... Mr. Travis WILLIAMS
19 Chief of University Police ... Chief Donn PETERSON
41 Athletic Director ... Mr. Duncan ROBINS
39 Director of Housing ... Mr. Stephen ST. ONGE
13 Chief Information Officer ... Ms. Anna KIRCHER
36 Director Career Devel Center ... Ms. Kathy THORNHILL
28 Executive Director ODEI ... Dr. Cheryl JOHNSON
46 Dean of Research & Sponsored Prgms ... Mr. Steve KARP
104 Study Abroad Advisor ... Ms. Penelope SHAW
35 Dean Student Affairs ... Ms. Randi DARNALL BURKE
37 Director Student Financial Aid ... Ms. Peggy METZGER
96 Director of Contracts & Procurement ... Ms. Tawny FLEMING
90 Director ITS User Support ... Ms. Jeanne WIELGUS
14 Director ITS Enterprise Data ... Ms. Bethany RIZZARDI
23 Dir Health/Counseling/Psych Svcs ... Dr. Brian MISTLER
38 Director Counseling & Psy Svc ... Dr. Jennifer SANFORD
56 Dean of eLearning & Ext Education ... Mr. Carl F. HANSEN
79 Dean Col Arts/Humanities/Soc Sci ... Dr. Lisa BOND-MAUPIN
107 Dean College Professional Studies ... Dr. Manohar SINGH
81 Dean Col Natural Resources/Science ... Dr. Richard BOONE
21 Director Financial Services ... Vacant
06 Registrar eLearning & Ext Educ ... Mr. Christian GUILLEN
105 Web Manager ... Mr. Matt HODGSON
29 Alumni Relations Outreach ... Ms. Stephanie LANE
04 Administrative Asst to President ... Ms. Mary HACKETT
117 Dir of Risk Management & Safety ... Ms. Kimberly COMET

*San Diego State University (B)

5500 Campanile Drive, San Diego CA 92182-8000
County: San Diego FICE Identification: 001151
Unit ID: 122409
Telephone: (619) 594-5200 Carnegie Class: DU-Higher
FAX Number: (619) 594-8894 Calendar System: Semester
URL: www.sdsu.edu
Established: 1897 Annual Undergrad Tuition & Fees (In-State): $7,084
Enrollment: 34,254 Coed
Affiliation or Control: State IRS Status: 501(c)3
Highest Offering: Doctorate
Accreditation: WC, ART, AUD, CAATE, CACREP, #CIDA, CLPSY, CS, DIETD, ENG, HSA, JOUR, MFCD, MIDWF, NURSE, PH, PTA, SP, SPAA, SW, THEA

02 Interim President ... Ms. Sally ROUSH
05 Provost and Senior Vice President ... Dr. Chukuka S. ENWEMEKA
10 Vice President/CFO Business Affairs ... Mr. Tom MCCARRON
32 Vice President for Student Affairs ... Mr. Eric RIVERA
30 VP University Relations/Development ... Ms. Mary Ruth CARLETON
46 VP for Research & Graduate Dean ... Dr. Stephen WELTER
20 Assoc Vice Pres Academic Affairs ... Dr. Radmila PRISLIN
88 Assoc VP Real Estate Planning & Dev ... Mr. Robert SCHULZ
21 Assoc VP for Financial Operations ... Ms. Agnes WONG NICKERSON
15 Associate VP Administration ... Ms. Jessica RENTTO
85 Asst Vice President Intl Programs ... Dr. Alan R. SWEEDLER
26 Interim Chief Comm Officer ... Ms. Gina JACOBS
35 Assoc VP for Student Affairs ... Mr. Tony CHUNG
35 Assoc VP for Student Affairs ... Dr. Vitaliano FIGUEROA
35 Assoc VP for Student Affairs ... Dr. Antionette MARBRAY
35 Assoc VP for Student Affairs ... Ms. Christy SAMARKOS
88 Asst VP Special Projects ... Mr. James S. HERRICK
100 Chief of Staff President's Office ... Vacant
23 Interim Dir Student Health Services ... Dr. Darrell HESS
84 Assoc VP Enrollment Management ... Dr. Sandra COOK
38 Director Counseling/Psych Services ... Dr. Jennifer RIKARD
08 Dean Library/Information Access ... Dr. Gale ETSCHMAIER
110 Associate VP for Development ... Ms. Amy HARMON
45 Exec Director Research Foundation ... Ms. Michele GOETZ
51 Dean College of Extended Studies ... Dr. Joe SHAPIRO
58 Assoc Dean Graduate & Rsrch Affairs ... Dr. Edmund BALSDON
49 Assoc VP AA/Student Achievement ... Dr. Norah SHULTZ
79 Dean of College Arts & Letters ... Dr. Norma BOUCHARD
81 Dean of College of Sciences ... Dr. Stanley MALOY
54 Dean of College of Engineering ... Dr. Monte MEHRABADI
50 Dean of Fowler College of Business ... Dr. Lance NAIL
76 Interim Dean Col Health/Human Svcs ... Dr. Larry VERITY
53 Dean of College of Education ... Dr. Joseph JOHNSON
12 Dean of Imperial Valley Campus ... Dr. Gregorio PONCE
57 Dean Professional Studies/Fine Arts ... Dr. Joyce M. GATTAS
84 Sr Director Enrollment Services ... Ms. Sandra TEMORES-VALDEZ
88 Director of Emergency Services ... Mr. Lamine SECKA
28 Chief Diversity Officer ... Dr. Aaron I. BRUCE
06 Registrar ... Ms. Rayanne WILLIAMS
07 Director of Admissions ... Ms. Sabrina CORTELL
36 Executive Director Career Services ... Dr. James TARBOX
39 Director Office of Housing Admin ... Dr. Eric HANSEN
40 Assoc VP & CEO Aztec Shops ... Mr. Todd SUMMER
41 Director Intercollegiate Athletics ... Mr. John David WICKER
85 Dir International Student Center ... Mr. Noah HANSEN
88 Director Environ Health & Safety ... Mr. Terry GEE
13 Assoc Vice President & CIO ... Mr. Christopher XANTHOS
09 Dir Analytic Studies/Inst Research ... Ms. Jeanne STRONACH
31 Community Relations Manager ... Vacant
96 Mgr Contract/Procurement Mgmt ... Mr. Bruce PETROZZA
21 University Controller ... Mr. Chris BRONSDON
18 Director of Facilities Services ... Mr. John FERRIS
22 Dir Educational Opportunity Program ... Dr. Emilio ULLOA
37 Dir Financial Aid & Scholarships ... Ms. Rose PASENELLI
88 Ombudsman ... Ms. Marit BESSESEN
39 Director of Residential Education ... Dr. Kara BAUER
88 Director Student Disability Svcs ... Dr. Pamela STARR
88 Sr Director Enterprise Tech Svcs ... Mr. Rick NORNHOLM
29 Asst VP Alumni Engagement ... Mr. Dan MONTOYA

*San Francisco State University (C)

1600 Holloway Avenue, San Francisco CA 94132-1740
County: San Francisco FICE Identification: 001154
Unit ID: 122597
Telephone: (415) 338-1111 Carnegie Class: DU-Mod
FAX Number: (415) 338-2514 Calendar System: Semester
URL: www.sfsu.edu
Established: 1899 Annual Undergrad Tuition & Fees (In-State): $6,484
Enrollment: 30,256 Coed
Affiliation or Control: State IRS Status: 501(c)3
Highest Offering: Doctorate
Accreditation: WC, AAFCS, ART, CACREP, DIETD, DIETI, ENG, JOUR, MT, MUS, NRPA, NURSE, PH, PTA, SP, SPAA, SW, THEA

02 President ... Dr. Leslie E. WONG
05 Provost & VP Academic Affairs ... Dr. Sue V. ROSSER
111 Vice Pres University Advancement ... Mr. Robert J. NAVA
10 VP & CFO Administration and Finance ... Mr. Ronald S. CORTEZ
32 VP Student Affairs/Enroll Mgmt ... Dr. Luoluo HONG
43 University Counsel ... Mr. Daniel OJEDA
20 Assoc VP Academic Resources ... Dr. Alan JUNG
46 Assoc VP Research Sponsored Pgms ... Mr. Michael SCOTT
20 Assoc VP Academic Affairs Operation ... Dr. Brian BEATTY
85 Assoc VP International Education ... Dr. Yenbo WU
45 Assoc VP Capital Plan Design Const ... Mr. Simon Y. LAM
13 Interim AVP Info Tech Services ... Mr. Nish MALIK
84 Senior AVP Enrollment Management ... Dr. Jo VOLKERT
18 Sr Assoc VP Physical Plng & Develop ... Mr. Thomas LOLLINI
21 Assoc VP Fiscal Affairs ... Ms. Maureen PASAG
15 Sr Assoc VP Human Resources ... Ms. Ann M. SHERMAN
35 Assoc VP Student Affairs ... Mr. Gene CHELBERG
88 Int AVP Univ Property Management ... Ms. Jeny VALDEZ
100 Chief of Staff ... Ms. Alison SANDERS
50 Dean College Business ... Ms. Linda OUBRE
53 Dean College Education ... Dr. Judith MUNTER
88 Dean College Ethnic Studies ... Dr. Kenneth P. MONTEIRO
51 Interim AVP/Dean of CELIA ... Dr. Guido KRICKX
69 Int Dean Col Health & Soc Science ... Dr. Alvin ALVAREZ
79 Int Dean Col Lib & Creative Arts ... Dr. Andrew HARRIS
81 Dean College Science & Engineering ... Dr. Keith BOWMAN
88 Dean Faculty Affairs & Prof Dev ... Dr. Sacha BUNGE
58 Dean Graduate Studies ... Dr. Ann HALLUM
88 Dean Undergraduate Studies ... Dr. Jennifer SUMMIT
102 SF State President Foundation ... Mr. Robert J. NAVA
08 University Librarian ... Ms. Deborah C. MASTERS
90 Director Academic Technology ... Dr. Maggie BEERS
85 Director International Programs ... Ms. Hildy HEATH
30 Associate Vice Pres Development ... Ms. Anne HARRIS
86 Director Government & Community Rel ... Ms. Noriko SHINZATO
26 AVP University Communications ... Ms. Monique BEELER
117 Risk Manager ... Mr. Michael BEATTY
39 Director Resident Life ... Mr. David ROURKE
37 Director Student Financial Aid ... Ms. Barbara HUBLER
88 Director Student Outreach Services ... Ms. Ree'shema THORNTON
07 Interim Dir Undergrad Admissions ... Mr. Edward CARRIGAN
114 Director Univ Budget Planning ... Mr. Jay ORENDORFF
06 Registrar ... Ms. Renee MONTE
41 Director Athletics ... Mr. Charles GUTHRIE
38 Director Counseling & Psych Svcs ... Dr. Derethia DUVAL
88 Director Disability Pgms/Res Ctr ... Ms. Nicole BOHN
22 Dir Education Opportunity Program ... Mr. Oscar M. GARDEA
19 Int Chief Police/Dir Public Safety ... Chief Reginald PARSON
23 Medical Dir Student Health Svcs ... Dr. Alastair SMITH
35 Interim Dean of Students ... Dr. Mary Ann BEGLEY
96 Director Procurement Department ... Mr. Stephen C. SMITH
29 Director Alumni Relations ... Mr. Doug HUPKE
110 Chief of Operations Advancement ... Ms. Venesia THOMPSON
116 Dir Internal Audit/Audit & Adv Svcs ... Ms. Helen STORRS
36 Interim Director Career Center ... Ms. Mariko HINGSTON
88 Exec Dir Budget Adm & Oper ... Mr. Jay ORENDORFF
88 Dir Environmental Health & Safety ... Mr. Marc MAJEWSKI
109 Int AVP Facilities & Service Enter ... Mr. Frank FASANO

† Grants additional Doctoral degrees in cooperation with the UC-Berkeley and UC-San Francisco.

*San Jose State University (D)

One Washington Square, San Jose CA 95192-0001
County: Santa Clara FICE Identification: 001155
Unit ID: 122755
Telephone: (408) 924-1000 Carnegie Class: Masters/L
FAX Number: (408) 924-1018 Calendar System: Semester
URL: www.sjsu.edu
Established: 1857 Annual Undergrad Tuition & Fees (In-State): $7,418
Enrollment: 32,773 Coed
Affiliation or Control: State IRS Status: 501(c)3
Highest Offering: Doctorate
Accreditation: WC, ART, CAATE, CAEPN, CEA, CS, DANCE, DIETD, DIETI, ENG, IPSY, JOUR, LIB, MT, MUS, NAIT, NRPA, NURSE, OT, PH, PLNG, SP, SPAA, SW, THEA

02 President ... Dr. Mary PAPAZIAN
05 Provost/Sr Vice Pres Acad Affairs ... Dr. Andrew FEINSTEIN
10 Vice Pres Administration & Finance ... Mr. Charles FAAS
32 Int Vice President Student Affairs ... Ms. Sharon WILLEY
35 Assoc Vice Pres Student Services ... Mr. Romando NASH
13 Deputy CIO ... Ms. Terry VAHEY
45 AVP Academic Budgets/Planning ... Mr. Bradley OLIN
100 VP Org Development/Chief of Staff ... Ms. Jaye BAILEY
20 Int Assoc Vice Pres Faculty Affairs ... Dr. Michael KIMBAROW
09 Assoc VP Research ... Dr. Pamela STACKS
20 Assoc VP Grad/Undergrad Programs ... Dr. Thalia ANAGNOS
30 VP University Advancement ... Mr. Paul LANNING
21 Assoc VP Finance ... Ms. Marna GENES
18 Assoc VP for Facilities/Operations ... Vacant
15 Associate VP Human Resources ... Ms. Beth PUGLIESE
26 AVP Strategic Comm/Public Affairs ... Mr. Barry SHILLER
29 AVP Alumni Engagement and Giving ... Mr. Brian BATES
51 Dean Col of Intnl/Extended Studies ... Dr. Ruth HUARD
84 AVP Admin/Enrollment Services ... Vacant
08 Dean University Library ... Dr. Tracy ELLIOTT
28 Dir Equal Opportunity & Emp Rel ... Ms. Julie PAISANT
06 University Registrar ... Ms. Marian YAO
41 Director Intercollegiate Athletics ... Ms. Maria TUITE
96 Director Procurement Services ... Vacant
07 Dir Undergrad Admissions/Outreach ... Ms. Deanna GONZALES
40 Director Spartan Bookstore ... Mr. Ryland METZINGER
19 Chief of Police ... Mr. Peter DECENA
36 Interim Director Career Center ... Ms. Catherine VOSS PLAXTON
38 Director Counseling Services ... Mr. Kell FUJIMOTO
37 Director Financial Aid/Scholarships ... Ms. Coleetta MCELROY
39 Dir University Housing Services ... Mr. Kevin KINNEY
23 Director Student Wellness Center ... Dr. Roger ELROD
49 Dean College of Applied Sci & Art ... Dr. Mary SCHUTTEN
50 Dean College of Business ... Dr. Dan MOSHAVI
53 Interim Dean College of Education ... Dr. Paul CASCELLA
54 Dean College of Engineering ... Dr. Sheryl EHRMAN
79 Int Dean College of Humanities/Arts ... Dr. Shannon MILLER
81 Interim Dean College of Science ... Dr. Michael KAUFMAN
83 Dean College Social Sciences ... Dr. Walt JACOBS
04 Presidential Aide ... Ms. Zaynna TELLO

*Sonoma State University (A)

1801 E Cotati Avenue, Rohnert Park CA 94928-3609
County: Sonoma FICE Identification: 001156
Unit ID: 123572
Telephone: (707) 664-2880 Carnegie Class: Masters/L
FAX Number: (707) 664-2505 Calendar System: Semester
URL: www.sonoma.edu
Established: 1960 Annual Undergrad Tuition & Fees (In-State): $7,388
Enrollment: 9,408 Coed
Affiliation or Control: State IRS Status: 501(c)3
Highest Offering: Master's
Accreditation: WC, ART, CACREP, MUS, NUR

02 President .... Dr. Judy SAKAKI
05 Provost & Vice Pres Academic Affs .... Dr. Lisa VOLLENDORF
10 Vice Pres Administration & Finance .... Vacant
30 Vice President Advancement .... Vacant
32 Int VP of Student Affairs .... Dr. Michael YOUNG
20 Assoc VP for Faculty Affairs .... Dr. Deborah ROBERTS
09 Sr Dir Records/Report & Analytics .... Mr. Sean JOHNSON
13 Assoc VP CIO/Information Technology .... Mr. Jason WENRICK
08 Dean of Library .... Ms. Karen SCHNEIDER
79 Dean School of Arts & Humanities .... Dr. Thaine STEARNS
50 Dean Sch of Business/Economic .... Dr. William SILVER
53 Dean School of Education .... Dr. Carlos AYALA
81 Dean School Science & Tech .... Dr. Lynn STAUFFER
83 Dean of Social Sciences .... Dr. John D. WINGARD
56 Dean School of Extended Education .... Dr. Robert EYLER
38 Dir of Counseling/Psych Services .... Dr. Laura WILLIAMS
37 Director of Financial Aid .... Mrs. Susan GUTIERREZ
18 Assoc VP Facilities Services/CPDC .... Mr. Christopher DINNO
27 AVP Strategic Communications .... Vacant
41 Director Athletics .... Mr. William J. FUSCO
19 Interim Chief Police Services .... Mr. David DOUGHERTY
21 Director Seawolf Services .... Ms. Elizabeth O'BRIEN
88 Assoc VP Entrepreneurial Srvcs .... Mr. Neil MARKLEY
06 Registrar .... Ms. Lisa NOTO
07 Director of Admissions .... Ms. Natalie KALOGIANNIS
84 Director of Enrollment Management .... Mr. Gustavo FLORES
29 Dir Alumni Relations/Annual Giving .... Ms. Laurie OGG
28 Mg Dir Employee Rel/Comp Svcs .... Ms. Joyce SUZUKI
15 Sr Director Human Resources .... Ms. Tammy KENBER
96 Managing Dir for Purchasing .... Ms. Jenifer BARNETT
32 Assoc Student Affairs Officer .... Mr. Wilson HALL

California University of Management and Sciences (B)

721 North Euclid Street, Anaheim CA 92801
County: Orange FICE Identification: 041331
Unit ID: 460075
Telephone: (714) 533-3946 Carnegie Class: Not Classified
FAX Number: (714) 533-7778 Calendar System: Quarter
URL: www.calums.edu
Established: 1998 Annual Undergrad Tuition & Fees: $9,570
Enrollment: 565 Coed
Affiliation or Control: Independent Non-Profit IRS Status: 501(c)3
Highest Offering: Master's
Accreditation: ACICS

01 President .... David PARK
03 Vice President .... Jason SHIN
10 Finance Director .... Fred J. KIM
05 Academic Dean .... Silviu VELOVICI
20 Associate Academic Dean .... Sasha SAFARZADEH
11 Director of Administration .... Jeffrey BEASCA
07 Admissions Director .... Yukari NISHIOKA
84 Enrollment Director .... Andrew PRESS
32 Student Services Advisor .... Alena MARTYNENKO
08 Librarian .... Karine PARRY
06 Registrar .... Hongjun AHN
85 International Student Advisor .... Woojin HAN
101 Board Secretary .... Jong S. YOON
37 Financial Aid Officer .... Jeff BEASCA

California Western School of Law (C)

225 Cedar Street, San Diego CA 92101-3046
County: San Diego FICE Identification: 013103
Unit ID: 111391
Telephone: (619) 239-0391 Carnegie Class: Spec-4-yr-Law
FAX Number: (619) 525-7092 Calendar System: Trimester
URL: www.cwsl.edu
Established: 1924 Annual Graduate Tuition & Fees: N/A
Enrollment: 628 Coed
Affiliation or Control: Independent Non-Profit IRS Status: 501(c)3
Highest Offering: First Professional Degree; No Undergraduates
Accreditation: LAW

01 President & Dean .... Dean Neils SCHAUMANN
05 Vice Dean Academic Affairs .... Prof. Don SMYTHE
46 Associate Dean Research & Fac Devel .... Prof. Daniel YEAGER
88 Assoc Dean of Exper Learning .... Prof. Floralynn EINESMAN
32 Associate Dean of Student Life .... Ms. Wendy BASHANT
32 Asst Dean Students/Diversity Svcs .... Ms. Susan GARRETT FINSTER
36 Assistant Dean Career Services .... Ms. Courtney MIKLUSAK
88 Asst Dean Mission Development .... Mr. James M. COOPER
37 Exec Director Financial Aid .... Mr. William KAHLER
13 Exec Director Computer Services .... Vacant
18 Exec Dir Facilities Management .... Ms. Jolie L. CARTIER
88 Ex Dir Inst for Criminal Def Advoc .... Prof. Justin P. BROOKS
88 Dir Inst of Health Law Studies .... Prof. Joanna SAX
08 Assoc Dean Law Library/Info Res .... Prof. Philip T. GRAGG
10 Chief Financial Officer .... Ms. Pamela A. DUFFY
07 Assistant Dean Admissions .... Mr. Christopher E. BAIDOO
06 Registrar .... Ms. Sandra E. MOREAU
88 Director MCL/LLM Program .... Prof. Lisa BLACK
26 Director Marketing Communications .... Mr. Patrick RIEDLING
29 Director Alumni Relations .... Ms. Lori BOYLE
15 VP Human Resources .... Ms. Rikklyn S. UEDA
28 Director Diversity .... Ms. Marion E. CLOETE
21 Director Business Office .... Ms. Ruth GOULDING
04 Administrative Asst to President .... Ms. Marilyn L. JORDAN
43 Dir Legal Services/General Counsel .... Ms. Lisa JORDAN
30 Director of Development .... Mr. Brian DALY

Cambridge Junior College (D)

990-A Klamath Lane, Yuba City CA 95993-8978
County: Sutter FICE Identification: 038743
Unit ID: 446093
Telephone: (530) 674-9199 Carnegie Class: Spec 2-yr-Other
FAX Number: (530) 671-7319 Calendar System: Other
URL: www.cambridge.edu
Established: 2010 Annual Undergrad Tuition & Fees: N/A
Enrollment: 172 Coed
Affiliation or Control: Proprietary IRS Status: Proprietary
Highest Offering: Associate Degree
Accreditation: ACICS

05 Director of Education .... Ms. Sandy FOWLER

Carnegie Mellon University Silicon Valley Campus (E)

NASA Research Pk, Bld 23 MS 23-11,
Moffett Field CA 94035
Telephone: (650) 335-2810 Identification: 770149
Accreditation: &M

† Branch campus of Carnegie Mellon University, Pittsburgh, PA

*Carrington College - Administrative Office (F)

7801 Folsom Boulevard, Suite 210,
Sacramento CA 95826-2620
County: Sacramento Identification: 666086
Telephone: (916) 388-2800 Carnegie Class: N/A
FAX Number: (916) 381-1609
URL: www.carrington.edu

01 President Carrington Colleges .... Dr. Donna LORAINE
05 Provost/VP Academic Affairs .... Ms. Ravinder DAYAL
10 VP Accred & Profession .... Dr. Danika BOWEN
11 Chief Operating Officer .... Ms. Shelly DUBOIS
12 Vice President Operation .... Mr. Jim MURPHY
07 VP Enrollment & Mktg .... Mr. Mitch CHARLES
32 VP Admin & Student Svcs .... Dr. Scott SAND
10 Dir Finance & infrastructure .... Mr. Joshua OLMSTED
13 VP IT .... Mr. David MCMURTRY

*Carrington College - Sacramento (G)

8909 Folsom Boulevard, Sacramento CA 95826-3203
County: Sacramento FICE Identification: 009748
Unit ID: 125532
Telephone: (916) 361-1660 Carnegie Class: Spec 2-yr-Health
FAX Number: (916) 361-6666 Calendar System: Other
URL: www.carrington.edu
Established: 1983 Annual Undergrad Tuition & Fees: N/A
Enrollment: 1,272 Coed
Affiliation or Control: Proprietary IRS Status: Proprietary
Highest Offering: Associate Degree
Accreditation: WJ, DH, MAC

02 Regional Director of Operations .... Tara MICELI
06 Registrar .... Ryanne GREEN-QUARLES
36 Regional Dir of Career Services .... Joy SILVA
121 Student Success Center Manager .... Becky CARDWELL

**Carrington College - Citrus Heights* (H)

7301 Greenback Lane, Suite A,
Citrus Heights CA 95621-5591
Telephone: (916) 722-8200 Identification: 667042
Accreditation: &WJ, MAC, SURGT

† Regional accreditation is carried under the parent institution in Sacramento, CA.

**Carrington College - Pleasant Hill* (I)

380 Civic Drive, Suite 300, Pleasant Hill CA 94523-1984
Telephone: (925) 609-6650 Identification: 666043
Accreditation: &WJ, COARC, MAC, PTAA

† Regional accreditation is carried under the parent institution in Sacramento, CA.

**Carrington College - Pomona* (J)

901 Corporate Center Drive, #300, Pomona CA 91768
Telephone: (909) 868-5800 Identification: 770506
Accreditation: &WJ, MAC

† Regional accreditation is carried under the parent institution in Sacramento, CA.

**Carrington College - San Jose* (K)

5883 Rue Ferrari, Ste. 125, San Jose CA 95138
Telephone: (408) 960-0161 Identification: 666042
Accreditation: &WJ, DH, MAC, SURGT

† Regional accreditation is carried under the parent institution in Sacramento, CA.

**Carrington College - San Leandro* (L)

15555 E 14th Street, Suite 500,
San Leandro CA 94578-1977
Telephone: (510) 276-3888 Identification: 666751
Accreditation: &WJ, MAC

† Regional accreditation is carried under the parent institution in Sacramento, CA.

**Carrington College - Stockton* (M)

1313 W Robinhood Drive, Suite B,
Stockton CA 95207-5509
Telephone: (209) 956-1240 Identification: 666140
Accreditation: &WJ, MAC

† Regional accreditation is carried under the parent institution in Sacramento, CA.

Casa Loma College-Van Nuys (N)

6725 Kester Avenue, Van Nuys CA 91405
County: Los Angeles FICE Identification: 006731
Unit ID: 111638
Telephone: (818) 785-2726 Carnegie Class: Spec 2-yr-Health
FAX Number: (818) 785-2191 Calendar System: Other
URL: www.casalomacollege.edu
Established: 1966 Annual Undergrad Tuition & Fees: N/A
Enrollment: 356 Coed
Affiliation or Control: Independent Non-Profit IRS Status: 501(c)3
Highest Offering: Associate Degree
Accreditation: ABHES, PTAA

01 Campus Director/Controller .... Ms. Veronica PANTOJA
05 Dean of Education .... Dr. Stephanie SHELBURNE
66 Director of Nursing .... Ms. Stephanie AYO-AKINYEMI
06 Registrar .... Ms. Vicki KIM
07 Director of Admissions .... Mr. Nicholas WALSH-DAVIS
86 Director of Compliance .... Vacant
37 Director Student Financial Aid .... Vacant
08 Head Librarian .... Ms. Jennifer MEYER
106 Dir Online Education/E-learning .... Ms. Stephanie SHELBURNE
13 Chief Info Technology Officer .... Mr. Cyrill REISER
18 Chief Facilities/Physical Plant .... Ms. Veronica PANTOJA
36 Director Student Placement .... Ms. Desiree TERCERO

CBD College (O)

3699 Wilshire Boulevard, 4th Floor,
Los Angeles CA 90010
County: Los Angeles FICE Identification: 032503
Unit ID: 439367
Telephone: (213) 427-2200 Carnegie Class: Not Classified
FAX Number: (213) 427-9278 Calendar System: Other
URL: www.cbd.edu
Established: 1982 Annual Undergrad Tuition & Fees: N/A
Enrollment: 425 Coed
Affiliation or Control: Independent Non-Profit IRS Status: 501(c)3
Highest Offering: Associate Degree
Accreditation: ABHES, DMS, OTA, PTAA, SURTEC

01 President .... Mr. Alan HESHEL

Cedars-Sinai Medical Center Graduate Program in Biomedical Sciences and Translational Medicine (P)

8700 Beverly Boulevard, Los Angeles CA 90048
County: Los Angeles Identification: 667071
Telephone: (310) 423-8294 Carnegie Class: Not Classified
FAX Number: N/A Calendar System: Trimester
URL: www.cedars-sinai.edu
Established: 1902 Annual Graduate Tuition & Fees: N/A
Enrollment: N/A Coed
Affiliation or Control: Independent Non-Profit IRS Status: 501(c)3
Highest Offering: Doctorate; No Undergraduates
Accreditation: WC

01 President/CEO .... Mr. Thomas PRISELAC
05 Exec Vice Pres Academic Affairs .... Dr. Shlomo MELMED
10 Exec Vice Pres Finance/CFO .... Mr. Edward PRUNCHUNAS

Cerritos College (A)

11110 Alondra Boulevard, Norwalk CA 90650-6298
County: Los Angeles FICE Identification: 001161
Unit ID: 111887
Telephone: (562) 860-2451 Carnegie Class: Assoc/MT-VT-High Trad
FAX Number: (562) 467-5005 Calendar System: Semester
URL: www.cerritos.edu
Established: 1955 Annual Undergrad Tuition & Fees (In-District): $1,346
Enrollment: 22,043 Coed
Affiliation or Control: State/Local IRS Status: 501(c)3
Highest Offering: Associate Degree
Accreditation: WJ, ADNUR, DA, DH, PTAA

01 President .... Dr. Jose L. FIERRO
05 Vice President Academic Affairs ..... Mr. Edmund (Rick) MIRANDA
10 Vice President Business Services .... Mr. Felipe LOPEZ
32 Vice President Student Services .... Dr. Stephen JOHNSON
15 Vice President Human Resources ..Dr. Adriana FLORES-CHURCH
20 Dean of Academic Affairs .... Vacant
07 Dean of Admissions/Records & Svcs .....Ms. Stephanie MURGUIA
38 Dean of Counseling Services .... Dr. Renee DELONG
86 Dir College/Govt Rels & Pub Affs .... Ms. Miya WALKER
22 Dean Disabled Student Pgms & Svcs .... Dr. Lucinda ABORN
121 Dean of Student Support Services .... Ms. Kim WESTBY
50 Instr Dean Business/Humanities/SS .... Ms. Rachel MASON
57 Instr Dean Fine Arts/Communications .... Dr. Gary PRITCHARD
76 Instr Dean Health Occupations .... Ms. Sandra MARKS
83 Dean Academic Success .... Ms. Shawna BASKETTE
49 Instr Dean Liberal Arts .... Mr. David FABISH
68 Instr Dean Health/PE/Dance/Athletic .... Dr. Daniel SMITH
54 Instr Dean Science/Engineering/Math ..... Ms. Connie BOARDMAN
73 Instr Dean Technology .... Dr. Yannick REAL
13 Director Information Technology .... Mr. Patrick O'DONNELL
21 Director of Fiscal Services .... Mr. Noorali DELAWALLA
35 Dean of Student Services .... Ms. Elizabeth MILLER
36 Dir of Career/Assessment Services .... Ms. Theresa LOPEZ
18 Director Physical Plant & Const Svc .... Mr. David C. MOORE
102 Executive Director Foundation .... Mr. Steven RICHARDSON
88 Director Community Advancement .... Ms. Bellegran GOMEZ
96 Dir Purchasing/Contract Admin .... Mr. Mark LOGAN
16 Director Human Resources/Risk Mgmt .... Vacant
19 Chief of Campus Police .... Mr. Thomas GALLIVAN
28 Assoc Dn Adult Educ/Diversity Pgms .... Ms. Graciela VASQUEZ
31 Director Community Education .... Dr. Patricia ROBBINS SMITH
88 Director Child Development Center .... Ms. Debra WARD
88 Operations Manager .... Mr. Thomas RICHEY
88 Payroll Manager .... Ms. Deanna HART
114 Budget Manager .... Mr. Conrad SELORIO
14 Manager Information Technology .... Mr. Javier BANUELOS
23 Assoc Dean Student Health Wellness .... Dr. Hillary MENNELLA
88 Director of Student Program Svcs .... Ms. Norma RODRIGUEZ
09 Dir Inst Effec Research & Planning .... Dr. Kristi BLACKBURN
88 Director Adv Trans Tech Projects .... Ms. Jannet MALIG
22 Dir Diver/Compliance/Title IX Coord ....Ms. Valencia RAPHAEL
88 EOPS Assistant Director .... Ms. Yvette TAFOYA
19 Dir Educational Partnerships .... Ms. Colleen MCKINLEY
88 Dual Enrollment Manager .... Ms. Carla YORKE
88 Accounting Manager .... Ms. Kathy BURGOS
88 Facilities Manager .... Mr. Shannon KAVENEY

*Chabot-Las Positas Community College District (B)

7600 Dublin Blvd., 3rd Flr., Dublin CA 94568
County: Alameda Identification: 666925
Telephone: (925) 485-5208 Carnegie Class: N/A
FAX Number: (925) 485-5256
URL: www.clpccd.org

01 Chancellor .... Dr. Jannett N. JACKSON
10 Vice Chanc Business Svcs .... Mr. Lorenzo LEGASPI
05 Vice Chanc Educational Svcs .... Ms. Krista JOHNS
15 Vice Chanc Human Resource Svcs .... Mr. Wyman FONG
18 Vice Chanc Facilities/Bond Program .... Mr. Doug HORNER

*Chabot College (C)

25555 Hesperian Boulevard, Hayward CA 94545-2400
County: Alameda FICE Identification: 001162
Unit ID: 111920
Telephone: (510) 723-6600 Carnegie Class: Assoc/HT-High Trad
FAX Number: (510) 782-9315 Calendar System: Semester
URL: www.chabotcollege.edu
Established: 1961 Annual Undergrad Tuition & Fees (In-District): $1,138
Enrollment: 13,457 Coed
Affiliation or Control: State/Local IRS Status: 501(c)3
Highest Offering: Associate Degree
Accreditation: WJ, ART, DH, MAC

02 President .... Dr. Susan S. SPERLING
05 VP Academic Services .... Ms. Stacy THOMPSON
32 Vice President Student Services .... Dr. Matthew KRITSCHER
11 Vice Pres Administrative Services .... Vacant
10 Actg Chief Financial Officer .... Dr. Matthew KRITSCHER
04 Exec Asst to the College President .... Ms. Kirti REDDY
08 Librarian .... Ms. Kim MORRISON
38 Dean Counseling .... Mr. Valjean DALE
41 Dean Health/PE/Athletics .... Mr. Dale WAGONER
07 Dir Admissions & Records/Registrar .... Mrs. Paulette LINO
37 Director of Financial Aid .... Ms. Kathryn LINZMEYER
19 Director Safety & Security .... Sgt. Michael WOODS
09 Director of Institutional Research .... Dr. Carolyn ARNOLD
15 Director Human Resources .... Dr. Wyman FONG
18 Chief Facilities/Physical Plant .... Mr. Tim NELSON
30 Exec Dir Devel/Foundation .... Vacant
35 Dir Student Life/Student Services .... Mr. Arnold PAGUIO
96 Manager Purchasing/Warehouse Svcs .... Ms. Victoria LAMICA

*Las Positas College (D)

3000 Campus Hill Drive, Livermore CA 94551-7623
County: Alameda FICE Identification: 030357
Unit ID: 366401
Telephone: (925) 424-1000 Carnegie Class: Assoc/HT-High Trad
FAX Number: (925) 443-0742 Calendar System: Semester
URL: www.laspositascollege.edu
Established: 1975 Annual Undergrad Tuition & Fees (In-District): $1,138
Enrollment: 8,912 Coed
Affiliation or Control: State/Local IRS Status: 501(c)3
Highest Offering: Associate Degree
Accreditation: WJ, EMT

02 President .... Dr. Barry A. RUSSELL
05 Vice President Academic Svcs .... Ms. Roanna BENNIE
32 Vice President Student Svcs .... Mr. William L. GARCIA
11 Vice Pres Administrative Services .... Ms. Diane BRADY
04 Exec Assistant to the President .... Ms. Kelly ABAD
35 Dean of Student Services .... Ms. Barbara MORRISSEY
49 Dean Arts & Humanities .... Dr. Donald MILLER
81 Dean Math/Science/Eng/Public Safety .... Dr. Nan HO
50 Dean Bus/Health/Athletics/Work Exp .... Dr. Amir LAW
77 Dn Computing/Applied Tech/Soc Svcs .... Mr. Don CARLSON
07 Dean of Enrollment Services .... Ms. Sylvia RODRIGUEZ
45 Director of Research & Planning .... Mr. Rajinder SAMRA
37 Financial Aid/Veterans Assistance .... Ms. Andi SCHREIBMAN
19 Campus Safety Supervisor .... Mr. Sean PRATHER
08 Head Librarian .... Dr. Tina INZERILLA
102 Executive Director LPC Foundation .... Mr. Kenneth COOPER
41 Athletic Director .... Vacant
10 Associate Business Officer .... Ms. Natasha LANG
18 Project Planner/Manager Facilities .... Vacant
06 Registrar .... Ms. Sylvia RODRIGUEZ
88 Project Manager CTE .... Ms. Vicki SHIPMAN
88 Director Child Development Center .... Ms. Corinna CALICA

Chaffey College (E)

5885 Haven Avenue, Rancho Cucamonga CA 91737-3002
County: San Bernardino FICE Identification: 001163
Unit ID: 111939
Telephone: (909) 652-6000 Carnegie Class: Assoc/HT-High Trad
FAX Number: (909) 652-6006 Calendar System: Semester
URL: www.chaffey.edu
Established: 1883 Annual Undergrad Tuition & Fees (In-State): $1,169
Enrollment: 21,054 Coed
Affiliation or Control: State IRS Status: 501(c)3
Highest Offering: Associate Degree
Accreditation: WJ, ADNUR, DA, RAD

01 Superintendent/President .... Dr. Henry D. SHANNON
11 Vice Pres Administrative Affairs .... Ms. Melanie SIDDIQI
10 Assoc Supt Bus Svcs/Econ Dev .... Ms. Lisa BAILEY
05 Assoc Supt Instruction/Inst Effect .... Meridith RANDALL
09 Dean Inst Research/Research Dev .... Mr. Jim FILLPOT
29 Director Alumni Relations .... Ms. Janeth RODRIGUEZ
85 Int Director International Students .... Ms. Saba KAZMI
32 Dean Student Life .... Mr. Christopher BRUNELLE
07 Admin Admissions/Records .... Ms. Kathy LUCERO
21 Exec Director Business Services .... Ms. Kim ERICKSON
88 Director Technical Services .... Mr. Michael FINK
88 Director Childrens Center .... Ms. Birgit MONKS
23 Director Student Health Services .... Ms. Katherine PEEK
37 Director Financial Aid .... Ms. Patricia BOPKO
109 Director Auxiliary Services .... Vacant
26 Director Marketing/Public Relations .... Ms. Alisha ROSAS
21 Exec Dir Budgeting & Fiscal Svc ....Ms. Anita UNDERCOFFER
88 Director Museum Gallery .... Ms. Rebecca TRAWICK
18 Manager Facilities Development .... Ms. Sarah RILEY
12 Dean Chino Campus .... Dr. Teresa HULL
88 Dean Visual Performing Arts .... Dr. Jason CHEVALIER
50 Dean Bus & Applied Tech .... Ms. Joy HAERENS
81 Dean Mathematics & Science .... Mr. Theodore YOUNGLOVE
83 Dean Social & Behav Sci & PE .... Dr. Corene SCHWARTZ
88 Dean Language Arts & Health Science .... Mr. Anthony DISALVO
38 Dean Counseling & Matriculation .... Ms. Amy NEVAREZ
12 Int Dean Fontana Campus .... Dr. Yolanda FRIDAY
08 Dean Instruct Support/Library Svcs .... Ms. Laura HOPE
04 Exec Assistant Supt/Pres Office .... Ms. Kathy NAPOLI
88 Dean Discipline/Grievance .... Mr. Len CROW
41 Interim Director Athletics .... Mr. Jeff KLEIN
86 Manager Government Relations .... Ms. Lorena CORONA
15 Director Human Resources .... Ms. Susan HARDIE
102 Executive Director Foundation .... Ms. Lisa NASHUA

Chamberlain University-Sacramento (F)

10971 Sun Center Drive, Rancho Cordova CA 95670
Telephone: (916) 330-3410 Identification: 770978
Accreditation: &NH, NURSE

† Branch campus of Chamberlain University-Addison, Addison, IL

Chapman University (G)

One University Drive, Orange CA 92866-1099
County: Orange FICE Identification: 001164
Unit ID: 111948
Telephone: (714) 997-6815 Carnegie Class: Masters/L
FAX Number: (714) 997-6713 Calendar System: 4/1/4
URL: www.chapman.edu
Established: 1861 Annual Undergrad Tuition & Fees: $48,710
Enrollment: 8,305 Coed
Affiliation or Control: Christian Church (Disciples Of Christ)
IRS Status: 501(c)3
Highest Offering: Doctorate
Accreditation: WC, #ARCPA, CAATE, CAEPT, DANCE, LAW, MFCD, MUS, @PHAR, PTA, #SP, THEA

01 President .... Dr. Daniele C. STRUPPA
05 Provost & Exec VP Academic Affairs .... Dr. Glenn PFEIFFER
03 Executive Vice President & COO ......Mr. Harold W. HEWITT, JR.
30 Exec VP University Advancement .... Ms. Sheryl BOURGEOIS
32 VP & Dean of Students .... Dr. Jerry PRICE
84 VP/Dean Enrollment Management .... Mr. Michael PELLY
20 Assoc Provost of Academic Admin .... Dr. Kenneth E. MURPHY
09 Vice Provost Inst Eff & Fac Affairs .... Mr. Joseph SLOWENSKY
49 Dean Wilkinson Col Hum/Soc Sci .... Dr. Patrick FUERY
61 Dean School of Law .... Dr. Matthew J. PARLOW
50 Dean School Business/Economics .... Dr. Thomas TURK
67 Dean School of Pharmacy .... Dr. Ronald JORDAN
53 Dean College of Educational Studies .... Dr. Margaret GROGAN
88 Dean College of Film & Media Arts .... Mr. Robert BASSETT
88 Dean College of Performing Arts .... Dr. Guilio ONGARO
81 Dean Col of Science/Tech .... Dr. Janeen HILL
88 Dean/Artistic Dir Center for Arts .... Dr. William HALL
88 Director Ctr for Global Education .... Dr. James COYLE
97 Vice Provost Undergrad Education .... Dr. Nina LENOIR
45 Vice President Campus Planning .... Mr. Kris OLSEN
15 Vice President of Human Resources .... Ms. Becky CAMPOS
43 Assoc Vice Pres of Legal Affairs .... Ms. Janine DUMONTELLE
10 Assoc Vice President & Controller .... Mr. Behzad BINESH
07 Dir Undergraduate Admission ......Ms. Marcela MEJIA MARTINEZ
88 Assistant Provost .... Ms. Iris GERBASI
18 Assoc VP Facilities .... Mr. Rick TURNER
26 Director Public Relations .... Ms. Sheri LEDBETTER
08 Dean of Library .... Ms. Charlene BALDWIN
29 Asst VP Strategic Engagement/Dev .... Ms. Delite TRAVIS
13 VP/Chief Information Officer .... Ms. Helen NORRIS
09 Director of Institutional Research .... Dr. Marisol ARREDONDO
06 Registrar .... Ms. Jan MCCUEN
46 VP Research & Sponsored Pgms Admin .. Dr. Thomas PIECHOTA
28 Director of Diversity and Inclusion .... Ms. Erin PULLIN
37 Director Financial Aid .... Mrs. Gail TYRON-POLWEKTOW
85 Director Intl Student Services .... Ms. Susan SAMS
19 Chief of Public Safety .... Mr. Randy BURBA
39 Assoc Dean/Director Residence Life .... Ms. Deborah MILLER
41 Athletic Director .... Mr. Terry BOESEL
42 Dean of the Chapel .... Dr. Gail STEARNS
04 Associate to the President .... Dr. Christina MARSHALL
88 Exec Assistant to the Provost .... Ms. Shehani REEDER
23 Director Student Health Services .... Ms. Jacqueline DEATS
35 Director of Student Engagement .... Dr. Chris HUTCHISON
36 Asst Dir Career Education .... Ms. Brittany DENEAU
38 Assoc Dean/Dir Student Psych Couns .... Dr. Jeannie WALKER
96 Purchasing Coordinator .... Ms. Wendy SEIRUP
04 Executive Asst to the President .... Ms. Erika CURIEL
58 Vice Provost for Graduate Educ .... Dr. Richard REDDING
102 Dir Corporate/Foundation Relations .... Mr. Mike STRINGER
44 Dir Legacy Planning .... Mr. David MOORE
90 Dir Academic Tech/Digital Media .... Dr. Mary LITCH
104 Assoc Director Ctr for Global Educ .... Ms. Kristy BEAVERS
105 Webmaster .... Ms. Mandy THOMAS

Charles R. Drew University of Medicine & Science (H)

1731 E 120th Street, Los Angeles CA 90059-3025
County: Los Angeles FICE Identification: 010365
Unit ID: 111966
Telephone: (323) 563-4800 Carnegie Class: Spec-4-yr-Other Health
FAX Number: (323) 563-5987 Calendar System: Semester
URL: www.cdrewu.edu
Established: 1966 Annual Undergrad Tuition & Fees: $13,444
Enrollment: 533 Coed
Affiliation or Control: Independent Non-Profit IRS Status: 501(c)3
Highest Offering: Master's
Accreditation: WC, #ARCPA, NURSE, PH, RAD

01 President & CEO .... Dr. David M. CARLISLE
05 EVP Academic Affairs/Provost .... Dr. Steve O. MICHAEL
100 Chief of Staff .... Ms. Jackie BROWN
45 VP Research & Health Affairs .... Dr. Jadutt VADGAMA
111 VP for Strategic Advancement .... Ms. Angela L. MINNIEFIELD
15 Chief Human Resources Officer .... Mr. Elias MUNOZ
10 VP Finance/Chief Business Officer .... Mr. Carl MCLANEY
63 Dean College of Medicine .... Dr. Deborah PROTHROW-STITH
66 Interim Dean School of Nursing .... Dr. Margaret AVILA
76 Dean College of Science & Health .... Dr. Hector BALCAZAR
20 Asst Provost Faculty Affairs .... Dr. William SHAY
32 Dean Student Affairs .... Dr. Jinny OH
58 Director GME .... Dr. Sandra GONZALEZ
20 Sr Assoc Dean Academic Affairs .... Dr. Ronald A. EDELSTEIN
09 Director Inst Research & Effectiv ......Mr. Richard W. LINDSTROM
21 Chief Financial Officer .... Mr. John GERAGHTY

08 Director Health Sciences Library ...... Ms. Darlene PARKER-KELLY
06 Registrar ...... Ms. Raquel MUNOZ
07 Director of Enrollment Management ...... Ms. Vanessa RIGGINS

Charter College-Oxnard (A)

2000 Outlet Center Drive, Suite 150, Oxnard CA 93036
Telephone: (805) 973-1240　Identification: 666675
Accreditation: ACICS

† Branch campus of Charter College, Anchorage, AK.

Chicago School of Professional Psychology Los Angeles Campus (B)

617 West 7th Street, Los Angeles CA 90017
County: Los Angeles　FICE Identification: 021553
Unit ID: 455664
Telephone: (213) 615-2700　Carnegie Class: Spec-4-yr-Other Health
FAX Number: (213) 615-7274　Calendar System: Semester
URL: www.thechicagoschool.edu
Established: 2008　Annual Graduate Tuition & Fees: $13,050
Enrollment: 2,174　Coed
Affiliation or Control: Independent Non-Profit　IRS Status: 501(c)3
Highest Offering: Doctorate; No Undergraduates
Accreditation: WC

01 President ...... Dr. Michele NEALON
05 Vice Pres AA/Chief Academic Officer ...... Dr. Ted SCHOLZ
10 Sr Director of Business Operations ...... Mr. Chris JACKSON
32 Dean for Student Success ...... Ms. Jennifer STRIPE PORTILLO
15 Vice Pres Human Resources ...... Dr. David IWANE
106 Dean Online Programs ...... Dr. Tiffany MASSON
11 Chief Operating Officer ...... Dr. Michael FALOTICO
111 AVP Institutional Advancement ...... Ms. Mickie FARIS
26 AVP of Communications ...... Ms. Elinor GILBERT
04 Administrative Asst to President ...... Ms. Adriana KLEIMAN
06 National Registrar ...... Ms. Connie KUANG
08 Head Librarian ...... Mr. Oliver CUTSHAW
100 Chief of Staff ...... Ms. Shari MIKOS
101 Secretary of the Institution/Board ...... Ms. Patti TYRA
19 Manager/Director of Facilities ...... Mr. Dennia ROJAS
29 Associate Director Alumni Relations ...... Ms. Bel JOSEPH
37 Regional Assoc Director of Fin Aid ...... Mr. Seph RODRIGUEZ
124 AVP Retention Mgmt & Student Svcs ...... Dr. Jim CHITWOOD
09 Director of Institutional Research ...... Ms. Ericka KILBURN
108 Director Institutional Effectivenes ...... Ms. Virginia QUINONEZ

Chicago School of Professional Psychology-Irvine Campus (C)

4199 Campus Drive, Irvine CA 92612
Telephone: (949) 769-7700　Identification: 770492
Accreditation: &WC

China Evangelical Seminary North America (D)

1520 W. Cameron Avenue Ste 275,
West Covina CA 91790
County: Los Angeles　Identification: 667256
Telephone: (626) 917-9482　Carnegie Class: Not Classified
FAX Number: (626) 851-1371　Calendar System: Quarter
URL: www.cesna.edu
Established: 2007　Annual Graduate Tuition & Fees: N/A
Enrollment: N/A　Coed
Affiliation or Control: Non-denominational　IRS Status: 501(c)3
Highest Offering: Doctorate; No Undergraduates
Accreditation: THEOL

01 President ...... Dr. Katheryn LEUNG
05 Academic Dean ...... Dr. Gee LOWE
106 Dir Online Education/E-learning ...... Dr. Raymond HSU
11 Chief of Administration ...... Mr. Paiyi CHUANG
30 Chief Development/Advancement ...... Dr. Agnes CHIU
36 Director Student Placement ...... Dr. Alan CHAN
37 Director Student Financial Aid ...... Dr. Anita LIU
39 Director Student Housing ...... Mr. Paiyi CHUANG

Christian Witness Theological Seminary (E)

1975 Concourse Drive, San Jose CA 95131
County: Santa Clara　Identification: 667255
Telephone: (408) 433-2280　Carnegie Class: Not Classified
FAX Number: (408) 433-9855　Calendar System: Other
URL: www.cwts.edu
Established: 1978　Annual Graduate Tuition & Fees: N/A
Enrollment: N/A　Coed
Affiliation or Control: Interdenominational　IRS Status: 501(c)3
Highest Offering: Doctorate; No Undergraduates
Accreditation: THEOL

01 President ...... Rev. Jeffrey LU
03 Vice President ...... Rev. James IP
05 Dean ...... Lvshao CHANG
07 Director of Admissions ...... Dr. Luke TSAI

Church Divinity School of the Pacific (F)

2451 Ridge Road, Berkeley CA 94709-1217
County: Alameda　FICE Identification: 001165
Unit ID: 112127
Telephone: (510) 204-0700　Carnegie Class: Spec-4-yr-Faith
FAX Number: (510) 644-0712　Calendar System: Semester
URL: www.cdsp.edu
Established: 1893　Annual Graduate Tuition & Fees: N/A
Enrollment: 80　Coed
Affiliation or Control: Protestant Episcopal　IRS Status: 501(c)3
Highest Offering: Doctorate; No Undergraduates
Accreditation: THEOL

01 President & Dean ...... Dr. W. Mark RICHARDSON
05 Dean Academic Affairs ...... Dr. Ruth MEYERS
30 Int Dir Institutional Advancement ...... Ms. Christine RODRIGUES
32 Dean of Students ...... Rev. Andrew HYBL
06 Registrar ...... Ms. Mary MCCHESNEY-YOUNG
07 Director of Recruitment/Admissions ...... Mr. Jamie NELSON
10 Operations Manager ...... Mr. Melville HAYES-MARTIN
88 Program Manager ...... Ms. Alissa FENCSIK
37 Director of Financial Aid ...... Ms. Mary MCCHESENEY-YOUNG
11 Director Administration ...... Ms. Elsbeth WETHERILL
29 Director Alumni Relations ...... Vacant

Citrus College (G)

1000 W Foothill Boulevard, Glendora CA 91741-1899
County: Los Angeles　FICE Identification: 001166
Unit ID: 112172
Telephone: (626) 963-0323　Carnegie Class: Assoc/HT-High Trad
FAX Number: (626) 914-8618　Calendar System: Semester
URL: www.citruscollege.edu
Established: 1915　Annual Undergrad Tuition & Fees (In-District): $1,176
Enrollment: 12,999　Coed
Affiliation or Control: State/Local　IRS Status: 501(c)3
Highest Offering: Associate Degree
Accreditation: WJ, DA

01 Superintendent/President ...... Dr. Geraldine M. PERRI
05 Vice President Academic Affairs ...... Dr. Arvid SPOR
32 Vice President Student Services ...... Dr. Martha MCDONALD
10 Vice Pres Finance/Admin Services ...... Ms. Claudette E. DAIN
07 Dean Enrollment Services ...... Dr. Gerald SEQUEIRA
51 Dean Career/Technical/Continuing Ed ...... Dr. James LANCASTER
38 Dean of Counseling ...... Dr. Lucinda OVER
15 Director Human Resources ...... Dr. Robert L. SAMMIS
102 Director Foundation ...... Ms. Christina M. GARCIA
35 Dean of Students ...... Dr. Maryann TOLANO-LEVEQUE
18 Director Facilities & Construction ...... Mr. Fred DIAMOND
09 Director of Institutional Research ...... Dr. Lan HAO
06 Registrar ...... Mr. Brian DEAN
37 Director Financial Aid ...... Ms. Carol THOMAS
96 Director of Purchasing ...... Mr. Robert IVERSON
21 Director of Fiscal Services ...... Ms. Rosalinda BUCHWALD
28 Staff Diversity Officer ...... Mrs. Brenda FINK
13 Chief Information Services Officer ...... Mr. Robert HUGHES
19 Campus Security Supervisor ...... Mr. Benjamin MACIAS
83 Dean Social/Behavioral Sciences/DE ...... Dr. Dana HESTER
41 Dean Kinesiology/Athletics/Health ...... Ms. Jody WISE
79 Dean Language Arts & Library ...... Vacant
65 Dean Natural/Physical Sci & Health ...... Dr. Eric RABITOY
57 Dean Visual & Performing Arts ...... Mr. Robert SLACK
81 Dean Math & Business ...... Vacant
88 Director EOPS CARE CalWORKS ...... Ms. Sarah GONZALES-TAPIA
88 Project Director RACE to STEM ...... Dr. Marianne SMITH
101 Secretary of the Institution/Board ...... Ms. Christine A. LINK

City College of San Francisco (H)

33 Gough Street, San Francisco CA 94103-1292
County: San Francisco　FICE Identification: 001167
Unit ID: 112190
Telephone: (415) 239-3000　Carnegie Class: Assoc/MT-VT-Mix Trad/Non
FAX Number: (415) 239-3919　Calendar System: Semester
URL: www.ccsf.edu
Established: 1935　Annual Undergrad Tuition & Fees (In-District): $1,598
Enrollment: 23,391　Coed
Affiliation or Control: State/Local　IRS Status: 501(c)3
Highest Offering: Associate Degree
Accreditation: WJ, ACFEI, CAHIIM, DA, EMT, MAC, RAD, RTT

01 Chancellor ...... Dr. Mark ROCHA
10 Vice Chanc Finance/Administration ...... Dr. Mark ZACOVIC
05 Vice Chancellor Academic Affairs ...... Dr. Anna DAVIES
108 Dean of Institutional Effectiveness ...... Dr. Pam MERY
12 Dean Civic Center Campus ...... Mr. Carl JEW
12 Dean Southeast Campus ...... Mr. Torrance BYNUM
12 Dean Mission Campus ...... Mr. Jorge BELL
12 Dean Downtown/Business School ...... Dr. Geisce LY
32 Vice President Student Development ...... Mr. Samuel SANTOS
37 Dean Financial Aid & Scholarships ...... Ms. Elizabeth CORIA
07 Dean Admissions & Records ...... Ms. Marylou LEYBA-FRANK
20 Assoc Vice Chanc of Instruction ...... Mr. Tom BOEGEL
103 Assoc Vice Chanc Workforce Dev ...... Ms. Theresa ROWLAND
15 Assoc Vice Chanc Human Resources ...... Ms. Clara STARR
38 Dean/Dir Counseling/Student Support ...... Vacant
88 Assoc Dean Matriculation/Assessment ...... Ms. Margaret SANCHEZ
85 Dean Chinatown/Intl Educ/ESL ...... Dr. Minh-Hoa TA
88 Dean School of Visual & Performing ...... Vacant
83 Int Dean Behavioral/Social Sci ...... Ms. Jill YEE
81 Dean Science/Math/Technology/Engr ...... Mr. David YEE
68 Dean J Adams Campus/Sch Hlth Educ ...... Mr. Terry HALL
30 Assoc Vice Chanc Institutional Dev ...... Ms. Kristin CHARLES
13 Director Information Services ...... Mr. Doug RE
16 Director Employee Relations ...... Mr. Mickey BRANCA
18 Int Director Buildings/Grounds ...... Mr. Theodore ARANAS
14 Chief Technology Officer ...... Mr. Jay FIELD
96 Director of Purchasing ...... Ms. Kathy HENNIG
19 Chief of Police/Public Safety ...... Mr. Andre BARNES
88 ADA Compliance Officer ...... Dr. Leilani BATTISTE
21 Assoc Vice Chanc/CFO ...... Mr. David MARTIN
25 Int Dean Grants & Resource Dev ...... Ms. Ilona MCGRIFF
06 Assoc Dean Admission & Records ...... Ms. Monika LIU
88 Dean Faculty Support Svcs ...... Dr. Minh-Hoa TA
101 Liaison to the Board of Trustees ...... Ms. Linda SHAW
41 Athletic Director ...... Mr. Harold BROWN
43 Dir Legal Services/General Counsel ...... Mr. Steve BRUCKMAN
26 Director of External Affairs ...... Mr. Jeff HAMILTON

City of Hope (I)

1500 East Duarte Road, Duarte CA 91010-3000
County: Los Angeles　FICE Identification: 035924
Unit ID: 441238
Telephone: (626) 256-4673　Carnegie Class: Spec-4-yr-Med
FAX Number: (626) 301-8105　Calendar System: Semester
URL: www.cityofhope.org
Established: 1994　Annual Graduate Tuition & Fees: N/A
Enrollment: 74　Coed
Affiliation or Control: Independent Non-Profit　IRS Status: 501(c)3
Highest Offering: Doctorate; No Undergraduates
Accreditation: WC

01 President/CEO ...... Robert STONE
05 Provost/Chief Scientific Officer ...... Dr. Steven T. ROSEN
58 Dean of Graduate School ...... Dr. John J. ROSSI
06 Registrar ...... Queenie DU
07 Director of Admissions ...... Stephanie PATTERSON
08 Head Librarian ...... Andrea LYNCH

Claremont Lincoln University (J)

250 West First Street Ste 330, Claremont CA 91711
County: Los Angeles　Identification: 667215
Unit ID: 488387
Telephone: (909) 667-4400　Carnegie Class: Not Classified
FAX Number: (909) 399-3443　Calendar System: Quarter
URL: claremontlincoln.edu
Established: 2011　Annual Graduate Tuition & Fees: N/A
Enrollment: N/A　Coed
Affiliation or Control: Independent Non-Profit　IRS Status: 501(c)3
Highest Offering: Master's; No Undergraduates
Accreditation: WC

01 President ...... Dr. Eileen ARANDA
05 VP for Academic Affairs ...... Dr. Darrell EZELL
26 VP of Strategic Engage & Media Comm ...... Ms. Wendy DEAN
30 VP for External & Alumni Relations ...... Mr. Kerry NEAL
10 Chief Financial Officer ...... Ms. Linda RABITOY
32 Director of Student Services ...... Ms. Heather CASE
04 Executive Asst to President ...... Ms. Judy MORAVITZ
105 Director Web Services ...... Mr. Jon PIEHL
15 Director Human Resources ...... Ms. Nancy BARNES
37 Director Student Financial Aid ...... Ms. Deb BARKER-GARCIA

*Claremont University Consortium (K)

101 South Mills Avenue, Claremont CA 91711-5053
County: Los Angeles　Identification: 666003
Telephone: (909) 621-8026　Carnegie Class: N/A
FAX Number: (909) 621-8517
URL: www.cuc.claremont.edu

01 Chief Executive Officer ...... Mr. Stig LANESSKOG
10 Vice Pres for Bus Admin/Treasurer ...... Ms. Lori HUSEIN
32 Vice President of Student Affairs ...... Dr. Denise HAYES
26 Director of Communications ...... Ms. Kim LANE
19 Director Campus Safety ...... Mr. Stan SKIPWORTH
101 Sec to Brd of Overseers/Asst to CEO ...... Dr. Bonnie CLEMENS
08 Dean TCC Library ...... Dr. Kevin MULROY
15 Director Human Resources ...... Ms. Stephanie DORNES

*Claremont Graduate University (L)

150 E 10th Street, Claremont CA 91711-5909
County: Los Angeles　FICE Identification: 001169
Unit ID: 112251
Telephone: (909) 621-8000　Carnegie Class: DU-Higher
FAX Number: (909) 621-8390　Calendar System: Semester
URL: www.cgu.edu
Established: 1925　Annual Graduate Tuition & Fees: N/A
Enrollment: 2,136　Coed
Affiliation or Control: Independent Non-Profit　IRS Status: 501(c)3
Highest Offering: Doctorate; No Undergraduates
Accreditation: WC, PH

02 Interim President ...... Dr. Jacob ADAMS
04 Exec Asst to the President ...... Ms. Donna STANDLEA
05 Exec Vice President and Provost ...... Dr. Patricia EASTON
10 VP for Finance and Admin/Treasurer ...... Ms. Leslie NEGRITTO

111 Vice President for Advancement ... Mr. Ernie ISEMINGER
84 Dean of Admissions ... Mr. Tim COUNCIL
46 Vice Provost/Research ... Dr. Andrew CONWAY
108 Director Institutional Effectivenes ... Ms. Alana OLSCHWANG
15 Assoc VP for Human Resources ... Ms. Brenda LESWICK
47 Botany Center ... Dr. Lucinda MCDADE
50 Drucker-Ito Grad School of Mgt ... Dr. Jenny DARROCH
83 Behavioral & Organizational Sci ... Dr. Michelle BLIGH
69 Community & Global Health ... Dr. Kim REYNOLDS
53 Educational Studies ... Dr. Allen OMOTO
77 Center for Information Science ... Dr. Lorne OLFMAN
81 Mathematical Sciences Institute ... Dr. Marina CHUGUNOVA
82 Politics & Economics ... Dr. Michelle BLIGH
73 Arts and Humanities ... Dr. Patrick MASON
09 Institutional Research Officer ... Ms. Jeannette GURROLA
08 Head Librarian ... Dr. Kevin MULROY
19 Director of Campus Safety ... Mr. Stan SKIPWORTH
21 Assoc VP Finance/Admin ... Mr. Jim IRWIN
29 Director of Alumni Engagement ... Ms. Rachel JIMENEZ
26 Assoc VP Mktg & Communications ... Dr. Max BENAVIDEZ
32 Asst VP for Student Services ... Ms. Lisa FLORES GRIFFITH
35 Interim Dean of Students ... Ms. Quamina CARTER
36 Director of Career Development ... Dr. Christine KELLY
37 Director Student Financial Aid ... Vacant
85 Director of International Students ... Ms. Ariel CARPENTER
07 Assoc Director of Admissions ... Ms. Paige POINTKOWSKY
06 Registrar ... Ms. Lindsay STADLER
18 Director of Facilities ... Mr. Edward BRATHWAITE
90 AVP/Tech & Info Systems ... Mr. Manoj CHITRE
91 Director of Enterprise Infras ... Mr. Robert FORD
101 Secretary to the Board ... Ms. Cindy BIERMAN

*Claremont McKenna College (A)

500 E 9th Street, Claremont CA 91711-6400
County: Los Angeles — FICE Identification: 001170
Unit ID: 112260
Telephone: (909) 621-8000 — Carnegie Class: Bac-A&S
FAX Number: (909) 621-8790 — Calendar System: Semester
URL: www.claremontmckenna.edu
Established: 1946 — Annual Undergrad Tuition & Fees: $50,945
Enrollment: 1,349 — Coed
Affiliation or Control: Independent Non-Profit — IRS Status: 501(c)3
Highest Offering: Master's
Accreditation: **WC**

02 President and CEO ... Hiram E. CHODOSH
05 VP Academic Affs/Dean Faculty ... Peter UVIN
30 Vice President for Development ... Carroll STEVENS
10 Vice Pres Business Admin/Treasurer ... Robin J. ASPINALL
11 VP for Planning and Administration ... Matthew G. BIBBENS
32 VP Student Affs/Admissions/Fin Aid ... Jefferson HUANG
115 VP and Chief Investment Officer ... James J. FLOYD
29 Vice President for Alumni Relations ... Evan RUTTER
35 Dean of Students ... Sharon BASSO
07 AVP & Dean Admission/Financial Aid ... Georgette DEVERES
26 Assoc VP Public Affs/Communications ... Vacant
13 Assoc VP/Chief Technology Officer ... Cynthia HUMES
36 Assoc Dean/Dir Career Services ... Diana SEDER
06 Registrar/Dir Institutional Rsrch ... Elizabeth MORGAN
15 Director of Human Resources ... Andrea GALE
104 Director of Off-Campus Study ... Kristen MALLORY
41 Athletic Director ... Terry TUMEY
04 Special Assistant to the President ... Cheryl M. AGUILAR

*Claremont School of Theology (B)

1325 N College Avenue, Claremont CA 91711-3199
County: Los Angeles — FICE Identification: 001288
Unit ID: 124283
Telephone: (909) 447-2500 — Carnegie Class: Spec-4-yr-Faith
FAX Number: (909) 626-7062 — Calendar System: Semester
URL: www.cst.edu
Established: 1885 — Annual Graduate Tuition & Fees: N/A
Enrollment: 291 — Coed
Affiliation or Control: United Methodist — IRS Status: 501(c)3
Highest Offering: Doctorate; No Undergraduates
Accreditation: **WC**, THEOL

02 President ... Dr. Jeffrey KUAN
04 Exec Assistant to the President ... Ms. Maria Lise IANNUZZI
10 Vice Pres for Business Affairs/CFO ... Mr. Gamward QUAN
05 Vice Pres Academic Affairs & Dean ... Dr. Sheryl KUJAWA-HOLBROOK
20 Assoc Dean/VP Curriculum/ Assessment ... Rev. Belva Brown JORDAN
08 Dean of Library & Info Services ... Dr. Tom PHILLIPS
18 Facilities ... Vacant
32 Assoc Dean Student & Community Life ... Ms. Lea APPLETON
111 VP Advancement & Communications ... Ms. Sharalyn HAMILTON
26 Director of Communications ... Ms. Kimberly EDWARDS
29 Director of Alumni/ae Relations ... Ms. Noemi ORTEGA
21 Controller ... Mr. Haroon AHMED
07 Sr Dir Admissions/Enrollment Svcs ... Mr. Murad DIBBINI
37 Director Student Financial Services ... Ms. Brenda NIEVES
06 Registrar ... Ms. Jennie ALLEN
42 Director of Field Education ... Ms. Alma JOHNSON-HAWKINS
22 Campus Diversity Officer ... Ms. Christine WHANG

*Keck Graduate Institute (C)

535 Watson Drive, Claremont CA 91711-4817
County: Los Angeles — FICE Identification: 038533
Unit ID: 440031
Telephone: (909) 607-7855 — Carnegie Class: Masters/S
FAX Number: (909) 607-8086 — Calendar System: Semester
URL: www.kgi.edu
Established: 1997 — Annual Graduate Tuition & Fees: N/A
Enrollment: 429 — Coed
Affiliation or Control: Independent Non-Profit — IRS Status: 501(c)3
Highest Offering: Doctorate; No Undergraduates
Accreditation: **WC**, @PHAR

02 President/CEO ... Dr. Sheldon M. SCHUSTER
05 Chief Academic Officer ... Vacant
101 Assoc VP/Sec to Board of Trustees ... Elizabeth WRIGHT
10 Vice Pres for Finance & Operations ... Michael JONES
06 Registrar ... Melissa S. BROWN
84 Dean of Stdnt Engagement/Enrol Svcs ... Sofia TORO
32 Chief Student Affairs/Student Life ... Vacant
07 Director of Admissions ... Marcia PARKER
04 Executive Asst to President ... Patricia ROBIDOUX
15 Director Human Resources ... Cheryl MERRITT
18 Director of Facilities ... Spencer LAPLACA

CNI College (D)

702 West Town and Country Road, Orange CA 92868
County: Orange — FICE Identification: 032423
Unit ID: 433013
Telephone: (714) 437-9697 — Carnegie Class: Not Classified
FAX Number: (714) 437-9356 — Calendar System: Other
URL: www.cnicollege.edu
Established: 1994 — Annual Undergrad Tuition & Fees: N/A
Enrollment: 616 — Coed
Affiliation or Control: Proprietary — IRS Status: Proprietary
Highest Offering: Baccalaureate
Accreditation: **ABHES**, SURTEC

01 President ... Mr. James BUFFINGTON

*Coast Community College District Administration Offices (E)

1370 Adams Avenue, Costa Mesa CA 92626-5429
County: Orange — FICE Identification: 008711
Unit ID: 112376
Telephone: (714) 438-4600 — Carnegie Class: N/A
FAX Number: (714) 438-4882
URL: www.cccd.edu

01 Chancellor ... Dr. John WEISPFENNING
10 Vice Chancellor Finance & Adm Svcs ... Dr. Andrew DUNN
05 Vice Chanc Educ Svcs & Technology ... Dr. Andreea SERBAN
15 Vice Chanc Human Resources ... Dr. Cindy VYSKOCIL
26 Dir Public Affairs/Mktg/Govt ... Ms. Letitia CLARK
96 Director of Purchasing ... Mr. John ERIKSEN

*Coastline Community College (F)

11460 Warner Avenue, Fountain Valley CA 92708-2597
County: Orange — FICE Identification: 020635
Unit ID: 112385
Telephone: (714) 546-7600 — Carnegie Class: Assoc/HT-High Non
FAX Number: (714) 241-6277 — Calendar System: Semester
URL: www.coastline.edu
Established: 1976 — Annual Undergrad Tuition & Fees (In-District): $1,136
Enrollment: 11,525 — Coed
Affiliation or Control: State/Local — IRS Status: 501(c)3
Highest Offering: Associate Degree
Accreditation: **WJ**

02 President ... Dr. Loretta P. ADRIAN
05 Vice Pres of Instruction ... Mr. Vince RODRIGUEZ
10 VP of Administrative Services ... Ms. Christine NGUYEN
32 Vice Pres Student Services ... Mr. Ross MIYASHIRO
38 Dean Counseling/Matriculation ... Mr. Bruce KEELER
106 Assoc Dean of Distance Learning ... Mr. Bob NASH
12 Dean of Instruction Newport Beach ... Mr. Tom NEAL
12 Dean Instruct Tech Ed Garden Grove ... Ms. Nancy JONES
79 Dean Instruction Hum/Basic Skills ... Ms. Dana EMERSON
88 Dean Military Pgms/Contract Educ ... Ms. Joycelyn GROOT
26 Director Public Relations/Marketing ... Vacant
07 Director of Admissions/Records ... Ms. Jennifer MCDONALD
37 Director of Financial Aid ... Mr. Steve WOODYARD
18 Director Maintenance & Operations ... Mr. David CANT
21 Director Business Services ... Ms. Helen ROTHGEB
102 Exec Director College Foundation ... Ms. Mariam KHOSRAVANI
40 Director Bookstore ... Vacant
09 Director Research/Planning/Develop ... Mr. Aeron ZENTNER
24 Director of Electronic Media ... Ms. Judy GARVEY
15 Director of Personnel Services ... Ms. Renate AKINS
13 Exec Dean eLearning Research/IT ... Mr. Dan JONES
103 Dir Workforce & Economic Dev ... Vacant
35 Director Student Life ... Mr. Nathan BRAIS

*Golden West College (G)

15744 Golden West Street, Huntington Beach CA 92647-2748
County: Orange — FICE Identification: 001206
Unit ID: 115126
Telephone: (714) 892-7711 — Carnegie Class: Assoc/HT-High Trad
FAX Number: (714) 895-8243 — Calendar System: Semester
URL: www.gwc.info
Established: 1966 — Annual Undergrad Tuition & Fees (In-District): $1,176
Enrollment: 12,093 — Coed
Affiliation or Control: State/Local — IRS Status: Exempt
Highest Offering: Associate Degree
Accreditation: **WJ**, ADNUR

02 President ... Mr. Wes BRYAN
05 VP Instruction ... Mr. Omid POURZANJANI
32 Vice Pres Student Services ... Dr. Claudia LEE
11 Vice Pres Admin Services ... Ms. Janet M. HOULIHAN
83 Dean Counseling & Social Sciences ... Dr. Robyn BRAMMER
50 Dean Business & CTE ... Mr. Christopher WHITESIDE
81 Dean Math & Science ... Mr. Jeff COURCHAINE
49 Dean Arts & Letters ... Dr. David D. HUDSON
66 Dir School of Nursing ... Ms. Diane RESTELLI
23 Director Student Health Svcs ... Ms. Judy CHENG
09 Admin Dir Research/Plng/Inst Effect ... Dr. Kay NGUYEN
61 Dean Criminal Justice ... Mr. Ron LOWENBERG
35 Dean of Students ... Ms. Carla MARTINEZ
84 Dean Enrollment Management ... Ms. Christina RYAN RODRIGUEZ
103 Dean Econ Workforce Dev ... Dr. David GATEWOOD
88 Dean Learning Resource ... Dr. Alex MIRANDA
15 Director Human Resources ... Ms. Danielle HEINBUCH
10 Director Fiscal Services ... Mr. Paul WISNER
102 Director Foundation/Community Rels ... Mr. Bruce BERMAN
88 Coord Scholarships & Spec Events ... Ms. Valerie A. VENEGAS
07 Director of Admissions ... Ms. Jennifer L. ORTBERG
37 Director of Financial Aid ... Ms. Adrienne BURTON
18 Director Maintenance & Operations ... Mr. Joseph B. DOWLING
68 Dean Health PE & Athletics ... Mr. Albert GASPARIAN
04 Executive Asst to President ... Ms. Christina OJA
19 Dir Public Safety/Emerg Prep ... Mr. Jon ARNOLD
35 Dir Student Life & Leadership Dev ... Mr. Frank CIRIONI
88 Proj Dir Adult Block Ed Grant ... Ms. Larisa SERGEYEVA

*Orange Coast College (H)

2701 Fairview Road, POB 5005, Costa Mesa CA 92628-5005
County: Orange — FICE Identification: 001250
Unit ID: 120342
Telephone: (714) 432-0202 — Carnegie Class: Assoc/HT-High Trad
FAX Number: (714) 432-5609 — Calendar System: Semester
URL: www.orangecoastcollege.edu
Established: 1947 — Annual Undergrad Tuition & Fees (In-District): $1,184
Enrollment: 22,140 — Coed
Affiliation or Control: State/Local — IRS Status: 501(c)3
Highest Offering: Associate Degree
Accreditation: **WJ**, ACFEI, COARC, CVT, DA, DIETT, DMS, NDT, POLYT, RAD

02 President ... Dr. Dennis HARKINS
05 Vice President Instruction ... Mr. Kevin M. BALLINGER
32 Vice President Student Services ... Dr. Madjid NIROUMAND
10 Director of Fiscal Services ... Ms. Rachel KUBIK
11 Vice Pres Administrative Services ... Dr. Richard PAGEL
84 Dean Enrollment Services ... Dr. Kate MUELLER
38 Dean of Counseling ... Dr. Hue PHAM
35 Director Student Life ... Mr. Michael MORVICE
26 Director Marketing & PR ... Mr. Juan GUTIERREZ
111 Exec Dir Institutional Advancement ... Mr. Douglas BENNETT
09 Admin Dir Research/Planning/IE ... Ms. Sheri STERNER
07 Director Admiss/Records/Enroll Tech ... Mr. Efren GALVAN
15 Interim Director HR & Staff Develop ... Ms. Denise LEAT
06 Manager Enrollment Services ... Mr. James K. WEST
18 Interim Director M & O ... Mr. Randall CLARK
37 Director Financial Aid ... Ms. Tanisha BRADFIELD
13 Director Information Technology ... Ms. Rupa SARAN
23 Director Student Health Services ... Ms. Kelly DALY
88 Director Child Care Center ... Ms. Sue BIERLICH
41 Dean Kinesiology & Athletics ... Dr. Michael SUTLIFF
88 Dean Consumer Health & Sciences ... Dr. Jane MCLAUGHLIN
72 Dean of Technology ... Dr. Daniel SHRADER
50 Dean of Business & Computer Science ... Dr. Ronald JOHNSON
83 Dean of Social & Behavioral Science ... Dr. Kevin HENSON
88 Dean of Literature & Languages ... Dr. Michael MANDELKERN
81 Dean of Math & Sciences ... Dr. Tara GIBLIN
57 Dean of Visual & Performing Arts ... Ms. Larissa NAZARENKO
25 Director CTE/Grants ... Ms. Lisa KNUPPEL
19 Director Security/Safety ... Mr. John FARMER
40 Manager Bookstore ... Mr. Todd MURPHY
85 Assoc Dean Global Engagement Ctr ... Mr. Nathan JENSEN
121 Dean Student Success & Student Svcs ... Mr. Stephen TAMANAHA
04 Executive Asst to President ... Ms. Thuy N. NGUYEN
08 Dean Library & Learning Support ... Mr. John TAYLOR
102 Dir Foundation/Corporate Relations ... Mr. Douglas BENNETT

Cogswell Polytechnical College (I)

191 Baypointe Parkway, San Jose CA 95134-1697
County: Santa Clara — FICE Identification: 001177
Unit ID: 112394
Telephone: (408) 498-5100 — Carnegie Class: Bac-Diverse
FAX Number: (408) 877-7373 — Calendar System: Semester
URL: www.cogswell.edu
Established: 1887 — Annual Undergrad Tuition & Fees: $19,096
Enrollment: 633 — Coed
Affiliation or Control: Proprietary — IRS Status: Proprietary
Highest Offering: Baccalaureate
Accreditation: **WC**

01 Acting CEO ... Mr. Kenneth BANKS
05 Dean of the College ... Mr. Jerome SOLOMON
10 Chief Financial Officer ... Mr. Kenneeth BANKS
26 VP of Marketing ... Mr. Brian ROUCH
06 Registrar ... Ms. Angela ACUNA

08 Librarian & Resource Manager .... Ms. Jackie CORREA
07 Director of Admissions .... Mr. Richard HENSON
04 Executive Assistant to President .... Ms. Barbara GURNARI
09 Exec Director Inst Research & QA .... Ms. Milla ZLATANOV
13 VP of Information Technology .... Dr. Audrey FEDIN
32 Dean of Students .... Ms. Brittany BOGLE
36 Director of Career Services .... Mr. Nando GAPASIN
37 Financial Aid Manager .... Ms. Yariela PEREZ-GONZALEZ
88 Director of Compliance .... Ms. Nikki LOVE

The Colburn School (A)

200 S Grand Avenue, Los Angeles CA 90012-3007

County: Los Angeles | Identification: 666233
Telephone: (213) 621-2200 | Carnegie Class: Not Classified
FAX Number: (213) 621-2110 | Calendar System: Semester
URL: www.colburnschool.edu
Established: 2003 | Annual Undergrad Tuition & Fees: N/A
Enrollment: N/A | Coed
Affiliation or Control: Independent Non-Profit | IRS Status: 501(c)3
Highest Offering: Master's
Accreditation: MUS

01 President & CEO .... Mr. Sel KARDAN
05 Provost .... Dr. Adrian DALY
30 Sr VP Advancement/External Affairs .... Mr. Ed HORNER
26 Vice President Communications .... Dr. Mark A. BERRY
10 Chief Financial Officer .... Mr. Seth WEINTRAUB

† Full room, board, and tuition are provided to accepted students through the school's endowment.

Coleman University (B)

8888 Balboa Avenue, San Diego CA 92123-1506

County: San Diego | FICE Identification: 007296
Unit ID: 112446
Telephone: (858) 499-0202 | Carnegie Class: Spec-4-yr-Other Tech
FAX Number: (858) 499-0233 | Calendar System: Other
URL: www.coleman.edu
Established: 1963 | Annual Undergrad Tuition & Fees: $20,725
Enrollment: 399 | Coed
Affiliation or Control: Independent Non-Profit | IRS Status: 501(c)3
Highest Offering: Master's
Accreditation: @WC, ACICS

01 President/CEO .... Mr. Norbert J. KUBILUS
03 Vice President/COO .... Mr. Bruce F. GILDEN
32 Vice President Student Success .... Ms. Sara PIRAYESH
05 Dean of Education/CAO .... Mr. William S. REID
07 Director Admissions .... Ms. Jenny JONES
121 Director Academic Advising .... Mr. Kevin WOOLL
10 Chief Financial Officer .... Vacant
15 Director Human Resources .... Ms. Maria HAMZAVI
06 Registrar .... Mr. Jonathan RAMIREZ
37 Director Financial Aid .... Mr. Axel N. HERNANDEZ
36 Director Career Services .... Mr. Bob SWEIGART
21 Comptroller .... Ms. Laura SALES
08 Librarian .... Vacant
29 Alumni Relations Coordinator .... Vacant
14 Network Administrator .... Mr. Brian J. MORGAN
18 Facilities Manager .... Mr. Terry S. GLYNN
26 Director External Relations .... Mr. Rod P. WEISS
13 Chief Info Technology Officer (CIO) .... Vacant

College of the Canyons (C)

26455 Rockwell Canyon Road,
Santa Clarita CA 91355-1899

County: Los Angeles | FICE Identification: 008903
Unit ID: 111461
Telephone: (661) 259-7800 | Carnegie Class: Assoc/HT-High Non
FAX Number: (661) 259-8302 | Calendar System: Semester
URL: www.canyons.edu
Established: 1967 | Annual Undergrad Tuition & Fees (In-District): $1,154
Enrollment: 18,437 | Coed
Affiliation or Control: State/Local | IRS Status: 501(c)3
Highest Offering: Associate Degree
Accreditation: WJ, MLTAD

01 Chancellor SCCCD & President COC .... Dr. Dianne G. VAN HOOK
03 Deputy Chancellor .... Dr. Barry GRIBBONS
05 Asst Supt/Vice Pres Instruction .... Dr. Jerry BUCKLEY
10 Asst Supt/VP Business Services .... Ms. Sharlene COLEAL
15 Asst Supt/Vice Pres Human Resources .... Dr. Diane FIERO
18 Asst Supt/VP Facil Plan Op/Const .... Mr. Jim SCHRAGE
32 Asst Superintendent/VP Student Svcs .... Dr. Michael WILDING
103 VP Econ & Workforce Development .... Mr. Jeffrey FORREST
26 VP Public Info/Advoc/Ext Relations .... Mr. Eric HARNISH
13 Vice President Technology .... Dr. James TEMPLE
12 VP Canyon Country Campus and Grants .... Dr. Ryan THEULE
20 VP Academic Affairs .... Ms. Audrey GREEN
21 Assoc VP Business Services .... Ms. Cynthia GRANDGEORGE
57 Dean School of Visual and Perf Arts .... Dr. Carmen DOMINGUEZ
88 Dean Educ Tech/Lrng Resrc/Dist Educ .... Mr. James GLAPA-GROSSKLAG
35 Dean Student Services .... Mr. Michael JOSLIN
79 Dean School of Humanities .... Mr. Andy MCCUTCHEON
46 Dean Inst Research/Plng/Inst Effect .... Dr. Daylene MEUSCHKE
121 Dean Instr Support & Student Succ .... Ms. Denee PESCARMONA
72 Dean School of Applied Tech .... Dr. Ronald MCFARLAND
84 Dean Enrollment Services .... Dr. Jasmine RUYS
56 Dean Canyons Extension .... Ms. Diane STEWART
81 Dean School of Math/Sci & Health .... Mr. Omar TORRES
50 Dean School of Business .... Mr. Russell WALDON
68 Int Dean PE/Kinesiology and Athl .... Mr. Chuck LYON
83 Dean School Social/Behav Sci .... Mr. Paul WICKLINE
36 Act Dean Campus Ops CCC/Career Svs .... Mr. Anthony MICHAELIDES
21 Controller .... Mr. Jason HINKLE
102 COO COC Foundation/Int Dir UC .... Ms. Cathy RITZ
30 Chief Devel Officer COC Foundation .... Mr. Murray WOOD
88 Deputy Sector Navigator Adv Manuf .... Mr. Michael BASTINE
88 Deputy Sector Navigator ICT/DM .... Ms. Paula HODGE
88 Deputy Sector Navigator Health .... Mr. John CORDOVA
103 Director WorkSource Center .... Ms. Keri AAVER
88 Director Student Business Office .... Ms. Kathleen BENZ
37 Director Financial Aid .... Mr. Tom BILBRUCK
28 Dir Diversity/EEO/Title IX Pgms .... Ms. Karen CARR
88 Director Professional Development .... Ms. Leslie CARR
19 Director Campus Safety .... Ms. Tamela CASTOR
88 Director Fiscal Services .... Ms. Balbir CHANDI
85 Director International Students Pgm .... Dr. Jia-Yi CHENG-LEVINE
16 Director Human Resources .... Ms. Christina CHUNG
88 Dir Student Dev & Campus Activity .... Ms. Kelly DAPP
88 Dir Central Energy Syst/Reg Comp .... Mr. Carl EBAUGH
88 MESA Program Director .... Ms. Amy FOOTE
91 Director Mgmt Info Systems .... Mr. Mark GARCIA
96 Director Contracts Proc & Risk Mgmt .... Ms. April GRAHAM
88 Director Small Bus Devel Ctr .... Ms. Catherine GROOMS
14 Director Information Technology .... Mr. Mike GUNTHER
75 Director Career and Technical Educ .... Ms. Harriet HAPPEL
88 Director Technology Services .... Mr. Hsiawen HULL
88 Director Art Gallery .... Mr. Larry HURST
88 Dir Volunteer & Stdnt Employment .... Mr. Yasser ISSA
88 Director Facilities Projects .... Mr. William KARRAT
23 Director Student Health & Wellness .... Ms. Mary MANUEL
88 Director Payroll Services .... Ms. Maria MARTINEZ
88 Director Recruitment & Employee Sv .... Ms. Rian MEDLIN
88 Director Employee Training Inst .... Mr. John MILBURN
88 Director Public Relations & Sports .... Mr. Jesse MUNOZ
88 Director Grant & Categ Accounting .... Ms. Carolyn SHAW
88 Dir Outreach & School Relations .... Ms. Kari SOFFA
88 Director Reentry & Vet Affairs .... Mr. Renard THOMAS
27 Dir Advertising/Social Media .... Ms. Wendy TRUJILLO
106 Director Distance & Acc Learning .... Mr. Brian WESTON
88 Director Civic Center .... Mr. Robin WILLIAMS
25 Director Grants Development .... Ms. Theresa ZUZEVICH
88 Int Director TEACH Program .... Ms. Renee MARSHALL

College of the Desert (D)

43-500 Monterey Avenue, Palm Desert CA 92260-9399

County: Riverside | FICE Identification: 001182
Unit ID: 113573
Telephone: (760) 346-8041 | Carnegie Class: Assoc/HT-High Trad
FAX Number: (760) 341-8678 | Calendar System: Semester
URL: www.collegeofthedesert.edu
Established: 1958 | Annual Undergrad Tuition & Fees (In-District): $1,327
Enrollment: 10,466 | Coed
Affiliation or Control: State/Local | IRS Status: 501(c)3
Highest Offering: Associate Degree
Accreditation: WJ

01 Superintendent/President .... Dr. Joel L. KINNAMON
05 Vice President Student Learning .... Dr. Pamela RALSTON
121 Vice President Student Success .... Dr. Annebelle NERY
10 Vice President Admin Services .... Ms. Lisa HOWELL
15 Vice President Human Resources .... Dr. Mary Anne GULARTE
111 Exec Dir Institutional Advancement .... Ms. Pam HUNTER
102 Exec Dir of Foundation .... Vacant
13 Exec Dir Educational Technology .... Ms. Sherilyn WILLIS
18 Director of Maintenance/Operations .... Mr. Brandon TOEPFER
29 Director Alumni Relations .... Ms. Betsy YOUNG
37 Director Financial Aid .... Ms. Kristen MILLIGAN
21 Director of Fiscal Services .... Mr. John RAMONT
06 Director Admissions and Records .... Mr. Curt LUTTRELL
26 Director Community Relations .... Ms. Caroline MALONEY
103 Dir Workforce Solutions/Career Ctr .... Mr. Robert ST JULIANA, II
36 Dir Career/Col Access Pathways .... Ms. Michelle BLEZA
09 Director Institutional Research .... Dr. Daniel MARTINEZ
88 Director Education Centers .... Ms. Jessica ENDERS
19 Dir Pub Safety Dept/Emergency Prep .... Mr. Tim NAKAMURA
15 Director Human Resources .... Ms. Andrea STAEHLE

College of Marin (E)

835 College Avenue, Kentfield CA 94904-2590

County: Marin | FICE Identification: 001178
Unit ID: 118347
Telephone: (415) 457-8811 | Carnegie Class: Assoc/HT-Mix Trad/Non
FAX Number: (415) 456-6017 | Calendar System: Semester
URL: www.marin.edu
Established: 1926 | Annual Undergrad Tuition & Fees (In-District): $1,488
Enrollment: 5,490 | Coed
Affiliation or Control: State/Local | IRS Status: 501(c)3
Highest Offering: Associate Degree
Accreditation: WJ, DA

01 Superintendent/President .... Dr. David W. COON
05 Senior VP Student Svcs & Learning .... Mr. Jonathan ELDRIDGE
20 Asst VP Instructional Support .... Ms. Cari TORRES
10 Vice President Finance & Oper .... Mr. Greg NELSON
15 Exec Dir Human Res/Labor Relations .... Ms. Kristina A. COMBS
84 Dean Enrollment Services .... Mr. Jon HORINEK
32 Dean Student Success .... Ms. Lisa WEBB
49 Dean Arts & Humanities .... Dr. David SNYDER
103 Dean Career & Tech Education .... Ms. Elizabeth PRATT
81 Dean Math/Sciences .... Dr. Carol HERNANDEZ
21 Director Fiscal Services .... Ms. Peggy ISOZAKI
09 Exec Dir Plng/Research/Inst Plng .... Dr. Christina LEIMER
37 Asst Dean Enroll/Financial Aid .... Vacant
18 Dir Facil Planning & M&O .... Vacant
13 CIO & Director of IT .... Mr. Patrick EKOUE-TOTOU
35 Dir Student Activities/Advocacy .... Ms. Sadika SULAIMAN HARA
19 Chief of Police .... Mr. Jeff MAROZICK
68 Dir Kinesiolgy/Athletics .... Mr. Ryan BYRNE
76 Dean Health Sciences .... Dr. Marshall ALAMEIDA
51 Dir Cmty/Lifelong/Intl Education .... Ms. Carol HILDEBRAND
30 Exec Director of Development .... Dr. Linda FRANK
08 Director of Library Services .... Vacant
04 Exec Asst to Pres/Board .... Ms. Kathy JOYNER

College of the Redwoods Community College District (F)

7351 Tompkins Hill Road, Eureka CA 95501-9300

County: Humboldt | FICE Identification: 001185
Unit ID: 121707
Telephone: (707) 476-4100 | Carnegie Class: Assoc/HT-High Non
FAX Number: (707) 476-4400 | Calendar System: Semester
URL: www.redwoods.edu
Established: 1964 | Annual Undergrad Tuition & Fees (In-District): $1,142
Enrollment: 5,350 | Coed
Affiliation or Control: State/Local | IRS Status: 501(c)3
Highest Offering: Associate Degree
Accreditation: WJ, DA, EMT, NAIT

01 President/Superintendent .... Mr. Keith SNOW-FLAMER
05 Vice Pres Instruction/Student Dev .... Dr. Angela HILL
04 Exec Assistant to the President .... Ms. Cynthia PETRUSHA
10 VP Administrative Services .... Mr. Lee LINDSEY
31 Director Community Development .... Ms. Pru RATLIFF
15 Director Human Resources/EEO .... Ms. Wendy BATES
12 Director Del Norte Center .... Mr. Rory JOHNSON
68 Dean PE/Athletics/Health Occup .... Mr. Joseph HASH
37 Director Financial Aid .... Ms. Rianne CONNOR
88 Dir Special Pgms/Academic Support .... Mr. Kinte JOHNSON
22 Director Disabled Student Pgm Svcs .... Ms. Patricia BLAIR
18 Director Maintenance & Operations .... Mr. Garry PATRICK
26 Public Information Officer .... Mr. Marty COELHO
08 Learning Resource Center Director .... Ms. Cathy COX
07 Manager Admissions/Records .... Ms. Rianne CONNOR
19 Director of Public Safety .... Mr. Burke MCBRIDE
88 Director Administration of Justice .... Mr. Ron WATERS

College of the Sequoias (G)

915 S Mooney Boulevard, Visalia CA 93277-2234

County: Tulare | FICE Identification: 001186
Unit ID: 123217
Telephone: (559) 730-3700 | Carnegie Class: Assoc/MT-VT-High Trad
FAX Number: (559) 730-3894 | Calendar System: Semester
URL: www.cos.edu
Established: 1925 | Annual Undergrad Tuition & Fees (In-District): $1,388
Enrollment: 11,266 | Coed
Affiliation or Control: State/Local | IRS Status: 501(c)3
Highest Offering: Associate Degree
Accreditation: WJ, PTAA

01 Superintendent/President .... Mr. Stan A. CARRIZOSA
05 Vice President Academic Services .... Dr. Jennifer VEGA-LA SERNA
11 Vice President Administrative Svcs .... Ms. Christine STATTON
114 Dir Budgets & Categorical Accts .... Ms. Leangela MILLER-HERNANDEZ
32 Vice President Student Services .... Mr. Brent CALVIN
37 Dean Student Svcs/Financial Aid .... Ms. Jessica MORRISON
12 Provost Tulare Center .... Dr. Louann WALDNER
12 Provost Hanford Center .... Dr. Kristin ROBINSON
81 Dean Science/Math/Eng .... Dr. Robert URTECHO
76 Dean Allied Health/Phys Education .... Ms. Cindy DELAIN
49 Dean Arts & Letters .... Mr. Marshall FULLBRIGHT
15 Dean Human Resources/Legal Affairs .... Mr. John BRATSCH
18 Dean Facilities .... Mr. Byron WOODS
102 Director Foundation .... Mr. Tim FOSTER
66 Dir Nursing/Allied Health .... Ms. Belen KERSTEN
08 Dir Library/Instructional Tech .... Ms. Mary-Catherine OXFORD
09 Dean of Research .... Dr. Mehmet OZTURK
06 Registrar/Admissions Coordinator .... Ms. Velia RODRIGUEZ
41 Associate Dean/Athletic Director .... Mr. Brent DAVIS
19 Chief District Police .... Mr. Kevin MIZNER
40 Bookstore Manager .... Ms. Dorianna MENDIETTA
23 Coord Health Center .... Dr. Patricia ALVAREZ
35 Dir Student Activities/Affairs .... Ms. Debbie DOUGLASS
103 Dean CTE/Voc Ed .... Mr. Thad RUSSELL
88 Coord Welcome/Transfer Center .... Ms. Catherine MCGUIRE
26 Coord Mktg/Public Info .... Ms. Kristen FOSTER
04 Executive Asst to President .... Ms. Meghan TIERCE
13 Dean Info Technology .... Mr. Flen PROFETA

College of the Siskiyous (H)

800 College Avenue, Weed CA 96094-2899

County: Siskiyou | FICE Identification: 001187
Unit ID: 123484
Telephone: (530) 938-5555 | Carnegie Class: Assoc/MT-VT-High Non
FAX Number: (530) 938-5506 | Calendar System: Semester
URL: www.siskiyous.edu

Established: 1957 Annual Undergrad Tuition & Fees (In-District): $1,154
Enrollment: 2,203 Coed
Affiliation or Control: State/Local IRS Status: 501(c)3
Highest Offering: Associate Degree
Accreditation: WJ, EMT

01 Superintendent/President .... Dr. Stephen SCHOONMAKER
04 Exec Assistant II President & Board .... Ms. Sheila GRIMES
10 Vice President Administrative Svcs .... Ms. Darlene MELBY
05 Vice President Instruction .... Dr. Todd SCOTT
32 Vice President Student Services .... Ms. Melissa GREEN
09 Director Research & Evaluation .... Mr. Bart SCOTT
41 Assoc Dean Instruction/Dir Athletic .... Mr. Dennis ROBERTS
75 Dean Career & Technical Education .... Vacant
07 Director Admissions & Records .... Ms. Meghan WITHERELL
15 Assoc Vice Pres Human Resources .... Ms. Theresa RICHMOND
37 Director Financial Aid .... Ms. Janette HARRIS
18 Director Facilities .... Mr. Eric RULOFSON
30 Dir of Institutional Advancement .... Vacant
28 Director of Diversity .... Ms. Theresa RICHMOND
39 Director Student Housing .... Dr. Doug HAUGEN
26 Dir Comm Relations/Foundation .... Ms. Dawnie SLABAUGH

Columbia College Hollywood (A)

18618 Oxnard Street, Tarzana CA 91356-1411
County: Los Angeles FICE Identification: 021102
Unit ID: 112570
Telephone: (800) 785-0585 Carnegie Class: Spec-4-yr-Arts
FAX Number: (818) 345-9053 Calendar System: Quarter
URL: www.columbiacollege.edu
Established: 1952 Annual Undergrad Tuition & Fees: $21,105
Enrollment: 326 Coed
Affiliation or Control: Independent Non-Profit IRS Status: 501(c)3
Highest Offering: Baccalaureate
Accreditation: WC

01 President/CEO .... Mr. Bill SMITH
05 Vice Pres Academic Affairs .... Mr. Lex SANDERSON
32 Vice Pres Student Services .... Ms. Kelly PARKER
07 Vice Pres Admissions .... Ms. Jessica WILTGEN
11 Vice Pres Operations .... Mr. Patrick OLMSTEAD
101 Exec Asst to Board of Trustees .... Ms. Lisa ARNONE
22 Sr Compliance/Accreditation Manager .... Mr. Jan HASTINGS
10 Chief Financial Officer .... Mr. Richard CROWE
13 Director of IT and Production Svcs .... Mr. Ronald REEVES
37 Financial Aid Manager .... Ms. Maricela GUZMAN
36 Director Career Development .... Mr. Stephen HERRING
06 Registrar .... Ms. LaVona THOMAS

Community Christian College (B)

1849 N. Wabash, Redlands CA 92374
County: San Bernardino FICE Identification: 038744
Unit ID: 446163
Telephone: (909) 794-1084 Carnegie Class: Assoc/HT-High Trad
FAX Number: (909) 794-1093 Calendar System: Quarter
URL: www.cccollege.edu
Established: 1995 Annual Undergrad Tuition & Fees: $5,700
Enrollment: 87 Coed
Affiliation or Control: Independent Non-Profit IRS Status: 501(c)3
Highest Offering: Associate Degree
Accreditation: TRACS

01 President .... Mr. Joshua TURANSKY
05 Chief Academic Officer .... Dr. Steven AVALOS
07 Admissions Advisor .... Mr. David ZAMORA

Compton College (C)

1111 E Artesia Boulevard, Compton CA 90221-5393
County: Los Angeles FICE Identification: 001188
Unit ID: 112686
Telephone: (310) 900-1600 Carnegie Class: Assoc/HT-High Non
FAX Number: (310) 605-1458 Calendar System: Semester
URL: www.compton.edu
Established: 1927 Annual Undergrad Tuition & Fees (In-State): $1,142
Enrollment: 7,427 Coed
Affiliation or Control: State IRS Status: 501(c)3
Highest Offering: Associate Degree
Accreditation: WJ

01 President/CEO Compton Cmty Col Dist .... Dr. Keith CURRY
03 Vice President Compton College .... Ms. Barbara PEREZ
32 Vice President Student Services .... Ms. Elizabeth MARTINEZ
10 Vice Pres Finance/Admin Svcs .... Mr. Steven HAIGLER
15 Vice President Human Resources .... Mrs. Rachelle SASSER
05 Dean Academic Affairs .... Vacant
76 Dean Health/Human Services .... Ms. Wanda MORRIS
41 Dir Student Development/Athletics .... Mr. Junior DOMINGO
08 Director Learning Resources .... Mr. Rodney MURRAY
88 Director CalWORKs & DSPS .... Ms. Patricia BONACIC
22 Director EOP & S/CARE .... Ms. Christine ALDRICH
09 Director Institutional Research .... Vacant
37 Director Financial Aid .... Dr. Mytha PASCUAL
84 Int Dir Enrollment Management .... Ms. Nelly ALVARADO
21 Director Fiscal Affairs .... Mr. Ruben JAMES
18 Dir Facilities Plng/Operations .... Ms. Linda OWENS
13 Dir Information Technology Services .... Mr. Andrei YERMAKOV
07 Director Admissions & Records .... Ms. Richette BELL

† Regional accreditation is carried under the parent institution in Torrance, CA.

Concord Law School of Kaplan University (D)

10100 Santa Monica Boulevard #365,
Los Angeles CA 90067
Telephone: (800) 439-4794 FICE Identification: 041259
Accreditation: &NH

† Regional accreditation is carried under the parent institution in Davenport, IA.

Concorde Career College (E)

12951 Euclid Street, Suite 101,
Garden Grove CA 92840-1451
County: Orange FICE Identification: 008071
Unit ID: 123679
Telephone: (714) 703-1900 Carnegie Class: Spec 2-yr-Health
FAX Number: (714) 530-8421 Calendar System: Semester
URL: www.concorde.edu
Established: 1960 Annual Undergrad Tuition & Fees: N/A
Enrollment: 639 Coed
Affiliation or Control: Proprietary IRS Status: Proprietary
Highest Offering: Associate Degree
Accreditation: ACCSC, COARC, DH, PTAA

01 Campus President .... Mr. Nicholas EWELL

Concorde Career College (F)

12412 Victory Boulevard, North Hollywood CA 91606-3134
County: Los Angeles FICE Identification: 007607
Unit ID: 124937
Telephone: (818) 766-8151 Carnegie Class: Spec 2-yr-Health
FAX Number: (818) 766-1587 Calendar System: Quarter
URL: www.concorde.edu
Established: 1955 Annual Undergrad Tuition & Fees: N/A
Enrollment: 466 Coed
Affiliation or Control: Proprietary IRS Status: Proprietary
Highest Offering: Associate Degree
Accreditation: ACCSC, COARC, PTAA, SURGT

01 Campus President .... Carmen BOWEN
05 Academic Dean .... Weyland MORSE
07 Director of Admissions .... Allan GUECO
37 Director Student Financial Aid .... Cynthia STEIN

Concorde Career College (G)

201 E Airport Drive, San Bernadino CA 92408
County: San Bernardino FICE Identification: 008537
Unit ID: 124706
Telephone: (909) 884-8891 Carnegie Class: Spec 2-yr-Health
FAX Number: (909) 884-1831 Calendar System: Semester
URL: www.concorde.edu
Established: 1970 Annual Undergrad Tuition & Fees: N/A
Enrollment: 561 Coed
Affiliation or Control: Proprietary IRS Status: Proprietary
Highest Offering: Associate Degree
Accreditation: ACCSC, COARC, DH, NDT, POLYT, SURGT

01 Campus President .... DeWayne JOHNSON

Concorde Career College (H)

4393 Imperial Avenue, Suite 100,
San Diego CA 92113-1962
County: San Diego FICE Identification: 007930
Unit ID: 120661
Telephone: (619) 688-0800 Carnegie Class: Spec 2-yr-Health
FAX Number: (619) 220-4177 Calendar System: Other
URL: www.concorde.edu
Established: 1966 Annual Undergrad Tuition & Fees: N/A
Enrollment: 647 Coed
Affiliation or Control: Proprietary IRS Status: Proprietary
Highest Offering: Associate Degree
Accreditation: ACCSC, #COARC, DH, PTAA, SURGT

01 Campus President .... Ms. Rachel SAFFEL

Concordia University (I)

1530 Concordia W, Irvine CA 92612-3299
County: Orange FICE Identification: 020705
Unit ID: 112075
Telephone: (949) 854-8002 Carnegie Class: Masters/L
FAX Number: (949) 214-3520 Calendar System: Semester
URL: www.cui.edu
Established: 1972 Annual Undergrad Tuition & Fees: $32,780
Enrollment: 4,505 Coed
Affiliation or Control: Lutheran Church - Missouri Synod
IRS Status: 501(c)3
Highest Offering: Doctorate
Accreditation: WC, #CAATE, IACBE, NURSE

01 President .... Dr. Kurt J. KRUEGER
05 Exec Vice Pres Acad Affairs/Provost .... Dr. Peter SENKBEIL
32 Exec VP Student & Enroll Services .... Dr. Gary R. MCDANIEL
111 Exec VP Advancement .... Mr. Timothy J. JAEGER
10 Exec VP/Chief Finance Officer .... Mr. Kevin TILDEN
84 Assoc Provost/VP Enrollment Mgmt .... Dr. Doug GROVE
49 Dean School of Arts and Sciences .... Dr. Scott ASHMON
50 EVP Ext Rels/Dean Sch of Business .. Mr. Stephen CHRISTENSEN
50 Dean of Business Administration .... Mr. George WRIGHT
107 Dean School of Professional Studies .... Dr. Timothy PREUSS
53 Dean School of Education .... Dr. Deborah MERCIER
73 Dean Christ College .... Dr. Steven P. MUELLER
06 Dean of Academic Records/Registrar .... Vacant
09 Director of Institutional Research .... Mrs. Deborah LEE
35 Dean of Students .... Dr. Gilbert FUGITT
07 Director of Undergrad Admissions .... Mr. Doug WIBLE
123 Sr Director of Graduate Admissions .... Mr. Justin MOSCHINA
123 Sr Director of Graduate Admissions .... Mr. Jon O'NEILL, II
37 Director of Financial Aid .... Ms. Lori MCDONALD
113 Bursar .... Mr. Edgar LOPEZ
43 AVP & General Counsel .... Mr. Ronald VAN BLARCOM
15 Director of Human Resources .... Mrs. Penny MOCK
08 Director of Library Services .... Prof. Carolina BARTON
41 Athletic Director .... Mr. Mo ROBERSON
39 Director Residence Life .... Ms. Brianna SPRINGER
19 Director Security/Safety .... Mr. Steven RODRIGUEZ
29 Exec Director of Alumni Relations .... Mr. Michael BERGLER
24 Director Educational Media .... Prof. John RANDALL
36 Director of Career Services .... Mrs. Victoria JAFFEE
112 Director Major Gift Planning .... Mr. Dennis COX
85 Exec Director Global Programs .... Dr. Dan WAITE
13 Director of IT Services .... Mr. Chris HARRIS
28 Director of Inclusion/Diversity .... Dr. Terilyn JACKSON

*Contra Costa Community College District Office (J)

500 Court Street, Martinez CA 94553-1278
County: Contra Costa FICE Identification: 001189
Unit ID: 112817
Telephone: (925) 229-1000 Carnegie Class: N/A
FAX Number: (925) 370-2019
URL: www.4cd.edu

01 Chancellor .... Dr. Fred E. WOOD
05 Exec VC Education & Technology .... Vacant
11 Exec VC Administrative Services .... Mr. Eugene C. HUFF
20 Int Assoc Vice Chanc Education Svcs .... Mr. Gregory STOUP
18 Chief Facilities Planner .... Mr. Ray PYLE
10 Assoc Vice Chanc/CFO .... Mr. Johah NICHOLAS

*Contra Costa College (K)

2600 Mission Bell Drive, San Pablo CA 94806-3195
County: Contra Costa FICE Identification: 001190
Unit ID: 112826
Telephone: (510) 235-7800 Carnegie Class: Assoc/HT-High Non
FAX Number: (510) 236-6768 Calendar System: Semester
URL: www.contracosta.edu
Established: 1948 Annual Undergrad Tuition & Fees (In-District): $1,308
Enrollment: 6,355 Coed
Affiliation or Control: State/Local IRS Status: 501(c)3
Highest Offering: Associate Degree
Accreditation: WJ

02 President .... Ms. Mojdeh MEHDIZADEH
03 Vice President .... Mr. Kenneth SHERWOOD
05 Senior Dean of Instruction .... Dr. Tish YOUNG
32 Dean of Student Services .... Ms. Vicki FERGUSON
103 Dir Workforce & Econ Development .... Ms. Kelly SCHELIN
07 Director Admissions & Records .... Ms. Catherine FROST
10 Director Business Services .... Ms. Mariles MAGALONG
09 Director of Institutional Research .... Vacant
37 Financial Aid Supervisor .... Ms. Monica RODRIGUEZ
18 Manager Buildings & Grounds .... Mr. Bruce KING
04 Senior Exec Asst to the President .... Mr. Michael L. PETERSON
30 Development Officer .... Ms. Sara MARCELLINO
41 Athletic Director .... Mr. John WADE
26 Director of Marketing .... Ms. Brandy HOWARD

*Diablo Valley College (L)

321 Golf Club Road, Pleasant Hill CA 94523-1544
County: Contra Costa FICE Identification: 001191
Unit ID: 113634
Telephone: (925) 685-1230 Carnegie Class: Assoc/HT-Mix Trad/Non
FAX Number: (925) 685-1551 Calendar System: Semester
URL: www.dvc.edu
Established: 1949 Annual Undergrad Tuition & Fees (In-District): $1,308
Enrollment: 19,694 Coed
Affiliation or Control: State/Local IRS Status: 501(c)3
Highest Offering: Associate Degree
Accreditation: WJ, ACFEI, DA, DH

02 Interim President .... Mr. Ted WIEDEN
05 Vice President Instruction .... Ms. Rachel WESTLAKE
32 Vice President Student Services .... Dr. Newin ORANTE
10 Vice Pres Business & Admin Svcs .... Mr. John NAHLEN
20 Senior Dean of Curriculum & Instr .... Ms. Kimberely SCHENK
84 Dean Outreach/Enroll Mgt/
Matric .... Ms. Elizabeth HAUSCARRIAGUE
12 Dean San Ramon Campus .... Mr. Mike HOLZCLAW
41 Dean of PE/Athl/Dance/Athletic Dir .... Ms. Christine WORSLEY
62 Dean Library/Ed Tech & Learn Sup .... Mr. Rick ROBISON
26 Dir of Marketing & Communications .... Ms. Chrisanne KNOX
57 Interim Dean Applied & Fine Arts .... Ms. Toni FANNIN
54 Interim Dean Phys Sci/Engr/Bio Sci .... Mr. Joe GORGA
83 Dean English & Social Science .... Mr. Obed VAZQUEZ

50 Dean Business Ed/Math/Comp Sci ...... Ms. Despina PRAPAVESSI
06 Registrar/Admissions .... Ms. Stephanie ALVES
35 Dean Student Support Services .... Ms. Emily STONE

*Los Medanos College (A)

2700 E Leland Road, Pittsburg CA 94565-5197
County: Contra Costa　FICE Identification: 010340
Unit ID: 117894
Telephone: (925) 439-2181　Carnegie Class: Assoc/MT-VT-High Trad
FAX Number: (925) 427-1599　Calendar System: Semester
URL: www.losmedanos.edu
Established: 1973　Annual Undergrad Tuition & Fees (In-District): $1,308
Enrollment: 8,861　Coed
Affiliation or Control: State/Local　IRS Status: 501(c)3
Highest Offering: Associate Degree
Accreditation: WJ

02 President .... Dr. Bob KRATOCHVIL
04 Senior Executive Assistant .... Ms. Jennifer ADAMS
05 VP Instruction & Student Services .... Dr. Kevin HORAN
10 VP Business & Admin Services .... Mr. Alexander PORTER
32 Sr Dean Stdnt Svcs & Brentwood Ctr .... Ms. Gail NEWMAN
45 Sr Dean Plng & Inst Effectiveness .... Dr. Chialin HSIEH
28 Dean of Equity & Inclusion .... Dr. Sabrina T. KWIST
75 Dean Career Tech Educ & Social Sci .... Vacant
79 Dean of Liberal Arts .... Ms. Nancy YBARRA
81 Dean of Math & Sciences .... Dr. A'kilah MOORE
103 Dean Workforce & Econ Development .... Ms. Natalie HANNUM
38 Dean Counseling & Student Support .... Mr. Jeffrey BENFORD
121 Dean of Student Success .... Mr. David BELMAN
66 Assoc Dean Nursing & Allied Health .... Vacant
07 Director of Admissions & Records .... Ms. Robin ARMOUR
124 Dir Student Success/Retention Pgrms .... Ms. Carla ROSAS
36 Director Transfer & Career Services .... Vacant
88 Dir Student Life & Intl Student Pgm .... Ms. Teresea ARCHAGA
88 Director Early Childhood Lab School .... Ms. Kathryn NIELSEN
26 Director Marketing & Media Design .... Ms. Barbara CELLA
88 Asst Dir EOPS/CARE .... Mr. Steven FREEMAN, JR.
88 Outreach/Assessment Svcs Mgr .... Mr. Jorge CEA
40 Bookstore Manager .... Mr. Robert ESTRADA
88 Manager Disability Support Services .... Ms. Virginia RICHARDS
88 Prog Mngr Workforce & Econ Dev .... Mr. David WAHL
13 Technology Systems Manager .... Mr. Mike BECKER
18 Buildings & Grounds Manager .... Mr. Russ HOLT
88 Custodial Manager .... Vacant
37 Financial Aid Supervisor .... Ms. Jennifer MA
88 Office of Instruction Supervisor .... Ms. Eileen VALENZUELA
30 Foundation Development Officer .... Dr. Trinh NGUYEN
19 Police Services .... Lt. Chad WEHRMEISTER

Copper Mountain College (B)

6162 Rotary Way, Box 1398, Joshua Tree CA 92252-6102
County: San Bernardino　FICE Identification: 035424
Unit ID: 395362
Telephone: (760) 366-3791　Carnegie Class: Assoc/HT-High Trad
FAX Number: (760) 366-5255　Calendar System: Semester
URL: www.cmccd.edu
Established: 1999　Annual Undergrad Tuition & Fees (In-District): $1,112
Enrollment: 1,694　Coed
Affiliation or Control: State/Local　IRS Status: 170(c)1
Highest Offering: Associate Degree
Accreditation: WJ

01 Superintendent/President .... Mr. Jeff CUMMINGS
05 VP of Academic and Student Success .... Dr. David NORTON
20 Dean of Instruction .... Mr. Zachary GINDER
32 Assoc Dean Student Success/Equity .... Ms. Jane ABELL
15 Chief Human Resources Ofcr .... Ms. Bonnie BILGER
18 Director of Facilities & Operations .... Mr. Jerry PHIPPS
102 Executive Director of Foundation .... Ms. Sandy SMITH
10 Chief Business Officer .... Ms. Meredith PLUMMER
35 Associate Dean of Student Services .... Mr. Brian HEINEMANN
108 Dir of Institutional Effectiveness .... Mr. Jacob KEVARI
76 Dir Hlth Science-Registered Nursing .... Ms. Christi BLAUWKAMP
13 Director of Information Systems .... Mr. Steve KEMP
26 Public Relations & Event Specialist .... Ms. Jolie ALPIN
04 Executive Asst to the President .... Ms. Karen COGHILL
07 Admissions & Records Specialist .... Ms. Lynda BURNS
08 Head Librarian .... Ms. Carolyn HOPKINS
41 Athletic Director .... Mr. Devin AYE

Cuesta College (C)

PO Box 8106, San Luis Obispo CA 93403-8106
County: San Luis Obispo　FICE Identification: 001192
Unit ID: 113193
Telephone: (805) 546-3100　Carnegie Class: Assoc/HT-Mix Trad/Non
FAX Number: N/A　Calendar System: Semester
URL: www.cuesta.edu
Established: 1963　Annual Undergrad Tuition & Fees (In-District): $1,234
Enrollment: 9,600　Coed
Affiliation or Control: State/Local　IRS Status: 501(c)3
Highest Offering: Associate Degree
Accreditation: WJ, EMT

01 Superintendent/President .... Dr. Gilbert H. STORK
05 VP/Asst Supt Academic Affairs .... Dr. Deborah WULFF
10 VP/Asst Supt Administrative Svcs .... Mr. Dan TROY
32 VP/Asst Supt Student Svcs Col Ctrs .... Dr. Mark SANCHEZ
12 Dean North Co Campus/S Co Ctr .... Dr. Maria ESCOBEDO
35 Dean of Student Services .... Ms. Catherine RIEDSTRA
111 Exec Dir Found/Inst Advancement .... Ms. Shannon HILL
08 Director Library/Lrng Resources/DE .... Vacant
88 Coordinator Student Life/Leadership .... Dr. Anthony GUTIERREZ
13 Exec Director Info Sys and Tech .... Mr. Keith STEARNS
66 Director of Nursing .... Ms. Marcia SCOTT
15 Vice Pres Human Resource/Labor Rels .... Ms. Melissa RICHERSON
19 Director of Public Safety .... Mr. Bryan MILLARD
40 Director of Bookstore .... Ms. Trudy BELL
41 Director of Athletics .... Mr. Robert MARIUCCI
18 Dir Facilities Svcs/Plng/Cap Proj .... Mr. Terry REECE
38 Dir Counseling and Outreach .... Vacant
103 Dir Workforce Econ Devel Cmty Pgm .... Dr. Matthew GREEN
23 Coordinator of Health Services .... Ms. Joan DUFFY
81 Dean Acad Affs Sciences & Math .... Dr. Jason CURTIS
79 Dean Acad Affs Arts/Human/Soc Sci .... Ms. Madeline MEDEIROS
103 Dean Acad Affs Workforce Econ Dev .... Dr. John CASCAMO
07 Director of Admissions & Records .... Ms. Kristin PIMENTEL
09 Director of Institutional Research .... Dr. Ryan CARTNAL
21 Director Fiscal Services .... Mr. Chris GREEN
102 Director Foundation Programs .... Ms. Karen TACKET
88 Director Foundation Fiscal Services .... Mr. Richard CAMARILLO
25 Director of Grant Development .... Ms. Janet SHEPHARD
04 Executive Asst to President .... Mr. Todd FREDERICK

The Culinary Institute of America at Greystone (D)

2555 Main Street, Saint Helena CA 94574-9504
Telephone: (707) 967-1100　Identification: 666260
Accreditation: &M

† Regional accreditation is carried under the parent institution in Hyde Park, NY.

Deep Springs College (E)

HC 72 Box 45001, Via Dyer, NV 89010-9803
County: Inyo　FICE Identification: 001194
Unit ID: 113528
Telephone: (760) 872-2000　Carnegie Class: Not Classified
FAX Number: (760) 874-7077　Calendar System: Other
URL: www.deepsprings.edu
Established: 1917　Annual Undergrad Tuition & Fees: $0
Enrollment: N/A　Male
Affiliation or Control: Independent Non-Profit　IRS Status: 501(c)3
Highest Offering: Associate Degree
Accreditation: WJ

01 President .... Mr. David NEIDORF
05 Academic Dean .... Ms. Amity WILCZEK
88 Ranch Manager .... Mr. Tim GIPSON
10 Director of Operations .... Mr. Padraic MACLEISH
30 Development Director .... Mr. John DEWIS
06 Registrar/Librarian .... Ms. Gwen VON KLAN
21 Office Manager .... Ms. Niki FRISHMAN
88 Chef/BH Manager .... Ms. Martha CLARK
88 Farm Manager/Maintenance .... Mr. Noah BEYELER

† A scholarship covers the costs of tuition, room, and board for every student.

Dell'Arte International School of Physical Theatre (F)

P.O. Box 816, 131 H Street, Blue Lake CA 95525
County: Humboldt　FICE Identification: 030256
Unit ID: 113537
Telephone: (707) 668-5663　Carnegie Class: Spec-4-yr-Arts
FAX Number: (707) 668-5665　Calendar System: Other
URL: www.dellarte.com
Established: 1975　Annual Graduate Tuition & Fees: N/A
Enrollment: 38　Coed
Affiliation or Control: Independent Non-Profit　IRS Status: 501(c)3
Highest Offering: Master's; No Undergraduates
Accreditation: THEA

01 Executive Director .... Ms. Fran BEATTY
05 Producing Artistic Director .... Mr. Michael FIELDS
10 Chief Financial Officer .... Ms. Stephanie WITZEL
06 School Administrator/Registrar .... Vacant
07 Director of Admissions .... Mr. Matt CHAPMAN

Design Institute of San Diego (G)

8555 Commerce Avenue, San Diego CA 92121-2685
County: San Diego　FICE Identification: 022980
Unit ID: 113582
Telephone: (858) 566-1200　Carnegie Class: Spec-4-yr-Arts
FAX Number: (858) 566-2711　Calendar System: Semester
URL: www.disd.edu
Established: 1977　Annual Undergrad Tuition & Fees: $20,410
Enrollment: 148　Coed
Affiliation or Control: Proprietary　IRS Status: Proprietary
Highest Offering: Baccalaureate
Accreditation: ACICS, CIDA

01 President .... Mr. Arthur ROSENSTEIN
11 Campus Director/CEO .... Ms. Margot DOUCETTE
10 Chief Financial Officer .... Mr. Dennis DOUCETTE
05 Program Director .... Ms. Natalia WORDEN
07 Admissions .... Ms. Liz BARRY
37 Director Financial Aid .... Ms. Jackie GLORIA
32 Director of Student Services .... Ms. Tena MOIOLA
08 Librarian .... Ms. Lisa SCHATTMAN
06 Registrar .... Ms. Tracy GULINO
36 Director Student Placement .... Mr. Richard HESS

DeVry University - Pomona Campus (H)

901 Corporate Center Drive, Pomona CA 91768-2642
Telephone: (909) 622-8866　FICE Identification: 023329
Accreditation: &NH, ENGT

† Regional accreditation is carried under the parent institution in Downers Grove, IL.

Dominican School of Philosophy and Theology (I)

2301 Vine Street, Berkeley CA 94708-1816
County: Alameda　FICE Identification: 001296
Unit ID: 113704
Telephone: (510) 849-2030　Carnegie Class: Spec-4-yr-Faith
FAX Number: (510) 849-1372　Calendar System: Semester
URL: www.dspt.edu
Established: 1932　Annual Undergrad Tuition & Fees: N/A
Enrollment: 57　Coed
Affiliation or Control: Roman Catholic　IRS Status: 501(c)3
Highest Offering: Master's
Accreditation: WC, THEOL

01 President .... Fr. Peter ROGERS
05 Academic Dean .... Rev. Christopher M. RENZ
10 Vice Pres Finance/Administration .... Mr. Ian BROOKS
07 Director of Admissions/Recruitment .... Mr. Aaron ANDERSON
06 Registrar .... Sr. Francis Marie SEALE
105 Director of Communications .... Ms. Heidi MCKENNA
30 Director of Development .... Mr. Marc ROVETTI

Dominican University of California (J)

50 Acacia Avenue, San Rafael CA 94901-2298
County: Marin　FICE Identification: 001196
Unit ID: 113698
Telephone: (415) 457-4440　Carnegie Class: Masters/M
FAX Number: (415) 485-3205　Calendar System: Semester
URL: www.dominican.edu
Established: 1890　Annual Undergrad Tuition & Fees: $43,400
Enrollment: 1,863　Coed
Affiliation or Control: Independent Non-Profit　IRS Status: 501(c)3
Highest Offering: Master's
Accreditation: WC, #ARCPA, ART, NURSE, OT

01 President .... Dr. Mary B. MARCY
05 Vice President Academic Affairs .... Dr. Nicola PITCHFORD
10 Vice Pres Finance/Administration .... Ms. Tammi JACKSON
32 Dean of Student Affairs .... Dr. Paul RACCANELLO
84 Int Vice Pres Enrollment Mgmt .... Ms. Vickie ALLEMAN
20 Dean of General Studies .... Dr. Mojgan BEHMAND
06 AVP Academic Services & Registrar .... Ms. Marianne STICKEL
26 Senior Director of Marketing .... Ms. Kristen PEARCE
27 Director Comm & Media Relations .... Ms. Sarah GARDNER
04 Exec Assistant to the President .... Mrs. Sarita PURECE
100 Dir Board Relations/Special Events .... Ms. Jackie GENTILE
79 Dean Sch Arts/Humanities/Soc Sci .... Dr. Laura STIVERS
76 Dean Sch Health/Natural Sci .... Dr. Ruth RAMSEY
50 Dean Barowsky Sch Business .... Dr. Sam BELDONA
18 Exec Dir Facilities/Auxiliary Svcs .... Mr. Jacques CHARTON
08 University Librarian .... Mr. Gary GORKA
09 Director Institutional Research .... Mr. Christopher ANTONS
37 Director Financial Aid .... Ms. Shanon LITTLE
07 Director Undergrad Admissions .... Vacant
29 Alumni Relations Director .... Ms. Katherine KUNZ
15 Director Human Resources .... Ms. Wendy LEE
36 Career Services Manager .... Ms. Vanessa IOANNIDES
28 Dean Diversity and Equity .... Dr. Suresh APPAVOO
92 Director Honors Program .... Ms. Gigi GOKCEK
38 Director Counseling Center .... Dr. Diane SUFFRIDGE
85 Director of GEO .... Dr. Kati BELL
30 VP for Advancement .... Ms. Marly NORRIS
41 Director of Athletics .... Ms. Amy HENKELMAN
45 VP Public Affairs/University Rels .... Dr. Hanna RODRIGUEZ-FARRAR
102 Dir Foundation/Corp/Govt Relations .... Ms. Cyndi WEINGARD
108 Director of Assessment .... Dr. Matthew BRONSON

Dongguk University Los Angeles (K)

440 Shatto Place, 2nd floor, Los Angeles CA 90020
County: Los Angeles　FICE Identification: 031095
Unit ID: 122117
Telephone: (213) 487-0110　Carnegie Class: Spec-4-yr-Other Health
FAX Number: (213) 487-0527　Calendar System: Quarter
URL: www.dula.edu
Established: 1979　Annual Undergrad Tuition & Fees: N/A
Enrollment: 193　Coed
Affiliation or Control: Independent Non-Profit　IRS Status: 501(c)3
Highest Offering: Master's; No Lower Division
Accreditation: ACUP

01 President .... Dr. Seung Deok LEE
05 Dean of Academic Affairs .... Dr. John FANG

17 Clinic Director ..... Ms. Doris JOHNSON
10 Director Administrative Affairs ..... Mr. Albert KIM
21 Accounting Manager ..... Ms. Kelly KIM
04 Office Manager ..... Ms. Min PARK
06 Registrar ..... Mr. Stephen SEO
18 Facilities Manager ..... Mr. Arturo AGUIRRE

† Granted candidacy at the Doctorate level by ACAOM.

Eagle Rock College (A)

2607 Colorado Blvd, Los Angeles CA 90041
County: Los Angeles FICE Identification: 041192
Unit ID: 451005
Telephone: (323) 254-2203 Carnegie Class: Not Classified
FAX Number: (323) 254-2254 Calendar System: Semester
URL: eaglerockcollege.edu
Established: 2001 Annual Undergrad Tuition & Fees: N/A
Enrollment: N/A Coed
Affiliation or Control: Proprietary IRS Status: Proprietary
Highest Offering: Associate Degree
Accreditation: CNCE

01 President & CEO ..... Al MOAYERI
32 Exec Vice Pres Student Services ..... Ellie MIRAFTABI

East San Gabriel Valley Regional Occupational Program and Technical Center (B)

1501 W. Del Norte Street, West Covina CA 91790
County: Los Angeles FICE Identification: 031166
Unit ID: 413802
Telephone: (626) 472-5121 Carnegie Class: Assoc/HVT-High Non
FAX Number: (626) 472-5125 Calendar System: Semester
URL: www.esgvrop.org
Established: Annual Undergrad Tuition & Fees (In-District): N/A
Enrollment: 412 Coed
Affiliation or Control: State/Local IRS Status: 501(c)3
Highest Offering: Associate Degree
Accreditation: COE, MAC

01 Superintendent ..... Dr. Laurel ADLER
10 Chief Financial Officer ..... Ms. Josephine QUACH

El Camino College (C)

16007 Crenshaw Boulevard, Torrance CA 90506-0002
County: Los Angeles FICE Identification: 001197
Unit ID: 113980
Telephone: (310) 660-3670 Carnegie Class: Assoc/HT-High Trad
FAX Number: (310) 660-7798 Calendar System: Semester
URL: www.elcamino.edu
Established: 1947 Annual Undergrad Tuition & Fees (In-District): $1,142
Enrollment: 24,001 Coed
Affiliation or Control: State/Local IRS Status: 501(c)3
Highest Offering: Associate Degree
Accreditation: WJ, COARC, RAD

01 President ..... Dr. Dena P. MALONEY
05 Vice President Academic Affairs ..... Dr. Jean SHANKWEILER
11 Vice Pres Administrative Services ..... Ms. Jo Ann HIGDON
32 Vice Pres Student/Community Advance ..... Dr. Jeanie NISHIME
15 Vice Pres of Human Resources ..... Ms. Jane MIYASHIRO
111 Dean Community Advancement ..... Mr. Jose ANAYA
45 Director Research Planning ..... Ms. Irene GRAFF
72 Dean Industry & Technology ..... Dr. Stephanie RODRIGUEZ
81 Dean Math ..... Ms. Jacquelyn SIMS
50 Dean of Business ..... Dr. Virginia RAPP
83 Dean Behavioral & Social Science ..... Dr. Gloria MIRANDA
68 Dean Health/Exer/Science/Sport ..... Mr. Rory NATIVIDAD
57 Dean Fine Arts ..... Dr. Berkeley PRICE
76 Dean Natural Sciences ..... Dr. Amy GRANT
79 Dean Humanities ..... Ms. Elise GERAGHTY
121 Dean Counseling Matriculation Svcs ..... Dr. Dipte PALEL
121 Dean of Student Support Services ..... Ms. Idania REYES
13 Chief Technology Officer ..... Dr. Art LEIBLE
31 Director of Community Relations ..... Ms. Ann GARTEN
66 Director of Nursing ..... Dr. Wanda MORRIS
07 Dir Admissions/Records/Registrar ..... Mr. Bill MULROONEY
10 Chief Business Officer ..... Dr. Jo Ann HIGDON
26 Chief Public Relations Officer ..... Ms. Ann M. GARTEN
102 Executive Director Foundation ..... Ms. Andrea SALA
96 Director of Purchasing ..... Mr. Rocky BONURA
40 Director of Bookstore ..... Ms. Julie BOURLIER
19 Chief of Campus Police ..... Mr. Michael TREVIS
18 Director of Facilities Plng/Svcs ..... Mr. Tom BROWN
35 Director of Student Affairs ..... Dr. Gregory TOYA
37 Director Student Financial Aid ..... Ms. Melissa GUESS
06 Registrar ..... Mr. Bill MULROONEY
29 Director Alumni Relations ..... Ms. Andrea SALA
09 Director Institutional Research ..... Ms. Irene GRAFF
28 Director of Diversity ..... Dr. Jayne ISHIKAWA
21 Business Manager ..... Ms. Janice ELY
25 Resource Devel/Grants Coordinator ..... Ms. Andrea SALA
04 Executive Asst to President ..... Ms. Cynthia CONSTANTINO

Emperor's College of Traditional Oriental Medicine (D)

1807-B Wilshire Boulevard, Santa Monica CA 90403-5678
County: Los Angeles FICE Identification: 026090
Unit ID: 114114
Telephone: (310) 453-8300 Carnegie Class: Spec-4-yr-Other Health
FAX Number: (310) 829-3838 Calendar System: Quarter
URL: www.emperors.edu
Established: 1983 Annual Undergrad Tuition & Fees: N/A
Enrollment: 233 Coed
Affiliation or Control: Proprietary IRS Status: Proprietary
Highest Offering: Doctorate
Accreditation: ACUP

01 Chief Executive Officer/President ..... Yun KIM
05 Academic Dean ..... Jacques MORAMARCO
63 Dean of Clinical Education ..... Robert NEWMAN
10 CFO/Administrator ..... George PARK

Empire College (E)

3035 Cleveland Avenue, Santa Rosa CA 95403-2100
County: Sonoma FICE Identification: 009032
Unit ID: 114123
Telephone: (707) 546-4000 Carnegie Class: Assoc/HVT-High Trad
FAX Number: (707) 546-4058 Calendar System: Other
URL: www.empcol.edu
Established: 1961 Annual Undergrad Tuition & Fees: N/A
Enrollment: 442 Coed
Affiliation or Control: Proprietary IRS Status: Proprietary
Highest Offering: Master's
Accreditation: ACICS

01 President ..... Mr. Roy HURD
26 Vice Pres Marketing/Administration ..... Mrs. Sherie HURD

Epic Bible College & Graduate School (F)

4330 Auburn Boulevard, Sacramento CA 95841
County: Sacramento FICE Identification: 034033
Unit ID: 124487
Telephone: (916) 348-4689 Carnegie Class: Spec-4-yr-Faith
FAX Number: (916) 468-0866 Calendar System: Trimester
URL: www.EPIC.edu
Established: 1974 Annual Undergrad Tuition & Fees: $9,689
Enrollment: 186 Coed
Affiliation or Control: Independent Non-Profit IRS Status: 501(c)3
Highest Offering: Doctorate
Accreditation: TRACS

01 President ..... Dr. Ronald W. HARDEN
05 Vice President of Academics ..... Dr. Greg L. HARTLEY
58 Director Graduate Studies ..... Dr. Ed FUNK
73 Chair of Worship Arts ..... Dr. David YODER
08 Director Learning Resource ..... Rev. Dale SOLBERG
37 Director of Financial Services ..... Mr. David PINESCHI
06 Director of Records/Office Manager ..... Ms. Kathy CLARKE
106 Director of Online Program ..... Rev. John GALLEGOS
26 Director Enrollment/Marketing ..... Rev. Daniel HARDEN

Eternity Bible College (G)

2136 Winifred Street, Simi Valley CA 93063
County: Ventura Identification: 667045
Telephone: (805) 581-1233 Carnegie Class: Not Classified
FAX Number: (805) 581-1245 Calendar System: Semester
URL: www.eternitybiblecollege.com
Established: 2004 Annual Undergrad Tuition & Fees: N/A
Enrollment: N/A Coed
Affiliation or Control: Independent Non-Profit IRS Status: 501(c)3
Highest Offering: Baccalaureate
Accreditation: BI

01 President ..... Spencer MACCUISH
05 Academic Dean ..... Joshua WALKER
07 Director of Admissions ..... Mary Beth DRAGOUN
06 Registrar/Finance Manager ..... Ryan MCGLADDERY
32 Dir Student Life/Exec Asst ..... Nicole MCGLADDERY

Evangelia University (H)

2660 West Woodland Drive, Suite 200,
Anaheim CA 92801-2650
County: Orange Identification: 666640
Telephone: (714) 527-0691 Carnegie Class: Not Classified
FAX Number: (714) 527-0693 Calendar System: Other
URL: www.evangelia.edu
Established: 1999 Annual Undergrad Tuition & Fees: N/A
Enrollment: N/A Coed
Affiliation or Control: Reformed Presbyterian Church IRS Status: 501(c)3
Highest Offering: Doctorate
Accreditation: TRACS

01 President ..... Dr. David H. SHIN
05 Dean of Academic Affairs ..... Dr. Soo Young LEE
11 Dean Admin/Chief Operating Officer ..... Ki Won HAN
32 Dean of Student Affairs ..... Ki Won HAN
06 Registrar/Foreign Student Advisor ..... Charley LEE
57 Chair Masters of Arts Program ..... Cha Hi WON
106 Director of Distance Education ..... Soohae KANG

Ezra University (I)

2064 Marengo Street, Los Angeles CA 90033
County: Los Angeles Identification: 667316
Telephone: (323) 221-1024 Carnegie Class: Not Classified
FAX Number: (323) 221-1025 Calendar System: Quarter
URL: www.ezrauniversity.org
Established: 1997 Annual Undergrad Tuition & Fees: N/A
Enrollment: N/A Coed
Affiliation or Control: Independent Non-Profit IRS Status: 501(c)3
Highest Offering: Master's
Accreditation: @BI

01 President ..... Dr. John PYEON

Fashion Institute of Design and Merchandising-Orange County (J)

17590 Gillette Avenue, Irvine CA 92614-5610
Telephone: (888) 974-3436 Identification: 666004
Accreditation: &WC, ART

† Regional accreditation is carried under the parent institution in Los Angeles, CA.

Feather River College (K)

570 Golden Eagle Avenue, Quincy CA 95971-9124
County: Plumas FICE Identification: 008597
Unit ID: 114433
Telephone: (530) 283-0202 Carnegie Class: Assoc/HT-High Non
FAX Number: (530) 283-3757 Calendar System: Semester
URL: www.frc.edu
Established: 1968 Annual Undergrad Tuition & Fees (In-District): $1,461
Enrollment: 1,842 Coed
Affiliation or Control: State/Local IRS Status: 501(c)3
Highest Offering: Baccalaureate
Accreditation: WJ

01 Superintendent/President ..... Dr. Kevin TRUTNA
10 Chief Financial Officer ..... Mr. Jim SCOUBES
05 Chief Instructional Officer ..... Dr. Derek LERCH
32 Chief Student Services Officer ..... Ms. Carlie MCCARTHY
15 Director Human Resources/EEO ..... Mr. David BURRIS
18 Director of Facilities/CTO ..... Mr. Nick BOYD
06 Registrar/Dir of Admissions ..... Ms. Leslie MIKESELL
37 Director Student Financial Aid ..... Mr. Andre VAN DER VELDEN
96 Purchasing Agent ..... Ms. Tamara CLINE
04 Administrative Asst to President ..... Ms. Cynthia HALL
09 Director of Institutional Research ..... Dr. Agnes KOOS

FIDM/Fashion Institute of Design & Merchandising-San Diego (L)

350 10th Avenue, 3rd Floor, San Diego CA 92101
Telephone: (619) 235-2049 Identification: 666005
Accreditation: &WC, ART

† Regional accreditation is carried under the parent institution in Los Angeles, CA.

FIDM/Fashion Institute of Design and Merchandising-San Francisco (M)

55 Stockton Street, San Francisco CA 94108-5829
Telephone: (415) 675-5200 FICE Identification: 013041
Accreditation: &WC, ART

† Regional accreditation is carried under the parent institution in Los Angeles, CA.

FIDM/Fashion Institute of Design and Merchandising-Los Angeles (N)

919 S Grand Avenue, Los Angeles CA 90015-1421
County: Los Angeles FICE Identification: 011112
Unit ID: 114354
Telephone: (213) 624-1200 Carnegie Class: Spec-4-yr-Arts
FAX Number: (213) 624-9354 Calendar System: Quarter
URL: www.fidm.edu
Established: 1969 Annual Undergrad Tuition & Fees: $31,760
Enrollment: 2,814 Coed
Affiliation or Control: Proprietary IRS Status: Proprietary
Highest Offering: Baccalaureate
Accreditation: WC, ART

01 President ..... Ms. Tonian HOHBERG
10 Vice President Finance ..... Ms. Lynette WALKER
46 Vice President Planning ..... Ms. Vivien LOWY
05 Vice President Education ..... Ms. Barbara BUNDY
108 Dean of Accreditation ..... Ms. Lisa SCHOENING
08 Director Library ..... Ms. Kathy BAILON
06 Registrar ..... Mr. Michael GILBERT
37 Director Financial Aid ..... Mr. Chris JENNINGS
26 Director Public Rels/Publicity ..... Ms. Shirley WILSON
09 Dir Institutional Effectiveness ..... Dr. Andrea D. HELEKAR
38 Personal Counselor ..... Ms. Jessica CATTANI

96 Director College Services .... Ms. Ella VAN NORT
07 Exec Director of Admissions .... Ms. Susan ARONSON
13 Chief Info Technology Officer (CIO) .... Ms. Suzanna GRUESER
15 Human Resources Manager .... Ms. Julie Ann OTTESON
04 Executive Asst to President .... Ms. Megan NOWAK
104 Director International Affairs .... Ms. Sarah REPETTO
105 Director Web Mktg Ops/Publications .... Mr. Michael KAMINSKI
18 Director of FIDM Facilities .... Mr. John (Buddy) BOLOGNONE
19 Director of Security .... Mr. Todd J. ANDERSON
22 Title IX Coordinator .... Ms. Sheryl RABINOVICH
29 Director Alumni Relations .... Ms. Carrie SHAY
32 Director of Student Activities .... Ms. Caitlin MADDEN
36 Executive Director Industry Relati .... Ms. Sharon RYAN
39 Housing Administrator .... Ms. Sonialina ERWIN
53 Dean of Education .... Ms. Sheryl RABINOVICH
86 Director Government Relations .... Ms. Norine FULLER
90 Director Academic Computing .... Mr. Dave MELONE

Fielding Graduate University (A)

2020 De La Vina Street, Santa Barbara CA 93105-3538
County: Santa Barbara FICE Identification: 020961
Unit ID: 114549
Telephone: (800) 340-1099 Carnegie Class: DU-Mod
FAX Number: (805) 687-9793 Calendar System: Trimester
URL: www.fielding.edu
Established: 1974 Annual Graduate Tuition & Fees: N/A
Enrollment: 1,168 Coed
Affiliation or Control: Independent Non-Profit IRS Status: 501(c)3
Highest Offering: Doctorate; No Undergraduates
Accreditation: WC, CLPSY

01 President .... Dr. Katrina ROGERS
04 Exec Asst to President .... Ms. Maisee THAO
05 Provost & Senior Vice President .... Dr. Gerald PORTER
09 VP Strategic Initiative/Research .... Mr. Orlando TAYLOR
10 VP and Chief Financial Officer .... Ms. Lisa LEWIS
45 VP Institutional Planning & Effect .... Dr. Monique L. SNOWDEN
15 Vice President of Human Resources .... Ms. Amy RAMOS
06 Registrar/Dir Enrollment Services .... Ms. Bridget BRADY

Five Branches University, Graduate School of Traditional Chinese Medicine (B)

1885 Lundy Avenue, Suite 108, San Jose CA 95131
County: Santa Clara Identification: 667008
Telephone: (408) 260-0208 Carnegie Class: Not Classified
FAX Number: (408) 261-3166 Calendar System: Trimester
URL: www.fivebranches.edu
Established: 2005 Annual Undergrad Tuition & Fees: N/A
Enrollment: N/A Coed
Affiliation or Control: Proprietary IRS Status: Proprietary
Highest Offering: Doctorate; No Lower Division
Accreditation: ACUP

01 President/CEO .... Ron ZAIDMAN
05 VP Academic Affairs .... Joanna ZHAO
10 VP Finance .... Liana CHEN
13 VP Operations .... Gina HUANG
06 Registrar .... Ling ZHANG
58 Director of Doctoral Program .... Robyn GRIEVE
26 Director of Marketing .... Sean ZAIDMAN
37 Director of Financial Aid .... Daryl CULLEN
58 Associate Director Doctoral .... E-Sing HONG
84 Director of Enrollment .... Alex HU
56 Extension Program Admin .... Lykos YANG
23 Clinic Manager .... Joyce HE
88 Facility Manager .... Songsong GAO

Five Branches University, Graduate School of Traditional Chinese Medicine (C)

200 7th Avenue, Santa Cruz CA 95062-4669
County: Santa Cruz FICE Identification: 031313
Unit ID: 114585
Telephone: (831) 476-9424 Carnegie Class: Spec-4-yr-Other Health
FAX Number: (831) 476-8928 Calendar System: Trimester
URL: www.fivebranches.edu
Established: 1984 Annual Undergrad Tuition & Fees: N/A
Enrollment: 332 Coed
Affiliation or Control: Proprietary IRS Status: Proprietary
Highest Offering: Doctorate; No Lower Division
Accreditation: ACUP

01 President & CEO .... Ron ZAIDMAN
05 Vice President of Academic Affairs .... Joanna ZHAO
11 Director of Operations .... Gina HUANG
10 Chief Accounting Officer .... Liana CHEN
26 Dir of Marketing & Public Relations .... Ali POLK
08 Librarian .... Jim EMDY
17 Clinic Quality Control Director .... Sally LEWIS
06 Registrar .... Ling ZHANG
07 Admissions Director .... Eleonor MENDELSON
37 Director Student Financial Aid .... Mecca MATILDA
32 Director of Student Services .... Ana LOBATO
56 Director of Extension Programs .... Sumheda GOH
88 Student Accounts Manager .... Kayoko YAMAMOTO

*Foothill-De Anza Community College District System Office (D)

12345 El Monte Road, Los Altos Hills CA 94022-4597
County: Santa Clara FICE Identification: 009020
Unit ID: 114831
Telephone: (650) 949-6100 Carnegie Class: N/A
FAX Number: (650) 941-6289
URL: www.fhda.edu

01 Chancellor .... Dr. Judy C. MINER
10 Vice Chancellor Business Services .... Mr. Kevin MCELROY
15 Vice Chancellor Human Resources .... Ms. Dorene NOVOTNY
13 Vice Chancellor Technology .... Mr. Joseph MOREAU
18 Exec Dir Facilities/Operations .... Mr. Steve KITCHEN

*De Anza College (E)

21250 Stevens Creek Boulevard, Cupertino CA 95014-5793
County: Santa Clara FICE Identification: 004480
Unit ID: 113333
Telephone: (408) 864-5678 Carnegie Class: Assoc/HT-Mix Trad/Non
FAX Number: (408) 864-8238 Calendar System: Quarter
URL: www.deanza.edu
Established: 1967 Annual Undergrad Tuition & Fees (In-District): $1,549
Enrollment: 22,512 Coed
Affiliation or Control: State/Local IRS Status: 501(c)3
Highest Offering: Associate Degree
Accreditation: WJ, MLTAD

02 President .... Dr. Brian MURPHY
05 Vice Pres of Instruction .... Ms. Christina ESPINOSA-PIEB
32 Vice Pres of Student Services .... Dr. Stacey A. COOK
10 VP Finance/College Operations .... Ms. Susan CHEU
20 Assoc Vice Pres Instruction .... Ms. Lorrie RANCK
35 Dean Student Development/EOPS .... Ms. Michele LEBLEU BURNS
38 Dean Counseling & Matriculation .... Dr. Sheila WHITE-DANIELS
07 Dean Admissions & Records .... Ms. Tamika WARD
37 Director Student Financial Aid .... Ms. Lisa MANDY
15 Director Personnel Services .... Mr. Bret WATSON
18 Assoc Vice Pres College Operations .... Ms. Pam GREY
26 AVP Communications & External Rel .... Ms. Marisa SPATAFORE
102 Exec Director Foundation .... Ms. Tess CHANDLER
28 Director of Diversity .... Dr. Veronica NEAL
96 Director of Purchasing .... Ms. Annette PEREZ
36 Supervisor Student Placement .... Ms. Casie WHEAT
09 Institutional Researcher .... Dr. Mallory NEWELL
06 Supervisor Admissions and Records .... Mr. Barry JOHNSON
04 Administrative Asst to President .... Ms. Tina WOO
08 Head Librarian .... Mr. Tom DOLEN
13 Chief Info Technology Officer (CIO) .... Mr. Joe MOREAU
41 Athletic Director .... Mr. Kulwant SINGH
50 Dean Business/Comp Sys/Applied Tech .... Mr. Moaty FAYEK
86 Director Government Relations .... Dr. Jerry ROSENBERG

*Foothill College (F)

12345 El Monte Road, Los Altos Hills CA 94022-4599
County: Santa Clara FICE Identification: 001199
Unit ID: 114716
Telephone: (650) 949-7777 Carnegie Class: Assoc/HT-High Non
FAX Number: (650) 949-7375 Calendar System: Quarter
URL: www.foothill.edu
Established: 1957 Annual Undergrad Tuition & Fees (In-District): $1,551
Enrollment: 15,448 Coed
Affiliation or Control: State/Local IRS Status: 501(c)3
Highest Offering: Baccalaureate
Accreditation: WJ, COARC, DA, DH, DMS, EMT, RAD

02 President .... Ms. Thuy NGUYEN
04 Assistant to the President .... Mr. Peter CHOW
10 VP Finance & Admin Services .... Vacant
05 VP Instruction & Inst Research .... Dr. Kristy LISLE
32 VP Student Services .... Dr. Denise SWETT
20 Associate VP Instruction .... Dr. Andrew LAMANQUE
35 Associate VP Student Services .... Ms. Laureen BALDUCCI
21 Associate VP Finance & Admin Svcs .... Mr. Bret WATSON
35 Dean Student Affairs & Activities .... Vacant
38 Dean Counseling & Special Programs .... Ms. Lan TRUONG
12 Dean Sunnyvale Center .... Ms. Dawn GIRARDELLI
88 Dean Disabled Stdnt Svcs/Vet Pgms .... Ms. Teresa ONG
40 Director Bookstore .... Mr. Romeo PAULE
84 Dean Enroll Svcs & Intl Stdnt Pgm .... Ms. Nazy GALOYAN
37 Director Financial Aid .... Mr. Kevin HARRAL
26 Dir Marketing & Public Relations .... Ms. Andrea HANSTEIN
22 Director of Equity Programs .... Dr. Elaine KUO
23 Director Health Services .... Vacant
76 Dean Biology & Health Sciences .... Dr. Nanette SOLVASON
50 Dean Business & Social Sciences .... Mr. Kurt HUEG
106 Dean Foothill Online Learning .... Dr. Judy BAKER
57 Dean Fine Arts & Communications .... Mr. Simon PENNINGTON
79 Dean Language Arts & LRC .... Mr. Paul STARER
81 Dean Physical Sci/Math & Engr .... Mr. Ram SUBRAMANIAM
09 Supervisor Institutional Research .... Ms. Lisa LY
41 Athletic Director .... Mr. Mike TEIJEIRO
103 Associate VP Workforce .... Vacant

Franciscan School of Theology (G)

4050 Mission Avenue, Oceanside CA 92057
County: San Diego FICE Identification: 011792
Unit ID: 114734
Telephone: (760) 547-1800 Carnegie Class: Spec-4-yr-Faith
FAX Number: (760) 547-1806 Calendar System: Semester
URL: www.fst.edu
Established: 1968 Annual Graduate Tuition & Fees: N/A
Enrollment: 48 Coed
Affiliation or Control: Independent Non-Profit IRS Status: 501(c)3
Highest Offering: Master's; No Undergraduates
Accreditation: WC, THEOL

01 President .... Fr. Michael J. HIGGINS, TOR
05 VP for Academic Affairs and Rector .... Fr. Garrett GALVIN, OFM
06 Registrar .... Ms. Jackie GAMBLE
07 Co-Director of Recruitment .... Ms. Gigi BETANCOURT
07 Co-Director of Recruitment .... Ms. Christine AVELLA
30 Executive Director of Development .... Ms. Randi QUAID
10 Chief Financial Officer .... Ms. Kimberly RENNA

Fremont College (H)

18000 Studebaker Road, Suite 900A, Cerritos CA 90703
County: Los Angeles FICE Identification: 030399
Unit ID: 372073
Telephone: (562) 809-5100 Carnegie Class: Bac/Assoc-Assoc Dom
FAX Number: (562) 809-7100 Calendar System: Other
URL: www.fremont.edu
Established: 1985 Annual Undergrad Tuition & Fees: N/A
Enrollment: 350 Coed
Affiliation or Control: Proprietary IRS Status: Proprietary
Highest Offering: Baccalaureate
Accreditation: ACCSC

01 Chancellor/CEO .... Dr. Sabrina KAY
05 Chief Academic Officer .... Jonathan DAITCH
11 Director of Operations .... Tony WONG
36 Director of Student Placement .... Tasha SUA
37 Director of Financial Aid .... Joanne BRENNAN

Fremont College (I)

3440 Wilshire Blvd, 10th Floor, Los Angeles CA 90010
Telephone: (213) 355-7777 Identification: 770553
Accreditation: ACCSC

Fresno Pacific University (J)

1717 S Chestnut Avenue, Fresno CA 93702-4798
County: Fresno FICE Identification: 001253
Unit ID: 114813
Telephone: (559) 453-2000 Carnegie Class: Masters/L
FAX Number: (559) 453-2007 Calendar System: Semester
URL: www.fresno.edu
Established: 1944 Annual Undergrad Tuition & Fees: $29,320
Enrollment: 3,342 Coed
Affiliation or Control: Mennonite Brethren Church IRS Status: 501(c)3
Highest Offering: Master's
Accreditation: WC, NURSE, @SW, THEOL

01 President .... Dr. Joseph JONES
05 Interim Provost/Senior VP .... Dr. Dale SIMMONS
10 Vice President Finance .... Mr. Robert LIPPERT
26 Vice Pres Integrated Marketing .... Mrs. Diana BATES MOCK
11 Vice Pres of Operations .... Vacant
84 Vice Pres Enrollment Mgmt .... Mr. Jon ENDICOTT
111 VP for Advancement/Univ Relations .... Mr. Mark ISAAC
50 Interim Dean School of Business .... Dr. Susan COX
79 Dean Sch of Human/Rel/Soc Sci .... Dr. Ron HERMS
53 Dean School of Education .... Dr. Gary GRAMENZ
78 Dean School of Natural Sciences .... Dr. Karen CIANCI
42 Dean of Spiritual Formation .... Rev. Angulus WILSON
32 Vice President Student Life .... Dr. Randy WORDEN
06 Registrar .... Mr. Michael ALLEN
08 Director of Library .... Mr. Kevin ENNS-REMPEL
36 Director of Career Resource Center .... Ms. Alicia ANDRADE
15 Human Resources Director .... Mr. Brent CORSON
27 Publications Director .... Mr. Wayne STEFFEN
29 Director Alumni Development .... Ms. Ali SENA
37 Interim Director of Financial Aid .... Ms. Stacie BENEDICT
41 Athletic Director .... Mr. Aaron HENDERSON
19 Chief of Campus Safety .... Mr. Javier CAMPOS
26 Chief Public Relations Officer .... Mr. Wayne STEFFENS
104 Dir International Pgms/Svcs Ofc .... Vacant
07 Director of Admissions .... Mrs. Krista BROOKS
18 Facilities Manager .... Mr. Gary METCALF
04 Executive Asst to President .... Ms. Gwenevera E. BURKS
88 Seminary President .... Dr. Terry BRENSINGER
102 Dir Foundation/Corporate Relations .... Mr. Mark DEFFENBACHER
112 Director Major Gifts .... Mrs. Karin CHAO-BUSHOVEN
21 Controller .... Mr. Orren WANG
09 Director of Institutional Research .... Ms. Maribel VIVEROS
28 Director of Diversity .... Vacant
108 Assoc Prov Inst Effectiveness .... Dr. Cindy CARTER
13 Exec Director ITS .... Mr. Dave RICHERT
105 Director Web Services .... Mr. Justin GABLE
39 Director Student Housing .... Ms. Pam SCHOCK

Fuller Theological Seminary (K)

135 N Oakland, Pasadena CA 91182-1780
County: Los Angeles FICE Identification: 001200
Unit ID: 114840
Telephone: (626) 584-5200 Carnegie Class: Spec-4-yr-Faith
FAX Number: (626) 795-8767 Calendar System: Quarter
URL: www.fuller.edu

Established: 1947 Annual Graduate Tuition & Fees: N/A
Enrollment: 2,532 Coed
Affiliation or Control: Independent Non-Profit IRS Status: 501(c)3
Highest Offering: Doctorate; No Undergraduates
Accreditation: WC, CLPSY, THEOL

01 President Dr. Mark A. LABBERTON
05 Provost Dr. Joel B. GREEN
88 Senior Advisor Mr. Bill CLARK
10 Chief Financial Officer Mr. Lenny MOON
30 Vice President Development Mr. Jon YASUDA
26 Vice President Comm/Mktg & Admiss Mrs. Irene NELLER
88 Vice President/Chief of Leadership Dr. Tod BOLSINGER
73 Dean School of Theology Dr. Joel B. GREEN
83 Dean School of Psychology Dr. Mari L. CLEMENTS
88 Dean School Intercultural Studies Dr. Scott W. SUNQUIST
84 Assoc Prov Enroll Mgmt/Voc Form Dr. Kevin OSBORN
108 Accreditation Liaison Officer Dr. Mari L. CLEMENTS
09 Director of Institutional Research Dr. Dave SCOTT
88 Assoc Dean Doctor of Ministry Pgm Dr. Kurt FREDRICKSON
06 Registrar Mr. David E. KIEFER
15 Exec Director of HR & Org Dev Ms. Bernadette (BJ) BARBER
35 Assistant Dean of Students Mr. Sam BANG
07 Exec Director Admissions Mr. Steve SMITH
11 Director of Finance and Operations Mr. Al SEJCEK
39 Director of Housing Services Ms. Inge-Lise TITHERADGE
04 Assistant to President Mr. Mike DIMARCANGELO
18 Facilities Director Mr. Nathan MERRITT
109 Director of Auxiliary Services Mrs. Jeanne HANDOJO
43 General Counsel Mr. Brent S. KAMPE
85 Dir Student Affs/International Svcs Mr. Sam BANG
37 Director Student Financial Services Mr. David RICHARDS
106 Director Teaching and Learning Mr. Tommy LISTER
08 Director of the DAH Library Dr. Jeffrey A. WALDROP
19 Chief of Campus Safety Mr. Gary L. MEJIA
29 Director Alumni Engagement Ms. Bert JACKLITCH

Gateway Seminary (A)

3210 E. Guasti Rd, Ontario CA 91761-8642
County: San Bernadino FICE Identification: 001204
Unit ID: 115047
Telephone: (909) 687-1800 Carnegie Class: Not Classified
FAX Number: N/A Calendar System: Semester
URL: www.gs.edu
Established: 1944 Annual Graduate Tuition & Fees: N/A
Enrollment: N/A Coed
Affiliation or Control: Southern Baptist IRS Status: 501(c)3
Highest Offering: Doctorate; No Undergraduates
Accreditation: WC, THEOL

00 President Emeritus Dr. William O. CREWS
01 President/Chairman of the Faculty Dr. Jeff IORG
30 Vice Pres Institutional Advancement Dr. Jeff JONES
10 Vice Pres Strategic Services/CFO Mr. Gary GROAT
05 Vice President Academic Affairs Dr. D. Michael MARTIN
84 VP Enrollment/Student Svcs/Dn Stdts Dr. Adam GROZA
21 VP Business Services Mr. Tom HIXSON
21 Controller Mr. Harry WEAVER
06 Registrar Ms. Jennifer PEACH
08 Director of Library Services Dr. Bob PHILLIPS
12 Director PNW Campus Dr. Mark BRADLEY
12 Director Arizona Campus Dr. Dallas BIVINS
12 Director Rocky Mountain Campus Dr. Steve VETETO
13 Director Information Technology Mr. Steve POLCYN
15 Director Personnel Services Vacant
18 Chief Facilities/Physical Plant Mr. Robert DVORAK
44 Director of Development Mr. Jay BADRY
07 Director Enrollment Management Ms. Max STABENOW
32 Director of Student Life Mr. Shane TANIGAWA

Gavilan College (B)

5055 Santa Teresa Boulevard, Gilroy CA 95020-9599
County: Santa Clara FICE Identification: 001202
Unit ID: 114938
Telephone: (408) 848-4800 Carnegie Class: Assoc/HT-High Non
FAX Number: (408) 848-4801 Calendar System: Semester
URL: www.gavilan.edu
Established: 1919 Annual Undergrad Tuition & Fees (In-District): $1,166
Enrollment: 6,119 Coed
Affiliation or Control: State/Local IRS Status: 501(c)3
Highest Offering: Associate Degree
Accreditation: WJ

01 Superintendent/President Dr. Kathleen A. ROSE
05 Vice Pres Academic Affairs Dr. Michele BRESSO
11 Vice Pres Administrative Services Mr. Fred HARRIS
32 Vice President Student Services Ms. Kathleen MOBERG
06 Director of Admissions and Records Ms. Candice WHITNEY
08 Head Librarian Dr. Douglas ACHTERMAN
37 Director Student Financial Aid Ms. Veronica MARTINEZ
09 Director of Institutional Research Dr. Peter WRUCK
15 Director Human Resources Dr. Eric RAMONES
18 Director of Facilities and Maint Mr. Jeff GOPP
13 Int Dir Computing & Information Mgt Mr. Kyle BILLUPS
26 Director Public Information Ms. Jan CHARGIN
23 Student Health Nurse Ms. Alice DUFRESNE-REYES
41 Dean of Kinesiology and Athletics Mr. Ron HANNON
40 Manager Bookstore Ms. Laura JIMINEZ
49 Dean Liberal Art and Sciences Ms. Fran LOZANO
72 Dean Career Technical Education Ms. Sherrean CARR
07 Director of Admissions Ms. Candice WHITNEY
10 Chief Business Officer Ms. Wade ELLIS
96 Purchasing Specialist Ms. Jeanne ALAMADARI

Glendale Career College (C)

240 N. Brand Blvd, Lower Level, Glendale CA 91203
County: Los Angeles FICE Identification: 023385
Unit ID: 115010
Telephone: (818) 243-1131 Carnegie Class: Not Classified
FAX Number: (818) 243-6028 Calendar System: Semester
URL: www.glendalecareer.com
Established: 1946 Annual Undergrad Tuition & Fees: N/A
Enrollment: 287 Coed
Affiliation or Control: Proprietary IRS Status: Proprietary
Highest Offering: Associate Degree
Accreditation: ABHES, SURGT, SURTEC

01 Campus Director Mr. Rick HOKE

Glendale Community College (D)

1500 N Verdugo Road, Glendale CA 91208-2894
County: Los Angeles FICE Identification: 001203
Unit ID: 115001
Telephone: (818) 240-1000 Carnegie Class: Assoc/MT-VT-High Trad
FAX Number: (818) 549-9436 Calendar System: Semester
URL: www.glendale.edu
Established: 1927 Annual Undergrad Tuition & Fees (In-District): $1,175
Enrollment: 15,588 Coed
Affiliation or Control: State/Local IRS Status: 501(c)3
Highest Offering: Associate Degree
Accreditation: WJ

01 Superintendent/President Dr. David VIAR
11 Exec Vice Pres Administrative Svcs Dr. Anthony CULPEPPER
05 Vice Pres Instructional Services Mr. Michael RITTERBROWN
32 Vice President Student Services Dr. Ricardo PEREZ
51 Admn Dn Workforce Dev Cont/Cmty Ed Mr. Alfred RAMIREZ
15 Assoc VP Human Resources Ms. Teyanna WILLIAMS
45 Dean Research/Planning/Grants Dr. Edward KARPP
07 Director Admissions & Records Ms. Michelle MORA
20 Int Dean Instructional Services Ms. Agnes EGUARAS
103 Dean Workforce Development Ms. Jan SWINTON
32 Dean Student Affairs Dr. Paul SCHLOSSMAN
35 Dean of Student Services Dr. Robert HILL
37 Assoc Dean Stdnt Financial Aid Svcs Ms. Patricia HURLEY
10 Director Business Services Ms. Susan COURTEY
102 Exec Director College Foundation Ms. Lisa BROOKS

Golden Gate University (E)

536 Mission Street, San Francisco CA 94105-2968
County: San Francisco FICE Identification: 001205
Unit ID: 115083
Telephone: (415) 442-7000 Carnegie Class: Masters/L
FAX Number: (415) 495-2671 Calendar System: Trimester
URL: www.ggu.edu
Established: 1901 Annual Undergrad Tuition & Fees: $15,205
Enrollment: 2,735 Coed
Affiliation or Control: Independent Non-Profit IRS Status: 501(c)3
Highest Offering: Doctorate
Accreditation: WC, LAW

01 President Dr. David J. FIKE
05 VP of Academic Affairs Ms. Barbara H. KARLIN
10 VP of Business Affairs & CFO Mr. Bill LEE
30 VP of University Advancement Vacant
84 VP Enrollment Strategy & Services Mr. John REED
61 Dean School of Law Mr. Anthony NIEDWIECKI
50 Dean Ageno School of Business Dr. Gordon SWARTZ
88 Dean School Taxation & Accounting Mr. Fred SROKA
49 Dean Undergraduate Programs Dr. Nate HINERMAN
106 Director E-Learning Mr. Doug GEIER
32 Dean of Students & Student Affairs Ms. Kayla KRUPNICK
08 Director University Library Mr. James KRUSLING
08 Associate Dean Law Library Mr. Michael DAW
06 University Registrar Ms. Steven LIND
13 Director Information Technology Mr. Daniel FORTSON
26 Marketing Manager Mr. Ryan BADOWSKI
88 Director PLUS Program Dr. Karen MCROBIE
09 Dir Financial Planning/Analysis Mr. Sathyapal MENON
18 Director Business Svcs/Facilities Mr. Mike KOPERSKI
21 Controller Ms. Grace LEE
37 Director Student Financial Aid Ms. Gabriela DE LA VEGA
108 Director Institutional Assessment Ms. Lisa KRAMER
15 Head Human Resources Ms. S. Jamila BUCKNER

Golden State University (F)

9047 E. Florence Ave #L, Downey CA 90240
County: Los Angeles Identification: 667261
Telephone: (562) 622-3368 Carnegie Class: Not Classified
FAX Number: N/A Calendar System: Quarter
URL: www.goldenstateuniv.us
Established: Annual Graduate Tuition & Fees: N/A
Enrollment: N/A Coed
Affiliation or Control: Proprietary IRS Status: Proprietary
Highest Offering: Master's; No Undergraduates
Accreditation: @ACUP

01 President & Dean of Academics Sunny S. KIM
20 Assoc Dean of Academics Fataneh ZARGAR
07 Dean Admissions & Student Affairs Howard SUNGJI KIM

Golf Academy of America (G)

1950 Camino Vida Roble, Suite 125, Carlsbad CA 92008
Telephone: (760) 734-1642 FICE Identification: 015609
Accreditation: ACICS

† Branch campus of Virginia College, Birmingham, AL.

Grace Communion Seminary (H)

PO Box 875, Glendora CA 91740-0730
County: Los Angeles Identification: 667115
Telephone: (626) 650-2306 Carnegie Class: Not Classified
FAX Number: (626) 650-2307 Calendar System: Semester
URL: www.gcs.edu
Established: 2008 Annual Graduate Tuition & Fees: N/A
Enrollment: N/A Coed
Affiliation or Control: Independent Non-Profit IRS Status: 501(c)3
Highest Offering: Master's; No Undergraduates
Accreditation: DEAC

01 President/CEO Dr. Gary DEDDO
05 Dean of Faculty Dr. Michael MORRISON
06 Registrar Ms. Jillian CARANTO
10 CFO/Liaison Officer Dr. Russell DUKE

Grace Mission University (I)

1645 West Valencia Drive, Fullerton CA 92833-3860
County: Orange Identification: 666642
Unit ID: 481058
Telephone: (714) 525-0088 Carnegie Class: Spec-4-yr-Faith
FAX Number: (714) 525-0089 Calendar System: Semester
URL: www.gm.edu
Established: 1995 Annual Undergrad Tuition & Fees: $2,840
Enrollment: 214 Coed
Affiliation or Control: Presbyterian Church (U.S.A.) IRS Status: 501(c)3
Highest Offering: Doctorate
Accreditation: BI, THEOL, TRACS

01 President & CEO Dr. Kyunam CHOI
05 Academic Dean Dr. Hyun Wan KIM
10 Chief Financial Officer Dr. David Chang S. LEE
32 Dean of Students Dr. Dong Hyun HUH
11 Dir Administration/Financial Aid Mr. James KOO
06 Registrar Ms. Min KANG
08 Librarian Ms. Eun Ja SUH
07 Director of Admissions Ms. Won Ja KIM
111 Chief Development/Advancement Mrs. Soo Ok RHEE

Graduate Theological Union (J)

2400 Ridge Road, Berkeley CA 94709-1212
County: Alameda FICE Identification: 001207
Unit ID: 115214
Telephone: (510) 649-2400 Carnegie Class: Spec-4-yr-Faith
FAX Number: (510) 649-1417 Calendar System: Semester
URL: www.gtu.edu
Established: 1962 Annual Graduate Tuition & Fees: N/A
Enrollment: 208 Coed
Affiliation or Control: Independent Non-Profit IRS Status: 501(c)3
Highest Offering: Doctorate; No Undergraduates
Accreditation: WC, THEOL

01 President Dr. Riess POTTERVELD
05 Dean/Vice Pres Academic Affairs Dr. Uriah Y. KIM
10 Vice Pres Administration/Finance Mr. Steven G. ARGYRIS
30 Vice President for Advancement Vacant
32 VP Student Affairs/Dean Students Dr. Kathleen KOOK
07 Director of Admissions Dr. Andrea SHEAFFER
08 Interim Library Director Mr. Clay-Edward DIXON
06 Consortial Registrar Mr. John SEAL
13 Chief Information Officer Mr. Jeffrey DIGREORIO
18 Building & Grounds Engineer Mr. Curtis OSBORNE
15 Director Human Resources Ms. Deborah WALKER
37 Director of Financial Aid Ms. Denise MORITA
04 Executive Assistant to President Ms. Teresa JOYE

*Grossmont-Cuyamaca Community College District (K)

8800 Grossmont College Drive, El Cajon CA 92020-1799
County: San Diego FICE Identification: 007006
Unit ID: 115287
Telephone: (619) 644-7010 Carnegie Class: N/A
FAX Number: (619) 644-7936
URL: www.gcccd.edu

01 Chancellor Dr. Cindy MILES
10 Vice Chanc Business Services Ms. Sue REARIC
15 Vice Chanc Human Resources Mr. Tim CORCORAN

*Cuyamaca College (L)

900 Rancho San Diego Parkway, El Cajon CA 92019-4304
County: San Diego FICE Identification: 021113
Unit ID: 113218
Telephone: (619) 660-4000 Carnegie Class: Assoc/HT-Mix Trad/Non
FAX Number: (619) 660-4399 Calendar System: Semester
URL: www.cuyamaca.edu

Established: 1978 Annual Undergrad Tuition & Fees (In-District): $1,388
Enrollment: 9,000 Coed
Affiliation or Control: State/Local IRS Status: 501(c)3
Highest Offering: Associate Degree
Accreditation: WJ

02 President .... Dr. Julianna BARNES
05 Vice President Instruction .... Mr. Pat SETZER
32 Interim Vice Pres Student Services .... Mr. Aiden ELY
11 Vice Pres Admin Services .... Ms. Sahar ABUSHABAN
81 Dean of Math/Sci/Engineering .... Dr. Pam KERSEY
79 Int Dean of Arts/Human/Social Sci .... Ms. Alicia MUNOZ
72 Dean of Career Technical Education .... Mr. Larry MCLEMORE
08 Dean Learning/Technology Resources .... Ms. Kerry KILBER REBMAN
88 Interim Assistant Dean EOPS .... Ms. Cecelia BLANKS
41 Assoc Dean Athletics .... Dr. Ryan SHUMAKER
35 Assoc Dean Student Affairs .... Dr. Lauren VAKNIN
38 Dean Counseling Services .... Ms. Nicole JONES
37 Director of Financial Aid .... Mr. Ray REYES
07 Director Admissions & Records .... Mr. Gregory VEGA
18 Facilities Director .... Mr. Bruce FARNHAM
04 Executive Asst to President .... Ms. Valeri WILSON

*Grossmont College (A)

8800 Grossmont College Drive, El Cajon CA 92020-1799
County: San Diego FICE Identification: 001208
Unit ID: 115296
Telephone: (619) 644-7000 Carnegie Class: Assoc/HT-High Trad
FAX Number: (619) 644-7922 Calendar System: Semester
URL: www.grossmont.edu
Established: 1961 Annual Undergrad Tuition & Fees (In-District): $1,386
Enrollment: 18,159 Coed
Affiliation or Control: State/Local IRS Status: 501(c)3
Highest Offering: Associate Degree
Accreditation: WJ, ADNUR, CEA, COARC, CVT, OTA

02 President .... Dr. Nabil ABU-GHAZALEH
05 Vice Pres of Academic Affairs .... Dr. Katrina VANDERWOUDE
32 Int Sr Dean CPIE/Student Services .... Dr. Michael REESE
07 Dean Admissions/Records/Fin Aid .... Mr. Aaron STARCK
38 Dean Counseling Svcs .... Ms. Martha CLAVELLE
72 Dean Career & Technical Workforce .... Mr. Javier AYALA
81 Dean Math/Natural Sci/Phys Educ .... Dr. Cary WILLARD
60 Dean Arts/Languages/Comm .... Mr. Bill MCGREEVY
79 Dean English/Social & Behav Sci .... Mr. Agustin ALBARRAN
08 Int Dean of Learning Resources .... Ms. Nadra FARINA-HESS
35 Int Associate Dean Student Affairs .... Ms. Sarah VARGHESE
09 Director of Institutional Research .... Mr. Christopher TARMAN
10 Chief Business Officer .... Mr. Lorenze LEGASPI
15 Director Personnel Services .... Vacant
18 Chief Facilities/Physical Plant .... Mr. Loren HOLMQUIST
26 Chief Public Relations Officer .... Vacant
36 Director Student Placement .... Ms. Renee NASORI
37 Director Student Financial Aid .... Mr. Michael COPENHAVER
96 Director of Purchasing .... Ms. Linda BERTOLUCCI
04 Executive Assistant to President .... Ms. Bernadette BLACK

Gurnick Academy of Medical Arts (B)

2121 S. El Camino Real Bldg C200, San Mateo CA 94403
County: San Mateo FICE Identification: 041698
Unit ID: 459213
Telephone: (650) 685-6616 Carnegie Class: Not Classified
FAX Number: (650) 685-6640 Calendar System: Other
URL: www.gurnick.edu
Established: 2004 Annual Undergrad Tuition & Fees: N/A
Enrollment: 957 Coed
Affiliation or Control: Proprietary IRS Status: Proprietary
Highest Offering: Associate Degree
Accreditation: ABHES, PTAA, RAD

01 CEO .... Konstantin GOURJI
12 Campus Director .... Fred FARIDIAN
11 Chief Operating Officer .... Burke MALIN
05 Chief Academic Officer .... Larisa REVZINA

Hartnell College (C)

411 Central Avenue, Salinas CA 93901-1697
County: Monterey FICE Identification: 001209
Unit ID: 115393
Telephone: (831) 755-6700 Carnegie Class: Assoc/HT-High Trad
FAX Number: (831) 755-6751 Calendar System: Semester
URL: www.hartnell.edu
Established: 1920 Annual Undergrad Tuition & Fees (In-District): $1,420
Enrollment: 11,176 Coed
Affiliation or Control: State/Local IRS Status: 501(c)3
Highest Offering: Associate Degree
Accreditation: WJ, ADNUR, #COARC, PNUR

01 Superintendent/President .... Dr. Willard LEWALLEN
32 VP Student Affairs .... Dr. Romero JALOMO
10 VP Administrative Services .... Mr. Benjamin FIGUEROA
13 VP Information & Tech Systems .... Mr. David PHILLIPS
05 VP Academic Affairs .... Ms. Lori KILDAL
111 VP Advancement/Development .... Ms. Jackie CRUZ
15 Assoc VP Human Resources/EEO .... Ms. Terri PYER
21 Controller .... Vacant
18 Exec Dir Constr/Facilities Mgmt .... Mr. Joseph REYES
20 Dean Academic Aff Programs/Support .. Ms. Kathy MENDELSOHN
81 Dean Academic Affs Math/Science .... Ms. Shannon BLISS
35 Director of Student Life .... Mr. Augustine NEVAREZ
26 Director of Communications .... Ms. Esmeralda OWENS
22 Dir of Student Affairs EOPS/DSPS .... Mr. Paul CASEY
66 Dean Academic Affairs/Nursing .... Ms. Debra KACZMAR
83 Dean Acad Affs Soc/Fine Lang Arts .... Dr. Celine PINET
88 Dean South County Educ Programs .... Ms. Renata FUNKE
04 Senior Executive Assistant .... Ms. Lucille SERRANO
07 Dean of Student Affairs/Enrol Svcs .... Ms. Mary DOMINGUEZ
09 Director of Institutional Research .... Dr. Brian LOFMAN
101 Secretary of the Institution/Board .... Ms. Lucille SERRANO
35 Dean of Student Affairs .... Mr. Antonio ALARCON
41 Director Athletics .... Mr. Daniel TERESA
45 Dean Inst Planning and Effective .... Dr. Brian LOFMAN
103 Dir Workforce/Career Development .... Mr. Clint COWDEN
19 Director Public Safe/Emerg Mgmt .... Mr. Kenneth LAIRD

Harvey Mudd College (D)

301 Platt Boulevard, Claremont CA 91711-5990
County: Los Angeles FICE Identification: 001171
Unit ID: 115409
Telephone: (909) 621-8000 Carnegie Class: Bac-A&S
FAX Number: (909) 621-8360 Calendar System: Semester
URL: www.hmc.edu
Established: 1955 Annual Undergrad Tuition & Fees: $52,666
Enrollment: 825 Coed
Affiliation or Control: Independent Non-Profit IRS Status: 501(c)3
Highest Offering: Baccalaureate
Accreditation: WC, ENG

01 President .... Dr. Maria M. KLAWE
111 Vice President Advancement .... Mr. Daniel MACALUSO
10 Vice President Admin/Fin/Treasurer .... Mr. Andrew R. DORANTES
05 VP Acad Affairs/Dean of the Faculty .... Dr. Lisa SULLIVAN
07 Vice Pres Admissions/Financial Aid .... Ms. Thyra BRIGGS
32 VP Student Affairs/Dean of Students .... Dr. Jon JACOBSEN
13 VP/CIO .... Mr. Joseph VAUGHAN
15 Senior Director for Human Resources ...... Ms. Dana NAGENGAST
18 AVP Facilities/Physical Plant .... Ms. Theresa LAUER
28 Assoc Dean Institutional Diversity .... Vacant
06 Registrar .... Mr. Mark ASHLEY
26 Director of College Relations .... Ms. Stephanie GRAHAM
29 Director of Alumni Relations .... Ms. Jennifer GREEN
37 Director of Student Financial Aid .... Ms. Gilma LOPEZ
101 Director of Pres Ofc/Secy to Board .... Ms. Karen ANGEMI
100 Chief of Staff .... Ms. Karen ANGEMI
09 Director of Institutional Research .... Dr. Laura PALUCKI BLAKE

Henley-Putnam University (E)

2107 N. First Street, Suite 210, San Jose CA 95131
County: Santa Clara Identification: 666120
Telephone: (408) 453-9900 Carnegie Class: Not Classified
FAX Number: (775) 255-2741 Calendar System: Quarter
URL: www.henley-putnam.edu
Established: 2001 Annual Undergrad Tuition & Fees: N/A
Enrollment: N/A Coed
Affiliation or Control: Proprietary IRS Status: Proprietary
Highest Offering: Doctorate
Accreditation: DEAC

01 President .... Jim P. KILLIN
05 Chief Academic Officer .... Dr. Amy DIMAIO
10 Director of Finance .... Ray ASAD
07 Director of Admissions .... Nancy REGGIO

High Tech High Graduate School of Education (F)

2861 Womble Road, San Diego CA 92106-6025
County: San Diego Identification: 667118
Unit ID: 485403
Telephone: (619) 398-4902 Carnegie Class: Not Classified
FAX Number: (619) 758-1960 Calendar System: Other
URL: gse.hightechhigh.org
Established: 2007 Annual Graduate Tuition & Fees: N/A
Enrollment: 33 Coed
Affiliation or Control: Independent Non-Profit IRS Status: 501(c)3
Highest Offering: Master's; No Undergraduates
Accreditation: @WC

01 President .... Larry ROSENSTOCK
05 Academic Dean .... Ben DALEY
11 Chief Admin Officer/General Counsel .... Maria HEREDIA
12 Director of Clinical Sites .... Ben DALEY
32 Director Student Affairs .... Hayley MURUGESAN

Holy Names University (G)

3500 Mountain Boulevard, Oakland CA 94619-1699
County: Alameda FICE Identification: 001183
Unit ID: 115728
Telephone: (510) 436-1000 Carnegie Class: Masters/M
FAX Number: (510) 436-1199 Calendar System: Semester
URL: www.hnu.edu
Established: 1868 Annual Undergrad Tuition & Fees: $37,074
Enrollment: 1,049 Coed
Affiliation or Control: Independent Non-Profit IRS Status: 501(c)3
Highest Offering: Master's
Accreditation: WC, NURSE

01 Interim President .... Dr. Jeanie WATSON
05 Provost & VP for Academic Affairs .... Dr. Lizbeth MARTIN
10 Vice President for Finance/Admin .... Mr. Michael GROENER
32 Vice President for Student Affairs .... Mr. Michael S. MILLER
84 VP Strategic Enroll Mgmt .... Mr. Alan LIEBRECHT
06 Registrar .... Mr. Stephen STICKA
07 Director of Admissions .... Mr. Chris RASCON
08 Director of Library Services .... Ms. Nicole GREENLAND
37 Dir Student Financial Assistance .... Ms. Tam LEE-OPERARIO
31 Director Campus Services .... Mr. Luis GUERRA
42 Co-Director of Campus Ministry ...... Ms. Jenny GIRARD-MALLEY
42 Co-Director of Campus Ministry .... Fr. Sal RAGUSA
41 Director of Athletics .... Ms. Debbie SNELL
26 University Communications Manager .... Ms. Stephanie SILVA
29 Director of Alumni Relations .... Ms. Frances WILLIAMS
13 Director Information Technology .... Mr. Jay CASTILLO
15 Director Human Resources .... Ms. Patricia BARTON
04 Executive Asst to President .... Ms. Vicki TOM
09 Director of Institutional Research .... Mr. Francisco HERRERA
18 Chief Facilities/Physical Plant .... Mr. Luis GUERRA

Homestead Schools (H)

23800 Hawthorne Blvd, Torrance CA 90505
County: Los Angeles FICE Identification: 041497
Unit ID: 457086
Telephone: (310) 791-9975 Carnegie Class: Not Classified
FAX Number: (310) 791-0135 Calendar System: Other
URL: homesteadschools.net
Established: 2007 Annual Undergrad Tuition & Fees: N/A
Enrollment: 132 Coed
Affiliation or Control: Independent Non-Profit IRS Status: 501(c)3
Highest Offering: Baccalaureate
Accreditation: ABHES

01 President .... Mr. Vijay FADIA

Hope International University (I)

2500 E Nutwood Avenue, Fullerton CA 92831-3104
County: Orange FICE Identification: 001252
Unit ID: 120537
Telephone: (714) 879-3901 Carnegie Class: Masters/M
FAX Number: (714) 681-7451 Calendar System: 4/1/4
URL: www.hiu.edu
Established: 1928 Annual Undergrad Tuition & Fees: $30,550
Enrollment: 1,302 Coed
Affiliation or Control: Independent Non-Profit IRS Status: 501(c)3
Highest Offering: Master's
Accreditation: WC, BI, MFCD

01 President .... Dr. John L. DERRY
04 Exec Asst to the President .... Mrs. Sharon L. CARTER
05 Vice President for Academic Affairs .... Dr. Paul H. ALEXANDER
12 Dean Nebraska Christian College .... Dr. Mark KRAUSE
49 Dean College of Arts and Sciences .... Dr. Steve EDGINGTON
50 Dean College of Business & Mgmt ...... Dr. LaSharnda BECKWITH
53 Dean College of Education .... Dr. Douglas S. DOMENE
88 Dean Col of Ministry & Bible Stds .... Dr. Joe GRANA
83 Dean College of Psych & Counseling .... Dr. Laura L. STEELE
09 Director of Institutional Research .... Dr. Hector GALANO
08 Librarian .... Mrs. Robin HARTMAN
06 Registrar .... Mr. Ron ARCHER
10 Vice President for Business/Finance .... Mr. Frank SCOTTI
37 Director Student Financial Services ...... Mrs. Shannon O'SHIELDS
15 Director of Human Resources .... Mrs. Wende HOLTZEN
13 Director of Information Technology .... Mr. Darrell C. JONES
18 Director of Campus Facilities .... Mr. Steve MULLINS
30 Vice Pres Institutional Advancement .... Mr. Michael MULRYAN
26 Chief Public Relations Officer .... Mr. Michael MULRYAN
32 Vice President for Student Affairs .... Dr. Mark COMEAUX
36 Dean of Students .... Vacant
41 Athletic Director .... Mr. John G. TUREK
42 Chaplain/Director Campus Ministry .... Mr. Bryan A. SANDS
85 Director of International Students .... Mrs. Judy E. KIM
38 Director Student Counseling .... Dr. Laura L. STEELE
36 Dir Student Career Services .... Mrs. Kirsten M. MCCORMICK
84 Vice Pres for Enrollment Management .... Mrs. Teresa L. SMITH
07 Director Undergraduate Admissions .... Mrs. Barbara MOORE
106 Dir Learning Technology .... Ms. Micah N. ALSTON

Humphreys University (J)

6650 Inglewood Street, Stockton CA 95207-3896
County: San Joaquin FICE Identification: 001212
Unit ID: 115773
Telephone: (209) 478-0800 Carnegie Class: Bac-Diverse
FAX Number: (209) 478-8721 Calendar System: Quarter
URL: www.humphreys.edu
Established: 1896 Annual Undergrad Tuition & Fees: $14,004
Enrollment: 565 Coed
Affiliation or Control: Independent Non-Profit IRS Status: 501(c)3
Highest Offering: First Professional Degree
Accreditation: WC

01 President .... Dr. Robert G. HUMPHREYS, JR.
05 Dn Instruction/Dir Arts & Sciences .... Ms. Cynthia BECERRA
11 Dean Administration/Ofc Admin Pgm .... Ms. Wilma OKAMOTO-VAUGHN
09 Dean of Institutional Research .... Dr. Jess BONDS
61 Dean Law School .... Mr. Patrick L. PIGGOTT
20 Associate Dean of Instruction .... Dr. Lisa KOOREN

06 Registrar .... Ms. Maria GARCIA-MILLER
07 Director of Admissions .... Ms. Santa E. LOPEZ
26 Chief Public Relations Officer .... Vacant
08 Head Librarian .... Dr. Stanislav PERKNER
88 Director Court Reporting Program .... Mrs. Kay REINDL
10 Chief Business Officer .... Ms. Carol KRAMLICH
37 Director Student Financial Aid .... Ms. Rita FRANCO
13 Director of Information Services .... Mr. Fred WHITE

Hussian College-Relativity Campus California (A)

1201 West 5th St., Ste F10, Los Angeles CA 90017
Telephone: (800) 762-1993 Identification: 770969
Accreditation: ACCSC

† Branch campus of Hussian School of Art, Philadelphia, PA

Imperial Valley College (B)

380 E Aten Road, Imperial CA 92251-0158
County: Imperial FICE Identification: 001214
Unit ID: 115861
Telephone: (760) 352-8320 Carnegie Class: Assoc/HT-High Trad
FAX Number: (760) 355-2663 Calendar System: Semester
URL: www.imperial.edu
Established: 1922 Annual Undergrad Tuition & Fees (In-District): $1,142
Enrollment: 7,811 Coed
Affiliation or Control: Local IRS Status: 501(c)3
Highest Offering: Associate Degree
Accreditation: WJ, EMT

01 Superintendent/President .... Dr. Victor JAIME
05 Vice President Academic Services .... Dr. Nicholas AKINKUOYE
32 Vice President for Student Services .... Dr. Martha GARCIA
10 VP Administrative Services .... Mr. John LAU
15 Int Chief Human Resources Officer .... Mr. John LAU
103 Dean Economic & Workforce Develop .... Mr. Efrain SILVA
76 Dean of Health & Public Safety .... Mrs. Tina AGUIRRE
49 Dean Arts/Letters/Learning Svc .... Mr. David ZIELINSKI
35 Dean Student Svcs/Special Projects .... Dr. Lennor JOHNSON
07 Director of Admissions and Records .... Mrs. Vikki CARR
37 Director of Financial Aid .... Ms. Lisa SEALS
09 Dir Institutional Research .... Mr. Jose CARRILLO
59 Dir Child/Family/Consumer Sciences .... Ms. Rebecca GREEN
26 Chief Public Relations Officer .... Mr. Bill GAY
13 Chief Technology Officer .... Mr. Jeff ENZ
81 Dean of Math and Sciences .... Mr. David DRURY
96 Director of Purchasing .... Vacant

Institute for Business and Technology (C)

2400 Walsh Avenue, Santa Clara CA 95051
County: Santa Clara FICE Identification: 021283
Unit ID: 115931
Telephone: (404) 727-1060 Carnegie Class: Not Classified
FAX Number: N/A Calendar System: Semester
URL: www.ibttech.com
Established: 1965 Annual Undergrad Tuition & Fees: N/A
Enrollment: 408 Coed
Affiliation or Control: Proprietary IRS Status: Proprietary
Highest Offering: Associate Degree
Accreditation: ACCSC

01 President .... Peter MIKHAIL

Institute of Buddhist Studies (D)

2140 Durant Avenue, Berkeley CA 94704
County: Alameda Identification: 667312
Telephone: (510) 809-1444 Carnegie Class: Not Classified
FAX Number: N/A Calendar System: Semester
URL: www.shin-ibs.edu
Established: 1949 Annual Graduate Tuition & Fees: N/A
Enrollment: N/A Coed
Affiliation or Control: Independent Non-Profit IRS Status: 501(c)3
Highest Offering: Master's; No Undergraduates
Accreditation: @WC

01 President .... Rev. Kodo UMEZU
05 Provost & Vice Pres Academic Affs .... Rev. David MATSUMOTO
32 Dean of Students .... Mr. Scott MITCHELL
10 Director of Finance .... Ms. Linda SHIOZAKI

Institute of Technology (E)

564 West Herndon Avenue, Clovis CA 93612
County: Fresno FICE Identification: 030675
Unit ID: 431141
Telephone: (559) 297-4500 Carnegie Class: Assoc/HVT-High Non
FAX Number: (559) 297-5822 Calendar System: Semester
URL: www.iot.edu
Established: Annual Undergrad Tuition & Fees: N/A
Enrollment: 1,415 Coed
Affiliation or Control: Proprietary IRS Status: Proprietary
Highest Offering: Associate Degree
Accreditation: ACCSC, ACFEI

01 President .... Ron GARDNER

05 Director of Education .... Saechao MEUY
66 Director of Nursing .... Paula RICHARDS
32 Director of Student Services .... Melinda WOOD
07 Director of Admissions .... Marissa MARZAN
06 Registrar .... Anita RAMOS
37 Director of Financial Aid .... Sandi PUGH
36 Director of Career Services .... Tim KEARN
08 Librarian .... Laura HABERSTICH
18 Facilities Coordinator .... Tony LEON

Institute of Technology (F)

5601 Stoddard Road, Modesto CA 95356
Telephone: (209) 572-7800 Identification: 770554
Accreditation: ACCSC, ACFEI

Intercoast College (G)

388 West Cerritos Avenue, Bldg 7, Anaheim CA 92805
County: Orange FICE Identification: 025594
Unit ID: 366289
Telephone: (714) 712-7900 Carnegie Class: Spec 2-yr-Health
FAX Number: (714) 937-1983 Calendar System: Other
URL: www.intercoast.edu
Established: 1985 Annual Undergrad Tuition & Fees: N/A
Enrollment: 85 Coed
Affiliation or Control: Proprietary IRS Status: Proprietary
Highest Offering: Associate Degree
Accreditation: CNCE

01 President .... Geeta A. BROWN
12 Campus President .... Christine SANCHEZ

Interior Designers Institute (H)

1061 Camelback Road, Newport Beach CA 92660-3228
County: Orange FICE Identification: 025203
Unit ID: 116226
Telephone: (949) 675-4451 Carnegie Class: Spec-4-yr-Arts
FAX Number: (949) 759-0667 Calendar System: Quarter
URL: www.idi.edu
Established: 1984 Annual Undergrad Tuition & Fees: $19,350
Enrollment: 201 Coed
Affiliation or Control: Proprietary IRS Status: Proprietary
Highest Offering: Master's
Accreditation: ACCSC, CIDA

01 Executive Director .... Ms. Judy DEATON
37 Financial Aid Director .... Ms. Shanen FOYE

International Reformed University and Seminary (I)

125 S. Vermont Avenue, Los Angeles CA 90004
County: Los Angeles Identification: 667132
Telephone: (213) 381-0081 Carnegie Class: Not Classified
FAX Number: (213) 381-0010 Calendar System: Semester
URL: www.irus.edu
Established: 1977 Annual Undergrad Tuition & Fees: N/A
Enrollment: N/A Coed
Affiliation or Control: Independent Non-Profit IRS Status: 501(c)3
Highest Offering: Doctorate
Accreditation: BI

01 President .... Dr. Hun Sung PARK
05 Academic Dean .... Dr. Kwang Hoon LEE
32 Dean of Students .... Dr. Young Chung JIN
11 Dean of Administrative Services .... Dr. Joha OH
108 Director of Assessment & Planning .... Dr. Yumee RAH
88 Accreditation Liaison .... Dr. Grace KOOK
08 Librarian .... Ms. Hannah LEE
20 Director of Teaching & Learning Tec .... Ms. Hala SUN
88 Secretary .... Ms. Sunkyoung KIM

International Technological University (J)

2711 N. First Street, San Jose CA 95134
County: Santa Clara Identification: 667070
Unit ID: 443128
Telephone: (888) 488-4968 Carnegie Class: Masters/L
FAX Number: (408) 331-1026 Calendar System: Trimester
URL: www.itu.edu
Established: 1994 Annual Graduate Tuition & Fees: N/A
Enrollment: 1,176 Coed
Affiliation or Control: Independent Non-Profit IRS Status: 501(c)3
Highest Offering: Doctorate; No Undergraduates
Accreditation: WC, ACBSP

01 President and CEO .... Dr. Gregory O'BRIEN
05 Provost .... Dr. Barry RYAN
10 CFO .... Edward LAM
06 Registrar .... Nancy Jo BLACK
08 Head Librarian .... Marion HAYES
101 Board Liaison .... Angie LO
26 Dir Marketing/Comm/Admissions .... Vacant

International Theological Seminary (K)

3215-3225 Tyler Avenue, El Monte CA 91731-3355
County: Los Angeles Identification: 666360
Unit ID: 396985
Telephone: (626) 448-0023 Carnegie Class: Not Classified
FAX Number: (626) 350-6343 Calendar System: Quarter
URL: www.itsla.edu
Established: 1982 Annual Undergrad Tuition & Fees: N/A
Enrollment: N/A Coed
Affiliation or Control: Independent Non-Profit IRS Status: 501(c)3
Highest Offering: Doctorate
Accreditation: THEOL

01 President .... Dr. James S. LEE
05 Acting Vice Pres for Academics .... Dr. Pricilla ADOYO
11 Vice President for Administration .... Rev. Paul Zhaohui YANG
32 Dean of Students .... Dr. Premkumar DHARMARAJ
06 Registrar .... Dr. Grace KICHA
08 Librarian .... Ms. Susan LIU
26 Communication Director .... Rev. Sam BAIK

John F. Kennedy University (L)

100 Ellinwood Way, Pleasant Hill CA 94523-4817
County: Contra Costa FICE Identification: 004484
Unit ID: 116712
Telephone: (925) 969-3300 Carnegie Class: Masters/M
FAX Number: (925) 969-3399 Calendar System: Quarter
URL: www.jfku.edu
Established: 1964 Annual Undergrad Tuition & Fees: N/A
Enrollment: 1,111 Coed
Affiliation or Control: Independent Non-Profit IRS Status: 501(c)3
Highest Offering: Doctorate
Accreditation: WC, CLPSY, IACBE

01 President .... Ms. Debra BEAN
04 Administrative Asst to President .... Marie PAVONE
06 Registrar .... Diane CVETIC
07 Director of Admissions .... Catherine REED
09 Director of Institutional Research .... Dr. Mark KURAI
10 Chief Business Officer .... Jim MIRR
100 Chief of Staff .... Dr. Jack PADUNTIN
102 Dir Foundation/Corporate Relations .... Rhea JOHNSON
106 Dir Online Education/E-learning .... Matthew BRUCE
15 Director Personnel Services .... Dr. Robert JAKO
18 Chief Facilities/Physical Plant .... David SADLER
29 Director Alumni Relations .... Michael DAVIDSON
32 Chief Student Affairs/Student Life .... Dr. Judy CASTRO
37 Director Student Financial Aid .... Mindy BERGERON
38 Director Student Counseling .... Dr. Pilar EGUEZ GUEVARA

John Paul the Great Catholic University (M)

220 West Grand Avenue, Escondido CA 92025
County: San Diego FICE Identification: 041937
Unit ID: 462354
Telephone: (858) 653-6740 Carnegie Class: Bac-Diverse
FAX Number: (858) 653-3791 Calendar System: Quarter
URL: www.jpcatholic.com
Established: 2003 Annual Undergrad Tuition & Fees: $24,900
Enrollment: 317 Coed
Affiliation or Control: Independent Non-Profit IRS Status: 501(c)3
Highest Offering: Master's
Accreditation: WC

01 President .... Dr. Derry CONNOLLY
05 Chief Academic Officer .... Dr. Michael BARBER
10 Interim Chief Finance Officer .... Joan MAZIERE
11 VP for Administration .... Lidy CONNOLLY
07 VP of Admissions .... Martin HAROLD
13 VP for Technology & Real Estate .... Kevin MEZIERE
32 Dean of Students .... Julia CARRANO
37 Director of Financial Aid .... Lisa WILLIAMS
06 Registrar .... Nick HEYE
42 Director Campus Ministry .... Fr. Chase CROUSE
09 Director Institutional Research .... Clare OVEN
39 Director Student Life .... Joe CROSS

Kaiser Permanente School of Allied Health Sciences (N)

938 Marina Way South, Richmond CA 94804
County: Contra Costa Identification: 667152
Telephone: (510) 231-5000 Carnegie Class: Not Classified
FAX Number: (510) 231-5001 Calendar System: Quarter
URL: www.kpsahs.org
Established: 1989 Annual Undergrad Tuition & Fees: N/A
Enrollment: N/A Coed
Affiliation or Control: Proprietary IRS Status: Proprietary
Highest Offering: Baccalaureate
Accreditation: WC, DMS, NMT, RAD

01 Medical Director .... Dr. C. Darryl JONES
05 Dean of Academic Affairs .... Vacant
10 Assoc Director of Finance/CFO .... Pamela PRESSLEY
11 Regional School Administrator/CEO .... James FITZGIBBON
09 Dir Assessment/Inst Research .... Mr. Bert CHRISTENSEN

*Kern Community College District (O)

2100 Chester Avenue, Bakersfield CA 93301-4099
County: Kern FICE Identification: 006994
Unit ID: 436313
Telephone: (661) 336-5100 Carnegie Class: N/A
FAX Number: (661) 336-5134
URL: www.kccd.edu

01 Chancellor .... Mr. Thomas J. BURKE
05 Vice Chanc Educational Services .... Mr. John MEANS
15 Vice Chanc Human Resources .... Ms. Tonya DAVIS
30 Assoc Vice Chanc Govt/External Rels .... Vacant
10 Interim Chief Financial Officer .... Ms. Deborah MARTIN
13 Chief Technology Officer .... Mr. Gary MOSER
43 General Counsel .... Mr. Christopher HINE

*Bakersfield College (A)

1801 Panorama Drive, Bakersfield CA 93305-1299
County: Kern FICE Identification: 001118
Unit ID: 109819
Telephone: (661) 395-4011 Carnegie Class: Assoc/MT-VT-High Trad
FAX Number: (661) 395-4241 Calendar System: Semester
URL: www.bakersfieldcollege.edu
Established: 1913 Annual Undergrad Tuition & Fees (In-District): $1,326
Enrollment: 20,448 Coed
Affiliation or Control: State/Local IRS Status: 501(c)3
Highest Offering: Baccalaureate
Accreditation: WJ, EMT, RAD

02 President .... Dr. Sonya CHRISTIAN
05 Exec VP Instruction .... Ms. Nan GOMEZ-HEITZEBERG
10 VP Finance & Administrative Svcs .... Dr. Don CHRUSCIEL
32 Vice Pres Student Affairs .... Dr. Zavareh DADABHOY
30 Director Foundation & Development .... Mr. Tom GELDER
18 Dir Facilities/Maintenance/Ops .... Mr. Bill POTTER
12 Director Delano Center .... Mr. Rich MCCROW
37 Assistant Financial Aid Director .... Ms. Jennifer ACHAN
84 Director Enrollment Services .... Mrs. Suzanne A. VAUGHN
26 Dir Marketing & Public Relations .... Vacant
04 Admin Assistant to the President .... Ms. Jennifer MARDEN
13 Director Information Technology .... Mr. Todd COSTON
20 Interim Dean of Instruction .... Dr. Rich MCCROW
66 Dean of Instruction .... Ms. Cindy COLLIER
41 Director of Athletics .... Ms. Sandi TAYLOR
20 Dean of Instruction .... Ms. Liz ROZELL
20 Dean of Instruction .... Dr. Emmanuel MOURTZANOS

*Cerro Coso Community College (B)

College Heights Boulevard, Ridgecrest CA 93555-7777
County: Kern FICE Identification: 010111
Unit ID: 111896
Telephone: (760) 384-6100 Carnegie Class: Assoc/MT-VT-High Non
FAX Number: (760) 375-4776 Calendar System: Semester
URL: www.cerrocoso.edu
Established: 1973 Annual Undergrad Tuition & Fees (In-District): $1,290
Enrollment: 4,735 Coed
Affiliation or Control: State/Local IRS Status: 501(c)3
Highest Offering: Associate Degree
Accreditation: WJ

02 President .... Ms. A. Jill BOARD
05 Vice President Instruction .... Dr. Corey MARVIN
32 Vice President of Student Services .... Ms. Heather OSTASH
10 Vice Pres Finance/Admin Services .... Ms. Lisa COUCH
12 Dir Eastern Sierra College Center .... Ms. Deanna CAMPBELL
12 Dir of East Kern/Kern River Valley .... Ms. Lisa STEPHENS
75 Dean Career Technical Education .... Mr. Michael KANE
38 Dir of Counseling Svcs/SSSP .... Ms. Christine SMALL
07 Dir Admiss/Records/VA/Fin Aid .... Ms. Jennifer SAN NICOLAS
15 Human Resources Manager .... Ms. Resa HESS
88 Program Mgr Child Development Ctr .... Ms. Jessica KRALL
26 Mgr Public Rel/Marketing & Dev .... Ms. Natalie DORRELL
13 Director Information Technology .... Mr. Michael CAMPBELL
35 Dir Student Programs & Outreach .... Ms. Pam CAMPBELL
106 Director Distance Education .... Ms. Rebecca PANG
04 Administrative Asst to President .... Ms. Jennifer CURTIS
41 Athletic Director .... Mr. Kristopher DICKSON
88 Director of Access Programs .... Ms. Paula SUOREZ

*Porterville College (C)

100 E College Avenue, Porterville CA 93257-6058
County: Tulare FICE Identification: 001268
Unit ID: 121363
Telephone: (559) 791-2200 Carnegie Class: Assoc/HT-High Trad
FAX Number: (559) 784-4779 Calendar System: Semester
URL: www.portervillecollege.edu
Established: 1927 Annual Undergrad Tuition & Fees (In-District): $1,322
Enrollment: 4,074 Coed
Affiliation or Control: State/Local IRS Status: 501(c)3
Highest Offering: Associate Degree
Accreditation: WJ

02 Interim President .... Mr. William HENRY
05 Actg Vice President Instruction .... Mr. Sam AUNAI
32 Vice President Student Services .... Mr. Valentin GARCIA
10 Vice Pres Finance & Admin Services .... Dr. Arlitha WILLIAMS-HARMON
04 Administrative Asst to President .... Ms. Carol BROWN
20 Dean Instruction .... Ms. Kailani KNUTSON
76 Assoc Dean Health Careers .... Ms. Kim BEHRENS
18 Director Maintenance & Operations .... Mr. John WORD
84 Director Enrollment Management .... Ms. Erin CRUZ
15 Human Resources Manager .... Ms. Anne VANDERHORST
37 Assistant Director Financial Aid .... Ms. Tiffany HAYNES
09 Institutional Researcher .... Mr. Michael CARLEY
13 Director Information Technology .... Mr. Jay NAVARRETTE
35 Director Student Services .... Ms. Diane THOMPSON

21 Accounting Manager .... Ms. Sonia HUCKABAY
88 Program Manager Child Dev Center .... Ms. Karen BALL
08 Librarian .... Mr. Chris EBERT
26 Pub Relations/Mkting/Outreach Mgr .... Vacant
105 Web Content Editor .... Ms. Samantha SOUSA
41 Athletic Director .... Mr. Joseph CASCIO

Kernel University (D)

3319 W. Lincoln Avenue, Anaheim CA 92801
County: Orange Identification: 667308
Telephone: (714) 995-9988 Carnegie Class: Not Classified
FAX Number: (714) 995-9989 Calendar System: Semester
URL: www.kernel.edu
Established: 1995 Annual Undergrad Tuition & Fees: N/A
Enrollment: N/A Coed
Affiliation or Control: Independent Non-Profit IRS Status: 501(c)3
Highest Offering: Master's
Accreditation: @TRACS

01 CEO .... Samuel Y. LEE
05 Chief Academic Officer .... Jin HAN
10 Chief Financial Officer .... Joanne C. LEE

Kingston University (E)

3871 E. Colorado Blvd., Pasadena CA 91107
County: Los Angeles Identification: 667237
Telephone: (622) 229-9929 Carnegie Class: Not Classified
FAX Number: N/A Calendar System: Other
URL: www.kingstonuniversity.edu
Established: 2002 Annual Undergrad Tuition & Fees: N/A
Enrollment: N/A Coed
Affiliation or Control: Proprietary IRS Status: Proprietary
Highest Offering: Master's
Accreditation: ACICS

01 President .... Dr. Richard H. GAYER
05 Dean of Academics .... Gilbert SANCHEZ
11 Administrator/Student Affairs .... Rosalia HSIEH

La Sierra University (F)

4500 Riverwalk Parkway, Riverside CA 92515-8247
County: Riverside FICE Identification: 001215
Unit ID: 117627
Telephone: (951) 785-2000 Carnegie Class: Masters/S
FAX Number: (951) 785-2901 Calendar System: Quarter
URL: www.lasierra.edu
Established: 1922 Annual Undergrad Tuition & Fees: $31,590
Enrollment: 2,476 Coed
Affiliation or Control: Seventh-day Adventist IRS Status: 501(c)3
Highest Offering: Doctorate
Accreditation: WC, MUS, SW, THEOL

01 President .... Dr. Randal R. WISBEY
05 Provost .... Dr. Joy FEHR
10 Vice President for Finance .... Mr. David GERIGUIS
32 Vice President for Student Life .... Ms. Yamilet BAZAN
30 Vice Pres Advancement/Univ Rels .... Mr. Norman YERGEN
84 Vice Pres Enrollment Services .... Mr. David R. LOFTHOUSE
26 VP Communication/Integrated Mktg .... Dr. Marilyn THOMSEN
21 Associate Vice President Finance .... Ms. Pamela CHRISPENS
20 Interim Associate Provost .... Ms. Cindy PARKHURST
49 Dean College Arts/Sciences .... Dr. April SUMMITT
50 Dean School of Business .... Dr. John THOMAS
53 Dean School of Education .... Dr. Ginger KETTING-WELLER
73 Dean School of Divinity .... Dr. Friedbert NINOW
35 Dean of Students .... Ms. Marjorie ROBINSON
102 Exec Director University Foundation .... Mr. Larry GERATY
55 Director Adult Evening Program .... Ms. Nancy DITTEMORE
29 Alumni Director .... Ms. Julie NARDUCCI
15 Director Human Resources .... Ms. Dell Jean VAN FOSSEN
08 Director Library .... Ms. Kitty SIMMONS
37 Director Student Financial Services .... Ms. Esther KINZER
42 Director Campus Ministries .... Mr. Samuel E. LEONOR, JR.
13 Director Information Technology .... Mr. Geoff INGRAM
09 Director of Institutional Research .... Mr. Guru UPPALA
18 Director Physical Plant .... Mr. Al VALDEZ
38 Director Counseling Center .... Ms. Debra WRIGHT
92 Director Honors Program .... Dr. Douglas R. CLARK
07 Director of Admissions/Registrar .... Mr. Issmael NZAMUTUNA
36 Career Advisor .... Mr. William PENICK
41 Athletic Director .... Mr. Javier KRUMM

LACM, Los Angeles College of Music (G)

300 South Fair Oaks Avenue, Pasadena CA 91105
County: Los Angeles FICE Identification: 038684
Unit ID: 446385
Telephone: (626) 568-8850 Carnegie Class: Spec-4-yr-Arts
FAX Number: (626) 568-8854 Calendar System: Quarter
URL: www.lacm.edu
Established: 1996 Annual Undergrad Tuition & Fees: $24,004
Enrollment: 145 Coed
Affiliation or Control: Proprietary IRS Status: Proprietary
Highest Offering: Baccalaureate
Accreditation: MUS

01 President .... Tom AYLESBURY

05 EVP Academic Operations .... Mike PACKER
06 Registrar .... Jorge OJEDA
32 Dean of Students & Faculty .... Dave POZZI
37 Director of Financial Aid .... Mary OLMOS

Laguna College of Art & Design (H)

2222 Laguna Canyon Road,
Laguna Beach CA 92651-1136
County: Orange FICE Identification: 023305
Unit ID: 117168
Telephone: (949) 376-6000 Carnegie Class: Spec-4-yr-Arts
FAX Number: (949) 376-6009 Calendar System: Semester
URL: www.lcad.edu
Established: 1961 Annual Undergrad Tuition & Fees: $28,950
Enrollment: 607 Coed
Affiliation or Control: Independent Non-Profit IRS Status: 501(c)3
Highest Offering: Master's
Accreditation: WC, ART

01 President .... Dr. Jonathan BURKE
05 Vice President Academic Affairs .... Dr. Helene GARRISON
30 Vice Pres of Development .... Mr. Kevin CARTWRIGHT
07 Dean of Admissions .... Mr. Christopher BROWN
10 Chief Financial Officer .... Mr. Jim GODEK
06 Registrar .... Ms. Laura PATRICK
08 Library Director .... Ms. Jennifer WORMSER
04 Assistant to the President .... Ms. Jeni RICHARDS
37 Director Financial Aid .... Mr. Christopher BROWN
09 Director of Institutional Research .... Ms. Laura PATRICK
15 Human Resource Manager .... Ms. Caroline CARLSON
13 Chief Info Technology Officer (CIO) .... Mr. Matt MORTON
18 Chief Facilities/Physical Plant .... Vacant
26 Communications Manager .... Mr. Mike STICE
32 Chief Student Affairs/Student Life .... Mr. Doug DAVEE

Lake Tahoe Community College (I)

1 College Drive, South Lake Tahoe CA 96150-4524
County: El Dorado FICE Identification: 012907
Unit ID: 117195
Telephone: (530) 541-4660 Carnegie Class: Assoc/HT-High Non
FAX Number: (530) 541-7852 Calendar System: Quarter
URL: www.ltcc.edu
Established: 1975 Annual Undergrad Tuition & Fees (In-District): $1,224
Enrollment: 2,437 Coed
Affiliation or Control: State/Local IRS Status: 501(c)3
Highest Offering: Associate Degree
Accreditation: WJ

01 Superintendent/President .... Mr. Jeff DEFRANCO
04 Executive Assistant to President .... Ms. Lisa SHAFER
05 VP Academic Affairs .... Dr. Michelle RISDON
10 Vice Pres Administrative Svcs .... Ms. Russi EGAN
103 Dean of Workforce Development/Inst .... Mr. Brad DEEDS
32 Executive Dean of Student Success .... Ms. Sue GOCHIS
20 Dean of Instruction .... Ms. Michelle SOWER
08 Director of Library .... Vacant
13 Director Tech & Education Svcs .... Mr. Dave BURBA
84 Director Enrollment Services .... Ms. Steve BERRY
21 Director of Fiscal Services .... Ms. Andrea SALAZAR
15 Director of Human Resources .... Ms. Shelley HANSEN
18 Director of Facilities .... Mr. Randy JOSLIN
88 Int Dir Child Development Center .... Ms. Shawna SARVER
37 Director Financial Aid .... Ms. Julie CATHIE
09 Director of Institutional Research .... Mr. Jeremy BROWN
26 Public Information Officer .... Ms. Diane LEWIS
102 Foundation Director .... Ms. Nancy HARRISON
40 Bookstore Manager .... Mr. Trevor OSTENDORF
96 Purchasing Agent .... Ms. Heather CADE
41 Athletic Director .... Mr. Mike SPINA

Lassen Community College (J)

PO Box 3000, 478-200 Highway 139,
Susanville CA 96130-3000
County: Lassen FICE Identification: 001217
Unit ID: 117274
Telephone: (530) 257-6181 Carnegie Class: Assoc/HT-High Non
FAX Number: (530) 251-8872 Calendar System: Semester
URL: www.lassencollege.edu
Established: 1925 Annual Undergrad Tuition & Fees (In-District): $1,127
Enrollment: 2,241 Coed
Affiliation or Control: State/Local IRS Status: 501(c)3
Highest Offering: Associate Degree
Accreditation: WJ

01 District Superintendent/President .... Dr. Marlon R. HALL
04 Assistant to President .... Ms. Julie L. JOHNSTON
05 Interim VP Academic Services .... Dr. Larry BUCKLEY
11 Vice Pres Administrative Services .... Mr. Dave CLAUSEN
32 Dean of Student Services .... Mr. Patrick WALTON
08 Librarian .... Vacant
09 Assoc Dean Inst Effectiveness/Rsrch .... Mr. Brian MURPHY
37 Interim Director Financial Aid .... Mr. Davis MURPHY
35 Director Student Life .... Mr. Francis BEAUJON
41 Interim Athletic Director .... Mr. Glen YONAN
18 Chief Facilities/Physical Plant .... Mr. Gregory COLLINS
15 Director Human Resources .... Ms. Vickie RAMSEY
13 Director of Information Technology .... Mr. David CORLEY

Latin American Bible Institute (A)

14209 E. Lomitas Avenue, La Puente CA 91746

County: Los Angeles Identification: 667319
Telephone: (626) 968-1328 Carnegie Class: Not Classified
FAX Number: (626) 961-7253 Calendar System: Semester
URL: www.labi.edu
Established: 1926 Annual Undergrad Tuition & Fees: N/A
Enrollment: N/A Coed
Affiliation or Control: Independent Non-Profit IRS Status: 501(c)3
Highest Offering: Associate Degree
Accreditation: @BI

01 President .... Dr. Marty HARRIS

Laurus College (B)

81 Higuera Street, Ste 110, San Luis Obispo CA 93401

County: San Luis Obispo FICE Identification: 041414
Unit ID: 454786
Telephone: (805) 267-1690 Carnegie Class: Not Classified
FAX Number: (805) 352-1307 Calendar System: Quarter
URL: www.lauruscollege.com
Established: 2006 Annual Undergrad Tuition & Fees: N/A
Enrollment: 941 Coed
Affiliation or Control: Proprietary IRS Status: Proprietary
Highest Offering: Associate Degree
Accreditation: ACICS

00 President/CEO .... Dr. David AHN
01 School Chancellor .... Mr. Jeff REDMOND
32 Vice Pres Student Programs .... Ms. Cecilia MORTELA
37 Director Financial Aid .... Mr. Tim REDMOND
06 Registrar .... Mr. Brendan COYLE

Learnet Academy (C)

3251 W. 6th Street, 2nd Floor, Los Angeles CA 90020

County: Los Angeles Identification: 667223
Unit ID: 483221
Telephone: (213) 387-4242 Carnegie Class: Not Classified
FAX Number: (213) 387-5365 Calendar System: Other
URL: www.learnet.edu
Established: 1993 Annual Undergrad Tuition & Fees: N/A
Enrollment: 182 Coed
Affiliation or Control: Proprietary IRS Status: Proprietary
Highest Offering: Associate Degree
Accreditation: ACICS

01 Executive Director .... Ms. Tia SHIN

Life Chiropractic College West (D)

25001 Industrial Boulevard, Hayward CA 94545-2801

County: Alameda FICE Identification: 022285
Unit ID: 117520
Telephone: (510) 780-4500 Carnegie Class: Spec-4-yr-Other Health
FAX Number: (510) 780-4525 Calendar System: Quarter
URL: www.lifewest.edu
Established: 1976 Annual Undergrad Tuition & Fees: N/A
Enrollment: 565 Coed
Affiliation or Control: Independent Non-Profit IRS Status: 501(c)3
Highest Offering: First Professional Degree; No Lower Division
Accreditation: WC, CHIRO

01 President .... Dr. Ron OBERSTEIN
03 Executive Vice President .... Dr. Anatole BOGATSKI
05 Vice President of Academic Affairs .... Dr. Scott DONALDSON
09 Director of Institutional Research .... Dr. Dale JOHNSON
10 Interim Controller .... Angelito TOLENTINO
46 Director of Research .... Dr. Monica SMITH
30 Director Institutional Advancement .... Dr. Mark ZIEGLER
51 Director of Continuing Education .... Dr. Laurie ISENBERG
08 Director Learning Resource Center .... Ms. Annette OSENGA
29 Alumni Relations Coordinator .... Nancy MCKILLICAN
37 Director Financial Aid .... Ms. Brenda JOHNSON
06 Registrar .... Ms. Michelle MONTOYA
15 Manager Human Resources .... Sunita RANADIVE
32 Director of Student Life .... Mrs. Jackie BIRON
105 Webmaster .... Mr. Steve SARMIENTO
40 Bookstore Manager .... Mr. Michael BALDWIN
41 Athletic Director .... Mr. Adriann FERRIS
84 Dean of Enrollment .... Dr. Mary FLANNERY
30 Director of Development .... Raynell EWELL

Life Pacific College (E)

1100 W. Covina Boulevard, San Dimas CA 91773-3298

County: Los Angeles FICE Identification: 022706
Unit ID: 117104
Telephone: (909) 599-5433 Carnegie Class: Spec-4-yr-Faith
FAX Number: (909) 599-6690 Calendar System: Semester
URL: www.lifepacific.edu
Established: 1923 Annual Undergrad Tuition & Fees: $14,138
Enrollment: 612 Coed
Affiliation or Control: Other IRS Status: 501(c)3
Highest Offering: Master's
Accreditation: WC, BI

01 President .... Dr. Jim J. ADAMS
04 Exec Assistant to the President .... Mrs. Karli ALBANESE
05 Vice President Academic Affairs .... Dr. Michael SALMEIER
84 Vice President Enrollment Mgt .... Rev. Angie RICHEY
32 Director Student Development .... Mr. Joshua ARNOLD
10 CFO .... Mr. Todd ESKES
08 Librarian .... Mr. Gary MERRIMAN
06 Registrar .... Mr. Jeff GABLE
18 Director of Facilities .... Mr. Rick MEYER
37 Director of Financial Aid .... Mrs. Luci PEREZ
09 Dean Institutional Effectiveness .... Mr. Brian TOMHAVE
15 Human Resources Director .... Ms. Heidi BONADIE
39 Director Residence Life .... Mr. George BOSTANIC
41 Athletic Director .... Mr. Tim COOK
104 Director Study Abroad .... Dr. Karen TREMPER
13 IT Administrator (CIO) .... Mr. Marlon ESTELLA
111 Chief Development/Advancement .... Mr. Mike MEYER

Lincoln University (F)

401 15th Street, Oakland CA 94612-2801

County: Alameda FICE Identification: 006975
Unit ID: 117557
Telephone: (510) 628-8010 Carnegie Class: Spec-4-yr-Bus
FAX Number: (510) 628-8012 Calendar System: Semester
URL: www.lincolnuca.edu
Established: 1919 Annual Undergrad Tuition & Fees: $10,575
Enrollment: 574 Coed
Affiliation or Control: Independent Non-Profit IRS Status: 501(c)3
Highest Offering: Master's
Accreditation: PPPA

01 President/Rector .... Dr. Mikhail BRODSKY
11 Administrative Vice President .... Dr. Michael GUERRA
32 Dean of Students .... Mr. William HESS
07 Director of Admissions & Records .... Ms. Peggy AU
05 Provost .... Dr. Marshall J. BURAK
08 Head Librarian .... Ms. Nicole Y. MARSH
35 Director of Student Services .... Ms. Effie TORNETTA
13 Director Computer Laboratory .... Mr. Shakil SHRESTHA
37 Chief Financial Aid Director .... Mr. James PETERSON
06 Registrar .... Ms. Maggie HUA
10 CFO .... Ms. Sherry LIANG
20 Assistant Dean of Academic Affairs .... Ms. Mariya ORSHANSKY
88 Dir of Accreditation/Compliance .... Dr. Harpal DHILLON
09 Institutional Research Coordinator .... Dr. Igor HIMELFARB

Logos Evangelical Seminary (G)

9358 Telstar Avenue, El Monte CA 91731-2816

County: Los Angeles FICE Identification: 039454
Unit ID: 397553
Telephone: (626) 571-5110 Carnegie Class: Not Classified
FAX Number: N/A Calendar System: Semester
URL: www.logos-seminary.edu
Established: 1989 Annual Graduate Tuition & Fees: N/A
Enrollment: N/A Coed
Affiliation or Control: Other IRS Status: 501(c)3
Highest Offering: Doctorate; No Undergraduates
Accreditation: WC, THEOL

01 President .... Dr. Kuo-Liang LIN
05 Academic Dean .... Dr. Ekron CHEN
30 Director of Advancement .... Mr. Steven WU
32 Dean of Students .... Dr. Jonathan SIAH
04 Executive Asst to President .... Ms. Kathleen LIN
08 Head Librarian .... Mr. Sheng-Chung CHANG
09 Institutional Research Specialist .... Ms. Teresa KAO
13 Chief Info Technology Officer (CIO) .... Mr. Alex HUNG

Loma Linda University (H)

11139 Anderson Street, Loma Linda CA 92350

County: San Bernardino FICE Identification: 001218
Unit ID: 117636
Telephone: (909) 558-1000 Carnegie Class: Spec-4-yr-Med
FAX Number: (909) 558-0242 Calendar System: Quarter
URL: www.llu.edu
Established: 1905 Annual Undergrad Tuition & Fees: N/A
Enrollment: 4,490 Coed
Affiliation or Control: Seventh-day Adventist IRS Status: 501(c)3
Highest Offering: Doctorate
Accreditation: WC, ANEST, #ARCPA, CAHIIM, CLPSY, COARC, CVT, CYTO, DENT, DH, DIETC, DMS, IPSY, MED, MFCD, MT, NMT, NURSE, OPE, OT, PAST, PH, PHAR, PTA, PTAA, RAD, RADDOS, RTT, SP, SW

01 President .... Dr. Richard H. HART
05 Provost .... Dr. Ronald L. CARTER
10 Sr Vice President Financial Affairs .... Mr. Rodney NEAL
30 Sr Vice President Advancement .... Mrs. Rachelle BUSSELL
13 Vice President Information Systems .... Dr. David P. HARRIS
84 VP Enrollment Mgmt/Student Services .... Dr. Rick E. WILLIAMS
63 Dean of Medicine .... Dr. H. Roger HADLEY
52 Interim Dean of Dentistry .... Dr. Joseph CARUSO
69 Dean of Public Health .... Dr. Helen Hopp MARSHAK
66 Dean of Nursing .... Dr. Elizabeth (Becky) BOSSERT
76 Dean of Allied Health Professions .... Dr. Craig R. JACKSON
67 Dean School of Pharmacy .... Dr. Noreen Chan TOMPKINS
83 Dean School of Behavioral Health .... Dr. Beverly J. BUCKLES
73 Dean of School of Religion .... Dr. Jon PAULIEN
58 Exec Dir Faculty Graduate Studies .... Dr. Rafael CAÑIZALES
06 Director of Records .... Ms. Erin SEHEULT
08 Acting Dir University Libraries .... Mr. Jerry DALY
38 Director of Counseling .... Dr. William G. MURDOCH
43 General Legal Counsel .... Mr. Kent A. HANSEN
33 Dean of Men .... Mr. John NAFIE
34 Dean of Women .... Ms. Lynette BATES
37 Director Student Financial Aid .... Ms. Verdell SCHAEFER
09 Dir Educational Effectiveness .... Dr. Marilyn EGGERS
15 VP Human Resource Management .... Ms. Lizette NORTON
18 Director Campus Engineering .... Mr. Randy STEVENS
96 Director of Purchasing .... Mr. Tim HICKMAN
40 Campus Bookstore Manager .... Ms. Angela SERRANO
42 Campus Chaplain .... Pastor Terry SWENSON

Long Beach City College (I)

4901 E Carson Street, Long Beach CA 90808-1780

County: Los Angeles FICE Identification: 001219
Unit ID: 117645
Telephone: (562) 938-4111 Carnegie Class: Assoc/HVT-High Trad
FAX Number: (562) 938-4118 Calendar System: Other
URL: www.lbcc.edu
Established: 1927 Annual Undergrad Tuition & Fees (In-District): $1,182
Enrollment: 24,478 Coed
Affiliation or Control: State/Local IRS Status: 501(c)3
Highest Offering: Associate Degree
Accreditation: WJ, ADNUR

01 Superintendent-President .... Dr. Reagan ROMALI
45 Exec Vice Pres Econ & Resource Dev .... Lou Anne BYNUM
05 Vice Pres Academic Affairs .... Vacant
11 Vice Pres Administrative Services .... Ann-Marie GABEL
15 Vice President Human Resources .... Rose DELGAUDIO
16 Assoc VP Human Resources .... Gene DURAND
13 Chief Information Systems Officer .... Sylvia LYNCH
07 Interim Exec Dean Admissions/Record .... Robin DARCANGELO
20 Dean Academic Services .... Michelle GRIMES-HILLMAN
38 Dean Counseling/Stdnt Supp Svcs .... Nohel CORRAL
83 Interim Dean Social Sciences & Arts .... Elisabeth ORR
79 Dean of Language Arts .... Lee DOUGLAS
32 Dean Student Affairs .... Ramon KNOX
76 Dean School Health & Science .... Paul CREASON
09 Assoc Dean Inst Effectiveness .... Vacant
26 Dir Communications/College Adv .... John POPE
102 Exec Director Foundation .... Elizabeth MCCANN
96 Director Business Support Services .... Margie PADRON
18 Director of Facilities/Maint/Oper .... Tim WOOTTON
21 Director Fiscal Services & Payroll .... John THOMPSON
37 Dep Dir Enrollment Svcs/Fin Aid .... Juan MENJIVAR

Los Angeles Academy of Figurative Art (J)

16926 Saticoy Street, Van Nuys CA 91406

County: Los Angeles Identification: 667231
Telephone: (818) 708-9232 Carnegie Class: Not Classified
FAX Number: (818) 474-8679 Calendar System: Quarter
URL: www.laafa.edu
Established: 2002 Annual Undergrad Tuition & Fees: N/A
Enrollment: N/A Coed
Affiliation or Control: Proprietary IRS Status: Proprietary
Highest Offering: Baccalaureate
Accreditation: ART

01 President .... Maryam STORM

*Los Angeles Community College District Office (K)

770 Wilshire Boulevard, Los Angeles CA 90017

County: Los Angeles FICE Identification: 001221
Unit ID: 117681
Telephone: (213) 891-2000 Carnegie Class: N/A
FAX Number: N/A
URL: www.laccd.edu

01 Chancellor .... Dr. Francisco C. RODRIGUEZ
05 VC Educ Pgms/Inst Effective .... Dr. Ryan M. CORNNER
43 General Counsel .... Jeffrey M. PRIETO
10 VC Finance and Resource Development .... Dr. Robert B. MILLER
103 Vice Chanc Econ Workforce Devel .... Vacant
15 VC Human Resources .... Dr. Albert J. ROMAN
18 Chief Facilities Executive .... David SALAZAR
20 Deputy Chancellor .... Dr. Adriana D. BARRERA

*East Los Angeles College (L)

1301 Avenida Cesar Chavez,
Monterey Park CA 91754-6001

County: Los Angeles FICE Identification: 022260
Unit ID: 113856
Telephone: (323) 265-8650 Carnegie Class: Assoc/HT-High Trad
FAX Number: (323) 265-8763 Calendar System: Semester
URL: www.elac.edu
Established: 1945 Annual Undergrad Tuition & Fees (In-District): $1,220
Enrollment: 37,188 Coed
Affiliation or Control: State/Local IRS Status: 501(c)3
Highest Offering: Associate Degree
Accreditation: WJ, CAHIIM, COARC

02 President .... Mr. Marvin MARTINEZ
05 Interim VP Academic Affairs .... Mr. Ruben ARENAS

103 VP Workforce Educ/Academic Affairs ... Ms. Laura M. RAMIREZ
32 VP Student Services/Special Pgms ... Ms. Julie BENAVIDES
10 VP Administrative Services ... Dr. Ann TOMLINSON
51 VP Continuing Educ/Workforce Dev ... Dr. Armida ORNELAS
75 Dean Acad Affs/Career & Tech Educ ... Vacant
49 Dean Academic Affairs/Liberal Arts ... Mr. James KENNY
49 Dean Academic Affairs Liberal Arts ... Ms. Kerrin MCMAHAN
49 Dean Academic Affairs Liberal Arts ... Ms. Vi LY
07 Dean Admissions & Records ... Mr. Jeremy P. ALLRED
12 Dean Academic Affairs Southgate Ctr ... Mr. Alfonso RIOS
09 Dean Institutional Effectiveness ... Dr. Ryan CORNNER
35 Dean Student Services ... Mr. Jeremy ALLRED
88 Dean EOP&S/CARE ... Ms. Danelle FALLERT
88 Dean CFES ... Ms. Angelica TOLEDO
25 Assoc Dean Resource Development ... Mr. Paul DE LA CERDA
25 Assistant Dean Grants Management ... Ms. Martha ERMIAS
26 Chief Public Relations Officer ... Vacant
22 Affirmative Action Officer ... Ms. Maria E. YEPES
37 Director Financial Aid ... Ms. Lindy FONG
40 Director Student Store ... Ms. Joyce GARCIA
88 Director Vincent Price Art Museum . Ms. Pilar TOMPKINS RIVAS
41 Athletic Director (Men/Women) ... Mr. Allen J. CONE
28 Director of Diversity ... Ms. Maria Elena YEPES
88 Child Development Director ... Ms. Marcia CAGIGAS
38 Department Chair Counseling ... Mr. Daniel ORNELAS
21 College Fiscal Administrator ... Ms. Erlinda N. DEOCAMPO
08 Library Coordinator ... Ms. Choonhee L. RHIM
85 Foreign Student Advisement ... Ms. Nancy C. WONG

*Los Angeles City College (A)

855 N Vermont Avenue, Los Angeles CA 90029-9990
County: Los Angeles FICE Identification: 001223
Unit ID: 117788
Telephone: (323) 953-4000 Carnegie Class: Assoc/MT-VT-High Non
FAX Number: (323) 953-4013 Calendar System: Semester
URL: www.lacitycollege.edu
Established: 1929 Annual Undergrad Tuition & Fees (In-District): $1,220
Enrollment: 18,825 Coed
Affiliation or Control: Local IRS Status: 501(c)3
Highest Offering: Associate Degree
Accreditation: WJ, DT, RAD

02 President ... Mrs. Renee D. MARTINEZ
05 Vice President Academic Affairs ... Dr. Dan WALDEN
10 Vice President Administrative Svcs ... Dr. John AL-AMIN
32 Vice President of Student Services ... Dr. Regina SMITH
21 Asst Vice Pres Administrative Svcs ... Mr. Anil JAIN
20 Dean of Academic Affairs ... Dr. Thelma DAY
103 Dean Workforce Development ... Dr. A. Alex DAVIS
09 Dean of Institutional Effectiveness ... Dr. Anna BADALYAN
84 Dean of Enrollment Services ... Vacant
35 Dean Student Svcs Special Programs ... Dr. Randy ANDERSON
35 Dean of EOPS ... Ms. Jeannette MAGEE
37 Dean Financial Aid ... Dr. Jeremy VILLAR
35 Dean Office of Student Life ... Mr. Alen ANDRIASSIAN
40 Bookstore Manager ... Ms. Christi O'CONNOR
85 Director International Students ... Vacant
15 Human Resources Manager ... Vacant
66 Nursing Department Chair ... Ms. Christiana BASKARAN
38 Counseling Chairperson ... Mr. Boris LOPEZ
18 Facilities Director ... Vacant

*Los Angeles Harbor College (B)

1111 Figueroa Place, Wilmington CA 90744-2397
County: Los Angeles FICE Identification: 001224
Unit ID: 117690
Telephone: (310) 233-4000 Carnegie Class: Assoc/HT-High Trad
FAX Number: (310) 233-4223 Calendar System: Semester
URL: www.lahc.edu
Established: 1949 Annual Undergrad Tuition & Fees (In-District): $1,220
Enrollment: 10,115 Coed
Affiliation or Control: State/Local IRS Status: 501(c)3
Highest Offering: Associate Degree
Accreditation: WJ, ADNUR

02 President ... Dr. Otto LEE
04 Executive Assistant to President ... Ms. Sylvia FILES
05 Vice Pres Academic Affairs ... Dr. Bobbi VILLALOBOS
10 Vice Pres Administrative Services ... Mr. Robert E. SUPPELSA
32 Vice Pres Student Services ... Mr. Luis DORADO
21 Assoc Vice Pres Administrative Svcs ... Mr. Nestor TAN
09 Dean of Institutional Effectiveness ... Dr. Edward PAI
20 Dean of Academic Affairs ... Dr. Nicole ALBO-LOPEZ
20 Dean of Academic Affairs ... Dr. Stephanie ATKINSON-ALSTON
07 Dean Enrollment/Eve Ops ... Mr. Corey RODGERS
35 Dean of Student Services ... Ms. Mercedes YANEZ
25 Assoc Dean Grants Mgmt/ED ... Ms. Priscilla LOPEZ
103 Dean of Economic/Workforce Devel ... Ms. Sandra SANCHEZ
83 Div Chair Behavioral/Social Sci ... Mr. Son NGUYEN
50 Division Chairperson Business ... Mr. Stanley C. SANDELL
60 Div Chairperson Communications ... Ms. Ann WARREN
57 Div Chair Humanities/Fine Arts ... Mr. Juan BAEZ
81 Div Chairperson Math/Phys Science ... Ms. Farah SADDIGH
76 Div Chairperson Health Sciences ... Mrs. Lynn YAMAKAWA
68 Div Chairperson Physical Education ... Mr. Nabeel M. BARAKAT
88 Div Chair Sci & Fam/Consum Stds ... Dr. Basil IBE
08 Division Chairperson Library ... Mr. Jonathan LEE
38 Division Chairperson Counseling ... Ms. Joy FISHER
41 Athletic Director ... Mr. Dean DOWTY
37 Director Student Financial Aid ... Ms. Peggy LOEWY-WELLISCH
18 Facilities Manager ... Vacant

13 Manager Information Technology ... Mr. Ivan CLARKE
31 Community Services Manager ... Ms. Priscilla LOPEZ
85 International Student Program ... Ms. Jessica CRUZ
15 Payroll & Personnel Supervisor ... Ms. Claudette MCCLENNEY

*Los Angeles Mission College (C)

13356 Eldridge Avenue, Sylmar CA 91342-3244
County: Los Angeles FICE Identification: 012550
Unit ID: 117867
Telephone: (818) 364-7600 Carnegie Class: Assoc/HT-High Trad
FAX Number: (818) 364-7826 Calendar System: Semester
URL: www.lamission.edu
Established: 1975 Annual Undergrad Tuition & Fees (In-District): $1,220
Enrollment: 10,188 Coed
Affiliation or Control: State/Local IRS Status: 501(c)3
Highest Offering: Associate Degree
Accreditation: WJ

02 President ... Dr. Monte E. PEREZ
05 Vice President Academic Affairs ... Mr. Michael K. ALLEN
11 Vice President Administrative Svcs ... Mr. Daniel G. VILLANUEVA
32 Vice President of Student Services ... Dr. Christopher VILLA
20 Dean of Academic Affairs ... Ms. Darlene MONTES
35 Dean of Student Services ... Ms. Ludi VILLEGAS-VIDAL
88 Dean of CTE ... Ms. Marla ULIANA
35 Dean of Student Services ... Mr. Carlos R. GONZALEZ
09 Dean of Institutional Effectiveness ... Dr. Sarah L. MASTER
20 Dean of Academic Affairs ... Ms. Madelline HERNANDEZ
20 Dean DSP & S ... Dr. Larry RESENDEZ
26 Chief Public Relations Officer ... Mr. Alejandro GUZMAN
88 Director Child Development Center ... Ms. Diane STEIN
41 Athletic Director ... Mr. Steve RUYS
08 Head Librarian ... Ms. Donna AYERS
38 Counseling Chairperson ... Ms. Michong PARK
37 Financial Aid Manager ... Mr. Dennis J. SCHROEDER
31 Community Services Manager ... Mr. Dennis SOLARES
18 Facilities/Physical Plant Manager ... Mr. Walter J. BORTMAN
88 EOP & S/Care Director ... Ms. Ludi VILLEGAS-VIDAL
04 Administrative Asst to President ... Mrs. Oliva AYALA
10 Chief Business Officer ... Mr. Jerry HUANG
102 Dir Foundation/Corporate Relations ... Mr. Albert ALVAREZ
15 Personnel Services Assistant ... Mr. Pio CASTILLO
07 Director of Admissions/Records ... Ms. Rosalie TORRES
36 Director Student Placement ... Ms. Wendy RIVERA
84 Director Enrollment Management ... Mr. Michael ALLEN
96 Director of Purchasing ... Ms. Isabel RUIZ-MORENO

*Los Angeles Pierce College (D)

6201 Winnetka Avenue, Woodland Hills CA 91371-0001
County: Los Angeles FICE Identification: 001226
Unit ID: 117706
Telephone: (818) 710-4100 Carnegie Class: Assoc/HT-High Trad
FAX Number: (818) 710-4300 Calendar System: Semester
URL: www.piercecollege.edu
Established: 1947 Annual Undergrad Tuition & Fees (In-District): $1,220
Enrollment: 20,767 Coed
Affiliation or Control: State/Local IRS Status: 501(c)3
Highest Offering: Associate Degree
Accreditation: WJ

02 President ... Dr. Kathleen F. BURKE
05 Vice President Academic Affairs ... Ms. Sheri BERGER
11 Vice President Administrative Svcs ... Mr. Rolf SCHLEICHER
32 Vice President Student Services ... Dr. Earic DIXON-PETERS
10 Assoc Vice President Admin Services ... Mr. Bruce ROSKY
10 Assoc Vice President Admin Services ... Mr. Larry KRAUS
08 Chairman Library Services ... Ms. Paula PAGGI
38 Chair Student Counseling ... Mr. Rudy DOMPE
20 Dean of Academic Affairs ... Dr. Donna-Mae VILLANUEVA
20 Dean of Academic Affairs ... Ms. Mary Anne GAVARRA-OH
20 Dean of Academic Affairs ... Ms. Susan RHI-KLEINERT
20 Dean of Academic Affairs ... Mr. Jose Luis FERNANDEZ
20 Dean of Academic Affairs ... Mr. Tom VESSELLA
20 Dean of Academic Affairs ... Ms. Sharon DALMAGE
07 Dean Admissions/Records ... Mr. William MARMOLEJO
37 Director of Financial Aid ... Ms. Anafe ROBINSON
108 Dean Institutional Effectiveness ... Mr. Oleg BESPALOV
26 Public Information Officer ... Ms. Doreen CLAY
31 Director Community Services ... Ms. Cindy CHANG
102 Director of Foundation ... Vacant
18 Director of College Facilities ... Mr. Paul NIEMAN
41 Athletic Director ... Ms. Moriah VAN NORMAN
106 Dir Online Education/E-learning ... Ms. Wendy BASS KEER
35 Dean Student Services ... Dr. Kalynda WEBBER MCLEAN
35 Dean Student Services ... Mr. Juan Carlos ASTORGA
06 Registrar ... Ms. Lorena LOPEZ

*Los Angeles Southwest College (E)

1600 W Imperial Highway, Los Angeles CA 90047-4899
County: Los Angeles FICE Identification: 007047
Unit ID: 117715
Telephone: (323) 241-5225 Carnegie Class: Assoc/HT-High Non
FAX Number: (323) 241-5220 Calendar System: Semester
URL: www.lasc.edu
Established: 1967 Annual Undergrad Tuition & Fees (In-District): $1,220
Enrollment: 6,826 Coed
Affiliation or Control: State/Local IRS Status: 501(c)3
Highest Offering: Associate Degree
Accreditation: WJ

02 Interim President ... Dr. Denise NOLDON
05 Vice President Academic Affairs ... Dr. Lawrence BRADFORD
32 Vice President Student Services ... Dr. Howard IRVIN
10 Vice President Admin Services ... Mr. Daniel B. HALL
46 Dean Resource Development ... Vacant
111 Dean Institutional Advancement ... Mr. Jose Alfred GALLEGOS
103 Dean Career/Technical Education ... Mr. Rick HODGE
20 Dean Academic Affairs ... Dr. Tangelia ALFRED
20 Interim Dean Academic Affairs ... Mr. James E. STEVENSON
38 Chairperson Counseling ... Dr. Ralph DAVIS
08 Chairperson Library ... Mrs. Tim REAM
06 Registrar ... Ms. Kimberly CARPENTER
18 Director of Facilities ... Mr. Al MAH
37 Manager Student Financial Aid ... Ms. Marisol VELAZQUEZ
26 Chief Public Relations Officer ... Mr. Ben DEMERS

*Los Angeles Trade-Technical College (F)

400 W Washington Boulevard,
Los Angeles CA 90015-4108
County: Los Angeles FICE Identification: 001227
Unit ID: 117724
Telephone: (213) 763-7000 Carnegie Class: Assoc/HVT-Mix Trad/Non
FAX Number: (213) 763-5393 Calendar System: Semester
URL: www.lattc.edu
Established: 1925 Annual Undergrad Tuition & Fees (In-District): $1,220
Enrollment: 14,650 Coed
Affiliation or Control: State/Local IRS Status: 501(c)3
Highest Offering: Associate Degree
Accreditation: WJ, ACFEI

02 President ... Mr. Larry FRANK
11 VP Administrative Services ... Dr. Mary GALLAGHER
05 VP Academic Affs & Workforce Devel ... Ms. Leticia BARAJAS
32 Vice President Student Services ... Dr. Kaneesha TARRANT
21 Assoc Vice Pres Administrative Svcs ... Vacant
20 Dean Academic Affairs & Workforce ... Mr. Vincent JACKSON
20 Dean Academic Affairs & Workforce ... Ms. Cynthia MORLEY-MOWER
20 Dean Academic Affairs & Workforce ... Mr. Benjamin GOLDSTEIN
20 Dean Academic Affairs & Workforce ... Ms. Nicole ALBO-LOPEZ
37 Supervisor Financial Aid ... Ms. Ruth BLEDSOE
09 Dean Inst Effectiveness ... Vacant
35 Dean Student Services ... Ms. Dorothy SMITH
35 Dean Student Services ... Dr. Henan JOOF
18 Chief Facilities/Physical Plant ... Mr. Bill SMITH
06 Sr Supervisor Admission & Records ... Ms. Carolyn WALKER
10 Chief Business Officer ... Ms. Mary GALLAGHER
38 Chair Student Counseling ... Mr. Tom DAWKINS
102 Director Foundation/Corporate Rels ... Vacant
26 Public Relations Manager ... Mr. David YSAIS
13 Mgr College Information System ... Mr. Sang BAIK

*Los Angeles Valley College (G)

5800 Fulton Avenue, Valley Glen CA 91401-4096
County: Los Angeles FICE Identification: 001228
Unit ID: 117733
Telephone: (818) 947-2600 Carnegie Class: Assoc/HT-Mix Trad/Non
FAX Number: N/A Calendar System: Semester
URL: www.lavc.edu
Established: 1949 Annual Undergrad Tuition & Fees (In-District): $1,220
Enrollment: 18,838 Coed
Affiliation or Control: State/Local IRS Status: 501(c)3
Highest Offering: Associate Degree
Accreditation: WJ, ADNUR, COARC

02 President ... Dr. Erika A. ENDRIJONAS
05 Vice President Academic Affairs ... Ms. Karen DAAR
10 Vice Pres Administrative Services ... Mr. Mike C. LEE
32 Vice Pres Student Services ... Mr. Florentino MANZANO
11 Assoc Vice Pres Administrative Svcs ... Ms. Sarah SONG
45 Financial Anaylst ... Ms. Violet AMRIKHAS
20 Dean of Academic Affairs ... Dr. Laurie NALEPA
20 Dean of Academic Affairs ... Dr. Deborah A. DICESARE
20 Dean of Academic Affairs ... Mr. Matthew JORDAN
20 Dean of Academic Affairs ... Mr. Jermain PIPKINS
37 Financial Aid Manager ... Mr. Vernon D. BRIDGES
09 Dean of Institutional Effectiveness ... Ms. Michelle R. FOWLES
35 Dean of Student Life ... Dr. Elizabeth NEGRETE
88 Dean of Special Programs ... Dr. Sherri RODRIGUEZ
88 Associate Dean DSPS ... Mr. David M. GREEN
35 Assoc Dean of Student Services ... Ms. Annie G. REED
102 Executive Director of Foundation ... Mr. Raul V. CASTILLO
26 Public Relations Manager ... Ms. Jennifer C. BORUCKI
18 Director of College Facilities ... Mr. Tom LOPEZ
40 College Store Manager ... Ms. Mary JOHN
13 Manager College Info Svcs ... Ms. Hanh TRAN
31 Community Services Manager ... Mr. Michael B. ATKIN
38 Director Student Counseling ... Ms. Lynn BROWER
41 Athletic Director ... Mr. Jim FENWICK
06 Registrar ... Ms. Ashley DUNN
121 Dean Student Success & Support Svcs ... Mr. Marco DE LA GARZA
35 Associate Dean Student Services ... Dr. Llanet MARTIN
21 College Fiscal Administrator ... Vacant

*West Los Angeles College (H)

9000 Overland Avenue, Culver City CA 90230-5002
County: Los Angeles FICE Identification: 008596
Unit ID: 125471
Telephone: (310) 287-4200 Carnegie Class: Assoc/MT-VT-Mix Trad/Non

FAX Number: (310) 841-0396 Calendar System: Semester
URL: www.wlac.edu
Established: 1969 Annual Undergrad Tuition & Fees (In-District): $1,220
Enrollment: 11,141 Coed
Affiliation or Control: State/Local IRS Status: 501(c)3
Highest Offering: Baccalaureate
Accreditation: WJ, DH

02 President .... Dr. James M. LIMBAUGH
11 Vice President Administrative Svcs .... Ms. Iris INGRAM
05 Acting VP Academic Affairs .... Ms. Aracely AGUIAR
32 VP Student Services .... Dr. Roberto O. GONZALEZ
97 Dean General Education/Transfer .... Dr. Walter JONES
84 Dean Student Svcs/Enrollment .... Mr. Michael GOLTERMANN
75 Dean Career/Technology Educ .... Vacant
88 Dean of Student Support Services .... Dr. Shalamon DUKE
09 Dean of Institutional Effectiveness .... Ms. Rebecca TILLBERG
56 Dean Distance Learning/Inst Tech .... Mr. Eric ICHON
20 Dean of Academic Affairs .... Vacant
35 Interim Dean Student Services .... Dr. Celena ALCALA
11 Associate Dean Contract Education .... Mr. Barry SLOAN
88 Academic Senate President .... Ms. Holly BAILEY-HOFMANN
10 Chief Financial Administrator .... Ms. Rasel MENENDEZ
26 Dir Advtg/Marketing/Public Rels .... Ms. Michelle LONG-COFFEE
41 Athletic Director .... Mr. Ricardo HOOPER
18 Acting Facilities Manager .... Mr. Joachim MORERA
19 Sheriff/Deputy .... Mr. Leander DAVIS
37 Financial Aid Manager .... Mr. Glenn SCHENK
40 College Enterprise Manager .... Mr. Larry PACKHAM
88 Operations Manager .... Mr. Bruce HICKS
22 Compliance Officer .... Vacant
07 Sr Supervisor Admissions/Records .... Ms. Diana BAXTER
08 Head Librarian .... Ms. Susan TRUJILLO

Los Angeles County College of Nursing and Allied Health (A)

1237 N Mission Road, Los Angeles CA 90033-1083
County: Los Angeles FICE Identification: 006165
Unit ID: 117803
Telephone: (323) 226-4911 Carnegie Class: Spec 2-yr-Health
FAX Number: (323) 226-6343 Calendar System: Semester
URL: dhs.lacounty.gov/wps/portal/dhs/conah/
Established: 1895 Annual Undergrad Tuition & Fees (In-District): N/A
Enrollment: 196 Coed
Affiliation or Control: Local IRS Status: 501(c)3
Highest Offering: Associate Degree
Accreditation: WJ

01 Provost .... Ms. Vivian BRANCHICK
05 Acting Dean of Nursing Programs .... Ms. Leonece MYERS
32 Dean Administrative/Student Svcs .... Ms. Maria C. CABALLERO
53 Dean Education/Consulting Services .... Ms. Tammy BLASS
37 Director of Financial Aid .... Ms. Doris DEHART

Los Angeles Film School (B)

6363 Sunset Boulevard, Hollywood CA 90028
County: Los Angeles FICE Identification: 040373
Unit ID: 436429
Telephone: (323) 860-0789 Carnegie Class: Bac/Assoc-Assoc Dom
FAX Number: (323) 646-0770 Calendar System: Other
URL: www.lafilm.edu
Established: 1999 Annual Undergrad Tuition & Fees: N/A
Enrollment: 2,334 Coed
Affiliation or Control: Proprietary IRS Status: Proprietary
Highest Offering: Baccalaureate
Accreditation: ACCSC

01 President/CEO .... Ms. Diana DERYCZ-KESSLER

Los Angeles ORT College (C)

6435 Wilshire Boulevard, Los Angeles CA 90048
County: Los Angeles FICE Identification: 025703
Unit ID: 368780
Telephone: (323) 966-5444 Carnegie Class: Assoc/HVT-Mix Trad/Non
FAX Number: (323) 966-5455 Calendar System: Other
URL: www.laort.edu
Established: 1985 Annual Undergrad Tuition & Fees: N/A
Enrollment: 311 Coed
Affiliation or Control: Independent Non-Profit IRS Status: 501(c)3
Highest Offering: Associate Degree
Accreditation: CNCE

01 Director .... Mr. Joseph NEMAN

Los Angeles Pacific College (D)

3325 Wilshire Boulevard, Ste 550, Los Angeles CA 90010
County: Los Angeles Identification: 667143
Telephone: (213) 384-2318 Carnegie Class: Not Classified
FAX Number: (213) 384-0419 Calendar System: Semester
URL: www.lapacific.net
Established: 1989 Annual Undergrad Tuition & Fees: N/A
Enrollment: N/A Coed
Affiliation or Control: Proprietary IRS Status: Proprietary
Highest Offering: Associate Degree
Accreditation: COE, CEA

01 President .... Ms. Mary YOON
10 Controller .... Mr. Ho Sung YOON

*Los Rios Community College District Office (E)

1919 Spanos Court, Sacramento CA 95825-3981
County: Sacramento FICE Identification: 001231
Unit ID: 117900
Telephone: (916) 568-3021 Carnegie Class: N/A
FAX Number: (916) 561-0574
URL: www.losrios.edu

01 Chancellor .... Dr. Brian KING
04 Chancellor's Executive Assistant .... Ms. Jennifer DELUCCHI
10 Vice Chancellor Finance/Admin .... Ms. Theresa MATISTA
05 Vice Chancellor .... Dr. Jamey NYE
30 Vice Chanc Resource Development .... Ms. Paula ALLISON
26 Assoc Vice Chanc Comm/Media Rels .... Mr. Gabe ROSS
18 Assoc Vice Chanc Facilities Mgmt .... Mr. Pablo MANZO
15 Assoc Vice Chanc Human Resources .... Mr. Ryan COX
13 Interim Chief Information Officer .... Mr. Thomas DANFORD
20 Assoc Vice Chanc Instruction .... Vacant
32 Assoc Vice Chanc Student Services .... Dr. Victoria ROSARIO
43 General Counsel .... Mr. J.P SHERRY
37 Director Financial Aid .... Mr. Roy BECKHORN
96 Interim Director General Services .... Ms. Anita SINGH
09 Director Institutional Research .... Ms. Betty GLYER-CULVER

*American River College (F)

4700 College Oak Drive, Sacramento CA 95841-4286
County: Sacramento FICE Identification: 001232
Unit ID: 109208
Telephone: (916) 484-8011 Carnegie Class: Assoc/HT-High Trad
FAX Number: (916) 484-8674 Calendar System: Semester
URL: www.arc.losrios.edu
Established: 1955 Annual Undergrad Tuition & Fees (In-District): $1,104
Enrollment: 29,381 Coed
Affiliation or Control: State/Local IRS Status: 501(c)3
Highest Offering: Associate Degree
Accreditation: WJ, COARC, EMT, FUSER

02 President .... Dr. Thomas G. GREENE
10 Vice President Admin Services .... Ms. Kuldeep KAUR
05 Vice President Instruction .... Dr. Lisa LAWRENSON
32 Vice President Student Services .... Dr. Robin NEAL
20 Assoc VP Instruction .... Ms. Kate JAQUES
62 Assoc VP Instruction/Lrng Res .... Dr. Tammy MONTGOMERY
32 Assoc VP Student Services .... Ms. Christine THOMAS
88 Assoc VP Student Services (Grants) .... Dr. Jeff STEPHENSON
103 Int Assoc VP Workforce Development .... Dr. Frank KOBAYASHI
57 Dean Fine & Applied Arts .... Dr. Kale BRADEN
07 Dean Enrollment Services .... Mr. Parrish GEARY
83 Dean Behavioral & Social Science .... Mr. Carlos REYES
88 Dean English .... Mr. Doug HERNDON
79 Interim Dean Humanities .... Ms. Diana HICKS
68 Dean Kinesiology/Athletics .... Dr. Derrick BOOTH
81 Dean Mathematics .... Dr. Roger DAVIDSON
56 Dean McClellan Center .... Mr. Steve SEGURA
35 Dean Student Services .... Ms. Kolleen OSTGAARD
09 Dean Planning/Research/Technology .... Dr. Adam KARP
66 Dean Health & Education .... Ms. Jan DELAPP
81 Dean Science/Engineering .... Dr. Rina ROY
56 Interim Dean Natomas Center .... Ms. Nancy REITZ
88 Dean Equity Programs & Pathways .... Mr. Manuel PEREZ
50 Int Dean Business/Computer Science .... Ms. Raquel ARATA
75 Dean Technical Education .... Dr. Trish CALDWELL
04 Administrative Asst to President .... Ms. Sue MCCOY
11 Director Administrative Services .... Ms. Cheryl SEARS
111 Director College Advancement .... Ms. Kirsten DUBRAY
26 Public Information Officer .... Mr. Scott CROW
37 Financial Aid Supervisor .... Mr. Dimitry PROSHAK
88 Dean DE/Virtual Ed Center .... Ms. Marsha RESKE

*Cosumnes River College (G)

8401 Center Parkway, Sacramento CA 95823-5799
County: Sacramento FICE Identification: 007536
Unit ID: 113096
Telephone: (916) 691-7344 Carnegie Class: Assoc/MT-VT-High Trad
FAX Number: (916) 691-7375 Calendar System: Semester
URL: www.crc.losrios.edu
Established: 1970 Annual Undergrad Tuition & Fees (In-District): $1,104
Enrollment: 14,398 Coed
Affiliation or Control: State/Local IRS Status: 501(c)3
Highest Offering: Associate Degree
Accreditation: WJ, CAHIIM, DMS, MAC

02 President .... Dr. Edward C. BUSH
05 Int VP Instruction & Stdnt Lrng .... Dr. Robert MONTANEZ
11 VP Admin Svcs & Student Support .... Mr. Cory WATHEN
32 VP Student Svcs/Enrollment Mgmt .... Dr. Kimberly MCDANIEL
84 Dean Student Svcs/Enrollment .... Mr. Chad FUNK
20 Assoc VP Instruction/Student Lrng .... Mr. Torence POWELL
08 Dean Learning Res/College Tech .... Mr. Stephen MCGLOUGHLIN
38 Dean Counseling & Student Services .... Dr. Shannon COOPER
50 Dean Business & Family Science .... Vacant
79 Dean Humanities & Social Science .... Vacant
41 Dean Kinesiology & Athletics .... Mr. Collin PREGLIASCO
81 Dean Science/Math/Engineering .... Dr. Kathryn SORENSEN
72 Dean Careers & Technology .... Dr. Kimberly HARRELL
60 Dean Comm/Visual/Performing Arts .... Dr. Colette HARRIS-MATHEWS
45 Int Dean of Col Planning & Research .... Dr. Heather TILSON
06 Registrar/Admissions & Records .... Mr. Richard ANDREWS
18 Chief Facilities/Physical Plant .... Mr. Augustine CHAVEZ
26 Public Information Officer .... Ms. Kristie WEST
30 Chief Development/Advancement .... Vacant
121 Dean of Student Services and Equity .... Mr. Tadael EMIRU
40 Bookstore Manager .... Ms. Maria HYDE

*Folsom Lake College (H)

10 College Parkway, Folsom CA 95630-6798
County: Sacramento FICE Identification: 038713
Unit ID: 444219
Telephone: (916) 608-6500 Carnegie Class: Assoc/HT-High Trad
FAX Number: (916) 608-6584 Calendar System: Semester
URL: www.flc.losrios.edu
Established: 2004 Annual Undergrad Tuition & Fees (In-District): $1,104
Enrollment: 8,666 Coed
Affiliation or Control: State/Local IRS Status: 501(c)3
Highest Offering: Associate Degree
Accreditation: WJ, MLTAD

02 President .... Whitney YAMAMURA
11 Vice Pres Administration .... Kathleen KIRKLIN
05 Vice President Instruction .... Dr. Monica PACTOL
32 Vice President Student Services .... Melanie DIXON
20 Dean of Instruction RCC .... Brian ROBINSON
35 Int Dean Student Success .... Genevieve SIWABESSY
20 Int Dean Instruction/Technology CRC .... Greg MCCORMAC
20 Int Dean of Instruction EDC .... John ALEXANDER
57 Dean of Instruction VAPA/LALI .... Dr. Robert (BJ) SNOWDEN
09 Dean Planning & Research .... Molly SENECAL
35 Dean of Student Services .... Bernard GIBSON
88 Executive Director VAPAC .... David PIER
30 Director College Advancement .... Sally HOWARD
07 Admissions & Records Supervisor .... Christine WURZER
40 College Store Manager .... Rob MULLIGAN
10 Business Services Supervisor .... Joany HARMAN
88 Director of Administrative Services .... Melissa WILLIAMS
12 Educational Center Supervisor/EDC .... Adrienne ANDREWS
37 Financial Aid Supervisor .... Ali PADASH
26 Comm & Public Information Officer .... Kristy HART
04 Assistant to the President .... Sondra LEE
68 Dean of Instruction KHA .... Matt WRIGHT
72 Dean of Instruction CTE .... Victoria MARYATT
12 Educational Center Supervisor RCC .... Joyce HEILAND
88 Dir Mktg/Communications Harris Ctr .... Paul DORN

*Sacramento City College (I)

3835 Freeport Boulevard, Sacramento CA 95822-1386
County: Sacramento FICE Identification: 001233
Unit ID: 122180
Telephone: (916) 558-2111 Carnegie Class: Assoc/HT-High Trad
FAX Number: (916) 558-2449 Calendar System: Semester
URL: www.scc.losrios.edu
Established: 1916 Annual Undergrad Tuition & Fees (In-State): $1,104
Enrollment: 22,690 Coed
Affiliation or Control: State Related IRS Status: 501(c)3
Highest Offering: Associate Degree
Accreditation: WJ, DA, DH, OTA, PTAA

02 Interim President .... Dr. Michael GUTIERREZ
05 Vice Pres Instructional Institution .... Dr. Steven BOYD
10 Vice Pres Administrative Services .... Mr. Laduan SMEDLEY
32 Interim Vice Pres Student Services .... Mr. Michael POINDEXTER
20 Associate Vice Pres Instruction .... Ms. Gabriel MEEHAN
20 Associate Vice Pres Instruction .... Ms. Julia A. JOLLY
84 AVP Enrollment/Student Services .... Ms. Debra LUFF
13 Dean Information Technology .... Dr. Elaine ADER
37 Dean Financial Aid/Student Svcs .... Ms. Christine HERNANDEZ
46 Dean Planning/Research/Development .... Dr. Marybeth BUECHNER
08 Dean Learning Resources .... Mr. Kevin FLASH
36 Dean Counseling/Student Success .... Mr. Andre COLEMAN
88 Dean Student Equity/Success .... Ms. Molly SPRINGER
40 Director College Store .... Mr. Randy CLEM
66 Director Nursing .... Ms. Carel MOUNTAIN
18 Director College Operations .... Ms. Margaret LEDNICKY
30 Interim Dir College Advancement .... Mr. Dan MCCARTY
26 Public Information Officer .... Vacant
76 Dean Science & Allied Health .... Mr. James COLLINS
50 Dean Business .... Dr. Deborah SAKS
79 Dean Humanities/Fine Arts .... Mr. Chris IWATA
88 Dean Languages/Literature .... Dr. Albert GARCIA
72 Dean Advanced Technology .... Ms. Donnetta WEBB
41 Dean PE/Health/Athletics .... Mr. Mitchell L. CAMPBELL
81 Dean Statistics/Math/Engineering .... Dr. Daniel STYER
83 Int Dean Behavioral/Social Science .... Dr. Carl SJOVOLD
56 Interim Dean Davis Center .... Mr. Frank MALARET
56 Dean West Sacramento Ctr .... Mr. Art PIMENTEL
06 Records & Admissions Officer .... Ms. Kim GOFF
04 Administrative Asst to President .... Ms. Pamela MORRISON
88 Director HSI-SAGE .... Dr. Lorena RUEDAS

Loyola Marymount University (J)

1 LMU Drive, Los Angeles CA 90045-2659
County: Los Angeles FICE Identification: 011649
Unit ID: 117946
Telephone: (310) 338-2700 Carnegie Class: Masters/L
FAX Number: N/A Calendar System: Semester
URL: www.lmu.edu

Established: 1911 Annual Undergrad Tuition & Fees: $44,480
Enrollment: 9,392 Coed
Affiliation or Control: Roman Catholic IRS Status: 501(c)3
Highest Offering: Doctorate
Accreditation: WC, ART, CAEPN, DANCE, ENG, LAW, MUS, THEA, THEOL

01 President ... Dr. Timothy L. SNYDER
00 Chancellor ... Rev. Patrick J. CAHALAN, SJ
05 Exec Vice President & Provost ... Dr. Thomas POON
42 VP for Mission & Ministry ... Dr. John SEBASTIAN
20 Vice Provost for Academic Affairs ... Dr. Michael J. O'SULLIVAN
84 Vice Provost Enrollment Management ... Dr. Maureen WEATHERALL
10 Sr Vice Pres/Chief Financial Ofcr ... Mr. Tom O. FLEMING
30 Sr Vice Pres University Relations ... Mr. Dennis SLON
32 Sr Vice Pres for Student Affairs ... Dr. Elena M. BOVE
11 Sr Vice Pres for Administration ... Ms. Lynne B. SCARBORO
13 VP for Information Technology Svcs ... Mr. Patrick FRONTIERA
15 VP for Human Resources ... Ms. Rebecca CHANDLER
18 VP for Facilities Management ... Mr. Timothy HAWORTH
28 Vice Pres for Intercultural Affairs ... Dr. Abbie ROBINSON-ARMSTRONG
46 Assoc Provost Inst Effectiveness ... Dr. Margaret KASIMATIS
36 Assoc Provost Career & Professional ... Mr. Branden GRIMMETT
88 Assoc Provost for Faculty Affairs ... Dr. Deena GONZALEZ
88 Assoc Provost Rsrch Advance & Comp ... Dr. John CARFORA
109 Assoc VP Auxiliary Mgmt & Business ... Mr. Raymond DENNIS
100 Special Assistant to the President ... Dr. John PARRISH
08 Dean of University Library ... Ms. Kristine BRANCOLINI
06 University Registrar ... Ms. Kathy REED
61 Dean Loyola Law School/Sr VP ... Mr. Michael WATERSTONE
49 Dean College Liberal Arts ... Dr. Robbin D. CRABTREE
53 Dean Sch of Educ/Dean Graduate Educ ... Dr. Shane P. MARTIN
50 Dean College of Business Admin ... Dr. Dennis DRAPER
57 Dean Communication & Fine Arts ... Dr. Bryant ALEXANDER
54 Dean College of Science & Engineer ... Dr. Tina CHOE
88 Dean School of Film/Television ... Mr. Stephen G. UJLAKI
44 Ex Dir Dev Plnd Gvng/Princpal Gifts ... Ms. Joanie POHAS
07 Director of Admissions ... Mr. Matthew X. FISSINGER
37 Director of Financial Aid ... Ms. Darlene WILSON
41 Athletic Director ... Dr. William HUSAK
27 Assistant Director of Marketing ... Mr. Benjamin ALKALY
09 Interim Dir Institutional Research ... Ms. Christine CHAVEZ
108 Director of Assessment ... Dr. Laura MASSA
26 Vice Pres Marketing/Communications ... Mr. John KIRALLA
29 Executive Director of Alumni Rels ... Ms. Lisa FARLAND
23 Director of Student Health Services ... Ms. Katherine ARCE
104 Interim Director Study Abroad ... Mr. Adrian DOYLE
25 Dir Research & Sponsored Projects ... Dr. Joseph MCNICHOLAS
90 Director of Academic Technology ... Ms. Crista COPP
04 Executive Asst to President ... Ms. Debbie CAVANAGH
88 Administrative Specialist ... Ms. Rosa CALDERON
102 Exec Dir Corp/Foundation Relations ... Mr. David A. TILLIPMAN
19 Chief of Public Safety ... Mr. Hampton CANTRELL
22 EEO Officer and Title IX Coord ... Ms. Sara TRIVEDI
39 Director Student Housing ... Mr. Steven NYGAARD
43 General Counsel ... Mr. Harold A. BRIDGES
04 Sr Admin Coord to Ofc of the Pres ... Ms. Christine DENNIS

Marshall B. Ketchum University (A)

2575 Yorba Linda Boulevard, Fullerton CA 92831-1699
County: Orange FICE Identification: 001230
Unit ID: 123943
Telephone: (714) 870-7226 Carnegie Class: Spec-4-yr-Other Health
FAX Number: (714) 879-9834 Calendar System: Quarter
URL: www.ketchum.edu
Established: 1904 Annual Graduate Tuition & Fees: N/A
Enrollment: 460 Coed
Affiliation or Control: Independent Non-Profit IRS Status: 501(c)3
Highest Offering: Doctorate; No Undergraduates
Accreditation: WC, #ARCPA, OPT, OPTR, @PHAR

01 President ... Dr. Kevin L. ALEXANDER
111 Vice Pres University Advancement ... Ms. Joan RUBIO
100 Sr Vice President & Chief of Staff ... Dr. Julie A. SCHORNACK
32 Vice President for Student Affairs ... Dr. Carmen N. BARNHARDT
15 Vice Pres Human Resources ... Ms. Gail S. DEUTSCH
10 Vice Pres Admin & Finance ... Mr. Shawn MCCOWN
46 Associate Dean Research SCCO ... Dr. Jerry PAUGH
18 Director Campus Operations ... Mr. Gregory SMITH
51 Director Continuing Education ... Ms. Bonnie DELLATORRE
13 Director of Information Technology ... Mr. Samuel YOUNG
84 Sr Dir Enroll Mgmt & Financial Aid ... Ms. Tami A. SATO
37 Director Financial Aid ... Ms. Barbara BREFFLE
30 Dir Development/Alumni Affairs ... Vacant
08 Director of Library Services ... Ms. Donnajean MATTHEWS
23 Dir Special Clinic Programs ... Ms. Michele WHITECAVAGE
26 Dir Marketing/Communications ... Mrs. Katie SANTOS-COY
88 Dean for Optometry ... Dr. Eric J. BORSTING
67 Dean for Pharmacy ... Dr. Edward FISHER
76 Dean for Health Sciences ... Dr. Judy ORTIZ
108 Dir Institutional Effectiveness ... Dr. Ajoy KOOMER
04 Assistant to the President ... Ms. Carole JOLLY
23 Assoc Dean Clinics ... Dr. Mark E. NAKANO
24 Director Multi-Media Services ... Mr. Matt BRENEMAN
00 Chairman of the Board ... Ms. Carol NAJERA
29 Asst Director Alumni/Donar Relation ... Ms. Abigail MOORE
31 Director of Community Relations ... Mr. Wayne HEIDLE
109 Chief Auxiliary Services Manager ... Ms. Debra WOODS
06 Registrar ... Ms. Lisa CASSIDY
19 Director Campus Safety/Security ... Mr. Craig COOPER
38 Director Univ Student Counseling ... Ms. Alyse Sherman KIRSCHEN

Marymount California University (B)

30800 Palos Verdes Drive E,
Rancho Palos Verdes CA 90275-6299
County: Los Angeles FICE Identification: 010474
Unit ID: 118541
Telephone: (310) 377-5501 Carnegie Class: Bac-Diverse
FAX Number: (310) 377-6223 Calendar System: Semester
URL: www.marymountcalifornia.edu
Established: 1932 Annual Undergrad Tuition & Fees: $35,884
Enrollment: 1,099 Coed
Affiliation or Control: Roman Catholic IRS Status: 501(c)3
Highest Offering: Master's
Accreditation: WC

01 President ... Dr. Lucas LAMADRID
03 Executive Vice President ... Dr. Ariane SCHAUER
10 Vice Pres Finance/Administration ... Ms. Kathleen RUIZ
05 Provost/Dean of Faculty ... Dr. Ariane SCHAUER
30 Dean Institutional Development ... Ms. Jinny QUINONES
84 Vice President Enrollment Mgmt ... Mr. Roger JONES
32 Dean of Students ... Mr. Ryan ALCANTARA
20 Associate Academic Officer ... Ms. Susie MARTIN
08 Librarian ... Mr. Gary MEDINA
37 Director Student Financial Aid ... Mr. Pedro LADINO
15 Director Personnel Services ... Ms. Karen THORDARSON
18 Chief Facilities/Physical Plant ... Mr. Joel ZARBO
26 Chief Public Relations Officer ... Vacant
29 Director Alumni Relations ... Vacant
36 Director Student Placement ... Mr. Adam MITCHELL
38 Director Student Counseling ... Ms. Osmara REYES-OSARIO
96 Director of Purchasing ... Ms. Denise FESSENBECKER
06 Registrar ... Ms. Paula AVERY
35 Dir Student Life & Engagement ... Ms. Kimberly HERNANDEZ
09 Director of Institutional Research ... Mr. Michael SEMENOFF
21 Associate Business Officer ... Ms. Debra YAVAS
04 Administrative Asst to President ... Ms. Kimberly RAMSEY
19 Director Security/Safety ... Mr. Michael MACMENAMIE
39 Director Student Housing ... Ms. Laura DORFMAN
41 Athletic Director ... Ms. Courtney THOMSEN
104 Director Study Abroad ... Dr. David DRAPER
105 Director Web Services ... Mr. Maury HILLSTROM
13 Chief Info Technology Officer (CIO) ... Mr. Monte SCHMEISER
101 Secretary of the Institution/Board ... Ms. Kimberly RAMSAY
07 Director of Admissions ... Mr. Pedro LADINO
110 Assoc Dean Development ... Ms. Jinny QUINONES

The Master's University (C)

21726 Placerita Canyon Road,
Santa Clarita CA 91321-1200
County: Los Angeles FICE Identification: 001220
Unit ID: 117751
Telephone: (661) 259-3540 Carnegie Class: Masters/S
FAX Number: N/A Calendar System: Semester
URL: www.masters.edu
Established: 1927 Annual Undergrad Tuition & Fees: $31,970
Enrollment: 1,713 Coed
Affiliation or Control: Independent Non-Profit IRS Status: 501(c)3
Highest Offering: Doctorate
Accreditation: WC, MUS

01 President ... Dr. John MACARTHUR
03 Sr Vice President and Provost ... Dr. John STEAD
05 Vice President Academic Affairs ... Dr. John STEAD
32 Dean of Student Life ... Mr. Joe KELLER
58 Vice President Graduate School ... Mr. Rich GREGORY
11 Vice President of Operations ... Vacant
30 Vice President of Development ... Mr. Luke CHERRY
46 Vice Pres Institutional Research ... Dr. John HUGHES
10 Chief Financial Officer ... Mr. Jason HARTUNG
18 Chief of Operations ... Mr. Jason HARTUNG
06 Registrar ... Mr. Don GILMORE
08 Director Library Services ... Mr. John STONE
07 Director of Admissions ... Mr. Madison CURRIE
20 Associate Dean of Students ... Mr. David HULET
84 Director Enrollment ... Mr. Madison CURRIE
41 Athletic Director ... Mr. Steve WALDECK
37 Director Financial Aid ... Mr. Gary EDWARDS
35 Director Campus Activities ... Vacant
29 Director Alumni Affairs ... Ms. Shayna ANDERSON
09 Director of Institutional Research ... Mr. John M. WALTER
36 Director Student Placement ... Mr. Michael DAVIS
85 International Students Advisor ... Miss Lisa LAGEORGE
04 Administrative Asst to President ... Ms. Sharon STAATS
13 Chief Information Officer ... Mr. Paul SEDY
15 Director Personnel Services ... Mr. Kent HANEY
19 Director Security/Safety ... Mr. Chris POWELL

† The Master's Seminary is located at 13248 Roscoe Boulevard, Sun Valley, CA 91352.

Mayfield College (D)

35-325 Date Palm Drive, Suite 101,
Cathedral City CA 92234
County: Riverside FICE Identification: 041156
Unit ID: 454698
Telephone: (760) 328-5554 Carnegie Class: Spec 2-yr-Tech
FAX Number: (760) 328-5357 Calendar System: Semester
URL: www.mayfieldcollege.org
Established: 1997 Annual Undergrad Tuition & Fees: $13,079
Enrollment: 404 Coed
Affiliation or Control: Proprietary IRS Status: Proprietary
Highest Offering: Associate Degree
Accreditation: COE

01 Campus President ... Kevin HA

Mendocino College (E)

1000 Hensley Creek Road, Ukiah CA 95482-7821
County: Mendocino FICE Identification: 011672
Unit ID: 118684
Telephone: (707) 468-3000 Carnegie Class: Assoc/HT-High Non
FAX Number: (707) 468-3120 Calendar System: Semester
URL: www.mendocino.edu
Established: 1973 Annual Undergrad Tuition & Fees (In-District): $1,423
Enrollment: 4,290 Coed
Affiliation or Control: State/Local IRS Status: 501(c)3
Highest Offering: Associate Degree
Accreditation: WJ

01 Superintendent/President ... Mr. Arturo REYES
05 Int VP Education Pgms/Student Svcs ... Ms. Debra POLAK
10 Vice Pres Administrative Services ... Ms. Eileen CICHOCKI
08 Head Librarian ... Mr. John KOETZNER
20 Dean of Instruction ... Ms. Rebecca MONTES
20 Dean of Centers ... Ms. Debra POLAK
75 Dean Applied Academics ... Mr. Dennis ASELTYNE
38 Dean of Counseling/Student Programs ... Mr. Antonio LOPEZ
15 Director Human Resources ... Ms. Sabrina MEYER
18 Director of Facilities ... Mr. MacAdam LOJOWSKY
26 Director Communications & Cmty Rels ... Ms. Jessica SILVA
41 Director of Athletics ... Mr. Matthew GORDON
21 Director Fiscal Services ... Mr. Joe ATHERTON
13 Director Information Technology .. Ms. Karen CHRISTOPHERSON
09 Director of Institutional Research ... Ms. Minerva FLORES
07 Director Admissions/Registrar ... Ms. Anastasia SIMPSON-LOGG
37 Director of Financial Aid ... Mr. Ulises VELASCO
04 Administrative Asst to President ... Ms. Mary LAMB
12 Director of Lake Center ... Ms. Valerie JENSEN
102 Dir Foundation/Corporate Relations ... Ms. Katie FAIRBAIRN
88 MESA/Stem Success Director ... Ms. Amanda XU

Menlo College (F)

1000 El Camino Real, Atherton CA 94027-4301
County: San Mateo FICE Identification: 001236
Unit ID: 118693
Telephone: (800) 556-3656 Carnegie Class: Spec-4-yr-Bus
FAX Number: (650) 543-4085 Calendar System: Semester
URL: www.menlo.edu
Established: 1927 Annual Undergrad Tuition & Fees: $39,950
Enrollment: 787 Coed
Affiliation or Control: Independent Non-Profit IRS Status: 501(c)3
Highest Offering: Baccalaureate
Accreditation: WC

01 Acting President ... Dr. T. Geir RAMLETH
05 Provost ... Dr. Terri GIVENS
10 Exec VP Finance & Administration ... Mr. Steven WEINER
10 Dir Finance & Business Affairs ... Mr. Tim CHIOCHIOS
11 Director of Operations ... Ms. Linda TEUTSCHEL
13 Chief Information Officer ... Ms. Kristen DIETIKER
20 Dean for Academic/Prof Success ... Ms. Angela SCHMIEDE
84 Dean of Enrollment Mgmt/Admissions ... Ms. Priscila DESOUZA
08 Dean Library Services ... Ms. Linda SMITH
32 Dean of Student Affairs ... Ms. Andrea PEETERS
108 Assoc Director IR & Assessment ... Ms. Ivana IZVONAR
30 Sr Director Advancement Services ... Ms. Rosetta CLAY
15 Director of Human Resources ... Mr. Jay NAIDU
18 Director Facilities & Operations ... Mr. Robert TALBOTT
41 Director of Athletics ... Mr. Keith SPATARO
36 Director Internship Program ... Mr. Zach OSBORNE
26 Director of Communications ... Vacant
06 Registrar/Admissions/Enrol Mgmt ... Ms. Cristine RABAGO

Merced College (G)

3600 M Street, Merced CA 95348-2898
County: Merced FICE Identification: 001237
Unit ID: 118718
Telephone: (209) 384-6000 Carnegie Class: Assoc/MT-VT-High Trad
FAX Number: (209) 384-6043 Calendar System: Semester
URL: www.mccd.edu
Established: 1962 Annual Undergrad Tuition & Fees (In-District): $1,150
Enrollment: 10,389 Coed
Affiliation or Control: State/Local IRS Status: 501(c)3
Highest Offering: Associate Degree
Accreditation: WJ, DMS, RAD

01 President ... Mr. Chris VITELLI
04 Executive Assistant to President ... Ms. Stacey HICKS
05 Vice President Instruction ... Dr. Brian ELLISON
32 Acting Vice Pres Student Services ... Mr. Michael MCCANDLESS
12 Dean Los Banos Campus ... Dr. Brenda LATHAM
45 Dean Institutional Effectiveness ... Dr. Baba ADAM
81 Dean Science/Math/Engineering ... Dr. Douglas KAIN
79 Dean English & Humanities ... Mr. Vince PIRO
75 Dean Career Technical Education ... Mr. Jim ANDERSEN
50 Dean Business/Allied Health/Safety ... Dr. Bobby ANDERSON
83 Dean Social Sci/Fine-Perf Arts ... Mr. John ALBANO
103 Dean EWD/Cmty Service & Noncredit ... Mrs. Shelly CONNER
35 Dean of Student Services ... Ms. Angela TOS
22 Dean of Student Equity & Success ... Mr. Michael MCCANDLESS

26 Chief Public Relations Officer .... Vacant
06 Registrar & Dir Financial Aid .... Mrs. Sharon ALLRED
15 Director of Human Resources .... Ms. Tracie GREEN
07 Dir Admissions & Records .... Ms. Sherry ELMS

Meridian University (A)

47 Sixth Street, Petaluma CA 94952

County: Sonoma | Identification: 667300
Telephone: (707) 765-1836 | Carnegie Class: Not Classified
FAX Number: (707) 765-2351 | Calendar System: Other
URL: www.meridianuniversity.edu
Established: 1993 | Annual Graduate Tuition & Fees: N/A
Enrollment: N/A | Coed
Affiliation or Control: Proprietary | IRS Status: Proprietary
Highest Offering: Doctorate; No Undergraduates
Accreditation: WC

00 Chancellor .... Dr. Jean HOUSTON
01 CEO .... Dr. Aftab OMER
05 Vice President Academic Affairs .... Dr. Melissa SCHWARTZ
10 Chief Financial Officer .... Mr. Rob GALL
108 Dir of Assessment & Student Develop .... Ms. Courtney LUBELL

Merit University (B)

3699 Wilshire Blvd., Ste 970, Los Angeles CA 90010

County: Los Angeles | Identification: 667293
Telephone: (213) 325-2760 | Carnegie Class: Not Classified
FAX Number: (213) 325-2761 | Calendar System: Quarter
URL: www.meritu.edu
Established: | Annual Graduate Tuition & Fees: N/A
Enrollment: N/A | Coed
Affiliation or Control: Proprietary | IRS Status: Proprietary
Highest Offering: Master's; No Undergraduates
Accreditation: PPPA

01 President .... Dr. Jae D. KIM

Methodist Theological Seminary in America (C)

905 S. Euclid Street, Fullerton CA 92832

County: Orange | Identification: 667133
Telephone: (213) 386-0080 | Carnegie Class: Not Classified
FAX Number: (213) 386-5229 | Calendar System: Semester
URL: www.mtsamerica.org
Established: 1880 | Annual Undergrad Tuition & Fees: N/A
Enrollment: N/A | Coed
Affiliation or Control: Independent Non-Profit | IRS Status: 501(c)3
Highest Offering: Master's
Accreditation: @BI

01 President .... Rev. David LIM
00 Chairman of the Board .... Bis. Myung Ku JUN
03 Vice President .... Rev. Chan Hee KIM
05 Academic Dean .... Rev. Seong Joo LEE
32 Student Dean .... Rev. Hon Young CHO
20 Academic Director .... Rev. David AHN
35 Director of Student Affairs .... Rev. Michael LEE
06 Registrar .... Rev. David AHN
13 Chief Info Technology Officer (CIO) .... Mr. Seung Goo HAN
26 Marketing Coordinator .... Rev. Myung Kyun SHIN
42 Chaplain .... Rev. Inho JEONG

Middlebury Institute of International Studies at Monterey (D)

460 Pierce Street, Monterey CA 93940-2691

Telephone: (831) 647-4100 | FICE Identification: 001241
Accreditation: &EH, CEA

† Regional accreditation is carried under parent institution Middlebury College, VT.

Mills College (E)

5000 MacArthur Boulevard, Oakland CA 94613-1301

County: Alameda | FICE Identification: 001238
Unit ID: 118888
Telephone: (510) 430-2255 | Carnegie Class: Masters/L
FAX Number: (510) 430-2256 | Calendar System: Semester
URL: www.mills.edu
Established: 1852 | Annual Undergrad Tuition & Fees: $45,635
Enrollment: 1,397 | Female
Affiliation or Control: Independent Non-Profit | IRS Status: 501(c)3
Highest Offering: Doctorate
Accreditation: WC

01 President .... Ms. Elizabeth L. HILLMAN
05 Provost & Dean of Faculty .... Dr. Chinyere OPARAH
10 VP Finance & Administration .... Ms. Maria CAMMARATA
26 VP Communications/Chief of Staff .... Ms. Renee JADUSHLEVER
30 VP for Inst Advancement .... Dr. Jeffrey JACKANICZ
20 Associate Provost .... Dr. Maggie HUNTER
15 Chief HR Officer & Career Svcs Dir .... Vacant
84 VP for Enrollment Management .... Ms. Kathy BAUGHER
32 VP Student Life/Dean of Students .... Dr. Chicora MARTIN
07 Director of Undergraduate Admission .... Ms. Robynne LOFTON
09 Dir Acad Assess/Inst Research/Plng .... Dr. Alice B. KNUDSEN
101 Secretary of Board of Trustees .... Ms. Carrie HALL
18 Associate VP for Operations .... Ms. Linda ZITZNER
38 Asst Dir Counsel/Psych Svcs .... Ms. Ilana BARAKAT
41 Director of Athletics .... Ms. Themy-Jo ADACHI

MiraCosta College (F)

One Barnard Drive, Oceanside CA 92056-3899

County: San Diego | FICE Identification: 001239
Unit ID: 118912
Telephone: (760) 757-2121 | Carnegie Class: Assoc/HT-High Trad
FAX Number: (760) 795-6609 | Calendar System: Semester
URL: www.miracosta.edu
Established: 1934 | Annual Undergrad Tuition & Fees (In-District): $1,152
Enrollment: 15,062 | Coed
Affiliation or Control: State/Local | IRS Status: 501(c)3
Highest Offering: Baccalaureate
Accreditation: WJ, SURGT

01 Superintendent/President .... Dr. Sunita COOKE
04 Exec Assistant to Supt/President .... Ms. Evelyn CROGAN
04 Exec Assistant to Supt/President .... Ms. Jeanne SWANSON
05 Vice President Instructional Svcs .... Dr. Diane DIECKMEYER
32 Vice President Student Svcs .... Dr. Alketa WOJCIK
10 Vice President Business/Admin Svcs .... Mr. Charles NG
12 Dean San Elijo Campus-Letters/Comm .... Ms. Dana SMITH
20 Dean Academic Information Svcs .... Dr. Mario VALENTE
38 Dean Counseling/Student Devel .... Dr. Wendy STEWART
07 Dean Admissions/Student Support .... Mr. Freddy RAMIREZ
88 Associate Dean San Elijo Campus ... Ms. Cynthia RICE-CARROLL
51 Dean Community Education .... Dr. Nikki SCHAPER
49 Dean Arts/Intl Languages .... Mr. Jonathan FOHRMAN
81 Dean Math/Sciences .... Mr. Mike FINO
75 Dean Career/Technical Education .... Dr. Al TACCONE
88 Director Small Business Dev Ctr .... Mr. Sudershan SHAUNAK
31 Director Community Services .... Ms. Linda KUROKAWA
06 Registrar .... Ms. Jane SPARKS
09 Dean Institutional Research .... Dr. Chris HILL
26 Director Marketing/Communications .... Dr. Kristen HUYCK
102 Int Director Foundation/Fund Devel . Ms. Cynthia RICE-CARROLL
18 Director Facilities .... Mr. Tom MACIAS
37 Director Financial Aid .... Mr. Michael DEAR
117 Director Risk Management .... Mr. Joseph MAZZA
88 Director Cashiering Services .... Ms. Jo FERRIS
15 Director Human Resources .... Ms. Sheri WRIGHT
36 Director Career Center .... Ms. Donna DAVIS
88 Director Transfer Center .... Ms. Lise FLOCKEN
96 Director Purchasing/Material Mgmt .... Ms. Susan ASATO
124 Director Retention Services .... Dr. Edward POEHLERT
21 Director Fiscal Services .... Ms. Katie WHITE
19 Director Campus Police .... Chief Robert NORCROSS
106 Director Online Education .... Dr. James JULIUS

Monterey Peninsula College (G)

980 Fremont Street, Monterey CA 93940-4799

County: Monterey | FICE Identification: 001242
Unit ID: 119067
Telephone: (831) 646-4000 | Carnegie Class: Assoc/HT-High Non
FAX Number: (831) 655-2627 | Calendar System: Semester
URL: www.mpc.edu
Established: 1947 | Annual Undergrad Tuition & Fees (In-District): $1,174
Enrollment: 8,277 | Coed
Affiliation or Control: State/Local | IRS Status: 501(c)3
Highest Offering: Associate Degree
Accreditation: #WJ, ADNUR

01 Superintendent/President .... Dr. Walter TRIBLEY
05 Vice President of Academic Affairs .... Ms. Kiran KAMATH
11 Vice Pres Administrative Services .... Dr. Steven L. CROW
32 Vice President of Student Services .... Dr. Kim MCGINNIS
20 Interim Dean of Instruction .... Dr. Paul LONG
20 Dean of Instruction .... Dr. Jon KNOLLE
20 Dean of Instruction .... Ms. Judith CUTTING
20 Dean of Instruction .... Dr. Cathryn WILKINSON
35 Dean of Student Services .... Dr. Christine ERICKSON
09 Interim Dean of PRIE .... Ms. Catherine WEBB
15 Associate Dean of Human Resources .... Ms. Susan KITAGAWA
35 Dean of Student Services .... Mr. Larry WALKER
09 Director of Institutional Research .... Dr. Rosaleen RYAN
07 Director of Admissions & Records .... Ms. Nicole DUNNE
08 Librarian .... Vacant
37 Student Financial Services Director .... Mr. Francisco TOSTADO
41 Athletic Director .... Mr. Lyndon SCHUTZLER
18 Facilities Operations Supervisor .... Mr. Pete OLSEN
96 Purchasing Agent .... Ms. Mary WEBER
19 Director of Security .... Ms. Jo Anna BUTRON

Mount Saint Mary's University (H)

12001 Chalon Road, Los Angeles CA 90049-1599

County: Los Angeles | FICE Identification: 001243
Unit ID: 119173
Telephone: (310) 954-4000 | Carnegie Class: Masters/M
FAX Number: (310) 954-4379 | Calendar System: Semester
URL: www.msmu.edu
Established: 1925 | Annual Undergrad Tuition & Fees: $37,722
Enrollment: 3,431 | Female
Affiliation or Control: Roman Catholic | IRS Status: 501(c)3
Highest Offering: Doctorate
Accreditation: WC, NURSE, PTA

01 President .... Dr. Ann MCELANEY-JOHNSON
05 Provost .... Dr. Robert J. PERRINS
111 Vice Pres Institutional Advancement .... Dr. Stephanie CUBBA
10 Vice Pres Administration & Finance .... Mr. Chris MCALARY
13 VP Info Support Svcs .... Mr. Larry SMITH
32 Vice President Student Affairs .... Dr. Jane LINGUA
84 VP Enrollment Management .... Mr. Brian O'ROURKE
20 Associate Provost & ALO .... Dr. Michele STARKEY
09 Interim Dir Inst Planning/Research .... Ms. Maria NARVAEZ
35 Assoc VP Student Affairs .... Ms. Mari WADSWORTH
58 Graduate Dean .... Vacant
55 Dean of Weekend College .... Ms. Suzanne WILLIAMS
88 Asst VP Enrollment Management .... Mr. Dean KILGOUR
06 Registrar .... Ms. Rocio DELEON
26 Director Communications/Marketing .... Ms. Debbie REAM
15 Director of Human Resources .... Ms. Dana LOPEZ
18 Director of Facilities Mgmt .... Mr. Rick TORKELSON
37 Director of Student Financing .... Ms. La Royce HOUSLEY
08 Interim Director of MSMU Libraries .... Dr. Ruth JACKSON
28 Assoc VP Diversity and Inclusion .... Ms. Bernadette ROBERT
29 Director Alumni Relations .... Ms. Elizabeth ROBLES JIMENEZ
38 Director Student Counseling .... Dr. Susan SALEM
07 Director of Admissions .... Ms. Erika YAMASAKI
36 Director Career Services .... Ms. Marlene SIMON
04 Administrative Asst to President .... Ms. Lucille VILLEGAS
19 Director Security/Safety .... Mr. Michael MCFATRIDGE
35 Dean of Student Life .... Ms. Jessica CUEVAS
44 Director Individual Giving .... Ms. Maria SOLANO
104 Study Away Coordinator .... Ms. Jaime WOOD
105 Director Web Services .... Mr. Salvador RODRIGUEZ
106 Int Dir Online Education/E-learning .... Mr. Edgar CHABOLLA
39 Director of Residence Life .... Ms. Michelle SALDANA

Mt. San Antonio College (I)

1100 N Grand, Walnut CA 91789-1399

County: Los Angeles | FICE Identification: 001245
Unit ID: 119164
Telephone: (909) 594-5611 | Carnegie Class: Assoc/MT-VT-High Trad
FAX Number: (909) 598-2303 | Calendar System: Semester
URL: www.mtsac.edu
Established: 1946 | Annual Undergrad Tuition & Fees (In-District): $1,348
Enrollment: 28,991 | Coed
Affiliation or Control: State/Local | IRS Status: 501(c)3
Highest Offering: Associate Degree
Accreditation: WJ, COARC, EMT, HT, RAD

01 President/CEO .... Dr. William T. SCROGGINS
05 Vice President Instruction .... Dr. Irene M. MALMGREN
10 Vice President Administrative Svcs .... Mr. Michael D. GREGORYK
32 Vice President Student Services .... Dr. Audrey YAMAGATA-NOJI
15 Vice President Human Resources .... Mr. Ibrahim ALI
20 Assoc Vice Pres Instruction .... Dr. Joumana MCGOWAN
35 Dean Student Services .... Dr. Koji UESUGI
08 Dean Library/Learning Resources .... Dr. Meghan CHEN
38 Dean Counseling .... Mr. Tom MAUCH
13 Chief Technology Officer/Info Tech .... Mr. Dale VICKERS
84 Dean Enrollment Management .... Dr. George BRADSHAW
21 Assoc Vice Pres Fiscal Services .... Ms. Myeshia ARMSTRONG
102 Executive Director of Foundation .... Mr. Bill LAMBERT
37 Director Financial Aid .... Ms. Chau DAO
88 Director Risk Management .... Ms. Duetta LANGEVIN
46 Director Grants .... Ms. Adrienne PRICE
26 Director Marketing/Communications .... Ms. Uyen MAI
09 Dir Research & Inst Effectiveness .... Ms. Barbara MCNEICE-STALLARD
18 Director Facilities Planning & Mgmt .... Mr. Gary NELLESEN
35 Director Student Life .... Ms. Andrea SIMA
96 Purchasing Manager .... Ms. Teresa PATTERSON
50 Dean Business .... Ms. Jennifer GALBRAITH
68 Dean Kinesiology/Athletics/Dance .... Mr. Joe JENNUM
79 Dean Humanities & Social Science .... Dr. Karelyn HOOVER
72 Dean Tech/Health Science .... Ms. Jemma BLAKE-JUDD
65 Assoc Dean Natural Sciences .... Mr. Matthew JUDD
57 Dean Arts .... Dr. Susan LONG
51 Dean School of Continuing Education .... Dr. Madelyn ARBALLO
04 Exec Asst to President & BOT .... Ms. Carol NELSON

Mt. San Jacinto College (J)

1499 N State Street, San Jacinto CA 92583-2399

County: Riverside | FICE Identification: 001246
Unit ID: 119216
Telephone: (951) 487-6752 | Carnegie Class: Assoc/HT-High Trad
FAX Number: (951) 654-9712 | Calendar System: Semester
URL: www.msjc.edu
Established: 1962 | Annual Undergrad Tuition & Fees (In-District): $1,386
Enrollment: 15,010 | Coed
Affiliation or Control: State/Local | IRS Status: 501(c)3
Highest Offering: Associate Degree
Accreditation: WJ, DMS

01 Superintendent/President .... Dr. Roger W. SCHULTZ
04 Executive Assistant to President .... Ms. Kristen GRIMES
05 Vice Pres of Instruction .... Dr. Rudolph BESIKOF
32 Vice President Student Services .... Dr. John COLSON
10 Vice President Business Svcs .... Ms. Beth GOMEZ
15 Vice Pres of Human Resources .... Vacant
108 Executive Dean Inst Effect .... Mr. Brandon MOORE
19 Chief of Police .... Vacant
20 Dean of Academic Programs .... Dr. Jeremy BROWN
20 Dean of Academic Programs - SJC .... Dr. Carlos TOVARES
103 Dean Career Education .... Ms. Joyce JOHNSON
72 Dean Instruct Acad Success/Tech .... Mr. Micah ORLOFF

20 Dean of Academic Programs - MVC ..... Mr. Marc DONNHAUSER
21 Dean of Admin Services/Controller .... Ms. Julie VENABLE
13 Int Assoc Dean of Information Tech ...... Ms. Katherine STRATTON
18 Dean of Facilities Plng/Cap Constr .... Ms. Tina ELM
35 Dean Student Support Svcs .... Vacant
35 Dean Student Services .... Ms. Susan LOOMIS
84 Director Enrollment Services .... Ms. Cheri NAISH
41 Dean of Athletics .... Mr. Patrick SPRINGER
45 Dean Institutional Planning .... Ms. Rebecca TEAGUE
26 Public Information Officer .... Ms. Karin MARRIOTT
16 Int Assoc Dean of Human Resources .... Ms. Jeannine STOKES
37 Dean of Student Svcs/Financial Aid .... Ms. Dolores SMITH
66 Assoc Dean of Nursing/Allied Health .... Vacant
88 Dean of Instructional Support .... Dr. Jamail CARTER
18 Director Maint & Operations .... Mr. Brian TWITTY
09 Director of Research .... Mr. Nikilos 'Nik' MESARIS

Mt. Sierra College (A)

800 Royal Oaks Drive, Suite 101,
Monrovia CA 91016-3414

County: Los Angeles FICE Identification: 031287
Unit ID: 398130
Telephone: (626) 873-2100 Carnegie Class: Bac-Diverse
FAX Number: (626) 359-5528 Calendar System: Quarter
URL: www.mtsierra.edu
Established: 1991 Annual Undergrad Tuition & Fees: $15,688
Enrollment: 357 Coed
Affiliation or Control: Proprietary IRS Status: Proprietary
Highest Offering: Baccalaureate
Accreditation: ACCSC

01 President .... Dr. Eric TAO
10 Chief Financial Officer .... Ms. Lucy LI
05 Chief Academic Officer .... Dr. Eric TAO
07 Manager of Admissions .... Ms. Isabel MONROY
37 Director Student Financial Aid .... Ms. Lida CASTILLO

MTI College (B)

5221 Madison Avenue, Sacramento CA 95841-3037

County: Sacramento FICE Identification: 012912
Unit ID: 118198
Telephone: (916) 339-1500 Carnegie Class: Assoc/HVT-High Non
FAX Number: (916) 339-0305 Calendar System: Quarter
URL: www.mticollege.edu
Established: 1965 Annual Undergrad Tuition & Fees: N/A
Enrollment: 919 Coed
Affiliation or Control: Proprietary IRS Status: Proprietary
Highest Offering: Associate Degree
Accreditation: WJ

01 President .... Mr. John A. ZIMMERMAN
10 Vice Pres/Chief Financial Officer .... Mr. David W. ALLEN
12 Campus Director .... Mr. Malcolm CARLING SMITH
11 Director of Operations .... Mr. Michael ZIMMERMAN

Musicians Institute (C)

6752 Hollywood Boulevard, Hollywood CA 90028

County: Los Angeles FICE Identification: 021618
Unit ID: 119270
Telephone: (323) 462-1384 Carnegie Class: Spec-4-yr-Arts
FAX Number: (323) 462-1575 Calendar System: Quarter
URL: www.mi.edu
Established: 1977 Annual Undergrad Tuition & Fees: $24,030
Enrollment: 1,118 Coed
Affiliation or Control: Proprietary IRS Status: Proprietary
Highest Offering: Baccalaureate
Accreditation: MUS

01 President .... Mr. Donny GRUENDLER
108 Dean Compliance and Assessment .... Mr. Tom ENGFER

Napa Valley College (D)

2277 Napa-Vallejo Highway, Napa CA 94558-6236

County: Napa FICE Identification: 001247
Unit ID: 119331
Telephone: (707) 256-7000 Carnegie Class: Assoc/HT-High Trad
FAX Number: (707) 253-3015 Calendar System: Semester
URL: www.napavalley.edu
Established: 1942 Annual Undergrad Tuition & Fees (In-District): $1,142
Enrollment: 6,257 Coed
Affiliation or Control: State/Local IRS Status: 501(c)3
Highest Offering: Associate Degree
Accreditation: WJ, COARC, EMT

01 Superintendent/President .... Dr. Ronald D. KRAFT
05 Int Vice President Instruction .... Mr. Erik SHEARER
10 Vice Pres Admin Svcs/Asst Supt .... Mr. Robert PARKER
32 Vice Pres Student Svcs/Asst Supt .... Mr. Oscar DE HARO
38 Dean Counseling Svcs/Stdnt Success .... Mr. Howard WILLIS
20 Dean of Instruction .... Ms. Maria VILLAGOMEZ
08 Dean Library/Learning Resource Ctr .... Ms. Rebecca SCOTT
37 Dean Fin Aid/EOPS/Pre-Col TRIO Pgms .... Ms. Patricia MORGAN
103 Dean Career Tech Educ/Workforce Dev .... Ms. Miraglia GREGORY
13 Dean Institutional Technology .... Mr. Eric MOUCK
09 Dean Research Plng/Instl Effect .... Dr. Robyn WORNALL
36 Dean Counselor/WA III .... Mr. Howard WILLIS
12 Assoc Dean Upper Valley Campus .... Vacant

07 Assoc Dean Admissions/Records .... Ms. Jessica ERICKSON
15 Exec Director Human Resources .... Ms. Charo ALBARRAN
26 Chief Public Relations Officer .... Mr. Doug ERNST
18 Director Facilities .... Mr. Matt CHRISTENSEN
102 Exec Director NVC Foundation .... Ms. Anne BRANCH
19 Director College Police .... Mr. Kenneth L. ARNOLD
84 Enrollment Management .... Mr. Erik SHEARER
88 Coordinator Trans Center .... Ms. Marci SANCHEZ
28 Director of Equity & Inclusivity .... Dr. Craig ALIMO
29 Director Alumni Affairs/Advancement ...... Ms. Carolee CATTOLICA
96 Business Services Asst/Purchasing .... Ms. Solange KADAD
23 Director Student Health Services .... Ms. Nancy TAMARISK

National Career College (E)

14355 Roscoe Boulevard, Panorama City CA 91402

County: Los Angeles FICE Identification: 041460
Unit ID: 455868
Telephone: (818) 988-2300 Carnegie Class: Not Classified
FAX Number: (818) 988-9944 Calendar System: Semester
URL: www.nccusa.edu
Established: 2005 Annual Undergrad Tuition & Fees: N/A
Enrollment: 218 Coed
Affiliation or Control: Proprietary IRS Status: Proprietary
Highest Offering: Associate Degree
Accreditation: ABHES

01 President .... Gayane KHANOYAN
37 Director Student Financial Aid .... Anna TOVMASYAN

National Polytechnic College (F)

6630 Telegraph Rd., Ste 200, Commerce CA 90040

County: Los Angeles FICE Identification: 039104
Unit ID: 447759
Telephone: (323) 728-9636 Carnegie Class: Not Classified
FAX Number: (323) 728-0952 Calendar System: Semester
URL: www.npcollege.edu
Established: 1996 Annual Undergrad Tuition & Fees: N/A
Enrollment: 221 Coed
Affiliation or Control: Proprietary IRS Status: Proprietary
Highest Offering: Associate Degree
Accreditation: ACCSC, CEA

01 CEO and President .... Dariush (David) MADDAHI

National Test Pilot School (G)

PO Box 658, Mojave CA 93502-0658

County: Kern Identification: 667009
Telephone: (661) 824-2977 Carnegie Class: Not Classified
FAX Number: (661) 824-2943 Calendar System: Semester
URL: www.ntps.edu
Established: 1981 Annual Graduate Tuition & Fees: N/A
Enrollment: N/A Coed
Affiliation or Control: Independent Non-Profit IRS Status: 501(c)3
Highest Offering: Master's; No Undergraduates
Accreditation: ENG

01 President/CEO .... Dr. Al L. PETERSON
05 CAO/Head of Training .... Mr. Gregory V. LEWIS
11 Chief Operations Officer .... Mr. James BROWN
54 Director NFTI .... Mr. Marco LOTTERIO
13 Chief of Systems Academics .... Mr. Tom DREILICH
88 Chief of FW P&FQ Academics .... Dr. Gabriele DI FRANCESCO
88 Chief of RW P&FQ Academics .... Mr. Ilan ARUSH
88 Chief FW Test Pilot Instructor .... Mr. Rigel HEBMANN
88 Chief RW Test Pilot Instructor .... Mr. Nigel SPEEDY
06 Registrar .... Ms. Sindy STANTON
10 Business Manager .... Ms. Lynda MATOS

National University (H)

11255 N Torrey Pines Road, La Jolla CA 92037-1011

County: San Diego FICE Identification: 011460
Unit ID: 119605
Telephone: (858) 642-8000 Carnegie Class: Masters/L
FAX Number: (858) 642-8714 Calendar System: Other
URL: www.nu.edu
Established: 1971 Annual Undergrad Tuition & Fees: $13,016
Enrollment: 17,488 Coed
Affiliation or Control: Independent Non-Profit IRS Status: 501(c)3
Highest Offering: Master's
Accreditation: WC, ANEST, CAEPN, CS, IACBE, NURSE, PH, RTT

00 Chancellor .... Dr. Michael R. CUNNINGHAM
01 University President .... Dr. David ANDREWS
05 Provost .... Dr. Gangaram SINGH

New York Film Academy, Los Angeles (I)

3300 Riverside Drive, Burbank CA 91505

County: Burbank FICE Identification: 041188
Unit ID: 461148
Telephone: (818) 333-3558 Carnegie Class: Not Classified
FAX Number: (818) 333-3557 Calendar System: Semester
URL: www.nyfa.edu
Established: 2006 Annual Undergrad Tuition & Fees: $28,000
Enrollment: 1,948 Coed
Affiliation or Control: Proprietary IRS Status: Proprietary
Highest Offering: Master's
Accreditation: ART

01 Co-Director .... Mr. John SHERLOCK
01 Co-Director .... Mr. Dan MACKLER
05 Dean of College .... Mr. Sonny CALDERON
32 Dean of Students .... Ms. Kelly GARDNER
06 Registrar .... Mr. Vince VOSKANIAN
07 Director of Admissions .... Mrs. Amy ELLENBERGER
08 Head Librarian .... Mr. Josh MOORMON
39 Director Student Housing .... Mr. Brennan DILLION

NewSchool of Architecture and Design (J)

1249 F Street, San Diego CA 92101-6634

County: San Diego FICE Identification: 030439
Unit ID: 119775
Telephone: (619) 684-8800 Carnegie Class: Spec-4-yr-Arts
FAX Number: (619) 684-8880 Calendar System: Quarter
URL: www.newschoolarch.edu
Established: 1980 Annual Undergrad Tuition & Fees: $26,463
Enrollment: 515 Coed
Affiliation or Control: Proprietary IRS Status: Proprietary
Highest Offering: Master's
Accreditation: WC

01 President .... Mr. Marvin MALECHA
05 Chief Academic Officer .... Vacant
32 Dean Division of Student Affairs .... Dr. Sheila SULLIVAN
88 Dean School of Design .... Dr. Elena PACENTI
58 Graduate Architecture Program Chair .... Mr. Kurt HUNKER
48 Undergrad Architecture Pgm Chair .... Mr. Len ZEGARSKI
88 Construction Management Pgm Chair .... Mr. George WELCH
97 General Education Program Chair .... Mr. Bruce MATTHES
09 Director of Institutional Research .... Ms. Tiffany RODRIGUEZ
10 Finance Manager .... Ms. Julie CODINA
06 Registrar .... Mr. Allen MUTCHLER
26 Executive Director Public Relation .... Ms. Rachael LIGHTY
84 Director of Enrollment .... Mr. Dan STONE
37 Director of Financial Aid .... Mr. Bryan CHARBONNEAU
36 Director of Career/Alumni Services .... Ms. Lisa GANEM
15 Director of Human Resources .... Ms. Marcy MADIX
27 Director of Marketing .... Ms. Jessica NIELSEN
07 Admissions Manager .... Ms. Francesca GUIDALI
21 Business Office Manager .... Ms. Terre CORTEZ-FARAH
35 Student Life Manager .... Ms. Ashley WAGNER
08 Librarian .... Ms. Lucy CAMPBELL
88 Faculty Coordinator .... Mr. Dario MITICOCCHIO
121 Director Student Success .... Ms. Allison RILEY
13 Manager IT .... Mr. Joe SOSA
88 Materials Lab Manager .... Mr. David CONTRERAS

Nobel University (K)

505 Shatto Place #300, Los Angeles CA 90020

County: Los Angeles Identification: 667274
Telephone: (213) 382-1136 Carnegie Class: Not Classified
FAX Number: (213) 382-1187 Calendar System: Semester
URL: nobeluniversity.edu
Established: 2000 Annual Undergrad Tuition & Fees: N/A
Enrollment: N/A Coed
Affiliation or Control: Proprietary IRS Status: Proprietary
Highest Offering: Master's
Accreditation: ACICS

01 President .... Chong S. KIM

*North Orange County Community College District (L)

1830 W Romneya Drive, Anaheim CA 92801-1819

County: Orange FICE Identification: 009742
Unit ID: 120023
Telephone: (714) 808-4500 Carnegie Class: N/A
FAX Number: (714) 808-4791
URL: www.nocccd.edu

01 Chancellor .... Dr. Cheryl A. MARSHALL
10 Vice Chanc Finance/Facilities .... Mr. Fred WILLIAMS
15 Vice Chancellor Human Resources .... Ms. Irma RAMOS
05 Vice Chanc Educational Svcs/Tech .... Dr. Cherry LI-BUGG
26 Vice Chanc Public/Govt Affairs .... Ms. Kai STEARNS MOORE
04 Exec Admin Aide to Chancellor .... Ms. Alba RECINOS
22 Dist Director Diversity/Compliance .... Mr. Arturo OCAMPO

*Cypress College (M)

9200 Valley View, Cypress CA 90630-5897

County: Orange FICE Identification: 001193
Unit ID: 113236
Telephone: (714) 484-7000 Carnegie Class: Assoc/MT-VT-High Trad
FAX Number: (714) 527-8238 Calendar System: Semester
URL: www.cypresscollege.edu
Established: 1966 Annual Undergrad Tuition & Fees (In-District): $1,140
Enrollment: 16,187 Coed
Affiliation or Control: State/Local IRS Status: 501(c)3
Highest Offering: Baccalaureate
Accreditation: WJ, ADNUR, CAHIIM, DA, DH, DMS, FUSER, RAD

02 President .... Dr. JoAnna SCHILLING

05 Exec VP Educ Pgms/Student Svcs ... Dr. Santanu BANDYOPADHYAY
10 Vice Pres Admin/Business Svcs ... Vacant
08 Dean Library/Learning Resource Ctr ... Dr. Treisa CASSENS
88 Dean Language Arts ... Mr. Eldon YOUNG
07 Dean Counseling/Admiss & Records ... Dr. Paul DE DIOS
06 Registrar ... Mr. David BOOZE
26 Director Campus Communications ... Mr. Marc POSNER
102 Exec Dir Foundation/Community Rels ... Vacant
32 Dean Student Support Services ... Dr. Richard RAMS
22 Director Disabled Student Services ... Ms. Celeste PHELPS
90 Manager Systems Technology Svcs ... Vacant
37 Director Financial Aid ... Mr. Chinh PHAM
09 Dir Institutional Research/Planning ... Mr. Philip DYKSTRA
18 Director Physical Plant/Facilities ... Mr. Albert MIRANDA
19 Int Director Campus Safety ... Dr. Shirley SMITH
04 Executive Assistant to President ... Ms. Ty VOLCY
68 Dean Physical Education ... Dr. Richard RAMS
57 Dean Fine Arts ... Dr. Katy REALISTA
50 Dean Business/CIS ... Dr. Henry HUA
83 Interim Dean Social Sciences ... Dr. Lisa GAETJE
53 Dean Science Engineering & Math ... Dr. Richard FEE
76 Interim Dean Health Sciences ... Ms. Rebecca GOMEZ
75 Int Dean Career Technical Education ... Ms. Kathleen REILAND
88 Spec Proj Director Student Equity ... Ms. Ashley GRIFFITH
88 Manager SSSP ... Vacant
21 Bursar ... Ms. Dao DO
22 Director EOPS ... Vacant
88 Project Manager Campus Cap Proj ... Ms. Susan RITTEL

*Fullerton College (A)

321 E Chapman Avenue, Fullerton CA 92832-2095

County: Orange FICE Identification: 001201
Unit ID: 114859
Telephone: (714) 992-7000 Carnegie Class: Assoc/HT-High Trad
FAX Number: (714) 992-9930 Calendar System: Semester
URL: www.fullcoll.edu
Established: 1913 Annual Undergrad Tuition & Fees (In-District): $1,138
Enrollment: 24,613 Coed
Affiliation or Control: State/Local IRS Status: 501(c)3
Highest Offering: Associate Degree
Accreditation: WJ

02 Interim President ... Dr. Greg SCHULZ
05 Vice President Instruction ... Dr. Jose Ramon NUNEZ
32 Vice Pres Student Services ... Dr. Gilbert CONTRERAS
11 Vice Pres Administrative Svcs ... Mr. Rodrigo GARCIA
50 Dean Business & CIS ... Dr. Doug BENOIT
57 Interim Dean Fine Arts ... Mr. John TEBAY
79 Dean Humanities ... Mr. Dan WILLOUGHBY
81 Dean Math/Computer Science ... Mr. Mark GREENHALGH
88 Dean Natural Sciences ... Dr. Richard HARTMANN
68 Dean Physical Education ... Dr. David GROSSMAN
83 Dean Social Sciences ... Mr. Jorge GAMBOA
72 Dean Technology & Engr ... Mr. Kenneth STARKMAN
37 Director of Financial Aid ... Mr. Greg RYAN
23 Director Health Services ... Dr. Vanessa MILLER
18 Dir Facilities/Physical Plant ... Mr. Larry LARA
40 Director of Bookstore ... Mr. Nick KARVIA
35 Director Student Affairs ... Ms. Naomi ABESAMIS
06 Registrar ... Ms. Rena MARTINEZ STLUKA
19 Director Campus Safety ... Mr. Steve SELBY
38 Dean Counseling/Student Development ... Ms. Lisa CAMPBELL
08 Dean Library (LLR & ISPS) ... Ms. Dani WILSON
07 Dean Admissions & Records ... Mr. Albert ABUTIN
90 Academic Computing Technologies ... Mr. Co HO
09 Director Inst Research & Planning ... Mr. Carlos AYON
88 Director Cadena Transfer Center ... Ms. Cecilia ARRIAZA
26 Director Campus Communications ... Ms. Lisa MCPHERON
04 Exec Assistant to the President ... Ms. Melinda TAYLOR
88 Int Dean Student Support Services ... Dr. Elaine LIPIZ GONZALEZ

Northcentral University (B)

2488 Historic Decatur Rd, Suite 100, San Diego CA 92106

County: San Diego FICE Identification: 038133
Unit ID: 444130
Telephone: (866) 776-0331 Carnegie Class: DU-Mod
FAX Number: (844) 851-5889 Calendar System: Other
URL: www.ncu.edu
Established: 1996 Annual Undergrad Tuition & Fees: N/A
Enrollment: 11,029 Coed
Affiliation or Control: Proprietary IRS Status: Proprietary
Highest Offering: Doctorate
Accreditation: WC, ACBSP, CAEPT, MFCD

01 President ... Dr. George A. BURNETT
05 Provost/Chief Academic Officer ... Dr. David HARPOOL
20 Sr Vice Pres Academic Affairs ... Dr. John LANEAR
10 Chief Financial Officer ... Ms. Karen WHITNEY
13 Chief Information Officer ... Mr. Patrick PENDLETON
26 Chief Marketing Officer ... Mr. Russell NATOCE
43 General Counsel/Chief Compliance ... Mr. David HARPOOL
50 Dean School of Business & Tech Mgmt ... Dr. Peter BEMSKI
53 Dean School of Education ... Dr. John NEAL
76 Dean School of Health Sciences ... Dr. Laurie SHANDERSON
83 Dean Sch of Social/Behavioral Sci ... Dr. James BILLINGS
72 Dean School of Technology & Innovat ... Dr. Robert SAPP
09 Director Institutional Research ... Dr. John FULGINITI
108 Director Institutional Assessment ... Dr. Heather HUSSEY
06 Registrar ... Ms. Jennifer RACER
37 VP Student and Financial Services ... Dr. Ian COOPER

08 Associate Librarian ... Mr. Kristin BERNET
07 VP Enrollment ... Mr. Ken BOUTELLE
15 VP Human Resources ... Ms. Angie WALKER

Northwestern Polytechnic University (C)

47671 Westinghouse Drive, Fremont CA 94539-7474

County: Alameda Identification: 666759
Unit ID: 120166
Telephone: (510) 592-9688 Carnegie Class: Not Classified
FAX Number: (510) 657-8975 Calendar System: Trimester
URL: www.npu.edu
Established: 1984 Annual Undergrad Tuition & Fees: N/A
Enrollment: N/A Coed
Affiliation or Control: Independent Non-Profit IRS Status: 501(c)3
Highest Offering: Master's
Accreditation: ACICS

01 President ... Mr. Peter HSIEH
03 Executive Vice President ... Mr. Paul CHOI
05 Chief Academic Officer ... Ms. Nelly MANGAROVA

† ACICS scope of recognition as approved by US Dept of Education and CHEA includes diploma programs and degree programs through the Master's degree. However, NPU offers an ACICS accredited Doctorate of Computer Science and a Doctorate of Business.

Notre Dame de Namur University (D)

1500 Ralston Avenue, Belmont CA 94002-1908

County: San Mateo FICE Identification: 001179
Unit ID: 120184
Telephone: (650) 508-3500 Carnegie Class: Masters/L
FAX Number: (000) 000-0000 Calendar System: Semester
URL: www.ndnu.edu
Established: 1851 Annual Undergrad Tuition & Fees: $33,268
Enrollment: 1,855 Coed
Affiliation or Control: Independent Non-Profit IRS Status: 501(c)3
Highest Offering: Master's
Accreditation: WC, ACBSP

01 President ... Dr. Judith M. GREIG
05 Interim Provost ... Dr. John LEMMON
10 Vice Pres Finance & Administration ... Mr. Henry ROTH
32 Dean of Students ... Mr. Marsh-Allen SMITH
84 Vice Pres Enrollment Mgmt ... Mr. Jason MURRAY
111 Vice Pres for Advancement ... Mr. Dino HERNANDEZ
04 Exec Assistant to the President ... Ms. Alison LYON
49 Dean Arts & Sciences ... Dr. John LEMMON
50 Dean Business & Management ... Dr. Douglas RICE
53 Dean Education/Psychology ... Dr. Caryl HODGES
06 Registrar ... Mr. J. T BROWN
36 Director Career Development ... Ms. Carrie MCKNIGHT
37 Director Financial Aid ... Mr. Charles WALZ
38 Director Student Counseling ... Ms. Karin SPONHOLZ
41 Athletic Director ... Mr. Josh DOODY
42 Director Spirituality ... Ms. Diana ENRIQUEZ FIELD
19 Director of Public Safety ... Mr. William PALMINI, JR.
29 Director Alumni Relations ... Ms. Elizabeth VALENTE
26 Exec Dir Marketing/Communication ... Ms. Karen SCHORNSTEIN
15 Executive Director Human Resources ... Ms. Mary HAESLOOP
08 Director Library Services ... Ms. Mary WEGMANN
13 Director Office of Information Tech ... Mr. Merle MASON
18 Director Facilities ... Mr. Chris KORNAHRENS
20 Associate Provost ... Mr. Greg WHITE
21 Controller ... Ms. Emiko YAMADA
09 Director of Institutional Research ... Mr. John HOFMANN

Occidental College (E)

1600 Campus Road, Los Angeles CA 90041-3314

County: Los Angeles FICE Identification: 001249
Unit ID: 120254
Telephone: (323) 259-2500 Carnegie Class: Bac-A&S
FAX Number: (323) 259-2958 Calendar System: Semester
URL: www.oxy.edu
Established: 1887 Annual Undergrad Tuition & Fees: $51,070
Enrollment: 2,023 Coed
Affiliation or Control: Independent Non-Profit IRS Status: 501(c)3
Highest Offering: Master's
Accreditation: WC

01 President ... Dr. Jonathan VEITCH
05 VP Academic Affairs/Dean of College ... Dr. Wendy STERNBERG
10 Vice Pres/Chief Operating Officer ... Mr. Amos HIMMELSTEIN
07 VP Admissions/Financial Aid ... Mr. Vincent CUSEO
30 Vice Pres Inst Advancement ... Mr. Charlie CARDILLO
22 VP Inclusion/Equity/Chf Diversity ... Ms. Rhonda BROWN
32 VP Student Affairs/Dean of Students ... Mr. Rob FLOT
43 Interim General Counsel ... Ms. Rachel CRONIN
41 Assoc Vice Pres/Dir Athletics ... Ms. Jaime HOFFMAN
18 Assoc VP for Facilities Management ... Mr. Thomas POLANSKY
26 AVP Marketing/Communications ... Mr. Marty SHARKEY
13 AVP ITS/Chief Technology Officer ... Mr. James UHRICH
36 AVP/Exec Director Career Services ... Ms. Cherena JAMES WALKER
04 Int Exec Assistant to President ... Ms. Connie SANCHEZ
08 Acting Library Director ... Mr. Daniel CHAMBERLAIN
29 Director Alumni/Parent Engagement ... Ms. Monica MOORE
37 Director of Financial Aid ... Ms. Gina BECERRIL
15 Director of Human Resources ... Ms. Danita MAXWELL

27 Director of Communications ... Mr. Jim TRANQUADA
09 Director of Institutional Research ... Ms. Teresa KALDOR
19 Campus Safety Officer ... Mr. Leroy AVINGTON

Ohlone College (F)

43600 Mission Boulevard, Fremont CA 94539-0390

County: Alameda FICE Identification: 004481
Unit ID: 120290
Telephone: (510) 659-6000 Carnegie Class: Assoc/HT-Mix Trad/Non
FAX Number: N/A Calendar System: Semester
URL: www.ohlone.edu
Established: 1966 Annual Undergrad Tuition & Fees (In-District): $1,162
Enrollment: 10,193 Coed
Affiliation or Control: State/Local IRS Status: 501(c)3
Highest Offering: Associate Degree
Accreditation: WJ, ADNUR, COARC, PTAA

01 President/Superintendent ... Dr. Gari BROWNING
05 Vice President Academic Affairs ... Dr. Leta STAGNARO
10 Vice Pres Administrative Services ... Ms. Susan YEAGER
32 Vice President Student Services ... Dr. Minh-Hoa TA
13 Assoc Vice Pres Information Tech ... Dr. Chris DELA ROSA
15 Assoc Vice Pres Human Resources ... Ms. Shairon ZINGSHEIM
08 Dean Business & Career Tech Educ ... Ms. Lesley BUEHLER
38 Dean Counseling ... Vacant
09 Dean Institutional Research ... Mr. Michael BOWMAN
57 Dean Arts and Social Science ... Vacant
76 Dean Health Sciences & Env Studies ... Dr. Gale CARLI
83 Dean Language/Comm/Academic Success ... Mr. Mark LIEU
81 Dean Science/Engineering/Math ... Dr. Bob BRADSHAW
88 Dean Deaf Studies ... Ms. Darline GUNSAULS
102 Executive Director Foundation ... Mr. Binh NGUYEN
35 Director EOPS/Student Services ... Ms. Debra TRIGG
21 Director Business Services ... Mr. Farhad SABIT
30 Director College Advancement ... Ms. Patrice BIRKEDAHL
19 Chief Safety & Security ... Mr. John WORLEY
18 Director of Facilities ... Mr. Oscar GUILLEN
37 Director Financial Aid ... Ms. Deborah GRIFFIN
96 Director of Purchasing ... Mr. Alex LEBEDEFF
104 Director International Programs ... Mr. Bill SHARAR
88 Director Curriculum & Scheduling ... Ms. Kimberly ROBBIE
04 Administrative Asst to President ... Ms. Shelby FOSTER
07 Dean Enrollment Services ... Ms. Laura WEAVER
41 Dean Kinesiology/Athletics/Brdcstg ... Mr. Chris WARDEN

Oikos University (G)

7850 Edgewater Drive, Oakland CA 94621

County: Alameda Identification: 667212
Telephone: (510) 639-7879 Carnegie Class: Not Classified
FAX Number: (510) 639-7810 Calendar System: Semester
URL: www.oikos.edu
Established: 2004 Annual Undergrad Tuition & Fees: N/A
Enrollment: N/A Coed
Affiliation or Control: Independent Non-Profit IRS Status: 501(c)3
Highest Offering: Doctorate
Accreditation: TRACS

01 President ... Dr. Jongin KIM
05 Director of Academic Affairs ... Dr. Daeseop YI

Olivet University (H)

1025 Howard Street, San Francisco CA 94103

County: San Francisco Identification: 666176
Telephone: (415) 371-0002 Carnegie Class: Not Classified
FAX Number: (415) 371-0003 Calendar System: Quarter
URL: www.olivetuniversity.edu
Established: 1992 Annual Undergrad Tuition & Fees: N/A
Enrollment: N/A Coed
Affiliation or Control: Independent Non-Profit IRS Status: 501(c)3
Highest Offering: Doctorate
Accreditation: BI

01 University President ... Dr. Tracy DAVIS
03 Vice President ... Dr. Nathanael TRAN
05 Academic Dean ... Dr. Christy TRAN
10 Chief Financial Officer ... Mr. Barnabas JUNG
11 Chief Operating Officer ... Dr. Walker TZENG

Otis College of Art and Design (I)

9045 Lincoln Boulevard, Los Angeles CA 90045-3550

County: Los Angeles FICE Identification: 001251
Unit ID: 120403
Telephone: (310) 665-6800 Carnegie Class: Spec-4-yr-Arts
FAX Number: (310) 665-6805 Calendar System: Semester
URL: www.otis.edu
Established: 1918 Annual Undergrad Tuition & Fees: $44,020
Enrollment: 1,160 Coed
Affiliation or Control: Independent Non-Profit IRS Status: 501(c)3
Highest Offering: Master's
Accreditation: WC, ART

01 President ... Dr. Bruce FERGUSON
05 Provost ... Mr. Randall LAVENDER
10 VP of Admin & Financial Services ... Vacant
32 VP Student Success ... Dr. Laura KIRALLA
111 VP Institutional Advancement ... Ms. Susan POLLACK
15 Vice Pres Human Resources/Devel ... Vacant

20 Assoc Provost Academic Admin ... Ms. Kim RUSSO
35 Dean of Students ... Dr. Laura KIRALLA
51 Dean of Continuing Ed/Pre-Col Pgms ... Ms. Amy GANTMAN
07 Dean of Admissions & Financial Aid ... Mr. Matthew GALLAGHER
06 Registrar ... Ms. Anna MANZANO
08 Director of Library/Instruct Tech ... Ms. Sue MABERRY
37 Director of Financial Aid ... Ms. Jessika VASQUEZ
36 Director Career Services ... Ms. Donna Lee ODA
13 Chief Information Officer ... Mr. Ankush MAHINDRA
18 Chief Facilities/Operation Officer ... Mr. Claude NICA
26 VP of Communications and Marketing ... Mr. Jeffrey PERKINS
29 Director Alumni Relations ... Mr. Philip SCANLON
21 Controller ... Ms. Christine SANCHEZ
14 Director Tech Support Services ... Mr. Andrew ARMSTRONG
102 Board Relations Manager ... Ms. Mahtem SHIFERRAW
88 Director of Strategic Partnerships ... Ms. Christine LEAHEY
04 Executive Asst to President ... Ms. Doniell PETERS
09 Director of Inst Research & Effect ... Vacant
104 Director International Education ... Vacant
108 Assoc Provost for Assess & Accred ... Ms. Debra BALLARD
19 Chief Safety and Security Officer ... Mr. Rick GONZALEZ
28 Asst Dean of Stdnt Affs/Title IX ... Dr. Carol BRANCH
38 Director Student Health & Wellness ... Dr. Julie SPENCER
39 Director Housing & Res Life ... Ms. Morgan BROWN
90 Sr Director of End-User Computing ... Mr. Felipe GUTIERREZ
96 Director of Purchasing ... Ms. Barbara TECLE

Pacific College (A)

3160 Redhill Avenue, Costa Mesa CA 92626-3402
County: Orange   FICE Identification: 032993
Unit ID: 422695
Telephone: (800) 867-2243   Carnegie Class: Spec-4-yr-Other Health
FAX Number: (714) 662-1702   Calendar System: Semester
URL: www.pacific-college.edu
Established: 1993   Annual Undergrad Tuition & Fees: N/A
Enrollment: 252   Coed
Affiliation or Control: Proprietary   IRS Status: Proprietary
Highest Offering: Baccalaureate
Accreditation: WC, NURSE

01 President ... Mr. William L. NELSON
03 Vice President ... Ms. Donna WOO
11 Sr Vice Pres Operations ... Mr. Marcus TROMP
05 Vice Pres Education ... Mr. Brian CHILSTRON

Pacific College of Oriental Medicine (B)

7445 Mission Valley Road, #105,
San Diego CA 92108-4408
County: San Diego   FICE Identification: 030277
Unit ID: 378576
Telephone: (619) 574-6909   Carnegie Class: Spec-4-yr-Other Health
FAX Number: (619) 574-6641   Calendar System: Trimester
URL: www.pacificcollege.edu
Established: 1986   Annual Undergrad Tuition & Fees: $9,173
Enrollment: 517   Coed
Affiliation or Control: Proprietary   IRS Status: Proprietary
Highest Offering: Doctorate
Accreditation: WC, ACUP

01 President ... Mr. Jack MILLER
05 Vice Pres of Academic Affairs ... Ms. Stacy GOMES
10 Chief Operating Officer ... Mr. Malcolm YOUNGREN
37 Vice Pres of Financial Aid ... Ms. Beatrice SMITH
26 Vice President Marketing ... Ms. Gail VOGT
12 Campus Director NY Campus ... Mr. Malcolm YOUNGREN
12 Campus Director CH Campus ... Mr. Edward LAMADRID
07 Director Admissions ... Mr. Reza GARAJEEAGHI
06 Registrar ... Mr. Nayeli CORONA
23 Director of Clinical Services ... Mr. Greg LANE
08 Head Librarian ... Ms. Naomi BROERING
13 Information Technology Director ... Mr. Greg RUSSO
40 Bookstore Manager ... Ms. Patti HINES
21 Bursar ... Ms. Patti HINES
27 Pacific Symposium & Events Coord ... Ms. Tiffany MCCORT

Pacific Oaks College (C)

55 Eureka Street, Pasadena CA 91103
County: Los Angeles   FICE Identification: 001255
Unit ID: 120768
Telephone: (626) 529-8500   Carnegie Class: Spec-4-yr-Other
FAX Number: N/A   Calendar System: Semester
URL: www.pacificoaks.edu
Established: 1945   Annual Undergrad Tuition & Fees: N/A
Enrollment: 1,267   Coed
Affiliation or Control: Independent Non-Profit   IRS Status: 501(c)3
Highest Offering: Master's
Accreditation: WC

01 President ... Dr. Patricia A. BREEN
05 Dean Academic Affairs ... Dr. Terry RATCLIFF
11 Chief Operating Officer ... Ms. Melanie SAUER
32 Assoc Vice Pres Student Services ... Mr. Frank FRIAS
88 Exec Director Children's School ... Mr. Robert BOYMAN
15 Director of Human Resources ... Ms. Carolyn MATHIS
10 Director of Finance ... Ms. Yug Fon CHIQUITO
08 Campus Librarian ... Ms. Kelsey VUKIC
35 Dir Ctr Stdnt Achievmt/Res/Enrich ... Ms. Pat MEDA
07 Assoc Vice President Admissions ... Mr. Michael PATTON
13 IT Director ... Mr. Carlos BONILLA
04 Dir Pres Office & Board Affairs ... Ms. Amy SEYERLE
12 Campus Dean San Jose ... Dr. Marcia BANKIRER
88 Assoc Dean School of CFP ... Dr. Bree DAVIS
88 Assoc Dean School of HD ... Dr. Donald GRANT
30 Director Advancement ... Ms. Amy SEYERLE
26 Director Communications/Marketing ... Mr. Larry RENICK

Pacific School of Religion (D)

1798 Scenic Avenue, Berkeley CA 94709-1323
County: Alameda   FICE Identification: 001256
Unit ID: 120795
Telephone: (510) 849-8200   Carnegie Class: Spec-4-yr-Faith
FAX Number: (510) 845-8948   Calendar System: Semester
URL: www.psr.edu
Established: 1866   Annual Graduate Tuition & Fees: N/A
Enrollment: 159   Coed
Affiliation or Control: Independent Non-Profit   IRS Status: 501(c)3
Highest Offering: Doctorate; No Undergraduates
Accreditation: WC, THEOL

01 President ... Rev. David VASQUEZ-LEVY
05 Dean/VP Academic Affairs ... Dr. Mary Donovan TURNER
10 Chief Business Officer ... Mr. Patrick O'LEARY
30 Chief Advancement Officer ... Ms. Wanda SCOTT
06 Asst Dean Academic Pgms/Registrar ... Ms. Lyndsey REED
07 Admissions/Financial Aid Officer ... Mr. Ruben CORTEZ
15 Personnel Director ... Ms. Deborah WALKER
04 Executive Asst to President ... Ms. Jen GALL
26 Marketing/Communications Manager ... Ms. Erin BURNS

Pacific States University (E)

3424 Wilshire Boulevard, 12th Floor,
Los Angeles CA 90010
County: Los Angeles   FICE Identification: 031633
Unit ID: 120838
Telephone: (323) 731-2383   Carnegie Class: Spec-4-yr-Bus
FAX Number: (323) 731-7276   Calendar System: Quarter
URL: www.psuca.edu
Established: 1928   Annual Undergrad Tuition & Fees: $16,005
Enrollment: 170   Coed
Affiliation or Control: Independent Non-Profit   IRS Status: 501(c)3
Highest Offering: Master's
Accreditation: ACICS

01 President ... Mr. Hee Young AHN
05 Dean Academic Affairs ... Dr. Heidi CROCKER
88 Asst Dean General Affairs ... Miss Rosy LIM
32 Associate Dean Student Affairs ... Mr. Moonsik KIM
26 Asst Dean Public Rels/Intl Affs ... Ms. Sarah MIN
13 Dir General & Technology Services ... Mr. Kuang Kai LU
08 University Librarian ... Vacant
06 Registrar ... Mr. James CUMMINGS

Pacific Union College (F)

One Angwin Avenue, Angwin CA 94508-9797
County: Napa   FICE Identification: 001258
Unit ID: 120865
Telephone: (707) 965-6311   Carnegie Class: Bac-A&S
FAX Number: (707) 965-6390   Calendar System: Quarter
URL: www.puc.edu
Established: 1882   Annual Undergrad Tuition & Fees: $28,629
Enrollment: 1,555   Coed
Affiliation or Control: Seventh-day Adventist   IRS Status: 501(c)3
Highest Offering: Master's
Accreditation: WC, ADNUR, IACBE, MUS, NUR, SW

01 President ... Dr. Robert A. CUSHMAN, JR.
05 Academic Dean/VP Academic Admin ... Dr. Nancy LECOURT
10 VP Financial Administration/CFO ... Mr. Brandon C. PARKER
88 Vice President for Asset Management ... Dr. John COLLINS
32 Vice President Student Services ... Dr. Lisa BISSELL PAULSON
84 Vice Pres Enrollment Mgmt/Marketing ... Ms. Jennifer TYNER
30 Assoc Vice President Advancement ... Mr. Mark ISHIKAWA
33 Dean of Men ... Mr. James I. BOYD, JR.
34 Dean of Women ... Miss Janice R. WOOD
08 Director Library Services ... Mr. Adu WORKU
37 Director Student Financial Services ... Ms. Laurie WHEELER
13 Director Information Technology ... Mrs. Maria VANCE
06 Registrar ... Mrs. Marlo WATERS
15 Director Human Resources ... Ms. Iris CHUAH
21 Director Budgets & Fiscal Services ... Mrs. Joy L. HIRDLER
38 Director Counseling Center ... Mr. Michael JEFFERSON
18 Chief Facilities/Facil Management ... Mr. Dale WITHERS
20 Associate Academic Officer ... Mr. Edwin MOORE
07 Admissions Counselor ... Ms. Jordan THORNBURGH
09 Director of Institutional Research ... Mr. Serhii KALYNOVSKYI

Pacifica Graduate Institute (G)

249 Lambert Road, Carpinteria CA 93013-3019
County: Carpinteria   FICE Identification: 031268
Unit ID: 115746
Telephone: (805) 969-3626   Carnegie Class: Spec-4-yr-Other Health
FAX Number: (805) 565-1932   Calendar System: Quarter
URL: www.pacifica.edu
Established: 1974   Annual Graduate Tuition & Fees: N/A
Enrollment: 939   Coed
Affiliation or Control: Proprietary   IRS Status: Proprietary
Highest Offering: Doctorate; No Undergraduates
Accreditation: WC

01 Chancellor/Chief Executive Officer ... Dr. Stephen AIZENSTAT
05 Vice President/Provost ... Dr. Joseph CAMBRAY
10 Int Chief Financial Officer ... Ms. Cindy YOUNG
43 General Counsel ... Mr. Frank MICHAELSON
20 Sr Director Academic Services ... Mr. Alain DUSSERT
37 Director of Financial Aid ... Ms. Tracie TEAGUE
06 Registrar ... Ms. Francine MATAS
30 Dir of Institutional Advancement/PR ... Mr. Erik DAVIS
15 Director of Human Resources ... Ms. Norma MESA
39 Director of Guest Services ... Mr. Jeffrey ABRAHAM
29 Director of Alumni Relations ... Ms. Dianne TRAVIS-TEAGUE
08 Librarian ... Mr. Rick ABSHIER

Palmer College of Chiropractic, West Campus (H)

90 E Tasman Drive, San Jose CA 95134-1617
Telephone: (408) 944-6000   FICE Identification: 021849
Accreditation: &NH, &CHIRO

† Regional accreditation is carried under the parent institution in Davenport, IA.

Palo Alto University (I)

1791 Arastradero Road, Palo Alto CA 94304
County: San Mateo   FICE Identification: 021383
Unit ID: 120698
Telephone: (800) 818-6136   Carnegie Class: Spec-4-yr-Other Health
FAX Number: (650) 433-3888   Calendar System: Quarter
URL: www.paloaltou.edu
Established: 1975   Annual Undergrad Tuition & Fees: N/A
Enrollment: 1,131   Coed
Affiliation or Control: Independent Non-Profit   IRS Status: 501(c)3
Highest Offering: Doctorate
Accreditation: WC, CACREP, CLPSY

01 President ... Dr. Maureen O'CONNOR
05 Provost/Academic Vice President ... Dr. William FROMING
32 Vice President Student Services ... Ms. Elizabeth HILT
31 Vice Pres Community Development ... Ms. Helen TING
88 Vice President for Prof Development ... Dr. Luli EMMONS
10 Vice Pres Business Affairs/CFO ... Ms. June KLEIN
20 Dean of Academic Admin/Oper ... Dr. James BRECKENRIDGE
17 Dir of Clinical Training-PhD Pgm ... Dr. Rowena GOMEZ
17 Dir of Clinical Training-PsyD Pgm ... Dr. Kimberly HILL
23 Director of Gronowski Center ... Dr. Sandy MACIAS
06 Registrar ... Ms. Nora MARQUEZ
37 Director Financial Aid ... Ms. Jessica AYRES
42 Chaplain/Ombudsman ... Rev. Byron BLAND
08 University Librarian/Dir Acad Tech ... Mr. Scott HINES
30 Director of Advancement ... Ms. Elizabeth SHAUGHNESSY
07 Director of Admissions ... Ms. Eirian WILLIAMS
13 Chief Information Officer ... Mr. David LEAVITT
29 Director of Alumni Relations ... Ms. Kemper MITCHELL
09 Director Institutional Research ... Ms. Kristen GUY

Palo Verde College (J)

One College Drive, Blythe CA 92225-9561
County: Riverside   FICE Identification: 001259
Unit ID: 120953
Telephone: (760) 921-5500   Carnegie Class: Assoc/MT-VT-Mix Trad/Non
FAX Number: (760) 921-5590   Calendar System: Semester
URL: www.paloverde.edu
Established: 1947   Annual Undergrad Tuition & Fees (In-District): $1,288
Enrollment: 4,023   Coed
Affiliation or Control: State/Local   IRS Status: 501(c)3
Highest Offering: Associate Degree
Accreditation: WJ

01 Superintendent/President ... Dr. Donald WALLACE
05 Vice Pres Instructional/Stdnt Svcs ... Dr. Sean HANCOCK
04 Executive Asst to Supt/President ... Ms. Denise HUNT
66 Assoc Dean Nursing & Allied Health ... Vacant
08 Librarian ... Ms. June TURNER
07 Director of Admissions and Records ... Ms. Shelley HAMILTON
88 Site Supervsr Child Dev/Teacher Ctr ... Ms. Maria KEHL
09 Director of Institutional Research ... Mr. Adam HOUSTON
18 Facilities & Operations Director ... Mr. Shad LEE
13 Director of Information Technology ... Mr. Eric EGAN
26 Outreach & Events Coordinator ... Ms. Staci LEE
15 Chief Human Resources Officer/EEO ... Ms. Cecilia GARCIA
10 Int Vice Pres Administrative Svcs ... Ms. Maureen DAVIS
20 Instructional Service Manager ... Vacant
37 Director Student Financial Aid ... Ms. Diana MENDEZ
101 Exec Asst to Supt/President/Board ... Ms. Carrie MULLION
102 Executive Director Foundation ... Mr. Eugene HILL

Palomar College (K)

1140 W Mission Road, San Marcos CA 92069-1487
County: San Diego   FICE Identification: 001260
Unit ID: 120971
Telephone: (760) 744-1150   Carnegie Class: Assoc/HT-High Trad
FAX Number: (760) 744-8123   Calendar System: Semester
URL: www.palomar.edu
Established: 1946   Annual Undergrad Tuition & Fees (In-District): $1,338
Enrollment: 23,482   Coed
Affiliation or Control: State/Local   IRS Status: 501(c)3
Highest Offering: Associate Degree

Accreditation: WJ, ADNUR, DA, EMT

01 Superintendent/President ....Dr. Joi Lin BLAKE
05 Int Asst Supt/Vice Pres Instruction ....Dr. Jack KAHN
32 Asst Supt/VP Student Services ....Mr. Adrian GONZALES
10 Asst Supt/VP Finance/Admin Svcs ....Mr. Ron PEREZ
15 Asst Supt/VP Human Resources ....Vacant
04 Exec Assistant to the President ....Ms. Cheryl ASHOUR
79 Dean Languages & Literature ....Ms. Shayla SIVERT
81 Dean Math/Natural & Health Sciences ....Dr. Kathy KAILIKOLE
38 Dean Counseling Services ....Mr. Brian STOCKERT
75 Dean Career/Tech/Extended Educ ....Ms. Margie FRITCH
50 Dean Arts/Media/Bus & Comp Sci ....Vacant
83 Dean Social/Behavioral Sciences ....Vacant
13 Director Info Systems & Services ....Ms. Connie MOISE
84 Director Enrollment Svcs/Admissions ....Mr. Kendyl MAGNUSON
09 Sr Director Institutional Research ....Ms. Michelle BARTON
18 Director of Facilities ....Mr. Chris MILLER
35 Director Student Affairs ....Ms. Sherry TITUS
37 Director Student Financial Aid ....Ms. Adriana LEE
26 Dir Comm/Marketing/Public Affairs ....Ms. Laura GROPEN
102 Executive Director for Foundation ....Ms. Stacy RUNGAITIS
19 Chief of Police ....Mr. Chris MOORE
23 Director Health Services ....Ms. Judy HARRIS
41 Director Athletics ....Mr. Scott CATHCART

Pardee RAND Graduate School of Policy Studies (A)

1776 Main Street, Santa Monica CA 90407-2138
County: Los Angeles FICE Identification: 010441
Unit ID: 121628
Telephone: (310) 393-0411 Carnegie Class: Spec-4-yr-Other
FAX Number: (310) 451-6978 Calendar System: Quarter
URL: www.prgs.edu
Established: 1970 Annual Graduate Tuition & Fees: N/A
Enrollment: 107 Coed
Affiliation or Control: Independent Non-Profit IRS Status: 501(c)3
Highest Offering: Doctorate; No Undergraduates
Accreditation: WC

01 Dean/RAND VP Innovation ....Dr. Susan MARQUIS
05 Associate Dean Academics ....Ms. Rachel SWANGER
06 Registrar ....Ms. Mary PARKER
07 Asst Dean Admissions ....Ms. Stefanie HOWARD
10 Financial Aid/Budget Administrator ....Ms. Maggie CLAY

Pasadena City College (B)

1570 E Colorado Boulevard, Pasadena CA 91106-2041
County: Los Angeles FICE Identification: 001261
Unit ID: 121044
Telephone: (626) 585-7123 Carnegie Class: Assoc/HT-High Trad
FAX Number: (626) 585-7910 Calendar System: Semester
URL: www.pasadena.edu
Established: 1924 Annual Undergrad Tuition & Fees (In-District): $1,348
Enrollment: 27,050 Coed
Affiliation or Control: State/Local IRS Status: 501(c)3
Highest Offering: Associate Degree
Accreditation: WJ, DA, DH, DT, MAC, RAD

01 Superintendent-President ....Dr. Rajen VURDIEN
12 Senior VP Non-credit & Offsite Camp ....Dr. Robert H. BELL
05 VP Instruction ....Dr. Terry GIUGNI
10 VP Business & Administrative Svcs ....Dr. Richard STORTI
32 Vice President Student Services ....Dr. Cynthia OLIVO
21 Exec Dir Business & College Svcs ..Mr. Joseph W. SIMONESCHI
15 Vice President Human Resources ....Dr. Lisa NORMAN
09 Exec Dir Inst Research/Planning ....Ms. Crystal KOLLROSS
56 Director Extension ....Ms. Elaine CHAPMAN
38 Dean Counseling ....Mr. Armando DURAN
88 Dean Special Services ....Ms. Ketmani KOUANCHAO
07 Dean Admissions/Records ....Ms. Susan BRICKER
37 Director Financial Aid ....Mr. Manuel CERDA
13 Interim Exec Director Info Tech ....Mr. Matthew KIAMAN
26 Exec Dir Strategic Comm/Marketing ....Mr. Alex BOEKELHEIDE
18 Exec Dir Facilities Services ....Vacant
04 Exec Asst to President ....Ms. Monica MOLINA
19 Chief Police & Safety Services ....Mr. Steven MATCHAN
35 Dean Student Life ....Ms. Rebecca COBB
96 Director of Purchasing & Contracts ....Mr. George CHIDIAC

Patten University (C)

2100 Franklin Street, Suite 350, Oakland CA 94612
County: Alameda FICE Identification: 004490
Unit ID: 121071
Telephone: (415) 494-8240 Carnegie Class: Not Classified
FAX Number: N/A Calendar System: Semester
URL: www.patten.edu
Established: 1944 Annual Undergrad Tuition & Fees: N/A
Enrollment: N/A Coed
Affiliation or Control: Proprietary IRS Status: Proprietary
Highest Offering: Master's
Accreditation: WC

01 President ....Dr. Thomas STEWART
05 Vice Pres Academic Affairs ....Dr. Marc PORTER
10 VP Finance/Operations ....Mr. Ramon DOURADO
06 Registrar ....Mr. Aaron HIATT

Pepperdine University (D)

24255 Pacific Coast Highway, Malibu CA 90263-0001
County: Los Angeles FICE Identification: 010149
Unit ID: 121150
Telephone: (310) 506-4000 Carnegie Class: DU-Mod
FAX Number: (310) 506-4861 Calendar System: Semester
URL: www.pepperdine.edu
Established: 1937 Annual Undergrad Tuition & Fees: $50,022
Enrollment: 7,632 Coed
Affiliation or Control: Church Of Christ IRS Status: 501(c)3
Highest Offering: Doctorate
Accreditation: WC, CLPSY, DIETD, LAW, MUS

01 President ....Dr. Andrew K. BENTON
100 Chief of Staff ....Ms. Marnie D. MITZE
03 Executive Vice President ....Mr. Gary A. HANSON
04 Exec Assistant to the President ....Mrs. Cynthia PAVELL
05 Provost ....Dr. Rick MARRS
10 VP and Chief Financial Officer ....Mr. Paul B. LASITER
00 Chancellor ....Dr. Michael ADAMS
111 Sr VP Advancement & Public Affairs ....Mr. Keith HINKLE
115 Senior Vice President Investments ....Mr. Jeff PIPPIN
43 General Counsel ....Mr. Marc P. GOODMAN
11 VP of Administration ....Mr. Phil E. PHILLIPS
21 Chief Business Officer ....Mrs. Edna POWELL
13 Chief Information Officer ....Mr. Jonathan SEE
26 Chief Marketing Officer ....Mr. Rick GIBSON
21 Assoc VP Campus Ops/Business Svcs ....Mr. Alex PANG
06 Assoc VP & University Registrar ....Mr. Hung V. LE
104 Dean of International Programs ....Dr. Charles F. HALL
07 Dean of Admission/Enrollment Mgmt ....Dr. Kristy COLLINS
32 VP of Student Affairs ....Dr. Connie HORTON
08 Dean of Libraries ....Mr. Mark S. ROOSA
61 Dean of the School of Law ....Mr. Paul CARON
50 Dean Graziadio Sch Business & Mgmt ....Dr. Deryck VAN RENSBURG
53 Dean of Graduate School Educ/Psych ....Dr. Helen E. WILLIAMS
49 Dean of Seaver College ....Dr. Michael E. FELTNER
80 Dean of School of Public Policy ....Mr. Pete PETERSON
42 University Chaplain ....Ms. Sara BARTON
46 Vice Provost for Research and Strat ....Dr. Lee KATS
108 Assoc Provost Inst Effectiveness ....Dr. Lisa BORTMAN
29 Exec Director for Alumni Affairs ....Mr. Bob CLARK
15 Chief Human Resources Officer ....Mrs. Lauren COSENTINO
21 University Controller ....Mr. Brian THOMASON
88 Assistant Controller ....Mr. David BRANT
88 Director of Ministry Outreach ....Mr. Michael COPE
46 Director Research & Sponsored Pgm ....Vacant
39 Assoc Dean of Students/Housing ....Vacant
88 Managing Dir Center for the Arts ....Ms. Rebecca CARSON
88 Director of Special Programs ....Ms. Kanet THOMAS
85 Dir Intl Student Services ....Ms. Brooke CUTLER
27 Assoc VP IM Communications ....Mr. Matthew MIDURA
23 Director of Student Health Services ....Ms. Nancy SAFINICK
36 Assoc Dean of Students/Career Ctr ....Mr. Brad D. DUDLEY
41 Director of Athletics ....Dr. Steven POTTS
19 Assoc VP & Dir of Public Safety ....Mr. Lance BRIDGESMITH
18 Director Facilities Services ....Ms. Carly MISCHKE
86 Assoc VP Govt & Regulatory Affairs ....Ms. Rhiannon BAILARD
37 Dir of Seaver Financial Assistance ....Mrs. Janet LOCKHART
38 Assoc VP & Dir Student Counseling ....Dr. Connie HORTON
09 Director of Institutional Research ....Ms. Lily PANG
112 Exec Dir Estate and Gift Planning ....Mr. Curt PORTZEL
22 Director Disability Services ....Ms. Sandra HARRISON
116 Director of Auditing Services ....Ms. Norma IADEVAIA
102 Dir Corporate/Foundation Relations ....Ms. Shella D. KING

*Peralta Community Colleges District Office (E)

333 E Eighth Street, Oakland CA 94606-2889
County: Alameda FICE Identification: 001265
Unit ID: 121178
Telephone: (510) 466-7200 Carnegie Class: N/A
FAX Number: (510) 835-4078
URL: www.peralta.edu

01 Chancellor ....Dr. Jowel C. LAGUERRE
13 VC Information Technology ....Mr. Jason COLE
26 Exec Dir Public Info/Comm & Media ....Mr. Jeffrey HEYMAN

*Berkeley City College (F)

2050 Center Street, Berkeley CA 94704-1183
County: Alameda FICE Identification: 022427
Unit ID: 125170
Telephone: (510) 981-2800 Carnegie Class: Assoc/HT-High Non
FAX Number: (510) 841-7333 Calendar System: Semester
URL: www.berkeleycitycollege.edu
Established: 1974 Annual Undergrad Tuition & Fees (In-District): $1,232
Enrollment: 7,164 Coed
Affiliation or Control: State/Local IRS Status: 501(c)3
Highest Offering: Associate Degree
Accreditation: WJ

02 President ....Dr. Rowena M. TOMANENG
05 Vice President Instruction ....Ms. Tram VO-KUMAMOTO
32 Int Vice President Student Services ....Mr. Jason S. CIFRA
49 Dean Business Science MMART & AT ....Dr. Francisco GAMEZ
83 Dean Liberal Arts & Social Science ....Ms. Lisa R. COOK
35 Dean Student Support Services ....Ms. Brenda JOHNSON
10 Director Business Services & Admin ....Ms. Shirley SLAUGHTER
121 Int Assoc Dean Educational Success ....Mr. Andre SINGLETON
27 Public Information Officer ....Ms. Janice K. ADAM
15 Director Personnel Services ....Ms. Trudy LARGENT
18 Chief Facilities/Physical Plant ....Dr. Sadiq IKHARO
21 Associate Business Officer ....Mr. John PANG
26 Chief Public Relations Officer ....Mr. Jeffrey HEYMAN
04 Executive Assistant to President ....Ms. Cynthia REESE
36 Director Student Placement ....Ms. Gail PENDLETON
37 Director Student Financial Aid ....Ms. Loan NGUYEN
38 Director Student Counseling ....Ms. Susan TRUONG

*College of Alameda (G)

555 Ralph Appezzato Memorial Pkwy, Alameda CA 94501-2109
County: Alameda FICE Identification: 006720
Unit ID: 108667
Telephone: (510) 522-7221 Carnegie Class: Assoc/HT-High Non
FAX Number: (510) 337-0619 Calendar System: Semester
URL: www.alameda.peralta.edu
Established: 1968 Annual Undergrad Tuition & Fees (In-District): $1,232
Enrollment: 6,283 Coed
Affiliation or Control: State/Local IRS Status: 501(c)3
Highest Offering: Associate Degree
Accreditation: WJ, DA

02 President ....Mr. Tim KARAS
05 Int Vice President of Instruction ....Mr. Myron JORDAN
32 Vice President of Student Svcs ....Ms. Tina VASCONCELLOS
88 Dean Special Projects ....Ms. Toni COOK
26 Chief Public Relations Officer ....Vacant
84 Dean Enrollment Services ....Dr. Amy LEE
20 Dean Pathways/Student Success ....Mr. Myron JORDAN
103 Int Dean Workforce Development ....Ms. Lilia CELHAY
10 Business & Administrative Svcs Mgr ....Ms. Mary Beth BENVENUTTI
07 Admissions & Records Specialist ....Ms. Marcean BRYANT

*Laney College (H)

900 Fallon Street, Oakland CA 94607-4893
County: Alameda FICE Identification: 001266
Unit ID: 117247
Telephone: (510) 834-5740 Carnegie Class: Assoc/MT-VT-High Non
FAX Number: (510) 464-3528 Calendar System: Semester
URL: www.laney.edu
Established: 1953 Annual Undergrad Tuition & Fees (In-District): $1,232
Enrollment: 11,667 Coed
Affiliation or Control: State/Local IRS Status: 501(c)3
Highest Offering: Associate Degree
Accreditation: WJ

02 President ....Ms. Tammeil GILKERSON
05 Vice President of Instruction ....Mr. Zhanjing (John) YU
32 Dean of Student Success ....Ms. Jackie GRAVES
10 Director Business/Admin Services ....Ms. Phyllis CARTER
49 Dean Liberal Arts ....Dr. Chuen CHAN
81 Dean Mathematics and Science ....Ms. Denise RICHARDSON
75 Dean Career & Technical Educ ....Mr. Peter CRABTREE
23 Director Peralta Wellness Center ....Ms. Indra THADANI
84 Dean Enrollment Services ....Dr. Mildred LEWIS
79 Dean Humanities/Social Science ....Dr. Julianne KIRGIS
88 Dean Student Services ....Mr. Kevin WADE
04 Executive Assistant to President ....Ms. Maisha JAMESON
37 Financial Aid Supervisor ....Mr. Joseph KOROMA
41 Director Athletics ....Mr. John BEAM
88 Director Gateway to College Pgm ....Mr. Shawn TAYLOR
08 Head Librarian ....Ms. Evelyn LORD
35 Dir Student Activities/Campus Life ....Mr. Gary ALBURY

*Merritt College (I)

12500 Campus Drive, Oakland CA 94619-3196
County: Alameda FICE Identification: 001267
Unit ID: 118772
Telephone: (510) 531-4911 Carnegie Class: Assoc/HVT-High Non
FAX Number: (510) 436-2405 Calendar System: Semester
URL: www.merritt.edu
Established: 1953 Annual Undergrad Tuition & Fees (In-District): $1,232
Enrollment: 6,647 Coed
Affiliation or Control: State/Local IRS Status: 501(c)3
Highest Offering: Associate Degree
Accreditation: WJ, DIETT, HT, RAD

00 Chancellor ....Dr. Jowel LAGUERRE
02 Interim President ....Dr. Marie-Elaine BURNS
05 Vice President of Instruction ....Dr. Jeffrey LAMB
32 Vice President of Student Services ....Dr. Arnulfo CEDILLO
96 Vice Chancellor of General Services ....Dr. Sadiq IKHARO
15 Vice Chancellor for Human Resources ....Ms. Trudy LARGENT
20 Vice Chanc Educational Services ....Dr. Michael ORKIN
13 Assoc VC of Information Technology ....Mr. Calvin MADLOCK
26 Exec Dir Marketing/Public Rels/Comm ....Mr. Jeffrey HEYMAN
08 Head Librarian ....Mr. Timothy HACKETT
06 Registrar ....Ms. Susana DE LA TORRE
10 Director of Business/Admin Services ....Dr. Dativa DEL ROSARIO
35 Dir Student Activities/Campus Life ....Dr. Herbert KITCHEN
09 Director of Institutional Research ....Mr. Nathan PELLEGRIN
101 Board Clerk ....Ms. Brenda MARTINEZ
102 Interim Exec Dir Foundation ....Ms. Kaia BURKETT
18 Facilities Director/Physical Plant ....Mr. Ken BRICE
37 Director Student Financial Aid ....Vacant

Phillips Graduate University (A)

19900 Plummer Street, Chatsworth CA 91311
County: Los Angeles FICE Identification: 022372
Unit ID: 110307
Telephone: (818) 386-5600 Carnegie Class: Spec-4-yr-Other Health
FAX Number: (818) 386-5636 Calendar System: Semester
URL: www.pgu.edu
Established: 1971 Annual Graduate Tuition & Fees: N/A
Enrollment: 226 Coed
Affiliation or Control: Independent Non-Profit IRS Status: 501(c)3
Highest Offering: Doctorate; No Undergraduates
Accreditation: WC

05 Vice President Academic Affairs ... Dr. Ellie KAUCHER
32 Dean of Students ... Dr. Theresa WRAY

Pima Medical Institute-Chula Vista (B)

780 Bay Boulevard, Suite 101,
Chula Vista CA 91910-5261
Telephone: (619) 425-3200 Identification: 666272
Accreditation: ABHES, COARC, RAD

† Branch campus of Pima Medical Institute, Tucson, AZ.

Pitzer College (C)

1050 N Mills Avenue, Claremont CA 91711-6110
County: Los Angeles FICE Identification: 001172
Unit ID: 121257
Telephone: (909) 621-8129 Carnegie Class: Bac-A&S
FAX Number: (909) 621-8770 Calendar System: Semester
URL: www.pitzer.edu
Established: 1963 Annual Undergrad Tuition & Fees: $50,430
Enrollment: 1,067 Coed
Affiliation or Control: Independent Non-Profit IRS Status: 501(c)3
Highest Offering: Baccalaureate
Accreditation: WC

01 President ... Dr. Melvin L. OLIVER
05 Vice Pres Acad Affs/Dean of Faculty ... Dr. Nigel BOYLE
10 Treasurer/Vice Pres Administration ... Mr. Yuet LEE
30 Int Vice Pres College Advancement ... Ms. Pamela A. JONES-TINTLE
07 VP Admissions/Financial Aid ... Ms. Yvonne BERUMEN
32 Vice Pres Student Affairs ... Mr. Brian CARLISLE
26 VP Comm/Marketing/Public Relations ... Mr. Mark BAILEY
44 Assistant Vice Pres of Development ... Mrs. Pam JONES
20 Associate Dean of Faculty ... Ms. Kathleen YEP
20 Associate Dean of Faculty ... Mrs. Melinda HERROLD-MENZIES
06 Registrar ... Ms. Eva PETERS
37 Director Financial Aid ... Ms. Kara MOORE
09 Director of Institutional Research ... Mr. Marco Antonio CRUZ
15 Director Human Resources ... Ms. Marni BOBICH
18 Director Facilities ... Mr. Larry BURIK
21 Assoc VP Admin/Assoc Treasurer ... Ms. Lori YOSHINO
36 Director Career Services ... Mr. Brad THARPE
29 Sr Director Alumni Relations ... Ms. Nancy TRESER-OSGOOD
38 Director Student Counseling ... Dr. Rebecca KORNBLUH
04 Sr Executive Assistant to President ... Ms. Melanie LACY

Platt College (D)

1000 S Fremont Avenue, Bldg A10 S,
Alhambra CA 91803-8845
County: Los Angeles FICE Identification: 030627
Unit ID: 260789
Telephone: (626) 300-5444 Carnegie Class: Spec-4-yr-Other Health
FAX Number: (626) 457-8295 Calendar System: Other
URL: www.plattcollege.edu
Established: 1987 Annual Undergrad Tuition & Fees: $16,117
Enrollment: 639 Coed
Affiliation or Control: Proprietary IRS Status: Proprietary
Highest Offering: Baccalaureate
Accreditation: ACCSC, COARC, DMS

01 President ... Mr. Mike GIACOMINI

Platt College (E)

3700 Inland Empire Blvd, Ste 400, Ontario CA 91764-4906
Telephone: (909) 941-9410 Identification: 666056
Accreditation: ACCSC, COARC

† Branch campus of Platt College, Ahambra, CA.

Platt College (F)

6465 Sycamore Canyon Boulevard, Riverside CA 95207
Telephone: (951) 572-4300 Identification: 770561
Accreditation: ACCSC

Platt College (G)

6250 El Cajon Boulevard, San Diego CA 92115-3919
County: San Diego FICE Identification: 023043
Unit ID: 121275
Telephone: (619) 265-0107 Carnegie Class: Spec-4-yr-Arts
FAX Number: (619) 265-8655 Calendar System: Other
URL: www.platt.edu
Established: 1980 Annual Undergrad Tuition & Fees: $23,250
Enrollment: 255 Coed
Affiliation or Control: Proprietary IRS Status: Proprietary
Highest Offering: Baccalaureate
Accreditation: ACCSC

00 Chairman ... Mr. Robert D. LEIKER
01 President ... Mrs. Meg LEIKER
03 Vice President ... Mr. Alfred MEDRO
10 Chief Business Officer ... Ms. Marianne TAXTER
05 Director of Education ... Ms. Julio FRIZZA-POMPA

Point Loma Nazarene University (H)

3900 Lomaland Drive, San Diego CA 92106-2899
County: San Diego FICE Identification: 001262
Unit ID: 121309
Telephone: (619) 849-2200 Carnegie Class: Masters/L
FAX Number: (619) 849-2579 Calendar System: Semester
URL: www.pointloma.edu
Established: 1902 Annual Undergrad Tuition & Fees: $33,500
Enrollment: 3,663 Coed
Affiliation or Control: Church Of The Nazarene IRS Status: 501(c)3
Highest Offering: Beyond Master's But Less Than Doctorate
Accreditation: WC, ACBSP, CAATE, CAEPN, DIETD, EMT, MUS, NURSE, SW

01 President ... Dr. Bob BROWER
03 Executive Vice President ... Dr. Joe WATKINS
05 Provost/Chief Academic Officer ... Dr. Kerry FULCHER
10 VP Finance/Administrative Svcs ... Mr. George LATTER
32 VP Student Dev & Chief Title IX Ofc ... Dr. Caye SMITH
88 Vice Pres Spiritual Development ... Dr. Mary PAUL
15 Assoc VP for Human Resources ... Mr. Jeffrey HERMAN
37 Assoc Vice President for Finance ... Mrs. Cindy CHAPPELL
35 Assc VP Stdnt Dev/Chf Diversity Ofc ... Dr. Jeffrey CARR
21 Assoc VP for Budget/Accounting ... Ms. Janet CAPRARIO
84 Assoc VP Enrollment & Retention ... Dr. Scott SHOEMAKER
20 Vice Prov Academic Administration ... Dr. Mark PITTS
108 Vice Prov Accred & IE ... Dr. Karen LEE
35 Dean of Students ... Dr. Jeff BOLSTER
13 Chief Information Officer ... Mr. Corey FLING
09 Dir Institutional Research ... Mr. Brent GOODMAN
12 Director of Wesleyan Center ... Dr. Mark MANN
18 Director of Campus Facilities ... Mr. Bruce KUNKEL
36 Executive Dir Strengths & Vocation ... Ms. Rebecca SMITH
88 Exec Dir of Enrollment Mgmt ... Ms. Jeanne COCHRAN
86 Dir Public Affairs ... Ms. Jill MONROE
88 Director Center Pastoral Leadership ... Dr. John CALHOUN
42 Ld Con for Mission Res & Pst Rel ... Dr. Ron BENEFIEL
88 Director of Community Ministries ... Ms. Dana HOJSACK
88 Director of Worship Arts ... Mr. George WILLIAMSON
49 Dean College of Arts & Sciences ... Dr. Jim DAICHENDT
83 Dean College of Social Sciences ... Dr. Holly IRWIN
07 Director Undergraduate Admissions ... Ms. Shannon HUTCHISON-CARAVEO
08 Director of Ryan Library ... Dr. Frank QUINN
56 Dean Extended Learning ... Dr. Dave PHILLIPS
06 Dir Records/Institutional Research ... Ms. Cheryl GAUGHAN
26 Director Marketing/Creative Svcs ... Vacant
88 Assoc Dean Stdnt Success/Wellness ... Dr. Kim BOGAN
19 Director of Public Safety ... Mr. Mark GALBRAITH
29 Exec Director of Alumni Relations ... Ms. Sheryl SMEE
40 Bookstore Manager ... Ms. Katelyn MERRILL
85 Dir Multicultural/Intl Stdnt Svcs ... Mr. Sam KWAPONG
41 Athletic Director ... Mr. Ethan HAMILTON
88 Director of Nicholson Commons ... Mr. Milton KARAHADIAN
94 Dir Stevenson Ctr for Women's Stds ... Dr. Linda BEAIL
104 Director Study Abroad Program ... Ms. Sandy SOOHOO-REFAEI
88 Dir of Programs & Operations ... Mr. Nick WOLF
04 Exec Asst to President ... Ms. Myra FISHER
106 Dir Online Education/E-learning ... Dr. Dave PHILLIPS
39 Asst Dir Student Housing ... Ms. Molly PETERSEN
30 Sr Executive Director Advancement ... Ms. Kathy MEZA
88 Exec Dir Advancement Operations ... Ms. Christina GARDNER
50 Dean of Business ... Mr. Dan BOTHE
53 Dean of Education ... Ms. Deb ERICKSON
101 Secretary of the Institution/Board ... Dr. Joe WATKINS
28 Chief Diversity Officer ... Dr. Jeffrey CARR
44 Director Annual or Planned Giving ... Ms. Natalie LOPEZ

Pomona College (I)

550 N College Avenue, #206, Claremont CA 91711-6301
County: Los Angeles FICE Identification: 001173
Unit ID: 121345
Telephone: (909) 621-8000 Carnegie Class: Bac-A&S
FAX Number: (909) 621-8403 Calendar System: Semester
URL: www.pomona.edu
Established: 1887 Annual Undergrad Tuition & Fees: $49,352
Enrollment: 1,663 Coed
Affiliation or Control: Independent Non-Profit IRS Status: 501(c)3
Highest Offering: Baccalaureate
Accreditation: WC

01 President ... Dr. G. Gabrielle STARR
05 Vice President/Dean of College ... Dr. Audrey BILGER
13 Vice President Information ... Mr. William MORSE
10 Vice President/Treasurer ... Dr. Karen SISSON
111 VP for Institutional Advancement ... Ms. Pamela BESNARD
32 Vice President/Dean of Students ... Mrs. Miriam FELDBLUM
07 VP of Admissions & Financial Aid ... Mr. Seth ALLEN
26 VP & Chief Communications Ofcr ... Ms. Marylou FERRY
04 Special Assistant to President ... Dr. Teresa SHAW
06 Registrar ... Ms. Elisa C. ALBAN
27 Director Public Relations ... Mr. Mark WOOD
29 Assistant VP Alumni & Parent Engage ... Mr. Craig ARTEAGA-JOHNSON
37 Director Financial Aid ... Ms. Robin THOMPSON
36 Director Career Development ... Ms. Mary RAYMOND
15 Director Human Resources ... Ms. Brenda RUSHFORTH
41 Director Physical Education ... Ms. Lesley IRVINE
44 Director Annual Giving ... Mr. Michael SPICER
21 Assoc Treasurer/Controller ... Ms. Mary Lou WOODS
09 Director of Institutional Research ... Dr. Jennifer RACHFORD
18 Chief Facilities/Physical Plant ... Mr. Robert ROBINSON

Presbyterian Theological Seminary in America (J)

15605 Carmenita Rd., Santa Fe Springs CA 90670
County: Los Angeles FICE Identification: 041228
Telephone: (562) 926-1023 Carnegie Class: Not Classified
FAX Number: (562) 926-1025 Calendar System: Semester
URL: www.ptsa.edu
Established: 1977 Annual Undergrad Tuition & Fees: N/A
Enrollment: N/A Coed
Affiliation or Control: Presbyterian Church In America IRS Status: 501(c)3
Highest Offering: First Professional Degree
Accreditation: BI, @THEOL

01 President ... Dr. Sang Meyng LEE
05 Dean of Academic Affairs ... Rev. Kyung Mo KOO
11 Dean of Administration ... Vacant
32 Dean of Students/Student Ministry ... Rev. Choong Gi PARK
85 Dean/Dir of Intl Students/Fin Aid ... Mrs. Karen CHOI
08 Librarian ... Ms. Youngsook CHOI
10 Managing Treasurer/Accountant ... Mrs. Mihyun PARK
06 Registrar ... Mrs. Michelle YOON
106 Dir Online Education/E-learning ... Mr. Woo Joong KANG
13 IT Director ... Mr. Eliot LEE

Presidio Graduate School (K)

1202 Ralston Avenue, #300, San Francisco CA 94129
County: San Francisco Identification: 667150
Unit ID: 486433
Telephone: (415) 561-6555 Carnegie Class: Not Classified
FAX Number: (415) 561-6483 Calendar System: Semester
URL: www.presidio.edu
Established: 2003 Annual Graduate Tuition & Fees: N/A
Enrollment: 133 Coed
Affiliation or Control: Independent Non-Profit IRS Status: 501(c)3
Highest Offering: Master's; No Undergraduates
Accreditation: WC

01 President ... Suzanne FARVER
05 Dean Academic Pgms/Student Svcs ... Dr. Steven CRANE
07 Director of Admissions ... Kari DORTH

Professional Golfers Career College (L)

26109 Ynez Road, Temecula CA 92591-6013
County: Riverside FICE Identification: 033673
Unit ID: 437750
Telephone: (951) 719-2994 Carnegie Class: Spec 2-yr-Other
FAX Number: (951) 719-1643 Calendar System: Semester
URL: www.golfcollege.edu
Established: 1990 Annual Undergrad Tuition & Fees: $15,000
Enrollment: 162 Coed
Affiliation or Control: Proprietary IRS Status: Proprietary
Highest Offering: Associate Degree
Accreditation: ACICS

01 President ... Dr. Tim SOMERVILLE

Providence Christian College (M)

1539 E. Howard Street, Pasadena CA 91104
County: Los Angeles FICE Identification: 041539
Unit ID: 455770
Telephone: (866) 323-0233 Carnegie Class: Bac-A&S
FAX Number: (626) 696-4040 Calendar System: Semester
URL: www.providencecc.edu
Established: 2002 Annual Undergrad Tuition & Fees: $28,014
Enrollment: 147 Coed
Affiliation or Control: Non-denominational IRS Status: 501(c)3
Highest Offering: Baccalaureate
Accreditation: WC

01 President ... Dr. Jim BELCHER
05 Interim Chief Academic Officer ... Ann HAMILTON
10 VP Finance & Operations ... Dawn DIRKSEN
30 VP Advancement ... Michael KILEDJIAN
06 Registrar ... Patty TSAI
07 Director Admissions/Marketing ... Larissa KAMPS
39 Director Resident/Student Activity ... Mark RIPPETOE

*Rancho Santiago Community College District (N)

2323 N. Broadway, Santa Ana CA 92706-1640
County: Orange FICE Identification: 006991
Unit ID: 438665
Telephone: (714) 480-7300 Carnegie Class: N/A
FAX Number: (714) 796-3915
URL: www.rsccd.edu

01 Chancellor .... Dr. Raul RODRIGUEZ
10 Vice Chanc Business & Fiscal Svcs .... Mr. Peter HARDASH
05 Vice Chanc Educational Svcs .... Mr. Enrique PEREZ
15 Vice Chanc Human Resources .... Ms. Judy CHITLIK
19 Interim Chief of Security .... Ms. Toni BLAND
04 Exec Asst to the Chancellor .... Ms. Debra GERARD

*Santa Ana College (A)

1530 W 17th Street, Santa Ana CA 92706-3398
County: Orange FICE Identification: 001284
Unit ID: 121619
Telephone: (714) 564-6000 Carnegie Class: Assoc/HT-Mix Trad/Non
FAX Number: (714) 564-6379 Calendar System: Semester
URL: www.sac.edu
Established: 1915 Annual Undergrad Tuition & Fees (In-District): $1,142
Enrollment: 29,808 Coed
Affiliation or Control: State/Local IRS Status: 501(c)3
Highest Offering: Baccalaureate
Accreditation: WJ, ADNUR, IPSY, OTA

02 President .... Dr. Linda D. ROSE
05 Vice President Academic Affairs .... Carlos LOPEZ
10 Vice Chanc Bus Ops/Fiscal Svcs .... Mr. Peter HARDASH
51 Vice President Continuing Educ .... Dr. James KENNEDY
32 Dean Student Affairs .... Dr. Lilia TANAKEYOWMA
11 Vice Pres Administrative Svcs .... Dr. Michael COLLINS
07 Dean Enrollment Services .... Mark LIANG
06 Registrar .... Chris TRUONG
50 Dean Business Division .... Madeline GRANT
35 Assoc Dean Student Development .... Vacant
38 Dean Counseling .... Vacant
37 Director of Financial Aid .... Robert MANSON
41 Dean KinesiologyAthletics .... Dr. R. Douglas MANNING
57 Dean Fine & Performing Arts .... Eve KIKAWA
111 Exec Director College Advancement .... Christina ROMERO
18 Facilities Manager .... Vacant
79 Dean Humanities & Social Siences .... Shelly JAFFRAY
81 Dean Science/Math/Hlth Sci .... Dr. Michelle PRIEST
103 Dean Career Educ/Workforce Develop .... Bart HOFFMAN
56 Associate Dean EOPS .... Christine LEON
88 Associate Dean DSPS .... Dr. Veronica OFORLEA
04 Assistant to the President .... Kennethia J. VEGA
26 Public Information Officer .... Melissa UTSUKI
09 Director of College Research .... Janice LOVE
35 Assistant Dean Student Services .... Teresa MERCADO-COTA

*Santiago Canyon College (B)

8045 E Chapman Avenue, Orange CA 92869-4512
County: Orange FICE Identification: 036957
Unit ID: 399212
Telephone: (714) 628-4900 Carnegie Class: Assoc/HT-Mix Trad/Non
FAX Number: (714) 628-4723 Calendar System: Semester
URL: www.sccollege.edu
Established: 1997 Annual Undergrad Tuition & Fees (In-District): $1,142
Enrollment: 11,187 Coed
Affiliation or Control: State/Local IRS Status: 501(c)3
Highest Offering: Associate Degree
Accreditation: WJ

02 President .... Dr. John HERNANDEZ
04 Assistant to the President .... Ms. Esther ODEGARD
32 Int Vice President Student Services .... Ms. Ruth BABESHOFF
05 Vice President Academic Affairs .... Ms. Marilyn FLORES
51 Vice President Continuing Educ .... Mr. Jose VARGAS
11 Vice Pres Administrative Services .... Ms. Arleen SATELE
38 Interim Dean Counseling .... Dr. Jennifer COTO
41 Dean Math & Sciences/Athletic Dir .... Mr. Martin STRINGER
79 Dean Arts/Humanities/Social Science .... Mr. Dave VAKIL
36 Dean Business/Career Tech Educ .... Mr. Von LAWSON
108 Dean Institutional Effectiveness .... Mr. Aaron VOELCKER
20 Dean Instruction/Student Services .... Ms. Lori FASBINDER
37 Dean Enrollment and Support Svcs .... Mr. Syed RIZVI
20 Dean Instruction/Student Svcs .... Vacant
35 Interim Dean Student Affairs .... Ms. Loretta JORDAN
20 Int Assoc Dean Bus/Career Tech Educ .... Ms. Elizabeth ARTEAGA
07 Asst Dean of Admissions & Records .... Mr. Tuyen NGUYEN
37 Asst Dean Fin Aid/Scholarships .... Ms. Sheena TRAN
18 Facilities Manager .... Mr. Chuck WALES

Reach Institute for School Leadership (C)

1221 Preservation Park Way, Ste 100, Oakland CA 94612
County: Alameda Identification: 667313
Telephone: (510) 501-5075 Carnegie Class: Not Classified
FAX Number: (510) 868-2215 Calendar System: Semester
URL: www.reachinst.org
Established: 2007 Annual Graduate Tuition & Fees: N/A
Enrollment: N/A Coed
Affiliation or Control: Independent Non-Profit IRS Status: 501(c)3
Highest Offering: Master's; No Undergraduates
Accreditation: WC

01 Executive Director .... Ben SANDERS
05 Chief Academic Officer .... Liz BAHAN

Rio Hondo College (D)

3600 Workman Mill Road, Whittier CA 90601-1699
County: Los Angeles FICE Identification: 001269
Unit ID: 121886
Telephone: (562) 692-0921 Carnegie Class: Assoc/MT-VT-Mix Trad/Non
FAX Number: (562) 699-7386 Calendar System: Semester
URL: www.riohondo.edu
Established: 1960 Annual Undergrad Tuition & Fees (In-District): $1,360
Enrollment: 18,367 Coed
Affiliation or Control: State/Local IRS Status: 501(c)3
Highest Offering: Baccalaureate
Accreditation: WJ, NAIT

01 Superintendent/President .... Ms. Teresa DREYFUSS
05 Vice President Academic Svcs .... Dr. Laura RAMIREZ
10 Vice President Finance/Business .... Mr. Yulian LIGIOSO
32 Vice President Student Services .... Mr. Henry GEE
86 Dir Govt & Community Relations .... Mr. Russell CASTANEDA-CALLEROS
15 Executive Director Human Resources .... Mr. Loy NASHUA
26 Dir Marketing & Communications .... Ms. Ruthie RETANA
35 Dir Student Life & Leadership .... Ms. Shaina PHILLIPS
06 Dir Admin & Records/Registrar .... Ms. Leigh UNGER
38 Exec Dean Couns & Student Equity .... Dr. Mike MUNOZ
102 Executive Director RHC Foundation .... Mr. Howard KUMMERMAN
37 Director Financial Aid & Veteran's .... Ms. Yvonne GUTIERREZ-SANDOVAL
18 Director Facilities Services .... Vacant
96 Director of Purchasing .... Mr. Felix G. SARAO
04 Admin Assistant to President .... Ms. Sandy SANDELLO
09 Executive Dean Inst Res & Plng .... Mr. Howard KUMMERMAN
88 Dean Educational Centers .... Ms. Yolanda EMERSON

*Riverside Community College District (E)

3801 Market Street, Riverside CA 92501
County: Riverside Identification: 667039
Telephone: (951) 222-8000 Carnegie Class: N/A
FAX Number: (951) 682-5339
URL: www.rccd.edu

01 Chancellor .... Dr. Michael L. BURKE
05 VC Educ Svcs/Wrkforce Dev/Plng .... Vacant
10 VC Business & Financial Svcs .... Mr. Aaron BROWN
15 VC Div & Human Resources .... Dr. Terri HAMPTON
100 Chief of Staff & Facilities Devel .... Ms. Chris CARLSON
12 President Moreno Valley College .... Dr. Robin STEINBACK
12 President Norco College .... Dr. Bryan REECE
12 President Riverside City Col .... Dr. Wolde-Ab ISAAC

*Moreno Valley College (F)

16130 Lasselle Street, Moreno Valley CA 92551
County: Riverside FICE Identification: 041735
Unit ID: 460394
Telephone: (951) 571-6100 Carnegie Class: Assoc/MT-VT-Mix Trad/Non
FAX Number: N/A Calendar System: Semester
URL: www.mvc.edu
Established: 2010 Annual Undergrad Tuition & Fees (In-District): $1,416
Enrollment: 8,846 Coed
Affiliation or Control: State/Local IRS Status: 501(c)3
Highest Offering: Associate Degree
Accreditation: WJ, DA, DH, EMT

02 President .... Dr. Robin L. STEINBACK
05 Vice Pres Academic Affairs .... Vacant
10 Vice Pres Business Services .... Dr. Nathaniel JONES
32 Vice Pres of Student Services .... Mr. Dyrell FOSTER
20 Dean of Instruction .... Mrs. Anna Marie AMEZQUITA
84 Director Enrollment Services .... Ms. Jamie CLIFTON
37 Director Student Financial Services .... Ms. Sandra MARTINEZ
18 Director Facilities .... Mr. David COOPER

*Norco College (G)

2001 Third Street, Norco CA 92860
County: Riverside FICE Identification: 041761
Unit ID: 460464
Telephone: (951) 372-7000 Carnegie Class: Assoc/HT-Mix Trad/Non
FAX Number: N/A Calendar System: Semester
URL: www.norcocollege.edu
Established: 2010 Annual Undergrad Tuition & Fees (In-District): $1,416
Enrollment: 9,662 Coed
Affiliation or Control: State/Local IRS Status: 501(c)3
Highest Offering: Associate Degree
Accreditation: WJ

02 President .... Dr. Bryan REECE
05 Int Vice Pres Academic Affairs .... Dr. Sam LEE
32 Vice Pres Student Services .... Dr. Monica GREEN
04 Executive Asst to President .... Ms. Denise TERRAZAS
07 Dean Admissions & Records .... Mr. Mark DEASIS
09 Dean Institutional Effectiveness .... Dr. Greg AYCOCK
10 Int Vice Pres Business Services .... Mr. James REEVES
13 Dean Technology/Learning Resources .... Mr. Damon NANCE
18 Director Facilities .... Vacant
25 Dean Grants .... Dr. Gustavo OCEGUERA
37 Director Student Financial Services .... Ms. Maria GONZALEZ
20 Interim Dean Instruction .... Dr. Jason PARKS
75 Dean Instruction/CTE .... Dr. Kevin FLEMING

*Riverside City College (H)

4800 Magnolia Avenue, Riverside CA 92506
County: Riverside FICE Identification: 001270
Unit ID: 121901
Telephone: (951) 222-8000 Carnegie Class: Assoc/MT-VT-Mix Trad/Non
FAX Number: (951) 222-8036 Calendar System: Semester
URL: www.rcc.edu
Established: 1916 Annual Undergrad Tuition & Fees (In-District): $1,426
Enrollment: 19,086 Coed
Affiliation or Control: State/Local IRS Status: 501(c)3
Highest Offering: Associate Degree
Accreditation: WJ, ADNUR

02 President .... Dr. Wolde-Ab ISAAC
05 Vice Pres Academic Affairs .... Dr. Carol FARRAR
10 Vice Pres Business Services .... Vacant
45 Vice Pres Planning & Development .... Dr. Susan MILLS
32 Vice President Student Services .... Dr. FeRita CARTER
20 Int Dean Instr STEM/Kinesiology .... Dr. Arun GOYAL
66 Dean School of Nursing .... Dr. Sandy BAKER
83 Int Dean Instruction Hum/Soc Sci .... Dr. Kristi WOODS
57 Dean of Instr Fine & Perform Arts .... Dr. Scott BAUER
75 Dean of Career/Tech Educ .... Ms. Kristine DIMEMMO
88 Assoc Dean Academic Support .... Ms. Debbie WHITAKER
84 Dean Enrollment Services .... Vacant
35 Dean Student Services .... Ms. Cecilia ALVARADO
41 Interim Director Athletics .... Mr. James WOOLDRIDGE
23 Director Health Services .... Ms. Deborah CLOAN
19 Sergeant Safety & Police .... Mr. Robert KLEVENO

Rudolf Steiner College (I)

9200 Fair Oaks Boulevard, Fair Oaks CA 95628
County: Sacramento Identification: 667088
Unit ID: 122126
Telephone: (916) 961-8727 Carnegie Class: Not Classified
FAX Number: (877) 782-1884 Calendar System: Other
URL: www.rudolfsteinercollege.edu
Established: 1976 Annual Graduate Tuition & Fees: N/A
Enrollment: 72 Coed
Affiliation or Control: Independent Non-Profit IRS Status: 501(c)3
Highest Offering: Master's; No Undergraduates
Accreditation: @WC

01 Director .... Mr. Edmund KNIGHTON

Sacramento Ultrasound Institute (J)

2233 Watt Avenue #150, Sacramento CA 95825
County: Sacramento Identification: 667264
Telephone: (916) 877-7977 Carnegie Class: Not Classified
FAX Number: (916) 481-4032 Calendar System: Other
URL: www.sui.edu
Established: 2002 Annual Undergrad Tuition & Fees: N/A
Enrollment: N/A Coed
Affiliation or Control: Proprietary IRS Status: Proprietary
Highest Offering: Associate Degree
Accreditation: ABHES

01 President/CEO .... Mrs. Sima DERMISHYAN
11 Chief Operating Officer .... Mr. Samuel YARMAGYAN
07 Admissions Director .... Mr. Armine KOCHARYAN

SAE Expression College (K)

6601 Shellmound Street, Emeryville CA 94608-1021
County: Alameda FICE Identification: 039733
Unit ID: 447458
Telephone: (510) 654-2934 Carnegie Class: Spec-4-yr-Arts
FAX Number: (510) 658-3414 Calendar System: Quarter
URL: www.expression.edu
Established: 1999 Annual Undergrad Tuition & Fees: $23,899
Enrollment: 429 Coed
Affiliation or Control: Proprietary IRS Status: Proprietary
Highest Offering: Baccalaureate
Accreditation: ACCSC

01 Campus Director .... Mr. Elmo FRAZER
05 Director of Education .... Mr. Adam RUCH

SAE Institute - San Jose (L)

1751 Fox Drive, San Jose CA 95131
Telephone: (408) 620-3300 Identification: 770552
Accreditation: ACCSC

Saint John's Seminary (M)

5012 Seminary Road, Camarillo CA 93012-2500
County: Ventura FICE Identification: 001299
Unit ID: 123855
Telephone: (805) 482-2755 Carnegie Class: Spec-4-yr-Faith
FAX Number: (805) 482-3470 Calendar System: Semester
URL: www.stjohnsem.edu
Established: 1939 Annual Graduate Tuition & Fees: N/A
Enrollment: 116 Male
Affiliation or Control: Roman Catholic IRS Status: 501(c)3
Highest Offering: Master's; No Undergraduates
Accreditation: WC, THEOL

01 Rector .... Msgr. Marc V. TRUDEAU
05 Academic Dean .... Dr. Anthony LILLES
07 Director of Admissions .... Dr. Anthony LILLES
06 Registrar .... Mr. Kevin GODFREY

04 Administrative Asst to President .... Ms. Maria GAETA
10 Director of Finance .... Ms. Jackie ROTTER
15 Director Personnel Services .... Ms. Mary BISSINGER
18 Chief Facilities/Physical Plant .... Mr. Greg JULIUS
30 Chief Development/Advancement .... Ms. Julia SCALISE
32 Chief Student Affairs/Student Life .... Fr. Timothy KLOSTERMAN
96 Director of Purchasing .... Ms. Julie ALLYN

Saint Katherine College (A)

1637 Capalina Road, San Marcos CA 92069
County: San Diego Identification: 667263
Telephone: (760) 471-1316 Carnegie Class: Not Classified
FAX Number: (760) 704-1314 Calendar System: Semester
URL: www.skcca.edu
Established: Annual Undergrad Tuition & Fees: N/A
Enrollment: N/A Coed
Affiliation or Control: Independent Non-Profit IRS Status: 501(c)3
Highest Offering: Baccalaureate
Accreditation: WC

01 President & Founder .... Dr. Frank PAPATHEOFANIS
05 Dean of College/Chief Academic Ofcr .Dr. Fernando ARZOLA, JR.
10 Chief Financial Officer .... Ryan WEST
09 Dir of Inst Research/Effectiveness .... Christos KORGAN
07 Dean of Admissions/Registrar .... Marina KARAVOKIRIS
32 Dean of Students .... Bre WILLIAMS
08 Librarian .... Mike ANDERS HARRISON

St. Luke University (B)

1460 E. Holt Ave., Suite 72, Pomona CA 91767
County: Los Angeles Identification: 667299
Telephone: (909) 623-0302 Carnegie Class: Not Classified
FAX Number: (909) 623-0480 Calendar System: Semester
URL: www.sluedu.us
Established: 2004 Annual Undergrad Tuition & Fees: N/A
Enrollment: N/A Coed
Affiliation or Control: Independent Non-Profit IRS Status: 501(c)3
Highest Offering: Master's
Accreditation: @TRACS

01 Founder/President .... Rev. Young D. KIM
05 Chief Academic Officer .... Dr. Sungyi CHOI

Saint Mary's College of California (C)

1928 Saint Mary's Road, Moraga CA 94556-2744
County: Contra Costa FICE Identification: 001302
Unit ID: 123554
Telephone: (925) 631-4000 Carnegie Class: Masters/L
FAX Number: (925) 376-8497 Calendar System: 4/1/4
URL: www.stmarys-ca.edu
Established: 1863 Annual Undergrad Tuition & Fees: $44,360
Enrollment: 4,030 Coed
Affiliation or Control: Roman Catholic IRS Status: 501(c)3
Highest Offering: Doctorate
Accreditation: WC, MACTE

01 President .... Dr. James A. DONAHUE
05 Provost/Vice President Acad Affairs .... Dr. Bethami DOBKIN
32 Vice Provost Student Life .... Dr. Jane CAMARILLO
20 Vice Provost Undergrad Academics .... Dr. Richard M. CARP
10 VP for Finance & Administration .... Ms. Susan H. WALLACE
111 Vice President for Advancement .... Ms. Lisa MOORE
26 Asst VP College Communication .... Vacant
88 Vice President for Mission .... Dr. Carole SWAIN
84 Vice Provost Enrollment .... Mr. Hernan BUCHELI
107 Vice Prov Grad/Professionnal Stds .... Dr. Christopher SINDT
30 Assistant VP of Development .... Mr. Daniel G. LEWIS
43 General Counsel .... Mr. Larry NUTI
53 Dean School of Education .... Dr. Christopher SINDT
50 Dean School Econ & Business Admin .... Dr. Zhan LI
81 Dean School of Science .... Dr. Roy WENSLEY
49 Dean School Liberal Arts .... Dr. Sheila HUGHES
35 Dean of Students .... Dr. Evette CASTILLO CLARK
08 Dean Library & Academic Resources .... Ms. Patricia KREITZ
42 Director Mission & Ministry .... Ms. Karin MCCLELLAND
07 Interim Dean of Admissions .... Ms. Angelica MOORE
15 Associate VP Human Resources .... Vacant
29 Assistant VP of Alumni Engagement .... Ms. Mary POPPINGO
110 Assistant VP of Development ...... Ms. Carolyn OTIS CATANZARO
58 Interim Assoc Dean Graduate Pgms .... Dr. Yung Jae LEE
06 Interim Registrar .... Mr. Bill SULLIVAN
35 Associate Dean of Students .... Mr. Jim SCIUTO
37 Associate Director of Financial Aid .... Ms. Linda JUDGE
88 Director of Kinesiology .... Dr. Claire WILLIAMS
57 Director MFA in Creative Writing .... Dr. Matthew ZAPRUDER
102 Dir Corporate & Foundation Rels .... Mr. Jack PURDIE
14 Deputy CTO .... Mr. Lance HOURANY
13 Chief Technology Officer .... Mr. Peter GRECO
19 Director of Public Safety .... Mr. Adan TEJADA
38 Director of Counseling Center .... Ms. Dai L. TO
41 Dir of Athletic & Recreation Sports .... Vacant
88 Director Saint Mary's Art Museum .... Ms. Carrie BREWSTER
71 Director of January Term Program .... Ms. Anna NOVAKOV
18 Director of Facilities .... Mr. Michael VIOLA
88 Director of Office of Research .... Ms. Elizabeth GALLAGHER
36 Dir of Career Devel Center .... Ms. Beverly MCLEAN
23 Medical Director Health & Wellness .... Vacant
27 Director Media Relations .... Mr. Michael MCALPIN
86 Director Community & Govt Relations .... Mr. Tim FARLEY
94 Director Women's Resource Ctr .... Ms. Sharon SOBOTTA
88 Director of CILSA .... Dr. Jennifer PIGZA
88 Assistant Director of CILSA .... Mr. Ryan LAMBERTON
21 Controller .... Ms. Jeanne DEMATTEO
104 Director Ctr International Programs . Ms. M. Susan MILLER-REID
109 General Manager Sodexo .... Mr. Matt CARROLL
88 Director Meetings/Events/Conf Svcs .... Ms. Melissa GLICKMAN
121 Dir Student Engage & Academic Svcs .... Ms. Corliss WATKINS
28 Dir of Delphine Intercultural Ctr .... Ms. Desiree ANDERSON
09 Director of Institutional Research .... Mr. Gregg THOMSON
88 Dir New Student/Family Programs .... Ms. Jennifer HERZOG
96 Purchasing/Buyer .... Ms. Janie KLEIN
39 Director Student Housing .... Mr. Marcus WEEMES
04 Executive Asst to President ....Dr. David FORD

Saint Patrick's Seminary & University (D)

320 Middlefield Road, Menlo Park CA 94025-3596
County: San Mateo FICE Identification: 010074
Unit ID: 122250
Telephone: (650) 325-5621 Carnegie Class: Not Classified
FAX Number: (650) 322-0997 Calendar System: Semester
URL: www.stpatricksseminary.org
Established: 1894 Annual Undergrad Tuition & Fees: N/A
Enrollment: N/A Male
Affiliation or Control: Roman Catholic IRS Status: 501(c)3
Highest Offering: Master's
Accreditation: WC, THEOL

01 President/Rector .... Rev. George E. SCHULTZE, SJ
03 Vice Rector .... Rev. Daniel DONOHOO
05 Academic Dean .... Mrs. Karen CHAN
26 Vice President for External Affairs .... Rev. James MYERS
10 Vice President Administration .... Mr. Marc COLELLI
42 Dean of Spiritual Life .... Rev. Vincent BUI
08 Library Director .... Mr. David KRIEGH
06 Registrar .... Mr. Manvinder SHAHI

The Salvation Army College for Officer Training at Crestmont (E)

30840 Hawthorne Boulevard,
Rancho Palos Verdes CA 90275-5301
County: Los Angeles FICE Identification: 036954
Unit ID: 122269
Telephone: (310) 377-0481 Carnegie Class: Not Classified
FAX Number: (310) 541-1697 Calendar System: Quarter
URL: www.crestmont.edu
Established: 1878 Annual Undergrad Tuition & Fees: N/A
Enrollment: N/A Coed
Affiliation or Control: Other IRS Status: 501(c)3
Highest Offering: Associate Degree
Accreditation: WJ

01 Training Principal .... Major Brian SAUNDERS
03 Assistant Training Principal .... Major John BRACKENBURY
05 Director of Curriculum .... Major Brian JONES
10 Director of Business Administration .... Capt. Kelly NOLAN
32 Director of Campus Services .... Major Pamilla BRACKENBURY
04 Exec Secretary to Trng Principal .... Ms. Celeste SKINNER

Samuel Merritt University (F)

3100 Telegraph Avenue, Oakland CA 94609
County: Alameda FICE Identification: 007012
Unit ID: 122296
Telephone: (510) 869-6511 Carnegie Class: Spec-4-yr-Other Health
FAX Number: (510) 869-6525 Calendar System: Semester
URL: www.samuelmerritt.edu
Established: 1909 Annual Undergrad Tuition & Fees: N/A
Enrollment: 1,593 Coed
Affiliation or Control: Independent Non-Profit IRS Status: 501(c)3
Highest Offering: Doctorate
Accreditation: WC, ANEST, ARCPA, NURSE, OT, POD, PTA

01 President .... Dr. Sharon C. DIAZ
05 Academic Vice President/Provost .... Dr. Scot FOSTER
10 Vice Pres Finance/Admin/CFO .... Mr. Gregory GINGRAS
84 Vice President Enrollment Services .... Dr. Terrence NORDSTROM
20 Assistant Academic Vice President .... Dr. Celeste VILLANUEVA
20 Asst Academic Vice President .... Dr. Michael NEGRETE
04 Assistant to the President .... Ms. Margrette PETERSON
66 Dean & Professor of Nursing .... Dr. Audrey BERMAN
63 Dean Podiatric Medicine .... Dr. John VENSON
88 Chair Dept Physical Therapy .... Dr. Nicole CHRISTENSEN
88 Chair Dept Occupational Therapy .... Dr. Kate HAYNER
66 Chair ABSN Program .... Ms. Rene ENGELHART
88 Chair Physician Assistant Pgm .... Dr. Michael DEROSA
66 Chairperson Undergraduate Nursing .... Dr. Margaret EARLY
07 Dean Admission .... Mr. Timothy CRANFORD
15 Exec Director Human Resources .... Ms. Elaine LEMAY
45 Exec Dir Planning/Business Dev .... Ms. Cynthia ULMAN
26 Exec Dir Communications/Ext Rels .... Ms. Stephanie BANGERT
30 Exec Dir Development/Chf Dev Ofcr .... Ms. Susan VALENCIA
09 Director Institutional Research .... Ms. Nandini DASGUPTA
21 Finance Director .... Ms. Jill EMERSON
06 Registrar .... Ms. Anne SCHER
08 Library Director .... Ms. Hai-Thom SOTA
37 Director Financial Aid .... Mr. Tyler PRUETT
88 Dir Family Nurse Practitioner Pgm .... Ms. Rhonda RAMIREZ
29 Director of Alumni Relations .... Vacant
18 Director Facilities Management .... Ms. Lillian HARVIN
32 Asst Director Student Services .... Ms. Kathryn WARD
12 Site Manager Sacramento .... Ms. Rene ENGELHART
12 Site Manager San Mateo .... Dr. Mileva LEWIS SAULO
13 Dir of Information Technology Svcs .... Mr. Blair SIMMONS
28 Chief Diversity Officer .... Ms. Shirley STRONG

*San Bernardino Community College District (G)

114 S. Del Rosa Drive, San Bernardino CA 92401
County: San Bernardino Identification: 667040
Telephone: (909) 382-4091 Carnegie Class: N/A
FAX Number: (909) 382-0153
URL: www.sbccd.edu

01 Chancellor .... Bruce BARON
10 Vice Chanc Business/Fiscal Services .... Jose TORRES
15 Vice Chanc Human Resources .... Dr. Lisa NORMAN

*Crafton Hills College (H)

11711 Sand Canyon Road, Yucaipa CA 92399-1799
County: San Bernardino FICE Identification: 009272
Unit ID: 113111
Telephone: (909) 794-2161 Carnegie Class: Assoc/MT-VT-High Trad
FAX Number: (909) 794-0423 Calendar System: Semester
URL: www.craftonhills.edu
Established: 1972 Annual Undergrad Tuition & Fees (In-District): $1,142
Enrollment: 5,985 Coed
Affiliation or Control: State/Local IRS Status: 501(c)3
Highest Offering: Associate Degree
Accreditation: WJ, COARC, EMT

02 President .... Dr. Wei ZHOU
05 Int Vice Pres of Instruction .... Mr. Khetam BAKHIT
11 Vice President Administrative Svcs .... Mr. Mike STRONG
32 Vice President Student
Services .... Dr. Rebeccah WARREN-MARLATT
35 Dean Stdnt Svcs/Stdnt Development .... Mr. Joe CABRALES
49 Dean of Arts & Sciences .... Mr. Mark SNOWHITE
81 Dean Math/English/Reading/Inst Supp .... Mr. Robert D. BROWN
36 Dean Career Educ & Human Devel .... Mr. Daniel WORD
38 Dean Student Services/Counseling .... Ms. Kirsten S. COLVEY
09 Dean Inst Effect/Research/Planning .... Dr. Keith WURTZ
30 Director Resource Development .... Ms. Michelle RIGGS
40 Director Bookstore .... Ms. Gloriann CHAVEZ
88 Director EOPS/CARE .... Dr. Rejoice CHAVIRA
37 Director Financial Aid .... Mr. John W. MUSKAVITCH
35 Director Student Life .... Dr. Ericka PADDOCK
18 Director Facilities .... Mr. Larry COOK
13 Director Technology Services .... Mr. Wayne BOGH
26 Director Marketing/Public Relations .... Ms. Donna HOFFMANN
07 Director Admissions & Records .... Ms. April DALE-CARTER
04 Administrative Asst to President .... Mrs. Cyndie ST. JEAN

*San Bernardino Valley College (I)

701 S Mt. Vernon Avenue,
San Bernardino CA 92410-2798
County: San Bernardino FICE Identification: 001272
Unit ID: 123527
Telephone: (909) 384-4400 Carnegie Class: Assoc/MT-VT-High Trad
FAX Number: N/A Calendar System: Semester
URL: www.valleycollege.edu
Established: 1926 Annual Undergrad Tuition & Fees (In-District): $1,238
Enrollment: 13,136 Coed
Affiliation or Control: State/Local IRS Status: 501(c)3
Highest Offering: Associate Degree
Accreditation: WJ, ADNUR

02 President .... Ms. Diana RODRIGUEZ
05 Interim Vice President Instruction .... Dr. James SMITH
11 VP Administrative Services .... Mr. Scott STARK
32 VP Student Services .... Dr. Ricky SHABAZZ
72 Dean AT/TRANS/CULA .... Mr. Albert MANIAOL
79 Dean Arts & Humanities .... Dr. Kay WEISS
38 Dean Counseling/Matriculation .... Mr. Marco COTA
50 Interim Dean Math/Bus/Computer Tech .... Dr. Stephanie BRIGGS
09 Dean Research/Planning/Inst Effect .... Dr. James SMITH
81 Dean Sciences .... Dr. Susan BANGASSER
83 Dean SS/Human Development & PE .... Dr. Wallace JOHNSON
22 Int Dean Student Equity & Success .... Ms. Carmen RODRIGUEZ
07 Director Admissions/Records .... Ms. April DALE-CARTER
40 Director Bookstores .... Ms. Gloriann CHAVEZ
88 Director Child Development Ctr .... Mr. Mark MERJIL
31 Dir Dev Community Relations .... Ms. Karen CHILDERS
88 Director EOP&S/CARE .... Ms. Carmen RODRIGUEZ
37 Director Financial Aid .... Mr. Ernesto NERY
25 Dir Grant Development/Management .... Vacant
08 Dir Library/Learning Support Svcs .... Mr. Ron HASTINGS
26 Director Marketing/PR .... Mr. Paul BRATULIN
35 Director Student Life .... Mr. Raymond CARLOS
13 Director Technology Services .... Mr. Rick HRDLICKA
88 Mgr Cafeteria & Snack Bar .... Mr. Erik MORDEN
103 Mgr CalWORKS/Workforce Dev .... Ms. Shalita TILLMAN
66 Assoc Dean & Nursing Director .... Ms. Carol WELLS
68 Director Athletics .... Mr. Dave RUBIO
88 Director Police Academies .... Mr. Jeff KLUG
18 Dir Facilities M&O .... Mr. Robert JENKINS
88 Director DSP&S .... Mr. Marty MILLIGAN
88 AEBG Administrator .... Ms. Emma DIAZ

San Diego Christian College (A)

200 Riverview Parkway, Santee CA 92071

County: San Diego FICE Identification: 012031
Unit ID: 112084
Telephone: (619) 201-8700 Carnegie Class: Bac-Diverse
FAX Number: (619) 201-8749 Calendar System: Semester
URL: www.sdcc.edu
Established: 1970 Annual Undergrad Tuition & Fees: $29,550
Enrollment: 916 Coed
Affiliation or Control: Independent Non-Profit IRS Status: 501(c)3
Highest Offering: Master's
Accreditation: WC

01 President Dr. Paul E. AGUE
04 Exec Assistant to the President Mrs. Kelly BUCHANAN
10 VP for Finance Mr. Steve CHANEY
05 Interim VP for Academic Affairs Dr. Elizabeth STANTON
32 Dean of Students Rick ROOF
35 Director of Student Life Mr. Pete GOODMAN
06 Registrar Mrs. Tammy DALLY
37 Director of Financial Aid Mr. Daniel REED
07 Director of Admissions Ms. Christine ROBERTS
42 Director of Spiritual Life Mr. Steve JENKINS
30 Director of Advancement Mr. Chad CUNNINGHAM
30 VP for Advancement & Administration Mr. Robert JENSEN
15 Director of Human Resources Ms. Carolyn DELEON
08 Director of Library Services Ms. Ruth MARTIN
29 Manager of Alumni/Donor Relations Ms. Stephanie EDWARDS
09 Dean of Assessment and Planning Mrs. Lundie CARSTENSEN
41 Athletic Director Vacant
23 Director of Health Services Mrs. Malia JENKINS
28 Director of Diversity Mr. Carl CALDERSON

*San Diego Community College District Administrative Offices (B)

3375 Camino Del Rio South, San Diego CA 92108-3883

County: San Diego FICE Identification: 008895
Unit ID: 122320
Telephone: (619) 388-6500 Carnegie Class: N/A
FAX Number: (619) 388-6913
URL: www.sdccd.edu

01 Chancellor Dr. Constance M. CARROLL
10 Exec Vice Chanc Business Tech Svcs Dr. Bonnie Ann DOWD
32 Vice Chancellor Student Services Dr. Lynn C. NEAULT
15 Vice Chancellor Human Resources Mr. Will SURBROOK
18 Vice Chanc Facilities Management Mr. Christopher MANIS
05 Vice Chanc Instructional Svcs Dr. Stepahnie BULGER
26 Director Comm & Public Relations Mr. Jack BERESFORD
04 Exec Assistant to the Chancellor Ms. Margaret LAMB
13 Chief Info Technology Officer (CIO) Vacant
19 Chief of Police Mr. Raymund AGUIRRE

*San Diego City College (C)

1313 Park Boulevard, San Diego CA 92101-4787

County: San Diego FICE Identification: 001273
Unit ID: 122339
Telephone: (619) 388-3400 Carnegie Class: Assoc/HVT-High Trad
FAX Number: (619) 388-3063 Calendar System: Semester
URL: www.sdcity.edu
Established: 1914 Annual Undergrad Tuition & Fees (In-District): $1,142
Enrollment: 16,520 Coed
Affiliation or Control: State/Local IRS Status: 501(c)3
Highest Offering: Associate Degree
Accreditation: WJ, ADNUR

02 President Dr. Ricky SHABAZZ
04 Executive Asst to President Ms. Erin FLANAGAN
11 Vice President of Admin Services Ms. Seher AWAN
05 Acting Vice President Instruction Dr. Minou SPRADLEY
68 Dean Health/Exercise Sci/Athletics Mr. Randy BARNES
83 Dean Behav & Soc Sci/Consumer Stds Ms. Lori ERRECA
08 Dean Information/Learning Tech Mr. Robbi EWELL
79 Dean School of Arts/Humanities Ms. Trudy GERALD
50 Dean Sch Business/Info Tech Ms. Rose LAMURAGLIA
124 Dean Student Dev/Matriculation Ms. Nesha SAVAGE
32 Dean of Student Affairs Mr. Marciano PEREZ
54 Act Dean Engr & Tech/Math/Sci/Nurs Dr. Carlos DE LA LAMA
28 Dean of Student Equity Mr. Chris BAKER
22 Affirmative Action Officer Vacant
40 Bookstore Supervisor Ms. DeeDee PORTER
26 Public Information Officer Ms. Heidi BUNKOWSKE
88 PgmMgr Disabled Student Services Ms. Brianne KENNEDY
37 Financial Aid Supervisor Mr. Gregory SANCHEZ
88 Director EOPS Ms. Beverly WARREN
56 Director Off-Campus Programs Vacant
92 Director Honors Program Vacant
18 Chief Facilities/Physical Plant Mr. Derrall CHANDLER
07 Admissions & Records Supervisor Ms. Megan SOTO

*San Diego Mesa College (D)

7250 Mesa College Drive, San Diego CA 92111-4998

County: San Diego FICE Identification: 001275
Unit ID: 122375
Telephone: (619) 388-2721 Carnegie Class: Assoc/HT-High Trad
FAX Number: (619) 388-2929 Calendar System: Semester
URL: www.sdmesa.edu
Established: 1962 Annual Undergrad Tuition & Fees (In-District): $1,142
Enrollment: 24,208 Coed
Affiliation or Control: State/Local IRS Status: 501(c)3
Highest Offering: Associate Degree
Accreditation: WJ, CAHIIM, DA, PTAA, RAD

02 President Dr. Pamela T. LUSTER
05 Vice President Instruction Dr. Tim MCGRATH
32 Vice Pres Student Services Dr. Ashanti HANDS
11 Vice Pres Administrative Services Ms. Rachelle AGATHA
88 Acting Dean Student Development Ms. Aileen CRAKES
79 Dean Arts & Languages Ms. Leslie SHIMAZAKI
76 Dean Health Sciences/Public Svc Ms. Tina RECALDE
81 Dean School Math/Natural Sciences Ms. Susan TOPHAM
50 Dean Sch Business Technology Dr. Danene BROWN
62 Dean Lrng Res/Educational Tech Vacant
68 Dean PE/Health Educ/Athletics Dir Mr. Ryan SHUMAKER
79 Dean of Humanities Ms. Linda HENSLEY
83 Dean Social/Behav Sci/Mult Stds Dr. Charles ZAPPIA
35 Dean Student Affairs Ms. Victoria MILLER
93 Dean of Student Success/Equity Mr. Larry MAXEY
09 Dean Institutional Effectiveness Dr. Madeleine HINKES
26 Public Information Officer Ms. Jennifer KEARNS
37 Financial Aid Officer Ms. Gilda MALDONADO
07 Student Svcs Supervisor Admission Ms. Ivonne ALVAREZ
04 Exec Asst to the President Ms. Sara Beth CAIN

*San Diego Miramar College (E)

10440 Black Mountain Road, San Diego CA 92126-2999

County: San Diego FICE Identification: 011820
Unit ID: 122384
Telephone: (619) 388-7800 Carnegie Class: Assoc/MT-VT-Mix Trad/Non
FAX Number: (619) 388-7901 Calendar System: Semester
URL: www.sdmiramar.edu
Established: 1969 Annual Undergrad Tuition & Fees (In-District): $1,142
Enrollment: 13,008 Coed
Affiliation or Control: State/Local IRS Status: 501(c)3
Highest Offering: Associate Degree
Accreditation: WJ, MLTAD

02 President Dr. Patricia HSIEH
05 Int Vice President Instruction Dr. Paulette HOPKINS
32 Vice President Student Services Mr. Gerald RAMSEY
10 Vice President Admin Services Mr. Brett BELL
49 Dean Liberal Arts Dr. Lou ASCIONE
50 Dean Business/Tech/Workforce Init Ms. Lynne ORNELAS
81 Actg Dean Math/Bio/Exer/Phys Sci Dr. Fred GARCES
88 Dean Public Safety Mr. George BEITEY
108 Dean PRIE/Library & Technology Dr. Daniel MIRAMONTEZ
35 Dean Student Affairs Ms. Adela JACOBSON
124 Dean Matriculation & Student Dev Vacant
121 Assoc Dean Stdnt Equity & Success Dr. Jacqueline HONDA
04 Executive Assistant to President Ms. Briele WARREN
26 Public Information Officer Mr. Stephen QUIS
37 Financial Aid Officer Mr. Vincent NGO
07 Admissions & Records Officer Ms. Dana STACK

San Diego Global Knowledge University (F)

1095 K Street Suite B, San Diego CA 92101

County: San Diego Identification: 667294
Telephone: (619) 934-0797 Carnegie Class: Not Classified
FAX Number: N/A Calendar System: Semester
URL: www.sdgku.com
Established: Annual Undergrad Tuition & Fees: N/A
Enrollment: N/A Coed
Affiliation or Control: Proprietary IRS Status: Proprietary
Highest Offering: Master's
Accreditation: ACICS

01 President Dr. Miguel A. CARDENAS
05 Chief Academic Officer Dr. Miguel A. CARDENAS, JR.
13 Chief Technology Officer Mr. Joe BARRUS

San Francisco Art Institute (G)

800 Chestnut Street, San Francisco CA 94133-2206

County: San Francisco FICE Identification: 003948
Unit ID: 122454
Telephone: (415) 771-7020 Carnegie Class: Spec-4-yr-Arts
FAX Number: (415) 749-4590 Calendar System: Semester
URL: www.sfai.edu
Established: 1871 Annual Undergrad Tuition & Fees: $43,090
Enrollment: 599 Coed
Affiliation or Control: Independent Non-Profit IRS Status: 501(c)3
Highest Offering: Master's
Accreditation: WC, ART

00 Chair of the Board Christopher TELLIS
01 President Gordon KNOX
05 Dean of Academic Affairs Jennifer RISSLER
31 VP Exhibitions and Public Programs Hesse MCGRAW
30 VP Development & Alumni Relations Vacant
84 VP Enrollment and Student Affairs Mark CAMPBELL
26 Dir of Marketing & Communications Vacant
06 Registrar Delphine HWANG
123 Director of Grad Admissions Jana RUMBERGER
07 Director of Undergrad Admiss Colleen MULVEY
08 Head Librarian Vacant
09 Inst Research & Acad Planning Assoc Jose DE LOS REYES
11 Assoc VP Operations & Facilities Heather HICKMAN HOLLAND
13 Director of Technology Jeremy HOBBS
15 Director of Human Resources Vacant
18 Assistant Director of Facilities John SEDEN
21 Controller Adrian TRUJILLO
24 Director of Educational Media Vacant
88 Director of Academic Administration Jen SIKORA
29 Alumni Relations Manager Clea MASSIANI
32 Dean of Students Elizabeth TRAYNER
35 Assistant Dean of Students Galen CRAWFORD
37 Director of Financial Aid Annita ALLDREDGE
38 Director of Counseling Services Deb SCHNEIDER
39 Director of Housing and Res Life Alicia LEWIS
110 Assistant Director of Development Will LAMB
88 Director of Public Education Emily SHALLMAN
57 Chair of BA Programs Nicole ARCHER
58 Chair of MFA Programs Tony LABAT
58 Chair of MA Programs Claire DAIGLE
58 Director of Graduate Administration Zeina BARAKEH
85 Global Prog & Stdnt Engage Spec Dominic SHING
121 Interim Dir of Academic Advising Jen SIKORA
88 Director of Admissions Operations Jeremy SIMMONS
88 Director of BFA Studios Sherry KNUTSON
88 Director of City Studio JD BELTRAN
90 Director of Academic Computing Benjamin ASHLOCK
91 Technical Architect Andrew SIMAS
100 Chief of Staff Anne SHULOCK
101 Exec Assistant President and Board Jan-Marie BANNON

San Francisco Conservatory of Music (H)

50 Oak Street, San Francisco CA 94102-6011

County: San Francisco FICE Identification: 001278
Unit ID: 122506
Telephone: (415) 864-7326 Carnegie Class: Spec-4-yr-Arts
FAX Number: (415) 503-6299 Calendar System: Semester
URL: www.sfcm.edu
Established: 1917 Annual Undergrad Tuition & Fees: $43,410
Enrollment: 379 Coed
Affiliation or Control: Independent Non-Profit IRS Status: 501(c)3
Highest Offering: Beyond Master's But Less Than Doctorate
Accreditation: WC

01 President David STULL
05 Provost and Dean Kate SHEERAN
10 Vice Pres Finance & Administration Kathryn WITTENMYER
45 Vice Pres of Strategic Initiatives Susan MCCONKEY
20 Asst Dean Acad Affairs Jonas WRIGHT
32 Associate Dean of Student Life Jason SMITH
64 Asc Dean for New Media & Music Tech MaryClare BRZYTWA
15 Human Resources Manager Michael PATTERSON
07 Director of Admission Melissa COCCO-MITTEN
37 Director of Financial Aid Doris HOWARD
56 Director PreCollege/Extension Michael ROEST
26 Director of Communications Margot FREY
09 Director of IR and Registrar Rebecca SORELL
31 Director of Community Engagement Rachael SMITH
18 Chief Facilities Engineer David MITCHELL
35 Asst Director of Student Affairs Susannah WHITE
20 Assistant to the Dean Lisa NICKELS
29 Director Alumni Relations Vacant
04 Administrative Asst to President Marina KENNEDY
102 Dir Foundation/Corporate Relations Christian MILLS
19 Director Security/Safety Ali ASHRAF
30 Chief Development/Advancement Kathleen NICELY
44 Director Annual or Planned Giving Rhiannon LEWIS

San Francisco Theological Seminary (I)

105 Seminary Road, San Anselmo CA 94960-2997

County: Marin FICE Identification: 001279
Unit ID: 122603
Telephone: (415) 451-2800 Carnegie Class: Spec-4-yr-Faith
FAX Number: (415) 451-2852 Calendar System: Semester
URL: www.sfts.edu
Established: 1871 Annual Graduate Tuition & Fees: N/A
Enrollment: 156 Coed
Affiliation or Control: Presbyterian Church (U.S.A.) IRS Status: 501(c)3
Highest Offering: Doctorate; No Undergraduates
Accreditation: WC, PAST, THEOL

01 President Dr. James L. MCDONALD
05 Dean Seminary/VP Academic Affs Rev.Dr. Jana CHILDERS
30 Vice Pres Advancement Dr. Walter COLLINS
84 Vice Pres Enrollment Management Dr. David BEHRS
10 Vice Pres Finance/Operations Mr. Mike CAIRNS
32 Assoc Dean Student Svcs/Chaplain Rev. Scott CLARK
75 Assoc Dean for Vocations Rev. Elizabeth MCCORD
29 Int Director Alumni Relations Dr. David BEHRS
07 Director of Admissions Vacant
04 Exec Administrator to President Ms. Sheryn KLEIN
06 Registrar Ms. Susan LAWLOR
21 Controller Mr. Ron DEAN
18 Director of Facilities Mr. Dean HANSEN
91 Director of IT Mr. Larry PICKARD
35 Dir Student Services/Intl Programs Ms. Stephanie LAMONACA
15 Dir Human Resources Ms. Kathleen WATERS
44 Director of Annual Giving Vacant
26 Director of Marketing Ms. Liz HUNTINGTON

San Joaquin College of Law (A)

901 Fifth Street, Clovis CA 93612-1312
County: Fresno　FICE Identification: 025000
Unit ID: 122649
Telephone: (559) 323-2100　Carnegie Class: Spec-4-yr-Law
FAX Number: (559) 323-5566　Calendar System: Semester
URL: www.sjcl.edu
Established: 1969　Annual Graduate Tuition & Fees: N/A
Enrollment: 184　Coed
Affiliation or Control: Independent Non-Profit　IRS Status: 501(c)3
Highest Offering: Doctorate; No Undergraduates
Accreditation: WC

01 Dean .... Janice L. PEARSON
05 Academic Dean .... Justin ATKINSON
18 Facilities Manager .... Richard RODRIGUEZ
10 Chief Financial Officer .... Jill A. RANDLES
32 Director of Student Services .... Joyce K. MORODOMI
37 Financial Aid Administrator .... Jeannie M. LEWIS
08 Library Director .... Alicia DIAZ WREST
26 Public Relations Director .... Missy M. CARTIER
15 Chief of Personnel .... Beth PITCOCK
30 Chief Development .... Janice L. PEARSON
84 Director Enrollment Management .... Diane M. STEEL
61 Law Program Coordinator .... Pat A. SMITH

San Joaquin Delta College (B)

5151 Pacific Avenue, Stockton CA 95207-6370
County: San Joaquin　FICE Identification: 001280
Unit ID: 122658
Telephone: (209) 954-5151　Carnegie Class: Assoc/HT-High Trad
FAX Number: (209) 954-7001　Calendar System: Semester
URL: www.deltacollege.edu
Established: 1935　Annual Undergrad Tuition & Fees (In-District): $1,104
Enrollment: 17,895　Coed
Affiliation or Control: State/Local　IRS Status: 501(c)3
Highest Offering: Associate Degree
Accreditation: WJ, ADNUR

01 Superintendent/President .... Dr. Kathleen HART
05 Asst Supt/VP of Instruction .... Dr. Matt WETSTEIN
32 Asst Supt/VP of Student Svc .... Dr. Lisa COOPER
10 Vice Pres of Administrative Svcs .... Dr. Jeff MENGE
15 Vice Pres of Human Resources .... Vacant
11 Vice Pres of Operations .... Mr. Gerardo CALDERON
38 Dean Counseling & Special Svcs .... Mrs. Delecia NUNNALLY
09 Acting Director Inst Effectiveness .... Ms. Tina MERLINO
103 Dean Workforce/Economic Development .... Mr. Salvador VARGAS
108 Dean Student Learning & Assessment .... Dr. Ginger HOLDEN
08 Div Dean Library/Learning Res/Lang .... Ms. Sheli AYERS
12 Associate Dean of Tracy Center .... Dr. Jessie GARZA-RODERICK
26 Director of Marketing/Stdnt Outrch .... Ms. Shelly VALENTON
21 Controller .... Vacant
18 Director Facilities Management .... Vacant
07 Director of Admissions & Records .... Ms. Amy COURTRIGHT
37 Director of Financial Aid/Vet Svcs .... Ms. Tina LENT
96 Director of Purchasing .... Ms. Maria BERNARDINO
06 Registrar .... Ms. Karen SEA

San Joaquin Valley College, Inc. - Visalia (C)

8344 West Mineral King Avenue, Visalia CA 93291-9283
County: Tulare　FICE Identification: 021207
Unit ID: 122685
Telephone: (559) 651-2500　Carnegie Class: Assoc/HVT-High Non
FAX Number: (559) 651-0574　Calendar System: Other
URL: www.sjvc.edu/campuses/central-california/visalia
Established: 1977　Annual Undergrad Tuition & Fees: N/A
Enrollment: 5,605　Coed
Affiliation or Control: Proprietary　IRS Status: Proprietary
Highest Offering: Associate Degree
Accreditation: WJ, COARC, DH

01 President/Chief Executive Officer .... Mr. Michael PERRY
05 Campus Director .... Mr. Ben ALMAGUER
11 Vice President of Administration .... Ms. Wendy MENDES
88 Chief Administrative Officer .... Mr. Joseph HOLT
10 Chief Financial Officer .... Mr. Russ LEBO
37 VP Student Financial Services .... Mr. Kevin ROBINSON
96 Director of Purchasing .... Mr. Ralph ORTIZ

San Joaquin Valley College-Antelope Valley (Lancaster) (D)

42135 10th Street West, Ste 147, Lancaster CA 93534
Telephone: (661) 974-8282　Identification: 770968
Accreditation: &WJ

San Joaquin Valley College-Bakersfield (E)

201 New Stine Road, Bakersfield CA 93309-2668
Telephone: (661) 834-0126　FICE Identification: 023135
Accreditation: &WJ, COARC, SURGT

† Regional accreditation is carried under the parent institution in Visalia, CA.

San Joaquin Valley College-Fresno (F)

295 East Sierra Avenue, Fresno CA 93710-3616
Telephone: (559) 448-8282　Identification: 666008
Accreditation: &WJ, SURGT

† Regional accreditation is carried under the parent institution in Visalia, CA.

San Joaquin Valley College-Fresno Aviation Campus (G)

4985 East Andersen Avenue, Fresno CA 93727
Telephone: (559) 453-0123　Identification: 666009
Accreditation: &WJ

† Regional accreditation is carried under the parent institution in Visalia, CA.

San Joaquin Valley College-Hanford (H)

215 West 7th Street, Hanford CA 93230-4523
Telephone: (559) 584-8840　Identification: 770508
Accreditation: &WJ

San Joaquin Valley College-Modesto (I)

5380 Pirrone Road, Salida CA 95368-9090
Telephone: (209) 543-8800　Identification: 666128
Accreditation: &WJ

† Regional accreditation is carried under the parent institution in Visalia, CA.

San Joaquin Valley College-Ontario (J)

4580 Ontario Mills Parkway, Ontario CA 91764
Telephone: (909) 948-7582　Identification: 666096
Accreditation: &WJ, COARC

† Regional accreditation is carried under the parent institution in Visalia, CA.

San Joaquin Valley College-Rancho Cordova (K)

11050 Olson Drive, Suite 210,
Rancho Cordova CA 95670-5600
Telephone: (916) 638-7582　Identification: 666133
Accreditation: &WJ, COARC

† Regional accreditation is carried under the parent institution in Visalia, CA.

San Joaquin Valley College-Temecula (L)

27270 Madison Avenue, Suite 103, Temecula CA 92590
Telephone: (951) 296-6015　Identification: 770507
Accreditation: &WJ, #COARC

San Joaquin Valley College-Victor Valley (Hesperia) (M)

9331 Mariposa Road, Hesperia CA 92344-8000
Telephone: (760) 948-1947　Identification: 667044
Accreditation: &WJ

† Regional accreditation is carried under the parent institution in Visalia, CA.

*San Jose/Evergreen Community College District (N)

4750 San Felipe Road, San Jose CA 95135-1599
County: Santa Clara　FICE Identification: 029042
Unit ID: 122737
Telephone: (408) 274-6700　Carnegie Class: N/A
FAX Number: (408) 531-8722
URL: www.sjeccd.edu

01 Chancellor .... Dr. Deborah BUDD
11 Vice Chanc Administrative Services .... Mr. Douglas SMITH
15 Vice Chanc Human Resources .... Ms. Kim L. GARCIA
13 Vice Chanc Information Tech Svcs .... Dr. Ben SEABERRY
103 Interim Exec Dir of Workforce Inst .... Mr. William WATSON
09 Exec Dir Inst Effect/Stdnt Success .... Ms. Alice VAN OMMEREN
86 Exec Dir Government/External Affs .... Ms. Rosalie LEDESMA
18 Dir Facilities/Bond Program Mgmt .... Mr. Owen LETCHER
10 Director of Fiscal Services .... Mr. Peter FITZSIMMONS
26 Dir of Communications/Community Rel .... Mr. Sam HO

*Evergreen Valley College (O)

3095 Yerba Buena Road, San Jose CA 95135-1598
County: Santa Clara　FICE Identification: 012452
Unit ID: 114266
Telephone: (408) 274-7900　Carnegie Class: Assoc/HT-High Trad
FAX Number: (408) 238-3179　Calendar System: Semester
URL: www.evc.edu
Established: 1975　Annual Undergrad Tuition & Fees (In-District): $1,343
Enrollment: 8,691　Coed
Affiliation or Control: State/Local　IRS Status: 501(c)3
Highest Offering: Associate Degree
Accreditation: WJ, ADNUR

02 Interim President .... Mr. Keith AYTCH
05 Interim VP Academic Affairs .... Mr. Mark GONZALES
32 VP Student Services .... Ms. Adela SWINSON
10 VP Administrative Services .... Ms. Andrea ALEXANDER
50 Dean Business & Workforce .... Dr. Lena TRAN
66 Dean Nursing & Allied Health .... Dr. Antoinette HERRERA
62 Dean Library/Lrng Res .... Dr. Merryl KRAVITZ
81 Dean Math/Science/Engineering .... Vacant
83 Dean Soc Sci/PE/Arts/Humanities .... Mr. Mark GONZALES
84 Dean Enrollment Services .... Mr. Octavio CRUZ
79 Dean Language Arts .... Dr. Merryl KRAVITZ
121 Int Dean Student Success/Counseling .... Ms. Adriana AYALA
35 Assoc Dean Student Life & EOPS .... Dr. Victor GARZA, JR.
88 Associate Dean Noncredit Education .... Ms. Julie VO
37 Director Financial Aid .... Ms. Alma TANON
88 Director Student Life .... Ms. Raniyah JOHNSON
88 Director CalWorks/WIN .... Ms. Elizabeth TYRRELL
21 Supervisor Administrative Services .... Ms. Lauren MCKEE
13 Supervisor Campus Tech Svcs .... Mr. Eugenio CANOY
88 Student Success Supervisor .... Mr. Song-Ho TRAN

*San Jose City College (P)

2100 Moorpark Avenue, San Jose CA 95128-2799
County: Santa Clara　FICE Identification: 001282
Unit ID: 122746
Telephone: (408) 298-2181　Carnegie Class: Assoc/HVT-High Trad
FAX Number: (408) 298-1935　Calendar System: Semester
URL: www.sjcc.edu
Established: 1921　Annual Undergrad Tuition & Fees (In-District): $1,343
Enrollment: 8,445　Coed
Affiliation or Control: State/Local　IRS Status: 501(c)3
Highest Offering: Associate Degree
Accreditation: WJ, DA

02 President .... Dr. Byron BRELAND
05 Int Vice President Academic Affairs .... Mr. Roland MONTEMAYOR
11 Vice President Administrative Svcs .... Mr. Jorge ESCOBAR
32 Vice President Student Affairs .... Mr. Roland MONTEMAYOR
10 Chief Financial/Business Officer .... Ms. Marilyn MORIKANG
88 Director Support Programs .... Ms. Marilyn BRODIE
37 Financial Aid Director .... Mr. Takeo KUBO
92 Director Honors Program .... Mr. Sean ABEL
41 Dean of Athletics & Kinesiology .... Mr. Lamel HARRIS
04 Assistant to the President .... Ms. Lisa BRILLON
50 Act Dean Business/Workforce Devel .... Mr. Maniphore DICKERSON
79 Dean Humanities/Social Science .... Mr. Sean ABEL
38 Dean Counseling/Matriculation .... Dr. Eliazer AYALA-AUSTIN
49 Dean Language Arts .... Dr. Celia CRUZ-JOHNSON
81 Dean Mathematics/Sciences Division .... Dr. Mark NEWTON
09 Director of Institutional Research .... Dr. Joyce LUI

*San Mateo County Community College District Office (Q)

3401 CSM Drive, San Mateo CA 94402-3651
County: San Mateo　FICE Identification: 004697
Unit ID: 122782
Telephone: (650) 574-6500　Carnegie Class: N/A
FAX Number: (650) 574-6566
URL: www.smccd.edu

01 Chancellor .... Mr. Ron D. GALATOLO
03 Executive Vice Chancellor .... Ms. Kathy BLACKWOOD
15 Vice Chanc Human Res/Gen Couns .... Mr. Eugene WHITLOCK
05 Int Vice Chanc Educ Svcs/Plng .... Ms. Kimberlee MESSINA
18 Vice Chanc Facil Plng/Maint/Oper .... Mr. Jose NUNEZ
109 Vice Chanc Auxiliary Services .... Mr. Tom BAUER
104 Provost International Education .... Dr. Jing LUAN
10 Chief Financial Officer .... Ms. Bernata SLATER
13 Chief Technology Officer .... Mr. Bruce GRIFFIN

*Cañada College (R)

4200 Farm Hill Boulevard, Redwood City CA 94061-1099
County: San Mateo　FICE Identification: 006973
Unit ID: 111434
Telephone: (650) 306-3100　Carnegie Class: Assoc/MT-VT-High Non
FAX Number: (650) 306-3457　Calendar System: Semester
URL: www.canadacollege.edu
Established: 1968　Annual Undergrad Tuition & Fees (In-District): $1,344
Enrollment: 6,477　Coed
Affiliation or Control: State/Local　IRS Status: 501(c)3
Highest Offering: Associate Degree
Accreditation: WJ, RAD

02 President .... Dr. Jamillah MOORE
05 Interim VP Instruction .... Dr. David M. JOHNSON
32 Interim VP Student Services .... Mr. Phillip KING
11 Vice Pres Administrative Services .... Ms. Michelle MARQUEZ
10 College Business Officer .... Ms. Mary Chries CONCHA THIA
38 Interim Dean Counseling .... Ms. Gloria DARAFSHI
06 Registrar .... Ms. Ruth MILLER
26 Director Marketing .... Ms. Megan RODRIGUEZ ANTONE
45 Interim Dean PRIE .... Dr. Tracy HUANG
37 Director Financial Aid Services .... Ms. Margie CARRINGTON
18 Facilities Manager .... Ms. Karen PINKHAM
103 Interim Dean Bus Design & Workforce .... Ms. Leonor CABRERA
79 Int Dean Humanities & Soc Sci .... Vacant

81 Dean Science & Technology .... Dr. Janet STRINGER
41 Dean Ath/Kin/Learning Res .... Dr. Anniqua RANA

*College of San Mateo (A)

1700 W Hillsdale Boulevard, San Mateo CA 94402-3795
County: San Mateo FICE Identification: 001181
Unit ID: 122791
Telephone: (650) 574-6161 Carnegie Class: Assoc/HT-Mix Trad/Non
FAX Number: (650) 574-6680 Calendar System: Semester
URL: www.collegeofsanmateo.edu
Established: 1922 Annual Undergrad Tuition & Fees (In-District): $1,400
Enrollment: 8,889 Coed
Affiliation or Control: State/Local IRS Status: 501(c)3
Highest Offering: Associate Degree
Accreditation: WJ, DA

02 President .... Mr. Michael CLAIRE
05 Vice President Instruction .... Dr. Sandra Stefani COMERFORD
10 Vice Pres Administrative Services ....Ms. Jan ROECKS
32 Vice President Student Services .... Ms. Jennifer HUGHES
07 Dean Admissions & Records .... Dr. Henry VILLAREAL
38 Dean Counsel/Advis/Matriculation .... Ms. Krystal ROMERO
09 Dean Plng/Rsrch/Inst Effectiveness .... Dr. John J. SEWART
35 Dean Student Services/Counseling .... Ms. Marsha RAMEZANE
79 Dean Language Arts Division .... Dr. James CARRANZA
68 Dean Kinesiology/Athletics Division ....Mr. Andreas WOLF
81 Dean Math/Science Division .... Dr. Charlene FRONTIERA
83 Dean Creative Arts/Social Sci Div .... Dr. Laura DEMSETZ
50 Dean Business & Technology Division .... Ms. Heidi DIAMOND
06 Registrar ....Ms. Niruba SRINIVASAN
37 Director Financial Aid Services ....Ms. Claudia I. MENJIVAR
26 Dir Marketing/Comm/Public Relations ....Mr. Richard ROJO
18 Facilities Manager ....Ms. Michelle RUDOVSKY

*Skyline College (B)

3300 College Drive, San Bruno CA 94066-1698
County: San Mateo FICE Identification: 007713
Unit ID: 123509
Telephone: (650) 738-4100 Carnegie Class: Assoc/MT-VT-High Non
FAX Number: (650) 738-4338 Calendar System: Semester
URL: www.skylinecollege.edu
Established: 1969 Annual Undergrad Tuition & Fees (In-District): $1,446
Enrollment: 9,681 Coed
Affiliation or Control: State/Local IRS Status: 501(c)3
Highest Offering: Baccalaureate
Accreditation: WJ, ACBSP, COARC, SURGT

02 President ....Dr. Regina STANBACK STROUD
05 Vice President Instruction ....Mr. Aaron D. MCVEAN
32 Vice President Student Services .... Dr. Angelica GARCIA
84 Dean Enrollment Svcs/Financial Aid .... Mr. William MINNICH
09 Dean Plng/Rsrch/Inst Effective .... Vacant
10 Vice President Business Service ....Ms. Eloisa M. BRIONES
83 Dean Social Science/Creative Arts .... Dr. Tammy ROBINSON
50 Dean Business/Ed/Prof Pgm .... Ms. Christine ROUMBANIS
60 Dean Language Arts/Learning Res .... Ms. Mary GUTIERREZ
68 Dean Kinesiology/Athletics/Dance ....Mr. Joseph MORELLO, JR.
81 Dean Science/Math/Technology .... Mr. Raymond HERNANDEZ
38 Dean Counsel/Advis/Matric .... Dr. Luis ESCOBAR
103 Director SparkPoint at Skyline Col .... Mr. Chad THOMPSON
26 Director Marketing/Comm/PR ....Ms. Cherie COLIN
08 Director Learning Commons .... Dr. Pearl LY
103 Director Workforce Development ....Ms. Andrea VIZENOR
85 Dean Global Learning Programs .... Dr. Tammy ROBINSON
121 Dean Acad Support & Learning Tech .... Dr. James HOUPIS
06 Registrar .... Ms. Susan LORENZO
04 Administrative Asst to President .... Ms. Theresa TENTES
104 Director Study Abroad .... Mr. Zaid GHORI
18 Facilities Manager ....Mr. John DOCTOR
19 Chief Public Safety Officer .... Mr. Jim VANGELE
37 Director Student Financial Aid ....Ms. Regina MORRISON

Sanford Burnham Prebys Medical Discovery Institute (C)

10901 North Torrey Pines Road, La Jolla CA 92037
County: San Diego Identification: 667069
Unit ID: 481535
Telephone: (858) 646-3100 Carnegie Class: Spec-4-yr-Other Health
FAX Number: (858) 646-3199 Calendar System: Quarter
URL: www.sbpdiscovery.org
Established: 2005 Annual Graduate Tuition & Fees: N/A
Enrollment: 31 Coed
Affiliation or Control: Independent Non-Profit IRS Status: 501(c)3
Highest Offering: Doctorate; No Undergraduates
Accreditation: WC

01 President ....Dr. Kristiina VUORI
10 Chief Financial Officer ....Dr. Gary CHESSUM
05 Dean Grad Sch Biomedical Sciences ....Dr. Guy SALVESEN
15 Sr Vice Pres Human Resources .... Ms. Julie COOKE
88 Sr Vice Pres Drug Discovery/Devel ....Dr. Michael JACKSON
30 Vice Pres Business Development ....Dr. Lee BLUMENFELD
100 Vice Pres/Chief of Staff .... Dr. Elizabth SCHWARZBACH

The Santa Barbara and Ventura Colleges of Law (D)

4475 Market Street, Ventura CA 93003
County: Ventura Identification: 667229
Unit ID: 125037
Telephone: (805) 765-9300 Carnegie Class: Spec-4-yr-Law
FAX Number: (805) 658-0529 Calendar System: Semester
URL: www.collegesoflaw.edu
Established: 1969 Annual Graduate Tuition & Fees: N/A
Enrollment: 101 Coed
Affiliation or Control: Independent Non-Profit IRS Status: 501(c)3
Highest Offering: Doctorate; No Undergraduates
Accreditation: WC

01 Executive Director .... Dr. Matthew NEHMER
05 Dean .... Ms. Jackie GARDINA
07 Director of Admissions .... Mr. Shawn TAYLOR
06 Asst Dean & Registrar .... Ms. Barbara DOYLE
32 Student Services Coordinator .... Ms. Jennifer MACKIE
04 Administrative Asst to Executive .... Ms. Alexis BURDICK

Santa Barbara City College (E)

721 Cliff Drive, Santa Barbara CA 93109-2394
County: Santa Barbara FICE Identification: 001285
Unit ID: 122889
Telephone: (805) 965-0581 Carnegie Class: Assoc/HT-High Trad
FAX Number: (805) 963-7222 Calendar System: Semester
URL: www.sbcc.edu
Established: 1909 Annual Undergrad Tuition & Fees (In-District): $1,374
Enrollment: 17,920 Coed
Affiliation or Control: State/Local IRS Status: 501(c)3
Highest Offering: Associate Degree
Accreditation: WJ, ADNUR, CAHIIM, DMS, RAD

01 Superintendent/President ....Dr. Anthony E. BEEBE
05 Exec Vice Pres Educ Pgms .... Dr. Paul JARRELL
10 VP Business Services .... Ms. Lyndsay MAAS
15 VP Human Resources .... Ms. Monalisa HASSON
13 VP Information Technology .... Dr. Paul BISHOP
56 Int VP Sch of Extended Learning ....Dr. Melissa MORENO
72 Dean Educational Programs .... Mr. Arturo RODRIGUEZ
76 Dean Educational Programs ....Dr. Alan PRICE
81 Dean Educational Programs .... Dr. Jens-Uwe KUHN
57 Dean Educational Programs .... Dr. Alice PEREZ
72 Dean Educational Programs ....Mr. Kenley NEUFELD
07 Associate Dean Admissions .... Mr. Christopher JOHNSON
08 Librarian ....Ms. Elizabeth BOWMAN
102 Exec Dir Foundation for SBCC .... Mr. Geoff GREEN
09 Dir Institutional Research & Plng ....Dr. Z. REISZ
26 Exec Dir Public Affairs .... Ms. Luz REYES-MARTIN
37 Director of Student Financial Aid ....Mr. Saul QUIROZ
18 Interim Dir of Fac & Opers .... Mr. Robert MORALES
85 Director International Students .... Ms. Carola SMITH
06 Director of Records ....Mr. Michael MEDEL
96 Manager of Purchasing .... Mr. Robert MORALES
04 Executive Asst to President ....Ms. Angie ESQUEDA
19 Director Security/Safety ....Mr. Erik FRICKE
41 Athletic Director .... Mr. Rocco CONSTANTINO
84 Coordinator for Enrollment Services ....Ms. Vanessa PELTON
28 Director of Diversity .... Mr. Luis GIRALDO

Santa Clara University (F)

500 El Camino Real, Santa Clara CA 95053-0001
County: Santa Clara FICE Identification: 001326
Unit ID: 122931
Telephone: (408) 554-4000 Carnegie Class: Masters/L
FAX Number: (408) 554-2700 Calendar System: Quarter
URL: www.scu.edu
Established: 1851 Annual Undergrad Tuition & Fees: $47,112
Enrollment: 8,680 Coed
Affiliation or Control: Independent Non-Profit IRS Status: 501(c)3
Highest Offering: Doctorate
Accreditation: WC, CS, ENG, IPSY, LAW, THEOL

01 President .... Rev. Michael E. ENGH, SJ
05 Provost ....Dr. Dennis JACOBS
10 Int Vice President Finance/Admin .... Mr. Chris SHAY
43 General Counsel ....Mr. John OTTOBONI
111 Vice President University Relations .... Mr. James LYONS
100 Chief of Staff to the President .... Ms. Molly MC DONALD
49 Dean of Arts & Sciences .... Dr. Debbie TAHMASSEBI
50 Dean of Business ....Ms. Caryn BECK-DUDLEY
53 Dean Educ & Counseling Psych .... Dr. Sabrina ZIRKEL
54 Dean of Engineering ....Dr. Godfrey MUNGAL
61 Dean of Law .... Ms. Lisa KLOPPENBERG
73 Dean Jesuit School of Theology ....Rev. Kevin O'BRIEN, SJ
121 Dean Academic Support Services .... Ms. Kathryn PALMIERI
88 Presidential Prof Global Outreach ....Dr. Don C. DODSON
20 Sr Vice Provost Academic Affairs ....Dr. Diane E. JONTE-PACE
32 Vice Provost and Dean Student Life . Ms. Jeanne ROSENBERGER
84 Vice President for Enrollment Mgmt ....Mr. Mike B. SEXTON
45 Vice Prov Inst Effectiveness .... Dr. Ed RYAN
13 CIO/Vice Provost Info Services .... Dr. Robert OWEN
20 Assoc Vice Prov Undergrad Studies .... Dr. Philip R. KESTEN
20 Assoc Provost Undergraduate Studies .... Mr. Jim BENNETT
88 Sr Assoc Provost Rsrch Faculty Affs ....Dr. Amy M. SHACHTER
88 Assoc Vice Provost Faculty Devel ....Dr. Eileen R. ELROD
07 Dean Undergraduate Admission ....Ms. Eva BLANCO MASIAS
37 Dean University Financial Aid Svcs ....Ms. Nan MERZ
21 Assoc Vice President Finance ....Mr. Harry M. FONG
15 Asst Vice President Human Resources .....Mr. Charlie AMBELANG
30 Assoc Vice President Development .... Mr. Mike J. WALLACE
109 Asst Vice Pres Auxiliary Services ....Ms. Robin REYNOLDS
35 Assoc Dean for Student Life .... Mr. Matthew DUNCAN
06 University Registrar ....Ms. Monica L. AUGUSTIN
29 Asst Vice President Alumni Rels .... Ms. Kathy KALE
41 Director Athletics and Recreation ....Dr. Renee BAUMGARTNER
08 University Librarian ....Ms. Jennifer NUTEFALL
90 Deputy CIO Academic Technology ....Ms. Nancy CUTLER
36 Director Career Center .... Ms. Elspeth ROSSETTI
09 Director Institutional Research ....Ms. Barbara A. STEWART
25 Director Sponsored Projects ....Ms. Mary-Ellen FORTINI
38 Director Health & Counseling Svcs ....Dr. Jill ROVARIS
85 Assoc Provost International Pgm ....Ms. Susan POPKO
114 University Director Budget .... Vacant
115 Chief Investment Officer .... Mr. John E. KERRIGAN
21 Controller ....Ms. Ramona SAUTER
18 Director of Facilities ....Mr. Jeffrey R. CHARLES
96 Director University Support Service .... Mr. Ed MERRYMAN
19 Director Campus Safety Services ....Mr. Philip BELTRAN
40 General Manager Bookstore .... Ms. Deborah KENDALL
42 Director of Campus Ministry ....Ms. Lulu SANTANA
22 EEO & Title IX Coordinator ....Ms. Belinda GUTHRIE
88 Director de Saisset Museum .... Ms. Rebecca M. SCHAPP
88 Exec Dir Ignatian Ctr Jesuit Educ ......Rev. Dorian LLYWELYN, SJ
88 Exec Dir Miller Ctr Soc Entrepren ....Dr. Thane KREINER
88 Exec Dir Markkula Ctr Applied Ethic ....Mr. Kirk O. HANSON
110 Assoc Vice President Development ....Ms. Nancy T. CALDERON
28 Assoc Provost Diversity & Inclusion .... Mr. Aldo BILLINGSLEA
44 Asst Vice President Advance Svcs .... Mr. Jeff BEACHY
92 Director University Honors Program .... Dr. Leilani M. MILLER
94 Director Womens & Gender Studies ....Dr. Linda GARBER
93 Director Ethnic Studies .... Dr. Anna C. SAMPAIO

Santa Monica College (G)

1900 Pico Boulevard, Santa Monica CA 90405-1628
County: Los Angeles FICE Identification: 001286
Unit ID: 122977
Telephone: (310) 434-4000 Carnegie Class: Assoc/HT-High Trad
FAX Number: (310) 434-4386 Calendar System: Semester
URL: www.smc.edu
Established: 1929 Annual Undergrad Tuition & Fees (In-District): $1,142
Enrollment: 30,615 Coed
Affiliation or Control: State/Local IRS Status: 501(c)3
Highest Offering: Associate Degree
Accreditation: WJ, ADNUR

01 Superintendent/President ....Dr. Kathryn E. JEFFERY
10 Vice President Business/Admin .... Mr. Robert G. ISOMOTO
15 Vice President Human Resources ....Ms. Marcia WADE
05 Vice President Academic Affairs .... Dr. Georgia LORENZ
84 Vice Pres Enrollment Development .... Dr. Teresita RODRIGUEZ
32 Vice President Student Affairs ....Mr. Michael TUITASI
20 Dean Academic Affairs ....Ms. Erica LEBLANC
16 Dean Human Resources ....Ms. Sherri LEE-LEWIS
08 Dean Learning Resources .... Vacant
85 Dean International Education .... Ms. Kelley BRAYTON
56 Dean Noncredit/External Programs .... Ms. Dione CARTER
124 Dean Counseling/Retention .... Ms. Brenda BENSON
13 Chief Dir Information Technology ....Vacant
88 Interim Dean Education Enterprise ....Mr. Mitch HESKEL
43 Campus Counsel .... Mr. Robert MYERS
106 Assoc Dean Online Svcs & Support .... Ms. Julie YARRISH
51 Assoc Dean Emeritus College .... Ms. Gita RUNKLE
35 Dean Students ....Ms. Deyna HEARN
17 Associate Dean of Health Sciences ....Dr. Eve ADLER
26 Public Information Officer .... Ms. Grace SMITH
31 Dean Community & Academic Relations ..... Ms. Kiersten ELLIOTT
86 Sr Director Government Relations ....Mr. Don GIRARD
07 Dean of Admissions ....Dr. Esau TOVAR
37 Assoc Dean Financial Aid/Scholarshp .... Mr. William BLOOM
18 Chief Dir Facilities Management .... Mr. Bruce WYBAN
114 Budget Manager .... Ms. Veronica DIAZ
09 Dean Institutional Research ....Ms. Hannah LAWLER
104 Assoc Dean International Education .... Ms. Denise KINSELLA
41 Asst Director Athletics ....Mr. Reggie ELLIS
102 Associate Dean Grants .... Ms. Laurel MCQUAY-PENINGER
88 Director of Classified Personnel ....Ms. Carol LONG
88 Director Network Services ....Mr. Bob DAMMER
25 Director of Contracts .... Mr. Charlie YEN
96 Director of Purchasing .... Ms. Cynthia MOORE
19 Chief of Campus Police .... Mr. Johnnie ADAMS
04 Admin Asst to the President ....Ms. Letty KILIAN
14 Director Management Info Systems .... Ms. Rupinder BHATIA
24 Mgr Media & Reprographic Services .... Mr. Albert DESALLES
40 Bookstore Manager .... Mr. David DEVER
103 Dean Workforce Development ....Dr. Patricia RAMOS
101 Coordinator Board of Trustees ....Ms. Lisa ROSE
88 Interim Assoc Dean Student Life ....Ms. Nancy GRASS
88 Director Radio Station (KCRW) ....Ms. Jennifer FERRO
88 Director Facilities Programming ....Ms. Linda SULLIVAN
89 Dean First Year Programs ....Vacant
88 Dir Sustainability Coordination .... Mr. Ferris KAWAR
75 Dir Career & Contract Education ....Ms. Michelle KING
88 Assoc Dir Dual Enroll/Instr Svcs ....Ms. Maral HYELER
88 Dir Supplemental Instruct/Tutoring ....Ms. Wendi DEMORST
88 Director Student Equity & STEM Pgm . Ms. Melanie BOCANEGRA
88 Director Business Development ....Ms. Sasha KING
88 Assoc Dean Instruct/Stdnt Pgm .... Mr. Frank DAWSON
29 Dir Student and Alumni Rels .... Ms. Deirdre WEAVER
88 Special Assistant to the President ....Ms. Katharine MULLER
105 Web/Social Media Manager .... Ms. Regina IP

Santa Rosa Junior College (H)

1501 Mendocino Avenue, Santa Rosa CA 95401-4395
County: Sonoma FICE Identification: 001287
Unit ID: 123013
Telephone: (707) 527-4011 Carnegie Class: Assoc/MT-VT-High Trad

FAX Number: (707) 527-4816 Calendar System: Semester
URL: www.santarosa.edu
Established: 1918 Annual Undergrad Tuition & Fees (In-District): $1,340
Enrollment: 22,411 Coed
Affiliation or Control: State/Local IRS Status: 501(c)3
Highest Offering: Associate Degree
Accreditation: WJ, DA, DH, DIETT, EMT, RAD

01 Superintendent/President ....Dr. Frank CHONG
12 Vice President Petaluma Campus ..... Dr. Jane SALDANA-TALLEY
05 Sr VP Acad Affs/Asst Superintendent ...... Dr. Mary Kay RUDOLPH
10 Sr VP Finance & Administrative Svc ....Mr. Doug ROBERTS
32 VP Student Svcs/Asst Superintendent ....Mr. Pedro AVILA
15 VP Human Resources ....Ms. Karen FURUKAWA
88 Director Capital Projects ....Mr. Leigh SATA
04 Sr Executive Assistant to CEO/BOT ....Ms. Erin MAGEE
75 Dean Career/Tech Ed/Economic Dev ....Mr. Jerry MILLER
18 Interim Dean Facility Planning/Ops ....Mr. Paul BIELEN
88 Dean Curriculum/Education Support ....Dr. Abraham FARKAS
49 Dean Liberal Arts & Sciences ....Dr. Kris ABRAHAMSON
08 Dean Learning Res/Educ Tech ....Ms. Alicia VIRTUE
38 Interim Dean Counseling/Support Svc ....Mr. Martin LEE
88 Dean Public Safety ....Ms. April CHAPMAN
81 Dean Sci/Tech/Engr/Math ....Mr. Victor TAM
17 Dean Health Sciences ....Ms. Deborah CHIGAZOLA
50 Dean Business/Professional Studies ....Mr. Joshua ADAMS
79 Dean Arts & Humanities ....Ms. Anna SZABADOS
88 Dean Language Arts/Acad Foundation ....Mr. Robert HOLCOMB
41 Dean Kinesiology/Dance/Athletic Dir . Mr. Matthew MARKOVITCH
22 Dean Disabled Students Pgm & Svcs ....Ms. Patie WEGMAN
72 Dean Instruction & Enrollment Svcs ...... Ms. Catherine WILLIAMS
35 Dean Student Services Petaluma ....Ms. Vanessa SHANNON
88 Dean Child Dev & Teacher Education ....Ms. Yolanda GARCIA
121 Dean Student Success & Retention ....Ms. Li COLLIER
47 Int Dean Agri/Natural Resources ....Mr. Ron MYERS
19 Chief of Police ....Mr. Lorenzo DUENAS
13 Director Information Technology ....Mr. Scott CONRAD
103 Director Workforce Development ....Vacant
21 Director of Fiscal Services ....Ms. Kate JOLLEY
37 Director Student Financial Services ....Ms. Jana COX
18 Director Facilities Operations ....Vacant
23 Director Student Health Services ....Ms. Susan QUINN
09 Director Institutional Research ....Dr. KC GREANEY
35 Dir Student Affs/New Student Pgm ....Mr. Robert ETHINGTON
96 Director Purchasing & Graphics ....Ms. Laura RIVERA
40 Director Bookstore ....Vacant
102 Executive Director Foundation ....Ms. Kate MCCLINTOCK
66 Interim Director Nursing Program ....Ms. Anna VALDEZ
06 Dean Acad Records/Intl Admissions ....Ms. Freyja PEREIRA
07 Director Admissions/Enrollment Svcs ....Ms. Vayta SMITH
31 Director Community Education ....Mr. Jeffrey RHOADES
16 Director Human Resources ....Ms. Sarah HOPKINS
26 Director Public Relations Manager ....Ms. Ellen MAREMONT-SILVER
90 Manager Instructional Computing ....Mr. Michael ROTH
24 Manager Media Services Petaluma ....Mr. Matt PEARSON

Saybrook University (A)

475 14th Street, Oakland CA 94612
County: Alameda FICE Identification: 021206
Unit ID: 123095
Telephone: (510) 593-2900 Carnegie Class: Spec-4-yr-Other Health
FAX Number: (510) 455-7046 Calendar System: Semester
URL: www.saybrook.edu
Established: 1971 Annual Graduate Tuition & Fees: N/A
Enrollment: 558 Coed
Affiliation or Control: Independent Non-Profit IRS Status: 501(c)3
Highest Offering: Doctorate; No Undergraduates
Accreditation: WC

01 President ....Dr. Nathan LONG
05 VP Academics/Student Affs (CAO) ....Dr. Carol R. HUMPHREYS
84 VP Enrollment Mgmt/Chief Enroll Ofc ....Ms. Elizabeth O'BRIEN
06 Registrar ....Mr. Thomas CHAMPION
08 Librarian ....Mr. Noah LOWENSTEIN
04 Executive Assistant ....Ms. LaTanya O. HICKS
26 Dir Cmty Engagement/Strateg Partner ....Mr. Anthony MOLINAR
15 Director Business Operations ....Ms. Connie SHULMAN
13 IT Manager ....Mr. Alex SALTZBERG
32 Dir Student Success/Chf Stdnt Affs ....Ms. Julia SONDEJ

SBBCollege Bakersfield (B)

5300 California Ave, Bakersfield CA 93309-2139
County: Kern FICE Identification: 025779
Unit ID: 122834
Telephone: (661) 835-1100 Carnegie Class: Bac/Assoc-Mixed
FAX Number: (661) 835-0242 Calendar System: Other
URL: www.sbbcollege.edu
Established: 1982 Annual Undergrad Tuition & Fees: $14,435
Enrollment: 487 Coed
Affiliation or Control: Proprietary IRS Status: Proprietary
Highest Offering: Baccalaureate
Accreditation: ACICS

01 President ....Matthew JOHNSTON
26 Marketing Manager ....Monica RAYMOND

SBBCollege Rancho Mirage (C)

34275 Monterey Ave, Rancho Mirage CA 92270
Telephone: (760) 341-7602 Identification: 666582
Accreditation: ACICS

SBBCollege Santa Maria (D)

303 E Plaza Drive, Santa Maria CA 93454
County: Santa Barbara FICE Identification: 025780
Unit ID: 122852
Telephone: (805) 922-8256 Carnegie Class: Bac/Assoc-Assoc Dom
FAX Number: (805) 346-1857 Calendar System: Other
URL: www.sbbcollege.edu
Established: 1980 Annual Undergrad Tuition & Fees: $14,505
Enrollment: 166 Coed
Affiliation or Control: Proprietary IRS Status: Proprietary
Highest Offering: Baccalaureate
Accreditation: ACICS

01 President ....Matthew JOHNSTON
26 Marketing Manager ....Monica RAYMOND

SBBCollege Ventura (E)

4839 Market Street, Ventura CA 93003
County: Ventura FICE Identification: 009989
Unit ID: 433420
Telephone: (805) 339-2999 Carnegie Class: Bac/Assoc-Mixed
FAX Number: (805) 339-2994 Calendar System: Other
URL: www.sbbcollege.edu
Established: 2003 Annual Undergrad Tuition & Fees: $13,690
Enrollment: 516 Coed
Affiliation or Control: Proprietary IRS Status: Proprietary
Highest Offering: Baccalaureate
Accreditation: ACICS

01 President ....Matthew JOHNSTON
26 Marketing Manager ....Monica RAYMOND

Scripps College (F)

1030 Columbia, Claremont CA 91711-3948
County: Los Angeles FICE Identification: 001174
Unit ID: 123165
Telephone: (909) 621-8000 Carnegie Class: Bac-A&S
FAX Number: (909) 621-8323 Calendar System: Semester
URL: www.scrippscollege.edu
Established: 1926 Annual Undergrad Tuition & Fees: $50,982
Enrollment: 989 Female
Affiliation or Control: Independent Non-Profit IRS Status: 501(c)3
Highest Offering: Baccalaureate
Accreditation: WC

01 President ....Dr. Lara TIEDENS
05 VP Academic Affairs/Dean of Faculty ....Ms. Julia E. LISS
111 VP for Institutional Advancement ....Mr. Michael ARCHIBALD
10 VP for Business Affairs/Treasurer ....Mr. Dean CALVO
32 Vice President of Student Affairs ....Ms. Charlotte JOHNSON
07 Vice President for Enrollment ....Ms. Victoria ROMERO
26 VP for Communications & Marketing ....Ms. Binti HARVEY
29 Asst VP Alumnae & Parent Engagement ....Ms. Nikki KHURANA
101 VP/Secretary of Board of Trustees ....Ms. Denise NELSON NASH
04 Executive Asst to the President ....Ms. Christine COSTANZA
20 Associate Dean of Faculty ....Dr. Gretchen EDWALDS-GILBERT
15 Director of Human Resources ....Ms. Jennifer L. BERKLAS
09 Dir of Assessment/Inst Research ....Ms. Junelyn PEEPLES
08 Librarian ....Ms. Judy B. HARVEY-SAHAK
06 Registrar ....Ms. Kelly HOGENCAMP
37 Associate Director of Financial Aid ....Ms. Lindsay MORALES
36 Director of Career Planning ....Ms. Vicki P. KLOPSCH
13 Director of Information Technology ....Mr. Jeff SESSLER
18 Director of Facilities ....Mr. Josh REEDER
104 Director of Off-Campus Study ....Ms. Neva BARKER

The Scripps Research Institute (G)

10550 N Torrey Pines Road, TPC19,
La Jolla CA 92037-1000
County: San Diego FICE Identification: 033213
Unit ID: 435338
Telephone: (858) 784-8469 Carnegie Class: Not Classified
FAX Number: (858) 784-2802 Calendar System: Quarter
URL: www.scripps.edu
Established: 1989 Annual Graduate Tuition & Fees: N/A
Enrollment: N/A Coed
Affiliation or Control: Independent Non-Profit IRS Status: 501(c)3
Highest Offering: Doctorate; No Undergraduates
Accreditation: WC

01 President/CEO ....Dr. Peter G. SCHULTZ
43 Exec Vice Pres/General Counsel ....Mr. Douglas A. BINGHAM
05 VP Acad Affs/Dean Graduate Studies ....Dr. James R. WILLIAMSON
10 Chief Financial Officer/Treasurer ....Mr. Jared MACHADO

Shasta Bible College and Graduate School (H)

2951 Goodwater Avenue, Redding CA 96002-1544
County: Shasta FICE Identification: 023593
Unit ID: 123280
Telephone: (530) 221-4275 Carnegie Class: Spec-4-yr-Faith
FAX Number: (530) 221-6929 Calendar System: Semester
URL: www.shasta.edu
Established: 1972 Annual Undergrad Tuition & Fees: $12,060
Enrollment: 50 Coed
Affiliation or Control: Independent Non-Profit IRS Status: 501(c)3
Highest Offering: Master's
Accreditation: TRACS

01 President ....Dr. David R. NICHOLAS
04 Exec Assistant to the President ....Ms. Jane DEANGELO
05 Vice President of Academics ....Dr. Stephen G. BROWN
32 Vice President of Student Services ....Mr. George A. GUNN
18 Coordinator Grounds & Maintenance ....Mr. Gary KELLOGG
06 Registrar ....Mrs. Faith MCCARTHY
10 Director of Finance/Controller ....Mr. Eric BROWN
37 Director of Financial Aid ....Ms. Linda ILES
49 Dean Undergraduate Studies ....Mrs. Faith MCCARTHY
60 Library Sciences ....Mrs. Virginia M. WILLIAMS
39 Director Student Housing ....Mrs. Donna R. NICHOLAS

Shasta College (I)

PO Box 496006, 11555 Old Oregon Tr,
Redding CA 96049-6006
County: Shasta FICE Identification: 001289
Unit ID: 123299
Telephone: (530) 242-7500 Carnegie Class: Assoc/HT-Mix Trad/Non
FAX Number: (530) 225-4990 Calendar System: Semester
URL: www.shastacollege.edu
Established: 1950 Annual Undergrad Tuition & Fees (In-District): $1,183
Enrollment: 8,620 Coed
Affiliation or Control: State/Local IRS Status: Exempt
Highest Offering: Baccalaureate
Accreditation: WJ, DH

01 Superintendent/President ....Dr. Joe WYSE
04 Asst to Superintendent/President ....Ms. Andree BLANCHIER
102 Executive Director SC Foundation ....Mr. Scott THOMPSON
05 VP Instruction ....Dr. Frank NIGRO
10 VP Administrative Services ....Mr. Morris RODRIGUE
32 Asst Supt/VP of Student Services ....Dr. Kevin O'RORKE
84 Int AVP Student & Enrollment Svcs ....Mr. Timothy JOHNSTON
15 Assoc VP of Human Resources ....Mr. Gregory SMITH
103 AVP Economic/Workforce Development ....Ms. Eva JIMENEZ
13 Director of Information Technology ....Mr. James CRANDALL
21 Comptroller ....Ms. Jill AULT
57 Dean Arts/Communication/Soc Science ....Ms. Stacey BARTLETT
50 Dean Business/Ag/Ind/Tech/Safety ....Ms. Susan WYCHE
76 Dean Health Sciences ....Ms. Kathy ROYCE
81 Dean Science/Language Arts/Math ....Dr. John YU
56 Assoc Dean Extended Education ....Mr. Andy FIELDS
62 Dean Library Services/Educ Tech ....Mr. William BREITBACH
68 Dean Phys Education and Athletics ....Mr. Mike MARI
35 Interim Dean Student Services ....Ms. Sandra HAMILTON SLANE
28 Assoc Dean Access and Equity ....Dr. Sharon BRISOLARA
88 Dean Fndnl Skills/Inst Effectivenes ....Dr. Kate MAHAR
19 Director of Campus Safety ....Mr. Lonnie SEAY
37 Assoc Dean Student Services ....Ms. Becky MCCALL
109 Director Food Services ....Ms. Denise AXTELL
25 Director Grant Development ....Ms. Amy WEBB
18 Director Physical Plant ....Mr. George ESTRADA
39 Director Residence Life ....Mr. Nick WEBB

Shepherd University (J)

3200 N San Fernando Rd, Los Angeles CA 90065
County: Los Angeles Identification: 667056
Unit ID: 487667
Telephone: (323) 550-8888 Carnegie Class: Not Classified
FAX Number: (323) 550-1313 Calendar System: Semester
URL: shepherduniversity.edu
Established: 1999 Annual Undergrad Tuition & Fees: $19,889
Enrollment: 295 Coed
Affiliation or Control: Independent Non-Profit IRS Status: 501(c)3
Highest Offering: Doctorate
Accreditation: @WC, NURSE, THEOL

01 President ....Dr. Michael PICKETT
05 Vice Pres & Academic Dean ....Dr. Shalom Y. KIM

Sierra College (K)

5100 Sierra College Blvd., Rocklin CA 95677
County: Placer FICE Identification: 001290
Unit ID: 123341
Telephone: (916) 624-3333 Carnegie Class: Assoc/HT-High Trad
FAX Number: N/A Calendar System: Semester
URL: www.sierracollege.edu
Established: 1914 Annual Undergrad Tuition & Fees (In-District): $1,142
Enrollment: 18,218 Coed
Affiliation or Control: State/Local IRS Status: 501(c)3
Highest Offering: Associate Degree
Accreditation: WJ

01 Superintendent/President ....Mr. William H. DUNCAN
05 Supt/Vice President Instruction ....Dr. Debra SUTPHEN
10 Vice Pres Administrative Services ....Mr. Chris YATOOMA
32 Vice Pres Student Services ....Ms. Mandy DAVIES
04 Exec Assistant Presidents Office ....Ms. Jeannette BISCHOFF
08 Dean Library/Learning Resource Ctr ....Ms. Sabrina PAPE
50 Assoc Dean Business & Technology ....Ms. Darlene JACKSON
81 Dean Science & Mathematics ....Dr. Heather ROBERTS
49 Dean Liberal Arts ....Dr. Rebecca BOCCHICCHIO
68 Dean Phys Educ/Athletics Director ....Mr. Lucas MOOSMAN
09 Dean Planning/Research/Res Devel ....Mr. Erik COOPER

66 Dean Nursing .... Ms. Nancy SCHWAB
21 Director of Finance .... Ms. Linda FISHER
15 Director Human Resources .... Mr. Cameron ABBOTT
18 Dir of Facilities & Construction .... Ms. Laura DOTY
37 Manager Financial Aid .... Dr. Linda WILLIAMS
31 Community Education Pgm Manager .... Ms. Jill ALCORN
22 EEO Program Manager .... Mr. Cameron ABBOTT
26 Manager Marketing/Public Relations .... Ms. Sue MICHAELS
39 Residence Life Supervisor .... Ms. Cortney MAGORIAN
07 Manager of Admissions & Records .... Ms. Gail MODDER

Silicon Valley University (A)

2010 Fortune Drive, San Jose CA 95131

County: Santa Clara — FICE Identification: 038103
Unit ID: 444848
Telephone: (408) 435-8989 — Carnegie Class: Not Classified
FAX Number: (408) 955-0887 — Calendar System: Trimester
URL: www.svuca.edu
Established: 1997 — Annual Undergrad Tuition & Fees: N/A
Enrollment: N/A — Coed
Affiliation or Control: Independent Non-Profit — IRS Status: 501(c)3
Highest Offering: Master's
Accreditation: ACICS

01 Interim President .... Mr. Kevin CHENG
05 Academic Dean .... Mr. Aaron DONSKY

Simpson University (B)

2211 College View Drive, Redding CA 96003-8606

County: Shasta — FICE Identification: 001291
Unit ID: 123457
Telephone: (530) 224-5600 — Carnegie Class: Masters/S
FAX Number: (530) 226-4860 — Calendar System: Semester
URL: www.simpsonu.edu
Established: 1921 — Annual Undergrad Tuition & Fees: $25,950
Enrollment: 1,162 — Coed
Affiliation or Control: The Christian And Missionary Alliance
IRS Status: 501(c)3
Highest Offering: Master's
Accreditation: #WC, NURSE

01 President .... Dr. Robin K. DUMMER
11 Acting Chief Operating Officer .... Mr. Walter QUIRK
05 Provost .... Dr. Gayle COPELAND
10 Chief Financial Officer .... Ms. Natalie E. MCKENZIE
30 Director of Development .... Mr. Roger D. JANIS
32 Assoc VP of Student Dev/Title IX .... Dr. Michael J. LOOMIS
26 Director of Marketing .... Mr. Mark U. WOOD
88 Faculty President .... Dr. Cherry L. MCCABE
84 Senior Director of Admissions .... Mr. Dustin J. LOWE
07 Director of Undergrad Admissions .... Ms. Molly K. MCKEEVER
123 Director of Admiss for Adult & Grad .... Ms. Stacy BURGESS
88 Director of Admissions Data & Comm .... Ms. Amy I. HUEY
73 Dean AW Tozer Seminary .... Dr. Patrick A. BLEWETT
53 Dean School of Education .... Dr. Craig A. COOK
66 Dean School of Nursing .... Mrs. Kristie D. STEPHENS
107 Dean of Adult & Graduate Prof Stds .... Dr. Adeline R. JACKSON
88 Asst Dean of Adult & Grad Prof .... Mr. Andrew R. JESSON
88 Director of Veterans Success Center .... Mr. Justin R. SPEARS
18 Director of Facilities .... Mr. Merlin D. WEBER
13 Director of IT .... Mr. Michael F. SUMPTION
41 Director of Athletics .... Mr. Thomas J. GALBRAITH
39 Director of Residence Life .... Mr. Mark C. ENDRASKE
38 Director of Wellness Center .... Ms. Beverly G. KLAIBER
09 Dir Institutional Research/ALO .... Ms. Jennifer J. FOX
15 Director of Human Resources .... Mrs. Kori D. OECHSLI
109 Director of Campus Operations .... Mr. Paul R. DAVIS
37 Director Student Financial Services .... Mr. Gregory P. BAILEY
121 Director of Academic Success Center .... Mr. Louis E. BURKWHAT
35 Director of Student Engagement .... Ms. Isis C. MARTIN
08 Interim Director of Library Service .... Mr. Eric WHEELER
21 Controller .... Ms. Karen CAPFER
06 Registrar .... Mr. Harold E. LUND
88 Assoc Registrar for Records/Advis .... Ms. Cassandra A. HEATH
04 Exec Assistant to the President .... Mrs. Regina ERICKSON
19 Campus Safety Operations Coord .... Mr. Dennis SMITH
42 Campus Pastor .... Mr. Kevin M. BENNIE
40 Bookstore Manager .... Vacant

Sofia University (formerly Institute of Transpersonal Psychology) (C)

1069 E Meadow Circle, Palo Alto CA 94303-4231

County: Santa Clara — FICE Identification: 022676
Unit ID: 110778
Telephone: (650) 493-4430 — Carnegie Class: Spec-4-yr-Other Health
FAX Number: (650) 493-6835 — Calendar System: Quarter
URL: www.sofia.edu
Established: 1975 — Annual Undergrad Tuition & Fees: N/A
Enrollment: 296 — Coed
Affiliation or Control: Proprietary — IRS Status: Proprietary
Highest Offering: Doctorate
Accreditation: WC

01 President & CEO .... Dr. Qiaoyun (Liz) LI
05 Dean of Faculty .... Dr. Barbara HECKER
10 Accounting Manager .... Ms. Linyan LIU
07 Admissions and Marketing Manager .... Ms. Kimberly Anne YARBROUGH

32 Dean Student Services .... Ms. Rosalie COOK
15 Human Resources Manager .... Ms. Aida SMAILAGIC
37 Director Student Financial Aid .... Ms. Josephine MELTON
18 Facilities Manager .... Mr. Henry WU

Soka University of America (D)

1 University Drive, Aliso Viejo CA 92656-8081

County: Orange — FICE Identification: 038144
Unit ID: 399911
Telephone: (949) 480-4000 — Carnegie Class: Bac-A&S
FAX Number: (949) 480-4001 — Calendar System: Semester
URL: www.soka.edu
Established: 2001 — Annual Undergrad Tuition & Fees: $31,042
Enrollment: 444 — Coed
Affiliation or Control: Independent Non-Profit — IRS Status: 501(c)3
Highest Offering: Master's
Accreditation: WC

01 President/Professor of Economics .... Dr. Daniel Y. HABUKI
04 Exec Asst to the President .... Mr. Hiro SAKAI
05 Provost/Vice Pres Academic Affairs .... Dr. Edward M. FEASEL
10 Vice President Finance & Admin/CFO .... Mr. Archibald E. ASAWA
09 VP Inst Rsch/Dean of Graduate Sch .... Dr. Tomoko TAKAHASHI
20 Dean of Faculty/CAO .... Dr. Edward M. FEASEL
84 Dean of Enrollment Services .... Mr. Andrew WOOLSEY
32 Dean of Students .... Dr. Hyon J. MOON
19 Director Safety/Security/Events .... Mr. Craig LEE
31 Director of Community Relations ... Ms. Wendy WETZEL HARDER
41 Director of Athletics & Recreation .... Mr. Mike MOORE
35 Director of Student Services .... Mr. Brian DURICK
39 Dir Stdnt Activities/Resident Life .... Ms. Michelle HOBBY-MEARS
30 Director of Philanthropy .... Ms. Linda KENNEDY
13 Director Information Technology .... Mr. John MIN
44 Dir of International Development .... Ms. Toshiko SATO
15 Director of Human Resources .... Ms. Katherine KING
104 Dir Study Abroad & Intl Internships .... Mr. Alex H. OKUDA
06 Registrar .... Ms. Nancy YOSHIMURA
18 Chief of Operations .... Mr. Tom HARKENRIDER
08 Director of Library .... Mr. Hiroko TONONO

Solano Community College (E)

4000 Suisun Valley Road, Fairfield CA 94534-3197

County: Solano — FICE Identification: 001292
Unit ID: 123563
Telephone: (707) 864-7000 — Carnegie Class: Assoc/HT-Mix Trad/Non
FAX Number: (707) 864-0361 — Calendar System: Semester
URL: www.solano.edu
Established: 1945 — Annual Undergrad Tuition & Fees (In-District): $1,140
Enrollment: 9,964 — Coed
Affiliation or Control: State/Local — IRS Status: 501(c)3
Highest Offering: Associate Degree
Accreditation: WJ

01 Superintendent/President .... Dr. Celia ESPOSITO-NOY
05 VP Academic Affairs .... Dr. David WILLIAMS
10 Vice President Finance & Admin .... Mr. Yulian LIGIOSO
13 Interim Chief Technology Officer .... Mr. James (Kimo) CALILAN
32 Vice President Student Services .... Dr. Gregory BROWN
38 Dean Counseling/Special Services .... Vacant
37 Int Director Financial Aid .... Ms. Maureen MASON-MUYCO
09 Dean Research and Planning .... Mr. Peter CAMMISH
15 Human Resources Manager .... Vacant
18 Director Facilities .... Vacant
88 Director Children's Programs .... Ms. Christie SPECK
103 Assoc Dean Workforce Development .... Vacant
26 Outreach/Public Relations Manager .... Vacant
96 Purchasing Tech/Buyer .... Ms. Laura SCOTT
36 Career & Job Placement Coordinator .... Ms. Patricia YOUNG
49 Dean School of Liberal Arts .... Mr. Neil GLINES
83 Dean Sch of Social/Behav Science .... Dr. Sandy LAMBA
81 Dean School Math/Science .... Vacant
76 Dn Sch Career Tech Ed/Bus/Vcvl/TAFB .... Mrs. Maire MORINEC
12 Center Dean Vallejo .... Dr. Shirley LEWIS
76 Dean Health Sciences .... Dr. Robert GABRIEL
41 Director of Athletics .... Mr. Erik VISSER

South Baylo University (F)

1126 N Brookhurst Street, Anaheim CA 92801-1702

County: Orange — FICE Identification: 025973
Unit ID: 123633
Telephone: (714) 533-1495 — Carnegie Class: Spec-4-yr-Other Health
FAX Number: (714) 533-6040 — Calendar System: Quarter
URL: www.southbaylo.edu
Established: 1977 — Annual Undergrad Tuition & Fees: N/A
Enrollment: 672 — Coed
Affiliation or Control: Independent Non-Profit — IRS Status: 501(c)3
Highest Offering: Doctorate
Accreditation: ACUP

01 President .... Dr. Jason SHIN
05 Academic Dean .... Dr. Pia MELEN
07 Director of Admission .... Mr. Charles KIM
06 Registrar .... Ms. Sophia CENTENO
10 Director of Finance .... Ms. Michelle JANG
15 Operations/Personnel Director .... Dr. Yolanda JAINI
36 Program Student Advisor .... Dr. Henry CHOI
08 Director of Libraries .... Dr. Edwin FOLLICK
13 Dir Computer Information System .... Mr. James KIM
88 Director of Clinics .... Dr. Hyo Jeong KANG

37 Financial Aid Officer .... Ms. Mimi PARK
32 Stdnt/Alumni/English LG Coordinator .... Ms. Jillian FISHBACK
85 International Student Advisor .... Ms. Seon KIM
88 Doctoral Clerkship Coordinator .... Dr. Sheng LI
88 Doctoral Program Director .... Dr. Wayne CHENG
88 Master Program Director .... Dr. Hanjik KIM
18 Chief Facilities/Physical Plant .... Mr. Yong Hee PARK
38 CCE Coordinator .... Dr. Seongok KIM

South Coast College (G)

2011 W Chapman Avenue, Orange CA 92868-2609

County: Orange — FICE Identification: 022774
Unit ID: 123642
Telephone: (714) 867-5009 — Carnegie Class: Spec 2-yr-Other
FAX Number: (714) 867-5026 — Calendar System: Quarter
URL: www.southcoastcollege.com
Established: 1961 — Annual Undergrad Tuition & Fees: N/A
Enrollment: 315 — Coed
Affiliation or Control: Proprietary — IRS Status: Proprietary
Highest Offering: Associate Degree
Accreditation: ACICS

01 President .... Ms. Jean GONZALEZ
03 Vice President .... Ms. Lonnie SKELTON
10 Dean Finance & Operations .... Ms. Jila ANDELIBI
11 Director of Operations .... Mr. Kevin MAGNER
37 Director of Financial Aid .... Mr. Michael LY
06 Registrar .... Ms. Yoshiko IZUMI

*South Orange County Community College District (H)

28000 Marguerite Parkway, Mission Viejo CA 92692-3697

County: Orange — FICE Identification: 033433
Unit ID: 432144
Telephone: (949) 582-4850 — Carnegie Class: N/A
FAX Number: (949) 364-2726
URL: www.socccd.edu

01 Interim Chancellor .... Dr. Debra FITZSIMONS
05 Vice Chanc Technology/Learning Svcs .. Dr. Robert S. BRAMUCCI
15 Vice Chancellor Human Resources .... Vacant
10 Actg Vice Chancellor Business Svcs .... Ms. Kim MCCORD
26 Dir Public Affairs/Government Rels .... Ms. Tere FLUEGEMAN
84 Dean Enroll Svcs Irvine Valley Col .... Ms. Arleen ELSEROAD
84 Int Dean Enroll Svcs Saddleback Col .... Mr. Christian ALVARADO

*Irvine Valley College (I)

5500 Irvine Center Drive, Irvine CA 92618-4399

County: Orange — FICE Identification: 025395
Unit ID: 116439
Telephone: (949) 451-5100 — Carnegie Class: Assoc/HT-High Trad
FAX Number: (949) 451-5270 — Calendar System: Semester
URL: www.ivc.edu
Established: 1979 — Annual Undergrad Tuition & Fees (In-District): $1,142
Enrollment: 13,183 — Coed
Affiliation or Control: State/Local — IRS Status: 501(c)3
Highest Offering: Associate Degree
Accreditation: WJ

02 President .... Dr. Glenn R. ROQUEMORE
100 Manager Office of the President .... Ms. Sandy JEFFRIES
05 Vice President Instruction .... Dr. Christopher MCDONALD
32 Vice President Student Services .... Dr. Linda FONTANILLA
11 Vice President Admin Services .... Mr. Davit KHACHATRYAN
26 Exec Director Market/Comm/Broadcast .... Ms. Diane G. OAKS
102 Exec Director College Foundation .... Ms. Elissa ORANSKY
41 Dean Kinesiology/Health/Athletics .... Mr. Keith SHACKLEFORD
83 Dean Social & Behavioral Sciences .... Ms. Traci FAHIMI
38 Dean Counseling Services .... Dr. Elizabeth CIPRES
09 Dir Research/Planning/Accreditation .... Dr. Loris FAGIOLI
19 Chief of Police .... Mr. Will GLEN
79 Interim Dean Liberal Arts .... Dr. Brooke CHOO
103 Dean Instruction/EWD .... Dr. Corine DOUGHTY
50 Dean Business Sciences Online/Ex Ed .... Dr. Cathleen GREINER
81 Dean Math/Sciences and Engr .... Dr. Lianna ZHAO
57 Dean The Arts .... Mr. Joseph POSHEK
84 Dean of Enrollment Services .... Ms. Arleen ELSEROAD
23 Director Health and Wellness .... Ms. Nancy MONTGOMERY
37 Asst Dean Financial Aid/Student Sup .... Mr. Ken LIRA
85 Director International Student Prog .... Ms. Christina DELGADO
89 Director Outreach and Recruitment .... Mr. Dennis GORDON
18 Director IVC Facilities .... Mr. Jeffrey HURLBUT
44 Director Annual Giving/Dev Svs .... Ms. Karen ORLANDO
35 Director Student Life .... Ms. Anissa HEARD
121 Director Student Success/Support .... Mr. Deejay SANTIAGO
75 Director Econ and Workforce Develop .... Mr. William KERWIN
55 Director Noncredit/Adult/Comm Ed .... Ms. Debbie VANSCHOELANDT
13 Director Technology Services .... Mr. Bruce HAGAN
06 Registrar/Admissions/Records .... Mr. Ruben GUZMAN
88 Director Arts Production Management .... Mr. Patric TAYLOR

*Saddleback College (J)

28000 Marguerite Parkway, Mission Viejo CA 92692-3635

County: Orange — FICE Identification: 008918
Unit ID: 122205
Telephone: (949) 582-4500 — Carnegie Class: Assoc/HT-Mix Trad/Non
FAX Number: (949) 347-0438 — Calendar System: Semester
URL: www.saddleback.edu

Established: 1968 Annual Undergrad Tuition & Fees (In-District): $1,326
Enrollment: 19,552 Coed
Affiliation or Control: State/Local IRS Status: 501(c)3
Highest Offering: Associate Degree
Accreditation: WJ, ADNUR, CAHIIM, EMT

02 President ... Dr. Gregory ANDERSON
05 Vice President of Instruction ... Vacant
10 VP College Administrative Services ... Ms. Carol HILTON
32 Vice President of Student Services ... Dr. Juan AVALOS
04 Acting Mgr Office of the President ... Mr. Ryan BROOK
45 Director Planning/Research/Grants ... Ms. Jennifer KLEIN
06 Registrar ... Dr. James M. FEIGERT
84 Dean of Enrollment Services ... Mr. Christian ALVARADO
19 Chief Of Police ... Mr. Pat HIGA
26 Director Public Information ... Vacant
88 Director Outreach and Recruitment ... Dr. Lesley HUMPHREY
102 Director College Foundation ... Vacant
35 Director Student Life ... Mr. Christopher HARGRAVES
31 Dean Cmty Educ/El & K-12 Partnershp ... Dr. Estella CASTILLO-GARRISON
88 Director of Emeritus Institute ... Mr. Dan PREDOEHL
44 Director Annual/Planned Giving ... Ms. Erin MCHENRY
66 Director of Nursing ... Ms. Diane PESTOLESI
15 Director Human Resources ... Ms. Teddi LORCH
18 Dir Facilities/Maint/Operation ... Mr. James ROGERS
23 Director Student Health Center .. Dr. Jeanne HARRIS-CALDWELL
13 Director Technology Services ... Dr. Anthony MACIEL
37 Director Financial Assistance ... Ms. Amber GALLAGHER
96 Director of Purchasing ... Ms. Brandye D'LENA
85 Director of Intl Student Program ... Ms. Angela YANG
92 Honors Program ... Ms. Alannah ROSENBERG
38 Dean Counseling Svcs/Special Pgms ... Ms. Penny SKAFF
57 Dean Fine Arts ... Dr. Cadence WYNTER
50 Dean Bus/Science/Economic/Workforce ... Dr. John JARAMILLO
76 Dean Hlth Sci/Human Svcs & Emeritus ... Dr. Donna RANE-SZOSTAK
81 Dean Math/Science & Engineering ... Dr. Akira NITTA
79 Dean Liberal Arts/Learning Res ... Dr. Kevin O'CONNOR
106 Dean Online Education/Learning Res ... Dr. Marina AMINY
72 Dean Advance Tech Appl Science ... Dr. Anthony TENG
68 Dean Kinesiology/Athletic Director ... Mr. Daniel CLAUSS
83 Dean Social & Behavioral Sciences ... Dr. Christina HINKLE
88 Acting Director Learning Assistance ... Dr. Kim D'ARCY
71 Dean Transfer/Career/Special Pgms ... Dr. Georgina GUY
103 Dir Economic/Workforce Development ... Mr. Israel DOMINGUEZ
25 Director Fiscal Contract Services ... Dr. Roxanne METZ

Southern California Institute of Architecture (A)

960 E 3rd Street, Los Angeles CA 90013-1822
County: Los Angeles FICE Identification: 020758
Unit ID: 123952
Telephone: (213) 613-2200 Carnegie Class: Spec-4-yr-Arts
FAX Number: (213) 613-2260 Calendar System: Semester
URL: www.sciarc.edu
Established: 1972 Annual Undergrad Tuition & Fees: $42,900
Enrollment: 502 Coed
Affiliation or Control: Independent Non-Profit IRS Status: 501(c)3
Highest Offering: Master's
Accreditation: WC

01 Director ... Mr. Herman DIAZ ALONSO
04 Director's Assistant ... Ms. Jessica WHEELER
05 Vice Director/Chief Academic Ofcr ... Mr. John ENRIGHT
10 Chief Financial Officer ... Ms. Sue GOSNEY
11 Chief Administration Officer ... Mr. Paul HOLLIDAY
13 Chief Information Officer ... Mr. Vic JABRASSIAN
30 Assoc Director Development ... Ms. Maria ROBINSON GLOVER
58 Graduate Program Chair ... Ms. Elena MANFERDINI
88 Undergraduate Program Chair ... Mr. Tom WISCOMBE
04 Executive Assistant to Director ... Ms. Nicole FISHER
07 Admissions Director ... Ms. Angel MONTES
06 Registrar/International Advisor ... Ms. Lisa RUSSO
37 Sr Financial Aid Counselor ... Ms. Marisela DE LA TORRE
08 Library Manager ... Mr. Kevin MCMAHON
88 Wood & Metal Shop Manager ... Mr. Rodney ROJAS
18 Facilities Manager ... Ms. Cindy JOLLOTTA
88 Wood & Metal Shopmaster ... Mr. Katsumi MOROI
20 Academic Affairs Coordinator ... Ms. Andrea YOUNG

Southern California Institute of Technology (B)

525 North Muller Street, Anaheim CA 92801-5454
County: Orange FICE Identification: 031136
Unit ID: 399869
Telephone: (714) 300-0300 Carnegie Class: Spec-4-yr-Eng
FAX Number: (714) 300-0311 Calendar System: Quarter
URL: www.scitech.edu
Established: 1987 Annual Undergrad Tuition & Fees: $17,335
Enrollment: 559 Coed
Affiliation or Control: Proprietary IRS Status: Proprietary
Highest Offering: Baccalaureate
Accreditation: ACCSC

01 President ... Dr. Parviz SHAMS
03 Vice President ... Mrs. Nazila SHAMS
05 Dean of Education ... Mr. Saravana RAMAN
13 Director of Operations ... Mr. Arian SHAMS

Southern California Seminary (C)

2075 E Madison Avenue, El Cajon CA 92019-1108
County: San Diego FICE Identification: 033323
Unit ID: 117575
Telephone: (619) 201-8999 Carnegie Class: Spec-4-yr-Faith
FAX Number: (619) 201-8975 Calendar System: Trimester
URL: www.socalsem.edu
Established: 1946 Annual Undergrad Tuition & Fees: $14,245
Enrollment: 235 Coed
Affiliation or Control: Independent Non-Profit IRS Status: 501(c)3
Highest Offering: Doctorate
Accreditation: TRACS

00 Chancellor ... Dr. David JEREMIAH
01 President ... Dr. Gary F. COOMBS
05 Provost & Chief Academic Officer ... Dr. Gino PASQUARIELLO
83 Dean Grad Sch Behavioral Science ... Dr. Elizabeth ELENWO
73 Dean of Biblical Studies/Theology ... Mr. James I. FAZIO
06 Registrar ... Mrs. Cheryl OBST
32 Director of Student Services ... Mrs. Jillian HINES
37 Director of Financial Aid ... Mrs. Yuli MARTINEZ
08 Library Director ... Miss Jennifer EWING
07 Dean of Admissions Services ... Dr. Bob FREIBERG
06 Dean of Online Learning ... Dr. Joseph R. MILLER

Southern California University of Health Sciences (D)

16200 E Amber Valley Drive, Whittier CA 90604-4051
County: Los Angeles FICE Identification: 001229
Unit ID: 117672
Telephone: (562) 947-8755 Carnegie Class: Spec-4-yr-Other Health
FAX Number: (562) 947-5724 Calendar System: Trimester
URL: www.scuhs.edu
Established: 1911 Annual Undergrad Tuition & Fees: $9,012
Enrollment: 1,044 Coed
Affiliation or Control: Independent Non-Profit IRS Status: 501(c)3
Highest Offering: First Professional Degree
Accreditation: WC, ACUP, #ARCPA, CHIRO

01 President ... Dr. John SCARINGE
05 Vice Pres Academic Affairs ... Dr. Sheryl BERMAN
100 Chief of Staff/VP Operations ... Mr. Chuck SWEET
84 Int VP Enroll Mgmt/Student Affairs ... Mr. Chuck SWEET
10 VP Admin & Finance/CFO ... Mr. Thomas K. ARENDT
17 VP SCU Health Sys/Chief Clin Off ... Dr. Melissa KIMURA
20 Interim CSIH Dean ... Mrs. Carla SKORIN
06 Registrar ... Ms. Kate MCCUNE
37 Director of Financial Aid ... Mrs. Nina MARTINEZ
04 Exec Asst to President/BOR ... Mrs. Regina TORRES-ELLIS
20 AVPAA Teaching/Learning/Leadership ... Vacant
88 Dean of Chiropractic ... Dr. Jonathon EGAN
88 Int Dean College of Eastern Med ... Dr. Jenny YU
13 Chief Information Officer ... Mr. Tim FARRIS
21 Executive Director of Accounting ... Mrs. Kelly GALLO
109 Director of Auxiliary Services ... Mr. Joseph EGGLESTON
09 Dean OSIE ... Dr. Heather VANVOLKINBURG
32 Exec Director of Student Affairs ... Dr. Steven R. JAFFE
26 Executive Director of Marketing ... Mr. Luke PHILLIPS
08 Exec Dir of Seabury Learning Center ... Ms. Kathleen E. SMITH
96 Accounts Payable/Purchasing Coord ... Mrs. Catherine MCBRIDE
15 Human Resources ... Ms. Cindy SCHEIBEL
35 AVP Student Affairs/Enroll Mgt ... Vacant
18 Director of Physical Plant ... Mr. Bob HARRISON
88 Assistant Controller ... Mrs. Lupe YABUR

Southern California University School of Oriental Medicine & Acupuncture (E)

3460 Wilshire Boulevard, Suite 500, Los Angeles CA 90010
County: Los Angeles FICE Identification: 041720
Unit ID: 459222
Telephone: (213) 413-9500 Carnegie Class: Spec-4-yr-Other Health
FAX Number: (213) 413-5400 Calendar System: Quarter
URL: www.scusoma.edu
Established: 2000 Annual Undergrad Tuition & Fees: N/A
Enrollment: 69 Coed
Affiliation or Control: Proprietary IRS Status: Proprietary
Highest Offering: Master's
Accreditation: ACUP

01 President ... Ms. Judy OH
05 Academic Dean ... Dr. Katherine H S. CHO
06 Registrar/Student Services ... Mr. Andy HSU
37 Director of Financial Aid ... Mr. Samuel YOUNG
07 Director of Admissions ... Mr. Dave PARK

Southern States University (F)

1601 Dove Street, Suite 105, Newport Beach CA 92660
Telephone: (949) 833-8868 Identification: 770629
Accreditation: ACICS

Southern States University (G)

123 Camino de la Reina Ste 100 East, San Diego CA 92108
County: San Diego Identification: 667108
Telephone: (619) 298-1829 Carnegie Class: Not Classified
FAX Number: (619) 704-0175 Calendar System: Quarter
URL: www.ssu.edu
Established: 1985 Annual Undergrad Tuition & Fees: N/A
Enrollment: N/A Coed
Affiliation or Control: Proprietary IRS Status: Proprietary
Highest Offering: Master's
Accreditation: ACICS

01 Chancellor ... John D. TUCKER
05 Vice Chanc Academic Affairs/CAO ... Dr. Claudia ARAIZA
06 Univ Registrar/Compliance Officer ... Wendy DU
07 Dean Admissions/Academic Advising ... William AMOKE
08 University Librarian ... Jason ROGERS
11 Administrative Director ... Denise MASTRO

Southwestern College (H)

900 Otay Lakes Road, Chula Vista CA 91910-7299
County: San Diego FICE Identification: 001294
Unit ID: 123800
Telephone: (619) 421-6700 Carnegie Class: Assoc/HT-High Trad
FAX Number: (619) 482-6413 Calendar System: Semester
URL: www.swccd.edu
Established: 1961 Annual Undergrad Tuition & Fees (In-District): $1,336
Enrollment: 18,716 Coed
Affiliation or Control: State/Local IRS Status: 501(c)3
Highest Offering: Associate Degree
Accreditation: WJ, ADNUR, DH, EMT, MLTAD, SURGT

01 Superintendent/President ... Dr. Kindred MURILLO
05 Interim VP Academic Affairs ... Dr. Renee KILMER
10 VP Business & Financial Affairs ... Mr. Tim FLOOD
32 VP Student Affairs ... Dr. Angelica SUAREZ
12 Dn High Ed Ctr Otay Mesa/San Ysidro ... Ms. Silvia CORNEJO
12 Dn High Ed Ctr Natl City/Crown Cove ... Ms. Christine PERRI
79 Dean Language & Literature ... Dr. Joel LEVINE
81 Dean Math/Science Engineering ... Dr. Michael ODU
68 Dean Wellness/Ex Sci/Athletics ... Mr. James SPILLERS
50 Dean Business & Technology ... Dr. Mink STAVENGA
60 Int Dean Arts/Commun & Soc Sci ... Mr. William KINNEY
108 Dean Inst Effect/Dir of Foundation ... Ms. Linda GILSTRAP
51 Dean Inst Suppt Svcs/Continuing Ed ... Ms. Mia C. MCCLELLAN
38 Dean Couns/Student Support Pgms ... Dr. Jonathan KING
26 Chief Public Info/Govt Relations ... Ms. Lillian LEOPOLD
88 Director Payroll Services ... Ms. Janet TAYLOR
88 Dir Center Ops San Ysidro ... Ms. Cynthia K. NAGURA
88 Director Crown Cove Aq Ctr ... Ms. Patrice MILKOVICH
37 Director Financial Aid/Veterans ... Ms. Patti LARKIN
07 Director Admissions/Records ... Mr. Nicholas MONTEZ
96 Dir Procurement/Cntrl Svc/Risk Mgt ... Ms. Priya JEROME
35 Dean Student Services ... Dr. Malia FLOOD
88 Director EOPS ... Mr. Omar ORIHUELA
21 Director of Finance ... Mr. Wayne YANDA
88 Director Child Development Center ... Ms. Patricia BARTOW
04 Exec Asst to Superintendent ... Ms. Mary GANIO
19 Acting Police Chief ... Mr. Davis NIGHSWONGER
13 Chief Info Technology Officer (CIO) ... Mr. Daniel BORGES
28 Director Equity/Inclusion/Diversi ... Dr. Guadalupe CORONA
102 Director Foundation ... Ms. Zaneta ENCARNACION
88 Director Student Development ... Mr. Brett ROBERTSON
18 Director Facilities/Operations ... Ms. Charlotte ZOLEZZI

Southwestern Law School (I)

3050 Wilshire Boulevard, Los Angeles CA 90010-1106
County: Los Angeles FICE Identification: 001295
Unit ID: 123970
Telephone: (213) 738-6700 Carnegie Class: Spec-4-yr-Law
FAX Number: (213) 383-1688 Calendar System: Semester
URL: www.swlaw.edu
Established: 1911 Annual Graduate Tuition & Fees: N/A
Enrollment: 1,031 Coed
Affiliation or Control: Independent Non-Profit IRS Status: 501(c)3
Highest Offering: Master's; No Undergraduates
Accreditation: LAW

01 Chief Executive Officer ... Ms. Susan WESTERBERG PRAGER
10 Chief Financial Officer ... Mr. Paul KALUSH
04 Corporate Secretary ... Ms. Janis K. YOKOYAMA
03 Vice Dean ... Mr. Christopher CAMERON
32 Dean of Students & Div Aff ... Ms. Nydia DUENEZ
05 Dean Academic Affairs ... Ms. Susan WESTERBERG PRAGER
20 Sr Assoc Dean for Academic Admin ... Ms. Doreen E. HEYER
111 Assoc Dean for Institutional Advanc ... Ms. Debra L. LEATHERS
07 Asst Dean of Admissions ... Ms. Lisa L. GEAR
35 Assoc Dean of Student Affairs ... Dr. Robert MENA
37 Director of Financial Aid ... Ms. Lina BORJORQUEZ
11 Assoc Dean Administrative Services ... Ms. Marcie CANAL
06 Director of Reg and Academic Record ... Ms. Jessica JOHNSON
103 Director of Career Svcs ... Ms. Shahrzad POORMOSLEH
28 Dean of Students & Diversity Affair ... Ms. Nydia DUENEZ

Spartan College of Aeronautics and Technology (A)

8911 Aviation Blvd, Inglewood CA 90301
County: Los Angeles FICE Identification: 025964
Unit ID: 413680
Telephone: (310) 879-0554 Carnegie Class: Not Classified
FAX Number: N/A Calendar System: Other
URL: www.spartan.edu
Established: 2014 Annual Undergrad Tuition & Fees: N/A
Enrollment: 457 Coed
Affiliation or Control: Proprietary IRS Status: Proprietary
Highest Offering: Associate Degree
Accreditation: #COE

01 President .... Dennis MANZO

Stanbridge University (B)

2041 Business Center Dr., Suite 107, Irvine CA 92612
County: Orange FICE Identification: 038893
Unit ID: 446561
Telephone: (949) 794-9090 Carnegie Class: Spec-4-yr-Other Health
FAX Number: (949) 794-9098 Calendar System: Other
URL: www.stanbridge.edu
Established: 1996 Annual Undergrad Tuition & Fees: N/A
Enrollment: 1,134 Coed
Affiliation or Control: Proprietary IRS Status: Proprietary
Highest Offering: Master's
Accreditation: ACCSC, NURSE, OT, OTA, PTAA

01 Chief Executive Officer .... Yasith WEERASURIYA
10 Chief Financial Officer .... Nazi MASOUM
05 Vice Pres of Instruction .... Dr. Elizabeth RILEY
105 VP of Internet and Media Technology .... Monir BOKTOR
66 Director of Nursing .... Renee HYPOLITE
66 Program Director - RN .... Bobbie Ann MURPHY
66 BSN & MSN Program Director .... Dr. Janet BAGHOOMIAN
75 Director of Occupational Therapy .... Satch PURCELL
75 MSOT Program Director .... Dr. Janis DAVIS
88 Director of Physical Therapy .... Elizabeth PEYTON
106 Asst Director of Online Programs .... Jered MADRID
20 Dean of Instruction .... Tim POWERS
32 Dean of Students .... Elizabeth PEYTON
37 Director of Financial Aid .... Brian SILVANO
07 Director of Admissions .... Edward RIEPMA
74 Asst Program Director ASVT .... Emma CUSACK
74 Asst Program Director ASVT .... Karen HARTMAN
07 Director Admissions .... Edward RIEPMA
08 Librarian .... Frederick POLING
36 Career Services Coordinator .... Darleen HICKSON
29 Alumni & Community Service Coord .... Nataly MCBRIDE

Stanford University (C)

450 Serra Mall, Stanford CA 94305-2004
County: Santa Clara FICE Identification: 001305
Unit ID: 243744
Telephone: (650) 723-2300 Carnegie Class: DU-Highest
FAX Number: (650) 725-6847 Calendar System: Quarter
URL: www.stanford.edu
Established: 1885 Annual Undergrad Tuition & Fees: $47,940
Enrollment: 16,980 Coed
Affiliation or Control: Independent Non-Profit IRS Status: 501(c)3
Highest Offering: Doctorate
Accreditation: WC, ARCPA, ENG, IPSY, LAW, MED, PDPSY

01 President .... Dr. Marc TESSIER-LAVIGNE
43 Vice President & General Counsel .... Ms. Debra L. ZUMWALT
05 Provost .... Dr. Persis DRELL
30 Vice President for Development .... Mr. Martin SHELL
10 Vice President Business Affairs/CFO .... Mr. Randy LIVINGSTON
86 Vice President for Public Affairs .... Mr. David F. DEMAREST
88 Vice President SLAC Nat Accel Lab .... Dr. William J. MADIA
15 Vice President for Human Resources ... Ms. Elizabeth ZACHARIAS
26 Vice President for Communications .... Ms. Lisa A. LAPIN
29 President of Alumni Association .... Mr. Howard E. WOLF
46 Vice Provost/Dean of Research .... Dr. Ann ARVIN
20 Vice Provost for Academic Affairs .... Dr. Stephanie KALFAYAN
88 Vice Provost Faculty Development .... Ms. Karen COOK
20 Senior Vice Provost for Education .... Mr. Harry J. ELAM
18 Vice Provost for Land & Buildings .... Mr. Robert C. REIDY
114 Vice Provost Budget & Auxiliaries .... Mr. Timothy R. WARNER
32 Vice Provost Student Affairs .... Mr. Gregory E. BOARDMAN
100 Chief of Staff .... Ms. Megan PIERSON
63 Dean School of Medicine .... Dr. Lloyd MINOR
50 Dean Graduate School Business .... Dr. Jonathan LEVIN
65 Dean School of Earth Sciences .... Dr. Pamela A. MATSON
53 Dean School of Education .... Dr. Daniel SCHWARTZ
54 Dean School of Engineering .... Dr. Jennifer WIDOM
49 Dean School Humanities & Sciences .... Mr. Richard P. SALLER
61 Dean School of Law .... Ms. M. Elizabeth MAGILL
87 Dean Summer Session/Cont Stds ..... Dr. Charles L. JUNKERMAN
42 Dean for Religious Life .... Rev. Jane SHAW
88 Director Hoover Institution .... Dr. Thomas GILLIGAN
88 Director Stanford Lin Accelerator .... Mr. Chi-Chang KAO
13 Executive Director IT Services .... Mr. Bill CLEBSCH
08 University Librarian .... Mr. Michael A. KELLER
41 Athletic Director .... Mr. Bernard MUIR
07 Dean of Admission and Financial Aid .... Mr. Richard SHAW
88 CEO Stanford Management Company .... Mr. Robert WALLACE
118 Director of Compensation .... Ms. Linda S. LEE
21 AVP of Business Development .... Ms. Susan L. WEINSTEIN
06 Registrar .... Mr. Thomas BLACK
36 Director Career Development Center .... Mr. Farouk DEY
09 Dir Inst Research/Assessment .... Ms. Corrie POTTER
37 Director of Student Financial Aid .... Ms. Karen S. COOPER
27 Sr Director Stanford News Service .... Ms. Donna LOVELL
19 Director Public Safety .... Ms. Laura L. WILSON
96 Chief Procurement Officer .... Mr. Ben MORENO
35 Director of Student Activities .... Ms. Nanci HOWE
38 Director Student Counseling .... Dr. Ronald ALBURCHER
101 Secretary of the Board of Trustees .... Mr. Phil TAUBMAN
102 Dir Foundation/Corporate Relations .... Ms. Kathy VEIT
104 Director Study Abroad .... Ms. Irene KENNEDY
39 Director Student Housing .... Mr. Roger WHITNEY
88 Director Knight-Hennessy Scholars .... Dr. John L. HENNESSY

Starr King School for the Ministry (D)

2441 Le Conte Avenue, Berkeley CA 94709-1299
County: Alameda FICE Identification: 004080
Unit ID: 123916
Telephone: (510) 845-6232 Carnegie Class: Spec-4-yr-Faith
FAX Number: (510) 845-6273 Calendar System: Semester
URL: www.sksm.edu
Established: 1904 Annual Graduate Tuition & Fees: N/A
Enrollment: 85 Coed
Affiliation or Control: Unitarian Universalist IRS Status: 501(c)3
Highest Offering: Master's; No Undergraduates
Accreditation: THEOL

01 President .... Rev. Rosemary Bray MCNATT
30 Vice President Advancement .... Ms. Jessica CLOUD
10 VP for Finance & Admin .... Ms. Jane KOLMODIN
05 Dean of the Faculty .... Dr. Gabriella LETTINI
06 Registrar .... Rev. Sonsiris TAMAYO
07 Director of Admissions/Recruitment .... Mr. Jeremiah KALENDAE
106 Director Online Education .... Dr. Hugo CORDOVA QUERO
26 Communications Officer .... Mr. Matt VIOLET

*State Center Community College District (E)

1525 E Weldon Avenue, Fresno CA 93704-6398
County: Fresno FICE Identification: 001306
Unit ID: 123925
Telephone: (559) 244-5900 Carnegie Class: N/A
FAX Number: N/A
URL: www.scccd.edu

01 Chancellor .... Dr. Paul PARNELL
10 Vice Chancellor Finance & Admin .... Mr. Edwin ENG
05 VC Educ Svcs/Inst Effectiveness .... Mr. Jerome COUNTEE
15 Vice Chanc Human Resources .... Ms. Julianna MOSIER
11 Assc Vice Chanc Business/Operations . Ms. Christine MIKTARIAN
07 AVC Enroll Mgmt/Admiss & Records/IS .... Vacant
26 Exec Dir Pub/Legislative Rels .... Ms. Lucy RUIZ
102 Executive Director Foundation .... Mr. Rico GUERRERO
43 General Counsel .... Mr. Gregory TAYLOR
25 Dir Grants/External Funding .... Ms. Cherylyn CRILL-HORNSBY
16 Director Human Resources .... Ms. Samerah CAMPBELL
96 Director of Purchasing .... Mr. Randy VOGT
21 Director of Finance .... Mr. William SCHOFIELD
13 Director of Information Systems .... Mr. Scott OLDS
88 Director of Classified Personnel .... Ms. Elba GOMEZ

*Clovis Community College (F)

10309 N. Willow Avenue, Fresno CA 93730
County: Fresno Identification: 667125
Unit ID: 489201
Telephone: (559) 325-5200 Carnegie Class: Not Classified
FAX Number: (559) 499-6065 Calendar System: Semester
URL: www.cloviscollege.edu
Established: 2007 Annual Undergrad Tuition & Fees (In-District): $1,304
Enrollment: N/A Coed
Affiliation or Control: State/Local IRS Status: 501(c)3
Highest Offering: Associate Degree
Accreditation: WJ

02 President .... Dr. Lori BENNETT
05 VP Instruction & Student Services .... Ms. Kelly FOWLER
10 VP Administrative Services .... Ms. Lorrie HOPPER
79 Dean of Instruction .... Mr. James ORTEZ
75 Dean of Instruction CTE .... Dr. Roberta KUNKEL
88 Dean of Instruction .... Dr. John FORBES
32 Dean of Students .... Ms. Kira TIPPINS
13 Director of Technology .... Dr. John FORBES
26 Director of Marketing .... Ms. Stephanie BABB
88 Dir Student Success/Equity/Outrch .... Ms. Gurdeep HEBERT
09 Director of Institutional Research .... Dr. James ATKINSON
12 Director of Herndon Campus .... Mr. Charles FRANCIS
41 Athletic Director .... Ms. Susan YATES
37 Director of Financial Aid .... Vacant
07 Admissions & Records Manager .... Ms. Reynani HAWKINS
04 Assistant to the President .... Ms. Emilie GERETY

*Fresno City College (G)

1101 E University Avenue, Fresno CA 93741-0002
County: Fresno FICE Identification: 001307
Unit ID: 114789
Telephone: (559) 442-4600 Carnegie Class: Assoc/MT-VT-High Trad
FAX Number: (559) 499-6045 Calendar System: Semester
URL: www.fresnocitycollege.edu
Established: 1910 Annual Undergrad Tuition & Fees (In-District): $1,304
Enrollment: 22,697 Coed
Affiliation or Control: State/Local IRS Status: 501(c)3
Highest Offering: Associate Degree
Accreditation: WJ, CAHIIM, COARC, DH, RAD

02 President .... Dr. Carole GOLDSMITH
05 Int Vice President of Instruction .... Mr. Don LOPEZ
32 VP of Student Services .... Vacant
10 Vice Pres Administrative Services .... Ms. Cheryl SULLIVAN
07 District Dean Admissions & Records .... Ms. Mirna DUARTE
08 Dean Student Success/Learning .... Ms. Laurel PRYSIAZNY
50 Dean Business Division .... Mr. Rojelio VASQUEZ
57 Dean Fine Perform Commun Arts .... Mr. Neil VANDERPOOL
79 Dean Humanities Division .... Dr. Jennifer JOHNSON
54 Dean Math/Science/Engineering Div .... Ms. Shirley MCMANUS
83 Dean Social Sciences Division .... Dr. Margaret E. MERICLE
76 Dean Health Sciences Division .... Ms. Lorraine SMITH
72 Dean Applied Technology Division .... Ms. Becky BARABE
38 Dean Counseling-Guidance .... Ms. Monica CUEVAS
35 Dean of Student Services .... Mr. Sean HENDERSON
103 Dean Workforce Development & CTC .... Dr. Tim WOODS
75 Int Director FCC Training Institute .... Mr. Rob WEIL
22 Dir Disabled Student Pgms & Svcs .... Dr. Stephanie CROSBY
09 Director Institutional Research .... Dr. Lijuan ZHAI
88 Director Police Academy .... Mr. Gary FIEF
35 Int Director of Student Activities .... Mr. Ernie MARTINEZ
26 Director Marketing/Communications .... Ms. Cris M. BREMER
37 Director Financial Aid .... Ms. Mikki JOHNSON
27 Public Information Officer .... Ms. Kathleen BONILLA
41 Athletic Director .... Mr. Eric SWAIN
38 Dir Distance Education/Inst Tech .... Dr. Jodie STEELEY
72 Interim Director of Technology .... Mr. Harry ZAHLIS
36 Dir College Relations & Outreach .... Ms. Emilee SLATER
66 Director of Nursing .... Dr. Stephanie R. ROBINSON
88 Acting Director CalWORKs Program .... Ms. Mary Beth MOSSETTE
06 Director Admissions & Records .... Ms. Robin TORRES
88 Director TRIO Programs .... Mr. Perry ANGLE
88 Director EOPS/CARE .... Mr. Thomas GAXIOLA

*Reedley College (H)

995 N Reed Avenue, Reedley CA 93654-2099
County: Fresno FICE Identification: 001308
Unit ID: 117052
Telephone: (559) 638-0300 Carnegie Class: Assoc/MT-VT-High Trad
FAX Number: N/A Calendar System: Semester
URL: www.reedleycollege.edu
Established: 1926 Annual Undergrad Tuition & Fees (In-District): $1,304
Enrollment: 9,836 Coed
Affiliation or Control: State/Local IRS Status: 501(c)3
Highest Offering: Associate Degree
Accreditation: WJ

02 President .... Dr. Sandra CALDWELL
05 Vice President of Instruction .... Mr. Dale VAN DAM
11 Vice Pres Administrative Svcs .... Ms. Donna BERRY
32 Vice Pres of Student Services .... Ms. Renee CRAIG-MARIUS
12 Vice Pres Madera/Oakhurst Centers .... Dr. Claudia HABIB
20 Dean of Instruction/Agri/Nat Res .... Mr. David CLARK
79 Dean of Instruction/Humanities .... Dr. G. Todd DAVIS
81 Dean Instruct/Math/Sci/Tech/PE/Hlth .... Ms. Marie BYRD-HARRIS
88 Dean Instruct/Madera/Oakhurst Ctrs ..... Dr. Ganesan SRINIVASAN
35 Dean of Student Services .... Ms. Leticia CANALES
26 Dir Marketing/Communication .... Ms. Renee DELPORT
22 Dir Disabled Student Programs/Svcs .... Dr. Samuel MORGAN
22 Director EOPS .... Mr. Mario GONZALES
13 Director of Technology .... Mr. Gary SAKAGUCHI
37 Financial Aid Manager .... Ms. Chris CORTES
07 Admissions & Records Mgr/Registrar .... Ms. Veronica JURY
08 Librarian .... Ms. Shivon HESS

SUM Bible College and Theological Seminary (I)

735 105th Avenue, Oakland CA 94603-3603
County: Alameda FICE Identification: 037524
Unit ID: 447953
Telephone: (510) 567-6174 Carnegie Class: Spec-4-yr-Faith
FAX Number: (510) 568-1024 Calendar System: Trimester
URL: www.sum.edu
Established: 1999 Annual Undergrad Tuition & Fees: $10,144
Enrollment: 588 Coed
Affiliation or Control: Independent Non-Profit IRS Status: 501(c)3
Highest Offering: Master's
Accreditation: @WC, BI

01 President/Chancellor .... Rev. George NEAU
11 Vice President Cohort Development .... Dr. Elsie COOK
05 Chief Academic Officer .... Dr. Bruce COATS
10 Vice President Finance .... Mr. Robert HORNICK
26 Vice Pres Marketing/Enrollment .... Mr. Mike SAVAGE
42 Dean of Student Ministry .... Vacant
08 Director of the Library .... Ms. Catherine DIETERLY
32 Dean of Student Life .... Vacant
20 Assistant to the Vice President .... Mr. Joey Alan LE
06 Registrar/Institutional Research .... Ms. Lauren WALDROFF
37 Financial Aid Director .... Mrs. Rose STADLER
07 Director of Admissions .... Ms. Taia STEFOGLO
88 US Cohort Director .... Vacant

21 Business Administrator ....Ms. Judith LITTLETON

† Affiliated with School of Urban Missions-New Orleans, Gretna, LA.

Taft College (A)

29 Cougar Court, Taft CA 93268-2329
County: Kern FICE Identification: 001309
Unit ID: 124113
Telephone: (661) 763-7700 Carnegie Class: Assoc/HT-High Non
FAX Number: (661) 763-7703 Calendar System: Semester
URL: www.taftcollege.edu
Established: 1922 Annual Undergrad Tuition & Fees (In-District): $1,134
Enrollment: 4,449 Coed
Affiliation or Control: State/Local IRS Status: 501(c)3
Highest Offering: Associate Degree
Accreditation: WJ, DH

01 Superintendent/President ....Dr. Debra DANIELS
10 Exec Vice Pres/Administrative Svcs ....Mr. Brock MCMURRAY
05 Vice President of Instruction ....Mr. Mark WILLIAMS
32 Vice Pres of Student Services ....Mr. Severo BALASON, JR.
04 Assistant to the President ....Ms. Sarah CRISS
30 Director Foundation & Development ....Ms. Sheri HORN BUNK
13 Director Information Services ....Vacant
08 Research and Instruction Librarian ....Ms. Terri SMITH
46 Coord Inst Research/Assessment/Plng ....Mr. Oleg BESPALOV
41 Director Athletics ....Ms. Kanoe BANDY
15 Asst VP of Human Resources ....Dr. Robert METEAU
21 Director of Fiscal Services ....Ms. Amanda BAUER
07 Director of Admissions & Records ....Vacant
18 Supervisor Maintenance/Operations ....Mr. Michael CAPELA
37 Director Student Financial Aid ....Ms. Barbara AMERIO
88 Dean of Student Success ....Ms. Primavera ARVIZU

Taft Law School (B)

3700 South Susan Street, Office 200,
Santa Ana CA 92704-6954
County: Orange Identification: 666398
Telephone: (714) 850-4800 Carnegie Class: Not Classified
FAX Number: (714) 708-2082 Calendar System: Other
URL: www.taftu.edu
Established: 1976 Annual Undergrad Tuition & Fees: N/A
Enrollment: N/A Coed
Affiliation or Control: Proprietary IRS Status: Proprietary
Highest Offering: Doctorate
Accreditation: DEAC

01 Chancellor ....Mr. David L. BOYD
05 Dean ....Mr. Robert K. STROUSE
86 VP of Governmental Relations ....Ms. Joan L. SLAVIN
20 Associate Dean ....Ms. Melody JOLLY
37 Director of Financial Aid ....Ms. Tina M. SAXON

Teachers College of San Joaquin (C)

2857 Transworld Dr, Stockton CA 95206
County: San Joaquin Identification: 667087
Telephone: (209) 468-4926 Carnegie Class: Not Classified
FAX Number: (209) 468-9124 Calendar System: Semester
URL: teacherscollegesj.edu
Established: 2009 Annual Graduate Tuition & Fees: N/A
Enrollment: N/A Coed
Affiliation or Control: State IRS Status: 501(c)3
Highest Offering: Master's; No Undergraduates
Accreditation: WC

01 President ....Dr. Diane CARNAHAN
06 Registrar/Admissions ....Mr. Harold RUSSELL III
58 Director Graduate Studies ....Dr. Sylvia TURNER
04 Administrative Asst to President ....Ms. Victoria L. DE PRATER
10 Chief Business Officer ....Mr. Scott ANDERSON
07 Director of Admissions ....Ms. Michele BADOVINAC
09 Director of Institutional Research ....Dr. Sylvia TURNER

Theatre of Arts (D)

1536 N Highland Avenue, Hollywood CA 90028
County: Los Angeles Identification: 667098
Unit ID: 486123
Telephone: (323) 463-2500 Carnegie Class: Not Classified
FAX Number: (323) 463-2500 Calendar System: Trimester
URL: www.toa.edu
Established: 1927 Annual Undergrad Tuition & Fees: $19,800
Enrollment: 49 Coed
Affiliation or Control: Proprietary IRS Status: Proprietary
Highest Offering: Associate Degree
Accreditation: THEA

00 President ....Amir KORANGY
01 Executive Director ....Jason WEISS
84 Manager Enrollment Services ....Michael JURY
11 Chief of Administration ....Elizabeth INIGUEZ

Thomas Aquinas College (E)

10,000 Ojai Road, Santa Paula CA 93060-9621
County: Ventura FICE Identification: 023580
Unit ID: 124292
Telephone: (805) 525-4417 Carnegie Class: Bac-A&S
FAX Number: (805) 525-9342 Calendar System: Semester
URL: www.thomasaquinas.edu
Established: 1971 Annual Undergrad Tuition & Fees: $24,500
Enrollment: 377 Coed
Affiliation or Control: Independent Non-Profit IRS Status: 501(c)3
Highest Offering: Baccalaureate
Accreditation: WC

01 President ....Dr. Michael F. MCLEAN
04 Secretary to the President ....Miss Sarah J. KAISER
26 Asst to Pres/Dir College Relations ....Mrs. Anne S. FORSYTH
30 Vice President for Development ....Dr. Paul J. O'REILLY
43 General Counsel ....Mr. John Q. MASTELLER
10 Vice President for Admn & Finance ....Mr. Peter L. DELUCA
05 Academic Dean ....Dr. John GOYETTE
30 Director of Development ....Mr. Robert A. BAGDAZIAN
112 Director of Gift Planning ....Mr. Thomas J. SUSANKA
44 Director of the Annual Fund ....Mr. Paul LAZENBY
07 Director of Admissions ....Mr. Jonathan P. DALY
21 Supervisor Business/Finance ....Mr. Michael COLLINS
37 Director of Financial Aid ....Mr. Gregory J. BECHER
32 Asst Dean for Student Affairs ....Dr. Christopher DECAEN
06 Registrar/Dir of Student Placement ....Mr. Mark KRETSCHMER
08 Librarian ....Ms. Richena CURPHEY
42 Chaplain ....Fr. Paul RAFTERY, OP
27 Communications Manager ....Mr. Christopher WEINKOPF
88 Development Database Manager ....Mr. Aaron DUNKEL
102 Dir Foundation/Corporate Relations ....Mrs. Sharon REISER

Thomas Jefferson School of Law (F)

1155 Island Avenue, San Diego CA 92101
County: San Diego FICE Identification: 010854
Unit ID: 126049
Telephone: (619) 297-9700 Carnegie Class: Spec-4-yr-Law
FAX Number: (619) 961-4370 Calendar System: Semester
URL: www.tjsl.edu
Established: 1969 Annual Graduate Tuition & Fees: N/A
Enrollment: 700 Coed
Affiliation or Control: Independent Non-Profit IRS Status: 501(c)3
Highest Offering: Doctorate; No Undergraduates
Accreditation: @WC, LAW

01 President and Dean ....Dean Joan BULLOCK
05 Vice Dean & Assoc Dean Acad Affairs ....Dean Linda KELLER
43 Vice President and General Counsel ....Karin K. SHERR
04 Exec Asst to the President/Dean ....Jan DAUSS
10 VP and Chief Financial Officer ....Nancy VU
111 VP for Institutional Advancement ....Beth SAVAGE
26 Dir of Marketing and Communications ....Edgar HOPIDA
32 Assistant Dean for Student Affairs ....Lisa FERREIRA
88 Asst Dean for Prog Devel & Dist Ed ....Jason FISKE
84 Asst Dean of Enrollment
Mgmnt ....Michelle SLAUGHTER ALLISON
88 Asst Dir Recruitment and Outreach ....Leah STRALEY
08 Library Director ....Leigh INMAN
36 Director of Career Services ....Jeffrey CHINN
20 Director of Academic Administration ....Jody LASALLE
37 Director of Financial Assistance ....Marc BERMAN
06 Registrar ....Carrie KAZYAKA
21 Financial Operations Specialist ....Anh PHAN
88 Externship Director/Pro Bono ....Judybeth TROPP
15 Director of Human Resources ....Lisa CHIGOS
13 Director of IT ....Gil SUSANA
18 Director of Facilities ....Dennis SABLE

Touro College Los Angeles (G)

1317 N Crescent Heights Blvd,
West Hollywood CA 90046-4506
County: Los Angeles Identification: 770944
Unit ID: 459727
Telephone: (323) 822-9700 Carnegie Class: Not Classified
FAX Number: (310) 654-2086 Calendar System: Semester
URL: tcla.touro.edu/
Established: 2005 Annual Undergrad Tuition & Fees: $14,600
Enrollment: 880 Coed
Affiliation or Control: Independent Non-Profit IRS Status: 501(c)3
Highest Offering: Baccalaureate
Accreditation: WC

01 CEO ....Dr. Yoram NEUMANN
03 Provost ....Dr. Edith NEUMANN
05 Dean ....Rabbi David JACOBSON
07 Director of Admissions ....Ms. Leah MIZRAHI
09 Dir Inst Research/Assessment ....Dr. Aaron BROWNSTEIN
10 Chief Business Officer/Bursar ....Mr. Kamran MANUEL
06 Registrar & Fin Aid Coordinator ....Ms. Rivka WEINBERG

† Branch campus of Touro University Worldwide, Los Alamitos, CA.

Touro University California (H)

1310 Club Drive, Vallejo CA 94592
County: Solano FICE Identification: 041426
Unit ID: 459736
Telephone: (707) 638-5200 Carnegie Class: Spec-4-yr-Med
FAX Number: (707) 638-5255 Calendar System: Trimester
URL: www.tu.edu
Established: 1997 Annual Undergrad Tuition & Fees: N/A
Enrollment: 1,386 Coed
Affiliation or Control: Independent Non-Profit IRS Status: 501(c)3
Highest Offering: Doctorate
Accreditation: WC, ARCPA, NURSE, OSTEO, PH, PHAR

01 President & CEO Univ System ....Dr. Alan KADISH
12 Sr Provost/CEO Touro Western Div ....Hon. Shelley BERKLEY
05 Provost & COO ....Dr. Marilyn HOPKINS
32 Dean of Students ....Dr. Lisa WAITS
35 Associate Dean of Students ....Dr. James BINKERD
07 Director of Admissions ....Mr. Steven DAVIS
09 AVP Institutional Effectiveness ....Dr. Meiling TANG
10 Dir of Fiscal Affairs & Accounting ....Ms. Amber SHOMO
15 Director Human Resources ....Ms. Kathy LOWE
11 Associate VP of Administration ....Mr. Jay RITCHIE
08 Director University Library ....Ms. Tamara TRUJILLO
63 Dean College of Osteopathic Med ....Dr. Michael CLEARFIELD
67 Dean College of Pharmacy ....Dr. Rae MATSUMOTO
53 Dean Col of Education & Health Sci ....Dr. Jim O'CONNOR
13 Director of Information Technology ....Vacant
30 AVP Univ Advancement ....Ms. Andrea GARCIA
37 Financial Aid Director ....Ms. Kim KANE
35 Director of Campus Life ....Rabbi Elchonon TENENBAUM
23 Director of Student Health Center ....Ms. Judith CORTE
06 Registrar ....Mr. Ron TRAVENICK

Touro University Worldwide (I)

10601 Calle Lee Ste 179, Los Alamitos CA 90720
County: Orange FICE Identification: 041425
Unit ID: 459727
Telephone: (818) 575-6800 Carnegie Class: Masters/S
FAX Number: (818) 707-0316 Calendar System: Semester
URL: www.tuw.edu
Established: 2005 Annual Undergrad Tuition & Fees: $14,600
Enrollment: 880 Coed
Affiliation or Control: Independent Non-Profit IRS Status: 501(c)3
Highest Offering: Doctorate
Accreditation: WC

01 CEO ....Dr. Yoram NEUMANN
05 Provost & Chief Academic Officer ....Dr. Edith NEUMANN
10 Chief Financial Officer (CFO) ....Mr. Jayson CAPUNO
11 Chief Operating Officer (COO) ....Mr. Roy FINALY

Trident University International (J)

5757 Plaza Drive, Suite 100, Cypress CA 90630
County: Orange FICE Identification: 041279
Unit ID: 450979
Telephone: (714) 816-0366 Carnegie Class: DU-Mod
FAX Number: (714) 816-0367 Calendar System: Semester
URL: www.trident.edu
Established: 1998 Annual Undergrad Tuition & Fees: $9,000
Enrollment: 7,684 Coed
Affiliation or Control: Proprietary IRS Status: Proprietary
Highest Offering: Doctorate
Accreditation: WC

01 President/CEO ....Mr. Travis J. ALLEN
10 Chief Financial Officer ....Mr. David BARRETT
05 Interim Provost ....Dr. Afshin AFROOKHTEH
13 Exec Vice President/CIO ....Mr. Vahid SHARIAT
88 SVP/Chief Compliance Officer ....Dr. Afshin AFROOKHTEH
20 Dean of University Studies and Ext ....Vacant
50 Dean GJ Col Business/Info Systems ....Dr. Debra LOUIS
04 Executive Assistant ....Ms. Patricia PARKS
15 Director Human Resources ....Ms. Melissa ROTHMEYER
06 Registrar ....Ms. Abby DOLAN
37 Student Finance Manager ....Ms. Brittney DRAKE
09 Director of Institutional Research ....Dr. Heidi SATO
08 Librarian ....Ms. Leslie ANDERSEN
21 Director of Financial Operation ....Mr. Scott PAK
76 Dean Educ/Health Sciences ....Dr. Mickey SHACHAR
07 Vice President of Admissions ....Ms. Elizabeth HARRIS
18 Facilities Manager ....Mr. Fred WILSON
101 Board of Trustees Secretary ....Mr. Brian VAN KLOMPENBERG

Trinity Law School (K)

2200 N Grand Avenue, Santa Ana CA 92705
Telephone: (714) 836-7500 Identification: 770098
Accreditation: &NH

† Branch campus of Trinity International University, Deerfield, IL

Trinity School of Health and Allied Sciences (L)

1149 W. 190th St., Ste 2000, Gardena CA 90248
County: Los Angeles FICE Identification: 041601
Unit ID: 459161
Telephone: (310) 834-3065 Carnegie Class: Not Classified
FAX Number: (310) 834-6236 Calendar System: Semester
URL: www.tshas.edu
Established: 2002 Annual Undergrad Tuition & Fees: $23,587
Enrollment: 101 Coed
Affiliation or Control: Proprietary IRS Status: Proprietary
Highest Offering: Baccalaureate
Accreditation: ABHES

01 President/CEO ....Dr. Estrella AGUINALDO
05 COO/Academic Dean ....Violeta BELLO

Union University of California (A)

14200 Goldenwest Street, Westminster CA 92683
County: Orange Identification: 667269
Telephone: (714) 903-2762 Carnegie Class: Not Classified
FAX Number: N/A Calendar System: Semester
URL: www.uuc.edu
Established: 1986 Annual Graduate Tuition & Fees: N/A
Enrollment: N/A Coed
Affiliation or Control: Independent Non-Profit IRS Status: 501(c)3
Highest Offering: Master's; No Undergraduates
Accreditation: DEAC

01 President .... Dr. Linh DOAN
03 Senior Vice President .... Dr. Son Xuan NGUYEN
05 Vice President Academic Affairs .... Dr. Margaret SCOTT
32 Vice Pres Student Affairs .... Dr. Kim-Lien THI NGO
13 Chief Information Officer .... Mr. Thai-Hoa NGUYEN

United Education Institute (B)

6055 Pacific Boulevard, Huntington Park CA 90255
County: Los Angeles FICE Identification: 025593
Unit ID: 124681
Telephone: (323) 319-9500 Carnegie Class: Spec 2-yr-Other
FAX Number: (949) 788-2505 Calendar System: Other
URL: www.uei.edu
Established: 1986 Annual Undergrad Tuition & Fees: N/A
Enrollment: 624 Coed
Affiliation or Control: Proprietary IRS Status: Proprietary
Highest Offering: Associate Degree
Accreditation: CNCE

01 Executive Area President .... Mr. J.C RIVAS

United States University (C)

7675 Mission Valley Road, San Diego CA 92108
County: San Diego FICE Identification: 040053
Unit ID: 447050
Telephone: (629) 876-4250 Carnegie Class: Bac-Diverse
FAX Number: N/A Calendar System: Semester
URL: www.usuniversity.edu
Established: 1997 Annual Undergrad Tuition & Fees: $11,880
Enrollment: 365 Coed
Affiliation or Control: Proprietary IRS Status: Proprietary
Highest Offering: Master's
Accreditation: WC, NURSE

01 President and CEO .... Dr. Steven A. STARGARDTER
05 Provost/Chief Academic Officer .... Dr. Jennifer NEWMANN
07 VP of Enroll Mgmt/Stdnt Svcs/Mktg .... Vacant
10 Chief Financial Officer .... Will TITERA
88 Director of International Affairs .... Vacant
20 Assoc Provost Accred/Curriculum .... Dr. Elizabeth ARCHER
66 Dean College of Nursing .... Dr. Renee MCLEOD
06 Registrar .... Jennifer STROBEL
29 Director Alumni Relations .... Vacant
37 Director Student Financial Aid .... Natalie ROBINSON

Unitek College (D)

4670 Auto Mall Parkway, Fremont CA 94538
County: Alameda FICE Identification: 041697
Unit ID: 459204
Telephone: (888) 775-1514 Carnegie Class: Spec-4-yr-Other Health
FAX Number: (510) 249-9125 Calendar System: Other
URL: www.unitekcollege.edu
Established: 1992 Annual Undergrad Tuition & Fees: $33,110
Enrollment: 821 Coed
Affiliation or Control: Proprietary IRS Status: Proprietary
Highest Offering: Baccalaureate
Accreditation: ACCSC, NURSE

01 Director .... Mr. Benjamin ELIAS

University of Antelope Valley (E)

44055 Sierra Hwy, Lancaster CA 93534
County: Los Angeles FICE Identification: 034275
Unit ID: 442930
Telephone: (661) 726-1911 Carnegie Class: Bac/Assoc-Mixed
FAX Number: (661) 726-5158 Calendar System: Other
URL: www.uav.edu
Established: 1997 Annual Undergrad Tuition & Fees: N/A
Enrollment: 487 Coed
Affiliation or Control: Proprietary IRS Status: Proprietary
Highest Offering: Master's
Accreditation: WC, EMT

01 President .... Mr. Marco JOHNSON
10 Vice President/CFO .... Ms. Sandra JOHNSON
05 Assoc Dean of Academic Affairs .... Ms. Chonnea HARRIS
32 Dean of Student Affairs .... Mr. Ronald FELTS
37 Financial Aid Director .... Ms. Araceli JIMENEZ
09 Dir Institutional Effectiveness .... Ms. Crystal STEPHENS
13 Director Information Technology .... Mr. Noel SANCHEZ
36 Director Career Services .... Ms. Karyn FRAHM
07 Director of Admissions .... Ms. Mirna TURCIOS

*University of California Office of the President (F)

1111 Franklin Street, 12th Floor, Oakland CA 94607-5200
County: Alameda FICE Identification: 001311
Unit ID: 124557
Telephone: (510) 987-0700 Carnegie Class: N/A
FAX Number: (510) 987-0328
URL: www.ucop.edu

01 President .... Janet NAPOLITANO
05 Provost/EVP Academic Affairs .... Aimee DORR
10 EVP/Chief Financial Officer .... Nathan E. BROSTROM
11 EVP/Chief Operating Officer .... Rachael NAVA
17 Exec Vice Pres UC Health .... John D. STOBO
26 Sr Vice Pres External Relations .... Julie HENDERSON
86 SVP Government Relations .... Nelson PEACOCK
108 Sr Vice Pres Compliance/Audit .... Sheryl S. VACCA
47 VP Agriculture/Natural Resources .... Barbara H. ALLEN-DIAZ
45 VP Budget & Capital Resources .... Patrick J. LENZ
44 Vice President of Investments .... Jagdeep S. BACHHER
09 Vice Pres Inst Rsrch/Acad Planning .... Pamela BROWN
88 VP Office of National Laboratories .... Kimberly S. BUDIL
15 Vice Pres Human Resources .... Dwaine B. DUCKETT
43 General Counsel/VP Legal Affairs .... Charles F. ROBINSON
32 Vice President Student Affairs .... Judy K. SAKAKI
46 Interim VP Innovation Alliance Svcs .... William TUCKER
13 CIO Information Technology Svcs .... Tom ANDRIOLA
20 Vice Provost/Chief Outreach Officer .... Yvette GULLATT
20 Vice Provost Academic Personnel .... Susan CARLSON
21 Int Assoc VP Budget Analysis/Plng .... David ALCOCER

*University of California-Berkeley (G)

Berkeley CA 94720-0001
County: Alameda FICE Identification: 001312
Unit ID: 110635
Telephone: (510) 642-6000 Carnegie Class: DU-Highest
FAX Number: (510) 643-5499 Calendar System: Semester
URL: www.berkeley.edu
Established: 1868 Annual Undergrad Tuition & Fees (In-State): $13,509
Enrollment: 38,189 Coed
Affiliation or Control: State IRS Status: 501(c)3
Highest Offering: Doctorate
Accreditation: WC, CLPSY, CS, DIETD, ENG, IPSY, LAW, LSAR, OPT, OPTR, PCSAS, PH, PLNG, SCPSY, SW

02 Chancellor .... Carol CHRIST
05 Exec Vice Chancellor/Provost .... Paul ALIVISATOS
11 Int Vice Chancellor Finance/Admin .... Scott BIDDY
10 Vice Chancellor/CFO .... Rosemarie RAE
32 Int Vice Chancellor Student Affairs .... Steve SUTTON
26 Vice Chanc University Relations .... Scott BIDDY
18 Vice Chancellor Real Estate .... Bob LALANNE
22 Vice Chanc Equity & Inclusion .... Oscar DUBON
43 Chief Campus Counsel .... Christopher M. PATTI
100 Assc Exec Vice Chanc/Chief of Staff .... Phyllis HOFFMAN
25 Asst VC Research Admin & Compliance .... Patrick SCHLESINGER
13 Asst Vice Chanc Info Technology .... Lyle NEVELS
84 Assc Vice Chanc Admiss & Enrollment .... Anne DE LUCA
87 AVP/Dn Summer Session/Study Abroad .... Richard RUSSO
27 Assoc VP Comm/Public Affairs .... Diana HARVEY
21 Asst Vice Chanc Finance/Controller .... Delphine REGALIA
07 Asst VC & Dir Undergrad Admissions .... Amy JARICH
35 Assc Vice Chanc/Dean of Students .... Joseph D. GREENWELL
37 Asst VC & Dir Fin Aid & Scholarship .... Rachelle FELDMAN
08 University Librarian .... Thomas C. LEONARD
06 Associate Registrar .... Johanna METZGAR
38 Dir Counseling & Psychological Svcs .... Jeff PRINCE
36 Director Career Center .... Thomas C. DEVLIN
41 Director of Athletics .... Michael WILLIAMS
58 Dean of the Graduate Division .... Fiona M. DOYLE
61 Dean of Law .... Erwin CHEMERINSKY
88 Dean of Optometry .... John FLANAGAN
54 Dean School of Engineering .... S. Shankar SASTRY
88 Dean of Environmental Design .... Jennifer WOLCH
65 Dean of Natural Resources .... J. Keith GILLESS
50 Dean of Haas School of Business .... Richard K. LYONS
70 Dean of Social Welfare .... Jeffrey EDELSON
88 Dean School of Information .... AnnaLee SAXENIAN
69 Dean of Public Health .... Stefano BERTOZZI
53 Dean of Education .... Prudence CARTER
60 Dean of Journalism .... Ed WASSERMAN
88 Dean of Chemistry .... Douglas S. CLARK
80 Dean Goldman School Public Policy .... Henry E. BRADY
79 Dean of Arts and Humanities .... Anthony CASCARDI
88 Dean of Biological Sciences .... Michael R. BOTCHAN
81 Dean Mathematical/Physical Sciences .... Frances HELLMAN
83 Dean of Social Sciences .... Carla HESSE
97 Dean of the Undergrad Division .... Bob JACOBSON
56 Dean of University Extension .... Diana WU

*University of California-Davis (H)

One Shields Avenue, Davis CA 95616-5270
County: Yolo FICE Identification: 001313
Unit ID: 110644
Telephone: (530) 752-1011 Carnegie Class: DU-Highest
FAX Number: N/A Calendar System: Quarter
URL: www.ucdavis.edu
Established: 1905 Annual Undergrad Tuition & Fees (In-State): $14,046
Enrollment: 35,186 Coed
Affiliation or Control: State IRS Status: 501(c)3
Highest Offering: Doctorate
Accreditation: WC, ARCPA, CS, DIETD, DIETI, ENG, IPSY, LAW, LSAR, MED, MT, NURSE, PAST, PH, VET

02 Chancellor .... Dr. Gary MAY
05 Provost & Exec Vice Chancellor .... Dr. Ralph J. HEXTER
100 Associate Chancellor .... Mr. Karl M. ENGELBACH
26 Int Strategic Communication Leader .... Ms. Dana TOPOUSIS
46 Interim Vice Chancellor Research .... Dr. Cameron S. CARTER
30 Vice Chanc Dev/Alumni Relations .... Dr. Shaun B. KEISTER
32 Vice Chancellor Student Affairs .... Dr. Adela I. DE LATORRE
10 Int Lead Finance/Operation & Admin .... Ms. Kelly RATLIFF
63 Interim VC Human Health Sciences .... Dr. Thomas S. NESBITT
17 CEO UCD Medical Center .... Ms. Ann M. RICE
66 Assoc VC/Dean Sch of Nursing .... Dr. Heather M. YOUNG
22 Assoc Exec VC Campus Cmty Relations .... Mr. Rahim REED
21 Sr Assoc VC Finance & Resource .... Ms. Kelly RATLIFF
88 Exec Assoc VC Research .... Dr. Cindy M. KIEL
88 Assoc VC Research .... Dr. Paul DODD
88 Assoc VC Research .... Dr. Dushyant PATHAK
15 Interim Chief Human Resources .... Ms. Brenda REBMAN
88 Assoc VC Accounting/Financial Svcs .... Mr. J. Michael ALLRED
88 Assoc VC Development .... Mr. Jason L. WOHLMAN
88 Assoc VC Development .... Mr. Paul PROKOP
88 Assoc VC Development Health Sci .... Ms. Chong U. PORTER
39 Assoc VC Student Affairs .... Ms. Emily GALINDO
84 Assoc VC Student Affairs .... Mr. John CAMPBELL
35 Assoc VC Student Affairs .... Dr. Milton LANG
07 Assoc VC Admissions & Enrollment .... Mr. Walter A. ROBINSON
88 Assoc VC Safety Services .... Mr. Eric KVIGNE
88 Assoc VC Design & Construct .... Mr. Clayton HALLIDAY
18 Assoc VC Facilities Management .... Mr. Allen TOLLEFSON
86 Asst Chanc Govt & Comm Relations .... Ms. Marjorie M. DICKINSON
88 Asst Exec Vice Chanc Provost Ofc .... Mr. Karl MOHR
45 Asst VC Campus Plng & Environ Stwd .... Mr. Robert B. SEGAR
88 Asst VC Capital Plng & Real Estate .... Mr. Grant ROCKWELL
88 Asst VC Development Outreach .... Ms. Angela JOENS
88 Asst VC Development .... Ms. Beth BRENNER
112 Asst VC Planned Giving .... Mr. Brian CASEY
102 Asst VC Foundation & Corp Giving .... Ms. Shelley MADDEX
88 Asst VC Student Affairs .... Ms. Emily PRIETO-TSEREGOUNIS
29 AVC/Exec Director Alumni Relations .... Mr. Richard R. ENGEL
13 CIO & VP Info/Educ Tech .... Ms. Viji MURALI
88 VP & Dean Undergraduate Educ .... Dr. Carolyn THOMAS
58 VP Grad Education/Dean Grad Studies .... Dr. Prasant MOHAPATRA
20 Vice Provost Academic Affairs .... Dr. Phil KASS
104 VP & Assoc Chanc Global Affairs .... Dr. Joanna REGULSKA
88 Assoc Vice Provost Global Affairs .... Dr. Ermia KEBREAB
88 Assoc Vice Provost Global Affairs .... Dr. Fadi FATHALLAH
47 Dean Agricultural/Environ Sci .... Dr. Helene DILLARD
88 Dean Biological Sciences .... Dr. Mark WINEY
54 Dean Engineering .... Dr. Jennifer SINCLAIR CURTIS
63 Interim Dean School of Medicine .... Dr. Lars BERGLUND
83 Vice Dean Social Sciences .... Dr. Li ZHANG
81 Vice Dean Math & Physical Sciences .... Dr. Alexandra NAVROTSKY
79 Vice Dean Humanities/Arts & Culture .... Dr. Susan B. KAISER
61 Dean School of Law .... Dr. Kevin R. JOHNSON
50 Dean Grad School of Management .... Dr. H. Rao UNNAVA
74 Dean Veterinary Medicine .... Dr. Michael D. LAIRMORE
53 Dean School of Education .... Dr. Lauren LINDSTROM
56 Dean University Extension .... Dr. Paul M. MCNEIL
88 Exec Director Mondavi Center .... Dr. Don F. ROTH
23 Director Student Health Services .... Dr. Margaret TROUT
37 Director Financial Aid .... Ms. Deborah G. AGEE
38 Director Student Health Counseling .... Dr. Sarah HAHN
36 Director Internship & Career Center .... Ms. Marcie KIRK-HOLLAND
109 Dir Campus Rec/Unions & Stores .... Mr. Jason LORGAN
41 Dir Intercollegiate Athletics .... Mr. Kevin BLUE
116 Int Director Internal Audit Svcs .... Ms. Leslyn KRAUS
88 Director World Food Center .... Dr. Jan HOPMANS
19 Interim Chief of Police .... Chief Jennifer GARCIA
43 Interim Chief Campus Counsel .... Mr. Michael SWEENEY
06 Registrar .... Dr. Elias S. LOPEZ
08 University Librarian .... Ms. MacKenzie SMITH

*University of California-Hastings College of the Law (I)

200 McAllister Street, San Francisco CA 94102-4978
County: San Francisco FICE Identification: 003947
Unit ID: 110398
Telephone: (415) 565-4600 Carnegie Class: Spec-4-yr-Law
FAX Number: (415) 565-4865 Calendar System: Semester
URL: www.uchastings.edu
Established: 1878 Annual Graduate Tuition & Fees: N/A
Enrollment: 950 Coed
Affiliation or Control: State IRS Status: 501(c)3
Highest Offering: First Professional Degree; No Undergraduates
Accreditation: WC, LAW

02 Chancellor and Dean .... Mr. David L. FAIGMAN
05 Provost & Academic Dean .... Dr. Morris RATNER
43 General Counsel .... Ms. Elise TRAYNUM
10 Chief Financial Officer .... Mr. David SEWARD
20 Associate Academic Dean .... Dr. Jeffrey LEFSTIN
32 Asst Dean Student Services .... Mr. Jaime NYE
19 Acting Chief Public Safety .... Mr. Scott HALLAHAN
06 Registrar .... Ms. Gina BARNETT
07 Director of Admissions .... Mr. Bryan ZERBE
13 Chief Information Officer .... Mr. Jake HORNSBY
36 Asst Dean Career & Profess Devel .... Ms. Sari ZIMMERMAN
26 Dir Communications/Public Affairs .... Mr. Alex A G. SHAPIRO

22 Director LEOP .... Ms. Jan JEMISON
23 Student Health Manager/Admin Nurse ....Ms. Laurie BROOKNER
21 Controller .... Ms. Deborah TRAN
37 Director Financial Aid .... Mr. Victor HO
18 Property Manager .... Ms. Pansy MAR
96 Director of Purchasing .... Mr. Darryl SWEET
30 Chief Development Officer .... Mr. Eric DUMBLETON
108 Director of Accreditation & Assess .... Ms. Andrea BING
84 Sr Assistant Dean of Enrollment Mgm ....Ms. June SAKAMOTO

*University of California-Irvine (A)

Campus Drive, Irvine CA 92697-0001
County: Orange — FICE Identification: 001314
Unit ID: 110653
Telephone: (949) 824-5011 — Carnegie Class: DU-Highest
FAX Number: N/A — Calendar System: Quarter
URL: www.uci.edu
Established: 1965 — Annual Undergrad Tuition & Fees (In-State): $13,360
Enrollment: 30,836 — Coed
Affiliation or Control: State — IRS Status: 501(c)3
Highest Offering: Doctorate
Accreditation: WC, CEA, CS, ENG, IPSY, LAW, MACTE, MED, MT, NURSE, PH, PLNG, RADDOS

02 Chancellor .... Howard A. GILLMAN
05 Provost & Exec Vice Chancellor .... Enrique J. LAVERNIA
10 Vice Chanc Admin/Business Services .... Ronald CORTEZ
46 Vice Chancellor for Research .... Pramod KHARGONEKAR
32 Vice Chanc Student Affairs .... Thomas A. PARHAM
111 Vice Chanc Univ Advancement .... Brian T. HERVEY
45 Vice Chanc Planning & Budget .... Meredith MICHAELS
20 Vice Provost for Academic Planning ...... Judith STEPAN-NORRIS
88 Vice Provost for Academic Personnel .... Diane K. O'DOWD
28 Vice Provost for AED&Inclusion .... Douglas M. HAYNES
100 Associate Chancellor/Chief of Staff .... Michael R. ARIAS
20 Assoc Prov & Exec Vice Chancellor .... Jeff LEFKOFF
22 Assoc Chancellor ED & Inclusion .... Kirsten K. QUANBECK
15 Assoc Chancellor & Chief HR Exec .... Ramona AGRELA
29 Asst Vice Chanc Alumni Relations .... Barney ELLIS-PERRY
35 Interim Assoc VC Stdnt Affairs .... Brice K. KIKUCHI
35 Asst Vice Chanc/Dean of Students .... Rameen A. TALESH
84 Asst Vice Chanc Enrollment Services .... Brent W. YUNEK
06 University Registrar .... Elizabeth C. BENNETT
43 Chief Campus Counsel .... Diane F. GEOCARIS
51 Dean Continuing Educ/Summer Session .... Gary W. MATKIN
08 University Librarian .... Lorelei A. TANJI
36 Director Career Center .... Suzanne C. HELBIG
37 Director Financial Aid .... Rebecca SANCHEZ
41 Director Intercollegiate Athletics .... Michael A. IZZI
09 Asst Vice Chanc Inst Research .... Ryan M. CHERLAND
20 Dean Undergrad Education & VP .... Michael DENNIN
58 Dean Graduate Division & VP .... Frances M. LESLIE
23 Vice Chancellor of Health Affairs .... Howard FEDEROFF
49 Dean Arts .... Stephen BARKER
50 Dean Paul Merage School of Business ....Eric SPANGENBERG
53 Dean School of Education .... Richard ARUM
81 Dean Biological Sciences .... Frank LAFERLA
54 Dean School of Engineering .... Gregory WASHINGTON
79 Dean Humanities .... Georges VAN DEN ABBEELE
77 Dean Bren Sch of Info & Comp Sci ..... Marios PAPAEFTHYMIOU
61 Interim Dean of Law School .... Song RICHARDSON
63 Dean School of Medicine .... Michael STAMOS
81 Dean Physical Sciences .... Kenneth C. JANDA
83 Dean Social Ecology .... Nancy GUERRA
83 Dean School of Social Sciences .... William M. MAURER
88 Chair Academic Senate .... Maria PANTELIA
21 Assoc Vice Chanc Admin/Business Svc .... Richard COULON
13 CIO and Assoc Vice Chancellor IT .... Dana F. ROODE
26 Assoc Chanc Communications .... Ria M. CARLSON
07 Exec Director of Admissions .... Patricia MORALES

*University of California-Los Angeles (B)

405 Hilgard Avenue, Los Angeles CA 90095-1405
County: Los Angeles — FICE Identification: 001315
Unit ID: 110662
Telephone: (310) 825-4321 — Carnegie Class: DU-Highest
FAX Number: N/A — Calendar System: Quarter
URL: www.ucla.edu
Established: 1919 — Annual Undergrad Tuition & Fees (In-State): $12,920
Enrollment: 41,908 — Coed
Affiliation or Control: State — IRS Status: 501(c)3
Highest Offering: Doctorate
Accreditation: WC, CLPSY, CS, CYTO, DENT, DIETI, EMT, ENG, ENGR, IPSY, LAW, LIB, MED, NURSE, PAST, PCSAS, PH, PLNG, RAD, SW, THEA

02 Chancellor .... Gene D. BLOCK
05 Exec Vice Chancellor and Provost .... Scott WAUGH
11 Administrative Vice Chancellor .... Michael J. BECK
10 Vice Chancellor/CFO .... Steven A. OLSEN
15 Vice Chancellor Academic Personnel .... Carole E. GOLDBERG
28 VChanc Equity Diversity & Inclusion .... Jerry KANG
26 Vice Chancellor External Affairs .... Rhea TURTELTAUB
23 Vice Chancellor Health Sciences .... John MAZZIOTTA
43 Interim Vice Chanc Legal Affairs .... Louise C. NELSON
46 Interim Vice Chanc Research .... Ann R. KARAGOZIAN
32 Interim Vice Chanc Student Affairs .... Monroe GORDEN, JR.
58 Vice Provost & Dean Graduate Educ .... Robin L. GARRELL
20 Vice Provost & Dean Undergrad Educ .... Patricia A. TURNER
13 Vice Provost Information Technology .... James DAVIS
88 Vice Prov Inst of American Cultures .... David K. YOO
88 VProv Interdiscip/Cross-campus Affs .... Timothy BREWER
88 V Provost Intl Studies/Global Engmt .... C. Cindy FAN
88 V Provost New Collaborative Initiat .... Kathryn Ann ATCHISON
17 President UCLA Health .... Johnese Maria SPISSO
79 Dean of Humanities .... David SCHABERG
88 Dean of Life Sciences .... Victoria SORK
81 Dean of Physical Sciences .... Miguel GARCIA-GARIBAY
83 Dean of Social Sciences .... Darnell HUNT
52 Dean School of Dentistry .... Paul KREBSBACH
48 Interim Dean Sch of the Arts & Arch .... David ROUSSIVE
53 Dean Grad Sch Educ & Info Studies .... Marcelo M. SUAREZ-OROZCO
54 Dean Sch of Eng & App Sci .... Jayathi Y. MURTHY
61 Dean School of Law .... Jennifer L. MNOOKIN
50 Dean Grad Sch of Mgmt .... Judy D. OLIAN
63 Dean School of Medicine .... Kelsey C. MARTIN
64 Dean School of Music .... Judith L. SMITH
66 Dean School of Nursing .... Linda SARNA
80 Dean School of Public Affairs .... Gary SEGURA
69 Dean Sch of Public Health .... Jody HEYMANN
88 Dean School of Theater Film & TV .... Teri SCHWARTZ
51 Dean Continuing Ed and Extension .... Wayne SMUTZ
88 Assoc VC Academic Planning & Budget .... Jeff ROTH
29 Assoc VC Alumni Affairs/Advancemnt .... Julie SINA
16 Assoc VC Campus Human Resources .... Lubbe LEVIN
21 Assoc Vice Chancellor/Controller .... Allison BAIRD-JAMES
30 Assoc VC Development .... Kathryn CARRICO
30 Assoc VC Development .... Laura PARKER
84 Vice Provost Enrollment Management .... Youlonda COPELAND-MORGAN
14 Assoc VC Info Technology Services .... Andrew WISSMILLER
35 Asst VC of Student Development .... Suzanne SEPLOW
35 Asst VC of Campus Life .... Mick DELUCA
27 Assoc VC UCLA Comm/Public Outreach ....Kathryn KRANHOLD
20 Assistant Provost .... Maryann J. GRAY
20 Assistant Provost .... Margaret LEAL-SOTELO
18 Asst VC Facilities Management .... Kelly J. SCHMADER
86 Asst VC Govt/Community Relations .... Keith S. PARKER
39 Asst VC Housing & Hospitality Svcs .... Peter ANGELIS
25 Asst VC Research/Compliance .... Ann M. POLLACK
04 Executive Asst to the Chancellor .... Dawn SCHERER
88 Executive Director ASUCLA .... Robert WILLIAMS
09 Executive Director Inst Research .... Adam SUGANO
88 Director Volunteer Center .... Shannon Regan HICKMAN
96 Director Campus Purchasing & Payabl .... William S. PROPST
36 Director Career Center .... Wesley E. THORNE, II
85 Director Ctr for Intl Students .... Shideh HANASSAB
37 Director Financial Aid Office .... Ronald W. JOHNSON
41 Director Intercollegiate Athletics .... Daniel G. GUERRERO
90 Director Res Comp & Acad Tech Svcs .... William LABATE
38 Interim Exec Dir Couns & Psych Svcs .... Nicole GREEN
07 Director Undergraduate Admission .... Gary A. CLARK
06 Registrar .... Frank Y. WADA
08 University Librarian .... Virginia STEEL
19 Chief of Police .... James HERREN

*University of California-Merced (C)

5200 North Lake Road, Merced CA 95343
County: Merced — FICE Identification: 041271
Unit ID: 445188
Telephone: (209) 228-4400 — Carnegie Class: DU-Higher
FAX Number: (209) 228-4424 — Calendar System: Semester
URL: www.ucmerced.edu
Established: 2005 — Annual Undergrad Tuition & Fees (In-District): $13,262
Enrollment: 6,685 — Coed
Affiliation or Control: State/Local — IRS Status: 501(c)3
Highest Offering: Doctorate
Accreditation: WC, ENG

02 Chancellor .... Dr. Dorothy LELAND
88 Assoc Chancellor & Senior Advisor .... Luanna PUTNEY
05 Provost & Exec Vice Chancellor .... Dr. Tom PETERSON
11 Int Vice Chanc Business & Admin Svc .... Brian POWELL
30 Vice Chancellor Develop/Alumni Rels .... Vacant
32 Int Vice Chancellor Student Affairs .... Dr. Charles NIES
114 Vice Chancellor Budget/Planning .... Vacant
46 Vice Chancellor Research .... Dr. Samuel TRAINA
84 Assoc Vice Chanc Enrollment Mgmt .... Jill ORCUTT
26 Asst Vice Chanc Univ Communications .... Vacant
58 Vice Provost/Dean of Graduate Educ .... Marjorie ZATZ
20 Vice Provost UG Education .... Elizabeth WHITT
86 Exec Director of Govt Relations .... Cori LUCERO
04 Exec Assistant to the Chancellor .... Kim GARNER
13 Chief Information Officer .... Ann KOVALCHICK
65 Dean Natural Sciences .... Dr. Betsy DUMONT
79 Dean School of SSHA .... Dr. Jill ROBBINS
54 Dean Engineering .... Dr. Mark MATSUMOTO
07 Director of Admissions .... Encarnacion RUIZ
06 University Registrar .... Dr. Laurie HERBRAND
37 Director of Financial Aid .... Ron RADNEY
41 Director of Campus Athletics & Rec .... David DUNHAM
23 Assoc Vice Chanc Health & Wellness .... Dr. Fuji COLLINS
85 Director of International Programs .... Vacant
08 University Librarian .... Haipeng LI
39 Director of Housing and Residence .... Martin REED
43 Campus Counsel .... Elisabeth GUNTHER
100 Associate Chancellor/Chief of Staff .... Ed KLOTZBIER
19 Chief of Police .... Chou HER

*University of California-Riverside (D)

900 University Avenue, Riverside CA 92521
County: Riverside — FICE Identification: 001316
Unit ID: 110671
Telephone: (951) 827-1012 — Carnegie Class: DU-Highest
FAX Number: (951) 827-3800 — Calendar System: Quarter
URL: www.ucr.edu
Established: 1954 — Annual Undergrad Tuition & Fees (In-State): $13,581
Enrollment: 21,385 — Coed
Affiliation or Control: State — IRS Status: 501(c)3
Highest Offering: Doctorate
Accreditation: WC, CS, ENG, IPSY, MED, SCPSY

02 Chancellor .... Dr. Kim A. WILCOX
100 Associate Chancellor .... Ms. Christine VICTORINO
05 Exec Vice Chancellor/Provost .... Dr. Cynthia LARIVE
45 Vice Chanc Planning & Budget .... Vacant
32 Vice Chancellor Student Affairs .... Mr. James W. SANDOVAL
10 Vice Chanc Business & Admin Svcs .... Mr. Ron T. COLEY
111 Vice Chanc University Advancement ...... Mr. Peter A. HAYASHIDA
46 Vice Chancellor Research .... Dr. Michael J. PAZZANI
17 VC Hlth Affs/Dean School of Med .... Dr. Deborah DEAS
20 Vice Provost Academic Personnel .... Dr. Ameae WALKER
18 Assoc Vice Chanc Facil Plant Admin .... Vacant
84 Assoc Vice Chanc Enrollment .... Ms. LaRae LUNDGREN
30 Int Assoc Vice Chanc Development .... Mr. Hieu NGUYEN
09 Asst Vice Chanc Strat Acad Rsrch An .... Mr. Charles GREER
28 Asst Vice Chanc Affirm Action .... Vacant
58 Dean Graduate Division .... Dr. Shaun BOWLER
50 Dean School of Business Admin .... Dr. Yungzeng WANG
53 Dean Grad School of Educ .... Dr. Thomas SMITH
54 Dean Bourns College of Engineering .... Dr. Sharon WALKER
79 Dean College of Humanities Arts SS .... Dr. Milagros PENA
81 Dean Col of Nat and Agr Sciences .... Dr. Kathryn UHRICH
06 Registrar .... Ms. Bracken J. DAILEY
80 Dean School of Public Policy .... Dr. Anil DEOLALIKAR
36 Director Career Center .... Mr. Sean GILL
37 Director Financial Aid .... Mr. Jose A. AGUILAR
38 Director Counseling Center .... Ms. Elizabeth MONDRAGON
07 Director of Admissions .... Ms. Emily D. ENGELSCHALL
96 Director Material Management .... Mr. Russ LEWIS
08 Head Librarian .... Mr. Steve MANDEVILLE-GAMBLE
04 Executive Asst to Chancellor .... Ms. Suzette M. LYONS
41 Athletic Director .... Ms. Tamica SMITH JONES

*University of California-San Diego (E)

9500 Gilman Drive, La Jolla CA 92093-0014
County: San Diego — FICE Identification: 001317
Unit ID: 110680
Telephone: (858) 534-2230 — Carnegie Class: DU-Highest
FAX Number: (858) 534-6523 — Calendar System: Quarter
URL: www.ucsd.edu
Established: 1960 — Annual Undergrad Tuition & Fees (In-State): $13,645
Enrollment: 32,906 — Coed
Affiliation or Control: State — IRS Status: 501(c)3
Highest Offering: Doctorate
Accreditation: WC, AUD, CEA, CLPSY, DIETI, DMS, ENG, IPSY, MED, MT, PDPSY, PHAR

02 Chancellor .... Dr. Pradeep K. KHOSLA
05 Interim EVC Academic Affairs .... Dr. Peter COWHEY
10 VC and Chief Financial Officer .... Mr. Pierre-Yves OUILLET
32 VC Student Affairs .... Dr. Juan C. GONZALEZ
11 Vice Chanc Resource Mgmt/Planning .... Mr. Gary C. MATTHEWS
65 Vice Chancellor Marine Sciences .... Dr. Margaret LEINEN
63 VC Health Science/Dean Sch Med .... Dr. David A. BRENNER
46 Vice Chancellor Research .... Dr. Sandra BROWN
28 VC for Equity/Diversity & Inclusion .... Dr. Becky R. PETITT
111 Vice Chancellor Advancement .... Vacant
100 Assistant Chancellor/Chief of Staff .... Mr. Jeffrey P. GATTAS
22 Chief Ethics and Compliance Officer .... Ms. Judith BRUNER
56 Assoc VC Public Pgms/Dean Univ Ext ...... Dr. Mary L. WALSHOK
43 Chief Campus Counsel .... Mr. Daniel W. PARK
13 Chief Information Officer .... Mr. Vince KELLEN
21 AVC Business Fin Svcs/Controller .... Ms. Cheryl ROSS
08 University Librarian .... Mr. Brian E C. SCHOTTLAENDER
100 Assistant Chancellor .... Ms. Suzi M. STERNER
88 Director Policy Admin .... Ms. Paula J. JOHNSON, CRM
23 Exec Dir Student Health/Wellness .... Ms. Karen J. CALFAS
26 University Communications .... Vacant
20 Sr Assoc VC Academic Planning .... Dr. William S. HODGKISS
20 AVC Academic Affairs .... Dr. Barbara SAWREY
15 Asst VC Human Resources .... Ms. Catherine M. LEDFORD
88 Associate Vice Chancellor Research .... Dr. Miroslav KRSTIC
88 AVC Innovation & Commercialization .... Mr. Paul W. ROBEN
84 Assoc Vice Chanc Enrollment Mgmt ....Ms. Adele C. BRUMFIELD
06 University Registrar .... Vacant
23 CEO UCSD Medical Center .... Ms. Patty MAYSENT
29 Asst VC Student Life .... Ms. Sharon VAN BRUGGEN
96 Assoc Controller/Chief Procurement .... Mr. Ted JOHNSON
54 Dean Jacobs Sch of Engineering .... Dr. Albert P. PISANO
49 Dean Arts & Humanities .... Dr. Cristina DELLA COLETTA
81 Dean Div of Biological Sciences .... Dr. William MCGINNIS
83 Dean of Social Sciences .... Dr. Carol A. PADDEN
50 Dean Rady School of Management .... Mr. Robert S. SULLIVAN
82 Dean Div of Physical Science .... Dr. Steven E. BOGGS
82 Dean Global Policy and Strategy .... Dr. Gordon HANSON
58 Dean Graduate Studies .... Dr. Steven CASSEDY
12 Provost John Muir College .... Dr. John C. MOORE
12 Prov Thurgood Marshall Coll .... Dr. Leslie CARVER
12 Provost Earl Warren College .... Dr. Emily ROXWORTHY

12 Provost Revelle College ... Dr. Paul K. YU
12 Provost Eleanor Roosevelt College ... Dr. Ivan EVANS
12 Provost Sixth College ... Dr. Daniel J. DONOGHUE
38 Director Stdt Psych/Counseling Svcs ... Dr. Reina JUAREZ
18 AVC EH&S and Facilities Management ... Mr. Garry L. MAC PHERSON
41 Athletic Director ... Mr. Earl W. EDWARDS
19 Police Chief Community Safety ... Mr. David S. ROSE

*University of California-San Francisco (A)

513 Parnassus Avenue, Box 0402, San Francisco CA 94143

County: San Francisco FICE Identification: 001319
Unit ID: 110699
Telephone: (415) 476-9000 Carnegie Class: Spec-4-yr-Med
FAX Number: (415) 476-9634 Calendar System: Quarter
URL: www.ucsf.edu
Established: 1864 Annual Graduate Tuition & Fees: N/A
Enrollment: 3,107 Coed
Affiliation or Control: State IRS Status: 501(c)3
Highest Offering: Doctorate; No Undergraduates
Accreditation: WC, DENT, DIETI, IPSY, MED, MIDWF, NURSE, PAST, PHAR, PTA

02 Chancellor ... Dr. Samuel HAWGOOD
03 Executive Vice Chancellor & Provost ... Dr. Daniel H. LOWENSTEIN
100 Associate Chancellor ... Dr. Theresa O'BRIEN
10 VC and Chief Financial Officer ... Ms. Teresa COSTANTINIDIS
05 Vice Provost Academic Affairs ... Dr. Brian ALLDREDGE
63 Dean School of Medicine/VC Med Affs ... Dr. Talmadge E. KING, JR.
32 Vice Chanc Student Academic Affairs ... Dr. Elizabeth WATKINS
30 Vice Chanc Univ Develop & Alum Rels ... Mr. John FORD
88 VC Science Policy & Strategy ... Dr. Keith YAMAMOTO
26 VC Strat Communications & Univ Rels ... Ms. Barbara FRENCH
13 Assoc VC & Chief Info Officer ... Mr. Joseph BENGFORT
28 VC Diversity & Outreach ... Dr. Renee NAVARRO
109 Assoc VC Campus Life Services ... Ms. Clare SHINNERL
15 Assoc VC Human Resources ... Mr. David ODATO
18 Assoc VC Cap Pgms/Campus Architect ... Mr. Michael BADE
63 Vice Dean Academic Affairs ... Dr. Elena FUENTES-AFFLICK
37 Interim Dir Student Financial Svcs ... Mr. Jerry LOPEZ
43 Chief Campus Counsel ... Ms. Greta SCHNETZLER
08 University Librarian/Asst VC ... Mr. Chris SHAFFER
19 Chief of Police ... Mr. Michael DENSON
66 Interim Dean School of Nursing ... Dr. Sandra WEISS
52 Dean School of Dentistry ... Dr. John FEATHERSTONE
67 Dean School of Pharmacy ... Dr. B. Joseph GUGLIELMO
58 Dean Graduate Division ... Dr. Elizabeth WATKINS
32 Asst VC Student Life ... Dr. Carol TAKAO
96 Assoc VC/Chief Procurement Officer ... Mr. James HINE
06 Registrar/Asst VC Student Info ... Mr. Douglas CARLSON
88 Associate Registrar ... Ms. Jina SHAMIM
36 Exec Dir Career/Prof Development ... Mr. William LINDSTAEDT
23 Exec Dir Student Health Services ... Ms. Susan ROSEN
09 Director Institutional Research ... Dr. Ning WANG

*University of California-Santa Barbara (B)

552 University Road, Santa Barbara CA 93106-0001

County: Santa Barbara FICE Identification: 001320
Unit ID: 110705
Telephone: (805) 893-8000 Carnegie Class: DU-Highest
FAX Number: N/A Calendar System: Quarter
URL: www.ucsb.edu
Established: 1909 Annual Undergrad Tuition & Fees (In-State): $14,073
Enrollment: 23,497 Coed
Affiliation or Control: State IRS Status: 501(c)3
Highest Offering: Doctorate
Accreditation: WC, CS, DANCE, ENG, IPSY, PSPSY

02 Chancellor ... Dr. Henry T. YANG
04 Exec Assistant to the Chancellor ... Ms. Diane O'BRIEN
05 Executive Vice Chancellor ... Dr. David B. MARSHALL
114 Acting Asst Chanc Fin & Resourc Mgt ... Mr. Chuck HAINES
46 Interim Vice Chancellor Research ... Dr. Joe INCANDELA
11 Vice Chancellor Admin Services ... Mr. Marc FISHER
32 Vice Chancellor Student Affairs ... Ms. Margaret KLAWUNN
10 Exec Dir/Controller Bus & Fin Svc ... Mr. Jim R. CORKILL
15 Assoc Vice Chanc Acad Personnel ... Dr. Alison BUTLER
28 AVC Diversity/Equity/Acad Policy ... Dr. Maria HERRERA-SOBEK
20 Co-Interim AVC/Dean UG Education ... Dr. Jeffrey STOPPLE
20 Co-Interim AVC/Dean UG Education ... Dr. Linda ADLER-KASSNER
30 Assoc Vice Chancellor Development ... Ms. Beverly COLGATE
26 AVC Public Affairs & Communications ... Vacant
84 Acting AVC Enrollment Services ... Mr. Mike MILLER
88 Assoc Dean Student Acad Support Svc ... Ms. Lupe GARCIA
29 Asst Vice Chanc Alumni Affairs ... Mr. George THURLOW, III
88 Interim Dean Col Creative Studies ... Dr. Kathy FOLTZ
54 Dean College of Engineering ... Dr. Rod ALFERNESS
58 Dean Graduate Division ... Dr. Carol GENETTI
53 Dean Gevirtz Grad Sch Educ ... Dr. Jeffrey MILEM
65 Dean Bren School of Env Sci & Mgmt ... Dr. Steven D. GAINES
56 Dean UC Santa Barbara Extension ... Dr. Michael T. BROWN
35 Dean of Student Life ... Ms. Katya ARMISTEAD
79 Dean Humanities & Fine Arts ... Dr. John MAJEWSKI
81 Dean Math/Life & Physical Sciences ... Dr. Pierre WILTZIUS
87 Director Summer Sessions ... Mr. Blake NEMELKA
83 Interim Dean Social Sciences ... Dr. Leila RUPP
85 Dir International Students/Scholars ... Dr. Simran SINGH
06 Registrar ... Ms. Leesa BECK
16 Director Human Resources ... Ms. Cynthia SENERIZ
37 Director Financial Aid ... Dr. Michael MILLER
116 Acting Dir Audit & Advisory Service ... Ms. Jessie MASEK
07 Director Admissions ... Ms. Lisa PRZEKOP
09 Director Institutional Research ... Dr. Steven C. VELASCO
23 Exec Director Student Health Svcs ... Dr. Mary FERRIS
39 AVC Housing/Dining & Aux Enterpris ... Mr. Wilfred E. BROWN
40 Director of UCSB Bookstore ... Mr. Mark BEISECKER
19 Chief of Police ... Mr. Dustin OLSON
41 Director Intercollegiate Athletics ... Mr. John MCCUTCHEON
86 Dir Governmental Relations ... Ms. Kirsten DESHLER
21 Director Finance/Administration ... Mr. Eric J. SONQUIST
08 University Librarian ... Ms. Denise STEPHENS
89 Director Orientation Programs ... Ms. Tricia RASCON
88 Acting Director Capital Development ... Mr. Mark NOCCIOLO
88 Director Campus Planning & Design ... Ms. Alissa HUMMER
88 Director Arts & Lectures ... Ms. Celesta BILLECI
22 Director Disabled Students Pgm ... Mr. Gary R. WHITE
104 Dir Campus Education Abroad Program ... Dr. Juan E. CAMPO
88 Director Env Health & Safety ... Mr. John STERRITT
88 Director MultiCultural Center ... Ms. Zaveeni KHAN-MARCUS
38 Dir Counseling & Psychological Svcs ... Dr. Jeanne STANFORD
94 Director Women's Center ... Ms. Kim EQUINOA
88 Campus Ombuds ... Ms. Caroline ADAMS
88 Exec Dir Instructional Devel ... Mr. George H. MICHAELS
36 Director Career Services ... Mr. Ignacio GALLARDO
13 Chief Information Officer ... Mr. Matthew HALL
43 UCSB Legal Counsel ... Ms. Nancy G. HAMILL
22 Dir Equal Op & Discrim Prevention ... Mr. Ricardo ALCAINO
88 Acting Dir Design & Construction ... Mr. Ray ARONSON
88 Director Univ Center/Events Center ... Mr. Gary LAWRENCE
88 Director of Recreation ... Mr. Jeff HUSKEY
92 Honors Program Analyst ... Ms. Summer HOWATT-NAB

*University of California-Santa Cruz (C)

1156 High Street, Santa Cruz CA 95064-1077

County: Santa Cruz FICE Identification: 001321
Unit ID: 110714
Telephone: (831) 459-0111 Carnegie Class: DU-Highest
FAX Number: (831) 459-0146 Calendar System: Quarter
URL: www.ucsc.edu
Established: 1965 Annual Undergrad Tuition & Fees (In-State): $13,539
Enrollment: 17,868 Coed
Affiliation or Control: State IRS Status: 501(c)3
Highest Offering: Doctorate
Accreditation: WC, ENG, IPSY

02 Chancellor ... Dr. George R. BLUMENTHAL
05 Campus Provost/Exec Vice Chancellor ... Dr. Marlene TROMP
10 Vice Chanc Business/Admin Services ... Dr. Sarah LATHAM
45 Vice Chancellor Planning/Budget ... Dr. Peggy DELANEY
46 Vice Chancellor Research ... Dr. Scott BRANDT
30 Vice Chanc of University Relations ... Dr. Keith BRANT
13 Vice Chanc Information Technology ... Dr. Mary DOYLE
20 Vice Prov/Dean Undergrad Educ ... Dr. Richard HUGHEY
20 Vice Provost Academic Affairs ... Dr. Herbert LEE
84 Assoc VC Enrollment Mgmt ... Ms. Michelle WHITTINGHAM
16 Asst VC Academic Personnel ... Dr. Pamela PETERSON
18 Assoc VC & Campus Architect ... Mr. John BARNES
15 Assoc VC Staff Human Resources ... Mr. Steve STEIN
32 AVC Campus Life/Dn of Students ... Ms. Alma SIFUENTES
08 University Librarian ... Ms. Elizabeth COWELL
79 Dean of Humanities ... Dr. Tyler STOVALL
81 Dean Physical & Biological Sci ... Dr. Paul KOCH
49 Interim Dean of the Arts ... Dr. William LADUSAW
83 Dean of Social Sciences ... Dr. Sheldon KAMIENIECKI
54 Dean of Engineering ... Dr. Joseph KONOPELSKI
58 Vice Prov/Dean of Graduate Studies ... Dr. Tyrus MILLER
65 Director Institute Marine Sciences ... Dr. Gary B. GRIGGS
81 Director Institute Particle Physics ... Dr. Steven RITZ
88 Director UCO/Lick Observatory ... Dr. Claire MAX
12 Provost Stevenson College ... Dr. Alice YANG
12 Provost Cowell College ... Dr. Faye CROSBY
12 Provost Crown College ... Dr. Manel CAMPS
12 Provost Merrill College ... Dr. Elizabeth ABRAMS
12 Provost Porter College ... Dr. Sean KEILEN
12 Provost Kresge College ... Dr. Ben LEEDS CARSON
12 Provost College Eight ... Dr. Ronnie LIPSCHUTZ
12 Provost College Nine ... Dr. Flora LU
12 Provost College Ten ... Dr. Regina LANGHOUT
06 Registrar ... Mr. Tchad SANGER
09 Director Institutional Research ... Dr. Julian L. FERNALD
37 Director Financial Aid/Operations ... Mr. Patrick REGISTER
22 Staff Dir EEO/Affirmative Action ... Mr. Ashish SAHNI
29 Director of Alumni Relations ... Ms. Shayna KENT
26 Dir Marketing/Communications ... Ms. Lisa NIELSEN
86 Director Government Relations ... Ms. Donna M. BLITZER
38 Director Student Counseling ... Dr. Gary DUNN
07 Director of Admissions ... Mr. Michael MCCAWLEY
41 Athletic Director ... Mr. Cliff DOCHTERMAN
108 Asst Director for Assessment ... Dr. Anna SHER
102 Dir Foundation/Corporate Relations ... Ms. Lynne STOOPS

University of East-West Medicine (D)

595 Lawrence Expressway, Sunnyvale CA 94085

County: Santa Clara FICE Identification: 039953
Unit ID: 447801
Telephone: (408) 733-1878 Carnegie Class: Spec-4-yr-Other Health
FAX Number: (408) 636-7705 Calendar System: Trimester
URL: www.uewm.edu
Established: 1997 Annual Undergrad Tuition & Fees: N/A
Enrollment: 258 Coed
Affiliation or Control: Proprietary IRS Status: Proprietary
Highest Offering: Master's
Accreditation: ACUP

01 Acting President ... Dr. Doreen SIMMONS
03 Vice President ... Mr. Richard FRIBERG
32 VP Student/Academic Affairs ... Dr. Amy CHAN
07 Director of Admissions ... Dr. Sharon ZHOU

† Granted candidacy at the Doctorate level.

University of La Verne (E)

1950 Third Street, La Verne CA 91750-4443

County: Los Angeles FICE Identification: 001216
Unit ID: 117140
Telephone: (909) 593-3511 Carnegie Class: DU-Mod
FAX Number: (909) 593-0965 Calendar System: Semester
URL: www.laverne.edu
Established: 1891 Annual Undergrad Tuition & Fees: $39,900
Enrollment: 8,334 Coed
Affiliation or Control: Independent Non-Profit IRS Status: 501(c)3
Highest Offering: Doctorate
Accreditation: WC, CAATE, CAEPN, CLPSY, LAW, SPAA

01 President ... Dr. Devorah A. LIEBERMAN
05 Provost & Vice President ... Dr. Jonathan REED
88 Special Assistant to Provost ... Dr. Mark GOOR
10 Chief Financial Officer ... Mr. Avedis (Avo) KECHICHIAN
111 Vice President Univ Advancement ... Mrs. Sherri MYLOTT
84 Vice Pres Strategic Enroll & Comm ... Dr. Homa SHABAHANG
50 Dean College Business/Public Mgmt ... Dr. Ibrahim (Abe) HELOU
53 Dean College Educ/Org Ldrship ... Dr. Kimberly WHITE-SMITH
61 Dean College of Law ... Mr. Gilbert HOLMES
32 Dean Student Affairs ... Dr. Loretta RAHMANI
12 Dean Regional & Online Programs ... Dr. David SMITH
07 Interim Dean of Admissions ... Mr. Todd ECKEL
121 Assoc VP Academic Sppt/Retent Svcs ... Ms. Adeline CARDENAS-CLAGUE
21 Associate Vice President of Finance . Ms. Lori K. GORDIEN CASE
26 Assoc VP Strategic Communications ... Ms. Melissa ROBINSON-COGGINS
15 Interim Chief HR Officer ... Mr. Peter MALJIAN
18 Vice President of Facilities/Tech ... Dr. Clive K. HOUSTON-BROWN
35 Associate Dean Student Affairs ... Mrs. Ruby S. MONTANO-CORDOVA
88 Asst Dean Grad Acad Supp/Ret Svcs ... Ms. Jo Nell BAKER
88 Assoc VP & Chief Marketing Officer ... Mr. Fred A. CHYR
85 Director International Student Svcs ... Dr. Jeffrey NONEMAKER
18 Sr Dir Physical Plant Ops & Svcs ... Mr. Robert D. BEEBE
11 Director Admin & Operation ... Mr. Jason NEAL
27 Director of Public Relations ... Mr. Rod LEVEQUE
30 Asst VP Development & Campaign Dir ... Mr. Kevin DOODY
29 Sr Dir Advancement Oper & Services ... Ms. Bianca ROMERO
38 Dir Counseling & Psych Services ... Dr. Elleni R. KOULOS
88 Director Student Accounts ... Ms. Xochitl E. MARTINEZ
96 Director Purchasing & Procurement ... Mrs. Deborah S. DEACY
28 Director Multicultural Affairs ... Dr. Daniel L. LOERA
23 Dir Health Svcs/Svcs for Stds-Disab ... Ms. Cynthia K. DENNE
39 Assoc Dean of Stdnts/Dir Stdnt Hous ... Mr. Juan REGALADO
36 Asst Dean Student Career Support ... Ms. Mindy BAGGISH
88 Dir Center for Adv/Teaching & Lrng ... Dr. Sammy ELZARKA
88 Director Graduate Success Center ... Dr. Linda DE LONG
41 Athletic Director ... Ms. Julie KLINE
06 Registrar ... Ms. Marilyn S. DAVIES
08 University Librarian ... Dr. Vinaya L. TRIPURANENI
28 Chief Diversity Officer ... Dr. Beatriz GONZALEZ
09 Director of Institutional Research ... Dr. Leeshawn MOORE
42 Chaplain/Dir of Campus Ministry ... Dr. Zandra L. WAGONER
88 Director of La Verne Experience ... Dr. Kathleen WEAVER
90 Sr Dir Admission Oper/Tech Svcs ... Mrs. Loreto D'MONTE
88 Director High Desert ... Ms. Juli ROBERTS
88 Director Inland Empire ... Mr. Allen STOUT
88 Director Kern County ... Dr. Nora DOMINGUEZ
88 Director Orange County ... Dr. Todd ECKEL
88 Director Point Mugu NAWC ... Mr. Jamie DEMPSEY
88 Sr Ex Dir San Fernando Valley ... Dr. Nelly KAZMAN
88 Director Vandenberg AFB ... Ms. Kitt VINCENT
88 Director Ventura County ... Mr. Kevin LAACK
88 Director International Admission ... Mr. Adam WU
20 Vice Provost ... Dr. Beatriz GONZALEZ
88 Director of Civic Engagement ... Ms. Marisol MORALES
04 Special Asst to President ... Dr. Shannon HIGGINS

University of the Pacific (F)

3601 Pacific Avenue, Stockton CA 95211-0197

County: San Joaquin FICE Identification: 001329
Unit ID: 120883
Telephone: (209) 946-2011 Carnegie Class: DU-Mod
FAX Number: (209) 946-2845 Calendar System: Semester
URL: www.pacific.edu
Established: 1851 Annual Undergrad Tuition & Fees: $44,588
Enrollment: 6,281 Coed
Affiliation or Control: Independent Non-Profit IRS Status: 501(c)3
Highest Offering: Doctorate
Accreditation: WC, #ARCPA, ART, @AUD, CAATE, CAEPN, CS, DENT, DH, ENG, IPSY, LAW, MUS, PHAR, PTA, SP

01 President .... Dr. Pamela A. EIBECK
05 Provost/Exec VP Academic Affairs .... Dr. Maria G. PALLAVICINI
10 Vice President Business & Finance .... Ken MULLEN
32 Vice President Student Life .... Patrick DAY
30 VP Development & Alumni Relations .... G. Burnham 'Burnie' ATTERBURY
13 VP Technology/CIO .... Art SPRECHER
21 Assoc VP Business & Finance .... Ron ELLISON
84 Assoc VP & Vice Prov Enroll Mgmt .... J. Michael THOMPSON
26 Assoc VP Marketing & Communication .... Marge GREY
86 AVP External Relations .... Stacy MCAFEE
45 Assoc VP Planning .... Linda BUCKLEY
31 Assoc VP External Relations .... Dr. Stacy MCAFEE
119 Assoc VP Info Security/CISO .... Dr. James AUGUST
14 Assoc VP Tech Ops/COO .... Jack BROWN
115 Asst VP Treasury/Chief Invest Off .... Jol MANILAY
49 Dean College of the Pacific .... Rena FRADEN
50 Int Dean Eberhardt School Business .... David DAUWALDER
52 Dean Dugoni School of Dentistry .... Nader NADERSHAHI
53 Dean Benerd School of Education .... Vanessa SHEARED
54 Dean Sch of Eng/Comp Science .... Steven HOWELL
61 Dean McGeorge School of Law .... Michael SCHWARTZ
64 Dean Conservatory of Music .... Peter WITTE
67 Dean Long Sch Pharm/Hlth Sciences ... Phillip R. OPPENHEIMER
36 Assoc VP/Exec Dir Career Dev .... Tom VECCHIONE
08 Dean University Library .... Vacant
58 Dean Graduate School .... Thomas NAEHR
51 Dean University College .... Patricia CAMPBELL
25 Sponsored Pgms Administrator .... Vacant
29 Exec Dir of Alumni Relations .... Kelli PAGE
37 Director of Financial Aid .... Lynn FOX
07 Asst Vice Prov/Dir Admissions .... Chris KRZAK
06 University Registrar .... Vacant
09 Director Institutional Research .... Mike ROGERS
35 Director Student Activities .... Vacant
96 Director of Purchasing .... Ronda MARR
92 Director Honors Program .... Balint SZATARAY
93 Director Multicultural Affairs .... Ines RUIZ-HUSTON
94 Director Gender Studies .... Traci ROBERTS-CAMPS
38 Director of Counseling Services .... Stacie TURKS
39 Director of Housing .... Vacant
41 Director of Athletics .... Ted LELAND
42 University Chaplain .... Joel LOHR
15 Asst VP Human Resources .... Greg WALTERS
40 Director of Bookstore .... Nicole CASTILLO
19 Director of Public Safety .... Michael BELCHER
18 Exec Director Support Services .... Scott HEATON
82 Director School Intl Studies .... William HERRIN
102 AVP Foundation/Corporate Relations .... Scott BIEDERMANN
110 AVP Development .... Bill JOHNSON
100 President's Chief of Staff .... Vacant
104 Dir International Programs Services .... Ryan GRIFFITH
43 General Counsel/Secy Regents .... Kevin MILLS
12 Director Sacramento Campus .... Dr. Patrick FAVERTY
04 Exec Asst to the President .... Shim LACY
123 Director Graduate Admissions .... Oliva NASH
16 Director Human Resources .... Linda JEFFERS
117 Director Enterprise Risk Mgmt .... Roberta MARTOZA
116 Director Internal Audit .... Randy SCHWANTES
114 Director University Budget .... Jonallie PARRA
105 Director Web Services .... Vacant
108 Vice Prov Strategy & Educ Effectiv .... Cyd JENEFSKY

University of the People (A)

225 S. Lake Avenue, Suite 300, Pasadena CA 91101
County: Los Angeles — Identification: 667160
Telephone: (626) 264-8880 — Carnegie Class: Not Classified
FAX Number: N/A — Calendar System: Other
URL: www.uopeople.edu
Established: 2009 — Annual Undergrad Tuition & Fees: N/A
Enrollment: N/A — Coed
Affiliation or Control: Independent Non-Profit — IRS Status: 501(c)3
Highest Offering: Master's
Accreditation: DEAC

01 President & Founder .... Mr. Shai RESHEF
05 Provost .... Dr. David HARRIS COHEN
45 VP for Strategy & Planning .... Mr. Yoav VENTURA
84 Vice President Enrollment .... Mr. Asaf WOLFF
11 Sr Vice Pres Operations .... Mr. Rami ISH-HURVITZ
10 Chief Financial Officer .... Mr. Paul AFFUSO

University of Philosophical Research (B)

3910 Los Feliz Boulevard, Los Angeles CA 90027
County: Los Angeles — Identification: 666373
Telephone: (323) 663-2167 — Carnegie Class: Not Classified
FAX Number: (323) 663-9443 — Calendar System: Quarter
URL: www.uprs.edu
Established: 1998 — Annual Undergrad Tuition & Fees: N/A
Enrollment: N/A — Coed
Affiliation or Control: Independent Non-Profit — IRS Status: 501(c)3
Highest Offering: Master's
Accreditation: DEAC

01 President/Chief Executive Officer .... Dr. Greg SALYER
05 Dean & Chief Academic Officer .... Ms. Sharon WRIGHT
06 Registrar .... Mr. Matthew TAYLOR
10 Chief Financial Officer .... Mr. Gregory WILLIS

University of Phoenix Bay Area Campus (C)

3590 N First Street, San Jose CA 95134-1805
Telephone: (800) 266-2107 — Identification: 770193
Accreditation: &NH, ACBSP

† Branch campus of University of Phoenix, Tempe, AZ

University of Phoenix Central Valley Campus (D)

45 River Park Place West, Fresno CA 93720-1552
Telephone: (800) 266-2107 — Identification: 770190
Accreditation: &NH, ACBSP

† Branch campus of University of Phoenix, Tempe, AZ

University of Phoenix Sacramento Valley Campus (E)

2860 Gateway Oaks Drive, Sacramento CA 95833-4334
Telephone: (800) 266-2107 — Identification: 770191
Accreditation: &NH, ACBSP

† Branch campus of University of Phoenix, Tempe, AZ

University of Phoenix San Diego Campus (F)

9645 Granite Ridge Dr, Suite 200,
San Diego CA 92123-2658
Telephone: (800) 473-4346 — Identification: 770192
Accreditation: &NH, ACBSP

† Branch campus of University of Phoenix, Tempe, AZ

University of Phoenix Southern California Campus (G)

3090 Bristol Street, Suite 400, Costa Mesa CA 92626
Telephone: (800) 888-1968 — Identification: 770189
Accreditation: &NH, ACBSP

† Branch campus of University of Phoenix, Tempe, AZ

University of Redlands (H)

PO Box 3080, Redlands CA 92373-0999
County: San Bernardino — FICE Identification: 001322
Unit ID: 121691
Telephone: (909) 793-2121 — Carnegie Class: Masters/L
FAX Number: (909) 793-2029 — Calendar System: Semester
URL: www.redlands.edu
Established: 1907 — Annual Undergrad Tuition & Fees: $46,570
Enrollment: 5,215 — Coed
Affiliation or Control: Independent Non-Profit — IRS Status: 501(c)3
Highest Offering: Doctorate
Accreditation: WC, MUS, SP

01 President .... Dr. Ralph W. KUNCL
05 Provost/Chief Academic Officer .... Dr. Kathy OGREN
10 Vice Pres Finance/Administration .... Mr. Cory NOMURA
32 Vice President/Dean Student Life .... Vacant
84 Vice President for Enrollment .... Mr. Kevin M. DYERLY
111 Vice Pres for Advancement .... Ms. Anita WEST
26 Chief Communications Officer .... Ms. Wendy SHATTUCK
43 General Counsel .... Mr. Brent G. GERATY
100 Chief of Staff .... Ms. Michelle ROGERS
53 Dean School of Education .... Dr. Andrew WALL
50 Dean School of Business .... Dr. Thomas HORAN
49 Dean Arts & Sciences .... Dr. Kendrick BROWN
64 Dean School of Music .... Dr. Andrew GLENDENING
30 Assoc Vice Pres Development .... Mr. Ray WATTS
21 Director Financial Ops & Controller .... Ms. Patricia M. CAUDLE
28 Asc Dean Campus Diversity/Inclusion .Ms. Leela MADHAVA RAU
42 Chaplain .... Rev. John T. WALSH
06 Registrar .... Ms. Maria JOHNSON
104 Director Study Abroad .... Mr. Leo ROWLAND
37 Director of Financial Aid .... Ms. Emily BAKER
90 Director Academic Computing .... Mr. Shariq AHMED
81 Director Center of Sciences & Math .... Dr. Barbara M. MURRAY
88 Director of Environmental Programs .... Dr. Lamont C. HEMPEL
08 Int Director of Library Services .... Ms. Shana HIGGINS
15 Director of Human Resources .... Mr. Jeremy HAMMOND
09 Asst Provost Institutional Research .... Dr. Yan XIE
19 Chief of Public Safety .... Mr. Jeffrey TALBOTT
88 Director Administrative Services .... Mr. Brett TELFORD
18 Director of Facilities Management .... Mr. Roger CELLINI
29 Director of Alumni Relations .... Ms. Shelli STOCKTON
20 Asst Dean of Academic/Student Life .... Ms. Amy WILMS
38 Director Student Counseling Ctr .... Dr. Matt GRAGG
41 Director of PE & Athletics .... Mr. Jeffrey MARTINEZ
96 Office Services Manager .... Ms. Sandi TAYLOR
36 Director Student Employment .... Ms. Kathryn WOOD
07 Director of Admissions .... Ms. Belinda SANDOVAL
13 Exec Dir Information Tech Svcs .... Mr. Steve GARCIA
04 Executive Assistant to President .... Ms. Lauri GRIER
102 Director Foundation & Corp Rels .... Mr. Jerry YU
108 Director Assessment .... Ms. Sheila LLOYD
39 Director of Student Housing .... Ms. Cassandra MORTON
109 Director Event Services .... Mr. Toby BUSHEE
23 Director Student Health Center .... Ms. Elizabeth MEADE
112 Director Major Gifts .... Mr. Brandon MULDER
88 Dir Military & Veteran Services .... Ms. Monique POPE
44 Director Annual Giving .... Ms. Molly WIDDICOMBE
88 Dir Community Service Learning .... Mr. Tony MUELLER
103 Dir Professional Development .... Mr. Erik LARSEN

University of St. Augustine for Health Sciences (I)

700 Windy Point Drive, San Marcos CA 92069
County: San Diego — FICE Identification: 031713
Unit ID: 367954
Telephone: (706) 591-3012 — Carnegie Class: Spec-4-yr-Other Health
FAX Number: (706) 591-3068 — Calendar System: Trimester
URL: www.usa.edu
Established: 1979 — Annual Graduate Tuition & Fees: N/A
Enrollment: 2,140 — Coed
Affiliation or Control: Proprietary — IRS Status: Proprietary
Highest Offering: Doctorate; No Undergraduates
Accreditation: WC, OT, PTA

00 CEO .... Ms. Vivian SANCHEZ
01 President/Chief Academic Officer .... Dr. Wanda NITSCH
88 Sr VP Innovation/Emerg Strategies .... Dr. Susan SAXTON
05 Vice President Academic Operations .... Dr. Cindy MATHENA
32 Vice Pres Student Administration .... Dr. Jeremy WELLS
10 Executive Director of Finance .... Ms. Jennifer BRIAR
75 Dir Inst of Occupational Therapy .... Dr. Karen HOWELL
75 Program Dir Occupational Therapy-CA .... Dr. Erin SCHWIER
88 Int Chair Inst of Physical Therapy .... Dr. Annie BURKE-DOE
88 Dir Physical Therapy Program-FL .... Dr. Jeffrey ROT
88 Program Dir Physical Therapy-TX .... Dr. Manuel A. DOMENECH
88 Dir Trans Doctor Physical Therapy .... Dr. Jodi LIPHART
75 Chair Inst Physical Therapy .... Dr. Anne HULL
88 Director of DHSc/EdD Programs .... Dr. Betine A. MALHOTRA
06 Registrar .... Ms. Diane RONDINELLI
07 Director of Admissions .... Ms. Adrianne JONES
51 Director Continuing Prof Education .... Ms. Lori HANKINS
15 Director Human Resources .... Ms. Kristine ASONSO

University of San Diego (J)

5998 Alcala Park, San Diego CA 92110-2492
County: San Diego — FICE Identification: 010395
Unit ID: 122436
Telephone: (619) 260-4600 — Carnegie Class: DU-Mod
FAX Number: (619) 260-6833 — Calendar System: 4/1/4
URL: www.sandiego.edu
Established: 1949 — Annual Undergrad Tuition & Fees: $46,140
Enrollment: 8,251 — Coed
Affiliation or Control: Roman Catholic — IRS Status: 501(c)3
Highest Offering: Doctorate
Accreditation: WC, CACREP, CAEPN, CEA, ENG, IPSY, LAW, MFCD, NURSE

01 President .... Dr. James T. HARRIS
04 Special Assistant to the President .... Ms. Elaine ATENCIO
05 Vice President & Provost .... Dr. Gail F. BAKER
10 VP Finance/Chief Financial Officer .... Ms. Terry KALFAYAN
45 VP Inst Effectiveness & Strategic .... Dr. Andrew ALLEN
42 Vice President Mission & Ministry .... Msgr. Daniel J. DILLABOUGH
32 Vice President Student Affairs .... Ms. Carmen M. VAZQUEZ
30 Vice President Univ Relations .... Dr. Timothy L. O'MALLEY
11 Vice President of Operations .... Mr. Ky L. SNYDER
49 Dean College of Arts & Sciences .... Dr. Noelle NORTON
50 Dean School of Business Admin .... Dr. Jaime A. GOMEZ
54 Dean Shiley-Marcos School of Engr .... Dr. Chell ROBERTS
61 Dean School of Law .... Mr. Stephen C. FERRUOLO
53 Dean Sch Leadership/Educ Sciences .... Dr. Nicholas LADANY
66 Dean School Nursing/Health Science .... Dr. Sally B. HARDIN
88 Dean School of Peace Studies .... Dr. Patricia MARQUEZ
51 Dean Prof & Continuing Education .... Dr. Jason LEMON
08 Dean University Library .... Dr. Theresa BYRD
43 General Counsel .... Ms. Kelly C. DOUGLAS
20 Vice Provost .... Dr. Thomas R. HERRINTON
13 Vice Provost & Chief Info Officer .... Mr. Christopher W. WESSELLS
06 University Registrar .... Ms. Elizabeth SILVA
20 Associate Provost Academic Planning .... Vacant
28 Assoc Provost for Incl & Diversity .... Dr. Esteban DEL RIO
20 Assoc Provost International Affairs .... Dr. Denise DIMON
21 Assoc Vice Pres & Controller .... Ms. Katy ROIG
41 Assoc VP & Exec Dir of Athletics .... Mr. Bill MCGILLIS
84 Asst VP Enrollment Management .... Mr. Stephen F. PULTZ
15 AVP & Chief Human Resources Officer .... Ms. Karen BRIGGS
18 Asst VP Facilities Management .... Ms. Melissa PLASKONOS
26 Assoc Vice Pres Univ Communications .... Mr. Peter MARLOW
27 Asst Vice Pres Digital & Media Comm .... Ms. Pamela GRAY PAYTON
19 Asst VP & Chief Public Safety .... Mr. James MIYASHIRO
35 Asst VP & Dean of Students .... Dr. Donald R. GODWIN
109 Assoc VP Auxiliary Services .... Mr. Andre MALLIE
07 Director of Admissions & Enrollment .... Ms. Minh-Ha HOANG
09 Dir Inst Research & Planning .... Dr. Paula S. KRIST
90 Sr Director Academic Tech Services .... Ms. Shahra MESHKATY
91 Senior Director ERP Technologies .... Mr. Avi BADWAL
102 Sr Director Foundation Relations .... Ms. Annette KETNER
86 Sr Dir Community/Govt Relations .... Mr. Thomas R. CLEARY
112 Senior Director Planned Giving .... Mr. John A. PHILLIPS
29 Senior Director Alumni Relations .... Mr. Charles BASS
44 Director Annual Giving .... Mr. Philip GARLAND
36 Director Career Development Center .... Ms. Robin DARMON
38 Director Counseling Center .... Dr. Stephen D. SPRINKLE
37 Director Financial Aid .... Ms. Judith LEWIS LOGUE

92 Director Honors Program .... Dr. James O. GUMP
39 Asst Dean Residential Life .... Ms. Dayanne IZMIRIAN
85 Dir International Students/Scholars .... Ms. Chia-Yen LIN
104 Dir International Studies Abroad .... Dr. Kira A. ESPIRITU
93 Director Multicultural Center .... Dr. Mayte PEREZ-FRANCO
88 Director Digital Media & Communicat .... Ms. Elizabeth HARMAN
96 Director Procurement Services .... Ms. Dawn L. ANDERSON
25 Director Sponsored Programs .... Ms. Traci MERRILL
23 Director Student Health Center .... Ms. Pamela J. SIKES
106 Dir Online Education/E-learning .... Ms. Roxanne MORRISON
22 Dir Title IX/EEO .... Dr. Nicole SCHUESSLER

University of San Francisco (A)

2130 Fulton Street, San Francisco CA 94117-1080
County: San Francisco FICE Identification: 001325
Unit ID: 122612
Telephone: (415) 422-5555 Carnegie Class: DU-Mod
FAX Number: (415) 422-2303 Calendar System: 4/1/4
URL: www.usfca.edu
Established: 1855 Annual Undergrad Tuition & Fees: $44,494
Enrollment: 10,797 Coed
Affiliation or Control: Roman Catholic IRS Status: 501(c)3
Highest Offering: Doctorate
Accreditation: **WC**, IPSY, LAW, NURSE, PH, SPAA

01 President .... Rev. Paul J. FITZGERALD, SJ
00 Chancellor .... Rev. Stephen A. PRIVETT, SJ
05 Provost & Vice Pres Acad Affairs .... Dr. Donald HELLER
10 Vice President Business & Finance .... Mr. Charles E. CROSS
26 Vice Pres Marketing Communications .... Ms. Ellen RYDER
82 Vice Pres International Relations .... Dr. Stanley D. NEL
30 Vice President Development .... Mr. Peter J. WILCH
43 General Counsel .... Ms. Donna J. DAVIS
13 Vice President IT & CIO .... Mr. Opinder BAWA
20 Senior Vice Provost Acad Affairs .... Dr. Shirley MCGUIRE
32 Vice Provost Student Life .... Ms. Julie J. ORIO
28 Vice Prov Diversity & Community .... Dr. Mary J. WARDELL-GHIRARDUZZI
114 Vice Prov Inst Budget/Plan/Effect .... Dr. Jeff HAMRICK
84 Vice Provost Strategic Enroll Mgmt .... Mr. Michael BESEDA
12 Vice Prov Branch Campus .... Vacant
61 Dean of the School of Law .... Mr. John D. TRASVINA
49 Dean College Arts & Sciences .... Dr. Marcelo F. CAMPERI
08 Dean of University Library .... Dr. Tyrone H. CANNON
53 Dean School of Education .... Dr. Shabnam KOIRALA-AZAD
66 Dean School of Nursing & Health Pgm .... Dr. Margaret W. BAKER
50 Dean School of Management .... Dr. Elizabeth B. DAVIS
18 Assoc Vice Pres Facilities Mgmt .... Mr. Michael LONDON
21 Assoc Vice Pres Finance & Treasury .... Ms. Stacy LEWIS
15 Assoc Vice Pres Human Resources .... Ms. Martha A. PEUGH-WADE
21 Assoc Vice Pres Account & Bus Svcs .... Mr. Frank M. WASILEWSKI
88 Rector of Jesuit Community .... Rev. Timothy S. GODFREY, SJ
42 Director University Ministry .... Ms. Julia A. DOWD
88 Asst Vice Prov Digital Strat/Online .... Mr. John DEVOY
37 Assoc Vice Prov Student Fin Svcs .... Ms. Mary L. BOOKER
04 Exec Asst to President/Sec BOT .... Ms. Jaci E. NEESAM
27 Assoc VP Public Affairs/Media Rels .... Mr. Gary MCDONALD
88 Assoc Vice Prov Acad Affs/Historian .... Dr. Alan L. ZIAJKA
45 Assoc Vice Prov Planning and Budget .... Mr. Michael J. HARRINGTON
110 Sr Assoc VP Development .... Mr. Preston S. WALTON
06 Assoc Dean University Registrar .... Mr. Robert L. BROMFIELD
91 Assoc VP & Dir Application Svcs .... Mr. Way LEON
96 Dir Purchasing & Ancillary Svc .... Ms. Janet L. TEYMOURTASH
38 Senior Dir Counseling & Psych Svcs .... Dr. Barbara J. THOMAS
36 Senior Director Career Svcs .... Mr. Alex HOCHMAN
19 Senior Director of Public Safety .... Dr. Daniel L. LAWSON
88 Asst Vice Prov Graduate Enrollment .... Mr. Michael HUGHES
88 Asst Vice Prov Integ Enrol Data Mgt .... Mr. Shawn HICKS
104 Director Ctr for Global Education .... Ms. Sharon F. LI
07 Asst Vice Prov Undergrad Admissions .... Ms. April CRABTREE
85 Assoc Dir Intl Student/Scholar Svcs .... Ms. Marcella PITCHER DEPROTO
41 Director of Athletics .... Mr. Scott A. SIDWELL
29 Assoc VP Alumni & Donor Engagement .... Ms. Leslie THEODORE
44 Assoc VP Giving & Devel Svc & PR&M .... Ms. Jessica JORDAN
102 Director Corporate & Foundation Rel .... Mr. Johnny COOPER
29 Director University Initiatives .... Mr. Bill CARTWRIGHT
16 Dir Employment & Employee Relations .... Ms. Diane L. NELSON
09 Dir Inst Research and Analytics .... Mr. Theodore M. LYDON, JR.
39 Dir Student Housing/Resident Educ .... Vacant
24 Dir Ctr Learning Instruct & Tech .... Dr. John BANSAVICH
105 Sr Director Web Communications .... Ms. Marlene K. TOM
108 Dir Educ Effective/Assessment .... Ms. Deborah PANTER
25 Director Contracts/Grants Admin .... Mr. Donald CAMPBELL
88 Asst Dean/Director Disability Svcs .... Mr. Tom MERRELL

University of Southern California (B)

University Park, Los Angeles CA 90089-0012
County: Los Angeles FICE Identification: 001328
Unit ID: 123961
Telephone: (213) 740-2311 Carnegie Class: DU-Highest
FAX Number: (213) 740-8502 Calendar System: Semester
URL: www.usc.edu
Established: 1880 Annual Undergrad Tuition & Fees: $52,283
Enrollment: 43,401 Coed
Affiliation or Control: Independent Non-Profit IRS Status: 501(c)3
Highest Offering: Doctorate
Accreditation: **WC**, ANEST, ARCPA, CAEPN, CLPSY, CS, DENT, DH, @DIETC, DIETI, ENG, HSA, IPSY, JOUR, LAW, LSAR, MED, OT, PCSAS, PDPSY, PH, PHAR, PLNG, PTA, SPAA, SW

01 President .... Dr. C. L. M. NIKIAS
05 Provost and Sr VP Academic Affairs .... Dr. Michael QUICK
11 Sr VP Administration .... Mr. Todd R. DICKEY
10 Sr VP Finance & CFO .... Mr. James STATEN
26 Sr VP University Relations .... Mr. Thomas SAYLES
30 Sr VP University Advancement .... Mr. Albert R. CHECCIO
23 Sr VP & CEO for USC Health .... Mr. Thomas E. JACKIEWICZ
88 Chief Investment Officer .... Ms. Lisa MAZZOCCO
43 Senior VP Admin and General Counsel .... Ms. Carol MAUCH AMIR
32 VP for Student Affairs .... Dr. Ainsley CARRY
07 VP Admissions and Planning .... Dr. L. Katharine HARRINGTON
46 VP for Research .... Dr. Randolph W. HALL
88 VP for Athletic Compliance .... Mr. Michael BLANTON
88 VP Capital Construction/Facilities .... Mr. Lloyd SILBERSTEIN
88 VP for Health Sciences Development .... Mr. Dave CARRERA
27 VP Public Relations & Marketing .... Ms. Brenda K. MACEO
41 Athletic Director .... Mr. Lynn SWAN
100 Chief of Staff/Director of Protocol .... Mr. Dennis CORNELL
60 Dean Annenberg School Communication .... Dr. Willow C. BAY
48 Dean School of Architecture .... Mr. Milton S. CURRY
50 Dean Marshall School of Business .... Mr. James G. ELLIS
88 Dean School of Cinematic Arts .... Dr. Elizabeth M. DALEY
66 Dean Kaufman School of Dance .... Dr. Robert A. CUTIETTA
52 Dean Ostrow School of Dentistry .... Dr. Avishai SADAN
53 Dean Rossier School of Education .... Dr. Karen S. GALLAGHER
54 Dean Viterbi School of Engineering .... Dr. Yannis C. YORTSOS
57 Dean Roski School of Fine Arts .... Dr. Erica MUHL
88 Dean Davis School of Gerontology .... Dr. Pinchas COHEN
61 Dean Gould School of Law .... Dr. Andrew GUZMAN
63 Dean Keck School of Medicine .... Dr. Rohit VARMA
64 Dean Thornton School of Music .... Dr. Robert A. CUTIETTA
67 Dean School of Pharmacy .... Dr. Vassilios PAPADOPOULOS
70 Dean School of Social Work .... Dr. Marilyn L. FLYNN
88 Dean School of Dramatic Arts .... Mr. David BRIDEL
88 Dean Price School of Public Policy .... Dr. Jack H. KNOTT
49 Dean Dornsife Col Ltrs Arts & Sci .... Dr. Amber MILLER
42 Dean Religious Life .... Dr. Varun SONI
06 Registrar .... Dr. Frank CHANG
08 Dean University Libraries .... Ms. Catherine QUINLAN
07 Dean of Admission .... Mr. Timothy BRUNOLD
37 Dean of Financial Aid .... Mr. Thomas MCWHORTER
88 Assoc Sr VP Admin Operations .... Mr. David W. WRIGHT
29 Assoc Sr VP and Campaign Director .... Mr. Sam M. LOPEZ
28 Exec Dir of Equity/Diversity .. Ms. Gretchen DAHLINGER MEANS
38 Dir Counseling & Psychological Svcs .... Dr. Ilene ROSENSTEIN
88 Vice Provost and Senior Advisor .... Dr. Martin L. LEVINE
20 Vice Prov for Graduate Programs .... Dr. Sarah PRATT
20 Vice Prov for Undergraduate Program .... Dr. Andrea HODGE
13 Chief Information Officer .... Dr. Douglas SHOOK
88 Vice Prov Academic Ops .... Dr. Mark TODD
88 Exec Dir USC Stevens Ctr for Innov .... Ms. Jennifer DYER
88 VP of Global Initiatives .... Dr. Anthony BAILEY
20 Vice Prov for Acad/Faculty Affairs .... Dr. Elizabeth GRADDY

University of the West (C)

1409 Walnut Grove Avenue, Rosemead CA 91770-3709
County: Los Angeles FICE Identification: 036963
Unit ID: 449870
Telephone: (626) 571-8811 Carnegie Class: Bac-Diverse
FAX Number: (626) 571-1413 Calendar System: Semester
URL: www.uwest.edu
Established: 1991 Annual Undergrad Tuition & Fees: $11,412
Enrollment: 324 Coed
Affiliation or Control: Independent Non-Profit IRS Status: 501(c)3
Highest Offering: Doctorate
Accreditation: **WC**

01 President .... Dr. Stephen MORGAN
05 Chief Academic Officer .... Dr. Peter M. ROJCEWICZ
32 Dean of Student Affairs .... Ms. Vanessa KARAM
84 Dean of Enrollment .... Dr. Maria AYON
10 Chief Financial Officer .... Mr. Michael OERTEL
08 Director of Library .... Ms. Ling Ling KUO
06 Registrar .... Ms. Jeanette ANDERSON
35 Student Life Coordinator .... Mr. Eddie ESCALANTE
73 Chair of Religious Studies .... Dr. Jane IWAMURA
50 Chair of Business Admin .... Dr. Bill CHEN
97 Chair of General Education .... Dr. Peter ROJCEWICZ
83 Chair of Psychology .... Dr. Hiroshi SASASKI
88 Chair of English/ESL .... Mr. Michael GROSSO

University of West Los Angeles (D)

9800 La Cienga Blvd., 12th Floor, Inglewood CA 90301-4423
County: Los Angeles Identification: 667301
Unit ID: 484862
Telephone: (310) 342-5200 Carnegie Class: Not Classified
FAX Number: N/A Calendar System: Semester
URL: www.uwla.edu
Established: 1966 Annual Undergrad Tuition & Fees: N/A
Enrollment: N/A Coed
Affiliation or Control: Proprietary IRS Status: Proprietary
Highest Offering: First Professional Degree
Accreditation: **@WC**

01 President .... Robert BROWN
10 Chief Financial Officer .... Richard MIYAKE
61 Dean School of Law .... Jay FRYKBERG
09 Director Institutional Research .... Jesse ALDAVA

Valley College of Medical Careers (E)

8399 Topanga Canyon Blvd Ste 200, West Hills CA 91304
County: Los Angeles FICE Identification: 041145
Unit ID: 449445
Telephone: (818) 883-9002 Carnegie Class: Not Classified
FAX Number: (818) 883-9003 Calendar System: Semester
URL: www.vcmc.edu
Established: Annual Undergrad Tuition & Fees: N/A
Enrollment: 124 Coed
Affiliation or Control: Proprietary IRS Status: Proprietary
Highest Offering: Associate Degree
Accreditation: **ABHES**, SURTEC

01 Campus Director .... Mr. Ronny SUSSMAN

Vanguard University of Southern California (F)

55 Fair Drive, Costa Mesa CA 92626-6597
County: Orange FICE Identification: 001293
Unit ID: 123651
Telephone: (714) 556-3610 Carnegie Class: Masters/S
FAX Number: (714) 957-9317 Calendar System: Semester
URL: www.vanguard.edu
Established: 1920 Annual Undergrad Tuition & Fees: $31,430
Enrollment: 2,184 Coed
Affiliation or Control: Assemblies Of God Church IRS Status: 501(c)3
Highest Offering: Master's
Accreditation: **WC**, MUS, NURSE, THEA

01 President .... Dr. Michael J. BEALS
100 Dir Oper Strategic Plng/Spec Proj .... Ms. Shree CARTER
04 Exec Assistant to the President .... Mrs. Alexis SCHNOOR
05 Provost/Vice President Acad Affairs .... Dr. Doretha O'QUINN
49 Assoc Provost/Dean Col Arts & Sci .... Dr. Michael D. WILSON
107 Dean Professional Studies .... Vacant
73 Co-Director of Graduate Religion .... Dr. Roger HEUSER
73 Co-Director of Graduate Religion .... Dr. Doug PETERSEN
53 Director for Graduate Education .... Dr. Sylvia KANE
83 Director for Graduate Psychology .... Dr. Jerre WHITE
06 Registrar .... Ms. Judy HAMILTON
104 Director Global Outreach/Educ .... Ms. Kayli HILLEBRAND
09 Assoc Dir of Institutional Research .... Mr. John KIM
08 Head Librarian .... Ms. Pamela CRENSHAW
41 Athletic Director .... Mr. Rhett SOLIDAY
10 Chief Financial Officer .... Mr. Jeremy MOSER
21 Controller .... Ms. Jill ROBINSON
21 Director of Accounting Operations .... Ms. Krystal GOWENS
96 Director of Fiscal Management .... Ms. Katy MCINTOSH
19 Sr Dir of Campus Safety Services .... Mr. Paul TURGEON
13 Chief Information Officer .... Mr. Derek DENSBERGER
15 Senior Director of Human Resources .... Mr. Joe BAFFA
18 Director of Facility Operations .... Mr. Dan TORO
40 Bookstore Manager .... Ms. Stephanie BUNT
101 Board Professional .... Ms. Shree CARTER
42 University Campus Pastor .... Rev. Jonathan ALLBAUGH
32 Vice President of Student Life .... Dr. Tim YOUNG
39 Student Housing Coordinator .... Ms. Megan SISK
24 Dir Stdnt Success/Acad Res/Fam Rels .... Ms. Amanda LEBRECHT
38 Director of Counseling Services .... Dr. Doug HUTCHINSON
36 Career Planning Coordinator .... Ms. Kimberly GREENE
28 Chief Diversity Officer .... Dr. April HARRIS
84 VP for Enrollment Management .... Ms. Kim JOHNSON
07 Director of Undergrad Admissions .... Vacant
07 Dir of Grad/Prof Studies Admissions .... Mr. Matthew NIXON
37 Director of Student Financial Aid .... Ms. Crystal MADAULE
30 VP University Advancement .... Mr. Justin MCINTEE
44 Director of Annual Fund .... Mr. Brent THEOLBALD
29 Director of Alumni Engagement .... Mr. Joel GACKLE
26 Chief Communications Officer .... Ms. Linsey CARBONE
86 Director of Veteran/Government Rels .... Mr. Brent THEOBALD
102 Director of External Relations .... Mr. David VAZQUEZ
108 Director Institutional Assessment .... Ms. Ludmilla PRASLOVA

*Ventura County Community College District (G)

761 East Daily Drive, Suite 200, Camarillo CA 93010
County: Ventura FICE Identification: 006863
Unit ID: 125019
Telephone: (805) 652-5500 Carnegie Class: N/A
FAX Number: N/A
URL: www.vcccd.edu

01 Chancellor .... Dr. Greg GILLESPIE
101 Admin Officer to Chancellor/Board .... Ms. Patti BLAIR
05 Vice Chancellor Educ Services .... Mr. Rick POST
10 Vice Chanc Business Svcs/Fin Mgmt .... Dr. David EL FATTAL
15 Vice Chanc of Human Resources .... Mr. Michael SHANAHAN
13 Assoc Vice Chanc of IT .... Mr. Dave FUHRMANN
02 Moorpark College President .... Mr. Luis SANCHEZ
02 Oxnard College President .... Dr. Cynthia AZARI
02 Ventura College President .... Mr. David KEEBLER

*Moorpark College (A)

7075 Campus Road, Moorpark CA 93021-1695
County: Ventura FICE Identification: 007115
Unit ID: 119137
Telephone: (805) 378-1400 Carnegie Class: Assoc/HT-High Trad
FAX Number: (805) 378-1499 Calendar System: Semester
URL: www.moorparkcollege.edu
Established: 1967 Annual Undergrad Tuition & Fees (In-State): $1,388
Enrollment: 14,027 Coed
Affiliation or Control: State IRS Status: 501(c)3
Highest Offering: Associate Degree
Accreditation: WJ, ADNUR, RAD

02 President ... Mr. Luis P. SANCHEZ
05 Vice President Academic Affairs ... Dr. Julius SOKENU
10 Vice President Business Services ... Ms. Silvia BARAJAS
32 Vice President Student Services ... Dr. Amanuel GEBRU
04 Executive Assistant to President ... Ms. Linda RESENDIZ
20 Dean of Student Learning ... Mr. Howard DAVIS
20 Dean of Student Learning ... Dr. Jennifer KALFSBEEK-GOETZ
20 Dean of Student Learning ... Dr. Norman MARTEN
20 Dean of Student Learning ... Dr. Jane MORGAN
20 Dean of Student Learning ... Ms. Mary REES
20 Dean of Student Learning ... Ms. Lisa PUTNAM
20 Dean of Student Learning ... Dr. Helga WINKLER
109 College Business Services Manager ... Vacant
18 Director Maintainence/Operations ... Mr. John SINUTKO
13 Director Information Technology ... Mr. Dan MCMICHAEL
113 Bursar ... Ms. Lindy CHAU
23 Director Student Health Services ... Ms. Sharon MANAKAS
41 Athletic Director ... Mr. Vance MANAKAS
121 Director Student Success ... Dr. Jesus VEGA
06 Registrar ... Mr. David ANTER
37 Student Financial Aid Officer ... Ms. Kim KORINKE

*Oxnard College (B)

4000 S Rose Avenue, Oxnard CA 93033-6699
County: Ventura FICE Identification: 012842
Unit ID: 120421
Telephone: (805) 678-5800 Carnegie Class: Assoc/MT-VT-High Trad
FAX Number: (805) 986-5806 Calendar System: Semester
URL: www.oxnardcollege.edu
Established: 1975 Annual Undergrad Tuition & Fees (In-District): $1,388
Enrollment: 7,006 Coed
Affiliation or Control: State/Local IRS Status: 501(c)3
Highest Offering: Associate Degree
Accreditation: WJ, DH, IFSAC

02 President ... Dr. Cynthia AZARI
05 VP Acad Affairs/Student Learning ... Vacant
10 Vice President of Business Services ... Dr. Michael BUSH
32 Vice Pres Student Development ... Dr. Oscar COBIAN
79 Dean Liberal Studies ... Mr. Art SANDFORD
88 Dean Career & Technical Education ... Dr. Christina TAFOYA
81 Dean Math Science/Health ... Dr. Carolyn INOUYE
09 Dean Institutional Effectiveness ... Dr. Cynthia HERRERA
18 Director Maintenance/Operations ... Mr. Bob SUBE
41 Director of Athletics ... Mr. Jonas CRAWFORD
06 Registrar ... Mr. Joel DIAZ
88 Director STEM ... Dr. Eliseo GONZALEZ
37 Financial Aid Officer ... Ms. Linda FAASUA
109 College Services Supervisor ... Mr. Christopher RENBARGER

*Ventura College (C)

4667 Telegraph Road, Ventura CA 93003-3899
County: Ventura FICE Identification: 001334
Unit ID: 125028
Telephone: (805) 289-6000 Carnegie Class: Assoc/HT-High Trad
FAX Number: (805) 289-6466 Calendar System: Semester
URL: www.venturacollege.edu
Established: 1925 Annual Undergrad Tuition & Fees (In-District): $1,388
Enrollment: 12,989 Coed
Affiliation or Control: State/Local IRS Status: 501(c)3
Highest Offering: Associate Degree
Accreditation: WJ, ADNUR, EMT

02 President ... Dr. Greg GILLESPIE
05 Vice President Academic Affairs ... Dr. Kim HOFFMANS
32 Vice Pres Student Affairs ... Dr. Damien A. PENA
10 Vice Pres Business/Admin Services ... Mr. David KEEBLER
04 Exec Assistant to the President ... Ms. Laura BROWER
108 Dean Institutional Effectiveness ... Mr. Phillip BRIGGS
81 Dean Sciences ... Mr. Dan KUMPF
88 Dean Health/Kines/Ath/Perf Ar ... Mr. Tim HARRISON
83 Dean Vis Arts/Behav & Soc Sci/Lang ... Ms. Gwen HUDDLESTON
103 Dean Workforce/Economic Development ... Ms. Debbie NEWCOMB
81 Dean Eng/Math/Lrng Resources ... Ms. Lynn WRIGHT
102 Executive Director Foundation ... Vacant
06 Registrar ... Ms. Arlene REED
18 Director Maintenance/Operations ... Mr. Jay MOORE
35 Coordinator Student Activities ... Ms. Libby FATTA
37 Financial Aid Officer ... Ms. Alma RODRIGUEZ
09 Institutional Research ... Mr. Michael CALLAHAN
85 International Students ... Ms. Ellie YOO
84 Enrollment Management ... Ms. Connie BAKER
23 Director Student Health Center ... Ms. Mary JONES
19 Campus Police ... Sgt. Mike PALLOTO
26 Marketing Specialist ... Ms. Cindy JONES
41 Athletic Director ... Mr. Will COWEN

Veritas Evangelical Seminary (D)

3000 W. MacArthur Boulevard, Santa Ana CA 92704
County: Orange Identification: 667103
Telephone: (714) 966-8500 Carnegie Class: Not Classified
FAX Number: (714) 966-8500 Calendar System: Semester
URL: www.ves.edu
Established: 2008 Annual Graduate Tuition & Fees: N/A
Enrollment: N/A Coed
Affiliation or Control: Independent Non-Profit IRS Status: 501(c)3
Highest Offering: Master's; No Undergraduates
Accreditation: TRACS

00 Chancellor ... Norman L. GEISLER
01 President ... Joseph M. HOLDEN
06 Registrar/Dir of Admissions ... Vanessa ACOSTA
05 Chief Academic Officer ... Joel L. WINGO
08 Library Director ... Joe MCELROY
10 Chief Business Officer ... Deborah DELARGY
88 Director External Studies Program ... Scott MATSCHERZ
09 Dir Inst Effectiveness/Assessment ... Frank CORREA
32 Director Student/Alumni Affairs ... Deborah DELARGY

Victor Valley College (E)

18422 Bear Valley Road, Victorville CA 92395-5850
County: San Bernardino FICE Identification: 001335
Unit ID: 125091
Telephone: (760) 245-4271 Carnegie Class: Assoc/HT-High Trad
FAX Number: (760) 245-9019 Calendar System: Semester
URL: www.vvc.edu
Established: 1961 Annual Undergrad Tuition & Fees (In-District): $1,126
Enrollment: 11,669 Coed
Affiliation or Control: State/Local IRS Status: 501(c)3
Highest Offering: Associate Degree
Accreditation: WJ, COARC, EMT

01 Superintendent/President ... Dr. Roger W. WAGNER
05 Exec VP Instruction/Stdnt Svcs ... Dr. Peter MAPHUMULO
10 Vice President Admin Services ... Ms. Tracey RICHARDSON
15 Director Human Resources ... Mr. Raymond QUAN
76 Dean Health Science & Public Safety ... Vacant
79 Dean Acad Pgms Humanities/Soc Sci ... Dr. Patricia ELLERSON
21 Director Fiscal Services ... Ms. Shawntee MILTON
07 Director of Admissions ... Mrs. Greta MOON
26 Director Public Info/Marketing ... Mr. Robert SEWELL
41 Director Athletics/Athletic Trainer ... Mrs. Jaye TASHIMA
18 Exec Dir Facilities/Operations ... Mr. Stephen R. GARCIA
37 Director Financial Aid ... Mr. Jason JUDKINS
109 Director Auxiliary Services/ASB Adv ... Mrs. Deanna SANABRIA
32 Dean Student Services ... Mr. Arthur LOPEZ
18 Director Facilities Construction ... Vacant
19 Chief Campus Police ... Mr. Leonard KNIGHT
13 Chief Information Officer ... Mr. Kevin LEAHY
88 Director Child Development Center ... Vacant
88 Dir EOPS/CARE ... Mr. Carl SMITH
09 Exec Dean Inst Effectiveness ... Ms. Virginia MORAN
04 Executive Asst to President ... Ms. Victoria MARTINELLI
08 Head Librarian ... Ms. Leslie HUINER
102 Exec Dir Foundation ... Mrs. Catherine ABBOTT
104 Facilitator Study Abroad ... Dr. Hinrich KAISER

Weimar Institute (F)

20602 W. Paoli Lane, Weimar CA 95736
County: Placer Identification: 667302
Telephone: (530) 422-7927 Carnegie Class: Not Classified
FAX Number: N/A Calendar System: Semester
URL: www.weimar.edu
Established: Annual Undergrad Tuition & Fees: N/A
Enrollment: N/A Coed
Affiliation or Control: Independent Non-Profit IRS Status: 501(c)3
Highest Offering: Baccalaureate
Accreditation: @WC

01 President ... Neil NEDLEY
05 Vice President Academic Affairs ... Allen DAVIS
10 Chief Financial Officer ... Michael BERNARD
09 Director of Institutional Research ... Kristine BRUNKOW

West Coast Baptist College (G)

4010 E. Lancaster Boulevard, Lancaster CA 93535
County: Los Angeles Identification: 667268
Telephone: (661) 946-2274 Carnegie Class: Not Classified
FAX Number: (661) 946-4510 Calendar System: Semester
URL: www.wcbc.edu
Established: 1995 Annual Undergrad Tuition & Fees: N/A
Enrollment: N/A Coed
Affiliation or Control: Baptist IRS Status: 501(c)3
Highest Offering: Master's
Accreditation: @TRACS

01 Founder & President ... Dr. Paul CHAPPELL
03 Exec Vice President ... Dr. John GOETSCH
05 Chief Academic Officer ... Dr. Thomas SHEPHERD
11 Dean of Administrative Affairs ... Dr. Jerry GODDARD

West Coast Ultrasound Institute (H)

291 S. La Cienega Blvd, Ste 500, Beverly Hills CA 90211
County: Los Angeles FICE Identification: 036393
Unit ID: 441229
Telephone: (310) 289-5123 Carnegie Class: Spec 2-yr-Health
FAX Number: (310) 289-5136 Calendar System: Quarter
URL: www.wcui.edu
Established: 1998 Annual Undergrad Tuition & Fees: $21,300
Enrollment: 748 Coed
Affiliation or Control: Proprietary IRS Status: Proprietary
Highest Offering: Associate Degree
Accreditation: ACCSC

01 Campus Director ... Ms. Myra CHASON

West Coast Ultrasound Institute (I)

3700 E. Inland Empire Blvd, Ste 235, Ontario CA 91764
Telephone: (909) 483-3808 Identification: 770942
Accreditation: ACCSC

† Main campus is West Coast Ultrasound Institute in Los Angeles, CA.

West Coast University (J)

1477 South Manchester Avenue, Anaheim CA 92802
Telephone: (949) 783-4841 Identification: 770480
Accreditation: &WC, DH

West Coast University (K)

12215 Victory Boulevard, North Hollywood CA 91606-3206
County: Los Angeles FICE Identification: 036983
Unit ID: 443331
Telephone: (818) 299-5500 Carnegie Class: Spec-4-yr-Other Health
FAX Number: (818) 299-5545 Calendar System: Semester
URL: www.westcoastuniversity.edu
Established: 1909 Annual Undergrad Tuition & Fees: $33,675
Enrollment: 1,820 Coed
Affiliation or Control: Proprietary IRS Status: Proprietary
Highest Offering: Doctorate
Accreditation: WC, NURSE, OT, @PHAR, @PTA

01 Co-President ... Dr. Jeb EGBERT
01 Co-President ... Ms. Sandra PHAM
03 Executive Director ... Mr. Tim GRAMLING
05 Provost ... Mr. Arte LIBUNAO
10 Business Ops/Chief Financial Ofcr ... Ms. Sandra PHAM
66 Dean of Nursing Los Angeles Campus ... Dr. Robyn NELSON
20 Academic Dean ... Dr. Miriam KAHAN
76 Founding Dean Occupational Therapy ... Dr. Nicolaas VAN DEN HEEVER
67 Associate Dean School of Pharmacy ... Dr. Reza TAHERI
07 Director of Admissions ... Ms. Julie CHIN
37 Exec Director of Financial Aid ... Dr. Amanda SCHROEDER
75 Founding Dean of Physical Therapy ... Dr. Stan HARTGRAVES
81 Chair Science Department ... Dr. Evan PEPPER
32 Director of Student Affairs ... Ms. Rochelle ASANTI
08 Librarian ... Ms. Jan KUEBEL-HERNANDEZ
06 Registrar ... Mr. Steve BURNS
09 Director of Institutional Research ... Mr. Mahmoud ALBAWANEH

West Coast University (L)

2855 E Guasti Road, Ontario CA 91761
Telephone: (909) 467-6100 Identification: 770484
Accreditation: &WC

*West Hills Community College District (M)

9900 Cody Street, Coalinga CA 93210
County: Fresno Identification: 667041
Telephone: (559) 934-2180 Carnegie Class: N/A
FAX Number: (559) 934-2810
URL: www.westhillscollege.com

01 Chancellor ... Dr. Stuart VAN HORN
10 Deputy Chancellor ... Mr. Ken STOPPENBRINK
05 VC Educ Svcs/Workforce Development ... Dr. Linda THOMAS
90 Assoc VC Enr Mgmt & Inst Eff ... Ms. Rita GROGAN
13 Assoc VC Educ Svcs/Info Technology . Ms. Michelle KOZLOWSKI
21 Assoc VC of Business Services ... Ms. Tammy WEATHERMAN
46 Assoc VC of Connected Learning ... Dr. Kelly COOPER
15 Director of Human Resources ... Ms. Becky CAZARES
102 Exec Director WHCC Foundation ... Vacant
26 Dir of Marketing/Comm/Public Info ... Ms. Amber MYRICK
25 Director of Grants ... Ms. Anita WRIGHT
66 District Director of Health Careers ... Ms. Kathryn DEFEDE
88 Dir of Child Development Centers ... Ms. Conne CLEVELAND
103 Dir of Special Grant Programs ... Mr. David CASTILLO
103 Dir of Special Grant Programs ... Mr. Javier CAZARES
09 Dir of Accred/Research/Inst Eff ... Mr. Kyle CRIDER
04 Executive Assistant to Chancellor ... Ms. Donna ISAAC

*West Hills College Coalinga (N)

300 Cherry Lane, Coalinga CA 93210-1399
County: Fresno FICE Identification: 001176
Unit ID: 125462
Telephone: (559) 934-2000 Carnegie Class: Assoc/MT-VT-Mix Trad/Non
FAX Number: N/A Calendar System: Semester
URL: www.westhillscollege.com/coalinga
Established: 1932 Annual Undergrad Tuition & Fees (In-District): $1,380
Enrollment: 2,643 Coed
Affiliation or Control: State/Local IRS Status: Exempt
Highest Offering: Associate Degree

Accreditation: WJ

02 President Ms. Brenda THAMES
03 Executive Vice President Vacant
32 Assoc Dean of Student Services Mr. Mark GRITTON
05 Assoc Dean of Educational Services Mr. Robert PIMENTEL
41 Associate Dean of Athletics Mr. Eric MENDOZA
47 Director of Farm of the Future Mr. Clint COWDEN
85 Dir of International Student Svcs Mr. Daniel TAMAYO
88 Director of Title IV Projects Ms. Raquel RODRIGUEZ
88 Director of North District Center Ms. Bertha FELIX-MATA
37 Director of Financial Aid Vacant
04 Administrative Asst to President Ms. Lorna DAVIS
08 Head Librarian Mr. Matthew MAGNUSON
18 Dir of Maintenance & Operations Mr. Shaun BAILEY
39 Director of Residential Living Mr. Alex VILLALOBOS

*West Hills College Lemoore (A)

555 College Avenue, Lemoore CA 93245-9248
County: Kings FICE Identification: 041113
Unit ID: 448594
Telephone: (559) 925-3000 Carnegie Class: Assoc/HT-High Trad
FAX Number: (559) 924-1243 Calendar System: Semester
URL: www.westhillscollege.com/lemoore
Established: 2002 Annual Undergrad Tuition & Fees (In-District): $1,380
Enrollment: 3,853 Coed
Affiliation or Control: State/Local IRS Status: Exempt
Highest Offering: Associate Degree
Accreditation: WJ

02 President Dr. Kristin CLARK
05 Vice President of Educational Svcs Mr. James PRESTON
32 Vice President of Student Services Ms. Sylvia DORSEY-ROBINSON
20 Dean of Educational Svcs Ms. Sue WARNER
35 Dean of Student Services Mr. Joel RUBLE
75 Dean of Career Technical Education Ms. Kris COSTA
37 Director of Financial Aid Ms. Deborah SORIA
88 Assoc Dean of Categorical Programs Ms. Lataria HALL
41 Associate Dean of Athletics Mr. Christopher HAWKEN
08 Head Librarian Mr. Ron OXFORD
18 Dir of Maintenance & Operations Mr. Patrick SWEENEY
88 Director of Upward Bound Mr. Oscar VILLARREAL
04 Administrative Asst to President Ms. Amber AVITIA

*West Valley-Mission Community College District (B)

14000 Fruitvale Avenue, Saratoga CA 95070-5698
County: Santa Clara FICE Identification: 029139
Unit ID: 125222
Telephone: (408) 741-2011 Carnegie Class: N/A
FAX Number: (408) 867-8273
URL: www.wvm.edu

01 Chancellor Dr. Patrick SCHMITT
04 Exec Assist to Chancellor Ms. Brenda ROGERS
11 Vice Chancellor Admin Services Mr. Ed MADULI
15 Vice Chanc Human Resources Mr. Albert MOORE
13 Director Information Systems Mr. Ron SMITH
18 Director of Facilities Mr. Javier CASTRUITA
19 Chief of Police Mr. Kenneth TANAKA
111 Exec Director Advancement Vacant

*Mission College (C)

3000 Mission College Boulevard,
Santa Clara CA 95054-1897
County: Santa Clara FICE Identification: 021191
Unit ID: 118930
Telephone: (408) 988-2200 Carnegie Class: Assoc/HT-High Non
FAX Number: (408) 496-0462 Calendar System: Semester
URL: www.missioncollege.org
Established: 1976 Annual Undergrad Tuition & Fees (In-District): $1,185
Enrollment: 8,576 Coed
Affiliation or Control: State/Local IRS Status: 501(c)3
Highest Offering: Associate Degree
Accreditation: WJ

02 President Mr. Daniel A. PECK
05 Vice Pres of Instruction Dr. Leandra MARTIN
32 Vice President Student Services Dr. John MOSBY
11 Vice Pres Administrative Services Mr. Rick BENNETT
35 Dean of Student Support Services Mr. Richard ALFARO
20 Dean of Instruction Mr. Danny NGUYEN
26 Dir of Public Info & Graphic Design Vacant
20 Director of Marketing Mr. Niall ADLER
81 Dean Applied Science Ms. Mina JAHAN
19 Chief of Police Lt. Kenneth TANAKA
18 Manager of Facilities Mr. Don HOUSTON
07 Director of Admissions Mr. Asmare TADESSE
09 Director of Institutional Research Ms. Inge BOND
37 Dir Student Enroll & Financial Aid Ms. Maria ESCOBAR
04 Exec Assistant to the President Ms. Milani ZEPEDA
88 Language Arts Division Ms. Kathy HENDERSON
60 Communications Dept Mr. Rob DEWIS
81 Mathematics and Science Division Mr. Rick HOBBS
83 Liberal Studies Division Mr. Keith JOHNSON
35 Student Services Division Vacant

*West Valley College (D)

14000 Fruitvale Avenue, Saratoga CA 95070-5698
County: Santa Clara FICE Identification: 001338
Unit ID: 125499
Telephone: (408) 867-2200 Carnegie Class: Assoc/HT-High Non
FAX Number: (408) 867-5033 Calendar System: Semester
URL: www.westvalley.edu
Established: 1963 Annual Undergrad Tuition & Fees (In-District): $1,183
Enrollment: 8,799 Coed
Affiliation or Control: State/Local IRS Status: 501(c)3
Highest Offering: Associate Degree
Accreditation: WJ

02 President Mr. Bradley DAVIS
05 VP Instruction Ms. Kuni HAY
32 VP Student Services Dr. Victoria HINDES
11 VP Administrative Services Mr. Patrick FENTON
20 Dean Instruction Ms. Stephanie KASHIMA
30 Dean Advancement Ms. Cindy SCHELCHER
36 Dean Career Pgm/Wrkforce Dev Mr. Bradley WEISBERG
26 Director Marketing/Communications Mr. Scott LUDWIG
35 Dean of Student Services Mr. Matais POUNCIL
100 Associate Vice Chancellor Mr. Albert MOORE
57 Dean School of Art & Design Mr. Andrew CHANDLER
88 Director Student Equity & Success Ms. Herlisa HAMP
18 Chief Facilities/Physical Plant Mr. Bill TAYLOR
37 Dir Student Financial Aid/Admiss Ms. Maritza CANTARERO
09 Research Analyst Mr. Miqueas DIAL
35 Director Student Development Dr. Sean PEPIN
29 Director Alumni Relations Ms. Cindy SCHELCHER
106 Coord Instruct Tech/Distance Lrng Ms. Lisa KAAZ
04 Sr Executive Assistant to the Pres Ms. Gloria GUTIERREZ
41 Athletic Director Mr. John VLAHOS

Westcliff University (E)

4199 Campus Drive #650, Irvine CA 92612
County: Orange Identification: 667203
Telephone: (888) 491-8686 Carnegie Class: Not Classified
FAX Number: (888) 409-7306 Calendar System: Trimester
URL: www.westcliff.edu
Established: 1993 Annual Undergrad Tuition & Fees: N/A
Enrollment: N/A Coed
Affiliation or Control: Proprietary IRS Status: Proprietary
Highest Offering: Doctorate
Accreditation: @WC, DEAC

01 CEO/President Dr. Anthony LEE
05 CAO/Provost Dr. David C. MCKINNEY
10 Chief Financial Officer Mr. Sean MURRAY
06 Registrar Ms. Rebeca IARATE-CERVANTES

Western State University College of Law (F)

1 Banting, Irvine CA 92618-3601
Telephone: (714) 459-1101 FICE Identification: 010832
Accreditation: &WC, LAW

† Regional accreditation is carried under the parent institution, Argosy University in Orange, CA.

Western University of Health Sciences (G)

309 E 2nd Street, Pomona CA 91766-1854
County: Los Angeles FICE Identification: 024827
Unit ID: 112525
Telephone: (909) 623-6116 Carnegie Class: Spec-4-yr-Med
FAX Number: N/A Calendar System: Semester
URL: www.westernu.edu
Established: 1977 Annual Graduate Tuition & Fees: N/A
Enrollment: 3,876 Coed
Affiliation or Control: Independent Non-Profit IRS Status: 501(c)3
Highest Offering: Doctorate; No Undergraduates
Accreditation: WC, ARCPA, DENT, NURSE, OPT, OSTEO, PHAR, POD, PTA, VET

01 President Dr. Daniel R. WILSON
05 Provost/COO Dr. Gary GUGELCHUK
10 Treasurer/Chief Financial Officer Mr. Kevin SHAW
46 Exec Vice Provost for Academic Dev Dr. Elizabeth REGA
20 Vice Provost Dr. Sheree ASTON
32 Vice Pres Student Affs/Enroll Mgt Dr. Beverly SANKS GUIDRY
111 VP University Advancement Dr. Diane ABRAHAM
25 Asst VP Spnsrd Pgms/Contract Mgt Mr. Matthew KATZ
84 Asst VP Enroll Mgmt/Registrar Ms. Kimberly DEKRUIF
15 Executive Director Human Resources Ms. Linda EMILIO
18 Exec Dir Facilities/Physical Plant Mr. Todd CLARK
07 Director Admiss COP/CGN Ms. Kathy FORD
07 Director Admissions COMP/MSHS Ms. Susan HANSON
07 Director Admissions CO/CPM/CDM Ms. Marie ANDERSON
07 Director Admissions CVM/PT/PA Ms. Karen HUTTON-LOPEZ
11 Chief Administrative Officer Mr. Steve JASPERSON
08 Director of University Library Ms. Patricia VADER
37 Co-Director of Financial Aid Ms. Theresa POULLARD
37 Co-Director of Financial Aid Ms. Linda FRENZA
88 Dir Ctr Disability Issues/Hlth Prof Ms. Brenda PREMO
13 Exec Director Information Tech Ms. Denise WILCOX
96 Director of Procurement Services Mr. Michael BUTLER
26 Exec Director of Public Affs/Mrktg Mr. Jeff KEATING
121 Dir Learning Enhancement/Acad Devel Ms. Dagmar COFER
09 Director of Institutional Research Dr. Juan RAMIREZ
40 Bookstore Director Ms. Elizabeth GUERRA
52 Dean College of Dental Medicine Dr. Steven W. FRIEDRICHSEN
67 Dean College of Pharmacy Dr. Daniel C. ROBINSON
88 Founding Dean College of Optometry Dr. Elizabeth HOPPE
88 Interim Dean College of Podiatry Dr. Lester JONES
76 Dean College Allied Health Profess Dr. Stephanie BOWLIN
66 Dean Col of Graduate Nursing Dr. Mary LOPEZ
58 Dean Grad Col Biomedical Sciences Dr. Michel BAUDRY
74 Dean College of Veterinary Medicine Dr. Phil NELSON
63 Chr Dept Osteopath Manipulative Med Dr. Michael SEFFINGER
88 Chair Dept of Physical Therapy Dr. Dayle ARMSTRONG
76 Chair Dept of Health Sciences Dr. Gail EVANS
88 Chair Physician Assistant Program Mr. Roy GUIZADO
63 Chair Department Family Medicine Dr. Alan CUNDARI
06 Registrar Ms. Kimberly DEKRUIF
19 Director Security/Safety Ms. Brett BOSTON
29 Director Alumni Relations Mr. Russel HESKIN
04 Administrative Asst to President Ms. Liz PAWELL
102 Dir Foundation/Corporate Relations Mr. Kevin SWEENEY
44 Director of Annual Giving Ms. Susan TERRAZAS
86 Director Government Relations Ms. Brenda PREMO

Westminster Theological Seminary in California (H)

1725 Bear Valley Parkway, Escondido CA 92027-4128
County: San Diego FICE Identification: 022768
Unit ID: 125718
Telephone: (760) 480-8474 Carnegie Class: Spec-4-yr-Faith
FAX Number: (760) 480-0252 Calendar System: Semester
URL: www.wscal.edu
Established: 1979 Annual Graduate Tuition & Fees: N/A
Enrollment: 138 Coed
Affiliation or Control: Independent Non-Profit IRS Status: 501(c)3
Highest Offering: Master's; No Undergraduates
Accreditation: WC, THEOL

01 President Rev. Joel E. KIM
11 Vice President for Administration Dr. Marcus MCARTHUR
05 Academic Dean Dr. John FESKO
30 Vice President for Advancement Ms. Dawn DOORN
84 VP for Enrollment Management Mr. Mark MACVEY
10 Chief Financial Officer Ms. Phyllis PIZZUTO
32 Dean of Students Dr. Julius KIM
08 Library Director Mr. James LUND
06 Registrar Mr. Danny MARRIOTT

Westmont College (I)

955 La Paz Road, Santa Barbara CA 93108-1089
County: Santa Barbara FICE Identification: 001341
Unit ID: 125727
Telephone: (805) 565-6000 Carnegie Class: Bac-A&S
FAX Number: (805) 565-7006 Calendar System: Semester
URL: www.westmont.edu
Established: 1937 Annual Undergrad Tuition & Fees: $42,900
Enrollment: 1,297 Coed
Affiliation or Control: Independent Non-Profit IRS Status: 501(c)3
Highest Offering: Baccalaureate
Accreditation: WC, MUS

01 President Dr. Gayle D. BEEBE
05 Provost/Dean of Faculty Dr. Mark L. SARGENT
10 Vice President Finance Mr. Douglas W. JONES
11 Vice President for Administration Mr. Christopher D. CALL
32 VP Student Life/Dean of Students Dr. Edee SCHULZE
30 Vice President for Advancement Dr. Reed L. SHEARD
13 VP Information Technology & CIO Dr. Reed SHEARD
07 Dean of Admissions Mr. Silvio VAZQUEZ
35 Associate Dean of Students Mr. Timothy B. WILSON
88 Assoc Dean of Students for Res Life Mr. Stu CLEEK
06 Registrar Mrs. Michelle M. HARDLEY
08 Director Library/Information Svcs Ms. Mary LOGUE
09 Assoc Provost/Dir of Inst Research Dr. Patti HUNTER
15 Director of Human Resources Ms. Beth CAUWELS
18 Director of Physical Plant Mr. Thomas BEVERIDGE
21 Controller Mr. Paul V. LARSON
23 Director of Student Health Services Dr. David HERNANDEZ
19 Public Safety Director Mr. Thomas G. BAUER
26 Director of Public Events Ms. Joan M. WIMBERLY
29 Sr Director Alumni & Parent Rels Mrs. Teri BRADFORD ROUSE
36 Director of Career/Development Mr. Paul BRADFORD
44 Senior Director of Gift Planning Mrs. Kati BUEHLER
88 Director of Campus Life Ms. Angela L. D'AMOUR
88 Director of Internships/Practica Mrs. Jennifer TAYLOR
37 Director of Financial Aid Mr. Sean SMITH
38 Director Counseling Services Dr. Eric NELSON
39 Director of Housing/Parking Mr. David W. KING
40 Asst Director Bookstore Mrs. Joanne GISH
41 Athletic Director Mr. David ODELL
42 Campus Pastor Rev. Ben PATTERSON
45 Director of Campus Planning Mr. Randy JONES
96 Assc Dir Procurement/Auxiliary Svcs Mr. Bill GROENEVELD
28 Director of Intercultural Programs Mr. Jason CHA
43 College Counsel Ms. Toya COOPER
20 Associate Academic Officer Dr. Tatiana NAZARENKO
24 Coord Media Services/Asst Librarian Vacant

Whittier College (A)

13406 E Philadelphia St, PO Box 634,
Whittier CA 90608-4413
County: Los Angeles FICE Identification: 001342
Unit ID: 125763
Telephone: (562) 907-4200 Carnegie Class: Bac-A&S
FAX Number: (562) 907-4242 Calendar System: 4/1/4
URL: www.whittier.edu
Established: 1887 Annual Undergrad Tuition & Fees: $44,774
Enrollment: 2,187 Coed
Affiliation or Control: Independent Non-Profit IRS Status: 501(c)3
Highest Offering: Doctorate
Accreditation: WC, LAW, SW

01 President .... Dr. Sharon D. HERZBERGER
10 Vice Pres Finance & Administration .... Mr. James DUNKELMAN
05 VP Academic Affs/Dean of Faculty .... Dr. Darrin GOOD
61 Dean of Whittier Law School .... Ms. Judith DAAR
111 VP for Advancement .... Mr. Steve DELGADO
84 Vice President Dean of Enrollment .... Mr. Kieron MILLER
32 Dean of Students .... Dr. Joel JOEL PEREZ
37 Director of Student Financial Aid .... Mr. David CARNEVALE
08 Interim Library Director .... Mr. Mike GARABEDIAN
20 Dir Whtr Scholar Pgm/Assc Acad Dean .... Ms. Andrea REHN
26 Dir Public Relations/Communications .... Ms. Ana Lilia BARRAZA
13 Director of Computing Services .... Mr. Troy GREENUP
09 Dir of Institutional Research .... Mr. Gary WHISENAND
41 Director of Athletics .... Mr. Rob COLEMAN
62 Dir Lib Educ Pgm/Assoc Acad Dean .... Dr. Fritz SMITH
15 Director of Human Resources .... Ms. Cynthia JOSEPH
19 Director of Campus Safety .... Mr. Jose PADILLA
06 Registrar .... Mr. John T. HILL

William Jessup University (B)

2121 University Avenue, Rocklin CA 95765-3707
County: Placer FICE Identification: 001281
Unit ID: 122728
Telephone: (916) 577-2200 Carnegie Class: Bac-Diverse
FAX Number: (916) 577-2203 Calendar System: Semester
URL: www.jessup.edu
Established: 1939 Annual Undergrad Tuition & Fees: $28,700
Enrollment: 1,161 Coed
Affiliation or Control: Independent Non-Profit IRS Status: 501(c)3
Highest Offering: Master's
Accreditation: WC, BI

01 President .... Dr. John JACKSON
05 Provost/Chief Academic Officer .... Dr. Dennis JAMESON
84 Vice Provost .... Dr. Todd ERICKSON
10 Chief Financial Officer .... Mr. David PUNT
30 Chief Development Officer .... Mr. Eric HOGUE
13 Chief Operations Officer .... Mrs. Judy RENTZ
88 Accreditation Liaison Officer .... Dr. Kay LLOVIO
107 School of Professional Studies Dir .... Ms. Nancy THOMPSON
15 Human Resources Manager .... Ms. Linda GIUSTI
21 Controller .... Ms. Diane KIM
08 University Librarian .... Mr. Kevin PISCHKE
88 Director of Church Relations .... Mr. Jim JESSUP
32 Dean of Students .... Mr. Dave HEITMAN
06 Registrar .... Mrs. Tina PETERSEN
07 Director of Admission .... Mr. Steve JIN
09 Institutional Research Director .... Mrs. Karen LAMBRECHTSEN
42 Campus Pastor .... Mr. Ryan HAYNES
41 Athletic Director .... Mr. Lance VON VOGT
18 Facilities Director .... Vacant
35 Chief Student Life Officer .... Dr. Kay LLOVIO
12 Academic Director Bay Area Center .... Dr. Daniel ALBRECHT
04 Executive Asst to President .... Mrs. Janice NEWMAN
19 Director of Campus Safety .... Mr. Paul YBARRA
36 Director Student Placement .... Ms. Christy JEWELL
106 Dir Online Education/E-learning .... Ms. Sandra WOODSON
37 Director Student Financial Aid .... Mr. John SWAN

Woodbury University (C)

7500 North Glenoaks Boulevard, Burbank CA 91504-7520
County: Los Angeles FICE Identification: 001343
Unit ID: 125897
Telephone: (818) 767-0888 Carnegie Class: Masters/M
FAX Number: (818) 767-3470 Calendar System: Semester
URL: www.woodbury.edu
Established: 1884 Annual Undergrad Tuition & Fees: $37,906
Enrollment: 1,457 Coed
Affiliation or Control: Independent Non-Profit IRS Status: 501(c)3
Highest Offering: Master's
Accreditation: WC, ACBSP, ART, CIDA

01 President .... David M. STEELE-FIGUEREDO
101 Secretary of the Institution/Board .... Seta JAVOR
05 Senior Vice President .... Randy STAUFFER
10 VP Administration & Human Resources .... Natalie AVALOS
84 VP Enrollment Management .... Michael TRUSCHKE
30 VP University Advancement .... Eric GREENY
13 VP Information Technology .... Eric WANG
32 Vice Pres Student Development .... Vacant
35 Dean of Student Affairs .... Mauro DIAZ
50 Dean School of Business .... Joan MARQUES
48 Interim Dean School of Architecture .... Ingalill WAHLROOS-RITTER
07 Director of Admissions .... Sabrina TAYLOR
20 Dean of Faculty .... Kristen FUHS
88 Dean Institute of Transdisciplinary .... Douglas CREMER
09 Director of Institutional Research .... Vacant

World Mission University (D)

500 Shatto Place, Suite 600, Los Angeles CA 90020-1789
County: Los Angeles FICE Identification: 038683
Unit ID: 401223
Telephone: (213) 385-2322 Carnegie Class: Spec-4-yr-Faith
FAX Number: (213) 385-2332 Calendar System: Semester
URL: www.wmu.edu
Established: 1989 Annual Undergrad Tuition & Fees: $5,620
Enrollment: 332 Coed
Affiliation or Control: Independent Non-Profit IRS Status: 501(c)3
Highest Offering: First Professional Degree
Accreditation: BI, THEOL

01 President .... Dr. John M. SONG
05 Exec Vice Pres/Chief Acad Officer .... Dr. Sung Jin LIM
32 Dean of Student Affairs .... Ms. Yoon Jung CHOI
30 Director of Development/CFO .... Ms. Jung Ho LIM
10 Director of Business .... Vacant
06 Registrar .... Mrs. Jin Joo NAM
37 Dir Financial Aid/Admissions Coord .... Ms. KyungHae KIM

The Wright Institute (E)

2728 Durant Avenue, Berkeley CA 94704-1796
County: Alameda FICE Identification: 008846
Unit ID: 126012
Telephone: (510) 841-9230 Carnegie Class: Spec-4-yr-Other Health
FAX Number: (510) 841-0167 Calendar System: Trimester
URL: www.wi.edu
Established: 1969 Annual Graduate Tuition & Fees: N/A
Enrollment: 451 Coed
Affiliation or Control: Independent Non-Profit IRS Status: 501(c)3
Highest Offering: Doctorate; No Undergraduates
Accreditation: WC, CLPSY, IPSY

01 President .... Mr. Peter DYBWAD
05 Dean/Director Clinical Training .... Dr. Gilbert NEWMAN
10 VP of Finance & Administrative Affs .... Ms. Tricia O'REILLY
32 Dean of Students/Registrar .... Ms. Ginny MORGAN
07 Dir of Admissions/Student Services .... Mr. John PITTS
08 Library Director .... Mr. Jason STRAUSS
37 Director of Financial Aid .... Ms. Julia KALYAYEVA

Yeshiva Ohr Elchonon Chabad/ West Coast Talmudical Seminary (F)

7215 Waring Avenue, Los Angeles CA 90046-7660
County: Los Angeles FICE Identification: 022624
Unit ID: 126076
Telephone: (323) 937-3763 Carnegie Class: Spec-4-yr-Faith
FAX Number: (323) 937-9456 Calendar System: Semester
URL: www.yoec.edu
Established: 1953 Annual Undergrad Tuition & Fees: $13,900
Enrollment: 161 Male
Affiliation or Control: Independent Non-Profit IRS Status: 501(c)3
Highest Offering: Baccalaureate
Accreditation: RABN

01 Chief Executive Officer .... Rabbi Ezra B. SCHOCHET
03 Executive Vice President .... Rabbi Mendel SPALTER
05 Curriculum Suprv/Education Counsel .... Rabbi Shimon RAICHIK
37 Director Student Financial Aid .... Mrs. Hendy TAUBER
06 Registrar .... Rabbi Chaim CITRON
38 Director Student Counseling .... Rabbi Mendel SCHAPIRO
08 Head Librarian .... Rabbi Ben Zion OSTER

Yo San University of Traditional Chinese Medicine (G)

13315 W Washington Boulevard, Los Angeles CA 90066
County: Los Angeles FICE Identification: 030982
Unit ID: 401250
Telephone: (310) 577-3000 Carnegie Class: Spec-4-yr-Other Health
FAX Number: (310) 577-3033 Calendar System: Trimester
URL: www.yosan.edu
Established: 1989 Annual Undergrad Tuition & Fees: N/A
Enrollment: 175 Coed
Affiliation or Control: Independent Non-Profit IRS Status: 501(c)3
Highest Offering: Doctorate; No Lower Division
Accreditation: ACUP

01 President/CEO .... Dr. Lawrence LAU
10 Chief Financial Officer .... Tracy WANG
06 Director Operations & Registrar .... Tora FLINT
63 Dean MATCM Program .... Dr. Brady CHIN
63 Dean DAOM Program .... Dr. Laraine CRAMPTON
63 Dean Clinical Education .... Brian LEE
30 Director Development & Ext Affairs .... Brandon BLAIR
07 Director Enrollment & Students .... Joe DENEAL
21 Controller/Bursar .... Mariani MAY
37 Financial Aid Coordinator .... Ed MERVINE

*Yosemite Community College District (H)

PO Box 4065, Modesto CA 95352-4065
County: Stanislaus FICE Identification: 009146
Unit ID: 126100
Telephone: (209) 575-6509 Carnegie Class: N/A
FAX Number: (209) 575-6565
URL: www.yosemite.edu

01 Chancellor .... Mr. Henry YONG
10 Exec Vice Chancellor Fiscal Service .... Ms. Teresa M. SCOTT
15 Vice Chancellor Human Resources .... Ms. Gina LEGURIA
13 Int Vice Chancellor Info Tech .... Ms. Karen TRIMBLE

*Columbia College (I)

11600 Columbia College Drive, Sonora CA 95370-8580
County: Tuolumne FICE Identification: 007707
Unit ID: 112561
Telephone: (209) 588-5100 Carnegie Class: Assoc/MT-VT-Mix Trad/Non
FAX Number: (209) 588-5104 Calendar System: Semester
URL: www.gocolumbia.edu
Established: 1968 Annual Undergrad Tuition & Fees (In-District): $1,162
Enrollment: 2,424 Coed
Affiliation or Control: State/Local IRS Status: 501(c)3
Highest Offering: Associate Degree
Accreditation: WJ, ACFEI

02 President .... Dr. Angela FAIRCHILDS
05 Vice Pres Instruction .... Dr. Brian SANDERS
11 VP College & Administrative Svcs .... Vacant
72 Dean Instruct Svcs/Career Tech Educ .... Dr. Klaus TENBERGEN
49 Dean of Instruction/Arts & Sciences .... Dr. Joseph RYAN
24 Director of Info Tech & Media Svcs .... Mrs. Margo GUZMAN
41 Athletic Director .... Mr. Nate RIEN
37 Financial Aid Manager .... Ms. Marnie SHIVELY
26 Public Information Officer .... Vacant
31 Director Community Services .... Vacant
30 Director of Development .... Ms. Amy NILSON
06 Registrar .... Ms. Lesley MICHTAVY
09 Dir of Institutional Rsrch & Plng .... Ms. Diana SUNDAY
40 Bookstore Manager .... Mr. Jeff WHALEN
18 Manager Facilities/Operations .... Mr. Dave KEENER

*Modesto Junior College (J)

435 College Avenue, Modesto CA 95350-9977
County: Stanislaus FICE Identification: 001240
Unit ID: 118976
Telephone: (209) 575-6498 Carnegie Class: Assoc/MT-VT-High Trad
FAX Number: (209) 575-6630 Calendar System: Semester
URL: www.mjc.edu
Established: 1921 Annual Undergrad Tuition & Fees (In-District): $1,162
Enrollment: 17,739 Coed
Affiliation or Control: State/Local IRS Status: 501(c)3
Highest Offering: Baccalaureate
Accreditation: WJ, COARC, MAC

02 President .... Dr. Jill STEARNS
05 Vice President for Instruction .... Dr. Jennifer HAMILTON
32 Vice Pres for Student Services .... Dr. James TODD
11 VP College & Administrative Svcs .... Dr. Albert ALT
57 Div Dean Arts/Humanites/Comm .... Mr. Mike SUNDQUIST
83 Div Dean Business/Behav/Social Sci .... Vacant
76 Div Dean Inst/All Hlth/Fam/Con Sci .... Mr. Patrick BETTENCOURT
79 Div Dean Literature/Language Arts .... Ms. Jillian DALY
54 Div Dean Science/Math/Engineering .... Dr. Laura MAKI
47 Dean Agri/Envir Science/Tech Ed .... Dr. Donald BORGES
88 Dean Public Safety/Tech Ed/Cmty Ed .... Mr. Pedro MENDEZ
25 Int Dir Planning/Grants Development .... Ms. Jenni ABBOTT
09 Dir Institutional Effectiveness .... Ms. Jenni ABBOTT
07 Director Admissions & Records .... Ms. Angelica GUZMAN
37 Director Student Financial Aid .... Ms. Peggy FIKSE
26 Marketing/Public Information Ofcr .... Ms. Linda HOILE

*Yuba Community College District (K)

2088 North Beale Road, Marysville CA 95901
County: Yuba Identification: 666478
Unit ID: 126119
Telephone: (530) 741-6700 Carnegie Class: N/A
FAX Number: N/A
URL: www.yccd.edu

01 Chancellor .... Dr. Douglas B. HOUSTON
05 VC Educ Planning & Services .... Dr. Sandra MAYO
13 Chief Technology Officer .... Mr. Roger CLAGUE
102 Grants/Research/Development Officer .... Ms. Tonya MACK
15 Chief Human Resources Officer .... Mr. Jacques WHITFIELD
10 Chief Business Officer .... Mrs. Kuldeep KAUR

*Woodland Community College (L)

2300 East Gibson Road, Woodland CA 95776-5156
County: Yolo FICE Identification: 041438
Unit ID: 455512
Telephone: (530) 661-5700 Carnegie Class: Assoc/HT-High Trad
FAX Number: (530) 666-9028 Calendar System: Semester
URL: www.yccd.edu/woodland/
Established: 2008 Annual Undergrad Tuition & Fees (In-District): $1,144
Enrollment: 2,955 Coed

Affiliation or Control: State/Local IRS Status: 501(c)3
Highest Offering: Associate Degree
Accreditation: WJ

02 President .... Dr. Michael WHITE
05 Vice Pres Academic/Student Svcs .... Dr. Alfred B. KONUWA
04 Administrative Asst to President .... Ms. Ana L. VILLAGRANA

*Yuba College (A)

2088 N Beale Road, Marysville CA 95901-7699
County: Yuba FICE Identification: 001344
Unit ID: 126119
Telephone: (530) 741-6700 Carnegie Class: Assoc/HT-High Trad
FAX Number: (530) 741-3541 Calendar System: Semester
URL: https://yc.yccd.edu/
Established: 1927 Annual Undergrad Tuition & Fees (In-District): $1,144
Enrollment: 6,869 Coed
Affiliation or Control: State/Local IRS Status: 501(c)3
Highest Offering: Associate Degree
Accreditation: WJ, RAD

02 President .... Dr. G. H JAVAHERIPOUR
05 VP Academic/Student Services .... Dr. Sonja LOLLAND
32 Dean Student Services .... Dr. Delmy SPENCER
50 Dean Applied Academics .... Dr. Daren OTTEN
88 Dir Child Dev Center/Foster Care .... Ms. Karen STANIS
66 Director Nursing/Allied Health .... Dr. Clark SMITH
19 Director Public Safety .... Dr. Pete VILLARREAL
79 Dean of Humanities & Education .... Ms. Carla TWEED
07 Dir Admissions/Records/Fin Aid .... Mr. Martin GUTIERREZ
68 Director Athletics/Health/PE .... Mr. Erick BURNS
81 Dean STEM & Outreach Centers .... Dr. Karsten STEMMANN
88 Director Academic Excellence .... Ms. Kristina VANNUCCI

Zaytuna College (B)

2401 Le Conte Avenue, Berkeley CA 94709
County: Alameda Identification: 667230
Unit ID: 458575
Telephone: (510) 356-4760 Carnegie Class: Not Classified
FAX Number: (510) 327-2688 Calendar System: Semester
URL: www.zaytuna.edu
Established: 2009 Annual Undergrad Tuition & Fees: $19,350
Enrollment: 61 Coed
Affiliation or Control: Independent Non-Profit IRS Status: 501(c)3
Highest Offering: Baccalaureate
Accreditation: WC

01 President .... Hamza YUSUF
05 Provost .... Dr. Hatem BAZIAN
20 Dean of Faculty .... Dr. Mark Damien DELP
10 Head of Operations .... Cathrine HAMZE
108 Dir of Assessment & Accreditation .... Sumaira AKHATAR

COLORADO

Academy of Natural Therapy (C)

625 8th Avenue, Greeley CO 80631
County: Weld FICE Identification: 040933
Unit ID: 449454
Telephone: (970) 352-1181 Carnegie Class: Spec 2-yr-Health
FAX Number: (970) 352-1906 Calendar System: Quarter
URL: www.natural-therapy.com
Established: 1989 Annual Undergrad Tuition & Fees: N/A
Enrollment: 57 Coed
Affiliation or Control: Proprietary IRS Status: Proprietary
Highest Offering: Associate Degree
Accreditation: COMTA

01 President .... Mr. Jeremiah James MONGAN

Adams State University (D)

208 Edgemont Boulevard, Alamosa CO 81101-2320
County: Alamosa FICE Identification: 001345
Unit ID: 126182
Telephone: (719) 587-7011 Carnegie Class: Masters/L
FAX Number: (719) 587-7522 Calendar System: Semester
URL: www.adams.edu
Established: 1921 Annual Undergrad Tuition & Fees (In-State): $9,153
Enrollment: 3,404 Coed
Affiliation or Control: State IRS Status: 501(c)3
Highest Offering: Doctorate
Accreditation: #NH, CACREP, MUS, NURSE

01 President .... Dr. Beverlee J. MCCLURE
05 Interim Vice President for Academic .... Dr. Matt NEHRING
11 Chief Operations Officer .... Mr. Kurt CARY
84 Dir of Marketing & Enrollment Mgmt .... Ms. Karla HARDESTY
111 VP Institutional Advancement .... Vacant
18 Director of Facilities Services .... Mr. Scott TRAVIS
10 Chief Financial Officer .... Ms. Heather HEERSINK
20 Asst VP for Academic Affairs .... Ms. Margaret DOELL
32 VP for Student Services .... Mr. Kenneth L. MARQUEZ
09 Senior Research Analyst .... Mr. Victor SOE
08 Director Library .... Mr. Jeffrey BULLINGTON
37 Director Student Financial Aid .... Mr. Philip SCHROEDER
06 Registrar .... Ms. Belen MAESTAS
13 Chief Information Officer .... Mr. Kevin S. DANIEL
41 Athletic Director .... Mr. Larry MORTENSEN
26 Asst to President Communications .... Ms. Julie WAECHTER
109 Director of Auxiliary Services .... Mr. Bruce DEL TONDO
38 Director Counseling/Career Services .... Ms. Elisabeth TOMLIN
15 Director Human Resources .... Ms. Tracy ROGERS
102 Executive Director ASU Foundation .... Ms. Tammy L. LOPEZ
29 Director Alumni and Donor Relations .... Ms. Lori L. LASKE
96 Director of Purchasing .... Ms. Renee VIGIL
19 Dir Adams State Univ Police Dept .... Mr. Andrew MCPHERSON
40 Director Bookstore .... Ms. Shannon MADIGAN
27 Director of Creative Relations .... Mr. Mark SCHOENECKER
57 Chair English/Theatre/Communication .. Dr. David MACWILLIAMS
50 Chair Business & Economics .... Dr. Patrica ROBBINS
53 Chair Education .... Dr. Edward CROWTHER
77 Chair Chemistry/Computer Sci/Math .... Dr. Christina MILLER
81 Chair Biology/Earth Science .... Dr. Benita BRINK

Aims Community College (E)

Box 69, Greeley CO 80632-0069
County: Weld FICE Identification: 007582
Unit ID: 126207
Telephone: (970) 330-8008 Carnegie Class: Assoc/HVT-Mix Trad/Non
FAX Number: N/A Calendar System: Semester
URL: www.aims.edu
Established: 1967 Annual Undergrad Tuition & Fees (In-District): $1,835
Enrollment: 5,298 Coed
Affiliation or Control: Local IRS Status: 501(c)3
Highest Offering: Associate Degree
Accreditation: NH, ADNUR, EMT, IFSAC, SURGT

01 President .... Dr. Leah L. BORNSTEIN
10 VP Admin Services .... Mr. Chuck JENSEN
05 Vice President Academic Affairs .... Ms. Deborah KISH
32 Vice President Student Affairs .... Dr. Patricia MATIJEVIC
88 Vice President CCR .... Dr. Geri ANDERSON
49 Dean Arts & Sciences .... Mr. Scott REICHEL
50 Dean Business & Technology .... Mr. Jeff SMITH
88 Dean Public Services & Transp .... Mr. Robert ABERNATHY
35 Dean of Students .... Ms. Shannon MCCASLAND
102 Executive Director Foundation .... Ms. Kelly JACKSON
07 Exec Dir Admissions/Records .... Ms. Sarah ENER
15 Exec Director Human Resources .... Ms. Dee SHULTZ
09 Exec Dir Inst Research/Assessment .... Mr. William BROWN
114 Budget Director/Asst Controller .... Ms. Kailey BLOCK
18 Exec Director Facilities/Operations .... Mr. Michael MILLSAPPS
37 Executive Director Financial Aid .... Ms. Nancy GRAY
06 Registrar .... Mr. Stuart THOMAS
13 Exec Director IT Admin Services .... Ms. Andria ROGERS
21 Assistant VP/Controller .... Ms. Kara BERG
31 Exec Director Cmty & PIO .... Ms. Laura COALE
35 Exec Dir Student Leadership & Dev .... Vacant
12 Exec Campus Dir Loveland .... Ms. Heather LELCHOOK
12 Exec Campus Dir Windsor .... Ms. Mary GABRIEL
12 Exec Campus Dir Fort Lupton .... Vacant
103 Dean Workforce Dev/Cmty Prtnrshps .... Ms. Libby KLINGSMITH

Altierus Career College (F)

1815 Jet Wing Drive, Colorado Springs CO 80916
County: El Paso FICE Identification: 004503
Unit ID: 126401
Telephone: (719) 638-6580 Carnegie Class: Assoc/HVT-Mix Trad/Non
FAX Number: (719) 638-6818 Calendar System: Quarter
URL: www.alterius.org
Established: 1897 Annual Undergrad Tuition & Fees: $12,015
Enrollment: 209 Coed
Affiliation or Control: Independent Non-Profit IRS Status: 501(c)3
Highest Offering: Associate Degree
Accreditation: #ACICS, MAC

01 Campus Director .... Mr. Ivan NIKOLAEFF
05 Dean of Education .... Ms. Dawn KOTTKE
07 Director Admissions .... Mr. Dan MILNE
32 Director Student Success .... Mr. Dan MILNE

Altierus Career College (G)

9065 Grant Street, Denver CO 80229-4339
County: Adams FICE Identification: 004507
Unit ID: 127787
Telephone: (303) 457-2757 Carnegie Class: Assoc/HVT-High Non
FAX Number: (303) 457-4030 Calendar System: Other
URL: www.altierus.org
Established: 1895 Annual Undergrad Tuition & Fees: $12,510
Enrollment: 232 Coed
Affiliation or Control: Independent Non-Profit IRS Status: 501(c)3
Highest Offering: Associate Degree
Accreditation: ACCSC, ACICS, MAC, SURGT

01 Executive Director .... Ms. Carissa SERGER
05 Academic Dean .... Ms. Colleen LOTT
32 Director of Student Success .... Mr. Dan MILNE
36 Director of Career Services .... Ms. Diane BOOREN
06 Registrar .... Ms. Cindy STEERMAN
37 Manager of Student Finance .... Ms. Kim MARTINEZ

American Sentinel University (H)

2260 South Xanadu Way, Ste 310, Aurora CO 80014
County: Arapahoe FICE Identification: 041277
Unit ID: 460738
Telephone: (303) 991-1575 Carnegie Class: Not Classified
FAX Number: (303) 991-1577 Calendar System: Other
URL: www.americansentinel.edu
Established: 2000 Annual Undergrad Tuition & Fees: N/A
Enrollment: 2,949 Coed
Affiliation or Control: Proprietary IRS Status: Proprietary
Highest Offering: Doctorate
Accreditation: @NH, DEAC, NUR, NURSE

01 President .... Ms. Mary A. ADAMS
84 Sr VP Enrollment Services .... Mr. Mark COBB
66 Dean of Nursing .... Vacant
06 Registrar .... Ms. Sandie HUBBARD

Arapahoe Community College (I)

5900 S Santa Fe Drive, PO Box 9002,
Littleton CO 80160-9002
County: Arapahoe FICE Identification: 001346
Unit ID: 126289
Telephone: (303) 797-4222 Carnegie Class: Assoc/HVT-High Non
FAX Number: (303) 797-5935 Calendar System: Semester
URL: www.arapahoe.edu
Established: 1965 Annual Undergrad Tuition & Fees (In-State): $3,493
Enrollment: 10,004 Coed
Affiliation or Control: State IRS Status: 501(c)3
Highest Offering: Associate Degree
Accreditation: NH, ADNUR, CAHIIM, EMT, FUSER, MLTAD, PTAA

01 President .... Dr. Diana M. DOYLE
11 Vice President Admin Services .... Dr. Cindy SOMERS
05 Vice President Instruction and Prov .... Ms. Rebecca WOULFE
10 Chief Financial Officer .... Vacant
103 Dean Community/Workforce Partnershp .... Dr. Eric DUNKER
32 Vice President of Student Services .... Dr. Lisa MATYE EDWARDS
124 Director of Advising and Retention .... Mr. Michael MCMANUS
07 Director Admissions & Records .... Ms. Darcy BRIGGS
37 Dir of Student Financial Services .... Ms. Gail MCKINNEY
31 Exec Dir of Community/Workforce Pgm .... Ms. Kim LARSON-COONEY
83 Dean Legal/Comm/Soc & Behav Sci .... Dr. Vanessa ANDERSON
81 Dean Health/Math & Science .... Dr. Samuel DEVRIES
49 Dean Arts/Human/Business & Tech .... Vacant
102 Executive Director Foundation .... Ms. Courtney LOEHFELM
21 Controller .... Ms. Jill BECKER-LUTZ
19 Chief of Police .... Mr. Joseph MORRIS
09 Director Institutional Research .... Mr. Yared BELETE
08 Director Learning Resource Center .... Ms. Lisa GRABOWSKI
26 Dir of Marketing/Public Relations .... Ms. Tina GRIESHEIMER
35 Assoc Dean of Judicial Affairs .... Ms. Jennifer HUSUM
96 Purchasing Coordinator .... Mr. Daniel HOHN
18 Facilities Director .... Mr. David CRAWFORD
13 Chief Info Technology Officer (CIO) .... Vacant
15 Director Personnel Services .... Ms. Angela WILLIAMS
04 Executive Assistant .... Ms. Carol PATTERSON
108 Director Institutional Assessment .... Dr. Terry BARMANN

Argosy University, Denver (J)

7600 East Eastman Avenue, Denver CO 80231
Telephone: (303) 923-4110 Identification: 666654
Accreditation: &WC, ACBSP, CACREP, MFCD

† Regional accreditation is carried under the parent institution in Orange, CA.

The Art Institute of Colorado (K)

1200 North Lincoln Street, Denver CO 80203-2172
County: Denver FICE Identification: 020789
Unit ID: 126702
Telephone: (303) 837-0825 Carnegie Class: Spec-4-yr-Arts
FAX Number: (303) 860-8520 Calendar System: Quarter
URL: www.artinstitutes.edu/denver
Established: 1952 Annual Undergrad Tuition & Fees: $17,628
Enrollment: 1,145 Coed
Affiliation or Control: Proprietary IRS Status: Proprietary
Highest Offering: Baccalaureate
Accreditation: NH, ACFEI, CIDA

01 President .... Mr. James O. CALDWELL
05 Vice President/Dean Academic Affs .... Dr. Benjamin A. VALDEZ
07 Senior Director of Admissions .... Mr. Joshua JONES
32 Director of Student Services .... Mr. Daniel SNYDER
10 Director Financial Services .... Ms. Theresa BARGAS
06 Registrar .... Ms. Lisa BARRY
15 Human Resource Generalist .... Ms. Shandra ADAIR

Aspen University (L)

1660 S. Albion Street Suite 525, Denver CO 80222
County: Denver FICE Identification: 040803
Unit ID: 454829
Telephone: (303) 333-4224 Carnegie Class: DU-Mod
FAX Number: (303) 200-7428 Calendar System: Other
URL: www.aspen.edu
Established: 1987 Annual Undergrad Tuition & Fees: $4,200
Enrollment: 2,145 Coed
Affiliation or Control: Proprietary IRS Status: Proprietary
Highest Offering: Doctorate
Accreditation: DEAC, NURSE

01 Chairman & CEO .... Mr. Michael MATHEWS
05 Chief Academic Officer .... Dr. Cheri ST. ARNAULD
11 COO .... Mr. Gerard WENDOLOWSKI
10 CFO .... Ms. Janet GILL
06 Registrar .... Ms. Ashley MOSS

Auguste Escoffier School of Culinary Arts (A)

637 South Broadway, Ste H, Boulder CO 80305
County: Boulder FICE Identification: 037763
Unit ID: 454810
Telephone: (303) 494-7988 Carnegie Class: Not Classified
FAX Number: N/A Calendar System: Quarter
Established: Annual Undergrad Tuition & Fees: N/A
Enrollment: 369 Coed
Affiliation or Control: Proprietary IRS Status: Proprietary
Highest Offering: Associate Degree
Accreditation: CNCE, ACFEI

01 President .... Kim JENSEN

Augustine Institute (B)

6160 S. Syracuse Way #310,
Greenwood Village CO 80111
County: Arapahoe Identification: 667219
Telephone: (303) 937-4420 Carnegie Class: Not Classified
FAX Number: (303) 468-2933 Calendar System: Semester
URL: augustineinstitute.org
Established: 2005 Annual Graduate Tuition & Fees: N/A
Enrollment: N/A Coed
Affiliation or Control: Roman Catholic IRS Status: 501(c)3
Highest Offering: Master's; No Undergraduates
Accreditation: THEOL

01 President .... Mr. Tim GRAY
05 Academic Dean .... Dr. Christopher BLUM
11 Chief Operating Officer .... Mr. Darren WALSH
07 Director of Admissions .... Ms. Katie MURRAY

Bel-Rea Institute of Animal Technology (C)

1681 S Dayton Street, Denver CO 80247-3048
County: Arapahoe FICE Identification: 012670
Unit ID: 126359
Telephone: (800) 950-8001 Carnegie Class: Spec 2-yr-Health
FAX Number: (303) 751-9969 Calendar System: Quarter
URL: www.bel-rea.com
Established: 1971 Annual Undergrad Tuition & Fees: $11,963
Enrollment: 445 Coed
Affiliation or Control: Proprietary IRS Status: Proprietary
Highest Offering: Associate Degree
Accreditation: ACCSC

01 Director .... Cynthia MEDINA
05 Dean of Education .... Nolan RUCKER
37 Director Student Financial Aid .... Stasi BOTTINELLI
32 Director Student Services .... Cynthia MEDINA

College for Financial Planning (D)

9000 E. Nichols Avenue #200, Centennial CO 80112
County: Denver Identification: 666809
Unit ID: 126526
Telephone: (303) 220-1200 Carnegie Class: Not Classified
FAX Number: (303) 220-4940 Calendar System: Other
URL: www.cffp.edu
Established: 1972 Annual Graduate Tuition & Fees: N/A
Enrollment: N/A Coed
Affiliation or Control: Proprietary IRS Status: Proprietary
Highest Offering: Master's; No Undergraduates
Accreditation: NH

01 President .... Mr. John SEARS
05 Vice President Academic Affairs .... Mr. Jim PASZTOR
10 Vice President Business Development .... Mr. Dirk PANTONE
84 Director of Enrollment .... Ms. Alicia MEAD
06 Registrar .... Ms. Katie PEDERSON
32 Director Student Service Center .... Mr. Spencer CAMERON

CollegeAmerica Colorado Springs (E)

2020 N Academy Boulevard, Ste 100,
Colorado Springs CO 80909
Telephone: (719) 622-3600 Identification: 666293
Accreditation: ACCSC

† Branch campus of CollegeAmerica Denver, Denver, CO.

CollegeAmerica Denver (F)

1385 S Colorado Blvd, 5th Floor, Denver CO 80222
County: Denver FICE Identification: 025943
Unit ID: 126872
Telephone: (303) 300-8740 Carnegie Class: Spec-4-yr-Other Health
FAX Number: (303) 692-9156 Calendar System: Other
URL: www.collegeamerica.edu
Established: 1964 Annual Undergrad Tuition & Fees: $16,968
Enrollment: 299 Coed
Affiliation or Control: Independent Non-Profit IRS Status: 501(c)3
Highest Offering: Baccalaureate
Accreditation: ACCSC

01 Executive Director .... Ms. Suzanne SCALES
05 Academic Director .... Ms. Kacey JECHURA
37 Director of Financial Aid .... Ms. Sonia MARTINEZ
07 Director of Admissions .... Ms. Mary GORDY
06 Registrar .... Ms. Lauren ELI

CollegeAmerica Fort Collins (G)

4601 S Mason, Fort Collins CO 80525-3740
Telephone: (970) 225-4860 Identification: 666362
Accreditation: ACCSC

† Branch campus of CollegeAmerica Denver, Denver, CO.

Colorado Academy of Veterinary Technology (H)

2766 Janitell Road, Colorado Springs CO 80906
County: El Paso FICE Identification: 041850
Unit ID: 461953
Telephone: (719) 219-9636 Carnegie Class: Spec 2-yr-Health
FAX Number: (719) 302-5577 Calendar System: Quarter
URL: www.cavt.edu
Established: 2007 Annual Undergrad Tuition & Fees: $11,435
Enrollment: 67 Coed
Affiliation or Control: Proprietary IRS Status: Proprietary
Highest Offering: Associate Degree
Accreditation: COE

01 CEO/Admissions Officer/Registrar .... Dr. Steve RUBIN
05 Academic Officer .... Ms. Cat WIMUNC
38 Dir Student Counseling/Fin Aid .... Mrs. Traci THOMPSON

Colorado Christian University (I)

8787 W Alameda Avenue, Lakewood CO 80226-7499
County: Jefferson FICE Identification: 009401
Unit ID: 126669
Telephone: (303) 963-3000 Carnegie Class: Masters/M
FAX Number: (303) 963-3001 Calendar System: Semester
URL: www.ccu.edu
Established: 1914 Annual Undergrad Tuition & Fees: $29,360
Enrollment: 6,879 Coed
Affiliation or Control: Independent Non-Profit IRS Status: 501(c)3
Highest Offering: Master's
Accreditation: NH, CACREP, MUS, NURSE

01 President .... Dr. Donald W. SWEETING
10 VP for Business Affairs & CFO .... Mr. Daniel L. COHRS
05 VP Acad Affairs College UG Studies .... Dr. Cherri S. PARKS
30 VP for Development .... Vacant
31 Vice President .... Mr. Shannon DREYFUSS
32 VP for Student Development .... Mr. Jim S. MCCORMICK
20 VP of Acad Affairs/Dean CAGS .... Dr. Sarah SCHERLING
35 Asst VP Stdnt Pgm/Dean of Students .... Ms. Sharon M. FELKER
84 VP Enrollment for CAGS .... Ms. Allison SIEVERS
121 VP of Student Success .... Mr. Roger CHANDLER
50 Dean School of Business .... Dr. Gary EWEN
72 Dean of Business and Technology .... Dr. Mellani J. DAY
53 Dean School of Education .... Dr. Debora SCHEFFEL
83 Dean of Social Science & Humanities .... Dr. Debra HUDSON
53 Dean of Ed/Curriculum & Instruction .... Dr. Wendy WENDOVER
79 Dean Sch Humanities & Sciences .... Dr. William R. SAXBY
64 Dean School of Music .... Mr. Steven T. TAYLOR
73 Dean School of Theology .... Dr. David KOTTER
66 Dean of Nursing & Sciences .... Dr. Barbara WHITE
73 Dean of Biblical Studies & Theology .... Dr. Earl WAGGONER
07 Director of Admissions .... Ms. Jo Leda MARTIN
43 University Counsel .... Mr. Steven MILLER
21 Asst VP and Controller .... Ms. Karen FARRAND
06 Registrar .... Ms. Linda K. PERCIANTE
41 Athletic Director .... Mr. Brian WALL
38 Director of Counseling Services .... Ms. Alisa SHANKS
38 Director of Centennial Institute .... Mr. Jeff HUNT
110 Senior Director of Development .... Ms. Kathy PETTIT
18 Director of Facilities .... Mr. Mathew J. GOTHARD
37 Asst VP of Financial Aid .... Mr. Steve M. WOODBURN
23 Director of Health Services .... Ms. Mandy WILLIAMS
15 Director of Human Resources .... Mr. Rick GARRIS
13 Asst VP of Information Systems .... Ms. Renee MARTIN
08 Library Director .... Ms. Gayle C. GUNDERSON
36 Director of Life Directions Center .... Ms. Leah SMITH
39 Director of Residence Life .... Mr. Joseph BROOKS
19 Director of Security .... Mr. John MAXFIELD
26 Dir of University Communications .... Mr. Lance OVERSOLE
29 Director Alumni Relations .... Ms. Chrysandra BRUNSON
105 Asst VP of Creative Services .... Ms. Chris FRANZ
106 Asst VP of Technical Support .... Mr. Jordan HEERSINK
04 Executive Assistant to President .... Ms. Kerry BLEIKAMP

Colorado College (J)

14 E Cache La Poudre St.,
Colorado Springs CO 80903-3294
County: El Paso FICE Identification: 001347
Unit ID: 126678
Telephone: (719) 389-6000 Carnegie Class: Bac-A&S
FAX Number: (719) 634-4180 Calendar System: Other
URL: www.coloradocollege.edu
Established: 1874 Annual Undergrad Tuition & Fees: $50,892
Enrollment: 2,131 Coed
Affiliation or Control: Independent Non-Profit IRS Status: 501(c)3
Highest Offering: Master's
Accreditation: NH

01 President .... Dr. Jill TIEFENTHALER
05 Dean of College & Faculty .... Dr. Sandi WONG
100 Asst VP/Special Asst to the Pres .... Ms. Mary Frances KERR
10 Sr VP/Finance & Administration .... Mr. Robert G. MOORE
111 Vice Pres for Advancement .... Mr. Sean PIERI
84 Vice Pres Enrollment Management .... Mr. Mark HATCH
32 VP Student Life/Dean of Students .... Mr. Mike EDMONDS
13 VP for Information Management/CTO .... Mr. Brian YOUNG
45 Asst VP for Inst Planning & Eff .... Ms. Lyrae WILLIAMS
20 Assoc Dean of Academic Programs .... Dr. Emily CHAN
30 Asst VP Advancement Operations .... Ms. Molly BODNAR
35 Sr Assc VP for Student Life .... Mr. John LAUER
20 Assoc Dean of the Faculty .... Dr. Mike SIDDOWAY
35 Sr Associate Dean of Students .... Ms. Rochelle MASON
37 Director of Financial Aid .... Ms. Shannon AMUNDSON
06 Registrar .... Mr. Phillip C. APODACA
26 Vice President for Communications .... Ms. Jane TURNIS
41 Director of Athletics .... Mr. Ken RALPH
104 Director International Programs .... Dr. Inger BULL
15 Director Human Resource .... Ms. Barbara WILSON
07 Director of Admissions .... Mr. Carlos JIMENEZ
18 Assoc VP of Facilities .... Mr. Chris COULTER
19 Director Campus Safety .... Ms. Maggie SANTOS
08 Library Director .... Vacant
96 Director Administrative Svcs .... Mr. Don DAVIDSON
36 Director Career Center .... Ms. Megan NICKLAUS
28 Asst VP/Director of Butler Ctr .... Mr. Paul BUCKLEY
29 Director Alumni Relations .... Ms. Anita PARISEAU
09 Dir Assessment/Program Review .... Ms. Amanda UDIS-KESSLER
21 Assoc VP of Finance/Controller .... Ms. Stacy LUTZ-DAVIDSON
14 Asst VP for Information Technology .... Mr. Vish PARADKAR
105 Director Web & Digital .... Ms. Karen TO
114 Senior Budget Analyst .... Ms. Enid RUIZ-MATTEI
38 Director of Counseling Center .... Mr. Bill DOVE
22 Director Disability Services .... Ms. Jan EDWARDS
27 Director of News & Media Relations .... Ms. Leslie WEDDELL
90 Director Educational Solutions .... Mr. Matt GOTTFRIED
88 Dir Collab Cmty Engagement .... Ms. Jordan RADKE
46 College Research Professor .... Dr. Kevin RASK
42 Chaplain .... Dr. Kate HOLBROOK
04 Executive Asst to the President .... Ms. Lori HAMACHER
39 Assoc Dir Ofc of Housing & Conf .... Mr. Justin WEIS

Colorado Mesa University (K)

1100 North Avenue, Grand Junction CO 81501-3122
County: Mesa FICE Identification: 001358
Unit ID: 127556
Telephone: (970) 248-1020 Carnegie Class: Bac-Diverse
FAX Number: (970) 248-1076 Calendar System: Semester
URL: www.coloradomesa.edu
Established: 1925 Annual Undergrad Tuition & Fees (In-State): $7,835
Enrollment: 9,448 Coed
Affiliation or Control: State IRS Status: 501(c)3
Highest Offering: Doctorate
Accreditation: NH, #CAATE, MLTAD, MUS, NURSE, PNUR, RAD, SW

01 President .... Mr. Tim FOSTER
05 Vice Pres Academic Affairs .... Dr. Cynthia PEMBERTON
10 Vice President Financial/Admin Svcs .... Ms. Laura GLATT
31 Vice Pres Community College Affairs .... Mr. Dennis BAILEY
109 Asst Vice Pres Auxiliary Services .... Mr. Andy RODRIGUEZ
32 Vice Pres Student Services .... Mr. John MARSHALL
13 VP of Information Technology/Comm .... Mr. Jeremy BROWN
20 Provost .... Dr. Carol FUTHEY
08 Library Director .... Ms. Sylvia RAEL
30 Director of Development .... Ms. Liz MEYER
37 Director Financial Aid .... Mr. Curt MARTIN
26 Director of Media Relations .... Ms. Dana NUNN
06 Registrar .... Ms. Holly TEAL
07 Director of Admissions .... Ms. Sharaya SELSOR-COWAN
09 Dir of Inst Research/Assessment .... Ms. Sonia BRANDON
18 Chief Facilities/Physical Plant .... Mr. Kent MARSH
29 Director Alumni Relations .... Mr. Jared MEIER
84 Director Enrollment Management .... Mr. Michael POLL

Colorado Mesa University-Montrose Campus (L)

245 South Cascade Avenue, Montrose CO 81401
Telephone: (970) 249-7009 Identification: 770031
Accreditation: &NH

Colorado Mountain College (M)

802 Grand Avenue, Glenwood Springs CO 81602-3961
County: Garfield FICE Identification: 004506
Unit ID: 126711
Telephone: (970) 945-8691 Carnegie Class: Bac/Assoc-Mixed
FAX Number: (970) 947-8385 Calendar System: Semester
URL: www.coloradomtn.edu
Established: 1965 Annual Undergrad Tuition & Fees (In-District): $1,768
Enrollment: 5,806 Coed
Affiliation or Control: Local IRS Status: 501(c)3
Highest Offering: Baccalaureate
Accreditation: NH, ADNUR, EMT, NUR, NURSE

01 President .... Dr. Carrie BESNETTE HAUSER
05 VP Academic Affairs .... Ms. Kathy KISER-MILLER
10 CFO .... Ms. Mary BOYD
09 VP Institutional Effectiveness .... Dr. Debra LOPER
32 VP Student Affairs .... Mr. Shane LARSON
15 Vice President of Human Resources .... Vacant
26 Public Relations Officer .... Ms. Debbie CRAWFORD
13 Chief Information Officer .... Vacant
07 Dir Pre-Enrollment Svcs/Registrar .... Mr. Shane LARSON
37 Director of Financial Aid .... Mr. Thomas VALLER
18 Director of College Facilities .... Mr. Sean NESBITT
27 Director of Marketing/Publications .... Mr. Doug STEWART
96 Director of Purchasing .... Mr. Steve BOYD
88 Dean Sch of Transitional Education .... Ms. A. Yvette MYRICK
04 Administrative Asst to President .... Ms. Debbie NOVAK
100 Chief of Staff .... Mr. Matt GIANNESCHI
43 Dir Legal Services/General Counsel .... Mr. Richard GONZALES

***Colorado Mountain College Alpine Campus* (A)**

1275 Crawford Avenue, Steamboat Springs CO 80487

Telephone: (970) 870-4444 Identification: 770038

Accreditation: &NH

***Colorado Mountain College Aspen Campus* (B)**

0255 Sage Way, Aspen CO 81611

Telephone: (970) 925-7740 Identification: 770032

Accreditation: &NH

***Colorado Mountain College Roaring Fork Campus-Spring Valley* (C)**

690 Colorado Avenue, Carbondale CO 81623

Telephone: (970) 963-2172 Identification: 770035

Accreditation: &NH

***Colorado Mountain College Summit Campus-Breckinridge Center* (D)**

PO Box 2208, Breckinridge CO 80424

Telephone: (970) 453-6757 Identification: 770033

Accreditation: &NH

***Colorado Mountain College Timberline Campus* (E)**

27900 County Road 319, PO Box 897,
Buena Vista CO 81211

Telephone: (719) 395-8419 Identification: 770036

Accreditation: &NH

***Colorado Mountain College Vail Valley Campus at Edwards* (F)**

150 Miller Ranch Road, Edwards CO 81632

Telephone: (970) 569-2900 Identification: 770034

Accreditation: &NH, MAC

***Colorado Mountain College West Garfield Campus* (G)**

3695 Airport Road, Rifle CO 81650

Telephone: (970) 625-1871 Identification: 770037

Accreditation: &NH

Colorado Northwestern Community College (H)

500 Kennedy Drive, Rangely CO 81648-3598

County: Rio Blanco FICE Identification: 001359

Unit ID: 126748

Telephone: (970) 675-2261 Carnegie Class: Assoc/MT-VT-High Non

FAX Number: (970) 675-5046 Calendar System: Semester

URL: www.cncc.edu

Established: 1962 Annual Undergrad Tuition & Fees (In-District): $3,736

Enrollment: 1,178 Coed

Affiliation or Control: State/Local IRS Status: 170(c)1

Highest Offering: Associate Degree

Accreditation: NH, ADNUR, DH

01 President .... Mr. Ron GRANGER
12 Vice Pres Craig/Student Services .... Ms. Janell OBERLANDER
05 Vice Pres Instruction .... Dr. Holly BOOMER
10 Vice Pres Business/Administration .... Mr. Roger FICKEN
07 Director of Admissions/Registrar .... Ms. Kelly SCOTT
08 Library Director .... Ms. Leana COX
15 Human Resource Specialist .... Ms. Kim BENSE
26 Marketing Director .... Vacant
18 Facilities Director .... Mr. Roger FICKEN
09 Director of Institutional Research .... Ms. Susan BOLES
38 Director Student Counseling .... Ms. Caitlan MOORE
37 Financial Aid Technician .... Ms. Merrie BYERS
20 Dean of Instruction in Rangely .... Dr. Jeff GRUBBS
20 Dean of Instruction in Craig .... Ms. Donna THEIMER

***Colorado Northwestern Community College Craig* (I)**

2801 W 9th Street, Craig CO 81625

Telephone: (970) 824-1101 Identification: 770039

Accreditation: &NH

Colorado School of Mines (J)

1500 Illinois Street, Golden CO 80401-1843

County: Jefferson FICE Identification: 001348

Unit ID: 126775

Telephone: (303) 273-3000 Carnegie Class: DU-Higher

FAX Number: (303) 273-3278 Calendar System: Semester

URL: www.mines.edu

Established: 1874 Annual Undergrad Tuition & Fees (In-State): $17,842

Enrollment: 6,054 Coed

Affiliation or Control: State IRS Status: 501(c)3

Highest Offering: Doctorate

Accreditation: NH, ENG

01 President .... Dr. Paul C. JOHNSON
05 Provost .... Dr. Thomas BOYD
10 Executive Vice Pres Admin & Ops .... Ms. Kirsten VOLPI
100 Chief of Staff .... Mr. Peter HAN
32 Vice Pres Student LIfe .... Dr. Dan FOX
88 Sr VP Research & Tech Transfer .... Dr. Tony DEAN
88 Sr Vice Pres Strat Enterprises .... Dr. Nigel T. MIDDLETON
111 Pres for Institutional Advancement .... Mr. Brian WINKELBAUER
54 Dean Earth Resource Sci & Engr .... Dr. Romana GRAVES
54 Dean Engr & Computer Science .... Dr. Kevin MOORE
54 Dean Applied Sci & Engineering .... Dr. Michael KAUFMAN
43 Dir Legal Services/General Counsel .... Ms. Anne WALKER
84 AVP Enrollment Management .... Ms. Heather BOYD
20 Associate Provost .... Dr. Wendy ZHOU
11 AVP Administration .... Ms. Vicki NICHOL
35 AVP Student Life .... Ms. Rebecca FLINTOFT
18 AVP of Operations .... Mr. Gary BOWERSOCK
15 AVP Human Resources .... Mr. Michael DOUGHERTY
13 Chief Information Officer .... Mr. Michael ERICKSON
26 Exec Dir Integrated Marketing Comm .... Vacant
35 Dean of Students .... Mr. Derek MORGAN
88 Exec Dir for Strategic Development .... Ms. Deb LASICH
04 Spec Assistant to the President .... Ms. Tammy STRANGE
41 Athletic Director .... Mr. David HANSBURG
08 University Librarian .... Ms. Carol SMITH
88 Dir of Trefny Instructional Center .... Dr. Sam SPIEGEL
37 Director of Financial Aid .... Ms. Jill ROBERTSON
51 Director of Special Programs .... Dr. Barry MARTIN
88 Dir of WISEM .... Ms. Annette PILKINGTON
38 Director Student Counseling .... Ms. Sandra SIMMS
09 Director of Institutional Research .... Ms. Tricia DOUTHIT
36 Director Student Placement .... Ms. Jean MANNING-CLARK
19 Director Public Safety .... Mr. Greg BOHLEN
92 Director Honors Program .... Dr. Ken OSGOOD
06 Registrar .... Ms. Lara MEDLEY
93 Director Minority Engineering Pgm .... Ms. Andrea MORGAN
29 Director Alumni Relations .... Mr. Damian FRIEND
91 Director Enterprise Systems .... Mr. David LEE
104 Director of International Programs .... Ms. Kay GODEL-GENGENBACH
108 Sr Assessment Associate .... Ms. Megan SANDERS
96 Director of Purchasing .... Ms. Natalie MARTINEZ
44 Senior Director Annual Giving .... Ms. Sara POND
102 Dir Foundation/Corporate Relations .... Ms. Emily KELTON

Colorado School of Trades (K)

1575 Hoyt Street, Lakewood CO 80215-2996

County: Jefferson FICE Identification: 011572

Unit ID: 126784

Telephone: (800) 234-4594 Carnegie Class: Spec 2-yr-Tech

FAX Number: (303) 233-4723 Calendar System: Other

URL: www.schooloftrades.edu

Established: 1947 Annual Undergrad Tuition & Fees: N/A

Enrollment: 171 Coed

Affiliation or Control: Proprietary IRS Status: Proprietary

Highest Offering: Associate Degree

Accreditation: ACCSC

01 President .... Mr. Robert E. MARTIN

Colorado School of Traditional Chinese Medicine (L)

1441 York Street, Suite 202, Denver CO 80206-2127

County: Denver FICE Identification: 036863

Unit ID: 381352

Telephone: (303) 329-6355 Carnegie Class: Spec-4-yr-Other Health

FAX Number: (303) 388-8165 Calendar System: Trimester

URL: www.cstcm.edu

Established: 1989 Annual Undergrad Tuition & Fees: N/A

Enrollment: 101 Coed

Affiliation or Control: Proprietary IRS Status: Proprietary

Highest Offering: Master's

Accreditation: ACUP

01 Administrative Director .... Vladimir DIBRIGIDA
05 Academic Dean .... Camille RODRIQUEZ
20 Assistant Academic Dean .... Christopher SHIFLETT
20 Assistant Academic Dean .... Abigail MENSAH-BONSU
88 Clinic Director .... Parago JONES
37 Financial Aid Administrator .... Joel SPENCER
06 Registrar .... William WALLIN
07 Recruiting Director .... Chris DUXBURY-EDWARDS
88 Receptionist .... Kirsten WEEKS

*Colorado State University System Office (M)

475 17th Street, Suite 1550, Denver CO 80202

County: Denver FICE Identification: 033437

Telephone: (303) 534-6290 Carnegie Class: N/A

FAX Number: (303) 534-6298

URL: www.csusystem.edu

01 Chancellor .... Dr. Tony FRANK
03 Executive Vice Chancellor .... Ms. Amy PARSONS
05 Chief Academic Officer .... Dr. Rick MIRANDA
43 General Counsel .... Mr. Jason JOHNSON
10 Chief Financial Officer .... Mr. Lynn JOHNSON
26 Director of Public Relations .... Mr. Mike HOOKER
86 Government Relations Coordinator .... Mr. Rich SCHWEIGERT
04 Executive Asst to Chancellor .... Ms. Melanie GEARY

*Colorado State University (N)

200 W. Lake Street, Fort Collins CO 80523-0015

County: Larimer FICE Identification: 001350

Unit ID: 126818

Telephone: (970) 491-1101 Carnegie Class: DU-Highest

FAX Number: (970) 491-0501 Calendar System: Semester

URL: www.colostate.edu

Established: 1870 Annual Undergrad Tuition & Fees (In-State): $11,052

Enrollment: 30,614 Coed

Affiliation or Control: State IRS Status: 501(c)3

Highest Offering: Doctorate

Accreditation: NH, CACREP, CAEPT, CEA, CIDA, CONST, COPSY, DIETC, DIETD, ENG, ENGR, IPSY, JOUR, LSAR, MFCD, MUS, OT, PH, SW, VET

02 President .... Dr. Anthony A. FRANK
05 Senior Executive VP/Provost .... Dr. Rick MIRANDA
46 Vice President for Research .... Dr. Alan S. RUDOLPH
32 Vice Pres Student Affairs .... Ms. Blanche M. HUGHES
11 VP for University Operations .... Ms. Lynn JOHNSON
111 VP Advancement/Strategic Initiative .... Ms. Kim TOBIN
84 Vice Pres for Enrollment/Access .... Vacant
26 VP for External Relations .... Mr. Tom MILLIGAN
56 VP Engagement/Dir CO State Univ Ext .... Dr. Louis SWANSON
20 Vice Prov for Undergraduate Affairs .... Dr. Kelly LONG
58 Vice Provost Graduate Affairs .... Dr. Jodie R. HANZLIK
91 Director of Acad Comp/Network Svc .... Mr. Scott BAILY
15 Dir Human Resource Svcs .... Ms. Diana PRIETO
36 Director Career Services .... Mr. Jeremy PODANY
08 Dean of Libraries .... Vacant
07 Assoc VP Enroll/VP for Diversity .... Ms. Mary R. ONTIVEROS
29 Exec Director Alumni Relations .... Ms. Kristi BOHLENDER
41 Athletic Director .... Mr. Joe PARKER
43 Deputy General Counsel .... Mr. Jason L. JOHNSON
47 Dean Agriculture Sciences .... Dr. Ajay MENON
88 Dean Applied Human Sciences .... Dr. Jeff MCCUBBIN
50 Dean of Business .... Dr. Beth WALKER
54 Dean of Engineering .... Dr. David MCLEAN
49 Dean of Liberal Arts .... Dr. Ben WITHERS
62 VP for IT/Dean of Libraries .... Dr. Patrick BURNS
65 Dean of Natural Resources .... Dr. John HAYES
81 Dean of Natural Sciences .... Dr. Janice L. NERGER
74 Dean of Veterinary Med & Biomed Sci .... Dr. Mark STETTER
06 Registrar .... Mr. Chris SENG
18 Chief Facilities/Physical Plant .... Mr. Tom SATTERLY
22 Dir of Equal Opportunity .... Ms. Diana PRIETO
37 Director of Student Financial Aid .... Mr. Thomas BIEDSCHEID
39 Exec Dir Housing & Dining Services .... Dr. James DOLAK
40 Director of Bookstore .... Mr. John PARRY
96 Director of Purchasing .... Mr. Frank KRAPPES
92 Director University Honors Program .... Dr. Donald MYKLES
94 Dir Women & Gender Advocacy Center .... Ms. Kathy SISNEROS
09 Director of Institutional Research .... Dr. Laura JENSEN
100 Chief of Staff Office of the Pres .... Mr. Mark GILL

*Colorado State University-Global Campus (O)

7800 E Orchard Road, Suite 200,
Greenwood Village CO 80111

County: Arapahoe FICE Identification: 042087

Unit ID: 476975

Telephone: (800) 462-7845 Carnegie Class: Masters/L

FAX Number: N/A Calendar System: Trimester

URL: https://csuglobal.edu

Established: 2008 Annual Undergrad Tuition & Fees (In-State): N/A

Enrollment: 9,838 Coed

Affiliation or Control: State IRS Status: 170(c)1

Highest Offering: Master's

Accreditation: NH, ACBSP

02 President & CEO .... Dr. Becky TAKEDA-TINKER

*Colorado State University-Pueblo (P)

2200 Bonforte Boulevard, Pueblo CO 81001-4901

County: Pueblo FICE Identification: 001365

Unit ID: 128106

Telephone: (719) 549-2100 Carnegie Class: Masters/M

FAX Number: (719) 549-2650 Calendar System: Semester
URL: www.csupueblo.edu
Established: 1933 Annual Undergrad Tuition & Fees (In-State): $9,519
Enrollment: 7,563 Coed
Affiliation or Control: State IRS Status: 501(c)3
Highest Offering: Master's
Accreditation: NH, CAATE, CAEPT, ENG, ENGT, MUS, NUR, SW

02 President .... Dr. Timothy MOTTET
05 Provost/Exec VP for Academic Affs .... Dr. Rick KREMINSKI
10 VP Finance & Administration .... Mr. Karl SPIECKER
84 VP Enrollment Mgmt/Student Affairs .... Ms. Chrissy HOLLIDAY
18 Asst VP Facilities Management .... Mr. Craig CASON
20 Asst Provost Assess/Student Lrng .... Dr. Helen CAPRIOGLIO
13 Chief Information Officer .... Mr. Erich MATOLA
08 Dean Library .... Ms. Rhonda GONZALES
50 Dean Hasan School of Business .... Dr. Bruce RAYMOND
79 Dean Col of Humanities/Soc Sci .... Dr. William FOLKESTAD
54 Dean Col Engr/Educ/Prof Studies .... Dr. Sylvester KALEVELA
81 Dean Col Science/Math .... Dr. David LEHMPUHL
102 Executive Director Foundation .... Mr. Todd KELLY
26 Exec Director External Affairs .... Ms. Cora ZALETEL
09 Dir Institutional Research/Analysis .... Ms. Maureen O'KEEFE
21 Controller .... Mr. Robert GONZALES
37 Director Student Financial Services .... Mr. Justin STREATER
06 Registrar .... Ms. Amy ROBERTSHAW
36 Director Career Center .... Mrs. Michelle B. GJERDE
41 Director Athletics .... Mr. Joe FOLDA
15 Director Human Resources .... Mr. Ralph JACOBS
39 Dir Residence Life & Housing .... Ms. Gwendolyn YOUNG
109 Int Director Auxiliary Services .... Mr. Chris FENDRICH
23 Dir Student Health/Counseling .... Ms. Carolyn DAUGHERTY
29 Director Alumni Relations .... Ms. Tracy SAMORA
88 Director Center for Acad Enrichment .... Dr. Derek LOPEZ
85 Dir International Programs .... Ms. Annie WILLIAMS
04 Exec Asst to the President .... Ms. Niki WHITAKER
07 Director of Admissions .... Ms. Tiffany KINGREY
32 Dean of Student Affairs .... Dr. Marie HUMPHREY

Colorado Technical University (A)

3151 South Vaughn Way, Suite 150, Aurora CO 80014
Telephone: (303) 632-2300 Identification: 666732
Accreditation: &NH, ACBSP

† Regional accreditation is carried under the parent institution in Colorado Springs, CO.

Colorado Technical University (B)

4435 N Chestnut Street, Colorado Springs CO 80907-3896
County: El Paso FICE Identification: 010148
Unit ID: 126827
Telephone: (719) 598-0200 Carnegie Class: Masters/L
FAX Number: (719) 598-3740 Calendar System: Quarter
URL: www.coloradotech.edu
Established: 1965 Annual Undergrad Tuition & Fees: $10,540
Enrollment: 1,448 Coed
Affiliation or Control: Proprietary IRS Status: Proprietary
Highest Offering: Doctorate
Accreditation: NH, ACBSP, ENG, NURSE

00 Interim CEO .... Mr. Jack KOEHN
01 Campus President .... Mr. Andrew HURST
05 Chief Academic Officer/Provost .... Dr. Connie JOHNSON
10 Vice President Finance .... Ms. Erin KRAFT
07 Vice President of Admissions .... Mr. Keith ARMSTRONG
11 VP Univ Strategy/Operations .... Ms. Elise BASKEL
20 Vice Provost .... Dr. Douglas STEIN
20 Vice Provost .... Dr. Emma ZONE
36 Director of Career Services .... Ms. Belinda NICHOLS-ZONNO
08 Library Manager .... Ms. Nicole HULT
13 Manager of Information Systems .... Mr. Thomas LEIGH
53 Program Director General Education .... Dr. Tonya TROKA

Community College of Aurora (C)

16000 E Centre Tech Parkway, Aurora CO 80011-9036
County: Arapahoe FICE Identification: 022769
Unit ID: 126863
Telephone: (303) 360-4700 Carnegie Class: Assoc/MT-VT-High Non
FAX Number: (303) 360-4761 Calendar System: Semester
URL: www.ccaurora.edu
Established: 1983 Annual Undergrad Tuition & Fees (In-State): $3,702
Enrollment: 6,943 Coed
Affiliation or Control: State IRS Status: 501(c)3
Highest Offering: Associate Degree
Accreditation: NH, EMT

01 President .... Dr. Elizabeth OUDENHOVEN
05 Vice President of Academic Affairs .... Dr. Tricia JOHNSON
32 Vice President of Student Affairs .... Dr. Paulette DALPES
45 VP of Institutional Effectiveness .... Dr. Chris WARD
15 Director of Human Resources .... Ms. Cindy HESSE
21 Controller .... Ms. Xochil HERRERA
35 Dean of Students .... Ms. Tamara WHITE
20 Dean Academic Affairs .... Mr. Victor VIALPANDO
20 Dean Academic Affairs .... Dr. Ted SNOW
19 Director of Security .... Vacant
36 Director of Career Services .... Ms. LeeDel COHENOUR
13 Director Information Technology .... Mr. Sam THOMAS
18 Facilities Director .... Mr. John BOTTELBERGHE
26 Director Marketing/Communications .... Ms. Mary MEEKS
37 Director Financial Aid .... Mr. John YOUNG
06 Director Admissions & Registrar .... Ms. Kristen CUSACK
08 Director Library Services .... Mr. Dan LAWRENCE
09 Director of Institutional Research .... Vacant
124 Dean of Retention & Student Success .... Dr. Derrick HAYNES
27 Director Public & Media Relations .... Ms. Mary MEEKS
102 Exec Dir CCA Foundation .... Mr. John WOLFKILL
28 Director of Diversity .... Ms. Quill PHILLIPS

Community College of Denver (D)

Campus Box 250, PO Box 173363,
Denver CO 80217-3363
County: Denver FICE Identification: 009542
Unit ID: 126942
Telephone: (303) 556-2400 Carnegie Class: Assoc/MT-VT-Mix Trad/Non
FAX Number: (303) 556-8555 Calendar System: Semester
URL: www.ccd.edu
Established: 1967 Annual Undergrad Tuition & Fees (In-State): $3,702
Enrollment: 9,130 Coed
Affiliation or Control: State IRS Status: 501(c)3
Highest Offering: Associate Degree
Accreditation: NH, CSHSE, DH, RAD

01 President .... Dr. Everette FREEMAN
05 Provost/Chief Academic Officer .... Dr. Rhonda EPPER
10 Vice Pres Finance & Admin/CFO .... Mr. Duane RISSE
32 Vice Pres Student Affairs .... Ms. Judi DIAZ BONACQUISTI
75 Dean Career/Technical Education .... Mr. James KYNOR
49 Dean Language/Arts/Behavioral Sci .... Ms. Ruthanne ORIHUELA
124 Dean Student Development/Retention .... Mrs. Tina GARCIA
84 Dean of Enrollment Services .... Dr. Tami SELBY
35 Dean of Student Life .... Ms. Meloni RUDOLPH
37 Director Financial Aid .... Ms. Theresa CLAPHAM LAVIN
07 Int Dir Admissions/Recruit/Outreach .... Mr. Andrew GARCIA
15 Director Human Resources .... Ms. Patty DAVIES
13 Director IT Services .... Mr. Chris ARCARESE
09 Director Inst Research & Planning .... Vacant
06 Registrar .... Ms. Darla RUFF
18 Chief Facilities/Physical Plant .... Mr. Kevin SEILER

Concorde Career College (E)

111 N Havana Street, Aurora CO 80010-4314
County: Arapahoe FICE Identification: 008871
Unit ID: 126687
Telephone: (303) 861-1151 Carnegie Class: Spec 2-yr-Health
FAX Number: (303) 839-5478 Calendar System: Other
URL: www.concorde.edu
Established: 1969 Annual Undergrad Tuition & Fees: N/A
Enrollment: 578 Coed
Affiliation or Control: Proprietary IRS Status: Proprietary
Highest Offering: Associate Degree
Accreditation: ACCSC, COARC, DH, PTAA, RAD, SURGT

01 Campus President .... Mr. Thomas WICKE
05 Academic Dean .... Vacant
37 Director of Financial Aid .... Ms. Nancy DISANTE
07 Director of Admissions .... Mr. Nick HRUBY

Denver School of Nursing (F)

1401 19th Street, Denver CO 80202
County: Denver FICE Identification: 041483
Unit ID: 454856
Telephone: (303) 292-0015 Carnegie Class: Spec-4-yr-Other Health
FAX Number: (720) 974-0290 Calendar System: Quarter
URL: www.denverschoolofnursing.edu
Established: 2003 Annual Undergrad Tuition & Fees: N/A
Enrollment: 807 Coed
Affiliation or Control: Proprietary IRS Status: Proprietary
Highest Offering: Master's
Accreditation: NH, ADNUR, NUR

01 President .... Dr. Marcia BANKIRER
10 Director of Business Operations .... Ms. Renee MCMILLIN
32 Director of Student Services .... Mr. Michael RUSCHIVAL
05 Dean/Dir of Nursing Education Pgms ... Dr. Diana KOSTRZEWSKI
37 Director of Financial Aid .... Ms. Geri REICHMUTH
07 Director of Admissions .... Mr. Jeff JOHNSON
06 Senior Registrar .... Ms. Katie PEDERSON

Denver Seminary (G)

6399 S Santa Fe Drive, Littleton CO 80120-2912
County: Arapahoe FICE Identification: 001352
Unit ID: 126979
Telephone: (303) 761-2482 Carnegie Class: Spec-4-yr-Faith
FAX Number: (303) 761-8060 Calendar System: Semester
URL: www.denverseminary.edu
Established: 1950 Annual Graduate Tuition & Fees: N/A
Enrollment: 929 Coed
Affiliation or Control: Interdenominational IRS Status: 501(c)3
Highest Offering: Doctorate; No Undergraduates
Accreditation: NH, CACREP, PAST, THEOL

01 President .... Dr. Mark S. YOUNG
00 Chancellor .... Dr. Gordon MACDONALD
05 Provost/Dean .... Dr. Randolph M. MACFARLAND
10 Vice President of Finance .... Ms. Deborah KELLAR
111 Vice President of Advancement .... Mr. Chris JOHNSON
32 VP Student Life/Enrollment Mgmt .... Mr. Robert JONES
20 Associate Academic Dean .... Dr. W. David BUSCHART
06 Registrar .... Mrs. Sara RIESE
35 Dean of Students .... Mr. Rob FOLEY
07 Director of Admissions .... Mr. Michael MURPHY
30 Director of Development .... Vacant
109 Director of Auxiliary Services .... Mr. Kent B. QUACKENBUSH
13 Director of Information Systems .... Mr. Jason ADAMS
26 Director of Communications .... Mrs. Katie LARIC
90 Associate Dean of Ed Technology .... Mr. Aaron JOHNSON
18 Director of Facilities .... Mr. Rob BACHMAN
37 Director of Financial Aid .... Mrs. Mandy MUSSO
08 Director of Library .... Dr. Keith P. WELLS
73 Director of DMin Program .... Dr. Marshall SHELLEY
21 Controller/Dir Financial Services .... Ms. Diana SMITH
15 Director of Human Resources .... Ms. Zandy WENNERSTROM
28 Assoc Dean for Ethical Communities .... Mr. Wilmer RAMIREZ
56 Assoc Dean Innovation/Extension Ed .... Mr. Tim KOLLER
04 Executive Asst to the President .... Ms. Christy DIAMOND
19 Director Security/Safety .... Mr. Kent QUACKENBUSH

DeVry University - Westminster Campus (H)

1870 W 122nd Avenue, Westminster CO 80234-2010
Telephone: (303) 280-7400 Identification: 666227
Accreditation: &NH, ENGT

† Regional accreditation is carried under the parent institution in Downers Grove, IL.

Ecotech Institute (I)

1400 South Abilene Street, Aurora CO 80012
Telephone: (303) 586-5290 Identification: 770840
Accreditation: ACICS

† Branch campus of Virginia College, Birmingham, AL

Fort Lewis College (J)

1000 Rim Drive, Durango CO 81301-3999
County: La Plata FICE Identification: 001353
Unit ID: 127185
Telephone: (970) 247-7010 Carnegie Class: Bac-A&S
FAX Number: (970) 247-7175 Calendar System: Semester
URL: www.fortlewis.edu
Established: 1911 Annual Undergrad Tuition & Fees (In-State): $8,104
Enrollment: 3,707 Coed
Affiliation or Control: State IRS Status: 170(c)1
Highest Offering: Master's
Accreditation: NH, CAEPT, ENG, MUS

01 President .... Dr. Dene Kay THOMAS
05 Provost/Vice Pres Academic Affairs .... Dr. Barbara MORRIS
10 Vice Pres Finance & Administration .... Mr. Steven J. SCHWARTZ
111 Vice President for Advancement .... Mr. Mark A. JASTORFF
84 Assoc Vice Pres Enrollment Mgmt .... Dr. Carol SMITH
32 Vice President Student Affairs .... Dr. Glenna W. SEXTON
20 Assoc Vice Pres Academic Affairs .... Dr. Lisa M. SNYDER
21 Assoc Vics Pres Finance & Admin .... Ms. Michele PETERSON
06 Registrar .... Ms. Theresa E. RODRIGUEZ
21 Controller .... Ms. Cheryl WIESCAMP
25 Director of Grants Management .... Ms. Angela ROCHAT
37 Director Financial Aid .... Ms. Tracey PICCOLI
07 Director of Admission .... Vacant
38 Dir Counseling Center .... Ms. Karen NAKAYAMA
08 Director of the Library .... Ms. Martha A. TALMAN
15 Dir Human Resources/Equal Opptnty .... Mr. Greg MCCLURG
39 Dir Stdnt Housing/Conferences Svcs .... Ms. Julie N. LOVE
41 Athletic Director .... Mr. Gary HUNTER
13 Director Computing & Telecomm .... Mr. Matt MCGLAMERY
29 Director Alumni Engagement .... Vacant
96 Director of Purchasing .... Mr. Wayne J. HERMES
26 Chief Public Relations Officer .... Mr. Mitch DAVIS
40 Bookstore Manager .... Ms. Brooke INGLE
22 Coord Equal Opportun/Judicial Affs .... Dr. Haeryon KIM
83 Dean Arts and Science .... Dr. Darrell PETERS
50 Dean Sch of Business Admin .... Dr. Steven M. ELIAS
49 Assoc Dean Arts & Sciences .... Ms. Anne E. MCCARTHY
49 Assoc Dean Arts & Sciences .... Dr. Peter MCCORMICK
106 Dir Digital Innovation & eLearning .... Vacant
108 Dir Academic Effectiveness & Eval .... Dr. Lisa M. SNYDER
53 Director of Teacher Education .... Dr. Richard FULTON
101 Secretary of the Institution/Board .... Ms. Peggy SHARP

Front Range Community College (K)

3645 W 112th Avenue, Westminster CO 80031-2105
County: Adams FICE Identification: 007933
Unit ID: 127200
Telephone: (303) 404-5000 Carnegie Class: Assoc/MT-VT-High Non
FAX Number: (303) 466-1623 Calendar System: Semester
URL: www.frontrange.edu
Established: 1968 Annual Undergrad Tuition & Fees (In-State): $3,660
Enrollment: 18,747 Coed
Affiliation or Control: State IRS Status: 501(c)3
Highest Offering: Associate Degree
Accreditation: NH, ADNUR, CAHIIM, DA, MAC

01 President .... Mr. Andrew R. DORSEY
04 Asst to the President .... Ms. Denise BUCHER

05 Vice Pres Academic/Student Affairs .... Dr. Gillian MCKNIGHT-TUTEIN
10 Vice Pres Finance & Administration .... Dr. Joseph HARBOUK
12 VP Westminster Campus/Brighton Ctr .... Ms. Cathy PELLISH
12 Vice Pres Larimer Campus .... Dr. Jean RUNYON
12 Vice Pres Boulder County Campus .... Dr. Elena SANDOVAL-LUCERO
84 Assoc VP Enroll Mgmt & Student Svcs .... Dr. Kris BINARD
18 Assoc VP Facilities Planning/Mgmt .... Mr. Derek BROWN
20 Dean of Instruction Larimer .... Dr. Shashi UNNITHAN
106 Dean of Online Learning .... Ms. Tammy VERCAUTEREN
20 Dean of Instruction Larimer .... Ms. Darcy OROZCO
20 Dean of Instruction Boulder County .... Mr. Matt JAMISON
20 Dean of Instruction Westminster .... Ms. Francois JACOBS
32 Dean of Student Svcs Boulder County .... Ms. Carla STEIN
32 Dean of Student Svcs Westminster .... Mr. Aaron PRESTWICH
15 Exec Director of Human Resources .... Mr. Paul MEESE
09 Director of Institutional Research .... Ms. Kim WALLACE
114 Director of Budget & Auxiliary Svcs .... Ms. Patti ARROYO
06 Registrar .... Ms. Sonia GONZALES
07 Director of Admissions .... Ms. Cynthia FARMER
37 Dir of Financial Aid Larimer .... Ms. Carolee GOLDSMITH
08 Librarian .... Mr. Jeff WAHL
18 Director of Facilities Westminster .... Mr. Patrick O'NEILL
18 Director of Facilities Larimer .... Mr. Dennis DEREMER
35 Director Student Life Westminster .... Ms. Amy ROSDIL
35 Director Student Life Larimer .... Ms. Mary BRANTON-HOUSLEY
35 Dir Student Life Boulder County .... Ms. Amanda CLANCY
102 Exec Director of Foundation .... Mr. Ryan MCCOY
26 Lead Dir Marketing/Communications .... Ms. Marian MAHARAS
27 Public Information Officer .... Mr. John FEELEY
13 Dir of Information Technology Svcs .... Ms. Jeannine MENEFEE
19 Dir Campus Security/Preparedness .... Mr. Gordon GOLDSMITH

Front Range Community College-Boulder County Campus (A)

2190 Miller Drive, Longmont CO 80501
Telephone: (303) 678-3722 Identification: 770041
Accreditation: &NH

Front Range Community College Larimer Campus (B)

4616 S Shields Street, Fort Collins CO 80526
Telephone: (970) 226-2500 Identification: 770040
Accreditation: &NH, ADNUR

Holmes Institute of Consciousness Studies (C)

573 Park Point Drive, Golden CO 80401
County: Jefferson Identification: 666255
Telephone: (720) 496-1370 Carnegie Class: Not Classified
FAX Number: (303) 526-0913 Calendar System: Quarter
URL: www.holmesinstitute.edu
Established: 1972 Annual Graduate Tuition & Fees: N/A
Enrollment: N/A Coed
Affiliation or Control: Other IRS Status: 501(c)3
Highest Offering: Master's; No Undergraduates
Accreditation: DEAC

01 President .... Rev Dr. Robert DEEN
06 Registrar .... Ms. Maureen THURSTON
05 Academic Dean .... Rev Dr. Kim KAISER
56 Dean of Distance Education .... Rev Dr. Christina TILLOTSON

IBMC College (D)

6805 Corporate Drive, Suite 100,
Colorado Springs CO 80919
County: El Paso FICE Identification: 008635
Unit ID: 127839
Telephone: (719) 596-7400 Carnegie Class: Spec 2-yr-Health
FAX Number: (719) 596-2464 Calendar System: Other
URL: www.ibmc.edu
Established: 1966 Annual Undergrad Tuition & Fees: N/A
Enrollment: 344 Coed
Affiliation or Control: Proprietary IRS Status: Proprietary
Highest Offering: Associate Degree
Accreditation: MLTAB

01 Campus President .... Mr. Josh DRUCKER

IBMC College (E)

3842 South Mason Street, Fort Collins CO 80526
County: Larimer FICE Identification: 030063
Unit ID: 372329
Telephone: (970) 223-2669 Carnegie Class: Spec 2-yr-Health
FAX Number: (970) 223-2796 Calendar System: Quarter
URL: www.ibmc.edu
Established: 1987 Annual Undergrad Tuition & Fees: $12,600
Enrollment: 446 Coed
Affiliation or Control: Proprietary IRS Status: Proprietary
Highest Offering: Associate Degree
Accreditation: ACICS

00 CEO .... Mr. Steven STEELE
01 President .... Ms. Pat SCHLOTTER

IBMC College (F)

2863 35th Avenue, Greeley CO 80634-9421
Telephone: (970) 356-4733 Identification: 770631
Accreditation: ACICS

Iliff School of Theology (G)

2323 E. Iliff Ave, Denver CO 80210-4798
County: Denver FICE Identification: 001354
Unit ID: 127273
Telephone: (303) 744-1287 Carnegie Class: Spec-4-yr-Faith
FAX Number: (303) 777-3387 Calendar System: Quarter
URL: www.iliff.edu
Established: 1892 Annual Graduate Tuition & Fees: N/A
Enrollment: 340 Coed
Affiliation or Control: United Methodist IRS Status: 501(c)3
Highest Offering: Doctorate; No Undergraduates
Accreditation: NH, THEOL

01 President and CEO .... Dr. Thomas V. WOLFE
05 Vice Pres/Dean Academic Affairs .... Dr. Albert HERNANDEZ
10 Vice President for Business Affairs .... Vacant
111 VP Inst Advancement/Enrollment .... Mr. David WORLEY
26 Director of Communications .... Dr. Soon Beng YEAP
06 Registrar .... Ms. Carmen E. BACA-DOSTER
13 Dir of Academic and Info Technology ... Mr. Michael HEMENWAY
07 Director Admission/Financial Aid .... Ms. Peggy J. BLOCKER
28 Associate Dean of Diversities .... Dr. Edward ANTONIO
04 Executive Asst to President .... Mrs. Alisha ENO
18 Interim Dir of Facilities Mgmt .... Mr. Willie WATSON
29 Donor and Alumni Relations Director .. Ms. Caran WARE JOSEPH
15 Director of Human Resources .... Mrs. Janice TURNER

Institute of Business and Medical Careers (H)

2315 North Main Street, Longmont CO 80501
Telephone: (303) 651-6819 Identification: 770630
Accreditation: ACICS

Institute of Taoist Education and Acupuncture (I)

317 West South Boulder Road, Ste 5, Louisville CO 80027
County: Boulder FICE Identification: 041212
Unit ID: 454838
Telephone: (720) 890-8922 Carnegie Class: Spec-4-yr-Other Health
FAX Number: (720) 890-7719 Calendar System: Other
URL: www.itea.edu
Established: 1996 Annual Graduate Tuition & Fees: N/A
Enrollment: 41 Coed
Affiliation or Control: Independent Non-Profit IRS Status: 501(c)3
Highest Offering: Master's; No Undergraduates
Accreditation: ACUP

01 President .... Sandra LILLIE
05 Director .... Hilary SKELLON
06 Registrar .... Claudia O'NEILL
10 Financial Administrator .... Kathy KNAUS

IntelliTec College (J)

2315 E Pikes Peak Avenue,
Colorado Springs CO 80909-6096
County: El Paso FICE Identification: 022537
Unit ID: 128179
Telephone: (719) 632-7626 Carnegie Class: Assoc/HVT-High Trad
FAX Number: (719) 632-7451 Calendar System: Quarter
URL: www.intellitec.edu
Established: 1965 Annual Undergrad Tuition & Fees: N/A
Enrollment: 762 Coed
Affiliation or Control: Proprietary IRS Status: Proprietary
Highest Offering: Associate Degree
Accreditation: ACCSC

01 Campus Director .... Raymond ADA

IntelliTec College (K)

772 Horizon Drive, Grand Junction CO 81506-3994
County: Mesa FICE Identification: 030669
Unit ID: 128188
Telephone: (970) 245-8101 Carnegie Class: Assoc/HVT-High Non
FAX Number: (970) 243-8074 Calendar System: Quarter
URL: www.intelliteccollege.com
Established: 1984 Annual Undergrad Tuition & Fees: N/A
Enrollment: 591 Coed
Affiliation or Control: Proprietary IRS Status: Proprietary
Highest Offering: Associate Degree
Accreditation: ACCSC

01 President .... Mr. Wayne ZELLNER
05 Director .... Ms. Cheryl MORRIS

IntelliTec College (L)

3673 Parker Boulevard, Pueblo CO 81008-2211
Telephone: (719) 542-3181 Identification: 666366
Accreditation: ACCSC

Johnson & Wales University - Denver Campus (M)

7150 Montview Boulevard, Denver CO 80220-1866
Telephone: (303) 256-9300 Identification: 666411
Accreditation: &EH, DIETD

† Regional accreditation is carried under the parent institution in Providence, RI.

Lamar Community College (N)

2401 S Main, Lamar CO 81052-3999
County: Prowers FICE Identification: 001355
Unit ID: 127389
Telephone: (719) 336-2248 Carnegie Class: Assoc/MT-VT-High Non
FAX Number: (719) 336-2448 Calendar System: Semester
URL: www.lamarcc.edu
Established: 1937 Annual Undergrad Tuition & Fees (In-State): $3,720
Enrollment: 777 Coed
Affiliation or Control: State IRS Status: 501(c)3
Highest Offering: Associate Degree
Accreditation: NH, ADNUR

01 President .... Dr. Linda LUJAN
05 VP Academic Services/Student Svcs .... Ms. Cheryl SANCHEZ
11 VP Admin Svcs/Inst Effectiveness .... Mr. Chad DE BONO
20 Dean of Academic Services .... Dr. Annessa STAGNER
26 Director of Communication .... Ms. Anne-Marie CRAMPTON
06 Registrar .... Ms. Amber THOMPSON
08 Library Tech .... Ms. Ellen LOVELL
18 Director of Facilities .... Mr. Sean LIRLEY
15 Director Personnel Services .... Ms. Jennifer MORTIMEYER
39 Director Student Housing .... Mr. Michael PRESTIN
27 Director of Marketing .... Ms. Kristin LUBBERS
38 Director Student Counseling .... Vacant
96 Director of Purchasing .... Ms. Ava BAIR
41 Athletic Director .... Mr. Scott CRAMPTON
37 Director Financial Aid .... Ms. Teale HEMPHILL
07 Director of Admissions .... Ms. Jenna DAVIS
09 Coordinator Institutional Research .... Ms. Kim WALLACE
84 Coord for Concurrent Enrollment .... Mr. Del CHASE

Lincoln College of Technology (O)

11194 East 45th Avenue, Denver CO 80239
County: Denver FICE Identification: 007547
Unit ID: 126951
Telephone: (303) 722-5724 Carnegie Class: Spec 2-yr-Tech
FAX Number: (303) 778-8264 Calendar System: Semester
URL: www.lincolnedu.com
Established: 1963 Annual Undergrad Tuition & Fees: N/A
Enrollment: 1,054 Coed
Affiliation or Control: Proprietary IRS Status: Proprietary
Highest Offering: Associate Degree
Accreditation: ACCSC

01 Campus President .... Ms. Kelly THUMM MOORE
07 Senior Director Admissions .... Ms. Jennifer HASH
05 Academic Dean .... Mr. Dwayne ISBELL
20 Director of Education .... Mr. Ivan SMITH
04 Administrative Asst to President .... Ms. Melinda K. COWGER
06 Registrar .... Mr. Craig FITZPATRICK

McKinley College (P)

2001 Lowe Street, Fort Collins CO 80525-3474
County: Larimer Identification: 666237
Telephone: (970) 207-4550 Carnegie Class: Not Classified
FAX Number: (877) 599-5863 Calendar System: Other
URL: www.mckinleycollege.edu
Established: 2004 Annual Undergrad Tuition & Fees: N/A
Enrollment: N/A Coed
Affiliation or Control: Proprietary IRS Status: Proprietary
Highest Offering: Associate Degree
Accreditation: DEAC

01 President .... Ann ROHR
32 Vice President of Student Affairs .... Joyce LINDQUIST
05 Dean of Faculty .... Nancy HAMPSON
108 Director of Compliance/Fin Aid .... Janet PERRY
106 Dir Online Education/E-learning .... Leslie BALLENTINE
88 Applications Development Director .... Scott LYNCH
15 Human Resources Manager .... Joy DAVIS
26 Marketing Director .... Holly COOK
36 Graduate Services Supervisor .... Karen THOMPSON
37 Financial Aid Supervisor .... Jennifer BRIGGLE
84 Admissions Manager .... Jennifer MANNS

Metropolitan State University of Denver (Q)

PO Box 173362, Denver CO 80217-3362
County: Denver FICE Identification: 001360
Unit ID: 127565
Telephone: (303) 556-2400 Carnegie Class: Masters/M
FAX Number: (303) 556-3912 Calendar System: Semester
URL: www.msudenver.edu
Established: 1963 Annual Undergrad Tuition & Fees (In-State): $6,930
Enrollment: 20,676 Coed
Affiliation or Control: State IRS Status: 501(c)3
Highest Offering: Master's

Accreditation: NH, ART, CAATE, CS, #CSHSE, DIETD, ENGT, EXSC, MT, MUS, NRPA, NUR, SW, THEA

01 President .... Dr. Janine A. DAVIDSON
05 Vice President Academic Affairs .... Dr. Vicki GOLICH
10 Vice Pres Admin/Finance/Facilities .... Mr. Steve KREIDLER
30 VP University Advancement .... Vacant
43 General Counsel/Secretary to Board .... Vacant
13 AVP Info Technology Services/CIO .... Mr. Kevin TAYLOR
15 Director Human Resources .... Dr. Joshua MACKEY
84 Assoc VP Enrollment Services .... Ms. Lori KESTER
26 Chief of Staff/Marketing & Comm .... Ms. Catherine LUCAS
29 Dir of Alumni Relations/Giving .... Ms. Jamie HURST
50 Dean School Business .... Dr. Ann B. MURPHY
107 Dean School Professional Studies .... Dr. Sandra HAYNES
32 AVP Stdnt Engage & Well/Dean Stdnts .... Ms. Braelin PANTEL
06 Registrar .... Dr. James TISDALE
37 Director Financial Aid .... Ms. Cindy HEJL
41 Athletic Director .... Dr. G. Anthony GRANT
35 Assoc Director Student Activities .... Ms. Gretta MINCER
36 Director Career Services .... Ms. Bridgette COBLE
28 Assoc to Pres Inst Diversity .... Dr. Myron ANDERSON
07 Assoc Director of Admissions .... Mr. Patrick FAY
09 Director of Institutional Research .... Ms. Ellen BOSWELL

Morgan Community College (A)

920 Barlow Road, Fort Morgan CO 80701-4399
County: Morgan | FICE Identification: 009981 | Unit ID: 127617
Telephone: (970) 542-3100 | Carnegie Class: Assoc/HVT-High Non
FAX Number: (970) 542-3115 | Calendar System: Semester
URL: www.morgancc.edu
Established: 1967 | Annual Undergrad Tuition & Fees (In-State): $3,494
Enrollment: 1,647 | Coed
Affiliation or Control: State | IRS Status: Exempt
Highest Offering: Associate Degree
Accreditation: NH, ADNUR, @PTAA

01 President .... Dr. Curt FREED
10 Vice Pres Finance/Admin Services .... Ms. Susan CLOUGH
05 Vice President of Instruction .... Ms. Kathy FRISBIE
84 Vice President of Student Success .... Mr. Kent BAUER
04 Assistant to the President .... Ms. Jane FRIES
20 Dean for Instruction .... Dr. Misty STROUD
12 Director of Regional Outreach .... Ms. Kellie OVERTURF
12 Director of Regional Outreach .... Ms. Valerie RHOADES
09 Dir of Institutional Effectiveness .... Mr. Derek GRUBB
26 Dir of Communications & Marketing .... Ms. Katie BARRON
30 Director of Development .... Ms. Kari LINKER
37 Director of Financial Aid .... Ms. Sally SHAWCROFT
07 Dir Admissions/Regional Outreach .... Ms. Kim MAXWELL
15 Director of Human Resources .... Ms. Julie BEYDLER
08 Director of Learning Resources .... Ms. April AMACK
96 Director of Purchasing .... Ms. Trisha KEMBEL
40 Director of Bookstore .... Ms. Debbie CASTENEDA
18 Coordinator of M & O .... Mr. Seth NOBLE
36 Voc Guidance/Placement Counselor .... Mr. Dan MARLER
13 Director Information Technology .... Mr. Mark FRASCO

Naropa University (B)

2130 Arapahoe Avenue, Boulder CO 80302-6697
County: Boulder | FICE Identification: 021175 | Unit ID: 127653
Telephone: (303) 444-0202 | Carnegie Class: Masters/L
FAX Number: (303) 444-0410 | Calendar System: Semester
URL: www.naropa.edu
Established: 1974 | Annual Undergrad Tuition & Fees: $31,170
Enrollment: 942 | Coed
Affiliation or Control: Independent Non-Profit | IRS Status: 501(c)3
Highest Offering: Master's
Accreditation: NH

01 President .... Mr. Charles G. LIEF
04 Assistant to the President .... Ms. Rachel SOLUM
10 Vice President of Operations .... Mr. Tyler KELSCH
05 Provost/Vice Pres Academic Affs .... Dr. Janet CRAMER
26 Director of Marketing .... Ms. Michel REEVES
30 Director of Development .... Ms. Angela MADURA
88 Special Advisor to the Pres .... Ms. Cheryl BARBOUR
13 Director of IT .... Mr. David EDMINSTER
07 Asst Prov Marketing and Admiss .... Mr. Brian PRECIOUS
97 Dean Naropa College .... Ms. Carole CLEMENTS
32 Dean of Students .... Mr. Learie NURSE
28 Dir of Diversity & Inclusion .... Ms. Regina SMITH
38 Director Counseling Center .... Ms. Joy REDSTONE
06 Registrar .... Ms. Keely PRESTON
08 Library Director .... Vacant
18 Director of Safety/Facilities & Ops .... Mr. Aaron COOK
37 Dir Student Financial Services .... Ms. Jessica BREJC
15 Director of Human Resources .... Mr. Randall ARNOLD
106 Director of Online Education .... Mr. Jirka HLADIS
19 Asst Dir of Campus Security .... Ms. Karina SCOTT
36 Dir Career & Community Eng .... Vacant

National American University-Centennial (C)

8242 S University Blvd, Suite 100, Centennial CO 80122
Telephone: (303) 542-7000 | Identification: 770389
Accreditation: &NH, MAC, OTA

† Branch campus of National American University, Rapid City, SD

National American University-Colorado Springs (D)

1915 Jamboree Drive, Suite 185,
Colorado Springs CO 80920
Telephone: (719) 590-8300 | Identification: 770390
Accreditation: &NH, MAC

† Branch campus of National American University, Rapid City, SD

National American University-Colorado Springs South (E)

1079 Space Center Drive, Unit 140,
Colorado Springs CO 80915
Telephone: (719) 208-3800 | Identification: 770391
Accreditation: &NH

† Branch campus of National American University, Rapid City, SD

Northeastern Junior College (F)

100 College Avenue, Sterling CO 80751-2399
County: Logan | FICE Identification: 001361 | Unit ID: 127732
Telephone: (970) 521-6600 | Carnegie Class: Assoc/MT-VT-Mix Trad/Non
FAX Number: (970) 522-4945 | Calendar System: Semester
URL: www.njc.edu
Established: 1941 | Annual Undergrad Tuition & Fees (In-State): $4,710
Enrollment: 1,498 | Coed
Affiliation or Control: State | IRS Status: 501(c)3
Highest Offering: Associate Degree
Accreditation: NH, ADNUR

01 President .... Mr. Jay LEE
05 Vice President Academic Services .... Mr. Stanton GARTIN
10 Vice Pres Finance & Administration .... Ms. Lisa LEFEVRE
32 Vice President Student Services .... Mr. Steven SMITH
29 Alumni Director .... Mr. Jack ANNAN
102 Executive Director NJC Foundation .... Ms. Kathleen REINHARDT
06 Director Records/Admission Process .... Ms. Lisa SCHAEFER
37 Director of Financial Aid .... Ms. Alice WEINGARDT
39 Dir Resident Life & Student Activit .... Vacant
18 Physical Plant Director .... Mr. Tracey KNOX
15 Human Resources Director .... Ms. Jeri ESTRADA
41 Athletic Director .... Ms. Marci HENRY
96 Director of Purchasing .... Ms. Erin WAITLEY
09 Dir of Inst Research/Plng/Devel .... Ms. Leslie WEINSHEIM
26 Director of Marketing .... Ms. Sarah MATTHEWS
21 Controller .... Ms. Judy MCFADDEN
13 Director Information Technology .... Ms. Cherie BRUNGARDT
40 Bookstore Director .... Ms. Heather BRUNGARDT
04 Executive Asst to President .... Ms. Shawn ROSE
07 Director of Admissions .... Mr. Adam KUNKEL
106 Dir Online Education/E-learning .... Ms. Cyndi VANDENBARK
108 Director Institutional Assessment .... Ms. Misti PIERCE
25 Chief Contracts/Grants Admin .... Ms. Rebecca ROMERO

Otero Junior College (G)

1802 Colorado Avenue, La Junta CO 81050-3346
County: Otero | FICE Identification: 001362 | Unit ID: 127778
Telephone: (719) 384-6831 | Carnegie Class: Assoc/MT-VT-High Non
FAX Number: (719) 384-6933 | Calendar System: Semester
URL: www.ojc.edu
Established: 1941 | Annual Undergrad Tuition & Fees (In-State): $3,569
Enrollment: 1,410 | Coed
Affiliation or Control: State | IRS Status: 501(c)3
Highest Offering: Associate Degree
Accreditation: NH, ADNUR, MLTAD, PHLEB

01 President .... Mr. James T. RIZZUTO
11 Vice Pres Administrative Services .... Mr. Pat MALOTT
05 Vice Pres Instructional Services .... Ms. Kim GRIMSLEY
32 Vice President Student Services .... Mr. Jeff PAOLUCCI
84 Assoc VP Enrollment Management .... Mrs. Almabeth KAESS
20 Assoc VP Instructional Services .... Mr. Ryan TROSPER
08 Director Learning Resources .... Ms. Chelsea HEARASINGH
41 Athletic Director .... Mr. Gary ADDINGTON
15 Director of Human Resources .... Ms. Carol NOLL
18 Director of Physical Plant .... Mr. John CANADAY, JR.
40 Bookstore Coordinator .... Ms. Tiana EDDY
37 Director of Financial Aid .... Ms. Angela MOORE
109 Director of Auxiliary Services .... Ms. Desiree CARRILLO
26 Dir of Communications/Development .... Mrs. Sue SAMANIEGO
13 Director of Computer Services .... Mr. Mark ALLEN
09 Director of Institutional Research .... Ms. Rebecca GRANTHAM

Pikes Peak Community College (H)

5675 S Academy Boulevard,
Colorado Springs CO 80906-5498
County: El Paso | FICE Identification: 008896 | Unit ID: 127820
Telephone: (719) 502-2000 | Carnegie Class: Assoc/MT-VT-Mix Trad/Non
FAX Number: (719) 502-2201 | Calendar System: Semester
URL: www.ppcc.edu
Established: 1968 | Annual Undergrad Tuition & Fees (In-State): $3,536
Enrollment: 13,311 | Coed
Affiliation or Control: State | IRS Status: 501(c)3
Highest Offering: Associate Degree
Accreditation: NH, ACFEI, ADNUR, DA, EMT

01 President .... Dr. Lance BOLTON
04 Exec Assistant to the President .... Ms. Kimberly BARNETT
05 Vice Pres Instructional Services .... Dr. Josh BAKER
32 Vice President Student Services .... Mr. Homer WESLEY
10 Vice Pres Administrative Services .... Ms. Brenda LAUER
103 Vice Pres of Workforce Development .... Ms. Debbie SAGEN
35 Assoc Vice Pres of Student Services .... Ms. Jennifer SENGENBERGER
20 Director of Instructional Support .... Ms. Julie HAZEL
37 Director of Financial Aid .... Mr. Ronald SWARTWOOD
08 Director of Libraries .... Ms. Carole OLDS
15 Exec Dir of Human Resource Services .... Mr. Carlton BROOKS
26 Exec Dir Marketing/Communications .... Mr. Warren EPSTEIN
21 Director of Business Svcs .... Ms. Eileen HOGUE
06 Registrar/Coordinator of Records .... Ms. Twila HUMPHREY
07 Director of Admissions .... Mr. Kevin HUDGENS
102 Exec Director of Foundation .... Ms. Lisa JAMES
18 Dir Facilities and Operations .... Mr. Paul ROSS
13 Chief Technology Officer .... Mr. Cyrille PARENT
19 Dir Public Safety/Emergency Mgmt .... Mr. Jim BARRENTINE
09 Exec Dir of Inst Effectiveness .... Dr. Patrica DIWARA
36 Director of Advising & Testing .... Mr. Lincoln WULF
96 Director of Purchasing .... Ms. Rockie HURRELL
38 Director Counseling Center .... Ms. Yolanda HARRIS
88 Project Dir of Stdnt Support Svcs .... Mr. Michael COUILLARD
76 Dean Health and Science .... Ms. Kristen JOHNSON
81 Dean Mathematics & English .. Ms. Jacquelyn GAITERS-JORDAN
50 Dean Business/Public Service/SS .... Mr. Rob HUDSON
60 Dean Comm/Humanities/Tech Studies .... Ms. Fran HETRICK
88 Dean of High School Programs .... Ms. Chelsy HARRIS

Pima Medical Institute (I)

13750 E. Mississippi Avenue, Aurora CO 80012
County: Arapahoe | FICE Identification: 041771 | Unit ID: 461689
Telephone: (303) 368-7462 | Carnegie Class: Spec 2-yr-Health
FAX Number: N/A | Calendar System: Other
URL: pmi.edu
Established: 2012 | Annual Undergrad Tuition & Fees: N/A
Enrollment: 322 | Coed
Affiliation or Control: Proprietary | IRS Status: Proprietary
Highest Offering: Associate Degree
Accreditation: ABHES

01 Campus Director .... Mr. Michael BEATY

Pima Medical Institute-Colorado Springs (J)

3770 Citadel Drive North, Colorado Springs CO 80909
Telephone: (719) 482-7462 | Identification: 770516
Accreditation: ABHES

† Branch campus of Pima Medical Institute-Tucson, Tucson, AZ

Pima Medical Institute-Denver (K)

7475 Dakin Street, Denver CO 80221
Telephone: (303) 426-1800 | Identification: 666171
Accreditation: ABHES, COARC, OTA, PTAA, RAD

† Branch campus of Pima Medical Institute, Tucson, AZ.

Platt College (L)

3100 S Parker Road, Suite 200, Aurora CO 80014-3141
County: Arapahoe | FICE Identification: 030149 | Unit ID: 260813
Telephone: (303) 369-5151 | Carnegie Class: Spec-4-yr-Other Health
FAX Number: (303) 745-1433 | Calendar System: Quarter
URL: www.plattcolorado.edu
Established: 1986 | Annual Undergrad Tuition & Fees: $19,286
Enrollment: 216 | Coed
Affiliation or Control: Proprietary | IRS Status: Proprietary
Highest Offering: Baccalaureate
Accreditation: ACCSC, NUR

01 President/CEO .... Mr. Jerald B. SIRBU
05 Vice President of Academic Affairs .... Dr. Julie BASLER
10 Director of Financial Services .... Mr. Robert CRAVER
37 Director of Financial Aid/Registrar .... Ms. Margie ROSE
08 Head Librarian .... Ms. Laura CULLERTON
66 Dean College of Nursing .... Ms. Hollie CALDWELL
06 Registrar .... Ms. Katie DAHL
07 Admissions Representative .... Ms. Kylie IZIENICKI

Pueblo Community College (M)

900 W Orman Avenue, Pueblo CO 81004-1499
County: Pueblo | FICE Identification: 021163 | Unit ID: 127884
Telephone: (719) 549-3200 | Carnegie Class: Assoc/HVT-High Non
FAX Number: (719) 544-1179 | Calendar System: Semester
URL: www.pueblocc.edu
Established: 1933 | Annual Undergrad Tuition & Fees (In-State): $7,121
Enrollment: 5,673 | Coed
Affiliation or Control: State | IRS Status: 501(c)3
Highest Offering: Baccalaureate
Accreditation: NH, ACFEI, ADNUR, COARC, DH, EMT, OTA, PTAA, SURGT

01 President .... Dr. Patricia ERJAVEC
10 Chief Business Officer .... Mr. Jon BRUDE
05 Chief Academic Officer .... Dr. Todd ECKLUND
32 Chief of Student Services .... Dr. Heather SPEED
12 Exec Dean SWCCC Campus .... Ms. Tonya NELSON
12 Dean Fremont Campus .... Dr. Lana CARTER
76 Dean Health & Public Safety .... Ms. Mary CHAVEZ
49 Dean of Arts & Science .... Dr. Jeff ALEXANDER
50 Dean Business/Advance Technology .... Dr. Jennifer SHERMAN
31 Exec Dir Pueblo Corporate College .... Ms. Amanda CORUM
102 Director of PCC Foundation .... Ms. Martha SIMMONS
07 Dir Admissions & Records/Registrar .... Ms. Barbara BENEDICT
21 Controller .... Ms. Emma ALCALA
37 Director Financial Aid .... Ms. Monica HARDWICK
15 Director Human Resources .... Mr. Ken NUFER
13 Director Information Technology .... Mr. Bryan CRAWFORD
18 Director Facility Svcs/Capital Plng .... Vacant
88 Director Learning Center .... Mr. Ross BARNHART
08 Director Library Services .... Ms. Chris MCGRATH
26 Director Marketing/Communications .... Ms. Erin WHITE
35 Dir Student & Judicial Affairs .... Mr. Dennis JOHNSON
09 Dir Institutional Effectiveness .... Mr. Corey SHILLING
96 Director of Purchasing .... Mr. Edmond INIGUEZ
121 Director of Academic Advising .... Mr. Gage MICHAEL
04 Administrative Asst to President .... Ms. Julie JIMENEZ
106 Multimedia Tech Specialist .... Mr. Robin LEACH
06 Registrar .... Ms. Barbara BENEDICT

Pueblo Community College Fremont Campus (A)

51320 W Highway 50, Canon City CO 81212
Telephone: (719) 296-6100 Identification: 770042
Accreditation: &NH

Red Rocks Community College (B)

13300 W Sixth Avenue, Lakewood CO 80228-1255
County: Jefferson FICE Identification: 009543
Unit ID: 127909
Telephone: (303) 914-6600 Carnegie Class: Assoc/HVT-High Non
FAX Number: (303) 914-6666 Calendar System: Semester
URL: www.rrcc.edu
Established: 1969 Annual Undergrad Tuition & Fees (In-State): $3,685
Enrollment: 7,789 Coed
Affiliation or Control: State IRS Status: 501(c)3
Highest Offering: Master's
Accreditation: NH, ARCPA, MAC, RAD

01 President .... Dr. Michele HANEY
04 Exec Assistant to the President .... Ms. Kathy SCHISSLER
10 Vice Pres Administrative Services .... Ms. Peggy MORGAN
05 Vice President Instruction .... Ms. Linda COMEAUX
32 Vice Pres Stdnt Svc/Enrollment Mgt .... Vacant
35 Vice Pres Student Success .... Dr. Lisa FOWLER
103 Vice Pres Workforce/Community Devel .... Vacant
20 Dean Academic Services .... Ms. Kelly CIRCLE
20 Dean Instructional Services .... Ms. Nicole LACROIX
20 Dean Instructional Services .... Mr. Mike COSTE
13 Dean Technology CTE .... Ms. Dorothy WELTY
88 Dean of Instruct/Exec Dir RMEC-OSHA .... Ms. Joan SMITH
85 Director International Education .... Ms. Linda YAZDANI
07 Dir Student Recruit/Advising/Admiss .... Vacant
21 Controller .... Ms. Kathy KAOUDIS
37 Director Financial Aid .... Ms. Linda CROOK
06 Registrar/Dir Enrollment Services .... Dr. Dean RATHE
18 Director Facilities .... Mr. Mark BANA
15 Interim Director Human Resources .... Mr. Arnie OUDENHOVEN
102 Assoc VP of Inst Advancement .... Mr. Ron SLINGER
26 Director Marketing/Communications .... Ms. Kim REIN
35 Director Student Activities .... Ms. Carolyn MATTERN
88 Dir Childhood Ed & Support Svcs .... Vacant
09 Director Institutional Research .... Mr. Charles DUELL
28 Director of Diversity & Inclusion .... Ms. Jennifer MACKEN
96 Coordinator Purchasing .... Ms. Renee ARCHULETA
36 Director Student Outreach .... Vacant
46 Exec Dir Planning/Rsrch/Inst Effect .... Dr. Tim GRIFFIN

Red Rocks Community College Arvada Campus (C)

5420 Miller Street, Arvada CO 80002
Telephone: (303) 914-6010 Identification: 770045
Accreditation: &NH

Regis University (D)

3333 Regis Boulevard, Denver CO 80221-1099
County: Denver FICE Identification: 001363
Unit ID: 127918
Telephone: (303) 458-4100 Carnegie Class: Masters/L
FAX Number: (303) 964-5449 Calendar System: Semester
URL: www.regis.edu
Established: 1877 Annual Undergrad Tuition & Fees: $34,450
Enrollment: 8,725 Coed
Affiliation or Control: Roman Catholic IRS Status: 501(c)3
Highest Offering: Doctorate
Accreditation: NH, CACREP, CAHIIM, CS, MFCD, NURSE, PHAR, PTA

01 President .... Rev. John P. FITZGIBBONS, SJ
43 VP/General Counsel .... Ms. Erika M. HOLLIS
05 Provost .... Dr. Janet HOUSER
10 Sr Vice President/CFO .... Dr. Salvador D. ACEVES
30 Vice President Advancement .... Mr. Jason J. CANIGLIA
100 Vice Pres & Chief of Staff .... Ms. Jeanette GREY
88 Vice President Mission .... Dr. Kevin F. BURKE
84 VP Enrollment Management .... Mr. Robert BLUST
84 Assoc VP Enrollment Services .... Mr. Bill HATHAWAY-CLARK
50 Dean of Business .... Dr. Timothy KEANE
109 Assoc VP Auxiliary & Business Svcs .... Ms. Susan LAYTON
15 Assoc VP Human Resources .... Mr. Tony L. CROW
18 Assoc VP Physical Plant .... Mr. Michael J. REDMOND
26 Assoc VP Marketing/Communication .... Mr. Todd COHEN
20 Asst Provost/Chief of Staff Provost .... Mr. Steve JACOBS
102 Asst VP University Advancement .... Ms. Mary BROZOVICH
29 Asst VP Alumni Engagement Pgms .... Ms. Sarah BEHUNEK
13 Chief Information Officer .... Mr. Jaganmohan GUDUR
107 Dean Professional Studies .... Dr. Elisa ROBYN
77 Dean Computer & Info Sciences .... Dr. Shari PLANTZ-MASTERS
76 Assoc Dean Health Professions .... Dr. Tristen AMADOR
49 Dean of Regis College .... Dr. Thomas BOWIE
08 Dean of Libraries .... Dr. Janet LEE
32 Dean of Students .... Ms. Diane M. MCSHEEHY
07 Dean of Admissions .... Ms. Kim FRISCH
37 Director Financial Aid .... Ms. Elinor MILLER
06 Director Registration .... Ms. Cathy GORRELL
06 Director Academic Records .... Ms. Terry GAURMER
38 Int Dir Counseling/Personal Dev .... Dr. Chaney COOK
19 Director of Campus Safety .... Mr. Manuel AMADO
25 Director Academic Grants .... Mr. Donald BRIDGER
42 Director of University Ministry .... Ms. Kristi GONSALVES-MCCABE
36 Director of Career Services .... Mr. Richard DELLIVENERI
41 Director Athletics .... Ms. Whitney LAWLER
04 Assistant to the President .... Ms. Mary NIELSEN
09 Director of Institutional Research .... Ms. Cathy GORRELL
39 Director Student Housing .... Mr. Brent WALLER
112 Director Estate/Gift Planning .... Ms. Karen WILBREW

Rocky Mountain College of Art & Design (E)

1600 Pierce Street, Lakewood CO 80214-1433
County: Denver FICE Identification: 007649
Unit ID: 127945
Telephone: (303) 753-6046 Carnegie Class: Spec-4-yr-Arts
FAX Number: (303) 759-4970 Calendar System: Semester
URL: www.rmcad.edu
Established: 1963 Annual Undergrad Tuition & Fees: $17,170
Enrollment: 1,096 Coed
Affiliation or Control: Proprietary IRS Status: Proprietary
Highest Offering: Master's
Accreditation: NH, ART, CIDA

01 President .... Mr. Chris SPOHN
05 Senior Vice Pres Academic Affairs .... Ms. Neely PATTON
26 Senior Vice Pres of Marketing .... Mr. Daron RODRIGUEZ
07 Vice President of Admissions .... Mr. Marc ABRAHAM
32 Dean of Students .... Mr. Robert FLADRY

Rocky Vista University (F)

8401 South Chambers Road, Parker CO 80134
County: Douglas Identification: 667002
Unit ID: 480790
Telephone: (303) 373-2008 Carnegie Class: Spec-4-yr-Med
FAX Number: N/A Calendar System: Other
URL: www.rvu.edu
Established: 2006 Annual Graduate Tuition & Fees: N/A
Enrollment: 632 Coed
Affiliation or Control: Proprietary IRS Status: Proprietary
Highest Offering: Doctorate; No Undergraduates
Accreditation: NH, OSTEO

01 President .... Dr. Clint ADAMS
04 Executive Administrative Assistant .... Ms. Linda TERPENNING
09 VP for Institutional Effectiveness .... Dr. Jennifer WILLIAMS
88 Compliance Coordinator .... Ms. Laura DEMENT
05 Dean .... Dr. Thomas TOLD
10 Chief Operating Officer/CFO .... Mr. Peter FREYTAG
37 Dir Student Financial Svc .... Ms. Fran LATA
07 Exec Dir Admissions & Marketing .... Ms. Julie ROSENTHAL
32 Assoc Dean Student Affairs .... Ms. Amy SCHLUETER
06 Registrar .... Ms. Ashley MORAN
08 Director of Library Services .... Mr. Brian SCHWARTZ
19 Director Security/Safety .... Mr. Dan HAVENS
15 Director Personnel Services .... Mr. Jerry ARMSTRONG

St. John Vianney Theological Seminary (G)

1300 S Steele Street, Denver CO 80210-2526
County: Denver Identification: 666127
Telephone: (303) 282-3427 Carnegie Class: Not Classified
FAX Number: (303) 282-3453 Calendar System: Semester
URL: www.sjvdenver.edu
Established: 1999 Annual Graduate Tuition & Fees: N/A
Enrollment: N/A Male
Affiliation or Control: Roman Catholic IRS Status: 501(c)3
Highest Offering: Master's; No Undergraduates
Accreditation: THEOL

01 Rector .... V.Rev. Scott TRAYNOR
03 Vice Rector .... Rev. Jason WALLACE

05 Academic Dean .... Dr. Joel BARSTAD
10 Director of Finance .... Mr. Paul VILLAMARIA
07 Director of Admissions .... Mrs. Maricel CELIS
08 Library Director .... Mr. Stephen SWEENEY
06 Registrar .... Ms. Denise SEERY
04 Administrative Asst to President .... Mrs. Lynda FITZSIMMONS

Southwest Acupuncture College (H)

6630 Gunpark Drive Suite 200, Boulder CO 80301-3339
Telephone: (303) 581-9955 Identification: 666618
Accreditation: ACUP

† Branch campus of Southwest Acupuncture College, Santa Fe, NM.

Southwest Colorado Community College-East (I)

701 Camino del Rio, Durango CO 81301
Telephone: (970) 247-2929 Identification: 770043
Accreditation: &NH

Southwest Colorado Community College-West (J)

33057 Highway 160, Mancos CO 81328
Telephone: (970) 564-6200 Identification: 770044
Accreditation: &NH

Spartan College (K)

10851 W 120th Avenue, Broomfield CO 80021-3401
County: Broomfield FICE Identification: 007297
Unit ID: 126605
Telephone: (303) 466-1714 Carnegie Class: Spec 2-yr-Tech
FAX Number: (303) 496-0211 Calendar System: Other
URL: www.spartan.edu
Established: 1965 Annual Undergrad Tuition & Fees: $15,743
Enrollment: 450 Coed
Affiliation or Control: Proprietary IRS Status: Proprietary
Highest Offering: Associate Degree
Accreditation: ACICS

01 Campus President .... Mr. Nicholas BROWN
05 Campus Academic Dean .... Mr. Tim GUERRERO
07 Director of Admissions .... Mr. Eric PACHECO
06 Senior Registrar .... Ms. Vicki MIDDEKER

Trinidad State Junior College (L)

600 Prospect, Trinidad CO 81082-2396
County: Las Animas FICE Identification: 001368
Unit ID: 128258
Telephone: (719) 846-5011 Carnegie Class: Assoc/HVT-Mix Trad/Non
FAX Number: (719) 846-5667 Calendar System: Semester
URL: www.trinidadstate.edu
Established: 1925 Annual Undergrad Tuition & Fees (In-State): $4,723
Enrollment: 1,660 Coed
Affiliation or Control: State IRS Status: 501(c)3
Highest Offering: Associate Degree
Accreditation: NH, ADNUR, ENGR

01 President .... Dr. Carmen M. SIMONE
05 Vice President of Academic Affairs .... Ms. Lynette BATES
32 VP Student Services .... Ms. Kerry GABRIELSON
11 Vice Pres of Campus Operations .... Ms. Lorrie VELASQUEZ
49 Dean Arts & Sciences .... Vacant
35 Dean of Students/Dir of HR .... Mr. Robert MARTINEZ
37 Director Financial Aid .... Ms. Wilma ATENCIO
06 Registrar/Institutional Research .... Ms. Annette LUJAN
18 Director of Facilities .... Mr. Al MALESPINI
21 Controller .... Ms. Alana BEST
106 Dir Online Ed/Dir of Technology .... Mr. Doug BAK
04 Admin Asst to Pres/Cont Ed Coord .... Ms. Donna HADDOW
26 Director of Marketing .... Mr. Greg BOYCE
41 Athletic Director .... Mr. Mike SALBATO
10 VP of Business & Finance .... Vacant

Trinidad State Junior College San Luis Valley Campus (M)

1011 Main Street, Alamosa CO 81101
Telephone: (719) 589-7000 Identification: 770047
Accreditation: &NH

UCH Memorial Hospital School Of Radiologic Technology (N)

1400 East Boulder Street, Colorado Springs CO 80909
County: El Paso Identification: 667097
Telephone: (719) 365-8291 Carnegie Class: Not Classified
FAX Number: N/A Calendar System: Semester
URL: www.uchealth.org
Established: 1969 Annual Undergrad Tuition & Fees: N/A
Enrollment: N/A Coed
Affiliation or Control: Independent Non-Profit IRS Status: 501(c)3
Highest Offering: Associate Degree
Accreditation: RAD

01 Director .... Elaine R. IVAN
05 Dean of Education .... Jarad MUASAU

06 Registrar/Clinical Coordinator ..... Karen GEORGE
07 Director of Admissions ..... Elaine R. IVAN
08 Head Librarian ..... Char LONGWELL

*University of Colorado System Office (A)

1800 Grant Street, Suite 800, Denver CO 80203
County: Denver FICE Identification: 007996
Unit ID: 128300
Telephone: (303) 860-5600 Carnegie Class: N/A
FAX Number: (303) 860-5610
URL: www.cu.edu

01 President ..... Mr. Bruce D. BENSON
05 Vice Pres Academic Affairs ..... Dr. Michael LIGHTNER
100 Senior VP & Chief of Staff ..... Mr. Leonard DINEGAR
10 VP & Chief Financial Officer ..... Mr. Todd SALIMAN
43 VP University Counsel/Secy Board ..... Mr. Pat O'ROURKE
15 Sr AVP/Chief Human Resource Ofcr ..... Ms. Kathy NESBITT
86 VP Government Relations ..... Ms. Tanya KELLY-BOWRY
26 Assoc VP University Relations ..... Mr. Ken MCCONNELLOGUE
21 Asst VP & University Controller ..... Mr. Robert KUEHLER
13 Asst VP & Chief Information Ofcr ..... Mr. Scott MUNSON
31 Dir Business & Community Relations ..... Ms. Elizabeth COLLINS
27 Assistant VP External Relations ..... Ms. Michele MCKINNEY

*University of Colorado Boulder (B)

Regent Drive At Broadway, Boulder CO 80309-0001
County: Boulder FICE Identification: 001370
Unit ID: 126614
Telephone: (303) 492-1411 Carnegie Class: DU-Highest
FAX Number: N/A Calendar System: Semester
URL: www.colorado.edu
Established: 1876 Annual Undergrad Tuition & Fees (In-State): $11,531
Enrollment: 33,056 Coed
Affiliation or Control: State IRS Status: 501(c)3
Highest Offering: Doctorate
Accreditation: NH, AUD, CAEPN, CEA, CLPSY, CS, ENG, IPSY, JOUR, LAW, MUS, SP

02 Chancellor ..... Dr. Phillip P. DISTEFANO
05 Provost & Exec VC for Acad Affairs ..... Dr. Russell MOORE
10 Sr Vice Chanc/Chief Financial Ofcr ..... Ms. Kelly L. FOX
46 Vice Chancellor for Research ..... Dr. Terri FIEZ
11 Vice Chanc for Infrastruc/Safety ..... Mr. David KANG
32 Vice Chanc for Student Affairs ..... Ms. Christina GONZALES
28 Vice Chanc for Diversity/Equity ..... Dr. Robert BOSWELL
26 Vice Chanc for Strategic Relations ..... Ms. Frances DRAPER
114 Assoc VC for Budget & Planning ..... Ms. Louise VALE
13 Assoc VC for IT/Chief Info Officer ..... Dr. Lawrence M. LEVINE
100 Chief of Staff ..... Ms. Catherine SHEA
111 Vice Chanc for Advancement ..... Ms. Deb COFFIN
29 Asst Vice Chanc Alumni Relations ..... Mr. Ryan CHREIST
58 Dean of the Graduate School ..... Dr. Ann SCHMIESING
61 Dean of Law ..... Dr. James ANAYA
49 Interim Dean of Arts & Sciences ..... Dr. Jim WHITE
54 Dean of Engineering ..... Dr. Robert D. BRAUN
50 Dean of Business ..... Dr. Sharon MATUSIK
53 Dean of Education ..... Dr. Katherine SCHULTZ
64 Dean of Music ..... Dr. Robert S. SHAY
60 Dean Media/Communications/Info ..... Dr. Lori BERGEN
51 Dean of Division of Continuing Educ ..... Dr. Sara THOMPSON
08 Interim Dean of Libraries ..... Ms. Leslie REYNOLDS
35 Assoc VC/Dean of Students ..... Ms. Akirah BRADLEY
37 Director of Financial Aid ..... Ms. Gwen E. POMPER
07 Director of Admissions ..... Ms. Colleen NEWMAN
06 Registrar ..... Dr. Kristi WOLD-MCCORMICK
22 Exec Director Title IX Programs ..... Ms. Valerie SIMONS
09 Dir of Institutional Research ..... Mr. Robert STUBBS
25 Dir of Contracts and Grants ..... Ms. Denitta D. WARD
15 Chief Human Resources Ofcr ..... Ms. Charlotte Katherine ERWIN
41 Athletic Director ..... Mr. Rick GEORGE
19 Chief of Police ..... Mr. Kenneth KOCH
23 Exec Dir Student Health Ctr ..... Ms. Melissa LOWE
36 Director of Career Services ..... Dr. Lisa SEVERY
39 Exec Dir Housing Services ..... Ms. Amy D. BECKSTROM
88 Director of Museum ..... Dr. Patrick KOCIOLEK
104 Director of Education Abroad ..... Ms. Mary DANDO
43 Managing Assoc Univ Counsel ..... Ms. Elvira U. STREHLE-HENSON

*University of Colorado Colorado Springs (C)

1420 Austin Bluffs Parkway, Colorado Springs CO 80918
County: El Paso FICE Identification: 004509
Unit ID: 126580
Telephone: (719) 255-8227 Carnegie Class: Masters/L
FAX Number: (719) 255-3362 Calendar System: Semester
URL: www.uccs.edu
Established: 1965 Annual Undergrad Tuition & Fees (In-State): $8,042
Enrollment: 11,988 Coed
Affiliation or Control: State IRS Status: 501(c)3
Highest Offering: Doctorate
Accreditation: NH, CACREP, #CAEP, CLPSY, CS, DIETD, ENG, NURSE, SPAA

02 Chancellor ..... Dr. Venkat REDDY
05 Provost ..... Dr. Tom CHRISTENSEN
10 Vice Chanc Admin & Finance ..... Susan SZPYRKA
32 Vice Chanc Student Success ..... Dr. Sentwali BAKARI
30 Vice Chanc Univ Advancement ..... Martin WOOD
20 Sr Assoc VC Academic Affairs ..... Dr. David MOON
18 Chief Facilities/Physical Plant ..... Gary REYNOLDS
11 Assoc VC Admin & Finance ..... Carlos GARCIA
21 Director Resource Management ..... Gayanne SCOTT
43 Legal Counsel ..... Jennifer GEORGE
13 AVC Info Technology/CIO ..... Harper JOHNSON
46 Assoc Vice Chanc Research ..... Dr. Kelli KLEBE
25 Director of Sponsored Programs ..... Gwen GENNARO
84 Director of Enrollment Mgmt ..... Matthew COX
09 Director of Institutional Research ..... Dr. Robyn MARSCHKE
15 Director of Human Resources ..... Anja WYNNE
19 Interim Director Public Safety ..... Marc PINO
29 Director Alumni & Community Rels ..... Jennifer HANE
37 Director Financial Aid ..... Jevita ROGERS
26 Director Media Relations ..... Tom HUTTON
38 Director Student Counseling ..... Dr. Benek ALTAYLI
41 Director of Athletics ..... Nathan GIBSON
35 Dean of Students ..... Steve LINHART
49 Dean of Letters/Arts/Science ..... Dr. Peter BRAZA
50 Interim Dean of Business ..... Dr. Eric OLSON
53 Dean of Education ..... Dr. Valerie CONLEY
54 Interim Dean of Engineering ..... Dr. Charles ZHOU
80 Dean of Public Affairs ..... Dr. George REED
66 Dean Nursing/Health Sciences ..... Dr. Nancy SMITH
58 Dean of Graduate School ..... Dr. Kelli KLEBE
08 Dean of Library ..... Dr. Martin GARNAR
39 Director Campus Housing ..... Ralph GIESE
06 Registrar ..... Tracy BARBER
07 Dir of Admissions/Recruitment ..... Chris BEISWANGER
04 Executive Asst to the Chancellor ..... Brenda BONN
105 Director Web Services ..... Craig DECKER
40 Director of Bookstore ..... Paul DENISTON
104 Director Study Abroad ..... Dr. Mandy HANSEN

*University of Colorado Denver|Anschutz Medical Campus (D)

1250 14th Street, Denver CO 80204
County: Denver FICE Identification: 004508
Unit ID: 126562
Telephone: (303) 556-2400 Carnegie Class: DU-Higher
FAX Number: N/A Calendar System: Semester
URL: www.ucdenver.edu
Established: 1912 Annual Undergrad Tuition & Fees (In-State): $9,228
Enrollment: 23,671 Coed
Affiliation or Control: State IRS Status: 501(c)3
Highest Offering: Doctorate
Accreditation: NH, AA, ARCPA, CACREP, CAEPN, CLPSY, CS, DENT, DMS, ENG, HSA, IPSY, LSAR, MED, MIDWF, MUS, NURSE, PAST, PH, PHAR, PLNG, PTA, SPAA

02 Chancellor ..... Dr. Don ELLIMAN
03 VP Health Affairs/Exec VC AMC ..... Ms. Lilly MARKS
46 Vice Chancellor for Research ..... Dr. Richard TRAYSTMAN
10 Sr Vice Chanc Admin/Finance ..... Ms. Terri C. CARROTHERS
17 VC Health Affairs/Dean of Medicine ..... Dr. John REILLY
26 Vice Chanc of Univ Communications ..... Ms. Leanna CLARK
05 Provost & VC Academic/Student Affs ..... Dr. Roderick NAIRN
30 Vice Chanc of Development Anschutz ..... Mr. Scott ARTHUR
30 Vice Chanc of Development Denver ..... Mr. Matthew WASSERMAN
52 Dean School of Dental Medicine ..... Dr. Denise KASSEBAUM
66 Dean College of Nursing ..... Dr. Sarah THOMPSON
67 Dean School of Pharmacy ..... Dr. Ralph ALTIERE
69 Dean CO School of Public Health ..... Dr. David GOFF
58 Interim Dean Graduate School ..... Dr. Terry POTTER
64 Dean College of Arts/Media ..... Dr. Laurence KAPTAIN
80 Dean School of Public Affairs ..... Dr. Paul TESKE
49 Dean College Liberal Arts & Sci ..... Dr. Pamela JANSMA
48 Dean College of Arch/Planning ..... Mr. Mark GELERNTER
50 Dean Business School ..... Ms. Sueann AMBRON
53 Dean School of Education ..... Dr. Rebecca KANTOR
54 Dean College of Engineering ..... Dr. Marc INGBER
46 Assoc VC for Research ..... Dr. Robert DAMRAUER
20 Assoc VC Academic Affairs ..... Dr. Laura GOODWIN
32 Assoc VC Student Affairs ..... Dr. Raul CARDENAS
28 Assoc VC Diversity/Inclusion ..... Dr. Brenda ALLEN
21 Assoc VC Finance/Controller ..... Ms. E. Kim HUBER
18 Assoc VC Facilities Management ..... Mr. David C. TURNQUIST
88 Assoc VC of Academic Planning ..... Dr. Terry POTTER
15 Asst VC Human Resources ..... Mr. Kevin JACOBS
13 Asst VC Information Technology Svcs ..... Mr. Russell POOLE
88 Asst VC Academic Tech/Extd Learning ..... Mr. Robert TOLSMA
84 Asst VC UG Admissions/K-12 Outreach ..... Mr. Chris DOWEN
09 Asst VC Institutional Research ..... Dr. Christine STROUP-BENHAM
88 Asst VC Student Success ..... Ms. Peggy LORE
88 Interim Asst VC University Life ..... Mr. Sam KIM
06 Registrar ..... Ms. Ingrid ESCHHOLZ
08 Director Auraria Library ..... Dr. Mary SOMERVILLE
08 Interim Dir Health Sciences Library ..... Ms. Melissa DESANTIS
27 Director PR/Media Relations ..... Vacant
37 Interim Director Financial Aid Svcs ..... Mr. Justin JARAMILLO
19 Chief of Police ..... Mr. Doug ABRAHAM
29 Director Alumni Relations ..... Ms. Joy FRENCH
43 Assistant University Counsel ..... Mr. Christopher PUCKETT
35 Interim Dean of Students ..... Dr. Kristin KUSHMIDER
104 Director International Education ..... Mr. John SUNNYGARD
45 Chief Institutional Planning ..... Mr. Michale DEL GIUDICE

University of Denver (E)

2199 S. University Blvd., Denver CO 80208-0001
County: Denver FICE Identification: 001371
Unit ID: 127060
Telephone: (303) 871-2000 Carnegie Class: DU-Higher
FAX Number: (303) 871-3301 Calendar System: Quarter
URL: www.du.edu
Established: 1864 Annual Undergrad Tuition & Fees: $46,422
Enrollment: 11,797 Coed
Affiliation or Control: Independent Non-Profit IRS Status: 501(c)3
Highest Offering: Doctorate
Accreditation: NH, ART, CEA, CLPSY, COPSY, ENG, IPSY, LAW, LIB, MUS, SW

01 Chancellor ..... Dr. Rebecca CHOPP
05 Provost & Exec Vice Chancellor ..... Dr. Gregg O. KVISTAD
43 Vice Chanc Legal Affairs/Gen Couns ..... Mr. Paul H. CHAN
32 Vice Chanc Campus Life/Inclus Excel ..... Dr. Liliana RODRIGUEZ
10 Vice Chanc Business/Financial Affs ..... Mr. Craig WOODY
41 Vice Chanc Athletics and Recreation ..... Ms. Peg BRADLEY-DOPPES
111 Vice Chanc University Advancement ..... Mr. Armin AFSAHI
26 Vice Chancellor Communications ..... Ms. Renell WYNN
13 Vice Chancellor/Chief Info Officer ..... Mr. Donald HARRIS
84 Int Vice Chancellor for Enrollment ..... Mr. Todd RINEHART
37 Asst Vice Chanc Enroll/Dir Fin Aid ..... Mr. John E. GUDVANGEN
04 Exec Assistant to the Chancellor ..... Ms. Allison RIOLA
20 Associate Provost Academic Program ..... Dr. Jennifer KARAS
07 Assoc Vice Chanc Enrollment ..... Mr. Todd RINEHART
88 Assoc Vice Chancellor IE ..... Ms. Johanna LEYBA
28 Sr Advisor to Chancellor/Provost ..... Dr. Frank TUITT
58 Int Assoc Provost Graduate Studies ..... Dr. Corinne LENGSFELD
08 Dean/Dir University Libraries ..... Mr. Michael LEVINE-CLARK
34 Interim Dean CO Women's College ..... Dr. Linda OLSON
20 Senior Assoc Provost Academic Admin ..... Dr. Linda KOSTEN
88 Assoc Vice Chanc Global Networks ..... Mr. Brandon BUZBEE
30 Asst Vice Chanc Development ..... Ms. Kellie FISCHER
06 Registrar ..... Mr. Dennis M. BECKER
21 Assoc Vice Chancellor Finance ..... Mr. Andrew CULLEN
36 Director of Career Services ..... Ms. Cindy HYMAN
22 Title IX Coordinator ..... Mr. Eric BUTLER
18 Assoc Vice Chanc Facilities ..... Mr. James ROSNER
09 Asst Provost Institutional Research ..... Mr. Mike FURNO
15 Vice Chanc Human Resources ..... Ms. Laura MARESCA
19 Director Campus Safety ..... Mr. Donald ENLOE
88 Dir Student Financial Services ..... Ms. Janet BURKHARDT
88 Asst Vice Chanc Enterprise Services ..... Ms. Susan LUTZ
38 Dir of Counseling Services ..... Dr. Jacaranda PALMATEER
54 Dean Engr/Computer Science ..... Mr. J.B HOLSTON
79 Dean Arts/Humanities/Social Science ..... Dr. Daniel MCINTOSH
81 Dean Natural Science/Math ..... Dr. Andrei KUTATELADZE
50 Dean College of Business ..... Dr. Brent CHRITE
61 Dean College of Law ..... Dr. Bruce SMITH
82 Dean Graduate Sch of Intl Studies ..... Mr. Christopher R. HILL
70 Dean Graduate School of Social Work ..... Dr. Amanda MCBRIDE
55 Dean University College ..... Mr. Michael MCGUIRE
53 Dean College of Education ..... Dr. Karen RILEY
64 Director Lamont School of Music ..... Ms. Nancy COCHRAN
31 Exec Dir Special Community Programs ..... Dr. Cathy GRIEVE
57 Director School of Art/Art History ..... Dr. Sarah GJERTSON
07 Director of Enrollment Services ..... Ms. Anne GROSS
35 Exec Director of Campus Life ..... Mr. Carl JOHNSON
101 Secretary of the Institution/Board ..... Ms. Claire BROWNELL
105 Senior Digital Design and Architect ..... Mr. Matt ESCHENBAUM
106 Director of Web-based Learning ..... Ms. Kathy KEAIRNS
108 Director of Assessment ..... Dr. Christina PAGUYO

University of Northern Colorado (F)

501 20th Street, Greeley CO 80639-6900
County: Weld FICE Identification: 001349
Unit ID: 127741
Telephone: (970) 351-1890 Carnegie Class: DU-Higher
FAX Number: (970) 351-1880 Calendar System: Semester
URL: www.unco.edu
Established: 1889 Annual Undergrad Tuition & Fees (In-State): $8,888
Enrollment: 12,216 Coed
Affiliation or Control: State IRS Status: 501(c)3
Highest Offering: Doctorate
Accreditation: NH, ART, AUD, CAATE, CACREP, CEA, COPSY, DIETD, DIETI, IPSY, MUS, NURSE, PH, SCPSY, SP, THEA

01 President ..... Ms. Kay NORTON
05 Provost/Vice Pres Academic Affairs ..... Dr. Robbyn WACKER
11 Vice President Administration ..... Ms. Michelle QUINN
43 Vice President & University Counsel ..... Mr. Dan SATRIANA
26 VP External & University Relations ..... Mr. Dan WEAVER
30 Vice Pres Development/Alumni Rels ..... Ms. Allie STEG HASKETT
28 VP for Campus Community & Climate ..... Dr. Katrina RODRIGUEZ
58 Dean Grad School ..... Ms. Linda BLACK
20 Ast VP Undergrad Stds/Dean Univ Col ..... Dr. Thomas SMITH
114 Asst Vice President Budgets/Analysi ..... Ms. Susan SIMMERS
13 Asst Vice President Info Technology ..... Mr. Bret NABER
84 Asst Vice Pres for Enrollment Mgmt ..... Mr. Tobias GUZMAN
26 AVP Marketing ..... Mr. Jason HUGHES
88 AVP for Equity and Inclusion ..... Ms. Fleurette KING
79 Dean Humanities/Social Sciences ..... Dr. Laura CONNOLLY
50 Dean Business ..... Dr. Paul BOBROWSKI
53 Dean Education/Behavioral Sciences ..... Dr. Eugene SHEEHAN
76 Dean Natural & Health Sciences ..... Dr. Ellen GREGG
57 Dean Performing Visual Arts ..... Dr. Leo WELCH
08 Dean University Libraries ..... Ms. Helen REED
32 Dean of Students ..... Dr. Gardiner TUCKER

102 President University Foundation Mr. Rod ESCH
06 Registrar Mr. Charlie COUCH
07 Director of Admissions Dr. Sean M. BROGHAMMER
25 AVP Sponsored Pgms/Research Dr. Robert HOUSER
37 Dir Student Financial Resources Mr. Marty SOMERO
36 Director of Career Services Ms. Renee WELCH
15 Director of Human Resources Mr. Marshall PARKS
29 Asst VP Alumni Relations Ms. Lyndsey CRUM
18 Director Facilities Management Mr. Kirk LEICHLITER
41 Director of NCAA Athletics Mr. Darren DUNN
39 Director of Residential Education Mr. Montez BUTTS
38 Director Student Counseling Ms. Kim WILCOX
19 Chief of University Police Mr. Dennis PUMPHREY
44 Acting Director of Annual Giving Mr. Alex STERN
27 Dir News & Public Relations Mr. Nate HAAS
96 Director of Purchasing Ms. Cristal SWAIN
85 Director Ctr for International Educ Ms. Maureen ULEVICH
104 Director Study Abroad Ms. Teneisha ELLIS
108 Director Institutional Assessment Ms. Kim BLACK
04 Administrative Asst to President Ms. Elaine QUAM
100 Chief of Staff Ms. Gloria REYNOLDS
101 Secretary of the Institution/Board Ms. Victoria NICCUM
105 Director Web Services Mr. Jesse CLARK
106 Dir Online Education/E-learning Ms. Jeanie YORK
22 Dir Affirmative Action/EEO Mr. Larry LOFTEN

University of Phoenix Colorado Main Campus (A)

1000H Park Meadows Drive, Lone Tree CO 80124-5453
Telephone: (303) 755-9090 Identification: 770195
Accreditation: &NH, ACBSP

† No longer accepting campus-based students.

University of the Rockies (B)

1201 16th Street, Suite 200, Denver CO 80202
County: Denver FICE Identification: 035453
Unit ID: 441308
Telephone: (866) 621-0124 Carnegie Class: Spec-4-yr-Other Health
FAX Number: (303) 446-5884 Calendar System: Other
URL: www.rockies.edu
Established: 1998 Annual Graduate Tuition & Fees: N/A
Enrollment: 1,425 Coed
Affiliation or Control: Proprietary IRS Status: Proprietary
Highest Offering: Doctorate; No Undergraduates
Accreditation: NH

01 President Dr. Dawn IWAMOTO
05 Provost Dr. Jeremy MORELAND
10 Vice Pres Finance & Operations Mr. Steve MANSDOERFER
21 Director of Financial Services Ms. Jamie ESQUIBEL
15 Director of Human Resources Ms. Barbara HENRY-QUINN
06 Registrar/Dir Univ Svcs Ms. Joy ONSTAD
28 Director of Diversity Vacant

U.S. Career Institute (C)

2001 Lowe Street, Fort Collins CO 80525
County: Larimer Identification: 666776
Telephone: (970) 207-4500 Carnegie Class: Not Classified
FAX Number: (970) 223-1678 Calendar System: Other
URL: www.uscareerinstitute.edu
Established: 1981 Annual Undergrad Tuition & Fees: N/A
Enrollment: N/A Coed
Affiliation or Control: Proprietary IRS Status: Proprietary
Highest Offering: Associate Degree
Accreditation: DEAC

01 President Ms. Ann ROHR
32 Vice President Student Affairs Ms. Joyce LINDQUIST
26 Vice Pres Stdnt Relations/Marketing Ms. Holly COOK
05 Vice Pres of Academics/Compliance Ms. Janet PERRY
106 Dean of Curriculum Ms. Leslie BALLENTINE

Western Colorado Community College-Tilman M. Bishop Campus (D)

2508 Blichmann Avenue, Grand Junction CO 81505
Telephone: (970) 255-2600 Identification: 770030
Accreditation: &NH

Western State Colorado University (E)

600 North Adams, Gunnison CO 81231-0001
County: Gunnison FICE Identification: 001372
Unit ID: 128391
Telephone: (970) 943-0120 Carnegie Class: Masters/S
FAX Number: (970) 943-7069 Calendar System: Semester
URL: www.western.edu
Established: 1901 Annual Undergrad Tuition & Fees (In-State): $9,193
Enrollment: 2,722 Coed
Affiliation or Control: State IRS Status: 501(c)3
Highest Offering: Master's
Accreditation: NH, MUS

01 President Dr. Greg SALSBURY
11 Exec Vice Pres and COO Mr. Brad BACA
05 Int Vice Pres for Academic Affairs Dr. Bill NIEMI
10 Chief Financial Officer Ms. Julie FEIER
32 Vice President for Student Affairs Mr. Gary PIERSON
26 Vice President Marketing/Enrollment Mr. John KAWAUCHI
20 Assoc Vice Pres Academic Affairs Dr. Kathleen KINKEMA
35 Assoc Vice Pres for Student Affairs Mr. Chris LUEKENGA
06 Registrar Ms. Ginny HAYES
37 Director of Financial Aid Ms. Carrie SHAW
104 Dir Intl Student Pgms/Study Abroad Ms. Katie WHEATON
41 Athletic Director Mr. Miles VAN HEE
15 Director of Human Resources Ms. Kim GAILEY
40 Director Retail Operations Ms. Teri HAUS
13 Chief Information Ofcr/IT Director Mr. Chad ROBINSON
08 Director Library Services Mr. Dustin FIFE
51 Director Extended Studies Ms. Erica BOUCHER
39 Director of Residence Life Ms. Shelley JANSEN
36 Career Services Coordinator Ms. Mariah GREEN
26 Director of Public Relations Vacant
29 Director of Alumni Relations Ms. Tonya VANHEE
44 Director Annual & Special Gifts Vacant
09 Director Institutional Research Mr. Doug DRIVER
28 Director of Multicultural Center Ms. Sally ROMERO
07 Int Dir Recruitment/Admissions Ms. Amanda ARAGON
96 Business Services Manager Ms. Sherry FORD

William Howard Taft University (F)

3333 South Wadsworth Blvd, Lakewood CO 80227
County: Jefferson FICE Identification: 041004
Unit ID: 454689
Telephone: (303) 867-1155 Carnegie Class: Spec-4-yr-Bus
FAX Number: (303) 867-1156 Calendar System: Other
URL: www.taft.edu
Established: 1976 Annual Undergrad Tuition & Fees: $3,410
Enrollment: 851 Coed
Affiliation or Control: Proprietary IRS Status: Proprietary
Highest Offering: Doctorate
Accreditation: DEAC

01 President Dr. Neil A. JOHNSON
03 Chief Operating Officer Mr. Robert K. STROUSE
11 Director of Administration Ms. Christine A. BALDWIN

† Tuition varies by degree program.

CONNECTICUT

Albertus Magnus College (G)

700 Prospect Street, New Haven CT 06511-1189
County: New Haven FICE Identification: 001374
Unit ID: 128498
Telephone: (203) 773-8550 Carnegie Class: Masters/M
FAX Number: (203) 773-9539 Calendar System: Semester
URL: www.albertus.edu
Established: 1925 Annual Undergrad Tuition & Fees: $30,526
Enrollment: 1,515 Coed
Affiliation or Control: Independent Non-Profit IRS Status: 501(c)3
Highest Offering: Master's
Accreditation: EH, IACBE

01 President Dr. Marc M. CAMILLE
05 Vice Pres Academic Affairs Dr. Sean O'CONNELL
10 Vice President Finance/Treasurer Vacant
13 VP Information Technology Services Mr. Steven GSTALDER
30 VP Development/Alumni Relations Ms. Carolyn A. BEHAN KRAUS
32 Vice President for Student Services Mr. Andrew FOSTER
35 Asst Dean Campus Activities/Orien Ms. Erin MORRELL
06 Registrar Mrs. Melissa DELUCIA
08 Director Library/Information Svcs Ms. Anne LEENEY-PANAGROSSI
09 Inst Research & Assessment Analyst Ms. Viola SIMPSON
37 Director Financial Aid Mrs. Michelle COCHRAN
90 Director Academic Computing Vacant
41 Director of Athletics Mr. James ABROMAITIS
58 Director MALS Program Ms. Julia COASH
89 Director of Freshmen Advising Ms. Heather WOTTON
92 Director of Honors Program Dr. Christine ATKINS
96 Asst VP Purch/Pub Safety/Spec Proj Mr. James A. SCHAFRICK
15 Director Human Resources Ms. Renee SULLIVAN
26 Dir Communications/Community Rels Ms. Rosanne ZUDEKOFF
36 Director Career Services Mr. Patrick CLIFFORD
42 Coord of Dominican Ministries Sr. Joan SCANLON
18 Supervisor of Facilities Services Mr. Dan SECOR
04 Administrative Asst to President Ms. Lynne M. HENNESSY

Charter Oak State College (H)

55 Paul Manafort Drive, New Britain CT 06053-2142
County: Hartford FICE Identification: 029171
Unit ID: 128780
Telephone: (860) 515-3800 Carnegie Class: Bac-A&S
FAX Number: (860) 606-9615 Calendar System: Other
URL: www.charteroak.edu
Established: 1973 Annual Undergrad Tuition & Fees (In-State): $7,671
Enrollment: 1,735 Coed
Affiliation or Control: State IRS Status: 501(c)3
Highest Offering: Master's
Accreditation: EH, CAHIIM

01 President Mr. Edward KLONOSKI
05 Provost Dr. Shirley M. ADAMS
10 Chief Financial/Administrative Ofcr Mr. Michael J. MORIARTY
13 Chief Information Officer Mr. George F. CLAFFEY, JR.
09 Dir Institutional Effectiveness Mr. Michael BRODERICK
06 Registrar Ms. Jennifer WASHINGTON
37 Dir Financial Aid/Veterans Benefits Mr. Ralph BRASURE, III
20 Director Academic Services Ms. Wanda WARSHAUER
07 Director Admissions Ms. Lori GAGNE PENDLETON
88 Coord Prior Learning Assessment Pgm Ms. Linda WILDER
26 Director Marketing/Public Relations Ms. Carolyn HEBERT
04 Administrative Asst to President Ms. Carol HALL
102 Dir Foundation/Corporate Relations Ms. Carol HALL
105 Director Web Services Mr. Daniel RUSSELL
15 Director Personnel Services Ms. Rowena MCGOLDRICK
29 Director Alumni Relations Ms. Carol HALL

*Connecticut Board of Regents for Higher Education (I)

61 Woodland Street, Hartford CT 06105-2345
County: Hartford Identification: 666656
Unit ID: 129011
Telephone: (860) 723-0000 Carnegie Class: N/A
FAX Number: (860) 723-0009
URL: www.ct.edu

01 President CTCU Mr. Mark E. OJAKIAN
05 Provost/SVP Acad & Student Affairs Dr. Jane McBride GATES
12 Vice President for CSU Dr. Elsa NUNEZ
12 Vice President for CCC Dr. David LEVINSON
15 VP for Human Resources Mr. Steve WEINBERGER
26 Director PR & Mktg Mr. Michael KOZLOWSKI
10 Chief Financial Officer Ms. Erika STEINER
13 Chief Information Officer Mr. Joseph TOLISANO
101 Assoc Director Board Affairs Ms. Erin FITZGERALD
04 Administrative Assist to President Ms. Judith S. NOSAL
100 Chief of Staff Dr. Alice PRITCHARD
09 Director of Institutional Research Dr. William GAMMELL
18 VP Facilities/RE/Infrastruct Plng Mr. Keith EPSTEIN
43 Dir Legal Services/General Counsel Ms. Ernestine WEAVER
27 Director of Communications Ms. Maribel LA LUZ

*Central Connecticut State University (J)

1615 Stanley Street, New Britain CT 06050-4010
County: Hartford FICE Identification: 001378
Unit ID: 128771
Telephone: (860) 832-3200 Carnegie Class: Masters/L
FAX Number: N/A Calendar System: Semester
URL: www.ccsu.edu
Established: 1849 Annual Undergrad Tuition & Fees (In-State): $9,741
Enrollment: 12,086 Coed
Affiliation or Control: State IRS Status: 501(c)3
Highest Offering: Doctorate
Accreditation: EH, ANEST, ANEST, CAATE, CACREP, CAEPN, CONST, CS, ENG, ENGT, EXSC, MFCD, MUS, NAIT, NURSE, SW

02 President Dr. Zulma R. TORO
04 Admin Assistant to the President Ms. Courtney MCDAVID
05 Interim Provost/VP Academic Affs Dr. Susan E. PEASE
30 Vice Pres Institutional Advancement Dr. Chris GALLIGAN
32 Vice President Student Affairs Dr. Laura TORDENTI
35 Associate Dean Student Affairs Mr. Ramon HERNANDEZ
20 Associate VP Academic Affairs Dr. Joseph P. PAIGE
58 Associate VP Graduate Studies Dr. Glynis A. FITZGERALD
26 Assoc VP Marketing/Communications Dr. Mark W. MCLAUGHLIN
43 University Counsel Ms. Carolyn MAGNAN
11 Chief Administrative Officer Dr. Richard R. BACHOO
10 Chief Financial Officer Mrs. Charlene CASAMENTO
15 Chief Human Resources Officer Mrs. Anna SUSKI-LENCZEWSKI
28 Chief Diversity Officer Ms. Rosa RODRIGUEZ
49 Int Dean Liberal Arts/Soc Sciences Dr. Brian SOMMERS
50 Dean School of Business Dr. Ken COLWELL
53 Dean School Educ & Prof Studies Dr. Michael P. ALFANO
54 Int Dean School Engr/Science/Tech Dr. Zdzislaw KREMENS
82 Dir Center International Education Dr. Momar NDIAYE
51 Dir Continuing Educ/Comm Engagement Ms. Christa STERLING
07 Director Admissions & Recruitment Mr. Lawrence HALL
41 Director Athletics Mr. Paul SCHLICKMANN
39 Director Residence Life Ms. Jean ALICANDRO
19 Director Public Safety Mr. Gregory SNEED
37 Director Student Financial Aid Mr. Richard BISHOP
44 Director Institutional Advancement Ms. Lisa BIGELOW
27 Media Relations Officer Ms. Janice PALMER
08 Director Library Services Mr. Carl ANTONUCCI
36 Int Dir Career Success Center Mr. Paul ROSSITTO
23 Dir Student Wellness Svcs Dr. Jacqueline HARRIS
06 Registrar Mr. Patrick TUCKER
38 Coordinator Office Wellness Educ Mr. Jonathan POHL
18 Asst Chief Admin Ofcr/Dir Facil Mgt Mr. Salvatore CINTORINO
21 University Controller Ms. Kimberly MARTOHUE
96 Purchasing Manager Mr. Thomas BRODEUR
09 Director of Institutional Research Ms. Yvonne KIRBY

*Eastern Connecticut State University (K)

83 Windham Street, Willimantic CT 06226-2295
County: Windham FICE Identification: 001425
Unit ID: 129215
Telephone: (860) 465-5000 Carnegie Class: Masters/S
FAX Number: (860) 465-4485 Calendar System: Semester

URL: www.easternct.edu
Established: 1889 Annual Undergrad Tuition & Fees (In-State): $10,500
Enrollment: 5,261 Coed
Affiliation or Control: State IRS Status: 501(c)3
Highest Offering: Master's
Accreditation: EH, CAEPN, SW

02 President .... Dr. Elsa M. NUNEZ
05 Provost .... Dr. Dimitrios C. PACHIS
10 VP Finance/Administration .... Mr. James R. HOWARTH
32 Vice Pres Student Affairs .... Mr. Walter DIAZ
111 Vice Pres Institutional Advance .... Mr. Kenneth J. DELISA
28 Assoc VP Equity & Diversity .... Dr. Stacey CLOSE
35 Dean of Students .... Ms. Michelle DELANY
09 Asst Dir of Institutional Research .... Dr. Brian R. LASHLEY
41 Director of Athletics .... Ms. Lori RUNKSMEIER
08 Director of Library Services .... Ms. Janice WILSON
84 Dir of Enrollment Mgmt/Fin Aid .... Dr. Jennifer HORNER
36 Director of Career Services .... Mr. Clifford MARRETT
29 Director of Alumni Affairs .... Mr. Michael STENKO
06 Registrar .... Ms. Jennifer HUOPPI
19 Director of Public Safety .... Mr. Jeffrey A. GAREWSKI
39 Director Housing/Residence Life .... Mr. Lamar COLEMAN
40 Director of Bookstore .... Ms. Allyson HALL
42 Director of Campus Ministry .... Rev. Laurence LAPOINTE
18 Dir of Facilities Mgmt/Planning .... Ms. Renee KEECH
26 Director University Relations .... Mr. Edward H. OSBORN
49 Dean of Arts & Sciences .... Dr. Carmen R. CID
51 Assoc Dean Continuing Education .... Dr. Indira PETOSKEY
58 Dean Educ/Prof Studies/Grad Pgm .... Dr. Jacob EASLEY
96 Assoc Dir Fiscal Affs/Acquisition .... Ms. Terry O'BRIEN
38 Director Counseling/Psych Svcs .... Dr. Joseph CHEREPON
15 Vice Pres for Human Resources .... Vacant
07 Director of Admissions .... Mr. Christopher DORSEY

*Southern Connecticut State University (A)

501 Crescent Street, New Haven CT 06515-0901
County: New Haven FICE Identification: 001406
Unit ID: 130493
Telephone: (203) 392-7278 Carnegie Class: Masters/L
FAX Number: N/A Calendar System: Semester
URL: www.southernct.edu
Established: 1893 Annual Undergrad Tuition & Fees (In-State): $10,054
Enrollment: 10,473 Coed
Affiliation or Control: State IRS Status: 501(c)3
Highest Offering: Doctorate
Accreditation: EH, CAATE, CACREP, CAEPN, CS, EXSC, MFCD, NURSE, PH, SP, SW

02 President .... Dr. Joe BERTOLINO
04 Admin Assistant to the President .... Ms. Charmaine R. LLOYD
05 Provost/Vice Pres Acad Affairs .... Dr. Robert PREVANT
10 EVP for Finance & Administration .... Mr. Mark ROZEWSKI
32 Vice Pres Student Affairs .... Dr. Tracy TYREE
30 Vice President Inst Advancement .... Mr. Robert L. STAMP
84 Assoc VP for Enrollment Management .... Dr. Terricita E. SASS
15 Chief Human Resources Officer .... Ms. Diane MAZZA
18 Assoc VP Capital Budgeting/Fac Ops .... Mr. Robert G. SHEELEY
13 Chief Info Tech Officer .... Dr. Robert RENNIE
49 Dean School Arts & Sciences .... Mr. Steven BREESE
50 Dean School of Business .... Dr. Ellen DURNIN
53 Dean School Education .... Dr. Stephen HEGEDUS
58 Dean School Graduate Studies .... Dr. Christine BROADBRIDGE
70 Interim Dean School Health/Human Sv .... Dr. Sandra BULMER
41 Director of Athletics .... Mr. Jay MORAN
26 Director of Public Affairs .... Mr. Patrick DILGER
29 Director Alumni Affairs .... Ms. Michelle JOHNSTON
07 Director Admissions .... Ms. Alexis HAAKONSEN
06 Registrar .... Ms. Alicia CARROLL
08 Director of Library Services .... Dr. Christina BAUM
19 Director of Public Safety .... Mr. Joseph M. DOOLEY
25 Director of Sponsored Research .... Ms. Amy TAYLOR
37 Director of Financial Aid .... Ms. Gloria LEE
23 Director of Health Services .... Dr. Diane S. MORGENTHALER
35 Dean of Student Affairs .... Dr. Jules TETREAULT
46 AVP for Institutional Effectiveness .... Dr. Richard RICCARDI
38 Director of Counseling Services .... Dr. Jeffrey VANLONE
21 University Controller .... Vacant
92 Director of Honors Program .... Dr. Terese GEMME
94 Director of Women's Studies .... Dr. Yi-Chun Tricia LIN
88 Dir of Academic & Career Advising .... Mr. Frank LADORE
39 Director of Residence Life .... Mr. Robert C. DEMEZZO

*Western Connecticut State University (B)

181 White Street, Danbury CT 06810-6885
County: Fairfield FICE Identification: 001380
Unit ID: 130776
Telephone: (203) 837-8200 Carnegie Class: Masters/M
FAX Number: (203) 837-8276 Calendar System: Semester
URL: www.wcsu.edu
Established: 1903 Annual Undergrad Tuition & Fees (In-State): $10,017
Enrollment: 5,826 Coed
Affiliation or Control: State IRS Status: 501(c)3
Highest Offering: Doctorate
Accreditation: EH, CACREP, CAEPN, MUS, NURSE, SW, THEA

02 President .... Dr. John B. CLARK
05 Provost/Vice Pres Academic Affairs .... Dr. Missy ALEXANDER
10 Assoc VP Finance & Administration .... Mr. Sean LOUGHRAN
111 VP Inst Advancement .... Vacant
32 VP Student Affairs .... Dr. Keith BETTS
88 Dean of Visual/Performing Arts .... Mr. Brian VERNON
35 Dean of Student Affairs .... Dr. Walter CRAMER
49 Int Dean Macricostas Sch Arts & Sc .... Dr. Josephine HAMER
50 Dean of Ancell Sch of Business .... Dr. David MARTIN
107 Int Dean Sch of Prof Studies .... Dr. Patricia IVRY
15 Chief Human Resources Officer .... Mr. Frederic W. CRATTY
13 Director of Info Systems .... Mr. John DEROSA
21 Director Fiscal Affairs/Controller .... Mr. Peter ROSA
44 Director of Development .... Ms. Lynne LEBARRON
28 Chief Diversity Officer .... Ms. Jesenia MINIER-DELGADO
06 Registrar .... Mr. Keith R. GAUVIN
08 Director of Library Services .... Ms. Veronica KENAUSIS
09 Director Inst Research/Assessment .... Dr. Jerome WILCOX
25 Director of Grant/Programs .... Ms. Gabrielle E. JAZWIECKI
38 Director of Counseling Svcs .... Dr. Rée GUNTER
37 Director of Financial Services .... Ms. Melissa STEPHENS
36 Director Career Development Center .... Ms. Kathleen LINDENMAYER
26 Director Univ & Cmty Relations .... Mr. Paul STEINMETZ
39 Director Housing & Residence Life .... Mr. Ron MASON
35 Director Student Life .... Dr. Paul M. SIMON
41 Director of Athletics .... Ms. Lori MAZZA
29 Director of Alumni Relations .... Mr. Thomas CRUCITTI
07 Director of Admissions .... Vacant
45 Dir of Facilities Plng & Engr .... Mr. Peter VISENTIN
11 Director of Administrative Services .... Mr. Mark R. CASE
18 Assoc VP Facilities .... Mr. Luigi MARCONE
88 Dir Facil Utilization & Promotion .... Mr. John MURPHY
114 Director of Fin Planning & Budgets .... Ms. Mary Ann DEASE
27 Assoc Dir of Public Relations .... Ms. Sherri HILL
88 Chief of Police .... Mr. Roger CONNOR
04 Administrative Asst to President .... Ms. Janet MCKAY
84 Assoc VP Enrollment Services .... Mr. Jay MURRAY
90 Director Media Svcs & Acad Comput .... Ms. Rebecca WOODWARD

*Asnuntuck Community College (C)

170 Elm Street, Enfield CT 06082-3800
County: Hartford FICE Identification: 011150
Unit ID: 128577
Telephone: (860) 253-3000 Carnegie Class: Assoc/HVT-Mix Trad/Non
FAX Number: (860) 253-3014 Calendar System: Semester
URL: www.asnuntuck.edu
Established: 1972 Annual Undergrad Tuition & Fees (In-State): $4,208
Enrollment: 1,571 Coed
Affiliation or Control: State IRS Status: 501(c)3
Highest Offering: Associate Degree
Accreditation: EH

02 President .... Dr. James P. LOMBELLA
05 Dean of Academic Affairs .... Mr. Michael STEFANOWICZ
10 Interim Dean of Administration .... Mr. Gennaro DEANGELIS
32 Interim Dean of Student Services .... Mr. Tim ST. JAMES
15 Interim Director of HR .... Ms. Cheryl A. CYR
84 Director of Enrollment Management .... Vacant
06 Registrar .... Ms. Diane CLOKEY
37 Interim Director of Financial Aid .... Ms. Beth-Anne EGAN
09 Director of Institutional Research .... Ms. Qing L. MACK
111 Director Institutional Advancement .... Mr. Keith MADORE
103 Dean Workforce Dev/Cont Educ .... Ms. Eileen PELTIER
18 Bldg Superintendent II/Phys Plant .... Mr. Joseph MULLER
26 Coord of Mktg/Business/Industry .... Mr. Gary CARRA
04 Executive Asst to President .... Ms. Margret G. VAN COTT
07 Interim Director of Admissions .... Ms. Jennifer ANILOWSKI
13 Director of Information Technology .... Ms. Lynn D. GREGOR
38 Dir Ctr for Advising/Stdnt Achieve .... Ms. Jill RUSHBROOK

*Capital Community College (D)

950 Main Street, Hartford CT 06103-1207
County: Hartford FICE Identification: 007635
Unit ID: 129367
Telephone: (860) 906-5000 Carnegie Class: Assoc/HT-Mix Trad/Non
FAX Number: (860) 520-7906 Calendar System: Semester
URL: www.ccc.commnet.edu
Established: 1967 Annual Undergrad Tuition & Fees (In-State): $4,236
Enrollment: 3,503 Coed
Affiliation or Control: State IRS Status: 501(c)3
Highest Offering: Associate Degree
Accreditation: EH, ADNUR, EMT, #MAC, RAD

02 President .... Dr. Wilfredo NIEVES
32 Dean of Student Services .... Ms. Doris B. ARRINGTON
11 Dean of Administration .... Mr. Lester PRIMUS
51 Dean Continuing Educ/Community Svcs .... Ms. Linda GUZZO
09 Director of Institutional Research .... Ms. Jenny WANG
10 Director Finance/Administration .... Mr. Ted HALE
06 Registrar .... Mr. Argelio MARRERO
08 Director of Library Services .... Ms. Eileen RHODES
07 Director of Admissions .... Mr. Gregg GORNEAULT
37 Director of Financial Aid .... Ms. Margaret MALASPINA
13 Director of Computer Services .... Mr. Roger FERRARO
66 Dir Cont Educ Nurse/Allied Health .... Ms. Ruth KREMS
36 Dir of Career Planning/Development .... Ms. Linda DOMENITZ
26 Director of Information/Marketing .... Ms. Jane BRONFMAN
15 Director of Human Resources .... Ms. Josephine AGNELLO-VELEY
20 Associate Academic Officer .... Mr. C. Raymond HUGHES
111 Director Institutional Advancement .... Mr. John MCNAMARA

*Gateway Community College (E)

20 Church St., New Haven CT 06510-5970
County: New Haven FICE Identification: 008037
Unit ID: 130396
Telephone: (203) 285-2000 Carnegie Class: Assoc/HT-Mix Trad/Non
FAX Number: (203) 285-2018 Calendar System: Semester
URL: www.gwcc.commnet.edu
Established: 1968 Annual Undergrad Tuition & Fees (In-State): $4,168
Enrollment: 7,980 Coed
Affiliation or Control: State IRS Status: 501(c)3
Highest Offering: Associate Degree
Accreditation: EH, ADNUR, DIETT, DMS, NMT, RAD, RTT

02 President .... Dr. Paul BROADIE, II
11 Dean of Administrative Services .... Vacant
46 Dean of Devel/Community Partnership .... Ms. Mary Ellen CODY
05 Dean of Academics .... Dr. Mark KOSINSKI
51 Dean of Cont Educ/Workforce Develop .... Ms. Victoria BOZZUTO
15 Director Personnel/Contract Admin .... Ms. Lucille BROWN
04 Executive Assistant to President .... Vacant
09 Director Institutional Research .... Dr. Vincent P. TONG
26 Director Public Info & Marketing .... Ms. Evelyn GARD
10 Director Finance & Admin Svcs .... Ms. Jill MCDOWELL
30 Director Institutional Advancement .... Vacant
08 Director Library .... Ms. Clara OGBAA
84 Director of Enrollment Management .... Mr. Joseph CARBERRY
36 Director Career Services .... Ms. Kellie BYRD-DANSO
37 Director Financial Aid .... Mr. Raymond ZEEK
38 Director Student Counseling .... Mr. Michael BUCCILLI
32 Interim Dir of Student Activities .... Mr. Marc HARTMANN
24 Director Educational Technologies .... Vacant
25 Grants Facilitator .... Vacant
13 Director Computer Services .... Mr. Lawrence SALAY
24 Director Early Learning Center .... Ms. Sarah CHAMBERS
121 Coord Center for Education Svcs .... Ms. Clara MENA
50 Chair Business Department .... Mr. Richard REES
79 Chair Humanities Department .... Mr. Chester H. SCHNEPF
83 Chair Social Sciences Department .... Mr. Jonah COHEN
88 Coord Early Childhood Education .... Ms. Carmelita E. VALENCIA-DAYE
88 Coord Drug/Alcohol Rehab Counseling .... Vacant
67 Coordinator Pharmacy Tech Program .... Ms. Louise A. PETROKA
81 Chair Math/Natural Sci Department .... Mr. Rocky TREMBLAY
50 Director Business & Industry Svcs .... Ms. Marilee BAKER-ROUSSAT
88 Director Dietetic Technician Pgm .... Ms. Marcia DORAN
76 Director Allied Health .... Ms. Sheila SOLERNOU
20 Associate Dean of Learning .... Vacant
54 Dir Engineering/Applied Technology .... Mr. Eric F. FLYNN
18 Chief Facilities/Physical Plant .... Mr. Lucian SIMONE
06 Registrar .... Ms. Maribel LOPEZ

*Housatonic Community College (F)

900 Lafayette Boulevard, Bridgeport CT 06604-4704
County: Fairfield FICE Identification: 004513
Unit ID: 129543
Telephone: (203) 332-5000 Carnegie Class: Assoc/HT-High Trad
FAX Number: (203) 332-5123 Calendar System: Semester
URL: www.housatonic.edu
Established: 1967 Annual Undergrad Tuition & Fees (In-State): $4,168
Enrollment: 5,369 Coed
Affiliation or Control: State IRS Status: 501(c)3
Highest Offering: Associate Degree
Accreditation: EH

02 President .... Dr. Paul BROADIE, II
05 Acting Academic Dean .... Dr. William Terry BROWN
11 Acting Dean of Administration .... Dr. Rose ELLIS
32 Acting Dean of Students .... Mr. James D. CONNOLLY
20 Associate Dean Academics .... Vacant
06 Registrar .... Mr. James CONNOLLY
07 Director of Admissions .... Mr. Earl GRAHAM
08 Librarian .... Ms. Shelly STROHM
37 Director of Financial Aid .... Vacant
26 Public Relations Associate .... Vacant
19 Director of Security .... Mr. Christopher GOUGH
09 Director Institutional Research .... Ms. Jan SCHAEFFLER
13 Director of Computer Services .... Mr. Anthony VITOLA
15 Director Personnel/Labor Relations .... Ms. Theresa EISENBACH
30 Exec Dir University Advancement .... Mr. Richard DUPONT
35 Director of Student Life .... Dr. Kelly HOPE
10 Director of Finance/Admin Svcs .... Ms. Teresa ORAVETZ
18 Coordinator of Facilities .... Mr. Richard HENNESSEY
04 Executive Asst to President .... Ms. Camilla COSTANTINI
38 Director Student Counseling .... Mr. Hernan YEPES

*Manchester Community College (G)

PO Box 1046, Great Path, Manchester CT 06045-1046
County: Hartford FICE Identification: 001392
Unit ID: 129695
Telephone: (860) 512-3000 Carnegie Class: Assoc/HT-High Trad
FAX Number: (860) 512-3631 Calendar System: Semester
URL: www.manchestercc.edu
Established: 1963 Annual Undergrad Tuition & Fees (In-State): $4,168
Enrollment: 6,891 Coed
Affiliation or Control: State IRS Status: 501(c)3
Highest Offering: Associate Degree
Accreditation: EH, ACFEI, COARC, DA, MUS, OTA, RAD, RTT, SURGT

02 President ....Dr. Gena GLICKMAN
05 Int Provost/Chief Academic Officer . Dr. Tanya MILLNER-HARLEE
32 Dean of Student Affairs ....Dr. G. Duncan HARRIS
11 Dean of Administrative Affairs ....Mr. James MCDOWELL
30 Dean of Advancement ....Ms. Susan ALSTON
51 Dean of Continuing Education ....Ms. Melanie HABER
20 Associate Dean of Academic Affairs ....Dr. Pamela MITCHELL-CRUMP
10 Director Finance & Admin Services ....Ms. Regina FERRANTE
07 Assoc Director of Admissions ....Ms. Cynthia ZELDNER
06 Registrar ....Ms. Anita SPARROW
08 Dir Library Svcs/Educational Tech ....Ms. Deborah HERMAN
13 Director of Information Technology ....Mr. Barry GRANT
09 Director Plng/Research & Assessment ....Mr. David NIELSEN
15 Director of Human Resources ....Ms. Patricia LINDO
18 Dir Facilities Management/ Planning ....Ms. Darlene MANCINI-BROWN
26 Dir Marketing and Public Relations ....Ms. Charlene TAPPAN
37 Director of Financial Aid ....Ms. Anna TORRES
72 Director Business/Engineering/Tech ....Vacant
83 Director Social Science/Hospitality ....Dr. Tuesday COOPER
81 Int Dir Math/Science/Health Careers ....Ms. Sharale GOLDING
79 Director of Liberal Arts ....Ms. Samantha GONZALEZ
35 Director of Student Life ....Mr. Trent J. BARBER
44 Director of Development ....Ms. Diana REID
38 Dir Counseling and Career Svcs ....Ms. Julia GREENE
84 Director of Enrollment Management ....Mr. Peter HARRIS
31 Director of Community Outreach ....Ms. Sara VINCENT
103 Int Director of Business & Industry ....Mr. Miguel PIGOTT
90 Director of Academic Support Ctr ....Mr. Brian CLEARY
85 Dir Multicultural/Intl Affairs ....Mr. Joseph MESQUITA
28 Chief Diversity Officer ....Ms. Debra FREUND
96 Assoc Director of Purchasing ....Mr. Paul MOUNDS
29 Director of Alumni Affairs ....Ms. Diana REID

*Middlesex Community College (A)

100 Training Hill Road, Middletown CT 06457-4889
County: Middlesex FICE Identification: 008038
Unit ID: 129756
Telephone: (860) 343-5800 Carnegie Class: Assoc/HT-Mix Trad/Non
FAX Number: (860) 344-7488 Calendar System: Semester
URL: www.mxcc.commnet.edu
Established: 1966 Annual Undergrad Tuition & Fees (In-State): $4,168
Enrollment: 2,902 Coed
Affiliation or Control: State IRS Status: 501(c)3
Highest Offering: Associate Degree
Accreditation: EH, OPD, RAD

02 President ....Vacant
05 Dean of Academics ....Dr. Steven MINKLER
11 Dean of Administration ....Ms. Kimberly HOGAN
32 Dean of Students ....Dr. Adrienne MASLIN
51 Dean Continuing Education ....Vacant
08 Director Library Services ....Ms. Lan LIU
37 Director Financial Aid ....Ms. Irene MARTIN
30 Associate Dean of Development ....Ms. Cheryl DUMONT-SMITH
09 Director of Institutional Research ....Dr. Paul CARMICHAEL
13 Director Information Technology ....Ms. Annie SCOTT
18 Chief Facilities/Physical Plant ....Mr. Steven CHESTER
15 Director Personnel Services ....Ms. Anastasia PYCH
20 Academic Division Director ....Dr. Lin LIN
20 Academic Division Director ....Mr. Jaime FLORES
124 Retention Specialist ....Ms. Judy MAZGULSKI
88 Disability Services Coordinator ....Ms. Hilary PHELPS
81 Division Director Math ....Vacant
84 Director of Enrollment Management ....Ms. Gayle BARRETT
06 Associate Registrar ....Ms. Joanne FAUST

*Naugatuck Valley Community College (B)

750 Chase Parkway, Waterbury CT 06708-3089
County: New Haven FICE Identification: 006982
Unit ID: 129729
Telephone: (203) 575-8044 Carnegie Class: Assoc/MT-VT-High Trad
FAX Number: (203) 575-8096 Calendar System: Semester
URL: www.nv.edu
Established: 1964 Annual Undergrad Tuition & Fees (In-State): $4,208
Enrollment: 6,976 Coed
Affiliation or Control: State IRS Status: 501(c)3
Highest Offering: Associate Degree
Accreditation: EH, ADNUR, COARC, ENGT, PTAA, RAD

02 President ....Dr. Daisy Cocco DE FILIPPIS
05 Provost/Senior Dean Administration ....Mr. James TROUP
30 Associate Dean of Development ....Ms. Angela CHAPMAN
32 Dean of Student Services ....Ms. Sarah GAGER
26 Dean of Community Engagement ....Mr. Waldemar KOSTRZEWA
13 Assoc Dean Information Technology ....Mr. Conal LARKIN
20 Dean of Academic Affairs ....Ms. Irene RIOS-KNAUF
06 Registrar ....Ms. Lourdes CRUZ
37 Director of Financial Aid ....Ms. Catherine HARDY
84 Assoc Dean of Enrollment Management ....Ms. Noel ROSAMILIO
22 Affirmative Action Officer ....Mr. Ron CLYMER
08 Director Learning Resource Ctr ....Ms. Jamie HAMMOND
10 Director of Finance/Admin Services ....Ms. Lisa PALEN
35 Director of Student Activities ....Ms. Karen BLAKE
18 Chief Facilities/Physical Plant ....Mr. Robert DIVJAK
09 Int Dir of Institutional Research ....Ms. Lisa RODRIGUES-DOOLABH
121 Dir of Student Development Services ....Ms. Bonnie GOULET
15 Director of Human Resources ....Ms. Kimberly CAROLINA
26 Director of Marketing ....Ms. Sydney VOGHEL-OCHS
27 Public Relations Associate ....Ms. Claudia WARD-DE LEON

*Northwestern Connecticut Community-Technical College (C)

Park Place E, Winsted CT 06098-1798
County: Litchfield FICE Identification: 001398
Unit ID: 130040
Telephone: (860) 738-6300 Carnegie Class: Assoc/HT-Mix Trad/Non
FAX Number: (860) 738-6488 Calendar System: Semester
URL: www.nwcc.commnet.edu/
Established: 1965 Annual Undergrad Tuition & Fees (In-State): $4,168
Enrollment: 1,521 Coed
Affiliation or Control: State IRS Status: 501(c)3
Highest Offering: Associate Degree
Accreditation: EH, ADNUR, MAC

02 President ....Dr. Michael ROOKE
11 Dean of Administration ....Dr. Steven R. FRAZIER
05 Dean of Academic & Student Affairs ....Dr. Patricia A. BOUFFARD
07 Associate Dean of Enrollment ....Mr. Darryl REOME
08 Director of Library Services ....Mr. James PATTERSON
06 Registrar ....Ms. Debra ZAVATKAY
15 Director of Human Resources ....Ms. Wendy BOVIA
37 Financial Aid Officer ....Mr. Louis BRISTOL
13 Director of Computer Services ....Mr. Joseph DANAJOVITS
32 Dir of Student Development ....Ms. Ruth GONZALEZ
09 Director of Institutional Research ....Ms. Caitlin BOGER-HAWKINS
26 Director Marketing/Public Relations ....Mr. Grantley ADAMS
10 Director Financial/Admin Services ....Ms. Kimberly DRAGAN

*Norwalk Community College (D)

188 Richards Avenue, Norwalk CT 06854-1655
County: Fairfield FICE Identification: 001399
Unit ID: 130004
Telephone: (203) 857-7000 Carnegie Class: Assoc/HT-Mix Trad/Non
FAX Number: (203) 857-7287 Calendar System: Semester
URL: www.norwalk.edu
Established: 1961 Annual Undergrad Tuition & Fees (In-State): $4,188
Enrollment: 6,054 Coed
Affiliation or Control: State IRS Status: 501(c)3
Highest Offering: Associate Degree
Accreditation: EH, ADNUR, COARC, MAC, PTAA

02 President ....Dr. David L. LEVINSON
32 Dean of Students ....Dr. Calvin MCFADDEN
05 Interim Dean of Academics ....Mr. Michael BUTCARIS
30 Executive Director of Development ....Ms. Ann ROGERS
103 Int Assoc Dn Ext Stds/Workforce Dev ....Dr. Kristina TESTA-BUZZEE
08 Director of Library Services ....Ms. Linda LERMAN
37 Director Financial Aid ....Mr. Luis GUAMAN
66 Int Director of Nursing Education ....Ms. Katherine FRIES
06 Registrar ....Mr. Steve MENDES
15 Director Human Resources ....Ms. Therese MARROCCO
26 Director of Public Relations ....Ms. Madeline K. BARILLO
38 Director Student Counseling ....Ms. Catherine MILLER
07 Acting Director of Admissions ....Mr. William CHAGNON
10 Director Finance/Administration ....Ms. Carrie MCGEE-YUROF
18 Chief Facilities/Physical Plant ....Mr. Craig CARLSON
28 Chief Diversity Officer ....Ms. Cheryl DEVONISH
04 Administrative Asst to President ....Mrs. Thomasina L. CALISE

*Quinebaug Valley Community College (E)

742 Upper Maple Street, Danielson CT 06239-1440
County: Windham FICE Identification: 010530
Unit ID: 130217
Telephone: (860) 932-4000 Carnegie Class: Assoc/MT-VT-High Trad
FAX Number: (860) 932-4306 Calendar System: Semester
URL: www.qvcc.edu
Established: 1971 Annual Undergrad Tuition & Fees (In-State): $4,198
Enrollment: 1,680 Coed
Affiliation or Control: State IRS Status: 501(c)3
Highest Offering: Associate Degree
Accreditation: EH, MAC

02 President ....Dr. Carlee DRUMMER
05 Dean Academic Affs & Student Svcs ....Mr. Alfred WILLIAMS
11 Dean of Administrative Services ....Mr. Paul MARTLAND
08 Director of Library Services ....Ms. Jennifer COURNOYER
37 Director of Student Financial Aid ....Ms. Kim RICH
09 Director of Institutional Research ....Dr. Donna SOHAN
10 Dir Finance/Administrative Svcs ....Ms. Alessandra LUNDBERG
18 Chief Facilities/Physical Plant ....Mr. Martin CHARETTE
26 Chief Public Relations Officer ....Ms. Susan BREAULT
111 Dir of Institutional Advancement ....Ms. Monique WOLANIN
32 Dir of Student Services/Registrar ....Ms. Amy KACERIK
27 Coordinator of Marketing ....Ms. Margie HUOPPI
07 Associate Director of Admissions ....Ms. Sarah HENDRICK
04 Administrative Asst to President ....Ms. Jennifer GREEN
13 Chief Info Technology Officer (CIO) ....Mr. Jarrod BOREK
15 Director Personnel Services ....Ms. Karla DESJARDINS
29 Director Alumni Relations ....Ms. Elle GOSLIN

*Three Rivers Community College (F)

574 New London Turnpike, Norwich CT 06360
County: New London FICE Identification: 009765
Unit ID: 129808
Telephone: (860) 215-9000 Carnegie Class: Assoc/HT-High Trad
FAX Number: (860) 215-9901 Calendar System: Semester
URL: www.trcc.commnet.edu
Established: 1963 Annual Undergrad Tuition & Fees (In-State): $4,208
Enrollment: 4,259 Coed
Affiliation or Control: State IRS Status: 501(c)3
Highest Offering: Associate Degree
Accreditation: EH, ACBSP, ADNUR

02 President ....Dr. Mary Ellen JUKOSKI
05 Academic Dean ....Dr. Jerry T. ICE
11 Dean of Administration/HR and IT ....Mr. Stephen H. GOETCHIUS
84 Dn Student Svcs/Enrol Mgt/Wrkf Dev ....Mr. Stephan FINTON
13 Dir of Information Technology ....Mr. Larry DAVENPORT
30 Dir Institutional Advancement ....Ms. Betty BAILLARGEON
06 Acting Registrar ....Ms. Betty WILLIAMSON
10 Dir of Finance/Admin Svcs ....Ms. Gayle O'NEILL
38 Director of Student Development ....Ms. Margaret STROUP
08 Director Library Services ....Ms. Mildred HODGE
37 Actg Dir Student Financial Aid ....Mr. Kenneth BRIGGS
18 Director of Facilities ....Mr. Arnie DELAROSSA
09 Office of Institutional Research ....Ms. Laura QIN
26 Dir of Marketing/Public Relations ....Ms. Kathryn GAFFNEY
14 Dir Information Tech Support ....Ms. Cathy DAVENPORT
14 Dir of Educational Technology ....Mr. Kem BARFIELD
35 Dir of Student Success ....Ms. Christine LANGUTH
04 Exec Assistant to President ....Ms. April HODSON
07 Director of Admissions ....Ms. Peg STROUP
32 Director of Student Programs ....Ms. Rhonda SPAZIANI
103 Assoc Dean Workforce Dev ....Ms. Marjorie VALENTIN

*Tunxis Community College (G)

271 Scott Swamp Road, Farmington CT 06032-3187
County: Hartford FICE Identification: 009764
Unit ID: 130606
Telephone: (860) 773-1300 Carnegie Class: Assoc/HT-Mix Trad/Non
FAX Number: N/A Calendar System: Semester
URL: www.tunxis.edu/
Established: 1969 Annual Undergrad Tuition & Fees (In-State): $4,208
Enrollment: 4,055 Coed
Affiliation or Control: State IRS Status: 501(c)3
Highest Offering: Associate Degree
Accreditation: EH, ACBSP, DA, DH

02 Interim President ....Dr. James P. LOMBELLA
05 Dean of Academic Affairs ....Dr. David ENGLAND
32 Dean of Student Affairs ....Dr. Kirk PETERS
11 Dean of Administration ....Mr. Charles CLEARY
10 Dir Finance/Administrative Services ....Ms. Nancy ESCHENBRENNER
30 Dir of Institutional Advancement ....Ms. Leigh E. KNOPF
15 Director Human Resources ....Vacant
08 Director Library Services ....Dr. Lisa LAVOIE
13 Director Information Technology ....Mr. Robert WAHL
07 Director of Admissions ....Ms. Tamika DAVIS
06 Registrar ....Ms. Susan WINN
35 Director Academic Support Center ....Ms. Kathleen SCHWAGER
09 Director of Institutional Research ....Vacant
37 Director Financial Aid Services ....Mr. David WELSH
18 Director of Facilities ....Mr. John LODOVICO
90 Coord Academic Info Technology ....Mr. Steven MEAD
91 Coord Admin Information Technology ....Mrs. Mary Ann DIORIO
26 Public Relations Associate ....Ms. Melissa LAMAR

Connecticut College (H)

270 Mohegan Avenue, New London CT 06320-4125
County: New London FICE Identification: 001379
Unit ID: 128902
Telephone: (860) 447-1911 Carnegie Class: Bac-A&S
FAX Number: (860) 439-2700 Calendar System: Semester
URL: www.conncoll.edu
Established: 1911 Annual Undergrad Tuition & Fees: $50,940
Enrollment: 1,922 Coed
Affiliation or Control: Independent Non-Profit IRS Status: 501(c)3
Highest Offering: Master's
Accreditation: EH

01 President ....Ms. Katherine BERGERON
05 Dean of the Faculty ....Ms. Abigail A. VANSLYCK
10 Vice Pres Finance and Admin ....Mr. Richard MADONNA
30 Vice President College Advancement ....Vacant
08 Vice Pres of Info Svcs/Librarian ....Dr. W. Lee HISLE
26 Vice President Communications ....Ms. Pamela DUMAS SERFES
07 VP of Admission & Financial Aid ....Mr. Andrew STRICKLER
15 Asst VP HR/Professional Development ....Ms. Cheryl L. MILLER
20 Dean of the College ....Jefferson SINGER
32 Dean of Student Life ....Dr. Victor J. ARCELUS
28 Dean of Institution Equity and Incl ....Mr. Jonathan MCNIGHT
20 Associate Dean of Faculty ....Prof. Jeffrey COLE
06 Registrar ....Ms. Elisabeth S. LABRIOLA
09 Director of Institutional Research ....Dr. John D. NUGENT
21 Controller ....Ms. Amanda B. MAYFIELD
37 Director of Financial Aid ....Mr. Sean MARTIN
41 Director of Athletics ....Mr. Fran SHIELDS
29 Director of Alumni Relations ....Ms. Bridget MCSHANE

38	Director Student Counseling Service	Dr. Janet D. SPOLTORE
96	Director of Purchasing	Vacant
88	Secretary of the College	Ms. Bonnie WELLS
04	Executive Asst to the President	Wendy MAHON
102	Dir Foundation/Corporate Relations	Naima GHERBI
13	Asst VP Enterprise/Tech Systems	Jean KILBRIDE
19	Director Security/Safety	Vacant
22	Dir Affirmative Action/EEO	John MCKNIGHT
36	Director Student Placement	Persephone HALL
39	Director Student Housing	Sara ROTHENBERGER
44	Director Annual or Planned Giving	Matt GLASZ

Fairfield University (A)

1073 N Benson Road, Fairfield CT 06824-5195

County: Fairfield FICE Identification: 001385
Unit ID: 129242
Telephone: (203) 254-4000 Carnegie Class: Masters/L
FAX Number: (203) 254-4101 Calendar System: Semester
URL: www.fairfield.edu
Established: 1942 Annual Undergrad Tuition & Fees: $46,000
Enrollment: 5,138 Coed
Affiliation or Control: Roman Catholic IRS Status: 501(c)3
Highest Offering: Doctorate
Accreditation: **EH**, ANEST, CACREP, CAEPN, ENG, MFCD, NURSE

01	University President	Dr. Mark R. NEMEC
42	Univ Chaplain/Special Asst to Pres	Rev. Charles H. ALLEN, SJ
11	Exec VP & Chief Operating Officer	Mr. Kevin P. LAWLOR
05	Interim Provost	Dr. Christine SIEGAL
100	Exec Asst to Pres/Chief of Staff	Mr. Michael TORTORA
111	Vice Pres Univ Advancement	Mr. Wally HALAS
15	Vice President of Human Resources	Mr. Scott ESPOSITO
32	Sr Vice President Student Affairs	Dr. Thomas C. PELLEGRINO
88	Vice Pres for Mission and Identity	Dr. Nancy DALLAVALLE
26	VP Marketing and Communications	Ms. Jennifer ANDERSON
84	VP Enrollment Management	Ms. Karen A. PELLEGRINO
20	Assoc Vice Pres Academic Affairs	Dr. Mary Frances MALONE
20	Senior VP for Academic Affairs	Dr. Christine SIEGEL
18	Assoc Vice Pres Facilities Mgmt	Mr. David W. FRASSINELLI
38	Asst Vice Pres/Dir Counseling Svcs	Dr. Susan N. BIRGE
35	Asst Vice Pres Student Affairs	Mr. James D. FITZPATRICK
09	Dir Institutional Research/Plng	Ms. Amy BOCZER
123	Director of Graduate Admission	Ms. Marianne L. GUMPPER
06	University Registrar	Mr. Robert C. RUSSO
13	Chief Information Officer	Mr. Jonathan CARROLL
37	Director of Financial Aid	Ms. Diana M. DRAPER
36	Dir Career/Leadership & Prof Dev	Ms. Cathleen M. BORGMAN
29	Asst Vice Pres of Alumni Relations	Ms. Janet A. CANEPA
42	Director of Campus Ministry	Rev. Mark SCALESE
19	Director of Public Safety	Mr. Todd A. PELAZZA
41	Director of Athletics	Mr. Eugene P. DORIS
49	Dean College Arts & Science	Dr. Richard GREENWALD
50	Dean Charles F Dolan Sch of Bus	Dr. Donald E. GIBSON
54	Dean School of Engineering	Dr. Bruce BERDANIER
66	Dean School of Nursing/Health Stds	Dr. Meredith W. KAZER
53	Dean Grad Sch Educ/Allied Prof	Dr. Robert HANNAFIN
35	AVP Student Affs/Dean of Students	Ms. Karen A. DONOGHUE
88	Dir of Conference/Event Management	Mr. Matthew A. DINNAN
35	Assoc Dean of Students	Mr. William H. JOHNSON
39	Assoc Dean/Dir Resid Life	Dr. Ophelie ROWE-ALLEN
104	Dir Study Abroad/Intl Programs	Ms. Jennifer EWALD
92	Co-Director of Honors Program	Dr. Laura NASH
92	Co-Director of Honors Program	Dr. Giovanni RUFFINI
08	Univ Librarian/Dir of Library Svcs	Dr. Brent A. MAI
23	Director of Student Health Center	Ms. Julia A. DUFFY
16	Director Human Resources	Mr. Mark J. GUGLIELMONI
96	Purchasing Manager	Mr. Peter PEREZ
88	Dean Acad & Career Develop	Ms. Heather PETRAGLIA

Goodwin College (B)

One Riverside Drive, East Hartford CT 06118-2777

County: Hartford FICE Identification: 022449
Unit ID: 129154
Telephone: (860) 528-4111 Carnegie Class: Spec-4-yr-Other Health
FAX Number: (860) 291-9550 Calendar System: Semester
URL: www.goodwin.edu
Established: 1999 Annual Undergrad Tuition & Fees: $20,400
Enrollment: 3,549 Coed
Affiliation or Control: Independent Non-Profit IRS Status: 501(c)3
Highest Offering: Baccalaureate
Accreditation: **EH**, ADNUR, COARC, DH, HT, MAAB, MAC, NURSE, OPD, #OTA, @SW

01	President	Mr. Mark E. SCHEINBERG
03	Executive Vice President/Provost	Ms. Ann B. CLARK
05	VP Academic Affs/Dean Faculty	Ms. Danielle WILKEN
10	Vice President for Finance/CFO	Mr. Eddie MEYER
45	Vice Pres for Inst Effectiveness	Dr. Henriette PRANGER
30	Vice Pres Economic/Strategic Dev	Mr. Todd J. ANDREWS
18	Vice Pres Facilities/Technology	Mr. Bryant L. HARRELL
84	Vice Pres Enrollment/Mrktg/Comm	Mr. Daniel NOONAN
30	Vice President for Advancement	Ms. Brooke PENDERS
20	Asst Vice Pres Academic Affairs	Ms. Danielle S. WILKEN
32	AVP Stdnt Affs/Dean of Students	Ms. Tamara ODAY-STEVENS
09	Asst VP Institutional Effectiveness	Dr. Henriette M. PRANGER
88	Asst VP Strategy/Business Devel	Dr. Clifford THERMER
84	Asst VP Enrollment Services	Mr. Nicholas LENTINO
08	Director of Library Services	Ms. Susan HANSEN
56	Dean of Magnet Schools	Vacant
36	Director of Career Services	Ms. Patricia SHAW

26	Dir Marketing/Communications	Mr. Phil MOORE
44	Director Advancement	Ms. Holly WINTERS
21	Director of Finance/Controller	Mr. Bryan SOLTIS
13	Director Information Technology	Mr. John RUGGIRELLO
37	Director of Financial Aid	Ms. Bonnie SOLTZ-KNOWLTON
07	Director of Admissions	Mr. Dan WILLIAMSON
09	Dir Inst Research/Educ Assessment	Ms. Melissa QUINLAN
106	Director of Online Learning	Ms. Lisa MANLEY
06	Registrar	Ms. Allison MISKY
29	Alumni Relations Coordinator	Ms. Vanessa PERGOLIZZI
04	Executive Assistant to President	Ms. Ann ZAJCHOWSKI
66	Dept Chair/Director Nursing	Ms. Janice WATTS

Hartford Seminary (C)

77 Sherman Street, Hartford CT 06105-2260

County: Hartford FICE Identification: 001387
Unit ID: 129491
Telephone: (860) 509-9500 Carnegie Class: Spec-4-yr-Faith
FAX Number: (860) 509-9509 Calendar System: Semester
URL: www.hartsem.edu
Established: 1834 Annual Graduate Tuition & Fees: N/A
Enrollment: 128 Coed
Affiliation or Control: Independent Non-Profit IRS Status: 501(c)3
Highest Offering: Doctorate; No Undergraduates
Accreditation: **EH**, THEOL

01	President	Dr. Heidi HADSELL
05	Academic Dean	Dr. Scott THUMMA
11	Director of Admin and Facilities	Ms. Roseann LEZAK JANOW
30	Chief Development Officer	Mr. Samuel LOCKE
07	Director of Recruitment/Admissions	Ms. Tina DEMO
88	Director of Islamic Center	Vacant
08	Library Director	Dr. Steven BLACKBURN
10	Chief Business Officer	Mr. Michael SANDNER
06	Registrar	Ms. Danielle LAVINE
04	Exec Assistant to the President	Ms. Heather HOLDA
26	Director of Communications	Ms. Susan SCHOENBERGER

Holy Apostles College and Seminary (D)

33 Prospect Hill Road, Cromwell CT 06416-2027

County: Middlesex FICE Identification: 001389
Unit ID: 129534
Telephone: (860) 632-3010 Carnegie Class: Spec-4-yr-Faith
FAX Number: (860) 632-3030 Calendar System: Semester
URL: www.holyapostles.edu
Established: 1956 Annual Undergrad Tuition & Fees: $7,750
Enrollment: 442 Coed
Affiliation or Control: Roman Catholic IRS Status: 501(c)3
Highest Offering: Beyond Master's But Less Than Doctorate
Accreditation: **EH**, THEOL

01	President & Rector	V.Rev. Douglas L. MOSEY
11	VP External Affs/Govt Compliance	Dr. Sebastian MAHFOOD
05	Academic Dean/Chief Academic Ofcr	Rev. Peter KUCER
32	Director of Student Services	Mrs. Laura BROWN
10	Chief Financial Officer	Mr. William RUSSELL
08	Director of Library Services	Ms. Clare ADAMO
07	Director Graduate Admissions	Dr. Elizabeth REX

Lincoln College of New England (E)

2279 Mount Vernon Road, Southington CT 06489-1057

County: Hartford FICE Identification: 009407
Unit ID: 128683
Telephone: (860) 628-4751 Carnegie Class: Bac/Assoc-Assoc Dom
FAX Number: (860) 628-6444 Calendar System: Semester
URL: www.lincolncollegene.edu
Established: 1966 Annual Undergrad Tuition & Fees: $20,050
Enrollment: 619 Coed
Affiliation or Control: Proprietary IRS Status: Proprietary
Highest Offering: Baccalaureate
Accreditation: **EH**, CAHIIM, DA, DH, FUSER, NURSE, #OTA

01	President	Ms. Denise LEWICKI
04	Executive Assistant to President	Ms. Elaine WALD
05	VP Academic Affairs	Dr. Mark ANDERSON
11	VP Operations & Student Affairs	Vacant
10	Dir Business Admin Services	Mr. Stephen PERMAR
36	Director of Career Services	Ms. Jenifer RAHUSEN
32	Dean of Student Services	Mrs. Cynthia A. CLARK
20	Dean of Academic Affairs	Mr. Chris DI STISO
06	Registrar	Ms. Stephanie CROMBIE
07	Director of Admissions	Ms. Edmund LIZOTTE
08	Director of Library Services	Mr. Shawn FIELDS
37	Director of Financial Aid	Mrs. Gina D. SWENTON
09	Director of Institutional Research	Mr. Jon DALY
19	Director Campus Safety & Security	Mr. David C. ALLING
13	IT Administrator-Southington	Mr. Edward D. CONNELLY

Mitchell College (F)

437 Pequot Avenue, New London CT 06320-4498

County: New London FICE Identification: 001393
Unit ID: 129774
Telephone: (860) 701-5000 Carnegie Class: Bac-Diverse
FAX Number: (860) 701-5090 Calendar System: Semester
URL: www.mitchell.edu
Established: 1938 Annual Undergrad Tuition & Fees: $31,780
Enrollment: 723 Coed
Affiliation or Control: Independent Non-Profit IRS Status: 501(c)3
Highest Offering: Baccalaureate
Accreditation: **EH**

01	President	Ms. Janet STEINMAYER
05	VP Acad Affs/Dean of the College	Dr. Catherine WRIGHT
10	Sr VP Administration & Finance	Ms. Dyann J. BAKER
32	VP Student Affairs/Dean of Students	Dr. Sandra WIRTH
111	VP Advancement	Ms. Endia DECORDOVA
84	VP for Enrollment Management	Mr. Jamie ROMEO
15	VP for Human Resources	Mr. Jonathan HOWELL
45	VP for Strategic Initiatives	Ms. Amanda LJUBICIC
41	Director of Athletics	Ms. Dana FULMER
06	Registrar	Ms. Amy VAN OOT
88	Director of Thames @ Mitchell	Ms. Tracy GEARY
13	Chief Information Officer	Ms. Joanne KOSSUTH
90	Director of Academic Technologies	Mr. Rich WALL
37	Director of Financial Aid	Ms. Jacklyn C. STOLTZ
89	Assistant Dean 1st Year Experience	Ms. Jennifer R. WELSH
27	Director of Communications	Ms. Colleen GRESH
39	Asst Director of Residence Life	Mr. Curtis CLARK
18	Director of Facilities	Mr. Joseph PARDEE
113	Bursar	Ms. Leah BRENNAN
04	Office Administrator to President	Ms. Kristen TRAINI
38	Director Health & Wellness	Ms. Stacey TORPEY
19	Director Security/Safety	Mr. James GILMAN
26	Director of Marketing	Ms. Lisa STINSON
36	Director Career Services	Mr. Paul DUNN

Paier College of Art (G)

20 Gorham Avenue, Hamden CT 06514-3902

County: New Haven FICE Identification: 007459
Unit ID: 130110
Telephone: (203) 287-3031 Carnegie Class: Spec-4-yr-Arts
FAX Number: (203) 287-3021 Calendar System: Semester
URL: www.paiercollegeofart.edu
Established: 1946 Annual Undergrad Tuition & Fees: $15,450
Enrollment: 128 Coed
Affiliation or Control: Proprietary IRS Status: Proprietary
Highest Offering: Baccalaureate
Accreditation: **ACCSC**

01	President	Mr. Jonathan E. PAIER
03	Vice President	Mr. Daniel L. PAIER
05	Dean of the College	Mr. Daniel L. PAIER
10	Director Finance	Mrs. Maureen E. PAIER
57	Director Design/Graphics	Mr. Peter MISERENDINO
102	Director Foundation/Arts	Mr. Robert E. ZAPPALORTI
97	Director of Academics	Mr. Francis COOLEY
08	Librarian	Ms. Beth HARRIS
37	Director Student Financial Aid	Mr. John DE ROSE
32	Director of Student Services	Mrs. Angela DEROSE
20	Assistant to the Dean	Ms. Angela DEROSE
88	Director Interior Design	Mr. Pierre STRAUCH
88	Director Photography	Mr. Peter BENSON
07	Admissions Secretary	Ms. Lynn PASCALE

Post University (H)

800 Country Club Road, Waterbury CT 06723-2540

County: New Haven FICE Identification: 001401
Unit ID: 130183
Telephone: (203) 596-4500 Carnegie Class: Masters/L
FAX Number: (203) 756-5810 Calendar System: Semester
URL: www.post.edu
Established: 1890 Annual Undergrad Tuition & Fees: $16,510
Enrollment: 7,429 Coed
Affiliation or Control: Proprietary IRS Status: Proprietary
Highest Offering: Master's
Accreditation: **EH**, ACBSP

00	Chief Executive Officer	Mr. John L. HOPKINS
01	President	Dr. Donald W. MROZ
11	Chief Operations Officer	Mr. Bobby REESE
10	Chief Financial Officer	Mr. Scott T. ALLEN
26	Chief Marketing Officer	Mr. Richard SCHECHTER
13	Chief Information Officer	Mr. Greg THEISEN
88	VP Operations Analysis	Mr. Shane LIVELY
05	Provost	Dr. Elizabeth JOHNSON
06	Registrar	Vacant
32	Dean of Students	Ms. Erica PERYGA
124	Dir of Acad Success & Retention	Ms. Megan LUCIA
07	Director Admissions Main Campus	Vacant
07	Director Admissions-ADP	Ms. Jeanna SINN
123	Director Grad Admiss-ADP	Ms. Gina WELLMAN
88	Dir of Military Field Enrollment	Mr. Charles YOUNG
41	Director of Athletics	Mr. Ronnie PALMER
49	Dean of School of Arts & Sciences	Dr. Jeremi BAUER
50	Acting Dean of School of Business	Mr. Christopher SZPRYNGEL
80	Dean John P Burke Sch Pub Svcs & Ed	Vacant
08	Library Director	Ms. Tracy RALSTON
37	Director Financial Aid	Mr. Michael GREER
113	Director of Student Accounts	Ms. Michelle ORBE
88	Director of Compliance	Ms. Jillian DIAZ
04	Executive Asst to the CEO	Ms. Melissah KOCHERA
04	Executive Asst to the President	Ms. Patricia JENNINGS
16	Human Resources Director	Ms. Madelaine KELSEY
19	Director of Campus Safety	Mr. Robert TANSLEY
38	Director Student Counseling	Ms. Lisa ANTEL
36	Director Career Services	Dr. Mary RIGALI
09	Dir Inst Rsrch/Assess/Effectiveness	Dr. Zvi GOLDMAN
18	Facilities Manager	Mr. Bill DAVIS

Quinnipiac University (A)

275 Mount Carmel Avenue, Hamden CT 06518-1908
County: New Haven FICE Identification: 001402
Unit ID: 130226
Telephone: (203) 582-8200 Carnegie Class: Masters/L
FAX Number: (203) 582-4703 Calendar System: Semester
URL: www.quinnipiac.edu
Established: 1929 Annual Undergrad Tuition & Fees: $43,940
Enrollment: 9,654 Coed
Affiliation or Control: Independent Non-Profit IRS Status: 501(c)3
Highest Offering: First Professional Degree
Accreditation: EH, AA, ANEST, ARCPA, CAATE, CAEPN, CS, LAW, MED, NURSE, OT, PA, PERF, PTA, RAD, SW

01 President .... Dr. John L. LAHEY
03 Vice President/Exec Assoc to Pres .... Ms. Jean L. HUSTED
05 Executive Vice President/Provost .... Dr. Mark A. THOMPSON
10 VP Finance/Chief Financial Ofcr .... Mr. Mark VARHOLAK
26 Vice President for Public Affairs .... Ms. Lynn M. BUSHNELL
18 Vice Pres Facilities & Capital Plng .... Mr. Salvatore FILARDI
15 VP for Human Resources .... Ms. Jean L. HUSTED
07 Vice Pres for Admissions & Fin Aid .... Ms. Joan I. MOHR
37 Assoc VP for Admissions & Fin Aid ... Mr. Gregory E. EICHHORN
114 Assoc VP Budget & Fin Planning .... Mr. Sandip PATEL
30 Vice Pres Devel & Alumni Affairs .... Mr. Donald J. WEINBACH
32 Vice President & Dean of Students .... Dr. Monique DRUCKER
13 VP/Chief Info & Tech Officer .... Mr. Fred E. TARCA
20 Assoc VP Academic & Strategic Plng .... Dr. Annalisa ZINN
27 VP & Chief Digital Comm Officer .... Mr. Keith RHODES
27 Assoc VP for Public Relations .... Mr. John MORGAN
06 Registrar .... Mr. Joshua BERRY
106 VP & COO for QU Online .... Ms. Cynthia GALLATIN
28 AVP Acad Affs/Chief Diversity Ofcr .... Dr. Diane M. ARIZA
35 Assoc VP Student Affairs .... Ms. Cindy LONG PORTER
39 Director of Resident Life .... Mr. Mark DEVILBISS
35 Asst Dean Stdnt Affairs/Campus Life .... Vacant
23 Dir of Student Health Services .... Ms. Christy CHASE
38 Director of Health & Wellness .... Ms. Kerry PATTON
19 Chief of Public Safety .... Mr. Edgar RODRIGUEZ
08 Director of Arnold Bernhard Library .... Mr. Robert JOVEN
41 Director of Athletics & Recreation .... Mr. Greg AMODIO
40 Campus Store Manager .... Ms. Margaret SAMUL
104 Director for Global Education .... Ms. Andrea HOGAN
21 Assoc VP for Finance/Controller .... Mr. Daniel R. JOHNSON
96 Manager of Strategic Sourcing .... Ms. Daniella VIZZIELLO
109 Assoc VP for Auxiliary Services .... Mr. John MERIANO
29 Sr Dir Parent/Family Development .... Ms. Melinda FORMICA
110 Sr Assoc VP Devel & Alumni Affairs .... Vacant
37 Assoc VP & Univ Director of Fin Aid .... Mr. Dominic YOIA
108 Assoc Dir Acad Assessment/Research .... Ms. Sungah KIM
90 Director of Academic Technology .... Ms. Lauren ERARDI
66 Dean School of Nursing .... Dr. Jean LANGE
50 Dean School of Business .... Dr. Matthew L. O'CONNOR
49 Dean College of Arts & Sciences .... Dr. Robert SMART
76 Dean School of Health Sciences .... Dr. William C. KOHLHEPP
61 Dean School of Law .... Ms. Jennifer BROWN
61 Associate Dean School of Law .... Mr. Neal R. FEIGENSON
60 Dean School of Communications .... Mr. Lee KAMLET
53 Dean School of Education .... Dr. Anne M. DICHELE
63 Dean School of Med & VP Health Affs .... Dr. Bruce KOEPPEN
54 Dean School of Engineering .... Dr. Justin KILE
94 Director of Women's Studies .... Dr. Jennifer SACCO

Rensselaer at Hartford (B)

275 Windsor Street, Hartford CT 06120-2991
Telephone: (860) 548-2400 FICE Identification: 002804
Accreditation: &M

† Regional accreditation is carried under the parent institution, Rensselaer Polytechnic Institute, NY.

Sacred Heart University (C)

5151 Park Avenue, Fairfield CT 06825-1000
County: Fairfield FICE Identification: 001403
Unit ID: 130253
Telephone: (203) 371-7999 Carnegie Class: Masters/L
FAX Number: (203) 365-7652 Calendar System: Semester
URL: www.sacredheart.edu
Established: 1963 Annual Undergrad Tuition & Fees: $38,300
Enrollment: 8,235 Coed
Affiliation or Control: Independent Non-Profit IRS Status: 501(c)3
Highest Offering: Doctorate
Accreditation: EH, #ARCPA, CAATE, CAEPN, CEA, NURSE, OT, PTA, @SP, SW

01 President & CEO .... Dr. John J. PETILLO
11 Sr VP Finance & Administration .... Mr. Michael J. KINNEY
05 Provost/VP Academic Affairs .... Dr. Rupendra PALIWAL
32 Sr VP Student Affairs & Athletics .... Mr. James M. BARQUINERO
15 VP Human Resources .... Mr. Robert M. HARDY
26 VP Marketing & Communication .... Mr. Michael L. IANNAZZI
88 Interim VP Mission/Catholic ID .... Fr. Anthony CIORRA
10 VP Finance .... Mr. Philip J. MCCABE
13 VP Information Tech & Security .... Mr. Michael D. TRIMBLE
111 VP University Advancement .... Mr. William REIDY
43 University General Counsel .... Mr. Michael D. LAROBINA
49 Dean College of Arts & Sciences .... Mrs. Robin CAUTIN
50 Dean College of Business .... Dr. John CHALYKOFF
76 Dean College of Health Professions .... Dr. Patricia W. WALKER
53 Interim Dean College of Education .... Dr. Thomas FORGET
66 Dean College of Nursing .... Ms. Mary Alice DONIUS
108 President University Acad Assembly .... Dr. Patrick MORRIS
07 Exec Director Undergrad Admissions .... Mr. Kevin O'SULLIVAN
06 Registrar .... Ms. Dona PERRONE

St. Vincent's College (D)

2800 Main Street, Bridgeport CT 06606-4292
County: Fairfield FICE Identification: 006191
Unit ID: 130448
Telephone: (203) 576-5235 Carnegie Class: Spec-4-yr-Other Health
FAX Number: (203) 576-5893 Calendar System: Semester
URL: www.stvincentscollege.edu
Established: 1991 Annual Undergrad Tuition & Fees: $14,870
Enrollment: 675 Coed
Affiliation or Control: Independent Non-Profit IRS Status: 501(c)3
Highest Offering: Baccalaureate
Accreditation: EH, ADNUR, NUR, RAD

01 President/CEO .... Dr. Michael GARGANO, JR.
10 Chief Financial Officer .... Mr. Christopher GIVEN
05 VP Academic Affairs/Dean of Faculty .... Vacant
13 Director MIS/Student Affairs .... Mrs. Anet SURRRUSCO
09 Institutional Researcher .... Vacant
29 Director Alumni Relations/Devel .... Vacant
84 Dir Enroll Mgmt & Financial Svcs .... Mrs. Dorothy MARTIN-HATCHER
06 Registrar .... Mr. Vincent B. CATAUDELLA
51 Director of Continuing Education .... Ms. Tatiana RAMPINO
08 Librarian .... Ms. Deborah GUERRA
66 Associate Dean of Nursing .... Dr. Maryanne DAVIDSON
88 Chair of Radiography .... Ms. Terry HINE
97 Chair of General Education .... Vacant
88 Chair of Medical Assisting .... Vacant
113 Director Student Accounts .... Mrs. Dorothy MARTIN-HATCHER
88 Chair of Healthcare Administration .... Vacant

Trinity College (E)

300 Summit Street, Hartford CT 06106-3100
County: Hartford FICE Identification: 001414
Unit ID: 130590
Telephone: (860) 297-2000 Carnegie Class: Bac-A&S
FAX Number: (860) 297-5359 Calendar System: Semester
URL: www.trincoll.edu
Established: 1823 Annual Undergrad Tuition & Fees: $52,760
Enrollment: 2,397 Coed
Affiliation or Control: Independent Non-Profit IRS Status: 501(c)3
Highest Offering: Master's
Accreditation: EH, ENG

01 President .... Dr. Joanne BERGER-SWEENEY
05 Dean of Faculty/VP Academic Affairs .... Dr. Timothy CRESSWELL
10 Vice Pres Finance/CFO .... Mr. Dan HITCHELL
13 Vice Pres Information Svcs/CIO .... Ms. Suzanne ABER
30 Vice Pres College Advancement .... Mr. Michael CASEY
32 Vice Pres Stdnt Affs/Dean Stdnts .... Mr. Joseph DICHRISTINA
84 Vice Pres Enrollment/Stdnt Success .... Dr. Angel B. PEREZ
26 VP of Marketing/Communications .... Ms. Angela SCHAEFFER
101 Secretary of the College .... Mr. Dickens MATHIEU
37 AVP/Director of Financial Aid .... Mr. Michael LIGHT
100 Chief of Staff .... Mr. Jason ROJAS
07 Director of Admissions .... Mr. Anthony T. BERRY
28 Dean Multicultural Affs/Sr Div Ofcr .... Ms. Karla SPURLOCK-EVANS
20 Associate Academic Dean .... Dr. Sonia CARDENA
20 Associate Academic Dean .... Dr. Melanie STEIN
27 Director of Media Relations .... Ms. Kathy ANDREWS
31 Community Relations Manager .... Ms. Julia RIVERA
06 Registrar .... Ms. Patricia MCGREGOR
18 Director of Facilities .... Mr. Chuck MCKAY
15 Director of Human Resources .... Ms. Beth IACAMPO
21 Director of Business Operations .... Mr. Michael ELLIOTT
21 Budget Director .... Ms. Marcia PHELAN JOHNSON
19 Director of Campus Safety .... Mr. Brian HEAVREN
44 Director of Development .... Mr. Christopher FRENCH
44 Director of Annual Giving .... Mr. William KNAPP
36 Assoc Director Career Development .... Mr. Jett MCALISTER
21 Comptroller .... Mr. Guy DRAPEAU
41 Int Director of Athletics .... Ms. Kristin NOONE
09 Director of Institutional Research .... Dr. James J. HUGHES
39 Director of Residential Life .... Ms. Susan SALISBURY
42 College Chaplain .... Rev. Allison READ
38 Director Student Counseling .... Dr. Randolph LEE
96 Director of Purchasing .... Mr. Michael S. ELLIOTT
88 Dean of Urban and Global Studies .... Dr. Xiangming CHEN
29 Director of Alumni Relations .... Mr. Steve DONOVAN
08 Head Librarian .... Ms. Janine S. KINEL
04 Administrative Asst to President .... Ms. Patrice A. LEMOINE

University of Bridgeport (F)

126 Park Avenue, Bridgeport CT 06604-5620
County: Fairfield FICE Identification: 001416
Unit ID: 128744
Telephone: (203) 576-4000 Carnegie Class: Masters/L
FAX Number: (203) 576-4653 Calendar System: Semester
URL: www.bridgeport.edu
Established: 1927 Annual Undergrad Tuition & Fees: $31,630
Enrollment: 5,433 Coed
Affiliation or Control: Independent Non-Profit IRS Status: 501(c)3
Highest Offering: Doctorate
Accreditation: EH, ACBSP, ACUP, ARCPA, ART, CHIRO, DH, ENG, MT, NATUR, NURSE

01 President .... Mr. Neil Albert SALONEN
04 Executive Assistant to President .... Ms. Joan E. FLORCZAK
05 Provost & VP for Academic Affairs .... Dr. Stephen E. HEALEY
10 VP Administration & Finance .... Dr. Susan D. WILLIAMS
88 Vice Pres International Programs .... Dr. Thomas J. WARD
30 Vice Pres for University Relations .... Mr. Robert P. COTTLE
18 VP of Facilities .... Mr. George ESTRADA
09 Exec Asst Pres Plng/Inst Research ... Ms. Barbara A. GABIANELLI
07 Associate VP for Enrollment .... Ms. Karissa L. PECKHAM
32 Dean of Students .... Ms. Edina R. OESTREICHER
08 University Librarian .... Ms. Deborah L. DULEPSKI
15 Dir Human Resources/Affirm Act Ofcr .. Dr. Melitha R. PRZYGODA
21 Controller .... Mr. Thomas A. DEBRIZZI, JR.
13 Systems Architect & CIO .... Mr. Matanya ELCHANANI
37 Director Student Financial Services .Ms. Christine E. FALZERANO
90 Director of Academic Computing .Mr. Abdelshakour A. ABUZNEID
19 Exec Director of Campus Security .... Ms. April J. VOURNELIS
38 Director of Counseling Services .... Ms. Amy L. SCEERY
06 University Registrar .... Vacant
85 Director of Intl Student Affairs .... Ms. Yumin WANG
39 Dir Housing/Res Life/Comm Standards .... Mr. Robert VASS
96 Director of Purchasing .... Ms. Jacqueline A. REEVES
35 Dir Campus Activity & Civic Engmt .... Ms. Kelli A. MEYER
12 Director of Waterbury Center .... Ms. Karen K. RINGWOOD
12 Director of Stamford Center .... Ms. Maureen L. MALONEY
29 Director Alumni Relations .... Ms. Aimee R. MARCELLA
26 Dir Public Info & Media Affairs .... Ms. Leslie H. GEARY
43 University Counsel .... Ms. Carolyn R. LINSEY
41 Athletic Director .... Mr. Anthony VITTI
107 Dean School of Professional Studies . Mr. Michael J. GIAMPAOLI
23 Director of Health Center .... Ms. Melissa H. LOPEZ
88 Director of Acupuncture Institute .... Dr. Jennifer BRETT
40 Manager of the Bookstore .... Mr. Richard HEBERT
36 Director of Career Services .... Mr. Keith HASSELL
54 VP Grad Stds/Research & Dean Engr .... Dr. Tarek M. SOBH
49 Dean Arts & Sciences .... Dr. Manyul IM
53 Dean School of Education .... Dr. Allen P. COOK
88 Dean College of Chiropractic .... Dr. Michael A. CIOLFI
88 Dean College Naturopathic Medicine .. Dr. Marcia A. PRENGUBER
50 Dean Ernest C Trefz Sch of Business .... Dr. Lloyd G. GIBSON
17 Vice President for Health Sciences .... Dr. David M. BRADY
97 Director Div of General Studies .... Dr. Edward V. GEIST
121 Director Academic Resource Center .... Ms. Roxie L. RAY
52 Dean Fones Sch of Dental Hygiene ..... Dr. Marcia H. LORENTZEN
106 Director for Distance Learning .... Mr. Kris BICKELL
24 Media Services Coordinator .... Ms. Lynn DORSEY
57 Dir Shintaro Akatsu Sch of Design .... Mr. Richard W. YELLE
88 Dir Physician Assistant Institute .... Dr. Monica LOCKWOOD
44 Director Annual Giving .... Ms. Arielle M. PURCELL

University of Connecticut (G)

352 Mansfield Road, Storrs CT 06269-1048
County: Tolland FICE Identification: 001417
Unit ID: 129020
Telephone: (860) 486-2337 Carnegie Class: DU-Highest
FAX Number: (860) 486-2627 Calendar System: Semester
URL: www.uconn.edu
Established: 1881 Annual Undergrad Tuition & Fees (In-State): $14,066
Enrollment: 27,043 Coed
Affiliation or Control: State IRS Status: 501(c)3
Highest Offering: Doctorate
Accreditation: EH, ART, AUD, CAATE, CACREP, CAEPN, CEA, CGTECH, CLPSY, CS, DIETC, DIETD, DIETI, DMOLS, ENG, IPSY, JOUR, LAW, LSAR, MFCD, MT, MUS, NURSE, PHAR, PTA, SCPSY, SP, SPAA, SW

01 President .... Susan HERBST
100 Chief of Staff .... Rachel RUBIN
05 Int Provost/Exec VP Academic Affs .... Jeremy TEITELBAUM
17 Exec VP for Health Affairs .... Andrew AGWUNOBI
10 Exec VP for Admin and CFO .... Scott JORDAN
32 Vice President for Student Affairs .... Michael GILBERT
46 Vice President for Research .... Radenka MARIC
101 Executive Secretary to the Board .... Rachel RUBIN
26 Vice Pres for Communications .... P. Tysen KENDIG
41 Director of Athletics .... David BENEDICT
43 Asst Attorney General .... Holly BRAY
43 Vice President and General Counsel .... Richard ORR
13 Vice Provost & Chief Info Officer .... Michael MUNDRANE
114 Assoc VP for Budget & Planning .... Katrina SPENCER
19 Chief of Police/Int Pub Safety Dir .... Hans RHYNHART
28 Assoc VP & Chief Diversity Officer .... Joelle MURCHISON
88 Assoc VP for Institutional Equity .... Elizabeth CONKLIN
09 Assoc VProv for Inst Rsrch & Effect .... Lloyd BLANCHARD
102 Pres Univ of Connecticut Foundation .... Joshua NEWTON
20 Vice Provost for Academic Affairs .... John VOLIN
20 Vice Provost Academic Operations .... Amy DONAHUE
84 VP Enrollment Planning & Mgmt .... Wayne LOCUST
08 Int Vice Prov for Univ Library .... Holly JEFFCOAT
12 Director Stamford Campus .... Terrence CHENG
12 Director Avery Point Campus .... Annemarie SEIFERT
12 Director Waterbury Campus .... William J. PIZZUTO
12 Interim Director Hartford Campus .... Nina ROVINELLI HELLER
92 AVProv Enrich Pgms/Dir Honors Pgms .... Jennifer LEASE BUTTS
25 AVP Research/Sponsored Pgm Svcs .... Michael GLASGOW
86 Sr Director Government Relations .... Joann LOMBARDO
86 Dir Govt Relations/Health Affairs .... Andrea KEILTY
06 Registrar .... Lauren DIGRAZIA
07 Director Undergrad Admissions .... Nathan FUERST
37 Int Director Student Financial Aid .... Wayne LOCUST

29 Asst Vice Pres Alumni Relations .... Montique COTTON KELLY
23 Exec Director Student Health Svcs .... Suzanne ONORATO
15 Director of Human Resources .... Aliza WILDER
96 Dir Procurement/Logistical Svcs .... Matthew LARSON
47 Dean Col of Agric/Natural Resources .... Gregory WEIDEMANN
50 Dean School of Business .... John ELLIOTT
53 Dean Neag School of Education .... Richard SCHWAB
54 Dean of Engineering .... Kazem KAZEROUNIAN
88 Assoc Vice Prov Excell Teach/Lrng .... Peter DIPLOCK
57 Dean of Fine Arts .... Anne D'ALLEVA
58 Vice Prov Grad Ed/Dean Grad Sch .... Kent HOLSINGER
61 Dean School of Law .... Timothy FISHER
49 Int Dean Col of Lib Arts/Sciences .... Davita SILFEN GLASSBERG
66 Dean School of Nursing .... E. Carol POLIFRONI
67 Dean School of Pharmacy .... James HALPERT
70 Dean School of Social Work .... Nina ROVINELLI HELLER
52 Dean of Dental Medicine .... R. Lamont MACNEIL
63 Dean School of Medicine .... Bruce LIANG
38 Dir Student Counslg/Mental Hlth Svc .... Elizabeth CRACCO
39 Executive Director Residential Life .... Pamela SCHIPANI
88 Deputy Chief of Staff .... Michael KIRK
88 Master Planner/Chief Architect .... Laura CRUICKSHANK
88 Vice Provost for Global Affairs .... Daniel WEINER
36 Asst VProv/Exec Dir Career Services .... James R. LOWE
121 Asst VProvost for Student Success .... Maria D. MARTINEZ
27 Director Marketing Communications .... Patricia FAZIO
88 Ombuds .... James WOHL
88 Dir Institute for Materials Science .... Steven L. SUIB
04 Executive Asst to President .... Debra MERRITT
104 Director Study Abroad .... Sarah O'LEARY
18 Assoc VP Facilities Ops & Bldg Svcs .... P. Michael JEDNAK
30 Vice President for Development .... Brian OTIS
112 Director of Planned Giving .... Gregory KNOTT
106 Dir Online Education/E-learning .... Peter DIPLOCK
88 Dir Vet Affs & Military Programs .... Alyssa KELLEHER

University of Connecticut Health Center (A)

263 Farmington Avenue, Farmington CT 06030-1827
Telephone: (860) 679-2000 FICE Identification: 009867
Accreditation: &EH, DENT, MED, PH

† Regional accreditation is carried under the parent institution in Storrs, CT.

University of Connecticut School of Law (B)

55 Elizabeth Street, Hartford CT 06105-2290
Telephone: (860) 570-5000 Identification: 770108
Accreditation: &EH, LAW

University of Hartford (C)

200 Bloomfield Avenue, West Hartford CT 06117-1599
County: Hartford FICE Identification: 001422
Unit ID: 129525
Telephone: (860) 768-4100 Carnegie Class: DU-Mod
FAX Number: (860) 768-4070 Calendar System: Semester
URL: www.hartford.edu
Established: 1877 Annual Undergrad Tuition & Fees: $37,790
Enrollment: 6,912 Coed
Affiliation or Control: Independent Non-Profit IRS Status: 501(c)3
Highest Offering: Doctorate
Accreditation: EH, ART, CAEPN, CLPSY, COARC, DANCE, ENG, ENGT, MUS, NURSE, OPE, PTA, RAD, THEA

01 President .... Dr. Gregory S. WOODWARD
05 Interim Provost .... Dr. Frederick SWEITZER
10 Vice Pres Finance & Administration .... Mr. Arosha JAYAWICKREMA
111 Int Vice Pres Institutional Advance .... Ms. Kate PENDERGAST
32 Vice Pres Student Affs/Dean Stdnts .... Dr. J. Lee PETERS
26 Vice Pres of Univ Relations .... Vacant
21 Asst Vice Pres Finance/Controller .... Ms. Laura WHITNEY
35 Asst Vice Pres Student Development .... Ms. DeLois LINDSEY
04 Senior Advisor to the President .... Ms. Susan FITZGERALD
35 Assoc Vice Pres for Student Life .... Vacant
21 Assoc Vice Pres/Treasurer .... Mr. Brett CARROLL
43 Vice Pres/Gen Counsel & Secretary .... Ms. Maria FEELEY
84 Sr Assoc Provost/Dean Enroll Mgmt .... Dr. Guy C. COLARULLI
58 Int Assoc Prov/Dean of Grad Studies .... Dr. Clark SAUNDERS
07 Dean of Admission .... Mr. Richard A. ZEISER
04 Exec Assistant to the President .... Ms. Ilena ROSENSTEIN
15 Exec Dir Human Resources & Devel .... Ms. Lisa BELANGER
08 Director University Libraries .... Ms. Randi L. ASHTON-PRITTING
37 Director Student Financial Aid .... Ms. Victoria HAMPTON
06 Registrar .... Ms. Natalie DURANT
38 Dir Counsel & Personal Development .... Mr. Nick PINKERTON
36 Director Career Center .... Mr. John KNIERING
13 Chief Information Officer .... Mr. Andrew HILLBERRY
19 Director Public Safety .... Mr. John SCHMALTZ
23 Director Health Services .... Ms. Mary NORRIS
24 Director User Services .... Mr. Sebastian SORRENTINO
25 Dir Inst Prtnrshp/Sponsored Rsrch .... Dr. Peter LISI
29 Director Alumni Relations .... Ms. Heather CORBETT
18 Assoc Vice Pres for Facilities/Mgmt .... Mr. Norman YOUNG
41 Director Athletics .... Ms. Mary Ellen GILLESPIE
104 Director International Studies ...... Ms. Nicole KURKER-STEWART
108 Dir Institutional Effectiveness .... Ms. Debra HAGEN-FOLEY
94 Director of Women's Center .... Ms. Kenna GRANT
88 Director of Judicial Process .... Ms. Kristy SEVERINO
96 Director of Purchasing .... Ms. Lisa CONDON
92 Director of University Honors .... Dr. Donald JONES
106 Asst Prov Online Lrng/Dean Univ Pgm .... Dr. R. J. MCGIVNEY
57 Dean Hartford Art School .... Dr. Nancy M. STUART
72 Dean College Engineer/Tech/Arch .... Dr. Louis MANZIONE
49 Dean College Arts & Science .... Dr. Katherine BLACK
50 Dean Barney School of Business .... Dr. Martin ROTH
53 Int Dean Col of Educ/Nurs/Hlth Prof . Dr. David H. GOLDENBERG
64 Dean Hartt School .... Ms. Elizabeth COOPER
12 Dean Hillyer College .... Dr. David H. GOLDENBERG
39 Asst Vice Pres for Residential Life .... Mr. Michael MALONE
27 Dir of Marketing/Communications .. Mr. Jonathan EASTERBROOK
102 Dir Foundation/Corporate Relations .... Ms. Keeley PATRICK
103 Dir Workforce/Career Development .... Ms. Linda SCHULTZ
112 Director Planned Giving .... Ms. Lauren PARDA

University of New Haven (D)

300 Boston Post Road, West Haven CT 06516-1916
County: New Haven FICE Identification: 001397
Unit ID: 129941
Telephone: (203) 932-7000 Carnegie Class: Masters/L
FAX Number: (203) 931-6060 Calendar System: 4/1/4
URL: www.newhaven.edu
Established: 1920 Annual Undergrad Tuition & Fees: $37,060
Enrollment: 6,786 Coed
Affiliation or Control: Independent Non-Profit IRS Status: 501(c)3
Highest Offering: Doctorate
Accreditation: EH, ART, CS, DH, DIETD, @DIETI, ENG, FEPAC

01 President .... Dr. Steven H. KAPLAN
05 Provost/Senior VP of Acad Affairs .... Dr. Daniel MAY
10 VP of Finance & Administration .... Mr. George S. SYNODI
111 VP of Advancement .... Mr. Stephen J. MORIN
84 VP of Enrollment Management .... Mr. Walter F. CAFFEY
15 VP of Human Resources .... Ms. Caroline KOZIATEK
26 VP of Marketing & Communication .... Ms. Lyn CHAMBERLIN
100 Chief of Staff & Univ Secretary .... Ms. Gayle S. TAGLIATELA
18 Associate VP for Facilities .... Mr. Louis ANNINO
20 Assoc Provost Strategic Initiatives .... Dr. Stuart SIDLE
21 Associate VP for Finance .... Mr. Patrick TORRE
13 Assoc VP for Information Technology .... Mr. Vincent P. MANGIACAPRA
32 VP Student Affairs/Dean of Students ... Ms. Rebecca D. JOHNSON
07 Assoc VP Enrollment Management .... Mr. Kevin J. PHILLIPS
41 Associate VP Athletics/Recreation .... Mr. Duane BAILEY
37 Associate VP for Financial Aid .... Ms. Karen FLYNN
88 Associate Provost Undergrad Stds .... Dr. Gordon SIMERSON
08 University Librarian .... Ms. Hanko H. DOBI
110 Associate VP for Development .... Ms. Roslyn REABACK
06 University Registrar .... Ms. Lynn KOHRN
30 Exec Dir of Advancement Operations .... Mr. Carl PITRUZZELLO
07 Senior Assoc VP of Grad Enrollment .... Ms. Shobi SIVADASAN
85 Exec Dir of International Programs .... Ms. Kathy KAUTZ
29 Director of Alumni Relations .... Ms. Jennifer PJATAK
09 Director Institutional Research .... Ms. Susan TURNER
19 Chief of University Police .... Chief Tracy MOONEY
35 Exec Dir of Student Activities .... Mr. Gregory OVEREND
96 Director of Procurement Services .... Mr. Robert STEVENS
85 Director International Admissions .... Mr. Joseph SPELLMAN
88 Dir Student Accounts/Risk Manager .... Mr. Marc MANIATIS
49 Dean College Arts & Sciences .... Dr. Lourdes ALVAREZ
50 Dean College Business .... Dr. Brian KENCH
54 Dean Tagliatela Col Engineering ...... Dr. Ronald HARICHANDRAN
88 Dean Col Crim Justice/Forensic Sci .... Dr. Mario GABOURY
103 Exec Director of Career Development ...... Mr. Matthew CAPORALE
104 Director of International Study .... Vacant
39 Associate Dean of Residential Life .... Ms. Nicole MCGRATH
108 Director of Academic Assessment .... Dr. Kristy HUNTLEY
04 President's Office Coordinator .... Ms. Jennifer FAZEKAS
91 Dir Enterprise Applications .... Mr. Todd MCINERNEY
28 Director of Myatt Ctr for Diversity .... Mr. Juan HERNANDEZ

University of Saint Joseph (E)

1678 Asylum Avenue, West Hartford CT 06117-2791
County: Hartford FICE Identification: 001409
Unit ID: 130314
Telephone: (860) 232-4571 Carnegie Class: Masters/L
FAX Number: (860) 232-6927 Calendar System: Semester
URL: www.usj.edu
Established: 1932 Annual Undergrad Tuition & Fees: $36,870
Enrollment: 2,553 Coed
Affiliation or Control: Roman Catholic IRS Status: 501(c)3
Highest Offering: Doctorate
Accreditation: EH, #ARCPA, CACREP, CAEPN, DIETD, DIETI, MFCD, NURSE, PHAR, SW

01 President .... Dr. Rhona C. FREE
05 Provost .... Dr. Michelle KALIS
10 Sr VP Finance and Strategy .... Mr. Shawn M. HARRINGTON
30 VP Inst Advancement .... Ms. Marjorie PINNEY
84 VP Enrollment Management .... Ms. Kimberly CRONE
32 VP Student Affairs/Dean of Students .... Vacant
21 Assoc VP of Finance/Controller .... Mr. William HAWKINS
15 Director of Human Resources .... Ms. Deborah SPENCER
58 Dean Sch of Grad & Prof Studies .... Dr. Daniel NUSSBAUM
67 Dean School of Pharmacy .... Dr. Joseph OFOSU
53 Dean School of Education .... Dr. Daniel NUSSBAUM
76 Dean School of Health/Nat Sci .... Dr. Raouf BOULES
79 Dean School of Humanities/Soc Sci .... Dr. Wayne STEELY
08 Librarian .... Mr. Tim SALM
06 Registrar .... Vacant
41 Dir of Athletics/AVP Student Affair .... Mr. William CARDARELLI
26 Dir of Marketing & Communications .... Ms. Diana SOUSA
18 Director of Facilities .... Mr. Andrew LEVESQUE
29 Dir of Alumni Rels/Annual Giving .... Ms. Sarah BLANCHARD
37 Director of Financial Aid .... Ms. Ashley DUTTON
36 Director Career Development Ctr .... Mr. Breton BOUDREAUX
39 Director of Residential Life .... Mr. Frank KUSTER
09 Director of Institutional Research .... Ms. Kathleen NEAL
13 Director of Info Tech (CIO) .... Mr. Joe GLEASON
19 Director of Public Safety .... Mr. Paul LOMBARDO
38 Director of Counseling & Wellness .... Dr. Meredith YUHAS
23 Director of Health Services .... Ms. Elizabeth COCOLA
04 Exec Asst to President .... Ms. Ruth FOXMAN
07 Director of Admissions .... Ms. Molly DEVER

Wesleyan University (F)

45 Wyllys Avenue, Middletown CT 06459
County: Middlesex FICE Identification: 001424
Unit ID: 130697
Telephone: (860) 685-2000 Carnegie Class: Bac-A&S
FAX Number: (860) 685-2001 Calendar System: Semester
URL: www.wesleyan.edu
Established: 1831 Annual Undergrad Tuition & Fees: $50,912
Enrollment: 3,138 Coed
Affiliation or Control: Independent Non-Profit IRS Status: 501(c)3
Highest Offering: Doctorate
Accreditation: EH

01 President .... Dr. Michael S. ROTH
05 Provost/Vice Pres Academic Affairs .... Dr. Joyce JACOBSEN
10 Vice Pres Finance/Administration .... Dr. Nathan D. PETERS
100 Vice Pres/Chief of Staff .... Mr. Andrew TANAKA
26 Vice President University Relations .... Ms. Barbara-Jan WILSON
28 Vice President for Equity and Incl .... Mr. Antonio FARIAS
32 Vice Pres of Student Affairs .... Mr. Michael J. WHALEY
13 VP Information Technology/CIO .... Dr. David BAIRD
27 Assoc VP University Relations .... Ms. Gemma F. EBSTEIN
30 Development Officer .... Mr. Stephen KIRSCHE
20 Associate Provost .... Dr. Mark HOVEY
18 Asst Vice President for Facilities .... Ms. Joyce TOPSHE
35 Asst Vice Pres/Dean of Students .... Mr. Richard CULLITON
07 Dean of Admissions & Financial Aid .... Ms. Nancy HARGRAVE MEISLAHN
58 Dir Cont Stds/Graduate Liberal Stds .... Ms. Jennifer CURRAN
06 Registrar .... Ms. Anna VAN DER BURG
08 University Librarian .... Mr. Dan CHERUBIN
09 Director of Institutional Research .... Mr. Michael E. WHITCOMB
37 Director Financial Aid .... Mr. Robert D. COUGHLIN
36 Director Career Development .... Ms. Sharon CASTONGUAY
15 Chief Human Resources Officer .... Ms. Julia HICKS
19 Director Public Safety .... Mr. Scott ROHDE
31 Dir Community Svcs/Volunteerism .... Ms. Catherine CRIMMINS LECHOWICZ
41 Director of Athletics .... Mr. Michael WHALEN
45 Director of Strategic Initiatives .... Dr. Charles G. SALAS

Yale University (G)

New Haven CT 06520
County: New Haven FICE Identification: 001426
Unit ID: 130794
Telephone: (203) 432-4771 Carnegie Class: DU-Highest
FAX Number: N/A Calendar System: Semester
URL: www.yale.edu
Established: 1701 Annual Undergrad Tuition & Fees: $49,480
Enrollment: 12,385 Coed
Affiliation or Control: Independent Non-Profit IRS Status: 501(c)3
Highest Offering: Doctorate
Accreditation: EH, ARCPA, CLPSY, ENG, IPSY, LAW, MED, MIDWF, NURSE, PAST, PH, THEOL

01 President .... Peter SALOVEY
05 Provost .... Benjamin POLAK
86 Vice Pres & Dir New Haven/State Aff .... Bruce D. ALEXANDER
32 Secretary & VP Student Affairs .... Kimberly GOFF-CREWS
10 Vice Pres Finance & CFO .... Stephen MURPHY
30 Vice President Development .... Joan E. O'NEILL
43 Vice President & General Counsel .... Alexander DREIER
15 Vice Pres/Chief HR Officer .... Janet LINDNER
46 Vice Provost of Research .... Peter SCHIFFER
20 Deputy Provost .... Emily P. BAKEMEIER
20 Deputy Prov Health Affairs and Acad .... Stephanie SPANGLER
20 Deputy Provost Academic Resources .... J. Lloyd SUTTLE
18 Assoc VP Facilities .... John H. BOLLIER
26 Vice President for Communications .... Eileen O'CONNOR
96 Assoc VP & Chief Procurement Ofcr .... John A. MAYES
102 Assoc VP/Dir Corp & Found Rels .... Patricia E. PEDERSEN
08 Univ Librarian & Deputy Provost .... Susan GIBBONS
09 Asst VP for Strategic Analysis .... Tim PAVLIS
13 Assoc VP & Chief Information Ofcr .... John BARDEN
19 Chief University Police .... Ronnell A. HIGGINS
06 University Registrar .... Vacant
07 Dean Undergraduate Admissions .... Jeremiah QUINLAN
35 Sr Assoc Dean & Dean Student Affs .... Mark SCHENKER
29 Exec Director Assoc of Yale Alumni .... Weili CHENG
37 University Director Financial Aid .... Caesar T. STORLAZZI
22 Dir Ofc Equal Opportunities .... Valarie J. STANLEY
23 Director University Health Services .... Dr. Paul GENECIN
25 Exec Dir Sponsored Projects .... Lisa MOSLEY
36 Director Career Services .... Jeanine DAMES
112 Univ Director Planned Giving .... Eileen B. DONAHUE
39 Dir Grad & Prof Student Housing ...... George E. LONGYEAR, JR.

41 Director Athletics ... Thomas A. BECKETT
42 University Chaplain ... Sharon KUGLER
85 Director Intl Students & Scholars ... Ann KUHLMAN
48 Dean of the School of Architecture ... Deborah BERKE
49 Dean of Yale College ... Marvin CHUN
50 Acting Dean School of Management ... Anjani JAIN
54 Dean School of Engineering ... Ms. T. Kyle VANDERLICK
57 Dean of the School of Art ... Marta KUZMA
58 Dean of Grad Sch Arts & Science ... Lynn COOLEY
57 Dean of the School of Drama ... James A. BUNDY
61 Dean of the Law School ... Heather GERKEN
64 Dean of the School of Music ... Robert L. BLOCKER
65 Dean Sch of Forestry & Environ Stds ... Indy BURKE
73 Dean of the Divinity School ... Gregory E. STERLING
88 Director Inst of Sacred Music ... Martin D. JEAN
63 Dean of School of Medicine ... Dr. Robert J. ALPERN
66 Dean of the School of Nursing ... Ann KURTH
69 Dean of Public Health ... Sten VERMUND
28 Chief Diversity Officer ... Deborah STANLEY-MCAULAY
104 Dean Intl & Professional Experience ... Jane EDWARDS
100 Chief of Staff ... April Joy MCGRATH

DELAWARE

Delaware College of Art and Design (A)

600 N Market Street, Wilmington DE 19801-3007
County: New Castle FICE Identification: 041398
Unit ID: 432524
Telephone: (302) 622-8000 Carnegie Class: Spec 2-yr-A&S
FAX Number: (302) 622-8870 Calendar System: Semester
URL: www.dcad.edu
Established: 1997 Annual Undergrad Tuition & Fees: $24,830
Enrollment: 153 Coed
Affiliation or Control: Independent Non-Profit IRS Status: 501(c)3
Highest Offering: Associate Degree
Accreditation: M, ART

01 Interim President ... Mr. John HAWKINS
06 Registrar ... Ms. Krista ROTHWELL
05 Interim Dean ... Ms. Krista ROTHWELL
08 Library Director ... Ms. Megan JOHNSON
13 Information Technology Coordinator ... Mr. Bates CARTER
30 Director of Development ... Ms. Renee GARNICK
37 Director Student Financial Aid ... Ms. Nicole LITTLE
32 Director of Student Services ... Mr. Jason MOKAR
26 Director of Communications ... Ms. Susan COULBY
11 Chief Administrative Officer ... Mr. Bill SCHOELL
07 Director of Admissions ... Ms. Jane CAMPBELL
108 Director Institutional Assessment ... Ms. Pamela MACPHERSON

Delaware State University (B)

1200 N DuPont Highway, Dover DE 19901-2275
County: Kent FICE Identification: 001428
Unit ID: 130934
Telephone: (302) 857-6001 Carnegie Class: Masters/M
FAX Number: (302) 857-6069 Calendar System: Semester
URL: www.desu.edu
Established: 1891 Annual Undergrad Tuition & Fees (In-State): $7,532
Enrollment: 4,288 Coed
Affiliation or Control: State IRS Status: 501(c)3
Highest Offering: Doctorate
Accreditation: M, CAEPN, @DIETC, NUR, SW

01 President ... Dr. Harry L. WILLIAMS
04 Executive Asst to the President ... Ms. Georgeann HAYWARD
05 Associate Provost ... Dr. Saundra DELAUDER
10 Sr VP & Chief Operating Officer ... Dr. Teresa HARDEE
30 VP Inst Advancement ... Dr. Vita C. PICKRUM
32 Vice Pres Student Affairs ... Dr. Stacy L. DOWNING
46 Vice President for Research ... Vacant
13 Assoc VP Information Technology ... Vacant
09 AVP Inst Research/Planning/Analysis ... Dr. Kimberly R. SUDLER
15 Vice Pres Human Resources ... Ms. Irene HAWKINS
43 General Counsel ... Mr. David SHEPPARD
18 Director of Facilities ... Vacant
06 Registrar ... Mr. Terrell HOLMES
07 Director of Admissions ... Vacant
62 Dean of Library Services ... Ms. Rebecca BATSON
37 Director of Financial Aid ... Ms. Desiree BARNES
29 Executive Director Alumni Relations ... Dr. Marcia TAYLOR
36 Director Career Services ... Vacant
19 Director of Public Safety ... Mr. Harry W. DOWNES
38 Director of Student Counseling ... Mr. Ralph ROBINSON
26 News Director ... Mr. Carlos HOLMES
41 Director of Athletics ... Mr. Louis PERKINS
44 Director Annual Giving ... Mrs. Charity SHOCKLEY
86 Director Government Relations ... Mr. Victor SANTOS

Delaware Technical Community College, George Campus (C)

300 N. Orange Street, Wilmington DE 19801
Telephone: (302) 571-5300 Identification: 770855
Accreditation: &M, ACBSP, CAHIIM, COARC, DH, DMS, MAC, OTA, PTAA

Delaware Technical Community College, Owens Campus (D)

21179 College Drive, Georgetown DE 19947-0610
Telephone: (302) 259-6000 FICE Identification: 007053
Accreditation: &M, ACBSP, ADNUR, COARC, CSHSE, DMS, ENGT, MLTAD, OTA, PNUR, PTAA, RAD

Delaware Technical Community College, Stanton Campus (E)

400 Stanton-Christiana Road, Newark DE 19713-2197
Telephone: (302) 454-3900 FICE Identification: 021449
Accreditation: &M, ACFEI, ADNUR, CSHSE, ENGT, HT, NMT, RAD

Delaware Technical Community College, Terry Campus (F)

100 Campus Drive, Dover DE 19904-1383
County: Kent FICE Identification: 011727
Unit ID: 130907
Telephone: (302) 857-1000 Carnegie Class: Assoc/HT-High Trad
FAX Number: (302) 857-1096 Calendar System: Semester
URL: www.dtcc.edu/terry
Established: 1972 Annual Undergrad Tuition & Fees (In-State): $4,607
Enrollment: 13,471 Coed
Affiliation or Control: State IRS Status: 501(c)3
Highest Offering: Baccalaureate
Accreditation: M, ACBSP, ACFEI, ADNUR, CSHSE, EMT, PNUR, SURGT

01 Vice President & Campus Director ... Dr. June S. TURANSKY
05 Dean Instruction ... Mr. John M. BUCKLEY
32 Dean Student Affairs ... Ms. Jennifer P. PIRES
04 Director Communication and Planning ... Ms. Dana L. SAWYER
103 Director Workforce Development ... Dr. Lisa STRUSOWSKI
15 Director of Human Resources ... Ms. Charlotte T. LISTER
11 Director of Administrative Services ... Mr. Ray PARSONS
10 Director Business Services ... Ms. Noelle SUGALSKI
88 Asst Director of Admin Services ... Mr. Allan NELSON
20 Assistant Dean of Instruction ... Mr. Bill J. MORROW

Goldey-Beacom College (G)

4701 Limestone Road, Wilmington DE 19808-0551
County: New Castle FICE Identification: 001429
Unit ID: 130989
Telephone: (302) 998-8814 Carnegie Class: Spec-4-yr-Bus
FAX Number: (302) 998-8631 Calendar System: Semester
URL: www.gbc.edu
Established: 1886 Annual Undergrad Tuition & Fees: $23,400
Enrollment: 1,997 Coed
Affiliation or Control: Independent Non-Profit IRS Status: 501(c)3
Highest Offering: Master's
Accreditation: M, ACBSP

01 President ... Dr. Gary L. WIRT
03 Executive Vice President ... Ms. Kristine M. SANTOMAURO
05 Vice President for Academic Affairs ... Ms. Alison Boord WHITE
10 Exec Dir of Finance/HR ... Ms. Susan M. MANNERING
32 Dean of Students ... Mr. Charles A. HAMMOND
84 Dean Enrollment Mgmt/Registrar ... Ms. Jane H. LYSLE
13 Dean of Information Technology/ACC ... Ms. Emily S. JACKSON
07 Director of Admissions ... Mr. Larry EBY
39 Director of Residence/Student Life ... Mr. Kevin MARTIN
41 Director of Athletics ... Dr. Thomas M. BRENNAN
30 Director of External Affairs ... Ms. Janine SORBELLO
18 Director of Facilities/Operations ... Mr. Meezie FOSTER
08 Director of Library/Learning Center ... Mr. Russell MICHALAK
72 Director of Information Technology ... Mr. Peter RYSAVY
09 Dir Institutional Research/Training ... Dr. Monica RYSAVY
36 Career Service Coordinator ... Ms. Elizabeth KIRKER

Irish American University (H)

404 East Savannah Road, Lewes DE 19958
County: Sussex Identification: 667120
Telephone: (302) 793-1101 Carnegie Class: Not Classified
FAX Number: (808) 334-0443 Calendar System: Semester
URL: www.acd.ie
Established: 1993 Annual Undergrad Tuition & Fees: N/A
Enrollment: N/A Coed
Affiliation or Control: Independent Non-Profit IRS Status: 501(c)3
Highest Offering: Master's
Accreditation: M

01 President/CEO ... Dr. Donald E. ROSS
03 Executive Vice President ... Mr. Christopher SARAFIAN
05 Academic Dean ... Dr. Rory MCENTERGART
30 Provost Institutional Advancement ... Mr. Joseph A. ROONEY

University of Delaware (I)

104 Hullihen Hall, Newark DE 19716
County: New Castle FICE Identification: 001431
Unit ID: 130943
Telephone: (302) 831-2000 Carnegie Class: DU-Highest
FAX Number: (302) 831-8000 Calendar System: 4/1/4
URL: www.udel.edu
Established: 1743 Annual Undergrad Tuition & Fees (In-State): $12,830
Enrollment: 22,852 Coed
Affiliation or Control: State Related IRS Status: 501(c)3
Highest Offering: Doctorate
Accreditation: M, CAATE, CAEPN, CEA, CLPSY, CSHSE, DIETD, DIETI, ENG, IPSY, MT, MUS, NURSE, PCSAS, PTA, @SP, SPAA

01 President ... Dr. Dennis ASSANIS
05 Provost ... Dr. Domenico GRASSO
03 Exec VP & Univ Treasurer ... Mr. Alan BRANGMAN
107 Senior Vice Prov Grad/Prof Educ ... Dr. Ann ARDIS
30 Interim VP Devel & Alumni Relations ... Ms. Beth BRAND
26 VP Comm & Marketing ... Mr. Glenn CARTER
13 Interim VP Information Technologies ... Mr. Jason CASH
08 Vice Prov Libraries & Museums ... Mr. Trevor A. DAWES
43 Vice Pres and General Counsel ... Ms. Laure ERGIN
101 Vice Pres & Univ Secretary ... Mr. Jeffrey W. GARLAND
28 Vice Provost for Diversity ... Dr. Carol E. HENDERSON
88 Vice Provost for Faculty Affairs ... Dr. Matt KINSERVIK
18 VP Facilities/Real Est/Aux Svcs ... Mr. Peter KRAWCHYK
84 Vice Pres Enrollment Management ... Mr. Christopher LUCIER
20 Deputy Provost Academic Affairs ... Dr. Lynn OKAGAKI
10 Vice Pres Finance/Dept Treasurer ... Mr. Gregory S. OLER
41 Dir Intercol Athletics & Rec Svcs ... Ms. Christine RAWAK
45 VP Strategic Planning & Analysis ... Ms. Mary M. REMMLER
46 VP Research/Scholarship/Innovation ... Dr. Charles RIORDAN
32 Vice Pres for Student Life ... Ms. Dawn M. THOMPSON
47 Dean Agric & Natural Resources ... Dr. Mark RIEGER
49 Dean Arts & Sciences ... Dr. George H. WATSON
50 Dean Lerner Col Business & Econ ... Dr. Bruce W. WEBER
65 Interim Dean Earth Ocean & Environ ... Dr. Mohsen BADIEY
53 Dean Educ & Human Development ... Dr. Carol VUKELICH
54 Dean Engineering ... Dr. Babatunde A. OGUNNAIKE
76 Dean Health Sciences ... Dr. Kathleen S. MATT
100 Assoc Provost & Chief of Staff ... Ms. Margaret B. BOTTORFF
51 Assoc Vice Prov Prof Cont Studies ... Dr. James K. BROOMALL
88 Assoc Prov Inst Research & Effec ... Dr. John E. SAWYER
09 Director Institutional Research ... Dr. Heather A. KELLY
108 Int Director Ctr for Educ Effectiv ... Ms. Kathleen L. PUSECKER
29 Int AVP Alumni Engagemt/Ann Giving ... Ms. Lauren M. SIMIONE
104 Director Inst for Global Studies ... Dr. Cynthia SCHMIDT-CRUZ
37 Director Student Financial Services ... Ms. Melissa STONE
36 Director Career Services ... Mr. Nathan ELTON
19 Exec Dir Campus & Public Safety ... Mr. Albert J. HOMIAK, JR.
92 Director University Honors Program ... Dr. Michael A. ARNOLD
07 Director Undergraduate Admissions ... Dr. William D. ZANDER
58 Director of Graduate Admissions ... Mr. Michael ALEXO
15 Chief Human Resources Officer ... Mr. Thomas LAPENTA
96 Manager Purchasing Services ... Mr. George WALUEFF
06 University Registrar ... Mr. Jeff L. PALMER
114 Chief Budget Officer ... Ms. Mandy MINNER
22 Dir Inst Diversity/Title IX Coord ... Dr. Susan L. GROFF
35 Dean of Students ... Dr. José-Luis RIERA
38 Director Ctr for Couns/Student Dev ... Dr. Charles L. BEALE
39 Exec Director Res Life & Housing ... Dr. Kathleen G. KERR
85 Director Intl Students & Scholars ... Mr. Ravi AMMIGAN
23 Director Student Health Services ... Dr. Timothy F. DOWLING
04 Assistant to the President ... Ms. Susan L. WILLIAMS

Wesley College (J)

120 N State Street, Dover DE 19901-3876
County: Kent FICE Identification: 001433
Unit ID: 131098
Telephone: (302) 736-2300 Carnegie Class: Bac-Diverse
FAX Number: (302) 736-2301 Calendar System: Semester
URL: www.wesley.edu
Established: 1873 Annual Undergrad Tuition & Fees: $25,646
Enrollment: 1,650 Coed
Affiliation or Control: United Methodist IRS Status: 501(c)3
Highest Offering: Master's
Accreditation: M, CAEPN, NUR

01 President ... Mr. Robert E. CLARK, II
05 Provost & VP for Academic Affairs ... Dr. Jeffrey GIBSON
10 VP Finance/COO/CFO ... Ms. Belinda BURKE
111 Vice Pres Institutional Advancement ... Mr. William PRITCHARD
84 VP of Enrollment Management ... Mr. Christopher DEARTH
32 Dean of Students ... Ms. Wanda ANDERSON
42 Dir Spiritual Life and Comm Involv ... Pastor Bonnie MULLEN
21 CPA/Controller ... Mr. James LEWIS
43 General Counsel ... Vacant
06 Registrar/Dir Student Acad Records ... Ms. Patricia SEUNARINE
12 Admin Coord DAFB ... Ms. Tracey LUNDBLAD
08 Director of Parker Library ... Ms. Martha BOYD
07 Dir of Admissions Operations ... Ms. Sue HOUSER
88 Dir of Admissions Communication ... Ms. Cassandra HYNSON
121 Ex Dir Student Success/Retention ... Ms. Christine MCDERMOTT
26 Dir Communications & Marketing ... Ms. Jessica COOK
09 Director of Institutional Research ... Ms. Jessica HANSEN
46 Data & Strat Res Specialist ... Mr. Abdul HAMEED
07 Assoc Director of Admissions ... Mr. Christopher JESTER
41 Exec Dir of Sports & Recreation ... Mr. Mike DRASS
18 Director of the Physical Plant ... Mr. Tom IDNURM
40 Director of the Bookstore ... Mr. Kris MCGLOTHIN
19 Director of Safety/Security ... Mr. Walter BEAUPRE
23 Director Student Health Services ... Dr. Jill MASER
30 Dir of Advancement Services ... Ms. Amanda DOWNES
39 Asst Dean of Students/Dir Res Life ... Vacant
35 Director of Campus Life ... Mr. Mark BERRY
37 Dir of Student Financial Planning ... Mr. Michael HALL
38 Director of Counseling Service ... Ms. Ann ROGGE
85 Director of International Programs ... Ms. Rebecca MILLER
29 Director Alumni Affairs ... Ms. Laura MAYSE
04 Assistant to the President ... Ms. Ellen COLEMAN
88 Supervisor Business Operations ... Ms. Adele FLAMM
103 Dir for Career Development ... Vacant

13 Chief Info Technology Officer (CIO) .... Mr. Paul COPELAND
15 Human Resources Director .... Ms. Heather SCHALK
104 Director Study Abroad .... Ms. Rebecca SCHRODER

Widener University Delaware Law School (A)

PO Box 7474, Wilmington DE 19803-0474
Telephone: (302) 477-2100 FICE Identification: 012962
Accreditation: &M, LAW

† Branch campus of Widener University in Pennsylvania. This listing reflects the administrators for the school of law for the Harrisburg (PA) and Delaware campuses.

Wilmington University (B)

320 N Dupont Highway, New Castle DE 19720-6491
County: New Castle FICE Identification: 007948
Unit ID: 131113
Telephone: (302) 356-4636 Carnegie Class: DU-Mod
FAX Number: (302) 328-5902 Calendar System: Trimester
URL: www.wilmu.edu
Established: 1967 Annual Undergrad Tuition & Fees: $10,670
Enrollment: 15,002 Coed
Affiliation or Control: Independent Non-Profit IRS Status: 501(c)3
Highest Offering: Doctorate
Accreditation: M, CACREP, CAEPN, IACBE, NURSE

01 President .... Dr. LaVerne T. HARMON
04 Executive Asst to President .... Ms. Donna M. QUINN
10 Senior VP/CFO Financial Affairs .... Ms. Heather A. O'CONNELL
11 Senior Vice President/COO .... Dr. Erin DIMARCO
03 University Vice President .... Ms. Carole D. PITCHER
26 Vice President External Affairs .... Dr. Peter A. BAILEY
05 Vice President Academic Affairs .... Dr. James D. WILSON, JR.
11 Vice Pres Admin & Legal Affairs .. Dr. Christian A. TROWBRIDGE
84 Vice Pres Enrollment Management .... Dr. Eileen G. DONNELLY
88 Asst Vice Pres/Dean of Locations ..... Dr. Bonnie L. KIRKPATRICK
21 Asst Vice President/Controller .... Mr. David R. LEWIS
43 Asst VP of Admin & Legal Affairs .... Mr. P. Donald HAGERMANN
27 Asst Vice Pres Public Relations .... Mr. Christopher G. PITCHER
108 Asst Vice President .... Dr. Angela C. SUCHANIC
106 Asst VP Admin Affs/Dean Online .... Dr. Sallie A. REISSMAN
32 VP Student Affairs/Alumni Rel .... Dr. Tina M. BARKSDALE
20 Asst Vice Pres Academic Affairs .... Dr. Sheila M. SHARBAUGH
19 Asst VP/University Safety/Athletic .... Dr. Jack L. CUNNINGHAM
111 VP Institutional Advancement .... Dr. Jacque R. VARSALONA
88 Asst VP Academic Support Services .... Ms. Peg P. MITCHELL
15 Chief Human Resources Officer .... Dr. Nicole ROMANO
18 Sr Director Buildings/Maintenance .... Mr. William P. QUINN
105 Sr Director of Web Communications .... Mr. Kevin G. BARRY
36 Sr Dir Career Svcs/Student Life .... Dr. Regina C. ALLEN-SHARPE
37 Sr Dir Student Financial Services .... Ms. Trudy E. HITE
88 Sr Dir University Partnership Ctr .... Dr. Stefanie A. WHITBY
44 Sr Director Annual Fund .... Ms. Gloria R. JOHNSON
06 Registrar .... Dr. Elizabeth P. JORDAN
08 Director Library .... Mr. James M. MCCLOSKEY
88 Dir Administrative Services .... Mr. Bryan E. STEINBERG
41 Director Athletics .... Ms. Linda M. ANDRZJEWSKI
07 Director of Admissions .... Ms. Laura M. MORRIS
78 Director Cooperative Learning .... Mr. David C. CAFFO
09 Director of Institutional Research .... Dr. Dana S. SANTORO
86 Director Government Relations .... Ms. Simone M. GEORGE
96 Purchasing Specialist .... Mr. Mark S. PARIS
50 Dean College of Business .... Dr. Robert W. RESCIGNO
53 Dean College of Education .... Dr. John C. GRAY
76 Dean College of Health Professions . Ms. Denise Z. WESTBROOK
49 Dean College of Arts and Sciences .... Dr. Doreen B. TURNBO
83 Dean College of Soc & Beh .... Dr. Edward L. GUTHRIE
72 Dean College of Technology .... Dr. Mary Ann K. WESTERFIELD
88 Senior Dir External Affairs .... Ms. Melanie C. BALDWIN
14 Senior Dir Information Technology .... Mr. Brian C. BEARD
120 Dir Online Learning Ed Tech .... Dr. Matthew H. DAVIS
121 Dir Student Success Center .... Ms. Sally J. HEALY
37 Director Financial Aid .... Ms. Nicole L. MCDANIEL-SMITH
88 Sr Dir Recruitment .... Mr. Robert P. MILLER
88 Dir University Information Center .... Ms. Felicia K. QUINN
88 Dir Center for Teaching Excellence .... Dr. Patricia A. RAMONE
16 Dir Human Resources .... Ms. Karen A. SHEATS
14 Sr Dir Information Technology .... Mr. Bryan E. STEINBERG
88 Sr Dir University Relations .... Mr. Bill F. SWAIN
29 Director Alumni Relations .... Mr. Stuart J. HANF

DISTRICT OF COLUMBIA

American University (C)

4400 Massachusetts Avenue, NW, Washington DC 20016
FICE Identification: 001434
Unit ID: 131159
Telephone: (202) 885-1000 Carnegie Class: DU-Higher
FAX Number: N/A Calendar System: Semester
URL: www.american.edu
Established: 1893 Annual Undergrad Tuition & Fees: $44,853
Enrollment: 13,198 Coed
Affiliation or Control: United Methodist IRS Status: 501(c)3
Highest Offering: Doctorate
Accreditation: M, CAEPN, CLPSY, IPSY, JOUR, LAW, MUS, SPAA

01 President .... Ms. Sylvia M. BURWELL
05 Provost .... Dr. Scott A. BASS
30 Vice President Development & Alumni .... Ms. Courtney SURLS
10 Vice President Finance & Treasurer ..... Mr. Douglas KUDRAVETZ
32 Interim Vice President Campus Life .... Dr. Fanta AW
43 Acting VP General Counsel .... Ms. Bethany BRIDGHAM
11 Vice Provost for Academic Admin .... Ms. Violeta ETTLE
18 Asst VP Facilities Management .... Mr. Vincent HARKINS
35 Asst Vice Pres and Dean of Students .... Dr. Robert HRADSKY
35 Asst Vice President Campus Life .... Dr. Fanta AW
108 Asst Provost Inst Rsrch/ Assessment .... Ms. Karen L. FROSLID JONES
29 Asst Vice Pres of Alumni Relations .... Ms. Raina LENNEY
21 Asst Vice President of Treasury .... Ms. Laura MCANDREW
84 Vice Provost Undergrad Enrollment .... Dr. Sharon ALSTON
13 Vice President and CIO .... Mr. David L. SWARTZ
100 Chief of Staff Office of President .... Mr. David E. TAYLOR
20 Dean Acad Affs/Sr Vice Provost .... Dr. Mary L. CLARK
58 Vice Provost Res/Dean Grad Studies ..... Dr. Jonathan G. TUBMAN
20 Vice Provost Undergrad Studies .... Dr. Jessica WATERS
49 Dean College Arts & Sciences .... Dr. Peter STARR
60 Dean Sch of Communication .... Dr. Jeffrey RUTENBECK
50 Dean Kogod Sch of Business .... Dr. John T. DELANEY
61 Dean Washington College of Law .... Dr. Camille A. NELSON
82 Interim Dean School of Intl Service .... Dr. Christine CHIN
107 Dean School of Prof & Extended Stds .... Dr. Carola WEIL
80 Int Dean School of Public Affairs .... Dr. Vicky WILKINS
15 Asst VP of Human Resources .... Ms. Beth MUHA
36 Exec Director Career Center .... Mr. Gihan FERNANDO
88 Assoc Vice Provost/Acad Admin .... Ms. Prita PATEL
26 Vice President of Communication .... Dr. Teresa (Terry) FLANNERY
06 University Registrar .... Mr. Charles (Doug) MCKENNA
08 University Librarian .... Ms. Nancy DAVENPORT
21 Controller .... Ms. Nicole BRESNAHAN
88 Dir Student Account Operations .... Mr. Darrell COOK
114 Asst VP Budget & Finance Res Ctr .... Ms. Nana AN
42 Interim University Chaplain .... Rev. Mark SCHAEFER
19 AVP Risk/Safety/Transportation .... Mr. Daniel NICHOLS
37 Asst Vice Provost Financial Aid .... Mr. Brian LEE SANG
38 Director of Counseling Center .... Dr. Traci CALLANDRILLO
96 Sr Dir Procurement and Contracts .... Mr. Brian BLAIR
07 Asst Vice Provost UG Adm .... Dr. Andrea FELDER
85 Director Intl Student/Scholar Svcs .... Ms. Senem BAKAR
92 Dir Univ Honors Program .... Dr. Christopher TUDGE
41 Director Athletics & Recreation .... Dr. William (Billy) WALKER
28 Sr Dir Ctr Diversity & Inclusion .... Ms. Tiffany SPEAKS
104 Director AU Abroad .... Ms. Sara E. DUMONT
45 Asst VP Planning/Project Mgmt .... Mr. David DOWER
88 Asst VP Univ Programs/Development .... Ms. Lee HOLSOPPLE
39 Asst VP Housing and Dining Programs .... Mr. Chris MOODY
07 Asst Vice Provost Ops/Enrollment .... Mr. Robert LINSON
04 Exec Asssistant to the President .... Ms. Margaret CLEMMER
22 Sr Dir Employee Relations/Recruitr .... Ms. Deadre JOHNSON
90 Assoc Chief Information Officer .... Ms. Kamalika SANDELL
25 Interim Dir Sponsored Programs .... Dr. Ashley ALEXANDER
09 Asst Provost Inst Res & Assessment .... Ms. Karen L. FROSLID JONES
103 Interim Dir Performance & Learning ...... Ms. Michelle FREDERICK
112 Exec Director Planned Giving .... Mr. Seth SPEYER
53 Dean School of Education .... Dr. Cheryl HOLCOMB-MCCOY
109 Asst VP External Rel/Auxiliary Svcs .... Ms. Linda ARGO
91 Director Network Operations .... Mr. Hassan MARVI

The Catholic University of America (D)

620 Michigan Avenue, NE, Washington DC 20064-0002
FICE Identification: 001437
Unit ID: 131283
Telephone: (202) 319-5100 Carnegie Class: DU-Higher
FAX Number: (202) 319-4441 Calendar System: Semester
URL: www.cua.edu
Established: 1887 Annual Undergrad Tuition & Fees: $42,536
Enrollment: 6,521 Coed
Affiliation or Control: Roman Catholic IRS Status: 501(c)3
Highest Offering: Doctorate
Accreditation: M, CAEPN, CLPSY, CS, ENG, IPSY, LAW, LIB, MUS, NURSE, SW, THEOL

01 President .... Mr. John H. GARVEY
100 VP University Rels/Chief of Staff .... Mr. Frank G. PERSICO
05 Provost .... Dr. Andrew V. ABELA
10 Vice Pres Finance & Treasurer .... Mr. Robert M. SPECTER
32 Vice President Student Affairs .... Dr. Michael S. ALLEN
84 Vice Pres Enroll Mgmt/Marketing .... Mr. Christopher P. LYDON
108 Vice Provost/Dean of Assessment .... Dr. Duilia DE MELLO
88 Vice Provost for Policy .... Ms. Lucia SILECCHIA
11 Vice Provost for Administration .... Mr. Victor NAKAS
35 Assoc VP Student Life/Dean Students ... Mr. Jonathan C. SAWYER
43 University Counsel .... Mr. Lawrence J. MORRIS
15 Assoc VP/Chief Human Resources .... Ms. Maureen BROOKBANK
18 Assoc VP Facilities Operations .... Ms. Margaret CARNEY
41 Assoc VP & Director Athletics .... Mr. Sean M. SULLIVAN
88 Executive Director for Housing .... Mr. Timothy CARNEY
30 Vice Pres for Univ Advancement .... Mr. Scott REMBOLD
44 Assoc VP Univ Advancement .... Ms. Deborah BROWN
44 Assoc VP University Advancement .... Mr. William WARREN
25 Assoc Prov Sponsored Research .... Mr. Ralph ALBANO
26 Assoc VP Marketing/Communications .. Ms. Jacquelyn MALCOLM
106 Assoc Vice Prov Online Education .... Dr. James MONAGHAN
58 Dean Graduate Studies .... Dr. J. Steven BROWN
48 Dean of Architecture .... Mr. Randall OTT
49 Dean of Arts & Sciences .... Dr. Aaron DOMINGUEZ
50 Dean School of Business/Economics .... Mr. William BOWMAN
54 Dean of Engineering .... Dr. John JUDGE
61 Dean of Law .... Mr. Daniel F. ATTRIDGE
64 Dean of Music .... Dr. Grayson WAGSTAFF
70 Dean Natl Catholic Sch Social Svcs .... Dr. William RAINFORD
66 Dean of Nursing .... Dr. Patricia MCMULLEN
73 Dean Theology/Religious Studies ...... VRev. Mark MOROZOWICH
107 Dean Metro Sch Professional Studies .... Dr. Vincent KIERNAN
79 Dean of Philosophy .... Dr. John C. MCCARTHY
88 Dean of Canon Law .... Msgr. Ronny JENKINS
07 Dean of Undergrad Admissions .Mr. James DEWEY-ROSENFELD
13 Chief Information Officer .... Mr. Matthew MCNALLY
27 Exec Director Univ Communications .... Ms. Elise ITALIANO
08 Director of Libraries .... Mr. Stephen CONNAGHAN
06 Registrar .... Ms. Julie ISHA
36 Director of Career Services .... Mr. Anthony CHIAPPETTA
29 Asst VP Alumni Relations & Univ Adv .... Ms. Kyra A. LYONS
19 Assoc VP Public Safety & Emergency .. Ms. Thomasine JOHNSON
38 Director of Counseling Center .... Dr. T. Monroe RAYBURN
23 Medical Director of Health Center .... Dr. Loretta STAUDT
37 Dir Student Financial Assistance .... Vacant
39 Assoc Dean of Students .... Ms. Heidi E. ZEICH
44 Director of the CUA Fund .... Mr. Patrick DAVEY
42 Dir Univ Campus Ministry .... Rev. Jude DEANGELO, OFM CONV
09 Assoc VP Fin Plng/Inst Res/Assess .... Mr. Brian A. JOHNSTON
88 Vice Provost & Assoc Dean Undergrad .... Dr. Lynn MAYER
96 Assoc VP for Strategic Sourcing .... Vacant
22 Title IX Coordinator/EOO .... Mr. Frank VINIK
88 Compliance and Ethics Officer .... Mr. Vincent A. LACOVARA
40 Manager Bookstore .... Mr. Brett MCMICHAEL

Chicago School of Professional Psychology-Washington DC (E)

901 15th Street NW, Washington DC 20005
Telephone: (202) 706-5000 Identification: 770493
Accreditation: &WC, CLPSY

† Branch campus of Chicago School of Professional Psychology Los Angeles Campus, Los Angeles, CA

Daniel Morgan Academy (F)

1620 L Street NW, 7th Floor, Washington DC 20036
Identification: 667304
Telephone: (202) 759-4988 Carnegie Class: Not Classified
FAX Number: (202) 759-0908 Calendar System: Semester
URL: dmgs.org
Established: 2014 Annual Graduate Tuition & Fees: N/A
Enrollment: N/A Coed
Affiliation or Control: Independent Non-Profit IRS Status: 501(c)3
Highest Offering: Master's; No Undergraduates
Accreditation: @M

Educatore School of Education (G)

1701 K Street NW, Ste 250, Washington DC 20036
Identification: 667305
Telephone: (844) 283-2246 Carnegie Class: Not Classified
FAX Number: N/A Calendar System: Other
URL: teach-now.com
Established: 2012 Annual Graduate Tuition & Fees: N/A
Enrollment: N/A Coed
Affiliation or Control: Proprietary IRS Status: Proprietary
Highest Offering: Master's; No Undergraduates
Accreditation: DEAC

01 President .... Dr. Philip A. SCHMIDT
05 Chief Academic Officer .... Dr. Donna A. GOLLNICK
10 Chief Financial Officer .... Mr. Richard FEISTRITZER

Gallaudet University (H)

800 Florida Avenue, NE, Washington DC 20002-3695
FICE Identification: 001443
Unit ID: 131450
Telephone: (202) 651-5000 Carnegie Class: Masters/M
FAX Number: (202) 651-5508 Calendar System: Semester
URL: www.gallaudet.edu
Established: 1864 Annual Undergrad Tuition & Fees: $16,078
Enrollment: 1,477 Coed
Affiliation or Control: Independent Non-Profit IRS Status: 501(c)3
Highest Offering: Doctorate
Accreditation: M, ACBSP, AUD, CACREP, CAEPN, CEA, CLPSY, SP, SW

01 President .... Ms. Roberta (Bobbi) CORDANO
05 Provost .... Dr. Carol J. ERTING
10 Vice Pres Admin & Finance .... Mr. Paul KELLY
30 Vice Pres Dev & Alumni Relations .... Mr. Paul JULIN
28 VP for Diversity/Equity/Inclusion .... Dr. Elavie NDURA
12 Int Chf Admin Ofcr LClerc Natl Ctr .... Ms. Nicole SUTCLIFFE
20 Int CAO Laurent Clerc Natl Ctr .... Ms. Marianne BELSKY
11 Asst Vice Pres Administration .... Mr. Fred WEINER
101 Spec Asst to Pres/Board Liaison .... Ms. Rita JENOURE
100 Chief of Staff President .... Ms. Heather HARKER
09 Exec Dir Strategic Planning .... Ms. Susan JACOBY
53 Int Dean Sch Educ/Bus/Human Svcs .... Dr. Khadijat RASHID
58 Dean Graduate School .... Dr. Guarav MATHUR
32 Dean Student Affs/Academic Support .... Mr. Dwight BENEDICT
49 Dean College Arts & Sciences .... Dr. Genie GERTZ
121 Assoc Prov Stdnt Succ/Acad Quality .... Dr. Thomas HOREJES
21 Executive Director Finance .... Ms. Jean CIBUZAR
96 Exec Dir Business Support Services .... Mr. Gary ALLER
18 Director Facilities .... Mr. Amon BROWN
112 Dir Major Gifts .... Mr. David REEKERS
26 Dir Communications .... Ms. Kaitlin LUNA

09 Director Institutional Research ... Ms. Lindsay BUCHKO
29 Exec Director Alumni Relations ... Mr. Samuel SONNENSTRAHL
15 Director Human Resources Svcs ... Ms. Christina SHEN-AUSTIN
13 Exec Director Technology Services ... Mr. Earl PARKS
14 Dir Enterprise Info Systems ... Mr. James KING
08 Director Library Public Services ... Ms. Sarah HAMRICK
88 University Ombuds ... Ms. Elizabeth STONE
08 Dir Library Deaf Collection/Archive ... Mr. Michael OLSON
22 Director Equal Opportunity Programs ... Ms. Sharrell MCCASKILL
06 Registrar ... Ms. Elice PATTERSON
07 Director of Admissions ... Mr. Young Hae PARK
37 Director Student Financial Aid ... Ms. Shondra DICKSON

George Washington University (A)

2121 I Street, NW, Washington DC 20052-0002
FICE Identification: 001444
Unit ID: 131469
Telephone: (202) 994-1000 Carnegie Class: DU-Highest
FAX Number: (202) 994-0458 Calendar System: Semester
URL: www.gwu.edu
Established: 1821 Annual Undergrad Tuition & Fees: $51,950
Enrollment: 26,212 Coed
Affiliation or Control: Independent Non-Profit IRS Status: 501(c)3
Highest Offering: Doctorate
Accreditation: M, ARCPA, ART, CACREP, CAEPN, CIDA, CLPSY, CS, ENG, #FEPAC, HSA, IPSY, LAW, MED, MT, NURSE, PH, PTA, SP, SPAA

01 President ... Dr. Thomas J. LEBLANC
100 Chief of Staff President's Office ... Vacant
05 Provost & Exec VP Academic Affairs ... Dr. Forrest MALTZMAN
30 Vice Pres for Dev/Alumni Relations ... Mr. Aristide J. COLLINS
10 Exec Vice President & Treasurer ... Mr. Louis H. KATZ
43 Senior Vice Pres & General Counsel ... Ms. Beth NOLAN
26 Vice President External Relations ... Ms. Lorraine A. VOLES
20 Deputy Provost Academic Affairs ... Dr. Teresa MURPHY
84 Vice Provost for Enrollment Mgmt ... Ms. Laurie KOEHLER
114 Vice Provost of Budget and Finance ... Ms. Rene S. O'NEAL
28 Vice Provost Diversity & Inclusion ... Ms. Caroline LAGUERRE-BROWN
88 Sen Assoc Prov for Intl Strategy ... Dr. Douglas B. SHAW
15 Int Chief Human Resources Officer ... Mr. Dale A. MCLEOD
13 Chief Information Officer ... Ms. Loretta EARLY
20 Vice Provost Faculty Affairs ... Dr. Christopher A. BRACEY
11 Senior Assoc VP of Operations ... Ms. Alicia M. O'NEIL KNIGHT
32 Senior Assoc VP & Dean of Students ... Dr. Peter A. KONWERSKI
89 Assoc VP & Dean of Freshmen . Ms. Helen CANNADAY SAULNY
90 Assoc VP for Acad Technologies ... Ms. P. B. GARRETT
88 Assoc VP of Acad Plng & Assessment ... Dr. Cheryl BEIL
46 Vice President for Research ... Dr. Leo M. CHALUPA
88 AVP Budget & Financial Mgmt ... Ms. Stella G. APEKEY
21 University Comptroller ... Ms. Sharon HEINLE
09 Director Inst Research & Planning ... Mr. Joachim W. KNOP
86 Asst VP Government Relations ... Ms. Renee MCPHATTER
104 Associate VP for International Pgms ... Dr. Donna SCARBORO
08 University Librarian ... Ms. Geneva HENRY
27 Asst VP for Communications ... Ms. Sarah GEGENHEIMER BALDASSARO
27 Interim Exec Dir of Media Relations ... Ms. Maralee B. CSELLAR
29 Sr Associate VP Development ... Mr. David B. ANDERSON
06 Registrar ... Ms. Elizabeth A. AMUNDSON
07 Director of Undergrad Admissions ... Dr. Costas SOLOMOU
38 Director Counseling Center ... Vacant
37 Assoc VP & Director Financial Aid ... Mr. Daniel E. SMALL
36 Asst Provost Career Center ... Ms. Rachel A. BROWN
85 Director International Services ... Ms. Jennifer H. DONAGHUE
19 Sr Assoc VP Safety & Security ... Mr. Darrell L. DARNELL
22 Dir EEO & Affirmative Action ... Ms. Vickie FAIR
23 Director Student Health Services ... Dr. Isabel GOLDENBERG
40 Director GW Bookstore ... Ms. Janet F. UZZELL
107 Dean Col of Professional Studies ... Dr. Ali ESKANDARIAN
49 Dean Columbian Col Arts/Sciences ... Dr. Ben VINSON
63 Dean Medicine & Health Sciences ... Dr. Jeffrey S. AKMAN
69 Dean School of Public Health ... Dr. Lynn R. GOLDMAN
61 Dean Law School ... Dr. Blake D. MORANT
54 Dean Engineer/Applied Science ... Dr. David DOLLING
53 Dean Education/Human Development ... Dr. Michael J. FEUER
50 Interim Dean School of Business ... Dr. Vivek CHOUDHURY
82 Dean Elliott School Intl Affairs ... Dr. Reuben E. BRIGETY
66 Dean School of Nursing ... Dr. Pamela R. JEFFRIES
12 Dean GW Virginia Sci/Tech Campus ... Dr. Ali ESKANDARIAN
41 Director Athletics/Recreation ... Mr. Patrick NERO
92 Director University Honors Program ... Dr. Maria H. FRAWLEY
93 Director Multicultural Student Svc ... Mr. Michael R. TAPSCOTT
39 Director Student Housing ... Mr. Seth D. WEINSHEL

Georgetown University (B)

37th & O Streets, NW, Washington DC 20057-1947
FICE Identification: 001445
Unit ID: 131496
Telephone: (202) 687-0100 Carnegie Class: DU-Highest
FAX Number: N/A Calendar System: Semester
URL: www.georgetown.edu
Established: 1789 Annual Undergrad Tuition & Fees: $50,547
Enrollment: 18,459 Coed
Affiliation or Control: Roman Catholic IRS Status: 501(c)3
Highest Offering: Doctorate
Accreditation: M, ANEST, CEA, HSA, LAW, MED, MIDWF, NURSE, PAST

01 President ... Dr. John (Jack) J. DEGIOIA
46 Sr VP Research/Chief Technology Off ... Dr. Spiros DIMOLITSAS
101 Secretary of the University ... Mr. Edward M. QUINN
100 Chief of Staff ... Mr. Joseph FERRARA
05 Provost ... Dr. Robert M. GROVES
17 Exec Vice Pres Health Sciences ... Dr. Edward B. HEALTON
61 Exec Vice Pres/Dean of Law School ... Dr. William M. TREANOR
30 Vice Pres for Advancement ... Mr. R. Bartley MOORE
42 Vice Pres for Mission and Ministry ... Rev. Mark BOSCO, SJ
10 Vice Pres Finance & Univ Treasurer ... Mr. David RUBENSTEIN
13 Interim Vice Pres/CIO ... Mr. Judd NICHOLSON
15 VP Human Resources ... Ms. Brenda R. MALONE
26 VP Public Affairs & Strategic Dev ... Mr. Erik SMULSON
27 Assoc VP Communications ... Vacant
18 VP Planning & Facilities Mgmt ... Mr. Robin MOREY
32 VP Student Affairs ... Dr. Todd OLSON
28 VP for Inst Diversity & Equity ... Ms. Rosemary KILKENNY
19 Chief of Police Dept Public Safety ... Mr. Jay GRUBER
43 VP & General Counsel ... Ms. Lisa M. BROWN
88 VP for Global Engagement ... Dr. Thomas BANCHOFF
11 VP & COO Main Campus ... Mr. Darryl E. CHRISTMON
29 Associate VP Alumni Relations ... Mr. William G. REYNOLDS
109 Assoc VP for Auxiliary Services ... Ms. Joelle D. WIESE
118 Assc VP Benefits/Chief Benefits Off ... Mr. Charles E. DESANTIS
90 AVP Acad Sys/Chief Enterprise Arch ... Ms. Beth BERGSMARK
20 Vice Provost Education ... Dr. Randall BASS
88 Vice Provost Research ... Dr. Janet MANN
20 Vice Provost Faculty ... Dr. Reena AGGARWAL
21 Assoc Vice President for Operations ... Ms. Christina ROBERTS
114 Asst VP Finance Planning & Budget ... Mr. Matthew C. GREAVES
06 Assoc VP & University Registrar ... Ms. Annamarie BIANCO
07 Dean Undergraduate Admissions ... Mr. Charles A. DEACON
35 Assoc VP Student Affairs ... Dr. Jeanne F. LORD
23 Asst VP for Student Health ... Dr. Vince C. WINKLERPRINS
08 University Librarian ... Ms. Artemis G. KIRK
88 Ex Dir Ctr New Designs Lrng/Schlrs ... Dr. Edward J. MALONEY
37 Dean Student Financial Svcs ... Ms. Patricia A. MCWADE
25 Senior Research Compliance Officer ... Ms. Mary E. SCHMIEDEL
49 Dean Georgetown College ... Dr. Christopher CELENZA
82 Dean School Foreign Service ... Dr. Joel HELLMAN
50 Dean School of Business ... Dr. Paul A. ALMEIDA
63 Dean Medical School ... Dr. Edward B. HEALTON
66 Dean Sch of Nurs/Health Stds ... Dr. Patricia CLOONAN
51 Dean Continuing Studies ... Dr. Kelly OTTER
58 Dean of Grad School ... Dr. Norberto M. GRZYWACZ
80 Dean McCourt School Public Policy ... Dr. Michael A. BAILEY
86 Asst to President Federal Relations ... Mr. Scott S. FLEMING
31 Director Partnerships & Cmty Engage ... Ms. Brenda ATKINSON-WILLOUGHBY
96 Asst VP Procurement ... Mr. O.T WELLS
85 Director of Global Services ... Ms. Vanessa MEYERS
104 Director of Global Education ... Mr. Craig RINKER
36 Exec Director Career Center ... Dr. Mike SCHAUB
22 Director Affirmative Action Pgm ... Mr. Michael W. SMITH
24 Exec Dir Classroom Educ/Tech Svcs ... Mr. Mark J. COHEN
38 Director Counseling Center ... Dr. Philip W. MEILMAN
41 Director Athletics ... Mr. Lee REED
39 Director of Residence Life ... Ms. Stephanie J. LYNCH
108 Asst Dir CNDLS/Assessment ... Ms. Mindy MCWILLIAMS
102 Dir Found & Corp Relations ... Ms. Carma FAUNTLEROY
112 Exec Director Gift Planning ... Mr. Stephen LINK

Howard University (C)

2400 Sixth Street, NW, Washington DC 20059-0001
FICE Identification: 001448
Unit ID: 131520
Telephone: (202) 806-6100 Carnegie Class: DU-Higher
FAX Number: (202) 806-5934 Calendar System: Semester
URL: www.howard.edu
Established: 1867 Annual Undergrad Tuition & Fees: $24,908
Enrollment: 10,002 Coed
Affiliation or Control: Independent Non-Profit IRS Status: 501(c)3
Highest Offering: Doctorate
Accreditation: M, #ARCPA, ART, CAEPN, CLPSY, COPSY, CS, DENT, DH, DIETC, ENG, IPSY, JOUR, LAW, MED, MT, MUS, NURSE, OT, PHAR, PTA, RTT, SP, SW, THEA, THEOL

01 President ... Dr. Wayne FREDERICK
05 Provost/Chief Academic Officer ... Dr. Anthony K. WUTOH
101 Interim Secretary of University ... Ms. Florence PRIOLEAU
43 General Counsel ... Ms. Florence PRIOLEAU
10 Chief Financial Officer ... Mr. Michael MASCH
26 Vice President for External Affairs ... Ms. Gracia HILLMAN
15 VP for Human Resources ... Ms. Carrolyn J. BOSTICK
30 Vice President Development ... Mr. David P. BENNETT
17 CEO University Hospital ... Mr. James DICGEL
46 Assoc Provost Research & Graduates ... Dr. Gary L. HARRIS
20 Associate Provost ... Dr. Joseph P. REIDY
20 Assoc Provost Undergraduate Studies ... Dr. Melanie CARTER
32 Vice President Student Affairs ... Mr. Kenneth M. HOLMES
88 AVP Regulatory/Research Compliance .. Dr. Thomas O. OBISESAN
88 AVP for Research and Faculty ... Dr. Kristy F. WOODS
13 Chief Information Officer ... Mr. Rick WATTS
100 Chief of Staff ... Ms. LaRue BARKWELL
58 Dean Graduate School ... Dr. Gary L. HARRIS
49 Dean College Arts/Sciences ... Dr. Bernard A. MAIR
50 Dean School of Business ... Dr. Barron H. HARVEY
61 Dean School of Law ... Ms. Danielle R. HOLLEY-WALKER
63 Dean Medicine/VP Clinical Affairs ... Dr. Hugh E. MIGHTY
52 Dean College of Dentistry ... Dr. Dexter A. WOODS
54 Dean Col Engr/Arch/Comp Sc ... Dr. Achille MESSAC
53 Interim Dean School of Education ... Dr. Dawn WILLIAMS
60 Dean School Communications ... Dr. Gracie LAWSON-BORDERS
88 Int Dean Nursing/Allied Hlth Sc ... Dr. Mary HILL
70 Dean School of Social Work ... Dr. Sandra CREWE
73 Dean School of Divinity ... Dr. Yolanda PIERCE
67 Dean School of Pharmacy ... Dr. Toyin TOFADE
48 Director School of Architecture ... Prof. Hazel EDWARDS
76 Assoc Dean/Div Allied Health Sci ... Dr. Shirley J. JACKSON
66 Assoc Dean/Div of Nursing ... Ms. Tammi L. DAMAS
57 Assoc Dean/Division of Fine Arts ... Dr. Gwendolyn H. EVERETT
81 Assoc Dean/Div Natural Sciences ... Dr. Robert CATCHINGS
83 Interim Assoc Dean/Social Sciences ... Dr. Terri ADAMS
79 Associate Dean Humanities ... Dr. James J. DAVIS
23 Associate VP for Clinical Affairs ... Dr. Hugh E. MIGHTY
06 Registrar ... Ms. LaTrice BYAM
37 Director Financial Aid ... Vacant
07 Director of Admissions ... Ms. Latrice BYAM
42 Dean Andrew Rankin Chapel ... Dr. Bernard L. RICHARDSON
35 Dean Student Life & Activities ... Vacant
39 Dean of Residence Life ... Mr. Wilson T. BLAND
36 Director Career Services Office ... Dr. Joan M. BROWNE
08 Executive Director Libraries ... Ms. Rhea BALLARD-THROWER
88 Director Health Sciences Library ... Ms. Fatima BARNES
88 Interim Director Law Library ... Ms. Eileen SANTOS
24 Dir Teaching Learning & Assmnt Ctr ... Dr. Helen BOND
16 Senior Director Human Resources ... Mr. Michael MCFADDEN
22 Dir Equal Employment Opportunity ... Mr. Antwan LOFTON
30 Director for Advancement Services ... Mr. David P. BENNETT
29 Senior Director Alumni Relations ... Mr. Charles GIBBS
44 Principal Gift Officer ... Mr. Ken ASHWORTH
27 AVP of External Affairs ... Ms. Cynthia BROCK-SMITH
18 AVP Facilities ... Vacant
88 Director Campus Planning ... Mr. Derrek NIEC-WILLIAMS
19 Chief of Campus Police ... Mr. Alonzo F. JOY
31 Director HU Community Association ... Ms. Maybelle T. BENNETT
109 Director Auxiliary Enterprises ... Mr. Antwan D. CLINTON
92 Director of Honors Program ... Dr. Daniel A. WILLIAMS, III
41 Athletics Director ... Mr. Kery DAVIS
23 Director Student Health Center ... Dr. David BOWMAN
40 Gen Manager Barnes & Noble at HU ... Mr. Alex BAMFO
94 Director of Women's Studies ... Vacant
18 Director Physical Facilities ... Mr. Victor MCNAUGHTON
108 Director Institutional Assessment ... Dr. Gerunda B. HUGHES
88 Director Events & Protocol ... Mr. Andrew RIVERS

The Institute of World Politics (D)

1521 16th Street, NW, Washington DC 20036-1464
FICE Identification: 041144
Unit ID: 455804
Telephone: (202) 462-2101 Carnegie Class: Spec-4-yr-Other
FAX Number: (202) 464-0335 Calendar System: Semester
URL: www.iwp.edu
Established: 1990 Annual Graduate Tuition & Fees: N/A
Enrollment: 107 Coed
Affiliation or Control: Independent Non-Profit IRS Status: 501(c)3
Highest Offering: Master's; No Undergraduates
Accreditation: M

01 President ... Dr. John LENCZOWSKI
03 Executive Vice President ... Lawrence COSGRIFF
05 Academic Dean ... Dr. MacKubin OWENS
10 Chief Financial Officer ... Elaine PINDER
120 SVP Cyber Intelligence Init ... Dean LANE
88 SVP Professional Affiliations ... CAPT. Chris GLASS
111 VP Institutional Advancement ... Tom ATWOOD
32 VP Student Affairs and Admissions ... Jason JOHNSRUD
06 Registrar & Institutional Research ... Hasanna BENSON-TYUS
84 Director Student Recruitment ... Tim STEBBINS
29 Alumni/Communications Officer ... Katie BRIDGES
36 Director Career Services ... Derrick DORTCH
37 Director Financial Aid ... Thelbert SNOWDEN
26 Director Marketing and Comm ... MaryAnne GARNER
08 Library Manager ... Dmitry KULIK

Inter-American Defense College (E)

210 B Street SW, Bldg 52, Ft McNair,
Washington DC 20319-5008
Identification: 667275
Telephone: (202) 646-1337 Carnegie Class: Not Classified
FAX Number: N/A Calendar System: Semester
URL: www.colegio-id.org
Established: 1962 Annual Graduate Tuition & Fees: N/A
Enrollment: N/A Coed
Affiliation or Control: Independent Non-Profit IRS Status: 501(c)3
Highest Offering: Master's; No Undergraduates
Accreditation: ACICS

01 Director ... RAdm. Martha HERB
05 Chief of Studies ... BGen. Arturo GONZALEZ
03 Vice Director ... MjGen. Rolemberg CUNHA
06 Registrar ... Ms. Laura SÁ FREIRE

Pontifical Faculty of the Immaculate Conception at the Dominican House of Studies (F)

487 Michigan Avenue, NE, Washington DC 20017-1585
FICE Identification: 012803
Unit ID: 131405
Telephone: (202) 495-3820 Carnegie Class: Spec-4-yr-Faith
FAX Number: (202) 495-3873 Calendar System: Semester
URL: www.dhs.edu
Established: 1902 Annual Graduate Tuition & Fees: N/A
Enrollment: 90 Coed

Affiliation or Control: Roman Catholic IRS Status: 501(c)3
Highest Offering: Master's; No Undergraduates
Accreditation: M, THEOL

01 President .... Fr. John LANGLOIS, OP
05 Vice President/Academic Dean .... Fr. Thomas PETRI, OP
20 Secretary of Studies .... Fr. Brian CHRZASTEK, OP
08 Librarian .... Fr. John Martin RUIZ, OP
18 Director of Facilities .... Ms. Shauna ROYE
42 Chaplain to Commuter Students .... Fr. Aquinas GUILBEAU, OP
06 Registrar .... Fr. Albert TRUDEL, OP
10 Treasurer/Director of Financial Aid .... Ms. Shauna ROYE
30 Assistant Director of Advancement .... Mr. George CERVANTES
13 IT Director .... Mr. Carlos MOLINA
36 Director of Career Placement .... Dr. Jem SULLIVAN
04 Executive Assistant .... Mrs. Patricia WORK
88 Administrative Secretary .... Ms. Sharon SMITH

Pontifical John Paul II Institute for Studies on Marriage and Family (A)

620 Michigan Ave, NE, McGivney Hall,
Washington DC 20064

FICE Identification: 041427
Unit ID: 455813
Telephone: (202) 526-3799 Carnegie Class: Spec-4-yr-Faith
FAX Number: (202) 269-6090 Calendar System: Other
URL: www.johnpaulii.edu
Established: 1988 Annual Graduate Tuition & Fees: N/A
Enrollment: 65 Coed
Affiliation or Control: Roman Catholic IRS Status: 501(c)3
Highest Offering: Doctorate; No Undergraduates
Accreditation: M

01 President .... RevMsg. Pierangelo SEQUERI
03 Vice President .... Carl A. ANDERSON
05 Provost/Dean .... Fr. Antonio LOPEZ
20 Associate Dean for Academic Affairs .... David S. CRAWFORD
11 Assoc Dean Progams & Administration .... Nick J. BAGILEO
07 Director of Admissions .... Sara L. TRUDEAU

† Affiliated with The Catholic University of America, DC.

Strayer University (B)

1133 15th Street, NW, Washington DC 20005-2710

FICE Identification: 001459
Unit ID: 131803
Telephone: (202) 408-2400 Carnegie Class: Masters/M
FAX Number: (202) 419-1423 Calendar System: Quarter
URL: www.strayer.edu
Established: 1892 Annual Undergrad Tuition & Fees: $12,975
Enrollment: 1,203 Coed
Affiliation or Control: Proprietary IRS Status: Proprietary
Highest Offering: Master's
Accreditation: M, ACBSP, CAEPT, NURSE

01 President .... Mr. Brian W. JONES
05 Provost/Chief Academic Ofcr .... Dr. Andrea BACKMAN
20 Vice Provost of Academics/Faculty .... Ms. Lily GARCIA
32 Senior Vice Provost Student Affairs .... Ms. Chandra QUAYE
08 University Librarian .... Mr. David A. MOULTON
06 University Registrar .... Mr. Alan SMITH
106 Global Online Campus Dean .... Vacant
20 Chamblee Campus Dean .... Mr. Ross BOGASH
12 Chamblee Campus Director .... Mr. Richard WYLIE
20 Chesterfield Campus Dean .... Dr. Carol WILLIAMS
20 Newport News Campus Dean .... Mr. Terrell MASON
12 Chesterfield Campus Director .... Ms. Amy BREEDEN
12 Newport News Campus Director .... Mr. Ryan ALLEN
20 North Charlotte Campus Dean .... Dr. Jeffrey ROMANCZUK
12 North Charlotte Campus Director .... Ms. Christine VITO
20 Owings Mills Campus Dean .... Ms. Latoya HALE
12 Owings Mills Campus Director .... Ms. Oleida WILLIAMS
20 Roswell Campus Dean .... Ms. Donna KILGORE LY
12 Roswell Campus Director .... Mr. Travis NORRIS
20 Shelby Oaks Campus Dean .... Dr. Clinton MILLER
12 Shelby Oaks Campus Director .... Mr. Sam THOMAS
20 Maitland Assoc Campus Dean .... Ms. Sunshine JINGOZIAN
20 Prince Georges Campus Dean .... Ms. Shanee MAJOR-KELLY
12 Prince Georges Campus Director .... Ms. Candy COLLINS
20 Research Triangle Park Campus Dean .... Dr. William DENNING
12 Research Triangle Park Campus Dir .... Mr. Pashuan ARMOND
20 Rockville Campus Dean .... Mr. Steve HARRIS
12 Rockville Campus Director .... Ms. Tamara DORSEY
20 South Charlotte Campus Dean .... Dr. Miranda CARLTON-CAREW
12 South Charlotte Campus Director .... Ms. Janet BEAMER
20 Virginia Beach Campus Dean .... Ms. Ashley CASTLE
12 Virginia Beach Campus Director .... Mr. Tom LOTITO
12 Maitland Campus Director .... Ms. Ann POHIRA VIETH
12 Takoma Park Campus Director .... Ms. Carolene BLOOMFIELD
20 Takoma Park Campus Dean .... Dr. Twila LINDSAY
20 Tampa East Campus Dean .... Ms. DeNeen ATTORD
12 Tampa East Campus Director .... Mr. Jeffrey KEITH
20 Tampa Westshore Campus Dean .... Ms. DeNeen ATTORD
12 Tampa Westshore Campus Director .... Mr. Jeffrey KEITH
20 Woodbridge Campus Dean .... Dr. Ras ACOLASTE
12 Woodbridge Campus Director .... Mr. Haroon MOKEL
12 Thousand Oakes Campus Director .... Ms. Nedra BROWN
20 Thousand Oaks Campus Dean .... Dr. William CARMICHAEL
20 Miramar Campus Assoc Dean .... Mr. B. Nate SMITH
20 Washington Campus Dean .... Dr. Richelle RESTO
12 Washington Campus Director .... Mr. D'Andre WILSON
20 White Marsh Campus Dean .... Ms. Tafadzwa NHIRA
12 White Marsh Campus Director .... Mr. Leator KNUCKLES
20 Arlington Campus Dean .... Dr. Isaac MOONZWE
12 Arlington Campus Director .... Ms. Breanne WINTER
20 Alexandria Campus Dean .... Dr. Angela AGBOLI-ESEDEBE
12 Alexandria Campus Director .... Ms. Cardene BLOOMFIELD
20 Center City Campus Dean .... Dr. R. Renee THOMPSON
12 Center City Campus Director .... Mr. Isaac WALTERS
12 Miramar Campus Director .... Ms. Trish ADIA
20 Anne Arundel Campus Dean .... Ms. Aerin GILBERT
12 Anne Arundel Campus Director .... Ms. Cristen JONES
12 Birmingham Campus Director .... Ms. Kendra GOODE
20 Birmingham Campus Dean .... Mr. Keith JOHNSON
20 Chesapeake Campus Dean .... Ms. Ashley CASTLE
12 Chesapeake Campus Director .... Ms. Jeanne POINDEXTER
20 Huntsville Assoc Campus Dean .... Mr. Dustin VICK
12 Huntsville Campus Director .... Ms. Julie PRYOR
20 Little Rock Campus Dean .... Dr. Elizabeth DELONE
12 Little Rock Campus Director .... Ms. Angela MILLER
20 Orlando East Assoc Campus Dean .... Ms. Sunshine JINGOZIAN
20 Baymeadows Assoc Campus Dean .... Ms. Sarah FRADEN
12 Baymeadows Campus Director .... Ms. Kristina HILLIARD
12 Orlando East Campus Director .... Ms. Kristin HILLIARD
20 Palm Beach Gardens Campus Dean .... Dr. Joann RAPHAEL
12 Palm Beach Gardens Campus Director .... Ms. Trish ADIA
20 Ft. Lauderdale Assoc Campus Dean .... Mr. Nate SMITH
12 Ft. Lauderdale Campus Director .... Mr. Geoffrey RAMGOLAM
20 Sand Lake Assoc Campus Dean .... Ms. Sunshine JINGOZIAN
12 Sand Lake Campus Director .... Ms. Ann POHIRA VIETH
20 Augusta Campus Dean .... Dr. Lezlie BANKS
12 Augusta Campus Director .... Mr. Louis DAVIS
20 Columbus GA Campus Dean .... Dr. Stephani DUNSTON
12 Columbus GA Campus Director .... Ms. Georgette CURRY
20 Douglasville Campus Dean .... Dr. A. Fitzgerald JONES
12 Douglasville Campus Director .... Ms. Tracey MARTIN
20 Lithonia Campus Dean .... Dr. Tonya MOORE
12 Lithonia Campus Director .... Mr. Paul LAWSON
20 Savannah Campus Dean .... Dr. Denise OGDEN
12 Savannah Campus Director .... Mr. Paul LAWSON
20 Christiana Campus Dean .... Dr. R. Renee THOMPSON
20 Jackson Campus Dean .... Dr. Dana EVANS
12 Jackson Campus Director .... Ms. Angela MILLER
20 Cherry Hill Campus Dean .... Dr. R. Renee THOMPSON
12 Cherry Hill Campus Director .... Ms. Mary Kate HODOWANEC
20 Piscataway Campus Dean .... Mr. Khioverny DUARTE
12 Piscataway Campus Director .... Mr. Roger GASPAR
20 Warrendale Campus Director .... Ms. Amy CESTONE
20 Warrendale Campus Dean .... Mr. Timothy GRIFFIN
20 Willingboro Assoc Campus Dean .... Mr. Khioverny DUARTE
12 Willingboro Campus Director .... Ms. Mary Kate HODOWANEC
12 Christiana Campus Director .... Ms. Amy CESTONE
20 Huntersville Campus Dean .... Dr. Jonita HENRY POWELL
12 Huntersville Campus Director .... Ms. Stephanie JOHNSON
20 South Raleigh Assoc Campus Dean .... Ms. Kimberly WILLIAMS
12 South Raleigh Campus Director .... Ms. Mara JEFFERSON
20 Allentown Assoc Campus Dean .... Ms. Holli QUINN
12 Allentown Campus Director .... Ms. Lauren PLINER
20 Knoxville Campus Dean .... Dr. Dasie SCHULZ
12 Knoxville Campus Director .... Ms. Marilyn MAYE
20 Cedar Hill Campus Dean .... Mr. Jay CULLINS
12 Cedar Hill Campus Director .... Ms. Marisol GREENWOOD
20 Charleston Campus Dean .... Dr. Deborah HILL
20 Irving Campus Dean .... Ms. Tretha HARRIS
12 Irving Campus Director .... Ms. Marisol GREENWOOD
20 North Austin Campus Dean .... Dr. Samuel GOODING
12 North Austin Campus Director .... Mr. Sean HOFER
20 North Dallas Campus Dean .... Ms. Tretha HARRIS
12 North Dallas Campus Director .... Ms. Marisol GREENWOOD
20 Northwest Houston Campus Dean .... Ms. Charity LANIER
12 Northwest Houston Campus Director .... Mr. Derrell SHEELOR
12 Charleston Campus Director .... Ms. Chiwana CUMMINGS
20 Plano Campus Dean .... Ms. Tretha HARRIS
12 Plano Campus Director .... Ms. Marisol GREENWOOD
20 San Antonio Campus Dean .... Dr. Samuel GOODING
12 San Antonio Campus Director .... Mr. Sean HOFER
20 Stafford Campus Dean .... Dr. Charity LANIER
12 Stafford Campus Director .... Mr. Derrell SHEELOR
20 Teays Valley Campus Dean .... Ms. Amber EAKIN
12 Teays Valley Campus Director .... Ms. Christine VITO
20 Cobb County Campus Dean .... Dr. Amona WASHINGTON
12 Cobb County Campus Director . Ms. Kedicia RITCHIE-MITCHELL
20 Columbia Campus Dean .... Mr. Lamont JOHNSON
12 Columbia Campus Director .... Mr. Ryan BUCKSON
20 Delaware County Campus Dean .... Ms. Cornelia ZAVADSKY
12 Delaware County Campus Director .... Mr. Alex HARRIS
20 Fredericksburg Campus Dean .... Ms. Jenelle THORMAN
12 Fredericksburg Campus Director .... Mr. Duan BUTLER
20 Greensboro Campus Dean .... Dr. Joel GOLDSTEIN
12 Greensboro Campus Director .... Ms. Dorenda CRAIGG
20 Henrico Campus Dean .... Ms. Nell MESHCHERYAKO
12 Henrico Campus Director .... Ms. Lorisa KERTAMUS
20 Lower Bucks Campus Dean .... Dr. Byron WESS
12 Lower Bucks Campus Director .... Ms. Lauren PLINER
20 Greenville Campus Dean .... Dr. William DUERR
12 Greenville Campus Director .... Ms. Ashley MILLS
20 Loudoun Campus Dean .... Ms. April HUDSON
12 Loudoun Campus Director .... Ms. Ashley COLLINS
20 Manassas Campus Dean .... Dr. Peter DEDOMINICI
12 Manassas Campus Director .... Mr. Rizwan CHOUDHRY
20 North Raleigh Campus Dean .... Dr. Pang-Jen CRAIG KUNG
12 North Raleigh Campus Director .... Ms. Sharon POMEROY
20 Morrow Campus Dean .... Dr. Angela WILLIAMS
12 Morrow Campus Director .... Ms. Stephanie GOWER
20 Nashville Campus Dean .... Dr. Lendozia EDWARDS
12 Nashville Campus Director .... Ms. Marilyn MAYE

Trinity Washington University (C)

125 Michigan Avenue, NE, Washington DC 20017-1090

FICE Identification: 001460
Unit ID: 131876
Telephone: (202) 884-9000 Carnegie Class: Masters/L
FAX Number: (202) 884-9229 Calendar System: Semester
URL: www.trinitydc.edu
Established: 1897 Annual Undergrad Tuition & Fees: $23,250
Enrollment: 2,161 Female
Affiliation or Control: Roman Catholic IRS Status: 501(c)3
Highest Offering: Master's
Accreditation: M, CAEPN, NURSE, OT, #OTA

01 President .... Ms. Patricia A. MCGUIRE
04 Special Assistant to the President .... Dr. Kim ELDRIDGE
05 Provost .... Dr. Carlota OCAMPO
84 Vice Pres Enrollment Services .... Dr. Stephanie L. KRUSEMARK
30 Vice Pres Institutional Advancement .... Ms. Ann PAULEY
11 Vice President Administration .... Mr. Michael MALEWICKI
32 Vice President for Student Affairs .... Dr. Karen GERLACH
44 Vice President of Development .... Ms. Kathleen ZEIFANG
49 Dean College of Arts & Science .... Dr. Sita RAMAMURTI
53 Dean School of Education .... Dr. Janet STOCKS
107 Dean School of Professional Studies .... Dr. Peggy LEWIS
66 Dean Sch Nursing/Health Professions .... Dr. Mary ROMANELLO
35 Dean of Student Services .... Ms. Michelle BOWIE
15 Director for Human Resources .... Ms. Tracey PRINCE ROSS
41 Athletic Director .... Ms. Amy OLSON
42 Director of Campus Ministry .... Sr. Ann HOWARD
18 Director Facilities Services .... Mr. Matthew LAPOINTE
29 Director Alumnae Affairs .... Ms. Margy REAGAN
06 Registrar .... Ms. Susie POWERS
07 Director of Admissions .... Ms. Germel CLARKE
08 Head Librarian .... Ms. Trisha SMITH
10 Controller/Business Officer .... Mr. Jared BASCO
13 Chief Info Technology Officer (CIO) .... Mr. Michael BURBACK

University of the District of Columbia (D)

4200 Connecticut Avenue, NW,
Washington DC 20008-1174

FICE Identification: 001441
Unit ID: 131399
Telephone: (202) 274-6016 Carnegie Class: Masters/S
FAX Number: (202) 274-5304 Calendar System: Semester
URL: www.udc.edu
Established: 1976 Annual Undergrad Tuition & Fees (In-District): $5,612
Enrollment: 4,805 Coed
Affiliation or Control: Local IRS Status: 501(c)3
Highest Offering: Master's
Accreditation: M, ACBSP, CACREP, CAEPN, COARC, CS, DIETD, ENG, LAW, NUR, SP, SW

01 President .... Mr. Ronald MASON, JR.
05 Provost/Vice Pres Academic Affairs .... Dr. Carl MOORE
32 Chief Student Development & Success .... Dr. William LATHAM
15 Vice President Human Resources .... Ms. Patricia JOHNSON
18 VP Facilities & Real Estate .... Mr. Erik THOMPSON
88 Executive Asst to the Provost .... Mr. Herman PRESCOTT
10 Chief Financial Officer .... Ms. Shaina COOPER
49 Dean Arts & Sciences .... Dr. April MASSEY
50 Dean Sch Business & Public Admin .... Dr. Mo SEPEHRI
61 Dean School of Law .... Ms. Shelley BRODERICK
54 Dean Engineering/Applied Scis .... Dr. Devdas SHETTY
56 Dean Agric/Urban Sustainabilty .... Dr. Sabine O'HARA
06 University Registrar .... Ms. Rapheael GASAWAY
37 Director Student Financial Aid .... Ms. Nailah WILLIAMS
26 Dir Marketing & Communications .... Mr. John GORDON
20 Interim Dean Learning Resources .... Ms. Melba BROOME
25 Director Grants Administration .... Ms. Cassandra PARKER
41 Athletic Director .... Ms. Patricia A. THOMAS
43 General Counsel .... Ms. Karen M. HARDWICK
88 General Manager UDC Cable TV .... Mr. Edward JONES, JR.
88 Dir of Operations and Maintenance .... Mr. Darron MCCLAIN
11 Vice President for Advancement .... Mr. Rodney TRAPP
09 Director of Institutional Research .... Mrs. Jackie XU
38 Director Student Counseling .... Dr. Sislena LEDBETTER
88 Director Student Achievement .... Ms. Hermina P. PETERS
103 Dean Workforce Development .... Mr. Tony JOHNSON
19 Dir Public Safety/Chief of Police .... Mr. Marieo FOSTER
36 Director Career Services .... Mr. Jared E. MOFFETT
86 Director State & Local Affairs .... Mr. Thomas E. REDMOND
11 Deputy Chief Operating Officer .... Mr. David FRANKLIN
88 Director STEM .... Ms. Barbara J. HOLMES
29 Director Alumni Affairs .... Mr. Joseph LIBERTELLI
97 Assistant Director of General Educ .... Ms. Kimberly CREWS
102 Director Sponsored Programs .... Ms. Jovita WELLS
13 Dir Information Technology .... Mr. Michael ROGERS
07 Director Admissions/TRIO Programs .... Ms. Saundra CARTER
101 Exec Secretary Office the Board .... Ms. Beverly FRANKLIN
28 Director of Labor & Employee Rels .... Ms. Jennifer MATTHEWS
124 Director of Advising & Retention .... Mr. Timothy L. HATCHETT

University of Phoenix Washington DC Campus (A)
25 Massachusetts Avenue, NW,
Washington DC 20001-1431
Telephone: (202) 471-3728 Identification: 770196
Accreditation: &NH, ACBSP

† No longer accepting campus-based students.

University of the Potomac (B)
1401 H Street NW, Suite 100, Washington DC 20005
FICE Identification: 032183
Unit ID: 384412
Telephone: (202) 274-2303 Carnegie Class: Spec-4-yr-Bus
FAX Number: N/A Calendar System: Semester
URL: www.potomac.edu
Established: 1991 Annual Undergrad Tuition & Fees: $13,884
Enrollment: 155 Coed
Affiliation or Control: Proprietary IRS Status: Proprietary
Highest Offering: Master's
Accreditation: M

01 President/Chief Executive Officer ....Dr. Clinton GARDNER
108 VP Assessment/Inst Effectiveness ....Walter PERSON
08 Director of Learning Resource Ctr ....Edward ROBINSON
07 Director of Admissions ....Vacant
26 Chief Marketing Officer ....Ron HENDRICKS

Wesley Theological Seminary (C)
4500 Massachusetts Avenue, NW,
Washington DC 20016-5690
FICE Identification: 001464
Unit ID: 131973
Telephone: (202) 885-8600 Carnegie Class: Spec-4-yr-Faith
FAX Number: (202) 885-8605 Calendar System: Semester
URL: www.wesleyseminary.edu
Established: 1882 Annual Graduate Tuition & Fees: N/A
Enrollment: 589 Coed
Affiliation or Control: United Methodist IRS Status: 501(c)3
Highest Offering: Doctorate; No Undergraduates
Accreditation: M, THEOL

01 President ....Dr. David MCALLISTER-WILSON
04 Special Assistant to the President ....Dr. Josie HOOVER
10 Vice Pres Finance/CFO ....Mr. Jeffrey STRAITS
11 Vice President for Administration ....Rev. Terry BRADFIELD
24 Director of Educational Technology ....Ms. Berkeley COLLINS
30 Vice President for Development ....Rev. Laura NORVELL
05 Interim Dean ....Dr. Bruce BIRCH
32 Assoc Dean for Community Life ....Dr. Asa LEE
35 Program Administrator Community Lif ....Ms. Octavia YOUNG
88 Vice President of Intl Relations ....Dr. Kyunglim SHIN LEE
45 Vice Pres of Strategic Initiatives ....Rev. Beth LUDLUM
07 Associate Dean of Admissions ....Rev. William D. ALDRIDGE
20 Associate Dean Academic Affairs ....Dr. Michael KOPPEL
06 Registrar ....Mr. Joseph E. ARNOLD
15 Director Human Resources ....Ms. Yasmin LEWIS-WHITE
18 Chief Facilities/Physical Plant ....Mr. Randall ADAMS
37 Director Student Financial Aid ....Mr. Dane SMITH
08 Director of Library ....Dr. James ESTES
26 Director of Communications/Marketin ....Ms. Sheila GEORGE
29 Development Specialist/Alumni Rels ....Mr. David SHANK
39 Director of Housing ....Ms. Monica PETTY
28 Diversity Officer ....Berkeley COLLINS

FLORIDA

Academy for Five Element Acupuncture (D)
305 SE Second Avenue, Gainesville FL 32601-6811
County: Alachua FICE Identification: 035243
Unit ID: 451079
Telephone: (352) 335-2332 Carnegie Class: Spec-4-yr-Other Health
FAX Number: (352) 337-2535 Calendar System: Trimester
URL: www.acupuncturist.edu
Established: 1998 Annual Graduate Tuition & Fees: N/A
Enrollment: 57 Coed
Affiliation or Control: Independent Non-Profit IRS Status: 501(c)3
Highest Offering: Master's; No Undergraduates
Accreditation: ACUP

01 President ....Ms. Misti OXFORD-PICKERAL
11 Vice President Administration ....Ms. Joanne EPSTEIN
05 Academic Dean ....Mr. Chuck GRAHAM
10 Finance Director ....Ms. Odalis CRUZ
37 Financial Aid Director ....Mr. Glenn MORRIS
06 Registrar ....Ms. Kimberly MCCALL
07 Admissions Counselor ....Ms. Isabelle WINZELER

Academy for Nursing and Health Occupations (E)
5154 Okeechobee Blvd #201, West Palm Beach FL 33417
County: Palm Beach FICE Identification: 033463
Unit ID: 412173
Telephone: (561) 683-1400 Carnegie Class: Spec 2-yr-Health
FAX Number: (561) 683-6773 Calendar System: Other
URL: www.anho.edu
Established: 1978 Annual Undergrad Tuition & Fees: N/A
Enrollment: 360 Coed
Affiliation or Control: Independent Non-Profit IRS Status: 501(c)3
Highest Offering: Associate Degree
Accreditation: COE

01 President ....Dr. Lois M. GACKENHEIMER
05 Assistant Director/Dean ....Renee WERNER
06 Registrar ....Elizabeth RODRIGUEZ
07 Admissions Specialist ....Angela STILES

Acupuncture & Massage College (F)
10506 N Kendall Drive, Miami FL 33176-1509
County: Miami-Dade FICE Identification: 034145
Unit ID: 439969
Telephone: (305) 595-9500 Carnegie Class: Spec-4-yr-Other Health
FAX Number: (305) 595-2622 Calendar System: Semester
URL: www.amcollege.edu
Established: 1983 Annual Undergrad Tuition & Fees: $10,765
Enrollment: 149 Coed
Affiliation or Control: Proprietary IRS Status: Proprietary
Highest Offering: Master's
Accreditation: ACCSC, ACUP

01 President ....Dr. Gabriel GLIKSBERG
05 Academic Dean ....Dr. Sylvia SANTANA
17 Clinic Director ....Dr. Hailan WU
37 Financial Aid Director ....Ms. Christy WOOD
07 Admissions Director ....Mr. Joe CALARESO
06 Registrar/Student Services ....Ms. Maria GARCIA

Advance Science College (G)
3750 West 12 Avenue, Hialeah FL 33012
County: Miami-Dade FICE Identification: 037573
Unit ID: 444334
Telephone: (305) 827-5452 Carnegie Class: Not Classified
FAX Number: (305) 557-2268 Calendar System: Semester
URL: asimedschool.com
Established: 1998 Annual Undergrad Tuition & Fees: N/A
Enrollment: 44 Coed
Affiliation or Control: Proprietary IRS Status: Proprietary
Highest Offering: Associate Degree
Accreditation: ACCSC

01 President ....Pablo PEREZ

Adventist University of Health Sciences (H)
671 Winyah Drive, Orlando FL 32803-1204
County: Orange FICE Identification: 031155
Unit ID: 133872
Telephone: (407) 303-9798 Carnegie Class: Spec-4-yr-Other Health
FAX Number: (407) 303-5671 Calendar System: Trimester
URL: www.adu.edu
Established: 1992 Annual Undergrad Tuition & Fees: $13,480
Enrollment: 1,984 Coed
Affiliation or Control: Seventh-day Adventist IRS Status: 501(c)3
Highest Offering: Doctorate
Accreditation: SC, ANEST, #ARCPA, DMS, NMT, NUR, OT, OTA, @PTA, RAD

01 President ....Dr. Edwin I. HERNANDEZ
05 Provost ....Vacant
10 Sr VP for Finance/CFO ....Mr. Ruben O. MARTINEZ
32 Sr VP for Student Services ....Mr. Stephen H. ROCHE
26 VP Marketing & Public Relations ....Mr. Lonnie MIXON
106 VP Educational Tech/Distance Educ ....Dr. Dan LIM
20 VP for Academic Administration ....Dr. Len ARCHER
09 Dir of Institutional Effec & Accred ....Dr. Roy LUKMAN
37 Director of Financial Aid ....Ms. Daisy TABACHOW
06 Registrar ....Dr. Janet CALDERON
88 Dir Ctr for Academic Achievement ....Dr. Ndala BOOKER
88 Library Director ....Ms. Deanna L. FLORES
88 Office of Mission ....Dr. Don WILLIAMS
07 Director of Enrollment Services ....Ms. Yoouhenky HICKMAN
21 Chief Accountant ....Mr. Grayson GOODMAN
39 Director of Residence Hall ....Mr. David A. BRYANT
30 Director of Philanthropy ....Dr. Carol BRADFIELD
15 Director of Human Resources ....Mr. Fred W. STEPHENS
13 Director of Information Technology ....Mr. Travis WOOLEY
04 Executive Asst to the President ....Mr. Viviana CALANDRA
88 Chief Compliance Officer ....Ms. Starr S. BENDER
88 COO for Online Education ....Ms. Deena SLOCKETT
29 Director Alumni Relations ....Ms. Dawn H. CREFT

American College for Medical Careers (I)
5959 Lake Ellenor Drive, Orlando FL 32809
Telephone: (407) 738-4488 Identification: 770842
Accreditation: ACICS, #COARC, DMS

† Branch campus of Salter College, West Boylston, MA

American Medical Academy (J)
12215 SW 112th Street, Miami FL 33186
County: Miami-Dade FICE Identification: 041921
Unit ID: 475714
Telephone: (305) 271-6555 Carnegie Class: Spec 2-yr-Health
FAX Number: (305) 271-6556 Calendar System: Semester
URL: www.ama.edu
Established: 2006 Annual Undergrad Tuition & Fees: N/A
Enrollment: 318 Coed
Affiliation or Control: Proprietary IRS Status: Proprietary
Highest Offering: Associate Degree
Accreditation: ABHES

01 Chief Executive Officer ....Mr. Eduardo GUTIERREZ

Ana G. Mendez University System Metro Orlando Campus (K)
5601 S Semoran Boulevard, #55, Orlando FL 32822
Telephone: (407) 207-3363 Identification: 770921
Accreditation: &M

† Branch campus of Sistema Universitario Ana G. Mendez, Rio Piedras, PR

Ana G. Mendez University System South Florida Campus (L)
3520 Enterprise Way, Miramar FL 33025
Telephone: (954) 885-5595 Identification: 770922
Accreditation: &M

† Branch campus of Sistema Universitario Ana G. Mendez, Rio Piedras, PR

Ana G. Mendez University System Tampa Bay Campus (M)
3655 West Waters Avenue, Tampa FL 33614
Telephone: (813) 932-7500 Identification: 770923
Accreditation: &M

† Branch campus of Sistema Universitario Ana G. Mendez, Rio Piedras, PR

Argosy University, Sarasota (N)
5250 17th Street, Sarasota FL 34235-8246
Telephone: (941) 379-0404 FICE Identification: 025906
Accreditation: &WC, ACBSP, CACREP

† Regional accreditation is carried under the parent institution in Orange, CA.

Argosy University, Tampa (O)
1403 N. Howard Avenue, Tampa FL 33607
Telephone: (813) 393-5290 Identification: 666082
Accreditation: &WC, ACBSP, CLPSY

† Regional accreditation is carried under the parent institution in Orange, CA.

The Art Institute of Fort Lauderdale (P)
1799 SE 17th Street, Fort Lauderdale FL 33316-3000
County: Broward FICE Identification: 010195
Unit ID: 132338
Telephone: (954) 463-3000 Carnegie Class: Spec-4-yr-Arts
FAX Number: (954) 523-7676 Calendar System: Quarter
URL: www.aifl.edu
Established: 1968 Annual Undergrad Tuition & Fees: $17,700
Enrollment: 1,274 Coed
Affiliation or Control: Proprietary IRS Status: Proprietary
Highest Offering: Baccalaureate
Accreditation: #ACICS, ACFEI, CIDA

01 President ....Carolyn PIERCE
32 Dean of Student Affairs ....Vacant
05 Dean of Academic Affairs ....Eric WATSON
06 Registrar ....Vacant
07 Senior Director of Admissions ....Debra BARTKOWSKI
37 Director Student Financial Services ....Yudi NIN CECYN
15 Human Resources Generalist ....Samantha GORDON

The Art Institute of Tampa (Q)
4401 North Himes Avenue, Suite 150, Tampa FL 33614
Telephone: (813) 873-2112 Identification: 770935
Accreditation: &SC, ACFEI

† Branch campus of Miami International University of Art & Design, Miami, FL.

ATA Career Education-Spring Hill (R)
7351 Spring Hill Drive, Suite 11, Spring Hill FL 34606
Telephone: (352) 684-3007 Identification: 770521
Accreditation: ABHES

† Branch campus of ATA College, Louisville, KY

Atlantic Institute of Oriental Medicine (S)
100 E Broward Boulevard, Suite 100,
Fort Lauderdale FL 33301-3510
County: Broward FICE Identification: 034296
Unit ID: 439446

Telephone: (954) 763-9840 Carnegie Class: Spec-4-yr-Other Health
FAX Number: (954) 763-9844 Calendar System: Trimester
URL: www.atom.edu
Established: 1994 Annual Graduate Tuition & Fees: N/A
Enrollment: 158 Coed
Affiliation or Control: Independent Non-Profit IRS Status: 501(c)3
Highest Offering: Doctorate; No Undergraduates
Accreditation: **ACUP**

01 President ... Johanna C. YEN
11 Executive Director ... Dort BIGG
05 Academic Dean ... Yan CHENG
03 Executive Vice President ... Di FU
10 Financial Officer ... Celia MUNOZ
06 Registrar ... Milagros FERREIRA
08 Head Librarian ... Jeanne THOMAS

† Granted candidacy at the Doctorate level.

Atlantis University (A)

1442 Biscayne Boulevard, Miami FL 33132
County: Miami-Dade FICE Identification: 042339
Unit ID: 485768
Telephone: (305) 377-8817 Carnegie Class: Not Classified
FAX Number: (305) 377-9557 Calendar System: Semester
URL: www.atlantisuniversity.edu
Established: 1975 Annual Undergrad Tuition & Fees: $4,928
Enrollment: 201 Coed
Affiliation or Control: Proprietary IRS Status: Proprietary
Highest Offering: Master's
Accreditation: **ACCSC**, CEA

01 Executive Director ... Ms. Carol PALACIOS

Ave Maria School of Law (B)

1025 Commons Circle, Naples FL 34119
County: Collier FICE Identification: 036914
Unit ID: 442295
Telephone: (239) 687-5300 Carnegie Class: Spec-4-yr-Law
FAX Number: (239) 353-3173 Calendar System: Semester
URL: www.avemarialaw.edu
Established: 2000 Annual Graduate Tuition & Fees: N/A
Enrollment: 269 Coed
Affiliation or Control: Roman Catholic IRS Status: 501(c)3
Highest Offering: First Professional Degree; No Undergraduates
Accreditation: **LAW**

01 President and Dean ... Mr. Kevin CIEPLY
04 Executive Assistant to the Dean ... Ms. Pamela KRAMER
05 Assoc Dean Academic Affairs ... Mr. Timothy TRACEY
08 Director of the Law Library ... Mr. Ulysses JAEN
42 Chaplain ... Msgr. Frank MCGRATH
06 Registrar ... Ms. Mary RUGGERI
37 Director of Financial Aid ... Mr. Kevin MCGOWAN
30 Chief Advancement/Comm Officer ... Ms. Donna HEISER
07 Director of Admissions ... Ms. Claire O'KEEFE
36 Director of Career Services ... Ms. Jennifer LUCAS-ROSS
10 Assoc Dean Student/Admin Affairs ... Ms. Kaye CASTRO
40 Bookstore Manager ... Ms. Kathryn LOVE

Ave Maria University (C)

5050 Ave Maria Boulevard, Ave Maria FL 34142-9505
County: Collier FICE Identification: 039413
Unit ID: 446048
Telephone: (239) 280-2500 Carnegie Class: Bac-A&S
FAX Number: (239) 352-2392 Calendar System: Semester
URL: www.avemaria.edu
Established: 2003 Annual Undergrad Tuition & Fees: $19,128
Enrollment: 1,110 Coed
Affiliation or Control: Independent Non-Profit IRS Status: 501(c)3
Highest Offering: Doctorate
Accreditation: **SC**

00 Chancellor ... Mr. Thomas S. MONAGHAN
01 President/CEO ... Mr. James TOWEY
03 Executive Vice President ... Mr. Dennis GRACE
05 VP Academic Affairs ... Dr. Roger NUTT
10 VP Finance/Administration ... Mr. Robert FARNHAM
13 Chief Information Officer ... Mr. Eddie DEJTHAI
30 VP Institutional Advancement ... Mr. Brian COUCH
32 Vice President Student Affairs ... Ms. Kimberly KING
07 Director of Admissions ... Ms. Karen FULL
06 Registrar ... Ms. Chelsea KOZISEK
09 Coordinator Institutional Research ... Vacant
37 Director Financial Aid ... Mrs. Anne HART
41 Athletic Director ... Mr. John LAMANNA
42 Director of Campus Ministry ... Fr. Amedeo GUIDA
44 Major Gift Officer ... Mr. John DE COLA
35 Director of Student Life ... Mr. Noah BLANCHARD
88 Director of Mission/Outreach ... Mr. Jeff FOX
08 Director of Library Services ... Ms. Jennifer NODES
15 Director of Human Resources ... Ms. Kathy PHELPS
18 Director Physical Plant ... Mr. Jason SYLVESTER
38 Director Counseling Services ... Ms. Ana Maria LI-ROSI
39 Director Resident Life ... Mrs. Vivian CROCKETT
19 Asst Director Security/Safety ... Mr. Bradley JOHNSON
43 General Counsel ... Vacant

Aviator College of Aeronautical Science & Technology (D)

3800 St. Lucie Boulevard, Fort Pierce FL 34946
County: Saint Lucie FICE Identification: 039863
Unit ID: 447847
Telephone: (772) 466-4822 Carnegie Class: Spec 2-yr-Tech
FAX Number: (772) 462-4886 Calendar System: Semester
URL: www.aviator.edu
Established: 1984 Annual Undergrad Tuition & Fees: $71,882
Enrollment: 152 Coed
Affiliation or Control: Proprietary IRS Status: Proprietary
Highest Offering: Associate Degree
Accreditation: **ACCSC**, CEA

01 President ... Mr. Michael E. COHEN
10 Sr Vice Pres/Chief Financial Ofcr ... Ms. T.J METE
05 Director of Education ... Mr. Pierre LAVIAL
06 Registrar/Director Student Services ... Ms. Lisa KREAMER
37 Financial Aid Officer ... Ms. Amy ROTH
43 Legal Counsel ... Mr. Kendall PHILLIPS

Azure College (E)

550 W Cypress Creek Rd #200, Fort Lauderdale FL 33876
County: Highlands Identification: 667116
Unit ID: 483762
Telephone: (954) 500-2987 Carnegie Class: Not Classified
FAX Number: N/A Calendar System: Quarter
URL: www.azure.edu
Established: 2004 Annual Undergrad Tuition & Fees: N/A
Enrollment: 236 Coed
Affiliation or Control: Proprietary IRS Status: Proprietary
Highest Offering: Baccalaureate
Accreditation: **ABHES**

11 Assoc VP of Regional Opers ... Ms. Shirley SAWYER

The Baptist College of Florida (F)

5400 College Drive, Graceville FL 32440-3306
County: Jackson FICE Identification: 021596
Unit ID: 132408
Telephone: (850) 263-3261 Carnegie Class: Spec-4-yr-Faith
FAX Number: (850) 263-9026 Calendar System: Semester
URL: www.baptistcollege.edu
Established: 1943 Annual Undergrad Tuition & Fees: $10,800
Enrollment: 481 Coed
Affiliation or Control: Southern Baptist IRS Status: 501(c)3
Highest Offering: Master's
Accreditation: **SC**, MUS

01 President ... Dr. Thomas A. KINCHEN
30 Vice President for Development ... Dr. Charles R. PARKER
05 Academic Dean ... Dr. G. Robin JUMPER
06 Registrar ... Ms. Stephanie W. ORR
32 Director of Student Life/Marketing ... Mrs. Sandra K. RICHARDS
09 Director of Institutional Research ... Dr. Ed SCOTT
37 Director of Financial Aid & VA ... Mrs. Stephanie E. POWELL
07 Director of Admissions ... Mrs. Sandra K. RICHARDS
18 Maintenance Director ... Mr. Huie G. WILSON
10 Associate Business Officer ... Ms. Polly K. FLOYD
04 Administrative Asst to President ... Ms. Laura L. TICE
08 Head Librarian ... Mr. John E. SHAFFETT
84 Director Enrollment Management ... Ms. Sandra K. RICHARDS
39 Director Student Housing ... Mrs. Rose A. STRICKLAND
41 Athletic Director ... Mr. Edward C. BOOTH

Barry University (G)

11300 NE Second Avenue, Miami Shores FL 33161-6695
County: Dade FICE Identification: 001466
Unit ID: 132471
Telephone: (305) 899-3000 Carnegie Class: DU-Mod
FAX Number: (305) 899-3054 Calendar System: Semester
URL: www.barry.edu
Established: 1940 Annual Undergrad Tuition & Fees: $28,800
Enrollment: 7,971 Coed
Affiliation or Control: Roman Catholic IRS Status: 501(c)3
Highest Offering: Doctorate
Accreditation: **SC**, ANEST, ARCPA, CAATE, CACREP, HT, LAW, MACTE, MT, NURSE, OT, PERF, POD, SW, THEOL

01 President ... Sr. Linda BEVILACQUA
04 Executive Asst to the President ... Ms. Mary Ellen LETSCHE
00 President Emerita ... Sr. Jeanne O'LAUGHLIN
05 Provost ... Dr. John D. MURRAY
10 Vice Pres Business & Finance ... Mrs. Susan ROSENTHAL
15 Vice Pres Human Resources ... Mrs. Jennifer N. BOYD-PUGH
20 Vice Provost ... Dr. Christopher STARRATT
32 Vice President Student Affairs ... Dr. Scott F. SMITH
13 VP Technology/CIO ... Ms. Yvette KOOTTUNGAL
43 General Counsel ... Mr. David DUDGEON
49 Dean College of Arts/Sciences ... Dr. Karen A. CALLAGHAN
50 Dean School of Business ... Dr. Tomislav MANDAKOVIC
53 Dean School of Education ... Dr. Jill FARRELL
76 Dean College of Health Sciences ... Dr. John MCFADDEN
61 Dean School of Law ... Dr. Leticia M. DIAZ
63 Dean School of Pod Med ... Dr. Albert ARMSTRONG
51 Assoc Vice Provost/Dean PACE ... Dr. Andrea KEENER
20 Associate Vice Provost ... Dr. Victor ROMANO
70 Dean School of Social Work ... Dr. Phyllis SCOTT
35 Assoc VP Student Affs/Dean Students ... Dr. Maria L. ALVAREZ
35 Assoc Vice Pres Student Affairs ... Dr. Eileen MCDONOUGH
29 Assoc VP Alum Rels & Annual Giving ... Mr. Matthew BLAIR
84 Assoc Vice Pres Recruit & Admission ... Ms. Roxanna CRUZ
105 Assoc VP Enrollment Mkt Strategy ... Mr. Michel SILY
19 Director Public Safety & Emerg Mgt ... Mr. John BUHRMASTER
08 Director Library Services ... Vacant
42 Chaplain ... Fr. Cristobal TORRES
112 Assoc VP Major Gifts Develop ... Vacant
06 University Registrar ... Ms. Cynthia A. CHRUSZCZYK
39 Director Housing and Residence Life .. Mr. Matthew R. CAMERON
36 Director Career Services ... Mr. John MORIARTY
37 Director Financial Aid ... Mrs. Aida CLARO
92 Director Honors Program ... Dr. Pawena SIRIMANGKALA
38 Director Student Counseling Center ... Sr. Anastasia MAGUIRE
26 Assoc VP Brand Mkt & Communications ... Vacant
07 Director of Graduate Admission ... Ms. Betsy THOMAS
09 Director Institutional Research ... Ms. Shaunette GRANT
14 AVP & Chief Technology Officer ... Mr. Hernan LONDONO
41 Director of Athletics ... Mr. Michael COVONE
102 Dir Foundation Rels & Major Gifts ... Mr. Frank SAAVEDRA
105 Director Mkt for Prod Dev & Design ... Mr. Miguel RAMIREZ
109 Dir Student Union & Food Services ... Mr. Mickie VOUTSINAS
25 Director Grant & Sponsored Programs . Mrs. Sandra L. MANCUSO
40 Manager Bookstore ... Ms. Claudia HADJEZ
96 Dir Procurement & Accounts Payable ... Ms. Monica SOTO

Beacon College (H)

105 E Main Street, Leesburg FL 34748-5162
County: Lake FICE Identification: 033733
Unit ID: 384254
Telephone: (352) 787-7660 Carnegie Class: Bac-Diverse
FAX Number: (352) 787-0721 Calendar System: Semester
URL: www.beaconcollege.edu
Established: 1989 Annual Undergrad Tuition & Fees: $36,172
Enrollment: 274 Coed
Affiliation or Control: Independent Non-Profit IRS Status: 501(c)3
Highest Offering: Baccalaureate
Accreditation: **SC**

01 President ... Dr. George J. HAGERTY
05 Provost ... Dr. Shelly CHANDLER
32 Dean of Student Affairs ... Dr. Kerry GREENSTEIN
30 VP of Institutional Development ... Mr. Stephen MULLER
10 VP of Finance & Administration ... Mr. Otis VANCE
06 Registrar ... Mr. David BROWN
18 Director of Facilities ... Vacant
37 Director of Financial Aid ... Ms. Shawna WELLS-BOOTH
08 Director of Library Resources ... Ms. Tiffany REITZ
13 Director of Information Technology ... Mr. Tim PAIGE
04 Exec Assistant to the President ... Ms. Tamara SYNDER
15 Director of Human Resources ... Mr. Tom BROWN
07 Dean of Admissions Enrollment Mgmt ... Ms. Dale HEROLD
101 Admin Asst to the Board ... Ms. Tamara SNYDER
103 Dir Workforce/Career Development ... Ms. Dinorah RAMOS
29 Director Alumni Relations ... Ms. Chelsea EUBANK
23 Executive Director Student Health ... Ms. Monika RANKIN
19 Chief of Campus Security ... Mr. Ryan NESBITT
39 Director Student Housing ... Ms. Sara BAILEY

Bethesda College of Health Sciences (I)

3800 S Congress Avenue, Suite 9,
Boynton Beach FL 33426
County: Palm Beach Identification: 667258
Telephone: (561) 364-3064 Carnegie Class: Not Classified
FAX Number: (561) 364-3059 Calendar System: Semester
URL: www.BethesdaCollege.net
Established: 2011 Annual Undergrad Tuition & Fees: N/A
Enrollment: N/A Coed
Affiliation or Control: Independent Non-Profit IRS Status: 501(c)3
Highest Offering: Associate Degree
Accreditation: **ACICS**, RAD

01 Dean ... Amanda MURPHY

Bethune Cookman University (J)

640 Dr. Mary McLeod Bethune Blvd,
Daytona Beach FL 32114-3099
County: Volusia FICE Identification: 001467
Unit ID: 132602
Telephone: (386) 481-2000 Carnegie Class: Bac-A&S
FAX Number: (386) 481-2010 Calendar System: Semester
URL: www.cookman.edu
Established: 1904 Annual Undergrad Tuition & Fees: $14,410
Enrollment: 3,831 Coed
Affiliation or Control: United Methodist IRS Status: 501(c)3
Highest Offering: Master's
Accreditation: **SC**, ACBSP, CAEPN, ENG, MUS, NUR

01 Interim President ... Judge Hubert L. GRIMES
10 Vice President Fiscal Affairs ... Mr. George GALL
32 VP Student Affairs ... Mr. Jason E. GLENN
111 Vice Pres Institutional Advancement ... Dr. Hakim J. LUCAS
43 VP/General Counsel ... Mr. Hubert GRIMES
13 VP Info Tech/Chief Info Officer ... Mr. Franklin PATTERSON

41 VP of Intercollegiate Athletics ... Mr. Lynn THOMPSON
88 VP Business & Community Development ... Dr. Aubrey LONG
15 Vice President Human Resources ... Dr. Nan FISHER-WILLIAMS
05 Provost for Academic Affairs ... Dr. Helena WALROND
21 Assoc Vice Pres Business Affairs ... Mr. Gabe CASSANOVA
84 Associate VP Enrollment Management ... Mr. Warren HEUSNER
100 Chief of Staff ... Mr. Fontaine DAVIS
39 Asst VP Resident Life/Judicial Affs ... Ms. Bonisha PORTER
30 Director of Advancement ... Ms. Sophia HUGER
26 Director of Communications ... Ursla JAMES
36 Dir Academic and Career Development ... Ms. Davita BONNER
08 Chief Librarian Dean of Library/LRC ... Dr. Tasha LUCAS-YOUMANS
06 Registrar ... Ms. Patricia KRESL
07 Director Admissions ... Ms. Manicia FINCH
37 Director Financial Aid ... Ms. Salina HAMILTON
23 Director Health Services/Counsling ... Ms. Nadine HEUSNER
42 Chaplain/Dir of Religious Life ... Rev. John BALDWIN
19 Director of Campus Safety ... Chief Gregory ELDER
18 VP Capital Assets and Planning ... Mr. Graham GILCHRIST
66 Dean School of Nursing ... Dr. Sandra TUCKER
50 Dean of College of Business ... Dr. Ida WRIGHT
53 Acting Dean College of Education ... Dr. Stephanie PASLEY-HENRY
49 Dean School of Liberal Arts ... Dr. Janice ALLEN-KELSEY
81 Dean Sch Science/Engineering/Math ... Dr. Herbert THOMPSON
107 Dean School of Professional Studies ... Dr. Arletha MCSWAIN
58 Dean of Graduate Studies ... Dr. Adrienne COOPER
97 Dean of Undergrad Studies ... Dr. Kimberly BURGESS
76 Exec Dean School of Health Sci ... Dr. Deanna WATHINGTON
04 Executive Asst to President ... Mrs. Valerie WILT
90 Director Administrative Systems ... Ms. Anna HEIN
88 Dean of Chapel ... Rev. John BALDWIN
20 Associate Provost ... Dr. Adrienne COOPER
35 Asst Vice Pres for Student Life ... Dr. Clyde WILSON, JR.
38 Asst VP Counseling & Disability Svc ... Ms. Nadine HEUSNER
88 Director of Testing ... Mr. James LAI
108 Executive Director of Assessment ... Mr. Cory POTTER
29 Alumni Affairs Manager ... Ms. Marah BELTZ
44 Annual Giving Manager ... Ms. Ashley PORTERFIELD

Broward College (A)

111 E Las Olas Boulevard,
Fort Lauderdale FL 33301-2298
County: Broward FICE Identification: 001500
Unit ID: 132709
Telephone: (954) 201-7350 Carnegie Class: Bac/Assoc-Assoc Dom
FAX Number: (954) 201-7576 Calendar System: Trimester
URL: www.broward.edu
Established: 1959 Annual Undergrad Tuition & Fees (In-State): $2,753
Enrollment: 43,078 Coed
Affiliation or Control: State IRS Status: 501(c)3
Highest Offering: Baccalaureate
Accreditation: **SC**, ADNUR, ART, CAHIIM, COARC, DA, DH, DMS, EMT, MAC, MUS, NMT, NURSE, OPD, PTAA, RAD, RTT

01 President ... Mr. J. David ARMSTRONG, JR.
10 Sr Vice Pres Finance/Administration ... Mr. Thomas OLLIFF
84 Vice Pres Enrollment Mgmt ... Dr. Marielena DESANCTIS
26 VP Public Affairs and Marketing ... Mr. Don COOK
11 Vice President of Operations ... Mr. John DUNNUCK
111 VP Advanc/Exec Dir BC Foundation ... Ms. Nancy BOTERO
13 Vice President Info Technology ... Ms. Patti BARNEY
86 VP Govt Policy/Regulatory Affairs ... Mr. Gregory A. HAILE
103 Executive Director Workforce Educ ... Ms. Mildred COYNE
100 Chief of Staff ... Ms. Adriana FAZZANO FICANO
12 Campus President BC Online ... Dr. David SHULMAN
12 Campus President Central Campus ... Dr. Marielena DESANCTIS
12 Campus President North Campus ... Dr. Avis PROCTOR
12 Campus President South Campus ... Dr. Rolando GARCIA
21 Chief Financial Officer ... Mr. Jayson IROFF
18 Chief Facilities/Physical Plant ... Mr. Sean DEVANEY
09 Dean Institutional Research ... Ms. Pauline ANDERSON
45 Dean Inst Planning/Effectiveness ... Dr. Deborah POSNER
08 Dean of Libraries/Learning Res ... Ms. Sarah WIGGINS
37 Director of Student Financial Svcs ... Ms. Theresa COWAN
15 Exec Director Human Res & Equity ... Dr. Denese EDSALL
06 Registrar ... Ms. Rochelle MOORE
29 Director Alumni Relations ... Ms. Mary WORKMAN
04 Sr Exec Asst to the President ... Mrs. Avis M. MCCOY
19 Director Security/Safety ... Mr. Peter AGNESI
25 Chief Contracts/Grants Admin ... Ms. Kareen TORRES
96 Director of Purchasing ... Dr. Judy SCHMELZER

Cambridge College (B)

5150 Linton Boulevard, Suite 340, Delray Beach FL 33484
County: Palm Beach FICE Identification: 040834
Unit ID: 454865
Telephone: (561) 381-4990 Carnegie Class: Spec 2-yr-Health
FAX Number: (561) 381-4992 Calendar System: Other
URL: www.cambridgehealth.edu
Established: Annual Undergrad Tuition & Fees: N/A
Enrollment: 453 Coed
Affiliation or Control: Proprietary IRS Status: Proprietary
Highest Offering: Associate Degree
Accreditation: **ABHES**, DMS

01 President ... Mr. Terry LAPIER

Cambridge Institute of Allied Health & Technology-Altamonte Springs (C)

460 E. Altamonte Drive, Third Floor,
Altamonte Springs FL 32701
County: Seminole FICE Identification: 038425
Unit ID: 446109
Telephone: (407) 265-8383 Carnegie Class: Not Classified
FAX Number: (407) 265-8384 Calendar System: Other
URL: www.cambridgehealth.edu
Established: Annual Undergrad Tuition & Fees: N/A
Enrollment: 223 Coed
Affiliation or Control: Proprietary IRS Status: Proprietary
Highest Offering: Baccalaureate
Accreditation: **ABHES**

01 President ... Dr. Terrance LAPIER
12 Campus Director ... Vicente QUINONES
07 Director of Admissions ... Gordon HUNT
06 Registrar ... Kristie MCCARTHY
37 Financial Aid Manager ... Monica ROBLES
36 Careers Services Director ... Theresa MANTOVANI

Carlos Albizu University Miami Campus (D)

2173 NW 99th Avenue, Miami FL 33172-2209
Telephone: (305) 593-1223 Identification: 666814
Accreditation: **&M**, CLPSY, SP

† Regional accreditation is carried under the parent institution in San Juan, PR.

Center of Cinematography, Art & Television (E)

1637 NW 27th Avenue, Miami FL 33125
Telephone: (305) 634-0550 Identification: 770562
Accreditation: **ACCSC**

† Branch campus of Colegio de Cinematografia, Artes y Television, Bayamon, PR

Chamberlain University-Jacksonville (F)

5200 Belfort Road, Suite 100, Jacksonville FL 32256
Telephone: (904) 251-8100 Identification: 770501
Accreditation: **&NH**, NURSE

† Branch campus of Chamberlain University-Addison, Addison, IL

Chamberlain University-Miramar (G)

2300 SW 145th Avenue, Miramar FL 33027
Telephone: (954) 885-3510 Identification: 770498
Accreditation: **&NH**, NURSE

† Branch campus of Chamberlain University-Addison, Addison, IL

Chipola College (H)

3094 Indian Circle, Marianna FL 32446-3065
County: Jackson FICE Identification: 001472
Unit ID: 133021
Telephone: (850) 526-2761 Carnegie Class: Bac/Assoc-Mixed
FAX Number: (850) 718-2388 Calendar System: Semester
URL: www.chipola.edu
Established: 1947 Annual Undergrad Tuition & Fees (In-District): $3,120
Enrollment: 2,133 Coed
Affiliation or Control: State/Local IRS Status: 501(c)3
Highest Offering: Baccalaureate
Accreditation: **SC**, ADNUR, NUR

01 President ... Dr. Sarah CLEMMONS
05 VP of Instructional Affairs ... Dr. Pam RENTZ
10 Vice Pres of Admin & Business Svcs ... Mr. Steve YOUNG
32 Vice Pres of Student Affairs ... Dr. Jayne ROBERTS
15 Assoc VP of HR & Equity ... Mrs. Karan P. DAVIS
13 Associate VP Information Systems ... Mr. Dennis F. EVERETT
108 Dean Assessment/Compliance & Grant ... Dr. Matthew HUGHES
18 Dir Facilities & Campus Operations ... Vacant
26 Director Public Relations ... Dr. Bryan C. CRAVEN
07 Dir of Enrollment Services ... Ms. Stacey HINSON
37 Director of Financial Aid ... Ms. Beverly HAMBRIGHT
41 Director of Athletics ... Mr. Jeffrey JOHNSON
06 Registrar ... Ms. Kathy REHBERG
04 Administrative Asst to President ... Ms. Jan CUMMINGS
103 Dir Workforce/Career Development ... Mr. Darwin GILMORE
08 Dir of Learning Resources ... Ms. Vikki MILTON
102 Dir Foundation/Corporate Relations ... Ms. Julie FUQUA

City College (I)

177 Montgomery Road, Altamonte Springs FL 32714
County: Seminole FICE Identification: 030799
Unit ID: 417327
Telephone: (407) 831-9816 Carnegie Class: Assoc/HVT-Mix Trad/Non
FAX Number: (407) 831-1147 Calendar System: Quarter
URL: www.citycollegeorlando.edu
Established: 1997 Annual Undergrad Tuition & Fees: $13,098
Enrollment: 329 Coed
Affiliation or Control: Independent Non-Profit IRS Status: 501(c)3
Highest Offering: Associate Degree
Accreditation: **ABHES**, ACICS, EMT, SURTEC

01 President ... Mrs. Esther FIKE-CURRY
05 Executive Director ... Dr. P. Michael LANOUETTE
07 Director Admissions ... Ms. Tara DORSEY

City College (J)

2000 W Commercial Boulevard,
Fort Lauderdale FL 33309-1916
County: Broward FICE Identification: 025154
Unit ID: 244233
Telephone: (954) 492-5353 Carnegie Class: Bac/Assoc-Mixed
FAX Number: (954) 958-9257 Calendar System: Quarter
URL: www.citycollege.edu
Established: 1983 Annual Undergrad Tuition & Fees: $13,098
Enrollment: 490 Coed
Affiliation or Control: Independent Non-Profit IRS Status: 501(c)3
Highest Offering: Baccalaureate
Accreditation: **ACICS**, EMT, SURTEC

01 President ... Esther FIKE-CURRY
03 Executive Director ... Steve BROOKS
36 Director of Career Development ... Holly MCFADDEN
05 Director of Education ... Anie BONILLA
07 Director of Admissions ... Rob CARUSO
13 Director of Technologies ... Jeffrey CLAYTON
08 Director of Library ... Torri KELLOG
06 Registrar ... Sanchia WILLIAMS
15 Human Resources Generalist ... Virginia LLANO
37 Director Student Financial Aid ... Patty PATTERSON
106 Dir Online Education/E-learning ... Dr. Suzanne MORRISON-WILLAIMS
108 Director Institutional Assessment ... Heather PAYNE
18 Chief Facilities/Physical Plant ... Donna VARELA

City College (K)

7001 NW Fourth Boulevard, Gainesville FL 32607
Telephone: (352) 335-4000 Identification: 666413
Accreditation: **ACICS**, EMT

† Branch campus of City College, Fort Lauderdale, FL.

City College (L)

6565 Taft Street, Hollywood FL 33024
Telephone: (954) 744-1777 Identification: 770674
Accreditation: **ACICS**

City College (M)

9300 S Dadeland Blvd, Suite 200, Miami FL 33156
Telephone: (305) 666-9242 Identification: 666414
Accreditation: **ACICS**, EMT, SURTEC

† Branch campus of City College, Fort Lauderdale, FL.

College of Business and Technology (N)

8700 W. Flagler Street, Miami FL 33174
County: Miami-Dade FICE Identification: 030716
Unit ID: 417318
Telephone: (305) 273-4499 Carnegie Class: Bac/Assoc-Mixed
FAX Number: (305) 270-0779 Calendar System: Semester
URL: www.cbt.edu
Established: 1988 Annual Undergrad Tuition & Fees: $13,052
Enrollment: 9 Coed
Affiliation or Control: Proprietary IRS Status: Proprietary
Highest Offering: Associate Degree
Accreditation: **ACICS**

01 CEO/President ... Ms. Monica LLERENA
05 Regional Director of Education ... Mrs. Gladys P. LLERENA
10 Finance Director ... Ms. Maricel SPEZZACATENA
11 Director of Operations ... Mr. Stephen BREWSTER
12 Acting Campus Director ... Mr. Hector DUENAS
20 Director of Academic Operations ... Mr. Hector DUENAS
20 Asst Director Academic Operations ... Ms. Carolyn SMITH
37 Financial Aid Director ... Mrs. Yazmin PALMA
36 Career Services Director ... Vacant
26 Marketing Manager ... Mr. Hamlet ARIAS
08 Head Librarian ... Ms. Jennifer ROMA
15 HR Manager ... Ms. Alma TROCHE
88 Compliance Manager ... Mr. Ken KISTNER

College of Business and Technology - Cutler Bay (O)

19151 South Dixie Highway, Cutler Bay FL 33157
Telephone: (305) 273-4499 Identification: 770677
Accreditation: **ACICS**, CAHIIM

College of Business and Technology - Flagler (P)

8230 W Flagler Street, Miami FL 33144
Telephone: (305) 273-4499 Identification: 770676
Accreditation: **ACICS**

College of Business and Technology - Hialeah Campus (A)

935 West 49th Street, Hialeah FL 33012
Telephone: (305) 273-4499 Identification: 770675
Accreditation: ACICS

College of Business and Technology - Miami Gardens (B)

5190 NW 167 Street, Suite 200, Miami Gardens FL 33014
Telephone: (786) 693-8801 Identification: 770612
Accreditation: ACICS

College of Central Florida (C)

3001 S.W. College Road, Ocala FL 34474
County: Marion FICE Identification: 001471
Unit ID: 132851
Telephone: (352) 237-2111 Carnegie Class: Bac/Assoc-Assoc Dom
FAX Number: (352) 291-4450 Calendar System: Semester
URL: www.cf.edu
Established: 1957 Annual Undergrad Tuition & Fees (In-District): $2,570
Enrollment: 7,452 Coed
Affiliation or Control: Local IRS Status: 501(c)3
Highest Offering: Baccalaureate
Accreditation: SC, ADNUR, CAHIIM, DA, EMT, NUR, PTAA, SURGT

01 President .... Dr. James D. HENNINGSEN
10 Vice Pres Administration & Finance .... Mr. Francis J. MAZUR, III
05 Vice President Academic Affairs .... Dr. Mark PAUGH
32 Vice President Student Affairs .... Dr. Saul REYES
12 Vice President Regional Campuses .... Dr. Vernon LAWTER, JR.
43 General Counsel & Dir Govt Rels .... Vacant
09 VP Inst Effectiveness/College Rels .... Dr. Jillian RAMSAMMY
26 Director Marketing/Public Relations .. Ms. Lois BRAUCKMULLER
102 Executive Director Foundation .... Mr. Christopher KNIFE
21 Assistant VP for Finance .... Mr. Steven ASH
12 Provost Levy Center .... Dr. Rayanne GIDDIS
88 Dean Public Service/Criminal Just .... Mr. Charles MCINTOSH
75 Dean Bus Tech Careers & Tech Educ .... Dr. Rob WOLF
35 Dean Student Services .... Dr. Henri BENLOLO
49 Dean Liberal Arts & Sciences .... Mr. Allan DANUFF
35 Dean Student Success .... Ms. Debbie BOWE
53 Dean Arts and Education .... Dr. Jennifer FRYNS
84 Dean Enrollment Management .... Vacant
76 Dean Health Sciences .... Dr. Stephanie CORTES
106 Dean E-learning & Learning Resource .... Dr. Tamara VIVIANO-BRODERICK
37 Director Financial Aid .... Ms. Maureen ANDERSON
09 Dir Institutional Effectiveness .... Dr. Lawrence J. KUSZYNSKI
07 Director Admissions/Records .... Mrs. Teri LITTLE-BERRY
18 Director Facilities .... Mr. Tommy MORELOCK
15 Director Human Resources .... Ms. Jennifer KLEPFER
35 Director Student Life .... Ms. Marjorie MCGEE
88 Director Student Support Services .... Ms. Lisa SMITH
41 Director Athletics/Wellness .... Mr. Bob ZELINSKI
88 Director Access and Counsel Service .... Ms. Victoria COLLELI
121 Dir Stdnt Success & Educ Outreach .... Dr. Leonard EVERETT
88 Director Appleton Museum of Art .... Ms. Cindi MORRISON
25 Director Grants Funding .... Mr. Matt MATTHEWS
96 Dir Purchasing & Risk Mgmt .... Mr. Stewart TRAUTMAN
08 Library Director .... Ms. Teresa FAUST
19 Manager Public Safety .... Mr. Lewis PREVATT
109 Manager Printing & Postal Service .... Mr. Andrew LOWREY
109 Manager Conference & Food Service .... Ms. Cheryl CROSBY
13 Associate VP Information Technology .... Mr. Henry GLASPIE
06 Registrar .... Ms. Devona SEWELL
30 Director of Development .... Ms. Traci MASON

Concorde Career Institute (D)

7259 Salisbury Road, Jacksonville FL 32256
County: Duval FICE Identification: 020896
Unit ID: 133845
Telephone: (904) 725-0525 Carnegie Class: Spec 2-yr-Health
FAX Number: (904) 721-9944 Calendar System: Semester
URL: www.concorde.edu
Established: 1988 Annual Undergrad Tuition & Fees: N/A
Enrollment: 483 Coed
Affiliation or Control: Proprietary IRS Status: Proprietary
Highest Offering: Associate Degree
Accreditation: ACCSC, COARC, PTAA, SURGT

01 Campus President .... Melissa RYAN

Concorde Career Institute (E)

10933 Marks Way, Miramar FL 33025
County: Broward FICE Identification: 022751
Unit ID: 133854
Telephone: (954) 731-8880 Carnegie Class: Spec 2-yr-Health
FAX Number: (954) 484-2961 Calendar System: Other
URL: www.concorde.edu
Established: 1989 Annual Undergrad Tuition & Fees: N/A
Enrollment: 467 Coed
Affiliation or Control: Proprietary IRS Status: Proprietary
Highest Offering: Associate Degree
Accreditation: ACCSC, COARC, OTA, PTAA, SURGT

01 Campus President .... Matthew DIACONT

Concorde Career Institute (F)

3444 McCrory Place, Orlando FL 32803
Telephone: (407) 812-3060 Identification: 770563
Accreditation: ACCSC, SURGT

Concorde Career Institute (G)

4202 West Spruce Street, Tampa FL 33607-4127
County: Hillsborough FICE Identification: 021727
Unit ID: 133863
Telephone: (813) 874-0094 Carnegie Class: Spec 2-yr-Health
FAX Number: (813) 872-6884 Calendar System: Other
URL: www.concorde.edu
Established: 1978 Annual Undergrad Tuition & Fees: N/A
Enrollment: 272 Coed
Affiliation or Control: Proprietary IRS Status: Proprietary
Highest Offering: Associate Degree
Accreditation: ACCSC, COARC, SURGT

01 Campus President .... Mr. Rod KIRKWOOD

Daytona College (H)

425 South Nova Road, Ormond Beach FL 32174-8449
County: Volusia FICE Identification: 039396
Unit ID: 447014
Telephone: (386) 267-0565 Carnegie Class: Spec 2-yr-Health
FAX Number: (386) 267-0567 Calendar System: Semester
URL: www.daytonacollege.edu
Established: 1996 Annual Undergrad Tuition & Fees: N/A
Enrollment: 246 Coed
Affiliation or Control: Proprietary IRS Status: Proprietary
Highest Offering: Associate Degree
Accreditation: ACCSC

01 President .... Mr. Roger BRADLEY
05 Director .... Mr. Justin BERKOWITZ

Daytona State College (I)

PO Box 2811, Daytona Beach FL 32120-2811
County: Volusia FICE Identification: 001475
Unit ID: 133386
Telephone: (386) 506-3000 Carnegie Class: Bac/Assoc-Mixed
FAX Number: (386) 506-4440 Calendar System: Semester
URL: www.DaytonaState.edu
Established: 1957 Annual Undergrad Tuition & Fees (In-District): $3,112
Enrollment: 14,292 Coed
Affiliation or Control: State/Local IRS Status: 501(c)3
Highest Offering: Baccalaureate
Accreditation: SC, ADNUR, CAHIIM, COARC, DA, DH, EMT, ENGT, MAC, NUR, OTA, PTAA, SURGT

01 President .... Dr. Thomas LOBASSO
03 Executive Vice President .... Mr. Brian T. BABB
05 Provost .... Dr. Amy LOCKLEAR
10 Chief Business Officer .... Ms. Isalene MONTGOMERY
13 VP Information Technology .... Mr. Roberto LOMBARDO
15 AVP Human Resources .... Ms. Robin BARR
84 VP Enrollment Services .... Mr. Kenneth MATTHEWS
08 Head Librarian .... Ms. Mercedes CLEMENT
49 AVP Arts & Science .... Dr. Alycia EHLERT
69 AVP College of Health .... Dr. Linda MILES
106 Exec Dir Instructional Resources .... Dr. Rob SAUM
32 VP Student Development .... Mr. Keith KENNEDY
18 AVP Facilities Planning .... Mr. Christopher WAINWRIGHT
53 AVP College of Education .... Dr. Alycia EHLERT
09 Exec Dir Inst Research .... Mr. Robert WILKINSON
37 Director Financial Aid .... Ms. Aileen MORRISSEY
88 Dean School of Health & Wellness .... Mr. Will DUNNE
19 Director Campus Safety .... Mr. Bill TILLARD
12 Dean DeLand & Deltona Campuses .... Mr. Neil CLEMONS
12 Dean New Smryna Beach Campus .... Mr. Clarence MCCLOUD
43 College Counsel .... Mr. Brian BABB
51 Director Ctr for Business/Industry .... Mr. Frank MERCER
32 Asst Dean Student Activities .... Mr. Bruce COOK
121 Director Academic Advising .... Ms. LeeAnn DAVIS
07 Director Admissions/Recruitment .... Ms. Karen SANDERS
22 Director of Equity & Inclusion .... Mr. Lonnie THOMPSON
21 AVP Accounting .... Ms. Tina MYERS
06 Director Student Accounts .... Ms. Amy IVERSON
26 Director of Marketing .... Ms. Laurie WHITE
09 Dean Institutional Effectiveness .... Dr. Karla MOORE
102 Executive Director Foundation .... Ms. Lorene KING
29 Director Alumni Relations .... Ms. Suzette CAMERON
96 Director of Purchasing .... Ms. Elaine THIEL

DeVry University - Miramar Campus (J)

2300 SW 145th Avenue, Miramar FL 33027-4150
Telephone: (954) 499-9775 Identification: 666196
Accreditation: &NH, ENGT

† Regional accreditation is carried under the parent institution in Downers Grove, IL.

DeVry University - Orlando Campus (K)

7352 Greenbriar Pkwy, Orlando FL 32819-8934
Telephone: (407) 345-2800 Identification: 666112
Accreditation: &NH, ENGT

† Regional accreditation is carried under the parent institution in Downers Grove, IL.

Dragon Rises College of Oriental Medicine (L)

1000 NE 16th Ave., Building F, Gainesville FL 32601-4557
County: Alachua FICE Identification: 038883
Unit ID: 449481
Telephone: (352) 371-2833 Carnegie Class: Not Classified
FAX Number: (352) 244-0003 Calendar System: Semester
URL: www.dragonrises.edu
Established: 2001 Annual Undergrad Tuition & Fees: N/A
Enrollment: 46 Coed
Affiliation or Control: Independent Non-Profit IRS Status: 501(c)3
Highest Offering: Master's
Accreditation: ACUP

01 Director/CEO .... Dr. George VALCOURT
05 Academic Dean .... Dr. George VALCOURT
23 Clinic Director .... Mr. Jerrod FLETCHER
32 Director of Student Services .... Ms. Ruth HAYES-MORRISON
37 Financial Aid Administrator .... Ms. Karen MARTIN-BROWN

East West College of Natural Medicine (M)

3808 N Tamiami Trail, Sarasota FL 34234-5362
County: Sarasota FICE Identification: 034297
Unit ID: 439394
Telephone: (941) 355-9080 Carnegie Class: Spec-4-yr-Other Health
FAX Number: (941) 355-3243 Calendar System: Trimester
URL: www.ewcollege.edu
Established: 1994 Annual Undergrad Tuition & Fees: $10,675
Enrollment: 116 Coed
Affiliation or Control: Proprietary IRS Status: Proprietary
Highest Offering: Master's
Accreditation: ACICS, ACUP

01 President/CEO .... Mr. Russell BATTIATA
05 Academic Dean .... Mr. Kevin PIERCE
07 Director of Admissions .... Mr. Russell BATTIATA

Eastern Florida State College (N)

3865 N. Wickham Road, Melbourne FL 32935
County: Brevard FICE Identification: 001470
Unit ID: 132693
Telephone: (321) 632-1111 Carnegie Class: Bac/Assoc-Assoc Dom
FAX Number: (321) 633-4565 Calendar System: Semester
URL: www.easternflorida.edu
Established: 1960 Annual Undergrad Tuition & Fees (In-District): $2,496
Enrollment: 15,593 Coed
Affiliation or Control: Local IRS Status: 501(c)3
Highest Offering: Baccalaureate
Accreditation: SC, ADNUR, #COARC, DA, DH, DMS, EMT, MLTAD, @PTAA, RAD

01 President .... Dr. James H. RICHEY
10 Chief Financial Officer .... Mr. Mark CHERRY
11 VP Operations .... Mr. Richard LAIRD
05 VP Academic & Student Affairs/CLO .... Dr. Linda L. MIEDEMA
41 Assoc Vice Pres of Athletics .... Mr. Jeffrey CARR
18 AVP Facilities & Special Projects .... Mr. Stockton WHITTEN
15 VP/Exec Dir Human Resources .... Ms. Darla FERGUSON
86 VP External Affairs .... Mr. Jack PARKER
26 AVP Communications .... Mr. John GLISCH
12 Provost Palm Bay Campus .... Dr. Wayne STEIN
12 Provost Melbourne/AVP Enr Mgmt .... Ms. Sandy HANDFIELD
12 Provost Cocoa Campus .... Dr. Dedra SIBLEY
12 Provost Titusville Campus/eLearning .... Dr. Philip SIMPSON
103 Dean/Workforce Trng & Devel .... Mr. Stephen TAYLOR
37 Director Student Financial Aid .... Ms. Eileen BRZOZOWSKI
07 Dir Collegewide Admissions .... Ms. Michelle LOUFEK
04 Executive Asst to the President .... Ms. Gina CLINE
06 Registrar .... Ms. Stephanie BURNETTE
09 Coordinator Institutional Research .... Dr. Mark QUATHAMER
108 AVP Planning & Assessment .... Dr. Jayne GORHAM
22 Dir Affirmative Action/EEO .... Ms. Darla FERGUSON
29 Director Alumni & Donor Relations .... Ms. Jennie KRIETE
36 Exec Dir Career Plng/Development .... Dr. Cathy CADY

Eckerd College (O)

4200 54th Avenue S, Saint Petersburg FL 33711-4700
County: Pinellas FICE Identification: 001487
Unit ID: 133492
Telephone: (727) 867-1166 Carnegie Class: Bac-A&S
FAX Number: (727) 864-1877 Calendar System: 4/1/4
URL: www.eckerd.edu
Established: 1958 Annual Undergrad Tuition & Fees: $41,538
Enrollment: 2,023 Coed
Affiliation or Control: Presbyterian Church (U.S.A.) IRS Status: 501(c)3
Highest Offering: Baccalaureate
Accreditation: SC

01 President .... Dr. Donald R. EASTMAN, III
05 VP/Dean of Faculty .... Dr. Suzan HARRISON
10 VP Business and Finance .... Mr. Christopher P. BRENNAN
03 VP and Secretary of the College .... Dr. Lisa A. METS
111 Vice President Advancement .... Mr. Matthew S. BISSET
51 VP/Dean for Executive Education .... Mr. Kelly KIRSCHNER
32 VP/Dean for Student Life .... Dr. James J. ANNARELLI

84 VP Enrollment Management Mr. John SULLIVAN
20 Assoc Dean Faculty Development Dr. Kathryn J. WATSON
26 VP Marketing and Communications Ms. Valerie GLIEM
110 Assoc VP Advancement Mr. Tom SCHNEIDER
105 Dir Web/Marketing/Communication Mr. Michel FOUGERES
88 Director of ASPEC Mr. Ken WOLFE
104 Director of International Education Ms. Diane L. FERRIS
85 Dir International Student Programs Mr. Olivier DEBURE
13 Director of Information Technology Dr. John A. DUFF
09 Exec Director Instl Effectiveness Ms. Jacqueline MACNEIL
06 Registrar Ms. Amy APICERNO
08 Director of Library Ms. Lisa JOHNSTON
38 Acting Director Counseling Services Dr. Trajana THOMAS
29 Director Alumni Relations Vacant
19 Director Campus Safety Mr. Adam COLBY
37 Director Financial Aid Dr. Pat E. WATKINS
41 Acting Athletic Director Mr. Tom RYAN
07 Director of Admission Mr. Jacob BROWNE
42 Chaplain Rev. Doug MCMAHON
25 Director of Grant Development Ms. Anna RUTH
21 Controller Ms. Robin SMALLEY
124 Asst Dean Students for Engagement Mr. Fred SABOTA
87 Dir Conferences and Summer School Ms. Cheryl GOLD
04 Administrative Asst to President Ms. JoAnn TOWNSEND

ECPI University College of Nursing (A)

660 Century Point, Ste 1050, Lake Mary FL 32746
Telephone: (407) 562-9100 Identification: 770566
Accreditation: &SC, NURSE

† Branch campus of ECPI University, Virginia Beach, VA

Edward Waters College (B)

1658 Kings Road, Jacksonville FL 32209-6199
County: Duval FICE Identification: 001478
Unit ID: 133526
Telephone: (904) 470-8000 Carnegie Class: Bac-Diverse
FAX Number: (904) 470-8039 Calendar System: Semester
URL: www.ewc.edu
Established: 1866 Annual Undergrad Tuition & Fees: $13,525
Enrollment: 2,254 Coed
Affiliation or Control: African Methodist Episcopal IRS Status: 501(c)3
Highest Offering: Baccalaureate
Accreditation: SC, IACBE

01 President Dr. Nathaniel GLOVER
03 Executive Vice President/COO Dr. Anna HAMMOND
88 Special Assistant to the President Mr. George DANDELAKE
05 VP Academic Affairs Dr. Marvin GRANT
10 VP Business & Finance Mr. Randolph MITCHELL
32 Int VP Student Affs/Enrollment Mgmt Dr. Eric JACKSON
30 VP Institutional Advancement Ms. Jennifer SILVA
21 Assoc VP/Business and Finance Ms. Jacqueline DOWDY
15 Director Human Resources Ms. Geree LOCKETT
88 Accreditation Coordinator Dr. Phyllis WALKER
25 Dir Title III & Sponsored Pgms Mrs. Lisa WILLIAMS
06 Coord of Records/Registration Dr. Andrew GORDON
20 Asst VP Academic Affairs Dr. Stephanie CAMPBELL
37 Director Financial Aid Ms. Janice NOWAK
09 Dir Inst Research & Assessment Ms. Bernice PARKER-BELL
88 Director Upward Bound Dr. Delacy SANFORD
36 Career Services Director Mr. Antonio STARKE
44 Director Development Ms. Anita WALTON
07 Director of Admissions Mr. Joel WALKER
88 Int Director of Support Services Dr. Sabrina EDWARDS
31 Dir Community Resource Center Mrs. Marie HEATH
88 Director of CTL Dr. Kenesha BRACELY
88 Director of FAME Mrs. Gladys CLAY
41 Interim Director of Athletics Mr. Stanley CROMATIE
13 Director IT Mr. David SIMFUKWE
08 Library Director Ms. Carmella MARTIN
101 Secy of the College/Clerk of Board Mrs. Linda FOSTER
26 Coordinator of Public Relations Ms. Dee REGISTRE
29 Director of Alumni Affairs Ms. Anita WALTON
38 Director Counseling Center Ms. Ragan SUMMERS
39 Dean of Students/Residence Life Dr. Karen BUCKMAN
96 Purchasing Clerk Ms. Susie MATTISON

Embry-Riddle Aeronautical University (C)

600 S Clyde Morris Boulevard,
Daytona Beach FL 32114-3900
County: Volusia FICE Identification: 001479
Unit ID: 133553
Telephone: (386) 226-6000 Carnegie Class: Masters/L
FAX Number: N/A Calendar System: Semester
URL: www.erau.edu
Established: 1926 Annual Undergrad Tuition & Fees: $33,886
Enrollment: 5,806 Coed
Affiliation or Control: Independent Non-Profit IRS Status: 501(c)3
Highest Offering: Doctorate
Accreditation: SC, AAB, ACBSP, CEA, CS, ENG, IFSAC

01 President Dr. Barry BUTLER
05 Interim SVP Acad Affairs & Research Dr. Maj MIRMIRANI
10 SVP for Finance and CFO Dr. Randy B. HOWARD
11 SVP for Administration & Planning Mr. Rodney J. CRUISE
15 VP/Chief Human Resources Officer Mr. Brandon L. YOUNG
13 Chief Information Officer Ms. Becky L. VASQUEZ
09 Exec Dir of Institutional Research Ms. Maria FRANCO
29 Exec Director of Alumni Relations Mr. William G. THOMPSON
39 Dir of Housing & Residence Life Mr. Steven LOGAN
41 Director of Athletics Mr. John M. PHILLIPS
43 Vice President & General Counsel Mr. Charlie W. SEVASTOS
04 Senior Executive Asst to President Ms. Chantal C. CRISWELL
06 Registrar Ms. M.J CARO
84 Dean of Enrollment Management Mr. Robert J. ADAMS
104 Dir Office of Global Engagement Mrs. Sue A. MACCHIARELLA
108 Director of Academic Assessment Ms. Tiffany D. PHAGAN
18 Dir of Univ Planning & Construction Mr. Chris C. HARDESTY
19 Director of Campus Safety & Securit Mr. Kevin A. MANNIX
30 Interim SVP Dev & Alumni Relations Ms. Lee WILLIAMS
32 Dean of Students Ms. Lisa S. KOLLAR
36 Executive Director of Career Svcs Ms. Alicia SMYTH
37 Director Student Financial Aid Ms. Barbara DRYDEN
50 Dean College of Business Dr. Michael J. WILLIAMS
54 Dean College of Engineering Dr. Maj MIRMIRANI

Embry-Riddle Aeronautical University-Worldwide (D)

600 S Clyde Morris Boulevard,
Daytona Beach FL 32114-3900
Telephone: (800) 522-6787 Identification: 666089
Accreditation: &SC, AAB, ACBSP

† Regional accreditation is carried under the parent institution in Daytona Beach, FL.

Emergency Educational Institute (E)

3111 N. University Dr., Ste 300, Coral Springs FL 33065
County: Broward Identification: 667310
Telephone: (954) 753-6869 Carnegie Class: Not Classified
FAX Number: (954) 755-9050 Calendar System: Other
URL: www.eei.edu
Established: 2002 Annual Undergrad Tuition & Fees: N/A
Enrollment: N/A Coed
Affiliation or Control: Proprietary IRS Status: Proprietary
Highest Offering: Associate Degree
Accreditation: ABHES

01 CEO Michelle UGALDE

Everglades University (F)

5002 T-Rex Avenue, Suite 100,
Boca Raton FL 33431-4493
County: Palm Beach FICE Identification: 031085
Unit ID: 385619
Telephone: (888) 772-6077 Carnegie Class: Bac-Diverse
FAX Number: (561) 912-1191 Calendar System: Semester
URL: www.evergladesuniversity.edu
Established: 1990 Annual Undergrad Tuition & Fees: $16,400
Enrollment: 1,498 Coed
Affiliation or Control: Independent Non-Profit IRS Status: 501(c)3
Highest Offering: Master's
Accreditation: SC

01 President/CEO Ms. Kristi L. MOLLIS
05 Vice President of Academic Affairs Dr. Jayne MOSCHELLA
37 Regional Director of Financial Aid Mrs. Seeta SINGH MOONILALL
26 Director of Marketing Ms. Christina OAKLEY
09 Director Inst Effectiveness Chee PIOG
88 Program Dir of Aviation Ms. Vickie RAMOS
84 Gegional Dir Enrollment Management Ms. Marci TULLT
10 Chief Financial Officer Mr. Joseph BERARDINELLI

Express Training Services (G)

3911 Newberry Road, Suite B, Gainesville FL 32607
County: Alachua Identification: 667276
Telephone: (352) 338-1193 Carnegie Class: Not Classified
FAX Number: (352) 240-1530 Calendar System: Other
URL: www.expresstrainingservices.com
Established: 2004 Annual Undergrad Tuition & Fees: N/A
Enrollment: N/A Coed
Affiliation or Control: Proprietary IRS Status: Proprietary
Highest Offering: Associate Degree
Accreditation: ACICS

07 Director of Admissions Tony KALISHMAN
08 Librarian Sammi HARMON

FCC-Anthem College (H)

989 N Semoran Boulevard, Orlando FL 32807
Telephone: (888) 852-7272 Identification: 770613
Accreditation: ACICS

Flagler College (I)

74 King Street, Saint Augustine FL 32084-4342
County: Saint Johns FICE Identification: 007893
Unit ID: 133711
Telephone: (904) 829-6200 Carnegie Class: Bac-Diverse
FAX Number: (904) 824-6017 Calendar System: Semester
URL: www.flagler.edu
Established: 1968 Annual Undergrad Tuition & Fees: $17,500
Enrollment: 2,701 Coed
Affiliation or Control: Independent Non-Profit IRS Status: 501(c)3
Highest Offering: Master's
Accreditation: SC

01 President Dr. Joseph G. JOYNER
00 Chancellor Dr. William L. PROCTOR
10 Vice President Business Services Mr. David L. CARSON
111 Vice President Inst Advancement Dr. Beverly C. CARMICHAEL
05 Vice President Academic Affairs Dr. Alan WOOLFOLK
26 Exec Director College Relations Ms. Donna DELORENZO
21 Executive Director of Finance Mr. Jeff KNIGHT
09 Director Analytics/Planning/Rsrch Dr. Greg HAWKINS
27 Director of News and Information Mr. Brian L. THOMPSON
84 Vice Pres for Enrollment Mgmt Ms. Deborah L. THOMPSON
32 Vice President of Student Services Dr. Daniel P. STEWART
20 Assoc VP of Academic Affairs Dr. Yvan J. KELLY
35 Dean of Student Services Dr. Dirk HIBLER
38 Director of Counseling Dr. Amy FALVO
06 Registrar Mrs. Miriam C. ROBERSON
37 Director of Financial Aid Ms. Sheia I. PLEASANT-DOINE
36 Director of Career Services Ms. Tara STEVENSON
08 Director of Library Services Mr. Brian NESSELRODE
41 Director Intercollegiate Athletics Mr. Jud DAMON
19 Director of Safety & Security Mr. Creig DOYLE
40 Bookstore Manager Mr. Bob SMITH
24 Director Educational Media Services Mr. Steven I. SKIPP
13 Director Technology Services Mr. Joseph S. PROVENZA
39 Director of Residence Life Ms. Michelle HOLLAND
35 Director of Student Activities Mr. Timothy MELLON
12 Dean Flagler College - Tallahassee Dr. Donald K. PARKS
22 Dir of Disability Services Ms. Eva Lynn FRANCISCO
18 Superintendent of Plant & Grounds Mr. Victor CHENEY
04 Assistant to the President Ms. Mary Jane DILLON
21 Director of Business Services Mr. Larry D. WEEKS
29 Director Alumni Relations Ms. Margo BROWN
44 Assitant Director Annual Fund Ms. Kristy KUROWSKI
15 Director Human Resources Ms. Tricia KRISTOFF-RAMPATA
88 Senior Woman Admin Athletic Dept Ms. Karen HUDGINS
07 Director of Admissions Ms. Rachel U. BRANCH
104 Director Study Abroad Ms. Julia GALAN
105 Director Web Services Ms. Holly L. HILL
106 Dir Online Education/E-learning Dr. Jessica HOWELL

Florida Career College (J)

1743 N Congress Avenue, Boynton Beach FL 33426
Telephone: (561) 634-7400 Identification: 770678
Accreditation: ACICS

Florida Career College (K)

3750 West 18th Avenue, Hialeah FL 33012-7028
Telephone: (786) 534-0940 Identification: 666624
Accreditation: ACICS

Florida Career College (L)

6600 Youngerman Circle, Jacksonville FL 32244
Telephone: (904) 573-1900 Identification: 770679
Accreditation: ACICS

Florida Career College (M)

3383 North State Road 7,
Lauderdale Lakes FL 33319-5617
Telephone: (954) 908-4700 Identification: 666622
Accreditation: ACICS

Florida Career College - Margate Campus (N)

3271 North State Road 7, Margate FL 33063
Telephone: (954) 935-7921 Identification: 770681
Accreditation: ACICS

Florida Career College (O)

1321 SW 107th Avenue, Suite 201B,
Miami FL 33174-2521
County: Miami-Dade FICE Identification: 023058
Unit ID: 133997
Telephone: (786) 534-0500 Carnegie Class: Bac/Assoc-Assoc Dom
FAX Number: (786) 534-0558 Calendar System: Quarter
URL: www.careercollege.edu
Established: 1982 Annual Undergrad Tuition & Fees: N/A
Enrollment: 278 Coed
Affiliation or Control: Proprietary IRS Status: Proprietary
Highest Offering: Associate Degree
Accreditation: ACICS

01 President/CEO Mr. David KNOBEL
12 Campus Director Mr. Louis RODRIGUEZ
06 Registrar Ms. Cheyla DAVILA

Florida Career College (P)

7891 Pines Boulevard, Pembroke Pines FL 33024-6916
Telephone: (954) 399-4801 Identification: 666025
Accreditation: ACICS

Florida Career College (A)
9950 Princess Palm Ave, Suite 100, Tampa FL 33619
Telephone: (813) 621-5775 Identification: 770682
Accreditation: ACICS

Florida Career College (B)
6058 Okeechobee Boulevard, West Palm Beach FL 33417
Telephone: (561) 689-0550 Identification: 770683
Accreditation: ACICS

Florida Coastal School of Law (C)
8787 Baypine, Jacksonville FL 32256-8528
County: Duval FICE Identification: 033743
Unit ID: 434715
Telephone: (904) 680-7700 Carnegie Class: Spec-4-yr-Law
FAX Number: (904) 680-7777 Calendar System: Semester
URL: www.fcsl.edu
Established: 1995 Annual Graduate Tuition & Fees: N/A
Enrollment: 955 Coed
Affiliation or Control: Proprietary IRS Status: Proprietary
Highest Offering: First Professional Degree; No Undergraduates
Accreditation: LAW

01 President ... Mr. Dennis STONE
05 Dean ... Mr. Scott DEVITO
07 Associate Dean of Admissions ... Mr. Tony CARDENAS
29 Dir of Alumni Affairs ... Lauren GRIFFITH
32 Assistant Dean of Student Affairs ... Mr. James ARTLEY
20 Associate Dean of Academic Affairs ... Ms. Jennifer REIBER
15 Sr Director of Human Resources ... Mrs. Susie PONTIFF STRINGER
62 Assoc Dean of Library & Technology .. Ms. Korin MUNSTERMAN
106 Assoc Dean of Strategy & Innovation .... Ms. Margaret IOANNIDES
28 Dir of Diversity/Equity/Inclusion ... Ms. Tammy HODO
88 Director of Clinical Programs ... Ms. Ericka CURRAN
09 Mgr of Institutional Effectiveness ... Ms. Karen EUBANKS
18 Dir of Security & Facilities ... Vacant
88 Process Partner ... Ms. Lisa VERVYNCK
04 Exec Asst to the Dean & President ... Ms. Kelly HARRIS

Florida College (D)
119 N Glen Arven Avenue,
Temple Terrace FL 33617-5578
County: Hillsborough FICE Identification: 001482
Unit ID: 133809
Telephone: (813) 988-5131 Carnegie Class: Bac/Assoc-Mixed
FAX Number: (813) 899-6772 Calendar System: Semester
URL: www.floridacollege.edu
Established: 1944 Annual Undergrad Tuition & Fees: $16,550
Enrollment: 550 Coed
Affiliation or Control: Independent Non-Profit IRS Status: 501(c)3
Highest Offering: Baccalaureate
Accreditation: SC, MUS

01 President ... Dr. Harry E. PAYNE, JR.
05 Vice Pres of Acad & Student Affairs ... Dr. Daniel W. PETTY
20 Dean of Academics ... Dr. Brian L. CRISPELL
32 Dean of Student Services ... Dr. Jason S. LONGSTRETH
10 Chief Business Officer ... Mr. Jamie LEWIS
37 Director Student Financial Aid ... Mr. Stephen BLAYLOCK
07 Dir of Admissions & Retention Svcs ... Mr. Paul CASEBOLT
09 Director of Institutional Research ... Dr. M. Thaxter DICKEY
88 Director of Advising ... Mrs. Holly CABINA
06 Registrar ... Ms. Beth A. GRANT
08 Director of Library ... Mrs. Wanda DICKEY
90 Director of Academic Computing ... Vacant
91 Director of Information Technology ... Mr. Jon RAE
30 Director of Development ... Mr. Martin ADAMS
29 Director of Alumni Relations ... Mr. Adam J. OLSON
26 Director of Marketing/Info Officer ... Mr. Jared M. BARR
40 Manager of Bookstore ... Mrs. Amy CASEBOLT
88 Events Coordinator ... Mrs. Sharon L. CLARK

Florida College of Health Science (E)
6000 South Rio Grande Avenue, Orlando FL 32809
County: Orange Identification: 667265
Telephone: (407) 601-0411 Carnegie Class: Not Classified
FAX Number: (407) 601-6983 Calendar System: Quarter
URL: www.floridacollegeofhealth.com
Established: Annual Undergrad Tuition & Fees: N/A
Enrollment: N/A Coed
Affiliation or Control: Proprietary IRS Status: Proprietary
Highest Offering: Associate Degree
Accreditation: ABHES

01 President ... Mr. Max PAUL

Florida College of Integrative Medicine (F)
7100 Lake Ellenor Drive, Orlando FL 32809-5721
County: Orange FICE Identification: 032383
Unit ID: 434441
Telephone: (407) 888-8689 Carnegie Class: Spec-4-yr-Other Health
FAX Number: (407) 888-8211 Calendar System: Semester
URL: www.fcim.edu
Established: 1990 Annual Undergrad Tuition & Fees: N/A
Enrollment: 95 Coed
Affiliation or Control: Proprietary IRS Status: Proprietary
Highest Offering: Master's; No Lower Division
Accreditation: ACUP

01 President ... Mr. Lincoln Z. ZHAO
03 Vice President ... Ms. Jenjen HAN
108 Chief Quality Officer ... Ms. Yuan-Yuan HAN
05 Dean of Academic Affairs ... Ms. Tara REED
10 Director of Finance ... Ms. Susan HOEH
07 Admissions Representative ... Ms. Michelle COLON
37 Director of Financial Aid ... Ms. Mary SIMMONS

Florida College of Natural Health (G)
2600 Lake Lucien Drive, Suite 140,
Maitland FL 32751-7253
Telephone: (407) 261-0319 Identification: 666513
Accreditation: ACCSC

† Branch campus of Florida College of Natural Health, Pompano Beach, FL.

Florida College of Natural Health (H)
7925 NW 12th Street, Suite 201, Miami FL 33126-1821
Telephone: (305) 597-9599 Identification: 666514
Accreditation: ACCSC

† Branch campus of Florida College of Natural Health, Pompano Beach, FL.

Florida College of Natural Health (I)
2001 W Sample Road, Suite 100,
Pompano Beach FL 33064-1342
County: Broward FICE Identification: 030086
Unit ID: 387925
Telephone: (954) 975-6400 Carnegie Class: Assoc/HVT-High Non
FAX Number: (954) 975-9633 Calendar System: Other
URL: www.fcnh.com
Established: 1986 Annual Undergrad Tuition & Fees: N/A
Enrollment: 206 Coed
Affiliation or Control: Proprietary IRS Status: Proprietary
Highest Offering: Associate Degree
Accreditation: ACCSC

01 President ... Ms. Paris ZUPANCIC
05 Vice President of Education ... Ms. Karina ROLNIK
22 Vice President of Compliance ... Ms. Melissa WADE
37 Financial Aid Officer ... Mr. Jesse SHEPHERD

Florida Gateway College (J)
149 SE College Place, Lake City FL 32025-2007
County: Columbia FICE Identification: 001501
Unit ID: 135160
Telephone: (386) 752-1822 Carnegie Class: Bac/Assoc-Assoc Dom
FAX Number: (386) 755-1521 Calendar System: Semester
URL: www.fgc.edu
Established: 1947 Annual Undergrad Tuition & Fees (In-State): $3,100
Enrollment: 2,860 Coed
Affiliation or Control: State IRS Status: 501(c)3
Highest Offering: Baccalaureate
Accreditation: SC, ADNUR, EMT, NURSE, PTAA

01 President ... Dr. Lawrence BARRETT
10 Vice President Business Services ... Vacant
04 Assistant to the President ... Ms. Karyn CONGRESSI
05 Vice President for Academic Pgms ... Dr. Brian DOPSON
84 VP Enroll Mgmt & Student Affairs ... Ms. Jennifer PRICE
20 Dean of Academic Pgm & Bacc Liaison ... Dr. Paula GAVIN
13 Exec Dir Info Technology/CIO ... Mr. Mike DAVIS
72 Exec Dir of Tech Pgm & Public Svcs ... Mr. John JEWETT
15 Executive Director Human Resources ... Ms. Sharon BEST
53 Exec Dir Teacher Prep Programs ... Ms. Pamela CARSWELL
30 Exec Director Resource Development ... Mr. Lee PINCHOUCK
26 Exec Dir Media & Community Info ... Mr. Mike MCKEE
37 Director Financial Aid ... Mrs. Becky WESTBERRY
26 Dir Recruitment & Communication ... Ms. Kacey SCHRADER
06 Registrar & Dir of Enrollment Svcs ... Ms. Gayle HUNTER
21 Director Business Services ... Ms. Michelle HOLLOWAY
25 Director of Grants & Grant Mgmt ... Ms. Sandra JOHNSTON
09 Director of Inst Effect & Assess ... Ms. Rebecca VANHOEK
66 Exec Director Nursing ... Ms. Melody CORSO
18 Director Facilities ... Mr. Ed D'AVI
96 Director Procurement & Contracts ... Ms. Misty TAYLOR
121 Director Advising ... Ms. Laurie ALBURY
36 Director of Career Services ... Ms. Audrey JACKSON
88 Director of Public Service Programs ... Mr. Jay SWISHER
08 Director Library ... Ms. Christine BOATRIGHT

Florida Institute of Technology (K)
150 W University Boulevard, Melbourne FL 32901-6975
County: Brevard FICE Identification: 001469
Unit ID: 133881
Telephone: (321) 674-8000 Carnegie Class: DU-Higher
FAX Number: (321) 984-8461 Calendar System: Semester
URL: www.fit.edu
Established: 1958 Annual Undergrad Tuition & Fees: $40,446
Enrollment: 6,631 Coed
Affiliation or Control: Independent Non-Profit IRS Status: 501(c)3
Highest Offering: Doctorate
Accreditation: SC, AAB, CLPSY, CS, ENG, IACBE

01 President ... Dr. T. Dwayne MCCAY
04 Exec Asst to Pres ... Ms. Rebecca CROOK
05 Sr VP Accred/Acad/Student Affs/CAO ... Dr. Monica BALOGA
10 Sr Vice Pres Financial Affairs/CFO ... Ms. Cathy WOOD
88 Sr Advisor to the President ... Capt. Winston SCOTT
100 Chief of Staff/Govt Relations ... Mr. Frank KINNEY
88 Dean College of Aeronautics ... Dr. Korhan OYMAN
50 Dean College of Business ... Dr. Theodore RICHARDSON
54 Dean College of Engineering ... Dr. Marco CARVALHO
83 Dean Col of Psychology/Liberal Arts ... Dr. Mary Beth KENKEL
81 Dean College of Science ... Dr. Hamid RASSOUL
08 Dean of Libraries ... Dr. Sohair WASTAWY
29 VP Alum Rel/Exec Dir Alum Assn ... Mr. Albino P. CAMPANINI
30 Vice President Development ... Mr. Gary GRANT
84 Vice Pres Enrollment Mgmt ... Mr. Gary HAMME
18 Vice Pres Facilities Operations ... Mr. Chad SHOULTZ
13 Vice Pres IT/CIO ... Mr. Eric KLEDZIK
26 Vice Pres Marketing & Communication .. Mr. Wesley D. SUMNER
106 Vice Pres Online Learning ... Mr. Brian EHRLICH
88 Vice President Orlando Center ... Ms. Leslie HIELEMA
46 Vice President Research ... Dr. S. Ann BECKER
32 Vice President Student Affairs ... Dr. Randall L. ALFORD
102 Assoc VP Corp Sponsored Programs ... Ms. Gretchen SAUERMAN
21 Assoc Vice Pres Financial Services ... Ms. Brenda BROWN
35 Assoc VP Student Affs/Dean of Stdnt ... Mr. Rodney BOWERS
109 Asst VP Business & Ret Operation ... Mr. Greg GRAHAM
28 Chief Diversity Officer/Title IX ... Dr. Joni OGLESBY
06 Registrar ... Mr. David MICUS
88 Director Academic Support Services ... Mr. Rodd NEWCOMBE
41 Director Athletics ... Mr. William K. JURGENS
19 Director Campus Security ... Mr. Kevin GRAHAM
36 Director Career Services ... Ms. Dona E. GAYNOR
38 Dir Counseling/Psychological Svcs ... Dr. Robyn TAPLEY
88 Director Creative Services ... Ms. Judith E. TINTERA
88 Dir Environ & Regulatory Compliance ... Mr. Henry PEEBLES
18 Director Facilities Operations ... Mr. John M. MILBOURNE
37 Director Financial Aid ... Mr. Jay LALLY
123 Director Graduate Admissions ... Ms. Cheryl-Ann BROWN
123 Director Grad Adm Online/Off-Campus .. Ms. Carolyn P. FARRIOR
58 Director Graduate Programs ... Dr. Rosemary LAYNE
15 Director Human Resources ... Ms. Karen GATHERCOLE
09 Director Institutional Research ... Ms. Leslie L. SAVOIE
85 Director Intl Students/Scholar Svcs ... Ms. Judith BROOKE
104 Director Study Abroad ... Ms. Heather WAUTLET
07 Director Undergraduate Admission ... Mr. Michael PERRY
88 Director University Museums ... Ms. Carla FUNK
90 Executive Director Ellucian ... Ms. Rebecca ARCHER

Florida Keys Community College (L)
5901 College Road, Key West FL 33040-4397
County: Monroe FICE Identification: 001485
Unit ID: 133960
Telephone: (305) 296-9081 Carnegie Class: Assoc/MT-VT-Mix Trad/Non
FAX Number: (305) 292-5155 Calendar System: Trimester
URL: www.fkcc.edu
Established: 1963 Annual Undergrad Tuition & Fees (In-District): $3,276
Enrollment: 1,081 Coed
Affiliation or Control: State/Local IRS Status: 501(c)3
Highest Offering: Baccalaureate
Accreditation: SC

01 President ... Dr. Jonathan GUEVERRA
05 Vice President Academic Affairs ... Mrs. Brittany SYNDER
10 Vice Pres Business & Admin Svcs ... Ms. Jean MAUK
111 Vice President Advancement ... Dr. Frank WOOD
35 Dean Student Affairs ... Vacant
84 Int Assoc Dean Enrollment Mgmt ... Mrs. Michelle CHERRY
88 Dir Institute for Public Safety ... Mrs. Cathy TORRES
04 Director President's Office ... Mrs. Debbie LEONARD
26 Dir College and Public Relations .. Mrs. Amber ERNST-LEONARD
06 Registrar ... Vacant
08 Director Learning Resources ... Ms. Lori KELLY
37 Director Financial Aid ... Ms. Beryl MORGAN
18 Dir Purchasing & Plant Operations ... Mr. Douglas PRYOR
13 Director of IT ... Mrs. Michelle ADAM
15 Director Human Resources ... Ms. Kathleen DANIEL
21 Interim Controller ... Ms. Heather GARCIA
09 Director Institutional Research ... Vacant
30 Director Development/Alumni Rels ... Vacant
76 Dean of Science & Nursing ... Mr. Mark ROBY
103 Dean Business and Marine Tech ... Mr. Jack SUEBERT
49 Dean Arts & Sciences ... Mr. Michael MCPHERSON
32 Dean Student Affairs/Campus Life ... Ms. Erika HEFFERNAN

Florida Memorial University (M)
15800 NW 42nd Avenue, Miami Gardens FL 33054-6199
County: Miami-Dade FICE Identification: 001486
Unit ID: 133979
Telephone: (305) 626-3600 Carnegie Class: Bac-Diverse
FAX Number: (305) 626-3769 Calendar System: Semester
URL: www.fmuniv.edu
Established: 1879 Annual Undergrad Tuition & Fees: $15,536
Enrollment: 1,467 Coed
Affiliation or Control: Independent Non-Profit IRS Status: 501(c)3
Highest Offering: Master's
Accreditation: SC, AAB, ACBSP, CS, MUS, SW

01 Interim President ... Dr. Michelle HOWARD-VITAL

05 Executive VP and Provost .... Dr. Michelle HOWARD-VITAL
20 Associate Provost .... Dr. Denise CALLWOOD-BRATHWAITE
04 Assistant to President .... Ms. Rachel TURNER
49 Interim Dean of Arts and Sciences .... Dr. William E. HOPPER
10 Exec VP Finance/Administration .... Ms. Cynthia CURRY
84 Interim Director of Enrollment Mgmt .... Mr. Francis FRANCOIS
111 Vice Pres University Advancement .... Mr. Marcus BURGESS
45 Assc VP Institutional Effectiveness ... Dr. William E. HOPPER, JR.
88 Chair Aviation and Safety .... Dr. Arnold J. TOLBERT
50 Dean School of Business .... Dr. Abbass ENTESSARI
53 Dean School of Education .... Dr. Idriss ABDOULAYE
81 Chair Health and Natural Sciences .... Dr. Rose Mary STIFFIN
83 Interim Chair Social Sciences .... Vacant
64 Interim Chair Visual/Perf Arts .... Mr. Melvin WHITE
77 Chair Comp Science/Math & Tech .... Dr. Ben WONGSAROJ
79 Chair Humanities .... Vacant
124 Dir Ctrs Acad Support & Reten .... Ms. Jamila LYN
08 Interim Director Library Services .... Ms. Cheryl WILCHER
37 Director Financial Aid .... Ms. Faye RODNEY
06 Registrar .... Mrs. Lelia EFFORD
09 Director of Institutional Research .... Dr. Carlos CANAS
15 Int Dir Human Resources Management .... Mr. Sam HINES
41 Director Intercollegiate Athletics .... Mr. Rodney CARTER
36 Director Career Development .... Vacant
39 Director Residential Life .... Ms. Lovely DURHAM
19 Chief of Campus Safety .... Chief Edgar CLARK
18 Dir Facility Mgmt/Plant Operations .... Mr. David JACCARINO
42 Dean of Campus Ministry .... Dr. Jeffrey D. SWAIN
29 Director Alumni Affairs .... Mrs. Shelia POWELL-COHEN
35 Director Student Activities .... Ms. Sharhonda FORD
85 International Student Advisor .... Mr. Trevor LEWIS
13 CIO .... Mr. Christopher BROMFIELD
32 Dean of Students .... Dr. Michael GARY
108 Director Institutional Assessment .... Dr. Richard YAKLICH
07 Assistant Director of Admissions ..... Mr. Gerald RICHARDSON, II
105 Web Master .... Mr. Gerald PATTILO
26 VP Public Relations/Marketing .... Dr. Ceeon SMITH
38 Director Student Development .... Dr. Angela BRINSON-BROWN
96 Director of Procurement Management .... Mrs. Cheryl PHILLIP

Florida National University Hialeah Campus (A)

4425 W. Jose Regueiro (20th) Ave,
Hialeah FL 33012-4108

County: Dade FICE Identification: 025476
Unit ID: 408844
Telephone: (305) 821-3333 Carnegie Class: Bac/Assoc-Mixed
FAX Number: (305) 362-0595 Calendar System: Semester
URL: www.fnu.edu
Established: 1982 Annual Undergrad Tuition & Fees: $13,250
Enrollment: 2,492 Coed
Affiliation or Control: Proprietary IRS Status: Proprietary
Highest Offering: Master's
Accreditation: SC, COARC, NURSE, PTAA

01 President/CEO .... Dr. Maria C. REGUEIRO
09 VP of Assessment & Research/FA Dir .... Mr. Omar SANCHEZ
11 Vice President of Operations .... Mr. Frank ANDREU
05 Vice President of Academic Affairs .... Dr. Caridad HERNANDEZ
10 Controller .... Dr. Lourdes NIEVES
88 Accreditation Liaison .... Dr. Barbara J. RODRIGUEZ
07 Director of Admissions .... Mr. Robert LOPEZ
06 University Registrar .... Mr. Jose L. VALDES
32 Director of Student Services .... Ms. Maria HOFFMAN
106 Director of Distance Learning .... Mrs. Sandra LOMENA
12 Campus Dean .... Dr. Jorge ALFONSO
35 Student Services Officer .... Mr. John FERRARI
50 Business & Economics Division Head .... Dr. James BULLEN
76 Allied Health Division Head .... Dr. Loreto ALMONTE
79 Humanities and Fine Arts Division .... Dr. Barbara RODRIGUEZ
88 ESL Division Head .... Mr. Oscar PEREZ
66 RN Program Director .... Mrs. Maida BURGOS
66 BSN Program Director .... Mr. Ruben COLL
66 MSN Program Director .... Dr. Marlene CESAR-BERRO
15 Human Resources Director .... Mr. Edward ZALDIVAR
41 Athletic Director/Head Men's Soccer . Mr. Fernando VALENZUELA
20 Assistant Campus Dean .... Mr. Harold FLORES
20 Assistant Campus Dean .... Mrs. Yedi CEPERO
07 Admissions Supervisor Distance .... Mrs. Yolanda NAVARRO
07 Admissions Supervisor .... Mrs. Virginia RABELO
121 Academic Advisor .... Mrs. Carol ROMERO
121 Academic Advisor .... Dr. Rosa HERNANDEZ
31 Director Community Relations .... Mrs. Rachel TOURGEMAN
36 Job Placement Officer .... Mrs. Vanessa PEREZ
26 Social Media/Marketing Rep .... Mr. Kevin MARTINEZ
108 Director Institutional Assessment .... Mr. Rodrigo LOAIZA

Florida National University South Campus (B)

11865 SW 26th Street Unit H-3, Miami FL 33175
Telephone: (305) 226-9999 Identification: 666691
Accreditation: &SC

† Regional accreditation is carried under the parent institution Florida National College, Hialeah, FL.

Florida National University Training Center (C)

4206 West 12th Avenue, Hialeah FL 33012
Telephone: (305) 231-3326 Identification: 666690
Accreditation: &SC

† Regional accreditation is carried under the parent institution Florida National College, Hialeah, FL.

Florida Southern College (D)

111 Lake Hollingsworth Drive, Lakeland FL 33801-5698
County: Polk FICE Identification: 001488
Unit ID: 134079
Telephone: (863) 680-4111 Carnegie Class: Masters/S
FAX Number: (863) 680-4112 Calendar System: Semester
URL: www.flsouthern.edu
Established: 1883 Annual Undergrad Tuition & Fees: $33,150
Enrollment: 2,869 Coed
Affiliation or Control: United Methodist IRS Status: 501(c)3
Highest Offering: Doctorate
Accreditation: SC, MUS, NURSE

01 President .... Dr. Anne B. KERR
05 Provost .... Dr. Kyle FEDLER
30 Vice President Advancement .... Dr. Robert H. TATE
10 Vice President Finance & Admin .... Mr. Terry DENNIS
84 VP Enrollment Management .... Mr. John GRUNDIG
20 Assoc Provost Experiential Educ .... Dr. Mary L. CROWE
102 Asst VP Advancement .... Ms. Heather PHARRIS
44 Asst VP for Annual Giving .... Ms. Kathy ELLIS
35 Asst Dean of Student Development .... Mr. Mike CRAWFORD
42 Chaplain Director Campus Ministry .... Rev. Timothy S. WRIGHT
13 Chief Information Officer .... Mr. John L. THOMAS
21 Controller .... Ms. Judy ROBINSON
108 Coordinator Assessment/Compliance .. Mr. Matthew K. DESANTIS
104 Coordinator Student Travel .... Ms. Bridgette MCARTHUR
49 Dean Art and Sciences .... Dr. Brad E. HOLLINGSHEAD
50 Dean Business and Free Enterprise .... Dr. James FENTON
53 Dean Education .... Dr. Tracey D. TEDDER
66 Dean Nursing and Health Science .... Dr. Linda S. COMER
121 Dean of Student Success .... Dr. Susan FREEMAN
32 Dean of Student Development .... Mr. Bill C. LANGSTON, II
07 Director of Admissions .... Ms. Arden MITCHELL
123 Director of Adult & Graduate Educ .... Ms. Kristen PLACEK
29 Director of Alumni Relations .... Ms. Jennifer OLIVIER
41 Director of Athletics .... Mr. Peter E. MEYER
36 Director of Career Development .... Ms. Cara CIMA
39 Director of Community Living .... Mr. Marc A. TUSCHEN
23 Director of Health Services .... Dr. Paige MCCRANEY
112 Director of Major Gifts .... Ms. Sara OLSON
92 Director of Honors Program .... Dr. Gabriel J. LANGFORD
15 Director of Human Resources .... Ms. Katherine PAWLAK
09 Dir Inst Research/Effectiveness .... Ms. Jazmine ESPARZA
119 Director of IT Services .... Ms. Francine NEILING
08 Director of the Library .... Mr. Randall M. MACDONALD
28 Director Life and Cultural Center .... Ms. Brenda LEWIS
26 Director of Marketing and Comm .... Vacant
18 Director of Operations .... Mr. Jon P. CAMP
06 Registrar .... Ms. Sally L. THISSEN
19 Director of Security/Safety .... Mr. William CAREW
38 Director of Student Counseling .... Dr. Carol BALLARD
37 Director of Student Financial Aid .... Mr. William L. HEALY
105 Director of Web Services .... Mr. James JARRETT
04 Executive Asst to President .... Ms. Lynn M. DENNIS
40 Manager Bookstore .... Mr. James BAUER

Florida SouthWestern State College (E)

8099 College Parkway, SW, Fort Myers FL 33919-5566
County: Lee FICE Identification: 001477
Unit ID: 133508
Telephone: (239) 489-9300 Carnegie Class: Bac/Assoc-Mixed
FAX Number: (239) 489-9103 Calendar System: Semester
URL: www.fsw.edu
Established: 1961 Annual Undergrad Tuition & Fees (In-State): $3,401
Enrollment: 15,709 Coed
Affiliation or Control: State IRS Status: 501(c)3
Highest Offering: Baccalaureate
Accreditation: SC, ADNUR, CAHIIM, COARC, CVT, DH, EMT, NUR, RAD

01 President .... Dr. Jeffery ALLBRITTEN
100 Chief of Staff .... Dr. Henry PEEL
12 Regional VP/Pres Charlotte Campus .... Dr. Denis WRIGHT
12 Regional VP/Pres Collier Campus .... Dr. Robert JONES
05 Provost & VP Acad Affairs .... Dr. Jeff STEWART
32 VP Student Affairs & Enroll Mgmt .... Dr. Christine DAVIS
11 VP Administrative Services .... Dr. Gina DOEBLE
111 VP Institutional Advancement .... Dr. Lou TRAINA
20 Associate VP Academic Affairs .... Dr. Eileen DELUCA
43 General Counsel .... Mr. Mark LUPE
50 Dean Business & Technology .... Vacant
76 Dean Health Professions .... Dr. Marie COLLINS
53 Dean Education and Charter Schools .... Dr. Lawrence MILLER
79 Dean Arts/Hum & Social Sci .... Dr. Deborah TEED
49 Dean Pure & Applied Sci .... Dr. Martin MCCLINTON
86 Director Governmental Relations .... Mr. Matthew HOLLIDAY
41 Director Intercollegiate Athletics .... Mr. Carl MCALOOSE
114 Asst VP Budget & Financial Svcs .... Mr. Tobias DISCENZA
84 Asst VP Enrollment/Student Success .... Dr. Laura ANTCZAK
88 Campus Dean Stdnt Affs & Acad Svcs .... Dr. Christy GILFERT
88 Campus Dean Stdnt Affs & Acad Svcs .... Ms. Gail MURPHY
88 Assoc Dean Stdnt Affs HG Center .... Ms. Michelle FANSLAU
35 Dean of Students .... Mr. Mark BUKOWSKI
06 Registrar .... Mr. Garnett SALMON
13 Chief Information Officer .... Mr. Jason DUDLEY
08 Library Coordinator/Head Librarian .... Mr. William SHULUK
102 Sr Director Admin & Dev/Foundation .... Mr. Kevin MILLER
110 Asst VP Institutional Advancement .... Ms. Susan ELLIS
26 Dir Comm & Public Info Officer .... Ms. Teresa ARAQUE

108 Dir Assessment & Effectiveness .... Dr. Joseph VAN GAALEN
09 Dir Institutional Research .... Ms. Kelli DUNLAP
12 Director Hendry/Glades Center .... Ms. Amanda LEHRIAN
113 Bursar .... Ms. Kristine BAXTER
19 Director Public Safety .... Mr. Richard PARFITT
109 Director Auxiliary Services .... Ms. Judith PULTRO
37 Director Student Financial Aid .... Mr. Matthew SANCHEZ
15 Director Human Resources .... Ms. Susan BRONSTEIN
07 Director Admissions .... Ms. Amber MCCOWN
18 Dir Facilities Plng & Dev .... Mr. Ron COPASS
88 Director Academic Support Programs .... Ms. Monica MOORE
39 Dir Housing & Res Life .... Mr. Justin LONG
88 Director Adaptive Services .... Ms. Angela HARTSELL
36 Assoc Dir Advising & Career Svcs .... Mr. Andrae JONES
96 Director of Procurement Services .... Ms. Lisa TUDOR
88 Director Testing Services .... Ms. Denise SWAFFORD
29 Coordinator Alumni Relations .... Mr. Joseph TURNER
22 Title IX Coord Equity Officer .... Ms. Jana SABO
88 Director DSO Finance .... Ms. Kathleen PORTER
88 Director Corporate Sponsorships .... Mr. Kevin ANDERSON
88 Director Prof Dev & Training .... Dr. Melissa RIZZUTO
88 Director Development .... Mr. Joseph KRAMP
88 Director Exhibitions & Collections .... Mr. Jade DELLINGER
89 Director First Year Experience .... Ms. Whitney RHYNE
88 Director Corp Training & Services .... Mr. Adrian KERR
88 Director Simulation Education .... Ms. Lynne CRANDALL
88 Director Risk & Counsel .... Ms. Susan MARCY

Florida State College at Jacksonville (F)

501 W State Street, Jacksonville FL 32202-4097
County: Duval FICE Identification: 001484
Unit ID: 133702
Telephone: (904) 646-2300 Carnegie Class: Bac/Assoc-Mixed
FAX Number: N/A Calendar System: Semester
URL: www.fscj.edu
Established: 1965 Annual Undergrad Tuition & Fees (In-District): $2,878
Enrollment: 26,164 Coed
Affiliation or Control: Local IRS Status: Exempt
Highest Offering: Baccalaureate
Accreditation: SC, ACBSP, ACFEI, ADNUR, CAHIIM, COARC, CVT, DA, DH, EMT, FUSER, HT, MLTAD, NUR, OTA, PTAA, SURGT

01 College President .... Dr. Cynthia A. BIOTEAU
10 Vice Pres of Business Services .... Mr. Albert LITTLE
43 College General Counsel .... Dr. Colin C. MAILLOUX
05 Provost/Vice President Academics .... Dr. John WALL
32 Vice President Student Services .... Dr. Christopher HOLLAND
12 Campus President North .... Dr. Sandy ROBINSON
108 VP Institutional Effectiveness .... Dr. Marie F. GNAGE
49 Assoc Provost Liberal Arts/Sciences .... Dr. Ian NEUHARD
120 VP Online/Workforce Education .... Ms. Jana KOOI
103 AVP Workforce Development .... Dr. Cedrick GIBSON
84 Exec Director Academic Operations .... Mr. Rich TURNER
56 Assoc Provost Outreach & Extension .... Dr. Nancy K. WEBSTER
20 Assoc Prov Curriculum/Instruction .... Dr. Kathleen CIEZ-VOLZ
21 AVP Finance .... Ms. Anita KOVACS
35 AVP Student Success .... Ms. Melanie MILLER
45 AVP Institutional Effectiveness .... Dr. Carrie HENDERSON
103 AVP Workforce Educ/Econ Development ..... Ms. Linda WOODARD
15 Chief Human Resource Officer .... Mr. Mark LACEY
21 Chief Business Affairs Officer .... Mr. Laurence I. SNELL
13 Chief Information Tech Officer .... Ms. Karen HEINEMANN
22 Exec Dir Employee Rels/Equity .... Ms. Lisa J. MOORE
18 Exec Dir Facilities Mgmt/
Construct .... Mr. Charles M. STRATMANN
88 Exec Director Artist Series .... Dr. Milton A. RUSSOS
88 Executive Director College Data Rep .... Ms. Theresa LOTT
88 Executive Director Talent Acquis .... Ms. Barbara HUNTER
88 Executive Director Enterprise App .... Mr. Chris MARTIN
62 Executive Dean of Library Services .... Dr. Tom MESSNER
14 Exec Dir Computer Infrastructure .... Mr. Ron SMITH
19 Executive Director Public Safety .... Mr. James W. STEVENSON
12 Executive Director of Nassau Center .... Ms. Donna MARTIN
102 Executive Director Foundation .... Mr. Cleve WARREN
12 Executive Director Cecil Center .... Mr. Paul MCNAMARA
96 Executive Director Purchasing .... Ms. Randi BROKVIST
86 Dir Government/Cmty Engagement .... Ms. Jennifer SILVA
88 Director of Student Onboarding .... Dr. Roland BULLARD
19 Director of Security .... Mr. Gordon BASS
37 Director Financial Aid .... Ixchel BAKER-TATE
41 Director of Athletics .... Ms. Ginny ALEXANDER
25 Director of Resource Development .... Ms. Jennifer PETERSON
06 Registrar .... Ms. Jamie DIGESARE
09 Director Student Analytics/Research .... Mr. Gregory MICHALSKI
26 Director Marketing/Communications .... Ms. Jill K. JOHNSON

Florida Technical College (G)

1199 S Woodland Boulevard, Deland FL 32720-7415
Telephone: (386) 734-3303 Identification: 666419
Accreditation: ACICS

Florida Technical College (H)

3831 West Vine Street, Kissimmee FL 34741
Telephone: (407) 483-5700 Identification: 770684
Accreditation: ACICS, ACFEI

Florida Technical College **(A)**

4715 South Florida Avenue, Suite 4,
Lakeland FL 33813-2101
Telephone: (866) 967-8822 FICE Identification: 025981
Accreditation: ACICS

Florida Technical College (B)

12900 Challenger Parkway, Orlando FL 32826
County: Orange FICE Identification: 022187
Unit ID: 134112
Telephone: (407) 447-7300 Carnegie Class: Bac/Assoc-Assoc Dom
FAX Number: (407) 447-7301 Calendar System: Quarter
URL: www.ftccollege.edu
Established: 1982 Annual Undergrad Tuition & Fees: N/A
Enrollment: 4,575 Coed
Affiliation or Control: Proprietary IRS Status: Proprietary
Highest Offering: Baccalaureate
Accreditation: ACICS

00 President/CEO ... Mr. James BURKETT
01 Executive Director ... Ms. Linda ROBERTS
11 Executive Administrator ... Ms. Megan ALLEN
05 Director of Education ... Dr. David PENN
07 Director of Admissions ... Ms. Lorraine COLLINS
37 Director of Financial Aid ... Ms. Ivette LUGO

Florida Technical College **(C)**

12520 Pines Boulevard, Pembroke Pines FL 33027
Telephone: (954) 556-1900 Identification: 770685
Accreditation: ACICS

Fortis College (D)

700 Blanding Boulevard, Suite 16, Orange Park FL 32065
County: Clay FICE Identification: 034343
Unit ID: 439792
Telephone: (904) 269-7086 Carnegie Class: Spec 2-yr-Health
FAX Number: (904) 269-6664 Calendar System: Semester
URL: www.fortis.edu
Established: 1985 Annual Undergrad Tuition & Fees: $14,709
Enrollment: 362 Coed
Affiliation or Control: Proprietary IRS Status: Proprietary
Highest Offering: Associate Degree
Accreditation: ACICS, SURGT

01 Campus President ... Mr. Wyman DICKEY

Fortis Institute-Port St. Lucie **(E)**

9022 South Federal Highway/US-1,
Port St. Lucie FL 34952
Telephone: (772) 221-9799 Identification: 770527
Accreditation: ABHES

† Branch campus of Fortis Institute, Baton Rouge, LA.

Full Sail University (F)

3300 University Boulevard, Winter Park FL 32792
County: Orange FICE Identification: 023621
Unit ID: 134237
Telephone: (407) 679-0100 Carnegie Class: Masters/L
FAX Number: (407) 679-9685 Calendar System: Other
URL: www.fullsail.edu
Established: 1979 Annual Undergrad Tuition & Fees: $23,116
Enrollment: 20,025 Coed
Affiliation or Control: Proprietary IRS Status: Proprietary
Highest Offering: Master's
Accreditation: ACCSC

01 President ... Mr. Garry JONES
07 Vice President of Admissions ... Mr. Matt PENGRA

Galen College of Nursing **(G)**

11101 Roosevelt Blvd N, Suite 100,
St. Petersburg FL 33716
Telephone: (727) 577-1497 Identification: 770539
Accreditation: &SC, ADNUR

† Branch campus of Galen College of Nursing, Louisville, KY

Golf Academy of America **(H)**

510 South Hunt Club Blvd., Apopka FL 32703
Telephone: (800) 342-7342 Identification: 666186
Accreditation: ACICS

† Branch campus of Virginia College, Birmingham, AL.

Gordon-Conwell Theological Seminary-Jacksonville **(I)**

7235 Bonneval Road, Jacksonville FL 32256
Telephone: (904) 354-4800 Identification: 770111
Accreditation: &EH, THEOL

† Branch campus of Gordon-Conwell Theological Seminary, South Hamilton, MA

Gulf Coast State College (J)

5230 W Highway 98, Panama City FL 32401-1058
County: Bay FICE Identification: 001490
Unit ID: 134343
Telephone: (850) 769-1551 Carnegie Class: Bac/Assoc-Assoc Dom
FAX Number: (850) 913-3319 Calendar System: Semester
URL: www.gulfcoast.edu
Established: 1957 Annual Undergrad Tuition & Fees (In-State): $2,370
Enrollment: 5,453 Coed
Affiliation or Control: State Related IRS Status: 501(c)3
Highest Offering: Baccalaureate
Accreditation: SC, ACFEI, ADNUR, COARC, DA, DH, EMT, NURSE, PTAA, RAD, SURGA, SURGT

01 President ... Dr. John R. HOLDNAK
10 Vice Pres Administration & Finance ... Mr. John D. MERCER
05 VP Academic Affairs ... Dr. Holly KUEHNER
32 VP Student Affairs ... Dr. Melissa LAVENDER
45 VP Institutional Effect/Stratg Plng ... Dr. Cheryl L. FLAX-HYMAN
13 Chief Information Officer ... Ms. Rhonda BARKER
08 Director of Library ... Ms. Lori DRISCOLL
84 Dean of Enrollment Services ... Ms. Sharon O. TODD
15 Exec Director of Human Resources ... Vacant
26 Exec Director Marketing & Comm ... Mr. Christopher P. THOMES
103 Dean Workforce Education ... Mr. Al MCCAMBRY
96 Director Procurement ... Mr. Fred BROWN
37 Exec Director Student Financial Svc ... Mr. Christopher J. WESTLAKE
09 Institutional Research Analyst ... Ms. Amber COKER
04 Executive Asst to President ... Ms. Dottie TERRYN

Health Career Institute (K)

1764 N. Congress Avenue, West Palm Beach FL 33409
County: Palm Beach Identification: 667104
Telephone: (561) 586-0121 Carnegie Class: Not Classified
FAX Number: (561) 471-4010 Calendar System: Semester
URL: www.hci.edu
Established: 1993 Annual Undergrad Tuition & Fees: N/A
Enrollment: N/A Coed
Affiliation or Control: Proprietary IRS Status: Proprietary
Highest Offering: Associate Degree
Accreditation: ACCSC

01 President ... Brenda GREEN
10 Business Manager ... Angela MOECKES

Herzing University **(L)**

1865 SR 436, Winter Park FL 32792
Telephone: (407) 478-0500 Identification: 666422
Accreditation: &NH, ADNUR, NURSE, PTAA

† Regional accreditation is carried under the parent institution in Madison, WI.

Hillsborough Community College (M)

PO Box 31127, 39 Columbia Drive, Tampa FL 33631-3127
County: Hillsborough FICE Identification: 007870
Unit ID: 134495
Telephone: (813) 253-7000 Carnegie Class: Assoc/HT-High Trad
FAX Number: (813) 253-7183 Calendar System: Semester
URL: www.hccfl.edu
Established: 1968 Annual Undergrad Tuition & Fees (In-State): $2,506
Enrollment: 26,571 Coed
Affiliation or Control: State IRS Status: 501(c)3
Highest Offering: Associate Degree
Accreditation: SC, ACFEI, ADNUR, COARC, CSHSE, DA, DH, DIETT, DMS, EMT, MUS, NMT, OPD, RAD, RTT

01 President ... Dr. Ken ATWATER
10 VP Administration/CFO ... Mr. Al ERDMAN
05 VP for Academic Affairs ... Dr. Ginger CLARK
13 VP Information Technology ... Mr. Daya PENDHARKAR
32 VP Student Services/Enrollment Mgt ... Dr. Ken RAY
12 Campus President Dale Mabry ... Dr. Robert CHUNN
12 Campus President Ybor City Campus ... Dr. Shawn ROBINSON
12 Campus President Plant City Campus ... Dr. Martyn CLAY
12 Campus President Brandon Campus ... Dr. Nancee SORENSON
12 Campus President South Shore Campus ... Dr. Allen WITT
22 Asst to Pres Equity/Special Pgms ... Dr. Joan HOLMES
26 Exec Dir Marketing/Public Relations ... Ms. Ashley CARL
09 Spc Asst to Pres Strat Plng & Analy ... Dr. Paul NAGY
102 Exec Director HCC Foundation ... Mr. Stephen SHEAR
43 College Attorney ... Ms. Martha Kaye KOEHLER
15 Exec Dir Human Resources ... Ms. Kristin SMUDER
21 Controller ... Ms. Kimberly MCMILLON
75 Director Technical Programs ... Dr. Brian MANN
88 Director Assoc in Arts Programs ... Dr. Karen GRIFFIN
90 Director of Academic Technology ... Mr. Mark LEWIS
20 Dean of Academic Affairs ... Dr. Keith BERRY
88 Dean of Acad Affairs - Plant City ... Dr. Anthony BORRELL
88 Dean of AS Programs - Brandon ... Dr. Alessandro ANZALONE
88 Dean of Arts & Sciences-Dale Mabry ... Dr. Mary BENDICKSON
88 Dean of AS Programs - Dale Mabry ... Dr. Elizabeth JOHNSON
81 Dean AA Math/Science - Dale Mabry ... Dr. James WYSONG
76 Dean Health/Wellness & Sports Tech ... Mr. Leif PENROSE
37 Financial Aid Director ... Ms. Tierra SMITH
06 Registrar ... Nevaler DAVIS
18 Director Facilities/Physical Plant ... Mr. Ben MARSHALL

96 Director of Purchasing ... Ms. Vonda MELCHIOR
31 Dir of Community & Govt Relations ... Mr. Eric JOHNSON
19 Director Security/Safety ... Mr. Jeff COPELAND

Hobe Sound Bible College (N)

11298 SE Gomez Avenue, Hobe Sound FL 33455
County: Martin FICE Identification: 021889
Unit ID: 134510
Telephone: (772) 545-1400 Carnegie Class: Spec-4-yr-Faith
FAX Number: (772) 545-1422 Calendar System: Semester
URL: www.hsbc.edu
Established: 1960 Annual Undergrad Tuition & Fees: $6,320
Enrollment: 228 Coed
Affiliation or Control: Independent Non-Profit IRS Status: 501(c)3
Highest Offering: Baccalaureate
Accreditation: BI

01 President ... Dr. P. Daniel STETLER
05 Academic Dean ... Dr. Clifford W. CHURCHILL
10 Director of Finances ... Mr. Rick HUFF
11 Director of Administration ... Mr. Wesley HOLDEN
32 Dean of Students ... Mr. John S. JONES
33 Dean of Men ... Mr. Jonathan STRATTON
08 Librarian ... Mr. Phil JONES
26 Public Relations Director ... Mr. Paul STETLER
06 Registrar ... Mr. Lucas RYDER
07 Director of Admissions ... Ms. Pam DAVIS
51 Dean of External Studies ... Mr. Dalbert N. WALKER

Hodges University (O)

2655 Northbrooke Drive, Naples FL 34119-7932
County: Collier FICE Identification: 030375
Unit ID: 367884
Telephone: (239) 513-1122 Carnegie Class: Masters/S
FAX Number: (239) 598-6253 Calendar System: Trimester
URL: www.hodges.edu
Established: 1990 Annual Undergrad Tuition & Fees: $13,700
Enrollment: 1,723 Coed
Affiliation or Control: Independent Non-Profit IRS Status: 501(c)3
Highest Offering: Master's
Accreditation: SC, CACREP, IACBE

01 President ... Dr. Donald WORTHAM
32 Sr Vice Pres Student Service ... Ms. Carol MORRISON
11 Exec Vice Pres of Operations ... Ms. Erica VOGT
05 Exec Vice Pres Academic Affairs ... Mr. John D. MEYER
07 Vice Pres Strategic Implementation ... Mr. Brent PASSEY
35 Dean of Students ... Dr. Marcia TURNER
111 Acting Vice Pres Advancement ... Mr. Timothy HALL
26 Chief Marketing Officer ... Ms. Karen GREBING
09 Dir Institutional Effective/Rsrch ... Dr. Diane BALL
28 Chief Diversity Officer ... Ms. Gail WILLIAMS
29 Director of Alumni Affairs ... Vacant
76 Dean School of Allied Health ... Dr. William GRIZ
72 Dean Fisher School of Technology ... Dr. Al BALL
50 Dean Johnson School of Business ... Dr. Aysegul TIMUR
107 Dean Nichols School of Prof Studies ... Dr. Mary NUOSCE
97 Dean School of Liberal Studies ... Dr. Elsa ROGERS
04 Executive Asst to President ... Ms. Marian KLINK
06 Chief Processing Officer ... Ms. Jessica PAUTZ
08 Director of the Library ... Ms. Gayle HARING
13 Director of Information Technology ... Mr. Carlos PADILLA
15 Director of Human Resources ... Ms. Kim UPTON
18 Dir Facilities Mgmt/Campus Security ... Mr. Skip CAMP

Hope College of Arts & Sciences (P)

1200 SW 3rd Street, Pompano Beach FL 33317
County: Broward FICE Identification: 042517
Unit ID: 488332
Telephone: (954) 532-9614 Carnegie Class: Not Classified
FAX Number: N/A Calendar System: Other
URL: www.hcas.us
Established: 2011 Annual Undergrad Tuition & Fees: N/A
Enrollment: N/A Coed
Affiliation or Control: Proprietary IRS Status: Proprietary
Highest Offering: Associate Degree
Accreditation: ACICS

05 Dean of Academic Affairs ... Dr. Chantal DESIR

Indian River State College (Q)

3209 Virginia Avenue, Fort Pierce FL 34981-5596
County: Saint Lucie FICE Identification: 001493
Unit ID: 134608
Telephone: (772) 462-4772 Carnegie Class: Bac/Assoc-Mixed
FAX Number: (772) 462-4796 Calendar System: Semester
URL: www.irsc.edu
Established: 1960 Annual Undergrad Tuition & Fees (In-District): $2,764
Enrollment: 18,204 Coed
Affiliation or Control: Local IRS Status: 501(c)3
Highest Offering: Baccalaureate
Accreditation: SC, ADNUR, CAHIIM, COARC, DA, DH, EMT, MAC, MLTAD, NUR, PTAA, RAD, SURGT

01 President ... Dr. Edwin MASSEY
84 Vice President Enrollment Services ... Dr. Christina HART
103 Vice President Science & Tech ... Dr. Pamela WELMON

45 Vice Pres Institutional Effectiv .... Dr. Patricia PROFETA
05 Vice President Academic Affairs .... Dr. Marta CRONIN
10 Vice President Financial Services .... Ms. Sheryl VITTITOE
32 Vice President Student Affairs .... Mr. Frank WATKINS
13 Vice President Institutional Tech .... Mr. Paul O'BRIEN
17 Dean Health Science .... Dr. Ann HUBBARD
12 Dean Northwest Center .... Mr. Andre HAWKINS
08 Dean Learning Resources .... Dr. Akos DELNEKY
75 Dean Industrial Education .... Ms. Donna RIVETT
12 Provost Pt St Lucie/St Lucie W .... Dr. Harvey ARNOLD
12 Provost Okeechobee County .... Mr. Russ BROWN
12 Provost Martin County .... Ms. Elizabeth GASKIN
12 Provost Indian River County .... Mr. Casey LUNCEFORD
102 Executive Director Foundation .... Ms. Ann DECKER
83 Dean Communication & Social Science .... Dr. Bruce FRASER
66 Dean Nursing .... Dr. Patricia GAGLIANO
11 Dean Administrative Services .... Vacant
80 Dean Public Service Education .... Mr. Evan BERRY
50 Dean Business Technology .... Mr. Ray CARPENTER
72 Dean Advanced Technology .... Mr. Kevin COOPER
53 Dean School of Education .... Dr. Kelly AMATUCCI
15 Dean Human Resources .... Mrs. Melissa WHIGHAM
18 Dean Facilities & Sustainability .... Mr. Sean DONAHUE
07 Dean Enrollment & Student Services .... Ms. Eileen STORCK
49 Dean Arts & Sciences .... Mr. Paul HORTON
21 Dean Finance .... Ms. Edith PACACHA
14 Dean Enterprise Systems .... Dr. Meredith COUGHLIN
41 Director Athletics .... Mr. Scott KIMMELMAN
106 Director Virtual Campus .... Ms. Kendall ST. HILAIRE
93 Director Minority Affairs .... Mrs. Adriene JEFFERSON
26 Director Executive Communications ...... Mr. Andrew TREADWELL
111 Director Institutional Advancement .... Ms. Michelle ABALDO
88 Director Enrollment Management .... Mr. Douglas DORAN
121 Director Instructional Advising .... Ms. Dale HAYES
36 Director Career & Transfer Services .... Ms. Flossie JACKSON
37 Director Financial Aid .... Ms. Mary LEWIS
35 Director Student Affairs .... Ms. Sharon LOWE
22 Equity Officer .... Ms. Adriene JEFFERSON
96 Purchasing Agent .... Mr. Don WINDHAM
19 Director Safety/Security .... Mr. Alan MONTGOMERY

International College of Health Sciences (A)

2300 S. Congress Avenue #105, Boynton Beach FL 33426
County: Palm Beach — Identification: 667238
Telephone: (561) 202-6333 — Carnegie Class: Not Classified
FAX Number: (561) 296-9647 — Calendar System: Semester
URL: www.ihep.edu
Established: — Annual Undergrad Tuition & Fees: N/A
Enrollment: N/A — Coed
Affiliation or Control: Proprietary — IRS Status: Proprietary
Highest Offering: Associate Degree
Accreditation: ACICS, CVT

01 Campus President .... Karyn J. VIDAL

Jacksonville University (B)

2800 University Boulevard N, Jacksonville FL 32211-3394
County: Duval — FICE Identification: 001495
Unit ID: 134945
Telephone: (904) 256-8000 — Carnegie Class: Masters/L
FAX Number: N/A — Calendar System: Semester
URL: www.ju.edu
Established: 1934 — Annual Undergrad Tuition & Fees: $33,930
Enrollment: 4,048 — Coed
Affiliation or Control: Independent Non-Profit — IRS Status: 501(c)3
Highest Offering: Doctorate
Accreditation: SC, AAB, DANCE, DENT, MUS, NURSE, @SP

01 President .... Mr. Timothy P. COST
05 Senior VP Univ & Academic Affairs .... Dr. Donnie HORNER
10 Senior VP Finance .... Mr. David HEALY
07 Chief Admissions Officer .... Mr. Tom TAGGART
32 Senior VP Student Affairs .... Dr. Kristie GOVER
30 Chief Advancement Officer .... Ms. Kimberly JONES
84 Sr VP Enroll Mgmt/Communications .... Ms. Margaret DEES
13 Chief Information Officer .... Mr. Tom HALL
04 Exec Assistant to the President .... Ms. Ellita BLACK
06 Registrar .... Ms. Carolyn BARRETT
09 Coord of Research & Assessment .... Ms. Christina VERCRUYSSE
08 Director of the Library .... Ms. Jessica COLLOGAN
35 Associate Dean of Students .... Mr. Luke MORRILL
36 Director of Career Resource Center .... Ms. Toni HIGGS
37 Director of Financial Aid .... Mr. Charles MOORE
21 Controller .... Ms. Liza MULLINS
11 Exec Dir Budgets/Business Opers .... Ms. Ellen PAIGE
96 Exec Director of Campus Services .... Mr. Michael BOBBIN
40 Director of the Bookstore .... Mr. Patrick JONES
42 Campus Minister .... Mr. Lance BEAUCHAMP
15 Director of Human Resources .... Mr. James V. WILLIAMS, JR.
57 Dean of Fine Arts .... Dr. Henry RINNE
49 Dean College of Arts & Sciences .... Dr. Henry RINNE
50 Dean College of Business .... Dr. Don CAPENER
76 Dean College of Health Science .... Dr. Christine SAPIENZA
64 Chairman Division of Music .... Dr. Tim SNYDER
79 Chair Division of Humanities .... Dr. Scott KIMBROUGH
81 Chair Division of Science & Math .... Dr. Brian LANE
38 Director Counseling Center .... Dr. Kristin ALBERTS
83 Chair Division of Social Science .... Dr. Sherri JACKSON
88 Chair Division of Naval Science .... Capt. Neil KARNES
88 Division Chair Dance & Theatre .... Mr. Brian PALMER
57 Chair Division Visual Arts .... Mr. Dana TUPA
18 Sr Director of Facilities Services .... Ms. Keri ZEIGLER
19 Director of Campus Security .... Mr. Kevin BENNETT
102 Dir Corporate/Foundation Relations .... Ms. Michele QUERRY
29 Director Alumni Relations .... Ms. Kim GRANT
39 Director of Residential Life .... Mr. Lucas MULLIN
44 Director Major Gifts/Planned Giving .... Ms. Maria PELLEGRINO-YOKITIS
25 Dir Research & Sponsored Pgms .... Ms. Renee ROSSI

Johnson & Wales University (C)

1701 NE 127th Street, North Miami FL 33181-2518
Telephone: (305) 892-7000 — Identification: 666423
Accreditation: &EH

† Regional accreditation is carried under the parent institution in Providence, RI.

Johnson University Florida (D)

1011 Bill Beck Boulevard, Kissimmee FL 34744-5301
Telephone: (407) 847-8966 — FICE Identification: 021567
Accreditation: &SC, &BI

† Branch campus of Johnson University, Knoxville, TN

Jose Maria Vargas University (E)

10131 Pines Boulevard, Pembroke Pines FL 33026
County: Broward — FICE Identification: 041620
Unit ID: 461281
Telephone: (954) 322-4460 — Carnegie Class: Spec-4-yr-Other
FAX Number: (954) 322-4131 — Calendar System: Semester
URL: www.jmvu.edu
Established: 2003 — Annual Undergrad Tuition & Fees: $10,480
Enrollment: 237 — Coed
Affiliation or Control: Proprietary — IRS Status: Proprietary
Highest Offering: Master's
Accreditation: ACICS

01 President .... Dr. Alicia F. PARRA
06 Registrar .... Ms. Lelis ORTIZ PARRA

Keiser University (F)

1800 Business Park Blvd, Daytona Beach FL 32114
Telephone: (386) 274-5060 — Identification: 770900
Accreditation: &SC, ACBSP, DMS, MAC, OTA, RAD

Keiser University (G)

1500 NW 49th Street, Fort Lauderdale FL 33309-3700
County: Broward — FICE Identification: 021519
Unit ID: 135081
Telephone: (954) 776-4476 — Carnegie Class: Bac/Assoc-Mixed
FAX Number: N/A — Calendar System: Semester
URL: www.keiseruniversity.edu
Established: 1977 — Annual Undergrad Tuition & Fees: $18,368
Enrollment: 16,579 — Coed
Affiliation or Control: Independent Non-Profit — IRS Status: 501(c)3
Highest Offering: Doctorate
Accreditation: SC, ACBSP, ADNUR, #ARCPA, CAHIIM, COARC, @DIETI, DMS, MLTAD, NURSE, OT, OTA, PTAA, RAD

01 Chancellor .... Dr. Arthur KEISER
03 Executive Vice Chancellor .... Mr. Peter CROCITTO
05 Vice Chancellor of Academic Affairs .... Dr. John SITES
31 Vice Chancellor of Community Rels .... Mrs. Belinda KEISER
84 Vice Chancellor of Enrollment Mgmt .... Mr. Brian WOODS
10 Sr Vice Chancellor of Finance .... Mr. Joseph BERARDINELLI
85 Vice Chancellor International Affs .... Mr. Zhanjun YANG
26 Reg Dir Media & Public Relations .... Ms. Kimberly DALE
06 Registrar .... Ms. Jazmine FERNANDEZ
09 Director of Institutional Research .... Dr. Margaret SULLIVAN
29 Director Alumni Relations .... Mr. John HOATSON
32 Chief Student Affairs/Student Life .... Mr. Ryan REIS

Keiser University (H)

9100 Forum Corporate Pkwy, Fort Myers FL 33905
Telephone: (239) 277-1336 — Identification: 770901
Accreditation: &SC, ACBSP, DMS, OTA

Keiser University-Jacksonville Campus (I)

6430 Southpoint Pkwy, Jacksonville FL 33216
Telephone: (904) 296-3440 — Identification: 770902
Accreditation: &SC, ACBSP, ADNUR, OTA, PTAA, RAD

Keiser University (J)

2400 Interstate Drive, Lakeland FL 33805
Telephone: (863) 682-6020 — Identification: 770903
Accreditation: &SC, ACBSP, ADNUR, DIETC, NMT, PTAA, RAD

Keiser University (K)

900 South Babcock Street, Melbourne FL 32901
Telephone: (321) 409-4800 — Identification: 770904
Accreditation: &SC, ACBSP, ACFEI, ADNUR, @DIETC, DMS, OTA, @PTAA, RAD

Keiser University (L)

2101 NW 117th Avenue, Miami FL 33172
Telephone: (305) 596-2226 — Identification: 770905
Accreditation: &SC, ACBSP, ADNUR, OTA, PTAA, RAD

Keiser University (M)

6014 US Hwy 19 North, Ste 250, New Port Richey FL 34652
Telephone: (727) 484-3110 — Identification: 770854
Accreditation: &SC, DMS

Keiser University (N)

5600 Lake Underhill Road, Orlando FL 32807
Telephone: (407) 381-1233 — Identification: 770906
Accreditation: &SC, ACBSP, ADNUR, HT, MLTAD, OTA

Keiser University (O)

1640 SW 145th Avenue, Pembroke Pines FL 33027
Telephone: (954) 431-4300 — Identification: 770907
Accreditation: &SC, ACBSP, DIETC, HT, OTA

Keiser University (P)

10330 S Federal Highway, Port Saint Lucie FL 34952-5605
Telephone: (772) 398-9990 — Identification: 666289
Accreditation: &SC, ACBSP, DIETC

† Regional accreditation is carried under the parent institution Keiser University, Fort Lauderdale, FL.

Keiser University (Q)

6151 Lake Osprey Drive, Sarasota FL 34240
Telephone: (941) 907-3900 — Identification: 770908
Accreditation: &SC, ACBSP, ACFEI, ADNUR, PTAA, RAD

Keiser University (R)

1700 Halstead Blvd, Bldg 2, Tallahassee FL 32309
Telephone: (850) 906-9494 — Identification: 770909
Accreditation: &SC, ACBSP, ACFEI, ADNUR, OTA

Keiser University (S)

5002 West Waters Ave, Tampa FL 33634
Telephone: (813) 885-4900 — Identification: 770910
Accreditation: &SC, ACBSP, ADNUR, OTA, SURGT

Keiser University (T)

2085 Vista Parkway, West Palm Beach FL 33411-2719
Telephone: (561) 471-6000 — Identification: 667032
Accreditation: &SC, ACBSP, ADNUR, OTA, PTAA

† Regional accreditation is carried under the parent institution Keiser University, Fort Lauderdale, FL.

Keiser University at Clearwater (U)

16120 US Hwy 19 N, Clearwater FL 33764
Telephone: (727) 576-6500 — Identification: 666758
Accreditation: SC, SURGT

Key College (V)

1040 Bayview Drive, Suite 200, Fort Lauderdale FL 33304
County: Broward — FICE Identification: 023251
Unit ID: 134422
Telephone: (754) 312-2898 — Carnegie Class: Spec 2-yr-Other
FAX Number: (954) 900-3446 — Calendar System: Quarter
URL: www.keycollege.edu
Established: 1982 — Annual Undergrad Tuition & Fees: $11,085
Enrollment: 49 — Coed
Affiliation or Control: Proprietary — IRS Status: Proprietary
Highest Offering: Associate Degree
Accreditation: PPPA

01 President .... Mr. Ronald H. DOOLEY
05 EVP/Director of Academic Affairs .... Ms. Marella DOOLEY
07 Director of Admissions .... Mr. Ron DOOLEY
37 Director of Financial Aid .... Ms. Traci ANDREWS
06 Registrar .... Mr. Guy ETIENNE
08 Librarian .... Mr. John C. COPELAND
20 Academic Coordinator .... Ms. Ursala CLARKE
106 Online IT Support .... Mr. Mark ROSE

Knox Theological Seminary (W)

5555 N Federal Highway, Fort Lauderdale FL 33308-3209
County: Broward — FICE Identification: 039923
Unit ID: 484288
Telephone: (954) 771-0376 — Carnegie Class: Not Classified
FAX Number: (954) 351-3343 — Calendar System: Semester
URL: www.knoxseminary.edu
Established: 1989 — Annual Undergrad Tuition & Fees: N/A
Enrollment: N/A — Coed
Affiliation or Control: Independent Non-Profit — IRS Status: 501(c)3

Highest Offering: Doctorate
Accreditation: THEOL

01 President & CEO .... Dr. Samuel LAMERSON
11 Vice President of Administration .... Dr. Timothy SANSBURY
05 Dean of Faculty/Dean of Students .... Dr. Scott MANOR
106 Director of Distance Education .... Dr. Tim FOX
30 Director of Development .... Mr. Charles BURGE
06 Registrar .... Ms. Lori GOTTSHALL
08 Head Librarian .... Mr. Alan WIBBELS
04 Administrative Asst to President .... Ms. Laura KASTENSMIDT
07 Dir of Admissions & Communications .... Ms. Stephany GALLO

Lake Erie College of Osteopathic Medicine Bradenton (A)

5000 Lakewood Rance Boulevard, Bradenton FL 34211
Telephone: (941) 756-0690　Identification: 770160
Accreditation: &M, DENT, OSTEO, PHAR

† Branch campus of Lake Erie College of Osteopathic Medicine, Erie, PA

Lake-Sumter State College (B)

9501 US Highway 441, Leesburg FL 34788-8751
County: Lake　FICE Identification: 001502
Unit ID: 135188
Telephone: (352) 787-3747　Carnegie Class: Bac/Assoc-Assoc Dom
FAX Number: (352) 365-3548　Calendar System: Semester
URL: www.lssc.edu
Established: 1962　Annual Undergrad Tuition & Fees (In-District): $3,172
Enrollment: 4,641　Coed
Affiliation or Control: State/Local　IRS Status: 501(c)3
Highest Offering: Baccalaureate
Accreditation: SC, ADNUR, CAHIIM

01 President .... Dr. Stanley SIDOR
10 VP Admin/Business Services .... Dr. Heather BIGARD
05 VP Academic Affairs .... Dr. Douglas A. WYMER
84 VP Enrollment & Student Affairs .... Dr. Claire BRADY
21 Assoc VP for Business Affairs .... Ms. Vicki WARD
97 Assoc VP General Studies .... Mr. Thom KIEFT
15 Exec Director Human Resources .... Ms. Fran PISTILLI
13 Chief Information Officer .... Mr. Douglas GUILER
111 AVP Inst Advancement/Foundation .... Dr. Laura BYRD
18 Exec Director Facilities .... Mr. David WILDES
08 Director Libraries .... Ms. Katie SACCO
32 Dean of Students .... Ms. Carolyn SCOTT
21 Director Accounting .... Ms. Diana BILLINGHAM
81 Dean Math & Science .... Ms. Karen HOGANS
66 Director Nursing .... Ms. Nicole TINNY
08 Interim Director Learning Center .... Mr. Khoy STOUTT
26 Dir Marketing/College Relations .... Mr. Kevin YURASEK
37 Director Financial Aid .... Ms. Katrina BENNETT
06 Registrar .... Ms. Caitlin MOORE
41 Athletic Director .... Mr. Michael K. MATULIA
106 Director Distance Learning .... Mr. Mike NATHANSON
07 Director Enrollment Mgmt .... Ms. Jenni KOTOWSKI
28 Equity/Diversity Officer .... Ms. Araina MUNIZ
96 Asst Director of Purchasing .... Mr. Bill PONKO
04 Executive Asst to the President .... Ms. Claudia MORRIS
103 Dean Workforce Programs .... Dr. Luis PIZARRO

Larkin Health Sciences Institute (C)

18301 North Miami Avenue, Suite 1, Miami FL 33169
County: Miami-Dade　Identification: 667288
Telephone: (305) 760-7500　Carnegie Class: Not Classified
FAX Number: N/A　Calendar System: Semester
URL: ularkin.org
Established:　Annual Graduate Tuition & Fees: N/A
Enrollment: N/A　Coed
Affiliation or Control: Independent Non-Profit　IRS Status: 501(c)3
Highest Offering: Doctorate; No Undergraduates
Accreditation: @PHAR

01 President .... Ms. Sandy SOSA-GUERRERO
67 Vice President/Dean of Pharmacy .... Dr. Gary M. LEVIN
88 Vice Pres Patient Care Services .... Ms. Mercedes PEREZ
13 Director of Technology .... Dr. Jorge E. MACHADO

Lincoln College of Technology (D)

2410 Metrocentre Boulevard,
West Palm Beach FL 33407-3155
County: Palm Beach　FICE Identification: 022808
Unit ID: 136066
Telephone: (561) 842-8324　Carnegie Class: Bac/Assoc-Mixed
FAX Number: (561) 842-9503　Calendar System: Other
URL: www.lincolncollegeoftechnology.com
Established: 1982　Annual Undergrad Tuition & Fees: $13,770
Enrollment: 567　Coed
Affiliation or Control: Proprietary　IRS Status: Proprietary
Highest Offering: Baccalaureate
Accreditation: ACICS, ACFEI

01 President .... Mr. Mike CLULING

Lynn University (E)

3601 N Military Trail, Boca Raton FL 33431-5598
County: Palm Beach　FICE Identification: 001505
Unit ID: 132657
Telephone: (561) 237-7000　Carnegie Class: Masters/L
FAX Number: (561) 237-7100　Calendar System: Semester
URL: www.lynn.edu
Established: 1962　Annual Undergrad Tuition & Fees: $36,650
Enrollment: 2,693　Coed
Affiliation or Control: Independent Non-Profit　IRS Status: 501(c)3
Highest Offering: Doctorate
Accreditation: SC, IACBE, MUS

01 President .... Dr. Kevin M. ROSS
00 President Emeritus .... Dr. Donald E. ROSS
11 Sr Vice President Administration .... Mr. Gregory J. MALFITANO
05 Vice President Academic Affairs .... Dr. Gregg COX
84 Vice Pres Enrollment Management .... Dr. Gareth FOWLES
10 Vice President Business & Finance .... Ms. Laurie LEVINE
32 Vice President for Student Life .... Dr. Anthony ALTIERI
30 Vice Pres Development/Alumni Affs .. Mr. Gregory J. MALFITANO
13 Chief Information Officer .... Mr. Chris G. BONIFORTI
26 Chief Marketing Officer .... Mrs. Sherrie WELDON
88 Dean of Administration .... Mr. Thomas J. HEFFERNAN
35 Dean of Students .... Mr. Gary MARTIN
43 General Counsel .... Mr. Michael ANTONELLO
88 Exec Dir Stdnt Administrative Svcs .... Ms. Evelyn C. NELSON
39 Director Housing & Residence Life .... Ms. Meagan ELSBERRY
36 Executive Director Career Develop .... Ms. Barbara CAMBIA
41 Director of Athletics .... Mr. Devin CROSBY
109 Director Auxiliary Services .... Mr. Matthew P. CHALOUX
23 Director Health Center .... Ms. Rita ALBERT
27 Director of Marketing and Comm .... Ms. Stephanie BROWN
112 Asst Director of Major Gifts .... Ms. Ashleigh FOWLES
29 Director Alumni Affairs .... Ms. Barbara SAGEMAN
42 Chaplain .... Fr. Martin C. DEVEREAUX
07 Dir Undergraduate Admissions .... Mr. Stefano PAPALEO
37 Dir of Financial Aid .... Mr. John CHAMBERS
38 Director of the Counseling Center .... Ms. Nicole R. OVEDIA
96 Director of Purchasing .... Mr. Alfredo H. BONIFORTI
06 Registrar .... Ms. Jenifer MOSLEY
21 Director of Accounting .... Mr. Michael C. BOLDUC
123 Dir Graduate & UG Evening Admiss .... Mr. Steven PRUITT
09 Director of Institutional Research .... Mrs. Lara MARTIN
15 Director of Employee Services .... Mr. Aaron GREENBERG
40 Bookstore Manager .... Ms. Rita D. LOUREIRO
50 Dean College Business & Management .... Mr. RT GOOD
49 Dean College of Arts & Sciences .... Dr. Katrina CARTER-TELLISON
88 Dean School of Aeronautics .... Dr. Jeffrey C. JOHNSON
53 Dean Ross College of Education .... Dr. Kathleen WEIGEL
60 Dean College Intl Communications .... Dr. David L. JAFFE
64 Dean Conservatory of Music .... Dr. Jon H. ROBERTSON
88 Exe Dir Inst Achievement Learning .... Mr. Shaun EXSTEEN
08 Director of the Library .... Ms. Amy FILIATREAU
104 Director of International Programs .... Mrs. Erin GARCIA
19 Chief .... Mr. Larry RICKARD

Med-Life Institute-Lauderdale Lakes (F)

4000 N. State Road 7, Suite 301,
Lauderdale Lakes FL 33319
County: Broward　Identification: 667221
Telephone: (954) 943-8667　Carnegie Class: Not Classified
FAX Number: (954) 943-0984　Calendar System: Quarter
URL: www.medlifeinstitute.com
Established: 2003　Annual Undergrad Tuition & Fees: N/A
Enrollment: N/A　Coed
Affiliation or Control: Proprietary　IRS Status: Proprietary
Highest Offering: Associate Degree
Accreditation: ABHES

01 President/CEO .... Dr. Lemuel PIERRE

Med-Life Institute-Naples (G)

4995 Tamiami Trail E, Naples FL 34113
County: Collier　Identification: 667220
Telephone: (239) 732-1300　Carnegie Class: Not Classified
FAX Number: (239) 417-5110　Calendar System: Semester
URL: www.medlifeinstitute.com
Established: 2003　Annual Undergrad Tuition & Fees: N/A
Enrollment: N/A　Coed
Affiliation or Control: Proprietary　IRS Status: Proprietary
Highest Offering: Associate Degree
Accreditation: ABHES

01 President .... Mr. Cleophat TANIS

Medical Career Institute (H)

27975 Old 41 Road, Suite 201, Bonita Springs FL 34135
County: Lee　Identification: 667266
Telephone: (239) 992-4624　Carnegie Class: Not Classified
FAX Number: (239) 405-8024　Calendar System: Semester
URL: www.medicalcareerinstitute.org
Established: 2008　Annual Undergrad Tuition & Fees: N/A
Enrollment: N/A　Coed
Affiliation or Control: Proprietary　IRS Status: Proprietary
Highest Offering: Associate Degree
Accreditation: ABHES

01 President/CEO .... Mr. Richard GONZALEZ
17 Medical Director .... Dr. Antonio GANDIA

Medical Prep Institute (I)

2304 Busch Boulevard, Tampa FL 33613
County: Hillsborough　Identification: 667267
Telephone: (813) 932-1710　Carnegie Class: Not Classified
FAX Number: (813) 762-1325　Calendar System: Other
URL: www.medicalprepinstitute.org
Established:　Annual Undergrad Tuition & Fees: N/A
Enrollment: N/A　Coed
Affiliation or Control: Proprietary　IRS Status: Proprietary
Highest Offering: Baccalaureate
Accreditation: ABHES

01 Director .... Thomas NAZZANT
05 Dean of Academics .... Rochelle L. LEFLER

Mercy Hospital College of Nursing (J)

3663 South Miami Ave Ste 1500, Miami FL 33133
County: Miami-Dade　Identification: 667222
Unit ID: 419217
Telephone: (305) 285-2777　Carnegie Class: Not Classified
FAX Number: (305) 285-2671　Calendar System: Semester
URL: www.mercymiami.com/professionals/college-of-nursing
Established: 2008　Annual Undergrad Tuition & Fees: N/A
Enrollment: 83　Coed
Affiliation or Control: Proprietary　IRS Status: Proprietary
Highest Offering: Associate Degree
Accreditation: ABHES, ADNUR, PNUR

66 Dean .... Ms. Elizabeth HERNANDEZ

Meridian College (K)

7020 Professional Pkwy E, Sarasota FL 34240
County: Sarasota　FICE Identification: 023268
Unit ID: 244279
Telephone: (941) 377-4880　Carnegie Class: Spec 2-yr-Health
FAX Number: (941) 378-2842　Calendar System: Other
URL: www.meridian.edu
Established: 1982　Annual Undergrad Tuition & Fees: N/A
Enrollment: 161　Coed
Affiliation or Control: Proprietary　IRS Status: Proprietary
Highest Offering: Associate Degree
Accreditation: ACCSC

01 Campus Director .... Mr. Patrick MCDERMOTT
05 Director of Education .... Mr. André DODSON
07 Director of Admissions .... Ms. Kim MILES
36 Director Student Placement .... Ms. Tracy FORDHAM

Miami Dade College (L)

300 NE Second Avenue, Miami FL 33132-2204
County: Miami-Dade County　FICE Identification: 001506
Unit ID: 135717
Telephone: (305) 237-8888　Carnegie Class: Bac/Assoc-Assoc Dom
FAX Number: (305) 237-7913　Calendar System: Semester
URL: www.mdc.edu
Established: 1960　Annual Undergrad Tuition & Fees (In-State): $2,834
Enrollment: 62,332　Coed
Affiliation or Control: State　IRS Status: 501(c)3
Highest Offering: Baccalaureate
Accreditation: SC, ADNUR, ARCPA, ART, CAHIIM, COARC, DANCE, DH, DMS, EMT, FUSER, HT, MLTAD, MUS, NUR, NURSE, OPD, PTAA, RAD, THEA

01 College President .... Dr. Eduardo J. PADRON
05 Executive Vice President & Provost .... Dr. Lenore RODICIO
11 Sr Vice Provost/COO .... Ms. Gloria BAEZ
10 Sr Vice Provost Business Affairs .... Mr. E. H. LEVERING
13 Vice Provost Information Technology .... Dr. Wendy CHANG
18 Interim Vice Provost Facilities .... Vacant
15 Vice Provost Human Resources .... Ms. Iliana CASTILLO-FRICK
09 Vice Provost Inst Effectiveness .... Dr. Archieval CUBARRUBIA
12 Campus President Hialeah/Wolfson .... Dr. Joaquin MARTINEZ
12 Campus President Kendall/West .... Dr. Beverly MOORE-GARCIA
12 Campus President Medical .... Dr. Richard PRENTISS
12 Campus President Wolfson .... Vacant
12 Campus President North/InterAmerica .... Ms. Malou HARRISON
12 Campus President Homestead .... Dr. Jeanne JACOBS
21 Assoc Vice Prov Business Affs .... Ms. Delilah ALMEDA
32 Vice Provost Student Services .... Dr. Kathy MAALOUF
102 Executive Dir MDC Foundation .... Mr. Mark COLE
37 Assoc VP Student Financial Services .... Ms. Mercedes AMAYA
07 Interim Collegewide Dir Admissions .... Ms. Ferne CREARY
26 Chief Public Rels Officer/Dir Comm .... Mr. Juan MENDIETA
29 Director Alumni Relations .... Mr. Adlar GARCIA
35 Director Student Life .... Ms. Lauren ADAMO
88 Dir Testing Admin/Pgm Evaluation .... Mr. Silvio RODRIGUEZ
22 Dir Equal Opportunity Pgm/ADA Coord .... Dr. Joy C. RUFF
121 Director Student Advisement .... Ms. Marie BERNARDINE
84 Director Enrollment Management .... Mr. Harry LINENBERG
96 Director of Purchasing .... Mr. Roman MARTINEZ
41 Director Athletics & Student Life .... Mr. Anthony FIORENZA
09 Director of Institutional Research .... Vacant
43 Legal Counsel .... Mr. Javier LEY-SOTO
86 Director Governmental Affairs .... Ms. Victoria HERNANDEZ
100 Chief of Staff .... Mr. George ANDREWS
103 Exec Dir Workforce Educ & Partnrshp .... Vacant
104 Director Study Abroad .... Ms. Carol REYES
105 College Webmaster .... Mr. Andrew SEAGA

08 Head Librarian/Dir Lrng Resources .... Mr. Erick DOMINICIS
85 Director Intl Student Services .... Ms. Cristina FLOREZ

Miami International University of Art & Design (A)

1501 Biscayne Boulevard, Suite 100,
Miami FL 33132-1418

County: Miami-Dade FICE Identification: 008878
Unit ID: 134811
Telephone: (305) 428-5700 Carnegie Class: Spec-4-yr-Arts
FAX Number: (305) 374-7946 Calendar System: Quarter
URL: www.artinstitutes.edu/miami
Established: 1965 Annual Undergrad Tuition & Fees: $17,700
Enrollment: 2,478 Coed
Affiliation or Control: Proprietary IRS Status: Proprietary
Highest Offering: Master's
Accreditation: #SC, CIDA

01 President .... Ms. Erika FLEMING
05 Dean of Academic Affairs .... Dr. Paul COX
10 Dir Admin & Financial Services .... Ms. Leslie THEROULDE
32 Dean of Student Affairs .... Mr. John OSBORNE
07 Senior Director of Admissions .... Mr. Kevin RYAN
08 Librarian .... Ms. Kiara NOLAN

Miami Regional University (B)

700 S. Royal Poinciana Blvd, Miami Springs FL 33166

County: Miami-Dade FICE Identification: 041284
Unit ID: 451103
Telephone: (305) 442-9223 Carnegie Class: Spec 2-yr-Health
FAX Number: (305) 442-8723 Calendar System: Other
URL: www.mru.edu
Established: 1996 Annual Undergrad Tuition & Fees: N/A
Enrollment: 943 Coed
Affiliation or Control: Proprietary IRS Status: Proprietary
Highest Offering: Master's
Accreditation: ACICS

01 President & CEO .... Ophelia SANCHEZ
03 Executive Vice President .... Vacant
05 Sr Vice President Academic Affairs .... Jay OBER
07 Director of Admissions .... Vacant
08 Librarian .... Tammy OLIVERA
10 Chief Business Officer .... Vacant
15 VP Employment Affairs .... Mitsy SOUSA
36 Director Career Services .... Randy BREITER
37 Director Student Financial Aid .... Vacant

Millennia Atlantic University (C)

3801 NW 97th Avenue, Doral FL 33178

County: Miami-Dade FICE Identification: 041825
Unit ID: 461883
Telephone: (786) 331-1000 Carnegie Class: Spec-4-yr-Bus
FAX Number: (305) 503-9680 Calendar System: Semester
URL: www.maufl.edu
Established: Annual Undergrad Tuition & Fees: $10,340
Enrollment: 280 Coed
Affiliation or Control: Proprietary IRS Status: Proprietary
Highest Offering: Master's
Accreditation: ACICS

01 President .... Dr. Aristides MAZA-DUERTO
00 Chancellor .... Mr. Luis E. MARTINEZ
10 CFO .... Mrs. Orianna M. MOSS
05 Director of Academic Programs .... Mrs. Teresa FITZGERALD
06 Registrar .... Ms. Natasha ALEONG
37 Financial Aid Manager .... Ms. Maria VELAR
26 Coord of Marketing & Public Rels .... Mr. Sergio CUBILLOS
36 Student Services and Placement Mgr .... Ms. Jakelin MIRANDA
07 Director of Admissions .... Mr. Juan Carlos RODRIGUEZ
08 Librarian .... Dr. Otis ALEXANDER
88 Bursar .... Mrs. Jenice MAZA-DUERTO

North Florida Community College (D)

325 NW Turner Davis Drive, Madison FL 32340-1610

County: Madison FICE Identification: 001508
Unit ID: 136145
Telephone: (850) 973-2288 Carnegie Class: Assoc/MT-VT-Mix Trad/Non
FAX Number: (850) 973-1696 Calendar System: Semester
URL: www.nfcc.edu
Established: 1958 Annual Undergrad Tuition & Fees (In-State): $3,054
Enrollment: 1,243 Coed
Affiliation or Control: State IRS Status: 501(c)3
Highest Offering: Associate Degree
Accreditation: SC, EMT

01 President .... Mr. John GROSSKOPF
05 Dean of Academic Affairs/CAO .... Ms. Frances ADLEBURG
10 Dean Administrative Svcs & CBO .... Mr. Andrew BARNES
84 Dean of Enrollment/Student Services .... Ms. Kay HOGAN
09 Manager of Networking Systems .... Mr. Nick SKIPPER
15 Director of Personnel Services .... Mr. Bill HUNTER
08 Head Librarian .... Ms. Lynn WYCHE
88 SSS and Disability Coordinator .... Ms. Sheila NOBLES
88 Director of Public Safety Academy .... Mr. Rick DAVIS
06 Registrar .... Ms. Lori PLEASANT
18 Chief Facilities/Physical Plant .... Mr. Dale HACKLE
26 Public Information Officer .... Ms. Kim SCARBORO
102 Dir Foundation/Alumni Relations .... Dr. Cheryl JAMES
37 Director Student Financial Aid .... Ms. Karen SURLES
28 Director of Diversity .... Ms. Denise BELL
96 Director of Purchasing .... Ms. Sarah NEWSOME
04 Executive Asst to President .... Ms. Cindy M. GAYLARD
103 Dir Workforce/Career Development .... Mr. David DUNKLE
19 Director Security/Safety .... Mr. Skip JAMES

Northwest Florida State College (E)

100 College Boulevard, Niceville FL 32578-1295

County: Okaloosa FICE Identification: 001510
Unit ID: 136233
Telephone: (850) 678-5111 Carnegie Class: Bac/Assoc-Mixed
FAX Number: (850) 729-5215 Calendar System: Semester
URL: www.nwfsc.edu
Established: 1963 Annual Undergrad Tuition & Fees (In-State): $3,123
Enrollment: 5,905 Coed
Affiliation or Control: State IRS Status: 501(c)3
Highest Offering: Baccalaureate
Accreditation: SC, ADNUR, DA, EMT, NURSE

01 President .... Dr. Devin STEPHENSON
05 Vice Pres for Academic Affairs .... Dr. Sasha JARRELL
11 Vice Pres Administrative Services .... Mr. Randy WHITE
30 Vice Pres College Advancement .... Mrs. Cristie KEDROSKI
13 Chief Information Officer .... Mr. Greg ELLER
10 Controller .... Ms. Pamela KABY
09 Director of Institutional Research .... Dr. Diane W. HODGINS
15 Director Human Resources/Diversity .... Ms. Roberta MACKEY
07 Director of Admissions .... Ms. Karyn COOPER
29 Assoc Director for Resource/Alumni .... Ms. Carla REINLIE
41 Athletic Director .... Mr. Ramsey ROSS
37 Director Financial Aid/Veteran Affs .... Ms. Patricia BENNETT
18 Facilities Director .... Mr. Sam JONES
08 Director Learning Resources Center .... Ms. Janice HENDERSON
26 Director Strategic Communications .... Ms. Stephanie PETTIS
32 Dean of Students .... Dr. Aimee WATTS
04 Executive Assistant to President .... Ms. Julie SCHRODT
06 Director of Records/Registrar .... Ms. Bree DURHAM
106 Director of Online Education .... Mr. Syed HASNAIN
75 Dean of Career & Technical Educ .... Mr. Dennis SHERWOOD
97 Dean of Education .... Dr. Anne SOUTHARD
35 Director of Student Life .... Mr. Sam HILL
19 Director Security/Safety .... Mr. William LOOPER
25 Director of Grant Development .... Mr. Michael LUCCHESI

Nova Southeastern University (F)

3301 College Avenue, Fort Lauderdale FL 33314-7796

County: Broward FICE Identification: 001509
Unit ID: 136215
Telephone: (800) 541-6682 Carnegie Class: DU-Higher
FAX Number: (954) 262-3800 Calendar System: Trimester
URL: www.nova.edu
Established: 1964 Annual Undergrad Tuition & Fees: $28,736
Enrollment: 23,236 Coed
Affiliation or Control: Independent Non-Profit IRS Status: 501(c)3
Highest Offering: Doctorate
Accreditation: SC, AA, ACAE, ARCPA, AUD, CAATE, CAEPN, CLPSY, #COARC, CVT, DENT, DMS, IACBE, IPSY, LAW, MFCD, NURSE, OPT, OPTR, OSTEO, OT, PH, PHAR, PTA, SCPSY, SP, SPAA

01 President & CEO .... Dr. George L. HANBURY, II
05 Provost & Exec VP Academic Affairs .... Dr. Ralph V. ROGERS
10 VP Finance/CFO .... Ms. Alyson SILVA
00 Chancellor Nova Southeastern Univ .... Mr. Ray FERRERO, JR.
17 Chancellor Health Professions Div .... Dr. Fred LIPPMAN
11 Exec Dean for Administration .... Dr. Irving ROSENBAUM
88 SVP Transitional Rsrch & Econ Dev .... Dr. H. Thomas TEMPLE
08 Interim VP Info Svcs/Univ Librarian .... Mr. James HUTCHENS
43 VP Legal Affairs .... Mr. Joel BERMAN
46 VP Research Tech Transfer .... Dr. Gary S. MARGULES
32 VP Student Affairs/Dean UG Studies .... Dr. Brad WILLIAMS
111 VP Inst Advancement ...... Dr. Jennifer O'FLANNERY ANDERSON
13 VP Info Tech/Chief Info Ofcr .... Mr. Tom WEST
15 VP Human Resources .... Mr. Robert J. PIETRYKOWSKI
84 VP Enrollment and Stdnt Svcs .... Dr. Stephanie BROWN
21 VP Business Services .... Mr. Marc CROCQUET
106 VP Reg Campus & Online Educ .... Mr. Ricardo BELMAR
18 Interim VP Facilities Mgmt .... Mrs. Jessica BRUMLEY
26 Exec Director Univ Relations .... Mr. Brandon HENSLER
19 Director Public Safety .... Mr. James EWING
09 VP Institutional Effectiveness .... Dr. Donald J. RUDAWSKY
20 Associate Provost .... Dr. Ronald CHENAIL
88 Director Accreditation .... Ms. Jane DUNCAN
24 Exec Dir Ed Tech/Digital Media Prod .... Ms. Diane LIPPE
25 Director Sponsored Programs .... Ms. Cathy HARLAN
86 Exec Dir Licensure/State Relations .... Dr. Greg F. STIBER
12 Headmaster University School .... Mr. William KOPAS
27 Director University Publications .... Mr. Ron RYAN
27 Director Public Affairs .... Ms. Julie SPECHLER
36 Director of Career Development .... Ms. Shari SAPERSTEIN
29 Director of Alumni Relations .... Mr. R.J STAMPER
06 Dir University Registrar's Office .... Ms. G. Elaine N. POFF
41 Director Athletics .... Mr. Michael MOMINEY
88 Director Campus Recreation .... Mr. Tom VITUCCI
116 Executive Dir Internal Auditing .... Mr. Ron MIDEI
88 Exec Dir Inst & Comm Engagement ... Dr. Barbara PACKER-MUTI
88 VP Compliance/Chief Integrity Ofcr .... Ms. Robin SUPLER
88 Dir Museum of Art .... Ms. Bonnie CLEARWATER
63 Dean College Osteopathic Medicine .... Ms. Elaine WALLACE
67 Dean College Pharmacy .... Dr. Lisa DEZIEL
23 Vice Pres Clinical Operations .... Mr. Kelly GREGG
88 Dean College Optometry .... Dr. David LOSHIN
76 Dean College of Hlth Care Sciences .... Dr. Stanley WILSON
54 Dean College of Engineering/Comp .... Dr. Yong TAO
61 Dean Shepard Broad Law Center .... Mr. Jon GARON
65 College of Natural Sci/Oceanography .... Dr. Richard DODGE
66 Dean College of Nursing .... Dr. Marcella M. RUTHERFORD
50 Huizenga College of Bus/Entr .... Dr. J. Preston JONES
92 Dean Farquhar Honors College .... Dr. Donald ROSENBLUM
88 Dean College of Psychology .... Dr. Karen GROSBY
83 Dean College Arts/Humani/Social Sci .... Dr. Honggang YANG
88 Dean Mailman Ctr for Human Devel .... Dr. Roni LEIDERMAN
63 Dean College of Medical Sciences .... Dr. Harold LAUBAUCH
52 Dean of Dental Medicine .... Dr. Linda NIESSEN
53 Int Dean Fischler College of Educ .... Dr. Kimberly DURHAM
88 Dean College Allopathic Med .... Dr. Johannes VIEWEG

Orion College (G)

51 North State Road 7, Plantation FL 33317

County: Broward FICE Identification: 041359
Unit ID: 454883
Telephone: (866) 251-3244 Carnegie Class: Spec 2-yr-Health
FAX Number: (877) 493-7416 Calendar System: Other
URL: www.orioncollege.org
Established: 2004 Annual Undergrad Tuition & Fees: $12,312
Enrollment: 336 Coed
Affiliation or Control: Proprietary IRS Status: Proprietary
Highest Offering: Associate Degree
Accreditation: ABHES

01 President .... Jennifer ANGLIN
03 Vice President .... Sondra GERHOFF

Orlando Medical Institute (H)

6220 S. Orange Blossom Tr, Ste 410, Orlando FL 32809

County: Orange Identification: 667127
Telephone: (407) 251-0007 Carnegie Class: Not Classified
FAX Number: (407) 251-0352 Calendar System: Semester
URL: www.omi.edu
Established: 2004 Annual Undergrad Tuition & Fees: N/A
Enrollment: N/A Coed
Affiliation or Control: Proprietary IRS Status: Proprietary
Highest Offering: Associate Degree
Accreditation: ABHES

01 President .... Felix J. MARQUEZ, JR.
11 Vice Pres/Director Operations .... Abigail MARQUEZ

Palm Beach Atlantic University (I)

901 S. Flagler Drive, West Palm Beach FL 33401

County: Palm Beach FICE Identification: 008849
Unit ID: 136330
Telephone: (561) 803-2000 Carnegie Class: Masters/L
FAX Number: (561) 803-2186 Calendar System: Semester
URL: www.pba.edu
Established: 1968 Annual Undergrad Tuition & Fees: $28,520
Enrollment: 3,918 Coed
Affiliation or Control: Interdenominational IRS Status: 501(c)3
Highest Offering: Doctorate
Accreditation: SC, #CAATE, IACBE, MUS, NURSE, PHAR, @THEOL

01 President .... Mr. William M. FLEMING
05 Provost .... Dr. E. Randolph RICHARDS
10 Sr VP for Finance Admin & Plng .... Mr. John KAUTZ, III
30 Vice President Development .... Mrs. Vicki PUGH
07 Vice President for Admissions .... Mr. Tim WORLEY
09 Asst Provost Rsrch/Effectiveness .... Mrs. Carolanne BROWN
13 Assoc VP Campus Information Svcs .... Mr. Phillip MAJOR
26 Assoc VP Univ Relations & Marketing ...... Mrs. Rebecca PEELING
51 Dean MacArthur School of Leadership .... Dr. Craig DOMECK
49 Dean School of Arts & Sciences .... Dr. Robert LLOYD
50 Dean School of Business .... Dr. Leslie TURNER
53 Dean School of Education .... Dr. Gene SALE
57 Dean School of Music/Fine Arts .... Dr. Lloyd MIMS
66 Dean School of Nursing .... Dr. Joanne MASELLA
67 Dean Gregory School of Pharmacy .... Dr. Jeff LEWIS
60 Dean School Communication/Media .... Dr. J. Duane MEEKS
73 Dean School of Ministry .... Dr. Jonathan GRENZ
06 Registrar .... Ms. Audrey SCHOFIELD
08 Dean of the Library .... Mr. Steven BAKER
20 Associate Provost for Instruction .... Dr. Nathan LANE
15 Assoc VP of Human Resources .... Ms. Mona L. HICKS
32 Dean of Students .... Mr. Kevin ABEL
18 Director of Physical Plant .... Mr. Matt STEVENS
21 Controller .... Mrs. Carla CROW
29 AVP Alumni Relations/Annual Fund .... Mrs. Delesa MORRIS
31 Dir of Campus and Community Events .... Mrs. Mary WARD
35 Assistant Dean of Students .... Mr. Bob LUTZ
37 Director of Financial Aid .... Mrs. Jen MCMAHON
40 Director of Campus Store .... Mrs. Abbie ROSEMEYER
41 Director of Athletics .... Mrs. Carolyn STONE
42 Director of Campus Ministries .... Mr. Mark KAPRIVE
92 Director of Supper Honors Program .... Dr. Tom ST. ANTOINE
19 Director Security/Safety .... Mr. Wayne BUCHANAN

Palm Beach State College (A)

4200 Congress Avenue, Lake Worth FL 33461-4796

County: Palm Beach FICE Identification: 001512
Unit ID: 136358
Telephone: (561) 967-7222 Carnegie Class: Bac/Assoc-Assoc Dom
FAX Number: (561) 868-3504 Calendar System: Semester
URL: www.palmbeachstate.edu
Established: 1933 Annual Undergrad Tuition & Fees (In-State): $2,444
Enrollment: 29,616 Coed
Affiliation or Control: State IRS Status: 501(c)3
Highest Offering: Baccalaureate
Accreditation: SC, ACBSP, ADNUR, CAHIIM, COARC, DA, DH, DMS, EMT, MAC, NUR, RAD, SURGT

01 President .... Ms. Ava L. PARKER
05 Vice President Academic Affairs .... Dr. Roger YOHE
10 Vice President Admin/Business Svcs .... Mr. Richard A. BECKER
32 Vice President Student Services .... Dr. Peter BARBATIS
13 Vice President Information Svcs .... Dr. Ginger L. PEDERSEN
31 Exec Director Community Engagement .... Ms. Rachael E. ONDRUS
43 General Counsel .... Mr. Kevin A. FERNANDER
102 Exec Director Foundation .... Ms. Suellen MANN
12 Provost Belle Glade .... Dr. Maria M. VALLEJO
12 Provost Boca Raton .... Dr. Bernadette MENDONEZ RUSSELL
12 Provost Palm Beach Gardens .... Dr. Holly L. BENNETT
12 Provost Lake Worth .... Dr. Jean WIHBEY
75 Dean Bus/Trade & Indus & Pub Safety ...... Ms. Patricia V. RICHIE
76 Acting Dean Health Science .... Mr. Ed W. WILLEY
97 Dean Academic Affairs Lake Worth .... Dr. Irving BERKOWITZ
97 Dean Academic Affairs PB Gardens .... Mr. Edward W. WILLEY
97 Dean Academic Affairs Belle Glade .... Dr. Roy M. VARGAS
97 Dean Academic Affairs Boca Raton .... Dr. Tunjarnika L. COLEMAN-FERRELL
88 Dean Bachelor Degree Programs .... Dr. Anita S. KAPLAN
20 Dean Curriculum .... Dr. Velmarie ALBERTINI
35 Dean Student Services Lake Worth .... Ms. Penny J. MCISAAC
35 Dean Student Services Boca Raton .... Dr. Sheri E. GOLDSTEIN
35 Dean Student Services PB Gardens .... Mr. Scott MACLACHLAN
35 Asst Dean Student Svc Belle Glade .... Ms. Latanya L. MCNEAL
84 Dean Enrollment Management .... Mr. Chuck H. ZETTLER
37 Director Financial Aid .... Mr. Eddie VIERA
41 Interim Athletics Director .... Mr. John SCARPINO
09 Exec Dir Inst Rsrch/Effectiveness .... Dr. Donald W. TAYLOR
18 Facilities Director .... Mr. John T. WASUKANIS
15 Exec Director Human Resources .... Ms. Barbara MATIAS
26 Dir College Relations & Marketing .... Dr. Grace H. TRUMAN
21 Controller .... Mr. James E. DUFFIE
06 College Registrar .... Ms. Amy L. MCDONALD
96 Procurement Director .... Mr. David CHOJNACKI
13 Chief Information Officer .... Mr. Ken LIBUTTI
25 Dir Resource & Grant Development .... Ms. Maureen CAPP
106 E-Learning Director .... Mr. Sidney BEITLER
108 Assessment Director .... Dr. Karen D. PAIN
19 Security & Risk Management Director .... Mr. John E. SMITH

Palmer College of Chiropractic, Florida Campus (B)

4777 City Center Parkway, Port Orange FL 32129-4153

Telephone: (386) 763-2709 Identification: 666330
Accreditation: &NH, &CHIRO

† Regional accreditation is carried under the parent institution in Davenport, IA.

Pasco-Hernando State College (C)

10230 Ridge Road, New Port Richey FL 34654-5199

County: Pasco FICE Identification: 010652
Unit ID: 136400
Telephone: (727) 847-2727 Carnegie Class: Bac/Assoc-Assoc Dom
FAX Number: (727) 816-1815 Calendar System: Semester
URL: www.phsc.edu
Established: 1972 Annual Undergrad Tuition & Fees (In-District): $3,155
Enrollment: 11,387 Coed
Affiliation or Control: State/Local IRS Status: 501(c)3
Highest Offering: Baccalaureate
Accreditation: SC, ADNUR, DH, EMT, NURSE, SURGT

01 President .... Dr. Timothy L. BEARD
05 VP Acad Affs & Fac Dev/Col Provost ..... Dr. Stanley M. GIANNET
32 VP Stdnt Affairs/Enrollment Mgmt .... Dr. Robert E. BADE
10 Vice Pres Administration & Finance .... Mr. Kenneth R. BURDZINSKI
12 Provost of the East Campus .... Dr. Lisa A. RICHARDSON
12 Provost North Campus .... Dr. Donna R. BURDZINSKI
12 Provost Spring Hill Campus .... Dr. Amy ANDERSON
12 Provost Porter Campus at Wiregrass .... Dr. Kevin F. O'FARRELL
103 Dean of Workforce Development .... Dr. Edwin G. GOOLSBY
120 VP of Technology & Distance Educ .... Dr. Melissa L. HARTS
84 Dean Stdnt Dev & Enroll Mgmt .... Ms. Chiquita A. HENDERSON
20 Assoc Dean of Acad Aff & Inst Accr .... Ms. Sonia B. THORN
49 Dean Arts and Sciences .... Dr. Patricia R. CAMPBELL
21 Asst VP Admin/Finance/Comptroller .... Mr. Brian S. HORN
09 Dean Institutional Effectiveness .... Dr. Gerardine K. COCHRAN
13 Exec Dir Management Info Svcs .... Ms. Janice L. SCOTT
111 Asst VP Inst Advance/Exec Dir Fnd .... Dr. William J. SHUSTOWSKI, JR.
66 Associate Dean of Nursing .. Dr. Barbara SOUTHWORTH-FISHER
07 Dir Admissions & Student Records .... Mr. Chris BIBBO
37 Dean Financial Aid .... Ms. Rebecca SHANAFELT
43 Asst VP of Policy/General Counsel . Mr. Stephen C. SCHROEDER
08 Director of Libraries .... Mr. Raymond J. CALVERT
41 Athletics Director/Instructor .... Mr. Stephen A. WINTERLING
26 Exec Dir Marketing/Public Relation .... Ms. Lucy T. MILLER
18 Director of Facilities .... Mr. Keith V. BRAUN
15 Exec Director of Human Resources .... Ms. Vivian M. FRIEND
109 Auxiliary Services Manager .... Mr. John D. COLLINS
35 Asst Dean Stdnt Aff/Engage/Spec Svc .... Vacant
22 Dir of Global & Multi Aware & Spec .... Mr. Imani D. ASUKILE
96 Purchasing Agent .... Ms. Michelle L. SWINGLE
04 Executive Asst to President & DBOT .... Ms. Rhonda M. DODGE
29 Director Alumni & Donor Relations .... Ms. Michelle L. BULLWINKEL

Pensacola Christian College (D)

250 Brent Lane, Pensacola FL 32503

County: Escambia Identification: 667101
Telephone: (850) 478-8496 Carnegie Class: Not Classified
FAX Number: (850) 479-6577 Calendar System: Semester
URL: www.pcci.edu
Established: 1974 Annual Undergrad Tuition & Fees: N/A
Enrollment: N/A Coed
Affiliation or Control: Independent Non-Profit IRS Status: 501(c)3
Highest Offering: Doctorate
Accreditation: TRACS, ENG, NURSE

01 President .... Dr. Troy SHOEMAKER
05 Academic Vice President .... Dr. Raylene COCHRAN
32 Vice Pres Student Life .... Dr. Tim MCLAUGHLIN
10 Chief Financial Officer .... Mr. Gary EAST
06 Registrar .... Ms. Linda TROUTMAN

Pensacola State College (E)

1000 College Boulevard, Pensacola FL 32504-8998

County: Escambia FICE Identification: 001513
Unit ID: 136473
Telephone: (850) 484-1000 Carnegie Class: Bac/Assoc-Assoc Dom
FAX Number: (850) 484-1826 Calendar System: Semester
URL: www.pensacolastate.edu
Established: 1948 Annual Undergrad Tuition & Fees (In-District): $2,704
Enrollment: 9,840 Coed
Affiliation or Control: Local IRS Status: 501(c)3
Highest Offering: Baccalaureate
Accreditation: SC, ACFEI, ADNUR, CAHIIM, DH, EMT, MAC, NUR, NURSE, PNUR, #PTAA, RAD, SURGT

01 President .... Dr. Ed MEADOWS
05 VP Academic and Student Affairs .... Dr. Erin SPICER
11 VP Administrative Services .... Mr. Tom GILLIAM
10 VP Business Affairs .... Mrs. Gean Ann EMOND
103 Dean Workforce Educ/Vocational Supp .... Mr. Dan BUSSE
12 Dean Milton Campus .... Ms. Anthea AMOS
12 Dean Warrington Campus .... Dr. Dusti SLUDER
28 Assoc VP Inst Diversity .... Dr. Gael FRAZER
102 Exec Director College Foundation .... Ms. Andrea KRIEGER
13 Exec Director ITS .... Mr. Bert MERRITT
86 Assoc VP Govt Relations .... Ms. Sandy RAY
26 Director Marketing & College Info .... Ms. Sheila NICHOLS
06 Registrar .... Ms. Susan DESBROW
108 Dean Inst Effectiveness & Grants .... Dr. Debbie DOUMA
18 Director Physical Plant .... Ms. Diane BRACKEN
14 Director Technology Support .... Ms. Liz GOMEZ
15 Director Human Resources .... Ms. Tammy HENDERSON
37 Dir Fin Aid/Veteran Svcs/Scholrshps .... Ms. Nan JACKSON
75 Coordinator Career & Technical Ed .... Ms. Kayla RILEY
19 Director Public Safety .... Mr. Sean FAGAN
43 General Counsel .... Mr. Thomas J. GILLIAM
08 District Dept Head Libraries .... Ms. LisaMarie BARTUSIK
96 Director Purchasing .... Ms. Ted YOUNG
21 Comptroller .... Ms. Jackie PADILLA
29 Exec Director Alumni Affairs .... Ms. Patrice WHITTEN
07 Director Admissions .... Ms. Debbie GERARD
36 Director Advising & Career Svcs .... Dr. Monique COLLINS
41 Director Athletics .... Mr. Bill HAMILTON
32 Dean Student Services .... Ms. Kathy DUTREMBLE
12 Director South Santa Rosa Center .... Ms. Karen MCCABE
12 Director Century Center .... Ms. Paula BYRD
51 Coordinator Continuing Education .... Mr. Michael LISTAU
04 Exec Assistant to the President .... Ms. Patricia S. CREWS
106 Director Distributed Learning .... Dr. Bill WATERS
09 Director Institutional Research .... Mr. Michael JOHNSTON

Polk State College (F)

999 Avenue H, NE, Winter Haven FL 33881-4299

County: Polk FICE Identification: 001514
Unit ID: 136516
Telephone: (863) 297-1000 Carnegie Class: Bac/Assoc-Mixed
FAX Number: (863) 297-1065 Calendar System: Trimester
URL: www.polk.edu
Established: 1964 Annual Undergrad Tuition & Fees (In-District): $3,366
Enrollment: 10,657 Coed
Affiliation or Control: Local IRS Status: 501(c)3
Highest Offering: Baccalaureate
Accreditation: SC, ADNUR, COARC, CVT, DMS, EMT, NUR, OTA, PTAA, RAD

01 President .... Dr. Angela FALCONETTI
10 Vice Pres Administrative Svcs/CFO .... Mr. Peter ELLIOTT
05 Interim Vice Pres Academic Affairs .... Dr. Donald PAINTER
32 Vice Pres Student Services .... Mr. Reginal WEBB
111 Vice Pres Inst Advanc/Exec Dir PSCF .... Ms. Tracy PORTER
13 VP Strategic Initiatives/Innov/CIO .... Dr. Naomi BOYER
12 Campus Provost-LK .... Mr. Stephen HULL
12 Campus Provost-WH .... Dr. Martha SANTIAGO
26 AVP Communications & Public Affs ...... Ms. Tamara SAKAGAWA
20 District Dean Academic Affairs .... Dr. Orathai NORTHERN
15 Director Human Resources .... Ms. Jill HALL
35 Dean Student Services-WH .... Mr. Lawrence PAKOWSKI
35 Dean Student Services-LK .... Mr. Sylvester LITTLE
20 Dean Academic Affairs-WH .... Ms. April ROBINSON
20 Dean Academic Affairs-LK .... Mr. Donald PAINTER
21 Controller .... Ms. Teresa VOROUS
84 Director Stdnt Enrollment/Registrar .... Ms. Kathy BUCKLEW
37 Director Student Financial Svcs .... Ms. Ronshetta HOWELL
66 Director Nursing .... Dr. Annette HUTCHERSON
102 Director Financial Affs/PSC Found .... Mr. Lynn WILSON
18 Director Facilities .... Mr. George URBANO
22 Director Equity & Diversity .... Ms. Valparisa BAKER
103 Director Corporate College .... Mr. Howard DRAKE
88 Principal Chain of Lakes CHS .... Ms. Bridget FETTER
88 Principal Lakeland Col HS .... Mr. Rick JEFFRIES
88 Center Director JDA .... Mr. Andy OGUNTOLA
41 Athletic Director .... Mr. Bing TYUS
96 Director Purchasing .... Mr. Mark LILLQUIST
04 Administrative Asst to President .... Mrs. Christine LEE
104 Director Study Abroad .... Ms. Kim SIMPSON
106 Dir Online Education/E-learning .... Mr. Nathan NEUMAN
108 Dir Strategic Plng & Assessment .... Dr. Kevin JONES
19 Director Security/Safety .... Ms. Denise ANDREU
25 Chief Contracts/Grants Admin .... Ms. Jennifer FIORENZA
29 Director Alumni Relations .... Mrs. Marianne GEORGE
38 Director Student Counseling .... Ms. Kim PEARSALL
43 Dir Legal Services/General Counsel .... Mr. Don WILSON
44 Director Annual Giving .... Ms. Tracy PORTER
50 Program Director Business .... Ms. Maria LOHOCZKY
53 Program Director Education .... Dr. Patty LINDER
54 Program Director Engineering Tech .... Dr. Mori TOOSI

Polytechnic University of Puerto Rico (G)

8180 NW 36th Street, Suite 401, Miami FL 33166-6674

Telephone: (305) 418-8000 Identification: 666238
Accreditation: &M

† Regional accreditation is carried under the parent institution, Universidad Politecnica de Puerto Rico, San Juan, PR.

Polytechnic University of Puerto Rico-Orlando Campus (H)

550 N Econlockhatchee Trail, Orlando FL 32825

Telephone: (407) 677-7000 Identification: 770172
Accreditation: &M

† Branch campus of Universidad Politecnica De Puerto Rico, San Juan, PR

The Praxis Institute (I)

1850 SW 8th Street, 4th Floor, Miami FL 33135

County: Miami-Dade FICE Identification: 031147
Unit ID: 430582
Telephone: (305) 642-4104 Carnegie Class: Not Classified
FAX Number: N/A Calendar System: Semester
URL: the-praxisinstitute.com
Established: 1988 Annual Undergrad Tuition & Fees: N/A
Enrollment: 378 Coed
Affiliation or Control: Proprietary IRS Status: Proprietary
Highest Offering: Associate Degree
Accreditation: COE, OTA, PTAA

01 Executive Director .... Rebeca ALFIE

Premiere International College (J)

2055 Central Avenue, Fort Myers FL 33901

County: Palm Beach Identification: 667295
Telephone: (239) 454-5000 Carnegie Class: Not Classified
FAX Number: (239) 454-0456 Calendar System: Quarter
URL: www.premierecollege.com
Established: 2009 Annual Undergrad Tuition & Fees: N/A
Enrollment: N/A Coed
Affiliation or Control: Proprietary IRS Status: Proprietary
Highest Offering: Associate Degree
Accreditation: ACICS

01 President .... Cynthia RUE

Professional Hands Institute (K)

3383 NW 7th Street, Suite 200, Miami FL 33125

County: Miami-Dade FICE Identification: 041431
Unit ID: 454908
Telephone: (305) 442-6011 Carnegie Class: Not Classified
FAX Number: (305) 442-6013 Calendar System: Semester
URL: www.prohands.edu
Established: 2004 Annual Undergrad Tuition & Fees: N/A
Enrollment: 111 Coed
Affiliation or Control: Proprietary IRS Status: Proprietary
Highest Offering: Associate Degree
Accreditation: COE

12 Campus Director .... Ms. Caridad TRIANA

Rasmussen College - Fort Myers (A)

9160 Forum Corporate Parkway, Fort Myers FL 33905
Telephone: (239) 477-2100 Identification: 667062
Accreditation: &NH, MAAB

† Regional accreditation is carried under the parent institution in Saint Cloud, MN. The tuition figure is an average, actual tuition may vary.

Rasmussen College - Land O'Lakes (B)

18600 Fernview Street, Land O'Lakes FL 34638
Telephone: (813) 435-3601 Identification: 770488
Accreditation: &NH, PNUR

† Regional accreditation carried under the parent institution in Saint Cloud, MN. The tuition figure is an average, actual tuition may vary.

Rasmussen College - New Port Richey (C)

8661 Citizens Drive, Suite 300, New Port Richey FL 34654
Telephone: (727) 942-0069 Identification: 666425
Accreditation: &NH, ADNUR, MAAB

† Regional accreditation is carried under parent institution in Saint Cloud, MN. The tuition figure is an average, actual tuition may vary.

Rasmussen College - Ocala (D)

4755 SW 46th Court, Ocala FL 34474
Telephone: (352) 629-1941 FICE Identification: 008501
Accreditation: &NH, ADNUR, MAAB

† Regional accreditation carried under the parent institution in Saint Cloud, MN. The tuition figure is an average, actual tuition may vary.

Rasmussen College - Tampa/Brandon (E)

4042 Park Oaks Boulevard, Tampa FL 33610
Telephone: (813) 246-7600 Identification: 667067
Accreditation: &NH, MAAB

† Regional accreditation is carried under the parent institution in Saint Cloud, MN. The tuition figure is an average, actual tuition may vary.

Reformed Theological Seminary (F)

1231 Reformation Drive, Oviedo FL 32765-7197
Telephone: (407) 366-9493 Identification: 666628
Accreditation: &SC, THEOL

† Regional accreditation is carried under the parent institution in Jackson, MS.

Remington College Online (G)

500 International Pkwy, Suite 200,
Heathrow FL 33612-5627
Telephone: (407) 562-5671 Identification: 770567
Accreditation: ACCSC, CAHIIM, OTA

† Branch campus of Remington College-Dallas Campus, Garland, TX

Ringling College of Art and Design (H)

2700 N Tamiami Trail, Sarasota FL 34234-5895
County: Sarasota FICE Identification: 012574
Unit ID: 136774
Telephone: (941) 351-5100 Carnegie Class: Spec-4-yr-Arts
FAX Number: (941) 359-7517 Calendar System: Semester
URL: www.ringling.edu
Established: 1931 Annual Undergrad Tuition & Fees: $43,040
Enrollment: 1,262 Coed
Affiliation or Control: Independent Non-Profit IRS Status: 501(c)3
Highest Offering: Baccalaureate
Accreditation: SC, ART, CIDA

01 President .... Dr. Larry R. THOMPSON
04 Executive Assistant to the Pres .... Ms. Kerry SCHAFFER
100 Special Assistant to the Pres .... Ms. Jaime COFFEY
05 VP for Academic Affairs .... Dr. Peter MCALLISTER
20 Assoc VP for AA/Dean of Faculty .... Mr. David H. JACKSON
20 Assoc VP for AA/Dean of UG Studies .... Mr. Jeff SCHWARTZ
20 Assoc VP for Collab Enterprises .... Ms. Cynthia GRAVINO
51 Asst VP/Dir Cont Stds/Special Pgms .... Vacant
06 Registrar .... Mr. Justin SELPH
36 Director Career Services .... Mr. Charles KOVACS
08 Dir of Library Services .... Dr. Kristina KEOGH
26 Int Dir Marketin/Digital Strategies .... Ms. Lisa MOODY
27 Editorial & PR Manager .... Ms. Stephanie LEDERER
108 Director of Assessment .... Ms. Kelly BEACHLER
111 VP for Advancement .... Ms. Stacey CORLEY
110 Asst VP for Constituent Engagement .... Ms. Lisa INTAGLIATA
112 Asst VP for Strategic Philanthropy .... Ms. Terry MARKS
29 Dir Alumni Relations/Annual Giving .... Ms. Susan BOROZAN
10 VP for Finance & Administration .... Ms. Tracy A. WAGNER
21 Asst VP for Fin & Admn/Controller .... Ms. Monica K. WAID
18 Asst VP/Dir Facilities Operations .... Mr. Jeffrey A. POLESHEK
19 Director of Public Safety .... Mr. Richard E. TUBBS
37 Dir of Financial Aid .... Mr. Lee HARRELL
15 VP for Human/Organizational Dev .... Ms. Christine C. DEGEORGE
09 Asst VP for Planning & IE .... Dr. Pat MIZAK
16 Dir of Human Resources .... Mr. Darren MATHEWS
32 VP for Student Life/Dean Stdnts .... Dr. Tammy S. WALSH
39 Assoc Dean of Students/Res Life .... Mr. Chris SHAFFER
35 Assoc Dean of Students/Student Dev .... Mr. Jekeyma ROBINSON
23 Dir Student Health Services .... Dr. Erin ROBINSON
07 Dean of Admissions .... Mr. James H. DEAN
07 Director of Admissions .... Mr. Gregg PRIGERSON
13 Dir of Institutional Technology .... Ms. Mahmoud PEGAH
90 Dir of Academic Computing .... Ms. Karissa MILLER
91 Dir of Administrative Computing .... Ms. Kris PEGAH

The Robert E. Webber Institute for Worship Studies (I)

4001 Hendricks Ave, Jacksonville FL 32207
County: Duval Identification: 666616
Telephone: (904) 264-2172 Carnegie Class: Not Classified
FAX Number: (904) 379-5534 Calendar System: Semester
URL: www.iws.edu
Established: 1998 Annual Graduate Tuition & Fees: N/A
Enrollment: N/A Coed
Affiliation or Control: Independent Non-Profit IRS Status: 501(c)3
Highest Offering: Doctorate; No Undergraduates
Accreditation: BI

01 Chief Executive Officer .... Dr. James R. HART
05 Chief Academic Officer .... Dr. Dinelle FANKLAND
10 Chief Financial Officer .... Ms. Christi G. MATTESON
06 Registrar .... Vacant
84 VP of Enrollment Management .... Mr. Mark J. MURRAY
08 Library Director .... Ms. Susan A. MASSEY
29 Director Alumni Relations .... Dr. Kent L. WALTERS
42 VP of Spiritual Life .... Dr. Darrell A. HARRIS
24 Dir of Technical Services .... Mr. Samuel L. HOROWITZ
04 Asst to the President .... Vacant
32 Dir Student Services/Office Admin .... Ms. Sandy E. DINKINS
45 Dir Strategic Plng/Accred/Assess .... Dr. Steve E. HUNTLEY
13 Coordinator of Info Technology .... Dr. James Kenneth RUSHING
26 Dir of Missional Relations .... Dr. Frank FORTUNATO
111 Director of Advancement .... Vacant

Rollins College (J)

1000 Holt Avenue, Winter Park FL 32789-4499
County: Orange FICE Identification: 001515
Unit ID: 136950
Telephone: (407) 646-2000 Carnegie Class: Masters/L
FAX Number: (407) 646-2600 Calendar System: Semester
URL: www.rollins.edu
Established: 1885 Annual Undergrad Tuition & Fees: $46,520
Enrollment: 3,260 Coed
Affiliation or Control: Independent Non-Profit IRS Status: 501(c)3
Highest Offering: Doctorate
Accreditation: SC, CACREP, MUS

01 President .... Dr. Grant H. CORNWELL
05 VP Acad Affairs/Provost .... Dr. Susan R. SINGER
32 Vice President Student Affairs .... Dr. Mamta M. ACCAPADI
10 Vice President Business/Finance .... Mr. Jeffrey EISENBARTH
13 Chief Information Officer .... Dr. Pat SCHOKNECHT
20 Dean of the Faculty .... Dr. Jennifer CAVENAUGH
35 Asst VP Stdnt Affs & Dean of Stdnts .... Dr. Meghan HARTE WEYANT
84 VP of Enrollment Mgmt and Marketing .... Dr. Faye F. TYDLASKA
50 Dean Crummer Grad Sch of Business .... Dr. Deborah F. CROWN
42 Dean of Religious Life .... Rev. Katrina JENKINS
21 Assoc VP Finance/Asst Treasurer .... Mr. William SHORT
26 Chief Marketing & Comm Rels Officer .... Mr. Sam STARK
15 Assoc VP Human Res/Risk Management .... Ms. Maria MARTINEZ
108 Asst Provost Inst Effectiveness .... Dr. Toni STROLLO HOLBROOK
41 Athletic Director .... Ms. Pennie PARKER
37 Director of Financial Aid .... Mr. Steve BOOKER
09 Director of Institutional Research .... Mr. Udeth LUGO
104 Director of International Programs .... Ms. Giselda BEAUDIN
07 Dean of Admission .... Ms. Zaire MCCOY
39 Sr Dir Res Life & Explorations .... Mr. Leon HAYNER
36 Asst VP of Career & Life Planning .... Ms. Lisa JOHNSON
18 AVP of Facilities Management .... Mr. Scott BITIKOFER
19 Assistant VP Public Safety .... Mr. Ken MILLER
29 Sr Assoc Director Alumni Relations .... Ms. Elaine LILES
111 VP for Institutional Advancement .... Ms. Laurie HOUCK
102 Director of Foundation Relations .... Mr. Joseph MONTI
06 Registrar .... Ms. Robin MATEO
40 Manager of Bookstore .... Ms. Mary VITELLI
04 Exec Assistant to the President .... Ms. Jillian SCHUMM
23 Director of Wellness .... Ms. Connie BRISCOE
25 Director Contracts/Grants Admin .... Ms. Devon MASSOT
35 Asst VP Student Affairs/Community .... Ms. Michele MEYER
16 Director of Human Resources .... Mr. Matt HAWKS
08 Interim Director of Olin Library .... Mr. Wenxian ZHANG

Saber College (K)

3990 West Flagler Street, Ste 103, Miami FL 33134
County: Miami-Dade FICE Identification: 036964
Unit ID: 449506
Telephone: (305) 443-9170 Carnegie Class: Spec 2-yr-Health
FAX Number: (305) 443-8441 Calendar System: Other
URL: www.sabercollege.com
Established: 1972 Annual Undergrad Tuition & Fees: N/A
Enrollment: 553 Coed
Affiliation or Control: Independent Non-Profit IRS Status: 501(c)3
Highest Offering: Associate Degree
Accreditation: COE, PTAA

01 Director Nursing Program .... Ms. Angela GAUD
05 Dean of Academic Affairs .... Ms. Amarilis SOMOZA

St. John Vianney College Seminary (L)

2900 SW 87th Avenue, Miami FL 33165-3244
County: Miami-Dade FICE Identification: 008075
Unit ID: 137272
Telephone: (305) 223-4561 Carnegie Class: Spec-4-yr-Faith
FAX Number: (305) 223-0650 Calendar System: Semester
URL: www.sjvcs.edu
Established: 1959 Annual Undergrad Tuition & Fees: $21,100
Enrollment: 90 Male
Affiliation or Control: Roman Catholic IRS Status: 501(c)3
Highest Offering: Baccalaureate
Accreditation: SC

01 Rector & President .... RevMsg. Roberto GARZA
32 Vice Rector/Dean of Students .... Rev. Scott CIRCE
05 Academic Dean .... Dr. Ramon SANTOS
06 Registrar/Office Manager .... Mrs. Bonnie DE ANGULO
10 Comptroller .... Mr. Carlos CALMET
08 Director of Library .... Mrs. Maria RODRIGUEZ
09 Office Institutional Research Dir .... Dr. Jose ORTA
42 Spiritual Director .... Rev. Joseph KOTTOYIL

St. Johns River State College (M)

5001 St. Johns Avenue, Palatka FL 32177-3897
County: Putnam FICE Identification: 001523
Unit ID: 137281
Telephone: (386) 312-4200 Carnegie Class: Bac/Assoc-Assoc Dom
FAX Number: (386) 312-4229 Calendar System: Semester
URL: www.sjrstate.edu
Established: 1958 Annual Undergrad Tuition & Fees (In-District): $2,880
Enrollment: 7,091 Coed
Affiliation or Control: State/Local IRS Status: 501(c)3
Highest Offering: Baccalaureate
Accreditation: SC, ADNUR, CAHIIM, COARC, NUR

01 President .... Mr. Joe PICKENS
43 Senior VP/General Counsel .... Dr. Melissa C. MILLER
32 Vice President Student Affairs .... Dr. Gilbert L. EVANS, JR.
05 VP & CAO/Exec Dir St Augustine .... Dr. Melanie A. BROWN
10 Vice President Finance & Admin/CFO .... Dr. Lynn POWERS
30 Vice Pres Develop/External Affairs .... Mrs. Caroline D. TINGLE
108 VP Assessment/Research & Tech .... Dr. Rosalind M. HUMERICK
103 VP Workforce/Exec Dir Orange Park .... Dr. Anna M. LEBESCH
20 Associate VP Academic Affairs .... Dr. Edward K. JORDAN
15 Associate VP Human Resources .... Mrs. Ginger C. STOKES
13 Chief Information Officer .... Mr. Paul M. HAWKINS
49 Dean of Arts & Sciences .... Mr. Mike KELLER
19 Dean of Crim Justice/Public Safety .... Ms. Angela A. SOCKWELL
57 Dean of Florida School of the Arts .... Mr. Alain R. HENTSCHEL
08 Dean of Library Services .... Dr. Christina WILL
66 Dean Nursing .... Dr. Mary A. LANEY
55 Dean of Adult Education .... Dr. Melissa PERRY
53 Dean of Teacher Education .... Dr. Myrna L. ALLEN
76 Associate Dean of Allied Health .... Dr. Holly COULLIETTE
88 Exec Dir TH Center for the Arts .... Mr. Denton J. YOCKEY
50 Director of Business Education .... Mr. Joel C. ABO
103 Director of Workforce Services .... Mrs. Melissa E. O'CONNELL
51 Dir of Dual Enroll & College Access .... Mrs. Meghan DEPUTY
26 Director of Public Relations .... Mrs. Susan B. KESSLER
121 Director of Academic Advising .... Ms. Karen THOMAS
88 Director of Testing & Stdnt Support .... Mr. Todd DIXON
06 Registrar .... Mrs. Susanne B. LINEBERGER
21 Controller .... Mr. Randall PETERSON
37 Interim Director of Financial Aid .... Ms. Suzanne M. EVANS
106 Director of eLearning .... Mr. Jack C. HALL

Saint Leo University (N)

33701 State Road 52 W, Saint Leo FL 33574-6665
County: Pasco FICE Identification: 001526
Unit ID: 137032
Telephone: (352) 588-8200 Carnegie Class: Masters/L
FAX Number: (352) 588-8654 Calendar System: Semester
URL: www.saintleo.edu
Established: 1889 Annual Undergrad Tuition & Fees: $21,440
Enrollment: 15,800 Coed
Affiliation or Control: Roman Catholic IRS Status: 501(c)3
Highest Offering: Doctorate
Accreditation: SC, ACBSP, CEA, IACBE, SW

01 President .... Dr. William J. LENNOX, JR.
05 VP Academic Affairs .... Vacant
32 VP Student Affairs/Campus Operation .... Dr. Edward DADEZ
26 VP Marketing & Enrollment .... Mr. Christian SCHINDLER
10 VP Business Affairs .... Mr. Eric WEEKES
111 VP University Advancement .... Mr. Denny MOLLER
88 VP Business Development .... Mr. Robert QUINN
88 VP Saint Leo Univ Worldwide .... Ms. Melanie STORMS
04 Assistant to the President .... Ms. Molly-Dodd ADAMS
13 Assoc VP/Chief Information Officer .... Mr. Vijay SONTY
20 Associate VP Academic Affairs .... Dr. Jeffrey ANDERSON
20 Assoc VP Learning & Innovation .... Dr. Jeff BORDEN
88 Associate VP Regional Accreditation .... Vacant
108 Director of Academic Assessment .... Vacant
43 Associate VP/General Counsel .... Ms. Kelly HILL

84 Senior Director Campus Enrollment ... Mr. John LAROSA
88 Asst VP Academic Worldwide Liaison ... Dr. Carol WALKER
42 Chaplain for University Ministries ... Fr. Kyle SMITH
35 Associate VP Student Affairs ... Mr. Kenneth POSNER
38 Director Counseling Services ... Mr. Lawson JOLLY
49 Dean School of Arts & Sciences ... Dr. Mary SPOTO
53 Dean School of Educ/Social Svcs ... Dr. Susan KINSELLA
50 Dean School of Business ... Dr. Balbir BAL
58 Dir Grad Studies Criminal Justice ... Dr. Robert DIEMER
58 Dir Grad Studies in Education ... Dr. Fern AEFSKY
58 Dir Grad Studies in Social Work ... Dr. Cindy LEE
58 Dir Graduate Studies in Theology ... Dr. Randall WOODARD
58 Director Graduate Creative Writing ... Dr. Steven KISTULENTZ
06 Registrar ... Mrs. Karen HATFIELD
08 Director Library Services ... Mr. Brent SHORT
07 Assoc VP of Enrollment/Support Svcs ... Mr. Jeffrey WALSH
88 Director Enrollment Info Systems ... Mr. Mark JONES
88 Asst VP of Learning Design ... Dr. Karen HAHN
88 Director Student Learning ... Ms. Erica HICKS
39 Dir Residence Life & Leadership ... Ms. Kimberly MCCONNELL
11 Director Academic Administration ... Mr. Joseph TADEO
41 Director Intercollegiate Athletics ... Mr. Francis REIDY
26 Assoc VP Integrated Marketing ... Mr. Nick TEMNICK
88 Director Market Research ... Mr. William HAMILTON
18 Director Facilities Management ... Mr. Jose CABAN
19 Director Campus Security & Safety ... Mr. Vincent D'AMBROSIO
23 Director Health Services ... Vacant
22 Director Accessibility Services ... Ms. Christine GEORGALLIS
35 Assoc VP for Student Success ... Ms. Ana DI DONATO
29 Director Alumni Engagement ... Ms. Elizabeth BARR
44 Exec Director Development ... Ms. Dawn PARISI
88 Director Advancement Services ... Mr. Stephen KUBASEK
88 Grant & Scholarship Officer ... Ms. Victoria REECE
85 Exec Director Student Success . Ms. Paige RAMSEY-HAMACHER
88 Dir Military Affairs & Services ... Ms. Pamela MARTIS
15 Associate VP Human Resources ... Ms. Sheri NESHIEM
36 Director of Career Planning ... Vacant
21 Senior Assoc VP Finance ... Mr. James DETUCCIO
96 Mgr Accts Payable/Sponsor Billing ... Ms. Laura SOLBERG
88 Director of Budgets ... Mr. Mark WILLIAMS
88 Director Internal Audit Services ... Ms. Monica MOYER
12 Asst VP Military Center Operations ... Dr. John CAIN
12 Asst VP Central Region ... Ms. Candis WHITFIELD
12 Asst VP Tampa Region ... Mr. Tyler UPSHAW
12 Asst VP Florida Region ... Ms. Katie DEGNER
103 Director Talent Development ... Mr. Joseph ARNER
109 Director Dining Services ... Mr. Rich VOGEL
88 Executive Officer ... Ms. Marcia MALIA
37 Associate VP of Financial Aid ... Ms. Melinda CLARK
27 Director University Communications ... Ms. Lucia RAATMA

St. Petersburg College (A)

PO Box 13489, Saint Petersburg FL 33733-3489
County: Pinellas | FICE Identification: 001528 | Unit ID: 137078
Telephone: (727) 341-4772 | Carnegie Class: Bac/Assoc-Mixed
FAX Number: (727) 341-3318 | Calendar System: Semester
URL: www.spcollege.edu
Established: 1927 | Annual Undergrad Tuition & Fees (In-District): $3,385
Enrollment: 31,767 | Coed
Affiliation or Control: Local | IRS Status: 501(c)3
Highest Offering: Baccalaureate
Accreditation: SC, ADNUR, CAHIIM, CEA, COARC, DH, EMT, FUSER, NURSE, PTAA, RAD

01 President ... Dr. Tonjua L. WILLIAMS
05 Sr VP Instruction/Academic Pgm ... Dr. Anne M. COOPER
32 Sr Vice Pres Student Affairs ... Vacant
10 Sr VP Admin/Bus Svcs & Info Tech ... Brian MILES
18 Assoc VP Facilities Plng/Inst Svcs ... James WAECHTER
15 Human Resources/Dir of Operations ... Desiree WORONER
30 VP Inst Advance/Exec Dir Foundation ... Frances NEU
21 Budget/Compliance Director ... Janette HUNT
84 Assoc VP Enrollment Services ... Dr. Pat RINARD
37 Assoc VP Financial Asst Svcs ... Michael J. BENNETT
20 Assoc VP Academic Affs/Partnership ... Catherine C. KENNEDY
20 Assoc Provost ... Heather DISLER
26 Exec Dir Marketing/Public Info ... Diana SABINO
103 Director Workforce Services ... Dr. Jason KRUPP
43 General Counsel ... Suzanne GARDNER
12 Provost Allstate Center ... Dr. Scott FRONRATH
12 Provost Clearwater Campus ... Dr. Stanley VITTETOE
12 Provost/Health Education Center ... Dr. Eric CARVER
12 Provost St Petersburg Campus ... Jamelle CONNER
12 Provost Seminole Campus/eCampus ... Mark STRICKLAND
12 Provost Tarpon Springs Campus ... Dr. Marvin BRIGHT
12 Provost Downtown Center ... Dr. Kevin GORDON
22 Dir Equal Access/Equal Opp/Title IX ... Pam SMITH
96 Dir Procurement & Asset Mgmt ... Joe C. SMITH
38 Dir Student Success ... Joe DVORACSEK
88 Dean College of Public Safety Admin ... Dr. Brian FRANK
88 Dean Col of Policy Ethics/Leg Stds ... Dr. Susan S. DEMERS
83 Dean Social & Behavioral Sciences ... Dr. Joseph SMILEY
88 Principal St Pete Collegiate High ... Starla METZ
88 President Faculty Senate ... Dr. Richard MERCADANTE
50 Dean College of Business ... Dr. Greg NENSTIEL
81 Dean Mathematics ... Jimmy CHANG
65 Dean Natural Science ... Dr. Natavia MIDDLETON
79 Dean Humanities/Fine Arts ... Dr. Jonathan STEELE
53 Dean College of Education ... Dr. Kimberly HARTMAN
60 Dean Communications ... Joseph LEOPOLD
76 Dean College of Health Sciences ... Dr. Rebecca LUDWIG
74 Dean Sch of Veterinary Technology ... Dr. Richard FLORA
72 Dean College of Comp & Info Tech ... Dr. Sharon SETTERLIND
66 Dean College of Nursing ... Dr. Susan BAKER
08 Exec Director Learning Resources ... Matthew BODIE
04 Executive Admin Svcs Specialist ... Rebecca TURNER
07 Director of Admissions and Records ... Eva CHRISTENSEN
09 Director of Institutional Research ... Edward SIEGEL
100 Chief of Staff ... Deborah BOYLE
104 Director International Programs ... Ramona KIRSCH
106 Associate VP Online Learning/Svcs ... Dr. Susan COLARIC
108 Director Assessment ... Magaly TYMMS
13 Senior Director Enterprise Systems ... Zoran STANISIC
19 Director College Security Services ... Daniel BARTO
25 Exec Dir of Grants Development ... Jackie SKRYD
86 Director Government Relations ... Edward W. WOODRUFF, JR.

St. Thomas University (B)

16401 NW 37th Avenue, Miami Gardens FL 33054-6498
County: Miami-Dade | FICE Identification: 001468 | Unit ID: 137476
Telephone: (305) 625-6000 | Carnegie Class: Masters/L
FAX Number: (305) 628-6510 | Calendar System: Semester
URL: www.stu.edu
Established: 1961 | Annual Undergrad Tuition & Fees: $28,800
Enrollment: 4,918 | Coed
Affiliation or Control: Roman Catholic | IRS Status: 501(c)3
Highest Offering: Doctorate
Accreditation: SC, LAW, @THEOL

01 President ... Msgr. Franklyn M. CASALE
05 Univ Provost/Chief Academic Ofcr ... Dr. Irma BECERRA
10 VP Administration/Chief Fin Ofcr ... Mr. Terrence L. O'CONNOR
61 Dean of Law School ... Mr. Alfredo GARCIA
30 Vice Pres University Advancement ... Ms. Hilda FERNANDEZ
45 Vice Pres for Enrollment Services ... Ms. Carmen A. BROWN
20 Assoc Provost Academic Support Svcs ... Dr. Susan ANGULO
84 Dean Enrollment ... Mr. Celso ALVAREZ
26 Director University Marketing ... Burcu AYRIM
06 Executive Associate Registrar ... Mrs. Maria ABDEL
37 Assoc Director Financial Aid ... Ms. Yaidany RIVERO
08 University Librarian ... Mr. Lawrence TREADWELL, IV
21 Controller ... Mrs. Maribel SMITH
18 Director Facilities/Physical Plant ... Mr. Juan M. ZAMORA
09 Dir Institutional Research/Effect ... Dr. Susan DONOFF
88 Assoc Dir Emergency/Risk Management .. Ms. Monique BRIJBASI
41 Athletic Director ... Mrs. Laura J. COURTLEY-TODD
07 Director of Admissions ... Mr. Celso J. ALVAREZ
32 Dean of Students ... Vacant
15 Assoc Director Human Resources ... Ms. Lenore M. PRADO
25 Director for Prospect Research ... Ms. Jacqueline HOUSE
73 Dean School of Theology ... RevMsg. Terrance E. HOGAN
12 Int Dean Biscayne College ... Dr. Pamela CINGEL
13 Chief Information Officer ... Mr. Rudy IBARRA
29 Director Alumni Affairs ... Ms. Yisel CABRERA
44 Director Annual Giving ... Vacant
11 Dir Administration/Budget Analyst ... Mrs. Sylvia L. RODRIGUEZ

St. Vincent De Paul Regional Seminary (C)

10701 S Military Trail, Boynton Beach FL 33436-4899
County: Palm Beach | FICE Identification: 008223 | Unit ID: 136701
Telephone: (561) 732-4424 | Carnegie Class: Spec-4-yr-Faith
FAX Number: (561) 737-2205 | Calendar System: Semester
URL: www.svdp.edu
Established: 1963 | Annual Graduate Tuition & Fees: N/A
Enrollment: 145 | Coed
Affiliation or Control: Roman Catholic | IRS Status: 501(c)3
Highest Offering: Master's; No Undergraduates
Accreditation: SC, THEOL

01 Rector/President ... Rev. David L. TOUPS
03 Vice Rector ... Rev. Remek BLASZKOWSKI
05 Academic Dean ... Rev. Alfredo HERNANDEZ
10 Treasurer ... Mr. Keith PARKER
08 Director of the Library ... Mr. Arthur QUINN
04 Administrative Asst to President ... Mrs. Herminia C. GARCIA
09 Dir Inst Research/Assessment ... Dr. Mary FROEHLE
111 Chief Development/Advancement ... Ms. Daniella COY
06 Registrar ... Mrs. Alicia RUEFF

San Ignacio University (D)

10395 NW 41st Street, Suite 125, Doral FL 33178
County: Miami-Dade | Identification: 667130 | Unit ID: 486239
Telephone: (305) 629-2929 | Carnegie Class: Not Classified
FAX Number: (305) 629-2910 | Calendar System: Semester
URL: www.sanignaciocollege.edu
Established: 2007 | Annual Undergrad Tuition & Fees: $10,350
Enrollment: 102 | Coed
Affiliation or Control: Proprietary | IRS Status: Proprietary
Highest Offering: Master's
Accreditation: ACICS

01 President ... Luis LAUREDO
11 Vice Pres of Administration ... Marisol SALCEDO
05 Director Academic Affairs ... Dr. Hector MIRABILE
08 Head Librarian ... Silvia LOPEZ
15 Human Resources Senior Coordinator ... Ivette BAJANDAS
37 Financial Aid Director ... Elba CASTANOS
26 Marketing Director ... Maria Carolina LANDAETA

Santa Fe College (E)

3000 NW 83rd Street, Gainesville FL 32606-6200
County: Alachua | FICE Identification: 001519 | Unit ID: 137096
Telephone: (352) 395-5000 | Carnegie Class: Bac/Assoc-Assoc Dom
FAX Number: (352) 395-5581 | Calendar System: Semester
URL: www.sfcollege.edu
Established: 1965 | Annual Undergrad Tuition & Fees (In-District): $2,563
Enrollment: 14,767 | Coed
Affiliation or Control: Local | IRS Status: 501(c)3
Highest Offering: Baccalaureate
Accreditation: SC, ADNUR, CAHIIM, COARC, CONST, CVT, DA, DH, DMS, EMT, MT, NMT, NURSE, POLYT, @PTAA, RAD, SURGT

01 President ... Dr. Jackson N. SASSER
05 Provost/Vice Pres Academic Affairs ... Dr. Edward BONAHUE
10 Chief Financial Ofcr/VP Admin Affs ... Ms. Ginger GIBSON
32 Vice President Student Affairs ... Dr. Naima BROWN
111 Vice President Ofc for Advancement ... Mr. Chuck CLEMONS
108 VP Assessment/Research/Technology ... Dr. Lisa ARMOUR
04 Assistant to the President ... Ms. Cathy KEEN
20 Assoc Vice Pres Academic Affairs ... Dr. Jodi LONG
20 Assoc Vice Pres Academic Affairs ... Dr. Stefanie WASCHULL
104 Assoc VP Academic Affairs ... Dr. Vilma FUENTES
13 Assoc VP Information Tech Services ... Mr. Bill PENNEY
18 Assoc VP Facilities Services ... Mr. Gary COTHREN
35 Assoc VP Student Affairs ... Dr. Dan RODKIN
88 Dean Educational Centers ... Dr. Cheryl CALHOUN
25 Director Grants/Projects ... Ms. Kathryn LEHMAN
35 Asst Vice Pres Student Affairs ... Dr. Beatrice AWONIYI
43 Legal Counsel ... Ms. Patti P. LOCASCIO
06 College Registrar ... Mr. Mike HUTLEY
88 Dir High Sch Dual Enrollment Pgm ... Ms. Jennifer HOMARD
121 Director Advisement Center ... Ms. Kimberly FUGATE-ROBERTS
41 Athletic Director ... Mr. Jim KEITES
08 Director Library Service ... Ms. Myra STERRETT
19 Director Institute of Public Safety ... Mr. Tom ACKERMAN
35 Director of Student Life ... Dr. Tracey REEVES
96 Director of Purchasing ... Mr. David SHLAFER
28 Coordinator Col Achievement Pgm ... Ms. Dana LINDSEY
37 Director Student Financial Aid ... Ms. Kamia MWANGO
15 Director Human Resources ... Ms. Lela FRYE
09 Director of Institutional Research ... Mr. Gary HARTGE
07 Coordinator for Admissions ... Ms. Gayle JONES
26 Chief Public Relations/Marketing ... Ms. Teri MCCLELLAN
102 Assoc VP Advace/Dep Exec Dir Found ... Mr. Mike CURRY
106 Asst VP Academic Technologies ... Dr. Lisa CIARDULLI
86 Asst to President Govt Relations ... Mr. Liam MCCLAY

Schiller International University (F)

8560 Ulmerton Road, Largo FL 33771
County: Pinellas | FICE Identification: 023141 | Unit ID: 404338
Telephone: (727) 736-5082 | Carnegie Class: Spec-4-yr-Bus
FAX Number: (727) 734-0359 | Calendar System: Semester
URL: www.schiller.edu
Established: 1964 | Annual Undergrad Tuition & Fees: $14,360
Enrollment: 131 | Coed
Affiliation or Control: Proprietary | IRS Status: Proprietary
Highest Offering: Master's
Accreditation: ACICS

01 Campus Director ... Mr. Fabian FERNANDEZ
05 Provost ... Dr. Carlos DE AQUINO
07 Director of Admissions ... Ms. Tara AUGUSTINE

Seminole State College of Florida (G)

100 Weldon Boulevard, Sanford FL 32773-6199
County: Seminole | FICE Identification: 001520 | Unit ID: 137209
Telephone: (407) 708-4722 | Carnegie Class: Bac/Assoc-Assoc Dom
FAX Number: (407) 708-2139 | Calendar System: Semester
URL: www.seminolestate.edu
Established: 1965 | Annual Undergrad Tuition & Fees (In-District): $3,131
Enrollment: 17,741 | Coed
Affiliation or Control: Local | IRS Status: 501(c)3
Highest Offering: Baccalaureate
Accreditation: SC, ADNUR, CAHIIM, COARC, EMT, PTAA

01 President ... Dr. E. Ann MCGEE
10 Executive VP/CFO ... Dr. Joseph SARNOVSKY
05 VP Academic Affairs/CAO ... Dr. Laura ROSS
32 Interim VP Student Affairs/CSAO ... Dr. Dick HAMANN
13 VP Information Resources/CIO ... Dr. Dick T. HAMANN
30 VP Resource Develop & Economic Dev ... Dr. John GYLLIN
21 AVP Finance & Budget ... Ms. Judi COOPER
35 AVP Student Development ... Dr. Jan LLOYD
12 Dean of Students Altamonte Springs ... Ms. Lynn GARRETT
12 Dean of Students Oviedo Campus ... Mr. Randy PAWLOWSKI
08 Dean Learning Resources ... Ms. Barbara HILDERBRAND
36 AVP Career Programs ... Dr. Angela M. KERSENBROCK
54 Dean Engineering and Design ... Mr. Michael STALEY
88 Dean Academic Foundations ... Mr. Frank BONJIONE
26 Dir College & Community Relations ... Ms. Deborah RICHARD
91 Director Networks ... Mr. Julio VALENTIN

38 Director Counseling and Advising .... Ms. Deborah LYNCH
20 Director Curriculum .... Ms. Carlene MCNEIL
15 AVP Human Resources .... Ms. Mae KLINE
07 Dir Enrollment Svcs/Registrar .... Ms. Kathy VOUDRY
37 Director Student Financial Aid .... Ms. Roseann AMATO
09 AVP Institutional Effectiveness .... Dr. Mark MORGAN
41 Director Intercollegiate Athletics .... Mr. Kurt ESSER
84 AVP Student Recruitment .... Mrs. Pamela MENNECHEY
36 Director Career Development .... Ms. Heather ENGELKING
14 AVP Information Technology .... Ms. Pilar ACOSTA
106 Dir Online Education/E-learning .... Ms. Michelle FRANZ
28 Director of Diversity .... Ms. Janet BALANOFF
102 Dir Foundation Finance & Operations ..... Ms. Christina BEHRENS
110 Assistant Director of Development .... Ms. Amber COX

South Florida Bible College (A)

1100 South Federal Highway, Deerfield Beach FL 33441
County: Broward FICE Identification: 032643
Unit ID: 366003
Telephone: (954) 545-4500 Carnegie Class: Spec-4-yr-Faith
FAX Number: (954) 719-3780 Calendar System: Semester
URL: www.sfbc.edu
Established: 1985 Annual Undergrad Tuition & Fees: $6,560
Enrollment: 218 Coed
Affiliation or Control: Interdenominational IRS Status: 501(c)3
Highest Offering: Master's
Accreditation: BI

01 President .... Dr. Mary A. DRABIK
03 Vice President .... Josiah STEPHAN
05 Chief Academic Officer .... Dr. John STEVENSON
10 Chief Financial Officer .... Zil WENCESLAU
06 Registrar .... Dr. Becky EMERSON
08 Librarian .... Paula STEVENSON
20 Dean of Faculty .... Dr. Esa AUTERO
32 Dean of Students .... Refik OZBAY
29 Director Alumni Relations .... George T. SHARP
84 Director Enrollment Management .... John MEZZACAPPA
13 Chief Info Technology Officer (CIO) .... Joshua DRABIK
111 Chief Development/Advancement .... Wayne RICHARDSON
04 Administrative Asst to President .... Deanna STEPHAN
09 Director of Institutional Research .... Daniel DRABIK

South Florida State College (B)

600 W College Drive, Avon Park FL 33825-9399
County: Highlands FICE Identification: 001522
Unit ID: 137315
Telephone: (863) 453-6661 Carnegie Class: Bac/Assoc-Assoc Dom
FAX Number: (863) 453-0165 Calendar System: Trimester
URL: www.southflorida.edu
Established: 1965 Annual Undergrad Tuition & Fees (In-District): $3,165
Enrollment: 2,659 Coed
Affiliation or Control: Local IRS Status: 501(c)3
Highest Offering: Baccalaureate
Accreditation: SC, ADNUR, DA, DH, EMT, NUR, RAD

01 President .... Dr. Thomas C. LEITZEL
05 Vice Pres Educational/Stdnt Svcs .... Dr. Sidney VALENTINE
10 Controller .... Ms. Melissa LEE
11 Vice Pres Administrative Services .... Mr. Glenn W. LITTLE
75 Dean Applied Science & Tech .... Mr. Erik CHRISTENSEN
49 Int Dean Arts & Sciences .... Mr. Lynn MACNEILL
88 Director Cultural Programs .... Ms. Cynthia GARREN
45 Dean Resource Development .... Ms. Jamie BATEMAN
32 Dean Student Services .... Dr. Timothy WISE
12 Director DeSoto Campus .... Ms. Asena MOTT
12 Director Hardee Campus .... Ms. Teresa CRAWFORD
12 Director Lake Placid Center .... Mr. Randall K. PAEPLOW
26 Director Community Relations .... Ms. Deborah LATTER
106 Director eLearning .... Mrs. Melanie M. JACKSON
15 Director Human Res/EA-EO & ADA
Ofcr .... Mr. Donald KESTERSON
18 Dir Remodeling/Reno & Maint .... Dr. Robert E. FLORES
06 Registrar .... Dr. Deborah M. FUSCHETTI
41 Athletic Director .... Mr. Richard J. HITT
36 Director Career Development Center .... Mrs. Colleen RAFATTI
37 Director Financial Aid .... Mr. Jerry DONNA
13 Chief Information Officer .... Dr. Christopher VAN DER KAAY
38 Chair Counseling .... Mrs. Carla ELLERKER
08 Library Services .... Ms. Lena PHELPS
96 Coordinator Purchasing .... Mrs. Deborah OLSON
07 Director of Admissions .... Ms. Lynn HINTZ
76 Dean Division of Health Services .... Dr. Michele HESTON

South University (C)

9801 Belevedere Road, Royal Palm Beach FL 33411
Telephone: (561) 273-6500 Identification: 666117
Accreditation: &SC, ACBSP, CACREP, NURSE, #OTA, PTAA

† Regional accreditation is carried under the parent institution in Savannah, GA.

South University (D)

4401 North Himes Ave Ste 175, Tampa FL 33614-7095
Telephone: (813) 393-3800 Identification: 770913
Accreditation: &SC, ACBSP, ARCPA, NURSE, OTA, PTAA

† Branch campus of South University, Savannah, GA

Southeastern College (E)

17395 NW 59th Avenue, Miami Lakes FL 33015-5111
Telephone: (305) 820-5003 Identification: 666290
Accreditation: ACCSC, SURGT

† Branch campus of Southeastern College, West Palm Beach, FL.

Southeastern College (F)

2081 Vista Parkway, Suite 100B,
West Palm Beach FL 33411
County: Palm Beach FICE Identification: 031239
Unit ID: 428170
Telephone: (561) 433-2330 Carnegie Class: Spec 2-yr-Health
FAX Number: (561) 433-9025 Calendar System: Other
URL: www.sec.edu
Established: 1988 Annual Undergrad Tuition & Fees: $18,288
Enrollment: 1,063 Coed
Affiliation or Control: Proprietary IRS Status: Proprietary
Highest Offering: Associate Degree
Accreditation: ACCSC, MAAB, SURGT

01 Vice President .... Ms. Dana HUPPON

Southeastern University (G)

1000 Longfellow Boulevard, Lakeland FL 33801-6099
County: Polk FICE Identification: 001521
Unit ID: 137564
Telephone: (863) 667-5000 Carnegie Class: Masters/M
FAX Number: (863) 667-5200 Calendar System: Semester
URL: www.seu.edu
Established: 1935 Annual Undergrad Tuition & Fees: $24,160
Enrollment: 4,538 Coed
Affiliation or Control: Assemblies Of God Church IRS Status: 501(c)3
Highest Offering: Doctorate
Accreditation: SC, ACBSP, NURSE, SW

01 President .... Dr. Kent INGLE
03 Executive Vice President .... Dr. James (Chris) OWEN
05 Provost .... Dr. William C. HACKET, JR.
32 VP for Student Development .... Mrs. Bethany THOMAS
84 VP for Enrollment Management .... Mr. Roy ROWLAND, IV
09 VP Inst Research/Effectiveness .... Dr. Andrew H. PERMENTER
10 VP for Finance .... Mr. Jeff SPEAR
88 VP for Unrestricted Education .... Mr. Nicholas WALLSTEADT
08 Dean of Library Services .... Mrs. Amy HARRIS
06 Dir Student Records/Registrar .... Mrs. Melissa MAISENBACHER
37 Exec Dir Student Financial Services .... Mr. Michael YOHE
88 Director of Hispanic Learning Ctr .... Ms. Betania TORRES
07 Director of Admissions .... Mrs. Sarah E. CLARK
15 Director Human Resources .... Ms. Betty KELLEY
26 Director External Relations .... Mr. Edward L. MANER
18 Exec Dir Facilities/Physical
Plant .... Mr. Norman (Mike) M. ALDERMAN
20 Director Academic Auxiliary Svcs .... Mrs. Laura BROWN
36 Sr Dir Center for Calling & Career .... Mrs. Pamela CROSBY
10 Exec Director of Finance .... Mr. Frederick S. GORE
84 Director Enrollment Marketing .... Mr. Brandt MERRITT
38 Dir Counseling/Health & Wellness .... Mrs. Paula WHITAKER
56 Exec Dir School of Extended Educ .... Mr. Andrew MILLER
13 Chief Info Technology Officer (CIO) .... Mr. Jerry RAINS
19 Director Security/Safety .... Mr. Richard DAVIS

Southern Technical College (H)

1685 Medical Lane, Fort Myers FL 33907-1158
County: Lee FICE Identification: 022788
Unit ID: 366553
Telephone: (239) 939-4766 Carnegie Class: Bac/Assoc-Mixed
FAX Number: (239) 790-2118 Calendar System: Quarter
URL: www.southerntech.edu
Established: 1974 Annual Undergrad Tuition & Fees: $14,940
Enrollment: 1,023 Coed
Affiliation or Control: Proprietary IRS Status: Proprietary
Highest Offering: Baccalaureate
Accreditation: ACICS, CAHIIM, SURTEC

01 Executive Director .... Mr. Alex RODRIGUEZ
05 Director Education .... Mr. Esmail DARIAROW

Southern Technical College (I)

2910 South Orlando Drive, Sanford FL 32773
County: Seminole FICE Identification: 039035
Unit ID: 446552
Telephone: (407) 323-4141 Carnegie Class: Not Classified
FAX Number: (407) 323-4221 Calendar System: Semester
URL: www.southerntech.edu
Established: 1956 Annual Undergrad Tuition & Fees: N/A
Enrollment: 1,254 Coed
Affiliation or Control: Proprietary IRS Status: Proprietary
Highest Offering: Associate Degree
Accreditation: ACICS

01 Executive Director .... Ms. Sherry PARKER

Southern Technical College-Auburndale (J)

298 Havendale Boulevard, Auburndale FL 33823
Telephone: (863) 551-1112 Identification: 770705
Accreditation: ACICS

Southern Technical College-Brandon (K)

608 E Bloomingdale Avenue, Brandon FL 33511
Telephone: (813) 654-8800 Identification: 770707
Accreditation: ACICS

Southern Technical College-Mount Dora (L)

2799 W Old US Highway 441, Mount Dora FL 32757
Telephone: (352) 383-4242 Identification: 770706
Accreditation: ACICS

Southern Technical College-Orlando (M)

1485 Florida Mall Avenue, Orlando FL 32809
Telephone: (407) 438-6000 Identification: 770704
Accreditation: ACICS

Southern Technical College-Port Charlotte (N)

950 Tamiami Trail, Unit 109, Port Charlotte FL 33953
Telephone: (239) 274-5860 Identification: 770709
Accreditation: ACICS, SURTEC

Southern Technical College-Tampa (O)

3910 RIGA Boulevard, Tampa FL 33619-1269
Telephone: (813) 630-4401 Identification: 770708
Accreditation: ACICS, DMS, SURTEC

State College of Florida, Manatee-Sarasota (P)

PO Box 1849, Bradenton FL 34206-7046
County: Manatee FICE Identification: 001504
Unit ID: 135391
Telephone: (941) 752-5000 Carnegie Class: Bac/Assoc-Assoc Dom
FAX Number: (941) 727-6230 Calendar System: Semester
URL: www.scf.edu
Established: 1957 Annual Undergrad Tuition & Fees (In-District): $3,074
Enrollment: 10,532 Coed
Affiliation or Control: Local IRS Status: 501(c)3
Highest Offering: Baccalaureate
Accreditation: SC, ADNUR, DH, NUR, OTA, PTAA, RAD

01 President .... Dr. Carol F. PROBSTFELD
04 Exec Assistant to President .... Ms. Susan MARROCCO
10 VP Finance/Admin Services .... Ms. Julie JAKWAY
05 VP Academic Affairs .... Mr. Gary T. RUSSELL
84 VP Strategic Enrollment .... Dr. Richard BARNHOUSE
108 VP Planning/Inst Effectiveness .... Dr. Scott PARKE
32 Dean Student Services .... Ms. Jaquelyn MCNEIL
12 Dean Venice .... Mr. Ryan HALE
35 Director Student Services .... Ms. MariLynn J. LEWY
12 Dean Bradenton .... Mr. Mike KIEFER
102 Executive Director SCF Foundation .... Ms. Cassandra HOLMES
38 Director Student Development .... Ms. Lynn DREES
12 Dean Lakewood Ranch .... Ms. Daisy VULOVICH
45 Director Planning & Inst Effect .... Mr. Bradley W. DAVIS
18 Director Facilities Manager .... Mr. Chris WELLMAN
103 Director Workforce Services .... Ms. Lee KOTWICKI
21 Director Business Services .... Mr. Josef RILL
22 Equity Officer .... Mr. Ed HENRY
08 Director Library Services .... Ms. Margaret E. HAWKINS
09 Director Institutional Research .... Ms. Su-hua MEN
13 Director IT Operations .... Ms. Karla LAUER
37 Director Financial Aid .... Mr. Thomas VO
07 Director of Admissions .... Ms. Stacey SHARPLES
36 Director Career Resource Center .... Ms. Denise D. GATCH
41 Director Athletics .... Mr. Matt ENNIS
43 General Counsel .... Mr. Steve PROUTY
88 Head of SCF Collegiate School .... Ms. Kelly MONOD
106 Director Online Learning .... Mr. Gary BAKER
26 Director Communications & Marketing .... Ms. Jamie M. SMITH
19 Manager Public Safety .... Mr. Shawn PATTEN
15 Director Human Resources .... Ms. Jennifer LAHURD
29 Alumni Coordinator .... Ms. Erica WUORIO

*State University System of Florida, Board of Governors (Q)

325 W Gaines Street, Suite 1614,
Tallahassee FL 32399-0400
County: Leon FICE Identification: 008068
Unit ID: 137449
Telephone: (850) 245-0466 Carnegie Class: N/A
FAX Number: (850) 245-9685
URL: www.flbog.edu

01 Chancellor .... Mr. Marshall M. CRISER, III
05 Vice Chanc Academic/Student Affairs .... Dr. Jan IGNASH
10 Vice Chanc Budget & Finance .... Mr. Tim JONES
43 General Counsel .... Ms. Vikki SHIRLEY
22 Inspector General & Compliance .... Mr. Joseph MALESZEWSKI
101 Corporate Secretary .... Ms. Vikki SHIRLEY
86 Assoc Vice Chanc Govt Relations .... Mr. Brian LOGAN
04 Assistant to the Chancellor .... Ms. Shannon M. TRUE
26 Director of Communications .... Ms. Brittany DAVIS

13 Chief Info Technology Officer (CIO) ... Mr. Gene KOVACS
15 Assist Director Personnel Services ... Ms. Abigail MARTIN
18 Chief Facilities/Physical Plant ... Mr. Chris KINSLEY

*Florida Agricultural and Mechanical University (A)

1601 S. Martin Luther King Jr. Blvd, Tallahassee FL 32307
County: Leon FICE Identification: 001480
Unit ID: 133650
Telephone: (850) 599-3000 Carnegie Class: DU-Higher
FAX Number: (850) 599-3952 Calendar System: Semester
URL: www.famu.edu
Established: 1887 Annual Undergrad Tuition & Fees (In-State): $5,785
Enrollment: 9,928 Coed
Affiliation or Control: State IRS Status: 501(c)3
Highest Offering: Doctorate
Accreditation: SC, ACBSP, CAEPN, CAHIIM, COARC, CS, ENG, ENGT, JOUR, LAW, NUR, #OT, PH, PHAR, PTA, SW

00 Chair Board of Trustees ... Mr. Kelvin LAWSON
02 Interim President ... Dr. Larry ROBINSON
05 Provost/VP Academic Affairs ... Mr. Rodner WRIGHT
10 Interim VP Finance & Administration ... Dr. Wanda FORD
32 Vice President Student Affairs ... Dr. William HUDSON, JR.
25 VP Research ... Dr. Timothy E. MOORE
111 VP University Advancement ... Mr. George COTTON, SR.
116 VP Audit and Compliance ... Mr. Richard GIVENS
45 VP Strategic Planning/Analysis/IE ... Dr. Maurice EDINGTON
43 Int VP Legal Affairs/Gen Counsel ... Ms. Shira THOMAS
101 Spec Asst to President/BOT Liaison ... Ms. Linda BARGE-MILES
41 Director Athletics ... Mr. Milton OVERTON
26 Executive Assoc Dir Communications ... Ms. Kathy TIMES
86 Director Governmental Relations ... Ms. Barbara PIPPIN
04 Executive Asst to the President ... Ms. Ora S. MUKES
53 Interim Dean Education ... Dr. Patricia GREEN-POWELL
67 Interim Dean Pharmacy ... Dr. Seth ABLORDEPPEY
72 Interim Dean Science & Technology ... Dr. Sonya STEPHENS
47 Dean Agriculture & Food Sciences ... Dr. Robert TAYLOR
83 Dean Social Sci/Arts & Humanities ... Dr. Valencia E. MATTHEWS
54 Dean FAMU-FSU Engineering ... Dr. J. Murray GIBSON
61 Interim Dean College of Law ... Mr. Leroy F. PERNELL
48 Int Dean Architecture & Engr Tech ... Mr. Andrew CHIN
76 Dean Allied Health Sciences ... Dr. Cynthia HUGHES HARRIS
50 Dean Business and Industry ... Dr. Shawnta FRIDAY-STROUD
60 Int Dean Journalism/Graphic Comm ... Dr. Dhyana ZIEGLER
65 Dean School of the Environment ... Dr. Victor IBEANUSI
66 Dean Nursing ... Dr. Henry TALLEY
58 Assoc Provost & Dean Grad Studies ... Dr. David JACKSON, JR.
08 Dean University Libraries ... Ms. Faye WATKINS
20 Assoc Provost for Undergrad Educ ... Dr. Carl GOODMAN
88 Assoc Provost Faculty ... Dr. Genyne BOSTON
06 University Registrar ... Dr. Agatha ONWUNLI
37 Director Financial Aid ... Ms. Lisa STEWART
07 Director Admissions ... Ms. Barbara COX
19 Chief of Police/Dir Public Safety ... Mr. Terence CALLOWAY
35 Associate VP Student Affairs ... Dr. Angela COLEMAN
88 University Ombudsman & Spec Asst VP ... Mr. Bryan F. SMITH
35 Interim Associate VP Student Life ... Mr. Bryan F. SMITH
84 Assoc VP Enrollment Management ... Mr. Nigel EDWARDS
13 Associate VP/CIO Info Tech Svcs ... Mr. Ronald HENRY
18 Assoc VP Facilities/Construction ... Mr. Sameer KAPILESHWARI
15 Associate VP Human Resources ... Ms. Joyce A. INGRAM
88 Assoc VP Research ... Dr. Charles WEATHERFORD
88 Assoc VP Strategic Planning/Analy ... Ms. Beverly BARRINGTON
102 Assoc VP University Advancement ... Ms. Mechelle ENGLISH
09 Asst VP Institutional Research ... Dr. Kwadwo OWUSU-ADUEMIRI
21 Asst VP/University Controller ... Ms. Tiffany HOLMES
104 Asst VP International Educ & Dev ... Dr. William HYNDMAN, III
88 Asst VP Strategic Planning ... Dr. Lewis JOHNSON
88 Exec Director Title III Programs ... Dr. Charles WEATHERFORD
88 Director Office of Animal Welfare ... Dr. Tanise JACKSON
105 Director ITS Services & Telcomm ... Vacant
36 Director Career Center ... Ms. Shereada HARRELL
88 Director Technology Transfer ... Mr. Reis ALSBERRY
88 Director Sponsored Programs ... Ms. Glory BROWN
25 Director Contracts & Grants ... Ms. Pamela BLOUNT
39 Director Student Housing ... Dr. Jennifer WILDER
38 Director Counsel Services ... Ms. Anika FIELDS
96 Director Purchasing ... Ms. Stephany FALL
23 Director Student Health Services ... Ms. Tanya TATUM
108 Actg Director Univ Assessment ... Dr. Franz RENEAU
30 Business Manager Univ Development ... Ms. Juanita JOHNSON
29 Executive Director Alumni Affairs ... Ms. Carmen CUMMINGS
22 Director EEO ... Ms. Carrie GAVIN
51 Director Continuing Education ... Ms. Phyllis WATSON
106 Director Instr Tech & Distance Ed ... Ms. Franzetta FITZ
109 Director Business & Auxiliary Svc ... Mr. Bryon WILLIAMS
109 Asst VP Administrative Services ... Ms. Rebecca BROWN
88 Director Veteran and Military Affs ... Mr. Louis DILBERT
88 Director Center for Disability ... Mr. Jovany FELIX
121 Director Student Success/Dev Stds ... Dr. Tamaria WILLIAMS

*Florida Atlantic University (B)

PO Box 3091, 777 Glades Road,
Boca Raton FL 33431-0991
County: Palm Beach FICE Identification: 001481
Unit ID: 133669
Telephone: (561) 297-3000 Carnegie Class: DU-Higher
FAX Number: (561) 297-3942 Calendar System: Semester
URL: www.fau.edu
Established: 1961 Annual Undergrad Tuition & Fees (In-State): $4,831
Enrollment: 30,380 Coed
Affiliation or Control: State IRS Status: 501(c)3
Highest Offering: Doctorate
Accreditation: SC, CACREP, CAEP, CS, ENG, IPSY, MED, MUS, NURSE, PLNG, SP, SPAA, SW

02 President ... Dr. John KELLY
05 Provost/VP Academic Affairs ... Dr. Gary W. PERRY
10 VP Finance/Chief Fiscal Officer ... Mr. Jeffrey ATWATER
32 Vice Pres Student Affairs ... Dr. Corey KING
46 Vice President Research ... Dr. Daniel FLYNN
11 VP Admin Affairs ... Ms. Stacy VOLNICK
102 Inst Advancement & CEO FAU Fdn ... Ms. Danita NIAS
13 Assoc Provost IT/CIO ... Mr. Jason BALL
29 Asst Vice Pres Alumni Relations ... Vacant
35 Assoc VP Student Affairs ... Dr. Larry FAERMAN
43 General Counsel ... Mr. David KIAN
22 Exec Dir Equity/Inclusion/Compl ... Ms. Katrina OLIVER
84 Asst Provost Enrollment Mgmt ... Ms. Tracy BOULUKOS
63 Dean C E Schmidt Col of Medicine ... Dr. Phillip BOISELLE
20 Vice Provost Academic Affairs ... Dr. Michele HAWKINS
80 Dean of Design/Social Inquiry ... Dr. Wesley E. HAWKINS
49 Dean of Arts & Letters ... Dr. Michael HORSWELL
50 Dean of Business ... Dr. Daniel GROPPER
53 Dean of Education ... Dr. Valerie BRISTOR
54 Dean of Engineering/Comp Sci ... Dr. Stella BATALAMA
66 Dean of Nursing ... Dr. Marlaine SMITH
92 Dean of Honors College ... Dr. Ellen GOLDEY
20 Dean Undergraduate Studies ... Dr. Edward E. PRATT
81 Dean College of Science ... Dr. Ata SARAJEDINI
58 Dean of Graduate Studies ... Dr. Deborah FLOYD
88 Asst Dean/PK-12 Sch/Educational Pgm ... Mr. Joel HERBST
90 Director Enterprise Computing Svcs . Mr. Mehran BASIRATMAND
91 Dir Univ Administrative Systems ... Ms. Kay RECKTENWALD
25 Associate VP Research ... Dr. Karen SCARPINATO
09 Asst Prov Inst Effective/Analysis ... Mr. Jeffery HOYT
06 Registrar ... Mr. Brian HODGE
08 Dean University Libraries ... Ms. Carol HIXSON
15 Asst Vice Pres Human Resources ... Mr. David TOMANIO
41 Vice Pres for Athletics ... Mr. Patrick CHUN
39 Exec Director Student Housing ... Dr. Larry FAERMAN
36 Dir Career Devel Ctr/Student Place ... Ms. Sandra JAKUBOW
85 Director Intl Students/Scholar Svcs ... Dr. Mihaela METIANU
37 Director Student Financial Aid ... Ms. Tracy BOULUKOS
07 Director of Admissions ... Ms. Jessica LOPEZ-ACEVEDO

*Florida Gulf Coast University (C)

10501 FGCU Boulevard S, Fort Myers FL 33965-6565
County: Lee FICE Identification: 032553
Unit ID: 433660
Telephone: (239) 590-1000 Carnegie Class: Masters/L
FAX Number: (239) 590-1166 Calendar System: Semester
URL: www.fgcu.edu
Established: 1991 Annual Undergrad Tuition & Fees (In-State): $6,118
Enrollment: 14,833 Coed
Affiliation or Control: State IRS Status: 501(c)3
Highest Offering: Doctorate
Accreditation: SC, ANEST, #ARCPA, CAATE, CACREP, CAEPN, ENG, IPSY, MT, MUS, NURSE, OT, PTA, SPAA, SW

02 President ... Dr. Michael V. MARTIN
05 Provost & VP Academic Affairs ... Dr. Ronald B. TOLL
10 Vice Pres Admin Services/Finance ... Mr. Steve L. MAGIERA
30 VP Univ Advance/Exec Dir Foundation ... Mr. Christopher (Chris) J. SIMONEAU
32 Vice President Student Affairs ... Dr. J. Michael ROLLO
100 Vice President & Chief of Staff ... Ms. Susan EVANS
43 Vice President & General Counsel ... Ms. Vee LEONARD
20 Assoc VP Academic/Curriculum Sppt ... Dr. Cathy DUFF
45 Sr Asc Prov/Asc VP Plng & Inst Perf ... Dr. Paul SNYDER
58 Assoc VP Research/Dean Grad Studies ... Dr. T. C YIH
26 AVP Communications & Marketing ... Ms. Deborah WILTROUT
04 Asst to Pres/University Ombudsman ... Ms. Monique MCKAY
21 Assoc VP Admin Svcs & Finance ... Mr. Joseph MCDONALD
13 Asst VP Business Technology Svcs ... Ms. Mary BANKS
15 Asst Vice Pres Human Resources ... Vacant
20 Assoc Provost/Assoc VP Acad Affs ... Dr. Tony BARRINGER
21 Controller ... Ms. June GUTKNECHT
35 Dean Student Affairs ... Dr. Michele YOVANOVICH
49 Dean College Arts & Sciences ... Dr. Robert (Bob) GREGERSON
20 Dean of Undergraduate Studies ... Dr. Dawn LATTA KIRBY
50 Dean Lutgert College of Business ... Dr. Robert BEATTY
53 Dean College of Education ... Dr. Eunsook HYUN
76 Dean College of Health/Human Svcs ... Dr. Mitchell CORDOVA
54 Dean U.A. Whitaker Col Engineering ... Dr. Richard A. BEHR
62 Dean Library Services ... Dr. Kathleen MILLER
45 Asst Dir Planning/Inst Performance ... Ms. Kristen VANSELOW
38 Dir Counselng/Student Health Svcs ... Dr. Jon L. BRUNNER
43 Asst Dean Judicial Affairs ... Mr. Chad TRISLER
07 Director of Admissions ... Mr. Marc LAVIOLETTE
96 Director of Procurement Services ... Ms. Maryan EGAN
19 Director Campus Police & Safety ... Chief Steven C. MOORE
18 Director Facilities Planning ... Mr. Tom MAYO
37 Director Student Financial Aid ... Mr. Jorge LOPEZ-ROSADO
06 University Registrar ... Ms. Susan BYARS
23 Dir Student Health Services/Med Dir ... Dr. Kevin COLLINS
41 Director Intercollegiate Athletics ... Mr. Kenneth KAVANAGH
28 Director Title IX Compliance ... Ms. Precious GUNTER
85 Director International Services ... Dr. Elaine HOZDIK
106 Director Instructional Technology ... Mr. David JAEGER
72 Director Academic & Event Tech ... Ms. Pat O'CONNOR-BENSON
36 Director Career Development Svcs ... Mr. Reid LENNERTZ
31 Dir Cmty Engagement/Svc Learning ... Ms. Jessica RHEA
29 Director Alumni Relations ... Ms. Kimberly WALLACE
92 Director Honors Program ... Dr. Clay MOTLEY
09 Director Inst Research/Analysis ... Dr. Robert VINES
21 Director University Budgets ... Mr. David VAZQUEZ
39 Director University Housing ... Dr. Brian FISHER
86 Director Government Relations ... Ms. Jennifer GOEN
88 Dir Environmental Health/Safety ... Ms. Rhonda HOLTZCLAW
51 Exec Dir Cont Educ/Off-Campus Pgms ... Dr. Paul THORNTON
88 General Manager/WGCU ... Mr. Rick JOHNSON
40 Manager The University Store ... Ms. Laura JENSEN
88 Dir Emergent Technologies Inst ... Dr. John WOOLSCHLAGER
88 Dir Ctr for Academic Achievement ... Dr. P. Brandon JOHNSON
88 Chief Compliance/Ethics Officer ... Ms. Stacey CHADOS

*Florida International University (D)

University Park, 11200 SW 8 Street, Miami FL 33199-0001
County: Miami-Dade FICE Identification: 009635
Unit ID: 133951
Telephone: (305) 348-2000 Carnegie Class: DU-Highest
FAX Number: N/A Calendar System: Semester
URL: www.fiu.edu
Established: 1965 Annual Undergrad Tuition & Fees (In-State): $6,556
Enrollment: 49,782 Coed
Affiliation or Control: State IRS Status: 501(c)3
Highest Offering: Doctorate
Accreditation: SC, ANEST, #ARCPA, ART, CAATE, CACREP, CAEPN, CIDA, CLPSY, CONST, CS, DIETC, DIETD, @DIETI, ENG, FEPAC, HSA, IPSY, JOUR, LAW, LSAR, MED, MUS, NURSE, OPE, OT, PH, PTA, SP, SPAA, SW, THEA

02 President ... Dr. Mark ROSENBERG
100 Chief of Staff ... Mr. Javier MARQUES
03 Executive VP & COO ... Dr. Kenneth FURTON
88 VP for Engagement ... Mr. Saif ISHOOF
05 Vice President Academic Affairs ... Dr. Elizabeth BEJAR
10 CFO & Sr VP for Administration ... Dr. Kenneth JESSELL
111 Vice President for Advancement ... Mr. Howard LIPMAN
32 VP Student Affairs ... Dr. Larry LUNSFORD
09 Interim VP Analysis/Info Mgmt ... Dr. Hiselgis PEREZ
46 Vice President of Research ... Dr. Andres GIL
13 Vice President/CIO ... Mr. Robert GRILLO
12 Vice Prov Biscayne Bay Campus ... Mr. Stephen MOLL
84 Int VP Enrollment Mgmt ... Dr. Kevin COUGHLIN
35 Assoc VP and Dean of Students ... Dr. Cathy AKENS
15 Vice President Human Resources ... Dr. Jaffus HARDRICK
18 Assoc VP Facilities Operations ... Mr. John CAL
07 Dir Undergraduate Admissions ... Ms. Jody GLASSMAN
49 Dean Col Arts/Sciences/Educ ... Dr. Michael HEITHAUS
50 Dean College Business Admin ... Dr. Joanne LI
54 Dean Col Engineering/Computing ... Dr. John VOLAKIS
53 Director College of Education ... Dr. Laura DINEHART
88 Dean Sch Hospitality Management ... Dr. Mike HAMPTON
82 Dean School Intl/Pub Affairs ... Dr. John STACK
66 Dean Col Nursing/Health Science ... Dr. Ora STRICKLAND
69 Dean College of Public Health ... Dr. Tomas GUILARTE
61 Int Dean College of Law ... Dr. Tawia ANSAH
63 Dean College of Medicine ... Dr. John ROCK
92 Int Dean Honors College ... Dr. Juan Carlos ESPINOSA
48 Dean Col Comm/Architecture/Arts ... Dr. Brian SCHRINER
77 Dir Sch Computing/Info Sciences ... Dr. Sundararaj IYENGAR
38 Asst VP Stdnt Hlth & Counseling ... Dr. Cheryl NOWELL
22 Director Equal Opportunity Program ... Ms. Shirlyon J. MCWHORTER
88 Director School Accounting ... Dr. Ruth MCEWEN
88 Dir Multicultural Programs Admin ... Dr. Dorret SAWYERS
62 Dean of Libraries ... Dr. Anne PRESTAMO
41 Athletics Director ... Mr. Pete GARCIA
86 VP for Government Relations ... Ms. Michelle PALACIO
06 Int University Registrar ... Dr. Andrea JAY
31 AVP Community Rel/Special Events ... Ms. Dania ADAMS
37 Director Student Financial Aid ... Mr. Francisco VALINES
36 Director Career Services ... Dr. Fernando FIGUEREDO
23 Dir Student Health Services ... Dr. Oscar LOYNAZ
39 Dir of Housing/Residential Life ... Ms. Lynn HENDRICKS, JR.
22 Director Disability Student Svcs ... Ms. Amanda NIGUIDULA
116 Chief Audit Executive ... Mr. Allen VANN
24 Dir University IT/Media Support ... Mr. Matthew HAGOOD
21 Associate VP and Univ Controller ... Ms. Katharine BROPHY
88 Dir Environmental Health/Safety ... Ms. Yenny DIAZ
19 Chief of Police ... Chief Alexander CASAS
26 Director Media Relations ... Ms. Maydel SANTANA-BRAVO
43 General Counsel ... Mr. Carlos CASTILLO
85 Dir International Student Svcs ... Ms. Nancy HERNANDEZ
25 Assistant VP for Research ... Mr. Roberto GUTIERREZ
04 Assistant Chief of Staff ... Ms. Claudia GONZALEZ
44 Exec Dir Dev/Foundation Relations ... Ms. Jill BASSETT
102 Sr Dir Corporate/Found Relations ... Ms. Karla HERNANDEZ

*Florida Polytechnic University (E)

4700 Research Way, Lakeland FL 33805-8531
County: Polk Identification: 667279
Unit ID: 482936
Telephone: (863) 583-9050 Carnegie Class: Not Classified
FAX Number: N/A Calendar System: Semester
URL: www.floridapolytechnic.org
Established: 2012 Annual Undergrad Tuition & Fees (In-State): $4,940
Enrollment: 924 Coed
Affiliation or Control: State IRS Status: 501(c)3
Highest Offering: Master's
Accreditation: SC

02 President Dr. Randy K. AVENT
05 Provost Dr. Terry PARKER
20 Vice Pres Academic Affairs Dr. Elhami NASR
30 Vice President Advancement Mr. Kevin ASPEGREN

*Florida State University (A)

222 S. Copeland Street, Tallahassee FL 32306

County: Leon FICE Identification: 001489
Unit ID: 134097
Telephone: (850) 644-2525 Carnegie Class: DU-Highest
FAX Number: (850) 644-9936 Calendar System: Semester
URL: www.fsu.edu
Established: 1851 Annual Undergrad Tuition & Fees (In-State): $6,507
Enrollment: 40,830 Coed
Affiliation or Control: State IRS Status: 501(c)3
Highest Offering: Doctorate
Accreditation: SC, AAFCS, ANEST, #ARCPA, ART, CAATE, CACREP, CIDA, CLPSY, CS, DANCE, DIETD, DIETI, ENG, IPSY, LAW, LIB, MED, MFCD, MUS, NURSE, PH, PLNG, PSPSY, SP, SPAA, SW, THEA

02 President Mr. John E. THRASHER
05 Prov/Exec VP Academic Affairs Dr. Sally E. MCRORIE
10 Vice Pres Finance & Admin Mr. Kyle CLARK
32 Vice President Student Affairs Dr. Amy HECHT
46 Vice President Research Dr. Gary K. OSTRANDER
26 Vice Pres University Relations Ms. Kathleen DALY
45 VP Planning and Programs Vacant
111 VP University Advancement Mr. Thomas W. JENNINGS
102 Exec VP FSU Foundation Mr. Andy A. JHANJI
20 Vice Pres Faculty Development Dr. Janet KISTNER
100 Chief of Staff to President Mr. David COBURN
88 Assoc Vice President for Research Dr. Ross ELLINGTON
18 Associate VP for Facilities Mr. Dennis A. BAILEY
21 Assoc VP Finance & Admin Mr. Michael WILLIAMS
20 Asst VP for Academic Affairs Mr. Paul HARLACHER
15 Asst Vice Pres for Human Resources Ms. Renisha L. GIBBS
11 Asst VP for Administrative Services Mr. Steven CONNER
84 Asst VP Enrollment Mgmt Mr. John BARNHILL
27 Asst VP of University Communication Ms. Browning BROOKS
88 Dir Academic Pgm Professional Svcs Mr. Bill LINDNER
49 Dean Arts & Sciences Dr. Sam HUCKABA
50 Dean Business Dr. Michael HARTLINE
53 Dean Education Dr. Marcy P. DRISCOLL
59 Dean Human Sciences Dr. Michael DELP
88 Dean Communication & Information Dr. Larry DENNIS
66 Dean Nursing Dr. Judith MCFETRIDGE-DURDLE
88 Dean Criminology Dr. Thomas BLOMBERG
61 Dean Law Dr. Erin O'HARA O'CONNOR
83 Dean Social Sciences Dr. Timothy CHAPIN
70 Dean Social Work Dr. Clark JAMES
88 Dean Motion Picture Arts Mr. Reb BRADDOCK
64 Dean Music Dr. Patricia J. FLOWERS
57 Int Dean Fine Arts Dr. Scott SHAMP
54 Dean Engineering Dr. Murray GIBSON
63 Dean Medicine Dr. John FOGARTY
58 Int Dean Graduate School Dr. Mark RILEY
88 Dean Undergraduate Studies Dr. Karen L. LAUGHLIN
35 Dean of Students Dr. Victoria DOBIYANSKI
12 Dean Panama City Branch Campus Dr. Randy HANNA
06 University Registrar Dr. Kimberly BARBER
07 Director Admissions Ms. Hege FERGUSON
92 Dir University Honors Program Dr. Mark KEARLEY
37 Director Student Financial Aid Mr. Darryl MARSHALL
08 Director Libraries Ms. Julia ZIMMERMAN
13 Chief Information Officer Mr. Michael BARRETT
90 Sr Director Enterprise Applications Mr. Byron MENCHION
43 General Counsel Ms. Carolyn EGAN
104 Director International Programs Dr. James E. PITTS
88 Chief Budget Officer Mr. Michael P. LAKE
09 Director Institutional Research Dr. James HUNT
86 Director Governmental Relations Ms. Kathy MEARS
41 Athletic Director Mr. Stan WILCOX
38 Director Student Counseling Dr. Carlos J. GOMEZ
19 Director Public Safety Mr. David L. PERRY
23 Director University Health Services Dr. Amy MAGNUSON
36 Director Career Center Ms. Myrna HOOVER
29 President Alumni Association Mr. Scott ATWELL
116 Chief Audit Officer Dr. Sam MCCALL
28 Dir Diversity/Equal Opportunity Ms. Michelle DOUGLAS
96 Director of Purchasing Mr. Ian ROBBINS
39 Director Student Housing Ms. Shannon STATEN
88 Director Business Services Mr. Charles FRIEDRICH, II
106 Int Director Distance Learning Mr. Robert FUSELIER
25 Director Sponsored Research Ms. Pamela RAY
14 Director Information Technology Mr. Kenneth JOHNSON

*New College of Florida (B)

5800 Bay Shore Road, Sarasota FL 34243-2109

County: Sarasota FICE Identification: 001507
Unit ID: 262129
Telephone: (941) 487-4100 Carnegie Class: Bac-A&S
FAX Number: (941) 487-4101 Calendar System: 4/1/4
URL: www.ncf.edu
Established: 1960 Annual Undergrad Tuition & Fees (In-State): $6,916
Enrollment: 861 Coed
Affiliation or Control: State IRS Status: 501(c)3
Highest Offering: Master's
Accreditation: SC

02 President Dr. Donal E. O'SHEA
05 Provost Dr. Barbara FELDMAN
10 Vice Pres Finance & Administration Mr. John U. MARTIN
79 Chair of Humanities Dr. Miriam WALLACE
81 Chair of Natural Sciences Dr. Katherine WALSTROM
83 Chair of Social Sciences Dr. Richard COE
08 Dean Cook Library Dr. Brian DOHERTY
84 Dean of Enrollment & Info Tech Ms. K. Joy HAMM
32 Dean of Students Dr. Robin WILLIAMSON
07 Associate Dean of Admissions Ms. Sonia WU
20 Associate Academic Officer Dr. Robert ZAMSKY
21 Associate Business Officer Ms. Kimberly BENDICKSON
13 Actg Dir of Information Technology Mr. Ben FOSS
14 Director of Technology Support Mr. Jeff SMITH
29 Director Alumnae/i Association Ms. Jessica ROGERS
06 Registrar Mr. Brian SCHOLTEN
26 Director Public Affairs Ms. Jessica ROOD
38 Director Counseling Dr. Anne E. FISHER
09 Director of Institutional Research Ms. Hui-Men WEN
100 Chief of Staff President's Office Dr. Bradley THIESSEN
15 Director Personnel Services Mr. Daniel RICHARDSON
18 Chief Facilities/Physical Plant Mr. Alan BURR
28 Director of Diversity Ms. Autumn HARRELL
96 Director of Purchasing Ms. Jean HARRIS
37 Director Student Financial Aid Ms. Tara KARAS
43 Director Legal Svcs/General Counsel Mr. Mike PIERCE
25 Contract Administrator Ms. Lee Ann RODRIGUEZ
30 Chief Development Ms. MaryAnne YOUNG
19 Chief of Police Sgt. Michael KESSIE
39 Director Student Housing Dr. Mark STIER
41 Athletic Director Mr. Colin JORDAN
86 Director Government Relations Ms. Suzanne JANNEY
04 Administrative Asst to President Ms. Shelley WILBUR

*University of Central Florida (C)

PO Box 160000, Orlando FL 32816-0001

County: Orange FICE Identification: 003954
Unit ID: 132903
Telephone: (407) 823-2000 Carnegie Class: DU-Highest
FAX Number: N/A Calendar System: Semester
URL: www.ucf.edu
Established: 1963 Annual Undergrad Tuition & Fees (In-State): $6,368
Enrollment: 62,953 Coed
Affiliation or Control: State IRS Status: 501(c)3
Highest Offering: Doctorate
Accreditation: SC, CAATE, CACREP, CAEPN, CAHIIM, CEA, CLPSY, CS, ENG, HSA, IPSY, MED, MT, MUS, NURSE, PTA, SP, SPAA, SW, THEA

02 President Dr. John C. HITT
05 Provost/Executive Vice President Dr. A. Dale WHITTAKER
100 Vice President and Chief of Staff Dr. John SCHELL
10 Vice Pres Admin & Finance/CFO Mr. William F. MERCK, II
26 Vice President University Relations Dr. Daniel HOLSENBECK
43 Vice President/General Counsel Mr. W. Scott COLE
32 VP Student Dev/Enrollment Svcs Dr. Maribeth EHASZ
30 VP Dev/Alum Rels/Foundation CEO Mr. Michael J. MORSBERGER
31 Vice President Emerita Comm Rels Ms. Helen DONEGAN
63 VP Medical Affairs/Dean Med College Dr. Deborah GERMAN
41 Vice Pres & Dir of Athletics Mr. Danny WHITE
49 Dean College of Arts & Humanities Mr. Jeffrey MOORE
50 Dean College of Business Admin Dr. Paul JARLEY
53 Dean College of Education Dr. Pamela S. CARROLL
54 Dean College of Engr/Comp Sci Dr. Michael GEORGIOPOULOS
76 Dean College of Hlth/Pub Affs Dr. Michael FRUMKIN
88 Dean Rosen College Hospitality Mgt Dr. Abraham PIZAM
66 Dean College of Nursing Dr. Mary L. SOLE
88 Dean/Dir Col of Optics & Photonics Dr. Bahaa SALEH
81 Dean College of Sciences Dr. Michael D. JOHNSON
92 Interim Dean Burnett Honors Col Dr. Martin DUPUIS
13 Vice Provost & CIO Info Tech/Res Dr. Joel L. HARTMAN
12 Vice Provost Regional Campuses Dr. Jeff JONES
58 Vice Pres Res/Dean Grad Studies Dr. Elizabeth KLONOFF
97 Vice Provost/Dean Undergrad Studies Dr. Elizabeth A. DOOLEY
82 VP Fac Exc/Intl Affs/Global Strat Dr. Cynthia Y. YOUNG
09 Assoc Prov APQ and Assoc VP IKM Dr. M. Paige BORDEN
18 Assoc VP Facilities and Safety Ms. Lee KERNEK
29 Sr Assoc Vice Pres Alumni Relations Ms. Julie C. STROH
86 Sr Assoc VP University Relations Mr. Fred KITTINGER
30 AVP of Col/Univ Advancement Mr. Jeff COATES
46 Assoc VP Rsrch & Commercialization Mr. Tom O'NEAL
20 Assoc Prov/Chief Staff Acad Affairs Dr. Ronnie KOROSEC
84 Assoc VP Enrollment Services Dr. Gordon CHAVIS
27 VP Communications & Marketing Mr. Grant HESTON
37 Dir Student Financial Asst Ms. Alicia KEATON
06 University Registrar Mr. Brian BOYD
08 Director Libraries Mr. Barry BAKER
15 Assoc VP HR/Chief HR Officer Ms. Maureen BINDER
19 Assoc VP Safety & Chief of Police Mr. Richard BEARY
93 Director Multicul Acad Suppt Svcs Mr. Wayne JACKSON
14 Chief Technology Officer Mr. Robert YANCKELLO
14 AVP/CIO UCF IT Mr. Michael SINK
38 Director Counseling Center Dr. Karen HOFMANN
22 Dir Office of Institutional Equity Ms. Nancy MYERS
23 Director Health Services Dr. Michael G. DEICHEN
39 Exec Dir Housing and Residence Life Mrs. Christi HARTZLER
28 Chief Diversity Officer Ms. Karen MORRISON
96 Director of Purchasing Mr. Gregory ROBINSON
36 Exec Director Career Services Ms. Lynn HANSEN

*University of Florida (D)

235 Tigert Hall, Gainesville FL 32611-9500

County: Alachua FICE Identification: 001535
Unit ID: 134130
Telephone: (352) 392-3261 Carnegie Class: DU-Highest
FAX Number: (352) 392-8735 Calendar System: Semester
URL: www.ufl.edu
Established: 1853 Annual Undergrad Tuition & Fees (In-State): $6,381
Enrollment: 50,645 Coed
Affiliation or Control: State IRS Status: 501(c)3
Highest Offering: Doctorate
Accreditation: SC, ARCPA, ART, AUD, CAATE, CACREP, CEA, CIDA, CLPSY, CONST, COPSY, DANCE, DENT, DIETD, DIETI, ENG, ENGR, HSA, IPSY, JOUR, LAW, LSAR, MED, MIDWF, MUS, NURSE, OT, PH, PHAR, PLNG, PTA, SCPSY, SP, THEA, VET

02 President Dr. W. Kent FUCHS
05 Provost & Senior Vice President Dr. Joseph GLOVER
47 Sr Vice Pres Agric/Natural Res Dr. Jack M. PAYNE
17 Sr Vice Pres Health Affairs Dr. David S. GUZICK
10 VP/Chief Financial Ofcr Mr. Michael MCKEE
11 Sr Vice Pres/Chief Operating Ofcr Dr. Charles E. LANE
111 Vice President Advancement Mr. Thomas J. MITCHELL
21 Vice President Business Affairs Mr. Curtis REYNOLDS
32 Vice President Student Affairs Mr. David PARROTT
26 Vice President Univ Relations Ms. Jane A. ADAMS
15 Vice Pres Human Resources Ms. Jodi D. GENTRY
46 Vice President Research Dr. David P. NORTON
43 Interim VP/General Counsel Ms. Amy M. HASS
13 Vice President & CIO Mr. Elias G. ELDAYRIE
84 Vice Pres Enroll Mgmt/Assoc Provost Dr. Zina EVANS
86 Assoc VP Government Relations Ms. Marion S. HOFFMAN
88 Associate Provost Teaching & Tech Dr. William A. MCCOLLOUGH
27 Asst Vice Pres Marketing Ms. Nicole YUCHT
27 Asst VP Media Rels/Public Affairs Ms. Janine SIKES
27 Senior Director Media Relations Mr. Stephen F. ORLANDO
21 Business Affs/Finance/Admin AVP Mr. Craig R. HILL
18 Asst VP/Fac/Plng/Construction Mr. Carlos DOUGNAC
20 Associate Provost Academic Affairs Dr. Angel KWOLEK-FOLLAND
20 Assoc Provost Undergrad Affairs Dr. Angela LINDNER
09 Asst Provost/Dir Inst Research/Plng Dr. Marie ZEGLEN
35 Dean Students/Assoc VP Student Affs Dr. Jen D. SHAW
08 Dean University Libraries Ms. Judith RUSSELL
50 Dean of Business Administration Dr. John KRAFT
49 Dean of Liberal Arts & Science Mr. David E. RICHARDSON
68 Dean of Health/Human Performance Dr. Michael B. REID
61 Dean of Law Ms. Laura A. ROSENBURY
66 Dean of Nursing Dr. Anna M. MCDANIEL
67 Dean of Pharmacy Dr. Julie A. JOHNSON
54 Dean of Engineering Dr. Cammy ABERNATHY
47 Dean Agricultural/Life Sciences Dr. R. Elaine TURNER
60 Dean of Journalism/Communications Ms. Diane H. MCFARLIN
76 Dean Pub Health/Health Professions Dr. Michael PERRI
53 Dean of Education Dr. Glenn GOOD
47 Dean IFAS Extension Dr. Nick T. PLACE
74 Dean of Veterinary Medicine Dr. James W. LLOYD
57 Dean of Fine Arts Ms. Lucinda LAVELLI
48 Dean Design Construction Planning Dr. Chimay ANUMBA
63 Dean of Medicine Dr. Michael L. GOOD
46 Dean of IFAS Research Dr. Jacqueline BURNS
52 Dean of Dentistry Dr. Isabel GARCIA
58 Dean Graduate School Dr. Henry T. FRIERSON
65 Dir School Natural Res/Envir Dr. Thomas K. FRAZER
06 University Registrar Mr. Stephen J. PRITZ
23 Director of Student Health Dr. Guy NICOLETTE
38 Director of Counseling Center Dr. Sherry BENTON
37 Director Student Financial Aid Mr. Richard D. WILDER
36 Director of Career Resource Center Ms. Heather B. WHITE
14 Director of Computer Center Mr. Timothy J. FITZPATRICK
19 Director of University Police Ms. Linda J. STUMP
24 Director of Academic Technology Dr. Fedro S. ZAZUETA
65 Director of Forestry Dr. Timothy L. WHITE
39 Director of Housing Mr. Norbert W. DUNKEL
41 Athletic Director Mr. Jeremy N. FOLEY
29 Exec Director Alumni Affairs Ms. Danita NIAS
28 Director of Diversity Ms. Tamara COHEN
96 Director of Purchasing Ms. Lisa DEAL
07 Director of Admissions Mr. Patrick C. HERRING
04 Executive Asst to President Ms. Beth BOONE
106 Dir Online Education/E-learning Ms. Evangeline CUMMINGS
108 Director Institutional Assessment Dr. Timothy S. BROPHY

*University of North Florida (E)

1 UNF Drive, Jacksonville FL 32224-7699

County: Duval FICE Identification: 009841
Unit ID: 136172
Telephone: (904) 620-1000 Carnegie Class: Masters/L
FAX Number: (904) 620-2414 Calendar System: Semester
URL: www.unf.edu
Established: 1965 Annual Undergrad Tuition & Fees (In-State): $6,394
Enrollment: 15,675 Coed
Affiliation or Control: State IRS Status: 501(c)3
Highest Offering: Doctorate
Accreditation: SC, ANEST, ART, CAATE, CACREP, CAEPN, CONST, CS, DIETD, DIETI, ENG, ENGR, EXSC, HSA, JOUR, MT, MUS, NURSE, PH, PTA, SPAA, SW

02 President Mr. John A. DELANEY
05 Provost Dr. Earle C. TRAYNHAM
100 VP/Chief of Staff Dr. Thomas S. SERWATKA
86 VP Governmental Affairs Ms. Janet D. OWEN
43 VP/General Counsel Ms. Karen J. STONE
15 VP Human Resources Ms. Rachelle GOTTLIEB
10 VP Administration/Finance Ms. Shari A. SHUMAN
30 VP Development Alumni Aff Mr. Joshua D. MERCHANT

32 VP Student & International Affairs ... Dr. Mauricio GONZALEZ
20 Associate Provost ... Dr. Bob J. COLEMAN
84 Assoc VP Enrollment Svs ... Dr. Albert N. COLOM
07 Director of Admissions ... Ms. Karen LUCAS
88 Assoc VP/Compliance Officer ... Dr. Joann N. CAMPBELL
21 Assoc VP Admin & Finance ... Mr. Scott BENNETT
13 Assoc VP Chief Info Officer ... Mr. Reggie BRINSON
35 Assoc VP Student Affairs ... Mr. Everett J. MALCOLM, III
45 Asst VP Research ... Dr. John KANTNER
110 Asst VP Development ... Ms. Ann S. MCCULLEN
26 VP Public Relations ... Ms. Sharon ASHTON
35 Asst VP Student Affairs ... Dr. Lucy S. CROFT
49 Int Dean College of Arts and Sci ... Dr. Daniel C. MOON
58 Dean of the Graduate School ... Dr. John KANTNER
08 Dean of the Library ... Dr. Elizabeth A. CURRY
88 Dean of Undergraduate Studies ... Dr. Karen B. PATTERSON
50 Dean Coggin College of Business ... Dr. Mark DAWKINS
53 Dean College of Education ... Dr. Diane YENDOL-HOPPEY
76 Dean Brooks College of Health ... Dr. Pam CHALLY
77 Dean Computing Engineering & Constr ... Dr. Mark A. TUMEO
22 Dir Equal Opportunity Programs ... Ms. Cheryl N. GONZALEZ
88 Dir Professional Dev Training ... Ms. Kelly G. HARRISON
114 Chief Budget Officer ... Mrs. Devany GROVES
21 Controller ... Ms. Valerie O. STEVENSON
88 Dir of Compliance ... Ms. Donna R. KIRK
88 Dir Environment Health/Safety ... Mr. Daniel D. ENDICOTT
22 Dir ADA Compliance ... Ms. Rocelia T. GONZALEZ
14 Dir IT Networking ... Mr. Jeffrey A. DURFEE
21 Treasurer ... Mr. Michael S. NEGLIA
18 Dir Univ Facilities Planning ... Mr. Zak OVADIA
88 Dir University Center ... Mr. George ANDROUIN
29 Asst VP Alumni Engagement ... Mr. Christopher M. DECENT
19 Dir Safety Security ... Mr. Francis J. MACKESY
36 Dir Career Development Services ... Mr. Rick ROBERTS
88 Dir Child Development Ctr ... Ms. Mahreen N. MIAN
23 Chief Medical Officer ... Dr. Lisa DYNAN-DOBBERTIEN
38 Dir Univ Counseling Center ... Dr. Andrew B. KING
85 Dir The International Center ... Dr. Timothy ROBINSON
39 Dir Housing Residence Life ... Mr. Robert J. BOYLE
41 Athletic Director ... Mr. Lee L. MOON
88 Dir Faculty Enhancement ... Dr. Dan RICHARD
108 Director of Assessment ... Ms. Megan S. POSSINGER
37 Dir Student Financial Aid ... Mrs. Anissa AGNE
06 Registrar ... Mrs. Megan R. KUEHNER
09 Dir Institutional Research ... Ms. Abby WILLCOX
88 Exec Dir FL Inst of Education ... Dr. Cheryl A. FOUNTAIN
88 Dir Small Business Dev Ctr ... Ms. Janice W. DONALDSON
96 Dir Purchasing ... Ms. Shawn ASMUTH
51 Int Dean Continuing Education ... Mr. Abdullah E. EDYTHE
106 Dir Center for Instr & Res Tech ... Ms. Deb MILLER
90 Director Academic Technology ... Dr. Gordon F. RAKITA

*University of South Florida (A)

4202 E Fowler Avenue, Tampa FL 33620-6100

County: Hillsborough FICE Identification: 001537
Unit ID: 137351
Telephone: (813) 974-2011 Carnegie Class: DU-Highest
FAX Number: N/A Calendar System: Semester
URL: www.usf.edu
Established: 1956 Annual Undergrad Tuition & Fees (In-State): $6,410
Enrollment: 42,067 Coed
Affiliation or Control: State IRS Status: 501(c)3
Highest Offering: Doctorate
Accreditation: SC, ANEST, #ARCPA, ART, AUD, CAATE, CACREP, CAEPN, CEA, CLPSY, CS, DANCE, @DIETI, ENG, ENGR, HSA, IPSY, LIB, MED, MUS, NURSE, PCSAS, PH, PHAR, PTA, SCPSY, SP, SPAA, SW, THEA

02 President ... Dr. Judy L. GENSHAFT
04 Special Assistant to the President ... Mr. John L. PRUGH, JR.
11 Chief Operating Officer & Sr VP ... Mr. John W. LONG
100 Chief of Staff/President's Office ... Dr. Cynthia S. VISOT
43 General Counsel ... Mr. Gerard SOLIS
05 Prov/Exec Vice Pres Academic Affs ... Dr. Ralph WILCOX
15 Vice Provost for HR and Space Plng ... Dr. Kofi GLOVER
20 Vice Provost for Plng/Perf & Acct ... Dr. Theresa H. CHISOLM
20 Vice Provost and AVP USF World ... Dr. Roger BRINDLEY
104 Director Education Abroad ... Dr. Amanda C. MAURER
46 Sr Vice Pres Research & Innovation ... Dr. Paul SANBERG
17 Sr Vice Pres USF Health ... Dr. Charles LOCKWOOD
23 Sr System VP & COO USF Health ... Dr. Edmund F. FUNAI
58 Sr Vice Provost/Dean Grad School ... Dr. Dwayne SMITH
10 Vice Pres Business & Finance ... Mr. Nick TRIVUNOVICH
88 Assistant Treasurer ... Ms. Dawn M. RODRIGUEZ
11 Vice Pres Administrative Services ... Mr. Calvin WILLIAMS
18 Asst VP Physical Plant ... Mr. Chris DUFFY
102 CEO USF Foundation Inc ... Mr. Joel MOMBERG
32 Asst VP and Dean of Students ... Ms. Danielle MCDONALD
13 Vice Pres Information Technology ... Mr. Sidney FERNANDES
14 AVP Information Technology ... Ms. Jenny PAULSEN
14 AVP Information Technology ... Swapna CHACKRAVARTHY
105 Director Web Services ... Mr. Christopher L. AKIN
29 Assoc Vice Pres Alumni Affairs ... Mr. Bill MCCAUSLAND
22 Chief Diversity Officer ... Dr. Jose HERNANDEZ
121 Vice Provost for Student Success ... Dr. Paul J. DOSAL
16 Assoc Vice Pres Human Resources ... Ms. Donna KEENER
86 Asst Vice Pres Government Rels ... Mr. Mark WALSH
88 University Ombuds ... Mr. Steven D. PREVAUX
39 Asst VP Housing/Residential Educ ... Ms. Ana HERNANDEZ
83 Dean Behavioral/Community Sci ... Dr. Julianne SEROVICH
50 Dean Business Administration ... Dr. Moez LIMAYEM
53 Int Dean College of Education ... Dr. Roger BRINDLEY
54 Dean Engineering ... Dr. Robert H. BISHOP
57 Dean College of the Arts ... Dr. James S. MOY
67 Dean College of Pharmacy ... Dr. Kevin B. SNEED
49 Dean Arts & Sciences ... Dr. Eric EISENBERG
92 Dean Honors College ... Dr. Charles H. ADAMS
88 Dean Marine Science ... Dr. Jacqueline DIXON
69 Dean Public Health ... Dr. Donna PETERSEN
88 Int Dean Global Sustainability ... Dr. Richard BERMAN
89 Interim Dean Undergraduate Studies ... Dr. Williams CUMMINGS
106 Asst Vice Provost Innovative Educ ... Dr. Cynthia A. DELUCA
48 Dir Sch of Architecture/Cmty Design ... Mr. Robert MACLEOD
12 Regional Chanc Sarasota-Manatee ... Dr. Sandra STONE
12 Int Reg Chanc USF St Petersburg ... Dr. Martin TADLOCK
21 Controller ... Ms. Jennifer CONDON
26 Director of Media Relations ... Ms. Lara WADE
07 Director Admissions ... Mr. David HENRY
06 Registrar ... Ms. Lois PALMER
114 University Budget Officer ... Ms. Nell PETERSON
84 Assoc VP Enrollment Management ... Ms. Billie Jo HAMILTON
38 Director Counseling Center ... Dr. Ann JARONSKI
36 Asst Vice President Career Services ... Mr. Russ COUGHENAIR
19 Interim Chief University Police ... Mr. Chris DANEIL
08 USF Libraries Dean ... Dr. Todd CHAVEZ
41 Director of Athletics ... Mr. Mark HARLAN
28 Director of Diversity & Inclusion ... Ms. Patsy FELICIANO
96 Int Director Purchasing & Property ... Mr. George COTTER
09 Asst VP Office of Decision Support ... Dr. Valeria GARCIA

*University of South Florida St. Petersburg (B)

140 7th Avenue S, Saint Petersburg FL 33701-5016

County: Pinellas FICE Identification: 009016
Unit ID: 448840
Telephone: (727) 873-4873 Carnegie Class: Masters/M
FAX Number: (727) 873-4131 Calendar System: Semester
URL: www.usfsp.edu
Established: 1956 Annual Undergrad Tuition & Fees (In-District): $5,821
Enrollment: 4,739 Coed
Affiliation or Control: State/Local IRS Status: 501(c)3
Highest Offering: Master's
Accreditation: SC, CAEPN, JOUR

02 Interim Regional Chancellor ... Dr. Martin TADLOCK
05 Reg Vice Chanc Academic Affairs ... Dr. Martin TADLOCK
10 Reg Vice Chanc Admin/Financial Svcs ... Dr. Joseph TRUBACZ
86 Reg Vice Chanc Government Relations ... Dr. Helen LEVINE
32 Reg Assoc Vice Chanc Student Affs ... Dr. Patricia HELTON
11 Reg Asst Vice Chanc Administration ... Dr. Chitra IYER
84 RVC Enrollment/Mktg & Comm ... Ms. Holly KICKLITER
111 Reg Vice Chanc Advancement ... Ms. Deborah READ
53 Dean College of Education ... Dr. Allyson WATSON
50 Dean College of Business ... Dr. Sridhar SUNDARAM
49 Dean College of Arts & Sciences ... Dr. Frank BIAFORA
08 Dean of the Library ... Ms. Catherine CARDWELL
19 Chief of Police ... Dr. David HENDRY
13 Director of Campus Computing ... Mr. Jeff REISBERG
15 Assoc Director Human Resources ... Ms. Denelta ADDERLY-HENRY
37 Director of Financial Aid ... Ms. Erin DUNN
06 Registrar ... Ms. Shari SCHWARTZ
18 Dir Facil Plng/Construction Svcs ... Mr. John DICKSON
96 Purchasing Manager ... Mr. Bill BENJAMIN
114 Budget Director ... Mr. David EVERINGHAM
26 Communications Director ... Ms. Jessica BLAIS
30 Asst Director Development ... Ms. Alexis SEARFOSS
105 Director Web Services ... Mr. Patrick BAXTER
28 Chief Diversity Officer ... Dr. Cecil HOWARD

*University of South Florida Sarasota-Manatee (C)

8350 Tamiami Trail, Sarasota FL 34243-2049

County: Manatee Identification: 667058
Unit ID: 451671
Telephone: (941) 359-4200 Carnegie Class: Masters/S
FAX Number: N/A Calendar System: Semester
URL: www.usfsm.edu
Established: 1956 Annual Undergrad Tuition & Fees (In-State): $5,587
Enrollment: 2,030 Coed
Affiliation or Control: State IRS Status: 501(c)3
Highest Offering: Master's; No Lower Division
Accreditation: SC, CAEPN

02 Interim Regional Chancellor ... Dr. Terry OSBORN
10 Vice Chancellor Business & Finance ... Mr. Ben ELLINOR
05 Vice Chancellor Academic Affairs ... Dr. Terry OSBORN
111 Vice Chancellor Advancement ... Vacant
09 AVP Institutional Research ... Dr. Bonnie J. JONES
49 Dean College of Lib Arts & Soc Sci ... Dr. Jane ROSE
50 Dean College of Business ... Dr. James CURRAN
81 Dean College of Science & Math ... Dr. Paul KIRCHMAN
88 Dean College of Hosp & Tourism Mgmt ... Dr. Patrick MOREO
09 Director of Institutional Research ... Ms. Laura HOFFMAN
13 Chief Info Technology Officer (CIO) ... Mr. Bryan MUDD
07 Director of Admissions ... Mr. Andrew TELATOVICH
96 Director of Purchasing ... Ms. Michelle KRUEGER
32 Director Student Engagement ... Ms. Kimberly MONES
04 Administrative Asst to President ... Ms. Tiffany JACKSON
08 Head Librarian ... Ms. Diane FULKERSON
20 Assoc Dir Academic Affairs & Reg ... Ms. Lynn LYNCH
106 Dir Online Education/E-learning ... Ms. Timi HAGAER
15 Assoc Dir Admin Services ... Ms. Carolyn DYSON
26 Director Information Services ... Mr. Charlie TERENZIO

*University of West Florida (D)

11000 University Parkway, Pensacola FL 32514-5750

County: Escambia FICE Identification: 003955
Unit ID: 138354
Telephone: (850) 474-2000 Carnegie Class: DU-Mod
FAX Number: (850) 474-3131 Calendar System: Semester
URL: uwf.edu
Established: 1963 Annual Undergrad Tuition & Fees (In-State): $6,360
Enrollment: 12,763 Coed
Affiliation or Control: State IRS Status: 501(c)3
Highest Offering: Doctorate
Accreditation: SC, CAATE, CAEPN, ENG, EXSC, MT, MUS, NURSE, PH, SW

02 President ... Dr. Martha D. SAUNDERS
05 Interim Provost ... Dr. George B. ELLENBERG
10 Vice President and CFO ... Dr. Steven CUNNINGHAM
32 Sr Assoc Vice Pres Student Affairs ... Dr. James R. HURD
84 Vice Pres Enrollment & Student Affs ... Dr. Joffery GAYMON
116 Asc VP Internal Audit/Mgmt Consultg ... Ms. J. Betsy BOWERS
15 Associate Director Human Resources ... Mr. Jeff COMEAU
15 Assoc Director Human Resources ... Ms. Jamie SPRAGUE
16 Asst Director HR ... Ms. Christine DILLARD
96 Director Procurement & Contracts ... Ms. Angela JONES
43 General Counsel ... Ms. Pam LANGHAM
35 Assistant VP/Dean of Students ... Dr. Brandon FRYE
50 Dean of Business ... Dr. Timothy O'KEEFE
49 Dean Arts/Social Sci/Humanities ... Dr. Steven BROWN
107 Dean Education & Prof Studies ... Dr. William CRAWLEY
08 Dean University Libraries ... Mr. Robert DUGAN
35 Associate Dean of Students ... Dr. LuSharon WILEY
21 Asst VP Financial Services ... Ms. Colleen M. ASMUS
13 Executive Director & CTO ITS ... Mrs. Melanie J. HAVEARD
26 Exec Dir University Communication ... Ms. Megan GONZALEZ
07 Director of Admissions ... Ms. Katherine CONDON
92 Director of Kugleman Honors Program ... Dr. Greg LANIER
37 Director of Financial Aid ... Ms. Shana GORE
19 Director of University Police ... Mr. John S. WARREN
39 Director of Housing/Residence Life ... Dr. Ruth L. DAVISON
38 Assistant VP Counseling Center ... Dr. Rebecca E. KENNEDY
29 Director of Alumni Relations ... Ms. Melissa H. GRACE
41 Athletic Director ... Mr. David L. SCOTT
81 Dean Science/Engineering/Health ... Dr. Michael HUGGINS
76 Dean College of Health ... Dr. Ermalynn KIEHL
20 Vice President Academic Engagement ... Dr. Kimberly LEDUFF
30 Assoc Vice Pres of Development ... Dr. Meredith BRUNEN
109 Director Business/Auxiliary Svcs ... Ms. Ellen P. TILL
06 Registrar ... Ms. Kelly BRUNDAGE

Stetson University (E)

421 N Woodland Boulevard, DeLand FL 32723-0001

County: Volusia FICE Identification: 001531
Unit ID: 137546
Telephone: (386) 822-7000 Carnegie Class: Masters/M
FAX Number: (386) 822-8832 Calendar System: 4/1/4
URL: www.stetson.edu
Established: 1883 Annual Undergrad Tuition & Fees: $43,240
Enrollment: 4,330 Coed
Affiliation or Control: Independent Non-Profit IRS Status: 501(c)3
Highest Offering: Doctorate
Accreditation: SC, CACREP, CAEP, LAW, MUS

01 President ... Dr. Wendy B. LIBBY
05 Exec VP & Provost ... Dr. Noel PAINTER
10 Exec Vice Pres & CFO ... Mr. F. Robert HUTH
111 VP for Devel & Alumni Engagement ... Mr. Jeffrey ULMER
84 VP Enrollment Management ... Mr. Joel BAUMAN
26 VP for University Marketing ... Mr. Bruce CHONG
32 Vice Pres for Student Affairs ... Dr. Lua HANCOCK
61 Dean College of Law ... Mr. Christopher PIETRUSZKIEWICZ
49 Dean of College of Arts & Sciences ... Dr. Karen RYAN
50 Dean of School of Business Admin ... Dr. Neal P. MERO
64 Dean of School of Music ... Dr. Thomas G. MASSE
08 Dean of duPont-Ball Library ... Ms. Susan RYAN
20 Assoc Provost for Faculty Devlpmnt ... Dr. Rosalie RICHARDS
06 Registrar ... Mr. Robert BERWICK
41 Director of Athletics ... Mr. Jeffrey P. ALTIER
13 Assoc VP & CIO ... Dr. Jose BERNIER
15 Assoc VP for Human Resources ... Ms. Drew MACAN
18 Assoc Vice Pres Facilities Mgmt ... Mr. Al ALLEN
21 Assoc Vice Pres for Finance ... Mr. Jeffrey MARGHEIM
114 Assoc VP Budget ... Ms. Melissa PETERS
88 Spec Advsr to Pres for Philanthropy ... Ms. Linda P. DAVIS
35 Dean of Students ... Ms. Lynn SCHOENBERG
36 Exec Dir Career Dev & Advising ... Mr. Timothy STILES
09 Dir Institutional Research ... Dr. Resche HINES
104 Director of International Learning ... Ms. Paula HENTZ
110 Assoc VP Development ... Dr. Paul GLEASON
30 Asst VP Development ... Ms. Katheryn P. PEARCE
112 Asst VP for Devel/Alumni Engagement ... Ms. Rina TOVAR
30 Asst VP Dev & Communications ... Ms. Amy GIPSON
29 Asst VP Alumni/Parent Engagement ... Mr. Woody O'CAIN
07 Exec Dir of Admissions ... Vacant
37 Dir Student Financial Aid ... Ms. Beth Anne KIEFT
39 Dir of Res Educ & Housing ... Dr. Larry CORRELL-HUGHES
16 Director Human Resources ... Ms. Betty WHITEMAN
96 Director of Purchasing ... Ms. Valinda WIMER
19 Chief Public Safety ... Mr. Robert MATUSICK
04 Executive Asst to President ... Ms. Joan BEASLEY
102 Dir Ofc of Grants/Sponsored Rsrch ... Ms. Carol BUCKELS
38 Director Counseling Ctr ... Dr. Leigh BAKER

Sullivan and Cogliano Training Centers (A)
4760 NW 167th Street, Miami FL 33014
County: Miami-Dade FICE Identification: 040393
Unit ID: 433466
Telephone: (305) 694-2401 Carnegie Class: Not Classified
FAX Number: (786) 871-7525 Calendar System: Other
URL: sctrain.edu
Established: 1997 Annual Undergrad Tuition & Fees: N/A
Enrollment: 518 Coed
Affiliation or Control: Proprietary IRS Status: Proprietary
Highest Offering: Associate Degree
Accreditation: COE

01 President & CEO .... Herb COGLIANO

Suncoast College of Health (B)
6513 14th Street West #103, Bradenton FL 34207
County: Manatee Identification: 667296
Telephone: (941) 727-2273 Carnegie Class: Not Classified
FAX Number: (941) 727-2274 Calendar System: Quarter
URL: www.suncoastcollege.edu
Established: Annual Undergrad Tuition & Fees: N/A
Enrollment: N/A Coed
Affiliation or Control: Proprietary IRS Status: Proprietary
Highest Offering: Baccalaureate
Accreditation: ACICS

01 President .... Lori BARNES

Tallahassee Community College (C)
444 Appleyard Drive, Tallahassee FL 32304-2895
County: Leon FICE Identification: 001533
Unit ID: 137759
Telephone: (850) 201-6200 Carnegie Class: Assoc/HT-High Trad
FAX Number: (850) 201-8682 Calendar System: Semester
URL: www.tcc.fl.edu
Established: 1966 Annual Undergrad Tuition & Fees (In-District): $2,026
Enrollment: 12,445 Coed
Affiliation or Control: Local IRS Status: 501(c)3
Highest Offering: Baccalaureate
Accreditation: SC, ADNUR, COARC, DA, DH, EMT, SURGT

01 President .... Dr. Jim MURDAUGH
10 Vice Pres Administrative Svcs/CFO .... Dr. Barbara WILLS
13 VP Information Technology .... Mr. Bret INGERMAN
05 Provost and VP for Academic Affairs .... Dr. Feleccia MOORE-DAVIS
32 Vice President for Student Affs .... Dr. Sheri ROWLAND
103 Vice Pres Workforce Development .... Ms. Kimberly MOORE
26 VP Communications and Marketing .... Mr. Al MORAN
108 Assoc VP Inst Effectiveness .... Dr. Lei WANG
100 Chief of Staff .... Mr. Scott BALOG
79 Dean Communications & Humanities .... Dr. Tracy WOODARD-MEYERS
83 Dean Behavioral/Social Science/Educ .... Dr. Richard MURGO
72 Dean Business Industry & Technology .. Mr. Stephen DUNNIVANT
88 Dean Transitional Studies .... Ms. Sharisse TURNER
08 Director of Library Services .... Ms. Deborah P. ROBINSON
76 Dean Health Care Professions .... Ms. Stephanie SOLOMON
37 Director of Financial Aid .... Mr. William SPIERS
124 Dir of Student Success & Retention .... Dr. Shanna AUTRY
15 Director of Human Resources .... Ms. Nyla DAVIS
102 Director of TCC Foundation .... Ms. Heather MITCHELL
41 Director of Athletics .... Mr. Rob CHANEY
35 Dir of Campus & Civic Engagement .... Mr. Mike COLEMAN
88 Exec Dir Florida Public Safety Inst .... Mr. E. E. EUNICE
18 Dir Facilities/Construction/Plng .... Mr. Don HERR
21 Controller .... Ms. Patricia MANNING
45 Director of Educational Research .... Dr. Barbara J. GILL
09 Director of Institutional Research .... Ms. Margaret WINGATE
106 Dir Center for Distance Learning .... Dr. Marilyn DICKEY
88 Dir Ctr for Teach/Learn/Ldrshp .... Dr. Karinda BARRETT
85 International Students Advisor .... Ms. Li PON
14 Director of User Services .... Mr. Chip SINGLETARY
14 Director of Enterprise Systems .... Mr. Mike ROBECK
25 Contracts and Grants Manager .... Ms. Vanessa WRIGHT
88 Director Grants & Special Projects .... Mr. Steven SOLOMON
96 Purchasing Manager .... Mr. Bobby HINSON
19 Chief of Police .... Mr. Christopher SUMMERS
06 Registrar .... Ms. Brenda KNIGHT
20 Dean of Curriculum and Instruction .... Mrs. Calandra STRINGER
36 Director of Career Services .... Ms. Catie GOODMAN
04 Administrative Asst to President .... Ms. Lenda KLING
43 Dir Legal Services/General Counsel .... Mr. Craig KNOX

Talmudic College of Florida (D)
4000 Alton Road, Miami Beach FL 33140
County: Dade FICE Identification: 025089
Unit ID: 137777
Telephone: (305) 534-7050 Carnegie Class: Spec-4-yr-Faith
FAX Number: (305) 534-8444 Calendar System: Semester
URL: www.talmudicu.edu
Established: 1974 Annual Undergrad Tuition & Fees: $13,250
Enrollment: 53 Male
Affiliation or Control: Independent Non-Profit IRS Status: 501(c)3
Highest Offering: Doctorate
Accreditation: RABN

01 President .... Rabbi Yitzchak ZWEIG
05 Dean/Vice President .... Rabbi Yochanan ZWEIG
06 Registrar .... Rabbi Yitzchak WINKLER
37 Director Student Financial Aid .... Ms. Sharon BRECHER
20 Director Educational Programs .... Rabbi Yeshaya GREENBERG
07 Director of Admissions .... Rabbi Yaakov BURSTYN

Taylor College (E)
5190 SE 125th Street, Belleview FL 34420
County: Marion FICE Identification: 041166
Unit ID: 449524
Telephone: (352) 245-4119 Carnegie Class: Spec 2-yr-Health
FAX Number: (352) 245-0276 Calendar System: Other
URL: taylorcollege.edu
Established: 1999 Annual Undergrad Tuition & Fees: $11,951
Enrollment: 132 Coed
Affiliation or Control: Proprietary IRS Status: Proprietary
Highest Offering: Associate Degree
Accreditation: COE, PTAA

01 President .... Dianne HAMMOND

Trinity Baptist College (F)
800 Hammond Boulevard, Jacksonville FL 32221-1398
County: Duval FICE Identification: 031019
Unit ID: 137953
Telephone: (904) 596-2400 Carnegie Class: Spec-4-yr-Faith
FAX Number: (904) 596-2532 Calendar System: Semester
URL: www.tbc.edu
Established: 1974 Annual Undergrad Tuition & Fees: $11,040
Enrollment: 441 Coed
Affiliation or Control: Baptist IRS Status: 501(c)3
Highest Offering: Master's
Accreditation: TRACS

00 Chancellor .... Dr. Thomas C. MESSER
01 President/CEO .... Mr. Mac HEAVENER
05 Senior Vice President .... Dr. Matthew BEEMER
32 Dean of Students .... Mr. Jeremiah STANLEY
84 VP Enrollment Mgmt & Development .... Mr. Matthew HEAVENER
37 Director of Financial Aid .... Mr. Mark ELKINS
04 Administrative Asst to President .... Mrs. Sherry LENTZ
06 Registrar .... Dr. John CASH
08 Head Librarian .... Dr. John LUCY
10 Chief Business Officer .... Mr. Mike AKINS
41 Athletic Director .... Mr. John JONES
18 Chief Facilities/Physical Plant .... Mr. Roger CHASTAIN
19 Director Security/Safety .... Mr. John CASH, JR.
29 Director Alumni Relations .... Vacant

Trinity College of Florida (G)
2430 Welbilt Boulevard, Trinity FL 34655-4401
County: Pasco FICE Identification: 030282
Unit ID: 137962
Telephone: (727) 376-6911 Carnegie Class: Spec-4-yr-Faith
FAX Number: (727) 376-0781 Calendar System: Semester
URL: www.trinitycollege.edu
Established: 1932 Annual Undergrad Tuition & Fees: $15,690
Enrollment: 205 Coed
Affiliation or Control: Independent Non-Profit IRS Status: 501(c)3
Highest Offering: Baccalaureate
Accreditation: BI

01 President .... Dr. Mark T. O'FARRELL
32 Vice President Student Affairs .... Rev. Al DEPOUTOT
05 Vice President Academic Affairs .... Dr. Dennis COX
111 Vice President for Advancement .... Dr. Charlie MARTIN
10 Vice Pres for Business & Finance .... Mr. Paul S. WILLARD
06 Registrar .... Mrs. Shannon T. RANES
26 Asst VP Marketing/Communications .... Vacant
07 Director of Admissions .... Mrs. Rachel NOBLE
04 Administrative Asst to President .... Mrs. Billie SKINNER
08 Head Librarian .... Mrs. Cindy T. HYER

Trinity International University, Florida Regional Center (H)
8190 W State Road 84, Davie FL 33324-4611
Telephone: (954) 382-6400 FICE Identification: 012314
Accreditation: &NH

† Regional accreditation is carried under the parent institution in Deerfield, IL.

UAC School of Global Management (I)
7955 NW 12th Street, Suite 119, Miami FL 33126
County: Miami-Dade Identification: 667277
Telephone: (305) 325-9090 Carnegie Class: Not Classified
FAX Number: (305) 507-4344 Calendar System: Other
URL: www.uac.edu
Established: Annual Undergrad Tuition & Fees: N/A
Enrollment: N/A Coed
Affiliation or Control: Proprietary IRS Status: Proprietary
Highest Offering: Master's
Accreditation: ACICS

01 President .... Ramses VARGAS
07 Admissions Director .... Jairo CRUZ
37 Financial/Admin Director .... Ligia BARRIOS
06 Registrar/Asst Admin .... Heidy DAVILA

Ultimate Medical Academy-Clearwater (J)
1255 Cleveland Street, Clearwater FL 33756
County: Pinellas FICE Identification: 035493
Unit ID: 441371
Telephone: (727) 298-8685 Carnegie Class: Spec 2-yr-Health
FAX Number: (727) 446-2489 Calendar System: Semester
URL: www.ultimatemedical.edu
Established: 1998 Annual Undergrad Tuition & Fees: N/A
Enrollment: 259 Coed
Affiliation or Control: Proprietary IRS Status: Proprietary
Highest Offering: Associate Degree
Accreditation: ABHES

01 Campus Director .... Mr. Mark GUTMANN

Ultimate Medical Academy Online-Tampa (K)
3101 W Martin Luther King Boulevard, Tampa FL 33607
Telephone: (813) 386-6350 Identification: 770528
Accreditation: ABHES, CAHIIM

Unilatina International College (L)
3130 Commerce Pkwy, Miramar FL 33025
County: Broward Identification: 667155
Unit ID: 486354
Telephone: (954) 607-4344 Carnegie Class: Not Classified
FAX Number: (954) 357-1766 Calendar System: Quarter
URL: www.unilatina.edu
Established: 2001 Annual Undergrad Tuition & Fees: $8,907
Enrollment: 50 Coed
Affiliation or Control: Proprietary IRS Status: Proprietary
Highest Offering: Associate Degree
Accreditation: ACICS

01 President .... Lydia B. BAUTISTA MOLLER
05 Academic Director .... Angelica MOYANO

Universal Career School (M)
10720 W. Flagler Street Ste 21, Sweetwater FL 33174
County: Miami-Dade FICE Identification: 038563
Unit ID: 446589
Telephone: (305) 485-7700 Carnegie Class: Not Classified
FAX Number: (305) 485-8515 Calendar System: Semester
URL: www.ucs.edu
Established: Annual Undergrad Tuition & Fees: N/A
Enrollment: 126 Coed
Affiliation or Control: Proprietary IRS Status: Proprietary
Highest Offering: Associate Degree
Accreditation: COE

University of Fort Lauderdale (N)
4069 NW 16th Street, Lauderhill FL 33313-5809
County: Broward FICE Identification: 041563
Unit ID: 457402
Telephone: (954) 486-7728 Carnegie Class: Spec-4-yr-Faith
FAX Number: (954) 486-7667 Calendar System: Other
URL: www.uftl.edu
Established: Annual Undergrad Tuition & Fees: $7,410
Enrollment: 31 Coed
Affiliation or Control: Non-denominational IRS Status: 501(c)3
Highest Offering: Doctorate
Accreditation: TRACS

01 Chancellor and CEO .... Dr. Henry B. FERNANDEZ
10 Chief Financial Officer .... Mr. Brian HANKERSON
05 Vice Pres for Academic Affairs/CAO .... Dr. Chelsea HANSEN
09 VP Institutional Effect/Compliance .... Ms. Chloris UNDERWOOD
06 Registrar .... Ms. Lenice BARNETT
07 Director of Admissions .... Vacant

University of Miami (O)
1252 Memorial Drive, Coral Gables FL 33124
County: Miami-Dade FICE Identification: 001536
Unit ID: 135726
Telephone: (305) 284-2211 Carnegie Class: DU-Highest
FAX Number: N/A Calendar System: Semester
URL: www.miami.edu
Established: 1925 Annual Undergrad Tuition & Fees: $47,004
Enrollment: 16,825 Coed
Affiliation or Control: Independent Non-Profit IRS Status: 501(c)3
Highest Offering: Doctorate
Accreditation: SC, ANEST, CAATE, CEA, CLPSY, COPSY, DENT, ENG, HSA, IPSY, LAW, MED, MUS, NURSE, PH, PTA

01 President .... Dr. Julio FRENK
05 Executive Vice President & Provost .... Dr. Jeffrey DUERK
10 Exec VP Business & Finance and CFO .... Dr. Jacqueline TRAVISANO

111 Int VP Advancement/External Affairs .... Ms. Donna ARBIDE
84 VP Enrollment Management .... Mr. John G. HALLER
115 AVP Treasury .... Mr. Charmel MAYNARD
18 VP Real Estate & Facilities .... Mr. Larry D. MARBERT
26 VP University Communications .... Ms. Jacqueline R. MENENDEZ
15 VP Human Resources .... Ms. Nerissa E. MORRIS
43 VP/General Counsel .... Ms. Aileen M. UGALDE
32 VP Student Affairs .... Dr. Patricia A. WHITELY
00 Chairman Board of Trustees .... Mr. Richard D. FAIN
100 President's Chief of Staff .... Mr. Rodolfo J. FERNANDEZ
20 Sr Vice Provost/Dean Undergrad Educ .... Dr. William S. GREEN
46 Vice Provost Research .... Dr. John L. BIXBY
20 Vice Provost Faculty Affairs .... Dr. David J. BIRNBACH
41 Director Athletics .... Mr. Blake JAMES
29 Assoc VP Advancement & Alumni Rels .... Ms. Donna A. ARBIDE
31 AVP Community Relations .... Ms. Sarah N. ARTECONA
17 Exec VP Health Affairs/CEO UHealth .. Dr. Steve M. ALTSCHULER
105 AVP Communications and Marketing ... Mr. Todd M. ELLENBERG
16 Associate Vice President/Med HR .... Vacant
27 Executive Director Comm & PR .... Ms. Megan M. ONDRIZEK
19 Chief of Police .... Major David A. RIVERO
63 Dean School of Medicine .... Dr. Edward ABRAHAM
49 Dean College of Arts & Sciences .... Dr. Leonidas G. BACHAS
48 Dean School of Architecture .... Dr. Rodolphe EL-KHOURY
50 Dean Business Administration .... Dr. John A. QUELCH
60 Dean School Communication .... Dr. Gregory J. SHEPHERD
53 Dean Education/Human Development . Dr. Isaac PRILLELTENSKY
54 Dean College of Engineering .... Dr. Jean Pierre BARDET
61 Dean School of Law .... Ms. Patricia WHITE
64 Dean School of Music .... Dr. Shelton G. BERG
65 Dean Marine & Atmospheric Science .... Dr. Roni AVISSAR
66 Dean Nursing & Health Studies .... Dr. Cindy L. MUNRO
58 Dean Graduate School .... Dr. Guillermo PRADO
35 AVP Stdnt Affs & Dean of Students .... Dr. Ryan C. HOLMES
07 Associate Dean Enrollment .... Mr. Mark REID
38 Director Student Counseling .... Dr. Rene MONTEAGUDO
85 Director Intl Services .... Ms. Teresa S. DE LA GUARDIA
39 Exec Director Student Housing .... Mr. James G. SMART
96 Executive Director Purchasing .... Ms. Susan R. MONTES
88 Associate VP Enterprise App .... Mr. Jack J. GEORGE
119 Assoc VP and CISO .... Ms. Theresa SEMMENS
90 Asst VP Chief Academic Tech Offic .... Mr. Allan GYORKE
14 Assoc VP Information Technology .... Mr. Brad ROHRER
109 Executive Director Auxiliary Svcs .... Ms. Ana ALVAREZ
51 Dean Continuing Education .... Dr. Rebecca MACMILLAN FOX
40 Director Bookstore .... Ms. Wendy SMITH
06 Registrar .... Ms. Karen J. BECKETT
08 Dean Libraries .... Dr. Charles ECKMAN
101 Acting University Secretary .... Ms. Leslie DELLINGER ACEITUNO
102 Exec Director Foundation Relations .... Ms. Joanna DE VELASCO
36 Assoc Dean Career Services .... Mr. Christian GARCIA
104 Director Study Abroad .... Ms. Devika M. MILNER
22 AVP Workplace Equity .... Ms. Beverly PRUITT
25 AVP Business Services .... Mr. Humberto M. SPEZIANI
37 Assoc Dean Financial Aid .... Mr. Raymond E. NAULT
13 VP Information Technology & CIO .... Mr. Steve CAWLEY
44 Executive Director Annual Giving .... Mr. Troy ODOM
114 AVP Budget & Planning .... Ms. Aintzane CELAYA
04 Administrative Manager to President .... Ms. Alicia BLATCHFORD
86 Sr VP for Pub Affairs & Comm .... Mr. Rodolfo J. FERNANDEZ
116 AVP Chief Audit/Compliance Officer .... Ms. Blanca MALAGON
117 Executive Director Risk Management .... Ms. Andrea ORANGE

University of Phoenix Central Florida Main Campus (A)

8325 South Park Circle Ste 100, Orlando FL 32819

Telephone: (407) 345-8868 Identification: 770932

Accreditation: &NH, ACBSP

† No longer accepting campus-based students.

University of Phoenix North Florida Campus (B)

4500 Salisbury Road, Jacksonville FL 32216-0959

Telephone: (904) 636-6645 Identification: 770197

Accreditation: &NH, ACBSP

† No longer accepting campus-based students.

University of Phoenix South Florida Main Campus (C)

2400 SW 145th Avenue, Miramar FL 33207-4145

Telephone: (954) 382-5303 Identification: 770237

Accreditation: &NH, ACBSP

† No longer accepting campus-based students.

University of St. Augustine for Health Sciences (D)

One University Boulevard, St. Augustine FL 32086

Telephone: (904) 826-0084 Identification: 770939

Accreditation: &WC, OT, PTA

† Branch campus of University of St. Augustine for Health Sciences, San Marcos, CA.

University of Tampa (E)

401 W Kennedy Boulevard, Tampa FL 33606-1490

County: Hillsborough FICE Identification: 001538

Unit ID: 137847

Telephone: (813) 253-3333 Carnegie Class: Masters/L

FAX Number: (813) 258-7207 Calendar System: Other

URL: www.ut.edu

Established: 1931 Annual Undergrad Tuition & Fees: $27,740

Enrollment: 7,959 Coed

Affiliation or Control: Independent Non-Profit IRS Status: 501(c)3

Highest Offering: Master's

Accreditation: SC, CAATE, CS, FEPAC, MUS, NUR

01 President .... Dr. Ronald L. VAUGHN
05 Provost/Vice Pres Academic Affairs .... Dr. David STERN
10 Vice Pres Administration/Finance .... Mr. Richard W. OGOREK
84 Vice President Enrollment .... Mr. Dennis L. NOSTRAND
30 Vice Pres Develop & Univ Relations .... Mr. L. Keith TODD
44 Vice Pres Capital Campaign .... Mr. Daniel T. GURA
45 Vice Pres Operations & Planning .... Dr. Linda W. DEVINE
88 Chief Information Security Officer .... Ms. Tammy L. CLARK
21 Assistant Vice Pres Admin/Finance .... Mr. T. Kevin LAFFERTY
32 Dean of Students .... Ms. Stephanie R. KREBS
20 Assoc Provost & Dean of Acad Svcs .... Dr. Katharine H. COLE
06 Registrar .... Ms. Michelle PELAEZ
08 Director of the Library .... Ms. Marlyn PETHE-COOK
29 Director of Alumni Relations .... Mr. James HARDWICK
37 Director of Financial Aid .... Ms. Jacqueline LATORELLA
26 Director of Public Information .... Mr. Eric D. CARDENAS
18 Director of Facilities Management .... Ms. Jennifer ISENBECK
15 Exec Director of Human Resources .... Ms. Donna B. POPOVICH
07 Dir Enr Management/Admissions .... Mr. Brent W. BENNER
41 Athletic Director .... Mr. Larry J. MARFISE
40 Manager Campus Store .... Ms. Angela M. O'CONNOR
39 Director of Residence Life .... Vacant
22 Affirmative Action Officer .... Ms. Donna B. POPOVICH
19 Director Safety & Security .... Mr. Kevin A. HOWELL
23 Dir Health Center/Stdnt Counseling .... Ms. Sharon P. SCHAEFER
38 Director Student Counseling .... Ms. Sharon P. SCHAEFER
96 Director of Procurement .... Ms. Cyn D. EZELL
09 Dir Institutional Effectiveness .... Dr. Jeanne M. ROBERTS
92 Director of Honors Program .... Dr. Gary S. LUTER
50 Dean College of Business .... Dr. F. Frank GHANNADIAN
83 Dean Social Science/Math Education .... Dr. Jack M. GELLER
81 Dean College Natural/Health Sci .... Dr. Paul GREENWOOD
57 Dean College of Arts/Letters .... Dr. David GUDELUNAS
51 Assoc Dean Graduate/Continuing Stds .... Dr. Donald D. MORRILL
89 Dir First Year/Baccalaureate Exp .... Ms. Edesa SCARBOROUGH
36 Assoc Dean Career Dev & Engagement .... Mr. Timothy HARDING
104 Assoc Dean International Programs .... Dr. Marca BEAR
04 Executive Asst to President .... Ms. Madelyn CASTRO

Valencia College (F)

PO Box 3028, Orlando FL 32802-3028

County: Orange FICE Identification: 006750

Unit ID: 138187

Telephone: (407) 299-5000 Carnegie Class: Bac/Assoc-Assoc Dom

FAX Number: (407) 426-8970 Calendar System: Semester

URL: www.valenciacollege.edu

Established: 1967 Annual Undergrad Tuition & Fees (In-State): $2,474

Enrollment: 44,050 Coed

Affiliation or Control: State IRS Status: 501(c)3

Highest Offering: Baccalaureate

Accreditation: SC, ADNUR, CEA, CVT, DH, DMS, EMT, RAD

01 President .... Dr. Sanford C. SHUGART
05 VP Academic Affairs & Planning .... Dr. Susan E. LEDLOW
10 VP Business Ops & Finance .... Mr. Loren J. BENDER
88 VP Educational Partnerships .... Dr. Joyce C. ROMANO
107 VP Global/Prof & Cont Education .... Mr. Joe N. BATTISTA
13 VP Info Technology and CIO .... Mr. John J. SLOT, JR.
15 VP Org Dev & Human Resources .... Dr. Amy N. BOSLEY
43 VP Policy & General Counsel .... Dr. Bill J. MULLOWNEY
26 VP Public Affairs & Marketing .... Mr. Jay R. GALBRAITH, II
32 VP Student Affairs .... Dr. Kim W. SEPICH
07 Asst VP Admissions & Records .... Dr. Linda K. HERLOCKER
14 Asst VP Application .... Dr. Jamie D. ROST
114 Asst VP Budgets & Analysis .... Mr. Oscar J. CRISTANCHO MERCADO
103 Asst VP Career & Workforce Educ .... Dr. Nasser HEDAYAT
88 Asst VP College Transition .... Dr. Amy KLEEMAN
108 Asst VP Curriculum & Assessment .... Dr. Karen Marie BORGLUM
18 Asst VP Fac Plng/Real Est Dev .... Mr. Jose A. FERNANDEZ
37 Interim Asst VP Fin Aid/Vet Affairs .... Ms. Brenda WRIGHT
21 Asst VP Financial Services .... Ms. Jackie D. LASCH
51 Asst VP Global & Cont Educ .... Ms. Lisa G. ELI
27 Asst VP Marketing .... Ms. Traci A. THORNTON
19 Asst VP Operations .... Mr. Paul ROONEY
16 Asst VP Org Dev & Incl .... Mr. Ryan D. KANE
88 Asst VP Prof & Cont Ed .... Dr. Carolyn R. MCMORRAN
25 Asst VP Resource Development .... Ms. Kristeen R. CHRISTIAN
35 Asst VP Student Affairs .... Dr. Sonya F. JOSEPH
16 Asst VP Talent Acq/Total Rew .... Ms. Mary Beth CLIFTON
88 Asst VP Teaching & Learning .... Dr. Wendi M. DEW
12 Campus President East/Winter Park .... Dr. Stacey R. JOHNSON
12 Campus President Osceola/LNC/PNC .... Dr. Kathleen A. PLINSKE
12 Campus President West/Downtown .... Dr. Falecia D. WILLIAMS
88 Executive Dean Downtown .... Mr. Eugene G. JONES
88 Executive Dean Lake Nona .... Dr. Mike BOSLEY
88 Executive Dean Poinciana .... Dr. Jennifer ROBERTSON
88 Executive Dean School Public Safety .... Dr. Jeff W. GOLTZ
88 Executive Dean Winter Park .... Dr. Terri G. DANIELS
102 Foundation President and CEO .... Dr. Geraldine M P. GALLAGHER
20 Campus Dean Academic Affairs East .... Ms. Michelle R. FOSTER
20 Campus Dean Academic Affairs West .... Dr. Nicholas J. BEKAS
97 Campus Dean Learning Support East .... Dr. Leonard C. BASS
97 Campus Dean Learning Supprt Osceola .... Dr. Landon P. SHEPHARD
97 Campus Dean Learning Support West .... Dr. Karen L. REILLY
35 Dean of Students East/WP .... Mr. Joe M. SARRUBBO
35 Dean of Students Osceola .... Dr. Jill M. SZENTMIKLOSI
35 Dean of Students West .... Dr. Ben C. LION
76 Dean Allied Health .... Ms. Penny L. CONNERS
49 Dean Arts/Entertainment East .... Ms. Wendy L. GIVOGLU
49 Dean Arts & Humanities West .... Ms. Ana J. CALDERO FIGUEROA
83 Dean Behav/Social Science West .... Dr. Molly MCINTIRE
50 Dean Business & Hospitality Office .... Dr. Terry L. ALLCORN
50 Dean Bus/Info Tech/Pub Svc East .... Dr. Carin M. GORDON
75 Dean Career & Tech Prgms .... Dr. James R. MCDONALD
60 Dean Communications East .... Ms. Linda R. NEAL
60 Dean Comm/Languages Osceola .... Ms. Jenni L. CAMPBELL
60 Dean Communications West .... Dr. Elizabeth S. RENN
54 Dean Engr/Computer Pgm & Tech .... Dr. Lisa R. MACON
79 Dean Humanities/Foreign Lang East .... Mr. David O. SUTTON
79 Dean Humanities/Soc Science .... Dr. Thomas T. TAKAYAMA
81 Dean Math East .... Dr. Maryke LEE
81 Dean Math Osceola .... Dr. Melissa D. PEDONE
81 Interim Dean Math West .... Ms. Amy J. COMERFORD
66 Dean Nursing .... Ms. Rise W. SANDROWITZ
49 Dean Science East .... Ms. Jennifer L. SNYDER
81 Dean Science Osceola .... Dr. Anitza M. SAN MIGUEL
49 Dean Science West .... Dr. Bob F. GESSNER
83 Dean Social Science .... Dr. Lee L. THOMAS
08 Campus Director Library W .... Ms. Ruth S. SMITH
29 Director Alum Engage/Annual Giving .... Dr. Jennifer V. MEZQUITA
40 Director Aux Svcs Campus Store .... Ms. Yaremis P. FULLANA
96 Director Auxiliary Svcs Contracts .... Mr. Jeffrey D. FILKO
116 Director Compliance & Audit .. Ms. Cynthia SANTIAGO-GUZMAN
88 Director Corporate Partnerships .... Mr. Brian B. HENTIES
88 Director Curriculum Initiatives .... Ms. Robyn BRIGHTON
84 Director Enrollment Services .... Ms. Jacquelyn F. THOMPSON
22 Director Eq Op & Emp Relations .... Ms. Lauren E. KELLY
92 Director Honors Program .... Dr. Cheryl ROBINSON
119 Director Information Security .... Mr. John E. KNIGHTS
108 Director Institutional Assessment .... Dr. Laura N. BLASI
108 Director Inst Effectiveness .... Mr. Darren A. SMITH
09 Director Institutional Research .... Mr. Daryl J. DAVIS
120 Director Learn Tech/Proj Mgmt Svcs .... Mr. Todd A. TREECE
106 Director Online Teaching/Learning .... Ms. Page A. JERZAK
105 Director Web and Portal Services .... Mr. James FLANAGAN
18 Mgng Director Plant Ops .... Mr. Shaun D. ANDREWS
19 Mgng Director Safety & Security .... Mr. Mike D. FAVORIT
44 Sr Engagement/Special Gifts Officer .... Ms. Barbara B. SHELL
04 Executive Assistant Senior .... Ms. Barbara E. HALSTEAD

Virginia College (G)

5940 Beach Boulevard, Jacksonville FL 32207

Telephone: (904) 520-7400 Identification: 770839

Accreditation: ACICS, ACFEI

† Branch campus of Virginia College, Birmingham, AL

Virginia College (H)

312 East Nine Mile Road, Suite 34, Pensacola FL 32514-1475

Telephone: (850) 436-8444 FICE Identification: 031005

Accreditation: ACICS, SURGT

† Branch campus of Virginia College, Birmingham, AL.

Warner University (I)

13895 Highway 27, Lake Wales FL 33859-2549

County: Polk FICE Identification: 008848

Unit ID: 138275

Telephone: (863) 638-1426 Carnegie Class: Bac-Diverse

FAX Number: (863) 638-1472 Calendar System: Semester

URL: www.warner.edu

Established: 1968 Annual Undergrad Tuition & Fees: $20,712

Enrollment: 1,183 Coed

Affiliation or Control: Church Of God IRS Status: 501(c)3

Highest Offering: Master's

Accreditation: SC, SW

01 President .... Dr. David A. HOAG
88 Senior Director of Special Projects .... Dr. James G. MOYER
05 VP and Chief Academic Officer .... Dr. Steven DARR
10 Vice Pres for Finance & Business .... Mr. Greg A. RODDEN
111 Vice President for Advancement .... Mrs. Andrea THIES
84 VP for Enrollment Mgmt & Marketing .... Mrs. Dawn M. RAFOOL
07 Assoc VP Admissions .... Mr. Kevin JONES
32 Dean of Students .... Rev. Dawn MEADOWS
06 Registrar .... Mrs. Sara F. KANE
88 Dean of Admissions .... Mr. Bob MOBLEY
37 Director Student Financial Aid .... Mrs. Lorrie STEEDLEY
21 Controller .... Mr. Dean MEADOWS
08 Librarian .... Mrs. Sherill HARRIGER
29 Director Alumni Relations .... Miss Kareen PICKETT
18 Chief Facilities/Physical Plant .... Mr. Bill BROWN
97 Director of General Studies .... Mrs. Kelly MILLS
20 Dean of Faculty .... Dr. Michael SANDERS
40 Director Bookstore .... Ms. Monica HAMILTON
13 Director of Institutional Tech .... Mr. Mark THOMAS
19 Director Campus Security .... Mr. Brian ROWLES
36 Director Career Counseling .... Mrs. Dawn MEADOWS
88 Director Academic Skills Ctr .... Mrs. Kelly MORGAN
106 Director Online Services .... Mr. Shawn TAYLOR

107 Dean Adult Prof Div & Grad Studies .... Mr. Thomas MALCOLM
04 Administrative Asst to President .... Mrs. Alane RICHARDVILLE

Webber International University (A)

1201 Scenic Highway N/P.O. Box 96,
Babson Park FL 33827-0096

County: Polk FICE Identification: 001540
Unit ID: 138293
Telephone: (863) 638-1431 Carnegie Class: Bac-Diverse
FAX Number: (863) 638-2823 Calendar System: Semester
URL: www.webber.edu
Established: 1927 Annual Undergrad Tuition & Fees: $25,358
Enrollment: 733 Coed
Affiliation or Control: Independent Non-Profit IRS Status: 501(c)3
Highest Offering: Master's
Accreditation: SC, IACBE

01 President .... Dr. H. Keith WADE
05 Academic Dean .... Dr. Charles SHIEH
10 Vice President Finance .... Ms. Christina JORDON
32 Dean of Student Life .... Mr. Jay CULVER
06 Registrar/Dir of Financial Aid .... Mrs. Kathy A. WILSON
26 Director Cmty Rels & Marketing .... Mrs. Devyn MONTALVO
08 Head Librarian .... Ms. Sue DUNNING
41 Athletic Director .... Mr. Darren RICHIE
13 Director Information Technology .... Mr. Bob M. WEIS
18 Director of Campus Svcs/Maintenance .... Mr. Matt YENTES
40 Director of Bookstore .... Ms. Ruby FERNANDEZ
07 Director of Admissions .... Mr. Ryan PICARD
09 Director of Institutional Effectiv .... Dr. Nelson MARQUEZ
50 Chair of Business Education .... Dr. Jeanette EBERLE
53 Chair of General Education Division .... Dr. Charles WUNKER
04 Executive Asst to President .... Ms. Gerlinde DANCY
19 Director Security/Safety .... Mr. Michael RITTER
29 Dir Annual Fund/Alumni Relations .... Ms. Jennifer MUELLER

West Coast University - Miami (B)

9250 NW 36th Street, Doral FL 33178

Telephone: (786) 501-7070 Identification: 770936
Accreditation: &WC

† Branch campus of West Coast University, North Hollywood, CA.

WMU - Cooley Law School Tampa Bay Campus (C)

9445 Camden Field Parkway, Riverview FL 33578

Telephone: (813) 419-5100 Identification: 770290
Accreditation: &NH

† Branch campus of Western Michigan University Cooley Law School, Lansing, MI

Wolford College (D)

1336 Creekside Boulevard, Suite 2,
Naples FL 34108-1931

County: Collier FICE Identification: 039393
Unit ID: 451130
Telephone: (239) 513-1135 Carnegie Class: Spec-4-yr-Other Health
FAX Number: (239) 513-1368 Calendar System: Semester
URL: www.wolford.edu
Established: 2004 Annual Graduate Tuition & Fees: N/A
Enrollment: 188 Coed
Affiliation or Control: Independent Non-Profit IRS Status: 501(c)3
Highest Offering: Master's; No Undergraduates
Accreditation: ANEST

01 President/CEO .... Ms. Lynda WATERHOUSE
00 Chancellor Emeritus .... Dr. Thomas COOK
05 Program Director .... Dr. Lauren CORDER
37 Director of Financial Aid Services .... Mr. Gilbert CHANG
84 Dir Enrollment & Student Services .... Ms. Lori ELLISON
04 Executive Coordinator .... Ms. Margie MAZEFFA

WyoTech (E)

470 Destination Daytona Lane, Ormond Beach FL 32174

County: Volusia FICE Identification: 023462
Unit ID: 132268
Telephone: (386) 255-0295 Carnegie Class: Spec 2-yr-Tech
FAX Number: (386) 252-3523 Calendar System: Quarter
URL: www.wyotech.edu
Established: Annual Undergrad Tuition & Fees: N/A
Enrollment: 234 Coed
Affiliation or Control: Independent Non-Profit IRS Status: 501(c)3
Highest Offering: Associate Degree
Accreditation: ACCSC

01 Campus Director/Academic Dean .... Mr. Chris BARTON

Yeshiva Gedolah Rabbinical College (F)

1140 Alton Road, Miami Beach FL 33139-4708

County: Dade FICE Identification: 032563
Unit ID: 363712
Telephone: (305) 653-8770 Carnegie Class: Not Classified
FAX Number: (305) 653-6790 Calendar System: Semester
URL: www.lecfl.com
Established: 1973 Annual Undergrad Tuition & Fees: $8,400
Enrollment: 31 Male
Affiliation or Control: Independent Non-Profit IRS Status: 501(c)3
Highest Offering: Master's
Accreditation: RABN

01 Executive Vice President .... Rabbi Benzion KORF
05 Dean .... Rabbi Abraham KORF
06 Registrar .... Ayelet BORTUNK
07 Director of Admissions .... Rabbi Benche KORF

GEORGIA

Abraham Baldwin Agricultural College (G)

ABAC 1 - 2802 Moore Highway, Tifton GA 31793-2601

County: Tift FICE Identification: 001541
Unit ID: 138558
Telephone: (229) 391-5001 Carnegie Class: Bac/Assoc-Mixed
FAX Number: (229) 391-5002 Calendar System: Semester
URL: www.abac.edu
Established: 1908 Annual Undergrad Tuition & Fees (In-State): $3,453
Enrollment: 3,393 Coed
Affiliation or Control: State IRS Status: 501(c)3
Highest Offering: Baccalaureate
Accreditation: SC, ADNUR, NUR

01 President .... Dr. David BRIDGES
05 VP for Academic Affairs .... Dr. Jerry BAKER
10 VP for Fiscal Affairs & Opers .... Mr. Paul WILLIS
111 Interim VP Ext Affairs/Advancement .... Mr. Paul WILLIAMS
08 Director of Library Services .... Ms. Tamatha LAMBERT
32 Dean of Students .... Ms. Bernice HUGHES
41 Athletic Director .... Mr. Alan KRAMER
06 Registrar .... Dr. Amy WILLIS
38 Director of Student Development .... Dr. Maggie MARTIN
37 Director of Student Financial Svcs .... Mr. Michael WRIGHT
15 Director of Human Resources .... Mr. Richard SPANCAKE
26 Director of Public Relations .... Ms. Lindsey ROBERTS
108 Director of Assessment .... Vacant
84 Director Enrollment Management .... Ms. Donna WEBB
96 Director of Procurement .... Ms. Teri MATHIS
19 Chief of Police .... Mr. Frank STRICKLAND
04 Administrative Asst to President .... Ms. Pam LEONARD
39 Director of Student Housing .... Dr. Chris S. KINSEY
13 Chief Info Technology Officer .... Mr. Robert GERHART

† Part of the University System of Georgia.

Agnes Scott College (H)

141 E. College Avenue, Decatur GA 30030-3770

County: DeKalb FICE Identification: 001542
Unit ID: 138600
Telephone: (404) 471-6000 Carnegie Class: Bac-A&S
FAX Number: (404) 471-6067 Calendar System: Semester
URL: www.agnesscott.edu
Established: 1889 Annual Undergrad Tuition & Fees: $38,472
Enrollment: 902 Female
Affiliation or Control: Presbyterian Church (U.S.A.) IRS Status: 501(c)3
Highest Offering: Baccalaureate
Accreditation: SC

01 President .... Dr. Elizabeth KISS
05 VP for Academic Affairs .... Dr. Kerry E. PANNELL
32 VP for Student Life .... Dr. Karen GOFF
10 VP Business & Finance .... Mr. John P. HEGMAN
111 VP for College Advancement .... Dr. Robiaun R. CHARLES
84 VP for Enrollment & Dean of Admiss .... Ms. Alexa GAETA
26 VP for Communications & Mkt .... Vacant
101 Associate VP & Board Secretary .... Ms. Lea Ann HUDSON
13 Assoc VP Technology .... Ms. LaNeta COUNTS
20 Assoc Dean of the College .... Vacant
06 Registrar .... Ms. Gail N. MEIS
08 Director of Library Services .... Ms. Elizabeth BAGLEY
29 Senior Director Alumnae Relations .... Ms. Kimberly VICKERS
18 Director of Facilities .... Mr. Dave MARDER
15 Associate VP for Human Resources .... Ms. Karen GILBERT
42 Chaplain .... Rev. Kate COLUSSY-ESTES
37 Director of Financial Aid .... Mr. Patrick BONONES
09 Director of Institutional Research .... Dr. Corey DUNN
07 Director of Admissions .... Ms. Aimee S. KAHN-FOSS
23 Executive Director Wellness Center .... Ms. Juanita G. MOTTLEY
19 Director of Public Safety .... Mr. Henry HOPE
36 Director Student Placement .... Ms. Dawn KILLENBERG

Albany State University (I)

504 College Drive, Albany GA 31705-2796

County: Dougherty FICE Identification: 001544
Unit ID: 138716
Telephone: (229) 430-4600 Carnegie Class: Masters/M
FAX Number: (229) 430-4830 Calendar System: Semester
URL: www.asurams.edu
Established: 1903 Annual Undergrad Tuition & Fees (In-State): $5,490
Enrollment: 3,492 Coed
Affiliation or Control: State IRS Status: 501(c)3
Highest Offering: Beyond Master's But Less Than Doctorate
Accreditation: SC, ACBSP, CACREP, CAEPN, CAHIIM, DH, DMS, EMT, FEPAC, HT, MLTAD, NUR, RAD, SPAA, SW

01 President .... Dr. Arthur N. DUNNING
100 Senior Advisor/Spec Asst to Pres .... Ms. Cynthia HOKE
26 Spec Asst to Pres .... Mrs. Wendy WILSON
43 Legal Counsel/Title IX Coord .... Ms. Rowena DANIELS
05 Provost/VP Academic Affairs .... Dr. Olufunke FONTENOT
10 Vice President Fiscal Affairs .... Mr. Shawn MCGEE
13 VP Information Technology .... Mr. Del KIMBROUGH
111 VP Institutional Advancement .... Dr. Cynthia GEORGE
32 VP Student Affairs & Success .... Dr. Danette SAYLOR
46 Assoc Prov Sponsored Pgms .... Dr. Louise WRENSFORD
58 Graduate School Dean .... Dr. Louise WRENSFORD
84 Assoc VP Enrollment Management .... Vacant
45 Asst VP Inst Effect/Research & Plng .... Dr. Kellei SAMUELS
06 Registrar .... Ms. Victoria EILAND
19 Chief of Police .... Mr. John FIELDS
21 Controller .... Ms. Dorothy MARTIN
83 Dean Arts & Humanities .... Dr. Marilyn SPEARMAN
50 Dean College of Business .... Dr. Alicia JACKSON
53 Interim Dean College of Education .... Dr. Thomas THOMPSON
88 Dean Sciences & Health Professions .... Dr. Joyce JOHNSON
41 Director of Athletics .... Dr. Richard WILLIAMS
116 Director Internal Audits .... Ms. Katherine LASTER
88 Director Title III .... Ms. Saundrette MOODY
114 Director Budgets and Contracts .... Mrs. Marion RYANT
109 Director Business Services .... Ms. Lori W. BURNETT
18 Interim Dir Facilities Management .... Mr. Robert LAWSON
15 Interim Dir Human Resources Mgmt .... Ms. Kimberly CARTER
16 Asst Director Human Resources
Mgmt .... Ms. Cassandra ALEXANDER
88 Director Infrastructure Services .... Mr. Lonnie WORMLEY
91 Director Application Services .... Mr. Amitabh SINGH
88 Dir Academic On-Line Instruction .... Ms. LaQuata SUMTER
92 Director Honors Program .... Dr. Melvin SHELTON
104 Director Global Programs .... Dr. Nneka-Nora OSAKWE
26 Director University Communications .... Ms. Landera CARROLL
29 Director Alumni Affairs .... Ms. Sue POLITE-SOLOMON
36 Director Career Services .... Ms. Tracy S. WILLIAMS
88 Director Sports Information .... Mr. Stanley MCCORMICK
35 Interim Dir Student Life .... Ms. Charity STARR
88 Director Judicial Affairs .... Ms. Angelnique JORDAN
38 Director Counseling/Disability
Svcs .... Dr. Stephanie HARRIS-JOLLY
23 Director Student Health Services .... Dr. Vicki PHILLIPS
88 Exec Asst Ctr African American Male .... Mr. Antonio LEROY
07 Interim Director of Admissions .... Mr. Allan CASE
37 Director Financial Aid .... Mrs. Stephanie LAWRENCE
124 Dir of Academic Advising/Retention .... Dr. Ouida MCAFEE
25 Director Sponsored Programs .... Mrs. Melissa WIDNER
88 Director Undergrad Research Ctr .... Dr. Zephyrinus OKONKWO
08 Director Library Services .... Dr. LaVerne MCLAUGHLIN
88 Director Academic Success Unit .... Mrs. Flo HILL
88 Director Quality Enhancement Plan .... Dr. Clancy THOMAS
88 Director Water Policy Center .... Dr. Mark MASTERS
09 Director Institutional Research .... Dr. Frank ARCHER, III
30 Director of Development .... Mr. Andrew FLOYD
40 Director Bookstore .... Ms. Tara JOHNSON
88 Food Service Director .... Mr. Henry WARD

† Part of the University System of Georgia.

Albany Technical College (J)

1704 S Slappey Boulevard, Albany GA 31701-3587

County: Dougherty FICE Identification: 005601
Unit ID: 138682
Telephone: (229) 430-3500 Carnegie Class: Assoc/HVT-Mix Trad/Non
FAX Number: (229) 430-3594 Calendar System: Semester
URL: www.albanytech.edu
Established: 1961 Annual Undergrad Tuition & Fees (In-State): $2,654
Enrollment: 3,331 Coed
Affiliation or Control: State IRS Status: 501(c)3
Highest Offering: Associate Degree
Accreditation: SC, ADNUR, DA, EMT, MAC, RAD, SURGT

01 President .... Dr. Anthony O. PARKER
05 Exec Vice Pres Academic Affairs .... Dr. Tanjula PETTY
32 VP Student Affairs/Enrollment Mgmt .... Dr. Sherry AAKER
46 Vice President Economic Development .... Mr. Matt TRICE
10 Vice Pres Administrative Services .... Ms. Kathy SKATES
45 Vice Pres of Inst Effectiveness .... Dr. Kimberly LEE
55 Vice Pres of Adult Education .... Mrs. Linda COSTON
04 Special Assistant to the President .... Mr. Joe NAJJAR
06 Registrar .... Ms. Suzann CULPEPPER
37 Director of Financial Aid .... Ms. Helen CATT
36 Dir of Job Placement/Career Svcs .... Ms. Judy JIMMERSON
21 Director of Accounting Services .... Ms. Janet HAYES
20 Dean of Academic Affairs .... Dr. Debra JONES
20 Dean of Academic Affairs .... Ms. Joy KNIGHTON
20 Dean of Academic Affairs .... Dr. Emmett GRISWOLD
55 Dean of Evening Administration .... Dr. Ed COOPER
88 Director of Business & Industry Svc .... Vacant
51 Director of Continuing Education .... Ms. Valerie WILLIAMS
09 Director of Institutional Research .... Mr. Joe NAJJAR
26 Exec Dir Public Relations/Marketing .... Ms. Wendy HOWELL
13 Director of Computer/Info Systems .... Mr. Bruce HOPKINS
88 Director of Special Programs .... Vacant
18 Director of Facilities .... Mr. Lavon ACKLEY
56 Dir Spec Proj/Tech in Curriculum .... Ms. Troycia WEBB
35 Director Student Activities .... Dr. Mary RICHARDSON
07 Director of Admissions .... Dr. Alexander EDWARD
15 Director Human Resources .... Ms. Lola EDWARDS

American InterContinental University (A)
6600 Peachtree Dunwoody Road, Atlanta GA 30328
Telephone: (404) 965-6500 Identification: 666723
Accreditation: &NH, ACBSP

† Regional accreditation is carried under the parent institution in Schaumburg, IL.

Andrew College (B)
501 College Street, Cuthbert GA 39840-5550
County: Randolph FICE Identification: 001545
Unit ID: 138761
Telephone: (229) 732-2171 Carnegie Class: Assoc/HT-High Trad
FAX Number: (229) 732-2176 Calendar System: Semester
URL: www.andrewcollege.edu
Established: 1854 Annual Undergrad Tuition & Fees: $15,770
Enrollment: 311 Coed
Affiliation or Control: United Methodist IRS Status: 501(c)3
Highest Offering: Baccalaureate
Accreditation: SC

01 President .... Dr. Linda R. BUCHANAN
05 Int Dean of Academic Affairs .... Dr. Richard MCCALLUM
10 Vice President for Finance .... Mrs. Julie CADLE
111 Vice President for Advancement .... Vacant
84 Vice President for Enrollment .... Mr. Andy GEETER
21 Controller .... Mrs. Lola MOSES
32 Dean of Student Affairs .... Ms. Whitney MOSLEY
41 Athletic Director .... Mr. Blake WILLIAMS
42 Chaplain .... Vacant
08 Director of Library Services .... Ms. Mckenzie RAGAN
40 Director of Bookstore .... Ms. Allyson KING
26 Dir of Communications & Marketing .... Ms. Sheri MICHAELS
06 Registrar .... Ms. Tekesha JACKSON
18 Director of Maintenance .... Mr. Andrew LOWERY
19 Chief of Police .... Mr. Freddie JENKINS
39 Director of Residence Life .... Ms. Lakenya DRAYTON
105 Web Services .... Mr. Brice HERRIN
88 FOCUS Director .... Mrs. Bennie MATTOX
09 Director of Student Success Ctr/IR .... Ms. Julia WILLIAMS
37 Director of Financial Aid .... Mr. Letherio ZEIGLER
15 Director of Human Resources .... Mrs. Jennifer MITCHELL

Argosy University, Atlanta (C)
980 Hammond Drive, Suite 100, Atlanta GA 30328-6162
Telephone: (770) 671-1200 Identification: 666735
Accreditation: &WC, ACBSP, CACREP, CLPSY

† Regional accreditation is carried under the parent institution in Orange, CA.

Armstrong State University (D)
11935 Abercorn Street, Savannah GA 31419-1997
County: Chatham FICE Identification: 001546
Unit ID: 138789
Telephone: (912) 344-2576 Carnegie Class: Masters/L
FAX Number: N/A Calendar System: Semester
URL: www.armstrong.edu
Established: 1935 Annual Undergrad Tuition & Fees (In-State): $5,360
Enrollment: 7,103 Coed
Affiliation or Control: State IRS Status: 501(c)3
Highest Offering: Doctorate
Accreditation: SC, CAEPN, COARC, CS, DMS, HSA, MT, MUS, NMT, NURSE, PH, PTA, RAD, RTT, SP

01 President .... Dr. Linda M. BLEICKEN
05 Provost & VP Academic Affairs .... Dr. Robert SMITH
10 Vice President Business & Finance ... Mr. Christopher CORRIGAN
32 Vice President Student Affairs .... Dr. Georj LEWIS
111 Vice President for Advancement .... Mr. William KELSO
100 Chief of Staff .... Dr. Amy HEASTON
43 University Counsel .... Mr. Lee DAVIS
13 CIO .... Mr. Timothy MOODY
14 Associate CIO .... Ms. Pamela CULBERSON
21 Associate VP Business & Finance .... Vacant
76 Interim Dean Health Professions .... Dr. Anne THOMPSON
53 Dean College of Education .... Vacant
49 Dean College of Liberal Arts .... Dr. Chris CURTIS
72 Dean Science and Technology .... Dr. Delana NIVENS
08 University Librarian .... Mr. Doug FRAZIER
06 Registrar .... Ms. Kathleen PLATT
19 Interim Chief Campus Police .... Ms. Tiffany LAND
41 Athletic Director .... Ms. Lisa SWEANY
07 Director of Admissions .... Ms. Tobe FRIERSON
88 Director Faculty Development .... Dr. Nancy REMLER
37 Director Financial Aid .... Vacant
89 Director First Year Experience .... Mr. Gregory ANDERSON
92 Director Honors Program .... Dr. Jonathan ROBERTS
36 Director of Career Services .... Mr. Glenn GIBNEY
09 Director Institutional Research .... Ms. Laura J. MILLS
85 Director of Intl Education .... Dr. Dorothee MERTZ-WEIGEL
104 Asst Director International Educ .... Dr. Kristin KASTING
35 Interim Dean of Students .... Mr. Andrew DIES
12 Director Liberty Center .... Ms. Dorothy KEMPSON
15 Interim Director of Human Resources .... Ms. Willette STEVENS
18 Director Facility Services .... Ms. Katie TWINING
38 Director Counseling Services .... Ms. Jeanne MCGOWAN
39 Director Housing & Residence Life .... Mr. Nick SHRADER
28 Director Multicultural Affairs .... Ms. Nashia WHITTENBURG
35 Assistant Dean of Students .... Vacant
29 Director Alumni Development .... Ms. Cheryl ANDERSON
30 Assistant Vice President of Develop .... Ms. Julie GERBSCH
26 Director Marketing & Communications .... Dr. Allison HERSH
105 Manager of Web Communications .... Ms. Janice STANFORD
04 Executive Asst to President .... Ms. Trina SMITH
108 Director Assessment .... Ms. Angeles EAMES
22 Dir Affirmative Action/EEO .... Ms. Deidra DENNIE
25 Int Dir Grants & Sponsored Research .... Dr. Brent FESKE
86 Director Government Relations .... Col. Peter HOFFMAN

† Part of the University System of Georgia.

The Art Institute of Atlanta (E)
6600 Peachtree Dunwoody Road, Atlanta GA 30328-1635
County: Fulton FICE Identification: 009270
Unit ID: 138813
Telephone: (770) 394-8300 Carnegie Class: Spec-4-yr-Arts
FAX Number: (770) 394-0008 Calendar System: Quarter
URL: www.artinstitutes.edu/atlanta/
Established: 1949 Annual Undergrad Tuition & Fees: $17,592
Enrollment: 2,249 Coed
Affiliation or Control: Proprietary IRS Status: Proprietary
Highest Offering: Baccalaureate
Accreditation: #SC, ACFEI, CIDA

01 President .... Mr. Newton MYVETT
05 Provost/Dean of Academic Affairs .... Dr. Linda WOOD
10 Director of Financial Services .... Ms. Audry SANBDIMANIE
07 Senior Director of Admissions .... Ms. Phyllis HORTON-MACK
32 Dean of Student Affairs .... Mr. Nadraqua DAWES
37 Director of Student Financial Svcs .Ms. Precious PRENDERGAST
09 Dir of Inst Effectiveness/Research .... Vacant
08 Librarian .... Mr. Robert SARWARK
06 Registrar .... Ms. Sheldon WOODS
36 Director of Career Services .... Mr. Enrique (Leo) ORTIZ
26 Director of Campus Relations .... Ms. Vivian LETT
18 Director of Facilities .... Ms. Stacey CARMICHAEL
04 Exec Assistant to the President .... Ms. Sophia PITTMAN
15 Human Resources Manager .... Ms. Mary HARRIEL

Ashworth College (F)
6625 The Corners Parkway, Suite 500,
Norcross GA 30092-3406
County: Gwinnett Identification: 666106
Telephone: (770) 729-8400 Carnegie Class: Not Classified
FAX Number: (770) 729-9296 Calendar System: Semester
URL: www.ashworthcollege.edu
Established: 2000 Annual Undergrad Tuition & Fees: N/A
Enrollment: N/A Coed
Affiliation or Control: Proprietary IRS Status: Proprietary
Highest Offering: Master's
Accreditation: DEAC

01 President .... Mr. Robert KLAPPER
05 Chief Academic Officer .... Mr. William KAKISH

Athens College of Ministry (G)
PO Box 7593, Athens GA 30604
County: Clarke Identification: 667306
Telephone: (706) 769-1472 Carnegie Class: Not Classified
FAX Number: (706) 769-1479 Calendar System: Semester
URL: www.acmin.org
Established: 2012 Annual Undergrad Tuition & Fees: N/A
Enrollment: N/A Coed
Affiliation or Control: Interdenominational IRS Status: 501(c)3
Highest Offering: Master's
Accreditation: @TRACS

01 President .... Dr. Marcia WILBUR
05 Chief Academic Officer .... Dr. Raymond MORRIS
32 Director of Student Affairs .... Mr. Paul COOKE

Athens Technical College (H)
800 US Highway 29 N, Athens GA 30601-1500
County: Clarke FICE Identification: 005600
Unit ID: 246813
Telephone: (706) 355-5000 Carnegie Class: Assoc/HVT-Mix Trad/Non
FAX Number: (706) 369-5753 Calendar System: Semester
URL: www.athenstech.edu
Established: 1958 Annual Undergrad Tuition & Fees (In-State): $2,794
Enrollment: 4,199 Coed
Affiliation or Control: State IRS Status: 501(c)3
Highest Offering: Associate Degree
Accreditation: SC, ACBSP, ADNUR, CAHIIM, DA, DH, EMT, PTAA, RAD, SURGT

01 President .... Dr. Andrea D. DANIEL
05 Vice President Academic Affairs .... Ms. Caroline ANGELO
32 Vice President Student Affairs .... Ms. Jennifer BENSON
10 Vice Pres Administrative Services .... Ms. Kathryn S. THOMAS
45 Vice President Economic Development .... Dr. Ilka MCCONNELL
13 Vice Pres Information Technology .... Mr. Dennis ASHWORTH
88 Vice President Adult Education .... Ms. Stephanie G. BENSON
72 Dean Technology/Engineering/Manufac .... Mr. James PRICE
76 Dean Life Sciences/Public Safety .... Mr. Glenn HENRY
50 Dean Business and Education .... Mr. Nick CHAPMAN
06 Director Registration & Records .... Ms. Kala MCNAIR
07 Director Admissions .... Ms. Justin MCCALLA
08 Director Library Services .... Ms. Carol STANLEY
36 Director Student Support/Career Dev .... Ms. Keli FEWOX
37 Director Financial Aid .... Mr. Dustin MCDANIEL
12 Exec Dir Greene & Walton Co Campus .... Mr. Lenzy REID, III
35 Student Activities Director .... Mr. Alvie COES
15 Director Human Resources .... Ms. Becky BURTON
18 Facilities Director .... Mr. Jim WALTER
30 Director Institutional Advancement .... Ms. Jennifer GRIFFETH
21 Director of Accounting .... Mr. Ryan STANLEY
19 Chief of Police .... Mr. John GAISSERT
26 Director Public Relations .... Mr. Antoine BOYNTON
108 Director Institutional Effectivenes .... Dr. Bobbi JOHNSTONE
106 Dean General Ed and Online Learning .... Dr. Mary Clare DIGIACOMO

Atlanta Metropolitan State College (I)
1630 Metropolitan Parkway, SW, Atlanta GA 30310-4498
County: Fulton FICE Identification: 012165
Unit ID: 138901
Telephone: (404) 756-4000 Carnegie Class: Bac/Assoc-Assoc Dom
FAX Number: (404) 756-4460 Calendar System: Semester
URL: www.atlm.edu
Established: 1974 Annual Undergrad Tuition & Fees (In-State): $3,250
Enrollment: 3,129 Coed
Affiliation or Control: State IRS Status: 501(c)3
Highest Offering: Baccalaureate
Accreditation: SC, ACBSP

01 President .... Dr. Gary A. MCGAHA, SR.
05 Vice Pres Academic Affairs .... Dr. Michael HEARD
10 Vice President Fiscal Affairs .... Mr. Kwabena BOAKYE
32 Vice President Student Affairs .... Dr. Maria LUMPKIN
111 Vice Pres Institutional Advancement .... Vacant
21 Associate Financial/BusinessOfficer .... Ms. Arisa BURGEST
50 Dean Div Business/Computer Sci .... Dr. Vincent MANGUM
79 Dean Div Humanities/Fine Arts .... Dr. Frank JOHNSON
81 Dean Div of Sci/Math/Health Profess .... Dr. Bryan MITCHELL
83 Dean Div of Social Sciences .... Dr. Vance GRAY
06 Dir Enrollment Services/Registrar .... Mrs. Candace PERRY
15 Director of Human Resources .... Ms. Regina Ray SIMMONS
08 Director of the Library .... Mr. Robert QUARLES
35 Director of Student Activities .... Ms. Iris SHANKLIN
37 Director of Financial Aid .... Mrs. Anna ENGLISH
38 Director Counseling/Disability Svcs .... Ms. Dorothy WILLIAMS
13 Chief Information/Tech Officer .... Mr. Antonio TRAVIS
108 Director Inst Effectiveness .... Dr. Mark CUNNINGHAM
19 Director of Campus Safety .... Mr. Antonio LONG
35 Dir of Student Outreach & Access .... Mr. Stephen WOODALL
18 Dir Plant Operations/Facilities .... Mr. Keith WILLIAMS
40 Bookstore Manager .... Ms. Gloria MCCLAIN
26 Media Relations Director/Marketing .... Ms. Sheila TENNEY
41 Athletic Director .... Mr. Robert PRICHETT

† Part of the University System of Georgia.

Atlanta Technical College (J)
1560 Metropolitan Parkway, SW, Atlanta GA 30310-4446
County: Fulton FICE Identification: 008543
Unit ID: 138840
Telephone: (404) 225-4400 Carnegie Class: Assoc/HVT-Mix Trad/Non
FAX Number: (404) 225-4445 Calendar System: Semester
URL: www.atlantatech.edu
Established: 1967 Annual Undergrad Tuition & Fees (In-State): $2,756
Enrollment: 3,789 Coed
Affiliation or Control: State IRS Status: 501(c)3
Highest Offering: Associate Degree
Accreditation: SC, ACFEI, CAHIIM, DA, DH, EMT, MAC, PTAA, RAD, SURGT

01 President .... Dr. Alvetta P. THOMAS
05 Exec VP Academic & Student Affairs .... Dr. Caroline ANGELO
11 Vice Pres Administrative Services .... Ms. Teresa BROWN
30 Vice President Economic Development .... Ms. Yulonda DARDEN-BEAUFORD
04 Assistant to the President .... Dr. Joni WILLIAMS
26 Director Communications & Marketing .... Ms. Lauretta HANNON
37 Director of Financial Aid .... Mr. LaMario PRIMAS
07 Director of Admissions .... Mr. Vory BILLUPS
88 Dean Industrial and Transportation .... Ian TOPPEN
51 Director of Continuing Education .... Curtis HALTON
36 Director Career Placement .... Mr. Michael BURNSIDE
50 Dean Business and Public Services .... Ms. Phoebe COQUEREL
88 Dean Health and Public Safety .... Katrina WALKER
06 Registrar .... Ms. Niya EADY
15 Director Human Resources .... Ms. Marilyn SMITH-ROBINSON
18 Director of Facilities .... Ms. Marlon ELLIS
09 Director of Institutional Research .... Vacant
49 Dean Arts and Sciences .... Ms. Sonya MCCOY-WILSON
08 Director of Library Services .... Ms. Tosha BUSSEY
106 AVP of Evening/Weekend/Online .... Mr. Shawn ADAMS
13 Director of Information Technology .... Vacant
19 AVP of Operations .... Mr. Fred HAMMETT
25 Director of Sponsored Programs .... Ms. Faye EVANS
96 Procurement Officer .... Ms. Ella SIZEMORE

Atlanta's John Marshall Law School (K)
1422 West Peachtree Street NW, Atlanta GA 30309
County: Fulton FICE Identification: 031733
Unit ID: 138929
Telephone: (678) 916-2600 Carnegie Class: Spec-4-yr-Law

FAX Number: (404) 873-3802 Calendar System: Semester
URL: www.johnmarshall.edu
Established: 1933 Annual Graduate Tuition & Fees: N/A
Enrollment: 522 Coed
Affiliation or Control: Proprietary IRS Status: Proprietary
Highest Offering: First Professional Degree; No Undergraduates
Accreditation: LAW

01 Dean/CEO Mr. Malcolm L. MORRIS
32 Assoc Dean of Students Ms. Sheryl E. HARRISON-MERCER
10 Assoc Dean of Finance Mr. Allan BREZEL
06 Registrar Ms. Cheryl FEREBEE
26 Asst Dir Marketing & Communications Ms. Hilary WALDO
07 Director of Admissions Mrs. Rebecca MILTER
37 Director of Financial Aid Mr. Montre EVERETT
29 Alumni Director Mrs. Erika S. MURRAY
36 Asst Dean of Career Development Mrs. Ivonne BETANCOURT
05 Assoc Dean for Academic Program Mr. Jace GATEWOOD
20 Assoc Dean of Academic Admin Ms. Judith BARGER
08 Director of Law Library Mr. Michael LYNCH
58 Assoc Dean of Graduate Programs Mr. Jace GATEWOOD
04 Executive Assistant to the Dean/CEO Mrs. Erika S. MURRAY

Augusta Technical College (A)

3200 Augusta Tech Drive, Augusta GA 30906-3399
County: Richmond FICE Identification: 005599
Unit ID: 138956
Telephone: (706) 771-4000 Carnegie Class: Assoc/HVT-High Trad
FAX Number: (706) 771-4016 Calendar System: Semester
URL: www.augustatech.edu
Established: 1961 Annual Undergrad Tuition & Fees (In-District): $2,704
Enrollment: 4,490 Coed
Affiliation or Control: State/Local IRS Status: 501(c)3
Highest Offering: Associate Degree
Accreditation: SC, COARC, CVT, DA, ENGT, MAC, OTA, PNUR, RAD, SURGT

01 President Mr. Terry D. ELAM
05 Sr Vice President Academic Affairs Dr. C. Rick HALL
10 Vice Pres Administrative Services Ms. Sheila M. HILL
32 Vice Pres Student Affairs Dr. Nichole KENNEDY
88 Vice President Economic Development Dr. Lisa PALMER
12 Dean/Director Waynesboro Campus Mr. Greg COURSEY
37 Director Financial Aid Ms. Beverly SMYRE HINES
07 Director Admissions Ms. Christine BALL
111 Director Institutional Advancement Ms. Beverly PELTIER
06 Interim Registrar Mr. Najhee JACKSON
108 Sr Vice Pres Inst Effectiveness Dr. Melissa F. ALSTON
21 Director Accounting Ms. Sherrick L. JOHNSON
26 Dir Marketing/Public Relations Ms. Kimberly HOLDEN
15 Director Human Resources Ms. Shannon PATTERSON
12 Dean Director Thomson Campus Ms. Julie LANGHAM
84 Enrollment Manager Ms. Jeanette LOWE
36 Director Career Services Ms. Donna WENDT
88 High School Coordinator Mrs. Evett DAVIS
76 Dean Allied Health Science Dr. Gwen TAYLOR
50 Dean Business/Public Safety Ms. Elizabeth A. JULIAN
97 Dean Gen Educ & Learning Support Mr. John RICHARDSON
54 Dean Industrial & Engineering Tech Mr. James PRICE
08 Head Librarian Vacant
106 Dir Online Education/E-learning Mrs. Tammy O'BRIEN
18 Chief Facilities/Physical Plant Mr. Garry STEPHENS
19 Director Security/Safety Mr. Mike ANCHOR
04 Administrative Asst to President Mrs. Charlene LEWIS
13 Chief Info Technology Officer (CIO) Mr. Pete WILKINSON

Augusta University (B)

1120 Fifteenth Street, Augusta GA 30912-0004
County: Richmond FICE Identification: 001579
Unit ID: 482149
Telephone: (706) 721-0211 Carnegie Class: DU-Higher
FAX Number: N/A Calendar System: Semester
URL: www.augusta.edu
Established: 1828 Annual Undergrad Tuition & Fees (In-State): $8,282
Enrollment: 8,333 Coed
Affiliation or Control: State IRS Status: 501(c)3
Highest Offering: Doctorate
Accreditation: SC, ANEST, ARCPA, ART, CACREP, CAEPN, CAHIIM, COARC, DENT, DH, DIETI, EMT, IPSY, MED, MIL, MT, MUS, NMT, NURSE, OT, PH, PTA, RTT, SPAA, SW

01 President Dr. Brooks A. KEEL
05 Exec VP for Acad Affairs/Provost Dr. Gretchen CAUGHMAN
10 Chief Business Ofcr/EVP Admin & Fin Mr. Anthony E. WAGNER
26 EVP Strategic Comm/Chf Mrktng Ofcr Ms. Karla LEEPER
31 Exec VP External Rel/Chief of Staff Mr. Russell KEEN
43 General Counsel Mr. Chris MELCHER
17 EVP Medical Affairs/Dean Medicine Dr. David HESS
86 EVP Stratregic Partnrshps/Econ Dev Mr. W. Michael SHAFFER
46 Senior Vice President for Research Dr. Michael DIAMOND
30 Sr VP Advance/Cmty Relations/CDO Vacant
15 Enterprise VP Human Resources Ms. Susan A. NORTON
20 VP Academic & Faculty Affairs Dr. Kathy BROWDER
28 VP Acad Plng/Strategic Initiative Vacant
32 Interim VP Enrollment/Student Affs Dr. Scott WALLACE
09 VP Institutional Effectiveness Mrs. Beth P. BRIGDON
18 VP Facilities Service Mr. Philip HOWARD
27 VP Communications & Marketing Mr. Jack EVANS
21 Vice Pres Finance Mr. Lee FRUITTICHER
58 Dean The Graduate School Dr. Mitchell WATSKY
76 Int Dean College of Allied Health Dr. Lester PRETLOW
52 Dean College of Dental Med Dr. Carol LEFEBVRE
66 Dean College of Nursing Dr. Lucy N. MARION
50 Dean Hull College of Business Dr. Richard M. FRANZA
49 Dean College of Arts/Hum/Soc Sci Dr. Elna C. GREEN
53 Dean College of Education Dr. Zach KELEHEAR
81 Int Dean College of Science & Math Dr. John SUTHERLAND
88 Chief Audit Officer Mr. Clay SPROUSE
88 Chief Integrity Officer Mr. James RUSH, JR.
13 VP Information Technology/CIO Mr. Charles ENICKS
88 Interim Director Cancer Center Dr. John K. COWELL
06 Registrar Ms. Heather B. METRESS
88 Bursar Ms. Beth WELSH
41 Director of Athletics Mr. Clint BRYANT
19 Director of Public Safety Chief James LYON
08 Director of Libraries Dr. Brenda SEAGO
96 Senior Manager Supply Management Mr. Greg WOODLIEF
109 Director of Auxiliary Services Mr. Karl MUNSCHY
37 Director of Financial Aid Ms. Debra TURNER
07 Director of Admissions Ms. Maura FLASCHNER
04 Exec Admin Asst to President Mrs. Jacqueline B. STEPHENS
104 Director Study Abroad Ms. Maria DARLEY
22 Dir Affirmative Action/EEO Mr. Glenn POWELL
29 Director Alumni Affairs Ms. Kim KOSS
36 Director Career Services Ms. Julie GOLEY
38 Director Student Counseling Dr. Mark F. PATISHNOCK
39 Director Student Housing Dr. Heather SCHNELLER
84 Asst VP Enrollment Services Mr. David BARRON

† Part of the University System of Georgia.

Bainbridge State College (C)

2500 E Shotwell Street, PO Box 990, Bainbridge GA 39818-0990
County: Decatur FICE Identification: 011074
Unit ID: 139010
Telephone: (229) 243-6000 Carnegie Class: Assoc/HVT-High Trad
FAX Number: (229) 248-2623 Calendar System: Semester
URL: www.bainbridge.edu
Established: 1970 Annual Undergrad Tuition & Fees (In-State): $3,227
Enrollment: 2,401 Coed
Affiliation or Control: State IRS Status: 501(c)3
Highest Offering: Baccalaureate
Accreditation: SC, ADNUR

01 Interim President Dr. Stuart RAYFIELD
05 Vice Pres Academic & Student Affs Dr. Rodney CARR
10 Interim VP of Business & Operations Mr. Justin JANNEY
49 Dean School of Arts & Sciences Ms. Joann SIMPSON
107 Int Dean Sch Hlth Sci/Profess Stds Mr. Jason RUBENBAUER
32 Associate Dean of Student Affairs Mr. Spencer STEWART
08 Director Library Ms. Michelle BARSOM
26 Chief Public Relations Officer Vacant
37 Interim Director of Financial Aid Ms. Haley HOOKS
21 Interim Comptroller Ms. Leslie JUDKINS
18 Director of Plant Operations Mr. Wayne QUINN
13 Chief Information Officer Mr. Scott DUNN
35 Assistant Dean of Student Affairs Mr. Sam MAYHEW
111 Exec Director of Inst Advancement Ms. Lauren HARRELL
07 Director of Admissions Ms. Melanie CLEVELAND
19 Director of Public Safety Mr. James SPOONER
06 Assistant Registrar Mr. Robert THOMPSON

† Part of the University System of Georgia.

Berry College (D)

2277 Martha Berry Highway, NW, Mount Berry GA 30149
County: Floyd FICE Identification: 001554
Unit ID: 139144
Telephone: (706) 232-5374 Carnegie Class: Masters/S
FAX Number: (706) 236-2238 Calendar System: Semester
URL: www.berry.edu
Established: 1902 Annual Undergrad Tuition & Fees: $33,556
Enrollment: 2,245 Coed
Affiliation or Control: Independent Non-Profit IRS Status: 501(c)3
Highest Offering: Beyond Master's But Less Than Doctorate
Accreditation: SC, MUS, NURSE

01 President Dr. Stephen R. BRIGGS
05 Provost Dr. Mary K. BOYD
10 Vice President Finance Mr. Brian I. ERB
32 VP Student Affairs and Enrollment Ms. Debbie HEIDA
111 Vice Pres Institutional Advancement Ms. Bettyann O'NEILL
84 VP of Enrollment Management Dr. Andrew BRESSETTE
26 VP Marketing & Communications Ms. Nancy REWIS
100 Chief of Staff Dr. Gary WATERS
42 Chaplain Rev. Jonathan HUGGINS
35 Assoc Vice Pres Student Affairs Ms. Lindsey TAYLOR
11 Assistant Provost of Administration Dr. Thomas D. KENNEDY
50 Dean Campbell School of Business Dr. Joyce HEAMES
53 Dean Charter School of Education Dr. Jackie MCDOWELL
79 Dean School Humanities/Arts/Soc Sci Dr. Thomas D. KENNEDY
66 Director of Nursing Dr. Pam DUNAGAN
81 Dean School of Math/Nat Sci Dr. Gary BRETON
78 Dean Stdnt Work/Experiential Lrng Mr. Rufus MASSEY
20 Dean Academic Services Dr. David SLADE
07 Asst Vice Pres Admissions Mr. Brett E. KENNEDY
30 Asst VP Campaign/Leadership Giving Mr. Scott BREITHAUPT
08 Director of the Library Ms. Sherre Lee HARRINGTON
29 Director of Alumni Affairs Ms. Jennifer SCHAKNOWSKI
13 Chief Information Officer Ms. Penny EVANS-PLANTS
38 Director of Counseling Center Dr. J. Marshall JENKINS
37 Director of Financial Aid Ms. Donna CHILDRES
36 Director of Career Center Mrs. Sue TARPLEY
09 Dir Institutional Research Dr. Bryce DURBIN
46 Dir Research & Sponsored Programs Mrs. Donna DAVIN
18 Director Physical Plant Mr. Mark HOPKINS
89 Director First Year Experience Mrs. Katherine POWELL
92 Co-Director Honors Program Dr. Todd TIMBERLAKE
92 Co-Director Honors Program Dr. Lauren HELLER
94 Director Women's Studies Dr. Susan CONRADSEN
96 Director Purchasing Mr. Brad BARRIS
85 Director International Programs Mr. Christopher BORDA
15 Director Human Resources Mr. Wayne PHIPPS
43 Director of Legal Services Mr. Danny PRICE
28 Director of Multicultural Affairs Dr. Tasha TOY
06 Registrar Dr. Bryce DURBIN
41 Director of Athletics Mr. Todd BROOKS
121 Director of Academic Success Center Ms. Wilma MAYNARD
44 Dir of Annual Giv & Specialty Pgms Ms. Sharma TURNER

Beulah Heights University (E)

892 Berne Street, SE, PO Box 18145, Atlanta GA 30316-1873
County: Fulton FICE Identification: 030763
Unit ID: 139153
Telephone: (404) 627-2681 Carnegie Class: Spec-4-yr-Faith
FAX Number: (404) 627-0702 Calendar System: Semester
URL: www.beulah.edu
Established: 1918 Annual Undergrad Tuition & Fees: $9,510
Enrollment: 701 Coed
Affiliation or Control: Other Protestant IRS Status: 501(c)3
Highest Offering: Doctorate
Accreditation: BI, TRACS

01 President Dr. Benson M. KARANJA
04 Administrative Asst to President Ms. Kimberly WIGLEY
11 Vice Pres Operations Mr. Peter KARANJA
05 Vice Pres/Dean Academic Affairs Dr. Mark HARDGROVE
106 Dean of Distance Education Dr. Dennis C. MALONE
06 University Registrar Ms. Georgia SKINNER
10 Director of Finance/Comptroller Ms. Bernadette ASHER
37 Director of Financial Aid Ms. Tamika TAYLOR
07 Director of Admissions Ms. Jasmine DOUGLAS
88 Vice Pres Asian Affairs Dr. John KIM
73 Chair Religious Studies Dr. Rodney JACKSON
26 Director of Marketing Vacant
08 Director of Library Services Mr. Pradeep K. DAS
15 Director Personnel Services (HR) Ms. Trish STATON
42 Dean of Chapel Rev. Billy JOHNSON

Brenau University (F)

500 Washington Street, SE, Gainesville GA 30501-3668
County: Hall FICE Identification: 001556
Unit ID: 139199
Telephone: (770) 534-6299 Carnegie Class: Masters/L
FAX Number: (770) 534-6114 Calendar System: Semester
URL: www.brenau.edu
Established: 1878 Annual Undergrad Tuition & Fees: $27,152
Enrollment: 2,883 Coed
Affiliation or Control: Independent Non-Profit IRS Status: 501(c)3
Highest Offering: Doctorate
Accreditation: SC, ACBSP, CAEPN, CIDA, NURSE, OT, @PTA

01 President Dr. Ed L. SCHRADER
03 Executive VP/CFO Dr. David L. BARNETT
05 Provost & VP For Academic Affairs Dr. Jim ECK
100 Chief of Staff Ms. Jody Y. WALL
10 Vice President Financial Services Mr. Toby R. HINTON
84 Vice Pres Enrollment Management Mr. Ray TATUM
111 Vice Pres External Relations Mr. J. Matthew THOMAS
13 Vice Pres Information Technology Mr. Chip L. ANDREWS
26 VP Communications/Publications Mr. David MORRISON
32 VP for Student Services Dr. Amanda LAMMERS
09 Director of Research & Planning Dr. Robert E. CUTTINO
37 Assoc VP & Dir Financial Aid Ms. Pam J. BARRETT
21 Asst VP Financial Svcs/Controller Ms. Holly REYNOLDS
15 Director of Human Resources Ms. Kelley L. MADDOX
36 Director of Career Services Mr. George BAGEL
24 Director of Learning Center Dr. Vince J. YAMILKOSKI
41 Athletic Director Mr. Mike LOCHSTAMPFOR
53 Dean College of Education Dr. Eugene WILLIAMS
76 Dean College of Health Sciences Dr. Gale H. STARICH
50 Dean College Business/Mass Comm Dr. Suzanne ERICKSON
79 Dean College of Fine Arts & Human Dr. Andrea C. BIRCH
08 Dean of Library Svcs & SACS Liaison Ms. Marlene GIGUERE
07 Executive Director for Admissions Mr. Nathan R. GOSS
06 Registrar & Dir of Student Records Ms. Barbara WILSON
29 Exec Director Alumni Ms. Ashley CARTER
19 Director Campus Safety & Security Ms. Paula DAMPIER
104 Director Study Abroad Ms. Jordan ANDERSON

Brewton-Parker College (G)

201 David-Eliza Fountain Circle, Mount Vernon GA 30445-0197
County: Montgomery FICE Identification: 001557
Unit ID: 139205
Telephone: (912) 583-2241 Carnegie Class: Bac-Diverse
FAX Number: (912) 583-4498 Calendar System: Semester
URL: www.bpc.edu
Established: 1904 Annual Undergrad Tuition & Fees: $16,960
Enrollment: 616 Coed

Affiliation or Control: Baptist IRS Status: 501(c)3
Highest Offering: Baccalaureate
Accreditation: SC

01 President ... Dr. Steven F. ECHOLS
04 Executive Asst to President ... Ms. Laura HAY
03 Exec Vice Pres & Dir of Advancement ... Mr. Ray SULLIVAN
43 General Counsel ... Mr. Thomas EVERETT
10 Chief Financial Officer ... Dr. Nicole SHEPARD
05 Provost ... Dr. Robert M. BRIAN
121 Assoc Provost Student Engagement ... Dr. Beverly ROBINSON
32 VP of Student Services and Athletic ... Mr. Daniel PREVETT
07 VP of Enrollment Services ... Mr. Chris DOOLEY
11 Director of Operations ... Mr. Ted TOWNS
15 Director Human Resources ... Ms. Nikki BELL
37 Director of Financial Aid ... Ms. Loretta WATSON
07 Director of Admissions ... Ms. Michelle HARTER
38 Dir Counseling Services ... Mr. Thadeus HOLLOWAY
08 Librarian ... Mr. Daryl FLETCHER
06 Registrar ... Ms. Elizabeth ADAMS
09 Dir of IER ... Dr. Angie BAUMAN
26 Dir Public Relations and Marketing ... Vacant
88 Textbook Coordinator ... Ms. Lynn ADDISON
29 Director Alumni Relations ... Ms. Kim LAJINESS
22 Dir Affirmative Action/EEO ... Mr. Forrest RICH
50 Chair Business and Communication ... Dr. James WEST
53 Co-Chair Education and Behav Sci ... Dr. Angie BAUMAN
53 Co-Chair Education and Behav Sci ... Dr. Justin RUSSELL
79 Chair Christian Studies Humanities ... Dr. Grant LILFORD
81 Chair Math and Natural Sci ... Dr. Helene PETERS
42 Campus Pastor ... Mr. Steve EDWARDS
88 Director of Baptist Col Ministry ... Mr. Madison HERRIN

Brown College of Court Reporting (A)

1100 Spring Street NW, Suite 101, Atlanta GA 30309
County: Fulton FICE Identification: 020609
Unit ID: 139214
Telephone: (404) 876-1227 Carnegie Class: Not Classified
FAX Number: (404) 876-4415 Calendar System: Quarter
URL: www.bccr.edu
Established: 1972 Annual Undergrad Tuition & Fees: $12,900
Enrollment: 226 Coed
Affiliation or Control: Proprietary IRS Status: Proprietary
Highest Offering: Associate Degree
Accreditation: COE

01 President ... Russell FREEMAN
03 Director ... Marita CAREY
07 Director of Admissions ... Carlette JENNINGS
05 Director of Education ... Julie MORRIS
06 Registrar ... Lisa LOWE

Cambridge Institute of Allied Health & Technology (B)

5673 Peachtree Dunwoody Rd, Ste 100, Atlanta GA 30342
Telephone: (404) 255-4500 Identification: 770938
Accreditation: ABHES, DMS

† Branch campus of Cambridge Institute of Allied Health and Technology, Delray Beach, FL.

Carver College (C)

3870 Cascade Road SW, Atlanta GA 30331-2184
County: Fulton FICE Identification: 036353
Unit ID: 139287
Telephone: (404) 527-4520 Carnegie Class: Spec-4-yr-Faith
FAX Number: (404) 527-4524 Calendar System: Semester
URL: www.carver.edu
Established: 1943 Annual Undergrad Tuition & Fees: $10,460
Enrollment: 120 Coed
Affiliation or Control: Independent Non-Profit IRS Status: 501(c)3
Highest Offering: Baccalaureate
Accreditation: #BI

01 President and CEO ... Mr. Robert W. CRUMMIE
05 Academic Dean ... Dr. Benjamin JACKS
30 Director of Advancement ... Ms. Linda BROWN
32 Dean of Students ... Mr. David PATRICK
84 Dir Enrollment Management ... Mrs. Margarie PATRICK
06 Registrar ... Mrs. Olive JACKS
09 Dir Institutional Effectiveness ... Ms. Oronda M. SMITH
29 Director Alumni Affairs ... Ms. Cathy REYNOLDS
42 Director of Chapel Services ... Mr. David PATRICK
73 Director of Bible/Theology Studies ... Dr. Brien MARTIN
97 Director of General Studies ... Mrs. Amber HAMILTON BOGLIN
107 Director of Professional Studies ... Dr. John A. JENKINS
08 Director of Library Services ... Ms. Debra A. MILLIGAN
83 Director of Psychology Studies ... Ms. Patricia WESLEY BROWN
50 Director of Business Studies ... Dr. Robert BARNES
18 Director of Physical Plant ... Mr. Herman PATE
41 Athletic Director ... Mr. Martin CARTER
40 Director of Bookstore ... Vacant
04 Assistant to the President ... Ms. Iverna SHELTON
19 Chief of Police ... Capt. Ray COLLINS
26 Public Relations/Sports Information ... Mr. Augustus HOWARD

Central Georgia Technical College (D)

3300 Macon Tech Drive, Macon GA 31206
County: Bibb FICE Identification: 005763
Unit ID: 140304
Telephone: (478) 757-3400 Carnegie Class: Not Classified
FAX Number: (478) 757-3454 Calendar System: Quarter
URL: www.centralgatech.edu
Established: 1966 Annual Undergrad Tuition & Fees (In-State): N/A
Enrollment: N/A Coed
Affiliation or Control: State IRS Status: 501(c)3
Highest Offering: Associate Degree
Accreditation: SC, CVT, DH, EMT, MLTAD, POLYT, RAD

01 President ... Dr. Ivan ALLEN
05 Vice President Academic Affairs ... Dr. Amy HOLLOWAY
10 Vice President Admin/Fin Svcs ... Ms. Michelle SINIARD
32 Vice President Student Affairs ... Mr. Craig JACKSON
31 Vice President Economic Development ... Ms. Andrea GRINER
11 AVP Facilities/Ancillary Svcs ... Mr. Jimmy FAIRCLOTH
13 Chief Information Officer ... Mr. Brian SNELGROVE
12 VP for Satellite Operations ... Ms. Dana DAVIS
35 Dean of Student Affairs ... Vacant
06 Registrar ... Ms. Sonja JENKINS
30 Asst VP for Advancement ... Ms. Tonya MCCLURE
08 Director Library & Media Services ... Mr. Neil MCARTHUR
15 Executive Director Human Resources ... Ms. Carol JONES
18 Facilities Director ... Mr. Robert DOMINY
51 Director of Continuing Education ... Mr. Clay TEAGUE

Central Georgia Technical College (E)

80 Cohen Walker Drive, Warner Robins GA 31088-2729
County: Houston FICE Identification: 025086
Unit ID: 483045
Telephone: (478) 988-6800 Carnegie Class: Not Classified
FAX Number: (478) 988-6813 Calendar System: Quarter
URL: www.centralgatech.edu
Established: 1973 Annual Undergrad Tuition & Fees (In-State): $2,714
Enrollment: 7,832 Coed
Affiliation or Control: State IRS Status: 501(c)3
Highest Offering: Associate Degree
Accreditation: SC, DH, RAD, SURGT

01 President ... Dr. Ivan H. ALLEN
03 Executive Vice President ... Mr. Jeffrey SCRUGGS
05 Vice President for Academic Affairs ... Dr. Amy L. HOLLOWAY
32 Vice President for Student Affairs ... Mr. Craig JACKSON
09 VP Economic Development ... Ms. Andrea GRINER
11 VP Administrative Services ... Mrs. Michelle SINIARD
55 Vice President for Adult Education ... Ms. Brenda L. BROWN
26 Asst VP Enrol Svcs/Marketing/PR ... Mrs. Janet H. KELLY
30 Asst VP of Advancement ... Ms. Tonya L. MCCLURE
84 Director of Enrollment Services ... Ms. Brandi MITCHEN
37 Director of Financial Aid ... Ms. Shirley GLOVER
06 Registrar ... Ms. Sonja JENKINS
08 Exec Director of Library Services ... Mr. Neil MCARTHUR
15 Exec Director of Human Resources ... Ms. Carol F. JONES
18 Asst VP Facilities/Ancillary Svcs ... Mr. Jimmy FAIRCLOTH

Chamberlain University-Atlanta (F)

5775 Peachtree-Dunwoody Rd NE,A100, Atlanta GA 30342
Telephone: (404) 250-8500 Identification: 770504
Accreditation: &NH, NURSE

† Branch campus of Chamberlain University-Addison, Addison, IL

Chattahoochee Technical College (G)

980 South Cobb Drive, Marietta GA 30060
County: Cobb FICE Identification: 030290
Unit ID: 140331
Telephone: (770) 528-4545 Carnegie Class: Assoc/HVT-Mix Trad/Non
FAX Number: (770) 975-4126 Calendar System: Quarter
URL: www.chattahoocheetech.edu
Established: 1981 Annual Undergrad Tuition & Fees (In-State): $2,746
Enrollment: 9,817 Coed
Affiliation or Control: State IRS Status: 501(c)3
Highest Offering: Associate Degree
Accreditation: SC, ACFEI, ADNUR, EMT, MAC, MLTAD, OTA, PTAA, RAD, SURGT

01 President ... Dr. Ron NEWCOMB
04 Administrative Asst to President ... Ms. Tammy COLLUM
05 Vice President for Academics ... Dr. Jason TANNER
11 Vice Pres for Administrative Svcs ... Ms. Catrice HUFSTETLER
13 VP Student Affairs/Technology ... Dr. Trina BOTELER
32 VP Student Affairs/External Affairs ... Ms. Jennifer NELSON
18 Vice President for Facilities ... Mr. David SIMMONS
15 Vice President Human Resources ... Mr. Ron PRICE
26 Exec Dir External Affs/Brd Liaison ... Ms. Jennifer NELSON

Clark Atlanta University (H)

223 James P. Brawley Drive, SW, Atlanta GA 30314-4391
County: Fulton FICE Identification: 001559
Unit ID: 138947
Telephone: (404) 880-8000 Carnegie Class: DU-Higher
FAX Number: N/A Calendar System: Semester
URL: www.cau.edu
Established: 1988 Annual Undergrad Tuition & Fees: $22,396
Enrollment: 3,661 Coed
Affiliation or Control: United Methodist IRS Status: 501(c)3
Highest Offering: Doctorate
Accreditation: SC, CACREP, CAEPN, SPAA, SW

01 President ... Dr. Ronald A. JOHNSON
05 Provost/VP for Acad Affairs ... Dr. Peter O. NWOSU
111 VP for Inst Advance/Univ Rels ... Mr. Getchel CALDWELL
10 Exec VP and CFO ... Ms. Lucille MAUGE
32 VP Student Affairs/Dean of Students ... Vacant
46 Int VP Research & Sponsored Pgms ... Ms. Carol JOHNSON
20 Int Assoc Provost ... Dr. Calvin BROWN
13 Assoc VP/Chief Info Ofcr ... Mr. Rodney FOWLKES
21 Interim Assoc VP/Controller ... Mr. Leighton O'SULLIVAN
09 Asst VP Planning Assess/Inst Rsrch ... Dr. Narendra H. PATEL
43 General Counsel ... Mr. Lance DUNNINGS
06 University Registrar ... Ms. Susan GIBSON
26 Assoc VP Strategic Communications ... Ms. Donna BROCK
84 AVP Enrollment Services ... Dr. Michael MARSHALL
29 Director Alumni Relations ... Ms. Gay-linn JASHO
15 AVP/Chief HR Officer ... Ms. Debra HOYT
07 Dir Recruitment & Admissions ... Ms. Lori RICE-SADDLER
38 Director University Counseling Ctr ... Dr. Joy BRADFORD
35 Assoc Dean of Students/Student Dev ... Mr. Andre MCKINNEY
37 Director Student Financial Aid ... Mr. James STOTTS
96 Director of Purchasing ... Ms. Donna BYRD
41 Director of Athletics ... Mr. J. Lin DAWSON
49 Dean Arts & Sciences ... Dr. Danille K. TAYLOR
50 Interim Dean School of Business ... Dr. Ed L. DAVIS
53 Dean School of Education ... Dr. Moses NORMAN
70 Dean School of Social Work ... Dr. Jenny L. JONES
19 Chief of Public Safety ... Chief Joe LITTLE
23 Director Health Services ... Ms. Janet SINGLETON
25 Dir Accts Payable Grants/Contracts ... Ms. Rotesha HARRIS
39 Director of Residence Life ... Mr. Tarome ALFORD
88 Director Instructional Media ... Mr. Frank EDWARDS
101 Coordinator for Board Relations ... Ms. Natalie BAKER
104 Coordinator Multicultural Affairs ... Ms. Gwen WADE
22 University Compliance Officer ... Mr. Robert CLARK
18 Asst Director of Facilities ... Mr. Steve LESTER
108 Exec Dir Institutional Assessment ... Dr. Lauren LOPEZ
04 Executive Asst to President ... Ms. Crista MONSON
100 Chief of Staff ... Ms. Marilynn DAVIS
102 Corp Relations and Special Giving ... Mr. Magnus CHRISTON

Clayton State University (I)

2000 Clayton State Boulevard, Morrow GA 30260-0285
County: Clayton FICE Identification: 008976
Unit ID: 139311
Telephone: (678) 466-4000 Carnegie Class: Masters/M
FAX Number: (770) 961-3700 Calendar System: Semester
URL: www.clayton.edu
Established: 1969 Annual Undergrad Tuition & Fees (In-State): $5,340
Enrollment: 7,012 Coed
Affiliation or Control: State IRS Status: 501(c)3
Highest Offering: Master's
Accreditation: SC, CAEPN, DH, EXSC, MUS, NURSE

01 President ... Dr. Tim HYNES
05 Provost/Vice Pres Academic Affairs ... Dr. Kevin DEMMITT
10 VP for Operations/Planning/Budget ... Ms. Corlis CUMMINGS
32 Vice President for Student Affairs ... Dr. Elaine MANGLITZ
26 Vice President External Affairs ... Ms. Kate TROELSTRA
13 Vice Pres Information Tech & Svcs ... Mr. Bill GRUSZKA
20 Associate Provost ... Dr. Jill L. LANE
35 Assistant Vice Pres Student Affairs ... Dr. Allen WARD
84 AVP for Enrollment Management ... Dr. Stephen SCHULTHEIS
41 Executive Director of Athletics ... Mr. Tim DUNCAN
88 Executive Director of Spivey Hall ... Mr. Samuel DIXON
15 Exec Dir Human Resources & Services ... Vacant
49 Dean of Arts & Sciences ... Dr. Nasser MOMAYEZI
36 Dir Retention & Stdnt Placement ... Mr. Eric TACK
50 Dean of Business ... Dr. Avinandan MUKHERJEE
76 Dean of Health Sciences ... Dr. Lisa EICHELBERGER
81 Dean Information/Mathematical Sci ... Dr. Lila ROBERTS
08 Dean of Library Services ... Dr. Gordon BAKER
88 Dir Center for Instructional Dev ... Mr. Justin MAYS
51 Director of Continuing Education ... Ms. Karen LAMARSH
06 University Registrar ... Ms. Rebecca GMEINER
07 Director of Admissions ... Mr. Stephen JENKINS
109 Director of Auxiliary Services ... Ms. Carolina AMERO
27 Asst VP Marketing/Communications ... Ms. Maritza FERREIRA
18 AVP of Facilities Management ... Mr. Harun BISWAS
19 Director of Public Safety ... Mr. Bobby HAMIL
30 Director of Development ... Mr. Thomas GIFFIN
09 Director of Institutional Research ... Dr. Narem REDDY
24 Director Media Services ... Mr. Paul BAILEY
38 Director of Counseling Services ... Dr. Christine SMITH
37 Director Student Financial Aid ... Ms. Pat BARTON
96 Director of Purchasing ... Ms. Marcia JONES
29 Director Alumni Relations ... Ms. Leila TATUM
21 AVP Budget & Finance/Comptroller ... Mr. Donal CHRISTIAN

† Part of the University System of Georgia.

Coastal Pines Technical College (J)

1701 Carswell Avenue, Waycross GA 31503-4016
County: Ware FICE Identification: 005511
Unit ID: 485458
Telephone: (912) 287-6584 Carnegie Class: Not Classified
FAX Number: N/A Calendar System: Semester
URL: www.coastalpines.edu
Established: 1965 Annual Undergrad Tuition & Fees (In-State): $4,785
Enrollment: 2,445 Coed
Affiliation or Control: State IRS Status: 501(c)3
Highest Offering: Associate Degree
Accreditation: SC, COARC, EMT, MAC, MLTAD, RAD, SURGT

01 President ... Dr. Glenn DEIBERT
03 Provost ... Mr. Lonnie ROBERTS
05 Vice Pres for Academic Affairs ... Ms. Amanda MORRIS
11 VP of Administrative Services ... Ms. Melissa LAMB
46 Vice Pres for Economic Development ... Dr. Pete SNELL
32 Vice President for Student Affairs ... Ms. Karla EUBANKS
06 Registrar ... Ms. Tara EICHFIELD
111 Executive Dir Inst Advancement ... Ms. Melinda LAAGER
18 Facilities Director ... Mr. Chad BOYETT
36 Career Placement & Develop Coord ... Mr. Buck THIGPEN
37 Director Student Financial Aid ... Ms. Tina MANNING
108 VP for Institutional Effectiveness ... Dr. Teresa ALLEN
07 Director of Admissions ... Mr. Chris JEANCAKE
15 Human Resources Coordinator ... Ms. Cynthia LINDER
04 Administrative Asst to President ... Ms. Natasha KING
08 Director of Library Services ... Ms. Cassie CLEMONS
13 Chief Info Technology Officer (CIO) ... Mr. Derrell HARRIS
38 Director Student Counseling ... Ms. Cathy MONTGOMERY

College of Coastal Georgia (A)

One College Drive, Brunswick GA 31520-3632
County: Glynn FICE Identification: 001558
Unit ID: 139250
Telephone: (912) 279-5700 Carnegie Class: Bac/Assoc-Mixed
FAX Number: (912) 262-3072 Calendar System: Semester
URL: www.ccga.edu
Established: 1961 Annual Undergrad Tuition & Fees (In-State): $3,821
Enrollment: 3,131 Coed
Affiliation or Control: State IRS Status: 501(c)3
Highest Offering: Baccalaureate
Accreditation: SC, ACFEI, ADNUR, CAEPN, NUR, RAD

01 Interim President ... Dr. Margaret AMSTUTZ
05 Interim Provost/VPAA ... Ms. Kay S. HAMPTON
111 Vice President Advancement ... Mr. Kevin SALAWAY
10 Vice President Business Affairs ... Mr. Jeffrey H. PRESTON
32 VP Student Affairs & Enrollment ... Dr. Jason W. UMFRESS
20 Asst VP Academic Affairs ... Dr. German VARGAS
20 Asst VP Academic Affairs ... Dr. Laura LYNCH
21 Asst VP Business Affairs ... Mr. C. Tom SAUNDERS
84 Asst VP Recruitment & Admissions ... Dr. Amy CLINES
13 Chief Information Officer ... Mr. Alan OURS
19 Chief of Police ... Mr. Bryan SIPE
08 Dean of Library Services ... Ms. Debra HOLMES
35 Dean of Students ... Dr. Michael BUTCHER
49 Interim Dean Sch Arts & Sciences ... Dr. Victor VEGA-VAZQUEZ
50 Dean Sch of Business & Public Mgmt ... Dr. William MOUNTS
53 Dean School of Education & Teacher ... Vacant
66 Dean School of Nursing & Health Sci ... Dr. Patricia KRAFT
41 Director of Athletics ... Dr. William CARLTON
12 Director Camden Center ... Vacant
106 Director of E-Learning ... Dr. Lisa MCNEAL
09 Director Institutional Effectivenes ... Dr. James LYNCH
104 Int Dir International Initiatives ... Dr. James LYNCH
15 Director of Human Resources ... Ms. Phyllis BROADWELL
18 Director of Facilities and Plant Op ... Mr. Gary STRICKLAND
26 Director of Marketing & Public Rels ... Vacant
37 Director Student Financial Aid ... Ms. Terral HARRIS
06 Registrar ... Ms. Lisa LESSEIG
07 Associate Director of Admissions ... Ms. Aerial DICKERSON
04 Executive Assistant President's Off ... Ms. Judy JOHNSTON
88 Coordinator Faculty & Admin Svcs ... Ms. Connie HIOTT
96 Purchasing Officer ... Ms. Karen O. MARTIN
36 Director Career Development ... Mr. Brian WEESE
38 Dir Counseling & Disability Svcs ... Ms. Jennifer ZAK

† Part of the University System of Georgia.

Columbia Theological Seminary (B)

P.O. Box 520, 701 S Columbia Drive,
Decatur GA 30031-0520
County: DeKalb FICE Identification: 001560
Unit ID: 139348
Telephone: (404) 378-8821 Carnegie Class: Spec-4-yr-Faith
FAX Number: (404) 377-9696 Calendar System: 4/1/4
URL: www.ctsnet.edu
Established: 1828 Annual Graduate Tuition & Fees: N/A
Enrollment: 189 Coed
Affiliation or Control: Presbyterian Church (U.S.A.) IRS Status: 501(c)3
Highest Offering: Doctorate; No Undergraduates
Accreditation: SC, THEOL

01 President ... Dr. Leanne VAN DYK
05 Interim VP Academic Affairs ... Dr. Christine R. YODER
28 VP Equity/Diversity & Inclusion ... Dr. Deborah F. MULLEN
10 VP Business and Finance ... Mr. Martin SADLER
32 Dean of Students ... Rev. Brandon MAXWELL
111 VP Institutional Advancement ... Mr. Steven P. MILLER
20 Academic Administrator ... Dr. Ann Clay ADAMS
13 Assoc Dean Info Svcs/Dir of Library ... Dr. Kelly D. CAMPBELL
107 Assoc Dean Advanced Prof Studies ... Dr. Kevin PARK
06 Registrar ... Mr. Mike MEDFORD
07 Assoc Dir Admissions/Financial Aid ... Rev. Lucy STRONG
26 Director of Communications ... Mr. Michael THOMPSON
106 Dir Online Education ... Dr. Israel GALINDO

Columbus State University (C)

4225 University Avenue, Columbus GA 31907-5645
County: Muscogee FICE Identification: 001561
Unit ID: 139366
Telephone: (706) 507-8800 Carnegie Class: Masters/L
FAX Number: (706) 568-2123 Calendar System: Semester
URL: www.columbusstate.edu
Established: 1958 Annual Undergrad Tuition & Fees (In-State): $6,031
Enrollment: 8,440 Coed
Affiliation or Control: State IRS Status: 501(c)3
Highest Offering: Doctorate
Accreditation: SC, ART, CACREP, CAEPN, MUS, NURSE, THEA

01 President ... Dr. Chris MARKWOOD
05 Interim Provost/VP Academic Affairs ... Dr. Tina BUTCHER
10 Vice President Business & Finance ... Dr. Tom HELTON
32 VP Student Affairs & Enrollment Mgt ... Dr. Gina SHEEKS
30 VP University Advancement ... Dr. Rocky KETTERING
13 Chief Information Officer ... Mr. Abraham GEORGE
84 Asst VP for Enrollment Mgmt ... Mr. John MCELVEEN
26 Assoc VP for University Relations ... Dr. John LESTER
50 Dean College of Business & Comp Sci ... Dr. Linda HADLEY
08 Dean of Libraries ... Mr. Mark FLYNN
35 AVP Student Affs/Dean of Students ... Mr. Aaron J. REESE
15 Human Resources Director ... Ms. Laurie S. JONES
09 Director Institutional Research ... Dr. Sri SITHARAMAN
41 Athletic Director ... Mr. Todd REESER
37 Director Financial Aid ... Mr. Russ ROMANDINI
07 Director of Admissions ... Ms. Viola ALEXANDER

† Part of the University System of Georgia.

Columbus Technical College (D)

928 Manchester Expressway, Columbus GA 31904-6572
County: Muscogee FICE Identification: 005624
Unit ID: 139357
Telephone: (706) 649-1800 Carnegie Class: Assoc/HVT-Mix Trad/Non
FAX Number: (706) 649-1885 Calendar System: Semester
URL: www.columbustech.edu
Established: 1961 Annual Undergrad Tuition & Fees (In-State): $2,704
Enrollment: 3,800 Coed
Affiliation or Control: State IRS Status: 501(c)3
Highest Offering: Associate Degree
Accreditation: SC, ADNUR, COARC, DA, DH, DMS, MAC, RAD, SURGT

01 President ... Ms. Lorette M. HOOVER
11 VP Administrative Services ... Ms. Karen THOMAS
05 Vice President Academic Affairs ... Dr. Melanie THORNTON
32 Vice President Student Affairs ... Ms. Tara ASKEW
18 Vice President Operations ... Mr. Tommy WILSON
46 VP Institutional Effectiveness ... Mr. David FLETCHER
88 Vice President Economic Development ... Mr. James LOYD
51 Director of Adult Education ... Ms. April HOPSON
15 Director of Human Resources ... Ms. Patricia HOOD
26 Exec Dir Community/College Rels ... Ms. Cheryl MYERS
37 Associate VP of Financial Aid ... Ms. Debbie HENSHAW
13 Director Information Technology ... Mr. Daniel RAGAN
30 Director Institutional Advancement ... Mr. David FLETCHER

Covenant College (E)

14049 Scenic Highway, Lookout Mountain TN 30750-4164
County: Dade FICE Identification: 003484
Unit ID: 139393
Telephone: (706) 820-1560 Carnegie Class: Bac-A&S
FAX Number: (706) 820-2165 Calendar System: Semester
URL: www.covenant.edu
Established: 1955 Annual Undergrad Tuition & Fees: $32,230
Enrollment: 1,102 Coed
Affiliation or Control: Presbyterian Church In America IRS Status: 501(c)3
Highest Offering: Master's
Accreditation: SC

01 President ... Dr. J. Derek HALVORSON
05 Vice Pres of Academic Affairs ... Dr. Jeffrey B. HALL
30 Vice President of Development ... Mr. Jeff SANDHOFF
32 Vice Pres of Student Development ... Mr. Brad VOYLES
10 Vice Pres of Finance & Operations ... Mr. Dan WYKOFF
08 Director of Library Services ... Mr. John HOLBERG
06 Dean of Records and Registrar ... Mr. Rodney E. MILLER
42 Chaplain ... Mr. Grant LOWE
58 Dean of Master of Education Pgm ... Dr. Jim DREXLER
21 Controller ... Mr. Robert E. HARBERT
88 Campus Architect ... Mr. David NORTHCUTT
37 Director of Financial Aid ... Mrs. Beth BAILEY
15 Director of Human Resources ... Ms. Renee TIMMERMAN
41 Director of Athletics ... Mr. Tim SCEGGEL
13 Director of Technology Services ... Ms. Marjorie CROCKER
29 Director of Alumni Relations ... Ms. Kim COLLINS
23 Director of Health Services ... Ms. Tina HOLT
07 Director of Admissions ... Mr. Scott SCHINDLER
09 Director of Institutional Research ... Dr. Karen NELSON
26 Dir of Marketing & Communications ... Mr. David PETERSON
20 Director of Academic Support ... Mrs. Janet HULSEY
36 Dir of Center for Calling & Career ... Mr. John PLATING
04 Admin Asst to Office of President ... Mrs. Cassandra JONES
19 Director of Safety & Security ... Mr. Keith MCCLEARN
109 Director of Business Operations ... Mr. Tom SCHREINER
100 Dir of Admin Office of President ... Ms. Jen ALLEN
104 Director of Global Education ... Ms. Christiana FITZPATRICK

Dalton State College (F)

650 College Drive, Dalton GA 30720-3797
County: Whitfield FICE Identification: 003956
Unit ID: 139463
Telephone: (706) 272-4436 Carnegie Class: Bac/Assoc-Mixed
FAX Number: (706) 272-4588 Calendar System: Semester
URL: www.daltonstate.edu
Established: 1963 Annual Undergrad Tuition & Fees (In-State): $3,503
Enrollment: 5,044 Coed
Affiliation or Control: State IRS Status: 501(c)3
Highest Offering: Baccalaureate
Accreditation: SC, ADNUR, CAEPN, COARC, MLTAD, NUR, PHLEB, RAD, SW

01 President ... Dr. Margaret VENABLE
05 VP for Academic Affairs ... Dr. Pat CHUTE
10 Vice President Fiscal Affairs ... Mr. Nick HENRY
84 VP Student Affairs & Enroll Mgmt ... Dr. Jodi S. JOHNSON
37 Director of Financial Aid/Vet Svcs ... Ms. Carol JONES
08 Director Library Services ... Ms. Melissa WHITESELL
09 Director Inst Research & Planning ... Dr. Henry M. CODJOE
18 Interim Director Plant Opers ... Mr. George BREWER
26 Director Marketing & Communication ... Ms. Pam PARTAIN
102 Director Foundation ... Mr. David ELROD
32 Dean of Students ... Ms. Jami HALL
15 Director Human Resources ... Ms. Lori MCCARTY
96 Purchasing Coordinator ... Ms. Penny CORDELL
13 Director Computing & Info Services ... Mr. Terry BAILEY
19 Director Public Safety ... Mr. Michael MASTERS
29 Director Alumni Relations ... Mr. Josh WILSON
39 Director Student Housing ... Mr. Tim REILLY
50 Dean School of Business ... Dr. Larry JOHNSON
53 Dean School of Education ... Dr. Sharon HIXON
49 Dean School of Liberal Arts ... Ms. Mary NIELSEN
81 Dean School of Science/Tech/Math ... Dr. Randall GRIFFUS
76 Dean Health Professions ... Dr. Gina KERTULIS-TARTAR
06 Registrar ... Mr. Rob WINGFIELD
04 Administrative Asst to President ... Mrs. Mary Ellen GURLEY
07 Director of Admissions ... Mrs. Katherine LOGAN
22 Dir Affirmative Action/EEO ... Ms. Lori MCCARTY
41 Athletic Director ... Mr. Jon JAUDON

† Part of the University System of Georgia.

DeVry University - Decatur Campus (G)

One West Court Square, Ste. 100,
Decatur GA 30030-2556
Telephone: (404) 270-2700 FICE Identification: 009224
Accreditation: &NH, ENGT

† Regional accreditation is carried under the parent institution in Downers Grove, IL.

East Georgia State College (H)

131 College Circle, Swainsboro GA 30401-3643
County: Emanuel FICE Identification: 010997
Unit ID: 139621
Telephone: (478) 289-2000 Carnegie Class: Bac/Assoc-Assoc Dom
FAX Number: (478) 289-2038 Calendar System: Semester
URL: www.ega.edu
Established: 1973 Annual Undergrad Tuition & Fees (In-State): $3,067
Enrollment: 3,001 Coed
Affiliation or Control: State IRS Status: 501(c)3
Highest Offering: Baccalaureate
Accreditation: SC

01 President ... Dr. Robert G. BOEHMER
05 Vice President for Academic Affairs ... Dr. Deborah L. VESS
10 Vice President for Business Affairs ... Mr. Cliff GAY
32 Vice Pres for Student Affairs ... Dr. Donald AVERY
13 Vice Pres Information Technology ... Mr. Mike ROUNTREE
100 Chief of Staff/Legal Counsel ... Mrs. Mary C. SMITH
04 Executive Assistant to President ... Mrs. Susan GRAY
08 Librarian ... Mrs. Kelly ANSLEY
06 Registrar ... Ms. Tabithia ROSS
12 Director of EGSC-Augusta ... Mr. Nick KELCH
09 Director of Institutional Research ... Mr. David GRIBBIN
84 Assoc Vice Pres Enrollment Mgmt ... Mrs. Karen S. JONES
15 Director of Human Resources ... Mrs. Tracy WOODS
111 Vice Pres Institutional Advancement ... Ms. Elizabeth GILMER
11 Director of Business Operations ... Mrs. Michelle GOFF
110 Assoc VP Institutional Advancement ... Ms. Norma KENNEDY
12 Assoc VP External Campuses ... Ms. Caroline JOYNER
19 Dir Public Safety/Chief of Police ... Mr. Wiley GAMMON
35 Director of Student Life ... Ms. Vicki SHERROD
07 Director of Admissions ... Ms. Georgia MATHEWS
38 Dir Counseling/Disability Services ... Dr. Odey P. EGBE
39 Director of Housing ... Ms. Angela STORCK
41 Director of Athletics ... Mr. Chuck WIMBERLY
88 Dir Sudie A Fulford Cmty Lrng Ctr ... Mrs. Jean D. SCHWABE
18 Director of Plant Operations ... Mr. David STEPTOE
21 Director of Accounting Services ... Ms. Becky FOSKEY
106 Assoc Dean of Teaching and Learning ... Dr. Dee MCKINNEY
88 Director of Academic Advisement ... Ms. Deborah KITTRELL-MIKELL
88 Director Acad Ctr for Excellence ... Ms. Kristin WATERS
109 Director of Auxiliary Services ... Mrs. Ruth UNDERWOOD
88 Director of Student Conduct ... Ms. Sherrie HELMS
81 Dean of Mathematics & Sciences ... Dr. Jim WEDINCAMP
79 Dean of Humanities ... Dr. Carmine PALUMBO
83 Dean of Social Sciences ... Dr. Lee CHEEK
81 Chair of Biology Department ... Dr. David CHEVALIER
88 Dir of FESA ... Ms. Beverley WALKER
66 Director of Nursing ... Dr. Sylvia ROZIER
88 Dir of Military Resource Center ... Ms. Stacey GRANT
25 Director Financial Accounting ... Ms. Sheial D. WENTZ

† Part of the University System of Georgia.

Emmanuel College (A)

181 Springs Street, Franklin Springs GA 30639
County: Franklin FICE Identification: 001563
Unit ID: 139630
Telephone: (706) 245-7226 Carnegie Class: Bac-Diverse
FAX Number: (706) 245-4424 Calendar System: Semester
URL: www.ec.edu
Established: 1919 Annual Undergrad Tuition & Fees: $19,330
Enrollment: 884 Coed
Affiliation or Control: Pentecostal Holiness Church IRS Status: 501(c)3
Highest Offering: Baccalaureate
Accreditation: SC

01 President Dr. Ronald WHITE
32 Vice President for Student Life Dr. Tracy REYNOLDS
05 Vice President for Academic Affairs Dr. John R. HENZEL, JR.
10 Vice President for Finance Mr. Greg K. HEARN
30 Vice President for Development Mr. W. Brian JAMES
84 Vice Pres Enrollment Mgmt/Marketing Ms. Donna QUICK
08 Director of Library Services Ms. Deborah MILLIER
06 Registrar Mrs. Debra F. GRIZZLE
37 Director of Financial Aid Mrs. Niki STINSON
13 Director of Information Technology Mr. Glenn TONEY
11 Assoc VP of Campus Operations Mr. Matt MCREE
41 Athletics Director Mr. Nate MOORMAN
42 Dir Spiritual Life/Campus Pastor Mr. Chris MAXWELL
15 Director of Human Resources Mrs. Joann HARPER
26 Chief Public Relations Officer Mrs. Ashley WESTBROOK
96 Director of Accounting Services Mrs. Anita RAY
18 Physical Plant Director Mr. Wayne CRIDER
09 Director of Institutional Research Ms. Sharon SYNAN
29 Director Alumni Relations Mr. Harrell W. QUEEN
36 Dir Career Svcs/Student Counseling Mr. Jason CROY
04 Administrative Asst to President Mrs. Mary BEADLES
19 Director Security/Safety Mr. Joel SWAILS
39 Director Student Housing Mrs. Ginni MAXWELL
07 Director of Admissions Ms. Lyquaia PURCELL
106 Dir Online Education/E-learning Ms. Sharon SYNAN

Emory University (B)

201 Dowman Drive, Atlanta GA 30322-0001
County: DeKalb FICE Identification: 001564
Unit ID: 139658
Telephone: (404) 727-6123 Carnegie Class: DU-Highest
FAX Number: (404) 727-5997 Calendar System: Semester
URL: www.emory.edu
Established: 1836 Annual Undergrad Tuition & Fees: $47,954
Enrollment: 13,788 Coed
Affiliation or Control: United Methodist IRS Status: 501(c)3
Highest Offering: Doctorate
Accreditation: SC, AA, ANEST, ARCPA, CLPSY, DENT, IPSY, LAW, MED, MIDWF, NURSE, PAST, PCSAS, PH, PTA, RAD, THEOL

01 President Dr. Claire E. STERK
05 Provost/Exec VP Acad Affs Dr. Dwight A. MCBRIDE
11 Exec VP for Business/Admin Mr. Christopher AUGOSTINI
17 Exec Vice Pres Health Affairs Dr. Jonathan S. LEWIN
101 VP/Secretary of the University Ms. Alllison K. DYKES
04 VP/Deputy to the President Dr. Gary S. HAUK
43 Sr Vice Pres & General Counsel Mr. Stephen D. SENCER
30 Sr Vice Pres Devel/Alumni Rels Ms. Susan CRUSE
32 Sr Vice President/Dean Campus Life Dr. Ajay NAIR
88 Vice Provost International Affairs Dr. Philip WAINWRIGHT
46 Vice President for Research Admin Dr. David L. WYNES
10 Vice President for Finance/CFO Ms. Carol KISSAL
58 Vice Provost/Dean Graduate Sch Dr. Lisa A. TEDESCO
15 AVP Human Resources Ms. Theresa MILAZZO
15 AVP Human Resources Ms. Del KING
26 Interim Sr VP Comm/Public Affairs Mr. Vincent DOLLARD
88 VP Strategic Research Initiatives Dr. Lanny S. LIEBESKIND
86 Vice Pres Govt and Cmty Affairs Ms. Cameron TAYLOR
18 Vice President Campus Services Mr. Matthew EARLY
29 Sr Assoc Vice Pres Alumni Affairs Ms. Sarah COOK
25 Assoc Vice Pres for Research Admin Ms. Kathleen BIENKOWSKI
21 Assoc VP Finance & Controller Ms. Allison S. BERG
28 Vice Provost Equity/Inclusion Ms. Lynell CADRAY
20 Sr Vice Prov Academic Affairs Dr. Lynn ZIMMERMAN
84 Interim Vice Prov Enrollment Svcs Ms. Heather MUGG
08 Enterprise CIO/Sr VP Lib Svcs Mr. Richard A. MENDOLA
07 AVP Undergrad Enroll/Dean of Admiss Dr. John LATTING
114 Chief Univ Budget Officer Mr. Michael ANDRECHAK
49 Interim Dean of Emory College Dr. Michael A. ELLIOTT
12 Dean & CEO Oxford College Dr. Douglas A. HICKS
63 Interim Dean of Medicine Dr. David S. STEPHENS
66 Dean of Nursing Dr. Linda MCCAULEY
73 Dean of Theology Dr. Jan LOVE
61 Interim Dean of Law Mr. Judson GRAVES
50 Dean of Business School Ms. Erika JAMES
69 Dean of Public Health Dr. James W. CURRAN
85 Dir Intl Student Scholar Program Ms. Shinsaeng KO
80 Pres & CEO of the Carter Center Ms. Mary Ann PETERS
42 Dean of the Chapel & Spiritual Life Rev. Bridgette YOUNG ROSS
06 University Registrar Ms. JoAnn MCKENZIE
27 AVP Communications & Marketing Vacant
36 Exec Director Career Service Mr. Paul FOWLER
19 Assistant VP Public Safety Mr. Craig T. WATSON
41 Director Athletics/Recreation Dr. Michael VIENNA
12 Director Yerkes Research Ctrs Dr. Paul JOHNSON
49 Director Institute Liberal Arts Dr. Michael RISJORD
88 Director M C Carlos Museum Ms. Bonnie SPEED
40 Director Bookstore Mr. Bruce COVEY
39 Service Supervisor Housing Mr. Kenneth JONES, JR.
38 Assistant VP Counseling/Psych Svcs Dr. Wanda COLLINS
09 Director Institutional Research Dr. Melissa BOLYARD
96 Director Contract Admin/Compliance Mr. Rex HARDAWAY
44 Executive Director of Annual Giving Ms. Kimberly JULIAN BOWDEN
45 Vice Provost University Strategies Vacant
88 Director Operations Ms. Carol A. FLOWERS
37 Director Student Financial Aid Mr. John LEACH
100 Chief of Staff Mr. Michael P. KLOSS
108 Dir Institutional Effectiveness Dr. David M. JORDAN

Fort Valley State University (C)

1005 State University Drive, Fort Valley GA 31030-4313
County: Peach FICE Identification: 001566
Unit ID: 139719
Telephone: (478) 825-6211 Carnegie Class: Masters/S
FAX Number: (478) 825-6394 Calendar System: Semester
URL: www.fvsu.edu
Established: 1895 Annual Undergrad Tuition & Fees (In-State): $5,594
Enrollment: 2,696 Coed
Affiliation or Control: State IRS Status: 501(c)3
Highest Offering: Beyond Master's But Less Than Doctorate
Accreditation: SC, AAFCS, CACREP, CAEPN, ENGT, @SW

01 President Dr. Paul JONES
05 Provost/VP for Academic Affairs Dr. Ramon STUART
10 VP Business & Finance Ms. Mary LOOMIS
111 Interim VP External Affairs Dr. Chanta HAYWOOD
84 Vice Pres Enroll Mgmt/Stdnt Success Mr. Jessie KANE
09 VP Inst Research/Plng & Effec Mr. Frank ARCHER
88 Assoc VP for Land Grant Affair Dr. Mark LATTIMORE
49 Dean Arts & Sciences Dr. Josephine DAVIS
21 Interim Comptroller Ms. Akwai AGOONS
06 Registrar Mrs. Sharee LAWRENCE
43 Chief Legal Officer/Dir Govt Rels Mr. Charles JONES
13 Director for Information Technology Mr. Chad HEBNER
08 Director Hunt Memorial Library Mr. Frank MAHITAB
07 Director Admissions Ms. Calandra WRIGHT
37 Director Financial Aid Ms. Kimberly MORRIS
29 Director Alumni Affairs Mr. Ed BOSTON
15 Director of Human Resources Ms. Carole CLERIE
19 Director Campus Safety Mr. Ken MORGAN
47 Dean Agriculture Dr. Gavindarajan KANNAN
23 Dir Student Health & Behav Coun Mrs. Jacqueline CASKEY-JAMES
18 Director Plant & Maintenance Mr. Joseph THOMAS
36 Director Counsel/Career Development Ms. Simmons ROMELDA
26 Director Marketing/Communications Mr. Cedric MOBLEY
41 Director of Athletics Dr. Darryl POPE
124 Exec Dir Retention Services Dr. Stevie LAWRENCE
53 Int Dean College of Education Dr. Rebecca MCMULLEN
22 Dir Affirmative Act/EEO/Diversity Mrs. Patrice TERRELL
25 Director of Sponsored Programs Vacant
39 Director Student Housing Mr. Shawn MODENA
102 Director Foundation Mrs. Kristie KENNEY
50 Director Business Dr. Samuel GYAPONG
54 Director Engineering Mr. Archie WILLIAMS
96 Director of Purchasing Ms. Becky HORTON

† Part of the University System of Georgia.

Georgia Christian University (D)

6789 Peachtree Industrial Boulevard, Atlanta GA 30360
County: DeKalb FICE Identification: 041565
Unit ID: 461236
Telephone: (770) 279-0507 Carnegie Class: Bac-Diverse
FAX Number: (770) 279-0308 Calendar System: Semester
URL: www.gcuniv.edu
Established: 1995 Annual Undergrad Tuition & Fees: $5,125
Enrollment: 239 Coed
Affiliation or Control: Independent Non-Profit IRS Status: 501(c)3
Highest Offering: Doctorate
Accreditation: THEOL, TRACS, CEA

01 President Dr. Paul C. KIM
45 Prov & Exec Dir Strat/Innovation Dr. Rick YI
111 Vice Pres for Inst Advancement Dr. Hee Sook SONG
05 Vice President for Academic Affairs Dr. Howoo LEE
07 Director of Admissions Ms. Mi Hee LEE
88 Assistant of Academic Affairs Dr. Mia KANG
45 Director Of Planning Mr. Justin PARK
21 Chief Financial Officer Ms. Eunice KIM
12 Dir of New Jersey Teaching Site Ms. Sun Hee CHOI
12 Dir of Virginia Teaching Site Dr. Nam Hong CHO
12 Dir of California Teaching Site Dr. Haejinn HAHN
13 Senior Director of IT Mr. Deok Joo MOO
14 Assistant of IT Mr. William QUEIROZ
24 Director Literature & Information Dr. Hyun Sung CHO
18 Chief Facilities/Physical Plant Rev. Min Soo KIM
19 Director Security/Safety Mr. Samuel KIM
21 Director of Business Affairs Mr. Daniel KIM
88 Assistant of Business Affairs Mr. Hyun Seok JO
88 Director of ESOL Mr. Alain GALLIE
29 Director Alumni Relations Dr. Chang Sun PYO
26 Chief Public Relations Officer Vacant
06 Registrar Ms. Sara KIM
37 Director Student Financial Aid Ms. Laura PERRONE
50 Dean School of Business Dr. William STAUFF
73 Dean School of Christianity Dr. Hyun Sung CHO
73 Dean School of Divinity Dr. Ho Woo LEE
64 Dean School of Music Ms. Kyung Mi YANG
88 Director of Doctoral Programs Dr. Eun Moo LEE
63 Dean School of Oriental Medicine Dr. Soo Hyun HONG
88 International Student Advisor Ms. Laura PERRONE
108 Dir of Institutional Effectiveness Dr. Hee Sook SONG
42 Chaplain Dr. Hyun Sung CHO
08 Director of the Library Ms. Hyongsig SONG
04 Administrative Asst to President Ms. Chawook BAE
32 Director of Student Affairs Dr. Soo Hyun HONG
69 MMT Program Coordinator Ms. Sherry MURY

Georgia College & State University (E)

231 West Hancock Street, Milledgeville GA 31061-0490
County: Baldwin FICE Identification: 001602
Unit ID: 139861
Telephone: (478) 445-5004 Carnegie Class: Masters/L
FAX Number: (478) 445-1191 Calendar System: Semester
URL: www.gcsu.edu
Established: 1889 Annual Undergrad Tuition & Fees (In-State): $9,202
Enrollment: 6,889 Coed
Affiliation or Control: State IRS Status: 501(c)3
Highest Offering: Doctorate
Accreditation: SC, CAATE, CAEPN, CS, MUS, NUR, NURSE, SPAA

01 President Dr. Steve M. DORMAN
04 Special Assistant to the President Ms. Monica STARLEY
05 Provost/VP for Acad Affairs Dr. Kelli BROWN
10 VP Finance/Administration Ms. Susan ALLEN
32 Vice President for Student Affairs Dr. Bruce HARSHBARGER
111 VP for University Advancement Ms. Monica DELISA
88 Dir of Econ Dev/External Relations Mr. Johnny GRANT
20 Sr Assoc Provost/Dir Grad Studies Dr. Costas SPIROU
121 Assoc Provost for Student Success Dr. Carolyn DENARD
45 Assoc VP for Strategic Initiatives Dr. Mark PELTON
35 Dean of Students Dr. Andy LEWTER
26 Assoc VP Strategic Communications Mr. Omar ODEH
84 Assoc VP for Enrollment Management Ms. Suzanne PITTMAN
109 Asst VP for Auxiliary Services Mr. Kyle CULLARS
114 Sr Dir for Budget Planning & Admin Mr. Russ WILLIAMS
49 Dean College of Arts & Sciences Mr. Ken PROCTER
50 Dean College of Business Dr. Dale YOUNG
53 Dean College of Education Dr. Joseph PETERS
76 Dean College of Health Sciences Dr. Sandra GANGSTEAD
39 Exec Director of University Housing Mr. Larry CHRISTENSON
88 Univ Architect/Dir Facilities Plng Mr. Michael RICKENBAKER
18 Asst VP of Facilities Operations Mr. Mark DUCLOS
19 Chief of Police & Dir of Pub Safety Mr. Don CHALLIS
09 Asst VP of Institutional Research Dr. Chris FERLAND
13 Chief Information Officer Mr. Robert ORR
08 Interim Director of Libraries Dr. Shaundra WALKER
36 Director Career Center Ms. Mary ROBERTS
15 Chief Human Resources Officer Ms. Leslie PIERCE
28 Chief Diversity Officer Dr. Veronica WOMACK
07 Director of Admissions Mr. Ramon BLAKLEY
06 Registrar Ms. Kay ANDERSON
41 Director of Athletics Mr. Wendell STATON
29 Dir Alumni Relations/Annual Giving Mrs. Mindy MILLER
43 Director of Legal Affairs Ms. Qiana WILSON
38 Director of Counseling Services Dr. Stephen WILSON
37 Director of Financial Aid Ms. Cathy CRAWLEY
88 Sr Dir Materials Mgmt/Central Svcs Mr. Mark MEEKS
116 Dir of Internal Audit Ms. Stacy MULVANEY
35 Exec Director of Campus Life Mr. Tom MILES
104 Asst VP for International Educ Dr. Eric SPEARS

Georgia Gwinnett College (F)

1000 University Center Lane, Lawrenceville GA 30043
County: Gwinnett FICE Identification: 041429
Unit ID: 447689
Telephone: (678) 407-5000 Carnegie Class: Bac-Diverse
FAX Number: N/A Calendar System: Semester
URL: www.ggc.edu
Established: 2005 Annual Undergrad Tuition & Fees (In-District): $5,558
Enrollment: 11,468 Coed
Affiliation or Control: State/Local IRS Status: 501(c)3
Highest Offering: Baccalaureate
Accreditation: SC, CAEPN

01 President Dr. Stanley PRECZEWSKI
05 SVP for Academic Affairs/Provost Dr. T.J ARANT
111 Vice Pres Advancement Ms. Lori BUCKHEISTER
10 VP of Business & Finance/CFO Ms. Laura MAXWELL
26 Vice Pres Strategic Communications Ms. Renee BYRD-LEWIS
100 Chief of Staff Mr. Dan NOLAN
04 Executive Asst to President Mrs. Luann CAUSLAND
50 Dean School of Business Dr. Tyler YU
53 Dean School of Education Dr. Cathy D. MOORE
49 Dean School of Liberal Arts Dr. Adolfo SANTOS
81 Dean School Science and Technology Dr. Thomas MUNDIE
66 Dean School of Health Sciences Dr. Diane WHITE
121 Dean School of Transitional Studies Dr. Justin JERNIGAN

Georgia Highlands College (G)

3175 Cedartown Highway SE, Rome GA 30161-3897
County: Floyd FICE Identification: 009507
Unit ID: 139700
Telephone: (706) 802-5000 Carnegie Class: Bac/Assoc-Assoc Dom
FAX Number: (706) 295-6341 Calendar System: Semester
URL: www.highlands.edu
Established: 1970 Annual Undergrad Tuition & Fees (In-State): $3,245

Enrollment: 5,746 Coed
Affiliation or Control: State IRS Status: 501(c)3
Highest Offering: Baccalaureate
Accreditation: SC, ADNUR, DH, NUR

01 President .... Dr. Donald J. GREEN
05 Vice President Academic Affairs .... Dr. Renva WATTERSON
10 Vice Pres Finance/Administration .... Mr. Jeff DAVIS
32 Vice President Student Affairs .... Dr. Todd JONES
15 Vice President Human Resources .... Ms. Ginni SILER
111 VP Advanc/Exec Dir GHS Foundation .... Ms. Mary TRANSUE
13 VP Information Technology/CIO .... Mr. Jeff PATTY
37 Director Financial Aid .... Ms. Melinda KING
08 Interim Dean Libraries/Col Testing .... Ms. Susan VINES
12 Dean Floyd .... Dr. Todd JONES
12 Dean Cartersville .... Ms. Leslie JOHNSON
12 Dean Marietta .... Mr. Ken REAVES
12 Dean Paulding .... Ms. Joy HAMBRICK
12 Dean Douglasville .... Ms. Julia AREH
04 Executive Asst to the President .... Ms. Tammy NICHOLSON
41 Director of Athletics .... Mr. Phillip GAFFNEY
18 Director Plant Operations .... Mr. Phillip KIMSEY
06 Registrar .... Ms. Sandra DAVIS
09 Research/Planning & Accreditation .... Dr. Cathy LEDBETTER
19 Police Chief of Campus Safety .... Mr. David HORACE
26 Sr Dir of Marketing & Commnications .... Ms. Sheila JONES
28 Director of Diversity/Asst Prof .... Dr. Sean CALLAHAN
29 Alumni Affairs Specialist .... Ms. Alison LAMPKIN
38 Dir Student Support & Counseling .... Ms. Angela WHEELUS
96 Purchasing Manager .... Ms. Cynthia PARKER

† Part of the University System of Georgia.

Georgia Institute of Technology (A)

225 North Avenue, NW, Atlanta GA 30332-0002
County: Fulton FICE Identification: 001569
Unit ID: 139755
Telephone: (404) 894-2000 Carnegie Class: DU-Highest
FAX Number: (404) 894-1277 Calendar System: Semester
URL: www.gatech.edu
Established: 1885 Annual Undergrad Tuition & Fees (In-State): $12,212
Enrollment: 25,034 Coed
Affiliation or Control: State IRS Status: 501(c)3
Highest Offering: Doctorate
Accreditation: SC, ART, CEA, CS, ENG, IPSY, OPE, PLNG

01 President .... Dr. G. P. (Bud) PETERSON
05 Provost/Exec VP Academic Affairs .... Dr. Rafael BRAS
10 Exec VP Administration/Finance .... Mr. Steven SWANT
46 Executive Vice President Research .... Dr. Stephen CROSS
100 Assistant Vice Pres/Chief of Staff .... Ms. Lynn DURHAM
30 Vice President Development .... Mr. Barrett H. CARSON
26 Vice Pres Communications/Marketing .... Mr. Michael L. WARDEN
32 VP Student Life & Dean of Students .... Mr. John STEIN
88 VP/Director GA Tech Res Inst .... Dr. Andrew GERBER
46 Vice President Research .... Ms. Jilda GARTON
86 Vice Pres Government/Cmty Relations .... Mr. Dene SHEHEANE
88 VP Enterprise Innovation Inst .... Mr. Chris DOWNING
29 President Georgia Tech Alumni Assoc .... Mr. Joseph IRWIN
58 Vice Prov Grad Educ/Faculty Affairs .... Dr. Susan COZZENS
84 Vice Prov Enrollment Services .... Dr. Paul KOHN
20 Vice Prov Undergraduate Education .... Dr. Colin POTTS
43 Vice Pres Legal Affairs/Risk Mgmt .... Mr. Patrick MCKENNA
28 Vice President Institute Diversity .... Dr. Archie ERVIN
15 Assoc VP Human Resources .... Dr. Kim HARRINGTON
18 Vice President Facilities .... Mr. Charles G. RHODE
11 Vice President Campus Services .... Mr. Paul STROUTS
13 Interim VP Information Tech/CIO .... Mr. Mark HOETING
41 Director of Athletics .... Mr. Todd STANSBURY
22 Sr Director Diversity Management .... Ms. Pearl ALEXANDER
12 Dean Ivan Allen Col Liberal Arts .... Dr. Jacqueline J. ROYSTER
48 Dean College of Design .... Dr. Steve FRENCH
77 Dean College of Computing .... Dr. Zvi GALIL
54 Dean College of Engineering .... Dr. Gary S. MAY
08 Dean Libraries/Vice Prov Acad Eff .... Ms. Catherine MURRAY-RUST
82 Dean Scheller College of Business .... Dr. Maryam ALAVI
81 Dean College of Sciences .... Dr. Paul GOLDBART
06 Registrar .... Ms. Reta PIKOWSKY
40 Director Georgia Tech Bookstore .... Ms. Leah ANTONIAZZI
19 Director of Security & Police .... Mr. Robert CONNOLLY
107 Dean Professional Education .... Dr. Nelson BAKER
36 Executive Director Career Develop .... Dr. Michelle TULLIER
37 Director Student Financial Aid .... Ms. Marie MONS
23 Sr Director Student Health Svcs .... Dr. Gregory MOORE
39 Executive Director Housing .... Mr. Michael BLACK
09 Asst VP Institutional Res/EDM .... Ms. Sandra J. BRAMBLETT
85 Vice Prov International Initiatives .... Dr. Yves BERTHELOT
104 Exec Dir International Education .... Ms. Amy HENRY
38 Director Counseling Center .... Dr. Ruperto PEREZ
109 Senior Director Auxiliary Services .... Mr. Richard STEELE
07 Director Undergraduate Admission .... Mr. Richard CLARK
96 Director of Procurement Services .... Mr. Frans BARENDS
114 Asst VP Inst Budget Plng & Admin .... Mr. James KIRK
88 Asst VP Capital Planning/Space Mgmt .... Mr. Howard WERTHEIMER
88 Exec Director Strategic Consulting .... Dr. Sonia ALVAREZ-ROBINSON
113 Bursar .... Mr. Terry FAIR
21 Interim VP Financial Services .... Mr. James FORTNER

† Part of the University System of Georgia.

Georgia Military College (B)

201 E Greene Street, Milledgeville GA 31061-3398
County: Baldwin FICE Identification: 001571
Unit ID: 485111
Telephone: (478) 387-4900 Carnegie Class: Not Classified
FAX Number: N/A Calendar System: Quarter
URL: www.gmc.edu
Established: 1879 Annual Undergrad Tuition & Fees: $6,128
Enrollment: 7,876 Coed
Affiliation or Control: Independent Non-Profit IRS Status: 501(c)3
Highest Offering: Baccalaureate
Accreditation: SC

01 President .... LtGen. William B. CALDWELL, IV
03 Executive Vice President/COO .... BGEN. Curt RAUHUT
05 Chief Academic Ofcr/Dn of Faculty .... Dr. Phillip M. HOLMES
10 Chief Financial Officer .... COL. James WATKINS
32 Commandant/Dean of Students .... COL. Patrick BEER
30 Chief College Relations Officer .... Mr. Mark STROM
13 VP Info Technology/Online Campus .... Mr. Jody YEARWOOD
15 VP Human Resources .... Ms. Jill ROBBINS
21 Assoc Vice Pres Resource Management .... Ms. Susan MEEKS
06 Associate VP Academic Records .... Mrs. Robin KNIGHT
09 Director Institutional Research .... Dr. Susan ISAAC
41 Athletic Director .... Mr. Bert WILLIAMS
18 Director Facilities/Engineer .... Mr. Jeff GRAY
08 Director of Library Services .... Ms. Erin NEWTON
19 Chief Security/Safety/Campus Police .... Mr. James HODNETT
26 Chief Public Relations/Marketing .... Mr. Jay BENTLEY
20 Associate Academic Officer .... Mr. Derek STONE
84 Director of Enrollment Management .... Mr. Jody YEARWOOD
04 Administrative Asst to President .... Ms. Joelle TRUMBO
37 Director Student Financial Aid .... Ms. Alisa STEPHENS

Georgia Northwestern Technical College (C)

One Maurice Culberson Drive, Rome GA 30161
County: Floyd FICE Identification: 005257
Unit ID: 139384
Telephone: (706) 295-6963 Carnegie Class: Assoc/HVT-Mix Trad/Non
FAX Number: (706) 295-6944 Calendar System: Semester
URL: www.gntc.edu
Established: 1966 Annual Undergrad Tuition & Fees (In-State): $2,764
Enrollment: 5,874 Coed
Affiliation or Control: State IRS Status: 501(c)3
Highest Offering: Associate Degree
Accreditation: SC, ADNUR, CAHIIM, COARC, DA, DMS, EMT, MAC, RAD, SURGT

01 President .... Dr. Pete MCDONALD
05 Provost .... Vacant
11 Vice Pres Administrative Services .... Ms. Kelly BARNES
30 Vice Pres Econ Development .... Ms. Mardi JACKSON
20 Vice President Academic Affairs .... Dr. Mindy MCCANNON
09 Exec Vice Pres Inst Effectiveness .... Ms. Heidi POPHAM
51 Vice President Adult Education .... Ms. Kerri HOSMER
32 Exec Vice Pres Student Affairs .... Ms. Selena MAGNUSSON
06 Registrar .... Ms. Selena MAGNUSSON
08 Director of Library Services .... Mr. John LASSITER
19 Director Safety & Security .... Mr. Bill BYARS
37 Exec Director of Financial Aid .... Mr. Stephen ANDERSEN
18 Director Facilities Management .... Mr. Jeffrey AGAN
26 Dir Marketing/Public Relations .... Ms. Amber JORDAN
15 Director of Human Resources .... Ms. Peggy CORDELL

Georgia Piedmont Technical College (D)

495 N Indian Creek Drive, Clarkston GA 30021-2397
County: DeKalb FICE Identification: 005622
Unit ID: 244446
Telephone: (404) 297-9522 Carnegie Class: Assoc/HVT-Mix Trad/Non
FAX Number: (404) 297-4234 Calendar System: Semester
URL: www.gptc.edu
Established: 1961 Annual Undergrad Tuition & Fees (In-State): $2,850
Enrollment: 3,908 Coed
Affiliation or Control: State IRS Status: 501(c)3
Highest Offering: Associate Degree
Accreditation: SC, EMT, ENGT, MAC, MLTAD

01 President .... Dr. Jabari SIMAMA
04 Exec Dir & Spec Asst to President .... Mr. Keith SAGERS
05 Exec Vice Pres Academic/Stdnt Affs .... Dr. Ivan HARRELL
10 Vice Pres Business/Financial Svcs .... Mr. Mark KOMDAT
31 VP Economic Devel/Cmty Engagement .... Ms. Cynthia EDWARDS
30 VP Institutional Advancement .... Mr. Anthony NEAL
20 Assoc Vice Pres Academic Affairs .... Dr. Debra GORDON
37 Assistant VP of Financial Aid .... Ms. Lakisha SANDERS
32 Dean of Student Affairs .... Dr. Candice JONES
20 Dean of Academic Affairs .... Mr. Marcus HICKS
35 Dean of Student Affairs .... Ms. Candice JONES
108 Dean of Quality Initiatives .... Vacant
15 Director of Human Resources .... Ms. Lolita MORRISON
26 Dir Marketing/Public Relations .... Ms. Martha PACINI
06 Registrar .... Ms. Joana BLANKSON
07 Director Admissions/Recruiting .... Mr. Corey PARKER
51 Director Continuing Education .... Ms. Consuelo GODDEN
18 Director Facilities/Auxiliary Svcs .... Vacant
36 Dir Adv/Career & Retention Svcs .... Ms. Angela CUMMINGS
13 Director of Information Technology .... Mr. Keith PERRY

Georgia Southern University (E)

PO Box 8033, Statesboro GA 30460-8033
County: Bulloch FICE Identification: 001572
Unit ID: 139931
Telephone: (912) 478-4636 Carnegie Class: DU-Mod
FAX Number: N/A Calendar System: Semester
URL: www.georgiasouthern.edu
Established: 1906 Annual Undergrad Tuition & Fees (In-State): $6,273
Enrollment: 20,459 Coed
Affiliation or Control: State IRS Status: 501(c)3
Highest Offering: Doctorate
Accreditation: SC, ART, CAATE, CACREP, CAEPN, CIDA, CLPSY, CONST, CS, DIETD, DIETI, ENG, ENGT, IPSY, MUS, NRPA, NURSE, PH, SPAA, THEA

01 President .... Dr. Jaimie HEBERT
05 Interim Provost .... Dr. Diana CONE
10 Vice Pres Business & Finance .... Mr. Rob WHITAKER
32 VP Student Affairs & Enroll Mgmt .... Dr. Teresa THOMPSON
111 VP Univ Advancement & External Affs .... Mr. Trip ADDISON
13 Chief Information Officer .... Mr. Ron STALNAKER
09 Assoc VP Strategic Rsrch & Analysis .... Dr. Jayne PERKINS BROWN
20 Vice Provost .... Vacant
35 Dean of Students .... Dr. Patrice BUCKNER JACKSON
43 Assoc Vice Pres for Legal Affairs .... Ms. Maura COPELAND
30 Assoc VP University Advancement .... Mr. Michael SHIPPAM
04 Exec Associate to the President .... Ms. Leigh PRICE
07 Director of Admissions .... Ms. Amy SMITH
58 Dean College of Graduate Studies .... Vacant
50 Dean College Business Admin .... Dr. Allen AMASON
53 Dean College Education .... Dr. Thomas KOBALLA
76 Dean College Health/Human Sci .... Dr. Barry JOYNER
49 Dean Col Liberal Arts/Social Sci .... Dr. Curtis RICKER
81 Dean College Science & Mathematics .... Dr. Martha ABELL
54 Dean AEP Col Engr/Info Tech .... Dr. Mohammad DAVOUD
51 Exec Director Continuing Educ .... Dr. Belkis CAPELES
69 Dean College of Public Health .... Dr. R. Gregory EVANS
62 Dean University Library .... Dr. Bede MITCHELL
88 Dir NCAA Compliance .... Mr. Keith ROUGHTON
116 Chief Audit & Advisory Services .... Ms. Jana BRILEY
26 Assoc VP Mktg & Comm .... Ms. Jan BOND
121 Director Academic Success Center .... Vacant
37 Director Financial Aid .... Ms. Tracey MINGO
06 Registrar .... Dr. Velma BURDEN
109 Assoc VP Auxiliary Services .... Mr. Edward D. MILLS
21 Senior Assoc VP/Controller .... Ms. Kim THOMPSON BROWN
15 Assoc VP Human Resources .... Ms. Rebecca CARROLL
41 Athletic Director .... Mr. Tom KLEINLEIN
18 Interim Assoc VP Facilities .... Ms. Wendy WOODRUM
19 Director Public Safety .... Ms. Laura MCCULLOUGH
36 Director Career Services .... Mr. Philip BRUCE
38 Director Counseling Services .... Dr. Jodi K. CALDWELL
23 Director Health Services .... Ms. Elissa NORRIS
39 Director University Housing .... Mr. Peter BLUTREICH
28 Dir Multicultural Student Center .... Ms. Takeshia BROWN
88 Director Leadership/Outreach Pgms .... Dr. Todd DEAL
88 Director Advancement IT .... Ms. Jill GERIG
29 Sr Director Alumni Relations .... Mr. Wendell TOMPKINS, JR.
88 Director Botanic Garden .... Ms. Carolyn ALTMAN
14 Director Technical Services .... Mr. Joey REEVES
90 Director Info Tech for Acad Affairs .... Ms. Pamela DEAL
88 Director Museum .... Dr. Brent THARP
88 Director Wildlife Educ/Raptor Ctr .... Mr. Steven M. HEIN
96 Director of Procurement & Contract .... Mr. John OGLESBY
28 Dir Equal Opp/Title IX .... Mr. Joel WRIGHT
89 Director First-Year Experience .... Dr. Chris CAPLINGER
92 Director Univ Honors Program .... Dr. Steven ENGEL
119 Chief Information Tech Security Ofc .... Mr. Michael FOX
88 Director Centers for Teaching & Tec .... Dr. Rachel SCHWARTZ
22 Dir Stdnt Affs/Disability Res Ctr .... Mrs. Deborah J. PEREZ-LOPEZ
102 Director Foundation Acct .... Ms. Jodi COLLINS

† Part of the University System of Georgia.

Georgia Southwestern State University (F)

800 GA Southwestern State Univ Dr,
Americus GA 31709-4693
County: Sumter FICE Identification: 001573
Unit ID: 139764
Telephone: (877) 871-4594 Carnegie Class: Masters/M
FAX Number: N/A Calendar System: Semester
URL: www.gsw.edu
Established: 1906 Annual Undergrad Tuition & Fees (In-State): $5,262
Enrollment: 2,755 Coed
Affiliation or Control: State IRS Status: 501(c)3
Highest Offering: Beyond Master's But Less Than Doctorate
Accreditation: SC, CAEPN, NURSE

01 President .... Dr. Neal WEAVER
05 Int Vice President Academic Affairs .... Ms. Lynda L. PURVIS
10 Vice Pres Business & Finance .... Mr. W. Cody KING
32 Vice President for Student Affairs .... Dr. Samuel T. MILLER
84 Vice Pres Enroll Mgmt/Dir Admiss .... Dr. Gaye HAYES
09 Director Institutional Research .... Dr. Lisa A. COOPER
08 Dean Library Services .... Ms. Ru STORY-HUFFMAN
13 Dir Information Technology/CIO .... Mr. Royce HACKETT
102 GSW Foundation Executive Director .... Ms. Reda K. ROWELL
06 Registrar .... Ms. Krista SMITH
36 Director Career Services Center .... Ms. Sandra FOWLER

37 Director Student Financial Aid .... Dr. Angela V. BRYANT
26 Director University Relations .... Mr. Stephen E. SNYDER
35 Assistant Dean of Students .... Dr. Darcy BRAGG
41 Athletic Director .... Mr. Mike LEEDER
29 Coord Alumni Relations/Annual Fund .... Ms. Kimberly COMER
15 Director of Human Resources .... Ms. Gena WILSON
19 Director of Public Safety .... Mr. Michael TRACY
04 Exec Assistant to the President .... Ms. Angela SMITH
108 Dir Institutional Effectiveness .... Dr. Bryan P. DAVIS
38 Director Counseling Services .... Ms. Alma G. KEITA
96 Director of Purchasing .... Ms. Michelle W. UNDERWOOD

† Part of the University System of Georgia.

Georgia State University (A)

PO Box 3999, Atlanta GA 30302-3999

County: Fulton FICE Identification: 001574
Unit ID: 139940
Telephone: (404) 413-2000 Carnegie Class: DU-Highest
FAX Number: (404) 413-1380 Calendar System: Semester
URL: www.gsu.edu
Established: 1913 Annual Undergrad Tuition & Fees (In-State): $8,974
Enrollment: 32,058 Coed
Affiliation or Control: State IRS Status: 501(c)3
Highest Offering: Doctorate
Accreditation: SC, ADNUR, ART, CACREP, CAEPN, CEA, CLPSY, COARC, COPSY, DH, DIETC, EXSC, HSA, IPSY, LAW, MUS, NURSE, PH, PTA, SCPSY, SP, SPAA, SW

01 President .... Dr. Mark P. BECKER
05 Sr VP Academic Affairs & Provost .... Dr. Risa I. PALM
10 Sr VP Finance & Administration .... Dr. Jerry J. RACKLIFFE
84 Vice Provost & VP Enroll Mgt .... Dr. Timothy M. RENICK
12 Vice Provost/Dean Perimeter College .... Dr. Peter LYONS
46 Vice President Research & Econ Dev .... Dr. James A. WEYHENMEYER
32 Vice President Student Affairs .... Dr. Douglass F. COVEY
30 Vice President Development .... Mr. Walter T. MASSEY
26 VP PR & Mktg Communications .... Mr. Don HALE
43 University Attorney .... Dr. Kerry L. HEYWARD
49 Dean Arts & Sciences .... Dr. Sara ROSEN
50 Dean Business .... Dr. Richard D. PHILLIPS
53 Dean Education & Human Development .... Dr. Paul A. ALBERTO
66 Dean Nursing/Health Professions .... Dr. Nancy P. KROPF
69 Dean Public Health .... Dr. Michael P. ERIKSEN
61 Interim Dean Law .... Dr. Wendy HENSEL
80 Interim Dean Policy Studies .... Dr. Sally WALLACE
92 Dean Honors College .... Dr. Larry S. BERMAN
08 Dean Libraries .... Mr. Jeff STEELY
88 Assoc Provost Strategic Initiatives .... Dr. Mary Beth WALKER
58 Assoc Provost Grad Programs .... Dr. Lisa P. ARMISTEAD
09 Assoc Provost Inst Effectiveness .... Dr. Michael GALCHINSKY
82 Assc Prov International Initiatives .... Dr. Wolfgang SCHLOER
20 Assoc Provost Faculty Affairs .... Dr. Kavita PANDIT
88 Assistant Provost Admin Operations .... Mr. Christopher D. HILL
45 Assoc VP Research Integrity .... Dr. Brenda J. CHAPMAN
88 Assoc VP Tech Lic/Commercial .... Dr. Chester A. BISBEE
88 Chief Innovation Officer for IT .... Mr. Phil VENTIMIGLIA
13 AVP IS&T/Chief Technology Ofcr .... Vacant
18 Assoc VP Facilities .... Mr. Ramesh VAKAMUDI
21 Assoc Vice President Finance .... Ms. Elizabeth R. JONES
21 Assoc VP Finance & Comptroller .... Mr. Bruce R. SPRATT
88 Assoc VP Central Development .... Ms. Tabatha MICHEL
30 Assoc VP Constituent Programs Dev .... Mr. Michael J. WORLEY
88 Asst VP Campaign Strategy .... Ms. Susan BOYETTE
102 Assoc VP GSU Foundation .... Mr. Dale J. PALMER
35 Assoc VP Stdnt Affs/Dean Students .... Dr. Darryl B. HOLLOMAN
27 Assoc VP Public Relations .... Ms. Andrea JONES
07 Asst VP Undergraduate Admissions .... Mr. Scott M. BURKE
124 Asst VP Student Retention .... Dr. Allison CALHOUN-BROWN
29 Asst VP Alumni Relations .... Ms. Christina C. MILLION
15 Asst VP Human Resources .... Ms. Linda J. NELSON
22 Asst VP Opp Dev/Diversity Educ .... Ms. Linda J. NELSON
19 Asst VP/Chief University Police .... Mr. Joseph SPILLANE
06 Registrar .... Ms. Tarrah N. MIRUS
85 Dir Intl Students/Scholars Svcs .... Ms. Heather L. HOUSLEY
39 Director University Housing .... Mr. Randy D. BROWN, JR.
38 Director Psychological & Health Svc .... Dr. Jill LEE-BARBER
28 Director Diversity Programs .... Mr. John R. DAY
88 Director Application Engineering .... Mr. John M. BANDY, JR.
14 Director Technology Engineering .... Mr. Keith E. CAMPBELL
88 Interim Dir Research Computing .... Mr. Davide GAETANO
36 Director University Career Svcs .... Ms. Catherine NEINER
37 Interim Director Financial Aid .... Mr. Anthony CARTER
96 Director of Business Services .... Mr. Michael E. DAVIDSON
116 Dir Univ Auditing & Advisory Svcs .... Mr. Sterling ROTH
88 Director Emergency Management .... Mr. Keith P. SUMAS
31 Director Govt & Community Affairs .... Ms. Julia M. KERLIN
41 Athletic Director .... Mr. Charles G. COBB
88 Special Advisor to President .... Mr. Thomas C. LEWIS
04 Assistant to the President .... Ms. Ethel M. BROWN

† Part of the University System of Georgia.

Gordon State College (B)

419 College Dr., Barnesville GA 30204-1746

County: Lamar FICE Identification: 001575
Unit ID: 139968
Telephone: (678) 359-5555 Carnegie Class: Bac/Assoc-Mixed
FAX Number: (678) 359-5080 Calendar System: Semester
URL: www.gordonstate.edu
Established: 1852 Annual Undergrad Tuition & Fees (In-State): $3,974
Enrollment: 4,084 Coed
Affiliation or Control: State IRS Status: 501(c)3
Highest Offering: Baccalaureate
Accreditation: SC, ADNUR, CAEPN, NUR

01 President .... Dr. Max BURNS
05 Provost & VP Academic Affairs .... Dr. Jeffery KNIGHTON
10 VP Finance and Administration .... Mrs. Kristen ALBRITTON
32 VP Student Affairs .... Dr. Dennis R. CHAMBERLAIN
111 VP Institutional Advancement .... Mrs. Rhonda TOON
04 Administrative Asst to President .... Mrs. Dolores BELL
20 Associate VP Academic Affairs .... Dr. Richard BASKIN
108 Asst VP Institutional Effectiveness .... Mrs. Teresa BETKOWSKI
08 Library Director .... Dr. Sonya GAITHER
09 Director of Institutional Research .... Mr. Britt LIFSEY
49 Int Dean School of Arts & Sciences .... Dr. Susan FINAZZO
53 Dean School of Education .... Dr. Michael MAHAN
66 Dean School of Nursing .... Dr. Anne PURVIS
121 Director of Student Success Center .... Mr. Peter J. HIGGINS
21 Assistant VP/Controller .... Mr. Walter GREEN
15 Asst VP Human Resources .... Mrs. Laura BOWEN
113 Bursar .... Mr. Kenneth HUTTO
114 Dir of Budgets & Aux Operations .... Mr. Justin WHITE
18 Director of Facilities .... Mr. Richard VEREEN
37 Director of Financial Aid .... Mrs. Jody DEFORE
13 Director of Information Technology .... Mr. Jeff HAYES
19 Director of Public Safety .... Chief Jeff MASON
07 Int Director of Admissions .... Mrs. Valerie CALHOUN
41 Interim Athletic Director .... Mr. Gary SHARPE
38 Director of Counseling Services .... Ms. Alicia DORTON
39 Director of Residence Life .... Mrs. Tonya R. COLEMAN
35 Director of Student Activities .... Ms. Sharon LLOYD
06 Registrar .... Mrs. Janet BARRAS
30 Development Officer .... Mr. Skipper BURNS
26 Chief Public Information Officer .... Mrs. Tamara BOATWRIGHT
40 Bookstore Manager .... Mrs. Connie H. WADE

† Part of the University System of Georgia.

Gupton Jones College of Funeral Service (C)

5141 Snapfinger Woods Drive, Decatur GA 30035-4022

County: DeKalb FICE Identification: 010771
Unit ID: 139995
Telephone: (770) 593-2257 Carnegie Class: Spec 2-yr-A&S
FAX Number: (770) 593-1891 Calendar System: Quarter
URL: www.gupton-jones.edu
Established: 1920 Annual Undergrad Tuition & Fees: $11,700
Enrollment: 194 Coed
Affiliation or Control: Independent Non-Profit IRS Status: 501(c)3
Highest Offering: Associate Degree
Accreditation: FUSER

01 President .... Mr. Antonio WALLACE
05 Dean .... Mr. Duane PIEL
06 Registrar .... Ms. Felicia SMITH

Gwinnett College (D)

4230 Highway 29, Suite 11, Lilburn GA 30047-3447

County: Gwinnett FICE Identification: 025830
Unit ID: 140003
Telephone: (770) 381-7200 Carnegie Class: Assoc/HVT-High Non
FAX Number: (770) 381-0454 Calendar System: Other
URL: www.gwinnettcollege.com
Established: 1976 Annual Undergrad Tuition & Fees: $9,925
Enrollment: 306 Coed
Affiliation or Control: Proprietary IRS Status: Proprietary
Highest Offering: Associate Degree
Accreditation: ACICS

01 President .... Mr. Michael DAVIS
05 Director of Education .... Ms. Lisa MCLARIO

Gwinnett College-Marietta (E)

1130 North Chase Parkway, Suite 100, Marietta GA 30067

County: Cobb FICE Identification: 038044
Unit ID: 444714
Telephone: (770) 859-9779 Carnegie Class: Spec 2-yr-Health
FAX Number: (770) 859-9778 Calendar System: Quarter
URL: www.medtech.edu
Established: Annual Undergrad Tuition & Fees: N/A
Enrollment: 195 Coed
Affiliation or Control: Proprietary IRS Status: Proprietary
Highest Offering: Associate Degree
Accreditation: COE

01 Campus President .... Mr. Michael DAVIS

Gwinnett College-Sandy Springs (F)

6690 Roswell Rd, NE, Ste 2200, Sandy Springs GA 30328

County: Fulton FICE Identification: 034183
Unit ID: 425250
Telephone: (770) 457-2021 Carnegie Class: Not Classified
FAX Number: (404) 574-2234 Calendar System: Other
URL: www.risingspirit.edu
Established: 1994 Annual Undergrad Tuition & Fees: N/A
Enrollment: 96 Coed
Affiliation or Control: Proprietary IRS Status: Proprietary
Highest Offering: Associate Degree
Accreditation: ACCSC

01 President .... Mr. Michael DAVIS
04 Assistant to President .... Mr. Ty DAVIS

Gwinnett Technical College (G)

5150 Sugarloaf Parkway, Lawrenceville GA 30043-5702

County: Gwinnett FICE Identification: 022884
Unit ID: 140012
Telephone: (770) 962-7580 Carnegie Class: Assoc/HVT-High Trad
FAX Number: (770) 962-7985 Calendar System: Semester
URL: www.gwinnetttech.edu
Established: 1984 Annual Undergrad Tuition & Fees (In-State): $2,796
Enrollment: 6,959 Coed
Affiliation or Control: State IRS Status: 501(c)3
Highest Offering: Associate Degree
Accreditation: SC, ACFEI, ADNUR, CAHIIM, COARC, CVT, DA, DMS, EMT, MAC, RAD, SURGT

01 President .... Dr. Glen D. CANNON
10 VP Economic Development .... Mr. David WELDEN
05 VP of Academic Affairs .... Ms. Rebecca ALEXANDER
11 VP Administrative Services .... Ms. Sonya MCDANIEL
13 VP Technology & Operations .... Mr. Galen MARTIN
111 VP of Institutional Advancement .... Ms. Mary Beth BYERLY
32 VP of Student Affairs .... Dr. Julie POST
84 Exec Dir Enrollment Support .... Ms. Betsy HARRIS-BRACKETT
07 Exec Dir Enrollment Processing .... Mr. Kohle PAUL
103 Director State Workforce Programs .... Ms. Ann SECHRIST
09 Dir Inst Research & Effectiveness .... Dr. Carla MORELON
36 Director of Career Services .... Ms. Ave MILLER
53 Dean of Adult Education .... Ms. Stephanie ROOKS
37 Director of Financial Aid .... Ms. Lisa MARTIN
06 Dir of Admissions & Registrar .... Dr. Jymmyca WYATT
15 Director of Human Resources .... Ms. LaShanta' COX
04 Exec Assistant to the President .... Ms. Melissa FLANAGAN
18 Supervisor of Facilities Operation .... Ms. Janice BOLTON
19 Chief of Campus Police & Security .... Mr. Mike BLOUIN
08 Manager of Library Services .... Ms. Elissa CHECOV

Helms College (H)

5171 Eisenhower Pkwy, Macon GA 31206-5309

County: Bibb FICE Identification: 042064
Unit ID: 481155
Telephone: (478) 471-4394 Carnegie Class: Not Classified
FAX Number: N/A Calendar System: Quarter
URL: helms.edu
Established: 2007 Annual Undergrad Tuition & Fees: $16,259
Enrollment: 151 Coed
Affiliation or Control: Independent Non-Profit IRS Status: 501(c)3
Highest Offering: Associate Degree
Accreditation: CNCE

01 President .... James STIFF

Herzing University (I)

3393 Peachtree Road NE, Suite 1003, Atlanta GA 30326-1332

Telephone: (404) 816-4533 FICE Identification: 020897
Accreditation: &NH, NURSE

† Regional accreditation is carried under the parent institution in Madison, WI.

Interactive College of Technology (J)

5303 New Peachtree Road, Chamblee GA 30341-2818

County: DeKalb FICE Identification: 022843
Unit ID: 138655
Telephone: (770) 216-2960 Carnegie Class: Assoc/HVT-High Trad
FAX Number: (678) 287-3474 Calendar System: Semester
URL: www.ict.edu
Established: 1986 Annual Undergrad Tuition & Fees: $9,458
Enrollment: 467 Coed
Affiliation or Control: Proprietary IRS Status: Proprietary
Highest Offering: Associate Degree
Accreditation: COE

01 President .... Mr. Elmer R. SMITH
03 Executive Vice President .... Mr. Michael K. POWER
05 Dean of the College .... Mr. Thomas A. BLAIR
12 Campus Director Pasadena Texas .... Mr. Todd PATTERSON
12 Campus Dir SW Houston Texas .... Ms. Cynthia BRYSON
12 Campus Dir North Houston Texas .... Mr. Harry MAUZ
12 Campus Director - Newport KY .... Mr. William K. MCGUIRE
12 Campus Director - Morrow GA .... Mr. Greg KOCH
12 Campus Director - Gainesville GA .... Ms. Sofia LUKAS
04 Administrative Asst to President .... Ms. Karen A. MILLER
88 Senior Administrative Assistant .... Ms. Liesa PEAVY
26 Vice President/Marketing .... Mr. Jim C. HARRIS
36 Director Student Placement .... Mr. Andre GIPSON
06 Registrar .... Ms. Rosalind HOLT

Interactive College of Technology (K)

2323-C Browns Bridge Road, Gainesville GA 30504

Telephone: (678) 456-0550 Identification: 770533
Accreditation: COE

Interactive College of Technology (A)

1580 Southdale Parkway, Suite C, Morrow GA 30260
Telephone: (770) 960-1298 Identification: 770534
Accreditation: COE

Interdenominational Theological Center (B)

700 Martin L. King, Jr. Drive, SW, Atlanta GA 30314-4143
County: Fulton FICE Identification: 001568
Unit ID: 140146
Telephone: (404) 527-7700 Carnegie Class: Spec-4-yr-Faith
FAX Number: (404) 527-0901 Calendar System: Semester
URL: www.itc.edu
Established: 1958 Annual Graduate Tuition & Fees: N/A
Enrollment: 256 Coed
Affiliation or Control: Interdenominational IRS Status: 501(c)3
Highest Offering: Doctorate; No Undergraduates
Accreditation: SC, THEOL

01 President ... Dr. Edward LORENZA WHEELER
05 VP for Academic Services/Provost ... Dr. Maisha HANDY
11 VP of Administrative Services ... Mr. Alfred NORRIS
10 Int Vice Pres Financial Services ... Mr. Thomas POITIER
30 Int VP Institutional Advancement ... Ms. Rochelle REEDER
84 AVP Enrollment Management/Registrar ... Ms. Bobbie HALL
32 AVP Student Services ... Mr. Willie F. GOODMAN
37 Financial Aid Director ... Mr. Johnny NIMES
15 Chief Human Resources Officer ... Ms. Idell HENDERSON
07 Director of Admissions/Recruitment ... Ms. Michelle DAVIS
42 Chaplain ... Dr. Keith SLAUGHTER

Kennesaw State University (C)

585 Cobb Avenue NW, MD #0101,
Kennesaw GA 30144-5563
County: Cobb FICE Identification: 001577
Unit ID: 486840
Telephone: (470) 578-6033 Carnegie Class: DU-Mod
FAX Number: (470) 578-9117 Calendar System: Semester
URL: www.kennesaw.edu
Established: 1963 Annual Undergrad Tuition & Fees (In-State): $6,060
Enrollment: 33,252 Coed
Affiliation or Control: State IRS Status: 501(c)3
Highest Offering: Doctorate
Accreditation: SC, ART, CAEPN, CGTECH, CONST, CS, CSHSE, ENG, ENGR, ENGT, MACTE, MUS, NURSE, SPAA, SW, THEA

01 President ... Mr. Sam OLENS
10 Chief Business Officer ... Ms. Julie PETERSON
05 Provost/Vice Pres Academic Affs ... Dr. W. Ken HARMON
32 Vice Pres Student Affairs ... Dr. Kathleen C. WHITE
09 Interim VP for Research ... Dr. Donald MCGAREY
26 VP of Marketing ... Vacant
88 VP Economic Dev/Community Engage ... Mr. Charles ROSS
20 Senior Vice Provost Academic Affs ... Dr. John OMACHONU
43 Chief Legal Affairs Officer ... Mr. Jeff MILSTEEN
20 Assoc Vice Pres for Curriculum ... Dr. Valerie D. WHITTLESEY
97 Dean University College ... Dr. Lynn DISBROW
15 Chief Human Resources Officer ... Ms. Ann BURRIS
13 Chief Information Officer ... Ms. Lectra LAWHORNE
84 Assoc Vice Pres Enrollment Services ... Mr. Kim WEST
106 AVP Technology Enhanced Learning ... Dr. Elke LEEDS
88 Asst VP Strategic Comm & Issues Mgt ... Ms. Tammy DEMEL
30 Asst VP Development ... Ms. Melisa BALDWIN
88 Asst VP University Comm ... Mr. James COOPER
08 Asst Vice Pres for Library Services ... Dr. J. David EVANS
18 Asst Vice Pres Facilities Services ... Mr. John A. ANDERSON
27 Asst VP of Marketing ... Mr. Ronald RAMOS
46 Asst VP Institutional Research ... Dr. Robert SMITH
35 Asst VP Student Life Operations ... Ms. Katherine E. ALDAY
79 Dean Humanities/Social Science ... Dr. Robert DORFF
81 Dean Science & Mathematics ... Dr. Mark R. ANDERSON
53 Dean Bagwell College of Education ... Dr. Arlinda EATON
50 Dean Coles College of Business ... Dr. Kathy S. SCHWAIG
76 Dean WellStar Col Health/Human Svcs ... Dr. Mark TILLMAN
49 Dean College of the Arts ... Dr. Patricia S. POULTER
48 Dean Architecture/Construction Mgmt ... Dr. Richard COLE
77 Interim Dean CCSE ... Dr. Jon PRESTON
58 Dean Graduate College ... Dr. Mike DISHMAN
92 Dean Honors College ... Dr. Rita BAILEY
51 Dean Continuing/Professional Educ ... Ms. Barbara S. CALHOUN
35 Assoc VP Student Affairs ... Dr. Michael L. SANSEVIRO
07 Sr Exec Director Enrollment Svcs ... Ms. Susan N. BLAKE
121 Assoc VP/Dir Student Success Svcs ... Dr. Bob J. MATTOX
28 Chief Diversity Officer ... Dr. Erik MALEWSKI
06 Registrar ... Mr. Kim WEST
14 Assoc CIO/CTO ... Dr. John L. ISENHOUR
91 Exec Dir Enterprise Systems & Svcs ... Ms. Rifka MAYANI
37 Director Student Financial Aid ... Mr. Rondall H. DAY
07 Exec Dir Undergraduate Programs ... Dr. Angela J. EVANS
25 Director Procurement & Contracting ... Mr. Robert FORBES
88 Exec Dir Internships & Coops ... Ms. Ana BAIDA
41 Athletics Director ... Mr. Vaughn A. WILLIAMS
29 Director Alumni Relations ... Ms. Pierrette MAILLET
110 Director University Development ... Dr. Joan DUNCAN
19 AVP Public Safety/Chief of Police ... Mr. Roger STEARNS
100 Exec Admin to Pres/Chf of Protocol ... Ms. Lynda K. JOHNSON
104 Education Abroad Progam Coordinator ... Ms. Nicole MEANOR
105 Dir Web Services/Mobile Development ... Mr. Chris WARD
108 Vice Provost Inst Effectiveness ... Dr. Jorge PEREZ
39 Director University Housing ... Mr. Christopher BRUNO
54 Dean of Engineering/Eng Technology ... Dr. Thomas CURRIN
86 Director Government Relations ... Vacant
116 Chief Internal Auditor ... Ms. Lesley NETTER-SNOWDEN
88 Director Ethics & Compliance ... Mr. Clay DEAN
102 Interim COO Foundation ... Mr. James DUNN

† Part of the University System of Georgia.

LaGrange College (D)

601 Broad Street, La Grange GA 30240-2999
County: Troup FICE Identification: 001578
Unit ID: 140234
Telephone: (706) 880-8000 Carnegie Class: Bac-A&S
FAX Number: (706) 880-8358 Calendar System: 4/1/4
URL: www.lagrange.edu
Established: 1831 Annual Undergrad Tuition & Fees: $28,490
Enrollment: 1,028 Coed
Affiliation or Control: United Methodist IRS Status: 501(c)3
Highest Offering: Master's
Accreditation: SC, ACBSP, NUR

01 President ... Dr. Dan MCALEXANDER
04 Executive Assistant to President ... Mrs. Carla RHODES
41 VP of Athletics ... Mrs. Jennifer D. CLAYBROOK
05 VP Academic Affairs ... Dr. Karen AUBREY
32 VP of Student Engagement ... Dr. Mark SHOOK
06 Registrar ... Ms. Cindy SAINES
08 Director of Library Services ... Mrs. Charlene BAXTER
09 Director Inst Effectiveness ... Dr. Carol YIN
36 Director Career Development Center ... Dr. Karen PRUETT
38 Director Counseling Center ... Mrs. Pamela TREMBLAY
20 Associate Provost ... Dr. Maranah SAUTER
39 Director Res Educ & Housing ... Mr. Vernon JAMES
30 VP of External Relations ... Mrs. Rebecca ROTH NICKS
26 Sr Director Communications/Mktg ... Mr. Dean A. HARTMAN
37 Director Student Financial Aid ... Mrs. Michelle REEVES
110 Director of Development ... Ms. Rebecca DAVIS
29 Director Alumni & Cmty Relations ... Mrs. Martha PIRKLE
84 VP of Enrollment ... Mr. Joseph C. MILLER
112 Major Gift Officer ... Mr. Mark DAVIS
07 Director of Admission ... Mrs. Leslie TRAYLOR
105 Asst Director Communications & Mktg ... Vacant
10 VP of Finance & Operations ... Mr. Martin E. PIRRMAN
21 Director of Finance ... Mrs. Patti D. HOXSIE
15 VP of Human Resources ... Mrs. Dawn COKER
18 Manager Facilities/Physical Plant ... Mr. Michael CONIGLIO
19 Director of Security ... Mr. Michael A. THOMAS
13 Sr Director Information Technology ... Mr. James BLACKWOOD
42 Director Spiritual Life & Chaplain ... Dr. Adam ROBERTS
106 Director Online Instruction ... Dr. Jon ERNSTBERGER
91 Database Administrator ... Mr. Brandon MOBLEY
88 Events Coordinator ... Ms. Tammy ROGERS

Lanier Technical College (E)

2990 Landrum Education Drive, Oakwood GA 30566-3405
County: Hall FICE Identification: 005254
Unit ID: 140243
Telephone: (770) 533-7000 Carnegie Class: Assoc/HVT-High Trad
FAX Number: (678) 989-3107 Calendar System: Semester
URL: www.laniertech.edu
Established: 1964 Annual Undergrad Tuition & Fees (In-State): $3,169
Enrollment: 3,646 Coed
Affiliation or Control: State IRS Status: 501(c)3
Highest Offering: Associate Degree
Accreditation: SC, DA, DH, EMT, MAC, PTAA, RAD, SURGT

01 President ... Dr. Ray PERREN
03 Executive Vice President ... Mr. Tim MCDONALD
103 Vice President Economic Development ... Mr. Carl ROGERS
05 Vice President Academic Affairs ... Dr. Tavarez HOLSTON
45 Vice President IE & Operations ... Dr. Joanne P. TOLLESON
32 Vice President Student Affairs ... Ms. Nancy BEAVER
10 Vice Pres Administrative Services ... Mr. Les SALTER
13 Vice Pres Information Technology ... Mr. Robbie VICKERS
04 Executive Assistant to President ... Ms. Karen MINOR
75 Dean Business Tech/Professional Svc ... Ms. Donna BRINSON
72 Dean of Applied Technology ... Mr. Christian TETZLAFF
97 Dean of General Education ... Dr. Cheree M. WILLIAMS
76 Dean of Allied Health ... Dr. Deanne COLLINS
50 Dean of Barrow Campus ... Ms. Lisa MALOOF
72 Dean of Dawson Campus ... Mr. Troy LINSEY
97 Dean of Jackson Campus ... Dr. Howard LEDFORD
09 Dir of Institutional Effectiveness ... Mr. Brad GADBERRY
111 Exec Dir Institutional Advancement ... Mr. Dennis STOCKTON
26 Director of Marketing ... Mr. Dave PARRISH
07 Director of Admissions ... Ms. Sue CRONIC
06 Registrar ... Ms. Caroline FRICK
37 Director Student Financial Aid ... Ms. Kimberly KELLEY
21 Director Administrative Services ... Ms. Mary FOWLER
15 Director of Human Resources ... Ms. Jill CANTRELL
18 Director of Facilities ... Mr. Guy ABBS
36 Career Services Specialist ... Ms. Melissa LAWRENCE
22 Disability Services Coordinator ... Ms. Mallory SAFLEY
08 Library Services Director ... Ms. Kathryn S. THOMPSON
19 College Police Chief ... Mr. Jeff STRICKLAND
96 Purchasing Agent ... Ms. Kathy PHAGAN

Life University (F)

1269 Barclay Circle, Marietta GA 30060-2996
County: Cobb FICE Identification: 020748
Unit ID: 140252
Telephone: (770) 426-2600 Carnegie Class: Spec-4-yr-Other Health
FAX Number: (770) 429-4819 Calendar System: Quarter
URL: www.life.edu
Established: 1974 Annual Undergrad Tuition & Fees: $11,220
Enrollment: 2,710 Coed
Affiliation or Control: Independent Non-Profit IRS Status: 501(c)3
Highest Offering: Doctorate
Accreditation: SC, #CAATE, CHIRO, DIETD, DIETI

00 Chancellor ... Dr. Guy F. RIEKEMAN
01 President ... Dr. Rob SCOTT
10 Exec VP for Finance ... Mr. William JARR
05 Vice Provost & VP Academic Affairs ... Dr. Tim GROSS
111 VP of University Advancement ... Mr. Greg HARRIS
32 VP for Student Services ... Dr. Marc SCHNEIDER
11 VP of Operations ... Mr. John MCGEE
84 VP of Enrollment & Mktg ... Dr. Cynthia BOYD
88 VP of Professional Relations ... Dr. Gilles LAMARCHE
41 Director of Athletics ... Ms. Jayme PENDERGAST
15 Director of Human Resources ... Ms. Stella PETERSON
13 Chief Information Officer ... Mr. John ALTIKULAC
14 Director Information Technology ... Mr. Thorton MUIR
104 Director of Global Initiatives ... Dr. John DOWNES
76 Dean College of Chiropractic ... Dr. Leslie KING
88 Dean College of Grad and Undergrad ... Dr. Jana W. HOLWICK
88 Assoc Dean Grad & Undergrad Studies ... Dr. Michael D. SMITH
23 Assistant Dean for Clinics ... Dr. Bernadette LAVENDER
88 Assoc Dean College of Chiropractic ... Dr. Michael CLUSSERATH
06 Registrar ... Ms. Heather HOFFMAN
07 Director of Admissions Operations ... Ms. Detrenyona CHESTER
106 Assoc Dean Online Education ... Dr. Richard BELCASTRO
08 Director of Learning Resources ... Ms. Karen PRESTON
46 Director of Sponsored Research ... Dr. Olivia SCRIVEN
29 Alumni Relations Manager ... Ms. Mary Ellen LEFFARD
108 Director of Inst Effectiveness ... Dr. Vince ERARIO
09 Director of Institutional Research ... Dr. Howard WRIGHT
18 Director Facilities/Physical Plant ... Mr. Larry RIDDLE
121 Director Student Success ... Dr. Lisa RUBIN
37 Director Student Financial Aid ... Ms. Jessica MAGAZU
35 Exec Dir of Student Services ... Ms. Jennifer VALTOS
36 Director of Career Planning ... Ms. Susan DUDT
88 Dir of Student Administrative Svcs ... Ms. Melissa WATERS
114 Budget Director ... Ms. Amy MCILVANE
30 Director of Development ... Ms. Erin DANCER
27 Director of Marketing ... Ms. Shelly BATCHER
44 Director of Advancement Services ... Ms. Lauren NIELSON
88 Director of Life Force ... Dr. Cierra HOFFMAN
101 Board Secretary ... Ms. Nita LOONEY
96 Director of Purchasing ... Mr. Mel BURTON
88 Director of Student Advisement ... Ms. Tameka GLASS
88 Director of Student Conduct ... Mr. Andre CLANTON
88 Director of Grounds ... Mr. John WHEELER
88 Director CETL ... Mr. William WATSON
88 Controller ... Ms. Jo Ann MILLER
88 Director Wellness Center ... Ms. Pat BANKS
88 Exec Director Neurolife Institute ... Dr. Micheal HALL
88 Director of Clinic Services ... Dr. Mark MAIYER

Luther Rice College and Seminary (G)

3038 Evans Mill Road, Lithonia GA 30038-2454
County: DeKalb FICE Identification: 031009
Unit ID: 135364
Telephone: (770) 484-1204 Carnegie Class: Spec-4-yr-Faith
FAX Number: (770) 484-1155 Calendar System: Semester
URL: www.lutherrice.edu
Established: 1962 Annual Undergrad Tuition & Fees: $6,800
Enrollment: 1,154 Coed
Affiliation or Control: Independent Non-Profit IRS Status: 501(c)3
Highest Offering: Doctorate
Accreditation: BI, TRACS

01 President ... Dr. James L. FLANAGAN
10 Vice President Financial Affairs ... Mr. Louis B. HARDCASTLE
32 Director for Student Affairs ... Mr. Steve PRAY
05 Vice President for Academic Affairs ... Dr. Evan POSEY
07 Director of Admissions and Comm ... Mr. Russell L. SORROW
08 Director of Library Services ... Mr. Prasada SAJJA
37 Director Student Financial Aid ... Mr. Casey W. KUFFREY
85 Asst to the Pres Global Strategy ... Dr. Ronald B. LONG
58 Director Doctor of Ministry Program ... Dr. Ron K. COBB
11 Executive Vice President ... Mr. Steven STEINHILBER
13 Chief Info Technology Officer (CIO) ... Mr. Ken STOKES

Mercer University (H)

1501 Mercer University Drive, Macon GA 31207-0003
County: Bibb FICE Identification: 001580
Unit ID: 140447
Telephone: (478) 301-2700 Carnegie Class: DU-Mod
FAX Number: (478) 301-2108 Calendar System: Semester
URL: www.mercer.edu
Established: 1833 Annual Undergrad Tuition & Fees: $35,130
Enrollment: 8,600 Coed
Affiliation or Control: Independent Non-Profit IRS Status: 501(c)3
Highest Offering: Doctorate
Accreditation: SC, ARCPA, CACREP, CS, ENG, LAW, MED, MFCD, MUS, NURSE, PH, PHAR, PTA, THEOL

01 President and CEO ... Mr. William D. UNDERWOOD
125 Chancellor ... Dr. R. Kirby GODSEY
03 Executive VP for Admin & Finance ... Dr. James S. NETHERTON

100 Senior VP and Chief of Staff ... Mr. Larry D. BRUMLEY
05 Provost ... Dr. D. Scott DAVIS
88 VP for Strategic Initiatives ... Ms. Kellie APPEL
111 Sr VP for University Advancement ... Mr. John A. PATTERSON
84 Sr Vice Pres Enrollment Management ... Dr. Penny L. ELKINS
43 Vice President and General Counsel ... Mr. William G. SOLOMON
13 Assoc VP & Chief Technology Officer ... Mr. Michael R. BELOTE
41 Athletic Director ... Mr. Jim COLE
46 Sr V Prov Research/Exec Assoc Dean ... Dr. Wayne C. GLASGOW
09 Vice Provost for Inst Effectiveness ... Dr. Susan C. MALONE
21 Assoc VP Finance & Treasurer ... Ms. Julia T. DAVIS
18 Assoc Vice President for Facilities ... Mr. Russell VULLO
15 Assoc Vice Pres for Human Resources ... Ms. Rhonda W. LIDSTONE
26 Sr Asst VP Marketing Communications ... Mr. Richard L. CAMERON
37 Assoc VP Student Financial Planning ... Ms. Maria A. HAMMETT
32 VP Stdnt Affairs & Dean of Students ... Dr. Doug R. PEARSON
36 Assoc Dean of Student Services ... Dr. Stephen R. BROWN
39 Director of Student Housing ... Mr. Jeff TAKAC
49 Dean College of Liberal Arts ... Dr. Anita O. GUSTAFSON
61 Dean School of Law ... Ms. Cathy COX
67 Dean of Pharmacy ... Dr. Brian CRABTREE
63 Dean School of Medicine ... Dr. Jean R. SUMNER
54 Int Dean School of Engineering ... Dr. Laura W. LACKEY
50 Dean Sch Business/Econ ... Dr. Susan P. GILBERT
73 Dean School of Theology ... Dr. Jeffrey G. WILLETTS
53 Int Dean College of Education ... Dr. D. Scott DAVIS
66 Dean College of Nursing ... Dr. Linda A. STREIT
51 Dean Penfield College ... Dr. Priscilla R. DANHEISER
64 Dean School of Music ... Dr. C. David KEITH
76 Dean Col of Health Professions ... Dr. Lisa M. LUNDQUIST
08 Dean of University Libraries ... Ms. Elizabeth D. HAMMOND
42 Univ Minister/Dean of Chapel ... Dr. Craig T. MCMAHAN
06 Registrar ... Ms. Lucy P. WILSON
19 Chief Police Department ... Mr. Gary COLLINS
09 Director of Institutional Research ... Ms. Sarah E. MAY
96 Director of Purchasing ... Mr. Charles MIZE
04 Administrative Asst to President ... Ms. Vonne SHEFFIELD
29 Assoc VP & Exe Dir Alumni Assn ... Ms. Jill H. KINSELLA
86 VP for Government Relations ... Mr. Hugh D. SOSEBEE, JR.
112 Director of Planned Giving ... Mr. Richard C. SPIVEY

Middle Georgia State University (A)

100 University Parkway, Macon GA 31206-5145
County: Bibb FICE Identification: 007728
Unit ID: 482158
Telephone: (478) 471-2700 Carnegie Class: Bac-Diverse
FAX Number: (478) 471-2846 Calendar System: Semester
URL: www.mga.edu
Established: 1884 Annual Undergrad Tuition & Fees (In-State): $3,890
Enrollment: 7,676 Coed
Affiliation or Control: State IRS Status: 501(c)3
Highest Offering: Master's
Accreditation: SC, ADNUR, CAEPN, COARC, CS, NUR, OTA

01 President ... Dr. Christopher BLAKE
05 Provost ... Dr. Melanie HATCH
10 Exec VP Finance & Operations ... Ms. Nancy STROUD
32 VP Student Affairs ... Dr. Jennifer BRANNON
111 VP Univ Advancement/Exec Dir Fdn ... Vacant
20 Vice Provost Academic Initiatives ... Dr. Pamela BEDWELL
20 Vice Provost for Acad Integrity ... Vacant
88 Assoc Provost Regional Campus Coord ... Dr. Deepa ARORA
108 Asst Provost Acad Planning/Policy ... Dr. Mary WEARN
100 Chief of Staff ... Mr. Albert J. ABRAMS
13 Chief Information Officer ... Mr. Roger DIXON
43 Dir Legal Services/General Counsel ... Ms. Frances DAVIS
26 VP Recruit/Mktg & Chief Mktg Ofcr ... Ms. Cheryl CARTY
15 Exec Dir Human Resources ... Ms. Vicky SMITH
112 Exec Dir Major and Planning Giving ... Ms. Julie DAVIS
35 Asst VP Student Affairs ... Dr. Michael STEWART
18 Asst VP Facilities ... Mr. David SIMS
19 Asst VP Risk Mgmt and Police Svcs ... Mr. Shawn DOUGLAS
21 Controller ... Mr. Brian STANLEY
06 Registrar ... Ms. Brenda HOGAN
07 Director of Admissions ... Ms. Margo WOODHAM
29 Director Alumni Relations ... Ms. Natalie RISCHBIETER
41 Director Athletics/Rec/Wellness ... Mr. Chip SMITH
109 Director Auxiliary Services ... Mr. Ryan GREENE
40 Director Campus Stores ... Ms. Jessica HALL
38 Director Counseling ... Ms. Predita HOWARD
37 Director Financial Aid ... Ms. LeeAnn KIRKLAND
25 Director Grants and Contracts ... Ms. Barbara RATZLAFF
09 Director Institutional Research ... Dr. Michael GIBBONS
104 Director International Educ ... Dr. Laura THOMASON
08 Director Library Services ... Ms. Pat BORCK
96 Director Purchasing ... Ms. Barbara BURNS
39 Director of Residence Life ... Mr. Brian HARRELL
12 Director Cochran/Eastman Campuses ... Mr. Henry WHITFIELD
12 Director Warner Robins Campus ... Ms. Pella MURPHY
58 Dean Graduate Studies ... Dr. Kevin CANTWELL
49 Dean Arts & Sciences ... Dr. Ron WILLIAMS
88 Dean Aviation ... Mr. Adon CLARK
50 Dean of Business ... Dr. M. Kenneth HOLT
53 Dean of Education ... Dr. David FULLER
76 Dean Health Sciences ... Dr. Tara UNDERWOOD
72 Dean Information Technology ... Dr. Alex KOOHANG

† Part of the University System of Georgia.

Miller-Motte Technical College (B)

621 NW Frontage Road, Augusta GA 30907
Telephone: (706) 396-8000 Identification: 770710
Accreditation: ACICS

† Branch campus of Miller-Motte Technical College, Clarksville, TN

Miller-Motte Technical College (C)

1800 Box Road, Columbus GA 31907
Telephone: (706) 225-5000 Identification: 770711
Accreditation: ACICS

† Branch campus of Miller-Motte Technical College, Clarksville, TN

Miller-Motte Technical College (D)

175 Tom Hill Sr Boulevard, Macon GA 31210
Telephone: (478) 257-3912 Identification: 770844
Accreditation: ACICS

† Branch campus of McCann School of Business & Technology, Pottsville, PA

Morehouse College (E)

830 Westview Drive SW, Atlanta GA 30314-3773
County: Fulton FICE Identification: 001582
Unit ID: 140553
Telephone: (404) 681-2800 Carnegie Class: Bac-A&S
FAX Number: (404) 681-2650 Calendar System: Semester
URL: www.morehouse.edu
Established: 1867 Annual Undergrad Tuition & Fees: $26,742
Enrollment: 2,167 Male
Affiliation or Control: Independent Non-Profit IRS Status: 501(c)3
Highest Offering: Baccalaureate
Accreditation: SC, MUS

01 Interim President ... Mr. Harold MARTIN, JR.
04 Executive Asst to the President ... Nakia WASHINGTON
116 Chief Audit Officer ... Ms. Undria STALLING
05 Interim Provost ... Dr. Michael HODGE
100 Chief of Staff ... Vacant
10 VP for Business & Finance/CFO ... Dr. Alan D. ROBERTSON, SR.
32 VP for Student Development ... Dr. Timothy SAMS
43 Interim General Counsel ... Ms. Joy WHITE
111 VP for Institutional Advancement ... Mr. Phillip HOWARD
13 Interim VP of Technology & CIO ... Mr. Mauise RICARD
19 Chief of Campus Police ... Chief Valerie DALTON
15 AVP for Human Resource ... Mrs. Amanda BAILEY
84 AVP of Enrollment Management ... Mr. Terrance DIXON
39 AVP for Student Services ... Mr. Maurice WASHINGTON
96 AVP/Chief Procurement Mgr ... Mr. Ralph JOHNSON
21 AVP & Controller ... Ms. Tonya JACKSON
42 Dean Martin Luther King Jr Chapel ... Dr. Lawrence E. CARTER
06 Dean/Registrar ... Ms. Kasimira ROBINSON
35 Assoc Dean for Student Life ... Mr. Kevin BOOKER
07 Director Admissions & Recruitment ... Mr. Darryl ISOM
37 Director of Financial Aid ... Ms. Sheryl SPIVEY
29 Director of Alumni Relations ... Mr. Henry GOODGAME
41 Athletic Director ... Mr. Andre PATTILLO
85 Interim Director Andrew Young Ctr ... Dr. Julius COLES
38 Director for Student Counseling ... Dr. Gary WRIGHT
105 Director Web Services ... Ms. Kara WALKER
88 Title IX Coordinator ... Ms. Terraine BAILEY

Morehouse School of Medicine (F)

720 Westview Drive, SW, Atlanta GA 30310-1495
County: Fulton FICE Identification: 024821
Unit ID: 140562
Telephone: (404) 752-1500 Carnegie Class: Spec-4-yr-Med
FAX Number: (404) 752-1027 Calendar System: Semester
URL: www.msm.edu
Established: 1975 Annual Graduate Tuition & Fees: N/A
Enrollment: 452 Coed
Affiliation or Control: Independent Non-Profit IRS Status: 501(c)3
Highest Offering: Doctorate; No Undergraduates
Accreditation: SC, MED, PH

01 President ... Dr. Valerie MONTGOMERY RICE
05 Dean ... Dr. Valerie MONTGOMERY RICE
10 Sr Vice Pres Finance/CFO ... Dr. John CASE
43 Sr Vice President/General Counsel ... Ms. Almeta COOPER
30 Sr Vice President of Institutional ... Dr. Bennie L. HARRIS
100 Chief of Staff/VP Strategic Plng ... Dr. David HEFNER
26 VP of Marketing & Communications ... Ms. Pamela SIMMONS
15 Associate VP of Human Resources ... Ms. Denise BRITT
102 Assoc VP Development/Advance ... Dr. Ernie HUGHES
20 Sr Assoc Dean Educational Affairs ... Dr. Martha ELKS
88 Sr Assoc Director Clinical Research ... Dr. Elizabeth OFILI
20 Assoc Dean Faculty Affairs ... Dr. Erika BROWN
86 Exec Director of Government Affairs ... Mr. Daniel DAWES
37 Director Student Fiscal Affairs ... Ms. Cynthia H. HANDY
08 Library Manager ... Mr. Joe SWANSON, JR.
09 Director II Planning & IR/Title 3 ... Vacant
25 Exec Director of Grants & Contracts ... Ms. Sandi PHILLIPS
29 Dir Alumni Constituent Engagement ... Ms. Samra COOTE
07 Asoc Dean Admissions/Student Affs ... Dr. Ngozi F. ANACHEBE
96 Director Purchasing ... Mr. Philmon THOMAS
22 Chief Compliance Officer ... Ms. Desiree RAMIREZ
13 Chief Information Officer ... Ms. Annemarie EADES
06 Registrar ... Ms. Angela FREEMAN
19 Chief of Police ... Mr. Joseph CHEVALIER, JR.

North Georgia Technical College (G)

PO Box 65, Clarkesville GA 30523-0065
County: Habersham FICE Identification: 005619
Unit ID: 140678
Telephone: (706) 754-7700 Carnegie Class: Assoc/HVT-High Trad
FAX Number: (706) 754-7777 Calendar System: Semester
URL: www.northgatech.edu
Established: 1943 Annual Undergrad Tuition & Fees (In-State): $2,734
Enrollment: 2,665 Coed
Affiliation or Control: State IRS Status: 501(c)3
Highest Offering: Associate Degree
Accreditation: SC, ACFEI, MAC, MLTAD

01 President ... Dr. Mark IVESTER
05 Vice President for Academic Affairs ... Kathie IVESTER
32 Vice President for Student Affairs ... Dr. Michael KING
11 Vice President for Administration ... Carol CARSON
30 Vice Pres of Economic Development ... Rick STORY
06 Registrar ... Dr. Michele SHIRLEY
07 Director of Admissions ... Dr. Michele SHIRLEY
15 Human Resources Coordinator ... Lorna CHAPMAN
18 Chief Facilities/Physical Plant ... Michael BOYD
26 Chief Public Relations Officer ... Amy HULSEY
29 Director Alumni Relations ... Cynthia BROWN
35 Campus Life Director ... Sherry SEAL
36 Director for Job Placement ... Patrick LEDFORD
37 Financial Aid Director ... Audra JIMENEZ
96 Procurement Officer ... Jeannie BARRETT
09 Institutional Research Analyst ... Hamilton SCOTT
46 Institutional Effectiveness Dir ... Janet LOVELL
20 Dean for Academic Affairs ... Dan PRESSLEY
20 Dean for Academic Affairs ... Leslie MCFARLIN
20 Dean for Academic Affairs ... Mindy GLANDER
106 Distance Education Specialist ... Dr. Renee DEIBERT
13 Information Technology Director ... Savonda TURNER
19 Chief of Police ... Stan LOVELL

Oconee Fall Line Technical College-North Campus (H)

1189 Deepstep Road, Sandersville GA 31082-9337
County: Washington FICE Identification: 031555
Unit ID: 420431
Telephone: (478) 553-2050 Carnegie Class: Assoc/HVT-High Non
FAX Number: (478) 553-2118 Calendar System: Semester
URL: www.oftc.edu
Established: 1996 Annual Undergrad Tuition & Fees (In-State): $2,624
Enrollment: 1,569 Coed
Affiliation or Control: State IRS Status: 501(c)3
Highest Offering: Associate Degree
Accreditation: SC

01 President ... Dr. Lloyd HORADAN
05 Vice Pres Academic/Student Affs ... Ms. Erica HARDEN
10 Vice Pres Administrative Services ... Ms. Rosemary SELBY
30 Vice Pres Economic Development ... Ms. Kim DAVID
49 Dean Arts & Sciences/Business Svcs ... Ms. Michele STRICKLAND
06 Registrar ... Ms. Geri CLEMENTS
07 Director of Admissions ... Ms. Raydor CONEWAY
15 Director Human Resources ... Ms. Sharon O'NEAL
21 Director of Administrative Services ... Ms. Penny KITCHENS
18 Director Facilities/Physical Plant ... Mr. Jim HARRISON
37 Financial Aid Director ... Ms. Betty YOUNG
28 Dir of Spec Populations/Stdnt Life ... Ms. Susan HAMMOCK

Oconee Fall Line Technical College-South Campus (I)

560 Pinehill Road, Dublin GA 31021-1599
County: Laurens FICE Identification: 022795
Unit ID: 140076
Telephone: (478) 275-6589 Carnegie Class: Not Classified
FAX Number: (478) 275-6642 Calendar System: Semester
URL: www.oftc.edu
Established: 1984 Annual Undergrad Tuition & Fees (In-State): N/A
Enrollment: N/A Coed
Affiliation or Control: State IRS Status: 501(c)3
Highest Offering: Associate Degree
Accreditation: SC, COARC, EMT, MAC, RAD

01 President ... Dr. Lloyd HORADAN
09 Vice Pres Inst Effectiveness ... Dr. Katie DAVIS
32 Dean Student Affairs ... Mr. Jay MULLIS
18 Director Facilities ... Mr. Ragan GREEN
30 Exec Dir Institutional Advancement ... Mrs. Jenny SHUMAN
19 Chief Security & Facilities ... Mr. Mark ROGERS
36 Director of Career Development ... Vacant
76 Dean Allied Health/Prof Svcs ... Ms. Tammy BAYTO
37 Asst Director Financial Aid ... Ms. Teresa CRAFTON
08 Director Library Services ... Ms. Wendi MORRIS
07 Director of Admissions ... Mr. Raydor CONEWAY

Ogeechee Technical College (J)

One Joseph E. Kennedy Boulevard,
Statesboro GA 30458-8049
County: Bulloch FICE Identification: 030300
Unit ID: 366465

Telephone: (912) 681-5500 Carnegie Class: Assoc/HVT-High Trad
FAX Number: (912) 486-7704 Calendar System: Semester
URL: www.ogeecheetech.edu
Established: 1986 Annual Undergrad Tuition & Fees (In-State): $2,872
Enrollment: 2,068 Coed
Affiliation or Control: State IRS Status: 170(c)1
Highest Offering: Associate Degree
Accreditation: SC, CAHIIM, DA, DMS, FUSER, MAC, OPD, RAD, SURGT

01 President .... Ms. Lori S. DURDEN
04 Exec Assistant to the President .... Ms. Karen MOBLEY
05 Int VP for Academic Affairs .... Dr. Ryan FOLEY
88 Vice President Economic Development .... Ms. Jan MOORE
108 VP Institutional Effectiveness .... Ms. Brandy TAYLOR
32 Vice President Student Affairs .... Dr. Ryan FOLEY
10 Vice President for Administration .... Ms. Eyvonne HART
13 VP Technology & Institutional Supp .... Mr. Jeff DAVIS
111 VP for College Advancement .... Mr. Barry TURNER
09 Director Inst Research & Planning .... Ms. YLonne HODGES
08 Director for Library Services .... Ms. Lisa LANIER
51 Dir Continuing Educ & Ind Training .... Ms. Kathleen KOSMOSKI
07 Director for Admissions .... Ms. Molly BICKERTON
06 Registrar .... Ms. Michelle STUBBS
37 Director for Financial Aid .... Ms. Kristie SANDERS
15 Director for Human Resources .... Mr. Steve MILLER
109 Exec Director Auxiliary Services .... Mr. J.J ALTMAN
18 Director for Plant Operations .... Mr. Buddy SAPP
19 Director Campus Safety & Security .... Mr. Stan YORK
20 Dean for Academic Affairs .... Dr. Paul MIZELL
97 Dean Distance & General Education .... Ms. Jennifer WITHERINGTON
20 Dean for Academic Affairs .... Ms. Kelly KINGRY
21 Asst VP for Administration .... Ms. Tonya VICKERS

Oglethorpe University (A)

4484 Peachtree Road, NE, Atlanta GA 30319-2797
County: DeKalb FICE Identification: 001586
Unit ID: 140696
Telephone: (404) 261-1441 Carnegie Class: Bac-A&S
FAX Number: (404) 364-8500 Calendar System: Semester
URL: www.oglethorpe.edu
Established: 1835 Annual Undergrad Tuition & Fees: $35,280
Enrollment: 1,155 Coed
Affiliation or Control: Independent Non-Profit IRS Status: 501(c)3
Highest Offering: Baccalaureate
Accreditation: SC

01 President .... Dr. Lawrence M. SCHALL
05 Provost/VP Academic Affairs .... Dr. Glenn SHARFMAN
10 Vice Pres for Business & Finance .... Mr. Norman MCKAY
30 Vice Pres Devel & Alumni Relations .... Ms. Robyn FURNESS-FALLIN
84 VP Enrollment/FinancialAid .... Ms. Lucy LEUSCH
26 VP Marketing/Communications .... Mr. Todd BENNETT
32 Dean of Students/VP Campus Life .... Ms. Michelle HALL
20 Assistant Provost .... Mr. Brian COLDREN
04 Exec Assistant to the President .... Ms. Colleen D'ALESSANDRO
08 Int Univ Librarian/Library Director .... Mr. Eli ARNOLD
06 Registrar .... Mr. Brian COLDREN
09 Director of Institutional Research .... Mr. Todd CRAIG
41 Athletic Director .... Ms. Becky HALL
37 Director of Financial Aid .... Mr. Chris SUMMERS
39 Director of Residence Life .... Dr. Amy PALDER
21 Director of Finance/Controller .... Mr. Mark BERGER
13 Chief Information Officer .... Mr. Michael GONSALVES
27 Dir University Communications .... Ms. Renee VARY KEELE
29 Director of Alumni/Donor Relations .... Ms. Mary RINALDI WINN
36 Director of Career Development .... Ms. Erin SHERRILL
44 Director of Major Gifts .... Mr. John CARR
15 Director Human Resources .... Ms. Sandy BUTLER
31 Director A_LAB for Civic Engagement .... Ms. Beth CONCEPCION
18 Director Facilities/Physical Plant .... Mr. Lance KNIGHT
07 Associate Director of Admissions .... Ms. Whitney LEWIS
40 Bookstore Manager .... Mr. Justin GAMBLE

Pacific Institute of Technology (B)

1388 Southlake Plaza Drive, Morrow GA 30260
County: Clayton Identification: 667239
Telephone: (678) 610-5900 Carnegie Class: Not Classified
FAX Number: (678) 610-5008 Calendar System: Quarter
URL: www.pacifictech.edu
Established: 1999 Annual Undergrad Tuition & Fees: N/A
Enrollment: N/A Coed
Affiliation or Control: Proprietary IRS Status: Proprietary
Highest Offering: Associate Degree
Accreditation: ACICS

01 President .... Mr. Frank WEBSTER

Paine College (C)

1235 Fifteenth Street, Augusta GA 30901-3182
County: Richmond FICE Identification: 001587
Unit ID: 140720
Telephone: (706) 821-8200 Carnegie Class: Bac-A&S
FAX Number: (706) 821-8373 Calendar System: Semester
URL: www.paine.edu
Established: 1882 Annual Undergrad Tuition & Fees: $14,224
Enrollment: 555 Coed
Affiliation or Control: Multiple Protestant Denominations
IRS Status: 501(c)3
Highest Offering: Baccalaureate
Accreditation: #SC, ACBSP, CAEPN

01 President .... Dr. Jerry L. HARDEE
04 Office Manager/President's Office .... Mrs. Juanita HARPS
05 Provost/VP Academic Affairs .... Dr. Cheryl EVANS JONES
32 Dean Student Affairs & Enroll Mgt .... Mr. R. Wayne WOODSON
10 VP Administrative & Fiscal Affairs .... Ms. Mary MORALE
30 Asst VP Institutional Development .... Ms. Helene CARTER
42 Campus Pastor .... Dr. Luther FELDER
41 Director of Athletics .... Mrs. Selina KOHN
20 Exec Asst to Provost/VP AA .... Ms. Frances WIMBERLY
21 Director Fiscal Affairs/Treasurer .... Ms. Veronica STREETMAN
50 Chair Business Dept .... Dr. Okoroafor NZEH
53 Interim Chair Education Dept .... Dr. Gloria BENNETT
79 Chair Humanities Dept .... Vacant
81 Chair Math Sci Tech Dept .... Dr. Raul PETERS
60 Chair Media Studies Dept .... Ms. Teri BURNETTE
83 Chair Social Sciences Dept .... Vacant
107 Pgm Coord Ctr for Adv Prof Studies .... Mrs. Symphoni WIGGINS
09 Dir Inst Research/Qual Enhance Plan .... Mrs. Alice M. SIMPKINS
08 Director Library/LRC .... Mrs. Alana LEWIS
06 Registrar .... Mrs. Tanika BEARD
36 Director Career Services .... Mrs. April EWING
38 Int Dir Counseling & Wellness Ctr .... Ms. Jenease HORSTEAD
39 Director of Residence Life .... Vacant
19 Chief of Police .... Chief Leroy MORGAN, JR.
18 Dir Facilities Mgmt/Environ Svcs .... Mr. Yewston CURRY
13 Interim Dir Information Technology .... Mr. Jeffrey OWENS
37 Director of Financial Aid .... Ms. Consuelo QUINN
15 Director Human Resources .... Vacant
29 Director Alumni Relations .... Vacant
26 Dir Communications & Marketing .... Vacant
25 Inter Dir Sponsored Prog/Title III .... Mrs. Tamekia S. GREEN
88 Director of Tutorial Services .... Dr. Sezilee REID
108 Director of Assessment & Eval .... Vacant
24 Info Tech Mgr Learning Resources .... Mrs. Rosa L. MARTIN
07 Admissions Coordinator .... Mrs. Felicia FENNER
88 Sr Women's Athletics Administrator .... Ms. Kisha LUCETTE
88 Asst Ath Dir Compliance/Com .... Mr. Ruben R. PEREZ, JR.
88 Asst Ath Dir External Relations .... Vacant

Philadelphia College of Osteopathic Medicine Georgia Campus (D)

625 Old Peachtree Road NW, Suwanee GA 30024
Telephone: (678) 225-7500 Identification: 770165
Accreditation: &M, OSTEO, PHAR

† Branch campus of Philadelphia College of Osteopathic Medicine, Philadelphia, PA

Piedmont College (E)

PO Box 10, Demorest GA 30535-0010
County: Habersham FICE Identification: 001588
Unit ID: 140818
Telephone: (706) 778-3000 Carnegie Class: Masters/L
FAX Number: (706) 776-0701 Calendar System: Semester
URL: www.piedmont.edu
Established: 1897 Annual Undergrad Tuition & Fees: $23,112
Enrollment: 2,264 Coed
Affiliation or Control: United Church Of Christ IRS Status: 501(c)3
Highest Offering: Doctorate
Accreditation: SC, ACBSP, CAATE, CVT, NUR

01 President .... Dr. James F. MELLICHAMP
05 Vice Pres Academic Affairs .... Dr. Perry RETTIG
10 Vice Pres Administration & Finance .... Mr. Kenneth JONES
30 Vice President for Advancement .... Ms. Amy AMASON
13 AVP of Information Technology .... Dr. Shahryar HEYDARI
88 Special Assistant to the President .... Ms. Jane KIDD
04 Assistant to the President .... Ms. Kristen GRAY
32 Dean of Student Engagement .... Ms. Emily PETTIT
07 Dean of Admiss/Undergrad Enrol Mgmt .... Ms. Cynthia L. PETERSON
08 Dean of Libraries/College Librarian .... Mr. Robert GLASS, JR.
06 Registrar .... Mr. Anthony COX
09 Director of Institutional Research .... Ms. Kim LOVELL
84 Director Graduate Enrollment Mgmt .... Ms. Kathleen CARTER
07 Director Undergraduate Admissions .... Ms. Brenda BOONSTRA
37 Director of Financial Aid .... Mr. David MCMILLION
42 Campus Minister .... Rev. Timothy GARVIN-LEIGHTON
15 Human Resources Manager .... Ms. Rose Mariee ALLISON
26 Director of Public Relations .... Mr. David E. PRICE
41 Dir of Intercollegiate Athletics .... Mr. Jim PEEPLES
21 Compliance & Treasury Officer .... Ms. Leesa P. ANDERSON
19 Director Security/Campus Police .... Ms. Marie G. TAYLOR
66 Dean School of Nursing/Health Sci .... Dr. Julie BEHR
50 Dean School of Business Admin .... Dr. Edward TAYLOR
49 Dean School of Arts & Sciences .... Dr. Steven NIMMO
53 Dean School of Education .... Dr. Donald GNECCO

Point University (F)

507 West 10th St, West Point GA 31833
County: Troup FICE Identification: 001547
Unit ID: 138868
Telephone: (706) 385-1000 Carnegie Class: Bac-Diverse
FAX Number: (706) 645-9473 Calendar System: Semester
URL: www.point.edu
Established: 1937 Annual Undergrad Tuition & Fees: $19,200
Enrollment: 1,582 Coed
Affiliation or Control: Christian Churches And Churches of Christ
IRS Status: 501(c)3
Highest Offering: Master's
Accreditation: SC, CAEPN

01 President .... Mr. Dean C. COLLINS
05 Chief Academic Officer .... Dr. W. Darryl HARRISON
11 Chief Operations Officer .... Mr. Lance FRANCIS
108 Vice Pres for Inst Effectiveness .... Dr. Dennis GLENN
10 Interim Vice Pres of Finance .... Ms. Wendy BARNHART
58 Vice Pres Graduate & Prof Studies .... Mr. Chris DAVIS
107 Asst Vice Pres Prof Studies .... Mr. Leon REESE
84 Vice Pres for Enrollment Management .... Dr. Stacy BARTLETT
07 Asst Vice President of Enrollment .... Mrs. Tiffany WOOD
07 Executive Director of Enrollment .... Mr. Rusty HASSELL
26 Communications Manager .... Ms. Katherine HAMILTON
06 Interim Registrar .... Mr. Obie KILLCREAS
106 Dir OL Learning and Instruc Design .... Ms. Valarie WILLIAMS
113 Director of Student Finance .... Mr. John LANIER
37 Director of Financial Aid .... Ms. Janifer MORGAN
88 Director of Student Accounts .... Ms. Yolanda STEELE
32 Dean of Students .... Ms. Laura SCHAAF
41 Athletic Director .... Mr. Alan WILSON
109 Dir of Auxiliary Services .... Mr. Troy HIGDON
19 Chief of Security .... Mr. Eric FLOURNOY
18 Dir of Facilities and Maintenance .... Mr. Terry HOPPE
15 Director of Human Resources .... Ms. Margaret HODGE
42 Vice Pres for Spiritual Formation .... Mr. Wye HUXFORD
08 Library Director .... Mr. Michael BAIN
13 Vice Pres for Info Technology .... Mr. Bill DORMINY
111 Vice President of Advancement .... Mr. Joshua HARRELSON
30 Director of Development .... Mr. Richard BUMPERS
26 Dir of University Relations .... Mr. Chris BEIRNE

† Formerly Atlanta Christian College

Reformed University (G)

1724 Atkinson Road, Lawrenceville GA 30043
County: Gwinnett Identification: 667247
Telephone: (770) 232-2717 Carnegie Class: Not Classified
FAX Number: N/A Calendar System: Semester
URL: www.trsusa.org
Established: 1992 Annual Undergrad Tuition & Fees: N/A
Enrollment: N/A Coed
Affiliation or Control: Presbyterian Church In America IRS Status: Exempt
Highest Offering: Master's
Accreditation: TRACS

01 President .... Dr. Joshua PARK

Reinhardt University (H)

7300 Reinhardt Circle, Waleska GA 30183-2981
County: Cherokee FICE Identification: 001589
Unit ID: 140872
Telephone: (770) 720-5600 Carnegie Class: Bac-Diverse
FAX Number: (770) 720-5602 Calendar System: Semester
URL: www.reinhardt.edu
Established: 1883 Annual Undergrad Tuition & Fees: $21,644
Enrollment: 1,364 Coed
Affiliation or Control: United Methodist IRS Status: 501(c)3
Highest Offering: Master's
Accreditation: SC, MUS

01 President .... Dr. Kina S. MALLARD
04 Executive Assistant to President .... Mrs. Bonnie H. DEBORD
05 Provost .... Dr. Mark A. ROBERTS
10 Chief Financial Officer .... Mrs. Stephanie R. OWENS
111 VP for Advancement & Marketing .... Mr. Timothy A. NORTON
32 Dean of Students .... Vacant
84 VP for Enrollment Mgmt .... Mrs. Julie C. FLEMING
41 Director of Athletics .... Mr. William C. POPP
20 Assoc VP Acad Svcs/Grad Studies .... Dr. Margaret M. MORLIER
101 Asst Secretary Board of Trustees .... Mrs. Bonnie H. DEBORD
18 Director of Physical Plant .... Mrs. Missy H. DAYOUB
26 Chief Marketing Officer .... Ms. Mary B. LEIDIG
13 Dir of Info Tech/Chief Tech Officer .... Mr. David G. DOSTER
88 Exec Director of Funk Heritage Ctr .... Dr. Joseph H. KITCHENS
07 Director of Admissions .... Ms. Lacey L. SATTERFIELD
06 Registrar .... Ms. Janet M. RODNING
09 Dir Inst Research/Effectiveness .... Mr. Daniel TEODORESCU
08 Director of Library Services .... Mr. Joel C. LANGFORD
19 Director of Public Safety .... Mr. Jay R. DUNCAN
30 Dir Development & Alumni Relations .... Vacant
42 Campus Pastor .... Rev. Jamie HUDGINS
21 Controller .... Mr. Scott WATSON
37 Director Student Financial Aid .... Mrs. Angie D. HARLOW
15 Director Human Resources .... Mrs. Teresa MCPHERSON
39 Director Residence Life .... Mr. Eric W. BOOTH
23 University Nurse .... Mrs. Alicia C. MILES
35 Asst Dean of Students/Dir Stdnt Act .... Dr. Walter P. MAY
38 Director of Counseling Svcs .... Mr. Derek L. STRUCHTEMEYER
121 Dir Center for Student Success .... Dr. Catherine B. EMANUEL
36 Dir Vocation & Career Services .... Mrs. Karen W. MATHEWS
40 Bookstore Manager .... Mrs. Janet SWEENEY
106 Coordinator Online Education .... Dr. Katherine E. HYATT
49 Dean School of Arts & Humanities .... Dr. Arthur W. GLOWKA
81 Dean School of Maths & Sciences .... Dr. Jake P. HARNEY
50 Int Dean McCamish School Business .... Dr. Jake P. HARNEY
53 Int Dean Price School of Education .... Dr. Nancy J. MARSH
64 Dean School of Performing Arts .... Dr. Fredrick A. TARRANT
107 Int Dean Sch Professional Studies .... Mr. Lester W. DRAWDY
66 Dean School Nursing/Health Sciences .... Dr. Glynis D. BLACKARD

SAE Institute Atlanta (A)

215 Peachtree Street NE, Suite 300,
Atlanta GA 30303-1739

County: Fulton FICE Identification: 042066
Unit ID: 476948
Telephone: (404) 526-9366 Carnegie Class: Spec 2-yr-Tech
FAX Number: (404) 526-9367 Calendar System: Semester
URL: atlanta.sae.edu
Established: 1976 Annual Undergrad Tuition & Fees: N/A
Enrollment: 370 Coed
Affiliation or Control: Proprietary IRS Status: Proprietary
Highest Offering: Associate Degree
Accreditation: ACICS

01 Campus Director .... Mr. Todd CLARK
05 Director of Education .... Vacant

Savannah College of Art and Design (B)

342 Bull Street, PO Box 3146, Savannah GA 31402-6263

County: Chatham FICE Identification: 021415
Unit ID: 140951
Telephone: (912) 525-5000 Carnegie Class: Spec-4-yr-Arts
FAX Number: (912) 525-6263 Calendar System: Quarter
URL: www.scad.edu
Established: 1978 Annual Undergrad Tuition & Fees: $35,690
Enrollment: 11,861 Coed
Affiliation or Control: Independent Non-Profit IRS Status: 501(c)3
Highest Offering: Master's
Accreditation: SC, CIDA

01 President .... Mrs. Paula WALLACE
11 COO .... Mr. Glenn WALLACE
10 Senior VP for Finance .... Mr. J.J WALLER
88 VP for Student Financial Services .... Mr. Scott LINZEY
05 Chief Academic Officer .... Dr. Gokhan OZAYSIN
20 AVP for Acad Support/Legal Affairs .... Ms. Hannah FLOWER
12 Vice President for SCAD Atlanta .... Dr. Teresa GRIFFIS
12 Vice President for SCAD Hong Kong .... Mr. David PUGH
84 Sr VP Admission/Student Success .... Dr. Philip ALLETTO
13 VP for Information Technology .... Mr. Brad GRANT
106 VP for SCAD Savannah .... Mr. John Paul ROWAN
15 VP for Human Resources .... Ms. Lesley HANAK
09 VP for Institutional Effectiveness .... Ms. Erin O'LEARY
07 VP for Admission .... Mr. Steve MINEO
20 Dean of Academic Svcs Atlanta .... Mr. Dale CLIFFORD
26 Director of Univ Communications .... Ms. Ally HUGHES
18 Exec Dir of Physical Resources .... Ms. Helen MORGAN
08 Senior Director of Library Services .... Mr. Darrell NAYLOR-JOHNSON
37 Director of Financial Aid .... Ms. Kim BEVERIDGE
07 Exec Dir Adm Recruitment .... Ms. Jenny JAQUILLARD
19 VP for University Safety .... Mr. John BUCKOVICH
41 Athletics Director .... Mr. Doug WOLLENBURG
38 Dir Counseling/Student Support Svc .... Mr. Christopher CORBETT
58 Sr Dir of Grad Studies & Registrar .... Ms. Sarah MCCARN
88 Dean of School of Building Arts .... Mr. Ivan CHOW
88 Dean of School Communication Arts .... Mr. Anthony FISHER
88 Dean of School of Design .... Mr. Victor ERMOLI
88 Dean of School of Digital Media .... Ms. Marilynn ALMY
57 Dean of School of Fine Arts .... Ms. Maureen GARVIN
49 Dean of School of Liberal Arts .... Dr. Geoffrey TAYLOR
88 Dean School of Fashion .... Mr. Michael FINK
88 Dean School of Foundation Studies .... Ms. Maureen GARVIN
88 Dean of Entertainment Arts .... Mr. Andra REEVE-RABB
36 Exec Dir of Career & Alumni Success .... Ms. Kimberly LOPEZ
44 Exec Director of Giving .... Ms. Tish CAMPBELL
20 AVP of Academic Services .... Mr. Jesus ROJAS
35 Dean of Students Atlanta .... Mr. Art MALLOY
35 Dean of Students Savannah .... Mr. David BLAKE
104 Assoc Director SCAD Study Abroad .... Ms. Stephanie JACKSON
39 Assoc Dean/Dir of Residence Life .... Mr. Jason RIGSBEE
43 Sr VP Operations & Gen Cousel .... Ms. Brian ROSENTHAL

Savannah State University (C)

3219 College Street, Savannah GA 31404-5308

County: Chatham FICE Identification: 001590
Unit ID: 140960
Telephone: (912) 358-3004 Carnegie Class: Masters/S
FAX Number: N/A Calendar System: Semester
URL: www.savannahstate.edu
Established: 1890 Annual Undergrad Tuition & Fees (In-State): $5,644
Enrollment: 4,800 Coed
Affiliation or Control: State IRS Status: 501(c)3
Highest Offering: Master's
Accreditation: SC, ENGT, JOUR, SPAA, SW

01 University President .... Dr. Cheryl DOZIER
05 Interim Provost/VP Academic Affairs .... Dr. Carl WALTON
10 Vice Pres Business & Finance .... Mr. Edward B. JOLLEY, JR.
32 Vice President Student Affairs .... Dr. Carl WALTON
30 VP Advancement/Exec Dir SSU Found .... Mr. Phillip D. ADAMS
13 Chief Information Officer .... Dr. Mable MOORE
50 Dean College Business Admin .... Dr. Mostafa SARHAN
81 Dean Col Science & Technology .... Dr. Jonathan LAMBRIGHT
49 Dean Col Liberal Arts/Soc Sci .... Dr. Julius SCIPIO
53 Dean School of Teacher Education .... Dr. Mary KROPIEWNICKI
07 Director of Admissions for Recruit .... Mr. Brian DAWSEY
26 Director Marketing/Communications .... Ms. Loretta HEYWARD
15 Assistant VP Human Resources .... Dr. Sandra M. BEST
08 Librarian .... Mrs. MaryJo FAYOYIN
19 Chief of Police .... Mr. James BARNWELL
18 Director Facilities/Physical Plant .... Mr. Ervin OGDEN
43 Dir Legal Services/General Counsel .... Mr. Joseph STEFFEN
09 Interim Dir Inst Rsrch/Plng/Assess .... MS. Nijah E. BRYANT
29 Director Alumni Relations .... Ms. Barbara S. MYERS
37 Director Financial Aid .... Mr. Kenneth WILSON
41 Director Athletics .... Mr. Sterling STEWARD, JR.
35 Director of Student Development .... Ms. Jacqueline AWE
06 Interim Registrar .... Ms. Cynthia STEPHENS
04 Exec Asst to President .... Ms. Lisa JONES
39 Director Student Housing .... Dr. Priscilla WILLIAMS
100 Chief of Staff .... Dr. David SMITH
106 Dir Online Education/E-learning .... Dr. Frank WILLIAMS

† Part of the University System of Georgia.

Savannah Technical College (D)

5717 White Bluff Road, Savannah GA 31405-5521

County: Chatham FICE Identification: 005618
Unit ID: 140942
Telephone: (912) 443-5700 Carnegie Class: Assoc/HVT-Mix Trad/Non
FAX Number: (912) 443-5705 Calendar System: Semester
URL: www.savannahtech.edu
Established: 1967 Annual Undergrad Tuition & Fees (In-State): $2,704
Enrollment: 4,196 Coed
Affiliation or Control: State IRS Status: 501(c)3
Highest Offering: Associate Degree
Accreditation: SC, ACFEI, DA, DH, EMT, ENGT, MAC, SURGT

01 President .... Dr. Kathy S. LOVE
05 Vice Pres Academic Affairs .... Dr. Al CUNNINGHAM
11 Vice Pres Administrative Services .... Mr. Marc MASCOLO
32 Vice President Student Affairs .... Ms. Terrie O. SELLERS
45 Vice Pres Economic Development .... Mr. Kevin WERNTZ
108 VP Institutional Effectiveness .... Dr. Vic BURKE
111 Exec Director Inst Advance & Comm .... Ms. Gail EUBANKS
13 Exec Director Information Tech .... Mr. Jamie DAVIS
07 Director Admissions .... Ms. Gwendolyn MOORE
37 Director Financial Aid .... Ms. Faith ANDERSON
06 Registrar .... Ms. Regina THOMAS-WILLIAMS
18 Director Facilities .... Mr. Gary STRICKLAND
37 Exec Dir Student Financial Services .... Vacant
15 Director Human Resources .... Ms. Melissa BANKS
88 Director Learning Enrichment Center .... Dr. Ethel BERKSTEINER
08 Library Services Director .... Mr. Jim BURCH
26 Director of Communications .... Ms. Amy SHAFFER
12 Campus Dean Liberty Campus .... Mr. Lonnie GRIFFIN
12 Campus Dean Effingham Campus .... Mr. Robert SOLOMON
96 Purchasing Manager .... Mr. Kevin CHIEVES
88 Dean Public Services .... Mr. Anthony FAUST
76 Dean Health Science .... Ms. Kathleen BOMBERY
50 Dean Business and Technology .... Mr. Brendan FERRARA
97 Dean General Studies .... Vacant
88 Dean Industrial Technology .... Mr. Joseph POWELL
88 Dean Aviation .... Mr. Tal LOOS
56 Adult Education Coordinator .... Mr. Brent STUBBS
88 Military Outreach Coordinator .... Mr. Jeff ASHMEN
88 Dir of Enterprise Tech Specialist .... Ms. Tammy BRANNEN
19 Chief of Police .... Mr. Mark GERBINO

Shorter University (E)

315 Shorter Avenue, Rome GA 30165-4298

County: Floyd FICE Identification: 001591
Unit ID: 140988
Telephone: (706) 291-2121 Carnegie Class: Bac-Diverse
FAX Number: (706) 236-1515 Calendar System: Semester
URL: www.shorter.edu
Established: 1873 Annual Undergrad Tuition & Fees: $21,730
Enrollment: 1,472 Coed
Affiliation or Control: Baptist IRS Status: 501(c)3
Highest Offering: Master's
Accreditation: SC, MUS, NURSE

01 President .... Dr. Donald V. DOWLESS
05 Executive Vice President & Provost .... Dr. Donald L. MARTIN
11 VP for Administrative Affairs .... Vacant
10 VP for Finance & CFO .... Ms. Susan ZEIRD
84 Vice Pres Enrollment Management .... Dr. Emily MESSER
30 Vice President for Advancement .... Vacant
32 VP Student Affairs/Dean of Students .... Mr. Corey HUMPHRIES
26 Assoc VP University Communications .... Dr. Dawn C. TOLBERT
104 Asst Vice Pres International Pgms .... Mrs. Linda PALUMBO-OLSZANSKI
06 Registrar .... Mr. Justin MITCHELL
29 Director of Alumni Relations .... Mrs. Melissa WILLIAMS
35 Director of Student Life & Conduct .... Mr. Anthony CHATMAN
08 Director of Libraries .... Ms. Linda FLOYD
09 Director of Inst Planning/Research .... Vacant
37 Director of Financial Aid .... Ms. Colleen LASSITER
15 Director Human Resources .... Mrs. Stacy HARDY
90 Director of Academic Computing .... Mr. Anthony J. NICHOLS
56 Director Special Programs .... Vacant
13 Director of Information Technology .... Mr. Jeff BRAMLETTE
18 Director of Facilities Management .... Mr. Bob BAGLEY
38 Director of Student Support Svcs .... Dr. Chris WHEELUS
23 Director of Health Services .... Mrs. Mary SHOTWELL SMITH
41 Athletic Director .... Vacant
44 Director of Annual Giving .... Vacant
07 Director of Admissions .... Mr. Patrick MCELHANEY
39 Director Residence Life .... Mr. Anthony CHATMON
40 Bookstore Manager .... Ms. Julie BINKLEY
57 Dean School of the Arts .... Dr. John REAMS
50 Interim Dean College of Business .... Mr. Heath HOOPER
49 Dean College of Arts & Sciences .... Dr. Kathi VOSEVICH
53 Dean School of Education .... Dr. Norma HARPER
66 Dean School of Nursing .... Dr. Roxanne JOHNSTON
106 Dean Online Programs .... Mr. Legari PRICE
81 Chair of Natural Sciences .... Mr. Clint HELMS
73 Chair Dept of Christian Studies .... Vacant
77 Chair Dept of Mathematics .... Dr. Diana SWANAGAN
60 Chair Dept of Communication Arts .... Vacant
83 Chair Dept of Social Sciences .... Dr. Barsha PICKELL
42 Campus Minister .... Rev. David E. ROLAND

South Georgia State College (F)

100 W College Park Drive, Douglas GA 31533-5098

County: Coffee FICE Identification: 001592
Unit ID: 482699
Telephone: (912) 260-4394 Carnegie Class: Bac/Assoc-Assoc Dom
FAX Number: (912) 260-4454 Calendar System: Semester
URL: www.sgsc.edu
Established: 1906 Annual Undergrad Tuition & Fees (In-State): $3,211
Enrollment: 2,648 Coed
Affiliation or Control: State IRS Status: 501(c)3
Highest Offering: Baccalaureate
Accreditation: SC, ADNUR, NUR

01 President .... Dr. Ingrid THOMPSON-SELLERS
05 Vice Pres Academic/Student Affs .... Dr. Robert PAGE
84 Interim Exec Dir Enrollment Mgmt .... Mr. Jimmy HARPER
10 Vice Pres Fiscal Affairs & Admin .... Mr. Mark LATHAM
13 Chief Info Technology Officer .... Mr. Jimmy HARPER
08 Director of Libraries .... Ms. Jacqueline VICKERS
06 Registrar .... Ms. Ame WILKERSON
37 Director of Financial Aid .... Vacant
15 Director of Human Resources .... Mr. Ryan SCONYERS
07 Interim Director of Admissions .... Ms. Ame WILKERSON
88 Dir of Entry Programs and Planning .... Ms. Valerie WEBSTER
40 Bookstore Manager .... Ms. Daphne FRENCH
32 Dean of Students .... Dr. Greg TANNER
09 Dir of Inst Effectiveness & Rsrch .... Ms. Danielle SUTLIFF
19 Campus Poilice Chief .... Ms. Sonja MCCULLOCH
26 Marketing Coordinator .... Ms. Courtney SEARS

† Part of the University System of Georgia.

South Georgia Technical College (G)

900 South Georgia Tech Parkway,
Americus GA 31709-8167

County: Sumter FICE Identification: 005617
Unit ID: 141006
Telephone: (229) 931-2394 Carnegie Class: Assoc/HVT-Mix Trad/Non
FAX Number: (229) 931-2924 Calendar System: Semester
URL: www.southgatech.edu
Established: 1948 Annual Undergrad Tuition & Fees (In-State): $2,744
Enrollment: 1,668 Coed
Affiliation or Control: State IRS Status: 501(c)3
Highest Offering: Associate Degree
Accreditation: SC

01 President .... Dr. John WATFORD
11 Vice Pres Administrative Services .... Lea COE
10 Vice Pres Business & Industry Svcs .... Wally SUMMERS
05 Vice President for Academic Affairs .... David KUIPERS
09 Vice Pres of Institutional Support .... Karen J. WERLING
04 Special Assistant to the President .... Don SMITH
20 Dean of Academic Affairs .... Raymond HOLT
20 Dean of Academic Affairs .... Vanessa WALL
20 Dean of Academic Affairs .... Dr. Andrea OATES
20 Dean of Academic Affairs .... Dr. David FINLEY
26 Vice Pres Institutional Advancement .... Su Ann BIRD
13 Technology Director .... Dianne TRUEBLOOD
37 Director of Financial Aid .... Carrie WILDER
15 Director Personnel Services .... Sandy LARSON
32 Director of Campus Life .... Cynthia CARTER
21 Director of Accounting .... Robin BELL
88 Director of Administrative Services .... Mark BROOKS
06 Registrar .... Eulish KINCHENS
08 Librarian .... Jerry STOVALL
07 Director of Admissions .... Whitney CRISP
41 Athletic Director .... James FREY
29 Director Alumni Relations .... SuAnn BIRD
38 Director Student Counseling .... LaKenya JOHNSON
84 Dean Enrollment Management .... Julie PARTAIN
18 Chief Facilities/Physical Plant .... Don SMITH
96 Purchasing Agent .... Gail CLARY
19 Director Security/Safety .... Sammy STONE

South University (H)

709 Mall Boulevard, Savannah GA 31406-4881

County: Chatham FICE Identification: 013039
Unit ID: 139579
Telephone: (912) 201-8000 Carnegie Class: Masters/M
FAX Number: (912) 201-8070 Calendar System: Quarter
URL: www.southuniversity.edu
Established: 1899 Annual Undergrad Tuition & Fees: $17,016
Enrollment: 1,437 Coed
Affiliation or Control: Proprietary IRS Status: Proprietary
Highest Offering: Doctorate

Accreditation: #SC, AA, ACBSP, ARCPA, CACREP, MAC, NURSE, PHAR, PTAA

01 Chancellor ..... Mr. John T. SOUTH, III
12 President Ai Charlotte Campus ..... Mr. Christopher MESECAR
12 President Ai Raleigh-Durham Campus ..... Mr. Christopher MESECAR
12 President Ai Dallas Campus ..... Ms. Barbara JANOWSKI
12 President Montgomery Campus ..... Mr. Victor K. BIEBIGHAUSER
12 Int Pres West Palm Beach Campus ..... Mr. David MCGUIRE
12 President Columbia Campus ..... Dr. David SHOOP
12 President Novi Campus ..... Ms. Sheila MALEWSKA
12 President Richmond Campus ..... Mr. Troy RALSTON
12 President Tampa Campus ..... Mr. James F. MCCOY, JR.
12 President Virginia Beach Campus ..... Mr. Scot HAYNES
12 President Austin Campus ..... Ms. Shelby FRUTCHEY
12 President Cleveland Campus ..... Mr. Scott BEHMER
12 President High Point Campus ..... Mr. Derek KOEBEL
12 President Savannah Campus ..... Dr. Todd CELLINI
13 Assoc Chanc Information Technology ..... Mr. James FREYBURGER
14 Regional Director of Technology ..... Mr. Dustin BARRETT
11 Vice Chanc South Campuses ..... Mr. David MCGURE
106 Vice Chanc Online & Strat Operation ..... Mr. Steven READ
10 Vice Chancellor for Finance ..... Mr. John PAPP
05 Vice Chancellor Academic Affairs ..... Dr. Jay STUBBLEFIELD
20 Assoc Vice Chanc Academic Affairs ..... Dr. Destini COPP
20 Assoc Vice Chan Academic Affairs ..... Vacant
20 Assoc Vice Chan Academic Affairs ..... Dr. Devin BYRD
08 Interim Asst Vice Chanc Univ Libr ..... Ms. Nancy SPEISSER
06 University Registrar ..... Ms. Anita MACIAS
20 Asst Vice Chanc Academic Services ..... Dr. Tamara AVANT
09 Sr Director Inst Effectiveness ..... Dr. Frances W. OBLANDER
108 Director for Academic Assessment ..... Ms. Elizabeth DEVITA
20 Dir QEP & Academic Project Manager ..... Dr. Reinhold GERBSCH
49 Dean College of Arts and Sciences ..... Vacant
50 Dean College of Business ..... Dr. Cheryl NOLL
107 Dean College of Health Professions ..... Dr. Scott MCPHEE
66 Dean College of Nursing ..... Dr. Mable H. SMITH
67 Dean School of Pharmacy ..... Dr. Curtis JONES
57 Dean College Creative Art & Design ..... Vacant
73 Dean College of Theology ..... Dr. Robert R. REDMAN, JR.
07 Vice Chancellor for Admissions ..... Mr. Matthew MILLS
84 Regional Director of Admissions ..... Mr. Matt SWANSON
84 Regional Director of Admissions ..... Ms. Ashley WEEKS
28 ADA Training Manager ..... Vacant
15 Assoc Chancellor of Human Resources ..... Ms. Lynne HAINES
16 Human Resources Generalist ..... Ms. Jamie FRAZIER-HELD
32 Asst Chancellor for Student Affairs ..... Ms. Alisa KROUSE
36 University Director Career Services ..... Ms. Paula REISING
37 Asst Chanc Student Financial Svcs ..... Ms. Kacey ATKINSON
26 Vice Chancellor for Marketing ..... Mr. Jeff BEAMON
27 Digital Marketing Director ..... Ms. Kalani ROBINSON
27 Marketing Director SU Online ..... Mr. John MAASS

Southeastern Technical College (A)

3001 E First Street, Vidalia GA 30474-8817
County: Toombs — FICE Identification: 030665
Unit ID: 368911
Telephone: (912) 538-3100 — Carnegie Class: Assoc/HVT-Mix Trad/Non
FAX Number: (912) 538-3156 — Calendar System: Semester
URL: www.southeasterntech.edu
Established: 1989 — Annual Undergrad Tuition & Fees (In-State): $2,784
Enrollment: 1,667 — Coed
Affiliation or Control: State — IRS Status: 501(c)3
Highest Offering: Associate Degree
Accreditation: SC, DH, EMT, MAC, MLTAD, RAD

01 President ..... Mr. Larry CALHOUN
05 Vice Pres Academic Affairs ..... Ms. Teresa COLEMAN
11 Vice Pres Administrative Services ..... Ms. Denise POWELL
10 Vice President Fiscal Affairs ..... Vacant
32 Vice President Student Affairs ..... Dr. Barry DOTSON
84 Director Enrollment Services ..... Mr. Brad HART
06 Registrar ..... Ms. Karen VEREEN
37 Director Financial Aid ..... Mr. Mitchell FAGLER
36 Director Job Placement ..... Mr. Lance HELMS
103 Special Populations Coordinator ..... Ms. Helen THOMAS
40 Bookstore Manager ..... Ms. Stacy FREEMAN
26 Dir Marketing & Public Relations ..... Ms. Krysta RUSHING
08 Head Librarian ..... Mrs. Leah DASHER
19 Director Security/Safety ..... Mr. Travis AKRIDGE

Southern Crescent Technical College (B)

501 Varsity Road, Griffin GA 30223-2042
County: Spalding — FICE Identification: 005621
Unit ID: 139986
Telephone: (770) 228-7348 — Carnegie Class: Assoc/HVT-Mix Trad/Non
FAX Number: (770) 229-3227 — Calendar System: Semester
URL: www.sctech.edu
Established: 1963 — Annual Undergrad Tuition & Fees (In-State): $2,758
Enrollment: 4,867 — Coed
Affiliation or Control: State — IRS Status: 501(c)3
Highest Offering: Associate Degree
Accreditation: SC, COARC, COARCP, DA, EMT, MAC, SURGT

01 President ..... Dr. Alvetta PETERMAN THOMAS
03 Executive Vice President ..... Mr. Mark ANDREWS
05 Vice Pres for Academic Affairs ..... Dr. Dawn HODGES
04 Exec Admin Asst to President ..... Ms. Kim SANTERRE
32 Vice Pres for Student Affairs ..... Dr. Xenia JOHNS
10 Vice Pres Administrative Services ..... Ms. Miriam CASLIN
111 Vice President Advancement ..... Ms. Barbara Jo COOK
46 Vice Pres Inst Effectiveness ..... Ms. Melissa GORDON
18 Assoc VP Facilities & Opers ..... Mr. Alan STANFIELD
06 Registrar ..... Ms. Kathlyn BURDEN
26 Dir Marketing & Public Relations ..... Ms. Anna TAYLOR
37 Director of Financial Aid ..... Dr. Michelle CHAPMAN
49 Dean Arts & Sciences ..... Ms. Rebecca JOHNSON
76 Dean Allied Health & ParaMedicine ..... Mr. Michael MELVIN
75 Dean Film/Prof Svcs/Public Safety ..... Mr. Lemuel MERCADO
77 Dean Business Tech/CIS ..... Ms. Tempie KITCHENS
84 Director of Enrollment Management ..... Dr. Jasper FOUST
15 Director of Human Resources ..... Ms. Sharon HILL
35 Director of Student Affairs ..... Ms. Cherryl GILBERT
21 Director of Administrative Services ..... Ms. Gina BYRD
36 Director of Career Placement & Acad ..... Ms. Susan MURRAY
19 Campus Police Chief ..... Mr. Kenneth TROISI
13 Chief Information Officer ..... Mr. Michael SHIVER

Southern Regional Technical College (C)

15689 US Highway 19 N, Thomasville GA 31792-2622
County: Thomas — FICE Identification: 005615
Unit ID: 487162
Telephone: (229) 225-4096 — Carnegie Class: Assoc/HVT-Mix Trad/Non
FAX Number: (229) 225-4330 — Calendar System: Semester
URL: www.southernregional.edu
Established: 2015 — Annual Undergrad Tuition & Fees (In-State): $2,654
Enrollment: 3,490 — Coed
Affiliation or Control: State — IRS Status: 501(c)3
Highest Offering: Associate Degree
Accreditation: SC, ADNUR, EMT, MAC, MLTAD, RAD, SURGT

01 President ..... Dr. Craig R. WENTWORTH
11 Vice Pres Administrative Services ..... Mr. Ross COX
05 Vice Pres Academic Affairs ..... Mr. Jim GLASS
32 Vice President Student Affairs ..... Ms. Leigh WALLACE
30 Vice President Economic Development ..... Mr. Dennis LEE
09 VP Institutional Effectiveness ..... Dr. Debbie GOODMAN
76 Dean School of Health Sciences ..... Ms. Carla BARROW
50 Dean School of Bus/Industrial Tech ..... Ms. Abby CARTER
107 Dean School of Professional Svcs ..... Ms. Tina STRICKLAND
49 Dean School of Art and Sciences ..... Ms. Kathryn KENT
37 Executive Director Financial Aid ..... Ms. Judi LOVVORN
26 VP Marketing/Inst Devel/Pub Rels ..... Ms. Amy MAISON
88 Director Adult Education ..... Ms. Melissa BURTLE
07 Director of Admissions ..... Ms. Wanda HANCOCK
35 Director Student Affairs ..... Ms. Lisa GRIFFIN
06 Registrar ..... Ms. Wendi TOSTENSON
08 Executive Director Library Services ..... Ms. Udella SPICER
36 Dir Career Services & Counseling ..... Dr. Jeanine LONG
15 Director Human Resources ..... Mr. Michael HEARD
18 VP Operations ..... Mr. David EVANS

Spelman College (D)

350 Spelman Lane, SW, Atlanta GA 30314-4399
County: Fulton — FICE Identification: 001594
Unit ID: 141060
Telephone: (404) 681-3643 — Carnegie Class: Bac-A&S
FAX Number: N/A — Calendar System: Semester
URL: www.spelman.edu
Established: 1881 — Annual Undergrad Tuition & Fees: $27,314
Enrollment: 2,144 — Female
Affiliation or Control: Independent Non-Profit — IRS Status: 501(c)3
Highest Offering: Baccalaureate
Accreditation: SC, CAEPN, MUS

01 President ..... Dr. Mary SCHMIDT CAMPBELL
05 Provost & VP Academic Affairs ..... Dr. Sharon DAVIES
10 VP Business/Financial Affairs/ Treas ..... Mr. Robert D. FLANIGAN, JR.
32 Vice President for Student Affairs ..... Dr. Darnita KILLIAN
26 Vice President College Relations ..... Dr. Jane SMITH
84 Vice Pres Enrollment Management ..... Ms. Ingrid HAYES
111 VP of Institutional Advancement ..... Mr. Jessie BROOKS
09 VP of IR/Planning & Effectiveness ..... Dr. Myra BURNETT
114 Director of Budgets & Contracts ..... Ms. Rhonda HONEGAN
21 Controller ..... Ms. April AUSTIN
101 Secretary of College ..... Dr. Terri REED
27 Director Marketing & Communications ..... Ms. Joyce E. DAVIS
04 Executive Assistant ..... Ms. Jarvis RIDGES
13 VP of MIT & Chief Info Officer ..... Mr. Mario BERRY
88 Dir Bonner Comm Svcs/Student Dev ..... Ms. Jilo TISDALE
20 Dean of Undergraduate Studies ..... Dr. Desiree PEDESCLEAUX
42 Director Sisters Center for WISDOM ..... Dr. Lisa D. RHODES
06 Registrar ..... Mr. John BROWN
07 Director of Admissions ..... Ms. Tiffany NELSON
29 Director of Alumnae Affairs ..... Ms. Sharon OWENS
37 Director of Financial Aid ..... Ms. Lenora JACKSON
36 Director Career Planning/Devel ..... Mr. Harold BELL
78 Director of Cooperative Education ..... Mr. Keith WEBB
15 Director Human Resources ..... Ms. Bernadette COHEN
38 Director Counseling Services ..... Dr. Ave MARSHALL
108 Dir Inst Rsrch/Assessment/Planning ..... Ms. Jill TRIPLETT
88 Director Women's Resource Center ..... Dr. Beverly GUY-SHEFTALL
18 Director Facilities/Mgmt & Svcs ..... Mr. Arthur E. FRAZIER, III
19 Director of Public Safety ..... Mr. Steve BOWSER
24 Educational Technology Coordinator ..... Ms. Natasha BROWN
102 Dir of Corp & Foundation Relations ..... Ms. Shelese LANE
88 Director of Special Events ..... Ms. Heather HAWES
39 Director Housing & Residential Life ..... Ms. Alison CUMMINGS
86 Director Title III/Government Rels ..... Ms. Helga GREENFIELD
22 Coordinator of Inclusion Division ..... Ms. Letitia J. DENARD
85 Council on Intl Educ Exchange ..... Ms. Theresa METZGER
08 Library Director/CEO ..... Ms. Loretta PARHAM
23 Director Health Services ..... Dr. Brenda DALTON
25 Director Sponsored Programs ..... Dr. Claudia SCHOLZ
35 Dean of Students ..... Dr. Fran'Cee BROWN MCCLURE
40 Bookstore Manager ..... Ms. Tiffani HODGE
96 Dir Administrative Support Svcs ..... Ms. Jacqueline JAMES
21 AVP Business & Financial Affairs ..... Ms. Dawn ALSTON

Thomas University (E)

1501 Millpond Road, Thomasville GA 31792-7499
County: Thomas — FICE Identification: 001555
Unit ID: 141167
Telephone: (229) 226-1621 — Carnegie Class: Masters/S
FAX Number: (229) 226-1653 — Calendar System: Semester
URL: www.thomasu.edu
Established: 1950 — Annual Undergrad Tuition & Fees: $16,940
Enrollment: 1,182 — Coed
Affiliation or Control: Independent Non-Profit — IRS Status: 501(c)3
Highest Offering: Master's
Accreditation: SC, CACREP, IACBE, MT, NUR, SW

01 President ..... Dr. Andy SHEPPARD
05 Vice President of Academic Affairs ..... Dr. John MEIS
30 Vice Pres Institutional Advancement ..... Dr. Grady ENLOW
08 Univ Librarian/Dir Info Services ..... Ms. Lynn KELLY
06 Registrar ..... Mrs. Michelle WENDEL
09 Director of Institutional Research ..... Danae JOHNSON
84 VP Enrollment Management ..... Dr. Susan BACKOFEN
37 Director of Financial Aid ..... Mr. Clifton MITCHELL
41 Director of Athletics ..... Mr. Michael D. LEE
10 Controller ..... Ms. Sue STONE
32 Student Life/Athletics Coordinator ..... Vacant
44 Director of Annual Fund ..... Vacant
26 Director of Communications ..... Mrs. Cindy MONTGOMERY
04 Assistant to the President ..... Mrs. Linda M. HERNDON

Toccoa Falls College (F)

107 Kincaid Drive, Toccoa Falls GA 30598-0068
County: Stephens — FICE Identification: 001596
Unit ID: 141185
Telephone: (706) 886-6831 — Carnegie Class: Bac-Diverse
FAX Number: (706) 282-6005 — Calendar System: Semester
URL: www.tfc.edu
Established: 1907 — Annual Undergrad Tuition & Fees: $21,414
Enrollment: 937 — Coed
Affiliation or Control: The Christian And Missionary Alliance — IRS Status: 501(c)3
Highest Offering: Baccalaureate
Accreditation: SC, MUS

01 President ..... Dr. Robert M. MYERS
04 Sr Exec Administrative Assistant ..... Mrs. Paula S. ELKINS
32 VP Student Affairs ..... Vacant
111 VP for Advancement ..... Vacant
10 Vice President for Finance ..... Mr. R. Gregg SCHULTE
05 Provost/VP for Academic Affairs ..... Dr. W. Brian SHELTON
84 VP for Enrollment Services ..... Vacant
42 Director Spiritual Formation ..... Mr. Chris STRATTON
09 Director Institutional Research ..... Dr. Kieran CLEMENTS
106 Director of Distance Education ..... Ms. Anna MCCLATCHY
39 Director Residence/Community Life ..... Mrs. Faith NEWEY
29 Director Alumni Assoc/Col Relations ..... Mrs. Deborah WILKES
38 Dir Counseling/Career Svcs ..... Mr. Johnathan C. KERR
37 Director Student Financial Aid ..... Mrs. Wanda PICKENS
07 Director of Admissions ..... Mr. Ronnie STEWART
06 Registrar ..... Mr. Kelly G. VICKERS
41 Athletic Director ..... Mr. Kevin HALL
18 Chief Facilities/Physical Plant ..... Mr. Merlin SCHENCK
19 Director of Security/Safety ..... Mr. Stephen JOHANNES
15 Director Human Resources ..... Ms. Mary Kaye RITCHEY
88 Director of Business Services ..... Mrs. Helen GENTRY
66 Dean of Nursing ..... Mrs. Deborah ALVATER
11 Assistant VP of Operations ..... Mr. Merlin SCHENCK
08 Head Librarian ..... Mr. Armand TERNAK
108 Director Institutional Effectivenes ..... Ms. Allison BRADY

Truett McConnell University (G)

100 Alumni Drive, Cleveland GA 30528-1264
County: White — FICE Identification: 001597
Unit ID: 141237
Telephone: (706) 865-2134 — Carnegie Class: Bac-Diverse
FAX Number: (706) 243-4968 — Calendar System: Semester
URL: www.truett.edu
Established: 1946 — Annual Undergrad Tuition & Fees: $18,510
Enrollment: 2,017 — Coed
Affiliation or Control: Baptist — IRS Status: 501(c)3
Highest Offering: Master's
Accreditation: SC, MUS, NURSE

01 President ..... Dr. Emir CANER
05 Vice Pres Academic Services ..... Dr. Brad REYNOLDS
32 Vice President of Student Services ..... Mr. Chris EPPLING
10 VP Finance/Operations/Gen Counsel ..... Dr. Joe WIEGAND
04 Executive Assistant to President ..... Ms. Cindy ERBELE
41 Athletic Director ..... Mr. Johnny GARVILLA

06 Registrar/Dir Inst Research .... Mrs. Melissa FORTNER
37 Director of Financial Aid .... Mr. Truitt FRANKLIN
08 Director of Library Resources .... Mrs. Teresa HAYMORE
29 Director of Alumni Relations .... Dr. John YARBROUGH
07 Director of Admissions .... Mr. Andrew GAILEY
42 Director of Church Relations .... Dr. David DRAKE
40 Campus Store Director .... Mr. Eddie O'BRIEN
18 Director of Facilities .... Mr. Justin COALLEY

University of Georgia (A)

Athens GA 30602-0001
County: Clarke　FICE Identification: 001598
Unit ID: 139959
Telephone: (706) 542-3000　Carnegie Class: DU-Highest
FAX Number: N/A　Calendar System: Semester
URL: www.uga.edu
Established: 1785　Annual Undergrad Tuition & Fees (In-State): $11,634
Enrollment: 36,130　Coed
Affiliation or Control: State　IRS Status: 501(c)3
Highest Offering: Doctorate
Accreditation: SC, AAFCS, ART, CAATE, CACREP, CAEPN, CEA, CIDA, CLPSY, COPSY, CS, DANCE, DIETD, DIETI, ENG, JOUR, LAW, LSAR, MFCD, MUS, PCSAS, PH, PHAR, PLNG, SCPSY, SP, SPAA, SW, THEA, VET

01 President .... Mr. Jere W. MOREHEAD
100 Chief of Staff .... Dr. Kathy R. PHARR
04 Assistant to the President .... Dr. Kyle TSCHEPIKOW
04 Assistant to the President .... Mr. Arthur TRIPP, JR.
05 Sr VP Academic Affs/Provost .... Dr. Pamela WHITTEN
10 Sr Assoc VP Finance & Admin .... Mr. James SHORE
20 Vice Provost Academic Affairs .... Dr. Russ MUMPER
11 Vice Pres for Finance & Admin .... Mr. Ryan A. NESBIT
30 Vice Pres for Devel & Alumni Rels .... Mr. Kelly K. KERNER
20 Vice President for Instruction .... Dr. Rahul SHRIVASTAV
46 Vice President for Research .... Dr. David C. LEE
88 Vice Pres Public Svc/Outreach .... Dr. Jennifer L. FRUM
32 Vice President Student Affairs .... Dr. Victor K. WILSON
86 Vice President for Govt Relations .... Mr. J. Griffin DOYLE
26 Vice President for Marketing & Comm . Ms. Karri HOBSON-PAPE
13 VP for Information Technology .... Dr. Timothy M. CHESTER
92 Assoc Prov/Dir of Honors Program .... Dr. David S. WILLIAMS
104 Int Assoc Prov International Educ .... Dr. Noel FALLOWS
28 Assoc Prov/Chief Diversity Officer .... Dr. Michelle G. COOK
20 Assoc Provost Academic Programs .... Dr. Margaret AMSTUTZ
08 Assoc Provost/University Librarian .... Dr. Toby GRAHAM
88 Assoc Provost Faculty Affairs .... Ms. Sarah COVERT
07 Assoc VP Admissions/Enroll Mgmt .... Mr. Patrick WINTER
21 Assoc VP Univ Business & Acct Svcs .... Ms. Holley W. SCHRAMSKI
18 Assoc VP Facilities Management .... Mr. Ralph F. JOHNSON
15 Associate VP Human Resources .... Mr. Juan JARRETT
43 Executive Director Legal Affairs .... Mr. Michael RAEBER
49 Dean of Arts & Sciences .... Dr. Alan T. DORSEY
47 Dean of Agricultural & Environ Sci .... Dr. Samuel PARDUE
61 Dean of Law .... Mr. Peter RUTLEDGE
67 Dean of Pharmacy .... Dr. Svein OIE
65 Dean Forestry & Natural Resources .... Dr. Dale GREENE
53 Dean of Education .... Dr. Craig H. KENNEDY
58 Dean of the Graduate School .... Dr. Suzanne BARBOUR
50 Dean of Business .... Dr. Benjamin C. AYERS
60 Dean Journalism & Mass Comm .... Dr. Charles N. DAVIS
59 Dean of Family & Consumer Sci .... Dr. Linda K. FOX
74 Dean of Veterinary Medicine .... Dr. Lisa K. NOLAN
70 Dean of Social Work .... Dr. Anna M. SCHEYETT
48 Dean of Environment & Design .... Mr. Daniel J. NADENICEK
80 Dean Public/International Affs .... Dr. Matthew R. AUER
69 Dean of Public Health .... Dr. Phillip L. WILLIAMS
88 Dean School of Ecology .... Dr. John L. GITTLEMAN
88 Dean GRU/UGA Medical .... Dr. Shelley NUSS
54 Dean of Engineering .... Dr. Donald LEO
41 Athletic Director .... Mr. William G. MCGARITY
22 Director of Equal Opportunity .... Ms. E. Janyce DAWKINS
06 Interim Registrar .... Ms. Rosemary SEGRETI
19 Chief of Police .... Chief James E. WILLIAMSON
37 Director of Student Financial Aid .... Ms. Bonnie C. JOERSCHKE
36 Director of Career Services Center .... Mr. Scott T. WILLIAMS
39 Executive Director of Housing .... Dr. Gerard J. KOWALSKI
23 Exec Director of Health Services .... Dr. Jean E. CHIN
35 Dean of Students .... Dr. William M. MCDONALD
38 Dir Counseling/Psychological Svcs .... Dr. Ash THOMPSON
88 Director Georgia Center .... Dr. Dawn H. CARTEE
29 Exec Dir of Alumni Relations .... Ms. Meredith G. JOHNSON
110 Sr Assoc VP for Dev & Alumni Rel .... Mr. Jay STROMAN
09 Director of Institutional Research .... Mr. Paul KLUTE
121 Director of Academic Enhancement .... Dr. Thomas HAGOOD
94 Director Inst of Women's Studies . Dr. Juanita JOHNSON-BAILEY
96 Director of Purchasing .... Ms. Annette EVANS
106 Dir Online Education/E-learning .... Dr. Stephen P. BALFOUR
88 Sr Director for Accreditation .... Mr. Allan AYCOCK
44 Exec Dir Annual or Planned Giving .... Mr. David JONES
88 Director Office of Economic Dev .... Mr. Sean MCMILLAN

† Part of the University System of Georgia.

University of North Georgia (B)

82 College Circle, Dahlonega GA 30597-1001
County: Lumpkin　FICE Identification: 001585
Unit ID: 482680
Telephone: (706) 864-1400　Carnegie Class: Masters/M
FAX Number: (706) 864-1478　Calendar System: Semester
URL: ung.edu
Established: 1873　Annual Undergrad Tuition & Fees (In-State): $4,397
Enrollment: 17,289　Coed
Affiliation or Control: State　IRS Status: 501(c)3
Highest Offering: Doctorate
Accreditation: SC, ART, CAATE, CACREP, CAEPN, CSHSE, NUR, PTA

01 President .... Dr. Bonita JACOBS
05 Provost & Sr VP Academic Affairs .... Dr. Tom ORMOND
10 Sr VP Business & Finance .... Mr. Frank J. MCCONNELL
88 Sr VP Leadership & Global Engage .... Dr. Billy WELLS
32 VP Student Affairs .... Dr. Janet MARLING
12 VP of Gainesville Campus .... Dr. Richard OATES
111 VP of University Advancement .... Mr. Jeff TARNOWSKI
20 Vice Provost Academic Affairs .... Dr. Chaudron GILLE
108 Assoc Provost Inst Effectiveness .... Vacant
46 Assoc Prov & Chief Research Officer .... Dr. Andy NOVOBILSKI
20 Assoc VP & Dean Univ College .... Dr. Carol ADAMS
58 Assoc VP Graduate Studies .... Dr. Bill GASH
21 AVP Financial Svcs & Comptroller .... Ms. Donna CALDWELL
109 Assoc VP Aux Services & Real Estate .... Mr. Gerald SULLIVAN
13 Chief Information Officer .... Mr. Brandon HAAG
84 Assoc VP Enrollment Management .... Ms. Sallie MCMULLIN
35 Assoc VP Stdnt Aff & Dean of Stdnts .... Dr. Cara RAY
35 Asst VP Stdnt Affs & Dean of Stdnts .... Dr. Michelle BROWN
35 Asst VP Stdnt Affs & Dean of Stdnts .... Dr. Alyson PAUL
29 Director Alumni Relations & Annual .... Ms. Wendy HUGULEY
106 Dir Distance Educ/Tech Integration .... Dr. Irene KOKKALA
07 Director of Undergrad Admissions .... Ms. Molly POTTS
07 Director of Cadet Admissions .... Mr. Tony MOSS
92 Dean of Honors Program .... Dr. Tanya BENNETT
41 Director of Athletics .... Ms. Lindsay REEVES
88 Director of Internal Audit .... Ms. Jill HOLMAN
06 University Registrar .... Mr. Steve STUBBS
25 Director of Grants & Contracts .... Vacant
37 Director of Financial Aid .... Ms. Jill RAYNER
09 Director Institutional Research .... Ms. Linda ROWLAND
08 Dean of Libraries .... Dr. Deborah PROSSER
49 Dean College of Arts & Letters .... Dr. Christopher JESPERSEN
50 Dean M C College of Business .... Dr. Donna MAYO
53 Dean of College of Education .... Dr. Susan AYRES
81 Dean College of Sci & Mathematics .... Dr. Michael BODRI
76 Dean College of Health Sciences .... Dr. Teresa CONNER-KERR
104 Int Assoc VP International Programs .... Mr. Anthony FRITCHLE
15 Assoc VP Human Resources .... Ms. Beth ARBUTHNOT
18 Asst VP of Facilities .... Mr. Ken CROWE
19 Director of Public Safety .... Mr. Justin GAINES
14 Deputy CIO .... Mr. Steve MCLEOD
100 Chief of Staff .... Ms. Kate MAINE
35 Commandant Corp of Cadets .... Col. James PALMER
36 Director of Career Services .... Ms. Diane FARRELL
38 Director Counseling Services .... Dr. Simon CORDERY
39 Director of Residence Life .... Ms. Treva SMITH
23 Director of Student Health Services .... Ms. Karen TOMLINSON
12 Exec Dir Cumming Campus .... Mr. Jason PRUITT
12 Exec Director Oconee Campus .... Dr. Cyndee MOORE
108 Dir Accreditation & Assessment .... Ms. Betsy CANTRELL
51 Director Continuing Education .... Dr. Wendy ESTES
86 Exec Director External Relations .... Dr. Edward MIENIE
43 General Counsel & Dir Gov Relations .... Ms. Jenna COLVIN
96 Director Purchasing .... Ms. Beverly LONG
85 Dir Multicultural Student Affairs .... Dr. Robert ROBINSON
04 Admin Asst to the President .... Ms. Linda SMITH
28 Diversity Advisor to President .... Ms. Sheila CALDWELL
105 Director Web Services .... Ms. Joanie CHEMBARS
91 Asst CIO .... Mr. Rick CRAIN

† Part of the University System of Georgia.

University of Phoenix Atlanta Campus (C)

8200 Roberts Drive, Sandy Springs GA 30350-4147
Telephone: (678) 731-0555　Identification: 770200
Accreditation: &NH, ACBSP

† No longer accepting campus-based students.

University of Phoenix Augusta Campus (D)

3150 Perimeter Parkway, Augusta GA 30909-4583
Telephone: (706) 868-2000　Identification: 770198
Accreditation: &NH, ACBSP

† No longer accepting campus-based students.

University of Phoenix Columbus GA Campus (E)

7200 North Lake Drive, Columbus GA 31909
Telephone: (706) 320-1266　Identification: 770199
Accreditation: &NH, ACBSP

† No longer accepting campus-based students.

University of West Georgia (F)

1601 Maple Street, Carrollton GA 30118-0001
County: Carroll　FICE Identification: 001601
Unit ID: 141334
Telephone: (678) 839-5000　Carnegie Class: DU-Mod
FAX Number: N/A　Calendar System: Semester
URL: www.westga.edu
Established: 1906　Annual Undergrad Tuition & Fees (In-State): $6,143
Enrollment: 12,834　Coed
Affiliation or Control: State　IRS Status: 501(c)3
Highest Offering: Doctorate
Accreditation: SC, ART, CACREP, CAEPN, CS, MUS, NURSE, SP, SPAA, THEA

01 President .... Dr. Kyle MARRERO
05 Provost & VP for Academic Affairs .... Dr. Michael CRAFTON
10 Exec VP for Business & Finance .... Mr. Jim SUTHERLAND
32 VP for Student Affairs & Enroll Mgt .... Dr. Scott LINGRELL
111 VP for University Advancement .... Mr. Dave FRABONI
30 Director of Development .... Ms. Nichole FANNIN
84 AVP for Enrollment Management .... Dr. John HEAD
20 Associate VP for Academic Affairs .... Dr. Myrna GANTNER
21 University Controller .... Mr. Richard SEARS
83 Dean Social Sciences .... Dr. N. Jane MCCANDLESS
50 Dean Richards College of Business .... Dr. Faye S. MCINTYRE
53 Dean Education .... Dr. Dianne HOFF
79 Dean Arts & Humanities .... Dr. Pauline GAGNON
81 Dean Science & Mathematics .... Dr. Lok LEW YAN VOON
92 Dean Honors College .... Dr. Janet DONOHOE
06 Registrar .... Ms. Donna HALEY
07 Director Admissions .... Mr. Justin BARLOW
08 Interim Dean of Libraries .... Mr. Christopher HUFF
37 Director Financial Aid .... Ms. Leigh Ann HUSSEY
36 Director Career Services .... Ms. Keri BURNS
13 VP Info Tech Services/CIO .... Ms. Annemarie EADES
51 Director Continuing Education .... Mr. Marty DAVIS
15 Assoc VP of Human Resources .... Ms. Juanita HICKS
18 Asst VP Campus Planning/Facilities .... Mr. Brendan BOWEN
19 Interim Chief of University Police .... Lt. G. E WATSON
23 Interim Dir of Health Services .... Dr. Michael POSS
39 Director Housing & Residence Life .... Mr. Stephen WHITLOCK
41 Director of Athletics .... Mr. Daryl DICKEY
38 Director Counseling Center .... Dr. Lisa ADAMS SOMERLOT
109 Assoc VP Auxiliary Services .... Mr. Mark REEVES
108 AVP Inst Effectiveness & Assessment .... Dr. Catherine JENKS
29 Exec Dir of Alumni Relations .... Ms. Alison ROSBOROUGH
26 Assoc VP Communication & Marketing .... Ms. Jami BOWER
58 Assoc VP & Dean of Graduate School ...... Dr. Denise OVERFIELD
106 Dean USG eCore .... Dr. Melanie N. CLAY
110 Dir of Dev-Legacy Giving & Athletic .... Mr. Baylor BASSETT
24 Asst Director for Classroom Support .... Mr. Brian MCCRARY
43 University General Counsel .... Ms. Jane SIMPSON
102 Dir of Advancement Services .... Mr. Bart GILLESPIE
66 Dean Tanner School of Nursing .... Dr. Jennifer SCHUESSLER
14 Director of User Services .... Mr. Blake ADAMS
16 Dir of Human Resources Operations .... Mr. Rodney BYRD
96 Director of Purchasing .... Ms. Shelly PARKER
22 Social Equity Support Spec Title IX .... Ms. Kelsey STEPHENS
86 Spec Asst Pres Govt & External Rels . Mr. Russell CRUTCHFIELD
12 Sr Dir/Chief Admin Ofcr Off Cam Pgm ..... Dr. Robert HEABERLIN
105 Manager Web Innovations .... Mr. Denny CHASTEEN
40 Bookstore Manager .... Ms. Bettina A. ROBINSON
85 Dir International Services & Pgms .... Dr. Maria DOYLE
28 Senior Diversity Officer .... Ms. Yves-Rose PORCENA

† Part of the University System of Georgia.

*University System of Georgia Office (G)

270 Washington Street, SW, Atlanta GA 30334-9007
County: Fulton　FICE Identification: 008290
Telephone: (404) 962-3049　Carnegie Class: N/A
FAX Number: (404) 962-3013
URL: www.usg.edu

01 Chancellor .... Dr. Steve WRIGLEY
04 Executive Assistant to Chancellor .... Ms. Shelia ELDER
11 Exec Vice Chanc Administration .... Ms. Tricia CHASTAIN
05 Exec Vice Chanc/Chief Academic Ofcr .... Dr. Tristan DENLEY
10 Vice Chancellor Fiscal Affairs .... Ms. Shelley C. NICKEL
21 Chief Audit Officer .... Mr. Terry THOMPSON
18 Vice Chancellor Facilities .... Mr. Jim JAMES
43 Vice Chancellor Legal Affairs .... Mr. Sam BURCH
26 Vice Chanc Comm & Govt Relations .... Mr. Charles SUTLIVE
13 Vice Chanc/Chief Information Ofcr .... Dr. Robert LAURINE

Valdosta State University (H)

1500 N Patterson Street, Valdosta GA 31698-0010
County: Lowndes　FICE Identification: 001599
Unit ID: 141264
Telephone: (229) 333-5800　Carnegie Class: DU-Mod
FAX Number: (229) 333-7400　Calendar System: Semester
URL: www.valdosta.edu
Established: 1906　Annual Undergrad Tuition & Fees (In-State): $6,297
Enrollment: 11,302　Coed
Affiliation or Control: State　IRS Status: 501(c)3
Highest Offering: Doctorate
Accreditation: SC, ART, CAATE, CACREP, CAEP, CS, EXSC, LIB, MFCD, MUS, NURSE, SP, SPAA, SW, THEA

01 President .... Dr. Richard CARVAJAL
05 Provost & VPAA .... Dr. Robert T. SMITH
10 Vice President for Finance & Admin .... Ms. Traycee F. MARTIN
111 Vice President for Advancement .... Mr. John D. CRAWFORD
32 VP for Student Affairs .... Dr. Vince MILLER
58 Asst VP Rsrch & Grad Dean .... Dr. James T. LAPLANT
20 Assoc Provost Academic Affairs .... Dr. Sharon L. GRAVETT
20 Dean Undergrad Studies AA .... Dr. Lai K. ORENDUFF
30 Asst VP for Development .... Ms. Hilary H. GIBBS
49 Dean College of Arts & Sciences .... Dr. Connie L. RICHARDS
50 Dean College of Business Admin .... Dr. Wayne L. PLUMLY
57 Dean College of the Arts .... Mr. Arthur B. PEARCE
53 Int Dean College of Educ & Hum Svc .... Dr. Lynn C. MINOR
66 Dean College of Nursing .... Dr. Sheri R. NOVIELLO
92 Dean of Honors College .... Dr. Michael P. SAVOIE

08 University Librarian .... Dr. Alan BERNSTEIN
06 Registrar .... Mr. Stanley JONES
106 Dir of Office of Extended Learning .... Ms. Meg H. GIDDINGS
13 Chief Information Officer .... Mr. Brian HAUGABROOK
14 Chief Technology Officer .... Mr. Joseph A. NEWTON
124 Assoc VP of Student Success .... Mr. Tee MITCHELL
39 Dir Housing & Residence Life .... Dr. Zduy CHU
88 Director of Off-Campus Learning .... Dr. Joseph WEAVER
41 Director of Athletics .... Mr. Herb REINHARD
37 Director of Financial Aid .... Mr. Douglas R. TANNER
88 Dir of Creative Design Services .... Mr. Jeff GRANT
36 Director of Career Opportunities .... Dr. Gerald WILLIAMS
29 Director Alumni Relations .... Ms. Hilary GIBBS
15 Director of Human Resources .... Dr. Denise BOGART
88 Director Division Aerospace Studies .... LtCol. Melvin GREEN, III
22 Director of Social Equity .... Dr. Maggie J. VIVERETTE
43 University Attorney .... Mr. Tony G. THOMAS
18 Dir Phys Plant & Facilities Plng .... Mr. Ray SABLE
26 Ex Dir of Communications & Mktg .... Mr. Keith WARBURG
38 Director of Counseling Center .... Dr. Tricia A. HALE
88 Director of Centralized Advising .... Ms. Alicia ROBERSON
40 Manager of Bookstore .... Ms. Lee Ann JOHNSON
23 Director of Student Health Services .... Dr. Edwin L. HIATT
19 Int Dir Public Safety/Police Chief .... Mr. Alan ROWE
108 Director of Inst Effectiveness .... Dr. Michael M. BLACK
88 Dir of Info Tech Svcs for Adv Svcs .... Ms. Amelia REAMS
04 Special Assistant to the President .... Ms. Melinda CUTCHENS
96 Asst Director of Procurement .... Mr. Matthew R. WALL
09 Director Inst Research .... Mr. Barrie D. FITZGERALD

† Part of the University System of Georgia.

Virginia College (A)

2807 Wylds Road Extension, Suite B, Augusta GA 30909
Telephone: (706) 288-2500 Identification: 770833
Accreditation: **ACICS**, MAAB

† Branch campus of Virginia College, Birmingham, AL

Virginia College (B)

5601 Veterans Parkway, Columbus GA 31904
Telephone: (762) 207-1600 Identification: 770835
Accreditation: **ACICS**, SURGT

† Branch campus of Virginia College, Birmingham, AL

Virginia College (C)

1901 Paul Walsh Drive, Macon GA 31206
Telephone: (478) 803-4600 Identification: 770834
Accreditation: **ACICS**

† Branch campus of Virginia College, Birmingham, AL

Virginia College (D)

14045 Abercorn Street, Suite 1503, Savannah GA 31419
Telephone: (912) 721-5600 Identification: 770836
Accreditation: **ACICS**, ACFEI

† Branch campus of Virginia College, Birmingham, AL

Wesleyan College (E)

4760 Forsyth Road, Macon GA 31210-4462
County: Bibb FICE Identification: 001600
Unit ID: 141325
Telephone: (478) 477-1110 Carnegie Class: Bac-A&S
FAX Number: (478) 757-4030 Calendar System: Semester
URL: www.wesleyancollege.edu
Established: 1836 Annual Undergrad Tuition & Fees: $21,750
Enrollment: 708 Female
Affiliation or Control: United Methodist IRS Status: 501(c)3
Highest Offering: Master's
Accreditation: **SC**, MUS, NURSE

01 President .... Dr. Vivia L. FOWLER
05 Provost/VP for Academic Affairs .... Dr. Melody BLAKE
111 VP Institutional Advancement .... Ms. Andrea G. WILLIFORD
10 Vice Pres Finance/Treasurer .... Mrs. Dawn P. NASH
32 Vice Pres for Student Affairs .... Ms. Patricia M. GIBBS
84 VP for Strategic Enrollment .... Mr. Clinton G. HOBBS
06 Assistant Dean/Registrar .... Ms. Angie WRIGHT
04 Assistant to the President .... Mrs. Denise W. HOLLOWAY
04 Assistant to the President .... Mrs. Carol A. PAYTON
08 Library Director .... Ms. Kristi PEAVY
13 Director of Information Services .... Mr. Kevin L. ULSHAFER
29 Director of Alumnae Affairs .... Ms. Cathy C. SNOW
26 Director of Communications .... Ms. Mary Ann HOWARD
44 Director of Annual Fund .... Ms. Whitney DAVIS
37 Director of Financial Aid .... Mr. Courtney HAYNES
39 Director of Residence Life .... Ms. Emily JARVIS
18 Director of Physical Plant .... Mr. James FLEENOR
41 Athletic Director .... Ms. Patty GIBBS
42 Chaplain .... Rev. Tyler SCHWALLER
19 Director Security/Safety .... Ms. Patty GIBBS
15 Director Human Resources .... Ms. Meagon DAVIS
07 Director of Admissions .... Ms. Lisa SLOBEN
09 Director of Institutional Research .... Ms. Glenda FERGUSON
35 Chief Student Life Officer .... Ms. Ashley TOMLIN
36 Director Career Development .... Ms. Sarah SCHANCK
38 Director Student Counseling .... Ms. Jamie THAMES
96 Director of Purchasing .... Ms. Barbara MONTGOMERY
20 Associate Academic Officer .... Dr. Matthew R. MARTIN
21 Associate Business Officer .... Ms. Quintress HOLLIS
40 Bookstore Manager .... Ms. Barbara MONTGOMERY

West Georgia Technical College (F)

176 Murphy Campus Boulevard, Waco GA 30182-2407
County: Haralson FICE Identification: 010487
Unit ID: 139278
Telephone: (770) 537-6000 Carnegie Class: Assoc/HVT-Mix Trad/Non
FAX Number: (770) 537-7976 Calendar System: Semester
URL: www.westgatech.edu
Established: 1968 Annual Undergrad Tuition & Fees (In-State): $2,764
Enrollment: 6,431 Coed
Affiliation or Control: State IRS Status: 501(c)3
Highest Offering: Associate Degree
Accreditation: **SC**, ACBSP, ADNUR, CAHIIM, DH, MAC, MLTAD, RAD, SURGT

01 President .... Mr. Steve G. DANIEL
88 Executive VP High School Initiative .... Dr. Perrin ALFORD
11 Executive VP Admin Svcs .... Mr. Rick LEVEILLE
05 Vice President Academic Affairs .... Dr. Kristen DOUGLAS
32 Vice President Student Affairs .... Dr. Tonya F. WHITLOCK
111 VP Institutional Advancement .... Ms. Kim LEARNARD
09 VP Institutional Effectiveness .... Mr. John PARTON
20 Asst Vice Pres For Curriculum .... Dr. Sindi MCGOWAN
08 Exec Director Library Services .... Mr. Emanuel MITCHELL
06 Registrar .... Mrs. Laura THORNTON
13 Exec Dir Information Technology .... Mr. Sam JENKINS
07 Director of Admissions .... Mrs. Mary ADERHOLD
18 Director Facilities .... Mr. Michael JILES
04 Executive Asst to President .... Mrs. Julia WATSON
36 Manager Career Services .... Ms. Dawne WHITE
37 Director Student Financial Aid .... Mrs. Anna ENGLISH
41 Interim Athletic Director .... Mr. Todd PRATT
10 Chief Business Officer .... Ms. Carol REID
103 Executive VP Economic Development .... Ms. Laura B. GAMMAGE
15 Director Personnel Services .... Ms. Susan DANHAUSER
19 Chief of Police .... Mr. James PERRY
50 Dean Sch of Business & Public Svcs .... Ms. Babs RUSSELL
53 Dean Sch of Arts & Sciences .... Mr. Brian BARKLEY
54 Dean Sch of Trade & Technology .... Ms. Linda SULLIVAN

Wiregrass Georgia Technical College (G)

4089 Val Tech Road, Valdosta GA 31602
County: Lowndes FICE Identification: 005256
Unit ID: 141255
Telephone: (229) 333-2100 Carnegie Class: Assoc/HVT-High Non
FAX Number: (229) 333-2129 Calendar System: Semester
URL: www.wiregrass.edu
Established: 1963 Annual Undergrad Tuition & Fees (In-State): $2,744
Enrollment: 3,708 Coed
Affiliation or Control: State IRS Status: 501(c)3
Highest Offering: Associate Degree
Accreditation: **SC**, CAHIIM, DA, DH, EMT, MAC, RAD, SURGT

01 President .... Dr. Tina K. ANDERSON
05 Exec Vice Pres Academic Affairs .... Dr. Shawn UTLEY
10 Vice President Operations .... Ms. Lisa TOMBERLIN
46 VP Research/Strategic Initiatives .... Dr. Ron O'MEARA
11 VP for Administrative Services .... Ms. Keren WYNN
84 VP for Enrollment Management .... Ms. Angela HOBBY
09 Exec Dir for Inst Effectiveness .... Dr. Bonnie KELLY
31 VP Community Affs/Minority Recruit .... Mr. Alvin PAYTON
46 VP for Economic Development .... Ms. Lidell GREENWAY
13 Chief Info Technology Officer (CIO) .... Mr. Jarrod BROGDON
18 Chief of Facilities .... Mr. Michael FLETCHER
30 Exec Dir Advancement/Res Devel .... Dr. Penelope SCHMIDT
32 Dean of Student Affairs .... Ms. Shannon MCCONICO
26 Dir for Cmty/College Relations .... Ms. Lydia HUBERT
07 Director Recruitment .... Ms. Brooke JARAMILLO
04 Administrative Asst to President .... Ms. Cheryl ACREE
06 Assistant Registrar .... Ms. Julie DREXLER
08 Head Librarian .... Ms. Kathryn TOMLINSON
105 Director Web Services .... Ms. Mary Ann GARNER
106 Exec Director Online Education .... Ms. Sally DORMINY
15 Exec Dir of Human Resources .... Ms. Shalonda SANDERS
19 Chief of Police .... Mr. Tim ALLMOND
37 Financial Aid Coordinator .... Ms. Paula HERRING
96 Director of Purchasing .... Mr. Jim RAGO
50 Dean of Business/Education .... Ms. Lynn BOWEN
49 Dean of Arts and Science .... Ms. Lynn BOWEN
76 Dean of Allied Health .... Ms. DeAnnia CLEMENTS

Young Harris College (H)

1 College Street, Young Harris GA 30582-0098
County: Towns FICE Identification: 001604
Unit ID: 141361
Telephone: (706) 379-3111 Carnegie Class: Bac-A&S
FAX Number: (706) 379-4319 Calendar System: Semester
URL: www.yhc.edu
Established: 1886 Annual Undergrad Tuition & Fees: $29,012
Enrollment: 1,204 Coed
Affiliation or Control: United Methodist IRS Status: 501(c)3
Highest Offering: Baccalaureate
Accreditation: **SC**, MUS

01 Interim President .... Dr. Brooks SEAY
05 Interim Vice Pres Academic Affairs .... Dr. Benny FERGUSON
11 Senior VP for Finance & Admin .... Dr. Brooks SEAY
10 Controller .... Mr. Wade M. BENSON
32 Vice President for Student Affairs .... Ms. Angi SMITH
84 Vice Pres for Enrollment Management .... Mr. Clayton DANIELS
111 Vice President of Advancement .... Mr. Jimmy OWEN
45 VP for Planning and Assessment .... Ms. Rosemary R. ROYSTON
13 Vice President of Campus Technology .... Mr. Ken FANEUFF
29 Director of Alumni Relations .... Ms. Dana ENSLEY
20 Assoc VP for Academic Services .... Dr. Keith DEFOOR
08 Dean of Library Services .... Ms. Debra MARCH
38 Dir of Counseling & Psychological .... Ms. Lynne GRADY
06 Registrar .... Ms. Tammy GIBSON
37 Director of Financial Aid .... Ms. Linda ADAMS
15 Human Resources Director .... Mr. Vince ROBELOTTO
26 Dir of Communication & Marketing .... Ms. LeAnn WALDROUP
18 Interim Facilities General Manager .... Mr. Rusty ROYSTON
19 Director of Safety & Compliance .... Vacant
41 Director of Athletics .... Mr. Randy DUNN
42 Chaplain & Dean of the Chapel .... Rev. Blair TOLBERT
04 Administrative Asst to President .... Ms. Teresa KELLEY
39 Asst Dean of Students .... Mr. Stuart MILLER
07 Senior Assoc Director of Admissions .... Mr. Matthew MASHBURN
100 Chief of Staff .... Ms. Rosemary ROYSTON

HAWAII

Argosy University, Hawaii (I)

400 ABS Tower, 1001 Bishop Street, Honolulu HI 96813
Telephone: (808) 536-5555 Identification: 666787
Accreditation: **&WC**, ACBSP, CLPSY

† Regional accreditation is carried under the parent institution in Orange, CA.

Babel University Professional School of Translation (J)

1833 Kalakaua Avenue, #208, Honolulu HI 96815
County: Honolulu Identification: 666350
Telephone: (808) 946-3773 Carnegie Class: Not Classified
FAX Number: (808) 946-3993 Calendar System: Other
URL: www.babel.edu
Established: 2000 Annual Graduate Tuition & Fees: N/A
Enrollment: N/A Coed
Affiliation or Control: Proprietary IRS Status: Proprietary
Highest Offering: Master's; No Undergraduates
Accreditation: **DEAC**

01 Chancellor .... Dr. Miyoko YUASA
03 Vice Chancellor/Educational Dir .... Mr. Tomoki HOTTA
43 General Counsel .... Mr. Yoshiharu ISHIDA
05 Head of Deans .... Mr. Yoshiharu ISHIDA
11 Director of Administration .... Dr. Miyoko YUASA
32 Student Services Manager .... Ms. Yuji TATENO

Brigham Young University Hawaii (K)

55-220 Kulanui Street, Laie Oahu HI 96762-1294
County: Honolulu FICE Identification: 001606
Unit ID: 230047
Telephone: (808) 675-3211 Carnegie Class: Bac-Diverse
FAX Number: (808) 675-3329 Calendar System: Semester
URL: www.byuh.edu
Established: 1955 Annual Undergrad Tuition & Fees: $5,240
Enrollment: 2,718 Coed
Affiliation or Control: Latter-day Saints IRS Status: 501(c)3
Highest Offering: Baccalaureate
Accreditation: **WC**, CAEPT, SW

01 President .... Dr. John S. TANNER
05 Vice President for Academics .... Dr. John D. BELL
11 VP of Administration .... Vacant
32 VP for Student Development & Svcs .... Dr. Debbie HIPPOLITE WRIGHT
04 Admin Assistant to the President .... Mrs. Bettina FEKETE
108 Assoc Academic VP for Assessment .... Dr. Rosalind RAM
20 Assoc Academic VP for Instruction .... Dr. David BYBEE
20 Assoc Academic VP for Curriculum .... Vacant
81 Dean College of Math and Sciences .... Dr. Mark B. CANNON
50 Dean College of Bus/Computing/Govt .... Dr. James D. LEE
88 Dean College of Human Development .... Dr. Jennifer JANE
88 Dean College of Lang/Culture & Arts .... Dr. Phillip MCARTHUR
13 University Technology Officer .... Mr. Kevin SCHLAG
07 Director Enrollment Services .... Mr. James FAUSTINO
41 Director of Athletics .... Mr. Bradley JONES
08 University Librarian .... Mr. Michael ALDRICH
21 Director Budget Services .... Mr. Steven TUELLER
96 Director of Purchasing & Travel .... Mr. Robert OWAN
19 Director Safety/Security & Risk Mgt .... Mr. Earl MORRIS
15 Director of Human Resources .... Vacant
18 Director Facilities Management .... Mr. Randy SHARP
10 Director Financial Services .... Mr. Eric MARLER
23 Director Health Center .... Mrs. Laurie ABREGANO
116 Dir Compliance & Internal Audit .... Mr. Christopher BEARD
36 Director Career Services .... Mr. Mark MACDONALD
38 Director of Counseling Services .... Mrs. Leilani AUNA
35 Director Student Leadership & Honor .... Ms. Alison WHITING
109 Director Food Services .... Mr. David KEALA

26 Director Communications ... Mrs. Laura TEVAGA
88 Director Testing and Assessment ... Mr. Christopher WRIGHT
06 Registrar ... Mr. Daryl WHITFORD
39 Director Housing & Residential Life ... Mr. Edwin ROGERS
51 Manager of Educational Outreach ... Mr. Jacob NIHIPALI
40 Manager Bookstore ... Mr. David FONOIMOANA
85 Dir International Student Services ... Mr. Arapata MEHA
37 Director Student Financial Aid ... Mr. James FAUSTINO

† Affiliated with Brigham Young University, Provo, UT.

Chaminade University of Honolulu (A)

3140 Waialae Avenue, Honolulu HI 96816-1578
County: Honolulu FICE Identification: 001605
Unit ID: 141486
Telephone: (808) 735-4711 Carnegie Class: Masters/L
FAX Number: (808) 735-4870 Calendar System: Semester
URL: www.chaminade.edu
Established: 1955 Annual Undergrad Tuition & Fees: $23,310
Enrollment: 2,466 Coed
Affiliation or Control: Independent Non-Profit IRS Status: 501(c)3
Highest Offering: Master's
Accreditation: WC, CAEPT, CIDA, IACBE, MACTE, NURSE

01 President ... Dr. Lynn BABINGTON
88 Exec Director of Compliance & Pers ... Ms. Christine DENTON
05 Provost ... Dr. Helen WHIPPY
30 VP for Institutional Advancement ... Ms. Diane PETERS-NGUYEN
10 Vice President Finance/Facilities ... Ms. Aulani KAANOI
13 Dean of Info Technologies & Support ... Mr. Kyle JOHNSON
84 Dean of Enrollment Management ... Ms. Joy BOUEY
32 Dean of Students ... Ms. Allison JEROME
90 Director Network/Desktop Services ... Mr. Eddie PANG
51 Dir Professional & Continuing Educ ... Ms. Michelle COHEN
29 Director of Alumni Relations ... Ms. Be-Jay KODAMA
41 Director of Athletics ... Mr. William VILLA
42 Director of Campus Ministry ... Mr. Danny O'REGAN
36 Dir Career Develop/Job Placement ... Mrs. Megan ROBISON
18 Director of Facilities Operations ... Mr. Michael HAISEN
21 Director of Finance ... Mr. Choong LIM
08 Director of Library ... Ms. Sharon LEPAGE
19 Director of Security ... Mr. Robert WONG
38 Director of Student Counseling ... Dr. June YASUHARA
06 Registrar ... Mr. John MORRIS
37 Director of Financial Aid ... Ms. Amy TAKIGUCHI
09 Dir of Institutional Research ... Mr. Hieu NGUYEN
26 Senior Dir of Univ Communications ... Ms. Lisa FURUTA

Hawaii Medical College (B)

1221 Kapiolani Blvd PH 35, Honolulu HI 96814
County: Honolulu FICE Identification: 041822
Unit ID: 460756
Telephone: (808) 237-5140 Carnegie Class: Not Classified
FAX Number: N/A Calendar System: Other
URL: www.hmi.edu
Established: 2007 Annual Undergrad Tuition & Fees: $17,434
Enrollment: 510 Coed
Affiliation or Control: Proprietary IRS Status: Proprietary
Highest Offering: Associate Degree
Accreditation: CNCE

01 Executive Director ... Guy BENJAMIN
05 Director of Education ... Anita GRAHAM-ROY

Hawaii Pacific University (C)

1164 Bishop Street, Suite 800, Honolulu HI 96813-2882
County: Honolulu FICE Identification: 007279
Unit ID: 141644
Telephone: (808) 544-0200 Carnegie Class: Masters/L
FAX Number: (808) 544-1136 Calendar System: Semester
URL: www.hpu.edu
Established: 1965 Annual Undergrad Tuition & Fees: $23,440
Enrollment: 4,781 Coed
Affiliation or Control: Independent Non-Profit IRS Status: 501(c)3
Highest Offering: Master's
Accreditation: WC, CAEPT, NURSE, SW

01 President ... Mr. John GOTANDA
00 President Emeritus ... Mr. Chatt G. WRIGHT
05 Provost & VP Academic Affairs ... Mr. Matthew LIAO-TROTH
11 Exec Vice Pres Admin/Gen Counsel ... Ms. Janet BOIVIN
10 Sr VP/Chief Financial Officer ... Mr. Bruce EDWARDS
84 Vice Pres Enrollment Management ... Mr. Greg GRAUMAN
30 Vice Pres University Relations ... Mr. Samuel MOKU
20 Assoc VP Academic Affairs ... Mr. Joe SCHMIEDL
15 Int AVP of Human Resources ... Ms. Diana NILES-HANSEN
21 Associate VP/Controller ... Mr. James BRESE
50 Int Dean Business Administration ... Dr. Warren WEE
76 Actg Dean College Health Sciences ... Dr. Jayne SMITTEN
81 Dean Natural/Computational Sciences ... Dr. Brenda JENSEN
49 Dean College of Liberal Arts ... Dr. Allison GOUGH
89 Dean of Students ... Ms. Marites MCKEE
56 Dean Col Extended/Intrdiscipl Educ ... Mr. Mani SEHGAL
07 Assoc Dir International Admissions ... Mr. Jimmi HEMMENBACH
97 Assistant Dean General Education ... Dr. Valentina ABORDONADO
07 Director of Admissions ... Ms. Marissa BRATTON
104 Director Intl Exchange/Study Abroad ... Ms. Melissa MATSUBARA
36 Director Career Svcs Ctr/Co-op Educ ... Mr. Michael VAN LEAR
06 Asst University Registrar ... Ms. Leigh KOBAYASHI
37 Assoc Director Financial Aid ... Ms. Alyson MACHADO
41 Executive Athletic Director ... Mr. Vince BALDEMOR
51 Assoc Dir Adult Learning Program ... Ms. Jill MERL
105 Director Network/Infrastructure ... Mr. Ryan MONTGOMERY
08 Director of Libraries ... Ms. Nori LEONG
42 University Chaplain ... Rev. Dale BURKE
13 Director Computing Services ... Ms. Lisa CARPENTER
19 Assoc Director Security and Safety ... Mr. Wayne FERNANDEZ
18 Director Facilities Management ... Mr. John RUSSELL
29 Alumni/Parent Relations Coordinator ... Vacant
38 Dir Counseling/Behavioral Health ... Dr. Kevin BOWMAN
96 Procurement Director ... Mr. Kevin WETTER
26 Chief Information Ofcr/Vice Pres ... Dr. Sharon BLANTON
100 Chief of Staff ... Mr. Mark E. DELOS REYES DAVIS

Hawaii Tokai International College (D)

91-971 Farrington Hwy, Kapolei HI 96707
County: Honolulu FICE Identification: 037603
Telephone: (808) 983-4000 Carnegie Class: Not Classified
FAX Number: (808) 983-4107 Calendar System: Quarter
URL: www.htic.edu
Established: 1992 Annual Undergrad Tuition & Fees: N/A
Enrollment: N/A Coed
Affiliation or Control: Independent Non-Profit IRS Status: 501(c)3
Highest Offering: Associate Degree
Accreditation: WJ

01 Chancellor ... Dr. Naoto YOSHIKAWA
03 Vice Chancellor ... Dr. Elizabeth KEITH
05 Dean of Instruction ... Dr. Samantha HUME

Institute of Clinical Acupuncture and Oriental Medicine (E)

100 N Beretania Street, Suite 203 B,
Honolulu HI 96817-4709
County: Honolulu FICE Identification: 037353
Unit ID: 444699
Telephone: (808) 521-2288 Carnegie Class: Spec-4-yr-Other Health
FAX Number: (808) 521-2271 Calendar System: Semester
URL: www.orientalmedicine.edu
Established: 1996 Annual Graduate Tuition & Fees: N/A
Enrollment: 55 Coed
Affiliation or Control: Proprietary IRS Status: Proprietary
Highest Offering: Master's; No Undergraduates
Accreditation: ACUP

01 President ... Dr. Wai Hoa LOW
05 Chancellor Academic Affairs ... Dr. Edmund BERNAUER
32 Director of Student Affairs ... Dr. Craig TWENTYMAN
10 Director of Finance ... Dr. Catherine Yu-Ling LOW
06 Registrar ... Ms. Jeanne BERNAUER

Pacific Rim Christian University (F)

290 Sand Island Access Road, Honolulu HI 96819
County: Honolulu Identification: 667010
Unit ID: 457484
Telephone: (808) 853-1040 Carnegie Class: Bac-Diverse
FAX Number: (808) 853-1042 Calendar System: Semester
URL: www.pacrim.edu
Established: 1998 Annual Undergrad Tuition & Fees: $10,460
Enrollment: 117 Coed
Affiliation or Control: Independent Non-Profit IRS Status: 501(c)3
Highest Offering: Master's
Accreditation: BI

00 Founder ... Dr. Wayne CORDEIRO
01 President ... Dr. Kent KEITH
58 Dean Grad Sch/Pres Emeritus ... Dr. Randall FURUSHIMA
05 Vice Pres Academic Affairs ... Martha STINTON
32 Vice Pres Student Services ... Craig PANKOW
07 Director of Admissions ... Jade RANESES
08 Library Director ... Karen CLARKE
37 Director of Financial Aid ... Eli JENNINGS

Remington College-Honolulu Campus (G)

1111 Bishop Street, Suite 400, Honolulu HI 96813-2811
Telephone: (808) 942-1000 Identification: 666028
Accreditation: ACCSC

† Branch campus of Remington College, Mobile, AL.

*University of Hawaii System (H)

2444 Dole Street, Honolulu HI 96822
County: Honolulu FICE Identification: 007885
Unit ID: 141963
Telephone: (808) 956-8207 Carnegie Class: N/A
FAX Number: (808) 956-5286
URL: www.hawaii.edu

01 President ... Dr. David K. LASSNER
05 VP for Academic Planning & Policy ... Dr. Risa E. DICKSON
46 VP for Research and Innovation ... Dr. Vassilis L. SYRMOS
43 VP for Legal Affs/Univ Gen Counsel ... Ms. Carrie K. OKINAGA
10 VP for Budget and Finance/CFO ... Mr. Kalbert K. YOUNG
88 VP for Community Colleges ... Dr. John F. MORTON
11 VP for Administration ... Ms. Jan N. GOUVEIA
13 VP for Information Tech/CIO ... Mr. Garret T. YOSHIMI
32 Assoc VP Student Affairs ... Ms. Joanne K. ITANO
102 President & CEO UH Foundation ... Ms. Donna VUCHINICH
21 Director of Budget ... Mr. Michael M. NG
15 Interim Sys Dir Human Resources ... Ms. Donna F. KIYOSAKI
14 Director Management Info Systems ... Ms. Susan K. INOUYE
45 Interim Dir Ofc of Research Svcs ... Ms. Darcie S. YOSHINAGA
21 Dir Fin Mgmt & Controller ... Ms. Susan X. LIN
09 Director Data Govt & Operations ... Ms. Sandra K. FURUTO
22 Director EEO/AA ... Mr. Mark G. AU
88 Director Media Production ... Mr. Dan T. MEISENZAHL
26 Director of Communications ... Ms. Diane E. CHANG
101 Exec Administrator/Sec to the BOR ... Ms. Cynthia D. QUINN
86 Director Government Relations ... Ms. Stephanie C. KIM
100 Executive Asst to President ... Ms. Lynne K. MONACO
04 Administrative Asst to President ... Ms. Courtney N. DOMINGO

*University of Hawaii at Hilo (I)

200 W Kawili Street, Hilo HI 96720-4091
County: Hawaii FICE Identification: 001611
Unit ID: 141565
Telephone: (808) 932-7348 Carnegie Class: Masters/S
FAX Number: (808) 932-7338 Calendar System: Semester
URL: www.hilo.hawaii.edu
Established: 1947 Annual Undergrad Tuition & Fees (In-State): $7,650
Enrollment: 3,829 Coed
Affiliation or Control: State IRS Status: 501(c)3
Highest Offering: Doctorate
Accreditation: WC, CAEPT, CEA, NUR, NURSE, PHAR

02 Interim Chancellor ... Dr. Marcia SAKAI
05 Int Vice Chanc Academic Affairs ... Dr. Ken HON
10 Actg Vice Chanc Administrative Affs ... Mr. Kalei RAPOZA
46 Vice Chancellor for Research ... Vacant
32 Vice Chancellor Student Affairs ... Ms. Farrah-Marie GOMES
20 Asst VC for Academic Affairs ... Vacant
114 Budget Director ... Ms. Lois M. FUJIYOSHI
88 Director University Disability Svcs ... Ms. Susan SHIRACHI
15 Director Human Resources ... Mr. Kalei RAPOZA
18 Director Facilities Planning ... Mr. Lo-Li CHIH
26 Director University Relations ... Mr. Jerry CHANG
08 Interim University Librarian ... Ms. Helen ROGERS
24 Director Media Relations ... Ms. Alyson Y. KAKUGAWA-LEONG
07 Interim Director Admissions ... Mr. Zach STREET
38 Int Asst Director Counseling ... Mr. Andrew POLLOI
39 Exec Director Housing & Dining Svs ... Mr. Miles K. NAGATA
35 Director Campus Center ... Ms. Ellen I. KUSANO
37 Director Financial Aid ... Ms. Sherrie PADILLA
06 Interim University Registrar ... Ms. Chelsea KAY-WONG
49 Int Dean College of Arts & Sciences ... Dr. Michael BITTER
50 Int Dean Col of Business/Economics ... Dr. Tam VU
67 Interim Dean College of Pharmacy ... Dr. Carolyn MA
47 Int Dean Col Agri/For/Nat Res Mgmt ... Dr. Bruce MATHEWS
51 Int Dean Cont Educ/Community Svcs ... Dr. Farrahmarie GOMES
41 Director of Athletics ... Mr. Patrick J. GUILLEN
40 Bookstore Manager ... Mr. Jason K. TANAKA
85 Exex Dir Internatl Student Services ... Mr. James P. MELLON
36 Exec Director Career Services ... Ms. Kainoa ARIOLA-SUKISAKI
22 Director EEO/AA ... Dr. Jennifer STOTTER
09 Institutional Research Analyst ... Ms. Kelli OKUMURA
29 Director Marketing & Alumni ... Ms. Yu Yok PEARRING
30 Exec Director of Development ... Ms. Mariko MIHO
94 Coordinator Women's Center ... Ms. Leslie MCCLUNG
23 Asst Director Medical Services ... Ms. Heather HIRATA
88 Dir College of Hawaiian Language ... Ms. Keiki KAWAI`AE`A
19 Director Security/Safety ... Mr. Darrell MAYFIELD

*University of Hawaii at Manoa (J)

2500 Campus Road, Honolulu HI 96822-2217
County: Honolulu FICE Identification: 001610
Unit ID: 141574
Telephone: (808) 956-8111 Carnegie Class: DU-Highest
FAX Number: N/A Calendar System: Semester
URL: www.manoa.hawaii.edu
Established: 1907 Annual Undergrad Tuition & Fees (In-State): $11,732
Enrollment: 18,865 Coed
Affiliation or Control: State IRS Status: 501(c)3
Highest Offering: Doctorate
Accreditation: WC, CAATE, CACREP, CEA, CLPSY, DH, DIETD, ENG, IPSY, LAW, LIB, MED, MT, MUS, NURSE, PH, PLNG, SP, SPAA, SW

02 Interim Chancellor ... Dr. David LASSNER
10 Vice Chanc Admin/Finance/
Operations ... Ms. Kathleen D. CUTSHAW
05 Interim Vice Chanc Academic Affairs ... Dr. Michael BRUNO
32 Int Vice Chancellor for Students ... Ms. Lori IDETA
06 University Registrar ... Mr. Stuart LAU
08 Acting University Librarian ... Dr. Monica GHOSH
37 Director Financial Aid Services ... Ms. Jodie M. KUBA
38 Director Counsel/Student Devel Ctr ... Dr. Allyson M. TANOUYE
23 Director University Health Center ... Dr. Andrew W. NICHOLS
39 Director Student Housing ... Mr. Michael W. KAPTIK
40 Director Campus Svcs (Bookstore) ... Ms. Deborah T. HEUBLER
41 Athletic Director ... Mr. David MATLIN
86 Director of Cmty/Govt Affairs ... Mr. Elmer KAAI
28 Dir Stdnt Equity/Exclnce/Diversity ... Dr. Amefil AGBAYANI
36 Interim Dir Manoa Career Center ... Ms. Wendy SORA
15 Director Human Resources ... Ms. Tammy KUNIYOSHI
88 Director Cancer Center ... Dr. Michele CARBONE
88 Director Institute for Astronomy ... Dr. Guenther HASINGER

88 Director Waikiki Aquarium .... Dr. Andrew ROSSITER
88 Int Assc Dr Pac Biosci Research Ctr .... Dr. Marilyn DUNLAP
56 Int Dean Outreach College .... Dr. William G. CHISMAR
50 Dean Shidler College of Business .... Dr. V. Vance ROLEY
58 Dean Graduate Education .... Dr. Krystyna AUNE
88 Int Dean Sch of Travel Industry Mgt .... Dr. Tom BINGHAM
53 Dean College of Education .... Dr. Donald B. YOUNG
54 Interim Dean College of Engineering .... Dr. Ronald E. RIGGS
47 Int Dean Col Trop Agric & Human Res .... Dr. Rachel NOVOTNY
63 Dean John A Burns Sch of Med .... Dr. Jerris R. HEDGES
66 Dean Sch Nursing & Dental Hygiene .... Dr. Mary G. BOLAND
70 Dean M P Thompson Sch of Soc Work ... Dr. Noreen K. MOKUAU
61 Dean Wm S Richardson Sch of Law .... Mr. Aviam SOIFER
48 Dean School of Architecture .... Mr. Daniel S. FRIEDMAN
49 Dean College Arts & Humanities .... Mr. Peter ARNADE
65 Dean College Natural Sciences .... Dr. Aloysius HELMINCK
83 Dean College Social Sciences .... Dr. Denise E. KONAN
79 Int Dean College Lang/Ling & Lit .... Dr. Laura LYONS
88 Dean Sch Ocean & Earth Sci & Tech .... Dr. Brian TAYLOR
88 Dean Pacific and Asian Studies .... Dr. R. Anderson SUTTON
88 Interim Dean Sch Hawn Knowledge .... Dr. Jonhathan OSORIO
09 Director of Institutional Research .... Dr. Yang ZHANG

*University of Hawaii - West Oahu (A)

91-1001 Farrington Highway, Kapolei HI 96707

County: Honolulu — FICE Identification: 021078

Unit ID: 141981

Telephone: (808) 689-2770 — Carnegie Class: Bac-Diverse

FAX Number: (808) 689-2771 — Calendar System: Semester

URL: www.uhwo.hawaii.edu

Established: 1976 — Annual Undergrad Tuition & Fees (In-State): $7,440

Enrollment: 2,692 — Coed

Affiliation or Control: State — IRS Status: 501(c)3

Highest Offering: Baccalaureate

Accreditation: WC, ACBSP, CAEPN

02 Chancellor .... Dr. Maenette BENHAM
05 Vice Chanc Academic Affairs .... Dr. Jeffrey MONIZ
32 Vice Chanc for Student Affairs .... Dr. Judy OLIVEIRA
11 Vice Chanc for Administration .... Mr. Kevin ISHIDA
84 Director for Enrollment Services .... Mr. Jim CROMWELL
09 Assoc Dir of Institutional Research .... Mr. John STANLEY
26 Director of Communications .... Ms. Leila SHIMOKAWA
08 Librarian .... Ms. Michiko JOSEPH
06 Registrar .... Ms. Robyn OSHIRO
37 Financial Aid Officer .... Ms. Christina PADILLA
15 Director of Human Resources .... Ms. Nancy K. NAKASONE
10 Director of Budget .... Ms. Linda SAIKI

*University of Hawaii Community Colleges (B)

2444 Dole Street, Honolulu HI 96822-2411

County: Honolulu — FICE Identification: 006751

Unit ID: 420592

Telephone: (808) 956-7038 — Carnegie Class: N/A

FAX Number: (808) 956-9219

URL: www.hawaii.edu

01 Vice Pres for Community Colleges .... Dr. John F. MORTON
05 Assoc Vice Pres Academic Affairs .... Dr. Peter QUIGLEY
11 Assoc Vice Pres Admin/Cmty Col Oper .... Mr. Michael T. UNEBASAMI
04 Executive Assistant to the VP & Dir ..... Ms. Deborah NAKAGAWA
10 Director Budget & Planning .... Mr. Lance YAMAMOTO
15 Director Personnel Services .... Ms. Sandra UYENO
18 Director Facilities/Physical Plant .... Ms. Denise YOSHIMORI-YAMAMOTO
22 Dir Affirmative Action/EEO .... Ms. Mary PERREIRA
26 Director Marketing & Communications .... Ms. Susan LEE

*Kapiolani Community College (C)

4303 Diamond Head Road, Honolulu HI 96816-4221

County: Honolulu — FICE Identification: 001613

Unit ID: 141796

Telephone: (808) 734-9000 — Carnegie Class: Assoc/HT-Mix Trad/Non

FAX Number: (808) 734-9162 — Calendar System: Semester

URL: www.kapiolani.hawaii.edu

Established: 1957 — Annual Undergrad Tuition & Fees (In-State): $3,084

Enrollment: 7,816 — Coed

Affiliation or Control: State — IRS Status: 501(c)3

Highest Offering: Associate Degree

Accreditation: WJ, ACBSP, ACFEI, ADNUR, COARC, DA, EMT, MAC, MLTAD, OTA, PHLEB, PTAA, RAD, SURGT

02 Interim Chancellor .... Dr. Louise PAGOTTO
05 Interim VC Academic Affairs .... Ms. Susan KAZAMA
10 Vice Chancellor for Admin Services .... Mr. Brian FURUTO
32 Vice Chancellor for Student Affairs .... Dr. Brenda IVELISSE
49 Dean Arts and Sciences .... Mr. Nawa?a NAPOLEON
50 Dean Hospitality/Business/Legal .... Mr. John RICHARDS
66 Dean Health Programs .... Dr. Patricia O'HAGAN
51 Dir Continuing Educ & Training .... Vacant
04 Special Asst to the Chancellor .... Ms. Joanne WHITAKER
88 Dir Culinary Inst of the Pacific .... Mr. Conrad NONAKA
09 Dir Institutional Effectiveness .... Dr. Robert FRANCO
08 Interim Head Librarian .... Ms. Susan WEBER
06 Registrar .... Ms. Jerilyn ENOKAWA
37 Financial Aid Officer .... Ms. Jennifer BRADLEY

109 Auxiliary Services Officer .... Mr. Christopher EDMONDS
26 Dean College & Community Relations .... Dr. Carol HOSHIKO
30 Development Officer .... Ms. Linh HOANG POE
15 Director Personnel Office .... Ms. Kelli BRANDVOLD
21 Fiscal Officer .... Mr. Justin KASHIWAEDA

*University of Hawaii Hawaii Community College (D)

1175 Manono Street, Hilo HI 96720-5096

County: Hawaii — FICE Identification: 005258

Unit ID: 383190

Telephone: (808) 934-2500 — Carnegie Class: Assoc/MT-VT-High Trad

FAX Number: (808) 934-2501 — Calendar System: Semester

URL: www.hawaii.hawaii.edu

Established: 1941 — Annual Undergrad Tuition & Fees (In-State): $3,084

Enrollment: 3,087 — Coed

Affiliation or Control: State — IRS Status: 501(c)3

Highest Offering: Associate Degree

Accreditation: WJ, ACFEI, ADNUR

02 Chancellor .... Dr. Rachel H. SOLEMSAAS
05 Vice Chanc Academic Affairs .... Ms. Joni Y. ONISHI
10 Interim Vice Chanc Admin Affairs ... Mr. Kenneth K. KALEIWAHEA
32 Interim Vice Chanc Student Affairs .... Ms. Dorinna MANUEL-CORTEZ
51 Director Continuing Educ/Training .... Ms. Jessica YAMAMOTO
37 Student Financial Aid Officer .... Ms. Susan OLSEN
12 Director UH Center at West Hawaii . Dr. Kenneth Marty FLETCHER
15 Human Resource Manager .... Ms. Mari CHANG
07 Interim Registrar/A&R Mgr .... Ms. Sherise TIOGANGCO
21 Budget Analyst .... Ms. Jodi MINE
04 Private Secretary to the Chancellor .... Ms. Patricia A. FREEMAN
19 Campus Safety and Security Chief .... Mr. Jeffrey NEWSOME

*University of Hawaii Honolulu Community College (E)

874 Dillingham Boulevard, Honolulu HI 96817-4598

County: Honolulu — FICE Identification: 001612

Unit ID: 141680

Telephone: (808) 845-9211 — Carnegie Class: Assoc/HVT-Mix Trad/Non

FAX Number: (808) 845-9173 — Calendar System: Semester

URL: www.honolulu.hawaii.edu

Established: 1920 — Annual Undergrad Tuition & Fees (In-State): $3,054

Enrollment: 4,328 — Coed

Affiliation or Control: State — IRS Status: 501(c)3

Highest Offering: Associate Degree

Accreditation: WJ

02 Chancellor .... Ms. Erika LACRO
11 Vice Chancellor of Admin Svcs .... Mr. Derek INAFUKU
05 Vice Chancellor of Academic Affairs .... Ms. Katy HO
88 Director PCATT .... Mr. Steven AUERBACH
88 Dean Transport & Trades .... Vacant
27 Dean Communications & Services .... Mr. Kasey "Keala" CHOCK
08 Librarian in Charge .... Ms. Irene MESINA
37 Financial Aid Officer .... Ms. Heather FLORENDO
15 Human Resources Mgr/EEO/AA Coord ... Ms. Monique TINGKANG
32 Director Student Affairs .... Ms. Emily Ann KUKULIES
06 Registrar .... Ms. Josephine STENBERG
09 Director Management Info & Research .... Mr. Steven SHIGEMOTO
36 Dir Student Placement/Counselor .... Ms. Silvan CHUNG
20 Dean University College .... Ms. Marcia ROBERTS-DEUTSCH
07 Director of Admissions .... Ms. Josephine STENBERG
10 Acting Chief Business Officer .... Ms. Myrna PATTERSON
26 Chief Public Relations Officer .... Ms. Billie LUEDER
38 Director Student Counseling .... Ms. Lara SUGIMOTO
88 Dean of Academic Support .... Mr. Wayne SUNAHARA
96 Acting Director of Purchasing .... Ms. Myrna PATTERSON
88 Director Secondary Education Pgms .... Ms. Lara SUGIMOTO
13 Chief Info Technology Officer (CIO) .... Mr. Michael MEYER
35 Dean of Student Services .... Ms. Lara SUGIMOTO

*University of Hawaii Kauai Community College (F)

3-1901 Kaumualii Highway, Lihue HI 96766-9500

County: Kauai — FICE Identification: 001614

Unit ID: 141802

Telephone: (808) 245-8311 — Carnegie Class: Assoc/MT-VT-High Trad

FAX Number: (808) 245-8220 — Calendar System: Semester

URL: kauai.hawaii.edu/

Established: 1964 — Annual Undergrad Tuition & Fees (In-State): $3,132

Enrollment: 1,401 — Coed

Affiliation or Control: State — IRS Status: 501(c)3

Highest Offering: Associate Degree

Accreditation: WJ, ACFEI, ADNUR

02 Chancellor .... Dr. Helen COX
05 Vice Chanc Academic Affairs .... Dr. James DIRE
32 Int Vice Chanc Student Affairs .... Mr. Isaiah KAAUWAI
11 Vice Chanc Administrative Services ..... Mr. Brandon SHIMOKAWA
10 Chief Financial Officer .... Mr. Leighton ORIDE
20 Int Dir Acad Support/Univ Ctr Dir ..... Ms. Colleen KAIMINAAUAO
51 Director Continuing Educ/Training .... Mr. Calvin SHIRAI
08 Head Librarian .... Mr. Robert KAJIWARA
37 Financial Aid Officer .... Mr. Jeff ANDERSON
15 Human Resource Manager .... Ms. JoRae BAPTISTE
35 Counselor/Student Life Coordinator .... Mr. John CONSTANTINO
09 Institutional Researcher .... Mr. Jonathan KALK

*University of Hawaii - Leeward Community College (G)

96-045 Ala Ike, Pearl City HI 96782-3393

County: Honolulu — FICE Identification: 004549

Unit ID: 141811

Telephone: (808) 455-0011 — Carnegie Class: Assoc/HT-Mix Trad/Non

FAX Number: (808) 455-0471 — Calendar System: Semester

URL: www.leeward.hawaii.edu

Established: 1968 — Annual Undergrad Tuition & Fees (In-State): $3,084

Enrollment: 7,535 — Coed

Affiliation or Control: State — IRS Status: 501(c)3

Highest Offering: Associate Degree

Accreditation: WJ, ACFEI, CAEPT, CAHIIM

02 Chancellor .... Mr. Manuel J. CABRAL
05 Vice Chanc Academic Affairs .... Ms. Della TERAOKA
11 Vice Chancellor Admin Services .... Mr. Mark LANE
10 Fiscal Manager .... Ms. Cecilia LUCAS
49 Dean Arts & Sciences .... Mr. James GOODMAN
72 Dean Career & Tech Education .... Mr. Ron UMEHIRA
32 Dean Student Services .... Dr. Curtis WASHBURN
20 Dean of Academic Services .... Mr. Paul KUEHN
08 Librarian .... Mr. Wayde OSHIRO
06 Registrar .... Mr. Grant HELGESON
37 Financial Aid Officer .... Mr. Gregg YOSHIMURA
18 Aux & Facilities Services Mgr .... Mr. Grant OKAMURA
09 Dir Policy/Planning/Assessment .... Vacant
26 Marketing Director .... Ms. Kathleen CABRAL
15 Human Resources Mgr/EEO/AA Coord .... Ms. Lori Lei HAYASHI
13 Information Technology Coord .... Ms. Jennifer DEGIACINTO
12 Int Coord Waianae Education Center .... Mr. Danny WYATT
24 Media Coordinator .... Ms. Leanne RISELEY
35 Student Activities Coordinator .... Ms. Lexer CHOU

*University of Hawaii Maui College (H)

310 Kaahumanu Avenue, Kahului HI 96732-1644

County: Maui — FICE Identification: 001615

Unit ID: 141839

Telephone: (808) 984-3500 — Carnegie Class: Bac/Assoc-Assoc Dom

FAX Number: (808) 984-3546 — Calendar System: Semester

URL: maui.hawaii.edu

Established: 1931 — Annual Undergrad Tuition & Fees (In-State): $3,150

Enrollment: 3,593 — Coed

Affiliation or Control: State — IRS Status: 501(c)3

Highest Offering: Baccalaureate

Accreditation: WC, ACFEI, ADNUR, DH

02 Chancellor .... Dr. Lui HOKOANA
05 Vice Chanc Academic Affairs .... Dr. Jonathon MCKEE
32 Vice Chancellor of Student Affs .... Ms. Debra NAKAMA
10 Vice Chanc of Administrative Affs .... Mr. David TAMANAHA
20 Int Assistant Dean of Instruction .... Mr. David GROOMS
51 Director Continuing Educ/Training .... Ms. Karen HANADA
08 Librarian .... Ms. Ellen PETERSON
12 Director University Center Maui .... Ms. Tamone Karen HANADA
07 Director of Admissions/Registrar .... Ms. Flora MORA
09 Director of Institutional Research .... Dr. Jeannie PEZZOLI
15 Director Personnel Services .... Ms. Susan TOKUNAGA
18 Chief Facilities/Physical Plant .... Mr. Robert BURTON
21 Associate Fiscal Officer .... Ms. Cindy YAMAMOTO
30 Chief Development .... Ms. Cordy MACLAUGHLIN
36 Director Student Placement .... Ms. Debra NAKAMA
37 Interim Financial Aid Officer .... Ms. Davileigh NAE`OLE
38 Director Student Counseling .... Ms. Kulamanu ISHIHARA

*University of Hawaii Windward Community College (I)

45-720 Keaahala Road, Kaneohe HI 96744-3598

County: Honolulu — FICE Identification: 011220

Unit ID: 141990

Telephone: (808) 235-7400 — Carnegie Class: Assoc/HT-High Non

FAX Number: (808) 247-5362 — Calendar System: Semester

URL: www.wcc.hawaii.edu

Established: 1972 — Annual Undergrad Tuition & Fees (In-State): $3,064

Enrollment: 2,610 — Coed

Affiliation or Control: State — IRS Status: 501(c)3

Highest Offering: Associate Degree

Accreditation: WJ

02 Chancellor .... Mr. Doug DYKSTRA
05 Vice Chancellor Academic Affs .... Dr. Ardis ESHENBERG
32 Vice Chancellor Student Affairs .... Ms. Amy ROZEK
11 Vice Chanc Administrative Services .... Mr. Brian PACTOL
20 Dean of Academic Affairs Div I .... Ms. Colette HIGGINS
20 Dean of Academic Affairs Div II .... Mr. Charles SASAKI
75 Dir Vocational/Cmty Education .... Mr. Mike MOSER
08 Head Librarian .... Ms. Sarah Gilman SUR
06 Registrar .... Ms. Geri IMAI
09 Director of Institutional Research .... Mr. Jeffrey HUNT
37 Director Student Financial Aid .... Mr. Steven CHIGAWA
15 Personnel Officer .... Ms. Karen CHO
26 Marketing/Public Relations Dir .... Ms. Bonnie BEATSON

University of Phoenix Hawaii Campus (J)

745 Fort Street, Suite 2000, Honolulu HI 96813-3800

Telephone: (808) 536-2686 — Identification: 770202

Accreditation: &NH, ACBSP, CAEPN

† No longer accepting campus-based students.

World Medicine Institute (A)

1073 Hind Iuka Drive, Honolulu HI 96821
County: Honolulu FICE Identification: 030725
Unit ID: 141936
Telephone: (808) 373-2849 Carnegie Class: Spec-4-yr-Other Health
FAX Number: (808) 373-4341 Calendar System: Semester
URL: www.wmi.edu
Established: 1970 Annual Graduate Tuition & Fees: N/A
Enrollment: 41 Coed
Affiliation or Control: Independent Non-Profit IRS Status: 501(c)3
Highest Offering: Master's; No Undergraduates
Accreditation: **ACUP**

01 President .... Dr. Patrcia BRADY
05 Academic Dean .... Dr. Wasim SIDDIQUI
10 Chief Operating Officer .... Dr. Eric ONO
09 Director of Institutional Research .... Dr. Catharina ANG
37 Director Student Financial Aid .... Mr. Hansford CHOCK
07 Dir Admissions/Registrar/Enr Mgmt .... Dr. Gayle TODOKI
15 Chief Human Resources Officer .... Dr. Rodney YOUNG
18 Chief Facilities/Physical Plant .... Mr. Conrad LOMMEN
29 Director of Alumni Affairs .... Ms. Tia KLUG-WESSERL
32 Chief Student Affairs Officer .... Mr. Frank GONZALES
38 Director of Student Counseling .... Dr. Eric ONO

IDAHO

Boise Bible College (B)

8695 W Marigold Street, Boise ID 83714-1220
County: Ada FICE Identification: 022345
Unit ID: 142090
Telephone: (208) 376-7731 Carnegie Class: Spec-4-yr-Faith
FAX Number: (208) 376-7743 Calendar System: Semester
URL: www.boisebible.edu
Established: 1945 Annual Undergrad Tuition & Fees: $11,750
Enrollment: 150 Coed
Affiliation or Control: Christian Churches And Churches of Christ
IRS Status: 501(c)3
Highest Offering: Baccalaureate
Accreditation: **BI**

01 President .... Dr. Derek VOORHEES
05 Academic Dean .... Mr. Charles FABER
32 Dean of Students .... Dr. Cody CHRISTENSEN
10 Business Officer .... Mr. Mark STEVENS
30 Director of Development .... Mr. David DAVOLT
06 Registrar .... Mr. Ross KNUDSEN
07 Director of Admissions .... Mr. Chris WILSON
08 Librarian .... Mrs. Amber GROVE
37 Financial Aid Director .... Mrs. Joyce ANDERSON
18 Supt of Building & Grounds .... Mr. Jon SHINGLER
04 Executive Assistant .... Mrs. Rhonda HETHERINGTON

Boise State University (C)

1910 University Drive, Boise ID 83725-1000
County: Ada FICE Identification: 001616
Unit ID: 142115
Telephone: (208) 426-1000 Carnegie Class: DU-Mod
FAX Number: (208) 426-3765 Calendar System: Semester
URL: www.boisestate.edu
Established: 1932 Annual Undergrad Tuition & Fees (In-State): $7,080
Enrollment: 22,086 Coed
Affiliation or Control: State IRS Status: 501(c)3
Highest Offering: Doctorate
Accreditation: **NW**, ART, CAATE, CACREP, CAEP, COARC, CONST, CS, DMS, ENG, MUS, NURSE, RAD, SPAA, SW, THEA

01 President .... Dr. Robert W. KUSTRA
05 Provost/Vice Pres Academic Affairs .... Dr. Martin E. SCHIMPF
10 Vice Pres Finance & CFO .... Mr. Mark HEIL
32 VP Student Affairs/Enrollment Mgmt .... Dr. Leslie WEBB
111 Vice Pres University Advancement .... Ms. Laura SIMIC
43 VP/Chief Ops Officer/Spec Counsel .... Mr. Kevin SATTERLEE
20 Vice Provost for Acad Planning .... Dr. James MUNGER
92 Vice Provost/Dean of Honors .... Dr. Andrew FINSTUEN
21 Associate Vice Pres for Finance .... Ms. Jo Ellen DI NUCCI
35 Assoc Vice Pres Student Life .... Dr. Jeremiah SHINN
46 VP of Research .... Dr. Mark RUDIN
13 Assoc VP/Chief Info Tech .... Mr. Max DAVIS-JOHNSON
08 Dean of University Library .... Ms. Tracy BICKNELL-HOLMES
35 Dean of Students .... Dr. Chris WUTHRICH
84 Assoc VP Enrollment Services .... Mr. James ANDERSON
15 Assoc VP Human Resources .... Vacant
29 Executive Director Alumni Relations .... Ms. Lisa GARDNER
17 Dir Medical Services .... Dr. Vincent SERIO
06 Registrar .... Ms. Kristine COLLINS
18 Exec Dir of Public Safety .... Mr. John KAPLAN
40 Director Bookstore .... Ms. Nicole R. GOUVEA
09 Director Institutional Research .... Dr. Shari ELLERTSON
07 Director of Admissions .... Dr. Kelly TALBERT
26 Assoc Vice Pres Comm & Market .... Mr. Greg HAHN
41 Director Athletics .... Mr. Curt APSEY
22 EEO/AA Officer .... Ms. Gayla THOMAS-DABNEY
38 Director Counseling Services .... Dr. Matthew NIECE
37 Dir Financial Aid & Scholarships .... Ms. Diana FAIRCHILD
96 Director of Purchasing .... Ms. Terri SPINAZZA
51 Dean Extended Studies .... Mr. Mark WHEELER
49 Dean of Arts & Sciences .... Dr. Tony ROARK
50 Dean of Business & Economics .... Dr. Kenneth J. PETERSEN
53 Dean of Education .... Dr. Richard OSGUTHORPE
58 Dean of the Graduate College .... Dr. Tammi VACHA-HAASE
76 Dean of Health Sciences .... Dr. Tim DUNNAGAN
54 Dean of College of Engineering .... Dr. JoAnn LIGHTY
88 Dean Col of Innovation & Design .... Mr. Gordon JONES
104 Asst Prov for Global Educ .... Dr. Gonzalo BRUCE
88 Dean School of Public Service .... Dr. Corey COOK
04 Exec Asst to President .... Ms. Melissa JENSEN
100 Chief of Staff .... Ms. Randi MCDERMOTT
104 Dir Intl Learn Student Success .... Ms. Corrine HENKE
39 Director Housing and Res Life .... Dr. Dean KENNEDY
88 Director of Wellness .... Dr. Michelle IHMELS
36 Director Career Center .... Ms. Debbie KAYLOR
106 Exec Dir/e-campus Center .... Ms. Janet ATKINSON
28 Dir of Student Diversity/Inclusion .... Mr. Francisco SALINAS
102 Dir of Corporate & Foundation Rels .... Ms. Virginia PELLEGRINI
30 Senior Development Director .... Ms. Gertrude L. ARNOLD
105 Assoc VP Campus Operations .... Ms. Alicia ESTEY

Brigham Young University-Idaho (D)

525 South Center Street, Rexburg ID 83460
County: Madison FICE Identification: 001625
Unit ID: 142522
Telephone: (208) 496-1411 Carnegie Class: Bac-Diverse
FAX Number: (208) 496-1103 Calendar System: Semester
URL: www.byui.edu
Established: 1888 Annual Undergrad Tuition & Fees: $3,920
Enrollment: 43,803 Coed
Affiliation or Control: Latter-day Saints IRS Status: 501(c)3
Highest Offering: Baccalaureate
Accreditation: **NW**, ENG, MUS, NURSE, PTAA, SW

01 President .... Dr. Henry J. EYRING
05 Academic Vice President .... Mr. Kelly T. BURGENER
11 University Resources Vice President .... Mr. Jeffrey R. MORRIN
32 Student Life Vice President .... Mrs. Amy R. LABAUGH
106 Online Vice President .... Dr. Jon F. LINFORD
45 VP for Exec Strategy & Planning .... Mr. Rob J. GARRETT
20 Assoc Academic VP Instruction .... Mr. Rob I. EATON
20 Assoc Acad VP Curriculum .... Dr. Van D. CHRISTMAN
20 Assoc Acad VP F&IS .... Dr. Scott W. GALER
121 Assoc Acad VP Student Success .... Mr. Brian K. MEMMOTT
35 Dean of Students .... Mr. Kip B. HARRIS
88 Student Well-Being Mng Director .... Mr. Wynn N. HILL
13 Chief Information Officer .... Mr. Joe TAYLOR
09 Inst Research Managing Director .... Dr. Scott J. BERGSTROM
06 Student Records & Registration .... Mrs. Lauri D. ARENSMEYER
37 Int Stdnt Fin Aid/Scholarship Dir .... Mr. Ken L. JACKSON
08 University Librarian .... Mrs. Laurie S. FRANCIS
10 Univ Operations Managing Director .... Mr. Wayne N. CLARK
15 Human Resources Director .... Mr. Kevin L. PRICE
23 Student Health Services Director .... Mr. Shaun ORR
38 Student Counseling Center Director .... Mr. Reed J. STODDARD
19 University Public Safety Dir .... Mr. Stephen P. BUNNELL
07 Admissions Director .... Mr. Tyler R. WILLIAMS
29 Alumni Director .... Mr. Steven J. DAVIS
88 Student Activities Mng Director .... Mr. Derek R. FAY
26 University Relations Mng Director .... Mr. Merv R. BROWN
30 LDS Philanthropies Director .... Mr. Kelly REEVES
39 Housing & Student Living Director .... Dr. Troy J. DOUGHERTY
43 Legal Counsel .... Mr. Stephen CRAIG
21 Financial Services Mng Director .... Mr. Shane WEBSTER
88 Student Development Mng Director .... Mrs. Jill EVANS
96 Purchasing & Travel Director .... Mr. Mike B. THUESON
35 Student Svcs Managing Director .... Mr. Kyle R. MARTIN
40 University Store Director .... Mr. Ryan J. BUTTARS
104 Director of International Services .... Mr. Mike R. OSWALD
36 Career and Academic Advising Dir .... Mr. Sam R. BRUBAKER
109 Auxiliary Services Mng Director .... Mr. Brett COOK

Broadview University (E)

2750 East Gala Court, Meridian ID 83642
Telephone: (208) 577-2900 Identification: 770712
Accreditation: **ACICS**

† Branch campus of Broadview University, West Jordan, UT

Carrington College - Boise (F)

1122 N Liberty Street, Boise ID 83704-8741
Telephone: (208) 377-8080 FICE Identification: 022180
Accreditation: **&WJ**, DA, DH, MAAB, PNUR, PTAA

† Regional accreditation is carried under the parent institution in Sacramento, CA.

College of Eastern Idaho (G)

1600 S 25th E, Idaho Falls ID 83404-5788
County: Bonneville FICE Identification: 011133
Unit ID: 142179
Telephone: (208) 524-3000 Carnegie Class: Assoc/HVT-High Non
FAX Number: (208) 524-3007 Calendar System: Semester
URL: www.eitc.edu
Established: 1969 Annual Undergrad Tuition & Fees (In-State): $2,434
Enrollment: 688 Coed
Affiliation or Control: State IRS Status: 501(c)3
Highest Offering: Associate Degree
Accreditation: **NW**, MAC, SURGT

01 President .... Dr. Rick K. AMAN
10 Vice President of Finance and Admin .... Dr. Christian GODFREY
05 VP of Instruction & Student Affairs .... Dr. Sharee ANDERSON
06 Registrar .... Mrs. Rae Lynn PATTERSON
21 Controller .... Mr. Don E. BOURNE
103 Mgr Workforce Trng/Cmty Education .... Ms. Michelle M. HOLT
37 Financial Aid Director .... Mrs. Shayna SHARP
04 President Administrative Assistant .... Mrs. Kristina BUCHAN
26 Director of College Relations .... Mr. Todd WIGHTMAN
102 Foundation Director .... Mrs. Natalie J. HEBARD
07 Director of Admissions/Placement .... Mrs. Hailey MACK
50 Business/Office/Technology Div Mgr .... Mr. Leslie JERNBERG
97 General Education Division Manager .... Mrs. Peggy L. NELSON
76 Health Care Technology Div Manager .... Mr. Jared L. GARDNER
88 Trades/Industry Division Manager .... Mr. Kent E. BERGGREN
88 Adult Basic Education Div Manager .... Mrs. Theresa GROENEWOLD
09 Director of Institutional Research .... Mr. Lee STIMPSON
13 Chief Info Technology Officer .... Mrs. Karen FOSTER

The College of Idaho (H)

2112 Cleveland Boulevard, Caldwell ID 83605-9990
County: Canyon FICE Identification: 001617
Unit ID: 142294
Telephone: (208) 459-5011 Carnegie Class: Bac-A&S
FAX Number: (208) 454-2077 Calendar System: Other
URL: www.collegeofidaho.edu
Established: 1891 Annual Undergrad Tuition & Fees: $27,425
Enrollment: 1,065 Coed
Affiliation or Control: Independent Non-Profit IRS Status: 501(c)3
Highest Offering: Master's
Accreditation: **NW**

01 Interim President .... Dr. Robert HOOVER
05 Vice President Academic Affairs .... Dr. David DOUGLASS
10 Vice Pres Finance/Administration .... Mr. Richard ERNE
32 Vice President Student Affairs .... Dr. Paul BENNION
111 Vice President for Advancement .... Mr. Michael VANDERVELDEN
84 Vice President for Enrollment .... Dr. Lorna HUNTER
20 Associate Dean of Faculty .... Dr. Paul MOULTON
06 Registrar .... Mr. Mark HEIDRICH
41 Director of Athletics .... Ms. Reagan ROSSI
26 Dir of Marketing & Communications .... Vacant
29 Director of Alumni .... Ms. Sally SKINNER
44 Director of Boone Fund .... Ms. Sarah NASH
08 Director of Library .... Ms. Christine SCHUTZ
18 Director of Facilities .... Mr. Mike KALTENECKER
21 Controller .... Mr. Jesse HARRIS
37 Director of Financial Services .... Ms. Jennifer WORDEN
15 Human Resources Director .... Ms. Nancy JOHNSON-CASSULO
36 Director Student Placement .... Ms. Jennifer RIDDLE
92 Director of Honors Program .... Dr. Sue SCHAPER
39 Director of Residential Life .... Ms. Jen NELSON
93 Director of Multicultural Affairs .... Mr. Arnold HERNANDEZ
42 Campus Minister/Asc Dean Students .... Dr. Phil ROGERS
19 Director of Campus Safety .... Mr. Allan LAIRD
13 Director of Information Technology .... Mr. Fred WARR
09 Director Institutional Research .... Mr. Mark HEIDRICH
30 Director Development .... Mr. Jack CAFFERTY
07 Associate Director of Admissions .... Mr. Mike BURDINE
40 Bookstore Manager .... Mr. Kris PERDEW
38 Counselor .... Ms. Cynthia MAUZERALL
04 Executive Asst to President .... Ms. Maggie COLWELL

College of Southern Idaho (I)

PO Box 1238, 315 Falls Avenue,
Twin Falls ID 83303-1238
County: Twin Falls FICE Identification: 001619
Unit ID: 142559
Telephone: (208) 733-9554 Carnegie Class: Assoc/MT-VT-High Non
FAX Number: (208) 736-3015 Calendar System: Semester
URL: www.csi.edu
Established: 1965 Annual Undergrad Tuition & Fees (In-District): $3,120
Enrollment: 7,548 Coed
Affiliation or Control: Local IRS Status: 501(c)3
Highest Offering: Associate Degree
Accreditation: **NW**, ADNUR, DH, EMT, MAC, PTAA, RAD, SURGA, SURGT

01 President .... Dr. D. Jeff FOX
00 Chairman of the Board .... Mr. Karl KLEINKOPF
05 Exec VP/Chief Academic Officer .... Dr. Todd SCHWARZ
11 Vice President of Administration .... Mr. Jeff HARMON
13 Chief Technology Officer .... Mr. Kevin MARK
32 Assoc VP Student Services .... Dr. Michelle SCHUTT
09 Assoc Dean of IE/ALO .... Mr. Chris BRAGG
121 Dean of Student Success .... Mr. John HUGHES
04 Exec Admin Asst to President .... Ms. Kathy S. DEAHL
10 Chief Financial Officer .... Ms. Kristy CARPENTER
20 Instructional Dean .... Dr. Cindy R. BOND
20 Instructional Dean .... Mr. Terry L. PATTERSON
20 Instructional Dean HSHS .... Mr. Jayson LLOYD
35 Dean of Students .... Mr. Jason OSTROWSKI
56 Assoc Dean of Extended Studies .... Mr. Cesar PEREZ
15 Director Human Resources .... Mr. Eric NIELSON
06 Registrar .... Dr. Michele MCFARLANE
07 Director of Admissions .... Ms. Gail SCHULL
37 Director of Student Financial Aid .... Ms. Jennifer J. ZIMMERS
08 Director Library .... Ms. Teri L. FATTIG
102 Executive Director Foundation .... Ms. Debra J. WILSON
103 Director Workforce Development .... Ms. Brandi TURNIPSEED

14 Dir Application/Data Architecture ... Mr. Ed DITLEFSEN
14 Dir Systems/Network Architecture ... Mr. Bruce NUKAYA
41 Athletic Director ... Mr. Joel C. BATE
18 Director Physical Plant ... Mr. Allen SCHERBINSKE
19 Director Security & Safety ... Mr. James MUNN
26 Public Information Director ... Mr. Doug L. MAUGHAN
27 Public Information Specialist ... Ms. Kim LAPRAY
40 Bookstore Manager ... Ms. Jayme KETTERLING
92 Coordinator Honors Program ... Mr. Brian DOBBS
39 Director Student Housing ... Vacant

College of Western Idaho (A)

6056 Birch Lane, Nampa ID 83687
County: Canyon FICE Identification: 042118
Unit ID: 455114
Telephone: (208) 562-3000 Carnegie Class: Assoc/MT-VT-Mix Trad/Non
FAX Number: (888) 562-3216 Calendar System: Semester
URL: cwidaho.cc
Established: 2007 Annual Undergrad Tuition & Fees (In-District): $3,336
Enrollment: 8,391 Coed
Affiliation or Control: Local IRS Status: 501(c)3
Highest Offering: Associate Degree
Accreditation: NW, ADNUR, DA, EMT, MAC, PTAA, SURGT

01 President ... Dr. Bert GLANDON
05 Exec VP Instruction/Student Svcs ... Mr. David SHELLBERG
10 VP Finance & Administration ... Mr. Tony MEATTE
11 VP Operations ... Mr. Craig BROWN
20 Asst VP Academic Affairs ... Ms. Brenda PETTINGER
32 Asst VP Student Services ... Mr. Patrick TANNER
57 Dean Languages & Arts ... Ms. Laura STAVOE
81 Dean STEM ... Ms. Kae JENSEN
83 Dean Social Sciences & Public Aff ... Ms. Courtney SANTILLAN
50 Asst Dean Business/Info Tech ... Ms. Kelly STEELY
76 Asst Dean Health Professions ... Ms. Cathleen CURRIE
72 Asst Dean Trades & Technology ... Mr. Pat NEAL
21 Associate Controller ... Ms. Mary Jo HAYES
102 Executive Director CWI Foundation ... Mr. Mitch MINNETTE
18 Executive Director Facilities Mgmt ... Mr. Jeff FLYNN
15 Executive Director Human Resources ... Ms. Lillian TALLEY
26 Director Marketing ... Ms. Audrey ELDRIDGE
103 AVP Economic Development ... Ms. Christi ROOD
07 Director of Admissions & One Stop ... Mr. Luis CALOCA
88 Director Adult Basic Education ... Mr. Jac WEBB
88 Director Advising & New Students ... Ms. Autumn BRACKLEY
88 Director Center for Teach/Learn ... Ms. Courtney COLBY-BOND
88 Director Dual Cr/College Readiness ... Mr. Stephen CRUMRINE
37 Director Financial Aid ... Ms. Nicole MCMILLIN
08 Director Library Services ... Ms. Kim REED
88 Director Math Solutions Center ... Ms. Susan KNIGHTS
35 Dean Social Services ... Ms. Jenn CROWDER
88 Director WD Business & Manufact ... Mr. Marc SWINNEY
06 Registrar ... Ms. Connie BLACK

Idaho State University (B)

921 S 8th Ave, Pocatello ID 83209-0009
County: Bannock FICE Identification: 001620
Unit ID: 142276
Telephone: (208) 282-0211 Carnegie Class: DU-Mod
FAX Number: (208) 282-4000 Calendar System: Semester
URL: www.isu.edu
Established: 1901 Annual Undergrad Tuition & Fees (In-State): $6,956
Enrollment: 13,078 Coed
Affiliation or Control: State IRS Status: 501(c)3
Highest Offering: Doctorate
Accreditation: NW, ADNUR, ARCPA, AUD, CAATE, CACREP, CAEPN, CAHIIM, CLPSY, COARC, COMTA, DENT, DH, DIETD, DIETI, EMT, ENG, ENGR, ENGT, MAC, MT, MUS, NAIT, NURSE, OT, PH, PHAR, PTA, PTAA, RAD, SP, SW, THEA

01 President ... Dr. Arthur C. VAILAS
04 Executive Assistant to President ... Ms. Shereen AINSWORTH
05 Executive Vice President & Provost ... Dr. Laura WOODWORTH-NEY
10 Interim Chief Financial Officer ... Mr. Brian HICKENLOOPER
111 Vice Pres of University Advancement ... Dr. Kent M. TINGEY
32 Interim VP of Student Affairs ... Mr. Lowell RICHARDS
46 Vice President for Research ... Dr. Cornelis VAN DER SCHYF
17 VP Kasiska Division Health Sciences ... Dr. Rex FORCE
43 General Counsel/Chief Comp Officer ... Ms. Joanne HIRASE-STACEY
41 Athletic Director ... Mr. Jeff TINGEY
20 Vice Provo Acad Strat & Inst Effect ... Ms. Selena GRACE
20 Interim AVP for Academic Affairs ... Dr. Joanne TOKLE
84 AVP for Enrollment Management ... Mr. Scott SCHOLES
30 AVP for Development ... Ms. Pauline THIROS
18 AVP for Facilities Services ... Ms. Cheryl HANSON
58 Dean of Graduate School ... Dr. Cornelis VAN DER SCHYF
54 Interim Dean College Science & Eng ... Dr. Lyle W. CASTLE
67 Dean College of Pharmacy ... Dr. Paul S. CADY
50 Dean College of Business ... Dr. Thomas OTTAWAY
49 Dean College of Arts & Letters ... Dr. Kandi TURLEY-AMES
53 Interim Dean College of Education ... Dr. Karen APPLEBY
72 Dean College of Technology ... Mr. Scott RASMUSSEN
12 Dean of Academic Pgm ISU-Meridian ... Vacant
12 Interim Dir University Programs-IF ... Ms. Ann HOWELL
08 Dean & University Librarian ... Mr. Karl BRIDGES
06 Registrar & Dir of Undergrad Admiss ... Ms. Laura MCKENZIE
13 Chief Information Officer ... Mr. Randy GAINES
29 Associate Director Alumni Relations ... Mr. Ryan SARGENT
09 Director Institutional Research ... Mr. Vince MILLER
37 Director Student Finan Aid & Schol ... Mr. James R. MARTIN
15 Director Human Resources ... Mr. Brian SAGENDORF
23 Director Student Health Center ... Dr. Ronald SOLBRIG
22 Dir EEO/Affirm Action & Diversity ... Ms. Stacey GIBSON
19 Director Public Safety ... Mr. Lewis EAKINS
26 Assoc VP Marketing & Communication ... Mr. Stuart SUMMERS
86 Director Government Relations ... Mr. Kent KUNZ
88 Director Events Management ... Mr. George CASPER
35 Director of Student Life ... Mr. Kris CLARKSON
38 Director of Counseling & Testing ... Dr. Richard PONGRATZ
85 Interim Asst Dir of Intl Programs ... Mr. Shawn BASCOM
84 Director of Enrollment Services/IF ... Ms. Ann HOWELL
07 Director Admissions & Recruitment ... Ms. Nicole ROSEBERG
39 Director University Housing ... Mr. Craig THOMPSON
96 Director of Purchasing Services ... Mr. David BUCK
44 Director Annual Giving ... Ms. Kallee VALENTINE

Lewis-Clark State College (C)

500 8th Avenue, Lewiston ID 83501-2698
County: Nez Perce FICE Identification: 001621
Unit ID: 142328
Telephone: (208) 792-5272 Carnegie Class: Bac-Diverse
FAX Number: (208) 792-2831 Calendar System: Semester
URL: www.lcsc.edu
Established: 1893 Annual Undergrad Tuition & Fees (In-State): $6,120
Enrollment: 3,633 Coed
Affiliation or Control: State IRS Status: 501(c)3
Highest Offering: Baccalaureate
Accreditation: NW, CAEPN, EMT, IACBE, MAC, NURSE, PTAA, RAD, SW

01 President ... Dr. J. Anthony FERNANDEZ
05 Provost/VP Academic Affairs ... Dr. Lori STINSON
10 VP Finance and Administration ... Mr. Todd KILBURN
75 Dean Career & Technical Education ... Mr. Jeffrey OBER
51 Dean Community Programs ... Ms. Kathy MARTIN
20 Dean Academic Programs ... Ms. Mary FLORES
32 Vice President Student Affairs ... Dr. Andrew HANSON
08 Director of Library Services ... Ms. Johanna BJORK
103 Director of Workforce Training ... Dr. Linda STRICKLIN
07 Director of Admissions/Registrar ... Ms. Nikol ROUBIDOUX
09 Dir Planning/Research/Assessment ... Vacant
13 Chief Technology Officer ... Mr. Allen SCHMOOCK
41 Athletic Director ... Ms. Brooke CUSHMAN
15 Director of Human Resources ... Ms. Vikki SWIFT
26 Director Communications & Marketing ... Mr. Logan FOWLER
29 Director of Alumni Relations ... Ms. Renee OLSEN
37 Director of Student Financial Aid ... Ms. Laura HUGHES
30 Director of College Advancement ... Ms. Erika ALLEN
18 Director of Physical Plant ... Mr. Tom GARRISON
36 Director Career & Advising Services ... Ms. Debra LYBYER
96 Director of Purchasing ... Ms. Sheila KOM
19 Director Security/Safety ... Ms. Barbara PIERCE

New Saint Andrews College (D)

PO Box 9025, Moscow ID 83843-1525
County: Latah Identification: 666166
Unit ID: 440396
Telephone: (208) 882-1566 Carnegie Class: Not Classified
FAX Number: (208) 882-4293 Calendar System: Other
URL: www.nsa.edu
Established: 1994 Annual Undergrad Tuition & Fees: $12,100
Enrollment: N/A Coed
Affiliation or Control: Independent Non-Profit IRS Status: 501(c)3
Highest Offering: Master's
Accreditation: TRACS

01 President ... Dr. Ben MERKLE
05 Academic Dean ... Dr. Timothy EDWARDS
73 Director MA Program ... Mr. Douglas WILSON
53 Dir Classical Christian Studies Pgm ... Mr. Christopher SCHLECT
10 Chief Financial Officer ... Mr. Thomas BRAINERD
08 Head Librarian ... Mrs. Helen HOWELL
06 Registrar ... Mr. Jacob MOYA
07 Director of Recruitment ... Mrs. Brenda SCHLECT
30 Director Development ... Mr. Gabriel RENCH
32 Manager New Student Services ... Mr. John SAWYER
110 Director of Fundraising ... Mrs. Heather LLOYD
07 Recruitment Counselor ... Mrs. Grace HENDRIX

North Idaho College (E)

1000 W Garden Avenue, Coeur d'Alene ID 83814-2199
County: Kootenai FICE Identification: 001623
Unit ID: 142443
Telephone: (208) 769-3300 Carnegie Class: Assoc/MT-VT-High Trad
FAX Number: (208) 765-2761 Calendar System: Semester
URL: www.nic.edu
Established: 1933 Annual Undergrad Tuition & Fees (In-District): $3,288
Enrollment: 5,543 Coed
Affiliation or Control: Local IRS Status: 501(c)3
Highest Offering: Associate Degree
Accreditation: NW, ADNUR, MAC, PTAA, RAD

01 President ... Dr. Richard L. MACLENNAN
05 Vice President for Instruction ... Dr. Lita BURNS
10 VP for Finance & Business Affairs ... Mr. Christopher MARTIN
32 Vice President for Student Services ... Mr. Graydon STANLEY
86 Chief Cmty & Gov Relations Officer ... Ms. Laura RUMPLER
103 Dean of Career Tech/Workforce Educ ... Ms. Kassie SILVAS
97 Dean of General Studies ... Dr. Larry BRIGGS
76 Dean of Health Prof & Nursing ... Ms. Christy DOYLE
07 Director of Admissions/Registrar ... Ms. Tami HAFT
09 Director of Inst Effectiveness ... Ms. Ann LEWIS
08 Library Director ... Mr. George MCALISTER
13 Chief Information Officer ... Mr. Ken WARDINSKY
37 Director of Financial Aid ... Ms. Stephanie HOUSE
18 Director of Facilities ... Mr. Garry STARK
26 Director of Comm & Marketing ... Ms. Stacy HUDSON
30 Development Director ... Ms. Rayelle ANDERSON
35 Director Student Development ... Mr. Alex HARRIS
21 Controller ... Ms. Sarah GARCIA
72 Technology Coordinator ... Mr. Andy FINNEY
29 Alumni Relations Coordinator ... Mr. Taylor FORE
04 Sr Executive Assistant ... Ms. Shannon GOODRICH
106 Director of E-learning ... Mr. Thomas SCOTT
25 Grants Development Manager ... Ms. Sara FLADELAND
41 Athletic Director ... Mr. Alvin WILLIAMS
19 Supervisor Security ... Mr. Patrick MURRAY

Northwest Nazarene University (F)

623 S. University Boulevard, Nampa ID 83686-5897
County: Canyon FICE Identification: 001624
Unit ID: 142461
Telephone: (208) 467-8011 Carnegie Class: Masters/L
FAX Number: (208) 467-8099 Calendar System: Semester
URL: www.nnu.edu
Established: 1913 Annual Undergrad Tuition & Fees: $28,650
Enrollment: 2,207 Coed
Affiliation or Control: Church Of The Nazarene IRS Status: 501(c)3
Highest Offering: Doctorate
Accreditation: NW, ACBSP, CACREP, CAEPN, ENG, MUS, NURSE, SW, @THEOL

01 President ... Mr. Joel K. PEARSALL
05 Vice Pres Academic Affairs/Dean ... Dr. Brad KURTZ-SHAW
10 Vice Pres Financial Affairs ... Vacant
32 Vice President Student Development ... Dr. Carey W. COOK
88 Exec Dir for Univ Ministry & Miss ... Dr. Fred C. FULLERTON
111 Vice Pres for External Relations ... Mr. Mark WHEELER
07 Assoc Vice Pres for Admissions ... Mr. Shawn A. BLENKER
06 Registrar ... Mrs. Nancy A. AYERS
08 Director of the Library ... Dr. Sharon I. BULL
29 Director of Alumni Relations ... Mr. Darl L. BRUNER
51 Dir Center for Professional Devel ... Mr. Dave R. COVINGTON
42 Dean of the Chapel ... Rev. Dustin METCALF
40 Bookstore Manager ... Ms. Gail D. WALKER
39 Director of Residential Life ... Mrs. Karen L. PEARSON
38 Director of Wellness Center ... Mrs. Terri BLACKBURN
21 Controller ... Mrs. Macey CROW
35 Director of Community Life ... Mr. Grant T. MILLER
36 Director of Career Center ... Ms. Amanda F. MARBLE
13 Exec Director of Info Technology ... Vacant
37 Director of Financial Aid ... Mrs. Ann CRABB
15 Director of Human Resources ... Ms. Sherry L. HARTMAN
41 Athletic Director ... Ms. Kelli LINDLEY
91 Dir of Administrative Computing ... Mr. Brian C. STILLMAN
18 Chief Facilities/Physical Plant ... Mr. Jade ANDERSON
04 Administrative Asst to President ... Ms. Jill D. JONES

Stevens-Henager College (G)

901 Pier View Drive, Suite 105, Idaho Falls ID 83404
Telephone: (205) 522-0887 Identification: 770573
Accreditation: ACCSC

† Branch campus of Stevens-Henager College, Ogden, UT

Stevens-Henager College-Boise (H)

1444 S. Entertainment Avenue, Boise ID 83709
Telephone: (208) 383-4540 Identification: 666329
Accreditation: ACCSC, COARC

† Branch campus of Stevens-Henager College, Ogden, UT

University of Idaho (I)

875 Perimeter Drive, Moscow ID 83844
County: Latah FICE Identification: 001626
Unit ID: 142285
Telephone: (208) 885-6111 Carnegie Class: DU-Higher
FAX Number: N/A Calendar System: Semester
URL: www.uidaho.edu
Established: 1889 Annual Undergrad Tuition & Fees (In-State): $7,232
Enrollment: 11,372 Coed
Affiliation or Control: State IRS Status: 501(c)3
Highest Offering: Doctorate
Accreditation: NW, ART, CAATE, CACREP, CAEPN, CEA, CIDA, CS, DIETC, ENG, IPSY, JOUR, LAW, LSAR, MUS, NAIT, NRPA

01 President ... Dr. Chuck A. STABEN
05 Provost & Executive VP ... Dr. John M. WIENCEK
10 VP Finance ... Mr. Brian R. FOISY
111 VP University Advancement ... Ms. Mary Kay MCFADDEN
03 VP Infrastructure ... Mr. Dan EWART
46 VP Research & Econ Dev ... Dr. Janet NELSON
84 Vice Provost Strategic Enroll Mgmt ... Mr. Dean KAHLER
112 Special Asst/Principal Gift Ofcr ... Mr. Michael C. PERRY
88 Special Asst/Agriculture Initiative ... Dr. John FOLTZ
26 Executive Dir of Mktg & Comm ... Ms. Stefany BALES
41 Athletic Director ... Dr. Robert SPEAR

43 General Counsel .... Mr. Kent E. NELSON
86 Special Asst State Govt Relations .... Mr. Joe STEGNER
28 Chf Diversity Ofr/Ex Dir Tribal Rel .... Dr. Yolanda BISBEE
08 Dean Library Services .... Ms. Lynn N. BAIRD
49 Dean Col of Letters/Arts Soc Sci .... Dr. Andrew KERSTEN
47 Dean College of Agric/Life Sci .... Dr. Michael PARRELLA
50 Dean College of Business & Econ .... Dr. Marc CHOPIN
53 Dean College of Education .... Dr. Alison CARR-CHELLMAN
54 Dean College of Engineering .... Dr. Larry STAUFFER
58 Dean Graduate Studies .... Dr. Jerry MCMURTY
65 Dean College of Natural Resources .... Dr. Kurt PREGITZER
61 Dean College of Law .... Mr. Mark ADAMS
48 Int Dean College of Art & Arch .... Dr. Shauna CORRY
81 Assoc Dean College of Science .... Dr. Mark NIELSEN
20 Vice Provost for Faculty .... Dr. Jeanne M. STEVENSON
109 Asst VP Auxiliary Services .... Mr. Alan COKER
15 Executive Director Human Resources .... Mr. Wesley MATTHEWS
45 Budget Director .... Ms. Trina MAHONEY
12 Executive Officer Couer d'Alene .... Dr. Charles BUCK
12 Executive Officer Boise Center .... Mr. Michael SATZ
12 Executive Officer Idaho Falls Ctr .... Dr. Marc SKINNER
18 Assistant Vice President Facilities .... Mr. Brian D. JOHNSON
13 AVP ITS/CIO .... Mr. Daniel EWART
19 Exec Dir Public Safety & Security .... Mr. Matt DORSCHEL
108 Dir Inst Effectiveness & Accred .... Dr. Dale PIETRZAK
37 Director Student Financial Aid .... Dr. Daniel D. DAVENPORT
07 Assistant Vice Provost SEM .... Ms. Bobbi J. GERRY
38 Director Counseling & Testing Ctr .... Dr. Gregory LAMBETH
42 Director Campus Christian Center .... Ms. Sharon A. KEHOE
39 Director University Residences .... Ms. Dee Dee KANIKKEBERG
44 Director Annual Giving .... Mr. James BROWNSON
92 Director Honors Program .... Ms. Sandra REINEKE
93 Dir Multicultural Affairs .... Mr. Jesse MARTINEZ
94 Director Women's Center .... Ms. Lysa SALSBURY
40 Director Bookstore .... Vacant
96 Director Purchasing Services .... Ms. Julia MCILROY
36 Director Career Services .... Mr. Christopher COOK
25 Director Research Admin .... Ms. Deborah SHAVER
32 Dean of Students .... Dr. Blaine ECKLES
103 Dir Academic Support and Access Pgm .... Ms. Cynthia CASTRO
06 Registrar .... Ms. Heather A. CHERMAK
29 Executive Dir Alumni Relations .... Ms. Kathy BARNARD
102 Actg Dir Found/Corp Relations .... Ms. Casey HANSON
106 Dir Distance & Extended Educ .... Vacant
87 Coord Summer & Dual Credit Pgm .... Ms. Linda GOLLBERG
22 Dir Civil Rights & Investigation .... Ms. Erin AGIDIUS
105 Director Enterprise Applications .... Mr. Brian BORCHERS
104 Exec Dir International Programs .... Dr. Susan BENDER
100 Chief of Staff President's Office .... Ms. Brenda HELBLING

ILLINOIS

Adler University (A)

17 North Dearborn Street, Chicago IL 60602
County: Cook FICE Identification: 020681
Unit ID: 142832
Telephone: (312) 662-4000 Carnegie Class: Spec-4-yr-Other Health
FAX Number: (312) 662-4099 Calendar System: Semester
URL: www.adler.edu
Established: 1952 Annual Graduate Tuition & Fees: N/A
Enrollment: 988 Coed
Affiliation or Control: Independent Non-Profit IRS Status: 501(c)3
Highest Offering: Doctorate; No Undergraduates
Accreditation: NH, CACREP, CLPSY, IPSY, MFCD

01 President .... Dr. Raymond E. CROSSMAN
101 Board Secy/Dir Ofc of the Pres .... Ms. Mitzi NORTON
11 Vice President Administration .... Mrs. Jo Beth CUP
05 Vice President Academic Affairs .... Dr. Wendy PASZKIEWICZ
10 Vice President Finance & IT .... Mr. Jeffrey GREEN
111 VP for Institutional Advancement .... Ms. Mary Jo LAMPARSKI
07 Vice President Admissions .... Mr. Craig HINES
26 Assoc Vice President Marketing .... Mr. Mark BRANSON
06 Registrar .... Ms. Sheba JONES
32 Assoc Vice President Student Affair .... Vacant
88 Ex Dir Inst Pub Safety/Soc Justice .... Dr. Elena QUINTARA
37 Director Student Financial Aid .... Mr. David NELSON
13 Associate VP Technology .... Mr. Paul COLLINS
12 Dean Vancouver Campus .... Mr. Bradley O'HARA
106 Executive Dean Online Campus .... Ms. Greta FERKEL
15 AVP Human Resources .... Ms. Susan YASECKO
29 Director Alumni Relations .... Mr. Michael ZAROBE
04 Administrative Asst to President .... Ms. Shana FAZAL
18 Chief Facilities/Physical Plant .... Mr. Tom ROHNER
43 Dir Legal Services/General Counsel .... Ms. Julie PROSCIA

Ambria College of Nursing (B)

5210 Trillium Boulevard, Hoffman Estates IL 60192
County: Cook FICE Identification: 041247
Unit ID: 457527
Telephone: (847) 397-0300 Carnegie Class: Spec 2-yr-Health
FAX Number: (847) 397-0313 Calendar System: Other
URL: www.ambria.edu
Established: 2006 Annual Undergrad Tuition & Fees: N/A
Enrollment: 452 Coed
Affiliation or Control: Proprietary IRS Status: Proprietary
Highest Offering: Baccalaureate
Accreditation: ACICS

01 President .... Jon OLIVEROS

American Academy of Art (C)

332 S Michigan Avenue, Chicago IL 60604-4302
County: Cook FICE Identification: 001628
Unit ID: 142887
Telephone: (312) 461-0600 Carnegie Class: Spec-4-yr-Arts
FAX Number: (312) 294-9570 Calendar System: Semester
URL: www.aaart.edu
Established: 1923 Annual Undergrad Tuition & Fees: $32,220
Enrollment: 317 Coed
Affiliation or Control: Independent Non-Profit IRS Status: 501(c)3
Highest Offering: Baccalaureate
Accreditation: NH, ACCSC

01 Director .... Mr. Richard H. OTTO
05 Academic Dean .... Mr. Duncan WEBB
06 Registrar .... Ms. Marcia R. THOMAS
36 Career Services Coordinator .... Ms. Lindsay SANDBOTHE
37 Financial Aid Director .... Ms. Ione FITZGERALD
07 Director of Admissions .... Mr. Stuart ROSENBLOOM

American InterContinental University (D)

231 North Martingale Rd, 6th Floor, Schaumburg IL 60173
County: Cook FICE Identification: 021136
Unit ID: 445027
Telephone: (877) 701-3800 Carnegie Class: Masters/L
FAX Number: N/A Calendar System: Quarter
URL: www.aiuonline.edu
Established: 1970 Annual Undergrad Tuition & Fees: $10,966
Enrollment: 11,560 Coed
Affiliation or Control: Proprietary IRS Status: Proprietary
Highest Offering: Master's
Accreditation: NH, ACBSP, CAEPT

00 Chancellor .... Dr. George P. MILLER
01 President .... Mr. John KLINE
05 Provost/Chief Academic Officer .... Dr. Ruki JAYARAMAN
32 Vice President Student Affairs .... Ms. Betsy BALACHANDRAN
37 Vice President Financial Aid .... Ms. Nicole STULL
07 Vice President Admissions .... Ms. Trisha GANGER
09 Dir of Institutional Effectiveness .... Mr. Chris PERRY

Argosy University, Chicago (E)

225 North Michigan Ave., Suite 1300, Chicago IL 60601
Telephone: (312) 777-7600 Identification: 666736
Accreditation: &WC, ACBSP, CACREP, CLPSY

† Regional accreditation is carried under the parent institution in Orange, CA.

Argosy University, Schaumburg (F)

999 N. Plaza Drive, Suite 111, Schaumburg IL 60173-5403
Telephone: (847) 969-4900 Identification: 666789
Accreditation: &WC, ACBSP, CACREP, CLPSY

† Regional accreditation is carried under the parent institution in Orange, CA.

Augustana College (G)

639 38th Street, Rock Island IL 61201-2296
County: Rock Island FICE Identification: 001633
Unit ID: 143084
Telephone: (309) 794-7000 Carnegie Class: Bac-A&S
FAX Number: (309) 794-7422 Calendar System: Trimester
URL: www.augustana.edu
Established: 1860 Annual Undergrad Tuition & Fees: $39,621
Enrollment: 2,478 Coed
Affiliation or Control: Evangelical Lutheran Church In America
IRS Status: 501(c)3
Highest Offering: Baccalaureate
Accreditation: NH, CAEPN, MUS

01 President .... Mr. Steven C. BAHLS
05 Dean of College .... Dr. Pareena G. LAWRENCE
10 Vice Pres Business & Finance .... Mr. Kirk D. ANDERSON
30 Vice President Advancement .... Mr. W. Kent BARNDS
32 Vice Pres/Dean of Student Services .... Dr. Evelyn S. CAMPBELL
84 VP Enrollment/Communication/Plng .... Mr. W. Kent BARNDS
20 Associate Dean of the College . Dr. Wendy S. HILTON-MORROW
20 Associate Dean of the College .... Dr. Kristin DOUGLAS
20 Associate Dean of the College .... Dr. Jeffrey RATLIFF-CRAIN
42 Chaplain .... Rev. Richard W. PRIGGIE
06 College Registrar .... Ms. Liesl A. FOWLER
09 Asst Dean/Director Inst Research .... Mr. Mark SALISBURY
08 Director of the Library .... Ms. Carla B. TRACY
36 Associate VP Careers & Prof Devel .... Vacant
13 Director of ITS .... Mr. Chris VAUGHAN
37 Director of Student Financial Aid .... Ms. Susan STANDLEY
96 Director Financial Plng&Procurement .... Mr. Malhar SAHEED
19 Chief of Public Safety .... Mr. Thomas M. PHILLIS
41 Director of Athletics .... Mr. Mike ZAPOLSKI
15 Director Human Resources .... Mrs. Laura C. FORD
18 Director Facilities Services .... Mr. Joe SCIFO
38 Director Student Counseling .... Mr. Michael W. TENDALL
35 Assistant Dean of Student Life .... Ms. Laura L. SCHNACK
26 Assistant VP for Comm & Marketing .... Ms. Keri RURSCH
28 Director of Multicultural & Intl .... Mr. Samuel PAYAN
29 Director Alumni/Parent Relations .... Ms. Kelly NOACK
07 Director of Admissions/Recruitment .... Ms. Meghan M. COOLEY
04 Administrative Asst to President .... Ms. Jennifer MOON
104 Director Study Abroad .... Dr. Allen P. BERTSCHE
43 Dir Legal Services/General Counsel .... Ms. Sheri L. CURRAN
100 Chief of Staff .... Mr. Kai SWANSON
102 Dir Foundation/Corporate Relations .... Ms. Lori RODERICK
44 Associate VP of Development .... Ms. Nancy A. JOHNSON
39 Director of Residential Life .... Mr. Christopher BEYER
105 Director Web Services & New Media .... Leslie M. DUPREE

Aurora University (H)

347 S Gladstone Avenue, Aurora IL 60506-4892
County: Kane FICE Identification: 001634
Unit ID: 143118
Telephone: (630) 892-6431 Carnegie Class: Masters/L
FAX Number: (630) 844-5463 Calendar System: Semester
URL: www.aurora.edu
Established: 1893 Annual Undergrad Tuition & Fees: $22,830
Enrollment: 5,423 Coed
Affiliation or Control: Independent Non-Profit IRS Status: 501(c)3
Highest Offering: Doctorate
Accreditation: NH, CAATE, CAEPN, NURSE, SW

01 President .... Dr. Rebecca L. SHERRICK
30 Executive Vice President .... Mr. Theodore C. PARGE
05 Vice President for Academic Affairs .... Dr. Frank M. BUSCHER
10 Vice President for Finance .... Ms. Sharon MAXWELL
11 Vice President for Administration .... Dr. Carmella MORAN
84 Sr Vice President for Enrollment .... Dr. Donna DE SPAIN
32 Sr Vice President for Student Life .... Dr. Lora DE LACEY
26 VP University Communications .... Mr. Steven MCFARLAND
31 Vice President Community Relations .... Ms. Sarah R. RUSSE
30 VP for Development/Alumni Relations .... Ms. Teri TOMASZKIEWICZ
15 Vice President of Human Resources .... Ms. Mary WEIS
35 Assoc Vice Pres for Student Life .... Dr. Amy GRAY
37 Dean of Student Financial Services .... Ms. Heather L. GRANART
13 Vice President for Technology .... Mr. David W. DIEHL
06 Registrar .... Ms. Melody NABORS
08 Director University Library .... Ms. Kathy CLARK
19 Director of Campus Safety .... Mr. Joe BRANKIN
41 AVP Student Life/Athletic Director .... Mr. James HAMAD
38 Director of Counseling Center .... Dr. Marcie WISEMAN
66 Dean of Sch of Nursing/Allied Hlth .... Dr. Jan STROM
70 Dean School of Social Work .... Dr. Fred R. MCKENZIE
88 Dean of Faculty Development .... Dr. Alicia C. COSKY
49 Dean College of Art and Sciences .... Dr. Frank BUSCHER
68 Dean School of Educ/Human Perf .... Dr. Jennifer BUCKLEY
50 Dean Dunham Sch Bus/Public Policy .... Dr. Toby ARQUETTE
51 Dean of Online Enroll/Cont Educ .... Dr. Donna LILJEGREN
20 Dean Academic Administration .... Dr. Mary TARLING
07 Dean of General Educ/Dir of Admiss .... Dr. Jessica THURLOW
09 Director of University Analytics .... Ms. Katie THARP

Benedictine University (I)

5700 College Road, Lisle IL 60532-0900
County: DuPage FICE Identification: 001767
Unit ID: 145619
Telephone: (630) 829-6000 Carnegie Class: DU-Mod
FAX Number: (630) 960-1126 Calendar System: Semester
URL: www.ben.edu
Established: 1887 Annual Undergrad Tuition & Fees: $32,170
Enrollment: 5,954 Coed
Affiliation or Control: Roman Catholic IRS Status: 501(c)3
Highest Offering: Doctorate
Accreditation: NH, DIETD, DIETI, NURSE, PH

01 President .... Dr. Michael S. BROPHY
05 Provost/Vice Pres Academic Affs .... Dr. James PAYNE
10 VP Business & Finance .... Ms. Miroslava MEJIA KRUG
30 Vice President of Development .... Mr. Len A. BERTOLINI
32 Vice Pres Student Life .... Mr. Marco MASINI
20 Assoc Provost .... Vacant
42 Director University Ministry .... Ms. Carrie ROBERTS
84 VP of Admissions and Financial Aid .... Mr. Edward ROBINSON
06 Registrar .... Ms. Cindy LAMBERT
08 Director Library Services .... Mr. Jack FRITTS
37 Sr Associate Dean Financial Aid .... Ms. Diane BATTISTELLA
09 Director of Institutional Research .... Dr. Amy SHIN
36 Director Career Development .... Ms. Julie COSIMO
23 Director Health Services .... Ms. Pamela DEELY
26 Exec Dir Marketing/Communications .... Ms. Mercy ROBB
50 Dean College of Business .... Dr. Sandra GILL
81 Interim Dean College of Science .... Dr. Robin RYLAARSDAM
49 Interim Dean College of Lib Arts .... Dr. Tammy SARVER
51 VP Adult and Professional Programs .... Ms. Michelle KOPPITZ
53 Int Dean Col of Educ/Health Svcs .... Dr. Richard CAMPBELL
19 Chief of Police .... Mr. Derek FERGUSON
18 Director Campus Services .... Mr. Chet ILDEFONSO
31 Asst to the Pres for Cmty Relations .... Ms. Patricia ARIANO
15 Director of Personnel Resources .... Ms. Betsy RHINESMITH
35 Student Activ & Commuter Svcs Coord .... Ms. Katie BUELL
13 Chief Information Officer .... Mr. John JERIES
07 Assoc VP of Admissions and Fin Aid .... Mr. Anthony SCOLA
04 Administrative Asst to President .... Ms. Yvette KNOX
102 Dir Foundation/Corporate Relations .... Vacant
104 Director International Pgm and Svcs .... Dr. David KLEINBERG
105 Director Web Services .... Ms. Christine BOARD
108 Assoc Provost Institutional Assess .... Ms. Donna GRAY

29 Director Alumni Relations .... Ms. Trente ARENS
121 Director Student Advising .... Ms. Karen CAMPANA
39 Assoc Dean Student Life .... Mr. Jon MILLER
41 Director of Athletics .... Mr. Mark MCHORNEY
43 Chief Compliance Ofcr/Legal Counsel .... Ms. Nancy STOECKER
44 Director of Annual Giving .... Ms. Jill POSKIN
45 Exec Dir Facilities Mgmt and Plng .... Mr. Chad TREISCH
86 Assoc Compliance Officer .... Mr. Kevin RAPPEL

Benedictine University at Springfield (A)

1500 N 5th Street, Springfield IL 62702
Telephone: (217) 525-1420 Identification: 770067
Accreditation: &NH

Bexley Seabury (B)

1407 E 60th St, Chicago IL 60637
County: Cook FICE Identification: 037473
Unit ID: 443702
Telephone: (773) 380-6780 Carnegie Class: Spec-4-yr-Faith
FAX Number: (773) 380-6788 Calendar System: Semester
URL: www.bexleyseabury.edu
Established: 1824 Annual Graduate Tuition & Fees: N/A
Enrollment: 39 Coed
Affiliation or Control: Protestant Episcopal IRS Status: 501(c)3
Highest Offering: Master's; No Undergraduates
Accreditation: THEOL

01 Acting President .... Dean Therese DELISIO
05 VP Academic Affairs/Academic Dean .Rev. Thomas C. FERGUSON
10 Director of Finance .... Mr. Robert DOAK

Black Hawk College (C)

6600 34th Avenue, Moline IL 61265-5899
County: Rock Island FICE Identification: 001638
Unit ID: 143279
Telephone: (309) 796-5000 Carnegie Class: Assoc/MT-VT-High Non
FAX Number: (309) 792-5976 Calendar System: Semester
URL: www.bhc.edu
Established: 1946 Annual Undergrad Tuition & Fees (In-District): $4,410
Enrollment: 5,271 Coed
Affiliation or Control: Local IRS Status: 501(c)3
Highest Offering: Associate Degree
Accreditation: NH, ADNUR, EMT, PTAA

01 President .... Dr. Bettie TRUITT
05 VP of Instruction/Student Svcs .... Dr. Amy MAXEINER
10 VP Finance/Admin & Board Treasurer .... Mr. Steve FROMMELT
20 Executive Dean .... Dr. Betsey MORTHLAND
15 Director of Human Resources .... Ms. Stacey CARY
19 Chief of Police .... Mr. Shawn CISNA
09 Director Plng & Inst Effectiveness .... Ms. Kathy MALCOLM
26 Director Marketing/Public Relations .... Mr. John MEINEKE
13 Co-CIO/IT Systems Manager .... Mr. Ryan WHITE
13 Co-CIO/Manager of Admin Systems .... Ms. Sandy COX
102 Exec Dir BHC Foundation EC Campus .... Ms. Liz BREEDLOVE
102 Exec Dir BHC Foundation QC Campus .Ms. Maureen DICKINSON
51 Dean Adult/Continuing Educ .... Ms. Glenda NICKE
32 Dean of Student Services .... Mr. Luis MORENO
81 Academic Dean .... Mr. Ken NICKELS
04 Executive Asst to the President .... Ms. Heather BENNETT
36 Director Career Services Center .... Dr. Bruce STOREY
37 Director of Financial Aid .... Ms. Joanna DYE
41 Division Director Athletics/Coach .... Mr. Gary HUBER
08 Librarian .... Ms. Ashtin TRIMBLE
51 Director Adult Education .... Ms. Bianca PERKINS
06 Registrar .... Ms. Heather BJORGAN
40 Bookstore Manager Quad Cities .... Ms. Aimee MUHLEMAN
96 Purchasing Manager .... Mr. Mike MELEG
50 Dept Chair Business & Technology .... Ms. Carrie DELCOURT
57 Dept Chair Comm & Fine Arts ..Ms. Melissa HEBERT-JOHNSON
79 Dept Chair Human/Languages/Journal .... Mr. Bill DESMOND
81 Dept Chair Mathematics .... Ms. Connie MCLEAN
54 Dept Chair Natural Science/Engrng .... Mr. Brian GLASER
83 Dept Chair Social Sciences .... Mr. Mark ESPOSITO
47 Department Chair Agriculture .... Dr. Jeffrey HAWES
66 Dept Chair Nursing .... Ms. Trudy STARR
76 Dept Chair Allied Health/HPE .... Ms. Diane ABELS
88 Dept Chair Counseling .... Ms. Wendy BOCK
62 Dept Chair Lrg Resource Center .... Vacant
53 Dept Chair Psych/Sociology/Educ .... Dr. Traci DAVIS
72 Dept Chair Career Technologies .... Ms. Jamie HILL
18 Chief Facilities/Physical Plant .... Mr. Bob MCCHURCH

Black Hawk College East Campus (D)

26230 Black Hawk Road, Galva IL 61434
Telephone: (309) 854-1700 Identification: 770069
Accreditation: &NH

Blackburn College (E)

700 College Avenue, Carlinville IL 62626-1498
County: Macoupin FICE Identification: 001639
Unit ID: 143288
Telephone: (217) 854-3231 Carnegie Class: Bac-Diverse
FAX Number: (217) 854-5700 Calendar System: Semester
URL: www.blackburn.edu
Established: 1837 Annual Undergrad Tuition & Fees: $21,162
Enrollment: 585 Coed
Affiliation or Control: Presbyterian Church (U.S.A.) IRS Status: 501(c)3
Highest Offering: Baccalaureate
Accreditation: NH

01 President .... Dr. John COMERFORD
05 Provost .... Dr. John MCCLUSKY
10 Vice Pres Administration & Finance .... Mr. Steve MORRIS
111 VP for Institutional Advancement .... Ms. Sheryl RAY
32 Interim VP/Dean of Student Affairs .... Ms. Abbey HARDIN
101 Exec Asst to Pres/Sec Bd Trustees .... Ms. Shawna POE
07 Director of Admissions .... Ms. Alisha KAPP
88 Director of Transfer Admissions .... Mr. Brian HERRMANN
30 Sr Develop Ofcr/Alumni/Staff Rels .... Mr. Nate RUSH
37 Director of Financial Aid .... Ms. Jane KELSEY
08 Head Librarian .... Vacant
38 College Counselor .... Mr. Tim MORENZ
06 College Registrar .... Ms. Dianna RUYLE
15 Director Personnel Services .... Ms. Melissa JONES
36 Director Student Placement .... Ms. Suzanne KRUPICA
18 Director Physical Plant .... Mr. Sam HARDING
41 Dir of Athletics/Recreational Pgms .... Mr. John MALIN
42 Chaplain .... Vacant
26 Director of Public Relations .... Mr. Peter OSWALD
09 Director of Institutional Research .... Dr. Kristi NELMS
21 Controller .... Ms. Dawn SHRYOCK
44 Director of Annual Giving .... Dr. Mark ZOBEL
84 Enrollment Services Administrator .... Ms. Kathy RUITER
19 Director Security/Safety .... Mr. Morrison FRASER
28 Director of Diversity .... Vacant
13 Chief Info Technology Officer (CIO) .... Mr. Jason CLONINGER
88 Associate Dean of Work .... Mr. Rob WEIS

Blessing-Rieman College of Nursing & Health Sciences (F)

11th & Oak, PO Box 7005, Quincy IL 62305-7005
County: Adams FICE Identification: 006214
Unit ID: 143297
Telephone: (217) 228-5520 Carnegie Class: Spec-4-yr-Other Health
FAX Number: (217) 223-4661 Calendar System: Semester
URL: www.brcn.edu
Established: 1891 Annual Undergrad Tuition & Fees: N/A
Enrollment: 261 Coed
Affiliation or Control: Independent Non-Profit IRS Status: 501(c)3
Highest Offering: Master's
Accreditation: NH, #COARC, NURSE

01 President/CEO .... Dr. Brenda BESHEARS
05 Academic Dean .... Dr. Jan AKRIGHT
32 Dean of Student Services .... Ms. Jenna CRABTREE
06 Registrar .... Ms. Rachel CRAMSEY

Bradley University (G)

1501 W Bradley Avenue, Peoria IL 61625-0001
County: Peoria FICE Identification: 001641
Unit ID: 143358
Telephone: (309) 676-7611 Carnegie Class: Masters/M
FAX Number: N/A Calendar System: Semester
URL: www.bradley.edu
Established: 1897 Annual Undergrad Tuition & Fees: $32,120
Enrollment: 5,338 Coed
Affiliation or Control: Independent Non-Profit IRS Status: 501(c)3
Highest Offering: Doctorate
Accreditation: NH, ART, CACREP, CAEPN, CONST, DIETD, DIETI, ENG, ENGT, MUS, NURSE, PTA, SW, THEA

01 President .... Dr. Gary R. ROBERTS
05 Provost/Vice Pres Academic Affs .... Dr. Walter R. ZAKAHI
20 Interim Associate Provost .... Dr. Molly CLUSKEY
20 Assistant Provost Academic Affairs .... Mrs. Linda J. PIZZUTI
10 Vice President Business Affairs .... Mr. Gary M. ANNA
111 Vice President Advancement .... Mr. Jacob HEUSER
32 Vice President Student Affairs .... Mr. Nathan THOMAS
13 Chief Information Officer .... Mr. Zach GORMAN
26 Exec Dir Public Relations .... Ms. Renee CHARLES
84 Assoc VP Enrollment Management .... Mr. Justin BALL
58 Assoc Provost/Dean Res/Grad School .... Dr. Jeffrey BAKKEN
21 Assoc Business Officer/Controller .... Mrs. Pratima N. GANDHI
50 Dean Foster Col Business .... Dr. Darrell J. RADSON
57 Dean Slane Col Commun/Fine Arts .... Dr. Jeffrey H. HUBERMAN
53 Dean Educ & Health Sciences .... Dr. Joan SATTLER
54 Dean Engineering & Technology .... Dr. Lex A. AKERS
49 Dean Liberal Arts & Sciences .... Dr. Christopher JONES
08 Exec Director of the Library .... Ms. Barbara GALIK
39 Dir Ctr Residential Lvng/Ldrshp .... Mr. Ryan BAIR
36 Exec Dir Smith Career Center .... Mr. Jon NEIDY
29 Director of Alumni Relations .... Ms. Tory JENNETTEN
51 Executive Director Continuing Educ .... Ms. Janet LANGE
06 Registrar .... Mr. Andreas KINDLER
37 Director Financial Aid .... Ms. Debra JACKSON
19 Chief of Campus Police .... Mr. Brian JOSCHKO
15 Director of Human Resources .... Ms. Nena PEPLOW
18 Director Facilities Management .... Mr. Larry MCGUIRE
23 Medical Director Health Services .... Dr. Jessica HIGGS
27 Senior Director Public Relations .... Ms. Kathleen CONVER
41 Director Athletics .... Dr. Chris REYNOLDS
78 Director Springer Center .... Mrs. Dawn KOELTZOW
87 Dir Summer/Interim Sessions .... Ms. Janet LANGE
25 Exec Dir Sponsored Programs .... Vacant
22 Director Affirmative Action/EEO .... Ms. Nena PEPLOW
28 Exec Dir Diversity/Inclusion .... Mr. Norris CHASE
92 Director of Honors Program .... Dr. Kyle DZAPO
94 Dir of Women's Studies & Gender .... Dr. Amy SCOTT
09 Dir of Institutional Improvement .... Ms. Jennifer G. BURGE
40 Manager Bookstore .... Mr. Paul KROENKE
88 Dir of Health Prof Advising Ctr .... Dr. Valerie BENNETT
88 Dir Center for Legal Studies .... Ms. Jerelyn MAHER
07 Asst Dir Admissions .... Mr. Joshua JONES
104 Director Study Abroad .... Dr. Christine BLOUCH
38 Dir of Health Services .... Ms. Jessica HIGGS

Carl Sandburg College (H)

2400 Tom L. Wilson Boulevard, Galesburg IL 61401-9576
County: Knox FICE Identification: 007265
Unit ID: 143613
Telephone: (309) 344-2518 Carnegie Class: Assoc/MT-VT-High Non
FAX Number: (309) 344-1395 Calendar System: Semester
URL: www.sandburg.edu
Established: 1966 Annual Undergrad Tuition & Fees: $4,390
Enrollment: 2,082 Coed
Affiliation or Control: Independent Non-Profit IRS Status: 501(c)3
Highest Offering: Associate Degree
Accreditation: NH, ADNUR, DH, FUSER, PNUR

01 President .... Dr. Lori L. SUNDBERG
37 Director Financial Aid .... Ms. Lisa HANSON
88 Director of Recruitment .... Ms. Mollye CRATERFIELD
19 Director of Public Safety .... Mr. Kipton CANFIELD
07 Director of Admissions & Records .... Mr. Rick EDDY
41 Athletic Director .... Mr. Mike BAILEY
16 Director of Human Resources .... Ms. Gina KRUPPS
108 Dir Institutional Effectiveness .... Ms. Michelle JOHNSON
88 Director TRIO Upward Bound .... Mr. Tony BENTLEY
88 Director of TRIO SSS .... Ms. Autumn SCOTT
32 VP of Student Services .... Mr. Steve NORTON
12 Director of Branch Campus ...... Ms. Ellen HENDERSON-GASSER
66 Dean of Health Professions .... Ms. Mischelle MONAGLE
88 Director of Corporate & Leisure .... Ms. Stacey RUCKER
79 Assoc Dean Humanities/Fine Arts .... Mr. James HUTCHINGS
83 Assoc Dean Social & Behavioral Sci .... Ms. Jill JOHNSON
81 Assoc Dean Math/Natural Sciences .... Mr. Dave BURNS
75 Assoc Dean CTHE .... Ms. Diana HIGGINS
05 VP of Academic Services .... Ms. Julie GIBB
04 Sr Exec Assistant to President .... Ms. Lisa ZUCCO
10 Chief Financial Officer/Treasurer .... Ms. Lisa BLAKE
15 Dean HR/Institutional Effectiveness .... Dr. Constance THURMAN
111 Director of Advancement .... Ms. Stephanie HILTEN
26 Director Marketing/Public Relations .... Ms. Brittany GRIMES
13 Director of Technology Services .... Mr. Drew WITHERELL
35 Dean of Student Success .... Ms. Misty LYON

Carl Sandburg College The Branch Campus (I)

305 Sandburg Drive, Carthage IL 62321
Telephone: (217) 357-3129 Identification: 770071
Accreditation: &NH

Catholic Theological Union (J)

5401 S Cornell Avenue, Chicago IL 60615-5698
County: Cook FICE Identification: 009232
Unit ID: 143659
Telephone: (773) 371-5400 Carnegie Class: Spec-4-yr-Faith
FAX Number: (773) 324-8490 Calendar System: Semester
URL: www.ctu.edu
Established: 1968 Annual Graduate Tuition & Fees: N/A
Enrollment: 375 Coed
Affiliation or Control: Roman Catholic IRS Status: 501(c)3
Highest Offering: Doctorate; No Undergraduates
Accreditation: THEOL

01 President .... Rev. Mark R. FRANCIS, CSV
05 Vice President/Academic Dean .... Sr. Barbara E. REID, OP
10 Vice Pres Administration & Finance .... Mr. Michael W. CONNORS
30 Director of Development .... Ms. Colleen KENNEDY
26 Dir of Marketing & Communications .... Mr. Jeff KRAFT
08 Director of the Library .... Ms. Kristine VELDHEER
06 Registrar .... Mrs. Maria De Jesus LEMUS
07 Asst Director Admissions/Retention .... Mr. Patrick MCGOWAN
13 Director of Information Technology .... Mr. Darnell PAYNE
04 Assistant to the President .... Sr. Pam PAULOSKI, SP
84 Director Enrollment Management .... Ms. Christine HENDERSON

*Chamberlain University-Administrative Office (K)

3005 Highland Parkway, Downers Grove IL 60515
County: DuPage Identification: 667149
Telephone: (888) 556-8226 Carnegie Class: N/A
FAX Number: (630) 512-8888
URL: www.chamberlain.edu

01 President .... Dr. Susan GROENWALD
11 Sr Dir Campus Operations .... Elizabeth DUNLEVY
11 Sr Dir Campus Operations .... Kimberly LAMAR
11 Sr Dir Campus Operations .... Patrick ROMBALSKI
11 Sr Dir Campus Operations .... Kacie SPENCER
05 VP Academic Affairs .... Dr. Richard COWLING
10 VP Finance .... Sonya EVANOSKY
26 Director Marketing .... George ADKINS
07 VP Enrollment Management .... Larry VENSEY
32 VP Student Services .... June MARLOWE

† Part of DeVry University, IL.

*Chamberlain University-Addison (A)

1221 N. Swift Road, Addison IL 60101
County: DuPage FICE Identification: 006385
Unit ID: 454227
Telephone: (630) 953-3660 Carnegie Class: Not Classified
FAX Number: (630) 628-1154 Calendar System: Semester
URL: www.chamberlain.edu
Established: 1889 Annual Undergrad Tuition & Fees: $19,230
Enrollment: 23,250 Coed
Affiliation or Control: Proprietary IRS Status: Proprietary
Highest Offering: Doctorate
Accreditation: NH, NURSE

02 Campus President .... Dr. Jan SNOW
05 Dean Academic Affairs .... Terry BRENNAN
32 Manager Student Services .... Lisa PETSCHENKO
07 Director Admissions .... Roz CASTRO

† Master's and Doctorate programs are only offered online.

*Chamberlain University-Chicago (B)

3300 North Campbell Avenue, Chicago IL 60618
Telephone: (773) 961-3000 Identification: 770495
Accreditation: &NH, NURSE

*Chamberlain University-Tinley Park (C)

18624 West Creek Drive, Tinley Park IL 60477
Telephone: (708) 560-2000 Identification: 770496
Accreditation: &NH, NURSE

Chicago ORT Technical Institute (D)

5440 W. Fargo Avenue, Skokie IL 60077
County: Cook FICE Identification: 041184
Unit ID: 393180
Telephone: (847) 324-5588 Carnegie Class: Spec 2-yr-Other
FAX Number: (847) 324-5580 Calendar System: Other
URL: www.ortchicagotech.edu
Established: 1991 Annual Undergrad Tuition & Fees: N/A
Enrollment: 77 Coed
Affiliation or Control: Independent Non-Profit IRS Status: 501(c)3
Highest Offering: Associate Degree
Accreditation: CNCE

01 Executive Director .... Michelle MOVITZ
05 Academic Dean .... Roxanne WITTKAMP
07 Director of Admissions .... Michael THORNBER
37 Director of Financial Aid .... Anahi HUERTA

Chicago School of Professional Psychology-Chicago (E)

325 N Wells Street, Chicago IL 60654-8158
Telephone: (312) 329-6600 Identification: 770349
Accreditation: &WC, CLPSY

† Branch campus of Chicago School of Professional Psychology Los Angeles Campus, Los Angeles, CA

Chicago State University (F)

9501 S King Drive, Chicago IL 60628-1598
County: Cook FICE Identification: 001694
Unit ID: 144005
Telephone: (773) 995-2000 Carnegie Class: Masters/M
FAX Number: (773) 995-2563 Calendar System: Semester
URL: www.csu.edu
Established: 1867 Annual Undergrad Tuition & Fees (In-State): $10,252
Enrollment: 4,767 Coed
Affiliation or Control: State IRS Status: 501(c)3
Highest Offering: Doctorate
Accreditation: NH, ACBSP, ART, CACREP, CAEPN, CAHIIM, MUS, NRPA, NUR, OT, PHAR, SW

01 Interim President .... Dr. Rachel LINDSEY
05 Provost/Sr VP for Academic Affairs .... Dr. Angela HENDERSON
11 Chief Administrative Officer .... Mr. Paul G. VALLAS
10 Int Chief Finance Officer .... Mrs. Arrileen PATAWARAN
114 Executive Director Budget/Resource .... Mrs. Arrileen PATAWARAN
13 Chief Information Officer .... Mr. Prashant SHINDE
84 Vice Pres of Enrollment Management .... Dr. Micheal ELLISON
09 Dir Inst Effectiveness & Research .... Dr. Latrice E. EGGLESTON WILLIAMS
32 Dean of Student Affairs & FYE .... Ms. Sheila COLLINS
49 Acting Dean Col of Arts & Sciences .... Dr. Justin AKUJIEZE, II
53 Int Assoc Col of Dean Education .... Dr. Jamilah JOR'DAN
67 Int Dean College of Pharmacy .... Dr. Carmita COLEMAN
76 Dean College of Health Sciences .... Dr. Leslie A. ROUNDTREE
50 Dean College of Business .... Mr. Derrick K. COLLINS
08 Dean of Library/Instruct Services .... Dr. Richard DARGA
51 Asst Dean Cont Educ Nontrad Pgms .... Ms. Nelly MAYNARD
06 Registrar .... Mrs. Shawnice AVILEZ
37 Assistant Director of Financial Aid .... Mr. James LUCKE
07 Director of Admissions and Outreach .... Vacant
29 Exec Director Alumni Affairs .... Mr. Louis WRIGHT
26 Dir of Marketing & Communications .... Mrs. Sabrina LAND
15 Int Director Human Resources .... Ms. Lindsay HAMILTON
36 Director of Career Development .... Vacant
18 Int Director Facilities/Physical Pl .... Ms. Monique HORTON
20 Assoc Provost Academic Affairs .... Dr. Bernard ROWAN
35 Dir of Student Activities .... Ms. MaToya MARSH
38 Director Counseling Center .... Vacant
20 Assoc Provost Academic Affairs .... Dr. Satasha GREEN
25 Int Assoc VP of Sponsored Programs .... Dr. David KANIS
43 Assoc VP Gen Counsel/Ethics Officer .... Ms. Robin HAWKINS
19 Chief of Police .... Vacant
39 Director Student Housing .... Mr. Timothy LEE
41 Assoc VP/Athletic Director .... Vacant

Chicago Theological Seminary (G)

1407 East 60th Street, Chicago IL 60637-1284
County: Cook FICE Identification: 001661
Unit ID: 144014
Telephone: (773) 896-2400 Carnegie Class: Spec-4-yr-Faith
FAX Number: (773) 643-1284 Calendar System: Semester
URL: www.ctschicago.edu
Established: 1855 Annual Graduate Tuition & Fees: N/A
Enrollment: 253 Coed
Affiliation or Control: United Church Of Christ IRS Status: 501(c)3
Highest Offering: Doctorate; No Undergraduates
Accreditation: NH, THEOL

01 President .... Dr. Alice HUNT
05 Academic Dean .... Dr. Ken STONE
10 Vice President for Finance & Admin .... Ms. Julie FISHER
111 Vice President for Advancement .... Vacant
06 Registrar .... Ms. Elena JIMENEZ
08 Director of the Lapp Learning Ctr .... Vacant
07 Director Recruitment/Admission .... Mr. Jason FREY
04 Assistant to the President .... Ms. Kim M. JOHNSON
26 Director of Communications .... Ms. Susan CUSICK
18 Facilities Coordinator .... Ms. Shauna WARREN

Christian Life College (H)

400 E Gregory Street, Mount Prospect IL 60056-2522
County: Cook FICE Identification: 031993
Unit ID: 260947
Telephone: (847) 259-1840 Carnegie Class: Spec-4-yr-Faith
FAX Number: (847) 259-3888 Calendar System: Semester
URL: www.christianlifecollege.edu
Established: 1950 Annual Undergrad Tuition & Fees: $11,000
Enrollment: 45 Coed
Affiliation or Control: Pentecostal/Charismatic Non-Denominational
IRS Status: 501(c)3
Highest Offering: Baccalaureate
Accreditation: TRACS

01 President .... Mr. Harry R. SCHMIDT
05 Academic Dean .... Mr. Wayne R. WACHSMUTH
08 Director of Library Services .... Vacant
10 Director of Finance .... Mr. Roger K. STEVENS
32 Dean of Students .... Vacant
06 Registrar .... Miss Haley BENSON

*City Colleges of Chicago (I)

226 W Jackson Boulevard, Chicago IL 60606-6998
County: Cook FICE Identification: 001647
Unit ID: 144500
Telephone: (312) 553-2500 Carnegie Class: N/A
FAX Number: (312) 553-2699
URL: www.ccc.edu

01 Chancellor .... Mr. Juan SALGADO
10 Vice Chanc Finance/Business/CFO .... Ms. Joyce CARSON
13 Vice Chanc/Chief Information Ofcr .... Vacant
09 Exec Vice Chanc/Chief Strategy Ofcr .... Vacant
11 Vice Chanc Administrative Services .... Ms. Diane MINOR
43 General Counsel .... Mr. John GASIOROWSKI
30 Exec Vice Chancellor/Sr Advisor .... Mr. Eric LUGO

*City Colleges of Chicago Harold Washington College (J)

30 E Lake Street, Chicago IL 60601-2449
County: Cook FICE Identification: 001652
Unit ID: 144209
Telephone: (312) 553-5600 Carnegie Class: Assoc/HT-Mix Trad/Non
FAX Number: (312) 553-5964 Calendar System: Semester
URL: www.ccc.edu
Established: 1962 Annual Undergrad Tuition & Fees (In-District): $3,506
Enrollment: 9,093 Coed
Affiliation or Control: State/Local IRS Status: 501(c)3
Highest Offering: Associate Degree
Accreditation: NH, ACBSP

02 Interim President .... Mr. Ignacio LOPEZ
05 Vice Pres Academic/Student Affairs .... Mr. Armen SARRAFIAN
10 Exec Dir of Business/Operations .... Mr. Kent LUSK
37 Director of Financial Aid .... Mr. Norberto VALENTIN
18 Chief Facilities/Physical Plant .... Mr. Jeremy GONZALEZ
88 Dean of College to Careers .... Mr. Paul THOMPSON, III
08 Librarian .... Mr. John KIERALDO
15 Human Resources Admin .... Vacant
20 Dean of Instruction .... Vacant
32 Dean of Student Services .... Mr. Wendell BLAIR
20 Associate Dean of Instruction .... Mr. Asif WILSON
13 Director Information Technology .... Ms. Ewa BEJNAROWICZ
35 Assoc Dean of Student Services .... Ms. Patricia CUEVAS
46 Asst Director Research/Planning .... Dr. George W. CALISTO
06 Registrar .... Ms. Courtney O'BRIEN
19 Director of Security .... Mr. Milton OWENS
09 Director Strategy/Initiatives .... Vacant

*City Colleges of Chicago Harry S Truman College (K)

1145 W Wilson Avenue, Chicago IL 60640-5691
County: Cook FICE Identification: 001648
Unit ID: 144184
Telephone: (773) 907-4700 Carnegie Class: Assoc/MT-VT-High Non
FAX Number: (773) 907-4464 Calendar System: Semester
URL: www.trumancollege.edu
Established: 1956 Annual Undergrad Tuition & Fees (In-District): $3,506
Enrollment: 9,467 Coed
Affiliation or Control: State/Local IRS Status: 501(c)3
Highest Offering: Associate Degree
Accreditation: NH

02 President .... Dr. Shawn L. JACKSON
03 Vice President .... Dr. Pervez RAHMAN
05 Dean of Instruction .... Ms. Susan MARCUS
06 Registrar .... Ms. My Linh TRAN
32 Dean of Student Services .... Ms. Mary Ann SOLEY
35 Associate Dean of Student Services .... Dr. Quincy PADEN
56 Dean of Adult Education .... Mr. Armanda MATA
51 Director of Continuing Education .... Ms. Kyla WILSON
20 Associate Dean of Instruction .... Dr. DeShaunta STEWART
20 Associate Dean of Instruction .... Mr. Derek LAZARSKI
20 Associate Dean of Instruction .... Ms. Maggie RICE AYALA
10 Exec Director Business Services .... Mr. Thomas DUNHAM
19 Director of Security .... Mr. Andres DURBAK
37 Director of Financial Aid .... Ms. Maria PINTO
15 Director Human Resource .... Mr. Michael ROBERTS
26 Director Public Relations/Marketing .... Mr. R. Scott BRIGHAM
109 Director Auxiliary Services .... Ms. Penelope VARNAVA
72 Director Information Technology .... Mr. Nick NICHOLSON
09 Asst Dir of Research & Planning .... Ms. Maureen PYLMAN
21 Business Manager .... Ms. Nina CAO
88 Director of Developmental Education .... Ms. Elizabeth ROSENTHAL
32 Dean of College to Careers .... Dr. Peggy KORELLIS
45 Director of Strategic Initiatives .... Dr. Cari Lynn HENNESSY
121 Dir of Student Development Projects .... Ms. Aubrey SCHEFFEY
103 Director of Workforce Development .... Ms. Danielle WALLINGTON-HARRIS
18 Director of Facilities Management .... Ms. Penelope VARNAVA
35 Director of Student Activities .... Mr. Anthony KWIATKOWSKI
35 Associate Dean of College to Career .... Ms. Allison ZURES
35 Assoc Dean of College to Careers .... Mr. Richard MORALES
36 Dir of Career Plng & Placement Ctr .... Ms. Wendy MATTHIS
41 Director Intercollegiate Athletics .... Ms. Alison GUENGERICH

*City Colleges of Chicago Kennedy-King College (L)

6301 South Halsted Street, Chicago IL 60621-3798
County: Cook FICE Identification: 001654
Unit ID: 144157
Telephone: (773) 602-5000 Carnegie Class: Assoc/HVT-High Non
FAX Number: N/A Calendar System: Semester
URL: www.ccc.edu/colleges/kennedy
Established: 1934 Annual Undergrad Tuition & Fees (In-District): $3,506
Enrollment: 3,989 Coed
Affiliation or Control: State/Local IRS Status: 501(c)3
Highest Offering: Associate Degree
Accreditation: NH

02 President .... Mr. Craig LYNCH
05 Vice President for Academic Affairs .... Vacant
32 Dean Student Services .... Vacant
12 Dean-Dawson Tech Institute .... Ms. Lucretzia JAMISON
36 Dean College to Careers .... Mr. Marshall SHAFKOWITZ
51 Dean Adult/Continuing Education .... Mr. Herny HORACE
20 Dean of Instruction .... Mr. Eddie PHILLIPS
35 Assoc Dean Student Services .... Ms. Zalika LANDRUM
35 Assoc Dean Student Services .... Mr. Isaac ZUNIGA
88 Dean Washburne Culinary Institute .... Ms. Jori ORSINI
37 Director Financial Aid .... Ms. Tabitha O'NEIL
121 Director Academic Support Services .... Ms. Shandria HOLMES
10 Exec Dir Business/Operations .... Mr. Baha AWADALLAH
06 Registrar .... Mr. Eric HAYES
09 Director of Institutional Research .... Vacant
18 Chief Facilities/Physical Plant .... Mr. Jerome DABNEY
26 Marketing Director .... Mr. Daniel STERNFIELD
15 Director Human Resources .... Mrs. Araceli CABRALES-MEDINA
27 Senior Director of Communications .... Ms. Katheryn HAYES
04 Assistant to the President .... Mrs. Roxanne BROWN
109 Director of Auxiliary Services .... Mr. Robert GRAHAM
45 Director Strategic Initiatives .... Mr. Patrick GIPSON
19 Director Security/Safety .... Mr. Hershey NORISE
41 Athletic Director .... Mr. Rodell DAVIS

*City Colleges of Chicago Olive-Harvey College (M)

10001 S Woodlawn Avenue, Chicago IL 60628-1645
County: Cook FICE Identification: 009767
Unit ID: 144175
Telephone: (773) 291-6100 Carnegie Class: Assoc/HVT-High Non
FAX Number: (773) 291-6304 Calendar System: Semester

URL: www.ccc.edu/colleges/olive-harvey/pages/default.aspx
Established: 1970 Annual Undergrad Tuition & Fees (In-District): $3,506
Enrollment: 3,465 Coed
Affiliation or Control: State/Local IRS Status: 501(c)3
Highest Offering: Associate Degree
Accreditation: NH

Code	Title	Name
02	Interim President	Ms. Felicia DAVIS
04	Executive Office Manager	Ms. Lexie TRIPP
05	VP Academic Affairs	Vacant
88	Dean STEM/Ctr Teaching & Lrng	Dr. Danielle LIUBIEICH
32	Dean Student Services	Ms. Michelle ADAMS
51	Dean Adult & Continuing Education	Mr. Robert REIMER
36	Assoc Dean of College to Career	Ms. LaTonya ARMSTRONG
35	Assoc Dean of Student Services	Ms. Tania WITTGENFELD
20	Dean of Instruction	Dr. Stephanie DECICCO
35	Assoc Dean of Student Services	Ms. Kay FRANCIS-GARLAND
36	Assoc Dean of College to Career	Ms. Glasetta BARKSDALE
10	Exec Dir Bus/Admin/Auxiliary Svcs	Ms. Angela ARRINGTON-JONES
13	Director Information Technology	Mr. Savio PINTO
12	Director of South Chicago Lrng Ctr	Vacant
37	Director Financial Aid	Vacant
06	Registrar	Vacant
19	Director Security	Vacant
88	Director Child Development Center	Ms. Caroline CASILLAS
41	Director of Athletics	Mr. Anthony BINION
15	Director Human Resources	Ms. Latasha LARRY
26	Director Public Relations	Vacant
38	Manager Wellness Center	Vacant
18	Chief Engineer	Mr. Tom SIEFERT

*City Colleges of Chicago Richard J. Daley College (A)

7500 S Pulaski Road, Chicago IL 60652-1299
County: Cook FICE Identification: 001649
Unit ID: 144193
Telephone: (773) 838-7500 Carnegie Class: Assoc/HVT-High Non
FAX Number: (773) 838-7524 Calendar System: Semester
URL: daley.ccc.edu
Established: 1960 Annual Undergrad Tuition & Fees (In-District): $3,506
Enrollment: 8,365 Coed
Affiliation or Control: State/Local IRS Status: 501(c)3
Highest Offering: Associate Degree
Accreditation: NH

Code	Title	Name
02	President	Dr. Jose M. AYBAR
05	Vice Pres Academic/Student Affs	Vacant
20	Dean of Instruction	Mr. Michael CRAWFORD
55	Dean Adult Education	Vacant
32	Dean of Student Services	Dr. Edwardo GARZA
51	Dean Continuing Education	Mrs. Jean JOHNSON
10	Exec Director Business Operations	Ms. Crystal WASHINGTON
18	Chief Engineer/Physical Plant	Mr. Tim SMITH
19	Director Security	Mr. Ronald MARTIN
35	Assoc Dean Student Services	Ms. Maria ACOSTA
35	Assoc Dean Student Services	Ms. Eileen LYNCH
06	Assistant Registrar	Mr. Victor SANCHEZ
15	Director Human Resources	Ms. Elinore MOORE
13	Director of Information Technology	Mr. Ronald VERSETTO
26	Senior Director of Marketing	Vacant
37	Director Student Financial Aid	Dr. Loucynda WHITE

*City Colleges of Chicago Wilbur Wright College (B)

4300 N Narragansett Avenue, Chicago IL 60634-1591
County: Cook FICE Identification: 001655
Unit ID: 144218
Telephone: (773) 777-7900 Carnegie Class: Assoc/MT-VT-High Non
FAX Number: (773) 481-8185 Calendar System: Semester
URL: www.ccc.edu/wright
Established: 1934 Annual Undergrad Tuition & Fees (In-District): $3,506
Enrollment: 10,770 Coed
Affiliation or Control: State/Local IRS Status: 501(c)3
Highest Offering: Associate Degree
Accreditation: NH, ACBSP, OTA

Code	Title	Name
02	President	Dr. David POTASH
05	VP of Academic & Student Affairs	Ms. Nicole REAVES
32	Dean of Student Services	Ms. Romell MURDEN-WOLDU
20	Dean of Instruction	Mr. James HOWLEY
121	Assoc Dean Student Svcs Advising	Ms. Maria LLOPIZ
07	Assoc Dean Student Svcs Admissions	Ms. Linda HUERTAS
20	Associate Dean of Instruction	Ms. Nancy KOLL
10	Executive Business Director	Ms. Phoebe WOOD
37	Director of Financial Aid	Ms. Inesha KELLY
09	Dir Institutional Research/Plng	Mr. Brian TRZEBIATOWSKI
13	Director Information Technology	Mr. Anthony GAMBOA
109	Director of Auxiliary Services	Ms. Dina LEILER
15	Human Resources Director	Ms. Griselda SILVA
38	Director of Wellness Center	Vacant
19	Director of Security	Mr. Jack MURPHY
06	Registrar	Vacant
41	Athletic Director	Mr. John MCDONNELL
51	Dean of Adult Education	Ms. Emily ANDERSON
51	Dean Professional & Personal Dev	Ms. Alba PEZZAROSSI
12	Dean of HPVEC	Mr. Kenneth SANTIAGO
31	Community Affairs Liaison	Ms. Iris MILLAN
04	Executive Office Manager	Ms. Margaret KLUZA
36	Dean of College to Careers (C2C)	Ms. Khallai TAYLOR

*Malcolm X College, One of the City Colleges of Chicago (C)

1900 W. Jackson Boulevard, Chicago IL 60612-3197
County: Cook FICE Identification: 001650
Unit ID: 144166
Telephone: (312) 850-7000 Carnegie Class: Assoc/HVT-High Non
FAX Number: (312) 850-7039 Calendar System: Semester
URL: www.ccc.edu/malcolmx
Established: 1911 Annual Undergrad Tuition & Fees (In-District): $3,506
Enrollment: 5,550 Coed
Affiliation or Control: State/Local IRS Status: 501(c)3
Highest Offering: Associate Degree
Accreditation: NH, ADNUR, COARC, DH, EMT, FUSER, @PTAA, RAD, SURGT

Code	Title	Name
02	Interim President	Mr. David A. SANDERS
05	Int Vice Pres Acad/Student Affairs	Dr. Kimberly HOLLINGSWORTH
32	Dean Student Services	Dr. Tasha WILLIAMS
10	Exec Director Business Operations	Ms. Tiffany DIXON
04	Executive Office Manager	Mrs. Alanna S. WITHERSPOON
15	Director of Human Resources	Mr. Stanley BEAMON
20	Interim Dean Instruction	Vacant
20	Assoc Dean Instruction	Mr. Byron A. JAVIER
13	Director Information Technology	Mr. Lonnie WASHINGTON
06	Registrar	Mr. Jeffery WONDERS
35	Assoc Dean Student Services	Mr. Mario DIAZ
37	Director Financial Aid	Ms. Tamika CARSON
88	Director Child Care Center	Ms. Aisha RUTHER
19	Director Security/Public Safety	Mrs. Angela HEARTS-GLASS
18	Chief Facilities/Physical Plant	Mr. John MORLEY
08	Librarian	Ms. CM WINTERS-PALACIO
21	Business Manager	Mr. Richard SLATER
76	Dean Health Sciences Programs	Mr. Roy WALKER, III
20	Assoc Dean Instruction	Dr. Carleta ALSTON
56	Dean Adult Education Programs	Ms. Pamela LYNCH
51	Dean Continuing Education	Vacant
66	Int Dean City Col Chicago/Nurs Pgm	Dr. James RICE
88	Assoc Dean Student Development	Ms. Lisa WILLIS
88	Assoc Dean Health Careers	Dr. Amy GRAY
36	Dir Career Planning/Placement	Ms. Toya JOHNSON
103	Director Workforce Partnerships	Ms. Rhonda HARDEMON
26	Director of Public Relations	Mr. Daniel STERNFIELD
46	Director of Strategic Initiatives	Vacant
109	Director of Auxiliary Services	Mrs. Jessica HOLLOWAY
88	Sr Mgr Accreditation and Compliance	Dr. Cherie N. MEADOR

College of DuPage (D)

425 Fawell Boulevard, Glen Ellyn IL 60137-6599
County: DuPage FICE Identification: 006656
Unit ID: 144865
Telephone: (630) 942-2800 Carnegie Class: Assoc/MT-VT-High Non
FAX Number: (630) 858-9399 Calendar System: Semester
URL: www.cod.edu
Established: 1965 Annual Undergrad Tuition & Fees (In-District): $4,050
Enrollment: 28,678 Coed
Affiliation or Control: State/Local IRS Status: 501(c)3
Highest Offering: Associate Degree
Accreditation: #NH, ACFEI, ADNUR, ART, CAHIIM, COARC, CSHSE, DH, DMS, MAC, NMT, POLYT, PTAA, RAD, SURGA, SURGT

Code	Title	Name
01	President	Dr. Ann RONDEAU
13	Vice Pres Information Technology	Mr. Chuck CURRIER
45	VP Planning & Inst Effectiveness	Mr. James BENTE
15	Vice President Human Resources	Ms. Linda SANDS-VANKERK
102	Interim Exec Dir COD Foundation	Ms. Karen KUHN
14	Asst VP Info Sys/Multimedia Svcs	Ms. Donna BERLINER
32	Vice President Student Affairs	Mr. Earl DOWLING
49	Dean Liberal Arts	Dr. Daniel LLOYD
51	Dean Cont Ed/Extended Learning	Dr. Joseph CASSIDY
32	Dean Student Affairs	Ms. Susan M. MARTIN
10	Interim Controller	Mr. Scott BRADY
18	Dir Facilities Planning and Dev	Mr. Bruce SCHMIEDL
06	Dean Admiss/Registration/Records	Ms. Jane L. SMITH
09	Director Research & Analytics	Mr. Eugene YE
116	Internal Auditor	Mr. James E. MARTNER
57	Director Performing Arts	Mrs. Diana MARTINEZ
41	Director Athletics	Mr. Paul ZAKOWSKI
25	Director of Grants	Ms. Barbara ABROMITIS
86	Director Legislative Relations	Ms. Mary Ann MILLUSH
19	Director & Chief COD Police Dept	Mr. Joseph MULLIN
79	Associate Dean Humanities	Dr. Sandra MARTINS
26	Dir Marketing & Creative Svcs	Ms. Laurie JORGENSEN
16	Director Labor & Emp Relations	Ms. Mia IGYARTO
83	Assoc Dean Social & Behav Sciences	Ms. Marianne HUNNICUTT
81	Assoc Dean Math & Physical Sciences	Mr. Thomas SCHRADER
07	Manager Admissions & Outreach	Ms. Tamara MCCLAIN

College of Lake County (E)

19351 W Washington Street, Grayslake IL 60030-1198
County: Lake FICE Identification: 007694
Unit ID: 146472
Telephone: (847) 543-2000 Carnegie Class: Assoc/HVT-High Non
FAX Number: N/A Calendar System: Semester
URL: www.clcillinois.edu
Established: 1967 Annual Undergrad Tuition & Fees (In-District): $3,780
Enrollment: 14,964 Coed
Affiliation or Control: Local IRS Status: 501(c)3
Highest Offering: Associate Degree
Accreditation: NH, ADNUR, CAHIIM, DH, MAC, PHLEB, RAD, SURGT

Code	Title	Name
01	Interim President	Dr. Richard J. HANEY
11	Vice Pres Administrative Affs	Mr. Kenneth GOTSCH
32	Interim Provost Student Devel	Ms. Karen HLAVIN
05	Interim Provost Educational Affairs	Ms. Alyssa O'BRIEN
06	Registrar	Ms. Jennifer MALLER
12	Dean Southlake Campus	Dr. Vicky CVITKOVIC
12	Dean Lakeshore Campus	Dr. Alphonso BALDWIN
08	Dean Library/Testing & Acad Success	Ms. Tanya WOLTMANN
10	Controller	Ms. Connie KRAVITZ
50	Dean of Business/Social Science Div	Dr. Jeffrey STOMPER
76	Dean Biological/Health Sciences	Ms. Maureen ROBINSON
79	Dean Comm Arts/Humanities/Fine Arts	Mr. Roland G. MILLER
54	Int Dean Engr/Math/Physical Science	Mr. Jeffrey ANDREWS
51	Dean Adult Basic Education/GED/ESL	Dr. Arlene SANTOS-GEORGE
38	Int Dean Counsel/Advising/Transfer	Ms. Sylvia JOHNSON
103	Exec Director Community Programming	Ms. Roneida MARTIN
26	Director Public Relations & Mktg	Ms. Anne O'CONNELL
35	Dean Student Life	Ms. Teresa AGUINALDO
102	Executive Director CLC Foundation	Ms. Karen SCHMIDT
15	Exec Director Human Resources	Ms. Julia GUINEY
88	Exec Dir James Lumber Ctr Perf Arts	Ms. Gwethalyn BRONNER
09	Exec Dir/Inst Effect/Plan/Research	Dr. Sean HOGAN
41	Director of Athletics/Title IX	Mr. Nic SCANDRETT
86	Dir Resource Dev/Legislative Affrs	Mr. Nick C. KALLIERIS
13	Chief Info Ofcr/Info Tech Svcs	Ms. Lynn BUTLER
14	Director User Services/User Spport	Mr. David AYKROID
109	Dir Business & Auxiliary Services	Ms. Michele REYNOLDS
88	Dir Application Svcs/Applic Develop	Mr. Jay MEYER
88	Director Student Services Lakeshore	Mr. David WEATHERSPOON
18	Director Facilities Administration	Mr. Mike WELCH
88	Dir Children's Learning Center	Ms. Sandra GROENINGER
22	Dir Ofc Students with Disabilities	Mr. Thomas CROWE
19	Chief of Police/CLC Police Dept	Mr. Thomas GUENTHER
36	Exec Dir Career/Placement Services	Ms. Sylvia M. JOHNSON JONES
66	Director Nursing Education	Vacant
88	Director Judicial Services	Vacant
23	Director Health Services	Ms. Michelle M. GRACE
37	Director Financial Aid	Ms. Erin FOWLES
88	Director Educational Technology	Mr. Scott RIAL
88	Director Professional Development	Ms. Carol EWING
88	Director Technical Services	Mr. James SENFT
100	Chief of Staff	Mr. Derrick HARDEN
07	Director Admissions/Recruitment	Mr. Jason SARNA

College of Lake County Lakeshore Campus (F)

33 North Genesee Street, Waukegan IL 60085
Telephone: (847) 543-2191 Identification: 770073
Accreditation: &NH

College of Lake County Southlake Campus (G)

1120 South Milwaukee Avenue, Vernon Hills IL 60061
Telephone: (847) 543-6501 Identification: 770072
Accreditation: &NH

Columbia College Chicago (H)

600 S Michigan Avenue, Chicago IL 60605-1996
County: Cook FICE Identification: 001665
Unit ID: 144281
Telephone: (312) 369-1000 Carnegie Class: Masters/M
FAX Number: (312) 369-8069 Calendar System: Semester
URL: www.colum.edu
Established: 1890 Annual Undergrad Tuition & Fees: $25,334
Enrollment: 8,961 Coed
Affiliation or Control: Independent Non-Profit IRS Status: 501(c)3
Highest Offering: Master's
Accreditation: NH, CIDA

Code	Title	Name
01	President and CEO	Dr. Kwang-Wu KIM
05	Sr VP Academic Affairs/Provost	Dr. Stanley WEARDEN
10	Sr VP Business Affairs/CFO	Mr. Jerry TARRER
43	VP Legal Affairs/General Counsel	Ms. Patricia BERGESON
30	VP Development/Alumni Relations	Mr. Shawn WAX
32	VP Student Affairs	Dr. Sharon WILSON-TAYLOR
49	Dean School Liberal Arts/Sciences	Dr. Steven COREY
57	Dean School of Fine/Performing Arts	Ms. Onye OZUZU
45	Planning and Compliance	Ms. Anne FOLEY
18	AVP Facilities/Operations	Mr. John KAVOURIS
35	Dean of Students	Mr. John PELRINE
19	AVP Safety & Security	Mr. Ronald SODINI
15	AVP of Human Res	Ms. Norma DE JESUS
09	AVP Institutional Effectiveness	Mr. Royal DAWSON
84	AVP Enrollment Management	Mr. Jeffrey MEECE
37	AVP Student Financial Svcs	Ms. Cynthia GRUNDEN
13	AVP Technology Services	Mr. Byron NASH
36	Assoc Dean Career Development	Mr. Erik FRIEDMAN
26	VP Marketing Communications	Ms. Deborah MAUE
96	Director of Purchasing	Mr. Thomas RUSSELL
35	Assistant Dean of Student Life	Ms. Sheila CARTER
85	Dir International Student Affairs	Ms. Gigi POSEJPAL
06	Registrar	Ms. Keri WALTERS
39	Director of Residence Life	Ms. Mary OAKES

Concordia University Chicago (I)

7400 Augusta Street, River Forest IL 60305-1499
County: Cook FICE Identification: 001666
Unit ID: 144351
Telephone: (708) 771-8300 Carnegie Class: Spec-4-yr-Other

FAX Number: (708) 209-3176 Calendar System: Semester
URL: www.cuchicago.edu
Established: 1864 Annual Undergrad Tuition & Fees: $30,630
Enrollment: 5,239 Coed
Affiliation or Control: Lutheran Church - Missouri Synod
IRS Status: 501(c)3
Highest Offering: Doctorate
Accreditation: NH, CACREP, CAEPN, MUS

01 President .... Dr. Daniel GARD
05 Sr Vice President for Academics .... Dr. John ZILLMAN
102 President for Foundation .... Mr. James M. MILLER
45 Sr VP for Planning & Research .... Dr. Alan E. MEYER
10 Vice President for Finance .... Mr. Tom HALLETT
11 Vice President for Administration .... Dr. Dennis E. WITTE
84 Sr VP Enrollment/Student Svcs .... Ms. Evelyn P. BURDICK
32 Vice President Student Services .... Mr. Jeff HYNES
88 Asst Vice President for Enrollment .... Ms. Gwen E. KANELOS
26 Asst Vice Pres Marketing .... Mr. Eric MATANYI
49 Dean College Arts & Sciences .... Dr. Rachel EELLS
53 Dean College Education .... Dr. Kevin BRANDON
50 Dean College of Business .... Dr. Claudia SANTIN
107 Dean Col of Innovation & Prof Pgms .... Dr. Thomas JANDRIS
09 Director Institutional Research .... Ms. Elizabeth OWOLABI
37 Director Student Financial Planning .... Ms. Aida ASENCIO-PINTO
06 Registrar .... Mr. Gilbert MARTINEZ
08 Director of Library Services .... Ms. Yana V. SERDYUK
88 Director of Degree Completion .... Dr. Carol J. REISECK
36 Director Career Services .... Mr. Gerald PINOTTI
15 Director of Human Resources .... Ms. Peg O'BRIEN
18 Director of Physical Plant .... Ms. Linda HOLOWICKI
88 Assistant VP of Administration .... Mr. Glen D. STEINER
29 Director of Alumni Relations .... Ms. Paige CRAIG
38 Director Schmieding Counseling Ctr .... Dr. Carol A. JABS
109 Director of Auxiliary Services .... Mr. Pete D. BECKER
41 Director of Athletics .... Mr. Peter D. GNAN
21 Director of Business Services .... Ms. Aileen POL
114 Director of Budget Services .... Ms. Tina NEPOMUCENO
39 Director University Housing .... Ms. Jessica KLINGBERG
42 University Pastor .... Rev. Jeffrey LEININGER
24 Dir of Media Production Services .... Mr. James A. KOSINSKY
19 Director of Public Safety .... Mr. David WITKEN
121 Director of Academic Advising ...... Ms. Rosemarie GARCIA-HILLS
96 Director of Purchasing .... Ms. Denise JAMES
91 Manager of Admin Information System .... Ms. Linda C. BERRY
85 International Student Coordinator .... Ms. Chyvonne GIBSON
123 Exec Director Graduate Admission .... Ms. Deborah NESS

Coyne College (A)

330 North Green Street, Chicago IL 60607-1300
County: Cook FICE Identification: 007549
Unit ID: 144485
Telephone: (773) 577-8100 Carnegie Class: Assoc/HVT-High Non
FAX Number: (312) 226-3818 Calendar System: Other
URL: www.coynecollege.edu
Established: 1899 Annual Undergrad Tuition & Fees: N/A
Enrollment: 522 Coed
Affiliation or Control: Proprietary IRS Status: Proprietary
Highest Offering: Associate Degree
Accreditation: ACCSC, MAAB

01 President .... Mr. Russell T. FREEMAN
05 Director of Education .... Virginia HANSON
07 Director of Admissions .... Claudia MACIAS-SILVERMAN
06 Registrar .... Vacant
08 Librarian .... Diana BARTHELEMY
36 Director of Career Services .... Jenny GONZALEZ
37 Director of Financial Aid .... Ashley TUCHTEN

Danville Area Community College (B)

2000 E Main Street, Danville IL 61832-5199
County: Vermilion FICE Identification: 001669
Unit ID: 144564
Telephone: (217) 443-3222 Carnegie Class: Assoc/HVT-High Non
FAX Number: (217) 443-8560 Calendar System: Semester
URL: www.dacc.edu
Established: 1949 Annual Undergrad Tuition & Fees (In-District): $4,425
Enrollment: 2,692 Coed
Affiliation or Control: State/Local IRS Status: 501(c)3
Highest Offering: Associate Degree
Accreditation: NH, ADNUR, CAHIIM, RAD

01 President .... Dr. Stephen D. NACCO
04 Admin Asst to the Pres/Board Sec .... Ms. Kerri L. THURMAN
05 VP Instruction & Student Svcs .... Mr. David L. KIETZMANN
15 Director Human Resources/AA Ofcr .... Ms. Jill A. CRANMORE
10 Chief Financial Officer .... Ms. Tammy L. CLARK-BETANCOURT
11 Director Administrative Services ... Mr. R. Michael CUNNINGHAM
84 Dean Student Services .... Ms. Stacy L. EHMEN
102 Foundation Executive Director .... Ms. Tracy D. WAHLFELDT
26 Director Marketing/Col Relations .... Ms. Lara L. CONKLIN
09 Dir Institutional Effectiveness .... Mr. Bob MATTSON
103 Executive Director of JTP .... Mr. Brian C. HENSGEN
21 Controller .... Ms. Debra L. KNIGHT
37 Director of Financial Aid .... Ms. Janet M. INGARGIOLA
91 Director of Admin Data Systems .... Mr. Kim H. COLWELL
90 Director Computer & Network Svcs .... Mr. Mark BARNES
88 Director of Adult Education .... Ms. Laura M. WILLIAMS
50 Dean Business & Technology .... Mr. Bruce M. RAPE
49 Dean Liberal Arts and Library Servi .... Dr. Penny J. MCCONNELL

81 Dean Math & Sciences .... Ms. Kathy R. STURGEON
41 Athletic Director .... Mr. Tim M. BUNTON
88 Director Small Business Development .... Ms. Carol NICHOLS
07 Director Admissions & Registrar .... Ms. Cindy J. PECK
121 Director Student Support Services .... Ms. Shanay M. WRIGHT
36 Coordinator Career Services .... Ms. Carla M. BOYD
88 Coordinator Recruitment .... Ms. Dawn S. NASSER
19 Director Security/Safety .... Mr. Greg FEGETT

DePaul University (C)

1 E Jackson Boulevard, Chicago IL 60604-2287
County: Cook FICE Identification: 001671
Unit ID: 144740
Telephone: (312) 362-8610 Carnegie Class: DU-Mod
FAX Number: (312) 362-5322 Calendar System: Quarter
URL: www.depaul.edu
Established: 1898 Annual Undergrad Tuition & Fees: $37,626
Enrollment: 23,539 Coed
Affiliation or Control: Roman Catholic IRS Status: 501(c)3
Highest Offering: Doctorate
Accreditation: NH, ANEST, CEA, CLPSY, LAW, MUS, NURSE, PH, SPAA, SW

01 President .... Dr. A. Gabriel ESTEBAN
00 Chancellor .... Rev. Dennis H. HOLTSCHNEIDER, CM
05 Provost .... Dr. Marten L. DENBOER
10 Executive Vice President .... Mr. Jeffrey BETHKE
101 Sec of Univ/VP Teaching & Learning .... Rev. Edward R. UDOVIC
32 VP Student Affairs .... Dr. Gene ZDZIARSKI
84 Sr Vice Pres Enroll Mgmt/Marketing .... Dr. David H. KALSBEEK
111 Sr Vice Pres for Advancement .... Ms. Erin MINNE
15 Vice President Human Resources .... Ms. Stephanie SMITH
18 Vice President Facilities Operation .... Mr. Robert J. JANIS
43 Vice President & General Counsel .... Dr. Jose D. PADILLA
29 Asst VP Alumni Engagement/Outreac .... Ms. Tracy KRAHL
28 VP Inst Diversity & Equity .... Dr. Elizabeth F. ORTIZ
26 VP Public Relations & Communication .... Ms. Linda BLAKLEY
20 Assoc Provost Academic Affairs .... Dr. Caryn CHADEN
106 Assoc VP Academic Affairs Online .... Dr. GianMario BESANA
45 VP Planning & Presidential Admin .... Dr. Jay BRAATZ
13 VP Information Services .... Mr. Robert MCCORMICK
35 Assoc Vice Pres Student Development .... Dr. Peggy BURKE
22 Assoc VP Diversity/Empowerment/Incl .... Mr. Rico TYLER
09 AVP Inst Research/Market Analytics .... Dr. Liz SANDERS
88 AVP Enrollment Management/ Marketing .... Mr. Jon BOECKENSTEDT
36 AVP Div Planning & Mgmt/Career Ctr .... Ms. Jane MCGRATH
42 Assoc VP University Ministry .... Mr. Mark LABOE
108 AVP Planning/Opers & Assess ...... Dr. Ellen MEENTS-DECAIGNY
27 Exec Dir News & Integrated Content .... Ms. Carol HUGHES
88 Senior Executive University Mission .... Rev. Edward R. UDOVIC, CM
21 Controller .... Ms. Sherri SIDLER
90 Dir Faculty Instructional Tech Svcs .... Dr. Sharon GUAN
37 Assoc Vice Pres Financial Aid .... Ms. Paula LUFF
25 VP for Research Services .... Dr. Lawrence HAMER
07 Associate Director of Admission .... Ms. Cass JOHNSON
19 Director Public Safety .... Mr. Robert WACHOWSKI
38 Director Student Counseling .... Dr. Jeffery LANFEAR
39 Director of Housing Operations .... Mr. Rick MORECI
41 Athletics Director .... Ms. Jean PONSETTO
06 Director of Registration/Records .... Ms. Patricia HUERTA
104 Director Study Abroad .... Ms. Nobi HAYASHI
123 Asst VP Grad & Adult Recruit & Adm ...... Ms. Suzanne DEPEDER
07 Dean of Undergraduate Admission .... Ms. Carlene KLAAS
77 Dean Computing & Digital Media .... Dr. David MILLER
49 Dean Liberal Arts & Social Sciences .... Dr. Guillermo VASQUEZ DE VELASCO
50 Int Dean Driehaus Business College .... Dr. Misty JOHANSEN
60 Dean Col of Communication .... Dr. Salma GHANEM
64 Dean School of Music .... Dr. Ronald CALTABIANO
61 Dean College of Law .... Ms. Jennifer R. PEREA
57 Dean Theatre School .... Mr. John CULBERT
53 Dean School of Education .... Dr. Paul ZIONTS
51 Int Dean School for New Learning .... Dr. Corinne ALICEA
76 Dean Col of Science & Health .... Dr. Gerald P. KOOCHER
08 Head Librarian .... Dr. Scott WALTER
04 Administrative Asst to President .... Ms. Phyllis GREGG
100 Deputy Chief of Staff .... Ms. Annette WILSON
86 Assoc VP Community & Govt Relations .... Mr. Peter COFFEY

*DeVry University - Home Office (D)

3005 Highland Parkway, Downers Grove IL 60515-5799
County: DuPage FICE Identification: 001672
Unit ID: 144777
Telephone: (800) 733-3879 Carnegie Class: N/A
FAX Number: (630) 571-0317
URL: www.devry.edu

01 President of DeVry University .... Mr. Robert PAUL
26 Chief Marketing Officer .... Ms. Melissa ESBENSHADE
11 Chief Operating Officer .... Mr. James BARTHOLOMEW
84 VP Enrollment Management .... Ms. Elise AWWAD
05 Provost/VP Academic Affs DVU .... Mr. Shantanu BOSE
20 Associate Provost .... Ms. Donna REKAU
10 VP Finance .... Ms. Kerry KOPERA
103 VP Workforce Solutions .... Mr. Joseph MOZDEN
15 Sr Director HR .... Mr. David BARNETT

*DeVry University - Chicago Campus (E)

3300 N Campbell Avenue, Chicago IL 60618-5916
County: Cook FICE Identification: 010727
Unit ID: 482477
Telephone: (773) 929-8500 Carnegie Class: Not Classified
FAX Number: (773) 348-1780 Calendar System: Semester
URL: www.devry.edu
Established: 1931 Annual Undergrad Tuition & Fees: $19,948
Enrollment: 22,273 Coed
Affiliation or Control: Proprietary IRS Status: Proprietary
Highest Offering: Master's
Accreditation: NH, CAHIIM, ENGT

02 Campus Dean .... Mr. Piotr LECHOWSKI
05 Group Dean Acad Excellence .... Mr. Timothy ZOREK
07 Director Admissions .... Mr. Drew LOGAN
32 Group Dir Student Central .... Mr. Brendan AUBIN
08 Regional Librarian .... Mr. Jason ROSSI

† Regional accreditation is carried under the parent institution in Downers Grove, IL.

Dominican University (F)

7900 W Division Street, River Forest IL 60305-1099
County: Cook FICE Identification: 001750
Unit ID: 148496
Telephone: (708) 366-2490 Carnegie Class: Masters/L
FAX Number: (708) 524-5990 Calendar System: Semester
URL: www.dom.edu
Established: 1901 Annual Undergrad Tuition & Fees: $31,570
Enrollment: 3,696 Coed
Affiliation or Control: Roman Catholic IRS Status: 501(c)3
Highest Offering: Doctorate
Accreditation: NH, #ARCPA, CAEPN, DIETC, DIETD, LIB, NURSE, SW

01 President .... Dr. Donna M. CARROLL
05 Interim Provost .... Dr. Jeffrey CARLSON
20 Associate Provost .... Dr. David H. KRAUSE
10 VP Finance/Business Affairs .... Mr. Mark TITZER
42 VP Mission & Ministry .... Dr. Claire NOONAN
111 VP University Advancement .... Ms. Grace J. CICHOMSKA
84 Interim VP Enrollment Management .... Ms. Pam JOHNSON
13 VP Technology & Opers/IT/CIO .... Ms. Jill ALBIN-HILL
07 AVP Enroll Mgt/Dir Undergrad Admiss .... Mr. Glenn HAMILTON
32 Dean of Students .... Ms. Trudi GOGGIN
50 Dean Brennan School of Business .... Dr. Roberto CURCI
62 Dean School of Info Studies .... Ms. Kate MAREK
53 Interim Exec Dir School of Educ .... Dr. Colleen REARDON
70 Dean School of Social Work .... Dr. Charles STOOPS
49 Interim Dean Rosary College .... Mr. Chad ROHMAN
107 Assistant Provost SPCS .... Mr. Matthew J. HLINAK
08 University Librarian .... Ms. Felice E. MACIEJEWSKI
06 Registrar .... Mr. Michael Patrick MILLER
36 Director Career Development .... Ms. Keli WOJCIECHOWSKI
29 Director Alumnae/i Relations .... Ms. Alysha BIEHL
09 Dir Institutional Rsrch/Assessment .... Ms. Elizabeth SILK
15 Exec Director Human Resources .... Ms. Roberta MCMAHON
18 Acting Dir Buildings & Grounds .... Mr. Guy MASON
07 Director Transfer/Adult Admission ...... Mr. Michael MORSOVILLO
37 Director Financial Aid .... Ms. Victoria SPIVAK
23 Director Wellness Center .... Ms. Elizabeth RITZMAN
41 Director Athletics .... Mr. Erick BAUMANN
104 Director International Studies .... Dr. Sue PONREMY
28 Chief Diversity Officer .... Dr. Sheila RADFORD-HILL

East-West University (G)

816 S Michigan Avenue, Chicago IL 60605-2185
County: Cook FICE Identification: 021686
Unit ID: 144883
Telephone: (312) 939-0111 Carnegie Class: Bac-A&S
FAX Number: (312) 939-0083 Calendar System: Quarter
URL: www.eastwest.edu
Established: 1980 Annual Undergrad Tuition & Fees: $20,820
Enrollment: 539 Coed
Affiliation or Control: Independent Non-Profit IRS Status: 501(c)3
Highest Offering: Baccalaureate
Accreditation: NH

01 Chancellor .... Dr. M. Wasiullah KHAN
05 Provost .... Dr. Madhu JAIN
20 Associate Provost .... Dr. Ekkehard T. WILKE
30 Dean Development/Univ Relations .... Mr. Zafar A. MALIK
32 Director Counseling/Student Affairs .... Ms. Chelious HIGGINS
07 Director of Admissions .... Vacant
37 Director of Financial Aid .... Mr. Cesar CAMPOS
06 Registrar .... Ms. Asma ADNAN
04 Assistant to the Chancellor .... Ms. Ghada MORRAR
19 Director of Security .... Mr. Tasleem RAJA
10 Director of Business .... Dr. Madhu JAIN
44 Dir Devel/Univ Rels/Publications .... Ms. Barbara ABRAJANO
26 Manager Public Relations .... Vacant
18 Facilities Manager .... Mr. Tasleem RAJA
85 International Student Advisor .... Mr. Rashed JAHANGIR
21 Associate Business Officer .... Ms. Deborah DEJI
84 Director Enrollment Management .... Mr. Gus PYROULIS

Eastern Illinois University (A)

600 Lincoln Avenue, Charleston IL 61920-3099
County: Coles FICE Identification: 001674
Unit ID: 144892
Telephone: (217) 581-5000 Carnegie Class: Masters/L
FAX Number: (217) 581-2722 Calendar System: Semester
URL: www.eiu.edu
Established: 1895 Annual Undergrad Tuition & Fees (In-State): $11,580
Enrollment: 8,520 Coed
Affiliation or Control: State IRS Status: 501(c)3
Highest Offering: Beyond Master's But Less Than Doctorate
Accreditation: NH, AAFCS, ART, #CAATE, CACREP, CAEPN, DIETD, DIETI, JOUR, MUS, NAIT, NRPA, NURSE, SP, THEA

01 President Dr. David M. GLASSMAN
05 Provost/Vice Pres Academic Affairs Dr. Jay D. GATRELL
10 Int Vice Pres Bus Affairs/Treasurer Mr. Paul A. MCCANN
32 Int Associate VP Student Affairs Ms. Lynette DRAKE
111 Vice Pres University Advancement Vacant
20 Associate VP Academic Affairs Mr. Jeffrey F. CROSS
35 Special Asst to VP Student Affairs Ms. Jennifer L. SIPES
13 Asst VP for Tech Svcs Mr. John HENDERSON
26 Asst VP Integ Marketing/Communic Vacant
08 Dean of Library Services Vacant
92 Dean Honors College Dr. Richard ENGLAND
15 Director Human Resources Vacant
43 General Counsel Mr. Robert L. MILLER
22 Int Director Civil Rights Dr. Shawn PEOPLES
45 Dir Planning/Budgeting/Research Vacant
07 Director of Admissions Ms. Kelly MILLER
37 Int Sr Assoc Dir of Financial Aid Ms. Amanda STARWALT
06 Registrar Ms. Amy J. LYNCH
29 Director Alumni Svc/Community Rels Mr. Steven W. RICH
18 Dir Facilities/Planning Mgmt Mr. Timothy P. ZIMMER
96 Dir Procur/Disburs/Contract Svc Ms. Kay E. MCELWEE
38 Director of Counseling Center Vacant
25 Director of Research & Grants Dr. Robert W. CHESNUT
41 Director of Athletics Mr. Thomas R. MICHAEL
93 Director of Minority Affairs Ms. Mona DAVENPORT
39 Director of Housing/Dining Service Mr. Mark A. HUDSON
21 Interim Director Business Services Ms. Linda C. HOLLOWAY
36 Asst Dir of Career Services Ms. Allison L. FREES-WILLIAMS
51 Dean Continuing Education Dr. Jeffrey F. CROSS
58 Int Dean Graduate School Dr. Ryan C. HENDRICKSON
81 Int Dean College Sciences Dr. Doug KLARUP
50 Dean Lumpkin Col Bus/Appl Sci Dr. Mahyar IZADI
79 Int Dean College Arts/Humanities Dr. Anita SHELTON
53 Int Dean College Education Mr. Doug J. BOWER

Elgin Community College (B)

1700 Spartan Drive, Elgin IL 60123-7193
County: Kane FICE Identification: 001675
Unit ID: 144944
Telephone: (847) 697-1000 Carnegie Class: Assoc/HVT-High Non
FAX Number: (847) 214-7995 Calendar System: Semester
URL: www.elgin.edu
Established: 1949 Annual Undergrad Tuition & Fees (In-District): $3,012
Enrollment: 10,336 Coed
Affiliation or Control: Local IRS Status: 501(c)3
Highest Offering: Associate Degree
Accreditation: NH, ADNUR, COMTA, CSHSE, DA, HT, MLTAD, PTAA, RAD, RADMAG, SURGT

01 President Dr. David SAM
10 Vice Pres Business/Finance Ms. Sharon KONNY
05 Int VP Teaching/Learning/Stdnt Dev Ms. Peggy HEINRICH
20 Asst VP Teach/Lrng/Stdnt Dev Ms. Marcy THOMPSON
20 Dean Academic Dev/Learning Resource Dr. Mi HU
88 Int Dean Sustain/Safety/Career Tech Mr. Marc BATTISTA
83 Dean Comm/Behavioral Sciences Dr. Ruixuan MAO
57 Dean Liberal/Visual/Performing Arts Ms. Mary HATCH
32 Dean of Student Services Dr. Gregory ROBINSON
51 Interim Dean Adult Basic Education Ms. Elizabeth HOBSON
76 Dean Hlth Prof/Int Dn Math/Sci/Eng Ms. Wendy MILLER
88 Assoc Dean Comm/Behavioral Sciences Dr. Mary PERKINS
106 Assoc Dean Inst Improve/Dist Lrng Mr. Timothy MOORE
88 Asc Dean TRIO/Reten/Stdnt Outreach Dr. L. Bruce AUSTIN
18 Managing Director Facilities Mr. Cal BYRD
13 Chief Information Officer Dr. Michael CHAHINO
26 Exec Director Communications Ms. Toya WEBB
30 Exec Dir Inst Advance/ECC Found Ms. Katherine SAWYER
88 Managing Dir Inst Comp/Curr Ms. Annamarie SCHOPEN
45 Sr Exec Dir Planning/Inst Effect Dr. Philip GARBER
09 Managing Dir Institutional Research Mr. David RUDDEN
37 Director Financial Aid/Scholarships Ms. Amy PERRIN
21 Controller Ms. Heather SCHOLL
84 Managing Director Enrollment Svcs Dr. Jennifer MCCLURE
90 Director Academic Computing Ms. Karin STACY
22 Paralegal/EEO/AA Title IX/FOIA Ofcr Ms. Marilyn PRENTICE
41 Director Athletics & Wellness Mr. Kent PAYNE
96 Director Business Services Ms. Melissa TAIT
36 Acad Advising/Transfer/Career Svcs Ms. Peggy GUNDRUM
27 Director of Marketing Ms. Heidi HEALY
35 Director Orientation/Student Life Ms. Amybeth MAURER
14 Sr Director Technology Services Mr. Phil HOWARD
86 Dir Cmty Engagemnt/Legislative Affs Ms. Paula AMENTA
04 Sr Exec Asst to Pres/Board Recorder Ms. Diane KERRUISH

Elmhurst College (C)

190 Prospect, Elmhurst IL 60126-3296
County: DuPage FICE Identification: 001676
Unit ID: 144962
Telephone: (630) 279-4100 Carnegie Class: Masters/M
FAX Number: (630) 617-3282 Calendar System: 4/1/4
URL: www.elmhurst.edu
Established: 1871 Annual Undergrad Tuition & Fees: $35,500
Enrollment: 3,298 Coed
Affiliation or Control: United Church Of Christ IRS Status: 501(c)3
Highest Offering: Master's
Accreditation: NH, NURSE, @SP

01 President Dr. Troy VANAKEN
10 VP of Finance & Administration/CFO Ms. Karen KISSEL
05 VP Acad Affs/Dean of Faculty Dr. April EDWARDS
13 VP and Chief Information Officer Mr. Kurt ASHLEY
30 VP for Development/Alumni Relations Ms. Valerie DAY
32 Interim Dean of Students Dr. Phil RIORDAN
07 VP for Admission Dr. Timothy RICORDATI
20 Associate Dean of Faculty Dr. Paul ARRIOLA
88 Exec Dir Center for Pro Excellence Dr. Lawrence B. CARROLL
18 Exec Director Facilities Management Mr. Bruce J. MATHER
42 Chaplain Rev. H. Scott MATHENEY
06 Interim Registrar Ms. Linda DUFORT
26 Sr Dir Communications/Public Affs Ms. Desiree CHEN-MENICHINI
08 Director of the Library Ms. Susan S. STEFFEN
36 Director of Career Education Ms. Peggy KILLIAN
21 VP for Finance & Admin Ms. Melinda GIESEKE
38 Director of Counseling Services Dr. Amy SWARR
28 Director of Intercultural Education Vacant
88 Director Development Services Mr. Rodney YOUNG
29 Director of Alumni Engagement Ms. Samantha KILEY
15 Director of Human Resources Vacant
19 Int Exec Dir of Campus Security Ms. Caroline KRAUSE
37 Director of Financial Aid Ms. Ruth PUSICH
07 Executive Director of Admissions Ms. Stephanie LEVENSON
123 Managing Dir Adult/Grad Admission Mr. Tim PANFIL
39 Director of Residence Life Vacant
41 Director Intercollegiate Athletics Mr. Paul KROHN
04 Administrative Asst to President Vacant
101 Assistant to the Board of Trustees Ms. Armaline MIRRETTI
104 Dir Intl Educ & Student Svcs Ms. Gail GILBERT
25 Chief Contracts/Grants Admin Ms. Jill MCWILLIAMS
110 Exec Dir of Development Ms. Meg HOWES
44 Director of Annual Giving Ms. Lori STEINER
50 Dir Ctr for Business & Economics Dr. Gary WILSON
53 Dept Chair Education Dr. Lisa BURKE
96 Director of Purchasing Ms. Donna MALANCA
108 Asst Dean for Assessment & Accred Dr. A. Andrew DAS
58 Asst Dean Grad & Special Programs Dr. Ruiying DING
88 Asst Dean For Faculty Development Dr. Kimberly LAWLER-SAGARIN
88 Asst Dean Programs & Curriculum Dr. Brian WILHITE

Erikson Institute (D)

451 N. Lasalle Street, Chicago IL 60654
County: Cook FICE Identification: 035103
Unit ID: 409254
Telephone: (312) 755-2250 Carnegie Class: Spec-4-yr-Other
FAX Number: (312) 755-0928 Calendar System: Semester
URL: www.erikson.edu
Established: 1966 Annual Graduate Tuition & Fees: N/A
Enrollment: 256 Coed
Affiliation or Control: Independent Non-Profit IRS Status: 501(c)3
Highest Offering: Master's; No Undergraduates
Accreditation: NH, SW

01 President/CEO Geoffrey A. NAGLE
05 Sr VP Academic Affs/Dean of Faculty Jie-Qi CHEN
10 Vice President Finance/CFO Patricia LAWSON
111 Vice Pres Institutional Advancement Cheryl L. MENDELSON
45 VP Inst Effectiveness and Planning Charles CHANG
84 Dean of Enrollment Management Michel FRENDIAN
32 Dean of Students Colette DAVISON
26 Chief Communications Officer Bonita BRODT
13 Chief Information Officer Jonathan FRANK
30 Dir Development/Alumni Relations Vacant
44 Asst Dir Data Systems/Donor Svcs Madeleine HOLDSWORTH

Eureka College (E)

300 E College Avenue, Eureka IL 61530-1500
County: Woodford FICE Identification: 001678
Unit ID: 144971
Telephone: (309) 467-3721 Carnegie Class: Bac-Diverse
FAX Number: (309) 467-6386 Calendar System: Semester
URL: www.eureka.edu
Established: 1855 Annual Undergrad Tuition & Fees: $21,120
Enrollment: 695 Coed
Affiliation or Control: Christian Church (Disciples Of Christ)
IRS Status: 501(c)3
Highest Offering: Baccalaureate
Accreditation: NH

01 President Dr. Jamel WRIGHT
04 Administrative Asst to President Mrs. Jyl ZUBIATE
05 Provost & Dean of the College Dr. Daniel BLANKENSHIP
10 VP Fin/Fac/Chief Financial Officer Mr. Marc PASTERIS
32 Dean of Students Mrs. Shari RICH
111 Vice Pres of Institutional Advance Mr. Michael MURTAGH
06 Registrar Ms. Kendi ONNEN
08 Library Director Mr. Tony GLASS
18 Director of Physical Plant Mr. Daryle EGE
42 Chaplain Rev. Bruce M. FOWLKES
36 Director of Career Services Vacant
13 Director of Computer Services Dr. Kanaka VIJITHA-KUMARA
37 Director of Financial Aid Mrs. Tammy CROTHERS
41 Athletic Director Mr. Steve THOMPSON
29 Director Alumni Relations Mrs. Shellie SCHWANKE
15 Director Personnel Services Mrs. Melody MOUNTS
39 Director Student Housing Mrs. Lisa ALLEN
28 Chief Diversity Officer Dr. Jamel WRIGHT
26 Director of Communications Mr. Bryan MOORE
07 Dean of Admissions Mrs. Pat PROSSER
108 Director Institutional Assessment Dr. Ann FULOP

Fox College (F)

6640 South Cicero Avenue, Bedford Park IL 60638
County: Cook FICE Identification: 025228
Unit ID: 145239
Telephone: (708) 444-4500 Carnegie Class: Spec 2-yr-Health
FAX Number: (708) 802-6585 Calendar System: Semester
URL: www.foxcollege.edu
Established: 1932 Annual Undergrad Tuition & Fees: $15,120
Enrollment: 331 Coed
Affiliation or Control: Proprietary IRS Status: Proprietary
Highest Offering: Associate Degree
Accreditation: NH, DH, MAAB, OTA, PTAA

01 President Mr. Teri TUCCI
08 Head Librarian Ms. Sierra CAMPBELL
36 Director Student Placement Ms. Lisa FENTON
37 Director Student Financial Aid Ms. Kerry DEMARS

Garrett-Evangelical Theological Seminary (G)

2121 Sheridan Road, Evanston IL 60201-3298
County: Cook FICE Identification: 001682
Unit ID: 145275
Telephone: (847) 866-3900 Carnegie Class: Spec-4-yr-Faith
FAX Number: (847) 866-3884 Calendar System: Semester
URL: www.garrett.edu
Established: 1853 Annual Graduate Tuition & Fees: N/A
Enrollment: 337 Coed
Affiliation or Control: United Methodist IRS Status: 501(c)3
Highest Offering: Doctorate; No Undergraduates
Accreditation: NH, THEOL

01 President Dr. Lallene J. RECTOR
05 Vice Pres Academic Affairs/Dean Dr. Luis J. RIVERA
30 Vice President for Development Dr. David L. HEETLAND
84 Vice Pres for Enrollment Management Rev. Becky J. EBERHART
10 Vice President Business Affairs/CFO Mr. Dale MCCLAIN
42 Dean of the Chapel Rev. Tercio JUNKER
45 Dir of Strategic Initiatives Ms. Erin B. MOORE
21 Controller Mr. Bob SUTTON
06 Registrar/Dir of Academic Studies Rev. Vince MCGLOTHIN-ELLER
08 Director of United Library Dr. Lucy CHUNG
18 Director of Buildings & Grounds Ms. Cheryl LARSEN
110 Director of Development Mrs. April MCGLOTHIN-ELLER
112 Director of Stewardship Ms. Ceciley AKINS
37 Director of Financial Aid Mr. Jason GILL
26 Exec Director of Communications Mr. Shane NICHOLS
32 Dean of Students Mr. Benjamin REYNOLDS

Governors State University (H)

1 University Parkway, University Park IL 60484-0975
County: Will FICE Identification: 009145
Unit ID: 145336
Telephone: (708) 534-5000 Carnegie Class: Masters/L
FAX Number: (708) 534-4107 Calendar System: Semester
URL: www.govst.edu
Established: 1969 Annual Undergrad Tuition & Fees (In-State): $10,516
Enrollment: 5,938 Coed
Affiliation or Control: State IRS Status: 501(c)3
Highest Offering: Doctorate
Accreditation: NH, ACBSP, CACREP, CAEPN, HSA, NUR, OT, PTA, SP, SPAA, SW

01 President Dr. Elaine P. MAIMON
05 Provost/VP Academic Affairs Dr. Deborah BORDELON
111 VP Advancement/CEO Foundation Mr. William DAVIS
13 Assoc VP/CIO Information Tech Svcs Mr. John BUENGER
43 Legal Counsel Ms. Alexis KENNEDY
22 Affirmative Action/EO Ms. Alexis KENNEDY
45 Director Budget Planning/Inst Rsrch Ms. Sandra ZURAWSKI
09 Assoc Dir of Institutional Research Mr. Marco KRCATOVICH, II
114 Director Budget & Financial Plng Ms. Kim LAMBERT-THOMAS
29 Director of Alumni Assoc Ms. Cheri GAREY
26 Asst VP of Marketing/Communication Ms. Keisha DYSON
50 Dean College of Business Dr. Jun ZHAO
49 Dean College Arts Sciences Dr. Andrae MARAK
76 Dean Col Health Professions Dr. Elizabeth CADA
53 Dean College Education Dr. Andrea EVANS
32 Dean Student Affairs & Services Dr. Aurelio VALENTE

08 Dean University Library ....Lydia MORROW RUETTEN
06 Registrar ....Mr. Christopher HUANG
37 Director Financial Aid ....Mr. John PERRY
20 Associate Provost/AVP Academic Affs ....Dr. Colleen SEXTON
15 Director Human Resources ....Ms. Joyce COLEMAN
18 Director Physical Plant ....Mr. Jim ZUMERCHIK
19 Int Director Dept Public Safety ....Mr. James MCGEE
38 Dir Student Devel/Counseling Center ....Ms. Kelly MCCARTHY
36 Director of Career Services ....Ms. Darcie R. CAMPOS
96 Dir of Procurement/Auxiliary Svcs ....Ms. Tracy SULLIVAN
04 Executive Asst to President ....Ms. Penny PERDUE
39 Director Student Housing ....Dr. Elizabeth JOSEPH
41 Athletic Director ....Mr. Anthony BATES
86 Director Government Relations ....Ms. Maureen KELLY

Greenville University (A)

315 E College, Greenville IL 62246
County: Bond　FICE Identification: 001684
Unit ID: 145372
Telephone: (618) 664-2800　Carnegie Class: Masters/S
FAX Number: (618) 664-6841　Calendar System: 4/1/4
URL: www.greenville.edu
Established: 1892　Annual Undergrad Tuition & Fees: $25,720
Enrollment: 1,321　Coed
Affiliation or Control: Free Methodist　IRS Status: 501(c)3
Highest Offering: Master's
Accreditation: NH, CAEPT, @SW

01 President ....Dr. Ivan FILBY
05 SVP/Provost/COO ....Dr. Edwin ESTEVEZ
101 Executive Assistant to the Board ....Mrs. Regina ROBART
20 Vice President for Academic Affairs ....Dr. Brian HARTLEY
30 Vice Pres for Development ....Mrs. Linda MYETTE
10 Vice President for Finance ....Mr. Tim DIETZ
29 VP for Intl and Alumni Relations ....Dr. Norman D. HALL
07 Dean of Undergraduate Admissions ....Mr. Karl HATTON
88 Dean of Adult Studies ....Dr. Dave HOLDEN
08 Director of Library ....Mrs. Georgann KURTZ-SHAW
06 Registrar ....Mrs. Michelle SUSSENBACH
37 Director of Financial Aid ....Mr. David KESSINGER
44 Director of Major & Planned Gifts ....Mr. Kent KROBER
42 Dean Chapel & Dir Spiritual Form ....Mrs. Lori GAFFNER
18 Director of Facilities ....Mr. Mark OWENS
26 Director of Marketing ....Vacant
49 Dean School Arts & Sciences ....Dr. Teresa HOLDEN
53 Dean School of Education ....Dr. Mark LAMB
41 Dean of Athletics ....Mr. Tom ACKERMAN
28 Dean of Diversity ....Dr. Eugene DUNKLEY
50 Interim Dean of School of Business ....Dr. Sandra LANG

Harper College (B)

1200 W Algonquin Road, Palatine IL 60067-7398
County: Cook　FICE Identification: 003961
Unit ID: 149842
Telephone: (847) 925-6000　Carnegie Class: Assoc/MT-VT-High Non
FAX Number: (847) 925-6034　Calendar System: Semester
URL: www.harpercollege.edu
Established: 1965　Annual Undergrad Tuition & Fees (In-District): $3,360
Enrollment: 14,532　Coed
Affiliation or Control: State/Local　IRS Status: 501(c)3
Highest Offering: Associate Degree
Accreditation: NH, ACBSP, ADNUR, CAHIIM, DH, DIETT, DMS, #MAC, MUS, PNUR, RAD

01 President ....Dr. Kenneth L. ENDER
100 Chf of Staff/VP Inst Plng Strag AI ....Dr. Maria COONS
05 Provost ....Dr. Judith MARWICK
10 Exec VP Finance & Admin Services ....Dr. Ron ALLY
111 VP and Chief Advancement Officer ....Ms. Laura BROWN
103 VP Wrkfrce Solutions/Assoc Provost ....Ms. Michele' SMITH
20 Assoc Provost/Interdis Student Succ ....Mr. Brian KNETL
15 Chief Human Resources Officer ....Mr. Roger SPAYER
13 Chief Information Officer ....Mr. Patrick BAUER
21 Controller ....Mr. Bret BONNSTETTER
18 Exec Dir of Facilities Management ....Mr. Darryl KNIGHT
84 Asst Provost/Dean Enrollment Svcs ....Ms. Maria MOTEN
32 Asst Provost/Dean Student Dev ....Ms. Sheryl OTTO
88 Asst VP Workfrc Dev/Exec Dean CE ....Dr. Mark MROZINSKI
45 Exec Dir Plng/Research/Inst Eff ......Ms. Darlene SCHLENBECKER
75 Dean Career & Technical Programs ......Dr. Mary Beth OTTINGER
76 Dean Health Careers ....Dr. Kimberly CHAVIS
08 Dean Resources for Learning ....Ms. Njambi KAMOCHE
35 Dean Student Affairs ....Dr. Travaris HARRIS
50 Dean Business & Social Science ....Ms. Kathryn ROGALSKI
81 Dean Mathematics & Sciences ....Dr. Kathy BRUCE
88 Assoc Dean Academy of Teaching Exce ....Dr. Michael BATES
103 Dean Workforce & Economic Devel ....Dr. Rebecca LAKE
49 Dean Liberal Arts ....Dr. Jennifer BERNE
102 Asc Exec Dir Found/Dir Major Gifts ....Ms. Heather ZOLDAK
88 Assoc Dean Interdisc Stdnt Success ....Ms. Darice TROUT
23 Director Health Services ....Dr. Bridget CAHILL
88 Dir New Student Prog/Women's Pgm ....Dr. Vicki ATKINSON
27 Director Marketing Services ....Mr. Mike BARZACCHINI
36 Director Job Placement Resource Ctr ......Ms. Kathleen CANFIELD
91 Director IT Client Services ....Ms. Sue CONTARINO
09 Director Institutional Research ....Dr. Katherine COY
88 Director Adult Educational Dev ....Ms. Andrea FIEBIG
88 Dir One Stop Center/Student Svcs ....Ms. Paula HANLEY
37 Dir Student Financial Assistance ....Ms. Laura MCGEE
66 Director Nursing ....Ms. Julie D'AGOSTINO

07 Dir Student Recruitment & Outreach ....Mr. Robert PARZY
121 Assoc Dean Acad Advising/Counseling ... Ms. Kristen HOFFHINES
41 Director of Athletics & Fitness ....Mr. Doug SPIWAK
19 Chief of Police ....Mr. Paul LEBRECK
88 Campus Architect ....Mr. Steve PETERSEN

Harrington College of Design (C)

200 W Madison, 2nd Floor, Chicago IL 60606-3433
County: Cook　FICE Identification: 020552
Unit ID: 145460
Telephone: (312) 939-4975　Carnegie Class: Spec-4-yr-Arts
FAX Number: (312) 939-8005　Calendar System: Semester
URL: www.harrington.edu
Established: 1931　Annual Undergrad Tuition & Fees: N/A
Enrollment: 154　Coed
Affiliation or Control: Proprietary　IRS Status: Proprietary
Highest Offering: Master's
Accreditation: NH

01 President ....Mr. Max S. SHANGLE

† School is in teach-out plan and plans to close in May, 2018. All of Harrington's classes have been transferred to Columbia College Chicago.

Heartland Community College (D)

1500 W Raab Road, Normal IL 61761-9446
County: McLean　FICE Identification: 030838
Unit ID: 384342
Telephone: (309) 268-8000　Carnegie Class: Assoc/HT-High Non
FAX Number: (309) 268-7999　Calendar System: Semester
URL: www.heartland.edu
Established: 1990　Annual Undergrad Tuition & Fees (In-District): $4,320
Enrollment: 5,298　Coed
Affiliation or Control: State/Local　IRS Status: 501(c)3
Highest Offering: Associate Degree
Accreditation: NH, ADNUR, PTAA, RAD

01 President ....Mr. Robert D. WIDMER
05 Vice Pres Learning/Student Success ....Dr. Rick PEARCE
10 Vice President Business Services ....Mr. Douglas MINTER
111 Vice Pres Cont Educ/Advancement ....Ms. Kelli HILL
20 Assoc VP for Academic Affairs ....Dr. Sarah DIEL-HUNT
88 Dean Student Success ....Ms. Anita MOORE
84 Dean Enrollment Services ....Mr. Padriac SHINVILLE
18 Executive Director of Facilities ....Mr. James HUBBARD
11 Director of Administrative Services ....Ms. Valerie CRAWFORD
13 Chief Information Officer ....Mr. Scott BROSS
21 Controller ....Ms. Sharon MCDONALD
37 Director of Financial Aid ....Mr. Todd BURNS
15 Exec Director Human Resources ....Mrs. Barb LEATHERS
41 Director of Athletics ....Mr. Ryan KNOX
29 Director College Engagement ....Ms. Colleen REYNOLDS
32 Director Student Success ....Ms. Kimberly KELLEY
06 Director of Records ....Ms. Cindy ALFANO
26 Director of Marketing ....Mr. Tim BILL
35 Director of Student Engagement ....Mr. Ian WILSON
36 Dir Advisement/Career Services ....Ms. Lindsay EICKHORST
07 Director of Admissions ....Ms. Candace BROWNLEE

Hebrew Theological College (E)

7135 N Carpenter Road, Skokie IL 60077-3263
County: Cook　FICE Identification: 001685
Unit ID: 145497
Telephone: (847) 982-2500　Carnegie Class: Spec-4-yr-Faith
FAX Number: (847) 674-6381　Calendar System: Semester
URL: www.htc.edu
Established: 1922　Annual Undergrad Tuition & Fees: $16,860
Enrollment: 526　Coordinate
Affiliation or Control: Independent Non-Profit　IRS Status: 501(c)3
Highest Offering: Master's
Accreditation: #NH

01 Chief Executive Officer ....Rabbi Shmuel SCHUMAN
05 Chief Academic Officer ....Dr. Zev ELEFF
100 Chief of Staff ....Ms. Cheryl KARP
20 Rosh Hayeshiva ....Rabbi Avraham FRIEDMAN
11 Vice President for Administration ....Rabbi Sender KUTNER
33 Mashgiach Ruchani-Dean ....Rabbi Zvi ZIMMERMAN
34 Menahel Ruchani-Dean ....Rabbi Binyamin OLSTEIN
34 Assistant Dean Blitstein Institute ....Ms. Rita LIPSHITZ
06 Registrar ....Rabbi Gavriel BACHRACH
07 Director of Admissions ....Rabbi Joshua ZISOOK
30 Director of Development ....Rabbi Gershon SEIF
44 Development Coordinator ....Rabbi Yaakov FRIEDMAN
08 Librarian ....Ms. Eti BERLAND

† Separate campuses for male and female students. Part of the Touro College and University System.

Highland Community College (F)

2998 W Pearl City Road, Freeport IL 61032-9341
County: Stephenson　FICE Identification: 001681
Unit ID: 145521
Telephone: (815) 235-6121　Carnegie Class: Assoc/MT-VT-High Non
FAX Number: (815) 235-6130　Calendar System: Semester
URL: www.highland.edu
Established: 1962　Annual Undergrad Tuition & Fees (In-District): $3,663
Enrollment: 1,804　Coed
Affiliation or Control: State/Local　IRS Status: 501(c)3
Highest Offering: Associate Degree
Accreditation: NH, MAC

01 President ....Mr. Tim HOOD
03 Executive Vice President ....Ms. Chris KUBERSKI
10 Vice Pres Administrative Services ....Ms. Jill M. JANSSEN
32 Vice Pres Student Dev & Support Svc ...Ms. Elizabeth L. GERBER
15 Associate VP Human Resources ....Ms. Rose A. FERGUSON
50 Dean Business & Technology ....Mr. Scott R. ANDERSON
79 Dean Humanities/Social Sci & FA ....Mr. Jim PHILLIPS
81 Assoc Dean Natural Science & Math ......Dr. Brendan C. DUTMER
66 Assoc Dean Nursing & Allied Health ....Ms. Jennifer GROBE
51 Director Adult Education ....Mr. Mark JANSEN
41 Director Athletics ....Mr. Peter E. NORMAN
84 Director of Enrollment & Records ....Mr. Jeremy BRADT
18 Director Facilities & Safety ....Mr. Kurt SIMPSON
37 Director Financial Aid ....Ms. Kathy BANGASSER
09 Director Institutional Research ....Dr. Michelle THRUMAN
88 Dir Learning & Transitional Educ ....Ms. Carolyn PETSCHE
26 Director Marketing & Cmty Relations ....Mr. Pete WILLGING
88 Director Retired & Senior Vol Pgm ....Ms. Cindi MIELKE
28 Director Title IV Student Support ....Mr. Anthony SAGO
21 Manager Accounting ....Ms. Mary J. LLOYD
40 Manager Bookstore ....Ms. Madonna KEENEY
101 Exec Asst to President/Board Sec ....Ms. Terri A. GRIMES
102 Executive Director Foundation ....Mr. James M. BERBERET

Illinois Central College (G)

1 College Drive, East Peoria IL 61635-0001
County: Tazewell　FICE Identification: 006753
Unit ID: 145682
Telephone: (309) 694-5422　Carnegie Class: Assoc/MT-VT-Mix Trad/Non
FAX Number: (309) 694-5450　Calendar System: Semester
URL: www.icc.edu
Established: 1966　Annual Undergrad Tuition & Fees (In-District): $4,200
Enrollment: 9,704　Coed
Affiliation or Control: State/Local　IRS Status: 501(c)3
Highest Offering: Associate Degree
Accreditation: NH, ACFEI, ADNUR, COARC, DH, EMT, MAC, MLTAD, MUS, OTA, PTAA, RAD, SURGT

01 President ....Dr. Sheila QUIRK-BAILEY
10 Exec VP Administration/Finance ....Mr. Bruce BUDDE
26 Vice President of Marketing & Comm ....Dr. Cheryl FLIEGE
05 Vice President of Academic Affairs ....Dr. Emmanuel AWUAH
102 Int Exec Dir Education Foundation ....Ms. Stephanie HOLMES
15 Vice President of Human Resources ....Ms. Marti BLOODSAW
28 VP of Diversity/Intl & Adult Educ ....Dr. Rita ALI
32 Vice President Student Services ....Dr. Tracy MORRIS
09 Exec Dir Inst Research & Planning ....Mr. David COOK
35 Dean of Students ....Ms. Emily POINTS
84 Dean of Enrollment Management ....Ms. Beth MCCLAIN
35 Dean of Student Services ....Ms. Angela DREESSEN
51 Dean Corporate/Community Education ....Ms. Ellen GEORGE
88 Assoc Dean Organizational Learning ....Ms. Janice KINSINGER
79 Dean Eng/Humanities/Lang ....Ms. Jennifer SWARTOUT
81 Dean Math/Science/Engineering ....Mr. Joe BERGMAN
50 Dean Business/Hospitality/Info Sys ....Ms. Julie HOWAR
57 Dean Arts & Communications ....Ms. Kari SCHIMMEL
47 Dean Agriculture/Industrial Tech ....Ms. Stacy GEHRIG
103 Dean Comm Outreach/Career Readiness ....Ms. Kay SUTTON
76 Dean Health Careers ....Ms. Wendee GUTH
106 Associate Dean Online Learning ....Dr. Patrice HESS
21 Director Business Services ....Ms. Kim MALCOLM
06 Registrar ....Ms. Nikisha WRIGHTANDERSON
29 Coordinator Alumni Relations ....Vacant
04 Administrative Asst to President ....Ms. Paula FRALEY
08 Director Library Services ....Ms. Cathryne KAUFMAN
19 Campus Police Chief ....Mr. Thomas LARSON
22 Dir Affirmative Action/EEO ....Dr. Rita ALI
25 Grants Development Officer ....Dr. Herbert DACOSTA
41 Athletic Director ....Ms. Sue SINCLAIR
104 Dir International Educ Program ....Dr. Barbara BURTON
88 Controller ....Mr. Ed BABCOCK
101 Secretary of the Institution/Board ....Ms. Paula FRALEY
86 Legislative Liaison ....Ms. Valerie WELSH

Illinois College (H)

1101 W College Avenue, Jacksonville IL 62650-2299
County: Morgan　FICE Identification: 001688
Unit ID: 145691
Telephone: (217) 245-3000　Carnegie Class: Bac-A&S
FAX Number: (217) 245-3034　Calendar System: Semester
URL: www.ic.edu
Established: 1829　Annual Undergrad Tuition & Fees: $31,610
Enrollment: 955　Coed
Affiliation or Control: Independent Non-Profit　IRS Status: 501(c)3
Highest Offering: Master's
Accreditation: NH

01 President ....Dr. Barbara A. FARLEY
05 Provost and Dean of the College ......Dr. Catharine E. O'CONNELL
10 Vice President of Business Affairs ....Mr. Tim WEIS
30 Vice President Development & Alumni ....Mr. Patrick WAGNER
84 Vice President of Enrollment ....Ms. Stephanie CHIPMAN
32 Dean of Students ....Dr. Malinda L. CARLSON
20 Dean of the Faculty ....Dr. Adam PORTER
20 Dean of Student Success ....Dr. Andrew JONES
09 Exec Dir for Inst Research ....Dr. Robert A. SWEATMAN
06 Registrar ....Ms. Helen KUHN
13 Chief Info Technology Officer (CIO) ....Mr. Patrick BROWN
07 Senior Assoc Director Admissions ....Mr. Richard L. BYSTRY

37 Assoc Director of Financial Aid ....Ms. Rebecca BIRDSELL
88 Associate Director of Admissions ....Ms. Kristen REED
29 Dir Annual Giving/Alumni Relations ....Ms. Kristin E. JAMISON
26 Director Marketing/Communications ....Mr. Bryan LEONARD
08 Library Director ....Mr. Luke BEATTY
18 Director of Facilities Operations ....Mr. Troy PETERS
36 Director of Career Services ....Ms. Susan K. DRAKE
21 Controller ....Ms. Melissa J. DYSON
35 Dir Center for Student Involvement ....Ms. Karen K. HOMOLKA
42 Chaplain ....Vacant
15 Director of Human Resources ....Ms. Angela VALUCK
38 Mental Health Counselor ....Mr. Zach WITTMANN
28 Director of Diversity ....Vacant
41 Athletic Director ....Mr. Mike SNYDER

Illinois College of Optometry (A)

3241 S Michigan Avenue, Chicago IL 60616-3878
County: Cook FICE Identification: 001689
Unit ID: 145628
Telephone: (312) 225-1700 Carnegie Class: Spec-4-yr-Other Health
FAX Number: (312) 225-1724 Calendar System: Quarter
URL: www.ico.edu
Established: 1872 Annual Graduate Tuition & Fees: N/A
Enrollment: 647 Coed
Affiliation or Control: Independent Non-Profit IRS Status: 501(c)3
Highest Offering: First Professional Degree; No Undergraduates
Accreditation: NH, OPT, OPTR

01 President ....Dr. Arol R. AUGSBURGER
05 Vice Pres for Academic Affairs/Dean ....Dr. Stephanie MESSNER
10 VP for Finance & Business/CFO ....Mr. John BUDZYNSKI
11 Vice President Administration ....Mrs. Laura L. ROUNCE
17 Vice Pres for Patient Care Services ....Dr. Leonard V. MESSNER
30 VP Student/Alumni/College Devel ....Dr. Mark COLIP
22 VP Compliance/Cmty Based Services ....Dr. Valarie CONRAD
06 Asst Dean Academic Admin/Registrar ....Mrs. Lavern YOUNG
07 Director of Admissions ....Ms. Teisha JOHNSON
32 Sr Director Student Development ....Ms. Beth KARMIS
37 Director Student Financial Aid ....Ms. Melissa BARTOLD
29 Director Alumni Relations ....Ms. Connie M. SCAVUZZO
18 Chief Facilities/Physical Plant ....Mr. Gary YOUNG
26 Director of Communications ....Ms. Jennifer SOPKO

*Illinois Eastern Community Colleges System Office (B)

233 E Chestnut Street, Olney IL 62450-2298
County: Richland FICE Identification: 009135
Unit ID: 443368
Telephone: (618) 393-2982 Carnegie Class: N/A
FAX Number: (618) 392-4816
URL: www.iecc.edu

01 Chief Executive Officer ....Mr. Terry BRUCE
05 Chief Academic Officer ....Dr. Jeff CUTCHIN
10 Chief Finance Officer/Treasurer ....Mr. Roger BROWNING
103 Dean Workforce Education ....Mr. Michael THOMAS
25 Pgm Dir of Grants/Compl & Outreach .... Dr. Ashlee SPANNAGEL
85 Pgm Dir Intl Std/Dir Dist Std Rctmt ....Ms. Pamela SWANSON-MADDEN
15 Director of Human Resources ....Mrs. Tara BUERSTER
88 Director TRIO Upward Bound ....Ms. Samantha WEIDNER
88 Pgm Dir Student Learning Assessment ....Mr. Brandon WEGER
88 Director TRIO Student Support Svcs ....Mr. Wain DAVIS

*Illinois Eastern Community Colleges Frontier Community College (C)

Frontier Drive, Fairfield IL 62837-9801
County: Wayne FICE Identification: 020744
Unit ID: 403469
Telephone: (618) 842-3711 Carnegie Class: Assoc/HVT-High Non
FAX Number: (618) 842-4425 Calendar System: Semester
URL: www.iecc.edu/fcc
Established: 1976 Annual Undergrad Tuition & Fees (In-District): $3,466
Enrollment: 2,229 Coed
Affiliation or Control: State/Local IRS Status: 501(c)3
Highest Offering: Associate Degree
Accreditation: &NH, ADNUR

02 President ....Dr. Gerald EDGREN, JR.
05 Dean of Instruction ....Mr. Paul BRUINSMA
32 Asst Dean of Student Services ....Mrs. Jan WILES
51 Director of Adult Education ....Ms. Cheryl HOLDER
10 Director of Business ....Mrs. Mary JOHNSTON
08 Director of Learning Resource Ctr ....Ms. Merna YOUNGBLOOD
41 Athletic Director ....Mr. Thomas KENT
88 Pgm Dir Emergency Preparedness Mgmt .... Mr. Scott MESEROLE
18 Supervisor of Building & Grounds ....Mr. Galen DUNN
37 Coordinator of Financial Aid ....Ms. Lori NOE
06 Coordinator of Registration/Records ....Ms. Amy LOSS

† Regional accreditation is carried under the parent institution Illinois Eastern Community Colleges System Office in Olney, IL.

*Illinois Eastern Community Colleges Lincoln Trail College (D)

11220 State Highway 1, Robinson IL 62454-5707
County: Crawford FICE Identification: 009786
Unit ID: 403478
Telephone: (618) 544-8657 Carnegie Class: Assoc/MT-VT-High Non
FAX Number: (618) 544-7423 Calendar System: Semester
URL: www.iecc.edu/ltc
Established: 1969 Annual Undergrad Tuition & Fees (In-District): $3,466
Enrollment: 1,010 Coed
Affiliation or Control: State/Local IRS Status: 501(c)3
Highest Offering: Associate Degree
Accreditation: &NH, ADNUR

02 President ....Dr. Ryan GOWER
05 Dean of the College ....Mr. Brent TODD
37 Coordinator of Financial Aid ....Ms. Destiny STAMBAUGH
32 Asst Dean of Student Services ....Ms. Julie HIGGINBOTHOM
08 Director of Learning Resource Ctr ....Ms. Vicky BONELLI
10 Director of Business ....Ms. Jamie HENRY
41 Athletic Director ....Mr. Kevin BOWERS
18 Groundskeeper ....Mr. Dan LEGGITT
26 Coord Public Information/Marketing ....Mr. Christopher FORDE

† Regional accreditation is carried under the parent institution Illinois Eastern Community Colleges System Office in Olney, IL.

*Illinois Eastern Community Colleges Olney Central College (E)

305 North West Street, Olney IL 62450-1099
County: Richland FICE Identification: 001742
Unit ID: 145707
Telephone: (618) 395-7777 Carnegie Class: Assoc/MT-VT-High Non
FAX Number: (618) 392-3293 Calendar System: Semester
URL: www.iecc.edu/occ
Established: 1962 Annual Undergrad Tuition & Fees (In-District): $3,466
Enrollment: 1,295 Coed
Affiliation or Control: State/Local IRS Status: 501(c)3
Highest Offering: Associate Degree
Accreditation: &NH, ADNUR, RAD

02 President ....Mr. Rodney RANES
05 Dean of Instruction ....Mr. Michael CONN
32 Assistant Dean Student Services ....Ms. Andrea PAMPE
76 Assoc Dean Nursing Allied Health .... Ms. Theresa MARCOTTE
08 Director Learning Skills Center/LRC ....Ms. Linda SHIDLER
88 Director Cosmetology ....Ms. Linda MILLER
10 Director Business ....Mr. Doug SHIPMAN
41 Athletic Director/Coach ....Mr. Dennis CONLEY
37 Financial Aid Coordinator ....Ms. Andrea PUCKETT

† Regional accreditation is carried under the parent institution Illinois Eastern Community Colleges System Office in Olney, IL.

*Illinois Eastern Community Colleges Wabash Valley College (F)

2200 College Drive, Mount Carmel IL 62863-2657
County: Wabash FICE Identification: 001779
Unit ID: 403487
Telephone: (618) 262-8641 Carnegie Class: Assoc/MT-VT-High Non
FAX Number: (618) 262-5347 Calendar System: Semester
URL: www.iecc.edu/wvc
Established: 1960 Annual Undergrad Tuition & Fees (In-District): $3,466
Enrollment: 4,274 Coed
Affiliation or Control: State/Local IRS Status: 501(c)3
Highest Offering: Associate Degree
Accreditation: &NH, ADNUR

02 President ....Mr. Matt FOWLER
05 Dean of Instruction ....Mr. Robert CONN
32 Assistant Dean Student Services ....Mrs. Tiffany COWGER
121 Director of Academic Advising ....Mr. Tim ZIMMER
08 Director of LRC ....Ms. Sandy CRAIG
60 Director of Broadcasting ....Mr. Kyle PEACH
41 Athletic Director ....Mr. Mike CARPENTER
10 Director of Business ....Mrs. Reilly BAUMGART
37 Financial Aid Coordinator ....Ms. Jane OWEN
18 Groundskeeper ....Mr. Adam ROESCH

† Regional accreditation is carried under the parent institution Illinois Eastern Community Colleges System Office in Olney, IL.

The Illinois Institute of Art (G)

350 N Orleans, Suite 136-L, Chicago IL 60654-1514
County: Cook FICE Identification: 012584
Unit ID: 148177
Telephone: (312) 280-3500 Carnegie Class: Spec-4-yr-Arts
FAX Number: (312) 777-8780 Calendar System: Quarter
URL: www.artinstitutes.edu/chicago
Established: 1916 Annual Undergrad Tuition & Fees: $17,484
Enrollment: 1,331 Coed
Affiliation or Control: Proprietary IRS Status: Proprietary
Highest Offering: Baccalaureate
Accreditation: NH, ACFEI, CIDA

01 President/Chicago ....Josh POND
05 Vice President Academic Affairs ....Dr. Donna L. GRAY
20 Dean of Academic Affairs ....Karen JANKO
07 Senior Director of Admissions ....Summer TOOMEY
06 Registrar ....Maja COLE
08 Librarian ....Sean MCCARTHY
79 Program Coordinator Humanities ....Karine BRAVAIS-SLYMAN
81 Program Coordinator Math/Science ....Deann GROSSI
10 Director of Financial Services ....Kim GORDON

37 Director Student Financial Aid ....Terry LEPPELLERE
32 Dean of Student Affairs ....Keith KRAMER
15 Human Resources Generalist ....Rae DEROSE
13 Director of Technology ....Vacant
29 Director Alumni Relations ....Vacant

The Illinois Institute of Art-Schaumburg (H)

1000 Plaza Drive, Suite 100, Schaumburg IL 60173-4913
Telephone: (847) 619-3450 Identification: 770074
Accreditation: &NH, CIDA

Illinois Institute of Technology (I)

10 West 35th Street, Chicago IL 60616-3793
County: Cook FICE Identification: 001691
Unit ID: 145725
Telephone: (312) 567-3000 Carnegie Class: DU-Higher
FAX Number: (312) 567-3004 Calendar System: Semester
URL: www.iit.edu
Established: 1890 Annual Undergrad Tuition & Fees: $45,214
Enrollment: 7,792 Coed
Affiliation or Control: Independent Non-Profit IRS Status: 501(c)3
Highest Offering: Doctorate
Accreditation: NH, CACREP, CLPSY, CS, ENG, LSAR

01 President ....Dr. Alan CRAMB
05 Provost ....Ms. Frances BRONET
84 Vice Pres Admission & Financial Aid ....Dr. Mike GOSZ
10 VP Finance/CFO and Treasurer ....Dr. Michael D. HORAN
18 VP Admin/Facilities/Pub Safety ....Mr. Bruce WATTS
111 Vice Pres Institutional Advancement ....Ms. Betsy HUGHES
88 Vice Pres International Affairs ....Dr. Darsh T. WASAN
86 Vice President External Affairs ....Mr. Jess GOODE
43 Vice President General Counsel ....Mr. Anthony D'AMATO
88 Sr VP & Dir IIT Research Inst ....Dr. David MCCORMICK
88 VP & Dir Inst Food Safety & Health ....Dr. Robert BRACKETT
13 Chief Information Officer ....Mr. Ophir TRIGALO
28 Vice Provost Student Diversity ....Mr. Gerald DOYLE
20 Vice Provost Academic Affairs ....Dr. Chris WHITE
32 Vice Provost Student Affairs ....Ms. Katherine MURPHY-STETZ
61 Dean Chicago-Kent College of Law ....Mr. Hal J. KRENT
49 Dean College of Science & Letters ....Dr. Russell BETTS
54 Dean Armour Col of Engineering ....Dr. Natacha DEPAOLA
50 Dean Stuart School of Business ....Dr. Harvey KAHALAS
48 Dean College of Architecture ....Mr. Wiel ARETS
83 Dean Lewis Col of Human Sciences ....Dr. Christine HIMES
12 Dean Institute of Design ....Mr. Denis WEIL
72 Dean School of Applied Technology ....Dr. Bob CARLSON
08 Dean of Libraries ....Ms. Sharon BOSTICK
22 Associate General Counsel ....Ms. Candida MIRANDA
21 Assoc VP Finance & Controller ....Mr. Ken JOHNSTON
15 Associate VP Human Resources ....Ms. Antoinette MURRIL
88 Assoc Vice Provost UG Acad Affairs ....Ms. Carole ORZE
88 Assoc Vice Provost Grad Acad Affs .....Ms. Holli PRYOR-HARRIS
41 AVP Director of Athletics ....Mr. Joseph HAKES
07 Assoc Vice Pres Enrollment Svcs ....Ms. Abby MCGRATH
07 Asst Vice Pres UG Admissions ....Ms. Toni RILEY
123 Asst VP Grad/Prof Admissions ....Mr. Rishab MALHOTRA
39 AVP Residence & Greek Life ....Ms. Slandie DIEUJUSTE
37 Director of Financial Aid ....Ms. Elizabeth WAHLSTROM HELGREN
06 Registrar ....Mr. Aubrey HALL
25 Director Sponsored Research ....Ms. Domenica G. PAPPAS
14 Director Enterprise Systems ....Mr. Vince BATTISTA
108 Director of Assessment ....Dr. Carol-Ann EMMONS
29 Sr Director Alumni & Donor Rels ....Mr. James ACTON
96 Director of Purchasing ....Mr. Frank FIORITO
22 Director Diversity/Inclusions/EE ....Ms. Lisa MONTGOMERY
88 Dir Environmental Health & Safety ....Ms. Cynthia CHAFFEE
23 Assoc VP Student Health & Wellness ....Ms. Anita OPDYCKE
105 Director Web Development/Services ....Mr. Brian BAILEY
106 Dir IIT Online Tech Svcs ....Ms. Lauren WOODS
04 Director President's Office ....Ms. Sandra LAPORTE
90 Manager Academic Computing ....Mr. Bill ORNT

Illinois Institute of Technology Downtown Campus (J)

565 W Adams Street, Chicago IL 60661
Telephone: (312) 906-5000 Identification: 770075
Accreditation: &NH, LAW

Illinois Institute of Technology Rice Campus (K)

201 East Loop Road, Wheaton IL 60189
Telephone: (630) 682-6000 Identification: 770077
Accreditation: &NH

Illinois State University (L)

School and North Streets, Normal IL 61790-0001
County: McLean FICE Identification: 001692
Unit ID: 145813
Telephone: (309) 438-2111 Carnegie Class: DU-Higher
FAX Number: (309) 438-2768 Calendar System: Semester
URL: www.ilstu.edu
Established: 1857 Annual Undergrad Tuition & Fees (In-State): $14,061
Enrollment: 20,760 Coed
Affiliation or Control: State IRS Status: 501(c)3
Highest Offering: Doctorate

Accreditation: NH, AAFCS, ART, AUD, CAATE, CAEPN, CAHIIM, CIDA, CONST, CS, DIETD, DIETI, ENGR, IPSY, MT, MUS, NAIT, NRPA, NURSE, SCPSY, SP, SW, THEA

01 President ... Dr. Larry DIETZ
05 Int VP Academic Affairs & Provost ... Dr. Jan MURPHY
10 VP Finance & Planning ... Mr. Daniel STEPHENS
32 VP Student Affairs ... Dr. Levester JOHNSON
111 VP University Advancement ... Mr. Pat VICKERMAN
20 Associate Provost ... Dr. Jim JAWAHAR
35 Assistant VP Student Affairs ... Dr. Danielle MILLER-SCHUSTER
21 Sr Assoc VP Finance & Planning ... Ms. Debra K. SMITLEY
90 Chief Academic Technology Officer ... Dr. Mark WALBERT
58 AVP Grad Stds/Research/Intl Educ ... Dr. John BAUR
84 Assoc VP Enrollment Management ... Ms. Jana ALBRECHT
15 Asst VP Human Resources ... Ms. Tammy CARLSON
08 Interim Dean University Libraries ... Dr. Sharon ZECK
06 University Registrar ... Mr. Jess D. RAY
07 Director Admissions ... Mr. Jeff MAVROS
20 Director University College ... Ms. Amelia NOEL-ELKINS
30 Exec Director of Development ... Ms. Joy D. HUTCHCRAFT
21 Senior Associate Comptroller ... Ms. JoEllen BAHNSEN
37 Director Financial Aid ... Ms. Bridget CURL
29 Exec Director Alumni Engagement ... Ms. Doris GROVES
18 Exec Director Facilities Management ... Mr. Charles SCOTT
19 Chief University Police ... Mr. Aaron WOODRUFF
28 Dir Ofc of Eq Opportunity & Access ... Mr. Anthony WALESBY
23 Director Student Health Services ... Ms. Laura KNOBLAUCH
39 Director University Housing ... Ms. Stacey MWILAMBWE
41 Director Intercollegiate Athletics ... Mr. Larry LYONS
85 Director International Studies ... Dr. Luis CANALES
92 Interim Director Honors Program ... Dr. Rocio RIVADENEYRA
94 Director Women's Studies ... Dr. Alison BAILEY
96 Director of Purchasing ... Ms. Judy JOHNSON
49 Dean College Arts & Sciences ... Dr. Gregory B. SIMPSON
50 Dean College Business ... Mr. Ajay SAMANT
53 Dean College Education ... Dr. Perry SCHOON
72 Dean College Applied Sci/Tech ... Dr. Todd MCLODA
57 Dean College Fine Arts ... Ms. Jean M K. MILLER
66 Dean Mennonite College ... Dr. Judy NEUBRANDER
35 Acting Dean of Students ... Dr. John DAVENPORT
88 Assoc VP Acad Admin ... Dr. Sam CATANZARO
88 Assoc VP Acad Fiscal Mgmt ... Dr. Alan LACY
88 Asst VP Administrative Technologies ... Mr. Charles EDAMALA
114 Dir of Budget Planning/Operations ... Ms. Sandra CAVI
44 Exec Dir Annual Giving ... Ms. Lora WEY
110 Asst VP University Advancement ... Ms. Jill JONES
27 Exec Dir University Marketing/Comm ... Mr. Brian BEAM
45 Dir Planning/Rsch/Policy Analysis ... Ms. Angela ENGEL
108 Director University Assessment ... Dr. Ryan SMITH
38 Director Student Counseling ... Dr. Sandy COLBS
43 General Counsel ... Ms. Lisa HUSON
105 Director Web & Interactive Comm ... Mr. Arturo RAMIREZ
86 Director State Government Relations ... Dr. Jonathan LACKLAND
90 Assoc VP Academic Technologies ... Dr. Mark WALBERT
04 Administrative Asst to President ... Mr. Dave BENTLIN

Illinois Valley Community College (A)

815 N Orlando Smith Road, Oglesby IL 61348-9692
County: La Salle — FICE Identification: 001705
Unit ID: 145831
Telephone: (815) 224-2720 — Carnegie Class: Assoc/HVT-High Non
FAX Number: (815) 224-3033 — Calendar System: Semester
URL: www.ivcc.edu
Established: 1966 — Annual Undergrad Tuition & Fees (In-District): $3,730
Enrollment: 3,310 — Coed
Affiliation or Control: Local — IRS Status: 501(c)3
Highest Offering: Associate Degree
Accreditation: NH, ADNUR, DA, EMT

01 President ... Dr. Jerry M. CORCORAN
05 Vice Pres for Academic Affairs ... Dr. Deborah L. ANDERSON
10 Vice Pres Business Svcs/Finance ... Ms. Cheryl E. ROELFSEMA
20 Assoc VP Acad Affs/Workforce Dev ... Ms. Bonnie L. CAMPBELL
32 Assoc Vice Pres Student Svcs ... Mr. Mark J. GRZYBOWSKI
24 Director of Learning Technologies ... Ms. Emily B. VESCOGNI
31 Director Cmty Relations & Marketing ... Mr. Francis R. BROLLEY
13 Dir of Information Technology Svcs ... Ms. Diann JABUSCH
51 Dir Cont Educ/Business Svcs ... Ms. Jennifer C. SCHERI
15 Director Human Resources ... Ms. Leslie A. HOFER
37 Director of Financial Aid ... Ms. Patricia A. WILLIAMSON
07 Director of Admissions/Records ... Mr. Quintin M. OVEROCKER
08 Head Librarian ... Ms. Frances A. WHALEY
30 Director of Development ... Mr. Francis R. BROLLEY
96 Director of Purchasing ... Ms. Michelle L. CARBONI
18 Director of Facilities ... Mr. Scott CURLEY
09 Director of Institutional Research ... Mr. Matthew P. SUERTH
81 Dean Natural Science/Business ... Mr. Ron W. GROLEAU
66 Dean Health Professions/Nursing ... Ms. Julie HOGUE
79 Int Dn Humanities/Fine Art/Soc Sci ... Dr. Robyn L. SCHIFFMAN
53 Dean English/Mathematics/Educ ... Dr. Robyn L. SCHIFFMAN

Illinois Wesleyan University (B)

PO Box 2900, 1312 Park Street,
Bloomington IL 61702-2900
County: McLean — FICE Identification: 001696
Unit ID: 145646
Telephone: (309) 556-1000 — Carnegie Class: Bac-A&S
FAX Number: (309) 556-3411 — Calendar System: Other
URL: www.iwu.edu
Established: 1850 — Annual Undergrad Tuition & Fees: $44,142
Enrollment: 1,842 — Coed
Affiliation or Control: Independent Non-Profit — IRS Status: 501(c)3
Highest Offering: Baccalaureate
Accreditation: NH, MUS, NURSE

01 President ... Dr. Eric R. JENSEN
05 Provost & Dean of Faculty ... Dr. Mark BRODL
10 Vice President Business & Finance ... Mr. Daniel P. KLOTZBACH
30 Vice President for Advancement ... Mr. Steve SEIBRING
27 Director for Communications ... Ms. Ann AUBRY
32 VP Student Affairs/Dean Students ... Dr. Karla CARNEY-HALL
84 VP of Enrollment & Marketing ... Ms. LeAnn HUGHES
07 Dean Admissions/AVP Enrollment Mgmt ... Mr. Greg KING
09 AVP Instl Research/Plng/Evaluation ... Dr. Michael THOMPSON
86 Dir Government/Community Relations ... Mr. Carl F. TEICHMAN
04 Exec Assistant to the President ... Dr. Molly MUNSON-DRYER
20 Int Assoc Prov Acad Plng/Standards ... Prof. Lynda DUKE
20 Int Assoc Dean Curricular/Fac Dev ... Prof. Kevin SULLIVAN
15 Assoc VP for Human Resources ... Ms. Catherine SPITZ
13 Asst Provost/Chief Technology Ofcr ... Mr. Trey SHORT
110 Associate Vice Pres Gift Planning ... Ms. Michele BRADY
29 Asst VP of Alumni Engagement ... Ms. Jodi ROWE
35 Assoc Dean of Students ... Ms. Darcy L. GREDER
38 Asst Dean/Dir Student Counseling ... Dr. Annorrah MOORMAN
35 Asst Dean Students/Dir Campus Life ... Dr. Brandon COMMON
08 University Librarian ... Dr. Karen SCHMIDT
06 Registrar ... Dr. Leslie BETZ
42 University Chaplain ... Rev. Elyse NELSON WINGER
21 Controller ... Mr. John BRYANT
37 Director of Financial Aid ... Mr. Scott SEIBRING
64 Director of School of Music ... Dr. Mario J. PELUSI
57 Director of School of Art ... Prof. Julie JOHNSON
57 Director of School of Theatre Arts ... Dr. Thomas QUINN
66 Director of School of Nursing ... Dr. Victoria FOLSE
41 Director of Athletics ... Prof. Mike WAGNER
29 Director of Alumni Relations ... Ms. Adriane POWELL
102 Dir Grants/Foundation Relations ... Mr. Dick FOLSE
44 Dir of Wesleyan Annual Fund ... Ms. Beth KEEGAN
36 Director of Career Center ... Mr. Warren KISTNER
18 Director of Physical Plant ... Mr. James J. BLUMBERG
88 Director of Sports Information ... Mr. Stewart I. SALOWITZ
93 Director of Diversity & Inclusion ... Ms. Greta FRANKLIN
35 Int Dir Student Act/Leadership Pgms ... Ms. Liz VALES
94 Dir of Women's & Gender Studies ... Dr. Carole MYSCOFSKI
104 Director of International Office ... Ms. Stacey SHIMIZU
40 Bookstore Manager ... Mr. Thaddeus SUTTER
26 Director of Marketing ... Mr. Andrew KREISS

Institute for Clinical Social Work (C)

401 South State Street, Suite 822, Chicago IL 60605
County: Cook — FICE Identification: 025737
Unit ID: 145886
Telephone: (312) 935-4232 — Carnegie Class: Spec-4-yr-Other Health
FAX Number: (312) 935-4255 — Calendar System: Semester
URL: www.icsw.edu
Established: 1981 — Annual Graduate Tuition & Fees: N/A
Enrollment: 116 — Coed
Affiliation or Control: Independent Non-Profit — IRS Status: 501(c)3
Highest Offering: Doctorate; No Undergraduates
Accreditation: NH

01 Dean/President ... Dr. Amy ELDRIDGE
11 Vice President of Operations ... Lynne GORDON
20 Director of Academic Administration ... Elizabeth OLLER
37 Director of Student Financial Svcs ... Sebastien BEAUDET

John A. Logan College (D)

700 Logan College Road, Carterville IL 62918-2500
County: Williamson — FICE Identification: 008076
Unit ID: 146205
Telephone: (618) 985-3741 — Carnegie Class: Assoc/HVT-High Non
FAX Number: (618) 985-2248 — Calendar System: Semester
URL: www.jalc.edu
Established: 1967 — Annual Undergrad Tuition & Fees (In-District): $3,510
Enrollment: 3,575 — Coed
Affiliation or Control: State/Local — IRS Status: 501(c)3
Highest Offering: Associate Degree
Accreditation: NH, CAHIIM, DA, DH, DMS, MLTAD, OTA, SURGT

01 President ... Dr. Ron HOUSE
05 Vice President Instruction Services ... Ms. Melanie PECORD
10 VP Business Svcs/College Facilities ... Mr. Brad MCCORMICK
32 Dean Student Services ... Mr. Tim WILLIAMS
21 Dean Financial Operations ... Ms. Stacy BUCKINGHAM
20 Dean Academic Affairs ... Dr. Stephanie HARTFORD
103 Dean Workforce Dev/Adult Education ... Ms. Kay FLLEMING
88 Dir for Term Faculty Instruction ... Ms. April STANLY
51 Dean for Continuing Education ... Dr. Barry HANCOCK
07 Assoc Dean of Admissions ... Ms. Christy STEWART
37 Director of Student Financial Asst ... Ms. Sherry SUMMARY
30 Dean for Institutional Effectivenes ... Vacant
84 Dir Recruit/Retention/Acad Advisor ... Dr. Steve O'KEEFE
35 Director of Student Activities ... Ms. Adrienne BARKLEY-GIFFIN
36 Dir of Career Services and Intl Ed ... Ms. Beth STEPHENS
102 Executive Director of Foundation ... Ms. Staci SHAFER
66 Director of Nursing ... Ms. Marilyn FALASTER
88 Director of Testing Services ... Ms. Christy MCBRIDE
15 Exec Dir of Human Resources/AAO ... Dr. Clay BREWER
18 Dir Buildings and Grounds ... Mr. Tim GIBSON
09 Director Institutional Research ... Mr. Eric PULLEY
04 Administrative Asst to President ... Ms. Sharyl MELVIN
101 Admin Asst Pres/Board of Trustees ... Ms. Susan MAY
28 Director of Diversity & Inclusion ... Ms. Toyin FOX
41 Athletic Director ... Mr. Greg STARRICK
88 Dir of Emergency Plng & Risk Mgmt ... Mr. Don PRIDDY
88 Bus Function Analyst in Stdnt Svcs ... Mr. Terry CRAIN
38 Director of Student Success ... Ms. Carolyn GALLEGLY
121 Director Academic Advisement ... Ms. Stacy HOLLOWAY
96 Dir of Purchasing/Auxilary Svcs ... Ms. Sue ZAMORA
88 CCR & R Director ... Ms. Lori LONGUEVILLE
88 Director of ASE ... Ms. Crystal HOSSELTON
56 Director of Adult Education ... Ms. Karla TABING
50 Director of Business & Industry ... Mr. Dennis WHITE
88 Director of Corporate Education ... Ms. Michelle HAMILTON
88 Exec Dir of Integrated Technology ... Mr. Scott ELLIOTT
88 Director of CHEC ... Mr. Bradley GRIFFITH
51 Director of Continuing Education ... Mr. Greg STETTLER
18 Director of Facility Services ... Mr. Chris NAEGELE
104 Coord of International Educ ... Dr. Sue TRAMMELL
105 WebMaster ... Mr. Phillip LANE
106 Assoc Dean of Education Technology ... Ms. Krystal REAGAN

John Marshall Law School (E)

315 S Plymouth Court, Chicago IL 60604-3968
County: Cook — FICE Identification: 001698
Unit ID: 146241
Telephone: (312) 427-2737 — Carnegie Class: Spec-4-yr-Law
FAX Number: (312) 427-8307 — Calendar System: Semester
URL: www.jmls.edu
Established: 1899 — Annual Graduate Tuition & Fees: N/A
Enrollment: 1,204 — Coed
Affiliation or Control: Independent Non-Profit — IRS Status: 501(c)3
Highest Offering: First Professional Degree; No Undergraduates
Accreditation: NH, LAW

01 Dean ... Ms. Darby DICKERSON
100 Chief of Staff Dean's Office ... Ms. Nicole VEAL
10 Chief Financial Officer ... Ms. Cynthia SAH
30 Exec Dir Development/Alum Rels ... Ms. Lauren PRIHODA-WEINER
13 Dir Library & IT Operations ... Mr. Ramsey DONNELL
15 Asst Dean Human Resources ... Mr. Martin D'AMBROSE
36 Asst Dean Career Services ... Ms. Chante SPANN
06 Registrar ... Vacant
26 Dir Marketing/Communications ... Mr. Michael HUGGINS
37 Director Student Financial Aid ... Ms. Yara SANTANA
09 Exec Dir of Institutional Affairs ... Ms. Anna KRUG
88 Assoc Dean for Advanced Studies ... Ms. Kathryn KENNEDY
88 Assoc Dn Professional/Career Strat ... Hon. Margaret O'Mara FROSSARD, RET.
28 Asst Dean for Diversity ... Mr. Troy RIDDLE
19 Director Security/Safety ... Mr. Ali HALEEM
88 Assoc Dean Faculty Development ... Ms. Julie SPANBAUER
11 Asst Dean for Administration ... Ms. Teresa DO
88 Assoc Dean for Faculty Development ... Ms. Andath HAMANN
32 Asst Dean Student Life/Leadership ... Dr. Jennifer POPE

John Wood Community College (F)

1301 S 48th Street, Quincy IL 62305-8736
County: Adams — FICE Identification: 012813
Unit ID: 146278
Telephone: (217) 224-6500 — Carnegie Class: Assoc/MT-VT-High Non
FAX Number: (217) 224-4208 — Calendar System: Semester
URL: www.jwcc.edu
Established: 1974 — Annual Undergrad Tuition & Fees (In-District): $4,710
Enrollment: 2,016 — Coed
Affiliation or Control: State/Local — IRS Status: 501(c)3
Highest Offering: Associate Degree
Accreditation: NH, SURGT

01 President ... Mr. Michael ELBE
05 Vice President for Instruction ... Dr. Laurel KLINKENBERG
10 Dean Business Svcs/Inst Effective ... Mr. Josh WELKER
32 Dean Student Services ... Vacant
49 Dean Arts and Sciences ... Mr. Mike TERRY
75 Dean Careers/Tech/Health Education ... Mr. William STUFLICK
84 Dean Enrollment Svcs/Dir Finan Aid ... Ms. Melanie LECHTENBERG
07 Director Admissions ... Mr. William SCHAFFER
06 Registrar/Dean of Students ... Mr. Cody BAGGETT
21 Director Fiscal Services ... Ms. Susan FIFER
35 Director Support Services ... Mr. Robert HODGSON
13 Director Information Technology ... Mr. Joshua BRUECK
08 Director Learning Resource Center ... Ms. Barbara LIEBER
26 Director Public Relations/Marketing ... Ms. Tracy ORNE
30 Director Advancement ... Ms. Barbara HOLTHAUS
15 Director Human Resources ... Ms. Dana KEPPNER
18 Director Physical Plant ... Mr. Lou BARTA
37 Director Financial Aid ... Ms. Melanie LECHTENBERG
19 Dean of Ops/Chief of Campus Police ... Mr. Bill LATOUR
41 Director Athletics ... Mr. Brad HOYT
40 Manager Campus Services ... Ms. Lynn BLICKHAN
96 Purchasing Coordinator ... Ms. Darla SNYDER
47 Dept Chair Ag Sciences ... Mr. Gary SHUPE
77 Dept Chair Ofc Technology/Comp Sci ... Ms. Barbara STOLL
50 Dept Chair Business ... Ms. Cathy STEPHENS
81 Department Chair Mathematics ... Ms. Shari HARRIS
65 Dept Chair Natural Sciences ... Dr. Christopher KAELKE
79 Dept Chair Lang/Lit/Hum/Fine Arts ... Ms. Christine WIEWEL
83 Dept Chair Social/Behavior Science ... Dr. Randall EGDORF
04 Executive Asst to President ... Ms. Leah BENZ
102 Dir Foundation/Corporate Relations ... Ms. Barbara HOLTHAUS

Joliet Junior College (A)

1215 Houbolt Road, Joliet IL 60431-8938

County: Will | FICE Identification: 001699
Unit ID: 146296
Telephone: (815) 729-9020 | Carnegie Class: Assoc/MT-VT-High Non
FAX Number: N/A | Calendar System: Semester
URL: www.jjc.edu
Established: 1901 | Annual Undergrad Tuition & Fees (In-District): $3,750
Enrollment: 14,944 | Coed
Affiliation or Control: State/Local | IRS Status: 501(c)3
Highest Offering: Associate Degree
Accreditation: NH, ACBSP, ACFEI, ADNUR, CAHIIM, DMS, MUS

01 President .... Dr. Judy MITCHELL
10 VP Administrative Services .... Mr. Rob GALICK
05 VP Academic Affairs .... Mr. Randy FLETCHER
13 Exec Dir Information Technology .... Mr. Jim SERR
32 VP Student Development .... Dr. Yolanda ISAACS
07 Director Admissions & Recruitment .... Ms. Jennifer KLOBERDANZ
88 Dir Adult & Family Services .... Ms. Emilie MCCALLISTER
37 Director Financial Aid .... Mr. Toron BALLARD
15 Exec Dir Human Resources .... Ms. Malinda CARTER
16 Assistant Director Human Resources .... Ms. Judy CONNELLY
06 Registrar .... Mr. Keith TILLMAN
18 Director Facility Services .... Mr. Patrick VAN DUYNE
109 Director Business/Auxiliary Svcs .... Ms. Janice REEDUS
26 Exec Dir Commun/External Rels .... Ms. Kelly ROHDER
36 Director Career Services .... Ms. Bridgett LARKIN-BEENE
41 Director Athletics .... Mr. Wayne KING
21 Director Financial Svcs/Controller .... Mr. Jeffrey HEAP
19 Dir Campus Safety & Police Chief .... Mr. Peter COMANDA
111 Ex Dir Inst Adv Exec Dir JJC Found .... Ms. Kristin MULVEY
09 Director of Institutional Research .... Mr. Joseph OFFERMANN
29 Alumni Relations & Fund Manager .... Ms. Kelly LARSON
49 Dean Arts & Sciences .... Ms. Sonya WILLIAMS
103 Dean Applied Arts/Wrkforce Ed & Trn .... Ms. Amy MURPHY
75 Dean CTE .... Ms. Patty ZUCCARELLO
88 Dean College & Career Readiness .... Ms. Sarena SCHOTT
108 Dean Academic Effectiveness .... Ms. Krisin CIESEMIER
88 Coord GSD .... Dr. Angie KAYSEN-LUZBETAK
74 Dept Chair Veterinary Medicine Tech .... Dr. Scott KELLER
38 Counselor/Dept Chair .... Ms. Jennifer KIMBAROVSKY
04 Senior Admin Asst to President .... Ms. Jennifer TENN
101 Secretary of the Institution/Board .... Ms. Joan TIERNEY
104 Coordinator Study Abroad .... Ms. Tamara BRATTOLI
106 Dir Online Education/E-learning .... Mr. Chris OSTWINKLE
84 Dean of Enrollment Management .... Mr. Trevell EDDINS
88 Asst Dir Resource Development .... Ms. Amanda QUINN

Judson University (B)

1151 N State Street, Elgin IL 60123-1498

County: Kane | FICE Identification: 001700
Unit ID: 146339
Telephone: (847) 628-2500 | Carnegie Class: Masters/S
FAX Number: (847) 628-1027 | Calendar System: Semester
URL: www.judsonu.edu
Established: 1913 | Annual Undergrad Tuition & Fees: $28,730
Enrollment: 1,274 | Coed
Affiliation or Control: American Baptist | IRS Status: 501(c)3
Highest Offering: Doctorate
Accreditation: NH

01 President .... Dr. Gene CRUME
04 Exec Assistant to the President .... Ms. Tena ROBOTHAM
05 Provost/Chief Academic Officer .... Dr. Wilbert FRIESEN
10 CFO & VP for Business Affairs .... Mr. Jeff EDER
06 Assoc VP and Univ Registrar .... Ms. Virginia GUTH
84 VP for Enrollment & Strategic Plan .... Ms. Nancy BINGER
13 VP for Info Systems & Technology .... Ms. Hasi SMITH
20 Assoc Provost/Academic Curriculum .... Dr. Lanette POTEETE-YOUNG
20 Assoc Provost of Faculty .... Dr. Jhennifer AMUNDSON
50 Dean Business & Professional Stds .... Vacant
32 VP for Student Life .... Ms. Lisa JAROT
08 Library Director .... Mr. Larry WILD
111 Senior VP for External Relations .... Mr. Devlin DONALDSON
30 Assoc VP for Development .... Ms. Kristen EGAN
88 Director of Advancement .... Ms. Lauryn MILLER
29 Director of Alumni Relations .... Ms. Bonnie BIENERT
37 Director of Financial Aid .... Ms. Diana WINTON
07 Director of Admissions .... Ms. Molly SMITH
26 Director of Comm & Marketing .... Ms. Mary DULABAUM
36 Career Development Coach .... Ms. Doris HAUGEN
38 Dir of Student Health & Wellness .... Mr. Elliott ANDERSON
19 Exec Dir of Campus Safety .... Mr. Nick SALZMANN
41 Athletic Director .... Mr. Chad GASSMAN
124 Director of Retention/Student Advoc .... Ms. Jaimee BARTHA
85 International Advisor .... Mr. Rafael HECK
35 Associate Dean of Students .... Ms. Casey SUNDSTEDT
23 Director of Health Center .... Ms. Susan WEBER
88 Tutor/ADA Compliance Coordinator .... Ms. Gineen VARGAS
92 Honors Director .... Dr. Craig KAPLOWITZ
15 Asst VP/Business Affairs & HR .... Mr. Wayne PEARSON
101 Asst Sec to Board of Trustees .... Ms. Tena ROBOTHAM
105 Webmaster .... Vacant
28 Assoc VP/Diversity & Spiritual Dev .... Dr. Curtis SARTOR
09 Director of Institutional Research .... Mr. Chad BRIGGS
39 Coordinator Student Housing .... Mr. Corey ASHLEY

Kankakee Community College (C)

100 College Drive, Kankakee IL 60901-6505

County: Kankakee | FICE Identification: 007690
Unit ID: 146348
Telephone: (815) 802-8100 | Carnegie Class: Assoc/HVT-High Non
FAX Number: (815) 802-8101 | Calendar System: Semester
URL: www.kcc.edu
Established: 1966 | Annual Undergrad Tuition & Fees (In-District): $4,260
Enrollment: 3,306 | Coed
Affiliation or Control: State/Local | IRS Status: 501(c)3
Highest Offering: Associate Degree
Accreditation: NH, ADNUR, COARC, MLTAD, PHLEB, PTAA

01 President .... Dr. John AVENDANO
04 Executive Secretary to President .... Ms. Karen SLAGER
05 VP of Instructional & Stdnt Success .... Dr. Michael BOYD
10 VP for Finance & Administration .... Ms. Vicki GARDNER
06 Registrar .... Mr. David HERMANN
32 Dean of Student Development .... Ms. Julia WASKOSKY
09 Director Institutional Research .... Dr. Purva DEVOL
31 Director Adult & Community Educ .... Ms. Margaret WOLF
103 Director of Workforce Development .... Ms. Dana WASHINGTON
37 Director Financial Aid .... Ms. Deanna LIACONE
41 Director Athletics .... Mr. Todd POST
15 Director Human Resources .... Mr. David CAGLE
10 Director Financial Affairs .... Ms. Beth NUNLEY
50 Assoc Dean Business & Technology .... Mr. Paul CARLSON
51 Asst Dean Cont Educ & Career Svcs .... Ms. Mary POSING
18 Dir Campus Facilities & Security .... Mr. Rich SODERQUIST
81 Assoc Dean Math/Science Division .... Dr. Francesca CATALANO
76 Assoc Dean Health Careers Div .... Ms. Sheri CAGLE
121 Director Student Advisement .... Ms. Meredith PURCELL
76 Director Respiratory Therapist Pgm .... Ms. Nancy OZEE
76 Director Medical Lab Technology .... Ms. Glenda FORNERIS
66 Director Nursing .... Ms. Kellee HAYES
88 Dir Physical Therapy Asst Pgm .... Ms. Nicole STOTTS
83 Assoc Dean Humanities/Social Sci .... Dr. Sheldon WALCHER
76 Director Radiology Technology Pgm .... Ms. Darla JEPSON
13 Director Information Tech Svcs .... Mr. Michael O'CONNOR
102 Exec Director of KCC Foundation .... Ms. Kelly MYERS
88 Director Institutional Tech/Fac Dev .... Mr. Craig KEIGHER
62 Director Learning Resource Center .... Ms. Karen BECKER
26 Director Marketing .... Ms. Kari NUGENT
101 Board Recording Secretary .... Ms. Karen SLAGER
88 Director Support Services .... Ms. Kimberlee HARPIN

Kaskaskia College (D)

27210 College Road, Centralia IL 62801-7878

County: Clinton | FICE Identification: 001701
Unit ID: 146366
Telephone: (618) 545-3000 | Carnegie Class: Assoc/HVT-High Non
FAX Number: (618) 532-1990 | Calendar System: Semester
URL: www.kaskaskia.edu
Established: 1940 | Annual Undergrad Tuition & Fees (In-District): $4,470
Enrollment: 4,472 | Coed
Affiliation or Control: State/Local | IRS Status: 501(c)3
Highest Offering: Associate Degree
Accreditation: NH, ADNUR, COARC, DA, EMT, MLTAD, PTAA, RAD, SURGT

01 President .... Dr. Penny QUINN
11 Vice Pres Administrative Services .... Mrs. Judy HEMKER
05 Vice Pres Instructional Services .... Dr. Gregory LABYAK
32 Vice President of Student Services .... Dr. Susan BATCHELOR
75 Dean Career & Technical Education .... Mr. George EVANS
49 Dean of Arts & Sciences .... Ms. Kellie HENEGAR
66 Associate Dean Nursing/Hlth Science .... Ms. Julie OBERMARK
09 Dean Institutional Effectiveness .... Mr. Jeffrey EBEL
15 Director of Human Resources .... Mrs. Beth JONES
18 Director Facilities/Physical Plant .... Mr. Jennings CARTER
96 Director Purchasing/Auxiliary Svcs .... Mr. Craig ROPER
37 Director of Financial Aid .... Ms. Jill KLOSTERMANN
76 Director of Radiologic Technology .... Ms. Mimi POLCZYNSKI
76 Dir Physical Therapist Asst Pgm .... Ms. Jane HERRMANN
13 Dean of Information Technology .... Ms. Gina SCHUETZ
26 Director of Marketing .... Mr. Travis HENSON
40 Bookstore Manager .... Ms. Cynthia WEBBER
41 Athletic Director .... Ms. Kimberly RAHAR
88 Director of Student Recruitment .... Ms. Amy TROUTT
07 Dir Admissions/Records & Dual Cred .... Mrs. Cheryl BOEHNE
111 Dir Inst Advancement Programs .... Mrs. Suzanne CHRIST
19 Director Security/Safety .... Ms. Deana BELCHER

Kendall College (E)

900 N North Branch Street, Chicago IL 60642

County: Cook | FICE Identification: 001703
Unit ID: 146393
Telephone: (312) 752-2000 | Carnegie Class: Bac-Diverse
FAX Number: (312) 752-2021 | Calendar System: Quarter
URL: www.kendall.edu
Established: 1934 | Annual Undergrad Tuition & Fees: $19,828
Enrollment: 1,275 | Coed
Affiliation or Control: Proprietary | IRS Status: Proprietary
Highest Offering: Baccalaureate
Accreditation: NH, ACFEI

01 President .... Mr. J. Paul LUSSOW
05 Provost .... Dr. Agueda BENITO
84 Director of Domestic Enrollment .... Vacant
04 Executive Assistant to President .... Mr. Scott BRANDEL
10 Executive Director of Finance & Ope .... Ms. Jennifer BRIAR
06 Registrar .... Mrs. Daniela LEOPALDI-ALEMAN
15 Senior Human Resources Manager .... Ms. Crystal KAMINSKI
29 Alumni Affairs .... Vacant
32 Exec Director of Student Services .... Ms. Kristen HODGES
08 Library Technician .... Ms. Alexis CARSCADDEN
37 Director of Financial Aid .... Mr. Lauren WALKER
39 Manager Student Life & Housing .... Ms. Vicki MULLALY
97 Director of General Education .... Mr. Ryan BARTELMAY
19 Director Campus Safety & Security .... Ms. Jeanette KONIECZKA
09 Director of Institutional Effective .... Mrs. Amanda MOLLER
96 Senior Procurement Manager .... Vacant
13 Manager of Information Technology .... Mr. James AMATO
53 Dean Education .... Mr. Paul BUSCENI

Kishwaukee College (F)

21193 Malta Road, Malta IL 60150-9600

County: De Kalb | FICE Identification: 007684
Unit ID: 146418
Telephone: (815) 825-2086 | Carnegie Class: Assoc/MT-VT-High Non
FAX Number: (815) 825-2072 | Calendar System: Semester
URL: www.kishwaukeecollege.edu
Established: 1968 | Annual Undergrad Tuition & Fees (In-District): $4,290
Enrollment: 4,064 | Coed
Affiliation or Control: State/Local | IRS Status: 501(c)3
Highest Offering: Associate Degree
Accreditation: NH, EMT, RAD

01 President .... Dr. Laurie BOROWICZ
108 VP Institutional Effectiveness .... Mr. Kevin J. FUSS
05 Vice President Instruction .... Ms. Joanne KANTNER
32 Vice President Student Services .... Ms. Michelle ROTHMEYER
83 Dean Arts/Communic/Social Science .... Ms. Jaime LONG
72 Dean Career Technologies .... Mr. Matt FEUERBORN
76 Dean Health & Education .... Ms. Bette CHILTON
35 Dean of Student Services .... Ms. Nancy PARTCH
81 Dean Math/Science/Business .... Mr. Chase BUDZIAK
10 Controller .... Ms. Jill HANSEN
102 Exec Dir Foundation Development .... Mr. Bill NICKLAS
07 Director Enrollment Services .... Ms. Sonia REISING
26 Exec Dir of Marketing & PR .... Ms. Kayte HAMEL
25 Director Accreditation & Grants .... Mr. Mark LANTING
37 Director Student Financial Aid .... Ms. Cynthia STONESIFER
13 Director Information Technology .... Mr. Robert MCGARRY
40 Bookstore Manager .... Ms. Jessica ANDERSON
08 Dir Acad Support & Lib Svcs .... Ms. Anne-Marie GREEN
15 Exec Director Human Resources .... Ms. Samantha DAILEY
88 Director Student Involvement .... Mr. Scott KAWALL
18 Director Campus Operations .... Mr. Keith LAMB
04 Executive Assistant to President .... Ms. Cindy MCCLUSKEY
09 Director Research & Data Mgmt .... Mr. Matthew CRULL
96 Purchasing Coordinator .... Ms. Kathleen JONES
103 Director Workforce & Cmty Educ .... Ms. Mary Ann KOLLS
50 Director Business & Training Part .... Ms. LaCretia KONAN

Knox College (G)

2 E South Street, Galesburg IL 61401-4999

County: Knox | FICE Identification: 001704
Unit ID: 146427
Telephone: (309) 341-7000 | Carnegie Class: Bac-A&S
FAX Number: (309) 341-7090 | Calendar System: Trimester
URL: www.knox.edu
Established: 1837 | Annual Undergrad Tuition & Fees: $43,285
Enrollment: 1,397 | Coed
Affiliation or Control: Independent Non-Profit | IRS Status: 501(c)3
Highest Offering: Baccalaureate
Accreditation: NH

01 President .... Dr. Teresa L. AMOTT
101 Secretary of the College .... Ms. Peggy J. WARE
05 VP Acad Affairs/Dean of College .... Dr. Michael A. SCHNEIDER
10 Vice Pres for Finance & Admin Svcs .... Mr. Keith A. ARCHER
111 Vice President for Advancement .... Ms. Beverly HOLMES
07 Vice Pres Enrollment/Dean of Admiss .... Mr. Paul R. STEENIS
32 VP for Student Development .... Dr. Anne R. EHRLICH
26 VP Communications .... Ms. Megan SCOTT
06 Registrar .... Dr. Timothy R. GRAY
32 Dean of Students .... Ms. Debbie SOUTHERN
20 Associate Dean of College .... Dr. Timothy J. FOSTER
37 Director Financial Aid .... Ms. Ann BRILL
08 Librarian .... Mr. Jeffrey A. DOUGLAS
36 Director Ctr Career Pre-Prof Dev .... Ms. Terrie SALINE
13 VP/CIO Information Technology Svcs .... Mr. Steven HALL
15 AVP Director Human Resources .... Ms. Crystal D. BOHN
18 Director Facilities Services .... Mr. Scott MAUST
21 Controller .... Ms. Bobby Jo MAURER
86 Dir Government & Community Relation .... Ms. Karrie HEARTLEIN
29 Dir Alumni & Constituent Programs .... Ms. Carol J. BROWN
38 Director of Counseling Services .... Ms. Janell J. MCGRUDER
19 Director Campus Safety .... Mr. Mark A. WELKER
09 Dir Institutional Research/Assess .... Mr. Charles L. CLARK
102 Dir Corporate/Foundation Relations .... Ms. Anne-Marie BERK
44 Director Annual or Planned Giving .... Mr. Scott PARK

Lake Forest College (H)

555 N Sheridan Road, Lake Forest IL 60045-2338

County: Lake | FICE Identification: 001706
Unit ID: 146481
Telephone: (847) 234-3100 | Carnegie Class: Bac-A&S
FAX Number: (847) 735-6291 | Calendar System: Semester
URL: www.lakeforest.edu

Established: 1857 Annual Undergrad Tuition & Fees: $44,116
Enrollment: 1,600 Coed
Affiliation or Control: Independent Non-Profit IRS Status: 501(c)3
Highest Offering: Master's
Accreditation: NH, IPSY

01 President .... Mr. Stephen D. SCHUTT
05 Provost/Dean of Faculty .... Dr. Michael ORR
10 VP for Finance/Planning & Treasurer .... Ms. Lori SUNDBERG
30 VP of Development & Alumni Pgms .... Mr. Philip HOOD
07 VP of Enrollment .... Mr. Chris ELLERTSON
32 Interim Dean of Students .... Ms. Erin HOFFMAN
21 Controller and Payroll .... Ms. Doris DUMAS
04 Executive Assistant to President .... Ms. Elizabeth A. PALM
35 Assoc Dean Dir of Residence Life .... Mr. Andrew POLLOM
28 Interim Dir Intercult Relations .... Ms. Jasmin ROBINSON
20 Asc Dean Facul/Dir Ctr Chicago Pgms .... Dr. Davis SCHNEIDERMAN
20 Assoc Dean Facul/Dir Lrng/Tchng Ctr .... Dr. Ann ROBERTS
31 Director of Community Education .... Mr. Dan LEMAHIEU
37 Associate VP of Financial Aid .... Mr. Gerard J. CEBRZYNSKI
41 Athletic Director .... Ms. Jacqueline SLAATS
08 Librarian & Director Info Svcs/Tech .... Mr. James R. CUBIT
06 Registrar .... Mr. BJ WHITE
38 Director of Counseling Services .... Dr. Jennifer JEZIORSKI
29 Assoc Vice Pres for Alumni Relation .... Ms. Kim FEIGH
09 Director of Institutional Research .... Ms. Lori H. SUNDBERG
15 Director of Human Resources .... Ms. Agnes STEPEK
36 Director of Career Services .... Ms. Lisa HINKLEY
18 Director of Facilities Management .... Mr. David J. SIEBERT
26 Assoc VP for Comm/Mktg .... Ms. Elizabeth LIBBY
19 Director of Public Safety .... Mr. Richard L. COHEN
101 Secretary of the Institution/Board .... Ms. Carol LUEDERS
104 Director Study Abroad .... Ms. Ashley SINCLAIR
44 Director Annual Giving .... Ms. Katie ROTH

Lake Forest Graduate School of Management (A)

1905 W Field Court, Lake Forest IL 60045-4824
County: Lake FICE Identification: 023192
Unit ID: 146490
Telephone: (847) 234-5005 Carnegie Class: Spec-4-yr-Bus
FAX Number: (847) 295-3656 Calendar System: Semester
URL: www.lfgsm.edu
Established: 1946 Annual Graduate Tuition & Fees: N/A
Enrollment: 401 Coed
Affiliation or Control: Independent Non-Profit IRS Status: 501(c)3
Highest Offering: Master's; No Undergraduates
Accreditation: NH

01 President .... Mr. Jeffrey J. ANDERSON
05 VP and Chief Academic Officer .... Dr. Bryan J. WATKINS
10 VP Finance & CFO .... Mr. Thomas PEROZZI
26 Senior Director of Marketing .... Ms. Barb SIEGEL
88 VP Corporate Learning Solutions .... Ms. Carrie BUCHWALD
13 VP IT & CIO .... Mr. Gregory KOZAK
20 Dean Faculty & Degree Programs .... Dr. Cheryl BONCUORE
20 Dean Educational Programs & Dev .... Dr. Neil HOLMAN
09 Asst Dir Institutional Research .... Ms. Jeanne KUETER
06 Registrar .... Ms. Christine L. PERLSTROM
37 Director of Financial Aid .... Ms. Connie ELDRIDGE
07 Senior Director of Admissions .... Ms. Carolyn BRUNE
32 Director of Student Services .... Ms. Currie GASCHE
11 Director of Campus Operations .... Ms. Kim PLACENTINO
04 Administrative Asst to President .... Ms. Dana KAECHELE

Lake Land College (B)

5001 Lake Land Boulevard, Mattoon IL 61938-9366
County: Coles FICE Identification: 007644
Unit ID: 146506
Telephone: (217) 234-5253 Carnegie Class: Assoc/HVT-High Non
FAX Number: (217) 234-5400 Calendar System: Semester
URL: www.lakeland.cc.il.us
Established: 1966 Annual Undergrad Tuition & Fees (In-District): $3,789
Enrollment: 5,241 Coed
Affiliation or Control: State/Local IRS Status: 501(c)3
Highest Offering: Associate Degree
Accreditation: NH, ADNUR, DH, PNUR, PTAA

01 President .... Dr. Josh BULLOCK
100 Senior Executive to the President .... Ms. Jean Anne GRUNLOH
04 Admin Asst to the President's Ofc .... Ms. Seirra LAUGHHUNN
10 VP for Business Services .... Mr. Bryan GLECKLER
05 VP for Academic Services .... Mr. Jon ALTHAUS
32 Vice President for Student Services .... Dr. Tina STOVALL
88 Dean of Correctional Pgms-South .... Mr. Brandon YOUNG
20 Assoc Vice Pres Educational Svcs .... Dr. Deb HUTTI
07 Dean of Admissions Services .... Mr. Jon VAN DYKE
88 Assoc Dean Corrections-Taylorville .... Mr. Robert EIFERT
88 Assoc Dean Corrections-Graham .... Vacant
88 Assoc Dean Corrections-Western .... Ms. Malea HARNEY
88 Assoc Dean Correction-IL River .... Mr. Michael CHASE
88 Assoc Dean Corrections-Southwestern ... Mr. Harvey GROENNERT
88 Assoc Dean Corrections-Jacksonville .... Mr. Steve BAHNEY
88 Assoc Dean Corrections-Lawrence .... Ms. Valerie PRATSCHER
88 Assoc Dean Corrections-Robinson .... Vacant
88 Assoc Dean Corrections-Vandalia .... Mr. Steve DRAKE
44 Exec Dir College Advance/Foundation .... Ms. Jacqueline JOINES
88 Site Director Corrections-Hill .... Vacant
88 Site Director Corr-Vienna & Shawnee .... Mr. Blake MCCONNELL

21 Comptroller .... Ms. Madge SHOOT
50 Dir Center for Business & Industry .... Ms. Bonnie MOORE
08 Director of Library Services .... Mr. Scott DRONE-SILVERS
26 Dir of Marketing/Public Relations .... Mrs. Kelly ALLEE
13 Dir of Information Systems/Services .... Mr. Lee SPANIOL
37 Dir of Financial Aid/Veteran Svcs .... Ms. Paula CARPENTER
15 Director of Human Resources .... Ms. Dustha WAHLS
88 Director of Learning Technologies .... Mr. Steve GARREN
25 Director of Grants Development .... Ms. Emily RAMAGE
35 Director Student Life .... Ms. Valerie LYNCH
109 Director of Auxiliary Services .... Ms. Christina KRAMER
29 Dir of Alumni Rels/Annual Giving .... Mr. Dave COX
36 Director of Career Services .... Ms. Tina MOORE
38 Chair of Counseling/Judicial Affs .... Ms. Emily HARTKE
18 Dir of Physical Plant Operations .... Mr. Scott RAWLINGS
41 Director of Athletics .... Mr. William JACKSON
09 Director of Institutional Research .... Dr. Mary BREER
84 Coordinator of Enrollment Services .... Ms. Paula SMITH
103 VP Workforce Solutions/Cmty Educ .... Dr. Jim HULL

Lakeview College of Nursing (C)

903 N Logan Avenue, Danville IL 61832-3788
County: Vermilion FICE Identification: 010501
Unit ID: 146533
Telephone: (217) 709-0920 Carnegie Class: Spec-4-yr-Other Health
FAX Number: (217) 709-0954 Calendar System: Semester
URL: www.lakeviewcol.edu
Established: 1987 Annual Undergrad Tuition & Fees: N/A
Enrollment: 316 Coed
Affiliation or Control: Independent Non-Profit IRS Status: 501(c)3
Highest Offering: Baccalaureate
Accreditation: NH, NURSE

01 President .... Ms. Sheila MINGEE
05 Interim Dean of Nursing .... Ms. Jessica SOTIRIOU
06 Registrar/Director of Enrollment .... Ms. Connie YOUNG
08 Library Director/IT Coordinator .... Ms. Miranda SHAKE
04 Administrative Asst to President .... Ms. Karlee THOMEN

Lewis and Clark Community College (D)

5800 Godfrey Road, Godfrey IL 62035-2466
County: Madison FICE Identification: 010020
Unit ID: 146603
Telephone: (618) 468-7000 Carnegie Class: Assoc/MT-VT-High Non
FAX Number: (618) 466-2798 Calendar System: Semester
URL: www.lc.edu
Established: 1970 Annual Undergrad Tuition & Fees (In-District): $3,264
Enrollment: 7,914 Coed
Affiliation or Control: State/Local IRS Status: 501(c)3
Highest Offering: Associate Degree
Accreditation: NH, ADNUR, DA, DH, EMT, MAAB, OTA

01 President .... Dr. Dale T. CHAPMAN
05 Vice President Academic Affairs .... Dr. Linda CHAPMAN
84 Vice President Enrollment Services .... Mr. Kent SCHEFFEL
32 Vice Pres Student Engagement .... Dr. Sean HILL
11 Vice President Administration .... Ms. Lori ARTIS
10 Vice President Finance .... Mrs. Mary SCHULTE
114 Chief Budget Officer .... Mrs. Nancy KAISER
88 Director Corp & Comm Learning .... Mrs. Kathy WILLIS
13 Chief Information Officer .... Vacant
09 Dir Institutional Res/Library Svcs .... Mr. Dennis KRIEB
06 Registrar .... Ms. Heidi SCOTT
41 Director Athletics .... Mr. Doug STOTLER
07 Director of Enrollment Center .... Ms. Delfina DORNES
15 Director Human Resources .... Mr. Gabe SPRINGER
18 Facilities Manager .... Mr. Mike RANDALL
19 Director Security .... Mr. Brad RAISH
26 Manager Media Services .... Ms. Laura INLOW
28 Coordinator Diversity & Inclusion .... Ms. Adrienne REED
30 Director of Development .... Ms. Debbie EDELMAN
37 Director Financial Aid .... Ms. Angela WEAVER

Lewis University (E)

One University Parkway, Romeoville IL 60446-2200
County: Will FICE Identification: 001707
Unit ID: 146612
Telephone: (815) 838-0500 Carnegie Class: Masters/L
FAX Number: (815) 838-9456 Calendar System: Semester
URL: www.lewisu.edu
Established: 1932 Annual Undergrad Tuition & Fees: $30,050
Enrollment: 6,679 Coed
Affiliation or Control: Roman Catholic IRS Status: 501(c)3
Highest Offering: Doctorate
Accreditation: NH, ACBSP, #CAATE, CAEPN, NURSE, SW

01 President .... Dr. David J. LIVINGSTON
05 Provost .... Dr. Stephany SCHLACHTER
32 Sr Vice President Student Services .... Mr. Joseph FALESE
10 Senior Vice Pres/CFO .... Vacant
84 Sr VP Enrollment Mgmt/Marketing .... Mr. Raymond KENNELLY
111 VP University Advancement .... Mr. Luigi AMENDOLA
07 Dean of Admission .... Ms. Ashley SKIDMORE
35 Dean of Student Services .... Ms. Katheryn SLATTERY
28 VP Mission & Academic Services .... Dr. Kurt SCHACKMUTH
49 Dean College Arts & Sciences .... Dr. Bonnie BONDAVALLI
50 Dean College Business .... Mr. Ryan BUTT

66 Dean Col Nursing/Health Professions .... Dr. Peggy RICE
53 Dean College of Education .... Dr. Pamela JESSEE
15 Assoc Vice Pres Human Resources .... Ms. Graciela DUFOUR
09 Assoc VP Inst Research/Planning .... Dr. Kang BAI
08 Director of Library .... Mr. Thomas URBANSKI
06 Registrar .... Ms. Jacqueline SCHMIDT
37 Director of Financial Aid .... Ms. Janeen DECHARINTE
26 Director Marketing/Communications ... Dr. Ramona LAMONTAGNE
41 Director of Athletics .... Dr. John PLANEK
38 Director of Counseling Services .... Ms. Michele MANASSAH
19 Chief of Police .... Mr. James MONTANARI
42 Director of University Ministry .... Mr. Steve ZLATIC
88 Dir of Meetings/Events/Conferences .... Ms. Julie PENNER
85 Director International Student Svcs .... Mr. Michael FEKETE
91 Director of Administrative Systems .... Mr. Charles PUSTZ
13 Associate Vice Pres/Technology .... Dr. LeRoy BUTLER
29 Executive Dir of Alumni Engagement ... Ms. Kathryn RISOR-HEISE
96 Director of Opers and Purchasing .... Ms. Jennifer SKVARLA
36 Exec Director of Career Services .... Ms. Mary MYERS
04 Administrative Asst to President .... Ms. Margaret KIENTOP
102 Dir Foundation & Corp Relations .... Ms. Jennifer DOHERTY
104 Director Study Abroad .... Mr. Christopher SWANSON
105 Director Web Services .... Mr. Sylvain GOYETTE
18 Assoc VP Facilities/Physical Plant .... Mr. Donald CASTELLO
25 Director of Sponsored Programs .... Mr. Jeffrey RITCHIE
23 Director Health Services .... Ms. Michele RONCHETTI
39 Director of Residence Life .... Mr. Fredrick GANDY
20 Assoc Provost for Acad Admin & Acc .... Dr. Kathy S. KREMER
21 Assistant Vice Pres for Business .... Mr. Aaron SCHEIWE

Lincoln Christian University (F)

100 Campus View Drive, Lincoln IL 62656-2167
County: Logan FICE Identification: 001708
Unit ID: 146667
Telephone: (217) 732-3168 Carnegie Class: Spec-4-yr-Faith
FAX Number: (217) 732-5914 Calendar System: Semester
URL: www.lincolnchristian.edu
Established: 1944 Annual Undergrad Tuition & Fees: $13,020
Enrollment: 878 Coed
Affiliation or Control: Christian Churches And Churches of Christ
IRS Status: 501(c)3
Highest Offering: Doctorate
Accreditation: NH, BI, CACREP, THEOL

01 President .... Dr. Donald GREEN
10 Vice President of Finance .... Mr. G. Steve POPENFOOSE
84 Vice Pres of Enrollment Services .... Dr. Silas MCCORMICK
32 VP of Student Services .... Mr. Randall INGMIRE
05 Vice President of Academics .... Dr. Rochelle SCHEUERMANN
111 VP of University Advancement .... Mr. Scott HURLEY
29 VP of Alumni Services .... Mr. Lynn LAUGHLIN
06 Registrar .... Mr. Shawn SMITH
08 Director of Library Services .... Ms. Nancy OLSON
37 Director of Financial Aid .... Ms. Nancy SIDDENS
101 Admin Asst to Pres/Secy Bd of Gov .... Mrs. Linda SEGGELKE
13 Director of Campus Technology .... Mr. Jeremiah PROCTOR
15 Director of Human Resources .... Mrs. Marla BENNETT
41 Athletic Director .... Mr. Nathaniel SMITH
18 Chief Facilities/Physical Plant .... Mr. Freddie TEDRICK
26 Associate Director of Marketing .... Mr. Nathan ROBERTS

Lincoln College (G)

300 Keokuk Street, Lincoln IL 62656-1699
County: Logan FICE Identification: 001709
Unit ID: 146676
Telephone: (217) 732-3155 Carnegie Class: Bac/Assoc-Mixed
FAX Number: (217) 732-8859 Calendar System: Semester
URL: www.lincolncollege.edu
Established: 1865 Annual Undergrad Tuition & Fees: $17,700
Enrollment: 1,194 Coed
Affiliation or Control: Independent Non-Profit IRS Status: 501(c)3
Highest Offering: Baccalaureate
Accreditation: NH, IACBE

01 President .... Dr. David M. GERLACH
05 Vice President for Academic Affairs .... Dr. A. Gigi FANSLER
30 Vice President for Advancement .... Ms. Debbie ACKERMAN
84 VP for Enroll Mgmt & Student Svcs .... Ms. Susan BOEHLER
10 Vice Pres Finance & Administration .... Mr. Greg A. EIMER
07 Dean of Enrollment Management .... Mr. Jason GARBER
32 Dean of Students .... Mrs. Bridgett THOMAS
107 Exec Dir Center for Adult Learning .... Mr. Vance LAINE
88 Director of Academic Advising .... Mr. Jacob HARNACKE
06 Registrar .... Mrs. Debra J. HARMON
08 Head Librarian .... Ms. Dorothy RYAN
13 Director of Information Technology .... Mr. David LOLLING
21 Controller .... Mrs. Katherine PAPESCH
15 Director of Human Resources .... Ms. Sara SCHWANTZ
18 Director of Building & Grounds .... Ms. Ronda PIATT
37 Director of Financial Aid .... Mr. Christopher JOHNSON
41 Athletic Director .... Mr. Dave KLEMM
40 Bookstore Manager .... Mrs. Donna HUTCHISON

Lincoln College - Normal (H)

715 W Raab Road, Normal IL 61761
Telephone: (309) 452-0500 Identification: 770078
Accreditation: &NH

Lincoln College of Technology (A)

8317 West North Avenue, Melrose Park IL 60160-1605
County: Cook FICE Identification: 010316
Unit ID: 146700
Telephone: (708) 344-4700 Carnegie Class: Spec 2-yr-Tech
FAX Number: (708) 345-4065 Calendar System: Semester
URL: www.lincolntech.edu
Established: 1950 Annual Undergrad Tuition & Fees: N/A
Enrollment: 676 Coed
Affiliation or Control: Proprietary IRS Status: Proprietary
Highest Offering: Associate Degree
Accreditation: ACCSC

01 Campus President Karen M. CLARK
05 Campus VP of Education Larry KESHNER
11 Director Administrative Services Karen STEPINA
36 Director of Career Services Keston EDWARDS
37 Director of Financial Aid Cliff DAVIS
04 Administrative Asst to President Mindy GUARINO
07 Director of Admissions Kevin FERGUSON
08 Head Librarian Karen MCELWAIN

Lincoln Land Community College (B)

5250 Shepherd Road, PO Box 19256,
Springfield IL 62794-9256
County: Sangamon FICE Identification: 007170
Unit ID: 146685
Telephone: (217) 786-2200 Carnegie Class: Assoc/HVT-High Non
FAX Number: (217) 786-2468 Calendar System: Semester
URL: www.llcc.edu
Established: 1967 Annual Undergrad Tuition & Fees (In-District): $3,024
Enrollment: 6,447 Coed
Affiliation or Control: Local IRS Status: 501(c)3
Highest Offering: Associate Degree
Accreditation: NH, ADNUR, COARC, NDT, OTA, PNUR, RAD, SURGT

01 President Dr. Charlotte J. WARREN
11 Vice President Administrative Svcs Mr. Todd MCDONALD
05 Vice President Academic Services Dr. Eileen G. TEPATTI
32 Vice President Student Services Ms. Lesley J. FREDERICK
103 VP Workforce Dev/Cmty Educ Dr. Judy JOZAITIS
13 Chief Information Officer Mr. Esteban CRUZ
15 AVP Human Resources Ms. Junell A. RANSDELL
84 AVP Enrollment Services Ms. Lisa COLLIER
10 AVP Finance Ms. Karie L. LONGHTA
86 Asst VP Corp/Govt Trng & Econ Devel Ms. Paula J. LUEBBERT
18 Assistant VP Construction Vacant
12 AVP LLCC Outreach Vacant
102 Exec Director LLCC Foundation Ms. Karen A. SANDERS
26 Exec Dir Public Relations/Marketing Ms. Lynn WHALEN
121 Exec Director Academic Success Mrs. Julie CLEVENGER
88 Director Small Business Devel Ctr Mr. Kevin LUST
07 Director Admissions/Records Mrs. Shanda R. BYER
22 Dir Employ Bnft Svc/Eq Opty Cmpl Of Ms. Nicole M. RALPH
09 Director Institutional Research Ms. Susan SIMPSON
45 Dir Institutional Effectiveness Ms. Tricia A. KUJAWA
19 Police Chief Mr. Bradley D. GENTRY
50 Dean Business & Technologies Mr. David A. GREEN
83 Dean Social Sciences Dr. Victor K. BRODERICK
20 AVP Academic Services Ms. Wendy L. HOWERTER
57 Dean Arts & Humanities Mr. J. Timothy HUMPHREY
81 Dean Mathematics and Sciences Mr. William D. BADE
76 Dean Health Professions Dr. Cynthia L. MASKEY
08 Assoc Dean Library Mrs. Tamara KUHN-SCHNELL
106 Dean ITDE Mrs. Becky PARTON
14 Director IT and Infrastructure Mr. Ben ROTH
14 Director IT Service and Support Mrs. Joni BERNAHL
41 Director Athletics Mr. Ron RIGGLE
109 Director Campus Services Mr. Andrew BLAYLOCK
35 Assistant VP Student Success Ms. Leslie R. JOHNSON
38 Dir Advising/Counseling/Career Svcs Ms. Mary Beth RAY
18 Director Facilities Mr. David BRETSCHER

Lindenwood University Belleville Campus (C)

2600 West Main Street, Belleville IL 62226
Telephone: (618) 239-6000 Identification: 770322
Accreditation: &NH, ACBSP

† Branch campus of Lindenwood University, Saint Charles, MO

Loyola University Chicago (D)

1032 W. Sheridan Road, Chicago IL 60660
County: Cook FICE Identification: 001710
Unit ID: 146719
Telephone: (773) 274-3000 Carnegie Class: DU-Higher
FAX Number: (312) 915-7003 Calendar System: Semester
URL: www.luc.edu
Established: 1870 Annual Undergrad Tuition & Fees: $42,032
Enrollment: 16,437 Coed
Affiliation or Control: Roman Catholic IRS Status: 501(c)3
Highest Offering: Doctorate
Accreditation: NH, CAEPN, CLPSY, COPSY, DENT, DIETI, EMT, FEPAC, LAW, MED, NURSE, PH, SCPSY, SW, THEA, @THEOL

00 Chancellor Rev. Michael J. GARANZINI, SJ
01 President Dr. Jo Ann ROONEY
17 Provost Health Sciences Dr. Margaret F. CALLAHAN
05 Provost Dr. John P. PELISSERO
10 Sr Vice President Finance & CFO Vacant
85 Vice Provost Acad Ctrs/Global Inits Dr. Patrick M. BOYLE
20 Vice Provost Academic & Faculty Res Dr. David P. PRASSE
111 Senior VP Advancement Dr. Damon CATES
45 Sr VP Cap Planning & Campus Mgmt Mr. Wayne MAGDZIARZ
11 Sr VP Admin Svcs Mr. Thomas M. KELLY
19 Director Campus Safety Mr. Thomas MURRAY
29 Director Alumni Relations Vacant
88 Dir of Advancement Communication Mr. Brendan KEATING
105 Director of Web Communication Mr. John DREVS
88 Director of Student Complex Ms. Dawn M. COLLINS
21 Director Financial Svcs & Payroll Ms. Rebecca GOMEZ
04 Administrative Asst to President Ms. Kate J. PETERSON
96 Director of Cash Management Mr. Corey O'BRIEN
18 Director of Facilities-HSD Mr. Tom EARLY
12 Interim VP & Director Rome Ctr Mr. Michael ANDREWS
12 General Manager LUREC & Cuneo Mr. Kevin GINTY
86 Vice President Government Affairs Mr. Philip P. HALE
13 Vice President Information Services Ms. Susan M. MALISCH
03 Vice Chancellor Rev. John COSTELLO, SJ
26 VP Marketing & Communications Vacant
88 Assoc VP Finance - HSD Ms. Lauren HAGAN
88 Assoc VP Informatics/System Devel Mr. Ronald N. PRICE
88 Asst VP Capital Planning Mr. Michael LOFTSGAARDEN
31 Assoc VP Campus/Community Planning Ms. Jennifer R. CLARK
114 Assoc VP for Budget & Finance Mr. Ben SMIGIELSKI
18 Associate VP of Capital Projects Ms. Kana WIBBENMEYER
88 Dir Retail/Residential Property Ast Mr. Brian T. O'LEARY
58 Dean Graduate School & Research Vacant
35 Assistant VP Student Development Dr. Jack MCLEAN
27 Dir Brand Marketing Ms. Katie HESSION
84 Assoc Provost Enrollment Management Mr. Paul G. ROBERTS
88 Assoc Provost Academic Admin Dr. Marian A. CLAFFEY
88 Assoc Provost for Mission & Identit Dr. John HARDT
62 Assoc Provost & Dir HSD Library Ms. Gail HENDLER
108 Asst Prov Institutional Effectivene Dr. David B. SLAVSKY
88 Assoc Provost Curriculum Dev Dr. Jo Beth D'AGOSTINO
96 Dir Purchasing Mr. Brian R. SLAVINKAS
88 Asst Provost & Dir Faculty Admin Ms. Anne C. REULAND
88 Asst Prov Educ Resources HSD Rev. Keith MUCCINO, SJ
121 Assistant Provost Academic Advising Vacant
100 Special Assistant to the President Ms. Lorraine G. FITZGERALD
62 Dean Libraries Ms. Marianne P. RYAN
50 Dean School of Business Admin Dr. Kevin STEVENS
49 Dean Arts & Sciences Mr. Thomas J. REGAN
51 Dean Continuing & Prof Studies Dr. Walter PEARSON
60 Dean School of Communication Dr. Donald B. HEIDER
61 Dean School of Law Mr. Michael J. KAUFMAN
63 Dean School of Medicine Dr. Steve GOLDSTEIN
66 Dean School of Nursing Dr. Vicki A. KEOUGH
70 Dean School of Social Work Dr. Goutham MENON
72 Dir Procedure Improvement & Tech Ad Ms. Danielle HANSON
53 Interim Dean School of Education Dr. David SLAVSKY
88 Dean & Exec Dir Arrupe College Rev. Stephen N. KATSOUROS, SJ
18 Superintendent Lakeside Facilities Mr. William SHERRY
88 Exec Director Conference Services Mr. Dana ADAMS
90 Director Academic Tech Services Mr. Bruce A. MONTES
88 Asst Prov Dir Academic Business Ops Ms. Joanna PAPPAS
88 Dir Enrollment Systems & Res Report Mr. Timothy HEUER
28 Dir Student Diversity & Multicultur Mr. Joseph SAUCEDO
30 VP of Development HSD Ms. Amy DAY
37 Director of Financial Aid Mr. Tobyn L. FRIAR
15 Director of Human Resources Ms. Joan C. STASIAK
90 Dir System Implement & Consulting Mr. Kevin J. SMITH
102 Dir of Corporate & Foundation Rels Vacant
06 Director of Registration & Records Ms. Clare M. KORINEK
88 Asst VP Advancement Info Services Mr. Mike HALVERSON
115 Treasurer & Chief Inv Officer Vacant
09 Director Institutional Research Dr. Richard S. HURST
07 Director Undergraduate Admissions Ms. Erin T. MORIATY
39 Director Residence Life Ms. Debrah SCHMIDT-ROGERS
101 Asst VP Trustee Relations Dr. Donna B. CURIN
104 Executive Director Intl Programs Dr. Jennifer ENGEL
106 Director Online Learning Ms. Sarah DYSART
18 Director Infrastructure Services Mr. Dan VONDER HEIDE
25 Assoc VP Finance Sponsored Pgm Acc Ms. Donna QUIRK
88 Dir Enterprise Architecture & Promo Mr. Jim SIBENALLER
36 Director Career Development Center Ms. Kathryn JACKSON
43 Vice President & General Counsel Ms. Pam COSTAS
38 Interim Director Wellness Center Ms. Joan HOLDEN
28 Dir Cultural Affairs & LUMA Vacant
88 Dir Facilities WTC Mr. Mark FEIEREISEL
32 Vice President Student Development Ms. Jane NEUFELD
42 Director Campus Ministry Dr. Lisa REITER
54 Director Engineering Sciences Dr. Gail BAURA
41 Athletic Director Mr. Steve WATSON
85 Director Chicago Center Mr. Jason OBIN
118 Director Compensation & Benefits Ms. Debra MEISTER
21 Dir General Accounting Ms. Maria ARAQUE
88 Director Faculty Admin-HSD Ms. Martha KING
102 Executive Director Corp Engagement Dr. Janet DEATHERIDGE
88 Dir Inst Environmental Sustain Dr. Nancy TUCHMAN
15 Vice President HR & CDO Dr. Winifred WILLIAMS
117 Director Strategic Financing/Risk Ms. Susan BODIN
24 Dir Communication & Media Mr. Steve CHRISTENSON
65 Director Environmental Services Mr. William CURTIN
88 Dir of Capital Business Operations Mr. David BEALL
88 Dean Institute Pastoral Studies Dr. Brian SCHMISEK
51 Director Adult & Transfer Center Ms. Jill SCHUR
88 Director Enrollment Marketing Ms. Heather TAYLOR

Loyola University Health Sciences Campus (E)

2160 S First Avenue, Maywood IL 60153
Telephone: (708) 216-9000 Identification: 770080
Accreditation: &NH, PAST

Loyola University Water Tower Campus (F)

820 N Michigan Avenue, Chicago IL 60611
Telephone: (312) 915-6000 Identification: 770079
Accreditation: &NH

Lutheran School of Theology at Chicago (G)

1100 E 55th Street, Chicago IL 60615-5199
County: Cook FICE Identification: 001712
Unit ID: 146728
Telephone: (773) 256-0700 Carnegie Class: Spec-4-yr-Faith
FAX Number: (773) 256-0782 Calendar System: Semester
URL: www.lstc.edu
Established: 1860 Annual Graduate Tuition & Fees: N/A
Enrollment: 214 Coed
Affiliation or Control: Evangelical Lutheran Church In America
IRS Status: 501(c)3
Highest Offering: Doctorate; No Undergraduates
Accreditation: NH, THEOL

01 President Dr. James NIEMAN
04 Assistant to the President Ms. Patti DEBIAS
108 Exec for Assessment and Planning Ms. Christine YUCHA
05 Dean for Academic Affairs Dr. Esther MENN
88 Director of the MDiv Programs Dr. Kathleen BILLMAN
88 Director of the MA Programs Vacant
58 Director of Advanced Studies Dr. Ben STEWART
42 Pastor to the Community Vacant
11 Vice President for Operations Mr. Bob BERRIDGE
111 Vice President for Advancement Mr. Mark H. VAN SCHARREL
10 Vice President for Finance Mr. Robert EDER
32 Dean of Student Services Dr. Scott CHALMERS
06 Registrar Ms. Patricia A. BARTLEY
26 Director of Communications/Mktg Ms. Janet BODEN
08 Director of Library Dr. Christine WENDEROTH
13 Dir of Information Technology Svcs Mr. Kenesa DEBELA

MacCormac College (H)

29 E Madison Street 2nd Floor, Chicago IL 60602-4405
County: Cook FICE Identification: 001716
Unit ID: 146816
Telephone: (312) 922-1884 Carnegie Class: Assoc/HVT-High Trad
FAX Number: (312) 922-4286 Calendar System: Semester
URL: www.maccormac.edu
Established: 1904 Annual Undergrad Tuition & Fees: $12,660
Enrollment: 235 Coed
Affiliation or Control: Independent Non-Profit IRS Status: 501(c)3
Highest Offering: Associate Degree
Accreditation: NH

00 Chancellor Dr. Marnelle ALEXIS STEPHENS
01 Interim President/Dean of Finance Mr. Matt GAWENDA
05 Dean of Academic & Student Affairs Mr. Roberto D. TORRES
06 Registrar Ms. Mariza SILVA
37 Director of Financial Aid Ms. Jamieta HOSKINS
84 Dean of Admission Mr. Joe PAINTER
26 Dir Communications/Public Relations Mr. Adam HITZEMAN

MacMurray College (I)

447 E College Avenue, Jacksonville IL 62650-2590
County: Morgan FICE Identification: 001717
Unit ID: 146825
Telephone: (217) 479-7000 Carnegie Class: Bac-Diverse
FAX Number: (217) 245-0405 Calendar System: 4/1/4
URL: www.mac.edu
Established: 1846 Annual Undergrad Tuition & Fees: $25,110
Enrollment: 570 Coed
Affiliation or Control: United Methodist IRS Status: 501(c)3
Highest Offering: Baccalaureate
Accreditation: #NH, NURSE, SW

01 President Dr. Mark J. TIERNO
10 CFO Ms. Kimberly STREIB
05 Provost Dr. Beverly RODGERS
32 Dean of Student Life Ms. Beth OBERG
07 Enrollment Manager Mr. Tressman GOODE
21 Controller Mr. Andrew SIDOCK
13 Director of IT/System Administrator Mr. Paul YOUNKER
06 Registrar Vacant
08 Librarian Ms. Susan EILERING
37 Director of One-Stop Student Svcs Ms. Laci ENGELBRECHT
36 Director of Career Services Ms. Anne GODMAN
29 Dir Alumni Relations/Annual Giving Ms. Rikki LANGAN
09 Director of Institutional Research Ms. Allison DECKER
18 Director of Facilities Mr. Jonathan JUMPER
26 Director of Communications & Mktg Ms. Marcy JONES
04 Executive Asst to President Ms. Sharon SEYMOUR
41 Athletic Director Mr. Justin FUHLER

McCormick Theological Seminary (A)

5460 S University Avenue, Chicago IL 60615-5108
County: Cook FICE Identification: 001721
Unit ID: 146977
Telephone: (773) 947-6300 Carnegie Class: Spec-4-yr-Faith
FAX Number: (773) 288-2612 Calendar System: 4/1/4
URL: www.mccormick.edu
Established: 1829 Annual Graduate Tuition & Fees: N/A
Enrollment: 195 Coed
Affiliation or Control: Presbyterian Church (U.S.A.) IRS Status: 501(c)3
Highest Offering: Doctorate; No Undergraduates
Accreditation: NH, THEOL

01 Interim President .... Mr. David CRAWFORD
00 Chair of the Board .... Dr. Melinda S. KREI
10 Exec Vice Pres/Chief Business Ofcr .... Mr. David CRAWFORD
05 Vice Pres Acad Affs/Dean Faculty .... Dr. Theodore HIEBERT
32 Vice President for Student Affairs .... Vacant
30 Vice Pres Seminary Rels/Development .... Ms. Lisa M. DAGHER
06 Registrar .... Ms. Chandra WADE
29 Dir of Alumni/ae & Church Rels .... Rev. Nannette BANKS
08 Director of JKM Library .... Dr. Christine WENDEROTH
15 Director Human Resources .... Ms. Ashley WOODFAULK
37 Dir Student Financial Aid/Planning .... Ms. Tabitha HIGHTOWER
07 Sr Director Admissions/Enrollment .... Ms. Veronica JOHNSON
04 Assistant to President & the Dean .... Ms. Jennifer OULD

McHenry County College (B)

8900 US Highway 14, Crystal Lake IL 60012-2796
County: McHenry FICE Identification: 007691
Unit ID: 147004
Telephone: (815) 455-3700 Carnegie Class: Assoc/MT-VT-High Non
FAX Number: (815) 455-3999 Calendar System: Semester
URL: www.mchenry.edu
Established: 1967 Annual Undergrad Tuition & Fees (In-District): $3,404
Enrollment: 6,561 Coed
Affiliation or Control: State/Local IRS Status: 501(c)3
Highest Offering: Associate Degree
Accreditation: NH, OTA

01 President .... Dr. Clinton E. GABBARD
111 Int VP Institutional Advancement .... Ms. Christina HAGGERTY
10 CFO/Treasurer .... Mr. Bob TENUTA
05 VP Academic & Student Affairs .... Dr. Chris GRAY
49 Interim AVP for Arts and Science .... Dr. Brock FISHER
75 Interim AVP Career Technical Ed .... Dr. Terri BERRYMAN
13 Chief Information Officer .... Dr. Allen P. BUTLER
04 Asst to the President/Board Liaison .... Mrs. Pat KRIEGERMEIER
19 Exec Dir Public Safety/Facilities .... Mr. Michael CLESCERI
26 Chief Communications Officer .... Mrs. Christina HAGGERTY
21 AVP of Finance .... Ms. Lynn COWLIN
15 AVP of Human Resources .... Vacant
79 Exec Dean Humanities & Soc Sciences .... Mr. Brock FISCHER
103 Exec Dean Workforce Comm .... Ms. Terri BERRMAN
102 Exec Director MCC Foundation .... Mr. Brian DIBONA
88 Exec Director of Adult Education .. Mr. Julio CAPELES-DELGADO
88 Dean of Academic Development .... Ms. Adriane HUTCHINSON
84 Dean Enrollment Services .... Ms. Marianne DEVENNY
08 Dean of Library .... Ms. Kate HARGER
35 Dean of Student Development .... Dr. Flecia THOMAS
66 Director Nursing .... Ms. Betsy SCHNOWSKE
16 Director Recruitment & Staffing .... Ms. Sandra HESS MOLL
108 Dir Institutional Effectiveness .... Ms. Patricia STEJSKAL
14 Director Software Solutions .... Mr. Todd SMITH
14 Director Technology Support Service .... Mr. Geary SMITH
40 Director Bookstore .... Ms. Karen SMITH
41 Director Athletics-Intramural & Rec .... Ms. Karen WILEY
51 Dir of Continuing Education .... Ms. Dori SULLINS
25 Director of Resource Development .... Mr. Mark DOUGHER
23 Director of Health and Wellness .... Ms. Lena KALEMBA
88 Director of Sustainability .... Ms. Kim HANKINS
109 Director Food Services .... Ms. Sandra JOHNSTON
96 Director of Business Services .... Ms. Jennifer JONES
37 Director of Financial Aid .... Ms. Leana DAVIS
06 Director of Registration & Records .... Ms. Amy HALLER
14 Director Infrastructure Operations .... Mr. Rob RASMUSSEN
106 Director of Online Learning .... Dr. Raymond LAWSON
09 Director of Institutional Research .... Dr. Amy HUMKE
18 Director Facilities .... Mr. Todd WHEELAND
88 Dir Fieldwork Occ Therapy Asst Pgm .... Ms. Marlene VOGT
88 Dir Health Info Technology Programs .... Ms. Chris COCLANIS-LODING
88 Assoc Dean College/Career Readiness .... Mr. Tony CAPALBO
88 Mgr IL Small Business Development .... Ms. Kristi PATTERSON
88 Manager of Customer Service .... Mr. Frank GELASI
88 Manager of Nursing Laboratory .... Ms. Ann STAUCHE
124 Manager New Student Transitions .... Ms. Kellie CARPER
15 Director of Human Resources .... Ms. Anita ROEWER
88 Manager Accounts & Production .... Mr. Ryan KLOS
22 Manager Access & Disability Service .... Ms. Lili O'CONNELL

McKendree University (C)

701 College Road, Lebanon IL 62254-9990
County: Saint Clair FICE Identification: 001722
Unit ID: 147013
Telephone: (618) 537-4481 Carnegie Class: Masters/L
FAX Number: (618) 537-6259 Calendar System: Semester
URL: www.mckendree.edu
Established: 1828 Annual Undergrad Tuition & Fees: $28,740
Enrollment: 3,001 Coed
Affiliation or Control: United Methodist IRS Status: 501(c)3
Highest Offering: Doctorate
Accreditation: NH, #CAATE, IACBE, NURSE

01 President .... Dr. James M. DENNIS
03 Senior Vice President .... Ms. Victoria A. DOWLING
04 Assistant to the President .... Ms. Patti J. DANIELS
05 Provost/Dean of the University .... Dr. Christine M. BAHR
10 Vice Pres Finance/Administration .... Mrs. Sally A. MAYHEW
07 Vice Pres Admission & Financial Aid .... Mr. Chris HALL
32 Vice President Student Affairs .... Dr. Joni BASTIAN
09 Vice Pres Research Plng & Tech .... Vacant
20 Associate Dean of the University .... Dr. Tami EGGLESTON
12 Assoc Dean McKendree-at-Scott .... Vacant
56 External Programs .... Dr. Joseph J. CIPFL
13 Director Technology Information .... Mr. George KRISS
06 Registrar/Asst Dean .... Ms. Debra LARSON
08 Director of Holman Library .... Ms. Paula MARTIN
21 Accounting Manager .... Mrs. Shari B. KEFFER
26 Exec Dir Marketing/Communications .... Mrs. Krysti H. CONNELLY
29 Director Alumni Relations .... Mr. PJ THOMPSON
44 Coordinator of Annual Giving .... Mr. Anthony VIVANO
37 Director Financial Aid .... Mrs. Elizabeth JUEHNE
36 Director Career Services .... Ms. Jennifer K. PICKERELL
18 Director of Operations .... Mr. Tom P. JENSEN
15 Director Human Resources .... Mrs. Shirley A. BAUGH
27 Director Media Relations .... Ms. Lisa K. BRANDON
39 Director of Residence Life .... Mrs. Samantha ENGLAR
35 Director of Campus Activities .... Mr. Craig L. ROBERTSON
41 Athletic Director .... Mr. Chuck BRUEGGEMANN
42 Chaplain/Director Church Relations .... Rev Dr. B. Timothy HARRISON
40 Bookstore Director .... Ms. Amy BLASDEL
30 Director of Advancement Services .... Mr. Scott L. BILLHARTZ
19 Director Safety & Security .... Mr. Ranodore M. FOGGS
112 Director of Major Gifts .... Mrs. Whitney STRONG
113 Director of Student Accounts .... Ms. Kristie JAQUES-ANGLIN
28 Director of Diversity .... Mr. Brent W. REEVES

Meadville Lombard Theological School (D)

610 South Michigan Avenue, Chicago IL 60605
County: Cook FICE Identification: 001723
Unit ID: 147031
Telephone: (773) 256-3000 Carnegie Class: Spec-4-yr-Faith
FAX Number: (312) 327-7002 Calendar System: Semester
URL: www.meadville.edu
Established: 1844 Annual Graduate Tuition & Fees: N/A
Enrollment: 98 Coed
Affiliation or Control: Unitarian Universalist IRS Status: 501(c)3
Highest Offering: Doctorate; No Undergraduates
Accreditation: THEOL

01 President .... Dr. Lee BARKER
05 Interim Provost .... Dr. Lee BARKER
10 Vice Pres Finance & Administration .... Ms. Cynthia REDMAN
06 Registrar .... Ms. Valencia PENN-HARGROVE

Methodist College (E)

7600 N. Academic Drive, Peoria IL 61615
County: Peoria FICE Identification: 006228
Unit ID: 147129
Telephone: (309) 672-5513 Carnegie Class: Spec-4-yr-Other Health
FAX Number: (309) 671-8303 Calendar System: Semester
URL: www.methodistcol.edu
Established: 2000 Annual Undergrad Tuition & Fees: $20,710
Enrollment: 606 Coed
Affiliation or Control: Independent Non-Profit IRS Status: 501(c)3
Highest Offering: Baccalaureate
Accreditation: NH, NURSE

01 Interim Chancellor/President .... Dr. Deborah GARRISON
05 Int Provost/VP Academic Affairs .... Dr. Pam FERGUSON
84 Vice Chanc Enrollment Management .... Dr. Keith BRANHAM
10 Director of Finance .... Mr. Barry SOFFIETTI
06 Registrar .... Ms. Melissa EARNEST
07 Director Admissions .... Ms. Alissa SELBURG
37 Director Financial Aid .... Ms. Angela ROBINSON
09 Institutional Research Coordinator .... Ms. Donnie JOHNSON

Midstate College (F)

411 W Northmoor Road, Peoria IL 61614-3558
County: Peoria FICE Identification: 004568
Unit ID: 147165
Telephone: (309) 692-4092 Carnegie Class: Bac/Assoc-Mixed
FAX Number: (309) 692-3893 Calendar System: Quarter
URL: www.midstate.edu
Established: 1888 Annual Undergrad Tuition & Fees: $16,230
Enrollment: 459 Coed
Affiliation or Control: Proprietary IRS Status: Proprietary
Highest Offering: Baccalaureate
Accreditation: NH, CAHIIM, MAC

01 President and CEO .... Meredith N. BUNCH
05 Dean of Academics .... Ruth E. SHAFFER
32 Dean of Students .... Vicki DRAKSLER
10 Controller .... Angie HATTEN
06 Registrar .... Angela K. KEPLER
37 Director of Financial Assistance .... Eric JOHNSON
15 Director of Human Resources .... Jessica R. REYLING
35 Director of Student Affairs .... Rhonda P. URBAN
36 Director of Career Services .... Jennie GREENAN
08 Director of Library Services .... Jane BRADBURY

Midwest College of Oriental Medicine (G)

1601 Sherman Avenue, Suite 300, Evanston IL 60202
Telephone: (773) 975-1295 Identification: 666090
Accreditation: ACUP

† Branch campus of Midwest College of Oriental Medicine, Racine, WI

Midwestern Career College (H)

20 N. Wacker Dr, Ste 3800, Chicago IL 60606
County: Cook FICE Identification: 041390
Unit ID: 457536
Telephone: (312) 236-9000 Carnegie Class: Not Classified
FAX Number: (312) 277-1007 Calendar System: Other
URL: mccollege.edu
Established: 2004 Annual Undergrad Tuition & Fees: N/A
Enrollment: 315 Coed
Affiliation or Control: Proprietary IRS Status: Proprietary
Highest Offering: Associate Degree
Accreditation: #COE

01 President/CEO .... Mr. Jeremy OBERFELD

Midwestern University (I)

555 31st Street, Downers Grove IL 60515-1200
County: DuPage FICE Identification: 001657
Unit ID: 143853
Telephone: (630) 969-4400 Carnegie Class: Spec-4-yr-Med
FAX Number: N/A Calendar System: Quarter
URL: www.midwestern.edu
Established: 1900 Annual Undergrad Tuition & Fees: N/A
Enrollment: 2,932 Coed
Affiliation or Control: Independent Non-Profit IRS Status: 501(c)3
Highest Offering: Doctorate
Accreditation: NH, ARCPA, CLPSY, DENT, @OPT, OSTEO, OT, PHAR, PTA, @SP

01 President/CEO .... Dr. Kathleen H. GOEPPINGER
03 Exec VP/Chief Operating Officer .... Dr. Arthur G. DOBBELAERE
10 Sr VP/Chief Financial Officer .... Mr. Gregory J. GAUS
21 Vice President Finance .... Mr. Dean P. MALONE
46 VP Research & Strategic Initiatives .... Dr. Theresa W. FOSSUM
26 Vice President University Relations .... Dr. Karen D. JOHNSON
05 VP/CAO Dental/Med/Veterinary Educ .... Dr. Dennis J. PAULSON
05 VP/CAO Pharmacy & Optometry .... Dr. Mary W L. LEE
05 VP/CAO Health Sci Ed & VP Clinic Op ... Dr. Kathleen N. PLAYER
11 VP Human Resources & Administration .... Ms. Angela L. MARTY
43 VP & General Counsel .... Ms. Barbara L. MCCLOUD
63 Dean Chicago Col of Osteo Medicine .... Dr. Karen J. NICHOLS
67 Dean Chicago College of Pharmacy .... Dr. Nancy F. FJORTOFT
76 Dean Col Health Sci Dowers Grove .... Dr. Fred D. ROMANO
88 Interim Dean Optometry .... Dr. Joshua C. BAKER
52 Dean College of Dental Medicine IL .... Dr. M. A. J. Lex MACNEIL
88 Dean Basic Sciences .... Dr. Kyle H. RAMSEY
58 Dean Postdoctoral Education .... Dr. Thomas A. BOYLE
32 Dean Student Services .... Dr. Teresa A. DOMBROWSKI
07 Director of Admissions .... Mr. Michael J. LAKEN
88 Director of Finance .... Mr. Gregory O'COYNE
30 Director Development/Alumni .... Ms. Barbara WYSOCKI
15 Director Human Resources .... Ms. Amy B. GIBSON
18 Director Campus Facilities .... Mr. Kevin M. MCCORMICK
13 Director Information Technology Svc .... Mr. Erik P. CARROLL
08 Director Library .... Ms. Rebecca A. CATON
09 Director of Institutional Research .... Dr. Kevin P. HYNES
06 Registrar .... Ms. Betty N. MORRISON
24 Director Media Resources .... Ms. Kathleen A M. DOOLEY
46 Director Research & Sponsored Pgms .... Dr. James M. WOODS
19 Director Security/Safety .... Mr. Paul R. CREEKMORE
27 Director of Communications .... Ms. Dana FAY
37 Director Student Financial Services .... Mr. Nathan ERNST

† Tuition varies by degree program.

Millikin University (J)

1184 W Main Street, Decatur IL 62522-2084
County: Macon FICE Identification: 001724
Unit ID: 147244
Telephone: (217) 424-6211 Carnegie Class: Bac-Diverse
FAX Number: (217) 424-3993 Calendar System: Semester
URL: www.millikin.edu
Established: 1901 Annual Undergrad Tuition & Fees: $31,824
Enrollment: 2,152 Coed
Affiliation or Control: Presbyterian Church (U.S.A.) IRS Status: 501(c)3
Highest Offering: Doctorate
Accreditation: NH, ACBSP, ANEST, CAATE, MUS, NURSE

01 President .... Dr. Patrick E. WHITE
05 Provost .... Dr. Jeffery P. APER
10 Vice Pres Finance/Business Affs .... Mrs. Ruby F. JAMES
111 Vice Pres University Development .... Mr. Charles J. HAHN
84 Vice President Enrollment/Marketing .... Ms. Sarah SHUPENUS
88 Assoc Vice Pres Alumni & Devel .... Ms. Gina BIANCHI
32 Dean of Student Development .... Mrs. Raphaella PRANGE
100 Chief of Staff/Board Secretary .... Ms. Marilyn S. DAVIS
49 Dean of Arts & Sciences .... Dr. Randy M. BROOKS

57 Dean of Fine Arts ... Ms. Laura LEDFORD
107 Dean Col of Professional Studies ... Dr. Deborah L. SLAYTON
50 Dean Tabor School Business ... Dr. Najiba BENABESS
06 Registrar ... Mr. Jason WICKLINE
29 Sr Director Alumni/Donor Engagement ... Mrs. Alyse KNUST
102 Dir Corp & Foundation Relations ... Mrs. Kim MANGAN
36 Director of Career Center ... Ms. Pamela M. FOLGER
13 Director of Technology ... Mrs. Amy BRILLEY
08 Director of the Library ... Ms. Cindy FULLER
30 Sr Director of Development ... Mrs. Amanda PODESCHI
41 Director of Athletics ... Dr. Craig WHITE
53 Director of School of Education ... Dr. Christina MAGOULIAS
88 Director Kirkland Fine Arts Center ... Mrs. Janiece L. SADDORIS-TRAUGHBER
28 Dir Inclusion/Student Engagement ... Mrs. Molly BERRY
104 Director Center for Intl Education ... Ms. Carrie TRIMBLE
15 Director Human Resources ... Ms. Diane L. LANE
21 Controller ... Mrs. Vicki A. WRIGLEY
38 Director of Counseling Services ... Mr. Kevin C. GRAHAM
92 Director of Honors Program ... Dr. Michael HARTSOCK
35 Director Student Development ... Mr. Z. Paul REYNOLDS
37 Director of Financial Aid ... Ms. Cheryl L. HOWERTON
58 Director of MBA Program ... Dr. Anthony F. LIBERATORE
64 Director School of Music ... Dr. Stephen B. WIDENHOFER
87 Director of Summer School ... Dr. Randy M. BROOKS
19 Dir Dept Public Safety/Chief Police ... Mr. Chris BALLARD
66 Director School of Nursing ... Dr. Pamela L. LINDSEY
07 Dean of Admission ... Mr. Kevin MCINTYRE
39 Director of Residence Life ... Mr. Paul LIDY
18 Director of Facilities Services ... Mr. Michael KUROPAS
26 Director of Marketing ... Mrs. Jodi SILOTTO
09 Coord of Institutional Research ... Mrs. Laura A. BIRCH
105 Web Developer ... Ms. Jessica LANDGREBE

Monmouth College (A)

700 E Broadway, Monmouth IL 61462-1963
County: Warren FICE Identification: 001725
Unit ID: 147341
Telephone: (800) 747-2687 Carnegie Class: Bac-A&S
FAX Number: (309) 457-2141 Calendar System: Semester
URL: www.monmouthcollege.edu
Established: 1853 Annual Undergrad Tuition & Fees: $35,300
Enrollment: 1,197 Coed
Affiliation or Control: Presbyterian Church (U.S.A.) IRS Status: 501(c)3
Highest Offering: Baccalaureate
Accreditation: NH

01 President ... Dr. Clarence R. WYATT
05 Dean of Faculty/Vice President ... Dr. David M. TIMMERMAN
10 Vice President Finance & Business ... Mr. Richard A. MARSHALL
32 Vice Pres Student Life/Dn Students ... Ms. Laura HUTCHINSON
84 Vice President for Enrollment Mgmt ... Mr. Trent GILBERT
13 Chief Information Officer ... Mr. Daryl B. CARR
06 Registrar ... Ms. Kristi HIPPEN
08 Director Hewes Library ... Mr. Richard SAYRE
30 Dir Devel/Alumni Engagement ... Ms. Hannah MAHER
26 Director College Communications ... Mr. Duane BONIFER
07 Assoc Vice President for Enrollment ... Mr. Nick SPAETH
15 Director of Personnel Services ... Mr. Mike MCNALL
18 Director Facilities Management ... Ms. Sarah YOUNG
20 Associate Dean of the Faculty ... Dr. Frank GERSICH
21 Controller ... Ms. Jessica R. JOHNSON

Moody Bible Institute (B)

820 N LaSalle Boulevard, Chicago IL 60610-3263
County: Cook FICE Identification: 001727
Unit ID: 147369
Telephone: (312) 329-4000 Carnegie Class: Spec-4-yr-Faith
FAX Number: (312) 329-4109 Calendar System: Semester
URL: www.moody.edu
Established: 1886 Annual Undergrad Tuition & Fees: $12,630
Enrollment: 3,922 Coed
Affiliation or Control: Independent Non-Profit IRS Status: 501(c)3
Highest Offering: First Professional Degree
Accreditation: NH, BI, MUS, THEOL

01 President ... Dr. J. Paul NYQUIST
05 Provost & Dean of Education ... Dr. Junias V. VENUGOPAL
11 Exec VP & Chief Operating Officer ... Mr. Steven A. MOGCK
10 Chief Financial Officer ... Mr. Ken HEULITT
43 VP & General Counsel ... Mrs. Janet A. STIVEN
20 VP & Associate Provost of Faculty ... Dr. Larry J. DAVIDHIZAR
13 VP of Information Systems ... Mr. Frank W. LEBER
15 VP of Human Resources ... Ms. Debbie ZELINSKI
26 Chief Marketing Officer ... Mr. Sam CHOY
20 VP & Dean of Undergraduate School ... Dr. James G. SPENCER
58 VP/Dean of Theol Sem & Grad School ... Dr. John A. JELINEK
106 VP & Dean of Dist Learning School ... Dr. Bryan O'NEAL
32 VP & Dean of Student Life ... Dr. Timothy E. ARENS
84 VP/Dean of Student/Enrollment Svcs ... Mr. Anthony TURNER
08 Department Manager Library ... Mr. James PRESTON
09 Director of Change Management ... Mr. Daniel M. HASSLER
108 Dir of Accreditation & Assessment ... Ms. Camille WARD
06 Registrar/Director of Acad Records ... Mr. George MOSHER
29 Exec Director Alumni Association ... Mrs. Nancy HASTINGS
39 Associate Dean Residence Life ... Mr. Bruce R. NORQUIST
35 Associate Dean of Students ... Ms. Rachel MONFETTE
36 Assoc Dean of Career Development ... Mr. Patrick FRIEDLINE
38 Associate Dean Counseling Services ... Mr. Steve BRASEL
35 Associate Dean for Student Programs ... Mr. Joseph M. GONZALES, JR.
104 Dean of International Study Program ... Dr. Gregg QUIGGLE
12 Campus Dean MBI Spokane WA ... Dr. Jack LEWIS
35 Dean of Student Svcs Spokane WA ... Mr. Daniel R. WARD
88 Pgm Mgr of Missionary Aviation Tech ... Mr. James A. CONRAD
88 Assc Dir of Faculty Development ... Mr. Andrew BEATY
88 Dir of Instructional Design MDL ... Mr. Kevin MAHAFFY
88 Director of Student Experience MDL ... Mr. John ENGELKEMIER
12 Campus Dean MTS Plymouth MI ... Mr. Christopher BROOKS
44 VP of Donor Dev & Channel Strategy ... Mr. Bruce EVERHART
30 VP of Stewardship ... Mr. James ELLIOTT
96 Manager of Procurement Services ... Mr. Paul BRACKLEY
102 Dir Foundation/Corporate Relations ... Ms. Mollie BOND
21 Controller ... Ms. Linda WAHR
37 Dean of Admissions & Financial Aid ... Mrs. Heather SHALLEY
14 Technology Services Director ... Mr. Michael JANCHENKO
18 Division Manager of Facilities ... Mr. Bill BIELAWSKI
19 Deputy Chief of Public Safety ... Mr. Brian M. STOFFER
41 Athletic Director ... Mr. Daniel DUNN
23 Admin of Health Service ... Ms. Ann MEYER
04 Executive Assistant to President ... Ms. Mary OLIVA
85 Asst Dean of International Stdnts ... Ms. Mary Evelyn CESAR
28 Asst Dean of Multicultural Stdnts ... Mr. Edward JONES

† Tuition is paid through donor contributions. Fees are $1,950.00 per year.

Moraine Valley Community College (C)

9000 W College Parkway, Palos Hills IL 60465-0937
County: Cook FICE Identification: 007692
Unit ID: 147378
Telephone: (708) 974-4300 Carnegie Class: Assoc/MT-VT-High Non
FAX Number: (708) 974-1184 Calendar System: Semester
URL: www.morainevalley.edu
Established: 1967 Annual Undergrad Tuition & Fees (In-District): $4,176
Enrollment: 15,016 Coed
Affiliation or Control: State/Local IRS Status: 501(c)3
Highest Offering: Associate Degree
Accreditation: NH, ACFEI, ADNUR, CAHIIM, COARC, COMTA, MAC, PHLEB, POLYT, RAD

01 President ... Dr. Sylvia JENKINS
05 Vice President Academic Affairs ... Dr. Pamela HANEY
32 Vice President Student Devel ... Dr. Normah SALLEH-BARONE
11 Vice Pres Administrative Services ... Mr. Richard J. HENDRICKS
10 Vice Pres Financial & Business Svcs ... Mr. Robert STERKOWITZ
13 Chief Information Officer ... Mr. Kamlesh SANGHVI
50 Dean Science/Business/Comp Tech ... Dr. Ryen NAGLE
49 Dean Liberal Arts ... Dr. Walter FRONCZEK
124 Dean Student Engagement ... Dr. Scott FRIEDMAN
84 Dean Enrollment Services ... Dr. Darryl WILLIAMS
51 Exec Dir Corporate/Cmty & Cont Educ ... Mr. Steven PAPPAGEORGE
36 Dean Career Programs ... Ms. Kiana BATTTLE
35 Dean Student Services ... Mr. Chester SHAW
88 Dean Learn Enrich & Col Readiness ... Mr. Michael MORSCHES
35 Dean of Students/Compliance Officer ... Mr. Kent MARSHALL
37 Director Financial Aid ... Ms. Carissa DAVIS
09 Dir Institutional Research/Planning ... Dr. Sadya KHAN
19 Chief of Police ... Mr. Patrick O'CONNOR
15 Director Human Resources ... Ms. Lynn HARRINGTON
07 Director of Admissions/Recruitment ... Mr. Andrew SARATA
18 Director Campus Operations ... Mr. Rick BRENNAN
109 Director Auxiliary Services ... Mr. Kashif SHAH
23 Director Health Education Well Ctr ... Mr. William FINN
85 Asst Dean Intl Student Admissions ... Ms. Diane VIVERITO
26 Director Marketing & Communications ... Ms. Clare BRINER
25 Dir Res Devel/Extended Programs ... Dr. Sharon KATTERMAN
21 Controller ... Ms. Theresa O'CARROLL
22 Director Center Disability Services ... Ms. Debbie SIEVERS
96 Director of Purchasing ... Ms. Jane BENTLEY
102 Executive Director Foundation ... Ms. Kristy MCGREAL
20 Dean Academic Development/Outreach ... Dr. Cynthia ANDERSON
20 Dean Academic Services ... Ms. Jennifer DAVIDSON
88 Dean Learning Resource Center ... Ms. Terra JACOBSON
121 Dean Student Success ... Dr. Jo Ann JENKINS
06 Registrar ... Mr. Emmanuel ESPERANZA, JR.
101 Secretary of the Institution/Board ... Ms. Dawn FREDRIKSON
108 Director Institutional Assessment ... Dr. Nancy GAYLEN

Morrison Institute of Technology (D)

701 Portland Avenue, Morrison IL 61270-2959
County: Whiteside FICE Identification: 008880
Unit ID: 147396
Telephone: (815) 772-7218 Carnegie Class: Spec 2-yr-Tech
FAX Number: (815) 772-7584 Calendar System: Semester
URL: www.morrisontech.edu
Established: 1973 Annual Undergrad Tuition & Fees: $15,791
Enrollment: 77 Coed
Affiliation or Control: Independent Non-Profit IRS Status: 501(c)3
Highest Offering: Associate Degree
Accreditation: COE, ENGT

01 Chief Executive Officer ... Mr. Christopher D. SCOTT
05 Vice President of Academic Affairs ... Mr. Greg J. TULLY
10 Vice President for Finance ... Mr. Richard PARKINSON
06 Registrar ... Ms. Dana VERDICK
07 Admissions Director ... Ms. Jodie EAKER

Morthland College (E)

202 East Oak St, PO Box 429, West Frankfort IL 62896
County: Franklin FICE Identification: 042279
Unit ID: 483984
Telephone: (618) 937-2127 Carnegie Class: Not Classified
FAX Number: (618) 937-2137 Calendar System: Semester
URL: www.morthland.edu
Established: 2009 Annual Undergrad Tuition & Fees: $14,780
Enrollment: 100 Coed
Affiliation or Control: Independent Non-Profit IRS Status: 501(c)3
Highest Offering: Baccalaureate
Accreditation: TRACS

01 President ... Dr. Tim MORTHLAND
03 Executive Vice President ... Ms. Emily HAYES
30 Campus Development ... Ms. Stephanie PARTON

Morton College (F)

3801 S Central Avenue, Cicero IL 60804-4398
County: Cook FICE Identification: 001728
Unit ID: 147411
Telephone: (708) 656-8000 Carnegie Class: Assoc/MT-VT-High Non
FAX Number: (708) 656-3297 Calendar System: Semester
URL: www.morton.edu
Established: 1924 Annual Undergrad Tuition & Fees (In-District): $3,892
Enrollment: 4,592 Coed
Affiliation or Control: State/Local IRS Status: 501(c)3
Highest Offering: Associate Degree
Accreditation: NH, ADNUR, PTAA

01 President ... Dr. Stanley FIELDS
05 Provost ... Dr. Keith MCLAUGHLIN
51 Dean Adult & Continuing Education ... Dr. Tom PIERCE
32 Student Activities & Workforce Dir ... Ms. Marisol VELASQUEZ
08 Dir Library & Instructional Tech ... Mr. Micheal KOTT
15 Exec Director of Human Resources ... Mr. Anthony RAY
51 Director of Continuing Education ... Ms. Susan FELICE
09 Director Institutional Research ... Ms. Magda BANDA
18 Director of Facilities & Operations ... Mr. John POTEMPA
37 Director of Financial Aid ... Ms. Yolanda FREEMON
06 Registrar ... Ms. Marlena AVALOS-THOMPSON
10 Director of Business Services ... Ms. Mireya PEREZ
11 Exec Director of Operations ... Mr. Frank MARZULLO

National-Louis University (G)

122 S Michigan Avenue, Chicago IL 60603
County: Cook FICE Identification: 001733
Unit ID: 147536
Telephone: (888) 658-8632 Carnegie Class: DU-Mod
FAX Number: N/A Calendar System: Quarter
URL: www.nl.edu
Established: 1886 Annual Undergrad Tuition & Fees: $10,380
Enrollment: 4,384 Coed
Affiliation or Control: Independent Non-Profit IRS Status: 501(c)3
Highest Offering: Doctorate
Accreditation: NH, CACREP, CAEPN, IACBE

01 President ... Dr. Nivine MEGAHED
05 Provost ... Dr. Alison HILSABECK
111 Vice Pres Institutional Advancement ... Ms. Carole WOOD
15 Vice President Human Resources ... Mr. Tom BERGMANN
10 Vice Pres Finance & Administration ... Mr. Marty MICKEY
84 Vice Pres Enrollment Mgmt ... Ms. Bobbi BIRINGER
26 Vice Pres Marketing/Communications ... Mr. Tom EHRHARDT
09 Vice Provost Institutional Effect ... Vacant
20 Vice Prov Acad Pgm & Fac Dev ... Dr. Ignacio LOPEZ
124 Exec Dir of Advising/Retention ... Mr. Stephen NEER
50 Dean CPSA ... Dr. Judah VIOLA
53 Dean NCE ... Dr. Robert MULLER
08 Dean University Library ... Dr. Robert MORRISON
32 VP Student Services ... Vacant
12 Exec Director Florida Regional ... Dr. Karen O'DONNELL
28 Director of Employment/Diversity ... Vacant
37 Director of Student Finance ... Ms. Rathenia HUNTER
07 Director of Admissions ... Mr. Ken KASPRZAK
51 Director Outreach Academic Pgm ... Ms. Karen HAWORTH
35 Director of Student Experience ... Ms. Danielle LABAN
04 Administrative Asst to President ... Ms. Diane M. TRAUSCH
06 Registrar ... Mr. Stephen NEER
108 Director Institutional Assessment ... Ms. Mital PATEL
13 Chief Info Technology Officer (CIO) ... Mr. Michael GRAHAM
18 Chief Facilities/Physical Plant ... Mr. Richard SORENSON
25 Assoc Dir of Grant Operations ... Ms. Lucille MORGAN
29 Director Alumni & Outreach Programs ... Vacant
91 Technical Director ... Mr. John MAZARIEGOS
96 Purchasing Coordinator ... Ms. Caryn SMITH
102 Exec Dir of IA ... Ms. Leslie VILLASENOR
103 Asst Dir Career Development ... Ms. Consiglia INTILE
106 Dir Online Operations ... Mr. Andi KORITARI
44 Director Annual or Planned Giving ... Ms. Brittany YANTOS

National-Louis University Elgin Campus (H)

620 Tollgate Road, Elgin IL 60123
Telephone: (800) 443-5522 Identification: 770083
Accreditation: &NH

National-Louis University Lisle Campus (A)

850 Warrenville Road, Lisle IL 60532
Telephone: (800) 443-5522 Identification: 770084
Accreditation: &NH

National-Louis University North Shore Campus (B)

5202 Old Orchard Road, Skokie IL 60077
Telephone: (800) 443-5522 Identification: 770085
Accreditation: &NH

National-Louis University Wheeling Campus (C)

1000 Capitol Drive, Wheeling IL 60090
Telephone: (800) 443-5522 Identification: 770086
Accreditation: &NH

National University of Health Sciences (D)

200 E Roosevelt Road, Lombard IL 60148-4583
County: DuPage FICE Identification: 001732
Unit ID: 147590
Telephone: (630) 629-2000 Carnegie Class: Spec-4-yr-Other Health
FAX Number: (630) 889-6600 Calendar System: Trimester
URL: www.nuhs.edu
Established: 1906 Annual Undergrad Tuition & Fees: N/A
Enrollment: 682 Coed
Affiliation or Control: Independent Non-Profit IRS Status: 501(c)3
Highest Offering: First Professional Degree
Accreditation: NH, ACUP, CHIRO, COMTA, NATUR

Code	Title	Name
01	President	Dr. Joseph P D. STIEFEL
05	Vice President Academic Services	Dr. Randy L. SWENSON
10	Vice President Business Services	Mr. Ron MENSCHING
11	Vice Pres Administrative Services	Ms. Tracy MCHUGH
76	Dean College Allied Health Sciences	Dr. Randy L. SWENSON
51	Dean Col Postprofessional Educ	Dr. Jenna GLENN
23	Dean of Clinics	Dr. Theodore JOHNSON
107	Dean Col Professional Studies FL	Dr. Daniel STRAUSS
107	Dean Col Professional Studies IL	Dr. Robert SHIEL
46	Dean of Research	Dr. Gregory D. CRAMER
32	Dean of Students	Ms. Yesenia MALDONADO
108	Dean Academic Assessment	Vacant
88	Dean Accreditation	Vacant
08	Director Learning Resource Center	Ms. Patricia GENARDO
06	University Registrar	Ms. Izabela DUBAK
07	Dir Communication/Enrollment Svcs	Ms. Victoria SWEENEY
21	Director of Financial Services	Ms. Sue UNGER
37	Director of Financial Aid	Mr. Marc YAMBO
18	Director Maintenance & Facilities	Mr. Mark GALVANONI
15	Director of Human Resources	Mr. Andrew WOZNIAK
26	Chief Public Relations Officer	Ms. Marie OLBRYSH
30	Dir Alumni Rels & Development	Mrs. Lynn NELSON
13	Dir Management Information Services	Mr. Ron MENSCHING
40	Bookstore Manager	Ms. Sue ROBERTSON
39	Coordinator of Housing	Ms. Marilyn FREAD

North Central College (E)

30 N Brainard Street, Naperville IL 60540-4607
County: DuPage FICE Identification: 001734
Unit ID: 147660
Telephone: (630) 637-5100 Carnegie Class: Masters/M
FAX Number: (630) 637-5121 Calendar System: Trimester
URL: www.northcentralcollege.edu
Established: 1861 Annual Undergrad Tuition & Fees: $36,654
Enrollment: 2,962 Coed
Affiliation or Control: United Methodist IRS Status: 501(c)3
Highest Offering: Master's
Accreditation: NH, CAATE

Code	Title	Name
01	President	Dr. Troy D. HAMMOND
04	Exec Secy/Assistant to President	Ms. Kimberly SALZBRUNN
05	Provost/VP Academic Affairs	Dr. Abiodun GOKE-PARIOLA
10	VP of Finance/CFO	Ms. Maryellen SKERIK
111	VP Institutional Advancement	Mr. Rick E. SPENCER
84	VP Enrollment Management/Athletics	Mr. Marty R. SAUER
32	VP Student Affairs/Dean of Students	Ms. Kimberly SLUIS
11	VP for Operations	Mr. Michael J. HUDSON
13	VP/Chief Information Officer	Mr. Matthew BURDEN
15	Asst Vice Pres Human Resources	Mr. John ACARDO
26	Asst Vice Pres Mktg/Communications	Mr. James GODO
20	Associate Academic Dean	Dr. Marti S. BOGART
07	Dean of Admissions	Ms. Martha A. STOLZE
58	Dean Graduate Pgms/Continuing Educ	Dr. Pamela MONACO
06	Registrar	Vacant
08	Director of the Library	Mr. John J. SMALL
36	Director of Career Development	Ms. Haydee NUNEZ
37	Director of Financial Aid	Vacant
23	Director of the Wellness Center	Ms. Tatiana SIFRI
31	Director of Cmty Educ/Conf/Camps	Mr. Troy BRISTOW
41	Athletic Director	Mr. James MILLER
21	AVP Finance/Controller	Mr. David S. MISSURELLI
39	Director of Residence Life	Ms. Sarah E. AVERY
42	Campus Chaplain	Rev. Eric DOOLITTLE
09	Director of Institutional Research	Mr. Peter S. BARGER
29	Director Alumni/Dev Relations	Mr. Adrian M. ALDRICH
28	Director of Multicultural Affairs	Ms. Dorothy J. PLEAS

North Park University (F)

3225 W Foster Avenue, Chicago IL 60625-4895
County: Cook FICE Identification: 001735
Unit ID: 147679
Telephone: (773) 244-6200 Carnegie Class: Masters/L
FAX Number: N/A Calendar System: Semester
URL: www.northpark.edu
Established: 1891 Annual Undergrad Tuition & Fees: $27,210
Enrollment: 3,159 Coed
Affiliation or Control: Evangelical Covenant Church Of America
IRS Status: 501(c)3
Highest Offering: Doctorate
Accreditation: NH, CAATE, IACBE, MUS, NURSE, THEOL

Code	Title	Name
01	Interim President	Mr. Carl E. BALSAM
05	Provost	Dr. Michael O. EMERSON
84	Vice Pres for Enrollment/Marketing	Vacant
30	Vice President for Development	Ms. Mary K. SURRIDGE
32	VP for Student Engagement	Dr. Jodi KOSLOW MARTIN
10	Vice Pres Finance & Admin/CFO	Mr. Scott STENMARK
73	Seminary Dean	Dr. David W. KERSTEN
49	Dean of College of Arts & Sciences	Dr. Gregor THUSWALDNER
107	Dean School of Professional Studies	Dr. Lori SCREMENTI
50	Dean School of Business & NFP Mgmt	Dr. Wesley LINDAHL
53	Dean School of Education	Dr. Rebecca NELSON
64	Dean School of Music	Dr. Craig JOHNSON
66	Dean School of Nursing	Dr. Linda DUNCAN
28	Director of Diversity	Ms. Jacqueline STRAPP
08	Dean Library & Academic Technology	Ms. Kathryn MAIER-O'SHEA
07	Director Undergraduate Enrollment	Mr. Brady MARTINSON
23	Director Health Services	Vacant
37	Director Financial Aid Services	Ms. Carolyn LACH
13	Director of Information Technology	Mr. Jeffrey K. LUNDBLAD
15	Director of Human Resources	Ms. Ingrid K. TENGLIN
18	Director of Physical Plant	Mr. Carl H. WISTROM
19	Director of Security	Mr. Daniel GOORIS
21	Director of Finance	Ms. Anne MCCULLAH
26	Dir Univ Marketing & Communications	Mr. Christopher CHILDERS
41	Athletic Director	Mr. Jack F. SURRIDGE
42	Director University Ministries	Mr. Anthony ZAMBLE
36	Senior Director of Career Planning	Ms. Pamela BOZEMAN-EVANS
06	Registrar	Mr. Aaron D. SCHOOF
29	Alumni Relations Director	Ms. Melissa VELEZ LUCE
04	Assistant to the President	Mrs. Karen P. MEARS
104	Director of International Office	Dr. Sumie SONG
39	Director Student Housing	Mr. Aidan HOWORTH
44	Annual Fund Manager	Vacant
108	Director Institutional Assessment	Ms. Hannah ANTHONY
106	Assoc Dean Center for Online Educ	Dr. Richard SCHULTZ

Northeastern Illinois University (G)

5500 N Saint Louis Avenue, Chicago IL 60625-4699
County: Cook FICE Identification: 001693
Unit ID: 147776
Telephone: (773) 583-4050 Carnegie Class: Masters/L
FAX Number: (773) 442-4900 Calendar System: Semester
URL: www.neiu.edu
Established: 1867 Annual Undergrad Tuition & Fees (In-State): $10,138
Enrollment: 9,891 Coed
Affiliation or Control: State IRS Status: 501(c)3
Highest Offering: Master's
Accreditation: NH, ART, CACREP, CAEPN, MUS, SW

Code	Title	Name
01	Interim President	Dr. Richard J. HELLDOBLER
05	Actg Provost & VP Academic Affairs	Dr. Wamucii NJOGU
10	Vice Pres Finance & Administration	Mr. Michael J. PIERICK
32	Vice President for Student Affairs	Dr. Daniel LOPEZ, JR.
30	Vice President Inst Advancement	Ms. Liesl V. DOWNEY
35	Dean of Students	Mr. Matthew F. SPECHT
07	Associate VP Enrollment Services	Dr. Janice M. HARRING-HENDON
21	Director of Univ Budgets	Ms. Ann M. MCNABB
08	Dean Libraries & Learning Res	Vacant
09	Exec Dir Inst Rsrch & Assessment	Mr. Blase E. MASINI
15	Dir of HR Empl & Labor Relations	Ms. Marta E. MASO
25	Director Sponsored Programs	Ms. Sharon K. TODD
26	Chief Communication Officer/Dir	Mr. Michael M. DIZON
37	Director Financial Aid	Ms. Maureen T. AMOS
50	Dean College Bus/Management	Dr. Michael D. BEDELL
58	Dean College Graduate Studies & Res	Dr. Michael J. STERN
53	Dean College of Education	Dr. Sandra BEYDA-LORIE
49	Dean College of Arts & Sciences	Dr. Katrina BELL-JORDAN
18	Asst Vice Pres Facilities Mgmt	Ms. Nancy MEDINA
19	Director University Police Dept	Mr. John ESCOLANTE
21	Director Controller's Office	Ms. Fe L. LENON
22	Dir Equal Opportunity/AA & Ethics	Ms. Leah HEINECKE-KRUMHUS
86	Executive Dir Government Relations	Dr. Suleyma PEREZ
06	University Registrar	Mr. Daniel R. WEBER
29	Director of Alumni Relations	Ms. Damaris TAPIA
36	Dir Student Counseling/Career Svcs	Dr. Susan R. STOCK
96	Asst VP Procurement & Support Svcs	Mr. Robert B. FILIPP
44	Director Institutional Advancement	Mr. John L. BUTLER
96	Director Purchasing	Ms. Rosalinda CASTILLO
23	Director of Student Health Services	Ms. Sharon HEIMBAUGH

Northern Illinois University (H)

1425 W. Lincoln Way, De Kalb IL 60115-2828
County: De Kalb FICE Identification: 001737
Unit ID: 147703
Telephone: (815) 753-1000 Carnegie Class: DU-Higher
FAX Number: (815) 753-0198 Calendar System: Semester
URL: www.niu.edu
Established: 1895 Annual Undergrad Tuition & Fees (In-State): $14,204
Enrollment: 20,130 Coed
Affiliation or Control: State IRS Status: 501(c)3
Highest Offering: Doctorate
Accreditation: NH, ART, AUD, #CAATE, CACREP, CAEPN, CLPSY, DIETD, DIETI, ENG, ENGT, IPSY, LAW, MFCD, MT, MUS, NAIT, NURSE, PH, PTA, SCPSY, SP, SPAA, THEA

Code	Title	Name
01	Acting President	Lisa C. FREEMAN
05	Actg Executive Vice Pres & Provost	Chris MCCORB
20	Vice Provost Inst Effectiveness	Carolinda DOUGLASS
10	VP Administration & Finance	Vacant
45	Vice Prov Resource Planning	Susan MINI
51	VP University Outreach	Anne C. KAPLAN
46	VP Research/Innovative Partnership	Jerry BLAZEY
26	VP Enroll Mgmt/Mktg/Communications	Sol JENSEN
43	Acting VP/General Counsel	Greg A. BRADY
102	Vice Pres University Advancement	Catherine SQUIRES
13	VP Chief Information Officer	Brett CORYELL
18	AVP Facilities Mgmt/Campus Services	John HECKMANN
15	Sr AVP for Human Resources	Laura ALEXANDER
35	Assoc VP Stdnt Affs & Dean of Stdnt	Kelly WESENER-MICHAEL
23	Director Health Services	Andrew DIGATE
28	Sr AVP Academic Diversity	Vernese EDGHILL-WALDEN
20	Vice Provost	Anne BIRBERICK
50	Dean of Business	Balaji RAJAGOPALAN
53	Dean of Education	Laurie ELISH-PIPER
54	Dean of Engineering/Engr Tech	Donald PETERSON
61	Interim Dean of Law	Mark CORDES
49	Dean Liberal Arts & Sciences	Vacant
76	Dean Health & Human Sciences	Derryl BLOCK
57	Dean Visual & Performing Arts	Paul KASSEL
58	Dean Grad Sch/AVP Grad Studies	Bradley BOND
85	Interim Sr International Affairs	Bradley BOND
88	Asst VP Outreach Rockford	Rena COTSONES
12	Director Lorado Taft Field Campus	Diana DENNIS
12	Director NIU Naperville	Gina KENYON
06	Director Registration & Records	Jerry MONTAG
09	Director of Institutional Research	J. Daniel HOUSE
36	Acting Exec Dir of Career Services	Brandon T. LAGANA
37	Director of Student Financial Aid	Rebecca BABEL
38	Exec Dir Counseling/Consultation	Brooke RUXTON
40	University Bookstore Manager	Don TURK
19	Police Chief/Public Safety	Thomas R. PHILLIPS, SR.
41	Athletic Director	Sean FRAZIER
39	Int Sr Dir Housing/Residential Svcs	Jennifer MANNING
22	Dir Disability Resources Center	Debra MILLER
29	Dir Alumni Relations/Univ Advance	Reggie BUSTINZA
96	Dir Procurement/Strategic Sourcing	Antoinette BRIDGES
07	Acting Director of Admissions	Katy SAALFELD

Northern Seminary (I)

410 Warrenville Road, Lisle IL 60532
County: DuPage FICE Identification: 001736
Unit ID: 147697
Telephone: (630) 620-2180 Carnegie Class: Spec-4-yr-Faith
FAX Number: (630) 620-2190 Calendar System: Quarter
URL: www.seminary.edu
Established: 1913 Annual Graduate Tuition & Fees: N/A
Enrollment: 187 Coed
Affiliation or Control: American Baptist IRS Status: 501(c)3
Highest Offering: Doctorate; No Undergraduates
Accreditation: THEOL

Code	Title	Name
01	President	Dr. William SHIELL
04	Executive Assistant to President	Mrs. Christine KOLB
05	Int Vice Pres of Academic Affairs	Dr. Jason GILE
30	Vice President of Advancement	Mr. David KRAUSE
10	Interim Comptroller	Mr. Nick NARDUCCI
07	Executive Director of Enrollment	Mr. Joshua MOORE
06	Registrar	Ms. Marilyn R. MAST HEWITT
88	Director Doctoral Studies	Dr. Jason GILE
32	Sr Exec Director Student Services	Rev. Linda OWENS
08	Director of Brimson Grow Library	Dr. Rena BAKER

Northwest Suburban College (J)

5999 S. New Wilke Road, Rolling Meadows IL 60008
County: Cook Identification: 667240
Unit ID: 488086
Telephone: (847) 290-6425 Carnegie Class: Not Classified
FAX Number: (847) 290-1441 Calendar System: Semester
URL: www.nwsc.edu
Established: 2008 Annual Undergrad Tuition & Fees: N/A
Enrollment: N/A Coed
Affiliation or Control: Independent Non-Profit IRS Status: 501(c)3
Highest Offering: Associate Degree
Accreditation: ACICS

Code	Title	Name
01	President	Dr. M. T. ALINIAZEE
11	Vice Pres/Chief Operating Officer	Dr. Mohammed FAHEEM
05	Provost/Dean of Acad & Student Affs	Dr. Maksood AKBAR

20 Assoc Dean Academic/Student Affairs .... Dr. Shazia ILYAS
07 Admissions Representative ....Ms. Molly KANE

Northwestern College (A)

9501 Technology Blvd; Suite 425, Rosemont IL 60018
County: Cook FICE Identification: 012362
Unit ID: 147749
Telephone: (847) 233-7700 Carnegie Class: Assoc/HVT-Mix Trad/Non
FAX Number: (847) 233-7705 Calendar System: Quarter
URL: www.nc.edu
Established: 1902 Annual Undergrad Tuition & Fees: $17,730
Enrollment: 239 Coed
Affiliation or Control: Proprietary IRS Status: Proprietary
Highest Offering: Associate Degree
Accreditation: NH, ACBSP, CAHIIM, MAC, RAD

01 President .... Mr. Lawrence SCHUMACHER
03 Executive VP of Operations .... Mrs. Gail SCHUMACHER
11 Chief Operations Officer ....Mr. Dimitrios KRIARAS
10 Controller ....Ms. Sheri PEKAR
05 Chief Academic Officer ....Mrs. Diane MAREK
13 Sr Director of CTO .... Mr. Omar BERNAL
86 Government and Public Relations Dir .....Ms. Laura POLLASTRINI
08 Director of Library Services ....Ms. Sarah DULAY
12 Director of Bridgeview Campus ....Ms. Mary REYNOLDS
12 Director of Chicago Campus ....Mrs. Jill MAKSYMEC
15 Director of Human Resources .... Mrs. Margie BENNECKE
37 Director of Financial Assistance .... Ms. Patricia KILIAN
105 Institutional Initiatives Director ....Ms. Lauren SCHUMACHER
38 Director of Counseling ....Vacant
106 Dean of Academic Operations .... Ms. Rakisha SLOANE
07 Enrollment Services Manager .... Mrs. Theresa VALDES
66 Dean of Nursing .... Ms. Ann AMAEFULE
06 Registrar ....Ms. Tina MARFOE
36 Career Development Coordinator .... Ms. Amy BUOSCIO
36 Career Development Coordinator ....Mr. Greg NORTON
97 Program Director - GE .... Mr. David COOPER
61 Program Director - LS ....Vacant
76 Program Director - SHS ....Ms. Chandra HURT
04 Executive Asst to President .... Ms. Vilma FRANCO

Northwestern College-SW Campus (B)

7725 S Harlem Avenue, Bridgeview IL 60455
Telephone: (888) 205-2283 Identification: 770089
Accreditation: &NH

Northwestern University (C)

633 Clark Street, Evanston IL 60208-3854
County: Cook FICE Identification: 001739
Unit ID: 147767
Telephone: (847) 491-8400 Carnegie Class: DU-Highest
FAX Number: (847) 491-7364 Calendar System: Quarter
URL: www.northwestern.edu
Established: 1851 Annual Undergrad Tuition & Fees: $50,855
Enrollment: 21,655 Coed
Affiliation or Control: Independent Non-Profit IRS Status: 501(c)3
Highest Offering: Doctorate
Accreditation: NH, ARCPA, AUD, CACREP, CLPSY, ENG, IPSY, LAW, MED, MFCD, MUS, OPE, PCSAS, PH, PTA, SP

01 President ....Dr. Morton O. SCHAPIRO
05 Provost .... Dr. Jonathan S. HOLLOWAY
11 Executive Vice President .... Mr. Nim S. CHINNIAH
32 Vice President Student Affairs .... Dr. Patricia TELLES-IRVIN
26 Vice President University Relations ....Mr. Alan K. CUBBAGE
45 Vice Pres Administration & Planning ....Ms. Marilyn MCCOY
13 Vice Pres Information Technology ....Mr. Sean B. REYNOLDS
30 Vice Pres for Alumni Rel & Devel .... Mr. Robert MCQUINN
46 Vice President Research ....Mr. Joseph T. WALSH
115 Vice Pres/Chief Investment Officer ....Mr. William H. MCLEAN
43 Vice President/General Counsel ....Mr. Philip L. HARRIS
18 VP for Facilities ....Mr. John DÆANGELO
84 Associate Provost Univ Enrollment .... Mr. Michael E. MILLS
53 Associate Provost Undergrad Educ ...Dr. Ronald R. BRAEUTIGAM
20 Associate Provost Faculty Affairs .Dr. Lindsay CHASE-LANSDALE
20 Assoc VP & Assoc Provost Academic .... Mr. Jake JULIA
21 Assoc Prov Budget/Facil/Analysis ....Ms. Jean E. SHEDD
86 Spec Asst to Pres for Govt Rels .... Mr. Bruce LAYTON
04 Assistant to the President .... Mr. Eugene Y. LOWE, JR.
100 Director Office of the President ....Ms. Judith V. REMINGTON
41 Vice Pres Athletics and Recreation .... Mr. James J. PHILLIPS
54 Dean Sch Engr/Applied Science .... Dr. Julio M. OTTINO
50 Dean Graduate School of Management .... Dr. Sally E. BLOUNT
60 Dean School of Journalism ....Dr. Bradley J. HAMM
64 Dean School of Music .... Dr. Toni-Marie MONTGOMERY
63 Dean School of Medicine .... Dr. Eric G. NEILSON
51 Dean/Assoc Prov SPS ....Dr. Thomas F. GIBBONS
58 Dean Graduate School ....Mr. Dwight A. MCBRIDE
60 Dean School of Communication .... Dr. Barbara J. O'KEEFE
53 Dean School of Educ & Social Policy ....Dr. David N. FIGLIO
49 Dean College Arts & Science ....Mr. Adrian RANDOLPH
61 Dean School of Law ....Dr. Daniel B. RODRIGUEZ
08 University Librarian ....Ms. Sarah M. PRITCHARD
36 Exec Dir of Univ Career Svcs .... Mr. Mark PRESNELL
35 Assistant VP of Student Engagement .... Ms. Kelly SCHAEFER
29 Assoc VP Alumni Relations & Develop ....Mr. David LIVELY
88 Assoc Vice President for Research ....Mr. Lewis SMITH
88 Assoc Vice President for Research .... Ms. Jian CAO
88 Assoc VP for Rsrch Innov & New Vent ....Ms. Alicia LOFFLER
88 Assoc Vice President for Research ....Ms. Ann ADAMS
88 Dean for Research .... Mr. Rex CHISHOLM
114 Assoc Vice Pres Budget Planning .... Mr. Paul CASTELLUCCI
15 Assoc Vice Pres for Human Resources .... Ms. Pamela BEEMER
21 Assoc Vice Pres Finance/Controller ....Ms. Ingrid S. STAFFORD
07 Dean of Undergraduate Admissions .... Mr. Christopher WATSON
88 Exec Dir Intl Research Partnerships .... Ms. Indrani MUKHARJI
23 Exec Director Health Services ....Dr. Robert PALINKAS
39 Asst Dean of Students ....Ms. Mary GOLDENBERG
38 Director of Counseling/Psych Svcs ....Dr. John H. DUNKLE
42 University Chaplain .... Dr. Timothy S. STEVENS
88 Asst VP for Information ....Mr. Amit PRACHAND
88 Dir Program Review/Spec Project ..... Ms. Megan BLACKWELDER
06 University Registrar ....Ms. Jacqualyn CASAZZA
37 Director Financial Aid ....Ms. Carolyn V. LINDLEY
16 Dir HR Consulting Svcs/Staffing ....Ms. Caroline M. ONAGAN
19 Chief of University Police .... Mr. Bruce LEWIS
116 Assoc VP of Audit & Advisory Svcs .... Ms. Marcia ISAACSON
22 Dir Equal Emply Opprty/Affirm Act ....Ms. Tasha SHELTON
96 Director University Svcs Purchasing .... Mr. Jim KONRAD
28 Assoc Provost Diversity & Inclusion .... Dr. Jabbar BENNETT

Oakton Community College (D)

1600 E Golf Road, Des Plaines IL 60016-1256
County: Cook FICE Identification: 009896
Unit ID: 147800
Telephone: (847) 635-1600 Carnegie Class: Assoc/MT-VT-High Non
FAX Number: (847) 635-1992 Calendar System: Semester
URL: www.oakton.edu
Established: 1969 Annual Undergrad Tuition & Fees (In-District): $3,621
Enrollment: 9,864 Coed
Affiliation or Control: Local IRS Status: 501(c)3
Highest Offering: Associate Degree
Accreditation: NH, ADNUR, CAHIIM, MLTAD, PTAA

01 President ....Dr. Joianne L. SMITH
05 Vice President Academic Affairs ....Dr. Ileo LOTT
20 Assistant VP Academic Affairs ....Dr. Nancy PRENDERGAST
20 Assistant VP Academic Affairs ....Dr. Michael CARR
32 Vice President Student Affairs ....Dr. Karl BROOKS
10 Vice President Business & Finance . Mr. Edwin CHANDRASEKAR
51 AVP Cont Ed/Trng/Wrkfrc Dev .... Dr. Colette HANDS
13 Vice Pres Information Technology ....Ms. Bonnie LUCAS
76 Dean Science & Health Careers ....Ms. Ruth WILLIAMS
81 Dean Math & Technology .... Dr. Robert SOMPOLSKI
60 Dean Language/Humanities & the Arts ....Ms. Linda KORBEL
83 Dean Social Science/Business ....Mr. Bradley WOOTEN
26 Director of College Relations .... Mr. Paul PALIAN
09 Executive Director Research ....Dr. Maya EVANS
30 Executive Director of Development .... Dr. Mary KNIGHT
08 Dean Library & On-line Learning ....Vacant
84 Dir of Student Recruitment/Outreach ....Ms. Michele BROWN
06 Director of Registrar Services ....Mr. Bruce OATES
35 Director of Student Life ....Ms. Ann Marie BARRY
121 Dean of Student Success .... Mr. Sebastian CONTRERAS, JR.
88 Dir of Student Learning/Engagement .... Ms. Leana CUELLAR
41 Director of Athletics ....Mr. Bruce OATES
103 Dir Cont Educ & Workforce Dev .... Dr. Ruben HOWARD, II
21 Controller ....Mr. Andy WILLIAMS
21 Director of Business Services .... Ms. Doreen SCHWARTZ
15 Chief Human Resources Officer .... Ms. Mums MARTENS
18 Director of Facilities ....Ms. Leah SWANQUIST
14 Director Systems & Network Svcs ....Mr. John WADE
14 Dir of Software & User Svcs .... Ms. Renee KOZIMOR
07 Director of Enrollment Services ....Ms. Cheryl WARMANN
25 Dir of Grants & Alternative Funding .... Ms. Roxann MARSHBURN
51 Dir of Operations and Admin .... Ms. Robyn BAILEY
28 Ethics Officer ....Ms. Mum MARTENS
38 Director of Counseling ....Dr. Mark KIEL
19 Chief of Police ....Vacant

Oakton Community College Ray Hartstein Campus (E)

7701 N Lincoln Avenue, Skokie IL 60077
Telephone: (847) 635-1600 Identification: 770091
Accreditation: &NH

Olivet Nazarene University (F)

One University Avenue, Bourbonnais IL 60914-2345
County: Kankakee FICE Identification: 001741
Unit ID: 147828
Telephone: (815) 939-5011 Carnegie Class: Masters/L
FAX Number: (815) 935-4998 Calendar System: Semester
URL: www.olivet.edu
Established: 1907 Annual Undergrad Tuition & Fees: $33,940
Enrollment: 4,892 Coed
Affiliation or Control: Church Of The Nazarene IRS Status: 501(c)3
Highest Offering: Doctorate
Accreditation: NH, #CAATE, CAEPN, DIETD, ENG, MUS, NURSE, SW

01 President .... Dr. John C. BOWLING
05 Vice President Academic Affairs .... Dr. Carol SUMMERS
10 Vice President for Finance ....Dr. Douglas E. PERRY
32 Vice President Student Development .... Dr. Walter W. WEBB
26 Vice Pres Institutional Advancement ....Dr. Brian ALLEN
88 Vice Pres of Strategic Expansion ....Mr. Ryan SPITTAL
20 Assoc VP for Academic Affairs ....Dr. Houston THOMPSON
29 Acting Dir Alumni & University Rels ....Mr. Erinn PROEHL
06 Dean of Inst Effect & Registrar .... Mr. Jonathan PICKERING
08 Interim Dean of Library Services ....Mrs. Pam GREENLEE
07 Director of Admissions ....Mrs. Susan WOLFF
37 Director of Financial Aid ....Mr. Greg BRUNER
13 Chief Information Officer ....Mr. Dennis SEYMOUR
41 Athletic Director ....Mr. Gary NEWSOME
42 Chaplain ....Rev. Mark HOLCOMB
30 Director of Development ....Mr. John MONGERSON
35 Director Student Activities ....Mrs. Kathy STEINACKER
38 Director Student Counseling ....Mrs. Lisa VANDER VEER
15 Director of Human Resources .... Mr. David PICKERING
18 Chief Facilities/Physical Plant ....Mr. Matt WHITIS
40 Bookstore Manager ....Mrs. Rachel PIAZZA
36 Assoc Director of Career Services ....Miss Poppy MILLER
85 International Student Advisor ....Dr. Mark MOUNTAIN
27 Director of Marketing .... Mr. Remington ANKSORUS
19 Director Security/Safety .... Mr. Dale NEWSOME
49 Dean College of Arts & Sciences ....Dr. Stephen LOWE
73 Dn Sch Theology/Christian Ministry .... Dr. Mark QUANSTROM
53 Dean School of Education ....Dr. Robert HULL
76 Dean School of Life/Health Sciences ....Mrs. Amber RESIDORI
64 Dean School of Music .... Dr. Don REDDICK
50 Dean School of Business ....Dr. Glen REWERTS
54 Dean School of Engineering ....Dr. Houston THOMPSON
58 Dean School Grad/Continuing Studies .... Dr. Jonathan BARTLING

Pacific College of Oriental Medicine (G)

65 East Wacker Place 21st Floor, Chicago IL 60601
Telephone: (888) 729-4811 Identification: 666615
Accreditation: &WC, ACUP

† Branch campus of Pacific College of Oriental Medicine, San Diego CA.

Parkland College (H)

2400 W Bradley Avenue, Champaign IL 61821-1899
County: Champaign FICE Identification: 007118
Unit ID: 147916
Telephone: (217) 351-2200 Carnegie Class: Assoc/HVT-High Non
FAX Number: (217) 351-2581 Calendar System: Semester
URL: www.parkland.edu
Established: 1966 Annual Undergrad Tuition & Fees (In-District): $4,710
Enrollment: 8,147 Coed
Affiliation or Control: State/Local IRS Status: 501(c)3
Highest Offering: Associate Degree
Accreditation: NH, ADNUR, COARC, DH, EMT, OTA, RAD, SURGT

01 President .... Dr. Thomas R. RAMAGE
04 Asst to President/Board of Trustees ..... Ms. Nancy R. WILLAMON
05 Vice President Academic Svcs .... Dr. Pam LAU
32 Vice President Student Services ....Dr. Mike TRAME
10 Vice Pres Administrative Svcs/ CFO ....Mr. Christopher M. RANDLES
111 Vice Pres Institutional Advancement ....Dr. Seamus REILLY
35 Dean of Students .... Ms. Marietta TURNER
09 Dean Institutional Effectiveness ....Mr. Kevin KNOTT
103 Dean Adult Basic Educ/Workforce Dev ...... Ms. Tawanna NICKENS
50 Dept Chair Bus & Agri Industries .... Mr. Jim MANSFIELD
77 Department Chair Comp Science & IT .... Mr. Derek DALLAS
54 Dept Chair Engineering Science/Tech .... Mr. Jim MANSFIELD
79 Dept Chair Humanities ....Mr. Matt HURT
57 Dean Fine & Applied Arts .... Ms. Nancy SUTTON
75 Dean Career and Technical Education .... Ms. Roberta SCHOLZE
81 Department Chair Mathematics ....Mr. Brian MERCER
65 Dept Chair Natural Sciences ....Mr. Scott SEICHEN
83 Dept Chair Social Sci & Human Svcs ....Mr. Joe WALWIK
121 Dir Center for Academic Success .... Ms. Tracey HICKOX
26 Dir Marketing & Public Relations ....Ms. Stephanie STUART
103 Exec Director Workforce Development .... Ms. Tawanna NICKENS
102 Exec Dir Foundation/Alumni Affairs .... Ms. Ellen SCHMIDT
08 Director Library .... Ms. Anna Maria S. WATKIN
31 Director Community Education ....Ms. Amy FLESHNER
25 Director Grants and Contracts .... Mr. Joshua BIRKY
07 Director Admissions/Enrollment Mgmt .... Ms. Julie MARLATT
41 Director Athletics ....Mr. Rod M. LOVETT
38 Dir Counseling & Advising Center .... Ms. Ellen ZIMMERMAN
37 Director Financial Aid .... Mr. Tim WENDT
19 Director Public Safety ....Mr. William COLBROOK
18 Director Physical Plant ....Mr. James BUSTARD
15 Director Human Resources .... Ms. Kathleen MCANDREW
21 Controller ....Mr. Dave DONSBACH
40 Manager of Bookstore ....Ms. Diane M. KIEST
88 Director Assessment Center ....Mr. Michael BEHRENS
101 Secretary of the Institution/Board ....Ms. Nancy WILLAMON

Prairie State College (I)

202 S Halsted Street, Chicago Heights IL 60411-8226
County: Cook FICE Identification: 001640
Unit ID: 148007
Telephone: (708) 709-3500 Carnegie Class: Assoc/HVT-High Non
FAX Number: (708) 755-2587 Calendar System: Semester
URL: www.prairiestate.edu
Established: 1957 Annual Undergrad Tuition & Fees (In-District): $3,804
Enrollment: 4,699 Coed
Affiliation or Control: State/Local IRS Status: 501(c)3
Highest Offering: Associate Degree
Accreditation: NH, ADNUR, DH, SURGT

01 President .... Dr. Terri L. WINFREE
10 Vice Pres Finance & Administration .... Dr. Thomas SABAN
05 Vice Pres Acad Affs/Dean Faculty ....Dr. Marie C. HANSEL
103 Vice Pres Community/Economic Devel .....Mr. Craig D. SCHMIDT

32 VP Student Affairs/Dean of Students .... Dr. Gregory A. THOMAS
49 Dean Liberal Arts/Social Sciences .... Mr. Elighie WILSON
50 Dean Math/Science/Curriculum .... Dr. Debra L. PRENDERGAST
76 Dean Allied Health/Emerg Services .... Ms. Carol FAWCETT
75 Dean Career and Tech Education .... Ms. Janice KAUSHAL
15 Exec Dir Human Resources .... Mr. David CRONAN
13 Exec Dir Info Technology Resources .... Mr. Gregory KAIN
56 Dean Adult Education .... Ms. Kim M. KUNCE
21 Controller/Dir of Business Svcs .... Ms. Marina KRTINIC
08 Int Assoc Dean/Learning Res/Assess .... Ms. Carolyn CIESLA
51 Dean Corporate/Continuing Education .... Ms. Kelly LAPETINO
35 Dean Student Dev/Campus Life .... Mr. Felix SIMPKINS
18 Exec Dir Facilities and Operations .... Mr. Timothy J. KOSIEK
111 Exec Dir Inst Advance & Foundation .... Ms. Deborah S. HAVIGHORST
07 Exec Dir Enrollment/Fin Aid Svcs .... Ms. Jaime M. MILLER
19 Dir Police/Campus Safe/Chief Police .... Mr. George PFOTENHAUER
37 Director Financial Aid .... Ms. Grace MCGINNIS
09 Director Inst Research/Planning .... Dr. Adane G. KASSA
88 Director Institutional Support Svcs .... Ms. Paulette A. MAURER
41 Director of Athletics .... Mr. Christopher ZORICH
04 Admin Dir Pres Office/Board .... Ms. Patricia G. TROST
89 Director First Year Experience .... Dr. Stephanie COLEMAN
108 Dir Plan Effectiveness and Accredit .... Ms. Jan BONAVIA

Principia College (A)

1 Maybeck Place, Elsah IL 62028-9799
County: Jersey FICE Identification: 001744
Unit ID: 148016
Telephone: (618) 374-2131 Carnegie Class: Bac-A&S
FAX Number: (618) 374-5500 Calendar System: Semester
URL: www.principiacollege.edu
Established: 1898 Annual Undergrad Tuition & Fees: $27,980
Enrollment: 460 Coed
Affiliation or Control: Independent Non-Profit IRS Status: 501(c)3
Highest Offering: Baccalaureate
Accreditation: NH

01 President .... Dr. Jonathan PALMER
05 Provost .... Dr. Joseph RITTER
115 Chief Investment Officer .... Mr. Howard E. BERNER, JR.
10 Vice President Finance & Operations .... Mr. Doug GIBBS
11 Vice President Administration .... Mrs. Karen D. GRIMMER
26 Vice President External Relations .... Mr. Peter STEVENS
111 Vice President of Advancement .... Mrs. Barbara BLACKWELL
20 Associate Dean of Academics .... Dr. Libby SCHEIERN
71 Dir Acad Special Programs .... Mr. James HEGARTY
43 Legal Counsel .... Mr. Lee BARRON
06 Registrar .... Ms. Alice DERVIN
32 Dean of Students .... Ms. Debra JONES
08 Director of Libraries .... Mrs. Lisa ROBERTS
13 Director Information Technology .... Mr. Chris HUFFORD
104 Director of Principia Abroad .... Dr. Gregory W. SANDFORD
41 Director of Athletics .... Mr. Pete PACIOREK
15 Human Resources Director .... Ms. SharonAnn SMITH
18 Director of Facilities .... Mr. Ed GOEWERT
21 Controller .... Mr. Don MILLER
29 Dir Alumni/Field Rels/Ann Giving .... Mrs. Donna GIBBS
07 Dir Admissions/Col Financial Aid .... Mrs. Tami GAVALETZ
96 Purchasing Agent .... Mrs. Susan CURRY
38 Director Academic Career Advising .... Mrs. Midge BROWNING
09 Institutional Research Officer .... Ms. Roz HIBBS
27 Dir Marketing & Communications .... Mrs. Laurel WALTERS

Quincy University (B)

1800 College Avenue, Quincy IL 62301-2699
County: Adams FICE Identification: 001745
Unit ID: 148131
Telephone: (217) 222-8020 Carnegie Class: Masters/M
FAX Number: (217) 228-5257 Calendar System: Semester
URL: www.quincy.edu
Established: 1860 Annual Undergrad Tuition & Fees: $27,128
Enrollment: 1,293 Coed
Affiliation or Control: Roman Catholic IRS Status: 501(c)3
Highest Offering: Master's
Accreditation: NH, CACREP

01 President .... Mr. Phillip CONOVER
05 VP for Academic Affairs .... Dr. Teresa REED
42 VP for Mission & Ministry .... Fr. John DOCTOR, OFM
10 VP for Business/Finance .... Mr. Mark STRIEKER
84 VP Student Enrollment & Engagement .... Mr. Tom OLIVER
41 VP for Athletics/Athletic Dir .... Mr. Marty BELL
111 VP for Univ Advancement .... Mrs. Julie BELL
13 Chief Information Officer .... Vacant
04 Exec Assistant to the President .... Mrs. Julie BUDINE
101 Corporate Secretary .... Fr. John DOCTOR, OFM
21 Assoc VP for Finance/Controller .... Mrs. Jean GREEN
06 Registrar .... Ms. Nancy GEISSLER
50 Dean School of Business .... Dr. Cynthia HALIEMUN
08 Dean Library/Info Resources .... Ms. Patricia TOMCZAK
79 Chair Division of Humanities .... Dr. Daniel STRUDWICK
81 Chair Division Science & Technology .... Dr. Lee ENGER
83 Chair Div Behavioral/Social Sci .... Vacant
57 Chair Div Communication/Fine Arts .... Mr. Karl WARMA
32 Dean of Students & Academic Success ...... Mrs. Christine TRACY
108 Director of Assessment .... Dr. David SHINN
92 Director Honors Program .... Dr. Daniel STRUDWICK
42 Director Campus Ministry .... Mr. Ray HEILMANN
30 Dir Development/Alum/Cmty Relations ..... Mr. Matthew BERGMAN

37 Director Financial Aid .... Ms. Lisa FLACK
18 Director Facilities Management .... Mr. Kevin BUSSEY
39 Asst Dir Residence Life/New Program .... Ms. Andrea GRUEGER
19 Director Safety & Security .... Mr. Sam LATHROP
15 Director Human Resources .... Mrs. Tanya MOORE
07 Director of Admissions .... Mr. Brittany ELLERMAN
36 Director Career Services .... Mrs. Kristen LIESEN
96 Purchasing .... Ms. Jennifer TRUITT
25 Grant Writer .... Mrs. Julie BOLL
40 Manager Bookstore .... Mr. Ben MEANS
88 Director of Student Teaching .... Dr. Glenda MCCARTY
09 Director of Institutional Research .... Mr. David SHINN

Rasmussen College - Aurora (C)

2363 Sequoia Drive, Suite 131, Aurora IL 60506
Telephone: (630) 888-3500 Identification: 667060
Accreditation: &NH, CAHIIM, MAAB

† Regional accreditation is carried under the parent institution in Saint Cloud, MN. The tuition figure is an average, actual tuition may vary.

Rasmussen College - Mokena/Tinley Park (D)

8650 W. Spring Lake Drive, Mokena IL 60448
Telephone: (815) 534-3300 Identification: 667064
Accreditation: &NH, MAAB

† Regional accreditation carried under the parent institution in Saint Cloud, MN. The tuition figure is an average, actual tuition may vary.

Rasmussen College - Rockford (E)

6000 E. State Street, 4th Floor, Rockford IL 61108
Telephone: (815) 316-4800 Identification: 667065
Accreditation: &NH, CAHIIM, MAAB

† Regional accreditation carried under the parent institution in Saint Cloud, MN. The tuition figure is an average, actual tuition may vary.

Rasmussen College - Romeoville/Joliet (F)

1400 West Normantown Road, Romeoville IL 60446
Telephone: (815) 306-2600 Identification: 667066
Accreditation: &NH, MAAB

† Regional accreditation carried under the parent institution in Saint Cloud, MN. The tuition figure is an average, actual tuition may vary.

Realtor University (G)

430 North Michigan Avenue, Chicago IL 60611
County: Cook Identification: 667270
Telephone: (855) 786-6546 Carnegie Class: Not Classified
FAX Number: N/A Calendar System: Semester
URL: www.realtors.edu
Established: 2003 Annual Graduate Tuition & Fees: N/A
Enrollment: N/A Coed
Affiliation or Control: Proprietary IRS Status: Proprietary
Highest Offering: Master's; No Undergraduates
Accreditation: DEAC

01 President .... Dale A. STINTON

Rend Lake College (H)

468 N Ken Gray Parkway, Ina IL 62846-9801
County: Jefferson FICE Identification: 007119
Unit ID: 148256
Telephone: (618) 437-5321 Carnegie Class: Assoc/HVT-High Non
FAX Number: (618) 437-5677 Calendar System: Semester
URL: www.rlc.edu
Established: 1967 Annual Undergrad Tuition & Fees (In-District): $3,750
Enrollment: 2,303 Coed
Affiliation or Control: State/Local IRS Status: 501(c)3
Highest Offering: Associate Degree
Accreditation: NH, CAHIIM, EMT, MAC, MLTAD, RAD

01 President .... Mr. Terry WILKERSON
05 VP Career Technical Education .... Mrs. Lori RAGLAND
10 VP of Finance & Administration .... Mrs. Angie KISTNER
32 VP of Student Services .... Mrs. Lisa PRICE
26 Director Marketing & Information .... Mr. Chad COPPLE
37 Director Student Financial Aid .... Ms. Cheri RUSHING
41 Athletic Director .... Mr. Tim WILLS
18 Director Physical Plant .... Mr. Donnie MILLENBINE
102 CEO of RLC Foundation .... Mrs. Kathleen ZIBBY-DAMRON
06 Director of Student Records .... Mrs. Kelly DOWNES
07 Director of Enrollment Services .... Mrs. Vickie SCHULTE

Resurrection University (I)

1431 N. Claremont Street, 6th Floor, Chicago IL 60622
County: Cook FICE Identification: 006250
Unit ID: 149763
Telephone: (773) 252-6464 Carnegie Class: Spec-4-yr-Other Health
FAX Number: (773) 227-5134 Calendar System: Semester
URL: www.resu.edu
Established: 1982 Annual Undergrad Tuition & Fees: N/A
Enrollment: 494 Coed
Affiliation or Control: Independent Non-Profit IRS Status: 501(c)3
Highest Offering: Master's
Accreditation: NH, CAHIIM, NURSE, RAD

01 President .... Dr. Therese A. SCANLAN
03 Executive Vice President .... Mr. Matthew HUGHES
05 Chief Academic Officer .... Mr. George ARNOLD
26 VP Marketing & Enrollment Mgmt .... Ms. Jeri BINGHAM
32 VP Student & Employee Affairs .... Mr. Brian BOLLENBACHER
35 Director of Student Development .... Ms. Esther WALLEN
90 Network Support Analyst .... Mr. Zbigniew KUSNIERZ
37 Student Financial Aid .... Ms. Shirley HOWELL
06 Registrar .... Mr. Michael SHERMAN
84 Director of Enrollment Mgmt .... Ms. Margaret WOOLWINE
08 Director of Library Services .... Ms. Liesl COTTRELL
66 Dean of Nursing .... Vacant
04 Administrative Asst to President .... Ms. Barbara BAILEY

Richland Community College (J)

One College Park, Decatur IL 62521-8513
County: Macon FICE Identification: 010879
Unit ID: 148292
Telephone: (217) 875-7200 Carnegie Class: Assoc/MT-VT-High Non
FAX Number: (217) 875-6961 Calendar System: Semester
URL: www.richland.edu
Established: 1971 Annual Undergrad Tuition & Fees (In-District): $4,230
Enrollment: 3,368 Coed
Affiliation or Control: State/Local IRS Status: 501(c)3
Highest Offering: Associate Degree
Accreditation: NH, ACFEI, ADNUR, CAHIIM, RAD, SURGT

01 President .... Dr. Cristobal (Cris) VALDEZ
10 Vice President of Finance & Admin .... Mr. Greg E. FLORIAN
05 Vice Pres Academic Services .... Dr. Denise CREWS
32 Vice Pres of Student Success .... Mr. Marcus BROWN
103 VP Econ Dev/Innov Wkfce Solutions .... Dr. Douglas BRAUER
106 Director Online Learning .... Mrs. Kona JONES
30 Exec Director Foundation & Devel .... Ms. Julie MELTON
29 Dir Scholarships/Alumni Development ... Mrs. Tricia CORDULACK
26 Exec Dir Public Info/Chief of Staff .... Ms. Lisa GREGORY
07 Director Admissions/Recruitment .... Ms. Cathy SEBOK
06 Director Advising & Registrar .... Mr. Richard KERR
35 Director Student Success .... Ms. Kathryn MAST
38 Director Student Development .... Mrs. Deborah MCGEE
36 Director Career Services .... Mr. Michael DIGGS
15 Director Human Resources .... Ms. Robin BOLLHORST
37 Asst Dir Financial Aid/Veteran Affs .... Ms. Jody BURTNETT
81 Dean Math & Sciences/Business Div .... Dr. Andy HYNDS
51 Dean Continuing & Prof Educ Div ...... Mrs. Darbe BRINKOETTER
57 Int Dean Comm/Fine Arts/Educ/Hum .... Dr. John CORDULACK
76 Dean of Health Professions .... Ms. Ellen COLBECK

Robert Morris University - Illinois (K)

401 South State Street, Chicago IL 60605-1225
County: Cook FICE Identification: 001746
Unit ID: 148335
Telephone: (312) 935-6800 Carnegie Class: Masters/L
FAX Number: (312) 935-6660 Calendar System: Other
URL: www.robertmorris.edu
Established: 1913 Annual Undergrad Tuition & Fees: $25,800
Enrollment: 3,056 Coed
Affiliation or Control: Independent Non-Profit IRS Status: 501(c)3
Highest Offering: Master's
Accreditation: NH, IACBE, MAC, NURSE, SURGT

00 Chancellor .... Michael P. VIOLLT
01 President .... Mablene KRUEGER
03 Executive Vice President .... Nicole CAFILLIO
10 Sr VP/Chief Financial Officer .... Arlene REGNERUS
05 VP of Curriculum & Instruction .... Larry NIEMAN
21 Controller .... Melanie CARLIN
15 VP of Human Resources .... Ann BRESINGHAM
88 VP of Academic Administration .... Kathleen SUHAJDA
13 VP of Information Systems .... Lisa CONTRERAS
32 VP of Student Affairs .... Angela JORDAN
37 Director of Financial Services .... Michelle HAYES
41 Director of Athletics .... Jared WILLIAMSON
26 Director of Marketing .... Michelle CASINI
20 Dean of Curriculum .... Lora TIMMONS
20 Dean of Instruction .... Basim KHARTABIL
06 Dean of Student Information .... Stella MACH
58 Dean of Morris Grad School of Mgmt .... Kayed AKKAWI
88 Dean of Academics MGSM .... Diane ALLEN
07 Dean of Admissions .... Andy BERGER
19 Director Security/Safety .... Paul HUERTA
11 Director of Administration .... Michelle HAYES
40 Director of Bookstore Operations .... Lynn RODGERS
102 Dir of Corporate Advancement .... Carlos VALE
35 Director of Student Engagement .... Carrie ROATH
53 Director of Education .... Kimberly WARFORD
53 Director of Education .... Jane WENDORFF-CRAPS
08 Institutional Library Director .... Sue DUTLER
18 Institutional Operations Director .... Nino RANDAZZO
14 Director of Networking Services .... Adrian CEPEDA
27 Director of Public Relations .... Nancy DONOHOE
91 Director of Data Administration .... Deana MUNOZ
88 Sr Dir of Academic Administration .... Kathleen VIOLLT
121 Dir of Student Support Services .... Angelica CASTANDEA
88 Director of Grant Advancement .... Lauren MILLER
88 Dir of Upward Bound and ETS .... Carolyn BASLEY
90 Director of Academic Programming .... Carmen CUEVAS
27 Director of Visual Strategy & Comm .... Deanna HO

Rock Valley College (A)

3301 N Mulford Road, Rockford IL 61114-5699
County: Winnebago FICE Identification: 001747
Unit ID: 148380
Telephone: (815) 921-7821 Carnegie Class: Assoc/MT-VT-High Non
FAX Number: N/A Calendar System: Semester
URL: www.rockvalleycollege.edu
Established: 1964 Annual Undergrad Tuition & Fees (In-District): $3,314
Enrollment: 7,651 Coed
Affiliation or Control: Local IRS Status: 501(c)3
Highest Offering: Associate Degree
Accreditation: NH, COARC, DH, SURGT

01 President ... Dr. Douglas J. JENSEN
05 Chief Academic Officer ... Ms. Susan BUSENBARK
10 Vice Pres Administrative Services ... Ms. Beth YOUNG
11 Chief Operating Officer ... Mr. Jim RYAN
32 VP Student Services ... Dr. Howard SPEARMAN
51 VP Career & Technical Education ... Vacant
15 Vice President of Human Resources ... Vacant
09 VP Institutional Effectiveness ... Dr. Lisa MEHLIG
30 Director of Development ... Ms. Brittany FREIBERG
35 Dean of Students ... Mr. Rick DANIELS
18 Director Facilities Planning & POM ... Ms. Janet TAYLOR
26 Exec Dir Col Comm/Marketing ... Mr. Dave COSTELLO
88 Director Theatre & Arts Park ... Mr. Christopher D. BRADY
19 Director Public Safety ... Mr. Joe DROUGHT
06 Registrar/Director Records/Rgstn ... Ms. Kelly COOPER
36 Manager Career Svcs/Placement ... Vacant
04 Assistant to the President ... Ms. Ann KERWITZ
41 Athletic Director ... Ms. Misty OPAT

Rockford Career College (B)

1130 S. Alpine Road, Suite 100, Rockford IL 61108
County: Winnebago FICE Identification: 008545
Unit ID: 148399
Telephone: (815) 965-8616 Carnegie Class: Assoc/HVT-High Non
FAX Number: (815) 965-0360 Calendar System: Quarter
URL: www.rockfordcareercollege.edu
Established: 1862 Annual Undergrad Tuition & Fees: $10,776
Enrollment: 513 Coed
Affiliation or Control: Proprietary IRS Status: Proprietary
Highest Offering: Associate Degree
Accreditation: ACICS

01 President/CEO ... Mr. Stephen TAVE
10 Vice President/Dir of Finance ... Mr. Guary BERNADELLE
05 Academic Dean ... Mr. Tom LEU
12 Campus President ... Mr. Mick O'HERRON
32 Dean of Students ... Ms. Danielle HARRIOTT
06 Registrar/Director of Compliance ... Ms. Heather SEIBERLICH
07 Director of Admissions ... Mr. Mike O'HERRON
15 Director of Human Resources ... Mr. Kent SHEPLER
36 Director Career Services ... Ms. Melissa RIDGEWAY
37 Director of Financial Aid ... Ms. Mari HUFFMAN
26 Director of College Relations ... Mr. Jeff SWANBERG
08 Library/Bookstore Coordinator ... Ms. Edith HILL

Rockford University (C)

5050 E State Street, Rockford IL 61108-2393
County: Winnebago FICE Identification: 001748
Unit ID: 148405
Telephone: (815) 226-4000 Carnegie Class: Masters/S
FAX Number: (815) 226-4119 Calendar System: Semester
URL: www.rockford.edu
Established: 1847 Annual Undergrad Tuition & Fees: $29,180
Enrollment: 1,274 Coed
Affiliation or Control: Independent Non-Profit IRS Status: 501(c)3
Highest Offering: Master's
Accreditation: NH, IACBE, NUR

01 President ... Dr. Eric W. FULCOMER
05 VP of Academic Affairs/Provost ... Dr. Michael MAHALYO
111 VP for Institutional Advancement ... Mr. Bernard SUNDSTEDT
30 AVP for Institutional Advancement ... Mrs. Denise NOE
10 Sr VP for Business/Operations/CFO ... Ms. Christina ANDERSON
21 Business Office Accounting Manager ... Mr. Justin KRUEGER
84 Int VP Enrollment Management ... Mr. Matthew PHILLIPS
07 Assoc VP Undergraduate Admission ... Ms. Jennifer NORDSTROM
37 Assistant VP for SAS ... Mr. Todd FISCHER-FREE
11 Director of Operations ... Mr. Ed TOMASZKIEWICZ
13 Director of Information Technology ... Mr. Ryan CUSHING
32 Dean of Students ... Ms. Lisa HETZEL
58 Director of MBA ... Vacant
58 Director of MAT ... Vacant
06 Registrar ... Ms. Anna J. JATTKOWSKI-HUDSON
04 Exec Assistant to the President ... Ms. Brenda PERRONE
04 Special Assistant to the President ... Ms. Teddy PHILLIPS
41 Director of Athletics ... Mr. Jason MULLIGAN
15 Director of Human Resources ... Ms. Monique LINDSTEDT
36 Director Career Services ... Mr. Maurice WEST, II
26 Director of Communications ... Ms. Rita ELLIOTT
09 Coordinator of IR ... Mr. Todd FISCHER-FREE
88 Director of Global Affairs ... Mr. Sam BANDY
38 Director Counseling ... Mrs. Sallyann ROBERTS
23 Director Health Services ... Mrs. Cecelia M. BRISTOL
18 Director Facilities/Custodial Svcs ... Mr. Steve CARSON
19 Int Dir Campus Safety & Security ... Mr. Jeffrey BOATWRIGHT
08 Head Librarian ... Ms. Kelly JAMES

Roosevelt University (D)

430 S Michigan Avenue, Chicago IL 60605-1394
County: Cook FICE Identification: 001749
Unit ID: 148487
Telephone: (312) 341-3500 Carnegie Class: Masters/L
FAX Number: (312) 341-3655 Calendar System: Semester
URL: www.roosevelt.edu
Established: 1945 Annual Undergrad Tuition & Fees: $28,119
Enrollment: 5,352 Coed
Affiliation or Control: Independent Non-Profit IRS Status: 501(c)3
Highest Offering: Doctorate
Accreditation: NH, ACBSP, CACREP, CAEPN, CLPSY, MUS, PHAR

01 President ... Dr. Ali MALEKZADEH
05 Exec Vice President/Univ Provost ... Dr. Lois BECKER
10 Interim Sr VP of Fin/Admin and CFO ... Ms. Tangella MADDOX
84 Interim VP Enrollment Mgmt ... Mr. Terry RICHARDS
100 Chief of Staff & Asst Secy to BOT ... Mr. Michael FORD
111 VP Inst Advancement ... Mr. Don JONES
30 Asst VP Institutional Advance ... Ms. Janice PARKIN
26 Assoc VP Marketing ... Ms. Nicole BARRON
32 Assoc VP Stdnt Affs/Dean Students ... Ms. Sharron EVANS
09 Assoc VP Inst Research ... Mr. Joseph P. REGAN
21 Acting Associate VP Finance ... Mr. Patrick ALFORQUE
18 Assoc VP Campus Planning & Op ... Mr. Steven A. HOSELTON
85 Asst Dir of International Programs ... Ms. Dawn HOUGLAND
13 Chief Information Officer ... Mr. Neeraj KUMAR
58 Assoc Provost Research ... Dr. Mike MALY
121 Assoc Provost Student Success ... Ms. Katrina COAKLEY
49 Dean College Arts & Sciences ... Dr. Bonnie GUNZENHAUSER
50 Interim Dean College Business ... Dr. Samuel ROSENBERG
64 Dean College of Performing Arts ... Mr. Henry FOGEL
53 Dean College of Education ... Dr. Thomas PHILION
67 Dean College of Pharmacy ... Dr. Melissa HOGAN
88 Exec Dir of Auditorium Theatre/ CEO ... Ms. Tania CASTROVERDE MOSKOLENKO
08 Interim Director of Libraries ... Mr. Estavan MONTANO
06 University Registrar ... Ms. Lakisha YOUNG
38 Director Counseling Center ... Dr. Mary GRIGAR
36 Director Career & Prof Development ... Ms. Jennifer WONDERLY
04 Senior Exec Asst to President ... Ms. Christine SPENCER
19 Director Campus Safety & Trans ... Ms. Maureen FRONCEK
88 Assoc VP Enroll Mgmt ... Mr. Michael CASSIDY
07 Director of Admissions ... Mr. Al NUNEZ
105 Senior Web Developer ... Mr. Eugene CHOI
96 Director of Purchasing ... Mr. Calvin LYONS

Rosalind Franklin University of Medicine & Science (E)

3333 Green Bay Road, North Chicago IL 60064-3095
County: Lake FICE Identification: 001659
Unit ID: 145558
Telephone: (847) 578-3000 Carnegie Class: Spec-4-yr-Med
FAX Number: (847) 578-3401 Calendar System: Quarter
URL: www.rosalindfranklin.edu
Established: 1912 Annual Undergrad Tuition & Fees: N/A
Enrollment: 2,214 Coed
Affiliation or Control: Independent Non-Profit IRS Status: 501(c)3
Highest Offering: Doctorate; No Lower Division
Accreditation: NH, ANEST, ARCPA, CLPSY, MED, PA, PHAR, POD, PTA

01 President/CEO ... Dr. Michael WELCH
05 Provost ... Dr. Wendy RHEAULT
67 Dean Col of Pharmacy ... Dr. Marc ABEL
107 Dean College Health Professions ... Dr. James CARLSON
58 Dean Sch Grad PostDoc Stds ... Dr. Joseph X. DIMARIO
63 Dean Scholl Col Podiatric Med ... Dr. Nancy L. PARSLEY
63 Dean Medical School ... Dr. James RECORD
26 VP Marketing/Brand Management ... Ms. Lee CONCHA
32 VP Student Affairs & Inclusion ... Ms. Rebecca DURKIN
46 Exec VP Research ... Dr. Ronald S. KAPLAN
88 Assoc Prov/Clinical Partnerships ... Dr. Sandra LARSON
13 Chief Information Officer ... Mr. Richard LOESCH
43 Chief Compliance Officer ... Mr. Bret MOBERG
84 VP Strategic Enrollment Management ... Dr. Bruce C. NEIMEYER
10 VP Finance & Admin ... Mr. John NYLEN
111 VP Institutional Advancement ... Mr. Chad RUBACK
103 Exec Dir Healthcare Workforce Dev ... Dr. William RUDMAN
20 VP Academic/Faculty Affairs ... Dr. Judith STOECKER
37 AVP Student Financial Services ... Ms. Maryann DECAIRE
88 AVP Faculty Development ... Dr. Rea KATZ
108 AVP Accreditation/Assessment ... Dr. Glenda GALLISATH
114 AVP Fin Plng & Analysis ... Ms. Christie TIPTON
101 Exec Administrator to the Board ... Ms. Donna AGNEW
35 Exec Dir Campus Life ... Ms. Shelly BRZYCKI
30 Exec Dir of Development ... Ms. Pamela LOWE
29 Exec Dir Alumni Relations ... Ms. Martha KELLY BATES
15 Exec Dir of Human Resources ... Ms. Sally J. MADDEN
30 Exec Dir of Development ... Mr. George RATTIN
21 Controller ... Mr. Thomas J. BUNS
06 Registrar ... Mr. Timothy CARROLL
100 Dir Office of the President ... Ms. Donna AGNEW
19 Dir Campus Security ... Mr. Gordon BLANCHARD
96 Dir Materials Management ... Mr. Vince BUTERA
102 Dir Foundation & Grant Relations ... Ms. Shella BLUE
28 Dir Training/Educational Programs ... Dr. Monica CUMMINGS
25 Dir Sponsored Research ... Ms. Dora ESPINOZA
09 Dir Institutional Research ... Ms. Renee FRANCISCO
121 Dir Academic Support ... Ms. Elizabeth FRIEDMAN
44 Dir Annual Giving ... Mr. Mark RUSSELL
07 Dir Admissions/Enrollment ... Ms. Tonishea TERRY-JACKSON
18 Dir Facilities Management ... Mr. Robert D. JACKSON
16 Asst Dir of Human Resources ... Ms. Mary TELL
118 Benefits Administrator ... Ms. Melissa HALEY
08 Library Director ... Mr. Scott THOMSON
04 Executive Administrative Assistant ... Ms. Jean MINA
39 Coordinator for Residence Life ... Ms. Amber WOYAK

Rush University (F)

600 S Paulina, Chicago IL 60612-3832
County: Cook FICE Identification: 009800
Unit ID: 148511
Telephone: (312) 942-7100 Carnegie Class: Spec-4-yr-Med
FAX Number: (312) 942-2219 Calendar System: Quarter
URL: www.rushu.rush.edu
Established: 1971 Annual Undergrad Tuition & Fees: N/A
Enrollment: 2,515 Coed
Affiliation or Control: Independent Non-Profit IRS Status: 501(c)3
Highest Offering: Doctorate
Accreditation: NH, ANEST, ARCPA, AUD, BBT, COARC, DIETI, DMS, HSA, IPSY, MED, MT, NURSE, OT, PAST, PERF, SP

01 CEO RUMC & Pres Rush University ... Dr. Larry J. GOODMAN
17 President & COO RUMC ... Mr. Michael DANDORPH
05 Provost ... Dr. Thomas A. DEUTSCH
26 Vice Pres Corp/External Affairs ... Mr. Terry PETERSON
10 Principal Business Officer ... Mr. Richard K. DAVIS
10 Senior Vice President Finance ... Mr. John MORDACH
30 Senior Vice President Philanthropy ... Ms. Diane M. MCKEEVER
13 Sr Vice Pres/Chief Information Ofcr ... Dr. Shafiq RAB
43 Vice President Legal Affairs ... Mr. Carl BERGETZ
15 Sr Vice President Human Resource ... Ms. Mary E. SCHOPP
25 Vice Pres Chief Compliance Office ... Dr. Cynthia E. BOYD
28 Int Dir Student Diversity/Multicul ... Mr. Greg MACVARISH
20 Sr Assc Provost Educational Affairs ... Dr. Gayle WARD
108 Assoc Prov Inst Res/Assess/Accred ... Dr. Rosemarie SUHAYDA
32 Chief Student Experience Officer ... Mr. Greg MACVARISH
76 Dean Col of Health Sciences ... Dr. Charlotte ROYEEN
58 Acting Dean Graduate College ... Dr. James L. MULSHINE
66 Dean College of Nursing ... Dr. Marquis D. FOREMAN
63 Dean Rush Medical College ... Dr. Ranga KRISHNAN
20 Sr Assoc Dean Medical College ... Dr. Elizabeth A. BAKER
27 Assoc VP Marketing & Comm ... Mr. Ryan NAGDEMAN
08 Director Library ... Ms. Jo CATES
35 Director Student Life & Engagement ... Ms. Angela BRANSON
37 Dir Student Financial Aid ... Ms. Jill GABLE
09 Director of Institutional Research ... Dr. Joshua JACOBS
38 Director Student Counsel Center ... Dr. Hilarie TEREBESSY
29 Director Alumni Relations ... Ms. Krista GIUFFI
96 Director of Purchasing ... Mr. Michael MULROE
18 Director University Facilities ... Mr. Chris KANAKIS
21 Manager of Financial Affairs ... Mr. Patrick MCNULTY
84 Chief Enroll Mgmt Ofcr/Registrar ... Ms. Brenda WEDDINGTON
102 Dir Foundation/Corporate Relations ... Ms. Sophia WOROBEC
105 Assoc VP IS Clinical Systems ... Mr. Steven P. WIGHTKIN
19 Director Security Services ... Mr. Lauris FREIDENFELDS
54 Director Med Ctr Engineering ... Mr. Mike WISNIEWSKI
101 Secretary of the Institution/Board ... Ms. Diane M. MCKEEVER

SAE Institute Chicago (G)

820 N. Orleans St., Ste 125, Chicago IL 60610
Telephone: (312) 300-5685 Identification: 770970
Accreditation: ACCSC

† Branch campus of SAE Institute Nashville, Nashville, TN

Saint Anthony College of Nursing (H)

5658 E. State Street, Rockford IL 61108
County: Winnebago FICE Identification: 009987
Unit ID: 149028
Telephone: (815) 282-7900 Carnegie Class: Spec-4-yr-Other Health
FAX Number: (815) 282-7901 Calendar System: Semester
URL: www.sacn.edu
Established: 1915 Annual Undergrad Tuition & Fees: $24,314
Enrollment: 322 Coed
Affiliation or Control: Roman Catholic IRS Status: 501(c)3
Highest Offering: Doctorate
Accreditation: NH, NURSE

01 President ... Dr. Sandie S. SOLDWISCH
66 Dean Undergraduate Affairs ... Dr. Elizabeth M. CARSON
58 Dean Graduate Affairs & Research ... Dr. Shannon K. LIZER
32 Associate Dean Support Services ... Ms. Nancy A. SANDERS
08 Library Supervisor ... Ms. Heather A. KLEPITSCH
37 Financial Aid Coordinator ... Ms. Serrita WOODS
04 Administrative Asst to President ... Ms. Teresa M. DAUGHERTY
84 Enrollment Management Coordinator ... Ms. April M. LIPNITZKY
09 Inst Effectiveness/Assessment Spec ... Ms. Elizabeth R. HARP
90 Educational Technology Coordinator ... Ms. Susan K. STAAB

St. Augustine College (I)

1333-45 W Argyle Street, Chicago IL 60640-3501
County: Cook FICE Identification: 021854
Unit ID: 148876
Telephone: (773) 878-8756 Carnegie Class: Bac/Assoc-Mixed
FAX Number: (773) 878-0937 Calendar System: Semester
URL: www.staugustine.edu
Established: 1980 Annual Undergrad Tuition & Fees: $13,200
Enrollment: 1,483 Coed
Affiliation or Control: Independent Non-Profit IRS Status: 501(c)3

Highest Offering: Baccalaureate
Accreditation: NH, COARC, SW

01 Interim President ... Dr. Bruno BONDAVALLI
05 VP of Academic Affairs & Operations ... Dr. Bruno BONDAVALLI
20 VP of Academic Affairs ... Ms. Madeline ROMAN-VARGAS
10 VP for Finance ... Ms. Saundra K. FLEMING
26 VP for Marketing ... Mr. Nicolas PIENOVI
103 VP Institute Workforce Development ... Mr. Norman RUANO
13 VP Technology/Research & Systems ... Mr. Paul HECK
37 Director of Financial Aid ... Ms. Maria ZAMBONINO
15 Director Human Resources ... Mr. Teofilo CALERO
07 Director of Admission ... Ms. Gloria QUIROZ
12 Director West Satellite ... Ms. Carmen RIVERA
12 Director South Satellite ... Dr. Beda LOPEZ SIERRA
12 Director of Southeast Satellite ... Ms. Patricia VEGA
12 Director of Aurora Satallite ... Ms. Elizabeth CARDENAS
08 Dir of Information Commons/Library ... Ms. Elizabeth MURPHY
84 Vice President of Enrollment Mgt ... Dr. Juan OJEDA

Saint Francis Medical Center College of Nursing (A)

511 NE Greenleaf Street, Peoria IL 61603-3783
County: Peoria FICE Identification: 006240
Unit ID: 148575
Telephone: (309) 655-2201 Carnegie Class: Spec-4-yr-Other Health
FAX Number: (309) 624-8973 Calendar System: Semester
URL: www.sfmccon.edu
Established: 1985 Annual Undergrad Tuition & Fees: N/A
Enrollment: 678 Coed
Affiliation or Control: Roman Catholic IRS Status: 501(c)3
Highest Offering: Doctorate
Accreditation: NH, NUR, NURSE

01 President of the College ... Dr. Patricia A. STOCKERT
05 Dean Undergraduate Program ... Dr. Sue C. BROWN
58 Dean Graduate Program ... Dr. Kimberly A. MITCHELL
32 Asst Dean of Support Services ... Mr. Kevin N. STEPHENS
07 Director of Admissions/Registrar .. Ms. Janice E. FARQUHARSON
08 Librarian ... Mr. William KOMANECKI
38 College Counselor ... Mrs. Jennifer CARLOCK
37 Coord Student Fin/Financial Assist .... Mrs. Nancy S. PERRYMAN
10 Coord Student Finance/Accts Rec .. Ms. Kimberly S. BUFFINGTON
04 Administrative Assistant ... Ms. Luann MORELOCK
108 Inst Effectiveness/Assessment Spec ... Mr. Ryan A. WILLIAMS

St. John's College (B)

729 E. Carpenter Street, Springfield IL 62702-5317
County: Sangamon FICE Identification: 030980
Unit ID: 148593
Telephone: (217) 525-5628 Carnegie Class: Spec-4-yr-Other Health
FAX Number: (217) 757-6870 Calendar System: Semester
URL: www.sjcs.edu
Established: 1991 Annual Undergrad Tuition & Fees: N/A
Enrollment: 121 Coed
Affiliation or Control: Independent Non-Profit IRS Status: 501(c)3
Highest Offering: Baccalaureate
Accreditation: NH, NUR

01 Chancellor ... Dr. Charlene S. AARON
05 Dean of Academic Affairs ... Dr. Judy SHACKELFORD
07 Admissions Officer/Registrar ... Ms. Britni CARUSO
30 Student Development Officer ... Ms. Abby MILLITELLO
51 Director of Continuing Education ... Dr. Mary Jo BROWN
37 Financial Aid Officer ... Mr. Timothy MARTEN

Saint Xavier University (C)

3700 W 103rd Street, Chicago IL 60655-3105
County: Cook FICE Identification: 001768
Unit ID: 148627
Telephone: (773) 298-3000 Carnegie Class: Masters/L
FAX Number: (773) 779-9061 Calendar System: Semester
URL: www.sxu.edu
Established: 1846 Annual Undergrad Tuition & Fees: $32,250
Enrollment: 3,949 Coed
Affiliation or Control: Roman Catholic IRS Status: 501(c)3
Highest Offering: Master's
Accreditation: NH, CAEPN, MUS, NURSE, SP

01 President ... Dr. Laurie M. JOYNER
05 Interim Provost ... Dr. Suzanne LEE
10 Vice President Business & Finance ... Mr. Robert H. FISHER
32 VP Student Affairs/Dean of Students ... Dr. Anthony CAMPBELL
09 Exec Dir Institutional Research ... Dr. Kathleen CARLSON
35 Asst Vice Pres Student Affairs ... Ms. Carrie SCHADE
26 AVP Marketing/Communications ... Ms. Deb RAPACZ
30 Assoc VP University Advancement ... Mr. John R. BASS
18 Director of Facilities Management ... Mr. Peter SKACH
20 Associate Provost ... Dr. Richard VENNERI
20 Asst Provost/Director Retention ... Ms. Maureen WOGAN
35 Dean of Students ... Dr. Eileen DOHERTY
13 Chief Information Officer ... Ms. Molly GAIK
109 Director Auxiliary Services ... Ms. Linda MORENO
37 Director Financial Aid ... Ms. Susan SWISHER
21 Controller ... Ms. Diane STALLMANN
43 General Counsel ... Ms. Kathleen A. RINEHART
07 Director of Admission ... Mr. Brian HOTZFIELD
24 Director CIDAT ... Mr. Christopher ZAKREWSKI
08 Director Library ... Mr. David STERN
06 Director Records/Registration Svcs ... Ms. Barbara SUTTON
19 Dir Public Safety/Chief of Police ... Mr. Jack TOUHY
41 Director Athletics ... Mr. Robert HALLBERG
85 Dir Center International Education ... Ms. Kelly REIDY-FOX
36 Director of Career Services ... Ms. Jean RIORDAN
49 Dean College Arts/Sciences ... Dr. Greg COUTTS
53 Dean School of Education ... Dr. Suzanne LEE
50 Dean Graham School of Management ... Dr. Asghar SABBAGHI
66 Dean School of Nursing ... Dr. Gloria JACOBSON
04 Executive Assistant to President ... Ms. Gail B. YOUNG

Saint Xavier University Orland Park Campus (D)

18230 Orland Parkway, Orland Park IL 60467
Telephone: (708) 802-6200 Identification: 770093
Accreditation: &NH

Sauk Valley Community College (E)

173 Illinois Route 2, Dixon IL 61021-9188
County: Lee FICE Identification: 001752
Unit ID: 148672
Telephone: (815) 288-5511 Carnegie Class: Assoc/HVT-High Non
FAX Number: (815) 288-1880 Calendar System: Semester
URL: www.svcc.edu
Established: 1965 Annual Undergrad Tuition & Fees (In-District): $3,586
Enrollment: 1,936 Coed
Affiliation or Control: State/Local IRS Status: 501(c)3
Highest Offering: Associate Degree
Accreditation: NH, RAD

01 President ... Dr. David M. HELLMICH
05 Vice Pres Academics/Student Svcs ... Mr. Jon D. MANDRELL
09 Vice Pres Research Plng/Info Affs ... Mr. Steve C. NUNEZ
76 Director of Health Professions ... Ms. Therese DITTO
10 Dean of Business Services ... Ms. Melissa DYE
18 Director Facilities ... Mr. Frank J. MURPHY
15 Director of Human Resources ... Ms. Kathryn C. SNOW
84 Director Enrollment Mgmt/Registrar ... Ms. Pamela S. MEDEMA
102 Dean Foundation/Grants/Govt Rels ... Ms. Lori A. CORTEZ
13 Director of Information Services ... Mr. Eric L. EPPS
41 Director of Athletics ... Vacant
37 Director of Financial Assistance ... Ms. Jennifer A. SCHULTZ
91 Instructional Technology Supp Spec ... Ms. Kathleen M. DIRKS

School of the Art Institute of Chicago (F)

37 S Wabash, Chicago IL 60603-3103
County: Cook FICE Identification: 001753
Unit ID: 143048
Telephone: (312) 899-5100 Carnegie Class: Spec-4-yr-Arts
FAX Number: (312) 263-0141 Calendar System: Semester
URL: www.saic.edu
Established: 1866 Annual Undergrad Tuition & Fees: $45,750
Enrollment: 3,591 Coed
Affiliation or Control: Independent Non-Profit IRS Status: 501(c)3
Highest Offering: Master's
Accreditation: NH, ART

01 President ... Dr. Elissa TENNY
05 Provost ... Mr. Craig BARTON
84 Vice Pres Enrollment Management ... Ms. Rose MILKOWSKI
111 VP for Institutional Advancement ... Ms. Cheryl JESSOGNE
10 Vice Pres Finance & Administration ... Mr. Brian ESKER
15 Vice President for Human Resources ... Mr. Michael NICOLAI
32 Vice Pres/Dean of Student Affairs ... Dr. Felice DUBLON
20 Vice Provost ... Mr. Paul COFFEY
18 Vice Pres Campus Operations ... Mr. Thomas BUECHELE
20 Dean of Faculty/VP Acad Affs ... Ms. Lisa WAINWRIGHT
35 Dean of Student Life ... Ms. Deborah MARTIN
21 Exec Dir Academic Accounting ... Ms. Sherry MISGEN
26 Exec Dir Enroll Mktg & Operations ... Ms. Maryann SCHAEFER
29 Exec Director Alumni Relations ... Ms. Ashley SPELL
38 Exec Director Wellness Center ... Dr. Joseph BEHEN
88 Exec Director Enrollment Services ... Ms. Jane BRUMITT
06 Director Registration & Records ... Ms. Christy MICELI
08 Exec Director of School Library ... Ms. Claire EIKE
36 Dean Career & Prof Experience ... Dr. Terri LONIER
07 Director of Undergrad Admissions ... Ms. Asia MITCHELL
123 Director of Graduate Admissions ... Ms. Nicole HALL
37 Director of Student Financial Svcs ... Mr. Patrick JAMES
28 Director of Multicultural Affairs ... Ms. Rashayla BROWN
88 Director of Learning Center ... Ms. Valerie ST. GERMAIN
49 Dean of Undergraduate Studies ... Ms. Tiffany HOLMES
58 Dean of Graduate Studies ... Mr. Arnold KEMP
28 Dir of Acad Affairs/Diversity/Incl ... Dr. Christina GOMEZ

Shawnee Community College (G)

8364 Shawnee College Road, Ullin IL 62992-2206
County: Pulaski FICE Identification: 007693
Unit ID: 148821
Telephone: (618) 634-3200 Carnegie Class: Assoc/MT-VT-High Non
FAX Number: (618) 634-3300 Calendar System: Semester
URL: www.shawneecc.edu
Established: 1967 Annual Undergrad Tuition & Fees (In-District): $3,648
Enrollment: 1,819 Coed
Affiliation or Control: Local IRS Status: 501(c)3
Highest Offering: Associate Degree
Accreditation: NH, CAHIIM, MLTAD, OTA, SURGT

01 President ... Dr. Peggy BRADFORD
05 Vice President Academic Affairs ... Dr. Vickie ARTMAN
32 Vice President Student Services ... Ms. Jipaum ASKEW-ROBINSON
04 Administrative Asst to President ... Ms. Becky CASPER LYNN
20 Dean Instructional Services ... Ms. Gabriele FARNER
51 Dean Adult Educ/Alternative Instruc ... Vacant
10 Vice President Financial Services ... Ms. Tiffiney RYAN
38 Student Support Services Director ... Ms. Amber SUGGS
35 Dean of Student Services ... Ms. Dee BLAKELY
37 Dir Fin Aid/Coord Vet & Mil Personl ... Dr. Tammy CAPPS
41 Athletic Director ... Mr. John SPARKS
13 Director of Information Technology ... Mr. Chris CLARK
12 Director Metropolis Ext Center ... Ms. Faye JOYNER-KEENE
66 Director of Nursing ... Ms. Denise GRIFFITH
08 Head Librarian ... Ms. Tracey JOHNSON
06 Registrar ... Ms. Danielle BOYD
102 Dir Resource Development/Foundation ... Vacant
21 Director of Business Services ... Ms. Brandy WOODS
18 Facilities Director ... Mr. Don KOCH
09 Director of Institutional Research ... Ms. Chris BARR
40 Director of the Bookstore ... Ms. Erica POAT
88 Accessibility & Resource Coord ... Ms. Heather CASNER
88 Director Economic Development ... Ms. Candy EASTWOOD
26 Public Relations Coordinator ... Ms. Katelynn ARMSTRONG
36 Career Services Coordinator ... Ms. Leslie WELDON
50 Div Chair Business/Occup/Tech Dp ... Ms. Ruth SMITH
81 Division Chair Math/Science ... Ms. Rhonda DILLOW
79 Div Chr Social Stds/Humanities/Comm ... Ms. Sharon WALKER
76 Div Chair Allied Health ... Ms. Tracy LOHSTROH
15 Human Resources Director ... Ms. Emily FORTHMAN
88 Director of Learning Resources ... Mr. Russ STOUP
56 Director Anna Extension Center ... Ms. Lindsay JOHNSON
88 Education Talent Search Director ... Ms. Deborah JOHNSON

South Suburban College of Cook County (H)

15800 S State Street, South Holland IL 60473-1270
County: Cook FICE Identification: 001769
Unit ID: 149365
Telephone: (708) 596-2000 Carnegie Class: Assoc/MT-VT-High Non
FAX Number: (708) 210-5710 Calendar System: Semester
URL: www.ssc.edu
Established: 1927 Annual Undergrad Tuition & Fees (In-District): $4,583
Enrollment: 4,205 Coed
Affiliation or Control: State/Local IRS Status: 501(c)3
Highest Offering: Associate Degree
Accreditation: NH, OTA, PHLEB

01 College President ... Mr. Don MANNING
05 Vice President Academic Services .... Dr. Linda STOKES-WILSON
11 Vice Pres Administration ... Mr. Martin LAREAU
32 Vice President Student Development ... Ms. Songie ADEBIYI
84 VP Enrollment/Community Education ... Mrs. Jane Ellen STOCKER
35 Dean Student Services ... Ms. Patrice BURTON
20 AVP Academic Svcs/Instl Effect ... Mr. Ronald KAWANNA, JR.
72 Dean Science/Technology/Engr/Math ... Ms. Anna HELWIG
76 Dean Allied Health/Career Programs ... Mr. Jeff WADDY
57 Dean Fine Arts/Soc & Behav Sci/Bus ... Mr. Tom GOVAN, JR.
66 Dean Nursing/Fine Arts/English/Hum ... Ms. Miriam ANTHONY
51 Director Continuing Education ... Ms. Shirley DREWENSKI
10 Treasurer/Controller ... Mr. Tim POLLERT
26 Director Public Rels/Pub & Found ... Mr. Patrick RUSH
13 Director Information Technology ... Mr. John SPEHAR
89 Dir New Student Ctr & Retenion Svcs ... Ms. Tiffane JONES
84 Director Enrollment Services ... Mrs. Robin RIHACEK
37 Director of Financial Aid ... Mr. John SEMPLE
18 Director Physical Plant Services ... Mr. Justin PAPP
24 Dir Communication Svcs/Media Design ... Mrs. Lisa MILLER
41 Athletic Director ... Mr. Steve RUZICH
09 Director of Institutional Research ... Mr. Kevin RIORDAN
15 Director Human Resources ... Ms. Kimberly PIGATTI
06 Manager for Registration/Records ... Ms. Tenial WHITTED
07 Mgr of Admissions/Recruitment ... Ms. Tiffane JONES

South Suburban College of Cook County University and College Center (I)

16333 Kilbourne Avenue, Oak Forest IL 60452
Telephone: (708) 225-6029 Identification: 770094
Accreditation: &NH

Southeastern Illinois College (J)

3575 College Road, Harrisburg IL 62946-4925
County: Saline FICE Identification: 001757
Unit ID: 148937
Telephone: (618) 252-5400 Carnegie Class: Assoc/MT-VT-High Non
FAX Number: (618) 252-3156 Calendar System: Semester
URL: www.sic.edu
Established: 1960 Annual Undergrad Tuition & Fees (In-District): $3,390
Enrollment: 2,034 Coed
Affiliation or Control: State/Local IRS Status: 501(c)3
Highest Offering: Associate Degree
Accreditation: NH, MLTAD

01 President ... Dr. Jonah RICE
05 Vice President Instruction ... Dr. Karen WEISS
10 Dean Administration/Business Affs ... Mr. David WRIGHT
32 Dean Student Servicess/Enrollment ... Mr. Chad FLANNERY
103 Assoc Dean Workforce & Cmty Educ ... Mrs. Lori COX

08 Librarian/LRC Director ... Mr. Gary JONES
84 Director Enrollment Services ... Ms. Kyla BURFORD
26 Marketing Coordinator ... Ms. Angela WILSON
37 Financial Aid Director ... Ms. Michelle METTEN
13 Chief Information Officer ... Mr. Greg MCCULLOCH
76 Director Allied Health & Nursing ... Ms. Amy MURPHY
04 Exec Asst to President ... Mrs. Lisa DYE
06 Registrar ... Ms. Kyla BURFORD
18 Director of Environmental Services ... Mr. Ed FITZGERALD
15 Director of Human Resources ... Mrs. Sky FOWLER

*Southern Illinois University System (A)

Stone Center - 1400 Douglas Drive, Carbondale IL 62901

County: Jackson
FICE Identification: 008237
Unit ID: 149240
Telephone: (618) 536-3331
Carnegie Class: N/A
FAX Number: (618) 536-3404
URL: www.siusystem.edu

01 President ... Dr. Randy J. DUNN
05 VP Academic Affairs ... Dr. Brad COLWELL
10 Sr VP Financial/Admin Affs/Bd Treas ... Dr. Duane STUCKY
117 Director Risk Management ... Ms. Chris GLIDEWELL
86 Exec Dir Governmental/Public Affs ... Mr. John CHARLES
116 Exec Dir of Internal Audits ... Ms. Kim LABONTE
43 General Counsel ... Mr. Lucas CRATER
04 Assistant to the President ... Ms. Paula S. KEITH

*Southern Illinois University Carbondale (B)

1265 Lincoln Drive, Carbondale IL 62901-6899

County: Jackson
FICE Identification: 001758
Unit ID: 149222
Telephone: (618) 453-2121
Carnegie Class: DU-Higher
FAX Number: (618) 453-3250
Calendar System: Semester
URL: siu.edu
Established: 1869
Annual Undergrad Tuition & Fees (In-State): $13,481
Enrollment: 17,292
Coed
Affiliation or Control: State
IRS Status: 501(c)3
Highest Offering: Doctorate
Accreditation: NH, AAB, ARCPA, ART, CACREP, CAEPN, CEA, CIDA, CLPSY, COPSY, CS, DH, DIETD, DIETI, DMS, ENG, ENGT, FUSER, IFSAC, IPSY, JOUR, LAW, MED, MUS, NAIT, #PH, PTAA, RAD, RADDOS, RADMAG, RTT, SP, SPAA, SW, THEA

02 Chancellor ... Dr. Carlo D. MONTEMAGNO
05 Provost & Vice Chancellor ... Vacant
32 Dean of Students ... Ms. Jennifer L. JONES-HALL
30 VC for Development & Alumni Rels ... Mr. Jim SALMO
46 Interim VC for Research ... Dr. James GARVEY
28 Interim Assoc Chancellor Diversity ... Vacant
102 CFO SIU Foundation ... Mr. Stephen NAGLE
13 Interim Chief Info Officer ... Mr. Scott D. BRIDGES
84 Asst Provost Enrollment Mgmt ... Vacant
20 Assoc Provost for Academic Admin ... Dr. David DILALLA
20 Assoc Provost for Academic Programs ... Dr. Lizette CHEVALIER
04 Assistant to the Chancellor ... Mr. Matthew BAUGHMAN
49 Dean Liberal Arts ... Dr. Meera KOMARRAJU
50 Dean College of Business ... Dr. Terry CLARK
53 Dean Educ & Human Services ... Dr. Matthew W. KEEFER
54 Dean Engineering ... Dr. John J. WARWICK
58 Dean Graduate School ... Dr. Yueh-Ting LEE
61 Dean School of Law ... Dr. Cynthia FOUNTAINE
81 Interim Dean College of Science ... Dr. Scott ISHMAN
63 Dean School of Medicine ... Dr. Jerry E. KRUSE
47 Dean Agricultural Sciences ... Dr. Mickey A. LATOUR
72 Dean Col Applied Sciences & Arts ... Dr. JuAn WANG
57 Interim Dean Mass Comm/Media Arts ... Dr. Deborah TUDOR
08 Dean Library Affairs ... Mr. John H. POLLITZ
37 Director Student Financial Aid ... Ms. Terri HARFST
29 Associate VC Alumni Services ... Ms. Michelle SUAREZ
09 Dir Institutional Research ... Vacant
10 Executive Dir for Admin & Finance ... Ms. Judith MARSHALL
26 Chief Marketing & Comm Officer ... Ms. Rae GOLDSMITH
15 Director Human Resources ... Ms. Jennifer WATSON
39 Director University Housing ... Mr. Jon L. SHAFFER
36 Director Univ Career Services . Mr. Douglas C. REICHENBERGER
85 Director International Education ... Mr. Andrew CARVER
18 Director Plant/Service Operations ... Mr. Brad DILLARD
19 Director of Public Safety ... Mr. Benjamin NEWMAN
23 Director Student Health Services ... Dr. Ted W. GRACE
41 Dir Intercollegiate Athletics ... Mr. Tommy BELL
106 Director Distance Education ... Dr. Mandara SAVAGE
06 Director Registrar's Office ... Ms. Tamara WORKMAN
38 Asst Dir Student Counseling Cntr ... Dr. Frank KOSMICKI
96 Director Procurement Services ... Ms. Debbie ABELL

*Southern Illinois University Edwardsville (C)

1 Hairpin Drive, Edwardsville IL 62026

County: Madison
FICE Identification: 001759
Unit ID: 149231
Telephone: (618) 650-2000
Carnegie Class: Masters/L
FAX Number: (618) 650-2270
Calendar System: Semester
URL: www.siue.edu
Established: 1957
Annual Undergrad Tuition & Fees (In-State): $11,008
Enrollment: 14,265
Coed
Affiliation or Control: State
IRS Status: 501(c)3
Highest Offering: Doctorate
Accreditation: NH, ANEST, ART, CAEPN, CONST, CS, DENT, ENG, EXSC, JOUR, MUS, NURSE, PHAR, SP, SPAA, SW, THEA

02 Chancellor ... Dr. Randall G. PEMBROOK
05 Provost & VC for Acad Affs ... Dr. P. Denise COBB
10 Vice Chancellor for Admin ... Mr. Richard WALKER
111 VC Univ Adv & CEO SIUE Foundation ... Ms. Rachel C. STACK
32 Vice Chanc for Student Affairs ... Dr. Jeffrey N. WAPLE
100 Chief of Staff ... Ms. Kimberly H. DURR
22 Dir Equal Opp/Access & Title IX ... Mr. Chad MARTINEZ
20 Assoc Prov Rsch/Dean Grad Sch ... Dr. Jerry B. WEINBERG
35 Assoc VC Stdnt Affs/Dean of Stdnts ... Dr. James W. KLENKE
35 Assoc VC for Student Affairs ... Ms. Lora MILES
13 Interim Assoc VC for IT & CIO ... Mr. Steven HUFFSTUTLER
28 Asc Chanc Inst Diversity/Inclusion ... Dr. Venessa BROWN
88 Asst Prov for Acad Innov & Eff ... Dr. Erin BEHNEN
41 Asst VC Athletic Dev/Dir Athletics ... Dr. Bradley L. HEWITT
84 Assoc VC for Enrollment Mgmt ... Dr. Scott BELOBRAJDIC
45 Asst VC for Planning & Budgeting ... Vacant
49 Dean College of Arts & Sciences ... Dr. Gregory BUDZBAN
50 Interim Dean School of Business ... Dr. Timothy SCHOENECKER
52 Dean Sch of Dental Medicine ... Dr. Bruce E. ROTTER
53 Int Dean Sch of Educ/Hlth Hum Behav ... Dr. Paul ROSE
54 Dean School of Engineering ... Dr. Cem KARACAL
66 Dean School of Nursing ... Dr. Laura BERNAIX
67 Dean School of Pharmacy ... Dr. Gireesh V. GUPCHUP
62 Dean Library & Information Services ... Dr. Regina MCBRIDE
114 Budget Director ... Mr. William F. WINTER, JR.
26 Exec Dir Univ Mktg & Comm ... Mr. Doug MCILHAGGA
88 Dir Grant Funded Pgm East StL Ctr ... Mr. Jesse DIXON
124 Dir Retention & Student Success ... Dr. Kevin THOMAS
07 Director Admissions ... Mr. Todd C. BURRELL
29 Dir Constituent Rel & Special Proj ... Ms. Cathy TAYLOR
36 Director Career Dev Center ... Ms. Susan SEIBERT
38 Interim Dir Counseling Services ... Ms. Jessica ULRICH
18 Director Facilities Management ... Mr. Paul FULIGNI
23 Director Health Service ... Ms. Riane B. GREENWALT
15 Director Human Resources ... Ms. Sherrie SENKFOR
09 Dir Institutional Rsrch & Studies ... Mr. Phillip M. BROWN
85 Exec Dir International Affairs ... Dr. Mary WEISHAAR
96 Director of Purchasing ... Ms. Shelly ALBERT
37 Dir Student Financial Aid ... Ms. Sally MULLEN
102 Dir Univ Advancement/Foundation Ops ... Mr. Kevin MARTIN
39 Director University Housing ... Mr. Michael J. SCHULTZ
19 Director University Police ... Mr. Kevin SCHMOLL
06 Registrar ... Ms. Laura A. STROM

*Southern Illinois University Carbondale School of Medicine (D)

PO Box 19620, Springfield IL 62794-9620

Telephone: (217) 545-8000
Identification: 770181
Accreditation: &NH

Southwestern Illinois College (E)

2500 Carlyle Avenue, Belleville IL 62221-5899

County: Saint Clair
FICE Identification: 001636
Unit ID: 143215
Telephone: (618) 235-2700
Carnegie Class: Assoc/HVT-High Non
FAX Number: (618) 277-0631
Calendar System: Semester
URL: www.swic.edu
Established: 1946
Annual Undergrad Tuition & Fees (In-District): $3,420
Enrollment: 9,943
Coed
Affiliation or Control: State/Local
IRS Status: 501(c)3
Highest Offering: Associate Degree
Accreditation: NH, ACFEI, ADNUR, CAHIIM, COARC, EMT, MAC, MLTAD, PTAA, RAD

01 President - District ... Dr. Georgia COSTELLO
10 VP Administrative Svcs/Treasurer ... Mr. Bernie J. YSURSA, JR.
05 Vice Pres Instruction ... Mr. Clay L. BAITMAN
31 Vice Pres Community Svcs ... Dr. Mark P. EICHENLAUB
15 Director Human Resources ... Ms. Anna MOYER
21 Controller ... Ms. Missy ROCHE
32 Vice Pres Student Development ... Ms. Staci G. CLAYBORNE
20 Assoc Dean Instructional Services ... Ms. Patricia POU
12 Executive Director SWGCC ... Ms. Nancy LEVAULT
12 Executive Director Red Bud Campus ... Vacant
37 Director of Financial Aid/Placement ... Mr. Robert TEBBE
13 Chief Information Officer ... Dr. James RIHA
18 Director of Physical Plant ... Mr. Ron R. HENDERSON
96 Director of Purchasing ... Mr. Mike R. THOMAS
76 Dean Hlth Sci and Homeland Security ... Ms. Julie A. MUERTZ
50 Dean of Business Division ... Dr. Janet S. FONTENOT
72 Dean of Technical Education ... Mr. Brad SPARKS
81 Dean of Math & Science ... Mr. Steve L. HOLMAN
49 Dean of Liberal Arts ... Mr. Richard SPENCER
51 Director Adult/Continued Education ... Ms. Lisa ATKINS
84 Dean of Enrollment Services ... Ms. Michelle L. BIRK
88 Treasurer IL Green Economy Network ... Mr. Robert J. HILGENBRINK
06 Specialist for Registration/Records ... Ms. Debra RAHN
102 Dir Foundation/Corporate Relations ... Ms. Haley THOMPSON

Spertus Institute for Jewish Learning and Leadership (F)

610 S Michigan Avenue, Chicago IL 60605-1994

County: Cook
FICE Identification: 001663
Unit ID: 148982
Telephone: (312) 322-1700
Carnegie Class: Spec-4-yr-Other
FAX Number: (312) 922-6406
Calendar System: Quarter
URL: www.spertus.edu
Established: 1924
Annual Graduate Tuition & Fees: N/A
Enrollment: 178
Coed
Affiliation or Control: Independent Non-Profit
IRS Status: 501(c)3
Highest Offering: Doctorate; No Undergraduates
Accreditation: NH

01 President ... Dr. Hal M. LEWIS
05 Provost/Vice President ... Dr. Dean BELL
20 Assistant Dean ... Ms. Beth SCHENKER
10 Controller ... Mr. Doug PETERSON
88 Director Nonprofit Admin Program ... Dr. Karen BAIRD
37 Financial Aid Manager ... Ms. Pamela FELTON
88 Dir Center for Jewish Leadership ... Mr. Tal ROSEN

Spoon River College (G)

23235 N County Road 22, Canton IL 61520-9801

County: Fulton
FICE Identification: 001643
Unit ID: 148991
Telephone: (309) 647-4645
Carnegie Class: Assoc/MT-VT-High Non
FAX Number: (309) 649-6235
Calendar System: Semester
URL: www.src.edu
Established: 1959
Annual Undergrad Tuition & Fees (In-District): $4,500
Enrollment: 1,665
Coed
Affiliation or Control: Local
IRS Status: 501(c)3
Highest Offering: Associate Degree
Accreditation: NH

01 President ... Mr. Curt OLDFIELD
05 Vice Pres Inst/Student Services ... Vacant
10 Vice Pres Administrative Services ... Mr. Brett STOLLER
04 Executive Asst to the President ... Ms. Julie HAMPTON
75 Dean Career & Technical Education ... Mr. Brad O'BRIEN
32 Dean Student Services ... Ms. Missy WILKINSON
66 Director Nursing ... Ms. Tamatha SCHLEICH
88 Dean Transfer Education ... Ms. Holly NORTON
06 Dir of Records & Admissions ... Ms. Melissa WILKINSON
18 Director Facilities ... Mr. Bob A. HAILE
55 Dir Adult and Outreach Education ... Mr. Chad MURPHY
08 Librarian ... Ms. Marla TURGEON
13 Chief Information Officer ... Mr. Raj SIDDARAJU
41 Director Athletics/Student Life ... Mr. John BASSETT
109 Director Business & Auxil Services ... Ms. Sarah GRAY
37 Director Financial Aid ... Ms. Salinda Jo BRANSON
15 Director Human Resources ... Ms. Michelle L. BUGOS
14 Director Technology Services ... Mr. Dean CLARY
84 Director Enrollment Services ... Ms. Janet MUNSON
09 Coord Institutional Reporting ... Ms. Anna YONTZ
26 Director Marketing ... Ms. Sherri RADER
27 Coordinator Public Information ... Ms. Sally SHIELDS
102 Director Foundation ... Mr. Colin DAVIS

Spoon River College-Macomb Campus (H)

208 S Johnston Street, Macomb IL 61455

Telephone: (309) 837-5727
Identification: 770097
Accreditation: &NH

Taylor Business Institute (I)

318 W Adams Street, Suite 500, Chicago IL 60606

County: Cook
FICE Identification: 011810
Unit ID: 149310
Telephone: (312) 658-5100
Carnegie Class: Assoc/MT-VT-High Non
FAX Number: (312) 658-0867
Calendar System: Quarter
URL: www.tbiil.edu
Established: 1962
Annual Undergrad Tuition & Fees: $14,175
Enrollment: 362
Coed
Affiliation or Control: Proprietary
IRS Status: Proprietary
Highest Offering: Associate Degree
Accreditation: NH

01 President ... Mrs. Janice C. PARKER

Telshe Yeshiva-Chicago (J)

3535 W Foster Avenue, Chicago IL 60625-5598

County: Cook
FICE Identification: 020732
Unit ID: 149329
Telephone: (773) 463-7738
Carnegie Class: Spec-4-yr-Faith
FAX Number: (773) 463-2849
Calendar System: Semester
Established: 1960
Annual Undergrad Tuition & Fees: $13,500
Enrollment: 82
Male
Affiliation or Control: Independent Non-Profit
IRS Status: 501(c)3
Highest Offering: Second Talmudic Degree
Accreditation: RABN

01 President ... Rabbi Avrohom C. LEVIN
03 Executive Vice President ... Rabbi Yitzchok LEVIN
05 Vice President ... Rabbi Chaim D. KELLER
05 Vice President ... Rabbi Moshe SCHMELCZER
11 Administrative Director/Secretary ... Rabbi Shmuel ADLER

Toyota Technological Institute at Chicago (K)

6045 South Kenwood Avenue, Chicago IL 60637

County: Cook
Identification: 666367
Unit ID: 445054
Telephone: (773) 834-2500
Carnegie Class: Not Classified
FAX Number: (773) 834-9881
Calendar System: Quarter

URL: www.ttic.edu
Established: 2003 Annual Graduate Tuition & Fees: N/A
Enrollment: 28 Coed
Affiliation or Control: Independent Non-Profit IRS Status: 501(c)3
Highest Offering: Doctorate; No Undergraduates
Accreditation: NH

01 President .... Dr. Sadaoki FURUI
05 Chief Academic Officer .... Dr. Avrim BLUM
10 Chief Financial Officer .... Ms. Jessica JOHNSTON
58 Admin Director of Graduate Studies .... Ms. Christina NOVAK

Tribeca Flashpoint Media Arts Academy (A)

28 North Clark Street, Suite 500, Chicago IL 60602
County: Cook Identification: 667083
Unit ID: 460747
Telephone: (312) 487-4743 Carnegie Class: Bac/Assoc-Assoc Dom
FAX Number: (312) 506-0708 Calendar System: Semester
URL: www.tribecaflashpoint.edu
Established: 2007 Annual Undergrad Tuition & Fees: $27,454
Enrollment: 288 Coed
Affiliation or Control: Proprietary IRS Status: Proprietary
Highest Offering: Baccalaureate
Accreditation: ACICS

01 President .... Bill VAN HUIS
05 Exec VP/Dean Academic Affairs .... Peter HAWLEY
10 Exec VP/Chief Financial Officer .... Erik PARKS
32 Vice President Student Affairs .... Kelly PARKER
88 AVP Institutional Compliance .... Darlene ULMER
07 VP Admissions .... Wendi FRANCZYK
12 Campus Director .... David DUNWORTH

Trinity Christian College (B)

6601 W College Drive, Palos Heights IL 60463-0929
County: Cook FICE Identification: 001771
Unit ID: 149505
Telephone: (708) 597-3000 Carnegie Class: Bac-Diverse
FAX Number: (708) 385-5665 Calendar System: 4/1/4
URL: www.trnty.edu
Established: 1959 Annual Undergrad Tuition & Fees: $27,675
Enrollment: 1,320 Coed
Affiliation or Control: Independent Non-Profit IRS Status: 501(c)3
Highest Offering: Master's
Accreditation: NH, ACBSP, NURSE, SW

01 President .... Mr. Kurt D. DYKSTRA
05 Provost .... Dr. Aaron KUECKER
10 Vice Pres for Finance & Admin .... Mr. James E. BELSTRA
32 Vice Pres for Student Life .... Mrs. Rebekah L. STARKENBURG
111 Vice Pres for Advancement .... Mr. Rick VAN DYKEN
08 Director of Library Services .... Mrs. Cathy MAYER
06 Registrar .... Ms. Jaynn TOBIAS-JOHNSON
07 Vice Pres for Enrollment .... Mr. Rick RIDDERING
36 Director of Vocation and Career Dev .... Mr. Jeff TIMMER
55 Dean Adult Studies & Grad Programs .... Dr. Rhoda MATTSON
29 Director of Alumni Relations .... Mr. Brad LANINGA
88 Senior Graphic Designer .... Mr. Pete VEGA
13 Director of Computer Services .... Mr. Joe VELDERMAN
41 Director of Athletics .... Mr. Bill SCHEPEL
31 Dir of Cmty Engage & Diversity Pgm .... Dr. Shaniqua JONES
42 Chaplain .... Dr. Willis VAN GRONINGEN
85 Director of Off-Campus Programs .... Dr. Burton J. ROZEMA
37 Director Financial Aid .... Mr. Ryan ZANTINGH
18 Director of Building/Grounds .... Mr. Tim TIMMONS
112 Director of Planned Giving .... Mr. Ken BOSS
21 Controller .... Mr. Mike TROCHUCK
28 Dir of Diversity/Dir AS Psychology .... Dr. Tiffany KING
92 Director of Honors Program .... Dr. Craig MATTSON
38 Director Cooper Ctr Counseling .... Vacant
09 Asst Registar for Inst Research .... Ms. Kimberly WILLIAMS
15 Human Resources Manager .... Ms. Julia FOUST
20 Assoc Dean Academics .... Dr. John FRY
04 Executive Assistant to President .... Ms. Deborah S. VINCENT
19 Director Security/Safety .... Mr. Tom KAZEN
102 Dir Foundation/Corporate Relations .... Mr. Dennis HARMS
105 Web Developer/Social Media Manager .... Ms. Diane BRUNSTING

Trinity College of Nursing & Health Sciences (C)

2122 25th Avenue, Rock Island IL 61201-5317
County: Rock Island FICE Identification: 006225
Unit ID: 146755
Telephone: (309) 779-7700 Carnegie Class: Spec-4-yr-Other Health
FAX Number: (309) 779-7748 Calendar System: Semester
URL: www.trinitycollegeqc.edu
Established: 1994 Annual Undergrad Tuition & Fees: $27,096
Enrollment: 271 Coed
Affiliation or Control: Independent Non-Profit IRS Status: 501(c)3
Highest Offering: Master's
Accreditation: NH, ADNUR, COARC, NURSE, RAD

01 Chancellor .... Dr. Tracy L. POELVOORDE
05 Dean of Nursing & Health Sci .... Dr. Christine KESSEL
06 Registrar .... Ms. Cara BANKS

Trinity International University (D)

2065 Half Day Road, Deerfield IL 60015-1284
County: Lake FICE Identification: 001772
Unit ID: 149514
Telephone: (847) 945-8800 Carnegie Class: DU-Mod
FAX Number: (847) 317-8090 Calendar System: Semester
URL: www.tiu.edu
Established: 1897 Annual Undergrad Tuition & Fees: $30,130
Enrollment: 2,237 Coed
Affiliation or Control: Evangelical Free Church Of America
IRS Status: 501(c)3
Highest Offering: Doctorate
Accreditation: NH, CAATE, CACREP, THEOL

01 President .... Dr. David S. DOCKERY
03 Exec Vice President & Provost .... Vacant
05 VP Education/Dean TEDS .... Dr. Graham COLE
05 VP Academic Admin/Dean TC & TGS .... Dr. Thomas CORNMAN
84 Sr VP Univ Svcs/Strat Initiatives .... Mr. Rich GRIMM
32 VP Stdnt Life/Univ Min/Dean Stdnts .... Mr. Felix THEONUGRAHA
13 Sr VP Information Technology/Plng .... Mr. Steven GEGGIE
30 Sr Vice Pres University Advancement .... Mr. Carl JOHNSON
10 Sr VP of Business & Finance/CFO .... Mr. Paul EISENMENGER
26 VP for University Communication .... Mr. Mark KAHLER
27 Asst VP University Communication .... Mr. Chris DONOTO
73 Assoc Academic Dean Divinity School .... Dr. H. Wayne JOHNSON
51 Director Adult Academic Programs .... Mr. Jay SIMALA
35 Assoc Dean of TC & TGS .... Dr. Don HEDGES
90 Director of Acad/Desktop Computing .... Mr. Chris MILLER
91 Director Administrative Computing .... Ms. Katie KEMP
61 Dean of Law School .... Mr. Eric HALVORSON
07 Director Undergraduate Admissions .... Mr. Jordan BRYANT
19 Director of Security Services .... Mr. Bob TOPOREK
96 Director of Facilities .... Ms. Julie WONG
15 Interim Director of Human Resources .... Mrs. Linda BRUNDIDGE
06 University Registrar .... Ms. Tiffany SELL
37 Executive Director Student Services .... Ms. Rachel RUSSIAKY
36 Director of Career Services .... Vacant
36 Director of Placement .... Dr. Phil SELL
08 University Librarian .... Ms. Rebecca DONALD
29 Director of Alumni Relations .... Mr. Michael GORSLINE
92 Director of Honors Program .... Dr. Joshua HELD
35 Director of Student Activities .... Ms. Heather CORDERO
21 Vice Pres for Business Services .... Dr. Jonathan DOCKERY
28 Director of Diversity .... Vacant
38 Director Student Care & Engagement .... Ms. Anne TOHME

Triton College (E)

2000 Fifth Avenue, River Grove IL 60171-1995
County: Cook FICE Identification: 001773
Unit ID: 149532
Telephone: (708) 456-0300 Carnegie Class: Assoc/MT-VT-High Non
FAX Number: (708) 583-3112 Calendar System: Semester
URL: www.triton.edu
Established: 1964 Annual Undergrad Tuition & Fees (In-District): $3,870
Enrollment: 11,684 Coed
Affiliation or Control: Local IRS Status: 501(c)3
Highest Offering: Associate Degree
Accreditation: NH, ADNUR, DMS, NMT, RAD, SURGT

01 President .... Ms. Mary-Rita MOORE
05 Vice President Academic Affairs .... Ms. Debra BAKER
32 Vice President Student Affairs .... Dr. Douglas OLSON
10 Vice President Business Services .... Mr. Sean SULLIVAN
26 Senior Executive of Public Affairs .... Mr. Randy BARNETTE
101 Secretary for Brd of Trustees .... Ms. Susan PAGE
13 Assoc VP Information Systems .... Mr. Michael GARRITY
21 Assoc VP Finance & Business .... Mr. Garrick ABEZETIAN
18 Assoc VP of Facilities .... Mr. John LAMBRECHT
15 Assoc VP Human Resources .... Mr. Joe KLINGER
20 Assoc VP Academic Affairs .... Ms. Cheryl ANTONICH
35 Dean of Student Services .... Mr. Corey WILLIAMS
84 Dean of Enrollment Services .... Dr. Amanda TURNER
49 Dean of Arts & Sciences .... Mr. Kevin LI
72 Dean of Business & Technology .... Dr. Henry "Chuck" BOHLEKE
51 Dean of Continuing Education .... Mr. Paul JENSEN
121 Dean of Academic Success .... Dr. Deborah BANESS KING
55 Dean of Adult Education .... Ms. Jacqueline LYNCH
37 Assoc Dean of Financial Aid .... Ms. Patricia ZINGA
21 Executive Director of Finance .... Mr. James REYNOLDS
27 Executive Director of Marketing .... Mr. Sam TOLIA
09 Executive Director of Research .... Dr. Kurian THARAKUNNEL
25 Exec Dir Grants Development .... Ms. Sacella SMITH
14 Sr Data and System Admin .... Ms. Elise RAPALA
86 Director Public Affairs .... Ms. Audrey JONAS
88 Special Assistant to the President .... Ms. Brenda JONES WATKINS

University of Chicago (F)

5801 S Ellis Avenue, Chicago IL 60637-1496
County: Cook FICE Identification: 001774
Unit ID: 144050
Telephone: (773) 702-1234 Carnegie Class: DU-Highest
FAX Number: N/A Calendar System: Quarter
URL: www.uchicago.edu
Established: 1890 Annual Undergrad Tuition & Fees: $53,649
Enrollment: 15,391 Coed
Affiliation or Control: Independent Non-Profit IRS Status: 501(c)3
Highest Offering: Doctorate
Accreditation: NH, IPSY, LAW, MED, SW, THEOL

01 President .... Mr. Robert J. ZIMMER
03 Executive Vice President .... Mr. David B. FITHIAN
05 Provost .... Mr. Daniel D. DIERMEIER
17 EVP for Medical Affairs/Dean of BSD .... Dr. Kenneth POLONSKY
100 VP/Secretary and Chief of Staff .... Ms. Katie CALLOW-WRIGHT
20 Vice Provost for Acad Affairs .... Mr. Ron THISTED
45 Vice Provost for Strategic Planning .... Mr. Michael HOPKINS
114 VP for Strategic Initiatives .... Mr. Darren REISBERG
46 EVP for Research/Natl Lab .... Mr. Eric D. ISAACS
10 VP and CFO .... Mr. Ivan SAMSTEIN
29 VP for Alumni Rels & Development .... Mr. Ken MANOTTI
43 Vice President & General Counsel .... Ms. Kim TAYLOR
115 Vice Pres/Chief Investment Officer .... Mr. Mark A. SCHMID
88 VP Global I&S/Sr Assoc Provost .... Mr. Balaji SRINIVASAN
84 VP for Enroll/Admissions/Aid .... Mr. James NONDORF
32 VP/Campus Life Student Services .... Ms. Michele RASMUSSEN
88 Director of Oriental Institute .... Mr. Christopher WOODS
88 Vice President for Civic Engagement .... Mr. Derek DOUGLAS
26 Vice Pres for Communications .... Mr. Paul M. RAND
49 Dean of the College .... Mr. John W. BOYER
81 Dean Physical Sciences Division .... Mr. Edward W. KOLB
83 Dean of SSD .... Vacant
20 Exec Vice Provost .... Mr. David NIRENBERG
42 Dean Rockefeller Memorial Chapel .... Ms. Elizabeth DAVENPORT
79 Dean of Humanities Division .... Ms. Anne W. ROBERTSON
54 Dean of Molecular Engineering .... Mr. Matthew TIRRELL
50 Dean of Booth School of Business .... Mr. Madhav RAJAN
61 Dean of the Law School .... Mr. Thomas MILES
73 Dean of the Divinity School .... Ms. Laurie ZOLOTH
51 Dean of Graham School .... Vacant
63 Dean Medicine .... Mr. Kenneth POLONSKY
80 Dean Harris Sch of Pub Pol .... Ms. Katherine BAICKER
70 Interim Dean Social Svcs Admin .... Ms. Deborah GORMAN-SMITH
21 AVP for Finance .... Mr. John R. KROLL
88 Assoc Provost and Budget Director .... Mr. David L. MURPHY
13 VP and CIO .... Mr. Cole W. CAMPLESE
15 Interim Associate VP HR .... Mr. Mike KNITTER
20 Senior Associate Provost .... Mr. Larry HILL
28 Vice Provost for Diversity .... Dr. Melissa GILLIAM
88 Vice Provost for Acad Initiatives .... Ms. Melina HALE
06 Registrar .... Mr. Scott CAMPBELL
37 Executive Director University Aid .... Ms. Amanda FIJAL
57 Executive Director of UChicago Arts .... Mr. Bill MICHEL
22 Asst Provost/Affirm Action Ofcr .... Ms. Bridget LE COUP COLLIER
09 Dir Institutional Research .... Mr. William GREENLAND
30 Senior AVP Alumni Rels & Develop .... Ms. Stephanie BANTA
36 Exec Dir Career Advancement .... Ms. Meredith DAW
41 Athletic Director .... Ms. Erin MCDERMOTT
08 Director University Library .... Ms. Brenda JOHNSON
38 Dir Student Counseling Services .... Mr. David ALBERT
96 Exec Dir Payroll/Procurement .... Mr. Mark FEHLBERG
39 Exec Director Student Housing .... Ms. Jennifer LUTTIG-KOMROSKY
18 Assoc VP for Facilities .... Mr. Jim MCCONNELL
19 Chief of Police .... Mr. Kenton W. RAINEY

*University of Illinois System (G)

506 S Wright Street, Urbana IL 61801-3689
County: Champaign FICE Identification: 008001
Unit ID: 149587
Telephone: (217) 333-6400 Carnegie Class: N/A
FAX Number: (217) 333-5733
URL: www.uillinois.edu

01 President .... Dr. Timothy L. KILLEEN
12 Chancellor/Vice President (Chicago) .... Dr. Michael AMIRIDIS
12 Chancellor/Vice President (Sprfld) .... Dr. Susan KOCH
12 Chancellor/Vice President (Urbana) .... Dr. Robert J. JONES
10 VP & Chief Financial Officer .... Mr. Walter KNORR
05 Exec Vice Pres and VPAA .... Dr. Barbara J. WILSON
88 Vice Pres for Econ Devel Innovation .... Dr. H. Edward SEIDEL
43 University Counsel .... Mr. Thomas R. BEARROWS
26 Exec Dir for University Relations .... Mr. Thomas P. HARDY
13 CIO & Sr Assoc VP .... Vacant
15 Interim Assoc VP Human Resources .... Ms. Jami PAINTER
101 Secretary Board of Trustees/Univ .... Ms. Dedra M. WILLIAMS
102 President/CEO Univ Foundation .... Mr. James H. MOORE, JR.
29 Pres UIAA/Assoc VC for Alumni Rel .... Ms. Jennifer NEUBAUER

*University of Illinois at Chicago (H)

601 S Morgan, M/C 102, Chicago IL 60607-7128
County: Cook FICE Identification: 001776
Unit ID: 145600
Telephone: (312) 996-7000 Carnegie Class: DU-Highest
FAX Number: (312) 413-3393 Calendar System: Semester
URL: www.uic.edu
Established: 1896 Annual Undergrad Tuition & Fees (In-State): $13,664
Enrollment: 29,048 Coed
Affiliation or Control: State IRS Status: 501(c)3
Highest Offering: Doctorate
Accreditation: NH, CAHIIM, CEA, CLPSY, CS, DENT, DIETC, DIETD, ENG, ENGR, FEPAC, HSA, IPSY, MED, MIDWF, MIL, NURSE, OT, PAST, PH, PHAR, PLNG, PTA, SPAA, SW

02 Chancellor .... Dr. Michael AMIRIDIS
05 Provost and Vice Chanc Acad Affs .... Dr. Susan POSER
32 Vice Chancellor Student Affairs .... Mr. Rex TOLLIVER
11 Int Vice Chanc for Admin Svcs .... Dr. Michael LANDEK
46 Vice Chancellor for Research .... Dr. Mitra DUTTA
26 Exec Assoc Chanc External Affairs .... Mr. Michael REDDING
17 Int CEO Hospital Administration .... Dr. Robert BARISH

29 Vice President Alumni Relations ... Vacant
30 Vice Chancellor Development ... Mr. Jeff NEARHOOF
84 Vice Prov Acad/Enrollment Svcs ... Mr. Kevin BROWNE
15 Vice Provost for Faculty Affairs ... Dr. Renee TAYLOR
20 Vice Prov Undergrad Affairs ... Dr. Nikos VARELAS
88 Vice Provost for Global Engagement ... Dr. Neal R. MCCRILLIS
114 Assoc Chanc for Resource Plng/Mgmt ... Ms. Janet PARKER
35 Assoc Vice Chanc/Dean Student Affs ... Dr. Linda DEANNA
27 Senior Exec Director Public Affairs ... Ms. Sherri MCGINNIS GONZALEZ
23 Vice Chancellor Health Affairs ... Dr. Robert BARISH
10 Interim Asst VP Business/Finance ... Ms. Gloria KEELEY
48 Dean Col of Architect/Design/Arts ... Dr. Steve EVERETT
50 Dean College of Business Admin ... Dr. Michael B. MIKHAIL
52 Dean College of Dentistry ... Dr. Clark STANFORD
53 Dean College of Education ... Dr. Alfred TATUM
54 Dean College of Engineering ... Dr. Peter C. NELSON
76 Dean Col Applied Health Sciences ... Dr. Bo FERNHALL
58 Dean Graduate College ... Dr. Karen COLLEY
92 Dean Honors College ... Dr. Ralph KEEN
49 Dean College Liberal Arts/Sciences ... Dr. Astrida O. TANTILLO
63 Acting Dean College of Medicine ... Dr. Charles RAY
66 Dean College of Nursing ... Dr. Terri E. WEAVER
67 Dean College of Pharmacy ... Dr. Jerry BAUMAN
70 Dean College of Social Work ... Dr. Creasie HAIRSTON
69 Dean School of Public Health ... Dr. Wayne GILES
27 Dean Urban Planning/Public Affairs ... Dr. Michael A. PAGANO
43 University Counsel ... Mr. Thomas R. BEARROWS
08 University Librarian ... Ms. Mary CASE
88 Asst Univ Librarian Health Sciences . Ms. Kathryn H. CARPENTER
07 Managing Director Admissions ... Ms. Malinda LORKOVICH
41 Director Athletics ... Mr. Garrett KLASSY
38 Director Counseling Services ... Dr. Joseph HERMES
39 Director of Campus Housing ... Ms. Susan TEGGATZ
37 Interim Director Financial Aid ... Ms. Shirley RODRIGUEZ-VEGA
09 Director of Institutional Research ... Mr. William C. HAYWARD
16 Assoc Vice Provost Faculty Affairs ... Ms. Angela L. YUDT
22 Director Access/Equity ... Ms. Caryn A. BILLS-WINDT
36 Director Career Services ... Mr. Thy NGUYEN
13 CIO/Exec Dir Acad Computing ... Ms. Cynthia E. HERRERA LINDSTROM
56 Int Exec Dir Extended Campus ... Ms. Janette SALAMANCA MALDONADO
06 Registrar ... Mr. Robert DIXON
96 Director of Purchasing ... Ms. Debra MATLOCK
18 Exec Dir Operations/Maintenance ... Mr. Clarence F. BRIDGES
28 Int Assoc Chanc & VP for Diversity ... Dr. Charu THAKRAL
100 Associate Provost/Chief of Staff ... Dr. Aisha EL-AMIN
104 Executive Director of Study Abroad ... Dr. Christopher DEEGAN

*University of Illinois at Springfield (A)

One University Plaza, Springfield IL 62703-5407

County: Sangamon FICE Identification: 009333
Unit ID: 148654
Telephone: (217) 206-6600 Carnegie Class: Masters/L
FAX Number: (217) 206-6511 Calendar System: Semester
URL: www.uis.edu
Established: 1969 Annual Undergrad Tuition & Fees (In-State): $11,413
Enrollment: 5,402 Coed
Affiliation or Control: State IRS Status: 501(c)3
Highest Offering: Doctorate
Accreditation: NH, CACREP, MT, SPAA, SW

02 Chancellor ... Dr. Susan KOCH
05 Vice Chancellor Acad Affs/Provost ... Dr. Dennis PAPINI
32 Vice Chancellor for Student Affairs ... Dr. Clarice FORD
20 Int Assoc Vice Chanc Undergrad Educ ... Dr. Robert BLANKENBERGER
29 Assoc Vice Chanc for Alumni Rels ... Mr. Charles SCHRAGE
30 Vice Chanc Dev/Sr VP UL Found ... Dr. Jeffrey D. LORBER
35 Asst Vice Chanc for Student Service ... Dr. Van VIEREGGE
18 Assoc Chanc Admin Affs/Facilities ... Mr. Charles CODERKO
22 Asc Chanc Access/Equal Opportunity ... Ms. Deanie BROWN
27 Assoc Chancellor for Public Affairs ... Mr. Ryan CROKE
21 Sr Assoc VP Business & Finance ... Mr. Jason BANE
49 Dean Col Liberal Arts/Science ... Dr. James ERMATINGER
50 Dean College Business/Management ... Dr. Ronald D. MCNEIL
80 Dean Col Public Affs/Admin ... Dr. Robert SMITH
53 Dean College Educ/Human Svcs ... Dr. Hanfu MI
15 Sr Director HR ... Ms. Melissa MLYNSKI
43 Legal Counsel ... Ms. Rhonda PERRY
08 Dean of Library ... Dr. Piotrowski PATTIE
26 Director Public Information ... Mr. Derek SCHNAPP
114 Assc Provost Budget and Admin Plng ... Dr. Jerry JOSEPH
19 Chief Campus Police Department ... Mr. Donald MITCHELL
06 Registrar ... Mr. Brian CLEVENGER
35 Director of Student Life ... Ms. Cynthia THOMPSON
41 Director of Athletics ... Mr. James SARRA
09 Director Institutional Research ... Ms. Laura DORMAN
96 Interim Director of Purchasing ... Ms. Janet FORD
37 Acting Dir Financial Assistance ... Ms. Carolyn SCHLOEMANN
38 Exec Director Counseling Center ... Dr. Judith SHIPP
85 Director International Programs .. Dr. Jonathan GOLDBERGBELLE
13 Director Information Technology ... Mr. Tulio LLOSA
39 Director Campus Housing ... Mr. John RINGLE
07 Director of Admissions ... Mr. Fernando PLANAS

*University of Illinois at Urbana-Champaign (B)

601 E John Street, Champaign IL 61820-5711

County: Champaign FICE Identification: 001775
Unit ID: 145637
Telephone: (217) 333-6677 Carnegie Class: DU-Highest
FAX Number: (217) 244-5639 Calendar System: Semester
URL: www.illinois.edu
Established: 1867 Annual Undergrad Tuition & Fees (In-State): $15,058
Enrollment: 45,842 Coed
Affiliation or Control: State IRS Status: 501(c)3
Highest Offering: Doctorate
Accreditation: NH, ART, AUD, CEA, CLPSY, COPSY, CS, DANCE, DIETD, DIETI, ENG, IPSY, JOUR, LAW, LIB, LSAR, MUS, NRPA, PCSAS, PH, PLNG, SP, SW, VET

00 Chief Executive Officer (President) ... Dr. Timothy L. KILLEEN
02 Chancellor ... Dr. Robert J. JONES
05 Int Prov/Vice Chanc Academic Affs ... Mr. John WILKIN
46 Vice Chancellor Research ... Dr. Peter E. SCHIFFER
32 Vice Chancellor Student Affairs ... Dr. Danita BROWN YOUNG
111 VC Inst Advancement/Found Admin ... Mr. Barry BENSON
88 Associate Chanc Corp Intl Relations ... Dr. Pradeep KHANNA
20 Vice Provost Academic Affairs ... Dr. William BERNHARD
88 Associate Chancellor ... Mr. Michael DELORENZO
28 Associate Chancellor for Diversity ... Dr. Assata ZERAI
26 Associate Chanc Public Affairs ... Ms. Robin KALER
15 Associate Provost Human Resources ... Ms. Elyne COLE
84 Int Assoc Prov Enrollment Mgmt ... Mr. Daniel MANN
114 Vice Prov for Budget & Resource Pln ... Dr. Paul ELLINGER
104 Vice Provost Intl Pgms/Studies ... Ms. Reitumetse MABOKELA
20 Vice Provost for Undergrad Educ ... Dr. Kevin PITTS
21 Exec Assoc Provost Budget Planning ... Ms. Vicky GRESS
09 Asst Provost Management Info ... Dr. Amy EDWARDS
49 Dean Liberal Arts & Sciences ... Dr. Feng Sheng HU
61 Dean Law ... Dr. Vikram AMAR
74 Dean Veterinary Medicine ... Dr. Peter CONSTABLE
54 Dean Engineering ... Dr. Andreas C. CANGELLARIS
47 Dean Agric/Consumer/Environ Sci ... Dr. Kim KIDWELL
50 Dean Business ... Dr. Jeffrey BROWN
57 Acting Dean Fine & Applied Arts ... Ms. Kathleen HARLEMAN
70 Dean School of Social Work ... Dr. Wynne S. KORR
68 Dean Col Applied Health Sciences ... Dr. Cheryl HANLEY-MAXWELL
60 Int Dean College of Media ... Dr. Wojciech CHODZKO-ZAJKO
58 Dean Graduate College ... Dr. Wojciech CHODZKO-ZAJKO
62 Dean School of Info Sciences ... Dr. Allen H. RENEAR
53 Dean Education ... Dr. James D. ANDERSON
63 Int Reg Dean Col Med/Urbana-Champ ... Dr. Janet JOKELA
16 Dean Labor & Employment Rels ... Dr. Fritz DRASGOW
08 University Librarian & Dean ... Mr. John P. WILKIN
13 Chief Information Officer ... Mr. Mark HENDERSON
35 Dean of Students ... Dr. Kenneth BALLOM
56 Assoc Dean Extension & Outreach ... Dr. George CZAPAR
41 Director Athletics ... Mr. Josh WHITMAN
10 Asst Vice Pres Bus/Fin Affairs ... Ms. Ginger VELAZQUEZ
43 Campus Legal Counsel ... Mr. Scott RICE
88 Deputy CIO Information Technology ... Mr. John M. ROSSI
22 Dir Equal Opportunity & Access ... Ms. Heidi JOHNSON
19 Director Public Safety ... Mr. Jeffrey T. CHRISTENSEN
18 Int Exec Director Facilities ... Ms. Helen COLEMAN
23 Director McKinley Health Center ... Dr. Robert D. PALINKAS
36 Director Career Services Center ... Dr. Gail ROONEY
37 Director Student Financial Aid ... Mr. Daniel R. MANN
38 Director Counseling Center ... Dr. Carla MCCOWAN
39 Director Housing Division ... Ms. Alma SEALINE
88 Dir Ctr Innovative Teaching/Lrng ... Dr. Michel BELLINI
06 Registrar ... Ms. Meghan HAZEN
07 Director of Admissions ... Ms. Nancy WALSH
101 Secretary of the Institution/Board ... Ms. Dedra WILLIAMS
108 Assoc Prov for Acad Effectiveness ... Dr. Staci J. PROVEZIS
100 Chief of Staff ... Ms. Laura CLOWER

*University of Illinois at Chicago College of Medicine at Peoria (C)

One Illini Drive, Peoria IL 61605

Telephone: (309) 671-3000 Identification: 770182
Accreditation: &NH

*University of Illinois College of Medicine at Rockford (D)

1601 Parkview Avenue, Rockford IL 61107

Telephone: (815) 395-0600 Identification: 770183
Accreditation: &NH, PHAR

*University of Illinois at Chicago College of Medicine at Urbana (E)

506 South Matthews Avenue, Urbana IL 61801

Telephone: (217) 333-5465 Identification: 770184
Accreditation: &NH

University of Phoenix Chicago Campus (F)

203 N. LaSalle Street, Chicago IL 60601-1210

Telephone: (312) 223-1101 Identification: 770205
Accreditation: &NH, ACBSP

† No longer accepting campus-based students.

University of St. Francis (G)

500 N Wilcox Street, Joliet IL 60435-6188

County: Will FICE Identification: 001664
Unit ID: 148584
Telephone: (815) 740-3400 Carnegie Class: Masters/L
FAX Number: (815) 740-4285 Calendar System: Semester
URL: www.stfrancis.edu
Established: 1920 Annual Undergrad Tuition & Fees: $30,840
Enrollment: 3,957 Coed
Affiliation or Control: Roman Catholic IRS Status: 501(c)3
Highest Offering: Doctorate
Accreditation: NH, ACBSP, CAEPN, NRPA, NURSE, RTT, SW

01 President ... Dr. Arvid C. JOHNSON
05 Provost/VP Academic Affairs ... Dr. Frank H. PASCOE
10 VP Administration & Finance ... Ms. Julee A. GARD
84 VP Admissions/Mktg/Enrollment Svcs ... Vacant
88 VP Mission Int & Univ Ministry ... Sr. Mary Elizabeth IMLER
32 VP Student & Alumni Affairs ... Mr. Damon N. SLOAN
13 VP Operations/Planning & IT ... Mr. Terrance L. COTTRELL
26 Exec Dir Mktg & Communications ... Vacant
30 Chief Development Officer ... Ms. Regina M. BLOCK
49 Dean Col Arts & Sciences ... Dr. Robert KASE
50 Dean Col Business/Health ... Dr. Orlando GRIEGO
53 Dean Col Education ... Dr. John S. GAMBRO
66 Dean Leach Col Nursing ... Dr. Carol J. WILSON
20 Dean Teaching & Learning Outcomes ... Dr. Pamela K. STEINKE
37 Exec Dir Financial Aid ... Mr. Bruce FOOTE
29 Dir Alumni Relations ... Ms. Aubrey L. KNIGHT
41 Dir Athletics ... Mr. Dave LAKETA
36 Dir Career Success Center ... Ms. Maribeth HEARN
38 Dir Counseling & Wellness ... Mr. Carlos AQUINO
15 Dir Human Resources ... Ms. Mary L. SPREITZER
28 Dir Institutional Diversity ... Ms. Allison HEARD
07 Dir Freshman Admissions ... Mr. Eric RUIZ
07 Dir Transfer Admissions ... Mr. Alan CHRISTENSEN
123 Dir Grad/Degree Completion Admiss ... Ms. Sandra L. SLOKA
104 Dir Intl Programs Office ... Ms. Angie MAFFEO
27 Dir Marketing Services ... Ms. Julie FUTTERER
14 Dir Network Support Services ... Mr. Mark T. SNODGRASS
18 Dir Operations & Facilities ... Mr. Mike DECMAN
39 Dir Residence Education ... Ms. Mollie ROCKAFELLOW
19 Dir Safety/Security ... Mr. Jason WILLIAMS
42 Dir University Ministry ... Mr. Joseph T. WYSOCKI
06 Registrar ... Ms. Laura A. KOGA
08 Head Librarian ... Ms. Shannon WENZEL
23 Coordinator of Health Services ... Ms. Phyllis M. PETERSON
09 Asst Dir Institutional Research ... Ms. Rebecca R. GARLAND

University of Saint Mary of the Lake-Mundelein Seminary (H)

1000 E Maple Avenue, Mundelein IL 60060-1174

County: Lake FICE Identification: 001765
Unit ID: 148885
Telephone: (847) 566-6401 Carnegie Class: Spec-4-yr-Faith
FAX Number: (847) 566-7330 Calendar System: Semester
URL: www.usml.edu
Established: 1844 Annual Graduate Tuition & Fees: N/A
Enrollment: 275 Male
Affiliation or Control: Roman Catholic IRS Status: 501(c)3
Highest Offering: Doctorate; No Undergraduates
Accreditation: THEOL

00 Chancellor ... Card. Blase CUPICH
01 Rector/President ... V.Rev. John KARTJE
11 Chief Operating Officer ... Mr. Jim HEINEN
03 Vice Rector for Formation ... Rev. Brian WELTER
05 Vice Rector for Academic Affairs ... V.Rev. Thomas A. BAIMA
73 Pres/Pontifical Faculty of Theology ... Rev. Brendan LUPTON
10 Vice President for Finance ... Mr. John F. LEHOCKY
30 Vice President Inst Advancement ... Mr. Ryan BUTTS
20 Assoc Acad Dean Sem/Grad Sch ... Dr. Christopher MCATEE
73 Director Pre-Theology Program ... Rev. Dennis SPIES
08 Library Director ... Vacant
06 Registrar ... Vacant
88 Director of Pastoral Internships ... Rev. Martin BARNUM
88 Director of Liturgy ... Rev. Bradley ZAMORA
42 Director of Spiritual Life ... Rev. Carlos RODRIGUEZ
85 Director of International Students ... Rev. Martin BARNUM
18 Chief Facilities/Physical Plant ... Mr. Clayton KALWEIT
07 Director of Admissions ... Rev. Edward PELRINE

VanderCook College of Music (I)

3140 S Federal Street, Chicago IL 60616-3731

County: Cook FICE Identification: 001778
Unit ID: 149639
Telephone: (312) 225-6288 Carnegie Class: Spec-4-yr-Arts
FAX Number: (312) 225-5211 Calendar System: Semester
URL: www.vandercook.edu
Established: 1909 Annual Undergrad Tuition & Fees: $27,180
Enrollment: 196 Coed
Affiliation or Control: Independent Non-Profit IRS Status: 501(c)3
Highest Offering: Master's
Accreditation: NH, MUS

01 President ... Dr. Roseanne K. ROSENTHAL
08 Head Librarian ... Mr. Robert DELAND
05 Dean of Undergraduate Studies ... Ms. Stacey L. DOLAN
58 Dean of Graduate Studies ... Mr. Robert L. SINCLAIR
07 Director of Admissions & Retention ... Ms. LeeAnn MEYER
10 Chief Financial Officer ... Ms. Michelle ANDERSON
37 Director of Financial Aid ... Ms. Sirena COVINGTON
13 Director Information Technologies ... Mr. Rick MALIK
04 President's Assistant ... Ms. Cindy TOVAR
51 Director of Continuing Education ... Mr. Patrick BENSON
09 Director of Institutional Reports ... Mr. Gregor MEYER
06 Registrar/EPO Director ... Mrs. Carolyn BERGHOFF

Vatterott College-Fairview Heights (A)
110 Commerce Lane, Fairview Heights IL 62208
Telephone: (618) 489-2400 Identification: 770943
Accreditation: ACCSC

† Branch campus of Vatterott College-NorthPark, Berkeley, MO

Vatterott College-Quincy (B)
3609 North Marx Drive, Quincy IL 62305
County: Adams FICE Identification: 020693
Unit ID: 148140
Telephone: (217) 224-0600 Carnegie Class: Assoc/HVT-High Non
FAX Number: (217) 223-6771 Calendar System: Other
URL: www.vatterott-college.edu
Established: 1995 Annual Undergrad Tuition & Fees: $12,513
Enrollment: 131 Coed
Affiliation or Control: Proprietary IRS Status: Proprietary
Highest Offering: Associate Degree
Accreditation: ACCSC

01 Campus Director .... Vacant
05 Director of Education .... Vacant
30 VP Regulatory Affs/Strategic Devel .... Mr. Aaron LACEY
43 General Counsel/Chief Administrator .... Mr. Scott CASANOVER

Waubonsee Community College (C)
Route 47 at Waubonsee Drive,
Sugar Grove IL 60554-9799
County: Kane FICE Identification: 006931
Unit ID: 149727
Telephone: (630) 466-7900 Carnegie Class: Assoc/MT-VT-High Non
FAX Number: (630) 466-7550 Calendar System: Semester
URL: www.waubonsee.edu
Established: 1966 Annual Undergrad Tuition & Fees (In-District): $3,024
Enrollment: 10,511 Coed
Affiliation or Control: Local IRS Status: 501(c)3
Highest Offering: Associate Degree
Accreditation: NH, ADNUR, ART, CAHIIM, EMT, MAC, SURGT

01 President .... Dr. Christine J. SOBEK
05 VP Educational Affairs .... Dr. Diane NYHAMMER
10 Exec VP Finance & Operations .... Mr. David QUILLEN
45 VP Strategic Development .... Dr. Jamal SCOTT
32 Vice Pres of Student Development .... Dr. Melinda L. TEJADA
21 Asst Vice President of Finance .... Ms. Darla S. CARDINE
106 Asst VP Online Lrng/Instruction Sup .... Dr. Renee TONIONI
36 Asst VP Workforce Sol/Comm Learning .... Mr. Gary KECSKÉS
75 Asst VP Career/Technical Education .... Ms. Suzette MURRAY
88 Asst VP Transfer/Development Educ .... Dr. Jonathan PAVER
13 Chief Information Officer .... Mr. Terence FELTON
35 Dean for Students .... Dr. Scott PESKA
15 Exec Director Human Resources .... Ms. Michele NEEDHAM
26 Exec Dir Marketing/Communications .... Ms. Amanda GEIST
76 Dean Health Professions/Public Svc .... Dr. Jess TOUSSAINT
83 Dean Social Sciences/Edu/World Lang .... Dr. Laura ORTIZ
79 Dean Communic/Humanities/Fine Arts .... Ms. Cynthia SPARR
81 Dean Mathematics/Sciences .... Ms. Mary Edith BUTLER
38 Dean Counseling/Careers/Student Sup .... Ms. Kelli SINCLAIR
56 Dean Adult Education .... Ms. Jeri L. DIXON
111 Chief Advancement Officer .... Mr. Robert BARTO
50 Dean Business/Career Technologies .... Ms. Ne'Keisha STEPNEY
103 Dean Workforce Development .... Ms. Lesa NORRIS
84 Dean Enrollment Management .... Ms. Faith LASHURE
31 Dean Community Education .... Mr. Douglas L. GRIER
04 Dir Pres Communications/Operations .... Ms. Kimberly CAPONI
37 Dir Student Financial Aid Services .... Dr. Charles BOUDREAU
09 Dean Inst Effective/Title V Proj .... Dr. Stacey RANDALL
88 Dir Governmental/Cmty Engagement ... Dr. Lourdes BLACKSMITH
19 Dir Emergency Management/Safety .... Mr. John WU
88 Dir Accounting/Business Services .... Mr. Bruce HARTMANN
18 Director Campus Operations .... Mr. Daniel LARSEN
06 Dir Registration/Records/Registrar .... Mr. Marc DALE
07 Admissions Manager .... Ms. Joy SANDERS

Western Illinois University (D)
1 University Circle, Macomb IL 61455-1390
County: McDonough FICE Identification: 001780
Unit ID: 149772
Telephone: (309) 298-1414 Carnegie Class: Masters/L
FAX Number: (309) 298-2400 Calendar System: Semester
URL: www.wiu.edu
Established: 1899 Annual Undergrad Tuition & Fees (In-State): $12,655
Enrollment: 11,094 Coed
Affiliation or Control: State IRS Status: 501(c)3
Highest Offering: Doctorate
Accreditation: NH, ART, CAATE, CACREP, CAEPN, CEA, DIETD, ENG, MUS, NAIT, NRPA, NURSE, SP, SW, THEA

01 President .... Dr. Jack THOMAS
05 Interim Provost/Academic VP .... Dr. Kathleen NEUMANN
20 Assoc Prov/Assoc VP Acad Affs .... Dr. Russell MORGAN
20 Assoc Provost/Undergrad & Grad .... Dr. Nancy P. PARSONS
10 VP Administrative Services .... Mr. Matthew J. BIERMAN
32 Vice President Student Services .... Dr. Ronald C. WILLIAMS
30 Vice Pres Advancement/Public Svcs .... Mr. Bradley BAINTER
29 Director Alumni Programs .... Ms. Amy SPELMAN
23 General Counsel Attorney .... Ms. Rica CALHOUN
39 Assoc Vice Pres Student Services .... Mr. John BIERNBAUM
45 VP for QC & Planning .... Dr. Joseph RIVES
86 Asst to Pres Government Relations .... Ms. Jeanette MALAFA
49 Dean College Arts/
Sciences .... Dr. Susan MARTINELLI-FERNANDEZ
50 Interim Dean College Business/Tech .... Dr. William C. BAILEY
53 Dean Col Educ & Human Svcs .... Dr. Erskine SMITH
57 Dean Fine Arts & Comm .... Mr. William T. CLOW
08 Dean University Libraries .... Dr. Michael LORENZEN
92 Dir Illinois Centennial Honors Col .... Dr. Richard J. HARDY
64 Director School of Music .... Dr. Tammie L. WALKER
06 Registrar .... Dr. Angela LYNN
13 Exec Dir University Technology/CIO .... Mr. Stephen L. FRAZIER
26 Director University Relations .... Ms. Darcie R. SHINBERGER
09 Director Inst Research & Planning .... Ms. Angela BONIFAS
22 Director Equal Opportunity & Access .... Ms. Andrea HENDERSON
37 Director Financial Aid .... Ms. Terri HARE
36 Director Placement .... Mr. Martin J. KRAL
15 Director Human Resources .... Ms. Pamela L. BOWMAN
18 Director Physical Plant .... Mr. Scott A. COKER
19 Director Public Safety .... Mr. Scott HARRIS
23 Director Health Center .... Ms. John W. SMITH
101 Int Dir Distance Learning/Outreach .... Dr. Jeffrey HANCKS
40 Interim Dir University Bookstore .... Ms. Ann COMERFORD
41 Director Athletics .... Mr. Matt TANNEY
102 Director WIU Foundation .... Mr. Bradley BAINTER
07 Director Admissions .... Mr. Seth MINER
38 Director Student Counseling .... Mr. James E. DITULIO
85 Int Dir Ctr International Studies .... Dr. Jeffrey HANCKS
88 Director Budget .... Mr. Matthew J. BIERMAN
100 Chief of Staff .... Dr. Paul SCHLAG

Western Illinois University Quad Cities (E)
3300 River Drive, Moline IL 61265
Telephone: (309) 762-9481 Identification: 770100
Accreditation: &NH

Wheaton College (F)
501 College Avenue, Wheaton IL 60187-5593
County: DuPage FICE Identification: 001781
Unit ID: 149781
Telephone: (630) 752-5000 Carnegie Class: Bac-A&S
FAX Number: (630) 752-5555 Calendar System: Semester
URL: www.wheaton.edu
Established: 1860 Annual Undergrad Tuition & Fees: $34,050
Enrollment: 2,929 Coed
Affiliation or Control: Independent Non-Profit IRS Status: 501(c)3
Highest Offering: Doctorate
Accreditation: NH, CACREP, CAEPN, CLPSY, MFCD, MUS

01 President .... Dr. Philip G. RYKEN
05 Provost .... Dr. Margaret DIDDAMS
10 Vice President for Finance .... Mr. Dale A. KEMP
32 Vice President Student Development .... Mr. Paul O. CHELSEN
111 VP Advancement/Alumni Rels .... Mr. Kirk FARNEY
13 Chief Information Officer .... Ms. Wendy WOODWARD
29 Sr Dir Vocation & Alum
Engagement .... Ms. Cindra STACKHOUSE TAETZSCH
04 Exec Asst to the President .... Miss Marilee A. MELVIN
58 Dean of the Graduate School .... Dr. Scott MOREAU
79 Int Dean Humanities/Theol Studies .... Dr. Lynn H. COHICK
64 Dean Conservatory/Arts & Comm .... Dr. Michael WILDER
83 Dean Natural & Social Sciences .... Dr. Dorothy F. CHAPPELL
104 Dean Global & Exper Learning .... Dr. Laura M. MONTGOMERY
35 Dean of Student Engagement .... Dr. Steve IVESTER
08 College Librarian .... Mrs. Lisa T. RICHMOND
21 Controller .... Mr. Craig SQUIRE
20 Executive Dir Billy Graham Center .... Dr. Ed STETZER
09 Dir Inst Research & Acad Support .... Dr. Gary N. LARSON
06 Registrar .... Mrs. Peggy KING
18 Director of Facilities .... Mr. Scott OKESSON
36 Dir Ctr Vocation & Career .... Ms. Dee PIERCE
15 Director of Human Resources .... Mrs. Karen TUCKER
07 Director Undergraduate Admissions .... Ms. Shawn B. LEFTWICH
123 Director Graduate Admissions .... Mr. Dusty DI SANTO
37 Director of Student Financial Aid .... Ms. Karen BELLING
41 Director of Athletics .... Ms. Julie DAVIS
39 Associate Dean of Residence Life .... Mr. Justin HETH
38 Director of Counseling .... Dr. Toussaint WHETSTONE
42 Chaplain .... Rev. Timothy BLACKMON
23 Director of Student Health Services .... Ms. Britt BLACK
26 Director Marketing Communications .... Ms. Kimberly MEDAGLIA
27 Director of Media Relations .... Ms. LaTonya TAYLOR
40 Manager of Bookstore .... Ms. Jennifer HAMPTON
19 Chief of Public Safety .... Mr. Robert F. NORRIS
93 Director Multicultural Development .... Mr. Rodney K. SISCO
96 Director of Purchasing .... Vacant
117 Director Risk Management .... Mr. Daniel CLARK
105 Director Web Communications .... Mrs. Rebecca LARSON
25 Academic Grants Officer .... Mrs. Virginia SHAFFER

Worsham College of Mortuary Science (G)
495 Northgate Parkway, Wheeling IL 60090-2646
County: Cook FICE Identification: 001783
Unit ID: 369455
Telephone: (847) 808-8444 Carnegie Class: Spec 2-yr-A&S
FAX Number: (847) 808-8493 Calendar System: Quarter
URL: www.worshamcollege.com
Established: 1911 Annual Undergrad Tuition & Fees: N/A
Enrollment: 100 Coed
Affiliation or Control: Proprietary IRS Status: Proprietary
Highest Offering: Associate Degree
Accreditation: FUSER

01 Director .... Ms. Stephanie J. KANN

INDIANA

American College of Education (H)
101 West Ohio Street, Suite 1200, Indianapolis IN 46204
County: Marion Identification: 666242
Unit ID: 449889
Telephone: (800) 280-0307 Carnegie Class: Spec-4-yr-Other
FAX Number: (877) 470-5896 Calendar System: Other
URL: www.ace.edu
Established: 2005 Annual Undergrad Tuition & Fees: N/A
Enrollment: 3,023 Coed
Affiliation or Control: Proprietary IRS Status: Proprietary
Highest Offering: Doctorate
Accreditation: NH, CAEPT

01 Interim President .... Dr. Shawntel D. LANDRY
05 Provost .... Dr. Shawntel D. LANDRY
32 Asst Provost Student Services .... Ms. Stephanie HINSHAW
11 Chief Operating Officer .... Mr. Dan HOLESTINE
84 SVP Enrollment Operations .... Ms. Monica CARSON
88 Dir Regulatory Affairs & Compliance .... Mr. Tom BROUWER
07 Director of Admissions .... Ms. Courtney SHELTON
09 Dir Inst Research/Effectiveness .... Dr. Kathryn TALLEY
04 Administrative Asst to President .... Ms. Jill ALGATE
08 Librarian .... Dr. Sandra QUIATKOWSKI
10 Chief Financial Officer .... Mr. Rick VOLK
13 Information Technology .... Mr. James ALDRIDGE
15 Director Human Resources .... Ms. KK BYLAND
20 Academic Dean .... Dr. Ronald KERN
108 Director Assessment & Accreditation .... Ms. Alison GILLINGS

American National University (I)
6131 N Clinton Street, Fort Wayne IN 46825
Telephone: (260) 483-1605 Identification: 770696
Accreditation: ACICS

† Branch campus of American National University, Lexington, KY

American National University (J)
1030 E Jefferson Boulevard, South Bend IN 46617
Telephone: (574) 307-7100 Identification: 770695
Accreditation: ACICS, MAC

† Branch campus of American National University, Lexington, KY

Anabaptist Mennonite Biblical Seminary (K)
3003 Benham Avenue, Elkhart IN 46517-1999
County: Elkhart FICE Identification: 001823
Unit ID: 151865
Telephone: (574) 295-3726 Carnegie Class: Spec-4-yr-Faith
FAX Number: (574) 295-0092 Calendar System: 4/1/4
URL: www.ambs.edu
Established: 1946 Annual Graduate Tuition & Fees: N/A
Enrollment: 102 Coed
Affiliation or Control: Mennonite Church IRS Status: 501(c)3
Highest Offering: Master's; No Undergraduates
Accreditation: NH, THEOL

01 President .... Dr. Sara W. SHENK
05 Academic Dean .... Dr. Rebecca SLOUGH
10 Vice President and CFO .... Mr. Ron RINGENBERG
30 Director of Development .... Ms. Missy K. SCHROCK
06 Registrar .... Mr. Scott JANZEN
08 Director of Library Services .... Mr. Karl STUTZMAN
84 Dir Enrollment Mgmt/Financial Aid .... Mr. Daniel GRIMES
73 Director of Inst Mennonite Studies .... Dr. Mary H. SCHERTZ

Ancilla College (L)
PO Box 1, Donaldson IN 46513-0001
County: Marshall FICE Identification: 001784
Unit ID: 150048
Telephone: (574) 936-8898 Carnegie Class: Assoc/HT-High Trad
FAX Number: (574) 935-1773 Calendar System: Semester
URL: www.ancilla.edu
Established: 1937 Annual Undergrad Tuition & Fees: $14,930
Enrollment: 504 Coed
Affiliation or Control: Roman Catholic IRS Status: 501(c)3
Highest Offering: Associate Degree
Accreditation: NH

01 President .... Dr. Ken ZIRKLE
04 Assistant to the President .... Ms. Diana CALDWELL
05 VP of Academic Affairs .... Mr. Sam SOLIMAN
10 VP of Finance & Admin .... Mr. Don HOLLAND
30 Vice President of Development .... Mr. Todd ZELTWANGER
84 Vice President of Enrollment Mgmt .... Vacant
42 Vice President Mission Integration .... Sr. Jolise MAY, PHJC
21 Director of Business Affairs .... Ms. Marcella HOPPLE
37 Director of Financial Aid .... Vacant
41 Athletic Director .... Mr. Robert REESE

Code	Title	Name
110	Development & Alumni Relations Mgr	Ms. Emily HUTSELL
13	Director of Information Technology	Mr. John LINBACK
18	Chief Facilities/Physical Plant	Mr. Tom NOWAK
06	Registrar/Institutiional Research	Ms. Tiffany FISHER
40	Bookstore Manager	Ms. Kim WEHR
08	Librarian	Ms. Cassaundra BASH
66	Director Nursing & Health Science	Vacant
26	Dir of Marketing & Social Media	Vacant
39	Director Student Services	Mr. Scott HORCH

Anderson University (A)

1100 E Fifth Street, Anderson IN 46012-3495

County: Madison — FICE Identification: 001785 — Unit ID: 150066
Telephone: (765) 649-9071 — Carnegie Class: Masters/M
FAX Number: (765) 641-3851 — Calendar System: Semester
URL: www.anderson.edu
Established: 1917 — Annual Undergrad Tuition & Fees: $28,650
Enrollment: 2,325 — Coed
Affiliation or Control: Church Of God — IRS Status: 501(c)3
Highest Offering: Doctorate
Accreditation: NH, ACBSP, CAATE, CAEP, MUS, NURSE, SW, THEOL

Code	Title	Name
01	President	Mr. John PISTOLE
05	Provost	Dr. Marie MORRIS
10	Vice President Finance/Treasurer	Mrs. Dana STUART
111	Vice President for Advancement	Vacant
84	VP Enrollment & Marketing	Vacant
73	Dean Sch of Theology/Christian Min	Dr. MaryAnn HAWKINS
50	Dean Falls School of Business	Dr. Terry TRUITT
53	Dean School of Education	Dr. Merribeth BRUNING
81	Dean Sch Humanities/Behavioral Sci	Dr. Joel SHROCK
64	Dean School Music/Theatre & Dance	Dr. Jeffrey WRIGHT
66	Dean Sch Nursing & Kinesiology	Dr. Lynn SCHMIDT
54	School of Science & Engineering	Dr. Chad WALLACE
42	Campus Pastor	Rev. Tamara SHELTON
32	Dean of Students	Dr. Christopher CONFER
06	University Registrar	Mr. Arthur LEAK
08	Director of Libraries	Dr. Janet BREWER
07	Director of Admissions	Ms. Kynan SIMISON
21	Assistant Treasurer/Controller	Mrs. Suahil HOUSHOLDER
36	Center for Career & Calling	Ms. Katie MITCHELL
13	Director of Info Technology Svcs	Mr. Michael TUCKER
37	Student Financial Services	Ms. Chaunta REDFIELD
18	Exec Dir Facilities & Property Mgmt	Mr. Joseph ROYER
15	Director of Human Resources	Ms. Shanna MCCLURE
19	Director Police & Security Services	Mr. Rick GARRETT
40	Bookstore Manager	Mr. Dustin MARTIN
41	Athletic Director	Ms. Marcie TAYLOR
38	Director Counseling Services	Ms. Christal HELVERING
29	Director of Alumni Engagement	Mr. Scott TILLEY
109	Manager Business & Auxiliary Svcs	Mrs. Whitney JIMENEZ
04	Executive Asst to the President	Mrs. Ronda REEMER
104	Director Study Abroad	Mrs. Aurora DOSTER
108	Director Institutional Assessment	Dr. Jaye ROGERS
39	Student Housing Coordinator	Ms. Stacey CARPENTER

The Art Institute of Indianapolis (B)

3500 Depauw Boulevard, Suite 1010,
Indianapolis IN 46268

Telephone: (317) 613-4800 — Identification: 666247
Accreditation: #ACICS

† Branch campus of The Art Institute of Phoenix, AZ.

Ball State University (C)

2000 W. University Avenue, Muncie IN 47306-1099

County: Delaware — FICE Identification: 001786 — Unit ID: 150136
Telephone: (765) 285-5555 — Carnegie Class: DU-Higher
FAX Number: (765) 285-1461 — Calendar System: Semester
URL: www.bsu.edu
Established: 1918 — Annual Undergrad Tuition & Fees (In-State): $9,654
Enrollment: 21,196 — Coed
Affiliation or Control: State — IRS Status: 501(c)3
Highest Offering: Doctorate
Accreditation: NH, AAFCS, ART, AUD, CAATE, CACREP, CAEPN, CEA, CIDA, COARC, CONST, COPSY, DANCE, DIETD, DIETI, IPSY, JOUR, LSAR, MUS, NURSE, PLNG, RAD, SCPSY, SP, SW, THEA

Code	Title	Name
01	President	Mr. Geoffrey S. MEARNS
05	Int Provost/EVP Academic Affairs	Dr. Marilyn BUCK
10	VP Business Affairs & Treasurer	Mr. Bernard M. HANNON
32	VP Stdnt Aff/Enr Mgt/Dean of Stdnts	Dr. Kay BALES
43	VP & General Counsel	Ms. Sali K. FALLING
13	Interim VP for IT	Mr. Loren MALM
86	VP Govt Relations Cmty Engagement	Vacant
102	President and CEO BSU Foundation	Ms. Cheri E. O'NEILL
41	Dir Intercollegiate Athletics	Mr. Mark SANDY
20	Int Assoc Provost/Dean Univ Col	Dr. Kecia THOMPSON
28	Associate Provost Diversity	Vacant
88	Assoc Prov Learning Initiatives	Vacant
50	Assoc Prov Entrepreneurial Learning	Ms. Jennifer BLACKMER
108	Asst Provost Inst Effectiveness	Dr. William KNIGHT
39	AVP Student Affairs/Dir of Housing	Dr. Alan HARGRAVE
26	Assoc VP Strategic Communications	Vacant
18	Assoc VP Facilities Planning/Mgmt	Mr. James LOWE
109	Assoc VP Business/Auxiliary Svcs	Ms. Julie HOPWOOD
14	Asst VP IT for Strategic/Fiscal Mgt	Mr. Donald KING, JR.
07	AVP of Enrollment/Ex Dir of Admiss	Mr. Christopher T. MUNCHEL
08	Dean University Libraries	Mr. Matthew SHAW
48	Dean Architecture/Planning	Mr. Phillip REPP
79	Dean Col of Science/Humanities	Dr. Maureen MCCARTHY
50	Dean Miller College of Business	Dr. Jennifer P. BOTT
53	Interim Dean of Teachers College	Dr. Roy WEAVER
57	Dean College of Fine Arts	Dr. Robert A. KVAM
58	Dean of Graduate School	Vacant
60	Dean Col of Comm/Info/Media	Mr. Roger LAVERY
88	Founding Dean College of Health	Dr. Mitchell WHALEY
92	Dean of Honors College	Dr. John EMERT
88	Chief Entrepreneurship Officer	Dr. Michael GOLDSBY
06	Reg/Dir Registration/Acad Pgms	Mrs. Nancy L. CRONK
37	Director Scholarships/Financial Aid	Dr. John MCPHERSON
15	Director of Human Resources Svcs	Ms. Kate STOSS
19	Director Public Safety	Mr. James DUCKHAM
25	Director Contracts & Grants	Vacant
44	Director Annual or Planned Giving	Mr. Phillip PURCELL
30	Senior VP for Development	Mr. Mark HELMUS
88	VP of Strategic Engagement and Com	Ms. Jean CROSBY
22	Assoc Dean of Students/Title IX	Ms. Katie SLABAUGH
106	Dir Online Education/E-learning	Ms. Staci DAVIS
38	Director Counseling/Health Services	Dr. Tim HESS
88	Dir Unified Technology Support	Mr. Dan LUTZ
36	Director Career Center	Mr. Jim MCATEE
96	Director of Purchasing Services	Mr. Roger HASSENZAHL
24	Dir of University Media Services	Mr. Allen GORDON
88	Dir of Economic Development Policy	Mr. David R. TERRELL
88	Dir Econ and Community Development	Mr. Dick HEUPEL
104	Exec Dir International Programs	Mr. Imara DAWSON
04	Exec Dir of Presidential Operations	Ms. Stephanie K. ARRINGTON
101	Secretary to the Board of Trustees	Ms. Anita KELSEY
105	Interim Chief Creative Officer	Ms. Mary BARR
45	Chief Institutional Planning	Ms. Jen GOINS

Bethany Theological Seminary (D)

615 National Road W, Richmond IN 47374-4019

County: Wayne — FICE Identification: 001637 — Unit ID: 143233
Telephone: (800) 287-8822 — Carnegie Class: Spec-4-yr-Faith
FAX Number: (765) 983-1840 — Calendar System: Semester
URL: www.bethanyseminary.edu
Established: 1905 — Annual Graduate Tuition & Fees: N/A
Enrollment: 53 — Coed
Affiliation or Control: Church Of The Brethren — IRS Status: 501(c)3
Highest Offering: Master's; No Undergraduates
Accreditation: NH, THEOL

Code	Title	Name
01	President	RevDr. Jeffrey W. CARTER
05	Academic Dean	Dr. Steven J. SCHWEITZER
10	Exec Director of Business Services	Ms. Brenda J. REISH
30	Exec Dir Institutional Advancement	Mr. Mark A. LANCASTER
20	Director of Academic Services	Ms. April VANLONDEN
26	Director of Communications	Mrs. Jennifer L. WILLIAMS
32	Dir Student Dev & Alumni Relations	Ms. Amy S. GALL RITCHIE
12	Director Brethren Academy	Ms. Janet L. OBER LAMBERT
88	Dir Peace/Cross Cultural Studies	Mr. Scott HOLLAND
88	Director of the MA Program	Ms. Denise KETTERING-LANE
88	Dir of Educational Technology	Mr. Dan POOLE
07	Dir of Admissions & Student Svcs	Ms. Lori M. CURRENT

Bethel College (E)

1001 Bethel Circle, Mishawaka IN 46545-5509

County: Saint Joseph — FICE Identification: 001787 — Unit ID: 150145
Telephone: (574) 807-7000 — Carnegie Class: Masters/S
FAX Number: (574) 807-7484 — Calendar System: Semester
URL: www.bethelcollege.edu
Established: 1947 — Annual Undergrad Tuition & Fees: $27,390
Enrollment: 1,719 — Coed
Affiliation or Control: Missionary Church — IRS Status: 501(c)3
Highest Offering: Master's
Accreditation: NH, ADNUR, CAEPN, MUS, NUR

Code	Title	Name
01	President	Dr. Gregg A. CHENOWETH
05	VP for Academic Services	Dr. Barbara K. BELLEFEUILLLE
111	VP for Advancement	Mr. Richard CUMMINS
10	VP for Business Services	Dr. David C. ARMSTRONG
32	VP for Student Development	Dr. Shawn M. HOLTGREN
121	Director of Student Success	Mrs. Rachel A. KENNEDY
84	Asst VP for Enrollment/Marketng	Vacant
13	Senior Director of IT	Ms. Patti J. FISHER
66	Dean of Nursing	Dr. Deborah GILLUM
49	Dean of Arts & Sciences	Dr. Janna MCLEAN
53	Dean of Education	Vacant
83	Dean of Humanities/Social Sciences	Dr. Bradley D. SMITH
35	Director of Student Life	Mrs. Julie BEAM
06	Registrar	Mrs. Jeanne E. FOX
36	Dir Career Devel & Global Engagemnt	Mr. Matthew STACKOWICZ
37	Director Financial Aid	Mrs. Cindi M. PEDERSEN
26	Director Public Relations	Mrs. Erin C. KINZEL
41	Director Athletics	Dr. Thomas VISKER
08	Director Library Services	Mr. Mark J. ROOT
88	Director Teacher Certification	Mrs. Kimberly J. MEYER
109	Sr Dir Auxiliary Svcs/Phys Plant	Vacant
09	Director Institutional Research	Dr. Raymond E. WHITEMAN
19	Director Campus Safety	Mr. Paul E. NEEL
85	Director International Students	Mrs. Susan A. MATTESON
91	Director Administrative Computing	Mr. Harold E. RODGERS
29	Director Alumni Services	Mrs. Emily S. SHERWOOD
07	Director of Admission	Mrs. Jill TYLER
15	Director Human Resources	Mr. Mike L. NICHOLAS
04	Administrative Asst to President	Mrs. Barbara J. RODGERS
104	Director Global & Comm Engagement	Mr. Tyler C. GRANT
44	Director Annual or Planned Giving	Vacant

Brightwood College (F)

7833 Indianapolis Boulevard, Hammond IN 46324-3347

County: Lake — FICE Identification: 022018 — Unit ID: 152415
Telephone: (219) 844-0100 — Carnegie Class: Not Classified
FAX Number: (219) 844-0105 — Calendar System: Quarter
URL: www.brightwood.edu
Established: 1969 — Annual Undergrad Tuition & Fees: N/A
Enrollment: 349 — Coed
Affiliation or Control: Proprietary — IRS Status: Proprietary
Highest Offering: Associate Degree
Accreditation: ACICS

Code	Title	Name
01	Campus President	Chris ARTIM
07	Director of Admissions	Wayne HAMPTON
36	Director Student Placement	Jennifer ROSS-ANDERSON
37	Director Student Financial Aid	MelodyAnn CLARK
05	Academic Dean	Andrea MONTELLA

Brightwood College (G)

4200 South East Street, Indianapolis IN 46227

Telephone: (317) 782-0315 — Identification: 770575
Accreditation: ACICS, MAAB

Brown Mackie College-Fort Wayne (H)

3000 E Coliseum Boulevard, Ste 100,
Fort Wayne IN 46805-1565

Telephone: (260) 484-4400 — Identification: 666435
Accreditation: ACICS, OTA, #PTAA

† In teach-out mode. Branch campus of Brown Mackie-South Bend, South Bend, IN.

Butler University (I)

4600 Sunset Avenue, Indianapolis IN 46208-3443

County: Marion — FICE Identification: 001788 — Unit ID: 150163
Telephone: (317) 940-8000 — Carnegie Class: Masters/L
FAX Number: (317) 940-9930 — Calendar System: Semester
URL: www.butler.edu
Established: 1855 — Annual Undergrad Tuition & Fees: $38,360
Enrollment: 4,797 — Coed
Affiliation or Control: Independent Non-Profit — IRS Status: 501(c)3
Highest Offering: Doctorate
Accreditation: NH, ARCPA, CACREP, CAEPN, DANCE, IPSY, MUS, PHAR, THEA

Code	Title	Name
01	President	Mr. James M. DANKO
05	Provost/VP Academic Affairs	Dr. Kathryn MORRIS
10	Vice President for Finance	Mr. Bruce E. ARICK
111	VP University Advancement	Ms. Jaci THIEDE
26	VP Marketing & Communication	Mr. Matthew S. MINDRUM
32	Vice President of Student Affairs	Dr. Frank E. ROSS, III
41	VP & Director of Athletics	Mr. Barry S. COLLIER
84	VP of Enrollment Management	Ms. Lori GREENE
100	Chief of Staff	Dr. Meagan BURTON-KRIEGER
43	General Counsel	Ms. Claire KONOPA AIGOTTI
20	Assoc Provost	Mr. Thomas PARADIS
57	Dean Jordan College Fine Arts	Dr. Michelle JARVIS
50	Dean College of Business	Dr. Stephen STANDIFIRD
49	Dean Liberal Arts & Science	Dr. Jay R. HOWARD
53	Dean Education	Dr. Ena M. SHELLEY
67	Dean Pharmacy & Health Sciences	Dr. Robert P. SOLTIS
60	Dean College of Communication	Dr. Jay R. HOWARD
08	Dean of Libraries	Dr. Julie L. MILLER
35	Dean Student Services	Dr. Sally E. CLICK
35	Dean Student Life	Dr. Anne G. FLAHERTY
38	Asst Dean & Director Counseling Ctr	Dr. Keith B. MAGNUS
18	Executive Director of Facilities	Mr. Richard MICHAL
112	Exec Dir Major Gifts/Planned Giving	Mr. Michael EIKENBERRY
15	Associate VP of Human Resources	Ms. Anila DIN
88	Exec Director Clowes Memorial Hall	Mr. Ty SUTTON
114	Executive Budget Director	Mr. Robert J. MARCUS
37	Director Financial Aid	Ms. Melissa J. SMURDON
88	Dir University Events	Ms. Beth A. ALEXANDER
39	Director Residence Life	Ms. Karla K. CUNNINGHAM
09	Director Institutional Research	Dr. Nandini RAMASWAMY
85	Director Global Education	Ms. Jill MCKINNEY
36	Director Career Services	Mr. Gary R. BEAULIEU
27	Director of Creative Services	Ms. Nancy LYZUN
28	Director of Diversity Programs	Ms. Valerie J. DAVIDSON
86	Director of External Relations	Mr. Michael KALTENMARK
07	Director of Admission	Ms. Aimee SCHEUERMANN
06	Registrar	Ms. Michele NEARY
13	Chief Information Officer	Mr. Peter WILLIAMS
21	Controller	Ms. Susan M. WESTERMEYER
40	Manager Bookstore	Ms. Janine L. FRAINIER
96	Manager of Purchasing	Ms. Shelly S. RABIDEAU

Calumet College of Saint Joseph (A)

2400 New York Avenue, Whiting IN 46394-2195
County: Lake FICE Identification: 001834
Unit ID: 150172
Telephone: (219) 473-7770 Carnegie Class: Masters/S
FAX Number: (219) 473-4259 Calendar System: Semester
URL: www.ccsj.edu
Established: 1951 Annual Undergrad Tuition & Fees: $17,570
Enrollment: 1,100 Coed
Affiliation or Control: Roman Catholic IRS Status: 501(c)3
Highest Offering: Master's
Accreditation: NH, CAEPN

01 President .... Dr. Amy MCCORMACK
05 Vice President Academic Affairs .... Dr. Ginger RODRIGUEZ
111 Dir of Institutional Advancement .... Ms. Ester DIAZ
10 VP Business & Finance .... Ms. Lynn MISKUS
32 VP of Student Affairs & Retention .. Ms. Dionne JONES-MALONE
06 Registrar .... Ms. Diana FRANCIS
08 Director of Library Services .... Ms. Qi CHEN
09 Institutional Researcher .... Mr. Darren HENDERSON
26 Dir of Marketing & Public Relations .... Ms. Linda GAJEWSKI
41 Athletic Director .... Mr. Enrique TORRES
42 Director of Campus Ministry .... Br. Jerry SCHWIETERMAN
18 VP of Facilities & Technology .... Mr. Gene KESSLER
84 Director of Enrollment Management .... Mr. Andy MARKS
37 Dir Financial Aid/Business Ofc Ops .... Ms. Gina PIRTLE
13 Director of Computer Services .... Mr. Kevin KRIEPS
121 Director of Academic Advising .... Ms. Sally LOBO-TORRES
105 Director Web Services .... Mr. Dan YOUNG

Caris College (B)

2780 Jefferson Centre Way, Ste 102,
Jeffersonville IN 47130
County: Clark Identification: 667314
Telephone: (812) 952-9791 Carnegie Class: Not Classified
FAX Number: N/A Calendar System: Quarter
URL: www.cariscollege.edu
Established: Annual Undergrad Tuition & Fees: N/A
Enrollment: N/A Coed
Affiliation or Control: Proprietary IRS Status: Proprietary
Highest Offering: Associate Degree
Accreditation: ABHES

01 President & CEO .... Mr. Bruce KEPLEY

Chamberlain University-Indianapolis Campus (C)

9100 Keystone Crossing, Suite 600, Indianapolis IN 46240
Telephone: (317) 816-7335 Identification: 770503
Accreditation: &NH, NURSE

† Branch campus of Chamberlain University-Addison, Addison, IL

Christian Theological Seminary (D)

1000 W. 42nd Street, Indianapolis IN 46208-3301
County: Marion FICE Identification: 001789
Unit ID: 150215
Telephone: (317) 924-1331 Carnegie Class: Spec-4-yr-Faith
FAX Number: (317) 923-1961 Calendar System: Semester
URL: www.cts.edu
Established: 1925 Annual Graduate Tuition & Fees: N/A
Enrollment: 152 Coed
Affiliation or Control: Christian Church (Disciples Of Christ)
IRS Status: 501(c)3
Highest Offering: Doctorate; No Undergraduates
Accreditation: NH, MFCD, THEOL

01 Interim President .... Dr. William KINCAID
05 Vice Pres of Academics .... Dr. Leah GUNNING-FRANCIS
30 Vice President Development .... Rev. Sarah LUND
32 Dean of Students .... Rev. Mary HARRIS
10 Vice President Finance and Business .... Mr. Curtis SHORT
04 Executive Administrator .... Ms. Sarah EVANS
07 Director of Admissions .... Rev. Brenda FREIJE
21 Director of Business Affairs .... Mr. Chuck CORBIN
08 Director of Library .... Mr. Anthony ELIA
06 Registrar .... Mr. Matt SCHLIMGEN
75 Director of Field Education .... Dr. William KINCAID
18 Director of Facilities .... Mr. Richard DAVIS
37 Int Dir of Student Financial Aid .... Mr. Rodney DUNN
26 Director of Communications .... Ms. Liz JOSS
40 Bookstore Manager .... Mr. Steve HORSMAN

College of Court Reporting, Inc. (E)

111 W 10th, Suite 111, Hobart IN 46342-5969
County: Lake FICE Identification: 026158
Unit ID: 150251
Telephone: (866) 294-3974 Carnegie Class: Spec 2-yr-Other
FAX Number: (219) 942-1631 Calendar System: Semester
URL: www.ccr.edu
Established: 1984 Annual Undergrad Tuition & Fees: $7,250
Enrollment: 229 Coed
Affiliation or Control: Proprietary IRS Status: Proprietary
Highest Offering: Associate Degree
Accreditation: ACICS

01 President .... Mr. Jeff T. MOODY
03 Executive Director .... Mr. Jay VETTICKAL
05 Director of Education .... Ms. Kay MOODY
07 Director of Admissions .... Ms. Nicky M. RODRIQUEZ
37 Director of Financial Aid .... Ms. Alice LEONARD
32 Director of Student Services .... Ms. Jennifer LEWIS

Concordia Theological Seminary (F)

6600 N Clinton Street, Fort Wayne IN 46825-4996
County: Allen FICE Identification: 020876
Unit ID: 150288
Telephone: (260) 452-2100 Carnegie Class: Spec-4-yr-Faith
FAX Number: (260) 452-2121 Calendar System: Quarter
URL: www.ctsfw.edu
Established: 1846 Annual Graduate Tuition & Fees: N/A
Enrollment: 338 Male
Affiliation or Control: Lutheran Church - Missouri Synod
IRS Status: 501(c)3
Highest Offering: Doctorate; No Undergraduates
Accreditation: NH, THEOL

01 President .... Dr. Lawrence R. RAST
05 Academic Dean .... Dr. Charles A. GIESCHEN
36 Dean Pastoral Education/ Placement .... Dr. Carl C. FICKENSCHER, II
32 Dean of Students .... Rev. Thomas P. ZIMMERMAN
11 Vice President of Operations .... Rev. Jon SCICLUNA
06 Registrar .... Mrs. Barbara A. WEGMAN
07 Director of Admissions .... Rev. John M. DREYER
08 Head Librarian .... Prof. Robert V. ROETHEMEYER

Crossroads Bible College (G)

601 N Shortridge Road, Indianapolis IN 46219-4912
County: Marion FICE Identification: 034567
Unit ID: 439613
Telephone: (317) 789-8255 Carnegie Class: Spec-4-yr-Faith
FAX Number: (317) 789-8253 Calendar System: Semester
URL: www.crossroads.edu
Established: 1980 Annual Undergrad Tuition & Fees: $12,400
Enrollment: 240 Coed
Affiliation or Control: Independent Non-Profit IRS Status: 501(c)3
Highest Offering: Baccalaureate
Accreditation: BI

01 President .... Dr. A. Charles WARE
11 Vice Pres Administration/Academics .... Mr. Marcus SCHRADER
05 Dean of Educational Svcs .... Dr. Joel BADAL
84 Dean of Enrollment Management .... Mr. Richard GREEN
07 Director of Admission/Retention .... Ms. Annetta COLEMAN
111 Dir of Institutional Advancement .... Mr. David SELVEY
37 Senior Director Financial Aid .... Ms. Phyllis DODSON

DePauw University (H)

313 S Locust Street, Greencastle IN 46135-1772
County: Putnam FICE Identification: 001792
Unit ID: 150400
Telephone: (765) 658-4800 Carnegie Class: Bac-A&S
FAX Number: (765) 658-4177 Calendar System: 4/1/4
URL: www.depauw.edu
Established: 1837 Annual Undergrad Tuition & Fees: $46,448
Enrollment: 2,265 Coed
Affiliation or Control: United Methodist IRS Status: 501(c)3
Highest Offering: Baccalaureate
Accreditation: NH, MUS

01 President .... Dr. Mark MCCOY
04 Executive Assistant to President .... Ms. Elizabeth DEMMINGS
45 VP for Strategic Initiatives .... Ms. Cindy A. BABINGTON
05 VP for Academic Affairs .... Dr. Anne HARRIS
32 VP Student Academic Life .... Mr. Alan P. HILL
10 VP for Finance/Administration .... Mr. Bob LEONARD
84 VP for Enrollment Management .... Mr. Robert ANDREWS
30 VP for Development .... Ms. Melanie NORTON
20 Dean of the Faculty .... Dr. Tamara M. BEAUBOEUF
88 Dean of Experiential Learning .... Mr. Alan HILL
64 Dean of the School of Music .... Dr. Mellasenah MORRIS
13 Chief Information Officer .... Ms. Carol L. SMITH
35 Dean of Campus Life .... Mr. Dorian SHAGER
06 Registrar .... Dr. Kenneth J. KIRKPATRICK
89 First Year Class Dean .... Ms. Cara SETCHELL
20 Dean of Academic Life .... Dr. David A. BERQUE
15 Director of Human Resources .... Ms. Jana L. GRIMES
37 Director of Financial Aid .... Mr. Elreo CAMPBELL
41 Director of Athletics .... Ms. Stevie BAKER-WATSON
110 Associate VP for Development .... Ms. Dana S. CUMMINGS
29 Associate VP for Alumni Engagement .... Mr. Steven J. SETCHELL
21 Assoc VP for Finance .... Mr. Travis W. LINNEWEBER
08 Director of Libraries .... Mr. Rick E. PROVINE
44 Director of Annual Giving .... Ms. Lee Ann JOURDAN
19 Director of Public Safety .... Ms. Angela D. NALLY
07 Director of Admission .... Ms. Rachel SCHMIDTKE
96 Director of Purchasing .... Vacant
18 Assoc VP for Facilities .... Mr. Warren WHITESELL
27 Exec Director of Media Relations .... Mr. Ken OWEN
09 Director of Institutional Research .... Dr. William M. TOBIN
38 Director of Student Counseling .... Dr. Julie D'ARGENT
39 Director of Housing .... Mr. Jean Carlos LOPEZ
28 Director of Diversity .... Ms. Renee MADISON
36 Director Student Placement .... Ms. Erin A. MAHONEY

26 VP of Communications and Marketing .... Ms. Deedie DOWDLE
105 Director Web Services .... Ms. Andrea ADAMCHAK
91 Director Administrative Computing .... Mr. Adam HUGHES

Earlham College and Earlham School of Religion (I)

801 National Road W, Richmond IN 47374-4095
County: Wayne FICE Identification: 001793
Unit ID: 150455
Telephone: (765) 983-1200 Carnegie Class: Bac-A&S
FAX Number: (765) 983-1304 Calendar System: Semester
URL: www.earlham.edu
Established: 1847 Annual Undergrad Tuition & Fees: $45,300
Enrollment: 1,067 Coed
Affiliation or Control: Friends IRS Status: 501(c)3
Highest Offering: Master's
Accreditation: NH, THEOL

01 President .... Alan C. PRICE
05 Vice President Academic Affairs .... Welling HALL
10 Vice President Business Affairs .... Sena LANDEY
88 Vice President School of Religion .... Jay MARSHALL
84 VP of Enrollment .... Priscilla ALICEA
32 VP/Dean of Student Life .... Earlhagi BRADLEY
20 Associate VP Academic Affairs .... Jay ROBERTS
20 Associate Academic Dean .... Lori WATSON
111 Assoc VP for Institutional Advance .... Kim TANNER
29 Director of Alumni Relations .... Gail CONNERLEY
21 Controller .... Cathy HABSCHMIDT
06 Registrar .... Vacant
121 Director Academic Support Services .... Donna KEESLING
07 Director of Admissions .... Joshua STEVENS
88 Admissions School of Religion .... Matt HISRICH
41 Athletic Director .... Mike BERGUM
13 Director of Computing Services .... Thomas STEFFES
37 Director of Financial Aid .... Katherine GOTTSCHALK
23 Director of Health Services .... Mary Ann STIENBARGER
15 Director of Human Resources/Ops .... Stephanie BISHOP
85 Director of International Programs .... Patty O'MALEY-LAMSON
18 Director of Physical Plant .... Ian SMITH
26 Director Marketing & Communications .... Jonathan GRAHAM
27 Director of Media Relations .... Brian ZIMMERMAN
19 Director of Public Safety .... Tom KEARNS
08 Director of Library .... Neal BAKER
35 Director Student Leadership .... Tracy DUBS
28 Director of Diversity & Inclusion .... Vacant
04 Executive Assistant .... Lyn THOMAS
39 Director Residence Life .... Shane PETERS
09 Director of Institutional Research .... Polly ALBRIGHT
38 Director Student Counseling .... Jessica SANFORD
102 Dir Foundation/Corporate Relations .... Sara PAULE
104 Director Study Abroad .... Patty LAMSON

Faith Bible Seminary (J)

5526 State Road 26 East, Lafayette IN 47905
County: Tippecanoe Identification: 667250
Telephone: (765) 448-1986 Carnegie Class: Not Classified
FAX Number: (765) 448-2985 Calendar System: Other
URL: www.faithlafayette.org/seminary
Established: 2005 Annual Graduate Tuition & Fees: N/A
Enrollment: N/A Coed
Affiliation or Control: Independent Non-Profit IRS Status: 501(c)3
Highest Offering: Master's; No Undergraduates
Accreditation: @BI

01 President .... Dr. Brent AUCOIN
06 Registrar .... Mr. Kirk FATOOL

Fortis College (K)

9001 N Wesleyan Road Suite 101, Indianapolis IN 46268
Telephone: (317) 808-4800 Identification: 770574
Accreditation: ACCSC, ADNUR, MAAB

† Branch campus of Fortis Colleg, Winter Park, FL.

Franklin College of Indiana (L)

101 Branigin Boulevard, Franklin IN 46131-2623
County: Johnson FICE Identification: 001798
Unit ID: 150604
Telephone: (317) 738-8000 Carnegie Class: Bac-A&S
FAX Number: (317) 736-6030 Calendar System: 4/1/4
URL: www.franklincollege.edu
Established: 1834 Annual Undergrad Tuition & Fees: $30,025
Enrollment: 1,087 Coed
Affiliation or Control: American Baptist IRS Status: 501(c)3
Highest Offering: Master's
Accreditation: NH, CAATE, CAEPN

01 President .... Dr. Thomas J. MINAR
04 Assistant to the President .... Ms. Janet D. SCHANTZ
10 Vice President of Finance .... Mr. Daniel SCHLUGE
05 Provost & Dean of College .... Dr. Lori SCHROEDER
07 VP/Dean of Admission/Financial Aid ... Mrs. Kathryn D. COFFMAN
30 VP of Development/Alumni Engagement .. Ms. Evelyn BUCHANAN
20 Associate Provost .... Dr. Denise BAIRD
32 VP Stdnt Affs/Dean of Students .... Mr. Ellis F. HALL
29 Director of Alumni Engagement .... Ms. Joanne SERGI

06 Registrar ..... Ms. Lisa MAHAN
18 Dir Facilities/Energy Management ..... Mr. Thomas PATZ
39 Director of Residence Life ..... Mr. Jacob E. KNIGHT
38 Director of Counseling Center ..... Dr. John R. SHAFER
35 Asst Dean Student Involvement ..... Ms. Keri ELLINGTON
46 Director of Research & Grants ..... Ms. Betsy SCHMIDT
44 Sr Dir Development/Planned Giving ..... Mr. Thomas W. ARMOR
37 Director of Financial Aid ..... Mr. James VINCENT-DUNN
42 Campus Minister ..... Dr. Hannah ADAMS-INGRAM
41 Director of Athletics ..... Mr. Kerry N. PRATHER
13 Dir of Information Tech Services ..... Mr. Larry J. STOFFEL
36 Dir Career Svcs/Asst Dean Students ..... Mr. Kirk J. BIXLER
88 Director of Leadership Development ..... Mr. Dale REBHORN
104 Dir Intercultural/Off-Campus Stds ..... Ms. Jennifer CATALDI
109 Director of Dining Services-Sodexo ..... Mr. Les PETROFF
44 Annual Fund Director ..... Vacant
07 Director of Admissions ..... Ms. Tara EVANS
27 Director of Communications ..... Ms. Deidra BAUMGARDNER
26 Director of Marketing ..... Ms. Theresa LEHMAN
08 Director of Library Services ..... Ms. Denise SHOREY
19 Director of Campus Security ..... Mr. Steve LEONARD
105 Website Administrator ..... Ms. Ann SMITH
15 Manager of Employee Resources ..... Vacant
22 Director Physical Facilities ..... Mr. Thomas PATZ
40 Asst Bookstore Manager ..... Mrs. Janet DOWTY
21 Business Office Manager ..... Mr. Bradley JONES
23 Coordinator Student Health Center ..... Ms. Catherine DECLEENE
28 Coord Multicultural/Diversity Svcs ..... Ms. Terri L. ROBERTS-LEONARD
50 Head Business/Computing/Math Div ..... Mr. Justin GASH
53 Head Education Division ..... Dr. Cindy PRATHER
79 Head Humanities Division ..... Dr. Susan CRISAFULLI
60 Head Journalism Division ..... Mr. Joel CRAMER
65 Head Natural Sciences Division . Dr. Sarah MORDAN-MCCOMBS
83 Head Social Sciences Division ..... Dr. Denise M. BAIRD
57 Head Fine Arts Division ..... Mr. Robin ROBERTS

Goshen College (A)

1700 S Main Street, Goshen IN 46526-4794

County: Elkhart FICE Identification: 001799
Unit ID: 150668
Telephone: (574) 535-7000 Carnegie Class: Bac-Diverse
FAX Number: (574) 535-7060 Calendar System: Semester
URL: www.goshen.edu
Established: 1894 Annual Undergrad Tuition & Fees: $33,200
Enrollment: 839 Coed
Affiliation or Control: Mennonite Church IRS Status: 501(c)3
Highest Offering: Doctorate
Accreditation: NH, CAEPN, NURSE, SW

01 President ..... Dr. Rebecca J. STOLTZFUS
03 Executive Vice President ..... Dr. Ken F. NEWBOLD
05 VP Academic Affairs/Academic Dean ..... Dr. Jo-Ann BRANT
10 Vice President for Finance ..... Ms. Deanna RISSER
111 Vice Pres Institutional Advancement ..... Mr. James K. CASKEY
84 VP for Enroll Management/Marketing ..... Vacant
28 Director of Intercultural Dev ..... Mr. Gilberto PEREZ, JR.
66 Director of Undergraduate Nursing ..... Ms. Brenda SROF
58 Director of Graduate Nursing ..... Dr. Ruth STOLTZFUS
70 Director of Social Work ..... Dr. Jeanne M. LIECHTY
53 Director of Elementary Teacher Educ ..... Dr. Kathryn MEYER REIMER
08 Library Director ..... Mr. Fritz HARTMAN
82 Director of International Education ..... Dr. Tom J. MEYERS
88 Director of Secondary Education ..... Ms. Suzanne EHST
13 Director of Information Tech Svcs ..... Mr. Michael SHERER
09 Director of Institutional Research ..... Mr. Justin HEINZEKEHR
06 Registrar ..... Ms. Jan KAUFFMAN
37 Director Student Financial Aid ..... Mr. Joel D. SHORT
26 Director of Communications ..... Ms. Jodi BEYELER
29 Director of Alumni/Parent Relations ..... Mr. Dan LIECHTY
42 Campus Minister ..... Mr. Robert E. YODER
36 Director of Career Services ..... Ms. Melissa KINSEY
18 Director of Facilities ..... Mr. Glenn GILBERT
15 Director of Human Resources ..... Mr. Norm BAKHIT
106 Director of Adult/Online Pgms ..... Vacant
39 Director of Residence Life ..... Mr. Chad COLEMAN
04 Exec Assistant to the President ..... Ms. Kathleen YODER
108 Director Institutional Assessment ..... Mr. Justin HEINZEKEHR
41 Athletic Director ..... Mr. Josh GLEASON
38 Director Student Counseling ..... Ms. Launa ROHRER
07 Dean of Admissions ..... Ms. Adela HUFFORD
102 Dir Foundation/Corporate Relations ..... Mr. Richard AGUIRRE

Grace College and Seminary (B)

200 Seminary Drive, Winona Lake IN 46590-1294

County: Kosciusko FICE Identification: 001800
Unit ID: 150677
Telephone: (574) 372-5100 Carnegie Class: Masters/S
FAX Number: (574) 372-5139 Calendar System: Semester
URL: www.grace.edu
Established: 1937 Annual Undergrad Tuition & Fees: $23,120
Enrollment: 2,303 Coed
Affiliation or Control: Fellowship Of Grace Brethren Churches
IRS Status: 501(c)3
Highest Offering: Doctorate
Accreditation: NH, CACREP, CAEPN, THEOL

01 President ..... Dr. William J. KATIP
04 Exec Assistant to the President ..... Mrs. Sarah E. PRATER
05 Provost ..... Dr. John R. LILLIS
88 Exec Assistant to the Provost ..... Mrs. Elma C. SHERMAN
20 Assistant Provost ..... Mr. John LOMMEL
73 VP & Dean Seminary & School of Min ..... Dr. Jeffery A. GILL
111 VP Advancement ..... Mr. Andrew R. FLAMM
11 VP Administration & Compliance ..... Dr. Carrie A. YOCUM
84 VP Enrollment Management/Marketing ..... Mrs. Cindy N. SISSON
10 VP Financial Affairs/CFO ..... Mr. Paul G. BLAIR
32 Dean of Students ..... Mr. Aaron T. CRABTREE
51 Dean of Community Education ..... Dr. Stephen A. GRILL
49 Dean of School of Arts & Sciences ..... Dr. Mark M. NORRIS
83 Dean of Sch of Behavioral Science ..... Dr. Thomas J. EDGINGTON
50 Dean of School of Business ..... Dr. Jeffrey K. FAWCETT
53 Dean of School of Education ..... Dr. Laurinda A. OWEN
106 Exec Dean School of Prof/Online Ed ..... Mr. Timothy J. ZIEBARTH
97 Dean of Core & Global Initiatives ..... Mrs. Jacqueline S. SCHRAM
42 Dean of Chapel ..... Mr. Brent MENCARELLI
06 Registrar ..... Mr. Steven T. CARLSON
08 Dir Library Services ..... Mrs. Tonya L. FAWCETT
13 Dir Information Technology ..... Mr. Donald W. FLUKE
23 Dir Student Health & Counseling ..... Dr. Debra S. MUSSER
37 Dir Student Financial Aid ..... Mrs. Charlette R. SAUDERS
15 Dir of Human Resource ..... Mrs. Lisa F. HARMAN
26 Dir of Marketing ..... Vacant
18 Director Physical Plant ..... Mr. Randy KLEINHANS
19 Director Security/Safety ..... Mr. Glenn GOLDSMITH
29 Director Alumni Engagement ..... Mr. Dennis L. DUNCAN
41 Director of Athletics ..... Mr. Chad BRISCOE
36 Director Career Connections ..... Mrs. Denise TERRY
09 Dir Institutional Effectiveness ..... Vacant
100 Chief of Staff ..... Dr. Carrie A. YOCUM

Hanover College (C)

PO Box 108, Hanover IN 47243-0108

County: Jefferson FICE Identification: 001801
Unit ID: 150756
Telephone: (812) 866-7000 Carnegie Class: Bac-A&S
FAX Number: (812) 866-2164 Calendar System: Other
URL: www.hanover.edu
Established: 1827 Annual Undergrad Tuition & Fees: $35,514
Enrollment: 1,133 Coed
Affiliation or Control: Presbyterian Church (U.S.A.) IRS Status: 501(c)3
Highest Offering: Baccalaureate
Accreditation: NH, CAEPN

01 President ..... Dr. Lake LAMBERT, III
04 Executive Asst to the President ..... Treva SHELTON
10 Vice President Business Affairs ..... J. Michael BRUCE
41 Director of Athletics ..... Lynn HALL
30 Vice President College Advancement ..... Melba RODRIGUEZ
05 Vice President Academic Affairs ..... Dr. Steve JOBE
84 Vice Pres Enrollment Management ..... Jon RIESTER
32 Vice President Student Life ..... Dr. Dewain LEE
88 Exec Dir Business Scholars Program ..... Diane MAGARY
88 Special Asst to the President ..... Chris GAGE
06 Registrar ..... Dr. Ken PRINCE
13 Chief Technology Officer ..... John COLLINS
35 Associate Dean of Students ..... Katy LOWE-SCHNEIDER
42 Chaplain ..... Catherine KNOTT
29 Director of Alumni Engagement ..... Christy HUGHES
19 Director of Campus Safety ..... Jim HICKERSON
36 Director of Career Center ..... Margaret KRANTZ
26 Dir of Communications & Marketing ..... Rhonda BURCH
08 Director of Duggan Library ..... Kelly JOYCE
37 Director of Financial Aid ..... Richard NASH
23 Director of Health Services ..... Sandi ALEXANDER-LEWIS
15 Director of Human Resources ..... Shelley PREOCANIN
18 Director of Physical Plant ..... Kevin BROWN
104 Director of Study Abroad ..... Uschi APPELT
38 Director of Student Counseling ..... Catherine LE SAUX
39 Director of Student Housing ..... Lindsay FAULSTICK
96 Director of Purchasing ..... Kevin BROWN

Harrison College - Anderson Campus (D)

140 E 53rd Street, Anderson IN 46013-1717

Telephone: (765) 644-7514 Identification: 666030
Accreditation: ABHES, MAC

† Regional accreditation is carried under the parent institution in Indianapolis (Downtown Campus), IN.

Harrison College - Columbus Indiana Campus (E)

2222 Poshard Drive, Columbus IN 47203-1843

Telephone: (812) 379-9000 Identification: 666428
Accreditation: ABHES, MAC

† Regional accreditation is carried under the parent institution in Indianapolis (Downtown Campus), IN.

Harrison College - Evansville Campus (F)

4601 Theater Drive, Evansville IN 47715-3901

Telephone: (812) 476-6000 Identification: 666429
Accreditation: ABHES, MAC

† Regional accreditation is carried under the parent institution in Indianapolis (Downtown Campus), IN.

Harrison College - Fort Wayne Campus (G)

6413 N Clinton Street, Fort Wayne IN 46825-4911

Telephone: (260) 471-7667 Identification: 666029
Accreditation: ABHES, MAC, SURTEC

† Regional accreditation is carried under the parent institution in Indianapolis (Downtown Campus), IN.

Harrison College - Indianapolis Downtown Campus (H)

550 E Washington Street, Indianapolis IN 46204-2611

County: Marion FICE Identification: 021584
Unit ID: 151166
Telephone: (317) 447-6200 Carnegie Class: Bac/Assoc-Mixed
FAX Number: (317) 686-9190 Calendar System: Quarter
URL: www.harrison.edu
Established: 1902 Annual Undergrad Tuition & Fees: $16,275
Enrollment: 3,040 Coed
Affiliation or Control: Proprietary IRS Status: Proprietary
Highest Offering: Baccalaureate
Accreditation: ABHES, ACFEI, MAC, NURSE

01 President ..... Dr. James D. HUTTON
12 Campus President ..... Mr. Ryon KAOPUIKI

† Includes online and The Chef's Academy.

Harrison College - Indianapolis East Campus (I)

8150 Brookville Road, Indianapolis IN 46239-8903

Telephone: (317) 375-8000 Identification: 666430
Accreditation: ABHES, ADNUR, MAC, MLTAD, SURGT, SURTEC

† Regional accreditation is carried under the parent institution in Indianapolis (Downtown Campus), IN.

Harrison College - Indianapolis Northwest Campus (J)

6300 Technology Center Drive,
Indianapolis IN 46278-6022

Telephone: (317) 873-6500 Identification: 666388
Accreditation: ABHES

† Regional accreditation is carried under the parent institution in Indianapolis (Downtown Campus), IN.

Harrison College - Lafayette Campus (K)

4705 Meijer Court, Lafayette IN 47905-4859

Telephone: (765) 447-9550 Identification: 666431
Accreditation: ABHES, MAC

† Regional accreditation is carried under the parent institution in Indianapolis (Downtown Campus), IN.

Harrison College - Terre Haute Campus (L)

1378 S State Road 46, Terre Haute IN 47803-9787

Telephone: (812) 877-2100 Identification: 666433
Accreditation: ABHES, MAC

† Regional accreditation is carried under the parent institution in Indianapolis (Downtown Campus), IN.

Holy Cross College (M)

PO Box 308, Notre Dame IN 46556-0308

County: Saint Joseph FICE Identification: 007263
Unit ID: 150774
Telephone: (574) 239-8400 Carnegie Class: Bac-A&S
FAX Number: (574) 239-8323 Calendar System: Semester
URL: www.hcc-nd.edu
Established: 1966 Annual Undergrad Tuition & Fees: $28,760
Enrollment: 578 Coed
Affiliation or Control: Roman Catholic IRS Status: 501(c)3
Highest Offering: Baccalaureate
Accreditation: NH

01 President ..... Rev. David D. TYSON, CSC
03 Senior Vice President ..... Dr. Michael GRIFFIN
05 Provost/CAO ..... Dr. Justin WATSON
11 VP for Administration ..... Vacant
111 VP for Advancement ..... Vacant
04 Executive Assistant ..... Ms. Jodie L. BADMAN
32 VP for Student Affairs ..... Vacant
26 Director of Communications ... Ms. Kristina BARROSO-BURRELL
45 VP for Strategic Initiatives ..... Vacant
06 Registrar ..... Mrs. Hiroko TEZUKA
84 Director of Enrollment Management ..... Vacant
37 Director of Financial Aid ..... Mr. Michael SCHMALTZ
38 Director of Student Counseling Svcs ..... Mr. Thomas DEHORN
13 Director of Campus Technology ..... Mr. Doug BLAIR
35 Dean of Students ..... Mr. William MCKENNEY
08 Director of Library Services ..... Mrs. Mary Ellen HEGEDUS
36 Director of Career Development ..... Mrs. Angela FITZPATRICK
42 Director of Campus Ministry ..... Mr. Andrew POLANIECKI
41 Athletic Director ..... Ms. Aimee NIESPODZIANY
09 Director of Institutional Research ..... Bro. Charles DREVON
10 Chief Financial/Business Officer ..... Mrs. Karen VARGO

15 Chief Human Resources Officer .... Mrs. Gwen DEMAEGD
18 Chief Facilities/Physical Plant .... Mr. Jeff JOZWIAK
21 Associate Business Officer .... Vacant
30 Director of Development .... Ms. Judeann HASTINGS
44 Director of Annual Giving .... Ms. Elizabeth FULNECKY
19 Chief Security Officer .... Mr. Greg RUNNELS

Horizon University (A)

7700 Indian Lake Road, Indianapolis IN 46231
County: Marion FICE Identification: 041405
Unit ID: 457226
Telephone: (800) 553-4674 Carnegie Class: Spec-4-yr-Faith
FAX Number: N/A Calendar System: Semester
URL: www.horizonuniversity.edu
Established: 1993 Annual Undergrad Tuition & Fees: $9,150
Enrollment: 29 Coed
Affiliation or Control: Independent Non-Profit IRS Status: 501(c)3
Highest Offering: Baccalaureate
Accreditation: BI

01 President .... Mr. Bill GOODRICH
05 Academic Dean & Exec Vice President .... Mr. Dave KOSOBUCKI
11 Dean of Administration .... Ms. Becky KIRSININKAS
10 Chief Financial Officer .... Ms. Debbie MARSHALL
32 Dean of Students .... Mr. Tracy GRAY

Huntington University (B)

2303 College Avenue, Huntington IN 46750-9986
County: Huntington FICE Identification: 001803
Unit ID: 150941
Telephone: (260) 356-6000 Carnegie Class: Bac-Diverse
FAX Number: (260) 359-4086 Calendar System: 4/1/4
URL: www.huntington.edu
Established: 1897 Annual Undergrad Tuition & Fees: $25,400
Enrollment: 1,252 Coed
Affiliation or Control: United Brethren Church IRS Status: 501(c)3
Highest Offering: Doctorate
Accreditation: NH, CAEPN, NURSE, OT, SW

01 President .... Dr. Sherilyn R. EMBERTON
05 VP Academic Affairs/Dean Faculty .... Dr. Michael K. WANOUS
10 VP for Business/Finance/Treasurer .... Mr. Gregory A. SMITLEY
84 VP Enrollment Mgmt & Marketing .... Mr. Daniel SOLMS
45 VP Strategy & Grad/Professionl Pgms .... Dr. Ann C. MCPHERREN
30 Vice President for Advancement .... Mr. Vincent D. HAUPERT
32 Vice President for Student Life .... Dr. Ron L. COFFEY
04 Administrative Asst to President .... Ms. Peg DEBOLT
42 Dean Spiritual Life/Campus Pastor .... Rev. Arthur L. WILSON
58 Dir of Grad & Professional Programs .... Mrs. Julie K. GOETZ
36 Assoc Dean Student Life/Career Dev .... Ms. Martha J. SMITH
35 Assoc Dean of Student Development .... Mr. Jesse M. BROWN
21 Controller/Dir of Fin Services .... Mrs. Connie C. BONNER
37 Director of Financial Aid .... Mr. Jerry W. DAVIS
06 Registrar .... Mrs. Sarah J. HARVEY
08 Director of Library Services .... Ms. Anita GRAY
13 Dir Information/Technology Services .... Mr. Adam L. SKILES
38 Director of Learning Assistance .... Mrs. Kris L. CHAFIN
41 Athletic Director .... Ms. Lori L. CULLER
18 Director of Physical Plant .... Mr. Jerry A. GRESSLEY
29 Director of Alumni Relations .... Mrs. Marcy T. HAWKINS
19 Director of Campus Police .... Mr. Barry A. COCHRAN
88 Dir of Horizon Leadership Program .... Mr. Jesse M. BROWN

Indiana State University (C)

200 N 7th Street, Terre Haute IN 47809-1902
County: Vigo FICE Identification: 001807
Unit ID: 151324
Telephone: (812) 237-6311 Carnegie Class: DU-Mod
FAX Number: (812) 237-2291 Calendar System: Semester
URL: web.indstate.edu
Established: 1865 Annual Undergrad Tuition & Fees (In-State): $8,746
Enrollment: 13,584 Coed
Affiliation or Control: State IRS Status: 501(c)3
Highest Offering: Doctorate
Accreditation: NH, #ARCPA, ART, #CAATE, CACREP, CAEPN, CIDA, CLPSY, CONST, COPSY, DIETC, ENGR, ENGT, MUS, NAIT, NUR, OT, @PTA, SCPSY, SP, SW

01 President .... Dr. Daniel J. BRADLEY
100 Chief of Staff .... Ms. Teresa D. EXLINE
86 Exec Dir of Government Relations .... Mr. Greg J. GOODE
45 Exec Dir Strat Initiatives .... Dr. Monica LOVE
05 Provost/Vice Pres Academic Affs .... Dr. Michael J. LICARI
10 Sr VP Finance & Admin/Univ Treas .... Ms. Diann E. MCKEE
84 Sr VP Enrollment Mgmt/Mktg/Comm .... Mr. John BEACON
32 VP Student Affairs .... Dr. Willie BANKS
88 Vice Pres Univ Engagement .... Dr. Nancy B. ROGERS
43 General Counsel Legal Affairs .... Ms. Bridget K. BUTWIN
20 Assoc VP Academic Affairs .... Dr. Susan POWERS
20 Assoc VP Academic Affairs .... Dr. Mark GREEN
20 Assoc VP Academic Affairs .... Dr. Joshua POWERS
13 Assoc VP Chief Info Officer .... Dr. Lisa SPENCE
18 Assoc VP Univ Facilities Management .... Mr. Kevin L. RUNION
26 Assoc VP Comm/Marketing .... Mr. Santhana NAIDU
07 Assoc VP Enroll/Mgmt/Adm/HS Rel .... Mr. Richard J. TOOMEY
29 Director of Alumni Affairs .... Mr. Rex KENDALL
15 Assoc VP Human Resources .... Mr. Wil DOWNS
14 Exec Dir Information Technology .... Mr. Yancy PHILLIPS
21 Assoc VP/Univ Controller .... Mr. Jeff JACSO
06 Registrar .... Ms. April HAY
22 Assoc VP for Inclusive Excellence .... Dr. Leah REYNOLDS
28 Exec Dir Multicultural Svcs & Pgms .... Ms. Elonda ERVIN
41 Director of Athletics .... Mr. Sherard CLINKSCALES
36 Executive Dir Career Svcs .... Mr. Brian LUBIC
25 Director Sponsored Programs .... Vacant
09 Director of Institutional Research .... Ms. Patty MCCLINTOCK
19 Director of Public Safety .... Mr. Joseph M. NEWPORT
96 Dir Purchasing/Central Receiving .... Mr. Kevin BARR
39 Executive Dir of Residential Life .... Ms. Amanda KNERR
38 Director of Student Counseling .... Dr. Kenneth CHEW
37 Director Student Financial Aid .... Vacant
49 Dean of Arts & Sciences .... Dr. Christopher OLSEN
50 Dean of Business .... Dr. Brien N. SMITH
53 Dean of Education .... Dr. Janet BUCKENMEYER
68 Dean Health & Human Svcs .... Dr. Caroline MALLORY
72 Interim Dean of Technology .... Dr. Kara HARRIS
58 Dean of Grad/Professional Studies .... Dr. Lynn MAURER
08 Dean of Library Services .... Dr. Robin CRUMRIN
56 Dean of Extended Learning .... Dr. Ken BRAUCHLE
30 Vice President Development .... Mr. Ron CARPENTER
35 Assoc VP Student Affairs .... Mr. Brooks MOORE

Indiana Tech (D)

1600 E Washington Boulevard, Fort Wayne IN 46803-1297
County: Allen FICE Identification: 001805
Unit ID: 151290
Telephone: (260) 422-5561 Carnegie Class: Spec-4-yr-Bus
FAX Number: (260) 420-1453 Calendar System: Semester
URL: www.IndianaTech.edu
Established: 1930 Annual Undergrad Tuition & Fees: $26,370
Enrollment: 7,542 Coed
Affiliation or Control: Independent Non-Profit IRS Status: 501(c)3
Highest Offering: Doctorate
Accreditation: NH, CAHIIM, ENG, #LAW

01 President .... Dr. Karl W. EINOLF
10 Exec VP Finance & Administration .... Ms. Judy K. ROY
05 Vice President for Academic Affairs .... Dr. John F. SHANNON
26 VP Marketing & Communications .... Mr. Brian W. ENGELHART
32 VP for Student Affairs .... Dr. Daniel J. STOKER
84 VP for Enrollment Management .... Mr. Steve A. HERENDEEN
100 Executive Operations Director .... Ms. Jennifer A. ROSS
21 Controller .... Ms. Shelly R. MUSOLF
15 Human Resources Director .... Ms. Julie A. HENDRYX
13 Director of Information Technology .... Mr. Jeff S. LEICHTY
18 Dir Security & Facilities Mgmt .... Mr. R. Michael TOWNSLEY
37 Financial Aid Director .... Mr. Scott W. THUM
54 Dean of Engineering/Computer Sci .... Mr. David A. ASCHLIMAN
50 Interim Dean of Business .... Dr. Joshua J. LONG
97 Dean of General Studies .... Dr. Joshua C. FRANCIS
58 Director Global Leadership Program .... Dr. Kenneth E. RAUCH
09 Director of Academic Research .... Mr. Christopher D. DOUSE
08 Director McMillen Library .... Ms. Constance E. SCOTT
06 Registrar .... Mr. Esaeas J. RODRIGUEZ
108 Director of Institutional Planning .... Mr. Henry D. KING
77 Assoc Dean of Computer Sciences .... Mr. Gary A. MESSICK
84 Enrollment Manager-Fort Wayne .... Mr. Yiani DEMITSAS
106 Director of Online Learning .... Dr. Y. Ben LEE
11 Associate VP for Operations .... Ms. Sharon LOKUTA
07 CPS Director of Admissions .... Mr. Duncan L. MCCORQUODALE
41 Athletic Director .... Ms. Debra P. WARREN
39 Assoc VP Student Services .... Mr. Chris M. DICKSON
35 Director Student Life .... Ms. Andrea G. CHECK
36 Director Career Center .... Ms. Cynthia P. VERDUCE
42 Faith Services Coordinator .... Mr. Gregory P. BYMAN
111 Associate VP Advancement .... Ms. Mary V. SLAFKOSKY
29 Dir Annual Fund & Alumni Relations .... Ms. Lauren A. ZUBER
88 Exec Dir C3 .... Ms. Crystal E. VANN WALLSTROM
102 Dir Foundation/Corporate Relations .... Ms. Tracina A. SMITH
44 Director Annual or Planned Giving .... Ms. Lisa M. BIERS

Indiana Tech-Elkhart (E)

3333 Middleburg Street, Elkhart IN 46516
Telephone: (574) 296-7075 Identification: 770102
Accreditation: &NH

Indiana Tech-Indianapolis (F)

3500 DePaul W Boulevard, Indianapolis IN 46268
Telephone: (317) 466-2121 Identification: 770103
Accreditation: &NH

*Indiana University (G)

107 S. Indiana Ave., Bryan Hall 200,
Bloomington IN 47405-7000
County: Monroe FICE Identification: 008002
Unit ID: 151351
Telephone: (812) 855-4613 Carnegie Class: N/A
FAX Number: (812) 855-9586
URL: www.indiana.edu

01 President .... Dr. Michael A. MCROBBIE
05 Exec Vice President/Provost IUB .... Ms. Lauren ROBEL
03 Exec Vice President IU .... Dr. Nasser PAYDAR
20 Exec VP Univ Academic Affairs .... Mr. John APPLEGATE
46 Vice Pres for Research .... Dr. Fred CATE
28 VP Diversity/Equity/Multicultural .... Dr. James WIMBUSH
18 Vice Pres Capital Planning & Facil .... Dr. Thomas MORRISON
10 Vice President/CFO .... Mr. John SEJDINAJ
86 Vice Pres Government Relations .... Mr. Michael SAMPLE
100 Chief of Staff .... Dr. Karen H. ADAMS
13 Vice President Info Tech/CIO .... Dr. Brad C. WHEELER
43 Vice Pres and University Counsel .... Ms. Jacqueline A. SIMMONS
104 Vice Pres for International Affairs .... Dr. David ZARET
88 Vice President for Engagement .... Mr. William B. STEPHAN
41 VP & Dir of Intercoll Athletics .... Mr. Fred GLASS
63 VP Univ Clinical Affs/Dean Sch Med .... Dr. Jay HESS
84 Vice Provost Enrollment Management .... Dr. David B. JOHNSON
21 University Treasurer .... Mr. Don LUKES
22 Director of Affirmative Action .... Ms. Julie KNOST
29 Exec Dir IU Alumni Association .... Mr. J. Thomas FORBES
102 President IU Foundation .... Dr. Dan SMITH
04 Executive Asst to President .... Ms. Nicole TODD
19 AVP Public Safety & Inst Assurance .... Mr. Mark S. BRUHN
25 Exec Dir Grant & Contract Services .... Mr. James BECKER
32 Dean of Students .... Dr. Lori REESOR
37 Univ Director of Financial Aid .... Ms. Jenny STEPHENS
06 Registrar .... Mr. Mark MCCONAHAY
07 Director of Admissions .... Ms. Sacha THIEME
08 Dean of University Libraries .... Ms. Carolyn WALTERS
09 Exec Dir of Inst Research & Report .... Mr. Todd J. SCHMITZ
101 Secretary of the Board .... Ms. Deborah A. LEMON
106 Director Online Education .... Dr. Chris J. FOLEY
39 Exec Dir Residential Pgms & Svcs .... Mr. Pat CONNOR
44 Director Annual Giving .... Ms. Lindsey PEARSEY
50 Dean of Business .... Dr. Idalene F. KESNER
53 Dean of Education .... Dr. Terrence C. MASON

*Indiana University Bloomington (H)

107 S. Indiana Avenue, Bloomington IN 47405-7000
County: Monroe FICE Identification: 001809
Unit ID: 151351
Telephone: (812) 855-4848 Carnegie Class: DU-Highest
FAX Number: (812) 855-5678 Calendar System: Semester
URL: www.iub.edu
Established: 1820 Annual Undergrad Tuition & Fees (In-State): $10,388
Enrollment: 48,514 Coed
Affiliation or Control: State IRS Status: 501(c)3
Highest Offering: Doctorate
Accreditation: NH, ART, AUD, CAATE, CACREP, CAEPN, CEA, CIDA, CLPSY, COPSY, DIETD, IPSY, JOUR, LAW, LIB, MUS, NRPA, OPT, OPTR, OPTT, PCSAS, PH, SCPSY, SP, SPAA, THEA

02 President .... Dr. Michael MCROBBIE
05 Exec VP & Provost .... Ms. Lauren ROBEL
03 Exec VP & Chanc IUPUI .... Mr. Nasser PAYDAR
05 Exec VP Univ Academic Affairs .... Mr. John S. APPLEGATE
10 VP & CFO .... Mr. John SEJDINAJ
63 VP University Clinical Affairs .... Dr. Jay L. HESS
18 VP Capital Planning & Facilities .... Mr. Thomas A. MORRISON
28 VP Diversity/Equity & Multicul Affs .... Mr. James WIMBUSH
46 VP for Research .... Mr. Fred H. CATE
26 VP for Public Affs & Govt Relations .... Mr. Mike SAMPLE
45 VP for Engagement .... Mr. William B. STEPHAN
32 VP Student Affairs/Dean of Students .... Ms. Lori REESOR
13 VP Info Technology & CIO .... Mr. Brad WHEELER
88 Vice Prov for Research .... Mr. Rick VAN KOOTEN
20 Vice Prov for Undergraduate Educ .... Mr. Dennis GROTH
20 Vice Prov Faculty & Academic Affs .... Ms. Eliza PAVALKO
09 Exec Dir of Institutional Research .... Mr. Todd SCHMITZ
84 Vice Prov Enrollment Mgmt .... Mr. David JOHNSON
88 Vice Prov Grad Educ & Health Sci .... Mr. David DALEKE
88 Vice Prov Finance and Strategy .... Dr. Munirpallam VENKATARAMANAN
28 Vice Prov Educ Inclusion/Diversity .... Mr. John NIETO-PHILLIPS
21 Assoc VP & Univ Controller .... Ms. Joan HAGEN
15 Assoc VP Univ Human Resources .... Mr. John WHELAN
58 Dean University Graduate School .... Mr. James WIMBUSH
102 Pres & CEO IU Foundation .... Mr. Daniel C. SMITH
85 Assoc VP for International Svcs .... Mr. Christopher VIERS
27 Assoc VP and Deputy CIO .... Ms. Laurie G. ANTOLOVIC
116 Assoc VP & Chief Audit Officer .... Mr. Stewart COBINE
49 Dean College Arts & Sciences .... Mr. Larry SINGELL
08 Ruth Lilly Dean Univ Libraries .... Ms. Carolyn WALTERS
63 Dean of Medical Sciences .... Dr. John B. WATKINS
50 Dean Kelley School of Business .... Ms. Idalene F. KESNER
53 Dean School of Education .... Mr. Terrence C. MASON
68 Dean School of Public Health .... Dr. Mohammed TORABI
88 Dean School of Optometry .... Dr. Joseph BONANNO
61 Dean School of Law .... Mr. Austen L. PARRISH
64 Dean Jacobs School of Music .... Mr. Gwyn RICHARDS
60 Dean Media School .... Mr. James SHANAHAN
57 Dean School of Art & Design .... Ms. Peg FAIMON
88 Dean Sch Informatics and Comp .... Mr. Raj ACHARYA
88 Dean School of Global and Intl Stds .... Mr. Lee FEINSTEIN
80 Dean SPEA .... Dr. John D. GRAHAM
66 Int Dean School of Nursing .... Ms. Desiree HENSEL
82 VP International Affairs .... Mr. David ZARET
92 Dean Hutton Honors College .... Ms. Andrea CICCARELLI
70 Director School of Social Work .... Ms. Karen ALLEN
29 Exec Dir IU Alumni Association .... Mr. J.T FORBES
39 Exec Dir Residential Pgm & Svcs .... Mr. Pat CONNOR
06 Assoc Vice Provost/Registrar .... Mr. Mark MCCONAHAY
23 Exec Dir IU Health Center .... Dr. Pete GROGG
43 VP & General Counsel .... Ms. Jacqueline SIMMONS
22 Director Affirmative Action .... Ms. Julie KNOST
19 Chief of Police .... Ms. Laury FLINT
88 Exec Dir Indiana Memorial Union .... Mr. Hank WALTER
88 Exec Dir Radio/TV Services .... Mr. Perry METZ
88 Director IU Auditorium .... Mr. Doug BOOHER

38 Director Counseling & Psych Svs ....Dr. Nancy STOCKTON
41 VP & Dir Intercollegiate Athletics ....Mr. Fred GLASS
96 Asst VP Procurement Services ....Ms. Jill SCHUNK
88 Director IU Art Museum ....Mr. David BRENNEMAN
07 Director of Admissions ....Ms. Sacha THIEME
100 Chief of Staff ....Ms. Karen ADAMS
101 Secretary of the Institution/Board ....Ms. Deborah A. LEMON
104 Assoc VP Overseas Study ....Ms. Kathleen SIDELI
106 Asst VP & Dir Online Education ....Mr. Chris FOLEY
88 Director of Healthy IU ....Ms. Patricia HOLLINGSWORTH
88 University Treasurer ....Mr. Don LUKES
88 Dir Office of Sustainability ....Mr. William BROWN
103 Exec Dir Career Development ....Mr. Patrick DONAHUE
37 Director Student Financial Aid . Ms. Jackie KENNEDY-FLETCHER
44 Assoc VP Gift Planning Svcs ....Mr. Brian D. YELEY
92 Director Wells Scholars Program ....Mr. Christoph IRMSCHER

*Indiana University East (A)

2325 Chester Boulevard, Richmond IN 47374-1289
County: Wayne FICE Identification: 001811
Unit ID: 151388
Telephone: (765) 973-8200 Carnegie Class: Masters/S
FAX Number: N/A Calendar System: Semester
URL: www.iue.edu
Established: 1946 Annual Undergrad Tuition & Fees (In-State): $7,073
Enrollment: 4,716 Coed
Affiliation or Control: State IRS Status: 501(c)3
Highest Offering: Master's
Accreditation: NH, ACBSP, CAEPN, NUR

02 Chancellor ....Dr. Kathryn CRUZ-URIBE
05 Vice Chanc Academic Affairs ....Dr. Michelle MALOTT
26 Vice Chanc External Affs/Marketing ....Mr. Jason TROUTWINE
10 Vice Chancellor Admin & Finance ....Mr. Dan DOOLEY
32 Interim Dean of Students ....Ms. Carrie REISNER
13 Director Information Technology ....Mr. Todd DUKE
30 Director of Gift Development ....Ms. Paula Kay KING
06 Registrar ....Mr. Dennis HICKS
08 Director Library/Media Services ....Dr. Frances YATES
15 Director Human Resources ....Ms. Evelyn GORDON
36 Career and Internship Coordinator ....Ms. Sally SAYDSHOEV
07 Director of Admissions ....Ms. Molly VANDERPOOL
37 Dir Fin Aid & Scholarships ....Ms. Sarah SOPER
20 Director University College ....Ms. Carrie REISNER
40 Manager of Barnes & Noble Bookstore ....Ms. Kristy FRASHER
35 Director of Campus Life ....Ms. Rebeckah HESTER
113 Interim Bursar ....Ms. Shelley DODSON
70 Director Social Work/Human Services ....Mr. Ed FITZGERALD
27 Director Communications & Marketing ....Mr. John DALTON
29 Director Alumni Relations ....Ms. Terry WIESEHAN
50 Dean Business/Technology ....Dr. Bob MULLIGAN
79 Interim Dean Humanities Social Sci ....Mr. T.J RIVARD
81 Dean Natural Science & Math ....Dr. Neil SABINE
66 Dean of Nursing ....Dr. Karen CLARK
53 Dean of Education ....Dr. Jerry WILDE
09 Director of Institutional Research ....Mr. Oniffe GRIZZLE
18 Director of Physical Facilities ....Mr. Gail SMOKER
41 Athletic Director ....Mr. Joe GRIFFIN

*Indiana University Kokomo (B)

2300 S Washington, Box 9003, Kokomo IN 46904-9003
County: Howard FICE Identification: 001814
Unit ID: 151333
Telephone: (765) 453-2000 Carnegie Class: Bac-Diverse
FAX Number: (765) 455-9444 Calendar System: Semester
URL: www.iuk.edu
Established: 1945 Annual Undergrad Tuition & Fees (In-State): $7,073
Enrollment: 4,090 Coed
Affiliation or Control: State IRS Status: 501(c)3
Highest Offering: Master's
Accreditation: NH, CAEP, NUR, NURSE, RAD

02 Chancellor ....Dr. Susan SCIAME-GIESECKE
05 Vice Chanc Academic Affairs ....Dr. Mark CANADA
20 Asst VC for Acad Aff/Stdnt Success ....Dr. Christina DOWNEY
20 Assoc Vice Chanc Academic Affairs ....Dr. Scott JONES
20 Asst VC for Acad Affs/Fac Dev ....Dr. Julie SAAM
32 Vice Chanc Student Affs/Enroll Mgmt ....Dr. Todd GAMBILL
111 Vice Chancellor for Advancement ....Ms. Jan HALPERIN
72 Director Purdue Polytechnic Inst ....Mr. Jeff GRIFFIN
08 Dean of the Library ....Ms. Polly BORUFF-JONES
37 Director Financial Aid ....Vacant
10 Vice Chanc of Finance ....Dr. Philemon YEBEI
26 Dir External Rels/Public Affairs ....Ms. Catherine VALCKE
06 Registrar ....Ms. Stacey THOMAS
100 Chief of Staff ....Ms. Sarah SARBER
36 Manager Career/Accessibility Center ....Ms. Tracy SPRINGER
27 Director Media & Marketing ....Ms. Marie LINDSKOOG
07 Director of Admissions ....Ms. Angie SIDERS
28 Coord Stdnt Life & Campus Diversity ....Ms. Kate AGUILAR
35 Dean of Students ....Ms. Audra DOWLING
18 Director Facilities/Physical Plant ....Mr. John SARBER
50 Dean School of Business ....Dr. Alan KRABBENHOFT
79 Dean Sch Humanities/Social Sciences ....Dr. Eric BAIN-SELBO
66 Inter Dean School of Nursing ....Dr. Mary BOURKE
53 Dean School of Education ....Dr. Leah NELLIS
81 Dean School of Sciences ....Dr. Christian CHAURET
09 Director of Institutional Research ....Ms. Angela SMITH
13 Chief Info Technology Officer (CIO) ....Ms. Beth VANGORDON
15 Director Human Resources ....Ms. Gabby VANALSTINE
41 Athletic Director ....Mr. Greg COOPER

*Indiana University Northwest (C)

3400 Broadway, Gary IN 46408-1197
County: Lake FICE Identification: 001815
Unit ID: 151360
Telephone: (219) 980-6500 Carnegie Class: Masters/M
FAX Number: (219) 980-6670 Calendar System: Semester
URL: www.iun.edu
Established: 1921 Annual Undergrad Tuition & Fees (In-State): $7,073
Enrollment: 5,848 Coed
Affiliation or Control: State IRS Status: 501(c)3
Highest Offering: Master's
Accreditation: NH, CAEPN, CAHIIM, DA, DH, NUR, RAD, RTT, SPAA

02 Chancellor ....Dr. William J. LOWE
04 Exec Asst to the Chancellor ....Mrs. Kathy MALONE
05 Exec VC Academic Affairs ....Dr. Victoria ROMAN-LAGUNAS
11 Exec Dir of Facilities/Operations ....Mr. Andrew KAPOCIUS
32 Vice Chanc Student Svcs/Enroll Mgmt ....Dr. Alexis S. MONTEVIRGEN
10 Campus Chief Financial Officer ....Ms. Michelle DICKERSON
111 Vice Chanc Advancement & Ext Affs ....Ms. Jeri Pat GABBERT
13 Chief Information Officer ....Ms. Beth VAN GORDON
20 Assoc Vice Chanc Academic Affs ....Dr. Cynthia O'DELL
09 Asst VC Inst Effectiveness & Rsrch ....Mr. John NOVAK
49 Dean College of Arts & Sciences ....Dr. Mark HOYERT
88 Dean Col of Health & Human Svcs ....Dr. Patrick BANKSTON
50 Dean School of Business & Economics ....Dr. Cynthia ROBERTS
53 Interim Dean School of Education ....Dr. Mark SPERLING
80 Dir Public & Environ Affs ....Dr. Karl BESEL
70 Director Social Work ....Dr. Darlene LYNCH
06 Registrar ....Mr. Peter ZACHOCKI
88 Director Pre-Professional Pgm ....Dr. Michael LAPOINTE
07 Director of Admissions ....Ms. Dorothy FRINK
37 Director Financial Aid ....Mr. Harold BURTLEY
36 Director Career & Placement ....Ms. Sharese DUDLEY
35 Director Student Activities ....Mr. Scott FULK
19 Director Security ....Mr. Wayne JAMES
29 Director Alumni Relations ....Ms. Paulette LAFATA-JOHNSON
66 Director Division of Nursing ....Dr. Linda DELUNAS
24 Director Instr Media ....Mr. Aaron PIGORS
08 Interim Director Library ....Ms. Latrice BOOKER
18 Director Physical Plant ....Vacant
21 Director of Accounting Services ....Ms. Susan SCHAEFER
25 Director Research/Sponsored Pgms ....Ms. T.J STOOPS
15 Director Human Resources ....Ms. Mianta' DIMING
28 Director Diversity Programming ....Mr. James WALLACE, JR.
38 Director of Counseling Services ....Ms. Barbara A. DAHL
22 Director Affirmative Action ....Ms. Aneesah ALI
88 Dir Schlrshp in Teaching & Learning ....Dr. Christopher YOUNG
88 Dir Urban & Regional Excellence ....Dr. Ellen SZARLETA
105 Director Web Services ....Ms. Myriam YOUNG
106 Dir Online Education/E-learning ....Mr. Christopher YOUNG
41 Athletic Director ....Mr. Ryan SHELTON

*Indiana University-Purdue University Fort Wayne (D)

2101 E Coliseum Boulevard, Fort Wayne IN 46805-1499
County: Allen FICE Identification: 001828
Unit ID: 151102
Telephone: (260) 481-6100 Carnegie Class: Masters/L
FAX Number: (260) 481-6880 Calendar System: Semester
URL: www.ipfw.edu
Established: 1964 Annual Undergrad Tuition & Fees (In-State): $8,213
Enrollment: 12,719 Coed
Affiliation or Control: State IRS Status: 501(c)3
Highest Offering: Doctorate
Accreditation: NH, ART, CAEPN, CS, DA, DH, DT, ENG, ENGT, MUS, NURSE, RAD, THEA

02 Chancellor ....Dr. Ronald ELSENBAUMER
05 Vice Chanc Academic Affs/Enrol Mgmt ....Dr. Carl DRUMMOND
10 Vice Chanc Financial/Admin Affairs ....Dr. David WESSE
32 Vice Chancellor Student Affairs ....Dr. George S. MCCLELLAN
111 Vice Chancellor for Advancement ....Ms. Angie FINCANNON
06 Assoc Vice Chanc/Registrar ....Mr. Patrick A. MCLAUGHLIN
07 Assoc Vice Chanc for Admissions ....Mr. Kenneth C. CHRISTMON
20 Assoc Vice Chanc Academic Programs ....Dr. Carol S. STERNBERGER
28 Assoc Vice Chancellor Diversity ....Mr. Kenneth C. CHRISTMON
100 Chief of Staff ....Ms. Kimberly WAGNER
13 Chief Information Ofcr/Dir IT Svcs ....Mr. Mitch DAVIDSON
18 Director Physical Plant ....Mr. Greg JUSTICE
29 Interim Director Alumni Relations ....Ms. Melissa EASTMAN
08 Library Dean ....Ms. Alexis MACKLIN
35 Chf Student Affs Ofcr/Dean Students ....Dr. Eric M. NORMAN
15 Dir Human Res/Institutional Equity ....Ms. Tamarah D. BROWNLEE
41 Dir of Athletics & Recreation ....Ms. Kelley HARTLEY
96 Director Purchasing ....Ms. Cynthia M. ELICK
19 Police Chief ....Mr. Stephen KIMBROUGH
22 Director Institutional Equity ....Ms. Christine M. MARCUCCILLI
85 Director International Program ....Mr. Brian MYLREA
37 Director Financial Aid ....Mr. David PETERSON
09 Director of Institutional Research ....Vacant
51 Exec Director Continuing Stds ....Ms. Karen VANGORDER
26 Interim Director of Marketing ....Ms. Kathryn HOPKINS
49 Dean Arts & Sciences ....Dr. Eric C. LINK
76 Dean Health and Human Services ....Dr. Ann OBERGFELL
72 Dean Engr Tech/Computer Sci ....Dr. Manoochehr ZOGHI
53 Dean Educ & Public Policy ....Dr. James BURG
50 Dean Business ....Dr. Melissa GRUYS
57 Dean Visual/Performing Arts ....Dr. John O'CONNELL

*Indiana University-Purdue University Indianapolis (E)

301 University Blvd., Suite 5010,
Indianapolis IN 46202-5146
County: Marion FICE Identification: 001813
Unit ID: 151111
Telephone: (317) 274-5555 Carnegie Class: DU-Higher
FAX Number: N/A Calendar System: Semester
URL: www.iupui.edu
Established: 1969 Annual Undergrad Tuition & Fees (In-State): $9,205
Enrollment: 30,105 Coed
Affiliation or Control: State IRS Status: 501(c)3
Highest Offering: Doctorate
Accreditation: NH, AA, ARCPA, ART, CACREP, CAHIIM, CIDA, CLPSY, COARC, CS, CYTO, DA, DENT, DH, DIETI, EMT, ENG, ENGT, FEPAC, HSA, HT, IPSY, LAW, MED, MT, MUS, NMT, NURSE, OT, PA, PAST, PH, PTA, RAD, RADDOS, RTT, SPAA, SW

02 Chancellor ....Dr. Nassar H. PAYDAR
100 Chief of Staff ....Ms. Christine FITZPATRICK
28 Vice Chanc Diversity/Equity/Incl ....Dr. Karen L. DACE
04 Assistant to Chancellor for Comm ....Dr. Becky WOOD
05 Exec Vice Chanc/Chief Acad Ofcr ....Dr. Kathy E. JOHNSON
10 Vice Chanc Admin & Finance ....Ms. Camy BROEKER
26 Vice Chanc Community Engagement ....Ms. Amy C. WARNER
32 Vice Chancellor Student Affairs ....Dr. Eric A. WELDY
46 Vice Chancellor Research ....Dr. Simon ATKINSON
13 Dean Information Technologies ....Dr. Anastasia MORRONE
08 Dean University Library ....Mr. David W. LEWIS
84 Director Enrollment Services ....Mr. Boyd A. BRADSHAW
06 Registrar ....Ms. Mary Beth MYERS
21 Bursar ....Mr. Dan YOUNGBLOOD
22 Interim Director Equal Opportunity ....Ms. Anne L. MITCHELL
38 Director Student Counseling ....Dr. Julie LASH
39 Director Campus Housing ....Mr. Aaron HART
40 Bookstore Manager ....Mr. Neil SCARBOROUGH
36 Career Services Council ....Mr. Joshua D. KILLEY
41 Athletic Director ....Dr. Roderick PERRY
29 Director Alumni Relations ....Ms. Andrea SIMPSON
27 Director News & Media ....Ms. Margie SMITH-SIMMONS
09 Director Institutional Research ....Ms. Michele J. HANSEN
07 Dir of Undergraduate Admissions ....Ms. Yohlunda MOSLEY
37 Director Student Financial Aid ....Mr. Marvin L. SMITH
15 Senior HR Dir/Dir Fin Services ....Ms. Juletta TOLIVER
23 Medical Director Student Health Svc ....Dr. Stephen F. WINTERMEYER
18 Director Campus Facility Services ....Ms. Emily C. WREN
19 Chief Campus Police ....Mr. Robert L. TRUE
92 Dean Honors College ....Dr. E. Jane LUZAR
96 Director Purchasing ....Mr. Robert HALTER
45 Senior Advisor/Academic Planning ....Dr. Stephen HUNDLEY
12 Dean Columbus Campus ....Dr. Reinhold R. HILL
76 Int Dean School Health/Rehab Sci ....Dr. Becky PORTER
57 Dean Herron School of Art ....Ms. Valerie EICKMEIER
52 Dean School of Dentistry ....Dr. John N. WILLIAMS
54 Dean School of Engr/Technology ....Dr. David J. RUSSOMANNO
88 Exec Assoc Dean of Informatics ....Dr. Mathew J. PALAKAL
61 Dean McKinney Sch of Law ....Mr. Andrew R. KLEIN
49 Dean School of Liberal Arts ....Dr. Thomas J. DAVIS
63 Dean School of Medicine ....Dr. Jay L. HESS
66 Dean School of Nursing ....Dr. Robin P. NEWHOUSE
68 Int Dean School of Physical Educ ....Dr. Rafael BAHAMONDE
81 Dean School of Science ....Dr. Simon RHODES
70 Dean School of Social Work ....Dr. Michael PATCHNER
69 Dean Fairbanks Sch of Public Health ....Dr. Paul K. HALVERSON
88 Dean Lilly Fam Sch of Philanthropy ....Dr. Amir PASIC
53 Exec Assoc Dean School of Education ....Dr. Robin L. HUGHES
80 Exec Assoc Dean Public/Environ Affs ....Dr. Lilliard RICHARDSON
85 Assoc Vice Chanc International Affs ....Dr. Gil LATZ
50 Assoc Dean School of Business ....Dr. Ken CAROW
58 Associate Dean Graduate School ....Dr. Janice S. BLUM
89 Dean University College ....Dr. James M. GLADDEN
43 Dir Legal Services/General Counsel ....Mr. Joseph M. SCODRO

*Indiana University South Bend (F)

1700 Mishawaka Avenue, South Bend IN 46634-7111
County: Saint Joseph FICE Identification: 001816
Unit ID: 151342
Telephone: (574) 520-4872 Carnegie Class: Masters/M
FAX Number: (574) 520-4834 Calendar System: Semester
URL: www.iusb.edu
Established: 1940 Annual Undergrad Tuition & Fees (In-State): $7,073
Enrollment: 7,574 Coed
Affiliation or Control: State IRS Status: 501(c)3
Highest Offering: Master's
Accreditation: NH, CACREP, CAEPN, DH, MUS, NURSE, RAD, SPAA

02 Chancellor ....Dr. Terry L. ALLISON
05 Exec Vice Chanc Acad Affairs ....Dr. Jann JOSEPH
10 Vice Chanc Admin & Finance ....Mr. Philip IAPALUCCI
26 Vice Chanc Public Affs/Univ Advance .Mr. Stephen W. STURMAN
13 Regional Chief Information Officer ....Ms. Elizabeth VAN GORDON
20 Int Assoc Vice Chanc Academic Affs ....Dr. Linda CHEN
32 Assoc Vice Chanc Student Services ....Ms. Karen L. WHITE
84 Assoc Vice Chanc Enrollment Svcs ....Ms. Cathy M. BUCKMAN
06 Registrar ....Mr. Keith DAWSON
35 Dir Student Activit Ctr/Athletics ....Mr. Steve BRUCE
18 Director Facilities Management ....Mr. Michael PRATER
19 Director of Safety & Security ....Mr. Kurt M. MATZ
15 Dir of Human Resources/Career Svcs ....Ms. Deb SCHMITT

24 Dir of Instructional Media Svcs ... Mr. Jim YOCOM
29 Dir Alumni Affs/Campus Ceremonies ... Ms. Moira DYCZKO
27 Director Communications/Marketing ... Mr. Kenneth W. BAIERL
52 Director of Dental Auxiliary Educ ... Ms. Kristyn QUIMBY
51 Director of Extended Learning ... Mr. Mike MANCINI
97 Director of General Studies ... Dr. David A. VOLLRATH
85 Director of International Programs ... Dr. Scott SERNAU
38 Director Student Counseling Ctr ... Mr. Kevin GRIFFITH
07 Director of Admissions ... Ms. Connie PETERSON-MILLER
09 Director of Institutional Research ... Mr. Biniam TESFAMARIAM
28 Director of Diversity ... Ms. Martha (Marty) MCCAMPBELL
30 Director of Development ... Ms. Dina HARRIS
39 Director of Student Housing ... Mr. Scott STRITTMATTER
21 Director of Accounting ... Ms. Kathleen PIZANA
37 Associate Director of Financial Aid ... Ms. Cyndi LANG
49 Dean of Liberal Arts & Science ... Dr. Elizabeth E. DUNN
50 Dean of Business & Economics ... Dr. Rick KOLBE
53 Interim Dean of Education ... Dr. Hope DAVIS
57 Dean of the Arts ... Dr. Marvin CURTIS
76 Dean Col of Health Sciences ... Dr. Thomas FISHER
08 Dean of Library Services ... Ms. Vicki BLOOM

*Indiana University Southeast (A)

4201 Grant Line Road, New Albany IN 47150-2158
County: Floyd FICE Identification: 001817
Unit ID: 151379
Telephone: (812) 941-2333 Carnegie Class: Masters/L
FAX Number: (812) 941-2475 Calendar System: Semester
URL: www.ius.edu
Established: 1941 Annual Undergrad Tuition & Fees (In-State): $7,073
Enrollment: 6,173 Coed
Affiliation or Control: State IRS Status: 501(c)3
Highest Offering: Master's
Accreditation: **NH**, CAEPN, NURSE

02 Chancellor ... Dr. Ray WALLACE
05 Executive VC Academic Affairs ... Dr. Uric DUFRENE
10 VC Administration/Finance ... Mr. Dana C. WAVLE
84 Int VC Enroll Mgmt/Student Affairs ... Ms. Amanda G. STONECIPHER
111 VC Advancement ... Ms. Betty S. RUSSO
20 Assoc VC Academic Affairs ... Dr. Angela M. SALAS
20 Asst VC Academic Affairs ... Dr. Annette M. WYANDOTTE
32 Asst VC Retention/Student Services ... Ms. Amanda G. STONECIPHER
13 Chief Information Officer ... Ms. Elizabeth VAN GORDON
07 Director Admissions ... Mr. Chris CREWS
04 Exec Secretary to the Chancellor ... Ms. Sarah R. JAMES
35 Dean for Student Life ... Dr. Seuth CHALEUNPHONH
06 Registrar ... Mr. James (Jay) MCTYIER
37 Director Student Financial Aid ... Ms. Traci ARMES
08 Director Library Services ... Mr. C. Martin ROSEN
36 Director Career Development ... Ms. Danielle LEFFLER
18 Exec Dir of Facility Operations ... Mr. Robert C. POFF
14 Dir IT Communications & Support ... Mr. Nicholas T. RAY
41 Director Athletics ... Mr. Joseph M. GLOVER
72 Dir Purdue College of Technology ... Andrew B. TAKAMI
15 Director Human Resources ... Mr. Ray KLEIN
09 Dir Institutional Effectiveness ... Mr. Ronald E. SEVERTIS, JR.
19 Chief Safety & Security ... Mr. Charles EDELEN
38 Dir Personal Counseling ... Dr. Michael DAY
26 Dir Marketing & Communications ... Ms. Nancy J. TRAFTON
97 Manager General Studies ... Ms. Saundra E. GORDON
79 Dean School Arts & Letters ... Mr. James HESSELMAN
81 Dean School Natural Sciences ... Dr. Elaine HAUB
83 Dean School Social Sciences ... Dr. Kelly A. RYAN
50 Dean School Business ... Dr. David EPLION
53 Dean School Education ... Dr. Doyin COKER-KOLO
66 Dean School Nursing ... Dr. Donna J. BOWLES
46 Dean for Research & Grad Studies ... Dr. Diane E. WILLE
28 Director Staff Equity & Diversity ... Ms. Darlene P. YOUNG
29 Dir Alumni and Community Relations ... Mr. J. T. DOUGLAS
88 Director of Advising ... Ms. Rebecca TURNER
88 Director Academic Accting Services ... Ms. Melissa D. HILL
88 Director Student Accting Services ... Ms. Ashley M. MCKAY
88 Academic Information Officer ... Mr. Steven KROLAK
121 Dean Student Success & Persistence ... Dr. Donna J. DAHLGREN
30 Dir Development ... Mr. David C. DEWITT
39 Int Dir Residence Life & Housing ... Ms. Abbie DUPAY

*_Indiana University-Purdue University Columbus_ (B)

4601 Central Avenue, Columbus IN 47203
Telephone: (812) 348-7390 Identification: 770185
Accreditation: &**NH**, NURSE

Indiana Wesleyan University (C)

4201 S Washington Street, Marion IN 46953-4999
County: Grant FICE Identification: 001822
Unit ID: 151801
Telephone: (765) 674-6901 Carnegie Class: Masters/L
FAX Number: (765) 677-2499 Calendar System: 4/1/4
URL: www.indwes.edu
Established: 1920 Annual Undergrad Tuition & Fees: $25,346
Enrollment: 14,730 Coed
Affiliation or Control: Wesleyan Church IRS Status: 501(c)3
Highest Offering: Doctorate
Accreditation: **NH**, CAATE, CACREP, CAEPN, EXSC, MFCD, MUS, NURSE, SW, THEOL

01 President ... Dr. David WRIGHT
05 Chief Academic Officer/Provost ... Dr. Stacy HAMMONS
88 Chancellor IWU-Marion ... Vacant
88 Chancellor IWU-National & Global ... Mrs. Audrey HAHN
28 VP for Multicultural Enrichment ... Ms. Diane MCDANIEL
10 Vice President Business Affs/CFO ... Mrs. Nancy SCHOONMAKER
88 President Wesley Seminary ... Dr. Colleen DERR
20 VP for Academic Affairs/CAPS ... Dr. Brock REIMAN
20 VP for Academic Affairs/SON ... Dr. Barbara IHRKE
111 VP for Advancement ... Dr. Chris YOUNG
20 Associate Provost ... Dr. Don SPROWL
84 VP Residential Enrollment Mgt ... Mr. Mike EGENREIDER
84 VP Enroll Mgmt & Mktg/Non-Resident ... Mr. David ROSE
88 VP Life Calling & Integrative Lrng ... Dr. Brandon HILL
11 VP of Operations/Residential Campus ... Mr. John JONES
04 Sr Counsel to the President/Ombudsm ... Mrs. Karen ROORBACH
58 Dean Graduate School ... Dr. Joanne BARNES
88 Dean of the Seminary ... Dr. David SMITH
76 Dean School of Health Sciences ... Dr. Martin RICE
88 Dean of Developmental Learning ... Mr. Andrew PARKER
37 Associate VP Financial Aid ... Mr. Thomas RATLIFF
08 Director Library Resources ... Mrs. Shelia CARLBLOM
08 Director Off-campus Library Svcs ... Mrs. Jule KIND
29 Director of Alumni ... Mr. Rick CARDER
07 Dir Admissions/Residential Educ ... Mr. Adam FARMER
36 Exec Dir Ctr for Student Success ... Mr. Nathan HERRING
15 Exec Director Human Resources ... Mr. Mark PEDERSON
06 University Registrar ... Mrs. Kim NICHOLSON
43 University Counsel ... Mr. Shawn MATTER
21 Controller ... Mrs. Tiffany LEWIS
41 Athletic Director ... Mr. Mark DEMICHAEL
42 Dean of the Chapel ... Dr. John BRAY
92 Dean Honors College ... Mr. David RIGGS
09 Director Institutional Research ... Mr. Tony PARANDI
18 AVP Facilities Services ... Mr. Don ROWLEY
19 Director Campus Police ... Mr. Chad BEIGHTS
25 Director of Research Support ... Dr. Ken BIELEN
13 Chief Info Technology Officer (CIO) ... Mr. Scott GILREATH
121 Dean Center for Student Success ... Mr. Nathan HERRING

International Business College (D)

5699 Coventry Lane, Fort Wayne IN 46804-9990
County: Allen FICE Identification: 004579
Unit ID: 151458
Telephone: (260) 459-4500 Carnegie Class: Bac/Assoc-Mixed
FAX Number: (260) 436-1896 Calendar System: Semester
URL: www.ibcfortwayne.edu
Established: 1889 Annual Undergrad Tuition & Fees: $13,920
Enrollment: 340 Coed
Affiliation or Control: Proprietary IRS Status: Proprietary
Highest Offering: Associate Degree
Accreditation: **ACICS**, MAC

01 President ... Ms. Kathy CHIUDIONI
11 Campus Administrator ... Ms. Amee AUGENSTEIN
05 Director of Education ... Ms. Catherine NOWICKI
07 Director of Admissions ... Ms. Gena HOPKINS
32 Student Services Director ... Ms. Roxanna SHULL
36 Director of Placement ... Ms. Marty BIANSKI
06 Registrar ... Ms. Christine ELLIS

International Business College (E)

7205 Shadeland Station, Indianapolis IN 46256-3997
Telephone: (317) 813-2300 Identification: 666929
Accreditation: **ACICS**, DA, MAC

*Ivy Tech Community College of Indiana-System Office (F)

50 W Fall Creek Parkway N Drive,
Indianapolis IN 46208-5752
County: Marion FICE Identification: 008546
Unit ID: 363563
Telephone: (317) 921-4882 Carnegie Class: N/A
FAX Number: (317) 921-4753
URL: www.ivytech.edu

01 President ... Dr. Sue J. ELLSPERMANN
05 Provost/Sr Vice President ... Dr. Steven TINCHER
102 Sr Vice Pres Ivy Tech Foundation ... Mr. John MURPHY
10 Sr Vice President/CFO ... Vacant
26 Sr Vice Pres Mktg/Comm/Stdnt Exp ... Mr. Jeff FANTER
20 Vice Pres Academic Affairs ... Dr. Russell D. BAKER
18 Vice President Facilities Planning ... Ms. Amanda WILSON
84 VP for Student Experience/Cust Svc ... Ms. Anne P. VALENTINE
06 Asst VP Student Records ... Mrs. Ann YATER
37 Chief Fin Student Resources Ofcr ... Mr. Ben BURTON
15 Executive Director Human Resources ... Ms. Julie LORTON-ROWLAND
21 Assistant Treasurer ... Mr. Mark A. HUSK
13 Chief Technology Officer ... Mr. Lige HENSLEY
103 Sr VP Workforce Alignment ... Mr. Chris LOWERY
19 Exec Dir Statewide Security/Safety ... Mr. Jon BAREFOOT
28 Exec Dir Statewide Diversity/Outrch ... Mr. Doran MORELAND
30 VP Fundraising ... Mr. Derek BERGER
32 Asst VP Student Life ... Dr. Carey TREAGER-HUBER
86 VP Government Relations ... Ms. Mary Jane MICHALAK

*Ivy Tech Community College of Indiana-Central Indiana (G)

50 W Fall Creek Parkway North Drive,
Indianapolis IN 46208-5752
County: Marion FICE Identification: 009917
Unit ID: 150987
Telephone: (317) 921-4882 Carnegie Class: Assoc/MT-VT-High Non
FAX Number: (317) 921-4753 Calendar System: Semester
URL: www.ivytech.edu/indianapolis/
Established: 1966 Annual Undergrad Tuition & Fees (In-State): $4,175
Enrollment: 81,668 Coed
Affiliation or Control: State IRS Status: 501(c)3
Highest Offering: Associate Degree
Accreditation: **NH**, ACBSP, ACFEI, ADNUR, ART, CAHIIM, COARC, CSHSE, ENGT, FUSER, MAC, NAIT, PNUR, RAD, SURGT

02 Chancellor ... Dr. Kathleen F. LEE
05 VC of Academic Affairs ... Dr. Frank MOMAN
32 Vice Chancellor of Student Affairs ... Dr. Darrell CAIN
10 Executive Director of Finance ... Mr. Corey BACK
15 Exec Director of Human Resources ... Ms. Sara MCKEE
11 Exec Dir of Administrative Services ... Mr. Aaron ROBERTS
103 Exec Dir Workforce & Economic Devel ... Vacant
30 Exec Director of Development ... Mrs. Danielle STILES-POLK
35 Asst Vice Chanc Student Affairs ... Mr. Jerry H. HARRELL
35 Asst Vice Chanc Student Affairs ... Dr. Tracy FUNK
84 Assoc Vice Pres Enrollment ... Ms. Anne P. VALENTINE
37 Director of Financial Aid ... Mr. Alex DELONIS
06 Registrar ... Mrs. Letha BROOKS
09 Director of Institutional Research ... Vacant
36 Director of Career Services ... Ms. Rebecca PATTEN-LEMONS
96 Director of Purchasing ... Mr. Jerry L. KOENIG
20 Asst Vice Chanc Academic Affairs ... Mr. Gary PELLICO
26 Director Marketing/Communications ... Ms. Kelli SCHNETZER
46 Director of Resource Development ... Ms. Christina COLLINS

*_Ivy Tech Community College of Indiana-Anderson_ (H)

104 West 53rd Street, Anderson IN 46013-1502
Telephone: (800) 644-4882 Identification: 770239
Accreditation: &**NH**, MAC

*_Ivy Tech Community College of Indiana-Bloomington_ (I)

200 N Daniels Way, Bloomington IN 47404-9772
Telephone: (812) 332-1559 FICE Identification: 035213
Accreditation: &**NH**, ACBSP, ACFEI, ADNUR, COARC, CSHSE, EMT, NAIT, PNUR, RTT

*_Ivy Tech Community College of Indiana-Columbus_ (J)

4475 Central Avenue, Columbus IN 47203-1868
Telephone: (812) 372-9925 FICE Identification: 010038
Accreditation: &**NH**, ART, ACBSP, ADNUR, CSHSE, DA, EMT, MAC, NAIT, PNUR, SURGT

*_Ivy Tech Community College of Indiana-East Central_ (K)

4301 Cowan Road, Muncie IN 47302-9448
Telephone: (765) 289-2291 FICE Identification: 009924
Accreditation: &**NH**, ACBSP, ACFEI, ADNUR, CSHSE, DA, DH, MAC, NAIT, PNUR, PTAA, RAD, SURGT

*_Ivy Tech Community College of Indiana-East Chicago_ (L)

410 East Columbus Drive, East Chicago IN 46312
Telephone: (219) 392-3600 Identification: 770240
Accreditation: &**NH**, ACFEI

*_Ivy Tech Community College of Indiana-Elkhart_ (M)

22531 County Road 18, Goshen IN 46528
Telephone: (574) 830-0375 Identification: 770241
Accreditation: &**NH**

*_Ivy Tech Community College of Indiana-Kokomo_ (N)

1815 E Morgan Street, Box 1373, Kokomo IN 46903-1373
Telephone: (765) 459-0561 FICE Identification: 010041
Accreditation: &**NH**, ACBSP, ADNUR, CSHSE, DA, EMT, MAC, NAIT, PNUR, SURGT

*_Ivy Tech Community College of Indiana-Lafayette_ (O)

3101 S Creasy Lane, Box 6299, Lafayette IN 47903-6299
Telephone: (765) 269-5000 FICE Identification: 010039
Accreditation: &**NH**, ACBSP, ADNUR, COARC, CSHSE, DA, MAC, NAIT, PNUR, SURGT

* Ivy Tech Community College of Indiana-Lawrenceburg-Riverfront (A)

50 Walnut Street, Lawrenceburg IN 47025
Telephone: (812) 537-4010 Identification: 770242
Accreditation: &NH, MAC

* Ivy Tech Community College of Indiana-Logansport (B)

1 Ivy Tech Way, Logansport IN 46947
Telephone: (866) 753-5101 Identification: 770243
Accreditation: &NH

* Ivy Tech Community College of Indiana-Marion (C)

261 S Commerce Drive, Marion IN 46953
Telephone: (800) 554-1159 Identification: 770244
Accreditation: &NH, MAC

* Ivy Tech Community College of Indiana-Michigan City (D)

3714 Franklin Drive, Michigan City IN 46360
Telephone: (219) 879-9137 Identification: 770245
Accreditation: &NH, ACFEI, MAC

* Ivy Tech Community College of Indiana-North Central (E)

220 Dean Johnson Boulevard, South Bend IN 46601-3415
Telephone: (574) 289-7001 FICE Identification: 008423
Accreditation: &NH, ART, ACBSP, ACFEI, ADNUR, COARC, CSHSE, DA, DH, EMT, MAC, MLTAD, NAIT, PNUR

* Ivy Tech Community College of Indiana-Northeast (F)

3800 N Anthony Boulevard, Fort Wayne IN 46805-1489
Telephone: (260) 482-9171 FICE Identification: 009926
Accreditation: &NH, ACBSP, ACFEI, ADNUR, CAHIIM, COARC, CSHSE, EMT, MAC, NAIT, PNUR

* Ivy Tech Community College of Indiana-Northwest (G)

1440 E 35th Avenue, Gary IN 46409-1499
Telephone: (219) 981-1111 FICE Identification: 010040
Accreditation: &NH, ACBSP, ADNUR, COARC, CSHSE, FUSER, NAIT, PNUR, PTAA, SURGT

* Ivy Tech Community College of Indiana-Richmond (H)

2357 Chester Boulevard, Richmond IN 47374-1298
Telephone: (765) 966-2656 FICE Identification: 010037
Accreditation: &NH, ACBSP, ADNUR, COARC, CSHSE, MAC, NAIT, PNUR

* Ivy Tech Community College of Indiana-Southeast (I)

590 Ivy Tech Drive, Madison IN 47250-1883
Telephone: (812) 265-2580 FICE Identification: 009923
Accreditation: &NH, ACBSP, ADNUR, CSHSE, EMT, MAC, NAIT, PNUR

* Ivy Tech Community College of Indiana-Southern Indiana (J)

8204 Highway 311, Sellersburg IN 47172-1897
Telephone: (812) 246-3301 FICE Identification: 010109
Accreditation: &NH, ACBSP, ADNUR, ART, COARC, CSHSE, MAC, MLTAD, NAIT, PNUR, PTAA

* Ivy Tech Community College of Indiana-Southwest (K)

3501 First Avenue, Evansville IN 47710-1881
Telephone: (812) 426-2865 FICE Identification: 009925
Accreditation: &NH, ACBSP, ADNUR, CSHSE, EMT, MAC, NAIT, PNUR, SURGT

* Ivy Tech Community College of Indiana-Valparaiso (L)

3100 Ivy Tech Drive, Valparaiso IN 46383
Telephone: (219) 464-8514 Identification: 770246
Accreditation: &NH

* Ivy Tech Community College of Indiana-Wabash (M)

277 N Thorne Street, Wabash IN 46992
Telephone: (260) 563-8828 Identification: 770247
Accreditation: &NH

* Ivy Tech Community College of Indiana-Wabash Valley (N)

8000 S. Education Drive, Terre Haute IN 47802-4833
Telephone: (812) 299-1121 FICE Identification: 008547
Accreditation: &NH, ACBSP, ADNUR, ART, COARC, CSHSE, DMS, EMT, MAC, MLTAD, NAIT, PNUR, RAD, SURGT

* Ivy Tech Community College of Indiana-Warsaw (O)

2545 Silreus Crossing, Warsaw IN 46582
Telephone: (574) 267-5428 Identification: 770248
Accreditation: &NH

Lincoln College of Technology (P)

7225 Winton Drive, Building 128,
Indianapolis IN 46268-4198
County: Marion FICE Identification: 007938
Unit ID: 151661
Telephone: (317) 632-5553 Carnegie Class: Spec 2-yr-Tech
FAX Number: (317) 851-3273 Calendar System: Semester
URL: www.lincolntech.edu
Established: 1962 Annual Undergrad Tuition & Fees: N/A
Enrollment: 1,103 Coed
Affiliation or Control: Proprietary IRS Status: Proprietary
Highest Offering: Associate Degree
Accreditation: ACCSC

01 Campus President .... Daniel RICHINS
05 Academic Dean .... Rodney ALLEE
11 Director of Administrative Services .... Andy RAHIMI
37 Director Student Financial Aid .... Sheila ANDREWS
07 Director of Adult Admissions .... Shannon BIGELOW
07 Director of High School Admissions .... John MARTIN
36 Director of Career Services .... Bryan FEILEN
13 IT Administrator .... Blake BROOKS
18 Facilities Manager .... Roger PARK
21 Business Office Coordinator .... Dawn KEMP

Manchester University (Q)

604 E College Avenue, North Manchester IN 46962-1225
County: Wabash FICE Identification: 001820
Unit ID: 151777
Telephone: (260) 982-5000 Carnegie Class: Bac-Diverse
FAX Number: (260) 982-5043 Calendar System: 4/1/4
URL: www.manchester.edu
Established: 1889 Annual Undergrad Tuition & Fees: $30,802
Enrollment: 1,536 Coed
Affiliation or Control: Church Of The Brethren IRS Status: 501(c)3
Highest Offering: Doctorate
Accreditation: NH, #CAATE, CAEPN, PHAR, SW

01 President .... Dr. David F. MCFADDEN
05 Vice President Academic Affairs .... Dr. Raylene M. ROSPOND
10 Chief Business Officer/VP Finance .... Mr. Clair W. KNAPP
30 Vice President College Advancement .... Mrs. Melanie B. HARMON
15 VP Human Res/Strategic Initiative .... Ms. Whitney A. CAUDILL
84 Asst VP for Enrollment/Marketing .... Mr. Adam R. HOHMAN
13 Asst Vice Pres/Chief Tech Ofcr .... Mr. Michael CASE
20 Associate Academic Dean .... Vacant
29 Exec Director of Alumni Relations .... Ms. Jennifer K. SHEPHERD
08 Director of the Library .... Ms. Jill LICHTSINN
06 Registrar .... Ms. Lila D. HAMMER
24 Director of Audio-Visual Services .... Mr. Stanley G. PITTMAN
38 Director of Counseling .... Ms. Danette NORMAN TILL
36 Dir Career/Professional Development .... Ms. Tish KALITA
39 Director of Residence Life .... Ms. Melanie E. LAWSON
42 University Pastor .... Mr. Bekah HOUFF
41 Athletic Director .... Mr. Rick ESPESET
19 Director of Security .... Mr. Harold NAPIER
44 Director of the Manchester Fund .... Ms. Janeen W. KOOI
37 Director of Student Financial Aid .... Ms. Sherri L. SHOCKEY
85 Dir Intercultural Svcs/Chf Div Ofcr .... Mr. Michael G. DIXON
26 Asst Director Media Relations .... Ms. Anne GREGORY
18 Director of Physical Plant/Grounds .... Mr. Pieter NARAGON
23 Director of Health Services .... Ms. Anna C. RICHISON
21 Senior Accountant .... Mr. Michael J. LECKRONE
32 Director Student Activities .... Ms. Shanon L. FAWBUSH
96 Director of Purchasing .... Mr. Quentin J. MOUDY
40 Campus Bookstore Manager .... Ms. Heather K. GOCHENAUR
04 Administrative Asst to President .... Mrs. Karen K. BRACE

Marian University (R)

3200 Cold Spring Road, Indianapolis IN 46222-1997
County: Marion FICE Identification: 001821
Unit ID: 151786
Telephone: (317) 955-6000 Carnegie Class: Masters/M
FAX Number: (317) 955-6448 Calendar System: Semester
URL: www.marian.edu
Established: 1851 Annual Undergrad Tuition & Fees: $31,500
Enrollment: 2,897 Coed
Affiliation or Control: Roman Catholic IRS Status: 501(c)3
Highest Offering: Doctorate
Accreditation: NH, ANEST, CAEPN, IACBE, NURSE, OSTEO

01 President .... Mr. Daniel J. ELSENER
05 Executive VP and Provost .... Dr. Thomas ENNEKING
45 VP Mission & Identity .... Mr. Adam SETMEYER
10 Sr VP Finance & Operations .... Mr. Greg GINDER
26 VP for Marketing Communications .... Mr. Mark APPLE
53 SVP Tchr Lrng Excel/Dn The Educ Col .... Dr. Kenith BRITT
32 VP Student Success & Engagement .... Ms. Ruth RODGERS
11 VP Administration/General Counsel .... Ms. Deborah LAWRENCE
111 VP Institutional Advancement .... Mr. John FINKE
63 VP and Dean College of Osteopathic .... Dr. Don SEFCIK
84 VP Enrollment Management .... Dr. Paul (PJ) WOOLSTON
20 Associate Provost .... Dr. Saib OTHMAN
20 Assistant Provost .... Mr. William HARTING
37 Director of Financial Aid .... Mr. Chad BIR
18 Exec Dir Facilities/Procurement .... Mr. Evan HAWKINS
41 Director of Athletics .... Mr. Steve DOWNING
29 Dir Alumni/Parent Engagement .... Ms. Cathy SILER
06 Registrar .... Ms. Jennifer SCHWARTZ
08 Library Director .... Ms. Rhonda HUISMAN
35 Student Activities Coordinator .... Mr. Candace LUEBBEHUSEN
19 Director of Safety & Police Svcs .... Mr. Scott RALPH
13 AVP & Chief Information Officer .... Mr. Ray STANLEY
27 Manager of Event Marketing and Spon .... Ms. Maggie KUCIK
36 Executive Director The Exchange .... Ms. Ellen WHITT
38 Director Academic Support Services .... Mrs. Marjorie BATIC
55 Exec Director Adult Programs .... Ms. Amy BENNETT
38 Director of Counseling Services .... Dr. Marla SMITH
23 Director of Health & Wellness Svcs .... Ms. Jan CARNAGHI
09 Director of Institutional Research .... Mr. William HARTING
15 Director of Human Resources .... Ms. Kimberly POHLMAN
21 Director of Business Services .... Ms. Alice SHELTON
40 Bookstore Manager .... Ms. Allison BONEZ
04 Executive Asst to President .... Ms. Cyndi KAMP

Martin University (S)

2186 North Sherman Drive, Indianapolis IN 46218
County: Marion FICE Identification: 021408
Unit ID: 151810
Telephone: (317) 543-3235 Carnegie Class: Bac-A&S
FAX Number: (317) 543-3257 Calendar System: Semester
URL: www.martin.edu
Established: 1977 Annual Undergrad Tuition & Fees: $12,536
Enrollment: 349 Coed
Affiliation or Control: Independent Non-Profit IRS Status: 501(c)3
Highest Offering: Master's
Accreditation: NH

01 President .... Dr. Eugene WHITE
05 Vice President Academic Affairs .. Dr. Charlesetta SMITH STALEY
09 VP of Institutional Effectiveness .... Dr. Brian STEUERWALD
10 VP Fiscal Affairs .... Mr. Michael MOOS
37 Director Financial Aid .... Ms. Virginia GOODWIN
32 Director Student & Enroll Services .... Tracey JACKSON
26 Dir of Univ Rels/Communications .... Ms. Jennifer MCCLOUD
113 Bursar .... Ms. Angela HARRINGTON-MARTIN

Mid-America College of Funeral Service (T)

3111 Hamburg Pike, Jeffersonville IN 47130-9630
County: Clark FICE Identification: 010618
Unit ID: 151962
Telephone: (812) 288-8878 Carnegie Class: Spec-4-yr-Other
FAX Number: (812) 288-5942 Calendar System: Quarter
URL: www.mid-america.edu
Established: 1980 Annual Undergrad Tuition & Fees: $11,150
Enrollment: 75 Coed
Affiliation or Control: Independent Non-Profit IRS Status: 501(c)3
Highest Offering: Baccalaureate
Accreditation: FUSER

01 President .... Dr. Mitch MITCHELL
32 Dean of Students/Financial Aid .... Ms. Alisa PERKINS
11 Office Manager .... Ms. Angela PERSINGER
08 Librarian .... Ms. Sonja PIERCE
07 Director of Admissions .... Mr. Michael MOELLER

Mid-America Reformed Seminary (U)

229 Seminary Drive, Dyer IN 46311-1069
County: Lake FICE Identification: 039893
Unit ID: 373030
Telephone: (219) 864-2400 Carnegie Class: Not Classified
FAX Number: (219) 864-2410 Calendar System: Semester
URL: www.midamerica.edu
Established: 1981 Annual Graduate Tuition & Fees: N/A
Enrollment: N/A Coed
Affiliation or Control: Independent Non-Profit IRS Status: 501(c)3
Highest Offering: Master's; No Undergraduates
Accreditation: THEOL, TRACS

01 President .... Dr. Cornelius VENEMA
32 Dean of Students .... Rev. Alan STRANGE
111 Vice President of Advancement .... Mr. Mike DECKINGA
11 Vice President of Operations .... Mr. Keith LEMAHIEU
36 Director of Apprenticeship Program .... Rev. Mark VANDERHART
84 Director of Enrollment Management .... Rev. Jeffrey DEBOER
108 Director Institutional Assessment .... Rev. Marcus MININGER
26 Manager Marketing/Digital/Pubs .... Mr. Jared LUTTJEBOER

National American University-Indianapolis (A)

3600 Woodview Terrace, Suite 200, Indianapolis IN 46268
Telephone: (800) 609-1430 Identification: 770393
Accreditation: &NH

† Branch campus of National American University, Rapid City, SD

Oakland City University (B)

138 N Lucretia Street, Oakland City IN 47660-1099
County: Gibson FICE Identification: 001824
Unit ID: 152099
Telephone: (812) 749-4781 Carnegie Class: Bac-Diverse
FAX Number: (812) 749-1233 Calendar System: Semester
URL: www.oak.edu
Established: 1885 Annual Undergrad Tuition & Fees: $23,400
Enrollment: 1,450 Coed
Affiliation or Control: Baptist IRS Status: 501(c)3
Highest Offering: Doctorate
Accreditation: NH, CAEPN, IACBE, THEOL

01 President ....Dr. Ray G. BARBER
11 Vice Pres Administration & Finance ....Dr. Susan LOCKWOOD
05 Provost ....Dr. Daniel DUNIVAN
10 Chief Financial Officer ....Mrs. Elizabeth BARBER
13 Assoc VP & Chief Info Officer ....Mr. Clint WOOLSEY
111 Vice President of Advancement ....Mr. Grady JONES
110 Assoc Vice Pres of Advancement ....Mr. Brian BAKER
20 Assistant Provost ....Mrs. Ely SENA-MARTIN
50 Dean School of Business ....Dr. Cathy ROBB
53 Dean School of Education ....Vacant
73 Dean Religious Studies ....Dr. Daniel DUNIVAN
49 Dean of Arts and Science ....Vacant
108 Director of Assessment ....Vacant
32 Director of Campus Life ....Mr. Brad KNOTTS
37 Director of Financial Aid ....Mrs. Nicole SHARP
56 Coordinator Adult Extend Learning ....Dr. Cathy ROBB
22 Compliance Officer ....Ms. Patricia ENDICOTT
88 Director of Correctional Education ....Mr. Theodore PEARSON
06 Registrar ....Mrs. Linda TIPTON
08 Director of Library ....Mrs. Denise PINNICK
26 Director of Mktg/Athletic Director ....Dr. Mike SANDIFAR
42 Campus Minister ....Vacant
18 Director of Maintenance ....Mr. Greg BURKE
15 Human Resources Coordinator ....Mrs. Cheryl YATES
19 Chief of Security ....Mr. Alec HENSLEY
29 Director of Alumni Affairs ....Ms. Susan SULLIVAN
36 Director of Directions Program ....Mrs. Charity JULIAN
35 Director Student Support Services ....Mrs. Tamara MILEY
21 Assistant Chief Financial Officer ....Mrs. Elizabeth CARLISLE
88 Supervisor of Collections ....Mrs. Anita MISKELL
88 Director of Housekeeping ....Mrs. Dorothy GRAPER
04 Administrative Asst to President ....Vacant
07 Director of Admissions ....Mr. Harrison CAMPBELL
105 Director Web Services ....Mrs. Andrea TURNER
28 Director of Diversity ....Mrs. Elisabet SENA-MARTIN

Purdue University Main Campus (C)

610 Purdue Mall, West Lafayette IN 47907-2040
County: Tippecanoe FICE Identification: 001825
Unit ID: 243780
Telephone: (765) 494-4600 Carnegie Class: DU-Highest
FAX Number: N/A Calendar System: Semester
URL: www.purdue.edu
Established: 1869 Annual Undergrad Tuition & Fees (In-State): $10,002
Enrollment: 40,472 Coed
Affiliation or Control: State IRS Status: 501(c)3
Highest Offering: Doctorate
Accreditation: NH, AAB, ART, AUD, CAATE, CACREP, CAEPN, CIDA, CLPSY, CONST, COPSY, CS, DIETC, DIETD, ENG, ENGR, ENGT, IPSY, LSAR, NAIT, NURSE, PHAR, SP, THEA, VET

01 President ....Mr. Mitchell E. DANIELS, JR.
10 Exec Vice President & Treasurer ....Mr. William E. SULLIVAN
05 Provost/Exec VP for Acad Affairs ....Dr. Debasish DUTTA
21 Sr VP Business Svcs/Asst Treas ....Mr. James S. ALMOND
13 Vice Pres Information Technology ....Dr. William G. McCARTNEY
15 Vice President Human Resources ....Mr. Denny DARROW
26 Vice President for Public Affairs ....Ms. Julie K. GRIFFITH
20 Int Vice Prov Student Acad Affairs ....Dr. Frank J. DOOLEY
20 Vice Pres Faculty Affairs ....Dr. Peter HOLLENBECK
08 Dean of Libraries ....Dr. James L. MULLINS
29 President & CEO Alumni Association ....Mr. Ralph AMOS
07 Dean Admiss/VP Enroll Mgmt ....Mr. Mitch WARREN
37 Director Financial Aid ....Mr. Ted E. MALONE

Purdue University North Central (D)

1401 S US 421, Westville IN 46391-9542
Telephone: (219) 785-5200 FICE Identification: 001826
Accreditation: &NH, ACBSP, CAEPN, ENG, ENGR, ENGT, NUR

† Branch Campus of Purdue University Northwest, Hammond, IN

Purdue University Northwest (E)

2200 169th Street, Hammond IN 46323-2094
County: Lake FICE Identification: 001827
Unit ID: 152248
Telephone: (219) 989-2370 Carnegie Class: Masters/L
FAX Number: (219) 989-2581 Calendar System: Semester
URL: www.pnw.edu
Established: 1946 Annual Undergrad Tuition & Fees (In-State): $7,478
Enrollment: 9,301 Coed
Affiliation or Control: State IRS Status: 501(c)3
Highest Offering: Doctorate
Accreditation: NH, CACREP, CAEPN, CEA, CS, ENG, ENGR, ENGT, MFCD, NAIT, NUR, @SW

01 Chancellor ....Dr. Thomas L. KEON
05 Vice Chanc Acad Affs & Provost ....Dr. Ralph O. MUELLER
10 Vice Chanc Finance & Admin ....Mr. Steve TURNER
111 Vice Chanc for Inst Advancement ....Dr. Regina D. BIDDINGS-MURO
13 Vice Chanc Info Services ....Mr. Tim WINDERS
32 Vice Chanc Enroll Mgmt & Stdnt Affs ....Dr. Carmen PANLILIO
46 Director of Research & Grad Stds ....Dr. Joy COLWELL
26 Assoc Vice Chanc Marketing ....Ms. Kris FALZONE
09 Int Exec Dir Ofc of Plng & Effectiv ....Dr. Becky STANKOWSKI
11 Asst Vice Chancellor for Admin Svcs ....Mr. Michael KULL
35 Assoc Vice Chanc Stdnt Affs/EOP ....Mr. Roy HAMILTON
15 Asst Vice Chanc Human Resources ....Ms. Susan MILLLER
79 Dean CHESS College of Humanities ....Ms. Elaine CAREY
54 Dean Col of Engr & Science ....Dr. Chris HOLFORD
72 Dean College of Technology ....Dr. Niaz LATIF
50 Dean College of Business ....Dr. Jane MUTCHLER
66 Dean College of Nursing ....Dr. Lisa HOPP
53 Dir School of Education ....Ms. Anne GREGORY
06 Registrar ....Ms. Cheryl ARROYO
114 Assc Comptroller Acct/Budget Svcs ....Ms. Donna ADELSPERGER
37 Int Exec Dir Fin Student Svcs ....Ms. Freda WHISENTON-COMER
41 Director of Athletics ....Mr. Richard J. COSTELLO
38 Director Counseling Center ....Dr. Kenneth JACKSON
08 Dir Research/Learning & Res Svcs ....Ms. Tammy GUERRERO
29 Dir Alumni Affairs & Advancement ....Ms. Megan DAVIS-OCHI
19 University Police ....Chief Patricia NOWAK
85 Asst Vice International Affairs ....Dr. Dallas KENNY
96 Dir of Procurement/General Services ....Mr. Philip BROWN
39 Director Housing Residential Educ ....Ms. Scott IVERSON
92 Dean Honors Program ....Dr. Rowan JOHN
84 Assoc Dean Enroll Mgmt & Grad Pgms ....Dr. Lori FELDMAN
04 Sr Exec Asst Strategic Initiatives ....Ms. Daphne D. ROBINSON
102 Dir Advance Resource/Donor Steward ....Ms. Mary Jane DOPP
104 Education Abroad Coordinator ....Ms. Judy MOORE
105 Int Dir Tech Infrastruc Services ....Ms. Heather ZAMOJSKI
25 Exec Director CVIS ....Dr. Chenn ZHOU
28 Director Ofc Equity & Diversity ....Ms. Linda B. KNOX
36 Director Career Dev & Services ....Ms. Natalie CONNORS
90 Asst Vice Chanc Lrng Tech ....Ms. Heather ZAMOJSKI
109 Dir of Procurement/Auxil Services ....Ms. Elizabeth DEPEW
88 Director of Public Safety ....Mr. Brian MILLER
88 Sr Direct Space Mgmt ....Ms. Michelle GRANT
88 Manager Strategic Events ....Ms. Ashley GERODIMOS
88 Lead Security Analyst ....Ms. Katie GUTIERREZ
88 Exec Dir Enterprise App Svcs ....Mr. Paul JOHANSEN
18 Chief Facilities/Physical Plant ....Mr. Steve TURNER

Radiological Technologies University-VT (F)

100 E. Wayne Street, Suite 140, South Bend IN 46601
County: St. Joseph Identification: 667156
Telephone: (574) 232-2408 Carnegie Class: Not Classified
FAX Number: (574) 232-2200 Calendar System: Semester
URL: www.rtuvt.com
Established: 2009 Annual Undergrad Tuition & Fees: N/A
Enrollment: N/A Coed
Affiliation or Control: Proprietary IRS Status: Proprietary
Highest Offering: Master's
Accreditation: ACICS, RADDOS

01 President ....Brent D. MURPHY
11 Dir of Administrative Services ....Betsy DATEMA

Rose-Hulman Institute of Technology (G)

5500 Wabash Avenue, Terre Haute IN 47803-3920
County: Vigo FICE Identification: 001830
Unit ID: 152318
Telephone: (812) 877-1511 Carnegie Class: Spec-4-yr-Eng
FAX Number: (812) 877-9925 Calendar System: Quarter
URL: www.rose-hulman.edu
Established: 1874 Annual Undergrad Tuition & Fees: $46,210
Enrollment: 2,354 Coed
Affiliation or Control: Independent Non-Profit IRS Status: 501(c)3
Highest Offering: Master's
Accreditation: NH, CS, ENG

01 President ....Dr. James C. CONWELL
10 Senior VP/Chief Admin Officer ....Mr. Robert A. COONS
05 Provost & Vice Pres Academic Affs ....Dr. Anne HOUTMAN
111 VP Inst Advancement ....Mr. Steven BRADY
32 VP Student Affs & Dean of Students ....Mr. Erik Z. HAYES
26 VP Communications/Marketing ....Ms. Mary W. ATTEBERRY
21 Assoc VP for Finance/Controller ....Mr. Matthew D. DAVIS
84 Vice President Enrollment Mgmt ....Mr. James A. GOECKER
88 Vice Pres of Corp Eng/Ventures ....Dr. Elizabeth M. HAGERMAN
88 Associate Dean of Innovation ....Dr. William KLINE
20 Dean of Faculty ....Dr. Russell L. WARLEY
88 Dir for Micronano Devices & Sys ....Dr. Azad SIAHMAKOUN
88 Associate Dean of Learning & Tech ....Dr. Kay C. DEE
104 Dir of Study Abroad/Intl Exchanges ....Ms. Maria DEL MAR APONTE
13 Vice Pres Info Tech and CIO ....Dr. Wayne DENNISON
18 Sr Director Facilities Operations ....Mr. Michael A. TAYLOR
36 Dir Career Services/Employer Rels ....Mr. Kevin L. HEWERDINE
07 Dean of Admissions ....Ms. Lisa M. NORTON
29 Executive Director Alumni Affairs ....Mr. Benjamin PAOLILLO
88 Int Dean of Cost Cutting Programs ....Dr. Julia M. WILLIAMS
15 Director of Human Resources ....Ms. Kimberly D. MILLER
37 Director of Financial Aid ....Ms. Melinda L. MIDDLETON
41 Director of Athletics ....Mr. Jeffrey L. JENKINS
28 Director Center for Diversity ....Ms. Janice FENN
30 Executive Director of Development ....Mr. Chris AIMONE
110 Exec Director Advancement Service ....Ms. Jennifer KENZOR
06 Registrar ....Ms. Jan PINK
08 Sr Director Logan Library & Info ....Ms. Bernadette EWEN
19 Director of Public Safety ....Mr. John S. WOLFE
40 Bookstore Manager ....Ms. Sheryl E. FULK
85 Dir of Intl Student Services ....Ms. Karen A. DEGRANGE
04 Exec Asst to the President/BOT ....Ms. Amy TIMBERMAN
88 Director of Business Operations ....Ms. Linda L. PRICE
88 Director Administrative Services ....Mr. Bryan T. BROMSTRUP
09 Director of Institutional Research ....Dr. Timothy CHOW
102 Dir of Corp & Foundation Relations ....Mr. Brandon M. ZOLLNER
35 Assoc VP & Dean of Student Affairs ....Mr. Thomas D. MILLER
35 Director of Student Services ....Ms. Kristen J. LOYD
44 Director of Donor Relations ....Ms. Tammy COONS
24 Instructional Technology Manager ....Ms. Cheryl DAVIDSON
24 Emerging Digital Technologies Mgr ....Mr. Alan WARD
38 Director of Counseling Services ....Dr. Michael LATTA
108 Int Sr Dir Inst Rsrch/Plng/Assess ....Dr. Matthew D. LOVELL

St. Anthony School of Echocardiography (H)

1201 S. Main Street, Crown Point IN 46307
County: Lake Identification: 667119
Telephone: (219) 757-6132 Carnegie Class: Not Classified
FAX Number: (219) 681-6725 Calendar System: Semester
URL: https://www.franciscanhealth.org/EchoSchoolNWI
Established: 2004 Annual Undergrad Tuition & Fees: N/A
Enrollment: N/A Coed
Affiliation or Control: Independent Non-Profit IRS Status: 501(c)3
Highest Offering: Associate Degree
Accreditation: DMS

01 Co-Program Director ....Lori HULT
05 Co-Program Director ....Karin KOLISZ

Saint Mary-of-the-Woods College (I)

1 St Mary of Woods College,
St Mary of the Woods IN 47876-1099
County: Vigo FICE Identification: 001835
Unit ID: 152381
Telephone: (812) 535-5151 Carnegie Class: Bac-Diverse
FAX Number: (812) 535-5231 Calendar System: Semester
URL: www.smwc.edu
Established: 1840 Annual Undergrad Tuition & Fees: $28,932
Enrollment: 873 Coed
Affiliation or Control: Roman Catholic IRS Status: 501(c)3
Highest Offering: Master's
Accreditation: NH, MUS, NURSE

01 President ....Dr. Dottie KING
30 VP for Advancement ....Ms. Karen DYER
10 CFO ....Ms. Jaclyn WALTER
05 Vice President for Academic Affairs ....Dr. Janet CLARK
11 Vice President for Operations ....Ms. Vicki KOSOWSKY
84 Vice Pres for Enrollment Management ....Mr. Brennan RANDOLPH
06 Registrar ....Ms. Deanna BABCOCK
08 Director of the Library ....Ms. Judy TRIBBLE
29 Senior Dir Advancement/Alumni Rels ....Ms. Susan TURNER
26 Executive Dir of College Relations ....Ms. Dee REED
07 Exec Director of Campus Admissions ....Mr. Ryan McDONALD
106 Director Woods Online Program ....Ms. Gwen HAGEMEYER
13 Sr Dir Information & Academic Svcs ....Ms. Mary SAMM
36 Director of Career Development ....Ms. Susan GRESHAM
15 Director Human Resources ....Ms. Diana WARREN
32 Director of Student Affairs ....Ms. Aimee JANSSEN-ROBINSON
37 Director Financial Aid ....Ms. Darla HOPPER
44 Dir Major and Planned Gifts ....Vacant
64 Dir Grad Pgm Music Therapy ....Ms. Tracy RICHARDSON
88 Dir Grad Pgm Art Therapy ....Ms. Kathy GOTSHALL
88 Dir Grad Pgm Leadership Development ....Ms. Susan DECKER
09 Director of Institutional Research ....Mr. Mike KING

Saint Mary's College (J)

Notre Dame IN 46556
County: Saint Joseph FICE Identification: 001836
Unit ID: 152390
Telephone: (574) 284-4000 Carnegie Class: Bac-A&S
FAX Number: (574) 284-4716 Calendar System: Semester
URL: www.saintmarys.edu
Established: 1844 Annual Undergrad Tuition & Fees: $38,880
Enrollment: 1,657 Female
Affiliation or Control: Roman Catholic IRS Status: 501(c)3
Highest Offering: Doctorate
Accreditation: NH, ART, CAEPN, MUS, NURSE, @SP, SW

01 President ....Ms. Janice A. CERVELLI
04 Special Asst to the President ....Ms. Kara KELLY

05 Int Provost/Sr VP Academic Affairs .... Dr. Nancy NEKVASIL
26 Vice President College Relations .... Ms. Shari M. RODRIGUEZ
32 Vice President for Student Affairs ....Ms. Karen A. JOHNSON
10 Vice Pres Finance & Administration .... Ms. Susan BOLT
84 Vice Pres for Enrollment Management .... Ms. Mona BOWE
88 Vice President for Mission .... Ms. Judith FEAN
89 Associate Dean for Advising .... Ms. Susan VANEK
06 Registrar .... Mr. Todd NORRIS
07 Director of Admission ....Ms. Sarah DVORAK
08 Director of Library ....Ms. Janet S. FORE
09 Director of Institutional Research ....Mr. Daniel FLOWERS
29 Director of Alumnae Relations .... Ms. Kara O'LEARY
37 Director of Financial Aid ....Ms. Kathleen M. BROWN
27 Director of Media Relations ....Vacant
38 Director of Women's Health ....Ms. Elizabeth FOURMAN
13 Chief Information Officer ....Mr. Michael BOEHM
15 Director of Human Resources .... Ms. Kris URSCHEL
19 Director of Safety & Security .... Mr. David GARIEPY
40 Manager Bookstore ....Ms. Judith MCKEE
41 Director of Athletics ....Ms. Julie SCHROEDER-BIEK
42 Director of Campus Ministry ....Ms. Regina WILSON
18 Director of Facilities .... Mr. Benjamin BOWMAN
96 Director of Purchasing ....Ms. Kathleen CARLSON
88 Director of Student Involvement ....Ms. Brittany HOUSE
85 Director of Multicultural Program ....Ms. Gloria JENKINS
43 College Counsel ....Vacant
04 Spec Asst to Pres Strategic Plng ....Mr. George KEEGAN
101 Secretary to the President .... Ms. Vicki BRIGGS

Saint Meinrad School of Theology (A)

200 Hill Drive, St. Meinrad IN 47577-1030

County: Spencer — FICE Identification: 007276
Unit ID: 152451
Telephone: (812) 357-6611 — Carnegie Class: Spec-4-yr-Faith
FAX Number: (812) 357-6964 — Calendar System: Semester
URL: www.saintmeinrad.edu
Established: 1861 — Annual Graduate Tuition & Fees: N/A
Enrollment: 195 — Coed
Affiliation or Control: Roman Catholic — IRS Status: 501(c)3
Highest Offering: Master's; No Undergraduates
Accreditation: NH, THEOL

01 President & Rector .... Rev. Denis ROBINSON, OSB
03 Vice Rector .... Rev. Tobias COLGAN, OSB
05 Academic Dean .... Dr. Robert ALVIS
42 Director of Spiritual Formation ....Rev. Peter MARSHALL
20 Dir of Graduate Theology Programs ....Sr. Jeana VISEL, OSB
30 Vice President of Development .... Mr. Michael ZIEMIANSKI
10 Business Manager & Treasurer ....Mrs. Lisa CASTLEBURY
08 Library Director ....Dr. Daniel KOLB
06 Registrar .... Mrs. Donna BALBACH
88 Dir of Clergy Formation Pgm .... Dr. Patrick COOPER
114 Director of Budget ....Mrs. Pam DOWLAND
37 Director of Student Financial Aid ....Mrs. Ruth KRESS
26 Director of Communications ....Mrs. Mary Jeanne SCHUMACHER
29 Director of Alumni Relations .... Mr. Christian MOCEK
38 Director of Student Counseling Ctr .... Sr. Diane PHARO, SCN
23 Director of Health Services ....Ms. Ann ROHLEDER
04 Executive Secretary .... Mrs. Karen SCHERZER
13 Chief Info Technology Officer (CIO) .... Mr. Dave GRAMELSPACHER
18 Chief Facilities/Physical Plant ....Mr. Andy HAGEDORN
110 Director of Development .... Mr. Duane SCHAEFER
112 Director of Planned Giving .... Mr. Darren SROUFE
105 Director Web Services ....Mrs. Mary Jeanne SCHUMACHER
106 Dir Online Education/E-learning ....Sr. Jeana VISEL, OSB
15 Director Human Resources .... Mr. Mike GRAMELSPACHER
19 Director Security/Safety ....Mr. Andy HAGEDONR
07 Director of Admissions ....Dr. John SCHLACHTER

St. Vincent College of Health Professions (B)

2001 West 86th Street, Indianapolis IN 46260

County: Marion — Identification: 667315
Telephone: (317) 338-3879 — Carnegie Class: Not Classified
FAX Number: (317) 338-3720 — Calendar System: Semester
Established: 2015 — Annual Undergrad Tuition & Fees: N/A
Enrollment: N/A — Coed
Affiliation or Control: Independent Non-Profit — IRS Status: 501(c)3
Highest Offering: Associate Degree
Accreditation: ABHES, EMT, RAD

01 President ....Dr. Jeffrey ROTHENBERG

Taylor University (C)

West 236 Reade Avenue, Upland IN 46989-1001

County: Grant — FICE Identification: 001838
Unit ID: 152530
Telephone: (765) 998-2751 — Carnegie Class: Bac-Diverse
FAX Number: (765) 998-4910 — Calendar System: 4/1/4
URL: www.taylor.edu
Established: 1846 — Annual Undergrad Tuition & Fees: $31,472
Enrollment: 2,168 — Coed
Affiliation or Control: Independent Non-Profit — IRS Status: 501(c)3
Highest Offering: Master's
Accreditation: NH, CAEPN, CEA, ENG, MUS, SW

01 President .... Dr. Paul Lowell HAINES
45 Special Assistant to the President .... Mr. Ron SUTHERLAND
05 Provost ....Dr. Jeffrey MOSHIER
111 VP for Advancement .... Mr. Rex BENNETT
32 VP Student Development ....Dr. Skip TRUDEAU
84 VP Enroll Mgmt & Marketing ....Mr. Stephen MORTLAND
10 VP for Business & Finance .... Mr. Stephen OLSON
20 Vice Provost ....Dr. Jeff GROELING
49 Dean Sch Hum/Arts & Biblical Stds ....Dr. Michael HAMMOND
83 Dean Sch of Soc Sci/Educ & Bus ....Dr. Rhoda SOMMERS
81 Dean Sch Natural & Applied Sciences .... Dr. William TOLL
104 Dean International Programs ....Dr. Charles BRAINER
13 Chief Information Officer .... Mr. Rob LINEHAN
41 Director of Athletics .... Mr. Kyle GOULD
20 Dean Faculty Development/Dir BCTLE .... Dr. Barb BIRD
88 Senior Director for Campaigns .... Mr. David RITCHIE
30 Exec Director of Development ....Mr. Mike FALDER
29 Exec Dir for Alumni Relations .... Ms. Dara BERKHALTER
37 Assoc Dean Enroll Mgmt/Dir Fin Aid .... Mr. Timothy NACE
08 University Librarian .... Mr. Daniel BOWELL
35 Dean of Students ....Mr. Jesse BROWN
44 Director Taylor Scholarship Fund ....Vacant
39 Dir Residence Life ....Mr. Scott BARRETT
36 Director Calling and Career Office ....Mr. Jeff AUPPERLE
06 Registrar ....Ms. Janet ROGERS
106 Director of Online Learning ....Ms. Carrie MEYER
42 Campus Pastor .... Mr. Jon CAVANAGH
15 Asst Director of Human Resources ....Ms. April EVANS
07 Exec Director Admissions .... Ms. Amy BARNETT
18 Director of Physical Plant .... Mr. Greg ELEY
38 Interim Dir of Counseling Ctr ....Ms. Caroline POLAND
19 Chief of Police/Taylor Police .... Mr. Jeff WALLACE
09 Director IR/Assoc Registrar ....Dr. Edwin WELCH
21 Controller ....Mr. David LLOYD
108 Director Assessment/Quality Improv ....Dr. Kim CASE
88 Payroll Manager ....Ms. Toni NEWLIN
114 University Bursar ....Ms. Cathy MOORMAN
35 Dean Experiential Learning ....Dr. Drew MOSER
105 Assoc Dir of Enterprise Systems .... Mr. Corey COOPER

TCM International Institute (D)

6337 Hollister Drive, Indianapolis IN 46224

County: Marion — Identification: 666333
Telephone: (317) 299-0333 — Carnegie Class: Not Classified
FAX Number: (317) 290-8607 — Calendar System: Semester
URL: www.tcmi.org
Established: 1991 — Annual Graduate Tuition & Fees: N/A
Enrollment: N/A — Coed
Affiliation or Control: Independent Non-Profit — IRS Status: 501(c)3
Highest Offering: Master's; No Undergraduates
Accreditation: NH

01 President ....Dr. Tony TWIST
05 Academic Affairs Manager ....Ms. Victoria BOJONCA
06 Registrar ....Ms. Victoria BOJONCA
10 Director of Finance .... Ms. Julie RICE

Trine University (E)

1 University Avenue, Angola IN 46703-1764

County: Steuben — FICE Identification: 001839
Unit ID: 152567
Telephone: (260) 665-4100 — Carnegie Class: Bac-Diverse
FAX Number: (260) 665-4292 — Calendar System: Semester
URL: www.trine.edu
Established: 1884 — Annual Undergrad Tuition & Fees: $30,960
Enrollment: 3,395 — Coed
Affiliation or Control: Independent Non-Profit — IRS Status: 501(c)3
Highest Offering: Doctorate
Accreditation: NH, ACBSP, CAEPN, ENG, PTA

01 President ....Dr. Earl D. BROOKS, II
03 Senior Vice President ....Mr. Mike BOCK
05 Vice President for Academic Affairs ....Dr. Allen HERSEL
10 Vice President Finance .... Ms. Jody GREER
84 Vice Pres Enrollment Management .... Mr. Scott GOPLIN
32 Vice President for Student Services ....Mr. Randy WHITE
26 VP Univ Marketing/Communications ....Mr. Dave JARZYNA
51 Asst Vice Pres for Adult Learning ....Dr. Jean DELLER
49 Dean Jannen School of Arts & Sci .... Ms. Amy NICHOLLS
107 Dean of Professional Studies ....Mr. Craig LAKER
15 Human Resources ....Ms. Jamie NORTON
41 Athletic Director ....Mr. Matt LAND
06 Registrar ....Ms. Debra F. HELMSING
04 Assistant to the President ....Ms. Gretchen MILLER
37 Director Student Financial Planning ....Ms. Kim BENNETT
08 Director of the Library ....Ms. Kristina BREWER
36 Director of Placement/Coop Educ .... Ms. Linda COOPER
09 Director Inst Planning/Analysis ....Ms. Christina ZUMBRUN

Union Bible College (F)

PO Box 900, Westfield IN 46074

County: Hamilton — Identification: 667253
Telephone: (317) 896-9324 — Carnegie Class: Not Classified
FAX Number: (317) 867-0784 — Calendar System: Semester
URL: www.ubca.org
Established: 1911 — Annual Undergrad Tuition & Fees: N/A
Enrollment: N/A — Coed
Affiliation or Control: Interdenominational — IRS Status: 501(c)3
Highest Offering: Baccalaureate
Accreditation: @BI

01 President .... C. Adam BUCKLER
05 Vice Pres Academic Affairs .... John WHITAKER
10 Int Finance Director .... C. Adam BUCKLER
11 Director of Operations ....Greg HOBELMAN
32 Dean of Student Life ....Joe CAREY
09 Director of Institutional Research ....Isabel RUNDELL
06 Registrar .... Lisa BURKET
07 Director of Admissions ....Phil HOARD

University of Evansville (G)

1800 Lincoln Avenue, Evansville IN 47722-1586

County: Vanderburgh — FICE Identification: 001795
Unit ID: 150534
Telephone: (812) 488-2000 — Carnegie Class: Masters/S
FAX Number: (812) 488-2320 — Calendar System: Semester
URL: www.evansville.edu
Established: 1854 — Annual Undergrad Tuition & Fees: $33,966
Enrollment: 2,495 — Coed
Affiliation or Control: United Methodist — IRS Status: 501(c)3
Highest Offering: Doctorate
Accreditation: NH, #ARCPA, CAATE, CAEP, CS, ENG, MUS, NUR, PTA, PTAA

01 President ....Dr. Thomas A. KAZEE
05 Exec VP Academic Affairs .... Dr. Michael AUSTIN
30 VP Development ....Ms. Abigail WERLING
10 VP Fiscal Affairs & Admin ....Ms. Donna TEAGUE
32 VP Student Affairs/Dean of Students .... Dr. Dana CLAYTON
84 Vice President Enrollment Services .... Dr. Shane DAVIDSON
20 Asst VP Academic Affairs ....Ms. Paula HELDT
20 Asst VP Academic Affairs ....Ms. Tracey FOLDEN
35 Asst VP Student Affs/Dir Res Life ....Mr. Michael A. TESSIER
13 Dir of Technology Services .... Mr. Michael SMITH
49 Dean of Arts & Sciences .... Dr. Ray LUTGRING
50 Dean of Business Administration ....Dr. Greg RAWSKI
53 Dean of Educ/Health Science .... Ms. Mary KESSLER
54 Dean Engineering/Computer Science .... Dr. Brian SWENTY
51 Director of Adult Education .... Ms. Lindsay ROBERTS
85 Exec Dir International Programs ....Dr. Wesley MILNER
41 Director of Athletics .... Mr. Mark SPENCER
88 Dir of Content Development .... Ms. Amanda CAMPBELL
09 Dir Institutional Effectiveness ....Mr. Chul LEE
06 University Registrar .... Ms. Jennifer BRIGGS
08 University Librarian .... Mr. Robb WALTNER
42 University Chaplain .... Rev. Tammy GIESELMAN
11 Director of Administrative Services ....Mr. Mark J. LOGEL
29 Director of Alumni/Parent Relations .... Ms. Sylvia Y. DEVAULT
36 Director of Career Svcs/Placement ....Mr. C. Gene WELLS
38 Director of Counseling/Health Educ .... Ms. Sylvia T. BUCK
37 Director of Financial Aid .... Ms. Cathleen WRIGHT
15 Director of Human Resources .... Mr. Keith GEHLHAUSEN
18 Dir of Facilities Mgmt & Planning ....Mr. Chad MILLER
19 Director of Safety & Security ....Mr. Harold P. MATTHEWS
104 Director of Harlaxton Programs .... Ms. Holly CARTER
40 Director of Bookstore .... Mr. Douglas GUSTWILLER
28 Chief Diversity Officer ....Ms. LaNeeca WILLIAMS
110 Director of Development ....Mr. Scott A. GILREATH
121 Director of Academic Advising ... Ms. Deborah A. KASSENBROCK
35 Director of Student Engagement ....Mr. Geoffrey M. EDWARDS
07 Director of Admissions ....Mr. Kenton HARGIS
04 Assistant to the President .... Ms. Patricia A. LIPPERT
101 Assistant Secretary of the Board ....Ms. Rebecca SIMPSON

University of Indianapolis (H)

1400 E Hanna Avenue, Indianapolis IN 46227-3697

County: Marion — FICE Identification: 001804
Unit ID: 151263
Telephone: (317) 788-3368 — Carnegie Class: Masters/L
FAX Number: (317) 788-3300 — Calendar System: Semester
URL: www.uindy.edu
Established: 1902 — Annual Undergrad Tuition & Fees: $27,420
Enrollment: 5,504 — Coed
Affiliation or Control: United Methodist — IRS Status: 501(c)3
Highest Offering: Doctorate
Accreditation: NH, ACBSP, ART, CAATE, CAEPN, CLPSY, COARC, EXSC, MIDWF, MUS, NURSE, OT, PTA, PTAA, SW

01 President ....Dr. Robert L. MANUEL
05 Exec VP Academic Affairs/Provost ....Dr. Stephen KOLISON
84 Exec VP for Campus Affs/Enroll Svcs ....Mr. Mark T. WEIGAND
10 VP of Business & Finance/Treasurer .... Mr. Michael L. HOLSTEIN
26 VP Communications & Marketing ....Dr. Jeanette DEDIEMAR
111 Vice President for Univ Advancement ....Mr. Christopher H. MOLLOY
31 Assoc VP of External Relations .... Mr. Corey WILSON
41 VP for Intercollegiate Athletics ....Dr. Sue C. WILLEY
42 Dean Ecumenical and Interfaith Pgm ....Dr. Michael G. CARTWRIGHT
43 Vice President & General Counsel ....Ms. Andrea NEWSOM
32 VP for Stdnt/Campus Affs/Dn of Std ....Ms. Kory M. VITANGELI
100 Special Asst to the President .... Ms. Lara G. MANN
04 Executive Administrative Asst .... Ms. Angela PRESNELL
36 Assoc VP of Professional Edge ....Mr. Corey L. WILSON
09 Asst VP of Inst Planning & Rsrch .... Dr. Patrick ALLES
35 Assistant Dean of Students ....Ms. Julie PAKENHAM
06 Registrar ....Ms. Josh HAYES
13 Associate VP Information Systems ......Mr. Steven R. HERRIFORD
49 Dean College of Arts & Sciences ....Dr. Travis MILLER
50 Dean School of Business ....Dr. Lawrence BELCHER
53 Dean School of Education .... Dr. Colleen MULHOLLAND
66 Dean School of Nursing .... Ms. Norma HALL

76 Dean College of Health Sciences .... Dr. Stephanie KELLY
51 Dean School of Adult Learning .... Dr. Lashun ARON
55 Dean Psychological Sciences .... Dr. Anita J. THOMAS
20 Assoc Provost for Academic Systems .... Dr. Mary Beth BAGG
20 Int Assoc Prov Rsrch/Grad/Acad Ptnr .... Ms. Ellen MILLER
108 Assoc VP for Accreditation .... Dr. Mary C. MOORE
07 Associate VP for Admissions .... Mr. Ronald W. WILKS
08 Library Director .... Vacant
15 Director Human Resources .... Mrs. Erin P. FARRELL
37 Assoc VP or Financial Aid .... Mrs. Linda B. HANDY
58 Director Graduate Business Pgms .... Mr. Stephen A. TOKAR
18 Executive Director Physical Plant .... Mrs. Pamela L. FOX
19 Director Safety & Police Services .... Mr. David K. SELBY
31 Director of Service Learning .... Dr. Marianna K. FOULKROD
42 Chaplain/Dir Lantz Center .... Rev. Jeremiah GIBBS
29 Assoc VP Alumni Engagement .... Mr. Andy M. KOCHER
85 Director International Division .... Ms. Marilyn O. CHASE
24 Asst VP of Information Systems .... Mr. Robert A. JONES
38 Director Counseling Center .... Dr. Kelly M. MILLER
40 Bookstore Manager .... Vacant
45 Director of Facilities & Planning .... Ms. Andrea NEWSOM

University of Notre Dame (A)

400 Main Building, Notre Dame IN 46556
County: Saint Joseph FICE Identification: 001840
Unit ID: 152080
Telephone: (574) 631-5000 Carnegie Class: DU-Highest
FAX Number: (574) 631-6700 Calendar System: Semester
URL: www.nd.edu
Established: 1842 Annual Undergrad Tuition & Fees: $49,685
Enrollment: 12,292 Coed
Affiliation or Control: Roman Catholic IRS Status: 501(c)3
Highest Offering: Doctorate
Accreditation: **NH**, ART, CLPSY, CS, ENG, IPSY, LAW, THEOL

01 President .... Rev. John I. JENKINS, CSC
05 Provost .... Dr. Thomas G. BURISH
03 Executive Vice President .... Dr. John F. AFFLECK-GRAVES
20 Vice Pres/Sr Associate Provost .... Dr. Christine M. MAZIAR
20 Vice Pres/Associate Provost .... Dr. Maura A. RYAN
89 VP/Assoc Prov/Dean First Year Stdts .... Dr. Hugh R. PAGE, JR.
82 VP/Provost Internationalization .... Dr. Michael PIPPENGER
32 Vice President for Student Affairs .... Ms. Erin HOFFMANN HARDING
10 Vice President for Finance .... Ms. Shannon B. CULLINAN
46 Vice President for Research .... Dr. Robert J. BERNHARD
43 Vice President & General Counsel .... Ms. Marianne CORR
115 Vice Pres/Chief Investment Ofcr .... Mr. Scott C. MALPASS
41 Vice Pres & Director of Athletics .... Mr. John 'Jack' B. SWARBRICK, JR.
15 Vice Pres Human Resources .... Mr. Robert K. MCQUADE
26 Vice President University Relations .... Mr. Louis M. NANNI
13 VP & Chief Information Officer .... Mr. Ronald D. KRAEMER
88 VP Mission Engagmnt/Church Affairs .... Rev. William M. LIES, CSC
58 VP/Assoc Prov/Dean Graduate Sch .... Dr. Laura CARLSON
45 VP Strategic Planning .... Mr. David C. BAILEY
100 Chief of Staff .... Ms. Ann M. FIRTH
28 Chief Diversity Officer .... Mr. Eric LOVE
84 Assoc VP Undergraduate Enrollment .... Mr. Donald C. BISHOP
18 VP Facilities & Design .... Mr. Douglas K. MARSH
06 Registrar .... Mr. Charles T. HURLEY
96 Director Procurement .... Mr. Vaibhav AGARWAL
50 Dean of College of Business .... Dr. Roger D. HUANG
61 Dean of Law School .... Prof. Nell J. NEWTON
54 Dean College of Engineering .... Dr. Peter K. KILPATRICK
49 Dean of Arts & Letters .... Dr. John T. MCGREEVY
81 Dean of Science .... Dr. Mary E. GALVIN
48 Dean of Architecture .... Dr. Michael N. LYKOUDIS
88 Dean First Year of Studies .... Dr. Hugh R. PAGE
29 Exec Director Alumni Assoc .... Ms. Dolly DUFFY
08 Dir of University Libraries .... Ms. Diane PARR WALKER
27 Chief Communications Executive .... Mr. Paul BROWNE
42 Director of Campus Ministry .... Rev. Peter M. MCCORMICK, CSC
37 Dir of Student Financial Aid .... Ms. Mary B. NUCCIARONE
36 Director of Career Center .... Vacant
38 Director of Counseling Center .... Dr. Susan C. STEIBE-PASALICH
19 Director of Security/Police .... Ms. Keri Kei SHIBATA
07 Director of Admissions .... Mr. Robert MUNDY
101 Secretary of the Institution/Board .... Ms. Beth SWIFT
09 Director of Institutional Research .... Ms. Eva NANCE
102 Dir Foundation/Corporate Relations .... Mr. Rudy REYES
104 Director Study Abroad .... Ms. Kathleen OPEL
39 Director Student Housing .... Ms. Karen M. KENNEDY
04 Administrative Asst to President .... Ms. Sarah A. GOTSCH
86 Director Government Relations .... Mr. Timothy D. SEXTON

University of Saint Francis (B)

2701 Spring Street, Fort Wayne IN 46808-3994
County: Allen FICE Identification: 001832
Unit ID: 152336
Telephone: (260) 399-7700 Carnegie Class: Masters/M
FAX Number: N/A Calendar System: Semester
URL: www.sf.edu
Established: 1890 Annual Undergrad Tuition & Fees: $28,310
Enrollment: 2,240 Coed
Affiliation or Control: Roman Catholic IRS Status: 501(c)3
Highest Offering: Doctorate
Accreditation: **NH**, ACBSP, ADNUR, ANEST, ARCPA, ART, CAEPN, @DIETC, MLTAD, NURSE, PTAA, RAD, SURGT, SW

01 President .... Sr. M. Elise KRISS, OSF
05 Vice President Academic Affairs .... Dr. J. Andrew PRALL
11 Vice President Administration .... Mrs. Teresa A. SORDELET
111 Vice Pres Institutional Advancement .... Dr. Matthew J. SMITH
10 Vice President Finance & Operations .... Mr. Richard A. BIENZ
20 Assoc VP Academic Affairs .... Dr. Joseph M. FRIONA
84 VP Enrollment Management .... Vacant
45 Assoc VP Inst Research/Planning .... Dr. Stephanie J. OETTING
26 Assoc Vice President Marketing .... Mrs. Trois K. HART
88 Assistant VP Mission Integration .... Sr. M. Anita HOLZMER, OSF
50 Dean Keith Busse School of Business .... Dr. Robert W. LEE
57 Int Dean School of Creative Arts .... Mrs. Colleen HUDDLESON
17 Dean School of Health Sciences .... Dr. Mindy J. YODER
49 Dean School Liberal Arts & Sciences .... Dr. Lance D. RICHEY
12 Dean Crown Point Site .... Dr. Marsha M. KING
32 Dean of Students .... Mr. Donald B. APPIARIUS
35 Associate Dean Campus Life .... Mrs. Elizabeth A. GROMAN
121 Assistant Dean Student Success .... Mrs. Linda A. JACKSON
21 Controller .... Mr. Craig M. TEETSEL
06 Registrar .... Mr. Francis P. CONNOR
42 Chaplain .... Fr. David L. MEINZEN
91 Interim Exec Dir Univ Technology .... Mr. Mark ROBBINS
106 Dir Adult/Online Enrollment Svcs .... Mrs. Michelle L. KUHLHORST
29 Director Alumni Relations .... Ms. Melissa S. EASTMAN
41 Director Athletics .... Mr. Michael H. MCCAFFREY
42 Director Campus Ministry .... Vacant
102 Dir Corp/Found Relations and Grants .... Mrs. Lynnette M. MCKENNA FRAZIER
30 Director Development .... Mr. Matthew C. ROWAN
88 Director Employer Relations .... Mrs. Natalie M. WAGONER
13 Dir Enterprise App/Tech Services .... Mr. A. Drew REPP
88 Dir Environ Health/Safety/Risk Mgt .... Mr. Randy D. TROY
37 Director Financial Aid .... Mrs. Michelle L. NISUN
97 Director General Education .... Mrs. Tricia J. VANDERLEE BUGAJSKI, OFS
88 Dir Hlth Sci Strategic Initiatives .... Dr. Lorene R. ARNOLD
15 Dir Human Resources & Org Develop .... Vacant
92 Dir John Duns Scotus Honors Program .... Dr. Kenneth A. BUGAJSKI
105 Dir Marketing & Creative Services .... Mrs. Carla S. PYLE
28 Dir Retention/Diversity Programming .... Mr. Garien L. HUDSON
88 Director Service & Social Action .... Mrs. Katrina P. BOEDEKER
88 Director Sports Information .... Mr. William J. SCOTT
88 Director Student Success .... Ms. Melissa J. REESMAN
08 Assoc Dir Information/Instruc Svcs .... Mrs. Maureen E. MCMAHAN
15 Assistant Dir Human Resources .... Mr. Andy MCKEE
53 Chair Department of Education .... Dr. Mary E. REIPENHOFF
19 Supervisor Campus Safety/Security .... Mr. Edward A. LAROCQUE
18 Supervisor Maintenance/Grounds .... Mr. Rex A. BERCOT
44 Senior Gift Officer .... Mrs. Tammy K. OAKES
09 Research/Assessment Analyst .... Mrs. Kim E. DIETRICH
04 Admin Liaison Office of Pres .... Miss Vicki L. JACOBS, OFS
109 Manager AVI Food Service .... Ms. Erhardt ERHARDT
40 Mgr Barnes & Noble Campus Shoppe .... Mrs. Robin HUFFMAN

University of Southern Indiana (C)

8600 University Boulevard, Evansville IN 47712-3596
County: Vanderburgh FICE Identification: 001808
Unit ID: 151306
Telephone: (812) 464-8600 Carnegie Class: Masters/L
FAX Number: (812) 464-1960 Calendar System: Semester
URL: www.usi.edu
Established: 1965 Annual Undergrad Tuition & Fees (In-State): $7,605
Enrollment: 10,671 Coed
Affiliation or Control: State IRS Status: 501(c)3
Highest Offering: Doctorate
Accreditation: **NH**, ART, CAEPN, CEA, COARC, DA, DH, DIETD, DMS, ENG, NURSE, OT, OTA, RAD, SW

01 President .... Dr. Linda L M. BENNETT
100 Exec Assistant to the President .... Ms. Miekka M. COX
05 Provost .... Dr. Ronald S. ROCHON
10 Vice President for Finance & Admin .... Mr. Steven J. BRIDGES
86 Vice Pres Govt and Univ Relations .... Ms. Cynthia S. BRINKER
84 VP for Enrollment Management .... Mr. Andrew W. WRIGHT
26 Assoc VP Marketing/Communications .... Mrs. Kindra L. STRUPP
56 Assoc Provost Outreach/Engagement .... Dr. Mark C. BERNHARD
20 Assoc Provost for Academic Affairs .... Dr. Shelly B. BLUNT
32 Assoc Provost for Student Affairs .... Dr. Marcia K. KIESSLING
21 AVP for Finance & Administration .... Ms. Mary A. HUPFER
09 Chief Data Officer .... Dr. Katherine A. DRAUGHON
58 Director of Graduate Studies .... Dr. Mayola ROWSER
06 Registrar .... Mrs. Sandy K. FRANK
07 Director of Undergrad Admission .... Mr. Rashad E. SMITH
08 Director of Library .... Ms. Marna M. HOSTETLER
30 VP for Development/USI Foundation .... Mr. David A. BOWER
92 Int Director Honors Program .... Dr. Shelly B. BLUNT
38 Director of Counseling .... Dr. B. Thomas LONGWELL
29 Dir Alumni Relations/Volunteer USI .... Mrs. Janet L. JOHNSON
37 Dir Student Financial Assistance .... Mrs. Mary J. HARPER
15 Exec Director of Human Resources .... Mr. Andrew R. LENHARDT
36 Director Career Svcs & Internships .... Mr. Philip L. PARKER
35 Dean of Students .... Dr. S. Bryan RUSH
85 Asst Provost Intl Programs & Svcs .... Ms. Heidi M. GREGORI-GAHAN
28 Director Multicultural Center .... Mrs. Pamela F. HOPSON
13 Chief Information Officer .... Mr. Richard J. TOENISKOETTER
90 Academic Services Coordinator .... Mr. Juzar AHMED
18 Dir of Facility Operations & Plng .... Mr. James E. WOLFE
96 Director Procurement Services .... Mr. Daniel R. MARTENS
27 Director of Univ Communications .... Mr. John A. FARLESS
19 Director of Public Safety .... Mr. Stephen G. WOODALL

39 Director of Housing/Residence Life .... Ms. Amy S. PRICE
40 Bookstore Manager .... Mr. Michael J. GOELZHAUSER
41 Athletic Director .... Mr. Jon Mark HALL
50 Dean Romain College of Business .... Dr. Mohammed KHAYUM
49 Dean College of Liberal Arts .... Dr. James M. BEEBY
66 Dean College Nursing/Health Profess .... Dr. Ann H. WHITE
81 Dean College of Sci/Engr/Educ .... Dr. Zane W. MITCHELL, JR.
51 Director of Lifelong Learning .... Ms. Dawn M. STONEKING
106 Asst Provost for Distance Learning .... Ms. Belle COWDEN

Valparaiso University (D)

1700 Chapel Drive, Valparaiso IN 46383-9978
County: Porter FICE Identification: 001842
Unit ID: 152600
Telephone: (219) 464-5000 Carnegie Class: Masters/L
FAX Number: (219) 464-5381 Calendar System: Semester
URL: valpo.edu
Established: 1859 Annual Undergrad Tuition & Fees: $37,450
Enrollment: 4,524 Coed
Affiliation or Control: Lutheran IRS Status: 501(c)3
Highest Offering: Doctorate
Accreditation: **NH**, CACREP, CAEPN, ENG, LAW, MUS, NURSE, SW

01 President .... Dr. Mark A. HECKLER
05 Provost/Exec VP for Acad Affs .... Dr. Mark BIERMANN
20 Assoc Prov International Affairs .... Dr. Jaishankar RAMAN
32 VP for Student Affairs .... Dr. Bonnie L. HUNTER
84 VP for Enrollment Mgt & Mktg .... Mr. Michael JOSEPH
58 Dean Grad School/Cont Educ .... Dr. Jennifer ZIEGLER
111 VP for Advancement .... Ms. Lisa HOLLANDER
30 AVP for Advancement .... Mr. Jason PETROVICH
26 AVP Integrated Marketing and Comm .... Ms. Nicole NIEMI
43 VP University Counsel .... Mr. Darron C. FARHA
10 VP for Finance & Administration .... Ms. Susan SCROGGINS
92 Interim Dean of Christ College .... Dr. Jeni PROUGH
49 Dean College Arts & Sciences .... Dr. Jon T. KILPINEN
61 Dean School of Law .... Dr. Andrea LYON
54 Dean College of Engineering .... Dr. Eric JOHNSON
50 Dean College of Business Admin .... Dr. James BRODZINSKI
66 Dean College of Nursing .... Dr. Karen ALLEN
08 Dean Library Services .... Dr. Bradford L. EDEN
35 Dean of Students .... Dr. Timothy S. JENKINS
88 AVP Enrollment Management .... Mr. David FEVIG
42 AVP for Mission & Ministry .... Rev. Brian T. JOHNSON
06 Registrar .... Ms. Stephanie MARTIN
19 Chief University Police .... Ms. Rebecca A. WALKOWIAK
39 Asst Dean Students/Residential Life .... Mr. Ryan BLEVINS
104 Assoc Dir of Study Abroad .... Ms. Erin KUNERT
85 Assoc Dir of International Program .... Ms. Janice LIN
29 Director Alumni Relations .... Ms. Linda ROETTGER
15 Dir Human Resource Services .... Mr. Scott HARRISON
18 Exec Dir of Facilities .... Mr. Jon VARNELL
36 Director Career Center .... Mr. Tom CATH
38 Director of Counseling Services .... Dr. Stewart E. COOPER
41 Director Athletics .... Mr. Mark LABARBERA
20 Asst Provost for Faculty Affairs .... Dr. Rick GILLMAN
21 Controller .... Ms. Diana BLANEY
28 Director of Multicultural Programs .... Mr. Byron MARTIN
96 Director of Procurement .... Ms. Nancy K. MURRAY
09 Exec Dir Inst Effectiveness .... Mr. Greg STINSON
42 University Pastor .... Rev. Charlene COX
42 University Pastor .... Rev. James WETZSTEIN
37 Director of Financial Aid .... Ms. Karen KLIMCZYK
100 Chief of Staff .... Mr. Rick AMRHEIN
04 Administrative Asst to President .... Ms. Gwen GRAHAM
07 Director of Admissions .... Ms. Barb LIESKE
101 Secretary of the Institution/Board .... Mr. Darron FARHA
102 Dir Foundation/Corporate Relations .... Ms. Kathy GROTH
13 Chief Info Technology Officer (CIO) .... Mr. Rick AMRHEIN
14 Director of Operations .... Ms. Diane NOE

Vincennes University (E)

1002 N First Street, Vincennes IN 47591-1504
County: Knox FICE Identification: 001843
Unit ID: 152637
Telephone: (812) 888-8888 Carnegie Class: Bac/Assoc-Assoc Dom
FAX Number: (812) 888-5868 Calendar System: Semester
URL: www.vinu.edu
Established: 1801 Annual Undergrad Tuition & Fees (In-State): $5,575
Enrollment: 18,711 Coed
Affiliation or Control: State IRS Status: 501(c)3
Highest Offering: Baccalaureate
Accreditation: **NH**, ACBSP, ADNUR, ART, CAEPN, CAHIIM, EMT, #FUSER, NUR, PNUR, PTAA, SURGT

01 President .... Dr. Charles R. JOHNSON
05 Provost/Vice Pres Instruct Svc .... Dr. Laurel A. SMITH
10 Vice Pres Financial Svcs/Govt Rels .... Mr. Phillip S. RATH
103 VP Workforce Dev/Comm Services .... Mr. David A. TUCKER
12 Assistant VP/Dean Jasper Campus .... Mr. Christian BLOME
21 Associate Vice President/Controller .... Ms. Linda L. WALDROUP
32 Asst Prov Student Aff/Dean Students .... Ms. Taja DAVIDSON
20 Asst Provost Curriculum & Inst .... Mr. Michael GRESS
35 Dean of Students .... Ms. Taja DAVIDSON
26 Sr Director External Relations .... Ms. Kristi R. DEETZ
07 Director of Admissions .... Ms. Heidi M. WHITEHEAD
08 Director of Learning Resources/Tech .... Mr. David M. PETER
09 Director of Institutional Research .... Ms. Kimela A. MEEKS
13 Director of Mgmt Information Center .... Mr. Carmin A. SCHNARR
27 Director Public Information .... Mr. Duane H. CHATTIN

88 Director of University Events ... Ms. Cynthia A. BEAMAN
36 Int Dir Ctr for Career & Empl Rel ... Ms. Donna TAYLOR-BOUCHIE
37 Director of Student Financial Aid ... Mr. Stanley J. WERNE
22 Director Disability Services ... Vacant
40 Manager of Bookstore ... Mr. Alan RAGGO
102 President of VU Foundation ... Mr. Bumper R. HOSTETLER
41 Athletic Director ... Mr. Harry L. MEEKS
88 Sr Dir Dual Credit Partnerships ... Ms. Heather MOFFAT
29 Director of Alumni Programs ... Ms. Jennifer D. GILMORE
28 Director Multicultural Affairs ... Mr. Diondraie L. ROBERTSON
18 Director of Physical Plant ... Mr. Andrew YOUNG
19 Director of Campus Police ... Vacant
113 Bursar ... Ms. Lori J. HOSTETLER
24 Director of Media Services ... Mr. Jay D. WOLF
06 Registrar ... Ms. Rebecca K. LITTLE
39 Director Residential Life ... Ms. Dawn M. BREWER
88 Director Marketing Services ... Ms. Andrea G. TSCHERTER
96 Director of Procurement ... Mr. Michael L. MORRISON
121 Director Student Success Ctr ... Ms. Michelle CUMMINS
88 Director Architectural Services ... Mr. Andrew YOUNG
15 Director Human Resources/AAO ... Ms. Regina L. MCCORD-FITHIAN
76 Dean College Health Sci/Human Perf ... Dr. Jana L. VIECK
50 Dean College of Business/Public Svc ... Ms. Anna MILLER
72 Dean College of Technology ... Mr. Ty FREED
81 Int Dean College of Sc/Engr/Math ... Mr. Curt COFFMAN
83 Dean Soc Sci/Perf Arts/Comm ... Mr. Robert T. EVANS
114 Budget Director ... Mr. Tim EATON
79 Dean College of Humanities ... Ms. Joan PUCKETT
88 Dir Avia Tech Ctr Indianapolis ... Mr. Michael D. GEHRICH
108 Int Dir Institutional Effectiveness ... Mr. Michael GRESS
88 Director Early College ... Ms. Nicole SHANKLE
88 Asst VP Outreach & Engagement ... Mr. Matthew J. SCHWARTZ
88 Director Veterans Affairs ... Ms. Kristen PHILLIPS
88 Dir Plainfield Logistics Center ... Mr. James E. DOLAN
04 Administrative Asst to President ... Ms. Patricia A. KONKLE
88 Director International Recruitment ... Dr. Zhe JI
23 Dir Univ Primary Care Clinic ... Ms. Denah PERRY
85 Dir International Affairs ... Dr. Zhe JI
51 Asst VP Lifelong Learning ... Ms. Shanni E. SIMMONS
101 Record Clerk Bd of Trustees ... Ms. Patricia A. KONKLE

Vincennes University-Jasper Center (A)

850 College Avenue, Jasper IN 47546
Telephone: (812) 482-3030 Identification: 770107
Accreditation: &NH

Wabash College (B)

301 W Wabash, PO Box 352,
Crawfordsville IN 47933-0352
County: Montgomery FICE Identification: 001844
Unit ID: 152673
Telephone: (765) 361-6100 Carnegie Class: Bac-A&S
FAX Number: (765) 361-6461 Calendar System: Semester
URL: www.wabash.edu
Established: 1832 Annual Undergrad Tuition & Fees: $41,050
Enrollment: 868 Male
Affiliation or Control: Independent Non-Profit IRS Status: 501(c)3
Highest Offering: Baccalaureate
Accreditation: NH

01 President ... Dr. Gregory D. HESS
05 Dean of the College ... Dr. Scott FELLER
10 Chief Financial Officer & Treasurer ... Ms. Kendra COOKS
32 Dean of Students ... Mr. Michael P. RATERS
111 Dean for Advancement ... Ms. Michelle L. JANSSEN
84 Dean for Enrollment Management ... Vacant
07 Assoc Dean of Enroll/Dir of Admiss ... Mr. Charles "Chip" TIMMONS
28 Dean Profess Dev & Malcolm X Inst ... Mr. Steven L. JONES
100 Chief of Staff ... Mr. James L. AMIDON
20 Sr Associate Dean of the College ... Dr. Todd F. MCDORMAN
08 Head Librarian & Dir Lilly Library ... Mr. John E. LAMBORN
06 Registrar and Assoc Dean ... Dr. Jonathon D. JUMP
13 Director of IT Services ... Mr. Bradley K. WEAVER
37 Director of Financial Aid ... Ms. Heidi A. CARL
35 Associate Dean of Students ... Mr. Marc WELCH
36 Director of Career Development ... Mr. Jacob PACTOR
29 Dir of Alumni & Parent Relations ... Mr. Steve HOFFMAN
109 Director of Business Auxiliaries ... Mr. Thomas E. KEEDY
41 Dir of Athletics & Campus Wellness ... Mr. Greg A. SHAHEEN
44 Associate Dean for Advancement ... Mr. Joseph R. KLEN
15 Director of Human Resources ... Ms. Catherine A. METZ
18 Director of Campus Services ... Mr. David MORGAN
21 Controller ... Ms. Cathy VANARSDALL
38 Director of Counseling Services ... Mr. Kevin C. SWAIM
88 Director of Inquiries CILA ... Dr. Charles F. BLAICH
88 Dir Wabash Ctr Teaching/Learning ... Dr. Nadine S. PENCE
19 Director of Safety and Security ... Mr. Richard G. WOODS
09 Director of Institutional Research ... Ms. Smitty WOOD
101 Secretary of the Institution/Board ... Mr. James L. AMIDON, JR.
102 Dir Foundation/Corporate Relations ... Ms. Deborah WOODS
104 Director International Programs ... Ms. Amy WEIR
26 Chief Public Relations/Marketing ... Ms. Kimberly JOHNSON
96 Director of Purchasing ... Mr. Thomas E. KEEDY

IOWA

Allen College (C)

1825 Logan Avenue, Waterloo IA 50703-1999
County: Black Hawk FICE Identification: 030691
Unit ID: 152798
Telephone: (319) 226-2000 Carnegie Class: Spec-4-yr-Other Health
FAX Number: (319) 226-2010 Calendar System: Semester
URL: www.allencollege.edu
Established: 1989 Annual Undergrad Tuition & Fees: $17,769
Enrollment: 611 Coed
Affiliation or Control: Independent Non-Profit IRS Status: 501(c)3
Highest Offering: Doctorate
Accreditation: NH, DMS, MT, NMT, NURSE, OT, RAD

01 Chancellor ... Dr. Jerry DURHAM
05 Vice Chancellor of Academic Affairs ... Dr. Nancy KRAMER
10 Dir Business/Administrative Svcs ... Ms. Denise HANSON
66 Dean School of Nursing ... Dr. Kendra WILLIAMS-PEREZ
76 Dean School of Health Sciences ... Dr. Peggy FORTSCH
32 Dean of Student Services ... Dr. Joanna RAMSDEN-MEIER
37 Director of Financial Aid ... Ms. Jobyna JOHNSTON
24 Media Specialist ... Ms. Robin NICHOLSON
06 Registrar ... Ms. Michelle KOEHN
08 Director of Library Services ... Dr. Ruth YAN
07 Director of Admissions ... Ms. Molly QUINN
09 Coord Inst Research/Effectiveness ... Vacant
04 Administrative Asst to President ... Ms. Rhonda GILBERT
28 Director of Diversity ... Dr. Doreen MINGO

Antioch School of Church Planting and Leadership Development (D)

2400 Oakwood Road, Ames IA 50014
County: Story Identification: 667026
Telephone: (515) 292-9694 Carnegie Class: Not Classified
FAX Number: (515) 292-1933 Calendar System: Other
URL: www.antiochschool.edu
Established: 2006 Annual Undergrad Tuition & Fees: N/A
Enrollment: N/A Coed
Affiliation or Control: Independent Non-Profit IRS Status: 501(c)3
Highest Offering: Doctorate
Accreditation: DEAC

01 President ... Jeff REED
05 Academic Dean ... Stephen KEMP

*Board of Regents, State of Iowa (E)

11260 Aurora Avenue, Urbandale IA 50322-7905
County: Polk FICE Identification: 033443
Telephone: (515) 281-3934 Carnegie Class: N/A
FAX Number: (515) 281-6420
URL: www.iowaregents.edu

01 President ... Dr. Michael RICHARDS
00 Executive Director & CEO ... Vacant
05 Interim Chief Academic Officer ... Dr. Rachel L. BOON
11 Chief Operating Officer ... Mr. Mark BRAUN
43 Board Counsel ... Mrs. Aimee K. CLAEYS
04 Administrative Asst to President ... Mrs. Laura M. DICKSON

*Iowa State University (F)

Ames IA 50011-0002
County: Story FICE Identification: 001869
Unit ID: 153603
Telephone: (515) 294-4111 Carnegie Class: DU-Highest
FAX Number: (515) 294-2592 Calendar System: Semester
URL: www.iastate.edu
Established: 1858 Annual Undergrad Tuition & Fees (In-State): $8,219
Enrollment: 35,714 Coed
Affiliation or Control: State IRS Status: 501(c)3
Highest Offering: Doctorate
Accreditation: NH, ART, CAATE, CIDA, COPSY, CS, DIETD, DIETI, ENG, IPSY, JOUR, LSAR, MUS, NAIT, PLNG, VET

02 Interim President ... Dr. Benjamin J. ALLEN
100 Chief Financial Off/Chief of Staff ... Mr. Miles LACKEY
04 Assistant to the President ... Ms. Shirley J. KNIPFEL
43 University Counsel ... Mr. Michael E. NORTON
05 Sr Vice President and Provost ... Dr. Jonathan A. WICKERT
10 Sr Vice Pres for University Svcs ... Ms. Katherine GREGORY
32 Sr Vice Pres for Student Affairs ... Dr. Martino HARMON
88 Vice Pres for Ec Dev/Bus Engagement ... Dr. Michael R. CRUM
46 Vice Pres Research ... Dr. Sarah M. NUSSER
56 Int Vice Pres Extension/Outreach ... Dr. John D. LAWRENCE
13 Vice President/Chief Info Officer ... Dr. Jim KURTENBACH
28 Vice Pres for Diversity & Inclusion ... Dr. Reginald C. STEWART
20 Associate Provost Academic Programs ... Dr. David K. HOLGER
20 Assoc Prov Faculty ... Dr. Dawn BRATSCH-PRINCE
21 Associate Vice President/Univ Sec ... Ms. Pam ELLIOTT CAIN
18 Assoc Vice Pres Facilities Planning ... Mr. Paul FULIGNI
15 Int Vice President Human Resources ... Ms. Kristi DARR
32 Assoc Vice Pres Student Affairs ... Dr. Martino HARMON
84 Assoc VP Stdnt Affs for Enroll Mgmt ... Ms. Laura J. DOERING
38 Int Dir for Student Counseling Svcs ... Dr. Joyce DAVIDSON
30 President of ISU Foundation ... Ms. Larissa HOLTMYER-JONES
29 President of Alumni Association ... Dr. Jeffrey W. JOHNSON
41 Director of Athletics ... Mr. Jamie B. POLLARD
26 Exec Director of University Rels ... Mr. John F. MCCARROLL
06 Interim Registrar ... Ms. Jennifer SUCHAN
37 Director of Financial Aid ... Ms. Roberta L. JOHNSON
07 Director of Admissions ... Ms. Katharine JOHNSON SUSKI
22 Director of Equal Opportunity ... Ms. Margo FOREMAN
09 Int Director of Inst Research ... Sandra W. GAHN
19 Director of Public Safety ... Mr. Michael R. NEWTON
35 Int Dean of Students ... Dr. Keith E. ROBINDER
23 Director of Student Health ... Ms. Erin BALDWIN
104 Director Study Abroad ... Dr. Trevor NELSON
39 Director of Residence ... Dr. Peter D. ENGLIN
91 Associate CIO ... Mr. David M. POPELKA
25 Assoc Director/Sponsored Pgm Admin ... Ms. Tamara R. POLASKI
88 Director Ames Laboratory ... Dr. Adam SCHWARTZ
96 Interim Director of Purchasing ... Mr. Cory L. HARMS
40 Director University Bookstore ... Ms. Rita M. PHILLIPS
58 Dean Graduate College ... Dr. David K. HOLGER
08 Dean of Library Services ... Ms. Mary E. MCNEIL
47 Dean College of Agriculture ... Dr. Wendy WINTERSTEEN
50 Dean College of Business ... Mr. David P. SPALDING
48 Dean College of Design ... Mr. Luis C. RICO-GUTIERREZ
53 Dean College of Human Sciences ... Dr. Laura JOLLY
54 Dean College of Engineering ... Dr. Sarah RAJALA
49 Dean Col of Lib Arts & Sciences ... Dr. Beate SCHMITTMANN
74 Int Dean College of Vet Medicine ... Dr. Parick G. HALBUR
102 Sr Dir Dev/Corporate Relations ... Mr. Mark BOECK
102 Sr Dir Dev/Foundation Relations ... Ms. Donna VAN PELT
44 Exec Dir of Annual & Special Giving ... Ms. Melissa ROWAN
27 Director of University Marketing ... Ms. Carole A. CUSTER

*University of Iowa (G)

Iowa City IA 52242-0001
County: Johnson FICE Identification: 001892
Unit ID: 153658
Telephone: (319) 335-3500 Carnegie Class: DU-Highest
FAX Number: (319) 335-0807 Calendar System: Semester
URL: www.uiowa.edu
Established: 1847 Annual Undergrad Tuition & Fees (In-State): $8,575
Enrollment: 30,844 Coed
Affiliation or Control: State IRS Status: 501(c)3
Highest Offering: Doctorate
Accreditation: NH, ANEST, ARCPA, AUD, CAATE, CACREP, CEA, CLPSY, COPSY, DANCE, DENT, DIETI, DMS, EMT, ENG, ENGR, HSA, IPSY, JOUR, LAW, LIB, MED, MUS, NMT, NURSE, PAST, PCSAS, PERF, PH, PHAR, PLNG, PTA, #RAD, #RTT, SCPSY, SP, SW, THEA

02 President ... Mr. Bruce HARRELD
05 Int Exec Vice President & Provost ... Dr. Susan J. CURRY
46 VP Research & Economic Development ... Dr. Daniel REED
10 SVP Fin & Ops/Chief Financial Ofcr ... Mr. Rod LEHNERTZ
32 Vice Pres Student Life ... Dr. Melissa SHIVERS
17 VP Med Affairs/Dean College of Med ... Dr. Jean E. ROBILLARD
30 Vice Pres & Development Officer ... Mr. David R. DIERKS
26 Asst VP External Affairs ... Ms. Jeneane BECK
27 Senior Director Marketing Comm ... Mr. Ben HILL
20 Associate Provost Faculty ... Dr. Kevin KREGEL
28 Chief Diversity Officer/AP ... Dr. Georgina DODGE
88 Assoc Provost/Dean Univ College ... Mr. Lon MOELLER
45 Assoc Vice President Research ... Dr. Richard D. HICHWA
11 Assoc VP/Dir of Admin and Planning ... Mr. Donald J. SZESZYCKI
15 Assoc VP Finance/Dir HR ... Ms. Cheryl REARDON
18 Assoc VP/Dir Facilities Management ... Mr. Donald J. GUCKERT
13 Assoc Vice President & CIO ... Mr. Steven R. FLEAGLE
23 Assoc VP/CEO Univ Hosp & Clinics ... Mr. Kenneth KATES
25 Exec Director Sponsored Programs ... Ms. Jennifer LASSNER
19 Asst VP & Director Public Safety ... Mr. Scott BECNKER
85 Dean International Programs ... Dr. Downing THOMAS
43 VP Legal Affairs & General Counsel ... Ms. Carroll REASONER
08 University Librarian ... Mr. John P. CULSHAW
102 President University Foundation ... Ms. Lynette L. MARSHALL
07 Director Admissions/Enrollment ... Mr. Kirk R. KLUVER
37 Director Student Financial Aid ... Mr. Mark S. WARNER
06 Registrar ... Mr. Lawrence J. LOCKWOOD
36 Director Career Center ... Mr. David A. BAUMGARTNER
38 Director Univ Counseling Services ... Dr. Sam V. COCHRAN, III
39 Director Residence Services ... Mr. Von STANGE
41 Director Athletics Administration ... Mr. Gary BARTA
49 Dean Col of Liberal Arts & Sciences ... Dr. Chaden DJALALI
50 Dean College of Business Admin ... Dr. Sarah GARDIAL
52 Dean College of Dentistry ... Dr. David C. JOHNSEN
53 Dean College of Education ... Dr. Daniel CLAY
54 Dean College of Engineering ... Dr. Alec SCRANTON
58 Dean Graduate College ... Dr. John C. KELLER
61 Dean College of Law ... Dr. Gail B. AGRAWAL
66 Interim Dean College of Nursing ... Dr. Kathleen BUCKWALTER
67 Dean College of Pharmacy ... Dr. Donald E. LETENDRE
69 Dean College of Public Health ... Dr. Susan CURRY
04 Special Assistant to President ... Dr. Thomas K. DEAN
22 Dir Equal Opportunity/Diversity ... Ms. Jennifer A. MODESTOU
86 Director State Relations ... Mr. Keith SAUNDERS
40 Director University Bookstore ... Mr. George E. HERBERT
96 Director Purchasing ... Ms. Deborah J. ZUMBACH
92 Director Honors Program ... Dr. Art L. SPISAK
87 Director Summer Session ... Dr. Marlys BOOTE
35 Dean of Students ... Dr. Lyn REDINGTON
84 Assoc VP/Enrollment Management ... Dr. Brent GAGE
100 Chief of Staff ... Mr. Peter MATTHES
104 Director Study Abroad ... Mr. Douglas LEE
09 Director of Institutional Research ... Mr. Daniel REED
44 Director Annual or Planned Giving ... Ms. Erin ALLEN

*University of Northern Iowa (A)

1227 W 27th Street, Cedar Falls IA 50614-0001
County: Black Hawk   FICE Identification: 001890
Unit ID: 154095
Telephone: (319) 273-2311   Carnegie Class: Masters/L
FAX Number: (319) 273-2885   Calendar System: Semester
URL: https://uni.edu/
Established: 1876   Annual Undergrad Tuition & Fees (In-State): $8,309
Enrollment: 11,981   Coed
Affiliation or Control: State   IRS Status: 501(c)3
Highest Offering: Doctorate
Accreditation: NH, CAATE, CACREP, CEA, CIDA, ENGT, MUS, NAIT, NRPA, SP, SW, THEA

Code	Title	Name
02	President	Dr. Mark A. NOOK
05	Exec VP & Provost	Dr. A. James WOHLPART
10	Sr VP Finance & Operations	Dr. Michael A. HAGER
32	Vice President for Student Affairs	Dr. Paula M. KNUDSON
111	Vice President for Univ Advancement	Ms. Lisa B. BARONIO
84	Assoc VP for Enrollment Management	Mr. Matthew D. KROEGER
18	Director Physical Plant Admin	Mr. Michael W. ZWANZIGER
26	Director Univ Relations	Mr. Scott A. KETELSEN
39	Asst VP & Exec Dir of Residence	Mr. Glenn P. GRAY
20	Interim Assoc Provost Acad Affairs	Dr. Patrick P. PEASE
20	Assoc Provost for Faculty	Dr. John F. VALLENTINE
13	Chief Information Officer	Ms. Marty L. MARK
09	Dir Inst Research & Effectiveness	Dr. Kristin M. MOSER
62	Dean of Library Services	Mr. Christopher N. COX
06	Interim University Registrar	Ms. Joyce S. MORROW
29	Director Alumni Relations	Ms. Leslie J. PRIDEAUX
37	Interim Director of Financial Aid	Mr. Timothy L. BAKULA
15	Dir Human Resource Services	Ms. Michelle C. BYERS
83	Dean Col Soc/Behav Sciences	Dr. Brenda L. BASS
53	Dean Col Education	Dr. Gadtane JEAN-MARIE
49	Dean Col Hum/Arts & Science	Dr. John E. FRITCH
51	Dean Cont Educ/Special Programs	Dr. Kent M. JOHNSON
58	Interim Dean Graduate College	Dr. Patrick P. PEASE
50	Dean Col Business Admin	Dr. Leslie K. WILSON
35	Dean of Students	Dr. Leslie K. WILLIAMS
38	Exec Dir Health & Rec Svcs	Ms. Shelley M. O'CONNELL
22	Asst to Pres Compliance/Equity Mgmt	Ms. Leah K. GUTKNECHT
41	Athletic Director	Mr. David W. HARRIS
21	Treas/Asst VP Finance & Operations	Ms. Kelly A. FLEGE
86	State Relations Officer	Ms. Mary C. BRAUN
104	Exec Director Intl Programs	Mr. Philip D. PLOURDE
88	Director Undergraduate Studies	Dr. Deirdre A. HEISTAD
19	Chief of Police/Dir Public Safety	Ms. Helen M. HAIRE
25	Dir Research & Sponsored Programs	Mr. Tolif R. HUNT
43	University Counsel	Mr. Timothy J. MCKENNA
88	Dir Business Operations/Controller	Ms. Tonya L. GERBRACHT
07	Director of Admissions	Ms. Kara M. HADLEY-SHAKYA
28	Asst to Pres/Chief Div Officer	Ms. Gwennette C. BERRY
124	Dir Student Success and Retention	Dr. Kristin L. WOODS
112	VP for Principal Gifts	Ms. Noreen M. HERMANSEN
36	Dir Career Services	Mr. Robert J. FREDERICK

Briar Cliff University (B)

3303 Rebecca Street, Sioux City IA 51104-2324
County: Woodbury   FICE Identification: 001846
Unit ID: 152992
Telephone: (712) 279-5321   Carnegie Class: Bac-Diverse
FAX Number: (712) 279-5410   Calendar System: 4/1/4
URL: www.briarcliff.edu
Established: 1929   Annual Undergrad Tuition & Fees: $28,788
Enrollment: 1,149   Coed
Affiliation or Control: Roman Catholic   IRS Status: 501(c)3
Highest Offering: Doctorate
Accreditation: NH, NURSE, @PTA, SW

Code	Title	Name
01	President	Dr. Hamid A. SHIRVANI
03	EVP/Acting President	Ms. Rachelle KARSTENS
05	VP Academic Affairs	Dr. Todd KNEALING
10	Vice President Finance & Treasurer	Mr. Ken RUETER
111	Vice Pres University Relations	Mrs. Tina STROUD
84	Interim VP Enrollment Management	Ms. Marcia NANCE
32	Vice President Student Development	Mrs. Louise PASKEY
06	Registrar	Mrs. Deidre ENGEL
08	Librarian/Dir Information Services	Mr. Julius FLESCHNER
13	Director Computer Center	Ms. Leah WARD
36	Director Career Development	Mr. Joshua COBBS
37	Director Financial Aid	Vacant
40	Director Bookstore	Ms. Nancy WATSON
41	Athletic Director	Mr. Nic NELSON
42	Director Campus Ministry	Sr. Janet MAY
18	Director Physical Plant	Ms. Angela WASHBURN
26	Director Marketing & Communications	Ms. Leslie HEYING
07	Director of Admissions	Vacant
15	Director Human Resources	Mr. Beau SUDTELGTE
39	Director Residence Life	Mr. Dave ARENS
38	Director Student Counseling	Mrs. Jeanette TOBIN
09	Director of Institutional Research	Ms. Deidre ENGEL
30	Director of Philanthropy	Mrs. Carolyn ELLWANGER
19	Director Security/Safety	Mr. Marty POTTEBAUM

Buena Vista University (C)

610 W Fourth Street, Storm Lake IA 50588-1798
County: Buena Vista   FICE Identification: 001847
Unit ID: 153001
Telephone: (712) 749-2351   Carnegie Class: Bac-Diverse
FAX Number: (712) 749-2037   Calendar System: 4/1/4
URL: www.bvu.edu
Established: 1891   Annual Undergrad Tuition & Fees: $32,210
Enrollment: 2,322   Coed
Affiliation or Control: Presbyterian Church (U.S.A.)   IRS Status: 501(c)3
Highest Offering: Master's
Accreditation: NH, CAATE, SW

Code	Title	Name
01	President	Mr. Joshua D. MERCHANT
04	Assistant to the President	Ms. Emily A. WILLIAMS
05	VP Academic Affairs/Dean of Faculty	Dr. James SALVUCCI
10	Vice President Business Services	Ms. Suzette RADKE
84	Vice Pres for Enrollment Management	Mr. Michael FRANTZ
32	VP Student Affairs/DOS	Mr. Dale SCULLY
111	Vice Pres for Inst Advancement	Mr. Kenneth L. CONVERSE
81	Dean School of Science	Mr. Ben DONATH
50	Dean HWS School of Business	Mr. Jim FALTER
53	Dean School of Education	Dr. Julie FINNERN
60	Dean School Communication & Arts	Dr. Anna ELSDEN
83	Dean School Social Sci/Phil/ Relig	Dr. Dixee BARTHOLOMEW-FEIS
20	Associate Dean of Faculty	Dr. Peter K. STEINFELD
20	AVP Acad Affs/Dn Graduate/Prof Stds	Dr. Jill RHEA
06	Registrar	Ms. Nila HOUSKA
07	Director of Admissions	Mr. Mike FOX
15	Human Resources Manager	Ms. Melissa BUTCHER
08	Actg Dir of Library/Ref Librarian	Ms. Jodie MORIN
26	Dir University Marketing & Comm	Ms. Jennifer FELTON
29	Director of Alumni Rels/Annual Fund	Ms. Amy J. JONES
13	Managing Director Univ Info Svcs	Mr. Bob WALKER
18	Director of Physical Plant	Mr. Keith E. SCHMIDT
36	Director of Career Services	Ms. Lori BERGLUND
37	Director of Financial Assistance	Ms. Leanne VALENTINE
28	Dir of Multicultural Engagement	Ms. Ebony KING
41	Athletic Director	Ms. Jack DENHOLM
42	Chaplain	Rev. Ken MEISSNER
19	Director of Campus Security	Mr. Mark KIRKHOLM
09	Institutional Researcher	Mr. James E. HEWETT
96	Purchasing Administrator	Ms. Tanya LANDGRAF

Central College (D)

812 University, Pella IA 50219-1999
County: Marion   FICE Identification: 001850
Unit ID: 153108
Telephone: (641) 628-9000   Carnegie Class: Bac-A&S
FAX Number: (641) 628-5316   Calendar System: Semester
URL: www.central.edu
Established: 1853   Annual Undergrad Tuition & Fees: $34,612
Enrollment: 1,274   Coed
Affiliation or Control: Reformed Church In America   IRS Status: 501(c)3
Highest Offering: Baccalaureate
Accreditation: NH, CAATE, MUS

Code	Title	Name
01	President	Dr. Mark L. PUTNAM
05	VP Academic Affairs/Dean of Faculty	Dr. Mary M. STREY
111	Vice President Advancement	Mrs. Sunny EIGHMY
84	Vice Pres Enrollment Management	Mrs. Carol WILLIAMSON
32	Vice Pres Student Development	Dr. Peggy FITCH
10	Vice Pres for Finance & Admin	Mr. Thomas JOHNSON
20	Director of Academic Resources	Mr. Eric JONES
35	Dean of Students	Mr. Charles STREY
07	Director of Admission	Mr. Chevy FREIBURGER
38	Director of Counseling	Ms. Michelle KELLAR
39	Assistant Dean of Students	Ms. Melissa SHARKEY
08	Director of Geisler Library	Ms. Beth MCMAHON
88	Associate Dean for Global Education	Ms. Lyn R. ISAACSON
36	Director of Career Center	Mrs. Patricia JOACHIM KITZMAN
29	Director of Alumni Relations	Mr. Kevin STITTSWORTH
37	Director Financial Aid	Mr. Wayne DILLE
104	Associate Director of Study Abroad	Mr. Mike HAMMOND
13	Chief Information Officer	Ms. Debra BRUXVOORT
42	Chaplain	Rev. Joe BRUMMEL
30	Dir Development/Planned Giving	Mr. Don MORRISON
15	Director of Human Resources	Ms. Paula RYAN
41	Athletics Director	Mr. Eric VAN KLEY
18	Dir Facilities Planning/Management	Mr. Mike LUBBERDEN
06	Registrar	Ms. Stephanie HENNING
04	Administrative Asst to President	Ms. Carma STURTZ
09	Institutional Research Director	Vacant

Clarke University (E)

1550 Clarke Drive, Dubuque IA 52001-3198
County: Dubuque   FICE Identification: 001852
Unit ID: 153126
Telephone: (563) 588-6300   Carnegie Class: Bac-Diverse
FAX Number: (563) 588-6789   Calendar System: Semester
URL: www.clarke.edu
Established: 1843   Annual Undergrad Tuition & Fees: $30,900
Enrollment: 1,075   Coed
Affiliation or Control: Roman Catholic   IRS Status: 501(c)3
Highest Offering: Doctorate
Accreditation: NH, CAATE, MUS, NURSE, PTA, SW

Code	Title	Name
01	President	Dr. Joanne M. BURROWS, SC
04	Exec Admin Assistant to President	Ms. Kathy TEIG
05	Vice Pres Academic Affs	Dr. Susan R. BURNS
111	Vice Pres Institutional Advancement	Mr. Bill BIEBUYCK
32	Vice President Student Life	Ms. Kate ZANGER
10	Vice President Business & Finance	Dr. Daisy HALVORSON
84	Vice President Enrollment Mgmt	Mr. Jay FEDJE
88	Assistant to the President	Ms. Megan STULL
06	Registrar	Ms. Kristi BAGSTAD
08	Director of Library	Ms. Susanne LEIBOLD
20	Dean of Undergraduate Studies	Vacant
58	Dir of Adm for Adult & Grad Studies	Ms. Kim ROUSH
37	Director of Financial Aid	Ms. Amy NORTON
26	Director of Marketing	Ms. Amy ERRTHUM
13	Chief Technology Officer	Mr. Andy BELLINGS
18	Exec Dir of Facilities Management	Mr. Steven KIRSCHBAUM
38	Asst Dir of Counseling/Career Svcs	Ms. Becky HERRIG
15	Director of Human Resources	Ms. Jody PFOHL
41	Director of Athletics	Mr. Curt LONG
42	Director of Campus Ministry	Mr. Hunter DARROUZET
40	Director of the Bookstore	Ms. Sarah HAAS
23	Director of Health Services	Ms. Tammy MOORE
90	Asst Dean Acad Affairs/Inst Supp	Mr. Pat MADDUX
07	Director of Admissions	Ms. Julie CIRKS
30	Exec Director of Development	Ms. Courtney LEONARD
29	Assoc Dir of Alumni Relations	Ms. Jodi HOOKS
85	International Students Advisor	Ms. Evelyn NADEAU
35	Dean of Students	Mr. Kevin UTT

Coe College (F)

1220 1st Avenue, NE, Cedar Rapids IA 52402-5092
County: Linn   FICE Identification: 001854
Unit ID: 153144
Telephone: (319) 399-8000   Carnegie Class: Bac-A&S
FAX Number: (319) 399-8830   Calendar System: Semester
URL: www.coe.edu
Established: 1851   Annual Undergrad Tuition & Fees: $41,000
Enrollment: 1,411   Coed
Affiliation or Control: Independent Non-Profit   IRS Status: 501(c)3
Highest Offering: Master's
Accreditation: NH, CAATE, MUS, NURSE

Code	Title	Name
01	President	Dr. David W. MCINALLY
03	Executive Vice President	Mr. Michael L. WHITE
05	Provost/Dean of Faculty	Dr. Paula O'LOUGHLIN
32	Vice President for Student Affairs	Mr. Erik ALBINSON
111	Vice President for Advancement	Mr. David HAYES
07	Associate VP/Dean of Admission	Ms. Julie STAKER
06	Registrar	Vacant
08	Director Library Services	Ms. Jill JACK
29	Director Alumni Programs	Vacant
09	Director of Institutional Research	Dr. Wendy L. DUNN
26	Dir of Marketing/Public Relations	Mr. Rod PRITCHARD
37	Director of Financial Aid	Ms. Barbara HOFFMAN
20	Associate Dean	Dr. Marty ST. CLAIR
35	Dean of Students	Mr. Tom HICKS
85	International Student Advisor	Mr. Peter GERLACH
42	Chaplain	Vacant
41	Director of Athletics	Vacant
18	Director of Physical Plant	Ms. Lisa CIHA
36	Dir of Internships/Career Services	Ms. Barb TUPPER
15	Director of Human Resources	Ms. Kristina BRIDGES
04	Administrative Asst to President	Ms. Kim PRIBYL
13	Chief Info Technology Officer	Mr. Anthony BATA
19	Director Security/Safety	Mr. Carlos VELEZ
44	Director Annual/Planned Giving	Ms. Mary SPRINGER

Cornell College (G)

600 First Street SW, Mount Vernon IA 52314-1098
County: Linn   FICE Identification: 001856
Unit ID: 153162
Telephone: (319) 895-4000   Carnegie Class: Bac-A&S
FAX Number: (319) 895-4492   Calendar System: Other
URL: www.cornellcollege.edu
Established: 1853   Annual Undergrad Tuition & Fees: $39,900
Enrollment: 1,037   Coed
Affiliation or Control: United Methodist   IRS Status: 501(c)3
Highest Offering: Baccalaureate
Accreditation: NH

Code	Title	Name
01	President	Mr. Jonathan BRAND
05	VP Acad Affairs/Dean of College	Dr. R. Joseph DIEKER
10	Vice President Business Affairs	Ms. Kay LANGSETH
84	Vice President for Enrollment	Ms. Colleen MURPHY
32	Vice President Student Affairs	Mr. John W. HARP
111	VP for Alumni & College Advancement	Ms. Pam GERARD
35	Dean of Students	Dr. Gwendolyn SCHIMEK
20	Associate Dean of the College	Dr. Erin DAVIS
09	Director of Institutional Research	Ms. Bethany MILLER
37	Director of Student Financial Asst	Ms. Pamela PERRY
06	Registrar	Ms. Megan HICKS
08	College Librarian	Mr. Gregory COTTON
29	Director of Alumni & Annual Giving	Mr. RJ HOLMES-LEOPOLD
30	Senior Director of Development	Ms. Kristi COLUMBUS
26	Senior Dir Marketing/Communications	Ms. Jen VISSER
42	Chaplain	Ms. Catherine M. QUEHL-ENGEL
22	Affirmative Action Officer	Ms. Lindsey HOTZ
41	Athletics Director	Mr. Keith HACKETT
18	Director of Facilities	Mr. Joel C. MILLER
36	Senior Dir Berry Career Institute	Ms. Jodi SCHAFER
38	Director Student Counseling	Dr. Brenda C. LOVSTUEN
15	Employee Relations Coordinator	Ms. Lindsey HOTZ
07	Director of Admission	Ms. Marie SCHOFER
13	Director of Information Technology	Mr. Jeff GIBSON
40	Manager Bookstore	Ms. Lee Ann GRIMLEY
04	Administrative Asst to President	Ms. RuthAnn SCHEER
101	Secretary to the Board of Trustees	Ms. RuthAnn SCHEER
19	Campus Safety Director	Mr. Mark WINDER

Des Moines Area Community College (A)

2006 S Ankeny Boulevard, Ankeny IA 50023-3993
County: Polk FICE Identification: 007120
Unit ID: 153214
Telephone: (515) 964-6200 Carnegie Class: Assoc/MT-VT-High Non
FAX Number: N/A Calendar System: Semester
URL: www.dmacc.edu
Established: 1966 Annual Undergrad Tuition & Fees (In-District): $4,410
Enrollment: 22,298 Coed
Affiliation or Control: State/Local IRS Status: 501(c)3
Highest Offering: Associate Degree
Accreditation: NH, ACBSP, ACFEI, ADNUR, COARC, DA, DH, EMT, FUSER, MAC, MLTAD, SURGT

01 President/CEO ... Dr. Rob DENSON
05 Exec Vice Pres Academic Affairs ... Dr. Kim LINDUSKA
10 Vice President Business Svcs ... Mr. Greg MARTIN
13 Exec Dir Information Solutions ... Mr. Mark CLARK
12 Provost Urban Campus ... Dr. Anne HOWSARE
12 Provost Boone Campus ... Mr. Andrew NELSON
12 Provost Carroll Campus ... Mr. Joel LUNDSTROM
12 Provost Newton Campus ... Dr. Joe DEHART
12 Provost West Campus ... Dr. Tony PAUSTIAN
32 Exec Dean Student Services ... Mr. Wade ROBINSON
15 Executive Director Human Resources ... Dr. Sandy TRYON
102 Executive Director Foundation ... Ms. Tara CONNOLLY
51 Exec Dir Continuing Education ... Mr. Michael HOFFMAN
50 Exec Dir Business Resources ... Ms. Kim DIDIER
37 Director Financial Aid ... Mr. Ean FREELS
26 Director of Marketing ... Mr. Todd JONES
25 Director Grants/Contracts ... Ms. Deb KOUA
06 Registrar ... Ms. Rachel ERKKILA
18 Chief Facilities/Physical Plant ... Mr. Ned MILLER
96 Director of Purchasing ... Mr. Tim HAGER
27 Media Liaison ... Mr. Dan IVIS
70 Dean Sciences & Humanities ... Mr. Jim STICK
72 Dean Industrial & Technology ... Mr. Scott OCKEN
76 Dean Health Service & Science ... Mr. Art BROWN
50 Dean Business/Mgmt/Information Tech ... Mr. MD ISLEY
55 Dean Evening & Weekend College ... Ms. Andrea ISEMINGER
08 Head Librarian ... Ms. Rebecca FUNKE
41 Athletic Director ... Mr. BJ MCGINN
101 Secretary of the Board ... Ms. Carolyn FARLOW

Des Moines Area Community College Boone Campus (B)

1125 Hancock Drive, Boone IA 50036
Telephone: (515) 432-7203 Identification: 770048
Accreditation: &NH

Des Moines Area Community College Carroll Campus (C)

906 North Grant Road, Carroll IA 51401-2525
Telephone: (712) 792-1755 Identification: 770049
Accreditation: &NH

Des Moines Area Community College Newton Campus (D)

600 N 2nd Avenue West, Newton IA 50208
Telephone: (641) 791-3622 Identification: 770051
Accreditation: &NH

Des Moines Area Community College Urban Campus (E)

1100 7th Street, Des Moines IA 50314
Telephone: (515) 244-4226 Identification: 770050
Accreditation: &NH

Des Moines Area Community College West Des Moines Campus (F)

5959 West Grand Avenue, West Des Moines IA 50266
Telephone: (515) 633-2407 Identification: 770052
Accreditation: &NH

Des Moines University (G)

3200 Grand Avenue, Des Moines IA 50312-4198
County: Polk FICE Identification: 001855
Unit ID: 154156
Telephone: (515) 271-1400 Carnegie Class: Spec-4-yr-Med
FAX Number: (515) 271-1532 Calendar System: Other
URL: www.dmu.edu
Established: 1898 Annual Graduate Tuition & Fees: N/A
Enrollment: 1,603 Coed
Affiliation or Control: Independent Non-Profit IRS Status: 501(c)3
Highest Offering: First Professional Degree; No Undergraduates
Accreditation: NH, #ARCPA, HSA, OSTEO, PH, POD, PTA

01 President/CEO ... Dr. Angela L. WALKER FRANKLIN
05 Provost ... Dr. Karen P. MCLEAN
84 VP Enrollment Mgmt/Student Svcs ... Ms. Kimberly BROWN
86 Chief External & Govt Affs Officer ... Ms. Susan HUPPERT
46 Vice President for Research ... Dr. Jeffrey GRAY
06 Registrar ... Ms. Kathy L. SCAGLIONE
08 Director of Library ... Ms. Natalie HUTCHINSON
15 Chief Human Resources Officer ... Ms. Becky LADE
13 Chief Information Officer ... Ms. Carolyn WEAVER
37 Director of Financial Aid ... Ms. Mary PAYNE
18 Director of Facilities Management ... Mr. Mark CHAMBERS
19 Director University Services ... Mr. Sebastian EISBACH
108 Chief Compliance Officer ... Ms. Erika LINDEN
10 Chief Financial Officer ... Mr. Mark J. PEIFFER
69 Director Public Health Program ... Dr. Rachel REIMER
26 Dir Marketing & Communication ... Mr. Mark DANES
121 Dir Center for Teaching & Learning ... Dr. Kerry GREGORYK
76 Dean College Health Sciences ... Dr. Jodi CAHALAN
63 Dean Col Podiatric Medicine/Surg ... Dr. Robert YOHO
63 Dean College Osteopathic Medicine . Dr. Gregory CHRISTIANSEN
04 Executive Asst to President ... Ms. Christina HENDERSON
07 Director of Admissions/Recruitment ... Ms. Molly MOELLER
32 Director of Student Services ... Ms. Alicia LYNCH
28 Director of Multicultural Affairs ... Dr. Richard SALAS
29 Director Alumni Relations ... Ms. Ronnette VONDRAK
30 Chief Development Officer ... Ms. Stephanie GREINER
101 Secretary of the Institution/Board ... Ms. Linda KADING
09 Institutional Research Manager ... Mr. Josh KVINLAUG

† Tuition varies by degree program.

Divine Word College (H)

102 Jacoby Drive, SW, PO Box 380, Epworth IA 52045-0380
County: Dubuque FICE Identification: 001858
Unit ID: 153241
Telephone: (563) 876-3353 Carnegie Class: Spec-4-yr-Faith
FAX Number: (563) 876-3407 Calendar System: Semester
URL: www.dwci.edu
Established: 1918 Annual Undergrad Tuition & Fees: $12,600
Enrollment: 81 Male
Affiliation or Control: Roman Catholic IRS Status: 501(c)3
Highest Offering: Baccalaureate
Accreditation: NH

01 President ... Fr. Thomas ASCHEMAN, SVD
05 Vice President Academic Affairs ... Dr. John SZUKALSKI, SVD
11 Vice President Operations ... Mr. Steven WINGER
32 Dean of Students ... Rev. Bang TRAN, SVD
07 Vice President for Admission ... Mr. Len UHAL
26 Public Relations Director ... Ms. Sandy WILGENBUSCH
08 Librarian ... Mr. Daniel C. WILLIAMS
06 Registrar ... Ms. Jolene ZIMMERMAN
38 Counselor ... Rev. Paul CHEN, SVD
104 Director Study Abroad ... Rev. Kenneth ANICH, SVD
13 Chief Info Technology Officer (CIO) ... Mr. Brad FLORENCE
45 Chief Institutional Planning ... Vacant
30 Development Director ... Rev. Linh PHAM, SVD
18 Chief Facilities/Physical Plant ... Mr. Steven WINGER

Dordt College (I)

498 4th Avenue, NE, Sioux Center IA 51250-1697
County: Sioux FICE Identification: 001859
Unit ID: 153250
Telephone: (712) 722-6000 Carnegie Class: Bac-Diverse
FAX Number: (712) 722-6035 Calendar System: Semester
URL: www.dordt.edu
Established: 1955 Annual Undergrad Tuition & Fees: $29,130
Enrollment: 1,458 Coed
Affiliation or Control: Christian Reformed Church IRS Status: 501(c)3
Highest Offering: Master's
Accreditation: NH, ENG, NURSE, SW

01 President ... Dr. Erik HOEKSTRA
05 Provost ... Dr. Eric A. FORSETH
111 Vice President College Advancement ... Mr. John BAAS
10 Exec Dir of Finance & Facilities ... Mr. Arlan NEDERHOFF
11 Vice President for Administration ... Mr. Howard WILSON
88 Director of Global Education ... Mr. Adam ADAMS
37 Director Financial Aid ... Mr. Harlan HARMELINK
06 Registrar ... Mr. James BOS
88 Director for Research & Scholarship ... Dr. Nathan TINTLE
20 Dean for Curriculum & Instruction ... Dr. Leah ZUIDEMA
58 Director Graduate Studies ... Dr. Steve HOLTROP
36 Career Services Coordinator ... Ms. Amy WESTRA
26 Marketing and Public Relations ... Ms. Sarah MOSS
18 Director Physical Plant ... Mr. Nate VAN NIEJENHUIS
32 Dean of Campus Life ... Mr. Robert TAYLOR
42 Dean of Chapel ... Rev. Aaron BAART
41 Director of Athletics ... Mr. Glenn BOUMA
40 Director Bookstore/Purchasing ... Ms. Lora DEVRIES
112 Director of Planned Giving ... Mr. Dave VANDER WERF
29 Director Alumni/External Relations ... Mr. Brandon HUISMAN
15 Director Human Resources ... Mrs. Sue DROOG
96 Director of Purchasing ... Mr. Fred HAAN
91 Director of Computer Services ... Mr. Brian VAN DONSELAAR
08 Director of Library Services ... Ms. Jennifer BREEMS
23 Director of Health Sciences ... Ms. Deb BOMGAARS
88 Director Academic Skills Center ... Ms. Sharon ROSENBOOM
04 Exec Admin Asst to President ... Mrs. LeeAnn MOERMAN
07 Director of Admissions ... Mr. Greg VAN DYKE

Drake University (J)

2507 University Avenue, Des Moines IA 50311-4505
County: Polk FICE Identification: 001860
Unit ID: 153269
Telephone: (515) 271-2011 Carnegie Class: Masters/L
FAX Number: (515) 271-3016 Calendar System: Semester
URL: www.drake.edu
Established: 1881 Annual Undergrad Tuition & Fees: $35,206
Enrollment: 4,991 Coed
Affiliation or Control: Independent Non-Profit IRS Status: 501(c)3
Highest Offering: Doctorate
Accreditation: NH, ART, CACREP, JOUR, LAW, MUS, PHAR

01 President ... Mr. Earl F. MARTIN
05 Provost ... Dr. Sue MATTISON
10 Chief Financial Officer ... Ms. Teresa KREJCI
11 Chief Administrative Officer ... Ms. Venessa MACRO
111 Vice Pres University Advancement ... Mr. John SMITH
07 Dean of Admission ... Ms. Anne KREMER
20 Associate Provost of Curriculum ... Mr. Art SANDERS
32 Associate Prov Student Affairs ... Ms. Melissa STURM-SMITH
35 Dean of Students ... Dr. Jerry PARKER
15 Human Resources Director ... Mr. Gary JOHNSON
13 Chief Tech Information Officer ... Mr. Chris GILL
18 Director Capital Projects ... Ms. Jolene SCHMIDT
09 Dir of Inst Research & Assessment ... Mr. Kevin SAUNDERS
06 Director of Student Records ... Mr. Kevin P. MOENKHAUS
08 Dean Cowles Library ... Mr. Rodney N. HENSHAW
85 Int Assoc Provost of Intl Programs ... Dr. Annique KIEL
19 Director Public Safety ... Mr. Scott LAW
26 Director University Communications ... Mr. Dave REMUND
29 Alumni/Parent Programs ... Mr. Andrew VERLENGIA
49 Dean Arts & Sciences ... Dr. Joseph LENZ
53 Dean School Education ... Dr. Janet M. MCMAHILL
61 Dean Law School ... Mr. Jerry ANDERSON
50 Dean Business/Public Administration ... Dr. Daniel CONNOLLY
67 Dean Pharmacy/Health Science ... Dr. Renae CHESNUT
60 Dean Journ/Mass Communications ... Ms. Kathleen RICHARDSON
41 Director Intercollegiate Athletics ... Ms. Sandy Hatfield CLUBB
37 Director Financial Aid ... Ms. Susan K. LADD
38 Director University Counseling Ctr ... Dr. Mark KLOBERDANZ
92 Assistant Director Honors Program ... Ms. Charlene SKIDMORE
94 Director Women's Studies ... Dr. Nancy REINCKE
31 Neighborhood & Comm Rel Mgr ... Mr. Nick VALDEZ
39 Director Office of Residence Life ... Ms. Lorissa LIEURANCE
04 Asst to President ... Ms. Cheryle ANANIA
100 Chief of Staff ... Mr. Nate REAGEN
30 Director of Development ... Mr. John AMATO
96 Director of Purchasing ... Ms. Caron FINDLEY

*Eastern Iowa Community College District (K)

306 W River Drive, Davenport IA 52801-1221
County: Scott FICE Identification: 004075
Unit ID: 153311
Telephone: (563) 336-3300 Carnegie Class: N/A
FAX Number: (563) 336-3350
URL: www.eicc.edu

01 Chancellor ... Dr. Donald S. DOUCETTE
30 Exec Dir Resource Development ... Dr. Ellen KABAT LENSCH
05 Vice Chanc for Education & Training ... Dr. Joan KINDLE
26 Associate Director for Marketing ... Ms. Karen FARLEY
09 Dir Institutional Effectiveness ... Ms. Laurie ADOLPH
27 Associate Director Communications ... Mr. Alan CAMPBELL
10 Chief Business Officer ... Mr. Suteesh TANDON
101 Secretary of the Institution/Board ... Ms. Honey BEDELL
15 Director Personnel Services ... Ms. Deb SULLIVAN
18 Chief Facilities/Physical Plant ... Mr. Matt SCHMIT
84 Director Enrollment Management ... Ms. Erin SNYDER

*Clinton Community College (L)

1000 Lincoln Boulevard, Clinton IA 52732-6299
County: Clinton FICE Identification: 001853
Unit ID: 153135
Telephone: (563) 244-7001 Carnegie Class: Not Classified
FAX Number: (563) 244-7107 Calendar System: Semester
URL: www.eicc.edu
Established: 1966 Annual Undergrad Tuition & Fees (In-District): N/A
Enrollment: N/A Coed
Affiliation or Control: State/Local IRS Status: 501(c)3
Highest Offering: Associate Degree
Accreditation: &NH, EMT

02 President ... Dr. Karen VICKERS
05 Dean of the College ... Mr. Ron SERPLISS
32 Dean of Student Development ... Ms. Lisa MILLER
102 Asst to Pres/Exec Dir Sharar Found ... Ms. Ann EISENMAN
04 Assistant to President/Admin ... Vacant

† Regional accreditation is carried under the parent institution Eastern Iowa Community College District in Davenport, IA.

*Muscatine Community College (M)

152 Colorado Street, Muscatine IA 52761-5396
County: Muscatine FICE Identification: 001882
Unit ID: 154040
Telephone: (563) 288-6001 Carnegie Class: Not Classified
FAX Number: (563) 288-6074 Calendar System: Semester
URL: www.eicc.edu
Established: 1929 Annual Undergrad Tuition & Fees (In-District): N/A
Enrollment: N/A Coed
Affiliation or Control: State/Local IRS Status: 501(c)3
Highest Offering: Associate Degree

Accreditation: &NH, EMT

02 President ... Dr. Naomi DEWINTER
04 Assistant to the President ... Ms. Lisa WIEGEL
05 Dean of the College ... Dr. Jeremy PICKARD
32 Dean of Student Development ... Ms. Shelly CRAM-RAHLF
06 Registrar ... Ms. Robin MITCHELL
08 Library Specialist ... Ms. Nancy LUIKART

† Regional accreditation is carried under the parent institution Eastern Iowa Community College District in Davenport, IA.

*Scott Community College (A)

500 Belmont Road, Bettendorf IA 52722-6804
County: Scott FICE Identification: 001885
Unit ID: 154314
Telephone: (563) 441-4001 Carnegie Class: Not Classified
FAX Number: (563) 441-4154 Calendar System: Semester
URL: www.eicc.edu
Established: 1966 Annual Undergrad Tuition & Fees (In-District): N/A
Enrollment: N/A Coed
Affiliation or Control: State/Local IRS Status: 501(c)3
Highest Offering: Associate Degree
Accreditation: &NH, CAHIIM, DA, EMT, NDT, RAD, SURGT

02 President ... Dr. Lyn BRODERSEN COCHRAN
32 Dean of Student Development/Affs ... Ms. LaDrina WILSON
103 Dean Career Assistance Center ... Mr. Scott SCHNEIDER
05 Dean of the College ... Dr. Gerald WICKHAM
08 Librarian ... Ms. Michelle BAILEY
11 Dean of Operations ... Dr. Matt SCHMIT
37 Director Student Financial Aid ... Ms. Jeannine INGELSON
36 Job Placement Specialist ... Mr. Wayne COLE

† Regional accreditation is carried under the parent institution Eastern Iowa Community College District in Davenport, IA.

Emmaus Bible College (B)

2570 Asbury Road, Dubuque IA 52001-3096
County: Dubuque FICE Identification: 023289
Unit ID: 153302
Telephone: (563) 588-8000 Carnegie Class: Spec-4-yr-Faith
FAX Number: (563) 588-1216 Calendar System: Semester
URL: www.emmaus.edu
Established: 1941 Annual Undergrad Tuition & Fees: $16,580
Enrollment: 247 Coed
Affiliation or Control: Independent Non-Profit IRS Status: 501(c)3
Highest Offering: Baccalaureate
Accreditation: #NH, BI

01 President ... Mr. Philip BOOM
10 VP for Administration and Finance ... Mr. Mark A. PRESSON
05 Vice President for Academic Affairs ... Mrs. Lisa L. BEATTY
111 Vice President for Advancement ... Mr. Jon W. GLOCK
32 Dean for Student Development ... Mr. Israel CHAVEZ
88 Dean for Biblical Studies ... Dr. David J. MACLEOD
08 Librarian ... Mr. John H. RUSH
37 Financial Aid Officer ... Mr. Steve C. SEEMAN
21 Controller ... Mr. Steve M. JENSEN
06 Registrar ... Mrs. Janice G. BENNETT
106 Dir Online Education/E-learning ... Vacant
108 Director Institutional Assessment ... Ms. Sherri L. POPP
29 Director Alumni Relations ... Mr. Jonathan J. ROUTLEY
41 Athletic Director ... Mr. Steve EDMONDSON
84 Director Enrollment Management ... Ms. Laurel R. RASMUSSEN
18 Chief Facilities/Physical Plant ... Mr. Jeremy MAU
26 Chief Public Relations/Marketing ... Mr. Jesse FULLAN
04 Administrative Asst to President ... Ms. Laura GUERRA
50 Chair Business Department ... Mr. Kim PARCHER

Faith Baptist Bible College and Seminary (C)

1900 NW 4th Street, Ankeny IA 50023-2152
County: Polk FICE Identification: 007121
Unit ID: 153320
Telephone: (515) 964-0601 Carnegie Class: Spec-4-yr-Faith
FAX Number: (515) 964-1638 Calendar System: Semester
URL: www.faith.edu
Established: 1921 Annual Undergrad Tuition & Fees: $16,766
Enrollment: 269 Coed
Affiliation or Control: Independent Non-Profit IRS Status: 501(c)3
Highest Offering: Master's
Accreditation: NH, BI

01 President ... Dr. James R. TILLOTSON
05 VP for Academic Services ... Dr. Kenneth D. RATHBUN
73 Dean of Seminary ... Dr. Douglas E. BROWN
10 VP for Business/CFO ... Mr. Paul BRAY
111 VP for Advancement/Church Rels ... Mr. Daniel H. BJOKNE
34 Dean of Women ... Mrs. Carrie A. AUGSBURGER
32 Dean of Students ... Mr. Lance A. AUGSBURGER
26 Director of Communications ... Mr. Kyle CLINE
06 Registrar ... Dr. Christopher E. ELLIS
37 Director Student Financial Aid ... Mr. Jordan SAUSER
08 Head Librarian ... Dr. Paul A. HARTOG
04 Administrative Assistant to President ... Miss Briana K. HARRIER
07 VP for Enrollment and Student Life ... Mr. Mark L. DAVIS
106 Dir Online Education/E-learning ... Dr. Christopher E. ELLIS
41 Athletic Director ... Mr. Brian S. FINCHAM
108 Director Institutional Assessment ... Dr. Donald LONG

Graceland University (D)

1 University Place, Lamoni IA 50140-1699
County: Decatur FICE Identification: 001866
Unit ID: 153366
Telephone: (641) 784-5000 Carnegie Class: Masters/M
FAX Number: (641) 784-5480 Calendar System: Trimester
URL: www.graceland.edu
Established: 1895 Annual Undergrad Tuition & Fees: $27,010
Enrollment: 2,300 Coed
Affiliation or Control: Other IRS Status: 501(c)3
Highest Offering: Doctorate
Accreditation: NH, #CAATE, CAEP

01 President ... Dr. Patricia H. DRAVES
05 Int VP Acad Affairs/Dean of Faculty ... Dr. Brian J. WHITE
108 VP Institutional Effectiveness ... Dr. Kathleen M. CLAUSON BASH
10 CIO/Vice Pres Business & Admin Svc ... Mr. Paul DAVIS
32 VP Student Life/Dean of Students ... Mr. Dave SCHAAL
84 Vice Pres Enrollment ... Mr. Scott BRIELL
111 Vice Pres Institutional Advancement ... Mr. Kelly EVERETT
51 Director Graduate/Continuing Educ ... Mr. Paul BINNICKER
39 Director of Residence Life ... Ms. Deb SKINNER
06 Registrar ... Mrs. M. Joyce LIGHTHILL
29 Director of Alumni Relations ... Mr. Paul J. DAVIS
36 Director Career/Acad/CAP Couns Ctr ... Ms. Catharine CRAIG
15 Director Human Resources ... Mrs. Ondrea DORY
04 Executive Asst to President ... Mrs. Jodi L. SEYMOUR
44 Director of Annual Fund/Stewardship .. Mrs. Peggy STURDEVANT
85 Director Intercultural Office ... Ms. Diana JONES
50 Dean School of Business ... Dr. Robert POULTON
53 Dean School of Education ... Dr. Lee BASH
66 Interim VP/Dean of Nursing ... Dr. Claudia HORTON
07 Director of Admissions ... Mr. Kevin BROWN
09 Director of Institutional Research ... Dr. James UHLENKAMP
124 Director of Retention ... Ms. Nicolle BRIELL

Grand View University (E)

1200 Grandview Avenue, Des Moines IA 50316-1599
County: Polk FICE Identification: 001867
Unit ID: 153375
Telephone: (515) 263-2800 Carnegie Class: Bac-Diverse
FAX Number: (515) 263-6095 Calendar System: Semester
URL: www.grandview.edu
Established: 1896 Annual Undergrad Tuition & Fees: $25,474
Enrollment: 1,988 Coed
Affiliation or Control: Evangelical Lutheran Church In America
IRS Status: 501(c)3
Highest Offering: Master's
Accreditation: NH, NURSE, @SW

01 President ... Mr. Kent L. HENNING
04 Exec Admin Asst to the President ... Ms. Corinna KING
05 Provost/Vice Pres Academic Affairs ... Dr. Carl MOSES
79 Dean College of Humanities & Educ ... Dr. Ross WASTVEDT
83 Dean College of Social/Nat Science ... Dr. Paul RIDER
10 Vice Pres Administration & Finance ... Mr. Adam J. VOIGTS
111 Vice President Advancement ... Mr. William H. BURMA
84 Vice Pres Enrollment Management ... Ms. Debbie M. BARGER
26 Vice Pres Marketing/Communications ... Ms. Kendall DILLON
32 Vice President Student Affairs ... Dr. Jay B. PRESCOTT
37 Director Financial Aid ... Ms. Michele A. DUNNE
20 Special Assistant to the Provost . Ms. Pamela M. CHRISTOFFERS
51 Dean Graduate/Adult Programs ... Dr. Patricia A. WILLIAMS
35 Associate VP for Student Affairs ... Mr. Jason K. BAUER
06 Registrar ... Ms. Debbie K. GANNON
42 Senior Campus Pastor ... Rev. Russell L. LACKEY
09 Director Inst Planning/Research ... Ms. Debbie M. BARGER
36 Director Career Center ... Ms. Susan M. STEARNS
91 Vice President Information Svcs/CIO ... Mr. Tim T. WHEELDON
08 Director of the Library ... Ms. Pamela D. REES
40 Director Bookstore & Campus Svcs ... Mr. Michael D. SHUPP
07 Director of Admissions ... Mr. Ryan THOMPSON
18 Director Buildings & Grounds ... Ms. Kim I. BUTLER
38 Director Leadership & Counseling ... Mr. Kent A. SCHORNACK
28 Dir Multicultural & Cmty Outreach ... Mr. Alex H. PIEDRAS
41 Athletic Director ... Mr. Troy A. PLUMMER
15 Human Resources Manager ... Ms. Erica L. KLUVER
88 Special Assistant to the President ... Mr. Robert BARRON

Grinnell College (F)

1121 Park Street, Grinnell IA 50112-1690
County: Poweshiek FICE Identification: 001868
Unit ID: 153384
Telephone: (641) 269-4000 Carnegie Class: Bac-A&S
FAX Number: (641) 269-3408 Calendar System: Semester
URL: www.grinnell.edu
Established: 1846 Annual Undergrad Tuition & Fees: $48,758
Enrollment: 1,705 Coed
Affiliation or Control: Independent Non-Profit IRS Status: 501(c)3
Highest Offering: Baccalaureate
Accreditation: NH

01 President ... Raynard S. KINGTON
100 Chief of Staff/VP Planning ... Angela VOOS
05 Vice Pres Acad Affs/Dean Col ... Michael LATHAM
30 Vice President Dev/Alumni Rel ... Vacant
115 Chief Investment Officer ... Scott L. WILSON
10 Vice President for Finance/Treas ... Kate E. WALKER
20 Associate Dean of College ... Maria TAPIAS
20 Associate Dean of College ... Mark LEVANDOSKI
20 Associate Dean of the College ... Shanna BENJAMIN
07 VP Enroll/Dean Adm & Fin Aid ... Joseph P. BAGNOLI
110 Director of Development Operations ... Adam LAUG
37 Dir Student Fin Aid & Asst VP Enrol ... Brad LINDBERG
15 Assistant VP of Human Resources ... Mary GREINER
26 Vice President for Communications ... Debra LUKEHART
06 Registrar ... Jason MAHER
08 Librarian ... Mark CHRISTEL
29 Director of Alumni Relations ... Jayn CHANEY
13 Chief Information Tech Officer ... Dave ROBINSON
09 Assoc VP Analytics/Inst Rsch ... Randy STILES
85 Director Intl Student Services ... Karen K. EDWARDS
40 Manager/Bookstore ... Cassandra J. WHERRY
41 Athletic Director ... Andrew HAMILTON
23 Dir Stdnt Health & Counsel Service ... Deb SHILL
121 Dean Student Success/Acad Advising ... Joyce STERN
18 Director Facilities Mgmt ... Richard WHITNEY
19 Dir of Campus Safety ... James SHROPSHIRE
42 Chaplain/Dean of Rel Life ... Deanna SHORB
102 Director Corp/Found/Govt Rels ... Susan FERRARI
32 Assoc VP Student Affairs ... Andrea CONNER
35 Dean of Students ... Sarah MOSCHENROSS
31 Dir Community Enhancement/Engagemnt . Monica CHAVEZ-SILVA
36 Dean & Director/Career Life & Svcs ... Mark PELTZ
04 Executive Asst to President ... Tammy PRUSHA
101 Secretary of the College ... Susan SCHOEN
104 Director of Off-Campus Study ... Alicia STANLEY
28 Asst VP and Chief Diversity Officer ... Lakesia JOHNSON
39 Director Residence Life ... John ROLON
44 Director Annual Giving ... Mae PARKER
96 Procurement Manager ... Amanda JONES

Hamilton Technical College (G)

1011 E 53rd Street, Davenport IA 52807-2616
County: Scott FICE Identification: 012064
Unit ID: 153427
Telephone: (563) 386-3570 Carnegie Class: Spec-4-yr-Other Tech
FAX Number: (563) 386-6756 Calendar System: Semester
URL: www.hamiltontechcollege.com
Established: 1969 Annual Undergrad Tuition & Fees: $14,250
Enrollment: 150 Coed
Affiliation or Control: Proprietary IRS Status: Proprietary
Highest Offering: Baccalaureate
Accreditation: ACCSC

01 President ... Mrs. Maryanne HAMILTON
32 Dean of Students ... Mr. Brian BEERT

Hawkeye Community College (H)

Box 8015, Waterloo IA 50704-8015
County: Black Hawk FICE Identification: 004595
Unit ID: 153445
Telephone: (319) 296-2320 Carnegie Class: Assoc/MT-VT-High Non
FAX Number: (319) 296-2874 Calendar System: Semester
URL: www.hawkeyecollege.edu
Established: 1966 Annual Undergrad Tuition & Fees (In-District): $4,786
Enrollment: 5,370 Coed
Affiliation or Control: State/Local IRS Status: 501(c)3
Highest Offering: Associate Degree
Accreditation: NH, COARC, DA, DH, EMT, MLTAD, OTA, PTAA

01 President ... Dr. Linda A. ALLEN
05 Provost & VP Academic Affairs ... Dr. Jane BRADLEY
10 Vice Pres Administration & Finance ... Mr. Dan GILLEN
84 Vice Pres Enrollment Services ... Ms. Kathy A. FLYNN
111 Exec Dir Institutional Advancement ... Ms. Holly JOHNSON
15 Exec Dir Human Resource Services ... Mr. John D. CLOPTON
81 Dean STEM & Business ... Dr. Cynthia BOTTRELL
79 Dean Comm/Humanities/Edu/SocSc/ Arts ... Ms. Catharine FREEMAN
75 Dean Applied Science/Eng Technology ... Mr. David GRUNKLEE
76 Dean Interprof Health & Safety Svcs ... Mr. Eugene LEUTZINGER
32 Dean of Students ... Ms. Nancy HENDERSON
07 Dir Admiss/Recruit/Athlet/Stdt Life ... Mr. Dave BALL
21 Director Business Services ... Ms. Julie THOMAS
13 Chief Information Officer ... Mr. Brian MCCORMICK
08 Director Library Services ... Ms. Candace HAVELY
51 Exec Director Business & Cmty Educ ... Mr. Aaron SAUERBREI
18 Director Plant & Facilities ... Ms. Lindsey NISSEN
06 Dir Student Records & Registration ... Ms. Patricia A. EAST
24 Director Teaching/Learning Services ... Mr. Robin GALLOWAY
09 Director Institutional Research ... Ms. Connie BUHR
26 Director Public Relations/Marketing ... Ms. Mary Pat MOORE
28 Director of Inclusion & Diversity ... Ms. Rhonda MCRINA
35 Assoc Director of Student Life ... Ms. Stephanie CHERRY
30 Development Officer ... Ms. Karen GEBEL
101 Board Secretary ... Ms. Denise A. DUNN
19 Dir Public Safety/Emergency Mgr ... Mr. John BECKMAN
88 Director Urban Ctrs/Adult Literacy ... Ms. Sandra JENSEN
88 Dean of Transitional Programs ... Mr. Tom MUELLER
103 Dir Workforce/Career Development ... Mr. Christopher HANNAN
37 Director Student Financial Aid ... Ms. Gisella BAKER
04 Assistant to President ... Ms. Donna S. MCNULTY

Indian Hills Community College (I)

525 Grandview Avenue, Ottumwa IA 52501-1398
County: Wapello FICE Identification: 008403
Unit ID: 153472
Telephone: (641) 683-5111 Carnegie Class: Assoc/MT-VT-High Non
FAX Number: (641) 683-5184 Calendar System: Quarter

URL: www.indianhills.edu
Established: 1966 Annual Undergrad Tuition & Fees (In-District): $3,960
Enrollment: 4,773 Coed
Affiliation or Control: State/Local IRS Status: 501(c)3
Highest Offering: Associate Degree
Accreditation: NH, ACFEI, CA, CAHIIM, DA, DH, EMT, MLTAD, OTA, PTAA, RAD

01 President Dr. Marlene SPROUSE
10 VP/Chief Financial Officer Mr. Bill MECK
05 Vice Pres Acad Affs/Instl Effect Dr. Matt THOMPSON
49 Executive Dean Arts & Sciences Ms. Darlas SHOCKLEY
103 Exec Dean Reg Economic Advancement Mr. Tom RUBEL
32 Exec Dean Student Services Mr. Chris BOWSER
103 Exec Dean Career/Workforce Educ Dr. Jill BUDDE
12 Dean Centerville Campus Mr. Joe STARCEVICH
86 Assoc Dean Govt Affs/Information Ms. Martha WICK
102 Dir Foundation/Community Relations Ms. Bianca MYERS
13 Chief Information Officer Mr. Shane MOLYNEUX
15 Director Human Resources Ms. Kristin PARKS
18 Director Maintenance Mr. Rick FOSDYCK
06 Registrar Ms. Joni KELLEY
41 Athletic Director Mr. Mike HAGEN
26 Director for Media/Public Rels Mr. Kevin PINK
88 Chair Aviation Programs Mr. Darren GRAHAM
07 Int Director of Admissions Mr. Chris BOWER
09 Director of Institutional Research Dr. Stephanie HOLLIMAN
29 Director of Alumni Relations Dr. Bianca MYERS
35 Chief Development Ms. Rhonda CONRAD

Indian Hills Community College Centerville (A)

721 N First Street, Centerville IA 52544
Telephone: (641) 856-2143 Identification: 770054
Accreditation: &NH

Inste Bible College (B)

2302 SW 3rd Street, Ankeny IA 50023-2453
County: Polk Identification: 666461
Telephone: (515) 289-9200 Carnegie Class: Not Classified
FAX Number: (515) 289-9201 Calendar System: Semester
URL: www.inste.edu
Established: 1982 Annual Undergrad Tuition & Fees: N/A
Enrollment: N/A Coed
Affiliation or Control: Interdenominational IRS Status: 501(c)3
Highest Offering: Baccalaureate
Accreditation: DEAC

01 President Dr. Nicholas VENDITTI
05 Executive Vice President Dr. Leona VENDITTI
20 Assistant Dean Rev. Victor COLON

Iowa Central Community College (C)

One Triton Circle, Fort Dodge IA 50501
County: Webster FICE Identification: 001865
Unit ID: 153524
Telephone: (515) 576-7201 Carnegie Class: Assoc/MT-VT-Mix Trad/Non
FAX Number: (515) 576-7207 Calendar System: Semester
URL: www.iowacentral.edu
Established: 1966 Annual Undergrad Tuition & Fees (In-District): $5,580
Enrollment: 5,634 Coed
Affiliation or Control: Local IRS Status: 501(c)3
Highest Offering: Associate Degree
Accreditation: NH, DH, EMT, MAC, MLTAD, RAD

01 President Dr. Daniel P. KINNEY
04 Assistant to the President Mrs. Karen L. LOMBARD
05 Vice President of Instruction Dr. Dreand R. JOHNSON
32 Vice Pres Enroll Mgmt/Student Devel Mr. Thomas J. BENEKE
10 Vice President of Business Affairs Mrs. Angela A. MARTIN
86 VP External Affairs/Govt Rels Mr. James B. KERSTEN
30 VP Development/Alumni Rels Mrs. Laurie M. HENDRICKS
50 Business & Ind Technology Dean Mr. Neale J. ADAMS
76 Health Sciences Dean Mrs. Trina J. STATON
49 Liberal Arts & Sciences Dean Mrs. Jennifer M. CONDON
106 Distance Learning Dean Mr. Timothy J. MARTIN
09 Institutional Effective Exec Dir Dr. Stacy L. MENTZER
103 Econ Wrkfrc Dev/Cont Educ Exec Dir Mrs. Shelly R. BLUNK
06 Registrar Ms. Courtney A. KOPP
07 Enrollment Management Director Mrs. Sara A. SCHARF
124 Retention Center Director Mrs. Tracy L. CRIPPIN-HAAKE
37 Financial Aid Director Mrs. Lindsey M. CHRISTIE
21 Business Office Director Mr. Luke J. GROVE
15 Human Resources Director Mrs. Kimberly N. WHITMORE
16 Human Resources Coordinator Ms. Sandi J. PIEPER
41 Intercollegiate Athletics Director Mr. Rick A. SANDQUIST
39 Housing Director Mr. Jeremy D. CONLEY
38 Mental Health Counselor Mrs. Kelli A. REUTER
35 Student Life & Activities Director Mr. David L. PEARSON
88 Academic Resource Services Director Ms. Lori L. WALTON
18 Physical Facilities Director Mr. Shan L. BEECHER
12 Storm Lake Center Director Mr. Dan J. ANDERSON
12 Webster City Center Director Vacant
26 Public Information Director Mr. Paul A. DECOURSEY
13 Institutional Technology Director Mr. Jeff A. NELSEN
13 Institutional Technology Director Mr. Troy D. CRAMPTON
14 Sr Computer System Analyst Mr. Warren K. BAUER
40 Bookstore Manager Mrs. Samantha E. MCCLAIN

Iowa Lakes Community College (D)

19 S Seventh Street, Estherville IA 51334-2234
County: Emmet FICE Identification: 001864
Unit ID: 153533
Telephone: (712) 362-2604 Carnegie Class: Assoc/MT-VT-High Non
FAX Number: (712) 362-8363 Calendar System: Semester
URL: www.iowalakes.edu
Established: 1967 Annual Undergrad Tuition & Fees (In-District): $5,900
Enrollment: 2,315 Coed
Affiliation or Control: State/Local IRS Status: 501(c)3
Highest Offering: Associate Degree
Accreditation: NH, MAC, SURGT

01 President Ms. Valerie K. NEWHOUSE
11 Vice President of Administration Mr. Robert A. LEIFELD
05 Exec Dean Estherville Campus Dr. Lisa STICH
12 Exec Dean Emmetsburg Campus Mr. Thomas S. BROTHERTON
26 Exec Director of Marketing Ms. Jane S. CAMPBELL
18 Exec Dir of Facilities Management Ms. Delaine S. HINEY
15 Exec Director Human Resources Ms. Kathy A. MULLER
31 Exec Dir Cmty & Business Relations Ms. Jolene R. ROGERS
10 Chief Financial Officer Mr. Jeff D. SOPER
32 Executive Dean of Students Ms. Julie R. WILLIAMS

Iowa Lakes Community College Emmetsburg Campus (E)

3200 College Drive, Emmetsburg IA 50536
Telephone: (712) 852-3554 Identification: 770055
Accreditation: &NH

Iowa Lakes Community College Spencer Campus (F)

Gateway N 1900 Grand Ave, Ste B-1, Spencer IA 51301
Telephone: (712) 262-7141 Identification: 770056
Accreditation: &NH

*Iowa Valley Community College District (G)

3702 S Center Street, Marshalltown IA 50158-4760
County: Marshall FICE Identification: 033436
Telephone: (641) 752-4643 Carnegie Class: N/A
FAX Number: (641) 754-1336
URL: www.iavalley.edu

01 Chancellor Dr. Christopher DUREE
11 Vice Chanc Administrative Services Ms. Colleen SPRINGER
51 Vice Chanc Continuing Educ/Training Ms. Jacque GOODMAN
10 Chief Financial Officer Ms. Kathleen PINK
13 Chief Information Officer Mr. Jim WILSON
12 Provost Ellsworth Community College Dr. Martin REIMER
12 Provost Marshalltown Community Col Dr. Robin SHAFFER LILIENTHAL
12 Dean of Iowa Valley Grinnell Ms. Mary Anne NICKLE
26 Director of Marketing Ms. Robin ANCTIL
09 Institutional Researcher Dr. Lisa BREJA
04 Admin Assistant to the Chancellor Ms. Barbara JENNINGS
86 Director of Government Affairs Ms. Cynthia SCHULTE

*Ellsworth Community College (H)

1100 College Avenue, Iowa Falls IA 50126-1199
County: Hardin FICE Identification: 001862
Unit ID: 153296
Telephone: (641) 648-4611 Carnegie Class: Assoc/HT-High Trad
FAX Number: (641) 648-3128 Calendar System: Semester
URL: https://www.iavalley.edu/
Established: 1890 Annual Undergrad Tuition & Fees (In-District): $4,536
Enrollment: 830 Coed
Affiliation or Control: State/Local IRS Status: 501(c)3
Highest Offering: Associate Degree
Accreditation: &NH, MAC

02 Provost Dr. Martin REIMER
05 Dean of Academic Affairs Dr. Lisa STOCK
32 Dean of Student Affairs Dr. Barb KLEIN
08 Library Service Mgr Ms. Sandra GREUFE
32 Director of Athletics/Student Life Mr. Nate FORSYTH
37 Director Financial Aid Ms. Tara MILLER
44 Dir Annual Plan Giving/Dir Alum Rel Ms. Kaitlyn BARTLING
07 Director of Admissions Ms. Adriane SIETSEMA

† Regional accreditation is carried under the parent institution Iowa Valley Community College District in Marshalltown, IA.

*Marshalltown Community College (I)

3700 S Center Street, Marshalltown IA 50158-4760
County: Marshall FICE Identification: 001875
Unit ID: 153922
Telephone: (641) 752-7106 Carnegie Class: Assoc/MT-VT-High Non
FAX Number: (641) 752-8149 Calendar System: Semester
URL: www.mcc.iavalley.edu
Established: 1927 Annual Undergrad Tuition & Fees (In-District): $4,536
Enrollment: 1,923 Coed
Affiliation or Control: State/Local IRS Status: 501(c)3
Highest Offering: Associate Degree
Accreditation: &NH, DA

02 Chancellor Dr. Christopher A. DUREE
05 Provost Dr. Robin SHAFFER LILIENTHAL
11 Vice Chanc Administrative Services Ms. Colleen SPRINGER
10 Chief Financial Officer Ms. Kathy PINK
51 Vice Chancellor of Cont Educ/Trng Jacque GOODMAN
20 Dean of Academic Affairs Mr. Patrick KENNEDY
32 Dean of Student Affairs Vacant
84 Dean Enrollment/Student Life Ms. Angie REDMOND
20 Dean of Students/Learning Svcs/TRIO Mr. Nate CHUA
06 Registrar/Dir of Operations Ms. Mandy BROWN
76 Assoc Dean of Health Occupations Ms. Linda HANSON
102 Executive Director MCC Foundation Ms. Carol GEIL
37 Financial Aid Administrator Mr. Matt DANIELS
26 Director of Marketing Vacant
09 Dir of Institutional Research Vacant
41 Athletic Director Ms. Kathleen BROWN
35 Dir Student Engagement/Res Life Mr. Chris BREES
38 Senior Student Success Specialist Mr. Dan KEY
08 Library Services Manager Ms. Joanna PRIMUS
40 MCC Bookstore Manager Mr. Aaron DEBOER

† Regional accreditation is carried under the parent institution Iowa Valley Community College District in Marshalltown, IA.

Iowa Wesleyan University (J)

601 N Main, Mount Pleasant IA 52641-1398
County: Henry FICE Identification: 001871
Unit ID: 153621
Telephone: (319) 385-8021 Carnegie Class: Bac-Diverse
FAX Number: (319) 385-6296 Calendar System: Semester
URL: www.iw.edu
Established: 1842 Annual Undergrad Tuition & Fees: $23,516
Enrollment: 457 Coed
Affiliation or Control: United Methodist IRS Status: 501(c)3
Highest Offering: Master's
Accreditation: NH, NUR

01 President Dr. Steven E. TITUS
10 VP for Finance and Treasurer Ms. Chris PLUNKETT
84 VP for Enrollment Management Mr. Nickolis BOONE
05 VP Academic Affairs Dr. DeWayne FRAZIER
30 VP for Strategic Initiatives Ms. Meg RICHTMAN
44 VP University Advancement Dr. Drew VAN HORN
32 VP for Student Development Dr. Wesley BROOKS
13 Assoc VP/Chief Information Officer Dr. Kit NIP
06 Registrar Ms. Megan HILLS
37 Director of Financial Aid Ms. Kristy JOHNSON
07 Director of Admissions Ms. Julie DUPLESSIS
21 Controller Ms. Deb LILLIE
20 Asst VP for Academic Affairs Ms. Paula KINNEY
15 Director of Human Resources Ms. Kathy MOOTHART
44 Director of Wesleyan Fund Ms. Jill YODER
26 Director of Marketing Ms. Lori BAERG
27 Creative Director Ms. Amanda RUNDQUIST
29 Director of Alumni/Parent Relations Ms. Holly JONES
41 Athletic Director Mr. Derek ZANDER
18 Director of Physical Plant Mr. Sean GRAY
35 Coordinator of Student Engagement Mr. Matthew KLUNDT
36 Director of Career Development Vacant
40 Bookstore Director Ms. Amy MABEUS
04 Asst to the President Ms. Mary NOTESTEIN
105 Webmaster Ms. Cindee VANDIJK
09 Director of Institutional Research Mr. Fred MILLER
102 Dir Corporate/Foundation Relations Mr. Jim PEDRICK

Iowa Western Community College (K)

2700 College Road, Council Bluffs IA 51503-0567
County: Pottawattamie FICE Identification: 004598
Unit ID: 153630
Telephone: (712) 325-3200 Carnegie Class: Assoc/MT-VT-Mix Trad/Non
FAX Number: (712) 325-3424 Calendar System: Semester
URL: www.iwcc.edu
Established: 1966 Annual Undergrad Tuition & Fees (In-District): $5,472
Enrollment: 6,472 Coed
Affiliation or Control: State/Local IRS Status: 501(c)3
Highest Offering: Associate Degree
Accreditation: NH, ACFEI, DA, DH, EMT, MAC, PTAA, SURGT

01 President Dr. Dan KINNEY
04 Assistant to the President Ms. Erin STOPAK
05 Vice President for Academic Affairs Dr. Marjorie WELCH
10 Vice President of Finance Mr. Edwin HOLTZ
32 Vice President for Student Services Mrs. Tori CHRISTIE
26 Vice Pres of Marketing/Public Rels Mr. Donald KOHLER
30 Vice Pres Institutional Advancement Mrs. Molly NOON
103 VP Economic/Workforce Devel Mr. Mark STANLEY
09 Dean Institutional Research/Accred Mrs. Barb GODDEN
07 Dean Admissions & Records Mr. Chris LAFERLA
84 Dean of Advising/Academic Support Mrs. Keri ZIMMER
35 Dean Student Life/Student Success Ms. Kimberly HENRY
106 Dean Distance Educ/Pathway Dev Mr. Matthew MANCUSO
81 Dean Science/Tech/Engineering/Math Mrs. Kim CARTER
79 Dean of Comm/Education/Fine Arts Mrs. Jenny KRUGER
76 Dean of Health & Sports Sciences Dr. Gina SCHOCHENMAIER
51 Dean of Continuing Education Vacant
50 Dean Ag/Bus/Computer Info/Soc Sci Mr. Rick MCFAYDEN
06 Registrar Mrs. Jill CLARK
15 Director of Human Resources Mrs. Kelly FISCHER
29 Director of Alumni Relations Mrs. Sarah SAAR
37 Director of Student Financial Aid Ms. Laura THAYER-MENCKE
21 Director Accounting Ms. Randi PAPE

13 Dir Information Technology .... Mr. James A. MAHLBERG
41 Athletic Director .... Mr. Jeremy CAPO
39 Director of Residence Life .... Mr. Spencer MATHEWS
18 Director Physical Plant .... Mr. Brian SUTTER
96 Director of Purchasing .... Mrs. Diane OSBAHR
40 College Store Manager .... Mrs. Maggie SOBCZYK-BARRON
88 Food Service Manager .... Mr. Bradley GROESSER

Kaplan University (A)

3165 Edgewood Parkway SW,
Cedar Rapids IA 52404-2998
Telephone: (319) 363-0481 FICE Identification: 004220
Accreditation: &NH, ACBSP, MAC

† Regional accreditation is carried under the parent institution in Davenport, IA.

Kaplan University (B)

1801 East Kimberly Road, Suite 1,
Davenport IA 52807-2095
County: Scott FICE Identification: 004586
Unit ID: 260901
Telephone: (563) 355-3500 Carnegie Class: Masters/L
FAX Number: (563) 355-1320 Calendar System: Quarter
URL: www.kaplanuniversity.edu/davenport-iowa.aspx
Established: 1937 Annual Undergrad Tuition & Fees: $14,325
Enrollment: 45,355 Coed
Affiliation or Control: Proprietary IRS Status: Proprietary
Highest Offering: Doctorate
Accreditation: NH, ACBSP, IFSAC, MAC, NURSE

01 Campus President .... Ms. Kacy WEBSTER
31 Campus Relations Manager .... Ms. Angela BOWERS
32 Director of Student Services .... Vacant
37 Director of Financial Aid .... Ms. Sharon BARBER
07 Director of Admissions .... Mr. Jason WILEBSKI
36 Employment Search Coordinator .... Ms. Sandra WAKEFIELD
06 Registrar .... Ms. Janet GEHRLS

Kaplan University (C)

Plaza West 2570 4th Street, SW,
Mason City IA 50401-3102
Telephone: (641) 423-2530 Identification: 666438
Accreditation: &NH, ACBSP

† Regional accreditation is carried under the parent institution in Davenport, IA.

Kaplan University (D)

4655 121st Street, Urbandale IA 50323-2311
Telephone: (515) 727-2100 Identification: 666437
Accreditation: &NH, ACBSP, MAC

† Regional accreditation is carried under the parent institution in Davenport, IA.

Kaplan University-Cedar Falls (E)

7009 Nordic Drive, Cedar Falls IA 50613
Telephone: (319) 277-0220 Identification: 770058
Accreditation: &NH, ACBSP

Kirkwood Community College (F)

6301 Kirkwood Blvd. SW, Cedar Rapids IA 52406
County: Linn FICE Identification: 004076
Unit ID: 153737
Telephone: (319) 398-5411 Carnegie Class: Assoc/MT-VT-High Non
FAX Number: (319) 398-1037 Calendar System: Semester
URL: www.kirkwood.edu
Established: 1966 Annual Undergrad Tuition & Fees (In-District): $4,362
Enrollment: 14,368 Coed
Affiliation or Control: Local IRS Status: 501(c)3
Highest Offering: Associate Degree
Accreditation: NH, ACFEI, CAHIIM, COARC, DA, DH, DT, EMT, MAC, NDT, OTA, PTAA, SURGT

01 President .... Dr. Mick STARCEVICH
51 VP Cont Education/Training Svcs .... Dr. Kim BECICKA
10 Vice President/Chief Fin/Oper Ofcr .... Mr. Jim CHOATE
30 Vice President Development .... Ms. Kathy HALL
05 Vice President Academic Affairs .... Dr. Bill LAMB
32 Vice President Student Services .... Mr. Jon BUSE
20 Assoc Vice President Acad Affairs .... Mr. John HENIK
12 Exec Dean Iowa City Campus .... Dr. Ann VALENTINE
35 Dean of Students .... Ms. Melissa PAYNE
15 Vice President Human Resources .... Mr. Wes FOWLER
13 Vice President IT .... Mr. Jon NEFF
09 VP Institutional Research .... Mr. Al ROWE
106 Exec Dean Distance Lrng .... Mr. Todd PRUSHA
84 Exec Dir Enrollment Services .... Mr. Patrick CLEMENCE
07 Director Admissions .... Mr. Douglas F. BANNON
18 VP Facilities & Security .... Mr. Troy MCQUILLEN
25 Director Grants & Fed Programs .... Ms. Heather CONLEY
41 Athletic Director .... Mr. Doug WAGEMESTER
06 Registrar .... Ms. Dena RAUCH
29 Scholarship & Alumni Director .... Ms. Jody DONALDSON
37 Financial Aid Director .... Mr. Matt FALDUTO
47 Dean Agriculture Science .... Mr. Scott ERMER
72 Dean Industrial Technology .... Mr. Dan MARTIN
79 Dean Humanities & English .... Ms. Jennifer BRADLEY
76 Dean Allied Health .... Ms. Nicky CLINE
83 Dean Social Sciences .... Dr. Brooke STRAHN-KOLLER
81 Dean Math/Science .... Mr. Marvin BAUSMAN
66 Dean Nursing .... Dr. Kathryn DOLTER
76 Dean Health Occupations .... Dr. Mike MCLAUGHLIN
50 Dean Business & Information Tech .... Ms. Colette ATKINS
88 Dean Learning Services/Dir Library .... Mr. Arron WINGS
04 Asst to President .... Ms. Carrie ANDERSON
104 Dean International Programs .... Ms. Dawn WOOD
19 Senior Director Security/Safety .... Ms. Melissa JENSEN
26 Exec Dir Communications/Marketing .... Mr. Kevin HANSEN
44 Director Annual or Planned Giving .... Ms. Jody PELLERIN
14 Exec Dir IT Services .... Mr. Darren ZABLOUDIL
21 Exec Director Finance .... Ms. Kris RILEY
103 Director Skills to Employment .... Ms. Carla ANDORF
88 Director Secondary Programs .... Mr. Marcel KIELKUCKI
108 Director Institutional Assessment .... Mr. Cort IVERSON

Kirkwood Community College Iowa City (G)

1816 Lower Muscatine Road, Iowa City IA 52240
Telephone: (819) 887-3658 Identification: 770062
Accreditation: &NH

Loras College (H)

1450 Alta Vista, Dubuque IA 52004-0178
County: Dubuque FICE Identification: 001873
Unit ID: 153825
Telephone: (563) 588-7100 Carnegie Class: Bac-Diverse
FAX Number: (563) 588-7964 Calendar System: Semester
URL: www.loras.edu
Established: 1839 Annual Undergrad Tuition & Fees: $31,525
Enrollment: 1,528 Coed
Affiliation or Control: Roman Catholic IRS Status: 501(c)3
Highest Offering: Master's
Accreditation: NH, CAATE, ENG, SW

01 President .... Mr. James E. COLLINS
05 VP Academic Affairs .... Dr. Donna N. HEALD
10 Treasurer .... Mr. Michael H. DOYLE
03 Senior Vice President .... Dr. Mary Ellen CARROLL
111 VP Institutional Advancement .... Mr. Michael H. DOYLE
32 VP Student Development .... Dr. Arthur W. SUNLEAF
04 Executive Assistant to President .... Ms. Heather L. JUNGBLUT
42 Dean of Campus Spiritual Life .... Rev. William M. JOENSEN
91 Sr Dir Technology Services .... Mr. Thomas D. KRUSE
29 Exec Dir Alumni/Communications .... Ms. Bobbi L. EARLES
15 Dir Human Resources .... Mr. Troy M. WRIGHT
09 Director of Institutional Research .... Vacant
38 Director Center for Counseling .... Ms. Tricia S. BORELLI
07 Admiss Dir of Recruit & Retention .. Mr. Kyle J. KLAPATAUSKAS
08 Library Director .... Ms. Joyce A. MELDREM
35 Assistant Dean of Students .... Ms. Molly A. BURROWS-SCHUMACHER
30 Assoc VP Institutional Advance .... Mr. Joshua D. BOOTS
41 Dir Intercollegiate Athletics .... Ms. Denise A. UDELHOFEN
18 Asst VP Physical Resources .... Mr. John R. MCDERMOTT
40 Director of Bookstore .... Ms. Renee A. MENNE
23 Director of Health Center .... Ms. Tammy S. MARTI
42 Campus Ministry/P&J Coordinator .... Ms. Anastacia M. MCDERMOTT
06 Registrar .... Mr. Michael P. FRIEND
19 Dir Res Life & Campus Safety .... Ms. Molly A. BURROWS-SCHUMACHER
35 Assoc Dean of Students .... Ms. Kimberly A. WALSH
37 Director of Financial Planning .... Ms. Julie A. DUNN
102 Dir Foundation/Gov Support .... Ms. Valorie A. WOERDEHOFF
26 Dir Communications/Marketing .... Mr. John D. SUTTER
96 Controller for Business Office .... Ms. Rennie A. ROOT
36 Academic Internship Coordinator .... Ms. Jennifer L. WEBER

Luther College (I)

700 College Drive, Decorah IA 52101-1045
County: Winneshiek FICE Identification: 001874
Unit ID: 153834
Telephone: (563) 387-2000 Carnegie Class: Bac-A&S
FAX Number: (563) 387-2158 Calendar System: 4/1/4
URL: www.luther.edu
Established: 1861 Annual Undergrad Tuition & Fees: $40,040
Enrollment: 2,337 Coed
Affiliation or Control: Evangelical Lutheran Church In America
IRS Status: 501(c)3
Highest Offering: Baccalaureate
Accreditation: NH, CAATE, CAEPN, MUS, NURSE, SW

01 President .... Dr. Paula J. CARLSON
05 Vice Pres Acad Affs/Dean of College .... Dr. Kevin KRAUS
20 Assistant Dean .... Ms. Arleen ORVIS
30 Vice President for Development .... Mr. James JERMIER
10 Vice President for Finance & Admin .... Mr. Eric RUNESTAD
32 Vice Pres/Dean for Student Life .... Mr. Corey LANDSTROM
84 Vice Pres Enrollment Management .... Mr. Scot SCHAEFFER
26 Vice Pres Communications/Marketing .... Vacant
13 Exec Dir Library & Information Svcs .... Mr. Paul R. MATTSON
88 Assoc VP and Dir of Admissions .... Mr. Derek HARTL
21 Controller .... Ms. Peggy LENSING
18 Director of Facilities Services .... Mr. Jay L. UTHOFF
91 Director Information Systems .... Ms. Marcia A. GULLICKSON
110 Senior Development Officer .... Mr. Doug NELSON
06 Registrar .... Dr. Kristin SWANSON
20 Associate Dean/Dir Faculty Devel .... Dr. Jeffrey WILKERSON
15 Director Human Resources .... Ms. Marsha WENTHOLD
41 Director Intercollegiate Athletics .... Ms. Renae HARTL
29 Exec Director of Alumni Relations .... Ms. Sherry B. ALCOCK
27 Director of Publications & Design .... Mr. Michael BARTELS
27 Director of Media Relations .... Ms. Julie TRYTTEN
04 Exec Assistant to the President .... Ms. Sally MING
35 Assistant Dean Student Life .... Ms. Kasey NIKKEL
36 Director Career Center .... Ms. Brenda RANUM
38 Director Counseling Service .... Ms. Meg HAMMES
37 Director Student Financial Planning .... Ms. Janice K. CORDELL
42 Dir Campus Ministry & Cong Rels .... Rev. Michael R. BLAIR
40 Director Book Shop/Union Services .... Ms. Deanna CASTERTON
39 Assistant Dean & Dir Res Life .... Ms. Kristine FRANZEN
85 Exec Dir Ctr Global Learn & Int Adm .... Mr. Jon LUND
23 Director Health Services .... Ms. Diane TAPPE
19 Director Security/Safety .... Mr. Robert HARRI
88 Director Campus Programming .... Mr. Paul ATKINS
22 Int Dean of Inst Equity & Inclusion .... Ms. Lisa M. SCOTT
09 Director Assessment/Inst Research .... Dr. Jon A. CHRISTY
07 Senior Assoc Director of Admissions .... Mr. Kirk NEUBAUER
35 Dir Stdnt Activities and the Union .... Ms. Trish NEUBAUER
88 Student Life Assistant Dean .... Ms. Janet HUNTER
45 Dean for Inst Planning & Mission .... Dr. Terry E. SPARKES
28 Director of Diversity Center .... Ms. Wintlett TAYLOR-BROWNE

Maharishi University of Management (J)

1000 N 4th Street, Fairfield IA 52557-0001
County: Jefferson FICE Identification: 011113
Unit ID: 153861
Telephone: (641) 472-7000 Carnegie Class: Masters/L
FAX Number: (641) 472-1179 Calendar System: Semester
URL: www.mum.edu
Established: 1971 Annual Undergrad Tuition & Fees: $27,530
Enrollment: 1,530 Coed
Affiliation or Control: Independent Non-Profit IRS Status: 501(c)3
Highest Offering: Doctorate
Accreditation: NH, IACBE

01 President .... Dr. John HAGELIN
03 Executive Vice President .... Dr. Craig PEARSON
45 Vice President of Expansion .... Mr. Thomas BROOKS
30 VP Development & Alumni Relations .... Mr. Brad MYLETT
05 Dean of Faculty .... Dr. Cathy GORINI
10 Treasurer .... Mr. Michael SPIVAK
88 International Vice President .... Dr. Michael DILLBECK
88 International Vice President .... Dr. Susan DILLBECK
11 Chief Administrative Officer .... Mr. David TODT
43 Legal Counsel/Dean Global Develop .... Mr. Bill GOLDSTEIN
07 Dean of Admissions .... Mr. Steve LANGERUD
07 Associate Dean of Admissions .... Ms. Aster HESSE
84 VP Enrollment Mgmt & Marketing .... Mr. Rod EASON
33 Associate Dean of Men .... Mr. Manyu HESSE
34 Associate Dean of Women .... Ms. Amellia HESSE
06 Registrar .... Ms. Taniya HALLMAN
26 Media Relations .... Mr. Norman ZIEROLD
51 Dir Distance Educ/Intl Programs .... Mr. Dennis HEATON
27 Director of Press .... Mr. Harry BRIGHT
39 Director of Housing .... Mr. Mahmood ALI
37 Director of Student Financial Aid .... Mr. Dan WASIELEWSKI
13 Director of Information Services .... Mr. Simon RODRIGUEZ
20 Dean Academic Programs .... Dr. Chris JONES
15 Director/Human Resources .... Mr. Stan LAMOTHE
29 Director Alumni .... Mr. Paul STOKSTAD
111 Co-Exec Director Inst Advancement .... Mr. Nick ROSANIA
111 Co-Exec Director Inst Advancement .... Ms. Sandra ROSANIA
36 Director Career Services .... Ms. Sheila SWANSON
18 Chief Facilities/Physical Plant .... Mr. Craig WAGNER
49 Dean College of Arts & Sciences .... Dr. Chris JONES
77 Dean College of Computer Sci & Math .... Mr. Gregory GUTHRIE
58 Dean of Graduate School .... Dr. Frederick TRAVIS
04 Administrative Asst to President .... Ms. Jane AIKENS
08 Head Librarian .... Ms. Rouzanna VARDANYAN
41 Athletic Director .... Mr. Ken DALEY
101 Secretary of the Board of Trustees .... Ms. Susan TRACY
19 Director of Security and Safety .... Ms. Beata NACSA
106 Dir Online Education/E-learning .... Ms. Cheryl MICHIE
38 Director Student Support Services .... Mr. Jonathan SHAPIRO
104 Director Study Abroad .... Dr. Cathy GORINI
105 Director Web Services .... Mr. Michael MATZKIN

Mercy College of Health Sciences (K)

928 Sixth Avenue, Des Moines IA 50309-1239
County: Polk FICE Identification: 006273
Unit ID: 153977
Telephone: (515) 643-3180 Carnegie Class: Spec-4-yr-Other Health
FAX Number: (515) 643-6698 Calendar System: Semester
URL: www.mchs.edu
Established: 1995 Annual Undergrad Tuition & Fees: $16,920
Enrollment: 789 Coed
Affiliation or Control: Roman Catholic IRS Status: 501(c)3
Highest Offering: Baccalaureate
Accreditation: NH, ADNUR, DMS, EMT, MAC, MT, NURSE, PTAA, RAD, SURGT

01 President .... Dr. Barbara Q. DECKER
05 VP of Academic Affairs and Provost .... Vacant

10 VP of Business & Regulatory Affairs .... Dr. Thomas LEAHY
84 VP Enroll Mgmt & Student Affairs .... Dr. Karen ANDERSON
66 Dean of Nursing .... Dr. Nancy KERTZ
49 Dean of Liberal Arts & Sciences .... Dr. Jeannine MATZ
76 Dean of Allied Health .... Dr. Robert LOCH
09 Dean Inst Rsrch & Effectiveness .... Dr. Jeanette MCGREEVY
08 Dir of Library and Media Services ....Mr. Roy MEADOR
06 Registrar ....Ms. Carolyn BUCKLIN
15 Human Resources Business Partner .... Ms. Anne DENNIS
37 Director of Financial Aid ....Mr. Joe BROOKOVER
121 Director of Student Success ....Vacant
13 Director of Information Technology ....Mr. David VON ARB
18 Facilities Manager ....Mr. David STEENHOEK
07 Director of Admissions ....Vacant
26 Director of Marketing Communication .... Mr. Jim TAGYE

Morningside College (A)

1501 Morningside Avenue, Sioux City IA 51106-1751
County: Woodbury FICE Identification: 001879
Unit ID: 154004
Telephone: (712) 274-5000 Carnegie Class: Masters/M
FAX Number: (712) 274-5101 Calendar System: Semester
URL: www.morningside.edu
Established: 1894 Annual Undergrad Tuition & Fees: $29,094
Enrollment: 2,797 Coed
Affiliation or Control: United Methodist IRS Status: 501(c)3
Highest Offering: Master's
Accreditation: NH, MUS, NURSE

01 President ....Mr. John C. REYNDERS
05 Provost .... Dr. William C. DEEDS
10 Vice President Business & Finance ....Mr. Ronald A. JORGENSEN
32 Vice Pres Student Life & Enrollment ....Mrs. Terri A. CURRY
111 Vice Pres Institutional Advancement ..Mrs. Kari L. WINKLEPLECK
35 Dean of Students ....Ms. Karmen TEN NAPEL
20 Associate Dean for Acad Affairs .... Dr. Alden STOUT
09 Assoc VP Grad Pgm & Inst Assessment ....Dr. John PINTO
121 Vice President Advising .... Dr. Lillian LOPEZ
06 Registrar ....Mrs. Jen DOLPHIN
37 Director Student Financial Planning .... Ms. Karen GAGNON
13 Exec Dir of Information Services ....Mr. Mike HUSMANN
26 Vice Pres Communications & Mktg ....Mr. Rick G. WOLLMAN
29 Director of Alumni Relations .... Mr. Shiran NATHANIEL
07 Director of Admissions ....Ms. Steph PETERS
18 Director of Physical Plant ....Mr. Jay MALIN
19 Director of Security ....Mr. Brett LYON
23 Director of Student Health ....Ms. Carol GARVEY
36 Director of Career Services ....Ms. Stacie HAYS
40 Director of Bookstore .... Mr. Duane BENSON
41 Athletic Director ....Mr. Tim JAGER
42 Campus Ministry ....Mr. Andy NELSON
112 Director of Gift Planning ....Mr. Jonathan BLUM
15 Director Human Resources .... Ms. Cindy WELP
21 Controller ....Mr. Paul TREFT
04 Administrative Asst to President .... Mrs. Lisa KROHN
102 Senior Writer & Foundation Mgr ....Mrs. Laura L. FLORIO
105 Digital Communications Mgr ....Mr. Kevin POTTEBAUM
39 Asst Director Residence Life .... Ms. Sheri HINEMAN
08 Library Director ....Mr. Adam FULLERTON
38 Personal Counselor ....Ms. Bobbi MEISTER
101 Secretary of the Institution/Board .... Mrs. Lisa KROHN
108 Director Institutional Assessment ....Dr. John PINTO
91 Director Administrative Computing ....Ms. Carla GREGG
106 Dir Online Education/E-learning .... Ms. Michelle E. LAUGHLIN
84 Director Enrollment Management ....Mrs. Terri A. CURRY

Mount Mercy University (B)

1330 Elmhurst Drive NE, Cedar Rapids IA 52402-4797
County: Linn FICE Identification: 001880
Unit ID: 154013
Telephone: (319) 363-8213 Carnegie Class: Masters/M
FAX Number: (319) 363-5270 Calendar System: 4/1/4
URL: www.mtmercy.edu
Established: 1928 Annual Undergrad Tuition & Fees: $29,696
Enrollment: 1,877 Coed
Affiliation or Control: Roman Catholic IRS Status: 501(c)3
Highest Offering: Master's
Accreditation: NH, MFCD, NURSE, SW

01 President ....Ms. Laurie HAMEN
05 Provost .... Dr. Janet HANDLER
10 VP of Finance ....Mr. Doug BROCK
84 VP Admin/Enrollment/Student Svcs .... Dr. Robert CALLAHAN
30 VP of Development/Alumni Relations .... Ms. Brenda HAEFNER
42 VP of Mission and Ministry .... Sr. Shari SUTHERLAND
20 Assoc Prov/Exec Dir Acad Innovation .... Dr. Tom CASTLE
07 Dean of Admissions ....Ms. Terri CRUMLEY
06 Registrar .... Mr. Chance MCWORTHY
08 Director of Library Services ....Ms. Marilyn MURPHY
36 Director of Career Services .... Ms. Cheryl TABARELLA-REDD
110 Asst VP for Development/Alumni Rel ...... Ms. Lonna DREWELOW
37 Director of Financial Aid .... Ms. Bethany DAVENPORT
26 Asst VP Marketing/Communications ....Ms. Jessica GORTNER
41 Director of Athletics .... Mr. Paul GAVIN
32 Asst VP/Dean of Students ....Mr. Will OPRISKO
88 Director of Faculty Development .... Dr. Mohammad CHAICHIAN
38 Director of Counseling ....Ms. Karol WHITE
13 Asst VP/Chief Information Officer ....Mr. Brian MCDONALD
19 Director of Public Safety ....Mr. Nicholas HEINTZ
24 Academic Technology Librarian .... Ms. Nadia GILLITZER
15 Director of Human Resources .... Mr. Thomas DOERMANN

18 Director of Facilities ....Mr. Dave DENNIS
92 Director of Honors Program .... Dr. Anna WATERMAN
40 Campus Store Manager ....Ms. Janie MILLS
04 Assistant to the President ....Ms. Kim BLANKENHEIM
09 Exec Dir of Institutional Research ....Ms. Lori HEYING

North Iowa Area Community College (C)

500 College Drive, Mason City IA 50401-7299
County: Cerro Gordo FICE Identification: 001877
Unit ID: 154059
Telephone: (641) 423-1264 Carnegie Class: Assoc/HVT-Mix Trad/Non
FAX Number: (641) 423-1711 Calendar System: Semester
URL: www.niacc.edu
Established: 1917 Annual Undergrad Tuition & Fees (In-District): $5,003
Enrollment: 2,947 Coed
Affiliation or Control: State/Local IRS Status: 501(c)3
Highest Offering: Associate Degree
Accreditation: NH, ADNUR, MAC, PTAA

01 President .... Dr. Steven D. SCHULZ
05 Vice President Academic Affairs .... Mr. David J. MASSEY
10 Vice Pres Administrative Services ....Mrs. Kathy M. GROVE
32 Vice President of Student Services ....Dr. Terri L. EWERS
30 Director of Inst Advancement ....Mrs. Molly H. KNOLL
88 Director of JPEC ....Mr. Timothy J. PUTNAM
15 VP Organiz Develop & Human Resource ....Dr. Shelly M. SCHMIT
06 Registrar ....Mrs. Michelle L. PETZNICK
83 Chair Humanities & Social Science .... Mr. Joe D. DAVIS
81 Chair Math & Wellness ....Dr. Kathy M. ROGOTZKE
76 Chair Health and Natural Science ....Ms. Nikae PERKINSON
72 Interim Chair Industrial Division .... Ms. Laura L. WOOD
50 Chair Business/Ag Division .... Ms. Laura L. WOOD
51 Dean of Continuing Education .... Mr. Terry W. SCHUMAKER
37 Director of Financial Aid .... Mrs. Mary E. BLOOMINGDALE
20 Director Learning Services .... Ms. Dalila A. SAJADIAN
13 Chief Information Officer ....Mr. Josh C. MACK
103 WIOA Title I Director Region 2 ....Ms. Patti HANSON
121 Dir Student Support Svcs/Devel .... Ms. Jennifer PATTERSON
40 Bookstore Manager .... Mrs. Rhonda K. NESHEIM-KAUFFMAN
41 Director of Athletics ....Mr. Dan J. MASON
18 Director of Facilities Management ....Mr. Tony A. PAPPAS
21 Director Business Services ....Ms. Mindy R. EASTMAN
39 Director Student Housing ....Mr. Travis J. HERGERT
08 Librarian .... Ms. Jennie VER STEEG
26 Dir Marketing/Public Rel/Govt
Affs ....Mrs. Valerie F. ZAHORSKI-SCHMIDT
88 Director Accelerator/Incubator .... Mr. Daniel J. WINEGARDEN
88 Director SBDC ....Mr. Brook S. BOEHMLER
88 Director of School Partnerships ....Mr. Brian M. WOGEN
88 Dir of Operations/Continuing Educ ..Mrs. Constance J. GLANDON
88 Director of Sales & Programming ....Mrs. Jody L. EAST
09 Director of Institutional Research ....Dr. Shelly M. SCHMIT
102 Grant Writer/Inst Fund Develop Spec ...... Ms. Jana T. BARRACKS
106 Instructional Tech Coordinator ....Mr. Bruce G. MCKEE
29 Director Alumni Relations ....Mrs. Molly H. KNOLL
07 Director of Admissions ....Mrs. Rachel L. MCGUIRE
28 Director of Diversity ....Dr. Shelly M. SCHMIT
04 Administrative Asst to President ....Ms. Ronda L. SMITH
101 Secretary of the Institution/Board ....Mrs. Kathy M. GROVE
22 Dir Affirmative Action/EEO ....Dr. Shelly M. SCHMIT

Northeast Iowa Community College (D)

Box 400, Calmar IA 52132-0400
County: Winneshiek FICE Identification: 004587
Unit ID: 154110
Telephone: (563) 562-3263 Carnegie Class: Assoc/HVT-High Non
FAX Number: (563) 562-3719 Calendar System: Semester
URL: www.nicc.edu
Established: 1966 Annual Undergrad Tuition & Fees (In-District): $5,012
Enrollment: 4,865 Coed
Affiliation or Control: Local IRS Status: 501(c)3
Highest Offering: Associate Degree
Accreditation: NH, CAHIIM, COARC, DA

01 President ....Dr. Liang C. WEE
10 Vice Pres Finance & Administration .... Mr. David W. DAHMS
05 Chief Acad Ofcr/VP Academic
Affairs .... Dr. Kathy J. NACOS-BURDS
46 Vice Pres Bus & Community
Solutions .... Dr. Wendy A. MIHM-HEROLD
12 Assoc Vice President for Operations .... Ms. Rhonda K. SEIBERT
51 Exec Dir of Inst Effectiveness ....Ms. Wendy S. KNIGHT
102 Exec Director of NICC Foundation ....Ms. Julie A. WURTZEL
21 Executive Director of Finance .... Mr. Thomas M. RIDOUT
15 Exec Director of Human Resources .... Ms. Connie KUENNEN
106 Director Distance Learning ....Mr. Kyle T. COLLINS
13 Director Computer Information Sys ....Mr. Craig R. MEIRICK
09 Director of Institutional Research .... Ms. Dolores M. MILLER
88 Director Economic Devel/Peosta ....Mr. Gregory A. WILLGING
37 Director of Financial Aid .... Mr. Randy D. MASHEK
06 District Registrar ....Ms. Karla R. WINTER
06 Dir of Advising/Registr/Persistence .... Ms. Sheila R. BECKER
36 Career Services Manager .... Mr. Chris E. ENTRINGER
07 Director of Admissions ....Ms. Kristi L. STRIEF
26 Dir Marketing/News/Publications .... Ms. Shea A. HERBST

Northwest Iowa Community College (E)

603 W Park Street, Sheldon IA 51201-1046
County: Sioux FICE Identification: 004600
Unit ID: 154129
Telephone: (712) 324-5061 Carnegie Class: Assoc/HVT-High Non
FAX Number: (712) 324-4136 Calendar System: Semester
URL: www.nwicc.edu
Established: 1966 Annual Undergrad Tuition & Fees (In-District): $5,760
Enrollment: 1,612 Coed
Affiliation or Control: State/Local IRS Status: 501(c)3
Highest Offering: Associate Degree
Accreditation: NH, CAHIIM

01 President ....Dr. Alethea F. STUBBE
05 VP Student & Academic Services .... Dr. John HARTOG
30 VP Inst Adv & External Affairs .... Dr. Jan E. SNYDER
10 VP Operations & Finance ....Mr. Mark BROWN
49 Dean Arts & Sci/Business/Health ....Dr. Rhonda R. PENNINGS
72 Dean Applied Technology .... Mr. Steve WALDSTEIN
53 Dean Center for Teaching &
Learning ....Ms. Gretchen G. BARTELSON
21 Director of Business Services ....Ms. Jessica WILLIAMS
37 Director Financial Aid ....Ms. Karna HOFMEYER
84 Director Enrollment Management ....Ms. Lisa L. STORY
08 Director of Library Services ....Ms. Molly D. GALM
13 Director of Technology & Info Svcs .... Mr. Mike OLDENKAMP
88 Director of TRIO ....Ms. Laurie L. EDWARDS
06 Registrar/Assoc Dean of
Students ....Ms. Beth SIBENALLER-WOODALL
15 Director of Human Resources ....Ms. Sandy BRUNS
88 Director of Alt HS/Learning Center ....Vacant
26 Director Community Relations ....Ms. Kristin E. KOLLBAUM
18 Director Physical Facilities ....Mr. Doug RODGER

Northeast Iowa Community College Peosta Campus (F)

8342 NICC Drive, Peosta IA 52068
Telephone: (800) 728-7367 Identification: 770063
Accreditation: &NH, EMT, MAC, RAD

Northwestern College (G)

101 Seventh Street, SW, Orange City IA 51041-1996
County: Sioux FICE Identification: 001883
Unit ID: 154101
Telephone: (712) 707-7000 Carnegie Class: Bac-Diverse
FAX Number: (712) 707-7247 Calendar System: Semester
URL: www.nwciowa.edu
Established: 1882 Annual Undergrad Tuition & Fees: $29,500
Enrollment: 1,210 Coed
Affiliation or Control: Reformed Church In America IRS Status: 501(c)3
Highest Offering: Master's
Accreditation: NH, CAATE, CAEPN, IACBE, NURSE, SW

01 President ....Mr. Gregory E. CHRISTY
32 Dean of Student Life .... Dr. Julie VERMEER ELLIOTT
10 Vice President Financial Affairs .... Mr. Doug D. BEUKELMAN
111 Vice President Advancement ....Mr. Jay WIELENGA
84 Dean of Enrollment Management ....Mr. Mark BLOEMENDAAL
42 Assoc Dean of Spiritual Formation .... Ms. Barb DEWALD
41 Director of Athletics ....Mr. Earl WOUDSTRA
08 Director of the Library ....Ms. Greta GROND
06 Registrar ....Ms. Sandy VAN KLEY
37 Director of Financial Aid ....Mr. Eric ANDERSON
13 Director of Computing Services .... Mr. Harlan R. JORGENSEN
26 Director of Public Relations ....Mr. Duane L. BEESON
36 Director of Career Development ....Mr. William C. MINNICK
38 Dir Student Counseling Services .... Dr. Sally EDMAN
18 Director of Maintenance/Operations ....Mr. Scott K. SIMMELINK
29 Director Alumni Relations ....Mr. Corky KOERSELMAN
15 Director of Human Resources .... Mrs. Deb SANDBULTE
09 Director of Institutional Research .... Mr. Michael WALLINGA
04 Administrative Asst to President ....Ms. Jill HAARSMA
19 Director Security/Safety .... Mr. Andrew VAN OMMEREN
07 Director of Admissions .... Ms. Jackie DAVIS

Palmer College of Chiropractic (H)

1000 Brady Street, Davenport IA 52803-5287
County: Scott FICE Identification: 012300
Unit ID: 154174
Telephone: (563) 884-5000 Carnegie Class: Spec-4-yr-Other Health
FAX Number: (563) 884-5409 Calendar System: Trimester
URL: www.palmer.edu
Established: 1897 Annual Undergrad Tuition & Fees: $8,919
Enrollment: 2,222 Coed
Affiliation or Control: Independent Non-Profit IRS Status: 501(c)3
Highest Offering: First Professional Degree
Accreditation: NH, CHIRO

01 Chancellor ....Dr. Dennis M. MARCHIORI
05 College Provost ....Dr. Daniel J. WEINERT
108 Vice Chancellor for Inst Effect ....Dr. Robert E. PERCUOCO
32 Vice Chancellor Student Success ......Dr. Kevin A. CUNNINGHAM
84 Vice Chancellor for Enrollment ....Mr. Thomas STEMPEK
10 Vice Chancellor for Administration ..Dr. James A. CHRISTOPHER
46 Vice Chancellor for Research .... Dr. Christine GOERTZ
26 Vice Chancellor for Mktg & Comm ....Mr. James O'CONNOR

111 VC for Institutional Advancement .... Barbara MELBOURNE
20 Dean of Academic Affairs .... Dr. Kevin PAUSTIAN
23 Dean of Clinics .... Dr. Ron BOESCH
88 Assoc Dean of Academic Affairs .... Dr. Michael TUNNING
88 Assoc Dean of Academic Affairs .... Dr. Michelle BARBER
29 Exec Director Alumni & Development .... Dr. Mickey G. BURT
111 Exec Dir Advancement .... Ms. Clare THOMPSON
06 Senior Director/Registrar ....Ms. Mindy S. LEAHY
09 Sr Dir Institutional Research & Eff ....Dr. Dustin C. DERBY
88 Sr Dir Accred & Licensure ....Dr. Mary FROST
21 Senior Dir for Financial Affairs ...... Ms. Alexis A. VANDER HORN
13 Senior Dir Information Services .... Mr. Mark WISELEY
15 Interim Senior Dir of HR .... Ms. Pat HARDAWAY
18 Senior Director of Facilities .... Mr. Michael ERNSTER
07 Sr Dir of Admissions & Recruitment ....Ms. Julie BEHN
37 Senior Dir of Financial Planning .... Ms. Abbey NAGLE-KUCH
108 Senior Director for Assessment .... Dr. Andrea HAAN
24 Sr Dir/Center for Teaching/Lrng ....Vacant
121 Sr Dir of Academic Support Services .... Dr. Alex MARGRAVE
08 Senior Director of Library ....Vacant
88 Sr Dir Quality Assurance/Sys Organ .... Ms. Earlye A. JULIEN
88 Sr Director Clinic Administration .... Dr. Julie SCHRAD
19 Sr Dir Campus Safety and Security .... Mr. Brian SHARKEY
101 Exec Director Board Affairs .... Ms. Lynne LINDSTROM
88 Director of Undergrad Studies .... Ms. Cathy EBERHART

St. Ambrose University (A)

518 W Locust Street, Davenport IA 52803-2898
County: Scott FICE Identification: 001889
Unit ID: 154235
Telephone: (563) 333-6000 Carnegie Class: Masters/L
FAX Number: (563) 333-6243 Calendar System: Semester
URL: www.sau.edu
Established: 1882 Annual Undergrad Tuition & Fees: $29,150
Enrollment: 3,266 Coed
Affiliation or Control: Roman Catholic IRS Status: 501(c)3
Highest Offering: Doctorate
Accreditation: NH, ACBSP, #ARCPA, CAEPT, ENG, NURSE, OT, PTA, SP, SW

01 President .... Sr. Joan LESCINSKI, CSJ
05 Provost & VP for ASA .... Dr. Paul KOCH
10 Vice President Finance ....Mr. Michael C. POSTER
42 Chaplain ....Rev. Charles A. ADAM
111 Vice President Advancement .... Mr. James R. STANGLE
84 Vice Pres Enrollment Management ....Mr. James P. LOFTUS
46 Assoc Vice Pres Assess/ Research .... Dr. Tracy SCHUSTER-MATLOCK
11 Director Administrative Services ....Ms. Carol A. GLINES
26 Asst Vice Pres Communications/Mktg ....Ms. Linda R. HIRSCH
32 Assoc VP Student Svs/Dean of Stdnts ....Mr. Timothy PHILLIPS
15 Director Human Resources .... Ms. Audrey D. BLAIR
13 Exec Dir of Information Resources ....Ms. Mary B. HEINZMAN
29 Director Alumni Rels & Spec Project ....Ms. Anne A. GANNAWAY
37 Director Financial Aid ....Ms. Julie A. HAACK
38 Director Counseling ....Vacant
18 Director Physical Plant .... Mr. Jim M. HANNON
06 Registrar ....Mr. Dan L. ZEIMET
23 Director of Health Services ....Ms. Nancy A. HINES
19 Director of Security ....Mr. Robert CHRISTOPHER
39 Director of Resident Life ....Mr. Matt B. HANSEN
08 Director Library ....Ms. Mary B. HEINZMAN
36 Director Career Development ....Ms. Kimberly MATTESON
41 Athletic Director ....Mr. Raymond J. SHOVLAIN
94 Director of Women's Studies ....Ms. Katy A. STRZEPEK
40 Manager of Bookstore .... Mr. Cory W. SAMBDMAN
104 Asst VP International Education ....Dr. Ryan D. DYE
88 Chair Masters Pastoral Studies ....Dr. Micah KIEL
88 Director Masters Criminal Justice ...... Dr. Chrisopher C. BARNUM
49 Dean College Arts & Sciences .... Dr. Paula M. MCNUTT
50 Dean College Business .... Dr. William J. LESCH
71 Dean Health & Human Services .... Dr. Sandra L. CASSADY
88 Dean Academic Adult & Graduate Pgm ....Dr. Regina M. MATHESON
54 Dir Industrial & Mechanical Engr ....Dr. Jodi E. PROSISE
57 Director Fine Arts .... Mr. Lance A. SADLEK
88 Director Occupational Therapy ....Dr. Lynn J. KILBURG
88 Director Masters of Accounting .... Dr. Rebekah A. HEATH
58 Director MBA Pgm ....Dr. David J. O'CONNELL
28 Director of Diversity ....Mr. Ryan C. SADDLER
04 Senior Asst to President .... Ms. Kathleen M. ANDERSON
09 Director Institutional Research .... Ms. Clare M. HOLLADAY
44 Assoc VP Legacy Giving/Campaign Dir .... Ms. Sally E. CRINO
53 Director Education ....Dr. Thomas CARPENTER
86 Director Government Relations ....Mr. Paul J. FOLEY
101 Secretary of the Institution/Board .... Sr. Joan LESCINSKI, CSJ
102 Dir Foundation/Corporate Relations .... Ms. Nikki J. DEFAUW
106 Dir Online Education/E-learning .... Dr. Regina M. MATHESON
108 Director Institutional Assessment .... Dr. Tracy SCHUSTER-MATLOCK
96 Director of Purchasing ....Ms. Carol A. GLINES
22 Dir Compliance & Title IX Coord .... Ms. Megan LEVETZOW

St. Luke's College (B)

2720 Stone Park Boulevard, Sioux City IA 51104-0010
County: Woodbury FICE Identification: 007291
Unit ID: 154262
Telephone: (712) 279-3149 Carnegie Class: Spec-4-yr-Other Health
FAX Number: (712) 233-8017 Calendar System: Semester
URL: www.stlukescollege.edu
Established: 1995 Annual Undergrad Tuition & Fees: $20,440
Enrollment: 244 Coed
Affiliation or Control: Independent Non-Profit IRS Status: 501(c)3
Highest Offering: Baccalaureate
Accreditation: NH, ADNUR, COARC, MT, NURSE, PAST, RAD

01 Chancellor ....Mr. Michael D. STILES
05 Chief Academic Officer .... Dr. Susan BOWERS
32 Dean Student Services ....Ms. Danelle D. JOHANNSEN
66 Dean Nursing Education .... Dr. Susan BOWERS
76 Dean Health Sciences .... Dr. Dan JENSEN
06 Registrar .... Ms. Michelle FITCH
113 Bursar .... Ms. Lori MEIER
26 Director of Communications ....Vacant
07 Enrollment Mgmt/Marketing Coord .... Ms. Sherry MCCARTHY
08 Dept Chair/Library .... Ms. Nancy ZUBROD
29 Alumni/Events Coordinator .... Ms. Monica HARVEY
37 Director Student Financial Aid ....Ms. Danelle JOHANNSEN

Shiloh University (C)

100 Shiloh Drive, Kalona IA 52247
County: Washington Identification: 667095
Unit ID: 480499
Telephone: (319) 656-2447 Carnegie Class: Spec-4-yr-Faith
FAX Number: (319) 656-2448 Calendar System: Trimester
URL: www.shilohuniversity.edu
Established: 2006 Annual Undergrad Tuition & Fees: $4,510
Enrollment: N/A Coed
Affiliation or Control: Independent Non-Profit IRS Status: 501(c)3
Highest Offering: Doctorate
Accreditation: DEAC

00 Chancellor .... Mr. Gary HARGRAVE
01 President .... Mr. Christopher REEVES
05 Vice President of Academics ....Dr. Wesley PINKHAM
24 Vice President of Instructional Svc .... Dr. Daniel SALVADOR
13 Vice President of Technology .... Mr. James WIRTHLIN
20 Dean Undergraduate .... Dr. John BUCKINGHAM
58 Dean Graduate .... Dr. Ana I. WOOD
06 Registrar ....Mrs. Judy BREWER
07 Admissions Coordinator .... Mr. Andy THOMPSON
08 Library Director ....Ms. Julie MCPHAIL
37 Director Student Financial Aid ....Mr. Andrew R. THOMPSON

Simpson College (D)

1450 SW Vintage Pkwy, Ankeny IA 50023
Telephone: (515) 965-9355 Identification: 770849
Accreditation: &NH

Simpson College (E)

701 North C Street, Indianola IA 50125-1297
County: Warren FICE Identification: 001887
Unit ID: 154350
Telephone: (515) 961-6251 Carnegie Class: Bac-A&S
FAX Number: (515) 961-1623 Calendar System: Other
URL: www.simpson.edu
Established: 1860 Annual Undergrad Tuition & Fees: $35,876
Enrollment: 1,690 Coed
Affiliation or Control: United Methodist IRS Status: 501(c)3
Highest Offering: Master's
Accreditation: NH, CAATE, MUS

01 President ....Dr. Jay K. SIMMONS
05 Vice Pres/Dean Academic Affairs .... Dr. Kent EATON
10 Vice President Business/Finance ....Ms. Cathy HOCH
111 Vice President College Advancement ....Mr. Robert J. LANE
32 Vice President Student Development .... Dr. Heidi LEVINE
84 Vice President Enrollment .... Ms. Deborah J. TIERNEY
13 VP Info Svcs/Chief Info Officer .... Ms. Kelley L. BRADDER
37 Asst VP Enrollment/Financial Aid .... Ms. Tracie PAVON
06 Registrar & Associate Dean .... Ms. Jody RAGAN
35 Dean of Students .... Mr. Luke BEHAUNEK
26 Vice President Marketing and PR ....Ms. Jill JOHNSON
08 Director of Library ....Ms. Cynthia M. DYER
44 Director of Annual Giving .... Vacant
15 Director of Human Resources .... Ms. Mary E. BARTLEY
36 Director of Career Services .... Vacant
07 Director of Admissions .... Ms. Alison SWANSON
41 Athletic Director .... Mr. Brian NIEMUTH
96 Director of Procurement .... Ms. Marilyn J. LEEK
35 Assistant Dean of Students .... Mr. Richard O. RAMOS
42 Chaplain .... Rev. Mara BAILEY
18 Director Campus Services ....Mr. John HARRIS
21 Controller ....Mr. Logan EDEL
19 Coordinator of Campus Security ....Mr. Chris FRERICHS
51 Associate Dean Adult Learning ....Ms. Amy GIESEKE
28 International Educ Coordinator .... Mr. Jay WILKINSON
04 Administrative Asst to President .... Ms. Brenda K. WICKETT
29 Director Alumni Relations ....Mr. Andy ENGLISH

Simpson College West Des Moines (F)

1415 28th Street, #250, West Des Moines IA 50266
Telephone: (515) 309-3099 Identification: 770064
Accreditation: &NH

Southeastern Community College (G)

1500 W Agency Road, PO Box 180,
West Burlington IA 52655-0180
County: Des Moines FICE Identification: 001848
Unit ID: 154378
Telephone: (319) 752-2731 Carnegie Class: Assoc/MT-VT-Mix Trad/Non
FAX Number: (319) 752-4957 Calendar System: Semester
URL: www.scciowa.edu
Established: 1966 Annual Undergrad Tuition & Fees (In-District): $5,220
Enrollment: 2,868 Coed
Affiliation or Control: State/Local IRS Status: 501(c)3
Highest Offering: Associate Degree
Accreditation: NH, COARC, EMT, MAC

01 President ....Dr. Michael ASH
05 Vice Pres of Academic Affairs .... Dr. Carole RICHARDSON
32 Vice President of Student Services ....Ms. Joan WILLIAMS
11 Vice Pres Administrative Services ....Mr. Kevin CARR
30 Exec Director for Inst Advancement ....Ms. Rebecca RUMP
37 Financial Aid Officer .... Ms. Renae ARMENTROUT
84 Enrollment Coordinator ....Ms. Dana CHRISMAN
06 Registrar .... Mr. Dennis MARINO
15 Director Human Resources ....Ms. Laurie HEMPEN
49 Dean Arts and Sciences ....Dr. Chris SEDLACK
12 Executive Dean .... Dr. Teresa GARCIA
75 Dean Career/Technical Education ....Ms. Susan DUNEK
26 Dir Marketing/Communications ....Mr. Jeff EBBING

Southeastern Community College Keokuk Campus (H)

335 Messenger Road, Keokuk IA 52632
Telephone: (319) 524-3221 Identification: 770065
Accreditation: &NH

Southwestern Community College (I)

1501 W Townline Street, Creston IA 50801-1098
County: Union FICE Identification: 001857
Unit ID: 154396
Telephone: (641) 782-7081 Carnegie Class: Assoc/MT-VT-High Non
FAX Number: (641) 782-3312 Calendar System: Semester
URL: www.swcciowa.edu
Established: 1966 Annual Undergrad Tuition & Fees (In-State): $5,490
Enrollment: 1,656 Coed
Affiliation or Control: State IRS Status: 501(c)3
Highest Offering: Associate Degree
Accreditation: NH

01 President/CEO ....Dr. Barbara J. CRITTENDEN
03 Vice President Economic Development ....Mr. Thomas L. LESAN
10 Chief Financial Officer .... Mrs. Tia SAMO
05 Vice President Instruction ....Mr. Bill TAYLOR
32 Dean Stdnt Svcs/Exec Dir Educ Fndn ....Ms. Beth KULOW
20 Asst Vice Pres of Instruction ....Mrs. Lindsay STOAKS
106 Director of Distance Education ....Mr. Doug GREENE
15 Director of Human Resources ....Mrs. Jolene GRIFFITH
26 Director Marketing/Enrollment Mgmt ....Mrs. Terri HIGGINS
08 Director Learning Resource Center ....Mrs. Ann COULTER
13 Director of Information Technology .... Mr. Scott HELM
37 Director of Financial Aid .... Mrs. Sarah FREESTONE
06 Registrar .... Ms. Alyssa RILEY
04 Administrative Asst to President ....Ms. Mary Jo SKARDA
07 Director of Admissions ....Ms. Caitlyn MAITLEN

University of Dubuque (J)

2000 University Avenue, Dubuque IA 52001-5099
County: Dubuque FICE Identification: 001891
Unit ID: 153278
Telephone: (563) 589-3000 Carnegie Class: Masters/S
FAX Number: (563) 589-3682 Calendar System: 4/1/4
URL: www.dbq.edu
Established: 1852 Annual Undergrad Tuition & Fees: $28,700
Enrollment: 2,179 Coed
Affiliation or Control: Presbyterian Church (U.S.A.) IRS Status: 501(c)3
Highest Offering: Doctorate
Accreditation: NH, AAB, #ARCPA, NURSE, THEOL

01 President ....Dr. Jeffrey F. BULLOCK
04 Exec Assistant to the President .... Mrs. Deborah L. BUOL
05 VPAA/Dean of the College ....Dr. Mark WARD
10 Vice Pres Finance/Auxiliary Servs ....Mr. James D. STEINER
84 Vice Pres Enrollment/Univ Rels .... Mr. Peter L. SMITH
32 Vice President/Dean of Student Life ....Dr. Mick H. MIYAMOTO
13 Director of Technology .... Ms. Sherry CUSICK
30 Sr AVP Enroll Mgmt/Univ Relations .... Mr. Jesse L. JAMES
06 Registrar ....Ms. Kim BAUMLER
08 University Librarian ....Ms. Mary Anne KNEFEL
15 Director of Human Resources ....Ms. Julie MACTAGGART
37 Dean of Student Financial Planning .... Mr. Timothy KREMER
09 Dir Institutional Research ....Ms. Keri SAMSON
36 Director of Vocation .... Dr. Amy BAUS
29 Director for Alumni Engagement ....Ms. Katie KRAUS
40 Director of Campus Stores ....Ms. Margo KETELS
41 Director of Athletics ....Mr. Dan RUNKLE
18 Director of Facilities ....Mr. Craig KLOFT
04 Special Assistant to the President .... Mr. Thomas J. ROBBINS
88 Executive Director Heritage Center .... Mr. Thomas J. ROBBINS
07 AVP & Dean of Admission ....Mr. Robert D. BROSHOUS

Upper Iowa University (K)

605 Washington, Box 1857, Fayette IA 52142-1857
County: Fayette FICE Identification: 001893
Unit ID: 154493
Telephone: (563) 425-5200 Carnegie Class: Masters/M
FAX Number: (563) 425-5271 Calendar System: Semester
URL: www.uiu.edu
Established: 1857 Annual Undergrad Tuition & Fees: $28,890

Enrollment: 4,797 Coed
Affiliation or Control: Independent Non-Profit IRS Status: 501(c)3
Highest Offering: Master's
Accreditation: NH, #CAATE, NURSE

01 President .... Dr. William R. DUFFY, II
05 Provost .... Dr. P. Joan POOR
10 CFO .... Mr. Murtuza SIDDIQUI
82 VP Student Life/International Pgms .... Mr. Ismael J. BETANCOURT VELEZ
84 VP Enrollment Management .... Ms. Kathy FRANKEN
30 VP of External Affairs .... Mr. Andrew WENTHE
09 Assoc Provost .... Ms. Janet SHEPHERD
88 Director of Military Affairs .... Mr. Wayne CONVERSE
36 Dean Students/Dir Residence Life .... Ms. Jean MERKLE
12 South Central Region Director .... Ms. Cynthia BENTLEY
12 Director North Central .... Ms. Jen WEBB
07 Int Exec Director of Admissions .... Ms. Kaisha MCCAFFREY
06 Registrar .... Mrs. Holly STREETER
08 Director Library Services .... Mr. Rob HUDSON
41 Director Athletics .... Mr. David MILLER
04 Exec Assistant to the President .... Ms. Holly D. WOLFF
105 Director Internet Development .... Mr. Joel KUNZE
21 Controller .... Ms. Linda GEBEL
36 Director of Career Development .... Ms. Hope TRAINOR
35 Director Student Activities .... Mr. Daryl GROVE
26 Exec Dir for Comm and Marketing .... Mr. Karl EASTTORP
86 Director External Affairs .... Mr. Andrew WENTHE
29 Director of Alumni Relations .... Mr. Andrew WENTHE
13 Director Information Technology .... Mr. Terry SMID
15 Director Human Resources .... Ms. Tiffany ADAMS
88 Director Sports Info Services .... Mr. Howard THOMPSON
18 Exec Director of Facilities .... Mr. Scott JUSTASON
40 Bookstore Manager .... Mr. Justin MARCHANT
37 Director Student Financial Aid .... Ms. Rachael CREQUE
38 Director Student Counseling .... Ms. Crystal COLE
96 Director of Purchasing .... Mr. Justin MARCHANT

Vatterott College-Des Moines (A)

7000 Fleur Drive, Des Moines IA 50321-2414
County: Polk FICE Identification: 026092
Unit ID: 373058
Telephone: (515) 309-9000 Carnegie Class: Assoc/HVT-High Non
FAX Number: (515) 309-0366 Calendar System: Other
URL: www.vatterott.edu
Established: 1997 Annual Undergrad Tuition & Fees: $12,419
Enrollment: 172 Coed
Affiliation or Control: Proprietary IRS Status: Proprietary
Highest Offering: Associate Degree
Accreditation: ACCSC, DA, MAAB

01 Campus Director .... Mr. Nick MOHR

Waldorf University (B)

106 S 6th Street, Forest City IA 50436-1713
County: Winnebago FICE Identification: 001895
Unit ID: 154518
Telephone: (641) 585-2450 Carnegie Class: Bac-Diverse
FAX Number: (641) 585-8194 Calendar System: Semester
URL: www.waldorf.edu
Established: 1903 Annual Undergrad Tuition & Fees: $21,260
Enrollment: 2,001 Coed
Affiliation or Control: Proprietary IRS Status: Proprietary
Highest Offering: Master's
Accreditation: NH

01 President .... Dr. Robert ALSOP
05 Dean of Col/Vice Pres Acad Affs .... Dr. Vincent BEACH
10 Vice President Business Affairs .... Mr. Mason HARMS
04 Assistant to the President .... Ms. Cindy CARTER
32 Dean of Students .... Mr. Jason RAMAKER
92 Dean of Honors Program .... Dr. Suzanne FALCK-YI
07 Director Admissions .... Mr. Scott PITCHER
08 Library Director .... Mr. Derrick BURTON
29 Director of Alumni Affairs .... Vacant
06 Registrar .... Mr. Darrell BARBOUR
37 Director of Financial Aid .... Mr. Duane POLSDOFER
18 Director of Facilities Services .... Mr. Tim SEVERSON
26 Marketing Director .... Ms. Kelli HARMS
44 Director of Annual Fund .... Ms. Nancy OLSON
38 Counselor .... Mr. James AMELSBERG
41 Athletic Director .... Mr. Denny JEROME
36 Director Student Placement .... Ms. Mary REISETTER
40 Bookstore Manager .... Ms. Karla SCHAEFER
15 Director Human Resources .... Ms. Dawn RAMAKER

Wartburg College (C)

PO Box 1003, 100 Wartburg Boulevard, Waverly IA 50677-0903
County: Bremer FICE Identification: 001896
Unit ID: 154527
Telephone: (319) 352-8200 Carnegie Class: Bac-A&S
FAX Number: (319) 352-8514 Calendar System: Other
URL: www.wartburg.edu
Established: 1852 Annual Undergrad Tuition & Fees: $38,380
Enrollment: 1,537 Coed
Affiliation or Control: Evangelical Lutheran Church In America
IRS Status: 501(c)3
Highest Offering: Baccalaureate
Accreditation: NH, CAEPN, MUS, SW

01 President .... Dr. Darrel D. COLSON
05 VP Acad Affairs/Dean Faculty .... Dr. Brian ERNSTING
32 VP Student Life/Dean Students .... Dr. Daniel KITTLE
10 VP for Finance and Administration .... Mr. Richard SEGGERMAN
111 Vice Pres Institutional Advancement .... Mr. Scott C. LEISINGER
84 Vice Pres Enrollment Management .... Dr. Edith J. WALDSTEIN
07 Asst VP Admissions .... Mr. Jay T. COLEMAN
06 Registrar .... Ms. Sheree S. COVERT
26 VP for Marketing & Communications .... Vacant
13 Asst VP for Information Tech/CIO .... Mr. Gary L. WIPPERMAN
08 College Librarian .... Vacant
29 Dir Alumni/Parent Rel/Annual Giving .... Ms. Renee VOVES
37 Director of Financial Aid .... Ms. Jen L. SASSMAN
41 Exec Dir of Athletics and Wellness .... Mr. Eric R. WILLIS
42 Dean of the Chapel .... Rev. Ramona S. BOUZARD
18 Director of Physical Plant .... Mr. Scott SHARAR
39 Dir Res Life/Chief Student Conduct .... Ms. Cassie HALES
36 Dir of Pathways/Career Svcs .... Mr. Derek N. SOLHEIM
38 Director of Counseling Svcs .... Ms. Stephanie R. NEWSOM
40 Store Mgr & Textbook Services Dir .... Ms. Janet HUEBNER
85 Director of International Programs .... Vacant
35 Director of Campus Programming .... Ms. Ashley LANG
88 Campus Pastor .... Rev. Brian A. BECKSTROM
21 Chief Business Officer & Treasurer .... Mr. Richard W. SEGGERMAN
15 Director of HR & Payroll .... Ms. Jamie HOLLAWAY
112 Senior Gift Planner .... Mr. Donald J. MEYER
92 Director Honors Program .... Dr. Leilani ZART
04 Executive Administrator Pres Ofc .... Ms. Janeen K. STEWART
20 Asst Dean of the Faculty .... Mr. Douglas D. KOSCHMEDER
28 Dir Student Diversity Programs .... Ms. Krystal MADLOCK
19 Director Campus Security & Safety .... Mr. John MYERS

Wartburg Theological Seminary (D)

333 Wartburg Place, Dubuque IA 52003
County: Dubuque FICE Identification: 001897
Unit ID: 154536
Telephone: (563) 589-0200 Carnegie Class: Spec-4-yr-Faith
FAX Number: (563) 589-0333 Calendar System: 4/1/4
URL: www.wartburgseminary.edu
Established: 1854 Annual Graduate Tuition & Fees: N/A
Enrollment: 115 Coed
Affiliation or Control: Evangelical Lutheran Church In America
IRS Status: 501(c)3
Highest Offering: Master's; No Undergraduates
Accreditation: NH, THEOL

01 President .... Rev. Louise N. JOHNSON
05 Academic Dean of the Seminary .... Dr. Craig L. NESSAN
10 Vice Pres for Finance & Operations .... Mr. Andy B. WILLENBORG
30 Vice President for Development .... Mr. Paul K. ERBES
07 Dean for Vocation .... Rev. Amy L. CURRENT
08 Library Director .... Ms. Susan J S. EBERTZ
06 Registrar/Admin Assistant to Dean .... Dr. Kevin L. ANDERSON
04 Asst to President .... Ms. Lynne BAUMHOVER
37 Director Student Financial Aid .... Ms. Barbara SIMON

Western Iowa Tech Community College (E)

PO Box 5199, 4647 Stone Avenue, Sioux City IA 51102-5199
County: Woodbury FICE Identification: 007316
Unit ID: 154572
Telephone: (712) 274-6400 Carnegie Class: Assoc/HVT-High Non
FAX Number: (712) 274-6412 Calendar System: Semester
URL: www.witcc.edu
Established: 1966 Annual Undergrad Tuition & Fees (In-District): $4,200
Enrollment: 6,152 Coed
Affiliation or Control: State/Local IRS Status: 501(c)3
Highest Offering: Associate Degree
Accreditation: NH, DA, EMT, MAC, PNUR, PTAA, SURGT

01 President .... Dr. Terry MURRELL
05 VP Learning .... Ms. Juline ALBERT
10 VP Finance/Administrative Svcs .... Mr. Troy JASMAN
15 Dean Human Resources .... Ms. Brenda BRADLEY
13 Dean of Information Technologies .... Mr. Steve BROWN
84 Dean of Completion/Students .... Dr. Tricia SUTHERLAND
88 Dean of Outreach .... Ms. Janet GILL
20 Executive Dean of Instruction .... Mr. Darin MOELLER
32 Director Student Support Services .... Ms. Sara KLATT
30 Exec Director College Development .... Mr. Jim BRAUNSCHWEIG
08 Library Manager .... Ms. Sharon DYKSHOORN
88 Director Small Business Devel Ctr .... Mr. Todd RAUSCH
18 Director Physical Plant .... Mr. Kyle HUESER
06 Registrar .... Ms. Lora VANDER ZWAAG
26 Director Marketing/Publications .... Ms. Emma HEWITT
37 Director of Financial Aid .... Ms. Merlyn KATHOL

William Penn University (F)

201 Trueblood Avenue, Oskaloosa IA 52577-1799
County: Mahaska FICE Identification: 001900
Unit ID: 154590
Telephone: (641) 673-1001 Carnegie Class: Masters/S
FAX Number: (641) 673-1396 Calendar System: Semester
URL: www.wmpenn.edu
Established: 1873 Annual Undergrad Tuition & Fees: $24,510
Enrollment: 1,635 Coed
Affiliation or Control: Friends IRS Status: 501(c)3
Highest Offering: Master's
Accreditation: NH, NURSE

01 President .... Mr. John OTTOSSON
05 Vice Pres for Academic Affairs .... Dr. Noel STAHLE
111 Vice Pres for Advancement .... Ms. Marsha RIORDAN
10 VP for Finance .... Ms. Bonnie JOHNSON
84 VP for Enrollment Management .... Ms. Kerra STRONG
106 VP of Online & Evening Programs .... Ms. Linda PARKER
108 Director of Assessment .... Dr. Jared PEARCE
06 Registrar .... Ms. DeAnne DOLL
37 Director of Financial Aid .... Ms. Cyndi PEIFFER
36 Career Services Coordinator .... Ms. Debbie STEVENS
08 Head Librarian .... Ms. Julie HANSEN
15 Human Resource Coordinator .... Ms. Angella DURIAN-GAMBELL
32 Director of Student Activities .... Mr. Levi TARBELL
09 Director of Institutional Research .... Mr. Michael EDWARDS
40 Bookstore Manager .... Ms. Heidi PARKER
83 Chair Div of Social/Behavioral Sci .... Dr. Michael COLLINS
72 Co-Chair Div of Applied Technology .... Dr. Jim DROST
72 Co-Chair Div of Applied Technology .... Mr. Jim HOEKSEMA
53 Chair Division of Education .... Ms. Cathy WILLIAMSON
50 Chair Div of Business Admin .... Mr. David MEINERT
79 Chair Division of Humanities .... Dr. Anita MEINERT
76 Chair Div of Health & Life Sciences .... Dr. Gary CHRISTOPHER
66 Chair Div of Nursing .... Dr. Brenda KROGH-DUREE
04 Executive Asst to President .... Ms. Angella DURIAN-GAMBELL
13 Director of Information Services .... Mr. Mike FOSTER
19 Director of Security .... Mr. Tim REYNOLDS
38 Campus Counselor .... Ms. Tyne SMITH
39 Co-Director of Residence Life .... Ms. Dianne BURNS
39 Co-Director of Residence Life .... Mr. Matt CROONQUIST
41 Athletic Director .... Mr. Nik RULE

KANSAS

Allen County Community College (G)

1801 N Cottonwood, Iola KS 66749-1698
County: Allen FICE Identification: 001901
Unit ID: 154642
Telephone: (620) 365-5116 Carnegie Class: Assoc/HVT-Mix Trad/Non
FAX Number: (620) 365-7406 Calendar System: Semester
URL: www.allencc.edu
Established: 1923 Annual Undergrad Tuition & Fees (In-District): $2,850
Enrollment: 2,382 Coed
Affiliation or Control: State/Local IRS Status: 501(c)3
Highest Offering: Associate Degree
Accreditation: NH

01 President .... Mr. John A. MASTERSON
05 Vice Pres for Academic Affairs .... Mr. Jon MARSHALL
10 Vice Pres for Finance & Operations .... Mr. Brian COUNSIL
32 Vice Pres Student Affairs .... Ms. Cynthia JACOBSON
12 Dean for the Iola Campus .... Mrs. Tosca HARRIS
12 Dean for the Burlingame Campus .... Mr. Bob REAVIS
106 Dean for Online Learning .... Mrs. Regena BAILEY-AYE
08 Director of Library .... Mrs. Sandy MOORE
13 Director of MIS .... Mr. Doug DUNLAP
37 Director of Financial Aid .... Mrs. Kim MURRY
18 Director of Physical Plant Opers .... Mr. Kent TOMSON
07 Director of Admissions .... Ms. Rebecca BILDERBACK
41 Director of Athletics .... Mr. Doug DESMARTEAU
40 Director of Bookstore .... Mrs. Reine LOFLIN
76 Allied Health Director .... Ms. Kattia ANDREWS
85 Foreign Student Advisor .... Mrs. Nichole PETERS
09 Director Inst Research/Assessment .... Vacant
35 Director Student Life .... Mr. Ryan BILDERBACK
06 Registrar .... Mrs. Bobbie HAVILAND
26 Public Relations Coordinator .... Mrs. Nancy FORD

Allen County Community College Burlingame Campus (H)

100 Bloomquist, Burlingame KS 66413
Telephone: (785) 654-2416 Identification: 770249
Accreditation: &NH

The Art Institutes International - Kansas City (I)

8208 Melrose Drive, Lenexa KS 66214
Telephone: (913) 217-4600 Identification: 666765
Accreditation: #ACICS

† Branch campus of The Art Institute of Phoenix, AZ. School is in teach-out plan.

Baker University (J)

618 Eighth Street, Baldwin City KS 66006-0065
County: Douglas FICE Identification: 001903
Unit ID: 154688
Telephone: (785) 594-6451 Carnegie Class: Masters/L
FAX Number: (785) 594-2522 Calendar System: 4/1/4
URL: www.bakeru.edu
Established: 1858 Annual Undergrad Tuition & Fees: $28,030
Enrollment: 2,689 Coed
Affiliation or Control: United Methodist IRS Status: 501(c)3
Highest Offering: Doctorate
Accreditation: NH, ACBSP, CAEPN, EXSC, MUS, NURSE

01 President ..... Dr. Lynne MURRAY
05 Interim Provost ..... Dr. Tes MEHRING
84 VP of Enrollment/Marketing ..... Ms. Danielle YEAROUT
13 CIO/VP Strateg Plng & Academic Res ..... Mr. Andy JETT
10 VP of Finance ..... Mr. David HOUCHEN
53 Dean School of Education ..... Dr. Marc CHILDRESS
66 Dean of School of Nursing ..... Dr. Bernadette M. FETTEROLF
49 Interim Dean of CAS ..... Ms. Martha HARRIS
107 Interim Dean SPGS ..... Dr. Emily FORD
41 Director Of Athletics ..... Ms. Theresa YETMAR
84 Director of Admissions ..... Ms. Cheryl MCCRARY
26 Director of Marketing & Comm ..... Ms. Erin CURTIS-DIERKS
31 Director of Corporate Relations ..... Mr. Ivan HUNTOON
06 University Registrar ..... Ms. Ruth MILLER
21 Chief Accounting Officer/Controller ..... Ms. Melissa VAN LEIDEN
18 Dir of Physical Plant & Facility Op ..... Mr. Jeremy PORTLOCK
42 Minister to the University ..... Rev. Kevin HOPKINS
37 Senior Director of Financial Aid ..... Ms. Jeanne MOTT
15 Chief Human Resources Officer ..... Ms. Connie DEEL
32 Dean of Students ..... Dr. Cassy BAILEY
09 Dir of Institutional Research ..... Mr. Eric HAYS
29 Dir of Alumni Relations ..... Mr. Doug BARTH
36 Director of Career Services ..... Ms. Susan WADE
38 Dir of Health & Counseling Center ..... Dr. Tim HODGES
08 Director of Library Services ..... Mr. Ray WALLING

Baker University School of Professional and Graduate Studies (A)

7301 College Boulevard, Suite 120,
Overland Park KS 66210-1856
Telephone: (913) 491-4432 Identification: 770250
Accreditation: &NH

Barclay College (B)

607 N Kingman, Haviland KS 67059-0288
County: Kiowa FICE Identification: 001917
Unit ID: 155070
Telephone: (620) 862-5252 Carnegie Class: Spec-4-yr-Faith
FAX Number: (620) 862-5242 Calendar System: Semester
URL: www.barclaycollege.edu
Established: 1917 Annual Undergrad Tuition & Fees: $15,990
Enrollment: 273 Coed
Affiliation or Control: Independent Non-Profit IRS Status: 501(c)3
Highest Offering: Master's
Accreditation: @NH, BI

01 President ..... Dr. Royce FRAZIER
00 Chancellor ..... Dr. Adrian HALVERSTADT
05 VP Academics ..... Dr. Jim LE SHANA
10 VP Business Services ..... Mr. Lee ANDERS
32 VP Student Services ..... Ms. Tiffany VAN DAME
30 VP Institutional Advancement ..... Mr. Larry LEWIS
06 VP Registration and Records ..... Dr. Glenn W. LEPPERT
37 Director Student Financial Aid ..... Mr. Ryan HAASE
07 Admissions Counselor ..... Mr. Justin KENDALL
08 Librarian ..... Vacant
29 Alumni Relations ..... Dr. Herb FRAZIER
106 Dir Online Education/E-learning ..... Mr. Aaron STOKES
13 Chief Info Technology Officer (CIO) ..... Mr. Trent MAGGARD
15 Director Personnel Services ..... Mrs. Gayle MORTIMER
18 Chief Facilities/Physical Plant ..... Mr. CD FITCH
19 Director Security/Safety ..... Ms. Tiffany VAN DAME
41 Athletic Director ..... Vacant
09 Director of Institutional Research ..... Dr. Keith WHITE
25 Chief Contracts/Grants Admin ..... Mr. Larry LEWIS

Barton County Community College (C)

245 NE 30th Road, Great Bend KS 67530-9107
County: Barton FICE Identification: 004608
Unit ID: 154697
Telephone: (620) 792-2701 Carnegie Class: Assoc/MT-VT-High Non
FAX Number: (620) 792-5624 Calendar System: Semester
URL: www.bartonccc.edu
Established: 1965 Annual Undergrad Tuition & Fees (In-District): $3,328
Enrollment: 4,815 Coed
Affiliation or Control: State/Local IRS Status: 501(c)3
Highest Offering: Associate Degree
Accreditation: NH, ADNUR, EMT, MLTAD

01 President ..... Dr. Carl R. HEILMAN
05 VP of Instruction ..... Mrs. Elaine SIMMONS
10 VP of Administration ..... Mr. Mark DEAN
32 VP of Student Services ..... Mrs. Angela MADDY
13 Chief Information Officer ..... Mrs. Michelle KAISER
20 Dean of Academics ..... Mr. Brian HOWE
88 Dean of Military Academic Services ..... Ms. Ashley ANDERSON
37 Assoc Dean Stdt Svcs/Dir Fin Aid ..... Mrs. Myrna PERKINS
111 Exec Dir Institutional Advancement ..... Mrs. Coleen CAPE
66 Exec Dir Nursing & Healthcare Educ ..... Dr. Kathy KOTTAS
50 Exec Dir of Business/Tech/Cmty Educ ..... Ms. Jane HOWARD
103 Exec Dir Workforce Trng & Cmty Educ ..... Ms. Mary FOLEY
26 Dir of Public Relations & Marketing ..... Mr. Brandon STEINERT
04 Assistant to President ..... Ms. Amye SCHNEIDER
41 Director of Athletics ..... Mr. Trevor ROLFS
08 Director of Library ..... Mrs. ReGina REYNOLDS-CASPER
15 Director of Human Resources ..... Mrs. Julie KNOBLICH
07 Director of Admissions ..... Ms. Tana COOPER
19 Coordinator of Facility Management ..... Mr. Jim IRELAND
25 Director of Grants ..... Ms. Cathie OSHIRO
06 Registrar ..... Mrs. Lori CROWTHER
40 Bookstore Manager ..... Mrs. Connie KERNS
09 Chief Inst Research Officer ..... Mrs. Caicey CRUTCHER
35 Director of Student Life ..... Mrs. Diane ENGLE
39 Coordinator of Student Housing ..... Mr. Jonathan DIETZ
23 Nurse ..... Mrs. Kathy BROCK
121 Dir Testing/Advisement/Career Svc ..... Mrs. Judy JACOBS
88 Dean Fort Riley Tech Ed & Military ..... Mr. Kurtis TEAL
108 Dean of Institutional Effectiveness ..... Mr. Charles PERKINS
106 Assoc Dean of Distance Learning ..... Mrs. Claudia MATHER

Benedictine College (D)

1020 N 2nd Street, Atchison KS 66002-1499
County: Atchison FICE Identification: 010256
Unit ID: 154712
Telephone: (913) 367-5340 Carnegie Class: Bac-Diverse
FAX Number: (913) 367-6566 Calendar System: Semester
URL: www.benedictine.edu
Established: 1858 Annual Undergrad Tuition & Fees: $27,480
Enrollment: 2,189 Coed
Affiliation or Control: Roman Catholic IRS Status: 501(c)3
Highest Offering: Master's
Accreditation: NH, #CAATE, CAEPN, ENG, MUS, NURSE

01 President ..... Mr. Stephen D. MINNIS
05 Dean of the College ..... Dr. Kimberly C. SHANKMAN
10 Chief Financial Officer ..... Mr. Ronald J. OLINGER
111 Vice President Advancement ..... Ms. Kelly J. VOWELS
84 Dean of Enrollment Management ..... Mr. Pete HELGESEN
32 Vice President of Student Life ..... Dr. Linda HENRY
35 Dean of Students ..... Dr. Joseph WURTZ
41 Athletic Director ..... Mr. Charles GARTENMAYER
26 Vice President for College Rels ..... Mr. Tom HOOPES
20 Assoc Dean & Registrar ..... Sr. Linda HERNDON, OSB
09 Director of Institutional Research ..... Ms. Mary T. HYNEK
58 Exec Dir of Grad Business Programs ..... Mr. Michael KING
58 Director of MASL/Asst Prof Educ ..... Dr. Cheryl REDING
37 Director of Student Financial Aid ..... Mr. Tony TANKING
27 Dir of Marketing & Communications ..... Mr. Steve JOHNSON
38 Director of Counseling Center ..... Mr. Kerry A. MARVIN
23 Director of Student Health Services ..... Ms. Janet ADRIAN
18 Director of Operations ..... Mr. Matt FASSERO
13 Dir of Tech & Information Sys ..... Mr. Randy ROWLAND
88 Director of International Program ..... Mr. Daniele MUSSO
08 Librarian ..... Mr. Steven GROMATZKY
39 Director of Residence Life ..... Mr. Sean MULCAHY
113 Bursar ..... Ms. Becky MILLER
36 Director of Career Development ..... Ms. Katie MCDOWELL
29 Director of Planned Giving & Alumni ..... Mr. Tim ANDREWS
04 Exec Assistant to the President ..... Ms. Abby BARTLETT
15 Int Director of Human Resources ..... Ms. Carolyn SANDERS
19 Security Account Manager ..... Mr. Danny FAIRLEY
53 Chair Education Department ..... Dr. Matthew RAMSEY
54 Chair Engineering Department ..... Dr. Darrin MUGGLI

Bethany College (E)

335 E Swensson Street, Lindsborg KS 67456-1895
County: McPherson FICE Identification: 001904
Unit ID: 154721
Telephone: (785) 227-3311 Carnegie Class: Bac-Diverse
FAX Number: (785) 227-2004 Calendar System: 4/1/4
URL: www.bethanylb.edu
Established: 1881 Annual Undergrad Tuition & Fees: $26,660
Enrollment: 699 Coed
Affiliation or Control: Evangelical Lutheran Church In America
IRS Status: 501(c)3
Highest Offering: Baccalaureate
Accreditation: NH, #CAATE, CAEPN, MUS

01 President ..... Mr. William JONES
05 Provost & Dean of the College ..... Mr. Robert CARLSON
10 VP for Finance and Operations ..... Ms. Jean HALL
06 Registrar ..... Ms. Cathy BRITTON
84 Dean of Admissions/Financial Aid ..... Mr. Matt PHANNENSTIEL
32 Dean of Student Development ..... Mr. Ryan VAN DUSEN
111 VP for Advancement ..... Mr. David EARLE
41 Dean of Athletics ..... Mr. Dane PAVLOVICH
09 Director of Institutional Research ..... Ms. Sarah B. ZEHNDER
21 Controller ..... Vacant
26 Director of Communications & Mktg ..... Vacant
07 Director of Admissions & Operations ..... Ms. Vicki CORNETT
37 Director of Financial Aid ..... Ms. Amy HOSS
08 Dir of Wallerstedt Learning Center ..... Ms. Denise K. CARSON
35 Assoc Dean for Student Development ..... Vacant
13 Director of Technology Services ..... Mr. Matthew CARVER
15 Director Human Resources/Title IX ..... Ms. Kristi HAYS
29 Dir Alumni Relations & Ann Giving ..... Ms. Erica KRUCKENBERG
27 Sports Information Director ..... Ms. Sara BLACKBURN
30 Director of Development ..... Mr. Clair OLEEN
35 Director Campus Activities ..... Ms. Roxie L. SJOGREN
38 Director of Clinical Counseling ..... Mr. David OLSEN
39 Director of Residential Education ..... Vacant
88 Director of Information Services ..... Ms. Christi PAULSEN
27 Director of Publications ..... Mr. Frank BALLEW
36 Director Career Services ..... Vacant
88 Academic Center for Excellence Dir ..... Mr. Dan CALLIHAN
20 Assistant Provost ..... Dr. Melody STEED
108 Institutional Assessment ..... Dr. Duke ROGERS
88 Director of Student Recruitment ..... Mr. Richard STRANGE
89 Dir of Ministry & 1st Yr Experience ..... Dr. Tyler ATKINSON
18 Director of Campus Facilities ..... Mr. Randy JIRAK
40 Bookstore Manager ..... Vacant
42 Campus Pastor ..... Ms. Amy TRUHE
04 Admin Assistant to President ..... Ms. Alissa JONES
88 Chair of Digital & Media Arts Dept ..... Mr. Ed POGUE
53 Program Director Teacher Education ..... Dr. Gretchen NORLAND
57 Chair of Theater Department ..... Mr. Greg LEGAULT
61 Chair of Criminal Justice Dept ..... Dr. Brian KINNAIRD
64 Music Department Co-Chair ..... Dr. Mark LUCAS
64 Music Department Co-Chair ..... Dr. Dan MASTERSON
73 Chair of Religion & Philosophy Dept ..... Dr. John MULLEN
76 Athletic Training Program Director ..... Ms. Laura STENLUND
81 Chair of Math/Science Depts ..... Dr. Lucas MCCORMICK
83 Chair of Psychology Department ..... Ms. Andrea RING
85 International Program Coordinator ..... Vacant
106 Director of Online & Outreach Ed ..... Dr. Jenni KINNAIRD
88 Director of Food Services ..... Mr. Kevin MCCOY
88 Work Control Coordinator ..... Ms. Renae ANDERSON
92 Honors Program Coordinator ..... Dr. Kristin VAN TASSEL

Bethel College (F)

300 E 27th Street, North Newton KS 67117-0531
County: Harvey FICE Identification: 001905
Unit ID: 154749
Telephone: (316) 283-2500 Carnegie Class: Bac-A&S
FAX Number: (316) 284-5286 Calendar System: 4/1/4
URL: www.bethelks.edu
Established: 1887 Annual Undergrad Tuition & Fees: $26,920
Enrollment: 525 Coed
Affiliation or Control: Mennonite Church IRS Status: 501(c)3
Highest Offering: Baccalaureate
Accreditation: NH, CAATE, CAEPN, NURSE, SW

01 Interim President ..... Dr. John K. SHERIFF
04 Assistant to the President ..... Ms. Rosa M. BARRERA
05 Vice President Academic Affairs ..... Dr. Robert W. MILLIMAN
32 Vice President Student Life ..... Mr. Aaron L. AUSTIN
41 Athletic Director ..... Mr. Tony HOOPS
111 Vice President Advancement ..... Mr. Eric SCHRAG
10 Vice President for Business Affairs ..... Mr. Allen WEDEL
26 VP for Marketing and Communications ..... Ms. Lori LIVENGOOD
07 Vice President for Admissions ..... Mr. Andrew W. JOHNSON
06 Registrar ..... Ms. Marcia K. MILLER
30 Director of Development ..... Vacant
37 Director of Financial Aid ..... Mr. Clark OSWALD
29 Director of Alumni Relations ..... Mr. Bradley KOHLMAN
08 Head Librarian ..... Ms. Gail STUCKY
42 Director of Church Relations ..... Mr. Andrew SCHMIDT
18 Chief Facilities/Physical Plant ..... Mr. Les GOERZEN
13 Chief Info Technology Officer (CIO) ..... Mr. Rus ROGERS
36 Dir Student Placement/Counseling ..... Ms. Joanna BJERUM

Brown Mackie College-Salina (G)

2106 S 9th Street, Salina KS 67401-7307
County: Saline FICE Identification: 006755
Unit ID: 154776
Telephone: (785) 825-5422 Carnegie Class: Spec-4-yr-Other Health
FAX Number: (785) 827-7623 Calendar System: Other
URL: www.brownmackie.edu
Established: 1892 Annual Undergrad Tuition & Fees: N/A
Enrollment: 366 Coed
Affiliation or Control: Proprietary IRS Status: Proprietary
Highest Offering: Baccalaureate
Accreditation: NH, OTA

01 President ..... Ms. Judy HOLMES
05 Dean of Academic Affairs ..... Vacant
06 Registrar ..... Vacant
36 Director of Career Services ..... Ms. Robin NASH

† In teach-out mode.

Bryan University (H)

1527 SW Fairlawn Road, Topeka KS 66604
County: Shawnee FICE Identification: 030662
Unit ID: 154794
Telephone: (785) 272-0889 Carnegie Class: Assoc/MT-VT-High Non
FAX Number: (785) 272-4538 Calendar System: Other
URL: www.bryanu.edu
Established: 1982 Annual Undergrad Tuition & Fees: $15,400
Enrollment: 89 Coed
Affiliation or Control: Proprietary IRS Status: Proprietary
Highest Offering: Associate Degree
Accreditation: ACICS

01 Executive Director ..... Mr. Wayne MAJOR

Butler Community College (I)

901 S. Haverhill Road, El Dorado KS 67042-3225
County: Butler FICE Identification: 001906
Unit ID: 154800
Telephone: (316) 321-2222 Carnegie Class: Assoc/HT-Mix Trad/Non
FAX Number: (316) 322-3109 Calendar System: Semester
URL: www.butlercc.edu
Established: 1927 Annual Undergrad Tuition & Fees (In-District): $2,750
Enrollment: 8,950 Coed
Affiliation or Control: Local IRS Status: 501(c)3
Highest Offering: Associate Degree

Accreditation: NH, ACBSP, ADNUR, ENGT

01 President Dr. Kimberly KRULL
05 Vice President of Academics Ms. Lori WINNINGHAM
10 Vice President of Finance Mr. Kent WILLIAMS
32 Vice President of Student Services Mr. Bill RINKENBAUGH
30 Vice President for Inst Advancement Ms. Stacy COFER
08 Reference Librarian Ms. Judy BASTIN
06 Registrar Ms. Willow DEAN
09 AVP of Research/Inst Effectiveness Dr. Esam MOHAMMAD
15 Assoc VP of Human Resources Ms. Shelley STULTZ
21 Associate Business Officer Ms. Kim SHERWOOD
29 Director Alumni Relations Vacant
36 Director Student Placement Vacant
37 Director Student Financial Aid Ms. Heather WARD
35 Associate VP of Student Services Ms. Jessica OHMAN
26 Director of Institutional Marketing Ms. Kelly SNEDDEN
18 Director Facilities Mr. Lynn UMHOLTZ
96 Director of Purchasing Ms. Yolanda HACKLER
07 Director of Admissions Ms. Kirsten ALLEN
38 Director Student Counseling Ms. Jessica OHMAN
13 VP of Digital Transformation Mr. Bill YOUNG
19 Director Security/Safety Mr. James BRYAN
39 Director Residence Life Mr. Andrew RAWLINGS
41 Athletic Director Mr. Todd CARTER

Butler of Andover (A)

1810 N Andover Road, Andover KS 67002
Telephone: (316) 733-0071 Identification: 770253
Accreditation: &NH

Butler of Council Grove (B)

131 West Main, Council Grove KS 66846
Telephone: (620) 767-5158 Identification: 770254
Accreditation: &NH

Butler of Marion (C)

701 E. Main, Hill Building, Marion KS 66861
Telephone: (620) 382-2183 Identification: 770255
Accreditation: &NH

Butler of McConnell (D)

Ed Ctr, Bldg 412, 53474 Lawrence Ct,
McConnell AFB KS 67221
Telephone: (316) 681-3522 Identification: 770257
Accreditation: &NH

Butler of Rose Hill (E)

712 Rose Hill Road, Rose Hill KS 67133
Telephone: (316) 776-9429 Identification: 770256
Accreditation: &NH

Central Baptist Theological Seminary (F)

6601 Monticello Road, Shawnee KS 66226-3513
County: Johnson FICE Identification: 001907
Unit ID: 154837
Telephone: (913) 667-5700 Carnegie Class: Spec-4-yr-Faith
FAX Number: (913) 371-8110 Calendar System: Semester
URL: cbts.edu
Established: 1901 Annual Graduate Tuition & Fees: $9,140
Enrollment: 359 Coed
Affiliation or Control: Baptist IRS Status: 501(c)3
Highest Offering: Doctorate; No Undergraduates
Accreditation: NH, THEOL

01 President Dr. Molly T. MARSHALL
05 Dean of the Seminary Dr. Robert E. JOHNSON
03 Executive Vice President Mr. George TOWNSEND
30 VP for Institutional Advancement Dr. John W. GRAVLEY
06 Associate Dean/Registrar Mr. Stephen GUINN
26 Director of Seminary Relations Ms. Robin SANDBOTHE

Central Christian College of Kansas (G)

1200 S Main, PO Box 1403, McPherson KS 67460
County: McPherson FICE Identification: 001908
Unit ID: 154855
Telephone: (620) 241-0723 Carnegie Class: Bac-Diverse
FAX Number: (620) 241-6032 Calendar System: 4/1/4
URL: www.centralchristian.edu
Established: 1884 Annual Undergrad Tuition & Fees: $16,850
Enrollment: 1,369 Coed
Affiliation or Control: Free Methodist IRS Status: 501(c)3
Highest Offering: Baccalaureate
Accreditation: NH

01 President Col. Hal HOXIE
05 Provost Dr. Leonard FAVARA, JR.
111 VP of Advancement Dr. Dean KROEKER
84 VP of Enrollment Management Mr. Joel FIGGS
10 VP of Finance Dr. Chris STOCKLIN
41 Athletic Director Mr. Steve REED
06 Registrar Mrs. Michele AUGUST
26 Marketing Director Mr. Tracy CASS
37 Associate Director of Financial Aid Mrs. Nichole CARVER
08 Library Director Ms. Bev KELLEY
20 Associate Dean Mr. Cheyenne KROEKER
18 Chief Facilities/Physical Plant Mr. Dan BRAND
42 Dir of Spiritual Formation Mr. Justin MOURN
04 Executive Assistant to President Mrs. Amanda ANDERSON
13 Chief Info Technology Officer (CIO) Mr. Doug VANDERHOOF
104 Dir International Student Progams Ms. Hatsue AIZAWA
29 Director Advance & Alumni Relations Ms. Karissa HOFFMAN
38 Campus Counselor Mrs. Kelly FRENCH

Cleveland University - Kansas City (H)

10850 Lowell Avenue, Overland Park KS 66210
County: Johnson FICE Identification: 020907
Unit ID: 177038
Telephone: (913) 234-0600 Carnegie Class: Spec-4-yr-Other Health
FAX Number: (913) 234-0904 Calendar System: Trimester
URL: www.cleveland.edu
Established: 1922 Annual Undergrad Tuition & Fees: $14,840
Enrollment: 456 Coed
Affiliation or Control: Independent Non-Profit IRS Status: 501(c)3
Highest Offering: First Professional Degree
Accreditation: NH, CHIRO

01 President Dr. Carl S. CLEVELAND, III
05 VP Academic Affairs Dr. Gery HOCHANADEL
10 Chief Operating Officer Mr. Jeff KARP
84 VP Enrollment Management Mr. Alex BACH
26 VP of Campus and Alumni Relations Dr. Clark BECKLEY
15 Vice Pres HR/Organizational Devel Mr. Dale MARRANT
30 Vice President Advancement Ms. Amy PIERSOL
20 Dean of Pre-Clinical Education Dr. Paul BARLETT
20 Dean of Chiropractic Education Dr. Julia BARTLETT
21 Controller Ms. Marla COPE
06 Director Academic Records/Support Mr. David FOOSE
37 Director of Financial Aid Ms. Caprice CALAMAIO
09 Director of Research Dr. Mark T. PFEFER
32 Director of Student Services Ms. Jalonna BOWIE
07 Director of Admissions Ms. Melissa DENTON
08 Library Director Ms. Simone BRIAND
18 Director of Facilities Management Mr. Frank HANEY
04 Assistant to the President Ms. Marjorie BRADSHAW

Cloud County Community College (I)

2221 Campus Drive, Concordia KS 66901-1002
County: Cloud FICE Identification: 001909
Unit ID: 154907
Telephone: (785) 243-1435 Carnegie Class: Assoc/HVT-High Non
FAX Number: (785) 243-1459 Calendar System: Semester
URL: www.cloud.edu
Established: 1965 Annual Undergrad Tuition & Fees (In-District): $2,970
Enrollment: 2,294 Coed
Affiliation or Control: State/Local IRS Status: 501(c)3
Highest Offering: Associate Degree
Accreditation: NH, ADNUR

01 President Dr. Danette TOONE
05 Vice President for Academic Affairs Ms. Nancy ZENGER-BENEDA
32 VP Student Affairs/Advancement Ms. Kimberly REYNOLDS
11 Vice Pres for Administrative Svcs Ms. Amy LANGE
13 Vice Pres Information Technology Mr. Shawn WALDEN
30 Director Institutional Advancement Vacant
07 Director of Admissions Mr. Shane OLSON
08 Director of Library Services Ms. Jennifer SCHROEDER
41 Athletic Director Mr. Matthew BECHARD
06 Registrar Mrs. Linda PETERSEN
18 Chief Facilities/Physical Plant Mr. Rex E. SICARD
26 Chief Public Relations Officer Ms. Jenny ACREE
102 Dir Cloud County Cmty College Fndn Ms. Heather GENNETTE
37 Director Student Financial Aid Ms. Suzi KNOETTGEN
38 Director Advising & Retention Ms. Amber KNOETTGEN
15 Director of Human Resources Ms. Christine WILSON
09 Director Institutional Research Dr. Mitch STIMERS

Cloud County Community College Geary County Campus (J)

631 Caroline Avenue, Junction City KS 66441
Telephone: (785) 238-8010 Identification: 770258
Accreditation: &NH

Coffeyville Community College (K)

400 W 11th Street, Coffeyville KS 67337-5064
County: Montgomery FICE Identification: 001910
Unit ID: 154925
Telephone: (620) 251-7700 Carnegie Class: Assoc/HVT-High Non
FAX Number: (620) 252-7098 Calendar System: Semester
URL: www.coffeyville.edu
Established: 1923 Annual Undergrad Tuition & Fees (In-District): $2,304
Enrollment: 1,740 Coed
Affiliation or Control: State/Local IRS Status: 501(c)3
Highest Offering: Associate Degree
Accreditation: NH, EMT, MAC

01 President Ms. Linda MOLEY
05 Vice President for Academic Service Ms. Aron POTTER
10 Vice Pres for Operations & Finance Mr. Jeff MORRIS
88 VP for Innovation/Bus Initiatives Mr. Marlon THORNBURG
12 Director Columbus Technical Campus Mrs. Cindy HARROLD
102 Exec Director-CCC Foundation Mr. Dickie ROLLS
32 Dean of Student Life Mr. Ryan MCCUNE
09 Dean Institutional Research/Records Mrs. Deborah OESTMANN
26 Director of Marketing Ms. Yvonne HULL
20 Director Academic Advising/SSC Mrs. Kim LAY
45 Director Institutional Effectivenes Mr. Marty EVENSVOLD
37 Director of Financial Aid Mrs. Pam FEERER
15 Director of Human Resources Mrs. Kelli BAUER
41 Athletics Director Mr. Jeff LEIKER
18 Director of Maintenance Ms. Vivian FROST
106 Director of Distance Learning Mr. Brad WEBER
40 Bookstore Manager Mrs. Karen STRIMPLE
07 Admissions Representative Ms. Kristin HORNER

Colby Community College (L)

1255 S Range, Colby KS 67701-4099
County: Thomas FICE Identification: 001911
Unit ID: 154934
Telephone: (785) 462-3984 Carnegie Class: Assoc/MT-VT-Mix Trad/Non
FAX Number: (785) 460-4699 Calendar System: Semester
URL: www.colbycc.edu
Established: 1964 Annual Undergrad Tuition & Fees (In-District): $3,150
Enrollment: 1,243 Coed
Affiliation or Control: State/Local IRS Status: 501(c)3
Highest Offering: Associate Degree
Accreditation: NH, ADNUR, PTAA

01 President Mr. Seth M. CARTER
05 Vice President of Academic Affairs Mr. Bradley BENNETT
32 Vice President of Student Affairs Dr. George MCNULTY
10 Vice President of Business Affairs Ms. Carolyn KASDORF
08 Librarian Ms. Tara SCHROER
26 Director of Public Information Mr. Doug JOHNSON
09 Director of Data Management Mrs. Angel MORRISON
37 Director of Financial Aid Mrs. Cindi KRISS
29 Director Alumni Relations Ms. Jennifer SCHOENFELD
41 Athletic Director Mr. Ryan STURDY
13 Director of IT Mr. Douglass MCDOWALL
04 Administrative Asst to President Ms. Penny CLINE

Cowley County Community College (M)

125 S Second, PO Box 1147,
Arkansas City KS 67005-1147
County: Cowley FICE Identification: 001902
Unit ID: 154952
Telephone: (620) 442-0430 Carnegie Class: Assoc/HT-Mix Trad/Non
FAX Number: (620) 441-5350 Calendar System: Semester
URL: www.cowley.edu
Established: 1922 Annual Undergrad Tuition & Fees (In-District): $2,759
Enrollment: 3,083 Coed
Affiliation or Control: Local IRS Status: 501(c)3
Highest Offering: Associate Degree
Accreditation: NH, EMT

01 President Dr. Dennis C. RITTLE
05 Vice President of Academic Affairs Dr. Harold ARNETT
10 Vice Pres of Finance/Administration Dr. Gloria WALKER
13 Vice Pres Information Technology Mr. Paul ERDMANN
30 Vice Pres Institutional Development Dr. Kori GREGG
20 AVP Secondary Partnerships/Acad Ms. Janice STOVER
84 Exec Director Enrollment Management Ms. Kristi SHAW
32 Executive Director of Student Life Mr. Jason O'TOOLE
41 Athletic Director Mr. Shane LARSON
35 Director of Student Affairs Mr. Landon WEST
103 AVP Business/Industry Advancement Ms. Tina GRILLOT
106 AVP Distance Learning & Site Mgmt Mr. Eddie ANDREO
26 Dir Inst Comm/Public Relations Mr. Rama PEROO
06 Registrar Mr. Devin GRAVES
15 Director of Human Resources Ms. Linda KREUTZER

Dodge City Community College (N)

2501 N 14th Avenue, Dodge City KS 67801-2399
County: Ford FICE Identification: 001913
Unit ID: 154998
Telephone: (620) 225-1321 Carnegie Class: Assoc/MT-VT-High Non
FAX Number: (620) 227-9366 Calendar System: Semester
URL: www.dc3.edu
Established: 1935 Annual Undergrad Tuition & Fees (In-District): $2,100
Enrollment: 1,779 Coed
Affiliation or Control: State/Local IRS Status: 501(c)3
Highest Offering: Associate Degree
Accreditation: NH, ADNUR

01 President Dr. Harold E. NOLTE, JR.
05 VP of Academic Affairs/Technology Dr. Adam JOHN
10 Vice Pres of Operations & Finance Ms. Vada HERMON
103 VP Aviation & Workforce Development Mr. Anthony LYONS
32 VP of Student Services Ms. Beverly TEMAAT
102 Exec Director of DCCC Foundation Ms. Christina HASELHORST
24 Director Adult Learning Center Mrs. Brandi FERGUSON
15 Director of Human Resources Mr. David WETMORE
07 Director of Admissions Vacant
08 Director Learning Resource Center Mrs. Shelly HUELSMAN

66 Director Nursing Allied Health ... Ms. Mechele HAILEY
41 Athletic Director ... Vacant
37 Director of Financial Aid ... Mr. Russ MCBEE
39 Director of Residence Life ... Vacant
18 Director of Facilities & Operations ... Mr. Tim RIEKENBERG
16 Asst Director of Human Resources ... Ms. Sheila BERGKAMP
04 Exec Assistant to the President ... Mrs. Carla PATEE
20 Dean Workforce Development/Title V ... Mr. Ryan AUSMUS
35 Dean of Students ... Ms. Stephanie LANNING
20 Dean of Academics ... Ms. Jane HOLWERDA
09 Dir of Inst Research/Accreditation ... Vacant
21 Comptroller ... Ms. Sandy MOORE
19 Director Security/Safety ... Mr. Joshua THOMPSON

Donnelly College (A)

608 N 18th Street, Kansas City KS 66102-4298
County: Wyandotte FICE Identification: 001914
Unit ID: 155007
Telephone: (913) 621-8700 Carnegie Class: Bac/Assoc-Mixed
FAX Number: (913) 621-8719 Calendar System: Semester
URL: www.donnelly.edu
Established: 1949 Annual Undergrad Tuition & Fees: $6,702
Enrollment: 382 Coed
Affiliation or Control: Roman Catholic IRS Status: 501(c)3
Highest Offering: Baccalaureate
Accreditation: #NH

01 President ... Msgr. Stuart SWETLAND
05 Vice President of Academics/Stdnts ... Mr. Pedro LEITE
111 Vice President of Advancement ... Mrs. Emily BUCKLEY
10 Vice President of Business Affairs ... Ms. Cheryl HICKS
32 Director Student Success ... Dr. Mary PFLANZ
06 Registrar ... Ms. Jennifer BALES
36 Career Center Coord/Library Dir ... Mrs. Jane BALLAGH DE TOVAR
37 Director of Financial Aid ... Mr. Michael PEPPLE
29 Alumni Relations ... Mr. Roger BERG

Emporia State University (B)

1 Kellogg Circle, Emporia KS 66801-5415
County: Lyon FICE Identification: 001927
Unit ID: 155025
Telephone: (620) 341-1200 Carnegie Class: Masters/L
FAX Number: (620) 341-5553 Calendar System: Semester
URL: www.emporia.edu
Established: 1863 Annual Undergrad Tuition & Fees (In-State): $6,179
Enrollment: 6,094 Coed
Affiliation or Control: State IRS Status: 501(c)3
Highest Offering: Doctorate
Accreditation: NH, ART, CAATE, CACREP, CAEPN, CEA, LIB, MUS, NUR

01 President ... Dr. Allison GARRETT
05 Provost/VP for Academic Affairs ... Dr. David CORDLE
11 VP Admin/Fiscal Affairs ... Ms. Diana E. KUHLMANN
32 Vice President Student Affairs ... Dr. James E. WILLIAMS
13 Assoc Vice Pres Info Technology ... Mr. Cory FALLDINE
09 Asst Provost Inst Research/Assess ... Dr. JoLanna KORD
85 Dean of International Education ... Mr. Mark DALY
35 Dean of Students ... Ms. Lynn M. HOBSON
102 President ESU Foundation ... Mr. Shane SHIVLEY
29 Director of Alumni/Govt Rels ... Mr. K. Tyler CURTIS
88 Director Natl Teachers Hall of Fame ... Ms. Carol STRICKLAND
22 Affirmative Action Officer ... Mr. Ray LAUBER
53 Dean/The Teachers College ... Dr. Kenneth WEAVER
49 Dean College of Liberal Arts/Sci ... Dr. R. Brent THOMAS
50 Dean School of Business ... Dr. Ed BASHAW
62 Dean School of Library/Info Mgmt ... Dr. Wooseob JEONG
58 Dean Graduate Studies ... Dr. James SPOTSWOOD
88 Exec Dir Jones Inst Educ Excel ... Dr. Roger CASWELL
06 Registrar ... Ms. M. Elaine HENRIE
08 Dean University Libraries/Archives ... Dr. Michelle HAMMOND
106 Director Distance Education ... Dr. James SPOTSWOOD
37 Director Student Financial Aid ... Ms. M. Elaine HENRIE
07 Director Admissions ... Dr. Shelly GEHRKE
36 Director Career Services ... Ms. June COLEMAN
38 Director Stdnt Wellness/Counseling ... Ms. Sally CRAWFORD-FOWLER
26 Exec Dir Marketing & Media Relation ... Vacant
41 Director Athletics ... Mr. Kent L. WEISER
18 Director Facilities/Physical Plant ... Mr. Mark S. RUNGE
15 Director Human Resources ... Mr. Ray LAUBER
23 Director Health Services ... Ms. Mary MCDANIEL
39 Dir Residential Life/Orientation ... Ms. Cass COUGHLIN
40 Manager Bookstore ... Mr. Michael MCRELL
19 Director Police & Safety ... Capt. Chris HOOVER
43 General Counsel ... Mr. Kevin JOHNSON
21 Controller ... Ms. Mary MINGENBACK
92 Associate Provost Honors College ... Dr. Gary WYATT
28 Director Diversity & Inclusion ... Mr. Jason BROOKS
04 Administrative Asst to President ... Ms. Sarah MCKERNAN
86 Director Government Relations ... Mr. Brian DENTON
91 Assoc CIO Academic & User Support ... Dr. Rob GIBSON

Flint Hills Technical College (C)

3301 W 18th Avenue, Emporia KS 66801-5957
County: Lyon FICE Identification: 005264
Unit ID: 155052
Telephone: (620) 343-4600 Carnegie Class: Assoc/HVT-Mix Trad/Non
FAX Number: (620) 343-4610 Calendar System: Semester
URL: www.fhtc.edu
Established: 1965 Annual Undergrad Tuition & Fees (In-District): $5,848
Enrollment: 944 Coed
Affiliation or Control: State/Local IRS Status: 501(c)3
Highest Offering: Associate Degree
Accreditation: NH, DA, DH

01 President ... Dr. Dean HOLLENBECK
05 Vice Pres Instructional Services ... Mr. Steve LOEWEN
32 Vice Pres Student Services ... Ms. Lisa KIRMER
10 Vice Pres Business Services ... Mrs. Nancy THOMPSON
15 Director Personnel Services ... Mrs. Jacinda KAHLE
37 Director Student Financial Aid ... Ms. Erica CLARK
84 Director Enrollment Management ... Ms. Brenda CARMICHAEL
04 Administrative Asst to President ... Ms. Jacqui ANDERSON
30 Chief Development/Advancement ... Mr. Mike CROUCH

Fort Hays State University (D)

600 Park Street, Hays KS 67601-4099
County: Ellis FICE Identification: 001915
Unit ID: 155061
Telephone: (785) 628-4000 Carnegie Class: Masters/L
FAX Number: (785) 628-4096 Calendar System: Semester
URL: www.fhsu.edu
Established: 1902 Annual Undergrad Tuition & Fees (In-State): $4,884
Enrollment: 14,210 Coed
Affiliation or Control: State IRS Status: 501(c)3
Highest Offering: Doctorate
Accreditation: NH, CAATE, CAEPN, MUS, NURSE, RAD, SP, SW

01 Interim President ... Dr. Andy TOMPKINS
05 Interim Provost ... Dr. Jeff BRIGGS
10 Vice Pres Administration & Finance ... Mr. Mike BARNETT
32 Vice Pres Student Affairs ... Dr. Joseph G. LINN
35 Asst Vice Pres Student Affairs ... Dr. Teresa CLOUNCH
20 Interim Asst Provost/Learning Tech ... Dr. Andrew FELDSTEIN
104 Int AVP Intl Programs ... Vacant
09 Asst VP Institutional Effectiveness ... Dr. Sangki MIN
58 Dean Graduate Studies ... Dr. Jennifer BONDS-RAACKE
35 Asst Vice Pres Student Affairs ... Dr. Kenton OLLIFF
06 Registrar ... Mr. Craig KARLIN
07 Admissions Director ... Ms. Tricia CLINE
29 Exec Director Alumni & Govt Rels ... Ms. Debra K. PRIDEAUX
45 Director Budget & Planning ... Mr. Robert MANRY
36 Director Career Services ... Mr. Daniel B. RICE
37 Dir Student Financial Aid ... Ms. Wendy ROHLEDER-SOOK
26 Director University Relations ... Mr. Lisa L. KARLIN
08 Dean Forsyth Library ... Ms. Deborah LUDWIG
15 Director Personnel Services ... Ms. Shannon LINDSEY
106 Director Virtual College ... Mr. Michael MICHAELIS
53 Dean College Education ... Dr. Paul ADAMS
49 Dean Col Arts/Humanities/Soc Sci ... Dr. Paul W. FABER
50 Dean Col Business/Entrepreneurship ... Dr. Mark BANNISTER
76 Int Dean Col Health & Sciences ... Mr. Glen MCNEIL
18 Co-Dir Chief Facil/Physical Plant ... Mr. Jim SCHREIBER
18 Co-Dir Chief Facil/Physical Plant ... Mr. Ken JACOBS
121 Dir Acad Advis/Career Exploration ... Dr. Patricia L. GRIFFIN
28 Director Inclusion and Diversity ... Ms. Taylor KRILEY
19 Director University Police ... Mr. Ed HOWELL
22 Univ Compliance Officer ... Ms. Amy SCHAFFER
102 President/CEO Foundation ... Mr. Jason WILLIBY
25 Chief Contracts/Grants Admin ... Ms. Leslie PAIGE
41 Athletic Director ... Mr. Curtis HAMMEKE
104 Director Study Abroad ... Ms. Andree BRISSON-FARLEY
43 General Counsel ... Ms. Kerry WASINGER
54 Dean College of Science/Tech/Math ... Dr. Greg FARLEY
84 Asst Vice Pres Enrollment Mgmt ... Mr. Dennis KING
13 Director Information Technology ... Mr. Mark GRIFFIN
96 Director of Purchasing ... Ms. Kathy HERRMAN
39 Director Residential Life ... Ms. Christina HURTADO

Fort Scott Community College (E)

2108 S Horton, Fort Scott KS 66701-3140
County: Bourbon FICE Identification: 001916
Unit ID: 155098
Telephone: (620) 223-2700 Carnegie Class: Assoc/HVT-High Non
FAX Number: (620) 223-4927 Calendar System: Semester
URL: www.fortscott.edu
Established: 1919 Annual Undergrad Tuition & Fees (In-District): $2,820
Enrollment: 1,758 Coed
Affiliation or Control: State/Local IRS Status: 501(c)3
Highest Offering: Associate Degree
Accreditation: NH, ADNUR

01 President ... Dr. Alysia JOHNSTON
05 VP of Academic Affairs ... Adam BORTH
10 Vice Pres of Finance and Operations ... Julie EICHENBERGER
32 Dean of Students ... Tom HAVRON
13 Director of Research & Technology ... Jacob REICHARD
07 Director Admissions ... Matt GLADES
08 Director of Library ... Susie ARVIDSON
06 Registrar ... Courtney METCALF
26 Director Public Relations ... Heather CUTSHALL
66 Director Nursing ... Bill RHOADS
14 Information Technology Director ... Jason SIMON
12 Dean Crawford County ... Santos MANRIQUE
12 Dean of Miami County Campus ... Buddy Jo TANCK
121 Dean of Student Support Services ... Janet FANCHER
15 Human Resource Director ... Juley MCDANIEL
30 Director of Development/Alumni ... Bob CABLE
37 Director Student Financial Aid ... Lillie GRUBB
88 Director of Gordon Parks Museum ... Jill WARFORD
21 Director Business Operations ... Mindy RUSSELL

04 Administrative Asst to President ... Darlene WOOD
39 Director Student Housing ... Marci MYERS
88 Program Industry Coordinator ... Nacoma OEHME
25 Director Grants & Special Projects ... Ralph BEACHAM

Friends University (F)

2100 W University Avenue, Wichita KS 67213-3397
County: Sedgwick FICE Identification: 001918
Unit ID: 155089
Telephone: (316) 295-5000 Carnegie Class: Masters/L
FAX Number: (316) 295-5060 Calendar System: Semester
URL: www.friends.edu
Established: 1898 Annual Undergrad Tuition & Fees: $26,865
Enrollment: 1,929 Coed
Affiliation or Control: Independent Non-Profit IRS Status: 501(c)3
Highest Offering: Master's
Accreditation: NH, CAEPN, MFCD, MUS

01 President ... Dr. Amy CAREY
04 Executive Asst to the President ... Ms. Natasha PEREZ
05 VP of Academic Affairs ... Dr. Jasper LESAGE
10 VP of Finance ... Ms. Marsha BEWERSDORF
32 VP of Student Affairs ... Dr. Carole OBERMEYER
111 Assoc VP of University Advancement ... Mr. David ALEXANDER
26 Assoc VP Marketing & Communications ... Ms. Deb STOCKMAN
11 VP of Administration ... Ms. Kelley WILLIAMS
84 VP of Enrollment Management ... Mr. Ken FAFFLER
06 University Registrar ... Mr. Mark BRITTON
49 Dean Col of Bus/Art/Sci & Educ ... Dr. Ken STOLTZFUS
107 Dean Col Adult/Prof Stds/Grad Sch ... Dr. David HOFMEISTER
50 Chair Business & IT ... Dr. Arlen HONTS
57 Chair Fine Arts ... Dr. Cecil RINEY
81 Chair Natural Science/Math ... Dr. Nora STRASSER
73 Chair Religion/Humanities ... Dr. Jeremy GALLEGOS
53 Chair Teacher Education ... Dr. Jan WILSON
83 Chair Social/Behavioral Science ... Dr. Tor WYNN
08 Director Library ... Ms. Anne CRANE
18 Chief Facilities/Physical Plant ... Mr. Paul WINCHESTER
96 Director of Business Operations ... Mr. Ryan ARCHER
07 Sr Dir Admissions & Fin Aid ... Vacant
37 Director Financial Aid ... Mr. Tony LUBBERS
42 Pastor & Dean Campus Ministries ... Dr. Guy CHMIELESKI
39 Director of Residence Life ... Ms. Kelley MARTIN
27 Director of Marketing ... Ms. Gisele MCMINIMY
29 Director of Alumni Relations ... Ms. Brie BOULANGER
12 Site Director - Topeka ... Vacant
12 Site Manager - Kansas City ... Ms. Monica HASHEMI-BOZARTH
112 Director of Planned Giving ... Vacant
09 Director of Institutional Research ... Mr. Aidan DUNLEAVY
19 Director Security/Safety ... Mr. Richard VINROE
106 Dir Online Education/E-learning ... Ms. Nancy ARTAZ

Garden City Community College (G)

801 Campus Drive, Garden City KS 67846-6398
County: Finney FICE Identification: 001919
Unit ID: 155104
Telephone: (620) 276-7611 Carnegie Class: Assoc/MT-VT-Mix Trad/Non
FAX Number: (620) 276-9573 Calendar System: Semester
URL: www.gcccks.edu
Established: 1919 Annual Undergrad Tuition & Fees (In-District): $2,880
Enrollment: 2,099 Coed
Affiliation or Control: Local IRS Status: 501(c)3
Highest Offering: Associate Degree
Accreditation: #NH, ADNUR, EMT

01 President ... Dr. Herbert SWENDER
11 Exec Vice Pres Admin Svcs ... Ms. Dee WIGNER
05 VP Instruction & Student Svcs/CAO ... Mr. Ryan RUDA
84 Director of Enrollment Management ... Ms. Tammy TABOR
06 Registrar ... Ms. Nancy UNRUH
13 Director of Information Technology ... Mr. Patrick PFEIFER
15 Director of Human Resources ... Ms. Sara KOEHN
18 Director of Facilities ... Mr. Derek RAMOS
26 Director Marketing & PR ... Ms. Kristi TEMPEL
37 Director Student Financial Aid ... Ms. Melinda HARRINGTON
39 Director Residential Life ... Ms. Christine DILLINGHAM
32 Dean of Student Services ... Mr. Colin LAMB
20 Dean of Academics ... Mr. Phil TERPSTRA
103 Director of Workforce Development ... Mr. Jerrad WEBB
04 Executive Assistant to President ... Ms. Debra ATKINSON
09 Director of Institutional Research ... Mr. Jeff SOUTHERN
10 Comptroller ... Ms. Debra NICHOLSON
19 Campus Police Chief ... Mr. Rodney DOZIER
08 Director Library Services ... Mr. Trent SMITH
41 Athletic Director ... Mr. John GREEN
44 Executive Director Endowment ... Mr. Jeremy GIGOT
121 Director of Student Success ... Ms. Leslie WENZEL
88 Coord Disability Svcs & Compliance ... Ms. Melanie HANDS
106 Coordinator Distance Learning ... Ms. Lecia SIMS

Grantham University (H)

16025 W 113th Street, Lenexa KS 66219
County: Johnson FICE Identification: 004283
Unit ID: 442569
Telephone: (888) 947-2684 Carnegie Class: Masters/L
FAX Number: (913) 309-4949 Calendar System: Other
URL: www.grantham.edu
Established: 1951 Annual Undergrad Tuition & Fees: $6,540
Enrollment: 11,721 Coed
Affiliation or Control: Proprietary IRS Status: Proprietary
Highest Offering: Master's

Accreditation: DEAC, ENGT, IACBE

01 President & CEO .... A. Scott ANDREWS
26 Chief Marketing Officer .... David EBY
10 Chief Financial Officer .... Lily CARPIO
05 Chief Academic Officer/Provost .... Dr. Niccole KOPIT
86 Vice President Government Relations .... Dr. Jeffrey CROPSEY
22 Chief Compliance Officer .... Harry DOTSON
84 Vice President Student Enrollment .... Jared PARLETTE
15 Vice President Human Resources .... Kip ESRY
13 VP of IT & Chief Information Ofcr .... Anthony SCHLINSOG
06 Associate Registrar .... Joshua CARCOPA
103 Director University Outreach .... Tabitha DAVIS
04 Administrative Asst to President .... Frances KLIPPER
07 Director of Admissions .... Lauren COOK
09 Director of Institutional Research .... Danielle GIBSON

Haskell Indian Nations University (A)

155 Indian Avenue, #5030, Lawrence KS 66046-4800
County: Douglas FICE Identification: 010438
Unit ID: 155140
Telephone: (785) 749-8404 Carnegie Class: Tribal
FAX Number: (785) 749-8406 Calendar System: Semester
URL: www.haskell.edu
Established: 1884 Annual Undergrad Tuition & Fees: $480
Enrollment: 799 Coed
Affiliation or Control: Federal IRS Status: Exempt
Highest Offering: Baccalaureate
Accreditation: NH, CAEPN

01 President .... Dr. Venida CHENAULT
05 Acting Vice Pres Academic Affairs .... Dr. Dan WILDCAT
11 Vice President University Services .... Ms. Tonia SALVINI
10 Chief Finance Officer .... Ms. Brenda RACEHORSE
13 Chief Information Officer .... Mr. Joshua ARCE
111 Acting Dir Academic Support Ctr .... Ms. Beverly FORTNER
39 Dir Resident Housing/Mgr Stdnt Life .... Vacant
37 Financial Aid Officer .... Ms. Carlene MORRIS
06 Registrar .... Ms. Lou HARA
07 Director of Admissions .... Ms. Dorothy D. STITES
09 Dir Instl Research/Sponsored Pgms .... Ms. Cynthia GROUNDS
36 Career Development Specialist .... Vacant
38 Director Student Counseling .... Vacant
15 Human Resources Liaison .... Ms. Mona FRANKLIN
96 Acquisitions .... Ms. Janice BEGAY
26 Executive Asst/Public Relations .... Mr. Stephen PRUE
18 Director Facilities Management .... Mr. Lee PAHCODDY, JR.

Hesston College (B)

Box 3000, Hesston KS 67062-2093
County: Harvey FICE Identification: 001920
Unit ID: 155177
Telephone: (620) 327-4221 Carnegie Class: Assoc/HT-High Trad
FAX Number: (620) 327-8300 Calendar System: Semester
URL: www.hesston.edu
Established: 1909 Annual Undergrad Tuition & Fees: $25,802
Enrollment: 412 Coed
Affiliation or Control: Mennonite Church IRS Status: 501(c)3
Highest Offering: Baccalaureate
Accreditation: NH, NURSE

01 President .... Mr. Joseph MANICKAM
05 Vice Pres of Academics .... Mr. Brent YODER
07 Vice President of Admissions .... Mrs. Rachel S. MILLER
10 Vice Pres Finance & Auxiliary Svcs .... Mr. Mark LANDES
32 Vice Pres of Student Development .... Mr. Rob RAMSEYER
29 Director of Alumni & Church Rels .... Mr. Dallas STUTZMAN
06 Registrar .... Mrs. Sheryl HODGE
21 Business Manager .... Mr. Karl BRUBAKER

Highland Community College (C)

606 W Main, Highland KS 66035-0068
County: Doniphan FICE Identification: 001921
Unit ID: 155186
Telephone: (785) 442-6000 Carnegie Class: Assoc/HVT-High Non
FAX Number: (785) 442-6100 Calendar System: Semester
URL: www.highlandcc.edu
Established: 1858 Annual Undergrad Tuition & Fees (In-District): $3,007
Enrollment: 3,343 Coed
Affiliation or Control: Local IRS Status: 501(c)3
Highest Offering: Associate Degree
Accreditation: NH

01 President .... Mr. David REIST
05 Vice President for Academic Affairs .... Dr. Erin SHAW
32 Vice President for Student Services .... Vacant
10 Vice Pres for Finance/Operations .... Mr. Randy WILLY
88 Director of Technical Education .... Mr. Lucas HUNZIGER
111 Vice Pres Institutional Advancement .... Dr. Craig E. MOSHER
06 Registrar .... Ms. Alice HAMILTON
37 Financial Aid Director .... Mr. Joshua NORTH
13 Director of Information Systems .... Mr. Josh BERRY
09 Director of Institutional Research .... Mr. Jeffrey HURN
38 Campus Counselor .... Vacant
41 Athletic Director .... Mr. Tyler NORDMAN
08 Library Director .... Vacant
18 Supervisor of Buildings & Grounds .... Mr. Rick BLEVINS
26 Chief Public Relations Officer .... Dr. Craig MOSHER
29 Director Alumni Relations .... Dr. Craig MOSHER
35 Director of Student Life .... Ms. Taylor ALLEN
15 Human Resource Manager .... Ms. Eileen C. GRONNIGER
40 Bookstore Coordinator .... Ms. Stephanie NORDMAN
07 Director of Admissions .... Ms. Stephanie PETERSON
106 Dir Online Education/E-learning .... Ms. Denise PETERS

Hutchinson Community College (D)

1300 N Plum Street, Hutchinson KS 67501-5894
County: Reno FICE Identification: 001923
Unit ID: 155195
Telephone: (620) 665-3500 Carnegie Class: Assoc/MT-VT-High Non
FAX Number: (620) 665-3310 Calendar System: Semester
URL: www.hutchcc.edu
Established: 1928 Annual Undergrad Tuition & Fees (In-District): $2,976
Enrollment: 5,546 Coed
Affiliation or Control: State/Local IRS Status: 501(c)3
Highest Offering: Associate Degree
Accreditation: NH, ACBSP, ADNUR, CAHIIM, #COARC, EMT, PNUR, PTAA, RAD, SURGT

01 President .... Dr. Carter FILE
05 Vice President of Academic Affairs .... Dr. Cindy HOSS
10 Vice President Finance/Operations .... Ms. Julie BLANTON
103 VP Workforce Development/Outreach .... Mr. Steve PORTER
32 Vice President of Students .... Mr. Brett BRIGHT
26 Director of Marketing & Info .... Mr. Denny STOECKLEIN
13 Chief Information Officer .... Mr. Loren L. MORRIS
06 Registrar .... Mrs. Christina LONG
41 Athletic Director .... Mr. Josh GOOCH
15 Director of Personnel .... Mr. Brooks E. MANTOOTH
37 Financial Aid Officer .... Mr. Nathan BUCHE
07 Director of Admissions .... Mr. Corbin STROBEL
18 Director of Plant Facilities .... Mr. Don ROSE
39 Director of Residence Life .... Ms. Dana HINSHAW
29 Director Alumni Relations .... Mrs. Cindy KEAST
08 Coordinator of Library Services .... Mr. Robert KELLY
09 Coord of Institutional Research .... Mr. Rex CHEEVER

Independence Community College (E)

1057 West College Avenue,
Independence KS 67301-0708
County: Montgomery FICE Identification: 001924
Unit ID: 155201
Telephone: (620) 331-4100 Carnegie Class: Assoc/HVT-High Non
FAX Number: (620) 331-5344 Calendar System: Semester
URL: www.indycc.edu
Established: 1925 Annual Undergrad Tuition & Fees (In-District): $3,728
Enrollment: 976 Coed
Affiliation or Control: State/Local IRS Status: 501(c)3
Highest Offering: Associate Degree
Accreditation: NH

01 President .... Dr. Daniel W. BARWICK
10 Contoller .... Ms. Wendy ISLE
32 VP Student Affairs/Athletics .... Ms. Tammie GELDENHUYS
13 Chief Information Officer .... Mr. Eric MONTGOMERY
26 Marketing Director/Instructor .... Mr. Brad HENDERSON
102 Foundation Director .... Ms. Lori SHAW
05 Chief Academic Officer .... Ms. Kara WHEELER
06 Registrar .... Ms. Sonja CONLEY
08 Director Library Services .... Ms. Sarah OWEN
18 Maintenance/Custodial Supervisor .... Ms. Kris KIPPENBERGER
07 Director of Admissions .... Ms. Brittany THORNTON
37 Financial Aid Director .... Ms. Laura ALLISON
09 Dir of Institutional Research .... Ms. Debbie PHELPS
04 Executive Asst to President .... Ms. Beverly HARRIS
40 Bookstore Manager .... Ms. Teresa VESTAL
88 Upward Bound Program Director .... Ms. Valon JONES
15 Human Resources Coordinator .... Ms. Keli TUSCHMAN
51 Interim Director Online/Cont Educ .... Ms. Jessica MORGAN-TATE
121 Associate Dean Acad Support Svcs .... Ms. Taylor CRAWSHAW
39 Student Housing General Manager .... Ms. Mary BAILEY

Johnson County Community College (F)

12345 College Boulevard, Overland Park KS 66210-1299
County: Johnson FICE Identification: 008244
Unit ID: 155210
Telephone: (913) 469-8500 Carnegie Class: Assoc/MT-VT-High Non
FAX Number: (913) 469-2559 Calendar System: Semester
URL: www.jccc.edu
Established: 1969 Annual Undergrad Tuition & Fees (In-District): $2,790
Enrollment: 19,091 Coed
Affiliation or Control: State/Local IRS Status: 501(c)3
Highest Offering: Associate Degree
Accreditation: NH, ACBSP, ACFEI, ADNUR, COARC, DH, EMT, IFSAC, NDT

01 President .... Dr. Joe SOPCICH
10 Exec Vice Pres Finance & Admin Svcs .... Dr. Barbara LARSON
05 Vice Pres Instruction/CAO .... Dr. Mickey MCCLOUD
11 Exec VP Administrative Services .... Ms. Barbara LARSON
32 Vice Pres Student Success/Engagemnt .... Dr. Randy WEBER
13 Vice President Information Services .... Mr. Tom PAGANO
04 Exec Asst to the President & Board .... Ms. Terri SCHLICHT
21 AVP Financial Services .... Ms. Rachel LIERZ
18 AVP Campus Services .... Mr. Rex HAYS
20 AVP Instruction .... Dr. Gurbhushan SINGH
96 AVP Business Services .... Mr. Mitch BORCHERS
14 Director Admin Computing Services .... Ms. Sandra WARNER
26 Exec Dir Mktg/Communications .... Mr. Chris GRAY
35 Dean Student Success .... Mr. Paul KYLE
84 Asst Dean Enrollment Management .... Ms. MargE SHELLEY
35 Asst Dean Student Life/Ldrshp Dev .... Ms. Pam VASSAR
37 Director Student Financial Aid .... Ms. Christal WILLIAMS
36 Director Testing and Assessment .... Ms. Mary Ann DICKERSON
06 Registrar .... Ms. Leslie QUINN
08 Director Library Services .... Mr. Mark DAGANAAR
07 Director of Admissions .... Mr. Peter BELK
41 Director of Athletics .... Mr. Randy STANGE
92 Program Facilitator Honors .... Ms. Anna PAGE
09 Director of Institutional Research .... Ms. Natalie ALLEMAN-BEYERS
38 Dean Learner Engagement & Success .... Mr. Richard MOEHRING

Kansas Christian College (G)

7401 Metcalf, Overland Park KS 66204-1995
County: Johnson Identification: 667134
Unit ID: 155308
Telephone: (913) 722-0272 Carnegie Class: Not Classified
FAX Number: (913) 601-3826 Calendar System: Semester
URL: www.kansaschristian.edu
Established: 1938 Annual Undergrad Tuition & Fees: $7,350
Enrollment: 34 Coed
Affiliation or Control: Independent Non-Profit IRS Status: 501(c)3
Highest Offering: Baccalaureate
Accreditation: BI

00 Chairman of the Board .... Rev. Rodney L. DAVIS
101 Secretary of the Board .... Mr. Dwight PURTLE
01 President .... Mr. Delbert L. SCOTT
05 Vice President of Academic Affairs .... Rev. Christopher W. SUMPTER
11 Vice President of Operations .... Mr. Chad POLLARD
106 Vice President of Adult and Online .... Rev. Matthew LEE
111 Vice President of Advancement .... Dr. James L. POTEET
32 Dean of Students .... Mr. David CARPENTER
18 Chief Facilities Officer .... Mr. Harold V. CARPENTER
07 Director of Admissions .... Mr. David PEDOTTO
08 Head Librarian .... Mrs. Dorie SCOFIELD

Kansas City Kansas Community College (H)

7250 State Avenue, Kansas City KS 66112-3003
County: Wyandotte FICE Identification: 001925
Unit ID: 155292
Telephone: (913) 334-1100 Carnegie Class: Assoc/HVT-Mix Trad/Non
FAX Number: (913) 288-7609 Calendar System: Semester
URL: www.kckcc.edu
Established: 1923 Annual Undergrad Tuition & Fees (In-District): $3,240
Enrollment: 5,625 Coed
Affiliation or Control: State/Local IRS Status: 501(c)3
Highest Offering: Associate Degree
Accreditation: NH, ACBSP, ADNUR, COARC, EMT, FUSER, MAC, PTAA

01 Acting President .... Dr. Jacqueline VIETTI
10 Chief Financial/Operations Officer .... Vacant
05 Interim Vice Pres Academic Affairs .... Dr. Edward KREMER
81 Dean Math/Sci/CompTech/Bus/CEB .... Dr. Edward KREMER
84 Assoc Dean Enrollment Management .... Dr. Stephen TERRY
51 Exec Director Adult Education .... Ms. Marisa GRAY
103 Exec Dir Entrep & Workforce Dev .... Ms. Alicia HOOKS
79 Dean Arts/Humanities/Social Science .... Dr. Cherilee WALKER
13 VP Information Services .... Mr. Baz ABOUELENEIN
09 Dean Institutional Services .... Dr. Sangki MIN
66 Dean Nursing/Allied Health .... Dr. Tiffany BOHM
32 Dean of Student Services .... Dr. Jonathan LONG
75 Dean Technical Operations .... Mr. Cliff SMITH
88 Exec Director Pioneer Career Ctr .... Mr. Cliff SMITH
88 Director of Academic Resource Ctr .... Ms. Amanda WILLIAMS
41 Director of Athletics .... Mr. Anthony (Tony) TOMPKINS
40 Interim Director of Bookstore .... Mr. Kasey MAYER
18 Director of Buildings/Grounds .... Mr. Jeff SIXTA
19 Director of Campus Police .... Chief Greg SCHNEIDER
14 Director of Computing .... Mr. James BENNETT
121 Director of Student Advising .... Mr. Shawn DERRITT
38 Director Counseling-Advocacy Ctr .... Ms. Linda WARNER
37 Director of Financial Aid .... Ms. Mary I. DORR
114 Director of Budget .... Ms. Marie BRANSTETTER
92 Director of Honors/Phi Theta Kappa .... Dr. Stacy TUCKER
28 Director of Intercultural Center .... Ms. Barbara CLARK-EVANS
08 Director of Library .... Vacant
24 Director Media Services Technology .... Mr. Randy ROYER
106 Director of Online Services .... Ms. Susan STUART
35 Director of Student Activities .... Ms. Andrica WILCOXEN
07 Director of Admissions .... Ms. Tami A. BARTUNEK
06 Registrar .... Ms. Theresa HOLLIDAY
15 Director Human Resources .... Mr. Alfonso ZARATE
88 Director Forensic Laboratory .... Ms. D.C BROIL
88 Director Wellness Center .... Mr. Rob M. CRANE
103 Director of Cultural Outreach .... Mr. Brian PATRICK
66 Director Nursing .... Ms. Sharon JACKSON
66 Director Practical Nursing .... Ms. Susan K. WHITE
88 Director Technical Programs .... Mr. Richard PIPER
88 Director Technical Programs Perkins .... Ms. Donna S. SHAWN
88 Asst Director Academic Resources .... Ms. Amanda WILLIAMS
88 Director Performing Arts Center .... Dr. Cherilee WALKER
04 Exec Admin Asst to President .... Ms. Peggy L. FRIEDMANN
105 Director Web Services .... Mr. Matthew FOWLER

22 Dir Affirmative Action/EEO ... Vacant
39 Director Student Housing ... Dr. Delfina WILSON
102 Exec Dir Foundation/Cmty Outreach ... Ms. Tami BARTUNEK

Kansas State University (A)

919 Mid-Campus Drive North, Manhattan KS 66506
County: Riley FICE Identification: 001928
Unit ID: 155399
Telephone: (785) 532-6250 Carnegie Class: DU-Highest
FAX Number: (785) 532-2120 Calendar System: Semester
URL: www.k-state.edu
Established: 1863 Annual Undergrad Tuition & Fees (In-State): $9,874
Enrollment: 24,146 Coed
Affiliation or Control: State IRS Status: 501(c)3
Highest Offering: Doctorate
Accreditation: NH, ART, CAATE, CACREP, CAEPN, CEA, CIDA, CONST, CS, DIETC, DIETD, ENG, IPSY, JOUR, LSAR, MFCD, MUS, NRPA, PH, PLNG, SP, SPAA, SW, THEA, VET

01 President ... Mr. Richard B. MYERS
04 Exec Asst to the President ... Ms. Dana M. HASTINGS
05 Provost and Senior Vice President ... Dr. April C. MASON
10 VP Admin & Finance ... Ms. Cindy A. BONTRAGER
46 VP for Research ... Dr. Peter K. DORHOUT
32 VP Student Life/Dean of Students ... Dr. Pat J. BOSCO
26 VP for Communications & Marketing ... Mr. Jeffery B. MORRIS
15 VP Human Capital ... Mr. Jay W. STEPHENS
102 President/CEO of Foundation ... Mr. Greg WILLEMS
29 Alumni Association President ... Ms. Amy Button RENZ
41 Athletics Director ... Mr. Gene TAYLOR
100 Chief of Staff/Dir Community Rels ... Dr. Jackie L. HARTMAN
86 Dir for Governmental Relations ... Dr. Susan K. PETERSON
88 Exec Dir Military/Veterans Affairs ... Dr. Arthur S. DE GROAT, II
43 General Counsel ... Ms. Cheryl G. STRECKER
20 Senior Vice Provost ... Dr. Ruth DYER
13 Interim Vice Provost Info Tech Svcs ... Mr. Rob CAFFEY
108 Assoc Prov Institutional Effectiv ... Dr. Brian A. NIEHOFF
28 Interim Assoc Prov for Diversity ... Dr. Zelia Z. WILEY
09 Director Planning & Analysis ... Dr. Brian A. NIEHOFF
08 Dean of Libraries ... Dr. Lori A. GOETSCH
47 Dean of Agriculture ... Dr. John FLOROS
48 Dean Architecture/Planning/Design ... Mr. Timothy DE NOBLE
49 Dean of Arts & Sciences ... Dr. Amitabha CHAKRABARTI
50 Dean of Business Admin ... Dr. Kevin P. GWINNER
51 Dean of Continuing Education ... Dr. Sue C. MAES
53 Dean of Education ... Dr. Debbie K. MERCER
54 Dean of Engineering ... Dr. Darren M. DAWSON
58 Dean of Graduate School ... Dr. Carol SHANKLIN
59 Dean of Human Ecology ... Dr. John B. BUCKWALTER
72 CEO/Dean of Technology & Aviation ... Dr. Verna M. FITZSIMMONS
74 Dean of Veterinary Medicine ... Dr. Tammy R. BECKHAM
12 CEO K-State Olathe ... Dr. Ralph C. RICHARDSON
18 Assoc VP Facilities Planning/Mgmt ... Mr. Ryan F. SWANSON
114 Asst VP for Budget Planning ... Mr. Ethan E. ERICKSON
19 Asst VP Univ Police & Public Safety ... Mr. Ronnie D. GRICE
96 Director of Purchasing ... Ms. Carla BISHOP
07 Assoc VP/Director of Admissions ... Mr. Lawrence E. MOEDER
06 Registrar ... Dr. Monty E. NIELSEN
37 Assoc VP/Dir Student Fin Assistance ... Mr. Lawrence E. MOEDER
39 Asst VP/Dir Housing & Dining Svcs ... Mr. Derek A. JACKSON
36 Exec Dir Career & Employment Svcs ... Ms. Kerri D. KELLER

Kansas State University Polytechnic, College of Technology and Aviation (B)

2310 Centennial Road, Salina KS 67401-8196
Telephone: (785) 826-2601 FICE Identification: 004611
Accreditation: &NH, AAB, ENGT

† Regional accreditation is carried under the parent institution in Manhattan, KS.

Kansas Wesleyan University (C)

100 E Claflin Avenue, Salina KS 67401-6196
County: Saline FICE Identification: 001929
Unit ID: 155414
Telephone: (785) 827-5541 Carnegie Class: Bac-Diverse
FAX Number: (785) 827-0927 Calendar System: Semester
URL: www.kwu.edu
Established: 1886 Annual Undergrad Tuition & Fees: $28,000
Enrollment: 748 Coed
Affiliation or Control: United Methodist IRS Status: 501(c)3
Highest Offering: Master's
Accreditation: NH, CAEPN

01 President and CEO ... Dr. Matthew R. THOMPSON
04 Executive Assistant to President ... Ms. Jan M. SHIRK
05 Interim Provost ... Dr. Damon KRAFT
32 Vice President Student Development ... Ms. Bridget R. WEISER
111 Vice Pres Institutional Advancement ... Mrs. Melanie B. OVERTON
10 Vice Pres Finance & Operations ... Ms. Karen TUMLINSON
84 Vice Pres Enrollment Management ... Dr. Mark A. BANDRE
21 Controller ... Mr. John W. COYKENDALL
37 Director Student Financial Planning ... Mrs. Lois MADSEN
06 Registrar ... Mrs. Karissa L. SWENSON
07 Director of Admissions ... Mr. Esteban PAREDES
20 Assistant Provost ... Dr. Kristine RODRIGUEZ
20 Assistant Provost ... Ms. Janeane HOUCHIN
88 Admin Assistant to EVP/Provost ... Ms. Kristan HERNANDEZ
29 Alumni Engagement Officer ... Mr. Bryan L. MCCULLAR
26 Sr Dir Marketing & Communications ... Mrs. Paula HERMANN
27 Asst Director of Market/Comm ... Ms. Amy ADAMS
36 Career Planning & Exper Educ Spec ... Vacant
35 Associate Director Student Develop ... Mr. Nate THIES
121 Dir Student Success/Testing Center ... Mrs. Jennifer BARRETT
08 Director of Library Svcs ... Ms. Kelley WEBER
24 Production Manager ... Mr. Paul GREEN
13 Director of Information Systems ... Mr. Jay C. KROB
19 Director of Emergency Management ... Dr. Lonnie BOOKER
18 Director of Plant Operations ... Mr. Dale WHITE
40 Manager Yotee's Bookstore ... Mr. Steve G. CARRIER
42 Chaplain Univ United Meth Church ... Vacant
41 Athletic Director ... Mr. Michael HERMANN
123 Assoc Dir Admissions MBA & Online ... Ms. Charlotte GARRETT
66 Director of Nursing Education ... Ms. Janeane HOUCHIN
53 Director of Teacher Education ... Dr. Kristine RODRIGUEZ
79 Division Chair Humanities ... Dr. Michael RUSSELL
49 Div Chair Applied Art & Sciences ... Prof. Bryan K. MINNICH
83 Division Chair Social Sciences ... Dr. Paul HEDLUND
57 Division Chair Fine Arts ... Prof. Barbara J. NICKELL
81 Division Chair Natural Sciences ... Dr. Dorothy HANNA
15 Human Resources Director ... Mr. Frank ROTH

Labette Community College (D)

200 S 14th, Parsons KS 67357-4299
County: Labette FICE Identification: 001930
Unit ID: 155450
Telephone: (620) 421-6700 Carnegie Class: Assoc/MT-VT-High Non
FAX Number: (620) 421-0921 Calendar System: Semester
URL: www.labette.edu
Established: 1923 Annual Undergrad Tuition & Fees (In-District): $2,760
Enrollment: 1,867 Coed
Affiliation or Control: Local IRS Status: 501(c)3
Highest Offering: Associate Degree
Accreditation: NH, ADNUR, COARC, DA, DMS, PTAA, RAD

01 President ... Dr. Mark WATKINS
04 Executive Assistant to President ... Ms. Megan A. FUGATE
05 Vice President Academic Affairs ... Mr. Joe BURKE
10 Vice President Finance & Operations ... Ms. Leanna J. DOHERTY
32 Vice President Student Affairs ... Ms. Tammy FUENTEZ
84 Assoc Dean Enrollment Mgmt ... Ms. Kathy JOHNSTON
20 Dean of Instruction ... Mr. Rick CARPENTER
13 Director of Information Technology ... Mrs. Jody BURZINSKI
30 Dir Resource Devel/Alumni Rels ... Mrs. Lindi D. FORBES
08 Director of Library Services ... Mr. Scott M. ZOLLARS
18 Director of Physical Plant ... Mr. Kevin DOHERTY
66 Director of Nursing ... Mrs. Delyna BOHNENBLUST
41 Athletic Director ... Mr. Aaron J. KEAL
26 Director of Public Relations ... Mrs. Bethany KENDRICK
06 Registrar/Dir Student Financial Aid ... Ms. Kathy JOHNSTON
15 Director of Human Relations ... Ms. Janice S. GEORGE
37 Director Student Financial Aid ... Ms. Kathy JOHNSTON
35 Student Life Coordinator ... Mrs. Melissa NANCE
40 Bookstore Specialist ... Mrs. Lois D. HEMBREE

Manhattan Area Technical College (E)

3136 Dickens Avenue, Manhattan KS 66503-2499
County: Riley FICE Identification: 005500
Unit ID: 155487
Telephone: (785) 587-2800 Carnegie Class: Assoc/HVT-High Non
FAX Number: (785) 587-2804 Calendar System: Semester
URL: www.manhattantech.edu
Established: 1965 Annual Undergrad Tuition & Fees (In-District): $5,640
Enrollment: 870 Coed
Affiliation or Control: State/Local IRS Status: 501(c)3
Highest Offering: Associate Degree
Accreditation: NH, ADNUR, DH, MLTAD

01 President/CEO ... Dr. Jim J. GENANDT
05 Vice Pres of Instructional Affairs ... Vacant
10 Vice Pres Administrative Services ... Mr. Keith ZACHARIASEN
32 Vice President of Student Services ... Ms. Sarah PHILLIPS
30 Assoc VP Institutional Advancement ... Dr. Richard FOGG
21 Chief Financial Officer ... Ms. Carmela JACOBS
13 Chief Information Officer ... Mr. Josh GFELLER
06 Registrar ... Ms. Rachel SHERLEY
15 Director Human Resources ... Vacant
07 Director of Admissions ... Mr. Neil ROSS
37 Director Financial Aid ... Ms. Laura WEISS-COOK

Manhattan Christian College (F)

1415 Anderson, Manhattan KS 66502-4081
County: Riley FICE Identification: 001931
Unit ID: 155496
Telephone: (785) 539-3571 Carnegie Class: Spec-4-yr-Faith
FAX Number: (785) 539-0832 Calendar System: Semester
URL: www.mccks.edu
Established: 1927 Annual Undergrad Tuition & Fees: $14,986
Enrollment: 308 Coed
Affiliation or Control: Christian Churches And Churches of Christ
IRS Status: 501(c)3
Highest Offering: Baccalaureate
Accreditation: NH, BI

01 President ... Mr. J. Kevin INGRAM
05 Vice President Academic Affairs ... Dr. Greg DELORT
10 Vice President Business Affairs ... Ms. LoriJo STANFIELD
32 Vice President Student Life ... Dr. Rick L. WRIGHT
06 Registrar ... Mr. Eric SANFORD
111 Director Institutional Advancement ... Mrs. Jolene K. RUPE
08 Director of Library Services ... Mrs. Mary Ann BUHLER
41 Athletic Director ... Mr. Shawn M. CONDRA
29 Alumni Relations Director ... Mrs. Genae DENVER
04 Admin Asst to President ... Mrs. April WENDT
07 Director of Admissions ... Mr. Paul WILSON
37 Financial Aid Counselor ... Mrs. Trish RUNION

McPherson College (G)

1600 E Euclid, PO Box 1402, McPherson KS 67460-1402
County: McPherson FICE Identification: 001933
Unit ID: 155511
Telephone: (620) 242-0400 Carnegie Class: Bac-Diverse
FAX Number: (620) 241-8443 Calendar System: 4/1/4
URL: www.mcpherson.edu
Established: 1887 Annual Undergrad Tuition & Fees: $26,498
Enrollment: 681 Coed
Affiliation or Control: Church Of The Brethren IRS Status: 501(c)3
Highest Offering: Master's
Accreditation: NH, CAEPN

01 President ... Mr. Michael P. SCHNEIDER
05 Provost/VP Academic Affairs ... Dr. Bruce CLARY
30 Vice President for Advancement ... Mr. Roger BRIMMERMAN
10 Vice President for Finance ... Mr. Rick TUXHORN
84 VP Enrollment Management/Marketing ... Ms. Christi HOPKINS
100 Chief of Staff ... Ms. Abby ARCHER-RIERSON
32 Assoc Dean of Students/Student Life ... Mr. Ben COFFEY
41 Athletic Director ... Mr. Doug QUINT
06 Registrar ... Ms. Tricia HARTSHORN
37 Director Financial Aid/Admissions ... Ms. Sara BRUBAKER
08 Director of Library Services ... Ms. Mary HESTER
29 Director Alumni Relations ... Vacant

MidAmerica Nazarene University (H)

2030 E College Way, Olathe KS 66062-1899
County: Johnson FICE Identification: 007032
Unit ID: 155520
Telephone: (913) 782-3750 Carnegie Class: Masters/M
FAX Number: (913) 971-3290 Calendar System: Semester
URL: www.mnu.edu
Established: 1966 Annual Undergrad Tuition & Fees: $28,150
Enrollment: 1,884 Coed
Affiliation or Control: Church Of The Nazarene IRS Status: 501(c)3
Highest Offering: Master's
Accreditation: NH, ACBSP, CAATE, CACREP, CAEPN, MUS, NURSE

01 President ... Dr. David J. SPITTAL
05 Provost and Chief Academic Officer ... Dr. Mary JONES
10 Vice President Finance ... Mr. Darrel ANDERSON
111 Vice Pres University Advancement ... Mr. Jon D. NORTH
32 VP Student Development ... Mrs. Kristi KEETON
42 University Chaplain ... Mr. Brady J. BRAATZ
58 Vice Provost/Dean SPGS ... Dr. Mark C. FORD
13 Associate VP for Instructional Tech ... Dr. Martin CROSSLAND
84 Assoc VP Enrollment Management ... Mr. Derry EBERT
09 Dir Institutional Effectiveness ... Mrs. Patricia J. WALSH
66 Dean Sch Nursing/Health Sci ... Dr. Karen D. WIEGMAN
50 Dean School of Business ... Mrs. Jamie MYRTLE
83 Dean Sch Behav Sci/Counseling ... Dr. Todd FRYE
49 Dean College of Arts & Sciences ... Dr. Nancy DAMRON
06 Registrar ... Mr. James R. GARRISON
08 Director Library ... Mr. Bruce FLANDERS
30 Assoc VP University Advancement ... Mr. Tim KEETON
29 Director of Alumni Relations ... Mr. Kevin S. GARBER
37 Director of Student Financial Svcs ... Mr. Cathy L. COLAPIETRO
41 Athletic Director ... Mr. Todd L. GARRETT
15 Director of Human Resources ... Ms. Nancy S. MERIMEE
26 Director of Marketing ... Mrs. Kimberly CAMPBELL
18 Director of Facility Services ... Mr. Jon N. SPENCE
40 Director MERC/Postmaster ... Mr. Nikos KELLEPOURIS
19 Director of Campus Safety ... Mr. Richard M. PACHECO
90 Associate VP Academic/Prof Success ... Dr. Richard HANSEN
04 Administrative Asst to President ... Mrs. Kelly GIBSON
103 Dir Workforce/Career Development ... Ms. Christine SNYDER
104 Director Study Abroad ... Mr. James GARRISON
106 Dir Online Education/E-learning ... Mrs. Amy SUDDUTH
25 Chief Contracts/Grants Admin ... Ms. Whitney GRAY
28 Director of Diversity ... Ms. Victoria HAYNES
39 Director Student Housing ... Mr. Daniel RINCONES

National American University-Overland Park (I)

10310 Mastin Street, Overland Park KS 66212
Telephone: (913) 981-8700 Identification: 770394
Accreditation: &NH, SURTEC

† Branch campus of National American University, Rapid City, SD

National American University-Wichita (J)

7309 E 21st Street, Suite G40, Wichita KS 67206
Telephone: (316) 448-5400 Identification: 770395
Accreditation: &NH, MAC, SURTEC

† Branch campus of National American University, Rapid City, SD

National American University-Wichita West (A)

8428 W 13th Street N, Suite 120, Wichita KS 67212
Telephone: (316) 448-3150 Identification: 770396
Accreditation: &NH

† Branch campus of National American University, Rapid City, SD

Nazarene Bible College (B)

17001 Prairie Star Parkway STE 300, Lenexa KS 66220
County: Johnson County FICE Identification: 013007
Unit ID: 127714
Telephone: (719) 884-5000 Carnegie Class: Spec-4-yr-Faith
FAX Number: (719) 884-5199 Calendar System: Trimester
URL: www.nbc.edu
Established: 1964 Annual Undergrad Tuition & Fees: $11,520
Enrollment: 783 Coed
Affiliation or Control: Church Of The Nazarene IRS Status: 501(c)3
Highest Offering: Baccalaureate
Accreditation: NH, BI

01 President Dr. Harold B. GRAVES
05 Vice President for Academic Affairs Dr. Alan D. LYKE
10 Vice President for Finance Mrs. Shirley A. CADLE
84 VP for Enrollment Management Dr. David M. CHURCH
37 Financial Aid Officer Rev. Wilbur E. MACKEY
06 Registrar Mr. Duane A. MATHIAS
13 Chief Information Officer Mr. Fred R. PHILLIPS
04 Executive Asst to President Rev. Susan P. MCKEITHEN
09 Institutional Research Rev. Lesley A. HANSHER
15 Director Personnel Services Mrs. Linda WHITNEY
29 Director Alumni Relations Mr. Mike ARRAMBIDE
90 Director Academic Computing Mr. David HERRON

Neosho County Community College (C)

800 W 14th Street, Chanute KS 66720-2699
County: Neosho FICE Identification: 001936
Unit ID: 155566
Telephone: (620) 431-2820 Carnegie Class: Assoc/HVT-High Non
FAX Number: (620) 431-0082 Calendar System: Semester
URL: www.neosho.edu
Established: 1935 Annual Undergrad Tuition & Fees (In-District): $4,522
Enrollment: 2,067 Coed
Affiliation or Control: Local IRS Status: 501(c)3
Highest Offering: Associate Degree
Accreditation: NH, ACBSP, ADNUR, CAHIIM, OTA, SURGT

01 President Dr. Brian L. INBODY
05 Vice President Student Learning Ms. Sarah ROBB
11 Vice President for Operations Mr. Benjamin J. SMITH
10 Chief Financial Officer Ms. Sondra K. SOLANDER
103 Dean Outreach/Workforce Development Ms. Brenda L. KRUMM
32 Dean of Student Services Ms. Kerrie COOMES
15 Director of Human Resources Ms. Karin JACOBSON
106 Dean for Ottawa & Online Campuses Ms. Marie GARDNER
13 Dean for Operations/CIO Mr. Kerry D. RANABARGAR
30 Director of Development/Alumni Rels Ms. Claudia CHRISTIANSEN
08 Coordinator of Library Services Mr. Todd KNISPEL
37 Director Student Financial Aid Ms. Jennifer DAISY
66 Director of Nursing Ms. Pamela COVAULT
105 Dir of Tech Services/Webmaster Mr. Jon SEIBERT
46 Director of Assessment/Research Mr. Nathan STANLEY
41 Athletic Director Mr. Mike SADDLER
85 Dir International Student Services Ms. Sarah CADWALLADER
06 Registrar Ms. Amy MORRIS
09 Coordinator/Institutional Research Ms. LuAnn HAUSER
40 Chanute Bookstore Coordinator Ms. Kara HALE
40 Ottawa Bookstore Coordinator Ms. Julie VINEYARD
26 Advertising/Media Coordinator Ms. Nancy ISAAC
39 Director of Residence/Student Life Ms. Allison OUELLETTE
04 AA to the President/Board Clerk Ms. Denise GILMORE
18 Director of Facilities Mr. Kyle SEUFERT
07 Director of Admissions Ms. Tristan JONES

Newman University (D)

3100 McCormick, Wichita KS 67213-2097
County: Sedgwick FICE Identification: 001939
Unit ID: 155335
Telephone: (316) 942-4291 Carnegie Class: Masters/M
FAX Number: (316) 942-4483 Calendar System: Semester
URL: www.newmanu.edu
Established: 1933 Annual Undergrad Tuition & Fees: $27,556
Enrollment: 3,595 Coed
Affiliation or Control: Roman Catholic IRS Status: 501(c)3
Highest Offering: Master's
Accreditation: NH, ANEST, CAEPN, COARC, NURSE, OTA, RAD, SW

01 President Dr. Noreen CARROCCI
04 Exec Assistant to the President Ms. Tracy MCGAREY
05 Provost & Vice Pres Acad Affairs Dr. Kimberly MCDOWALL LONG
111 Vice Pres University Advancement Mr. J.V JOHNSTON
10 Vice Pres Finance/Administration Ms. Jennifer GANTZ
32 VP Student Affairs/Dir Athletics Mr. Victor TRILLI
84 Vice Pres Enrollment Management Mr. Norm JONES
20 Assoc VP Academic Affairs Ms. Rosemary NIEDENS
42 Director of Campus Ministry Fr. John FOGLIASSO
29 Director of Alumni Relations Ms. Sarah STROLE
09 Director of Institutional Research Dr. Lori STEINER
08 Library Director Mr. Steve HAMERSKY
06 Registrar Ms. Shirley RUEB
37 Director of Financial Aid Ms. Myra PFANNENSTIEL
40 Director of Bookstore Mr. Larry WILLIAMS
13 Chief Information Officer Mr. Icer VAUGHAN
19 Director of Security Mr. Morris FLOYD
21 Controller Ms. Diana GRIBLIN
35 Dean of Students Mr. Levi ESSES
58 Dean College of Grad/Cont Studies Fr. Joseph GILE
49 Dean College of Undergrad Studies Dr. David SHUBERT
50 Dean School of Business Dr. Brett ANDREWS
104 Director Study Abroad Dr. Cheryl GOLDEN
18 Chief Facilities/Physical Plant Mr. Bruce SANDERSON
26 Chief Public Relations/Marketing Mr. Clark SCHAFER

North Central Kansas Technical College (E)

PO Box 507, Beloit KS 67420-0507
County: Mitchell FICE Identification: 005265
Unit ID: 155593
Telephone: (785) 738-2276 Carnegie Class: Assoc/HVT-High Non
FAX Number: (785) 738-2903 Calendar System: Semester
URL: www.ncktc.edu
Established: 1964 Annual Undergrad Tuition & Fees (In-District): $5,696
Enrollment: 900 Coed
Affiliation or Control: State/Local IRS Status: 501(c)3
Highest Offering: Associate Degree
Accreditation: NH, ADNUR

01 President Mr. Eric BURKS
05 Dean of Instruction Mr. Corey ISBELL
11 Dean of Administrative Services Mrs. Brandi ZIMMER
12 Dean of Hays Campus Mrs. Sandy GOTTSCHALK
06 Registrar Ms. Judy HEIDRICK
09 Coordinator Institutional Research Mrs. Jennifer BROWN
32 Dean of Student Services Ms. Angel PRESCOTT
37 Director Student Financial Aid Mr. Gary ODLE
04 Administrative Asst to President Ms. Kelly ROBERTS
102 Dir Foundation/Marketing Vacant
101 Secretary of the Institution/Board Ms. Kelly ROBERTS
13 Chief Info Technology Officer (CIO) Mr. Ian DRAEMEL

North Central Kansas Technical College (F)

2205 Wheatland Avenue, Hays KS 67601
Telephone: (785) 625-2437 Identification: 770259
Accreditation: &NH

Northwest Kansas Technical College (G)

1209 Harrison Street, PO Box 668, Goodland KS 67735-3441
County: Sherman FICE Identification: 005267
Unit ID: 155618
Telephone: (785) 890-3641 Carnegie Class: Assoc/HVT-Mix Trad/Non
FAX Number: (785) 899-5711 Calendar System: Semester
URL: www.nwktc.edu
Established: 1964 Annual Undergrad Tuition & Fees (In-District): N/A
Enrollment: 779 Coed
Affiliation or Control: State/Local IRS Status: 501(c)3
Highest Offering: Associate Degree
Accreditation: NH, COARC, MAC

01 President Mr. Ben SCHEARS
05 Vice Pres Academic/Student Affairs Mrs. Brenda L. CHATFIELD
11 Vice President for Operations Mrs. Sherri KNITIG
13 Vice Pres for Information Tech Mr. Brad BERGSMA
07 Director of Admissions Mrs. Kayla LUERA
18 Chief Facilities/Physical Plant Mr. Matt BANTA
41 Athletic Director Mr. Rory KLING
30 Director of Endowment/Career Svcs Mrs. Kelly JAMES

Ottawa University (H)

1001 S Cedar Street, Ottawa KS 66067-3399
County: Franklin FICE Identification: 001937
Unit ID: 155627
Telephone: (785) 242-5200 Carnegie Class: Bac-Diverse
FAX Number: (785) 229-1020 Calendar System: Semester
URL: www.ottawa.edu
Established: 1865 Annual Undergrad Tuition & Fees: $27,096
Enrollment: 664 Coed
Affiliation or Control: American Baptist IRS Status: 501(c)3
Highest Offering: Master's
Accreditation: NH, ACBSP, CAEPN, NURSE

01 President Mr. Kevin EICHNER
05 Exec VP & University Provost Dr. Terry HAINES
76 Dean of Health Sciences Dr. Dennis TYNER
10 Exec VP & Chief Financial Officer Mr. J. Clark RIBORDY
26 Sr Vice Pres Marketing & APOS Ms. Nancy WINGER
111 Vice Pres University Advancement Mr. Paul BEAN
32 Dean Student Affairs Mr. Tom TALDO
07 Director of Admissions Mr. Andy STILES
06 University Registrar Ms. Karen ADAMS
21 Director Finance/Controller Ms. Noelle TESTA
21 Director Business Operations Mr. Thomas CORLEY
15 Director Human Resources Ms. Joanna WALTERS
37 Director Financial Aid Mr. Howard FISCHER
29 Director Alumni Programs Ms. Janice TRIGG
08 Director Library Services Ms. Gloria CREED-DIKEOGU
41 Director Athletics Ms. Arabie CONNER
18 Chief Facilities/Physical Plant Mr. Herb ORR
04 Executive Assistant to President Ms. Gaynia MENNINGER
11 Chief Operations Officer Mr. Keith JOHNSON
20 Dean of Instruction Dr. Teresa KELLEY
53 Dean School of Education Dr. Amy HOGAN
84 Director of Enrollment Management Ms. Lydia MATLOCK
50 Dean Angell Snyder Sch of Business Dr. Kirk WESSEL
49 Dean School of Arts & Sciences Dr. Terry HAINES
86 Director Govt/Reg & Legal Affairs Ms. Carrie STEVENS

† The Online division is included in the institution's enrollment count.

Ottawa University Kansas City (I)

4370 W. 109th Street, Suite 200, Overland Park KS 66211-1302
Telephone: (913) 266-8600 Identification: 666083
Accreditation: &NH

† Regional accreditation is carried under the parent institution in Ottawa, KS.

Pittsburg State University (J)

1701 S Broadway, Pittsburg KS 66762-7500
County: Crawford FICE Identification: 001926
Unit ID: 155681
Telephone: (620) 231-7000 Carnegie Class: Masters/L
FAX Number: (620) 235-4080 Calendar System: Semester
URL: www.pittstate.edu
Established: 1903 Annual Undergrad Tuition & Fees (In-State): $6,910
Enrollment: 7,244 Coed
Affiliation or Control: State IRS Status: 501(c)3
Highest Offering: Doctorate
Accreditation: NH, CAEPN, CEA, ENGR, ENGT, MUS, NRPA, NURSE, SW

01 President Dr. Steven A. SCOTT
05 Provost & VP for Academic Affairs Dr. Lynette OLSON
11 CFO & VP Administration Mr. Doug BALL
111 VP University Advancement Ms. Kathleen FLANNERY
06 Registrar Ms. Debbie GREVE
32 VP Student Life Dr. Steve ERWIN
26 Assoc VP for Communication & Mktg Mr. Chris KELLY
84 Assoc VP Enroll Mgmt/Stdnt Success Dr. Howard SMITH
51 Dean Graduate & Continuing Studies Dr. Pawan KAHOL
49 Dean of Arts & Sciences Dr. Mary Carol POMATTO
50 Dean of Business Dr. Paul GRIMES
53 Dean of Education Dr. James TRUELOVE
72 Dean of Technology Dr. Tim DAWSEY
08 Dean of Library Services Mr. Randy ROBERTS
108 Director of Assessment Ms. Nora HATTON
27 Director of Media Relations Mr. Ron WOMBLE
29 Dir Alumni Rels/Constituent Svcs Mr. Jon A. BARTLOW
13 Chief Information Officer Ms. Angela NERIA
15 Director Human Resource Svcs/Budget Dr. Michele D. SEXTON
85 Interim Dir of Intl Affairs Mr. Aaron HURT
45 Chief Strategy Officer Dr. Shawn NACCARATO
18 Director of Trades & Landscape Svcs Mr. Tom AMERSHEK
18 Director Gen & Custodial Services Mr. Tim SENECAUT
19 Director of University Police Mr. Mike MCCRACKEN
22 Director of Institutional Equity Ms. Cindy JOHNSON
37 Director of Financial Aid Ms. Tammy HIGGINS
41 Direct of Intercollegiate Athletics Mr. Jim JOHNSON
07 Director of Admissions Ms. Melinda A. ROELFS
36 Director Career Services Ms. Mindy E. CLONINGER
09 Director of Institutional Research Dr. Dai LI
38 Dir University Counseling Services Dr. Steven MAYHEW
96 Director of Purchasing Mr. Jim HUGHES
28 Director of Diversity Ms. Deatrea ROSE
10 Controller Ms. Barbara J. WINTER
39 Director of University Housing Ms. Connie D. MALLE
100 Chief of Staff Ms. Jaime DALTON
43 General Counsel Dr. Jamie BROOKSHER

Pratt Community College (K)

348 NE SR 61, Pratt KS 67124-8432
County: Pratt FICE Identification: 001938
Unit ID: 155715
Telephone: (620) 672-2700 Carnegie Class: Assoc/HVT-High Non
FAX Number: (620) 450-2285 Calendar System: Semester
URL: www.prattcc.edu
Established: 1938 Annual Undergrad Tuition & Fees (In-District): $3,232
Enrollment: 1,189 Coed
Affiliation or Control: State/Local IRS Status: 501(c)3
Highest Offering: Associate Degree
Accreditation: NH, ACBSP

01 President Dr. Mike CALVERT
05 Vice President Instruction Dr. Michael FITZPATRICK
10 Vice President Finance/Operations Mr. Kent ADAMS
84 Vice Pres Student Enroll Management Ms. Lisa MILLER
30 Vice Pres of Inst Advancement Mr. Barry FISHER
41 Director of Athletics Mr. Bill WILSON
07 Director of Admissions Ms. Caitlin MILLER
06 Registrar Ms. Erin LACIO

13 Director of Information Technology .... Mr. Jerry SANKO
37 Director of Financial Aid .... Ms. Alicia NOVOTNY
08 Dir Linda Hunt Memorial Library .... Vacant
15 Director of Personnel .... Ms. Rita PINKALL
21 Controller ....Ms. Christy WRIGHT
18 Director of Buildings & Grounds ....Mr. Dan PETZ
39 Director of Residence Life .... Mr. Charles KEEFER
04 Administrative Asst to President ....Ms. Donna MEIER PFEIFER
29 Director Alumni Relations .... Mr. Barry FISHER
108 Director of Planning & Assessment .... Mr. David SCHMIDT
09 Director of Institutional Research .... Mr. Wayne MARCI
26 Chief Public Relations/Marketing .... Ms. Megan EATON
36 Director Student Placement .... Ms. Amy JACKSON

Rasmussen College-Kansas City/Overland Park (A)

11600 College Boulevard, Overland Park KS 66210
Telephone: (913) 491-7870 Identification: 770489
Accreditation: &NH, ADNUR, MAAB

† Regional accreditation carried under the parent institution in Saint Cloud, MN. The tuition figure is an average, actual tuition may vary.

Rasmussen College Topeka (B)

620 SW Governor View, Topeka KS 66606
Telephone: (785) 228-7320 Identification: 770490
Accreditation: &NH, MAAB

† Regional accreditation carried under the parent institution in Saint Cloud, MN. The tuition figure is an average, actual tuition may vary.

Saint Paul School of Theology (C)

4370 West 109th Street, Suite 300,
Overland Park KS 66211
County: Johnson FICE Identification: 002509
Unit ID: 179317
Telephone: (913) 253-5000 Carnegie Class: Spec-4-yr-Faith
FAX Number: (913) 253-5075 Calendar System: Semester
URL: www.spst.edu
Established: 1958 Annual Graduate Tuition & Fees: N/A
Enrollment: 156 Coed
Affiliation or Control: United Methodist IRS Status: 501(c)3
Highest Offering: Doctorate; No Undergraduates
Accreditation: #NH, THEOL

01 President ....Rev. Neil B. BLAIR
05 VP Academic Affairs/Dean ....Dr. Jeanne HOEFT
111 Vice President for Inst Advancement .... Dr. Angela SIMS
32 Associate Dean of Students .... Rev. Margaretta S. NARCISSE
15 Director of Human Resources .... Mr. Barney BARRY
06 Registrar ....Ms. Tahmeka THOMPSON
37 Dir of Student Financial Services ....Ms. Kim WARREN
07 Interim Dir Student Recruitment ....Ms. Deana BRINK
26 Director of Communications .... Mrs. Heather SNODGRASS
08 Librarian ....Ms. Maggie MUELLER
10 CFO .... Mr. Barney BARRY
101 Secretary of the Institution/Board .... Ms. Julie A. ROBINSON
88 Chair of the Institution/Board .... Dr. Michael PARMELY
100 Director of Seminary Operations .... Ms. Melissa WHALEN
50 Assoc Director Contextual Education .... Mr. Rick BURNS

Salina Area Technical College (D)

2562 Centennial Road, Salina KS 67401
County: Saline FICE Identification: 005499
Unit ID: 155830
Telephone: (785) 309-3100 Carnegie Class: Assoc/HVT-High Non
FAX Number: (785) 309-3101 Calendar System: Semester
URL: www.salinatech.edu
Established: 1965 Annual Undergrad Tuition & Fees (In-District): $6,493
Enrollment: 524 Coed
Affiliation or Control: State/Local IRS Status: 501(c)3
Highest Offering: Associate Degree
Accreditation: NH, DA

01 President ....Mr. Gregory A. NICHOLS
05 Vice Pres of Instruction ....Ms. Stephani JOHNS-HINES
11 Vice Pres of Operations .... Mr. Andrew MANLEY
32 Vice Pres of Student Services ....Mrs. Susan EBERWEIN
09 Director of Inst Research/Registrar ...... Mrs. Denise R. HOEFFNER
15 Director Human Resources ....Mrs. Tamera WILCOX
18 Director of Maintenance ....Mr. Dale CASTILLO
25 Director of Grants and Planning ....Vacant
102 Exec Dir of SATC Foundation ....Ms. Pam GEIHSLER
84 Director Enrollment Management ....Ms. Amanda FOUST
37 Student Financial Aid Specialist ....Ms. Anna KREIGHBAUM

Seward County Community College (E)

1801 N Kansas Avenue, Liberal KS 67901-2054
County: Seward FICE Identification: 008228
Unit ID: 155858
Telephone: (620) 624-1951 Carnegie Class: Assoc/MT-VT-High Trad
FAX Number: (620) 417-1169 Calendar System: Semester
URL: www.sccc.edu
Established: 1967 Annual Undergrad Tuition & Fees (In-District): $2,848
Enrollment: 1,971 Coed
Affiliation or Control: State/Local IRS Status: 501(c)3
Highest Offering: Associate Degree
Accreditation: NH, ACBSP, ADNUR, COARC, MLTAD, SURGT

01 President ....Dr. Ken J. TRZASKA
05 Vice President of Academic Affairs ....Dr. Todd CARTER
10 VP of Finance & Operations ....Mr. Dennis M. SANDER
32 Vice President of Student Services .... Ms. Celeste DONOVAN
51 Dean Industrial Tech/Cont Educ ....Vacant
06 Registrar .... Ms. Alaina M. RICE
13 Chief Information Officer .... Mr. J. J. WIDENER
37 Director of Financial Aid ....Mrs. Donna M. FISHER
26 Exec Dir of Marketing & PR ....Ms. Rachel C. COLEMAN
50 Director of Business & Industry ....Mrs. Norma Jean DODGE
24 Director of Multi-media Technology ....Mr. Doug BROWNE
08 Director of Library .... Mr. Matthew PANNKUK
41 Director of Athletics .... Mr. Roy ALLEN
18 Director of Facilities .... Mr. Roger SCHEIB
40 Director of Bookstore .... Ms. Jerri L. LYDDON
30 Executive Dir of Development .... Vacant
39 Director of Student Living Center .... Ms. Kate A. MULLIGAN
09 Institutional Research/Data Analyst .... Ms. Teresa WEHMEIER
19 Dir of Safety and Security ....Mr. Dennis K. MULANAX
15 Director of Human Resources .... Ms. Tanya DOWELL
07 Coordinator of Admissions/Marketing .... Mr. Chandler KIRKHART
38 Dir Counseling/Advising/Career Svcs ....Ms. Mariah CLINE
35 Dir of Student Life & Leadership .... Mr. Wade LYON
04 Executive Assistant .... Mrs. Lois B. MAGNER
66 Director of Nursing ....Ms. Susan INGLAND
105 Website and Portal Manager .... Mr. Craig DUSEK
84 Director of Admissions .... Mr. Bert LUALLEN
29 Exec Dir Alum Engagement/Grant Dev .... Ms. Charity HORINEK

Southwestern College (F)

100 College Street, Winfield KS 67156-2499
County: Cowley FICE Identification: 001940
Unit ID: 155900
Telephone: (620) 229-6000 Carnegie Class: Masters/M
FAX Number: (620) 229-6224 Calendar System: Semester
URL: www.sckans.edu
Established: 1885 Annual Undergrad Tuition & Fees: $27,250
Enrollment: 1,471 Coed
Affiliation or Control: United Methodist IRS Status: 501(c)3
Highest Offering: Doctorate
Accreditation: NH, CAATE, CAEP, MUS, NURSE

01 President ....Dr. Bradley J. ANDREWS
03 Executive Vice President .... Mr. Dean CLARK
05 VP Acad Affairs/Dean of the College ....Dr. Ross PETERSON-VEATCH
10 Vice President Finance .... Ms. Sheila R. KRUG
124 VP Student Retention & Success ....Dr. Dawn E. PLEAS
84 VP Enroll Mgmt Main Campus .... Mr. Adam JENKINS
45 Exec Dir Institute for Discipleship .... Dr. Stephen K. WILKE
111 Vice Pres Institutional Advancement ....Ms. DeAnn DOCKERY
26 Vice President Communications ... Ms. Kaydee RIGGS-JOHNSON
32 VP Student Life/Dean Students ....Mr. Dan FALK
29 Director Alumni Programs ....Mr. Charles MCKINZIE
08 Interim Library Director .... Ms. Marjorie SNIDER
37 Director Financial Aid .... Ms. Brenda D. HICKS
06 Registrar .... Ms. Linda WEIPPERT
09 Director of Institutional Research .... Ms. Joni RANKIN
41 Director Athletics ....Mr. Matthew A. SHELTON
15 Director Human Resources .... Ms. Lonnie BOYD
96 Director of Purchasing ....Mr. David H. DOLSEN
04 Exec Asst to President .... Ms. Doreen A. FAST
42 Campus Minister ....Rev. Benjamin C. HANNE

Sterling College (G)

125 W Cooper Street, Sterling KS 67579-1533
County: Rice FICE Identification: 001945
Unit ID: 155937
Telephone: (620) 278-2173 Carnegie Class: Bac-Diverse
FAX Number: N/A Calendar System: 4/1/4
URL: www.sterling.edu
Established: 1887 Annual Undergrad Tuition & Fees: $24,250
Enrollment: 704 Coed
Affiliation or Control: Presbyterian IRS Status: 501(c)3
Highest Offering: Baccalaureate
Accreditation: NH, CAATE, CAEPN

01 President ....Dr. Scott RICH
05 Vice President Academic Affairs .... Dr. Ken BROWN
111 Vice President for Inst Advancement .... Mr. Scott CARTER
32 Vice President Student Life .... Ms. Kimberly CHRISTIAN
11 Vice Pres Admin/Inst Initiatives .... Mr. David LANDIS
10 CFO .... Ms. Michelle HALL
41 Athletic Director .... Mr. Gary KEMPF
26 Dir Marketing/Pres Communications ....Mr. Brad EVENSON
21 Director of Finance & Admin ....Ms. Rita OWNBEY
37 Director of Financial Aid .... Ms. Mitzi SUHLER
06 Registrar ....Ms. Janet CAYWOOD
112 Director of Planned Giving ....Ms. Sheila BIRD
29 Alumni & Marketing Manager .... Ms. Susie CARNEY
18 Chief Facilities/Physical Plant .... Mr. Steven CAYWOOD
38 Director Student Counseling ....Ms. Loida LEONE
08 Library Director ....Ms. Laurell WATNEY
36 Director of Career Services ....Mr. Terry EHRESMAN
07 Vice President Enrollment ....Mr. Dennis DUTTON
04 Administrative Asst to President .... Ms. Erica FOSS
42 Chaplain .... Mr. Christian DASHIELL
108 Director Institutional Assessment .... Dr. Spencer WAGLEY
13 Chief Info Technology Officer (CIO) .... Mr. Mykeal PITTS
15 Director Personnel Services .... Ms. Becky VOTH

Tabor College (H)

400 S Jefferson Street, Hillsboro KS 67063-1753
County: Marion FICE Identification: 001946
Unit ID: 155973
Telephone: (620) 947-3121 Carnegie Class: Bac-Diverse
FAX Number: (620) 947-2607 Calendar System: 4/1/4
URL: www.tabor.edu
Established: 1908 Annual Undergrad Tuition & Fees: $26,590
Enrollment: 729 Coed
Affiliation or Control: Mennonite Brethren Church IRS Status: 501(c)3
Highest Offering: Master's
Accreditation: NH, #CAATE, CAEPN, MUS, NURSE, @SW

01 President ....Dr. Jules GLANZER
05 Vice President Academic Affairs ....Dr. Frank JOHNSON
10 Sr Vice President Business/Finance .... Mr. Norman HOPE
111 Vice President Advancement ....Mr. Ronald BRAUN
41 Vice President of Athletics .... Mr. Rusty ALLEN
32 Vice President of Student Life ....Dr. Jim PAULUS
06 Registrar .... Mr. Scott FRANZ
08 Director of Library Services ....Ms. Janet WILLIAMS
84 Director Enrollment Management .... Mr. Rusty ALLEN
37 Dir of Student Financial Services .... Ms. Tricia BROTHERS
29 Director Alumni Relations ....Mr. Rod HAMM
26 Director of Communications ....Ms. Amy DOANE
18 Director Facilities/Physical Plant .... Mr. Terry ENS
121 Director Student Success ....Mrs. Erica HAUDE
09 Institutional Research .... Mr. David FABER
13 Director IT Infastructure .... Mr. Chris GLANZER
14 Director of IT Operations .... Mr. Wayne KLIEWER
15 Human Resources Coordinator ....Mrs. Ruth FUNK

University of Kansas Main Campus (I)

1450 Jayhawk Boulevard, Room 230,
Lawrence KS 66045-7518
County: Douglas FICE Identification: 001948
Unit ID: 155317
Telephone: (785) 864-3131 Carnegie Class: DU-Highest
FAX Number: (785) 864-4120 Calendar System: Semester
URL: www.ku.edu
Established: 1866 Annual Undergrad Tuition & Fees (In-State): $11,455
Enrollment: 27,259 Coed
Affiliation or Control: State IRS Status: 501(c)3
Highest Offering: Doctorate
Accreditation: NH, ART, CAATE, CAEPN, CEA, CLPSY, COPSY, CS, ENG, HSA, IPSY, JOUR, LAW, MUS, PH, PHAR, PLNG, SCPSY, SP, SPAA, SW

01 Chancellor ....Dr. Douglas A. GIROD
05 Exec Vice Chancellor/Provost ....Dr. Neeli BENDAPUDI
12 Vice Chancellor/Dean Edwards Campus .... Dr. David COOK
26 Vice Chancellor for Public Affairs .... Vacant
04 Executive Assistant to Chancellor ....Ms. Mary G. BURG
43 General Counsel ....Mr. James P. POTTORFF, JR.
20 Sr Vice Provost Academic Affairs ....Dr. Stuart DAY
20 Vice Provost Faculty Development ....Dr. Christopher BROWN
10 Vice Provost Admin & Finance ....Ms. Diane H. GODDARD
32 Vice Provost for Student Affairs .... Dr. Tammara DURHAM
46 Vice Chancellor Research ....Dr. James W. TRACY
28 Vice Provost Diversity & Equity .... Dr. Jennifer F. HAMER
84 Vice Provost Enrollment Management .... Dr. Matt MELVIN
13 Chief Information Officer .... Vacant
58 Dean Graduate Studies ....Dr. Michael C. ROBERTS
104 Assoc VP International Programs .... Dr. Charles BANKART
11 Assoc Vice Provost of Operations .... Mr. Shannan D. NELSON
30 President Endowment Association .... Mr. Dale SEUFERLING
29 President Alumni Association ....Mr. Heath J. PETERSON
07 Director Admissions .... Ms. Lisa P. KRESS
10 Chief Business/Financial Plng Ofcr .... Ms. Leisa JULIAN
21 Comptroller .... Ms. Katrina M. YOAKUM
21 Assoc VP for Finance ....Mr. Richard L. MCKINNEY
06 University Registrar/Asst VP .... Ms. Cindy SANDERS
09 Exec Director Inst Research Plng .... Ms. Deborah J. TEETER
15 Assoc VP Human Resource Management .... Mr. Michael ROUNDS
85 Director International Student Svcs .... Dr. Chuck OLCESE
38 Director Counseling/Psych Services .... Dr. Michael MAESTAS
88 Director Design & Construction Mgmt ....Mr. James E. MODIG
37 Director Financial Aid/Scholarships ....Ms. Angela KARLIN
36 Exec Director Career Center .... Mr. David GASTON
41 Director Intercollegiate Athletics ....Dr. Sheahon ZENGER
18 Director Facilities Service .... Mr. Vince AVILA
22 Director Inst Oppty & Access .... Mr. Shane MCCREERY
28 Director Multicultural Affairs ....Ms. Precious PORRAS
23 Director Student Health Services .... Dr. Douglas C. DECHARIO
14 Director Info Tech Business Opers .... Mr. Chris CROOK
39 Director Student Housing .... Ms. Sarah WATERS
86 Director State Relations ....Ms. Kelly M. REYNOLDS
92 Director Honors Program .... Dr. C. Bryan YOUNG
86 Director Federal Relations .... Mr. Jack CLINE
40 Director KU Bookstore ....Ms. Jen O'CONNOR
51 Exec Dir Continuing Education ....Ms. Sharon D. GRAHAM
25 Assoc Dir Contract Negotiations ....Ms. Lucille MARINO
91 Project Coord Information Systems ....Mr. David M. GARDNER
49 Dean Liberal Arts/Science ....Dr. Carl W. LEJUEZ
61 Dean of Law .... Mr. Stephen W. MAZZA
54 Dean of Engineering .... Dr. Michael BRANICKY
48 Dean Architecture/Design/Planning .... Dr. Mahesh DAAS
50 Dean of Business ....Dr. L. Paige FIELDS
67 Dean of Pharmacy .... Dr. Kenneth L. AUDUS
60 Dean of Journalism ....Dr. Ann M. BRILL
53 Dean of Education .... Dr. Rick GINSBERG

64 Dean of Music ... Dr. Robert L. WALZEL, JR.
70 Dean of Social Welfare ... Dr. Michelle CARNEY
08 Dean Libraries ... Mr. Kevin L. SMITH
57 Assoc Dean School of the Arts ... Dr. Henry BIAL
19 Director Security/Safety ... Mr. Chris KEARY

† Medical Center and Main campus enrollments should be combined for the total institution enrollment.

University of Kansas Medical Center (A)

3901 Rainbow Boulevard, Kansas City KS 66160-0001
Telephone: (913) 588-5000 FICE Identification: 024579
Accreditation: **&NH**, ANEST, AUD, CAHIIM, COARC, DIETI, DMOLS, DMS, IPSY, MED, MIDWF, MT, NMT, NURSE, OT, PTA

† Enrollment at the Medical Center is included within the published enrollment for the University of Kansas Main Campus. Regional accreditation is carried under the parent institution in Lawrence, KS.

University of Saint Mary (B)

4100 S 4th Street Trafficway, Leavenworth KS 66048-5082
County: Leavenworth FICE Identification: 001943
Unit ID: 155812
Telephone: (913) 682-5151 Carnegie Class: Masters/M
FAX Number: (913) 758-6140 Calendar System: Semester
URL: www.stmary.edu
Established: 1923 Annual Undergrad Tuition & Fees: $26,650
Enrollment: 1,427 Coed
Affiliation or Control: Roman Catholic IRS Status: 501(c)3
Highest Offering: Doctorate
Accreditation: **NH**, CAEPN, CAHIIM, IACBE, NURSE, PTA

01 President ... Sr. Diane STEELE
05 Academic Vice President ... Dr. Bryan LEBEAU
10 Vice President for Finance ... Ms. Nancy BRAMLETT
30 Vice President of Development ... Vacant
07 VP Admissions & Marketing ... Mr. John SHULTZ
32 Dean of Students ... Ms. Lisa POTOKA
06 Registrar ... Mr. Russell PERKINS
08 Director of the Library ... Ms. Danielle DION
09 Data Analyst ... Ms. Veronica DONOVAN
29 Director of Alumni & Annual Fund ... Ms. Sharon CLAY
37 Director of Financial Aid ... Ms. Annissa EPPERSON
42 Director of Campus Ministry ... Mr. Jacob HAYDEN
112 Development Officer Planned Giving ... Ms. Jane LIEBERT
41 Athletic Director ... Mr. Rob MILLER
15 Director Human Resources ... Ms. Kelly GRISNIK
39 Director of Residence Life ... Ms. Kristen OWSLEY
21 Controller ... Ms. Sherry WELLS
38 Counselor ... Ms. Deborah SHADDY
18 Plant Manager ... Mr. Mark GIESEMAN
40 Bookstore Manager ... Ms. Cynthia FORRESTER
12 Site Coordinator Johnson County ... Ms. Patricia HOWARD
13 Coordinator of Computer Operations ... Mr. Kevin GANTT
04 Executive Administrative Assistant ... Ms. Kathy TATOM
19 Director of Campus Security ... Mr. Donald STUBBINGS

Vatterott College - Wichita (C)

8853 East 37th Street North, Wichita KS 67226-2018
Telephone: (316) 634-0066 Identification: 666583
Accreditation: **ACCSC**

† Branch campus of Vatterott College-North Park, Berkeley, MO.

Washburn University (D)

1700 SW College Avenue, Topeka KS 66621-0001
County: Shawnee FICE Identification: 001949
Unit ID: 156082
Telephone: (785) 670-1010 Carnegie Class: Masters/M
FAX Number: (785) 670-1089 Calendar System: Semester
URL: www.washburn.edu
Established: 1865 Annual Undergrad Tuition & Fees (In-District): $7,754
Enrollment: 6,615 Coed
Affiliation or Control: Local IRS Status: 501(c)3
Highest Offering: Doctorate
Accreditation: **NH**, ART, CAATE, CAEPN, CAHIIM, CEA, COARC, DMS, LAW, MUS, NURSE, OTA, PTAA, RAD, SW

01 President ... Dr. Jerry B. FARLEY
05 Vice Pres Academic Affairs ... Dr. JuliAnn MAZACHEK
10 Vice Pres Admin & Treasurer ... Mr. Jim MARTIN
32 Vice President for Student Life ... Dr. Eric GROSPITCH
04 Special Assistant to the President ... Ms. Cynthia HOLTHAUS
84 Director Enrollment Management ... Dr. Richard W. LIEDTKE
43 University Legal Counsel ... Mr. Marc FRIED
35 Assoc Vice Pres of Student Life ... Mr. Joel BLUML
20 Assoc Vice Pres Acad Affairs ... Dr. Nancy A. TATE
21 Assoc Vice Pres & Dir of Finance ... Mr. Bob CRUTSINGER
102 President WU Foundation ... Mr. Marshall MEEK
06 Registrar ... Mr. Steven GRENUS
08 Dean of Libraries ... Dr. Alan BEARMAN
37 Director Student Financial Aid ... Ms. Kandace MARS
07 Director of Admissions ... Vacant
15 Director of Human Resources ... Ms. Teresa LEE
90 Director Info Systems & Services ... Mr. Jim TAGLIARENI
09 Director Strategic Analysis & Rep ... Dr. Robert L. HANDLEY
49 Dean College Arts/Sciences ... Dr. Laura STEPHENSON
88 Dean School Applied Studies ... Dr. Pat MUNZER
61 Dean School of Law ... Mr. Thomas J. ROMIG
50 Dean School of Business ... Dr. David SOLLARS
66 Dean School of Nursing ... Dr. Monica S. SCHEIBMEIR
41 Director of Athletics ... Mr. Loren FERRE
22 Director Equal Opportunity ... Dr. Pam FOSTER
18 Director Facilities Services ... Mr. Rich CONNELL
23 Interim Director Health Services ... Ms. Tiffany MCMANUS
29 Alumni Association Director ... Ms. Susie HOFFMANN
92 Dean Honors Program ... Dr. Michael J. MCGUIRE
39 Director Student Housing ... Ms. Mindy P. RENDON
40 Director Bookstore ... Ms. Karen PETERSON
35 Director Student Activities ... Ms. Jessica BARRACLOUGH
38 Interim Director Student Counseling ... Ms. Crystal LEMING
26 Director of University Relations ... Mr. Patrick EARLY
36 Director Student Placement ... Mr. Kent MCANALLY
19 Director of Police ... Mr. Chris ENOS
101 Secretary of the Institution/Board ... Mr. Marc FRIED
28 Director of Diversity & Inclusion ... Ms. Danielle DEMPSEY-SWOPES
96 Director of Purchasing ... Ms. Sherry DRAPER

Wichita Area Technical College (E)

4004 N Webb Road, Wichita KS 67226-8101
County: Sedgwick FICE Identification: 005498
Unit ID: 156107
Telephone: (316) 677-9400 Carnegie Class: Assoc/HVT-High Non
FAX Number: (316) 677-9510 Calendar System: Semester
URL: www.watc.edu
Established: 1965 Annual Undergrad Tuition & Fees (In-District): $7,323
Enrollment: 3,318 Coed
Affiliation or Control: State/Local IRS Status: 501(c)3
Highest Offering: Associate Degree
Accreditation: **NH**, DA, SURGT

01 President ... Ms. Sheree UTASH
05 Chief of Academic Affairs ... Mr. Scott LUCAS
10 Vice Pres Finance/Administration ... Mr. Greg UNRUH
32 Vice President Student Services ... Mr. Justin PFEIFER
26 Dir Marketing/Community Outreach ... Mr. Andy MCFAYDEN
13 Exec Dir Tech/Inst Effectiveness ... Mr. Randy ROEBUCK
15 Exec Director Human Resources ... Ms. Judy MOUNT
20 CAO General Educ/Health Sciences ... Ms. Pam DOYLE

Wichita State University (F)

1845 N Fairmount, Wichita KS 67260-0001
County: Sedgwick FICE Identification: 001950
Unit ID: 156125
Telephone: (316) 978-3456 Carnegie Class: DU-Higher
FAX Number: (316) 978-3770 Calendar System: Semester
URL: www.wichita.edu
Established: 1895 Annual Undergrad Tuition & Fees (In-State): $7,895
Enrollment: 14,240 Coed
Affiliation or Control: State IRS Status: 501(c)3
Highest Offering: Doctorate
Accreditation: **NH**, ARCPA, ART, AUD, CAATE, CAEPN, CLPSY, CS, DANCE, DENT, DH, ENG, ENGT, IPSY, MT, MUS, NURSE, PTA, SP, SPAA, SW

01 President ... Dr. John W. BARDO
05 Provost/Senior VP Academic Affairs ... Dr. Anthony VIZZINI
10 VP Administration & Finance ... Mr. Werner M. GOLLING
32 VP Student Affairs ... Dr. Teri HALL
43 General Counsel ... Mr. David MOSES
26 VP Strategic Communications ... Mr. Lou HELDMAN
09 Chief Data Officer ... Dr. David WRIGHT
84 Senior VP Enrollment Management ... Dr. Richard D. MUMA
13 Chief Information Officer ... Mr. Toney FLACK
20 Assoc VP Academic Affairs ... Dr. Linnea GLENMAYE
46 VP Research & Technology Transfer ... Dr. John S. TOMBLIN
49 Dean Liberal Arts & Sciences ... Dr. Ronald R. MATSON
50 Dean Barton School of Business ... Dr. Anand DESAI
53 Dean Education ... Dr. Shirley LEFEVER-DAVIS
54 Dean Engineering ... Dr. Royce BOWDEN
57 Dean Fine Arts ... Dr. Rodney E. MILLER
76 Dean Health Professions ... Dr. Sandra BIBB
58 Dean Graduate School ... Dr. Dennis LIVESAY
08 Dean Libraries ... Ms. Kathy DOWNES
86 Exec Director Government Relations ... Mr. Andrew SCHLAPP
24 Dir Media Resources Center ... Mr. John JONES
102 CEO & President WSU Foundation ... Ms. Elizabeth H. KING
41 Director of Athletics ... Mr. Darron BOATRIGHT
15 Director Human Resources ... Ms. Judy ESPINOZA
114 Director Budgets ... Mr. David MILLER
06 Registrar ... Ms. Gina D. CRABTREE
07 Director Admissions ... Mr. Bobby GANDU
37 Director Financial Aid ... Ms. Sheelu M. SURENDER
36 Exec Director of Career Development ... Ms. Connie R. DIETZ
38 Director Counseling & Testing ... Dr. Maureen DASEY-MORALES
18 Director Physical Plant ... Mr. Bob SMITH, JR.
45 Director of Facilities Planning ... Mr. Eric KING
19 Campus Police Chief ... Ms. Sara B. MORRIS
23 Director Student Health Services ... Ms. Camille CHILDERS
39 Director Stdnt Housing & Resid Life ... Mr. Scott JENSEN
28 Director Diversity & Inclusion ... Ms. Alicia SANCHEZ
40 Manager Bookstore ... Mr. Kevin J. KONDA
21 Assoc VP Financial Operations ... Ms. Lois TATRO
42 Director of Student Ministries ... Mr. Jonathan FLESHER
96 Director of Purchasing ... Mr. Steven WHITE
29 Executive Director Alumni Assoc ... Ms. Courtney MARSHALL
22 Director of EEO ... Ms. Jane J. LINK
04 Assistant to President ... Ms. Anna LANIER
106 Dir Online Education/E-learning ... Mr. Mark D. PORCARO
88 Asst to President for Diversity ... Dr. Marceh FLEMING-RANDLE
88 Title IX Coordinator ... Dr. Natasha M. STEPHENS
105 Director Web Services ... Mr. Tim HART
30 Chief Development/Advancement ... Dr. Keith PICKUS
44 Director Annual or Planned Giving ... Mr. Michael LAMB

Wichita Technical Institute (G)

2051 South Meridian Avenue, Wichita KS 67213-1927
County: Sedgwick FICE Identification: 010503
Unit ID: 156134
Telephone: (316) 943-2241 Carnegie Class: Spec 2-yr-Tech
FAX Number: (316) 943-5438 Calendar System: Quarter
URL: www.wti.edu
Established: Annual Undergrad Tuition & Fees: N/A
Enrollment: 707 Coed
Affiliation or Control: Proprietary IRS Status: Proprietary
Highest Offering: Associate Degree
Accreditation: **ACCSC**

01 Director ... Mr. Rod MOORE

KENTUCKY

Alice Lloyd College (H)

Purpose Road, Pippa Passes KY 41844-9703
County: Knott FICE Identification: 001951
Unit ID: 156189
Telephone: (606) 368-2101 Carnegie Class: Bac-A&S
FAX Number: (606) 368-6212 Calendar System: Semester
URL: www.alc.edu
Established: 1923 Annual Undergrad Tuition & Fees: $11,550
Enrollment: 616 Coed
Affiliation or Control: Independent Non-Profit IRS Status: 501(c)3
Highest Offering: Baccalaureate
Accreditation: **SC**

01 President ... Dr. Joe A. STEPP
03 Executive Vice President ... Dr. Jim STEPP
05 Vice President Academic Affairs ... Dr. Claude CRUM
10 Vice President of Business Affairs ... Mr. David JOHNSON
32 Dean of Students & Community Life ... Mr. Scott CORNETT
07 Director of Admissions ... Ms. Angela PHIPPS
06 Registrar ... Ms. Dana DOTSON
08 Director of Library ... Ms. Jeannie GALLOWAY
37 Director of Financial Aid ... Mrs. Jacqueline STEWART
88 Director of Student Work Program ... Mr. Kerry RATLIFF
53 Director of Teacher Education ... Mr. Norman BISHOP
18 Director of Physical Plant ... Mr. Ryan GIBSON
39 Director of Student Housing ... Mr. John MILLS
29 Director of Alumni Relations ... Mrs. Teresa GRENDER
35 Director of Student Activities ... Ms. Christine STUMBO
26 Dir of Marketing & Communications ... Ms. Katelin HYLTON
09 Director of Institutional Research ... Mr. Norman BISHOP
30 Director of Development ... Mrs. Margo SPARKMAN
102 Dir Foundation/Corporate Relations ... Ms. Priscilla FRALEY
41 Athletic Director ... Mr. Gary STEPP

† Cost of tuition is guaranteed for students from 108 county territories.

American National University (I)

115 E Lexington Avenue, Danville KY 40422-1517
Telephone: (859) 236-6991 Identification: 666441
Accreditation: **ACICS**, MAC

† Branch campus of American National University, Indianapolis, IN

American National University (J)

8095 Connector Drive, Florence KY 41042-1466
Telephone: (859) 525-6510 Identification: 666442
Accreditation: **ACICS**, MAC, SURGT

† Branch campus of American National University, Indianapolis, IN

American National University (K)

2376 Sir Barton Way, Lexington KY 40509-2256
County: Fayette FICE Identification: 010489
Unit ID: 157021
Telephone: (859) 253-0621 Carnegie Class: Bac/Assoc-Assoc Dom
FAX Number: (859) 254-7664 Calendar System: Quarter
URL: www.ncbt.edu
Established: 1941 Annual Undergrad Tuition & Fees: $14,886
Enrollment: 780 Coed
Affiliation or Control: Proprietary IRS Status: Proprietary
Highest Offering: Baccalaureate
Accreditation: **ACICS**, MAC, SURGT

01 President ... Mr. Frank LONGAKER
05 Campus Director ... Ms. Kim THOMASSON
03 Vice President ... Ms. Charlotte BRINNEMAN
32 Director of Student Services ... Mr. Nicolas BARNES

† Branch campus of American National University, Indianapolis, IN

American National University (L)

4205 Dixie Highway, Louisville KY 40216-4147
Telephone: (502) 447-7634 Identification: 666443

Accreditation: **ACICS**, CAHIIM, MAC, SURGT

† Branch campus of American National University, Indianapolis, IN

American National University (A)

50 National College Boulevard, Pikeville KY 41501-3176
Telephone: (606) 478-7200 Identification: 666444
Accreditation: **ACICS**, MAC

† Branch campus of American National University, Indianapolis, IN

American National University (B)

125 S Killarney Lane, Richmond KY 40475-2309
Telephone: (859) 623-8956 Identification: 666445
Accreditation: **ACICS**, MAC

† Branch campus of American National University, Indianapolis, IN

Asbury Theological Seminary (C)

204 N Lexington Avenue, Wilmore KY 40390-1199
County: Jessamine FICE Identification: 001953
Unit ID: 156222
Telephone: (859) 858-3581 Carnegie Class: Spec-4-yr-Faith
FAX Number: N/A Calendar System: 4/1/4
URL: www.asburyseminary.edu
Established: 1923 Annual Graduate Tuition & Fees: N/A
Enrollment: 1,540 Coed
Affiliation or Control: Independent Non-Profit IRS Status: 501(c)3
Highest Offering: Doctorate; No Undergraduates
Accreditation: **SC**, CACREP, THEOL

01 President ....Dr. Timothy C. TENNENT
11 Sr Vice President/COO ....Mr. Robert S. LANDREBE
05 Provost/VP of Academic Affairs ....Dr. Douglas K. MATTHEWS
10 Vice Pres Finance/Admin/CFO ....Mr. Bryan P. BLANKENSHIP
30 Vice President of Advancement ....Mr. Jay MANSUR
31 Vice President Community Formation ....Dr. Marilyn ELLIOTT
84 Vice Pres Enrollment Management ....Mr. Kevin BISH
13 Chief Technology Officer ....Mr. Patrick GARDELLA
06 Registrar ....Dr. Christine L. JOHNSON
07 Director of Admissions ....Mr. Randy OZAN
37 Director of Student Financial Aid ....Mrs. Jenny BURKHART
18 Director of Physical Plant ....Mr. Lanny SPEARS
09 Dir Inst Effectiveness/Assessment ....Dr. Alexandra HENCHY
15 Director of Human Resources ....Mrs. Barbara ANTROBUS
29 Director Alumni/Church Relations ....Ms. Tammy CESSNA
73 Dean School of Theology & Formation ....Dr. James THOBABEN
88 Dean Beeson Center ....Dr. David GYERTSON
88 Dean ESJ School World of Missions ....Dr. Gregg OKESSON
88 Dean School Biblical Interpretation ....Dr. David BAUER
73 Int Dean School Practical Theology ....Dr. Chris KIESLING
88 Dean Advanced Research Programs ....Dr. Lalsangkima PACHUAU
04 Executive Asst to President ....Ms. Angela CLOYD
08 Exec Dir of Library Services ....Dr. Paul A. TIPPEY

Asbury University (D)

1 Macklem Drive, Wilmore KY 40390-1198
County: Jessamine FICE Identification: 001952
Unit ID: 156213
Telephone: (859) 858-3511 Carnegie Class: Masters/S
FAX Number: (859) 858-3921 Calendar System: Semester
URL: www.asbury.edu
Established: 1890 Annual Undergrad Tuition & Fees: $28,630
Enrollment: 1,915 Coed
Affiliation or Control: Independent Non-Profit IRS Status: 501(c)3
Highest Offering: Beyond Master's But Less Than Doctorate
Accreditation: **SC**, CAEPN, MUS, SW

01 President ....Dr. Sandra C. GRAY
05 Provost ....Dr. Jon S. KULAGA
10 Vice Pres Business Affs & Treasurer ....Mr. Glenn R. HAMILTON
84 Vice Pres for Enrollment Management ....Dr. William HALL, JR.
32 Vice Pres Student Dev/Dean Students ....Dr. Sarah T. BALDWIN
111 Vice Pres for Inst Advancement ....Dr. Mark R. TROYER
20 Academic Dean ....Dr. Timothy G. CAMPBELL
49 Dir of College of Arts & Sciences ....Dr. Stephen K. CLEMENTS
53 Interim Dean School of Education ....Dr. Bonnie BANKER
60 Dean of School of Comm Arts ....Dr. James R. OWENS
58 Dean School of Grad & Prof Studies ....Mr. T. Joshua FEE
50 Dean Howard Dayton Sch Business ....Dr. Michael KANE
110 Senior Advancement Director ....Rev. Stuart A. SMITH
37 Director of Financial Aid ....Mr. Ronald M. ANDERSON
42 Assoc Dean for Campus Ministries ....Rev. Gregory K. HASELOFF
39 Assoc Dean for Residence Life ....Mr. Joe W. BRUNER
06 Registrar ....Mrs. Sheryl VOIGTS
29 Dir of Alumni Relations/Parents Pgm ....Mrs. Lisa D. HARPER
08 Interim Dir of Library Services ....Mrs. Suzanne GEHRING
13 Director of Information Services ....Mr. Paul J. DUPREE
07 Director of Admissions ....Mr. Brandon COMBS
26 Dir of Marketing & Communications ....Mr. Brad JOHNSON
18 Director of Physical Plant ....Mr. Eric C. MCMILLION
23 Supervisor of Clinic ....Miss Carol J. AMEY
36 Dir Center for Career & Calling ....Ms. Michelle KRATZER
38 Assoc Dean of Wholeness & Wellness ....Mr. Kevin BELLEW
19 Dir of Security & Environ Safety ....Mr. David HAY
40 Manager of Bookstore ....Mr. C. David TRAMMELL
21 Associate Business Officer ....Mr. Gary E. HOWARD
04 Exec Assistant to the President ....Ms. Michelle CLARK
85 Coordinator of Intercultural Pgms ....Rev. Esther JADHAV
41 Athletics Director ....Mr. Mark PERDUE
09 Director of Institutional Research ....Dr. Gay HOLCOMB
104 Coordinator Global Engagement Ofc ....Mrs. Tina WEI SMITH
15 Dir of Human Resources/Risk Mgt ....Mrs. Jan CRAIGMILES
45 Director Institutional Planning ....Dr. Paul STEPHENS

ATA College (E)

10180 Linn Station Road, Ste A-200, Louisville KY 40223
County: Jefferson FICE Identification: 040383
Unit ID: 447935
Telephone: (502) 371-8330 Carnegie Class: Spec 2-yr-Health
FAX Number: (502) 371-8598 Calendar System: Quarter
URL: www.ata.edu
Established: 1994 Annual Undergrad Tuition & Fees: $11,545
Enrollment: 342 Coed
Affiliation or Control: Proprietary IRS Status: Proprietary
Highest Offering: Associate Degree
Accreditation: **ABHES**

01 President ....Mr. Donald A. JONES

Baptist Seminary of Kentucky (F)

400 E. College Street, Box 358, Georgetown KY 40324
County: Scott Identification: 667211
Telephone: (502) 863-8300 Carnegie Class: Not Classified
FAX Number: (502) 863-8300 Calendar System: Semester
URL: www.bsk.edu
Established: 2002 Annual Graduate Tuition & Fees: N/A
Enrollment: N/A Coed
Affiliation or Control: Independent Non-Profit IRS Status: 501(c)3
Highest Offering: Master's; No Undergraduates
Accreditation: **THEOL**

01 President ....Dr. David CASSADY
05 Academic Dean ....Dr. Dalen C. JACKSON
07 Int Director of Admissions ....Ms. Jessalynn CORNETT

Beckfield College (G)

16 Spiral Drive, Florence KY 41042-4866
County: Boone FICE Identification: 024911
Unit ID: 247065
Telephone: (859) 371-9393 Carnegie Class: Bac/Assoc-Assoc Dom
FAX Number: (859) 371-5096 Calendar System: Quarter
URL: www.beckfield.edu
Established: 1984 Annual Undergrad Tuition & Fees: $13,281
Enrollment: 662 Coed
Affiliation or Control: Proprietary IRS Status: Proprietary
Highest Offering: Baccalaureate
Accreditation: **ACICS**, NURSE

01 CEO/CFO ....Ms. Diane G. WOLFER
05 VP of Academics and Operations ....Dr. Rachel A. MCARTHUR
37 Director of Financial Aid ....Ms. Kimberly VILLAVERDE
13 VP of Information Technology ....Mr. Charles WILSON
07 Director Admissions ....Mr. Jeff BAKER
36 Director Career Services ....Ms. Karen SHELDON
22 Director of Compliance ....Mr. Lee FOLEY
06 Registrar ....Ms. Jocelyn ROY
08 Librarian ....Ms. Gayle ECABERT
50 Dean of Business/Technology ....Dr. Erica OKERE
66 Dean of Nursing ....Dr. Deborah SMITH-CLAY
76 Dean of Allied Health ....Ms. Dolores DOMINGUEZ
97 Dean of General Education ....Ms. Mindy HODGES
88 Dean of Criminal Justice ....Ms. Brandy EXELER
04 Assistant to the President ....Ms. Linda WOODALL

Bellarmine University (H)

2001 Newburg Road, Louisville KY 40205-0671
County: Jefferson FICE Identification: 001954
Unit ID: 156286
Telephone: (502) 272-8000 Carnegie Class: Masters/L
FAX Number: (502) 272-8033 Calendar System: Semester
URL: www.bellarmine.edu
Established: 1950 Annual Undergrad Tuition & Fees: $39,750
Enrollment: 3,846 Coed
Affiliation or Control: Independent Non-Profit IRS Status: 501(c)3
Highest Offering: Doctorate
Accreditation: **SC**, CAEPN, COARC, MT, NURSE, PTA

01 President ....Dr. Susan M. DONOVAN
05 Provost & Chief Academic Officer ....Dr. Carole PFEFFER
20 Vice Provost ....Dr. Graham ELLIS
20 Vice Provost - Faculty Development ....Dr. Anne BUCALOS
10 Vice President for Admin & Finance ....Mr. Robert L. ZIMLICH
32 Vice President for Student Affairs ....Dr. Helen G. RYAN
30 VP for Dev & Alumni Relations ....Mr. Glenn F. KOSSE
26 VP for Comm & Public Affairs ....Dr. Hunt C. HELM
84 Vice President for Enrollment Mgmt ....Dr. Sean J. RYAN
04 Administrative Asst to President ....Ms. Lucy BURNS
76 Vice Prov Col of Health Professions ....Dr. Mark WIEGAND
50 Dean Rubel School of Business ....Dr. Sharon KERRICK
107 Dean of Continuing and Prof Studies ....Dr. Sean J. RYAN
53 Dean Annsley Frazier Thornton Educ ....Dr. Robert B. COOTER
65 Dean Sch of Environmental Studies ....Dr. Robert KINGSOLVER
49 Dean Bellarmine College ....Dr. William E. FENTON
66 Dean Nursing & Clinical Sciences ....Dr. Nancy YORK
15 Chief Human Resources Officer ....Ms. Lynn M. BYNUM
21 Asst VP Business Affairs ....Ms. Denise BROWN-CORNELIUS
110 Associate VP Development ....Ms. Tina KAUFFMAN
35 Asst VP Student Affairs ....Mr. Patrick ENGLERT
85 Exec Dir Stdy Abroad & Intl Learn ....Dr. Gabriele W. BOSLEY
35 Dean of Students ....Dr. Sean MCGREEVEY
92 Director Honors Program ....Dr. Jonathan W. BLANDFORD
41 Athletic Director ....Mr. Scott P. WIEGANDT
18 Asst VP Facilities Management ....Mr. Jeffrey DEAN
07 Dean of Admission ....Mr. Timothy A. STURGEON
08 Director of the Library ....Dr. John K. STEMMER
19 Director of Safety & Security ....Ms. Debbie FOX
123 Dean of Graduate Admission ....Dr. Sara Y. PETTINGILL
06 Registrar ....Ms. Ann E. OLSEN
96 Purchasing Manager ....Mr. Patrick COONS
42 Director Campus Ministry ....Dr. Melanie P. SULLIVAN
39 Assoc Dean Stdnt/Dir Residence Life ....Ms. Leslie M. MAXIE-ASHFORD
13 Chief Information Officer/Vice Prov ....Mr. Eric SATTERLY
37 Director Student Financial Aid ....Ms. Heather BOUTELL
36 Director of Career Development ....Dr. Lilly MASSA-MCKINLEY
29 Executive Director Alumni Relations ....Mr. Peter W. KREMER
27 Director of News/Media/Social Netwk ....Mr. Jason A. CISSELL
38 Director of Counseling Center ....Dr. Gary PETIPRIN
92 Director of Brown Scholars Program ....Vacant
88 Dean Movement & Rehabilitation Sci ....Dr. Tony BROSKY
09 Director of Institutional Research ....Mr. Drew THIEMANN

Berea College (I)

101 Chestnut Street, Berea KY 40404-0003
County: Madison FICE Identification: 001955
Unit ID: 156295
Telephone: (859) 985-3000 Carnegie Class: Bac-A&S
FAX Number: (859) 985-3917 Calendar System: Semester
URL: www.berea.edu
Established: 1855 Annual Undergrad Tuition & Fees: $25,470
Enrollment: 1,643 Coed
Affiliation or Control: Independent Non-Profit IRS Status: 501(c)3
Highest Offering: Baccalaureate
Accreditation: **SC**, CAEPN, NURSE

01 President ....Dr. Lyle D. ROELOFS
10 Vice President Finance ....Mr. Jeff S. AMBURGEY
29 VP Alumni & College Relations ....Ms. Bernadine DOUGLAS
32 VP Labor and Student Life ....Mr. Virgil BURNSIDE
11 VP Operations and Sustainability ....Mr. Derrick SINGLETON
22 VP for Diversity and Inclusion ....Dr. Linda LEEK
45 VP Strategic Initiatives ....Ms. Teri THOMPSON
05 Academic VP/Dean of the Faculty ....Dr. Chad BERRY
26 Assoc VP of Int Marketing/Comm ....Ms. Kim BROWN
30 Assoc VP of Development Operations ....Ms. Joanne SINGH
35 Asst Vice Pres for Student Life ....Mr. Gus GERASSIMIDES
37 Dir of Student Financial Aid Svcs ....Ms. Theresa LOWDER
38 Dir Counseling/Psychological Svcs ....Ms. Sue REIMONDO
112 Executive Dir Major & Planned Gifts ....Ms. Teresa KASH DAVIS
108 Director of Academic Assessment ....Dr. Robert SMITH
20 Dean of Curriculum/Student Learning ....Dr. Scott STEELE
13 Chief Information Officer ....Ms. Huapei CHEN
07 Director of Admissions Operations ....Mr. Luke HODSON
88 Associate VP of Alumni Relations ....Ms. Jackie COLLIER
15 Director of Human Resources ....Mr. Steve LAWSON
18 Director of Facilities Management ....Mr. Wayne ORR
88 Director of Appalachian Center ....Mr. Chris GREEN
09 Director of Inst Rsrch/Assessment ....Ms. Judith WECKMAN
27 Publications and Project Manager ....Mr. J. MORGAN
08 Director of Library Services ....Ms. Anne CHASE
41 Dir Athletics/Seabury Ctr Complex ....Mr. Mark CARTMILL
42 Director Campus Christian Center ....Rev. Loretta REYNOLDS
43 General Counsel ....Mr. Judge WILSON
19 Director of Public Safety ....Mr. V. Lavoyed HUDGINS
28 Director Black Cultural Center ....Ms. Monica JONES
88 Dean of Labor ....Mr. David K. TIPTON
85 Director International Center ....Dr. Richard CAHILL
40 Retail Manager College Store ....Ms. Susan BUCKMASTER
96 Purchasing Manager ....Ms. Aurelia BRANDENBURG
24 Media Services Coordinator ....Vacant
121 Director of Academic Services ....Mr. Curtis SANDBERG
88 Center for Transformative Learning ....Ms. Leslie ORTQUIST-AHRENS
88 Woodson Center for Interracial Educ ....Dr. Alicestyne TURLEY
88 Director of CELTS ....Ms. Ashley COCHRANE
23 Director of Health and Wellness ....Ms. Jill GURTATOWSKI
88 Director of Internships ....Ms. Esther LIVINGSTON
103 Director of Career Development ....Ms. Amanda TUDOR
104 Education Abroad Adviser ....Ms. Ann BUTWELL
06 Registrar ....Ms. Judy GINTER
100 Executive Assistant to President ....Ms. Judy MOTT
105 Director Web Design/Development ....Mr. Charlie CAMPBELL

Brescia University (J)

717 Frederica Street, Owensboro KY 42301-3023
County: Daviess FICE Identification: 001958
Unit ID: 156356
Telephone: (270) 685-3131 Carnegie Class: Bac-Diverse
FAX Number: (270) 686-6422 Calendar System: Semester
URL: www.brescia.edu
Established: 1950 Annual Undergrad Tuition & Fees: $21,100
Enrollment: 1,060 Coed
Affiliation or Control: Roman Catholic IRS Status: 501(c)3
Highest Offering: Master's
Accreditation: **SC**, SW

01 President ... Rev. Larry HOSTETTER
05 Vice President & Academic Dean ... Dr. Cheryl CLEMONS
10 Vice President Business & Finance ... Mr. Dale CECIL
84 Vice President of Enrollment ... Mr. Christopher HOUK
30 Vice Pres Institutional Advancement ... Ms. Tracy NAYLOR
32 Vice Pres/Dean Student Development ... Mr. Joshua R. CLARY
39 Director Residence Life ... Mr. Issac DUNCAN
35 Director Stdnts Act/Leadership Dev ... Ms. Patricia LOVETT
06 Registrar ... Sr. Helena FISCHER, OSU
106 Director of BU Online ... Ms. Shanda LARUE
38 Director of Counseling Center ... Ms. Eva G. ATKINSON
08 Director of Library Services ... Sr. Judith N. RINEY, OSU
88 Director of UCTL ... Dr. Anna KUTHY
15 Director of Human Resources ... Ms. Tammy S. KELLER
13 Director of Information Technology ... Mr. Chris FORD
18 Director of Physical Plant ... Mr. Mike WARD
37 Director of Financial Aid ... Ms. Kristi EIDSON
41 Director of Athletics ... Mr. Brian SKORTZ
26 Director of Public Relations ... Ms. Kayla ALTMAN
29 Director of Alumni & Donor Rels ... Mr. Jake DAVIS
44 Director of Annual Giving ... Ms. Sydney WARREN
09 Director of Institutional Research ... Ms. Stephanie CLARY
58 Director of Graduate Program-MBA ... Dr. Sandra O. OBILADE
42 Director of Campus Ministry ... Sr. Pam MUELLER, OSU
07 Director of Admissions ... Ms. Christy ROHNER
21 Asst Director Business & Finance ... Mrs. Nancy W. REYNOLDS
36 Coordinator of Career Services ... Ms. Sarah INMAN
20 Associate Academic Dean for Online ... Mr. Jeffrey BARNETTE
40 Bookstore Manager ... Mrs. Beverly MCCANDLESS
25 Grants Writer/Special Asst to Pres ... Vacant

Brown Mackie College-Louisville (A)

3605 Fern Valley Road, Louisville KY 40219-1916
Telephone: (502) 810-6000 FICE Identification: 021082
Accreditation: ACICS, OTA

† In teach-out mode. Branch campus of Brown Mackie College-Findlay, Findlay, OH.

Campbellsville University (B)

1 Universty Drive, Campbellsville KY 42718-2799
County: Taylor FICE Identification: 001959
Unit ID: 156365
Telephone: (270) 789-5000 Carnegie Class: Masters/L
FAX Number: (270) 789-5050 Calendar System: Semester
URL: www.campbellsville.edu
Established: 1906 Annual Undergrad Tuition & Fees: $24,596
Enrollment: 3,128 Coed
Affiliation or Control: Baptist IRS Status: 501(c)3
Highest Offering: Doctorate
Accreditation: SC, CAEPN, IACBE, MFCD, MUS, NUR, SW

01 President ... Dr. Michael CARTER
10 Vice Pres Finance & Administration ... Mr. Otto TENNANT
05 Vice President Academic Affairs ... Dr. Donna HEDGEPATH
30 Vice President for Development ... Mr. Benji KELLY
07 VP for Enrollment ... Dr. Shane GARRISON
20 Associate Academic Officer ... Dr. Jeanette PARKER
21 Controller ... Mr. Tim JUDD
09 Director of Institutional Research ... Mrs. Anna PAVY
38 Director of Student Counseling ... Vacant
92 Director of Honors Program ... Dr. Craig L. ROGERS
41 VP for Athletics ... Mr. Rusty HOLLINGSWORTH
40 Director of Bookstore ... Mrs. Donna WRIGHT
42 Director of Campus Ministries ... Mr. Edwin C. PAVY
13 Director of Computing/Communication ... Mr. Eric SMITH
37 Director of Financial Aid ... Mrs. Chris MAPES
29 Director of Alumni Relations ... Mr. Darryl PEAVLER
08 Director of Library Services ... Vacant
15 Director of Personnel Services ... Mr. Terry VANMETER
18 Director of Maintenance ... Mr. Steve MORRIS
26 Director of News Information ... Mrs. Joan C. MCKINNEY
06 Director of Student Records ... Mrs. Rita A. CREASON
04 Assistant to the President ... Mrs. Kellie VAUGHN
96 Director of Purchasing ... Mrs. Lisa FERGUSON
88 Director of Custodial Services ... Mr. Bob STOTTS

Centre College (C)

600 W Walnut Street, Danville KY 40422-1394
County: Boyle FICE Identification: 001961
Unit ID: 156408
Telephone: (859) 238-5200 Carnegie Class: Bac-A&S
FAX Number: (859) 238-6977 Calendar System: Other
URL: www.centre.edu
Established: 1819 Annual Undergrad Tuition & Fees: $39,300
Enrollment: 1,367 Coed
Affiliation or Control: Independent Non-Profit IRS Status: 501(c)3
Highest Offering: Baccalaureate
Accreditation: SC

01 President ... Dr. John A. ROUSH
05 Vice President & Dean of College ... Dr. Stephanie L. FABRITIUS
10 Vice Pres/CFO & Treasurer ... Mr. Brian G. HUTZLEY
32 Vice Pres/Dean of Student Life ... Mr. Wm. Randy HAYS
30 VP Devel/Alumni Engagement ... Mr. Shawn LYONS
43 VP for Legal Affairs/Gift Planning ... Mr. James P. LEAHEY
53 Professor of Education ... Dr. Donna M. PLUMMER
28 Assoc Vice Pres Diversity/Acad Affs ... Dr. Rodmon C. KING
07 Dean of Admissions & Financial Aid ... Mr. Robert M. NESMITH
20 Associate Dean of the College ... Dr. Brian CUSATO
38 Director of Counseling Services ... Ms. Ann E. GOODWIN
45 Asst to the President for Planning ... Dr. J. Patrick NOLTEMEYER
104 Director of Global Citizenship ... Dr. Kyle D. ANDERSON
08 Director of Library Services ... Mr. Stanley R. CAMPBELL
04 Exec Assistant to the President ... Ms. Yvonne Y. MORLEY
37 Assoc Dean/Dir of Financial Aid ... Mr. Kevin D. LAMB
06 Registrar ... Mr. Timothy P. CULHAN
15 VP for Human Resources/Admin Svcs ... Mrs. Kay L. DRAKE
27 Director of Communications ... Dr. Michael P. STRYSICK
36 Dir Ctr for Career/Professional Dev ... Ms. Joy ASHER
39 Director Student Life & Housing ... Ms. Ann S. YOUNG
41 Director of Athletics & Recreation ... Mr. W. Bradley FIELDS
19 Co-Director of Public Safety ... Mr. Kevin S. MILBY
19 Co-Director of Public Safety ... Mr. Gary D. BUGG
09 Director of Institutional Research ... Dr. J. Patrick NOLTEMEYER
13 CIO & Director of ITS ... Mr. Andrew J. RYAN
24 Director Ctr for Teaching/Learning ... Dr. Sarah E. LASHLEY
18 Director of Facilities Management ... Mr. D. Wayne KING
21 Controller ... Mr. R. Scott OWENS
42 College Chaplain ... Dr. Richard D. AXTELL
96 Asst Dir Procurement/Capital Proj ... Ms. Ann T. SMITH
29 Director of Alumni Engagement ... Ms. Megan H. MILBY
57 Director Norton Center for Arts ... Mr. Steven A. HOFFMAN

Clear Creek Baptist Bible College (D)

300 Clear Creek Road, Pineville KY 40977-9754
County: Bell FICE Identification: 025356
Unit ID: 156417
Telephone: (606) 337-3196 Carnegie Class: Spec-4-yr-Faith
FAX Number: (606) 337-2372 Calendar System: Semester
URL: www.ccbbc.edu
Established: 1926 Annual Undergrad Tuition & Fees: $7,220
Enrollment: 151 Coed
Affiliation or Control: Southern Baptist IRS Status: 501(c)3
Highest Offering: Baccalaureate
Accreditation: SC, BI

01 President ... Dr. Donnie S. FOX
05 Academic Dean ... Dr. Jay SULFRIDGE
32 Dean of Student Affairs ... Rev. Charlie GOODMAN
11 Administrative Dean ... Mr. Jeremy ANDERSON
30 Dean of Institutional Advancement ... Mr. Shannon BENEFIEL
08 Director of Library ... Mrs. Lynn KAHKOLA
42 Director Christian Service ... Rev. Joshua SMITH
18 Director of Physical Plant ... Mr. Ronnie WASHAM
37 Director Financial Aid ... Mr. Sam RISNER
06 Registrar ... Mr. Jacob YATES
07 Director of Admissions ... Mr. Greg YOUNG
26 Director of College Relations ... Mr. David DOWELL
13 Dir of Information Technologies ... Mr. Shane KAHKOLA
56 Director of Distance Education ... Rev. Eric J. GREEN

Daymar College-Bowling Green (E)

2421 Fitzgerald Industrial Drive,
Bowling Green KY 42101-4071
Telephone: (270) 843-6750 Identification: 666439
Accreditation: ACICS

† Branch campus of Daymar College, Nashville, TN.

Eastern Kentucky University (F)

521 Lancaster Avenue, Richmond KY 40475-3102
County: Madison FICE Identification: 001963
Unit ID: 156620
Telephone: (859) 622-1000 Carnegie Class: Masters/L
FAX Number: (859) 622-1020 Calendar System: Semester
URL: www.eku.edu
Established: 1906 Annual Undergrad Tuition & Fees (In-State): $8,868
Enrollment: 16,844 Coed
Affiliation or Control: State IRS Status: 501(c)3
Highest Offering: Doctorate
Accreditation: SC, ADNUR, CAATE, CACREP, CAEPN, CAHIIM, CONST, CS, DIETD, EMT, ENGT, FEPAC, IFSAC, MT, MUS, NAIT, NRPA, NURSE, OT, PH, SP, SPAA, SW

01 President ... Dr. Michael BENSON
05 Interim Provost/VP Academic Affairs ... Dr. Deborah WHITEHOUSE
10 VP of Finance & Administration ... Mr. Barry POYNTER
30 VP Development & Alumni Relations ... Mr. Nick PERLICK
121 VP for Student Success ... Dr. Eugene PALKA
86 VP Engmt/Reg Stewardship & Gov Rel ... Dr. David MCFADDIN
32 Assoc VP & Chief Student Affs Ofcr ... Dr. Billy MARTIN
26 Asst VP Communications & Brand Mgmt ... Mr. Doug CORNETT
35 Dean of Students ... Ms. Kenna MIDDLETON
49 Interim Dean Letters/Arts/Soc Sci ... Dr. Sara ZEIGLER
76 Interim Dean Health Sciences ... Dr. Shelia PRESSLEY
81 Dean Science ... Dr. Tom OTIENO
50 Dean Business & Technology ... Dr. Thomas EREKSON
53 Dean Education ... Dr. Sherry POWERS
88 Dean Justice & Safety ... Dr. Victor KAPPELER
43 University Counsel ... Ms. Dana FOHL
19 Chief of Police ... Mr. Brian MULLINS
13 CIO & Dean of Libraries ... Ms. Betina GARDNER
06 Registrar ... Ms. Tina DAVIS
88 Director Advising ... Mr. Benton SHIREY
07 Director Admissions ... Ms. Stephanie WHALEY
36 Director Career Services & Coop Ed ... Mrs. Gladys MILLER
25 Director Sponsored Programs ... Mr. Gus BENSON
92 Director Honors Program ... Dr. David COLEMAN
09 Asst VP Inst Effectiveness & Res ... Dr. Tanlee WASSON
85 Director International Student Svcs ... Mr. Wenceslaus PORYEM
38 Director Counseling Center ... Dr. Melissa BARTSCH
39 Asst Dean of Students ... Ms. April BARNES
88 Director Student Conduct & Comm Std ... Mr. Robert BROWN
37 Dir Student Financial Assistance ... Mr. Bryan ERSLAN
23 Health Services Manager ... Vacant
40 Director Bookstore ... Mr. Timothy GOGNAT
15 Director Equity/Center Stdnt Access ... Ms. Lori DAVIS
14 Deputy Chief Technology Officer ... Ms. Jean MARLOW
112 Asst VP Principal Gifts ... Mrs. Kari MARTIN
18 Assoc VP Facilities Svcs & Cap Plng ... Mr. Robert GANNOE
28 Vice Provost Diversity ... Dr. Timothy FORDE
41 Athletic Director ... Mr. Stephen LOCHMUELLER
96 Director of Purchasing & Stores ... Ms. Andrea CASHELL
42 Chaplain ... Vacant
04 Admin Asst to the President ... Ms. Cassie MALICK
04 Exec Asst to the President & BOR ... Mr. Jeremy RAINES
58 Dean Graduate School & AVP Rsrch ... Dr. Jerry POGATSHNIK
20 Vice Provost ... Dr. Sherry ROBINSON
84 Exec Director Enrollment Mgmt ... Dr. Brett MORRIS
14 Deputy Chief Information Officer ... Mr. Jeff WHITAKER
29 Executive Director Alum Engagement ... Mr. Dan MCBRIDE
19 Exec Dir Public Safety & Risk Mgmt ... Mr. Bryan MAKINEN
116 Director of Internal Audit ... Ms. Beth BALLARD

Frontier Nursing University (G)

195 School Street, Hyden KY 41749
County: Leslie FICE Identification: 030070
Unit ID: 156727
Telephone: (606) 672-2312 Carnegie Class: Spec-4-yr-Other Health
FAX Number: (606) 672-3776 Calendar System: Quarter
URL: www.frontier.edu
Established: 1939 Annual Graduate Tuition & Fees: N/A
Enrollment: 1,605 Coed
Affiliation or Control: Independent Non-Profit IRS Status: 501(c)3
Highest Offering: Doctorate; No Undergraduates
Accreditation: SC, MIDWF, NUR

01 President ... Dr. Susan STONE
05 Associate Dean of Academic Affairs ... Dr. Anne COCKERHAM
66 Dean of Nursing ... Dr. Julie MARFELL
46 Associate Dean of Research ... Vacant
88 PM-DNP Director ... Dr. Joan JLAGER
88 Bridge Option Director ... Dr. Jacquelyne BROOKS
37 Director of Financial Aid ... Ms. Rainie BOGGS

Galen College of Nursing (H)

1031 Zorn Avenue, Louisville KY 40207-1064
County: Jefferson FICE Identification: 030837
Unit ID: 156471
Telephone: (502) 410-6200 Carnegie Class: Spec 2-yr-Health
FAX Number: (502) 568-1271 Calendar System: Quarter
URL: www.galencollege.edu
Established: 1989 Annual Undergrad Tuition & Fees: N/A
Enrollment: 1,045 Coed
Affiliation or Control: Proprietary IRS Status: Proprietary
Highest Offering: Baccalaureate
Accreditation: SC, ADNUR, NURSE

01 Chief Executive Officer ... Mr. Mark A. VOGT
05 Academic President ... Dr. Joan L. FREY
11 Executive VP/Chief Admin Ofcr ... Mr. Joseph R. PETERS
06 Director of Academic Records ... Ms. Jonda BRINNER
106 Dean of Online Programs ... Dr. Kathy BURLINGAME
88 Executive VP of Prelicensure Nurs ... Dr. Audria DENKER
88 Sr Dir of Ops and Reg Affairs ... Ms. Kathleen DWYER
84 VP of Enrollment Management ... Mr. Carter SMITH
66 Interim Dean of Main Campus ... Dr. Constance COOPER
10 VP of Finance ... Mr. Thomas DWYER
13 Director of Information Technology ... Mr. Duane HELLUMS
20 Executive VP and Provost ... Dr. Steve HYNDMAN
26 Director of Marketing ... Ms. Anna KITSON
15 VP of Human Resources and CCO ... Ms. Allyson WOLFE
88 Executive VP of Postlicensure Nurs ... Dr. Tracy ORTELLI
37 Director of Financial Aid ... Ms. Joni M. PENLAND
13 VP and Chief Strategy Officer ... Mr. David RAY
108 Director of Inst Effectiveness ... Dr. Carissa SHAFTO
07 Director of Admissions ... Ms. Terri THOMAS
18 Director of Facilities ... Ms. Layne MALONEY

Georgetown College (I)

400 E College Street, Georgetown KY 40324-1696
County: Scott FICE Identification: 001964
Unit ID: 156745
Telephone: (502) 863-8000 Carnegie Class: Bac-A&S
FAX Number: (502) 868-8891 Calendar System: Semester
URL: www.georgetowncollege.edu
Established: 1829 Annual Undergrad Tuition & Fees: $35,650
Enrollment: 1,364 Coed
Affiliation or Control: Baptist IRS Status: 501(c)3
Highest Offering: Master's
Accreditation: #SC, CAATE, CAEPN

01 President ... Dr. Dwaine GREENE
05 Provost/Dean of the College ... Dr. Rosemary ALLEN
10 Vice President/CFO/Treasurer ... Mr. David WILHITE
101 Asst to President/Board Secretary ... Mr. Robin OLDHAM
111 VP Institutional Advancement ... Dr. Todd RASBERRY

32 Dean of Students/Title IX Coord ... Ms. Laura JOHNSON
84 Vice President for Enrollment ... Dr. Jonathan SANDS WISE
13 Assoc VP for Info Tech Services ... Mr. Donald L. BLAKEMAN
26 Assoc VP for Comm & Marketing ... Mr. Jim ALLISON
21 Controller ... Mr. Brad KAUFMAN
06 Registrar ... Mr. Jason SNIDER
88 Dir Ctr for Culturally Rel Pedagogy ... Dr. Rebecca POWELL
15 Director of Human Resources ... Ms. Tracie SHAPIRO
53 Dean of Education ... Dr. Joy BOWERS-CAMPBELL
07 Director of Admissions ... Mr. Jeremiah TUDOR
37 Dir of Student Financial Planning ... Mr. Bob FULTZ
30 Director of Development ... Ms. Debbie SEWELL
09 Director of Institutional Research ... Dr. Jessica HEARN
08 Director of Library Services ... Mr. Benjamin RAWLINS
29 Director of Alumni Relations ... Ms. Laura OWSLEY
41 Director of Athletics ... Mr. Brian EVANS
26 Dir Comm/Mktg & Church Relations ... Mr. H.K KINGKADE
36 Dir Graves Ctr for Calling & Career ... Ms. Holly JAMES
19 Director Campus Safety ... Mr. Donald LUNDSFORD
38 Director of Counseling/Health Svcs ... Ms. Megan REDDITT
18 Dir Facilities and Grounds ... Mr. Bart HORNE
28 Director of Diversity Initiatives ... Ms. Robbi BARBER

Indiana Tech-Louisville (A)

11861 Commonwealth Drive, Louisville KY 40299
Telephone: (502) 708-2364 Identification: 770104
Accreditation: &NH

† Branch campus of Indiana Tech, Fort Wayne, IN

Interactive College of Technology (B)

76 Caruthers Road, Newport KY 41071
Telephone: (859) 282-8989 Identification: 770535
Accreditation: COE

† Branch campus of Interactive College of Technology, Chamblee, GA

Kentucky Christian University (C)

100 Academic Parkway, Grayson KY 41143-2205
County: Carter FICE Identification: 001965
Unit ID: 157100
Telephone: (606) 474-3000 Carnegie Class: Bac-Diverse
FAX Number: (606) 474-3189 Calendar System: Semester
URL: www.kcu.edu
Established: 1919 Annual Undergrad Tuition & Fees: $18,560
Enrollment: 606 Coed
Affiliation or Control: Christian Churches And Churches of Christ
IRS Status: 501(c)3
Highest Offering: Master's
Accreditation: SC, NURSE, SW

01 President/CEO ... Dr. Jeff K. METCALF
05 Executive Vice President ... Dr. Marvin L. ELLIOTT
30 Director of Development ... Vacant
88 Director of Church Relations ... Mr. Jeff W. GREENE
06 Registrar ... Mrs. Andrea L. STAMPER
13 Director of Campus Technology ... Mr. Greg C. RICHARDSON
08 Library Director ... Mrs. Naulayne R. ENDERS
108 Director Institutional Assessment ... Vacant
32 Director of Student Services ... Mr. William B. BAUMGARDNER
42 Campus Minister ... Mr. Larry W. MARSHALL
37 Director Financial Aid ... Mrs. Jennie M. BENDER
15 Human Resource Officer ... Mr. Terry L. YANKEY
38 Student Counseling Coordinator ... Mrs. Lori A. SMITH-WARD
41 Athletic Director ... Mr. Bruce W. DIXON
39 Director of Residence Services ... Vacant
18 Director of Facilities ... Mr. John R. SEAGRAVES
29 Alumni Relations Officer ... Mr. Jeff W. GREENE
58 Dean of the Graduate School ... Vacant
07 Director of Enrollment Services ... Mrs. Sheree GREER
40 Manager of Retail Operations ... Mrs. Julie M. BAUMGARDNER
105 Website Manager ... Mr. David A. BENNETT
10 Director of Business ... Mr. Daniel R. WHITE

*Kentucky Community and Technical College System (D)

300 N Main Street, Versailles KY 40383-1245
County: Woodford FICE Identification: 006724
Unit ID: 157854
Telephone: (859) 256-3100 Carnegie Class: N/A
FAX Number: (859) 256-3119
URL: www.kctcs.edu

01 President ... Dr. Jay BOX
00 Chancellor ... Dr. Rhonda TRACY
05 VC Academic Affairs ... Dr. Paul BLANKENSHIP
10 Vice President ... Mr. Wendell FOLLOWELL
13 Vice President ... Dr. Paul CZARAPATA
30 Vice President ... Mr. Timothy R. BURCHAM, CFRE
32 Vice President ... Dr. Gloria MCCALL
103 VC Econ Dev/Workforce Solutions ... Dr. Paul SCHREFFLER
09 VC Research and Analysis ... Dr. Alicia CROUCH
04 Sr Exec Assistant to the President ... Ms. Beth HILLIARD

*Ashland Community and Technical College (E)

1400 College Drive, Ashland KY 41101-3617
County: Boyd FICE Identification: 001990
Unit ID: 156231
Telephone: (606) 326-2000 Carnegie Class: Assoc/HVT-Mix Trad/Non
FAX Number: (606) 326-2187 Calendar System: Semester
URL: www.ashland.kctcs.edu
Established: 1938 Annual Undergrad Tuition & Fees (In-State): $3,936
Enrollment: 2,728 Coed
Affiliation or Control: State IRS Status: 501(c)3
Highest Offering: Associate Degree
Accreditation: SC, ADNUR, COARC, IFSAC, SURGT

02 President & CEO ... Dr. Kay ADKINS
32 Dean Student Success/Enroll Svcs ... Mr. Steven WOODBURN
10 Dean of Business Affairs ... Ms. Karen BLEVINS
30 Dean Resource Dev/External Affairs ... Ms. Willie MCCULLOUGH
09 Dean Inst Plng/Research/Effective ... Mr. Steve FLOUHOUSE
86 Dean of Public Service ... Mr. John MCGLONE
05 Assoc Dean of Academic Affairs ... Dr. Keith BRAMMELL
49 Division Chair of Arts & Sciences ... Dr. Nicole GRIFFITH-GREEN
26 Director of Marketing ... Ms. Allison GOBLE
08 Director of Library Services ... Ms. Pamela KLINEPETER
07 Director of Admissions/Registrar ... Ms. Robin LEWIS
13 Assoc Dean Information Technology ... Mr. Farnoosh RAFIEE
28 Director of Cultural Diversity ... Mr. Alvin BAKER
15 Director of Human Resources ... Ms. Kellie ALLEN
37 Director of Financial Aid ... Mr. Adam ABSHIRE
103 Director of Workforce Solutions ... Dr. Karen COBURN
121 Director of Student Support Svcs ... Ms. Megan HORNE
51 Director of Adult Education ... Ms. Penny QUALLS

*Big Sandy Community and Technical College (F)

1 Bert T. Combs Drive, Prestonburg KY 41653-9502
County: Floyd FICE Identification: 001996
Unit ID: 157553
Telephone: (606) 886-3863 Carnegie Class: Assoc/HVT-High Non
FAX Number: (606) 886-2677 Calendar System: Semester
URL: www.bigsandy.kctcs.edu
Established: 1964 Annual Undergrad Tuition & Fees (In-State): $3,936
Enrollment: 4,938 Coed
Affiliation or Control: State IRS Status: 501(c)3
Highest Offering: Associate Degree
Accreditation: SC, COARC, DH

02 Interim President/CEO ... Dr. Alan SCHEIBMEIR
11 Chief Institutional Officer ... Mr. Bobby MCCOOL
05 Provost ... Vacant
32 Dean of Student Affairs ... Mr. Jimmy WRIGHT
10 Chief Business Affairs Officer ... Ms. Michelle MEEK
08 Director of Library Services ... Ms. Kathy LOWE
15 Director of Human Resources ... Ms. Bryen GOBLE
06 Registrar ... Mr. Jeffrey T. HICKS
37 Director of Financial Aid ... Ms. Cathy HURD-CRANK
09 Dean of Institutional Effectiveness ... Dr. Chris DANIEL
13 Dean of Information Technology ... Vacant
18 Dir Facil/Safety/Auxiliary Svcs ... Mr. John HERALD
40 Bookstore Manager ... Ms. Stephanie WEST
26 Dean Public Relations/Strat Comm ... Mr. Joshua BALL
30 Director of Advancement ... Vacant
20 Dean of Academic Affairs ... Ms. Myra ELLIOTT
28 Director of Cultural Diversity ... Ms. Greta SLONE
103 Dean of Tech Ed/Workforce Solutions ... Ms. Kelli HALL
04 Exec Admin Asst to President ... Ms. Teresa MCCOART

*Bluegrass Community and Technical College (G)

470 Cooper Drive, Lexington KY 40506-0001
County: Fayette FICE Identification: 009707
Unit ID: 156392
Telephone: (859) 246-6200 Carnegie Class: Assoc/HVT-High Trad
FAX Number: (859) 246-4664 Calendar System: Semester
URL: www.bluegrass.kctcs.edu
Established: 1965 Annual Undergrad Tuition & Fees (In-State): $4,016
Enrollment: 10,388 Coed
Affiliation or Control: State IRS Status: 501(c)3
Highest Offering: Associate Degree
Accreditation: SC, ADNUR, COARC, DH, IFSAC, MAC, RAD, SURGT

02 President & CEO ... Dr. Augusta A. JULIAN
13 VP of Information Technology ... Mr. Ren BATES
05 VP of Academics/WFD ... Dr. Gregory FEENEY
32 VP Student Dev/Enrollment Svcs ... Dr. Palisa WILLIAMS RUSHIN
10 VP Finance & Administration ... Ms. Lisa G. BELL
28 VP Multiculturalism & Inclusion ... Ms. Charlene WALKER
111 VP Advancement & Org Development ... Mr. Mark MANUEL
20 Dean Academics ... Dr. Karen MAYO
20 Dean Academics ... Ms. Tammy LILES
103 Dean of Academics/Workforce Devel ... Ms. Pam HATCHER
121 Dean of Academic Support ... Dr. Rebecca SIMMS
06 Registrar ... Ms. Becky HARP-STEPHENS
37 Financial Aid Director ... Ms. Runan PENDERGRAST
07 Admissions Director ... Ms. Shelbie HUGLE
110 Associate VP Institutional Develop ... Ms. Deborrah L. CATLETT
26 PR and Marketing Coordinator ... Ms. Jennifer TYSON
44 Assoc Vice Pres for Advancement ... Ms. Laurel MARTIN
79 Assistant Dean Humanities ... Ms. Angella KING
76 Asst Dean Allied Health/Nat Science ... Dr. Yasemin CONGLETON
66 Assistant Dean Nursing ... Ms. Tammy LILES
81 Asst Dean Mathematics/Statistics ... Ms. Jackie WISEMAN
77 Asst Dean Business/CIS ... Dr. Steven WHITE
72 Asst Dean Advanced Mfg and Trade ... Mr. Ralph POTTER
83 Asst Dean Comm/Hist/Lang/Social Sci ... Ms. Vicki WILSON
08 Director Learning Resources Center ... Mr. Robert CAMPBELL
51 Director Adult Education ... Mr. David STURGILL
106 Assistant Dean Distance Learning ... Dr. Kevin DUNN
18 Director of Maintenance/Operations ... Mr. Michael BALL

*Elizabethtown Community and Technical College (H)

600 College Street Road, Elizabethtown KY 42701
County: Hardin FICE Identification: 001991
Unit ID: 156648
Telephone: (270) 769-2371 Carnegie Class: Assoc/HVT-Mix Trad/Non
FAX Number: (270) 769-0736 Calendar System: Semester
URL: www.elizabethtown.kctcs.edu
Established: 1963 Annual Undergrad Tuition & Fees (In-State): $3,936
Enrollment: 6,301 Coed
Affiliation or Control: State IRS Status: 501(c)3
Highest Offering: Associate Degree
Accreditation: SC, ADNUR, COARC, IFSAC, RAD

02 President ... Dr. Juston PATE
05 Provost/CAO ... Dr. Tiffany EVANS
32 Chief Student Affairs Officer ... Dr. Dale BUCKLES
11 Chief Operations ... Vacant
12 Campus Education Center Director ... Mr. Darrin POWELL
103 Dean of Workforce Development ... Dr. Thomas DAVENPORT
10 Dean of Business Affairs ... Vacant
20 Dean of Instruction/Prof Develop ... Vacant
15 Director of Human Resources ... Ms. Kris WOOD
06 Registrar ... Mr. Bryan SMITH
13 Director of Information Technology ... Mr. Chris LEE
37 Director of Financial Aid ... Mr. Michael BARLOW
30 Chief Development ... Vacant
26 Director of Public Relations ... Ms. Mary Jo KING
24 Learning Center Coordinator ... Ms. Pam HARPER
36 Counselor ... Ms. Sharon SPRATT
38 Counselor ... Ms. Suzanne DARLAND
40 Bookstore Manager ... Mr. Michael GESSNER
108 Director Inst Effectiveness ... Ms. Sarah EDWARDS
18 Maintenance/Operations Supervisor ... Mr. Charles COBB
57 Chair Div of Arts/Humanities ... Ms. Jacqueline HAWKINS
81 Chair Div of Biological Science ... Ms. Tiffany MCFALLS-SMITH
81 Chair Div of Physical Science ... Dr. Shawn KELLIE
75 Chair Div Occupational Technology ... Mr. Mike HAZZARD
83 Chair Div Social & Behavioral Sci ... Ms. Ramona BARROW
28 Director of Diversity ... Ms. Felicia TOLIVER
109 Campus Administrative Coordinator ... Dr. David DONATHAN

*Gateway Community and Technical College (I)

500 Technology Way, Florence KY 41042
County: Boone FICE Identification: 005273
Unit ID: 157438
Telephone: (859) 441-4500 Carnegie Class: Assoc/HVT-Mix Trad/Non
FAX Number: (859) 341-6859 Calendar System: Semester
URL: www.gateway.kctcs.edu
Established: 1961 Annual Undergrad Tuition & Fees (In-State): $4,016
Enrollment: 4,581 Coed
Affiliation or Control: State IRS Status: 501(c)3
Highest Offering: Associate Degree
Accreditation: SC, CAHIIM, EMT, IFSAC

02 President/CEO ... Dr. Fernando FIGUEROA
04 Executive Assistant to President ... Ms. Jane FRANTZ
05 VP Academic Affairs ... Dr. Teri VONHANDORF
49 Dean of Arts and Sciences ... Dr. Susan SANTOS
50 Dean of Business/IT/Prof Services ... Dr. Amy CARRINO
76 Dean of Health Professions ... Ms. Amber CARTER
72 Dean of Manufacturing & Engineering ... Mr. Dee WRIGHT
75 Dean of Transportation Technologies ... Mr. Sam COLLIER
30 VP Devel & Strategic Partnerships ... Dr. Amber DECKER
32 VP Student Development ... Ms. Ingrid WASHINGTON
35 Associate VP for Student Dev ... Ms. Mallis GRAVES
20 Associate VP Academic Services ... Mr. Doug PENIX
38 Director of Counseling ... Ms. Tiffany MINARD
10 VP Admin & Business Affairs ... Mr. James YOUNGER
84 Dean of Enrollment Services ... Mr. Andre WASHINGTON
06 Registrar ... Mr. Andre WASHINGTON
15 Director of Human Resources ... Ms. Phyllis YEAGER
18 Director Maintenance & Operations ... Mr. George HALL
19 Director Security/Safety ... Mr. Tim CHESSER
26 Director of Communications ... Ms. Michelle SJOGREN
37 Director of Financial Aid ... Ms. Zana SMITH
13 Director of Information Services ... Ms. Melissa SEARS
66 Director of Nursing ... Ms. Melani STALLKAMP
89 Director Early College Initiatives ... Ms. Shelby KRENTZ
08 Director Library/Information Svcs ... Ms. Denise FRITSCH
25 Director of Grants/Special Projects ... Ms. Sandy ORTMAN-TOMLIN
27 Creative Strategies Coordinator ... Mr. Patrick LAMPING

*Hazard Community and Technical College (J)

One Community College Drive, Hazard KY 41701-2402
County: Perry FICE Identification: 006962
Unit ID: 156790
Telephone: (606) 436-5721 Carnegie Class: Assoc/HVT-High Trad
FAX Number: (606) 439-2988 Calendar System: Semester
URL: www.hazard.kctcs.edu

Established: 1968 Annual Undergrad Tuition & Fees (In-State): $3,936
Enrollment: 3,238 Coed
Affiliation or Control: State IRS Status: 501(c)3
Highest Offering: Associate Degree
Accreditation: SC, CAHIIM, DMS, IFSAC, PTAA, RAD, SURGT

02 President/CEO Dr. Jennifer LINDON
05 Int Provost/Vice Pres of Acad Svcs Ms. Germaine SHAFFER
32 Vice President of Student Affairs Ms. Germaine SHAFFER
10 Chief Financial Officer Ms. Connie WATTS
04 Asst to President Special Projects Ms. Delcie COMBS
13 Chief Information Officer Ms. Donna ROARK
15 Senior Director of Human Resources Ms. Vickie COMBS
21 Dean of Business Services Ms. Jackie HALL
08 Director Library Services Mrs. Cathy BRANSON
97 Dean General Education Ms. Leila SMITH
75 Dean Occupational Technologies Mr. Tony BACK
76 Dean Allied Health Science Tech Ms. Anna NAPIER
56 Dean Distance Learning Ms. Ella STRONG
26 Director of Public Relations Mrs. Evelyn WOOD
37 Director of Financial Aid Mr. Charles ANDERSON, JR.
06 Registrar Ms. Libby PETERS
07 Director of Admissions Mr. Scott GROSS
108 Dir of Effect/Planning & Research Ms. Alexis MALEPEAI
18 Dir of Maintenance and Operations Mr. Stu FUGATE

*Henderson Community College (A)

2660 S Green Street, Henderson KY 42420-4699
County: Henderson FICE Identification: 001993
Unit ID: 156851
Telephone: (270) 827-1867 Carnegie Class: Assoc/MT-VT-High Non
FAX Number: (270) 831-9600 Calendar System: Semester
URL: www.henderson.kctcs.edu
Established: 1960 Annual Undergrad Tuition & Fees (In-State): $3,936
Enrollment: 1,561 Coed
Affiliation or Control: State IRS Status: 501(c)3
Highest Offering: Associate Degree
Accreditation: SC, ADNUR, DH, MAC, MLTAD

02 President Dr. Kris WILLIAMS
05 Chief Academic Officer Dr. Reneau WAGGONER
32 Chief Student Officer Mr. Keith SAYLES
10 Chief Business Officer Ms. Christina STINSON
08 Library Director Mr. Mike W. KNECHT
13 IT Coordinator Mr. Joe HEERDINK
15 Director of Human Resources Ms. Doris J. LAKE
57 Director of Preston Arts Center Vacant
06 Registrar Mr. Chad PHILLIPS
66 Director of Nursing Dr. Lori DONAHOO
88 Dean Success Grants Ms. Pamala P. WILSON
28 Director of Cultural Diversity Mr. William DIXON
30 Chief Advancement Officer Ms. Jennifer PRESTON
09 Dir Institutional Research & Effect Mr. Brian MCMURTRY
18 Maintenance/Oper Supervisor Mr. Lance CONYERS
36 Career Services Coordinator Ms. Angela WATSON
37 Director Financial Aid Mr. Andrew ZELLERS
84 Assoc Dean for Enrollment Mgmt Mr. Cary CONLEY
49 Div Chair Liberal Arts/Prof Studies Ms. Sharon BURTON
76 Div Chair Allied Health Dr. Carole MATTINGLY
81 Div Chair STEM Mr. Eugene PATSALIDES
04 Administrative Asst to President Ms. Malinda S. HUDSON
103 Dir Community/Workforce/Econ Dev Dr. Anne MATTHEW

*Hopkinsville Community College (B)

720 North Drive, PO Box 2100,
Hopkinsville KY 42241-2100
County: Christian FICE Identification: 001994
Unit ID: 156860
Telephone: (270) 707-3700 Carnegie Class: Assoc/MT-VT-High Trad
FAX Number: (270) 886-0237 Calendar System: Semester
URL: www.hopkinsville.kctcs.edu
Established: 1965 Annual Undergrad Tuition & Fees (In-State): $3,936
Enrollment: 3,120 Coed
Affiliation or Control: State IRS Status: 501(c)3
Highest Offering: Associate Degree
Accreditation: SC, ADNUR

02 President Dr. Alissa YOUNG
04 Exec Admin Asst to President Ms. Janice JONES
05 Int Chief Academic Affairs Officer Mr. James HUNTER
06 Registrar Ms. Tiffanie WITT
08 Director Library Services Ms. Ann NICHOLS
09 Dir Institutional Effectiveness Mr. James HUNTER
10 Chief Business Affairs Officer Mr. Jeff HORTON
12 Director Fort Campbell Campus Ms. Allisha LEE
13 Director Information Technology Mr. Tony NELSON
15 Director Human Resources Ms. Yvonne GLASMAN
18 Director Maintenance/Operations Mr. Dan HAMBY
19 Safety and Security Director Vacant
21 Associate Dean Business Affairs Ms. Ann T. HOLLAND
26 Director Marketing & Communication Ms. Rena YOUNG
28 Cultural Diversity Director Ms. Deloria SCOTT
30 Chief Institutional Advancement Ofc Ms. Yvette EASTHAM
32 Chief Student Affairs Officer Dr. Jason D. WARREN
36 Coordinator Career Services Ms. Kanya ALLEN
37 Director Financial Aid Ms. Janet GUNTHER
38 Advising Center Director Ms. Deloria SCOTT
40 Bookstore Director Ms. Diane CUNNINGHAM
57 Arts and Sciences Division Chair Dr. Ken CASEY
72 Professional & Technical Studies Mr. Gregory BRIDGEMAN

76 Allied Health Div Chair Ms. Peggy I. BOZARTH
81 Mathematics & Sciences Div Chair Mr. Ted H. WILSON
103 Chief Cmty/Workforce/Economic Dev Ms. Carol KIRVES

*Jefferson Community and Technical College (C)

109 E Broadway, Louisville KY 40202-2000
County: Jefferson FICE Identification: 006961
Unit ID: 156921
Telephone: (502) 213-5333 Carnegie Class: Assoc/HVT-High Trad
FAX Number: (502) 213-2115 Calendar System: Semester
URL: www.jefferson.kctcs.edu
Established: 1967 Annual Undergrad Tuition & Fees (In-State): $4,016
Enrollment: 12,138 Coed
Affiliation or Control: State IRS Status: 501(c)3
Highest Offering: Associate Degree
Accreditation: SC, ACFEI, ADNUR, CAHIIM, COARC, IFSAC, MAC, MLTAD, OTA, PTAA, RAD, SURGT

02 President Dr. Ty J. HANDY
05 VP of Academic & Student Affairs Dr. Diane CALHOUN-FRENCH
10 VP of Administration and CFO Mr. Gary DRYDEN
45 VP of College Advancement/Planning Mr. Don SCHIEMAN
21 Controller Ms. Norma NORTHERN
20 Dean Academic Affs Tech Pgms Dr. Telly SELLARS
97 Dean of General Education/Transfer Dr. Randy DAVIS
12 Coordinator Shelby Campus Ms. Maia LANGLEY
32 Dean Student Affairs/Enrollment Mgm Dr. Laura SMITH
08 Library Services Director Ms. Sheree WILLIAMS
13 Chief Information Technology Office Mr. Thomas ROGERS
09 Institutional Effectiveness Dr. Jo ZAUSCH
06 Registrar Ms. Amanda TINDALL
26 Public Relations/Marketing Mr. Ben JACKEY
15 Director of Human Resources Ms. Toni WHALEN
18 Facilities Director Mr. Craig TURPIN
37 Director of Financial Aid Ms. Angela JOHNSON
30 Inst Advance/Development Coord Ms. Karla HALL
103 VP Workforce Sol CE/CS/Bus/Industry Vacant
38 Student Counseling Ms. Rhonda GUMMER
96 Director of Purchasing Ms. Pamela DUMM
12 Director of Carrollton Campus Ms. Susan CARLISLE
12 Dean of Extended Campuses/Academic Ms. Donna MILLER
24 Learning Commons Ms. Hillary SORTOR
04 Administrative Asst to President Ms. Teresa B. HARPER
106 Dir Online Education/E-learning Dr. Claver HATEGEKIMANA
25 Chief Contracts/Grants Admin Ms. Joanna LYNCH
19 Int Chief Campus Safety/Security Mr. Gary DRYDEN

*Madisonville Community College (D)

2000 College Drive, Madisonville KY 42431-9199
County: Hopkins FICE Identification: 009010
Unit ID: 157304
Telephone: (270) 821-2250 Carnegie Class: Assoc/HVT-High Non
FAX Number: (270) 824-1866 Calendar System: Semester
URL: www.madisonville.kctcs.edu
Established: 1968 Annual Undergrad Tuition & Fees (In-State): $3,936
Enrollment: 4,261 Coed
Affiliation or Control: State IRS Status: 501(c)3
Highest Offering: Associate Degree
Accreditation: SC, ADNUR, COARC, EMT, IFSAC, MLTAD, OTA, PTAA, RAD, SURGA, SURGT

02 President Dr. Cynthia S. KELLEY
05 Provost Vacant
10 Chief Business Affairs Officer Mr. Ray GILLASPIE
11 Vice Pres Quality Assurance & Admin Dr. Jay PARRENT
32 Dean of Student Affairs Ms. Cathy A. VAUGHAN
72 Division Chair Applied Technology Mr. Matt LUCKETT
66 Div Chr Nursing/Related Tech Ms. Shannon ALLEN
79 Div Chr Humanities/Related Tech Dr. Mary B. WERNER
83 Div Chr Social Science/Related Tech Ms. Natalie F. COOPER
81 Div Chr Mathematics and Sciences Dr. John D. LOWBRIDGE
76 Div Chr Allied Health/Related Tech Ms. Stephanie A. TAYLOR
08 Director of Library Services Ms. Cherry L. BERGES
06 Registrar Ms. Tiffanie WITT
15 Director of Human Resources Ms. May F. WRIGHT
36 Director of Counseling Services Ms. Cathy A. VAUGHAN
111 Director of Advancement Mr. Chris WOODALL
37 Director of Financial Aid Ms. Martha PHELPS
26 Public Relations Director Ms. Joyce RIGGS
56 Extended Campus Director Ms. Betsy ALLEN
25 Dir Grants/Planning & Effectiveness Mr. David A. SCHUERMER
28 Director of Cultural Diversity Mr. James H. BOWLES
103 Director Workforce Solutions Mr. Mike DAVENPORT
20 Dean of Academic Affairs Ms. Lisa A. HOWERTON
21 Dean of Business Affairs Mr. Michael L. JOHNSON
40 Bookstore Manager Ms. Sonya L. PARKER
84 Dean of Enrollment Management Ms. Aimee J. WILKERSON

*Maysville Community and Technical College (E)

1755 US Highway 68, Maysville KY 41056-8910
County: Mason FICE Identification: 006960
Unit ID: 157331
Telephone: (606) 759-7141 Carnegie Class: Assoc/HVT-High Non
FAX Number: (606) 759-7176 Calendar System: Semester
URL: www.maysville.kctcs.edu
Established: 1968 Annual Undergrad Tuition & Fees (In-State): $3,936
Enrollment: 3,158 Coed
Affiliation or Control: State IRS Status: 501(c)3

Highest Offering: Associate Degree
Accreditation: SC, COARC, IFSAC, MAC, NAIT

02 President Dr. Stephen VACIK
05 Provost Dr. Thomas WARE
10 Chief Finance Officer Ms. Barbara CAMPBELL
84 Chief Ofcr Enrollment/Student Svc Ms. Jessica KERN
20 Assoc Dean Academic Support Svc Dr. Dana CALLAND
09 Assoc Dean Institutional Rsch/Plng Ms. Pam STAFFORD
08 Director Library Services Ms. Sonja EADS
13 Director Information Technology Mr. Brett CABLE
30 Dir Resource Development/Foundation Ms. Cara CLARKE
37 Director Financial Aid Ms. Sandy POWER
06 Registrar Ms. Lori GAUNCE
28 Director of Diversity Ms. Millicent HARDING
15 Director of Human Resources Ms. Sandi L. ESTILL
106 Coordinator Distance Learning Ms. Kim SPARKS
50 Div Chr Business/Info Technologies Ms. Natasha MADDOX
49 Div Chair Liberal Arts/Education Ms. Kathleen MELLENKAMP
81 Div Chair Math/Science/Agriculture Dr. Angela FULTZ
76 Division Chair of Health Sciences Ms. Deborah NOLDER
72 Division Chair Industrial Tech Mr. Tony WALLACE

*Owensboro Community and Technical College (F)

4800 New Hartford Road, Owensboro KY 42303-1899
County: Daviess FICE Identification: 030345
Unit ID: 247940
Telephone: (270) 686-4400 Carnegie Class: Assoc/HVT-Mix Trad/Non
FAX Number: (270) 686-4496 Calendar System: Semester
URL: www.octc.kctcs.edu
Established: 1986 Annual Undergrad Tuition & Fees (In-State): $3,936
Enrollment: 3,974 Coed
Affiliation or Control: State IRS Status: 501(c)3
Highest Offering: Associate Degree
Accreditation: SC, ACBSP, EMT, IFSAC, RAD, SURGT

02 President Dr. Scott WILLIAMS
04 Assistant to the President Ms. Kittridge MIDKIFF
05 Interim VP of Academic Affairs Mr. Mike RODGERS
32 VP of Student Affairs Mr. Kevin BEARDMORE
10 VP of Business Affairs Ms. Sarah PRICE
13 VP Information Technology Mr. James HARTZ
103 VP Workforce Solutions Ms. Cynthia FIORELLA
08 Library Services Director Ms. Donna ABELL
06 Registrar Ms. Christy ELLIS
15 Director of Human Resources Ms. Victoria HOHIEMER
37 Financial Aid Director Dr. Andrea BORREGARD
111 Int Dir Institutional Advancement Mr. Michael RODGERS
26 Director of Public Relations Ms. Bernadette TOYE-HALE
28 Director of Diversity Mr. Lewatis MCNEAL
38 Director Student Counseling Ms. Barbara TIPMORE
84 Director Enrollment Management Mr. Kevin BEARDMORE
96 Director of Purchasing Ms. Sarah PRICE
40 Bookstore Manager Ms. Sonya SOUTHARD
88 TV Production Manager Mr. John BRYENTON
07 Senior Admissions Advisor Ms. Linda CALHOUN
36 Career Resource/Placemnt Ctr Coord Ms. Katie BALLARD
79 Associate Dean Humanities Dr. Julia LEDFORD
49 Int Academic Dean Arts & Sciences Dr. Marc MALTBY
81 Assoc Dean Math/Science/Social Sci Dr. Veena SALLAN
75 Assoc Dean Prof/Tech Studies Mr. Dean AUTRY
66 Associate Dean Nursing Ms. Terri LANHAM
20 Interim Dean Acad Affs Prof/Tech Dr. Stacy EDDS-ELLIS
09 Coord Institutional Effectiveness Ms. Joy BOWLDS
19 Director Security/Safety Mr. Jeff HENDRICKS

*Somerset Community College (G)

808 Monticello Street, Somerset KY 42501-2973
County: Pulaski FICE Identification: 001997
Unit ID: 157711
Telephone: (877) 629-9722 Carnegie Class: Assoc/HVT-High Trad
FAX Number: N/A Calendar System: Semester
URL: somerset.kctcs.edu
Established: 1965 Annual Undergrad Tuition & Fees (In-State): $3,936
Enrollment: 6,386 Coed
Affiliation or Control: State IRS Status: 501(c)3
Highest Offering: Associate Degree
Accreditation: SC, ADNUR, COARC, EMT, IFSAC, MLTAD, PTAA, RAD, SURGT

02 President/CEO Dr. Jo MARSHALL
05 Provost Dr. Tony L. HONEYCUTT
10 Chief Business Affairs Officer Ms. Jill MEECE
11 Chief Operations Officer Mr. Larry ABBOTT
49 Dean of Arts and Sciences Vacant
76 Dean for Health Sciences Ms. Nancy L. POWELL
88 Dean of Applied Technology Mr. Roger L. ANGEVINE
09 Dir of Institutional Effectiveness Dr. Clint HAYES
32 Chief Student Affairs Officer Ms. Tracy L. CASADA
106 Assoc Dean for Distance Education Ms. Linda D. BOURNE
103 Chief Cmty Wkfc & Economic Dev Ofc Ms. Alesa JOHNSON
30 Chief Inst Advancement Officer Ms. Cindy D. CLOUSE
79 Assoc Dean Humanities/Fine Arts/SS Mr. Jon BURLEW
81 Assoc Dean Math/Natural Science Dr. Elaine KOHRMAN
88 Assoc Dean Career/Technical Mr. Daniel C. BURNETT
50 Assoc Dean Bus/IT/Crim Just/Ed/ Cons Ms. Lois A. MCWHORTER
121 Dean Academic Support Services Mr. Bruce GOVER
20 Assoc Dean for Learning Vacant
37 Director of Financial Aid Mr. Patrick MAYER

06 Registrar ..... Ms. Paula J. LATHAM
15 Director of Human Resources ..... Ms. Jill N. MEECE
26 Director of Public Relations ..... Ms. Cindy D. CLOUSE
28 Director of Cultural Diversity ..... Ms. Elaine WILSON
12 Director of McCreary Center ..... Mr. Steve HAMMONS
12 Director of Clinton Center ..... Ms. Judy TALLENT
12 Director of Casey Center ..... Ms. Judy SAPP
12 Director of Russell Center ..... Ms. Winfrey BATES

*Southcentral Kentucky Community and Technical College (A)

1845 Loop Drive, Bowling Green KY 42101-9202
County: Warren FICE Identification: 005271
Unit ID: 156338
Telephone: (270) 901-1000 Carnegie Class: Assoc/HVT-Mix Trad/Non
FAX Number: (270) 901-1145 Calendar System: Semester
URL: www.bowlinggreen.kctcs.edu
Established: 1939 Annual Undergrad Tuition & Fees (In-State): $3,936
Enrollment: 3,962 Coed
Affiliation or Control: State IRS Status: 501(c)3
Highest Offering: Associate Degree
Accreditation: SC, COARC, DMS, IFSAC, RAD, SURGT

02 President & CEO ..... Dr. Phillip W. NEAL
05 Provost ..... Dr. Maggie SHELTON
32 Int VP Student/Organization Success ..... Ms. Brooke JUSTICE
10 Vice President Finance/Admin ..... Mr. Chris CUMENS
31 Int Vice Pres Outreach/Cmty Dev ..... Dr. James B. MCCASLIN
06 Registrar ..... Ms. Amy CANNON
15 Director of Human Resources ..... Ms. Sherri L. FORESTER
26 Director of Public Relations ..... Mr. Mark D. BROOKS
111 Director of Inst Advancement ..... Ms. Heather ROGERS
37 Director of Financial Aid ..... Ms. Jennifer WELLS
09 Director Institution Effectiveness ..... Mr. Mark GARRETT

*Southeast Kentucky Community and Technical College (B)

700 College Road, Cumberland KY 40823-1099
County: Harlan FICE Identification: 001998
Unit ID: 157739
Telephone: (606) 589-2145 Carnegie Class: Assoc/HVT-High Non
FAX Number: (606) 589-3175 Calendar System: Semester
URL: www.southeast.kctcs.edu
Established: 1960 Annual Undergrad Tuition & Fees (In-State): $3,936
Enrollment: 3,111 Coed
Affiliation or Control: State IRS Status: 501(c)3
Highest Offering: Associate Degree
Accreditation: SC, ADNUR, COARC, MLTAD, PTAA, SURGT

02 President ..... Dr. Vic ADAMS
05 Chief Academic Officer ..... Dr. Joel MICHAELIS
111 Chief Inst Advancement Officer ..... Ms. Michelle DYKES-ANDERSON
10 Chief Business Affairs Officer ..... Ms. Angela SIMPSON
15 Director Human Resources ..... Ms. Billie FRANKS
08 Head Librarian ..... Ms. Lynn COX
13 Director of Information Technology ..... Mr. Merrill GALLOWAY
28 Director of Diversity ..... Ms. Carolyn SUNDY
32 Chief Student Affairs Officer ..... Dr. Rebecca PARROTT
07 Director of Admissions ..... Ms. Felicia CARROLL
37 Coordinator Financial Aid ..... Ms. Charlotte LOCKABY
04 Administrative Asst to President ..... Mr. Paul BRYANT
06 Registrar ..... Ms. Anita BARNHILL
09 Director of Institutional Research ..... Dr. Rick MASON
103 Dir Workforce/Career Development ..... Ms. Sherri CLARK
18 Chief Facilities/Physical Plant ..... Mr. Lige BUELL
26 Chief Public Relations/Marketing ..... Ms. Amelia SIMPSON

*West Kentucky Community and Technical College (C)

4810 Alben Barkley Drive, Paducah KY 42002-7380
County: McCracken FICE Identification: 001979
Unit ID: 157483
Telephone: (270) 554-9200 Carnegie Class: Assoc/HVT-Mix Trad/Non
FAX Number: (270) 554-6217 Calendar System: Semester
URL: www.westkentucky.kctcs.edu
Established: 1909 Annual Undergrad Tuition & Fees (In-State): $3,936
Enrollment: 5,980 Coed
Affiliation or Control: State IRS Status: 501(c)3
Highest Offering: Associate Degree
Accreditation: SC, ACBSP, ACFEI, ADNUR, DA, DMS, IFSAC, MLTAD, PNUR, PTAA, RAD, SURGT

02 President ..... Dr. Anton REECE
103 VP of Workforce Solutions ..... Mr. Kevin O'NEILL
05 VP of Academic Affairs ..... Dr. David HEFLIN
32 VP of Student Development ..... Dr. Belinda DALTON-RUSSELL
11 VP of Administrative Services ..... Vacant
10 VP Business Affairs ..... Ms. Susan GRAVES
111 VP Institutional Advancement ..... Ms. Lee EMMONS
84 VP of Enrollment ..... Mr. Nate SLATON
08 Interim Library Services Director ..... Ms. Amy SULLIVAN
37 Financial Aid Director ..... Ms. Angel RHODES
26 Public Relations Director ..... Ms. Janett BLYTHE
13 Director Information Technology ..... Ms. Ruby RODGERS
15 Director Human Resources ..... Ms. Bridget CANTER
40 Bookstore Manager ..... Mr. Todd MITCHELL
06 Registrar/Dir of Admissions ..... Ms. Jess PUFFENBARGER
35 Student Activities Coordinator ..... Ms. Amy ELMORE
79 Dean Humanities/Fine Arts/Soc Sci ..... Mr. Britton SHURLEY
66 Dean Nursing Division ..... Ms. Shari GHOLSON
50 Dean Business/Comp Related Tech Div ..... Ms. Tammy POTTER
76 Dean Allied Health Division ..... Ms. Carrie HOPPER
75 Dean Applied Tech Division ..... Ms. Stephanie MILLIKEN
81 Dean Science & Math Division ..... Dr. Karen HLINKA
09 Associate VP of IE ..... Dr. Renea AKIN
04 Administrative Asst to President ..... Ms. Barbara MAXEY
19 Director Security/Safety ..... Mr. David WALLACE
28 Director of Diversity ..... Ms. Chevene DUNCAN-HERRING

Kentucky Mountain Bible College (D)

855 Highway 541, Jackson KY 41339
County: Breathitt FICE Identification: 030021
Unit ID: 157030
Telephone: (606) 693-5000 Carnegie Class: Spec-4-yr-Faith
FAX Number: (888) 742-1124 Calendar System: Semester
URL: www.kmbc.edu
Established: 1931 Annual Undergrad Tuition & Fees: $7,610
Enrollment: 68 Coed
Affiliation or Control: Interdenominational IRS Status: 501(c)3
Highest Offering: Baccalaureate
Accreditation: BI

01 President ..... Dr. Philip E. SPEAS
05 Academic Dean/Exec Vice Pres ..... Rev. Thomas H. LORIMER
10 Chief Business Manager/CIO ..... Mr. Steve A. LORIMER
32 Dean of Student Affairs ..... Mr. Jim NELSON
08 Head Librarian ..... Ms. Patricia A. BOWEN
06 Registrar ..... Dr. Richard E. ENGLEHARDT
07 Chief Admissions Counselor ..... Mr. David W. LORIMER
37 Director Student Financial Aid ..... Mrs. Adelle SEMROW
32 Dean of Students ..... Mr. James H. NELSON
18 Chief Facilities/Physical Plant ..... Mr. Jonathan MATHES
20 Associate Academic Officer ..... Mrs. Sara BAGBY
29 Director of Alumni Relations ..... Ms. Donna WOODRING
106 Dir Online Education/E-learning ..... Mr. Jason GOBEN
88 Title 9 Coordinator ..... Mr. Robert ENGLAND
108 Director Institutional Assessment ..... Mr. Zane DARLAND
96 Director of Purchasing ..... Mr. David BOLERATZ

Kentucky State University (E)

400 E Main Street, Frankfort KY 40601-2355
County: Franklin FICE Identification: 001968
Unit ID: 157058
Telephone: (502) 597-6000 Carnegie Class: Bac-Diverse
FAX Number: (502) 597-6490 Calendar System: Semester
URL: www.kysu.edu
Established: 1886 Annual Undergrad Tuition & Fees (In-State): $7,754
Enrollment: 1,586 Coed
Affiliation or Control: State IRS Status: 501(c)3
Highest Offering: Doctorate
Accreditation: SC, ACBSP, ADNUR, CAEPN, MUS, NUR, SPAA, SW

01 President ..... Dr. M. Christopher BROWN, II
10 Sr VP of Finance & Administration ..... Mr. Kevin APPLETON
05 Provost & VP of Academic Affairs ..... Dr. Debbie G. THOMAS
32 VP Student Engagement & Campus Life ..... Dr. Thomas J. CALHOUN
84 VP Enrollment Mgmt & Brand Identity ..... Ms. Clara R. ROSS STAMPS
26 VP External Relations & Development ..... Mr. Rickey W. SMITH
43 General Counsel ..... Mr. Gordon A. ROWE
20 Associate VP Academic Affairs ..... Dr. Deneia M. THOMAS
13 Chief Information Officer ..... Ms. Wendy D. DIXIE
116 Internal Auditor ..... Mr. Ingram L. QUICK
20 Assistant VP Acad Support Svcs ..... Dr. Erin R. WHEELER
35 Assistant VP Student Affairs ..... Mr. Christopher D. CRIBBS
18 Capital Project Sr Manager ..... Mr. Joseph W. GRONEFELD
65 Director Land Grant ..... Dr. Kirk W. POMPER
47 Chair Div of Aquaculture ..... Dr. James H. TIDWELL
50 Chair School of Business ..... Dr. Abdul M. TURAY
57 Chair Fine Arts ..... Dr. Roosevelt O. SHELTON
81 Chair Math & Science ..... Dr. Fariba BIGDELI JAHED
77 Chair Computer Science ..... Dr. Chi SHEN
107 Chair Professional Studies ..... Dr. Jo Anne RAINEY
88 Chair Literature/Language/Phil ..... Mr. David SHABAZZ
92 Chair Honors ..... Dr. Cynthia L. SHELTON
25 Director Grants Sponsored Programs ..... Mr. Derrick C. GILMORE
58 Director Graduate Studies ..... Dr. James B. OBIELODAN
41 Director Athletics ..... Mr. William H. GRAHAM
15 Director Human Resource Svcs ..... Ms. Rayla L. SMOOT
04 Executive Asst to President ..... Ms. Sonia SANDERS
21 Director Accounting Services ..... Ms. Michelle D. SUTTON
06 Registrar ..... Ms. Marquiettia D. BIVENS
113 Int Coord Collection Manager ..... Ms. Natalie T. TURNER
114 Director Budget ..... Mr. Raymont GRIFFITH
08 Director Library ..... Ms. Sheila A. STUCKEY
121 Exec Dir for Student Success ..... Ms. Brittany S. MOTLEY
09 Dir Inst Research & Effectiveness ..... Ms. Yuliana SUSANTO
07 Director Admissions ..... Mr. Justin J. MATHIS
37 Director Financial Aid ..... Ms. Qiana M. HALL
96 Purchasing Manager ..... Ms. Alecia R. OLDHAM
29 Director Alumni Relations ..... Mr. Wendell C. THOMAS
106 Director Online Programs ..... Ms. Jennifer P. MILES
19 Chief of Police ..... Mr. Michael D. BRENNAMAN
39 Associate Dean Student Life ..... Ms. Monesca R. SMITH
88 Associate Dean Student Conduct ..... Mr. Daryl LOWE

Kentucky Wesleyan College (F)

3000 Frederica Street, Owensboro KY 42301
County: Daviess FICE Identification: 001969
Unit ID: 157076
Telephone: (270) 926-3111 Carnegie Class: Bac-Diverse
FAX Number: (270) 926-3112 Calendar System: Semester
URL: www.kwc.edu
Established: 1858 Annual Undergrad Tuition & Fees: $24,050
Enrollment: 693 Coed
Affiliation or Control: United Methodist IRS Status: 501(c)3
Highest Offering: Baccalaureate
Accreditation: SC, IACBE

01 President ..... Dr. Bart DARRELL
05 VP Acad Affairs/Dean of the College ..... Dr. Paula DEHN
10 Vice President of Finance ..... Ms. Cindra K. STIFF
32 VP of Exec Initiatives & Retention ..... Mr. Scott E. KRAMER
35 Assoc Dean of Student Services ..... Ms. Rebecca MCQUEEN
13 Dir Information Tech Services ..... Mr. Kevin PAYNE
111 Vice President for Advancement ..... Mr. Thomas W. KEITH
07 VP of Admissions and Financial Aid ..... Mr. Jeremy PITTMAN
06 Registrar ..... Ms. Lindsey CROWE
09 Dir of Institutional Effective/Rsch ..... Mr. Wesley WHISTLE
15 Director of Human Resources ..... Mrs. Linda B. KELLER
37 Director of Financial Aid ..... Ms. Crystal HAMILTON
89 Director of the PLUS Center ..... Vacant
08 Director of Library Learning Center . Mrs. Patricia G. MCFARLING
41 Director of Athletics ..... Mr. Rob MALLORY
21 Controller ..... Ms. Stephanie SNYDER
26 Director of Public Relations ..... Ms. Kathy RUTHERMAN
42 Director of Campus Ministries ..... Mr. Shawn TOMES
30 Dir Development/Donor Rels ..... Mr. M. Blake HARRISON
04 Assistant to President ..... Ms. Chanda F. PRATER
106 Assoc Dean/Dir Online Education ..... Mrs. Rebecca FRANCIS
36 Dir of Career Dev & Service Lrng ..... Ms. Margaret CAMBRON

Lexington Theological Seminary (G)

230 Lexington Green Circle, Ste 300, Lexington KY 40503
County: Fayette FICE Identification: 001971
Unit ID: 157207
Telephone: (859) 252-0361 Carnegie Class: Spec-4-yr-Faith
FAX Number: (859) 281-6042 Calendar System: Semester
URL: www.lextheo.edu
Established: 1865 Annual Graduate Tuition & Fees: N/A
Enrollment: 81 Coed
Affiliation or Control: Christian Church (Disciples Of Christ)
IRS Status: 501(c)3
Highest Offering: Doctorate; No Undergraduates
Accreditation: THEOL

01 President ..... Dr. Charisse L. GILLETT
05 VP Academic Affairs/Dean ..... Dr. Richard WEIS
111 Vice President for Advancement ..... Mr. Mark V. BLANKENSHIP
10 Chief Financial Officer ..... Mrs. Karen C. WAGERS
06 Registrar ..... Ms. Windy KIDD
08 Librarian ..... Ms. Dolores YILIBUW
13 Director Information Services ..... Mr. Ben WYATT
07 Director Admission ..... Rev. Erin CASH
15 Director Personnel Services ..... Ms. Karen C. WAGERS
18 Chief Facilities/Physical Plant ..... Ms. Karen C. WAGERS
29 Director Alumni Relations ..... Mr. Mark V. BLANKENSHIP
37 Director Student Financial Aid ..... Ms. Windy KIDD
96 Director of Purchasing ..... Ms. Robin VARNER

Lindsey Wilson College (H)

210 Lindsey Wilson Street, Columbia KY 42728-1298
County: Adair FICE Identification: 001972
Unit ID: 157216
Telephone: (270) 384-2126 Carnegie Class: Masters/L
FAX Number: (270) 384-8200 Calendar System: Semester
URL: www.lindsey.edu
Established: 1903 Annual Undergrad Tuition & Fees: $23,762
Enrollment: 2,651 Coed
Affiliation or Control: United Methodist IRS Status: 501(c)3
Highest Offering: Doctorate
Accreditation: SC, CACREP, CAEPN, IACBE, NURSE

01 President ..... Dr. William T. LUCKEY, JR.
00 Chancellor ..... Dr. John B. BEGLEY
05 Vice President Academic Affairs ..... Dr. Patricia PARRISH
10 Vice President Administration ..... Mr. Mark COLEMAN
111 Vice President Advancement ..... Mr. Kevin A. THOMPSON
04 Executive Assistant ..... Mrs. Amy THOMPSON-WELLS
32 Vice Pres Student Svcs/Enroll Mgmt ..... Dr. Dean ADAMS
37 VP Educ Outreach/Stdnt Finan Svcs ..... Mrs. Denise G. FUDGE
35 Dean of Students ..... Mr. Christopher SCHMIDT
88 Dean of Chapel ..... Dr. Terry W. SWAN
07 Dean of Admissions ..... Mrs. Traci M. POOLER
07 Director of Admissions ..... Mrs. Charity F. FERGUSON
55 Director of Evening College ..... Ms. Regina HAUGEN
41 Athletic Director ..... Mr. Willis POOLER, III
06 Registrar ..... Vacant
15 Director of Human Resources ..... Mrs. Karen F. WRIGHT
31 Dir of Civic Engagement & Std Ldrsp ..... Ms. Natalie VICKOUS
36 Director Career Services ..... Mrs. Laura BURWASH
08 Librarian ..... Mr. C. Phil HANNA
18 Director of Physical Plant ..... Mr. Michael L. NEWTON
109 Director of Auxiliary Services ..... Mr. Jeff WILLIS
40 Bookstore Manager ..... Mrs. Amy M. COOPER

35 Director of Student Activities .... Ms. Lafawn NETTLES
85 Dir International Student Programs .... Ms. Sabine EASTHAM
14 Director Information Services .... Mrs. Harriet B. GOLD
13 Director of Information Systems .... Mr. Anthony MOORE
26 Public Relations Officer .... Mrs. Venus POPPLEWELL
29 Assistant to Pres Alumni Affairs .... Mr. Randy BURNS
19 Director Safety/Security .... Mr. Michael STATEN
42 Chaplain .... Rev. Troy A. ELMORE
37 Director Student Financial Services .... Ms. Marilyn RADFORD
38 Director Student Counseling .... Dr. Jeff CRANE
66 Director of Nursing .... Vacant

Louisville Presbyterian Theological Seminary (A)

1044 Alta Vista Road, Louisville KY 40205-1798
County: Jefferson FICE Identification: 001974
Unit ID: 157298
Telephone: (502) 895-3411 Carnegie Class: Spec-4-yr-Faith
FAX Number: (502) 895-1096 Calendar System: 4/1/4
URL: www.lpts.edu
Established: 1853 Annual Graduate Tuition & Fees: N/A
Enrollment: 170 Coed
Affiliation or Control: Presbyterian Church (U.S.A.) IRS Status: 501(c)3
Highest Offering: Doctorate; No Undergraduates
Accreditation: SC, MFCD, THEOL

01 President .... Dr. Michael JINKINS
111 VP Institutional Advancement .... Ms. Sally PENDLETON
10 Vice President & CFO .... Mr. Patrick A. CECIL
05 Dean of the Seminary .... Dr. Susan R. GARRETT
32 Dean of Students .... Rev. Kilen GRAY
06 Registrar/OIRE .... Dr. Steve COOK
29 Director of Church Relations .... Ms. Sandra MOON
44 Director of Seminary Fund .... Ms. Erin HAMILTON
14 Director of Data Management .... Ms. Heather GRIFFIN
26 Director of Communications .... Mr. Chris WOOTON
08 Director of Library Services .... Dr. Matthew COLLINS
21 Controller .... Ms. Angela TRAYLOR
51 Director of DMin & Continuing Ed .... Vacant
07 Director of Recruitment & Admiss .... Ms. Emily MILLER
13 Director of IT Services .... Mr. Jack SHARER
18 Director of Facilities .... Mr. Tim WILLIAMS
04 Administrative Asst to President .... Ms. Susan A. DILUCA

Midway University (B)

512 E Stephens Street, Midway KY 40347-1120
County: Woodford FICE Identification: 001975
Unit ID: 157377
Telephone: (859) 846-4421 Carnegie Class: Masters/S
FAX Number: (859) 846-5349 Calendar System: Semester
URL: www.midway.edu
Established: 1847 Annual Undergrad Tuition & Fees: $23,350
Enrollment: 1,055 Coed
Affiliation or Control: Christian Church (Disciples Of Christ)
IRS Status: 501(c)3
Highest Offering: Master's
Accreditation: SC, ADNUR, NUR

01 President .... Dr. John P. MARSDEN
05 VP of Academic Affairs .... Dr. Mary E. STIVERS
04 Exec Assistant to the President .... Ms. Sheila K. HOLSCLAW
10 Vice President of Finance .... Mrs. Leah B. RICE
111 Vice President of Advancement .... Ms. Linda S. MEDLEY
84 VP of Enrollment Management .... Ms. Kelly S. GOSNELL
26 Vice Pres of Marketing & Comm .... Mrs. Ellen D. GREGORY
20 Associate VP Academic Affairs .... Vacant
32 Asst VP of Student Affairs .... Ms. Sarah G. MUDD
07 Exec Dir of Admissions and Prtnrshp .... Dr. Matthew B. COURTNEY
88 Dir of Admiss Data and Reporting .... Mrs. Jessica NEALEY
13 Chief Information Officer .... Dr. Salah SHAKIR
06 Registrar .... Ms. Susie POWERS
08 Director of Library Services .... Vacant
41 Athletic Director .... Mr. William "Rusty" KENNEDY, II
14 Technical Support Specialist .... Mr. Eric ASHCRAFT
15 Director of Human Resources .... Ms. Trish JONES
37 Director Student Financial Planning .... Mr. Justin CRISTELLO
18 Director of Facilities .... Mr. Greg HEIDEMAN
09 Director Compliance & Research .... Dr. Johnie DEAN
28 Dir Ofc of Multicultural & Int Affs .... Ms. Emily EVANS
50 Dean Business/Equine/Sport Stds .... Vacant
49 Dean School of Arts & Sciences .... Dr. Charles H. ROBERTS
76 Dean School of Health Sciences .... Dr. Barbara KITCHEN

Morehead State University (C)

150 University Boulevard, Morehead KY 40351-1689
County: Rowan FICE Identification: 001976
Unit ID: 157386
Telephone: (800) 585-6781 Carnegie Class: Masters/L
FAX Number: N/A Calendar System: Semester
URL: www.moreheadstate.edu
Established: 1887 Annual Undergrad Tuition & Fees (In-State): $8,496
Enrollment: 10,872 Coed
Affiliation or Control: State IRS Status: 501(c)3
Highest Offering: Doctorate
Accreditation: SC, ADNUR, ART, CAEPN, COARC, DMS, MUS, NAIT, NURSE, RAD, RADMAG, SPAA, SW, THEA

01 President .... Dr. Joseph A. MORGAN
05 Provost & VP Academic Affairs .... Dr. Steven M. RALSTON
10 Chief Financial Officer/VP AFS .... Ms. Beth G. PATRICK
32 Interim Vice Pres Student Success .... Mr. Russell F. MAST
111 Vice Pres for Univ Advancement .... Mr. James A. SHAW
20 Assoc VP UG Educ/Student Success .... Dr. Laurie L. COUCH
04 Assistant to the President .... Ms. Sharon S. REYNOLDS
06 Registrar .... Ms. Deborah ROSS
58 Assoc VP & Dean of Graduate School .... Dr. Michael C. HENSON
51 Asst VP Adult Educ & College Access .... Dr. Dan J. CONNELL
84 Asst Vice Pres Enrollment Services .... Mr. Tim RHODES
20 Asst VP Academic Affs/Inst Effectiv .... Ms. Jill C. RATLIFF
26 Asst VP Communication & Marketing .... Ms. Jami M. HORNBUCKLE
18 Asst VP Facilities Management .... Mr. Rick T. LINIO
109 Asst Vice Pres Auxiliary Services .... Mr. William REDWINE
29 Asst VP Alumni Relations & Develop .... Ms. Melinda C. HIGHLEY
13 Asst VP Technology .... Mr. Steve RICHMOND
35 AVP Student Life/Dean of Students .... Mr. Maxwell J. AMMONS
08 Dean of Library Services .... Dr. David L. GREGORY
07 Dir of Undergraduate Admissions .... Ms. Holly L. POLLOCK
09 Dir Inst Research & Analysis .... Dr. Jennifer S. TISON
15 Director of Human Resources .... Mr. Harold D. NALLY
19 Chief of Police .... Mr. Merrell J. HARRISON
21 Director Accounting/Financial Svcs .... Ms. Kelli D. OWEN
114 Exec Dir Budgets & Financial Plng .... Ms. Teresa C. LINDGREN
37 Director Financial Aid .... Ms. Denise M. TRUSTY
36 Director Career Services .... Ms. Julia L. HAWKINS
39 Director of Housing/Residence Educ .... Mr. Alan M. RUCKER
41 Director of Athletics .... Mr. Brian A. HUTCHINSON
43 General Counsel .... Dr. Jane FITZPATRICK
27 Media Relations Director .... Mr. Jason BLANTON
79 Director of DIIS .... Vacant
96 Director Procurement Services .... Ms. Ladonna M. PURCELL
38 Director of Counseling & Health Svc .... Dr. Shannon L. SMITH-STEPHENS
50 Dean Col of Business & Technology .... Dr. Robert ALBERT
53 Int Dean College of Education .... Dr. Chris MILLER
81 Dean College of Science .... Dr. Wayne C. MILLER
79 Interim Dean Arts/Hum/Soc Sciences .... Dr. John P. ERNST
105 Web Director .... Ms. April H. NUTTER
106 Interim Director Dist Educ & Instr .... Mr. David FLORA
108 Director Univ Assessment & Testing .... Dr. Shannon L. HARR
28 Chief Diversity Officer .... Mr. Charles HOLLOWAY

Murray State University (D)

218 Wells Hall, Murray KY 42071-3318
County: Calloway FICE Identification: 001977
Unit ID: 157401
Telephone: (270) 809-3011 Carnegie Class: Masters/L
FAX Number: (270) 809-3413 Calendar System: Semester
URL: www.murraystate.edu
Established: 1922 Annual Undergrad Tuition & Fees (In-State): $8,400
Enrollment: 10,998 Coed
Affiliation or Control: State IRS Status: 501(c)3
Highest Offering: Doctorate
Accreditation: SC, ANEST, ART, #CAATE, CACREP, CAEP, DIETD, DIETI, ENG, ENGR, ENGT, EXSC, JOUR, MUS, NURSE, SP, SW, THEA

01 President .... Dr. Robert O. DAVIES
101 Sr Exec Coord for Pres/Coord Bd Rel .... Ms. Jill HUNT
05 Provost/VP Academic Affairs .... Dr. Mark ARANT
10 VP Finance & Admin Svcs .... Ms. Jacklyn K. DUDLEY
32 VP Student Affairs .... Dr. Don E. ROBERTSON
30 VP Marketing & Outreach .... Dr. Adrienne KING
20 Assoc Provost Grad Educ & Research .... Dr. Robert PERVINE
20 Assoc Provost Undergrad Education .... Dr. Renae D. DUNCAN
35 Interim Assoc VP Student Affairs .... Mr. Michael E. YOUNG
26 Communications Director .... Mr. Shawn TOUNEY
43 General Counsel .... Mr. John P. RALL
50 Dean College of Business .... Dr. Timothy TODD
53 Dean Col of Education & Human Svcs .... Dr. David WHALEY
79 Dean Col Humanities & Arts .... Mr. David BALTHROP
81 Dean Col Science/Engineering & Tech .... Dr. Stephen H. COBB
47 Dean Hutson School of Agriculture .... Dr. Tony L. BRANNON
66 Dean School Nursing & Health Profes .... Dr. Marcia B. HOBBS
08 Dean University Libraries .... Ms. Ashley IRELAND
51 Associate Provost .... Dr. Brian W. VAN HORN
106 Interim Dean RAO .... Mr. Daniel A. LAVIT
97 Coordinator University Studies .... Vacant
92 Exec Dir Honors College .... Dr. Warren EDMINSTER
85 Assist VP Inst Internat Studies .... Dr. Guangming ZOU
104 Director Education Abroad .... Ms. Melanie C. MCCALLON
84 Assoc VP Enrollment Mgmt .... Mr. Fred K. DIETZ
07 Dir Undergrad Admin/Transf Ctr .... Ms. Maria ROSA
06 Registrar .... Ms. Tracy ROBERTS
37 Dir Student Financial Aid .... Vacant
39 Director Housing .... Dr. J. David WILSON
38 Dir University Counseling Services .... Dr. Angie TRZEPACZ
28 Dir Multicultural Affairs .... Mr. Sidney G. CARTHELL
36 Director Career Services .... Mr. Matt PURDY
23 Director Health Services .... Ms. Kimberly S. PASCHALL
96 Interim Dir Procurement Services .... Ms. Beth WARD
22 Ex Dir Inst Diversity/Equity/Access .... Ms. Camisha DUFFY
13 Chief Information Officer .... Mr. Keith WEBER
91 Dir Enterprise Application Services .... Mr. Brantly D. TRAVIS
90 Asst Dir Acad App Solutions .... Mr. Peter TERRY
09 Dir Institutional Effectiveness .... Dr. Kelley C. WEZNER
41 Athletic Director .... Mr. C. Allen WARD
18 Interim Chief Facilities Officer .... Mr. David BURDETTE
19 Dir Public Safety/Emergency Mgmt .... Mr. Jamie HERRING
40 Director University Store .... Ms. R. Karol HARDISON
25 Director Sponsored Programs .... Mr. John A. ROARK
29 Director Alumni Relations .... Ms. Carrie MCGINNIS
105 Manager Web Services .... Ms. Charley B. ALLEN
100 Chief of Staff .... Dr. K. Renee FISTER
102 President MSU Foundation .... Dr. Robert JACKSON
86 Director Government Relations .... Mr. Jordan SMITH
15 Director Human Resources .... Ms. Joyce GORDON

Northern Kentucky University (E)

Nunn Drive, Highland Heights KY 41099-0000
County: Campbell FICE Identification: 009275
Unit ID: 157447
Telephone: (859) 572-5100 Carnegie Class: Masters/L
FAX Number: (859) 572-5566 Calendar System: Semester
URL: www.nku.edu
Established: 1968 Annual Undergrad Tuition & Fees (In-State): $9,384
Enrollment: 14,699 Coed
Affiliation or Control: State IRS Status: 501(c)3
Highest Offering: Doctorate
Accreditation: SC, ANEST, CAATE, CACREP, CAEPN, COARC, CONST, ENGT, LAW, MUS, NUR, NURSE, RAD, SPAA, SW

01 Interim President .... Mr. Gerard ST. AMAND
04 Exec Asst to President .... Mr. Ben JAGER
05 Provost/Exec VP Academic Affairs .... Ms. Sue OTT ROWLANDS
10 Sr Vice Pres Admin & Finance .... Dr. Sue HODGES MOORE
32 Vice Pres Student Affairs .... Dr. Daniel NADLER
30 Vice Pres University Advancement .... Mr. Eric C. GENTRY
43 VP Legal Affairs & General Counsel .... Ms. Joan GATES
20 Vice Prov Undergrad Academic Affs .... Dr. Idna CORBETT
84 VP Enrollment/Degree Management .... Ms. Kimberly SCRANAGE
58 Vice Prov Grad Educ/Rsrch/ Outreach .... Ms. Samantha LANGLEY-TURNBAUGH
20 Assoc Provost Academic Affs/Admin .... Mr. Chad OGLE
13 Chief Information Officer .... Mr. Timothy FERGUSON
08 Assoc Provost Library Services .... Mr. Arne J. ALMQUIST
35 AVP Student Engage/Dean of Students .... Vacant
29 AVP Development & Alumni Relations .... Ms. Julie DIALS
49 Dean College of Arts & Sciences .... Dr. Diana MCGILL
50 Dean College of Business .... Dr. Rebecca PORTERFIELD
88 Dean College of Informatics .... Dr. Kevin KIRBY
53 Dean College of Ed/Human Svcs .... Dr. Cynthia REED
61 Dean Chase College of Law .... Mr. Jeffrey STANDEN
66 Dean College of Health Professions .... Dr. Dale SCALISE-SMITH
11 Director of Administration .... Ms. Karen SULLIVAN
18 Asst VP Facilities Management .... Mr. Syed ZAIDI
18 Director Operations & Maintenance .... Mr. Ray MIRIZZI
26 Asst VP Marketing & Communications .... Ms. Gina RITTINGER
21 Dir Fin & Operational Auditing .... Mr. Larry MEYER
109 Dir BusinessOps/Auxiliary Services .... Mr. Andy MEEKS
88 Dir Univ Architect/Design/Const Mgt .... Mr. Steve NIENABER
88 Director Campus Space and Planning .... Ms. Mary Paula SCHUH
15 Senior Director Human Resources .... Ms. Lori SOUTHWOOD
21 Comptroller .... Mr. Russell A. KERDOLFF
19 Director University Police .... Mr. John GAFFIN
96 Director Procurement Services .... Mr. Jeffrey STRUNK
92 Interim Director Honors Program .... Ms. Belle ZEMBRODT
07 Director Undergraduate Admissions .... Ms. Melissa GORBANDT
104 Exec Dir Intl Education Center .... Dr. Francois LEROY
06 Registrar .... Mr. W. Allen COLE, III
37 AVP Enrollment & Financial Aid .... Ms. Leah STEWART
78 Exec Dir Ctr for Civic Engagement .... Mr. Mark NEIKIRK
51 Director Community Connections .... Ms. Melinda SPONG
25 Director Research/Grants/Contracts .... Ms. Mary UCCI
89 Director First Year Programs .... Ms. Jeanne PETTIT
21 Chief Financial Officer .... Mr. Mike HALES
09 Exec Dir Planning/Inst Research .... Mr. Shawn RAINEY
88 Assoc Dir Institutional Research .... Mr. Cori HENDERSON
88 Director Campus Recreation .... Mr. Matthew HACKETT
38 Assoc Dir Health/Counseling/Prev .... Ms. Lisa BARRESI
35 Director of Student Engagement .... Ms. Tiffany MAYSE
22 Dir Hlth/Counseling/Stdnt Wellness .... Mr. Ben ANDERSON
36 Director Career Services .... Mr. Bill FROUDE
41 Dir of Intercollegiate Athletics .... Mr. Ken BOTHOF
22 Sr Advisor to Pres Inclusive Excell .... Dr. Kathleen ROBERTS

Simmons College of Kentucky (F)

1018 South 7th Street, Louisville KY 40203-3322
County: Jefferson FICE Identification: 041780
Unit ID: 461759
Telephone: (502) 776-1443 Carnegie Class: Spec-4-yr-Faith
FAX Number: (502) 776-2227 Calendar System: Semester
URL: www.simmonscollegeky.edu
Established: 1879 Annual Undergrad Tuition & Fees: $5,310
Enrollment: 216 Coed
Affiliation or Control: Baptist IRS Status: 501(c)3
Highest Offering: Baccalaureate
Accreditation: BI

01 President .... Dr. Kevin W. COSBY
03 Executive Vice President .... Dr. Frank M. SMITH, JR.
03 Executive Vice President .... Dr. Ken B. JOBST
05 Vice Pres Academic Affairs .... Dr. Brian J. WELLS
32 Vice Pres Student Affs/Dir Admiss .... Dr. Christine COSBY-GAITHER
06 Registrar .... Ms. Deborah THOMAS

The Southern Baptist Theological Seminary (A)

2825 Lexington Road, Louisville KY 40280-2899
County: Jefferson FICE Identification: 001982
Unit ID: 157748
Telephone: (502) 897-4011 Carnegie Class: Spec-4-yr-Faith
FAX Number: (502) 899-1770 Calendar System: Other
URL: www.sbts.edu
Established: 1859 Annual Undergrad Tuition & Fees: $17,916
Enrollment: 3,671 Coed
Affiliation or Control: Southern Baptist IRS Status: 501(c)3
Highest Offering: Doctorate
Accreditation: SC, MUS, THEOL

Code	Title	Name
01	President	Dr. R. Albert MOHLER, JR.
100	Chief of Staff to the President	Mr. Jonathan AUSTIN
04	Sr Admin Asst Office of President	Mrs. Celeste EAGLE
05	Sr VP Academic Administration	Dr. Randy STINSON
111	Sr VP Institutional Advancement	Mr. Craig PARKER
11	Vice President of Operations	Mr. Andrew VINCENT
26	Vice President Communications	Mr. Steve WATTERS
13	VP Campus Technology	Mr. Jason HEATH
20	Vice President Academic Services	Dr. Matthew HALL
106	Assoc VP Online Education	Dr. Timothy Paul JONES
108	Assoc VP Institutional Assessment	Dr. Joseph C. HARROD
84	Assoc VP Enrollment Management	Mr. Matt MINIER
15	Director Human Resources	Mr. Richard MCRAE
18	Chief Facilities/Physical Plant	Mr. Ken RICHARDSON
41	Director of Health & Recreation	Mr. Billy WARD
07	Director of Admissions	Mr. Kody GIBSON
08	Librarian	Dr. Berry DRIVER
37	Manager of Financial Aid	Mrs. Ana WILLIAMS
73	Dean of School of Theology	Dr. Greg WILLS
88	Dean Missions Evang Ch Growth	Mr. Adam GREENWAY
12	Dean Boyce College	Dr. Matthew HALL
06	Registrar	Mr. Norm CHUNG
39	Director Student Housing	Mr. Tyler CLARK

Spalding University (B)

845 S Third Street, Louisville KY 40203-2213
County: Jefferson FICE Identification: 001960
Unit ID: 157757
Telephone: (502) 585-9911 Carnegie Class: DU-Mod
FAX Number: (502) 585-7158 Calendar System: Other
URL: www.spalding.edu
Established: 1814 Annual Undergrad Tuition & Fees: $24,388
Enrollment: 2,202 Coed
Affiliation or Control: Independent Non-Profit IRS Status: 501(c)3
Highest Offering: Doctorate
Accreditation: SC, CAATE, CAEPN, CLPSY, IACBE, NURSE, OT, SW

Code	Title	Name
01	President	Ms. Tori MURDEN MCCLURE
05	Provost	Dr. Joanne BERRYMAN
111	Chief Advancement Officer	Mr. Bert GRIFFIN
32	Dean of Students	Dr. Richard HUDSON
10	Chief Financial Officer	Mr. Rush SHERMAN
43	General Counsel	Ms. Emily NORRIS
84	Dean of Enrollment Management	Mr. Chris HART
53	Associate Dean of College of Educ	Dr. Chris WALSH
83	Assoc Dean College Social Sci/Hum	Dr. Melissa CHASTAIN
88	Director Adult Accelerated Program	Ms. Katherine WALKER-PAYNE
26	Chief Marketing Officer	Mr. Rick BARNEY
88	Director Academic Resource Center	Mr. Sam MEYER
121	Director Academic Advising Center	Ms. Katherine WALKER-PAYNE
06	Registrar	Ms. Jennifer GOHMANN
13	Chief Information Officer	Mr. Ezra KRUMHANSL
08	Director Library	Mr. Tony HOPKINS
37	Director Financial Aid	Ms. Michelle STANDRIDGE
15	Human Resources Manager	Ms. Jennifer BROCKHOFF
09	Dir of Institutional Effectiveness	Ms. Kay VETTER
41	Director of Athletics	Mr. Roger BURKMAN
88	Admin Dir/Mstr Fine Arts in Writing	Ms. Karen MANN
21	Controller	Ms. Katherine WEYHING
18	JLL Facilities Manager	Mr. Kevin WEBER
40	Bookstore Manager	Vacant
50	Dir Masters Business Communications	Dr. Robin HINKLE
07	Director of Admissions	Dr. Matthew ELDER

Spencerian College (C)

2355 Harrodsburg Rd, Lexington KY 40504
Telephone: (859) 223-9608 Identification: 666448
Accreditation: ACICS, MAC, MLTAB, RAD

† Branch campus of Spencerian College, Louisville, KY.

Spencerian College (D)

4627 Dixie Highway, Louisville KY 40216-2605
County: Jefferson FICE Identification: 004618
Unit ID: 157766
Telephone: (502) 447-1000 Carnegie Class: Spec-4-yr-Other Health
FAX Number: (502) 447-4574 Calendar System: Quarter
URL: www.spencerian.edu
Established: 1892 Annual Undergrad Tuition & Fees: $20,400
Enrollment: 497 Coed
Affiliation or Control: Proprietary IRS Status: Proprietary
Highest Offering: Baccalaureate
Accreditation: ACICS, COARC, COMTA, MAC, MLTAB, RAD, SURGT

Code	Title	Name
01	Executive Director	Ms. Jan M. GORDON
05	Academic Dean	Ms. Linda BLAIR
06	Registrar	Mr. Rob SUKALA
37	Director of Financial Planning	Ms. Jill SCHULER
07	Director of Admissions	Ms. Charmaine POWELL
36	Director of Career Services	Ms. Rachel GIMBEL-JAGGERS
32	Director of Student Services	Ms. Cherise MINGUS

Sullivan College of Technology and Design (E)

3901 Atkinson Square Drive, Louisville KY 40218-4549
County: Jefferson FICE Identification: 012088
Unit ID: 157270
Telephone: (502) 456-6509 Carnegie Class: Spec-4-yr-Arts
FAX Number: (502) 456-2341 Calendar System: Quarter
URL: www.sctd.edu
Established: 1961 Annual Undergrad Tuition & Fees: $20,680
Enrollment: 406 Coed
Affiliation or Control: Proprietary IRS Status: Proprietary
Highest Offering: Baccalaureate
Accreditation: ACICS, CIDA

Code	Title	Name
00	Chancellor	Dr. A. R. SULLIVAN
01	President	Mr. Glenn D. SULLIVAN
11	Chief Operations Officer	Mr. Thomas F. DAVISSON
05	Dean of Academic Affairs	Mr. Vincent TINEBRA
10	Vice President Finance	Mr. Shelton BRIDGES
84	Vice Pres Enrollment Management	Mr. James CRICK
12	Executive Director	Mr. Chris ERNST
13	Chief Technology Officer	Ms. Jody GILLENWATER
55	Evening Division Dean	Ms. Brittany LEACH
06	Registrar	Mr. Ryan SEARS
07	Director of Admissions	Ms. Ashley AUSTIN
37	Dir of Student Financial Planning	Ms. Michelle SMITH
08	Head Librarian	Ms. Jill SHERMAN
36	Director Career Services	Ms. Donna REED
21	Business Officer	Ms. Sherri WILSON
29	Director Alumni Relations	Ms. Hazel MATTHEWS

Sullivan University (F)

3101 Bardstown Road, Louisville KY 40205-3000
County: Jefferson FICE Identification: 004619
Unit ID: 157793
Telephone: (502) 456-6504 Carnegie Class: Masters/L
FAX Number: (502) 456-0040 Calendar System: Quarter
URL: www.sullivan.edu
Established: 1962 Annual Undergrad Tuition & Fees: $19,740
Enrollment: 3,797 Coed
Affiliation or Control: Proprietary IRS Status: Proprietary
Highest Offering: Doctorate
Accreditation: SC, ACFEI, #ARCPA, CAHIIM, MAC, NURSE, PHAR

Code	Title	Name
00	Chancellor	Dr. A. R. SULLIVAN
01	President	Mr. Glenn D. SULLIVAN
03	Chief Executive Officer	Dr. Jay D. MARR
05	Provost	Dr. Diana LAWRENCE
11	Senior Vice President/COO	Mr. Thomas F. DAVISSON
10	Vice President Finance	Mr. Shelton BRIDGES
07	Vice President of Admissions	Ms. Nina MARTINEZ
58	Assoc Provost/Dean Graduate School	Dr. Tim SWENSON
32	Dean of Students	Mr. Gabe GHAMMACHI
88	Dir Natl Ctr Hospitality Studies	Mr. David DODD
06	Registrar	Ms. Kim MITCHELL
08	Librarian	Mr. Charles BROWN
13	Chief Technology Officer	Mr. Mike GROSSE
36	Director of Career Services	Mr. Sam MANNINO
37	Director Student Financial Planning	Ms. Angela MILLER
55	Director Evening Division	Mr. James TAYLOR
40	Bookstore Manager	Mr. Bryan NEEDY
12	Director Lexington Branch	Mr. David KEENE
96	Director of Purchasing	Ms. Ann VEST
56	Director of Extension Campus	Ms. Barbara DEAN
88	University Ombudsman	Mr. Jim KLEIN
29	Director Alumni Relations	Ms. Hazel MATTHEWS
09	Director Institutional Research	Dr. Mark WILJANEN
18	Manager Campus Facilities	Mr. Mike FOWLER
35	Student Life Coordinator	Ms. Kim ATWOOD
67	Dean College of Pharmacy	Dr. Cindy STOWE
50	Dean College of Business Admin	Dr. Ken MORAN
72	Dean Col Information/Computer Tech	Dr. Emmanuel UDOH
26	Chief Public Relations/Marketing	Mr. Michael JOHNSON

Thomas More College (G)

333 Thomas More Parkway,
Crestview Hills KY 41017-3495
County: Kenton FICE Identification: 002001
Unit ID: 157809
Telephone: (859) 341-5800 Carnegie Class: Masters/S
FAX Number: (859) 344-3345 Calendar System: Semester
URL: www.thomasmore.edu
Established: 1921 Annual Undergrad Tuition & Fees: $29,450
Enrollment: 1,909 Coed
Affiliation or Control: Roman Catholic IRS Status: 501(c)3
Highest Offering: Master's
Accreditation: SC, ACBSP, CAEPN, NUR

Code	Title	Name
01	President	Mr. David A. ARMSTRONG
04	Assistant to the President	Ms. Charlene BARLOW
10	CFO	Mr. Jeff BRIGGS
05	Vice President for Academic Affairs	Dr. Kathleen JAGGER
30	Vice Pres Institutional Advancement	Ms. Robyn HOFFMAN
11	Vice Pres of Operations/Cmty Affs	Vacant
32	Dean of Students	Mr. Kevin REYNOLDS
09	Dir of Inst Planning/Effectiveness	Ms. Kelly FRENCH
06	Registrar	Ms. Michelle VEZINA
08	Director of Library	Ms. Leoma DUNN
37	Director of Financial Aid	Mr. Mark MESSINGSCHLAGER
13	Director of IT	Mr. Sean KAPSAL
26	Dir Communications/Media Relations	Ms. Nicole DOLL
38	Director of Counseling	Ms. Veronica A. LUBBE
42	Chaplain	Rev. Gerald E. TWADDELL
84	AVP of Enrollment Management	Dr. Christopher POWERS
41	Athletic Director	Mr. Terry D. CONNOR
19	Director of Campus Safety	Mr. William WILSON
15	Director of Human Resources	Ms. Laura CUSTER
18	Director of Facilities	Mr. Eric WILKYMACKY
29	Director of Alumni	Ms. Leisa MULCAHY
36	Dir of Career Planning/Coop Educ	Ms. Emily HELLMANN
73	Director of Campus Ministry	Mr. Andrew COLE
21	Controller	Mr. Mark GOSHORN
51	Director of Lifelong Learning	Mr. Nathan HARTMAN
92	Director of Honors Program	Dr. Catherine SHERRON
44	Dir Annual Giving/Special Events	Vacant
07	Associate Director of Admissions	Mr. Justin VOGEL
35	Director of Student Engagement	Ms. Becky MULLINS
39	Coordinator of Residence Life	Vacant

Transylvania University (H)

300 N Broadway, Lexington KY 40508-1797
County: Fayette FICE Identification: 001987
Unit ID: 157818
Telephone: (859) 233-8300 Carnegie Class: Bac-A&S
FAX Number: (859) 233-8797 Calendar System: Other
URL: www.transy.edu
Established: 1780 Annual Undergrad Tuition & Fees: $35,830
Enrollment: 1,053 Coed
Affiliation or Control: Christian Church (Disciples Of Christ)
IRS Status: 501(c)3
Highest Offering: Baccalaureate
Accreditation: SC, CAEPN

Code	Title	Name
01	President	Dr. Seamus CAREY
05	Vice Pres & Dean of the University	Dr. Laura BRYAN
10	Vice President Finance & Business	Mr. Marc MATHEWS
07	VP for Enrollment & Student Affairs	Dr. Holly SHEILLEY
111	VP for Advancement	Mr. Martin SMITH
13	VP for Information Technology	Vacant
26	Vice President for Marketing & Comm	Ms. Michele SPARKS
28	Dir Diversity/Incl & Intl Students	Vacant
06	Registrar	Ms. Michelle RAWLINGS
08	Librarian	Ms. Susan M. BROWN
09	Director of Institutional Research	Mr. Rhyan M. CONYERS
104	Director of Study Abroad	Ms. Kathryn C. SIMON
36	Director of Career Development	Ms. Susan S. RAYER
15	Assoc VP & Director Human Resources	Mr. Jeff MUDRAK
18	Chief Facilities/Physical Plant	Mr. Darrell BANKS
19	Director Security/Safety	Mr. Gregg MURAVCHICK
96	Director of Purchasing	Ms. Shawn T. SINGLETON
39	Director Residence Life	Mr. Kevin FISHER
37	Director of Financial Aid	Ms. Jennifer PRIEST
29	Director Alumni Relations	Ms. Natasa PAJIC
04	Executive Assist to President	Ms. Kristin MILAM
100	Chief of Staff	Ms. Rachel MILLARD
41	Athletic Director	Ms. Mary STRUCKHOFF

Union College (I)

310 College Street, Barbourville KY 40906-1499
County: Knox FICE Identification: 001988
Unit ID: 157863
Telephone: (606) 546-4151 Carnegie Class: Masters/M
FAX Number: (606) 546-1217 Calendar System: Other
URL: www.unionky.edu
Established: 1879 Annual Undergrad Tuition & Fees: $25,135
Enrollment: 1,088 Coed
Affiliation or Control: United Methodist IRS Status: 501(c)3
Highest Offering: Master's
Accreditation: SC, #CAATE, CAEPN, NURSE

Code	Title	Name
01	President	Dr. Marcia HAWKINS
05	VP for Academic Affairs	Dr. David JOHNS
111	Vice President of Advancement	Vacant
84	VP for Enrollment Management	Mr. Craig GROOMS
32	Dean of Students	Mr. Justin KITTS
53	Head of Educational Studies Dept	Dr. Jason REEVES
35	Assistant Director of Campus Life	Ms. Fernanda C. FREY
10	Chief Business Officer	Mr. Steve HOSKINS
21	Controller	Ms. Elisabeth RICHARDSON
06	Registrar	Ms. Kathy INKSTER
18	Director of Physical Plant (NMRC)	Mr. James JAMERSON
41	Athletic Director	Mr. Tim CURRY
29	Director of Alumni Relations	Vacant
09	Director of Institutional Research	Ms. Anisa JAMES
26	Chief Communications Officer	Mr. Andy POWELL
88	Director of Sports Information	Mr. John GATTO
121	Associate Dean for Student Success	Ms. Stephanie SMITH
08	Head Librarian	Ms. Tara L. COOPER

42 College Minister .... Rev. David MILLER
37 Director of Financial Aid .... Ms. Andra BUTLER
118 Benefits Coordinator .... Ms. Lynn SMITH
19 Safety Team Leader .... Mr. Jurgin MCRIGHT
50 Chair Department of Business .... Dr. Carolyn PAYNE
88 Chair Dept Wellness/Human Perf/Rec .... Dr. Jennifer HATFIELD
79 Chair Dept Engr/Comm/Language .... Dr. Shayne CONFER
88 Chair Dept History/Rel Studies .... Dr. Joseph PEARSON
81 Chair Dept of Natural Sciences .... Dr. Dan COVINGTON
83 Chair Dept Social/Behav Science .... Dr. Robert ARMOUR
57 Chair Dept Fine/Performing Arts .... Dr. Virginia Gay GANDY
04 Assistant to the President .... Ms. Sherry PARTIN
102 Dir Foundation/Corporate Relations .... Vacant
105 Director Web Services .... Mr. Phillip HORN
108 Director Institutional Effectivenes .... Dr. Barry PELPHREY

University of the Cumberlands (A)

6191 College Station Drive, Williamsburg KY 40769-1372
County: Whitley FICE Identification: 001962
Unit ID: 156541
Telephone: (606) 549-2200 Carnegie Class: DU-Mod
FAX Number: (606) 539-4280 Calendar System: Semester
URL: www.ucumberlands.edu
Established: 1888 Annual Undergrad Tuition & Fees: $23,000
Enrollment: 6,276 Coed
Affiliation or Control: Baptist IRS Status: 501(c)3
Highest Offering: Doctorate
Accreditation: SC, #ARCPA, CACREP, CAEPN, NURSE

01 President .... Dr. Larry L. COCKRUM
100 Exec Vice President/Chief of Staff .... Ms. Jamirae HAMMONS
05 Vice President Academic Affairs .... Dr. Barbara KENNEDY
32 Vice President Student Services .... Dr. Emily COLEMAN
23 Director Medical Services .... Dr. Eddie PERKINS
10 Chief Financial Officer .... Mr. Chris ROLPH
11 Director of Operations .... Mr. Travis WILSON
37 Director of Financial Aid .... Mr. Larry RECTOR
41 Athletic Director .... Mr. Chris KRAFTICK
13 VP for Information Technology .... Dr. Donnie GRIMES
84 VP for Enrollment & Communication .... Dr. Jerry JACKSON
06 Registrar .... Mr. Charles DUPIER
20 Associate Dean .... Dr. Thomas E. FISH
26 Director of Communications .... Mrs. Leslie RYSER
35 Dean Student Life .... Ms. Linda CARTER
15 Director of Human Resources .... Mr. Steve ALLEN
42 Director of Church Relations .... Dr. Rick FLEENOR
36 Director of Career Services .... Ms. Debbie HARP
08 Director of Library .... Ms. Jan WREN
58 Director of Graduate Advising .... Mrs. Shonda POWERS
29 Director Alumni Relations .... Mr. Paul STEPP
18 Director of Physical Plant .... Mr. David ROOT
21 Bursar .... Ms. Jo DUPIER
07 Director of Admissions .... Mrs. Erica HARRIS
30 Director of Development .... Mr. Bill STOHLMAN

University of Kentucky (B)

101 Main Building, Lexington KY 40506-0003
County: Fayette FICE Identification: 001989
Unit ID: 157085
Telephone: (859) 257-9000 Carnegie Class: DU-Highest
FAX Number: (859) 257-4000 Calendar System: Semester
URL: www.uky.edu
Established: 1865 Annual Undergrad Tuition & Fees (In-State): $11,484
Enrollment: 29,727 Coed
Affiliation or Control: State IRS Status: 501(c)3
Highest Offering: Doctorate
Accreditation: SC, AAFCS, #ARCPA, ART, CAATE, CACREP, CAEPN, CIDA, CLPSY, COPSY, CS, DENT, DIETC, DIETD, DIETI, ENG, HSA, IPSY, JOUR, LAW, LIB, LSAR, MED, MFCD, MT, MUS, NURSE, PAST, PCSAS, PH, PHAR, PTA, SCPSY, SP, SPAA, SW, THEA

01 President .... Dr. Eli I. CAPILOUTO
46 Vice President Research .... Dr. Lisa A. CASSIS
05 Provost .... Dr. Tim S. TRACY
100 Chief of Staff .... Dr. Bill K. SWINFORD
11 Exec VP Finance/Administration .... Mr. Eric N. MONDAY
17 Executive VP for Health Affairs .... Dr. Michael KARPF
32 Assoc Provost Student/Academic Life .... Dr. Greg HEILEMAN
13 Interim Chief Information Officer .... Ms. Karen WILLMOTT
35 Int VP Stdnt Affs/Dean of Students .... Dr. Victor A. HAZARD
28 Assistant VP Institutional Equity .... Mr. Terry D. ALLEN
30 Vice President for Development .... Dr. D. Michael RICHEY
10 VP Health Affs/Chief Financial Ofcr .... Mr. Murray B. CLARK
45 VP Financial Planning & CBO .... Ms. Angela S. MARTIN
18 VP Facilities Mgmt & Chief Facil .... Ms. Mary S. VOSEVICH
28 Assoc VP Institutional Diversity .... Dr. Sonja M. FEIST-PRICE
26 VP University Relations .... Mr. Thomas W. HARRIS
15 VP Human Resources Admin & CHRO .. Ms. Kimberly P. WILSON
88 Asst Vice Pres Public Safety .... Mr. Anthony BEATTY
109 Exec Director Auxiliary Services .... Ms. Sarah F. NIKIRK
21 Assoc VP Res Admin & Fiscal Affs .... Mr. Jack SUPPLEE, JR.
25 Exec Director Sponsored Projects .... Ms. Kim C. CARTER
88 Assoc VP UKHC/EVPHA .... Mr. Joe CLAYPOOL
58 Interim Dean of Graduate School .... Dr. Brian A. JACKSON
88 Assoc Provost Faculty Advancement .... Dr. Gene T. LINEBERRY
84 Assoc Provost Enroll Mgmt/Registrar .... Mr. Don E. WITT
08 Dean of Libraries .... Dr. Terry L. BIRDWHISTELL
27 Exec Director Public Relations .... Mr. Jay D. BLANTON
27 Director University Press .... Ms. Leila W. SALISBURY
43 General Counsel .... Mr. William E. THRO
41 Director Athletics .... Mr. Mitch S. BARNHART
37 Director Student Financial Aid .... Dr. Nimmi K. WIGGINS
09 Director of Institutional Research .... Dr. Craig P. RUDICK
36 Asst Dean for Career & Academic Exp .... Mr. Ray R. CLERE
38 Director Counseling & Testing .... Dr. Mary C. BOLIN
29 Director Alumni Affairs .... Mr. Stan R. KEY
21 Controller .... Ms. Ronda S. BECK
47 Dean of Agriculture/Food & Envir .... Dr. Nancy M. COX
19 Chief of Police .... Mr. Joseph W. MONROE
88 Dean of Design .... Ms. Mitzi VERNON
88 Exec Director Student Center .... Mr. John H. HERBST
49 Dean of Arts & Sciences .... Dr. Mark L. KORNBLUH
50 Dean of Business & Economics .... Dr. David W. BLACKWELL
53 Dean of Education .... Dr. Mary John O'HAIR
54 Interim Dean of Engineering .... Mr. Larry HOLLOWAY
57 Dean of Fine Arts .... Mr. Mark SHANDA
60 Dean of Communication/Information .... Dr. H. Dan O'HAIR
61 Dean of Law .... Dr. David A. BRENNEN
70 Interim Dean of Social Work .... Dr. Ann VAIL
76 Dean of Health Sciences .... Dr. Scott M. LEPHART
52 Dean of Dentistry .... Dr. Stephanos KYRKANIDES
63 Dean of Medicine/VP Clinical Affs .... Dr. Robert DIPAOLA
66 Dean of Nursing .... Dr. Janie H. HEATH
67 Interim Dean of Pharmacy .... Dr. Kelly M. SMITH
69 Dean Public Health .... Dr. Donna ARNETT
96 Exec Director Purchasing & CPO .... Mr. Barry SWANSON
108 Director of Assessment .... Ms. Tara A. ROSE
44 Director Annual Giving .... Ms. Anne V. LICHTENBERG

University of Louisville (C)

2301 S Third Street, Louisville KY 40292-0001
County: Jefferson FICE Identification: 001999
Unit ID: 157289
Telephone: (502) 852-5555 Carnegie Class: DU-Highest
FAX Number: (502) 852-7013 Calendar System: Semester
URL: www.louisville.edu
Established: 1798 Annual Undergrad Tuition & Fees (In-State): $11,264
Enrollment: 21,294 Coed
Affiliation or Control: State IRS Status: 501(c)3
Highest Offering: Doctorate
Accreditation: #SC, AUD, CACREP, CAEP, CIDA, CLPSY, COPSY, CS, DENT, DH, ENG, EXSC, IPSY, LAW, MED, MFCD, MUS, NURSE, PH, PLNG, SP, SPAA, SW, THEA

01 Interim President .... Dr. Gregory POSTEL
05 Int Provost/VP Academic Affairs .... Dr. Dale B. BILLINGSLEY
17 Exec Vice Pres for Health Affairs .... Dr. Gregory C. POSTEL
46 Executive VP for Research .... Dr. Bill PIERCE
10 Interim Sr VP Finance/Admin & COO .... Mr. Lee SMITH
30 Vice Pres Univ Advancement .... Mr. Keith INMAN
13 Vice Pres Information Tech .... Vacant
86 VP for Community Engagement .... Mr. Daniel HALL
15 Vice Pres Human Resources .... Ms. Jeanell HUGHES
41 Vice President for Athletics .... Mr. Tom JURICH
44 Sr Assoc VP Advancement .... Ms. Rebecca SIMPSON
18 Assoc VP Facilities/Physical Plant .... Mr. James SEARS
29 Assoc VP for Alumni Relations .... Ms. Deborah DIETZLER
100 Chief of Staff for the President .... Ms. Trisha W. SMITH
43 Associate University Counsel .... Ms. Rebecca STAHL
20 Vice Prov Undergraduate Affairs .... Dr. Dale B. BILLINGSLEY
58 Dean Graduate School .... Dr. Beth A. BOEHM
28 Vice Prov for Diversity/Intl Affs ... Dr. Mordean TAYLOR-ARCHER
09 Vice Provost IR Effect & Analytics .... Mr. Robert S. GOLDSTEIN
84 Vice Provost Enrollment Management .... Mr. James BEGANY
106 Assoc Univ Provost Distance Ed/Delp .... Dr. Gale RHODES
88 Asst Prov for Accreditation .... Ms. Connie C. SHUMAKE
21 Interim Assoc VP Controller .... Mr. John T. FAULSTICH
07 Executive Director Admissions .... Ms. Jenny L. SAWYER
06 University Registrar .... Mr. Scott A. BURKS
37 Director Financial Aid .... Ms. Sandra NEEL
26 Director of Comm/Marketing .... Mr. John DREES
25 Assoc VP Business Services .... Mr. Mark J. WATKINS
16 Dir of Staff Dev/Employee Rel .... Ms. Mary E. MILES
19 Director Public Safety .... Mr. Wayne HALL
09 Exec Director Inst Res & Plng .... Ms. Becky PATTERSON
45 Exec Director Inst Effectiveness .... Dr. Cheryl B. GILCHRIST
39 Director Student Housing .... Ms. Julie WEBER
105 Director of Digital Media .... Mr. Jeffery A. RUSHTON
27 Director Media Relations .... Mr. Mark HEBERT
88 Interim Assoc VP Audit Services .... Ms. Cheri JONES
14 Exec Dir IT Infrastructure .... Vacant
92 Exec Director of Honors Program .... Dr. Joy HART
96 Asst Director Purchasing .... Mr. Curtis MONROE
88 Dir Planning/Design & Construction .... Mr. Kenneth DIETZ
36 Director Career Development .... Mr. Trey LEWIS
38 Director Counseling Center .... Ms. Aesha UQDAH
08 Dean of University Libraries .... Mr. Robert FOX
49 Dean College Arts & Sciences .... Dr. Kimberly KEMPF-LEONARD
50 Dean College of Business .... Dr. Todd MOORADIAN
52 Dean School of Dentistry .... Dr. Thomas G. BRADLEY
53 Dean Col of Educ/Human Develop .... Dr. Ann LARSON
70 Dean Kent School Social Work .... Dr. David A. JENKINS
64 Dean School of Music .... Dr. Christopher DOANE
61 Int Dean Brandeis School of Law .... Ms. Susan DUNCAN
66 Dean School of Nursing .... Dr. Marcia J. HERN
54 Act Dean Speed School Engineering .... Mr. John S. USHER
63 Dean School of Medicine .... Dr. Toni GANZEL
69 Dean Public Health/Information Sci .... Dr. Craig H. BLAKELY
35 Dean of Students/Assoc VP Stdnt Aff .... Dr. Michael MARDIS
04 Assistant to the President .... Mr. Denny CRUM
104 Director Study Abroad .... Ms. Virginia HOSONO
11 Int Chief Admin Officer .... Mr. David ADAMS

University of Phoenix Louisville Campus (D)

10400 Linn Station Road, Louisville KY 40223-3839
Telephone: (502) 423-0149 Identification: 770207
Accreditation: &NH, ACBSP

† No longer accepting campus-based students.

University of Pikeville (E)

147 Sycamore Street, Pikeville KY 41501-1194
County: Pike FICE Identification: 001980
Unit ID: 157535
Telephone: (606) 218-5250 Carnegie Class: Bac-A&S
FAX Number: (606) 218-5269 Calendar System: Semester
URL: www.upike.edu
Established: 1889 Annual Undergrad Tuition & Fees: $19,600
Enrollment: 2,531 Coed
Affiliation or Control: Presbyterian Church (U.S.A.) IRS Status: 501(c)3
Highest Offering: Doctorate
Accreditation: SC, NUR, @OPT, OSTEO, SW

00 Chancellor .... Mr. Paul E. PATTON
01 President .... Dr. Burton J. WEBB
05 Provost .... Dr. Lori WERTH
49 Dean College Arts/Sciences .... Dr. Thomas R. HESS
88 Dean College of Optometry .... Dr. Andrew BUZZELLI
50 Dean College of Business .... Dr. Howard V. ROBERTS
10 Vice Pres Finance/Business Affairs .... Mr. Barry BENTLEY
111 Vice President for Advancement .... Mr. David HUTCHENS
26 Director of Public Affairs .... Mrs. Laura DAMRON
63 VP Health Affairs/Dean KYCOM .... Dr. Boyd R. BUSER
32 Dean of Students .... Dr. Justin OWENS
07 Director of Admissions .... Mr. John YANCEY
08 Director of Library Services .... Ms. Karen S. CHAFIN-EVANS
06 University Registrar .... Mrs. Gia POTTER
09 Director of Institutional Research .... Dr. Meg SIDLE
13 Senior Info Services Administrator .... Vacant
18 Asst VP for Facilities .... Mr. John HOLMAN
37 Director of Student Financial Svcs .... Ms. Jennifer BATES
15 Director of Human Resources .... Mr. Michael PACHECO
04 Executive Asst to President .... Mrs. Sherrie MARRS
19 Director Security/Safety .... Mr. Allen ABSHIRE
41 Athletic Director .... Mr. Robert STAGGS
105 Coordinator of New Media .... Vacant
25 Chief Contracts/Grants Admin .... Mrs. Tiffany THACKER
29 Director Alumni Relations .... Ms. Lisa BLACKBURN
121 Director Student Success .... Dr. Mathys MEYER
39 Housing Operations Supervisor .... Mr. Chris ROBINSON
44 Director Annual or Planned Giving .... Mr. Ronald DAMRON
53 Dean College of Education .... Vacant
90 Director Academic Computing .... Mrs. Corrine BOLT

Western Kentucky University (F)

1906 College Heights Blvd, Bowling Green KY 42101-3576
County: Warren FICE Identification: 002002
Unit ID: 157951
Telephone: (270) 745-0111 Carnegie Class: Masters/L
FAX Number: (270) 745-5387 Calendar System: Semester
URL: www.wku.edu
Established: 1906 Annual Undergrad Tuition & Fees (In-State): $9,912
Enrollment: 20,063 Coed
Affiliation or Control: State IRS Status: 501(c)3
Highest Offering: Doctorate
Accreditation: SC, ADNUR, ART, CACREP, CAEPN, CAHIIM, DANCE, DH, DIETD, DIETI, ENG, JOUR, MUS, NAIT, NRPA, NURSE, PH, PTA, SP, SPAA, SW, THEA

01 President .... Dr. Timothy C. CABONI
04 Executive Administrative Assistant .... Ms. Torie COCKRIEL
04 Executive Administrative Assistant .... Ms. Shelia E. HOUCHINS
05 Provost/VP Academic Affairs .... Dr. David LEE
46 Assoc Provost for Research .... Dr. Cheryl DAVIS
26 VP for Public Affairs .... Ms. Robbin M. TAYLOR
30 VP Development & Alumni Rels .... Mr. Marc ARCHAMBAULT
29 Executive Director Alumni Relations .... Anthony MCADOO
32 Vice President Student Affairs .... Mr. Brian KUSTER
10 Senior VP Finance & Admin .... Ms. K. Ann MEAD
100 Chief of Staff/General Counsel .... Ms. Deborah T. WILKINS
20 Vice Provost Academic Affairs .... Dr. Richard C. MILLER
07 Director Recruitment & Admissions .... Dr. Jace T. LUX
84 Chief Enrollment/Grad Officer .... Dr. Brian MEREDITH
106 Assoc VP Ext Learning & Outreach .... Dr. Beth LAVES
79 Dean Arts & Letters .... Dr. Larry SNYDER, JR.
50 Dean Business .... Dr. Jeffrey KATZ
53 Dean Education/Behavioral Sci .... Dr. Sam EVANS
76 Dean Health & Human Services .... Dr. Neale R. CHUMBLER
81 Dean Science/Engineering .... Dr. Cheryl L. STEVENS
58 Dean Graduate School .... Dr. Scott LYONS
97 Assc Provost Regional Hgh Ed/Dean .... Dr. Dennis K. GEORGE
62 Dean Libraries .... Ms. Connie FOSTER
108 Assoc VP Enrichment & Effectiveness .... Dr. Doug MCELROY
88 Assoc VP Planning & Program Develop .... Dr. Sylvia GAIKO
21 Chief Financial Officer .... Mr. Jim CUMMINGS
114 Budget Director .... Ms. Kimberly REED
88 Assoc VP Academic Budgets & Admin ... Dr. Ladonna L. HUNTON
06 University Registrar .... Ms. Tiffany ROBINSON
13 Chief Information Tech Officer .... Mr. Gordon L. JOHNSON
15 Director Human Resources .... Mr. Tony L. GLISSON
18 Director Facilities Management .... Vacant
12 Regional Chancellor .... Dr. Sally RAY

12 Regional Chancellor ... Dr. Evelyn ELLIS
12 Regional Chancellor ... Dr. Gene E. TICE
27 Director of Media Relations ... Mr. Bob SKIPPER
105 Dir Web Svcs & Digital Media ... Dr. Corie MARTIN
86 VP/Dir Govt & Community Relations ... Ms. Jennifer B. SMITH
90 Director Academic Technology ... Mr. John BOWERS
121 Assoc Dir Advising & Retention Ctr ... Mr. Christopher JENSEN
39 Assistant VP Housing & Res Life ... Dr. Mike REAGLE
19 Interim Chief of Police ... Mr. Mitch WALKER
102 President College Heights Found ... Dr. Donald L. SMITH
112 Associate VP Major Gifts ... Mr. John P. BLAIR
36 Director Ctr for Career & Prof Dev ... Mr. Robert UNSELD, JR.
37 Dir Student Financial Assistance ... Ms. Cindy BURNETTE
88 Director Student Support Svcs ... Mr. Chris GEORGE
103 Dir Continuing & Professional Dev ... Mr. Derek OLIVE
40 Director WKU Store ... Ms. Ann FLORESCA
09 Director Institutional Research ... Dr. Tuesdi HELBIG
22 Equal Oppty/ADA/Compliance Director ... Mr. Joshua HAYES
24 Director Public Radio Services ... Mr. David BRINKLEY
41 Dir Intercollegiate Athletics ... Mr. Todd M. STEWART
85 Exec Dir Intl Enrollment Mgmt ... Ms. Stephanie SIEGGREEN
92 Executive Director Honors College ... Dr. Craig COBANE
96 Director Purchasing/Accts Payable ... Mr. Ken BAUSHKE
104 Dir Study Abroad/Global Learning ... Ms. Laura M. MONARCH

LOUISIANA

Baton Rouge School of Computers (A)

9352 Interline Avenue, Baton Rouge LA 70809-1909
County: East Baton Rouge FICE Identification: 021975
Unit ID: 158343
Telephone: (225) 923-2524 Carnegie Class: Spec 2-yr-Tech
FAX Number: (225) 923-2979 Calendar System: Other
URL: www.brsc.edu
Established: 1979 Annual Undergrad Tuition & Fees: N/A
Enrollment: 58 Coed
Affiliation or Control: Proprietary IRS Status: Proprietary
Highest Offering: Associate Degree
Accreditation: ACCSC

01 President/Director ... Mrs. Betty D. TRUXILLO
05 Chief Academic Officer ... Ms. Pauline ROBERTS
06 Registrar ... Ms. Cheryl DIFFEY

Cameron College (B)

2740 Canal Street, New Orleans LA 70119-5500
County: Orleans FICE Identification: 022340
Unit ID: 158440
Telephone: (504) 821-5881 Carnegie Class: Spec 2-yr-Health
FAX Number: (504) 822-3467 Calendar System: Other
URL: www.cameroncollege.com
Established: 1981 Annual Undergrad Tuition & Fees: N/A
Enrollment: 18 Coed
Affiliation or Control: Proprietary IRS Status: Proprietary
Highest Offering: Associate Degree
Accreditation: COE

01 Director ... Ms. James KEEN

Centenary College of Louisiana (C)

PO Box 41188, Shreveport LA 71134-1188
County: Caddo FICE Identification: 002003
Unit ID: 158477
Telephone: (318) 869-5011 Carnegie Class: Bac-A&S
FAX Number: (318) 869-5010 Calendar System: Semester
URL: www.centenary.edu
Established: 1825 Annual Undergrad Tuition & Fees: $35,430
Enrollment: 588 Coed
Affiliation or Control: United Methodist IRS Status: 501(c)3
Highest Offering: Master's
Accreditation: SC, CAEPT, MUS

01 President ... Dr. Christopher HOLOMAN
04 Exec Assistant to the President ... Mrs. Connie WHITTINGTON
05 Provost & Dean of the College ... Dr. Jenifer WARD
10 Vice President for Finance/Admin ... Mr. Bob BLUE
50 Dean of the School of Business ... Vacant
64 Dean of the School of Music ... Dr. Gale ODOM
30 Vice Pres for Development ... Mr. Fred LANDRY
84 Vice President Enrollment & Mktg ... Mr. Calhoun ALLEN
20 Vice Provost for Academic Affairs ... Dr. Karen SOUL
13 Director of Information Technology ... Mr. Scott MERRITT
21 Business Manager ... Mrs. Monica POWELL
41 Director of Athletics & Recreation ... Mr. Robert BUNNELL
32 Dean of Students ... Mr. Mark MILLER
38 Director of Counseling ... Ms. Tina FELDT
37 Director of Financial Aid ... Mrs. Lynette VISKOZKI
06 Registrar ... Ms. Nicole SHELBY
08 Librarian ... Ms. Christy WRENN
26 Dir of Strategic Communications ... Mrs. Kate PEDROTTY
29 Director Alumni/Family Relations ... Ms. Saige SOLOMON
36 Director of Professional Success ... Mrs. Rachael PETERS
18 Director of Facilities ... Mr. Chris SAMPITE
25 Director Sponsored Research ... Ms. Patty J. ROBERTS
07 Assoc Dir Admissions/Recruitment ... Ms. Lauren CARLETON
15 Human Resources Director ... Ms. Edie CUMMINGS
19 Director of Public Safety ... Mr. Eddie WALKER
104 Director Study Abroad ... Mrs. Rachel DRISKILL
39 Director Student Housing ... Mr. Montgomery MEWERS

Delta School of Business & Technology, DBA Delta Tech (D)

517 Broad Street, Lake Charles LA 70601-4334
County: Calcasieu FICE Identification: 020555
Unit ID: 158723
Telephone: (337) 439-5765 Carnegie Class: Assoc/HVT-Mix Trad/Non
FAX Number: (337) 436-5151 Calendar System: Quarter
URL: www.deltatech.edu
Established: 1970 Annual Undergrad Tuition & Fees: $9,685
Enrollment: 178 Coed
Affiliation or Control: Proprietary IRS Status: Proprietary
Highest Offering: Associate Degree
Accreditation: PPPA

01 Chief Executive Officer ... Mr. Jeff EDWARDS
05 Dean Academics/Compliance Officer ... Ms. Michelle EDWARDS
11 Director of Operations ... Mr. Allen MCLAUGHLIN
07 Admissions Director ... Ms. Barbara HOLT

Dillard University (E)

2601 Gentilly Boulevard, New Orleans LA 70122-3097
County: Orleans FICE Identification: 002004
Unit ID: 158802
Telephone: (504) 283-8822 Carnegie Class: Bac-A&S
FAX Number: N/A Calendar System: Semester
URL: www.dillard.edu
Established: 1869 Annual Undergrad Tuition & Fees: $17,064
Enrollment: 1,185 Coed
Affiliation or Control: United Methodist IRS Status: 501(c)3
Highest Offering: Baccalaureate
Accreditation: SC, NUR

01 President ... Dr. Walter M. KIMBROUGH
111 Vice Pres Inst Advancement ... Mr. Marc BARNES
05 Provost/Sr VP for Academic Affairs ... Dr. Yolanda PAGE
32 Vice President for Student Success ... Dr. Roland BULLARD
43 VP for Legal Affairs ... Dr. Denise WALLACE
10 VP for Business & Finance ... Mrs. Janel GREEN
20 Associate Provost ... Dr. Christopher JEFFRIES
07 Asst VP of Admissions & Programming ... Ms. Monica WHITE
18 Assoc Vice Pres Facilities Mgmt ... Mr. Adonis WOODS
36 Director of Career/Prof Services ... Ms. Caretta COOKE
06 Dir of Records & Registration ... Mr. Robert MITCHELL, JR.
37 Int Dir Financial Aid/Scholarships ... Ms. Shannon NEAL
46 Assoc VP Research & Spons Programs ... Mr. Theodore CALLIER
30 Director of Development ... Ms. Kimberly WOODARD
04 Exec Assistant to the President ... Ms. Kathy TAYLOR
09 Director of Institutional Research ... Dr. Willie KIRKLAND
31 Director Community Development ... Mr. Nick L. HARRIS
19 Chief of Police ... Mr. Julian COAXUM
15 Director of Human Resources ... Mrs. Brittany RICHARDSON
26 Dir of Marketing Communications ... Ms. Alina HERNANDEZ
08 Interim Dean of Library/Learning ... Ms. Cynthia CHARLES
49 Dean of College of Arts & Sciences ... Dr. Eartha JOHNSON
96 Purchasing Officer ... Ms. Anlatear KIRKLIN
103 Dir Workforce/Career Development ... Ms. Caretta COOKE
105 Director Web Services ... Mr. Norward SEARS
13 Chief Info Technology Officer (CIO) ... Mr. Cederic KONYAOLE
22 Dir Affirmative Action/EEO ... Ms. Sheila JUDGE
25 Chief Contracts/Grants Admin ... Mr. Theodore CALLIER
39 Director Student Housing ... Ms. Danette GREEN
41 Athletic Director ... Dr. Kiki BAKER-BARNES
50 Dean of Business ... Dr. Richard IGWIKI
29 Director Alumni Relations ... Mrs. Adrian GUY-ANDERSON
44 Director Annual or Planned Giving ... Mr. Christian PRYOR
84 Director Enrollment Management ... Mr. David PAGE

Fortis College (F)

9255 Interline Avenue, Baton Rouge LA 70809
County: East Baton Rouge FICE Identification: 034803
Unit ID: 439738
Telephone: (225) 248-1015 Carnegie Class: Spec 2-yr-Health
FAX Number: (225) 248-9517 Calendar System: Other
URL: www.fortis.edu
Established: 1991 Annual Undergrad Tuition & Fees: $14,337
Enrollment: 395 Coed
Affiliation or Control: Proprietary IRS Status: Proprietary
Highest Offering: Associate Degree
Accreditation: ABHES, MLTAD, RAD, SURGT, SURTEC

01 Campus President ... Mr. Darrell JOY
37 Financial Aid Director ... Ms. Mary RICAUD

Franciscan Missionaries of Our Lady University (G)

5414 Brittany Drive, Baton Rouge LA 70808
County: East Baton Rouge FICE Identification: 031062
Unit ID: 160074
Telephone: (225) 768-1700 Carnegie Class: Spec-4-yr-Other Health
FAX Number: (225) 768-0811 Calendar System: Semester
URL: www.ololcollege.edu
Established: 1923 Annual Undergrad Tuition & Fees: $12,046
Enrollment: 1,651 Coed
Affiliation or Control: Roman Catholic IRS Status: 501(c)3
Highest Offering: Doctorate
Accreditation: SC, ANEST, ARCPA, COARC, @DIETI, MT, NUR, PTAA, RAD

01 President ... Dr. Tina HOLLAND
05 Vice Pres for Academic Affairs ... Br.Dr. Edward VIOLETT
30 VP for Institutional Advancement ... Ms. Judith ROBERSON
10 Vice Pres Operations & Finance ... Vacant
84 VP Stdnt Affairs/Enrollment Mgmt ... Ms. Rebecca CANNON
88 VP for Mission Identity ... Sr. Martha Ann ABSHIRE
66 Dean School of Nursing ... Dr. Amy HALL
76 Dean School of Health Professions ... Dr. Susan STEELE-MOSES
32 Dean of Students ... Dr. Alison WELLS
49 Dean of School of Arts & Sciences ... Dr. Brian RASH
37 Director Financial Aid ... Mr. Terry MARTIN
06 Registrar ... Ms. Kimberly JONES-JAMES
88 Director Physician Asst Studies ... Ms. Sarah DEYO
88 Director Nurse Anesthesia Program ... Dr. Aimee BADEAUX
76 Director Radiologic Technology ... Ms. Nicole ST. GERMAIN
76 Director Clinical Lab Sciences ... Dr. Debbie FOX
76 Director Physical Therapist Asst ... Ms. Leah GEHEBER
88 Dir Health Service Administration ... Dr. Riaz FERDAUS
76 Director Respiratory Therapy ... Ms. Sue DAVIS
88 Director Writing Center ... Mr. Angus WOODWARD
13 Director of Information Systems ... Mr. Edward LEWIS
07 Director of Admissions ... Vacant
09 Dir Institutional Effectiveness ... Ms. Candi MCELHENY
04 Executive Asst to President ... Ms. Kimberly MELANCON

Herzing University (H)

2500 Williams Boulevard, Kenner LA 70062
Telephone: (504) 733-0074 Identification: 666450
Accreditation: &NH, MAAB, SURTEC

† Regional accreditation is carried under the parent institution in Madison, WI.

ITI Technical College (I)

13944 Airline Highway, Baton Rouge LA 70817-5998
County: East Baton Rouge FICE Identification: 021662
Unit ID: 159197
Telephone: (225) 752-4230 Carnegie Class: Spec 2-yr-Tech
FAX Number: (225) 756-0903 Calendar System: Quarter
URL: www.iticollege.edu
Established: 1973 Annual Undergrad Tuition & Fees: $10,575
Enrollment: 816 Coed
Affiliation or Control: Proprietary IRS Status: Proprietary
Highest Offering: Associate Degree
Accreditation: ACCSC

01 President ... Mr. Earl Joe MARTIN, III
03 Vice President ... Mr. Mark WORTHY
05 Dean of Education ... Ms. Lisa LAUNEY
88 Director of Compliance ... Mr. Michael CHAMPAGNE
06 Registrar ... Ms. Teresa MAYEUX
07 Director of Admissions ... Mr. Shawn NORRIS
37 Director Student Financial Aid ... Ms. Connie ROUBIQUE

Louisiana College (J)

1140 College Drive, Pineville LA 71359-0001
County: Rapides FICE Identification: 002007
Unit ID: 159568
Telephone: (318) 487-7000 Carnegie Class: Masters/M
FAX Number: (318) 487-7800 Calendar System: Semester
URL: www.lacollege.edu
Established: 1906 Annual Undergrad Tuition & Fees: $15,978
Enrollment: 1,092 Coed
Affiliation or Control: Southern Baptist IRS Status: 501(c)3
Highest Offering: Master's
Accreditation: SC, ACBSP, #CAATE, CAEPT, MUS, NURSE, PTAA, SW

01 President ... Dr. Rick BREWER
03 VP Integration Faith/Learning ... Dr. Philip CAPLES
05 Interim Vice Pres Academic Affairs ... Dr. Cheryl CLARK
10 Vice President for Business Affairs ... Mr. Randall HARGIS
111 VP Inst Advancement/New Projects ... Mr. Byron MCGEE
32 Dean of Students ... Mr. Vince SMITH
06 Registrar ... Ms. Eileen DEBOER
84 VP Enrollment Mgmt/Admissions ... Vacant
37 Director of Financial Aid ... Mr. Jeremy TREME
08 Director of the Library ... Mr. Howard TRYON
26 VP Comm/Integrative Marketing ... Mr. Norman MILLER
13 Director Computer Services ... Mr. Shane DAVIS
18 Director of Physical Plant ... Mr. Randall HARGIS
21 Director of Business Office ... Ms. Beverly INGRAM
39 Director of Housing ... Vacant
41 Athletic Director ... Mr. Reni MASON
42 Baptist Student Union Director ... Mr. Thomas WORSHAM
35 Director Student Activities ... Ms. K. B THOMAS
36 Director Career Development ... Mrs. Leneil MERCER
09 Coor of Institutional Research ... Ms. Lisa PRICE
38 Director Student Counseling ... Ms. Leneil MERCER
07 Director of Admissions ... Ms. Renee MELDER
15 Director Personnel Services ... Ms. Shannon TASSIN
40 Bookstore Manager ... Ms. Linda BILLINGSLEY
29 Director of Alumni Relations ... Ms. Kathy OVERTURF
19 Coordinator of Safety & Security ... Mr. Charles ROBERTSON
23 Coordinator of Health Services ... Ms. Janet SANDERS
04 Executive Asst to the President ... Ms. Karen WATKINS

*Louisiana Community & Technical College System (A)

265 S Foster Drive, Baton Rouge LA 70806-4104
County: East Baton Rouge Identification: 666188
Telephone: (225) 922-2800 Carnegie Class: N/A
FAX Number: (225) 922-2392
URL: www.lctcs.edu

01 President Dr. Monty SULLIVAN
10 Chief Operations Officer Mr. Joseph F. MARIN
30 Chief External Affairs Officer Mr. David HELVESTON
26 Exec Director Media Relations Mr. Quintin TAYLOR

*Baton Rouge Community College (B)

201 Community College Drive,
Baton Rouge LA 70806-4156
County: East Baton Rouge FICE Identification: 037303
Unit ID: 437103
Telephone: (225) 216-8000 Carnegie Class: Assoc/HT-Mix Trad/Non
FAX Number: (225) 216-8100 Calendar System: Semester
URL: www.mybrcc.edu
Established: 1998 Annual Undergrad Tuition & Fees (In-District): $4,221
Enrollment: 7,641 Coed
Affiliation or Control: State/Local IRS Status: 501(c)3
Highest Offering: Associate Degree
Accreditation: SC, ACBSP, ACFEI, ADNUR, CONST, DMS, NAIT, SURGT

02 Chancellor Dr. Larissa LITTLETON-STEIB
04 Asst to the Chancellor Ms. Tuesday A. GRAY
26 Exec Dir of PR & Marketing Ms. Kizzy PAYTON
05 Vice Chanc Academic/Student Affs Ms. Deborah LEA
09 Int VC Inst Effect/Strategic Init Dr. Vladimir APPEANING
103 Vice Chanc for Workforce Devel Mr. Charles FREEBURGH
30 Vice Chanc for Inst Adv/Foundation Mr. Philip L. SMITH, JR.
46 Dir of Business Process Improv Ms. Dionne ANDRUS
10 Vice Chanc for Finance & Admin Ms. Helen HARRIS
21 Director of Acct & Finance Mr. Corlin LEBLANC
21 Director of Budgets Ms. Quintesah SYAS
13 Chief Information Officer Mr. Ronald SOLOMON
15 Interim Chief HR Officer Ms. Mary GLOSTON
19 Chief of Police Ms. Genoria TILLEY
25 Dir Grants Resource Center Ms. Ann ZANDERS
18 Exec Dir of Facilities/Env Safety Mr. Bill SMITH
29 Alumni Relations Manager Ms. Georgia SCOBEE
32 Exec Dir of Student Development Dr. Teresa A. JONES
35 Assoc Dean of Students Ms. Stacia HARDY
36 Director of Career Services Ms. Lisa HIBNER
37 Director of Financial Aid Ms. Miracle DAVIS
41 Athletic Director Vacant
38 Director of Student Success Ms. Wendy DEVALL
88 Dir of Academic Learning Center Ms. Jeanne STACY
88 Upward Bound Program Director Ms. Darica SIMON
35 Int Dir of Student Services Center Mr. Johnny MANELA
96 Director of Purchasing Vacant
06 Registrar Ms. Erin BLAKE
88 Asst Director of Financial Aid Ms. Kimberly ZANDERS

*Bossier Parish Community College (C)

6220 E Texas Street, Bossier City LA 71111-6922
County: Bossier FICE Identification: 020554
Unit ID: 158431
Telephone: (318) 678-6000 Carnegie Class: Assoc/HT-Mix Trad/Non
FAX Number: (318) 678-6389 Calendar System: Semester
URL: www.bpcc.edu
Established: 1966 Annual Undergrad Tuition & Fees (In-District): $4,079
Enrollment: 7,839 Coed
Affiliation or Control: State/Local IRS Status: 501(c)3
Highest Offering: Associate Degree
Accreditation: SC, ACFEI, ADNUR, COARC, EMT, MAC, NAIT, OTA, PHLEB, PTAA, SURGT

02 Chancellor Dr. Douglas R. BATEMAN
05 VC for Academic Affairs Ms. Lesa TAYLOR DUPREE
11 Exec VC Business Affs Mr. Tom WILLIAMS
32 VC of Student Services Ms. Karen RECCHIA
103 VC of Econ & Workforce Devl Dr. Gayle FLOWERS
10 Assoc VC Finance Mr. Raymond ABRAHAM
45 Assoc VC Inst Planning & Assessment Dr. Holly FRENCH-HART
51 Dean of Workforce Develop/Cont Educ Ms. Lisa WARGO
08 Dean of Learning Resources Ms. Brenda BRANTLEY
21 Comptroller Vacant
37 Director Student Financial Aid Ms. Vicki TEMPLE
06 Registrar Mr. Richard COCKERHAM
26 Director of Public Relations Ms. Tracy MCGILL
15 Director of Human Resources Ms. Teri BASHARA
35 Director of Student Life Ms. Marjoree HARPER
13 Chief Information Officer Vacant
22 Diversity/Multicultural Affairs Ms. Marjoree HARPER
72 Director of Educational Technology Mr. Charley CAMERON
18 Dir Physical Plant & Maintenance Vacant
30 Director Institutional Advancement Vacant
25 Director of Grants Ms. Jennifer LAWRENCE
96 Director of Purchasing Ms. Gayle DOUCET
04 Exec Assistant to Chancellor Ms. Christy MOORE
07 Dean of Enrollment Management Ms. Kathy VERCHER
108 Dir Institutional Effectiveness Ms. Allison MARTIN
19 Director Security/Safety Mr. Mike MAY
60 Dean of Comm & Performing Arts Dr. Ray Scott CRAWFORD
50 Dean of Business Ms. Peggy FULLER
54 Dean of TEM Ms. Sandra PARTAIN
66 Dean of Sci/Nursing/Allied Health Ms. Carolyn BURROUGHS
49 Dean of Liberal Arts Ms. Vicki DENNIS
83 Dean of Behavioral Social Sciences Ms. Kay BOSTON
121 Dean of Acad Advising Ms. Peggy FULLER
09 Int Dir of Inst Research/Assessment Ms. Staci PHILLIPS
41 Athletic Director Mr. John RENNIE

*Central Louisiana Technical College Avoyelles Campus (D)

508 Choupique Street, Cottonport LA 71327-3743
County: Avoyelles FICE Identification: 008317
Unit ID: 158237
Telephone: (318) 876-2401 Carnegie Class: Not Classified
FAX Number: (318) 876-2634 Calendar System: Semester
URL: www.cltcc.edu
Established: 1938 Annual Undergrad Tuition & Fees (In-District): N/A
Enrollment: N/A Coed
Affiliation or Control: State/Local IRS Status: 501(c)3
Highest Offering: Associate Degree
Accreditation: COE

02 Campus Dean Ms. Jacqueline AUSBON

*Central Louisiana Technical College Oakdale Campus (E)

117 Highway 1152, Oakdale LA 71463-3536
County: Allen FICE Identification: 030026
Unit ID: 160047
Telephone: (318) 335-3944 Carnegie Class: Not Classified
FAX Number: (318) 335-3347 Calendar System: Quarter
URL: www.cltcc.edu
Established: 1999 Annual Undergrad Tuition & Fees (In-District): N/A
Enrollment: N/A Coed
Affiliation or Control: State/Local IRS Status: 501(c)3
Highest Offering: Associate Degree
Accreditation: COE

02 Campus Dean Ms. Kim ANDREWS

*Central Louisiana Technical Community College (F)

4311 S. MacArthur Drive, Alexandria LA 71301
County: Rapides FICE Identification: 005489
Unit ID: 158088
Telephone: (318) 487-5443 Carnegie Class: Assoc/HVT-High Non
FAX Number: (318) 487-5970 Calendar System: Trimester
URL: www.cltcc.edu
Established: 1965 Annual Undergrad Tuition & Fees (In-State): $4,089
Enrollment: 2,445 Coed
Affiliation or Control: State IRS Status: 501(c)3
Highest Offering: Associate Degree
Accreditation: COE

02 Chancellor Dr. James (Jimmy) R. SAWTELLE, III
05 Vice Chanc Academic Affairs Mr. William TULAK
10 Vice Chanc of Finance/Admin Ms. Lee MOORE
32 Exec VC Stdnt Affs/Enroll Mgmt Ms. Heather POOLE

*Central Louisiana Technical & Community College-Huey P. Long Campus (G)

5960 Highway 167 N, Winnfield LA 71483-5075
County: Winn FICE Identification: 005480
Unit ID: 159090
Telephone: (318) 628-4342 Carnegie Class: Not Classified
FAX Number: (318) 628-7768 Calendar System: Semester
URL: www.cltcc.edu
Established: 1938 Annual Undergrad Tuition & Fees (In-District): N/A
Enrollment: N/A Coed
Affiliation or Control: State/Local IRS Status: 501(c)3
Highest Offering: Associate Degree
Accreditation: COE

02 Campus Dean Mr. Jeff JOHNSON

*Delgado Community College (H)

615 City Park Avenue, New Orleans LA 70119-4399
County: Orleans FICE Identification: 004625
Unit ID: 158662
Telephone: (504) 671-5000 Carnegie Class: Assoc/MT-VT-High Trad
FAX Number: (504) 361-6699 Calendar System: Semester
URL: www.dcc.edu
Established: 1921 Annual Undergrad Tuition & Fees (In-District): $3,911
Enrollment: 16,131 Coed
Affiliation or Control: State/Local IRS Status: 501(c)3
Highest Offering: Associate Degree
Accreditation: SC, ACBSP, ACFEI, ADNUR, CAHIIM, COARC, DMS, EMT, ENGT, FUSER, MLTAD, NAIT, NMT, OTA, PHLEB, POLYT, PTAA, RAD, RTT, SURGT

02 Chancellor Ms. Joan Y. DAVIS
10 VC Business/Admin Affairs Mr. Ralph W. JOHNSON
05 Int VC Acad Affs/Col Provost Ms. Joan Y. DAVIS
103 Int VC Workforce Dev/Tech Educ Dr. Stanton F. MCNEELY, III
111 VC Inst Advancement/Public Rels Dr. Stanton F. MCNEELY, III
66 Exec Dean Charity School of Nursing Dr. Cheryl MYERS
76 Dean Allied Health Mr. Harold GASPARD
50 Dean Business & Technology Mr. Warren PUNEKY
60 Int Dean Communication Division Ms. Emily COSPER
81 Dean Science & Math Mr. Thomas GRUBER
79 Dean Arts and Humanities Ms. Patrice MOORE
106 Dean Distance Lrng/Instruct Tech Dr. Jeanne SAMUEL
12 Exec Dean West Bank Campus Dr. Peter CHO
12 Exec Dean City Park/VC Stdnt Affs Dr. Arnel COSEY
12 Exec Dean Sidney Collier Dr. Tamika DUPLESSIS
15 Asst Vice Chanc for Human Resources Ms. Carla MAJOR
13 AVC Information Technology Mr. Thomas LOVINCE
21 Asst VC Financial Services Mr. Ronald RUSSO
18 Asst VC Facilities & Planning Mr. James ROYER
21 Asst VC/Controller Ms. Garnette LISTI
04 Executive Asst to the Chancellor Ms. Traci SMOTHERS
72 Asst Dean Business & Technology Ms. Karen MUHSIN
09 Institutional Research Manager Mr. Brian AURITI
88 Exec Dir Curriculum & Pgm Devel Mr. Timothy STAMM
08 Dean Library Mr. Timothy STAMM
37 Director Financial Aid Ms. Rhonda KING
41 Athletic Director Mr. Joe SCHEUERMANN
06 College Registrar Ms. Maria CISNEROS
07 Director Admissions/Enrollment Svcs Ms. Gwen BOUTTE
44 Director Restricted Funds Ms. Sarah CAMANIA
35 Director Student Life Mrs. Michelle GRECO
121 Director Advising & Testing Ms. Tania CARRADINE
96 Director Purchasing Ms. Susan VARBLE
19 Interim Director Campus Police Mr. Ralph W. JOHNSON

*L.E. Fletcher Technical Community College (I)

1407 Highway 311, Schriever LA 70395
County: Terrebonne FICE Identification: 005761
Unit ID: 160481
Telephone: (985) 448-7900 Carnegie Class: Assoc/HVT-High Non
FAX Number: (985) 446-3308 Calendar System: Semester
URL: www.fletcher.edu
Established: 1948 Annual Undergrad Tuition & Fees (In-State): $3,951
Enrollment: 1,951 Coed
Affiliation or Control: State IRS Status: Exempt
Highest Offering: Associate Degree
Accreditation: SC, ADNUR, COARC, NAIT, PHLEB, PNUR

02 Chancellor Dr. Kristine STRICKLAND
05 Vice Chancellor of Academic Affairs Dr. Regina VERDIN
10 Vice Chancellor of Finance Mr. Matthew SWANSON
103 Associate VC of Workforce Ms. Tandra LEMAY
06 Registrar Ms. Lisa HIDALGO
09 Director of Inst Research & Effect Ms. Carrie CORTEZ
21 Director of Accounting Mr. Andrew BOYNE
32 Associate VC Student Services Dr. Becky MCBRIDE
66 Dean of Nursing and Allied Health Ms. Sonia CLARKE
07 Director of Admissions Ms. Ana NANNEY
15 Director of Human Resources Ms. Gina MARCEL
37 Director of Financial Aid Mr. Derrick PROCELL
04 Assistant to the Chancellor Ms. Brenda FAUCHEUX
08 Head Librarian Vacant
30 Interim Exec Dir Inst Advancement Mrs. Nicol BLANCHARD
49 Dean Art and Sciences Mrs. Donna ESTRADA
25 Director Grant Writing Initiatives Mrs. Catherine BARBER
96 Director of Purchasing Ms. Nancy CLEMENT

*Louisiana Delta Community College (J)

7500 Millhaven Road, Monroe LA 71203
County: Ouachita Parish FICE Identification: 041301
Unit ID: 483212
Telephone: (318) 345-9000 Carnegie Class: Assoc/HVT-High Trad
FAX Number: N/A Calendar System: Semester
URL: www.ladelta.edu
Established: 2001 Annual Undergrad Tuition & Fees (In-District): $4,158
Enrollment: 2,080 Coed
Affiliation or Control: State/Local IRS Status: 501(c)3
Highest Offering: Associate Degree
Accreditation: SC, ADNUR, NAIT

02 Chancellor Mr. William D. EPPS
05 Vice Chanc of Academic Affairs Vacant
10 VC of Finance & Administration Mr. Wendell COPLIN
84 Dir of Enrollment Mgmt/Registrar Mr. Adam ABERCROMBIE
32 Vice Chanc Academics/Student Affs Dr. John TURNER
30 Exec Dir of Dev/Alumni Relations Mr. James JOPLING
13 Chief Information Officer Mr. Bradley MASTERS
26 Director of Public Relations Ms. Darian ATKINS

*Northshore Technical Community College (K)

1710 Sullivan Drive, Bogalusa LA 70427-5866
County: Washington FICE Identification: 006756
Unit ID: 160667
Telephone: (985) 732-6640 Carnegie Class: Assoc/HVT-High Non
FAX Number: (985) 732-6603 Calendar System: Semester
URL: www.northshorecollege.edu
Established: 1930 Annual Undergrad Tuition & Fees (In-District): $4,103

Enrollment: 3,655 Coed
Affiliation or Control: State/Local IRS Status: 501(c)3
Highest Offering: Associate Degree
Accreditation: COE

02 Chancellor .... Dr. William S. WAINWRIGHT
05 Provost/Vice Chancellor of Academic .... Dr. Daniel ROBERTS
10 Vice Chancellor Finance & Admin .... Mr. Marc CHAUVIN
45 Vice Chancellor Strategic Initiativ .... Dr. Tina TINNEY
108 Vice Prov Assessment & Plng .... Ms. Sheila SINGLETARY
32 Vice Provost Student Affairs .... Ms. Christy MONTGOMERY
20 Associate Provost Academics .... Dr. Jim CARLSON
76 Assoc Provost Health Sci/Nursing .... Dr. Kenneth TILLMAN
75 Associate Provost Technical Studies .... Mr. Dewayne LAMBERT
06 Assistant Provost Compliance/Record .... Mr. Paul DONALDSON
12 Dean of Campus Administration .... Ms. Kim FINCH
12 Dean of Campus Administration .... Ms. Bridget LABORDE
15 Human Resources Director .... Ms. Joanna DILLMAN
18 Director of Facilities .... Mr. Kelly PERRIN
08 Director of Library Services .... Ms. Margaret KELLER
37 Financial Aid Director .... Ms. Nichole LABAT
13 Director Information Tech/Elearning .... Mr. Khiem NGO
09 Assoc Director Institutional Rsrch .... Ms. Darriona LEE

*Northwest Louisiana Technical College Northwest Campus (A)

9500 Industrial Drive, Minden LA 71055
County: Webster FICE Identification: 009975
Unit ID: 160010
Telephone: (318) 371-3035 Carnegie Class: Assoc/HVT-High Non
FAX Number: (318) 371-3026 Calendar System: Trimester
URL: www.nwltc.edu
Established: 1952 Annual Undergrad Tuition & Fees (In-District): $2,976
Enrollment: 2,924 Coed
Affiliation or Control: State/Local IRS Status: 501(c)3
Highest Offering: Associate Degree
Accreditation: COE

02 Director .... Mr. Earl MEADOR
15 Chief Human Resources Officer .... Ms. Amber SAUNDERS
10 Chief Financial Officer .... Ms. Jennifer PYE
37 Director of Financial Aid .... Ms. Sheri BUTLER
32 Director of Student Affairs .... Mr. Stephen LONG
09 Director of Institutional Research .... Mr. David RHODES
103 Director of Workforce Development .... Ms. Dianne CLARK
05 Chief Academic Officer .... Vacant

*Nunez Community College (B)

3710 Paris Road, Chalmette LA 70043-1297
County: Saint Bernard FICE Identification: 021661
Unit ID: 158884
Telephone: (504) 278-6200 Carnegie Class: Assoc/HVT-High Non
FAX Number: (504) 278-6480 Calendar System: Semester
URL: www.nunez.edu
Established: 1992 Annual Undergrad Tuition & Fees (In-District): $4,103
Enrollment: 2,629 Coed
Affiliation or Control: State/Local IRS Status: 501(c)3
Highest Offering: Associate Degree
Accreditation: SC, EMT, NAIT

02 Chancellor .... Dr. Thomas R. WARNER
05 Vice Chanc Academic & Student Affs .... Vacant
30 VC for Institutional Advancement .... Ms. Teresa L. SMITH
10 Chief Financial Officer .... Mr. David HUFF
15 Dir Human Res/Exec Asst to Chanc .... Mr. Richard GREENE
20 Dean of Academic Affairs .... Ms. Tonia LORIA
32 Dean for Student Affairs .... Ms. Becky MAILLET
45 Dean Planning/Inst Effectiveness .... Mr. Leonard UNBEHAGEN
103 Director Workforce Development .... Mr. Ernest T. FRAZIER, JR.
06 Registrar .... Ms. Meg GREENFIELD
07 Director of Admissions .... Mrs. Brittney BARRAS
37 Director Financial Aid .... Ms. Maria SANCHEZ
26 Public Information Officer .... Ms. Lindsey JAKIEL DIULUS
18 Coordinator of Facilities .... Ms. Dawn HART-THORE
25 Director of Sponsored Programs .... Vacant
13 IT Manager .... Mr. Jason HOSCH

*River Parishes Community College (C)

PO Box 2367, Gonzales LA 70707
County: Ascension FICE Identification: 037894
Unit ID: 436304
Telephone: (225) 743-8500 Carnegie Class: Assoc/MT-VT-High Non
FAX Number: (225) 644-8210 Calendar System: Semester
URL: www.rpcc.edu
Established: 1999 Annual Undergrad Tuition & Fees (In-District): $4,079
Enrollment: 1,956 Coed
Affiliation or Control: State/Local IRS Status: 501(c)3
Highest Offering: Associate Degree
Accreditation: SC, NAIT

02 Chancellor .... Dr. Dale DOTY
10 VC Business/Finance/Administration .... Khalli HAGAN
05 VC of Academic & Student Affairs .... Dr. Abigail STONEROCK
103 VC Workforce Development .... Dr. Bruce WAGUESPACK
111 Director Institutional Advancement .... Glen DUCAN
32 Chief Student Affairs Officer .... Melvin HARRISON
37 Interim Director Financial Aid .... Christina OCMAND
38 Director Student Counseling .... Shalither CUSHENBERRY
08 Director of Library Services .... Wendy JOHNSON
15 Human Resource Manager .... Donna WHITTINGTON
09 Director of Institutional Research .... Melba KENNEDY
06 Registrar .... Arthur GILLIS

*South Central Louisiana Technical College Young Memorial Campus (D)

900 Youngs Road, Morgan City LA 70380-2931
County: Saint Mary FICE Identification: 005526
Unit ID: 160913
Telephone: (985) 380-2957 Carnegie Class: Spec 2-yr-Tech
FAX Number: (985) 380-2440 Calendar System: Semester
URL: www.scl.edu
Established: 1965 Annual Undergrad Tuition & Fees (In-District): $2,996
Enrollment: 2,669 Coed
Affiliation or Control: State/Local IRS Status: 501(c)3
Highest Offering: Associate Degree
Accreditation: COE

02 Interim College Director .... Dr. Willie SMITH
05 Chief Academic Officer .... Ms. Melanie HENRY
07 Dir of Admissions/Student Affairs .... Ms. Tammie L. MOORE
09 Director of Institutional Research .... Ms. Nadja HAYNIE
15 Director Human Resources .... Ms. Pam MILLER
103 Chief Workforce Development Ofcr .... Mr. Anthony L. BAHAM

*South Louisiana Community College (E)

1101 Bertrand Drive, Lafayette LA 70506-4124
County: Lafayette FICE Identification: 039563
Unit ID: 434061
Telephone: (337) 521-9000 Carnegie Class: Assoc/HVT-High Non
FAX Number: (337) 521-9061 Calendar System: Semester
URL: www.solacc.edu
Established: 1998 Annual Undergrad Tuition & Fees (In-District): $4,205
Enrollment: 6,958 Coed
Affiliation or Control: State/Local IRS Status: 501(c)3
Highest Offering: Associate Degree
Accreditation: SC, ACFEI, ADNUR, EMT, MLTAD, NAIT

02 Chancellor .... Dr. Natalie HARDER
04 Sr Exec Assistant to the Chancellor .... Ms. Kelly GREENE
09 Vice Chanc Strategic Initiatives .... Dr. Micheal GLISSON
10 Vice Chanc Finance & Administration .... Mr. Bryan GLATTER
103 Vice Chanc Economic & Workforce Dev .... Vacant
32 Vice Chanc for Student Services .... Dr. Vincent JUNE
37 Asst Director of Financial Aid .... Ms. Janelle MANUEL
08 Director of Library Services .... Ms. Katherine ROLFES
88 Director of Student Accounts .... Ms. Katrina HEARD
21 Director of Accounting .... Ms. Carla ORTEGO
18 Director of Facilities .... Mr. Edwin LOPEZ
15 Dir Administration/Human Resources .... Ms. Alicia HULIN
06 Registrar .... Ms. Connie CHOPIN
19 Director Security/Safety .... Mr. Stephen NORTH
26 Communications & Marketing Director .... Ms. Christine PAYTON
84 Director Enrollment Management .... Ms. Debbie TABCHOURI

*Sowela Technical Community College (F)

PO Box 16950, Lake Charles LA 70616-6950
County: Calcasieu FICE Identification: 005467
Unit ID: 160579
Telephone: (337) 421-6565 Carnegie Class: Assoc/HVT-High Trad
FAX Number: (337) 491-2135 Calendar System: Semester
URL: www.sowela.edu
Established: 1938 Annual Undergrad Tuition & Fees (In-District): $4,185
Enrollment: 3,722 Coed
Affiliation or Control: State/Local IRS Status: 501(c)3
Highest Offering: Associate Degree
Accreditation: SC, ACFEI, NAIT

02 Chancellor .... Dr. Neil ASPINWALL
04 Assistant to the Chancellor .... Ms. Mary REEDER
05 Vice Chancellor Academic Affairs .... Ms. Paula HELLUMS
10 Vice Chancellor Finance .... Ms. Jeanine NEWMAN
103 Exec Dir of Workforce Solutions .... Mr. David HAYES
13 Chief Info Res & Tech Officer .... Dr. Martha J. SCHEXNEIDER
84 Exec Dir Enroll Mgmt/Stdnt Affs .... Ms. Anna DAIGLE
21 Controller .... Mr. Francis PORCHE, JR.
37 Director of Financial Aid .... Ms. Allison DERING
08 Director of Library Services .... Ms. Mary Frances SHERWOOD
15 Director of Human Resources .... Dr. FitzPatrick ANYANWU
35 Director of Student Support Svcs .... Ms. Christine COLLINS
18 Director Facilities Planning & Mgmt .... Mr. Davidson DARBONE
09 Exec Director Planning & Analysis ... Dr. Fitzpatrick U. ANYANWU
111 Exec Dir Institutional Advancement .... Ms. Marianne WHITE

*Northwest Louisiana Technical College Natchitoches Campus (G)

6587 Highway 1 Bypass, Natchitoches LA 71458-0657
Telephone: (318) 357-3162 FICE Identification: 021602
Accreditation: COE

† Branch campus of Northwest Louisiana Technical College Northwest Campus, Minden, LA.

*Northwest Louisiana Technical College Shreveport Campus (H)

Box 78527, 2010 N Market Street, Shreveport LA 71137-8527
Telephone: (318) 676-7811 FICE Identification: 005469
Accreditation: COE

† Branch campus of Northwest Louisiana Technical College Northwest Campus, Minden, LA.

*South Central Louisiana Technical College Lafourche Campus (I)

1425 Tiger Drive, Thibodaux LA 70301-4336
Telephone: (985) 447-0924 FICE Identification: 030091
Accreditation: COE, SURGT

† Branch campus of South Central Louisiana Technical College Young Memorial Campus.

*South Central Louisiana Technical College Reserve Campus (J)

181 Regala Park Road, Reserve LA 70084-0542
Telephone: (985) 536-4418 FICE Identification: 023334
Accreditation: COE, NAIT

† Branch campus of South Central Louisiana Technical Colege Young Memorial Campus.

Louisiana Culinary Institute (K)

10550 Airline Highway, Baton Rouge LA 70816-4109
County: East Baton Rouge FICE Identification: 041123
Unit ID: 449612
Telephone: (225) 769-8820 Carnegie Class: Spec 2-yr-A&S
FAX Number: (225) 769-8792 Calendar System: Semester
URL: www.lci.edu
Established: 2002 Annual Undergrad Tuition & Fees: $14,575
Enrollment: 207 Coed
Affiliation or Control: Proprietary IRS Status: Proprietary
Highest Offering: Associate Degree
Accreditation: COE, ACFEI

01 Chief Executive Officer .... Keith RUSH

*Louisiana State University Administration (L)

3810 W Lakeshore Drive, Baton Rouge LA 70808-4600
County: East Baton Rouge FICE Identification: 002009
Unit ID: 159638
Telephone: (225) 578-2111 Carnegie Class: N/A
FAX Number: (225) 578-5524
URL: www.lsu.edu

01 President .... Dr. F. King ALEXANDER
05 VP Academic Affairs/Tech Trans .... Dr. Richard J. KOUBEK
17 Exec VP HC/Med Educ Redesign .... Dr. Frank OPELKA
10 Vice Chancellor Finance/Admin .... Mr. John HARMAN
18 System Director Facility Planning .... Mr. Danny MAHAFFEY
43 LSU Lead Counsel .... Mr. Thomas SKINNER
15 System Dir Human Resource/Risk Mgt ... Ms. Sharyon LIPSCOMB
21 System Director Internal Audit .... Mr. Chad BRACKIN

*Louisiana State University and Agricultural and Mechanical College (M)

Baton Rouge LA 70803-0100
County: East Baton Rouge FICE Identification: 002010
Unit ID: 159391
Telephone: (225) 578-3202 Carnegie Class: DU-Highest
FAX Number: (225) 578-6400 Calendar System: Semester
URL: www.lsu.edu
Established: 1860 Annual Undergrad Tuition & Fees (In-State): $10,814
Enrollment: 31,524 Coed
Affiliation or Control: State IRS Status: 501(c)3
Highest Offering: Doctorate
Accreditation: SC, ART, CAATE, CACREP, CAEPN, CIDA, CLPSY, CONST, CS, DIETD, ENG, IPSY, JOUR, LAW, LIB, LSAR, MUS, SCPSY, SP, SPAA, SW, THEA, VET

02 President .... Dr. King ALEXANDER
05 Exec Vice Pres/Provost .... Dr. Richard KOUBEK
43 General Counsel .... Mr. Thomas SKINNER
26 Int VP Strategic Communication .... Dr. Jason DRODDY
10 Exec Vice Pres Finance & Admin/CFO .... Mr. Daniel LAYZELL
46 Vice Pres Research & Econ Dev .... Dr. Kalliat T. VALSARAJ
45 Vice Pres Strategic Initiatives .... Dr. Isiah M. WARNER
32 Vice Pres Student Affairs .... Dr. Kurt J. KEPPLER
102 President/CEO LSU Foundation .... Mr. Bryan BENCHOFF
28 Vice Prov Office of Diversity .... Mr. Dereck ROVARIS
20 Sr Vice Prov Academic Affairs .... Dr. Jane CASSIDY
20 Assoc Vice Pres Academic Programs .... Dr. Matt LEE
15 Assoc VP Human Resources Mgmt .... Mr. A.G MONACO
84 Chief Enrollment Officer .... Mr. Jose AVILES
111 Exec Director Inst Advancement .... Ms. Bunnie CANNON
86 Exec Dir Pub Policy & Ext Affairs .... Dr. Jason DRODDY

85 Assoc VP International Programs Dr. Hector ZAPATA
37 Assoc Dir Student Aid/Scholarships Ms. Amy MARIX
08 Dean LSU Libraries Mr. Stanley WILDER
79 Dean College of Hum & Soc Sciences Dr. Stacia HAYNIE
58 Dean of Graduate School Dr. Michelle MASSE
54 Dean College of Engineering Dr. Judy WORNAT
47 Dean College of Agriculture Dr. William RICHARDSON
50 Dean Ourso College of Business Dr. Richard D. WHITE
64 Dean College Music & Dramatic Arts Mr. Todd QUEEN
81 Dean College of Science Dr. Cynthia PETERSON
62 Dean Sch of Library & Info Science Dr. Carol BARRY
53 Dean College of Human Sci & Educ Dr. Damon P. ANDREW
57 Dean College of Art & Design Mr. Alkis TSOLAKIS
74 Dean Veterinary Medicine Dr. Joel D. BAINES
60 Dean Manship Sch of Mass Comm Dr. Jerry CEPPOS
92 Dean Honors College Dr. Jonathan H. EARLE
65 Dean Sch of Coast & Environ Dr. Christopher D'ELIA
88 Int Exec Dir University College Ms. Andrea JONES
35 Assc Dean of Student/Dir Greek Life Ms. Angela GUILLORY
88 Sr Ex Dir SN Ctr Security Rsch Trng Mr. Jeff MOULTON
88 Exec Director Center Energy Stds Mr. David DISMUKES
51 Exec Director Continuing Education Mr. Douglas P. WEIMER
29 President LSU Alumni Association Mr. Cliff VANNOY
88 Exec Director LSU Museum of Art Dr. Daniel STETSON
18 Exec Director Facility Services Mr. Tony LOMBARDO
13 Assoc VP & Chief Technology Officer Ms. Andrea BALLINGER
75 Int Dir Sch Human Res Ed & Wk Dev Dr. Reid BATES
80 Director Public Admin Institute Dr. Jared L. LORENS
88 Director LSU Press Ms. MaryKatherine CALLAWAY
41 Vice Chancellor/Athletic Director Mr. Joe ALLEVA
06 Assoc Vice Provost & Univ Registrar Mr. Robert K. DOOLOS
36 Director Olinde Career Center Mr. Jesse G. DOWNS
09 Director of Institutional Research Mr. Bernie BRAUN
93 Director Multicultural Affairs Ms. Andrea E. GRANT
94 Director Women's Center Ms. Summer STEIB
65 Director Museum of Natural Science Mr. Robb T. BRUMFIELD
88 Director Rural Life Museum Mr. David FLOYD
96 Exec Director Purchasing & Property Ms. Sally MCKECHNIE
07 Director of Admissions Mr. Danny BARROW
19 Acting Chief of LSU Police Dept Mr. Bart THOMPSON
39 Exec Director Residential Life Mr. Steve WALLER
101 Assoc Vice President for the Board Dr. Jason DRODDY
104 Director Study Abroad Mr. Harold LEDER
105 Director Web Services Ms. Lori MARTIN

*Louisiana State University at Alexandria (A)

8100 Highway 71 S, Alexandria LA 71302-9121
County: Rapides FICE Identification: 002011
Unit ID: 159382
Telephone: (318) 445-3672 Carnegie Class: Bac-A&S
FAX Number: (318) 473-6418 Calendar System: Semester
URL: www.lsua.edu
Established: 1959 Annual Undergrad Tuition & Fees (In-State): $6,668
Enrollment: 3,104 Coed
Affiliation or Control: State IRS Status: 501(c)3
Highest Offering: Baccalaureate
Accreditation: SC, ADNUR, MLTAD, NUR, RAD

02 Chancellor Dr. Guiyou HUANG
05 Vice Chanc Academic & Student Affs Dr. Barbara S. HATFIELD
10 Int Vice Chanc Finance/Admin Svcs Mr. Deron THAXTON
111 Director Institutional Advancement Ms. Melinda F. ANDERSON
20 Asst VC Academic/Student Affairs Dr. Eamon HALPIN
21 Asst VC Finance/Admin Services Vacant
50 Int Dept Chair Business Admin Mr. Kent LACHNEY
49 Dept Chair Arts/English/Humanities Dr. Holly WILSON
83 Dept Chair Behavioral & Social Sci Dr. Jerry SANSON
81 Dept Chair Math & Physical Sciences Dr. Nathan PONDER
53 Department Chair Education Dr. Patsy JENKINS
76 Department Chair Allied Health Dr. Haywood JOINER
66 Department Chair Nursing Dr. Cathy CORMIER
49 Dept Chair Biological Sciences Dr. Carol CORBAT
18 Director of Facility Services Mr. Chad GAUTHIER
08 Director Library Services Vacant
37 Director of Financial Aid Mr. Jeff MASSEY
13 Exec Dir Info Educational Tech Svcs Mr. Deron THAXTON
15 Director Human Resource Management Ms. Lynette BURLEW
51 Director Continuing Education Ms. Christi NATION
88 Director of Advising Dr. Eamon HALPIN
09 Dir Inst Research/Effectiveness Dr. Steve COX
96 Dir Procurement Svcs/Property Mgmt Vacant
41 Director Athletics Mr. Adam JONSON
07 Director of Admissions & Recruiting Ms. Shelly KIEFFER
06 Registrar Ms. Leana WILSON
19 Dir Public Safety/Chief of Police Mr. Dwayne ROGERS

*Louisiana State University at Eunice (B)

2048 Johnson Highway, Eunice LA 70535-6726
County: Acadia FICE Identification: 002012
Unit ID: 159407
Telephone: (337) 457-7311 Carnegie Class: Assoc/HT-High Trad
FAX Number: (337) 546-6620 Calendar System: Semester
URL: www.lsue.edu
Established: 1964 Annual Undergrad Tuition & Fees (In-State): $4,392
Enrollment: 2,508 Coed
Affiliation or Control: State IRS Status: 501(c)3
Highest Offering: Associate Degree
Accreditation: SC, ADNUR, COARC, DMS, RAD

02 Chancellor Dr. Kimberly A. RUSSELL
05 Vice Chancellor Academic Affairs Dr. Renee ROBICHAUX
84 Vice Chancellor Enrollment Mgmt Vacant
10 Vice Chancellor Business Affairs Ms. Arlene C. TUCKER
26 Director of Public Relations Mr. Van REED
08 Director of the Library Vacant
06 Registrar/Dir of Admissions Dr. Kenneth ELLIOTT
37 Director of Financial Aid Ms. Jacqueline LA CHAPELLE
30 Dir Foundation & Institutional Dev Vacant
09 Dir Inst Effect/Devel Educ Dr. Paul FOWLER
51 Director Continuing Education Mr. Launey P. GRIFFITH
18 Director Physical Plant Mr. Michael BROUSSARD
15 Director Personnel Services Ms. Angel MCGEE
81 Head Division of Sciences Dr. John HAMLIN
50 Head Div Bus/Nursing/Allied Health Ms. Dotty MCDONALD
49 Head Division of Liberal Arts Vacant
13 Chief Info Technology Officer (CIO) Vacant
41 Athletic Director Mr. Jeff WILLIS

*Louisiana State University Health Sciences Center-New Orleans (C)

433 Bolivar Street, New Orleans LA 70112-2223
County: Orleans FICE Identification: 002014
Unit ID: 159373
Telephone: (504) 568-4808 Carnegie Class: Spec-4-yr-Med
FAX Number: N/A Calendar System: Semester
URL: www.lsuhsc.edu
Established: 1931 Annual Undergrad Tuition & Fees (In-State): N/A
Enrollment: 2,791 Coed
Affiliation or Control: State IRS Status: 501(c)3
Highest Offering: Doctorate
Accreditation: SC, ANEST, ARCPA, AUD, CACREP, COARC, CVT, DENT, DH, DT, IPSY, MED, MT, NURSE, OT, PH, PTA, SP

02 Chancellor Dr. Larry H. HOLLIER
05 Vice Chanc Acad Aff/Dean Grad Stds Dr. Joseph M. MOERSCHBAECHER
10 Vice Chancellor Finance/Admin Mr. John HARMAN
31 Vice Chanc Cmty/Minority Affairs Mr. Edwin MURRAY
17 Vice Chanc Clinic Affairs Dr. J. Chris WINTERS
43 General Counsel Ms. Katherine MUSLOW
63 Dean Medicine NO Dr. Steve NELSON
52 Dean School of Dentistry Dr. Henry GREMILLION
66 Dean of Nursing Dr. Demetrius PORCHE
69 Dean of Public Health Dr. Dean SMITH
76 Dean Allied Health Professions Dr. Jim R. CAIRO
04 Assistant to the Chancellor Mrs. Christine MANALLA
86 Director of International Services Ms. Remy E. ALLEN
14 Director Computer Services Ms. Bettina OWENS
13 Director Information Services Ms. Leslie L. CAPO
08 Director Library Administration Ms. Debra H. SIBLEY
15 Director Human Resource Mgmt Dr. Rosalynn MARTIN
06 Registrar Mr. William Bryant FAUST
37 Assoc Dir Student Financial Aid Ms. Kimberly BRUNO
18 Chief Facilities/Physical Plant Mr. John BALL
96 Exec Director of Purchasing Mr. Brent HEROLD
26 Director of External Relations Mr. Christopher VIDRINE

*Louisiana State University Health Sciences Center at Shreveport (D)

1501 Kings Highway, Shreveport LA 71103
County: Caddo FICE Identification: 008067
Unit ID: 435000
Telephone: (318) 675-5240 Carnegie Class: Spec-4-yr-Med
FAX Number: (318) 675-5244 Calendar System: Semester
URL: www.lsuhscshreveport.edu
Established: 1969 Annual Undergrad Tuition & Fees: N/A
Enrollment: 891 Coed
Affiliation or Control: Other IRS Status: Exempt
Highest Offering: Doctorate
Accreditation: SC, #ARCPA, COARC, DENT, MED, MT, OT, PH, PTA, SP

02 Chancellor & Dean SOM Dr. Ghali E. GHALI
11 Vice Chancellor Administration Dr. Roxane TOWNSEND
46 Vice Chancellor Research Affairs Dr. Chris KEVIL
05 Vice Chancellor Academic Affairs Dr. Jane EGGERSTEDT
10 Chief Financial Officer Ms. Sheila FAOUR
43 Senior Legal Counsel Ms. Susan ARMSTRONG
76 Dean Sch Allied Health Professions Dr. Joseph MCCULLOCH
58 Dean School of Graduate Studies Dr. Sandra C. ROERIG
88 Vice Chancellor Clinical Affairs Dr. David F. LEWIS
88 Exec Director of Campus Operations Mr. Joseph MICIOTTO
86 Exec Dir Government Affairs Mr. Donald HAINS
26 Exec Dir Comm/Public Relations Ms. Lisa BABIN
13 Chief Info Technology Officer (CIO) Mr. Kenneth BROWN
07 Asst Dean for Admissions SOM Dr. Frank S. KENNEDY
32 Asst Dean for Student Affairs SOM Dr. Mark PLATT
15 Exec Director of Human Resources Ms. Lisa EBARB
88 Executive Director Medical Services Ms. Leisa OGLESBY
18 Chief Facilities/Physical Plant Mr. Marc GIBSON
19 Director Security/Safety Mr. Willie BUFFINGTON
09 Director of Institutional Planning Mr. Jeffrey D. HOWELLS
25 Director of Sponsored Programs Ms. Annella NELSON
06 Registrar Ms. Kim CARMEN
08 Interim Head Librarian Mr. William OLMSTADT
37 Director Student Financial Aid Ms. Sherry GLADNEY
28 Director of Diversity Dr. Debbie CHANDLER
29 Director Alumni Relations Ms. Bridget VERRET
16 Asst Director of Human Resources Vacant
96 Director of Purchasing Ms. Mary A. TEMPLETON

† Tuition varies by degree program.

*Louisiana State University in Shreveport (E)

One University Place, Shreveport LA 71115-2399
County: Caddo FICE Identification: 002013
Unit ID: 159416
Telephone: (318) 797-5000 Carnegie Class: Masters/M
FAX Number: (318) 797-5180 Calendar System: Semester
URL: www.lsus.edu
Established: 1967 Annual Undergrad Tuition & Fees (In-State): $7,146
Enrollment: 4,428 Coed
Affiliation or Control: State IRS Status: 501(c)3
Highest Offering: Doctorate
Accreditation: SC, CAEPN, CS, PH

02 Chancellor Mr. Lawrence S. CLARK
05 Interim Provost/VC Academic Affairs Dr. Julie LESSITER
10 Vice Chancellor Business Affairs Ms. Barbie CANNON
32 Assoc VC Student Development Mrs. Paula ATKINS
102 Executive Director LSUS Foundation Ms. Laura PERDUE
29 Director Alumni Affairs Ms. Dianne B. HOWELL
09 Director Planning/Inst Research Dr. Julie LESSITER
06 Registrar Ms. Darlenna M. ATKINS
15 Director of Human Resource Mgmt Mr. Bill WOLFE
08 Interim Dean Noel Memorial Library Mr. Brian SHERMAN
37 Director of Student Financial Aid Ms. Chelsea CHANCE
07 Director of Admissions Mrs. Mary Catherine HARVISON
38 Director Counseling Services Mrs. Paula ATKINS
13 Assoc VC & CIO/IT Mr. Shelby C. KEITH
40 Director of Bookstore Ms. Brenda P. BARTLEBAUGH
96 Director of Purchasing Mr. Bill WOLFE
26 Director of Media/Public Relations Mrs. Brooke H. RINAUDO
04 Assistant to the Chancellor Mrs. Kim RAMSEY
19 Dir of University Police Mr. Donald W. WRAY
41 Athletic Director Mr. Lucas MORGAN
49 Dean of Arts and Sciences Dr. Larry ANDERSON
58 Dean of Graduate Studies Dr. Sanjay T. MENON
51 Exec Dir Continuing Education Mr. Brent WALLACE
53 Dean Business/Ed/Human Dev Dr. Nancy MILLER

*University of New Orleans (F)

2000 Lakeshore Drive, New Orleans LA 70148-2000
County: Orleans FICE Identification: 002015
Unit ID: 159939
Telephone: (504) 280-6000 Carnegie Class: DU-Higher
FAX Number: (504) 280-5522 Calendar System: Semester
URL: www.uno.edu
Established: 1958 Annual Undergrad Tuition & Fees (In-State): $8,484
Enrollment: 8,423 Coed
Affiliation or Control: State IRS Status: 501(c)3
Highest Offering: Doctorate
Accreditation: SC, ART, CACREP, CAEPN, CS, ENG, MUS, PLNG, SPAA, THEA

02 President Dr. John W. NICKLOW
05 Provost/VP Academic Affairs Dr. Mahyar AMOUZEGAR
10 VP Business Affairs Dr. Gregg LASSEN
32 Dean of Students Dr. Brett KEMKER
13 Chief Information Officer Mr. David DUPREE
85 Asst Provost International Educ Ms. Alea COT
19 Asst Vice Chanc for Public Safety Mr. Thomas HARRINGTON
50 Dean of Business Administration Dr. John A. WILLIAMS
54 Dean of Engineering Dr. Emir MACARI
49 Dean Liberal Arts & Education Dr. Kim MARTIN LONG
08 Director Learning Resource Center Ms. Margaret WILLIAMSON
81 Dean of Sciences Dr. Steve JOHNSON
06 University Registrar Mr. Rajni SOHARU
29 Director Alumni Affairs Mr. Anthony ENTERANTE
26 Chief Communications Officer Mr. Adam NORRIS
96 Director of Purchasing Ms. Heather CASSELL
41 Director Athletics Mr. Derek MOREL
39 Director Student Housing Mr. Roy BRAUNINGER

Loyola University New Orleans (G)

6363 Saint Charles Avenue, New Orleans LA 70118-6195
County: Orleans FICE Identification: 002016
Unit ID: 159656
Telephone: (504) 865-2011 Carnegie Class: Masters/L
FAX Number: (504) 865-3851 Calendar System: Semester
URL: www.loyno.edu
Established: 1912 Annual Undergrad Tuition & Fees: $38,754
Enrollment: 4,087 Coed
Affiliation or Control: Roman Catholic IRS Status: 501(c)3
Highest Offering: Doctorate
Accreditation: SC, CACREP, JOUR, LAW, MUS, NURSE

01 President Rev. Kevin W. WILDES, SJ
101 Exec Asst to Pres for Board Rels Ms. Kristine D. LELONG
04 Executive Assistant to President Ms. Gail HOWARD
05 Provost/Vice Pres Academic Affs Dr. David BOROFSKY
10 Vice Pres Finance/Administration Mr. John J. CALAMIA
111 Vice Pres Institutional Advance Mr. Chris WISEMAN
32 VP Student Affairs/Assoc Provost Dr. Marcia L. PETTY
88 Vice Pres for Mission & Ministry Dr. John SEBASTIAN
84 Vice Pres for Enrollment Management Ms. Roberta KASKEL
13 Vice Prov Information Tech/CIO Mr. Bret JACOBS
21 Assoc Vice Pres Financial Affairs Mr. Leon MATHES

26 VP Marketing/Communications ... Ms. Laura KURZU
11 Asst Vice Pres Administration ... Mr. Thomas J. RAYMOND
35 Asst Vice Pres of Student Affairs ... Mr. Robert A. REED
09 Sr Dir Inst Rsrch/Student Success ... Dr. Brad PETITFILS
42 Director of University Ministry ... Mr. Kurt BINDEWALD
108 Coord Internal Reporting/Assessment ... Ms. Donna BOURGEOIS
27 Assoc Dir Public Affs/External Rels ... Ms. Patricia MURRET
43 General Counsel ... Vacant
29 Director Alumni Engagement ... Ms. Laurie LEIVA
06 Dir Stdnt Records/Registration Svcs ... Ms. Kathy R. GROS
15 Director of Human Resources ... Mr. Ross D. MATTHEWS
40 Bookstore Manager ... Ms. Maleta WILSON
41 Director Athletics & Wellness ... Mr. Brett SIMPSON
36 Director Career Development Center ... Ms. Tamara BAKER
23 Director of Student Health Services ... Dr. Alicia BOURQUE
19 Director University Police ... Mr. Patrick X. BAILEY
37 Director Scholarships/Financial Aid ... Ms. Carrie GLASS
08 Director of the Law Library ... Mr. P. Michael WHIPPLE
104 Dir Center for International Educ ... Ms. Debra DANNA
86 Dir Govt Relations & Legal Affairs ... Mr. Tommy SCREEN
38 Director Student Counseling ... Dr. Alicia BOURQUE
96 Director of Purchasing ... Mr. Robert NELSON
06 Dir Admin Services/Student Records ... Mr. Michael RACHAL
39 Director of Residential Life ... Ms. Amy BOYLE
08 Dean of Libraries ... Ms. Deborah POOLE
79 Dean Humanities/Natural Science ... Dr. Maria CALZADA
61 Interim Dean of Law ... Rev. Lawrence MOORE, SJ
64 Dean of Music and Fine Arts ... Mr. Kern MAASS
50 Dean of Business ... Dr. William LOCANDER
83 Dean of Social Sciences ... Dr. Roger WHITE
88 Int Director of Service Learning ... Ms. Jennifer N. JEANFREAU
88 Director of Women's Resource Ctr ... Ms. Patricia BOYETT
92 Dir of University Honors Program ... Ms. Naomi YAVNEH
88 Dir of Common Curriculum ... Dr. Lydia VOIGT
35 Director of Student Services ... Ms. Maria MCBRIDE
109 Director of Campus Dining ... Ms. Heather BACQUE
07 Director of Admissions ... Ms. Susan OAKES
18 Chief Facilities/Physical Plant ... Mr. Charles B. MARSHALL
25 Chief Contracts/Grants Admin ... Dr. Heidi L. DAVIS
28 Interim Chief Diversity Officer ... Dr. Liv KNEWMAN

McCann School of Business and Technology (A)

2319 Louisville Avenue, Monroe LA 71201-6126
County: Ouachita FICE Identification: 026068
Unit ID: 367112
Telephone: (318) 323-2889 Carnegie Class: Assoc/HVT-High Non
FAX Number: (318) 324-9883 Calendar System: Quarter
URL: www.careertc.edu
Established: 1988 Annual Undergrad Tuition & Fees: $10,100
Enrollment: 587 Coed
Affiliation or Control: Proprietary IRS Status: Proprietary
Highest Offering: Associate Degree
Accreditation: **ACICS**, MAC

01 Campus Director ... Ms. Cheryl P. LOKEY

McCann School of Business and Technology (B)

1227 Shreveport-Barksdale Highway,
Shreveport LA 71105
Telephone: (318) 629-2889 Identification: 770723
Accreditation: **ACICS**, MAC

† In teach-out mode.

NationsUniversity (C)

650 Poydras St., Ste 1400, PMB 133,
New Orleans LA 70130
County: Orleans Identification: 667257
Telephone: (866) 617-6446 Carnegie Class: Not Classified
FAX Number: N/A Calendar System: Other
URL: www.nationsu.edu
Established: 1996 Annual Undergrad Tuition & Fees: N/A
Enrollment: N/A Coed
Affiliation or Control: Independent Non-Profit IRS Status: 501(c)3
Highest Offering: Master's
Accreditation: **DEAC**

01 President/CEO ... Dr. Mac LYNN

New Orleans Baptist Theological Seminary (D)

3939 Gentilly Boulevard, New Orleans LA 70126
County: Orleans FICE Identification: 002019
Unit ID: 159948
Telephone: (504) 282-4455 Carnegie Class: Spec-4-yr-Faith
FAX Number: (504) 283-3631 Calendar System: Semester
URL: www.nobts.edu
Established: 1917 Annual Undergrad Tuition & Fees: $7,380
Enrollment: 2,871 Coed
Affiliation or Control: Southern Baptist IRS Status: 501(c)3
Highest Offering: Doctorate
Accreditation: **SC**, MUS, THEOL

01 President ... Dr. Charles S. KELLEY, JR.
05 Provost ... Dr. Suzanne DAVIS
09 Dir Institutional Effectiveness ... Dr. Jimmy DUKES
10 Vice President for Business Affairs ... Mr. Clay L. CORVIN
30 Vice President for Development ... Mr. Randy DRIGGERS
58 Dean Graduate Studies ... Dr. Margie BUTLER
12 Dean Leavell College ... Dr. L. Thomas STRONG, III
32 Dean of Students ... Dr. Emily SLOANE
07 Dean of Admissions & Registrar ... Dr. Paul E. GREGOIRE, JR.
08 Dean of Libraries ... Dr. Jeff D. GRIFFIN
18 Associate VP of Facilities ... Dr. Jim O. PARKER
13 Assoc VP Information Technology ... Dr. Laurie S. WATTS
73 Assoc Dean Prof Doctoral Pgms ... Dr. Reggie R. OGEA
106 Associate Dean of Online Learning ... Dr. Matthew BRYANT
58 Assoc Dean Research Doctoral Pgms ... Dr. Charles A. RAY, JR.
35 Assoc Dean Students/Retention Dir ... Ms. Amy MORGAN
15 Director of Human Resources ... Ms. Pattie SHOENER
26 Chief Public Relations Officer ... Mr. Gary D. MYERS
29 Director of Alumni Relations ... Dr. Dennis L. PHELPS
36 Director of Student Enlistment ... Mr. Michael REED
37 Director of Student Financial Aid ... Mr. Michael WANG
38 Director of Testing & Counseling ... Dr. Jeffery W. NAVE
88 Director of Innovative Learning ... Dr. Donna B. PEAVEY
39 Director Student Housing ... Mrs. Julie BARENTINE
41 Athletic Director ... Mr. Brad WINTER

Notre Dame Seminary, Graduate School of Theology (E)

2901 S Carrollton Avenue, New Orleans LA 70118-4391
County: Orleans FICE Identification: 002022
Unit ID: 160029
Telephone: (504) 866-7426 Carnegie Class: Spec-4-yr-Faith
FAX Number: (504) 866-3119 Calendar System: Semester
URL: www.nds.edu
Established: 1923 Annual Undergrad Tuition & Fees: N/A
Enrollment: 198 Coed
Affiliation or Control: Roman Catholic IRS Status: 501(c)3
Highest Offering: Master's
Accreditation: **SC**, THEOL

01 President - Rector ... V.Rev. James A. WEHNER, STD
05 Academic Dean ... Dr. Rebecca S. MALONEY
08 Director of Library ... Mr. Thomas B. BENDER, IV
09 Director IE/Planning/Faculty Devel ... Dr. Rebecca S. MALONEY
10 Business Manager ... Ms. Michelle W. KLEIN

Remington College-Baton Rouge Campus (F)

4520 S Sherwood Forrest Blvd #001,
Baton Rouge LA 70816
Telephone: (225) 236-3200 Identification: 666449
Accreditation: **ACCSC**

† Branch campus of Remington College, Cleveland, OH.

Remington College-Lafayette Campus (G)

303 Rue Louis XIV, Lafayette LA 70508-5700
Telephone: (337) 981-4010 FICE Identification: 005203
Accreditation: **ACCSC**

† Branch campus of Remington College, Cleveland, OH.

Remington College-Shreveport (H)

2106 Bert Kouns Industrial Loop, Shreveport LA 71118
Telephone: (318) 671-4000 Identification: 666302
Accreditation: **ACCSC**

† Branch campus of Remington College, Cleveland, OH.

Saint Joseph Seminary College (I)

75376 River Road, Saint Benedict LA 70457-9999
County: Saint Tammany FICE Identification: 002027
Unit ID: 160409
Telephone: (985) 867-2232 Carnegie Class: Spec-4-yr-Faith
FAX Number: (985) 867-2270 Calendar System: Semester
URL: www.sjasc.edu
Established: 1891 Annual Undergrad Tuition & Fees: $16,913
Enrollment: 140 Male
Affiliation or Control: Roman Catholic IRS Status: 501(c)3
Highest Offering: Baccalaureate
Accreditation: **SC**

01 President - Rector ... V.Rev. Gregory M. BOQUET, OSB
05 Academic Dean ... Dr. Daniel P. BURNS
03 Vice-Rector ... Rev. Matthew CLARK, OSB
08 Librarian ... Ms. Bonnie WOOD
10 Business Officer ... Mrs. Jennifer WHITEHOUSE
37 Director Financial Aid ... Ms. Caroline BIZOT
29 Director of Alumni Affairs ... Rev. Matthew CLARK, OSB
30 Director of Development ... Mr. Scott WALLACE
26 Director of Communications ... Mr. James SHIELDS
32 Dean of Students ... Rev. Jonathan WALLIS, OSB
06 Registrar ... Ms. Caroline BIZOT
108 Director Institutional Assessment ... Dr. Dianna LAURENT
13 Chief Info Technology Officer (CIO) ... Mr. Todd RUSSELL
18 Chief Facilities/Physical Plant ... Mr. Jim ROBEAUU

*Southern University and Agricultural & Mechanical College System (J)

JS Clark Admin Building, 4th Floor,
Baton Rouge LA 70813-0001
County: East Baton Rouge Parish FICE Identification: 009637
Unit ID: 160533
Telephone: (225) 771-4680 Carnegie Class: N/A
FAX Number: (225) 771-5522
URL: www.sus.edu

01 President-Chancellor ... Dr. Ray L. BELTON
10 System VP/Finance/Business Affairs ... Mr. Flandus MCCLINTON
05 Chief Academic Officer ... Dr. Luria YOUNG
32 Int VC Student Affairs/Enroll Mgmt ... Dr. Luria YOUNG
13 Assoc VP/Information Technology ... Dr. Gabriel FAGBEYIRO
15 Assoc VP/Human Resources ... Mr. Lester A. POURCIAU
84 System Dir Enroll/Online Processes ... Ms. Michelle HILL
30 CEO SU System Foundation ... Mr. Alfred E. HARRELL, III
43 General Counsel to the System/Board ... Ms. Tracie J. WOODS
04 Exec Assoc to President-Chancellor ... Ms. Robyn M. MERRICK
26 System Director of Communications ... Mr. Henry J. TILLMAN
18 System Dir of Facilities Planning ... Mr. Eli GUILLORY
116 System Director of Internal Audit ... Ms. Linda H. CATALON
09 System Dir/Institutional Research ... Ms. Sheila D. DEROEUN
06 Interim Registrar ... Ms. Velena JOHNSON
07 Director of Admissions ... Ms. Dianna GILBERT
104 Dean of International Education ... Dr. Barbara CARPENTER
19 Director Security/Safety ... Ms. Joycelyn JOHNSON
29 Exec Dir Alumni Federation ... Mr. Derrick V. WARREN
36 Director of Career Services ... Ms. Tamara F. MONTGOMERY
37 Director Student Financial Aid ... Ms. Ursula SHORTY
38 Director Student Counseling ... Dr. ValaRay IRVIN
39 Director Student Housing ... Ms. Tracie A. ABRAHAM
41 Athletic Director ... Mr. Roman BANKS, JR.
50 Dean College of Business ... Dr. Donald ANDREWS
53 Director of Education ... Dr. VerJanis PEOPLES
54 Dean College of Sci/Engineering ... Dr. Patrick CARRIERE
96 Director of Purchasing ... Ms. Linda ANTOINE

*Southern University and A&M College (K)

Harding Boulevard, Baton Rouge LA 70813-0001
County: East Baton Rouge FICE Identification: 002025
Unit ID: 160621
Telephone: (225) 771-4500 Carnegie Class: Masters/L
FAX Number: (225) 771-2018 Calendar System: Semester
URL: www.subr.edu
Established: 1880 Annual Undergrad Tuition & Fees (In-State): $9,332
Enrollment: 6,401 Coed
Affiliation or Control: State IRS Status: 501(c)3
Highest Offering: Doctorate
Accreditation: **SC**, AAFCS, CACREP, CAEPN, CS, DIETI, ENG, ENGT, JOUR, MUS, NURSE, SP, SPAA, SW

02 President/Chancellor ... Dr. Ray BELTON
05 Int EVP for AA & Provost ... Dr. Luria YOUNG
32 Vice Chanc Stdnt Affs/Enroll Mgmt ... Dr. Brandon DUMAS
10 Vice Chanc of Finance & Admin ... Mr. Benjamin PUGH
46 VC Research & Strategic Initiative ... Dr. Michael A. STUBBLEFIELD
13 AVP for IT/Chief Information Ofcr ... Dr. Gabriel FAGBEYIRO
21 Assoc Vice Chanc of Finance & Admin ... Mrs. Monica MEALIE
25 Assoc Controller for Sponsored Pgm ... Ms. Famika SARGENT
88 Assoc Controller for Financial Op ... Mrs. Cary HOLLINS
26 Director of Communications ... Mr. Henry TILLMAN
45 Dir Planning Assess/Inst Research ... Dr. Christopher GUILLORY
29 Dir Alumni Aff/Exec Dir SU Alum Fed ... Mr. Derrick WARREN
15 Director Human Resources ... Mr. Lester POURCIAU
06 Int Registrar ... Mrs. Velena JOHNSON
07 Exec Dir Admissions/Recruitment ... Mr. Anthony JACKSON
35 Dean of Students ... Mr. Marcus A. COLEMAN
39 Director Residential Housing ... Ms. Tracie A. ABRAHAM
37 Director of Financial Aid ... Ms. Ursula SHORTY
51 Dir Intl Educ/Dir Svc Learning/CE ... Dr. Barbara CARPENTER
41 Athletic Director ... Mr. Roman BANKS
18 Dir Facilities Svcs/Physical Plant ... Mr. Eli G. GUILLORY, III
88 Director School of Accountancy ... Dr. Ghirmay GHEBREYSUS
96 Director of Purchasing ... Mrs. Linda B. ANTOINE
38 Director Student Counseling ... Dr. ValaRay IRVIN
62 Dean of Libraries ... Mrs. Emma BRADFORD-PERRY
88 Dean University College ... Dr. Dana CARPENTER
92 Dean of Honors College ... Dr. Diola BAGAYOKO
58 Dean of the Graduate School ... Dr. Habib P. MOHAMADIAN
54 Dn Col of Sciences/Engineering ... Dr. Patrick CARRIERE
50 Dean College of Business ... Dr. Donald R. ANDREWS
53 Dean College of Education ... Dr. Verjanis PEOPLES
66 Dean College of Nursing/Allied Hlth ... Dr. Janet RAMI
83 Int Dean Col Social/Behavioral Sci ... Dr. Albert SAMUELS
49 Dn Col of Ag & Family/Consumer Sci ... Dr. Bobby R. PHILLS
48 Dn Col of Human/Interdis Studies ... Dr. Cynthia D. BRYANT
50 Dn Nelson Mandela Col of Gov/Soc Sc ... Dr. Damien EJIGIRI
59 Chair Dept Family/Consumer Sciences ... Dr. Kasundra CYRUS
48 Coordinator School of Architecture ... Mr. Lonnie WILKINSON

*Southern University at New Orleans (L)

6400 Press Drive, New Orleans LA 70126-1009
County: Orleans FICE Identification: 002026
Unit ID: 160630

Telephone: (504) 286-5000 Carnegie Class: Masters/M
FAX Number: (504) 286-5131 Calendar System: Semester
URL: www.suno.edu
Established: 1956 Annual Undergrad Tuition & Fees (In-State): $6,421
Enrollment: 2,792 Coed
Affiliation or Control: State IRS Status: 501(c)3
Highest Offering: Master's
Accreditation: SC, AAFCS, CAEPN, CAHIIM, SW

Code	Title	Name
02	Chancellor	Dr. Lisa MIMS-DEVEZIN
04	Exec Assoc to the Chancellor	Mr. Harry DOUGHTY
05	VC for Academic Affairs & SACS	Dr. David S. ADEGBOYE
10	VC for Admin & Finance	Mr. Jullin RENTHROPE
32	VC Student Affs & Enroll Management	Dr. Donna GRANT
46	VC for Research/Title III Programs	Dr. Brenda W. JACKSON
111	Chf Admn Ofcr Cmty Outrch/Alumni/ PR	Mrs. Gloria B. MOULTRIE
09	Dir IR/IE & Strategic Planning	Mrs. Ada KWANBUNBUMPEN
108	Learning Outcomes/Assessment Coord	Ms. Mallory MARTIN
25	Dir Grants & Sponsored Programs	Dr. William R. BELISLE
06	Registrar	Ms. Gilda DAVIS
21	Comptroller	Ms. Shawn M. CHARLES
07	Director of Admissions	Mr. C. Maxille MOULTRIE
08	Director of Library	Mrs. Shatiqua A. MOSBY-WILSON
36	Dir Career Counseling & Vet Liaison	Mr. Joseph MARION
13	Director of Information Technology	Mr. Edmond M. CUMMINGS
15	Director of Human Resources	Ms. Evelyn MASTERS-DUBUCLET
19	Police Captain Campus Police	Mr. Bruce ADAMS
20	Assoc VC Academic Affairs Faculty	Mr. Wesley T. BISHOP
41	Interim Director of Athletics	Mr. Yhann PLUMMER
26	Director of Public Relations	Ms. Tammy BARNEY
96	Director of Purchasing	Ms. Marilyn G. MANUEL
106	Director of E-Learning	Ms. Shelia WOOD
70	Dean School of Social Work	Dr. Rebecca CHAISSON
50	Dean College of Business/Pub Admin	Dr. Igwe E. UDEH
88	Director of Museum Studies	Mr. Haithum EID
58	Dean of Graduate Studies	Vacant
49	Dean College of Arts & Sciences	Dr. Evelyn HARRELL
53	Interim Dean College of Education	Dr. Willie JONES
22	Dir Services for Students w/Disab	Ms. Yolanda L. MIMS
32	Dir of Student Activities/Orgs	Mrs. Mary JACKSON
38	Dir of Student Development Center	Mrs. Josephine OKORONKWO
121	Dir Student Support Services Pgm	Ms. Linda D. FREDERICK
88	Dir Ctr for African & American Stds	Dr. Clyde ROBERTSON
18	Director of Facilities Management	Mr. Shaun M. LEWIS
37	Director Student Financial Aid	Ms. LaCharlotte GARRETT
88	Director Quality Enhancement Plan	Mr. Ashu BENJAMIN

*Southern University at Shreveport-Louisiana (A)

3050 Martin Luther King Drive, Shreveport LA 71107-4795
County: Caddo FICE Identification: 007686
Unit ID: 160649
Telephone: (318) 670-6000 Carnegie Class: Assoc/MT-VT-High Trad
FAX Number: (318) 670-6374 Calendar System: Semester
URL: www.susla.edu
Established: 1964 Annual Undergrad Tuition & Fees (In-State): $3,996
Enrollment: 3,174 Coed
Affiliation or Control: State IRS Status: 501(c)3
Highest Offering: Associate Degree
Accreditation: SC, ADNUR, CAHIIM, #COARC, DH, MLTAD, PHLEB, RAD, SURGT

Code	Title	Name
02	Chancellor	Dr. Rodney A. ELLIS
26	Spec Asst to Chanc IR/Div Univ Rels	Mr. Theron JACKSON
05	Vice Chanc Academic Affairs	Dr. Sharon HERRON-WILLIAMS
32	Vice Chanc Student Affairs	Ms. Melva WILLIAMS
10	Vice Chanc Finance/Administration	Mr. Benjamin W. PUGH
103	VC Cmty Outreach/Workforce Develop	Mrs. Janice B. SNEED
32	Asst Vice Chanc Student Affairs	Dr. Fatina ELLIOTT
84	Asst Vice Chanc Enrollment Mgmt	Mr. Terence VINSON
20	Asst Vice Chanc for Academic Affs	Dr. Regina ROBINSON
21	Chief Financial Officer	Mrs. Brandy JACOBSEN
113	Bursar	Ms. Tomeka K. BROWN
06	Registrar	Dr. Lalita ROGERS
08	Library Director	Mrs. Jane O'RILEY
35	Director of Student Activities	Mrs. Rebecca GILLIAM
51	Director of Continuing Education	Mrs. Beverly J. PARKER
07	Director of Admission & Recruitment	Ms. Annie MOSS
37	Director of Financial Aid	Ms. Katraya WILLIAMS
27	Dir Office of University Relations	Ms. Krystle GRINDLEY
19	Chief University Police	Mr. Marshall NELSON
13	Dir Information Technology Center	Dr. Gabriel FAGBEYIRO
88	Director Student Support Services	Ms. Karen COCO
75	Director Aerospace Technology	Mr. David FOGLEMAN
38	University Counselor	Ms. Kaye L. WASHINGTON
15	Director Human Resources	Mr. Wayne H. BRYANT
96	Director of Purchasing	Ms. Sophia JACKSON-LEE
18	Dir Maintenance & Grounds	Mr. Layne CHENEVERT
21	University Budget Officer	Ms. Regina WINN
72	Director Radiologic Technology	Ms. Sheila SWIFT
88	Exec Dir TRIO Community Outreach	Ms. Betty C. FAGBEYIRO
88	Director Dental Hygiene	Mrs. Kheysia H. WASHINGTON
88	Director Biomedical Research Devel	Dr. Joseph ORBAN
09	Director Inst Plng/Assessment/Rsrch	Mr. Martin FORTNER
66	Director of Nursing	Dr. Tiffany VARNER
79	Division Chair for Humanities	Ms. Wanda M. WALLER
72	Dean Business/Science & Technology	Dr. Barry C. HESTER
76	Div Chair Allied Health Sci	Mrs. JoAnn BROWN
83	Div Ch Behav Sci/Educ/Bus Standards	Dr. Rosalyn J. HOLT

*Southern University Law Center (B)

PO Box 9294, Baton Rouge LA 70813
County: East Baton Rouge Identification: 667233
Unit ID: 440916
Telephone: (225) 771-2552 Carnegie Class: Spec-4-yr-Law
FAX Number: N/A Calendar System: Semester
URL: www.sulc.edu
Established: 1947 Annual Graduate Tuition & Fees: N/A
Enrollment: 618 Coed
Affiliation or Control: State IRS Status: 501(c)3
Highest Offering: First Professional Degree; No Undergraduates
Accreditation: SC, LAW

Code	Title	Name
02	Chancellor	Mr. John K. PIERRE
05	Chief Academic Officer	Mr. Roederick C. WHITE
06	Registrar	Mrs. D'Andrea J. LEE
07	Director of Admissions	Ms. Andrea LOVE
09	VC Inst Accountability/Assessment	Ms. Alfreda DIAMOND
10	Assoc Vice Chanc for Financial Affs	Mr. Terry HALL
18	Chief Facilities/Physical Plant	Ms. Angela GAINES
26	Chief Public Relations Officer	Vacant
29	Director of Alumni Affairs	Ms. Cynthia REED
30	Chief Development Officer	Ms. Tonya FREEMAN
32	Chief Student Affairs Officer	Mr. Roederick WHITE
36	Director of Student Placement	Mr. Tavares WALKER
37	Director of Student Financial Aid	Ms. Calaundra CLARKE
84	Director Enrollment Management	Ms. D'Andrea J. LEE
21	Associate Business Officer	Ms. Demetria GEORGE
96	Director of Purchasing	Ms. Michele B. MCKEE

Southwest University (C)

2200 Veterans Memorial Boulevard,
Kenner LA 70062-4005
County: Jefferson Identification: 666310
Telephone: (504) 468-2900 Carnegie Class: Not Classified
FAX Number: (504) 468-3213 Calendar System: Semester
URL: www.southwest.edu
Established: 1982 Annual Undergrad Tuition & Fees: N/A
Enrollment: N/A Coed
Affiliation or Control: Proprietary IRS Status: Proprietary
Highest Offering: Master's
Accreditation: DEAC

Code	Title	Name
01	President	Dr. Grayce LEE
05	Vice Pres Academic Affairs	Dr. Glenn ZUERN
11	Chief Administrative Officer	Mr. Neil FESER
50	Dean of Business & Management	Dr. David BOUVIN

Tulane University (D)

6823 St. Charles Avenue, New Orleans LA 70118-5698
County: Orleans FICE Identification: 002029
Unit ID: 160755
Telephone: (504) 865-5000 Carnegie Class: DU-Highest
FAX Number: (504) 865-5202 Calendar System: Semester
URL: www.tulane.edu
Established: 1834 Annual Undergrad Tuition & Fees: $51,010
Enrollment: 12,485 Coed
Affiliation or Control: Independent Non-Profit IRS Status: 501(c)3
Highest Offering: Doctorate
Accreditation: SC, CAEPT, DIETI, ENG, ENGR, HSA, IPSY, LAW, MED, PH, SCPSY, SW

Code	Title	Name
01	President	Mr. Michael A. FITTS
05	Sr Vice Pres Acad Affairs/Provost	Prof. Robin FORMAN
111	Sr Vice Pres for Advancement	Ms. Ginny WISE
108	Sr VP Strategic Init/Inst Effectiv	Mr. Richard MATASAR
11	Chief Operating Officer	Mr. Patrick NORTON
63	Sr Vice Pres/Dn School of Medicine	Dr. L. L. HAMM
43	General Counsel	Ms. Victoria D. JOHNSON
13	VP Information Technology/CTO	Mr. Charles P. MCMAHON
115	Chief Investment Officer	Mr. Jeremy T. CRIGLER
20	Senior Associate Provost	Dr. Ana LOPEZ
32	VP Student Affairs	Dr. J. Davidson PORTER
76	Assoc Provost Health Sciences	Dr. M. A. 'Tonette' KROUSEL-WOOD
58	Assoc Prov Graduate Studies	Dr. Michael CUNNINGHAM
100	Sr VP and Chief of Staff	Ms. Tania TETLOW
22	VP Inst Equity/Asst to Pres Dvrsity	Ms. Deborah E. LOVE
84	Vice Pres Enrollment Mgmt	Mr. Satya DATTAGUPTA
18	VP Facilities Management	Mr. Randolph PHILIPSON
26	Vice Pres University Communications	Ms. Deborah L. GRANT
46	Vice President for Research	Dr. Laura LEVY
30	Vice Pres Constituency Programs	Ms. Luann D. DOZIER
86	Assoc VP Government Relations	Ms. Sharon P. COURTNEY
109	Assoc VP Auxiliary Svcs/Student Ctr	Mr. Robert C. HAILEY
37	Assoc Vice President Financial Aid	Mr. Michael GOODMAN
114	Director Budgets & Planning	Ms. Judy VITRANO
29	VP for Alumni Affairs	Mr. James STOFAN
21	Controller	Mr. Frank (Doug) HARRELL
19	Director of Public Safety	Mr. Jon BARNWELL
08	Dean Library & Academic Information	Mr. David BANUSH
38	Exec Dir Educ Resources/Couns	Dr. Donna BENDER
36	Exec Director Career Svcs Ctr	Dr. Amjad AYOUBI
12	Dir Tulane Natl Primate Res Ctr	Mr. Jim BLANCHARD
27	Executive Director Public Relations	Mr. Michael J. STRECKER
39	Assoc VP Housing Services/Residence	Dr. Brian JOHNSON
96	Director Central Procurement Svcs	Mr. William VAN CLEAVE
91	Asst VP Academic & Admin Computing	Ms. Mary T. WALSH
41	Director Athletics	Mr. Troy DANNEN
51	Dean Sch Cont Stds/Summer Sch	Dr. Suri DUITCH
49	Dean School of Liberal Arts	Dr. Carole HABER
49	Dean Newcomb-Tulane College	Dr. James MACLAREN
61	Dean School of Law	Mr. David D. MEYER
69	Dean Sch Public Health/Trop Med	Dr. Pierre BUEKENS
54	Dean School Science & Engineering	Dr. Nicholas J. ALTIERO
48	Dean School of Architecture	Mr. Kenneth SCHWARTZ
50	Dean AB Freeman School of Business	Dr. Ira SOLOMON
70	Dean School of Social Work	Dr. Patrick BORDNICK
09	Director of Institutional Research	Mr. Shawn POTTER
88	Exec Dir of CELT	Dr. Susann LUSNIA
85	Assoc Dean Ctr for Global Education	Dr. Scott PENTZER
35	Assoc VP Student Affairs	Dr. John NONNAMAKER
88	CPS Executive Director	Dr. Agnieszka NANCE
04	Senior Aide to the President	Ms. Jennifer JUMONVILLE
07	Director of Admissions	Mr. Jeffrey SCHIFFMAN
06	Registrar	Ms. Colette RAPHEL
101	Secretary to the Board	Ms. Cyndy ENGLISH

University of Holy Cross (E)

4123 Woodland Drive, New Orleans LA 70131-7399
County: Orleans FICE Identification: 002023
Unit ID: 160065
Telephone: (504) 394-7744 Carnegie Class: Bac-Diverse
FAX Number: (504) 391-2421 Calendar System: Semester
URL: www.uhcno.edu
Established: 1916 Annual Undergrad Tuition & Fees: $11,632
Enrollment: 1,135 Coed
Affiliation or Control: Roman Catholic IRS Status: 501(c)3
Highest Offering: Doctorate
Accreditation: SC, CACREP, CAEPN, IACBE, NUR, RAD

Code	Title	Name
01	President	Dr. David M. LANDRY
05	Provost/VP Academic Affairs	Dr. Victoria DAHMES
10	Vice Pres for Finance & Operations	Mrs. Arlean WEHLE
30	Vice Pres for Philanthropy/Planning	Mr. David CATHERMAN
84	VP Enrollment Management	Mr. Kobi SLOANE
32	VP Student Engagement/Advising	Ms. Meredith REED
88	VP for Mission Integration	Sr. Rochelle PERRIER
08	Director of Library Services	Ms. Diana SCHAUBHUT
83	Dean Couns/Educ/Business	Dr. Carolyn WHITE
66	Dean Nursing/Allied Health	Dr. Patricia PRECHTER
49	Dean Liberal Arts and Science	Dr. Michael LABRANCHE
32	Director Student Life	Ms. Heather DUCHARME
06	Registrar	Ms. Traci REES
09	Director Inst Research & Planning	Dr. Jacques DETIEGE
42	Director of Campus Ministry	Vacant
15	Human Resources Manager	Ms. Cathy WAGUESPACK
44	Director of Annual Fund	Mr. David CATHERMAN
13	Director of Technology Services	Ms. Rosalind CHESTER
37	Director of Financial Aid	Mr. Hayden WAGAR
04	Administrative Asst to President	Ms. Peggy BOURGEOIS
19	Director Security/Safety	Mr. Bernard NELSON
26	Director Communications	Ms. Erin SULLIVAN
29	Director Alumni Relations	Mr. Steve MORGAN
106	Distance Education Coordinator	Dr. Tess O'NEILL

*University of Louisiana System Office (F)

1201 N Third Street, Suite 7-300,
Baton Rouge LA 70802-5243
County: East Baton Rouge FICE Identification: 033444
Unit ID: 247083
Telephone: (225) 342-6950 Carnegie Class: N/A
FAX Number: (225) 342-6473
URL: www.ulsystem.net

Code	Title	Name
01	President	Dr. James B. HENDERSON
05	Provost and VP for Academic Affairs	Dr. Jeannine KAHN
10	VP of Business and Finance	Dr. Edwin LITOLFF
26	VP of External Affairs	Ms. Rachel KINCAID
32	VP for Student Affairs & Governance	Ms. Erica CALAIS

*Grambling State University (G)

403 Main Street, Grambling LA 71245
County: Lincoln FICE Identification: 002006
Unit ID: 159009
Telephone: (318) 247-3811 Carnegie Class: Masters/L
FAX Number: (318) 274-6172 Calendar System: Semester
URL: www.gram.edu
Established: 1901 Annual Undergrad Tuition & Fees (In-State): $7,371
Enrollment: 4,541 Coed
Affiliation or Control: State IRS Status: 501(c)3
Highest Offering: Doctorate
Accreditation: SC, CAEPN, CS, ENGT, MUS, NRPA, NUR, SPAA, SW, THEA

Code	Title	Name
02	President	Mr. Richard GALLOT, JR.
05	Provost/VP Academic Affairs	Dr. Ellen SMILEY
10	Vice President for Finance and Admn	Mr. Leon SANDERS
32	Vice Pres Student Affairs	Dr. David C. PONTON, JR.
18	Int Director Facilities Management	Mr. Fredrick CARR
13	Assoc VP of Info Technology	Ms. Peggy HANLEY
09	Director of Institutional Research	Ms. Ulrica S. EDWARDS
19	University Police Chief	Mr. Howard CAVINESS
15	AVP of Human Resources	Mrs. Monica BRADLEY
50	Dean College of Business	Dr. Donald WHITE
53	Int Col of Educ/Prof & Grad Stds	Dr. Andolyn HARRISON
49	Dean College of Arts & Sci	Dr. Stacey D. DUHON
92	Dean Honors College	Dr. Ellen SMILEY

41 Director of Athletics ... Dr. Paul BRYANT
22 EEO Officer & Wage & Salary Officer ... Mrs. Monica BRADLEY
07 Director of Admissions ... Ms. DeVaria HUDSON
06 University Registrar ... Mrs. Patricia J. HUTCHERSON
37 Dir Student Financial Aid ... Dr. Gavin HAMMS
04 Executive Asst to the President ... Mr. Lemelle MARTIN
29 Exec Director of Alumni Affairs ... Ms. Carolyn COLLIER
23 Director of Health Services ... Mrs. Patrice OUTLEY
38 Director Counseling Center ... Dr. Coleen SPEED
39 Director of Residential Life ... Ms. Dana K. HOWARD
42 Director of Campus Ministry ... Vacant
96 Director of Purchasing ... Mr. Alvin BRADLEY
40 Manager University Bookstore ... Mr. Elliot JONES
106 Director of Distance Learning ... Mr. Eldrie HAMILTON
88 Special Assistant to Provost and VP ... Mrs. JoAnn BROWN
36 Director of Career Services ... Dr. Shelia FOBBS

*Louisiana Tech University (A)

PO Box 3168, Ruston LA 71272-0001

County: Lincoln — FICE Identification: 002008
Unit ID: 159647
Telephone: (318) 257-0211 — Carnegie Class: DU-Mod
FAX Number: (318) 257-2928 — Calendar System: Quarter
URL: www.latech.edu
Established: 1894 — Annual Undergrad Tuition & Fees (In-State): $9,117
Enrollment: 12,371 — Coed
Affiliation or Control: State — IRS Status: 501(c)3
Highest Offering: Doctorate
Accreditation: SC, AAB, AAFCS, ADNUR, ART, AUD, CACREP, CAEPN, CAHIIM, CIDA, COPSY, CS, DIETD, DIETI, ENG, ENGT, MUS, SP

02 President ... Dr. Leslie K. GUICE
05 Vice Pres Academic Affairs ... Dr. Terry M. MCCONATHY
32 Vice Pres for Student Advancement ... Dr. Jim M. KING
11 AVP of Administration & Facilities ... Mr. Sam G. WALLACE
30 Vice President for Univ Advancement ... Mr. Brooks HULL
10 AVP of Finance & Comptroller ... Mrs. Lisa L. COLE
50 Dean of Business ... Dr. Chris MARTIN
49 Dean of Liberal Arts ... Dr. Don KACZVINSKY
53 Dean of Education ... Dr. Don N. SCHILLINGER
54 Dean of Engineering & Science ... Dr. Hisham HEGAB
65 Dean of Applied & Natural Sciences ... Dr. James LIBERATOS
84 Dean of Enrollment Management ... Mrs. Pamela R. FORD
26 Exec Dir University Communications ... Vacant
07 Director of Admissions ... Mr. Tree GEORGE
13 Director of Computer Center ... Mr. Roy S. WATERS
37 Director Student Financial Aid ... Ms. Aimee F. BAXTER
09 Director Institutional Research ... Mrs. Lori C. THEIS
06 Registrar ... Mr. Robert D. VENTO
08 Director of Libraries ... Ms. Rita FRANKS
15 Director of Human Resources ... Mrs. Sheila TRAMMEL
29 Director of Alumni Relations ... Mr. Wesley CAVIN
36 Dir Career Ctr/Student Counseling ... Mr. Ron CATHEY
89 Director of Freshmen Studies ... Vacant
92 Director of Honors Program ... Dr. Rick SIMMONS
93 Director of Multicultural Affairs ... Vacant
96 Director of Purchasing ... Ms. Melissa HUGHES
18 Chief Facilities/Physical Plant ... Vacant
41 Athletics Director ... Mr. Thomas H. MCCLELLAND, II

*McNeese State University (B)

4205 Ryan Street, Lake Charles LA 70609-4510

County: Calcasieu — FICE Identification: 002017
Unit ID: 159717
Telephone: (337) 475-5000 — Carnegie Class: Masters/L
FAX Number: (337) 475-5012 — Calendar System: Semester
URL: www.mcneese.edu
Established: 1939 — Annual Undergrad Tuition & Fees (In-State): $7,310
Enrollment: 8,153 — Coed
Affiliation or Control: State — IRS Status: 501(c)3
Highest Offering: Beyond Master's But Less Than Doctorate
Accreditation: SC, ART, #CAATE, CACREP, CAEPN, CS, DIETD, DIETI, ENG, MT, MUS, NURSE, RAD

02 President ... Dr. Daryl BURCKEL
05 Provost/VP Acad Affairs/Enroll Mgmt ... Vacant
10 VP Business Affairs/University Svcs ... Mr. Eddie P. MECHE
30 Vice Pres University Advancement ... Mr. Richard H. REID
84 Assoc VP Enrollment Management ... Ms. Stephanie B. TARVER
32 AVP University Services ... Dr. Christopher THOMAS
81 Dean College of Science ... Dr. George F. MEAD, JR.
50 Dean College Business ... Vacant
53 Dean of College of Education ... Dr. Wayne R. FETTER
49 Dean College Liberal Arts ... Vacant
54 Dean Col of Engr & Engr Technology ... Dr. Nikos KIRITSIS
66 Dean College of Nursing/Health Sci ... Dr. Peggy L. WOLFE
18 Director Facilities & Plant Opers ... Mr. Richard R. RHODEN
13 Chief Information Technology ... Mr. Chad THIBODEAUX
31 Dir Community Service and Outreach ... Mrs. Betty H. ANDERSON
15 Dir Human Res/Student Employment ... Ms. Charlene R. ABBOTT
09 Director Institutional Research ... Vacant
37 Director Student Financial Aid ... Ms. Taina J. SAVOIT
08 Director of Library ... Ms. Debbie L. JOHNSON-HOUSTON
19 University Police Chief ... Mr. Robert SPINKS
29 Director Alumni Affairs ... Ms. Joyce D. PATTERSON
88 Director of Scholarships ... Ms. Ralynn F. CASTETE
07 Dir of Admissions and Recruiting ... Ms. Kourtney ISTRE
41 Athletic Director ... Mr. F. Bruce HEMPHILL
45 Dir Inst Research and Effectiveness ... Ms. Jessica HUTCHINGS
96 Director Purchasing/Property Cntrl ... Ms. Roxane FONTENOT
92 Director of Honors College ... Dr. Scott E. GOINS
14 Director of Univ Computing Services ... Mr. Stanley HIPPLER
46 Dir Ofc of Research/Sponsored Pgm ... Vacant
85 Internat Stdnt Advisor/Dir Int Pgm ... Ms. Preble GIRARD
26 Director Public Relations ... Ms. Candace V. TOWNSEND
23 RN Supervisor-Student Health ... Vacant
40 Bookstore Manager ... Ms. Donna MARTIN
106 Director of Electronic Learning ... Mr. Kyle BOUDREAUX
28 Chief Diversity Officer ... Dr. Michael T. SNOWDEN
04 Administrative Asst to President ... Ms. Lisa SULLIVAN
06 Registrar ... Ms. Catrina BOENIG
38 Director Student Counseling/Health ... Ms. Ramie THIBODEAUX

*Nicholls State University (C)

University Station, Thibodaux LA 70310-0001

County: Lafourche — FICE Identification: 002005
Unit ID: 159966
Telephone: (985) 446-8111 — Carnegie Class: Masters/M
FAX Number: (985) 448-4920 — Calendar System: Semester
URL: www.nicholls.edu
Established: 1948 — Annual Undergrad Tuition & Fees (In-State): $7,641
Enrollment: 6,158 — Coed
Affiliation or Control: State — IRS Status: 501(c)3
Highest Offering: Beyond Master's But Less Than Doctorate
Accreditation: SC, AAFCS, ART, CAATE, CACREP, CAEPN, DIETD, DIETI, ENGR, JOUR, MUS, NAIT, NURSE

02 President ... Dr. Bruce T. MURPHY
05 Provost/VP for Academic Affairs ... Dr. Lynn GILLETTE
32 Vice Pres Student Affairs ... Dr. Eugene A. DIAL
30 VP for University Advancement ... Dr. Neal WEAVER
18 Superint Facility/Proj Manager ... Mr. Stan SILVERII
10 AVP for Finance & Administration ... Mr. Terry BRAUD
45 Exec Dir of Planning/Effectiveness ... Mrs. Renee G. HICKS
49 Dean of Arts & Sciences ... Dr. John DOUCET
66 Dean of Nursing and Allied Health ... Dr. Velma S. WESTBROOK
50 Int Dean Business Administration ... Dr. Marilyn MACIK-FREY
53 Dean of Education ... Dr. Leslie JONES
20 Director of Academic Services ... Mr. David ZERANGUE
09 Dir Assess/Institutional Research ... Mrs. Leslie B. DISHMAN
08 Co-Director of Library ... Dr. Van VIATOR
08 Co-Director of Library ... Ms. Anke TONN
08 Co-Director of Library ... Mr. Clifton THERIOT
19 Director of University Police ... Mr. Craig M. JACCUZZO
36 Director of Career Services ... Ms. Kristie R. TAUZIN
37 Director of Student Financial Aid ... Ms. Casie TRICHE
13 Director of Computing Center ... Mr. Charles R. ORDOYNE
15 Director of Human Resources ... Mr. Steven KENNEY
26 Director of University Relations ... Vacant
51 Dir of Continuing Education ... Mr. Jason EIERMANN
41 Athletic Director ... Mr. Matt ROAN
29 Exec Dir Alumni & External Affairs ... Miss Monique CROCHET
06 Director Records & Registration ... Mr. Kelly J. RODRIGUE
07 Director of Admissions ... Mrs. Becky L. DUROCHER
23 Director University Health Services ... Mrs. Adrienne BOLTON
35 Dean of Student Services ... Dr. Michele E. CARUSO
39 Director Residence Life ... Vacant
84 Director of Enrollment Services ... Mrs. Courtney CASSARD
96 Director of Purchasing ... Mr. Terry G. DUPRE
46 Director Research & Sponsored Pgms ... Mrs. Debra BENOIT
58 Director of Graduate Programs ... Mrs. DesLey PLAISANCE
88 Director of Printing & Design ... Mr. Bruno RUGGIERO
109 Director of Auxiliary Services ... Mrs. Brenda HASKINS
88 Coordinator of Veterans Services ... Mr. Gilberto BURBANTE
106 Dir Online Education/E-learning ... Dr. Andrew SIMONCELLI
100 Chief of Staff ... Mr. Alex ARCENEAUX

*Northwestern State University (D)

310 Sam Sibley Drive, Suite 223,
Natchitoches LA 71497-0002

County: Natchitoches — FICE Identification: 002021
Unit ID: 160038
Telephone: (318) 357-6011 — Carnegie Class: Masters/L
FAX Number: (318) 357-4223 — Calendar System: Semester
URL: www.nsula.edu
Established: 1884 — Annual Undergrad Tuition & Fees (In-State): $7,620
Enrollment: 9,179 — Coed
Affiliation or Control: State — IRS Status: 501(c)3
Highest Offering: Doctorate
Accreditation: SC, AAFCS, ADNUR, ART, CACREP, CAEPN, ENGT, MUS, NURSE, RAD, SW, THEA

02 President ... Dr. Chris MAGGIO
05 Interim Provost/VP Academic Affairs ... Dr. Vickie GENTRY
11 Exec VP University & Business Affs ... Dr. Marcus JONES
26 Vice President for External Affairs ... Mr. Jerry D. PIERCE
46 VP for Tech/Innovation/Econ Dev ... Dr. Darlene WILLIAMS
10 Vice President Business Affairs ... Mr. Carl JONES
32 VP for the Student Experience ... Dr. Chris MAGGIO
35 Dean of Students ... Mrs. Frances CONINE
53 Dean Col of Education/Human Dev ... Dr. Vickie GENTRY
49 Interim Dean Col of Arts & Sciences ... Dr. Greg HANDEL
66 Dean Col of Nursing & Allied Health ... Dr. Dana CLAWSON
50 Interim Dean Col of Business & Tech ... Dr. Margaret KILCOYNE
13 Chief Information Officer ... Mr. Ron WRIGHT
92 Director Scholars' College ... Dr. Kirsten BARTELS
12 Director CENLA Campus ... Mr. Jason PARKS
09 Director Institutional Research ... Ms. Maria MIRANDA
06 Registrar ... Mrs. Lillie F. BELL
08 Director of Libraries ... Ms. Abbie LANDRY
111 Asst VP External Affs/Univ Advance ... Mr. Drake OWENS
37 Director Student Financial Aid ... Ms. Lauren JACKSON
88 Dir Creative & Performing Arts ... Dr. Greg HANDEL
27 Director NSU Press ... Mrs. Leah JACKSON
36 Director Counseling & Career Svcs ... Mrs. Rebecca BOONE
41 Athletic Director ... Mr. Greg BURKE
23 Director of Health Services ... Mrs. Stephanie CAMPBELL
07 Director of University Recruiting ... Mrs. Jana LUCKY
15 Director Human Resources ... Mr. Cecil KNOTTS
18 Physical Plant Director ... Mr. Dale WOHLETZ
96 Director of Purchasing ... Mr. Dale MARTIN
21 Associate Business Officer ... Ms. Rita GRAVES

*Southeastern Louisiana University (E)

548 Ned McGehee Drive, Hammond LA 70402-0001

County: Tangipahoa — FICE Identification: 002024
Unit ID: 160612
Telephone: (985) 549-2000 — Carnegie Class: Masters/L
FAX Number: (985) 549-2061 — Calendar System: Semester
URL: www.southeastern.edu
Established: 1925 — Annual Undergrad Tuition & Fees (In-State): $7,773
Enrollment: 14,581 — Coed
Affiliation or Control: State — IRS Status: 501(c)3
Highest Offering: Doctorate
Accreditation: SC, AAFCS, ART, CAATE, CACREP, CAEPN, CS, ENGR, ENGT, MUS, NAIT, NURSE, SP, SW

02 President ... Dr. John L. CRAIN
05 Interim Provost/VP Academic Affairs ... Dr. Tena GOLDING
10 VP Administration/Finance ... Mr. Sam DOMIANO
111 Vice Pres University Advancement ... Ms. Wendy LAUDERDALE
32 Vice President Student Affairs ... Dr. Eric SUMMERS
84 Asst VP Enrollment Services ... Dr. Kay MAURIN
13 Chief Information Officer ... Dr. Mike M. ASOODEH
86 Exec Asst Public & Govt Affairs ... Ms. Erin K. COWSER
21 Controller ... Ms. Nettie L. BURCHFIELD
06 Director Records & Registration ... Ms. Paulette M. POCHE
08 Director of Library ... Mr. Eric W. JOHNSON
36 Director Career Development Svcs ... Mr. Ken W. RIDGEDELL
109 Director Auxiliary Services ... Ms. Connie DAVIS
29 Director of Alumni Services ... Ms. Michelle BIGGS
39 Dir Student Housing & Resident Svcs ... Vacant
15 Director Human Resources ... Ms. Tara DUPRE
19 Director University Police ... Mr. Harold TODD
46 Dir Sponsored Research/Programs ... Ms. Cheryl HALL
41 Athletic Director ... Mr. Jay ARTIGUES
18 Director Facility Planning ... Mr. Ken D. HOWE
92 Director Honors Program ... Dr. Kent NEUERBURG
23 Director Health Services ... Ms. Michelle REED
38 Director Counseling Center ... Vacant
37 Director Financial Aid ... Mr. Charles CAMBRE
09 Director Inst Research/Assessment ... Dr. Michelle HALL
26 Director Public Information ... Mr. Rene G. ABADIE
96 Dir Purchasing/Property Control ... Mr. Richard HIMBER
85 Int Dir Multicultl/Intl Stdnt Affs ... Mr. Gabe WILLIS
22 Coordinator EEO/ADA ... Mr. Gene E. PREGEANT
49 Int Dn Col Arts/Human/Soc Sciences ... Dr. Karen FONTENOT
50 Int Dean of College of Business ... Dr. Antoinette PHILLIPS
53 Interim Dean College Education ... Dr. Shirley JACOB
66 Dean Col of Nursing & Health Sci ... Dr. Ann CARRUTH
72 Dean Col of Science & Technology ... Dr. Daniel MCCARTHY

*University of Louisiana at Lafayette (F)

104 University Circle, Lafayette LA 70503-0001

County: Lafayette — FICE Identification: 002031
Unit ID: 160658
Telephone: (337) 482-1000 — Carnegie Class: DU-Higher
FAX Number: (337) 482-6195 — Calendar System: Semester
URL: www.louisiana.edu
Established: 1898 — Annual Undergrad Tuition & Fees (In-State): $9,450
Enrollment: 17,508 — Coed
Affiliation or Control: State — IRS Status: 501(c)3
Highest Offering: Doctorate
Accreditation: SC, ART, #CAATE, CACREP, CAEPN, CAHIIM, CIDA, CS, DIETD, ENG, JOUR, MUS, NAIT, NURSE, SP

02 President ... Dr. E. Joseph SAVOIE
05 Provost/VP for Academic Affairs ... Dr. David DANAHAR
10 VP Administration & Finance ... Mr. Jerry L. LEBLANC
32 Vice President for Student Affairs ... Ms. Patricia COTTONHAM
30 VP University Advancement ... Mr. John BLOHM
46 Vice President for Research ... Dr. Ramesh KOLLURU
84 VP for Enrollment Management ... Dr. DeWayne BOWIE
13 Chief Information Officer ... Mr. Gene FIELDS
11 Director of Administrative Services ... Ms. Lisa C. LANDRY
21 Asst Vice Pres Financial Services ... Ms. Debra CALAIS
108 Asst VP Institutional Plng & Effect ... Vacant
20 Asst VP Academic Affairs ... Dr. Ellen D. COOK
35 Dean of Students ... Ms. Margarita PEREZ
35 Assoc Dean Students/Dir Stdnt Life ... Ms. Heidie LINDSEY
25 Director of Research/Sponsored Pgms ... Ms. Abby GUILLORY
91 Director of Information Systems ... Mr. Sam F. BULLARD
14 Director Computing Support Services ... Mr. Patrick LANDRY
08 Dean of University Libraries ... Dr. Charles W. TRICHE, III
07 Dir of UN Admissions & Recruitment ... Mr. Andy BENOIT
88 Director Information Networks ... Mr. Stephen J. MAHLER
09 Director of Institutional Research ... Ms. Lisa LORD
55 Director University Connection ... Ms. Amanda DOYLE
37 Director of Financial Aid ... Ms. Cindy SHOWS-PEREZ

96 Director Purchasing ... Ms. Marie FRANK
27 Assoc Director Publications ... Ms. Kathleen A. THAMES
36 Director Career Services ... Ms. Kim A. BILLEAUDEAU
19 Chief of Police ... Chief Joey STURM
23 Director Student Health Svcs .. Ms. Madeline HUSBAND-ARDOIN
49 Dean Liberal Arts ... Dr. Jordan KELLMAN
54 Dean of Engineering ... Dr. Mark E. ZAPPI
53 Dean of Education ... Dr. Nathan ROBERTS
66 Dean of Nursing ... Dr. Gail P. POIRRIER
58 Dean of Graduate School ... Dr. Mary FARMER-KAISER
50 Dean of Business Administration ... Dr. Bret BECTON
81 Dean of Sciences ... Dr. Azmy ACKLEH
97 Dean of University College ... Dr. Bobbie DECUIR
57 Dean College of the Arts ... Mr. H. Gordon BROOKS, II
77 Director Ctr Adv Computer Studies ... Dr. Magdy A. BAYOUMI
18 Director Physical Plant ... Mr. William J. CRIST
43 Director of Operational Review ... Ms. Megan BREAUX
39 Director Housing ... Mr. Jules BREAUX
40 Manager Bookstore ... Mr. Robert RICHARD
24 Director Univ Media/Printing Svcs ... Mr. Steve MAHLER
41 Athletic Director ... Dr. Bryan MAGGARD
85 Director Office of Intl Affairs ... Dr. Rose HONEGGER
51 Director of Continuing Education ... Ms. Dawn PROVOST
31 Dean of Community Service ... Mr. David YARBROUGH
26 Chief Communications Officer ... Mr. Aaron MARTIN
29 Director Alumni Affairs ... Ms. Jennifer LEMEUNIER
112 Planned Giving Officer ... Mr. David P. COMEAUX
38 Director Counseling and Testing ... Mr. Brian FREDERICK
15 Director of Human Resources ... Mr. Paul THOMAS
06 Registrar ... Mr. Mickey DIEZ
106 Director of Distance Learning ... Dr. Luke DOWDEN
92 Director of Honors Program ... Dr. Julia FREDERICK
89 Director of First-Year Experience ... Dr. Jennifer FAUST
28 Director of Diversity ... Ms. Taniecea MALLERY
108 Director Institutional Assessment ... Ms. Alise HAGAN

*University of Louisiana at Monroe (A)

700 University Avenue, Monroe LA 71209-0001
County: Ouachita
FICE Identification: 002020
Unit ID: 159993
Telephone: (318) 342-1000
Carnegie Class: DU-Mod
FAX Number: (318) 342-5161
Calendar System: Semester
URL: www.ulm.edu
Established: 1931
Annual Undergrad Tuition & Fees (In-State): $8,284
Enrollment: 8,804
Coed
Affiliation or Control: State
IRS Status: 501(c)3
Highest Offering: Doctorate
Accreditation: SC, CACREP, CAEPN, CONST, CS, DH, EXSC, MFCD, MT, MUS, NURSE, OT, OTA, #PHAR, RAD, SP, SW

02 President ... Dr. Nick J. BRUNO
03 Executive VP ... Dr. Stephen P. RICHTERS
10 Chief Business Officer ... Dr. William T. GRAVES
32 Vice President for Student Affairs ... Mr. Camile CURRIER
05 Vice President for Academic Affairs ... Dr. Eric A. PANI
26 Chief Communication Officer ... Mrs. Lisa R. MILLER
20 Associate VP Academic Affairs ... Dr. Michael CAMILLE
07 Director Enrollment & Scholarship ... Ms. Mary SCHMEER
41 Director of Athletics ... Dr. Brian WICKSTROM
27 Director Marketing/Communications ... Dr. Julia LETLOW
88 Director Internal Audit ... Mr. Kirby D. CAMPBELL
49 Dean Arts/Education & Sciences ... Dr. Sandra M. LEMOINE
50 Dean Business and Social Sciences ... Dr. Ronald BERRY
67 Dean Health and Pharmaceutical Sci ... Dr. Benny BLAYLOCK
58 Director Graduate School ... Dr. Sushma KRISHNAMURTHY
108 Director Assessment and Evaluation .. Mrs. Allison L. THOMPSON
09 Exec Dir Univ Planning/Analysis ... Ms. Kelsey BOHL
08 Interim Dean of the Library ... Mrs. Cynthia ROBERTSON
106 Director eULM ... Ms. Paula THORNHILL
06 Registrar ... Mr. Anthony MALTA
37 Director Financial Aid Services ... Mrs. Frankie EVERETT
85 Dir Intl Student Program and Svcs ... Ms. Arely CASTILLO
124 Director of University Retention ... Mrs. Barbara MICHAELIDES
102 Executive Director Foundation ... Mrs. Susan CHAPPELL
39 Director Residential Life ... Ms. Tresea L. BUCKHAULTS
45 Budget Officer ... Mrs. Gail C. PARKER
21 Controller ... Ms. Sarah WALKER
15 Director Human Resources ... Ms. Melissa DUCOTE
13 Director Computer Center ... Mr. Chance W. EPPINETTE
109 Exec Dir Auxiliary Enterprises ... Mr. Tommy WALPOLE
40 Manager University Bookstore ... Ms. Karen LONGINO
18 Director Physical Plant Admin ... Mr. Robert KARAM
18 Facilities Planning Officer ... Mr. Michael DAVIS
35 Spec Projects Ofcr/Title IX Coord ... Ms. Treina LANDRUM
38 Director Counseling Center ... Ms. Karen FOSTER
19 Director of University Police ... Mr. Tom TORREGROSSA
36 Director Career Connections ... Ms. Roslynn POGUE
88 Dir Recreational Svcs/Facilities ... Mr. Brandon BRUSCATO
88 Technology and Comm Liaison ... Mr. Lindsey S. WILKERSON
29 Director of Alumni Affairs ... Miss Sarah MOUTON
30 Senior Development Officer ... Vacant
100 Special Assistant to President ... Mr. Ron HOGAN

Virginia College (B)

9501 Cortana Place, Baton Rouge LA 70815-8604
Telephone: (225) 236-3900
Identification: 770826
Accreditation: ACICS, ACFEI, SURGT

† Tuition varies by degree program. Branch campus of Virginia College, Birmingham, AL.

Virginia College (C)

2950 East Texas Street, Suite C, Bossier City LA 71111
Telephone: (888) 342-0014
Identification: 770827
Accreditation: ACICS

† Branch campus of Virginia College, Birmingham, AL

Xavier University of Louisiana (D)

One Drexel Drive, New Orleans LA 70125-1098
County: Orleans
FICE Identification: 002032
Unit ID: 160904
Telephone: (504) 486-7411
Carnegie Class: Masters/S
FAX Number: (504) 520-7904
Calendar System: Semester
URL: www.xula.edu
Established: 1925
Annual Undergrad Tuition & Fees: $23,046
Enrollment: 2,969
Coed
Affiliation or Control: Roman Catholic
IRS Status: 501(c)3
Highest Offering: Doctorate
Accreditation: SC, ACBSP, CACREP, CAEPN, MUS, PHAR

01 President ... Dr. C. Reynold VERRET
05 Provost and Sr VP Academic Affairs ... Dr. Ann MCCALL
46 Assoc VP Research/Sponsored Pgms ... Dr. Deborah MARSHALL
32 Vice President for Student Services ... Mr. Joseph K. BYRD
111 Vice President for Inst Advancement ... Mrs. Gia SOUBLET
10 Vice President for Finance ... Mr. Edward PHILLIPS
13 VP for Office of Technology ... Mr. Tony MOORE
45 VP Planning Inst Res & Assessment ... Dr. Ronald R. DURNFORD
18 Vice President Facilities Planning ... Mr. Marion BRACY
20 Assoc VP for Academic Affairs ... Dr. Marguerite GIGUETTE
07 Director of Admissions ... Dr. Monica SCOTT
06 Registrar ... Ms. Avis STUARD
42 University Chaplain ... Fr. Etido S. JEROME
21 Director of Accounting ... Ms. Joyce SANDIFER
21 Director of Operations ... Ms. Lori GIE
116 Dir Fin Reporting & External Audit ... Mrs. Ingenue S. SCHEXNIDER-FIELDS
15 Assoc VP of Human Resources ... Mr. Kevin WOLF
49 Dean of Arts & Sciences ... Dr. Anil KUKREJA
67 Dean of College of Pharmacy ... Dr. Kathleen KENNEDY
89 Director of Freshmen Studies ... Dr. Wendy GAUDIN
108 Dir of Inst Effectiv & Assessment ... Dr. Danielle DUFFOURC
09 Director for Institutional Research ... Dr. Clair WILKINS GREEN
88 Dir Inst Compliance & Plng Init ... Dr. Treva A. LEE
08 Director of the Library ... Vacant
36 Director of Career Services ... Mrs. Carolyn D. THOMAS
37 Director of Financial Aid ... Ms. Emily LONDON-JONES
19 Director of Campus Police ... Mr. Jacques BATTISTE
23 Med Dir Student Health Services ... Dr. Robert MERCADEL
38 Director of Counseling Services ... Mrs. Shirley LABBE
29 Director of Alumni Relations ... Ms. Kimberly REESE
40 Manager Bookstore ... Ms. Rose NAQUIN
41 Athletic Director ... Mr. Jason HORN
04 Administrative Asst to President ... Mrs. Amelia JENKINS
101 Secretary of the Institution/Board ... Mrs. Isabella THOMPSON
104 Director Study Abroad ... Mr. Torian LEE
106 Dir Online Education/E-learning ... Dr. Karen NICHOLS
39 Director Student Housing ... Mrs. Judy BRACY
44 Annual Fund Manager ... Ms. Lacrecia JAMES
105 Director Web Services ... Mr. Brian BOWERS
26 Chief Public Relations/Marketing ... Mr. Richard TUCKER
84 VP Enrollment Management ... Ms. Keyana SCALES

MAINE

Bates College (E)

2 Andrews Road, Lewiston ME 04240-6047
County: Androscoggin
FICE Identification: 002036
Unit ID: 160977
Telephone: (207) 786-6255
Carnegie Class: Bac-A&S
FAX Number: (207) 786-6123
Calendar System: Other
URL: www.bates.edu
Established: 1855
Annual Undergrad Tuition & Fees: $50,310
Enrollment: 1,792
Coed
Affiliation or Control: Independent Non-Profit
IRS Status: 501(c)3
Highest Offering: Baccalaureate
Accreditation: EH

01 President ... Dr. A. Clayton SPENCER
05 Interim VPAA/DOF ... Dr. Kathryn LOW
10 VP Finance & Admin/Treasurer ... Mr. Geoffrey SWIFT
08 Interim VPILS & Librarian ... Mr. Andrew WHITE
111 VP Advancement ... Ms. Sarah R. PEARSON
32 Dean of Students ... Mr. Joshua MCINTOSH
21 Asst Vice Pres Financial Planning ... Mr. Douglas W. GINEVAN
20 Assoc Dean of Faculty ... Ms. Aslaug ASGEIRSDOTTIR
20 Assoc Dean of Faculty ... Dr. Margaret A. IMBER
31 Director of Community Partnerships ... Ms. Darby K. RAY
06 Registrar ... Ms. Mary MESERVE
09 Dir Inst Rsch/Analysis and Planning ... Ms. Anne Marie T. RUSSELL
15 Asst VP Human Resources ... Ms. Shanna HINES
18 Dir of Facilities Svcs Operations ... Mr. Jay PHILLIPS
88 Dir Capital Planning/Construction ... Ms. Pamela J. WICHROSKI
07 Dean of Admissions & Financial Aid ... Ms. Leigh WEISENBURGER
19 Acting Dir Security & Campus Safety ... Mr. Paul MENICE
23 Assoc Dir Student Health Support ... Ms. Cynthia VISBARAS
26 Asst VP Communications/Media Rels ... Mr. Sean T. FINDLEN
37 Dir Student Financial Services ... Ms. Wendy G. GLASS
40 Dir Bookstore/Contract Officer ... Ms. Gail S. ST. PIERRE
36 Dir of Career Services ... Mr. David MCDONOUGH
91 Dir Sys Development & Integration ... Ms. Eileen P. ZIMMERMAN
24 Dir of Academic Technology Services ... Mr. Andrew W. WHITE
41 Director of Athletics ... Mr. Jason FEIN
42 College Chaplain ... Ms. Brittany LONGSDORF
39 Asst Dean of Students/Housing ... Ms. Erin FOSTER ZSIGA
102 Dir of the Office for External Grnt ... Ms. Rachel WRAY
104 Assoc Dean of Students/Study Abroad ... Ms. Tina MANGIERI
100 Chief of Staff ... Mr. Michael HUSSEY
28 AVP and Chief Diversity Officer ... Ms. Crystal WILLIAMS
88 Sr Assoc Dn Admiss/Dir Intl Enroll ... Mr. Scott ALEXANDER
04 Exec Assistant to the President ... Ms. Claire B. SCHMOLL
101 Secretary of the Institution/Board ... Mr. Michael HUSSEY

† Tuition figure is a comprehensive fees figure.

Beal College (F)

99 Farm Road, Bangor ME 04401-6831
County: Penobscot
FICE Identification: 005204
Unit ID: 160995
Telephone: (207) 947-4591
Carnegie Class: Assoc/HVT-High Non
FAX Number: (207) 947-0208
Calendar System: Other
URL: www.bealcollege.edu
Established: 1891
Annual Undergrad Tuition & Fees: N/A
Enrollment: 331
Coed
Affiliation or Control: Proprietary
IRS Status: Proprietary
Highest Offering: Associate Degree
Accreditation: ACICS, CAHIIM, MAC

01 President ... Ms. Sheryl L. DEWALT
03 Chief Operations Officer ... Mr. Stephen H. VILLETT
11 Director of Operations ... Mr. Corey LEIGHTON
10 Director of Finance ... Ms. Renee DUNTON
05 Director of Education ... Ms. Deborah CROCKETT
07 Director of Admissions ... Ms. Sue BORDEN
37 Director Student Financial Aid ... Ms. Maggie MAGEE
32 Director of Student Affairs ... Ms. Stephanie MISHOU
08 Chief Librarian ... Ms. Tegan C. MILLS
18 Superintendent Physical Plant ... Mr. Kevin HARDY
88 Dir Early Child Ed/Hospitality Svcs ... Ms. Susan XIRINACHS
76 Director Allied Health ... Ms. Barbara MARCHELLETTA
40 Director Bookstore ... Ms. Wandamae CLEAVES
36 Director Student Placement ... Ms. Donna GILLETTE
06 Registrar ... Ms. Ellen EDWARDS
50 Director Business Studies ... Ms. Katrin TEEL
83 Director Social & Human Svcs Asst ... Ms. Susan POLYOT
75 Director Welding Technology ... Mr. Jesse CROSBY

Bowdoin College (G)

3500 College Station, Brunswick ME 04011-8448
County: Cumberland
FICE Identification: 002038
Unit ID: 161004
Telephone: (207) 725-3000
Carnegie Class: Bac-A&S
FAX Number: (207) 725-3123
Calendar System: Semester
URL: www.bowdoin.edu
Established: 1794
Annual Undergrad Tuition & Fees: $49,900
Enrollment: 1,799
Coed
Affiliation or Control: Independent Non-Profit
IRS Status: 501(c)3
Highest Offering: Master's
Accreditation: EH

01 President ... Dr. Clayton ROSE
11 Int Sr VP Finance/Admin/Treasurer ... Mr. Matthew ORLANDO
30 Sr VP Devel & Alumni Relations ... Mr. Scott MEIKLEJOHN
26 Sr VP Communications/Public Affairs ... Mr. Scott W. HOOD
13 SVP/Chief Information Officer ... Vacant
15 Vice President of Human Resources ... Ms. Tamara D. SPOERRI
32 Dean of Student Affairs ... Mr. Timothy W. FOSTER
05 Dean for Academic Affairs ... Dr. Elizabeth MCCORMACK
07 Dean of Admissions/Financial Aid ... Ms. E. Whitney SOULE
09 VP Inst Rsrch/Analytics Consulting ... Dr. Christina M. FINNERAN
29 Director Alumni Relations ... Ms. Rodie F. LLOYD
08 College Librarian ... Ms. Marjorie HASSEN
37 Director of Student Aid ... Mr. Michael D. BARTINI
06 Registrar ... Ms. Martina DUNCAN
19 Director of Security ... Mr. Randall NICHOLS
36 Director of Career Planning ... Mr. Timothy DIEHL
38 Director of Counseling Service ... Dr. Bernie HERSHBERGER
41 Director of Athletics ... Mr. Timothy M. RYAN
23 Director of Health Services ... Dr. Jeffrey MAHER
18 Director Facilities Ops/Maintenance ... Mr. Theodore R. STAM
24 Instructional Media Librarian ... Ms. Carmen M. GREENLEE
39 Director of Residential Life ... Ms. Meadow DAVIS
109 Dir Dining & Bookstore Services ... Ms. Mary M. KENNEDY
35 Director of Student Activities ... Mr. Nate HINTZE
35 Dean of Students ... Ms. Janet LOHMANN
88 Co-Dir of the Museum of Art ... Ms. Anne GOODYEAR
88 Co-Dir of the Musuem of Art ... Mr. Frank GOODYEAR
18 Director of Capital Projects ... Mr. Donald V. BORKOWSKI
20 Assoc Dean for Academic Affairs ... Dr. Charles DORN

Colby College (H)

4000 Mayflower Hill, Waterville ME 04901-8840
County: Kennebec
FICE Identification: 002039
Unit ID: 161086
Telephone: (207) 859-4000
Carnegie Class: Bac-A&S
FAX Number: (207) 859-4603
Calendar System: 4/1/4
URL: www.colby.edu
Established: 1813
Annual Undergrad Tuition & Fees: $50,960

Enrollment: 1,857 Coed
Affiliation or Control: Independent Non-Profit IRS Status: 501(c)3
Highest Offering: Baccalaureate
Accreditation: EH

01 President Dr. David A. GREENE
05 Provost and Dean of Faculty Dr. Margaret T. MCFADDEN
10 Vice President Admin & CFO Mr. Douglas C. TERP
111 VP College Advancement Dr. Daniel G. LUGO
32 Dean of the College Dr. Karlene A. BURRELL-MCRAE
26 Vice President for Communications Ms. Ruth JACKSON
07 Vice Pres/Dean Admiss & Fin Aid Dr. Matthew PROTO
45 Vice President of Planning Mr. Brian J. CLARK
100 VP and Gen Couns/Sec of the Col Mr. Richard Y. UCHIDA
20 Assoc Provost & Dean of Faculty Dr. Russell R. JOHNSON
35 Dean of Students Ms. Barbara E. MOORE
06 Registrar Ms. Elizabeth N. SCHILLER
08 Interim Director of Libraries Darlyne M. PROVOST
36 VP and Dean of Student Advancement Dr. C. Andrew MCGADNEY
88 Director of Special Programs Mr. Brian BRAY
37 Director of Financial Aid Vacant
29 Dir Alumni Experience and Networks Vacant
15 Director Human Resources Mr. Mark CROSBY
19 Director of Security Mr. Peter S. CHENEVERT
13 Chief Information Officer Ms. Cindy J. MITCHELL
18 Asst VP Facilities and Campus Plng Ms. Minakshi M. AMUNDSEN
23 Medical Director Dr. Paul D. BERKNER
38 Director of Counseling Services Mr. Eric S. JOHNSON
41 Director of Athletics Mr. Jake OLKKOLA
09 Dir Inst Research & Assessment Ms. Rebecca H. BRODIGAN
21 Controller Mr. Ruben L. RIVERA
40 Director of the Bookstore Ms. Barbara C. SHUTT
104 Director of Off-Campus Study Dr. Nancy DOWNEY
102 Director of Grants Mr. William C. LAYTON, III

College of the Atlantic (A)

105 Eden Street, Bar Harbor ME 04609-1198
County: Hancock FICE Identification: 011385
Unit ID: 160959
Telephone: (207) 288-5015 Carnegie Class: Bac-A&S
FAX Number: (207) 288-3780 Calendar System: Trimester
URL: www.coa.edu
Established: 1969 Annual Undergrad Tuition & Fees: $43,542
Enrollment: 348 Coed
Affiliation or Control: Independent Non-Profit IRS Status: 501(c)3
Highest Offering: Master's
Accreditation: EH

01 President Dr. Darron COLLINS
05 Academic Dean Dr. Ken HILL
10 Administrative Dean Mr. Andy GRIFFITHS
32 Dean for Student Life Ms. Sarah LUKE
30 Dean Institutional Advancement Ms. Lynn BOULGER
07 Dean of Admission Ms. Heather ALBERT-KNOPP
06 Registrar Ms. Judy ALLEN
08 Director of Thorndike Library Ms. Jane HULTBERG
21 Comptroller Mrs. Melissa COOK
37 Director of Financial Aid Mr. Bruce HAZAM
36 Director of Internship/Career Svcs Ms. Jill BARLOW-KELLEY
26 Public Relations Manager Mr. Rob LEVIN

Husson University (B)

1 College Circle, Bangor ME 04401-2929
County: Penobscot FICE Identification: 002043
Unit ID: 487524
Telephone: (207) 941-7000 Carnegie Class: Masters/M
FAX Number: (207) 941-7139 Calendar System: Semester
URL: www.husson.edu
Established: 1898 Annual Undergrad Tuition & Fees: $17,035
Enrollment: 3,416 Coed
Affiliation or Control: Independent Non-Profit IRS Status: 501(c)3
Highest Offering: Doctorate
Accreditation: EH, CACREP, IACBE, NURSE, OT, PHAR, PTA

01 President Dr. Robert A. CLARK
05 VP for Academic Affairs/Provost Dr. Lynne COY-OGAN
10 VP Finance & Admin/Treasurer Craig HADLEY
111 Vice President for Advancement Sara C. ROBINSON
84 VP Enrollment Management Jonathan HENRY
50 Dean College of Business Dr. Marie HANSEN
67 Dean School of Pharmacy Dr. Rodney LARSON
53 Dean College of Health & Education Dr. Rhonda WASKIEWICZ
49 Dean Science/Humanities Dr. Patricia BIXEL
26 Exec Dir of Marketing and Comm Eric GORDON
32 Dean of Student Life Carl STILES
53 Director School of Education Barbara MOODY
07 Director of Admissions John CHAMPOLI
37 Director of Financial Aid Anne TABOR
13 Exec Dir of Information Resources Garth CORMIER
06 Registrar Nancy FENDERS
09 Director of Institutional Research Dr. Gail TUDOR
108 Director Institutional Assessment Travis E. ALLEN
106 Dir Online and Extended Learning Dr. David HAUS
36 Director Career Services James WESTHOFF
41 Director of Athletics Francis PERGOLIZZI
31 Dir of Comm and Student Engagement Julie GREEN
15 Human Resources Director Janet KELLE
29 Director of Alumni Relations Amanda CUMMINGS
18 Director of Maintenance Gary GEROW
08 Librarian Susanna PATHAK
88 Dir of Special Programs Mike FOSTER
30 Director of Advancement Services Paige HOLMES
04 Administrative Asst to President Kandi HALE
100 Chief of Staff Mary Ann HAAS
19 Director Safety and Security Ray BESSETTE
38 Director of Counseling Services Colleen OWENS
105 Website Manager & Social Media Dir Matthew GREEN-HAMANN
109 Assoc Vice President for Auxil Thomas WARREN

Institute for Doctoral Studies in the Visual Arts (C)

130 Neal Street, Portland ME 04102
County: Cumberland FICE Identification: 041888
Unit ID: 462044
Telephone: (207) 879-8757 Carnegie Class: Bac-A&S
FAX Number: N/A Calendar System: Semester
URL: www.idsva.org
Established: 2007 Annual Graduate Tuition & Fees: N/A
Enrollment: 64 Coed
Affiliation or Control: Independent Non-Profit IRS Status: 501(c)3
Highest Offering: Doctorate; No Undergraduates
Accreditation: EH

01 President George SMITH
10 Exec Vice President/CFO Amy CURTIS
05 Vice Pres Acad Affs/Dir of School Dr. Simonetta MORO

Kaplan University-Augusta (D)

14 Marketplace Drive, Augusta ME 04330
Telephone: (207) 213-2500 Identification: 770060
Accreditation: &NH

† Branch campus of Kaplan University, Davenport, IA

Kaplan University-Lewiston (E)

475 Lisbon Street, Lewiston ME 04240
Telephone: (207) 333-3300 Identification: 770061
Accreditation: &NH, MAC

† Branch campus of Kaplan University, Davenport, IA

Kaplan University-Maine (F)

265 Western Avenue, South Portland ME 04106
Telephone: (207) 774-6126 FICE Identification: 009292
Accreditation: &NH, ACBSP

† Regional accreditation is carried under the parent institution in Davenport, IA.

The Landing School (G)

286 River Road, Arundel ME 04046
County: York FICE Identification: 023613
Unit ID: 161208
Telephone: (207) 985-7976 Carnegie Class: Spec 2-yr-Tech
FAX Number: (207) 985-7942 Calendar System: Semester
URL: www.landingschool.edu
Established: 1978 Annual Undergrad Tuition & Fees: $22,296
Enrollment: 74 Coed
Affiliation or Control: Independent Non-Profit IRS Status: 501(c)3
Highest Offering: Associate Degree
Accreditation: ACCSC

01 President Dr. Richard J. SCHUHMANN
05 Director of Education Mr. Richard WOODMAN
10 Dir of Administration & Finance Ms. Kristy LANK
07 Director of Admissions Mr. Matthew BARRY
37 Director Student Financial Aid Ms. Jennifer BECHARD

Maine College of Art (H)

522 Congress St, Portland ME 04101
County: Cumberland FICE Identification: 011673
Unit ID: 161509
Telephone: (207) 699-5521 Carnegie Class: Spec-4-yr-Arts
FAX Number: (207) 775-5087 Calendar System: Semester
URL: www.meca.edu
Established: 1882 Annual Undergrad Tuition & Fees: $32,922
Enrollment: 468 Coed
Affiliation or Control: Independent Non-Profit IRS Status: 501(c)3
Highest Offering: Master's
Accreditation: EH, ART

01 President Ms. Laura FREID
03 Executive Vice President Ms. Beth ELICKER
05 VP Academic Affairs/Dean of College Mr. Ian ANDERSON
30 VP for Institutional Advancement Ms. Rebecca CONRAD
06 Registrar Ms. Anne DENNISON
32 Director of Student Life Ms. Adrea JAEHNIG
07 Director of Admissions Ms. Megan LLOYD
13 Director Technology Mr. Seth CLAYTER
26 Dir of Marketing & Communications Mr. Raffi DER SIMONIAN
10 Director of Business Services Mr. Phil STEVENS
37 Director of Financial Aid Ms. Carri FRECHETTE
51 Director Continuing Studies Ms. Courtney COOK
18 Director of Facilities Mr. Douglas DOERING
08 Library Director Ms. Shiva DARBANDI
04 Executive Assistant Ms. Melissa SULLIVAN
29 Director Alumni Relations Ms. Jill DALTON
36 Director of Artists at Work Ms. Jessica TOMLINSON

Maine College of Health Professions (I)

70 Middle Street, Lewiston ME 04240-7027
County: Androscoggin FICE Identification: 006305
Unit ID: 161022
Telephone: (207) 795-2840 Carnegie Class: Spec 2-yr-Health
FAX Number: (207) 795-2849 Calendar System: Semester
URL: www.mchp.edu
Established: 1891 Annual Undergrad Tuition & Fees: $12,310
Enrollment: 199 Coed
Affiliation or Control: Independent Non-Profit IRS Status: 501(c)3
Highest Offering: Associate Degree
Accreditation: EH, ADNUR, NMT, RAD

01 President Dr. Monika BISSELL
10 Director of Financial Affairs Ms. Lesa ROSE
05 Director of Med Imaging/Gen Ed Mrs. Judith RIPLEY
07 Director of Admissions Ms. Erica WATSON
06 Registrar Mrs. Kathleen C. JACQUES
37 Student Financial Aid Specialist Mrs. Nicole DEBLOIS
66 Interim Director of Nursing Ms. Heather FRASER

*Maine Community College System (J)

323 State Street, Augusta ME 04330-7131
County: Kennebec Identification: 666092
Unit ID: 409713
Telephone: (207) 629-4000 Carnegie Class: N/A
FAX Number: (207) 629-4048
URL: www.mccs.me.edu/

01 President Mr. Derek LANGHAUSER
05 Chief Academic Officer Ms. Janet SORTOR
10 Chief Financial Officer/Vice Pres Mr. David DAIGLER

*Central Maine Community College (K)

1250 Turner Street, Auburn ME 04210-6498
County: Androscoggin FICE Identification: 005276
Unit ID: 161077
Telephone: (207) 755-5100 Carnegie Class: Assoc/MT-VT-High Trad
FAX Number: (207) 755-5491 Calendar System: Semester
URL: www.cmcc.edu
Established: 1964 Annual Undergrad Tuition & Fees (In-State): $3,540
Enrollment: 2,984 Coed
Affiliation or Control: State IRS Status: 501(c)3
Highest Offering: Associate Degree
Accreditation: EH, ADNUR

02 President Dr. Scott E. KNAPP
05 Dean Academic Affairs Ms. Betsy LIBBY
06 Registrar Ms. Sonya SAMPSON
10 Dean of Finance and General Service Ms. Pamela REMIERES-MORIN
37 Director of Financial Aid Mr. John BOWIE
31 Dir Workforce & Professional Dev Ms. Michelle HAWLEY
32 Dean of Student Services Mr. Nicholas HAMEL
26 Dean of Planning & Public Affairs Mr. Roger PHILIPPON
07 Director of Admissions Mr. Andrew MORONG
08 Head Librarian Ms. Judith FROST
18 Chief Physical Plant Mr. Raymond MASSE
22 Affirmative Action Officer Ms. Barbara OWEN
39 Director of Housing/Athletic Dir Mr. David GONYEA
40 Director of Bookstore Ms. Christine MORIN
15 Dean of Human Resources Ms. Barbara OWEN
27 Director of Communications Ms. Heather B. SEYMOUR
09 Director of Institutional Research Mr. Ronald BOLSTRIDGE

*Eastern Maine Community College (L)

354 Hogan Road, Bangor ME 04401-4280
County: Penobscot FICE Identification: 005277
Unit ID: 161138
Telephone: (207) 974-4600 Carnegie Class: Assoc/HVT-High Non
FAX Number: (207) 974-4608 Calendar System: Semester
URL: www.emcc.edu
Established: 1966 Annual Undergrad Tuition & Fees (In-State): $3,676
Enrollment: 2,732 Coed
Affiliation or Control: State IRS Status: 501(c)3
Highest Offering: Associate Degree
Accreditation: EH, ADNUR, EMT, MAC, RAD, SURGT

02 President Dr. Lisa LARSON
05 VP of Academic Affairs Ms. Elizabeth RUSSELL
10 Dir Finance & Auxiliary Services Mr. Jerry HAYMAN
32 Dean of Student Life Mr. E. J. ROACH
09 Dean Inst Research/Enrollment Mgmt Mr. Daniel CROCKER
88 Professional Services Coordinator Ms. Francesca DESANCTIS
07 Director of Admissions Ms. Stacy GREEN
15 Director of Human Resources Ms. Jody VAIL
08 Librarian Ms. Janet ELVIDGE
37 Director of Financial Aid Ms. Candace WARD
13 Dean of Communication/Info Tech Mr. Timothy CONROY
18 Dir Facilities Mgmt/Student Life Vacant
111 Dir of Institutional Advancement Ms. Jenn KHAVARI

20 Assistant Academic Dean .... Vacant
04 Admin Asst to the President .... Ms. Terri ADAM

*Kennebec Valley Community College (A)

92 Western Avenue, Fairfield ME 04937-1367
County: Somerset FICE Identification: 009826
Unit ID: 161192
Telephone: (207) 453-5000 Carnegie Class: Assoc/MT-VT-High Non
FAX Number: (207) 453-5010 Calendar System: Semester
URL: www.kvcc.me.edu
Established: 1970 Annual Undergrad Tuition & Fees (In-State): $3,790
Enrollment: 2,450 Coed
Affiliation or Control: State IRS Status: 501(c)3
Highest Offering: Associate Degree
Accreditation: **EH**, ACBSP, ADNUR, CAHIIM, COARC, EMT, MAC, OTA, PTAA, RAD

02 President .... Dr. Richard HOPPER
05 Academic Dean .... Ms. Kathy ENGLEHART
13 Dean of Tech/Chief Security Officer .... Mr. Kevin CASEY
32 VP of Student Affairs/Public Rels .... Ms. Karen NORMANDIN
10 Dean of Finance & Administration .... Vacant
84 Asst Dean of Enrollment Management .... Mr. Crichton MCKENNA
06 Registrar .... Mr. Christian HANSEN
30 Director of Development .... Ms. Michelle WEBB
37 Director of Financial Aid .... Ms. Anne CONNORS
09 Director of Institutional Research .... Ms. Karen GLEW

*Northern Maine Community College (B)

33 Edgemont Drive, Presque Isle ME 04769-2099
County: Aroostook FICE Identification: 005760
Unit ID: 161484
Telephone: (207) 768-2700 Carnegie Class: Assoc/HVT-Mix Trad/Non
FAX Number: (207) 768-2831 Calendar System: Semester
URL: www.nmcc.edu
Established: 1961 Annual Undergrad Tuition & Fees (In-State): $3,464
Enrollment: 931 Coed
Affiliation or Control: State IRS Status: 501(c)3
Highest Offering: Associate Degree
Accreditation: **EH**, ACBSP, ADNUR, EMT, MAC

02 President .... Mr. Timothy D. CROWLEY
05 Academic Dean .... Dr. Dorothy MARTIN
32 Dean of Students .... Dr. William G. EGELER
10 Dean of Finance .... Mr. Michael WILLIAMS
51 Asst Dean Continuing Education .... Ms. Leah BUCK
30 Dean of Development/Public Affairs .... Vacant
07 Director of Admissions .... Ms. Wendy BRADSTREET
06 Registrar .... Ms. Betsy A. HARRIS
37 Director for Financial Aid .... Ms. Norma M. SMITH
39 Director of Housing & Resident Life .... Mr. Jon A. BLANCHARD
38 Director of Counseling .... Ms. Tammy NELSON
18 Dean of Tech and Facilities .... Mr. Barry INGRAHAM
21 Business Manager .... Ms. Wendy CAVERHILL
40 College Store Manager .... Ms. Rebecca A. MAYNARD
08 Head Librarian .... Ms. Gail ROY
19 College Safety/Security Officer .... Mr. Peter GOHEEN
15 Human Resource Coordinator .... Ms. Beth HUMMEL

*Southern Maine Community College (C)

2 Fort Road, South Portland ME 04106-1698
County: Cumberland FICE Identification: 005525
Unit ID: 161545
Telephone: (207) 741-5500 Carnegie Class: Assoc/MT-VT-High Trad
FAX Number: (207) 741-5751 Calendar System: Semester
URL: www.smccme.edu
Established: 1946 Annual Undergrad Tuition & Fees (In-State): $3,760
Enrollment: 6,045 Coed
Affiliation or Control: State IRS Status: 501(c)3
Highest Offering: Associate Degree
Accreditation: **EH**, ACFEI, ADNUR, COARC, DIETT, EMT, MAAB, RAD

02 President/CEO .... Ronald G. CANTOR
05 Dean of Academics .... Charles J. GREGORY
32 Dean of Student Life/Affirm Action .... Tiffanie L. BENTLEY
84 Dean Enrollment & Student Success .... Kaylene MITCHELL
04 Asst to the Pres/Strategic Initiat .... Darla JEWETT
04 Exec Assistant to the President .... Lori HALL
12 Dean of the Midcoast Campus .... James WHITTEN
10 Dean of Finance .... Robert COOMBS
13 Dean of Information Technology/CIO .... Timothy DUNNE
88 Int Dean Bus & Cmty Partnerships .... Julie CHASE
20 Associate Dean of Academic Affairs .... Paul CHARPENTIER
06 Asst Dean of Records/Retention .... Jeremy DILL
114 Director of Budget & Financial Rpt .... Shaun GRAY
37 Director of Financial Aid Systems .... Michel LUSSIER
07 Director of Admissions .... Amy LEE
121 Assistant Dean of Student Success .... Kathleen DOAN
39 Dir of Residence Life & Stdnt Dev .... Jason SAUCIER
19 Director Campus Security .... Joseph MANHARDT
41 Associate Dean of Student Life .... Matthew RICHARDS
18 Plant Maintenance Engineer III .... James RENY
40 Manager Campus Store .... Katharine DUCHETTE
113 Business Mgr Student Billing/Bursar .... Leslie GUERRETTE
15 HR & Benefits Manager .... Denise RENY
38 Dir Counseling & Disability Svcs .... Sandra LYNHAM
27 Director of Communications .... Clarke CANFIELD
102 Dir Foundation Corporate Relations .... Joan COHEN
105 Director Web Services .... Ken POOLEY
103 Dir Workforce/Career Development .... Charles COLLINS
106 Dir Online Education/E-learning .... Michael HART

*Washington County Community College (D)

One College Drive, Calais ME 04619-9704
County: Washington FICE Identification: 009231
Unit ID: 161581
Telephone: (207) 454-1000 Carnegie Class: Assoc/HVT-Mix Trad/Non
FAX Number: (207) 454-1092 Calendar System: Semester
URL: www.wccc.me.edu
Established: 1969 Annual Undergrad Tuition & Fees (In-State): $3,719
Enrollment: 482 Coed
Affiliation or Control: State IRS Status: 501(c)3
Highest Offering: Associate Degree
Accreditation: **EH**, MAC

02 President .... Mr. Joseph CASSIDY
05 Dean of Academic Affairs .... Dr. Alexander CLIFFORD
10 Dean of Finance .... Ms. Desiree THOMPSON
15 Dir of HR/Devel/Communications .... Mrs. Tina ERSKINE
84 Dean Enrollment Mgmt/Student Svcs .... Mrs. Susan MINGO
37 Financial Aid Director .... Mrs. Linda FITZSIMMONS
39 Director of Res Life .... Ms. Karen GOOKIN
04 Exec Asst to the Pres/HR Coord .... Mrs. Robyn LEIGHTON
21 Business Manager .... Mr. Tom MOHOLLAND
18 Facilities Manager .... Mr. Richard RAMSEY
13 IT Director .... Mr. William CODY
06 Assistant to the Academic Dean .... Mrs. Donna GEEL
113 Student Accounts .... Mrs. Heather SMALE
08 Dir of Library & Learning Resources .... Mrs. Elizabeth PHILLIPS
09 Instructor/Institutional Research .... Mr. Darin MCGAW
22 Instructional Technologist/AAO .... Ms. Tatiana OSMOND

*York County Community College (E)

112 College Drive, Wells ME 04090-0529
County: York FICE Identification: 031229
Unit ID: 420440
Telephone: (207) 646-9282 Carnegie Class: Assoc/HT-Mix Trad/Non
FAX Number: (207) 646-9675 Calendar System: Semester
URL: www.yccc.edu
Established: 1994 Annual Undergrad Tuition & Fees (In-State): $3,540
Enrollment: 1,758 Coed
Affiliation or Control: State IRS Status: 501(c)3
Highest Offering: Associate Degree
Accreditation: **EH**

02 President .... Dr. Barbara FINKELSTEIN
05 Vice President/Academic Dean .... Ms. Paula GAGNON
32 Dean of Students .... Mr. Jason AREY
10 Dean of Finance & Administration .... Mr. Samuel ELLIS
26 Dir of Marketing/Communications .... Ms. Stacy CHILICKI
31 Dir of Business/Community Programs .... Dr. Stefanie BOURQUE
04 Special Asst to the Pres/Dir Dev .... Ms. Erin HAYE
20 Associate Academic Dean .... Dr. Doreen ROGAN
08 Director Library/Learning Resources .... Ms. Amber TATNALL
88 Faculty Development Coordinator .... Vacant
07 Director of Admissions .... Mr. Fred QUISTGARD
84 Director of Enrollment Services .... Ms. Jessica MASI
37 Director Financial Aid .... Mr. David DAIGLE
13 Director of Technology .... Mr. Eric BOURQUE
21 Business Manager .... Mr. Paul GURNEY
15 Human Resources & Benefits Manager .... Ms. Ellen HARFORD
18 Manager of Facilities .... Mr. Dana PETERSEN
09 Assoc Dean of Inst Research .... Dr. Nicholas GILL

Maine Maritime Academy (F)

Pleasant Street, Castine ME 04420-0001
County: Hancock FICE Identification: 002044
Unit ID: 161299
Telephone: (207) 326-4311 Carnegie Class: Bac-Diverse
FAX Number: (207) 326-2218 Calendar System: Semester
URL: www.mma.edu
Established: 1941 Annual Undergrad Tuition & Fees (In-State): $13,078
Enrollment: 1,028 Coed
Affiliation or Control: State IRS Status: 501(c)3
Highest Offering: Master's
Accreditation: **EH**, ENG, ENGT

01 President .... Dr. William J. BRENNAN
05 Provost .... Dr. David GARDNER
11 VP Financial & Institutional Svcs .... Ms. Petra CARVER
84 VP Stdnt Svcs/Enrollment Mgmt .... Dr. Elizabeth TRUE
111 Vice President for Advancement .... Mr. Christopher HALEY
15 Human Resource Officer .... Mrs. Carrie MARGRAVE
35 Dean of Student Services .... Ms. Deidra DAVIS
36 Placement Director .... Mr. Timothy LEACH
07 Director of Admissions .... Mrs. Kelly GUALTIERI
06 Registrar .... Ms. Christina STEPHENS
29 Director Alumni Relations .... Mr. Jeff WRIGHT
37 Director Student Financial Aid .... Ms. Kathy HEATH
38 Director Student Counseling .... Mr. Paul FERREIRA
08 Head Librarian .... Ms. Lauren GARGANI
10 Chief Business Officer .... Ms. Diana SNAPP
18 Chief Facilities/Physical Plant .... Mr. Adam POTTER
20 Associate Academic Dean .... Dr. Susan LOOMIS
26 Chief Public Relations Officer .... Mrs. Jennifer DEJOY
39 Director of Residential Life .... Ms. Amanda MANNING
09 Director of Institutional Research .... Mr. Ryan KING
96 Director of Purchasing .... Mrs. Alice HERRICK
04 Executive Asst to President .... Ms. Rhonda VARNEY
13 Chief Info Technology Officer (CIO) .... Mrs. Lisa ROY
19 Director Security/Safety .... Mr. Ryan KUHL
41 Athletic Director .... Mr. Stephen PEED

Saint Joseph's College of Maine (G)

278 Whites Bridge Road, Standish ME 04084-5236
County: Cumberland FICE Identification: 002051
Unit ID: 161518
Telephone: (207) 892-6766 Carnegie Class: Masters/L
FAX Number: (207) 893-7861 Calendar System: Semester
URL: www.sjcme.edu
Established: 1912 Annual Undergrad Tuition & Fees: $33,600
Enrollment: 2,581 Coed
Affiliation or Control: Roman Catholic IRS Status: 501(c)3
Highest Offering: Master's
Accreditation: **EH**, CAHIIM, NURSE, @SW

01 President .... Dr. James S. DLUGOS
05 VP & Chief Officer of Learning .... Dr. Michael PARDALES
30 VP & Chief Advancement Officer .... Ms. Joanne BEAN
84 VP Enrollment .... Ms. Lynne ROBINSON
88 VP for Sponsorship & Mission .... Dr. Michael SANDERL
10 VP/Int Chief Financial Officer .... Mr. Stuart KOOP
13 AVP Chief Information Officer .... Mr. Chip STILES
32 Asst Director Student Activities .... Mr. Matthew GAWEL
06 Director Academic Records/Registrar .... Mr. Kevin PAQUETTE
08 Director Library .... Ms. Shelly DAVIS
23 Director of Student Health Center .... Ms. Sheri PIERS
15 AVP/Chief Human Resources Officer .... Ms. Kristine AVERY

Thomas College (H)

180 W River Road, Waterville ME 04901-5097
County: Kennebec FICE Identification: 002052
Unit ID: 161563
Telephone: (207) 859-1111 Carnegie Class: Masters/S
FAX Number: (207) 859-1114 Calendar System: Semester
URL: www.thomas.edu
Established: 1894 Annual Undergrad Tuition & Fees: $25,150
Enrollment: 1,367 Coed
Affiliation or Control: Independent Non-Profit IRS Status: 501(c)3
Highest Offering: Master's
Accreditation: **EH**

01 President .... Ms. Laurie G. LACHANCE
03 Executive Vice President .... Mr. Bernie OUELLETTE
05 Provost .... Dr. Thomas EDWARDS
10 Senior Vice President/CFO/Treasurer .... Ms. Beth B. GIBBS
30 Senior Vice Pres Advancement .... Mr. Robert M. MOORE
32 Vice President Student Affairs .. Ms. Lisa DESAUTELS-POLIQUIN
13 Vice Pres Information Services/CIO .... Mr. Christopher RHODA
84 Vice Pres Enrollment Management .... Mr. Jonathan KENT
44 Assistant Vice Pres Advancement .... Ms. Erin BALTES
35 Dean of Students .... Ms. Hannah GLADSTONE
20 Assistant Academic Dean .... Ms. Merlene SANBORN
15 Chief Human Resources Officer .... Ms. Michelle JOLER-LABBE
08 Director Library Services .... Ms. Lisa AURIEMMA
37 Director Student Financial Services .... Ms. Jeannine BOSSE
29 Director Alumni/Career Services .... Mr. Corey PELLETIER
18 Director Physical Plant .... Vacant
06 Registrar .... Ms. Lindsey NELSON
45 Director of Stategic Initiatives .... Ms. Mikaela ZIOBRO
04 Executive Asst to President .... Ms. Leta BILODEAU
41 Director of Athletics .... Ms. Shanda NESS
26 Director of Publications .... Ms. Jennifer BUKER

Unity College (I)

90 Quaker Hill Road, Unity ME 04988-9502
County: Waldo FICE Identification: 006858
Unit ID: 161572
Telephone: (207) 509-7100 Carnegie Class: Bac-Diverse
FAX Number: (207) 512-1192 Calendar System: Semester
URL: www.unity.edu
Established: 1965 Annual Undergrad Tuition & Fees: $27,570
Enrollment: 665 Coed
Affiliation or Control: Independent Non-Profit IRS Status: 501(c)3
Highest Offering: Master's
Accreditation: **EH**

01 President .... Dr. Melik Peter KHOURY
100 Chief of Staff .... Dr. John ZAVODNY
05 Chief Academic Officer .... Dr. Erika LATTY
10 Chief Business Officer .... Ms. Holli COSTEDIO
30 Chief Fundraising Officer .... Ms. Erica HUTCHINSON
13 Chief Information Officer .... Mr. Bert AUDETTE
26 Chief Marketing Officer .... Vacant
106 Chief Distance Education Officer .... Dr. Amy ARNETT
88 Chief Sustainability Officer .... Ms. Jennifer DEHART
101 Secretary to Board .... Ms. Christine MELANSON
04 Executive Assistant .... Mrs. Sharon PICARD
06 Registrar .... Vacant
32 Dean of Student .... Mr. Ray PHINNEY

07 Director of Admissions .... Mr. Joseph SALTALAMACHIA
09 Director of Institutional Research .... Ms. Holly HEIN
41 Director of Athletics & Wellness .... Mr. Timothy LECRONE
109 Director Dining Services .... Ms. Lorey DUPREY
36 Dean of Career Services .... Dr. Robert SCOTT
18 Director Facilities Management Offi .... Mr. James KAUPPILA
37 Director Financial Aid .... Mr. Rand E. NEWELL
23 Director Student Health Services .... Ms. Anna MCGALLIARD
15 Director Human Resources .... Ms. Bethany DRIGGS
121 Dean of Academic Support .... Ms. Bobette THOMAS
08 Director Library & Information Res .... Ms. Katherine RUSSELL
88 Director Outdoor Adventure Center .... Ms. Jessica STEELE
39 Director Residence Life .... Mr. Stephen S. NASON
88 Director Student Accounts .... Ms. Jeri ROBERTS
88 ADA Coordinator/Learning Specialis .... Vacant
53 Director of Teacher Education .... Dr. Jennifer CARTIER
27 Assoc Dir College Communications .... Ms. Michaela BEDELL
19 Director of Public Safety .... Mr. Steven DRAKE
88 Internship Coordinator .... Ms. Reeta BENEDICT
40 Manager Bookstore .... Ms. Leigh JUSKEVICE
28 Chief Diversity & Inclusion Officer .... Dr. Rana JOHNSON

*University of Maine System (A)

15 Estabrooke Drive, Orono ME 04469
County: Penobscot FICE Identification: 008012
Unit ID: 161280
Telephone: N/A Carnegie Class: N/A
FAX Number: N/A
URL: www.maine.edu

01 Chancellor .... Dr. James H. PAGE
05 Vice Chancellor Academic Affairs .... Dr. Robert NEELY
10 Vice Chanc for Finance & Treasurer .... Mr. Ryan LOW
43 University Counsel .... Mr. James B. THELEN
86 Dir of Comm/Governmental Rels .... Ms. Samantha C. WARREN
101 Clerk of the Board .... Ms. Ellen DOUGHTY
32 Chief Student Affairs Officer .... Ms. Rosa REDONNETT
13 Chief Information Officer .... Dr. David DEMERS
18 Chief General Services Officer .... Mr. M. F. Chip GAVIN
15 Chief Human Resources Officer .... Ms. Lynda DEC
26 Exec Director of Public Affairs .... Mr. Daniel DEMERITT

*University of Maine (B)

168 College Avenue, Orono ME 04469-0001
County: Penobscot FICE Identification: 002053
Unit ID: 161253
Telephone: (207) 581-1110 Carnegie Class: DU-Higher
FAX Number: (207) 581-1604 Calendar System: Semester
URL: www.umaine.edu
Established: 1865 Annual Undergrad Tuition & Fees (In-State): $10,628
Enrollment: 10,922 Coed
Affiliation or Control: State IRS Status: 501(c)3
Highest Offering: Doctorate
Accreditation: EH, ART, CAATE, CAEPN, CEA, CLPSY, CS, DIETD, DIETI, ENG, ENGT, IPSY, MUS, NURSE, SP, SW

02 President .... Dr. Susan J. HUNTER
05 Exec VP Academic Affairs/Provost .... Dr. Jeffrey E. HECKER
10 Assoc VC & Chief Financial Officer .... Mr. Ryan LOW
102 Pres Univ of Maine Foundation .... Dr. Jeffery N. MILLS
32 VP Student Affs/Dean of Students .... Dr. Robert Q. DANA
46 Vice President for Research .... Dr. Kody VARAHRAMYAN
84 Int VP Enrollment Management .... Dr. Joe LEE
88 VP Innovation/Economic Development .... Mr. James WARD, IV
15 Vice President of Human Resources .... Mr. Chris LINDSTROM
21 Chief Business Officer .... Mrs. Claire I. STRICKLAND
20 Sr Assoc Prov/Dean Undergrad Educ .... Dr. Jeffrey E. ST. JOHN
100 Chief of Staff .... CAPT. Jim D. SETTELE
08 Dean of Libraries .... Ms. Joyce V. RUMERY
13 Director ITS Project Management Of .... Ms. Robin SHERMAN
18 Exec Dir Facilities/Capital Mgt Svc .... Mr. Stewart A. HARVEY
26 Sr Dir Univ Relations/Operations .... Ms. Margaret A. NAGLE
109 Exec Director of Auxiliary Services .... Mr. Daniel H. STURRUP
25 Dir Research & Sponsored Programs .... Mr. Michael M. HASTINGS
06 Registrar .... Ms. Kimberly D. PAGE
07 Asst Dir Graduate Enrollment Svcs .... Ms. Sharon M. OLIVER
37 Director of Financial Aid .... Ms. Sarah DOHENY
36 Director of Career Center .... Ms. Crisanne BLACKIE
09 Director Institutional Studies .... Mr. Ted T. COLADARCI
85 Int Director International Programs .... Ms. Sarah JOUGHIN
41 Athletic Director .... Mr. Karlton W. CREECH
28 Director Equal Employment Diversity .... Vacant
19 Chief Police Dept .... Chief Roland J. LACROIX
29 President/Exec Dir Alumni Assn .... Mr. John N. DIAMOND
40 Interim Director of Bookstore .... Mr. Richard YOUNG
96 Director of Procurement Services .... Mr. Kevin CARR
38 Director Student Counseling .... Mr. Douglas P. JOHNSON
27 Director Strategic Communications .... Vacant
49 Dean Liberal Arts & Sciences .... Dr. Emily A. HADDAD
50 Dean Maine Business School .... Dr. Ivan M. MANEV
53 Dean Educ/Human Development .... Dr. Timothy G. REAGAN
54 Dean Engineering .... Dr. Dana N. HUMPHREY
65 Dean Natural Science/Forestry/Agric .... Dr. Frederick A. SERVELLO
51 Dean Lifelong Learning .... Dr. Monique M. LAROCQUE
58 Dean Graduate School .... Dr. Kody VARAHRAMYAN

*University of Maine at Augusta (C)

46 University Drive, Augusta ME 04330-9410
County: Kennebec FICE Identification: 006760
Unit ID: 161217
Telephone: (207) 621-3000 Carnegie Class: Bac-Diverse
FAX Number: (207) 621-3116 Calendar System: Semester
URL: www.uma.edu
Established: 1965 Annual Undergrad Tuition & Fees (In-State): $7,448
Enrollment: 4,683 Coed
Affiliation or Control: State IRS Status: 501(c)3
Highest Offering: Baccalaureate
Accreditation: EH, ADNUR, DA, DH, MLTAD, NUR

02 President .... Dr. Rebecca M. WYKE
05 Vice President/Provost .... Dr. Joe S. SZAKAS
10 Chief Business Officer .... Mr. Tim BROKAW
11 Exec Director of Admin Services .... Ms. Sheri R. STEVENS
30 VP for Univ Advance/Chief of Staff .... Ms. Joyce BLANCHARD
84 VP Stdnt Engagement/Enroll Mgt .... Dr. Claire GOOD
08 Int Director of UMA Library Svcs .... Mr. Ben TREAT
32 Dean of Students .... Ms. Sheri FRASER
107 Dean College of Prof Studies .... Ms. Brenda MCALEER
37 Director of Financial Aid .... Ms. Sherry MCCOLLETT
06 Registrar .... Ms. Ann CORBETT
15 Director of Human Resources .... Ms. Amie PARKER
18 Chief Facilities/Physical Plant .... Mr. Peter ST. MICHEL
38 Director of Counseling .... Ms. Jennifer MASCARO
07 Dir of Enrollment Svcs & Advising .... Ms. Tricia DYER
40 Director Bookstore .... Mr. Jerry GARTHOFF
26 Exec Dir of Marketing & Pub Rel .... Vacant
49 Dean College of Arts & Sciences .... Mr. Greg FAHY

*University of Maine at Farmington (D)

224 Main Street, Farmington ME 04938-1911
County: Franklin FICE Identification: 002040
Unit ID: 161226
Telephone: (207) 778-7000 Carnegie Class: Bac-Diverse
FAX Number: (207) 778-7247 Calendar System: Semester
URL: www.umf.maine.edu
Established: 1864 Annual Undergrad Tuition & Fees (In-State): $8,695
Enrollment: 2,016 Coed
Affiliation or Control: State IRS Status: 501(c)3
Highest Offering: Master's
Accreditation: EH, CAEPN

02 President .... Dr. Kathryn A. FOSTER
05 Vice Pres Academic Affairs/Provost .... Dr. Eric BROWN
10 Exec Dir Finance & Administration .... Ms. Laurie A. GARDNER
32 Vice Pres Student & Community Svcs .... Ms. Celeste BRANHAM
84 Vice Pres for Enrollment .... Mr. Jared CASH
88 Sustainability Coordinator .... Dr. Lucas C. KELLETT
53 Assoc Provost & Dean of Education .... Dr. Katherine W. YARDLEY
20 Assoc Provost .... Dr. Nicolas KOBAN
92 Director of Honors Program .... Dr. John D. MESSIER
121 Dir of Learning Assistance Center .... Ms. Jessica BERRY
37 Financial Aid Director .... Mr. Ronald P. MILLIKEN
21 Director of Finance .... Ms. Kathleen P. FALCO
124 Dir Center for Student Development .... Mr. Robert A. PEDERSON
27 Assoc Director of Media Relations .... Ms. April C. MULHERIN
13 IT Operations Manager .... Ms. Nicole HAGGAN
41 Dir Athletics/Fitness & Recreation .... Ms. Julie A. DAVIS
88 Dir Fitness & Recreation Center .... Mr. James D. TONER
35 Director Student Life .... Mr. Brian K. UFFORD
23 Director Student Health Center .... Dr. Susan E. COCHRAN
18 Director of Facilities Management .... Mr. Jeffrey MCKAY
19 Director of Public Safety .... Mr. Brock E. CATON
26 Dir of Marketing and Communications .... Ms. Jennifer A. ERIKSEN

*University of Maine at Fort Kent (E)

23 University Drive, Fort Kent ME 04743-1292
County: Aroostook FICE Identification: 002041
Unit ID: 161235
Telephone: (207) 834-7500 Carnegie Class: Bac-Diverse
FAX Number: (207) 834-7503 Calendar System: Semester
URL: www.umfk.maine.edu
Established: 1878 Annual Undergrad Tuition & Fees (In-State): $7,575
Enrollment: 1,559 Coed
Affiliation or Control: State IRS Status: 501(c)3
Highest Offering: Baccalaureate
Accreditation: EH, IACBE, NURSE

02 President .... Dr. John N. SHORT
05 Vice President Academic Affairs .... Dr. Steven GAMMON
10 Chief Business Officer .... Mrs. Pamela ASHBY
31 Dean of Community Education .... Mr. Scott A. VOISINE
121 Assistant Dean of Student Success .... Ms. Christine NUNEMAKER
06 Registrar .... Mr. Mark SCHENK
15 Senior HR Business Partner .... Vacant
66 Nursing Division Director .... Ms. Erin SOUCY
08 Dir of Information Svcs/Library .... Ms. Leslie E. KELLY
07 Director of Admissions .... Ms. Jill CAIRNS
37 Director of Financial Aid .... Ms. Lisa MICHAUD
18 Director of Facilities Management .... Mr. Andrew C. JACOBS
29 Director Alumni Relations .... Vacant
32 Assoc Dean Student Life/Development .... Mr. Raymond R. PHINNEY
09 Assoc Dir of Institutional Research .... Mr. Joseph R. BJERKLIE
30 Development Officer .... Ms. Linda DEPREY

*University of Maine at Machias (F)

116 O'Brien Avenue, Machias ME 04654-1397
County: Washington FICE Identification: 002055
Unit ID: 161244
Telephone: (207) 255-1200 Carnegie Class: Bac-A&S
FAX Number: (207) 255-4864 Calendar System: Semester
URL: www.umm.maine.edu
Established: 1909 Annual Undergrad Tuition & Fees (In-State): $7,530
Enrollment: 786 Coed
Affiliation or Control: State IRS Status: 501(c)3
Highest Offering: Baccalaureate
Accreditation: EH, NRPA

02 President .... Dr. Susan J. HUNTER
05 VP Academic Affairs/Head of Campus .... Dr. Kay KIMBALL
10 Chief Business/Financial Officer .... Ms. Claire STRICKLAND
32 Dean of Students .... Mr. Daniel GARDNER
06 Registrar .... Ms. Mary STOVER
08 Director Library .... Ms. Marianne THIBODEAU
15 Director Human Resources .... Ms. Michelle HALE
37 Assoc Director Financial Aid .... Ms. Shelbie ROSS
18 Director Physical Facilities .... Mr. Robert FARRIS
26 Director Public Relations/Marketing .... Ms. Penny GUISINGER
41 Director Athletics .... Mr. Christopher HART
07 Associate Director Admissions .... Ms. Ashley MCCOUBREY
13 IT Operations Manager .... Mr. Tom DRAKE

*University of Maine at Presque Isle (G)

181 Main Street, Presque Isle ME 04769-2888
County: Aroostook FICE Identification: 002033
Unit ID: 161341
Telephone: (207) 768-9400 Carnegie Class: Bac-Diverse
FAX Number: (207) 768-9608 Calendar System: Semester
URL: www.umpi.edu
Established: 1903 Annual Undergrad Tuition & Fees (In-State): $7,436
Enrollment: 1,289 Coed
Affiliation or Control: State IRS Status: 501(c)3
Highest Offering: Baccalaureate
Accreditation: EH, #CAATE, MLTAD, PTAA, SW

02 President .... Dr. Raymond J. RICE
05 Vice President Academic Affairs .... Vacant
10 Campus Business Officer .... Mr. Benjamin SHAW
49 Dean of Arts and Sciences .... Dr. Jason JOHNSTON
107 Dean of Professional Programs .... Ms. Barbara BLACKSTONE
111 Exec Dir for University Advancement .... Ms. Debbie ROARK
32 Interim Dean of Students .... Ms. Vanessa PEARSON
07 Director of Admissions .... Ms. Erin V. BENSON
06 Registrar .... Mr. Alexander MYHRE
15 HR Business Partner/AA/EEO .... Ms. Dorianna PRATT
08 Director of Library Services .... Mr. Roger GETZ
36 Director of Career Preparation .... Ms. Nicole FOURNIER
39 Director Residence Life .... Vacant
41 Director of Athletics .... Mr. Daniel C. KANE
26 Director of Media Relations .... Ms. Rachel RICE
37 Director Financial Services .... Mr. Christopher BELL
18 Director of Facilities Management .... Mr. Gregg BOUCHARD
19 Director Security/Safety .... Mr. Frederick A. THOMAS
121 Director of Student Success .... Vacant

*University of Southern Maine (H)

96 Falmouth Street, PO Box 9300,
Portland ME 04101-9300
County: Cumberland FICE Identification: 002054
Unit ID: 161554
Telephone: (207) 780-4141 Carnegie Class: Masters/L
FAX Number: (207) 780-4933 Calendar System: Semester
URL: www.usm.maine.edu
Established: 1878 Annual Undergrad Tuition & Fees (In-State): $7,796
Enrollment: 7,739 Coed
Affiliation or Control: State IRS Status: 501(c)3
Highest Offering: Doctorate
Accreditation: EH, ART, #CAATE, CACREP, CAEPT, CS, ENG, EXSC, LAW, MUS, NAIT, NURSE, OT, PH, SW

02 President .... Dr. Glenn T. CUMMINGS
05 Provost/VPAA .... Dr. Jeannine UZZI
10 Chief Financial Officer/VP Admin .... Mr. Buster NEEL
84 VP Enrollment Management .... Ms. Nancy D. GRIFFIN
102 President USM Foundation .... Mr. George CAMPBELL
09 Assoc Dir Institutional Research .... Ms. Patricia DAVIS
18 Exec Director Facilities Management .... Mr. John SOUTHER
08 University Librarian .... Mr. David NUTTY
108 Director Academic Assessment Ctr .... Ms. Susan L. KING
38 Director of Health & Counseling .... Dr. Kristine BERTINI
15 Chief Human Resources Office .... Ms. Natalie JONES
26 Executive Director Public Affairs .... Mr. Bob STEIN
37 Director of Financial Aid .... Mr. Keith DUBOIS
32 Executive Director Student Success .... Ms. Elizabeth HIGGINS
07 Director Admissions .... Mr. Andrew KING
06 Registrar .... Ms. Karin PIRES
72 Director CTEL .... Mr. Paul COCHRANE
41 Director of Athletics & Rec Sports .... Mr. Al BEAN
39 Director of Residential Life .... Mr. Jason SAUCIER
40 Director of USM Bookstore .... Ms. Catherine JOHNSON
61 Dean School of Law .... Ms. Danielle CONWAY
50 Dean College of Mgmt/Human Svcs .... Dr. Joanne WILLIAMS
72 Dean College of Sci/Tech & Health .... Dr. James GRAVES
49 Dean Arts/Humanities/Soc Sci .... Dr. Adam TUCHINSKY
12 Dean Lewiston-Auburn College .... Dr. Joyce GIBSON
88 Director of Community-Based Lrng .... Dr. Susan MCWILLIAMS
94 Director of Women's Studies .... Dr. Lisa WALKER
27 Director of Marketing .... Ms. Traci ST. PIERRE
102 President & CEO USM Foundation .... Mr. George CAMPBELL
46 Director of Research .... Ms. Kris SAHONCHIK

University of New England (A)

11 Hills Beach Road, Biddeford ME 04005-9988
County: York FICE Identification: 002050
Unit ID: 161457
Telephone: (207) 283-0171 Carnegie Class: Masters/L
FAX Number: (207) 282-6379 Calendar System: Semester
URL: www.une.edu
Established: 1831 Annual Undergrad Tuition & Fees: $35,630
Enrollment: 7,794 Coed
Affiliation or Control: Independent Non-Profit IRS Status: 501(c)3
Highest Offering: Doctorate
Accreditation: EH, ACBSP, ANEST, ARCPA, CAATE, DENT, DH, NUR, OSTEO, OT, #PH, PHAR, PTA, SW

01 President ... Dr. James HERBERT
04 Executive Asst to the President ... Ms. Holly HAMMOND NASS
05 Interim Provost ... Dr. Michael SHELDON
06 Registrar ... Ms. Kathy DAVIS
07 Dean of University Admissions ... Mr. Scott STEINBERG
45 VP Strategic Initiatives ... Dr. Ellen BEAULIEU
18 Vice Pres of Operations ... Mr. William BOLA
17 Vice President Clinical Affairs ... Dr. Dora MILLS
10 Vice Pres Finance and Admin ... Ms. Nicole TRUFANT
111 Vice Pres Institutional Advancement ... Mr. Bill CHANCE
15 Exec Dir Human Resources ... Ms. Sharen BEAULIEU
82 VP Global Affairs & Communications ... Dr. Anouar MAJID
46 VP for Research & Scholarship ... Dr. Edward BILSKY
20 Associate Provost ... Dr. Dennis LEIGHTON
106 Dean College of Grad/Prof Studies ... Dr. Martha WILSON
49 Dean College Arts & Sciences ... Dr. Jeanne HEY
17 Interim Dean Health Professions ... Dr. Karen PARDUE
63 Dean College Osteopathic Medicine ... Dr. Jane CARREIRO
67 Interim Dean College of Pharmacy ... Dr. Karen HOUSEKNECHT
52 Dean of College Dental Medicine ... Dr. Jon RYDER
62 Dean Library Services ... Mr. Andrew GOLUB
88 Assoc Dean College Health Prof ... Dr. Karen PARDUE
49 Assoc Dean College Arts & Sciences ... Dr. Susan GRAY
29 Director Alumni Relations ... Ms. Amy HAILE
35 Assistant Vice Pres Student Life ... Ms. Jennifer DEBURRO
09 Director for Institutional Research ... Ms. Margaret MOREMEN
88 Director Campus Planning ... Mr. Alan THIBEAULT
19 Director Campus Safety & Security ... Mr. Donald CLARK
96 Director Purch/Risk Mgmt/Contract ... Mr. William BOLA
08 Director Reference Services ... Ms. Barbara SWARTZLANDER
28 Assoc Dir Multicult Affs/ Diversity ... Mr. Richard ANDERSON MARTINEZ
25 Director Sponsored Programs ... Mr. Nicholas GERE
38 Director Student Counseling ... Dr. John LANGEVIN
37 Exec Director Student Fiscal Svcs ... Mr. Paul HENDERSON
100 Senior Advisor to the President and ... Mr. John TUMIEL
104 Director Study Abroad/Global Educ ... Ms. Emily DRAGON
13 Chief Info Technology Officer (CIO) ... Mr. Craig LOFTUS
36 Director Career Services ... Mr. Jeff NEVERS
102 Dir Foundation/Corporate Relations ... Ms. Ellen RIDLEY
108 Director Institutional Assessment ... Ms. Margaret MOREMENT
26 Chief Public Relations/Marketing ... Ms. Crystal CANNEY
41 Interim Athletic Director ... Mr. Curt SMYTH

MARYLAND

Allegany College of Maryland (B)

12401 Willowbrook Road, SE,
Cumberland MD 21502-2596
County: Allegany FICE Identification: 002057
Unit ID: 161688
Telephone: (301) 784-5000 Carnegie Class: Assoc/MT-VT-High Trad
FAX Number: (301) 784-5050 Calendar System: Semester
URL: www.allegany.edu
Established: 1961 Annual Undergrad Tuition & Fees (In-District): $3,750
Enrollment: 3,091 Coed
Affiliation or Control: Local IRS Status: 501(c)3
Highest Offering: Associate Degree
Accreditation: M, ADNUR, COARC, CSHSE, DH, MAC, MLTAD, OTA, PTAA, #RAD

01 President ... Dr. Cynthia S. BAMBARA
05 Vice Pres Instructional Affairs ... Dr. Kurt HOFFMAN
10 Vice President Finance ... Ms. Christina KILDUFF
30 VP Advancement/Community Rels ... Mr. David R. JONES

Ana G. Mendez University System Capital Area Campus (C)

11006 Veirs Mill Road, Wheaton MD 20902
Telephone: (301) 949-2224 Identification: 770924
Accreditation: &M

† Branch campus of Sistema Universitario Ana G. Mendez, Rio Piedras, PR

Anne Arundel Community College (D)

101 College Parkway, Arnold MD 21012-1895
County: Anne Arundel FICE Identification: 002058
Unit ID: 161767
Telephone: (410) 777-2222 Carnegie Class: Assoc/HT-Mix Trad/Non
FAX Number: (410) 777-2489 Calendar System: Semester
URL: www.aacc.edu
Established: 1961 Annual Undergrad Tuition & Fees (In-District): $4,564
Enrollment: 14,689 Coed
Affiliation or Control: State/Local IRS Status: 501(c)3
Highest Offering: Associate Degree
Accreditation: M, ACFEI, ADNUR, ARCPA, CAHIIM, CSHSE, EMT, MAC, MLTAD, PTAA, RAD, SURGT

01 President ... Dr. Dawn S. LINDSAY
05 VP for Learning ... Dr. Michael H. GAVIN
10 VP Learning Resources Management ... Ms. Melissa A. BEARDMORE
84 VP for Learner Support Services ... Ms. Felicia L. PATTERSON
106 Dean of Virtual Campus ... Dr. Colleen EISENBEISER
20 Associate VP for Learning ... Dr. Alycia MARSHALL
30 Director of Development ... Mr. Vollie D. MELSON
32 Dean of Student Services ... Dr. Jacqueline S. JACKSON
76 Dean School Health/Wellness/Phys Ed ... Dr. Elizabeth H. APPEL
66 Director of Nursing ... Ms. Beth Anne BATTURS
49 Dean School of Liberal Arts ... Dr. Alicia MORSE
50 Dean School of Business & Law ... Ms. Karen COOK
81 Dean School of Science & Technology ... Dr. Lance BOWEN
51 Dean Sch Cont Educ & Workforce Dev ... Dr. Faith A. HARLAND-WHITE
22 Controller ... Ms. Martha D. ROTHSCHILD
21 Executive Director of Finance ... Mr. Andrew P. LITTLE
13 Chief Technology Officer/Info Svcs ... Ms. Shirin M. GOODARZI
08 Director of Library ... Ms. Cynthia K. STEINHOFF
06 Registrar ... Ms. Nancy A. BEIER
09 Dean Plng/Rsrch/Inst Assess ... Dr. Ricka K. FINE
15 Exec Director of Human Resources ... Ms. Suzanne L. BOYER
26 Exec Director PR & Marketing ... Mr. Daniel B. BAUM
37 Director of Financial Aid ... Mr. Richard C. HEATH
07 Dir Admissions/Enroll Development ... Mr. Thomas J. MCGINN, III
11 Exec Dir of Administrative Services ... Mr. Maury L. CHAPUT, JR.
35 Asst Dean Student Devel & Success ... Dr. Tiffany F. BOYKIN
07 Dean Enrollment Services ... Dr. John F. GRABOWSKI
36 Dir Counseling/Advising/Reten Svcs ... Ms. Bonnie J. GARRETT
35 Director of Student Life ... Ms. Christine M. STORCK
22 Federal Compliance Officer ... Ms. Karen COOK
40 College Bookstore Manager ... Mr. Steven M. PEGG
19 Director Public Safety ... Mr. Sean KAPFHAMMER
96 Director Purchasing/Contracting ... Ms. Melanie L. SCHERER
29 Manager Major Giving ... Ms. Jenny CRAWFORD
23 Coordinator Health Services ... Ms. Beth A. MAYS
41 Athletic Director ... Mr. Duane HERR
28 Coordinator of Minority Recruitment ... Mr. James T. JACKSON, JR.
94 Coordinator of Women's Studies ... Dr. Suzanne J. SPOOR
88 Director of Environmental Center ... Dr. M. Stephen AILSTOCK
88 Director Center Study Local Issues ... Dr. Daniel D. NATAF
88 Dir Homeland Sec/Crim Justice Inst ... Dr. Tyrone POWERS
53 Director TEACH Institute ... Ms. Stacie BURCH
88 Director Hosp/Cul Arts/Tourism Inst ... Ms. Mary Ellen MASON
38 Coordinator Inst for the Future ... Mr. Steven T. HENICK
88 Dir Sarbanes Center/Pub & Cmty Svc ... Ms. Cathleen H. DOYLE
28 Chief Diversity Officer ... Vacant
04 Administrative Asst to President ... Ms. Judy HEATH
18 Dir Facilities Planning & Construc ... Mr. James TAYLOR
25 Director Sponsored Programs ... Ms. Deborah A. MERCADO

Bais HaMedrash & Mesivta of Baltimore (E)

6823 Old Pimlico Road, Baltimore MD 21209
County: Baltimore FICE Identification: 041884
Unit ID: 476601
Telephone: (410) 486-0006 Carnegie Class: Spec-4-yr-Faith
FAX Number: (410) 602-9738 Calendar System: Semester
Established: 1997 Annual Undergrad Tuition & Fees: $12,400
Enrollment: 58 Male
Affiliation or Control: Independent Non-Profit IRS Status: 501(c)3
Highest Offering: First Talmudic Degree
Accreditation: RABN

01 Rosh Yeshiva ... Rabbi Zvi Dov SLANGER

Baltimore City Community College (F)

2901 Liberty Heights Avenue, Baltimore MD 21215-7893
County: Baltimore City FICE Identification: 002061
Unit ID: 161864
Telephone: (410) 462-8300 Carnegie Class: Assoc/HT-Mix Trad/Non
FAX Number: (410) 462-7795 Calendar System: Semester
URL: www.bccc.edu
Established: 1947 Annual Undergrad Tuition & Fees (In-State): $2,578
Enrollment: 4,060 Coed
Affiliation or Control: State IRS Status: 501(c)3
Highest Offering: Associate Degree
Accreditation: M, ACBSP, ADNUR, CAHIIM, COARC, DH, PTAA, SURGT

01 President and CEO ... Dr. Gordon F. MAY
10 VP Business & Finance ... Mr. Calvin HARRIS, JR.
32 VP for Student Affairs ... Dr. Marguerite WEBER
05 VP Academic Affairs ... Dr. Tonja RINGGOLD
51 Interim VP Business & Cont Educ ... Mr. Vincent WHITMORE
84 Dean of Enrollment Management ... Ms. Sylvia ROCHESTER
46 VP of Research & Strategic Planning ... Vacant
111 Int VP of Advance & Strategic Partn ... Ms. Dawn KIRSTAETTER
18 Dir Facilities/Plng/Operations ... Mr. Maurice HOWELL
21 Int Controller/Chief of Accounting ... Ms. Eileen WAITSMAN
37 Director Student Financial Aid ... Ms. Vera BROOKS
13 Int Chief Information Tech Officer ... Dr. Hamid BARGHI
08 Director Library/Media Services ... Mr. David-Xudong JIN
06 Exec Director Records/Registrar ... Ms. Wendy HARRIS
15 Director of HR ... Ms. Michelle WILLIAMS
09 Director of Institutional Research ... Ms. Eileen HAWKINS
96 Int Chief Procurement Officer ... Ms. Benita SCOTT
04 Executive Asst to the President ... Ms. Valerie LEVERETTE
07 Director of Admissions ... Ms. Deneen DANGERFIELD
106 Director of E-Learning ... Dr. Diana ZILBERMAN
19 Director of Public Safety ... Mr. Leonard WILLIS
36 Coordinator Job Placement ... Mr. Vincent WHITMORE
41 Director Intercollegiate Athletics ... Ms. Tara OWENS
86 Director Government Relations ... Vacant
29 Director Alumni Relations ... Ms. Marie HINTON
43 General Counsel ... Mr. Bryan PERRY

Brightwood College (G)

1520 S Caton Avenue, Baltimore MD 21227-1063
County: Baltimore City FICE Identification: 007491
Unit ID: 163736
Telephone: (410) 644-6400 Carnegie Class: Spec 2-yr-Tech
FAX Number: (410) 644-6481 Calendar System: Quarter
URL: www.brightwood.edu
Established: 1956 Annual Undergrad Tuition & Fees: N/A
Enrollment: 566 Coed
Affiliation or Control: Proprietary IRS Status: Proprietary
Highest Offering: Associate Degree
Accreditation: ACICS

01 Campus President ... Mr. Kevin BEAVER
05 Academic Dean ... Ms. Jennifer WELCH

Brightwood College (H)

4600 Powder Mill Road, Suite 500,
Beltsville MD 20705-2649
County: Prince Georges FICE Identification: 020836
Unit ID: 164058
Telephone: (301) 586-4000 Carnegie Class: Assoc/HVT-Mix Trad/Non
FAX Number: (301) 937-5327 Calendar System: Quarter
URL: www.brightwood.edu
Established: 1956 Annual Undergrad Tuition & Fees: N/A
Enrollment: 448 Coed
Affiliation or Control: Proprietary IRS Status: Proprietary
Highest Offering: Associate Degree
Accreditation: ACICS

01 Campus President ... Mr. Dale TURNER

Brightwood College (I)

803 Glen Eagles Court, Towson MD 21286-2201
County: Baltimore FICE Identification: 010410
Unit ID: 161776
Telephone: (410) 828-2600 Carnegie Class: Assoc/HVT-Mix Trad/Non
FAX Number: (410) 296-5356 Calendar System: Quarter
URL: www.brightwood.edu
Established: 1956 Annual Undergrad Tuition & Fees: N/A
Enrollment: 270 Coed
Affiliation or Control: Proprietary IRS Status: Proprietary
Highest Offering: Associate Degree
Accreditation: ACICS

01 President ... Mr. Jeremiah STAROPOLI
07 Director of Admissions ... Mr. Dru YOKUM

Capitol Technology University (J)

11301 Springfield Road, Laurel MD 20708-9759
County: Prince Georges FICE Identification: 001436
Unit ID: 162061
Telephone: (301) 369-2800 Carnegie Class: Spec-4-yr-Eng
FAX Number: (301) 953-1442 Calendar System: Semester
URL: www.captechu.edu
Established: 1927 Annual Undergrad Tuition & Fees: $24,272
Enrollment: 804 Coed
Affiliation or Control: Independent Non-Profit IRS Status: 501(c)3
Highest Offering: Doctorate
Accreditation: M, ENG, ENGT, IACBE

01 President ... Dr. Bradford L. SIMS
05 Vice President for Academic Affairs ... Dr. W. Vic MACONACHY
10 Sr VP Finance/Administration/COO ... Jeffrey L. WILLIAMS
84 Sr VP for Enrollment Mgmt & Mktg ... Dianne M. O'NEILL
111 Vice President Advancement ... Vacant
20 Dean Academics & AVP Acad Assessmnt ... Dr. Helen G. BARKER
32 AVP Student Engagement & Univ Devel ... Melinda A. BUNNELL-RHYNE
54 Chair Electrical Engineering ... Dr. Nayef ABU-AGEEL
06 Director of Registration & Records ... Greg HUGHES
08 Dir Library/Information Literacy ... Beth EMMERLING
15 Dir Human Resources/Administration ... Katy DEHART
26 Director Communications ... Robert HERSCHBACH
30 Director Development/Alumni ... Vacant
07 Director Admissions ... Meghan YOUNG
37 Director of Financial Aid ... Kim WITTLER
21 Director of Finance ... Kathleen WERNER
51 Director of Continuing Education ... Vacant
90 Director Academic Computing ... Allen EXNER
18 Director of Facilities ... Casar DE LA ROSA
04 Executive Admin Asst to President ... Aletha R. WADE
103 Asst Dir Career Service ... Sarah ALSPAW
106 Dir Online Education/E-learning ... Ken MAYER

13 Supervisor Information Services ... Michael AUGUSTSON
39 Dir Student Life & Residential ... Brandi MCKEE

Carroll Community College (A)

1601 Washington Road, Westminster MD 21157-6913
County: Carroll FICE Identification: 031007
Unit ID: 405872
Telephone: (410) 386-8000 Carnegie Class: Assoc/HT-High Trad
FAX Number: (410) 386-8181 Calendar System: Semester
URL: www.carrollcc.edu
Established: 1993 Annual Undergrad Tuition & Fees (In-District): $3,850
Enrollment: 3,542 Coed
Affiliation or Control: Local IRS Status: 501(c)3
Highest Offering: Associate Degree
Accreditation: M, PTAA

01 President ... Dr. James D. BALL
10 Exec Vice Pres Administration ... Mr. Alan M. SCHUMAN
05 Vice Pres of Acad & Student Affs ... Dr. Rosalie MINCE
45 Vice Pres of Plng/Mktg & Assessment ... Dr. Craig A. CLAGETT
51 Vice Pres of Cont Educ/Training ... Ms. Karen L. MERKLE
30 Exec Dir Inst Devel/College Found ... Mr. Steven WANTZ
28 Compliance & Integrity Advoc ... Mr. Jonathan ROWE
26 Chief Public Rel/Communication ... Ms. Patricia CARROLL
50 Div Chair Business & Technology ... Mr. Robert BROWN
60 Div Chair English & Modern Language ... Ms. Siobhan WRIGHT
76 Div Chair Allied Health ... Dr. Nancy PERRY
83 Div Chair Social Sciences ... Dr. Michael STOVALL
54 Div Chair Mathematics/Engineer ... Ms. Maria BURNESS
81 Div Chair Sciences ... Dr. Raza KHAN
53 Div Chair Educ & Trans Studies ... Ms. Susan SIES
79 Div Chr Humanities/Music/Perf Arts ... Dr. Robert YOUNG
57 Div Chair Applied & Theater Arts ... Mr. Scott GORE
32 Dean of Student Affairs ... Dr. Kristie CRUMLEY
06 Sr Dir of Records/Stdnt Data Analy ... Ms. Laurie SHIELDS
38 Dir Advise/Transfer/Stdnt Placement ... Dr. April HEARRING
07 Sr Director Enrollment Development ... Ms. Candace EDWARDS
37 Director of Financial Aid ... Mr. John GAY
08 Sr Dir Library/Media/Dist Learning ... Vacant
106 Director Distance Learning Programs ... Vacant
27 Director Publications/Comm Design ... Dr. Maya DEMISHKEVICH
09 Director Institutional Research ... Dr. Natalie CRESPO
103 Sr Dir CET/Wkforce Trng & Bus Svcs ... Ms. Libby TROSTLE
31 Sr Dir Lifelong Lrng/Pgm Supp Sys ... Ms. Jean MARRIOTT
105 Director of Network & Tech Services ... Ms. Patti DAVIS
21 Director Fiscal Affairs ... Mr. Timothy LEAGUE
15 Director Human Resources ... Ms. Lisa KUHN
18 Director Facilities Management ... Ms. Terry BOWEN
19 Chief of Public Safety & Security ... Mr. Steve DRUMMOND
20 Assoc VP Program Dev/Partnerships ... Dr. Melody MOORE
22 Director Disability Support Svcs ... Mr. Joseph TATELA
20 Assoc VP Curriculum & Assessment ... Dr. Michelle KLOSS

Cecil College (B)

One Seahawk Drive, North East MD 21901-1999
County: Cecil FICE Identification: 008308
Unit ID: 162104
Telephone: (410) 287-6060 Carnegie Class: Assoc/HT-High Trad
FAX Number: (410) 287-1026 Calendar System: Semester
URL: www.cecil.edu
Established: 1968 Annual Undergrad Tuition & Fees (In-District): $3,870
Enrollment: 2,591 Coed
Affiliation or Control: State/Local IRS Status: 501(c)3
Highest Offering: Associate Degree
Accreditation: M, ADNUR, EMT, MAC, PTAA

01 President ... Dr. Mary WAY BOLT
05 Vice President Academic Programs ... Dr. Christy DRYER
10 Vice President Finance ... Mr. Daniel THOMPSON
32 VP Students/Inst Effectiveness ... Dr. Kimberly JOYCE
13 CIO ... Mr. Peter SHOUDY
111 Vice Pres Institutional Advancement ... Ms. Chris Ann SZEP
15 Executive Director Human Resources ... Ms. Colleen CASHILL
20 Dean of Academic Programs ... Vacant
31 Dean of Career/Community Education ... Mr. Miles DEAN
66 Dean Nursing Ed/Alld Hlth/Hlth Sci ... Dr. Veronica DOUGHERTY
18 Director of Facilities ... Mr. Ken MACINTIRE
37 Director of Financial Aid Services ... Ms. Amanda SOLECKI
26 Director of Marketing ... Ms. Charlene CONOLLY
84 Director of Enrollment Management ... Ms. Cindy MISHOE
93 Director Minority Student Services ... Ms. Laney HOXTER
09 Director of Institutional Research ... Mr. Dan STOICESCU
06 Director of Records & Registration ... Ms. S. Tomeka SWAN
08 Director of Library Services ... Ms. Lorraine MARTORANA
41 Director Athletics ... Mr. Ed DURHAM
29 Coordinator Alumni Relations ... Ms. Mary MOORE
04 Exec Assistant to the President ... Ms. Sherry PISTOR
21 Controller ... Mr. Craig WHITEFORD
19 Director Security/Safety ... Mr. John CAPOZZOLI

Chesapeake College (C)

PO Box 8, 1000 College Circle, Wye Mills MD 21679-0008
County: Queen Annes FICE Identification: 004650
Unit ID: 162168
Telephone: (410) 822-5400 Carnegie Class: Assoc/HT-High Trad
FAX Number: (410) 827-5875 Calendar System: Semester
URL: www.chesapeake.edu
Established: 1965 Annual Undergrad Tuition & Fees (In-District): $3,820
Enrollment: 2,264 Coed
Affiliation or Control: State/Local IRS Status: 501(c)3
Highest Offering: Associate Degree
Accreditation: M, ADNUR, EMT, PTAA, RAD, SURGT

01 President ... Dr. Barbara A. VINIAR
05 Vice President for Academic Affairs ... Dr. Clay RAILEY
11 VP for Administrative Services ... Mr. Tim JONES
111 VP of Institutional Advancement ... Ms. Lucie HUGHES
106 Dean for Acad Admin & Online Lrng ... Ms. Chandra M. GIGLIOTTI
20 Dean for Teaching and Learning ... Mr. David HARPER
32 Dean for Students and Learning ... Ms. Melina BAER
18 Director of Facilities ... Mr. Paul RENSHAW
15 Director of Human Resources ... Ms. Susan A. CIANCHETTA
37 Director of Financial Aid ... Ms. Mindy M. SCHAFFER
09 Dir Inst Planning/Research & Assmnt ... Mr. Vincent MARUGGI
26 Director of Public Information ... Ms. Marcie A. MOLLOY
06 Registrar ... Mr. James A. DAVIDSON
35 Dean for Student Development ... Ms. Joan M. SEITZER
101 Exec Assoc to Pres/Board ... Mrs. Jane THOMAS

College of Southern Maryland (D)

PO Box 910, La Plata MD 20646-0910
County: Charles FICE Identification: 002064
Unit ID: 162122
Telephone: (301) 934-2251 Carnegie Class: Assoc/HT-High Trad
FAX Number: (301) 934-7698 Calendar System: Semester
URL: www.csmd.edu
Established: 1958 Annual Undergrad Tuition & Fees (In-District): $3,631
Enrollment: 8,166 Coed
Affiliation or Control: Local IRS Status: 501(c)3
Highest Offering: Associate Degree
Accreditation: M, ACBSP, ADNUR, EMT, MLTAD, PNUR, PTAA

01 President ... Dr. Maureen MURPHY
05 Vice Pres Academic Affairs ... Dr. Eileen ABEL
12 Vice President Leonardtown Campus ... Dr. Tracy HARRIS
12 VP Prince Frederick Campus ... Dr. Richard FLEMING
103 VP Cmty Educ & Workforce Dev ... Dr. Daniel MOSSER
10 VP Financial & Admin Services ... Mr. Tony JERNIGAN
32 VP Student/Instruc Support Svcs ... Dr. William COMEY
111 Vice President for Advancement ... Ms. Michelle GOODWIN
43 Vice President/General Counsel ... Mr. Craig PATENAUDE
20 Assoc VP Academic Affairs ... Mr. Rob FARINELLI
09 Assoc VP Plng/Inst Effective/Rsrch ... Dr. Kelly MCMURRAY
84 Assoc VP Enrollment Mgmt Team ... Dr. Jessica CHAMBERS
13 Assoc VP Info Management ... Mr. James FINGER
18 Director of Facilities ... Mr. Ron TOWARD
15 Assoc VP of Human Resources ... Vacant
26 Asst Vice Pres Community Relations ... Ms. Karen SMITH-HUPP
37 Director Financial Assistance ... Mr. Christian ZIMMERMANN
06 Registrar ... Ms. Carol HARRISON
08 Director of Library ... Mr. Thomas REPENNING
66 Chair Nursing Dept ... Dr. Laura POLK
35 Director of Athletics/Student Life ... Ms. Michelle RUBLE
40 General Mgr College Store ... Ms. Marcy GANNON
07 Director Admissions Department ... Mr. Brian HAMMOND
36 Director Advisement/Career Services ... Ms. Helene CAMERON
96 Director of Procurement ... Mr. Joe PICCOLO
28 Assoc VP Diversity/Equal Oppty ... Dr. Carmen PHELPS
04 Exec Asst to President & Board ... Ms. Kim YELLMAN
19 Exec Director Security/Safety ... Mr. Bill BESSETTE
25 Grants Coordinator ... Ms. Becky COCKERHAM
30 Director Development ... Ms. Chelsea BROWN
27 Exec Dir Marketing & Communications ... Mr. Trovon WILLIAMS

The Community College of Baltimore County (E)

7201 Rossville Blvd., Baltimore MD 21237-3899
County: Baltimore FICE Identification: 002063
Unit ID: 434672
Telephone: (443) 840-2222 Carnegie Class: Assoc/HT-High Trad
FAX Number: (443) 840-1100 Calendar System: Semester
URL: www.ccbcmd.edu
Established: 1957 Annual Undergrad Tuition & Fees (In-District): $3,868
Enrollment: 22,179 Coed
Affiliation or Control: Local IRS Status: 501(c)3
Highest Offering: Associate Degree
Accreditation: M, ACBSP, ADNUR, ART, CAHIIM, COARC, COMTA, CSHSE, DH, EMT, FUSER, MAC, MLTAD, MUS, OTA, POLYT, RAD, RTT, SURGT, THEA

01 President ... Dr. Sandra L. KURTINITIS
111 Vice Pres Institutional Advancement ... Mr. Kenneth WESTARY
10 Vice Pres Finance/Administration ... Ms. Melissa HOPP
05 Vice Pres Instruction ... Dr. Mark MCCOLLOCH
84 VP Enrollment & Student Services ... Dr. Richard LILLEY
26 Sr Director for Public Relations ... Ms. Mary DELUCA
15 Senior Director Human Resources ... Ms. Penny MILSOM

Faith Theological Seminary (F)

529 Walker Avenue, Baltimore MD 21212
County: Baltimore City Identification: 667016
Unit ID: 212452
Telephone: (410) 323-6211 Carnegie Class: Spec-4-yr-Faith
FAX Number: (410) 323-6331 Calendar System: Semester
URL: FTS.edu
Established: 1937 Annual Undergrad Tuition & Fees: $5,870
Enrollment: 150 Coed
Affiliation or Control: Non-denominational IRS Status: 501(c)3
Highest Offering: Doctorate; No Lower Division
Accreditation: TRACS

01 President ... Rev.Dr. Norman J. MANOHAR
05 Academic Dean ... Dr. Stephen T. HAGUE
06 Registrar ... Ms. Aruna S. MANOHAR
07 Director of Admissions ... Dr. John LEPERA
08 Head Librarian ... Mrs. Anita TAYLOR
108 Director IE ... Mrs. Margaret P. PROCH
10 Business Manager ... Ms. Julie MORRIS
13 IT Manager/Financial Aid Advisor ... Mr. John MANOHAR

Fortis College (G)

4351 Garden City Drive, Landover MD 20785
Telephone: (301) 459-3650 Identification: 770731
Accreditation: ACICS, DH, MLTAD

† Branch campus of Fortis Institute, Erie, PA

Frederick Community College (H)

7932 Opossumtown Pike, Frederick MD 21702-2097
County: Frederick FICE Identification: 002071
Unit ID: 162557
Telephone: (301) 846-2400 Carnegie Class: Assoc/HT-High Trad
FAX Number: (301) 846-2498 Calendar System: Semester
URL: www.frederick.edu
Established: 1957 Annual Undergrad Tuition & Fees (In-District): $3,450
Enrollment: 6,197 Coed
Affiliation or Control: State/Local IRS Status: 501(c)3
Highest Offering: Associate Degree
Accreditation: M, ADNUR, COARC, NMT, SURGT

01 President ... Ms. Elizabeth BURMASTER
11 Chief of Operations ... Mr. John WICHSER
05 Provost/VP for Academic Affairs ... Dr. Tony HAWKINS
51 VP for CE/Workforce Development ... Mr. David CROGHAN
10 VP for Finance & Human Resources ... Ms. Dana MCDONALD
32 VP for Learning Support ... Dr. Wayne BARBOUR
111 Exec Dir Institutional Advancement ... Ms. Deborah POWELL
13 Chief Information Officer ... Mr. Joseph MCCORMICK
20 AVP of Academic Affairs ... Dr. Alanka BROWN
84 AVP for Enrollment Management ... Ms. Laura MEARS
15 AVP for Human Resources ... Ms. Maryrose WILSON
21 Director Fiscal Services ... Ms. Patricia HOYT
21 AVP for Fiscal Services ... Mr. Bill GRUTZKUHN
06 Exec Dir of Welcome Center/ Registar ... Ms. Deirdre WEILMINSTER
49 AVP/Dean of Arts & Science ... Dr. Brian STIPELMAN
20 AVP Teaching/Learning ... Dr. Kelly TRIGGER
35 AVP/Dean of Students ... Mr. Jerry HAYNES
35 Director of Student Engagement ... Ms. Jeanni WINSTON-MUIR
88 Spec Asst to President Inst Effect ... Mr. Gerald L. BOYD
18 Director Facilities Planning ... Mr. John ANZINGER
08 Director of Library Services ... Ms. Colleen MCKNIGHT
108 Exec Dir Assessment and Research ... Dr. Gohar FARAHANI
26 Director of Marketing ... Mr. Michael BAISEY
88 Director of Special Projects ... Mr. Michael PRITCHARD
37 Exec Dir Financial Aid ... Ms. Brenda DAYHOFF
04 Exec Assoc to the President & BOT ... Ms. Kari MELVIN
103 Director Workforce Training ... Ms. Patricia MEYER
88 Exec Director Emergency Management ... Ms. Kathy FRANCIS
14 Exec Dir of Enterprise Application ... Mr. Adam RENO
41 Director of Athletics ... Mr. Rodney BENNETT
88 Director Children's Center ... Ms. Teri BICKEL
106 Exec Director Distributed Learning ... Mr. Jurgen HILKE
38 Exec Dir Counseling & Advising ... Dr. Chad ADERO
88 Director Office of Adult Services ... Ms. Janice BROWN
22 Director Students w/Disabilities ... Ms. Kate KRAMER-JEFFERSON
07 Director of Admissions ... Ms. Lisa FREEL
105 Director Web Services ... Ms. Cindy OSBON
88 Coordinator Veterans Services ... Ms. Rachel NACHLAS
109 Exec Director Auxiliary Services ... Mr. Frederick HOCKENBERRY
88 Director Administrative Projects ... Ms. Linda SEEK
88 Scholarship Manager ... Mr. Michael THORNTON
109 Director Dining Services ... Ms. Donna S. SOWERS

Garrett College (I)

687 Mosser Road, McHenry MD 21541
County: Garrett FICE Identification: 010014
Unit ID: 162609
Telephone: (301) 387-3000 Carnegie Class: Assoc/HT-High Trad
FAX Number: N/A Calendar System: Semester
URL: www.garrettcollege.edu
Established: 1966 Annual Undergrad Tuition & Fees (In-District): $3,780
Enrollment: 712 Coed
Affiliation or Control: State/Local IRS Status: 501(c)3
Highest Offering: Associate Degree
Accreditation: M, EMT

01 President ... Dr. Richard MIDCAP
04 Executive Assistant to President ... Ms. Marcia KNEPP
10 VP of Admin & Financial Services ... Mr. Randall BITTINGER
05 VP of Instruction & Student Svcs ... Dr. Sarah GARRETT
20 Dean of Academic Affairs ... Dr. Qing YUAN
51 Dean of Cont Educ/Workforce Devel ... Ms. Julie YODER
13 Director of IT ... Vacant
30 Dir Develop/Exec Dir Foundation ... Ms. Cherie KRUG
06 Director of Records & Registration ... Ms. Kim DEGIOVANNI
37 Director of Financial Aid ... Ms. Cissy VANSICKLE
08 Dir of Library/Learning Commons ... Dr. Robert KERNS
21 Director of Business Office ... Ms. Katherine BROWNING
15 Director of Human Resources ... Ms. Janis BUSH
32 Director of Student Development ... Ms. Tracie ELLIS

65 Dir of Natural Res/Wildlife Tech .... Mr. Kevin DODGE
41 Director of Athletics .... Mr. Dennis GIBSON
18 Director of Facilities .... Ms. Kathy MEAGHER
121 Coord of Student Advis & Acad Supp .... Ms. Ashley RUBY
96 Purchasing/Accounts Payable .... Ms. Bonnie BROADWATER
09 Coord of Institutional Research .... Ms. Kelli SISLER
40 Interim Bookstore Manager .... Ms. Lois ANDERSON
84 Director of Enrollment Management .... Vacant
45 Dean of Inst Effectiveness .... Mr. James ALLEN, JR.
105 Web Developer .... Mr. David LANTZ
88 Director of Adventure Sports .... Mr. Michael LOGSDON
106 Coordinator of Distance Learning .... Ms. Denise FRIEND
19 Coordinator of Security/Safety .... Ms. Shelley MENEAR
26 Coordinator of Marketing and PR .... Ms. Stacy HOLLER

Goucher College (A)

1021 Dulaney Valley Road, Baltimore MD 21204-2780
County: Baltimore — FICE Identification: 002073
Unit ID: 162654
Telephone: (410) 337-6000 — Carnegie Class: Bac-A&S
FAX Number: N/A — Calendar System: Semester
URL: www.goucher.edu
Established: 1885 — Annual Undergrad Tuition & Fees: $43,416
Enrollment: 2,141 — Coed
Affiliation or Control: Independent Non-Profit — IRS Status: 501(c)3
Highest Offering: Master's
Accreditation: M

01 President .... Dr. Jose A. BOWEN
05 Provost .... Dr. Leslie W. LEWIS
45 Sr VP for Strategic Initiatives .... Mr. Marty SWEIDEL
32 Vice Pres/Dean of Students .... Dr. Bryan F. COKER
111 Vice Pres Advancement .... Ms. Trishana E. BOWDEN
10 VP for Finance & Administration .... Ms. Lynne LOCHTE
26 Exec Dir Marketing & Communications .... Ms. Stephanie COLDREN
13 VP for Technology and Planning .... Mr. Bill LEIMBACH
43 General Counsel .... Ms. Barbara STOB
20 Assoc Provost for UG Studies & Prof .... Ms. La Jerne CORNISH
104 Assoc Prov Experiential & Ext Pgm .... Mr. Eric SINGER
88 Asst VP for Integrative Learning .... Ms. Emily PERL
15 Vice President for Human Resources .... Ms. Deborah LUPTON
21 Controller .... Mr. Alex ANTKOWIAK
07 Director of Admissions .... Mr. Carlton E. SURBECK, III
08 Librarian .... Vacant
29 Exec Dir for Alumnae/i Engagement .... Ms. Jennifer PAWLO - JOHNSTONE
36 Director of Career Development .... Ms. Traci MARTIN
58 Asst Prov Grad Program in Education .... Ms. Phyllis SUNSHINE
06 Registrar .... Mr. Andrew WESTFALL
09 Senior Dir for Inst Effectiveness .... Ms. Shuang LIU
109 Dir Business/Auxiliary Services .... Vacant
18 Dir Facilities Management Services .... Mr Terence MCCANN, JR.
37 Director Financial Aid .... Ms. Stephanie BENDER
105 Webmaster .... Mr. John PERRELLI
106 Dir Online Education/E-learning .... Vacant
28 Asst Dean Stdnts Intercultural Affs .... Vacant
39 Director Student Housing .... Vacant
41 Director of Phys Ed and Athletics .... Mr. Geoff MILLER
04 Executive Asst to President .... Ms. Lillian JOHNSON
19 Director of Public Safety .... Mr. David HEFFER
38 Director Student Counseling Center .... Ms. Monica NEEL

Hagerstown Community College (B)

11400 Robinwood Drive, Hagerstown MD 21742-6590
County: Washington — FICE Identification: 002074
Unit ID: 162690
Telephone: (240) 500-2000 — Carnegie Class: Assoc/MT-VT-Mix Trad/Non
FAX Number: (301) 393-3682 — Calendar System: Semester
URL: www.hagerstowncc.edu
Established: 1946 — Annual Undergrad Tuition & Fees (In-District): $3,564
Enrollment: 4,276 — Coed
Affiliation or Control: State/Local — IRS Status: 501(c)3
Highest Offering: Associate Degree
Accreditation: M, ADNUR, DA, DH, EMT, PNUR, RAD

01 President .... Dr. Guy ALTIERI
05 VP of Academic Affs & Student Svcs .... Dr. David WARNER
10 Vice Pres Administration/Finance .... Vacant
32 Dean of Students .... Ms. Christine OHL-GIGLIOTTI
09 Dean of Plng/Inst Effectiveness .... Vacant
51 Dean Continuing Educ/Bus Svcs .... Ms. Theresa M. SHANK
18 Dir Facilities Management & Plng .... Mr. Jonathan G. METCALF
07 Dir of Admissions & Enrollment Mgmt .... Mr. Kevin CRAWFORD
111 Exec Director College Advancement .... Ms. Stacey L. CRAWFORD
26 Director Marketing/Public Info .... Ms. Elizabeth L. KIRKPATRICK
37 Director of Financial Aid & Records .... Vacant
106 Dean Academic Services/Online Educ .... Dr. Julian K. HORTON
21 Director of Finance .... Mr. David C. BITTORF
21 Director of Business Services .... Ms. Lita J. ORNER
66 Director of Nursing .... Ms. Karen S. HAMMOND
15 Director of Human Resources .... Ms. Jennifer A. KNIGHT
41 Dir Athletics/Phys Ed/Leisure Stds .... Mr. Robert ROHAN
13 Director of Information Technology .... Mr. Craig M. FENTRESS

Harford Community College (C)

401 Thomas Run Road, Bel Air MD 21015-1698
County: Harford — FICE Identification: 002075
Unit ID: 162706
Telephone: (443) 412-2000 — Carnegie Class: Assoc/HT-High Trad
FAX Number: (443) 412-2120 — Calendar System: Semester
URL: www.harford.edu
Established: 1957 — Annual Undergrad Tuition & Fees (In-District): $3,571
Enrollment: 6,520 — Coed
Affiliation or Control: Local — IRS Status: 501(c)3
Highest Offering: Associate Degree
Accreditation: M, ADNUR, EMT, HT, MAC

01 President .... Dr. Dianna G. PHILLIPS
05 Vice President Academic Affairs .... Dr. Steven L. THOMAS
10 AVP Finance & Accounting .... Mr. Stephen PHILLIPS
32 VP Student Affairs/Inst Effective .... Dr. Jacqueline JACKSON
100 Chief of Staff .... Ms. Brenda M. MORRISON
13 Chief Information Officer .... Dr. Thomas FRANZA
96 Asst Vice Pres Procurement .... Vacant
84 Assoc VP Enrollment Services .... Mr. Patrick ELLIOTT
35 Assoc VP Student Development .... Dr. Diane L. RESIDES
21 AVP for Finance & Accounting .... Mr. Stephen S. PHILLIPS
51 Int AVP Continuing Educ & Training .... Mr. John MAYHORNE
18 Assoc VP Campus Operations .... Mr. Stephen P. GAREY
37 Director Financial Aid .... Ms. Amy R. SPINNATO
06 Assistant Registrar .... Ms. Samantha SAUNDERS-CONSROE
26 Dir Marketing & Public Relations .... Ms. Nancy J. DYSARD
15 Dir Human Resources/Employee Dev .... Ms. Pamela STELL
30 Director College/Alumni Development .... Ms. Denise M. DREGIER
08 Director Library & Info Resources .... Ms. Carol M. ALLEN
106 Dir eLearning & Instr Resources .... Dr. Karen M. REGE
09 Dir Inst Research/Plng/Effective .... Ms. Valerie T. SWAIN
38 Dir Advising/Career/Transfer Svcs .... Ms. J. Bonnie SULZBACH
40 Coordinator College Store .... Ms. Linda L. FIFE
07 Dir for Admissions and Registrar .... Ms. Megan CORNETT
110 Asst Dir for Development .... Ms. Lanell PATRICK
81 Int Dean Science/Tech/Engr/Math .... Ms. Jaclyn MADDEN
83 Dean Behavioral & Social Sciences .... Vacant
79 Dean Humanities .... Vacant
57 Dean Visual/Performing/Applied Arts .... Mr. James MCFARLAND
50 Dean Bus/Ed/Computing/Applied Tech .... Mr. John F. MAYHORNE
66 Dean Nursing & Allied Health Profs .... Ms. Laura C. PRESTON

Hood College (D)

401 Rosemont Avenue, Frederick MD 21701-8575
County: Frederick — FICE Identification: 002076
Unit ID: 162760
Telephone: (301) 663-3131 — Carnegie Class: Masters/L
FAX Number: (301) 694-7653 — Calendar System: Semester
URL: www.hood.edu
Established: 1893 — Annual Undergrad Tuition & Fees: $36,540
Enrollment: 2,289 — Coed
Affiliation or Control: Independent Non-Profit — IRS Status: 501(c)3
Highest Offering: Doctorate
Accreditation: M, ACBSP, CAEPN, CS, NURSE, SW

01 President .... Dr. Andrea E. CHAPDELAINE
05 Provost/VP Academic Affairs .... Dr. Deborah RICKER
10 Vice Pres Finance .... Mr. Charles G. MANN
111 VP for Institutional Advancement .... Ms. Nancy E. GILLECE
32 VP Student Life/Dean of Students .... Dr. Olivia G. WHITE
84 VP Undergrad/Grad Enrollment .... Mr. William BROWN
07 Director of Admissions .... Vacant
58 Interim Dean of Graduate School .... Dr. April BOULTON
20 Director CAAR .... Mr. Matthew HOLSAPPLE
26 Exec Dir Marketing/Communications .... Mr. Dave DIEHL
29 Sr Director of Alumnae/i Programs .... Ms. Linda ROTH
06 Registrar .... Mrs. Nanette MARKEY
08 Interim Director of Library Service .... Mr. Toby PETERSON
37 Director of Financial Aid .... Ms. Brenda DISORBO
15 Director of Human Resources .... Ms. Carol M. WUENSCHEL
18 Director of Facilities .... Mr. James THOMAS
13 Chief Technology Officer .... Vacant
09 Dir Inst Research & Assessment .... Ms. Cynthia M. EMORY
04 Executive Asst to President .... Ms. Diane K. WISE
104 Director Study Abroad .... Vacant
19 Director Security/Safety .... Mr. Thurmond MAYNARD
38 Director Student Counseling .... Ms. Delores GRIGSBY
39 Director Student Housing .... Mr. Matthew TROUTMAN
41 Athletic Director .... Mr. Tom DICKMAN
102 Dir Foundation/Corporate Relations .... Ms. Jaime CACCIOLA

Howard Community College (E)

10901 Little Patuxent Parkway, Columbia MD 21044-3197
County: Howard — FICE Identification: 008175
Unit ID: 162779
Telephone: (443) 518-1000 — Carnegie Class: Assoc/HT-High Trad
FAX Number: N/A — Calendar System: Semester
URL: www.howardcc.edu
Established: 1966 — Annual Undergrad Tuition & Fees (In-District): $3,755
Enrollment: 9,632 — Coed
Affiliation or Control: State/Local — IRS Status: 501(c)3
Highest Offering: Associate Degree
Accreditation: M, ACFEI, ADNUR, CVT, DH, DMS, EMT, MLTAD, MUS, PNUR, PTAA, RAD

01 President .... Dr. Kathleen B. HETHERINGTON
32 Vice President of Student Services .... Dr. Cynthia J. PETERKA
05 Vice Pres of Academic Affairs .... Dr. Jean M. SVACINA
10 Vice Pres of Administration/Finance .... Ms. Lynn C. COLEMAN
13 Vice Pres Information Technology .... Mr. Thomas J. GLASER
51 Acting AVP Cont Ed/Workforce Dev .... Ms. Minah WOO
84 Assoc Vice Pres Enrollment Services .... Ms. Alison BUCKLEY
35 Assoc Vice Pres for Student Devel .... Ms. Janice L. MARKS
15 Associate Vice Pres Human Resources .... Mr. Dave JORDAN
21 Associate Vice Pres of Finance .... Ms. Janet L. CULLISON
18 Exec Dir Capital Proj/Facilities .... Mr. Charles NIGHTINGALE
101 Executive Associate to President .... Ms. Linda EMMERICH
88 Dir of Student Finance and Acctng .... Ms. Verna BERNOI
114 Dir of Budget & Accounting .... Mr. Chris HESTON
30 Director of Development .... Ms. Melissa MATTEY
109 Director Auxiliary Services .... Mr. Kevin COLLINS
19 Acting Director of Public Safety .... Mr. G. William DAVIS
35 Director Student Life .... Ms. Schnell R. GARRETT
04 Exec Assistant to the President .... Ms. Farida P. GUZDAR
96 Director of Procurement .... Ms. Elizabeth H. MOSS
06 Registrar .... Ms. Catherine MUND
07 Director of Admissions & Advising .... Ms. Dorothy B. PLANTZ
104 Director of International Education .... Ms. Christele N. CAIN
105 Web Enterprise Services Manager .... Mr. Roger F. STOTT
37 Director of Financial Aid Services .... Ms. Dawn LOWE
41 Athletics Director .... Ms. Diane E. SCHUMACHER
26 Exec Dir Public Relations/Mktg .... Ms. Elizabeth S. HOMAN
09 Exec Dir Plng/Research & Org Dev .... Ms. Zoe A. IRVIN

Johns Hopkins University (F)

3400 N. Charles Street, Baltimore MD 21218-2680
County: Independent City — FICE Identification: 002077
Unit ID: 162928
Telephone: (410) 516-8000 — Carnegie Class: DU-Highest
FAX Number: N/A — Calendar System: Semester
URL: www.jhu.edu
Established: 1876 — Annual Undergrad Tuition & Fees: $50,410
Enrollment: 22,686 — Coed
Affiliation or Control: Independent Non-Profit — IRS Status: 501(c)3
Highest Offering: Doctorate
Accreditation: M, BBT, CACREP, CAEPN, CS, DIETC, DMS, ENG, ENGR, HSA, IPSY, MED, MIL, NMT, NURSE, PH

01 President .... Mr. Ronald J. DANIELS
100 Sr Vice President/Chief of Staff .... Ms. Kerry A. ATES
05 Provost & Sr VP Acad Affs .... Dr. Sunil KUMAR
17 CEO Johns Hopkins Medicine .... Dr. Paul D. ROTHMAN
10 Sr VP Finance & Administration .... Mr. Daniel G. ENNIS
29 VP for Development & Alum Relations .... Mr. Fritz SCHROEDER
26 Vice Pres for Communications .... Ms. Susan RIDGE
43 Vice Pres/General Counsel .... Mr. Paul PINEAU
86 Vice Pres Govt/Community Affairs .... Mr. Thomas LEWIS
18 Vice Pres Real Estate/Campus Svcs .... Mr. Robert MCLEAN
15 Vice Pres Human Resources .... Ms. Heidi CONWAY
21 Vice Pres Finance & CFO .... Ms. Helene GRADY
115 Vice Pres Chief Investment Officer .... Mr. Jason PERLIONI
117 Chief Risk Officer .... Dr. Jonathan LINKS
32 Vice Provost Student Affairs .... Dr. Kevin SHOLLENBERGER
20 Vice Provost Faculty Affairs .... Dr. Susan COURTNEY
20 Vice Provost Academic Services .... Mr. Philip TANG
07 Vice Provost Admiss & Fin Aid .... Mr. David PHILLIPS
88 Vice Provost Education .... Dr. Kelly GEBO
13 Vice Provost Info Technology/CIO .... Ms. Stephanie REEL
22 Vice Provost Institutional Equity .... Ms. Kimberly HEWITT
46 Vice Provost Research .... Dr. Denis WIRTZ
09 Vice Provost Institutional Research .... Dr. Ratna SARKAR
88 Asst Prov International Services .... Mr. James BRAILER
06 Registrar .... Ms. Mary Ellen FLAHERTY
82 Dean Nitze School Adv Intl Studies .... Dr. Vali NASR
49 Dean Krieger School Arts & Sciences .... Dr. Beverly WENDLAND
50 Dean Carey Business School .... Dr. Bernard FERRARI
53 Dean School of Education .... Dr. Christopher MORPHEW
54 Dean Whiting Sch Engineering .... Dr. Ed SCHLESINGER
63 Dean School of Medicine .... Dr. Paul ROTHMAN
66 Dean School of Nursing .... Dr. Patricia DAVIDSON
69 Dean Bloomberg School Public Health .... Dr. Michael J. KLAG
08 Dean Sheridan Libraries and Museums .... Mr. Winston G. TABB
64 Director Peabody Institute .... Mr. Fred BRONSTEIN
81 Director Applied Physics Lab .... Mr. Ralph SEMMEL
96 Director Purchasing .... Mr. Paul N. BEYER
21 Controller .... Mr. Scott JONAS
19 Exec Director Safety & Security .... Mr. Leroy "Lee" JAMES
116 Exec Director Internal Audits .... Mr. James JARRELL
27 Exec Director Comm & Public Affairs .... Mr. Dennis O'SHEA
88 Exec Director JH Real Estate .... Mr. Brian B. DEMBECK
104 Director Study Abroad .... Dr. Lori A. CITTI
28 Chair Diversity Leadership Council .... Mr. Ashley J. LLORENS
36 Executive Director Career Center .... Ms. Ann GARNER
41 Athletic Director .... Ms. Alanna SHANAHAN

Kaplan University (G)

18618 Crestwood Drive, Hagerstown MD 21742-2797
Telephone: (301) 766-3600 — FICE Identification: 007946
Accreditation: &NH, ACBSP, MAC

† Regional accreditation is carried under the parent institution in Davenport, IA.

Lincoln College of Technology (H)

9325 Snowden River Parkway, Columbia MD 21046
County: Howard — FICE Identification: 007936
Unit ID: 163028
Telephone: (410) 290-7100 — Carnegie Class: Assoc/HVT-Mix Trad/Non
FAX Number: (410) 290-7880 — Calendar System: Quarter
URL: www.lincolntech.com
Established: 1978 — Annual Undergrad Tuition & Fees: N/A
Enrollment: 711 — Coed
Affiliation or Control: Proprietary — IRS Status: Proprietary
Highest Offering: Associate Degree
Accreditation: ACCSC

01 Campus President .... Mr. Cory HUGHES

Loyola University Maryland (A)

4501 N Charles Street, Baltimore MD 21210-2694
County: Independent City FICE Identification: 002078
Unit ID: 163046
Telephone: (410) 617-2000 Carnegie Class: Masters/L
FAX Number: (410) 322-2768 Calendar System: Semester
URL: www.loyola.edu
Established: 1852 Annual Undergrad Tuition & Fees: $46,430
Enrollment: 6,050 Coed
Affiliation or Control: Roman Catholic IRS Status: 501(c)3
Highest Offering: Doctorate
Accreditation: M, CACREP, CAEPN, CLPSY, CS, ENG, MACTE, SP

01 President ... Rev. Brian F. LINNANE, SJ
03 VP/Special Asst to the President ... Dr. Rob KELLY
04 Executive Asst to the President ... Ms. Amy VERNON
05 Int Vice President Academic Affairs ... Dr. Amanda THOMAS
10 Vice Pres for Finance & Treasurer ... Mr. Randall GENTZLER
30 Sr Vice President Advancement ... Dr. Terrence SAWYER
32 VP Student Development ... Dr. Donalda COOK
20 Int Assoc Vice Pres Academic Affs ... Ms. Jenny LOWRY
28 Asst VP Academic Affrs/Diversity ... Dr. Martha L. WHARTON
84 Asst Vice Pres of Enrollment Mgmt . Mr. Mark L. LINDENMEYER
09 Director of Institutional Research ... Ms. Nicole JACOBS
18 Assoc VP Facilities/Campus Services ... Ms. Helen SCHNEIDER
13 Asst VP of Technology Services/CIO ... Ms. Louise FINN
26 Dir Marketing and Communications ... Ms. Rita BUETTNER
15 Assoc Vice Pres for Human Resources ... Ms. Kathleen PARNELL
110 Asst Vice Pres for External Affairs ... Ms. Joan FLYNN
27 Asst VP Marketing/Communications ... Ms. Sharon HIGGINS
41 Asst VP/Director of Athletics ... Ms. Donna WOODRUFF
38 VP Student Development ... Dr. Donelda COOK
07 Director Undergraduate Admissions ... Vacant
07 Director of Graduate Admissions ... Ms. Maureen FAUX
06 Director of Records ... Ms. Rita L. STEINER
85 Dean of International Programs ... Dr. Andre COLOMBAT
08 Director of Library ... Ms. Barbara PREECE
42 Director of Campus Ministry ... Mr. Sean BRAY
88 Dir CCSJ/York Road Initiative ... Ms. Erin O'KEEFE
36 Director of the Career Center ... Ms. Jennifer KACZKOWSKI
88 Sexual Violence Prev & Educ Coord ... Ms. Melissa LEES
88 Director Recreational Sports ... Mr. Bryan HAUNERT
35 Director Student Activities ... Mr. Mark C. BRODERICK
88 Director ALANA Services ... Mr. Rodney PARKER
21 Asst VP Controller ... Vacant
45 Director Budget & Planning ... Mr. Sean FRANCIS
109 Director Event Svcs/Auxiliary Mgmt ... Mr. Joseph BRADLEY
88 Director of Project Management ... Mr. Laszlo PELY
88 Director Environment Health/Safety ... Mr. Thomas HETTLEMAN
19 Dir of Public Safety/Campus Police ... Mr. Timothy FOX
29 Director Alumni Relations ... Mr. Thomas BRUSH
30 Asst VP Advancement ... Ms. Jo Ann DOLAN
88 Director of Creative Services ... Mr. Brian HATCHER
88 Director Advancement Services ... Mr. Ian WEBSTER
49 Dean College of Arts & Sciences ... Dr. Steve FOWL
50 Dean Sellinger Sch Business & Mgmt ... Dr. Kathleen GETZ
49 Assoc Dean Social Sciences/Graduate ... Dr. Jeffrey BARNETT
50 Asst Dean for Business Programs ... Ms. Susan HASLER
88 Asst Vice Pres Student Development ... Ms. Michelle CHEATEM
18 Dir Facilities Management ... Ms. Kiki WILLIAMS
44 Director of Annual Giving ... Ms. Dianne THOMPSON
88 Asst Vice Pres Academic Operations ... Ms. Lorie HOLTGRAVE
88 Director of Bangkok Programs ... Vacant
105 Dir Web Communications ... Ms. Amy FILARDO

Maple Springs Baptist Bible College & Seminary (B)

4130 Belt Road, Capitol Heights MD 20743-5712
County: Prince Georges FICE Identification: 038224
Unit ID: 446394
Telephone: (301) 736-3631 Carnegie Class: Spec-4-yr-Faith
FAX Number: (301) 735-6507 Calendar System: Semester
URL: www.msbbcs.edu
Established: 1986 Annual Undergrad Tuition & Fees: $4,488
Enrollment: 89 Coed
Affiliation or Control: Baptist IRS Status: 501(c)3
Highest Offering: Doctorate
Accreditation: TRACS

01 President ... Dr. David CLARK
05 Vice President Academic Affairs ... Dr. Betty BOOKER
11 Vice Pres Administration & Finance ... Dr. Quentin COLEMAN
73 Academic Dean College Division ... Dr. Carl KEELS
06 Director Records and Admissions ... Dr. Esther BIRCH
09 Dir Institutional Plng/Assessment ... Dr. David CLARK
10 Director Business Affairs ... Mrs. Fannie G. THOMPSON
32 Director Student Affairs ... Mr. Jeffrey BATES
08 Dir Library/Instruc Resource Center ... Mr. Darren JONES
37 Financial Aid Coordinator ... Mrs. Patricia JONES

Maryland Institute College of Art (C)

1300 W. Mount Royal Avenue, Baltimore MD 21217-4191
County: Independent City FICE Identification: 002080
Unit ID: 163295
Telephone: (410) 669-9200 Carnegie Class: Spec-4-yr-Arts
FAX Number: (410) 669-9206 Calendar System: Semester
URL: www.mica.edu
Established: 1826 Annual Undergrad Tuition & Fees: $45,400
Enrollment: 2,197 Coed
Affiliation or Control: Independent Non-Profit IRS Status: 501(c)3
Highest Offering: Master's
Accreditation: M, ART

01 President ... Mr. Samuel HOI
05 Vice Pres Academic Affairs/Provost ... Dr. David BOGEN
10 Vice Pres Operations/Finance/COO ... Mr. Douglas MANN
30 Vice Pres Advancement ... Ms. Rita WALTERS
32 Vice Pres Student Affairs ... Mr. Michael PATTERSON
07 VP Admissions/Financial Aid ... Ms. Theresa BEDOYA
13 Vice Pres Technology Systems & Svcs ... Ms. Alexa KIM
11 Vice Pres Strategic Iniatives ... Mr. Mike MOLLA
97 Vice Provost Open Studies ... Mr. David GRACYALNY
46 Vice Provost Research/Grad Studies ... Ms. Gwynne KEATHLEY
04 Executive Assistant to President ... Ms. Lisa SHEPPLEY
37 Assoc VP Financial Aid ... Ms. Diane PRENGAMAN
14 Assoc VP Dev/Constituent Rels ... Ms. Lillian BURKE
14 Assoc VP Tech/Systems/Services ... Ms. Susan MILTENBERGER
18 Assoc VP Facilities Management ... Mr. Timothy MILLNER
15 Human Resources Director ... Ms. Laura ROSSI
20 Dean Academic Services ... Ms. Cynthia BARTH
53 Dean Art Education ... Ms. Karen CARROLL
35 Assoc Dean Stdnt Life/Judicial Affs ... Vacant
88 Assoc Dean Student Health Wellness ... Vacant
07 Assoc Dean Undergraduate Admissions ... Vacant
07 Director of Graduate Admissions ... Mr. Christopher HARRING
51 Assoc Dn Cont Studies/Open Studies ... Mr. Peter DUBEAU
06 Assoc Dean Enrollment Svs/Registrar ... Ms. Christine PETERSON
28 Asst Dean Diversity Intercultur Dev ... Mr. Clyde JOHNSON, JR.
21 Director Accounting ... Ms. Jessica RURKA
88 Director Budget ... Ms. Brigitte SULLIVAN
26 VP for Strategic Communications ... Ms. Debra RUBINO
39 Director Residence Life ... Mr. Scott STONE
36 Director Career Development ... Ms. Megan MILLER
31 Director Community Engagement ... Ms. Karen STULTS
38 Director Counseling Center ... Ms. Patricia FARRELL
35 Director Student Activities ... Ms. Karol MARTINEZ-DOANE
88 Director Admissions Operations ... Ms. Cheryl ISSOD
08 Director & Head Librarian ... Vacant
88 Director Annual Fund ... Vacant
88 Director Advancement Services ... Ms. Dana COSTELLO
88 Research & Stewardship Manager ... Ms. Nayeli MOWBRAY
88 Director Exhibitions ... Mr. Gerald ROSS
85 Director International Affairs ... Ms. Mary ALLEN
88 Director Writing St/Learn Res Ctr ... Mr. Daniel GUTSTEIN
88 Dir Data Mgmt/Registration Cont Std ... Ms. Sarah MARAVETZ
84 Dir Enroll Svcs/Stdnt Records/Rsrch ... Mr. Hadley GARBART
19 Director of Campus Safety ... Mr. Marlon BYRD
88 Director Events ... Mr. Jon LIPITZ
88 Director Operation Services ... Mr. Chris BOHASKA
29 Director Alumni & Parent Relations ... Ms. Lindsay DORRANCE
102 Director Corp/Found/Govt Relations ... Ms. Sara WARREN
105 Director of Web Communications ... Mr. Justin CODD
24 Director Technical Support Services ... Mr. John RHODES
91 Director Administrative Systems ... Vacant
105 Director Network Services ... Mr. David APAW
90 Dir Instructional Advance & Tech ... Ms. Pamela STEFANUCA
40 Manager College Store ... Ms. Kerri LITZ

Maryland University of Integrative Health (D)

7750 Montpelier Road, Laurel MD 20723-6010
County: Howard FICE Identification: 025784
Unit ID: 164085
Telephone: (410) 888-9048 Carnegie Class: Spec-4-yr-Other Health
FAX Number: (410) 888-9004 Calendar System: Trimester
URL: www.muih.edu
Established: 1981 Annual Graduate Tuition & Fees: N/A
Enrollment: 1,077 Coed
Affiliation or Control: Independent Non-Profit IRS Status: 501(c)3
Highest Offering: Doctorate; No Undergraduates
Accreditation: M, ACUP

01 President & CEO ... Dr. Steven COMBS
05 Provost/VP Academic Affairs ... Dr. Christina SAX
26 VP University Relations ... Ms. Gail DOERR
10 VP Finance & Admin/CFO & COO ... Mr. Marc LEVIN
20 Assoc Provost Academic Operations ... Ms. Mary Ellen HRUTKA
108 Asst Provost Acad Assessment & Accr ... Ms. Deneb FALABELLA
09 Asst Provost Research ... Mr. James SNOW
84 Assoc VP Enrollment Management ... Mr. Chad EGRESI
76 Acad Dir Acupuncture/Oriental Med ... Mr. Jeffrey MILLISON
76 Academic Director Herbal Programs ... Dr. Michael TIMS
76 Academic Director Nutrition ... Dr. Kathleen WARNER
37 Director Student Financial Aid ... Ms. Kristina DEAN
08 Director of Library Services ... Ms. Jenifer KIRIN
29 Director Alumni Affairs ... Ms. Patricia DELORENZO
06 Registrar ... Ms. Ashley ANDERSON
88 Meetings & Events Planner ... Ms. Olga MADIOU-BEALE
07 Assoc Director of Admissions ... Mr. Nicholas HOWLEY
27 Director Marketing ... Ms. Beth HANDY
13 Director IT ... Mr. Lesly ELVARD
19 Manager Security/Safety ... Ms. Jennifer YOCUM
32 Director Student Affairs ... Mr. Jan SHERRILL
28 Assoc Provost Values & Diversity ... Ms. Cheryl WALKER SHAPERO
20 Assoc Provost Acad Innov & Support ... Mr. Witt SALLEY
15 Director Human Enrichment ... Ms. Melissa L. CAHILL

McDaniel College (E)

2 College Hill, Westminster MD 21157-4390
County: Carroll FICE Identification: 002109
Unit ID: 164270
Telephone: (410) 848-7000 Carnegie Class: Bac-A&S
FAX Number: (410) 857-2279 Calendar System: Semester
URL: www.mcdaniel.edu
Established: 1867 Annual Undergrad Tuition & Fees: $40,580
Enrollment: 3,003 Coed
Affiliation or Control: Independent Non-Profit IRS Status: 501(c)3
Highest Offering: Master's
Accreditation: M, CAEPN, SW

01 President ... Dr. Roger N. CASEY
100 Chief of Staff ... Mr. Geoff PEARSON
05 Provost/Dean of Faculty ... Dr. Julia JASKEN
10 Vice Pres Administration & Finance ... Mr. Thomas PHIZACKLEA
111 Interim Vice President Advancement ... Ms. Vicky SHAFFER
32 Vice Pres/Dean of Student Affairs ... Ms. Beth R. GERL
84 VP Enroll Mgt/Dean of Admissions ... Ms. Florence W. HINES
13 Chief Information Officer ... Mr. Andrew LAWLOR
26 Assoc Vice Pres Comm/Marketing ... Ms. Gina PIELLUSCH
58 Dean Graduate/Professional Stds ... Dr. Michael TYLER
20 Assoc Dean/International Programs ... Dr. Amy MCNICHOLS
88 Assoc Dean/Student Academic Life ... Ms. Lisa BRESLIN
89 Assoc Dean/First Year Program ... Dr. Karen VIOLANTI
35 Assoc Dean/Student Affairs ... Ms. Elizabeth TOWLE
112 Executive Director of Major/Planned ... Mr. Robert CONRAD
29 Executive Director of Alumni Relati ... Ms. Heather WILENSKY
102 Dir Corp & Foundation Relations ... Ms. Bonnie CATON
08 Director of Library ... Ms. Jessame E. FERGUSON
37 Director Financial Aid ... Ms. Zhanna GOLTSER
06 Registrar ... Ms. Sandra CLARK
41 Director Athletics ... Mr. Paul MOYER
36 Director Center for Exper and Opp ... Mr. Joshua AMBROSE
124 Director Student Engagement ... Ms. Christine WORKMAN
39 Director of Residence Life ... Mr. Michael ROBBINS
21 Director Financial Services/Treas ... Mr. Arthur S. WISNER
15 Director Human Resources ... Ms. Jennifer GLENNON
45 Dir Facility Plng/Capital Projects ... Mr. Edgar S. SELL, JR.
18 Director Physical Plant ... Mr. James COONS
19 Director of Campus Safety ... Mr. James HAMRICK
40 Manager Bookstore ... Mr. Kyle MELOCHE
109 Dir Conferences/Auxiliary Services ... Ms. Mary J. COLBERT
28 Director of Diversity and Inclusion ... Mr. Jose MORENO
92 Director of Honors Program ... Dr. Bryn UPTON
96 Director of Purchasing/Receiving ... Ms. Ellen RUGEMER
88 Coord of Deaf Education Program ... Dr. Mark M. RUST
09 Director Institutional Research ... Vacant
86 Director of Government Relations ... Dr. Herbert C. SMITH
07 Director of Admissions ... Ms. Heidi REIGEL
104 Director of International Programs ... Ms. Elizabeth DAVIS
105 Director Digital Comm/Social Media ... Mr. Vince BUSCEMI
25 Director Academic/Government Grants ... Ms. Robin DEWEY

Montgomery College (F)

9221 Corporate Boulevard, Rockville MD 20850
County: Montgomery FICE Identification: 006911
Unit ID: 163426
Telephone: (240) 567-5000 Carnegie Class: Assoc/HT-Mix Trad/Non
FAX Number: (240) 567-9129 Calendar System: Semester
URL: www.montgomerycollege.edu
Established: 1946 Annual Undergrad Tuition & Fees (In-District): $4,902
Enrollment: 25,320 Coed
Affiliation or Control: Local IRS Status: 501(c)3
Highest Offering: Associate Degree
Accreditation: M, ADNUR, CAHIIM, DMS, MUS, POLYT, PTAA, RAD, SURGT

01 President ... Dr. DeRionne P. POLLARD
05 Sr VP for Academic Affairs ... Dr. Sanjay RAI
32 Sr VP for Student Affairs ... Dr. Monica R. BROWN
11 Sr VP for Admin & Fiscal Svcs ... Dr. Janet WORMACK
111 Sr VP for Advance & Comm Engagement ... Mr. David SEARS
100 Chief of Staff/Chief Strategy Ofcr ... Dr. Stephen D. CAIN
88 Deputy Chief of Staff and Strategy ... Dr. Michelle T. SCOTT
35 Assoc SVP for Student Affairs ... Dr. Melissa GREGORY
21 Assoc SVP for Admin & Fiscal Svcs ... Ms. Nadine PORTER
21 Assoc SVP for Admin & Fiscal Svcs ... Ms. Donna SCHENA
20 Assoc SVP for Academic Affairs ... Ms. Carolyn TERRY
86 Chief Government Relations Officer ... Ms. Susan MADDEN
43 Interim General Counsel ... Mr. Timothy D. DIETZ
04 Assistant to the President ... Ms. Ida BRITTON
101 Mgr of Bd of Trustees Svcs & Ops ... Ms. Lily LEE
12 VP & Provost Rockville Campus ... Dr. Kimberly KELLEY
12 VP & Provost Germantown Campus ... Ms. Margaret LATIMER
12 VP & Prov Takoma Pk/Silver Spring C ... Dr. Brad J. STEWART
103 VP/Prov App Tech/Tech Ed/WD&CE ... Mr. George M. PAYNE
13 VP of Instructional & IT/CIO ... Mr. Carl E. WHITMAN
88 Deputy CIO Performance Mgmt Svcs ... Mr. Chris WILKINS
14 Chief Technology Officer ... Mr. Anwar KARIM
15 Interim Chief Human Res Officer ... Mr. Robert G. ROOP
18 VP of Facilities & Security ... Mr. Marvin MILLS
26 VP of Communications ... Mr. Ray GILMER
106 VP E-Learning/Innov/Teaching Exc ... Dr. Michael MILLS
50 Dean Acct/BusAdmin/Econ/Paralegal . Ms. Katherine MICHAELIAN
88 Dean Eng/Dev Eng/Reading ... Dr. Rodney REDMOND
83 Dean Anthro/Crim Just/Ed/Psych/Soc ... Dr. Darrin CAMPEN
81 Dean Biology/Biotech/Chemistry ... Dr. James SNIEZEK
54 Dean Eng/Comp Sci/Netwk/Cyber Sec ... Dr. Muhammad KEHNEMOUYI
81 Dean Math/Dev Math/Statistics ... Mr. John HAMMAN
76 Dean Mgmt/Mental Health/Health&PE ... Ms. Angie PICKWICK
88 Dean AELP Writing/Reading/ Speech ... Dr. Monica PARRISH TRENT
79 Dean Hist/PolSci/World Lang/AmSign ... Dr. Sharon FECHTER
75 Dean Applied Tech & Gudelsky Inst ... Mr. Ed ROBERTS
50 Dean Bus Info/Tech/Safety ... Mr. Steve GREENFIELD

51 Dean Cmty Educ & Extended Learning .... Ms. Dorothy UMANS
51 Dean Adult Eng Lang & GED Programs ...... Dr. Donna KINERNEY
57 Dean Art/Comp App/Dance/Film .... Dr. Deborah PRESTON
124 Dean Student Engagement/Affairs .... Dr. Clemmie SOLOMON
88 Dean Student Access/Affairs .... Dr. Jamin BARTOLOMEO
121 Dean Student Success/Services .... Dr. Tonya MASON
53 Dir School of Education .... Ms. Debra POESE
41 Athletic Director .... Ms. Tarlough GASQUE
102 Dir of MC Foundation/Dir of Dev .... Ms. Carol ROGNRUD
112 Major and Planned Gifts Director .... Ms. Francene WALKER
88 Exec Dir Hercules Pinkney Life SP .. Ms. Martha SCHOONMAKER
09 Dir Inst Research & Effectiveness .... Dr. Robert LYNCH
96 Dir of Procurement .... Mr. Patrick JOHNSON
37 Collegewide Dir of Financial Aid .... Ms. Judith M. TAYLOR
84 Dir Enroll Svcs & College Registrar .... Mr. Ernest CARTLEDGE
19 Dir Public Safety/Emergency Mgmt .... Ms. Shawn HARRISON
28 Chief Equity & Diversity Officer .... Ms. Sharon BLAND
108 Dir of Assessment .... Dr. Cassandra JONES
25 Dir Grants & Sponsored Programs .Ms. Rose GARVIN AQUILINO
102 Interim Dir Foundation & Corp Rels .... Mr. Stuart TART
29 Alumni Coordinator .... Mr. John LIBBY
08 Dir College Libraries & Info Svcs .... Mr. Tanner WRAY
22 Dir Employee & Labor Relations .... Ms. Heather PRATT
104 Coord of Travel & Study Abroad .... Dr. Gregory MALVEAUX
18 Plant Maint & Ops Officer .... Mr. James GILLIS
110 Assoc SVP for Adv & Comm Engagement .... Ms. Nancy NUELL

Morgan State University (A)

1700 East Cold Spring Lane, Baltimore MD 21251-0001
County: Independent City FICE Identification: 002083
Unit ID: 163453
Telephone: (443) 885-3333 Carnegie Class: DU-Mod
FAX Number: (443) 885-3698 Calendar System: Semester
URL: www.morgan.edu
Established: 1867 Annual Undergrad Tuition & Fees (In-State): $7,636
Enrollment: 7,725 Coed
Affiliation or Control: State IRS Status: 501(c)3
Highest Offering: Doctorate
Accreditation: M, CAEPN, DIETD, ENG, ENGR, LSAR, MT, MUS, NURSE, PH, PLNG, SW

01 President .... Dr. David WILSON
05 Provost/Vice Pres Academic Affs .... Dr. Gloria GIBSON
88 VP Academic Outreach and Engagement .... Dr. Maurice TAYLOR
10 Vice Pres Finance & Management .... Mr. Sidney EVANS
13 Chief Information Officer .... Dr. Adebisi OLADIPUPO
32 Vice Pres Student Affairs .... Dr. Kevin BANKS
30 Vice Pres Institutional Advancement .... Ms. Cheryl Y. HITCHCOCK
84 VP for Enroll Mgmt/Student Success .... Dr. Kara TURNER
21 Asst Vice President for Finance .... Mr. Bickram JANAK
35 Associate VP Student Affairs .... Ms. Tanya RUSH
100 Chief of Staff .... Dr. Don-Terry VEAL
49 Acting Dean College of Liberal Arts .... Dr. Mbare NGOM
50 Dean School Business & Management .... Dr. Fikru BOGHOSSIAN
53 Dean School of Education .... Dr. Patricia WELCH
54 Dean School of Engineering .... Dr. Michael SPENCER
58 Dean of the Graduate School .... Dr. Mark GARRISON
48 Dean School of Architecture .... Dr. Mary Anne AKERS
70 Dean School of Social Work .... Dr. Anna MCPHATTER
69 Dean School of Community Health .... Dr. Kim SYDNOR
37 Director of Financial Aid .... Ms. Tanya WILKERSON
38 Director of Counseling Services ..... Ms. Nina DOBSON-HOPKINS
08 Director of Library .... Dr. Richard BRADBERRY
06 Director of Records/Registration .... Mr. Hans COOPER
07 Director of Admissions .... Ms. Shonda GRAY
36 Director of Placement .... Ms. Seana COULTER
15 Director Human Resources .... Mrs. Armada GRANT
29 Director Alumni Association .... Mrs. Joyce BROWN
14 Director Computer Center .... Mr. Gilbert MORGAN
86 Director State Relations .... Mr. Claude E. HITCHCOCK
09 Director of Institutional Research .... Ms. Cheryl ROLLINS
18 Acting Director Physical Plant ..... Mr. Premdat KOKILEPERSAUD
26 Director Public Relations .... Mr. Clinton R. COLEMAN
84 Director Enrollment Management .... Vacant
96 Interim Director of Purchasing .... Ms. Lois WHITAKER
28 Director of Diversity .... Ms. Tanyka BARBER

Mount St. Mary's University (B)

16300 Old Emmitsburg Road, Emmitsburg MD 21727-7799
County: Frederick FICE Identification: 002086
Unit ID: 163462
Telephone: (301) 447-6122 Carnegie Class: Masters/M
FAX Number: (301) 447-5634 Calendar System: Semester
URL: www.msmary.edu
Established: 1808 Annual Undergrad Tuition & Fees: $39,000
Enrollment: 2,257 Coed
Affiliation or Control: Roman Catholic IRS Status: 501(c)3
Highest Offering: Master's
Accreditation: M, CAEPN, CEA, IACBE, THEOL

01 President .... Dr. Timothy W. TRAINOR
03 Vice President/Rector .... Msgr. Andrew R. BAKER
84 VP Enrollment Mgmt/Stdnt Affairs .... Mr. Michael POST
100 Vice President University Affairs ...... Ms. Pauline ENGLESTATTER
05 Interim Provost .... Dr. Jenny HUNTER-CEVERA
10 Vice Pres for Business & Finance .... Mr. William E. DAVIES
111 Vice President for Advancement .... Mr. Robert J. BRENNAN
20 Assoc Provost .... Dr. David MCCARTHY
50 Dean Richard J Bolte Sr Sch of Bus .... Vacant
81 Dean School Natural Science & Math .... Vacant
49 Dean College of Liberal Arts .... Dr. Peter DORSEY
41 Director of Athletics .... Ms. Lynne P. ROBINSON
42 Chaplain .... Fr. Brian NOLAN
32 Dean of Students .... Mr. Kenneth MCVEARRY
51 Assoc Prov Continuing/Online Educ .... Vacant
08 Dean of the Library .... Mr. Charles KUHN
09 Director Institutional Research .... Ms. Linda K. SITES
06 Registrar .... Mr. Chris WEBER
50 Asst Director Grad/Adult Business .... Ms. Carol RINKOFF
88 Manager Conferences/Special Pgms .... Ms. Danielle GRACE
23 Director of Health Services .... Dr. Bonnie PORTIER
24 Director of Media Systems .... Mr. John B. BREWER, JR.
37 Director of Financial Aid .... Mr. David C. REEDER
36 Director Career Center .... Ms. Claire TAURIELLO
26 VP Marketing and Communications .... Mr. Jack J. CHIELLI
15 Director of Human Resources .... Ms. Kristin HURLEY
19 Director of Public Safety .... Mr. Rodney GRAYS
29 Director of Alumni Engagement .... Ms. Emily MYERS
18 Director of Physical Plant .... Ms. Kimberly KLABE
88 Director Office of Social Justice .... Mr. Ian VANANDEN
28 Director Ctr for Student Diversity .... Ms. Tirrani THURMOND
35 Dir Campus Activ/Student Ldrshp .... Mr. Joe ENSTE
92 Director of the Honors Program .... Dr. Jennifer STAIGER
40 Manager of College Store .... Ms. Amanda CASALE
96 Purchasing Agent .... Ms. Maria L. TOPPER
07 Director of Admissions .... Mr. Eric DANIELSON
13 Chief Transformation Officer .... Mr. Simon BLACKWELL
38 Director Student Counseling .... Mr. Gerald T. ROOTH

Ner Israel Rabbinical College (C)

400 Mount Wilson Lane, Baltimore MD 21208-1198
County: Baltimore FICE Identification: 002087
Unit ID: 163532
Telephone: (410) 484-7200 Carnegie Class: Spec-4-yr-Faith
FAX Number: (410) 484-3060 Calendar System: Semester
Established: 1933 Annual Undergrad Tuition & Fees: $11,400
Enrollment: 515 Male
Affiliation or Control: Independent Non-Profit IRS Status: 501(c)3
Highest Offering: Doctorate
Accreditation: RABN

01 President .... Rabbi Sheftel M. NEUBERGER
05 Chief Academic Officer .... Rabbi Aharon FELDMAN
88 Executive Director .... Mr. Jerome H. KADDEN
03 Vice President .... Rabbi Boruch NEUBERGER
07 Director of Admissions .... Rabbi Beryl WEISBORD
11 Director of Administrative Services .... Mr. Larry RIBAKOW
06 Registrar .... Rabbi Chaim D. LAPIDUS
85 Foreign Student Advisor .... Rabbi Eliyahu HAKKAKIAN
30 Director of Development .... Rabbi Louis HOFFMAN
45 Director of Planning .... Rabbi Leonard OBERSTEIN
37 Director Student Financial Aid .... Rabbi Shmuel SCHACHTER
18 Chief Physical Plant .... Mr. David FRIEDMAN
08 Head Librarian .... Rabbi Avrohom SHNIDMAN
39 Director of Student Housing .... Rabbi Emanuel GOLDFEIZ
29 Associate Director Alumni Relations .... Rabbi Eli GREENGART

Notre Dame of Maryland University (D)

4701 N Charles Street, Baltimore MD 21210-2404
County: Independent City FICE Identification: 002065
Unit ID: 163578
Telephone: (410) 435-0100 Carnegie Class: Masters/L
FAX Number: (410) 532-5791 Calendar System: Semester
URL: www.ndm.edu
Established: 1873 Annual Undergrad Tuition & Fees: $35,019
Enrollment: 2,612 Female
Affiliation or Control: Roman Catholic IRS Status: 501(c)3
Highest Offering: Doctorate
Accreditation: M, ACBSP, CAEPN, PHAR

01 President .... Dr. Marylou YAM
05 Int Vice President Academic Affairs .... Dr. Clarenda PHILLIPS
32 Assoc Vice President Student Life .... Ms. Kelly HOOVER
111 Vice Pres Institutional Advancement .... Dr. Tanya EASTON
84 Vice Pres Enrollment Management .... Mr. Terry WHITTUM
10 Vice Pres for Finance & Admin .... Mr. Sean DELANEY
20 Associate VP Academic Affairs .... Dr. Kathryn DOHERTY
37 Assoc VP Scholarships & Fin Aid .... Ms. Breanne SIMKIN
100 Chief of Staff .... Mr. Gregory FITZGERALD
06 Interim Registrar .... Ms. Jill EIGENBRODE
36 Director Career Center .... Mr. Ammad SHEIKH
13 Director Information Technology .... Mr. Warren SZELISTOWSKI
29 Director of Alumnae Relations .... Ms. Aliza ROSS
08 Librarian .... Ms. Barbara PREECE
85 Director International Education .... Ms. Margo CUNNIFFE
07 Interim Director of Admissions .... Ms. Marci LEADBETER
09 Dir Inst Research/Effectiveness .... Ms. Luz CACEDA
15 Director of Human Resources .... Ms. Theresa ARNOVE
18 Director of Facility Management .... Mr. Martin KAJIC
21 Controller .... Ms. Barbara MORRIS
38 Director Counseling Center .... Ms. Amy PROVAN
19 Director of Public Safety .... Mr. Jeff MUNCHEL
40 Bookstore Manager .... Ms. Emily WARNER
41 Athletic Director .... Ms. Erin FOLEY
42 Director Campus Ministry & Service .... Sr. Mary KERBER
67 Dean School of Pharmacy .... Dr. Anne LIN
07 Director Pharmacy Admissions .... Mr. Larry SHATTUCK
25 Chief Contracts/Grants Admin .... Mr. Carroll GALVIN
26 Chief Public Relations/Marketing .... Mr. Christian KENDZIERSKI

Prince George's Community College (E)

301 Largo Road, Largo MD 20774-2199
County: Prince Georges FICE Identification: 002089
Unit ID: 163657
Telephone: (301) 546-7422 Carnegie Class: Assoc/HT-High Trad
FAX Number: N/A Calendar System: Semester
URL: www.pgcc.edu
Established: 1958 Annual Undergrad Tuition & Fees (In-District): $3,650
Enrollment: 13,228 Coed
Affiliation or Control: Local IRS Status: 501(c)3
Highest Offering: Associate Degree
Accreditation: M, ADNUR, CAHIIM, COARC, EMT, NMT, RAD

01 President .... Dr. Charlene M. DUKES
05 Vice Pres Academic Affairs .... Dr. Sandra F. DUNNINGTON
32 Interim Vice Pres Student Affairs .... Ms. Cathryn CAMP
10 Vice Pres Administrative Services ... Ms. Terri BACOTE-CHARLES
103 Assoc VP Workforce Devel/Cont Educ ..... Dr. Yvette J. SNOWDEN
72 Vice Pres Enterprise Technology ..... Dr. Rhonda SPELLS FENTRY
20 Sr Acad Admin to VP for Acad Affs .... Ms. Catherine LAPALOMBARA
38 Dean Student Success/ Engagement .... Dr. Scheherazade W. FORMAN
84 Dean of Student Enrollment .... Ms. Carol E. MCKINNON
09 Exec Dir Research/Assessment/Effect .... Vacant
15 Executive Director Human Resources .... Ms. Lark T. DOBSON
21 Exec Director Financial Affairs .... Ms. Sabrina WELLS
100 Chief of Staff .... Ms. Alonia C. SHARPS
08 Director Library .... Ms. Priscilla C. THOMPSON
06 Registrar .... Ms. Margaret K. OMWENGA
07 Director Recruitment .... Vacant
18 Exec Dir Facilities Planning/Mgmt .... Dr. David C. MOSBY
88 Director Physical Facilities .... Dr. Melodye BATTEN-MICKENS
86 Dir Government Affairs & Compliance .... Vacant
30 Exec Dir Institutional Advancement .... Ms. Brenda S. MITCHELL
26 Dir Communications & Marketing .... Ms. Annie CREWS
13 Chief Technology Officer .... Dr. Rhonda SPELLS-FENTRY
96 Interim Director of Procurement .... Mrs. LaTonya HOLLAND
37 Director Financial Aid .... Ms. Thelma L. ROSS
36 Manager Career & Job Services .... Ms. Stephanie S. PAIR-CUNNINGHAM
79 Dean Humanities/English/Social Sci .... Vacant
76 Dean Health Sci/Business/Public Svc .. Ms. Angela D. ANDERSON
81 Dean Science/Tech/Engr/Math .... Dr. Christine E. BARROW

St. John's College (F)

60 College Avenue, Annapolis MD 21401
County: Anne Arundel FICE Identification: 002092
Unit ID: 163976
Telephone: (410) 263-2371 Carnegie Class: Bac-A&S
FAX Number: (410) 626-2886 Calendar System: Semester
URL: www.sjc.edu
Established: 1784 Annual Undergrad Tuition & Fees: $50,353
Enrollment: 451 Coed
Affiliation or Control: Independent Non-Profit IRS Status: 501(c)3
Highest Offering: Master's
Accreditation: M

01 President .... Mr. Peter KANELOS
30 VP for Development and Alumni .... Ms. Laurie REINHARDT
05 Dean of College .... Mr. Joseph MACFARLAND
10 Treasurer/Financial Officer .... Vacant
06 Registrar .... Ms. Melissa STEINER
07 Director of Admissions .... Mr. Benjamin BAUM
102 Director Corporate/Foundation Rels .... Ms. Susan BORDEN
37 Director of Financial Aid .... Mr. Steven BELL
08 Library Director .... Ms. Catherine DIXON
15 Director of Human Resources .... Ms. Lynn HOBBS
18 Director of Buildings and Grounds .... Mr. Jim BRANHAM
19 Director of Public Safety .... Mr. Robert MUECK
23 Director of Student Health .... Ms. Nancy CALABRESE
26 Assoc Director of Communications .... Mr. Gregory SHOOK
32 Director of Student Services .... Ms. Taylor WATERS
20 Assistant to the Dean .... Ms. Heather LATHAM
36 Director of Career Services .... Ms. Jaime DUNN
40 Bookstore Manager .... Mr. Robin DUNN
41 Athletics &Recreation Coordinator .... Mr. Christopher KRUEGER
58 Assoc Dean for Graduate Program .... Ms. Emily LANGSTON
21 Controller .... Ms. Sarah MACDONALD
29 Director of Alumni Relations .... Vacant
04 Executive Asst to President .... Ms. Ashleigh CADMUS

† See Affiliate: St. John's College at Santa Fe, NM.

St. Mary's College of Maryland (G)

47645 College Drive, Saint Mary's City MD 20686-3001
County: Saint Mary's FICE Identification: 002095
Unit ID: 163912
Telephone: (240) 895-2000 Carnegie Class: Bac-A&S
FAX Number: (240) 895-4462 Calendar System: Semester
URL: www.smcm.edu
Established: 1840 Annual Undergrad Tuition & Fees (In-State): $14,192
Enrollment: 1,735 Coed
Affiliation or Control: State IRS Status: 501(c)3
Highest Offering: Master's
Accreditation: M

01 President .... Dr. Tuajuanda C. JORDAN

05 Provost/Dean of Faculty ... Dr. Michael R. WICK
10 VP Business & Finance ... Mr. Charles C. JACKSON
111 VP for Institutional Advancement ... Ms. Carolyn S. CURRY
84 Vice Pres Enrollment Management ... Mr. David L. HAUTANEN
21 Asst Vice President for Finance ... Mr. Christopher J. TRUE
11 Asst VP for Campus Operations ... Mr. Derek K. THORNTON
101 Exec Assoc to President ... Ms. Cynthia A. GROSS
26 Asst VP of Marketing/Communication . Mr. Michael L. BRUCKLER
29 Director Alumni Relations ... Mr. David M. SUSHINSKY
09 Assoc Dir Institutional Research ... Mr. Ross P. CONOVER
06 Registrar ... Mr. Nickolas B. TULLEY
20 Assoc Dean of Faculty ... Dr. Katherine L. GANTZ
37 Int Director of Financial Aid ... Mr. Ray A. CEO
07 Director of Admissions ... Ms. Kristina C. ANDERSON
32 VP for Student Affairs ... Mr. Leonard E. BROWN, JR.
38 Exec Dir of the Wellness Center ... Dr. Kyle K. BISHOP
41 Director of Athletics/Recreation ... Mr. Scott W. DEVINE
20 Int Assoc Dean of Curriculum ... Dr. Christine A. WOOLEY
20 Assoc Dean of Academic Services ... Dr. Donald R. STABILE
18 Assoc VP Planning & Facilities ... Ms. Annette V. ANGUEIRA
19 Director of Public Safety ... Ms. Tressa A. SETLAK
40 Director of the Campus Store ... Mr. Richard T. WAGNER
15 Director of Human Resources ... Ms. Shannon K. JARBOE
23 Director of Health Services ... Ms. Linda L. SKUTKA
35 Assoc Dean Retention/Stdnt Success ... Ms. Joanne A. GOLDWATER
13 Asst VP of Information Technology ... Mr. Christopher L. BURCH
44 Sr Devel Ofcr Annual Giving ... Mr. Richard J. EDGAR
08 Director of the Library/Media Svcs ... Ms. Katherine E. PITCHER
102 Director of Corporate and Found ... Ms. Lauren K. SAMPSON
21 Comptroller/Director of Accounting ... Mr. Gabriel A. MBOMEH
43 Assistant Attorney General ... Ms. Allison J. BOYLE
22 Affirm Act/Equal Opportunity Office .. Mr. Melvin A. MCCLINTOCK
25 Director of Sponsored Research ... Dr. Sabine DILLINGHAM
109 Procurement Ofcr/Dir of Auxiliary ... Mr. Patrick G. HUNT
71 Director DeSousa Brent Scholars Pgm ... Dr. Frederico J. TALLEY
88 Director Events and Conferences ... Ms. Linda T. JONES
44 Sr Devel Ofcr Major Gifts ... Ms. Karen C. RALEY
104 Director of International Education ... Ms. Katherine L. SUMNER
36 Dir of Career Development ... Ms. Kate A. SHIREY
04 Administrative Asst to President ... Ms. Vivian R. JORDAN
90 Learning Technologist ... Ms. April N. RYAN
91 Director Administrative Computing ... Mr. Partha P. CHANDA
39 Director of Residence Life ... Mr. Derek M. YOUNG
88 Dir of Title IX Compliance ... Mr. Michael K. DUNN
09 Director of Institutional Research ... Dr. Anne Marie BRADY
28 Assoc VP of Diversity and Inclusion ... Dr. Kortet G. MENSAH
105 Director Web Services ... Ms. Jeannette L. MODIC

Saint Mary's Seminary and University (A)

5400 Roland Avenue, Baltimore MD 21210-1994
County: Independent City | FICE Identification: 002096
Unit ID: 163842
Telephone: (410) 864-4000 | Carnegie Class: Not Classified
FAX Number: (410) 864-4278 | Calendar System: Semester
URL: www.stmarys.edu
Established: 1791 | Annual Undergrad Tuition & Fees: N/A
Enrollment: N/A | Coed
Affiliation or Control: Roman Catholic | IRS Status: 501(c)3
Highest Offering: First Professional Degree
Accreditation: M, THEOL

01 President/Rector ... Rev. Phillip J. BROWN
10 Vice President for Finance ... Mr. Richard G. CHILDS
30 Vice Pres Advancement/Human Res ... Mrs. Elizabeth L. VISCONAGE
05 Dean School Theology ... Rev. Thomas BURKE
73 Dean Ecumenical Institute Theology ... Dr. D. Brent LAYTHAM
73 Dean Ecclesiastical Faculty ... Rev. Thomas BURKE
06 University Registrar ... Ms. Paula M. THIGPEN
37 Director Financial Aid ... Mrs. Victoria F. GAUNT
08 Director of Knott Library ... Mr. Thomas RASZEWSKI
13 Director Information Services ... Mr. Arryn MILNE

The SANS Technology Institute (B)

8120 Woodmont Avenue, Suite 310, Bethesda MD 20814
County: Montgomery | Identification: 667006
Telephone: (301) 654-7267 | Carnegie Class: Not Classified
FAX Number: (301) 951-0140 | Calendar System: Other
URL: www.sans.edu
Established: 2006 | Annual Graduate Tuition & Fees: N/A
Enrollment: N/A | Coed
Affiliation or Control: Proprietary | IRS Status: Proprietary
Highest Offering: Master's; No Undergraduates
Accreditation: M

01 President ... Mr. Alan PALLER
03 Executive Director ... Mr. Eric PATTERSON
05 Provost ... Dr. Toby GOUKER

Stevenson University (C)

1525 Greenspring Valley Road, Stevenson MD 21153-0641
County: Baltimore | FICE Identification: 002107
Unit ID: 164173
Telephone: (410) 486-7000 | Carnegie Class: Masters/M
FAX Number: (410) 486-3552 | Calendar System: Semester
URL: www.stevenson.edu
Established: 1947 | Annual Undergrad Tuition & Fees: $33,168
Enrollment: 4,185 | Coed
Affiliation or Control: Independent Non-Profit | IRS Status: 501(c)3
Highest Offering: Master's
Accreditation: M, CAEPN, CSHSE, MT, NURSE

01 President ... Dr. Elliot HIRSHMAN
04 Assistant to President ... Ms. Ruth HUBBARD
05 Exec VP Academic Affairs/Provost ... Dr. Susan T. GORMAN
10 Exec Vice Pres/Chief Financial Ofcr .. Mr. Timothy M. CAMPBELL
30 Vice Pres University Advancement ... Mr. Steve CLOSE
84 Vice Pres Enrollment Management ... Mr. Mark J. HERGAN
32 Int Vice President Student Affairs ... Mr. Jeffrey M. KELLY
26 VP Marketing/Digital Communications ... Mr. John BUETTNER
15 Vice Pres for Human Resources ... Ms. Pamela BARKETT
100 Vice President & Chief of Staff ... Ms. Sue B. KENNEY
36 Vice Pres for Career Services ... Ms. Anne SCHOLL-FIEDLER
20 Asst VP for Academic Affairs ... Dr. Bridget H. BRENNAN
28 Asst VP Multicultural Experience ... Ms. Natalie GILLARD
58 Dean Graduate/Professional Studies ... Ms. Joyce K. BECKER
50 Interim Dean School of Business ... Mr. Aris MELISSARATOS
81 Dean School of Science ... Dr. Meredith DURMOWICZ
83 Dean Sch of Humanities/Social Sci ... Vacant
88 Dean School of Design ... Ms. Amanda HOSTALKA
53 Dean School of Education ... Dr. Deborah KRAFT
66 Dept Chair Nursing Education ... Ms. Ellen CLAYTON
23 Assoc Dean/Dir of Wellness Center ... Ms. Linda REYMANN
66 Associate Dean GPS Nursing ... Dr. Judith FEUSTLE
106 Associate Dean Distance Education ... Dr. Barbara ZIRKIN
18 Asst VP Facilities & Campus Svcs ... Mr. Leland R. BEITEL
21 Asst VP Financial Affs/Controller ... Ms. Melanie M. EDMONDSON
37 Asst VP Financial Aid ... Ms. Barbara L. MILLER
35 Assoc VP/Dean of Students ... Dr. Jeffrey M. KELLY
13 Assoc VP Information Technology/CIO ... Mr. Tom ALLEN
09 Director Institutional Research ... Dr. Bonnie THOMAS
108 Director for Assessment ... Dr. Natasha MILLER
08 Director of Library Services ... Ms. Susan H. BONSTEEL
06 Registrar ... Ms. Tracy L. BOLT
19 Director of Safety & Security ... Mr. Timothy OSTENDARP
41 Director Athletics ... Mr. Brett C. ADAMS
109 Director Auxiliary Services ... Mr. Robert REED
29 Director Alumni Relations ... Mr. Jamie M. MYERS
88 Dir of Disability Services ... Ms. Abigail S. HURSON

Stratford University Baltimore Campus (D)

210 S. Central Avenue, Baltimore MD 21202
Telephone: (410) 752-4710 | Identification: 770616
Accreditation: ACICS, ACFEI

† Branch campus of Stratford University, Falls Church, VA

University of Phoenix Maryland Campus (E)

8830 Stanford Boulevard, Suite 100, Columbia MD 21045-5423
Telephone: (410) 872-9001 | Identification: 770210
Accreditation: &NH, ACBSP

† No longer accepting campus-based students.

*The University System of Maryland Office (F)

3300 Metzerott Road, Adelphi MD 20783
County: Prince George's | FICE Identification: 007959
Unit ID: 164146
Telephone: (301) 445-2740 | Carnegie Class: N/A
FAX Number: N/A
URL: www.usmd.edu

01 Chancellor ... Dr. Robert L. CARET
05 Sr VC Academic Affairs ... Dr. Joann BOUGHMAN
10 COO/Vice Chanc Admin & Finance ... Mr. Joseph F. VIVONA
111 VC Advancement & CEO USM Foundation ... Mr. Leonard R. RALEY
86 VC Governmental Relations ... Mr. Patrick N. HOGAN
26 VC for Communications ... Mr. Jeff NEAL
100 USM Chief of Staff ... Ms. Janice B. DOYLE
20 Assoc Vice Chanc Academic Affairs ... Ms. Teri HOLLANDER
13 Assoc VC & CIO ... Mr. Donald Z. SPICER
116 Director Internal Audit ... Mr. David MOSCA
114 Director Budget Analysis ... Ms. Monica WEST

*University of Maryland College Park (G)

1101 Main Administration Building, College Park MD 20742
County: Prince Georges | FICE Identification: 002103
Unit ID: 163286
Telephone: (301) 405-1000 | Carnegie Class: DU-Highest
FAX Number: (301) 314-9560 | Calendar System: Semester
URL: www.umd.edu
Established: 1856 | Annual Undergrad Tuition & Fees (In-State): $10,181
Enrollment: 38,140 | Coed
Affiliation or Control: State | IRS Status: 501(c)3
Highest Offering: Doctorate
Accreditation: M, AUD, CAEPN, CEA, CLPSY, COPSY, DANCE, DIETD, DIETI, ENG, IACBE, IPSY, JOUR, LIB, LSAR, MFCD, MUS, PCSAS, PH, PLNG, SCPSY, SP, SPAA

02 President ... Dr. Wallace D. LOH
05 Senior Vice President & Provost ... Dr. Mary Ann RANKIN
100 Asst President & Chief of Staff ... Ms. Michele A. EASTMAN
10 Vice President for Admin & Finance ... Mr. Carlo COLELLA
32 Vice President for Student Affairs ... Dr. Linda M. CLEMENT
111 Vice President University Relations ... Ms. Jacqueline A. LEWIS
46 Vice President for Research ... Dr. Laurie LOCASCIO
13 Interim Chief Information Officer ... Dr. Jeffrey K. HOLLINGSWORTH
43 Vice President and General Counsel ... Mr. Michael R. POTERALA
47 Dean Col Agriculture/Natl Resources ... Dr. Craig BEYROUTY
48 Dean Sch Architecture/Plng/Preserv ... Dr. Sonia HIRT
79 Dean College Arts & Humanities ... Dr. Bonnie T. DILL
83 Dean Col Behavioral/Social Sciences ... Dr. Gregory F. BALL
50 Dean Smith School of Business ... Dr. Alexander J. TRIANTIS
81 Interim Dean Col Comp/Math/Nat Sci .. Dr. Gerald S. WILKINSON
53 Dean College of Education ... Dr. Jennifer K. RICE
54 Dean Clark School of Engineering ... Dr. Darryll J. PINES
69 Dean School of Public Health ... Dr. Boris D. LUSHNIAK
60 Dean Merrill College of Journalism ... Ms. Lucy A. DALGLISH
62 Dean College of Information Studies ... Dr. Keith MARZULLO
80 Dean School of Public Policy ... Dr. Robert C. ORR
20 Dean Undergraduate Studies ... Dr. William A. COHEN
58 Dean Graduate School ... Dr. Juan URIAGEREKA
08 Interim Dean Libraries ... Dr. Babak HAMIDZADEH
28 Assoc VP & Chief Diversity Officer ... Dr. Roger WORTHINGTON
104 Assoc VP International Affairs ... Dr. Ross D. LEWIN
108 Assoc Provost Acad Planning & Pgms ... Dr. Elizabeth J. BEISE
84 Assoc VP Enrollment Management ... Ms. Barbara A. GILL
56 Assoc VP Extended Studies ... Mr. Chuck A. WILSON
20 Assoc Provost Faculty Affairs ... Dr. John BERTOT
106 Assoc Provost Learning Initiatives ... Dr. Ben BEDERSON
20 Assoc VP Innovation & Entrepreneur ... Dr. Dean CHANG
20 Assoc VP Acad Aff Finance Personnel ... Ms. Cynthia R. HALE
20 Assoc Provost Academic Affairs ... Dr. Steve FETTER
09 Asst VP Inst Research & Planning ... Ms. Sharon A. LA VOY
21 Assoc VP & Chief Financial Officer ... Mr. Paul S. DWORKIS
18 Assoc VP & Chief Facilities Officer ... Mr. Charles R. REUNING
96 Asst VP Procurement Str Sourcing ... Mr. James P. HALEY, SR.
15 Asst VP University Human Resources ... Ms. Jewel WASHINGTON
88 Asst VP Real Estate ... Mr. Edward MAGINNIS, JR.
19 Dir Pub Safety/Chief Campus Police ... Mr. David B. MITCHELL
117 Exec Dir Env Safety/Sustain/Risk ... Ms. Maureen KOTLAS
35 Asst VP Student Affairs ... Dr. John ZACKER
35 Asst VP Student Affairs ... Dr. Mary HUMMEL
35 Asst VP Student Affairs ... Dr. Warren KELLEY
26 Assoc VP Communications & Marketing ... Dr. Joel SELIGMAN
30 Assoc VP University Development ... Ms. Mary BURKE
102 Assoc VP Found/Corporate Relations ... Mr. Brian P. DARMODY
110 Asst VP Univ Rel Administration ... Mr. Michael KING
112 Interim Asst VP Univ Relations ... Ms. Veronica MEINHARD
29 Exec Director Alumni Association ... Ms. Amy EICHHORST
88 Assoc VP Research Administration ... Ms. Denise CLARK
88 Assc VP Innovation Econ Development ... Ms. Julie LENZER
88 Asst VP Research Development ... Mr. Eric CHAPMAN
07 Director Undergraduate Admissions ... Ms. Shannon GUNDY
37 Director Financial Aid ... Ms. Monique BOYD
85 Dir Intl Student & Scholar Services ... Ms. Susan-Ellis DOUGHERTY
64 Director School of Music ... Dr. Jason GEARY
92 Executive Director Honors College ... Dr. Susan J. DWYER
06 University Registrar ... Dr. Adrian R. CORNELIUS
113 Bursar/Assoc Comptroller ... Ms. Alisa ABADINSKY
36 Director University Career Center ... Mr. Kelley BISHOP
39 Director Resident Life ... Dr. Deborah F. GRANDNER
109 Director Stamp Student Union ... Dr. Marsha A. GUENZLER-STEVENS
23 Director University Health Center ... Dr. David MCBRIDE
38 Director Counseling Center ... Dr. Sharon E. KIRKLAND-GORDON
31 Asst Director Community Service ... Dr. Craig SLACK
41 Director Athletics ... Mr. Kevin ANDERSON
86 Exec Director Government Relations ... Mr. Ross STERN
90 Asst VP Academic Tech & Innovation ... Dr. Marcio A. OLIVEIRA

*University of Maryland, Baltimore (H)

620 W. Lexington Street, Baltimore MD 21201-1508
County: Independent City | FICE Identification: 002104
Unit ID: 163259
Telephone: (410) 706-7004 | Carnegie Class: Spec-4-yr-Med
FAX Number: (410) 706-0500 | Calendar System: Semester
URL: www.umaryland.edu
Established: 1807 | Annual Undergrad Tuition & Fees (In-State): N/A
Enrollment: 6,329 | Coed
Affiliation or Control: State | IRS Status: 501(c)3
Highest Offering: Doctorate
Accreditation: M, ANEST, DENT, DH, DIETI, IPSY, LAW, MED, MT, NURSE, PA, PH, PHAR, PTA, RADDOS, SW

02 President ... Dr. Jay A. PERMAN
05 Sr VP/Chief Acad & Research Officer ... Dr. Bruce E. JARRELL
11 VP Operations & Planning/Vice Dean ... Dr. Roger J. WARD
17 Vice President Medical Affairs/Dean ... Dr. E. Albert REECE
10 Chief Admin & Finance Officer/VP ... Ms. Dawn M. RHODES
25 VP/Chf Enterprise & Econ Dev Ofc ... Mr. James L. HUGHES
13 VP/Chief Information Officer ... Dr. Peter J. MURRAY
46 Sr VP/Chief Acad & Research Officer ... Dr. Bruce E. JARRELL
26 Chief Communications Officer/VP ... Ms. Jennifer B. LITCHMAN
30 Chief Development Officer/VP ... Mr. Thomas J. SULLIVAN
86 Chief Govt Affairs Officer/AVP ... Mr. Kevin P. KELLY
43 Chief University Counsel ... Ms. Susan GILLETTE
19 Chief of Police/AVP Public Safety ... Vacant
88 Chief Accountability Officer ... Dr. Roger J. WARD
32 Sr Assoc Dean/AVP Acad & Stdnt Affs ... Dr. Flavius R. LILLY

18 Assoc VP Facilities & Operations ... Vacant
15 Assoc VP Human Resources ... Mr. Matthew LASECKI
37 Assoc VP Student Financial Asst ... Ms. Patricia A. SCOTT
110 Assoc VP Development ... Mr. Thomas HOFSTETTER
113 Assoc VP Budget & Finance ... Mr. Scott BITNER
27 Assoc VP Communications & Pub Aff ... Ms. Laura A. KOZAK
88 Deputy Chief Accountability Ofc AVP ... Ms. Susan BUSKIRK
14 Asst VP Information Technology ... Mr. Christopher G. PHILLIPS
09 Asst VP Inst Rsrch & Accountability .. Mr. Gregory C. SPENGLER
96 AVP Strategic Sourcing & Acquis ... Mr. Joseph EVANS
45 AVP Real Estate Planning Space Mgt ... Ms. Angela FOWLER-YOUNG
88 AVP Sponsored Projects Accounting ... Ms. Lynn M. MCGINLEY
88 AVP ORD Marketing & Operations ... Ms. Linda KENDERDINE
88 AVP ORD Sponsored Programs Admin ... Mr. Dennis PAFFRATH
88 AVP ORD Technology Transfer ... Mr. Philip ROBILOTTO
88 AVP ORD Center for Clinical Trials ... Mr. Michael ROLLOR
88 AVP ORD Economic Development ... Ms. Jane SHAAB
102 Treasurer & Dir of Operations UMBF ... Ms. Pamela HECKLER
08 Exec Dir Health Sci/Human Svc Libr ... Ms. Mary J. TOOEY
90 Exec Dir Enterprise Applications ... Mr. Michael SMITH
31 Exec Dir Cmty Initiatives/Engage ... Ms. Ashley R. VALIS
06 Director Records & Registration ... Mr. Ryan HOLTZ
88 Director Benefits & Compensation ... Ms. Patricia HOFFMAN
22 Director EEO/Affirmative Action ... Ms. Sheila GREENWOOD-BLACKSHEAR
28 Dir Diversity and Inclusion ... Ms. Mikhel A. KUSHNER
85 Director International Services ... Ms. Amy RAMIREZ
38 Director Counseling ... Ms. Emilia K. PETRILLO
41 Director Univ Recreation & Fitness ... Mr. William P. CROCKETT
23 Director Student Health Center ... Dr. James BARONAS
35 Director Student Services ... Ms. Cynthia E. RICE
39 Director of UM Housing ... Ms. Margaret SCHOTTO
88 Director of Financial Services ... Ms. Susan E. MCKECHNIE
106 Dir Online Education/E-learning ... Dr. Flavius R. LILLY
105 Dir Web Dev Interactive Media ... Mr. Amir CHAMSAZ
52 Dean School of Dentistry ... Dr. Mark A. REYNOLDS
58 Dean Graduate School ... Dr. Bruce E. JARRELL
61 Dean School of Law ... Mr. Donald TOBIN
63 Dean School of Medicine ... Dr. E. Albert REECE
66 Dean School of Nursing ... Dr. Jane M. KIRSCHLING
67 Dean School of Pharmacy ... Dr. Natalie D. EDDINGTON
70 Dean School of Social Work ... Dr. Richard P. BARTH

*University of Maryland Baltimore County (A)

1000 Hilltop Circle, Baltimore MD 21250-0001
County: Baltimore — FICE Identification: 002105
Unit ID: 163268
Telephone: (410) 455-1000 — Carnegie Class: DU-Higher
FAX Number: (410) 455-1210 — Calendar System: 4/1/4
URL: www.umbc.edu
Established: 1966 — Annual Undergrad Tuition & Fees (In-State): $11,264
Enrollment: 13,839 — Coed
Affiliation or Control: State — IRS Status: 501(c)3
Highest Offering: Doctorate
Accreditation: M, CAEPN, CLPSY, CS, DANCE, DMS, EMT, ENG, IPSY, MUS, SW

02 President ... Dr. Freeman A. HRABOWSKI
05 Provost/Sr Vice Pres Acad Affs ... Dr. Philip ROUS
10 Vice Pres Finance/Administration ... Ms. Lynne SCHAEFER
32 Vice President Student Affairs ... Dr. Nancy YOUNG
111 Vice Pres Institutional Advancement ... Mr. Gregory SIMMONS
13 Vice Pres Information Technology ... Mr. Jack J. SUESS
46 Vice President of Research ... Dr. Karl V. STEINER
49 Dean Col of Arts/Humanities/Soc Sci ... Dr. Scott CASPER
81 Dean Col Natural/Math Sciences ... Dr. William LACOURSE
54 Dean College of Engr/Info Tech ... Dr. Julia ROSS
84 Asst Dean Graduate Enrollment Mgmt ... Ms. K. Jill BARR
20 Vice Provost/Dean Undergrad Educ ... Dr. Diane M. LEE
107 Int Vice Provost for Prof Studies ... Dr. Christopher STEELE
20 Vice Provost Academic Affairs ... Dr. Antonio R. MOREIRA
58 Dean/Vice Provost for Graduate Educ ... Dr. Janet RUTLEDGE
15 Vice Provost Faculty Affairs ... Dr. Patrice MCDERMOTT
84 Vice Provost Enrollment Mgmt ... Dr. Yvette MOZIE-ROSS
21 Assoc VP Financial Services ... Mr. Benjamin LOWENTHAL
26 Assistant to Pres/Assoc VP Mktg/PR ... Ms. Lisa G. AKCHIN
11 Assoc VP Administrative Services ... Ms. Terry COOK
16 Associate VP for Human Resources ... Ms. Valerie A. THOMAS
29 Director Alumni Relations ... Ms. Stanyell BRUCE
88 Asst VP New Media/Instruction Tech ... Mr. John FRITZ
18 Asst VP Facilities Management ... Mr. Lenn CARON
04 Senior Advisor to the President ... Dr. Peter HENDERSON
96 Director of Procurement ... Vacant
92 Director Honors College ... Dr. Simon STACEY
41 Director Physical Educ & Recreation ... Dr. Tim HALL
19 Director University Police ... Mr. Mark SPARKS
36 Asst VP Career & Corp Partnership ... Ms. Caroline BAKER
23 Int Director Health Services ... Dr. Bruce HERMAN
37 Director Financial Aid ... Ms. Jane HICKEY
25 Asst Director Sponsored Programs ... Mr. Stanley JACKSON
40 Director of UMBC Bookstore ... Mr. Robert J. SOMERS
85 Assoc Vice Prov International Educ ... Dr. David DIMARIA
08 Director Library ... Mr. Patrick DAWSON
06 Registrar ... Ms. Pamela HAWLEY
35 Int Director Student Life ... Ms. Jennifer DRESS
43 General Counsel ... Mr. David GLEASON
07 Assistant Vice Provost ... Mr. Dale BITTINGER
39 Director Residential Life ... Mr. John FOX
09 Director of Institutional Research ... Dr. Connie PIERSON
38 Director Student Counseling ... Dr. Bruce HERMAN
100 Chief of Staff President's Office ... Ms. Elyse ASHBURN

*University of Maryland Center for Environmental Science (B)

PO Box 775, Cambridge MD 21613
County: Dorchester — Identification: 667159
Telephone: (410) 228-9250 — Carnegie Class: Not Classified
FAX Number: (410) 228-3843 — Calendar System: Semester
URL: www.umces.edu
Established: 1925 — Annual Graduate Tuition & Fees: N/A
Enrollment: N/A — Coed
Affiliation or Control: State — IRS Status: 501(c)3
Highest Offering: Doctorate; No Undergraduates
Accreditation: M

02 President ... Dr. Peter GOODWIN
05 Vice Pres for Education ... Dr. Larry SANFORD
10 Vice President for Finance ... Ms. Lynn REHN

*University of Maryland Eastern Shore (C)

11868 Academic Oval, Princess Anne MD 21853-1299
County: Somerset — FICE Identification: 002106
Unit ID: 163338
Telephone: (410) 651-2200 — Carnegie Class: DU-Mod
FAX Number: (410) 651-6105 — Calendar System: Semester
URL: www.umes.edu
Established: 1886 — Annual Undergrad Tuition & Fees (In-State): $7,804
Enrollment: 4,465 — Coed
Affiliation or Control: State — IRS Status: 501(c)3
Highest Offering: Doctorate
Accreditation: M, CACREP, CAEPN, CONST, DIETD, DIETI, ENG, PHAR, PTA

02 President ... Dr. Juliette B. BELL
03 Executive Vice President ... Ms. Kimberly C. DUMPSON
05 Acting Provost/VP Academic Affairs ... Dr. Kimberly WHITEHEAD
10 Vice Pres Administrative Affs/CFO ... Mr. Kevin APPLETON
32 Int Vice President Student Affairs ... Dr. J. Michael HARPE
13 Chief Information Officer ... Vacant
20 Int Vice Provost Academic Affairs ... Dr. Latosha WADE
88 Asst to VP Administrative Affairs ... Dr. Maurice C. NGWABA
21 Asst VP Admin Affs/Budget Director ... Ms. Michelle MARTIN
15 Asst VP Human Resources ... Ms. Marie H. BILLIE
35 Assoc VP Student Affairs ... Dr. James M. WHITE
91 Director Administrative Computing ... Mr. Kenneth GASTON
56 Int Assoc Extension Administrator ... Dr. Enrique N. ESCOBAR
29 Director Alumni Affairs ... Mr. James G. LUNNERMON, II
08 Dean Library Services ... Ms. Adrienne WEBBER
37 Director Financial Aid ... Mr. Alvin J. DORSETT
23 Director Student Health Services ... Ms. Sharone V. GRANT
96 Director Procurement ... Ms. Jacqueline M. COLLINS
07 Actg Dir Admiss & Recruitment ... Ms. Jinawa A. MCNEIL
06 Registrar ... Ms. Cheryl HOLDEN-DUFFY
12 Gen Mgr Richard A Henson Center ... Ms. Kimberly A. MILLS
36 Director Career Services ... Dr. Theresa QUEENAN
09 Director Inst Research/Plng/Assess ... Dr. Stanley M. NYIRENDA
19 Interim Director Public Safety ... Mr. Mark TYLER
18 Director Physical Plant ... Mr. Kenny B. BELTON
39 Director Residence Life ... Mr. Marvin L. JONES
41 Athletic Director ... Mr. Keith S. DAVIDSON
21 Comptroller ... Ms. Bonita E. BYRD
46 Director Sponsored Research ... Ms. Catherine BOLEK
88 Director Student Retention & Svcs ... Dr. Angela L. WILLIAMS
88 Director Upward Bound ... Dr. Nicole L. GALE
35 Director Student Activities ... Ms. Qiana J. DRUMMOND
88 Director Title III Program ... Dr. Frances H. MCKINNEY
26 Director Public Relations ... Mr. William ROBINSON
44 Director Development ... Dr. Veronique L. DIRIKER
88 Director Advancement Services ... Ms. Chenita R. REDDICK
51 Coordinator Continuing Education ... Ms. Gretchen M. BOGGS
38 Coordinator Counseling Services ... Dr. Patricia E. TILGHMAN
58 Interim Dean Graduate Studies ... Dr. Lakeisha L. HARRIS
47 Dean School Agric/Natural Sciences ... Dr. Moses T. KAIRO
49 Int Dean School Art/Professions ... Mr. Christopher HARRINGTON
50 Dean School Business & Technology ... Dr. Ayodele J. ALADE
67 Int Dean Sch Pharmacy/Health Prof ... Dr. Rondall E. ALLEN

*University of Maryland University College (D)

3501 University Boulevard East, Adelphi MD 20783-7998
County: Prince Georges — FICE Identification: 011644
Unit ID: 163204
Telephone: (301) 985-7000 — Carnegie Class: Masters/L
FAX Number: (301) 985-7678 — Calendar System: Semester
URL: www.umuc.edu
Established: 1947 — Annual Undergrad Tuition & Fees (In-State): $7,176
Enrollment: 50,248 — Coed
Affiliation or Control: State — IRS Status: 501(c)3
Highest Offering: Doctorate
Accreditation: M, CAEPN, CAHIIM, NURSE

02 President ... Mr. Javier MIYARES
11 SVP/Chief Business Officer ... Mr. George SHOENBERGER
10 Vice Pres Chief Financial Officer ... Mr. Eugene D. LOCKETT, JR.
05 Interim Provost ... Ms. Blakely POMIETTO
26 Sr Vice President Communications ... Mr. Michael FREEDMAN
45 Sr VP Institutional Effectiveness ... Vacant
88 Sr VP Global Military Operations ... Mr. Lloyd MILES
13 Sr Vice Pres Analytics/Plng/Tech ... Mr. Peter C. YOUNG
43 Vice President & General Counsel ... Ms. Maureen DAVID
15 VP/Chief Human Resources Officer ... Mr. John PETROV
86 Vice Pres Federal Govt Relations ... Vacant
111 Vice Pres Inst Advancement ... Ms. Cathy SWEET
28 Ombudsman/VP Diversity Programs ... Dr. Blair HAYES
18 Associate Vice President Facilities ... Mr. George TRUJILLO
86 Director of State Govt Relations ... Ms. Erin FAVAZZA
37 AVP Student Financial Aid ... Ms. Cheryl STORIE
58 Acting Dean The Graduate School ... Ms. Kathryn KLOSE
08 Assoc Provost of Library Services ... Mr. Stephen MILLER
06 Assoc Vice Provost/Registrar ... Ms. Joellen SHENDY
49 Dean The Undergrad School ... Dr. Matthew PRINEAS
09 Sr Director Institutional Research ... Wei ZHOU
07 Director of Admissions ... Vacant
84 Sr VP Strategic Enrollment Mgmt ... Ms. Erika ORRIS
100 Chief of Staff ... Mr. Frank PRINCIPE

*Bowie State University (E)

14000 Jericho Park Road, Bowie MD 20715-3318
County: Prince Georges — FICE Identification: 002062
Unit ID: 162007
Telephone: (301) 860-4000 — Carnegie Class: Masters/L
FAX Number: (301) 860-3510 — Calendar System: Semester
URL: www.bowiestate.edu
Established: 1865 — Annual Undergrad Tuition & Fees (In-State): $7,880
Enrollment: 5,430 — Coed
Affiliation or Control: State — IRS Status: 501(c)3
Highest Offering: Doctorate
Accreditation: M, ACBSP, CACREP, CAEPN, CS, NUR, SPAA, SW

02 President ... Dr. Aminta BREAUX
05 Provost/Vice Pres Academic Affs ... Dr. Weldon JACKSON
10 Vice Pres Finance & Administration ... Dr. Karl B. BROCKENBROUGH
111 Vice Pres Institutional Advancement ... Dr. Richard LUCAS, JR.
32 VP Student Affairs/Campus Life ... Dr. Artie L. TRAVIS
43 Vice Pres & General Counsel ... Ms. Karen JOHNSON SHAHEED
35 Int Coord Student Code of Conduct ... Mrs. Anne VALENTINE
13 VP Office of Information Technology ... Mr. E. Wayne ROSE
84 Asst VP Enrollment Management ... Mr. Troy MILLER
88 Asst to Prov Institutional Effec ... Ms. Gayle M. FINK
06 University Registrar ... Ms. Patricia MITCHELL
08 Assoc Library Dir/Interim Dean ... Ms. Marian RUCKER-SHAMU
36 Director Career Services ... Ms. April JOHNOSON
15 Sr Director of Human Resources ... Ms. Sheila HOBSON
19 Chief of Campus Police ... Mr. Ernest WAITERS
58 Int Dean Sch of Grad Stds/Research ... Dr. Cosmos NWOKEAFOR
49 Dean College of Arts & Sciences ... Dr. George ACQUAAH
50 Dean College of Business ... Dr. Anthony NELSON
53 Interim Dean College of Education .. Dr. Rhonda JETER-TWILLEY
107 Int Dean College of Profess Studies ... Dr. Elliott PARRIS
92 Director UCE Honors Program ... Dr. Monika GROSS
23 Director University Wellness Center ... Dr. Rita WUTOH
41 Director Athletics ... Mr. Clyde DOUGHTY, JR.
26 Dir University Relations/ Marketing ... Ms. Cassandra M. ROBINSON
88 Director University Wiseman Centre ... Mr. Frank WALLER
37 Director Financial Aid ... Ms. Deborah STANLEY
18 Director Facilities ... Mr. Darryl WILLIFORD
07 Director Undergraduate Admissions ... Mr. Derrick DAVIS
29 Director of Alumni Relations ... Ms. Anette WEDDERBURN
96 Director of Purchasing ... Mr. Steve A. JOST
09 Director of Institutional Research ... Ms. Shama AKHTAR
04 Administrative Asst to President ... Ms. Denise WARD
108 Director Institutional Assessment ... Dr. Becky VERZINSKI
38 Director Student Counseling ... Dr. Tonya SWANSON
39 Interim Director Student Housing ... Mr. Rodney PETERS

*Coppin State University (F)

2500 W North Avenue, Baltimore MD 21216-3698
County: Baltimore City — FICE Identification: 002068
Unit ID: 162283
Telephone: (410) 951-3000 — Carnegie Class: Masters/S
FAX Number: (410) 333-5369 — Calendar System: Semester
URL: www.coppin.edu
Established: 1900 — Annual Undergrad Tuition & Fees (In-State): $7,438
Enrollment: 3,108 — Coed
Affiliation or Control: State — IRS Status: 501(c)3
Highest Offering: Doctorate
Accreditation: M, ACBSP, CACREP, CAEPN, CAHIIM, NURSE, SW

02 President ... Dr. Maria THOMPSON
05 Int Provost/VP Academic Affairs ... Dr. Keith WILLIAMSON
111 VP Institutional Advancement ... Mr. Douglas DALZELL
10 VP Administration & Finance ... Mr. Steve DANIK
32 Vice Pres Stdnt Affairs/Enroll Mgmt ... Dr. Michael FREEMAN
13 VP Information Systems/CIO ... Dr. Ahmed EL-HAGGAN
84 Assoc VP Enrollment Management ... Vacant
45 Assoc VP Planning/Assessment ... Mr. Michael BOWDEN
20 Assoc Vice Pres Academic Affs ... Vacant
18 Assoc VP Capital Plng/Constr & Cont ... Vacant
86 Assoc VP of Pub Policy & Govt Rel ... Vacant
15 Asst VP of Human Resources ... Dr. Lisa EARLY
07 Director of Admissions ... Mr. Sha-Ron E. JONES
06 Registrar ... Ms. Karen BARLAND
21 Controller ... Mrs. Crystal MOSLEY
08 Director of the Library ... Dr. Mary WANZA
37 Director of Financial Aid ... Dr. Marcus BYRD
36 Director of Career Services Center ... Mrs. Linda BOWIE
19 Chief of Public Safety ... Mr. Leonard HAMM
39 Director of Housing/Residence Life ... Ms. Jacquelyn WONSEY

41 Director of Athletics .... Mr. Derek CARTER
112 Director Major Gifts/Planned Giving .... Ms. Esperance SUTTON
96 Asst Vice President .... Mr. Thomas E. DAWSON, JR.
26 Director of University Relations .... Vacant
88 Director Client Computing Services .... Mr. Emmanuel OWUSU-SEKYERE
35 Director of Student Activities .... Vacant
14 Deputy Info Technology Officer .... Mr. Claude K. RADER
105 Senior Web Developer .... Ms. Melissa C. RIGBY
92 Dean Honors College & McNair Pgms .... Mr. Ronnie L. COLLINS, SR.
58 Dean Graduate School .... Dr. Mary E. OWENS-SOUTHHALL
66 Dean of Nursing .... Dr. Tracey L. MURRAY
04 Executive Assistant to President .... Mrs. Sherie JOHNSON
88 Chair Interdisciplinary Studies .... Vacant
97 Chair General & Adult Education .... Dr. Jacqueline H. WILLIAMS
88 Chair Applied Psych/Rehab Counsel .... Dr. Michelle POINTER
61 Chair Crim Justice/Law Enforcement .... Dr. Elgin KLUGH
53 Chair Curriculum & Instruction .... Dr. Glynis BARBER
57 Chair Fine Arts .... Dr. Garey HYATT
82 Chair History Geography/Global Stds .... Dr. Katherine BANKOLE-MEDINA
79 Interim Chair Humanities .... Dr. Douglas REARDON
50 Chr Col of Business Mgmt/Mktg .... Dr. Victoria MILLER
50 Chr Col of Bus/Sports/Ent Mgmt .... Dr. Surjeet BAIDWAN
50 Chr College Of Bus Acct/Info Syst .... Dr. Emmanuel ANOURO
77 Chair Math & Computer Science .... Dr. Nicholas EUGENE
65 Chair Natural Sciences .... Dr. Mintesinot JIRU
83 Chair Social Sciences .... Dr. Elgin KLUGH
70 Chair Social Work .... Dr. Kesslyn BRADE-STENNIS
68 Chair Health/Physical Education .... Vacant
88 Chair Teaching and Learning .... Dr. Daniel P. JOSEPH
09 Director of Institutional Research .... Mr. Beryl HARRIS
29 Director Alumni Relations .... Ms. Marcia CEPHAS
38 Director Student Counseling .... Ms. Michelle REYNOLDS

*Frostburg State University (A)

101 Braddock Road, Frostburg MD 21532-2303
County: Allegany — FICE Identification: 002072
Unit ID: 162584
Telephone: (301) 687-4000 — Carnegie Class: Masters/L
FAX Number: (301) 687-4737 — Calendar System: Semester
URL: www.frostburg.edu
Established: 1898 — Annual Undergrad Tuition & Fees (In-State): $8,702
Enrollment: 5,756 — Coed
Affiliation or Control: State — IRS Status: 501(c)3
Highest Offering: Doctorate
Accreditation: M, CAATE, CAEPN, ENG, EXSC, NRPA, NURSE, SW

02 President .... Dr. Ronald NOWACZYK
05 Provost & VP Academic Affairs .... Dr. Liz THROP
32 VP Student/Education Svcs .... Dr. Thomas BOWLING
10 Vice President for Admin & Finance .... Mr. David C. ROSE
111 Vice Pres Univ Advancement .... Mr. John SHORT
84 Assoc VP for Enrollment Management .... Mr. Wray BLAIR
15 Vice President Human Resources .... Ms. Katherine SNYDER
43 University Counsel .... Mr. Brad NIXON
20 Vice Provost .... Dr. John BOWMAN
20 Interim Asst Provost .... Dr. Doris SANTAMARIA-MAKANG
21 Assoc VP Finance & Controller .... Mr. Richard A. REPAC
35 Asst VP Student Affairs .... Dr. Jeff GRAHAM
30 Associate VP Univ Advancement .... Ms. Colleen STUMP
45 Assoc Director Budget & Planning .... Ms. Denise MURPHY
49 Dean Col Liberal Arts & Science .... Dr. Joseph M. HOFFMAN
50 Int Dean College of Business .... Dr. Sudhir SINGH
53 Interim Dean College of Education .... Dr. Boyce WILLIAMS
08 Director of the Library .... Ms. Lea MESSMAN-MANDICOTT
37 Director of Financial Aid .... Mrs. Angela L. HOVATTER
108 Director of PAIR .... Ms. SaraBeth BITTINGER
25 Dir of Research/Sponsored Programs .... Mr. Aaron HOEL
58 Director of Graduate Services .... Ms. Vickie MAZER
18 Director Facilities/Physical Plant .... Mr. Robert BOYCE
26 Director News & Media Services .... Ms. Elizabeth MEDCALF
36 Director Career Services .... Dr. Robbie L. CORDLE
38 Director Counseling & Psyc Svcs .... Vacant
40 Asst Mgr Bookstore & ID Services .... Mr. Kenneth EMERICK
41 Athletic Director .... Mr. Troy DELL
19 Chief University Police .... Col. Cynthia SMITH
13 Chief Information Officer .... Mr. Troy DONOWAY
91 Director of Technology Services .... Ms. Beth KENNEY
29 Director of Alumni .... Ms. Shannon L. GRIBBLE
22 Director of AA/EEO .... Mrs. Beth HOFFMAN
07 Director of Admissions .... Ms. Trisha GREGORY
28 Director of Diversity .... Ms. Robin WYNDER
44 Major Gifts Officer .... Mr. Jason ANDRICK
14 Dir Networking/Telecommunications .... Vacant
96 Coord Procurement/Material Handling .... Mr. Alan R. SNYDER
23 Director Health Services .... Ms. Darlene SMITH
39 Director Residence Life .... Mr. Dana A. SEVERANCE
06 Registrar .... Dr. Jay HEGEMAN
90 Director Academic Computing .... Ms. Beth KENNEY

*Salisbury University (B)

1101 Camden Avenue, Salisbury MD 21801-6860
County: Wicomico — FICE Identification: 002091
Unit ID: 163851
Telephone: (410) 543-6000 — Carnegie Class: Masters/L
FAX Number: (410) 548-2587 — Calendar System: Semester
URL: www.salisbury.edu
Established: 1925 — Annual Undergrad Tuition & Fees (In-State): $9,364
Enrollment: 8,671 — Coed
Affiliation or Control: State — IRS Status: 501(c)3
Highest Offering: Doctorate
Accreditation: M, CAATE, CAEPN, COARC, EXSC, MT, MUS, NURSE, SW

02 President .... Dr. Janet E. DUDLEY-ESHBACH
05 Int Provost & Sr VP of Acad Affairs .... Dr. Karen L. OLMSTEAD
100 Chief of Staff .... Ms. Amy S. HASSON
10 Interim VP Admin and Finance .... Mr. Marvin L. PYLES
32 Vice Pres of Student Affairs .... Dr. Dane R. FOUST
111 Vice Pres Advancement/External Affs .... Mr. Jason E. CURTIN
84 Asst VP of Enrollment Management .... Mr. Aaron M. BASKO
28 Chief Diversity Officer .... Mr. Humberto X. ARISTIZABAL
35 Associate VP of Student Affairs .... Vacant
20 Associate Provost .... Dr. Richard T. WILKENS
20 Assoc Vice Pres Academic Affairs .... Dr. Melissa M. BOOG
18 Assoc VP Facilities & Cap Mgmt .... Mr. Eric J. BERKHEIMER
35 Asst VP Student Affs/Dean Students .... Ms. Valerie J. RANDALL-LEE
13 Chief Information Officer .... Mr. Ken F. KUNDELL
26 Director of Public Relations .... Mr. Richard W. CULVER
41 Director of Athletics .... Dr. Gerard R. DIBARTOLO
92 Director Honors Program .... Dr. James J. BUSS
06 Registrar .... Ms. Jacqueline M. MAISEL
07 Director of Admissions .... Ms. Elizabeth A. SKOGLUND
09 Special Asst to Pres/UARA .... Dr. Kara O. SIEGERT
08 Dean of Libraries & Instr Resources .... Dr. Beatriz B. HARDY
38 Director of Counseling Center .... Dr. Kathleen J. SCOTT
36 Director of Career Services .... Dr. Kevin C. FALLON
37 Director of Financial Aid .... Ms. Barri E. ZIMMERMAN
15 Assoc VP for HR .... Mr. Kevin A. VEDDER
29 Dir Alumni Relations & Gift Develop .... Mr. Jayme E. BLOCK
23 Director of Student Health Services .... Ms. Victoria A. LENTZ
35 Director Ct For Student Inv & Lead .... Ms. Tricia G. SMITH
86 Dir of Govt & Community Relations .... Mr. Eli J. MODLIN
43 General Counsel .... Ms. Karen A. TREBER
39 Director Housing/Residence Life .... Mr. David P. GUTOSKEY
19 Director of Public Safety .... Mr. Edwin L. LASHLEY
40 Director of Bookstore .... Ms. Lisa G. GRAY
18 Director of Physical Plant .... Mr. Kevin J. MANN
96 Director of Purchasing .... Mr. Jeff H. CANADA
75 Int Dean Henson Sch Science/Tech .... Dr. Michael S. SCOTT
50 Dean Perdue School of Business .... Dr. Christy H. WEER
49 Dean Fulton School of Liberal Arts .... Dr. Maarten L. PEREBOOM
53 Int Dean Seidel Sch Ed/Prof Studies .... Dr. Kelly A. FIALA
58 Dean Graduate Studies/Research .... Dr. Clifton P. GRIFFIN
88 Dir Ctr for Student Achievement .... Dr. Heather W. HOLMES

*Towson University (C)

8000 York Road, Baltimore MD 21252-0001
County: Baltimore — FICE Identification: 002099
Unit ID: 164076
Telephone: (410) 704-2000 — Carnegie Class: Masters/L
FAX Number: N/A — Calendar System: 4/1/4
URL: www.towson.edu
Established: 1866 — Annual Undergrad Tuition & Fees (In-State): $9,408
Enrollment: 22,284 — Coed
Affiliation or Control: State — IRS Status: 501(c)3
Highest Offering: Doctorate
Accreditation: M, ARCPA, AUD, CAATE, CAEPN, CS, DANCE, FEPAC, IPSY, MUS, NURSE, OT, SP, THEA

02 President .... Dr. Kim SCHATZEL
05 Provost/Vice Pres Acad Affairs .... Dr. Timothy CHANDLER
10 Vice Pres Admin & Finance .... Mr. Joseph J. OSTER
30 Vice Pres University Advancement .... Mr. Brian J. DEFILIPPIS
32 Vice President Student Affairs .... Dr. Deb MORIARTY
46 Interim VP Innovation/Applied Rsrch .... Ms. Daraius IRANI
100 Chief of Staff .... Vacant
88 Deputy Chief of Staff .... Vacant
22 VP of Equity and Inclusion .... Dr. Leah COX
20 Vice Provost .... Dr. S. Maggie REITZ
84 Assoc VP Enrollment Mgmt/Registrar .... Mr. Robert GIORDANI
44 Assoc Vice President Development .... Vacant
26 VP Univ Marketing/Communications .... Ms. Marina COOPER
29 Assoc Vice Pres Alumni Relations .... Ms. Lori B. ARMSTRONG
13 Assoc Vice President OTS/CIO .... Mr. Jeffrey SCHMIDT
109 Assoc Vice Pres Auxiliary Svcs .... Mr. Daniel SLATTERY
18 Assoc VP Facilities Management .... Mr. Kevin PETERSEN
21 Assoc VP Fiscal Planning & Svcs .... Mr. Robert CAMPBELL
15 Assoc Vice Pres Human Resources .... Vacant
35 Assoc Vice Pres Student Affairs .... Dr. Jana VARWIG
45 Assoc Prov Academic Res & Plng .... Dr. Gary LEVY
88 Assoc Vice President Campus Life .... Vacant
28 Asst VP Student Affairs/Diversity .... Mr. Santiago SOLIS
39 Asst VP Housing & Residence Life .... Ms. Antoinette CANDIA-BAILEY
37 Director for Financial Aid .... Mr. David HORNE
25 Asst VP Sponsored Programs/Research .... Ms. Amy L. TAYLOR
07 Director of Admissions .... Mr. David FEDORCHAK
19 Asst VP Public Sfty/Chief of Police .... Chief Bernard GERST
53 Dean College of Education .... Dr. Laurie MULLEN
50 Dean College of Business/Economics .. Dr. Shohreh A. KAYNAMA
49 Dean College of Liberal Arts .... Dr. Terry COONEY
81 Dean J&M Fisher Col of Science/Math .... Dr. David VANKO
57 Dean Col Fine Arts/Communications .... Ms. Susan PICINICH
76 Dean College of Health Professions .... Dr. Lisa PLOWFIELD
43 University Counsel .... Ms. Traevena BYRD
08 Dean of University Libraries .... Ms. Deborah NOLAN
104 Director Study Abroad .... Ms. Liz SHEARER
94 Chair Women's & Gender Studies .Dr. Cindy H. GISSENDANNER
09 Director Institutional Research .... Mr. Tim BIBO, JR.
27 Dir Communications/Media Relations .... Mr. Raymond C. FELDMANN
41 Director of Athletics .... Mr. Timothy LEONARD

23 Director of Health Services .... Dr. Matthias GOLDSTEIN
40 Director of University Store .... Ms. Stacey ELOFIR
96 Director of Procurement .... Ms. Lucy SLAICH
38 Director Counseling Center .... Dr. Gregory REISING
36 Director of Career Center .... Ms. Lorie LOGAN-BENNETT
06 Assoc Director Records/Registration .... Ms. Susan HYMAN

*University of Baltimore (D)

1420 N Charles Street, Baltimore MD 21201-5779
County: Independent City — FICE Identification: 002102
Unit ID: 161873
Telephone: (410) 837-4200 — Carnegie Class: Masters/L
FAX Number: N/A — Calendar System: Semester
URL: www.ubalt.edu
Established: 1925 — Annual Undergrad Tuition & Fees (In-State): $8,596
Enrollment: 6,229 — Coed
Affiliation or Control: State — IRS Status: 501(c)3
Highest Offering: Doctorate
Accreditation: M, LAW, SPAA

02 President .... Mr. Kurt L. SCHMOKE
05 Executive Vice President & Provost .... Ms. Darlene B. SMITH
10 Sr VP Admin & Finance .... Mr. Harry SCHUCKEL
32 Vice Pres Student Affairs .... Ms. Shelia BURKHALTER
84 Chief Enrollment Manager .... Ms. Victoria REID
111 Vice Pres Institutional Advancement .... Ms. Theresa SILANSKIS
86 VP Government & Community Relations ... Ms. Anita HAREWOOD
18 VP Facil Mgmt/Capital Planning .... Mr. Neb SERTSU
13 Vice Pres Technology/CIO .... Mr. David BOBART
15 Asst Vice Pres Human Resources .... Ms. Mary MAHER
20 Vice Provost .... Ms. Catherine ANDERSEN
09 Asst Provost Institutional Research .... Mr. Paul MONIODIS
35 Dean of Students .... Ms. Kathleen ANDERSON
28 Dir Diversity and Culture Center .... Ms. Karla M. SHEPHERD
07 Actg Executive Director Admissions .... Ms. Janet WHELAN
08 Dean of Llibrary .... Ms. Lucy HOLMAN
19 Chief of Police .... Mr. Samuel D. TRESS
88 AVP Enrollment Services .... Mr. Mark JACQUE
96 Director of Procurement & Supply .... Mr. Blair BLANKINSHIP
44 Dir Annual Giving/Alumni Relations .... Ms. Kate CRIMMINS
38 Director Counseling Services .... Dr. Myra WATERS
36 Director Career & Professional Dev .... Ms. Lakeisha MATHEWS
06 Assistant Registrar .... Ms. Brenda DER
26 Manager Public Information .... Mr. Chris HART
80 Dean College of Public Affairs .... Dr. Roger HARTLEY
49 Dean College of Arts & Sci .... Dr. Christine SPENCER
61 Dean of the School of Law .... Dr. Ronald WEICH
50 Dean School of Business .... Mr. Murray DALZIEL
88 Dir Center for Education Access .... Ms. Karyn SCHULZ
21 AVP Admin & University Budget Dir .... Ms. Barbara AUGHENBAUGH
29 Director Alumni Relations .... Ms. Alli HEDDEN
37 Director Student Financial Aid .... Vacant

Washington Adventist University (E)

7600 Flower Avenue, Takoma Park MD 20912-7794
County: Montgomery — FICE Identification: 002067
Unit ID: 162210
Telephone: (301) 891-4000 — Carnegie Class: Masters/M
FAX Number: (301) 270-1618 — Calendar System: Semester
URL: www.wau.edu
Established: 1904 — Annual Undergrad Tuition & Fees: $23,400
Enrollment: 1,044 — Coed
Affiliation or Control: Seventh-day Adventist — IRS Status: 501(c)3
Highest Offering: Master's
Accreditation: M, MUS, NURSE, #RAD

01 President .... Dr. Weymouth SPENCE
05 Provost .... Dr. Cheryl HARRIS KISUNZU
10 Exec Vice Pres Finance .... Mr. Patrick FARLEY
11 Chief of Operations & Compliance .... Ms. Janette NEUFVILLE
32 Vice Pres Student Life .... Mr. Bruce PEIFER
84 VP Marketing & Enrollment .... Mr. William JACKSON
42 Vice President Ministry .... Dr. Baraka MUGANDA
13 VP Information Technology .... Vacant
15 Assoc VP of Human Resources .... Ms. Rythee JONES
58 Dean Sch Grad/Professional Studies .... Ms. Nicole CURRIER
88 Dean of Student Success .... Dr. Ralph JOHNSON
06 Registrar .... Ms. Juanita WOMACK
33 Dean of Men .... Mr. Tim NELSON
34 Dean of Women .... Ms. Sabrina ETIENNE
08 Library Director .... Mr. Don ESSEX
30 Director of Development .... Vacant
19 Director Safety & Security .... Mr. Edwin MONGE
41 Athletic Director .... Mr. Patrick CRAREY, II
07 Director of Admissions/Recruitment .... Ms. Wanda COLON-CANALES
29 Director of Alumni .... Ms. Ellie BARKER
26 Director Corporate Communications .... Ms. Angie CREWS
78 Dir Coop Educ/Acad Support & Test .... Mr. Fitzroy THOMAS
18 Chief Facilities/Physical Plant .... Mr. Steve LAPHAM
37 Director Student Financial Aid .... Ms. Sharon CONWAY
38 Campus Counseling .... Dr. Grethel BRADFORD
40 Manager the College Bookstore .... Mr. Lloyd YUTUC
85 Director of International Students .... Dr. Beulah MANUEL
66 Director of Nursing .... Dr. Nancie CRESPIE
04 Executive Asst to President .... Ms. Lydée BATTLE
09 Director of Institutional Research .... Mr. Jonathan PETER

Washington College (A)

300 Washington Avenue, Chestertown MD 21620-1197
County: Kent FICE Identification: 002108
Unit ID: 164216
Telephone: (410) 778-2800 Carnegie Class: Bac-A&S
FAX Number: (410) 778-7850 Calendar System: Semester
URL: www.washcoll.edu
Established: 1782 Annual Undergrad Tuition & Fees: $43,842
Enrollment: 1,427 Coed
Affiliation or Control: Independent Non-Profit IRS Status: 501(c)3
Highest Offering: Master's
Accreditation: M

01 President .... Mr. Kurt M. LANDGRAF
05 Int Provost/Dean of College .... Dr. Patrice DIQUINIZO
45 VP Planning & Policy/Chief of Staff .... Mr. Victor SENSENIG
10 Vice Pres Finance/Administration .... Dr. Rahel ROSNER
100 Deputy to the President .... Ms. Denise RAMONAS
30 Vice Pres College Advancement .... Ms. Andrea TRISCIUZZI
44 Sr AVP College Advancement .... Mrs. Barbara H. HECK
84 Int Vice Pres Enrollment Management .... Ms. Cindy CHILDS
26 VP College Relations/Marketing .... Mr. Rolando IRIZARRY
32 VP Student Affairs/Dean of Students .... Dr. Sarah FEYERHERM
29 Dir Alumni Rels/Ldrship Annual Gvng .... Ms. Rebekah L. HARDY
09 Director Institutional Research .... Mr. Matthew KIBER
20 Asst Dean Academic Initiatives .... Dr. Andrea G. LANGE
31 Director of Campus Special Events .... Ms. Gina RALSTON
41 Director of Athletics .... Mr. Thad MOORE
06 Registrar .... Ms. Ashley TURLINGTON
08 Director of Miller Library .... Dr. Ruth C. SHOGE
13 Chief Information Officer .... Mr. Scott COWDREY
91 Director of Admin Computing .... Mr. Kenneth W. SUTTON
58 Director of Graduate Program .... Dr. Andrea G. LANGE
21 Controller .... Ms. Penelope L. FARLEY
18 Director of Physical Plant .... Ms. Valerie RICHARD
15 Director of Human Resources .... Ms. Carolyn BURTON
19 Director of Public Safety .... Mr. Gerald K. RODERICK
07 Dir Admissions Communications .... Ms. Aundra ANDERSON
37 Director of Financial Aid .... Ms. Doryann BARNHARDT
39 Dir Resid Life/Assoc Dean of Stdnts .... Mr. Carl CROWE
23 Clinical Director Health Services .... Mrs. Lisa M. MARX
38 Director of Counseling Center .... Ms. Miranda ALTMAN
36 Director of Career Development .... Mr. James M. ALLISON, JR.
28 Asst Dean Students/Dir Intcult Affs .... Mr. Jean-Pierre LAURENCEAU-MEDINA
40 Bookstore Manager .... Ms. Shannon WYBLE

Women's Institute of Torah Seminary (B)

6602 Park Heights Avenue, Baltimore MD 21215
County: Baltimore Identification: 667271
Telephone: (410) 358-3144 Carnegie Class: Not Classified
FAX Number: (866) 990-1983 Calendar System: Semester
URL: www.witbaltimore.org
Established: 1998 Annual Undergrad Tuition & Fees: N/A
Enrollment: N/A Female
Affiliation or Control: Jewish IRS Status: 501(c)3
Highest Offering: Baccalaureate
Accreditation: AIJS

01 President .... Dr. Aviva WEISBORD
05 Academic Dean .... Dr. Leslie G. KLEIN

Wor-Wic Community College (C)

32000 Campus Drive, Salisbury MD 21804-1486
County: Wicomico FICE Identification: 020739
Unit ID: 164313
Telephone: (410) 334-2800 Carnegie Class: Assoc/HT-High Trad
FAX Number: (410) 334-2951 Calendar System: Semester
URL: www.worwic.edu
Established: 1975 Annual Undergrad Tuition & Fees (In-District): $2,952
Enrollment: 3,128 Coed
Affiliation or Control: Local IRS Status: 501(c)3
Highest Offering: Associate Degree
Accreditation: M, ACFEI, EMT, OTA, PTAA, RAD

01 President .... Dr. Murray K. HOY
05 Vice Pres Academic Affairs .... Dr. Kristin L. MALLORY
84 Vice Pres Enroll Mgmt & Student Aff .... Mr. Bryan NEWTON
10 Vice Pres Administrative Services .... Ms. Jennifer A. SANDT
26 Vice Pres Institutional Affairs .... Dr. Reenie MCCORMICK
51 Dean Continuing Education .... Mrs. Ruth E. BAKER
97 Dean General Education .... Dr. Colleen C. DALLAM
75 Dean Occupational Education .... Dr. Trevor H. JONES
07 Director Admissions .... Mr. Richard C. WEBSTER
13 Senior Director Info Technology .... Ms. Ruth GILL
36 Director Career Services .... Ms. Lori SMOOT
37 Director Financial Aid .... Ms. Deborah D. JENKINS
21 Director Finance .... Mr. Thomas N. TYSON
15 Senior Director Human Resources .... Ms. Karen BERKHEIMER
38 Director Counseling .... Ms. Annette BROWN
27 Director Marketing .... Ms. Janet S. KENNINGTON
09 Director Institutional Research .... Ms. Carol A. MENZEL
30 Director Development .... Mr. Michelangelo INFURNARI
06 Registrar .... Ms. Kelly HEWETT
32 Sr Director of Student Development .... Ms. Deirdra G. JOHNSON
08 Director of Library Services .... Ms. Cheryl MICHAEL
18 Sr Director Facilities Management .... Mr. Gregory D. GREY
96 Director Purchasing & Auxiliary Svc .... Ms. Allison M. CANADA
105 Webmaster .... Mr. Joshua W. TOWNSEND
19 Director Public Safety .... Mr. Linnie VANN

Yeshiva College of the Nation's Capital (D)

1216 Arcola Avenue, Silver Spring MD 20902-3408
County: Montgomery FICE Identification: 039373
Unit ID: 434937
Telephone: (301) 649-7077 Carnegie Class: Spec-4-yr-Faith
FAX Number: (301) 649-7053 Calendar System: Semester
Established: 1995 Annual Undergrad Tuition & Fees: $9,700
Enrollment: 29 Male
Affiliation or Control: Independent Non-Profit IRS Status: 501(c)3
Highest Offering: Second Talmudic Degree
Accreditation: RABN

01 President .... Rabbi Yitzchok MERKIN
05 Rosh Yeshiva .... Rabbi Aaron LOPIANSKY
37 Financial Aid Director .... Ms. Maryanna WALLS
11 Administrator .... Rabbi Yitzi LABELL

MASSACHUSETTS

American International College (E)

1000 State Street, Springfield MA 01109-3155
County: Hampden FICE Identification: 002114
Unit ID: 164447
Telephone: (413) 737-7000 Carnegie Class: DU-Mod
FAX Number: (413) 205-3084 Calendar System: Semester
URL: www.aic.edu
Established: 1885 Annual Undergrad Tuition & Fees: $33,140
Enrollment: 3,539 Coed
Affiliation or Control: Independent Non-Profit IRS Status: 501(c)3
Highest Offering: Doctorate
Accreditation: EH, IACBE, NURSE, OT, PTA

01 President .... Dr. Vincent M. MANIACI
05 Exec Vice Pres Academic Affairs .... Vacant
11 Exec VP Administration .... Vacant
15 Sr VP for Human Resources .... Ms. Nicolle M. CESTERO
13 Chief Information Officer .... Ms. Mimi ROYSTON
09 VP for Institutional Effectiveness .... Dr. Gregory T. SCHMUTTE
32 VP for Student Affairs .... Mr. Brian J. O'SHAUGHNESSY
10 Vice President for Finance .... Vacant
111 VP for Institutional Advancement .... Mr. Donovan BREUNIG
26 VP Mktg & Communications .... Mr. Robert COLE
123 Dean of Graduate Admissions .... Ms. Kerry BARNES
07 Dean of UG Admissions .... Mr. Jonathan SCULLY
41 Athletic Director .... Mr. Matthew JOHNSON
76 Dean Health Sciences .... Dr. Cesarina THOMPSON
49 Dean Business/Arts/Sciences .... Dr. Susanne SWANKER
53 Dean of Education .... Dr. Sylvia MASON
18 Director of Facilities .... Mr. Jeffrey BEDNARZ
06 Registrar .... Mr. Paul KLESCHICK
08 Director of Library .... Ms. Estelle H. SPENCER
35 Dean of Students .... Mr. Matthew SCOTT
38 Director Counseling Center .... Dr. Rose L. ANDREJCZYK
36 Dir of Career Services .... Mr. J. A. MARSHALL
76 Director Physical Therapy Program .... Vacant
66 Director of Division of Nursing .... Dr. Karen S. ROUSSEAU
50 Director of Business Programs .... Dr. Robyn POOLE
37 Director for Financial Aid .... Ms. Sage CRARY-STACHOWIAK
21 Comptroller .... Mr. Christopher GARRITY
04 Admin Asst to President .... Ms. Lani KRETSCHMAR
19 Director Security/Safety .... Mr. David KUZMESKI
91 Director Academic Computing .... Vacant

Amherst College (F)

PO Box 5000, Amherst MA 01002-5000
County: Hampshire FICE Identification: 002115
Unit ID: 164465
Telephone: (413) 542-2000 Carnegie Class: Bac-A&S
FAX Number: (413) 542-2621 Calendar System: Semester
URL: www.amherst.edu
Established: 1821 Annual Undergrad Tuition & Fees: $52,476
Enrollment: 1,795 Coed
Affiliation or Control: Independent Non-Profit IRS Status: 501(c)3
Highest Offering: Baccalaureate
Accreditation: EH

01 President .... Dr. Carolyn (Biddy) A. MARTIN
100 Chief of Staff/Sec of the Board .... Ms. Susan PIKOR
05 Dean of the Faculty .... Dr. Catherine A. EPSTEIN
32 Chief Student Affairs Officer .... Dr. Suzanne R. COFFEY
07 Dean Admission/Financial Aid .... Ms. Katharine L. FRETWELL
37 Dean of Financial Aid .... Ms. Gail W. HOLT
20 Associate Dean of the Faculty .... Dr. John CHENEY
20 Associate Dean of the Faculty .... Dr. Austin D. SARAT
10 Chief Financial Officer .... Mr. Kevin C. WEINMAN
111 Chief Advancement Officer .... Vacant
43 Chief Policy Ofcr/General Counsel .... Ms. Lisa H. RUTHERFORD
06 Registrar .... Vacant
15 Director of Human Resources .... Ms. Maria-Judith RODRIGUEZ
21 Controller .... Mr. Stephen M. NIGRO
09 Director of Institutional Research .... Mr. Jesse D. BARBA
26 Chief Communications Officer .... Dr. Peter F. MACKEY
08 College Librarian .... Mr. Bryn GEFFERT
13 Chief Information Officer .... Mr. David L. HAMILTON
23 Director of Student Health Services .... Dr. Emily M. JONES
38 Director of Counseling Center .... Dr. Jacqueline ALVAREZ
36 Director of the Career Center .... Ms. Emily GRIFFEN
41 Director of Athletics .... Mr. Donald R. FAULSTICK
18 Chief of Campus Operations .... Mr. James D. BRASSORD
19 Chief of Campus Police .... Mr. John B. CARTER
109 Director of Dining Services .... Mr. Charles G. THOMPSON

Andover Newton Theological School (G)

210 Herrick Road, Newton Centre MA 02459-2243
County: Middlesex FICE Identification: 002116
Unit ID: 164474
Telephone: (617) 964-1100 Carnegie Class: Spec-4-yr-Faith
FAX Number: (617) 965-9756 Calendar System: Semester
URL: www.ants.edu
Established: 1807 Annual Graduate Tuition & Fees: N/A
Enrollment: 234 Coed
Affiliation or Control: Independent Non-Profit IRS Status: 501(c)3
Highest Offering: Doctorate; No Undergraduates
Accreditation: EH, THEOL

01 President .... Rev. Martin COPENHAVER
05 Dean of Faculty/VP Academic Affs .... Dr. Sarah B. DRUMMOND
10 Chief Financial Officer .... Mr. Brian D. BOYCE
29 Alumni/ae & Development Officer .... Mr. Ned A. PARKER
06 Registrar .... Ms. Nayda G. AGUILA
08 Co-Director of the Library .... Rev. Nancy LOIS
32 Dean of Students .... Dr. Mikel SATCHER
04 Assistant to the President .... Mr. David AMES
18 Director Physical Plant .... Mr. Frank CAVACO
13 Chief Information Officer .... Mr. Mugur ROZ
37 Coordinator Financial Aid .... Ms. Rosemary TURANO
39 Director Housing & Events Planning .... Mr. Frank NOVO

Anna Maria College (H)

50 Sunset Lane, Paxton MA 01612-1198
County: Worcester FICE Identification: 002117
Unit ID: 164492
Telephone: (508) 849-3333 Carnegie Class: Masters/M
FAX Number: (508) 849-3311 Calendar System: Semester
URL: www.annamaria.edu
Established: 1946 Annual Undergrad Tuition & Fees: $36,110
Enrollment: 1,451 Coed
Affiliation or Control: Roman Catholic IRS Status: 501(c)3
Highest Offering: Beyond Master's But Less Than Doctorate
Accreditation: EH, MUS, NUR, SW

01 President .... Ms. Mary Louise RETELLE
10 Vice President/Chief Financial Ofcr .... Mr. David M. ROSATI
11 Vice Pres/Chief Operations Officer .... Mr. David K. BREEN
05 VP for Academic Affairs .... Dr. Christine L. HOLMES
32 VP for Student Affairs .... Mr. Andrew O. KLEIN
111 VP for Institutional Advancement .... Ms. Sharon M. DAVENPORT
07 VP for Enrollment .... Mr. John HAMEL
26 Director of College Relations .... Vacant
09 Dean of Institutional Research .... Ms. Irene IRUDAYAM
06 Registrar .... Ms. Julie DIX
88 Director of the Learning Center .... Mr. Dennis VANASSE
23 Director of Health Services .... Ms. Linda ARONSON
08 Director of Library .... Ms. Janice WILBUR
44 Executive Director of Annual Giving .. Ms. Jodi BRIGGS-PICKETT
36 Director Career Counsel/Placement .... Vacant
37 Director Financial Aid .... Ms. Sandra PEREIRA
13 Chief Information Officer .... Mr. Michael MIERS
04 Executive Asst to the President .... Ms. Kay FLICK
18 Director Physical Plant .... Mr. Matthew SIMPSON
41 Athletic Director .... Mr. Serge DEBARI
42 Director Campus Ministry .... Fr. Manuel CLAVIJO
15 Interim Director of Human Resources .... Ms. Jan RUGGIERI
88 Dean of Mission Effectiveness .... Sr. Rollande QUINTAL
35 Dean of Student Life .... Vacant
51 Director Grad/Continuing Educ .... Mr. William PURNELL
19 Director Security/Safety .... Lt. Mark SAVASTA

Assumption College (I)

500 Salisbury Street, Worcester MA 01609-1296
County: Worcester FICE Identification: 002118
Unit ID: 164562
Telephone: (508) 767-7000 Carnegie Class: Bac-A&S
FAX Number: (508) 767-7169 Calendar System: Semester
URL: www.assumption.edu
Established: 1904 Annual Undergrad Tuition & Fees: $36,260
Enrollment: 2,675 Coed
Affiliation or Control: Roman Catholic IRS Status: 501(c)3
Highest Offering: Beyond Master's But Less Than Doctorate
Accreditation: EH, CACREP

01 President .... Dr. Francesco C. CESAREO
10 VP for Finance and Administration .... Mr. Peter D. WELLS
05 Provost/Academic Vice Pres .... Dr. Louise Carroll KEELEY
32 Vice President for Student Affairs .... Dr. Catherine M. WOODBROOKS
111 Vice Pres Institutional Advancement .... Mr. Timothy R. STANTON
42 Vice President Mission .... Rev. Dennis M. GALLAGHER, AA
84 Vice Pres for Enrollment Management .... Mr. Evan E. LIPP

43 General Counsel .... Dr. Michael H. RUBINO
20 Associate Provost .... Dr. Kimberly A. SCHANDEL
51 Dir of Career & Continuing Educ .... Mr. Dennis BRAUN
07 Dir of Admission/Recruitment .... Mr. Michael DIPIAZZA
20 Dean of Undergraduate Studies .... Dr. Eloise KNOWLTON
89 Assistant Dean for the First Year .... Dr. Jennifer K. MORRISON
42 Director of Campus Ministry .... Mr. Paul F. COVINO
38 Director of Counseling Services .... Ms. Marta CARLSON
08 Director of Library Services .... Ms. Doris Ann SWEET
10 Director of Finance .... Ms. Cathleen R. CULLEN
09 Director Inst Research and Ac Asst .... Mr. Stuart J. MUNRO
107 Director Opers Grad & Prof Studies .... Vacant
06 Registrar .... Mr. David W. AALTO
13 Exec Dir Info Tech & Media Svcs .... Dr. Dawn M. THISTLE
15 Director of Human Resources .... Ms. Robin PELLEGRINO
26 Executive Director of Communication . Mr. Michael K. GUILFOYLE
29 Director of Alumni Experiences .... Ms. Linda ROSELUND
44 Director of Assumption Fund .... Mr. Timothy R. MARTIN
121 Director of Academic Support Center .... Dr. Allen A. BRUEHL
35 Dean of Campus Life .... Mr. Conway CAMPBELL
39 Assoc Dean Campus Life/Dir Res Life .... Mr. Joseph ZITO
41 Director of Athletics .... Mr. Nichloas A. SMITH
19 Director of Public Safety .... Mr. Steven B. CARL
23 Director of Health Services .... Ms. Elizabeth DREXLER-HINES
24 Director of Media Services .... Mr. Ted HALEY
37 Director of Financial Aid .... Vacant
21 Director of Business Services .... Mr. Todd DERDERIAN
25 Director of Grant Development .... Vacant
35 Dean of Students .... Mr. Robert G. RAVENELLE
28 Director Cross Cultural Center .... Ms. Beatriz PATINO
96 Director of Purchasing .... Ms. Gail M. RACINE
86 Exec Asst for Govt/Cmty Relations .... Mr. Daniel F. DITULLIO
36 Director of Career Services .... Ms. Shannon CURTIS
04 Exec Admin Asst to President .... Ms. Sharon A. MAHONEY

Babson College (A)

231 Forest Street, Babson Park MA 02457-0310
County: Norfolk FICE Identification: 002121
Unit ID: 164580
Telephone: (781) 235-1200 Carnegie Class: Spec-4-yr-Bus
FAX Number: (781) 239-5231 Calendar System: Semester
URL: www.babson.edu
Established: 1919 Annual Undergrad Tuition & Fees: $48,288
Enrollment: 3,057 Coed
Affiliation or Control: Independent Non-Profit IRS Status: 501(c)3
Highest Offering: Master's
Accreditation: EH

01 President .... Dr. Kerry MURPHY HEALEY
12 CEO Babson Global .... Dr. Shahid ANSARI
05 Provost .... Dr. Michael D. JOHNSON
10 Chief Administrative Officer .... Ms. Katherine CRAVEN
100 Dpty Chief of Staff/Ops/Governance .... Ms. Marni D. ALLEN
18 AVP Facilities Mgmt & Construction .... Ms. Janet FISHSTEIN
31 VP Programming/Community Outreach .... Ms. Jane EDMONDS
44 Senior VP for Advancement .... Mr. Edward CHIU
30 Vice President of Development .... Ms. Diana P. ZAIS
45 VP Strat Initiatives/Chief of Staff .... Ms. Kelly LYNCH
15 Vice Pres Human Resources .... Ms. Donna BONAPARTE
43 VP and General Counsel .... Mr. Michael D. LAYISH
13 VP & Chief Information Officer .... Mr. Phillip KNUTEL
26 VP/Chief Marketing Officer .... Mr. Greg GORDON
32 VP/Dean of Students .... Dr. Lawrence P. WARD
36 Dir Graduate Center for Career Dev .... Ms. Cheri PAULSON
06 Registrar .... Ms. Linda KEAN
36 Dir Ungrad Center for Career Dev .... Ms. Donna SOSHOWSKI
27 Director of Public Relations .... Mr. Michael CHMURA
20 Dean of Faculty .... Ms. Carolyn HOTCHKISS
07 Dean Undergraduate Admissions .... Ms. Courtney MINDEN
58 Dean Graduate School .... Dr. Will LAMB
97 Dean Undergraduate School .... Dr. Ian LAPP
107 Dean of Babson Exec Education .... Ms. Elaine EISENMAN
37 Assoc Dean UG Sch/Dir Std Fin Svcs .... Ms. Melissa J. SHAAK
94 Exec Dir Ctr for Wms Entrep Lship .... Dr. Susan DUFFY
07 Director Graduate Admissions .... Ms. Petia WHITMORE
09 Director of Institutional Research .... Ms. Anne Marie DELANEY
96 Director of Business Services .... Ms. Teresa PITARO
28 Chief Diversity & Inclusion Officer .... Dr. Sadie BURTON-GOSS
19 Director Public Safety .... Mr. James POLLARD
41 Director of Athletics .... Mr. Josh MACARTHUR

Bard College at Simon's Rock (B)

84 Alford Road, Great Barrington MA 01230-9702
County: Berkshire FICE Identification: 009645
Unit ID: 167792
Telephone: (413) 644-4400 Carnegie Class: Bac-A&S
FAX Number: (413) 528-7365 Calendar System: Semester
URL: www.simons-rock.edu
Established: 1964 Annual Undergrad Tuition & Fees: $52,870
Enrollment: 329 Coed
Affiliation or Control: Independent Non-Profit IRS Status: 501(c)3
Highest Offering: Baccalaureate
Accreditation: EH

01 President .... Dr. Leon BOTSTEIN
03 Executive Vice President .... Mr. Dimitri PAPADIMITRIOU
05 Vice President/Provost .... Dr. Ian BICKFORD
88 Asst to Vice President & Provost .... Ms. Deborah TREADWAY
32 Dean of the College .... Ms. S. Rebecca THOMAS
20 Dean of Academic Affairs .... Dr. Patricia SHARPE
35 Dean of Students .... Ms. Bethany NOHLGREN
10 Director of Finance/Admin/HR .... Mr. Bryant MORGAN
20 Dean of Academic Engagement .... Dr. Sue LYON
26 Director of Communications .... Ms. Kimberly ROCK
111 VP Development/Advancement .... Ms. Debra PEMSTEIN
07 Director of Admissions .... Mr. Mackie SIEBENS
06 Registrar .... Ms. Heidi ROTHBERG
08 Library Director .... Mr. Brian MIKESELL
37 Director of Financial Aid .... Ms. Denise Ann ACKERMAN
18 Director Physical Plant .... Mr. Gerard NESEL
38 Director Campus Wellness Ctr .... Ms. Sharon HARTUNIAN
13 Director of Information Technology .... Ms. Janice GILDAWIE
19 Director of Security .... Mr. Kenneth GEREMIA
39 Director of Residence Life .... Mr. Ali GONZALEZ TORRES
44 Director of Annual Fund/Alumni .... Mr. Richard MONTONE
41 Athletic Director .... Ms. Kristen HALL
57 Division Head Arts .... Mr. Ben KRUPKA
81 Division Head Science/Math/Computer .... Dr. David MYERS
83 Division Head Social Studies .... Dr. Brian CONOLLY
79 Division Head Language/Literature .... Dr. Brendan MATHEWS
103 Dir of Academic Trans & Career Dev .... Ms. Manat WOOTEN
28 Dir of Equity & Inclusion .. Ms. Gwendolyn HAMPTON VANSANT

Bay Path University (C)

588 Longmeadow Street, Longmeadow MA 01106-2292
County: Hampden FICE Identification: 002122
Unit ID: 164632
Telephone: (413) 565-1000 Carnegie Class: Masters/L
FAX Number: (413) 565-1105 Calendar System: Semester
URL: www.baypath.edu
Established: 1897 Annual Undergrad Tuition & Fees: $32,739
Enrollment: 3,107 Female
Affiliation or Control: Independent Non-Profit IRS Status: 501(c)3
Highest Offering: Doctorate
Accreditation: EH, ARCPA, OT

01 President .... Dr. Carol A. LEARY
05 Vice Pres Academic Affairs/
Provost .... Dr. Melissa MORRISS-OLSON
10 VP Finance/Administrative Services .... Mr. Michael GIAMPIETRO
30 VP Univ Relations & Board Liaison .... Ms. Kathleen BOURQUE
88 Chief Strategy Officer Springfield .... Ms. Caron T. HOBIN
04 Assistant to the President .... Ms. Laurie THIVIERGE
88 Deputy Chief Ops Effectiveness/TAWC .... Ms. Amanda GOULD
21 Controller .... Mr. John O'ROURKE
88 Dean Research & Academic Resource .... Ms. Ann DOBMEYER
12 Director of the Concord Campus .... Ms. Karen CARLSON
26 Director of Univ Communications .... Ms. Kathleen WROBLEWSKI
37 Exec Dir of Student Financial Svcs .... Ms. Stephanie KING
36 Exec Dir Career & Life Planning .... Ms. Laureen CIRILLO
08 Director of the Library .... Mr. Michael MORAN
06 Registrar .... Mr. Marshall BRADWAY
29 Dir of Alumni Relations .... Ms. Amanda SBRISCIA
23 Director of Health Services .... Ms. Deborah BAKER
19 Captain Campus Public Safety .... Mr. Danilo FELICIANO
15 Asst VP & Dir of Human
Resources .... Ms. Kathleen HALPIN-ROBBINS
18 Director Facilities/Campus Svcs .... Mr. Paul E. STANTON
13 Exec Director Info Technology .... Mr. Douglas SLAVAS
14 Mgr of Info Systems and Telecommun .... Mrs. Linda A. SIMONDS
41 Director of Athletics .... Mr. Steven J. SMITH
88 Executive Director Brand Strategy .... Ms. Karen WOODS
32 Asst Dean of Students .... Ms. Angela WATSON
88 Dir Business Programs TAWC .... Ms. Jamie LITCHFIELD
88 Dir MBA Entrepr Thnkg/Innov Practic .... Mr. Mo SATTAR
88 Dir Grad Pgms Nonprofit Mgmt/
Philan .... Ms. Sylvia DE HAAS PHILLIPS
20 Vice Provost/Chief Educ Compliance .... Ms. Kathleen MARTIN
88 Dir Center for Teaching & Learning .... Dr. Charlotte BRIGGS
96 Exec Dir of Purchasing/Office Svcs .... Mr. Ted LETH-STEENSEN
102 Dir Foundation/Corporate Relations .... Ms. Janine MCVAY
53 Dean School Educ/Human/Hlth Sci .... Dr. Elizabeth FLEMING
49 Dean School Art/Science/Mgmt .... Dr. Thomas LOPER
88 Dir Occupational Therapy Program .... Dr. Beverly ST. PIERRE
123 Dean Graduate Admissions .... Ms. Diane RANALDI
57 Director MFA Program .... Ms. Leanna JAMES BLACKWELL
53 Director ABA Program .... Dr. Susan AINSLEIGH
88 Director PA Program .... Ms. Theresa RIETHLE
44 Dir of Annual Giving & Alumni Rel .... Ms. Amanda SBRISCIA
88 Director of Cybersecurity Program .... Mr. Lawrence SNYDER
88 Dir Higher Education Administration .... Ms. Lauren WAY
88 Director Accounting Program .... Ms. Kara STEVENS
88 Director MS Leadership/Negotiation .... Mr. Joshua WEISS
88 Dir Ctr Excellence Women in Science .... Ms. Gina SEMPREBON
88 Executive Director Enrollment Mktg .... Ms. Rebecca CAPUANO
88 Exec Dir Ctr Online & Digital Lrng .... Mr. Peter TESTORI
88 Dean Liberal Studies .... Ms. Kristine BARNETT
88 Director Graduate Psychology Pgm .... Mr. Mark BENANDER
88 Director MS Applied Data Science .... Ms. Ning JIA
88 Director Neuroscience Program .... Ms. Princy MENNELLA

Bay State College (D)

122 Commonwealth Avenue, Boston MA 02116-2975
County: Suffolk FICE Identification: 003965
Unit ID: 164641
Telephone: (617) 217-9000 Carnegie Class: Bac/Assoc-Mixed
FAX Number: (617) 249-0400 Calendar System: Semester
URL: www.baystate.edu
Established: 1946 Annual Undergrad Tuition & Fees: $22,320
Enrollment: 1,069 Coed
Affiliation or Control: Proprietary IRS Status: Proprietary
Highest Offering: Baccalaureate
Accreditation: EH, ADNUR, MAAB, PTAA

01 President .... Dr. Stacy L. SWEENEY
05 Vice President of Academic Affairs .... Dr. William CARROLL
10 Vice Pres Administration & Finance .... Meg TRANT
32 Vice Pres Student Affs/Dean Stdnts .... Kate O'HARA
84 Vice Pres Enrollment Management .... Senthil KUMAR
26 VP of Marketing/Communications .... Chip BERGSTROM
37 Director Student Financial Services .... Jeanne DEVANI
06 Registrar .... Sarah WOOD
08 Librarian .... Jessica NEAVE
07 Director of Admissions .... Clancy KRUEGER
21 Student Account Administrator .... Melissa PEDERSEN
36 Director Career Services .... Diann LLOYD-DENNIS
38 Director Student Counseling .... Cheryl RAICHE
15 Director Human Resources .... Donna GAFFEY
35 Asst Dir Student Activities .... Kristin STAINE
18 Facilities Manager .... Vacant

Bay State College (E)

101 Industrial Park Road, Taunton MA 02780
Telephone: (617) 217-9829 Identification: 770927
Accreditation: &EH, MAAB

† Main campus is Bay State College in Boston, MA.

Becker College (F)

61 Sever Street, Worcester MA 01609-2165
County: Worcester FICE Identification: 002123
Unit ID: 164720
Telephone: (508) 791-9241 Carnegie Class: Bac-Diverse
FAX Number: (508) 796-2693 Calendar System: Semester
URL: www.becker.edu
Established: 1784 Annual Undergrad Tuition & Fees: $37,272
Enrollment: 2,153 Coed
Affiliation or Control: Independent Non-Profit IRS Status: 501(c)3
Highest Offering: Master's
Accreditation: EH, ADNUR, NUR

01 President .... Dr. Nancy P. CRIMMIN
10 Executive Vice President & CFO .... Dr. David A. ELLIS
05 VP for Academic Affairs .... Dr. Amber L. VAILL
32 Interim VP of Student Affairs .... Mr. Frank MILLERICK
111 Interim VP of Inst Advancement .... Mrs. Christine MEOLA
84 Vice President Enrollment Mgmt .... Mr. Greg W. POTTS
26 Exec Director Marketing & Comms .... Ms. Carolyn ASSA
13 Chief Information Officer .... Ms. Patricia L. PATRIA
19 Campus Police Chief .... Mr. David J. BOUSQUET
100 Chief of Staff/Spec Asst to Pres .... Vacant
15 Associate VP Human Resources .... Ms. Kathleen M. GARVEY
41 Asst VP & Athletic Director .... Mr. Francis E. MILLERICK
11 Assistant VP for Administration .... Mr. Kenneth CAMERON
07 Dean of Admissions .... Mr. Michael PERRON
57 Dean School of Design & Technology .... Mr. Alan RITACCO
66 Dean Sch of Nursing & Beh Sciences .... Vacant
74 Dean School of Animal Studies .... Dr. Julie A. BAILEY
32 Assistant Dean of Student Affairs .... Dr. Tracey A. PAKSTIS
88 Executive Director MassDIGI .... Mr. Timothy LOEW
88 Exec Director of Global
Initiatives .... Dr. Debra PALLATTO-FONTAINE
36 Exec Dir Career Educ & Advising .... Mr. Richard DAVINO
38 Director of Counseling Services .... Dr. Chantelle PSEEKOS
114 Dir Budget & Business Services .... Mr. Michael MONGEON
08 Director of the Libraries .... Ms. Donna M. SIBLEY
29 Dir Alumni Relations & Annual Fund .... Ms. Elizabeth FLEMING
53 Director of Education Programs .... Ms. Nina MAZLOFF
88 Director of Equestrian Center .... Ms. Nicole EASTMAN
09 Dir Inst Research & Assessment .... Ms. Vera MAUK
39 Dir Resid Life & Student Conduct .... Mr. Joseph A. LOMASTRO
37 Director Financial Aid .... Ms. Heather E. RULAND
18 Director of Facilities .... Mr. Richard ROODBEEN
109 Director of Dining Services .... Mr. Robert WILDER
88 Director Yunis Social Bus
Centre .... Dr. Debra PALLATTO-FONTAINE
88 Dir Col Learning Ctr/ADA/Disability .... Ms. Mary-Lou ROBERTS
50 Director of Business Programs .... Dr. Vaughn A. CALHOUN
85 Dir Intl Students & Title IX .... Ms. Michelle FATCHERIC
113 Director of Student Accounts/Bursar . Mr. Alexander M. HARTMAN
23 Director of Health Services .... Ms. Catherine MELOCHE
16 Associate Director Human Resources . Mr. Steven J. BOURGAULT
88 Manager Creative Services .... Ms. Judith TONELLI-BROWN
40 General Manager Bookstore .... Ms. Randie FARMELANT
90 Helpdesk Manager .... Mr. Steven J. BIGDA
88 Mgr Auxiliary & Safety Services .... Ms. Diana JOHNSON
104 Coordinator of Study Abroad .... Mr. Daniel W. CHAPMAN
06 Registrar .... Ms. Nikki ANDREWS
21 Controller .... Mr. Richard N. NAYLOR
04 Exec Asst to Pres/Liaison to Board .... Ms. Patricia KALINOWSKI

Benjamin Franklin Institute of Technology (G)

41 Berkeley Street, Boston MA 02116-6296
County: Suffolk FICE Identification: 002151
Unit ID: 165884
Telephone: (617) 588-1368 Carnegie Class: Spec-4-yr-Other Tech
FAX Number: (617) 482-3706 Calendar System: Semester
URL: www.bfit.edu
Established: 1908 Annual Undergrad Tuition & Fees: $16,950
Enrollment: 596 Coed
Affiliation or Control: Independent Non-Profit IRS Status: 501(c)3
Highest Offering: Baccalaureate

Accreditation: EH, OPD

01 President .... Anthony BENOIT
05 Dean of Academic Affairs .... Larson ROGERS
10 Chief Financial Officer .... Maureen JOYCE
32 Dean of Student Services .... Jackie CORNOG
06 Registrar .... James KLASEN
08 Librarian .... Sharon B. BONK
07 Dean of Recruitment .... Marvin LOISEAU
30 Chief Development Officer .... Kimberly FREEDMAN
121 Director of Student Success .... Shawn AYALA
09 Director of Institutional Research .... James KLASEN
15 Director Human Resources .... Shelley DROPKIN
19 Director of Facilities .... Myftar MYRTAJ
36 Director of Career Services .... Emily LEOPOLD
37 Director Student Financial Services .... Jamie SANTIAGO
04 Administrative Asst to President .... Nakia COCANOUGHER

Bentley University (A)

175 Forest Street, Waltham MA 02452-4705
County: Middlesex FICE Identification: 002124
Unit ID: 164739
Telephone: (781) 891-2000 Carnegie Class: Masters/L
FAX Number: (781) 891-2569 Calendar System: Semester
URL: www.bentley.edu
Established: 1917 Annual Undergrad Tuition & Fees: $45,760
Enrollment: 5,552 Coed
Affiliation or Control: Independent Non-Profit IRS Status: 501(c)3
Highest Offering: Doctorate
Accreditation: EH

01 President .... Ms. Gloria C. LARSON
43 General Counsel/Secretary to Corp .... Ms. Judith MALONE
05 Acting Provost .... Dr. Lynne ROSANSKY
102 Dir Corp Foundation Relations .... Mr. Paul CARBERRY
10 VP Admin/Finance/Treas .... Mr. Kenneth CODY
30 VP University Advancement .... Mr. William TORREY
32 VP Student Affairs .... Dr. J. Andrew SHEPARDSON
13 Chief Information Officer .... Mr. Bob WITTSTEIN
84 VP Enrollment Management .... Ms. Carolina FIGUEROA
49 Dean of Arts and Sciences .... Dr. Daniel EVERETT
50 Dean of Business/Grad Sch .... Dr. Roy WIGGINS
20 Associate Provost .... Dr. Vicki LAFARGE
121 Assoc Dean Academic Services .... Ms. Catherina CARLSON
58 Director GSAS .... Ms. Colleen MURPHY
29 Exec Director of Adv Relations .... Vacant
26 Chief Marketing Officer .... Ms. Val FOX
15 Assoc VP of Human Resources .... Ms. Ann DEXTER
11 Assoc Dean of Business Programs .... Dr. Dorothy FELDMANN
21 Assoc VP Finance .... Ms. Nancy ANTUNES
06 Registrar .... Ms. Patricia ROGERS
22 Spec Advisor to the Pres/Ombudsman .... Dr. Earl AVERY
38 Director of Counseling Center .... Dr. Peter FORKNER
41 Director of Athletics .... Mr. Robert DEFELICE
09 Director of Institutional Research .... Ms. Kelly GIARDULLO
39 Assoc Dean Student Affairs/Res Ctr .... Mr. John PIGA
08 Dir Library .... Ms. Hope HOUSTON
19 Executive Director of Public Safety .... Mr. Ernest LEFFLER
90 Director Academic Tech Center .... Mr. Gaurav SHAH
36 Assoc VP Univ Career Services .... Ms. Susan BRENNAN
23 Asst Dean/Dir Health & Wellness .... Ms. Geraldine TAYLOR
25 Director of Sponsored Programs .... Ms. Susan RICHMAN
88 Assoc VP Enrollment Management .... Ms. Donna KENDALL
07 Exec Director Undergrad Admission . Ms. Suzanne CUCCURULLO
28 Dir Diversity and Inclusion .... Ms. Katie LAMPLEY
123 Asst Dean/Dir of Grad Admission .... Ms. Sharon HILL
88 Director of MBA Programs .... Dr. David SCHWARZKOPF
18 Exec Director Facilities Management .... Mr. Thomas KANE
96 Exec Dir Purchasing/Adm & Camp Svcs .... Ms. Julianne BRITT
44 Sr Assoc Dir Annual Giving .... Mr. Brian READ
35 Dir of Student Prog & Engagement .... Ms. Nicole CHABOT-WIEFERICH
04 Exec Asst to President .... Ms. Sharon M. WILLIAMS-DYER
104 Director of International Education .... Ms. Natalie SCHLEGEL

Berklee College of Music (B)

1140 Boylston Street, Boston MA 02215-3693
County: Suffolk FICE Identification: 002126
Unit ID: 164748
Telephone: (617) 266-1400 Carnegie Class: Spec-4-yr-Arts
FAX Number: (617) 247-6878 Calendar System: Semester
URL: www.berklee.edu
Established: 1945 Annual Undergrad Tuition & Fees: $41,398
Enrollment: 5,289 Coed
Affiliation or Control: Independent Non-Profit IRS Status: 501(c)3
Highest Offering: Master's
Accreditation: EH

01 President .... Roger H. BROWN
100 Chief of Staff .... Melissa HOWE
12 Exec Dir Boston Conservatory .... Cathy YOUNG
05 Sr VP Academic Affairs/Provost .... Lawrence J. SIMPSON
84 Sr VP Student Enrollment/Engagement .... Betsy NEWMAN
84 VP Enrollment Marketing/Management .... Mike KING
111 Sr VP Institutional Advancement .... Cindy ALBERT LINK
10 Chief Financial Officer .... Richard M. HISEY
88 VP Innovation/Strategy .... Panos A. PANAY
13 VP Technology Resources .... David GREGORY
15 VP Human Resources .... Eileen ALVITI
88 VP Educ Outreach/Social Entrepren .... Vacant
88 Assoc VP Global Initiatives .... Matthew NICHOLL
20 VP Academic Affairs/Vice Provost .... Jay KENNEDY
26 VP for External Affairs .... Tom RILEY
88 Ad Int Dean of Prof Performance Div .... Ron SAVAGE
88 Dean Prof Writing Div/Music Tech .... Kari JUUSELA
53 Dean of Prof Education Division .... Darla S. HANLEY
06 Registrar .... Jeffrey KINNAMON
39 Dir Residential/Housing Operations .... Rosemary DOWLING
37 Asst VP Student Financial Services .... Tod OLIVIERE
38 Director of Counseling Center .... Felix PIZZI
07 Dean of Admissions .... Damien S. BRACKEN
36 Ad Int Asst VP Career Strategy/Svcs .... Stefanie HENNING
18 Senior Director of Physical Plant .... Kevin ANDERSON
08 Dean of Learning Resources .... Heather REID
09 Dir Inst Research/Assessment .... Sharon KRAMER
19 Sr Director Public Safety Services .... Mark LOUNEY
28 VP Student Affs/Diversity/ Inclusion .... Christopher KANDUS-FISHER
29 Director of Alumni Affairs .... Fritz KUHNLENZ
96 Dir Procurement/Campus Business .... Dennis FOX
104 Asst Director Study Abroad .... Tracey MELLOR
105 Sr Dir Marketing/Communications .... Janelle BROWNING
106 Sr VP Online Learning/Continuing Ed .... Deborah CAVALIER

Boston Architectural College (C)

320 Newbury Street, Boston MA 02115-2795
County: Suffolk FICE Identification: 003966
Unit ID: 164872
Telephone: (617) 262-5000 Carnegie Class: Spec-4-yr-Arts
FAX Number: (617) 585-0111 Calendar System: Semester
URL: www.the-bac.edu
Established: 1889 Annual Undergrad Tuition & Fees: $20,666
Enrollment: 770 Coed
Affiliation or Control: Independent Non-Profit IRS Status: 501(c)3
Highest Offering: Master's
Accreditation: EH, CIDA, LSAR

01 President .... Mr. Glen S. LEROY
05 Provost .... Ms. Diana RAMIREZ-JASSO
10 Vice President for Finance/Admin .... Mr. Mark VIRELLO
111 VP Institutional Advancement .... Mr. Evan GALLIVAN
84 VP of Enrollment Management .... Mr. James RYAN
18 Associate VP of Facilities .... Mr. Arthur BYERS
32 Assoc Vice Pres/Dean of Students .... Mr. Richard M. GRISWOLD
88 Dean of School of Interior Design .... Mr. Crandon GUSTAFSON
88 Dean School of Landscape Architect .... Ms. Maria BELLALTA
88 Dean School of Design Studies .... Mr. Donald HUNSICKER
48 Dean School of Architecture .... Ms. Karen L. NELSON
88 Dean & Faculty of Practice .... Mr. Len CHARNEY
13 Director of Information Technology .... Mr. Jason O'BRIEN
88 Dir of Master's Thesis Arch .... Mr. Ian TABERNER
88 Director of Design Media .... Mr. Aidan ACKERMAN
88 Dir of Applied Learning in Practice .... Ms. Beth GARVER
88 Director of Media Arts .... Mr. Luis MONTALVO
110 Assoc Director of Advancement Svcs .... Mr. Geoff WHALEY
08 Library Director .... Ms. Susan A. LEWIS
07 Director of Admissions .... Ms. Meredith SPINNATO
37 Director of Financial Aid .... Mr. Janice WILKOS-GREENBERG
06 Assoc Registrar .... Ms. Katherine KWOLEK
11 Dir of Administrative Operations .... Ms. Patti VAUGHN
121 Dean of Advising Services .... Ms. Rebecca CHABOT-WIEFERICH
88 Director of Foundation Studies .... Mr. Lee PETERS
35 Dean of Student Svcs & Registrar .... Mrs. Bethany FANTASIA
15 Director of Human Resources .... Ms. Lorri MAYER
29 Assoc Dir of Special Events & Alum .... Ms. Catalina IANETTA
21 Controller .... Ms. Patricia FARINO
88 Director Foundation Student Support .... Mr. Michael DANIELS
88 Director of Liberal Studies .... Ms. Victoria HALLINAN
04 Administrative Asst to President .... Ms. Janna ATCHESON
26 Dir of Marketing & Communications .. Ms. Betsy BUTTERWORTH
39 Coordinator of Student Life Housing .... Ms. Winny KWONG-SITO

Boston Baptist College (D)

950 Metropolitan Avenue, Boston MA 02136-4000
County: Suffolk FICE Identification: 032483
Unit ID: 164614
Telephone: (617) 364-3510 Carnegie Class: Spec-4-yr-Faith
FAX Number: (775) 245-1498 Calendar System: Semester
URL: www.boston.edu
Established: 1976 Annual Undergrad Tuition & Fees: $12,600
Enrollment: 85 Coed
Affiliation or Control: Baptist IRS Status: 501(c)3
Highest Offering: Baccalaureate
Accreditation: TRACS

01 President .... Rev. David V. MELTON
32 Vice President for Student Services .... Rev. Kenneth D. GILLMING
11 Vice President for Operations .... Mr. Randall WARD
84 Director of Enrollment Services .... Mrs. Rebekah BUTLER
07 Director of Admissions .... Mrs. Carolina WOUNDY
08 Head Librarian .... Mr. Fred TATRO

Boston College (E)

140 Commonwealth Avenue, Chestnut Hill MA 02467-3934
County: Middlesex FICE Identification: 002128
Unit ID: 164924
Telephone: (617) 552-8000 Carnegie Class: DU-Highest
FAX Number: (617) 552-8828 Calendar System: Semester
URL: www.bc.edu
Established: 1863 Annual Undergrad Tuition & Fees: $51,296
Enrollment: 14,354 Coed
Affiliation or Control: Roman Catholic IRS Status: 501(c)3
Highest Offering: Doctorate
Accreditation: EH, ANEST, CAEPT, COPSY, LAW, NURSE, SW, THEOL

01 President .... Rev. William P. LEAHY, S.J.
05 Provost & Dean of Faculties .... Dr. David QUIGLEY
03 Executive Vice President .... Mr. Michael J. LOCHHEAD
30 Senior VP University Advancement .... Mr. James J. HUSSON
04 Vice Pres/Exec Asst to President .... Mr. Kevin J. SHEA
10 Financial Vice President/Treasurer .... Mr. John D. BURKE
32 Vice Pres Student Affairs .... Dr. Barbara JONES
15 Vice President for Human Resources .... Mr. David P. TRAINOR
13 Vice Pres Information Technology .... Mr. Michael J. BOURQUE
88 Vice Pres Univ Mission & Ministry .... Rev. John T. BUTLER, S.J.
86 Vice Pres Govt/Community Affairs .... Mr. Thomas J. KEADY
18 Vice Pres Facilities Management .... Mr. Daniel F. BOURQUE
45 Vice Pres Planning & Assessment .... Dr. Kelli J. ARMSTRONG
20 Vice Provost for Undergrad Affairs .... Dr. Akua SARR
46 Vice Provost for Research .... Dr. Thomas CHILES
84 Vice Prov for Enrollment Management .... Ms. Nanci TESSIER
20 Vice Provost for Faculties .... Dr. Billy SOO
44 Vice President for Development .... Ms. Beth MCDERMOTT
09 VP Inst Research/Plng/Assessment .... Dr. Kelli J. ARMSTRONG
20 Assoc Vice Provost Undergrad Acad .... Dr. J. Joseph BURNS
18 Assoc VP Capital Projects .... Ms. Mary S. NARDONE
29 Associate VP Alumni Relations .... Ms. Joy MOORE
16 Assoc VP Human Resources .... Mr. William MURPHY
109 Assoc VP Auxiliary Services .... Ms. Patricia A. BANDO
49 Dean College Arts & Sciences .... Rev. Gregory KALSCHEUR, S.J.
87 Dean Col Adv Stds/Summer Session .... Rev. James R. BURNS
53 Dean School of Education .... Dr. Stanton WORTHAM
61 Dean Law School .... Mr. Vincent D. ROUGEAU
50 Dean School of Management .... Dr. Andrew C. BOYNTON
66 Dean of School of Nursing .... Dr. Susan GENNARO
70 Dean Grad School of Social Work .... Dr. Gautam N. YADAMA
73 Dean School of Theology & Ministry .... Rev. Thomas STEGMAN, SJ
84 Dean of Enrollment Management .... Mr. Robert S. LAY
35 Assoc VP Student Affairs Engagement .... Dr. Katherine G. O'DAIR
08 University Librarian .... Dr. Thomas WALL
28 Director Institutional Diversity .... Ms. Patricia LOWE
06 Exec Director Student Services .... Dr. Louise M. LONABOCKER
07 Director of Admission .... Mr. John L. MAHONEY, JR.
27 Assoc VP Marketing & Communication .... Mr. John B. DUNN
102 Assoc VP School Development .... Mrs. Ginger K. SAARIAHO
41 Director Athletic Department .... Mr. Martin JARMOND
36 Assoc VP Career Center .... Mr. Joseph DUPONT
42 Assoc VP Campus Ministry .... Rev. Anthony PENNA
31 Director of Community Affairs .... Mr. William R. MILLS
38 Assoc VP Univ Counseling Svcs .... Vacant
37 Director Financial Aid .... Ms. Mary S. MCGRANAHAN
23 Director Health Services .... Dr. Thomas I. NARY
39 Assoc VP Residential Life .... Mr. George A. AREY
25 Dir Pre-Award Admin Sponsored Pgms .... Mrs. Sharon COMVALIUS-GODDARD
19 Dir Public Safety/Chief of Police .... Mr. John M. KING
40 Director Bookstore .... Mr. Robert STEWART
43 General Counsel .... Mr. Joseph M. HERLIHY
24 Director Media Technology Services .... Mr. David CORKUM
85 Director International Programs .... Dr. Nick GOZIK
88 Director Presidential Scholars Pgms .. Rev. James F. KEENAN, SJ
93 Director AHANA Student Programs .... Dr. Ines MATURANA SENDOYA
86 Director Governmental Relations .... Ms. Jeanne LEVESQUE
96 Director Procurement Services .... Mr. Paul MCGOWAN
09 Director Inst Research & Assessment .... Dr. Jessica A. GREENE

Boston Graduate School of Psychoanalysis (F)

1581 Beacon Street, Brookline MA 02446-4602
County: Norfolk FICE Identification: 031943
Unit ID: 164915
Telephone: (617) 277-3915 Carnegie Class: Spec-4-yr-Other Health
FAX Number: (617) 277-0312 Calendar System: Semester
URL: www.bgsp.edu
Established: 1973 Annual Graduate Tuition & Fees: N/A
Enrollment: 143 Coed
Affiliation or Control: Independent Non-Profit IRS Status: 501(c)3
Highest Offering: Doctorate; No Undergraduates
Accreditation: EH

01 President .... Dr. Jane SNYDER
10 Vice President Finance .... Dr. Carol PANETTA
58 Dean of Graduate Studies .... Dr. Lynn PERLMAN
07 Director of Admissions .... Dr. Paula BERMAN
06 Registrar .... Ms. Allison WILLIAMS
37 Director of Financial Aid .... Ms. Stephanie WOOLBERT
21 Controller .... Ms. Gayle DOLAN
08 Head Librarian .... Ms. Amy COHEN-ROSE
09 Director of the Center for Research .... Dr. Stephen SOLDZ

Boston University (G)

One Silber Way, Boston MA 02215-1700
County: Suffolk FICE Identification: 002130
Unit ID: 164988
Telephone: (617) 353-2000 Carnegie Class: DU-Highest
FAX Number: (617) 353-2053 Calendar System: Semester
URL: www.bu.edu
Established: 1839 Annual Undergrad Tuition & Fees: $50,240
Enrollment: 32,158 Coed
Affiliation or Control: Independent Non-Profit IRS Status: 501(c)3
Highest Offering: Doctorate

Accreditation: EH, #ARCPA, ART, CAATE, CACREP, CAHIIM, CEA, CLPSY, COPSY, DENT, DIETD, DIETI, ENG, FEPAC, HSA, IPSY, LAW, MED, MUS, OT, PCSAS, PH, PTA, SP, SW, THEOL

01 President ... Robert A. BROWN
05 University Provost ... Jean MORRISON
17 Provost Med Campus/Dean Sch of Med ... Karen H. ANTMAN
100 VP & Chief of Staff to President ... Douglas A. SEARS
04 Admin Asst to the President ... Megan S. COHEN
49 Dean Col/Grad Sch Arts & Sciences ... Ann CUDD
60 Dean College of Communication ... Thomas FIEDLER
53 Interim Dean School of Education ... Catherine O'CONNOR
54 Dean College of Engineering ... Kenneth R. LUTCHEN
57 Interim Dean College of Fine Arts ... Lynne ALLEN
97 Dean College General Studies ... Natalie MCKNIGHT
88 Dean School of Hospitality Admin ... Arun UPNEJA
61 Dean of School of Law ... Maureen A. O'ROURKE
50 Dean Questrom School of Business ... Kenneth W. FREEMAN
42 Dean of Marsh Chapel ... Robert A. HILL
51 Dean Metropolitan College/Ext Ed ... Tanya ZLATEVA
76 Dean SAR Health & Rehab Sciences ... Christopher A. MOORE
70 Interim Dean School of Social Work ... Judith G. GONYEA
73 Dean School of Theology ... Mary Elizabeth MOORE
88 Dean Pardee Sch of Global Studies ... Adil NAJAM
52 Dean Goldman Sch of Dental Medicine ... Jeffrey W. HUTTER
69 Dean School of Public Health ... Sandro GALEA
32 Associate Provost/Dean of Students ... Kenneth ELMORE
46 VP & Assoc Provost Research ... Gloria WATERS
58 Assoc Provost Graduate Affairs ... Daniel L. KLEINMAN
88 Assoc Provost Budget & Planning ... Patricia O'BRIEN
88 Assc Prov Strateg Init/Chief of Stf ... Nicole HAWKES
20 Assoc Provost Undergraduate Affairs ... Elizabeth LOIZEAUX
20 Assoc Provost for Faculty Affairs ... Julie H. SANDELL
28 Assoc Provost Diversity & Inclusion ... Crystal A. WILLIAMS
106 Asoc Prov Digital Lrng & Innovation ... Chris DELLAROCAS
101 Sr VP/Sr Counsel & Board Secy ... Todd L C. KLIPP
18 Senior Vice President Operations ... Gary W. NICKSA
26 Senior VP External Affairs ... Stephen P. BURGAY
30 Senior VP Devel/Alumni Relations ... Scott G. NICHOLS
10 Senior Vice Pres/CFO & Treasurer ... Martin J. HOWARD
109 Vice President Auxiliary Services ... Peter SMOKOWSKI
43 VP & General Counsel ... Erika GEETTER
86 Vice President Federal Relations ... Jennifer GRODSKY
18 VP Real Estate & Facility Services ... Michael DONOVAN
110 Vice President Development ... Karen ENGELBOURG
114 VP Budget and Capital Planning ... Derek HOWE
88 VP/Assoc Provost Global Programs ... Willis G. WANG
13 VP Information Services & Tech ... Tracy SCHROEDER
84 VP/Assoc Prov Enroll & Stdnt Admin ... Christine W. MCGUIRE
86 VP Government & Community Rel ... Robert DONAHUE
11 Vice Pres Administrative Services ... Peter FIEDLER
29 VP Alumni Relations ... Steven A. HALL
27 VP For Marketing And Creative Svcs ... Amy HOOK
115 Chief Investment Officer ... Lila HUNNEWELL
19 Exec Dir Pub Safety/Chief of Police ... Kelly A. NEE
39 Exec Director of Housing/Dining ... Marc ROBILLARD
103 Exec Dir Career Development ... Louis V. GAGLINI
15 Chief Human Resources Officer ... Diane M. TUCKER
07 Assoc VP/Exec Dir Undergraduate Adm ... Kelly A. WALTER
35 Assoc VP Enroll & Student Affairs ... Denise MOONEY
25 Assoc VP Sponsored Programs ... Diane BALDWIN
44 Assoc VP Sch-based Dev & Alum Rels ... Adam K. WISE
88 Assoc VP Budget & Capital Planning ... Ines GARRANT
88 Assistant Dean Summer Term ... Donna SHEA
35 Asst Dean Stdnts/Ex Dir Stdnt Activ ... John BATTAGLINO, JR.
44 Asst VP Annual Giving ... Daniel E. ALLENBY
09 Asst VP Institutional Research ... Melanie MADAIO-O'BRIEN
41 Asst VP & Director of Athletics ... Drew MARROCHELLO
06 Asst VP/University Registrar ... Christine S. PAAL
96 Asst VP/Chief Procurement Officer ... Randall MOORE
104 Exec Director Study Abroad ... Gareth MCFEELY
37 Exec Dir Financial Assistance ... Julie WICKSTROM
09 Director Institutional Research ... Linette A. DECARIE
88 Exec Director Physical Ed Rec/Dance ... Timothy MOORE
85 Director Intl Student/Scholars Ofc ... Jeanne KELLEY
28 Director Howard Thurman Center ... Katherine J. KENNEDY
22 Dir Equal Opportunity ... Kim RANDALL
36 Director Student Employment ... Mary Ann FRENCH
108 Director Institutional Assessment ... Gillian PIERCE
08 University Librarian ... Robert E. HUDSON
88 Dir Ugrd Research Opportunities Pgm ... John CELENZA
88 General Manager Agganis Arena ... Kristoffer W. BRASSIL
23 Director Student Health Services ... Judy T. PLATT
35 Senior Assoc Dir Student Activities ... Bryan ADAMS

Brandeis University (A)

415 South Street, Waltham MA 02453

County: Middlesex — FICE Identification: 002133
Unit ID: 165015
Telephone: (781) 736-2000 — Carnegie Class: DU-Highest
FAX Number: (781) 736-8699 — Calendar System: Semester
URL: www.brandeis.edu
Established: 1948 — Annual Undergrad Tuition & Fees: $51,245
Enrollment: 5,752 — Coed
Affiliation or Control: Independent Non-Profit — IRS Status: 501(c)3
Highest Offering: Doctorate
Accreditation: EH

01 President ... Dr. Ronald D. LIEBOWITZ
05 Provost ... Dr. Lisa M. LYNCH
10 Exec VP for Finance/Administration ... Mr. Stewart URETSKY
111 Sr Vice Pres Inst Advancement ... Vacant
32 Sr Vice Pres for Students/Enroll ... Mr. Andrew FLAGEL
43 Sr VP and General Counsel ... Mr. Steven S. LOCKE
26 Sr VP Comm and External Relations ... Mr. Ira JACKSON
28 Chief Diversity Officer ... Dr. Mark BRIMHALL-VARGAS
18 Vice Pres for Operations ... Mr. James W. GRAY
13 Chief Information Officer ... Mr. James LACRETA
15 Vice Pres Human Resources ... Ms. Robin NELSON-BAILEY
45 VP Planning/Institutional Research ... Mr. Dan FELDMAN
49 Dean of Arts & Sciences ... Dr. Susan J. BIRREN
70 Dn Heller Sch Social Pol & Mgt ... Dr. David WEIL
50 Int Dean International Business Sch ... Dr. Peter A. PETRI
06 University Registrar ... Dr. Mark S. HEWITT
08 Interim University Librarian ... Mr. Matthew SHEEHY
07 Dean of Admissions ... Ms. Jennifer WALKER
09 Director of Institutional Research ... Ms. Judith A. JAFFE
102 Asst VP Corp & Foundation Relations ... Mr. Michael DETTELBACH
36 Exec Director Hiatt Career Center ... Ms. Andrea B. DINE
37 Exec Director Student Financial Svc ... Ms. Sherri M. AVERY

Cambridge College (B)

1000 Massachusetts Avenue, Cambridge MA 02138-5304

County: Middlesex — FICE Identification: 021829
Unit ID: 165167
Telephone: (800) 877-4723 — Carnegie Class: Masters/L
FAX Number: (617) 349-3545 — Calendar System: Trimester
URL: www.cambridgecollege.edu
Established: 1971 — Annual Undergrad Tuition & Fees: $14,436
Enrollment: 2,800 — Coed
Affiliation or Control: Independent Non-Profit — IRS Status: 501(c)3
Highest Offering: Doctorate
Accreditation: EH, CAEPT

01 President ... Deborah C. JACKSON
05 Interim Provost ... Dr. Gilda GELY
15 VP of Human Resources ... Lauretta SIGGERS
10 CFO/VP of Finance & Administration ... John SPINARD
111 VP of Institutional Advancement ... Carson BERGLUND
26 VP Marketing/Communications and PR ... Jacqueline CONRAD
86 VP of Strategic Partnerships ... Phillip PAGE
45 VP of Innovation/Strat Initiatives ... Mark ROTONDO
43 Acting General Counsel ... Judith SIZER
13 Director of Information Technology ... Achal KHATRI
37 Director of Financial Aid ... Frank LAUDER
21 Controller ... Dorothy WHALEN
06 Registrar ... Amy CAVALIER
88 Dir of Student Financial Services ... Sabrina HARLAN
112 Director of Major Gifts ... Alex MORR
12 Asst Director of Lawrence MA ... Brooks WINCHELL
29 Dir Annual Fund/Alumni Engagement ... Erik RYAN
09 Director of Institutional Research ... Dr. Tracy MCLAUGHLIN-VOLPE
12 Director of Puerto Rico ... Dr. Santiago MENDEZ-HERNANDEZ
12 Director of Southern California ... Rita CLEMONS
12 Asst Director of Lawrence MA ... Melissa Sue FRASCA
12 Director Springfield MA ... Teresa (Terrie) FORTE
07 Director of Admissions ... Carol LOMBARDI
102 Dir Foundation/Corporate Relations ... Sonnya ESPINAL
20 Dean Undergraduate Studies ... James LEE
54 Dean School of Psychology ... Dr. Niti SETH
32 Dean Student Affairs/Student Life ... Regina ROBINSON
53 Dean School of Education ... Dr. Sheila WRIGHT
50 Dean School of Management ... Mary Ann JOSEPH
88 Academic Affairs Chief of Staff ... Nelleen CHANDLER KNIGHT
88 Liaison to the Board of Trustees ... Kevin WONG
04 Administrative Asst to President ... Robyn CARROLL

Clark University (C)

950 Main Street, Worcester MA 01610-1477

County: Worcester — FICE Identification: 002139
Unit ID: 165334
Telephone: (508) 793-7711 — Carnegie Class: DU-Mod
FAX Number: (508) 793-7780 — Calendar System: Semester
URL: www.clarku.edu
Established: 1887 — Annual Undergrad Tuition & Fees: $43,150
Enrollment: 3,485 — Coed
Affiliation or Control: Independent Non-Profit — IRS Status: 501(c)3
Highest Offering: Doctorate
Accreditation: EH, CLPSY

01 President ... Dr. David P. ANGEL
03 Executive Vice President ... Ms. Julie L. DOLAN
115 Chief Investment Officer ... Mr. James E. COLLINS
05 Provost & Vice Pres Academic Affs ... Dr. Davis BAIRD
111 Vice Pres University Advancement ... Mr. Jeffrey GILLOOLY
26 Vice Pres Marketing & Communication ... Ms. Paula DAVID
13 Vice Pres for Information Tech/CIO ... Ms. Pennie TURGEON
86 VP Government/Cmty Affs/Campus Svcs ... Mr. John FOLEY
32 Dean of Students ... Dr. Frances MAGEE
46 Interim Dean Research/Assoc Provost ... Dr. Yuko AOYAMA
58 Assoc Provost/Dean Graduate Studies ... Dr. William FISHER
49 Assoc Provost/Dean of College ... Dr. Matthew MALSKY
50 Dean Graduate School Mgmt ... Dr. Catherine USOFF
07 Dean of Admissions & Financial Aid ... Mr. Donald HONEMAN
37 Director of Financial Aid ... Ms. Mary Ellen SEVERANCE
08 University Librarian ... Dr. Gwendolynne ARTHUR
10 Controller ... Ms. Katherine CANNON
36 Director Career Services ... Ms. Victoria COX-LANYON
06 Registrar ... Ms. Rebecca HUNTER
15 Interim Dir of HR/Affirm Act ... Mr. David EVERITT
18 Director of Physical Plant ... Mr. Daniel RODERICK
41 Director of Athletics ... Ms. Trish CRONIN
19 Chief of Campus Police ... Mr. Stephen P. GOULET
23 Director of Health Services ... Ms. Robin MCNALLY
28 Chief Officer Diversity/Inclusion ... Ms. Sheree MARLOWE
04 Assistant to the President ... Ms. Joanne MILLER
21 Business Manager ... Mr. Paul WYKES
09 Dir Strat Analytics/Instit Research ... Ms. Elissa LU
104 Director Study Abroad ... Ms. Alissa KRAMER
39 Director Student Housing ... Mr. Adam KEYES
110 Asst Vice Pres Univ Advancement ... Ms. Lindsay ALLEN
22 Title IX Coord/Asst Dean Wellness ... Ms. Lynn LEVEY

College of the Holy Cross (D)

1 College Street, Worcester MA 01610-2322

County: Worcester — FICE Identification: 002141
Unit ID: 166124
Telephone: (508) 793-2011 — Carnegie Class: Bac-A&S
FAX Number: (508) 793-3030 — Calendar System: Semester
URL: www.holycross.edu
Established: 1843 — Annual Undergrad Tuition & Fees: $48,940
Enrollment: 2,729 — Coed
Affiliation or Control: Roman Catholic — IRS Status: 501(c)3
Highest Offering: Baccalaureate
Accreditation: EH, THEA

01 President ... Rev. Philip L. BOROUGHS, SJ
04 Special Assistant to the President ... Ms. Jane CORR
05 VP Academic Affairs/Dean of Col ... Dr. Margaret FREIJE
10 VP Admin & Finance/Treasurer ... Ms. Dottie HAUVER
115 Chief Investment Officer ... Mr. Timothy JARRY
32 VP Student Affairs/Dean of Students ... Ms. Michelle MURRAY
30 VP for Development/Alumni Relations ... Ms. Tracy BARLOK
42 Vice President for Mission ... Rev. William R. CAMPBELL, SJ
20 Associate Dean of the College ... Mr. Ronald JARRET
21 Director of Finance/Asst Treasurer ... Ms. Elizabeth DIONNE
06 Registrar ... Ms. Patricia RING
07 Director of Admissions ... Ms. Ann B. MCDERMOTT
08 Director of Library Services ... Mr. Mark SHELTON
37 Director of Financial Aid ... Ms. Lynne M. MYERS
25 Director of Sponsored Research ... Ms. Stacy RISEMAN
42 Director Ofc of College Chaplains ... Ms. Marybeth KEARNS-BARRETT
71 Director Ctr Interdisc/Spec Studies ... Dr. Richard E. MATLAK
36 Director of Career Planning ... Ms. Amy MURPHY
13 Director Information Tech Services ... Dr. Ellen J. KEOHANE
26 VP for Communications ... Mr. Dan KIM
29 Director of Alumni Relations ... Ms. Kristyn M. DYER
19 Director of Public Safety ... Vacant
35 Director of Campus Center ... Mr. Jeremiah O'CONNOR
18 Director of Physical Plant ... Mr. Scott M. MERRILL
41 Director of Athletics ... Mr. Nathan PINE
21 Controller ... Ms. Charlene BELLOWS
38 Director Counseling Center ... Dr. Paul GALVINHILL
23 Director Student Health Services ... Ms. Martha SULLIVAN
15 Director Human Resources ... Mr. David ACHENBACH
96 Manager of Purchasing ... Ms. Joan E. ANDERSON
09 Ofc of Assessment/Research ... Dr. Denise BELL
86 Dir of Govt/Cmty Relations ... Mr. Jamie D. HOAG
43 General Counsel ... Ms. Elizabeth SMALL
28 Chief Diversity Officer ... Mr. Amit TANEJA

College of Our Lady of the Elms (E)

291 Springfield Street, Chicopee MA 01013-2839

County: Hampden — FICE Identification: 002140
Unit ID: 167394
Telephone: (413) 594-2761 — Carnegie Class: Masters/S
FAX Number: (413) 592-4871 — Calendar System: Semester
URL: www.elms.edu
Established: 1928 — Annual Undergrad Tuition & Fees: $33,412
Enrollment: 1,712 — Coed
Affiliation or Control: Roman Catholic — IRS Status: 501(c)3
Highest Offering: Doctorate
Accreditation: EH, IACBE, NURSE, SW

01 President ... Dr. Harry E. DUMAY
05 Vice President of Academic Affairs ... Dr. Walter C. BREAU
10 Vice Pres Finance/Administration ... Brian E. DOHERTY
32 Dean of Students ... Teresa WINTERS
111 Vice Pres of Inst Advancement ... Dr. Carla OLESKA
07 Director of Admissions ... Joseph WAGNER
28 Dir of Diversity & Inclusion ... Javier VENTURA
121 Dean of Stdnt Success & Strat Init ... Dr. Joyce HAMPTON
06 Registrar ... Brooke ANDERSEN
08 Director of Library ... Anthony FONSECA
26 Director of Institutional Marketing ... Nancy FARRELL
37 Director of Financial Aid ... Kristin HMIELESKI
13 Director Information Technology ... Mary KASELOUSKAS
15 Director Human Resources/Personnel ... Deborah METHE
36 Dir of Career Development ... Phyllis WILLIAMS-THOMPSON
04 Assistant to President ... Sandra C. TALBOT
09 Dir of Institutional Research ... Karalee YVON
101 Clerk to Board of Trustees ... Sandra TALBOT
108 Dir of Institutional Assessment ... Karalee YVON
44 Dir of Annual Giving ... Ruth ROY
18 Chief Facilities & Physical Plant ... Michael SULLIVAN
39 Dir of Student Housing ... Dominick UGUCCIONI
19 Director Security & Safety ... Thomas FOLEY
29 Dir of Alumni Relations ... Jessica COLSON
36 Director Student Placement ... Vacant
41 Athletic Director ... Ellen MCEWEN
30 Asst VP of Inst Advancement ... Bernadette NOWAKOWSKI

66 Dean School of Nursing .... Dr. Kathleen SCOBLE
58 Dean Grad & Prof Studies .... Dr. Elizabeth HUKOWICZ

Conway School of Landscape Design (A)

332 S Deerfield Road, PO Box 179,
Conway MA 01341-0179

County: Franklin FICE Identification: 022743
Unit ID: 165495
Telephone: (413) 369-4044 Carnegie Class: Spec-4-yr-Arts
FAX Number: (413) 369-4032 Calendar System: Trimester
URL: www.csld.edu
Established: 1972 Annual Graduate Tuition & Fees: N/A
Enrollment: 24 Coed
Affiliation or Control: Independent Non-Profit IRS Status: 501(c)3
Highest Offering: Master's; No Undergraduates
Accreditation: EH

01 Executive Director .... Mr. Bruce STEDMAN
05 Academic Director .... Mr. Ken BYRNE
10 Finance Director .... Vacant
11 Senior Adminstrator .... Ms. Priscilla NOVITT
06 Registrar .... Ms. Nancy BRAXTON
07 Director of Admissions .... Ms. Kate CHOLOKIS
18 Chief Facilities/Physical Plant .... Mr. David WEBER
29 Director Alumni Relations .... Ms. Nancy BRAXTON

Curry College (B)

1071 Blue Hill Avenue, Milton MA 02186-2395

County: Norfolk FICE Identification: 002143
Unit ID: 165529
Telephone: (617) 333-0500 Carnegie Class: Masters/M
FAX Number: (617) 979-3540 Calendar System: Semester
URL: www.curry.edu
Established: 1879 Annual Undergrad Tuition & Fees: $37,835
Enrollment: 2,950 Coed
Affiliation or Control: Independent Non-Profit IRS Status: 501(c)3
Highest Offering: Master's
Accreditation: EH, NURSE

01 President .... Mr. Kenneth K. QUIGLEY, JR.
05 Vice President Academic Affairs .... Dr. David SZCZERBACKI
111 VP Institutional Advancement .... Mr. Christopher LAWSON
10 Chief Financial Officer .... Mr. Eric NORMAN
07 VP Admission & Dean Undergrad Admis .... Ms. Jane P. FIDLER
32 VP of Student Affairs .... Ms. Maryellen M. KILEY
45 VP of Institutional Planning .... Dr. Susan W. PENNINI
04 Assistant to the President .... Ms. Amy M. BIANCHI
08 Director Library .... Mr. Garrett EASTMAN
13 Chief Information Officer .... Ms. Deborah GELCH
35 VP of Human Resources .... Mirlen MAL
06 Registrar .... Ms. June KOUKOL
18 Director of Buildings & Grounds .... Mr. Robert G. O'CONNELL
30 Assoc VP of Institutional Advance .... Ms. Frances L. JACKSON
36 Director of Student Placement .... Ms. Kerrie ABORN
37 Assoc VP of Finance for SFS .... Ms. Stephanny J. ELIAS
38 Director of Student Counseling .... Dr. Alison W. MARKSON
09 Director of Institutional Research .... Ms. Jennifer DUNNE
105 Director Web Services .... Mr. John EAGAN
41 Athletic Director .... Mr. Vincent ERUZIONE
39 Director Student Housing .... Ms. Jennifer MAITINO

Dean College (C)

99 Main Street, Franklin MA 02038-1994

County: Norfolk FICE Identification: 002144
Unit ID: 165574
Telephone: (508) 541-1508 Carnegie Class: Bac/Assoc-Mixed
FAX Number: (508) 541-8726 Calendar System: Semester
URL: www.dean.edu
Established: 1865 Annual Undergrad Tuition & Fees: $36,660
Enrollment: 1,363 Coed
Affiliation or Control: Independent Non-Profit IRS Status: 501(c)3
Highest Offering: Baccalaureate
Accreditation: EH

01 President .... Dr. Paula M. ROONEY
100 Chief of Staff .... Ms. Sandra CAIN
05 VP Academic Affairs .... Dr. Michael FISHBEIN
10 Vice Pres Financial Svcs/Treasurer .... Mr. Dan MODELANE
84 VP Enrollment & Retention .... Ms. Cindy T. KOZIL
111 Vice Pres Institutional Advancement .... Ms. Coleen RESNICK
13 VP/Chief Information Officer .... Mr. Darrell KULESZA
15 VP/Chief Human Resources Officer .... Dr. Gary CONVERTINO
44 Assoc Vice Pres Leadership Gifts .... Mr. Ryan MCDONALD
21 Assoc VP/Controller/Asst Treasurer .... Ms. Kathleen MCGUIRE
07 Assoc VP Enrollment/Dean Admission .... Ms. Iris GODES
121 Assc VP Student Success/Career Plng .... Ms. Wendy ADLER
20 Asst VP Academic Affairs .... Ms. Melissa READ
18 Asst VP Capital Planning/Facilities .... Mr. Brian KELLY
26 VP Marketing & Business Development .... Mr. Gregg CHALK
32 Dean of Students .... Mr. David DRUCKER
51 Dean School of Continuing Studies .... Mr. Paul RESTEN
50 Dean School of Business .... Dr. P. Gerard SHAW
49 Dean Sch of Liberal Arts/Sciences .... Dr. Dawn POIRIER
57 Dean School of Dance/Arts .... Mr. Marc ARENTSEN
06 Registrar .... Vacant
19 Dir Law Enforcement Services .... Mr. Ken CORKRAN
08 Director of the Library .... Mr. Ted BURKE
41 Athletic Director .... Mr. Todd A. VASEY
39 Assistant Dean of Students .... Ms. Shannon VALVERDE
35 Dir Orientation/Community Service .... Ms. Jennifer POLIMER
40 Director of Bookstore .... Ms. Jackie CALDERONE
37 Dean Student & Financial Plng/Svcs .... Mr. Frank MULLEN
88 Director Enrollment Operations .... Ms. Kathleen RYAN
36 Dir Career Planning/Internships .... Ms. Thea CERIO
38 Director of Counseling Services .... Ms. Mary Ann SILVESTRI
29 Director Alumni Relations .... Ms. Lindsay MCHUGH

Eastern Nazarene College (D)

23 E Elm Avenue, Quincy MA 02170-2999

County: Norfolk FICE Identification: 002145
Unit ID: 165644
Telephone: (617) 745-3000 Carnegie Class: Masters/S
FAX Number: (617) 745-3907 Calendar System: 4/1/4
URL: www.enc.edu
Established: 1918 Annual Undergrad Tuition & Fees: $30,815
Enrollment: 1,101 Coed
Affiliation or Control: Church Of The Nazarene IRS Status: 501(c)3
Highest Offering: Master's
Accreditation: EH, SW

01 President .... Vacant
05 Provost & Chief Operating Officer .... Dr. Timothy T. WOOSTER
10 Vice President for Finance .... Mr. David CALDWELL
32 Vice Pres Student Development .... Mr. Jeff KIRKSEY
84 Associate Director of Enrollment .... Ms. Ashley RUDEEN
111 Vice President Inst Advancement .... Dr. Larry BOLLINGER
39 Dir of Residential Life & Housing .... Dr. Elizabeth MOREAU
06 Registrar .... Mr. Edward WICHROWSKI
37 Asst Dean of Student Financial Aid .... Dr. Delinda HALL
08 Director of Library Services .... Ms. Amy HWANG
19 Director Safety/Security/Risk Mgmt .... Mr. John GELORMINI
38 Dir Counseling & Career Services .... Mr. Bradford E. THORNE
58 Asst Dean of Graduate Studies .... Ms. Melinda SMITH
41 Athletic Director .... Mr. Bradford ZARGES
18 Director of Facilities .... Mr. Michael JOHNSTON
45 Supervisor Instructional Resources .... Ms. Patricia VASQUEZ
21 Controller .... Ms. Patricia CONSTANTINO
22 Director Human Resources .... Ms. Lauren BOWEN
40 Director Bookstore .... Ms. Keri LEWIS
13 Chief Information Officer .... Mr. Charles BURT
88 Admin Assistant to the Provost .... Mrs. Sheryl WEISEN
93 Dir of Multicultural Affairs .... Mr. Robert BENJAMIN
09 Director of Institutional Research .... Mr. Kevin WELLS
29 Alumni Relations Coordinator .... Mrs. Kimberly POLSGROVE
36 Director Student Placement .... Ms. Krista BOGERTMAN
20 Associate Dean for Academic Affairs .... Dr. Linda SCOTT

Emerson College (E)

120 Boylston Street, Boston MA 02116-4624

County: Suffolk FICE Identification: 002146
Unit ID: 165662
Telephone: (617) 824-8500 Carnegie Class: Masters/L
FAX Number: (617) 824-8511 Calendar System: Semester
URL: www.emerson.edu
Established: 1880 Annual Undergrad Tuition & Fees: $42,908
Enrollment: 4,479 Coed
Affiliation or Control: Independent Non-Profit IRS Status: 501(c)3
Highest Offering: Doctorate
Accreditation: EH, SP

01 President .... Mr. M. Lee PELTON
43 Vice President & General Counsel .... Ms. Christine HUGHES
10 Vice President for Admin & Finance .... Ms. Maureen MURPHY
05 Vice President for Academic Affairs .... Ms. Michaele WHELAN
13 VP for Information Technology .... Dr. William GILLIGAN
26 Vice Pres Communications/Marketing .... Mr. Michael SARRA
28 VP Diversity & Inclusion .... Ms. Sylvia SPEARS
84 Vice Pres Enrollment Management .... Ms. Ruthanne MADSEN
07 Assoc VP & Dean of Admissions .... Mr. Eric SYKES
21 Assoc Vice Pres for Finance .... Mr. Marc MILLER
15 Assoc Vice Pres for Human Resources .... Ms. Alexa JACKSON
111 AVP Inst Advance/Dir Alumni Affrs .... Ms. Barbara RUTBERG
86 Assoc Vice Pres Govt/Community Rels .... Ms. Margaret Ann INGS
58 Dean Grad Studies/AVP Acad Affairs .... Ms. Jan ROBERTS-BRESLIN
32 Vice Pres/Dean of Students .... Mr. James HOPPE
107 Exec Director Professional Studies .... Ms. Lesley NICHOLS
08 Exec Director of Library Services .... Mr. Robert FLEMING
07 Director of Graduate Admission .... Ms. Leanda FERLAND
36 Director of Career Services .... Ms. Carol SPECTOR
38 Director Counseling Center .... Dr. Elise HARRISON
41 Director Athletics .... Ms. Patricia NICOL
85 Director International Student Affs .... Ms. Virga MOHSINI
96 Director Purchasing/Risk Management .... Ms. Margaret ROGAN
39 Assoc Dean Campus Life .... Mr. Erik MUURISEPP
21 Controller .... Mr. Jonathan PEARSALL
06 Registrar .... Mr. William DEWOLF
42 Campus Chaplain .... Mr. Harrison BLUM
101 Exec Asst to the Board of Trustees .... Ms. Anne SHAUGHNESSY
18 Director of Facilities .... Mr. Joseph KNOLL
37 Director Financial Aid .... Ms. Angela GRANT
09 Director of Institutional Research .... Mr. Michael DUGGAN
04 Administrative Asst to President .... Ms. Maggie MELANSON
104 Director Study Abroad .... Mr. David GRIFFIN
19 Director Security/Safety .... Mr. Robert SMITH
25 Chief Contracts/Grants Admin .... Mr. Eric ASETTA
30 Chief Development/Advancement .... Mr. Ronald KORVAS

Emmanuel College (F)

400 The Fenway, Boston MA 02115-5798

County: Suffolk FICE Identification: 002147
Unit ID: 165671
Telephone: (617) 277-9340 Carnegie Class: Bac-A&S
FAX Number: (617) 735-9877 Calendar System: Semester
URL: www.emmanuel.edu
Established: 1919 Annual Undergrad Tuition & Fees: $37,540
Enrollment: 2,201 Coed
Affiliation or Control: Roman Catholic IRS Status: 501(c)3
Highest Offering: Master's
Accreditation: EH, NURSE

01 President .... Sr. Janet EISNER, SND
100 Exec Asst to the President .... Ms. Michelle ERICKSON
04 Senior Assistant to the President .... Ms. Lori SIMMONS
10 VP of Finance/Treasurer (CFO) .... Sr. Anne DONOVAN, SND
05 VP Academic Affairs & Dean .... Dr. William LEONARD
32 VP of Student Affairs .... Dr. Patricia RISSMEYER
30 AVP of Development & Alumni Rels .... Ms. Kristen CONROY
37 Assoc VP for Student Financial Svcs .... Ms. Jennifer PORTER
42 VP of Mission & Ministry .... Fr. John SPENCER, SJ
26 VP of Marketing & Communication .... Mr. Robert MCDONALD
84 Dean of Enrollment .... Ms. Sandra ROBBINS
35 Dean of Students .... Dr. Joseph ONOFRIETTI
06 Assoc VP for Inst Rsrch/Registrar .... Ms. Elizabeth ROSS
20 Assoc Dean Academic Administration .... Ms. Cindy O'CALLAGHAN
88 Asst Dean Cmty Stdrds & Family Pgms .... Ms. Mary Beth THOMAS
121 Assoc Dean of Academic Advising .... Sr. Susan THORNELL, SND
79 Assoc Dean Humanities/Soc Science .... Ms. Lisa STEPANSKI
66 Assoc Dean Nursing .... Ms. Diane SHEA
88 Dean Strategic Pgms & Partnership .... Dr. Josef KURTZ
08 Assoc Dn of Library/Lrng Resources .... Ms. Karen STORIN LINITZ
36 Executive Director Career Ctr .... Ms. Maureen ASHBURN
15 Director of Human Resources .... Ms. Erin FARMER NOONAN
41 Director of Athletics & Recreation .... Ms. Alexis MASTRONARDI
38 Director of Counseling .... Dr. Brenda HAWKS
90 Director of Academic Resource Ctr .... Ms. Wendy LABRON
09 Director of Institutional Research .... Ms. Alison VALLEREUX
13 Chief Info Technology Officer (CIO) .... Mr. Sean PHILPOTT
19 Director Security/Safety .... Mr. John KELLY
29 Director Alumni Relations .... Ms. Molly M. ZUCCARINI

Endicott College (G)

376 Hale Street, Beverly MA 01915-2098

County: Essex FICE Identification: 002148
Unit ID: 165699
Telephone: (978) 927-0585 Carnegie Class: Masters/L
FAX Number: (978) 927-0084 Calendar System: 4/1/4
URL: www.endicott.edu
Established: 1939 Annual Undergrad Tuition & Fees: $31,312
Enrollment: 4,695 Coed
Affiliation or Control: Independent Non-Profit IRS Status: 501(c)3
Highest Offering: Doctorate
Accreditation: EH, ART, CAATE, CIDA, NUR

01 President .... Dr. Richard E. WYLIE
03 Executive Vice President .... Ms. Lynne O'TOOLE
05 Vice President & Academic Dean .... Dr. Laura ROSSI-LE
10 Vice President Finance .... Mr. Tony FERULLO
84 Vice Pres Admissions/Financial Aid .... Mr. Thomas J. REDMAN
58 VP/Dean Graduate & Prof Stds .... Dr. Mary HUEGEL
111 Vice Pres Institutional Advancement .... Mr. David VIGNERON
20 VP/Dean of Academic Resources .... Dr. Kathleen BARNES
26 Assistant Vice President PR .... Ms. Joanne L. WALDNER
90 Assoc Dean of Academic Technology .... Mr. Kent BARCLAY
07 Associate Dean of Admission .... Mr. George M. SHERMAN
45 Executive Director of Research .... Mr. Peter L. HART
15 Director Human Resources .... Ms. Sally ARNOLD
21 Controller .... Mr. Andy VIDAL
06 Registrar .... Ms. Rosa CADENA
08 Library Director .... Mr. Brian COURTEMANCHE
37 Dean of Financial Aid .... Ms. Marcia D. TOOMEY
41 Director of Athletics .... Dr. Brian WYLIE
91 Chief Information Systems Officer .... Mr. Gary F. KELLEY
38 Director Counseling Center .... Ms. Karen TOMPKINS
18 Director of Physical Plant .... Mr. Dennis MONACO
27 Director Communications .... Ms. Carol RAICHE
36 Director of Career Services .... Ms. Dale MCLENNAN
36 Dean of Internship & Career Center .... Mr. Eric HALL
09 Director of Institutional Research .... Mr. Donny FEMINO
96 Director of Purchasing .... Ms. Susan AYERS
85 Dean of International Education .... Dr. Warren JAFERIAN
49 Dean of Arts & Sciences .... Dr. Gene WONG
53 Dean of Education .... Dr. Sara QUAY
57 Dean of Visual & Performing Arts .... Mr. Mark TOWNER
59 Dean of Hospitality Management .... Dr. William H. SAMENFINK
68 Dean of Sports Science/Fitness Stds .... Dr. Deborah SWANTON
66 Dean of Nursing .... Dr. Kelly FISHER
50 Dean of Business .... Dr. Michael PAIGE
60 Dean of Communication .... Dr. Laurel HELLERSTEIN
88 Director Internship .... Ms. Cindy RICHARD
101 Executive Administrative Assistant .... Ms. Amy ASTOLFI
105 Director Web Development .... Ms. Jeanne COMMETTE
19 Director of Public Safety/Chief .... Mr. Charles FEMINO
43 General Counsel .... Ms. Karen ABBOTT
104 Director Study Abroad .... Ms. Alicia VINAL
29 Director of Alumni Relations .... Ms. Jessica JACOBS
32 Dean of Students .... Ms. Brandi JOHNSON
44 Director of Annual Giving .... Ms. Sarah EARNEST
04 Administrative Asst to President .... Ms. Amy ASTOLFI
39 Director Student Housing .... Ms. Caitlin COURTNEY-BIEDRZYCKI

FINE Mortuary College (A)

150 Kerry Place, Norwood MA 02062
County: Norfolk　FICE Identification: 033164
Unit ID: 436599
Telephone: (781) 762-1211　Carnegie Class: Spec 2-yr-A&S
FAX Number: (781) 762-7177　Calendar System: Quarter
URL: www.fmc.edu
Established: 1996　Annual Undergrad Tuition & Fees: $19,980
Enrollment: 95　Coed
Affiliation or Control: Proprietary　IRS Status: Proprietary
Highest Offering: Associate Degree
Accreditation: FUSER

01 President .... Mrs. Sherry JONES
03 Executive Vice President .... Mr. Kevin KOCH
05 Program Director .... Mr. Peter MASUZZO
11 Campus Manager .... Mr. Jason KELLER

Fisher College (B)

118 Beacon Street, Boston MA 02116-1500
County: Suffolk　FICE Identification: 002150
Unit ID: 165802
Telephone: (617) 236-8800　Carnegie Class: Bac/Assoc-Mixed
FAX Number: (617) 236-8858　Calendar System: Semester
URL: www.fisher.edu
Established: 1903　Annual Undergrad Tuition & Fees: $29,640
Enrollment: 1,959　Coed
Affiliation or Control: Independent Non-Profit　IRS Status: 501(c)3
Highest Offering: Master's
Accreditation: EH, CAHIIM, NURSE

01 President .... Dr. Alan RAY
05 Vice President Academic Affairs .... Dr. Janet KUSER
10 VP for Finance .... Mr. Steven RICH
84 VP of Enrollment Management .... Mr. Robert MELARAGNI
11 General Counsel/VP Operations .... Ms. Carolina AVELLANEDA
32 Dean of Students .... Ms. Shiela LALLY
88 Dean Intl Acad Oper/Curriculum Dev .... Ms. Nancy PITHIS
49 Asst Dean School of Liberal Arts .... Vacant
06 College Registrar .... Vacant
41 Director of Athletics .... Vacant
21 Director of Accounting .... Mr. Jeffrey CONRAD
13 Director of Information Services .... Mr. Jonathan BARTSCH
18 Director of Facilities .... Mr. Paul MCBRINE
37 Director of Financial Aid .... Ms. Laura BIECHLER
45 VP of Strategy and Planning .... Dr. Melinda COOK
20 Assistant Dean for Academic Affairs .... Mr. Carla DELUCIA
19 Chief Dept of Public Safety .... Ms. Deborah CRAFTS
36 Director of Career Services .... Ms. Barbara ZERILLO
88 Director of Accessibility Service .. Dr. Wanda CAMACHO-MARON
113 College Bursar .... Ms. Kristen MARTINEZ
08 College Librarian .... Mr. Joshua MCKAIN
29 Dir Student Activ & Alumni Affairs .... Ms. Amanda MATARESE
09 Director of Institutional Research .... Mr. Alex WAGNER
58 Dean Grad Studies .... Dr. Neil TROTTA
39 Director Student Housing .... Mr. Kyle GRENIER
04 Manager Office of President/HR Mgr .... Ms. Ellen LYONS

Franklin W. Olin College of Engineering (C)

Olin Way, Needham MA 02492-1200
County: Norfolk　FICE Identification: 039463
Unit ID: 441982
Telephone: (781) 292-2300　Carnegie Class: Spec-4-yr-Eng
FAX Number: (781) 292-2210　Calendar System: Semester
URL: www.olin.edu
Established: 1997　Annual Undergrad Tuition & Fees: $49,986
Enrollment: 370　Coed
Affiliation or Control: Independent Non-Profit　IRS Status: 501(c)3
Highest Offering: Baccalaureate
Accreditation: EH, ENG

01 President .... Dr. Richard K. MILLER
04 Asst to President .... Ms. Nancy SULLIVAN
05 Provost/Dean of Faculty .... Dr. Vincent P. MANNO
32 Dean of Student Affairs .... Ms. Rae-Anne BUTERA
06 Assoc Dean Student Life & Registrar .... Ms. Linda T. CANAVAN
07 Dean of Admission and Financial Aid . Ms. Emily ROPER-DOTEN
37 Director of Financial Aid .... Ms. Jean RICKER
08 Library Director .... Mr. Jeff GOLDENSON
03 Executive Vice President .... Mr. Stephen P. HANNABURY
10 VP for Financial Affairs & CFO .... Ms. Patricia GALLAGHER
13 Chief Information Officer .... Mr. Rick OSTERBERG
26 Chief Marketing Officer .... Ms. Michelle DAVIS
09 Asst Provost for Inst Research .... Mr. Jeremy GOODMAN
30 VP Development/Family & Alumni Rel .... Ms. Catherine DIDION

† All admitted students who enroll at Olin College receive an Olin Scholarship covering half tuition during the eight semesters of the baccalaureate program.

Gordon College (D)

255 Grapevine Road, Wenham MA 01984-1899
County: Essex　FICE Identification: 002153
Unit ID: 165936
Telephone: (978) 927-2300　Carnegie Class: Bac-A&S
FAX Number: (978) 867-4659　Calendar System: Semester
URL: www.gordon.edu
Established: 1889　Annual Undergrad Tuition & Fees: $36,060
Enrollment: 2,045　Coed
Affiliation or Control: Independent Non-Profit　IRS Status: 501(c)3
Highest Offering: Master's
Accreditation: EH, MUS, SW

01 President .... Dr. D. Michael LINDSAY
03 Exec VP and Chief of Staff .... Mr. Daniel TYMANN
05 Provost .... Dr. Janel CURRY
10 VP for Finance and Administration .... Mr. Michael J. AHEARN
07 AVP Enrollment .... Ms. June BODONI
32 Vice President for Student Life .... Mrs. Jennifer JUKANOVICH
26 VP of Marketing and Communications .... Mr. Rick SWEENEY
111 Chief Devel Ofcr/Sr VP Advancement .... Mr. Paul EDWARDS
08 Director of Library Services .... Mr. Myron SCHIRER-SUTER
06 Registrar .... Mrs. Alice A. FALCONE
13 AVP of Technology & Operations .... Mr. Christopher JONES
37 Sr Dir of Student Financial Svcs .... Mr. Daniel O'CONNELL
15 Director of Human Resources .... Ms. Nancy ANDERSON
18 Dir of Plant Operations and Sustain .... Mr. Paul HELGESEN
21 Controller .... Ms. Kim MATHER
30 AVP College Relations & Annual Fund .... Mrs. Britt CARLSON
36 Director of Career Services .... Ms. Pam LAZARAKIS
96 Dir of Purchasing and Distribution .... Mr. Michael NAWOICHIK
09 Exec Dir Institutional Research .... Mr. Robert VAN CLEEF
19 Director Security/Safety .... Mr. Glenn DECKERT
30 Dir of Development Information Tech .... Mr. Rick HOUSTON
41 Director of Athletics .... Mr. Jon TYMANN
105 Creative Dir and Web Team Lead .... Mr. Stephen DAGLEY
39 Director of Residence Life .... Mr. Michael CURTIS
35 Dean of Student Engagement .... Dr. Nicholas ROWE
121 Dean of Student Success .... Mr. Christopher CARLSON
04 Special Assistant to the President .... Miss Claire CAMPBELL

Gordon-Conwell Theological Seminary (E)

130 Essex Street, South Hamilton MA 01982-2317
County: Essex　FICE Identification: 009747
Unit ID: 165945
Telephone: (978) 468-7111　Carnegie Class: Spec-4-yr-Faith
FAX Number: (978) 468-6691　Calendar System: Semester
URL: www.gordonconwell.edu
Established: 1884　Annual Graduate Tuition & Fees: N/A
Enrollment: 1,924　Coed
Affiliation or Control: Independent Non-Profit　IRS Status: 501(c)3
Highest Offering: Doctorate; No Undergraduates
Accreditation: EH, THEOL

01 President .... Dr. Dennis HOLLINGER
10 Vice Pres Finance/Operations .... Mr. Jay S. TREWERN
05 Vice Pres for Academic Affairs .... Dr. Richard LINTS
111 Vice President of Advancement .... Mr. Kurt W. DRESCHER
12 Asst Dean of Boston Campus .... Dr. Seoung H. PARK
12 Chief Operations Charlotte Campus .... Dr. H. Neely GASTON
32 Dean of Students .... Ms. Michelle D. WILLIAMS
15 Exec Dir of Human Resources .... Ms. Robin HIGLE
13 Chief Information Officer .... Dr. Alex KOH
84 Dean Enrollment Mgmt .... Mr. Scott B. POBLENZ
18 Director of Physical Plant .... Mr. Timothy INGRAHAM
08 Director of Goddard Library .... Mr. James DARLACK
42 Dir Doctor of Ministry Programs .... Dr. David CURRIE
37 Director of Financial Aid .... Mr. Stacey T. GLIDDEN
40 Director of Support Services .... Mr. David SHOREY
19 Director of Campus Safety .... Mr. Cabot W. DODGE
26 Dir of Communications & Marketing .... Vacant
07 Asst Director of Admissions .... Ms. Sarah SOTELO
21 Controller & Dir Financial Svcs .... Mr. Gregg HANSEN
110 Chief Advancement Ofcr Charlotte .... Dr. H. Neely GASTON
06 Registrar .... Mr. Scott B. POBLENZ
29 Director Alumni Relations .... Mrs. Rhonda GIBSON
39 Director Student Housing .... Mr. Jason STRZEPEK
88 Dean of Hamilton Campus .... Dr. Thomas PFIZENMAIER

Hampshire College (F)

893 West Street, Amherst MA 01002-3372
County: Hampshire　FICE Identification: 004661
Unit ID: 166018
Telephone: (413) 549-4600　Carnegie Class: Bac-A&S
FAX Number: (413) 559-5584　Calendar System: 4/1/4
URL: www.hampshire.edu
Established: 1965　Annual Undergrad Tuition & Fees: $50,238
Enrollment: 1,410　Coed
Affiliation or Control: Independent Non-Profit　IRS Status: 501(c)3
Highest Offering: Baccalaureate
Accreditation: EH

01 President .... Dr. Jonathan LASH
101 Secretary of the College .... Ms. Beth I. WARD
05 Vice President & Dean of Faculty .... Dr. Eva RUESCHMANN
32 VP Student Affairs/Dean of Students .... Mr. Byron MCCRAE
10 Vice Pres for Finance & Admin .... Mr. Mary MCENEANY
15 Assoc Vice Pres Human Resources ..... Ms. Ann Michele RUOCCO
111 Chief Advancement Officer .... Mr. Clay BALLANTINE
84 Dean of Enrollment/Retention .... Ms. Meredith TWOMBLY
08 Director of Library/Info Services .... Ms. Jennifer KING
06 Director of Central Records .... Ms. Roberta P. STUART
37 Director of Financial Aid .... Ms. Jennifer G. LAWTON
09 Director of Institutional Research .... Ms. Meredith TWOMBLY
18 Director of Facilities and Grounds .... Mr. Larry ARCHEY
20 AVP of Academic Affairs .... Ms. Yaniris FERNANDEZ
26 Chief Creative Officer .... Mr. David GIBSON
29 Director Alumni & Family Relations ...... Ms. Melissa MILLS-DICK
36 Director Student Placement .... Ms. Carin RANK
38 Director Student Counseling .... Dr. Eliza MCARDLE
100 Chief of Staff .... Ms. Joanna OLIN
28 Chief Diversity Officer .... Ms. Diana FERNANDEZ

Harvard University (G)

1350 Massachusetts Ave, Cambridge MA 02138-3800
County: Middlesex　FICE Identification: 002155
Unit ID: 166027
Telephone: (617) 495-1000　Carnegie Class: DU-Highest
FAX Number: (617) 495-0500　Calendar System: Semester
URL: www.harvard.edu
Established: 1636　Annual Undergrad Tuition & Fees: $47,074
Enrollment: 29,652　Coed
Affiliation or Control: Independent Non-Profit　IRS Status: 501(c)3
Highest Offering: Doctorate
Accreditation: EH, CLPSY, DENT, ENG, IPSY, LAW, LSAR, MED, PCSAS, PH, PLNG, THEOL

01 President .... Drew FAUST
05 Provost .... Alan GARBER
49 Dean Arts and Sciences .... Michael D. SMITH
58 Dean Graduate School of A&S .... Xiao-Li MENG
50 Dean Harvard Business School .... Nitin NOHRIA
49 Dean Harvard College .... Rakesh KHURANA
56 Dean Continuing Educ and Extension .... Huntington D. LAMBERT
52 Dean School of Dental Medicine .... R. Bruce DONOFF
48 Dean Graduate School of Design .... Moshen MOSTAFAVI
73 Dean Harvard Divinity School .... David N. HEMPTON
53 Dean Graduate School of Education .... James E. RYAN
54 Dean Engineering/Applied Sciences .... Francis J. DOYLE
80 Dean Kennedy School of Government .... Douglas ELMENDORF
61 Dean Harvard Law School .... John F. MANNING
63 Dean Harvard Medical School .... George Q. DALEY
69 Dean School of Public Health .... Michelle A. WILLIAMS
88 Dean Inst for Advanced Studies .... Lizabeth COHEN
88 Treasurer .... Paul J. FINNEGAN
03 Executive Vice President .... Katherine N. LAPP
43 Sr VP and General Counsel .... Robert IULIANO
29 VP Alumni Affairs/Development .... Tamara ROGERS
10 VP for Finance and CFO .... Thomas HOLLISTER
101 VP and Secretary of the University .... Marc GOODHEART
88 VP for Strategy and Programs .... Leah ROSOVSKY
26 VP Public Affairs and Communication .... Paul ANDREW
15 VP for Human Resources .... Vacant
45 VP Planning and Project Management .... Vacant
08 VP for the Harvard Library .... Sarah E. THOMAS
13 VP and CIO .... Anne MARGULIES
18 VP for Campus Services .... Meredith WEENICK

Hebrew College (H)

160 Herrick Road, Newton Centre MA 02459-2237
County: Middlesex　FICE Identification: 002157
Unit ID: 166045
Telephone: (617) 559-8600　Carnegie Class: Spec-4-yr-Faith
FAX Number: (617) 559-8601　Calendar System: Semester
URL: www.hebrewcollege.edu
Established: 1921　Annual Undergrad Tuition & Fees: N/A
Enrollment: 191　Coed
Affiliation or Control: Independent Non-Profit　IRS Status: 501(c)3
Highest Offering: Beyond Master's But Less Than Doctorate
Accreditation: EH

01 President .... Rabbi Daniel LEHMANN
10 Vice Pres Finance & Administration .... Mr. Keith DROPKIN
05 Provost .... Mr. Michael SHIRE
84 Director of Enrollment Management .... Mr. Bob GIELOW
06 Registrar/Dir Student Financial Aid .... Ms. Marilyn JAYE
15 Director Personnel Services .... Ms. Steffi BOBBIN
04 Assistant to the President .... Mr. Micah ROYER
13 Director Information Technology .... Mr. Jim KEEN
26 Marketing Communications Manager .... Ms. Sharon KATZ

Hellenic College-Holy Cross Greek Orthodox School of Theology (I)

50 Goddard Avenue, Brookline MA 02445-7496
County: Norfolk　FICE Identification: 002154
Unit ID: 166054
Telephone: (617) 731-3500　Carnegie Class: Spec-4-yr-Faith
FAX Number: (617) 850-1460　Calendar System: Semester
URL: www.hchc.edu
Established: 1937　Annual Undergrad Tuition & Fees: $22,490
Enrollment: 193　Coed
Affiliation or Control: Greek Orthodox　IRS Status: 501(c)3
Highest Offering: Master's
Accreditation: EH, THEOL

01 President .... RevDr. Christopher T. METROPULOS
73 Dean School of Theology .... Dr. James SKEDROS
05 Dean Hellenic College .... Dr. Demetrios KATOS
32 Interim Dean of Students .... Mr. Antonios PAPATHANASIOU
10 Chief Financial Officer .... Mr. Kevin DERRIVAN
07 Director of Admissions & Records .... Mr. Gregory FLOOR
08 Director Library .... Rev. Joachim COTSONIS
37 Financial Aid Director .... Mr. Michael KIRCHMAIER
06 Registrar .... Mr. Jay OSTROSKY
13 Director Computing/Information Mgmt .... Vacant

111 Director Institutional Advancement ... Mr. Kosta ALEXIS
29 Director of Alumni Office ... Vacant
21 Controller ... Vacant
40 Bookstore Manager ... Ms. Nikoleta MAIDOU
39 Director of Housing/Security ... Vacant
15 Director of Human Resources ... Mr. David VOLZ
44 Director Annual or Planned Giving ... Ms. Frances LEVAS
45 Director Strategic Initiatives ... Mr. Gary ALEXANDER

Hult International Business School (A)

One Education Street, Cambridge MA 02141-1805
County: Middlesex FICE Identification: 041432
Unit ID: 164368
Telephone: (617) 746-1990 Carnegie Class: Spec-4-yr-Bus
FAX Number: (617) 746-1991 Calendar System: Other
URL: www.hult.edu
Established: 1964 Annual Undergrad Tuition & Fees: $36,450
Enrollment: 1,158 Coed
Affiliation or Control: Proprietary IRS Status: Proprietary
Highest Offering: Doctorate
Accreditation: EH

01 President ... Dr. Stephen J. HODGES
05 Chief Academic Officer ... Prof. Johan ROOS
88 Chief Innovation Officer ... Dr. Mukul KUMAR
11 Chief Operations Officer ... Mr. Chris HOLMES
20 Dean of Faculty ... Mr. Nick AMDUR
12 Dean Boston Campus ... Dr. Emmett TRACY
12 Dean San Francisco Campus ... Ms. Mona DHILLON
84 Regional Director Enrollment ... Mr. Steve WYNN
36 Dir of Career Services Boston ... Ms. Maggie DALEY
32 Dir Student Services Boston ... Ms. Nayeli VIVANCO
06 Senior Registrar Boston Campus ... Mr. Richard LESTAGE
06 Registrar San Francisco Campus ... Ms. Megan MOOSE
37 Director Student Financial Aid ... Ms. Karen VAN DYNE

Laboure College (B)

303 Adams Street, Milton MA 02186-4253
County: Suffolk FICE Identification: 006324
Unit ID: 165264
Telephone: (617) 322-3500 Carnegie Class: Spec-4-yr-Other Health
FAX Number: (617) 296-7947 Calendar System: Semester
URL: www.laboure.edu
Established: 1892 Annual Undergrad Tuition & Fees: $35,298
Enrollment: 803 Coed
Affiliation or Control: Roman Catholic IRS Status: 501(c)3
Highest Offering: Baccalaureate
Accreditation: EH, ADNUR, CAHIIM, NDT, NURSE, RTT

01 Interim President ... Lea A. JOHNSON
05 Interim Vice Pres Academic Affairs ... Marilyn GARDNER
84 Vice Pres Enrollment Management ... Matthew GREGORY
04 Senior Executive Asst to President ... Megan D. CURRIVAN
06 Registrar ... John SACCO
07 Director of Admissions ... Erin HANLON
08 Director of Library ... Andrew CALO
10 Controller ... William MCDONALD
13 Chief Information Officer ... Quintin LATIN
15 Chief Human Resource Officer ... Martha DOVE
26 Chief Marketing Officer ... Katelyn DWYER

Lasell College (C)

1844 Commonwealth Avenue, Newton MA 02466-2716
County: Middlesex FICE Identification: 002158
Unit ID: 166391
Telephone: (617) 243-2000 Carnegie Class: Masters/M
FAX Number: (617) 243-2389 Calendar System: Semester
URL: www.lasell.edu
Established: 1851 Annual Undergrad Tuition & Fees: $33,600
Enrollment: 2,160 Coed
Affiliation or Control: Independent Non-Profit IRS Status: 501(c)3
Highest Offering: Master's
Accreditation: EH, ACBSP, CAATE, EXSC

01 President ... Michael B. ALEXANDER
88 VP/Special Asst to President ... Pamela FARIA
05 VP Academic Affairs ... James OSTROW
10 VP Admin & Finance/CFO ... Michael HOYLE
84 VP Enrollment Management ... Kathleen O'CONNOR
88 President/Lasell Village ... Anne DOYLE
32 VP Student Affairs ... Diane AUSTIN
58 VP Graduate & Prof Studies ... Eric TURNER
30 VP Development & Alumni Relations ... Dean HICKEY
21 Assoc VP Admin & Finance ... Diane PARKER
20 Assoc VP/Dean UG Educ ... Steven BLOOM
07 Asst VP/Dean UG Admission ... James TWEED
107 Dean Grad & Prof Studies ... Joan DOLAMORE
89 Dean Advis & First Year Programs ... Helena SANTOS
35 Dean Student Affairs ... David HENNESSEY
37 Dir Student Financial Planning ... Michele KOSBOTH
09 Dir Institutional Research ... Eric LANTHIER
06 Registrar ... Dianne POLIZZI
18 Director Plant Operations ... Wayne LAMOUREUX
27 Dir Communications ... Vacant
29 Dir Alumni Relations ... Lauren MCCAUSLIN
35 Dir Student Act & Orientation ... Jennifer GRANGER
23 Dir Health Services ... Vacant
08 Dir Library ... Vacant
41 Dir Athletics ... Kristy WALTER
15 Dir Human Resources ... Marymichele DELANEY
38 Dir Counseling Center ... Janice FLETCHER
123 Dir Graduate Enrollment ... Adrienne FRANCIOSI
13 Chief Information Officer ... Jonathan GORHAM
39 Dir Residential Life ... Woodrow FREESE
19 Director Security/Safety ... Robert WINSOR
43 Dir Legal Services/General Counsel ... Jennifer OKEEFFE

Lesley University (D)

29 Everett Street, Cambridge MA 02138-2790
County: Middlesex FICE Identification: 002160
Unit ID: 166452
Telephone: (617) 868-9600 Carnegie Class: DU-Mod
FAX Number: (617) 349-8717 Calendar System: Semester
URL: www.lesley.edu
Established: 1909 Annual Undergrad Tuition & Fees: $25,875
Enrollment: 5,067 Coed
Affiliation or Control: Independent Non-Profit IRS Status: 501(c)3
Highest Offering: Doctorate
Accreditation: EH, ART, CAEPT

01 President ... Mr. Jeff A. WEISS
05 Interim Provost ... Dr. Richard HANSEN
11 Vice President for Administration ... Ms. Marylou BATT
10 Vice President/CFO ... Ms. Bernice BRADIN
111 Interim VP of Advancement ... Mr. Timothy CROSS
84 VP of Enrollment Management ... Mr. Timothy ROBISON
114 VP for Budgeting & Fin Planning ... Ms. M. L. DYMSKI
43 General Counsel ... Ms. Shirin PHILIPP
45 VP Strategy & Implementation ... Dr. MaryPat LOHSE
20 Associate Provost ... Dr. Lisa IJIRI
58 Dean Grad Sch Arts & Social Sci ... Dr. David KATZ
53 Dean School of Education ... Dr. Jack GILLETTE
32 Dean of Student Life & Academic Dev ... Dr. Nathaniel MAYS
49 Dean College of Liberal Arts & Sci ... Dr. Steven SHAPIRO
57 Dean of College of Art and Design ... Dr. Richard ZAUFT
13 Chief Information Officer ... Ms. Amy DONOVAN
123 Director of Graduate Admissions ... Ms. Barbara SELMO
15 Director of Human Resources ... Ms. Jane JOYCE
37 Director of Financial Aid ... Mr. Scott JEWELL
21 Controller ... Mr. Stephen MICARELLI
08 Dean of Libraries ... Mr. Hedi BENAICHA
07 Dir Undergrad Admissions ... Ms. Deb KOCAR
09 Dir of Assessment/Inst Research ... Dr. Linda PURSLEY
04 Assistant to the President ... Ms. Kathleen SAMMARTINO
06 Registrar ... Ms. Adrianne ZONDERMAN
28 Dir Equal Opportunity & Inclusion ... Vacant

Longy School of Music of Bard College (E)

27 Garden Street, Cambridge MA 02138
Telephone: (617) 876-0956 Identification: 770137
Accreditation: &M

† Branch campus of Bard College, Annandale-On-Hudson, NY

*Massachusetts Board of Higher Education (F)

One Ashburton Place, Room 1401,
Boston MA 02108-1696
County: Suffolk FICE Identification: 029283
Unit ID: 166531
Telephone: (617) 994-6950 Carnegie Class: N/A
FAX Number: (617) 727-6397
URL: www.mass.edu

01 Commissioner ... Dr. Carlos SANTIAGO
45 Chief Strategy Officer ... Mr. David C. CEDRONE
05 Assoc Comm Academic Affs/Stdnt Succ ... Dr. Winifred M. HAGAN
09 Sr Comm Research/Planning ... Dr. Jonathan KELLER
43 General Counsel ... Ms. Constantia PAPANIKOLAOU
10 Dep Comm Administration and Finance ... Mr. Sean NELSON
37 Sr Dep Comm Student Financial Aid ... Dr. Clantha MCCURDY

*University of Massachusetts System Office (G)

One Beacon Street, 31st Floor, Boston MA 02108
County: Suffolk FICE Identification: 008017
Unit ID: 166665
Telephone: (617) 287-7050 Carnegie Class: N/A
FAX Number: (617) 287-7167
URL: www.umassp.edu

01 President ... Mr. Martin T. MEEHAN
03 Exec VP/Chief Operating Officer ... Mr. James JULIAN
05 Sr VP Acad Affs/Stdnt & Intl Affs ... Dr. Marcellette WILLIAMS
10 Sr VP Admin/Finance & Treasurer ... Ms. Lisa CALISE
111 Vice President for Advancement ... Mr. Charles PAGNAM
26 Vice President for Communications ... Mr. Jeff COURNOYER
11 Deputy Chief Operating Officer ... Ms. Susan KELLY
86 Special Asst to Pres Govt Relation ... Mr. David MCDERMOTT
43 General Counsel ... Ms. Deirdre HEATWOLE
13 CIO ... Vacant
101 Secretary to Board of Trustees ... Ms. Zunilka BARRETT
116 Director for University Auditing ... Mr. Kyle DAVID
15 Human Resources Officer ... Mr. Andrew RUSSELL
106 Interim CEO UMass Online ... Dr. John CUNNINGHAM

*University of Massachusetts (H)

Amherst MA 01003-0001
County: Hampshire FICE Identification: 002221
Unit ID: 166629
Telephone: (413) 545-0111 Carnegie Class: DU-Highest
FAX Number: N/A Calendar System: Semester
URL: www.umass.edu
Established: 1863 Annual Undergrad Tuition & Fees (In-State): $14,971
Enrollment: 29,269 Coed
Affiliation or Control: State IRS Status: 501(c)3
Highest Offering: Doctorate
Accreditation: EH, ART, AUD, CAEPN, CLPSY, DIETD, DIETI, ENG, IPSY, LSAR, MUS, NURSE, PH, PLNG, SCPSY, SP

02 Chancellor ... Dr. Kumble R. SUBBASWAMY
05 Sr VC/Provost Academic Affairs ... Dr. Katherine S. NEWMAN
10 Vice Chancellor Admin/Finance ... Mr. Andrew MANGELS
30 VC Development & Alumni Relations ... Mr. Michael A. LETO
46 Vice Chancellor Research ... Dr. Michael F. MALONE
32 VC Student Affairs & Campus Life ... Ms. Enku GELAYE
26 Vice Chanc University Relations ... Mr. John KENNEDY
41 Director of Athletics ... Mr. Ryan BAMFORD
43 Senior Counsel ... Mr. Brian W. BURKE
13 VC Information Services & CIO ... Ms. Julie L. BUEHLER
22 Executive Director EO&D ... Ms. Debora D. FERREIRA
28 Faculty Adv Diversity & Excellence ... Dr. Anna BRANCH
20 Vice Provost for Academic Affairs ... Dr. Elizabeth R. DUMONT
20 Vice Provost Undegrad & Cont Educ ... Dr. Carol A. BARR
58 Vice Provost/Dean of Grad School ... Dr. John J. MCCARTHY
88 Assoc Provost Academic Personnel ... Mr. Michael J. EAGEN
85 Exec Dir International Programs ... Dr. Kalpen TRIVEDI
84 Assoc Provost Enrollment Management ... Dr. James ROCHE
45 Assoc Chancellor/Chf Planning Ofcr ... Dr. Bryan C. HARVEY
20 Asst Provost Advising/Acad Advising ... Dr. Pamela R. MARSH-WILLIAMS
09 Int Dir Institutional Research ... Dr. Krisztina FILEP
108 Asst Provost Assessment/Educ Effect ... Dr. Martha L. STASSEN
51 Vice Provost Cont Professional Educ ... Dr. Geraldine N. DE BERLY
07 Director Undergraduate Admissions ... Vacant
37 Director Financial Aid Services ... Ms. Suzanne PETERS
06 University Registrar ... Mr. Patrick SULLIVAN
92 Dean Commonwealth Honors College ... Dr. Gretchen GERZINA
79 Dean Col Humanities & Fine Arts ... Dr. Julie C. HAYES
81 Dean Col Natural Science ... Dr. Tricia R. SERIO
53 Dean School of Education ... Dr. Cynthia GERSTL-PEPIN
54 Dean College of Engineering ... Dr. Timothy J. ANDERSON
50 Dean School of Management ... Dr. Mark A. FULLER
66 Dean School of Nursing ... Dr. Stephen CAVANAGH
69 Dean Sch Public Health/Health Sci ... Dr. C. Marjorie AELION
08 Director of Libraries ... Dr. Simon NEAME
56 Director of Extension ... Ms. Nancy GARRABRANTS
47 Dir Stockbridge School Agriculture ... Dr. Wesley AUTIO
88 Director Fine Arts Center ... Dr. Willie L. HILL, JR.
15 Asst Vice Chanc Human Resources ... Vacant
21 Assoc VC Finance & Budget Director ... Mr. Andrew P. MANGELS
18 Assoc VC Facilities & Campus Svcs ... Mr. Shane R. CONKLIN
19 Asst Vice Chancellor/Chief Police ... Mr. Tyrone PARHAM
96 Director Procurement & Campus Svcs ... Mr. John O. MARTIN
40 Manager Univ Store/Retail Services ... Mr. Scott C. WRIGLEY
35 VC Student Affairs/Campus Life ... Ms. Enku GELAYE
39 Exec Director Residential Life ... Mr. Edward C. HULL
23 Director University Health Services ... Dr. George A. COREY
38 Director Mental Health/Health Svcs ... Dr. Harry S. ROCKLAND-MILLER
36 Director Career Services ... Ms. Candice J. SERAFINO
29 Exec Director Alumni Relations ... Dr. JC SCHNABL
86 Exec Dir Public/Constituent Rels ... Mr. Christopher DUNN
31 Assoc VC for University Relations ... Dr. Nancy BUFFONE
25 Acting Dir Grant & Contract Admin ... Ms. Carol SPRAGUE
91 Project Manager SPIRE Futures ... Ms. Heidi DOLLARD
90 Assoc Dir OIT Academic Computing ... Mr. Fred ZINN
24 Asst Dir AIMS Tech Classroom Sppt ... Mr. Stephen PIELOCK
105 Web Manager ... Ms. Nina SOSSEN

*University of Massachusetts Boston (I)

100 Morrissey Boulevard, Boston MA 02125-3393
County: Suffolk FICE Identification: 002222
Unit ID: 166638
Telephone: (617) 287-5000 Carnegie Class: DU-Higher
FAX Number: (617) 265-7173 Calendar System: Semester
URL: www.umb.edu
Established: 1964 Annual Undergrad Tuition & Fees (In-State): $13,435
Enrollment: 17,030 Coed
Affiliation or Control: State IRS Status: 501(c)3
Highest Offering: Doctorate
Accreditation: EH, CACREP, CAEPT, CLPSY, COPSY, CS, NURSE, SCPSY

02 Interim Chancellor ... Dr. Barry MILLS
05 Provost ... Dr. Emily MCDERMOTT
20 Associate Provost ... Ms. Cheryl NIXON
10 Vice Chanc for Admin & Finance ... Ms. Kathleen KIRLEIS
111 Int VC for University Advancement ... Ms. Allison DUFFY
84 Vice Chanc Enrollment Mgmt ... Ms. Lisa JOHNSON
32 Vice Chancellor for Student Affs ... Ms. Gail DISABATINO
41 VC for Athletics & Special Projects ... Mr. Charlie TITUS
86 VC for Govt Rel/Public Aff ... Mr. Edward LAMBERT
13 Vice Provost Info Tech/CIO ... Mr. Robert WEIR
15 Vice Chanc for Human Resources ... Ms. Marie BOWEN
20 Assoc Provost Assess and Planning ... Dr. Peter LANGER

53 Dean Col of Educ & Human Dev .... Mr. Joseph BERGER
107 Dean Col of Advancing & Prof Stds .... Dr. Philip DISALVIO
81 Dean of Math & Science .... Dr. Andrew GROSOVSKY
79 Dean of Liberal Arts .... Dr. David TERKLA
50 Dean College of Management .... Arindam BANDOPADHYAYA
66 Dean College of Nursing .... Dr. Linda THOMPSON ADAMS
80 Int Dean of Col Public & Cmty Svc .... Ms. Stephanie HARTWELL
81 Dean School for the Environment .... Ms. Robyn HANNIGAN
80 Dean John W. McCormack Grad School .... Mr. David CASH
26 Director of Communications .... Mr. DeWayne LEHMAN
09 Assoc Prov Institutional Research .... Mr. James J. HUGHES
08 Interim Dean of Univ Libraries .... Joanne RILEY
22 Chief Diversity Officer-ODI .... Ms. Georgianna MELENDEZ
92 Dean of Honors College .... Ms. Rajini SRIKANTH
88 Dean Sch Global Incl & Social Dev .... Mr. William KIERNAN
121 Vice Prov for Academic Support Svcs .... Ms. Joan BECKER
100 Director of Management Initiatives .... Ms. Anne RILEY
58 VP Research & Dean of Grad Studies .... Mr. Bala SUNDARAM

*University of Massachusetts Dartmouth (A)

285 Old Westport Road, North Dartmouth MA 02747-2300
County: Bristol FICE Identification: 002210
Unit ID: 167987
Telephone: (508) 999-8000 Carnegie Class: DU-Higher
FAX Number: (508) 999-8901 Calendar System: Semester
URL: www.umassd.edu
Established: 1895 Annual Undergrad Tuition & Fees (In-State): $13,188
Enrollment: 8,916 Coed
Affiliation or Control: State IRS Status: 501(c)3
Highest Offering: Doctorate
Accreditation: EH, ART, CS, ENG, LAW, MT, NURSE

02 Interim Chancellor .... Dr. Peyton HELM
05 Provost/VC Acad & Student Affairs .... Dr. Mohammad KARIM
10 VC Admin & Finance/CFO .... Mr. James SHEEHAN
111 VC Advancement .... Mr. Joseph MEDINA
04 Executive Office Director .... Ms. Lori NICKERSON
51 Exec Dir Univ Extension .... Mr. David PEDRO
20 Vice Provost for Academic Affairs .... Dr. Magali CARRERA
58 Assoc Provost Grad Studies .... Dr. Tesfay MERESSI
84 Assc VC Enrollment Management .... Mr. Ian DAY
21 Assoc Vice Chancellor Finance .... Ms. Mary Louise NUNES
18 Associate VC Facilities Management .... Mr. Peter DUFFY
58 Dir Graduate Studies/Admissions .... Mr. Scott WEBSTER
22 Assoc VC Diversity/Equity/Inc .... Ms. Deborah MAJEWSKI
121 Assistant VC Student Success .. Ms. Carol SPENCER-MONTEIRO
32 Assoc Vice Chanc Student Affairs .... Dr. David M. MILSTONE
13 Assoc VC IT/CIO .... Mr. Holger DIPPEL
88 Asst VC for Pgm Planning/Fiscal Mgt .... Ms. Joanne ZANELLA-LITKE
49 Dean College Arts & Science .... Dr. Jeannette RILEY
50 Dean Charlton Col of Business .... Dr. Angappa GUNASEKARAN
54 Dean College of Engineering .... Dr. Robert PECK
66 Dean College of Nursing .... Dr. Kimberly CHRISTOPHER
57 Dean College Visual Perform Arts .... Mr. David KLAMEN
88 Dean School Marine Science/Tech .... Dr. Steven LOHRENZ
61 Interim Dean School of Law .... Dr. Eric MITNICK
96 Asst VC for Administrative Services .... Mr. Michael LAGRASSA
21 Interim Financial Controller .... Ms. Suzanne AUDET
88 Director Faculty Development .... Dr. Catherine GARDNER
94 Dir Center Women/Gender/Sexuality .... Dr. Juli PARKER
88 Dir Academic Advising Center .... Ms. Suzanne MELLONI
06 University Registrar .... Ms. Audra CALLAHAN
07 Director of Admissions .... Ms. Hanan KHAMIS
09 Director of Institutional Research .... Ms. Tammy A. SILVA
08 Dean Library Services .... Mr. Terrance BURTON
19 Dir Public Safety/Chief of Police .... Col. Emil FIORAVANTI
36 Director Career Development Center .... Ms. Linda KENT DAVIS
37 Director Financial Aid .... Ms. Korrine PETERSON
38 Dir Counseling/Stdnt Develop Ctr .... Mr. Robert MARON
90 Exec Dir IT Quality Assurance .... Ms. Margaret S. DIAS
29 Director of Alumni Relations .... Ms. Nancy VANASSE
15 Asst VC Human Resources .... Ms. Carol SANTOS
18 Director Facilities/Physical Plant .... Mr. Jeffrey LOURO
41 Director of Athletics .... Ms. Amanda VAN VOORHIS
23 Director of Health Services .... Ms. Sheila DORGAN
39 Director of Housing/Residence Life .... Ms. Lucinda POUDRIER-AARONSON
44 Asst VC for Annual Giving .... Ms. Lindsay ROTH
26 Vice Chancellor for Univ Marketing .... Ms. Renee BUISSON
113 Bursar .... Ms. Kathleen L. EUBANKS
35 Asst VC Student Affairs .... Ms. Cynthia CUMMINGS
35 Associate Dean of Students .... Ms. Shelly METIVIER SCOTT
104 Asst Director Study Abroad Pgms .... Ms. Gina REIS
85 Dir International Student Center .... Ms. Christina M. BRUEN
93 Director Fred Douglas Unity House .... Ms. Nicole WILLIAMS
88 Director Academic Resource Center .... Mr. Sokratis KOUMAS
105 Webmaster .... Mr. Donald KING
88 Assistant Chancellor .... Mr. John HOEY
88 Senior VC Strategic Management .... Mr. Gerard KAVANAUGH
103 Dir Experiential Learning & Intern .... Ms. Amelia ALBURN
106 Dir Center for Access & Success .... Ms. Wendi CHAKA
25 Dir Sponsored Projects Admin .... Ms. Elena GLATMAN
28 Equal Opportunity Spec/Investigator .... Mr. David GOMES
45 Asst VC Campus Master Planning/Cap .... Mr. Michael HAYES

*University of Massachusetts Lowell (B)

1 University Avenue, Lowell MA 01854-2881
County: Middlesex FICE Identification: 002161
Unit ID: 166513
Telephone: (978) 934-4000 Carnegie Class: DU-Higher
FAX Number: (978) 934-3000 Calendar System: Semester
URL: www.uml.edu
Established: 1894 Annual Undergrad Tuition & Fees (In-State): $14,307
Enrollment: 18,047 Coed
Affiliation or Control: State IRS Status: 501(c)3
Highest Offering: Doctorate
Accreditation: EH, ART, CAEPN, @DIETC, ENG, ENGR, ENGT, MT, MUS, NURSE, PTA

02 Chancellor .... Dr. Jacqueline F. MOLONEY
05 Provost .... Dr. Michael E. VAYDA
10 Sr VC Financial Opers & Stat Plng .... Ms. Joanne YESTRAMSKI
26 VC University Relations .... Ms. Patricia MCCAFFERTY
46 VC of Research & Innovation .... Dr. Julie CHEN
111 Vice Chancellor for Advancement .... Mr. John FEUDO
15 Sr Assoc VC Human Resources & EOO .... Ms. Lauren TURNER
88 Sr AVC Entrepreneurship Econ Dev .... Mr. Steven TELLO
21 Assoc Vice Chancellor for Finance .... Mr. Steven O'RIORDAN
18 Assoc VC Facilities Management .... Mr. Thomas DREYER
32 Assoc VC Student Affs/Univ Events .... Mr. Larry SIEGEL
20 Vice Provost Faculty Success .... Dr. Beth MITCHNECK
103 Vice Prov Innov & Workforce Dev .... Dr. Scott LATHAM
121 Vice Provost Student Success .... Dr. Julie NASH
84 Dean Enrollment & Student Success .... Mr. Thomas TAYLOR
41 Director of Athletics .... Mr. Dana SKINNER
106 Dean Online/Cont Education .... Ms. Catherine KENDRICK
49 Dean Col Fine Arts/Hum/Soc Sci .... Dr. Luis FALCON
81 Dean Kennedy College of Sciences ... Dr. Nourreddine MELIKECHI
53 Dean College of Education .... Dr. Eleanor ABRAMS
54 Dean Francis College of Engineering .... Dr. Joseph HARTMAN
76 Dean College of Health Sciences .... Dr. Shortie MCKINNEY
50 Dean Manning School of Business .. Dr. Sandra RICHTERMEYER
09 Director of Institutional Research .... Dr. Julie ALIG
08 Director of Libraries .... Mr. George HART
88 Dean Academic Services .... Ms. Kerry DONOHOE
06 Registrar .... Ms. Mai NGUYEN
37 Assoc Dean Enrollment/Dir Fin Aid .... Ms. Joyce MCLAUGHLIN
38 Director of Counseling Svcs .... Dr. Christopher A. FRAZER
29 Exec Dir Alumni & Donor Relations .... Ms. Heather MAKREZ
19 Chief Univ Police Dir Public Safety .... Mr. Randolph BRASHEARS
123 Dir Graduate Admissions .... Ms. Linda SOUTHWORTH
96 Chief Procurement Officer .... Mr. Thomas HOOLE
88 Dir Outreach & Recruitment .... Mr. Michael BELCHER
07 Assoc Dean Enroll & Dir UG Admiss .... Ms. Kerri JOHNSTON
119 Dir Security Tech & UCAPS .... Mr. Jon VICTORINE
22 Dir Equal Opportunity & Outreach .... Ms. Clara ORLANDO
36 Asst Dean Student Affs/Career Dev .... Mr. Gregory DENON
88 Dir Student Disability Services .... Ms. Jody GOLDSTEIN
35 Dean Student Affairs & Enrichment .... Mr. James KOHL
23 Assoc Dir Student Health Svcs .... Ms. Diana WALKER MOYER
108 Director of Assessment .... Ms. Paula HAINES
35 Dean Student Affairs & Event Svcs .... Ms. Brenda EVANS
13 Chief Information Officer .... Mr. Michael CIPRIANO
85 Exec Dir Intl Administration .... Ms. Maria CONLEY
104 Director Intl Exper/Study Abroad .... Ms. Fern MACKINNON

*University of Massachusetts Medical School (C)

55 Lake Avenue N, Worcester MA 01655-0001
County: Worcester FICE Identification: 009756
Unit ID: 166708
Telephone: (508) 856-8989 Carnegie Class: Spec-4-yr-Med
FAX Number: (508) 856-8181 Calendar System: Semester
URL: www.umassmed.edu
Established: 1962 Annual Graduate Tuition & Fees: N/A
Enrollment: 1,079 Coed
Affiliation or Control: State IRS Status: 501(c)3
Highest Offering: Doctorate; No Undergraduates
Accreditation: EH, MED, NURSE

02 Chancellor & SVP Health Sciences .... Dr. Michael F. COLLINS
05 Dean Provost & Exec Dep Chancellor .... Dr. Terence R. FLOTTE
10 Exec VC Administration & Finance .... Mr. John LINDSTEDT
88 Exec VC Innovation and Business Dev .... Dr. Brendan O'LEARY
111 VC for Advancement .... Mr. John J. HAYES
88 Exec Vice Chancellor MassBiologics .... Dr. Mark D. KLEMPNER
11 Exec VC Commonwealth Medicine .... Ms. Joyce A. MURPHY
15 VC Diversity & Inclusion .... Dr. Deborah L. PLUMMER
86 VC Government/Community Relations .... Mr. James LEARY
26 Vice Chancellor of Communications .... Ms. Jennifer BERRYMAN
20 Vice Provost Faculty Affairs .... Dr. Luanne THORNDYKE
53 Sr Assoc Dean Educational Affairs .... Dr. Michele P. PUGNAIRE
63 Sr Assc Dean Clin Aff/Assc Dean GME .... Dr. Deborah DEMARCO
66 Dean Graduate School of Nursing .... Dr. Joan VITELLO
32 Vice Provost of Student Affairs .... Dr. Sonia CHIMIENTI
58 Dean Grad School Biomedical Science .... Dr. Anthony CARRUTHERS
06 Registrar .... Mr. Michael F. BAKER
13 Chief Information Officer .... Mr. Greg WOLF
07 Assoc Dean for Admissions .... Dr. Mariann M. MANNO
37 Director Financial Aid .... Mr. Shawn MORRISSEY
08 Director of Library .... Dr. Mary PIORUN
100 Asst VC for Mgmt/Chief of Staff .... Mr. Brendan H. CHISHOLM
04 Spec Assistant to the Chancellor .... Mr. Sean MACALUSO
88 Vice Provost for Clin/Trans Science .... Dr. Katherine LUZURIAGA
20 Exec Asst Dean Provost & Exec Dep .... Ms. Kimberly LAPERLE
88 Assc Provost Basic Sci Research .... Dr. Jean KING

*Bridgewater State University (D)

131 Summer Street, Bridgewater MA 02325-0001
County: Plymouth FICE Identification: 002183
Unit ID: 165024
Telephone: (508) 531-1000 Carnegie Class: Masters/L
FAX Number: N/A Calendar System: Semester
URL: www.bridgew.edu
Established: 1840 Annual Undergrad Tuition & Fees (In-State): $9,603
Enrollment: 11,089 Coed
Affiliation or Control: State IRS Status: 501(c)3
Highest Offering: Master's
Accreditation: EH, AAB, ART, CAATE, CACREP, CAEPN, CS, MUS, @SP, SPAA, SW

02 President .... Mr. Frederick CLARK
05 Provost & VP Academic Affairs .... Dr. Karim ISMAILI
88 Special Advisor to the President .... Vacant
10 Vice President and CFO .... Mr. Doug SHROPSHIRE
32 Int VP Student Affs/Enrollment Mgmt .... Dr. Margaret JABLONSKI
30 VP University Advancement .... Dr. Brenda MOLIFE
15 VP Human Resources & Talent Mgmt .... Ms. Keri POWERS
26 VP Marketing & Communication .... Mr. Paul JEAN
28 VP of Student Success & Diversity .... Dr. Sabrina GENTLEWARRIOR
11 Vice President Operations .... Ms. Karen W. JASON
111 Int Vice President External Affairs .... Dr. Deniz LEUENBERGER
100 Chief of Staff .... Dr. Deniz ZEYNEP LEUENBERGER
22 Director Title IX Coordinator .... Ms. Erin DEBOBES
15 Director HR & Talent Management .... Mr. Brian SALVAGGIO
35 AVP Student Affs/Dean of Students .... Ms. Denine ROCCO
84 Assoc Dean for Enrollment Services .... Mr. Todd AUDYATIS
20 Assoc Provost Faculty Affairs .... Dr. Pamela RUSSELL
45 Sr Assoc Provost/Chief Data Officer .... Dr. Michael YOUNG
79 Int Dean Col Humanities/Social Sci .... Dr. Arnaa ALCON
53 Dean Col Education/Allied Stds .... Dr. Lisa BATTAGLINO
51 Dean Col of Continuing Studies .... Dr. David CRANE
50 Dean Ricciardi College of Business .... Dr. Elmore ALEXANDER
07 Dean of University Admissions .... Mr. Gregg A. MEYER
13 VP & Chief Information Officer .... Mr. Raymond LEFEBVRE
06 Registrar .... Mr. Joseph WOLK
88 Director Academic Achievement Ctr .... Ms. Alicia D'OYLEY
29 Director Alumni Relations .... Ms. Shana MURRELL
30 Director Development .... Ms. Betsy DUBUQUE
41 Director Athletics/Recreation .... Dr. Marybeth LAMB
21 Director University Services .... Ms. Margarida VIEIRA
19 Chief of Police .... Mr. David TILLINGHAST
36 Director Career Services .... Mr. John PAGANELLI
37 Director of Financial Aid .... Ms. Janet GUMBRIS
23 Senior Director Wellness Center .... Vacant
08 Director Library Administration .... Mr. Michael SOMERS
22 Director Multicultural Affairs .... Ms. Sydne M. MARROW
27 Asst Dir Creative Svcs/Publications .... Ms. Jaime KNIGHT
25 Director Grants/Sponsored Projects .... Ms. Mia ZOINO
96 Director of Procurement Services .... Dr. Jennifer PACHECO
28 Director of Institutional Diversity .... Dr. Luis F. PAREDES
81 Dean Bartlett Col Science & Math .... Dr. Kristen PORTER-UTLEY
58 Dean College of Graduate Studies .... Dr. Lisa KRISSOFF BOEHM
09 Director of Institutional Research .... Dr. Kate MCLAREN
88 Director Teaching and Learning .... Dr. Roben TOROSYAN
46 Asst Prov High Impact Ed Practices .... Dr. Jenny SHANAHAN
85 Dir International Students/Scholar .... Vacant
88 Director Regional Partnerships .... Vacant
104 Director Study Abroad .... Mr. Michael SANDY
91 Dir Administrative Systems .... Ms. Kelley BARAN
88 Assoc VP Infrastructure Network Sys .... Mr. Steven ZUROMSKI
105 Director of Web Development .... Ms. Eileen O'SULLIVAN
26 Asst VP & Chief Marketing Officer .... Ms. Eva GAFFNEY
27 Director of University News .... Mr. John WINTERS
38 Asst Clinical Dir Counseling Center .... Mr. Philip ROBERTS
39 Dir Residence Life and Housing .... Ms. Beth MORIARTY
108 Director of Assessment .... Dr. Ruth SLOTNICK
88 Exec Dir Inst for Social Justice .... Dr. Kelly BROTZMAN
88 Dir Institute for Global Engagement .... Dr. Derek LEUENBERGER
04 Staff Associate to the President .... Ms. Kelly HESS SALISBURY
43 General Counsel .... Vacant
97 Dean of Undergraduate Studies .... Dr. Rita MILLER
50 Assoc Dean College of Business .... Dr. Jeanean DAVIS-STREET
53 Assoc Dean College of Education .... Dr. Jo HOFFMAN

*Fitchburg State University (E)

160 Pearl Street, Fitchburg MA 01420-2697
County: Worcester FICE Identification: 002184
Unit ID: 165820
Telephone: (978) 345-2151 Carnegie Class: Masters/L
FAX Number: (978) 665-3693 Calendar System: Semester
URL: www.fitchburgstate.edu
Established: 1894 Annual Undergrad Tuition & Fees (In-State): $10,135
Enrollment: 6,598 Coed
Affiliation or Control: State IRS Status: 501(c)3
Highest Offering: Master's
Accreditation: EH, CAEPN, CS, CSHSE, IACBE, NURSE

02 President .... Dr. Richard S. LAPIDUS
05 Provost/VP Academic Affairs .... Dr. Alberto CARDELLE
10 Vice Pres Finance & Administration .... Mr. Jay BRY
20 Associate VP Academic Affairs .... Dr. Catherine CANNEY
32 Vice President Student Affairs .... Dr. Laura BAYLESS
53 Dean of Education .... Dr. Bruno HICKS
111 Vice President of Inst Advancement .... Mr. Christopher HENDRY
35 Assistant Dean for Student Devel .... Dr. Henry C. PARKINSON, III
06 Registrar .... Ms. Linda DUPELL

Code	Title	Name
09	Director of Institutional Research	Mr. Anthony WILCOX
08	Interim Director Library	Dr. Sean GOODLETT
41	Director Athletics	Ms. Sue M. LAUDER
07	Director of Admissions	Vacant
36	Director of Career Services	Ms. Erin C. KELLEHER
38	Director Counseling	Dr. Robert HYNES
23	Director Student Health Services	Ms. Martha FAVRE
29	Asst Director of Alumni Relations	Ms. Emily AUSTIN-BRUNS
19	Director of Campus Police	Chief Michael CLOUTIER
44	Director of Annual Giving	Ms. Tanya CROWLEY
15	Asst VP of Human Resources/Payroll	Ms. Jessica MURDOCH
18	Dir of Operations & Maint	Mr. Richard MCCLUSKEY
88	Dir Capital Planning & Construction	Mr. Doug THOMAS
25	Director Grants & Sponsored Pgm	Ms. Karen FRANK MAYS
37	Director Financial Aid	Ms. Denise BRINDLE
106	Dir Online Education/E-learning	Dr. Michael B. LEAMY
108	Director Institutional Assessment	Vacant
13	Chief Info Technology Officer (CIO)	Mr. Stephen E. SWARTZ
39	Director Student Housing	Ms. Kristin MURPHY
04	Special Asst to President	Ms. Gail M. DOIRON
81	Dean of Health & Natural Science	Dr. John SCHAUMLOFFEL
58	Dean of Graduate & Cont Educ	Dr. Becky COPPER GLENZ
49	Dean of Arts & Sciences	Dr. Franca BARRICELLI

*Framingham State University (A)

100 State Street, PO Box 9101,
Framingham MA 01701-9101

County: Middlesex
FICE Identification: 002185
Unit ID: 165866
Telephone: (508) 620-1220
Carnegie Class: Masters/L
FAX Number: (508) 626-4592
Calendar System: Semester
URL: www.framingham.edu
Established: 1839
Annual Undergrad Tuition & Fees (In-State): $9,340
Enrollment: 6,398
Coed
Affiliation or Control: State
IRS Status: 501(c)3
Highest Offering: Master's
Accreditation: EH, ART, CAEPN, DIETC, DIETD, NURSE

Code	Title	Name
02	President	Dr. F. Javier CEVALLOS
03	Executive Vice President	Dr. Dale M. HAMEL
05	Vice President Academic Affairs	Dr. Linda VADEN-GOAD
32	Vice Pres Enrollment & Student Dev	Dr. Lorretta HOLLOWAY
43	Vice President/General Counsel	Ms. Rita COLUCCI
20	Associate Vice President	Dr. Scott B. GREENBERG
13	Associate Vice President	Mr. Patrick LAUGHRAN
18	Assistant Vice President	Mr. Warren FAIRBANKS
84	Dean of Enrollment Management	Mr. Jeremy SPENCER
35	Dean of Student Affairs	Dr. Melinda K. STOOPS
39	Associate Dean Student Affairs	Mr. Glenn COCHRAN
07	Associate Dean Undergrad Admissions	Ms. Shayna EDDY
35	Assistant Dean Student Affairs	Mr. David N. BALDWIN
35	Assistant Dean Student Affairs	Dr. Christopher GREGORY
06	Executive Director/Registrar	Mr. Mark R. POWERS
15	Director Human Resources	Ms. Erin NECHIPURENKO
19	Chief Public Safety	Mr. Brad MEDEIROS
88	Director Academic Support	Ms. LaDonna BRIDGES
108	Director Assessment	Dr. Mark NICHOLAS
41	Director Athletics	Mr. Thomas KELLEY
36	Director Career Services	Mrs. Dawn ROSS
37	Director Financial Aid	Ms. Deborah ALTSHER
10	Director Financial Services	Ms. Rachel TRANT
89	Director First Year Programs	Mr. Benjamin J. TRAPANICK
23	Director Health Services	Ms. Ilene HOFRENNING
104	Director International Education	Ms. Jane DECATUR
08	Director Library Services	Mrs. Bonnie MITCHELL
38	Director Counseling Center	Dr. Paul WELCH
35	Director Student Involvement	Ms. Rachel LUCKING
88	Director Student Accounts	Mr. Gregory JACKSON
30	Director Development	Mr. Eric GUSTAFSON
25	Director Grants Sponsored Programs	Mr. Jonathan LEE
09	Director Institutional Research	Ms. Ann CASO
04	Administrative Assistant	Ms. Katie HEBERT
22	Director of Equal Opportunity	Ms. Kimberly DEXTER
58	Dean of Graduate Studies	Dr. Yasar NAJJAR
26	Chief Public Relations Officer	Mr. Daniel MAGAZU
28	Chief Diversity & Inclusion Officer	Mr. Sean HUDDLESTON
29	Director of Alumni Relations	Mr. Steve WHITTEMORE

*Massachusetts College of Art and Design (B)

621 Huntington Avenue, Boston MA 02115-5882

County: Suffolk
FICE Identification: 002180
Unit ID: 166674
Telephone: (617) 879-7000
Carnegie Class: Spec-4-yr-Arts
FAX Number: (617) 566-4034
Calendar System: Semester
URL: www.massart.edu
Established: 1873
Annual Undergrad Tuition & Fees (In-State): $12,200
Enrollment: 1,990
Coed
Affiliation or Control: State
IRS Status: 501(c)3
Highest Offering: Master's
Accreditation: EH, ART

Code	Title	Name
02	President	Dr. David NELSON
10	Executive VP of Admin & Finance	Mr. Kurt STEINBERG
11	Associate VP of Administration	Mr. Robert PERRY
05	Provost/Vice Pres Academic Affairs	Mr. Ken STRICKLAND
32	Vice President Student Development	Dr. Maureen KEEFE
111	Vice Pres Institutional Advancement	Ms. Marjorie O'MALLEY
09	Assoc VP for Planning/Research	Ms. Kathleen KEENAN
21	Asst Vice Pres of Fiscal Affairs	Mr. Donald ARPINO
100	Chief of Staff President's Office	Ms. Susana SEGAT
07	Dean of Admissions/Enrollment	Mr. Christopher WRIGHT
88	Assoc VP/Dean Multi-Cultural Affs	Dr. Jamie COSTELLO
06	Registrar	Mr. Jonathan RAND
37	Director of Financial Aid	Mr. Aurelio RAMIREZ
88	Dir Curatorial Pgms/Prof Galleries	Ms. Lisa TUNG
08	Director Library	Ms. Rachel RESNICK
15	Director Human Resources	Ms. Velda MCRAE-YATES
22	Dir Civil Rights Compliance/Dvrsty	Ms. Mercedes EVANS
18	Exec Dir Facilities/Physical Plant	Mr. Howie LAROSEE
88	Director of Administrative Services	Mr. James MCDAID
26	Exec Dir Marketing/Communications	Ms. Ellen CARR
13	Chief Info Technology Officer	Mr. Patrick O'CONNOR
19	Director Security/Safety	Mr. Dwayne FARLEY
104	Director Study Abroad	Ms. Erica PUCCIO O'BRIEN
38	Director Student Counseling	Dr. Betsy SMITH
29	Director Alumni Communications	Ms. Darlene GILLAN
39	Director Student Housing	Ms. Danielle LICITRA

*Massachusetts College of Liberal Arts (C)

375 Church Street, North Adams MA 01247-4100

County: Berkshire
FICE Identification: 002187
Unit ID: 167288
Telephone: (413) 662-5000
Carnegie Class: Bac-A&S
FAX Number: (413) 662-5010
Calendar System: Semester
URL: www.mcla.edu
Established: 1894
Annual Undergrad Tuition & Fees (In-State): $9,875
Enrollment: 1,641
Coed
Affiliation or Control: State
IRS Status: 501(c)3
Highest Offering: Master's
Accreditation: EH, CAATE

Code	Title	Name
02	President	Dr. James F. BIRGE
03	Executive Vice President	Ms. Denise RICHARDELLO
05	VP Academic Affairs	Dr. Cynthia F. BROWN
10	VP Administration & Finance	Mr. Lawrence M. BEHAN
32	VP Student Affairs	Dr. Catherine B. HOLBROOK
111	Int VP Institutional Advancement	Ms. Molly F. WILLIAM
20	Dean Academic Affairs	Dr. Monica JOSLIN
58	Dean Graduate & Continuing Educ	Dr. Howard EBERWEIN
15	Director Human Resources	Ms. Barbara CHAPUT
35	Associate Dean Student Affairs	Ms. Theresa M. O'BRYANT
121	Associate Dean Student Success	Dr. Catherine MCKEEN
08	Associate Dean Library Services	Ms. Maureen HORAK
20	Associate Dean Academic Affairs	Dr. Adrienne WOOTTERS
04	Assistant to President	Ms. Ginger MENARD
07	Director Admissions	Ms. Gina PUC
41	Director Athletics	Ms. Laura MOONEY
06	Assistant Dean Registrar	Mr. Steven KING
13	Director Information Technology	Mr. Ian BERGERON
18	Director Facilities Management	Mr. Aldo TORTORELLI
29	Dir Alumni Relations & Development	Ms. Christine NAUGHTON
21	Director Fiscal Affairs	Ms. Laura BROWN
113	Director Student Accounts/Bursar	Ms. Bonnie J. HOWLAND
23	Director Health Services	Ms. Jacki KRZANIK
26	Director Marketing & Communications	Ms. Bernadette LUPO
19	Director Public Safety	Mr. Daniel J. COLONNO
37	Director Financial Aid	Ms. Elizabeth PETRI
38	Director Counseling Services	Ms. Heidi A. RIELLO
39	Director Residential Programs	Ms. Dianne M. MANNING
108	Director Assessment	Ms. Erin M. MILNE
09	Institutional Research Analyst	Mr. Jason G. CANALES
51	Director DGCE Programs	Ms. Barbara EMANUEL
105	Web and Applications Manager	Mr. Steven J. PESOLA
120	Associate Dir Academic Technology	Dr. Gerol C. PETRUZELLA
27	Social Media and Marketing Manager	Ms. Francesca SHANKS

*Massachusetts Maritime Academy (D)

101 Academy Drive, Buzzards Bay MA 02532-3400

County: Barnstable
FICE Identification: 002181
Unit ID: 166692
Telephone: (508) 830-5000
Carnegie Class: Masters/S
FAX Number: (508) 830-5004
Calendar System: Semester
URL: www.maritime.edu
Established: 1891
Annual Undergrad Tuition & Fees (In-State): $8,004
Enrollment: 1,674
Coed
Affiliation or Control: State
IRS Status: 501(c)3
Highest Offering: Master's
Accreditation: EH, IACBE

Code	Title	Name
02	President	RADM. Francis X. MCDONALD
05	Vice President/Dean	CAPT. Brad LIMA
10	Vice Pres Finance	Ms. Rose CASS
30	Vice Pres Advancement	Ms. Holly KNIGHT
27	Vice President/CIO	Ms. Anne Marie FALLON
32	Vice Pres Student Services	CAPT. Edward ROZAK
36	Assoc Dir Career/Professional Svcs	CDR. Maryanne RICHARDS
84	Vice Pres Enrollment Management	CAPT. Elizabeth STEVENSON
06	Director Student Records/Registrar	Mr. Michael CUFF
08	Director Library	Ms. Susan BERTEAUX
108	Dir of Institutional Effectiveness	Dr. Marlene CLAPP
15	Dean Human Resources	Mrs. Elizabeth BENWAY
18	Vice President Operations	Mr. Paul O'KEEFE
26	Chief Public Relations Officer	Mr. Christopher RYAN
29	Director Alumni Relations	Mr. Ian MACLEOD
37	Director Student Financial Aid	Mrs. Cathy KEDSKI
96	Director of Purchasing	Mr. Paul AIROZO
41	Athletic Director	Mr. Garin VERIS

*Salem State University (E)

352 Lafayette Street, Salem MA 01970-5353

County: Essex
FICE Identification: 002188
Unit ID: 167729
Telephone: (978) 542-6000
Carnegie Class: Masters/L
FAX Number: (978) 542-6970
Calendar System: Semester
URL: www.salemstate.edu
Established: 1854
Annual Undergrad Tuition & Fees (In-State): $9,736
Enrollment: 9,215
Coed
Affiliation or Control: State
IRS Status: 501(c)3
Highest Offering: Master's
Accreditation: EH, ART, CAATE, CAEPN, CS, MUS, NMT, NURSE, OT, SW, THEA

Code	Title	Name
02	President	Mr. John KEENAN
05	Provost & Academic VP	Dr. David J. SILVA
84	VP Enrollment Mgmt & Student Life	Dr. Scott JAMES
111	VP Institutional Advancement	Ms. Cynthia MCGURREN
10	VP Finance and Business	Ms. Karen HOUSE
28	VP Diversity and Inclusion	Dr. Lisa MCBRIDE
43	Gen Counsel & VP Adminisration	Vacant
100	Chief of Staff	Ms. Beth A. BOWER
26	Asst VP Marketing/Creative Svcs	Mr. Corey CRONIN
13	CIO-CISO	Mr. Curt KING
21	Assoc VP Financial Svcs	Mr. Joseph DONOVAN
15	Assistant VP for HR & EEO	Mr. Mark R. QUIGLEY
20	Assoc Provost and Dean Human Svcs	Dr. Neal DECHILLO
86	Director of External Affairs	Ms. Adria LEACH
08	Director Librarian & Lrng Support	Ms. Elizabeth MCKEIGUE
50	Interim Dean School of Business	Dr. Kathleen HESS
53	Dean of Education	Dr. Joseph CAMBONE
51	Interim Dean Sch Grad & Pro Studies	Dr. Emerson BAKER
49	Dean School of Arts & Sciences	Dr. Gail GASPARICH
32	Dean of Students	Dr. Carla PANZELLA
110	Assoc VP Institutional Advancement	Ms. Cheryl CROUNSE
101	Sr Asst to Pres/Asst Secy to BOT	Ms. Katrina SADOWSKI
19	Director Public Safety	Mr. Gene R. LABONTE
41	Director Athletics	Ms. Peggy CARL
06	Registrar	Ms. Megan M. MILLER
07	Assistant VP for Enroll Mgmt	Ms. Bonnie GALINSKI
18	Director of Facilities	Mr. Gualter ALMEIDA
28	Dir Diversity & Multicult Affairs	Ms. Rebecca COMAGE
29	Director Alumni Affairs	Ms. Mandy RAY
37	Director of Financial Aid	Ms. Judy CRAMER
38	Asst Dean of Students/Wellness	Ms. Elisa CASTILLO
96	Director Purchasing & Vendor Rel	Ms. Evelyn WILSON
25	Dir Sponsored Programs & Res Adm	Ms. Mary MADER
07	Director of Admissions	Ms. Mary DUNN
45	Exec Dir Strategic Planning	Dr. Chunju CHEN
102	Dir Foundation/Corporate Relations	Ms. Lisa MCFADDEN
39	Director Residence Life	Mr. Neil ANDRITO

*Westfield State University (F)

577 Western Avenue, Westfield MA 01086-1630

County: Hampden
FICE Identification: 002189
Unit ID: 168263
Telephone: (413) 572-5300
Carnegie Class: Masters/M
FAX Number: (413) 572-8147
Calendar System: Semester
URL: www.westfield.ma.edu
Established: 1838
Annual Undergrad Tuition & Fees (In-State): $9,275
Enrollment: 6,496
Coed
Affiliation or Control: State
IRS Status: 501(c)3
Highest Offering: Beyond Master's But Less Than Doctorate
Accreditation: EH, #CAATE, CAEPN, CS, EXSC, MUS, NURSE, SW

Code	Title	Name
02	President	Dr. Ramon S. TORRECILHA
100	Chief of Staff	Dr. Diane PRUSANK
05	Provost/VP Academic Affairs	Dr. Parviz ANSARI
32	Vice Pres Student Affairs	Dr. Carlton PICKRON
84	VP Enrollment Management	Mr. Dan FORSTER
10	VP Administration & Finance	Mr. Stephen TAKSAR
111	VP Institutional Advancement	Dr. Erica BROMAN
21	Assoc VP Administration/Finance	Ms. Lisa FREEMAN
18	Dir Capital Planning/Facilities	Mr. Robert HENRY
15	Interim Asst VP Human Resources	Ms. Evie SOUCIE
20	Interim Dean of Faculty	Dr. Susan LEGGETT
49	Interim Dean of Undergrad Studies	Dr. Christina SWAIDAN
58	Dean Graduate/Continuing Educ	Dr. Shelley TINKHAM
53	Dean of Education	Dr. Cheryl STANLEY
35	Dean of Students	Ms. Susan LAMONTAGNE
06	Registrar	Mr. John OHOTNICKY
09	Assoc Dean Inst Research/Assess	Dr. Lisa PLANTEFABER
88	Assoc Dean Academic Achievement	Ms. Maureen MCCARTNEY
08	Dean Acad Info Svcs/Dir Library	Mr. Thomas RAFFENSPERGER
39	Exec Director Residential Life	Dr. Jon CONLOGUE
19	Director Public Safety	Mr. Tony CASCIANO
36	Director Career Services	Mr. Junior DELGADO
90	Exec Director Acad Tech Services	Mr. Christopher HIRTLE
72	Director Information Technology	Mr. Alan BLAIR
91	Director Admin Systems	Mr. Rudolph HEBERT
18	Director Facilities/Operations	Vacant
41	Director Athletics	Mr. Richard LENFEST
38	Director Counseling Center	Ms. Tammy BRINGAZE
23	Director Health Services	Ms. Patricia BERUBE
37	Director of Financial Aid	Ms. Catherine RYAN
07	Director of Admissions	Dr. Kelly HART
96	Director of Purchasing	Mr. Chris RAYMOND
25	Director Grants Sponsored Programs	Ms. Louann D'ANGELO
102	Director of WSU Foundation	Vacant
04	Executive Assistant to President	Ms. Dominique CHAPMAN
101	Admin Asst to Board of Trustees	Ms. Jean BEAL

104 Director of International Program .... Ms. Cynthia SIEGLER
28 Director of Diversity & Inclusion .... Ms. Ashiah RICHEME
88 Veteran & Military Svcs Coord .... Ms. Lisa DUCHARME
106 Dir Center for Instructional Tech ....Ms. Lynn ZAYAC
22 Dir Non-Discrimination Compliance ... Mr. Lawrence P. JOHNSON
26 Director of Campus Communications ....Ms. Tricia OLIVER
29 Director Alumni Relations ....Ms. Katheryn BRADFORD
86 Director Government Relations ....Mr. Brent BEAN

*Worcester State University (A)

486 Chandler Street, Worcester MA 01602-2597
County: Worcester FICE Identification: 002190
Unit ID: 168430
Telephone: (508) 929-8000 Carnegie Class: Masters/L
FAX Number: (508) 929-8191 Calendar System: Semester
URL: www.worcester.edu
Established: 1874 Annual Undergrad Tuition & Fees (In-State): $9,202
Enrollment: 6,306 Coed
Affiliation or Control: State IRS Status: 501(c)3
Highest Offering: Master's
Accreditation: EH, CAEPT, NMT, NURSE, OT, SP

02 President ....Mr. Barry M. MALONEY
05 Provost/VP of Academic Affairs .... Dr. Lois A. WIMS
10 Vice Pres Administration & Finance ... Ms. Kathleen EICHELROTH
32 Dean of Student Affairs ....Ms. Julie KAZARIAN
111 Vice Pres University Advancement ....Mr. Thomas MCNAMARA
84 Vice Pres for Enrollment Management ....Dr. Ryan FORSYTHE
20 Assoc VP for Academic Affairs .... Dr. Henry THERIAULT
21 Assoc VP Administration & Finance ....Ms. Robin QUILL
13 Assoc VP/CIO Univ Technology Svcs ....Dr. Anthony ADADE
58 Assoc VP CE & Dean Grad Stds .... Dr. Roberta KYLE
108 Asst VP for Assessment & Planning .... Dr. Sarah STROUT
22 Dir Diversity/Inclusion & Eq Op ....Mr. Isaac TESFAY
53 Dean Sch of Educ/Health/Nat Sci .... Dr. Linda LARRIVEE
79 Dean Sch of Human & Social Sciences ....Dr. Russ POTTLE
88 Assoc Dean Education ....Dr. Raynold LEWIS
66 Associate Dean of Nursing ....Vacant
51 Assoc Dean of Grad/Cont Educ .... Ms. Sara GRADY
35 Assoc Dean & Dir Stdnt Ctr/Activ ....Vacant
93 Asst Dean/Dir Multicultural Affairs ....Ms. Marcela URIBE-JENNINGS
19 Chief of Campus Police .... Mr. Jason KAPURCH
86 Asst to Pres for Intl/Cmty & Govt ....Mr. Carl HERRIN
26 Asst to Pres for Camp Communication ....Ms. Renae LIAS CLAFFEY
08 Executive Director of the Library ....Mr. Matthew BEJUNE
29 Exec Dir Univ Advancement & Alumni .... Ms. Karen SHARPE
15 Asst VP of HR/Payroll/Aff Act/Eq .... Ms. Stacey LUSTER
18 Director of Facilities ....Ms. Sandra OLSON
37 Director of Financial Aid ....Ms. Jayne MCGINN
07 Director of Admissions ....Mr. Joseph DICARLO
06 Registrar ....Ms. Julie CHAFEE
39 Director Residence Life & Housing ....Mr. Adrian GAGE
113 Manager of Student Accounts .... Ms. Julie CARMEL
96 Dir Procurement/Business Manager .... Ms. Brenda BUSSEY
09 Director of Institutional Research ....Mr. Kenneth SMITH
38 Director Student Counseling ....Ms. Laura MURPHY
85 Director of International Students .... Ms. Katey PALUMBO
36 Director of Career Services ....Ms. Jillian ANDERSON
41 Director of Athletics ....Mr. Michael A. MUDD
24 Director of Media Services ....Mr. Thomas R. WHITE
109 Director of Admin Support Services .... Ms. Nancy M. RAMSDELL

*Berkshire Community College (B)

1350 West Street, Pittsfield MA 01201-5786
County: Berkshire FICE Identification: 002167
Unit ID: 164775
Telephone: (413) 499-4660 Carnegie Class: Assoc/HT-High Trad
FAX Number: (413) 447-7840 Calendar System: Semester
URL: www.berkshirecc.edu
Established: 1960 Annual Undergrad Tuition & Fees (In-State): $5,010
Enrollment: 2,111 Coed
Affiliation or Control: State IRS Status: 501(c)3
Highest Offering: Associate Degree
Accreditation: EH, ADNUR, COARC, PTAA

02 President ....Dr. Ellen KENNEDY
05 Int Vice Pres for Academic Affairs .... Dr. Maura DELANEY
10 Vice Pres Admin/Finance/CFO ....Mr. John LAW
32 Vice Pres Student Affs/Enroll Svcs ....Vacant
30 Vice Pres Institutional Advancement .... Mr. Craig SMITH
103 VP Community Educ/Workforce Devel ....Vacant
15 VP Human Res/Affirm Action Officer ....Ms. Deborah COTE
66 Int Dean Nursing/Allied Health ....Dr. Chris AYLESWORTH
84 Dir Enrollment Services/Registrar .... Mr. Adam EMERSON
102 Exec Dir BCC Foundation .... Mr. Craig SMITH
13 Director Information Technology ....Mr. Richard WIXSOM
07 Dir Marketing/Student Recruitment ....Vacant
37 Director Student Financial Aid ....Ms. Anne MOORE
38 Senior Academic Counselor .... Ms. Lisa MATTILA
04 Assistant to the President .... Ms. Kim BROOKMAN

*Bristol Community College (C)

777 Elsbree Street, Fall River MA 02720-7395
County: Bristol FICE Identification: 002176
Unit ID: 165033
Telephone: (508) 678-2811 Carnegie Class: Assoc/HT-High Trad
FAX Number: (508) 730-3270 Calendar System: Semester
URL: www.bristolcc.edu
Established: 1965 Annual Undergrad Tuition & Fees (In-State): $4,464
Enrollment: 8,761 Coed
Affiliation or Control: State IRS Status: 501(c)3
Highest Offering: Associate Degree
Accreditation: EH, ADNUR, CAHIIM, COMTA, DH, MAC, MLTAD, OTA

02 President .... Dr. Laura L. DOUGLAS
03 Executive Vice President ....Mr. David F. FEENEY
05 Vice President of Academic Affairs ....Mr. Greg SETHARES
50 Dean of Business & Info Tech .... Mr. William BERARDI
79 Dean of Humanities & Education .... Dr. Ulli RYDER
83 Dean of Behavioral & Soc Sciences ....Dr. Kathleen PEARLE
76 Dean of Health Sciences ....Ms. Lynne BRODEUR
81 Dean of Math/Science & Engineering ....Dr. Sarmad SAMAN
10 VP of Administration & Finance ....Mr. Steven KENYON
30 VP of Resource Development ....Ms. Elizabeth K. MCCARTHY
84 VP of Students and Enrollment Mgt .... Mr. Steve OZUG
13 VP of Information Technology .... Ms. Jo-Ann M. PELLETIER
103 Acting VP of Workforce Development ....Mr. Paul VIGEANT
32 Director Student Engagement ....Ms. Kathleen BURNS
07 Dean of Admissions ....Mr. John MCLAUGHLIN
12 Dean of New Bedford Campus .... Mr. Jim DANIELS
12 Dean of Attleboro Center .... Mr. Rodney CLARK
06 Acting Registrar ....Ms. Joanne CARROLL-CONNOR
08 Associate Dean Library Sciences .... Mr. Robert REZENDES
25 Dean of Grant Development .... Ms. Jennifer MENARD
37 Dean of Financial Aid & Technology ....Mr. David ALLEN
38 Director Counseling Services ....Mr. Michael BENSINK
15 Acting VP of HR/Affirm Action ....Ms. Lisa TARANTINO
18 Director of Facilities Management .... Mr. Leo RACINE
19 Director of Public Safety ....Mr. Wayne WOOD
21 Comptroller ....Mr. Keith TONI
11 Associate VP of Administration ....Mr. Mark CARMODY
20 Assoc VP of Academic Affairs .... Mr. Anthony UCCI
20 Assoc VP of Academic Affairs .... Dr. Ana GAILLAT
07 Acting VP Enrollment Services ....Ms. Kathleen TORPEY GARGANTA
26 VP College Communications .... Ms. Joyce BRENNAN
29 Assoc VP Development Alumni Affairs ....Vacant
44 Assoc VP Major Gifts Annual Fund ....Vacant
22 Dean Disability Svcs & Student Engm ....Ms. Susan BOISSONEAULT
78 Director Coop Education .... Ms. Nicole HEANEY
31 Dean Ctr Workforce/Community Educ .... Ms. Carmen AGUILAR
23 Health Services Coordinator .... Ms. Carol CONSTANTINE
56 Asst Dean Instructional Lrng Tech .... Ms. April BELLAFIORE
09 VP Inst Research/Plng & Assessment ....Ms. Rhonda GABOVITCH
92 Director Honors Program ....Ms. Susan MCCOURT
96 Director of Purchasing ....Ms. Philicia PACHECO
36 Coord Career Planning Placement .... Ms. Patricia CONDON
41 Athletic Director ....Mr. Derek VIVEIROS
04 Executive Assistant to President ....Ms. Kathleen A. WORDELL
88 Dean Access and Transition ....Ms. Sarah MORRELL

*Bunker Hill Community College (D)

250 New Rutherford Avenue, Boston MA 02129-2925
County: Suffolk FICE Identification: 011210
Unit ID: 165112
Telephone: (617) 228-2000 Carnegie Class: Assoc/HT-Mix Trad/Non
FAX Number: (617) 228-2050 Calendar System: Semester
URL: www.bhcc.mass.edu
Established: 1973 Annual Undergrad Tuition & Fees (In-State): $3,888
Enrollment: 13,142 Coed
Affiliation or Control: State IRS Status: 501(c)3
Highest Offering: Associate Degree
Accreditation: EH, ADNUR, COARC, DMS, MLTAD, RAD, SURGT

02 President ....Dr. Pam Y. EDDINGER
10 VP of Administration and Finance ....Mr. John PITCHER
05 VP Academic Affairs/Student Service ....Dr. James F. CANNIFF
28 Director Diversity & Inclusion .... Mr. Thomas L. SALTONSTALL
20 Associate Dean Academic Affairs .... Ms. Liya ESCALERA-KELLEY
32 Dean of Students ....Ms. Julie B. ELKINS
26 Exec Director of Communications ....Ms. Karen NORTON
18 Director Facilities Management .... Mr. Gary BIGELOW
81 Int Dean Mathematics/Behav Sciences .... Dr. Maria K. PUENTE
79 Dean of Humanities ....Ms. Lori A. CATALLOZZI
54 Dean Science/Engineering ....Dr. Laurie K. MCCORRY
107 Dean of Professional Studies .... Dr. Michelle ELIAS BLOOMER
66 Dean Nurse Education ....Vacant
12 Associate Provost Chelsea Campus .... Dr. Alice MURILLO
21 Comptroller .... Ms. Champa NAGAGE
25 Director of Grants Development ....Mr. Steven A. ROLLER
84 Director Enrollment Systems ....Ms. Debra A. BOYER
06 Executive Director and Registrar ....Ms. Marika HAMILTON
08 Director Library/Info Center ....Dr. Vivica D. PIERRE
13 Chief Information Officer ....Mr. Tim OGAWA
15 Dir Human Resources/Labor Relations .... Ms. Molly B. AMBROSE
27 Executive Director of Marketing .... Ms. Karen M. NORTON
19 Director of Public Safety .... Mr. Robert BARROWS
37 Director of Financial Aid ....Ms. Melissa HOLSTER
96 Manager Purchasing ....Mr. Mukti RAUT
07 Assoc Dean Enrollment ....Ms. Anne BROWN
30 Executive Director of Development .... Ms. Marilyn KUHAR
100 Exec Asst to the President ....Mr. George HALLSMITH
09 Exec Dir Institutional Research ....Mr. David LEAVITT
04 Administrative Asst to President ....Ms. Frances H. JARVIS
102 Dir Foundation/Corporate Relations .... Ms. Marilyn KUHAR
103 Dir Workforce/Career Development .... Mr. Darrell LEMAR
105 Director of Digital Communications ....Ms. Nicole MORO
22 Dir Affirmative Action/EEO .... Mr. Thomas L. SALTONSTALL

*Cape Cod Community College (E)

2240 Iyannough Road, West Barnstable MA 02668-1599
County: Barnstable FICE Identification: 002168
Unit ID: 165194
Telephone: (508) 362-2131 Carnegie Class: Assoc/HT-Mix Trad/Non
FAX Number: (508) 362-3988 Calendar System: Semester
URL: www.capecod.edu
Established: 1960 Annual Undergrad Tuition & Fees (In-State): $4,320
Enrollment: 3,627 Coed
Affiliation or Control: State IRS Status: 501(c)3
Highest Offering: Associate Degree
Accreditation: EH, ADNUR, DH, MAC

02 President ....Dr. John L. COX
05 Vice Pres Academic/Student Affairs ....Dr. Susan MILLER
10 Vice President Finance & Operations .... Ms. Lisa KOPECKY
18 Director Facilities ....Mr. Jeffrey MARCOTTE
49 Dean Arts & Humanities ....Dr. Lore DEBOWER
81 Dean Science/Tech/Math/Business ....Vacant
121 Dean Learning Res & Student Success ....Mr. David ZIEMBA
84 Dean Enroll Mgmt/Advising Services ......Ms. Christine MCCAREY
83 Dean Health/Social Sci/Human Svcs ....Ms. Susan MADDIGAN
15 Associate VP Human Resources .... Mr. Paul ALEXANDER
08 Assoc Dean Library ....Ms. Jeanmarie FRASER
13 Director of Network & Client Svcs .... Mr. Chuck PHELAN
07 Director Admissions ....Mr. Matthew CORMIER
37 Director of Financial Aid ....Ms. Sherry ANDERSEN
26 Director College Communications .... Mr. Michael GROSS
06 Registrar ....Ms. Lucina HOLMES
19 Chief Public Safety ....Ms. Maria PADILLA
04 Exec Assistant to President ....Ms. Mia HAZLETT
36 Coord Career Plng & Placement ....Vacant
09 Dir Institutional Research & Effec ....Ms. Maureen O'SHEA
41 Athletic Director ....Vacant

*Greenfield Community College (F)

1 College Drive, Greenfield MA 01301-9739
County: Franklin FICE Identification: 002169
Unit ID: 165981
Telephone: (413) 775-1000 Carnegie Class: Assoc/HT-High Trad
FAX Number: (413) 774-4676 Calendar System: Semester
URL: www.gcc.mass.edu
Established: 1962 Annual Undergrad Tuition & Fees (In-State): $5,330
Enrollment: 2,050 Coed
Affiliation or Control: State IRS Status: 501(c)3
Highest Offering: Associate Degree
Accreditation: EH, ADNUR, MAC

02 President ....Dr. Robert L. PURA
05 Chief Academic/Student Affairs Ofcr ....Dr. Catherine SEAVER
10 Chief Financial Officer .... Mr. Barry BRAIM
103 Dean of Workforce Dev & Cmty Educ ....Ms. Alyce STILES
84 Dean of Enrollment Services ....Ms. Elaine LAPOMARDO
79 Dean Humanities ....Mr. Leo HWANG
81 Dean Engr/Math/Nurs & Sciences .. Ms. Mary Ellen FYDENKEVEZ
50 Dean Bus/IT/Soc Sci/Prof Stds .... Ms. Kathleen VRANOS
15 Exec Dir of Human Resources .... Mr. Peter SENNETT
30 Exec Director Resource Development ....Ms. Regina CURTIS
13 Chief Information Officer .... Mr. Michael ASSAF
28 Chief Diversity Officer .... Mr. Peter SENNETT
18 Director Physical Plant ....Mr. Jeffrey MARQUES
07 Admissions Director .... Mr. Mark HUDGIK
37 Director Financial Aid ....Ms. Linda DESJARDINS
19 Director Public Safety ....Mr. Alex WILTZ
96 Director of Purchasing .... Mr. Ryan AIKEN
08 Director Library ....Ms. Deborah CHOWN
21 Comptroller .... Ms. Karen PHILLIPS
06 Registrar ....Ms. Holly FITZPATRICK
38 Co-Coord Learning Asst Programs ....Ms. Cynthia SNOW
38 Co-Coord Learning Asst Programs ....Mr. Norman BEEBE
88 Coordinator of Student Assessment ....Ms. Catherine DEVLIN
32 Coordinator of Student Activities ....Ms. Mary MCENTEE
04 Staff Assistant to President ....Ms. Shannon LARANGE
108 Director Institutional Assessment ....Ms. Marie BREHENY
26 Marketing Coordinator ....Ms. Elizabeth CARROLL

*Holyoke Community College (G)

303 Homestead Avenue, Holyoke MA 01040-1099
County: Hampden FICE Identification: 002170
Unit ID: 166133
Telephone: (413) 538-7000 Carnegie Class: Assoc/HT-High Trad
FAX Number: (413) 552-2045 Calendar System: Semester
URL: www.hcc.edu
Established: 1946 Annual Undergrad Tuition & Fees (In-State): $4,502
Enrollment: 6,285 Coed
Affiliation or Control: State IRS Status: 501(c)3
Highest Offering: Associate Degree
Accreditation: EH, ACFEI, ADNUR, MUS, RAD

02 President ....Dr. Christina ROYAL
11 Vice Pres Administration & Finance .... Mr. William FOGARTY
05 Vice President Academic Affairs ....Ms. Monica PEREZ
32 Vice President Student Affairs .... Ms. Yanina VARGAS
30 Vice Pres Institutional Development ....Ms. Amy DOPP
28 Assistant Vice Pres of Diversity ....Ms. Idelia SMITH
08 Dean Library ....Ms. Mary DIXEY
84 Dean of Enrollment Management .... Ms. Renee TASTAD
15 Dean Human Resources ....Ms. Clara ELLIOTT
36 Dean Coop Education & Career Svcs ....Vacant

06 Registrar Ms. Christine HOLBROOK
37 Director of Financial Aid Ms. Karen DEROUIN
91 Director Administrative Computing Vacant
18 Dir Facilities & Engineering Svcs Mr. Dan CAMPBELL
10 Comptroller Ms. Marcia MITCHELL
13 Chief Information Officer Ms. Linda SZALANKIEWICZ
21 Dir Business Services/Purchasing Ms. Karen DESJEANS
09 Director Institutional Research Ms. Veena DHANKHER
26 Dir of Marketing/Public Relations Ms. JoAnne ROME
29 Dir Alumni Relations/Special Events Ms. Bonnie ZIMA DOWD
35 Dean of Student Services Mr. Tony SBALBI
20 Director of Academic Administration Ms. Idelia SMITH
19 Director Security/Safety Mr. Jose RIVERA

*Massachusetts Bay Community College (A)

50 Oakland Street, Wellesley Hills MA 02481-5357
County: Norfolk FICE Identification: 002171
Unit ID: 166647
Telephone: (781) 239-3000 Carnegie Class: Assoc/MT-VT-Mix Trad/Non
FAX Number: (781) 237-1061 Calendar System: Semester
URL: www.massbay.edu
Established: 1961 Annual Undergrad Tuition & Fees (In-State): $4,808
Enrollment: 4,859 Coed
Affiliation or Control: State IRS Status: 501(c)3
Highest Offering: Associate Degree
Accreditation: EH, ADNUR, RAD, SURGT

02 President Dr. David PODELL
04 Executive Director Ofc of the Pres Ms. Karen BRITTON
05 VP for Academic Affairs and Provost Dr. Lynn HUNTER
10 VP for Finance & Administration Mr. Neil BUCKLEY
15 Int Director of Human Resources Mr. Jim BROWN
111 VP of Inst Advance & Alumni Rels Ms. Mary SHIA
84 Asst VP Enrollment Management Ms. Lisa SLAVIN
32 VP for Student Development Dr. Elizabeth BLUMBERG
45 Dean of Planning & Inst Effectivene Dr. Courtney JACKSON
13 Chief Information Officer Mr. Michael LYONS
50 Dean Business & Prof Studies Dr. Susan MAGGIONI
88 Director of Corp Partnerships Ms. Elizabeth WATSON
76 Dean Health Sciences Division Dr. Lynne DAVIS
79 Dean Humanities & Social Sciences Dr. Christopher LA BARBERA
81 Dean STEM Division Dr. Chitra JAVDEKAR
06 Registrar Mr. Ali GUVENDIREN
21 Assoc VP for Finance & Admin Ms. Eileen GERENZ
114 Int Budget Associate Ms. Deborah GEORGOPOULOS
88 Int Dir Academic Achievement Center Ms. Barbara BERNARD
121 Director of Academic Advising Ms. Sarah SALERNO
91 Director Administrative Computing Mr. Terry KRAMER
07 Director of Admissions Ms. Alison MCCARTY
88 Special Asst to the President Mr. Bill RAYNOR
36 Director of Career & Internship Svc Ms. Julie GINN
38 Director of Counseling Mr. Jon EDWARDS
88 Director CTLTI Dr. Linda GRISHAM
37 Int Director of Financial Aid Mr. Curtis COURMIER
18 Director of Facilities Mr. Joseph DELISLE
08 Director of Learning Services Mr. Timothy RIVARD
25 Director of Grants Development Ms. Laura BROWN
26 Dir Marketing & Inst Communications Ms. Lee KOH
19 Director of Public Safety Mr. Charles (Chuck) FURGAL
124 Director of Retention Mr. Richard WILLIAMS
35 Coordinator of Student Activities Ms. Julie SCHLEICHER

*Massasoit Community College (B)

1 Massasoit Boulevard, Brockton MA 02302-3996
County: Plymouth FICE Identification: 002177
Unit ID: 166823
Telephone: (508) 588-9100 Carnegie Class: Assoc/HT-Mix Trad/Non
FAX Number: (508) 427-1202 Calendar System: Semester
URL: www.massasoit.mass.edu
Established: 1966 Annual Undergrad Tuition & Fees (In-State): $4,680
Enrollment: 7,637 Coed
Affiliation or Control: State IRS Status: 501(c)3
Highest Offering: Associate Degree
Accreditation: EH, ADNUR, COARC, DA, MAC, RAD

02 President Dr. Charles WALL
05 VP Academic Affairs Dr. Barbara MCCARTHY
10 VP Administration/CFO Mr. William MITCHELL
32 VP Student Svcs/Enroll Mgmt Mr. David TRACY
12 Senior VP/VP Canton/Advancement Mr. Nicholas PALANTZAS
15 Exec Director of Human Resources Ms. Margaret GAZZARA HESS
28 Exec Director Diversity & Inclusion Ms. Yolanda DENNIS
13 Interim CIO/Dir Enterprise Systems Mr. William MORRISON
09 Assoc Dean Institutional Research Ms. Mary GOODHUE LYNCH
25 Assoc Dean of Grants & Sustain Ms. Hollyce STATES
04 Exec Dir External Affs/Asst to Pres Mr. Phillip SHEPPARD
26 Exec Director of Communications Ms. Laurie MAKER
84 Dean of Enrollment Management Ms. Shilo HENRIQUES
35 Interim Dean of Students Mr. Alvin RILEY
07 Director of Admissions Ms. Michelle HUGHES
37 Director Student Financial Aid Mr. Todd HUGHES
06 Registrar Ms. Jannie GILSON
38 Acting Dean of Advising Ms. Christine DYMENT
21 Comptroller Ms. Patricia MARCELLA
36 Director of Career Placement Ms. Kathryn PRYLES
18 Director Facilities/Physical Plant Mr. Richard HADLEY
96 Director of Purchasing Mr. Richard PISHKIN

41 Director of Athletics Ms. Julie MULVEY
29 Director Alumni Relations Mr. Steven MURPHY
108 Dean Planning & Inst Effectiveness Ms. Ingrid VARGAS
50 Dean Business & Technology Ms. Lynda THOMPSON
79 Dean Humanities/Fine Arts Ms. Deanna YAMEEN
76 Dean Allied Health Dr. Anne SCALZO-MCNEIL
83 Dean Public Svc/Social Science Ms. Karyn BOUTIN
81 Dean Science & Math Mr. Douglas BROWN
72 Dean of Emergent Technologies Ms. Carine SAUVIGNON

*Middlesex Community College (C)

591 Springs Road, Bedford MA 01730-1197
County: Middlesex FICE Identification: 009936
Unit ID: 166887
Telephone: (781) 280-3200 Carnegie Class: Assoc/HT-High Trad
FAX Number: (781) 275-0741 Calendar System: Semester
URL: www.middlesex.mass.edu
Established: 1969 Annual Undergrad Tuition & Fees (In-State): $4,730
Enrollment: 9,021 Coed
Affiliation or Control: State IRS Status: 501(c)3
Highest Offering: Associate Degree
Accreditation: EH, ADNUR, DA, DH, DMS, DT, MAC, MLTAD, RAD

02 President Dr. James C. MABRY
05 Provost/VP of Academic Affairs Mr. Philip J. SISSON
03 Executive Vice President Vacant
84 VP Enrollment Svcs/Rsrch & Plng Vacant
10 Executive Director of Finance/CFO Mr. Frank NOCELLA
04 Assistant to the President Vacant
20 Associate Provost Vacant
32 Dean of Students Ms. Pamela B. FLAHERTY
79 Dean Humanities and Social Sciences Mr. Matthew OLSON
72 Dean of Business/Education & Publi Ms. Judith HOGAN
17 Dean of Health and STEM Ms. Kathleen J. SWEENEY
88 Dean Professional/Instructional Dev Ms. Susan ANDERSON
22 Asst Dir HR/Affirm Action Officer Mr. Reginald NICHOLS
11 Chief Administrative Officer Ms. Colleen COX
12 Dir Fac Mgmt/Bedford Campus Mgr Mr. John LYONS
84 Dean of Enrollment Services Ms. Audrey NAHABEDIAN
26 Dean External Affs/Col Advancement Mr. Dennis MALVERS
07 Dean of Admissions Ms. Marilynn GALLAGAN
35 Associate Dean of Students Ms. Patricia BRUNO
09 Assoc Dean Institutional Planning Vacant
27 Exec Director Public Affairs Mr. Patrick COOK
27 Director Marketing Communication Ms. Jennifer M. ARADHYA
29 Director of Alumni Affairs Ms. Amy LEE
15 Director Human Resources Ms. Mary EMERICK
37 Director of Financial Aid Mr. Robert BAUMEL
21 Comptroller Ms. Kathy RICH
21 Bursar Mr. Christopher FIORI
08 Director Library Services Ms. Maryann NILES
23 Director of Health Services Vacant
06 Registrar Mr. Daniel MOYNIHAN
96 Coordinator of Purchasing Ms. Maureen HUDSON

*Mount Wachusett Community College (D)

444 Green Street, Gardner MA 01440-1000
County: Worcester FICE Identification: 002172
Unit ID: 166957
Telephone: (978) 632-6600 Carnegie Class: Assoc/MT-VT-High Trad
FAX Number: (978) 632-6155 Calendar System: Semester
URL: www.mwcc.edu
Established: 1963 Annual Undergrad Tuition & Fees (In-State): $5,188
Enrollment: 4,074 Coed
Affiliation or Control: State IRS Status: 501(c)3
Highest Offering: Associate Degree
Accreditation: EH, ADNUR, DA, DH, MAC, MLTAD, PNUR, PTAA

02 President Dr. James L. VANDER HOOVEN
84 Exec VP & VP of Enrollment Services Ms. Ann M. MCDONALD
05 Vice Pres of Academic Affairs Dr. Melissa FAMA
51 VP Lifelong Learning/Workforce Dev Ms. Jacqueline BELROSE
10 VP Finance & Administration Mr. Robert LABONTE
15 VP HR/Affirmative Action Officer Ms. Diane RUKSNAITIS
26 Vice Pres Marketing/Communications Ms. Lea Ann SCALES
111 Assoc VP Institutional Advancement Mr. Joseph STISO
12 Dean Leominster Campus Mr. John WALSH
72 Dean Academic & Inst Technology Mr. Vincent IALENTI
76 Dean School of Health Sciences Ms. Eileen COSTELLO
08 Dean Library and Academic Support Mr. Jess MYNES
09 Asst Dean of Records/Instl Research Ms. Rebecca FOREST
18 Director Maintenance/Mechanical Sys Mr. William SWIFT
68 Director Fitness & Wellness Center Mr. Stephen WASHKEVICH
19 Chief Public Safety & Security Ms. Karen KOLIMAGA
32 Assistant Dean of Student Services Mr. Gregory CLEMENT
38 Director of Counseling Vacant
06 Registrar Ms. Rebecca FOREST

*North Shore Community College (E)

1 Ferncroft Road, PO Box 3340, Danvers MA 01923-0840
County: Essex FICE Identification: 002173
Unit ID: 167312
Telephone: (978) 762-4000 Carnegie Class: Assoc/MT-VT-High Trad
FAX Number: (978) 762-4020 Calendar System: Semester
URL: www.northshore.edu
Established: 1965 Annual Undergrad Tuition & Fees (In-State): $4,848
Enrollment: 6,961 Coed
Affiliation or Control: State IRS Status: 501(c)3
Highest Offering: Associate Degree
Accreditation: EH, ADNUR, COARC, MAC, OTA, PNUR, PTAA, RAD, SURGT

02 President Dr. Patricia A. GENTILE
05 Vice Pres Academic Affairs Dr. Karen HYNICK
10 Vice Pres Administration/Finance Ms. Janice M. FORSSTROM
32 Vice Pres Student Affairs Mr. Jermaine WILLIAMS
114 Asst Vice Pres Budget/Planning Ms. Mariflor UVA
15 Vice President Human Res/Affirm Act Ms. Madeline WALLIS
103 Dean Workforce Dev/Corp Educ Ms. Dianne PALTER-GILL
90 Dean Academic Technology Mr. Michael BADOLATO
07 Dean of Enrollment Services Mr. John DUFF
37 Asst VP Student Financial Svcs/Comp Mr. Stephen CREAMER
08 Director Library/Tutoring Mr. Rex KRAJEWSKI
13 Dir of Networking/Info Services Mr. Gary HAM
37 Director of Financial Aid Ms. Susan SULLIVAN
09 Asst Vice Pres Planning & Research Ms. Laurie LACHAPELLE
18 Asst Vice Pres Facilities Mgmt Mr. Richard RENEY
19 Campus Police Chief Mr. Douglas P. PUSKA
21 Comptroller Ms. Patricia CALLAHAN
26 Director Public Relations/New Media Ms. Linda BRANTLEY
35 Chief Student Life Officer Ms. Lisa MILSO
36 Director Student Placement Ms. Lynn MARCUS
121 Director Student Support & Advising Mr. Daniel O'NEILL
27 Director Marketing Communications Ms. Samantha MCGILLOWAY
40 Bookstore Manager Mr. Shawn CRONIN
06 Registrar Ms. Mel POTOCZAK

*Northern Essex Community College (F)

100 Elliott Street, Haverhill MA 01830-2399
County: Essex FICE Identification: 002174
Unit ID: 167376
Telephone: (978) 556-3000 Carnegie Class: Assoc/HT-High Trad
FAX Number: (978) 556-3723 Calendar System: Semester
URL: www.necc.mass.edu
Established: 1960 Annual Undergrad Tuition & Fees (In-State): $4,776
Enrollment: 6,628 Coed
Affiliation or Control: State IRS Status: 501(c)3
Highest Offering: Associate Degree
Accreditation: EH, ADNUR, COARC, CSHSE, DA, EMT, MAC, MLTAD, PNUR, POLYT, RAD

02 President Dr. Lane A. GLENN
05 Vice President of Academic Affairs Dr. William HEINEMAN
30 Vice Pres Institutional Advancement Ms. Jean C. POTH
10 VP of Administration & Finance/CFO Mr. Michael R. MCCARTHY
15 Vice President of Human Resources Mr. Stephen W. FABBRUCCI
07 Dean of Enroll Services Ms. Tina FAVARA
12 Exec Dir of Lawrence Campus Dr. Noemi CUSTODIA-LORA
09 Dean of Institutional Research Ms. Kelly SARETSKY
44 Dean of Development Ms. Wendy SHAFFER
121 Dean of Acad Support/Transfer Ms. Grace YOUNG
103 Exec Dir Workforce Devel/Cont Educ Mr. George MORIARTY
13 Chief Information Officer Mr. Jeffrey BICKFORD
06 Registrar Ms. Sue SHAIN
37 Director of Financial Aid Ms. Alexis FISHBONE
26 Director of Public Relations Ms. Ernestine GREENSLADE
29 Director Alumni Relations Ms. Lindsey GRAHAM
32 Dir Student Life & Student Conduct Mr. Daniel MALAVE
18 Chief Facilities/Physical Plant Vacant
96 Director of Purchasing Vacant
04 Sr Exec Asst to President Ms. Cheryl GOODWIN

*Quinsigamond Community College (G)

670 W Boylston Street, Worcester MA 01606-2092
County: Worcester FICE Identification: 002175
Unit ID: 167534
Telephone: (508) 853-2300 Carnegie Class: Assoc/HT-High Trad
FAX Number: (508) 852-6943 Calendar System: Semester
URL: www.qcc.edu
Established: 1963 Annual Undergrad Tuition & Fees (In-State): $5,394
Enrollment: 8,064 Coed
Affiliation or Control: State IRS Status: 501(c)3
Highest Offering: Associate Degree
Accreditation: EH, ADNUR, COARC, CSHSE, DA, DH, MAC, OTA, PNUR, RAD, SURGT

02 President Dr. Luis PEDRAJA
05 Interim VP of Academic Affairs Dr. Nancy SCHOENFELD
10 VP of Administration Mr. Stephen T. MARINI
32 VP of Student Enrollment/Develop Dr. Lillian M. ORTIZ
15 VP of Human Resources Ms. Elizabeth AUSTIN
20 Assistant VP Academic Affairs Ms. Jane SHEA
04 Executive Assistant to President Ms. Selina M. BORIA
21 Asst VP for Finance/Comptroller Ms. Debra A. LAFLASH
79 Dean Humanities & Education Dr. Clarence ATES
76 Interim Dean Health Care Mr. C. Pat SCHMOHL
50 Dean Business/Engineer/Technology Ms. Kathleen RENTSCH
81 Dean Science & Mathematics Dr. Leslie HORTON
06 Assoc Dean Enrollment/Registrar Ms. Tara F. JENKINS
62 Dean of Library Services Ms. Andrea MACRITCHIE
09 Dean of Inst Research/Planning Dr. Ingrid SKADBERG
84 Dean of Enrollment Management Ms. Michelle TUFAU-AFRIYIE
13 Interim Dean of Academic and On-Lin Mr. Ken DWYER
56 Asst VP Ext Campus Operations Mr. Victor SOMMA
35 Director Student Life & Leadership Mr. Michael BEANE
18 Director of Facilities Mr. Don HALL

37 Director Student Financial Aid .... Ms. Karen GRANT
96 Purchasing Manager .... Ms. Juliana ESPOSITO
19 Chief of Campus Police .... Mr. Kevin RITACCO
26 Dir Institutional Communications .... Mr. Joshua MARTIN
22 Dean for Employment & Equity .... Ms. Anita BOWDEN
38 Social Worker/Mental Health Couns .... Ms. Tina WELLS
28 Director Disability Services .... Ms. Kristen PROCTOR
35 Dean of Students .... Ms. Elizabeth WOODS
07 Director of Admissions .... Ms. Mishawn DAVIS-EYENE
30 Chief Development/Advancement .... Ms. Karen RUCKS

*Roxbury Community College (A)

1234 Columbus Avenue,
Roxbury Crossing MA 02120-3423
County: Suffolk FICE Identification: 011930
Unit ID: 167631
Telephone: (617) 427-0060 Carnegie Class: Assoc/HT-High Trad
FAX Number: (617) 541-5351 Calendar System: Semester
URL: rcc.mass.edu
Established: 1973 Annual Undergrad Tuition & Fees (In-State): $4,414
Enrollment: 2,257 Coed
Affiliation or Control: State IRS Status: 501(c)3
Highest Offering: Associate Degree
Accreditation: EH, ADNUR, RAD

02 President .... Dr. Valerie R. ROBERSON
04 Executive Asst to the President .... Ms. Martha LAMBERT
05 VP Academic And Student Affairs .... Ms. Cecile REGNER
30 VP Advancement/Cmty Engagement .... Ms. Lorita WILLIAMS
10 Vice President of Admin & Finance .... Mr. Kevin HEPNER
13 Chief Information Tech Officer .... Mr. Patrick JEAN-LOUIS
15 Chief Human Res/Affirm Action Ofcr .... Ms. Patricia WEST
41 Director of RLTAC .... Mr. A. Keith MCDERMOTT
08 Director of Library .... Mr. William HOAG
23 Director of Health Services .... Ms. Ruth HINES
30 Dir Development/Alumni/Foundation .. Mr. Richard M. IACOBUCCI
06 Registrar .... Ms. Cheryl MARTIN
32 Director of Student Life .... Ms. Erica RIVERS
26 Director Marketing/Communications .... Mr. Jordan SMOCK
57 Dir of Visual/Performing/Media Arts .... Mr. Marshall HUGHES
88 Director of the Writing Center Lab .... Ms. Judith KAHALAS
37 Assoc Director Financial Aid .... Ms. Tanya JEAN-JACQUES
25 Grants Research Specialist .... Ms. Yvonne E. ANTHONY

*Springfield Technical Community College (B)

Armory Square, Springfield MA 01105-1296
County: Hampden FICE Identification: 008078
Unit ID: 167905
Telephone: (413) 781-7822 Carnegie Class: Assoc/HT-High Trad
FAX Number: (413) 755-6309 Calendar System: Semester
URL: www.stcc.edu
Established: 1967 Annual Undergrad Tuition & Fees (In-State): $5,736
Enrollment: 6,286 Coed
Affiliation or Control: State IRS Status: 501(c)3
Highest Offering: Associate Degree
Accreditation: EH, ADNUR, CAHIIM, COARC, DA, DH, DMS, ENGT, MAC, MLTAD, OTA, PTAA, RAD, SURGT

02 President .... Dr. John B. COOK
05 VP of Academic Affairs .... Dr. Arlene RODRIGUEZ
10 VP of Administration/CFO .... Mr. Joseph DASILVA
32 VP Student/Multicultural Affairs .... Mr. Kamari COLLINS
84 Dean of Enrollment Management .... Mr. Matthew GRAVEL
04 Assistant to the President .... Mr. Michael J. SUZOR
50 Dean Business/Info Tech .... Dr. Leona R. ITTLEMAN
66 Director of Nursing .... Ms. Lisa FUGIEL
72 Dean Engineering Tech/Mathematics .... Dr. Adrienne SMITH
76 Dean Health and Patient Simulation .... Mr. Christopher D. SCOTT
79 Dean Arts/Humanities/Social Sci .... Dr. Anne BONEMERY
81 Dean Sciences/Engineering Transfer .... Dr. Robert DICKERMAN
51 Senior Director of Business Service .... Dr. Debbie BELLUCCI
35 Asst VP Stdnt Affs/Dean of Stdnts .... Mr. LaRue A. PIERCE
07 Dean of Admissions .... Ms. Louisa M. DAVIS FREEMAN
108 VP of Institutional Effectiveness .... Dr. Barb CHALFONTE
06 Registrar .... Theresa REMILLARD
41 Director of Athletics .... Mr. J. Vincent GRASSETTI
103 Assistant VP Workforce .... Mr. Gerardo ZAYAS, JR.
19 Chief of Police/Dir Public Safety .... Ms. E. Shawn DEJONG
18 AVP of Administration/Facilities .... Mrs. Maureen SOCHA
121 Director of Advising .... Ms. Jessica HILL
23 Coordinator of Health Services .... Mr. Jonathan L. MILLER
26 Director of Marketing .... Ms. Joan GRAVEL
36 Director of Coop/Career Placement .... Ms. Pamela WHITE
15 Senior Director of Human Resources .... Ms. Joan D. MURPHY
16 Director of Human Resources .... Ms. Cheryl ROGERS
37 Dean of Student Financial Services .... Mr. Jeremy GREENHOUSE
88 Fiscal/Financial Project Manager .... Mr. Jason COHEN
35 Coord Student Activities/Devel .... Ms. Andrea TARPEY
27 Coordinator of Media Relations .... Mr. James DANKO
114 Senior Director Finance/Budgets .... Mrs. Cathy OLSON
14 Sr Director of IT Applications .... Mr. Clifton PORTER
08 Interim Dean Library Services .... Ms. Erica EYNOUF
21 Controller .... Mr. Jonathan TUDRYN
09 Dean of Institutional Research .... Ms. Suzanne SMITH
108 Director of Assessment .... Dr. Tracey TROTTIER
25 Director of Grants Research & Eval .... Ms. Samantha DANA
96 Director of Purchasing .... Mr. Roger BESSETTE
88 Director of Access/Student Success .Mr. Jose LOPES-FIGUEROA
88 Director of Gateway to College .... Ms. Jennifer SANCHEZ
102 Director of Foundation .... Ms. Jessica PROKOP
88 Director of Facilities Quality and .... Ms. Kerri KANE
113 Director of Student Accounts .... Ms. Dorothy UNGERER
88 Director of Grants Development & Ad .... Ms. Kimberley BRODERICK

Massachusetts Institute of Technology (C)

77 Massachusetts Avenue, Cambridge MA 02139-4307
County: Middlesex FICE Identification: 002178
Unit ID: 166683
Telephone: (617) 253-1000 Carnegie Class: DU-Highest
FAX Number: N/A Calendar System: 4/1/4
URL: web.mit.edu
Established: 1861 Annual Undergrad Tuition & Fees: $48,452
Enrollment: 11,331 Coed
Affiliation or Control: Independent Non-Profit IRS Status: 501(c)3
Highest Offering: Doctorate
Accreditation: EH, CS, ENG, PLNG

01 President .... Dr. L. Rafael REIF
88 Chairman of the Corporation .... Mr. Robert B. MILLARD
05 Provost .... Prof. Martin A. SCHMIDT
00 Chancellor .... Prof. Cynthia BARNHART
46 Vice President for Research .... Prof. Maria T. ZUBER
106 Vice President for Open Learning .... Prof. Sanjay SARMA
10 Exec Vice President & Treasurer .... Mr. Israel RUIZ
101 Senior VP & Secretary of the Corp .... Mr. R. Gregory MORGAN
30 VP for Resource Development .... Ms. Julie LUCAS
20 Chancellor for Academic Advancement .. Mr. W. Eric L. GRIMSON
43 Vice President & General Counsel .... Mr. Mark DIVINCENZO
88 Vice President .... Dr. Kirk D. KOLENBRANDER
26 VP for Communications .... Mr. Nate NICKERSON
29 Exec VP & CEO Alumni Association .... Ms. Judith M. COLE
115 President MIT Investment Mgmt Co .... Mr. Seth ALEXANDER
88 Deputy Executive Vice President .... Mr. Anthony P. SHARON
15 VP for Human Resources .... Ms. Lorraine A. GOFFE-RUSH
13 Vice President IS&T .... Mr. John CHARLES
21 Vice President for Finance .... Mr. Glen SHOR
48 Dean Sch of Architecture & Planning .... Prof. Hashim SARKIS
54 Dean School of Engineering .... Prof. Anantha CHANDRAKASAN
79 Dean Sch Hum/Arts/Soc Sciences .... Prof. Melissa NOBLES
81 Dean School of Science .... Prof. Michael SIPSER
50 Dean Sloan School of Management .... Prof. David C. SCHMITTLEIN
20 Associate Provost .... Dr. Karen GLEASON
20 Associate Provost .... Prof. Philip S. KHOURY
20 Associate Provost .... Prof. Richard K. LESTER
08 Director of Libraries .... Ms. Chris BOURG
28 Institute Community & Equity Ofcr .... Prof. Edmund BERTSCHINGER
88 Vice Chancellor .... Prof. Ian A. WAITZ
58 Interim Dean Graduate for Education .... Ms. Blanche E. STATON
88 Dean for Undergraduate Education .... Prof. Dennis FREEMAN
32 VP and Dean for Student Life .... Dr. Suzy NELSON
88 Director Lincoln Laboratory .... Dr. Eric D. EVANS
86 Director MIT Washington Office .... Mr. David GOLDSTON
07 Dean of Admissions/Student Fin Svcs .... Mr. Stuart SCHMILL
23 Medical Dir & Head MIT Medical .... Dr. Cecilia Warpinski STUOPIS
18 Director Campus Services and Chief .... Chief John DI FAVA
45 Director of Campus Planning .... Vacant
102 Exec Dir Foundation Relations .... Ms. Lindley HUEY
25 Dir Office of Sponsored Programs .... Ms. Michelle D. CHRISTY
96 Dir of Strategic Sourcing/Contracts .... Ms. Christina T. LO
41 Director of Athletics .... Ms. Julie SORIERO
09 Director of Institutional Research .... Mrs. Lydia S. SNOVER
85 Assoc Dean & Dir Intl Students Ofc .... Mr. David ELWELL
36 Exec Dir Global Educ/Career Dev Ctr .... Ms. Melanie L. PARKER
93 Associate Dean and Director OME .... Ms. DiOnetta CRAYTON
06 Registrar .... Ms. Mary CALLAHAN
88 Director MIT Press .... Ms. Amy BRAND
39 Assoc Director Housing Assignments .... Ms. Jennifer HAPGOOD-WHITE
42 Interim Institute Chaplain .... Rev. John WUESTNECK
38 Sr Assoc Dean Student Support .... Mr. David RANDALL
94 Women's and Gender Studies Director .... Prof. Helen Elaine LEE
104 Associate Dean Global Education .... Ms. Malgorzata HEDDERICK
24 Manager Audio Visual .... Mr. Louis W. GRAHAM, JR.
90 Dir Platform & Systems Integration .... Mr. Garry P. ZACHEISS
04 Exec Assistant to the President .... Ms. Karla CASEY

Massachusetts School of Law at Andover (D)

500 Federal Street, Andover MA 01810-1094
County: Essex FICE Identification: 032353
Unit ID: 369002
Telephone: (978) 681-0800 Carnegie Class: Spec-4-yr-Law
FAX Number: (978) 681-6330 Calendar System: Semester
URL: www.mslaw.edu
Established: 1988 Annual Graduate Tuition & Fees: N/A
Enrollment: 363 Coed
Affiliation or Control: Independent Non-Profit IRS Status: 501(c)3
Highest Offering: Doctorate; No Undergraduates
Accreditation: EH

00 Dean Emeritus .... Mr. Lawrence R. VELVEL
01 Dean .... Prof. Michael COYNE
10 Chief Financial Officer .... Mr. Clifford ABELSON
37 Director Student Financial Aid .... Ms. Lynn BOWAB
06 Registrar .... Ms. Louise ROSE
07 Director of Admissions .... Mr. Rohit BHASIN
26 Director of Media .... Ms. Kathryn VILLARE
05 Dir Academic Svcs/Career Devel .. Ms. Paula COLBY-CLEMENTS
13 Director of Technology .... Mr. Michael COYNE

MCPHS University (E)

179 Longwood Avenue, Boston MA 02115-5896
County: Suffolk FICE Identification: 002165
Unit ID: 166656
Telephone: (617) 732-2800 Carnegie Class: Spec-4-yr-Other Health
FAX Number: (617) 732-2801 Calendar System: Semester
URL: www.mcphs.edu
Established: 1823 Annual Undergrad Tuition & Fees: $31,560
Enrollment: 7,074 Coed
Affiliation or Control: Independent Non-Profit IRS Status: 501(c)3
Highest Offering: Doctorate
Accreditation: EH, ARCPA, DH, NMT, NURSE, OPT, #PHAR, PTA, RAD, RTT

01 President .... Mr. Charles F. MONAHAN, JR.
05 VP for Academic Affairs/Provost .... Dr. George HUMPHREY
10 Exec Vice President/COO & CFO .... Mr. Richard J. LESSARD
111 VP for Advancement & Chief of Staff ... Ms. Marguerite JOHNSON
20 Assoc VP Academic Affs/Assoc Prov .... Dr. Michael MONTAGNE
20 Assoc Provost Acad & Prof Affairs .... Dr. Jeanine MOUNT
20 Assoc Prov Acad & Intl Affairs .... Dr. Caroline ZEIND
106 Assoc Provost Online Education/CEO .... Dr. Barbara MACAULAY
43 VP/General Counsel & CCO .... Ms. Deborah A. O'MALLEY
32 Dean of Students .... Dr. Craig MACK
67 Dean of Pharmacy Boston .... Dr. Paul DIFRANCESCO
67 Dean of Pharmacy Wor/Man .... Dr. Anna MORIN
08 Dean Library & Learning Resources .... Mr. Richard KAPLAN
49 Dean School of Arts and Sciences .... Dr. Delia C. ANDERSON
66 Dean School of Nursing Graduate .... Dr. Carol ELIADI
66 Dean School of Nursing Boston .... Ms. Kathleen PAYNE
52 Dean Forsyth Sch of Dental Hygiene .... Dr. Linda D. BOYD
88 Director of Physical Therapy .... Dr. Frances KISTNER
88 Director of PA Studies Boston .... Mr. Christopher COOPER
88 Director of PA Studies Wor/Man .... Ms. Kristy ALTONGY-MAGEE
88 Director Master of Public Health .... Ms. Carly LEVY
88 Dean of Optometry .... Dr. Morris BERMAN
88 Dean of Acupuncture & Oriental Med .... Ms. Meredith ST JOHN
75 Director of Occupational Therapy .... Dr. Douglas SIMMONS
15 Chief Human Resources Officer .... Mr. Kevin DOLAN
06 Admin Dean/University Registrar .... Ms. Stacey TAYLOR
13 Director of Information Services .... Mr. Tom SCANLON
21 Chief Business Officer .... Mr. Keith BELLUCCI
12 Exec Director Wor/Manch Campuses .... Dr. Seth P. WALL
88 Title IX Coordinator .... Ms. Dawn BALLOU
84 Chief Enrollment Officer .... Ms. Kathleen RYAN
96 Director of Purchasing .... Ms. Peg CRAWFORD
38 Exec Dir Counseling Services .... Ms. Molly PAYNE
26 Director of Communications .... Mr. Michael RATTY
18 Director of Facilities .... Mr. Jeff WARD
19 Chief of Public Safety .... Mr. Jack KELLY
105 Manager of Web Services .... Ms. Charlene ROBERTSON
09 Dir Inst Research & Assessment .... Mr. Rajiv MALHOTRA
04 Special Assistant to the President .... Ms. Sheryl CHEAL

MCPHS-Worcester Campus (F)

19 Foster Street, Worcester MA 01608-1715
Telephone: (508) 890-8855 Identification: 770112
Accreditation: &EH

Merrimack College (G)

315 Turnpike Street, North Andover MA 01845-5800
County: Essex FICE Identification: 002120
Unit ID: 166850
Telephone: (978) 837-5000 Carnegie Class: Masters/M
FAX Number: (978) 837-5222 Calendar System: Semester
URL: www.merrimack.edu
Established: 1947 Annual Undergrad Tuition & Fees: $38,825
Enrollment: 3,620 Coed
Affiliation or Control: Roman Catholic IRS Status: 501(c)3
Highest Offering: Master's
Accreditation: EH, CAATE, ENG

01 President .... Dr. Christopher E. HOPEY
03 Executive Vice President .... Mr. Jeffrey DOGGETT
04 Director Office of the President .... Ms. Lisa JEBALI
05 Provost & Sr VP Academic Affairs .... Dr. Allan T. WEATHERWAX
10 Vice Pres Finance & Budget/CFO .... Mr. William KLINE
04 Special Assistant to the President .... Dr. Russell MAYER
11 VP of Administration & Campus Svcs .... Mr. Mark COLLINS
84 Vice Pres Enrollment Management .... Mr. Anthony ERWIN
42 Vice Pres Mission & Ministry .... Rev. Raymond DLUGOS, OSA
30 Sr VP Development & Alumni Affairs .... Ms. Sara Jane BRAZDA
45 VP Institutional Effectiveness .... Dr. Nancy LUDWIG
88 Assoc VP/Chief of Staff to Provost .... Mr. Mark GOULD
100 Chief of Staff .... Mr. James CHIAVELLI
86 AVP Campus Planning & Development .... Mr. Felipe SCHWARZ
20 Senior Vice Provost .... Dr. Cynthia MCGOWAN
43 Vice President & General Counsel .... Mr. Nicholas MCDONALD
27 Asst VP for Marketing .... Ms. Zoe COHEN
21 Asst VP & Controller Fiscal Affairs .... Ms. Paula CONNOLLY
29 Assoc VP Develop & Alumni Relations .... Ms. Joanne MERMELSTEIN
35 AVP Student Affairs/Dean Students .... Ms. Allison GILL
104 AVP Intl/Grad/Multicul Students .... Ms. Lauren BENT

36 Assoc VP Corporate & Career Engage .... Dr. Heather MAIETTA
50 Dean Girard School of Business .... Dr. Mark CORDANO
54 Dean Science & Engineering .... Dr. Alan WEATHERWAX
49 Dean of Liberal Arts .... Dr. Kathleen TIEMANN
53 Dean School of Education .... Dr. Dan BUTIN
88 AVP for Wellness/Dean of Students ....Ms. Stephanie KENDALL
37 Director Financial Aid ....Ms. Adrienne MONTGOMERY
13 Chief Information Officer ....Mr. Peter HASTINGS
07 Assoc VP/Dean of Admission .... Mr. Darren CONINE
41 Director of Athletics .... Mr. Jeremy GIBSON
09 Dir Institutional Research & Plng ....Ms. Kristen SULLIVAN
15 Director Human Resources .... Ms. Denice BAKER
08 Director of the Library ....Ms. Kathryn GEOFFRION-SCANNELL
42 Director of Campus Ministry .... Rev. Keith HOLLIS
23 Director Counseling & Health Svcs ....Vacant
39 Director of Residence Life .... Mr. Cameron SMITH
19 Director of Police Services .... Mr. Michael DELGRECO
31 Dir of Stevens Service Learning Ctr .... Ms. Mary MCHUGH
24 Dir of Media Instructional Services .... Mr. Kevin SALEMME
96 Director of Purchasing ....Mr. Michael MAGNER
105 Director of Web Services .... Ms. Stacie BOWMAN
28 Director Diversity Education ....Mr. J. Scott GAGE
88 Special Asst Acad Affairs/Provost ....Mr. Michael ACCARDI

MGH Institute of Health Professions (A)

36 1st Avenue, Boston MA 02129-4557
County: Suffolk FICE Identification: 022316
Unit ID: 166869
Telephone: (617) 726-2947 Carnegie Class: Spec-4-yr-Other Health
FAX Number: (617) 726-3716 Calendar System: Semester
URL: www.mghihp.edu
Established: 1977 Annual Undergrad Tuition & Fees: N/A
Enrollment: 1,112 Coed
Affiliation or Control: Independent Non-Profit IRS Status: 501(c)3
Highest Offering: Doctorate
Accreditation: EH, #ARCPA, NURSE, OT, PTA, SP

01 President ....Dr. Paula MILONE-NUZZO
05 Provost ....Dr. Alex JOHNSON

† Tuition varies by degree program.

Montserrat College of Art (B)

23 Essex Street, Beverly MA 01915-4508
County: Essex FICE Identification: 020630
Unit ID: 166911
Telephone: (978) 921-4242 Carnegie Class: Spec-4-yr-Arts
FAX Number: (978) 922-4268 Calendar System: Semester
URL: www.montserrat.edu
Established: 1970 Annual Undergrad Tuition & Fees: $30,800
Enrollment: 371 Coed
Affiliation or Control: Independent Non-Profit IRS Status: 501(c)3
Highest Offering: Baccalaureate
Accreditation: EH, ART

01 President ....Dr. Stephen D. IMMERMAN
05 Dean of Academic Affairs .... Mr. Brian PELLINEN
32 Dean of Students .... Ms. Maureen WARK
30 Dean of Development ....Vacant
26 Dean College Rels/Spec Asst to Pres ....Ms. Jo BRODERICK
10 Chief Financial Officer .... Ms. Cara CALLANAN
13 Director of Information Technology .... Ms. Ari GROSVENOR
08 Librarian ....Ms. Cheri COE
06 Registrar ....Mrs. Theresa SKELLY
37 Director of Financial Aid .... Ms. Emma PUGLISI
15 Human Resources Generalist .... Ms. Christin BOURANIS
07 Director of Admissions .... Mr. Jeffrey NEWELL
04 Executive Asst to the President .... Ms. Margaret WAUGH

Mount Holyoke College (C)

50 College Street, South Hadley MA 01075-1424
County: Hampshire FICE Identification: 002192
Unit ID: 166939
Telephone: (413) 538-2000 Carnegie Class: Bac-A&S
FAX Number: (413) 538-2391 Calendar System: Semester
URL: www.mtholyoke.edu
Established: 1837 Annual Undergrad Tuition & Fees: $45,866
Enrollment: 2,215 Female
Affiliation or Control: Independent Non-Profit IRS Status: 501(c)3
Highest Offering: Master's
Accreditation: EH

01 President .... Sonya STEPHENS
05 VP Acad Affairs/Dean of Faculty ....Jon WESTERN
10 VP Finance and Administration ....Shannon GUREK
84 VP Enrollment/Dean of Admissions .... Gail BERSON
111 VP for Advancement ....Kassandra JOLLEY
32 VP Student Life/Dean of Students .... Marcella RUNELL HALL
26 VP for Communications and Marketing ....Vacant
101 Secretary of the College .... Lenore REILLY
06 Registrar .... Elizabeth PYLE
13 Chief Information Officer .... Alex WIRTH-CAUCHON
100 Chief of Staff ....Kathleen C. PERTZBORN
04 Administrative Asst ....Lynne SULLIVAN
29 Exec Director Alumnae Association .... Nancy PEREZ

Mount Ida College (D)

777 Dedham Street, Newton MA 02459
County: Middlesex FICE Identification: 002193
Unit ID: 166948
Telephone: (617) 928-4500 Carnegie Class: Bac-Diverse
FAX Number: (617) 928-4746 Calendar System: Semester
URL: www.mountida.edu
Established: 1899 Annual Undergrad Tuition & Fees: $33,820
Enrollment: 1,345 Coed
Affiliation or Control: Independent Non-Profit IRS Status: 501(c)3
Highest Offering: Master's
Accreditation: EH, ART, CIDA, DH, FUSER

01 President .... Mr. Barry BROWN
05 Provost and Chief Academic Officer .... Mr. Ronald E. AKIE
111 Vice President for Advancement ....Ms. Jill WIERBICKI ABRAHAMS
10 Vice Pres & Chief Financial Officer ....Mr. Jason POTTS
32 Vice President of Student Affairs .... Ms. Laura DEVEAU
21 Controller .... Ms. Diane WOLFF
88 Asst Dean Student Engage/Leadership .... Mr. Patrick ROMERAO-ALDAZ
06 Registrar .... Ms. Kathy POSEY
22 Director of Disability Services ....Vacant
29 Dir Alumni Relations/Annual Giving ....Vacant
37 Director Financial Aid ....Ms. Dyan TEEHAN
36 Director of Career Services ....Vacant
15 Director of Human Resources ....Vacant
26 Assoc VP Marketing & Communication .... Ms. Fran BERGER
85 Dir Ctr Gbl Connections/Cont Educ .... Ms. Robin MELAVALIN
41 Athletic Director ....Mr. Matthew BURKE
19 Acting Director of Public Safety ....Mr. John KENNEDY
18 Director of Facilities .... Mr. Andrew PAIGE
09 Director of Institutional Research .... Mr. Jerome DEAN
35 Dean of Student Services ....Ms. Mary Anne MILLER
24 Director of Educational Media .... Mr. Manouche MADANIPOUR
96 Director of Business Services .... Ms. Leah WEBBER
07 Dean of Admissions .... Mr. Jeff CUTTING
28 Asst Director Diversity & Inclusion ....Vacant
13 VP of Technology .... Ms. Mary CORCORAN
23 Director Student Health Services .... Ms. Beth GRAMPETRO
58 Assistant Dean Graduate Studies .... Mr. Scott BURKE
04 Administrative Asst to President .... Ms. Grace J. BELTRAME
43 Dir Legal Services/General Counsel .... Mr. Joshua GRUBMAN

The National Graduate School of Quality Management (E)

186 Jones Road, Falmouth MA 02540-2908
County: Barnstable FICE Identification: 035043
Unit ID: 441478
Telephone: (800) 838-2580 Carnegie Class: Spec-4-yr-Bus
FAX Number: (508) 457-5347 Calendar System: Other
URL: www.ngs.edu
Established: 1993 Annual Undergrad Tuition & Fees: N/A
Enrollment: 225 Coed
Affiliation or Control: Independent Non-Profit IRS Status: 501(c)3
Highest Offering: Doctorate
Accreditation: EH

01 Interim President ....Dr. Robert V. ANTONUCCI
05 Dean of Academic Affairs .... Dr. Eileen SULLIVAN
10 Chief Financial Officer .... Mr. Charles RITCH
84 Dean Enrollment Management ....Mr. John ALONSO
19 Campus Security .... Mr. Jay BEIRNE
30 Director of Development ....Mr. Allan WILSON

New England College of Business and Finance (F)

10 High Street, Suite 204, Boston MA 02110
County: Suffolk FICE Identification: 039653
Unit ID: 164438
Telephone: (617) 603-6900 Carnegie Class: Spec-4-yr-Bus
FAX Number: (877) 469-6961 Calendar System: Other
URL: www.necb.edu
Established: 1909 Annual Undergrad Tuition & Fees: $11,240
Enrollment: 1,158 Coed
Affiliation or Control: Proprietary IRS Status: Proprietary
Highest Offering: Master's
Accreditation: EH

01 President ....Mr. Howard E. HORTON
05 Provost .... Ms. Debra LEAHY
10 Sr VP Operations/Finance ....Mr. Dennis J. MADIGAN
106 VP Center for eLearning Excellence ....Ms. Paula BRAMANTE
21 Controller ....Ms. Cassie LAMPSHIRE
20 Asst Provost/Dean of UG Studies .... Mr. Roger PAO
88 Program Chair MBE .... Ms. Deborah SEMENTA
88 Program Chair MBA .... Dr. Carla PATALANO
04 Asst to the President/Office Mgr .... Ms. Kathy CANTALUPA
06 Registrar .... Mr. Robert WAGSTAFF
32 Dean of Students .... Ms. Caitrin BRISSON
84 Director of Enrollment ....Ms. Kirsten THOMPSON
37 Student Finance Supervisor .... Ms. Renee JORDON
108 Director Institutional Assessment ....Ms. Lydia CAVIEUX
26 Chief Public Relations/Marketing .... Mr. Kacey CLARK
88 Vice President of Business Develop ....Mr. John HOPE

New England College of Optometry (G)

424 Beacon Street, Boston MA 02115-1129
County: Suffolk FICE Identification: 002164
Unit ID: 167093
Telephone: (617) 266-2030 Carnegie Class: Spec-4-yr-Other Health
FAX Number: (617) 424-9202 Calendar System: Semester
URL: www.neco.edu
Established: 1894 Annual Undergrad Tuition & Fees: N/A
Enrollment: 511 Coed
Affiliation or Control: Independent Non-Profit IRS Status: 501(c)3
Highest Offering: Doctorate
Accreditation: EH, OPT, OPTR

01 President ....Dr. Clifford SCOTT
05 Interim Dean of Academic Affairs .... Dr. Sandra MOHR
10 Sr VP Finance/Admin/CFO ....Ms. Traci LOGAN
17 Exec Dir of Clinical Training .... Dr. Tony CAVALLERANO
32 Assoc Dean Students ....Ms. Barbara MCGINLEY
07 Director of Admissions .... Ms. Kristen TOBIN
37 Director Student Financial Aid ....Ms. Carol RUBEL
15 Exec Dir of Human Resources ....Ms. Elizabeth DAVIES
06 Registrar .... Ms. Glenda UNDERWOOD
08 Director of Library Services .... Ms. Heather EDMONDS
04 Executive Asst to the President .... Ms. Marie HILL

New England Conservatory of Music (H)

290 Huntington Avenue, Boston MA 02115-5018
County: Suffolk FICE Identification: 002194
Unit ID: 167057
Telephone: (617) 585-1100 Carnegie Class: Spec-4-yr-Arts
FAX Number: (617) 262-0500 Calendar System: Semester
URL: www.necmusic.edu
Established: 1867 Annual Undergrad Tuition & Fees: $44,755
Enrollment: 789 Coed
Affiliation or Control: Independent Non-Profit IRS Status: 501(c)3
Highest Offering: Doctorate
Accreditation: EH

01 Interim President .... Mr. Thomas NOVAK
05 Provost/Dean of the College .... Mr. Thomas NOVAK
10 Sr Vice Pres Finance/Operations .... Mr. Edward R. LESSER
111 Vice Pres Institutional Advancement .... Ms. Kathleen KELLY
26 Vice Pres Marketing/Communications ....Vacant
100 Chief of Staff .... Ms. Kairyn RAINER
32 Dean of Students .... Ms. Suzanne HEGLAND
07 Asst Dean for Admissions ....Mr. Alex POWELL
21 Controller .... Ms. Kristina MARTIN
18 Exec Dir Facilities/Engrng/Constr ....Mr. Michael RYAN
06 Registrar .... Mr. Robert WINKLEY
08 Director of Libraries ....Mr. Alan KARASS
37 Director Financial Aid ....Ms. Lauren URBANEK
39 Director Residence Life .... Ms. Perry DOHERTY
29 Director of Alumni Relations ....Vacant
15 Director of Human Resources ....Vacant
13 Director ITS ....Mr. Charles MEMBRINO
09 Director of Research and Management .... Ms. Sarah DOW
35 Associate Dean of Students ....Ms. Rebecca TEETERS
38 Director Student Counseling .... Ms. Jan LERBINGER
88 Dir of Entrepreneurial Musicianship .... Ms. Rachel ROBERTS
88 Asst Dean of Campus Life ....Ms. Ashlee CARTER

The New England Institute of Art (I)

10 Brookline Place West, Brookline MA 02445-7295
County: Norfolk FICE Identification: 007486
Unit ID: 167321
Telephone: (617) 739-1700 Carnegie Class: Spec-4-yr-Arts
FAX Number: (617) 582-4500 Calendar System: Semester
URL: www.artinstitutes.edu/boston
Established: 1952 Annual Undergrad Tuition & Fees: N/A
Enrollment: 262 Coed
Affiliation or Control: Proprietary IRS Status: Proprietary
Highest Offering: Baccalaureate
Accreditation: EH

01 President ....Dr. John LAY

† In teach-out mode.

New England Law | Boston (J)

154 Stuart Street, Boston MA 02116-5687
County: Suffolk FICE Identification: 008916
Unit ID: 167215
Telephone: (617) 451-0010 Carnegie Class: Spec-4-yr-Law
FAX Number: (617) 422-7333 Calendar System: Semester
URL: www.nesl.edu
Established: 1908 Annual Undergrad Tuition & Fees: N/A
Enrollment: 688 Coed
Affiliation or Control: Independent Non-Profit IRS Status: 501(c)3
Highest Offering: First Professional Degree
Accreditation: LAW

01 Dean .... Mr. John F. O'BRIEN
05 Associate Dean ....Ms. Judith GREENBERG
11 Associate Dean of Administration .... Ms. Susan S. CALAMARE

07 Director of Admission ....Ms. Michelle L'ETOILE
10 Chief Financial Officer ....Mr. David M. ROSATI
08 Director of the Law Library ....Ms. Anne ACTON
36 Director Career Services ....Ms. Mandie A. LEBEAU
37 Director of Financial Aid ....Mr. Eric A. KRUPSKI
06 Registrar ....Mr. David M. BERTI
18 Director of Facilities/Security ....Mr. Miguel ALVARADO
32 Director of Student Services ....Ms. Jacqueline PILGRIM
30 Dir of Development/Alumni Rels ....Ms. Jocelyn J. COLETTI

New England School of Acupuncture (A)

150 California Street, Newton MA 02458-1005
County: Middlesex FICE Identification: 025798
Unit ID: 167181
Telephone: (617) 558-1788 Carnegie Class: Spec-4-yr-Other Health
FAX Number: (617) 558-1789 Calendar System: Trimester
URL: www.nesa.edu
Established: 1975 Annual Undergrad Tuition & Fees: N/A
Enrollment: 167 Coed
Affiliation or Control: Independent Non-Profit IRS Status: 501(c)3
Highest Offering: Master's; No Lower Division
Accreditation: ACUP

01 Executive Director ....Susan L. GORMAN
05 Academic Dean ....Meredith ST. JOHN
10 Controller ....Katherine DECELLES
07 Asst Director of Recruitment ....Patrick CAMERON
06 Managing Registrar ....Greg TILTON
13 Chief Information Officer ....Tom SCANLON

† Affiliate of MCPHS University.

Newbury College (B)

129 Fisher Avenue, Brookline MA 02445-5796
County: Norfolk FICE Identification: 007484
Unit ID: 167251
Telephone: (617) 730-7000 Carnegie Class: Bac-Diverse
FAX Number: (617) 731-9618 Calendar System: Semester
URL: www.newbury.edu
Established: 1962 Annual Undergrad Tuition & Fees: $33,510
Enrollment: 865 Coed
Affiliation or Control: Independent Non-Profit IRS Status: 501(c)3
Highest Offering: Baccalaureate
Accreditation: EH

01 President ....Dr. Joseph L. CHILLO
05 Vice President Academic Affairs ....Dr. Frank SARGENT
10 Vice President Finance/CFO ....Ms. Joyce HANLON
100 Chief of Staff ....Mr. Paul MARTIN
111 Vice President for Advancement ....Ms. Clare MCCULLY
84 Vice Pres Enrollment Management ....Mr. Paul VACCARO
121 Dean of Student Success ....Ms. Anne-Marie KENNEY
08 Director of Library Services ....Mr. Anthony VIOLA
37 Director of Student Financial Aid ....Ms. Jenny AGUIAR
06 Registrar ....Mr. Jesse AVALOS
15 Director Human Resources ....Ms. Amy DOWNING
36 Director of Career Services ....Ms. Larinda COLE
38 Director Counseling/Health Educ ....Ms. Susan CHAMANDY
41 Director of Athletics ....Mr. Jonathan HARPER
07 Director of Admissions ....Mr. Yavuz KIREMIT
32 Interim Dean of Student Affairs ....Ms. Jennifer FORRY
04 Executive Asst to President ....Ms. Elizabeth SCHIERLOH
19 Director Campus Safety ....Mr. Daniel AMORIM
29 Alumni Relations Manager ....Ms. Tracy RICCIARDI

Nichols College (C)

Center Road, PO Box 5000, Dudley MA 01571-5000
County: Worcester FICE Identification: 002197
Unit ID: 167260
Telephone: (508) 213-1560 Carnegie Class: Spec-4-yr-Bus
FAX Number: N/A Calendar System: Semester
URL: www.nichols.edu
Established: 1815 Annual Undergrad Tuition & Fees: $33,400
Enrollment: 1,454 Coed
Affiliation or Control: Independent Non-Profit IRS Status: 501(c)3
Highest Offering: Master's
Accreditation: EH, IACBE

01 President ....Susan WEST ENGELKEMEYER
05 Vice President for Academic Affairs ....Mauri S. PE
10 Vice President Administration ....Michael J. STANTON
111 Vice President for Advancement ....William C. PIECZYNSKI
84 Vice President for Enrollment ....William BOFFI
32 Dean of Students ....Pamela J. BOGGIO
26 Assoc VP Marketing/Communications ....Cynthia G. BROWN
124 Assoc Dir of Enroll & Retention ....Katie MOULTON
13 Chief Information Officer ....Kevin F. BRASSARD
58 Exec Dir Graduate & Prof Studies ....Kerry CALNAN
04 Assistant to the President ....Lynn S. LOOBY
41 Director of Athletics ....Christopher COLVIN
07 Asst Dean for Enrollment ....Paul O. BROWER
06 Registrar ....Betin ROBICHAUD
08 Director of Library ....Jim DOUGLAS
15 Asst Director of Human Resources ....Katie CUSHING
29 Director of Alumni Relations ....Molly THIENEL
21 Controller ....Jamie SKOWYRA
35 Dir Student Activities/Orientation ....Brian QUINLAN
36 Director of Career Services ....Elizabeth HORGAN

37 Director of Financial Aid ....Jennifer BIANCO
38 Director Mental Health Services . Monica GOODRICH PELLETIER
27 Director of Public Relations ....Lorraine MARTINELLE
18 Assoc VP for Facilities Management ....Robert W. LAVIGNE
09 Dir of Inst Research & Reporting ....Emily REARDON
96 Director Procurement & Contract Svc ....Kay F. YOUNG
19 Director Public Safety ....Jack CAULFIELD
23 Director Health Services ....Katherine NICOLETTI
39 Director Residence Life ....Marney BUSS
104 Director Study Abroad ....Susan WAYMAN
105 Webmaster ....Dana ARMSTRONG

Northeastern University (D)

360 Huntington Avenue, Boston MA 02115-0195
County: Suffolk FICE Identification: 002199
Unit ID: 167358
Telephone: (617) 373-2000 Carnegie Class: DU-Highest
FAX Number: N/A Calendar System: Semester
URL: www.northeastern.edu
Established: 1898 Annual Undergrad Tuition & Fees: $47,653
Enrollment: 19,940 Coed
Affiliation or Control: Independent Non-Profit IRS Status: 501(c)3
Highest Offering: Doctorate
Accreditation: EH, ANEST, ARCPA, AUD, COPSY, ENG, ENGT, LAW, NURSE, PH, PHAR, PTA, SCPSY, SP, SPAA

01 President ....Dr. Joseph E. AOUN
04 Executive Asst to the President ....Ms. Susie C. GUSZCZA
05 Sr VP Academic Affairs and Provost ....Dr. James C. BEAN
100 Chief of Staff ....Mr. James HACKNEY
84 Sr VP Enroll Mgmt & CEO NUGN ..Dr. Philomena V. MANTELLA
111 Sr VP University Advancement ....Ms. Diane N. MACGILLIVRAY
43 Sr VP and General Counsel ....Mr. Ralph C. MARTIN, II
26 Sr VP External Affairs ....Mr. Michael A. ARMINI
11 Sr VP & Chief Operating Officer ....Vacant
12 Seattle Campus Dean & CEO ....Mr. Peter TEMES
12 Regional Dean & CEO Silicon Valley ....Dr. P.K AGARWAL
12 Charlotte Campus Dean & CEO ....Dr. Cheryl RICHARDS
08 Dean University Libraries ....Dr. Dan COHEN
46 Sr Vice Provost Research/Grad Educ ....Dr. Art KRAMER
20 Sr Vice Prov UG Ed & Exp Learning ....Dr. Susan AMBROSE
32 Sr Advisor Strategic Init ....Dr. Laura A. WANKEL
13 VP & CIO ....Vacant
88 VP Enrollment Management ....Mr. Sundar KUMARASAMY
35 VP Student Affs & Dean of Students ....Ms. Madeleine A. ESTABROOK
30 VP Development ....Ms. Luanne KIRWIN
15 VP Human Resources Management ....Ms. Jane MOYER
18 VP Facilities ....Vacant
86 VP Government Relations ....Mr. Tim E. LESHAN
88 VP Business Affs Graduate Campuses .Mr. M. Seamus HARREYS
110 VP Advancement & Campaign Director ....Mr. Joseph DONNELLY, JR.
31 VP City & Community Affairs ....Mr. John M. TOBIN
117 VP Enterprise Risk Management ....Ms. Sonya GRANAHAN
45 VP & Chief Campus Planning and Dev . Ms. Kathy SPIEGELMAN
20 Sr Vice Provost Academic Affairs ....Ms. Debra FRANKO
114 Vice Provost Budget/Planning/Admin ....Vacant
28 Vice Prov Inst Diversity & Inclsn ....Dr. John ARMENDARIZ
76 Dean Health Sciences ....Dr. Susan PARISH
37 Dean Student Financial Services ....Mr. Tony ERWIN
36 Assoc VP Career Services/Co-Op Educ ....Ms. Maria K. STEIN
88 Assoc VP & Deputy General Counsel ....Ms. Lisa SINCLAIR
58 AVP Graduate Affairs ....Dr. Phil HE
21 VP of Finance ....Dr. Anthony RINI
88 AVP Research Administration ....Ms. Dana CARROLL
09 AVP Inst Rsrch & Data Admin ....Ms. Rana GLASGAL
06 Asst VP & University Registrar ....Ms. Linda D. ALLEN
27 Asst VP Communications ....Ms. Renata NYUL
88 AVP Interdisc Initiatives/Spec Proj ....Mr. Robert DIETRICH
44 VP & Asst Treasurer ....Ms. Alysa GERLACH
92 Director University Honors Program ....Ms. Laurie KRAMER
42 Exec Dir Spirituality & Dialogue ....Mr. Alexander KERN
19 Director of Public Safety ....Mr. Michael DAVIS
41 Director of Athletics ....Mr. Peter P. ROBY
10 Sr VP Finance & Treasurer ....Mr. Thomas NEDELL
77 Dean Col Computer & Info Science ....Dr. Carla E. BRODLEY
54 Dean College of Engineering ....Dr. Nadine AUBRY
81 Dean College of Science ....Dr. Kenneth HENDERSON
50 Dean D'Amore-McKim School of Bus ....Dr. Raj ECHAMBADI
57 Dean College of Arts/Media/Design ....Dr. Elizabeth HUDSON
61 Dean School of Law ....Dr. Jeremy PAUL
83 Dean Col of Soc Sci & Humanities ....Dr. Uta POIGER
107 Dean Col Prof Studies ....Dr. Mary LOEFFELHOLZ
12 Dean Toronto Campus ....Dr. John LABRIE
106 Dir Online Education/E-learning ....Mr. Chris MALLETT
29 VP Alumni Relations ....Mr. Rick DAVIS
39 Director Student Housing ....Mr. Robert JOSE

Northpoint Bible College (E)

320 South Main Street, Haverhill MA 01835
County: Essex FICE Identification: 035705
Unit ID: 217606
Telephone: (978) 478-3400 Carnegie Class: Spec-4-yr-Faith
FAX Number: (978) 478-3406 Calendar System: Semester
URL: www.northpoint.edu
Established: 1924 Annual Undergrad Tuition & Fees: $11,510
Enrollment: 313 Coed
Affiliation or Control: Assemblies Of God Church IRS Status: 501(c)3
Highest Offering: Master's
Accreditation: BI

01 President ....Rev Dr. David J. ARNETT
05 Academic Dean ....Rev Dr. Daniel HOWELL
32 Dean of Student Affairs ....Rev. David HANSHUMAKER
10 Director of Finance ....Mrs. Jaime RAGSDALE
07 Director of Enrollment ....Rev. Jonathan RAGSDALE
37 Director of Financial Aid ....Miss Patricia STAUFFER
06 Registrar ....Mrs. Amy MARANVILLE
13 Chief Info Technology Officer (CIO) ....Mr. Steve SIMMONS

Pine Manor College (F)

400 Heath Street, Chestnut Hill MA 02467-2332
County: Norfolk FICE Identification: 002201
Unit ID: 167455
Telephone: (617) 731-7000 Carnegie Class: Bac-A&S
FAX Number: (617) 731-7199 Calendar System: Semester
URL: www.pmc.edu
Established: 1911 Annual Undergrad Tuition & Fees: $28,780
Enrollment: 495 Coed
Affiliation or Control: Independent Non-Profit IRS Status: 501(c)3
Highest Offering: Master's
Accreditation: #EH

01 President ....Mr. Thomas O'REILLY
05 Dean of College ....Dr. Diane MELLO-GOLDNER
15 VP/Chief Human Resources Officer ....Ms. Shelleye DROPKIN
111 VP of Advancement ....Ms. Janine DAILEY
32 Dean of Student Affairs ....Ms. Staci WEBER
84 Dean of Enrollment & Admissions ....Mr. Samuel WHITE
06 Registrar/Dir Inst Research ....Mr. Jeffrey MEI
26 Dir Publications/Media Relations ....Ms. Efrat ZINNAR-SHAVIT
08 Library Director ....Ms. Sarah WOOLF

Pope St. John XXIII National Seminary (G)

558 South Avenue, Weston MA 02493-2699
County: Middlesex FICE Identification: 002202
Unit ID: 167464
Telephone: (781) 899-5500 Carnegie Class: Spec-4-yr-Faith
FAX Number: (781) 899-9057 Calendar System: Semester
URL: www.psjs.edu
Established: 1964 Annual Graduate Tuition & Fees: N/A
Enrollment: 61 Male
Affiliation or Control: Roman Catholic IRS Status: 501(c)3
Highest Offering: Master's; No Undergraduates
Accreditation: THEOL

01 Rector and President ....Rev. Brian R. KIELY
03 Executive Vice President ....Rev. Paul E. MICELI
05 Academic Dean ....Dr. Anthony KEATY
08 Librarian ....Sr. Jacqueline MILLER
10 Business Manager ....Mrs. Kyle RYAN
06 Registrar ....Dr. Anthony KEATY
30 Chief Development Officer ....Mr. Richard MURPHY
32 Chief Student Life Officer ....Rev. Paul MICELI

Quincy College (H)

1250 Hancock Street, Quincy MA 02169-4324
County: Norfolk FICE Identification: 002205
Unit ID: 167525
Telephone: (617) 984-1700 Carnegie Class: Assoc/HT-Mix Trad/Non
FAX Number: (617) 984-1779 Calendar System: Semester
URL: www.quincycollege.edu
Established: 1958 Annual Undergrad Tuition & Fees (In-District): $5,910
Enrollment: 4,732 Coed
Affiliation or Control: Local IRS Status: 501(c)3
Highest Offering: Associate Degree
Accreditation: EH, ADNUR, MLTAD, PNUR, PTAA, SURGT

01 President ....Dr. Peter H. TSAFFARAS
05 SVP Academic Affairs ....Dr. Mary E. BURKE
10 SVP Administration/Finance ....Mr. Joseph MERCURIO
100 Assistant to the President ....Mr. Stephen KEARNEY
04 Admin Asst to President ....Ms. Donna M. BRUGMAN
06 Dir of Student Records & Registrar ....Ms. Catherine MALONEY
66 Dean of Nursing ....Dr. Lori KOEHLER
49 Dean of Liberal Arts ....Dr. Robert BAKER
107 Dean of Professional Programs ....Mr. William BRENNAN
81 Dean of Natural & Health Sciences ....Capt. Vincent VANJOOLEN
21 Director of Finance ....Mr. Martin AHERN
13 VP Technology & Mission Support ....Mr. Tom C. PHAM
20 Assoc Dean for Academics Plymouth ....Mr. Robert BOSTROM
20 Assoc Dean for Admin Plymouth ....Ms. Laura BUCKLEY
37 Assoc VP for Financial Aid ....Ms. Rose M. DEVITO
18 Dir of Admin Services & Facilities ....Mr. William C. HALL
32 Assoc VP for Student Development ....Ms. Susan G. BOSSA
15 Vice Pres for Human Resources ....Vacant
26 Assoc VP of Comm & Marketing ....Mr. Taggart BOYLE
07 Director of Admissions ....Mr. Eric CLARK
121 Director of Academic Advising ....Mr. David CICHOCKI
85 Director of Intl Student Services ....Ms. Lisa STACK
111 Director Institutional Advancement ....Ms. Tina CAHILL
09 Senior Research Analyst ....Ms. Amanda COLLIGAN
35 Director of Student Development ....Ms. Amanda DECK
08 Director of Library Services ....Ms. Susan WHITEHEAD
106 Dean Online Programs & Inst Affairs ... Mr. Michael MARRAPODI
103 Dir Workforce Dev & Comm Engagement ....Ms. Kate LOPCI

Regis College (A)

235 Wellesley Street, Weston MA 02493-1571
County: Middlesex FICE Identification: 002206
Unit ID: 167598
Telephone: (781) 768-7000 Carnegie Class: Spec-4-yr-Other Health
FAX Number: (781) 768-8339 Calendar System: Semester
URL: www.regiscollege.edu
Established: 1927 Annual Undergrad Tuition & Fees: $39,040
Enrollment: 1,954 Coed
Affiliation or Control: Independent Non-Profit IRS Status: 501(c)3
Highest Offering: Doctorate
Accreditation: EH, ADNUR, NMT, NUR, RAD, SW

01 President .... Dr. Antoinette M. HAYS
10 Vice President Finance/Business .... Mr. Thomas G. PISTORINO
05 Vice President Academic Affairs .... Dr. Malcolm O. ASADOORIAN, III
07 Dean of Undergraduate Admission .... Dr. Laura BERTONAZZI
37 Director of Financial Aid .... Ms. Bonnie QUINN
06 Registrar .... Ms. Esther A. GHAZARIAN
09 Dean of Institutional Research .... Dr. Leslie GINDRO
15 Director of Human Resources .... Ms. Joan D. SULLIVAN
18 Director of Physical Plant .... Mr. Joseph SHAUGHNESSY
21 Director Finance & Business .... Ms. Nancy PLASKER
29 Director of Alumni Relations .... Mrs. Christina DUGGAN
32 VP Student Affairs & UG Enrollment .... Dr. Kara KOLOMITZ
23 Director of Health Services .... Ms. Dianna JONES
08 Director of Library .... Ms. Jane PECK
13 Chief Information Officer .... Ms. Kate KORZENDORFER
41 Dean of Athletics .... Ms. Pamela ROECKER
42 Director Campus Ministry .... Mr. Daniel LEAHY
96 Director of Purchasing .... Ms. Diep SHEEHAN
31 Director of Community Living .... Ms. Kelly TRESELER
35 Director of Student Programs .... Mr. Paul MURPHY
30 Chief Development Officer .... Ms. Miriam FINN-SHERMAN
104 Director Study Abroad .... Mr. David CRISCI

Saint John's Seminary (B)

127 Lake Street, Brighton MA 02135-3898
County: Suffolk FICE Identification: 002214
Unit ID: 167677
Telephone: (617) 254-2610 Carnegie Class: Spec-4-yr-Faith
FAX Number: (617) 787-2336 Calendar System: Semester
URL: www.sjs.edu
Established: 1884 Annual Undergrad Tuition & Fees: $22,650
Enrollment: 208 Coed
Affiliation or Control: Roman Catholic IRS Status: 501(c)3
Highest Offering: Master's
Accreditation: EH, THEOL

01 Rector .... Msgr. James MORONEY
03 Vice Rector .... Rev. Christopher K. O'CONNOR
05 Dean of Faculty .... Prof. Paul METILLY
32 Dean of Students .... Rev. Edward RILEY
07 Director of Admissions & Records .... Mrs. Maureen DEBERNARDI
08 Librarian .... Rev. Raymond VAN DE MOORTELL
10 Director Finance and Operations .... Mr. Richard A. FLAHERTY
73 Director Pre-Theology Program .... Rev. David PIGNATO
21 Asst Finance Director .... Mr. Armand DILANDO
108 Executive Institutional Assessment .... Mr. Kieran KELLY
44 Director Annual or Planned Giving .... Ms. Sandra BARRY

Salter College (C)

645 Shawinigan Drive, Chicopee MA 01020-3744
Telephone: (508) 853-1074 Identification: 770724
Accreditation: ACICS

Salter College (D)

184 West Boylston Street, West Boylston MA 01583
County: Worcester FICE Identification: 004666
Unit ID: 167738
Telephone: (774) 261-1500 Carnegie Class: Assoc/HVT-Mix Trad/Non
FAX Number: (774) 261-1554 Calendar System: Semester
URL: www.saltercollege-us.com
Established: 1937 Annual Undergrad Tuition & Fees: N/A
Enrollment: 348 Coed
Affiliation or Control: Proprietary IRS Status: Proprietary
Highest Offering: Associate Degree
Accreditation: ACICS, ACFEI

01 Campus Director .... Mr. Wade CHARLTON

Simmons College (E)

300 The Fenway, Boston MA 02115-5898
County: Suffolk FICE Identification: 002208
Unit ID: 167783
Telephone: (617) 521-2000 Carnegie Class: Masters/L
FAX Number: (617) 521-3065 Calendar System: Semester
URL: www.simmons.edu
Established: 1899 Annual Undergrad Tuition & Fees: $38,590
Enrollment: 5,662 Coordinate
Affiliation or Control: Independent Non-Profit IRS Status: 501(c)3
Highest Offering: Doctorate
Accreditation: EH, DIETD, DIETI, LIB, NURSE, PTA, SW

01 President .... Helen G. DRINAN
04 Assistant to the President .... Marianne FIGUEIREDO
05 Provost .... Sheila (Katie) CONBOY
10 Sr VP Finance/Administration .... Donna NG
26 VP Comm/Diversity & Inclusion .... Cheryl HOWARD
111 VP Advancement .... Marianne E. LORD
32 VP Student Affairs/Dean of Students .... Sarah NEILL
84 VP Enrollment Mgmt .... John F. DOLAN
20 Deputy Provost .... Stefan KRUG
62 Dean Grad Sch Library/Info Science .... Eileen G. ABELS
76 Dean Sch Nursing & Health Sciences .... Judy BEAL
50 Dean School of Management .... Patricia H. DEYTON
49 Dean College of Arts & Sciences .... Renee WHITE
104 Director of Study Abroad .... Joseph STANLEY
06 Asst VP Acad Operations & Registrar .... Vacant
08 Library Director .... Vivienne B. PIROLI
25 Director Sponsored Programs .... Jon KIMBALL
09 Director Institutional Research .... Lan GAO
36 Director Career Education Center .... Andrea WOLF
13 Executive Director Technology CIO .... Debra ORR
14 Sr Dir Enterprise Applications & Sv .... Michael PENNACHIO
19 Director Public Safety .... Sean COLLINS
96 Director Purchasing & Procurement .... Kathy PERONI-CALLAHAN
07 Director of Undergraduate Admission .... Ellen JOHNSON
123 Assistant VP Graduate Admissions .... Kristen HAACK
27 Sr Director Marketing .... Allyson IRISH
100 Chief of Staff .... Laura BRINK
88 Event Strategist .... Janice TAYLOR
42 Spiritual Life Program Manager .... Bonnie-Jeanne CASEY
38 Clinical Director Counseling Svcs .... Sherri ETTINGER
39 Director Residence Life .... Jessica FAULK
41 Director Athletics .... Ali KANTOR
32 Dean of Student Life .... Susan ANTONELLI
43 VP & General Counsel .... Kathleen R. ROGERS
15 Assistant VP Human Resources .... Sarah MILLER
29 Senior Director Alumni Engagement .... Elizabeth WEBSTER
28 Assistant Provost for Diversity .... Lisa SMITH-MCQUEENIE

Smith College (F)

Northampton MA 01063-0001
County: Hampshire FICE Identification: 002209
Unit ID: 167835
Telephone: (413) 584-2700 Carnegie Class: Bac-A&S
FAX Number: (413) 585-2123 Calendar System: Semester
URL: www.smith.edu
Established: 1871 Annual Undergrad Tuition & Fees: $47,904
Enrollment: 2,874 Female
Affiliation or Control: Independent Non-Profit IRS Status: 501(c)3
Highest Offering: Doctorate
Accreditation: EH, ENG, SW

01 President .... Kathleen MCCARTNEY
04 Executive Asst to the President .... Beth BERG
10 Vice Pres Finance & Administration .... Michael W. HOWARD
05 Provost & Dean of the Faculty .... Katherine ROWE
84 VP for Enrollment .... Audrey Y. SMITH
20 Dean for Academic Development .... Bill PETERSON
32 VP Campus Life/Dean of the College .... Donna LISKER
35 Dean of Students .... Julianne OHOTNICKY
70 Dean School for Social Work .... Marianne YOSHIOKA
39 Director of Residence Life .... Becky SHAW
85 Assoc Dean International Students .... Caitlin B. SZYMKOWICZ
30 VP for Development .... Beth RAFFELD
38 Director of Health and Wellness .... Pamela MCCARTHY
26 VP for Public Affairs .... Laurie FENLASON
29 VP Alum Rels/Exec Dir Alumnae Assn .... Jennifer S. CHRISLER
13 VP Information Technology .... Samantha EARP
09 Exec Dir Inst Research .... Cate ROWEN
08 Dean of Libraries .... Susan FLISS
15 Assoc VP for Human Resources .... Lawrence HUNT
07 Dean of Admission .... Debra D. SHAVER
37 Dir Student Financial Services .... David J. BELANGER
06 Registrar .... Gretchen B. HERRINGER
36 Director Career Development Office .... Stacie HAGENBAUGH
28 VP for Incl/Diversity and Equity .... Vacant
20 Associate Dean of Faculty .... Patricia DIBARTOLO
18 Assoc VP for Facilities Management .... Roger MOSIER
41 Director of Athletics .... Kristin HUGHES
42 Interim Director of Religious Life .... Matilda CANTWELL
96 Procurement Director .... Linda HIESIGER
104 Dean for International Study .... Rebecca HOVEY

Springfield College (G)

263 Alden Street, Springfield MA 01109-3797
County: Hampden FICE Identification: 002211
Unit ID: 167899
Telephone: (413) 748-3000 Carnegie Class: Masters/L
FAX Number: N/A Calendar System: Semester
URL: www.springfieldcollege.edu
Established: 1885 Annual Undergrad Tuition & Fees: $35,475
Enrollment: 3,241 Coed
Affiliation or Control: Independent Non-Profit IRS Status: 501(c)3
Highest Offering: Doctorate
Accreditation: EH, ARCPA, CAATE, CACREP, COPSY, EMT, EXSC, IACBE, NRPA, OT, PTA, SW

01 President .... Dr. Mary-Beth A. COOPER
05 Provost & VP Academic Affairs .... Dr. Martha POTVIN
111 VP Institutional Advancement .... Mr. Gary BLANCHETTE
10 Sr VP for Finance & Admin .... Mr. John MAILHOT
32 VP for Student Affairs .... Dr. Shannon FINNING
43 VP & General Counsel .... Mr. Christopher NERONHA
28 VP for Inclusion & Com Engagement .... Dr. Calvin R. HILL
20 Assoc VP Academic Affairs .... Dr. Mary Ann COUGHLIN
15 Director of Human Resources .... Ms. Miriam SIEGEL
30 Sr Assoc VP & Dir of Develop .... Ms. Julie TYSON
84 VP of Enrollment Management .... Mr. Stuart JONES
06 Registrar .... Mr. Keith INGALLS
08 Director of Library .... Ms. Andrea S. TAUPIER
29 Director of Alumni Relations .... Ms. Tamie KIDESS LUCEY
37 Director of Financial Aid .... Mr. Edward CIOSEK
36 Interim Director of Career Center .... Mr. Scott DRANKA
13 Chief Information Officer .... Mr. Danny DAVIS
90 Sr Dir Network/AC & Clnt Comp .... Mr. Thomas F. LARKIN
26 Exec Director Communications .... Mr. Stephen ROULIER
38 Director of Counseling Center .... Mr. Brian KRYLOWICZ
19 Exec Dir Public Safety/Chief .... Ms. Karen LEARY
85 Director of International Center .... Dr. Deborah ALM
42 Director Campus Ministry .... Mr. David MCMAHON
18 Director of Facilities & Campus Svc .... Mr. Gregory WALTERS
41 Director of Athletics .... Dr. Craig POISSON
96 Director of Purchasing .... Ms. Lita ADAMS

Stonehill College (H)

320 Washington Street, Easton MA 02357-6110
County: Bristol FICE Identification: 002217
Unit ID: 167996
Telephone: (508) 565-1000 Carnegie Class: Bac-A&S
FAX Number: (508) 565-1500 Calendar System: Semester
URL: www.stonehill.edu
Established: 1948 Annual Undergrad Tuition & Fees: $39,900
Enrollment: 2,400 Coed
Affiliation or Control: Roman Catholic IRS Status: 501(c)3
Highest Offering: Baccalaureate
Accreditation: EH

01 President .... Rev. John F. DENNING, CSC
100 Chief of Staff .... Mrs. Heather L. HEERMAN
05 Provost/VP for Acad Affairs .... Dr. Joseph FAVAZZA
10 Vice Pres for Finance & Treasurer .... Ms. Jeanne FINLAYSON
111 Vice President for Advancement .... Mr. Francis X. DILLON
32 Vice President of Student Affairs .... Ms. Pauline DOBROWSKI
88 Vice President for Mission .... Vacant
84 VP for Enrollment Mgmt & Marketing .... Mrs. Catherine CAPOLUPO
21 AVP for Finance & Operations .... Mr. Craig BINNEY
35 Assoc VP for Students Affairs .... Mr. Kevin PISKADLO
37 Asst VP/Dir of Student Aid/Finance .... Mr. William C. SMITH
04 Sr Executive Asst to the President .... Mrs. Jessica L. GRACIA
20 Assoc Prov Div/Fac/Dev/Assessment .... Dr. Maria CURTIN
121 Assoc Prov for Academic Achievement .... Dr. Craig ALMEIDA
43 General Counsel .... Mr. Thomas V. FLYNN
21 Controller .... Ms. Jennifer MATHEWS
07 Dean of Admissions .... Mr. Joe DACEY
06 Registrar .... Mr. John PESTANA
09 Dir of Inst Research/Assessment .... Mr. Brian M. OLES
08 Director of College Library .... Ms. Cheryl MCGRATH
26 Dir of Media Rels & Communications .... Mr. Martin P. MCGOVERN
29 Director of Alumni Affairs .... Ms. Anne M. SANT
15 Director of Human Resources .... Mrs. Lily A. KRENTZMAN
38 Dir of Counseling & Testing Center .... Ms. Maria A. KAVANAUGH
13 Chief Information Officer .... Ms. Tamara ANDERSON
19 Chief of Police .... Mr. Peter CARNES
42 Director Campus Ministry .... Rev. Anthony SZAKALY, CSC
90 Manager of Instructional Technology .... Ms. Janice HARRISON
45 Director of Academic Development .... Ms. Bonnie L. TROUPE
88 Dir of Enterprise Infrastructure .... Mr. Thomas MCGRATH
23 Director of Health Services .... Mrs. Maria SULLIVAN
36 Director of Career Services .... Mrs. Christina M. BURNEY
41 Dir of Intercollegiate Athletics .... Mr. Dean R. O'KEEFE
92 Director of Honors Program .... Prof. Allyson SHECKLER
30 Assoc VP for Advancement .... Mr. Douglas J. SMITH
20 Dir of Academic Svcs & Advising .... Mr. Joe WARANYUWAT
96 Director of Purchasing .... Mr. Gregory WOLFE
45 Asst VP for Planning & Budgeting .... Mr. Stephen BEAUREGARD
39 Director of Residence Life .... Ms. Kristen PIERCE
24 Dir of Media/Videography Services .... Mr. Michael PIETROWSKI
40 Manager of College Bookstore .... Mrs. Mary DUNCKLEE
97 Asst Dean Gen Educ & Acad Achievmnt .... Dr. Todd S. GERNES
18 Dir of Facilities Management .... Mr. Bruce BOYER
104 Director International Programs .... Ms. Jennifer E. JACKSON
31 Campus Minister Svc Immersion Pgm .... Ms. Mary Anne CAPPELLERI
28 Director of Intercultural Affairs .... Ms. Constanza CABELLO
49 Dean School of Arts and Sciences .... Dr. Peter N. UBERTACCIO
50 Dean of the School of Business .... Ms. Debra SALVUCCI

Suffolk University (I)

8 Ashburton Place, Boston MA 02108-2770
County: Suffolk FICE Identification: 002218
Unit ID: 168005
Telephone: (617) 573-8000 Carnegie Class: DU-Mod
FAX Number: (617) 573-8353 Calendar System: Semester
URL: www.suffolk.edu
Established: 1906 Annual Undergrad Tuition & Fees: $35,578
Enrollment: 7,922 Coed
Affiliation or Control: Independent Non-Profit IRS Status: 501(c)3
Highest Offering: Doctorate
Accreditation: EH, ART, CIDA, CLPSY, ENG, HSA, IPSY, LAW, RADDOS, RTT, SPAA

01 Acting President ... Dr. Marisa KELLY
05 Acting Provost ... Mr. Sebastian ROYO
10 Sr VP Finance/Admin/Treasurer ... Ms. Laura SANDER
30 Sr Vice Pres for Advancement ... Mr. Colm RENEHAN
84 Sr Vice Pres for Enrollment ... Mr. Michael CROWLEY
26 VP Communications ... Mr. Greg GATLIN
86 Sr VP External Affairs ... Mr. John A. NUCCI
20 Vice Prov Faculty Devel/Curriculum ... Mr. Jeffrey POKORAK
37 AVP/Dir of Financial Aid ... Ms. Christine M. PERRY
32 AVP/Dean of Students ... Dr. Ann C. COYNE
06 AVP/University Registrar ... Ms. Mary LALLY
100 Chief of Staff ... Dr. Carol S. STREIT
50 Dean Sawyer Business School ... Mr. William J. O'NEILL, JR.
61 Dean of the Law School ... Mr. Andrew PERLMAN
49 Dean College Arts & Science ... Dr. Maria TOYADA
22 Chief Diversity/Inclusion Officer ... Ms. Nicole G. PRICE
07 Director Undergraduate Admission ... Ms. Jeanne AVERSA
07 Director Graduate Admission ... Vacant
08 Director of Sawyer Library ... Ms. Sharon BRITTON
36 Exec Dir Career Development Center ... Ms. Teresa DIMAGNO
15 Chief Human Resources Officer ... Ms. Katherine WHIDDEN
29 Director of Alumni Affairs/Law Sch ... Ms. Caitlin HAUGHEY
13 Chief Information Officer ... Mr. Thomas LYNCH, III
19 Chief University Police ... Mr. Gerard COLETTA
35 Director of Student Activities ... Vacant
41 Director of Athletics ... Mr. Cary MCCONNELL
18 Sr Dir Facilities Plng & Mgmt ... Mr. Gordon B. KING
88 Asst Dean for Acad Svcs Law School ... Ms. Lorraine D. COVE
08 Director Law Library ... Mr. Richard BUCKINGHAM
20 Asst Dean Academic Services ... Ms. Melanie JENKINS

Tufts University (A)

419 Boston Avenue, Medford MA 02155
County: Middlesex FICE Identification: 002219
Unit ID: 168148
Telephone: (617) 628-5000 Carnegie Class: DU-Highest
FAX Number: N/A Calendar System: Semester
URL: www.tufts.edu
Established: 1852 Annual Undergrad Tuition & Fees: $52,430
Enrollment: 11,137 Coed
Affiliation or Control: Independent Non-Profit IRS Status: 501(c)3
Highest Offering: Doctorate
Accreditation: EH, ARCPA, ART, CS, DENT, DIETI, ENG, MED, OT, PH, PLNG, VET

01 President ... Dr. Anthony P. MONACO
100 Chief of Staff ... Mr. Michael BAENEN
03 Executive Vice President ... Ms. Patricia CAMPBELL
05 Provost & Senior Vice President ... Mr. David R. HARRIS
43 SVP Univ Relations & Gen Counsel ... Ms. Mary R. JEKA
111 SVP University Advancement ... Mr. Eric C. JOHNSON
11 Interim VP for Operations ... Ms. Barbara STEIN
10 Vice President Finance/Treasurer ... Mr. Thomas S. MCGURTY
15 VP for Human Resources ... Mr. Julien C. CARTER
13 VP & Chief Information Officer ... Mr. David J. KAHLE
26 Vice Pres Communications/Marketing ... Ms. Christine SANNI
20 Vice Provost ... Mr. Kevin DUNN
46 Associate Provost & Sr Intl Officer ... Ms. Diana CHIGAS
09 Associate Provost ... Dr. Dawn G. TERKLA
21 Administrative Associate Provost ... Ms. Celia K. CAMPBELL
30 Exec Dir University Advancement ... Ms. Margot BIGGIN
22 Assoc Prov/Chief Diversity Officer ... Vacant
23 Sr Director Health/Wellness Svcs ... Ms. Michelle D. BOWDLER
37 Director of Financial Aid ... Ms. Patricia REILLY
27 Executive Director Public Relations ... Mr. Patrick COLLINS
36 Executive Director Career Center ... Mr. Gregory J. VICTORY
08 Interim Director Tisch Library ... Ms. Dorothy MEANEY
18 Senior Facilities Director ... Mr. Stephen NASSON
28 Exec Director Equal Opportunity ... Ms. Jill A. ZELLMER
38 Director Mental Health Services ... Dr. Julie S. ROSS
19 Executive Director Public Safety ... Mr. Kevin C. MAGUIRE
49 Dean Arts & Sciences ... Mr. James GLASER
54 Dean of Engineering ... Dr. Jianmin QU
60 Dean SMFA ... Ms. Nancy BAUER
58 Dean Grad School of A&S ... Mr. Robert G. COOK
82 Dean Fletcher Sch Law & Diplomacy ... Adm. James STAVRIDIS
52 Dean of Dental Medicine ... Dr. Huw F. THOMAS
74 Dean Cummings Sch of Veterinary Med . Dr. Deborah KOCHEVAR
63 Dean Medical School ... Dr. Harris BERMAN
88 Dean Sackler School ... Dr. Naomi ROSENBERG
88 Dean Friedman School ... Dr. Dariush MOZAFFARIAN
88 Dean Tisch College ... Mr. Alan SOLOMONT
53 Dean Undergrad & Grad Educ ... Mr. John BARKER
88 Dean Academic Adv & Undergrad Study ... Dr. Carmen LOWE
32 Dean of Student Affairs ... Ms. Mary Pat MCMAHON
35 Dean of Student Services/Art & Sci ... Mr. Paul STANTON
07 Dean of Admissions/Enroll Mgmt ... Ms. Karen L. RICHARDSON
96 Sr Dir Purchasing & Strat Sourcing ... Mr. John HOMICH
41 Director Athletics ... Mr. John MORRIS
42 University Chaplain ... Rev. Gregory MCGONIGLE
102 Sr Dir Corp & Foundation Relations ... Ms. Ippolita A. CANTUTI-CASTELVETRI
104 Associate Dean Programs Abroad ... Ms. Sheila BAYNE
39 Director Residential Life ... Ms. Yolanda M. KING
112 Senior Director Gift Planning ... Ms. Brooke ANDERSON
31 Co-Director Community Relations ... Ms. Barbara G. RUBEL
31 Co-Director Community Relations ... Mr. Rocco DIRICO

University of Phoenix Boston Campus (B)

2 Adams Place, Suite 300, Quincy MA 02169
Telephone: (866) 867-3678 Identification: 770209
Accreditation: &NH, ACBSP

† No longer accepting campus-based students.

Urban College of Boston (C)

178 Tremont Street, Boston MA 02111-1006
County: Suffolk FICE Identification: 031305
Unit ID: 429128
Telephone: (617) 449-7070 Carnegie Class: Spec 2-yr-Other
FAX Number: (617) 423-4758 Calendar System: Semester
URL: www.urbancollege.edu
Established: 1993 Annual Undergrad Tuition & Fees: $7,124
Enrollment: 879 Coed
Affiliation or Control: Independent Non-Profit IRS Status: 501(c)3
Highest Offering: Associate Degree
Accreditation: EH

01 President ... Mr. Michael TAYLOR
05 Vice President Academic Affairs ... Ms. Nancy C. DANIEL
10 Dean of Administration/Finance ... Mr. Stephen LOZEN
84 Dean Enrollment Svcs & Registrar ... Mr. Avanti SEYMOUR
32 Dean of Students/Dir Student Affs ... Ms. Carmen PINEDA
37 Director of Financial Aid ... Ms. Mia TAYLOR
20 Instructional Coordinator ... Mr. Phoenix FENG
10 Business Manager ... Ms. Kathleen BARDELL

Wellesley College (D)

106 Central Street, Wellesley MA 02481-8203
County: Norfolk FICE Identification: 002224
Unit ID: 168218
Telephone: (781) 283-1000 Carnegie Class: Bac-A&S
FAX Number: (781) 283-3639 Calendar System: Semester
URL: www.wellesley.edu
Established: 1875 Annual Undergrad Tuition & Fees: $48,802
Enrollment: 2,510 Female
Affiliation or Control: Independent Non-Profit IRS Status: 501(c)3
Highest Offering: Baccalaureate
Accreditation: EH

01 President ... Paula A. JOHNSON
05 Provost & Dean of the College ... Andrew SHENNAN
30 VP for Resources & Public Affairs ... Cameran MASON
10 VP Finance Administration/Treasurer ... Ben HAMMOND
32 Vice Pres/Dean of Students ... Sheila SHAW HORTON
18 Asst VP Facilities Management/Plng ... David CHAKRABORTY
15 Asst VP/Director Human Resources/EO ... Carolyn SLABODEN
13 Chief Information Officer ... Elizabeth GILDERSLEEVE
07 Dean of Admission/Financial Aid ... Joy ST. JOHN
42 Dean Religious/Spiritual Life ... Tiffany L. STEINWERT
20 Dean of Academic Affairs ... Ann VELENCHIK
20 Dean of Faculty Affairs ... Kathryn LYNCH
09 Assc Provost Institutional Planning ... Pamela L. TAYLOR
28 Assc Prov/Acad Dir Dvrsty/Inclusion ... Robbin CHAPMAN
06 Registrar ... Carol SHANMUGARATNAM
29 Executive Director Alumnae Assn ... Missy SHEA
37 Director of Student Financial Svcs ... Scott JUEDES
36 Assoc Prov/Dir Exec Ctr Work/Svc ... Christine CRUZVERGARA
26 Chief Public Relations Officer ... Elizabeth T. GILDERSLEEVE
35 Assoc Director Student Involvement ... Megan K. JORDAN
38 Administrative Counseling Svcs ... Robin COOK-NOBLES
101 Clerk Board of Trustees ... Marianne B. COOLEY
96 Purchasing Manager ... Tina M. DOLAN

Wentworth Institute of Technology (E)

550 Huntington Avenue, Boston MA 02115-5998
County: Suffolk FICE Identification: 002225
Unit ID: 168227
Telephone: (617) 989-4590 Carnegie Class: Masters/M
FAX Number: (617) 989-4591 Calendar System: Semester
URL: www.wit.edu
Established: 1904 Annual Undergrad Tuition & Fees: $33,724
Enrollment: 4,576 Coed
Affiliation or Control: Independent Non-Profit IRS Status: 501(c)3
Highest Offering: Master's
Accreditation: EH, ART, CIDA, CONST, CS, ENG, ENGT, IACBE

01 President ... Dr. Zorica PANTIC
100 Chief of Staff ... Ms. Amy INTILLE
05 Senior Vice Pres of Academic Affs ... Dr. Eric OVERSTROM
10 Vice Pres Finance ... Mr. Robert TOTINO
11 Vice President Business ... Mr. David A. WAHLSTROM
111 Vice Pres Institutional Advancement ... Ms. Paula SAKEY
84 VP Enrollment Management ... Ms. Keiko BROOMHEAD
15 Interim Vice Pres Human Resources ... Ms. Margaret CARD
13 Int VP of Information Technology ... Mr. Les VAUGHAN
88 Exec Asst to the Chief of Staff ... Ms. Rebecca COAKLEY
20 Assoc Provost ... Vacant
32 VP Student Affairs/Dean of Stdnts ... Ms. Annamaria WENNER
21 Assoc Vice President Finance ... Mr. David GILMORE
88 Assoc VP of Enrollment Management ... Ms. Dianne PLUMMER
31 Assoc VP Community Affairs ... Ms. Sandra E. PASCAL
14 Assoc VP Information Technology ... Vacant
88 AVP Innovation & Entrepreneurship ... Ms. Monique FUCHS
20 Director Acad Operations ... Ms. Kelly PARRISH
51 Dean of College of Prof & Cont Educ ... Ms. Deborah WRIGHT
07 Executive Director of Admissions ... Ms. Maureen DISCHINO
06 Registrar ... Ms. Joan ROMANO
08 Director of Library ... Mr. Kevin KIDD
113 Dir Student Financial Services ... Ms. Patricia OSGOOD
18 Associate VP Physical Facilities ... Mr. Bob BURNS
26 Director of Publications ... Mr. Caleb COCHRAN
35 Assoc Vice President of Students ... Mr. Peter FOWLER
102 Dir Corp Foundation/Govt Rels ... Ms. Lori FRIEDMAN
37 Director Financial Aid ... Ms. Anne-Marie CARUSO
38 Director of Counseling ... Ms. Maura MULLIGAN
19 Director of Public Safety ... Mr. William POWERS
41 Associate Athletic Director ... Mr. William P. GORMAN
36 Dir Of Cooperative Educ/Career Svcs ... Ms. Robbin BEAUCHAMP
39 Director Housing & Residential Life ... Mr. Philip BERNARD
41 Director of Athletics ... Ms. Cheryl AARON
96 Director of Purchasing ... Vacant
09 Institutional Researcher ... Vacant
49 Dean for Arts & Sciences ... Dr. Patrick HAFFORD
48 Dean for Arch/Design & Const Mgmt ... Dr. Charles HOTCHKISS
54 Dean for Engineering & Technology ... Mr. Frederick DRISCOLL
18 Director of Physical Plant ... Mr. Robert FERRO
35 Director Office of Campus Life ... Ms. Carissa DURFEE
108 Director of Institutional Effective ... Ms. Cidhinnia TORRES CAMPOS

Western New England University (F)

1215 Wilbraham Road, Springfield MA 01119-2684
County: Hampden FICE Identification: 002226
Unit ID: 168254
Telephone: (413) 782-3111 Carnegie Class: Masters/M
FAX Number: (413) 782-1746 Calendar System: Semester
URL: www.wne.edu
Established: 1919 Annual Undergrad Tuition & Fees: $34,874
Enrollment: 3,912 Coed
Affiliation or Control: Independent Non-Profit IRS Status: 501(c)3
Highest Offering: Doctorate
Accreditation: EH, ENG, LAW, PHAR, SW

01 President ... Dr. Anthony S. CAPRIO
04 Executive Asst to President ... Ms. Robin SAVITT-KING
05 Provost/Vice Pres Academic Affairs ... Dr. Linda E. JONES
26 Vice Pres Marketing & External Affs ... Mrs. Barbara A. MOFFAT
10 Vice Pres Finance & Administration ... Mr. William J. KELLEHER
84 Vice President for Enrollment Mgmt ... Mr. Bryan J. GROSS
32 VP Student Affairs/Dean of Students ... Dr. Jeanne S. HART-STEFFES
111 Vice President Advancement ... Ms. Beverly J. DWIGHT
45 Vice Pres for Strategic Initiatives ... Dr. Richard S. KEATING
13 Asst Vice Pres Information Tech ... Mr. Scott J. COOPEE
15 Asst VP & Dir of Human Resources ... Ms. Joanne OLLSON
61 Dean of the School of Law ... Prof. Eric J. GOUVIN
67 Dean of the College of Pharmacy ... Dr. Evan ROBINSON
49 Dean of the College of Arts & Sci ... Dr. Saeed GHAHRAMANI
50 Dean of the College of Business ... Dr. Julie SICILIANO
54 Dean of the College of Engineering ... Dr. S. Hossein CHERAGHI
89 Dean First Year/Transfer Students ... Ms. Kerri P. JARZABSKI
08 Assoc Dean Law Library/Info Res ... Ms. Patricia NEWCOMBE
39 Asst Dean of Students and Res Life ... Mr. Jerry ROEDER
28 Asst Dean of Diversity Programs ... Mrs. Yvonne BOGLE
06 Registrar-Law ... Ms. Terese CHENIER
37 Director of Financial Aid ... Ms. Kathleen CHAMBERS
41 Director of Athletics ... Vacant
36 Director Career Development Center ... Ms. Andrea ST. JAMES
38 Director of Counseling Services ... Dr. Wayne D. CARPENTER
08 Director of D'Amour Library ... Mrs. Priscilla L. PERKINS
23 Director of Health Services ... Mrs. Kathleen A. REID
18 Director of Facilities Management ... Mr. C. Michael DUNCAN
90 Dir Educational Technology Center ... Mr. Steven NARMONTAS
91 Dir of Administrative Info Systems ... Mr. Anthony MUTTI
29 Director of Alumni Relations ... Ms. Katherine PAPPAS
102 Dir of Foundation Relations ... Mr. Matthew VANHEYNIGEN
42 Spiritual Life Coordinator ... Ms. Sheila HANIFIN
19 Director of Public Safety ... Mr. Adam WOODROW
11 Director Administrative Services ... Ms. Arlene M. ROCK
07 Dir of Undergraduate Admissions ... Mr. Christopher WYSTEPEK
20 Academic Scheduling Controller ... Dr. Linda M. CHOJNICKI
09 Director Inst Research & Planning ... Dr. Richard A. WAGNER
43 General Counsel ... Mrs. Cheryl SMITH

Wheaton College (G)

26 E Main Street, Norton MA 02766-2322
County: Bristol FICE Identification: 002227
Unit ID: 168281
Telephone: (508) 286-8200 Carnegie Class: Bac-A&S
FAX Number: (508) 286-8270 Calendar System: Semester
URL: www.wheatoncollege.edu
Established: 1834 Annual Undergrad Tuition & Fees: $49,012
Enrollment: 1,598 Coed
Affiliation or Control: Independent Non-Profit IRS Status: 501(c)3
Highest Offering: Baccalaureate
Accreditation: EH

01 President ... Dr. Dennis HANNO
05 Provost ... Dr. Renée T. WHITE
10 VP Finance/Administration ... Mr. Brian DOUGLAS
111 Vice President College Advancement ... Ms. Merritt CROWLEY
84 Vice President Enrollment ... Mr. Grant GOSSELIN
32 VP Student Affairs/Dean of Students ... Ms. Kate E. KENNY
26 VP Marketing and Communications ... Mr. Gene P. BEGIN
37 Asst VP Enroll/Stdnt Finan Svcs ... Ms. Robin RANDALL
26 Assistant VP for Communications ... Mr. Michael GRACA
06 Registrar/Dean Academic Systems ... Ms. Sally BUCKLEY
29 Dir Alumni Rels/Annual Giving ... Ms. Courtney SHURTLEFF
15 Asst VP/Director Human Resources ... Ms. Omaira ROY
38 Director Counseling Center ... Ms. Valerie TOBIA
07 Director of Admission ... Ms. Judy PURDY
18 Asst VP Business Svcs/Phys Plant ... Mr. John M. SULLIVAN
09 Director of Institutional Research ... Dr. Kimberly PUHALA
39 Director Stdnt Life/Housing ... Mr. Edward T. BURNETT

19 Director Public Safety ... Chief Christopher SANTIAGO
101 Asst to President/Sec Brd Trustees ... Ms. Kristen TURCOTTE
41 Athletic Director ... Mr. John SUTYAK
104 Dean Center for Global Education ... Ms. Gretchen YOUNG
13 Assistant VP Info Tech Services ... Mr. Joe LACASCIO
91 Dir Information Tech Services ... Ms. Regina CARVELL
36 Director of Career Services ... Ms. Lisa GAVIGAN
04 Administrative Assoc to President ... Ms. Pam VAZ
102 Dir Corporate & Foundation Rels ... Ms. Molly DESCHENES
44 Director Annual Fund ... Ms. Amy LAPREY

Wheelock College (A)

200 The Riverway, Boston MA 02215-4176
County: Suffolk FICE Identification: 002228
Unit ID: 168290
Telephone: (617) 879-2000 Carnegie Class: Masters/M
FAX Number: (617) 566-7369 Calendar System: Semester
URL: www.wheelock.edu
Established: 1888 Annual Undergrad Tuition & Fees: $34,825
Enrollment: 1,169 Coed
Affiliation or Control: Independent Non-Profit IRS Status: 501(c)3
Highest Offering: Beyond Master's But Less Than Doctorate
Accreditation: EH, CAEPN, SW

01 President ... Dr. David CHARD
04 Sr Exec Asst to Pres/Corp Secretary ... Ms. Valerie THORNHILL-HUDSON
11 VP Admin/Inst Effect/Innovation ... Vacant
05 VP for Academic Affairs ... Vacant
30 VP for Development/Alumni Affairs ... Ms. Jennifer RICE
10 VP/Chief Financial Officer ... Ms. Anne Marie MARTORANA
84 VP Student Success and Engagement ... Dr. Adrian K. HAUGABROOK
07 AVP Undergrad Admissions ... Mr. Cory MEYERS
86 Dir of Government and Ext Affairs ... Ms. Marta ROSA
32 Dean of Students ... Ms. Barbara MORGAN
49 Interim Dean of Arts & Sciences ... Dr. Detris Honora ADELABU
104 Dean International Pgms/Prtrnshp ... Dr. Linda DAVIS
53 Assoc Dean of Education ... Dr. Donna MCKIBBENS
70 Assoc Dean of Social Work ... Dr. Hope HASLAM STRAUGHAN
07 Director of Graduate Admissions ... Mr. Brian MINCHELLO
06 Registrar ... Ms. Michelle ORMEROD
08 Interim Director of Library ... Ms. Ann GLANNON
15 Director of Human Resources ... Ms. Michele CREWS
13 Director of Information Technology ... Mr. Jonathan LAPIERRE
36 Dir Center for Career Development ... Vacant
18 Chief Facilities/Physical Plant ... Mr. Ed JACQUES
38 Director Counseling Center ... Ms. Eileen THOMPSON
29 Dir of Development/Alumni Relations ... Ms. Lauren MARQUIS
09 Institutional Research Analyst ... Mr. Lance ANGELL
26 Marketing Manager ... Mr. Stephen DILL
41 Athletic Director ... Mr. Dwight DATCHER
42 Spiritual Life Coordinator ... Dr. Adrienne KISNER
39 Director of Residence Life ... Ms. Darcy DUBOIS
27 Communications Manager ... Ms. Beth KAPLAN
107 Interim Dean of Grad/Prof Programs . Dr. Linda BANKS-SANTILLI

William James College (B)

1 Wells Avenue, Newton MA 02459-3211
County: Norfolk FICE Identification: 021636
Unit ID: 166717
Telephone: (617) 327-6777 Carnegie Class: Spec-4-yr-Other Health
FAX Number: (617) 327-4447 Calendar System: Semester
URL: www.williamjames.edu
Established: 1974 Annual Graduate Tuition & Fees: N/A
Enrollment: 729 Coed
Affiliation or Control: Independent Non-Profit IRS Status: 501(c)3
Highest Offering: Doctorate; No Undergraduates
Accreditation: EH, CLPSY, IPSY, SCPSY

01 President ... Dr. Nicholas COVINO
04 Executive Asst to the President ... Ms. Lilly MANOLIS
10 VP Finance & Operations ... Mr. Daniel BRENT
111 Vice Pres Institutional Advancement ... Mr. Robert WHITTAKER
05 Vice Pres Academic Affairs ... Dr. Stanley BERMAN
46 Assoc VP for Research ... Dr. Edward DEVOS
37 Director Financial Aid ... Ms. Hilary BAXTER
06 Registrar ... Ms. Sonji PAIGE
32 Dean of Students ... Mr. Josh COOPER
07 Director of Admissions ... Mr. Mario MURGA
51 Director Continuing Prof Education ... Mr. Dean ABBY
27 Director of Marketing ... Mrs. Katie O'HARE
13 Dir Information Technology ... Mr. Jeff CHOO
08 Head Librarian ... Ms. Julia CLEMENT
15 Human Resource Director ... Mrs. Ellen COLLINS
18 Facilities Manager ... Mr. Kevin COSTELLO
29 Director Alumni Relations ... Dr. Alan BECK

† Formerly Massachusetts School of Professional Psychology

Williams College (C)

880 Main Street, Williamstown MA 01267
County: Berkshire FICE Identification: 002229
Unit ID: 168342
Telephone: (413) 597-3131 Carnegie Class: Bac-A&S
FAX Number: N/A Calendar System: 4/1/4
URL: www.williams.edu
Established: 1793 Annual Undergrad Tuition & Fees: $51,790
Enrollment: 2,171 Coed
Affiliation or Control: Independent Non-Profit IRS Status: 501(c)3
Highest Offering: Master's
Accreditation: EH

01 President ... Adam F. FALK
05 Dean of Faculty ... Denise K. BUELL
10 VP for Fin & Admin and Treasurer ... Frederick W. PUDDESTER
32 Vice President for Campus Life ... Stephen P. KLASS
28 VP for Inst Diversity & Equity ... Leticia HAYNES
111 VP for College Relations ... Megan MOREY
26 Chief Communications Officer ... Jim REISCHE
04 Asst to Pres/Secretary of the Col ... Keli A. GAIL
20 Dean of the College ... Marlene J. SANDSTROM
18 Exec Director Facilities Management ... Robert F. WRIGHT
06 Registrar ... Barbara A. CASEY
07 Director of Admission ... Richard L. NESBITT
37 Director of Financial Aid ... Paul J. BOYER
08 Librarian ... David M. PILACHOWSKI
21 Controller ... Susan S. HOGAN
29 Director Alumni Relations ... Brooks L. FOEHL
15 Director of Human Resources ... Martha R. TETRAULT
36 Director of Career Center ... Donald J. KJELLEREN
109 Director of Dining Services ... Robert P. VOLPI
13 Chief Technology Officer ... Barron KORALESKY
09 Director of Institutional Research ... Courtney WADE
23 Director of Health Admin Services ... Angie MARANO
35 Director Office of Student Life ... Douglas J. SCHIAZZA
41 Director of Athletics/PE ... Lisa M. MELENDY
42 Chaplain ... Richard E. SPALDING

Woods Hole Oceanographic Institution (D)

266 Woods Hole Road, Woods Hole MA 02543-1535
County: Barnstable FICE Identification: 002230
Unit ID: 166610
Telephone: (508) 289-2252 Carnegie Class: Not Classified
FAX Number: N/A Calendar System: 4/1/4
URL: www.whoi.edu
Established: 1930 Annual Graduate Tuition & Fees: N/A
Enrollment: N/A Coed
Affiliation or Control: Independent Non-Profit IRS Status: 501(c)3
Highest Offering: Doctorate; No Undergraduates
Accreditation: EH

01 President and Director ... Dr. Mark R. ABBOTT
09 Exec Vice Pres/Director of Research ... Dr. Laurence P. MADIN
05 VP of Academic Programs and Dean ... Dr. James A. YODER
10 Vice Pres of Operations/CFO ... Mr. Jeffrey FERNANDEZ
18 VP Marine Facilities/Operations ... Mr. Robert MUNIER
43 VP Legal Affairs/General Counsel ... Mr. Christopher LAND
30 Chief Development Officer ... Mr. Charles GAUVIN
20 Associate Dean ... Dr. Margaret K. TIVEY
06 Registrar ... Ms. Julia WESTWATER
08 Library Co-Director ... Ms. Lisa RAYMOND

Worcester Polytechnic Institute (E)

100 Institute Road, Worcester MA 01609-2280
County: Worcester FICE Identification: 002233
Unit ID: 168421
Telephone: (508) 831-5000 Carnegie Class: DU-Higher
FAX Number: (508) 831-5753 Calendar System: Semester
URL: www.wpi.edu
Established: 1865 Annual Undergrad Tuition & Fees: $46,994
Enrollment: 6,573 Coed
Affiliation or Control: Independent Non-Profit IRS Status: 501(c)3
Highest Offering: Doctorate
Accreditation: EH, ENG

01 President ... Dr. Laurie LESHIN
05 Sr Vice President and Provost ... Dr. Bruce BURSTEN
10 Executive Vice President & CFO ... Mr. Jeffrey S. SOLOMON
30 VP for University Advancement ... Mr. William J. MCAVOY
26 Chief Marketing Officer ... Ms. Amy M. MORTON
13 Chief Information Officer (CIO) ... Ms. Deborah C. SCOTT
03 Senior Vice President ... Ms. Kristin R. TICHENOR
18 Asst Vice President for Facilities ... Mr. Alfred DIMAURO, JR.
15 VP Talent Development/CDO ... Ms. Michelle JONES-JOHNSON
20 VP Academic & Corporate Devel ... Mr. Stephen P. FLAVIN
32 Vice President of Student Affairs ... Mr. Philip N. CLAY
22 AVP/Chief Compliance Officer ... Mr. Jon C. BARTELSON
36 Exec Director Career Devel Center ... Mr. Stefan KOPPI
100 Asst VP/Chief of Staff ... Ms. Stephanie PASHA
07 Director of Admissions ... Ms. Jennifer A. CLUETT
06 University Registrar ... Ms. Sarah L. MILES
27 Director of Research Communications ... Mr. Michael W. DORSEY
96 Director of Procurement Services ... Ms. Laurie COLELLA
21 University Controller ... Vacant
09 Assistant VP of Budget Planning ... Ms. Judith L. TRAINOR
38 Asst Dean of Stdnt Dev/Dir SDCC ... Mr. Charles C. MORSE
88 Associate Director LSBC ... Mr. Andrew BUTLER
37 Executive Director Student Aid ... Ms. Monica M. BLONDIN
19 Dir Environmental Health & Safety ... Mr. Daniel T. SARACHICK
28 Director of Multicultural Affair ... Ms. Charlana SIMMONS
29 Exec Director Lifetime Engagement ... Mr. Peter A. THOMAS

MICHIGAN

Adrian College (F)

110 S Madison Street, Adrian MI 49221-2575
County: Lenawee FICE Identification: 002234
Unit ID: 168528
Telephone: (517) 265-5161 Carnegie Class: Bac-Diverse
FAX Number: (517) 264-3331 Calendar System: Semester
URL: www.adrian.edu
Established: 1859 Annual Undergrad Tuition & Fees: $34,890
Enrollment: 1,715 Coed
Affiliation or Control: United Methodist IRS Status: 501(c)3
Highest Offering: Master's
Accreditation: NH, CAATE, CAEPT, SW

01 President ... Dr. Jeffrey R. DOCKING
05 Vice Pres/Dean for Academic Affairs ... Dr. Andrea MILNER
111 Vice Pres Institutional Advancement ... Mr. James MAHONY
84 Vice President of Enrollment ... Mr. Frank J. HRIBAR
10 Vice Pres Business Affairs/CFO ... Mr. Jerry WRIGHT
32 Dean of Student Affairs ... Mr. Troy SCHMIDLI
20 Asst Dean of Academic Affairs ... Ms. Bridgette WINSLOW
21 Asst Vice Pres of Business Affairs ... Mr. David DREWS
30 Director of Development ... Mr. Matt RHEINECKER
07 Associate Director of Admissions ... Ms. Erin DESMET
42 Chaplain/Director Church Relations .. Dr. Christopher P. MOMANY
06 Registrar ... Ms. Kristina SCHWEIKERT
35 Associate Dean for Student Life ... Ms. Grace WATERSTRADT
86 Dir of Govt & Foundation Relations ... Ms. Amy CAMPBELL
15 Director of Human Resources ... Ms. Renee BURCK
40 Bookstore Manager ... Ms. Rachelle M. DUFFY
93 Dir Multicultural Cultural Programs ... Ms. Shantay ERNST
29 Director Alumni Relations ... Mrs. Marsha FIELDER
41 Director of Athletics ... Mr. Michael DUFFY
19 Director of Campus Safety ... Mr. Wade BIETELCHIES
36 Director of Career Planning ... Mrs. Janna D'AMICO
88 Director of Conferences ... Ms. Denise HEIN
38 Director of Counseling ... Ms. Monique J. SAVAGE
08 Head Librarian ... Mr. David CRUSE
23 Director of Health Center ... Ms. Dawn MARSH
96 Director of Purchasing ... Ms. Donna WARD
37 Director of Financial Aid ... Mr. Steve BUCKLAND
18 Director of Facilities ... Mr. Chris STIVER
09 Director of Institutional Research ... Ms. Beth L. HEISS
88 Director of Academic Services ... Ms. Linda JACOBS
88 Asst Director of Academic Services ... Ms. Danielle WARD
04 Administrative Asst to President ... Mrs. Andrea BURT

Albion College (G)

611 E Porter Street, Albion MI 49224-1831
County: Calhoun FICE Identification: 002235
Unit ID: 168546
Telephone: (517) 629-1000 Carnegie Class: Bac-A&S
FAX Number: (517) 629-0509 Calendar System: Semester
URL: www.albion.edu
Established: 1835 Annual Undergrad Tuition & Fees: $41,040
Enrollment: 1,376 Coed
Affiliation or Control: United Methodist IRS Status: 501(c)3
Highest Offering: Baccalaureate
Accreditation: NH, CAATE, CAEPT, MUS

01 President ... Dr. Mauri A. DITZLER
10 Vice Pres Business & Finance ... Mr. Jerry WHITE
05 Provost ... Dr. Marc ROY
30 Vice Pres Institutional Advancement ... Mr. Robert ANDERSON
84 Vice Pres Enrollment Management ... Mr. Steven KLEIN
32 Vice Pres & Dean Student Affairs ... Dr. Sally J. WALKER
13 Assoc Vice Pres Info Svcs/CIO ... Mr. Michael DEVER
07 Director of Admissions ... Ms. Mandy DUBIEL
39 Director Residential Life ... Ms. Julie MCMAHON
08 Director of Libraries ... Dr. Michael VAN HOUTEN
26 Director of Communications ... Mr. John THOMPSON
29 Director of Alumni Engagement ... Vacant
38 Director of Counseling ... Dr. Frank KELEMEN
37 Director of Financial Aid ... Ms. Ann WHITMER
06 Registrar ... Dr. Andrew M. DUNHAM
109 Director Dining & Hospitality Svcs ... Mrs. Pat MILLER
18 Director of Facilities Operations ... Mr. Donald MASTERNAK
19 Director of Campus Safety ... Mr. Kenneth SNYDER
41 Athletic Director ... Mr. Matthew AREND
42 College Chaplain ... Rev. Donald PHILLIPS
15 Director of Human Resources ... Mrs. Lisa LOCKE
09 Director of Institutional Research ... Dr. Andrew DUNHAM
96 Director of Purchasing ... Mrs. Susan CLARK
20 Associate Academic Officer ... Dr. John WOELL
28 Assoc Director Multicultural Affs ... Ms. Keena WILLIAMS
40 Manager of Bookstore ... Mr. Todd SHAYLER

Alma College (H)

614 W Superior, Alma MI 48801-1599
County: Gratiot FICE Identification: 002236
Unit ID: 168591
Telephone: (989) 463-7111 Carnegie Class: Bac-A&S
FAX Number: (989) 463-7277 Calendar System: Other
URL: www.alma.edu
Established: 1886 Annual Undergrad Tuition & Fees: $37,310
Enrollment: 1,385 Coed
Affiliation or Control: Independent Non-Profit IRS Status: 501(c)3
Highest Offering: Baccalaureate
Accreditation: NH, #CAATE, CAEPT, MUS, NURSE

01 President ... Dr. Jeff ABERNATHY
05 Provost & Vice Pres for Acad Affs ... Dr. Michael L. SELMON
11 Chief Operating Office ... Mr. Alan GATLIN
111 Vice President for Advancement ... Mr. Matt VANDENBERG
84 Vice President for Enrollment ... Mr. Bob GARCIA
32 Vice President for Student Life ... Dr. Karl RISHE

26 Vice Pres Planning/Communication .... Ms. Ann HALL
04 Executive Asst to the President .... Ms. Sandee A. GADDE
06 Associate Provost & Registrar .... Ms. Julie WILLIAMS
20 Assistant Provost .... Ms. Susan M. DEEL
42 Chaplain .... Vacant
37 Director Financial Aid .... Ms. Michelle MCNIER
08 Director of Library .... Ms. Carol ZEILE
27 Associate VP for Communications .... Mr. Mike SILVERTHORN
13 Chief Technology Officer .... Dr. Keith R. NELSON
18 Director Facilities & Service Mgmt .... Mr. Douglas DICE
15 Director Human Resources .... Mr. Kenneth L. BORGMAN
21 Associate VP/Controller .... Mr. Dan HENRIS
36 Asst Dir Career & Internship Devel .... Ms. Amanda SLENSKI
35 Director Campus Life .... Mr. David K. BLANDFORD
38 Director Counseling & Wellness .... Ms. Anne K. LAMBRECHT
07 Assistant Vice President Enrollment .... Mr. Craig AIMAR
09 Director for Institutional Research .... Mr. John MACARTHUR
28 Director of Diversity & Inclusion .... Dr. Candy MCCORKLE
41 Athletic Director .... Mr. Steven RACKLEY

Alpena Community College (A)

665 Johnson Street, Alpena MI 49707-1495
County: Alpena FICE Identification: 002237
Unit ID: 168607
Telephone: (989) 356-9021 Carnegie Class: Assoc/MT-VT-High Trad
FAX Number: (989) 358-7553 Calendar System: Semester
URL: www.alpenacc.edu
Established: 1952 Annual Undergrad Tuition & Fees (In-District): $4,290
Enrollment: 1,493 Coed
Affiliation or Control: Local IRS Status: 501(c)3
Highest Offering: Baccalaureate
Accreditation: NH, ADNUR, MAC, PNUR

01 President .... Dr. Donald MACMASTER
05 Vice Pres of Instruction .... Ms. Deborah BAYER
10 Vice President Admin & Finance .... Mr. Richard SUTHERLAND
32 Dean of Students .... Ms. Nancy SEGUIN
21 Controller .... Ms. Lyn KOWALEWSKY
20 Dean Learning Resource Center .... Ms. Wendy BROOKS
25 Director of TAACCT Grants .... Ms. Dawn STONE
13 Co-Director Mgmt Info Systems .... Mr. Jeff BLUMENTHAL
13 Co-Director Mgmt Info Systems .... Mr. Mark GRUNDER
26 Dir Public Information/Marketing .... Mr. Jay WALTERREIT
40 Director of ACC Bookstore .... Mr. William MATZKE
102 Dir Dev/Exec Dir ACC Foundation .... Ms. Penny BOLDREY
18 Director of Facilities Management .... Mr. Nicholas BREGE
88 Volunteer Center Director .... Ms. Cathy GUTIERREZ-ABRAHAM
06 Registrar .... Ms. Lori DZIESINSKI
15 Director Human Resources .... Ms. Carolyn DAOUST
07 Director of Admissions .... Mr. Mike KOLLIEN
37 Director Financial Aid .... Mr. Robert ROOSE

Andrews University (B)

8975 U.S. 31, Berrien Springs MI 49104-0001
County: Berrien FICE Identification: 002238
Unit ID: 168740
Telephone: (269) 471-7771 Carnegie Class: DU-Mod
FAX Number: (269) 471-6900 Calendar System: Semester
URL: www.andrews.edu
Established: 1874 Annual Undergrad Tuition & Fees: $27,684
Enrollment: 3,366 Coed
Affiliation or Control: Seventh-day Adventist IRS Status: 501(c)3
Highest Offering: Doctorate
Accreditation: NH, CACREP, CAEPN, COPSY, CS, DIETD, DIETI, ENG, IACBE, MT, MUS, NUR, PH, PTA, @SP, SW, THEOL

01 President .... Dr. Andrea T. LUXTON
05 Provost .... Dr. Christon ARTHUR
20 Assistant Provost Inst Assessment .... Dr. Lynn MERKLIN
10 Vice President for Financial Admin .... Mr. Lawrence E. SCHALK
32 Vice Pres Student & Campus Life .... Dr. Frances M. FAEHNER
26 Vice Pres Marketing & Communication ..... Mr. Stephen D. PAYNE
84 Vice Pres for Enrollment Management .... Mr. Randy K. GRAVES
30 Vice President for Advancement .... Dr. David A. FAEHNER
43 General Counsel .... Ms. Gwendolyn POWELL BRASWELL
06 Registrar .... Ms. Aimee VITANGCOL REGOSO
49 Dean College Arts & Sciences .... Dr. Keith E. MATTINGLY
76 Dean School of Health Professions .... Dr. Emmanuel RUDATSIKIRA
50 Dean School of Business Admin .... Dr. Ralph TRECARTIN
53 Dean School of Education .... Dr. Robson MARINHO
48 Dean Sch Architect & Interior Des .... Mr. Carey CARSCALLEN
73 Dean of Theological Seminary .... Dr. Jiri MOSKALA
58 Dean School of Grad Studies .... Dr. Alayne THORPE
106 Dean Sch of Dist Educ/Intl Partners .... Dr. Alayne THORPE
08 Dean of Libraries .... Mr. Lawrence W. ONSAGER
21 Associate Business Officer .... Mr. Glenn A. MEEKMA
39 Dir of University Apartment Life .... Mr. Alfredo RUIZ
34 Dir of the Women's Residence Halls ..... Ms. Jennifer R. BURRILL
33 Dir of the Men's Residence Halls .... Mr. Spencer D. CARTER
85 Dir of International Student Svcs .... Mr. Robert BENJAMIN
92 Director of Honors Program .... Dr. L. Monique PITTMAN
15 Director of Human Resources .... Mr. Daniel E. AGNETTA
37 Director Student Financial Aid .... Ms. Elynda A. BEDNEY
07 Director of Undergrad Admissions .... Ms. Elivette DIAZ
07 Interim Dir of Graduate Admissions .... Ms. Justina CLAYBURN
27 Media Relations Specialist .... Ms. Becky ST. CLAIR
29 Director of Alumni Services .... Mr. Andriy KHARKOVYY
38 Dir of Counseling/Testing Center .... Dr. Judith FISHER
40 Manager of Bookstore .... Ms. Cynthia SWANSON

19 Director of Campus Safety .... Mr. Benjamin PANIGOT
23 Director of Medical Services .... Dr. Lowell HAMEL
42 University Chaplain .... Ms. June M. PRICE
09 Director Institutional Research .... Mr. James R. MASSENA
18 Director of Facilities Management .... Mr. Paul ELDER
04 Executive Asst to President .... Ms. Dalry B. PAYNE
41 Athletic Director .... Mr. David JARDINE
44 Director of Planned Giving .... Ms. Tari POPP
104 Director Study Abroad .... Dr. Pedro NAVIA
105 Director Web Services .... Mr. Jason STRACK
13 Chief Information Officer .... Ms. Lorena L. BIDWELL
28 Director of Diversity .... Vacant

Aquinas College (C)

1700 Fulton St. E, Grand Rapids MI 49506-1799
County: Kent FICE Identification: 002239
Unit ID: 168786
Telephone: (616) 632-8900 Carnegie Class: Masters/S
FAX Number: (616) 732-4469 Calendar System: Semester
URL: www.aquinas.edu
Established: 1886 Annual Undergrad Tuition & Fees: $30,062
Enrollment: 1,894 Coed
Affiliation or Control: Roman Catholic IRS Status: 501(c)3
Highest Offering: Master's
Accreditation: NH, CAATE, CAEPT

01 President .... Dr. Kevin G. QUINN
05 Provost/Dean of Faculty .... Dr. Stephen BARROWS
30 Vice Pres Foundation .... Ms. Patricia CASTIGLIONE
10 Interim Vice President Finance .... Ms. Stella A. SOROVIGAS
84 Vice Pres Enrollment Management .... Mr. Thomas MIKOWSKI
04 Chief Exec Assistant to President .... Ms. Lori ORLOWSKI
26 Assoc VP Marketing & Communication .... Mr. Carl APPLE
07 Assoc VP for Admissions .... Vacant
32 Assoc VP for Student Services .... Mr. Brian MATZKE
21 Controller .... Ms. Lynnsey MILBURN
09 Dean of Institutional Effectiveness .... Vacant
53 Dean of School of Education .... Vacant
06 Registrar .... Mrs. Cecelia MESLER
38 Director of Counseling Services .... Ms. Sharon E. SMITH
51 Director of Continuing Education .... Vacant
104 Assoc Dir International Educ Pgms .... Mr. Tim RAMSAY
94 Director of Women's Studies .... Ms. Amy DUNHAM STRAND
92 Director of Honors Program .... Dr. Michelle DEROSE
58 Director of Graduate Management .... Ms. Cynthia VANGELDEREN
08 Co-Director Woodhouse Library .... Ms. Shellie JEFFRIES
08 Co-Director Woodhouse Library .... Ms. Francine PAOLINI
18 Director of Maintenance .... Mr. Dale HAISMA
39 Director Residence Life .... Ms. Julie BLASZAK
07 Director of Admissions .... Ms. Angela SCHLOSSER-BACON
37 Director of Financial Aid .... Ms. Darcy KAMPFSCHULTE
41 Director Athletics .... Mr. Nick DAVIDSON
42 Director Campus Ministry .... Vacant
13 Dir Information Technology & Svcs .... Vacant
29 Director of Alumni Relations .... Ms. Alexa CAREY
35 Director of Campus Life .... Ms. Allie MARKLAND
44 Director of Major Gifts .... Ms. Cecelia CUNNINGHAM
102 Director of Corporate Giving .... Dr. Ali ERHAN
121 Director of Academic Advising .... Ms. Cecelia MESLER
28 Director of Diversity & Inclusion .... Ms. Latoya BOOKER
40 Director Bookstore .... Ms. Marian TODISH
24 Media Coordinator .... Ms. Francine PAOLINI
42 Campus Chaplain .... Rev. Stanley DRONGOWSKI, OP

The Art Institute of Michigan (D)

28175 Cabot Drive, Novi MI 48377
Telephone: (248) 675-3800 Identification: 666692
Accreditation: &NH, ACFEI

† Regional accreditation is carried under the parent institution The Illinois Institute of Art, Chicago, IL.

*Baker College System (E)

1050 W Bristol Road, Flint MI 48507-5508
County: Genesee Identification: 666923
Unit ID: 419572
Telephone: (810) 766-4280 Carnegie Class: N/A
FAX Number: (810) 766-4279
URL: www.baker.edu

01 CEO/President of System .... Dr. Bart DAIG
05 Vice President for Academics .... Dr. Denise A. BANNAN
13 Vice Pres Information Technology .... Ms. Jacqueline SPICER
15 Vice President of Human Resources .... Ms. Dana CLARK
26 Vice Pres Marketing/Admissions/PR .... Mr. Bruce LUNDEEN
10 Corporate Controller .... Mr. Michael MOORE
32 Vice President of Student Affairs .... Mr. Gerald MCCARTY
20 Assoc Provost of Academic Affairs .... Dr. Lesa LOUCH
36 Director of Career Services .... Mrs. Laura ZUCK
14 Director of IT Operations .... Mrs. Sheryl L. DEAN
08 Director of Library Services .... Mrs. Lynn STACEY
58 President Graduate Studies .... Dr. Jill LANGEN

*Baker College of Flint (F)

1050 W Bristol Road, Flint MI 48507-5508
County: Genesee FICE Identification: 004673
Unit ID: 168847
Telephone: (810) 766-4000 Carnegie Class: Bac/Assoc-Mixed
FAX Number: (810) 766-4293 Calendar System: Quarter
URL: www.baker.edu
Established: 1911 Annual Undergrad Tuition & Fees: $9,000
Enrollment: 23,790 Coed
Affiliation or Control: Independent Non-Profit IRS Status: 501(c)3
Highest Offering: Doctorate
Accreditation: NH, CAHIIM, CSHSE, ENG, IACBE, MAC, NURSE, OT, POLYT, PTAA, SURGT

02 President .... Mrs. Wen HEMINGWAY
05 Director of Academic Affairs .... Dr. Jason YOUNG
07 Vice President of Admissions .... Mr. Kevin PNACEK
15 Vice President of Human Resources .... Ms. Dana CLARK
32 Vice President of Student Services .... Mr. Gerald MCCARTY, II
50 Dir Business Admin/Early Child Educ .... Dr. John C. COTE
76 Dean of Health/Human Services .... Vacant
08 Director of Library Services .... Vacant
06 Co-Registrar .... Ms. Judi LANGOLF
06 Co-Registrar .... Ms. Jill PRICE
13 Director of Computer Operations .... Mr. Michael MYERS
18 Director of Facilities .... Mrs. Kim STODDARD
38 Director of Counseling/Assessment .... Mr. Paul ZANG
19 Director of Safety/Security .... Mr. John JOSEPH
40 Director of Bookstore .... Mr. Nick ANGLE
54 Dir Engineering/Computer Science .... Mrs. Anca SALA
26 Director Community Relations .... Vacant
10 Business Officer .... Mrs. Rebecca AYRE-BOGGS
36 Director of Career Services .... Mrs. Janie STEWART
37 Director Student Financial Aid .... Ms. Veta NORRIS
31 Director Corporate/Community Svcs .... Mr. Jeff MALLETS
23 Director of Health and Fitness .... Mrs. Maureen MILLER
39 Housing Coordinator .... Ms. Lauren PHILLIPS

**Baker College of Allen Park* (G)

4500 Enterprise Drive, Allen Park MI 48101-3033
Telephone: (313) 425-3700 Identification: 666996
Accreditation: &NH, CAHIIM, COMTA, CSHSE, IACBE, MAC, MLTAD, OTA, PTAA, SURGT

**Baker College of Auburn Hills* (H)

1500 University Drive, Auburn Hills MI 48326-2642
Telephone: (248) 340-0600 Identification: 666940
Accreditation: &NH, COARC, CSHSE, DMS, IACBE, MAC, PHLEB, PTAA

**Baker College of Cadillac* (I)

9600 E 13th Street, Cadillac MI 49601-9600
Telephone: (231) 876-3100 Identification: 666941
Accreditation: &NH, COMTA, CSHSE, IACBE, MAC, SURGT

**Baker College of Clinton Township* (J)

34950 Little Mack Avenue,
Clinton Township MI 48035-4701
Telephone: (586) 791-6610 Identification: 666942
Accreditation: &NH, CAHIIM, COMTA, CSHSE, DA, DH, EMT, IACBE, MAC, RAD, SURGT

**Baker College of Jackson* (K)

2800 Springport Road, Jackson MI 49202-1290
Telephone: (517) 788-7800 FICE Identification: 004680
Accreditation: &NH, CAHIIM, COMTA, CSHSE, IACBE, MAC, RTT, SURGT

**Baker College of Muskegon* (L)

1903 Marquette Avenue, Muskegon MI 49442-1490
Telephone: (231) 777-5200 FICE Identification: 002296
Accreditation: &NH, ACFEI, COMTA, CSHSE, EMT, IACBE, MAC, OTA, PTAA, RAD, SURGT

**Baker College of Owosso* (M)

1020 S Washington Street, Owosso MI 48867-4400
Telephone: (989) 729-3370 Identification: 666937
Accreditation: &NH, CAEPT, CSHSE, DMS, IACBE, MAC, OTA, RAD

**Baker College of Port Huron* (N)

3403 Lapeer Road, Port Huron MI 48060-2597
Telephone: (810) 985-7000 Identification: 666943
Accreditation: &NH, ACFEI, CSHSE, IACBE

Bay College West Campus (O)

PO Box 130, Iron Mountain MI 49801
Telephone: (906) 774-8547 Identification: 770262
Accreditation: &NH

Bay Mills Community College (P)

12214 W Lakeshore Drive, Brimley MI 49715-9750
County: Chippewa FICE Identification: 030666
Unit ID: 380359
Telephone: (906) 248-3354 Carnegie Class: Tribal
FAX Number: (906) 248-3351 Calendar System: Semester
URL: www.bmcc.edu
Established: 1984 Annual Undergrad Tuition & Fees: $3,040
Enrollment: 541 Coed
Affiliation or Control: Tribal Control IRS Status: 501(c)3
Highest Offering: Associate Degree
Accreditation: NH

01 President Michael C. PARISH
05 Vice President of Academic Affairs Samantha CAMERON
10 Vice Pres Business & Finance Laura POSTMA
32 Dean of Student Services Debra J. WILSON
13 Director Technology Chet KASPER
06 Registrar/Inst Info Systems Mgr Sherri SCHOFIELD
37 Director Student Financial Aid Tina MILLER
07 Director of Admissions Elaine LEHRE
88 Land Grant Director Stephen YANNI
30 Director of Development Kathy ADAIR
08 Library Director Megan CLARKE

Bay de Noc Community College (A)

2001 N Lincoln Road, Escanaba MI 49829-2510
County: Delta FICE Identification: 002240
Unit ID: 168883
Telephone: (906) 786-5802 Carnegie Class: Assoc/MT-VT-High Trad
FAX Number: (906) 789-6952 Calendar System: Semester
URL: www.baycollege.edu
Established: 1962 Annual Undergrad Tuition & Fees (In-District): $4,548
Enrollment: 1,853 Coed
Affiliation or Control: Local IRS Status: 501(c)3
Highest Offering: Associate Degree
Accreditation: NH, ADNUR

01 President Dr. Laura COLEMAN
11 VP of Operations Ms. Christine WILLIAMS
10 VP of Finance/Training & Develop Mr. Kevin CARLSON
05 VP of Academic Affairs Dr. Matthew BARRON
111 VP of College Advancement Ms. Kim CARNE
32 VP of Student Services Mr. Travis BLUME
50 Exec Dean of Business/Tech/WD Mr. Mark KINNEY
37 Director of Financial Aid Ms. Laurie SPANGENBERG
07 Director of Admissions Ms. Jessica LAMARCH
15 Director of Human Resources Ms. Bridget KENNEDY
18 Director of Buildings & Grounds Mr. Ralph CURRY
76 Dean of Allied Health Ms. Linda LEWANDOWSKI
32 Director of Student Life Mr. Dave LAUR
08 Head Librarian Mr. Oscar DELONG
04 Exec Admin Asst to President Mrs. Laura JOHNSON
06 Registrar Ms. Rebecca LANDENBERGER
106 Director of Online Learning Mr. Joseph MOLD
19 Security Officer Mr. Joseph PACHECO
41 Athletic Director Mr. Matt JOHNSON

Calvin College (B)

3201 Burton Street, SE, Grand Rapids MI 49546-4388
County: Kent FICE Identification: 002241
Unit ID: 169080
Telephone: (616) 526-6000 Carnegie Class: Bac-Diverse
FAX Number: (616) 526-8551 Calendar System: 4/1/4
URL: www.calvin.edu
Established: 1876 Annual Undergrad Tuition & Fees: $31,730
Enrollment: 3,990 Coed
Affiliation or Control: Christian Reformed Church IRS Status: 501(c)3
Highest Offering: Master's
Accreditation: NH, CAEPT, CS, ENG, MUS, NURSE, SP, SW

01 President Dr. Michael K. LE ROY
05 Provost Dr. Cheryl BRANDSEN
10 Vice Pres Admin/Finance Ms. Sally VANDER PLOEG
111 Vice President for Advancement Mr. Kenneth ERFFMEYER
84 Vice Pres Enrollment Management Mr. Russell J. BLOEM
32 Vice President Student Life Dr. Sarah VISSER
15 Vice President People/Strategy & IT Mr. Todd K. HUBERS
13 Assoc Vice President for IT Mr. Brian PAIGE
28 Exec Assoc for Diversity/Inclusion Dr. Michelle LOYD-PAIGE
42 College Chaplain Dr. Mary HULST
21 Director of Finance Ms. Barbara BOERS
08 Dean of the Library Mr. David MALONE
29 Director Alumni/Parent Relations Mr. Rick J. TREUR
06 Director Academic Svcs/Registrar Mr. Thomas L. STEENWYK
35 Dean of Students Mr. John WITTE
88 Dir of Commuter Life/Assessment Mr. C. Robert CROW
88 Dean of Students for Judicial Affs Ms. Jane E. HENDRIKSMA
46 Dean of Research & Scholarship Dr. Matthew WALHOUT
108 Dean Institutional Effectiveness Dr. Michael STOB
83 Acad Dean Lang/Soc Sci/Context Disc Dr. Elizabeth VANDERLEI
81 Acad Dean Educ/Kinesio/Nat Sci/Math Dr. Arlene HOOGEWERF
04 Senior Executive Associate Mr. Robert A. BERKHOF
36 Director of Career Development Ms. TaRita JOHNSON
09 Dir Institutional/Enroll Research Mr. Thomas A. VAN ECK
26 Dir Communications & Brand Strategy Mr. Timothy L. ELLENS
27 Director of Marketing Ms. Jeanne NIENHUIS
88 Director Social Research Center Dr. Neil CARLSON
19 Director of Campus Safety Mr. William T. CORNER
18 Director Physical Plant Mr. Philip D. BEEZHOLD
24 Director Instruc Resources Center Mr. Randal G. NIEUWSMA
38 Director Broene Counseling Center Vacant
23 Director Health Services Dr. Laura CHAMPION
92 Director Honors Program Dr. Bruce BERGLUND
41 Athletic Director Dr. James TIMMER, JR.
102 Dir Foundation/Corporate Relations Ms. Jodi OVERMAN
104 Director Study Abroad Dr. Donald DEGRAAF
105 Director Web Services Mr. Luke ROBINSON
37 Director Student Financial Aid Mr. Paul R. WITTE, III
44 Director Annual Giving & Engagement Mr. Rick TREUR
53 Dean of Education Dr. James ROOKS
07 Director of Admissions/Counseling Mr. Ben ARENDT
101 Secretary of the Institution/Board Ms. Sharolyn J. CHRISTIANS

Calvin Theological Seminary (C)

3233 Burton Street, SE, Grand Rapids MI 49546-4387
County: Kent FICE Identification: 002242
Unit ID: 169099
Telephone: (616) 957-6036 Carnegie Class: Spec-4-yr-Faith
FAX Number: (616) 957-8621 Calendar System: Semester
URL: www.calvinseminary.edu
Established: 1876 Annual Graduate Tuition & Fees: N/A
Enrollment: 300 Coed
Affiliation or Control: Christian Reformed Church IRS Status: 501(c)3
Highest Offering: Doctorate; No Undergraduates
Accreditation: THEOL

01 President Rev. Julius T. MEDENBLIK
05 Dean of Academic Programs Dr. Ronald J. FEENSTRA
20 Assoc Academic Dean Vacant
06 Registrar Ms. Joan BEELEN
32 Dean of Students Rev. Jeff SAJDAK
08 Theological Librarian Vacant
10 Controller Mr. David BARDOLPH
30 Director of Development Mr. Robert KNOOR
36 Director of Mentored Ministries Rev. Alvern GELDER
07 Dir of Admissions/Enrollment Mgmt Mr. Aaron EINFELD
37 Director of Financial Aid Mrs. Jennifer SETTERGREN

Career Quest Learning Center (D)

3215 S. Pennsylvania Avenue, Lansing MI 48910
County: Ingham FICE Identification: 039153
Unit ID: 446136
Telephone: (517) 318-3330 Carnegie Class: Assoc/HVT-High Non
FAX Number: (517) 318-3331 Calendar System: Other
URL: www.careerquest.edu
Established: 1995 Annual Undergrad Tuition & Fees: N/A
Enrollment: 273 Coed
Affiliation or Control: Proprietary IRS Status: Proprietary
Highest Offering: Associate Degree
Accreditation: COE

01 President & CEO Melissa SODEREERG

Central Michigan University (E)

1200 S. Franklin Street, Mount Pleasant MI 48859
County: Isabella FICE Identification: 002243
Unit ID: 169248
Telephone: (989) 774-4000 Carnegie Class: DU-Higher
FAX Number: (989) 774-3537 Calendar System: Semester
URL: www.cmich.edu
Established: 1892 Annual Undergrad Tuition & Fees (In-State): $12,150
Enrollment: 26,825 Coed
Affiliation or Control: State IRS Status: 501(c)3
Highest Offering: Doctorate
Accreditation: NH, ART, ARCPA, AUD, CAATE, CAEP, CIDA, CLPSY, DIETD, DIETI, ENG, EXSC, JOUR, #MED, MUS, NAIT, NRPA, PTA, SCPSY, SP, SPAA, SW

01 President Dr. George E. ROSS
05 Executive VP/Provost Dr. Michael A. GEALT
10 Vice Pres Finance/Admin Svcs Mr. Barrie J. WILKES
86 Vice Pres Govt & Ext Relations Ms. Kathleen M. WILBUR
84 Vice Pres Enrollment & Student Svcs Mr. Steven L. JOHNSON
111 Vice Pres Advancement Mr. Robert K. MARTIN
20 Vice Provost Academic Development Mr. Peter G. ROSS
13 Vice President Info Technology/CIO Dr. Roger E. REHM
21 AVP Fin Svcs & Reporting/Controller Ms. Mary M. HILL
26 AVP University Communications Ms. Sherry S. KNIGHT
18 Assoc Vice Pres Facilities Mgmt Mr. Jonathon WEBB
109 Interim Exec Dir Auxiliary Services Mr. Calvin H. SEELYE
39 Director Residence Life Ms. Kathleen GARDNER
28 Interim Assoc Vice Pres Diversity Dr. Traci GUINN
15 Assoc VP Human Resources Ms. Lori L. HELLA
108 Vice Provost Academic Effectiveness Dr. Claudia B. DOUGLASS
20 Sr Vice Provost Academic Admin Dr. Ray L. CHRISTIE
46 VP Rsrch & Dean Grad Stds Dr. David E. ASH
30 Asst Vice President Advancement Mr. Edward A. TOLCHER
08 Dean of Libraries Dr. Jeff LUZIUS
32 Assoc VP Student Affairs Mr. Anthony A. VOISIN
35 Executive Director Student Affairs Mr. Shaun HOLTGRIEVE
29 Exec Dir of Alumni Relations Ms. Marcie M. OTTEMAN
09 Exec Dir Institutional Research Dr. Robert M. ROE
22 Exec Dir Civil Rights/Inst Equity Ms. Katherine M. LASHER
07 Director Undergraduate Admissions Mr. Thomas W. SPEAKMAN
43 Vice President & General Counsel Dr. Manuel R. RUPE
06 Registrar Mr. Keith J. MALKOWSKI
37 Director Scholarships/Financial Aid Mr. Kirk M. YATS
36 Director Career Services Ms. Julia B. SHERLOCK
41 Interim Assoc VP/Dir of Athletics Ms. Marcy WESTON
38 Director Counseling Center Mr. Ross J. RAPAPORT
45 Director Financial Plan & Budgets Mr. Joseph L. GARRISON
27 Director Communications Ms. Heather L. SMITH
19 Chief of Police Mr. William YEAGLEY, JR.
40 Director CMU Bookstore Mr. Barry D. WATERS
81 Dean College of Sci & Engineering Dr. Ian R. DAVISON
76 Dean College of Health Professions Dr. Tom J. MASTERSON
63 Dean College of Medicine Dr. George E. KIKANO
83 Dean Col Hum/Soc/Behav Sci Dr. Pamela S. GATES
57 Dean College Comm/Fine Arts Dr. Janet HETHORN
50 Dean College of Business Admin Dr. Charles T. CRESPY
53 Dean College Education/Human Svcs Dr. Dale-Elizabeth PEHRSSON

04 Executive Assistant to President Ms. Mary Jane FLANAGAN
85 Exec Dir International Affairs Mr. William A. HOLMES
96 Dir Contract & Purchasing Svcs Ms. Anne PYBUS-THRUSH
92 Director Honors Program Dr. Phame M. CAMARENA
104 Director Study Abroad Ms. Dianne S. DESALVO
116 Director Internal Audit Mr. Scott M. STRONG
110 Assoc VP of Advancement Mr. Stephen KULL
44 Director of Annual Giving Mr. Bryan GRIFFIN
115 Assistant Controller Ms. Kim WAGESTER
25 Assistant Controller Ms. Julie MONTROSS
117 Dir/Risk Mgmt Envirn Hlth & Safety Mr. Benjamin S. COFFMAN
121 Director Student Success Dr. Evan MONTAGUE
124 Interim Assoc Vice Pres Enroll Mgmt Dr. Dave PATTON

Chamberlain University-Troy (F)

200 Kirts Blvd, Ste C, Troy MI 48084
Telephone: (248) 817-4140 Identification: 770851
Accreditation: &NH, NURSE

† Branch campus of Chamberlain University-Addison, Addison, IL

Cleary University (G)

3750 Cleary Drive, Howell MI 48843
County: Livingston FICE Identification: 002246
Unit ID: 169327
Telephone: (800) 686-1883 Carnegie Class: Spec-4-yr-Bus
FAX Number: N/A Calendar System: Semester
URL: www.cleary.edu
Established: 1883 Annual Undergrad Tuition & Fees: $17,600
Enrollment: 545 Coed
Affiliation or Control: Independent Non-Profit IRS Status: 501(c)3
Highest Offering: Master's
Accreditation: NH

01 President & CEO Mr. Jayson BOYERS
05 Provost & Chief Acad Officer Dr. Lance LEWIS
10 VP Finance & Administration Ms. Judy WALKER
26 VP Communications & Enrollment Mgmt Dr. Matt BENNETT
06 Asst Prov Academic Svcs/Registrar Ms. Dawn M. FISER
04 Exec Officer for Pres Ms. Darla HARGRAVES
20 Asst Prov Acad Affairs & Acad Dean Ms. Dawn MARKELL
09 Institutional Research Analyst Ms. Keeley K. SADLAK
37 Director Financial Aid Ms. Vesta SMITH-CAMPBELL
36 Dir Career Services & Placement Mr. Marcu MATTHEWS
40 Director Bookstore Services Ms. Sheila THOMPSON
07 Director of Admissions Vacant
41 Athletic Director Mr. Ward MULLENS

College for Creative Studies (H)

201 East Kirby Street, Detroit MI 48202-4034
County: Wayne FICE Identification: 006771
Unit ID: 169442
Telephone: (313) 664-7400 Carnegie Class: Spec-4-yr-Arts
FAX Number: (313) 872-8377 Calendar System: Semester
URL: www.collegeforcreativestudies.edu
Established: 1906 Annual Undergrad Tuition & Fees: $40,840
Enrollment: 1,487 Coed
Affiliation or Control: Independent Non-Profit IRS Status: 501(c)3
Highest Offering: Master's
Accreditation: NH, ART, CIDA

01 President Mr. Richard L. ROGERS
100 Exec Asst to Pres & Sec to Board Ms. Sandra WILSON
04 Admin Assistant to the President Ms. Brigette NEAL
05 Provost & VP for Academic Affairs Mr. Sooshin CHOI
10 Vice Pres Administration & Finance Ms. Anne D. BECK
84 Vice Pres Enrollment & Student Svcs Ms. Julie HINGELBERG
30 Vice Pres Institutional Advancement Ms. Nina HOLDEN
20 Assoc Provost Faculty Affairs Ms. Sharon PROCTER
58 Dean Graduate Studies Vacant
88 Dean Undergraduate Studies Mr. Vince CARDUCCI
32 Dean of Students Mr. Daniel LONG
06 Registrar & Acad Advising Director Ms. Nadine ASHTON
07 Director of Admissions Ms. Carla GONZALEZ
37 Director Financial Aid Ms. Kristin MOSKOVITZ
35 Director Student Life Mr. Michael COLEMAN
85 Director Intl Student Services Mr. Francisco LOPEZ
93 Dir of Student Diversity/Inclusion Mr. Cliff HARRIS
51 Dir Continuing & Precollege Studies Ms. Jane STEWART
31 Dir of Community Arts Partnerships Mr. Mikel BRESEE
08 Director Library Ms. Beth WALKER
19 Director of Safety & Security Mr. Michael BRUGGEMAN
18 Director Facilities & Admin Svcs Mr. Jamie LAESSLE
13 Director Information Technology Mr. Greg FRASER
90 Director of Academic Technologies Ms. Laurie EVANS
21 Director Business Services Ms. Kerri MCKAY
15 Director Human Resources Ms. Gina FINNEY
26 Director Marketing & Communications Mr. Marcus POPIOLEK
44 Dir Annual Giving/Donor Services Ms. Elizabeth KLOS
36 Director Career Services Ms. Terese NEHRA
29 Asst Dir Annual Giv/Alumni Rels Mr. Anthony SPANGLER
38 Personal Counselor Ms. Valerie WEISS
40 Manager Bookstore Ms. Glen MORREN
39 Director of Residence Life Mr. Ryan HARRISON
102 Dir Foundation/Corporate Relations Ms. Shannon MCPARTLON

Compass College of Cinematic Arts (I)

41 Sheldon Boulevard, SE, Grand Rapids MI 49503
County: Kent FICE Identification: 041633
Unit ID: 459417

Telephone: (616) 988-1000 Carnegie Class: Spec-4-yr-Arts
FAX Number: (616) 458-4676 Calendar System: Other
URL: www.compass.edu
Established: 2003 Annual Undergrad Tuition & Fees: $15,300
Enrollment: 116 Coed
Affiliation or Control: Independent Non-Profit IRS Status: 501(c)3
Highest Offering: Baccalaureate
Accreditation: ACCSC

01	President	Keri LOWE
03	VP of Institutional Affairs	Austin MORSE
05	Director of Education	Dr. Mark VANDERMEER
10	Finance Manager	Laura COULIER
26	Director Marketing & Recruiting	Tom LOWE
07	Admissions Manager	Amy HILLS

Concordia University Ann Arbor (A)

4090 Geddes Road, Ann Arbor MI 48105-2797
County: Washtenaw FICE Identification: 002247
Unit ID: 169363
Telephone: (734) 995-7300 Carnegie Class: Bac-Diverse
FAX Number: (734) 995-4610 Calendar System: Semester
URL: www.cuaa.edu
Established: 1962 Annual Undergrad Tuition & Fees: $27,710
Enrollment: 899 Coed
Affiliation or Control: Lutheran Church - Missouri Synod
IRS Status: 501(c)3
Highest Offering: Master's
Accreditation: NH, CAEPN

01	President	Rev. Patrick FERRY
03	Executive VP & Chief Oper Ofcr	Mr. Allen PROCHNOW
11	VP of Admin/Campus Chief Exec	Mr. Curt GIELOW
05	Sr VP Academic Affairs	Dr. William CARIO
10	Controller	Mr. William WOOD
07	Director of Admissions	Mr. Chance CHILDERS
32	Executive Director Student Life	Rev. John RATHJE
38	Director Student Counseling	Mrs. Gina VERSEMAN
39	Director Residence Life	Mr. Dauthan KEENER
41	Director of Athletics	Mr. Lonnie PRIES
42	Campus Pastor	Mr. Ryan PETERSON
18	Director Buildings & Grounds	Mr. Jerry NOVAK
19	Director Security/Safety	Mr. Dieter HERAN
13	Director IT Services	Mr. Christopher RAASCH
111	VP of Advancement	Rev. Roy PETERSON
09	Director of Institutional Research	Dr. Mae KELLER
08	Coordinator of Library Services	Ms. Elizabeth HARTIG
15	Human Resources Generalist	Mrs. Barb WALTHER
53	Campus Dean School of Education	Dr. Sandra HARRIS
50	Campus Dean School of Business	Dr. Suzanne SIEGLE
66	Campus Dean School of Nursing	Dr. Cynthia FENSKE
49	Campus Dean School Arts & Sciences	Dr. Robert MCCORMICK
20	Campus Dir of Acad Operations	Dr. Georgia KRIEGER
04	Administrative Asst to President	Ms. Laura TURNER
06	Registrar	Ms. Kendra ERNST
37	Director Student Financial Aid	Mr. Robert NOWAK

Cornerstone University (B)

1001 E Beltline Avenue, NE, Grand Rapids MI 49525-5897
County: Kent FICE Identification: 002266
Unit ID: 170037
Telephone: (616) 949-5300 Carnegie Class: Masters/L
FAX Number: (616) 222-1540 Calendar System: Semester
URL: www.cornerstone.edu
Established: 1941 Annual Undergrad Tuition & Fees: $26,860
Enrollment: 2,572 Coed
Affiliation or Control: Independent Non-Profit IRS Status: 501(c)3
Highest Offering: Doctorate
Accreditation: NH, CAEPT, MUS, SW, THEOL

01	President	Dr. Joseph M. STOWELL
03	Executive Vice President	Mr. Marc FOWLER
05	Chief Academic Officer	Dr. John VERBERKMOES
10	Chief Financial Officer	Mrs. Dee MOONEY
88	Vice President of Broadcasting	Mr. Chris LEMKE
32	Vice Pres Student Development	Mr. Gerald LONGJOHN
111	VP of Advancement	Mr. Bob SACK
20	Dean of Curriculum & Accreditation	Dr. Pete MUIR
73	Dean Grand Rpds Theol Seminary	Mr. John VER BERKMOES
108	Assoc Dean Assessment/Stdnt Success	Mrs. Emily GRATSON
35	Director of Student Services	Mr. Keith DEBOER
08	Director of Miller Library	Mr. Fred SWEET
37	Director Financial Services	Mrs. Carol CARPENTER
21	Controller	Mr. Scott STEWART
88	Director of Retention	Mrs. Kay LANDRUM
41	Athletic Director	Mr. Chip HUBER
15	Director of Human Resources	Mrs. Emilie AZKOUL
18	Director of Campus Services	Mr. Bob PRIOLO
19	Director of Campus Safety	Mr. Brandan BISHOP
29	Director of Alumni	Mrs. Amanda LAWRENCE
06	Registrar	Mrs. Gail DUHON
24	Director of Technical Support	Mr. Dan MILLS
38	Director of the Counseling Center	Mr. Scott COUREY
92	Director of Honors Program	Mr. Michael STEVENS
07	Director of Admissions	Mr. Dave EMERSON
04	Administrative Asst to President	Mrs. Beth LONGJOHN

Cranbrook Academy of Art (C)

39221 Woodward Avenue, PO Box 801,
Bloomfield Hills MI 48303-0801
County: Oakland FICE Identification: 002248
Unit ID: 169424
Telephone: (248) 645-3300 Carnegie Class: Spec-4-yr-Arts
FAX Number: (248) 645-3591 Calendar System: Semester
URL: www.cranbrook.edu
Established: 1932 Annual Graduate Tuition & Fees: N/A
Enrollment: 152 Coed
Affiliation or Control: Independent Non-Profit IRS Status: 501(c)3
Highest Offering: Master's; No Undergraduates
Accreditation: NH, ART

01	Director	Mr. Christopher SCOATES
06	Registrar/Fin Aid & Admiss Mgr	Ms. Leslie TOBAKOS

Davenport University (D)

6191 Kraft Avenue, S.E., Grand Rapids MI 49512
County: Kent FICE Identification: 002249
Unit ID: 169479
Telephone: (616) 698-7111 Carnegie Class: Masters/L
FAX Number: N/A Calendar System: Semester
URL: www.davenport.edu
Established: 1866 Annual Undergrad Tuition & Fees: $16,726
Enrollment: 8,142 Coed
Affiliation or Control: Independent Non-Profit IRS Status: 501(c)3
Highest Offering: Master's
Accreditation: NH, CAHIIM, IACBE, MAC, NUR, NURSE, OT, PNUR

01	President	Dr. Richard J. PAPPAS
111	Exec VP Advancement	Ms. Peg LUY
46	Exec VP of Quality & Effectiveness	Dr. Scott EPSTEIN
15	Exec VP Human/Organizational Devel	Mr. Dave VENEKLASE
07	Exec VP Admission & Student Svcs	Mr. Walter O'NEILL
10	Exec Vice President for Finance/CFO	Mr. Michael S. VOLK
05	Exec VP Academics/Provost	Dr. Linda RINKER
09	VP for Institutional Research	Dr. Kathy ABOUFADEL
50	Dean College of Business & Tech	Dr. Pamela IMPERATO
76	Dean College of Health Professions	Dr. Karen DALEY
49	Dean College of Arts and Sciences	Vacant
106	Dean Global Campus	Mr. Brian MILLER
107	Dean College of Urban Education	Ms. Susan GUNN
37	Exec Director Financial Aid	Mr. David DE BOER
26	Executive Dir of Communications	Mr. Robyn LUYMES
29	Director of Alumni Relations	Mr. Jason MADDON
21	Controller	Mr. Michael SLEVA
06	University Registrar	Ms. Donna MILHAM
41	Director of Athletics	Mr. Paul LOWDEN
04	Administrative Asst to President	Ms. Rose KARSTEN
28	Exec Dir Diversity/Equity/Inclusion	Dr. RhaeAnn BOOKER
18	VP Facilities Management	Mr. Damon P. GONZALES

Davenport University Holland (E)

643 S Waverly Road, Holland MI 49423
Telephone: (616) 395-4600 Identification: 770266
Accreditation: &NH

Davenport University Lansing (F)

220 E Kalamazoo, Lansing MI 48933
Telephone: (517) 484-2600 Identification: 770268
Accreditation: &NH, MAC

Davenport University Livonia (G)

19499 Victor Parkway, Livonia MI 48152
Telephone: (734) 943-2800 Identification: 770269
Accreditation: &NH

Davenport University Midland (H)

3555 E Patrick Road, Midland MI 48642
Telephone: (989) 835-5588 Identification: 770270
Accreditation: &NH

Davenport University Warren (I)

27650 Dequindre Road, Warren MI 48092
Telephone: (586) 558-8700 Identification: 770272
Accreditation: &NH

Delta College (J)

1961 Delta Rd., University Center MI 48710-0001
County: Bay FICE Identification: 002251
Unit ID: 169521
Telephone: (989) 686-9000 Carnegie Class: Assoc/MT-VT-Mix Trad/Non
FAX Number: (989) 667-0620 Calendar System: Semester
URL: www.delta.edu
Established: 1961 Annual Undergrad Tuition & Fees (In-District): $3,575
Enrollment: 9,291 Coed
Affiliation or Control: Local IRS Status: 501(c)3
Highest Offering: Associate Degree
Accreditation: NH, ADNUR, COARC, DA, DH, DMS, PTAA, RAD, SURGT

01	President	Dr. Jean GOODNOW
10	Vice President Finance/Treasurer	Ms. Debra K. LUTZ
32	Vice President Student & Educ Svcs	Ms. Margarita MOSQUEDA
05	VP Instruction/Learning Svcs	Dr. Reva CURRY
111	Ex Dir Delta Col Found/Inst Advance	Ms. Pam CLARK
20	Dean of Teaching & Learning	Dr. Martha CRAWMER
35	Dean of Students	Mr. Jonathan MILLER
36	Dean Career Educ/Learning Part	Ms. Ginny PRZYGOCKI
84	Dean of Enrollment Management	Dr. Russell CURLEY
26	Marketing & Public Info Director	Ms. Leanne GOVITZ
108	Dir Institutional Effectiveness	Ms. Andrea L. URSUY
101	Assistant to Pres/Board Secretary	Ms. Andrea URSUY
25	Director of Corporate Services	Ms. Jennifer CARROLL
37	Director of Student Financial Aid	Ms. Lisa BAKER
15	Director of Human Resources	Mr. Scott LEWLESS
18	Director of Facilities Management	Mr. Larry E. RAMSEYER
07	Dir of Admissions & Recruitment	Mr. Zachary WARD
19	Director of Public Safety	Mr. Robert BATTINKOFF
88	Director of Learning Centers	Ms. Kristy NELSON
38	Dir Counseling Advising/Career Svcs	Ms. Diana GUTIERREZ
21	Business Services Director	Ms. Barbara WEBB
09	Director of Institutional Research	Mr. Wm. Michael WOOD
06	Registrar	Ms. Terri GOULD
13	Chief Information Officer	Mr. Jason STAHL
40	Bookstore Manager	Ms. Barbara POWERS
08	Mgr of Library Programs & Services	Ms. Michele PRATT

Eastern Michigan University (K)

900 Oakwood St, Ypsilanti MI 48197-2207
County: Washtenaw FICE Identification: 002259
Unit ID: 169798
Telephone: (734) 487-1849 Carnegie Class: DU-Mod
FAX Number: (734) 481-1095 Calendar System: Semester
URL: www.emich.edu
Established: 1849 Annual Undergrad Tuition & Fees (In-State): $11,209
Enrollment: 21,824 Coed
Affiliation or Control: State IRS Status: 501(c)3
Highest Offering: Doctorate
Accreditation: NH, #ARCPA, ART, CAATE, CACREP, CAEPN, CEA, CIDA, CLPSY, CONST, DIETC, ENGT, MT, MUS, NURSE, OPE, OT, PLNG, SP, SPAA, SW

01	President	Dr. James M. SMITH
05	Provost and Executive VP	Dr. Rhonda LONGWORTH
10	Chief Financial Officer	Mr. Michael VALDES
26	Vice President Communications	Mr. Walter KRAFT
111	VP Advance/Exec Dir Foundation	Mr. William SHEPARD
101	VP & Sec to the Board of Regents	Ms. Vicki REAUME
41	Vice President/Dir Athletics	Mr. Scott WETHERBEE
32	Assoc Vice Pres Student Affairs	Mr. Calvin PHILLIPS
20	Assoc Prov/Assoc VP Acad Pgm Svcs	Vacant
11	Assoc Prov/Assoc VP Admin	Dr. James J. CARROLL, III
84	Vice Pres Enrollment Mgmt	Mr. Kevin KUCERA
86	Int Exec Dir Govt/Cmty Relations	Ms. Vicki REAUME
18	VP for Operations and Facilities	Mr. John P. DONEGAN
15	VP for University Human Resources	Mr. David TURNER
43	General Counsel/University Attorney	Ms. Gloria HAGE
13	Int Asst VP/CIO Info Technology	Mr. Ron WOODY
19	Exec Dir Public Safety	Mr. Robert HEIGHES
88	Advisor to the President	Mr. Leigh GREDEN
88	Dir Univ House & Special Events	Ms. Kelly BRENNAN
69	Dean Col Health & Human Svcs	Dr. Murali NAIR
49	Int Dean Col of Art & Sciences	Dr. Kathleen STACEY
50	Int Dean Col of Business	Dr. Anne BALAZS
53	Dean Col of Education	Dr. Michael SAYLER
72	Dean Col of Technology	Dr. Mohamad QATU
58	Int Assc Prov/AVP Grad Studies/Rsrc	Dr. Wade TORNQUIST
27	Assoc VP Marketing & Communication	Mr. Theodore G. COUTILISH
27	Executive Director Media Relations	Mr. Geoffrey LARCOM
23	Asst VP of Student Well-Being	Ms. Ellen GOLD
09	Asst VP & Exec Dir Inst Rsrch/Info	Dr. Bin NING
20	Asst VP Academic Affairs/AHR	Dr. David WOIKE
21	Asst VP Business Oper/Student Svcs	Mr. Brian KULPA
102	Exec Dir Foundation Operations/CFO	Ms. Laura WILBANKS
88	Ombuds	Dr. Chiara HENSLEY
29	Asst VP Alumni Engagement	Ms. Glenna MILLER
08	University Librarian	Vacant
88	Dir Charter Schools Program	Dr. Malverne WINBORNE
92	Director Honors College	Dr. Rebecca SIPE
39	Dir Housing & Residence Life	Ms. Jeanette ZALBA
114	Exec Dir Financial Plng & Budget	Mr. Todd OHMER
88	Dir University Convocation Center	Mr. Mark MONAHAN
30	Sr Development Officer/Central Svcs	Ms. Susan RINK
102	Assoc VP Advancement/Foundation	Ms. Jill HUNSBERGER
88	Exec Dir Integrated Content	Ms. Darcy GIFFORD
88	Gen Mgr WEMU-FM Public Rad	Ms. Mary MOTHERWELL
06	Registrar	Ms. Christina SHELL
37	Director Financial Aid	Ms. Donna HOLUBIK
28	Dir Diversity & Cmty Involvement	Mr. Steven P. BRYANT
22	Dir Diversity & Affirmative Action	Ms. Sharon ABRAHAM
96	Director Purchasing	Mr. Dean BACKOS
88	Title IX Investigator	Ms. Anika AWAI-WILLIAMS
88	Senior Assoc to CFO	Mr. Daniel KELLY
88	Controller	Ms. Doris M. CELIAN
88	Director Business Services	Mr. Bryan HOWARD
88	Dir Business Systems Support	Mr. Kenneth R. ADKINS
97	Interim Dir Undergraduate Studies	Mr. Michael TEW

Ecumenical Theological Seminary (L)

2930 Woodward Avenue, Detroit MI 48201-3035
County: Wayne FICE Identification: 040024
Unit ID: 247162
Telephone: (313) 831-5200 Carnegie Class: Spec-4-yr-Faith

FAX Number: (313) 831-1353 Calendar System: Quarter
URL: www.etseminary.edu
Established: 1980 Annual Undergrad Tuition & Fees: N/A
Enrollment: 152 Coed
Affiliation or Control: Independent Non-Profit IRS Status: 501(c)3
Highest Offering: Doctorate
Accreditation: THEOL

01 President ... Dr. Stephen B. MURRAY
05 Vice Pres Academic Affs/Acad Dean ... Rev. Tony C. HENDERSON
32 Vice Pres Administration/Stdnt Svcs ... Ms. Genetta Y. HATCHER
10 Finance Officer ... Ms. Porsha MALLETT
30 Dir Inst Advancement/Marketing ... Mr. John CUNNINGHAM
06 Registrar/Coord Acad Initiatives ... Ms. Barbara PYE
08 Library Director ... Mr. Joshua PIKKA
07 Director of Admissions/Recruitment ... Dr. Brandon GRAFIUS

Ferris State University (A)

1201 S. State Street, Big Rapids MI 49307-2295
County: Mecosta FICE Identification: 002260
Unit ID: 169910
Telephone: (231) 591-2000 Carnegie Class: Masters/M
FAX Number: (231) 591-3592 Calendar System: Semester
URL: www.ferris.edu
Established: 1884 Annual Undergrad Tuition & Fees (In-State): $11,290
Enrollment: 14,715 Coed
Affiliation or Control: State IRS Status: 501(c)3
Highest Offering: First Professional Degree
Accreditation: NH, ACBSP, CAEPT, CAHIIM, CEA, COARC, CONST, DH, DMOLS, DMS, ENG, ENGT, MLTAD, MT, NMT, NUR, OPT, OPTR, PHAR, RAD, SW

01 President ... Dr. David L. EISLER
05 Provost & VPAA ... Dr. Paul A. BLAKE
43 Vice President & General Counsel ... Mr. Miles J. POSTEMA
10 VP of Administration & Finance ... Mr. Jerry L. SCOBY
111 VP of Advancement & Mktg ... Ms. Shelly PEARCY
32 Vice President Student Affairs ... Dr. Jeanine WARD-ROOF
12 President of KCAD & VP of Ferris ... Dr. Leslie BELLAVANCE
56 Dean Extended and Intl Operations ... Dr. Steve REIFERT
28 VP for Diversity and Inclusion ... Dr. David PILGRIM
88 Assoc Provost of Accreditation ... Dr. Roberta TEAHEN
109 Assoc VP of Auxiliary Enterprises ... Ms. Gheretta HARRIS
21 Assistant VP of Finance ... Mr. Mike GRANDY
110 Assoc VP for Advancement ... Mr. Bob MURRAY
15 Assoc VP Human Resources ... Ms. Jan BLAIR
30 Assoc Vice Pres for Special Gifts ... Ms. Carla MILLER
18 Assoc VP Physical Plant ... Mr. Mike HUGHES
84 Associate Dean Enrollment Services ... Ms. Kathy LAKE
07 Dean of Enrollment Services ... Dr. Kristen SALOMONSON
114 Director Budget Planning/Analysis ... Ms. Sally DEPEW
13 Chief Technology Officer ... Mr. Jake MARTIN
19 Director of Public Safety ... Mr. Bruce BORKOVICH
88 Mgr Stdnt Empl & Financial Aid Adv ... Mr. John RANDLE
88 Director of University Center ... Mr. Mark SCHUELKE
38 Director Counseling & Health Center ... Ms. Lindsay BARBER
35 Dean of Student Life ... Ms. Joy PUFHAL
88 Dir Multicultural Student Svcs ... Dr. Matthew CHANEY
88 Director for CLACS ... Ms. Angela ROMAN
88 Director University Recreation ... Ms. Cindy HORN
29 Assoc VP for External Relations ... Mr. Jeremy MISHLER
09 Dir of Inst Research & Testing ... Ms. Mitzi DAY
39 Director Residential Life ... Mr. Brian MARQUARDT
40 Director Bookstore ... Ms. Karen BOHREN
41 Director of Athletics ... Mr. Perk WEISENBURGER
44 Dir Annual Giving & Advance Svcs ... Ms. Jennifer YONTZ
96 Director Purchasing ... Mr. Michael PETHICK
49 Dean of Arts & Sciences ... Dr. Kristi HAIK
50 Dean of Business ... Dr. David NICOL
53 Dean Educ & Human Svcs ... Mr. Arrick JACKSON
67 Dean of Pharmacy ... Dr. Steve DURST
76 Dean of Health Professions ... Dr. Matthew ADEYANJU
63 Dean Michigan College Optometry ... Dr. David DAMARI
72 Dean of Engineering Technology ... Mr. Larry SCHULT
08 Dean of FLITE ... Dr. Scott GARRISON
04 Executive Asst to the President ... Ms. Terri COOK
101 Secretary to the Board ... Ms. Karen HUISMAN
37 Director Financial Aid ... Ms. Heidi WISBY
06 Registrar ... Ms. Elise GRAMZA
104 Director Office of Intl Educ ... Dr. Piram PRAKASAM
105 Web Content Manager ... Mr. Theodore HALM
22 Director of Equal Opportunity ... Ms. Kylie PIETTE

Finlandia University (B)

601 Quincy Street, Hancock MI 49930-1882
County: Houghton FICE Identification: 002322
Unit ID: 172440
Telephone: (906) 482-5300 Carnegie Class: Bac-Diverse
FAX Number: (906) 487-7366 Calendar System: Semester
URL: www.finlandia.edu
Established: 1896 Annual Undergrad Tuition & Fees: $22,758
Enrollment: 536 Coed
Affiliation or Control: Evangelical Lutheran Church In America
IRS Status: 501(c)3
Highest Offering: Baccalaureate
Accreditation: NH, MAC, NURSE, PTAA

01 President ... Dr. Philip JOHNSON
10 Chief Financial Officer ... Ms. Angela PRICE
05 Vice Pres Academic Affairs ... Dr. Fredi DE YAMPERT
26 VP University Relations ... Ms. Karin VAN DYKE
04 Executive Administrative Assistant ... Ms. Doreen KORPELA
27 Director Marketing/Communications ... Mr. Michael BABCOCK
08 Librarian ... Ms. Rebecca DALY
32 Dean of Students ... Ms. Erin BARNETT
42 Campus Pastor ... Mr. Soren SCHMIDT
06 Registrar ... Mr. Jason SULLIVAN
13 Director Information Technology ... Mr. Scott BLAKE
41 Athletic Director ... Mr. Curtis WITTENBERG
18 Director of Plant and Facilities ... Mr. Curt HAHKA
37 Director Financial Services ... Ms. Sandra TURNQUIST
09 Institutional Research Analyst ... Mr. Hannu LEPPANEN
40 Bookstore Manager ... Ms. Alana NOLAN
96 Purchaser ... Ms. Janine NOTTKE
15 Human Resources Specialist ... Ms. Alyson DELANDSHEER
07 Director of Admissions ... Mr. Travis HANSON
19 Director of Campus Safety/Security ... Mr. Jim HARDEN
39 Coordinator Residence Life ... Ms. Leann FOGLE
49 Dean College of Arts & Sciences ... Dr. Jason OYADOMARI
57 Dean Intl School of Art & Design ... Ms. Denise VANDEVILLE
76 Dean College of Health Science ... Dr. Fredi DEYAMPERT
104 Dean Intl School of Business ... Mr. Kevin MANNINEN
15 Title IX Coordinator ... Ms. Karin VAN DYKE

Glen Oaks Community College (C)

62249 Shimmel Road, Centreville MI 49032-9719
County: Saint Joseph FICE Identification: 002263
Unit ID: 169974
Telephone: (269) 467-9945 Carnegie Class: Assoc/MT-VT-Mix Trad/Non
FAX Number: (269) 467-4114 Calendar System: Semester
URL: www.glenoaks.edu
Established: 1965 Annual Undergrad Tuition & Fees (In-District): $3,312
Enrollment: 1,134 Coed
Affiliation or Control: Local IRS Status: 501(c)3
Highest Offering: Associate Degree
Accreditation: NH, MAC

01 President ... Dr. David DEVIER
05 Dean of Academics/Extended Learning ... Dr. Patricia MORGENSTERN
10 Dean of Finance/Administrative Svcs ... Mr. Bruce ZAKRZEWSKI
32 Dean of Student Services ... Ms. Tonya HOWDEN
66 Dean of Nursing ... Mr. Bill LEDERMAN
84 Asst Dean Enrollment Svcs/Registrar ... Vacant
08 Director Learning Resources Center ... Ms. Betsy S. MORGAN
21 Accountant ... Ms. Jennifer DODSON
18 Director of Buildings/Grounds ... Mr. Larry DIEKMAN
07 Director of Admissions ... Ms. Adrienne SKINNER
37 Dir of Financial Aid/Scholarships ... Ms. Jean ZIMMERMAN
41 Director of Athletics ... Ms. Courtney IVAN
09 Institutional Effect/Rsrch Analyst ... Ms. Tammy RUSSELL
15 Personnel Coordinator ... Ms. Candy BOHACZ
26 Public Relations/Marketing ... Ms. Valorie JUERGENS

Gogebic Community College (D)

E4946 Jackson Road, Ironwood MI 49938-1366
County: Gogebic FICE Identification: 002264
Unit ID: 169992
Telephone: (906) 932-4231 Carnegie Class: Assoc/MT-VT-High Trad
FAX Number: (906) 932-5541 Calendar System: Semester
URL: www.gogebic.edu
Established: 1931 Annual Undergrad Tuition & Fees (In-District): $4,492
Enrollment: 1,112 Coed
Affiliation or Control: Local IRS Status: 501(c)3
Highest Offering: Associate Degree
Accreditation: NH, MAC

01 President ... Mr. James A. LORENSON
05 Dean of Instruction ... Mr. Ryon LIST
10 Dean of Business Services ... Mr. Erik M. GUENARD
32 Dean of Student Services ... Ms. Jeanne GRAHAM
37 Director Financial Aid ... Ms. Suzetta R. FORBES
76 Director of Allied Health Program ... Ms. Nicole ROWE
88 Director of Ski Area Management ... Mr. James VANDERSPOEL
08 Dir Learning Resource Center ... Ms. Kathryn MACIEJEWSKI
13 Director of Computer Services ... Mr. Steve SPETS
07 Dir of Admission/Public Information ... Ms. Kim ZECKOVICH
30 Dir of Institutional Development ... Ms. Kelly MARZCAK
15 Director of Human Resources ... Ms. Ashley PAQUETTE
88 Transfer Coord/Veterans Services ... Ms. Jennifer FORSHEY
09 Institutional Researcher ... Ms. Miranda LAWVER
04 Administrative Asst to President ... Ms. Linda M. GUSTAFSON

Grace Bible College (E)

1011 Aldon Street, SW, Grand Rapids MI 49509-1998
County: Kent FICE Identification: 002265
Unit ID: 170000
Telephone: (616) 538-2330 Carnegie Class: Bac/Assoc-Mixed
FAX Number: (616) 538-0599 Calendar System: Semester
URL: www.gbcol.edu
Established: 1939 Annual Undergrad Tuition & Fees: $12,644
Enrollment: 828 Coed
Affiliation or Control: Independent Non-Profit IRS Status: 501(c)3
Highest Offering: Master's
Accreditation: NH, BI

01 President ... Dr. Kenneth B. KEMPER
05 Provost ... Mrs. Kim PILIECI
10 Vice Pres Finance/Bus Operations ... Mr. Douglas VRIESMAN
11 Exec Vice President Operations ... Mr. Brian P. SHERSTAD
32 Assoc Vice Pres Community Life ... Mr. Kyle BOHL
04 Executive Assistant to President ... Mrs. Joyce A. STORMS
06 Registrar ... Ms. Linda K. SILER
111 Vice Pres Institutional Advancement ... Mr. Stephen GOWDY
08 Director Library Services ... Mr. Jeff BRODRICK
37 Director of Financial Aid ... Mr. Kurt POSTMA
13 Director of Information Technology ... Mr. Mark LOVE
18 Director of Maintenance ... Mr. Nathan JOHNSON
41 Athletic Director ... Mr. Gary BAILEY
42 Campus Ministry Coordinator ... Mr. Jim GAMBLE
26 Assoc Vice President of Marketing ... Mr. Zak SORENSEN
108 Director Institutional Assessment ... Mr. Timothy RUMLEY
15 Assoc Vice Pres of Human Resources ... Mrs. Sherea LACY
29 Alumni Services Coordinator ... Mrs. Julianne PRIOLO
07 Director of Admissions ... Mr. Alex BRADLEY

Grand Rapids Community College (F)

143 Bostwick Avenue, NE, Grand Rapids MI 49503-3295
County: Kent FICE Identification: 002267
Unit ID: 170055
Telephone: (616) 234-4000 Carnegie Class: Assoc/HT-Mix Trad/Non
FAX Number: (616) 234-4005 Calendar System: Semester
URL: www.grcc.edu
Established: 1914 Annual Undergrad Tuition & Fees (In-District): $3,789
Enrollment: 14,926 Coed
Affiliation or Control: Local IRS Status: 501(c)3
Highest Offering: Associate Degree
Accreditation: NH, ACFEI, ADNUR, ART, DA, DH, MAC, MUS, OTA, PNUR, RAD

01 President ... Dr. Bill PINK
05 Prov/Exec VP Academic Affairs ... Dr. Laurie CHESLEY
10 Exec VP Business/Financial Services ... Ms. Lisa FREIBURGER
13 VP & CIO Lrng Res/Tech Solutions ... Mr. David ANDERSON
111 Assoc VP Advancement/Exec Dir Found ... Dr. Kathryn MULLINS
88 Dean of Adult & Developmental Educ ... Dr. John COWLES
103 Director of Workforce Training ... Ms. Julie PARKS
32 Dean Student Affairs ... Dr. Tina OEN-HOXIE
09 Dean Inst Research & Planning ... Ms. Donna KRAGT
49 Dean School of Arts & Sciences ... Dr. Michael VARGO
103 Dean Workforce Development ... Dr. Amy KONING
26 Director of Communications ... Ms. Leah NIXON
37 Director of Financial Aid ... Ms. Ann ISACKSON
15 Executive Director Human Resources ... Ms. Cathy KUBIAK
06 Registrar ... Ms. Valerie BUTTERFIELD
35 Director Student Activities ... Mr. Eric MULLEN
36 Assoc Director Student Employment ... Ms. Luann WEDGE
08 Director of Library Services ... Ms. Pat INGERSOLL
18 Executive Director of Facilities ... Mr. Thomas J. SMITH
19 Chief of Campus Police ... Ms. Rebecca R. WHITMAN
43 General Counsel ... Ms. Kathy KEATING
96 Director Purchasing ... Mr. Mansfield MATTHEWSON
12 Dean of Lakeshore Campus & Outreach ... Mr. Daniel CLARK

Grand Valley State University (G)

1 Campus Drive, Allendale MI 49401-9403
County: Ottawa FICE Identification: 002268
Unit ID: 170082
Telephone: (616) 331-5000 Carnegie Class: Masters/L
FAX Number: (616) 331-3503 Calendar System: Semester
URL: www.gvsu.edu
Established: 1960 Annual Undergrad Tuition & Fees (In-State): $11,520
Enrollment: 25,325 Coed
Affiliation or Control: State IRS Status: 501(c)3
Highest Offering: Doctorate
Accreditation: NH, #ARCPA, ART, CAATE, CAEPN, CAHIIM, CS, CVT, @DIETC, DMS, ENG, IPSY, MT, MUS, NURSE, OT, PTA, RADDOS, RTT, @SP, SPAA, SW

01 President ... Dr. Thomas J. HAAS
05 Provost/Exec VP Acad & Student Affs ... Dr. Maria C. CIMITILE
10 Acting VP for Finance/Admin ... Mr. D. Scott RICHARDSON
26 Vice President University Relations ... Mr. Matthew E. MCLOGAN
84 Vice President Enrollment Develop ... Ms. Lynn M. BLUE
30 Vice President for Development ... Ms. Karen M. LOTH
28 Vice President Inclusion and Equity ... Dr. Jesse M. BERNAL
43 Vice President and General Counsel ... Mr. Thomas A. BUTCHER
100 Exec Assoc to the President ... Ms. Teri L. LOSEY
32 Acting V Prov/Dean Student Services ... Dr. Stephen GLASS
88 V Prov for Research Admin ... Dr. Robert SMART
20 V Prov Instruct Develop & Innov ... Dr. Christine RENER
23 V Prov for Health ... Dr. Jean NAGELKERK
20 Asst VP Academic Affairs ... Dr. Edward ABOUFADEL
20 Asst VP for Academic Affairs ... Dr. Suzeanne BENET
20 Asst VP Academic Affairs ... Dr. Chris PLOUFF
20 Asst VP Academic Affairs ... Ms. Bonnie BOWEN
21 Assoc VP Business/Finance ... Mr. Brian COPELAND
114 Asst VP for University Budgets ... Ms. Star RAYMOND
15 Assoc VP Human Resources ... Mr. D. Scott RICHARDSON
88 Assoc VP Institutional Marketing ... Ms. Rhonda LUBBERTS
27 Assoc VP for Univ Communications ... Ms. Mary Eilleen LYON
88 Assoc VP for Strategic Initiatives ... Mr. James BACHMEIER
18 Assoc VP Facilities Services ... Mr. Timothy THIMMESCH
88 Assoc VP for Facilities Planning ... Mr. James MOYER
12 Asst VP for Pew Campus Operations ... Ms. Lisa HAYNES
88 Asst VP for Inclusion & Equity ... Ms. Kathleen VANDERVEEN
35 Assoc VP Student Affs & Inclusion ... Dr. Marlene KOWALSKI-BRAUN
88 Assoc VP for Charter Schools ... Dr. Robert KIMBALL
49 Dean Col of Liberal Arts & Sciences ... Dr. Frederick ANTCZAK
50 Dean Seidman Col of Business ... Dr. Diana LAWSON

70 Dean College of Cmty/Public Service ... Dr. George GRANT
53 Dean College of Education ... Dr. Barry KANPOL
54 Dean Padnos Col Engr & Computing ... Dr. Paul PLOTKOWSKI
76 Dean College of Health Professions ... Dr. Roy OLSSON
88 Dean College Interdisciplin Studies ... Dr. Anne HISKES
66 Dean Kirkhof College of Nursing ... Dr. Cynthia MCCURREN
58 Dean of The Graduate School ... Dr. Jeffrey POTTEIGER
08 Dean University Libraries ... Dr. Annie BÉLANGER
07 Director of Admissions ... Ms. Jodi CHYCINSKI
29 Director of Alumni Relations ... Mr. Chris BARBEE
36 Director of Career Center ... Mr. Troy FARLEY
37 Director of Financial Aid ... Ms. Michelle RHODES
88 Director of Hauenstein Center ... Mr. Gleaves WHITNEY
39 Director of Housing & Res Life ... Dr. Andrew BEACHNAU
13 Director of Information Technology ... Ms. Sue KORZINEK
09 Director of Institutional Analysis ... Dr. Philip BATTY
28 Director of AA/EEO Equity Officer ... Mr. Scott AYOTTE
96 Director of Procurement Services ... Mr. Kim PATRICK
19 Director Public Safety/Police Chief ... Ms. Renee FREEMAN
38 Director Univ Counseling Center ... Dr. Amber ROBERTS
41 Athletic Director ... Ms. Keri BECKER
40 Bookstore Manager ... Mr. Jerrod NICKELS
85 Chief International Officer ... Dr. Mark SCHAUB
88 Controller ... Ms. Pam BRENZING
88 General Manager WGVU ... Mr. Michael WALENTA
06 Registrar ... Dr. Sherril SOMAN
22 Title IX Coordinator ... Ms. Theresa ROWLAND

Great Lakes Christian College (A)

6211 Willow Highway, Lansing MI 48917-1299
County: Eaton FICE Identification: 002269
Unit ID: 170091
Telephone: (517) 321-0242 Carnegie Class: Spec-4-yr-Faith
FAX Number: (517) 321-5902 Calendar System: Semester
URL: www.glcc.edu
Established: 1949 Annual Undergrad Tuition & Fees: $14,770
Enrollment: 158 Coed
Affiliation or Control: Christian Churches And Churches of Christ
IRS Status: 501(c)3
Highest Offering: Baccalaureate
Accreditation: NH

01 President ... Mr. Lawrence L. CARTER
10 Vice President Finance/Operations . Mr. William D. BROSSMANN
05 Vice President of Academic Affairs ... Mr. Michael C. HARRISON
111 Vice Pres Institutional Advancement ... Mr. Philip E. BEAVERS
06 Registrar ... Vacant
08 Director of Library Services ... Vacant
37 Financial Aid Director ... Prof. Ryan APPLE
32 Dean of Students/Dir Student Life ... Mr. Ryan BUSHNELL
41 Athletic Director ... Ms. Sasha LOCKWOOD
88 Director of Outreach Ministries ... Mrs. Judy BEAVERS
18 Maintenance Supervisor ... Mr. Chris ADLEMAN

Henry Ford College (B)

5101 Evergreen Road, Dearborn MI 48128-1495
County: Wayne FICE Identification: 002270
Unit ID: 170240
Telephone: (313) 845-9615 Carnegie Class: Assoc/HT-Mix Trad/Non
FAX Number: (313) 845-9658 Calendar System: Semester
URL: www.hfcc.edu
Established: 1938 Annual Undergrad Tuition & Fees (In-District): $2,822
Enrollment: 12,755 Coed
Affiliation or Control: Local IRS Status: 501(c)3
Highest Offering: Baccalaureate
Accreditation: NH, ACFEI, ADNUR, COARC, MAC, PTAA, RAD, SURGT

01 President ... Dr. Stanley C. JENSEN
10 Vice President Financial Services ... Dr. John SATKOWSKI
32 Vice President Student Services ... Vacant
05 Vice Pres Academic/Career Education ... Dr. Michael NEALON
30 Vice President of Development ... Mr. A. Reginald BEST, JR.
11 VP Admin Services/Chief of Staff ... Dr. Cynthia GLASS
45 Vice President Strategy and Info ... Ms. Becky J. CHADWICK
06 Exec Director Registration/Record ... Ms. Holly DIAMOND
38 Assoc Dean Counseling ... Vacant
50 Dean Business/Entrepreneurship/PD ... Ms. Patricia CHATMAN
08 Director Library ... Mr. Terrence POTVIN
13 Dir Network and Infrastructure ... Mr. Joseph ZITNIK
27 Dir Marketing/Communications ... Mr. Rhonda DELONG
37 Exec Director Student Financial Aid ... Mr. Kevin J. CULLER
92 Director Honors Program ... Dr. Michael DAHER
96 Director Purchasing ... Mr. Fred STEINER
40 Manager of College Store ... Ms. Pamela HALL
04 Administrative Asst to President ... Ms. Kathy DIMITRIOU
09 Director of Institutional Research ... Mr. Chris BUCZYNSKI
15 Director Personnel Services ... Vacant
19 Director Security/Safety ... Ms. Karen SCHOEN
41 Athletic Director ... Ms. Rochelle TAYLOR
43 Dir Legal Services/General Counsel ... Vacant

Hillsdale College (C)

33 East College Street, Hillsdale MI 49242-1298
County: Hillsdale FICE Identification: 002272
Unit ID: 170286
Telephone: (517) 437-7341 Carnegie Class: Bac-A&S
FAX Number: (517) 437-3923 Calendar System: Semester
URL: www.hillsdale.edu
Established: 1844 Annual Undergrad Tuition & Fees: $25,522
Enrollment: 1,526 Coed
Affiliation or Control: Independent Non-Profit IRS Status: 501(c)3
Highest Offering: Doctorate
Accreditation: NH

01 President ... Dr. Larry ARNN
05 Provost ... Dr. David WHALEN
11 VP & Chief Administrative Officer ... Mr. Rich PEWE
43 VP & General Counsel ... Mr. Robert NORTON
07 VP Admissions/Business Improvement ... Mr. Doug BANBURY
26 VP External Affairs ... Mr. Douglas JEFFREY
10 VP Finance ... Mr. Patrick FLANNERY
111 VP Institutional Advancement ... Mr. John CERVINI
88 VP Marketing ... Mr. Matt SCHLIENTZ
32 VP Student Affairs/Dean of Women ... Ms. Diane PHILIPP
27 Associate VP External Affairs ... Mr. Timothy CASPAR
100 Chief Staff Officer ... Mr. Mike HARNER
36 Executive Director Career Services ... Mr. Ken KOOPMANS
15 Executive Director HR ... Ms. Janet MARSH
90 Executive Director ITS ... Mr. Jason SHERRILL
29 Director Alumni Affairs ... Mr. Grigor HASTED
41 Director Athletics ... Mr. Don BRUBACHER
19 Director Campus Security ... Mr. William WHORLEY
40 Director College Bookstore ... Ms. Cindy WILLING
105 Director Digital and Social Media ... Vacant
37 Director Financial Aid ... Mr. Rich MOEGGENBERG
23 Director Health Services ... Mr. Brock LUTZ
08 Director Library ... Mr. Dan KNOCH
09 Director Institutional Research ... Mr. George ALLEN
27 Director Marketing ... Mr. Bill GRAY
18 Director Physical Plant ... Mr. Todd CLOW
35 Director Student Activities ... Ms. Ashlyn LANDHERR
42 Chaplain ... Rev. Adam RICK
21 Controller ... Ms. LeAnn CREGER
33 Dean of Men ... Mr. Aaron PETERSEN
06 Registrar ... Mr. Douglas MCARTHUR
04 Admin Assistant to the President ... Ms. Victoria BERGEN
20 Assistant to the Provost ... Mr. Mark MAIER

Hope College (D)

141 E 12th Street, Holland MI 49423-3607
County: Ottawa FICE Identification: 002273
Unit ID: 170301
Telephone: (616) 395-7000 Carnegie Class: Bac-A&S
FAX Number: (616) 395-7922 Calendar System: Semester
URL: www.hope.edu
Established: 1866 Annual Undergrad Tuition & Fees: $31,560
Enrollment: 3,392 Coed
Affiliation or Control: Reformed Church In America IRS Status: 501(c)3
Highest Offering: Baccalaureate
Accreditation: NH, ART, CAATE, CAEPT, DANCE, ENG, MUS, NURSE, SW, THEA

01 Interim President ... Dr. Dennis VOSKUIL
00 Chairman of the Board ... Mr. Karl DROPPERS
05 Provost ... Dr. Cady SHORT-THOMPSON
10 Vice Pres and Chief Fiscal Officer ... Mr. Thomas W. BYLSMA
07 Vice President for Admissions ... Mr. William VANDERBILT
30 VP for Develop & Alumni Engagement ... Mr. Jeffrey PUCKETT
32 VP Student Devel/Dean of Students ... Dr. Richard A. FROST
26 VP Public Affairs & Marketing ... Mrs. Jennifer FELLINGER
08 Librarian ... Ms. Kelly G. JACOBSMA
39 Dir of Residential Life & Housing ... Dr. John E. JOBSON
22 Assc Dn Stdnts/Dir Ctr Div & Incl ... Ms. Vanessa GREENE
94 Director of Women's/Gender Studies ... Ms. Virginia BEARD
81 Dean for Natural Sciences ... Dr. David G. VANWYLEN
79 Interim Dean for Arts & Humanities ... Dr. Sandra L. VISSER
83 Dean for Social Sciences ... Dr. Scott D. VANDER STOEP
88 Dean of the Chapel ... Rev. Trygve D. JOHNSON
06 Registrar/Dean for Academic Svcs ... Ms. Carol DEJONG
37 Director of Financial Aid ... Ms. Jill NUTT
36 Director Career Services ... Mr. Dale F. AUSTIN
21 Director of Finance & Business Svcs ... Mr. Douglas VAN DYKEN
11 Director of Operations ... Mr. Greg MAYBURY
88 Dir Systems and Innovation ... Mr. Carl E. HEIDEMAN
15 Director Human Resources ... Mrs. Lori MULDER
18 Director Physical Plant ... Ms. Kara SLATER
40 Manager of Bookstore ... Mr. Craig THELEN
29 Exec Director of Alumni Engagement ... Mr. Scott TRAVIS
41 Co-Director of Athletics ... Mr. Tim SCHOONVELD
41 Co-Director of Athletics ... Ms. Melinda LARSON
42 Senior Chaplain ... Rev. Paul H. BOERSMA
38 Asst Dean/Director Counseling Ctr ... Dr. Kristen GRAY
04 Administrative Asst to President ... Mrs. Jan SOMMERVILLE
19 Director Security/Safety ... Mr. Jeffrey HERTEL
25 Chief Contracts/Grants Admin ... Ms. Tracey NALLY
13 Dir Computing/Info Technology ... Mr. Jeff PESTUN
100 Chief of Staff ... Mrs. Mary REMENSCHNEIDER

Jackson College (E)

2111 Emmons Road, Jackson MI 49201-8399
County: Jackson FICE Identification: 002274
Unit ID: 170444
Telephone: (517) 787-0800 Carnegie Class: Bac/Assoc-Assoc Dom
FAX Number: (517) 796-8630 Calendar System: Semester
URL: www.jccmi.edu
Established: 1928 Annual Undergrad Tuition & Fees (In-District): $4,200
Enrollment: 5,440 Coed
Affiliation or Control: Local IRS Status: 501(c)3
Highest Offering: Baccalaureate
Accreditation: NH, ACBSP, COARC, DMS, EMT, MAC, RAD

01 President/CEO ... Dr. Daniel J. PHELAN
05 Provost ... Dr. Rebekah WOODS
10 Vice President of Finance/CFO ... Mr. Darrell NORRIS
32 Vice Pres of Student Services ... Mr. Jeremy FREW
11 Vice Pres of Administration ... Ms. Cindy ALLEN
102 President of JCC Foundation ... Mr. Jason VALENTE
04 Administrative Asst to President ... Ms. Deborah HOLT
06 Registrar ... Mr. Zakary MCNITT
07 Director of Admissions ... Ms. Karen CUZYDLO
08 Head Librarian ... Vacant
09 Exec Director of Inst Effectiveness ... Mr. Rob STIRTON
100 Chief of Staff ... Ms. Sara PERKINS
103 Dir Workforce/Career Development ... Ms. Tina MATZ
18 Chief Facilities/Physical Plant ... Mr. Jim JONES
19 Security/Safety Manager ... Mr. Jeffrey WHIPPLE
28 Director of Diversity ... Mr. Lee HAMPTON
29 Director Alumni Relations ... Ms. Brigette ROBINSON
37 Director Student Financial Aid ... Ms. Andrew SPOHN
39 Director of Housing ... Ms. Elizabeth ANDREWS
41 Athletic Director ... Ms. Heather BATEMAN

Kalamazoo College (F)

1200 Academy Street, Kalamazoo MI 49006-3295
County: Kalamazoo FICE Identification: 002275
Unit ID: 170532
Telephone: (269) 337-7000 Carnegie Class: Bac-A&S
FAX Number: (269) 337-7251 Calendar System: Quarter
URL: www.kzoo.edu
Established: 1833 Annual Undergrad Tuition & Fees: $44,857
Enrollment: 1,443 Coed
Affiliation or Control: Independent Non-Profit IRS Status: 501(c)3
Highest Offering: Baccalaureate
Accreditation: NH

01 President ... Dr. Jorge G. GONZALEZ
05 Provost ... Dr. Michael A. MCDONALD
10 Vice President Business & Finance ... Mr. James E. PRINCE
111 Vice President College Advancement ... Mr. Albert J. DESIMONE
32 VP Student Devel & Dean of Students ... Dr. Sarah B. WESTFALL
85 Associate Provost for Intl Pgms ... Dr. Margaret WIEDENHOEFT
13 Associate Provost for Info Services ... Mr. Gregory S. DIMENT
09 Asst Provost Inst Support/Research ... Ms. Anne T. DUEWEKE
35 Assoc Dean of Stdnts/1st Yr Exper ... Ms. Dana JANSMA
06 Registrar ... Ms. Nicole KRAGT
15 Human Resources Manager ... Ms. Renee E. BOELCKE
07 Dean of Admission and Financial Aid ... Mr. Eric P. STAAB
37 Director of Financial Aid ... Vacant
26 Director of College Communication ... Mr. James A. VANSWEDEN
18 Director of Facilities Management ... Mr. Paul W. MANSTROM
40 Director Bookstore ... Ms. Deborah L. THOMPSON
29 Director of Alumni Relations ... Ms. Kimberly J. ALDRICH
38 Director of Student Counseling ... Dr. Kenlanna FERGUSON
121 Director of Advising ... Ms. Lesley J. CLINARD
36 Dir Ctr Career/Professional Devel ... Ms. Joan C. HAWXHURST
20 Associate Provost ... Dr. Laura L. FURGE
04 Administrative Asst to President ... Ms. Melanie K. WILLIAMS
08 Head Librarian ... Dr. Stacy A. NOWICKI
102 Dir Foundation/Corporate Relations ... Ms. Ann M. JENKS
19 Director Security/Safety ... Mr. Timothy YOUNG
41 Athletic Director ... Vacant
88 Enrollment Data Specialist ... Ms. Linda WIRGAU
101 Secretary of the Institution/Board ... Ms. Melanie K. WILLIAMS

Kalamazoo Valley Community College (G)

6767 West O Avenue, PO Box 4070,
Kalamazoo MI 49003-4070
County: Kalamazoo FICE Identification: 006949
Unit ID: 170541
Telephone: (269) 488-4400 Carnegie Class: Assoc/MT-VT-Mix Trad/Non
FAX Number: (269) 488-4220 Calendar System: Semester
URL: www.kvcc.edu
Established: 1966 Annual Undergrad Tuition & Fees (In-District): $3,220
Enrollment: 8,836 Coed
Affiliation or Control: Local IRS Status: 501(c)3
Highest Offering: Associate Degree
Accreditation: NH, COARC, DH, EMT, MAC

01 President ... Dr. Marilyn J. SCHLACK
05 EVP Instruct/Student Success Svcs ... Dr. Dennis BERTCH
10 Vice President Finance & Business ... Ms. Louise ANDERSON
84 EVP Enrollment/Campus Operations ... Mr. Michael COLLINS
15 Vice President for Human Resources ... Vacant
13 Vice Pres for Admin Svc/Info Tech ... Mr. Tim WELSH
45 VP for Strategic Business/Cmty Dev ... Mr. Craig JBARA
121 Dean of Student Success ... Ms. Laura COSBY
88 VP for Analytics/Res/Compliance ... Ms. Kathy JOHNSON
19 Director of Public Safety ... Mr. Richard IVES
08 Director of Libraries ... Vacant
07 Dir Admissions/Registration/Records ... Ms. Sarah HUBBELL
09 Dir Planning/Research/Accred/Compl ... Mr. Dan MONDOUX
30 Director Development ... Mr. Steve DOHERTY
37 Director Financial Aid ... Ms. Alisha CEDERBERG
18 Dir Facilities/Construction Mgmt ... Vacant
96 Mgr of Purchasing ... Mr. Paul O'CONNELL
21 Director of Business Services ... Ms. Muriel HICE
66 Director of Nursing ... Ms. Patricia HENNING
28 Director of Diversity ... Mr. Trice BATSON
36 Director Student Placement ... Ms. Tracy QUADA
41 Athletic Director ... Mr. Russ PANICO
88 Director Enrollment Management ... Mr. EJ BAST

Kellogg Community College (A)

450 North Avenue, Battle Creek MI 49017-3397
County: Calhoun FICE Identification: 002276
Unit ID: 170550
Telephone: (269) 965-3931 Carnegie Class: Assoc/MT-VT-High Trad
FAX Number: (269) 962-4290 Calendar System: Semester
URL: www.kellogg.edu
Established: 1956 Annual Undergrad Tuition & Fees (In-District): $3,705
Enrollment: 5,081 Coed
Affiliation or Control: Local IRS Status: 501(c)3
Highest Offering: Associate Degree
Accreditation: NH, DH, EMT, PTAA, RAD

01 President .... Mr. Mark P. O'CONNELL
05 Vice President Instruction .... Mr. Kevin RABINEAU
11 Vice Pres Administration/Finance .... Vacant
32 Vice Pres Student & Community Svcs .... Dr. Kay KECK
10 Chief Financial Officer .... Mr. Richard SCOTT
57 Chair Arts & Communication Dept .... Ms. Barbara SUDEIKIS
81 Chair Math & Science Dept .... Ms. Carole DAVIS
49 Dean Arts and Sciences .... Ms. Tonya FORBES
102 Executive Director KCC Foundation .... Ms. Teresa DURHAM
96 Director Purchasing .... Ms. Angela CLEVELAND
06 Registrar .... Ms. Colleen WRIGHT
08 Director Library Services .... Ms. Michele REID
41 Director Athletics & PE .... Mr. Tom SHAW
12 Director of Grahl Center .... Ms. Roberta GAGNON
12 Director of Fehsenfeld Center .... Mr. Colin MCCALEB
15 Director Human Resources .... Ms. Ali ROBERTSON
18 Dir Inst Facilities/Public Safety .... Vacant
51 Director Lifelong Learning .... Ms. Mary GREEN
09 Director Inst Compliance Reporting .... Ms. Naomi LIVENGOOD
21 Director of Finance .... Ms. Tracy BEATTY
12 Director Regional Mfg Tech Center .... Mr. Tom LONGMAN
35 Dean Student & Community Services .... Ms. Terah ZAREMBA
26 Dir Public Information & Marketing .... Mr. Eric GREENE
07 Director of Admissions .... Ms. Meredith STRAVERS
40 Bookstore Manager .... Ms. Catherine JAMES
28 Director of Diversity .... Dr. Jorge ZEBALLOS
04 Executive Asst to President .... Ms. Rebecca GALLIMORE
103 Dean Workforce Development .... Dr. Jan KARAZIM
36 Director Career & Emp Services .... Mr. Patrick CASEY
37 Director Financial Aid .... Ms. Nikki JEWELL
121 Manager Academic Advising .... Ms. Donna MALASKI

Kendall College of Art & Design of Ferris State University (B)

17 Fountain Street, NW, Grand Rapids MI 49503
Telephone: (800) 676-2787 Identification: 770273
Accreditation: &NH, ART, CIDA

Kettering University (C)

1700 University Avenue, Flint MI 48504-6214
County: Genesee FICE Identification: 002262
Unit ID: 169983
Telephone: (810) 762-9500 Carnegie Class: Masters/M
FAX Number: (810) 762-9837 Calendar System: Semester
URL: www.kettering.edu
Established: 1919 Annual Undergrad Tuition & Fees: $39,790
Enrollment: 2,252 Coed
Affiliation or Control: Independent Non-Profit IRS Status: 501(c)3
Highest Offering: Master's
Accreditation: NH, ACBSP, CS, ENG, ENGR

01 President .... Dr. Robert K. MCMAHAN
04 Executive Assistant to President .... Ms. Evelyn YAEGER
04 Assistant to President .... Ms. Megan HANSON
05 Provost & VP Academic Affairs .... Dr. James ZHANG
10 VP Administration & Finance .... Mr. Tom AYERS
84 VP Enrollment Services .... Mr. Kip DARCY
32 VP Student Life & Dean of Students .... Ms. Betsy E. HOMSHER
111 VP Univ Advancement/Ext Relations .... Ms. Susan DAVIES
13 VP Instruct/Admin & Info Technology .... Ms. Viola SPRAGUE
106 VP Kettering Global .... Ms. Christine WALLACE
20 Associate Provost .... Dr. Kathryn SVINARICH
15 Director Human Resources .... Ms. Beth EWALD
102 Dir of Philanthropy Corp/Found .... Mr. Thomas SOMMER
29 Dir of Alumni Engagement .... Mr. Steven BANDURSKI
44 Dir of Philanthropy Indiv Giving .... Ms. Caroline ETHINGTON
19 Director of Campus Safety .... Mr. Paul CRANE
37 Director Student Financial Aid .... Ms. Diane K. KIMES
21 Controller .... Ms. Beth A. COVERS
09 Director Institution Effectiveness .... Dr. Mark WOODS
58 Director Graduate Programs .... Mr. Tom CREECH
18 Director Physical Plant .... Mr. Joseph ASPERGER
08 Director Library Services .... Dr. Charles D. HANSON
07 Director of Admissions .... Ms. Susan SLOAN
41 Director Athletics/Rec Service .... Mr. Michael L. SCHAAL
93 Director Minority Student Affairs .... Mr. L.B MCCUNE
104 Director International Office .... Dr. Basem ALZAHABI
109 Director Auxiliary Services .... Ms. Nadine L. THOR
26 Director of Marketing .... Ms. Julie A. ULSETH
06 Registrar .... Ms. Judi LANGOLF
23 Director Wellness Center .... Ms. Cristina REED
39 Director Residence Life .... Ms. Katherine BOSIO
78 Director Coop Educ & Career Svcs .... Ms. Venetia PETTEWAY
88 MI SBTDC Regional Director .... Ms. Marsha J. LYTTLE
96 Purchasing Manager .... Ms. Kathleen A. REMENDER
14 Director of IT Operations .... Mr. Daniel GARCIA
25 Contract/Grant Specialist .... Ms. Jodi L. DORR
105 Webmaster .... Ms. Donna WICKS
88 Dir Enrollment Events/Visitor Rels .... Ms. Sheila ADAMS COWES
88 Director Special Events .... Ms. Diane ALDERSON
121 Director Academic Success Center .... Dr. Natalie CANDELA
50 Dean Business .... Mr. Michael SMITH
54 Dean Engineering .... Mr. Craig HOFF
88 Dean Liberal Studies .... Ms. Laura VOSEJPKA

Keweenaw Bay Ojibwa Community College (D)

111 Beartown Rd, PO Box 519, Baraga MI 49908
County: Baraga FICE Identification: 041647
Unit ID: 461315
Telephone: (906) 353-4640 Carnegie Class: Tribal
FAX Number: (906) 353-8107 Calendar System: Semester
URL: www.kbocc.edu
Established: 1975 Annual Undergrad Tuition & Fees (In-District): $2,900
Enrollment: 102 Coed
Affiliation or Control: Local IRS Status: 501(c)3
Highest Offering: Associate Degree
Accreditation: NH

01 President .... Ms. Debra J. PARRISH
10 Vice Pres of Operations .... Ms. Cherie DAKOTA
05 Dean of Instruction .... Dr. Lynn AHO
07 Admissions Officer .... Mr. Patrick RACETTE
32 Student Services Assistant .... Ms. Betti SZAROLETTA
37 Director Financial Aid .... Ms. Liz JULIO

Kirtland Community College (E)

10775 N Saint Helen Road, Roscommon MI 48653-9721
County: Roscommon FICE Identification: 007171
Unit ID: 170587
Telephone: (989) 275-5000 Carnegie Class: Assoc/MT-VT-High Trad
FAX Number: (989) 275-6706 Calendar System: Semester
URL: www.kirtland.edu
Established: 1966 Annual Undergrad Tuition & Fees (In-District): $3,900
Enrollment: 1,628 Coed
Affiliation or Control: Local IRS Status: 501(c)3
Highest Offering: Associate Degree
Accreditation: NH, CVT

01 President .... Dr. Thomas QUINN
05 Vice Pres of Instructional Services .... Dr. Julie LAVENDER
32 Vice Pres of Student Svcs/Registrar .... Ms. Michelle VYSKOCIL
10 Vice Pres of Business Services .... Mr. Jason BROGE
13 Chief Info Ofcr/Title III Proj Dir .... Mr. Matt BIERMANN
97 Dean of General Education/Transfer .... Vacant
75 Dean of Occupational Programs .... Ms. Laura PERCIVAL
08 Director of Library & Tutoring Svcs .... Ms. Deb SHUMAKER
37 Director of Financial Aid .... Ms. Christin BATES
18 Director of Facilities .... Mr. Ron SHARPE
15 Dir of Human Resources/Talent Dev .... Mr. Nathan SUTTON
09 Director of Institutional Research .... Mr. Nick BAKER
102 Foundation Director .... Ms. Jennifer PAGE
26 Director of Public Information .... Ms. Sarah HOLECHECK
07 Admissions Coordinator .... Mr. Ryan MADDIS

Kuyper College (F)

3333 East Beltline Avenue, NE,
Grand Rapids MI 49525-9749
County: Kent FICE Identification: 002311
Unit ID: 171881
Telephone: (616) 222-3000 Carnegie Class: Bac-Diverse
FAX Number: (616) 988-3608 Calendar System: Semester
URL: www.kuyper.edu
Established: 1939 Annual Undergrad Tuition & Fees: $20,342
Enrollment: 260 Coed
Affiliation or Control: Independent Non-Profit IRS Status: 501(c)3
Highest Offering: Baccalaureate
Accreditation: NH, BI, SW

01 President .... Dr. Patricia HARRIS
05 Provost .... Vacant
06 Registrar .... Mr. Kyle WIGBOLDY
10 Controller/CFO .... Ms. Christine MULKA
30 Vice Pres College Advancement .... Mr. Ken CAPISCIOLTO
07 Director of Admissions .... Mr. Kevin GILLIAM
37 Financial Aid Director .... Ms. Agnes M. RUSSELL
44 Director Annual/Planned Giving .... Ms. Lisa RUSTICUS
04 Assistant to the President .... Ms. Alyssa BLOM
08 Librarian .... Ms. Dianne V. ZANDBERGEN
32 Director of Student Life .... Mr. Curt ESSENBURG
18 Director of Physical Plant .... Mr. Tim CHUPP
29 Director of Alumni/Public Relations .... Ms. Lisa RUSTICUS
15 Director Personnel Services .... Ms. Mary CARLSON
13 Director Computing/Info Management .... Mr. Keith TORNO
49 Arts and Sciences .... Mr. Andrew ZWART
70 Social Work .... Mr. Greg SCOTT
73 Theology .... Dr. Branson PARLER
85 International Student Services .... Ms. Jana POSPMA
50 Director of Business Leadership .... Mr. Marc ANDREAS
19 Director Security/Safety .... Mr. Curt ESSENBURG

Lake Michigan College (G)

2755 E Napier, Benton Harbor MI 49022-1899
County: Berrien FICE Identification: 002277
Unit ID: 170620
Telephone: (269) 927-1000 Carnegie Class: Bac/Assoc-Assoc Dom
FAX Number: N/A Calendar System: Semester
URL: www.lakemichigancollege.edu
Established: 1946 Annual Undergrad Tuition & Fees (In-District): $4,230
Enrollment: 4,172 Coed
Affiliation or Control: Local IRS Status: 501(c)3
Highest Offering: Baccalaureate
Accreditation: NH, ADNUR, DA, DMS, MAC, RAD

01 President .... Dr. Trevor A. KUBATZKE
11 VP Administrative Services .... Ms. Anne C. ERDMAN
111 VP Institutional Advance/Planning .... Vacant
10 Chief Financial Officer .... Ms. Kelli HAHN
04 Exec Assistant to the President .... Ms. Rebecca STEFFEN
05 VP Academics .... Dr. Leslie KELLOGG
103 Dean Career Education Workforce .... Dr. Ken FLOWERS
49 Dean Arts & Sciences .... Dr. Gary ROBERTS
76 Dean Health Sciences .... Ms. Marla CLARK
84 VP of Enrollment & Community Engage .... Mr. Doug SCHAFFER
56 VP Regional Campuses .... Ms. Barbara CRAIG
88 Manager Mainstage Services .... Mr. Mike NADOLSKI
18 Director Facilities Management .... Ms. Sara VANDERVEEN
13 Exec Dir Informational Technology .... Mr. Randall MELTON
26 Director Marketing & Communications .... Ms. Candice ELDERS
06 Registrar .... Ms. Sara SKINNER
102 President College Foundation .... Mr. Mike WELCH
96 Purchasing Manager .... Mr. Nathan MAIN
90 Director Teaching/Learning Center .... Mr. Mark KELLY
08 Head Librarian .... Ms. Diane BAKER
09 Director of Institutional Research .... Mr. John HULSEBUS
19 Director Security/Safety .... Mr. Steve SILCOX
39 Director Student Housing .... Mr. Matt KREVDA
41 Athletic Director .... Mr. Melissa GRAU
37 Director Financial Aid .... Ms. Kemmoree DUNCOMBE

Lake Michigan College Bertrand Crossing (H)

1905 Foundation Drive, Niles MI 49120
Telephone: (269) 695-1391 Identification: 770277
Accreditation: &NH

Lake Michigan College South Haven (I)

125 Veterans Boulevard, South Haven MI 49090
Telephone: (269) 639-8442 Identification: 770278
Accreditation: &NH

Lake Superior State University (J)

650 W Easterday Avenue,
Sault Sainte Marie MI 49783-1699
County: Chippewa FICE Identification: 002293
Unit ID: 170639
Telephone: (906) 632-6841 Carnegie Class: Bac-Diverse
FAX Number: (906) 635-2111 Calendar System: Semester
URL: www.lssu.edu
Established: 1946 Annual Undergrad Tuition & Fees (In-State): $11,019
Enrollment: 2,249 Coed
Affiliation or Control: State IRS Status: 501(c)3
Highest Offering: Baccalaureate
Accreditation: NH, ACBSP, CAATE, CAEPT, EMT, ENG, ENGT, IFSAC, NURSE

01 President .... Dr. Peter T. MITCHELL
05 Int Provost/VP Academic Affairs .... Dr. David FINLEY
32 Vice Pres Student Affs/Enroll Svcs .... Vacant
10 Int Vice President Finance .... Mr. Morrie WALWORTH
108 Assoc Provost Assess/Grad/Educ .... Dr. David MYTON
49 Dean ALSS .... Dr. Donna FIEBELKORN
81 Dean Natural & Math Sciences .... Dr. Barbara KELLER
66 Interim Dean Nursing .... Mr. Ronald HUTCHINS
50 Dean Business & Engineering .... Dr. David FINLEY
53 Asst Dean Education .... Dr. Donna FIEBELKORN
13 Director IT/Network Admin .... Mr. Scott OLSON
18 Director Physical Plant .... Mr. Steve GREGORY
06 Registrar .... Ms. Nancy NEVE
07 Director of Admissions .... Ms. Kellie GREENER
15 Int Director of Human Resources .... Ms. Wendy BEACH
36 Director of Career Services .... Vacant
37 Director of Financial Aid .... Ms. Deborah FAUST
38 Director of Counseling .... Ms. Kristin LARSON
39 Diversity Ofcr/Asst Dir Housing .... Mr. Derric KNIGHT
26 Director of Public Affairs .... Vacant
29 Director Alumni Relations .... Ms. Susan FITZPATRICK
102 Director of Foundation .... Mr. Tom COATES
96 Director of Purchasing .... Ms. Colleen RYE
23 Director Health Services .... Ms. Karen STOREY
28 Dir Native American Ctr/Diversity .... Ms. Stephanie SABATINE
41 Director of Athletics .... Dr. David PAITSON
35 Asst Director Student Life .... Ms. Sharmay WOOD
40 Bookstore Manager .... Ms. Amber MCLEAN
09 Institutional Research Analyst .... Mr. Pritish PONAKA

Lansing Community College (K)

610 N Capitol Avenue, Lansing MI 48933
County: Ingham FICE Identification: 002278
Unit ID: 170657
Telephone: (517) 483-1200 Carnegie Class: Assoc/MT-VT-Mix Trad/Non
FAX Number: (517) 483-1845 Calendar System: Semester
URL: www.lcc.edu
Established: 1957 Annual Undergrad Tuition & Fees (In-District): $3,350
Enrollment: 14,851 Coed
Affiliation or Control: Local IRS Status: 501(c)3

Highest Offering: Associate Degree
Accreditation: NH, ADNUR, COMTA, DH, DMS, EMT, IFSAC, RAD, SURGT

01 President ... Dr. Brent KNIGHT
05 Provost ... Dr. Richard PRYSTOWSKY
10 Sr VP Finance/Admin & Advancement ... Dr. Lisa WEBB SHARPE
21 Chief Financial Officer ... Mr. Don WILSKE
13 Chief Information Officer ... Mr. Kevin BUBB
11 Exec Dir Administrative Svcs ... Ms. Tim MARTZ
20 Associate VP Academic Affairs ... Dr. Vicki DEKETELAERE
30 Assoc VP External Affs/Development ... Ms. Toni GLASSCOE
88 Dean Health & Human Services ... Ms. Margie CLARK
103 Dean Community Educ/Workforce Dev ... Mr. Bo GARCIA
49 Dean Arts & Sciences ... Ms. Elaine POGONCHEFF
32 Dean Student Affairs ... Dr. Tanya MCFADDEN
72 Dean Technical Careers ... Mr. Mark COSGROVE
15 Exec Director Human Resources ... Ms. Ann KRONEMAN
28 Chief Diversity Officer ... Dr. Paul HERNANDEZ
26 Director Public Affairs ... Ms. Devon BRADLEY
77 Director Center for Data Science ... Mr. Matt FALL

Lawrence Technological University (A)

21000 W Ten Mile Road, Southfield MI 48075-1058
County: Oakland FICE Identification: 002279
Unit ID: 170675
Telephone: (248) 204-4000 Carnegie Class: Masters/L
FAX Number: (248) 204-3727 Calendar System: Semester
URL: www.ltu.edu
Established: 1932 Annual Undergrad Tuition & Fees: $31,140
Enrollment: 3,516 Coed
Affiliation or Control: Independent Non-Profit IRS Status: 501(c)3
Highest Offering: Doctorate
Accreditation: NH, ACBSP, ART, CIDA, ENG, IACBE

01 President and CEO ... Dr. Virinder K. MOUDGIL
04 Exec Assistant to the President ... Ms. Karen MCARDLE
05 Provost ... Dr. Maria J. VAZ
88 Exec Dir Marburger STEM Center ... Dr. Sibrina Nichelle COLLINS
10 Vice Pres Finance/Admin ... Ms. Linda L. HEIGHT
111 Vice Pres University Advancement ... Ms. Kristen R. DEVRIES
26 Vice Pres Mktg & Public Affairs ... Mr. Bruce J. ANNETT, JR.
20 Assistant Provost ... Mr. Jim JOLLY
84 Asst Provost Enrollment Management ... Ms. Lisa R. KUJAWA
48 Dean of Architecture & Design ... Mr. Karl DAUBMANN
49 Dean of Arts & Sciences ... Dr. Hsiao-Ping H. MOORE
54 Dean of Engineering ... Dr. Nabil F. GRACE
50 Dean of Management ... Dr. Bahman MIRSHAB
32 Dean of Students & Diversity Dir ... Mr. Kevin FINN
13 Chief Information Officer/IT Svcs ... Mr. Tim CHAVIS
07 Director of Admissions ... Ms. Jane T. ROHRBACK
06 University Registrar ... Ms. Noreen FERGUSON
08 Director Library ... Mr. Gary R. COCOZZOLI
18 Director of Campus Facilities ... Mr. Carey G. VALENTINE
14 Director Help Desk/Services ... Ms. Charlene RAMOS
37 Director of Financial Aid ... Ms. Susie POLI-SMITH
41 Dir of Rec/Athletics & Wellness ... Mr. Scott TRUDEAU
36 Director of Career Services ... Ms. Peg PIERCE
35 Assistant Dean of Students ... Ms. Cyndi SPOTTS
24 Director Audio Visual Media Svcs ... Mr. Walter G. BIZON
39 Director of Residence Life ... Ms. Kimberly JERDINE
86 Exec Dir Corp & Comm Partnerships ... Mr. Mark J. BRUCKI
102 Dir of Corp & Foundations Relations ... Mr. Howard DAVIS
112 Director of Major Gifts ... Ms. Julie VULAJ
15 Exec Director of Human Resources ... Ms. Deshawn JOHNSON
40 Manager Campus Bookstore ... Ms. Adria RAHN
109 Director of Dining Services ... Ms. Nancy THOMAS
27 Dir of Univ Comm & Academic Editor .. Ms. Anne M G. ADAMUS
88 Managing Editor Univ News Bureau ... Mr. Matt ROUSH
19 Director of Campus Safety ... Mr. Steven J. BOGDALEK
44 Director of Annual Giving ... Ms. Lauren N. SEEBOLD
31 Exec Dir of Outreach & Spec Events ... Ms. Robin LECLERC
110 Coordinator of Advancement Services ... Ms. Brande' OLIVER
88 University Architect ... Mr. Joseph C. VERYSER
121 Dir of Academic Achievement Center ... Dr. Gladys M. AVILES
09 Dir of Inst Research/Academic Plng ... Ms. Noreen FERGUSON
96 Purchasing Supervisor ... Ms. Michelle BUTKOVICH
105 Director of Web Services ... Mr. Christian FORREST
106 eLearning Architect & Pgm Producer ... Dr. Lynn MILLER-WIETECHA
108 Director Institutional Assessment ... Mr. Larry CHESTNUTT

Macomb Community College (B)

14500 Twelve Mile Road, Warren MI 48088-9896
County: Macomb FICE Identification: 008906
Unit ID: 170790
Telephone: (586) 445-7241 Carnegie Class: Assoc/MT-VT-High Non
FAX Number: (586) 445-7886 Calendar System: Semester
URL: www.macomb.edu
Established: 1954 Annual Undergrad Tuition & Fees (In-District): $3,282
Enrollment: 22,182 Coed
Affiliation or Control: Local IRS Status: 501(c)3
Highest Offering: Associate Degree
Accreditation: NH, ACFEI, ADNUR, CAHIIM, COARC, EMT, IFSAC, MAC, OTA, PTAA, SURGT

01 President ... Dr. James SAWYER
05 VP/Provost Learning Unit ... Vacant
10 Vice President for Business ... Ms. Elizabeth ARGIRI
15 Vice President for Human Resources ... Ms. Denise WILLIAMS
111 VP College Adv/Community Relations ... Dr. Casandra ULBRICH
26 Dean University Relations ... Mr. Kevin CHANDLER
32 Vice President for Student Services . Ms. Jill M. THOMAS-LITTLE
49 Dean Arts & Sciences ... Dr. Marie PRITCHETT
76 Dean Health/Public Services ... Ms. Charlene MCPEAK
54 Dean Engineering & Adv Tech ... Mr. Joseph PETROSKY
50 Dean Business & Info Technology ... Mr. David CORBA
35 Dean of Student Success ... Dr. Susan BOYD
45 Exec Director Planning & Research ... Ms. Gerri Lynn PAVONE
115 Director Finance & Investments ... Vacant
88 Director Public Service Institute ... Mr. John CALABRESE
27 Director Marketing & Recruitment ... Ms. Audrey TAKACS
09 Director Institutional Research ... Ms. Deirdre SYMS
88 Director Special Research Projects ... Mr. Randall HICKMAN
06 Registrar/Dir Enrollment Services ... Ms. Carrie JEFFERS
102 Director Macomb College Foundation ... Ms. Dawn MAGRETTA
38 Dir Counseling & Academic Advising ... Ms. Michelle KOSS
96 Purchasing Administrator ... Mr. Dennis COSTELLO
41 Manager Athletics/Sports Clubs ... Mr. Randall NELSON
18 Director Facilities Management ... Mr. Stevan ALTON
37 Director of Financial Aid ... Mr. Douglas LEVY
36 Director Career Employment Services ... Mr. Robert PENKALA
51 Dir Workforce Continuing Education ... Ms. Elise JOHNSON
13 CIO/Exec Dir Communications & IT ... Mr. Michael ZIMMERMAN
08 Dean Libraries/Learning Resources ... Mr. Michael BALSAMO
43 General Counsel/Exec Dir Col Police ... Mr. Hunter WENDT

Madonna University (C)

36600 Schoolcraft Road, Livonia MI 48150-1176
County: Wayne FICE Identification: 002282
Unit ID: 170806
Telephone: (734) 432-5300 Carnegie Class: Masters/L
FAX Number: (734) 432-5333 Calendar System: Semester
URL: www.madonna.edu
Established: 1937 Annual Undergrad Tuition & Fees: $19,500
Enrollment: 3,704 Coed
Affiliation or Control: Roman Catholic IRS Status: 501(c)3
Highest Offering: Doctorate
Accreditation: NH, ACBSP, CAEP, DIETD, DMS, FEPAC, NURSE, SW

01 President ... Dr. Michael GRANDILLO
05 Provost and VP for Academic Admin ... Dr. Lewis WALKER
10 Vice Pres for Finance/Operations ... Mr. David BOYD
32 Vice President for Student Affairs ... Dr. Connie TINGSON-GATUZ
84 VP Enrollmnt Mgt & Univ Advancement ... Dr. Cameron CRUICKSHANK
42 Director of Campus Ministry ... Mr. Patrick WATERS
06 Registrar ... Ms. Dina DUBUIS
07 Director of Admissions ... Mr. Mark SHROEDER
28 Director of BLG Program ... Mr. Brett JORDAN
08 Librarian ... Mr. Michael CUMMINGS
37 Director of Financial Aid ... Mr. Phillip HANG
13 Chief Info Technology Officer ... Mr. John MONTGOMERY
15 Director of Human Resources ... Ms. Tracey DURDEN
36 Director of Career Services ... Ms. Christine BRANT
88 Director of Special Events ... Ms. Katie ALEXANDER
19 Director Public Safety ... Ms. Nan GELMAN
41 Director of Athletics ... Mr. Scott KENNELL
40 Bookstore Manager ... Ms. Debbie MITCHELL
39 Director Residence Hall ... Ms. Sarah GOMBAR
24 Interim Dir Broadcast & Cinema ... Ms. Susan BOYD
23 Director Instruction Center ... Ms. Susan GREEN
09 Director of Institutional Research ... Dr. Phillip OLLA
18 Chief Facilities/Physical Plant ... Ms. Jody BATWAY
29 Director Alumni and Planned Giving ... Mr. Daniel CENTER
26 Director of Marketing ... Ms. Karen SANBORN
79 Int Dean/Chair Arts & Humanities ... Dr. Kevin EYSTER
50 Interim Dean School of Business ... Dr. Deborah DUNN
58 Dean Graduate Studies ... Dr. Deborah DUNN
66 Interim Co-Dean Nursing & Health ... Dr. Nancy O'CONNOR
66 Interim Co-Dean Nursing & Health ... Dr. Catherine GRIFFIN
83 Dean Natural & Social Sciences ... Dr. Karen ROSS
53 Dean Education ... Dr. Karen OBSNIUK
101 Secretary Board of Trustees ... Sr. Margaret KIJEK
30 Director of Development ... Mr. John DOYLE
104 Asst VP Academic Plan/Study Abroad ... Mr. John MAGEE
105 Director Web Services ... Ms. Sheryl HERRON
106 Dir Online Education/E-learning ... Dr. Elena QURESHI
04 Executive Asst to President ... Ms. Cheryll A. JOHNSON
100 Chief of Staff ... Mr. Neil NEIDHARDT

Marygrove College (D)

8425 W McNichols Road, Detroit MI 48221-2599
County: Wayne FICE Identification: 002284
Unit ID: 170842
Telephone: (313) 927-1200 Carnegie Class: Masters/L
FAX Number: (313) 927-1345 Calendar System: Semester
URL: www.marygrove.edu
Established: 1905 Annual Undergrad Tuition & Fees: $22,064
Enrollment: 1,380 Coed
Affiliation or Control: Roman Catholic IRS Status: 501(c)3
Highest Offering: Master's
Accreditation: NH, CAEPT, SW

01 President ... Dr. Elizabeth A. BURNS
111 Int VP Institutional Advancement ... Mr. Dennis HOWIE
04 Exec Assistant to the President ... Ms. Maryann S. KUMMER
05 Provost ... Dr. Sally WELCH
84 Vice President for Enrollment Mgmt ... Dr. Denise MALLETT
10 Interim VP Finance/Admin & CFO ... Mr. James L. MURDOCK
06 Registrar ... Ms. Gladys SMITH
07 Director of Admissions ... Ms. Sharon M. TOLES
08 Interim Director of the Library ... Dr. Mary KICKHAM-SAMY
09 Director of Institutional Research ... Vacant
11 Director of Administrative Services ... Mr. Horace DANDRIDGE
15 Director of Human Resources ... Ms. Tamiko OGBURN
19 Lieutenant Campus Safety ... Mr. Roosevelt LAWRENCE, JR.
20 Dean of the Faculty ... Dr. Frank D. RASHID
21 Controller ... Mr. David OTIS
29 Dir of Alumni Relations/Annual Giv ... Ms. Janice M. MACHUSAK
32 Dean of Students ... Dr. Reginald MOTLEY
36 Director of Career Services ... Vacant
37 Director Scholarships & Fin Aid ... Ms. Kimberly L. GOODEN
38 Director of Counseling ... Dr. Carolyn ROBERTS
41 Athletic Director ... Mr. Stephen BLOOMFIELD
42 Director of Mission Integration ... Mr. Jesse COX
26 Mgr of Marketing and Communications ... Ms. Renee AHEE
106 Director Online Education ... Dr. Mitali CHAUDHERY
100 Chief of Staff ... Ms. Jolene KNAPP
28 Director of Diversity ... Ms. Tamiko OGBURN

MIAT College of Technology (E)

2955 South Haggerty Road, Canton MI 48188
County: Wayne FICE Identification: 020603
Unit ID: 169655
Telephone: (734) 423-2139 Carnegie Class: Spec 2-yr-Tech
FAX Number: (734) 858-5000 Calendar System: Other
URL: www.miat.edu
Established: Annual Undergrad Tuition & Fees: $16,205
Enrollment: 541 Coed
Affiliation or Control: Proprietary IRS Status: Proprietary
Highest Offering: Associate Degree
Accreditation: ACCSC

01 Campus President ... Mr. Kevin BURCHETT

Michigan School of Professional Psychology (F)

26811 Orchard Lake Road,
Farmington Hills MI 48334-4512
County: Oakland FICE Identification: 021989
Unit ID: 169220
Telephone: (248) 476-1122 Carnegie Class: Spec-4-yr-Other Health
FAX Number: (248) 476-1125 Calendar System: Semester
URL: www.mispp.edu
Established: 1981 Annual Graduate Tuition & Fees: N/A
Enrollment: 141 Coed
Affiliation or Control: Independent Non-Profit IRS Status: 501(c)3
Highest Offering: Doctorate; No Undergraduates
Accreditation: NH, CLPSY

01 President/Chief Executive Officer ... Dr. Diane BLAU
03 Vice President/Chief Operating Ofcr ... Ms. Diane ZALAPI
05 Program Director/Chief Academic Ofc ... Dr. Fran BROWN
13 Director of Info Tech & Bldg Svcs ... Mr. Jeffrey CROSS
08 Head Academic Librarian ... Ms. Michelle WHEELER
06 Registrar ... Ms. Amanda MING
07 Admissions/Recruitment Coordinator ... Ms. Carrie HAUSER
11 Dir of Administrative Operations ... Ms. Laura LANE
23 Director of Clinical Training ... Dr. Heidi MARTIN

Michigan State University (G)

426 Auditorium Road, East Lansing MI 48824-1046
County: Ingham FICE Identification: 002290
Unit ID: 171100
Telephone: (517) 355-1855 Carnegie Class: DU-Highest
FAX Number: N/A Calendar System: Semester
URL: www.msu.edu
Established: 1855 Annual Undergrad Tuition & Fees (In-State): $14,062
Enrollment: 50,538 Coed
Affiliation or Control: State IRS Status: 501(c)3
Highest Offering: Doctorate
Accreditation: NH, ANEST, CAATE, CACREP, CAEPT, CEA, CIDA, CLPSY, CONST, CS, DIETD, DIETI, ENG, FEPAC, IPSY, JOUR, LAW, LSAR, MED, MFCD, MT, MUS, NURSE, OSTEO, PLNG, SCPSY, SP, SW, VET

01 President ... Dr. Lou Anna K. SIMON
05 Provost/Exec VP Academic Affairs ... Dr. June P. YOUATT
11 Exec Vice Pres for Admin Services ... Dr. Satish S. UDPA
101 Vice President/Secretary to Board ... Mr. William R. BEEKMAN
46 Vice President Research & Grad Stds ... Dr. Stephen HSU
32 VP Student Affairs & Svcs ... Dr. Denise B. MAYBANK
86 Vice President Governmental Affairs ... Mr. Mark A. BURNHAM
10 VP Finance Operations/Treasurer ... Mr. Mark HAAS
111 Vice Pres Univ Advancement ... Mr. Robert GROVES
43 VP Legal Affairs & General Counsel ... Mr. Robert A. NOTO
18 Assc VP Infrastructure Plng & Facil ... Mr. Dan BOLLMAN
109 Vice President Auxiliary Services ... Mr. Vennie GORE
26 VP Communication & Brand Strategy ... Ms. Heather C. SWAIN
22 Dir Incl/Intrcult Init/Sr Adv P Dvr ... Ms. Paulette GRANBERRY-RUSSELL
88 Assoc VP Research/Graduate Studies ... Dr. Paul M. HUNT
58 Assoc Prov and Dean Grad School ... Dr. Judith STODDART
20 Assoc Prov & Dean Ungrad Educ ... Dr. Sekhar CHIVUKULA
88 Assoc Prov Univ Outreach/Engagement ... Dr. Hiram E. FITZGERALD
88 Associate Provost Academic Svcs ... Dr. John D. GABOURY
16 Assoc Prov/VP Academic Human Res ... Mr. Theodore H. CURRY, II

45 Asst VP & Director of Plng/Budgets ... Mr. David S. BYELICH
15 Asst Vice Pres for Human Resources ... Ms. Sharon BUTLER
13 Assoc VP of Information and Tech ... Mr. Robert MCCURDY
88 Asst VP Ofc of Sponsored Programs ... Dr. Twila REIGHLEY
21 Controller ... Mr. Greg DEPPONG
07 Director of Admissions ... Mr. James W. COTTER
29 Assoc VP for Alumni Relations ... Mr. W. Scott WESTERMAN, III
25 Director Contract & Grant Admin ... Mr. Daniel T. EVON
36 Assoc Dir Career Services/Placement ... Dr. Phil GARDNER
38 Director Counseling Center ... Dr. Scott BECKER
88 Dir MI AgBioResearch ... Dr. Doug BUHLER
56 Assoc Dir MSU Extension ... Dr. Jeff DWYER
37 Director of Financial Aid ... Mr. Richard SHIPMAN
06 Registrar ... Vacant
85 Director Intl Students/Scholars ... Mr. James DORSETT
23 Director MSU Student Health Ctr ... Dr. Glynda M. MOORER
92 Dean Honors College ... Dr. Cynthia JACKSON-ELMOORE
41 Director Intercollegiate Athletics ... Mr. Mark J. HOLLIS
08 Director of Libraries ... Mr. Clifford H. HAKA
88 Dir Natl Supercond Cyclotron Lab ... Dr. Brad SHERRILL
19 Police Chf/Dir Police & Pub Safety ... Mr. James H. DUNLAP
88 Director Undergraduate Univ Div ... Dr. R. Sekhar CHIVUKULA
47 Dean Col Ag & Nat Resources ... Dr. Ronald HENDRICK
79 Dean College Arts & Letters ... Dr. Christopher P. LONG
79 Dean Res Col Arts/Humanities ... Dr. Stephen L. ESQUITH
50 Dean Eli Broad Col of Business ... Dr. Sanjay GUPTA
60 Dean Col Comm/Arts & Sci ... Dr. Prabu DAVID
53 Dean College of Education ... Dr. Robert FLODEN
54 Dean College of Engineering ... Dr. Leo KEMPEL
63 Dean College Human Medicine ... Dr. Norman BEAUCHAMP
82 Dean James Madison College ... Dr. Sherman W. GARNETT
61 Dean College of Law ... Mr. Lawrence PONOROFF
81 Dean Lyman Briggs College ... Dr. Elizabeth H. SIMMONS
64 Dean College of Music ... Mr. James FORGER
81 Dean College Natural Science ... Dr. R. James KIRKPATRICK
66 Dean College of Nursing ... Dr. Randolph RASCH
63 Dean College Osteopathic Medicine ... Dr. William D. STRAMPEL
83 Dean College of Social Sci ... Dr. Rachel CROSEN
74 Dean College Veterinary Medicine ... Dr. John C. BAKER
82 Dean Intl Studies & Programs ... Dr. Steven D. HANSON
04 Administrative Asst to President ... Ms. Lori BLANKENSHIP
100 Chief of Staff ... Ms. Jane MILLER

Michigan Technological University (A)

1400 Townsend Drive, Houghton MI 49931-1295
County: Houghton — FICE Identification: 002292
Unit ID: 171128
Telephone: (906) 487-1885 — Carnegie Class: DU-Higher
FAX Number: (906) 487-2935 — Calendar System: Semester
URL: www.mtu.edu
Established: 1885 — Annual Undergrad Tuition & Fees (In-State): $14,634
Enrollment: 7,218 — Coed
Affiliation or Control: State — IRS Status: 501(c)3
Highest Offering: Doctorate
Accreditation: NH, CAEPT, CEA, CONST, CS, ENG, ENGT

01 President ... Dr. Glenn D. MROZ
05 Provost/Vice Pres Academic Affairs ... Dr. Jacqueline E. HUNTOON
86 Vice Pres Governmental Relations ... Vacant
11 Vice President for Administration ... Ms. Ellen S. HORSCH
46 Vice President for Research ... Dr. David D. REED
32 VP for Student Affairs/Advancement ... Dr. Les P. COOK
84 Assc VP Enrollment & Univ Relations ... Dr. John B. LEHMAN
35 Dean of Students ... Dr. Bonnie B. GORMAN
10 Vice President for Finance ... Ms. Julie SEPPALA
26 Director Marketing/Communications ... Mr. Ian REPP
08 Director of the Library ... Ms. Ellen MARKS
09 Institutional Analysis ... Mr. Richard ELENICH
29 Exec Director Alumni Relations ... Ms. Brenda RUDIGER
06 Registrar ... Ms. Theresa K. JACQUES
07 Director Undergraduate Recruitment ... Ms. Allison A. CARTER
15 Director Human Resources ... Ms. Renee HILLER
37 Director of Financial Aid ... Mr. Joe J. COOPER
36 Director University Career Center ... Mr. Steve PATCHIN
18 Dir Facilities/Physical Plant ... Ms. Kerri SLEEMAN
21 Director Planning & Budgeting ... Ms. Deborah L. SHELDEN
38 Director Counseling Services ... Mr. Donald S. WILLIAMS
19 Director Public Safety ... Mr. Brian J. CADWELL
22 Director Affirmative Programs ... Dr. Jill HODGES
96 Director of Purchasing ... Mr. Raymond E. LASANEN
58 Dean Graduate School ... Dr. Pushpalatha MURTHY
50 Dean Business & Economics ... Dr. Dean L. JOHNSON
54 Dean of Engineering ... Dr. Wayne PENNINGTON
65 Dean of Forestry ... Dr. Terry SHARIK
49 Dean Sciences/Arts ... Dr. Bruce E. SEELY
72 Dean of Technology ... Dr. James FRENDEWEY, JR.
13 Chief Info Technology Officer (CIO) ... Mr. Joshua OLSON
41 Athletic Director ... Dr. Suzanne SANREGRET
25 Chief Contracts/Grants Admin ... Ms. Julie SEPPALA
30 Chief Development/Advancement ... Dr. Les P. COOK
39 Director Student Housing ... Mr. Travis L. PIERCE
04 Administrative Asst to President ... Ms. Roberta M. DESSELLIER

Mid Michigan Community College (B)

1375 S Clare Avenue, Harrison MI 48625-9447
County: Clare — FICE Identification: 006768
Unit ID: 171155
Telephone: (989) 386-6622 — Carnegie Class: Assoc/HT-Mix Trad/Non
FAX Number: (989) 386-2411 — Calendar System: Semester
URL: www.midmich.edu
Established: 1965 — Annual Undergrad Tuition & Fees (In-District): $3,786
Enrollment: 4,216 — Coed
Affiliation or Control: State/Local — IRS Status: 501(c)3
Highest Offering: Associate Degree
Accreditation: NH, MAC, PHLEB, PTAA, RAD

01 President ... Dr. Christine M. HAMMOND
05 Vice President of Academic Services ... Dr. Jennifer FAGER
32 VP Community/Student Relations ... Dr. Matt MILLER
10 Vice President for Admin & Finance ... Ms. Lillian K. FRICK
04 Executive Assistant to President ... Ms. Tonya M. CLAYTON
15 Exec Director of Personnel Services ... Ms. Lori FASSETT
26 College Info/Org Dev Officer ... Mr. Anthony FREDS
35 Exec Dean of Student Services ... Ms. Kimberly BARNES
103 Exec Dir Econ/Workforce Dev ... Mr. Scott GOVITZ
81 Dean of Math & Science ... Mr. Peter VELGUTH
69 Dean of Health Sciences ... Dr. Maggie MAGOON
49 Dean Liberal Arts ... Dr. Scott MERTES
75 Dean of Occupational Studies ... Mr. Shawn TROY
06 Registrar ... Mr. Charles "Hank" BRYAN
21 Director of Accounting ... Ms. Susan CALL
88 SBDC Director ... Mr. Anthony FOX
27 Dir of Marketing & Public Relations ... Ms. Meghan KEEN
08 Dir Library/Learning Services ... Mr. Corey GOETHE
37 Director of Financial Aid ... Mr. Gale M. CRANDELL
109 Director Auxiliary Services ... Ms. Kelly KOCH
18 Director of Facilities ... Mr. William D. WHITMAN
14 IT Systems Manager ... Mr. Chris KLIEWONEIT
13 Director IT ... Mr. Kirk A. LEHR
76 Director Radiology ... Ms. LouAnn GOODWIN
25 Dir Grants Mgmt & Resource Dev ... Ms. Carol DARLINGTON
88 Dir Of Educational Talent Search ... Ms. Marilee KUJAT
09 Director of Institutional Research ... Mr. Kim OREN
35 Student Advancement Coordinator ... Ms. Tammy ALVARO
07 Director of Admissions ... Mr. Brent MISHLER

Monroe County Community College (C)

1555 S Raisinville Road, Monroe MI 48161-9746
County: Monroe — FICE Identification: 002294
Unit ID: 171225
Telephone: (734) 242-7300 — Carnegie Class: Assoc/HT-High Non
FAX Number: (734) 242-9711 — Calendar System: Semester
URL: www.monroeccc.edu
Established: 1964 — Annual Undergrad Tuition & Fees (In-District): $3,880
Enrollment: 3,192 — Coed
Affiliation or Control: Local — IRS Status: 170(c)1
Highest Offering: Associate Degree
Accreditation: NH, ADNUR, COARC

01 President ... Dr. Kojo QUARTEY
05 Vice President of Instruction ... Dr. Grace B. YACKEE
10 Vice Pres of Admin ... Ms. Suzanne M. WETZEL
32 Vice Pres Student & Information Svc ... Mr. Randell W. DANIELS
72 Dean of Applied Sci & Eng Tech ... Mr. Parmeshwar COOMAR
50 Dean of Business ... Mr. Paul L. KNOLLMAN
76 Dean of Health Sciences ... Ms. Kimberly LINDQUIST
79 Dean of Humanities/Social Science ... Dr. Paul HEDEEN
81 Dean of Science/Mathematics ... Mr. Kevin COOPER
06 Registrar ... Ms. Tracy VOGT
07 Director of Admissions/Guidance ... Mr. Mark HALL
88 Director of Upward Bound ... Mr. Anthony QUINN
88 Director of Respiratory Therapy ... Ms. Bonnie BOGGS
21 Director of Financial Services ... Mr. Andrew FISCHER
18 Director Physical Plant ... Mr. Jack BURNS
109 Dir Auxiliary Services/Purchasing ... Ms. Jean FORD
14 Director Data Processing Services ... Mr. James A. ROSS
37 Director of Financial Aid ... Ms. Valerie CULLER
36 Dir Business Devel/Employment Svcs ... Mr. Barry C. KINSEY
51 Director of Lifelong Learning ... Ms. Tina PILLARELLI
13 Manager Information Services ... Mr. Brian K. LAY
26 Director of Marketing/Communication ... Mr. Joseph VERKENNES
15 Director of Human Resources ... Ms. Molly M. MCCUTCHAN
04 Executive Asst to President ... Ms. Penny R. DORCEY
09 Coord Inst Research/Eval & Assess ... Miss Jamie DELEEUW
102 Exec Director Foundation ... Mr. Joshua MYERS

Montcalm Community College (D)

2800 College Drive, Sidney MI 48885-9723
County: Montcalm — FICE Identification: 002295
Unit ID: 171234
Telephone: (989) 328-2111 — Carnegie Class: Assoc/HVT-High Trad
FAX Number: (989) 328-2950 — Calendar System: Semester
URL: www.montcalm.edu
Established: 1965 — Annual Undergrad Tuition & Fees (In-District): $4,440
Enrollment: 1,685 — Coed
Affiliation or Control: Local — IRS Status: 501(c)3
Highest Offering: Associate Degree
Accreditation: NH, MAC

01 President ... Mr. Robert C. FERRENTINO
05 Vice Pres for Student/Acad Affairs ... Mr. Robert SPOHR
10 VP Administrative Services ... Ms. Connie STEWART
102 Executive Director of Foundation ... Ms. Therese A. SMITH
32 Dean Student & Enrollment Svcs ... Ms. Debra ALEXANDER
37 Director of Financial Aid ... Ms. Jessica HERRICK
13 Director Information Tech Svcs ... Mr. Rodney C. MIDDLETON
09 Director Institutional Effectivenes ... Ms. Lisa LUND
26 Communications Director ... Ms. Shelly STRAUTZ-SPRINGBORN
15 Director of Human Resources ... Ms. Riki JENSEN
21 Director of Accounting ... Ms. Kire WIERDA
18 Director of Facilities ... Mr. Taylor MALE
66 Dean of Nursing & Health Careers ... Ms. Danielle ANDERSON
07 Recruitment Director ... Ms. Emily CARMEY
103 Dean Industrial Ed & Workforce Trng ... Ms. Susan HATTO
29 Director Community/Alumni Relations ... Ms. Melissa CHRISTENSEN
08 Librarian ... Ms. Katie ARWOOD

Moody Theological Seminary-Michigan (E)

41550 E Ann Arbor Trail, Plymouth MI 48170-4308
Telephone: (734) 207-9581 — FICE Identification: 031353
Accreditation: &NH, THEOL

† Regional accreditation is carried under the parent institution Moody Bible Institute, Chicago, IL.

Mott Community College (F)

1401 E Court Street, Flint MI 48503-2089
County: Genesee — FICE Identification: 002261
Unit ID: 169275
Telephone: (810) 762-0200 — Carnegie Class: Assoc/HT-Mix Trad/Non
FAX Number: (810) 762-0257 — Calendar System: Semester
URL: www.mcc.edu
Established: 1923 — Annual Undergrad Tuition & Fees (In-District): $3,785
Enrollment: 8,617 — Coed
Affiliation or Control: Local — IRS Status: 501(c)3
Highest Offering: Associate Degree
Accreditation: NH, ACBSP, ADNUR, COARC, DA, DH, OTA, PTAA

01 President ... Dr. Beverly WALKER-GRIFFEA
30 Assoc VP Institutional Advancement ... Mr. Dale WEIGHILL
05 Vice Pres Academic Affairs ... Dr. Amy FUGATE
32 VP Student Success ... Dr. Tanya MCFADDEN
10 Chief Financial Officer ... Mr. Larry GAWTHROP
15 Associate Vice President of HR ... Mr. Philip ESPINOSA
103 Assoc VP Workforce & Economic Dev ... Mr. Robert MATTHEWS
88 Exec Dean Regional Tech Ctr Project ... Mr. Tom CRAMPTON
51 Exec Dir Corporate Svcs & Cont Educ ... Vacant
35 Executive Dean Student Services ... Vacant
37 Exec Dir Student Financial Svcs ... Ms. Emily VARNEY
81 Dean of Math & Science ... Dr. Todd TROUTMAN
76 Dean of Health Sciences ... Dr. Rebecca MYSZENSKI
83 Dean Social Sciences & Fine Arts ... Ms. Mary CUSACK
50 Dean of Business ... Mr. Stephen SHUBERT
72 Dean of Technology ... Dr. Angelo BROWN
26 Exec Director Marketing & PR ... Vacant
13 Chief Technology Officer ... Ms. Cheryl SHELTON
06 Registrar ... Mr. Chris ENGLE
36 Int Dir Career Center/Job Placement ... Mr. Aron GERICS
62 Executive Director Library ... Mrs. Jill SODT
18 Int Exec Director Physical Plant ... Mr. Mike CIESLINSKI
41 Director Athletics/Campus Rec ... Mr. Al PERRY
09 Exec Dir Institutional Research ... Vacant
35 Student Life Coordinator ... Ms. Dawn VANNIMAN
96 Director of Purchasing ... Ms. Jody MICHAEL
04 Administrative Asst to President ... Ms. Melody BARTHOLOMEW
101 Board Relations Coordinator ... Mr. Michael SIMON

Muskegon Community College (G)

221 S Quarterline Road, Muskegon MI 49442-1493
County: Muskegon — FICE Identification: 002297
Unit ID: 171304
Telephone: (231) 773-9131 — Carnegie Class: Assoc/HT-Mix Trad/Non
FAX Number: (231) 777-0440 — Calendar System: Semester
URL: www.muskegoncc.edu
Established: 1926 — Annual Undergrad Tuition & Fees (In-District): $5,350
Enrollment: 4,506 — Coed
Affiliation or Control: Local — IRS Status: Exempt
Highest Offering: Associate Degree
Accreditation: NH, ADNUR, COARC, MAC

01 President ... Dr. Dale K. NESBARY
03 Executive Vice President & Provost ... Dr. John SELMON
05 VP for Academic Affairs ... Ms. Kelley CONRAD
32 Dean of Student Svcs & Registrar ... Ms. Jean ROBERTS
20 Dean of Instruction & Assessment ... Dr. Edward BREITENBACH
31 Dean of Community Outreach ... Ms. Trynette Lottie HARPS
10 Admin Director of Financial Svcs ... Mr. Kenneth LONG
13 Chief Information Officer ... Mr. Mike ALSTROM
37 Director Financial Aid ... Mr. Bruce WIERDA
09 Dir Institutional Research & Grants ... Mr. Eduardo BEDOYA
45 Director of Strategic Initiatives ... Ms. Tina DEE
15 Executive Director of HR ... Ms. Kristine ANDERSON
41 Dean of College Svcs & AD ... Mr. Marty MCDERMOTT
18 Physical Plant Director ... Mr. Gerald NYLAND
29 Alumni & Donor Relations Manager ... Ms. Rachel STEWART
04 Executive Assistant to President ... Ms. Cindy S. DEBOEF

North Central Michigan College (H)

1515 Howard Street, Petoskey MI 49770-8717
County: Emmet — FICE Identification: 002299
Unit ID: 171395
Telephone: (231) 348-6600 — Carnegie Class: Assoc/HT-High Trad
FAX Number: (231) 348-6628 — Calendar System: Semester
URL: www.ncmich.edu
Established: 1958 — Annual Undergrad Tuition & Fees (In-District): $3,728
Enrollment: 2,615 — Coed
Affiliation or Control: Local — IRS Status: 501(c)3
Highest Offering: Associate Degree
Accreditation: NH, EMT

01 President Dr. Cameron BRUNET-KOCH
05 VP Academic Affairs/Student Success Dr. Peter OLSON
10 VP of Finance & Facilities David HARTNETT
32 VP of Student Services Renee DEYOUNG
102 Executive Director Foundation Dr. Lisa WATSON
08 Librarian Vacant
37 Director of Financial Aid Virginia PANOFF
18 Director of Physical Plant Ernst RUSCHE
84 Dir Enrollment Services/Registrar Joseph BALINSKI
21 Director of Business Services Troy SLATER
39 Director of Campus Housing Leon NASH
15 Director of Human Resources Diana SOUZA
40 Bookstore Manager Julie WEAVER
09 Assoc Dean Research & Assessment Dr. Robert MARSH
49 Assoc Dean Liberal Arts Dr. Sara GLASGOW
66 Assoc Dean Nurs/Allied Hlth/Sci Rene BIEGANOWSKI
50 Assoc Dean Business/Manuf/Tech Dr. Gretchen CARROLL
26 Director of College Communications Carol LAENEN
07 Director of Student Outreach Wendy FOUGHT
13 Director of Information Services David BORING
88 Director of Resource Center Dallas CULVAHOUSE
04 Administrative Asst to President Megan VAN HORN

Northern Michigan University (A)

1401 Presque Isle Avenue, Marquette MI 49855-5301
County: Marquette FICE Identification: 002301
Unit ID: 171456
Telephone: (906) 227-1000 Carnegie Class: Masters/M
FAX Number: (906) 227-2204 Calendar System: Semester
URL: www.nmu.edu
Established: 1899 Annual Undergrad Tuition & Fees (In-State): $9,766
Enrollment: 8,303 Coed
Affiliation or Control: State IRS Status: 501(c)3
Highest Offering: Doctorate
Accreditation: NH, CA, CAATE, CGTECH, DMOLS, ENGT, MLTAD, MT, MUS, NURSE, RAD, SURGT, SW

01 President Dr. Fritz J. ERICKSON
05 Provost/VP Academic Affairs Dr. Kerri SCHUILING
10 VP for Finance & Administration Mr. R. Gavin LEACH
102 CEO NMU Foundation Mr. Brad CANALE
09 Assoc VP for Inst Research Mr. Jason NICHOLAS
106 VP Extended Lrng/Cmty Engagement Dr. Steve VANDENAVOND
20 Asc Provost Acad Affs/Undergrad Pgm Dr. Dale P. KAPLA
58 Interim Dir Graduate Education Dr. Lisa ECKERT
90 Dean Academic Information Services Dr. Leslie A. WARREN
32 Assistant VP/Dean of Students Dr. Christine G. GREER
49 Dean of Arts & Sciences Dr. Rob WINN
50 Dean Walker L Cisler Col Bus Dr. David RAYOME
06 Registrar Ms. Kim M. ROTUNDO
45 Asst to Pres Strategic Initiatives Ms. Cindy L. PAAVOLA
36 Dir of Acad & Career Advisement Mr. James G. GADZINSKI
37 Director of Financial Aid Mr. Michael R. ROTUNDO
38 Director Counseling Center Ms. Marie AHO
88 Director Glenn T Seaborg Center Mr. Chris STANDERFORD
41 Athletic Director Mr. Forrest KARR
19 Dir Public Safety/Police Services Mr. Michael J. BATH
39 Director Housing/Residence Life Mr. Jeff KORPI
07 Director of Admissions Ms. Gerri L. DANIELS
23 Chief of Staff/Physician Dr. David M. LUOMA
15 Director of Human Resources Ms. Rhea DEVER
26 Asst VP Marketing & Communications Mr. Derek HALL
88 Dir Multicult Educ/Resource Center Ms. Shirley A. BROZZO
92 Director of Honors Program Dr. David H. WOOD
88 Director of Support/Consulting Svcs Ms. Felecia J. FLACK
24 Director Broadcast & AV Services Mr. Eric L. SMITH
29 Exec Dir Alumni Ops/Annual Giving Ms. Robyn L. STILLE
40 Bookstore Manager Mr. Paul WRIGHT
18 Associate VP Eng & Plan/Facilities Ms. Kathy A. RICHARDS
13 Chief Technology Officer Mr. David W. MAKI
96 Manager of Purchasing Mr. Steven D. BROWN
86 Director of Government Relations Ms. Deanna HEMMILA
04 Executive Assistant to President Ms. Laura GLOVER
101 Secretary Board of Trustees Ms. Cathy NIEMI
22 Dir Affirmative Action/EEO Ms. Janet KOSKI
53 Dean Teacher Education/Dir of Educ Dr. Joe LUBIG
28 Chief Diversity Officer Dr. Jessica CRUZ

Northwestern Michigan College (B)

1701 E Front Street, Traverse City MI 49686-3061
County: Grand Traverse FICE Identification: 002302
Unit ID: 171483
Telephone: (231) 995-1000 Carnegie Class: Bac/Assoc-Assoc Dom
FAX Number: (231) 995-1339 Calendar System: Semester
URL: www.nmc.edu
Established: 1951 Annual Undergrad Tuition & Fees (In-District): $3,582
Enrollment: 4,264 Coed
Affiliation or Control: Local IRS Status: 501(c)3
Highest Offering: Baccalaureate
Accreditation: NH, ACFEI, ADNUR, DA, PNUR

01 President Mr. Timothy J. NELSON
05 VP for Educational Services Dr. Stephen N. SICILIANO
107 VP Lifelong/Professional Learning Ms. Marguerite C. COTTO
10 VP of Finance & Administration Ms. Vicki COOK
37 Director Student Financial Services Ms. Linda BERLIN
13 VP for Student Svcs & Technology Mr. Todd NEIBAUER
84 Associate Dean Enrollment Services Ms. Pam PALERMO
32 Dean of Students Ms. Lisa THOMAS
04 Exec Assistant to President & Board Ms. Holly J. GORTON
15 Director of Human Resources Mr. Mark LIEBLING
88 Exec Dir of Dennos Museum Center Mr. Eugene A. JENNEMAN
24 Director Educational Media Tech Ms. Terri GUSTAFSON
12 Supt Great Lakes Maritime Academy RAdm. Gerard ACHENBACH, USMS
20 Dir Academic Affairs/Business Div Dr. Susan DECAMILLIS
56 Director Extended Educ Services Mr. Don CUNNINGHAM
06 Registrar Ms. Sheila RUPP
23 Director of Health Services Ms. Renee R. JACOBSON
09 Dir Research Planning Effectiveness Ms. Joy EVANS
18 Director of Campus Services Mr. Paul PERRY
26 Exec Dir of PR/Marketing/Communic Ms. Diana FAIRBANKS LAWSON
102 Exec Dir of Resource Dev & Found Ms. Rebecca M. TEAHEN
29 Director Alumni Relations Ms. Betsy COFFIA
08 Director of Library Services Ms. Tina J. ULRICH
88 Director Great Lakes Culinary Inst Mr. Frederick L. LAUGHLIN
88 Director Training & Research Mr. Richard R. WOLIN
21 Controller Vacant
96 Purchasing Manager Mr. Donald LOEFFLER
19 Asst Dir Campus Safety & Security Mr. Jim WHITE
07 Director of Admissions Ms. Cathryn CLAERHOUT
92 Director of Learning Services Ms. Kari L. KAHLER
68 Coordinator Physical Education Mr. Peter W. LACOURSE
75 Director of Technical Division Mr. Ed BAILEY
88 Director of Aviation Mr. Alex BLOYE

Northwood University (C)

4000 Whiting Drive, Midland MI 48640-2398
County: Midland FICE Identification: 004072
Unit ID: 171492
Telephone: (989) 837-4200 Carnegie Class: Spec-4-yr-Bus
FAX Number: (989) 837-4111 Calendar System: Semester
URL: www.northwood.edu
Established: 1959 Annual Undergrad Tuition & Fees: $25,130
Enrollment: 3,337 Coed
Affiliation or Control: Independent Non-Profit IRS Status: 501(c)3
Highest Offering: Master's
Accreditation: NH, ACBSP

01 President & Chief Executive Officer Dr. Keith A. PRETTY
05 EVP/CAO/COO Dr. Kristin STEHOUWER
10 Vice President Finance & Treasurer Mr. W. Karl STEPHAN
88 SVP Strategic/Corporate Alliances Dr. Timothy G. NASH
84 Int VP Enrollment Management Ms. Rhonda ANDERSON
30 VP University Advancement & Alumni Mr. Justin W. MARSHALL
12 President Northwood Texas Dr. Kevin G. FEGAN
26 VP Marketing/Communications/PR Ms. Rachel VALDISERRI
51 Associate Dean Adult Degree Program Ms. Rhonda C. ANDERSON
32 Dean of Students Mr. Stephen A. CRIPE
85 Dean International Programs Ms. Mamiko REEVES
96 Director of Asset Management Mr. David L. BENDER
06 Registrar Dr. Marisa L. TOSCHKOFF
37 System Financial Aid Director Mr. Mark A. MARTIN
15 Director of Human Resources Ms. Pamela L. CHRISTIE
21 Business Office Mgr/System Director Ms. Susan M. RIDGWAY
29 Executive Director Alumni Relations Ms. Julie L. ADAMCZYK
41 Athletic Director Mr. David F. MARSH
19 Director Security/Safety Mr. Jason VONREICHBAUER

Oakland Community College (D)

2480 Opdyke Road, Bloomfield Hills MI 48304-2266
County: Oakland FICE Identification: 002303
Unit ID: 171535
Telephone: (248) 341-2000 Carnegie Class: Assoc/HT-High Non
FAX Number: (248) 341-2099 Calendar System: Semester
URL: www.oaklandcc.edu
Established: 1964 Annual Undergrad Tuition & Fees (In-District): $2,940
Enrollment: 21,061 Coed
Affiliation or Control: State/Local IRS Status: 501(c)3
Highest Offering: Associate Degree
Accreditation: NH, ACFEI, ADNUR, COARC, DH, DMS, MAC, RAD, SURGT

01 Interim Chancellor Dr. Peter PROVENZANO
05 Vice Chanc Academic & Student Affs Dr. Mary C. MAZE
10 Int Vice Chanc of Business/Finance Mr. Charles THOMAS
11 Int Vice Chanc Administrative Svcs Ms. Bobbie REMIAS
15 Vice Chancellor Human Resources Mr. William J. MACQUEEN
13 Vice Chanc Info Technologies/CIO Mr. Robert MONTGOMERY
20 Assoc Vice Chanc Academic Affairs Dr. Timothy SHERWOOD
20 Assoc Vice Chanc Academic Affairs Dr. Timothy L. TAYLOR
43 General Counsel Ms. Eileen K. HUSBAND
04 Exec Assistant to Chancellor Ms. Cherie A. FOSTER
12 President Highland Lakes Campus Dr. Cynthia ROMAN
12 President Royal Oak/Southfield Camp Dr. Steven J. REIF
12 President Auburn Hills Campus Dr. Timothy L. TAYLOR
12 Interim Pres Orchard Ridge Campus Dr. Steven J. REIF
09 Exec Dir Inst Research/Quality/Plng Ms. Nancy C. SHOWERS
88 Exec Dir Curriculum & Student Lrng Mr. Martin A. ORLOWSKI
84 Exec Director Enrollment Mgmt Mrs. Carla R. SIMS
66 Acad Dean Nursing/Health Profession Ms. Rosalind WOODSON
27 Exec Dir Marketing/Communications Ms. Janet E. ROBERTS
72 Exec Dir Information Technologies Mr. Chuck S. FLAGG
06 Registrar Mr. Stephen M. LINDEN
18 Director Physical Facilities Mr. Daniel P. CHEREWICK
19 Director Public Safety Mr. Terry L. MCCAULEY
21 Director Financial Services Ms. Sharon K. CONVERSE
21 Director Budget & Financial Plng Mrs. Renee OSZUST
22 Director Employee Relations Mr. Gary S. CASEY
102 Interim Director OCC Foundation Ms. Candy GEETER
36 Director Placement/Coop Education Mr. Willie L. LLOYD
41 Athletic Director Ms. Jamie CORONA
96 Int Director Purch/Auxiliary Svcs Ms. Sarah L. ROWLEY
37 Director Financial Res/Scholarships Ms. Wilma B. PORTER
16 Director Personnel Services Mrs. Margaret R. CARROLL
29 Director Alumni & Annual Giving Vacant
81 Academic Dean Math/Nat Life Sci Mr. Michael M. GOLDIN
54 Int Academic Dean Eng/Mfg/Ind Tech Ms. Deborah A. BAYER
80 Academic Dean Public Services/CREST Ms. Deborah A. BAYER
62 Academic Dean Learning Resources Ms. Mary Ann SHEBLE
83 Int Academic Dean Social Sciences Ms. Mary Ann SHEBLE
79 Acad Dean Humanities/Art & Design Mr. Henry Y. TANAKA
88 Academic Dean College Readiness Ms. Beverly J. STANBROUGH
60 Int Acad Dean English/Lit/Commun Ms. Beverly J. STANBROUGH
50 Acad Dean Bus & Info Technologies Mr. Tom M. HENDRICKS

Oakland Community College Auburn Hills (E)

2900Featherstone Road, Auburn Hills MI 48326-2845
Telephone: (248) 232-4100 Identification: 770281
Accreditation: &NH, EMT

Oakland Community College Highland Lakes (F)

7350 Cooley Lake Road, Waterford MI 48327-4187
Telephone: (248) 942-3100 Identification: 770285
Accreditation: &NH

Oakland Community College Orchard Ridge (G)

27055 Orchard Lake Road,
Farmington Hills MI 48334-4579
Telephone: (248) 522-3400 Identification: 770282
Accreditation: &NH

Oakland Community College Royal Oak (H)

739 South Washington, Royal Oak MI 48067-3898
Telephone: (248) 246-2400 Identification: 770283
Accreditation: &NH

Oakland Community College Southfield (I)

22322 Rutland Drive, Southfield MI 48075-4793
Telephone: (248) 233-2700 Identification: 770284
Accreditation: &NH

Oakland University (J)

371 Wilson Boulevard, Rochester MI 48309-4401
County: Oakland FICE Identification: 002307
Unit ID: 171571
Telephone: (248) 370-2100 Carnegie Class: DU-Mod
FAX Number: N/A Calendar System: Semester
URL: www.oakland.edu
Established: 1957 Annual Undergrad Tuition & Fees (In-State): $12,064
Enrollment: 20,261 Coed
Affiliation or Control: State IRS Status: 501(c)3
Highest Offering: Doctorate
Accreditation: NH, ANEST, CACREP, CAEPT, CS, DANCE, ENG, ENGR, MED, MUS, NURSE, PTA, SPAA, SW, THEA

01 President Dr. Ora PESCOVITZ
05 Sr VP Academic Affairs/Provost Dr. James P. LENITNI
32 VP Student Affairs Mr. Glenn MCINTOSH
11 Chief Operating Officer Mr. Scott G. KUNSELMAN
30 VP Dev/Alumni Relations Ms. Angie SCHMUCKER
10 VP Finance & Administration Mr. John W. BEAGHAN
86 VP Government & Comm Relations Ms. Rochelle A. BLACK
12 Exec Dir OU Macomb Ms. Julie TRUBE
66 Dean of Nursing Dr. Judy A. DIDION
54 Dean Engineering & Computer Science Dr. Louay M. CHAMRA
76 Dean School Health Sciences Dr. Kevin A. BALL
53 Dean Educ & Human Services Dr. Jon MARGERUM-LEYS
49 Dean College Arts & Sciences Dr. Kevin J. CORCORAN
50 Dean School of Business Admin Dr. Michael A. MAZZEO
63 Dean School of Medicine Dr. Robert FOLBERG
08 Dean University Library Mr. Stephen P. WEITER
20 Senior Associate Provost Dr. Susan M. AWBREY
46 Assoc VP for Research Dr. David A. STONE
24 Asst VP Classrm Spprt/Instruct Tech Mr. George T. PREISINGER
20 Asst VP Academic Affairs Ms. Peggy S. COOKE
88 Dir Ctr Excellence Tchg Lrng Dr. Judith ABLESER
88 Dir Eye Research Institute Dr. Frank GIBLIN
88 Director FAJRI Dr. Sayed NASSAR
21 Asst VP Finance & Administration Mr. Thomas P. LEMARBE
18 Assoc VP Facilities Management Ms. Patricia A. ENGLE
15 Asst VP University Human Resources Mr. Ronald P. WATSON
102 Campaign Director Ms. Alison K. GAUDREAU
35 Asst VP SA/Dean Students Ms. Nancy A. SCHMITZ
19 Chief of Police Mr. Mark B. GORDON
06 Registrar Mr. Steven J. SHABLIN
44 Dir Annual Giving Program Ms. Kelly N. BRAULT
37 Director of Financial Aid Ms. Cindy L. HERMSEN
29 Sr Dir of Engagement/Alumni Ms. Sue HELDEROP
26 VP Univ Communications & Marketing Mr. John O. YOUNG
41 Director of Athletics Mr. Jeffrey F. KONYA
16 AVP Academic Human Resources Ms. Joi M. CUNNINGHAM
39 Director of University Housing Mr. James R. ZENTMEYER

36 Director Career Services ....Mr. Wayne J. THIBODEAU
38 Director Counseling Center ....Dr. David J. SCHWARTZ
85 Director International Students ....Mr. David J. ARCHBOLD
22 Director Disability Support Svcs ....Vacant
96 Director of Purchasing ....Ms. Paula S. REYES
28 Sr Adv to Pres/Div Equity Incl ....Vacant
106 Int Dir E-Learning/Instr Support ....Mr. John COUGHLIN
108 Dir Inst Research & Assessment ....Ms. Laura A. SCHARTMAN
101 VP Legal Affairs & General Counsel ......Mr. Victor A. ZAMBARDI
13 Chief Information Officer ....Ms. Theresa M. ROWE
07 Director of Admissions ....Ms. Dawn M. AUBRY
58 Dean Graduate Education ....Dr. Claudia A. PETRESCU

Olivet College (A)

320 S Main Street, Olivet MI 49076-9406
County: Eaton FICE Identification: 002308
Unit ID: 171599
Telephone: (269) 749-7000 Carnegie Class: Bac-Diverse
FAX Number: (269) 749-7600 Calendar System: Semester
URL: www.olivetcollege.edu
Established: 1844 Annual Undergrad Tuition & Fees: $25,560
Enrollment: 1,014 Coed
Affiliation or Control: Independent Non-Profit IRS Status: 501(c)3
Highest Offering: Master's
Accreditation: NH, CAEPT

01 President ....Dr. Steven M. COREY
05 Provost and Dean of the College ....Dr. Maria DAVIS
10 Vice Pres Finance/Administration ....Ms. Jackie LOOSER
07 Vice Pres Admissions & Mktg ....Mr. Tim JOHNSTON
32 Vice President/Dean Student Life ....Dr. Linda LOGAN
111 Vice Pres Advancement ....Mr. William HULL
13 Asst Vice President Technology ....Mr. Suresh ACHARYA
06 Registrar ....Ms. Leslie SULLIVAN
41 Athletic Director ....Mr. Ryan SHOCKEY
42 Director of Campus Ministries ....Mr. Michael F. FALES
36 Dir Career Services Network ....Ms. Diane KIRKHAM
37 Director of Student Financial Aid ....Ms. Libby JEAN
18 Director of Facilities ....Mr. Frank SCHUMACHER
94 Director of Women's Resource Center ....Ms. Cynthia NOYES
39 Student Housing ....Ms. Shawn HOLT
15 Director of Human Resources ....Mrs. Terri GLASGOW
29 Director of Alumni Engagement ..Ms. Martha MASON JENNINGS
04 Executive Asst to President ....Ms. Barbara SPENCER
08 Head Librarian ....Ms. Julia FALES
19 Director Security/Safety ....Mr. Phil REED

Puritan Reformed Theological Seminary (B)

2965 Leonard Street NE, Grand Rapids MI 49525
County: Kent Identification: 667099
Telephone: (616) 977-0599 Carnegie Class: Not Classified
FAX Number: (616) 285-3246 Calendar System: Semester
URL: www.prts.edu
Established: 1995 Annual Graduate Tuition & Fees: N/A
Enrollment: N/A Coed
Affiliation or Control: Independent Non-Profit IRS Status: 501(c)3
Highest Offering: Doctorate; No Undergraduates
Accreditation: THEOL

01 President ....Dr. Joel R. BEEKE
05 Academic Dean/VP Academic Affairs ....Dr. Michael BARRETT
06 Registrar ....Mr. Jonathon BEEKE
10 Vice President for Operations ....Mr. Henk KLEYN
38 Dean of Students/Spiritual Form ....Rev. Mark KELDERMAN
04 Administrative Asst to President ....Ms. Ann C. DYKEMA
26 Chief Public Relations/Marketing ....Mr. Chris HANNA
07 Director of Admissions ....Mr. Jonathon D. BEEKE
08 Head Librarian ....Mrs. Laura LADWIG
106 Dir Online Education/E-learning ....Mr. Chris ENGELSMA

Rochester College (C)

800 W Avon Road, Rochester Hills MI 48307-2764
County: Oakland FICE Identification: 002288
Unit ID: 170967
Telephone: (248) 218-2000 Carnegie Class: Bac-Diverse
FAX Number: (248) 218-2025 Calendar System: Semester
URL: www.rc.edu
Established: 1959 Annual Undergrad Tuition & Fees: $21,662
Enrollment: 1,173 Coed
Affiliation or Control: Independent Non-Profit IRS Status: 501(c)3
Highest Offering: Master's
Accreditation: NH, NURSE

01 President ....Dr. Brian L. STOGNER
101 Sr VP/Special Asst to President ....Mr. Klint PLEASANT
10 Exec VP/Chief Financial Officer ....Mr. Tom RELLINGER
07 Dean of Enrollment ....Ms. Mackenzie RELLINGER
21 Controller ....Ms. Susan IDE
18 Director Operational Support ....Mr. Mark JOHNSON
50 Dir School of Bus/Prof Studies ....Mr. Danny CAGNET
79 Dean School of Humanities ....Dr. Catherine PARKER
15 Director of Human Resources ....Mrs. Ginny MAY
26 Dir of Communication Services ....Mr. Elliot JONES
32 Dean of Students ....Mr. Adam BARON
37 Director of Student Financial Svcs ....Ms. Jessica BRISTOW
08 Director of Library Services ....Mrs. Allison JIMENEZ
06 Registrar ....Ms. Rebekah PINCHBACK
108 Director of Assessment ....Mr. J. Mark MANRY
29 Director of Alumni ....Mr. Larry STEWART
35 Dir Student Ldrshp & Programs ....Mrs. Teri BUTCHER
41 Director of Athletics ....Mr. Klint PLEASANT
42 Asst Dean & Campus Minister ....Mr. Chris SHIELDS
19 Director of Safety & Security ....Mr. Shawn WESTAWAY
04 Assistant to the President ....Ms. Karen HART

Sacred Heart Major Seminary (D)

2701 Chicago Boulevard, Detroit MI 48206-1799
County: Wayne FICE Identification: 002313
Unit ID: 172033
Telephone: (313) 883-8500 Carnegie Class: Spec-4-yr-Faith
FAX Number: (313) 868-6440 Calendar System: Semester
URL: www.shms.edu
Established: 1919 Annual Undergrad Tuition & Fees: $18,746
Enrollment: 465 Coed
Affiliation or Control: Roman Catholic IRS Status: 501(c)3
Highest Offering: Master's
Accreditation: NH, THEOL

01 Rector & President ....Msgr. Todd LAJINESS
32 Vice Rector/Dean of Seminarians ....Rev. Stephen BURR
05 Dean of Studies ....Rev. Timothy LABOE
73 Dean of the Institute for Ministry ....Dr. Matthew GERLACH
10 Director Finance/Treasurer ....Ms. Ann Marie CONNOLLY
06 Registrar ....Mr. David TWELLMAN
35 Director Undergraduate Seminarians ....Rev. Clint MCDONELL
38 Graduate Spiritual Director ....Rev. Daniel TRAPP
08 Library Director ....Mr. Christopher SPILKER
58 Dir Graduate Pastoral Formation ....Rev. John VANDENAKKER
30 Dir Development/Stewardship ....Mr. David KELLEY
18 Facilities Director ....Mr. John DUNCAN
07 Director of Admissions ....Mr. Ryan CAHILL

Saginaw Chippewa Tribal College (E)

2274 Enterprise Drive, Mount Pleasant MI 48858-2335
County: Isabella FICE Identification: 037723
Unit ID: 441070
Telephone: (989) 775-4123 Carnegie Class: Tribal
FAX Number: (989) 775-4528 Calendar System: Semester
URL: www.sagchip.edu
Established: 1998 Annual Undergrad Tuition & Fees: $2,040
Enrollment: 116 Coed
Affiliation or Control: Tribal Control IRS Status: 501(c)3
Highest Offering: Associate Degree
Accreditation: NH

01 President ....Ms. Carla SINEWAY
05 Dean of Instruction ....Ms. Cheryl SWARTHOUT
32 Dean of Student Services ....Mr. Nathaniel LAMBERTSON
07 Admissions Officer/Registrar ....Ms. Amanda FLAUGHER
37 Financial Aid Officer ....Ms. Patricia ALONZO
09 Dean of Research ....Ms. Tracy REED
25 Grants and Special Projects Coord ....Ms. Gena QUALLS

Saginaw Valley State University (F)

7400 Bay Road, University Center MI 48710-0001
County: Saginaw FICE Identification: 002314
Unit ID: 172051
Telephone: (989) 964-4000 Carnegie Class: Masters/L
FAX Number: (989) 964-0180 Calendar System: Semester
URL: www.svsu.edu
Established: 1963 Annual Undergrad Tuition & Fees (In-State): $9,345
Enrollment: 9,633 Coed
Affiliation or Control: State IRS Status: 501(c)3
Highest Offering: Doctorate
Accreditation: NH, CAATE, CAEP, CEA, ENG, MT, MUS, NURSE, OT, SW

01 President ....Dr. Donald J. BACHAND
05 Provost/VP Academic Affairs ....Dr. Deborah R. HUNTLEY
10 Exec VP Admin & Business Affairs .....Mr. James G. MULADORE
29 Executive Director Alumni Relations ....Mr. James P. DWYER
32 Assoc Provost Student Affairs ....Dr. Sidney R. CHILDS
28 Spec Asst to Pres/Diversity Pgms ....Dr. Mamie T. THORNS
83 Assoc Dean Arts/Behavioral Sciences ....Dr. Carlos RAMET
49 Dean Arts/Behavioral Sciences ....Dr. Marc H. PERETZ
21 Assoc VP Admin & Business Affairs ....Mr. Ronald E. PORTWINE
43 AVP for ABA/General Counsel ....Dr. John DECKER
114 Budget Director ....Ms. Susan L. CRANE
13 Exec Dir Information Tech Svcs ....Mr. Larry K. EMMONS
07 Director of Admissions ....Ms. Jennifer K. PAHL
06 Registrar ....Dr. Clifford DORNE
36 Director Career Services ....Mr. Michael W. MAJOR
21 Director Business Services ....Ms. Connie J. SCHWEITZER
29 Director of Alumni Relations ....Mr. Kevin J. SCHULTZ
14 Dir Enterprise Applications & Devel ....Mr. Patrick C. SAMOLEWSKI
31 Dir Media & Community Relations ....Mr. J. J BOEHM
08 Int Dir of Melvin J Zahnow Library ....Ms. Anita DEY
25 Dir Sponsored Pgms/IRB Rsrch Compl .....Ms. Janet D. RENTSCH
15 Chief HR Ofcr/Asst General Counsel . Dr. Jack VANHOORELBEKE
37 Director Scholarships/Financial Aid ....Mr. Robert L. LEMUEL
22 Director of Disability Services ....Ms. Monica B. REYES
38 Dir Student Counseling Center ....Mr. Eddie V. JONES
41 Athletic Director ....Mr. Michael E. WATSON
27 Athletics Marketing/Devel Director ....Mr. Joseph A. VOGL
53 Dean College of Education ....Dr. Craig DOUGLAS
54 Dean College of Science/Eng/Tech ....Dr. Frank A. HALL
50 Dean College of Business/Management .. Dr. Anthony R. BOWRIN
88 Dir Environmental Health & Safety ....Mr. Robert J. TUTSOCK
88 Asst Registrar ....Dr. Shawn WILSON
20 Associate Provost ....Dr. David M. CALLEJO PEREZ
102 Executive Director SVSU Foundation ....Mr. Andrew J. BETHUNE
96 Purchasing Manager ....Mr. Joshua M. WEBB
35 Asst Dean Stdnt Life/Leadership Pgm ....Mr. Bryan E. CRAINER
76 Dean of Health & Human Services ....Dr. Judith P. RULAND
54 Assoc Dean College of Sci/Engr/Tech ....Dr. Andrew M. CHUBB
09 Director of Institutional Research ....Dr. Nicholas J. WAGNER
26 Chief Public Relations Officer ....Mr. Leo MIODUSZEWSKI
26 Exec Dir for Comm/External Affairs ....Mrs. Linda L. SIMS
101 Exec Asst to the Pres/Sec to Board ..... Mrs. Mary A. KOWALESKI
20 Assoc VP for Academic Affairs ....Dr. Joshua J. ODE
86 Director of Governmental Affairs ....Mr. John L. KACZYNSKI

St. Clair County Community College (G)

323 Erie Street, PO Box 5015, Port Huron MI 48061-5015
County: St. Clair FICE Identification: 002310
Unit ID: 172291
Telephone: (810) 984-3881 Carnegie Class: Assoc/HT-High Trad
FAX Number: (810) 984-4730 Calendar System: Semester
URL: www.sc4.edu
Established: 1923 Annual Undergrad Tuition & Fees (In-District): $3,843
Enrollment: 3,730 Coed
Affiliation or Control: Local IRS Status: 501(c)3
Highest Offering: Associate Degree
Accreditation: NH, ADNUR, CAHIIM, EMT, RAD

01 President ....Dr. Deborah SNYDER
05 CAO/VP Acad Svcs Arts & Sciences ....Mr. James NEESE
05 CAO/VP Acad Svcs Occupation Stds .... Ms. Julie ARMSTRONG
10 Chief Operating Officer ....Mr. Kirk A. KRAMER
32 Vice President Student Services ....Mr. Pete LACEY
09 VP Institutional Effectiveness ....Ms. Linda DAVIS
15 Vice President of Human Resources ....Ms. Bethany MAYEA
13 Chief Technology Officer ....Ms. Theresa M. STEVENS
101 Exec Assistant to the President ....Ms. Mary L. HAWTIN
66 Dean of Nursing/Health/Human Svcs ....Ms. Cindy NICHOLSON
37 Dir of Financial Assistance/Svcs ....Ms. Josephine R. CASSAR
06 Registrar ....Ms. Carrie BEARSS
21 Controller ....Ms. Mary K. BRUNNER
41 Director of Athletics ....Mr. Dale R. VOS
08 Director of Library Services ....Ms. Kendra LAKE

Schoolcraft College (H)

18600 Haggerty Road, Livonia MI 48152-2696
County: Wayne FICE Identification: 002315
Unit ID: 172200
Telephone: (734) 462-4400 Carnegie Class: Assoc/MT-VT-High Non
FAX Number: (734) 462-4507 Calendar System: Semester
URL: www.schoolcraft.edu
Established: 1961 Annual Undergrad Tuition & Fees (In-District): $3,836
Enrollment: 11,687 Coed
Affiliation or Control: Local IRS Status: 501(c)3
Highest Offering: Baccalaureate
Accreditation: NH, ACFEI, ADNUR, CAHIIM, MAC, PNUR

01 President ....Dr. Conway A. JEFFRESS
10 Vice Pres/Chief Financial Officer ....Dr. Glenn CERNY
05 Vice Pres/CAO ....Mr. Richard WEINKAUF
32 Vice Pres/Chief Student Affs Ofcr ....Dr. Cheryl M. HAGEN
26 VP & Chief Information Officer ....Mr. Patrick TURNER
49 Dean Liberal Arts & Sciences ....Dr. Cheryl HAWKINS
75 Dean Occupational Prog/Econ Dev ....Dr. Robert LEADLEY
20 Dean of Educ & Lrng Support ....Dr. Deborah DAIEK
88 Assoc Dean College Centers .... Dr. Bonnie HECKARD-FARMER
51 Assoc Dean Cont Educ/Prof Develop ....Dr. Leslie PETTY
38 Assoc Dean Counseling/Student Sppt .... Dr. Michael OLIVER
11 Assoc Dean Opers/Curriculum/Assess ....Ms. Cindy CICCHELLI
35 Dean of Students ....Mr. Martin HEATOR
53 Assoc Dean Education Programs ....Dr. Dennis GENIG
81 Assoc Dean Sciences ....Mr. Charles HAYES
88 Assoc Dean Public Safety Programs ......Mr. Gerald CHAMPAGNE
88 Assoc Dean Advising & Partnerships ....Ms. Laurie KATTUAH-SNYDER
72 Asst Dean Occupational Programs ....Ms. Amy JONES
15 Exec Director of Human Resources ....Ms. Laura SENSING
06 Registrar ....Ms. Nicole WILSON-FENNELL
37 Exec Dir Student Fin Svcs/Fin Aid ....Ms. Regina MOSLEY
19 Campus Police Authority Chief ....Mr. Steven KAUFMAN
96 Dir of Purchasing/Business Ops ....Mr. Matthew WILSON
21 Controller/Director of Finance ....Mr. Jon LAMB
84 Dean of Enrollment Services ....Ms. Stacey STOVER
88 Exec Dir Info Security & Networking ....Mr. Jeffrey BORTON
88 Exec Dir of Enterprise Applications ....Ms. Laura CULLEN
04 Executive Asst to President ....Ms. Karla W. FRENTZOS
18 Exec Dir/Facilities Operations ....Mr. John WRIGHT
27 Exec Dir Marketing & Advancement ....Mr. Frank RUGGIRELLO
41 Director of Athletics ....Mr. Sidney FOX
44 Director of Development ....Ms. Elizabeth KOHLER
91 Principal Software Developer ....Mr. Scott HEUSNER

Siena Heights University (I)

1247 Siena Heights Drive, Adrian MI 49221-1796
County: Lenawee FICE Identification: 002316
Unit ID: 172264
Telephone: (517) 263-0731 Carnegie Class: Masters/M
FAX Number: (517) 264-7704 Calendar System: Semester
URL: www.sienaheights.edu

Established: 1919 Annual Undergrad Tuition & Fees: $24,856
Enrollment: 2,707 Coed
Affiliation or Control: Roman Catholic IRS Status: 501(c)3
Highest Offering: Beyond Master's But Less Than Doctorate
Accreditation: NH, ART, CAEPT, NURSE, SW

01 President ... Dr. Peg ALBERT, OP
10 Sr Vice Pres for Business/Finance ... Dr. J. Lee JOHNSON
111 Vice President for Advancement ... Mr. Daniel PENA
05 Vice President for Academic Affairs ... Dr. Sharon R. WEBER, OP
84 Vice Pres of Enrollment Mgmt Svcs ... Mr. George WOLF
107 Dean of Professional Studies/Grad ... Dr. Cheri BETZ
49 Dean College of Arts and Science ... Dr. Matthew DRAUD
32 Dean for Students ... Mr. Michael ORLANDO
06 Registrar ... Ms. Joy GARROW
07 Director of Admissions ... Ms. Trudy MOHRE
08 Director of Library ... Vacant
13 Chief Information Officer ... Mr. Robert C. METZ
41 Director of Athletics ... Mr. Frederick M. SMITH
15 Human Resource Director ... Mr. Michael L. KARABETSOS
42 Director of Campus Ministry ... Fr. John GRACE
38 Director of Counseling Services ... Mrs. Sandy MORLEY
121 Director of Academic Advising ... Ms. Wiona PORATH
18 Supt of Buildings & Grounds ... Mr. Brian BERTRAM
09 Director of Institutional Research ... Mr. Jason HARTZ
39 Director of Residence Life ... Ms. Rachel RICKINGER
19 Director of Campus Security ... Mrs. Cindy A. BIRDWELL
23 Director of Health Services ... Sr. Sharon SPANBAUER
29 Director of Alumni Relations ... Vacant
36 Director of Career Services ... Ms. Sarah A. CHRENKO
28 Director of Immersion & Diversity ... Mrs. Sharese MATHIS
26 Dir of Integrated Univ Marketing ... Mr. Doug GOODNOUGH
37 Director Student Financial Aid ... Mrs. Lori KOSARUE
21 Controller ... Ms. Mary KRUSE
44 Coordinator of Annual Fund ... Mrs. Shawna WILSON
04 Executive Assistant to President ... Ms. Deborah KELLER

South University (A)

41555 Twelve Mile Road, Novi MI 48377
Telephone: (248) 675-0200 Identification: 770914
Accreditation: &SC, ACBSP, NURSE, PTAA

† Branch campus of South University, Savannah, GA

Southwestern Michigan College (B)

58900 Cherry Grove Road, Dowagiac MI 49047-9793
County: Cass FICE Identification: 002317
Unit ID: 172307
Telephone: (269) 782-1000 Carnegie Class: Assoc/HT-High Trad
FAX Number: (269) 782-8414 Calendar System: Semester
URL: www.swmich.edu
Established: 1964 Annual Undergrad Tuition & Fees (In-District): $4,891
Enrollment: 2,348 Coed
Affiliation or Control: State/Local IRS Status: 501(c)3
Highest Offering: Associate Degree
Accreditation: NH, ADNUR, CAHIIM

01 President ... Dr. David MATHEWS
100 Chief of Staff ... Mr. Thomas ATKINSON
10 Vice President/Chief Business Ofcr ... Ms. Susan COULSTON
05 Vice President of Instruction ... Dr. David FLEMING
26 Vice President of Mktg/Enrollment ... Mr. Michael O'BRIEN
32 Vice President of Student Services ... Ms. Christine PASSER
13 Director of IT and CIO ... Ms. Jeanne LUTHJOHAN
49 Dean of Arts and Sciences ... Dr. Scott TOPPING
50 Dean NAC/School of Business ... Dr. Stacy HORNER
66 Dean School Nursing/Human Services ... Ms. Rebecca JELLISON
07 Director of Admissions ... Mr. Jason SMITH
18 Director of Buildings & Grounds ... Mr. John EBERHART
30 Director of Development ... Ms. Eileen TONEY
88 Dir of Educational Talent Srch Pgm ... Ms. Kim LUTHRINGER
37 Director of Financial Aid ... Ms. Lauren MOW
15 Director of Human Resources ... Ms. Kate THOMAS
09 Director of Institutional Research ... Dr. Angela EVANS
08 Director of Library Services ... Ms. Colleen WELSCH
12 Director of Niles Campus ... Mr. Brent BREWER
06 Director of Records/Registrar ... Ms. Kristen MILLER
121 Director of Student Support Svcs ... Ms. Angela PALSAK
88 Dir of Student and Testing Services ... Ms. Charlotte MCGOWAN
39 Director of Student Housing ... Mr. Jeffery HOOKS
21 Controller ... Ms. Michelle KITE
88 Manager of Accounting ... Ms. Christy MANGUS
26 Manager of Marketing ... Ms. Michelle BOGUE
88 Manager of Student Activity Center ... Mr. William ROGGEMAN

Southwestern Michigan College Niles Area Campus (C)

33890 U.S. Highway 12, Niles MI 49120
Telephone: (800) 456-8675 Identification: 770286
Accreditation: &NH

Spring Arbor University (D)

106 E Main Street, Spring Arbor MI 49283-9799
County: Jackson FICE Identification: 002318
Unit ID: 172334
Telephone: (517) 750-1200 Carnegie Class: Masters/L
FAX Number: (517) 750-6620 Calendar System: 4/1/4
URL: www.arbor.edu
Established: 1873 Annual Undergrad Tuition & Fees: $26,730
Enrollment: 3,401 Coed
Affiliation or Control: Free Methodist IRS Status: 501(c)3
Highest Offering: Master's
Accreditation: NH, CACREP, MUS, NURSE, SW

01 University President ... Dr. Brent ELLIS
05 Provost/Chief Academic Officer ... Dr. Kimberly RUPERT
03 Executive Vice President ... Dr. Douglas A. WILCOXSON
10 Vice Pres Finance & Administration ... Mr. Keven W. ROSE
32 VP Student Success & Calling ... Dr. Kimberly K. HAYWORTH
100 Chief of Staff ... Mr. Damon M. SEACOTT
07 VP Enroll & Marketing ... Mr. Jon BAHR
12 Assistant Provost SAU Global ... Dr. Linda G. SHERRILL
15 Director of Human Resources ... Mrs. Melissa MONTGOMERY
91 Chief Technology Officer ... Vacant
20 Associate Provost ... Mr. Rod S. STEWART
30 Assistant VP Advancement Operations ... Mrs. Rhonda R. SAURBEK
49 Dean School Arts & Sciences ... Vacant
50 Dean Gainey School of Business ... Dr. Caleb K. CHAN
53 Dean School of Education ... Dr. Linda G. SHERRILL
88 Dean School of Human Services ... Mrs. Tamara L. DINDOFFER
35 Asst VP Student Development ... Mr. Dan VANDERHILL
06 Registrar ... Vacant
84 Director of Enrollment Operations ... Mr. Kevin BROWN
21 Assistant VP Financial Services ... Mrs. Dawn I. SCHNITKEY
44 Executive Director of Development ... Mrs. Linda SCHAUB
41 Athletic Director ... Mr. Ryan T. COTTINGHAM
42 Chaplain ... Mr. Ronald L. KOPICKO
37 Director of Financial Aid ... Mr. Herbert K. ROTICH
09 Director Institutional Research ... Mr. Thomas P. KORMAN
108 Director of Assessment ... Vacant
08 Director Library ... Mr. Robert D. BOLTON
18 Director of Physical Plant ... Mr. Marty FORTRESS
89 Director Retention & Fresh Programs ... Vacant
104 Director Cross Cultural Studies ... Mrs. Diane L. KURTZ
23 Exec Dir Student Health/Wellness ... Mrs. Mary BRODA
39 Asst Dean Students/Dir of Housing ... Mr. Robert C. PRATT
36 Director Career Svcs/Acad Advising ... Vacant
19 Director Campus Safety ... Mr. Scott L. KREBILL
106 Assoc Dean External/SAUonline ... Mr. Gary R. TUCKER
28 Director Intercultural Relations ... Mr. Eric A. BEDA
29 Director Alumni Relations ... Mr. Stephen CASTLE
105 Web Architect ... Vacant

SS. Cyril and Methodius Seminary (E)

3535 Indian Trail, Orchard Lake MI 48324-1623
County: Oakland FICE Identification: 037384
Unit ID: 260211
Telephone: (248) 683-0310 Carnegie Class: Not Classified
FAX Number: (248) 738-6735 Calendar System: Semester
URL: www.sscms.edu
Established: 1885 Annual Graduate Tuition & Fees: N/A
Enrollment: N/A Coed
Affiliation or Control: Roman Catholic IRS Status: 501(c)3
Highest Offering: Master's; No Undergraduates
Accreditation: THEOL

01 Rector/President ... RevMsg. Thomas MACHALSKI
05 Interim Academic Dean ... Rev. Leonard OBLOY
06 Registrar ... Ms. Joanna OLEJNICZAK-CAUSHAJ

University of Detroit Mercy (F)

4001 W McNichols Road, Detroit MI 48221-3038
County: Wayne FICE Identification: 002323
Unit ID: 169716
Telephone: (313) 993-1000 Carnegie Class: Masters/L
FAX Number: (313) 993-1229 Calendar System: Semester
URL: www.udmercy.edu
Established: 1877 Annual Undergrad Tuition & Fees: $39,882
Enrollment: 4,920 Coed
Affiliation or Control: Roman Catholic IRS Status: 501(c)3
Highest Offering: Doctorate
Accreditation: NH, ANEST, ARCPA, CACREP, CAEPT, CLPSY, DENT, DH, ENG, NURSE, SW

01 President ... Dr. Antoine M. GARIBALDI
05 Provost and VP for Academic Affairs ... Ms. Pamela ZARKOWSKI
10 VP for Business & Finance and CFO ... Mr. Vincent ABATEMARCO
111 VP for University Advancement ... Mr. Arnold D'AMBROSIO
84 VP Enrollment & Student Affairs ... Ms. Deborah STIEFFEL
101 University Secretary & Senior Atty ... Ms. Monica BARBOUR
18 Assoc Vice Pres Facil Management ... Ms. Tamara BATCHELLER
15 Associate Vice Pres Human Resources ... Mr. Steven J. NELSON
26 Assoc VP Marketing & Communications ... Mr. Gary ERWIN
13 Associate Vice President ITS ... Mr. Edward TRACY, II
06 Associate VP/Registrar ... Ms. Diane M. PRAET
44 Exec Director of Annual Giving ... Ms. Ann FISHER
112 Exec Director of Major Gifts ... Vacant
32 Dean of Students ... Ms. Monica WILLIAMS
08 Dean of Libraries ... Ms. Jennifer DEAN
09 Director of Institutional Research ... Ms. Shelley WAGNON
37 Director Scholarships & Fin Aid ... Ms. Jenny MCALONAN
35 Associate Director of Student Life ... Ms. Dorothy STEWART
41 Director of Athletics ... Mr. Robert VOWELS
49 Dean College of Liberal Arts/Ed ... Dr. Mark DENHAM
61 Dean School of Law ... Ms. Phyllis CROCKER
54 Interim Dean College Engr & Science ... Dr. Katherine SNYDER
48 Dean School of Architecture ... Mr. William WITTIG
50 Dean Col Business Admin ... Dr. Joseph EISENHAUER
52 Dean School of Dentistry ... Dr. Mert AKSU
76 Dean CHP/Nursing ... Dr. Christine PACINI
88 Dean Coop Education/Career Ctr ... Ms. Sheryl JOHNSON-ROULHAC
39 Director Residence Life ... Ms. Lanae GILL
04 Exec Asst to the President ... Ms. Lisa MACDONNELL
85 Dir of International Services ... Ms. Weihong SUN
38 Director of Wellness Center ... Ms. Annamaria SILVERI
92 Director of Honors Program ... Mr. J. Todd HIBBARD
96 Director of Procurement Services ... Ms. Tina A. MAITLAND
88 Coordinator of Advancement Systems ... Ms. Stephanie JONES
07 Executive Director of Admissions ... Ms. Tyra ROUNDS
108 Director Institutional Assessment ... Dr. Elizabeth ROBERTS-KIRCHOFF
19 Interim Director Public Safety ... Mr. Joel GALLIHUGH
25 Dir of Sponsored Research ... Ms. Catherine CALDWELL
53 Chair Education Department ... Dr. Lorri MACDONALD
106 Dir Online Education/E-learning ... Ms. Jennifer DEAN
102 Dir Foundation/Corporate Relations ... Ms. Yvonne LINDSTROM
22 Title IX & Equity/Compliance Coord ... Ms. Marjorie LANG
29 Director Alumni Relations ... Ms. Margaret PATTISON

University of Detroit Mercy Corktown Campus (G)

2700 Martin Luther King Jr. Blvd, Detroit MI 48208-2576
Telephone: (313) 494-6700 Identification: 770291
Accreditation: &NH

University of Detroit Mercy School of Law (H)

651 E Jefferson Avenue, Detroit MI 48226-4349
Telephone: (313) 596-0200 Identification: 770292
Accreditation: &NH, LAW

University of Michigan-Ann Arbor (I)

500 S. State Street, Ann Arbor MI 48109
County: Washtenaw FICE Identification: 002325
Unit ID: 170976
Telephone: (734) 764-1817 Carnegie Class: DU-Highest
FAX Number: N/A Calendar System: Trimester
URL: umich.edu
Established: 1817 Annual Undergrad Tuition & Fees (In-State): $14,402
Enrollment: 43,651 Coed
Affiliation or Control: State IRS Status: 501(c)3
Highest Offering: Doctorate
Accreditation: NH, ART, CAATE, CAEPT, CLPSY, CS, DANCE, DENT, DH, DIETD, DIETI, ENG, ENGR, HSA, IPSY, LAW, LIB, LSAR, MED, MIDWF, MUS, NURSE, PDPSY, PH, PHAR, PLNG, SW

01 President ... Dr. Mark S. SCHLISSEL
05 Interim Provost ... Dr. Paul N. COURANT
10 Exec VP/CFO ... Mr. Kevin P. HEGARTY
17 Exec VP for Medical Affairs ... Dr. Marschall S. RUNGE
30 Vice President Development ... Mr. Jerry A. MAY
32 Vice President Student Life ... Dr. E. Royster HARPER
46 Vice President for Research ... Dr. S. Jack HU
86 Vice Pres Governmental Relations ... Ms. Cynthia H. WILBANKS
26 Vice Pres Global Communications ... Ms. Lisa M. RUDGERS
43 Vice Pres/General Counsel ... Mr. Timothy G. LYNCH
101 Vice Pres/Sec of the University ... Ms. Sally J. CHURCHILL
04 Exec Asst to the President ... Ms. Erika J. HRABEC
100 Special Counsel to the Provost ... Ms. Kelly L. CUNNINGHAM
20 Vice Provost Acad/Budget Affairs ... Ms. Amy DITTMAR
20 Vice Provost Acad & Faculty Affairs ... Dr. Lori J. PIERCE
20 Vice Provost Acad & Faculty Affairs ... Dr. Sara B. BLAIR
58 Vice Provost Acad Affs/Grad Stds ... Dr. Carol A. FIERKE
104 Vice Provost Global & Engaged Educ ... Dr. James P. HOLLOWAY
28 Vice Prov Diversity/Eqty/Inclusion ... Dr. Rob M. SELLERS
20 Vice Prov Equity/Inclus & Acad Affs ... Dr. Robert M. SELLERS
20 Vice Prov Dig Educ & Univ Librarian ... Dr. James L. HILTON
84 Vice Provost for Enrollment Mgmt ... Dr. Kendra ISHOP
09 Assoc Vice Provost & Exec Dir OBP ... Ms. Tammy C. BIMER
07 Director Undergrad Admissions ... Ms. Erica L. SANDERS
15 Assoc Vice Provost & Sr Dr Acad HR ... Mr. Jeffery R. FRUMKIN
22 Assoc Vice Prov/Sr Dir Inst Equity ... Ms. Pamela HEATLIE
18 Assoc VP Facilities/Operations ... Mr. Henry D. BAIER
21 Assoc VP Finance ... Ms. Nancy A. HOBBS
88 Chief Investment Officer ... Mr. Erik LUNDBERG
30 Assoc VP for Development ... Mr. Dondi L. CUPP
17 Assoc VP for Medical Affairs ... Dr. John E. BILLI
46 Assoc VP for Research ... Dr. Volker SICK
46 Assoc VP for Research ... Dr. J. Brian FOWLKES
46 Assoc VP for Research ... Dr. Toni C. ANTONUCCI
46 Assoc VP for Research ... Mr. Daryl C. WEINERT
46 Assoc VP for Research ... Dr. Eric MICHIELSSEN
46 Assoc VP Research ... Mr. Kenneth J. NISBET
46 Assoc VP Research ... Dr. James A. ASHTON-MILLER
35 Assoc VP Student Life/Dean Stdnts ... Ms. Laura B. JONES
35 Assoc VP Student Life ... Ms. Anjali N. ANTURKAR
35 Assoc VP Student Life ... Dr. Simone HIMBEAULT-TAYLOR
35 Assoc VP Student Life ... Mr. Loren J. RULLMAN
16 Assoc VP for Human Resources ... Ms. Laurita E. THOMAS
13 Chief Information Officer ... Ms. Kelli TROSVIG
06 University Registrar ... Mr. Paul A. ROBINSON
96 Director Procurement Services ... Mr. Colin T. ANDERSON
38 Director Counseling & Psych Service ... Dr. Todd D. SEVIG
39 Director University Housing ... Ms. Marilyn TYUS
23 Director University Health Service ... Dr. Mike CORRIGAN
19 Exec Dir Pub Safety/Security ... Mr. Eddie L. WASHINGTON
37 Exec Director Financial Aid ... Ms. Pamela W. FOWLER
41 Director of Athletics ... Mr. Warde MANUEL
48 Int Dn Col Architecture/Urban Plng ... Mr. Robert FISHMAN

49 Dean Col Literature/Science/Arts .... Dr. Andrew D. MARTIN
54 Dean College of Engineering .... Dr. Alec D. GALLIMORE
61 Dean Law School .... Mr. Mark D. WEST
63 Dean Medical School .... Dr. Marschall S. RUNGE
67 Dean College of Pharmacy .... Dr. James T. DALTON
65 Dean Sch Natural Resrc/Environ .... Dr. Jonathan T. OVERPECK
64 Dean School Music Theatre & Dance ...... Mr. Aaron P. DWORKIN
57 Dean School of Art & Design .... Dr. Gunalan L. NADARAJAN
50 Dean School of Business .... Mr. Scott DERUE
52 Dean School of Dentistry .... Dr. Laurie K. MCCAULEY
53 Dean School of Education .... Dr. Elizabeth B. MOJE
62 Dean School of Information .... Dr. Thomas A. FINHOLT
68 Dean School of Kinesiology .... Dr. Lori PLOUTZ-SNYDER
66 Dean School of Nursing .... Dr. Patricia D. HURN
80 Dean School of Public Policy .... Mr. Michael S. BARR
70 Dean School of Social Work .... Ms. Lynn VIDEKA
69 Dean School of Public Health .... Dr. Martin A. PHILBERT
29 President Alumni Association .... Mr. Steve C. GRAFTON

University of Michigan-Dearborn (A)

4901 Evergreen Road, Dearborn MI 48128-1491
County: Wayne FICE Identification: 002326
Unit ID: 171137
Telephone: (313) 593-5000 Carnegie Class: Masters/L
FAX Number: (313) 593-5452 Calendar System: Trimester
URL: www.umd.umich.edu
Established: 1959 Annual Undergrad Tuition & Fees (In-State): $12,032
Enrollment: 9,066 Coed
Affiliation or Control: State IRS Status: 501(c)3
Highest Offering: Doctorate
Accreditation: NH, CAEPT, CEA, CS, ENG

01 Chancellor .... Dr. Daniel LITTLE
05 Prov/Vice Chanc Academic Affs .... Dr. Catherine A. DAVY
10 Vice Chancellor Business Affairs .... Mr. Jeffrey L. EVANS
84 Vice Chanc Enroll Mgmt .... Mr. Ray E. METZ
111 Vice Chanc Inst Advancement .... Ms. Mallory M. SIMPSON
31 Vice Chanc for External Relations .... Mr. Kenneth KETTENBEIL
21 Director of Financial Services .... Mr. Noel HORNBACHER
06 Registrar .... Ms. Janice LEWIS-BOYD
26 Director Communications/Marketing .... Ms. Beth MARMARELLI
86 Government Relations Manager .... Mr. Mike LATVIS
15 Director of Human Resources .... Ms. Keisha BLEVINS
29 Alumni Engagement .... Ms. Cristina FRENDO
20 Associate Provost Undergraduate .... Dr. Mitchel SOLLENBERGER
20 Associate Provost Graduate .... Dr. Ilir MITEZA
13 Int Dir IT Strategy/Operations .... Ms. Carrie SHUMAKER
08 Director of Library .... Ms. Elaine LOGAN
09 Int Dir of Institutional Research .... Dr. Mitchel SOLLENBERGER
84 Asst VC for Enrollment Management .... Dr. Monica PORTER
07 Director of Admissions .... Ms. Deb PEFFER
37 Director of Financial Aid .... Ms. Katherine ALLEN
38 Director of Counseling .... Dr. Debra HUTTON
36 Director of Career Services .... Ms. Regina M. STORRS
85 Director of International Affairs .... Vacant
32 Director of Student Engagement .... Ms. Reetha RAVEENDRAN
18 Exec Dir of Facilities Operations .... Ms. Carol GLICK
19 Chief of Police .... Mr. Kevin WILLIAMS
22 Institutional Equity Officer .... Ms. Anita GREEN
28 Sp Counsel to Chanc for Inclusion .... Dr. Ann LAMPKIN-WILLIAMS
49 Dean Col Arts/Science/Letters .... Dr. Martin HERSHOCK
54 Dean Col of Engr/Comp Sci .... Dr. A. W. ENGLAND
50 Dean College of Business .... Dr. Raju BALAKRISHNAN
53 Dean College of Ed/Health/HS .... Dr. Janine JANOSKY
88 Director of Enrollment Research .... Mr. Dan MERIAN
41 Athletic Director .... Mr. Matt BEAUDRY

University of Michigan-Flint (B)

303 E Kearsley Street, Flint MI 48502-1950
County: Genesee FICE Identification: 002327
Unit ID: 171146
Telephone: (810) 762-3000 Carnegie Class: Masters/L
FAX Number: (810) 762-5725 Calendar System: Semester
URL: www.umflint.edu
Established: 1956 Annual Undergrad Tuition & Fees (In-State): $10,344
Enrollment: 8,470 Coed
Affiliation or Control: State IRS Status: 501(c)3
Highest Offering: Doctorate
Accreditation: NH, ANEST, CAEPN, CEA, ENG, MUS, NURSE, PTA, RTT, SW

01 Chancellor .... Dr. Susan E. BORREGO
05 Provost/VC Academic Affairs .... Dr. Douglas KNERR
32 VC Campus Inclusion & Student Life .... Dr. Barbara J. AVERY
10 VC Business and Finance .... Mr. Michael J. HAGUE
111 VC University Advancement .... Ms. Kristin LINDSEY
35 Assoc VC & Dean of Students .... Dr. Julie SNYDER
121 Asst VC for Student Success .... Dr. Jonathan GRADY
58 Sr Vice Provost/Dean Grad Pgms .... Dr. Vahid LOTFI
20 Asst Prov/Dean Undergrad Studies .... Vacant
26 Director of News & Media .... Mr. Howard RAYMER
86 Director Government Relations .... Mr. David E. LOSSING
28 Director of Educational Oppty .... Vacant
08 Director of Library .... Mr. Robert L. HOUBECK, JR.
06 Registrar .... Ms. Karen A. ARNOULD
07 Admissions Director .... Vacant
37 Director Financial Aid .... Ms. Lori VEDDER
15 Director Human Res/Affirm Action .... Ms. Beth MANNING
49 Dean College Arts & Sciences .... Dr. Susan GANO-PHILLIPS
50 Dean School of Management .... Dr. Scott JOHNSON
66 Dean School of Nursing .... Dr. Margaret ANDREWS

76 Dean Sch Health Prof & Studies .... Dr. Donna FRY
53 Dean Sch Education & Human Svcs .... Dr. Robert BARNETT
51 Director of Extended Learning .... Ms. Deborah WHITE
19 Director of Public Safety .... Mr. Raymond D. HALL
18 Dir Facilities Mgmt/Auxiliary Svcs .... Mr. George HAKIM
13 Director Info Technology Services .... Mr. Scott ARNST
88 Director Student Success Center .... Dr. Fernando FLEURQUIN
46 Director of Research .... Dr. Kenneth SYLVESTER
21 Director of Financial Svcs & Budget .... Mr. Gerald GLASCO
88 Interim Dir University Outreach .... Ms. Paula NAS
96 Procurement Agent Senior .... Ms. Brenda ROTH
09 Director of Institutional Analysis .... Ms. Fawn SKARSTEN
38 Director CAPS .... Ms. Tamara MCKAY
39 Director Student Housing .... Mr. William WASHINGTON
100 Chief of Staff .... Dr. Tess BARKER
04 Executive Asst to the Chancellor .... Ms. Dru A. DORAN
29 Director Alumni Relations .... Dr. Mary Jo SEKELSKY
30 Director of Development .... Mr. Jay NUSSEL
92 Director Honors Program .... Dr. Maureen THUM
88 Sr Dir of Student Involv & Ldrship .... Dr. Michelle ROSYNSKY
91 Dir of Adm Info Mgmt Services .... Ms. Jay GANDHI
88 Dir Women's Educational Center .... Vacant
88 Dir Thompson Center for T&L .... Dr. Tracy WACKER

University of Phoenix Detroit Main Campus (C)

26261 Evergreen Road, Southfield MI 48076-4400
Telephone: (248) 675-3700 Identification: 770211
Accreditation: &NH

† No longer accepting campus-based students.

Van Andel Institute Graduate School (D)

333 Bostwick Avenue NE, Grand Rapids MI 49503
County: Kent Identification: 667085
Telephone: (616) 234-5708 Carnegie Class: Not Classified
FAX Number: (616) 234-5709 Calendar System: Semester
URL: vaigs.vai.org
Established: 2005 Annual Graduate Tuition & Fees: N/A
Enrollment: N/A Coed
Affiliation or Control: Independent Non-Profit IRS Status: 501(c)3
Highest Offering: Doctorate; No Undergraduates
Accreditation: NH

01 President/Dean of the Graduate Sch . Dr. Steven J. TRIEZENBERG
05 Associate Dean of Graduate School .... Dr. Julie D. TURNER
06 Enrollment and Records Admin .... Ms. Christy MAYO
04 Executive Asst to President .... Mrs. Susanne MILLER-SCHACHINGER
108 Director Institutional Assessment .... Dr. Patty FARRELL-COLE
32 Chief Student Affairs/Student Life .. Ms. Nancy SCHAPERKOTTER

Walsh College Novi Campus (E)

41500 Gardenbrook Road, Novi MI 48375-1313
Telephone: (248) 349-5454 Identification: 770293
Accreditation: &NH

Walsh College of Accountancy and Business Administration (F)

3838 Livernois Road, Box 7006, Troy MI 48007-7006
County: Oakland FICE Identification: 004071
Unit ID: 172608
Telephone: (248) 689-8282 Carnegie Class: Spec-4-yr-Bus
FAX Number: (248) 689-9066 Calendar System: Semester
URL: www.walshcollege.edu
Established: 1922 Annual Undergrad Tuition & Fees: N/A
Enrollment: 2,549 Coed
Affiliation or Control: Independent Non-Profit IRS Status: 501(c)3
Highest Offering: Doctorate
Accreditation: NH, ACBSP

01 President & CEO .... Ms. Marsha KELLIHER
05 Interim Exec VP/Chief Academic Ofc .... Dr. Michael A. RINKUS
10 Vice President/CFO/Treasurer . Ms. Helen C. KIEBA-TOLKSDORF
15 VP/Chief Human Resources/Admin Ofcr .... Ms. Elizabeth A. BARNES
30 Vice President/Chief Dev Officer .... Ms. Susan FOLEY
04 Exec Assistant to the President .... Ms. Stephanie M. WHEELER
32 Asst VP Student Services/Marketing ...... Ms. Victoria R. SCAVONE
106 Director Office of Online Learning .... Mr. Thomas PETZ
26 Asst VP/Director of Marketing .... Ms. Brenda MELLER
20 Director Academic Administration .... Ms. Monique CARDENAS
37 Director Financial Aid .... Ms. Catherine BERRAHOU
18 Director Facilities/Auxiliary Svcs .... Ms. Chris STOUT
21 Controller .... Mr. Ryan KUNZELMAN
07 Director Admissions/Acad Advising .... Ms. Heather RIGBY
06 Director of Records/Registrar .... Ms. Stacy JOHNSON
13 Exec Dir Ofc of Info Technology .... Mr. Jacob KLEIN
12 Director Novi Campus .... Mr. Jason SWEET
36 Director Career Services .... Ms. Brenda PAINE
88 Chair Management .... Dr. Sheila R. RONIS
88 Chair Business Comm .... Dr. Jenny TATSAK
88 Chair Marketing .... Dr. Michael LEVENS
88 Director Launchpad .... Ms. Carol GLYNN
29 Manager of Alumni Relations .... Ms. MiVida BURRUS
88 Chair Accounting/Taxation .... Mr. John BLACK
88 Chair Finance & Economics .... Mr. Greg TODD
88 Chair Decision Sciences .... Dr. Barbara CIARAMITARO

Washtenaw Community College (G)

4800 E Huron River Dr, Ann Arbor MI 48105-4800
County: Washtenaw FICE Identification: 002328
Unit ID: 172617
Telephone: (734) 973-3300 Carnegie Class: Assoc/MT-VT-High Non
FAX Number: (734) 677-5413 Calendar System: Semester
URL: www.wccnet.edu
Established: 1965 Annual Undergrad Tuition & Fees (In-District): $2,424
Enrollment: 12,211 Coed
Affiliation or Control: Local IRS Status: 501(c)3
Highest Offering: Associate Degree
Accreditation: NH, ACFEI, ADNUR, DA, PTAA, RAD, SURGT

01 President .... Dr. Rose BELLANCA
10 VP & Chief Financial Officer .... Mr. William JOHNSON
05 VP for Instruction .... Dr. Kimberly HURNS
15 VP Human Resources Mgmt .... Vacant
32 VP Student & Academic Services .... Ms. Linda BLAKEY
18 VP Facilities & Campus Safety .... Mr. Damon FLOWERS
111 AVP Pres of College Advancement .... Mr. Phil SNYDER
26 VP Economic/Community & College Dev .... Ms. Michelle MUELLER
07 AVP Recruitment & Enrollment .... Mr. Aamer CHAUDRI
45 Exec Dir Inst Effect Plng & Accred .... Dr. Julie MORRISON
20 Dean Supp Svcs & Student Advocacy .... Ms. Elizabeth ORBITS
08 Dean Learning Resources .... Vacant
50 Dean Business & Computer Tech .... Ms. Eva SAMULSKI
81 Dean Math/Sciene/Engineering .... Ms. Kristin GOOD
76 Dean Health Science .... Dr. Valerie GREAVES
36 Dean Career Svc/UA Programs .... Ms. Marilyn DONHAM
28 Dean Diversity & Inclusion .... Mr. Clarence JENNINGS
88 Dean Adv Tech/Public Service .... Mr. Brandon TUCKER
10 Controller .... Ms. Lynn GRACE
96 Dir Budget Purchasing Auxiliary Svc .... Ms. Barbara FILLINGER
16 Director Human Resource Svcs .... Ms. Christine MIHALY
37 Director Financial Aid .... Ms. Lori TRAPP
09 Director Institutional Research .... Dr. Roger MOURAD
19 Chief Public Safety .... Mr. Scott HILDEN
35 Dir Student Development/Activities .... Mr. Peter LESHKEVICH
84 Dean of Enrollment Management .... Mr. Larry AEILTS
86 Dir of Government Relations .... Vacant
43 General Counsel .... Mr. Larry BARKOFF
04 Exec Administrator to the President .... Ms. Vanessa BROOKS
100 Chief of Staff .... Vacant

Wayne County Community College District (H)

801 W Fort Street, Detroit MI 48226-3010
County: Wayne FICE Identification: 009230
Unit ID: 172635
Telephone: (313) 496-2600 Carnegie Class: Assoc/MT-VT-Mix Trad/Non
FAX Number: (313) 961-9439 Calendar System: Semester
URL: www.wcccd.edu
Established: 1967 Annual Undergrad Tuition & Fees (In-District): $2,838
Enrollment: 16,654 Coed
Affiliation or Control: State/Local IRS Status: 501(c)3
Highest Offering: Associate Degree
Accreditation: NH, DA, DH, EMT, SURGT

01 Chancellor .... Dr. Curtis L. IVERY
05 Int Dist VC Curric & Dist Lrng Pgm .... Dr. Patrick J. MCNALLY
51 Dist VC Sch Cont Ed/Wrkforce Dev .... Ms. Shawna FORBES
10 Dist VC Finance & Admin .... Ms. Kim DICARO
15 Dist VC HR/Accountability .... Mr. Mirza F. AHMED
108 Dist VC IE & Info Mgmt .... Ms. Johnesa HODGE
20 Int Dist VC Acad Acct & Polilcy .... Ms. CharMaine HINES
12 Campus President/CAO Downriver .... Mr. Anthony ARMINIAK
12 Campus President/CAO Downtown .... Ms. Denise SHANNON
12 Campus President/CAO Western .... Mr. Michael P. DOTSON
12 Campus President/CAO Northwest .... Dr. Letitia UDUMA
12 Campus President/Chief Student Svcs .... Ms. Mawine DIGGS
12 Provost University Center .... Dr. Sandra T. ROBINSON
76 Provost Health Sciences .... Dr. Abby FREEMAN

Wayne County Community College District Downriver Campus (I)

21000 Northline Road, Taylor MI 48180
Telephone: (734) 946-3500 Identification: 770297
Accreditation: &NH

Wayne County Community College District Downtown Campus (J)

1001 West Fort Street, Detroit MI 48226
Telephone: (313) 496-2758 Identification: 770926
Accreditation: @NH

Wayne County Community College District Eastern Campus (K)

5901 Conner, Detroit MI 48213
Telephone: (313) 922-3311 Identification: 770295
Accreditation: &NH

Wayne County Community College District Northwest Campus **(A)**

8200 West Outer Drive, Detroit MI 48219
Telephone: (313) 943-4000 Identification: 770296
Accreditation: &NH

Wayne County Community College District Ted Scott Campus **(B)**

9555 Haggerty Road, Belleville MI 48111
Telephone: (734) 699-7008 Identification: 770294
Accreditation: &NH, SURGA

Wayne State University (C)

656 W. Kirby Street, Room # 4070, Detroit MI 48202-4095
County: Wayne FICE Identification: 002329
Unit ID: 172644
Telephone: (313) 577-2424 Carnegie Class: DU-Highest
FAX Number: (313) 577-8154 Calendar System: Semester
URL: www.wayne.edu
Established: 1868 Annual Undergrad Tuition & Fees (In-State): $12,269
Enrollment: 27,140 Coed
Affiliation or Control: State IRS Status: 501(c)3
Highest Offering: Doctorate
Accreditation: NH, ANEST, ARCPA, AUD, CACREP, CAEPT, CLPSY, DANCE, DIETC, ENG, ENGT, FUSER, LAW, LIB, MED, MIDWF, MT, MUS, NURSE, OT, PA, PH, PHAR, PLNG, PTA, RAD, RTT, SP, SPAA, SW, THEA

01 President ... Dr. M. Roy WILSON
100 Chief of Staff/VP Marketing & Comm ... Mr. Michael G. WRIGHT
05 Provost ... Dr. Keith WHITFIELD
10 VP Finance & Business/Treasurer/CFO ... Mr. William DECATUR
43 Vice President and General Counsel ... Mr. Louis A. LESSEM
46 Vice President for Research ... Dr. Stephen M. LANIER
30 VP Development and Alumni Affairs ... Ms. Susan E. BURNS
86 VP Government and Community Affairs ... Mr. Patrick O. LINDSEY
20 Asst Provost for Academic Pgms ... Mr. R. Darin ELLIS
88 VP for Economic Development ... Mr. Ned STAEBLER
84 Int Assoc VP for Enrollment Mgmt ... Mr. Ahmad EZZEDDINE
101 Secretary to the BOG ... Ms. Julie H. MILLER
04 Assistant to the President ... Ms. Allison GUILLIOM
29 Exec Dir Alumni Relations ... Mr. Peter CABORN
15 Associate VP of Human Resources ... Ms. Alicia PENDELTON
18 Assoc VP Facilities/Planning/Mgmt ... Mr. Harry E. WYATT, JR.
21 Interim Assoc VP Budget ... Ms. Diana GOODE
44 Associate VP of Individual Gifts ... Mr. Michael MIRTO
32 Dean of Students ... Dr. David J. STRAUSS
07 Director Undergraduate Admissions ... Ms. Ericka JACKSON
26 Director of Communications ... Mr. Matthew T. LOCKWOOD
25 Asst VP Sponsored Program Admin ... Ms. Gail L. RYAN
37 Director of Student Financial Aid ... Ms. Catherine KAY
62 Dean University Library System ... Dr. Jon G. CAWTHORNE
06 University Registrar ... Ms. Linda K. FALKIEWICZ
49 Dean College of Liberal Arts/Sci ... Dr. Wayne RASKIND
61 Dean Law School ... Mr. Richard BIERSCHBACH
63 Dean School of Medicine ... Dr. Jack SOBEL
66 Dean College of Nursing ... Dr. Laurie LAUZON CLABO
54 Dean College of Engineering ... Dr. Farshad FOTOUHI
50 Dean Ilitch School of Business ... Dr. Robert E. FORSYTHE
70 Int Dean School of Social Work ... Dr. Jerrold BRANDELL
67 Acting Dean College of Pharmacy ... Dr. Deepak BHALLA
53 Dean College of Education ... Dr. R. Douglas WHITMAN
57 Dean College Fine/Perf & Comm Arts ... Dr. Matthew SEEGER
92 Dean Honors College ... Dr. Jerry HERRON
58 Dean Graduate School ... Dr. Ambika MATHUR
96 Assistant VP of Procurement ... Mr. Kenneth DOHERTY
104 Associate VP Outreach & Intl Pgms ... Dr. Ahmad EZZEDDINE
109 Assoc VP Business & Auxiliary Ops ... Mr. Timothy MICHAEL
88 Assoc VP Tech Commercialization ... Dr. Joan DUNBAR
13 Associate VP CIO ... Mr. Daren HUBBARD
41 Director of Athletics ... Mr. Robert FOURNIER
105 Director of Web Communications ... Mr. Nick DENARDIS
19 Chief of Police ... Mr. Anthony HOLT
22 Director Equal Opportunity ... Ms. Nikki WRIGHT
28 Assoc Provost Diversity & Inclusion ... Ms. Marquita CHAMBLEE
36 Director of Career Services ... Mr. Ronald KENT
39 Director Housing & Residential Life ... Ms. Jeanine BESSETTE
108 Director Institutional Assessment ... Dr. Catherine BARRETTE
38 Director Student Counseling ... Dr. Jeffrey KUENTZEL
09 Director Institutional Research ... Mr. Song YAN
102 Assoc VP Principal Gifts ... Ms. Tracy UTECH

West Shore Community College (D)

3000 N. Stiles Road, Scottville MI 49454-0277
County: Mason FICE Identification: 007950
Unit ID: 172671
Telephone: (231) 845-6211 Carnegie Class: Assoc/MT-VT-Mix Trad/Non
FAX Number: (231) 843-5803 Calendar System: Semester
URL: www.westshore.edu
Established: 1967 Annual Undergrad Tuition & Fees (In-District): $2,618
Enrollment: 1,235 Coed
Affiliation or Control: Local IRS Status: 501(c)3
Highest Offering: Associate Degree
Accreditation: NH

01 President ... Mr. Scott WARD
04 Executive Assistant to President ... Ms. Lisa STANKOWSKI
26 Exec Director of Communications ... Mr. Thomas A. HAWLEY
11 VP of Administrative Services ... Mr. Scott WARD
49 Dean of Arts and Sciences ... Dr. Brooke PORTMANN
13 Director of Information Technology ... Ms. Debra HINTZ
24 Media Svcs & Learning Tech Coord ... Mr. Craig PETERSON
119 Network Administrator ... Mr. Terrence JOHNSON
75 Dean of Occupational Programs ... Ms. Christy CHRISTMAS
32 Dean of Student Services ... Mr. Chad E. INABINET
06 Registrar ... Ms. Jill SWEET
09 Director of Institutional Research ... Mr. Steve SPARLING
40 Director of Bookstore & Food Svcs ... Ms. Cheryl HOGAN
37 Director Financial Aid ... Ms. Rebekah SCHAUB
91 Manager of Adm Computing Systems ... Ms. Bonnie CHALTRON
88 Director of Criminal Justice ... Mr. Dan DELLAR
41 Director of Recreational Services ... Mr. Michael A. MOORE
15 Director of Human Resources ... Ms. Debra CAMPBELL
16 Human Resources Specialist ... Ms. Sarah WAGNER
88 Director Student Resources ... Ms. Carla E. SHAY
08 Director of Library Services ... Ms. Renee SNODGRASS
23 Director of Wellness Center ... Ms. Julie PAGE-SMITH
10 Director of Accounting ... Ms. Kristen BIGGS
18 Facilities Maintenance Director ... Mr. Mark LIPPS
84 Director of Enrollment Services ... Mr. Marcus CROOK

Western Michigan University (E)

1903 West Michigan Avenue, Kalamazoo MI 49008-5202
County: Kalamazoo FICE Identification: 002330
Unit ID: 172699
Telephone: (269) 387-1000 Carnegie Class: DU-Higher
FAX Number: (269) 387-0958 Calendar System: Semester
URL: wmich.edu
Established: 1903 Annual Undergrad Tuition & Fees (In-State): $11,493
Enrollment: 23,529 Coed
Affiliation or Control: State IRS Status: 501(c)3
Highest Offering: Doctorate
Accreditation: NH, AAB, ARCPA, ART, AUD, #CAATE, CACREP, CAEPN, CEA, CIDA, CLPSY, COPSY, CS, DANCE, DIETD, DIETI, ENG, ENGT, MUS, NURSE, OT, SP, SPAA, SW, THEA

01 President ... Dr. Edward B. MONTGOMERY
05 Provost/Vice Pres Academic Affairs ... Dr. Timothy J. GREENE
10 Vice Pres Business & Finance/CFO ... Ms. Jan VAN DER KLEY
32 VP Student Affairs ... Dr. Diane K. ANDERSON
46 Vice President for Research ... Dr. Daniel M. LITYNSKI
30 VP Development & Alumni Relations ... Mr. Timothy TERRENTINE
43 General Counsel ... Dr. Carrick CRAIG
86 VP Govt Affairs & Univ Relations ... Mr. Gregory J. ROSINE
28 VP for Diversity and Inclusion ... Dr. Martha B. WARFIELD
13 Vice Prov Budget & Personnel/CIO ... Dr. James A. GILCHRIST
84 Assoc Provost Enrollment Mgmt ... Dr. Terrence M. CURRAN
09 Assoc Provost Inst Effectiveness ... Dr. Jody BRYLINSKY
108 Assoc Prov Assessment/UG Studies ... Dr. David S. REINHOLD
21 Assoc Vice Pres Business & Finance ... Ms. Patti VAN WALBECK
15 Assoc Vice Pres Human Resources ... Dr. Warren L. HILLS
18 Assoc Vice Pres Facilities Mgmt ... Mr. Peter J. STRAZDAS
35 Assoc VP of SA & Dean of Students ... Dr. Suzie NAGEL
35 Assoc VP for Student Affairs ... Mr. Vernon PAYNE
114 Exec Dir University Budgets ... Ms. Colleen SCARFF
31 Assoc VP for Community Outreach ... Mr. Robert MILLER
101 Secretary Board of Trustees ... Mr. Kahler B. SCHUEMANN
58 Dean Graduate College ... Dr. Susan R. STAPLETON
49 Dean of Arts & Sciences ... Dr. Carla M. KORETSKY
88 Dean of Aviation ... Capt. David M. POWELL
50 Interim Dean of Business ... Dr. Satish DESHPANDE
53 Dean of Education & Human Dev ... Dr. Ming LI
54 Dean of Engineer & Applied Sciences ... Dr. Houssam TOUTANJI
57 Dean of Fine Arts ... Mr. Daniel GUYETTE
76 Dean Health & Human Services ... Dr. Earlie WASHINGTON
92 Dean of Lee Honors College ... Dr. Gary H. BISCHOF
08 Dean of Libraries ... Ms. Julie A. GARRISON
26 Exec Dir of University Relations ... Ms. Cheryl ROLAND
36 Exec Dir Career & Student Empl Svcs ... Ms. Lynn C. KELLY-ALBERTSON
06 Registrar ... Ms. Carrie CUMMING
07 Director Admissions/Orientation ... Ms. Dachea HILL
37 Int Dir Student Financial Aid ... Dr. Terrell L. HODGE
38 Int Dir Counseling Services ... Dr. Brian J. FULLER
41 Dir Athletics ... Ms. Kathy B. BEAUREGARD
88 Int Assoc Prov for Global Education ... Dr. Jane BLYTH
85 Dir Intl Admissions & Services ... Mr. Juan TAVARES
106 Assoc Prov Extended Univ Programs ... Dr. Dawn M. GAYMER
14 Chief Technology Officer ... Mr. Thomas WOLF, JR.
22 Exec Dir Institutional Equity ... Dr. Evelyn B. WINFIELD-THOMAS
63 Dean School of Medicine ... Dr. Hal B. JENSON
104 Director Study Abroad ... Dr. Lee M. PENYAK
19 Dir Public Safety/Chief of Police ... Mr. Scott R. MERLO
25 Dir Grants/Contracts ... Ms. Betty J. MCKAIN
39 Director Residence Life ... Mr. Steven C. PALMER

Western Michigan University Cooley Law School (F)

300 S Capitol Avenue, Lansing MI 48933
County: Ingham FICE Identification: 012627
Unit ID: 172477
Telephone: (517) 371-5140 Carnegie Class: Spec-4-yr-Law
FAX Number: (517) 334-5718 Calendar System: Semester
URL: www.cooley.edu
Established: 1972 Annual Graduate Tuition & Fees: N/A
Enrollment: 1,444 Coed
Affiliation or Control: Independent Non-Profit IRS Status: 501(c)3
Highest Offering: First Professional Degree; No Undergraduates
Accreditation: NH, LAW

01 President ... Don LEDUC
04 Executive Asst to the President ... Cherie BECK
05 Dean ... Don LEDUC
10 Chief Financial Officer/COO ... Kathleen CONKLIN
07 Director of Admissions ... Brianne MYERS
08 Associate Dean Library/Info Svcs ... Duane STROJNY
20 Associate Dean Lansing Campus ... Michael MCDANIEL
108 Assoc Dean Planning/Accreditation ... Laura LEDUC
36 Assoc Dean Career Prof Development ... Charles TOY
32 Assoc Dean Students/Professionalism ... Amy TIMMER
43 Assoc Dean External Aff/Gen Counsel ... James ROBB
13 Assoc Dean for Information Tech/CIO ... Charles MICKENS
84 Assoc Dean for Enrollment Services ... Paul ZELENSKI
12 Associate Dean Grand Rapids ... Nelson MILLER
12 Associate Dean Tampa Bay ... Ronald SUTTON
12 Associate Dean Auburn Hills Campus ... Joan VESTRAND
88 Assistant Dean Auburn Hills Campus ... Lisa HALUSHKA
88 Assistant Dean Lansing Campus ... Mable MARTIN-SCOTT
88 Assistant Dean Grand Rapids Campus ... Tracey BRAME
88 Assistant Dean Tampa Bay Campus ... Katherine GUSTAFSON
06 Registrar/Dir of Student Records ... Mohammad SOHAIL
37 Director Financial Aid ... Richard BORUSZEWSKI
40 Bookstore Manager ... Joelle TOPP
21 Controller ... Ronda BECK
29 Director Alumni Donor Relations ... Pamela HEOS
26 Director Communications ... Terry CARELLA

Western Michigan University Cooley Law School Auburn Hills Campus **(G)**

2630 Featherstone, Auburn Hills MI 48326
Telephone: (248) 751-7800 Identification: 770288
Accreditation: &NH

Western Michigan University Cooley Law School Grand Rapids Campus **(H)**

111 Commerce Avenue, SW, Grand Rapids MI 49503
Telephone: (606) 301-6800 Identification: 770289
Accreditation: &NH

Western Michigan University Homer Stryker MD School of Medicine (I)

1000 Oakland Dr, Kalamazoo MI 49008-8010
County: Kalamazoo Identification: 667287
Telephone: (269) 337-4400 Carnegie Class: Not Classified
FAX Number: N/A Calendar System: Semester
URL: med.wmich.edu
Established: 2012 Annual Graduate Tuition & Fees: N/A
Enrollment: N/A Coed
Affiliation or Control: Independent Non-Profit IRS Status: 501(c)3
Highest Offering: Doctorate; No Undergraduates
Accreditation: @NH, #MED

01 Founding Dean ... Dr. Hal B. JENSON
05 Assoc Dean for Faculty Affairs ... Dr. Lisa GRAVES

Western Theological Seminary (J)

101 E 13th Street, Holland MI 49423-3622
County: Ottawa FICE Identification: 002331
Unit ID: 172705
Telephone: (616) 392-8555 Carnegie Class: Spec-4-yr-Faith
FAX Number: (616) 392-7717 Calendar System: Semester
URL: www.westernsem.edu
Established: 1866 Annual Graduate Tuition & Fees: N/A
Enrollment: 279 Coed
Affiliation or Control: Reformed Church In America IRS Status: 501(c)3
Highest Offering: Doctorate; No Undergraduates
Accreditation: THEOL

01 President ... Dr. Timothy BROWN
05 Academic Dean/VP Academic Affairs ... Dr. Alvin PADILLA
30 Vice Pres of Operations/Advancement ... Rev. Jeffrey MUNROE
10 Vice President of Finance ... Mr. Norman DONKERSLOOT
08 Interim Director of the Library ... Ms. Ann E. NIEUWKOOP
06 Registrar ... Ms. Tiffany NORDE
07 Director of Admissions ... Dr. Mark POPPEN
15 Director of Administration and HR ... Ms. Rayetta PEREZ

Yeshiva Beth Yehuda - Yeshiva Gedolah of Greater Detroit (K)

24600 Greenfield, Oak Park MI 48237-1544
County: Oakland FICE Identification: 023638
Unit ID: 247773
Telephone: (248) 968-3360 Carnegie Class: Spec-4-yr-Faith
FAX Number: (248) 968-8613 Calendar System: Semester
Established: 1985 Annual Undergrad Tuition & Fees: $6,800
Enrollment: 69 Male
Affiliation or Control: Independent Non-Profit IRS Status: 501(c)3
Highest Offering: Doctorate
Accreditation: RABN

01 Dean ... Rabbi Y. BAKST
05 Assistant Dean ... Rabbi M. S. BAKST
11 Executive Administrator ... Rabbi P. RUSHNAWITZ
37 Director of Financial Aid ... Rabbi Y. BLITZ

MINNESOTA

Academy College (A)

1600 W. 82nd Street, Suite 100, Bloomington MN 55431
County: Hennepin FICE Identification: 020503
Unit ID: 172866
Telephone: (952) 851-0066 Carnegie Class: Bac/Assoc-Mixed
FAX Number: (952) 851-0094 Calendar System: Quarter
URL: www.academycollege.edu
Established: 1936 Annual Undergrad Tuition & Fees: $17,409
Enrollment: 124 Coed
Affiliation or Control: Proprietary IRS Status: Proprietary
Highest Offering: Baccalaureate
Accreditation: ACICS

01 President ... Nancy GRAZZINI-OLSON
37 Director of Financial Aid ... Kellye MACLEOD

Adler Graduate School (B)

1550 E 78th Street, Richfield MN 55423
County: Hennepin FICE Identification: 030519
Unit ID: 374024
Telephone: (612) 861-7554 Carnegie Class: Spec-4-yr-Other Health
FAX Number: (612) 861-7559 Calendar System: Semester
URL: www.alfredadler.edu
Established: 1969 Annual Graduate Tuition & Fees: N/A
Enrollment: 311 Coed
Affiliation or Control: Independent Non-Profit IRS Status: 501(c)3
Highest Offering: Master's; No Undergraduates
Accreditation: NH

01 President ... Dr. Daniel HAUGEN
05 Academic Vice President ... Mr. Chris HELGESTAD
32 Director of Student Success Svcs ... Dr. Meg WHISTON
10 Director of Business ... Ms. Kathy BENGTSON
07 Director of Admissions ... Ms. Evelyn HAAS
37 Director of Student Financial Aid ... Ms. Jeanette MAYNARD NELSON
06 Registrar ... Ms. Debbie VELASCO
08 Head Librarian ... Ms. Nicole MARCHAND

American Academy of Acupuncture and Oriental Medicine (C)

1925 W County Road B2, Roseville MN 55113-2703
County: Ramsey FICE Identification: 038333
Unit ID: 446002
Telephone: (651) 631-0204 Carnegie Class: Spec-4-yr-Other Health
FAX Number: (651) 631-0361 Calendar System: Trimester
URL: www.aaaom.edu
Established: 1997 Annual Graduate Tuition & Fees: N/A
Enrollment: 66 Coed
Affiliation or Control: Proprietary IRS Status: Proprietary
Highest Offering: Master's; No Undergraduates
Accreditation: ACUP

01 President ... Dr. Changzhen GONG
11 Administrative Director ... Leila NIELSEN
37 Financial Aid Officer ... Cate LARSON

Argosy University, Twin Cities (D)

1515 Central Parkway, Eagan MN 55121-1756
Telephone: (888) 844-2004 FICE Identification: 007619
Accreditation: &WC, ACBSP, CLPSY, DH, DMS, HT, MAC, MFCD, MLTAD, MT, RTT

† Regional accreditation is carried under the parent institution in Orange, CA.

The Art Institutes International Minnesota (E)

15 S 9th Street, Minneapolis MN 55402-2808
County: Hennepin FICE Identification: 010248
Unit ID: 173887
Telephone: (612) 332-3361 Carnegie Class: Spec-4-yr-Arts
FAX Number: (612) 332-3934 Calendar System: Quarter
URL: www.artinstitutes.edu/minneapolis
Established: 1964 Annual Undergrad Tuition & Fees: N/A
Enrollment: 713 Coed
Affiliation or Control: Proprietary IRS Status: Proprietary
Highest Offering: Baccalaureate
Accreditation: #ACICS, ACFEI

† School is in teach-out plan through 2019.

Association Free Lutheran Bible School and Seminary (F)

3134 East Medicine Lake Blvd, Plymouth MN 55441
County: Hennepin Identification: 667235
Telephone: (763) 544-9501 Carnegie Class: Not Classified
FAX Number: (763) 412-2047 Calendar System: Semester
URL: www.aflbs.org
Established: 1964 Annual Graduate Tuition & Fees: N/A
Enrollment: N/A Coed
Affiliation or Control: Independent Non-Profit IRS Status: 501(c)3
Highest Offering: Master's; No Undergraduates
Accreditation: @TRACS

01 President ... Wade MOBLEY
03 Vice President/Dean ... Joel ROLF
05 Vice President Academic Affairs ... Mark OLSON
11 Vice President of Operations ... Larry MYHRER

Augsburg College (G)

2211 Riverside Avenue, Minneapolis MN 55454-1398
County: Hennepin FICE Identification: 002334
Unit ID: 173045
Telephone: (612) 330-1000 Carnegie Class: Masters/L
FAX Number: (612) 330-1649 Calendar System: Semester
URL: www.augsburg.edu
Established: 1869 Annual Undergrad Tuition & Fees: $36,415
Enrollment: 3,458 Coed
Affiliation or Control: Evangelical Lutheran Church In America
IRS Status: 501(c)3
Highest Offering: Doctorate
Accreditation: NH, ARCPA, MUS, NURSE, SW

01 President ... Dr. Paul C. PRIBBENOW
05 Provost and Chief Academic Officer ... Dr. Karen KAIVOLA
10 CFO/VP Finance & Admin ... Dr. Beth REISSENWEBER
111 VP Institutional Advancement ... Ms. Heather RIDDLE
84 VP Enrollment Management ... Vacant
32 VP Student Affairs ... Ms. Ann L. GARVEY
26 VP Marketing/Communication ... Ms. Rebecca JOHN
45 VP & Chief Strategy Officer ... Mr. Leif B. ANDERSON
30 AVP Institutional Advancement ... Ms. Sarah FOSSEN
30 AVP Institutional Advancement ... Ms. Amy ALKIRE
107 Dean of Professional Studies ... Dr. Monica C. DEVERS
49 AVP/Dean of Arts & Sciences ... Vacant
88 Asst Provost of Global Education ... Mr. Patrick MULVIHILL
35 Dean of Students ... Dr. Sarah GRIESSE
12 Director Rochester Program ... Vacant
41 Athletic Director ... Mr. Jeffrey F. SWENSON
42 Campus Pastor ... Rev. Sonja HAGANDER
28 Chief Diversity Officer/Dir CAO ... Ms. Joanne REECK
37 Director of Financial Aid ... Ms. Gina JONES
06 Registrar ... Ms. Crystal COMER
07 Director Undergraduate Admissions ... Mr. Rick ELLIS
123 Director Graduate Admissions ... Mr. Nathan GORR
18 Director of Facilities ... Mr. Dennis STUCKEY
13 Chief Information Officer ... Mr. Scott KRAJEWSKI
38 Director Ctr Wellness & Counseling . Ms. Nancy G. GUILBEAULT
15 Director & Chief HR Officer ... Ms. Lisa STOCK
08 Director Library Services ... Ms. Mary HOLLERICH
19 Director Public Safety & Risk Mgmt ... Mr. Scott BROWNELL
31 Director Community Relations ... Mr. Steve PEACOCK
88 Director StepUp Program ... Ms. Patrice SALMERI
85 Director International Student Svc ... Mr. James TRELSTAD-PORTER
114 Director of Budget ... Mr. Tom CARROLL
88 Director Event & Conf Planning ... Ms. Jodi COLLEN
20 Director of Academic Administration ... Dr. Nathan HALLANGER
27 Director News and Media Services ... Ms. Stephanie WEISS
27 Director Marketing Communication .... Mr. Stephen JENDRASZAK
36 Director Strommen Career Center ... Mr. Keith MUNSON
39 Director Residence Life ... Ms. Amanda ERDMAN
104 Director Global Initiatives ... Ms. Leah SPINOSA DE VEGA
25 Director Sponsored Programs ... Ms. Erica SWIFT
110 Asst Dir Leadership Gifts ... Ms. Amanda SCHERER
04 Executive Assistant to President ... Ms. Cyndi BERG
88 Admissions Operations Program Dir ... Ms. Keri VANOVERSCHELDE
40 Bookstore Manager ... Ms. Barbara HENDRICKS
09 Dir Inst Research & Effectiveness ... Ms. Kathryn HAHN
96 Manager of Purchasing & Central Svs ... Ms. Jill DAVENPORT

Bethany Global University (H)

6820 Auto Club Road, Suite C, Bloomington MN 55438
County: Hennepin Identification: 667136
Unit ID: 486284
Telephone: (952) 944-2121 Carnegie Class: Not Classified
FAX Number: (952) 829-2753 Calendar System: Semester
URL: www.bcom.org
Established: 1948 Annual Undergrad Tuition & Fees: $13,000
Enrollment: 179 Coed
Affiliation or Control: Interdenominational IRS Status: 501(c)3
Highest Offering: Master's
Accreditation: BI

01 President ... Dan BROKKE
03 Executive Vice President ... Tim FREEMAN
04 Administrative Asst to President ... Petra HARBOUR
11 Executive VP/Professor ... Dave HASZ
05 VP of Academic Affairs ... Paul HARTFORD
06 Registrar ... Jason HACHE
07 Director of Admissions ... Lori BEYER
08 Head Librarian ... Roger VANOOSTEN
101 Secretary of the Institution/Board ... Theresa HARTFORD
106 Dir Online Education/E-learning ... Jim RAYMO
13 Chief Info Technology Officer (CIO) ... Chris ERICKSON
15 Director Personnel Services ... Chelsey HOFFMEISTER
18 Chief Facilities/Physical Plant ... Mike MORCOMB
19 Director Security/Safety ... Matt ADAIR
26 Chief Public Relations/Marketing ... Dan SANCHEZ
29 Director Alumni Relations ... Marnie FUJII
30 Chief Development/Advancement ... Randy DIRKS
32 Chief Student Affairs/Student Life ... Derek BROKKE
37 Director Student Financial Aid ... Aaron HARRIS

Bethany Lutheran College (I)

700 Luther Drive, Mankato MN 56001-6163
County: Blue Earth FICE Identification: 002337
Unit ID: 173142
Telephone: (507) 344-7000 Carnegie Class: Bac-A&S
FAX Number: (507) 344-7376 Calendar System: Semester
URL: www.blc.edu
Established: 1911 Annual Undergrad Tuition & Fees: $25,890
Enrollment: 524 Coed
Affiliation or Control: Evangelical Lutheran Synod IRS Status: 501(c)3
Highest Offering: Baccalaureate
Accreditation: NH

01 President ... Dr. Gene R. PFEIFER
42 Dir Campus Spiritual Life/Chaplain .... Rev. Donald L. MOLDSTAD
05 Vice President of Academic Affairs ... Dr. Eric K. WOLLER
32 Vice President of Student Affairs ... Dr. Theodore E. MANTHE
10 VP of Finance & Administration ... Mr. Daniel L. MUNDAHL
111 Vice President of Advancement ... Mr. Arthur P. WESTPHAL
37 Director of Financial Aid ... Mr. Jeffrey W. YOUNGE
06 Registrar ... Ms. Stacy J. TOMHAVE
07 VP of Admissions & Enrollment ... Mr. Daniel P. TOMHAVE
15 Manager of Human Resources ... Ms. Mary Jo H. STARKSON
08 Interim Dir of Library Services ... Ms. Alyssa K. INNIGER
13 Director of Information Technology ... Mr. John M. SEHLOFF
26 Dir of Institutional Communication ... Mr. Lance W. SCHWARTZ
41 Director of Athletics ... Mr. Donald M. WESTPHAL
29 Manager of Alumni Relations ... Mr. Jacob C. KRIER
09 Mgr Acad & Institutional Research ... Ms. Lisa A. SHUBERT
40 Bookstore Manager ... Mr. Paul G. WOLD
21 Controller ... Mr. Gregory W. COSTELLO
28 Coord Ctr for Intercultural Develop ... Vacant
38 Coord of Student Counseling ... Vacant
18 Director of Facilities ... Mr. Juel O. MERSETH
108 Director of Assessment ... Dr. Theodore E. MANTHE
04 Executive Asst to President ... Ms. Lynette Y. MERSETH
106 Director Online Learning ... Mr. Kevin ZIMMERMAN

Bethel University (J)

3900 Bethel Drive, Saint Paul MN 55112-6999
County: Ramsey FICE Identification: 009058
Unit ID: 173160
Telephone: (651) 638-6400 Carnegie Class: Masters/L
FAX Number: (651) 638-6001 Calendar System: Semester
URL: www.bethel.edu
Established: 1871 Annual Undergrad Tuition & Fees: $35,160
Enrollment: 3,952 Coed
Affiliation or Control: Baptist IRS Status: 501(c)3
Highest Offering: Doctorate
Accreditation: NH, ACBSP, ARCPA, CAATE, CAEPT, MFCD, MIDWF, NURSE, SW, THEOL

01 President ... Dr. James H. BARNES, III
100 Special Assistant to President ... Dr. John A. ADDLEMAN
05 Executive Vice Pres and Provost ... Dr. Debra HARLESS
10 Chief Financial Officer ... Mr. Patrick BROOKE
46 Sr VP Strategic Plng & Opers Effect ... Mr. Joseph LALUZERNE
20 Associate Provost ... Dr. Randy BERGEN
26 Chief Marketing Officer ... Ms. Carmen SHIELDS
30 Sr VP University Relations ... Mr. Mark MILES
46 Chief Inst Data/Research Officer ... Mr. Daniel NELSON
90 VP for Facilities & Technology ... Mr. Mark POSNER
29 Exec Minister for Church Relations ... Mr. Ralph GUSTAFSON
32 Vice President Student Life ... Dr. William WASHINGTON
49 Vice President & Dean of CAS ... Dr. Deborah SULLIVAN-TRAINOR
73 VP and Dean BSSP ... Dr. David CLARK
84 VP for Enrollment Management ... Mr. Timothy EATON
79 Dean Arts & Humanities ... Dr. Barrett FISHER
108 Assoc Dean Inst Assess/Accred ... Dr. Joel FREDERICKSON
81 Dean Natural/Behavioral Sci ... Dr. Carole YOUNG
107 Dean Faculty Dev/Professional Pgms ... Vacant
104 Assoc Dean Off-Campus Programs ... Mr. Vincent PETERS
12 Actg Dn/Exec Ofcr BU Sem San Diego ... Dr. Arnell MOTZ
35 Dean of Students ... Ms. Miranda POWERS
08 Director of Libraries ... Mr. David R. STEWART
15 Director of Human Resources ... Ms. Cara WALD
41 Athletic Director ... Mr. Robert B. BJORKLUND
37 Financial Aid Officer ... Mr. Jeffery D. OLSON
42 Dean Campus Ministrs/Campus Pastor ... Ms. Laurel BUNKER
07 Director of CAS Admissions ... Mr. Bret HYDER
07 Director Seminary Admissions ... Vacant
07 Director of CAPS/GS Admissions ... Vacant
06 University Registrar ... Ms. Diane KRUSEMARK
36 Director Career Counsel/Placement ... Mr. Dave BROZA
19 Chief of Security and Safety ... Mr. Andrew LUCHSINGER
40 Director Campus Stores ... Ms. Jill SONSTEBY
23 Director of Health Services ... Mrs. Elizabeth K. MILLER
96 Director of Purchasing ... Vacant
38 Director Student Counseling ... Dr. Miriam HILL
18 Int Dir of Facilities Admin Ops ... Mr. Barry HOLST
18 Director Facilities Tech Ops ... Mr. Glenn HOFER
28 Chief Diversity Officer ... Dr. Ruben RIVERA

29 Director Alumni & Family Relations .... Mr. Jim BENDER

† The marriage and family therapy master's program at Bethel Seminary San Diego is accredited by the Commission on Accreditation for Marriage and Family Therapy Education (COAMFTE) of the American Association for Marriage and Family Therapy (AAMFT)

Bethlehem College & Seminary (A)

720 13th Avenue South, Minneapolis MN 55415

County: Hennepin Identification: 667249

Unit ID: 486053

Telephone: (612) 455-3420 Carnegie Class: Not Classified

FAX Number: N/A Calendar System: Semester

URL: bcsmn.edu

Established: 2009 Annual Undergrad Tuition & Fees: $6,080

Enrollment: 191 Coed

Affiliation or Control: Independent Non-Profit IRS Status: 501(c)3

Highest Offering: Master's

Accreditation: BI

01 President .... Dr. Timothy TOMLINSON
05 Academic Dean .... Dr. Brian TABB
11 VP of Administration .... Jason ABELL
111 VP of Advancement .... Rick SEGAL
07 Director of Admissions .... Daniel KLEVEN
04 Administrative Asst to President .... Lance M. KRAMER

Capella University (B)

225 S 6th Street, 9th Floor, Minneapolis MN 55402-4319

County: Hennepin FICE Identification: 032673

Unit ID: 413413

Telephone: (888) 227-3552 Carnegie Class: DU-Mod

FAX Number: (612) 977-5066 Calendar System: Other

URL: www.capella.edu

Established: 1993 Annual Undergrad Tuition & Fees: $13,998

Enrollment: 34,365 Coed

Affiliation or Control: Proprietary IRS Status: Proprietary

Highest Offering: Doctorate

Accreditation: NH, ACBSP, CACREP, CAEPN, CS, MFCD, NURSE, @SW

01 President .... Dr. Richard SENESE
05 VP Academic Affairs/CAO .... Dr. Richard SENESE
03 VP of Colleges & Univ Ops/COO .... Mr. Andrew WATT

Carleton College (C)

1 N College Street, Northfield MN 55057-4001

County: Rice FICE Identification: 002340

Unit ID: 173258

Telephone: (507) 222-4000 Carnegie Class: Bac-A&S

FAX Number: (507) 222-4204 Calendar System: Trimester

URL: www.carleton.edu

Established: 1866 Annual Undergrad Tuition & Fees: $50,874

Enrollment: 2,014 Coed

Affiliation or Control: Independent Non-Profit IRS Status: 501(c)3

Highest Offering: Baccalaureate

Accreditation: NH

01 President .... Mr. Steven G. POSKANZER, JR.
05 Dean of the College .... Ms. Beverly NAGEL
10 VP Business & Finance/Treasurer .... Mr. Fred A. ROGERS
111 Vice President External Relations .... Mr. Tommy BONNER
32 VP for Student Dev/Dean of Students .. Ms. Carolyn LIVINGSTON
07 VP and Dean of Admissions/Fin Aid .... Mr. Paul THIBOUTOT
100 Assoc Vice President/Chief of Staff .... Ms. Elise ESLINGER
30 Assoc VP External Relations .... Ms. Gayle MCJUNKIN
26 Assoc VP Ext Relations/Dir Col Comm .... Mr. Joe HARGIS
20 Associate Dean of the College .... Ms. Gretchen HOFMEISTER
20 Associate Dean of the College .... Mr. Andrew FISHER
88 Dir of Advising/Fac Div Rctmnt .... Mr. Alfred MONTERO
88 Director of Student Fellowships ....Ms. Marynel RYAN VAN ZEE
35 Associate Dean of Students .... Mr. Joseph BAGGOT
35 Associate Dean of Students .... Ms. Cathy CARLSON
37 Assoc Dean Admiss/Dir Stdnt Fin Svc .... Mr. Rod M. OTO
42 Chaplain .... Rev. Carolyn FURE-SLOCUM
06 Registrar .... Ms. Emy FARLEY
08 College Librarian .... Mr. Bradley SCHAFFNER
09 Dir of Inst Research and Assessment .... Vacant
44 Asst VP Alum/Par Rel/Annual Giving .... Ms. Becky ZRIMSEK
29 Director of Alumni Relations .... Ms. Sarah FORSTER
88 Director of Alumni Annual Fund .... Ms. Maggie PATRICK
110 Assoc VP for Development .... Mr. Dan RUSTAD
112 Director of Gift Planning .... Ms. Lynne WILMOT
13 Chief Technology Officer .... Ms. Janet SCANNELL
105 Dir Marketing Comm/Content Dvlpmt .... Ms. Jaye LAWRENCE
27 Director of Media/Public Relations .... Mr. Eric SIEGER
15 Director of Human Resources .... Ms. Kerstin CARDENAS
39 Director of Residential Life .... Ms. Andrea ROBINSON
88 Dir Intercult/International Life .... Vacant
104 Director of Off-Campus Studies .... Ms. Helena KAUFMAN
36 Director of the Career Center .... Ms. Kimberly BETZ
23 Dir Student Health and Counseling .... Ms. Marit LYSNE
18 Dir of Facilities/Capital Planning .... Mr. Steven SPEHN
21 Comptroller .... Ms. Linda THORNTON
102 Dir Corporate/Foundation Relations .... Mr. Mark GLEASON
88 Dir of Educational Research .... Ms. Andrea NIXON
88 Dir Center for Learning/Teaching .... Ms. Melissa EBLEN-ZAYAS
109 Director of Auxiliary Services .... Mr. Daniel BERGESON
41 Athletic Director .... Mr. Gerald YOUNG
19 Director of Security Services .... Mr. Wayne EISENHUTH

105 Director of Web Services .... Ms. Julie ANDERSON
88 Dir of Enterprise Information Svcs .... Ms. Julie CREAMER
88 Director of Technology Support .... Mr. Austin ROBINSON-COOLIDGE

Central Baptist Theological Seminary of Minneapolis (D)

900 Forestview Lane N, Plymouth MN 55441-5934

County: Hennepin Identification: 666050

Telephone: (763) 417-8250 Carnegie Class: Not Classified

FAX Number: (763) 417-8258 Calendar System: Semester

URL: www.centralseminary.edu

Established: 1956 Annual Undergrad Tuition & Fees: N/A

Enrollment: N/A Coed

Affiliation or Control: Baptist IRS Status: 501(c)3

Highest Offering: Doctorate

Accreditation: TRACS, @THEOL

01 President .... Dr. Matthew D. MORRELL
03 Provost .... Dr. Brett J. WILLIAMS
05 VP of Academic Affairs .... Dr. Jonathan R. PRATT
06 Registrar .... Dr. Jeff P. STRAUB

*College of Medicine, Mayo Clinic (E)

200 First Street, Rochester MN 55905-3712

County: Olmsted Identification: 666719

Telephone: (507) 284-2511 Carnegie Class: N/A

FAX Number: (507) 284-0999

URL: www.mayo.edu

01 Chief Executive Officer .... Dr. John H. NOSEWORTHY
05 Exec Dean for Education Mayo Clinic ...... Dr. Frederick B. MEYER
46 Exec Dean for Research Mayo Clinic .... Dr. Greg GORES
15 Chair of Human Resources .... Ms. Cathy FRASER
26 Chief Marketing Officer .... Mr. John H. WESTON
30 Exec Dean of Development .... Dr. Michael CAMILLERI
86 Chair Government Relations .... Vacant
37 Financial Aid Officer .... Mr. David L. DAHLEN
08 Executive Director of Libraries .... Ms. Anna Beth MORGAN
29 Director Mayo Clinic Alumni Center .... Ms. Judith ANDERSON

*Mayo Medical School (F)

200 1st Street, SW, Rochester MN 55905-0001

County: Olmsted FICE Identification: 011732

Unit ID: 173957

Telephone: (507) 538-4897 Carnegie Class: Spec-4-yr-Med

FAX Number: (507) 284-2634 Calendar System: Other

URL: www.mayo.edu/mms

Established: 1971 Annual Undergrad Tuition & Fees: N/A

Enrollment: 218 Coed

Affiliation or Control: Independent Non-Profit IRS Status: 501(c)3

Highest Offering: First Professional Degree

Accreditation: NH, MED

02 Dean .... Dr. Fredric B. MEYER
05 Assoc Dean Academic Affairs .... Dr. Darcy A. REED
32 Assoc Dean Student Affairs .... Dr. Alexandra P. WOLANSKYJ
20 Assoc Dean Faculty Affairs .... Dr. Geoffrey B. THOMPSON
11 Administrator for Mayo Med School .... Ms. Marcia ANDRESEN REID
22 Chief Human Resources .... Ms. Cathryn FRASER
26 Chief Mktg Ofcr/Chair Public Affs .... Mr. Chris W. GADE
88 Internatl Personnel Practice Group .... Ms. Ann H. LANCE
37 Director of Financial Aid .... Mr. David L. DAHLEN
08 Head Librarian .... Ms. Anna Beth MORGAN

*Mayo Clinic College of Medicine-Mayo Graduate School (G)

200 First Street, SW, Rochester MN 55905-0001

Telephone: (507) 538-1160 FICE Identification: 011516

Accreditation: &NH, DENT, PDPSY

† Regional accreditation is carried under College of Medicine, Mayo Clinic.

*Mayo School of Health Sciences (H)

200 First St. SW, Siebens Bldg 3, Rochester MN 55905-0001

Telephone: (507) 284-3293 FICE Identification: 008182

Accreditation: &NH, ANEST, COARC, CVT, CYTO, DIETI, DMS, HT, MT, NDT, NMT, PAST, PHLEB, PTA, RAD, RTT, SURGA

† Regional accreditation is carried under College of Medicine, Mayo Clinic.

College of Saint Benedict (I)

37 S College Avenue, Saint Joseph MN 56374-2099

County: Stearns FICE Identification: 002341

Unit ID: 174747

Telephone: (320) 363-5011 Carnegie Class: Bac-A&S

FAX Number: (320) 363-6099 Calendar System: Semester

URL: www.csbsju.edu

Established: 1913 Annual Undergrad Tuition & Fees: $42,271

Enrollment: 1,943 Coordinate

Affiliation or Control: Roman Catholic IRS Status: 501(c)3

Highest Offering: Baccalaureate

Accreditation: NH, CAEPN, DIETD, MUS, NURSE

01 President .... Dr. Mary HINTON
05 Provost Academic Affairs .... Dr. Richard ICE
32 Vice President Student Development .... Ms. Mary A. GELLER
111 VP Institutional Advancement .... Ms. Kathy HANSEN
45 VP Planning and Public Affairs .... Mr. Jon D. MCGEE
10 Vice Pres Finance/Administration .... Ms. Susan M. PALMER
07 VP Admission & Financial Aid .... Dr. Calvin MOSLEY
18 Exec Director Facilities .... Mr. Brad SINN
20 Academic Dean .... Dr. Barbara MAY
26 Chief Mktg & Comm Officer .... Ms. Tammy MOORE
34 Dean of Students .... Ms. Jody L. TERHAAR
06 Registrar .... Ms. Julie E. GRUSKA
08 Director Library .... Ms. Kathy PARKER
37 Exec Director Financial Aid .... Mr. Stuart PERRY
15 Director Human Resources .... Ms. Carol ABELL
38 Director of Counseling .... Dr. Mike J. EWING
42 Director of Campus Ministry .... Sr. Sharon NOHNER, OSB
41 Athletic Director .... Ms. Glennis WERNER
13 Director of Info Technology Svc .... Ms. Casey GORDON
19 Director of Security .... Mr. Darren SWANSON
21 Controller .... Ms. Anne OBERMAN
36 Director of Career Services .... Dr. Heidi HARLANDER
09 Assoc Dir of Institutional Research .... Ms. Karen KNUTSON
40 Director of Bookstores .... Ms. Tina STREIT
100 Chief of Staff/Lead Title IX Coord .... Dr. Kathryn ENKE
88 Director Student Human Rights .... Mr. Brandyn WOODARD
29 Asst Director Alumnae Relations .... Ms. Kristin LYMAN
30 Assoc VP Institutional Advancement .... Ms. Heather PIEPER-OLSON
27 Exec Director of Public Relations .... Mr. Michael HEMMESCH

The College of Saint Scholastica (J)

1200 Kenwood Avenue, Duluth MN 55811-4199

County: Saint Louis FICE Identification: 002343

Unit ID: 174899

Telephone: (218) 723-6000 Carnegie Class: Masters/L

FAX Number: (218) 723-6290 Calendar System: Semester

URL: www.css.edu

Established: 1912 Annual Undergrad Tuition & Fees: $35,326

Enrollment: 4,329 Coed

Affiliation or Control: Roman Catholic IRS Status: 501(c)3

Highest Offering: Doctorate

Accreditation: NH, #ARCPA, CAATE, CAEP, CAEPT, CAHIIM, NURSE, OT, PTA, SW

01 President .... Dr. Colette GEARY
10 Vice President Finance .... Ms. Susan KERRY
05 Vice Pres Academic Affairs .... Dr. Wolfgang NATTER
30 Vice Pres College Advancement .... Mr. John LABOSKY
32 Vice President for Student Affairs .... Mr. Steve LYONS
13 Chief Information Officer .... Mr. Xavier KNIGHT

Concordia College (K)

901 8th Street S, Moorhead MN 56562-0001

County: Clay FICE Identification: 002346

Unit ID: 173300

Telephone: (218) 299-4000 Carnegie Class: Bac-A&S

FAX Number: (218) 299-3947 Calendar System: Semester

URL: www.cord.edu

Established: 1891 Annual Undergrad Tuition & Fees: $36,878

Enrollment: 2,177 Coed

Affiliation or Control: Evangelical Lutheran Church In America

IRS Status: 501(c)3

Highest Offering: Master's

Accreditation: NH, #CAEP, DIETD, DIETI, MUS, NURSE, SW

01 President .... Dr. William J. CRAFT
05 Dean of College/VP Academic Affairs .... Dr. Eric J. ELIASON
10 Vice Pres Finance/Treasurer .... Ms. Linda J. BROWN
84 Vice Pres Enrollment and Marketing .... Mr. Karl A. STUMO
111 Vice Pres Advancement .... Ms. Teresa L. HARLAND
32 VP Student Dev and Campus Life .... Dr. Lisa SETHRE-HOFSTAD
28 Chief Diversity Officer .... Dr. Edward ANTONIO
100 Chief of Staff .... Ms. Tracey A. MOORHEAD
13 Chief Info Ofcr/Assoc Vice Pres .... Mr. Bruce W. VIEWEG
07 Exec Dir of Admission & Scholarship .... Ms. Carola THORSON
06 Registrar .... Ms. Ericka K. PETERSON
37 Assoc VP Enrollment & Financial Aid ..... Mr. Eric J. ADDINGTON
08 Library Director .... Mrs. Laura K. PROBST
15 Director Human Resources .... Ms. Peggy L. TORRANCE
29 Director Alumni Relations .... Mr. Eric P. JOHNSON
26 Assoc VP Commun & Chf Mktg Officer .... Mr. Josh D. LYSNE
18 Director of Facilities Management .... Mr. Wayne R. FLACK
41 Athletic Director .... Mr. Jeff BRETHERTON
42 Director Dovre Center .... Dr. Larry A. PAPENFUSS
42 Minister of Word and Sacrament .... Rev. Elizabeth C. MCHAN
42 Minister Faith/Spirit in Action .... Mr. Jon LEISETH
85 Associate Dean for Global Learning .... Dr. Per ANDERSON
19 Director of Public Safety .... Mr. William MACDONALD

Concordia University, St. Paul (L)

1282 Concordia Ave, Saint Paul MN 55104-5494

County: Ramsey FICE Identification: 002347

Unit ID: 173328

Telephone: (651) 641-8278 Carnegie Class: Masters/L

FAX Number: (651) 659-0207 Calendar System: Semester

URL: www.csp.edu

Established: 1893 Annual Undergrad Tuition & Fees: $21,250

Enrollment: 4,380 Coed

Affiliation or Control: Lutheran Church - Missouri Synod
IRS Status: 501(c)3
Highest Offering: Doctorate
Accreditation: **NH**, NURSE, OPE, PTA

Code	Title	Name
01	President	Rev.Dr. Thomas Karl RIES
03	Executive Vice President	Dr. Cheryl T. CHATMAN
05	Vice President Academic Affairs	Dr. Marilyn REINECK
10	Vice President for Finance	Rev.Dr. Michael H. DORNER
30	Vice President for Advancement	Mr. Mark HILL
11	Sr Vice Pres for Administration	Dr. Eric E. LAMOTT
84	Assoc VP Cohort Enrollment Mgmt	Ms. Kim CRAIG
07	Assc VP Traditional Enrollment Mgmt	Mrs. Kristin M. VOGEL
32	Assoc VP Student Life	Mr. Jason M. RAHN
108	Assoc VP for Assessment/Accred	Dr. Miriam LUEBKE
53	Dean College of Education & Science	Mr. Lonn MALY
49	Dean College of Arts & Letters	Dr. Paul HILLMER
58	Dean of Graduate School	Dr. Michael WALCHESKI
50	Dean College of Business	Dr. Kevin HALL
28	Dean of Diversity	Dr. Cheryl T. CHATMAN
39	Asst Director of Residence Life	Mr. Jake WAKEM
06	Registrar	Mrs. Toni SQUIRES
08	Director of Library Services	Dr. Charlotte M. KNOCHE
26	Dir Univ Communications/Mrktng	Mr. Brian EVANS
15	Director of Human Resources	Ms. Milissa M. BECKER
37	Director of Financial Aid	Ms. Jeanie PECK
04	Executive Assistant to President	Ms. Jill K. SIMON
42	University Pastor	Rev. Thomas GUNDERMANN
88	Director of Traditional Advising	Ms. Gretchen WALTHER
09	Director of Institutional Research	Ms. Beth C. PETER
29	Director of Alumni Relations	Mrs. Rhonda K. PALMERSHEIM
41	Director of Athletics	Mr. Mark MCKENZIE
18	Director of Operations	Mr. James P. ORCHARD
36	Coordinator of Placement	Ms. Jacquelyn MAGNUSON
40	Bookstore Manager	Mr. Chad L. MASTEL
90	Director of Computer Services	Mr. Jonathan S. BREITBARTH
91	Director Administrative Computing	Ms. Beth C. PETER
19	Risk Manager	Mrs. Sara K. MULSO
24	Help Desk Coordinator	Mr. Amrit MISRA

Crown College (A)

8700 College View Drive, Saint Bonifacius MN 55375-9001
County: Carver FICE Identification: 002383
Unit ID: 174862
Telephone: (952) 446-4100 Carnegie Class: Bac-Diverse
FAX Number: (952) 446-4149 Calendar System: Semester
URL: www.crown.edu
Established: 1916 Annual Undergrad Tuition & Fees: $24,700
Enrollment: 1,153 Coed
Affiliation or Control: The Christian And Missionary Alliance
IRS Status: 501(c)3
Highest Offering: Master's
Accreditation: **NH**, NURSE

Code	Title	Name
01	President	Dr. David J. WIGGINS
04	Exec Assistant to the President	Mrs. Shirley M. GRANLUND
10	Acting VP Finance	Dr. Scott MOATS
05	VP Academic Affairs/Provost	Dr. Scott MOATS
32	VP Student Development	Dr. Bill KUHN
84	VP Enrollment & Marketing Svcs	Mr. Bruce SNYDER
30	Director of External Relations	Ms. Jill OSBORN
20	Dean for Undergraduate Pgms	Dr. Scott MOATS
66	Director of Nursing	Mrs. Teresa NEWBY
21	Controller	Mr. Ronald STRAKA
41	Interim Athletic Director	Mr. Jamison ROSS
08	Director of Media Services	Dr. Dennis INGOLFSLAND
06	Registrar	Dr. Cheryl FISK
37	Director of Financial Aid	Mr. Jon ERICKSON
35	Dir Leadership Dev/Stdnt Activity	Ms. Kate JONES
07	Director of Graduate Admissions	Ms. Maggie UNGER
18	Director of Facilities Services	Mr. Rick LARSON
40	Director of Campus Store	Mrs. Sharie THOELKE
58	Dean Sch Online Studies/Grad School	Dr. Fawn MCCRACKEN
42	Chaplain	Mr. Bill KUHN
07	Dean of SAS Enrollment	Vacant
15	Director of Human Resources	Mrs. Amy LUESSE
36	Dir Career Services	Mr. Darren NOBLE
13	Director of Technology Services	Mr. Paul FLAGSTAD
26	Marketing/Communications Manager	Ms. Jessica ARTIBEE
29	Alumni Relations Coordinator	Vacant

Duluth Business University, Inc. (B)

4724 Mike Colalillo Drive, Duluth MN 55807-2723
County: Saint Louis FICE Identification: 009892
Unit ID: 173489
Telephone: (218) 722-4000 Carnegie Class: Bac/Assoc-Assoc Dom
FAX Number: (218) 628-2127 Calendar System: Quarter
URL: www.dbumn.edu
Established: 1891 Annual Undergrad Tuition & Fees: $18,975
Enrollment: 144 Coed
Affiliation or Control: Proprietary IRS Status: Proprietary
Highest Offering: Baccalaureate
Accreditation: **ACICS**, MAC

Code	Title	Name
01	President	Mr. James R. GESSNER
05	Campus Director	Mrs. Bonnie L. KUPCZYNSKI
20	Associate Director	Mr. David LUTZKA
08	Librarian	Ms. Joyce C. PETERSON
36	Career Services Manager	Mr. David E. COOK
37	Financial Aid Advisor	Mrs. Gloria G. COOLE

Dunwoody College of Technology (C)

818 Dunwoody Boulevard, Minneapolis MN 55403-1192
County: Hennepin FICE Identification: 004641
Unit ID: 175227
Telephone: (612) 374-5800 Carnegie Class: Bac/Assoc-Mixed
FAX Number: (612) 381-9620 Calendar System: Semester
URL: www.dunwoody.edu
Established: 1914 Annual Undergrad Tuition & Fees: $20,428
Enrollment: 1,094 Coed
Affiliation or Control: Independent Non-Profit IRS Status: 501(c)3
Highest Offering: Baccalaureate
Accreditation: **NH**, CIDA, ENGT, RAD

Code	Title	Name
01	President	Dr. Rich WAGNER
05	Provost	Mr. Jeff YLINEN
10	Chief Financial Officer	Mr. James MCDONALD
84	Vice President Enrollment Mgmt	Ms. Cynthia OLSON
111	VP of Institutional Advancement	Mr. Stuart LANG
15	Vice President of Human Resources	Ms. Patricia EDMAN

Gustavus Adolphus College (D)

800 W College Avenue, Saint Peter MN 56082-1498
County: Nicollet FICE Identification: 002353
Unit ID: 173647
Telephone: (507) 933-8000 Carnegie Class: Bac-A&S
FAX Number: (507) 933-7041 Calendar System: Semester
URL: www.gustavus.edu
Established: 1862 Annual Undergrad Tuition & Fees: $42,840
Enrollment: 2,379 Coed
Affiliation or Control: Evangelical Lutheran Church In America
IRS Status: 501(c)3
Highest Offering: Baccalaureate
Accreditation: **NH**, CAATE, NURSE

Code	Title	Name
01	President	Ms. Rebecca M. BERGMAN
05	Provost and Dean of the Faculty	Dr. Brenda S. KELLY
10	VP for Finance and Treasurer	Mr. Thomas J. ROONEY
07	AVP and Dean of Admission	Mr. Richard S. AUNE
30	VP for Institutional Advancement	Mr. Thomas W. YOUNG
32	VP for Student Life	Dr. JoNes R. VANHECKE
26	VP Marketing & Communication	Mr. Timothy R. KENNEDY
28	Director Diversity Center	Mr. Thomas G. FLUNKER
09	Director Institutional Research	Mr. David A. MENK
08	Head Librarian	Mr. Daniel J. MOLLNER
88	Director Church Relations	Rev. Grady I. ST. DENNIS
29	Dir Alumni and Parent Engagement	Mr. Glen D. LLOYD
36	Director Career Development	Ms. Cynthia L. FAVRE
06	Registrar	Ms. Kristianne R. WESTPHAL
13	Dir Gustavus Technology Services	Mr. Bruce N. AARSVOLD
18	AVP Facilities	Mr. Fath-Allah OUDGHIRI
37	AVP and Dean of Financial Aid	Mr. Doug O. MINTER
39	Director Residential Life	Mr. Lawrence C. POTTS
42	Chaplain	Rev. Siri C. ERICKSON
35	Associate Dean of Students	Dr. Stephen R. BENNETT
41	Athletics Director	Mr. Thomas W. BROWN
15	AVP Human Resources	Ms. Julie C. KLINE
19	Director Campus Security	Ms. Carol A. BREWER
40	Manager Book Mark	Ms. Molly L. YONKERS
27	Dir Media Relations/Internal Comm	Mr. Jacob J. AKIN
04	Asst to the Pres & Sec of the Board	Ms. Jolene D. CHRISTENSEN

Hamline University (E)

1536 Hewitt Avenue, Saint Paul MN 55104-1284
County: Ramsey FICE Identification: 002354
Unit ID: 173665
Telephone: (651) 523-2800 Carnegie Class: Masters/L
FAX Number: (651) 523-2899 Calendar System: 4/1/4
URL: www.hamline.edu
Established: 1854 Annual Undergrad Tuition & Fees: $39,181
Enrollment: 4,258 Coed
Affiliation or Control: United Methodist IRS Status: 501(c)3
Highest Offering: Doctorate
Accreditation: **NH**, CAEPN, MUS

Code	Title	Name
01	President	Dr. Fayneese S. MILLER
05	Provost	Dr. John MATACHEK
10	Sr VP Business/Finance/Technology	Ms. Margaret TUNGSETH
30	VP Development & Alumni Relations	Ms. Carrie ALBERS
32	Dean of Students	Ms. Patti KLEIN
43	VP HR/General Counsel	Ms. Catherine WASSBERG
13	Assoc VP/Dir IT	Mr. Mark KONDRAK
26	Assoc VP Marketing/Communications	Ms. Gail NOSEK
18	Assoc VP Facilities/Physical Plant	Mr. Lowell BROMANDER
50	Dean School of Business	Ms. Anne MCCARTHY
49	Dean College Liberal Arts	Ms. Marcela KOSTIHOVA
85	Ast Dn/Dir Multicult/Intl Stdt Affs	Mr. Carlos SNEED
06	Registrar Undergrad/Grad Schools	Ms. Gwen SHERBURNE
29	Exec Dir of Hamline Alumni Assn	Ms. Elizabeth L. RADTKE
37	Director Financial Aid	Ms. Lynette WAHL
07	Director Undergraduate Admission	Ms. Mai Nhia XIONG-CHAN
15	Director Human Resources	Ms. Lisa TODD
36	Interim Dir Career Development	Mr. Terry MIDDENDORF
41	Athletic Director	Mr. Jason VERDUGO
19	Director of Safety & Security	Ms. Andrea VIRCKS
23	Director Counseling & Health Center	Ms. Hussein RAJPUT
35	Dir Student Leadership & Activities	Vacant
42	Chaplain & Director	Ms. Nancy M. VICTORIN-VANGERUD
96	Director of Purchasing	Ms. Susan BORNUS
04	Exec Assistant to the President	Ms. Jane A. TELLEEN
09	Director of Institutional Research	Ms. Tracy WILLIAMS
08	Head Librarian	Mr. Terry METZ
39	Director Student Housing	Mr. Javier GUTIERREZ

Hazelden Betty Ford Graduate School of Addiction Studies (F)

PO Box 11 (CO9), Center City MN 55012-0011
County: Chisago FICE Identification: 040443
Unit ID: 173683
Telephone: (651) 213-4175 Carnegie Class: Spec-4-yr-Other Health
FAX Number: (651) 213-4710 Calendar System: Semester
URL: www.hazeldenbettyford.org
Established: 1999 Annual Graduate Tuition & Fees: N/A
Enrollment: 137 Coed
Affiliation or Control: Independent Non-Profit IRS Status: 501(c)3
Highest Offering: Master's; No Undergraduates
Accreditation: **NH**

Code	Title	Name
01	President and CEO	Mr. Mark MISHEK
05	Chief Academic Officer & Provost	Dr. Valerie SLAYMAKER
04	Asst to the Chief Academic Officer	Ms. Denell BELLE ISLE
20	Dean	Dr. Roy KAMMER
07	Mgr Enrollment & Student Services	Ms. LeAnn BROWN
06	Registrar	Ms. Debra MATTISON
09	Dir of Institutional Effectiveness	Dr. Timothy SHEEHAN
06	Registrar of Administrative Service	Ms. Twyla RAMSDELL

Herzing University (G)

5700 West Broadway, Minneapolis MN 55428
Telephone: (763) 535-3000 FICE Identification: 011017
Accreditation: **&NH**, DA, DH, NURSE, OTA

† Regional accreditation is carried under the parent institution in Madison, WI.

Institute of Production and Recording (H)

300 N. 1st Avenue, Suite 500, Minneapolis MN 55401
County: Hennepin FICE Identification: 041302
Unit ID: 454616
Telephone: (612) 244-2800 Carnegie Class: Spec 2-yr-Tech
FAX Number: (612) 244-2801 Calendar System: Other
URL: www.ipr.edu
Established: 2002 Annual Undergrad Tuition & Fees: $17,460
Enrollment: 232 Coed
Affiliation or Control: Proprietary IRS Status: Proprietary
Highest Offering: Baccalaureate
Accreditation: **ACCSC**

Code	Title	Name
01	Campus Director	Stacy SEVERSON
05	Dean of Education	Vacant
07	Assoc Director of Admissions	Peter YANG
36	Director of Career Services	Diana WILTER
08	Librarian	Tina HALFMANN

Leech Lake Tribal College (I)

6945 Little Wolf Rd., NW, Cass Lake MN 56633
County: Cass FICE Identification: 030964
Unit ID: 413626
Telephone: (218) 335-4200 Carnegie Class: Tribal
FAX Number: (218) 335-4282 Calendar System: Semester
URL: www.lltc.edu
Established: 1990 Annual Undergrad Tuition & Fees: $3,926
Enrollment: 348 Coed
Affiliation or Control: Tribal Control IRS Status: 501(c)3
Highest Offering: Associate Degree
Accreditation: **NH**

Code	Title	Name
01	Interim President	Dr. Patricia BROKER
05	Chief Academic Officer	Vikki HOWARD
10	Chief Financial Officer	Vacant
32	Dean of Student Services	Vacant
09	Director of Institutional Research	Tracy HENDRICKSON

Luther Seminary (J)

2481 Como Avenue, Saint Paul MN 55108-1496
County: Ramsey FICE Identification: 002357
Unit ID: 173896
Telephone: (651) 641-3456 Carnegie Class: Spec-4-yr-Faith
FAX Number: (651) 641-3425 Calendar System: Semester
URL: www.luthersem.edu
Established: 1869 Annual Graduate Tuition & Fees: N/A
Enrollment: 546 Coed
Affiliation or Control: Evangelical Lutheran Church In America
IRS Status: 501(c)3
Highest Offering: Doctorate; No Undergraduates
Accreditation: **NH**, THEOL

Code	Title	Name
01	President	Rev.Dr. Robin STEINKE
05	VP of Academic Affairs	Dr. Craig KOESTER
10	VP Administration & Finance	Mr. Michael MORROW
26	VP Seminary Relations	Ms. Heidi DROEGEMUELLER
32	VP Student Affs/Enroll/Dn Students	Ms. Carrie CARROLL
15	Director of Human Resources	Ms. Arnita WALLS

42 Seminary Pastor ... Dr. Justin LIND-AYRES
07 Director of Admissions ... Vacant
06 Registrar ... Ms. Diane DONCITS
27 Marketing/Communications Manager ... Ms. Melissa MAGGIO

Lutheran Brethren Seminary (A)

1036 Alcott Ave W, Fergus Falls MN 56537
County: Otter Tail Identification: 666644
Telephone: (218) 739-3375 Carnegie Class: Not Classified
FAX Number: (218) 739-1259 Calendar System: Semester
URL: www.lbs.edu
Established: 1903 Annual Graduate Tuition & Fees: N/A
Enrollment: N/A Coed
Affiliation or Control: Other IRS Status: 501(c)3
Highest Offering: Master's; No Undergraduates
Accreditation: TRACS

01 President ... Dr. David VEUM
05 Dean of the Seminary/CAO ... Dr. Eugene BOE
06 Registrar/Director Graduate Studies ... Dr. Gaylan MATHIESEN

Macalester College (B)

1600 Grand Avenue, Saint Paul MN 55105-1801
County: Ramsey FICE Identification: 002358
Unit ID: 173902
Telephone: (651) 696-6000 Carnegie Class: Bac-A&S
FAX Number: (651) 696-6689 Calendar System: Semester
URL: www.macalester.edu
Established: 1874 Annual Undergrad Tuition & Fees: $50,639
Enrollment: 2,172 Coed
Affiliation or Control: Presbyterian Church (U.S.A.) IRS Status: 501(c)3
Highest Offering: Baccalaureate
Accreditation: NH

01 President ... Dr. Brian C. ROSENBERG
05 Dean of the Faculty & Provost ... Dr. Karine F. MOE
115 Chief Investment Officer ... Mr. Gary D. MARTIN
111 VP Advancement ... Mr. Andrew BROWN
32 Vice President Student Affairs ... Ms. Donna LEE
10 Vice President for Admin/Finance ... Mr. David M. WHEATON
13 Associate VP ITS/CIO ... Mr. Jerry R. SANDERS
07 Interim Dean Admissions Fin Aid ... Mr. Jeffrey S. ALLEN
85 Dean Inst for Global Citizenship ... Dr. Donna K. MAEDA
20 Director of Academic Programs ... Ms. Ann M. MINNICK
28 Dean of Multicultural Life ... Mr. Chris A. MACDONALD-DENNIS
09 Director Inst Research ... Ms. Polly A. FASSINGER
35 Dean of Students ... Ms. DeMethra BRADLEY
37 Director Student Financial Aid ... Mr. Brian LINDEMAN
06 Registrar ... Ms. Jayne L. NIEMI
35 Assoc Dean for Student Services ... Ms. Denise WARD
15 Director Human Resources ... Mr. Bob GRAF
18 Director Facilities Management ... Mr. Nathan P. LIEF
41 Athletic Director ... Ms. Kim CHANDLER
04 Assistant to the President ... Ms. Cynthia L. HENDRICKS
21 Assistant Vice President Finance ... Ms. Patricia M. LANGER
26 Interim Dir Comm and PR ... Ms. Sara SUELFLOW
29 Exec Dir Alumni Engagement ... Ms. Katie LADAS
38 Director Health and Wellness Center ... Ms. Denise WARD
96 Dir Purchasing/Accounts Payable ... Mr. Matthew D. RUMPZA
105 Director Web Services ... Ms. Sara C. SUELFLOW
84 Manager of Enrollment Systems ... Mr. Abraham NOEL
08 Head Librarian ... Ms. Teresa FISHEL
102 Dir Foundation/Corporate Relations ... Ms. Michelle EPP
36 Dean of Career Development ... Ms. Mindy J. DEARDURFF
19 Assoc Director Security/Safety ... Mr. Bill S. COLLUMBIEN
108 Director Institutional Research ... Dr. Polly A. FASSINGER

Martin Luther College (C)

1995 Luther Court, New Ulm MN 56073-3300
County: Brown FICE Identification: 002361
Unit ID: 173452
Telephone: (507) 354-8221 Carnegie Class: Spec-4-yr-Other
FAX Number: (507) 354-8225 Calendar System: Semester
URL: www.mlc-wels.edu
Established: 1995 Annual Undergrad Tuition & Fees: $13,980
Enrollment: 900 Coed
Affiliation or Control: Wisconsin Evangelical Lutheran Synod
IRS Status: 501(c)3
Highest Offering: Master's
Accreditation: NH

01 President ... Rev. Mark G. ZARLING
05 Vice President for Academics ... Dr. Jeffery P. WIECHMAN
11 Vice President for Administration ... Prof. Steven R. THIESFELDT
32 Vice President Student Life ... Prof. Jeffrey L. SCHONE
53 Academic Dean Educational Ministry ... Prof. Benjamin P. CLEMONS
73 Academic Dean Pastoral Ministry ... Prof. Daniel N. BALGE
10 Director of Finance ... Mrs. Carla J. HULKE
08 Director of Library Services ... Mrs. Linda KRAMER
37 Director of Financial Aid ... Mr. Mark D. BAUER
07 Director of Admissions ... Prof. Mark A. STEIN
58 Director Graduate Studies/Cont Educ ... Prof. John E. MEYER
88 Director of Clinical Experiences ... Prof. Paul A. TESS
41 Director of Athletics ... Prof. James M. UNKE
42 Campus Pastor ... Rev. John C. BOEDER
13 Director of Technology ... Mr. James A. RATHJE
26 Director of Public Relations ... Prof. William A. PEKRUL
40 Bookstore Manager ... Mrs. Linette M. SCHARLEMANN

90 Director of Academic Computing ... Prof. Rachel M. FELD
29 Director Alumni Relations ... Mr. Stephen J. BALZA
108 Director Institutional Assessment ... Prof. Larry W. LOTITO

McNally Smith College of Music (D)

19 Exchange Street, Saint Paul MN 55101-2220
County: Ramsey FICE Identification: 030012
Unit ID: 367194
Telephone: (651) 291-0177 Carnegie Class: Spec-4-yr-Arts
FAX Number: (651) 291-0366 Calendar System: Semester
URL: www.mcnallysmith.edu
Established: 1985 Annual Undergrad Tuition & Fees: $27,940
Enrollment: 455 Coed
Affiliation or Control: Proprietary IRS Status: Proprietary
Highest Offering: Baccalaureate
Accreditation: MUS

01 President ... Harry CHALMIERS
10 Chief Financial Officer ... Kevin SULLIVAN
37 Financial Aid Director ... Jeffrey R. AALBERS
07 Admissions Director ... Matthew EDLUND
36 Director Career & Alumni Services ... Liz JENNINGS

Minneapolis Business College (E)

1711 W County Road B, Roseville MN 55113-4056
County: Ramsey FICE Identification: 004645
Unit ID: 174118
Telephone: (651) 636-7406 Carnegie Class: Assoc/HVT-High Trad
FAX Number: (651) 636-8185 Calendar System: Semester
URL: www.minneapolisbusinesscollege.edu
Established: 1874 Annual Undergrad Tuition & Fees: $14,720
Enrollment: 196 Coed
Affiliation or Control: Proprietary IRS Status: Proprietary
Highest Offering: Associate Degree
Accreditation: ACICS, MAC

01 President ... Mr. David WHITMAN
05 Director of Education ... Ms. Kate ADAMS
32 Director of Student Services ... Mrs. Marie MARTIN
36 Int Director of Placement ... Ms. Kelley RILEY

Minneapolis College of Art and Design (F)

2501 Stevens Avenue, Minneapolis MN 55404-4343
County: Hennepin FICE Identification: 002365
Unit ID: 174127
Telephone: (612) 874-3700 Carnegie Class: Spec-4-yr-Arts
FAX Number: (612) 874-3704 Calendar System: Semester
URL: www.mcad.edu
Established: 1886 Annual Undergrad Tuition & Fees: $36,548
Enrollment: 796 Coed
Affiliation or Control: Independent Non-Profit IRS Status: 501(c)3
Highest Offering: Master's
Accreditation: NH, ART

01 President ... Mr. Jay COOGAN
04 Executive Assistant to President ... Ms. Sarah HARDING
05 Vice President Academic Affairs ... Ms. Karen WIRTH
11 Vice President Administration ... Ms. Pam NEWSOME
30 AVP Institutional Advancement ... Ms. Cindy THEIS
84 Assoc VP Enrollment Management ... Ms. Melissa HUYBRECHT
18 Assoc VP Facilities/Public Safety ... Mr. Brock RASMUSSEN
13 Assoc Vice President Technology ... Mr. R. Hal WELLS
32 Dean of Student Affairs ... Ms. Jen ZUCCOLA
06 Registrar ... Mr. River GORDON
51 Director of Continuing Education ... Ms. Lara ROY
08 Director of Library ... Ms. Amy BECKER
24 Director Media Technology Services ... Mr. Scott BOWMAN
36 Director of Career Development ... Ms. Meghana SHROFF
29 Director Alumni and Annual Giving ... Mr. Seth GOODSPEED
39 Director Student Housing ... Mr. Nate K. LUTZ
26 Director Communications ... Ms. Ann BENRUD
37 Director Student Financial Aid ... Ms. Laura LINK
108 Director Accreditation & Assessment ... Mr. Colin O'NEILL
19 Director of Public Safety ... Mr. Steve MCLAUGHLIN

Minneapolis Media Institute (G)

4100 West 76th Street, Edina MN 55435
Telephone: (952) 897-1111 Identification: 770578
Accreditation: ACICS

† Branch campus of Madison Media Institute-College of Media Arts, Madison, WI

Minnesota School of Business (H)

1401 W 76th Street, Suite 500, Richfield MN 55423-3846
County: Hennepin FICE Identification: 004646
Unit ID: 174279
Telephone: (800) 752-4223 Carnegie Class: Masters/S
FAX Number: (612) 861-5548 Calendar System: Quarter
URL: www.msbcollege.edu
Established: 1877 Annual Undergrad Tuition & Fees: $14,940
Enrollment: 581 Coed
Affiliation or Control: Proprietary IRS Status: Proprietary
Highest Offering: Master's
Accreditation: ACICS

01 Campus Director ... Ms. Miriam WILLIAMS
05 Dean of Education ... Ms. Miriam WILLIAMS
32 Dean of Students ... Mr. Patrick SHAY
07 Director of Admissions ... Mr. Michael POSTER
36 Director of Career Services ... Mr. Dan WILSON
37 Director of Financial Aid ... Ms. Carol BARTA

† No longer enrolling students effective Sept 8 2016/under Show-Cause directive

*Minnesota State Colleges and Universities System Office (I)

30 7th Street East, Suite 350, Saint Paul MN 55101-4901
County: Ramsey FICE Identification: 009346
Unit ID: 428453
Telephone: (651) 201-1800 Carnegie Class: N/A
FAX Number: (651) 297-5550
URL: www.mnscu.edu

01 Interim Chancellor ... Devinder MALHOTRA
03 Vice Chancellor ... Mark CARLSON
05 Vice Chanc Academic/Student Affairs ... Ron ANDERSON
10 Vice Chanc Finance/CFO ... Laura M. KING
13 Vice Chanc Information Tech/CIO ... Ramon PADILLA
26 Chief Marketing/Communications Ofcr ... Noelle HAWTON
18 Assoc Vice Chancellor Facilities ... Brian D. YOLITZ
46 Assoc Vice Chanc Research/Planning ... Leslie K. MERCER
32 Assoc Vice Chanc Student Affairs ... Brent GLASS
100 Interim Chief of Staff ... Jaime SIMONSEN
15 Chief Human Resource Officer ... Jessica WHITE
28 Int Chief Diversity Officer ... Nickyia COGSHELL
102 Exec Dir System/Foundation Rels ... Maria R. MCLEMORE
43 General Counsel ... Gary CUNNINGHAM
45 Program Director for Planning ... Todd HARMENING

*Alexandria Technical & Community College (J)

1601 Jefferson Street, Alexandria MN 56308-2796
County: Douglas FICE Identification: 005544
Unit ID: 172918
Telephone: (320) 762-0221 Carnegie Class: Assoc/MT-VT-High Non
FAX Number: (320) 762-4501 Calendar System: Semester
URL: www.alextech.edu
Established: 1961 Annual Undergrad Tuition & Fees (In-State): $5,358
Enrollment: 2,702 Coed
Affiliation or Control: State IRS Status: 501(c)3
Highest Offering: Associate Degree
Accreditation: NH, MLTAD

02 President ... Dr. Laura URBAN
05 Exec VP Academic/Student Affairs ... Dr. Ross SANTELL
41 Vice Pres/Athletic Director ... Vacant
51 Dean of Customized Training ... Mr. Robert DEFRIES
10 Chief Financial Officer ... Mr. David BJELLAND
20 Sr Dean Academic Affairs & Students ... Mr. Gregg RAISANEN
32 Dean of Student Affairs ... Vacant
72 Dean of Technology ... Mr. Steve RICHARDS
20 Associate Dean of Academic Affairs ... Vacant
19 Dean of Law Enforcement ... Mr. Scott BERGER
37 Financial Aid Director ... Mr. Steve RICHARDS
22 Human Rights Officer ... Ms. Tamzin BUKOWSKI
36 Director Student Placement ... Mr. Patrick RUNNING
102 Foundation Executive Director ... Ms. Amy ALLEN
06 Registrar ... Ms. Debra LEDOUX
18 Director of Facilities ... Mr. Joel SEELA
15 Chief Human Resources Officer ... Ms. Shari MALONEY
09 Director of Institutional Research ... Ms. Rebekah SUMMER
07 Director of Admissions ... Ms. Amie ANDERSON
35 Director of Student Activities ... Ms. Michelle AHLQUIST
38 Director of K-12 Initiatives ... Ms. Mary LENZ
04 Asst to Pres/Dir of Office Services ... Ms. Annette PAVEK
21 Director of Financial Operations ... Ms. Julie FENLASON
40 Bookstore Manager ... Ms. Jan ANDERSON
44 Development Officer ... Ms. Linda DOLAN
88 Director of Support Services ... Ms. Kaye MADIGAN
28 Chief Diversity Officer ... Ms. Debra LEDOUX

*Anoka-Ramsey Community College (K)

11200 Mississippi Boulevard NW, Coon Rapids MN 55433-3499
County: Anoka FICE Identification: 002332
Unit ID: 172963
Telephone: (763) 433-1100 Carnegie Class: Assoc/HT-Mix Trad/Non
FAX Number: (763) 433-1121 Calendar System: Semester
URL: www.anokaramsey.edu
Established: 1965 Annual Undergrad Tuition & Fees (In-State): $4,979
Enrollment: 9,294 Coed
Affiliation or Control: State IRS Status: 501(c)3
Highest Offering: Associate Degree
Accreditation: NH, ADNUR, MUS, PTAA

02 President ... Dr. Kent HANSON
10 VP Finance & Administration ... Mr. Don LEWIS
05 VP Academic/Student Affairs ... Ms. Deidra PEASLEE
32 Dean of Student Affairs ... Ms. Lisa HARRIS
35 Dean of Student Affairs ... Mr. Steve CRITTENDEN
18 Physical Plant Manager ... Mr. Roger FREEMAN

15 Chief HR Director .... Mr. Jay NELSON
57 Dean of Arts & Letters .... Mr. Greg RATHERT
88 Dean CE/CT/Bus/Tech/Wellness .... Ms. Luanne KANE
35 Dean Student Life .... Vacant
76 Dean of Allied Health .... Ms. Natasha BAER
21 Director Fiscal & Auxiliary Svcs .... Ms. Marilyn SMITH
81 Interim Dean of STEM .... Ms. Melissa MILLS
09 Dean of Research & Assessment .... Ms. Nora MORRIS
28 Director of Multicultural Affairs .... Ms. Venoreen BROWNE-BOATSWAIN
102 Interim Director of Foundations .... Mr. Jamie BARTHEL
26 Director of Mktg/Public Relations .... Ms. Mary JACOBSON
19 Director of Safety & Security .... Mr. Cliff ANDERSON
35 Director of Student Life .... Ms. Joyce TRACZYK
13 Interim Director of Technology .... Mr. Tim ZONDLO
21 Business Manager .... Ms. Kim BIENFANG
37 Interim Director Financial Aid .... Ms. Brittany TWEED
04 Administrative Asst to President .... Ms. Margie SCHLUETER
06 Registrar .... Ms. Janine FORRER

*Anoka Technical College (A)

1355 W Highway 10, Anoka MN 55303-1590
County: Anoka FICE Identification: 007350
Unit ID: 172954
Telephone: (763) 576-4700 Carnegie Class: Assoc/HVT-High Trad
FAX Number: (763) 576-4715 Calendar System: Semester
URL: www.anokatech.edu
Established: 1967 Annual Undergrad Tuition & Fees (In-District): $5,534
Enrollment: 2,027 Coed
Affiliation or Control: State/Local IRS Status: 501(c)3
Highest Offering: Associate Degree
Accreditation: NH, CAHIIM, MAC, OTA, SURGT

02 President .... Dr. Kent HANSON
05 Vice Pres of Acad/Student Affs .... Dr. Elaina BLEIFIELD
13 Chief Information Officer .... Richard MALOTT
10 Vice Pres Finance & Admin .... Donald LEWIS
20 Academic Dean .... Sherry WICKSTROM
04 Assistant to the President .... Margie SCHLUETER
15 Chief Human Resource Officer .... Jay NELSON
26 Director of Marketing .... Mary JACOBSON
06 Director of Records .... Jamaica DELMAR
32 Dean of Student Affairs .... Sean JOHNS
37 Interim Financial Aid Director .... Brittany TWEED
08 Head Librarian .... Vacant
18 Chief Facilities/Physical Plant .... Roger FREEMAN
19 Director Security/Safety .... Clifford ANDERSON
84 Director of Enrollment Services .... Vacant
09 Director of Institutional Research .... Nora MORRIS
28 Director of Diversity .... Venoreen BROWNE-BOATSWAIN

*Bemidji State University (B)

1500 Birchmont Drive NE, Bemidji MN 56601-2699
County: Beltrami FICE Identification: 002336
Unit ID: 173124
Telephone: (218) 755-2001 Carnegie Class: Masters/S
FAX Number: N/A Calendar System: Semester
URL: www.bemidjistate.edu
Established: 1919 Annual Undergrad Tuition & Fees (In-State): $8,394
Enrollment: 5,081 Coed
Affiliation or Control: State IRS Status: 501(c)3
Highest Offering: Master's
Accreditation: NH, IACBE, MUS, NAIT, NURSE, SW

02 President .... Dr. Faith C. HENSRUD
05 Provost/VP Acad & Stdnt Affairs .... Dr. Tony PEFFER
10 VP Finance & Administration .... Ms. Karen SNOREK
84 Exec Dir of Enrollment Management .... Ms. Michelle FRENZEL
22 Affirmative Action & Accreditation .... Dr. Debra PETERSON
20 Interim Assoc VP Academic Affairs .... Dr. Randall WESTHOFF
08 Library & Library Services .... Ms. Dianne NARUM
09 Director Inst Rsrch/Effectiveness .... Mr. Douglas P. OLNEY
88 Director Ctr for Professional Devel .... Dr. Debbie GUELDA
92 Director Honors Program .... Dr. Season ELLISON
104 Director International Studies .... Dr. Thomas BEECH
85 Director International Program Ctr .... Ms. Cherish HAGEN-SWANSON
94 Director Gender Studies .... Vacant
79 Director Leadership Studies .... Dr. Dennis LUNT
49 Dean Arts & Sciences .... Dr. Colleen GREER
49 Asst Dean Arts & Sciences .... Dr. Vivian DELGADO
50 Interim Dean Business .... Dr. Bonnie HIGGINS
71 Exec Dir 360 Ctr of Excellence .... Mr. Jeremy LEFFELMAN
50 Directors MARS Program .... Dr. Kelly LA VENTURE
76 Dean Health Sci/Human Ecology .... Dr. Jim BARTA
32 Interim Dean of Students .... Dr. Jesse GRANT
88 Director American Indian Ctr .... Mr. Bill BLACKWELL
88 Director Campus Recreation .... Ms. Kierstin HOVEN
88 Director Hobson Memorial Union .... Ms. Nina JOHNSON
39 Director Housing & Res Life .... Dr. Randall LUDEMAN
38 Director Ctr for Health-Counseling ... Dr. Barb ERIKSSON-CAPES
106 Director Distance Learning .... Ms. Lynn JOHNSON
21 Business Manager .... Ms. Diane ILLIES
96 Director Procurement & Logistics .... Ms. Belinda S. LINDELL
18 Int Director Physical Plant .... Mr. Travis BARNES
19 Director Public Safety .... Mr. Casey J. MCCARTHY
15 Chief Human Resources Officer .... Ms. Megan ZOTHMAN
13 Acting Chief Information Officer .... Ms. Karen SNOREK
07 Director Admissions .... Mr. Paul MULLER
37 Director Financial Aid .... Ms. Lesa LAWRENCE
06 Interim Registrar .... Ms. Bev HODGSON

121 Director Advising Success Center .... Mr. Zak JOHNSON
36 Director Career Services .... Ms. Margie T. GIAUQUE
88 TRIO/SSS/UB/McNair .... Ms. Kelli STEGGALL
88 Disability Services .... Vacant
26 Director Communications & Marketing .... Mr. Scott FAUST
41 Athletic Director .... Mr. Tracy DILL
111 Exec Dir for University Advancement .... Ms. Marla PATRIAS
29 Director Alumni Relations .... Mr. Brett BAHR

*Central Lakes College (C)

501 W College Drive, Brainerd MN 56401-3900
County: Crow Wing FICE Identification: 002339
Unit ID: 173203
Telephone: (218) 855-8000 Carnegie Class: Assoc/MT-VT-High Non
FAX Number: (218) 855-8057 Calendar System: Semester
URL: www.clcmn.edu
Established: 1938 Annual Undergrad Tuition & Fees (In-State): $5,384
Enrollment: 4,274 Coed
Affiliation or Control: State IRS Status: 501(c)3
Highest Offering: Associate Degree
Accreditation: NH, DA, MAC

02 President .... Dr. Hara D. CHARLIER
05 VP Academic & Student Affairs .... Ms. Joy BODIN
11 VP Administrative Services .... Ms. Kari CHRISTIANSEN
12 Dean Staples Campus/CTE/Grants .... Ms. Tara KARELS
12 Dean Brainerd CTE/Cus Trng .... Ms. Rebekah KENT
47 Dean of Agricultural Studies .... Mr. Keith OLANDER
84 Dean of Enrollment/Student Success .Mr. Paul PREIMESBERGER
49 Dean of Liberal Arts .... Ms. Martha KUEHN
30 Director of Res Develop/CLC Found .... Ms. Jana SHOGREN
15 Director of Human Resources .... Ms. Nancy PAULSON
07 Director of Enrollment Services .... Mr. Nick HEISSERER
06 Registrar .... Ms. Michelle KANGAS
08 Librarian .... Mr. David BISSONETTE
37 Director Financial Aid .... Mr. Mike BARNABY
14 Director of Technology/Support .... Mr. Scott STREED
26 Director Marketing .... Mr. Kenn DOLS
109 Director of Business/Auxil Services .... Ms. Christina ANDERSON
88 Director of Trio Programs .... Mr. Charles BLACKLANCE
18 Director Physical Plant/Facilities .... Mr. James MCARDELL
28 Dean of Students/Equity/Inclusion .... Ms. Mary SAM
04 Executive Asst to President .... Ms. Jody LONGBELLA
09 Director of Institutional Research .... Ms. Wendy ADAMSON
88 Director Small Business Dev Center .... Mr. Greg BERGMAN
19 Director Security/Safety .... Mr. Ajeet YADAV
35 Director of Student Life .... Mr. Erich HEPPNER

*Century College (D)

3300 Century Avenue N, White Bear Lake MN 55110-1894
County: Ramsey FICE Identification: 010546
Unit ID: 175315
Telephone: (651) 779-3200 Carnegie Class: Assoc/MT-VT-High Trad
FAX Number: (651) 779-3417 Calendar System: Semester
URL: www.century.edu
Established: 1967 Annual Undergrad Tuition & Fees (In-State): $5,360
Enrollment: 8,996 Coed
Affiliation or Control: State IRS Status: 501(c)3
Highest Offering: Associate Degree
Accreditation: NH, ADNUR, DA, DH, EMT, MAC, MUS, RAD

02 President .... Ms. Angelia MILLENDER
05 VP Academic Affairs/CAO .... Mr. Michael BERNDT
32 VP Enroll Mgmt/Student Svcs .... Ms. Joyce COLEMAN
10 VP Finance & Administration .... Mr. Patrick OPATZ
13 Assoc VP Information Tech/Admn Svcs .... Mr. John ROHLEDER
96 Buyer Supervisor .... Ms. Suzanne WENNEN
21 Director of Finance .... Ms. Bonnie MEYERS
102 Executive Director Foundation .... Ms. Jill GREENHALGH
06 Registrar .... Ms. Kirsten FABOZZI
15 Director of Human Resources .... Ms. Mary NIENABER
07 Assistant Director of Admissions .... Mr. Robert BEAVER
45 Director of Resource Development .... Mr. Donald LONG
37 Director of Financial Aid .... Ms. Pam ENGEBRETSON
18 Mgr of Physical Plant/Super of Bld .... Mr. Michael HOUFER
19 Director of Public Safety .... Mr. Jason PHILIPP
66 Dean Nursing/Allied Health .... Ms. Beth HEIN
75 Dean .... Ms. Jane NICHOLSON
72 Dean Science/Technology .... Dr. Iddi ADAM
81 Dean English/ESOL/Reading/Math .... Mr. Andrew NESSET
83 Dean Soc & Beh Sci/Lang/Com .... Dr. Jesse MASON
35 Dean of Student Services .... Mr. Jason CARDINAL
35 Dean of Student Services .... Ms. Andrea RYSTROM
35 Dean of Student Services .... Ms. Kristin HAGEMAN
09 Dean of Institutional Effectiveness .... Ms. Nichole PETERSEN
04 Executive Assistant to President .... Ms. Christine MCGING
26 Director of Marketing .... Mr. James STUMNE
28 Interim Chief Diversity Officer .... Mr. Trumanue LINDSEY

*Dakota County Technical College (E)

145th Street E, Rosemount MN 55068-2999
County: Dakota FICE Identification: 010402
Unit ID: 173416
Telephone: (651) 423-8000 Carnegie Class: Assoc/HVT-Mix Trad/Non
FAX Number: (651) 423-8775 Calendar System: Semester
URL: www.dctc.edu
Established: 1970 Annual Undergrad Tuition & Fees (In-District): $5,662
Enrollment: 2,783 Coed
Affiliation or Control: State/Local IRS Status: 501(c)3
Highest Offering: Associate Degree
Accreditation: NH, DA, MAC

02 President .... Mr. Tim WYNES
05 VP Academic & Student Affairs .... Dr. Mike OPP
09 VP Strategic Alignment .... Ms. Suzanne BRUSOE
10 Chief Financial Officer .... Mr. Scott ERICKSON
09 Assoc VP Strategic Initiatives .... Ms. Carrie SCHNEIDER
88 Dean Transportation Indust Careers .... Mr. Chad SHEETS
49 Dean Academic Ops/Arts & Sciences .... Ms. Gayle LARSON
32 Director Student Success .... Mr. Patrick LAIR
06 Registrar/Enrollment Director .... Ms. Jodie SWEARINGEN
18 Director of Operations .... Mr. Paul DEMUTH
35 Director Student Life/Activities .... Ms. Nicole MEULEMANS
103 Dean Customized Training/Cont Educ .... Mr. Pat MCQUILLAN
07 Admissions Outreach Coordinator .... Ms. Karianne LOULA
30 Director Institutional Advancement .... Ms. Erin EDLUND
37 Director Financial Aid .... Mr. Scott ROELKE
15 Chief Human Resource Officer .... Ms. Suzanne BRUSOE
26 Director of Marketing/Communication .... Ms. Angela BURNS

*Fond du Lac Tribal and Community College (F)

2101 14th Street, Cloquet MN 55720-2984
County: Carlton FICE Identification: 031291
Unit ID: 380368
Telephone: (218) 879-0800 Carnegie Class: Tribal
FAX Number: (218) 879-0814 Calendar System: Semester
URL: www.fdltcc.edu
Established: 1987 Annual Undergrad Tuition & Fees (In-State): $5,257
Enrollment: 2,227 Coed
Affiliation or Control: State IRS Status: 501(c)3
Highest Offering: Associate Degree
Accreditation: NH

02 President .... Mr. Larry ANDERSON
05 Vice President of Academics .... Dr. Anna FELLEGY
10 Chief Financial Officer .... Ms. Stephanie HAMMITT
32 Dean of Student Affairs .... Mr. Russell SWAGGER
26 Director of Public Information .... Mr. Tom URBANSKI
06 Registrar .... Ms. Leah TOLLEFSON
88 Disability Services/Student Service .... Ms. Shelia SUMNER
13 Information Technology Specialist .... Mr. Loran WAPPES
37 Director of Financial Aid .... Mr. David SUTHERLAND
07 Director of Admissions .... Ms. Susan BUMANN
09 Director of Institutional Research .... Vacant
35 Dir of Student Support Services .... Ms. Peggy POITRA
62 Library Services .... Ms. Nancy BROUGHTON
30 Director of Development .... Mr. Larry ANDERSON
39 Director of Housing .... Mr. Jesse STIREWALT
15 Director of Human Resources .... Ms. Marisa HAGGY
18 Chief Facilities/Physical Plant .... Mr. Mark BERNHARDSON
40 Bookstore Coordinator .... Ms. Bonnie BERNHARDSON
04 Executive Assistant to President .... Ms. Mary SOYRING

*Hennepin Technical College (G)

9000 Brooklyn Boulevard, Brooklyn Park MN 55445-2399
County: Hennepin FICE Identification: 010491
Unit ID: 173708
Telephone: (952) 995-1300 Carnegie Class: Assoc/HVT-High Trad
FAX Number: (763) 488-2956 Calendar System: Semester
URL: www.hennepintech.edu
Established: 1972 Annual Undergrad Tuition & Fees (In-District): $5,130
Enrollment: 5,676 Coed
Affiliation or Control: State/Local IRS Status: 501(c)3
Highest Offering: Associate Degree
Accreditation: NH, ACBSP, ACFEI, DA, IFSAC, MAC

02 President .... Dr. Merrill IRVING, JR.
05 Provost .... Dr. Carmen COBALLES-VEGA
10 Vice Pres Finance and Operations .... Mr. Craig ERICKSON
06 Registrar .... Ms. Julie HIGDEM
15 Chief Human Resources Officer .... Ms. Sharon MOHR
28 Director of Diversity .... Ms. Jean MAIERHOFER
09 Dir of Institutional Effectiveness .... Ms. Donna S. STATZELL
30 Chief Advancement/Comm Officer .... Ms. Nairobi ABRAMS
37 Director of Financial Aid .... Mr. Tim JACOBSON
84 Dean of Enrollment .... Ms. Kristine RAMOS-WALKER
121 Dean of Student Success .... Ms. Dara HAGAN
04 Administrative Asst to President .... Ms. Lisa OPEM
13 Chief Info Technology Officer (CIO) .... Mr. Jason KOPP
08 Head Librarian .... Ms. Jennie SIMNING
22 Dir Affirmative Action/EEO .... Ms. Jean MAIERHOFER
19 Director Security/Safety .... Mr. Randy ROEHRICK
32 Director Student Life .... Ms. Jessica LAURITSEN
18 Director of Operations/Facilities .... Mr. Joe WIGHTKIN

*Hibbing Community College, A Technical and Community College (H)

1515 E 25th Street, Hibbing MN 55746-3300
County: Saint Louis FICE Identification: 002355
Unit ID: 173735
Telephone: (218) 262-7200 Carnegie Class: Assoc/MT-VT-High Trad
FAX Number: (218) 262-6717 Calendar System: Semester
URL: www.hibbing.edu
Established: 1916 Annual Undergrad Tuition & Fees (In-State): $5,262
Enrollment: 1,344 Coed
Affiliation or Control: State IRS Status: 501(c)3
Highest Offering: Associate Degree
Accreditation: NH, ADNUR, DA, MLTAD

02 President .... Mr. Bill MAKI
05 Provost .... Dr. Michael RAICH
32 Dean of Lib Arts & Student Affairs .... Ms. Lisa BESTUL
10 VP Finance & Administration .... Ms. Karen KEDROWSKI
09 Institutional Research .... Ms. Tracey ROY
37 Director Student Financial Aid .... Ms. Stephanie SKRABA
18 Plant Maintenance Engineer .... Mr. Jimmer HODGE
26 Marketing Specialist/Public Info .... Ms. Jessica MATVEY
06 Registrar .... Ms. Kari DOUCETTE
13 Chief Info Technology Officer (CIO) .... Ms. Linda RASKOVICH
39 Director Student Housing .... Ms. Angela KANG
41 Athletic Director .... Mr. Mike FLATEN
08 Head Librarian .... Ms. Rachel MILANI
28 Director of Diversity .... Ms. Miriam KERO

*Inver Hills Community College (A)

2500 80th Street E, Inver Grove Heights MN 55076-3224
County: Dakota FICE Identification: 009740
Unit ID: 173799
Telephone: (651) 450-3000 Carnegie Class: Assoc/HT-Mix Trad/Non
FAX Number: (651) 450-3679 Calendar System: Semester
URL: www.inverhills.edu
Established: 1970 Annual Undergrad Tuition & Fees (In-State): $5,285
Enrollment: 5,515 Coed
Affiliation or Control: State IRS Status: 501(c)3
Highest Offering: Associate Degree
Accreditation: NH, ACBSP, ADNUR, EMT

02 President .... Mr. Timothy WYNES
05 Int Provost/VP Academic Affs .... Ms. Tarryl CLARK
11 Vice Pres Administrative Services .... Mr. Patrick JACOBSON-SCHULTE
32 Vice Pres Student Affairs .... Dr. Wendy ROBINSON
10 Vice Pres/Chief Financial Officer .... Mr. Patrick JACOBSON-SCHULTE
45 Vice Pres Strategic Alignment .... Ms. Suzie BRUSOE
06 Registrar .... Mr. Scott KLAEHN
36 Dean of Career Programs .... Ms. Sabrina BUIVID
79 Dean of Liberal Arts .... Ms. Ann DEIMAN-THORNTON
81 Dean of STEM/Social Sciences .... Dr. Stephen L. STROM
102 Exec Dir of Foundation & Advancemnt .... Mrs. Gail MORRISON
15 Int Chief Human Resources Officer .... Ms. Laina CARLSON
103 Dean Ctr Prof/Workforce Development .... Vacant
08 Librarian .... Ms. Julie BENOLKEN
84 Director of Enrollment Services .... Vacant
88 Dir Paralegal Pgm/Ofc Sys-Legal .... Ms. Sally DAHLQUIST
90 Director Acad Tech/Computing Svcs .... Vacant
18 Director Facilities Plng/Management .... Mr. Paul DEMUTH
88 Int Dir Emergency Health Svcs .... Mr. Jeff MORGAN
28 Director of Equity & Inclusion .... Vacant
37 Int Director of Financial Aid .... Mr. Scott ROELKE
09 Director of Institutional Research .... Ms. Wendy MARSON
26 Dir of Inst Advance/Mktg & PR .... Vacant
35 Director of Student Life .... Ms. Nicole MEULEMANS

*Itasca Community College (B)

1851 E Highway 169, Grand Rapids MN 55744-3397
County: Itasca FICE Identification: 002356
Unit ID: 173805
Telephone: (800) 996-6422 Carnegie Class: Assoc/HT-High Trad
FAX Number: (218) 322-2332 Calendar System: Semester
URL: www.itascacc.edu
Established: 1922 Annual Undergrad Tuition & Fees (In-State): $5,277
Enrollment: 1,209 Coed
Affiliation or Control: State IRS Status: 501(c)3
Highest Offering: Associate Degree
Accreditation: NH

02 Chief Executive Officer .... Mr. William D. MAKI
03 Executive Vice President .... Ms. Karen KEDROWSKI
05 Provost .... Mr. Bart JOHNSON
20 Academic Dean .... Mr. Bart JOHNSON
10 Accounting Officer Finance .... Ms. Kristen LIND
84 Dir of Enrollment Mgmt/Admissions .... Mr. William MARSHALL
06 Registrar .... Ms. Allison GEISLER
29 Director of Alumni Relations .... Ms. Susan LYNCH
30 Director of College Development .... Vacant
37 Director of Student Financial Aid .... Mr. Nathan WRIGHT
08 Head Librarian .... Mr. Steve BEAN
18 Director of Facilities & Info Tech .... Mr. Chad HAATVEDT
40 Bookstore Manager .... Ms. Faith MCBRIDE
28 Director of Diversity .... Mr. Harold ANNETTE
09 Director of Institutional Research .... Ms. Tracey ROY
39 Director Student Housing .... Mr. Weldon BRAXTON
32 Dean of Student & Admin Services .... Mr. Richard KANGAS

*Lake Superior College (C)

2101 Trinity Road, Duluth MN 55811-3399
County: Saint Louis FICE Identification: 005757
Unit ID: 173461
Telephone: (218) 733-7600 Carnegie Class: Assoc/MT-VT-High Non
FAX Number: (218) 733-4921 Calendar System: Semester
URL: www.lsc.edu
Established: 1995 Annual Undergrad Tuition & Fees (In-State): $5,096
Enrollment: 4,862 Coed
Affiliation or Control: State IRS Status: 501(c)3
Highest Offering: Associate Degree
Accreditation: NH, ADNUR, COARC, DH, MAC, MLTAD, PNUR, PTAA, RAD, SURGT

02 President .... Dr. Patrick JOHNS
05 Vice Pres Academic/Student Affairs .... Mr. Michael SEYMOUR
10 Vice Pres Finance & Administration .... Mr. Al FINLAYSON
49 Dean of Liberal Arts & Sciences .... Ms. Hanna ERPESTAD
75 Dean of Business/Industry Division .... Ms. Jenni SWENSON
76 Dean of Allied Health & Nursing .... Ms. Laurie JENSEN
103 Interim Exec Dir of Workforce Dev .... Ms. Tamara ARNOTT
09 Dir IR/Accred Assessment/Research .... Mr. Kent RICHARDS
15 Director of Human Resources .... Ms. Becky WODZIAK
111 Dir of Institutional Advancement .... Mr. Daniel FANNING
84 Director of Enrollment Mgmt .... Ms. Melissa LENO
18 Building Maintenance Foreman .... Mr. Mark CARDINAL
32 Dean of Student Affairs .... Mr. Wade GORDON
36 Director Career Services .... Mr. Eric BRANDT
37 Director Student Financial Aid .... Ms. LaNita ROBINSON
21 Director Business Services .... Ms. Nickoel ANDERSON
13 Director Information Technology .... Mr. Steve FUDALLY
121 Director of Advising .... Mr. Keith TURNER
96 Purchasing Agent .... Mr. Michael FRANCISCO
04 Executive Asst to President .... Ms. Debbie JOHNSON

*Mesabi Range College (D)

1001 West Chestnut Street, Virginia MN 55792-3401
County: Saint Louis FICE Identification: 004009
Unit ID: 173993
Telephone: (218) 741-3095 Carnegie Class: Assoc/MT-VT-High Non
FAX Number: (218) 748-2419 Calendar System: Semester
URL: www.mesabirange.edu
Established: 1918 Annual Undergrad Tuition & Fees (In-State): $5,263
Enrollment: 1,206 Coed
Affiliation or Control: State IRS Status: Exempt
Highest Offering: Associate Degree
Accreditation: NH, EMT

02 President .... Mr. William MAKI
05 Provost .... Mrs. Shelly MCCAULEY JUGOVICH
10 Vice Pres Finance/Administration .... Mrs. Karen KEDROWSKI
32 Dean of Student Services .... Mr. David DAILEY
10 Director of Finance .... Mr. Roy TROUSDELL
15 Director Human Resources .... Mrs. Carmen BRADACH
37 Director Student Financial Aid .... Ms. Jodi PONTINEN
06 Registrar .... Mrs. Rebecca STEVINSON
07 Director of Admissions .... Ms. Brenda KOCHEVAR
09 Director of Institutional Research .... Ms. Tracey ROY
26 Chief Public Relations Officer .... Ms. Brenda KOCHEVAR
38 Director Student Counseling .... Ms. Kelly BAKK
36 Director Student Placement .... Ms. Shari CHRISTENSON
84 Director Enrollment Management .... Ms. Brenda KOCHEVAR
13 Chief Info Technology Officer (CIO) .... Mrs. Shelly MCCAULEY-JUGOVICH
41 Athletic Director .... Mrs. Joanne SCOTT

*Metropolitan State University (E)

700 E 7th Street, Saint Paul MN 55106-5000
County: Ramsey FICE Identification: 010374
Unit ID: 174020
Telephone: (651) 793-1300 Carnegie Class: Masters/L
FAX Number: (651) 793-1235 Calendar System: Semester
URL: www.metrostate.edu
Established: 1971 Annual Undergrad Tuition & Fees (In-State): $7,566
Enrollment: 8,424 Coed
Affiliation or Control: State IRS Status: 501(c)3
Highest Offering: Doctorate
Accreditation: NH, NURSE, SW

02 President .... Ms. Virginia ARTHUR
05 Executive VP and Provost .... Dr. Amy GORT
11 Int Vice Pres Administrative Affs .... Mr. Bruce BISER
111 Chief Advancement Officer .... Ms. Rita DIBBLE
84 Assoc VP Enrollment Management .... Ms. Amy DUNN
32 Dean of Students .... Mr. Herbert KING
13 VP & CIO IT Services .... Mr. Stephen REED
10 Business Manager .... Ms. Kristen LIND
15 Director Human Resources .... Ms. Deb GEHRKE
06 Registrar .... Mr. Daryl JOHNSON
37 Director Financial Aid .... Ms. Lois LARSON
26 Director Communications/Marketing .... Ms. Poh Lin KHOO
29 Director Alumni Relations .... Ms. Kristine HANSEN
28 Chief Diversity Officer .... Mr. Craig MORRIS
09 Director Institutional Research .... Ms. Cynthia DEVORE
07 Director of Admissions .... Mr. Julio VARGAS-ESSEX
81 Dean College of Sciences .... Dr. Kyle SWANSON
58 Dean of College of Management .... Dr. Kat LUI
88 Int Dean Col Cmty Stds/Urban Affs .... Dr. Francis SCHWEIGERT
88 Dean Col Individualized Stds .... Dr. Carl POLDING
88 Dean School of Urban Education .. Dr. Rene ANTROP-GONZALEZ
49 Int Dean College of Liberal Arts .... Dr. Craig HANSEN
66 Int Dean Col of Nursing/Health Sci .... Dr. Judith GRAZIANO
08 Dean Library and Learning Center .... Ms. Christine SCHAFER
96 Manager of Business Services .... Ms. Kora DULLEA

*Minneapolis Community and Technical College (F)

1501 Hennepin Avenue, Minneapolis MN 55403-9810
County: Hennepin FICE Identification: 002362
Unit ID: 174136
Telephone: (612) 659-6000 Carnegie Class: Assoc/MT-VT-High Trad
FAX Number: (612) 659-6210 Calendar System: Semester
URL: www.minneapolis.edu
Established: 1996 Annual Undergrad Tuition & Fees (In-State): $5,349
Enrollment: 8,621 Coed
Affiliation or Control: State IRS Status: 501(c)3
Highest Offering: Associate Degree
Accreditation: NH, ADNUR, DA, POLYT

02 President .... Dr. Sharon PIERCE
05 Vice Pres Academic Affairs .... Dr. Gail O'KANE
10 Vice Pres Finance/Operations .... Mr. Christopher RAU
32 Vice President Student Affairs .... Mr. Patrick TROUP
84 Dean of Enrollment Management .... Mr. Matthew CRAWFORD
49 Dean of Liberal Arts .... Mr. Derrick LINDSTROM
81 Int Dean of Science & Math .... Mr. Ed DILLON
51 Dean of Continuing Education .... Mr. Vincent THOMAS
66 Dean of Nursing & Allied Health .... Ms. Yvette TROTMAN
35 Dean of Students .... Ms. Becky NORDIN
43 CHRO and Director Legal Affairs .... Ms. Dianna CUSICK
13 Chief Information Officer .... Ms. Tiffni DEEB
06 Registrar .... Ms. Michele COPELAND
08 Librarian .... Mr. Tom ELAND
37 Financial Aid Director .... Ms. Angela CHRISTENSEN
09 Director of Institutional Research .... Ms. Jessica SHRAYCK
18 Director Facilities .... Mr. Roger BROZ
19 Director of Public Safety .... Mr. Curt SCHMIDT
26 Chief Public Relations Officer .... Ms. Deanna SHEELY
32 Chief Student Life Officer .... Ms. Tara MARTINEZ

*Minnesota State College Southeast (G)

1250 Homer Road, Winona MN 55987-4897
County: Winona FICE Identification: 002393
Unit ID: 175263
Telephone: (507) 453-2700 Carnegie Class: Assoc/HVT-High Trad
FAX Number: (507) 453-2715 Calendar System: Semester
URL: www.southeastmn.edu
Established: 1949 Annual Undergrad Tuition & Fees (In-District): $5,590
Enrollment: 2,059 Coed
Affiliation or Control: State/Local IRS Status: 501(c)3
Highest Offering: Associate Degree
Accreditation: NH, MLTAD, PNUR, RAD

02 President .... Dr. Dorothy DURAN
05 Vice President Academic Affairs .... Dr. Leslie BLESKACHEK
10 Vice Pres Finance/Administration .... Mr. Mike KROENING
13 Chief Information Officer .... Mr. Rick NAHRGANG
49 Dean of Liberal Arts & Sciences .... Ms. Jolene PONCELET
20 Dean of Trade & Technology .... Mr. Travis THUL
15 Chief Human Resource Officer .... Ms. Maryellen KANZ
06 Registrar .... Ms. Mary JOHNSON
07 Director of Admissions .... Ms. Gale LANNING
84 Director of Recruitment .... Ms. Shannon SCHELL
37 Director Financial Aid .... Dr. Tammy VONDRASEK
18 Chief Facilities/Physical Plant .... Mr. Thomas HOFFMAN
29 Director of Alumni Relations .... Ms. Casie JOHNSON
26 Director of Marketing .... Ms. Joanne THOMPSON
103 Director of Customized Training .... Ms. Jen OLSON
08 Director of Learning Resources .... Mr. Steve ZMYEWSKI
27 Director of Communications .... Ms. Katryn CONLIN
21 Accounting Supervisor .... Ms. Lisa POZANC
16 Associate Human Resources Officer .... Ms. Nicki ADANK
19 Director of Security .... Mr. Chris CICHOSZ
04 Assistant to President .... Ms. Mary DONLIN

*Minnesota State Community and Technical College (H)

1414 College Way, Fergus Falls MN 56537-1000
County: Otter Tail FICE Identification: 005541
Unit ID: 173559
Telephone: (218) 736-1500 Carnegie Class: Assoc/MT-VT-High Trad
FAX Number: (218) 736-1510 Calendar System: Semester
URL: www.minnesota.edu
Established: 1960 Annual Undergrad Tuition & Fees (In-State): $5,338
Enrollment: 6,391 Coed
Affiliation or Control: State IRS Status: 501(c)3
Highest Offering: Associate Degree
Accreditation: NH, CAHIIM, DA, MLTAD, RAD

02 President .... Dr. Peggy KENNEDY
05 Chief Academic Officer .... Dr. Carrie BRIMHALL
15 Chief of Human Resources .... Mrs. Dacia JOHNSON
06 Registrar .... Ms. Sharlene ALLEN
13 Chief Information Officer .... Mr. Dan KNUDSON
10 Chief Finance Officer .... Mr. Pat NORDICK
32 VP of Student Devel & Marketing .... Dr. Peter WIELINSKI
20 Assoc VP of Academic Affairs .... Dr. Jill ABBOTT
18 Director of College Facilities .... Mr. Matt SHEPPARD
121 Dean of Student Success .... Mr. Shawn ANDERSON
12 Academic Dean-Detroit Lakes .... Vacant
12 Acad Dean Lib Arts/Sci-Fergus Falls .... Mr. Matthew BORCHERDING
12 Academic Dean-Wadena .... Mr. Monty JOHNSON
103 Dean of CTS/BES .... Mr. G.L TUCKER
66 Dean of Health Careers .... Mrs. Jennifer JACOBSON
09 Dean of Inst Eff/Tech Programs .... Mr. Steve ERICKSON
07 Director of Admissions .... Mr. Kyle JOHNSTON
28 Chief Diversity Officer .... Vacant
30 Chief Development & Alum Officer .... Ms. Denise LAYMON
36 Career Services Director .... Ms. Sue ZURN
08 Head Librarian .... Ms. Paula DEMARS

*Minnesota State University, Mankato (A)

309 Wigley Administration Center,
Mankato MN 56001-6062

County: Blue Earth | FICE Identification: 002360
Unit ID: 173920
Telephone: (507) 389-1111 | Carnegie Class: Masters/L
FAX Number: (507) 389-6200 | Calendar System: Semester
URL: www.mnsu.edu
Established: 1868 | Annual Undergrad Tuition & Fees (In-State): $7,858
Enrollment: 15,313 | Coed
Affiliation or Control: State | IRS Status: Exempt
Highest Offering: Doctorate
Accreditation: NH, AAB, ART, CAATE, CACREP, CAEPN, CONST, DH, DIETD, ENG, ENGT, MUS, NRPA, NURSE, SP, SPAA, SW

02 President ... Dr. Richard DAVENPORT
05 Provost/Sr Vice Pres Academic Affs ... Dr. Marilyn WELLS
10 Vice Pres Finance & Administration ... Mr. Richard STRAKA
30 VP University Advancement ... Mr. Kent STANLEY
13 VP Technology/CIO ... Mr. Mark JOHNSON
88 VP Strategic/Bus/Ed/Reg Prtrshps ... Mr. Michael GUSTAFSON
32 VP for Student Affairs ... Dr. David JONES
20 VP for Academic Affairs ... Dr. Robert FLEISCHMAN
100 Executive Administrative Officer ... Ms. Sheri SARGENT
04 Exec Assistant to the President ... Ms. Juanita MILBRETT
20 AVP for Undergrad Education ... Dr. Ginger ZIERDT
28 Dean Institutional Diversity ... Mr. Henry MORRIS
18 Facilities Service Director ... Mr. David COWAN
06 University Registrar ... Mr. Marcius BROCK
07 Director of Admissions ... Mr. Brian JONES
08 Dean Library Services ... Dr. Joan ROCA
15 Director of Human Resources ... Mr. Steve BARRETT
36 Director Career Development ... Ms. Pamela WELLER-DENGEL
26 Director Media Relations ... Mr. Daniel BENSON
41 Dir of Intercollegiate Athletics ... Mr. Kevin BUISMAN
29 Director of Alumni Relations ... Mr. Ramon PINERO
22 Director Affirmative Action ... Ms. Cyrenthia JORDAN
37 Director Student Financial Services ... Ms. Jan MARBLE
58 AVP Graduate Studies/Research ... Dr. Barry RIES
79 Dean of Arts & Humanities ... Dr. Matt CECIL
53 Dean of Education ... Dr. Jean HAAR
50 Dean of Business ... Dr. Brenda FLANNERY
76 Dean Allied Health/Nursing ... Dr. Kristine RETHERFORD
81 Dean Science/Engineering/Technology ... Dr. Brian MARTENSEN
83 Dean Social/Behavioral Science ... Dr. Maria BEVACQUA
88 Dean Global Education ... Dr. Stephen STOYNOFF
56 Dean University Extended Education ... Dr. Tom NORMAN
38 Director Student Counseling ... Ms. Kari MUCH
09 Asst VP of Institutional Research ... Ms. Lynn AKEY
18 AVP Facilities Management ... Mr. Paul CORCORAN
21 AVP for Budget & Business Services ... Mr. Steve SMITH
19 Director Security/Safety ... Ms. Sandi SCHNORENBERG
39 Director Student Housing ... Ms. Cindy JANNEY
88 Director Ctr for Talent Dev ... Ms. Lou DICKMEYER

*Minnesota State University Moorhead (B)

1104 7th Avenue S, Moorhead MN 56563-2996

County: Clay | FICE Identification: 002367
Unit ID: 174358
Telephone: (218) 477-4000 | Carnegie Class: Masters/M
FAX Number: (218) 477-2168 | Calendar System: Semester
URL: www.mnstate.edu
Established: 1887 | Annual Undergrad Tuition & Fees (In-State): $8,114
Enrollment: 5,844 | Coed
Affiliation or Control: State | IRS Status: 501(c)3
Highest Offering: Doctorate
Accreditation: NH, ART, #CAATE, CACREP, CAEPN, CONST, DH, MUS, NAIT, NURSE, SP, SW

02 President ... Dr. Anne BLACKHURST
05 Int VP Academic Affairs ... Dr. Marsha L. WEBER
10 VP Finance & Administration ... Ms. Jean HOLLAAR
84 VP Enrollment Mgmt/Student Affairs ... Dr. Brenda AMENSON-HILL
29 VP Alumni Foundation ... Mr. Gary HAUGO
04 Assistant to the President ... Ms. Kathleen J. MCNABB
20 AVP Academic Affairs ... Dr. John (Jack) HEALY
28 Chief Diversity Officer ... Dr. Donna L. BROWN
09 Dir Institutional Effectiveness ... Mr. Kevin BROWN
41 Director of Athletics ... Mr. Doug D. PETERS
13 Chief Information Officer ... Mr. Daniel A. HECKAMAN
21 Comptroller ... Ms. Karen K. LESTER
50 Int Dean Business & Innovation ... Ms. Denise M. GORSLINE
49 Dean Arts/Media/Communication ... Dr. Ernest LAMB
53 Dean Educ/Human Svcs/Grad Stds ... Dr. Ok-Hee LEE
83 Dean Sciences/Health/Environ ... Dr. Jeffrey BODWIN
79 Dean of Col Humanities/Soc Sci ... Dr. Randy L. CAGLE
106 Dean Online/Extended Learning ... Dr. Julie ZALOUDEK
15 Director Human Resources ... Ms. Ann HIEDEMAN
06 Registrar ... Ms. Heather M. SOLEIM
26 Director Marketing/Communications ... Mr. David C. WAHLBERG
19 Director of Public Safety ... Mr. James SCHUMANN
37 Dir Financial Aid & Scholarships ... Ms. Carolyn F. ZEHREN
23 Int Dir Health/Wellness/Counseling ... Ms. Heather PHILLIPS
22 Director Disabilities ... Mr. Greg A. TOUTGES
36 Director of Career Development ... Mr. Troy NELLIS
07 Director of Admissions ... Mr. Tom REBURN
32 Exec Dir Student Union ... Mr. Layne ANDERSON
39 Dir Housing & Residential Life ... Ms. Heather PHILLIPS
85 Director International Student Affs ... Ms. Janet M. HOHENSTEIN
18 Manager Physical Plant ... Mr. Jeffrey D. GOEBEL
40 Bookstore Supervisor ... Ms. Kim M. SAMSON

*Minnesota West Community and Technical College (C)

1450 Collegeway, Worthington MN 56187

County: Nobles | FICE Identification: 005263
Unit ID: 173638
Telephone: (800) 658-2330 | Carnegie Class: Not Classified
FAX Number: (507) 372-5803 | Calendar System: Semester
URL: www.mnwest.edu
Established: 1985 | Annual Undergrad Tuition & Fees (In-State): $5,640
Enrollment: 3,026 | Coed
Affiliation or Control: State | IRS Status: 501(c)3
Highest Offering: Associate Degree
Accreditation: NH, ADNUR, DA, MAC, MLTAD, RAD, SURGT

02 President ... Dr. Terry GAALSWYK
05 College Provost ... Dr. Jeff WILLIAMSON
10 Vice Pres Finance/Facilities ... Ms. Jodi LANDGAARD
20 Interim Campus Dean ... Mr. Dan ROOS
106 Dean Technology/Distance Learning ... Ms. Kayla WESTRA
37 Dir Admission/Registr/Financial Aid ... Ms. Katie HERONIMUS
18 Chief Facilities/Physical Plant ... Vacant
06 Registrar ... Ms. Crystal STROUTH
15 Director Human Resources ... Ms. Karen MILLER
102 Foundation Director ... Mr. Michael VAN KEULEN
08 Library Director ... Mr. Kip THORSON
10 Business Manager ... Ms. Diana FLISS
26 Dir Marketing/Enrollment/Comm ... Ms. Amber LUINENBURG

*Normandale Community College (D)

9700 France Avenue S, Bloomington MN 55431-4399

County: Hennepin | FICE Identification: 007954
Unit ID: 174428
Telephone: (952) 358-8200 | Carnegie Class: Assoc/HT-Mix Trad/Non
FAX Number: (952) 358-8101 | Calendar System: Semester
URL: www.normandale.edu
Established: 1968 | Annual Undergrad Tuition & Fees (In-State): $5,730
Enrollment: 9,855 | Coed
Affiliation or Control: State | IRS Status: 501(c)3
Highest Offering: Associate Degree
Accreditation: NH, ACBSP, ADNUR, ART, DH, DIETT, MUS, THEA

02 President ... Dr. Joyce C. ESTER
04 Executive Assistant to President ... Vacant
10 Vice President Finance & Operations ... Dr. Lisa WHEELER
05 Vice President of Academic Affairs ... Mrs. Julie GUELICH
32 Vice President of Student Affairs ... Vacant
15 Chief Human Resources Officer ... Mrs. Dionne DOERING
09 Dir of Research & Planning ... Dr. Mark LEWIS
50 Dean of Business & Social Sci ... Mr. Michael KIRCH
79 Dean of Humanities ... Dr. Jeffrey JUDGE
81 Dean of STEME ... Dr. Cary KOMOTO
76 Dean of Health Sciences ... Dr. Colleen BRICKLE
08 Dean of Academic Svcs & Library ... Mrs. Erin DALY
21 Assoc VP Finance & Accounting ... Ms. Norma KONSCHAK
13 Chief Information Officer ... Mr. Stephen WINCKELMAN
16 Assistant Human Resources Director ... Ms. Victoria SCHWAB
18 Assoc Vice Pres of Operations ... Mr. Patrick BUHL
102 Executive Director of Foundation ... Mrs. Colleen SIMPSON
84 Dean Outreach & Enrollment ... Mr. Torrion AMIE
35 Dean of Students ... Mr. Greg MCCALLEY
26 Chief Public Relations Officer ... Mr. Steve GELLER
06 Registrar ... Ms. Tonya HANSON
07 Director of Admissions ... Ms. Nancy PATES
37 Director of Financial Aid & Scholar ... Mrs. Susan ANT
38 Assoc Director of Advising & Couns ... Ms. Kari RUSCH-CURL
19 Director of Public Safety ... Mr. Erik BENTLEY
106 Director of Online Learning ... Vacant
27 Director of Marketing Communication ... Mrs. Jennifer LEFLER
88 Accounting Supervisor ... Mrs. Cindy LADD
40 Bookstore Assistant Manager ... Mr. Greg LYONS
25 Grant Development Director ... Mrs. Angela ARNOLD

*North Hennepin Community College (E)

7411 85th Avenue N, Brooklyn Park MN 55445-2299

County: Hennepin | FICE Identification: 002370
Unit ID: 174376
Telephone: (763) 424-0702 | Carnegie Class: Assoc/HT-Mix Trad/Non
FAX Number: (763) 424-0929 | Calendar System: Semester
URL: www.nhcc.edu
Established: 1966 | Annual Undergrad Tuition & Fees (In-State): $4,367
Enrollment: 7,286 | Coed
Affiliation or Control: State | IRS Status: 501(c)3
Highest Offering: Associate Degree
Accreditation: NH, ACBSP, ADNUR, HT, MLTAD

02 President ... Dr. Barbara MCDONALD
05 Int VP Academic & Student Affairs ... Dr. Doris HILL
10 VP Finance & Facilities ... Mr. Stephen KENT
13 Chief Information Officer ... Mr. Joseph COLLINS
32 Dean Student Development ... Ms. Elena FAVELA
84 Dean of Enrollment ... Ms. Jackie OLSSON
08 Librarian ... Mr. Craig LARSON
06 Director of Admissions & Records ... Ms. Melissa LEIMBEK
15 Chief Human Resources Officer ... Ms. Victoria DEFORD
18 Director of Plant Services ... Mr. Joseph MORAN
102 Foundation Executive Director ... Mr. Dale FAGRE
28 Director Diversity/Multiculturalism ... Mr. Michael BIRCHARD
26 Dir Marketing/Communications ... Ms. Liz HOGENSON
09 Director of Institutional Research ... Ms. Dena COLEMER
19 Director of Public Safety ... Mr. Ibuchwa KISONGO
21 Business Manager ... Ms. Dawn BELKO
49 Dean of Liberal Arts ... Mr. Michael DUEÑES
50 Dean Business & Career Programs ... Ms. Tracey WYMAN
81 Int Dean of Math/Science ... Ms. Julie ZIEMINSKI
76 Int Dean of Health Sciences ... Ms. Julie ZIEMINSKI
60 Dean of Comm/Language & Fine Arts ... Ms. Jan MCFALL
121 Director Student Advising ... Ms. Sarah DOMAN-FLYGARE
04 Executive Assistant to President ... Ms. Nicole CARLSON
36 Director Student Placement ... Ms. Deb ATKINS
37 Director Student Financial Aid ... Mr. Steve YANG

*Northland Community and Technical College (F)

1101 Highway 1 E, Thief River Falls MN 56701-2598

County: Pennington | FICE Identification: 002385
Unit ID: 174473
Telephone: (218) 683-8800 | Carnegie Class: Assoc/HVT-Mix Trad/Non
FAX Number: (218) 683-8980 | Calendar System: Semester
URL: www.northlandcollege.edu
Established: 1965 | Annual Undergrad Tuition & Fees (In-State): $5,484
Enrollment: 3,573 | Coed
Affiliation or Control: State | IRS Status: 501(c)3
Highest Offering: Associate Degree
Accreditation: NH, ADNUR, COARC, EMT, OTA, PTAA, RAD, SURGT

02 President ... Dr. Dennis BONA
05 VP Academic Affairs/Student Svcs ... Mr. Carey CASTLE
10 VP of Admin Services/CFO ... Ms. Shannon JESME
04 Asst to President ... Ms. Julie FENNING
11 Campus Dean Administration ... Dr. Brian HUSCHLE
12 Dean Thief River Falls Campus ... Mr. Mike CURFMAN
32 Dean of Students East Grand Forks ... Dr. Mary FONTES
103 Dean Workforce & Econ Development ... Mr. James RETKA
66 Dean Health/Nursing & Public Svcs ... Ms. Jodi STASSEN
121 Academic Success Ctr Director ... Ms. Linnea SCHLUESSLER
38 Counselor ... Ms. Kelsy BLOWERS
38 Counselor ... Ms. Kate SCHMALENBERG
84 Dir of Enrollment Mgmt & Admission ... Ms. Nicki CARLSON
37 Director Student Financial Aid ... Mr. Gerald SCHULTE
09 Director of Institutional Research ... Dr. Mary FONTES
15 Chief Human Resource Officer ... Ms. Kristi LANE
18 Chief Facilities/Physical Plant ... Mr. Clinton CASTLE
26 Director of Marketing/Communication ... Mr. Chad SPERLING
06 Registrar ... Ms. Lisa BOTTEM
28 Diversity Coordinator ... Mr. Carey CASTLE
102 Executive Director of Foundation ... Ms. Sheila BRUHN
13 Director of Technology ... Ms. Stacey HRON
41 Director of Athletics ... Mr. Mike CURFMAN
102 Executive Director NCTC Foundation ... Mr. Lars DYRUD

*Northwest Technical College (G)

905 Grant Avenue, SE, Bemidji MN 56601-4907

County: Beltrami | FICE Identification: 005759
Unit ID: 173115
Telephone: (218) 333-6600 | Carnegie Class: Assoc/HVT-High Non
FAX Number: (218) 333-6694 | Calendar System: Semester
URL: www.ntcmn.edu
Established: 1966 | Annual Undergrad Tuition & Fees (In-State): $5,428
Enrollment: 1,128 | Coed
Affiliation or Control: State | IRS Status: 501(c)3
Highest Offering: Associate Degree
Accreditation: NH, DA

02 President ... Dr. Faith HENSRUD
09 Dir Inst Research/Effectiveness ... Mr. Doug OLNEY

*Pine Technical and Community College (H)

900 Fourth Street, SE, Pine City MN 55063-2198

County: Pine | FICE Identification: 005535
Unit ID: 174570
Telephone: (320) 629-5100 | Carnegie Class: Assoc/HVT-High Non
FAX Number: (320) 629-5101 | Calendar System: Semester
URL: www.pine.edu
Established: 1965 | Annual Undergrad Tuition & Fees (In-State): $4,029
Enrollment: 1,310 | Coed
Affiliation or Control: State | IRS Status: 501(c)3
Highest Offering: Associate Degree
Accreditation: NH, MAC

02 President ... Mr. Joe MULFORD
05 Int Chief Academic Officer ... Dr. Connie FRISCH
13 Chief Information Officer ... Mr. Kenneth RIES
10 Chief Financial Officer ... Ms. Janis WEGNER
32 Vice Pres Student Affairs ... Ms. Denine ROOD
51 Dean of Continuing Edu/Custom Trng ... Mr. Jason SPAETH
103 ETC Workforce Development ... Ms. Leslie PRICE
36 Exec Dir Employment/Training Ctr ... Mr. Dwayne GREEN
06 Registrar ... Ms. Darla CAVERLEY
15 Chief Human Resources Officer ... Ms. Amy KRUSE

26 Director Marketing/Enrollment .... Ms. Shawnda SCHELINDER
37 Director Student Financial Aid .... Mr. Shawn REYNOLDS
18 Physical Plant Supervisor .... Mr. Steven LANGE
04 Administrative Asst to President .... Ms. Sandra CARLISLE

*Rainy River Community College (A)

1501 Highway 71, International Falls MN 56649-2187
County: Koochiching FICE Identification: 006775
Unit ID: 174604
Telephone: (218) 285-7722 Carnegie Class: Assoc/HT-Mix Trad/Non
FAX Number: (218) 285-2239 Calendar System: Semester
URL: www.rrcc.mnscu.edu
Established: 1967 Annual Undergrad Tuition & Fees (In-State): $5,277
Enrollment: 341 Coed
Affiliation or Control: State IRS Status: 501(c)3
Highest Offering: Associate Degree
Accreditation: NH

02 Provost .... Dr. Roxanne KELLY
06 Registrar .... Ms. Berta HAGEN
37 Director of Financial Aid .... Mr. Scott T. RILEY
13 Dir Information Technology .... Ms. Shelly JUGOVICH
10 Business Manager .... Mrs. Emily AHRENS

*Ridgewater College (B)

PO Box 1097, 2101 15th Ave NW,
Willmar MN 56201-1097
County: Kandiyohi FICE Identification: 005252
Unit ID: 175236
Telephone: (320) 222-5200 Carnegie Class: Assoc/MT-VT-High Trad
FAX Number: (320) 222-5212 Calendar System: Semester
URL: www.ridgewater.edu
Established: 1961 Annual Undergrad Tuition & Fees (In-State): $5,370
Enrollment: 3,563 Coed
Affiliation or Control: State IRS Status: 501(c)3
Highest Offering: Associate Degree
Accreditation: NH, ADNUR, CAHIIM, EMT, MAC, PNUR

02 Interim President .... Dr. Joe OPATZ
05 Vice Pres Acad Affs/Student Svcs .... Dr. Betty J. STREHLOW
10 Vice President Finance & Operations .... Mr. Daniel F. HOLTZ
51 Dean of Cust Trng & Cont Education .... Mr. Sam BOWEN
20 Dean of Instruction/Technical Pgms .... Ms. Judy TEBBEN
20 Dean of Instruction .... Mr. Mike KUTZKE
20 Dean Instruction/Liberal Arts/Sci .... Mr. Alan STAGE
32 Dean of Student Services .... Ms. Heidi L. OLSON
21 Director of Business Services .... Ms. Cheryl A. NORLIEN
15 Int Chief Human Resource Officer .... Mr. Keith BALASKI
66 Director of Nursing .... Ms. C. Lynn JOHNSON
37 Director of Financial Aid .... Mr. James W. RICE
07 Admissions Director .... Ms. Sally KERFELD
41 Athletic Director .... Mr. Todd M. THORSTAD
06 Registrar .... Ms. Kelli S. KIENITZ
13 Chief Information Officer .... Mr. Timothy L. FURR
26 Director of Communication/Marketing .... Ms. Liz VANDERBILL
102 Foundation Executive Director .... Ms. Kelly J. MAGNUSON
09 Director of Institutional Research .... Dr. Ellen ROSTER
28 Multicultural Outreach/Academic Adv ...... Ms. Jehana SCHWANDT
18 Physical Plant Director .... Mr. Kip R. OVESON

*Riverland Community College (C)

1900 8th Avenue, NW, Austin MN 55912-1473
County: Mower FICE Identification: 002335
Unit ID: 173063
Telephone: (507) 433-0600 Carnegie Class: Assoc/MT-VT-Mix Trad/Non
FAX Number: (507) 433-0665 Calendar System: Semester
URL: www.riverland.edu
Established: 1940 Annual Undergrad Tuition & Fees (In-State): $5,507
Enrollment: 3,068 Coed
Affiliation or Control: State IRS Status: 501(c)3
Highest Offering: Associate Degree
Accreditation: NH, ACBSP, ADNUR, MAC, RAD

02 President .... Dr. Adenuga ATEWOLOGUN
05 VP of Academic & Student Affairs .... Dr. Kelly MCCALLA
10 Chief Financial Officer .... Mr. Brad DOSS
15 Chief Human Resources Officer .... Ms. Celeste RUBLE
66 Director of Nursing .... Ms. Laura BEASLEY
49 Dean Arts/Humanities/Soc Sciences .... Ms. Lisa SCHLOTTERHAUSEN
75 Dean Bus/Tech/Trade & Industry .... Mr. Matt BISSONETTE
32 Dean of Student Affairs .... Mr. Gary SCHINDLER
30 Dean for Institutional Advancement .... Mr. Steve BOWRON
06 Dir of Enrollment Svcs/Registrar .... Ms. Sue JECH
07 Dir of Admissions & New Student Rel .... Ms. Nel ZELLAR
26 Exec Dir Communications/Media/Mktg ..... Mr. James DOUGLASS
37 Director of Financial Aid .... Ms. Patty HEMANN
36 Dir of College Partnerships & Trans .... Ms. Jean KYLE
13 Director of Technology .... Mr. Dan HARBER
18 Facilities Supervisor .... Mr. Shawn O'CONNOR
96 Purchasing Agent .... Ms. Page PETERSEN
28 Reg DiversityTrainer/Investgtr .... Ms. Ricki WALTERS
08 Librarian .... Ms. Jeannie (Carol) KEARNEY
19 Safety Administrator .... Mr. Mike HOWE
29 Director Alumni Relations .... Ms. Attina EARL
41 Athletic Director-Men .... Mr. Doug WALDNER
41 Athletic Director-Women .... Ms. Helen JAHR

*Rochester Community and Technical College (D)

851 30th Avenue, SE, Rochester MN 55904-4999
County: Olmsted FICE Identification: 002373
Unit ID: 174738
Telephone: (507) 285-7210 Carnegie Class: Assoc/MT-VT-High Trad
FAX Number: (507) 285-7496 Calendar System: Semester
URL: www.rctc.edu
Established: 1915 Annual Undergrad Tuition & Fees (In-State): $5,588
Enrollment: 5,584 Coed
Affiliation or Control: State IRS Status: 501(c)3
Highest Offering: Associate Degree
Accreditation: NH, ACBSP, ADNUR, CAHIIM, DA, DH, PNUR, SURGT

02 Interim President .... Dr. Mary DAVENPORT
05 Executive VP of Academic Affairs .... Dr. Greg MOSIER
10 Vice Pres Finance and Facilities .... Mr. Steve SCHMALL
76 Dean Sciences/Health Professions .... Dr. Brian FORS
49 Dean of Liberal Arts .... Dr. Brenda FRAME
75 Dean of Career/Technical .... Ms. Michelle PYFFEROEN
15 Chief Human Resources Officer .... Mrs. Renee ENGELMEYER
13 Chief Information Officer .... Mr. Scott SAHS
32 Chief Student Affairs Officer .... Dr. Michael ANTHONY
88 Dir of Business/Econ Development .... Ms. Michelle PYFFEROEN
35 Student Life Coordinator .... Ms. Laura ENGELMAN
06 Registrar .... Ms. Nancy SHUMAKER
07 Director Admissions .... Ms. Alicia ZEONE
37 Director Financial Aid .... Ms. Beth DIEKMANN
09 Director of Institutional Research .... Dr. Priyank SHAH
04 Executive Assistant to President .... Mrs. Judy KINGSBURY
21 Business Office Supervisor .... Vacant
26 Chief Public Relations Officer .... Mr. Nate STOLTMAN
19 Security Officer .... Mr. Andrew HAMANN
40 Bookstore Coordinator .... Ms. Michelle DANIELSON
96 Purchasing Manager .... Ms. June MEITZNER
102 Foundation Executive Director .... Ms. Deb WARD
18 Chief Facilities/Physical Plant .... Mr. Mark FASS
38 Director Student Counseling .... Ms. Lisa MOHR
108 Dean .... Dr. Ginny BOYUM
08 Head Librarian .... Ms. Diane POLLOCK
22 Dir Affirmative Action/EEO .... Ms. Renee ENGELMEYER
41 Athletic Director .... Mr. Mike LESTER
105 Director Web Services .... Mr. Darin HOFFMAN
29 Director Alumni Relations .... Ms. Deb WARD

*St. Cloud State University (E)

720 4th Avenue S, Saint Cloud MN 56301-4498
County: Stearns FICE Identification: 002377
Unit ID: 174783
Telephone: (320) 308-0121 Carnegie Class: Masters/L
FAX Number: N/A Calendar System: Semester
URL: www.stcloudstate.edu
Established: 1869 Annual Undergrad Tuition & Fees (In-State): $7,910
Enrollment: 16,096 Coed
Affiliation or Control: State IRS Status: 501(c)3
Highest Offering: Doctorate
Accreditation: NH, ART, CAATE, CACREP, CAEPN, CS, ENG, ENGR, JOUR, MFCD, MT, MUS, NAIT, NURSE, SP, SW, THEA

02 Interim President .... Dr. Ashish VAIDYA
04 Interim Executive Asst to President .... Ms. Greta ABEL
05 Interim Provost/VP Academic Affairs .... Dr. Dan GREGORY
20 Dir of Academic Operations .... Dr. Michele MUMM
10 Vice Pres Finance/Admin .... Ms. Tammy L. MCGEE
21 Interim Assoc VP Finance/Admin .... Mr. Jeff WAGNER
117 AVP Safety/Risk Management .... Mr. Jesse CASHMAN
32 Vice Pres Student Life Development .... Dr. Wanda OVERLAND
111 Vice Pres University Advancement .... Mr. Matthew ANDREW
43 Special Advisor to the President .... Dr. Judith P. SIMINOE
22 Institutional Equity & Access .... Dr. Ellyn BARTGES
41 Athletic Director .... Ms. Heather WEEMS
86 Dir Univ Relations/Legislative Rel .... Mr. Bernie OMANN
45 Vice Pres Planning & Engagement .... Dr. Lisa FOSS
26 Asst VP Marketing & Communications .... Mr. Adam HAMMER
50 Dean Herberger Business School .... Dr. David HARRIS
53 Dean School of Education .... Dr. Jennifer MUELLER
76 Interim Dean Health/Human Service .... Dr. Shonda M. CRAFT
49 Dean College of Liberal Arts .... Dr. Mark SPRINGER
88 Dean School of Public Affairs .... Dr. King BANAIAN
81 Interim Dean Science & Engineering .... Dr. Adel ALI
51 Interim Director Continuing Studies .... Ms. Gail RUHLAND
08 Dean University Library .... Ms. Rhonda HUISMAN
46 Int AP for Research & Spons Pgm .... Dr. Latha RAMAKRISHNAN
88 Interim AP University College .... Dr. Glenn DAVIS
35 AP Faculty/Student Affairs ..... Dr. LaVonne CORNELL-SWANSON
84 AP Undergrad Recruit & Enrollment .... Dr. Amber SCHULTZ
06 Registrar .... Ms. Sue BAYERL
13 Dir Information Technology Services .... Mr. Phil THORSON
29 Director of Constituent Engagement .... Ms. Terri MISCHE
36 Executive Director Career Center .... Ms. Michelle SCHMITZ
37 Director of Financial Aid .... Mr. Mike T. URAN
38 Director of Counseling .... Dr. John M. EGGERS
39 Director of Student Housing .... Mr. Daniel T. PEDERSEN
09 Dir Analytics/Business Intelligence .... Mr. Brent DONNAY
15 Chief Human Resource Officer .... Mr. Michael FREER
18 AVP Facilities Management .... Mr. Phil MOESSNER
88 Director American Indian Center . Mr. Jim KNUTSON-KOLODZNE
88 Exec Director of Atwood Mem Ctr .... Mr. Mitchell KARSTENS
88 Director LGBT Resources .... Mr. Seth KAEMPFER
88 Director Lindgren Child Care Center .... Mr. Dennis MERGEN

88 Director Multicultural Student Svcs .... Mr. Shahzad AHMED
22 Director Student Disability Service .... Ms. Andria BELISLE
23 Director Student Health Services .... Ms. Corie BECKERMANN
88 Director Womens Center .... Ms. Jane OLSEN
19 Director Public Safety .... Mr. Kevin WHITLOCK
88 Director of International Studies .... Mr. Shahzad AHMAD
40 Bookstore Manager .... Mr. Ted MEARS

*Saint Cloud Technical and Community College (F)

1540 Northway Drive, Saint Cloud MN 56303-1240
County: Stearns FICE Identification: 005534
Unit ID: 174756
Telephone: (320) 308-5000 Carnegie Class: Assoc/HVT-High Trad
FAX Number: (320) 308-5981 Calendar System: Semester
URL: www.sctcc.edu
Established: 1948 Annual Undergrad Tuition & Fees (In-State): $5,295
Enrollment: 4,701 Coed
Affiliation or Control: State IRS Status: 501(c)3
Highest Offering: Associate Degree
Accreditation: NH, CAHIIM, CVT, DA, DH, DMS, EMT, PNUR, SURGT

02 Interim President .... Ms. Lori KLOOS
05 VP of Academic Affairs .... Ms. Carolyn OLSON
04 Assistant to the President .... Ms. Karen A. HIEMENZ
32 Vice President of Student Affairs .... Vacant
10 Vice Pres Admin/Chief Financial Ofc ...... Mr. Duane DAHLSTROM
75 Dean Trade/Industry .... Mr. Mike MENDEZ
81 Dean of Liberal Arts & Trans Stds .... Ms. Melissa LINDSEY
50 Dean of Business/Comm/Humanities .... Ms. Kristina KELLER
66 Dean of Nursing/Health .... Mr. Kelly HALVERSON
06 Registrar .... Ms. Lana L. FEDDEMA
15 Dir Personnel Svcs/Affirm Action .... Ms. Deb A. HOLSTAD
84 Dir of Enroll Management/Admissions .... Ms. Jodi M. ELNESS
08 Head Librarian .... Ms. Patricia AKERMAN
19 Security/Safety Officer .... Mr. Christopher LOOS
37 Director Student Financial Aid .... Ms. Anita G. BAUGH
36 Director Student Placement .... Ms. Jackie BAUER
40 Director Bookstore .... Mr. James SCHOLLA
35 Activ Dir/Chief Student Life Ofcr .... Ms. Melissa MAJERUS
18 Chief Facilities/Physical Plant .... Mr. Jason THEISEN
13 Chief Information Officer .... Ms. Viola BERGQUIST
21 Associate Business Officer .... Vacant
96 Director of Purchasing .... Ms. Susan MEYER
14 Director Library & Info Technology .... Ms. Viola BERGQUIST
22 Director Affirm Action/Equal Oppty .... Ms. Deb HOLSTAD
30 Chief Devel/Dir Annual/Planned Giv .... Ms. Arlene WILLIAMS
28 Director of Diversity .... Mr. Jonathan EICHTEN

*Saint Paul College-A Community & Technical College (G)

235 Marshall Avenue, Saint Paul MN 55102-1800
County: Ramsey FICE Identification: 005533
Unit ID: 175041
Telephone: (651) 846-1600 Carnegie Class: Assoc/HVT-Mix Trad/Non
FAX Number: (651) 846-1451 Calendar System: Semester
URL: www.saintpaul.edu
Established: 1910 Annual Undergrad Tuition & Fees (In-State): $5,458
Enrollment: 6,428 Coed
Affiliation or Control: State IRS Status: 501(c)3
Highest Offering: Associate Degree
Accreditation: NH, ACBSP, ACFEI, CAHIIM, COARC, MLTAD, PNUR

02 President .... Dr. Rassoul DASTMOZD
10 Vice President Finance & Operations .... Mr. Scott WILSON
32 Vice President of Student Affairs .... Dr. Laura KING
05 Vice President of Academic Affairs .... Dr. Kristen RANEY
27 Director of TRIO .... Ms. Mary VANG
103 Dean Workforce Trng/Continuing Educ .... Dr. Tracy WILSON
84 Dean Enrollment Management .... Ms. Sarah CARRICO
15 Chief Human Resources Officer .... Ms. Rachelle M. SCHMIDT
06 Dir Admissions/Registration .... Ms. Tarah BJORKLUND
09 Dean of Institutional Research .... Ms. Laura KING
29 Director of Alumni Relations .... Vacant
36 Director Student Placement .... Ms. Sheryl SAUL
38 Director Student Counseling .... Dr. Lisa HANES-GOODLANDER
96 Director of Purchasing .... Ms. Teresa SORENSEN
18 Director Facilities/Physical Plant .... Mr. Daniel KIRK
21 Business Manager .... Ms. Liz SCHMIDT
22 Director Equity/Inclusion .... Ms. Wendy ROBERSON
37 Director of Student Financial Aid .... Mr. Adam JOHNSON
102 Exec Dir of Foundation/Alumni Rels .... Vacant
13 Chief Information Officer .... Mr. Najam SAEED
26 Director of Marketing/Recruitment .... Ms. Audrey BERGENGREN
17 Dean of Health & Services .... Dr. Brendan ASHBY
81 Dean Science/Technology/Eng & Math .... Vacant
50 Dean Business/Career Tech Educ .... Mr. Frank BRASWELL
88 Dean Liberal & Fine Arts .... Dr. Milford MUSKETT
19 Director Security/Safety .... Mr. Thomas BERGS
108 Director Institutional Assessment .... Vacant
88 Dir One Stop Services .... Ms. Ali PICKENS-OPOKU

*South Central College (H)

1920 Lee Boulevard, PO Box 1920,
North Mankato MN 56003
County: Nicollet FICE Identification: 005537
Unit ID: 173911
Telephone: (507) 389-7200 Carnegie Class: Assoc/MT-VT-High Non
FAX Number: (507) 388-9951 Calendar System: Semester
URL: www.southcentral.edu

Established: 1946 Annual Undergrad Tuition & Fees (In-District): $5,369
Enrollment: 2,960 Coed
Affiliation or Control: State/Local IRS Status: 501(c)3
Highest Offering: Associate Degree
Accreditation: NH, DA, EMT, MAC, MLTAD

02 President Dr. Annette PARKER
04 Exec Assistant to the President Ms. Carol FREED
05 Vice Pres Student/Academic Affs Dr. Susan TARNOWSKI
10 VP Finance/Operations Mr. David ARMSTRONG
15 CHRO Ms. Dawn PEARSON
13 Vice Pres of Technology Dr. Mark BAAS
103 VP of Economic Development Ms. Marsha DANIELSON
09 Assoc VP Rsrch/Inst Effectiveness Dr. Narren BROWN
32 Dean of Student Affairs Ms. Judy ZEIGER
49 Dean of LAS Dr. Judy SHULTZ
75 Dean of Career & Technical Educ Ms. Barb EMBACHER
47 Dean of Agriculture Mr. Brad SCHLOESSER
66 Dean of Allied Health & Nursing Ms. Michele BRIELMAIER
26 Public Relations/Marketing Director Ms. Shelly MEGAW
28 Chief Diversity Officer Dr. Mitzi KENNEDY
37 Director of Financial Aid Ms. Jayne DINSE
19 Director of Safety & Security Mr. Al KLUEVER
08 Director of Library/Media Services Ms. Johnna HORTON
06 Registrar Ms. Deann SCHLOESSER

*Southwest Minnesota State University (A)

1501 State Street, Marshall MN 56258-1598
County: Lyon FICE Identification: 002375
Unit ID: 175078
Telephone: (507) 537-7678 Carnegie Class: Masters/M
FAX Number: (507) 537-7154 Calendar System: Semester
URL: www.smsu.edu
Established: 1963 Annual Undergrad Tuition & Fees (In-State): $8,347
Enrollment: 7,276 Coed
Affiliation or Control: State IRS Status: 501(c)3
Highest Offering: Master's
Accreditation: NH, MUS, NURSE, SW

02 President Dr. Connie J. GORES
05 Provost Dr. Dwight C. WATSON
10 VP Finance and Admin Ms. Debra KERKAERT
32 AVP Stdnt Affairs/Dean of Students Mr. Scott CROWELL
111 VP Advance/Foundation Ex Dir Mr. William MULSO
49 Dean Arts/Letters/Sciences Dr. Jan LOFT
50 Dean Bus/Ed/Grad/Prof Studies Dr. Raphael ONYEAGHALA
41 Athletic Director Mr. Christopher HMIELEWSKI
13 Chief Information Officer Mr. Dan BAUN
07 VP EMSS Mr. Rob FORGET
14 Director of Computer Services Mr. Shawn HEDMAN
06 Registrar Ms. Patricia CARMODY
19 Director University Public Safety Mr. Michael MUNFORD
28 Director Diversity & Inclusion Mr. Jay LEE
15 Chief Human Resources/Affirm Action Ms. Nancy OLSON
29 Director of Alumni Mr. Michael VANDREHLE
18 Facilities & Physical Plant Manager Ms. Cyndi HOLM
36 Director of Career Services Ms. Melissa SCHOLTEN
37 Director of Financial Aid Mr. David VIKANDER
38 Associate Professor of Counseling Ms. Sara FIER
96 Buyer Supervisor Ms. Barb BERKENPAS
21 Business Manager Mr. Eric RUNESTAD
26 Dir Communications/Marketing Mr. James TATE
04 Exec Admin Asst to President Ms. Chris ANDERSON
09 Director of Institutional Research Mr. Alan MATZNER
30 Director Development Ms. Stacy FROST
44 Director Annual or Planned Giving Mr. Erik VOGEL

*Vermilion Community College (B)

1900 E Camp Street, Ely MN 55731-1998
County: Saint Louis FICE Identification: 002350
Unit ID: 175157
Telephone: (218) 365-7200 Carnegie Class: Assoc/HT-High Trad
FAX Number: (218) 235-2173 Calendar System: Semester
URL: www.vcc.edu
Established: 1922 Annual Undergrad Tuition & Fees (In-State): $5,278
Enrollment: 655 Coed
Affiliation or Control: State IRS Status: 501(c)3
Highest Offering: Associate Degree
Accreditation: NH

02 Provost/Chief Academic Officer Mr. Shawn BINA
07 Director of Admissions/Student Affs Mr. Jeff NELSON
09 Director of Institutional Research Ms. Tracey ROY
15 Director of Human Resources Ms. Carmen BRADACH
32 Dir Student Life/Facil/Phy Plant Mr. Dave MARSHALL
36 Director of Student Placement Ms. Molly JOHNSTON
37 Director of Student Financial Aid Ms. Shannan HARDING
38 Director of Student Counseling Ms. Cindy ANDERSON-BINA
29 Director Alumni Relations Ms. Patti ZUPANCICH
28 Director of Diversity Ms. Patti ZUPANCICH
26 Chief Public Relations Officer Mr. Jeff NELSON
06 Registrar Ms. Chris HEGENBARTH

*Winona State University (C)

PO Box 5838, Winona MN 55987-0838
County: Winona FICE Identification: 002394
Unit ID: 175272
Telephone: (507) 457-5000 Carnegie Class: Masters/M
FAX Number: (507) 457-5586 Calendar System: Quarter
URL: www.winona.edu
Established: 1858 Annual Undergrad Tuition & Fees (In-State): $9,075
Enrollment: 8,490 Coed
Affiliation or Control: State IRS Status: 501(c)3
Highest Offering: Doctorate
Accreditation: NH, CAATE, CACREP, CAEPN, ENG, MT, MUS, NURSE, SW, THEA

02 President Dr. Scott R. OLSON
05 Provost/VP Academic Affairs/CAO Dr. Patricia ROGERS
10 VP Finance & Administration Mr. Scott ELLINGHUYSEN
30 VP University Advancement Mr. Ron DEMPSEY
32 VP Enrollment & Student Life & Dev Ms. Denise MCDOWELL
13 AVP Academic Affairs/CIO Mr. Kenneth JANZ
26 Asst VP Marketing & Communications Vacant
38 Director of Counseling Svcs Vacant
54 Dean Col of Science/Engr Dr. Charla MIERTSCHIN
49 Int Assoc Dean Col of Liberal Arts Dr. Peter MIENE
50 Dean College of Business Dr. Hamid AKBARI
53 Dean College of Education Dr. Tarrell PORTMAN
66 Dean Col of Nursing/Health Science Dr. William MCBREEN
35 Dean of Students Ms. Karen JOHNSON
06 Sr Associate Registrar Ms. Tania SCHMIDT
84 Director Warrior Success Center Vacant
37 Assistant Director of Financial Aid Ms. Charlene KREUZER
36 Associate Director Career Services Ms. Deanna GODDARD
07 Director of Admissions Vacant
39 Residential College Program Coord Ms. Sarah OLCOTT
51 Exec Dir Outreach/Continuing Educ Vacant
29 Associate Director Alumni Relations Mr. Mark REITAN
40 Bookstore Manager Ms. Karen KRAUSE
44 Director Development Ms. Debbie BLOCK
88 Director of International Svcs Ms. Kemale PINAR
19 Director of Security Mr. Christopher CICHOSZ
41 Athletic Director Mr. Eric SCHOH
18 Asst VP for Facilities Management Vacant
27 Director University Public Info Ms. Andrea NORTHAM
94 Director of Women's Studies Dr. Tamara BERG
96 Director of Purchasing Ms. Laura MANN
28 Director of Cultural Diversity Mr. Alexander HINES
15 Director of Human Resources Ms. Lori REED

*Anoka-Ramsey Community College Cambridge Campus (D)

300 Spirit River Drive South, Cambrdige MN 55008-5704
Telephone: (763) 433-1100 Identification: 770298
Accreditation: &NH

*Hennepin Technical College (E)

131000 College View, Eden Prairie MN 55347
Telephone: (952) 995-1300 Identification: 770299
Accreditation: &NH

*Mesabi Range College Eveleth (F)

1100 Industrial Park Drive, Eveleth MN 55734
Telephone: (218) 741-3095 Identification: 770300
Accreditation: &NH

*Minnesota State College-Southeast Technical Red Wing Campus (G)

308 Pioneer Road, Red Wing MN 55066
Telephone: (651) 385-6300 Identification: 770302
Accreditation: &NH

*Minnesota State Community and Technical College Detroit Lakes (H)

900 Highway 34 E, Detroit Lakes MN 56501
Telephone: (218) 846-3700 Identification: 770303
Accreditation: &NH

*Minnesota State Community and Technical College Moorhead (I)

1900 28th Avenue S, Moorhead MN 56560
Telephone: (218) 299-6500 Identification: 770304
Accreditation: &NH, SURGT

*Minnesota State Community and Technical College Wadena (J)

405 Colfax Avenue SW, Wadena MN 56482
Telephone: (213) 631-7800 Identification: 770305
Accreditation: &NH

*Minnesota West Community and Technical College Canby Campus (K)

1011 First Street, Canby MN 56220
Telephone: (507) 223-7252 Identification: 770306
Accreditation: &NH

*Minnesota West Community and Technical College Granite Falls Campus (L)

1593 11th Avenue, Granite Falls MN 56241
Telephone: (320) 564-5000 Identification: 770307
Accreditation: &NH

*Minnesota West Community and Technical College Jackson Campus (M)

401 West Street, Jackson MN 56143
Telephone: (547) 847-7920 Identification: 770308
Accreditation: &NH

*Minnesota West Community and Technical College Pipestone Campus (N)

1314 North Hiawatha Avenue, Pipestone MN 56164
Telephone: (507) 825-6800 Identification: 770309
Accreditation: &NH

*Minnesota West Community and Technical College Worthington Campus (O)

1450 College Way, Worthington MN 56187
Telephone: (507) 372-3400 Identification: 770310
Accreditation: &NH

*Northland Community and Technical College East Grand Forks Campus (P)

2022 Central Avenue NE, East Grand Forks MN 56721
Telephone: (218) 793-2800 Identification: 770311
Accreditation: &NH, @DIETT

*Ridgewater College Hutchinson Campus (Q)

2 Century Avenue SE, Hutchinson MN 55350
Telephone: (320) 234-8500 Identification: 770312
Accreditation: &NH

*Riverland Community College Albert Lea Campus (R)

2200 Riverland Drive, Albert Lea MN 56007
Telephone: (507) 379-3300 Identification: 770313
Accreditation: &NH

*South Central College Faribault Campus (S)

1225 Third Street SW, Faribault MN 55021
Telephone: (507) 332-5800 Identification: 770314
Accreditation: &NH

*Winona State University-Rochester (T)

859 30th Avenue SE, Rochester MN 55904
Telephone: (800) 366-5418 Identification: 770317
Accreditation: &NH

Mitchell Hamline School of Law (U)

875 Summit Avenue, Saint Paul MN 55105-3076
County: Ramsey FICE Identification: 002391
Unit ID: 175281
Telephone: (651) 227-9171 Carnegie Class: Spec-4-yr-Law
FAX Number: (651) 290-6414 Calendar System: Semester
URL: www.mitchellhamline.edu
Established: 1900 Annual Graduate Tuition & Fees: N/A
Enrollment: 738 Coed
Affiliation or Control: Independent Non-Profit IRS Status: 501(c)3
Highest Offering: First Professional Degree; No Undergraduates
Accreditation: LAW

01 President & Dean Mr. Mark GORDON
04 Exec Asst to President & Board Ms. Lynette FRACTION
05 Assoc Dean for Academic Affairs Mr. Peter KNAPP
46 Dean of Strategic Initiatives Mr. Greg DUHL
30 VP of Development Ms. Jodi GLASER
15 Director Human Resources Ms. Andrea BIEN
13 Director of Information Technology Mr. Andrew ALLEN
10 VP Finance & Administration Mr. Art BERMAN
11 VP Operations/Cmty Partnerships Ms. Christine SZAJ
08 Director of Law Library Ms. Barbara KALLUSKY
28 Program Mgr/Diversity & Inclusion Ms. Sharon VAN LEER
36 Dean for Career Development Ms. Leanne FUITH
07 Dean of Admissions Ms. Emily DUNSWORTH
06 Registrar Ms. Colleen CLISH
37 Director of Financial Aid Ms. Patty HARRIS
96 Purchasing Manager Ms. Paula B. MERTH
19 Director Security Mr. David HELLERMANN
32 Dean of Student Affairs Ms. Lynn LEMOINE
121 Dean of Academic Excellence Ms. Dena SONBOL

National American University-Bloomington (V)

7801 Metro Pkwy, Suite 200, Bloomington MN 55425
Telephone: (952) 356-3600 Identification: 770397
Accreditation: &NH, MAC

† Branch campus of National American University, Rapid City, SD

National American University-Brooklyn Center (A)

6200 Shingle Creek Pkwy, Suite 130,
Brooklyn Center MN 55430
Telephone: (763) 852-7500 Identification: 770398
Accreditation: &NH, MAC

† Branch campus of National American University, Rapid City, SD

National American University-Burnsville (B)

501 West Travelers Trail, #617, Burnsville MN 55337
Telephone: (952) 563-1250 Identification: 770399
Accreditation: &NH

† Branch campus of National American University, Rapid City, SD

National American University-Rochester (C)

3906 East Frontage Highway 52 Road,
Rochester MN 55901
Telephone: (866) 628-6387 Identification: 770400
Accreditation: &NH, MAC

† Branch campus of National American University, Rapid City, SD

National American University-Roseville (D)

1550 W Highway 36, Roseville MN 55113
Telephone: (651) 855-6300 Identification: 770401
Accreditation: &NH, MAC

† Branch campus of National American University, Rapid City, SD

North Central University (E)

910 Elliot Avenue, Minneapolis MN 55404-1391
County: Hennepin FICE Identification: 002369
Unit ID: 174437
Telephone: (612) 343-4400 Carnegie Class: Bac-Diverse
FAX Number: (612) 343-4778 Calendar System: Semester
URL: www.northcentral.edu
Established: 1930 Annual Undergrad Tuition & Fees: $22,240
Enrollment: 1,212 Coed
Affiliation or Control: Assemblies Of God Church IRS Status: 501(c)3
Highest Offering: Master's
Accreditation: NH, SW

01 President .... Rev. Scott A. HAGAN
04 Executive Assistant to President .... Mrs. Bridget KNISELY
05 VP Academic Affairs/Academic Dean .... Dr. Don L. TUCKER
10 Vice President Business/Finance .... Vacant
42 Vice President of Spiritual Life .... Dr. Doug GRAHAM
26 VP University Relations .... Mr. Andrew DENTON
57 Executive Director Fine Arts .... Dr. Larry C. BACH
21 Director of Accounting .... Mr. Bruce W. WHEELER
32 Dean of Students .... Dr. Lewis A. HATCHER
41 Director of Athletics .... Mr. Greg L. JOHNSON
37 Director of Financial Aid .... Mrs. Monica M. MUCHOW
08 Library Director .... Mrs. Judy PRUITT
13 Director of Information Technology .... Mr. Steve D. KRAHN
06 Registrar .... Ms. Mary MURPHY
09 Dir Inst Research/Effectiveness .... Mr. Greg LEEPER
07 Director of Admissions .... Mrs. Beth HARSHBARGER
121 Director of Student Success Center .... Mr. Todd MONGER
18 Director of Facility Management .... Mr. Jay VETTER
58 Director Graduate & Creative Educ .... Dr. Renea C. BRATHWAITE
15 Director of Human Resources .... Ms. Sue BENTLEY
19 Director Security/Safety .... Mr. James CRABTREE
29 Director Alumni Relations .... Ms. Aimee ROBERTSON
30 Director of Development .... Rev. Trent REDMANN

Northwestern Health Sciences University (F)

2501 W 84th Street, Bloomington MN 55431-1599
County: Hennepin FICE Identification: 012328
Unit ID: 174507
Telephone: (952) 888-4777 Carnegie Class: Spec-4-yr-Other Health
FAX Number: (952) 888-6713 Calendar System: Trimester
URL: www.nwhealth.edu
Established: 1941 Annual Undergrad Tuition & Fees: $10,396
Enrollment: 870 Coed
Affiliation or Control: Independent Non-Profit IRS Status: 501(c)3
Highest Offering: First Professional Degree
Accreditation: NH, ACUP, CHIRO, COMTA

01 President and CEO .... Dr. Christopher CASSIRER
05 Provost and Chief Academic Officer .... Dr. Deborah BUSHWAY
10 Chief Financial Officer .... Ms. Kathy PANCIERA
32 VP Student Affs/Dean of Students .... Vacant
15 VP of Human Resources .... Ms. Mary GALE
26 VP of Marketing & Events .... Ms. Kathy HAGENDS
11 Chief Operating Officer .... Vacant
07 Director of Admissions .... Ms. Erin KAHN
08 Director of Library Services .... Ms. Anne MACKERETH
29 Dir Alumni Relations .... Vacant
51 Manager of Continuing Education .... Ms. Jennifer BELL
13 Chief Information Officer .... Mr. Chad JOHNSON
38 University Counselor .... Ms. Becky LAWYER
18 Director Facilities Management .... Mr. Kevin WOLPERN
96 Director Bookstore & Purchasing .... Ms. Jan HALLEEN
04 Administrative Asst to President .... Ms. Nancy JOHNSON
28 Director of Diversity and Inclusion .... Dr. Alejandra DASHE
37 Director of Student Financial Svcs .... Ms. Karen SAMSTAD
76 Dean College of Health & Wellness .... Dr. Dale HEALEY
88 Dean College of Chiropractic .... Dr. Trevor FOSHANG
06 Registrar .... Ms. Susan NEPPL
108 Director Assessment & Inst Effectiv .... Mr. Yung-Chi SUNG

Oak Hills Christian College (G)

1600 Oak Hills Road SW, Bemidji MN 56601-8826
County: Beltrami FICE Identification: 009992
Unit ID: 174525
Telephone: (218) 751-8670 Carnegie Class: Spec-4-yr-Faith
FAX Number: (218) 751-8825 Calendar System: Semester
URL: www.oakhills.edu
Established: 1946 Annual Undergrad Tuition & Fees: $16,980
Enrollment: 119 Coed
Affiliation or Control: Interdenominational IRS Status: 501(c)3
Highest Offering: Baccalaureate
Accreditation: BI

01 President .... Dr. Martin GIESE
05 Interim Dean of Educ .... Dr. Susan GLIDDEN
111 Vice President for Advancement .... Mrs. Joan L. BERNTSON
84 VP Enrollment Management .... Mr. Mike RASCH
32 Dean of Student Life .... Mr. Brad DEJAGER
06 Registrar .... Mrs. Tammy MCCRAY
08 Library Director .... Mr. Keith BUSH
37 Director of Financial Aid .... Mr. Matt MYRICK
04 Administrative Asst to President .... Ms. Stacy NORVOLD
09 Director of Institutional Research .... Dr. Susan GLIDDEN
10 Chief Business Officer .... Mr. Bruce KAEHNE
41 Athletic Director .... Mr. Jeremy ANDERSON

Presentation College Fairmont (H)

115 S Park Street, Suite 117, Fairmont MN 56031
Telephone: (507) 235-4658 Identification: 770418
Accreditation: &NH

† Branch campus of Presentation College, Aberdeen, SD

*Rasmussen College Corporate Office (I)

8300 Norman Center Drive, Suite 300,
Bloomington MN 55437
County: Washington Identification: 667034
Unit ID: 17501405
Telephone: (952) 806-3910 Carnegie Class: N/A
FAX Number: (952) 831-0624
URL: www.rasmussen.edu

01 President .... Dr. Trenda BOYUM-BREEN

*Rasmussen College - St. Cloud (J)

226 Park Avenue South, Saint Cloud MN 56301-3713
County: Stearns FICE Identification: 008694
Unit ID: 175014
Telephone: (320) 251-5600 Carnegie Class: Bac/Assoc-Mixed
FAX Number: (320) 251-3702 Calendar System: Quarter
URL: www.Rasmussen.edu
Established: 1902 Annual Undergrad Tuition & Fees: $9,360
Enrollment: 5,385 Coed
Affiliation or Control: Proprietary IRS Status: Proprietary
Highest Offering: Master's
Accreditation: NH, CAHIIM, MAAB, MLTAD, NURSE, SURGT

02 Campus Director .... Ms. Mary SWINGLE

† Regional accreditation carried under the parent institution in Lake Elmo, MN.

**Rasmussen College - Blaine* (K)

3629 95th Avenue Northeast, Blaine MN 55014
Telephone: (763) 795-4720 Identification: 667061
Accreditation: &NH, MAAB

† Regional accreditation is carried under the parent institution in Saint Cloud, MN. The tuition figure is an average, actual tuition may vary.

**Rasmussen College - Bloomington* (L)

4400 W 78th St, 6th Floor, Bloomington MN 55435
Telephone: (952) 545-2000 FICE Identification: 011686
Accreditation: &NH, CAHIIM, MAAB

† Regional accreditation carried under the parent institution in Saint Cloud, MN. The tuition figure is an average, actual tuition may vary.

**Rasmussen College - Brooklyn Park* (M)

8301 93rd Avenue North, Brooklyn Park MN 55445-1512
Telephone: (763) 493-4500 Identification: 666769
Accreditation: &NH, CAHIIM, MAAB, @PTAA, SURGT

† Regional accreditation carried under the parent institution in Saint Cloud, MN. The tuition figure is an average, actual tuition may vary.

**Rasmussen College - Eagan* (N)

3500 Federal Drive, Eagan MN 55122-1346
Telephone: (651) 687-9000 FICE Identification: 004648
Accreditation: &NH, CAHIIM, MAAB

† Regional accreditation carried under the parent institution in Saint Cloud, MN. The tuition figure is an average, actual tuition may vary.

**Rasmussen College - Lake Elmo/Woodbury* (O)

8565 Eagle Point Circle, Lake Elmo MN 55042
Telephone: (651) 259-6600 Identification: 770486
Accreditation: &NH, CAHIIM, MAAB, MLTAD

† Regional accreditation carried under the parent institution in Saint Cloud, MN. The tuition figure is an average, actual tuition may vary.

**Rasmussen College - Mankato* (P)

130 Saint Andrews Drive, Mankato MN 56001
Telephone: (507) 625-6556 FICE Identification: 025033
Accreditation: &NH, CAHIIM, MAAB

† Regional accreditation carried under the parent institution in Saint Cloud, MN.

**Rasmussen College - Moorhead Park* (Q)

1250 29th Avenue South, Moorhead MN 56560
Telephone: (218) 304-6200 Identification: 770487
Accreditation: &NH, ADNUR, MLTAD, PNUR, SURGT

† Regional accreditation carried under the parent institution in Saint Cloud, MN. The tuition figure is an average, actual tuition may vary.

Red Lake Nation College (R)

15480 Migizi Dr PO Box 576, Red Lake MN 56671
County: Beltrami Identification: 667311
Telephone: (218) 679-2860 Carnegie Class: Not Classified
FAX Number: (218) 679-3870 Calendar System: Semester
URL: www.rlnc.edu
Established: 2014 Annual Undergrad Tuition & Fees: N/A
Enrollment: N/A Coed
Affiliation or Control: Tribal Control IRS Status: 501(c)3
Highest Offering: Associate Degree
Accreditation: @NH

01 President .... Dan RING
05 Vice Pres Opers & Academic Affs .... Mandy SCHRAM
32 Vice Pres Student Success .... Nokomis PAIZ
10 CFO .... Tami NISWANDER

St. Catherine University (S)

601 25th Avenue S, Minneapolis MN 55454
Telephone: (651) 690-6000 Identification: 770315
Accreditation: &NH

St. Catherine University (T)

2004 Randolph Avenue, Saint Paul MN 55105-1789
County: Ramsey FICE Identification: 002342
Unit ID: 175005
Telephone: (651) 690-6000 Carnegie Class: Masters/L
FAX Number: (651) 690-6024 Calendar System: 4/1/4
URL: www.stkate.edu
Established: 1905 Annual Undergrad Tuition & Fees: $36,820
Enrollment: 4,961 Female
Affiliation or Control: Roman Catholic IRS Status: 501(c)3
Highest Offering: Doctorate
Accreditation: NH, ADNUR, ARCPA, CAHIIM, COARC, DIETD, DMS, EXSC, LIB, NUR, OT, OTA, PHLEB, PTA, PTAA, RAD, SW

01 President .... Ms. ReBecca K. ROLOFF
05 Interim Provost .... Dr. Alan SILVA
10 EVP and CFO .... Ms. Angela RILEY
111 EVP and Chief Advancement Officer .... Ms. Elizabeth HALLORAN
04 Exec Assistant to the President .... Ms. Bryonie MOON
49 Int Dean Sch Humanities/Arts/Sci .... Dr. Lynda SZYMANSKI
76 Assoc Prov/Dean Sch Hlth/Grad Col .... Dr. Penelope MOYERS
50 Assoc Prov/Dn Sch Bus/Prof Stds/CFW .... Dr. Joann BANGS
51 Assoc Provost Col for Adults .... Dr. Anne WEYANDT
32 Assoc Provost Student Affairs .... Mr. Curt GALLOWAY
83 Interim Dean School of Social Work .... Dr. Corrine CARVALHO
08 Library Director .... Ms. Emily ASCH
84 SVP Enrollment Management/Athletics .... Mr. Daniel THOMPSON
30 Director of Development .... Ms. Elizabeth RIEDEL CARNEY
21 VP for Finance & Controller .... Ms. Tracey GRAN
13 VP and CIO .... Ms. Jean GUEZMIR
15 SVP for HR/Equity & Inclusion .... Ms. Patricia PRATT-COOK
06 Registrar .... Ms. Cynthia EGENESS
29 Director of Alumnae Relations .... Ms. Karen JOTHEN
26 Dir of Marketing & Communications .... Ms. Kristin CUMMINGS
07 Associate Dean of Admissions .... Ms. Cory PIPER-HAUSWIRTH
37 Associate Dean Enrollment/Fin Aid .... Ms. Elizabeth STEVENS
88 Assoc Dean Admiss/Market Devel .... Mr. Greg STEENSON
36 Director of Career Development .... Ms. Tina WAGNER
35 Associate Dean of Students .... Ms. Ellen RICHTER-NORGEL
16 Director of Human Resources .... Ms. Sarah SCHNELL
38 Director of Student Counseling .... Ms. Heide MALAT
92 Director of Honors Program .... Dr. Rafael CERVANTES

94 Director of Women's Studies .... Dr. Sharon DOHERTY
96 Director of Purchasing .... Mr. Michael HARA
09 Dir Inst Rsrch/Plng/Assessment . Dr. Jennifer ROBINSON KLOOS
18 VP Public Safety & Facilities ....Mr. Mark JOHNSON
28 Dir Multicultural/Intl Pgms & Svcs .... Ms. Donna HAUER

Saint John's University (A)

2850 Abbey Plaza, Box 2000, Collegeville MN 56321-2000

County: Stearns FICE Identification: 002379
Unit ID: 174792
Telephone: (320) 363-2011 Carnegie Class: Bac-A&S
FAX Number: (320) 363-2504 Calendar System: Semester
URL: www.csbsju.edu
Established: 1857 Annual Undergrad Tuition & Fees: $41,732
Enrollment: 1,869 Coordinate
Affiliation or Control: Roman Catholic IRS Status: 501(c)3
Highest Offering: Master's
Accreditation: NH, CAEPN, DIETD, MUS, NURSE, THEOL

01 President .... Dr. Michael HEMESATH
05 Provost Academic Affairs .... Dr. Richard ICE
20 Academic Dean .... Dr. Barbara MAY
111 Vice President for Inst Advancement .... Mr. Rob CULLIGAN
32 Vice President Student Development ... Fr. Douglas MULLIN, OSB
10 Vice Pres Finance/Admin Services .... Mr. Richard ADAMSON
46 VP Inst Plng/Research/Communication .... Mr. Jon MCGEE
07 Vice Pres Admissions/Financial Aid .... Dr. Cal MOSLEY
73 Dean School Theology .... Fr. Dale LAUNDERVILLE, OSB
35 Dean of Students .... Mr. Michael CONNOLLY
26 Exec Director of Public Relations .... Mr. Michael HEMMESCH
08 Director of Library .... Ms. Kathleen PARKER
06 Registrar .... Ms. Julie GRUSKA
36 Director of Career Services .... Ms. Heidi HARLANDER
37 Exec Director of Financial Aid .... Mr. Stuart PERRY
13 Director of Info Technology Svcs .... Ms. Casey GORDON
29 Director of Alumni Relations .... Mr. Adam HERBST
15 Director Human Resources .... Ms. Carol ABELL
09 Assoc Director Inst Research .... Ms. Karen G. KNUTSON

Saint Mary's University of Minnesota (B)

700 Terrace Heights, Winona MN 55987-1399

County: Winona FICE Identification: 002380
Unit ID: 174817
Telephone: (507) 452-4430 Carnegie Class: Masters/L
FAX Number: (507) 457-1633 Calendar System: Semester
URL: www.smumn.edu
Established: 1912 Annual Undergrad Tuition & Fees: $32,575
Enrollment: 5,931 Coed
Affiliation or Control: Roman Catholic IRS Status: 501(c)3
Highest Offering: Doctorate
Accreditation: NH, ANEST, COPSY, IACBE, MFCD, MUS, NMT, NURSE

01 President .... Bro. William MANN, FSC
18 Vice President of Facilities .... Mr. James BEDTKE
11 Exec VP & Chief Operating Officer .... Dr. John PYLE
30 Vice Pres for Devel & Alumni Rels .... Ms. Audrey KINTZI
32 Assoc Vice President of Campus Svcs .... Mr. Chris KENDALL
10 Vice President Financial Affairs .... Mr. Ben MURRAY
43 Exec Vice Pres/General Counsel .... Ms. Ann E. MERCHLEWITZ
05 Chief Academic Office & VP for SGPP .... Bro. Robert SMITH
26 Assistant VP of Brand Management .... Ms. Stacia VOGEL
20 Academic Dean/Assoc Vice President .... Ms. Sarah FERGUSON
42 Vice President for Mission .... Mr. Tim GOSSEN
04 Exec Assistant to the President .... Ms. Peggy WALTERS
06 Registrar .... Mr. Christopher VERCH
07 Director of Admissions .... Ms. Suzanne DERANEK
37 Director of Financial Aid .... Ms. Paul TERRIO
88 Director of Conferencing & Camps .... Ms. Kathy PEDERSON
36 Dir Career Services & Internships .... Mr. Michael HAGARTY
38 Director of Counseling Center .... Dr. Ruth MATHEWS
08 Director of Library .... Ms. Laura OANES
19 Director of Campus Security .... Mr. Jason MORK
18 Director of Physical Plant .... Mr. John SCHOLLMEIER
23 Director of Health Services .... Ms. Angela WEISBROD
29 Director Alumni Relations .... Mr. Robert FISHER
41 Director of Athletics .... Ms. Nicole FENNERN
15 Director of Human Resources .... Mr. Dave MILLIOTIS
09 Institutional Researcher .... Ms. Kara WENER
53 Dean School Education .... Dr. Rebecca HOPKINS
79 Dean School of the Arts .... Mr. Michael CHARRON
108 Director Institutional Assessment .... Mr. Robin HEMMINWAY
50 Dean School of Business .... Dr. Thomas MARPE
91 Director Administrative Computing .... Ms. Tianna JOHNSON
39 Director Student Housing .... Mr. Nathan WAGAR
44 Director Annual Giving .... Ms. Andrea PENGRA

St. Olaf College (C)

1520 St. Olaf Avenue, Northfield MN 55057-1098

County: Rice FICE Identification: 002382
Unit ID: 174844
Telephone: (507) 786-2222 Carnegie Class: Bac-A&S
FAX Number: N/A Calendar System: 4/1/4
URL: wp.stolaf.edu
Established: 1874 Annual Undergrad Tuition & Fees: $44,180
Enrollment: 3,046 Coed
Affiliation or Control: Evangelical Lutheran Church In America
IRS Status: 501(c)3
Highest Offering: Baccalaureate
Accreditation: NH, ART, DANCE, MUS, NURSE, SW, THEA

01 President .... Dr. David R. ANDERSON
05 Provost & Dean of the College .... Dr. Marci J. SORTOR
10 Vice Pres & Chief Financial Officer .... Ms. Janet K. HANSON
111 Vice Pres for Advancement .... Mr. Enoch BLAZIS
32 Vice Pres of Student Life .... Mr. Greg KNESER
84 Vice Pres Enrollment/Col Relations .... Mr. Michael KYLE
88 Vice Pres for Mission .... Dr. Jo M. BELD
15 Vice Pres for Human Resources .... Mr. Michael GOODSON
43 General Counsel .... Mr. Carl CROSBY LEHMANN
18 Asst Vice President for Facilities .... Vacant
28 Asst to the Pres for Inst Diversity .... Mr. Bruce KING
20 Associate Provost .... Dr. Dan DRESSEN
06 Asst VP/Registrar .... Dr. Steve MCKELVEY
89 Assoc Dean Interdisciplin/Gen Stds .... Dr. Dana GROSS
81 Assoc Dean Natural Sciences & Math .... Dr. Mary WALCZAK
79 Assoc Dean Humanities .... Dr. Corliss SWAIN
57 Assoc Dean Fine Arts .... Mr. Kent MCWILLIAMS
83 Assoc Dean Social Sciences .... Dr. Rebecca JUDGE
115 Asst VP/Chief Investment Officer .... Mr. Mark GELLE
114 Asst VP/Budget & Auxiliary Ops .... Ms. Angela MATHEWS
07 Dean of Admissions & Financial Aid .... Mr. Chris GEORGE
35 Dean of Students .... Dr. Rosalyn EATON
35 Assoc Dean of Students .... Mr. Justin FLEMING
35 Assoc Dean of Students .... Mr. Timothy SCHROER
42 Campus Pastor .... Dr. Matthew MAROHL
13 Director of IT and Libraries .... Ms. Roberta LEMBKE
19 Director of Public Safety .... Mr. Fred C. BEHR
41 Director of Athletics .... Mr. Ryan A. BOWLES
29 Dir of Engage/Alum/Parent Relations .... Mr. Brad HOFF
44 Director of Annual Giving .... Ms. Steph MCCLUSKEY
38 Director of Counseling .... Dr. Stephen O'NEILL
26 Chief Marketing Officer .... Ms. Katie WARREN
75 Dir Piper Ctr for Vocation & Career .... Ms. Leslie MOORE
36 Sr Assoc Dir Career Educ & Coaching .... Ms. Kirsten CAHOON
108 Assoc Dir of Eval & Assessment .... Ms. Kelsey THOMPSON
09 Director of Institutional Research .... Ms. Susan CANON
39 Director of Residence Life .... Ms. Pamela MCDOWELL
40 Bookstore Director .... Ms. Victoria BEUSSMAN
37 Director of Student Financial Aid .... Ms. Carly EICHHORST
102 Dir of Govt/Fndtn & Corp Relations .... Ms. Helen WARREN
104 Dir of Intl & Off Campus Studies .... Dr. Jodi MALMGREN
85 International Student Coordinator .... Vacant
04 Exec Assistant to the President .... Ms. Jennifer WHITSON

United Theological Seminary of the Twin Cities (D)

3000 5th Street, NW, New Brighton MN 55112-2598

County: Ramsey FICE Identification: 002386
Unit ID: 175139
Telephone: (651) 633-4311 Carnegie Class: Spec-4-yr-Faith
FAX Number: (651) 633-4315 Calendar System: Trimester
URL: www.unitedseminary.edu
Established: 1962 Annual Graduate Tuition & Fees: N/A
Enrollment: 110 Coed
Affiliation or Control: United Church Of Christ IRS Status: 501(c)3
Highest Offering: Doctorate; No Undergraduates
Accreditation: NH, THEOL

01 President .... Dr. Lewis P. ZEIDNER
05 VP for Academic Affairs/Dean .... Dr. Sharon M. TAN
10 VP for Finance and Administration .... Mr. Peter LEE
111 VP for Advancement .... Mr. Bradley O. REINERS
20 Associate Dean .... Dr. Paul CAPETZ
32 Asst Dean Students/Dir BCL Pgm .... Ms. Margaree LEVY
30 Director of Development .... Ms. Amy FISTLER
07 Director of Admissions .... Mr. Phil ROMINE
06 Registrar/Title IX Coordinator .... Mr. Christian ERIKSEN
08 Director of the Library .... Mr. Dale DOBIAS
108 Director of Assessment & Fin Aid .... Vacant
42 Chaplain .... Rev. John LEE
18 Director Physical Plant & Housing .... Mr. Brandon KROSCH
73 Dir Center for Arts/Faith/Culture .... Dr. Cindi Beth JOHNSON
29 Dir Alumni Relations and Dev Events ...... Ms. Kiely TODD ROSKA
15 Dir Human Resources & Operations .... Ms. Vonda PEARSON
26 Director of Community Engagement .... Ms. Katie LANGSTON
04 Admin Assistant to the President .... Ms. Gina LOTZER
20 Dir Academic Ops & Distance Educ ...... Mr. Matt STOLLENWERK
88 Dir Formation & Contextual Educ .... Ms. Sara WILHELM GARBERS
88 Dir Spir & Voc Devel/Field Educ .... Mr. Greg MELAND

University of Minnesota (E)

100 Church Street SE, 202 Morrill, Minneapolis MN 55455

County: Hennepin FICE Identification: 003969
Unit ID: 174066
Telephone: (612) 626-1616 Carnegie Class: DU-Highest
FAX Number: (612) 625-3875 Calendar System: Semester
URL: www.umn.edu
Established: 1851 Annual Undergrad Tuition & Fees (In-State): $14,142
Enrollment: 50,678 Coed
Affiliation or Control: State IRS Status: 501(c)3
Highest Offering: Doctorate
Accreditation: NH, ANEST, AUD, CAEPN, CEA, CIDA, CLPSY, COARC, CONST, COPSY, DANCE, DENT, DH, DIETC, DIETD, DIETI, ENG, ENGR, FUSER, HSA, IPSY, JOUR, LAW, LSAR, MED, MFCD, MIDWF, MT, MUS, NURSE, OT, PCSAS, PH, PHAR, PLNG, PTA, RTT, SCPSY, SP, SPAA, SW, VET

01 President .... Dr. Eric W. KALER
100 Chief of Staff .... Dr. Jon STEADLAND
05 Exec VP Academic Affairs/Provost .... Dr. Karen HANSON
17 Vice President for Health Sciences .... Dr. R. Brooks JACKSON
10 Sr VP Finance & Operations .... Mr. Brian BURNETT
46 Vice President for Research .... Dr. Al LEVINE
58 Vice Prov/Dean Graduate Education .... Dr. Scott LANYON
20 Vice Prov/Dean Undergrad Education .... Dr. Robert MCMASTER
15 Vice President Human Resources .... Ms. Kathryn F. BROWN
88 Vice Pres for University Services .... Mr. Michael BERTHELSEN
28 Interim VP/Equity and Diversity .... Dr. Michael GOH
13 VP/Chief Info Officer .... Mr. Bernard GULACHEK
43 General Counsel .... Mr. Doug PETERSON
102 President Univ Minnesota Foundation .... Ms. Katherine SCHMIDLKOFER
25 Assoc VP Sponsored Projects Admin .... Ms. Frances LAWRENZ
26 Vice Pres for University Relations .... Mr. Matt KRAMER
18 Int Assoc VP/Chief of Facilities .... Mr. Brian PAULUS
32 Int Vice Provost Student Affairs .... Ms. Maggie TOWLE
19 Asst VP Pub Safety/Chief of Police .... Mr. Matthew CLARK
08 University Librarian .... Dr. Wendy P. LOUGEE
06 Registrar .... Ms. Sue N. VAN VOORHIS
07 Director of Admissions .... Ms. Rachelle HERNANDEZ
09 Director of Institutional Research .... Dr. John KELLOGG
22 Director Equal Oppty/Affirm Action .... Ms. Tina MARISAM
37 Director of Student Finance .... Ms. Tina FALKNER
40 Director of the U of M Bookstores .... Mr. Ross ROSATI
39 Dir of Housing & Residential Life .... Ms. Laurie L. MCLAUGHLIN
48 Interim Dean College of Design .... Dr. Becky YUST
86 Director of Federal Relations .... Ms. Channing RIGGS
29 CEO Alumni Association .... Ms. Lisa LEWIS
38 Dir of Counseling & Consulting Srvc .... Dr. Glenn HIRSCH
87 Director of the Summer Session .... Ms. Michelle KOKER
114 Associate VP for Budget/Finance .... Ms. Julie A. TONNESON
96 Director of Purchasing .... Mr. Tim BRAY
49 Dean of the College of Liberal Arts .... Mr. John COLEMAN
51 Dean College of Continuing Educ .... Dr. Mary L. NICHOLS
61 Dean of the Law School .... Mr. Garry JENKINS
74 Dean College of Veterinary Medicine .... Dr. Trevor R. AMES
63 Dean of the Medical School .... Dr. Brooks JACKSON
66 Dean of the School of Nursing .... Dr. Connie J. DELANEY
53 Dean College Education/Human Devel .... Dr. Jean K. QUAM
52 Dean of the School of Dentistry .... Dr. Leon ASSAEL
69 Dean of the School Public Health .... Dr. John FINNEGAN
54 Dean College of Science/Engineering .... Dr. Samuel MUKASA
67 Dean of the College Pharmacy .... Dr. Marilyn K. SPEEDIE
50 Dean Carlson School of Management .... Dr. Srilata A. ZAHEER
80 Dean Humphrey Sch of Pub Aff .... Dr. Laura BLOOMBERG
81 Dean College of Biological Science .... Dr. Valery E. FORBES
47 Dean Col Food/Agric/Natural Res Sci .... Mr. Brian BUHR
41 Director Intercollegiate Athletics .... Mr. Mark COYLE
27 Deputy CoS Public Relations/URel .... Mr. Chuck TOMBARGE
27 Deputy CoS Marketing/URel .... Ms. Ann ARONSON

University of Minnesota Duluth (F)

1049 University Drive, Duluth MN 55812-3011

County: Saint Louis FICE Identification: 002388
Unit ID: 174233
Telephone: (218) 726-8000 Carnegie Class: Masters/L
FAX Number: (218) 726-6254 Calendar System: Semester
URL: www.d.umn.edu
Established: 1947 Annual Undergrad Tuition & Fees (In-State): $13,139
Enrollment: 10,878 Coed
Affiliation or Control: State IRS Status: 501(c)3
Highest Offering: Doctorate
Accreditation: NH, ART, CS, ENG, MUS, SP, SW

01 Chancellor .... Dr. Lendley C. BLACK
05 Exec Vice Chanc Acad Affairs .... Dr. Fernando DELGADO
32 Vice Chanc Stdnt Life/Dean Stdnts .... Dr. Lisa ERWIN
10 Vice Chanc Finance/Operations .... Mr. Stephen W. KETO
06 Registrar .... Ms. Carla L. BOYD
08 Director of Library .... Mr. Matt ROSENDAHL
37 Director Financial Aid .... Ms. Brenda H. HERZIG
36 Director Career Services .... Ms. Julie A. WESTLUND
13 Director Info Tech Sys/Services .... Dr. Jason DAVIS
09 Director Institutional Research .... Ms. Mary KEENAN
25 Senior Grant Administrator .... Ms. Elizabeth RUMSEY
51 Director Continuing Education .... Ms. Roxanne RICHARDS
41 Athletic Director .... Mr. Josh BERLO
15 Dir Human Resources/Equal Opp .... Ms. Karna KURTZ
07 Director Admissions .... Mr. Scott SCHULZ
18 Dir Facilities/Physical Plant .... Mr. John RASHID
29 Director Alumni Relations .... Mr. Matthew DUFFY
30 Director Development .... Ms. Tricia BUNTEN
114 Director of Budget and Analysis .... Mr. Greg SATHER
86 Dir University Marketing Public Rel .... Ms. Lynne WILLIAMS
63 Associate Dean School of Med .... Dr. Paula TERMUHLEN
81 Dean College Science/Engineering .... Dr. Joshua HAMILTON
49 Dean College Liberal Arts .... Dr. Susan MAHER
53 Dean Col Education/Human Svc Prof .... Dr. Jill PINKNEY-PASTRANA
50 Dean School of Business & Economics ...... Dr. Amy HIETAPELTO
57 Dean School Fine Arts .... Mr. William PAYNE
58 Director of Grad Programs .... Dr. Erik BROWN
19 Chief of Police .... Mr. Sean HULS

University of Minnesota-Crookston (G)

2900 University Avenue, Crookston MN 56716-5001

County: Polk FICE Identification: 004069
Unit ID: 174075
Telephone: (218) 281-6510 Carnegie Class: Bac-Diverse

FAX Number: (218) 281-8040 Calendar System: Semester
URL: www.crk.umn.edu
Established: 1965 Annual Undergrad Tuition & Fees (In-State): $11,700
Enrollment: 2,823 Coed
Affiliation or Control: State IRS Status: 501(c)3
Highest Offering: Baccalaureate
Accreditation: NH

01 Chancellor ... Dr. Mary HOLZ-CLAUSE
05 VC for Academic Affairs ... Dr. Barbara KEINATH
32 Assoc VC Student Affs/Enrollment ... Dr. Peter PHAIAH
18 Director Facilities/Operations ... Mr. Dave DANFORTH
10 Dir of Finance/University Services ... Ms. Tricia SANDERS
15 Director Human Resources ... Mr. Les JOHNSON
37 Director Financial Aid ... Ms. Melissa DINGMANN
26 Director of Communications ... Mr. Andrew SVEC
30 Dir Development/Alumni Relations ... Ms. Brandy CHAFFEE
08 Director Library ... Mr. Owen WILLIAMS
36 Director Career/Counseling ... Mr. Tim MENARD
49 Head of Arts/Humanities/Soc Sci ... Dr. Soo-Yin LIM-THOMPSON
47 Head Agriculture & Nat Resources ... Dr. Harouna MAIGA
81 Head Math/Science/Technology ... Dr. Tony KERN
50 Head Business ... Dr. Kevin THOMPSON
51 Director Center for Adult Learning ... Ms. Michelle CHRISTOPHERSON
06 Registrar ... Dr. Ken MYERS
07 Director of Admissions ... Ms. Carola THORSON
28 Director of Diversity ... Ms. Lorna HOLLOWELL
85 Dir of International Programs ... Dr. Kimberly GILLETTE

University of Minnesota-Morris (A)

600 E 4th Street, Morris MN 56267-2132
County: Stevens FICE Identification: 002389
Unit ID: 174251
Telephone: (320) 589-6035 Carnegie Class: Bac-A&S
FAX Number: (320) 589-6399 Calendar System: Semester
URL: www.morris.umn.edu
Established: 1959 Annual Undergrad Tuition & Fees (In-State): $12,846
Enrollment: 1,856 Coed
Affiliation or Control: State IRS Status: 501(c)3
Highest Offering: Baccalaureate
Accreditation: NH, CAEPN

01 Chancellor ... Dr. Michelle BEHR
05 Vice Chanc Academic Affs/Dean ... Dr. Bart FINZEL
32 Vice Chanc for Student Affairs ... Ms. Sandra OLSON-LOY
10 Vice Chanc for Finance & Facilities ... Mr. Bryan HERRMANN
21 Director for Finance ... Ms. Colleen MILLER
08 Head Librarian ... Ms. LeAnn DEAN
06 Registrar's Office ... Ms. Judy KORN
26 Director of Communications ... Ms. Melissa VANGSNESS
29 Director of Alumni Relations ... Ms. Carla RILEY
09 Director of Institutional Research ... Ms. Nancy HELSPER
36 Director Career Center ... Mr. Gary L. DONOVAN
13 Director Information Technology ... Mr. Matt SENGER
37 Director of Financial Aid ... Ms. Jill BEAUREGARD
93 Dir Multi Ethnic Student Program ... Ms. Hilda LADNER
24 Director Educational Media ... Mr. Michael CIHAK
07 Director of Admissions ... Ms. Jennifer ZYCH HERRMANN
108 Director of Institutional Effective ... Ms. Melissa BERT
53 Chair of Education Division ... Dr. Gwen RUDNEY
81 Chair of Science/Math Division ... Dr. Peh NG
79 Chair of Humanities Division ... Dr. Pieranno GARAVASO
83 Chair of Social Science Division ... Dr. Arne KILDEGAARD

University of Minnesota Rochester (B)

111 South Broadway, Suite 300, Rochester MN 55904
Telephone: (800) 947-0117 Identification: 770316
Accreditation: &NH, OT

University of Northwestern - St. Paul (C)

3003 Snelling Avenue N, Saint Paul MN 55113-1598
County: Ramsey FICE Identification: 002371
Unit ID: 174491
Telephone: (651) 631-5100 Carnegie Class: Masters/S
FAX Number: (651) 628-3339 Calendar System: Semester
URL: www.unwsp.edu
Established: 1902 Annual Undergrad Tuition & Fees: $29,460
Enrollment: 3,493 Coed
Affiliation or Control: Independent Non-Profit IRS Status: 501(c)3
Highest Offering: Master's
Accreditation: NH, MUS, NURSE

01 President ... Dr. Alan S. CURETON
05 Senior Vice Pres Academic Affairs ... Dr. Janet B. SOMMERS
26 Senior Vice President Media ... Mr. Jason R. SHARP
32 Vice Pres Student Life & Athletics ... Dr. Mathew B. HILL
111 Vice President Advancement ... Mr. Jim K. JOHNSON
10 Vice President Finance/CFO ... Mr. Douglas R. SCHROEDER
15 Assoc Vice President of HR ... Mr. Timothy A. RICH
18 Assoc VP Facility Ops & Planning ... Mr. Brian L. HUMPHRIES
79 Dean College of Arts & Humanities .. Dr. Jeremy W. KOLWINSKA
83 Dean College Behave & Nat Sciences ... Dr. Daniel R. CRANE
107 Dean College Professional Studies ... Dr. Susan E. JOHNSON
58 Dean Graduate/Online & Adult ... Dr. Tanya L. GROSZ
20 Sr Dean Academic Administration ... Dr. Fengling M. JOHNSON
35 Dean of Student Life ... Mr. Paul A. BRADLEY
13 CIO ... Mr. Chad N. MILLER
21 Controller ... Mr. Bryon D. KRUEGER
09 Institutional Researcher Rprt Spec ... Mr. Russell E. ERICKSON
38 Director of Counseling/Student Svcs . Ms. Dannette C. WILFAHRT
88 Director of Disability Services ... Mr. David P. GOLIAS
37 Director of Financial Aid ... Ms. Hannah K. BLAHNIK
23 Director of Health Services ... Mrs. Cynthia P. REEDSTROM
08 Director of Library Services ... Mrs. Ruth A. MCGUIRE
19 Director of Public Safety ... Mr. Peter L. SOLA
96 Manager of Purchasing ... Ms. Cheryl A. GLASS
40 Manager Campus Store ... Mrs. Julienne N. ENTINGER
101 Exec Secy to Pres & Bd of Trustees ... Mrs. Kathy M. SPARKS
04 Executive Admin Asst to President ... Mrs. Rachel A. MORGAN
102 Asst VP Advance/VP of NW Foundation ... Mr. Kirby R. STOLL
103 Director of Career Development ... Mrs. April C. STENSGARD
26 Director Marketing ... Mrs. Sara A. RING
108 Director of Assessment ... Mrs. Cheryl R. NORMAN
06 Registrar ... Mr. Andy L. SIMPSON
84 Vice President Enrollment Mgt ... Mr. Michael R. MORONEY
110 Sr Dir Advancement Relations ... Mr. Rich A. BRANHAM
29 Dir Alumni & Public Relations ... Mr. Scott D. ANDERSON
07 Dir Trad Enrollment Mgmt ... Mr. Erick P. KLEIN

† Formerly Northwestern College

University of Saint Thomas (D)

2115 Summit Avenue, Saint Paul MN 55105-1096
County: Ramsey FICE Identification: 002345
Unit ID: 174914
Telephone: (651) 962-5000 Carnegie Class: DU-Mod
FAX Number: (651) 962-6360 Calendar System: 4/1/4
URL: www.stthomas.edu
Established: 1885 Annual Undergrad Tuition & Fees: $39,594
Enrollment: 10,148 Coed
Affiliation or Control: Roman Catholic IRS Status: 501(c)3
Highest Offering: Doctorate
Accreditation: NH, CAEPN, COPSY, ENG, HSA, IPSY, LAW, MUS, SW, THEOL

01 President ... Dr. Julie H. SULLIVAN
05 EVP & Provost ... Dr. Richard G. PLUMB
88 Rector/VP School of Divinity ... Msgr. Aloysius R. CALLAGHAN
32 VP For Student Affairs ... Dr. Karen M. LANGE
10 VP For Business Affairs/CFO ... Mr. Mark D. VANGSGARD
86 VP Gov Relations/Special Projects ... Mr. Doug E. HENNES
13 VP Info Resources & Technology/CIO ... Dr. Edmund U. CLARK
20 Vice Provost For Academic Affairs ... Dr. Robert J. RILEY
84 VP Enrollment Management ... Mr. Allan L. COTRONE
21 Int AVP/Finance & Controller ... Ms. Terra K. PENNY
18 AVP For Facilities ... Mr. James M. BRUMMER
109 Int Exec Dir of Auxiliary Services ... Dr. Pamela L. PETERSON
49 Dean College Arts & Sciences ... Dr. Yohuru R. WILLIAMS
50 Dean Opus College of Business ... Dr. Stefanie A. LENWAY
53 Dean College of Education/Leadersh ... Dr. Joseph L. KREITZER
70 Int Dean School of Social Work ... Dr. Corrine I. CARVALHO
73 Academic Dean School of Divinity ... Dr. Kenneth D. SNYDER
61 Dean School of Law ... Mr. Robert K. VISCHER
35 Dean of Students ... Ms. Linda M. BAUGHMAN
88 Chair Grad School Prof Psychology ... Dr. Christopher S. VYE
58 Dir Graduate Programs/Business Comm .. Dr. Michael C. PORTER
88 Assoc Dean Opus College of Business ... Dr. Michael J. GARRISON
54 Dean School of Engineering ... Dr. Donald H. WEINKFAUF
30 VP Development & Alumni Relations ... Mr. Erik J. THURMAN
06 Director Student Data & Registrar ... Ms. Karen M. JULIAN
07 Exec Dir/Admissions & Financial Aid ... Ms. Kristin A. ROACH
09 Director of Institutional Research ... Ms. Kristine M. BAKER
35 Director Campus Life ... Ms. Margaret D. CAHILL
36 Director Career Development Center ... Ms. Linda M. SLOAN
26 Chief Marketing Officer ... Ms. Kymm MARTINEZ
41 Director Athletics ... Mr. Stephen J. FRITZ
40 Director Bookstore ... Mr. Stephen L. GRIFFIN
42 Director Campus Ministry ... Fr. Lawrence BLAKE
19 Director Safety/Security ... Mr. Daniel J. MEUWISSEN
38 Director Student Counseling ... Dr. Peter A. ZELLES
96 AVP Procurement Services ... Ms. Karen M. HARTHORN
28 AVP of Diversity & Inclusion ... Dr. Artika R. TYNER
88 Dean Dougherty Family College ... Mr. Alvin V. ABRAHAM
88 VP For Mission ... Fr. Larry J. SNYDER
15 AVP For Human Resources ... Ms. Michelle THOM
43 General Counsel ... Ms. Sara E. GROSS METHNER
125 President Emeritus ... Fr. Dennis J. DEASE
39 Director Residence Life ... Dr. Aaron M. MACKE

Walden University (E)

100 Washington Ave S, Suite 900, Minneapolis MN 55401
County: Hennepin FICE Identification: 025042
Unit ID: 125231
Telephone: (866) 492-5336 Carnegie Class: DU-Mod
FAX Number: (612) 338-5092 Calendar System: Other
URL: www.waldenu.edu
Established: 1970 Annual Undergrad Tuition & Fees: $12,075
Enrollment: 52,799 Coed
Affiliation or Control: Proprietary IRS Status: Proprietary
Highest Offering: Doctorate
Accreditation: NH, ACBSP, CACREP, CAEPN, CS, NURSE, SW

01 President/Chief Executive Officer ... Mr. Jonathan A. KAPLAN
05 Chief Academic Officer ... Dr. Eric RIEDEL
03 Vice President ... Dr. L. Ward ULMER
13 CIO ... Mr. Rob HILLIARD
10 CFO ... Mr. Roger MCKINNEY
46 Exec Dir Inst Research/Assessment ... Mr. Jim LENIO
32 Exec Dir Student Affairs ... Dr. Walter MCCOLLUM
121 Exec Dir Academic Ctr/Stdnt Success ... Ms. Susanna DAVIDSEN
88 Exec Dir Ctr for Faculty Excel ... Vacant
88 Exec Dir Ctr for Research Quality ... Dr. Laura LYNN
50 Dean College of Mgmt & Tech ... Dr. Karlyn BARILOVITS
15 SVP Human Resources ... Ms. Teri PARKER
07 Director of Admissions ... Mr. Peter SCANLAN
113 Bursar ... Ms. Linda ANTHONY
37 Director of Financial Aid ... Ms. Melvina JOHNSON
06 Exec Dir Registrar ... Ms. Devon EDMUND
09 Director of Institutional Research ... Ms. Nicole HOLLAND
108 Director Institutional Assessment ... Dr. Shari JORISSEN
29 Director Alumni Relations ... Ms. Valescia LEE-COLLICK
08 Director of Library Services ... Ms. Michelle HAJDER
88 Director of Program Review ... Dr. Mitchell PETERSON
43 Dir Legal Services/General Counsel ... Ms. Deborah ZIMIC
86 Director Government Relations ... Ms. Jeniffer BLUM

White Earth Tribal and Community College (F)

PO Box 478, Mahnomen MN 56557-0478
County: Mahnomen FICE Identification: 039214
Unit ID: 434751
Telephone: (218) 935-0417 Carnegie Class: Tribal
FAX Number: (218) 936-5814 Calendar System: Semester
URL: www.wetcc.edu
Established: 1997 Annual Undergrad Tuition & Fees: $4,281
Enrollment: 68 Coed
Affiliation or Control: Tribal Control IRS Status: 501(c)3
Highest Offering: Associate Degree
Accreditation: NH

01 Interim President ... Tracy CLARK
04 Executive Assistant ... Patty SCHULTZ
30 Development Director ... Lorna LAGUE
10 Finance Director ... Kami LHOTKA
05 Academic Dean ... Sheila MICHAELS
32 Dean of Student Services ... Melinda RUSTAD
56 Director of Extension ... Steve DAHLBERG
07 Admissions Coordinator ... Amber FOX
06 Registrar ... Sarah CASTLE
37 Financial Aid Coordinator ... Peggie CHISHOLM
15 Human Resources Technician ... Denise ASKELSON
18 Facilities Manager ... Paul PEMBERTON
13 IT Director ... Vacant
19 Security Coordinator ... Kurt HALVORSON
26 Marketing/Communications Specialist ... Joseph ALLEN
08 Head Librarian ... Tammi JALOWIEC

MISSISSIPPI

Alcorn State University (G)

1000 ASU Drive, #359, Lorman MS 39096-7500
County: Claiborne FICE Identification: 002396
Unit ID: 175342
Telephone: (601) 877-6100 Carnegie Class: Masters/M
FAX Number: (601) 877-2975 Calendar System: Semester
URL: www.alcorn.edu
Established: 1871 Annual Undergrad Tuition & Fees (In-State): $6,546
Enrollment: 3,518 Coed
Affiliation or Control: State IRS Status: 501(c)3
Highest Offering: Beyond Master's But Less Than Doctorate
Accreditation: SC, AAFCS, ACBSP, ADNUR, CAEP, #DIETD, MUS, NAIT, NUR, SW

01 President ... Dr. Alfred RANKINS, JR.
05 Provost/Exec VP Academic Affairs ... Dr. Donzell LEE
11 Sr VP for Univ Operations/COO ... Vacant
04 Exec Asst to the President ... Mrs. Karen R. SHEDRICK
116 Director of Internal Audit ... Ms. Tomeka L. MOORE
46 Chief Research Officer ... Dr. Babu P. PATLOLLA
10 VP for Finance & Administrative Svc ... Mrs. Carolyn DUPRE'
32 VP for Student Affairs ... Mr. Emanuel BARNES
10 Associate VP for Fiscal Affairs ... Mr. Bruce WILLIAMS
111 VP Institutional Advancement ... Mr. Marcus D. WARD
26 Interim VP Marketing/Communications ... Mr. Marcus D. WARD
20 Vice Provost Academic Affs/GS ... Dr. John IGWEBUIKE
18 Assoc VP for Facilities Management ... Dr. Jeff POSEY
39 Director of Residence Life ... Ms. Jessica L. FOXWORTH
28 Dir of Educational Equity/Inclusion ... Mrs. Lljuna WEIR
21 Director of Accounting ... Mrs. Cassandra B. LEWIS
96 Purchasing Agent ... Ms. Martha V. GEORGE
07 Director of Admissions/Recruiting ... Mrs. Katangela TENNER
37 Director of Financial Aid ... Mrs. Juanita RUSSELL-EDWARDS
06 Registrar ... Dr. John L. IGWEBUIKE
08 Dean University Libraries ... Dr. Blanche SANDERS
47 Dean School of Agriculture ... Dr. Edmond BUCKNER
49 Dean School of Arts & Science ... Dr. Babu P. PATLOLLA
50 Dean School of Business ... Dr. Donna WILLIAMS
53 Dean School of Education ... Dr. Robert CARR
66 Dean School of Nursing ... Dr. Debra SPRING
88 Dean University College ... Dr. Valerie THOMPSON
13 Int CIO for Ctr for Info Tech Svcs ... Mr. Desmond STEWART
15 Director of Human Resources ... Vacant
36 Director Career Services ... Dr. Joey MITCHELL
23 Director of Health & Disab Services ... Ms. Dorothy G. JACKSON-DAVIS
41 Director of Athletics ... Mr. Derek HORNE
40 Manager Barnes and Noble ... Mr. Domonic RABY

38 Director of Counseling & Testing ....Vacant
09 Director Institutional Res/Assess ....Dr. Ramesh MADDALI
108 Dir Institutional Effectiveness ....Dr. LaToya HART
19 Chief of Campus Police ....Mr. Douglas STEWART
88 General Manager Sodexo ....Mr. Corey D. YOUNG
102 Exec Dir ASU Foundation ....Mr. Marcus D. WARD
31 Dir Ctr Rural Life/Econ Dev ....Mr. Alfred GALTNEY
92 Director of Pre-Prof/Honors Program ....Dr. Thomas C. STURGIS
25 Grants/Contract Administrator ....Ms. Sallie GRIFFIN
88 Sp Asst to Pres Cmty & Econ Dev ....Dr. Ruth R. NICHOLS
88 Executive Director Vicksburg Expan ....Dr. Chris GILMER
104 Director Study Abroad ....Dr. Dovi ALIPOE
88 Asst VP Athletic Compl/Acad Svc ....Mr. Jason CABLE
100 Chief of Staff ....Mr. Tracy COOK

Antonelli College (A)

1500 N 31st Avenue, Hattiesburg MS 39401-3056
Telephone: (601) 583-4100 Identification: 666517
Accreditation: ACCSC

† Branch campus of Antonelli College, OH.

Antonelli College (B)

2323 Lakeland Drive, Jackson MS 39208-9549
Telephone: (601) 362-9991 Identification: 666518
Accreditation: ACCSC

† Branch campus of Antonelli College, OH.

Belhaven University (C)

1500 Peachtree Street, Jackson MS 39202-1798
County: Hinds FICE Identification: 002397
Unit ID: 175421
Telephone: (601) 968-5940 Carnegie Class: Masters/L
FAX Number: (601) 968-9998 Calendar System: Semester
URL: www.belhaven.edu
Established: 1883 Annual Undergrad Tuition & Fees: $23,016
Enrollment: 4,450 Coed
Affiliation or Control: Presbyterian Church (U.S.A.) IRS Status: 501(c)3
Highest Offering: Doctorate
Accreditation: SC, ART, DANCE, IACBE, MUS, NURSE, SW, THEA

01 President ....Dr. Roger PARROTT
05 Exec Vice President & Provost ....Dr. Dan FREDERICKS
111 Vice Pres Institutional Advancement ....Mr. Kevin RUSSELL
88 VP of Adult & Graduate Marketing ....Dr. Audrey KELLEHER
10 Chief Financial Officer ....Mrs. Virginia HENDERSON
32 VP for Student Affairs and Athletic ....Mr. Scott LITTLE
11 Asst Vice Pres Campus Operations ....Mr. David POTVIN
51 Assistant VP for Adult Studies ....Dr. Rick UPCHURCH
20 Assoc Provost ....Dr. Dennis WATTS
12 Academic Dean/Houston Campus ....Dr. Larry RUDDELL
12 Academic Dean/Mississippi ....Dr. Ken ELLIOTT
12 Academic Dean/Memphis Tennessee ....Dr. Paul CRISS
12 Academic Dean/Chattanooga-Atlanta ....Mr. Ron PIRTLE
50 Dean of the School of Business ....Dr. Chip MASON
35 Dean of Student Life ....Mr. Greg HAWKINS
08 Librarian ....Mr. Chris CULLNANE
07 Asst VP Trad & Online Admissions ....Mrs. Suzanne SULLIVAN
06 Registrar ....Mrs. Donna WEEKS
26 Director of Integrated Marketing ....Mr. Bryant BUTLER
88 Director of Student Leadership ....Ms. JoBeth PETTY
13 Director Institutional Technology ....Mr. Bo MILLER
19 Director Security/Safety ....Mr. Steve FARMER
40 Bookstore Manager ....Ms. Sheila LYONS

Blue Mountain College (D)

201 W Main Street, PO Box 160,
Blue Mountain MS 38610-0160
County: Tippah FICE Identification: 002398
Unit ID: 175430
Telephone: (662) 685-4771 Carnegie Class: Bac-Diverse
FAX Number: (662) 685-4776 Calendar System: Semester
URL: www.bmc.edu
Established: 1873 Annual Undergrad Tuition & Fees: $11,212
Enrollment: 483 Coed
Affiliation or Control: Southern Baptist IRS Status: 501(c)3
Highest Offering: Master's
Accreditation: SC

01 President ....Dr. Barbara C. MCMILLIN
04 Admin Assistant to the President ....Mrs. Pam BOWMAN
05 Vice President for Academic Affairs ....Dr. Sharon B. ENZOR
58 Dean Graduate Studies ....Dr. Jenetta WADDELL
09 Director of Institutional Research ....Mr. Robert E. RUCKER
08 Director of Library Services ....Dr. Derek J. CASH
06 Registrar ....Mrs. Sheila D. FREEMAN
88 Director Teaching & Learning Center ....Dr. Delise TEAGUE
32 VP for Student Services ....Mr. Jack T. MOSER
07 Vice Pres for Enrollment Services ....Mr. Lynn GIBSON
37 Director of Financial Aid ....Mrs. Beverly HICKEY
10 Chief Financial Officer ....Mr. Steve ROBBINS
11 Chief Operating Officer ....Mrs. Joyce PETERS
40 Campus Store Manager ....Mrs. Dot M. LOCKE
41 Athletic Director ....Mr. Will KOLLMEYER
42 Director Baptist Student Union ....Mrs. Tracy S. MOSER
13 Director of Information Services ....Mr. Kevin BAREFIELD
26 Dir of PR/Publications ....Ms. Emma L. AINSWORTH
29 Director of Alumni Affairs ....Mrs. Kayce BRAGG
30 Director of Development ....Mr. Jody HILL
88 Director of Church Relations ....Dr. Ronald MEEKS

Coahoma Community College (E)

3240 Friars Point Road, Clarksdale MS 38614-9700
County: Coahoma FICE Identification: 002401
Unit ID: 175519
Telephone: (662) 627-2571 Carnegie Class: Assoc/MT-VT-High Trad
FAX Number: (662) 627-9451 Calendar System: Semester
URL: www.coahomacc.edu
Established: 1949 Annual Undergrad Tuition & Fees (In-District): $2,603
Enrollment: 2,148 Coed
Affiliation or Control: State/Local IRS Status: 501(c)3
Highest Offering: Associate Degree
Accreditation: SC, ADNUR, COARC, EMT, POLYT

01 President ....Dr. Valmadge T. TOWNER
05 Dean of Academics ....Dr. Rolanda BROWN
10 Chief Financial Officer ....Ms. Deborah MCNEAL
32 Dir of Enrollment & Student Svcs ....Mrs. Karen DONE
09 Dir Inst Effectiveness/SACS Liaison ....Mrs. Margaret DIXON
30 Coordinator for Federal Programs ....Mrs. Marilyn STARKS
75 Dean of Career & Technical Educ ....Mrs. Anne SHELTON-CLARK
06 Registrar ....Mrs. Delores RICHARD
08 Dir Library/Instructional Resources ....Mrs. Rose LOCKETT
13 Director Computer Services ....Mr. Bow VIEWING
19 Director of Safety/Transportation ....Vacant
26 Chief Communication Officer ....Mrs. Brittany GREEN-DAVIS
37 Director of Financial Aid ....Mr. Luke HOWARD
15 Director of Employee Services ....Mr. Michael HOUSTON
18 Chief Facilities/Physical Plant ....Mr. Jerone SHAW
51 Director of Educational Outreach ....Ms. Letha RICHARDS
29 Director Alumni Relations ....Mr. Robert GILES
36 Director Student Placement ....Ms. Shanelle FRAZIER
38 Director Student Counseling ....Vacant
96 Director of Purchasing ....Ms. Deborah MCNEAL
04 Administrative Asst to President ....Ms. Yolanda D. MILLER
100 Chief of Staff ....Mr. Jerone SHAW
103 Dir Workforce/Career Development ....Mr. Steven JOSSELL
105 Director Web Services ....Mr. Ezra HOWARD
106 Dir Online Education/E-learning ....Mr. Joseph MCKEE
41 Athletic Director ....Mr. Reggie HANKERSON

Concorde Career College (F)

7900 Airways Boulevard, Suite 103, Southaven MS 38671
Telephone: (662) 429-9909 Identification: 770540
Accreditation: COE

† Branch campus of Concorde Career College, Memphis, TN

Copiah-Lincoln Community College (G)

PO Box 649, Wesson MS 39191-0649
County: Copiah FICE Identification: 002402
Unit ID: 175573
Telephone: (601) 643-5101 Carnegie Class: Assoc/MT-VT-High Trad
FAX Number: (601) 643-8212 Calendar System: Semester
URL: www.colin.edu
Established: 1928 Annual Undergrad Tuition & Fees (In-State): $2,730
Enrollment: 3,098 Coed
Affiliation or Control: State IRS Status: 501(c)3
Highest Offering: Associate Degree
Accreditation: SC, ADNUR, COARC, MLTAD, RAD

01 President ....Dr. Ronald E. NETTLES
04 Assistant to the President ....Mrs. Brenda J. PARRETT
10 Vice President Business Affairs ....Mr. Stan PATRICK
12 Vice Pres of the Wesson Campus ....Dr. Jane HULON
12 VP of the Simpson County Center ....Dr. Dewayne MIDDLETON
12 Vice Pres of the Natchez Campus ....Ms. Teresa BUSBY
20 Academic Dean ....Dr. Stephanie DUGUID
32 Dean of Student Services ....Mr. Chris WARREN
75 Dean Career & Technical Educ ....Ms. Jackie L. MARTIN
31 Dean of Community Programs ....Dr. Brenda B. ORR
41 Athletic Director ....Mr. Bryan NOBILE
38 Director of Counseling/Recruitment ....Mrs. Samantha SPEGG
35 Assistant Dean of Students ....Mr. Bryan NOBILE
37 Director Student Financial Aid ....Mrs. Leslie SMITH
40 Director Bookstore ....Mr. Charles HART
08 Director of Library Resources ....Mrs. Jacqueline QUINN
26 Director of Public Relations ....Mrs. Natalie DAVIS
13 Information Systems Specialist ....Ms. Deemie LETCHWORTH
19 Director of Security ....Mr. Alvin STARKEY
09 Dir Inst Effectiv/Facilities Plng ....Mrs. Tiffany PERRYMAN
07 Director of Admissions ....Mr. Chris WARREN
102 Executive Dir Foundation/Alumni ....Mr. D. J PREISS
18 Director of Physical Plant ....Mr. Daniel CASE
66 Director of Assoc Degree Nursing ....Ms. Mary Ann FLINT
06 Student Records Manager ....Mrs. Gay LANGHAM
57 Chair Fine Arts Division ....Mrs. Janet SMITH
50 Chair Business Division ....Mr. Richard BAKER
68 Chair Physical Education Division ....Mrs. Brenda SMITH
81 Chair Math/Computer Science Div ....Mr. Eddie BRITT
79 Chair Humanities Division ....Mrs. Mary WARREN
82 Chair Social Science Division ....Mr. David HIGGS
88 Chair Science Division ....Dr. Kevin MCKONE
96 Director of Purchasing ....Mrs. Erin LIKENS
106 Director of E-learning ....Ms. Vanessa ALEXANDER
108 QEP Director ....Ms. Glenda SILVERII
15 Human Resources Director ....Ms. Julia PARKER
39 Director Student Housing ....Mr. Allen KENT
91 Director of Technology/Info Systems ....Mr. James P. MCINNIS

Delta State University (H)

1003 W. Sunflower Rd., Cleveland MS 38733
County: Bolivar FICE Identification: 002403
Unit ID: 175616
Telephone: (662) 846-3000 Carnegie Class: Masters/L
FAX Number: (662) 846-4014 Calendar System: Semester
URL: www.deltastate.edu
Established: 1924 Annual Undergrad Tuition & Fees (In-State): $6,418
Enrollment: 3,454 Coed
Affiliation or Control: State IRS Status: 501(c)3
Highest Offering: Doctorate
Accreditation: SC, AAB, AAFCS, ACBSP, ART, CACREP, CAEPN, DIETC, MUS, NURSE, SW

01 President ....Dr. William (Bill) LAFORGE
05 Provost/VP Academic Affairs ....Dr. Charles MCADAMS
10 Vice President for Finance ....Mr. James RUTLEDGE
32 Vice President for Student Affairs ....Dr. Vernell BENNETT
100 Chief of Staff/VP Univ Relations ....Dr. Michelle A. ROBERTS
15 Director of Human Resources ....Ms. Lisa GIGER
41 Director of Athletics ....Mr. Ronnie MAYERS
84 Dean Enrollment Mgt/Director Ad Mkt ....Dr. Debbie S. HESLEP
29 Int Exec Dir of Alumni/Foundation ....Mr. Patrick HUNDLEY
49 Dean College of Arts & Sciences ....Dr. David BREAUX
50 Dean College of Business ....Dr. Billy MOORE
53 Dean College of Education ....Dr. Leslie GRIFFIN
66 Dean School of Nursing ....Dr. Vicki L. BINGHAM
08 Dean Library Services ....Mr. Jeff SLAGELL
58 Dean Grad/Cont Studies & Research ....Dr. Beverly MOON
06 Registrar ....Ms. Becky FINLEY
09 Dir of Inst Research & Planning ....Ms. Emily C. DABNEY
13 Chief Information Officer ....Mr. Edwin CRAFT
30 Chief Development Officer ....Mr. Gary BOUSE
21 Comptroller/Accounting ....Ms. Beverly LINDSEY
116 Internal Auditor ....Mrs. Mary Helen VARNER
88 Executive Director BPAC ....Ms. Laura HOWELL
121 Executive Director Student Success ....Ms. Christy RIDDLE
88 Director Coahoma County Higher Educ ....Ms. Jennifer WALLER
88 Coord Academic Support Services ....Ms. Rebecca POSEY
37 Director Student Financial Assist ....Ms. Christie ROCCONI
38 Director Counsel/Stdnt Health Svcs ....Dr. Richard HOUSTON
36 Director Career Services/Placement ....Mr. Davlon MILLER
19 Interim Director of Police Dept ....Mr. Jeffrey JOHNS
39 Director of Housing ....Ms. Julie JACKSON
26 Coordinator of Communication & Mktg ....Ms. Jennifer FARISH
29 Director of Alumni Affairs ....Mr. Jeffery FARRIS
25 Director Institutional Grants ....Ms. Heather MILLER
88 Director Student Business Svcs ....Mr. Kelvin DAVIS
88 Director Field Experiences ....Dr. Cheryl CUMMINS
106 Director of E-Learning ....Ms. Aimee HENDERSON
31 Director Delta Center Culture Learn ....Dr. Rolando HERTS
88 Director of Recruiting ....Ms. Caitlyn THOMPSON
88 Director of Enterprise Applications ....Mr. Chris GIGER
18 Director of Facilities Mgmt ....Mr. Charles BARKMAN
96 Assistant Comptroller ....Ms. Christina FARISH
35 Director Student Life ....Ms. Jeanna WILKES
40 Manager of Bookstore ....Ms. Tina GLADDEN
44 Director of Annual Giving ....Ms. Melissa PEARCE

East Central Community College (I)

PO Box 129, Decatur MS 39327-0129
County: Newton FICE Identification: 002404
Unit ID: 175643
Telephone: (601) 635-2111 Carnegie Class: Assoc/MT-VT-High Trad
FAX Number: (601) 635-4011 Calendar System: Semester
URL: www.eccc.edu
Established: 1928 Annual Undergrad Tuition & Fees (In-District): $2,290
Enrollment: 2,558 Coed
Affiliation or Control: Local IRS Status: 501(c)3
Highest Offering: Associate Degree
Accreditation: SC, ADNUR, EMT, SURGT

01 President ....Dr. Billy W. STEWART
05 Vice President for Instruction ....Dr. Teresa L. HOUSTON
10 Vice Pres for Business Operations ....Mr. Mickey VANCE
32 Vice President for Student Services ....Dr. Randall LEE
09 VP Institutional Research/Effective ....Mr. David CASE
26 Associate VP for Public Information ....Mr. Bill WAGNON
106 Dean of eLearning Education ....Dr. Christa WILHITE
08 Dean of Learning Resources ....Mr. Leslie HUGHES
20 Director of Academic & Cont Ed ....Ms. Misty SMITH
51 Director of ABE/HSE ....Mr. Ryan CLARKE
103 Director of Career & Tech Education ....Mr. Wayne EASON
07 Director Admissions and Records ....Dr. Stacey HOLLINGSWORTH
15 Dean of Personnel Svcs/Athletics ....Mr. Chris HARRIS
16 Director of Human Resources ....Mrs. Julie ROWZEE
18 Superintendent of Physical Plant ....Mr. Artie FOREMAN
13 Dean of Information Technology ....Mr. Derek PACE
14 Assoc Dir Information Technology ....Mrs. Regena BOYKIN
37 Director of Financial Aid ....Mrs. Brenda B. CARSON
19 Chief of Police ....Mr. John HARRIS
39 Director of Hous/Student Activities ....Dr. Amanda WALTON
29 Dir of Alumni Relations/Foundation ....Mr. David LEBLANC
57 Chairperson Fine Arts Division ....Mr. Chas EVANS
81 Chair Mathematics/Computer Science ....Ms. Cathryn MAY

83 Chairperson Social Sciences .... Mrs. Wanda HURLEY
76 Dean of Healthcare Education .... Dr. Sheryl ALLEN
81 Chairperson Science .... Mr. Curt SKIPPER
60 Chairperson Communications/ Language .... Mrs. Carol SHACKELFORD
04 Administrative Asst to President .... Ms. Carole H. GERMANY

East Mississippi Community College (A)

PO Box 158, Scooba MS 39358-0158
County: Kemper FICE Identification: 002405
Unit ID: 175652
Telephone: (662) 476-5000 Carnegie Class: Assoc/MT-VT-High Non
FAX Number: (662) 476-5058 Calendar System: Semester
URL: www.eastms.edu
Established: 1927 Annual Undergrad Tuition & Fees (In-District): $2,840
Enrollment: 4,259 Coed
Affiliation or Control: State/Local IRS Status: 501(c)3
Highest Offering: Associate Degree
Accreditation: SC, ADNUR, FUSER

01 President .... Dr. Thomas M. HUEBNER, JR.
11 Vice President for Administration .... Dr. Paul MILLER
32 Vice President for Student Life .... Mr. Mickey STOKES
10 Chief Financial Officer .... Ms. Melissa MOSLEY
103 VP Workforce & Cmty Services .... Dr. Raj SHAUNAK
84 VP Enrollment Management .... Mr. James GIBSON
04 Administrative Asst to President .... Mrs. Lauren CLAY
09 Special Assistant to the President .... Mr. Mark ALEXANDER
08 Director of Library Services .... Ms. Donna BALLARD
13 Director of Info Technology .... Mr. Michael TVARKUNAS
18 Director of Physical Plant .... Mr. Kyle YOUNGER
37 Director of Financial Aid .... Mr. Garry JONES
06 Registrar/Director of Admissions .... Mrs. Melinda SCIPLE
06 Registrar/Director of Admission .... Mrs. Faye MORGAN
40 Bookstore Manager .... Mrs. Ginnie CODY
26 Director of Public Information .... Mr. Rocky HIGGINBOTHAM
35 Campus Director/Dean of Students-SC .... Mr. Tony MONTGOMERY
35 Campus Director/Dean of Students-GT .... Mrs. Cathy KEMP
60 Athletic Director .... Dr. Randall BRADBERRY
12 Director Columbus Air Force Base .... Mrs. Jackie NEWTON
19 Chief of Police .... Mr. Archer SALLIS
91 Director Admin Comp/System Rpt .... Mr. Aaron BROOKS
15 Director Human Resources .... Ms. Theresa HARPOLE
111 Asst VP Institutional Advancement .... Mrs. Leia HILL
20 Associate Dean of Instruction-SC .... Mr. James RUSH
20 Associate Dean of Instruction-GT .... Mrs. Gina THOMPSON
20 Associate Dean of Instruction/CT .... Dr. Melanie SANDERS
106 Associate Dean of E-learning .... Mrs. Chris SQUARE

Hinds Community College (B)

PO Box 1100, Raymond MS 39154-1100
County: Hinds FICE Identification: 002407
Unit ID: 175786
Telephone: (601) 857-5261 Carnegie Class: Assoc/MT-VT-High Trad
FAX Number: (601) 857-3518 Calendar System: Semester
URL: www.hindscc.edu
Established: 1917 Annual Undergrad Tuition & Fees (In-District): $2,840
Enrollment: 11,935 Coed
Affiliation or Control: State/Local IRS Status: 501(c)3
Highest Offering: Associate Degree
Accreditation: SC, ADNUR, CAHIIM, COARC, DA, DMS, EMT, MAC, MLTAD, PTAA, RAD, SURGT

01 President .... Dr. Clyde MUSE
11 VP Admin Svcs/VP Utica/Vicksburg .. Dr. Debra MAYS-JACKSON
10 Vice President Business Services .... Mr. Russell SHAW
12 VP Raymond/NSG/AH/Parallel Pgm .... Dr. Theresa HAMILTON
12 VP Rankin/Jackson/Dir Occup Pgm .... Dr. Norman SESSION
18 VP Physical Plant/Auxiliary Svcs .... Mr. Thomas WASSON
111 VP Advancement .... Mr. Randall HARRIS
103 Vice Pres Workforce Development .... Dr. Chad STOCKS
35 Assoc Vice President for Students .... Dr. Tyrone JACKSON
84 Director of Enrollment Services .... Ms. Kathryn B. COLE
32 District Dean of Student Affairs .... Dr. Tyrone JACKSON
08 Dean of Learning Resources .... Ms. Mary Beth APPLIN
05 Academic Dean .... Dr. Benjamin G. CLOYD
15 Director of Human Resources .... Ms. Gay Lynn CASTON
37 Dir of Financial Aid & VA Affairs .... Mrs. Louanne LANGSTON
38 Director of Counseling Services .... Dr. Kashanta JACKSON
41 Athletic Director .... Mr. Gene MURPHY
09 Director of Institutional Research .... Ms. Carley DEAR
26 Public Relations Director .... Ms. Cathy C. HAYDEN
96 Director of Purchasing .... Mr. Samuel LEMONIS
04 Executive Secretary to President .... Mrs. Alesia PORCH
106 Dean Online Education/E-learning .... Mrs. Keri COLE
13 Chief Info Technology Officer (CIO) .... Mr. Hamp SHIVE
29 Alumni Coordinator .... Ms. Libby POSEY
39 Director Student Housing .... Mr. DeAndre HOUSE

Holmes Community College (C)

Hill Street, PO Box 369, Goodman MS 39079-0369
County: Holmes FICE Identification: 002408
Unit ID: 175810
Telephone: (662) 472-2312 Carnegie Class: Assoc/MT-VT-Mix Trad/Non
FAX Number: (662) 472-9152 Calendar System: Semester
URL: www.holmescc.edu
Established: 1925 Annual Undergrad Tuition & Fees (In-District): $2,740
Enrollment: 5,757 Coed
Affiliation or Control: Local IRS Status: 501(c)3
Highest Offering: Associate Degree
Accreditation: SC, ADNUR, EMT, #FUSER, OTA, @PTAA, SURGT

01 President .... Dr. Jim HAFFEY
09 VP Inst Research & Student Services .... Dr. Lindy MCCAIN
05 Vice Pres for Academic Programs .... Dr. Fran COX
12 Vice President Ridgeland Campus .... Dr. Don BURNHAM
12 Vice President Grenada Center .... Mrs. Michelle BURNEY
72 Director of Technical Education .... Dr. Amy WHITTINGTON
10 Vice Pres of Financial Services .... Mr. Sonny SPARKS
12 Dir Goodman Campus & Athletic Dir .... Mr. Andy WOOD
07 Director of Admissions & Records .... Mrs. Kay BATES
08 Librarian .... Mrs. Joan TIERCE
26 District Director of Communications .... Mr. Steve DIFFEY
31 Director Community/Workforce Devel ..... Dr. Mike BLANKENSHIP
37 Director Student Financial Aid .... Dr. Gail MUSE
15 Director Personnel Services .... Ms. Julia BROWN
09 Director of Institutional Research .... Mrs. Stephanie DIFFEY
18 Chief Facilities/Physical Plant .... Vacant
96 Director of Purchasing .... Mrs. Rosemary SELF
06 Registrar .... Mrs. Kay BATES
29 Director Alumni Relations .... Mrs. Katherine ELLARD
21 Business Manager .... Mr. Matt SURRELL

Itawamba Community College (D)

602 W Hill Street, Fulton MS 38843-1022
County: Itawamba FICE Identification: 002409
Unit ID: 175829
Telephone: (662) 862-8000 Carnegie Class: Assoc/HT-High Trad
FAX Number: (662) 862-8036 Calendar System: Semester
URL: www.iccms.edu
Established: 1948 Annual Undergrad Tuition & Fees (In-District): $2,620
Enrollment: 5,611 Coed
Affiliation or Control: Local IRS Status: 501(c)3
Highest Offering: Associate Degree
Accreditation: SC, ADNUR, CAHIIM, COARC, EMT, OTA, PTAA, RAD, SURGT

01 President .... Mr. Jay S. ALLEN
05 Vice President of Instruction .... Dr. Michelle SUMEREL
10 Exec Director of Finance .... Ms. Sandi SOUTH
32 Vice President of Student Services .... Mr. Buddy COLLINS
30 Vice Pres Dev/Plng/Telecom/Info Svc .... Mr. Wayne SULLIVAN
07 Dir Admission/Registration .... Ms. Cay LOLLAR
26 Director Community Relations .... Dr. Jan REID-BUNCH
37 Director of Financial Aid .... Mr. Terry BLAND
24 Director of Learning Resources .... Ms. Janet ARMOUR
08 Librarian/Tupelo .... Ms. Holly GRAY
51 Director of Adult & Continuing Educ .... Mr. Scott BLACKLEY
41 Athletic Director .... Ms. Carrie BALL-WILLIAMSON
102 Director of Foundation .... Mr. Jim INGRAM
18 Chief Facilities/Physical Plant .... Mr. Thomas BONDS
09 Director of Institutional Research .... Mrs. Elizabeth EDWARDS
15 Exec Director of Human Resources .... Mr. Timothy C. SENTER
106 Dean of eLearning .... Ms. Denise GILLESPIE
108 Director Strategic Planning and IE .... Mrs. Amy CAPPLEMAN
39 Director Student Housing .... Mr. Chad CASE

Jackson State University (E)

1400 J. R. Lynch Street, Jackson MS 39217
County: Hinds FICE Identification: 002410
Unit ID: 175856
Telephone: (601) 979-2121 Carnegie Class: DU-Higher
FAX Number: (601) 979-2358 Calendar System: Semester
URL: www.jsums.edu
Established: 1877 Annual Undergrad Tuition & Fees (In-State): $7,261
Enrollment: 9,802 Coed
Affiliation or Control: State IRS Status: 501(c)3
Highest Offering: Doctorate
Accreditation: SC, ART, CACREP, CAEPN, CLPSY, CS, ENG, MUS, NAIT, PH, PLNG, SP, SPAA, SW

01 President .... Dr. William BYNUM, JR.
05 Interim Provost/Sr VP Acad Affairs .... Dr. Ivory NELSON
10 Int VP for Business & Finance .... Ms. Dana BROWN
46 VP for Rsrch/Federal Relations .... Dr. Loretta A. MOORE
111 VP Institutional Advancement .... Ms. Sandra HODGE
13 VP for Information Management .... Dr. Deborah F. DENT
32 VP for Student Life .... Vacant
84 VP Enroll Mgmt/Inst Research .... Dr. Nicole EDWARDS-EVANS
43 General Counsel .... Mr. Matthew A. TAYLOR
116 Internal Auditor .... Ms. Ella HOLMES
18 Interim AVP for Fac/Const Mgmt .... Mr. Robert WATTS
21 Interim VP for Business & Finance .... Ms. Marvel A. TURNER
20 Assoc Provost for Academic Affairs .... Vacant
106 Asst Director JSU Online .... Ms. Tameka MOOREHEAD
35 Assoc VP for Student Life/Dean Std .... Vacant
46 Assoc VP for Research Development .... Vacant
88 Assoc VP for Research & Admin .... Mrs. Tracy STAPLETON
14 Assoc VP Information Tech .... Dr. Michael ROBINSON
100 Chief of Staff .... Dr. Debra MAYS-JACKSON
53 Dean College Educ/Human Devel .... Dr. Daniel WATKINS
58 Dean Division of Graduate Studies .... Dr. Dorris R. ROBINSON-GARDNER
89 Int Dean Division Undergrad Studies .... Dr. Marie O'BANNER/JACKSON
49 Dean College of Liberal Arts .... Dr. Mario AZEVEDO
85 Director JSU Global .... Dr. Thomas CALHOUN
50 Dean College of Business .... Vacant
80 Dean College of Public Service .... Dr. Ricardo BROWN
72 Dean College of Sci/Engr/Tech .... Dr. Richard ALO
51 Director of Lifelong Learning .... Dr. Carlos WILSON
08 Dean Div of Library & Info Res .... Dr. Melissa DRUCKREY
88 Interim Dean University College .... Dr. Marie O'BANNER-JACKSON
92 Assoc Dean Div of Honors College ... Dr. Loria BROWN GORDAN
31 Assoc Dir Ctr Svc & Comm/Eng Lrng .... Vacant
29 Int Dir Alumni/Constituency Rels .... Ms. Tabetha TERRELL-BROOKS
15 Executive Director Human Resources ... Mrs. Robin SPANN-PACK
110 Asst VP of Inst Advancement .... Mrs. Gwen CAPLES
39 Assc Director of Residence Life .... Vacant
37 Interim Director of Financial Aid .... Mrs. Glenda LATTIMORE
21 Dir Budget & Financial Analysis .... Mrs. Tammiko HARRISON
06 Registrar .... Mr. Alfred B. JACKSON
23 University Physician .... Dr. Robert SMITH
23 University Physician .... Dr. Samuel JONES
89 Director of First Year Experience .... Mrs. Meshonya WREN-COLEMAN
07 Dir Undergraduate Admissions .... Mrs. Janieth ADAMS
88 Int Director Student Recruitment .... Ms. Keiona MILLER
41 Director of Athletics .... Mr. Wheeler BROWN
88 Director of Title III .... Dr. Fredrick WHITE
88 Director MS Urban Research Ctr .... Dr. Melvin DAVIS
19 Director Public Safety .... Mr. Thomas ALBRIGHT
26 Director Communications .... Vacant
22 Int Dir for ADA Services .... Mr. Aaron RICHARDSON
88 Director of Planning & Construction .... Mr. Robert WATTS
40 Manager Bookstore .... Ms. Dyonne CONNER
09 Director Institutional Research .... Dr. Shemeka MCCLUNG
04 Administrative Asst to President ... Mrs. Joyce JORDAN-GOODEN
36 Executive Director Career Services .... Ms. Lashanda JORDAN
38 Director Student Counseling .... Ms. Shanice WHITE
21 Executive Director Business Office .... Ms. Jewell HARRIS
22 Chief Diversity Officer/EEO-AA Off .... Mr. Thomas HUDSON
105 Webmaster .... Mr. Gerard L. HOWARD
86 Exec Director Institutions of Govt .... Dr. Otha BURON
90 Director Academic IT .... Ms. Emily A. BISHOP
69 Dean School of Public Health .... Dr. Mohammad SHABAZZI
60 Dean School of Journalism .... Dr. Elayne ANTHONY
88 Dir Research/Federal Relations .... Dr. Loretta MOORE
104 Director Study Abroad .... Vacant

Jones County Junior College (F)

900 S Court Street, Ellisville MS 39437-3999
County: Jones FICE Identification: 002411
Unit ID: 175883
Telephone: (601) 477-4000 Carnegie Class: Assoc/MT-VT-High Trad
FAX Number: (601) 477-4875 Calendar System: Semester
URL: www.jcjc.edu
Established: 1927 Annual Undergrad Tuition & Fees (In-District): $3,000
Enrollment: 4,727 Coed
Affiliation or Control: State/Local IRS Status: Exempt
Highest Offering: Associate Degree
Accreditation: SC, ACBSP, ADNUR, EMT, RAD

01 President .... Dr. Jesse R. SMITH
05 VP Instructional Affs/Assessment .... Ms. Candace WEAVER
10 Vice President of Business Affairs .... Mr. Rick YOUNGBLOOD
32 Vice President of Student Affairs .... Dr. Sam JONES
111 VP of Institutional Advancement .... Mr. Charlie GARRETSON
13 Director of Information Technology .... Mr. Paul SPELL
26 Vice President of Marketing .... Ms. Finee RUFFIN
04 Assistant to the President .... Ms. Gwen MAGEE
11 Director of Campus Operations .... Mr. Michael BRADSHAW
35 Dean of Student Affairs .... Mr. Mark EASLEY
92 Dean of Arts and Honors .... Dr. Jason DEDWYLER
103 Director of the Adv Tech Center .... Mr. Greg BUTLER
07 Director of Admissions & Records .... Mr. Rick HAMILTON
88 Dir of Student Success Center .... Ms. Amanda MCLEOD
37 Director of Student Financial Aid .... Ms. Jennifer SUBER
39 Director of Housing-Women .... Ms. Michelle SHEARER
39 Director of Housing-Men .... Mr. Joseph TUGGLE
40 Bookstore Manager .... Mr. Kevin KUHN
41 Athletic Director .... Ms. Katie HERRINGTON
15 Human Resources Manager .... Mr. Luke HAMMONDS
96 Director of Purchasing .... Ms. Daphne YEAGER
106 Dean of eLearning .... Ms. Ashley BEARD
08 Head Librarian .... Mr. Andrew SHARP
19 Chief Campus Police .... Mr. Stan LIVINGSTON

Meridian Community College (G)

910 Highway 19 N, Meridian MS 39307-5890
County: Lauderdale FICE Identification: 002413
Unit ID: 175935
Telephone: (601) 483-8241 Carnegie Class: Assoc/MT-VT-High Trad
FAX Number: (601) 481-1305 Calendar System: Semester
URL: www.meridiancc.edu
Established: 1937 Annual Undergrad Tuition & Fees (In-District): $2,440
Enrollment: 3,381 Coed
Affiliation or Control: Local IRS Status: 501(c)3
Highest Offering: Associate Degree
Accreditation: SC, ADNUR, CAHIIM, COARC, DA, DH, EMT, MAC, MLTAD, PNUR, PTAA, RAD, SURGT

01 President .... Dr. Scott D. ELLIOTT
10 Vice President for Finance .... Mrs. Amy BRAND
07 Director of Admissions .... Dr. Angela PAYNE
09 Dir Institutional Effectiveness .... Mrs. Cathy PARKER
32 Dean of Students .... Ms. Soraya WELDEN
05 Dean of Academic Affs/General Educ ..... Mr. Michael THOMPSON

30	Assoc Vice Pres for Development	Mrs. Kathy BROOKSHIRE
18	Director Physical Plant	Mr. Adam FOREMAN
37	Director Financial Aid	Ms. Nedra BRADLEY
15	Director Human Resources	Ms. Angie PICKARD
41	Athletic Director	Mr. Sander ATKINSON
19	Chief of Security	Mr. Shane WILLIAMS
40	Bookstore Manager	Mrs. Cher WARREN
26	Dir Marketing/Public Relations	Mrs. Kay THOMAS
36	Career Center Development Director	Ms. Darlene MAYATT
103	Assoc Vice Pres for Workforce Educ	Dr. Richie MCALISTER
06	Registrar	Ms. Deborah OLDHAM
105	Director Web Services	Ms. Inga BASS
13	Chief Info Technology Officer (CIO)	Mr. Chris EDWARDS
39	Director Student Housing	Mr. Calvin BENNETT
106	Director of E-Learning	Mrs. Haley DUCK

Millsaps College (A)

1701 N State Street, Jackson MS 39210-0001

County: Hinds | FICE Identification: 002414 | Unit ID: 175980

Telephone: (601) 974-1000 | Carnegie Class: Bac-A&S

FAX Number: (601) 974-1059 | Calendar System: Semester

URL: www.millsaps.edu

Established: 1890 | Annual Undergrad Tuition & Fees: $37,110

Enrollment: 809 | Coed

Affiliation or Control: United Methodist | IRS Status: 501(c)3

Highest Offering: Master's

Accreditation: SC, CAEP

01	President	Dr. Rob PEARIGEN
05	VP/Dean of the College	Dr. Keith DUNN
10	Vice Pres of Finance	Mr. Dan HUNGERFORD
45	Vice Pres for Planning & Assessment	Ms. Terri HUDSON
111	VP for Institutional Advancement	Ms. Hope CARTER
32	VP Student Life/Dean Students	Dr. Brit KATZ
50	Dean of the School of Management	Dr. Kimberly G. BURKE
84	Vice Pres Enrollment/Communications	Dr. Robert ALEXANDER
79	Assoc Dean Arts & Letters	Dr. Laura FRANEY
81	Associate Dean Sciences Division	Dr. Timothy J. WARD
82	Assoc Dean International Education	Dr. George J. BEY
37	Director of Financial Aid	Mrs. Isabelle HIGBEE
20	Director Academic Support Services	Ms. Kia SMITH
51	Director of Continuing Education	Dr. Nola R. GIBSON
08	College Librarian	Ms. Jamie B. WILSON
36	Director of Career Center	Ms. Tonya CRAFT
41	Director of Athletics	Mr. Donnie BROOKS
15	Dir of Human Resource Services	Ms. Julie DANIELS
42	Chaplain	Vacant
21	Controller	Mrs. Whitney EMRICH
06	Registrar	Dr. Ken THOMPSON
09	Director of Institutional Research	Vacant
18	Director of Physical Plant	Mr. Michael SWITZER
29	Director Alumni Relations	Ms. Maribeth KITCHINGS
19	Director Security/Safety	Mr. John CONWAY
26	Director of Communications & Market	Mr. John SEWELL
07	Director of Admission	Vacant
04	Executive Asst to President	Mrs. Penta MOORE
100	Chief of Staff	Mr. Kenneth TOWNSEND
102	Dir Foundation/Corporate Relations	Mr. Lloyd GRAY
44	Director Annual Giving	Mr. Ryan PEMBERTON

Mississippi College (B)

200 W College Street, Clinton MS 39058-0001

County: Hinds | FICE Identification: 002415 | Unit ID: 176053

Telephone: (601) 925-3000 | Carnegie Class: Masters/L

FAX Number: (601) 925-3276 | Calendar System: Semester

URL: www.mc.edu

Established: 1826 | Annual Undergrad Tuition & Fees: $16,740

Enrollment: 5,036 | Coed

Affiliation or Control: Southern Baptist | IRS Status: 501(c)3

Highest Offering: Doctorate

Accreditation: SC, ACBSP, ARCPA, CACREP, CAEPN, CIDA, LAW, MUS, NURSE, SW

01	President	Dr. Lee G. ROYCE
04	Sr Exec Assistant to President	Ms. Shelia CARPENTER
10	Chief Financial Officer	Ms. Donna LEWIS
05	Vice President Academic Affairs	Dr. Ronald HOWARD
32	VP Enrollment Svcs/Dean of Students	Dr. Jim TURCOTTE
45	Vice President Planning/Assessment	Dr. Debbie NORRIS
42	Vice Pres Christian Development	Dr. Eric PRATT
111	VP Inst Advan/Alum/Leg Coun to Pres	Dr. Bill TOWNSEND
11	Vice Pres Admin/Government Rels	Dr. Steve STANFORD
84	Director Enrollment Services	Mr. Mark HUGHES
06	Registrar	Ms. Megan PRITCHETT
09	Director of Institutional Research	Ms. Cassandra SESSUMS
08	Librarian	Ms. Kathleen HUTCHISON
21	Comptroller	Ms. Allison ROOKER
13	Chief Information Officer	Mr. Bill CRANFORD
38	Director Counseling/Testing Center	Dr. Morgan BRYANT
15	Director Human Resources	Ms. Donna SMITH
29	Interim Director Alumni Affairs	Ms. Lori BOBO
26	Director Public Relations	Ms. Tracey HARRISON
18	Director of Physical Plant	Mr. Billy THORNTON
39	Coordinator of Residence Life	Ms. Sharia BROCK
37	Director Student Financial Aid	Ms. Karon MCMILLAN
07	Director of Admissions	Mr. Kyle BRANTLEY
35	Assoc Dir of Student Engagement	Ms. Becca BENSON
19	Director of Public Safety	Mr. Mike WARREN
41	Director of Athletics	Mr. Mike JONES
96	Director of Purchasing	Ms. Dana ELMORE
40	Manager Bookstore	Ms. Karen BARNES
36	Asst Director of Career Services	Mr. Jim MILLER
81	Dean School of Science/Mathematics	Dr. Stan BALDWIN
50	Dean School of Business Admin	Dr. Marcelo EDUARDO
79	Dean School of Humanities	Dr. Jonathan RANDLE
53	Dean School of Education	Dr. Cindy MELTON
73	Dean Sch Christian Studies/Fine Art	Dr. Wayne VAN HORN
61	Dean School of Law	Prof. Wendy SCOTT
58	Dean Grad School/Special Programs	Dr. Debbie NORRIS
66	Dean School of Nursing	Dr. Kimberly SHARP
86	Director Government Relations	Dr. Steve STANFORD

Mississippi Delta Community College (C)

PO Box 668, Moorhead MS 38761-0668

County: Sunflower | FICE Identification: 002416 | Unit ID: 176008

Telephone: (662) 246-6322 | Carnegie Class: Assoc/HT-Mix Trad/Non

FAX Number: (662) 246-6321 | Calendar System: Semester

URL: www.msdelta.edu

Established: 1926 | Annual Undergrad Tuition & Fees (In-District): $2,650

Enrollment: 2,402 | Coed

Affiliation or Control: Local | IRS Status: 501(c)3

Highest Offering: Associate Degree

Accreditation: SC, ADNUR, DH, MLTAD, RAD

01	President	Dr. Larry NABORS
03	Executive Vice President	Dr. Charles BARNETT
05	Vice President of Instruction	Mrs. Teresa WEBSTER
10	Vice President of Business Services	Mrs. Marsha LEE
32	Vice President of Student Services	Dr. Edward RICE
88	Dean of GHEC Operations	Ms. Linda CLARK
84	Associate Vice Pres of Enrollment	Dr. Brent GREGORY
111	Assoc VP College Advancement	Mr. Reed ABRAHAM
15	Director of Human Resources	Ms. Brenda VANLANDINGHAM
37	Director of Financial Aid	Ms. Amber KELLY
07	Director of Admissions	Dr. Brent GREGORY
13	Director Computer & Info Tech Svcs	Mr. Jim AYCOCK
08	Director of Library Services	Mrs. Kristi BARIOLA
07	Director Counseling/Recruiting	Mrs. Kate FAILING
18	Director of Maintenance	Mr. Don LEE
88	Director of Special Events	Mrs. Corey SMITH
09	Director of Institutional Research	Mrs. Rosemary LAMB
04	Admin Asst to the President	Mrs. Debra BAKER
41	Athletic Director	Mr. Jeff TATUM
19	Director Security/Safety	Mr. Henry MANUEL

Mississippi Gulf Coast Community College (D)

PO Box 609, Perkinston MS 39573-0012

County: Stone | FICE Identification: 002417 | Unit ID: 176071

Telephone: (601) 928-5211 | Carnegie Class: Assoc/MT-VT-High Trad

FAX Number: (601) 928-6386 | Calendar System: Semester

URL: www.mgccc.edu

Established: 1911 | Annual Undergrad Tuition & Fees (In-District): $3,272

Enrollment: 9,391 | Coed

Affiliation or Control: Local | IRS Status: 501(c)3

Highest Offering: Associate Degree

Accreditation: SC, ACFEI, ADNUR, EMT, MAC, MLTAD, PNUR, RAD, SURGT

01	President	Dr. Mary S. GRAHAM
05	Exec VP Teaching/Lrng/Student Svcs	Dr. Jason PUGH
10	VP Administration/Finance	Dr. Michael J. HEINDL
12	VP Perkinston Campus (PC)	Dr. Ladd TAYLOR
12	VP Jefferson Davis Campus (JDC)	Dr. Jonathan WOODWARD
12	VP Jackson County Campus (JCC)	Dr. Tammy FRANKS
84	Exec VP Enroll Mgmt/Student Success	Dr. Carmen WALTERS
75	AVP Cmty Campus/Career Tech Educ	Mr. John SHOWS
15	Assoc VP Human Resources	Mr. Jared BURNS
09	Director Inst Research & Planning	Mr. Adam SWANSON
41	College Dean for Athletics	Mr. Bert PICKARD
106	Director of Distance Learning	Ms. Jennifer LEIMER
50	Director of Business Services	Mr. Wayne KUNTZ
21	Comptroller	Ms. Shelly FORD
06	Records Clerk - PC	Ms. Latrice MCDONALD
06	Records Clerk - JCC	Ms. Amanda HESTER
06	Records Clerk - JDC	Vacant
20	Dean of Instruction - JCC	Dr. Cedric BRADLEY
20	Dean of Instruction - JDC	Mr. Larry MILLER
20	Dean of Instruction - PC	Dr. Jan MOODY
50	Dean of Business Services - PC	Dr. Vanessa DEDEAUX
50	Dean of Business Services - JCC	Ms. Tenesha BATISTE
50	Dean of Business Services - JDC	Dr. Suzi BROWN
66	Dean of Nursing/Allied Health	Dr. Joan HENDRIX
75	Dn Career Tech/Wrkfc/Cmty Ed - PC	Mr. Bobby GHOSAL
75	Dn Career/Tech/Wrkf/Cmty Ed - JDC	Dr. Beverly CLARK
75	Dn Career/Tech/Wrkf/Cmty Ed - JCC	Mr. Brock CLARK
08	Asst Dean LRC - PC	Dr. Brenda RIVERO
08	Asst Dean LRC - JCC	Dr. Pam ALEXANDER
08	Asst Dean LRC - JDC	Ms. Nancy WILCOX
32	Dn Stdnt Svcs/Enroll Mgmt - PC	Dr. Jason BEVERLY
32	Dn Stdnt Svcs/Enroll Mgmt - JCC	Ms. Michelle SEKUL
32	Dn Stdnt Svcs/Enroll Mgmt - JDC	Dr. Phil BONFANTI
88	Dean George County Center	Ms. Becky LAYTON
07	Director of Admissions/Rec - PC	Mr. Trey ROBERTSON
07	Director of Admissions/Rec - JCC	Mr. William EVERITT
07	Director of Admissions/Rec - JDC	Mr. Christopher BAGWELL
29	Coord College Events/Special Proj	Ms. Jenifer FRERIDGE
37	Financial Aid Director - JDC	Ms. Angela BRADLEY
37	Financial Aid Director - PC	Vacant
37	Financial Aid Director - JCC	Ms. LaShanda CHAMBERLAIN
96	Dir Purchasing/Property Control	Ms. Lynn DEEGEN
18	Construction Manager	Mr. Jason BRELAND
44	Director Institutional Development	Ms. Brenda DAVIS
04	Exec Assistant to the President	Ms. Tracey WALTERS

Mississippi State University (E)

Lee Boulevard, Mississippi State MS 39762-5708

County: Oktibbeha | FICE Identification: 002423 | Unit ID: 176080

Telephone: (662) 325-2323 | Carnegie Class: DU-Higher

FAX Number: (662) 325-7455 | Calendar System: Semester

URL: www.msstate.edu

Established: 1878 | Annual Undergrad Tuition & Fees (In-State): $7,780

Enrollment: 20,873 | Coed

Affiliation or Control: State | IRS Status: 501(c)3

Highest Offering: Doctorate

Accreditation: SC, AAFCS, ART, CACREP, CAEPN, CIDA, CLPSY, CS, DIETD, DIETI, ENG, LSAR, MUS, SCPSY, SPAA, SW, VET

01	President	Dr. Mark E. KEENUM
05	Provost/Executive VP	Dr. Judy BONNER
46	VP Research & Economic Development	Dr. David SHAW
88	VP Agric/Forestry & Veterinary Med	Dr. Gregory BOHACH
10	VP for Budget and Planning	Mr. Don ZANT
32	VP for Student Affairs	Dr. Regina HYATT
30	VP for Development and Alumni	Mr. John P. RUSH
18	VP for Campus Services	Ms. Amy TUCK
07	Assistant VP Enrollment	Dr. John DICKERSON
41	Athletic Director	Mr. John COHEN
43	General Counsel	Ms. Joan LUCAS
28	Chief Diversity Officer	Ms. Rasheda BODDIE-FORBES
15	Director Human Resources Mgmt	Ms. Judith SPENCER
26	Exec Dir External Affairs	Mr. Kyle STEWARD
27	Chief Communications Officer	Mr. Sid SALTER
86	Director Government Relations	Mr. Lee WEISKOPF
20	Assoc Provost Academic Affairs	Dr. Peter RYAN
13	Chief Information Officer	Mr. J. Mike RACKLEY
88	Exec Dir International Institute	Dr. Richard NADER
48	Dean of Architecture/Art/Design	Mr. James L. WEST
49	Dean Arts & Sciences	Dr. Rick TRAVIS
50	Dean College Business	Dr. Sharon OSWALD
53	Dean of Education	Dr. Richard L. BLACKBOURN
58	Dean of Graduate Studies	Dr. Lori BRUCE
54	Dean College of Engineering	Dr. Jason KEITH
65	Dean of Forest Resources	Dr. George M. HOPPER
47	Dean College Agriculture & Life Sci	Dr. George M. HOPPER
74	Dean of Veterinary Medicine	Dr. Kent H. HOBLET
12	Admin Dir & Head of Meridian Campus	Dr. Terry CRUSE
08	Dean of Libraries	Ms. Frances N. COLEMAN
92	Dean Honors College	Dr. Christopher SNYDER
56	Dir University Extension Service	Dr. Gary JACKSON
88	Dir Agricultural Experiment Station	Dr. George M. HOPPER
06	Registrar	Dr. John R. DICKERSON
106	Director Distance Education	Dr. Susan SEAL
36	Director Career Services/Coop Educ	Mr. Scott MAYNARD
35	Dean of Students	Dr. Thomas BOURGEOIS
38	Director Counseling Services	Ms. Luellyn SWITZER
37	Director Student Financial Aid	Mr. Paul MCKINNEY
39	Director Housing/Residence Life	Dr. Ann BAILEY
09	Director Institutional Research	Dr. Tim CHAMBLEE
23	Director Student Health Center	Mr. Robert K. CADENHEAD
29	Director of Alumni Association	Mr. Jeffrey DAVIS
112	Director of Planned Giving	Mr. Wes GORDON
25	Director Sponsored Projects	Mrs. Jennifer EASLEY
116	Director Internal Audit	Ms. Leisa ERVIN
96	Director Procurement/Contracts	Mr. Don BUFFUM
19	Police Chief	Mr. Vance RICE

Mississippi University for Women (F)

1100 College Street, Columbus MS 39701-5800

County: Lowndes | FICE Identification: 002422 | Unit ID: 176035

Telephone: (877) 462-8439 | Carnegie Class: Masters/S

FAX Number: (662) 329-7297 | Calendar System: Semester

URL: www.muw.edu

Established: 1884 | Annual Undergrad Tuition & Fees (In-State): $6,065

Enrollment: 2,673 | Coed

Affiliation or Control: State | IRS Status: 501(c)3

Highest Offering: Doctorate

Accreditation: SC, ACBSP, ADNUR, ART, CAEPN, MUS, NURSE, SP

01	President	Dr. Jim BORSIG
05	Provost/VP Academic Affairs	Dr. Thomas RICHARDSON
10	Sr Vice Pres Administration & CFO	Ms. Nora R. MILLER
26	Exec Dir of University Relations	Ms. Maridith GEUDER
32	Vice Pres for Student Affairs	Dr. Jennifer MILES
20	Assoc Vice Pres Academic Affairs	Dr. Martin HATTON
43	University Counsel	Ms. Karen CLAY
49	Dean College Arts/Sciences	Dr. Brian ANDERSON
50	Dean Business/Professional Studies	Dr. Scott TOLLISON
66	Dean College Nursing/SLP	Dr. Sheila V. ADAMS
08	Dean of Library Services	Ms. Amanda C. POWERS
58	Director Graduate Studies	Dr. Martin HATTON
88	Int Director Outreach & Innovation	Ms. Melinda LOWE
27	Chief Information Officer	Ms. Carla LOWERY
06	Registrar	Ms. Lynn DOBBS

09 Director Inst Research & Assessment .... Ms. Jennifer MOORE
92 Director Honors College .... Dr. Kim WHITEHEAD
25 Director Sponsored Programs .... Mr. James DENNEY
29 Director Alumni Relations .... Ms. Lyndsay CUMBERLAND
30 Exec Dir Development/Alumni Rels .... Ms. Andrea N. STEVENS
44 Director Annual Giving .... Ms. Brandy WILLIAMS
88 Director Public Affairs .... Ms. Anika M. PERKINS
105 Dir Web Development/Univ Webmaster .... Mr. Rich SOBOLEWSKI
21 Director University Accounting .... Ms. Susan SOBLEY
116 Internal Auditor .... Mr. Kenneth WIDNER
13 Director of Information Systems .... Ms. Lisa MCDANIEL
07 Director Admissions .... Ms. Shelley MCNEES MOSS
37 Director Financial Aid .... Ms. Nicole PATRICK
15 Director Human Resources .... Ms. Melanie H. FREEMAN
19 Chief of Police .... Mr. Danny PATTON
18 Director of Facilities Management .... Mr. Jody KENNEDY
96 Director Resources Management .... Ms. Angie S. ATKINS
35 Director Student Life .... Ms. Jessica HARPOLE
35 Dean of Students .... Ms. Sirena CANTRELL
41 Director Campus Recreation .... Ms. LeAnn ALEXANDER
40 Director Bookstore .... Ms. Helana ROBINSON
121 Director Student Success Center .... Dr. David BROOKING
109 General Manager of MUW Dining Svcs .... Mr. Alan JOHNSON
84 Enrollment Certification Officer .... Ms. Jody PETERS
14 Director of Systems & Networks .... Mr. Rodney GODFREY
104 Director Study Abroad .... Dr. Kim WHITEHEAD
39 Director Housing & Residence Life ... Mr. Andrew MONEYMAKER

Mississippi Valley State University (A)

14000 Highway 82 W, Itta Bena MS 38941-1400
County: Leflore FICE Identification: 002424
Unit ID: 176044
Telephone: (662) 254-9041 Carnegie Class: Masters/S
FAX Number: (662) 254-6709 Calendar System: Semester
URL: www.mvsu.edu
Established: 1950 Annual Undergrad Tuition & Fees (In-State): $6,116
Enrollment: 2,309 Coed
Affiliation or Control: State IRS Status: 501(c)3
Highest Offering: Master's
Accreditation: SC, ACBSP, ART, CAEPN, CS, MUS, SW

01 Acting President .... Dr. Jerryl BRIGGS, SR.
05 VP Academic Affairs .... Dr. Constance BLAND
32 Vice Pres for Student Affairs .... Dr. Jacqueline GIBSON
35 Int Dean Students/Dir Res Life .... Mr. Raynaldo GILLUS
20 Assoc VP Academic Affairs .... Dr. Elizabeth EVANS
09 Asst VP for IRE/Strat Planning .... Dr. Sharon FREEMAN
10 VP Business & Finance/CFO .... Ms. Joyce A. DIXON
100 Chief of Staff/Legislative Liaison .... Mrs. LaShon F. BROOKS
111 Int Vice Pres for Univ Advancement .... Mr. Dameon SHAW
106 Asst VP for Distance & Online .... Dr. Kenneth DONE
41 Director of Athletics .... Mrs. Dianthia FORD-KEE
06 Director of Student Records .... Mr. Jeff LOGGINS
07 Director Admission/Recruitment .... Ms. Jacqueline A. WILLIAMS
08 Head Librarian .... Ms. Mantra HENDERSON
15 Director of Human Resources .... Mrs. Elizabeth HURSSEY
13 Director of Information Technology .... Mr. Torrey MOORE
37 Director of Financial Aid .... Mr. Lloyd E. DIXON
29 Manager of Alumni Relations .... Ms. Latacha DAVIS-JACKSON
26 Director of Comm/Mktg .... Mrs. Maxine GREENLEAF
19 Director University Police .... Mr. Alex E. GRANDERSON
18 Director Facilities/Capital Project .... Mr. Terrence HURSSEY
39 Asst Director Residential Life .... Ms. Glenda RANSOM
36 Director Career Development .... Ms. Essie L. BRYANT
38 Director Student Counseling .... Dr. Yolanda JONES
50 Acting Chair of Business Department .... Dr. Curressia BROWN
53 Acting Chair of Education Dept .... Dr. Chukwuma AHANONU
65 Chair Nat Sci/Env Health Dept .... Dr. Julius O. IKENGA
88 Chair English/Foreign Language .... Dr. John ZHENG
57 Chair Fine Arts Department .... Dr. Alphonso SANDERS
68 Chair Health/Phys Ed/Rec Dept .... Dr. Gloria ROSS
81 Chair of Math/Computer Science Dept .... Dr. Latonya GARNER
54 Acting Chair of Engineering Tech .... Mr. Antonio BROWNLOW
60 Chair Mass Communication Dept .... Dr. Samuel OSUNDE
88 Chair Criminal Justice .... Dr. Emmanual AMADI
70 Chair Social Work Department .... Dr. Catherine SINGLETON-WALKER
96 Director of Purchasing .... Mr. Billy SCOTT
04 Executive Asst to President .... Mrs. Auguster WALLACE
25 Director Sponsored Pgm/Title III .... Mr. Samuel MELTON, JR.
30 Director of Development .... Mr. Kendall TANNER
84 Exec Director Enrollment Management .... Mr. Michael TAYLOR

Northeast Mississippi Community College (B)

101 Cunningham Boulevard, Booneville MS 38829-1731
County: Prentiss FICE Identification: 002426
Unit ID: 176169
Telephone: (662) 728-7751 Carnegie Class: Assoc/HT-High Trad
FAX Number: (662) 728-1165 Calendar System: Semester
URL: www.nemcc.edu
Established: 1948 Annual Undergrad Tuition & Fees (In-District): $2,732
Enrollment: 3,569 Coed
Affiliation or Control: State/Local IRS Status: 501(c)3
Highest Offering: Associate Degree
Accreditation: SC, ADNUR, COARC, DH, MAC, MLTAD, RAD

01 President .... Ricky G. FORD
03 Executive Vice President .... Craig-Ellis SASSSER
103 Vice Pres Wrkfrce Training/Econ Dev .... Nadara L. COLE
10 Vice President of Finance .... Chris MURPHY
26 Assoc Vice Pres of Public Info .... Tony FINCH
05 Vice President of Instruction .... Michelle BARAGONA
32 Vice President of Students .... David ROBBINS
35 Assoc Dean of Student Activities .... Rod COGGIN
08 Director Learning Resources .... Glenice STONE
96 Director of Purchasing .... Amber GARNER
37 Director of Financial Aid .... Greg WINDHAM
38 Director Student Counseling .... Joey WILLIFORD
13 Director Computer Center .... Gregory SMITH
18 Director Facilities/Maintenance .... Mark HATFIELD
39 Director Residential Housing .... Rod COGGIN
75 Director of Vocational Tech Educ .... Jason MATTOX
84 Dir of Enrollment Svcs/Registrar .... Chassie KELLY
15 Human Resources Officer .... Wesley FLOYD
04 Administrative Asst to President .... Misty DEVAUGHN
102 Dir Foundation/Corporate Relations .... Patrick D. EATON
106 Dir Online Education/E-learning .... Kim HARRIS
19 Director Security/Safety .... Randy A. BAXTER

Northwest Mississippi Community College (C)

4975 Highway 51 N, Senatobia MS 38668-1703
County: Tate FICE Identification: 002427
Unit ID: 176178
Telephone: (662) 562-3200 Carnegie Class: Assoc/MT-VT-High Trad
FAX Number: (662) 562-3911 Calendar System: Semester
URL: www.northwestms.edu
Established: 1927 Annual Undergrad Tuition & Fees (In-State): $2,800
Enrollment: 7,809 Coed
Affiliation or Control: State IRS Status: 501(c)3
Highest Offering: Associate Degree
Accreditation: SC, ADNUR, COARC, EMT, FUSER

01 President .... Dr. Gary Lee SPEARS
10 Vice President for Fiscal Affairs .... Mr. Gary MOSLEY
32 VP Student Affairs/Chief of Staff .... Mr. Dan SMITH
05 Vice Pres for Educational Affairs .... Mr. Richie LAWSON
20 Academic Dean .... Dr. Matthew S. DOMAS
103 Dean Career Tech Ed/Wrkfce Dev Trng .... Mr. David CAMPBELL
51 Dir Division of Continuing Educ .... Ms. Pam WOOTEN
84 Dean Enrollment Mgmt & Registrar .... Mrs. Aime ANDERSON
35 Director of Student Personnel .... Mr. Gerald BEARD
26 Director of Communications .... Mrs. Julie BAUER
37 Director of Financial Aid .... Ms. Jennifer LUNA
36 Dir Student Development Center .... Ms. Meg ROSS
08 Director of Learning Resources .... Dr. Melissa WRIGHT
13 Director Management Information Sys .... Mrs. Amy LATHAM
07 Director of Recruiting .... Mrs. Jere HERRINGTON
09 Director Planning/Inst Research .... Dr. Carolyn WARREN
18 Director of Physical Plant Building .... Mrs. Mary AYERS
19 Chief of Campus Security .... Mr. Zabe DAVIS
30 Director of Development/Alumni Rels .... Mrs. Sybil CANON
39 Director of Campus Life and Housing .... Ms. Tara DUNN
40 Director Bookstore .... Mr. Joel BOYLES
41 Director of Athletics/Intramurals .... Mr. Don SKELTON
96 Director of Purchasing .... Mrs. Barbara YOUNG
15 Personnel Officer .... Mrs. Erica STANFORD
29 Director Alumni Relations .... Ms. Patti GORDON
21 Business Manager .... Ms. Ruthie CASTLE

Pearl River Community College (D)

101 Highway 11 N, Poplarville MS 39470-2298
County: Pearl River FICE Identification: 002430
Unit ID: 176239
Telephone: (601) 403-1000 Carnegie Class: Assoc/MT-VT-High Trad
FAX Number: (601) 403-1339 Calendar System: Semester
URL: www.prcc.edu
Established: 1909 Annual Undergrad Tuition & Fees (In-District): $3,080
Enrollment: 4,379 Coed
Affiliation or Control: State/Local IRS Status: 501(c)3
Highest Offering: Associate Degree
Accreditation: SC, ADNUR, COARC, DA, DH, MLTAD, OTA, PTAA, RAD, SURGT

01 President .... Dr. Adam J. BREERWOOD
05 VP for General Educ & Technology .... Dr. Martha L. SMITH
10 VP for Business/Admn Services .... Mr. Roger A. KNIGHT
08 Director of College Libraries .... Ms. Tracy SMITH
26 Director of Public Relations .... Mr. Chuck ABADIE
84 Director of Admissions and Records .... Ms. Tonia MOODY
12 VP for Forrest County Operations .... Dr. Jana CAUSEY
18 Director of Physical Plant .... Mr. Craig TYNES
30 Director Development/Alumni Rels ...... Mr. Ernest L. LOVELL, JR.
37 Director Student Financial Aid .... Ms. Valerie HORNE
41 Athletic Director .... Mr. Jeff LONG
07 Director of Recruitment/Marketing .... Ms. Delana HARRIS
09 VP for Planning & Inst Research .... Dr. Jennifer SEAL
103 VP for Workforce & Economic Develop .... Dr. David S. ALSOBROOKS
04 Administrative Asst to President .... Ms. Marilyn DILLARD
105 Webmaster .... Mr. Eric REID
13 Chief Info Technology Officer (CIO) .... Mr. Matt LOGAN

Reformed Theological Seminary (E)

5422 Clinton Boulevard, Jackson MS 39209-3099
County: Hinds FICE Identification: 009193
Unit ID: 176284
Telephone: (601) 923-1600 Carnegie Class: Not Classified
FAX Number: (601) 923-1654 Calendar System: 4/1/4
URL: www.rts.edu
Established: 1965 Annual Graduate Tuition & Fees: N/A
Enrollment: N/A Coed
Affiliation or Control: Independent Non-Profit IRS Status: 501(c)3
Highest Offering: Doctorate; No Undergraduates
Accreditation: SC, MFCD, THEOL

00 Chancellor Emeritus .... Dr. Robert C. CANNADA, JR.
01 Chancellor/CEO .... Dr. J. Ligon DUNCAN
10 Chief Operations Financial Officer .... Mr. Bradley TISDALE
05 Provost and Chief Academic Officer .... Dr. Robert CARA
30 Sr Vice President for Development .... Mr. Matthew S. BRYANT
12 President Charlotte Campus .... Dr. Michael J. KRUGER
12 President Orlando Campus .... Dr. Scott R. SWAIN
12 President Jackson Campus .... Dr. Guy L. RICHARDSON
12 Executive Director Atlanta Campus .... Dr. Guy RICHARD
12 President Washington DC .... Dr. Scott REDD
106 Exec Dir RTS Global/Distance Educ .... Mr. David R. JOHN, III
06 Registrar Jackson Campus .... Ms. Kiama LEE
08 Library Director .... Mr. John CRABB
32 Director of Financial Aid .... Mr. Brian C. GAULT
04 Dir Operations/Asst to Pres Jackson .... Mrs. Wanda RUSHING
88 Dir Marriage/Family Therapy Jackson .... Dr. James B. HURLEY
18 Maintenance Director Jackson Campus .... Mr. Kyle SANDIDGE
108 Chief Institutional Assessment Ofcr .... Ms. Polly STONE
15 Director Personnel Svcs Jackson .... Ms. Linda COCHRAN
84 Director Enrollment Management .... Dr. Kevin COLLINS

Rust College (F)

150 Rust Avenue, Holly Springs MS 38635-2328
County: Marshall FICE Identification: 002433
Unit ID: 176318
Telephone: (662) 252-8000 Carnegie Class: Bac-Diverse
FAX Number: (662) 252-7119 Calendar System: Semester
URL: www.rustcollege.edu
Established: 1866 Annual Undergrad Tuition & Fees: $9,500
Enrollment: 856 Coed
Affiliation or Control: United Methodist IRS Status: 501(c)3
Highest Offering: Baccalaureate
Accreditation: SC, SW

01 President .... Dr. David L. BECKLEY
111 Vice President for College Relation .... Dr. Ishmell H. EDWARDS
10 Vice President for Finance .... Mr. Donald MANNING-MILLER
05 VP for Academic Affairs .... Dr. Sandra C. VAUGHN
06 Registrar .... Ms. Eleanor CLAYBORN
08 Library Director .... Mrs. Anita W. MOORE
13 Director Computer Center .... Ms. Barbara NAYLOR MOORE
32 Dean of Administrative Services .... Mr. Clarence E. SMITH
35 Director Student Activities .... Mr. Frederick TAYLOR
37 Director of Financial Aid .... Mr. Marlon JONES
25 Director Contracts & Grants .... Mrs. Christine L. RATCLIFF
29 Director Alumni Development .... Ms. Jo Ann SCOTT
89 Chair First Year Experience .... Dr. Vida MAYS
26 Director of Public Relations .... Vacant
21 Comptroller .... Ms. Glenda KING
84 Dean of Enrollment Services .... Mr. Braque TALLEY
23 Director Student Health Services .... Ms. Jannie LUELLEN
39 Director Student Housing .... Ms. Tanya K. KIRK
36 Director of Career Pathways .... Ms. Sandra BURKE
18 Director Physical Plant .... Mr. Robert CURRY
83 Division Chair Social Science .... Dr. Alfred J. STOVALL
15 Director Personnel Services .... Ms. Patricia PEGUES
19 Chief of Security .... Mr. Eric SCOTT
30 Director of Development .... Ms. Jo Ann SCOTT
40 Bookstore Manager .... Mrs. Patricia HARRIS
42 College Chaplain .... Mr. Kelvin KOSH
96 Director of Purchasing .... Ms. Ollie BOWENS
28 Director of Diversity .... Miss Patricia PEGUES
50 Division Chair Business .... Mr. Richard FREDERICK
53 Division Chair Education .... Dr. Leon HOWARD
79 Division Chair Humanities .... Dr. Margaret DELASHMIT
81 Chair Division Science & Math .... Dr. Doris WARD
70 Chair Department of Social Work .... Dr. Gemma BECKLEY
105 Director Web Services .... Vacant
41 Athletic Director .... Mr. Stanley STUBBS
101 Secretary of the Institution/Board .... Mrs. Willa TERRY
106 Dir Online Education/E-learning .... Dr. Helen OLIVER
38 Director Student Counseling .... Mr. Clarence E. SMITH
09 Director of Institutional Research .... Dr. Charles WILLIAMS
90 Director Academic Computing .... Mrs. Mollie PEGUES
91 Director Administrative Computing .... Mrs. Barbara N. MOORE

Southeastern Baptist College (G)

4229 Highway 15 N, Laurel MS 39440-1096
County: Jones FICE Identification: 002435
Unit ID: 176336
Telephone: (601) 426-6346 Carnegie Class: Spec-4-yr-Faith
FAX Number: (601) 426-6347 Calendar System: Semester
URL: www.southeasternbaptist.edu
Established: 1948 Annual Undergrad Tuition & Fees: $4,790
Enrollment: 38 Coed
Affiliation or Control: Baptist IRS Status: 501(c)3
Highest Offering: Baccalaureate
Accreditation: BI

01 Interim President .... Dr. Scott C. CARSON
05 Academic Dean .... Dr. Scott CARSON
32 Dean of Student Services .... Dr. Daryle COATS
13 Director Information Technology .... Mr. Hubert DYESS
07 Director of Admissions .... Mr. Ronnie KITCHENS
06 Registrar .... Mrs. Emma BOND
08 Director of Library .... Mrs. Amy E. HINTON

Southwest Mississippi Community College (A)

1156 College Drive, Summit MS 39666-9029
County: Pike FICE Identification: 002436
Unit ID: 176354
Telephone: (601) 276-2000 Carnegie Class: Assoc/MT-VT-High Trad
FAX Number: (601) 276-3888 Calendar System: Semester
URL: www.smcc.edu
Established: 1918 Annual Undergrad Tuition & Fees (In-District): $2,800
Enrollment: 1,884 Coed
Affiliation or Control: Local IRS Status: 501(c)3
Highest Offering: Associate Degree
Accreditation: SC, ADNUR, CAHIIM

01 President .... Dr. Steve BISHOP
05 Vice President of Academic Affairs .... Ms. Alicia SHOWS
10 Vice President of Financial Affairs .... Mr. Andrew ALFORD
32 Vice President of Student Affairs .... Dr. Bill ASHLEY
75 Vice Pres Career & Tech Education .... Mr. Jeremy SMITH
88 Vice Pres Physical Resources .... Mr. Bill TUCKER
06 Vice President Admissions/Registrar .... Mr. Matthew CALHOUN
37 Financial Aid Director .... Ms. Joni WILKINSON
09 Director of Institutional Research .... Ms. Lea TOUCHSTONE
08 Librarian .... Ms. Laura RIDDLE
39 Dir Student Activities/Housing .... Ms. Ashley GRAY

Tougaloo College (B)

500 West County Line Road, Tougaloo MS 39174-9999
County: Madison FICE Identification: 002439
Unit ID: 176406
Telephone: (601) 977-7730 Carnegie Class: Bac-A&S
FAX Number: (601) 977-7739 Calendar System: Semester
URL: www.tougaloo.edu
Established: 1869 Annual Undergrad Tuition & Fees: $10,600
Enrollment: 872 Coed
Affiliation or Control: United Church Of Christ IRS Status: 501(c)3
Highest Offering: Master's
Accreditation: SC

01 President .... Dr. Beverly W. HOGAN
05 Provost/VP for Acad & Stdnt Affs .... Dr. Asoka SRINIVASSAN
111 Vice Pres Institutional Advance .... Dr. Delores Bolden STAMPS
10 Vice Pres Finance Administration .... Dr. Cynthia MELVIN
18 Vice Pres for Facilities Management .... Mr. Kelle MENOGAN
84 Dean for Enrollment Management .... Ms. Linda DANIELS
20 Assoc Prov/VP for Acad & Stdnt Affs .... Dr. Robert BLAINE
08 Int Director of Library Services .... Ms. Susan SPRINGER
13 Chief Information Officer .... Ms. Denese CARROLL
37 Director of Student Financial Aid .... Ms. Maria THOMAS
09 Dir of Inst Effectiveness/Research .... Mr. Carlos SMITH
06 Registrar .... Ms. Carolyn L. EVANS
15 Director Human Resources .... Ms. Doretha PRESLEY
26 Dir Communications/Public Affairs .... Mr. Kendall G. LITTLE
29 Director of Alumni Affairs .... Mrs. Doris BRIDGEMAN
07 Admissions Manager .... Mr. Xavier AMOS
36 Director of Career Services .... Ms. Whitney MCDOWELL
44 Director of Advancement Services .... Ms. Valerie SMITH
46 Int Dir of Sponsored Pgms/Research .... Mr. Kerry THOMAS
88 Director of TRiO .... Dr. Valvia WILSON
38 Director of Counseling Services .... Dr. Rosie HARPER
96 Purchasing Agent .... Ms. Tracey MINOR
102 Asst VP for Foundation/Spons Pgms .... Dr. Motice BRUCE
19 Director Security/Safety .... Ms. Edna DRAKE
39 Director Student Housing .... Ms. Tracey PAUL
101 Secretary of the Institution/Board .... Mrs. Brenda H. WILSON
104 Director Study Abroad Educ .... Dr. Loye ASHTON
105 Director Web Services .... Ms. Virginia VARDAMAN
41 Athletic Director .... Dr. James C. COLEMAN

University of Mississippi (C)

P.O. Box 1848, University MS 38677
County: Lafayette FICE Identification: 002440
Unit ID: 176017
Telephone: (662) 915-7211 Carnegie Class: DU-Highest
FAX Number: (662) 915-7010 Calendar System: Semester
URL: www.olemiss.edu
Established: 1844 Annual Undergrad Tuition & Fees (In-State): $7,744
Enrollment: 23,212 Coed
Affiliation or Control: State IRS Status: 501(c)3
Highest Offering: Doctorate
Accreditation: SC, ART, CACREP, CAEPN, CLPSY, CS, DIETC, DIETD, ENG, FEPAC, JOUR, LAW, MUS, NRPA, PHAR, SP, SW, THEA

01 Chancellor .... Dr. Jeffrey S. VITTER
05 Senior Associate Provost .... Dr. Noel E. WILKIN
10 Vice Chanc Administration & Finance .... Mr. Larry D. SPARKS
26 Int VC for University Relations .... Dr. Alice CLARK
32 Vice Chancellor for Student Affairs .... Dr. Brandi HEPHNER LABANC
46 Int VC Research/Sponsored Programs .... Dr. Josh GLADDEN
28 Vice Chanc Diversity/Cmty Engagemnt .... Ms. Katrina M. CALDWELL
35 Asst VC Student Affs/Dean Students .... Dr. Melinda SUTTON
51 Assoc Prov/Dir Outreach/Cont Stds .... Dr. Tony AMMETER
06 Asst Provost & Registrar .... Dr. Charlotte Fant PEGUES
85 Ast Prov/Ast to Chanc Multicul Affs .... Dr. Donald R. COLE
08 Dean of Libraries .... Ms. Cecilia BOTERO
13 Chief Information Officer .... Dr. Kathryn F. GATES
30 Chief Development Officer .... Mr. Denson HOLLIS
29 Exec Director of Alumni Affairs .... Mr. Kurt PURDOM
37 Director of Financial Aid .... Mrs. Laura DIVEN-BROWN
36 Director of Career Center .... Ms. Toni D. AVANT
41 Director Intercollegiate Athletics .... Mr. Ross BJORK
15 AVC/Dir of Human Res & Contr Svcs .... Mr. Clayton H. JONES
18 Director of Facilities Management .... Mr. Ashton PEARSON
19 Dir/Chief Univ Police/Campus Safety .... Mr. Tim POTTS
38 Dir of University Counseling Center .... Dr. Quinton T. EDWARDS, JR.
23 Director University Health Services .... Dr. Travis W. YATES
39 AVC Student Affs/Dir Stdnt Housing .... Mr. Lionel MATEN
09 Director Institutional Research .... Ms. Katie BUSBY
22 Dir Equal Oppty/Reg Compliance .... Ms. Rebecca B. BRESSLER
100 Chief of Staff to the Chancellor .... Mrs. Sue T. KEISER
43 General Counsel .... Mr. Lee TYNER
96 Director of Procurement Services .... Ms. Rachel R. BOST
06 Associate Registrar .... Mrs. Denise KNIGHTON
21 Controller .... Mrs. Nina JONES
07 Director of Admissions .... Mr. Whitman SMITH
50 Dean School of Business Admin .... Dr. Kendall B. CYREE
49 Dean College of Liberal Arts .... Dr. Lee COHEN
81 Dean School of Applied Sciences .... Dr. Velmer S. BURTON, JR.
53 Dean School of Education .... Dr. David ROCK
54 Dean School of Engineering .... Dr. Alex CHENG
61 Interim Dean School of Law .... Dr. Deborah H. BELL
67 Dean of the School of Pharmacy .... Dr. David D. ALLEN
88 Dean School of Accountancy .... Dr. W. Mark WILDER
60 Dean Meek Sch Journalism/New Media .... Dr. H. Will NORTON
58 Int Dean of the Graduate School .... Dr. Christy M. WYANDT
92 Dean of SM Barksdale Honors College .... Dr. Douglass SULLIVAN-GONZALEZ
86 Spec Asst to Chanc Govt Affairs .... Mr. Perry SANSING
88 University Ombudsman .... Mrs. Brett HARRIS
116 Director of Audit .... Ms. Tanya SATTERFIELD

University of Mississippi Medical Center (D)

2500 N State Street, Jackson MS 39216-4505
County: Hinds FICE Identification: 004688
Unit ID: 176026
Telephone: (601) 984-1000 Carnegie Class: Not Classified
FAX Number: (601) 984-1013 Calendar System: Semester
URL: www.umc.edu
Established: 1955 Annual Undergrad Tuition & Fees (In-State): N/A
Enrollment: N/A Coed
Affiliation or Control: State IRS Status: 501(c)3
Highest Offering: Doctorate
Accreditation: SC, CAHIIM, DENT, DH, IPSY, MED, MT, NMT, NURSE, OT, PHAR, PTA, RAD, RADMAG

01 Vice Chancellor Health Affairs .... Dr. LouAnn WOODWARD
100 Chief of Staff to Vice Chancellor .... Dr. Brian RUTLEDGE
10 Chief Financial Officer .... Vacant
11 Chief Administrative Officer .... Dr. Jonathan WILSON
13 Chief Information Officer and CIMO .... Dr. Paul VEREGGE
46 Associate Vice Chanc Research .... Dr. Richard SUMMERS
05 Assoc VC for Academic Affairs .... Dr. Ralph H. DIDLAKE
23 Assoc Vice Chanc Clinical Affairs .... Dr. Charles O'MARA
17 CEO Univ Hosp & Health Systems .... Mr. Kevin COOK
88 Sr Advisor to VC for External Aff .... Dr. Claude BRUNSON
43 Chief Legal Officer .... Mr. Jeffrey WALKER
28 Chief Diversity & Inclusion Officer .... Dr. Juanyce TAYLOR
52 Vice Dean for Medical Educ SOM .... Dr. Loretta JACKSON-WILLIAMS
66 Dean School of Nursing .... Dr. Kim HOOVER
58 Dean Sch Grad Stds Health Sciences .... Dr. Joey GRANGER
76 Dean Sch Health Related Profess .... Dr. Jessica H. BAILEY
52 Dean of School of Dentistry .... Dr. David A. FELTON
66 Dean School Population Health .... Dr. Bettina BEECH
67 Assoc Dean for Clinical Affs/SOPH .... Dr. Leigh A. ROSS

University of Southern Mississippi (E)

118 College Drive, #5001, Hattiesburg MS 39406-0001
County: Forrest FICE Identification: 002441
Unit ID: 176372
Telephone: (601) 266-1000 Carnegie Class: DU-Higher
FAX Number: (601) 266-5756 Calendar System: Semester
URL: www.usm.edu
Established: 1910 Annual Undergrad Tuition & Fees (In-State): $7,659
Enrollment: 14,551 Coed
Affiliation or Control: State IRS Status: 501(c)3
Highest Offering: Doctorate
Accreditation: SC, AAFCS, ANEST, ART, AUD, CAATE, CAEPN, CIDA, CLPSY, CONST, COPSY, CS, DANCE, DIETD, DIETI, ENGT, JOUR, KIN, LIB, MFCD, MT, MUS, NURSE, PH, PHLEB, SCPSY, SP, SW, THEA

01 President .... Dr. Rodney D. BENNETT
04 Assistant to the President .... Ms. Christa MCLEOD
05 Provost & VP for Academic Affairs .... Dr. Steven MOSER
10 VP of Finance & Administration .... Vacant
12 VP for Gulf Coast Campus .... Dr. Steven G. MILLER
32 Vice President for Student Affairs .... Dr. Thomas BURKE
108 Assoc Prov Institutional Effect .... Dr. Doug MASTERSON
46 Vice President Research .... Dr. Gordon CANNON
84 Asst VP Enrollment Management .... Ms. Kate HOWARD
35 Assoc Vice President Student Affs .... Mr. Sid GONSOULIN
53 Dean College Education/Psychology .... Dr. Trent GOULD
49 Dean College Arts & Letters .... Dr. Maureen RYAN
50 Dean College Business .... Dr. Faye GILBERT
66 Dean College Nursing .... Dr. Kathy MASTERS
72 Dean College Science/Technology .... Dr. Chris WINSTEAD
92 Dean of Honors College .... Dr. Ellen WEINAUER
76 Interim Dean College Health .... Dr. Trent GOULD
58 Dean Graduate School .... Dr. Karen COATS
08 Dean/University Librarian .... Dr. John EYE
18 Asst VP Planning & Facilities Mgmt .... Dr. Chris CRENSHAW
13 Chief Information Officer .... Mr. David SLIMAN
41 Director Intercollegiate Athletics .... Mr. Jon GILBERT
06 Registrar .... Mr. Greg PIERCE
25 Asst VP for Research Administration .... Ms. Marcia LANDEN
09 Assoc Prov Institutional Research .... Dr. Michelle ARRINGTON
45 Dir of Institutional Effectiveness .... Mrs. Kathryn LOWERY
29 Alumni Activities/Exec Director .... Mr. Jerry DEFATTA
36 Director Career Services .... Mr. Russell ANDERSON
21 Asc VP for Finance & Controller .... Ms. Allyson EASTERWOOD
22 Title IX Coordinator .... Dr. Rebecca MALLEY
38 Director of Counseling Center .... Dr. Deena CRAWFORD
23 Director of Health Services .... Dr. Melissa ROBERTS
39 Director of Residence Life .... Dr. Scott BLACKWELL
15 Associate VP of Human Resources .... Mrs. Krystyna VARNADO
96 Director Procurement & Contracts .... Mr. Steve BALLEW
07 Interim Director of Admissions .... Ms. Susan W. SCOTT
26 Chief Communication Officer .... Mr. James P. COLL
88 Asst to Pres Military/Vet Stdnt Aff .... Gen. Jeff HAMMOND
102 Exec Dir USM Foundation .... Ms. Stace L. MERCIER
104 Assoc VP for Intl Programs .... Dr. Daniel NORTON
106 Dir Learn Enhancement Ctr .... Dr. Tom HUTCHINSON
19 Chief of Police .... Mr. Bob HOPKINS
43 Dir Legal Services/General Counsel .... Mr. Robert D. GHOLSON
86 Vice President for External Affairs .... Mr. Chad DRISKELL
37 Director Student Financial Aid .... Mr. David WILLIAMSON

Virginia College (F)

920 Cedar Lake Road, Biloxi MS 39532-2107
Telephone: (228) 546-9100 Identification: 666073
Accreditation: ACICS

† Branch campus of Virginia College, Birmingham, AL.

Virginia College (G)

5841 Ridgewood Road, Jackson MS 39211
Telephone: (601) 977-0960 Identification: 666032
Accreditation: ACICS, SURGT

† Branch campus of Virginia College, Birmingham, AL.

Wesley Biblical Seminary (H)

787 E Northside Drive, Jackson MS 39206-4945
County: Hinds FICE Identification: 025162
Unit ID: 176451
Telephone: (601) 366-8880 Carnegie Class: Spec-4-yr-Faith
FAX Number: (601) 366-8832 Calendar System: Semester
URL: www.wbs.edu
Established: 1974 Annual Graduate Tuition & Fees: N/A
Enrollment: 92 Coed
Affiliation or Control: Interdenominational IRS Status: 501(c)3
Highest Offering: Master's; No Undergraduates
Accreditation: THEOL

01 President .... Dr. John E. NEIHOF, JR.
05 VP Academic Affairs/Academic Dean .... Dr. Chris LOHRSTORFER
07 Exec VP Recruitment/Student Svcs .... Rev. Rob POCAI
30 Vice President Development .... Mr. Joshua FREIDEMAN
10 Director Business Affairs .... Ms. Peggy PRICE
08 Director of Library Services .... Ms. Grace ANDREWS
06 Registrar/Director Financial Aid .... Mr. Karl LUMAN

William Carey University (I)

710 William Carey Parkway, Hattiesburg MS 39401
County: Forrest FICE Identification: 002447
Unit ID: 176479
Telephone: (601) 318-6051 Carnegie Class: Masters/L
FAX Number: N/A Calendar System: Trimester
URL: www.wmcarey.edu
Established: 1892 Annual Undergrad Tuition & Fees: $11,700
Enrollment: 4,224 Coed
Affiliation or Control: Southern Baptist IRS Status: 501(c)3
Highest Offering: Doctorate
Accreditation: SC, CAEPN, IACBE, MUS, NURSE, OSTEO, @PTA

01 President/Chief Executive Officer .... Dr. Tommy KING
03 Provost .... Dr. Scott HUMMEL
05 Vice President of Academic Affairs .... Dr. Garry M. BRELAND
10 Vice Pres Business Affs/CFO .... Mr. Grant GUTHRIE
32 Vice Pres for Student Support .... Mrs. Valerie BRIDGEFORTH
46 Vice President Inst Effectiveness .... Dr. Bennie R. CROCKETT
63 Dean College Osteopathic Medicine .... Dr. James TURNER
12 Admin Dean Tradition Campus .... Mr. Gerald BRACEY
50 Dean School of Business .... Dr. Cheryl DALE
53 Dean School of Education .... Dr. Benjamin BURNETT
83 Dean Sch Natural/Behavioral Science .... Dr. Frank BAUGH
66 Dean School of Nursing .... Dr. Janet WILLIAMS
49 Dean School of Arts & Letters .... Dr. Myron NOONKESTER
64 Dean School of Music & Ministry .... Dr. Don ODOM
73 Chair School of Ministry Studies .... Dr. Daniel CALDWELL
84 Dean of Enrollment Management .... Mr. William N. CURRY
58 Dean of Graduate Studies .... Dr. Frank BAUGH
20 Academic Dean for Tradition .... Dr. Cassandra CONNOR

09 Director of Institutional Research ... Mrs. Susan CURRY
06 Registrar ... Mrs. Gayle KNIGHT
08 Director of Libraries ... Mr. Reese POWELL
29 Alumni Director ... Mrs. Pam SHEARER
26 Chief Public Relations Officer ... Vacant
13 Director of Information Technology ... Mr. Jeff ANDREWS
92 Director of Honors Program ... Dr. Jay RICHARDSON
114 Director of Budget Management ... Mr. Grant GUTHRIE
41 Athletic Director ... Mr. D. J PULLEY
18 Dir Facilities/Grounds/Maintenance ... Mr. Robert BLEVINS
21 Dir Business Svcs Tradition Campus ... Mr. Gerald BRACEY
12 Director of Keesler Center ... Ms. Amanda KNESAL
15 Associate VP of Human Resources ... Ms. Deidre SHOWS
19 Director Campus Security ... Mr. Bob BLEVINS
88 Coord of Instructional Technology ... Vacant
07 Director of Admissions ... Mrs. Alissa KING
04 Administrative Asst to President ... Mrs. Charlotte GREEN
106 E-Learning Coordinator ... Ms. Shanna MURRAY-LUKE

MISSOURI

A. T. Still University of Health Sciences (A)

800 W Jefferson Street, Kirksville MO 63501-1497
County: Adair — FICE Identification: 002477
Unit ID: 177834
Telephone: (660) 626-2391 — Carnegie Class: Spec-4-yr-Med
FAX Number: (660) 626-2672 — Calendar System: Semester
URL: www.atsu.edu
Established: 1892 — Annual Graduate Tuition & Fees: N/A
Enrollment: 3,357 — Coed
Affiliation or Control: Independent Non-Profit — IRS Status: 501(c)3
Highest Offering: First Professional Degree; No Undergraduates
Accreditation: NH, DENT, OSTEO, PH

01 President ... Dr. Craig PHELPS
05 Sr VP Academic Affairs ... Dr. Norman GEVITZ
63 Dean KCOM ... Dr. Margaret WILSON
32 VP Student Affairs ... Mrs. Lori HAXTON
111 VP University Advancement ... Dr. Shaun SOMMERER
43 VP & General Counsel ... Mr. Matthew HEEREN
46 VP Inst Res Grants & Info Systems ... Dr. John HEARD
52 Dean MO Sch of Dentistry/Oral Hlth ... Dr. Dwight MCLEOD
88 Dean Col of Graduate Hlth Studies ... Dr. Don ALTMAN
52 Dean AZ Sch of Dentistry/Oral Hlth ... Dr. Robert TROMBLY
76 Dean AZ Sch of Health Sciences ... Dr. Randy DANIELSEN
63 Dean Sch of Osteo Med in AZ ... Dr. Jeffrey MORGAN
10 VP Finance & Administration/CFO ... Mr. Rick RIEDER
35 Assoc VP AZ Student Affairs ... Mrs. Beth POPPRE
13 Asst VP Info Technologies/Services ... Mr. Bryan KRUSNIAK
07 Asst VP Admissions ... Dr. David KOENECKE
88 VP Strat Univ Partnershps/Diversity ... Dr. Gary CLOUD
45 Sr VP Strat Planning & Univ Init ... Dr. O.T WENDEL
25 Associate VP Sponsored Programs ... Mrs. Gaylah SUBLETTE
04 Asst to Pres & Secretary to BoT ... Mrs. Norine EITEL
06 Registrar ... Dr. Deanna HUNSAKER
08 Director Library ... Mr. Michael KRONENFIELD
15 Asst VP Human Resources/AA Ofcr . Mrs. Donna BROWN WYATT
18 Director Facilities/Plant Operation ... Mr. Robert EHRLICH
37 Dir Student Financial Assistance ... Mr. Steven JORDEN
38 Director Student Counseling ... Mr. Thomas VAN VLECK
96 Director Purchasing ... Mr. Corey LOUDER
19 Director Security ... Mr. Bob FRAIZER
28 Director of Diversity ... Mr. Clinton NORMORE
20 Associate VP/SVP Academic Affairs ... Dr. Ann BOYLE
110 Associate VP University Advancement ... Mr. Bob BEHNEN
88 Assistant VP/SVP Academic Affairs ... Dr. Leonard GOLDSTEIN
21 Assistant VP for Finance ... Mrs. Tonya GRIMM
09 Director AT Still Research Inst ... Dr. Brian DEGENHARDT
29 Director Alumni Relations ... Mrs. Kimberly BLACKMAN

† Arizona campus accreditation includes ARPCA, AUD, CAATE, DENT, OSTEO, OT, PTA.

American Business & Technology University (B)

1018 West Saint Maartens Drive, Saint Joseph MO 64506
County: Buchanan — FICE Identification: 041187
Unit ID: 457688
Telephone: (816) 279-7000 — Carnegie Class: Bac/Assoc-Assoc Dom
FAX Number: (888) 890-8190 — Calendar System: Other
URL: www.abtu.edu
Established: 2001 — Annual Undergrad Tuition & Fees: N/A
Enrollment: 299 — Coed
Affiliation or Control: Proprietary — IRS Status: Proprietary
Highest Offering: Master's
Accreditation: DEAC

01 President & CEO ... Mr. Sam ATIEH
11 Vice President ... Mr. Lute ATIEH
84 VP of Enrollment/Retention ... Mr. Eddie COLON
37 VP of Financial Aid ... Dr. Michael CAMPBELL
05 Chief Academic Officer ... Dr. Luanne HAGGARD
13 Chief Information Officer ... Mr. Ramsey ATIEH
10 Chief Financial Officer ... Mr. Dan MARLOW
20 Program Development Officer ... Dr. Donald LADER
108 Accreditation/Compliance Officer ... Mr. Chad BREAZILE
06 Registrar ... Mrs. Kourtney DRAKE
07 Director of Admissions ... Mr. Richard LINGLE

American Trade School (C)

3925 Industrial Drive, Saint Ann MO 63074
County: Saint Louis — FICE Identification: 041748
Unit ID: 461573
Telephone: (314) 423-1900 — Carnegie Class: Not Classified
FAX Number: (314) 423-1911 — Calendar System: Quarter
URL: www.americantradeschool.edu
Established: 2003 — Annual Undergrad Tuition & Fees: N/A
Enrollment: 97 — Coed
Affiliation or Control: Proprietary — IRS Status: Proprietary
Highest Offering: Associate Degree
Accreditation: ACCSC

01 President ... Mr. John VATTEROTT, JR.
03 Director ... Mr. Turner BROOKS

Aquinas Institute of Theology (D)

23 S Spring Avenue, Saint Louis MO 63108-3323
County: City of Saint Louis — FICE Identification: 001632
Unit ID: 176600
Telephone: (314) 256-8800 — Carnegie Class: Spec-4-yr-Faith
FAX Number: (314) 256-8888 — Calendar System: Semester
URL: www.ai.edu
Established: 1951 — Annual Graduate Tuition & Fees: N/A
Enrollment: 128 — Coed
Affiliation or Control: Roman Catholic — IRS Status: 501(c)3
Highest Offering: Doctorate; No Undergraduates
Accreditation: THEOL

01 President ... Rev. Sean MARTIN
05 Academic Dean ... Rev. Gregory HEILLE
111 VP Institutional Advancement ... Ms. Sue WALLACE
06 Registrar ... Mrs. Erin HAMMOND
84 Director Recruitment and Admissions ... Mr. Bernie BACKER
32 Director Student Services ... Mr. Kevin SWEENEY
29 Director Alumni ... Mr. David WERTHMANN
26 Dir Communications/Financial Aid ... Mrs. Jan LINGUA
90 Director Instructional Technology ... Mr. Daniel MOORE

The Art Institute of St. Louis (E)

1520 South Fifth Street, Suite 107,
Saint Charles MO 63303
Telephone: (636) 688-9281 — Identification: 770738
Accreditation: #ACICS

† In teach-out mode.

Assemblies of God Theological Seminary (F)

1435 N Glenstone Avenue, Springfield MO 65802-2131
County: Greene — FICE Identification: 012120
Unit ID: 176619
Telephone: (417) 268-1000 — Carnegie Class: Spec-4-yr-Faith
FAX Number: (417) 268-1001 — Calendar System: Semester
URL: www.agts.edu
Established: 1972 — Annual Graduate Tuition & Fees: N/A
Enrollment: 323 — Coed
Affiliation or Control: Assemblies Of God Church — IRS Status: 501(c)3
Highest Offering: Doctorate; No Undergraduates
Accreditation: THEOL

05 AGTS Dean/Vice President ... Dr. James H. RAILEY
20 Associate Dean ... Dr. Paul W. LEWIS
58 Dir Intercultural Doctoral Studies ... Dr. DeLonn L. RANCE
58 Dir PhD Biblical Interp & Theol ... Dr. James H. RAILEY
58 Director DMin Program ... Dr. Cheryl A. TAYLOR
42 Director of Spiritual Formation ... Dr. Jay P. TAYLOR
88 Director of Veteran Center ... Mrs. Stormy M. DAVIS
26 Director of Integrated Marketing ... Mrs. Robin L. STRATHDEE
08 Asst Director of Library Services ... Mr. Rick E. OLIVER
06 Seminary Registration/Degree Audit ... Mrs. Kathy L. HARRISON
37 Financial Aid Coordinator ... Mr. Brian L. HAWK
29 Coord of Institutional & Alum Rels ... Ms. Christina M. AYRES

† The Seminary continues to offer its educational programs as a distinct unit within the consolidated Evangel University, Springfield, MO.

Avila University (G)

11901 Wornall Road, Kansas City MO 64145-9990
County: Jackson — FICE Identification: 002449
Unit ID: 176628
Telephone: (816) 942-8400 — Carnegie Class: Masters/M
FAX Number: (816) 942-3362 — Calendar System: Semester
URL: www.avila.edu
Established: 1916 — Annual Undergrad Tuition & Fees: $27,312
Enrollment: 1,885 — Coed
Affiliation or Control: Roman Catholic — IRS Status: 501(c)3
Highest Offering: Master's
Accreditation: NH, IACBE, NURSE, RAD, SW

01 President ... Dr. Ron SLEPITZA
05 Provost/VP of Academic Affairs ... Dr. Cathryn PRIDAL
20 VP Instl Effectiveness/Info Svcs ... Dr. Sue KING
10 Vice Pres for Finance/Admin Svcs ... Mr. Paul TOLER
84 VP for Enrollment & Athletics ... Mr. Brandon JOHNSON
32 AVP Student Development/Success ... Darby GOUGH
13 Coordinator Information Management ... Mr. Jon GAMBILL
26 Sr Dir Marketing/Communications ... Mr. Darren ROUBINEK
30 Sr Director Development ... Ms. Deanna NELSON
06 Registrar/Director Student Records ... Ms. Michelle DRISCOLL
08 Director of Library ... Ms. Kathleen FINEGAN
37 Director of Financial Aid ... Ms. Crystal BRUNTZ
42 Dir Mission Effect & Campus Ministr ... Mr. David M. ARMSTRONG
21 Controller ... Mr. Joseph H. SJUTS
29 Director Alumni ... Mrs. Bailey CARR
41 Assistant Athletic Director ... Mrs. Cristina COWAN
15 Director of Human Resources ... Ms. Janet MCMANUS
18 Director Campus Services ... Mr. Mike STUCKEY
40 Bookstore Manager ... Mr. John A. TARANTO
38 Coord Counseling & Career Services ... Ms. Elizabeth MCKINLEY

Baptist Bible College (H)

628 E Kearney St, Springfield MO 65803-3498
County: Greene — FICE Identification: 013208
Unit ID: 176664
Telephone: (417) 268-6000 — Carnegie Class: Spec-4-yr-Faith
FAX Number: (800) 819-8330 — Calendar System: Semester
URL: www.gobbc.edu
Established: 1950 — Annual Undergrad Tuition & Fees: $10,536
Enrollment: 401 — Coed
Affiliation or Control: Baptist — IRS Status: 501(c)3
Highest Offering: First Professional Degree
Accreditation: #NH, BI

01 President ... Mr. Mark L. MILIONI
05 Vice President of Academic Affairs ... Dr. Greg T. CHRISTOPHER
10 Vice President of Financial Affairs ... Mr. Jason L. TODD
32 Vice President of Student Affairs ... Mr. Nathaniel S. HARMON
18 Chief Facilities/Physical Plant ... Mr. Chris C. WILLIAMS
06 Registrar ... Mr. Terry A. ALLCORN
07 Dir Enrollment Services ... Mr. John DECKER
37 Director of Financial Aid ... Mr. Brian RAINS
39 Director of Resident Life ... Mr. Bill J. LEVERGOOD
15 Director of Human Resources ... Miss Emily MILIONI
19 Director Security/Safety ... Mr. Glenn COZZENS
40 Virtual Bookstore ... Mrs. Julie BECK
08 Director of Library Services ... Mr. Jon JONES
51 Dean of Continuing Education ... Ms. Cheryl PAGE
04 Administrative Asst to President ... Mrs. Barbara MILIONI
09 Director of Institutional Research ... Mr. Shannon MULFORD

Bolivar Technical College (I)

1135 North Oakland Avenue, Bolivar MO 65613
Telephone: (417) 777-5062 — Identification: 667033
Accreditation: ACICS

Brookes Bible College (J)

10257 St. Charles Rock Road, St. Ann MO 63074
County: St. Louis — Identification: 667137
Telephone: (314) 773-0083 — Carnegie Class: Not Classified
FAX Number: (314) 736-6293 — Calendar System: Semester
URL: www.brookesbible.org
Established: 1909 — Annual Undergrad Tuition & Fees: N/A
Enrollment: N/A — Coed
Affiliation or Control: Independent Non-Profit — IRS Status: 501(c)3
Highest Offering: Associate Degree
Accreditation: @BI

00 Chairman of the Board ... Dr. James CLARK
01 President ... Rev. Robert D. THURMAN, JR.
05 Academic Dean ... Dr. Allan D. HENDERSON
07 Director of Admissions ... Mr. Joshua CLUTTERHAM
10 Chief Financial Officer ... Ms. Tamara SANDOVAL
08 Librarian ... Ms. Kathleen B. MILLIGAN
110 Comm & Development Coordinator ... Ms. Bethany BOYLE

Bryan University (K)

3215 LeMone Industrial Boulevard, Columbia MO 65201
Telephone: (573) 777-5550 — Identification: 770725
Accreditation: ACICS

† Branch campus of Bryan University, Springfield, MO.

Bryan University (L)

4255 Nature Center Way, Springfield MO 65804
County: Greene — FICE Identification: 030663
Unit ID: 369516
Telephone: (417) 862-5700 — Carnegie Class: Bac/Assoc-Mixed
FAX Number: (417) 865-7144 — Calendar System: Other
URL: www.bryanu.edu
Established: 1982 — Annual Undergrad Tuition & Fees: $15,400
Enrollment: 289 — Coed
Affiliation or Control: Proprietary — IRS Status: Proprietary
Highest Offering: Master's
Accreditation: ACICS

01 Executive Director ... Mr. Scott HAAR

Calvary University (M)

15800 Calvary Road, Kansas City MO 64147-1341
County: Cass — FICE Identification: 002450
Unit ID: 176789

Telephone: (816) 322-0110 Carnegie Class: Spec-4-yr-Faith
FAX Number: (816) 331-4474 Calendar System: Semester
URL: www.calvary.edu
Established: 1932 Annual Undergrad Tuition & Fees: $11,700
Enrollment: 319 Coed
Affiliation or Control: Independent Non-Profit IRS Status: 501(c)3
Highest Offering: First Professional Degree
Accreditation: **NH**, BI

01 President/CEO ... Dr. Christopher CONE
10 Chief Operating Officer/VP ... Mr. Randy GRIMM
05 Chief Academic Officer/VP ... Dr. Teddy BITNER
111 Chief Development Officer/VP ... Dr. Skip HESSEL
32 Vice President of Student Services ... Mr. Cory D. TROWBRIDGE
41 Athletic Director ... Miss Jeanette REGIER
100 Director of the President's Office ... Mr. Jeff CAMPA
97 Dean of the College ... Dr. Michel DODDS
73 Dean of the Seminary ... Dr. Thomas BAURAIN
58 Dean of the Graduate School ... Dr. Eric STRICKER
06 Registrar ... Mr. Gary ROGERS
13 Director Information Technology ... Mr. Aaron HEATH
07 Director of Admissions ... Mrs. Tania EDWARDS
19 Director of Security ... Mr. Glenn WILLIAMS
37 Director of Financial Aid ... Mr. Robert CRANK
08 Head Librarian ... Miss Tiffany SMITH
09 Institutional Research Coordinator ... Mr. Charles KURTZ
15 Human Resources Coordinator ... Mrs. Jolayne ROGERS
29 Alumni Relations Coordinator ... Mrs. Sara KLAASSEN
121 Director of The Academic Center ... Dr. Terri STRICKER
88 Director of Christian Ministries ... Mr. Joe EVERETT
109 Director of Food Service ... Mr. Joe DAPRA
105 Director Web Services ... Vacant
30 Executive Director of Advancement ... Mr. Mervin WAGNER
35 Asst Director of Student Services ... Miss Arely PEREZ
27 Marketing Manager ... Mr. Brian MASON
18 Director of Maintenance ... Vacant

Central Christian College of the Bible (A)

911 E Urbandale Drive, Moberly MO 65270-1997
County: Randolph FICE Identification: 022664
Unit ID: 176910
Telephone: (660) 263-3900 Carnegie Class: Spec-4-yr-Faith
FAX Number: (660) 263-3936 Calendar System: Semester
URL: www.cccb.edu
Established: 1957 Annual Undergrad Tuition & Fees: $13,700
Enrollment: 271 Coed
Affiliation or Control: Christian Churches And Churches of Christ
IRS Status: 501(c)3
Highest Offering: Baccalaureate
Accreditation: **BI**

01 President ... Dr. David B. FINCHER
05 Academic Dean ... Dr. Eric A. STEVENS
10 VP of Business & Finance ... Mrs. Lara LAWRENCE
07 Executive Director of Admissions ... Mr. Rocky CHRISTENSEN
88 Director of Stewardship ... Mr. Alan G. WILSON
04 Exec Assistant to the President ... Mrs. Sherry L. WALLIS
32 Exec Dir of Student Development ... Mr. Darryl C. AMMON
34 Dean of Women ... Ms. Anne P. MENEAR
41 Athletic Director ... Mr. Jack DEFREITAS
08 Head Librarian ... Mrs. Patty A. AGEE
06 Registrar ... Vacant
37 Director of Financial Aid ... Mrs. Rhonda J. DUNHAM
13 Director of Information Technology ... Mr. Aaron MERRITT
18 Physical Plant Manager ... Mr. Mark E. DUNHAM
40 Bookstore Manager ... Mrs. Kelly HARDING
35 Director of Student Services ... Mrs. Lori PETER
39 Residence Director - Women ... Mrs. Anne MENEAR
39 Residence Director - Men ... Mr. Rocky CHRISTENSEN
33 Dean of Men ... Mr. Aaron P. WELCH
101 Secretary of the Institution/Board ... Mr. Ronald SELF
106 Online Education Coordinator ... Mr. James FRANKE

† Onsite students accepted into a degree or certificate program will receive Full-Tuition Scholarship which equals cost of tuition up to 18 hrs/semester. Scholarship may be reduced from deficiencies in grades, Christian service, or chapel attendance.

Central Methodist University (B)

411 Central Methodist Square, Fayette MO 65248-1198
County: Howard FICE Identification: 002453
Unit ID: 445267
Telephone: (660) 248-3391 Carnegie Class: Masters/S
FAX Number: (660) 248-2287 Calendar System: Semester
URL: www.centralmethodist.edu
Established: 1854 Annual Undergrad Tuition & Fees: $5,400
Enrollment: 4,516 Coed
Affiliation or Control: United Methodist IRS Status: 501(c)3
Highest Offering: Master's
Accreditation: **NH**, CAATE, MUS, NURSE, @PTAA

01 President ... Dr. Roger D. DRAKE
05 Provost ... Dr. Rita GULSTAD
13 VP Technology & Planning ... Mr. Chad GAINES
111 VP Advancement/Alumni Rels ... Dr. Joshua JACOBS
32 VP Student Engagement ... Mr. Kenneth R. OLIVER
84 VP Enrollment Management ... Vacant
10 VP Finance & Administration ... Ms. Julee SHERMAN
08 Director of Information Resources ... Ms. Cynthia DUDENHOFFER
37 Director of Financial Assistance ... Vacant
29 Exec Dir Advancement & Alumni Pgm ... Mr. David HUTCHISON
44 Dir Annual Giving & Advance Opers ... Ms. Jackie JACKSON
07 Director of Admissions ... Ms. Aimee SAGE
106 Asst Dean Online Programs ... Ms. Stephanie BRINK
09 Coordinator Institutional Research ... Ms. Amber MONNIG
26 Exec Dir Marketing Communications ... Mr. Kent PROPST
04 Administrative Asst to President ... Ms. Catherine SHANAHAN
41 Athletic Director ... Mr. Brian SPIELBAUER
15 Director of Human Resources ... Ms. Kimberly THOMSON
06 Registrar ... Ms. Kathryn WINEGARD
18 Chief Facilities/Physical Plant ... Mr. Derry WISWALL
19 Safety Coordinator ... Mr. Wayne MORSE
36 Director Student Placement ... Ms. Nicolette YEVICH
40 Bookstore Manager ... Ms. Jill BARRINGHAUS
39 Associate Dean of Students ... Mr. Brad DIXON

Chamberlain University-St. Louis (C)

11830 Westline Industrial, Ste 106, St. Louis MO 63146
Telephone: (314) 991-6200 Identification: 770494
Accreditation: **&NH**, NURSE

† Branch campus of Chamberlain University-Addison, Addison, IL

City Vision University (D)

3101 Troost Ave. Suite 200, Kansas City MO 64109-1845
County: United States FICE Identification: 041191
Unit ID: 457697
Telephone: (816) 960-2008 Carnegie Class: Bac-Diverse
FAX Number: (816) 256-8471 Calendar System: Other
URL: www.cityvision.edu
Established: 1998 Annual Undergrad Tuition & Fees: $7,000
Enrollment: 106 Coed
Affiliation or Control: Other IRS Status: 501(c)3
Highest Offering: Master's
Accreditation: **DEAC**

01 Executive Director/President ... Dr. Andrew SEARS
50 Dean of School of Business ... Dr. Joy VANN-HAMILTON
88 Addiction Studies Department Chair ... Mrs. Lynda MITTON
10 Financial Accounting Manager ... Mrs. AnnMarie CAMERON-THOMPSON
07 Director of Admissions ... Ms. Nancy YOUNG

† Mail address is 31 Torrey St, Dorchester, MA 02124-3543.

College of the Ozarks (E)

PO Box 17, Point Lookout MO 65726-0017
County: Taney FICE Identification: 002500
Unit ID: 178697
Telephone: (417) 334-6411 Carnegie Class: Bac-Diverse
FAX Number: (417) 335-2618 Calendar System: Semester
URL: www.cofo.edu
Established: 1906 Annual Undergrad Tuition & Fees: $18,930
Enrollment: 1,441 Coed
Affiliation or Control: Independent Non-Profit IRS Status: 501(c)3
Highest Offering: Baccalaureate
Accreditation: **NH**, ACFEI, DIETD, NURSE

01 President ... Dr. Jerry C. DAVIS
03 Vice President ... Dr. Howell W. KEETER
05 VP for Academic Affairs ... Dr. Eric BOLGER
30 Director of Development ... Mrs. Natalie RASNICK
10 Chief Financial Officer ... Mr. Charles F. HUGHES
11 Dean of Administration ... Dr. Marvin SCHOENECKE
103 Dean of Work Education ... Dr. Marvin SCHOENECKE
32 Dean of Student Services ... Mr. Nick SHARP
07 VP for Patriotic Activities ... Dr. Marci LINSON
42 VP of Christian Ministries ... Dr. Justin CARSWELL
88 VP Cultural Affs/Dean Character Ed ... Dr. Sue HEAD
06 Registrar ... Dr. Fran FORMAN
29 Director of Alumni Affairs ... Mrs. Angela WILLIAMSON
36 Director of Career Placement ... Mr. Jim FREEMAN
37 Director of Financial Aid ... Mr. Jeff FORD
26 Director of Public Relations ... Mrs. Valorie COLEMAN
96 Director of Purchasing ... Mr. Kurt MCDONALD
38 Student Counseling ... Mrs. Pat MCLEAN
04 Administrative Asst to President ... Ms. Elizabeth HUDSON
13 Chief Info Technology Officer ... Ms. Debbie HENDERSON
18 Chief Facilities/Physical Plant ... Mr. Jody BRASWELL
41 Athletic Director ... Mr. Steve SHEPHERD
08 Head Librarian ... Ms. Gwen SIMMONS
19 Director Security/Safety ... Mr. Robert BRIDGES

Columbia College (F)

1001 Rogers Street, Columbia MO 65216-0001
County: Boone FICE Identification: 002456
Unit ID: 177065
Telephone: (573) 875-8700 Carnegie Class: Masters/L
FAX Number: (573) 875-7209 Calendar System: Semester
URL: www.ccis.edu
Established: 1851 Annual Undergrad Tuition & Fees: $20,936
Enrollment: 14,759 Coed
Affiliation or Control: Christian Church (Disciples Of Christ)
IRS Status: 501(c)3
Highest Offering: Master's
Accreditation: **NH**, NURSE

01 President ... Dr. Scott DALRYMPLE
04 Sr Exec Assistant to the President ... Ms. Mary BROWN
05 Provost/VP Academic Affairs ... Dr. David STARRETT
51 VP Adult Higher Education ... Dr. Jeff MUSGROVE
11 SVP/Chief Operations Officer ... Mr. Kevin PALMER
106 VP Online Educ/Online Campus ... Dr. Piyusha SINGH
10 Chief Financial Officer ... Mr. Bruce E. BOYER
32 Dean for Student Affairs ... Mr. Dave ROBERTS
30 Exec Director of Advancement ... Ms. Suzanne ROTHWELL
18 Exec Director of Plant/Facilities ... Mr. Cliff JARVIS
27 Executive Director of Marketing ... Mr. Brad WUCHER
07 Director of Admissions ... Ms. Stephanie JOHNSON
06 Registrar ... Ms. Jennifer THORPE
29 Director of Alumni Relations ... Ms. Ann MERRIFIELD
26 Exec Director of Public Relations ... Ms. Suzanne ROTHWELL
37 Director of Financial Aid ... Ms. Sharon A. ABERNATHY
08 Director of Stafford Library ... Ms. Janet CARUTHERS
35 Director of Student Activities ... Ms. Kim COKE
36 Director Career Services Center ... Mr. Dan GOMEZ-PALACIO
15 Executive Director Human Resources ... Ms. Patty FISCHER
23 Director of Health Services ... Ms. Judy WOOD
13 Chief Information Officer ... Mr. Gary STANOWSKI
55 Sr Dir Adult Higher Educ Acad Spprt ... Mr. Eric CUNNINGHAM
58 Associate Dean Graduate Studies ... Vacant
41 Athletic Director ... Mr. Bob P. BURCHARD
09 Director Institutional Research ... Ms. Misty HASKAMP
19 Director of Campus Safety ... Mr. Robert KLAUSMEYER
21 Bursar ... Mr. Randal SCHENEWERK

Conception Seminary College (G)

37174 State Highway VV, PO Box 502,
Conception MO 64433-0502
County: Nodaway FICE Identification: 002467
Unit ID: 177083
Telephone: (660) 944-3105 Carnegie Class: Spec-4-yr-Faith
FAX Number: (660) 944-2829 Calendar System: Semester
URL: www.conception.edu
Established: 1883 Annual Undergrad Tuition & Fees: $20,706
Enrollment: 96 Male
Affiliation or Control: Roman Catholic IRS Status: 501(c)3
Highest Offering: Baccalaureate
Accreditation: **NH**

01 Rector & President ... Rev. Brendan MOSS
11 Director of Administration ... Mrs. Amy K. SCHIEBER
32 Dean of Students ... Rev. Patrick G. YORK
05 Dean of Academic Affairs ... Dr. William BROWNSBERGER
10 Business Manager/Dir Auxiliary Svcs ... Bro. Jacob KUBAJAK
30 Development Director ... Rev. Macario MARTINEZ
07 Director of Admissions ... Mrs. Jeanette SCHIEBER
37 Director of Student Financial Aid ... Bro. Justin J. HERNANDEZ
06 Registrar ... Mrs. Jeanette SCHIEBER
29 Director of Alumni ... Bro. Thomas SULLIVAN
08 Librarian ... Mr. Chris BRITE
26 Director of Communications ... Mrs. Jenny HUARD
13 Director of Information Technology ... Mr. Tony MEISTER
38 Director of Counseling Services ... Rev. Duane REINERT
41 Director of Wellness Program ... Mr. Skip SHEAR
101 Secretary of the Institution/Board ... Mrs. Amy SCHIEBER
18 Chief Facilities/Physical Plant ... Mr. Mark WIEDERHOLT

Concorde Career College (H)

3239 Broadway Boulevard, Kansas City MO 64111-2407
County: Jackson FICE Identification: 023616
Unit ID: 155283
Telephone: (816) 531-5223 Carnegie Class: Spec-4-yr-Other Health
FAX Number: (816) 756-3231 Calendar System: Other
URL: www.concorde.edu
Established: 1986 Annual Undergrad Tuition & Fees: N/A
Enrollment: 435 Coed
Affiliation or Control: Proprietary IRS Status: Proprietary
Highest Offering: Baccalaureate
Accreditation: **ACCSC**, COARC, DH, PTAA

01 President ... Colleen MCDERMOTT
05 Academic Dean ... April RAHE
07 Director Student Recruitment ... Vacant

Concordia Seminary (I)

801 Seminary Place, Saint Louis MO 63105-3168
County: Saint Louis FICE Identification: 002457
Unit ID: 177092
Telephone: (314) 505-7000 Carnegie Class: Spec-4-yr-Faith
FAX Number: (314) 505-7001 Calendar System: Semester
URL: www.csl.edu
Established: 1839 Annual Graduate Tuition & Fees: N/A
Enrollment: 580 Coed
Affiliation or Control: Lutheran Church - Missouri Synod
IRS Status: 501(c)3
Highest Offering: Doctorate; No Undergraduates
Accreditation: **NH**, THEOL

01 President ... Rev Dr. Dale A. MEYER
03 Executive Vice President/COO ... Mr. Michael LOUIS
05 Provost ... Rev Dr. Jeffrey KLOHA
10 Sr VP for Finance/Administration ... Mr. Chad A. CATTOOR
111 Senior VP for Advancement ... Mrs. Vicki BIGGS
58 Dean of Advanced Studies ... Rev Dr. Gerhard BODE
06 Registrar ... Mrs. Beth R. MENNEKE

08 Director of Library Services .... Rev. Benjamin HAUPT
20 Director Curriculum Design & Devel .... Rev Dr. Jason BROGE
88 Director Center for Hispanic Study ....Rev Dr. Leopoldo A. SANCHEZ
15 Director of Human Resources .... Mr. Thomas MYERS
18 Director Campus Facilities .... Mr. Martin HAGUE
36 Director of Placement .... Rev Dr. Glenn NIELSEN
37 Director of Student Financial Aid .... Mrs. Laura HEMMER
13 Chief Information Officer .... Mr. John KLINGER
29 Sr Coor Alumni Relations .... Ms. Melodie BOSTIC
04 Executive Asst to President .... Ms. Pamela K. DAVITZ
07 Director of Admissions .... Rev. William WREDE
09 Director of Institutional Research .....Rev Dr. Alan BORCHERDING
44 Director Gift Operations .... Mrs. Valerie SOMMER

Cottey College (A)

1000 W Austin Boulevard, Nevada MO 64772-2763
County: Vernon FICE Identification: 002458
Unit ID: 177117
Telephone: (417) 667-8181 Carnegie Class: Bac/Assoc-Mixed
FAX Number: (417) 667-8103 Calendar System: Semester
URL: www.cottey.edu
Established: 1884 Annual Undergrad Tuition & Fees: $19,300
Enrollment: 326 Female
Affiliation or Control: Independent Non-Profit IRS Status: 501(c)3
Highest Offering: Baccalaureate
Accreditation: NH, MUS

01 President .... Dr. Jann WEITZEL
05 Vice President for Academic Affairs .... Dr. Chioma R. UGOCHUKWU
88 Dir Center Women's Leadership ....Ms. Denise C. HEDGES
36 Coord Career & Transfer Planning ....Ms. Renee HAMPTON
04 Executive Asst to President .... Mrs. Tricia BOBBETT
10 VP for Administration & Finance ....Mrs. Amy RUETTEN
111 Int VP Institutional Advancement .... Ms. Betsy MCREYNOLDS
32 VP for Student Life ....Dr. Mari Anne PHILLIPS
42 Dir Spiritual Life & Diversity .... Ms. Erica SIGAUKE
84 VP for Enrollment Management .... Ms. JoEllen LINDNER
30 Director of Development .... Ms. Staci KEYS
26 VP for Marketing/Comm .... Ms. Carla FARMER
07 Director of Admissions .... Ms. Angela MOORE
06 Registrar .... Ms. Marcia MORTON
08 Library Director .... Ms. Courtney TRAUTWEILER
18 Director Physical Plant/Security .... Mr. Neal R. SWARNES
19 Dir Campus Security & Title IX .... Mr. Mark BURGER
27 Director of Public Information .... Mr. Steve E. REED
105 Webmaster .... Ms. Donna LENHARTH
15 Director of Human Resources ....Ms. Betsy A. MCREYNOLDS
91 Director Administrative Computing .... Mr. Keith J. SPENCER
120 Instructional Technology Specialist .... Mr. Mike DOMBROSKI
37 Director of Financial Aid .... Mrs. Sherry R. PENNINGTON
90 Director Academic Computing .... Mr. Adam S. DEAN
39 Director of Student Housing .... Ms. Helen LODGE
41 Director of Athletics .... Ms. Stephanie BEASON
40 Bookstore Manager ....Mrs. Lois J. WITTE
09 Coordinator Institutional Research .... Mrs. Nancy KERBS
29 Director of Alumnae Relations ....Ms. Christi ELLIS
38 Coordinator of Counseling .... Ms. Jeanna BRAUER
88 Director of Food Service .... Mr. Michael RICHARDSON
88 Director of PEO Relations .... Ms. Margaret HAVERSTIC
121 Coordinator Academic Advising .... Ms. Stephanie MCGHEE
85 Coord International Student Svcs .... Vacant

Covenant Theological Seminary (B)

12330 Conway Road, Saint Louis MO 63141-8697
County: Saint Louis FICE Identification: 004707
Unit ID: 177126
Telephone: (314) 434-4044 Carnegie Class: Spec-4-yr-Faith
FAX Number: (314) 434-4819 Calendar System: 4/1/4
URL: www.covenantseminary.edu
Established: 1956 Annual Graduate Tuition & Fees: N/A
Enrollment: 535 Coed
Affiliation or Control: Presbyterian Church In America IRS Status: 501(c)3
Highest Offering: Doctorate; No Undergraduates
Accreditation: NH, THEOL

01 President .... Dr. Mark DALBEY
05 VP of Academics .... Dr. Jay SKLAR
10 VP of Business and Finance .... Ms. Alice EVANS
111 VP of Advancement .... Mr. John RANHEIM
88 VP of Strategic Academic Projects .... Dr. Daniel M. DORIANI
08 Library Director .... Rev. James C. PAKALA
20 Dean of Academic Administration .... Ms. Jessica SWIGART
32 Dean of Students .... Rev. Michael HIGGINS
18 Director of Facilities & Operations .... Mr. David BROWN
07 Director of Admissions ....Mr. Mark SANDVIG
13 Director of Information Technology .... Mr. Richard HIERS
37 Director of Financial Aid .... Ms. Melinda CONN
06 Registrar .... Ms. Betsy GASOSKE
29 Alumni/Placement Services Director .... Mr. Joel HATHAWAY
21 Controller .... Mr. Jason ROBEY
35 Associate Dean of Student Life .... Mr. Mark MCELMURRY
35 Associate Dean of Student Life .... Ms. Suzanne BATES
38 Associate Dean of Counseling .... Mrs. Sabrina HICKEL
88 Associate Dean of Academic Services ....Ms. Diane PRESTON
88 Director of Field Education .... Mr. Jeremy MAIN

Cox College (C)

1423 N Jefferson Avenue, Springfield MO 65802-1917
County: Greene FICE Identification: 020682
Unit ID: 176770
Telephone: (417) 269-3401 Carnegie Class: Spec-4-yr-Other Health
FAX Number: (417) 269-3581 Calendar System: Semester
URL: www.coxcollege.edu
Established: 1907 Annual Undergrad Tuition & Fees: $11,170
Enrollment: 871 Coed
Affiliation or Control: Independent Non-Profit IRS Status: 501(c)3
Highest Offering: Master's
Accreditation: NH, ADNUR, DIETI, DMS, NURSE, RAD

01 Interim President .... Dr. Robert LUNN
05 Vice Pres Acad Affairs/Inst Effect .... Dr. Amy DEMELO
09 Vice Pres College Svcs/Inst Rsrch .... Dr. Jim MOORE
10 Vice Pres Business/Finance .... Jayne BULLARD
32 VP Student Affs/Marketing/Comm/Dev .... Dr. Sonya HAYTER
58 Dean Interprof Graduate Studies ....Dr. Kathleen JACKSON
37 Director of Financial Aid .... Steve NICHOLS
07 Director of Admissions .... Antoinette MURPHY
08 Director Library Services .... Wilma BUNCH

Crowder College (D)

601 Laclede Avenue, Neosho MO 64850-9165
County: Newton FICE Identification: 002459
Unit ID: 177135
Telephone: (417) 451-3223 Carnegie Class: Assoc/HT-High Trad
FAX Number: (417) 455-5702 Calendar System: Semester
URL: www.crowder.edu
Established: 1963 Annual Undergrad Tuition & Fees (In-District): $2,448
Enrollment: 5,584 Coed
Affiliation or Control: Local IRS Status: 501(c)3
Highest Offering: Associate Degree
Accreditation: NH, ADNUR, EMT, OTA

01 President .... Dr. Jennifer METHVIN
10 Vice President of Finance .... Mrs. Amy RAND
05 Vice President of Academic Affairs .... Dr. Glenn COLTHARP
32 Vice President of Student Affairs .... Mrs. Tiffany SLINKARD
26 Assoc VP of Information Services .... Mrs. Mickie MAHAN
75 Assoc VP of Careers & Tech Educ .... Mr. Edward STEPHENS
07 Director of Admissions .... Mr. JP DICKEY
09 Director of Institutional Research .... Vacant
08 Director of Lee Library .... Mr. Eric DEATHERAGE
27 Director of Public Information .... Mrs. Cindy BROWN
41 Athletic Director .... Mr. John SISEMORE
37 Director of Financial Aid .... Mrs. Stephanie FERGUSON
15 Director of Human Resources ....Mrs. Michelle PAUL
111 Dir of Institutional Advancement .... Mrs. Cindy BRANSCUM
40 Bookstore Manager .... Ms. Colleen HOLLAND
36 Career Services Coordinator ....Ms. Abby TRIBBLE
13 Director of Information Technology .... Mr. Mitch CORDRAY

Culver-Stockton College (E)

One College Hill, Canton MO 63435-1257
County: Lewis FICE Identification: 002460
Unit ID: 177144
Telephone: (573) 288-6000 Carnegie Class: Bac-Diverse
FAX Number: (573) 288-6611 Calendar System: Semester
URL: www.culver.edu
Established: 1853 Annual Undergrad Tuition & Fees: $25,415
Enrollment: 1,066 Coed
Affiliation or Control: Christian Church (Disciples Of Christ) IRS Status: 501(c)3
Highest Offering: Master's
Accreditation: NH, #CAATE, IACBE, MUS

01 President ....Dr. Kelly M. THOMPSON
05 Vice Pres Academic Affs/Dean of Col ....Dr. Daniel K. SILBER
32 Dean of Student Life ....Dr. D. Christopher GILL
07 Director of Admission .... Mrs. Misty MCBEE
111 VP for Advancement .... Dr. Bill SHEEHAN
06 Registrar/Director Inst Research .... Mrs. Chris HUEBOTTER
08 Librarian ....Dr. Katherine MARNEY
26 Asst Director of Communications .... Mr. Brian KROEGER
37 Director Financial Aid .... Mrs. Tina WISEMAN
29 Director of Alumni Programs .... Mrs. Melissa DUBUQUE
91 Exec Dir Admin Systems & Service ....Mr. Joseph LIESEN
10 Chief Financial Officer .... Mrs. Diane BOZARTH
15 Director of Human Resources .... Mrs. Amy BAKER
35 Coordinator of Student Activities .... Mr. Bill BOXDORFER
42 Chaplain ....Rev. Amanda SORENSON
41 Athletic Director .... Mr. Patrick ATWELL
40 Wildcat Warehouse Manager .... Mrs. Sharon FARR
04 Assistant to the President .... Ms. Cindy FREELS
19 Director Campus Security & Facil .... Mr. Michael BRINGER
49 Chair Applied Liberal Arts/ Sciences .... Dr. Lauren SCHELLENBERGER
50 Chair Business Education & Law .... Dr. Kimberly GAITHER
57 Chair Fine Applied & Literary Arts .... Dr. Dylan MARNEY
20 Assoc Dean of Instruction .... Dr. Dell Ann JANNEY
92 Director of Honors Program .... Dr. Haidee HEATON
93 International Student Coordinator .... Ms. Alissa MURPHY
24 Media Coordinator .... Mrs. Julie WRIGHT
44 Director of the Annual Fund .... Mr. Steve MILLER
36 Coord of Career Services/Internship .... Ms. Kara MANDRELL
39 Director of Residential Life .... Ms. Megan CATALANO
121 Associate Dean Academic Success .Dr. Holly ANDRESS-MARTIN

38 Dir Counseling/Student Wellness .... Ms. Susan MOON
09 Director of Institutional Research ....Mrs. Karla MCREYNOLDS
30 Director of Advancement Operations ....Mrs. Marjorie ELLISON
104 Director Study Abroad .... Dr. C. Patrick HOTLE
28 Director of Diversity .... Mr. Ernest EVANS

DeVry University - Kansas City Campus (F)

1310 E. 104th St., 2nd Floor, Kansas City MO 64131
Telephone: (816) 943-7300 FICE Identification: 002455
Accreditation: &NH, ENGT

† Regional accreditation is carried under the parent institution in Downers Grove, IL.

Drury University (G)

900 N Benton Avenue, Springfield MO 65802-3791
County: Greene FICE Identification: 002461
Unit ID: 177214
Telephone: (417) 873-7879 Carnegie Class: Bac-A&S
FAX Number: (417) 873-7529 Calendar System: Semester
URL: www.drury.edu
Established: 1873 Annual Undergrad Tuition & Fees: $25,905
Enrollment: 3,688 Coed
Affiliation or Control: Independent Non-Profit IRS Status: 501(c)3
Highest Offering: Master's
Accreditation: NH, ACBSP, CAEPN, MUS

01 President .... Dr. Timothy CLOYD
05 Provost .... Dr. Beth HARVILLE
10 Vice President for Admin & CFO .... Mr. Rob FRIDGE
32 Vice President for Student Services .... Dr. Tijuana S. JULIAN
111 Executive VP for Advancement .... Mr. Wayne CHIPMAN
20 Assoc VP Academic Affairs Quality ...... Dr. Peter K. MEIDLINGER
84 Vice President Enrollment Mgt .... Mr. Kevin KROPF
51 Assoc VP Academic Affairs - CCPS .... Mr. Jana NEISS
20 Assoc VP Academic Affairs Operation .... Dr. Bruce CALLEN
06 Registrar .... Mrs. Cindy M. JONES
13 AVP Tech Svcs/Sr Dir Info Svcs .... Mr. Val SERAFIMOV
37 Director of Financial Aid .... Ms. Rebecca AHRENS
08 Director of FW Olin Library .... Mr. William GARVIN
36 Dir Career Planning & Development .....Ms. Emily BUCKMASTER
15 Director of Human Resources .... Ms. Scotti SIEBERT
09 Director of Institutional Research .... Dr. Justin LEINAWEAVER
14 Chief Info Technology Officer (CIO) .... Mr. David J. HINSON
18 Chief Facilities/Physical Plant ....Mr. Brandon GAMMILL
100 Chief of Staff .... Mr. Aaron JONES
38 Dir Counseling/Disability/Testing .... Mr. Ed DERR
19 Director Safety/Security .... Ms. Sarene DEEDS
35 Director of Orientation .... Ms. Jennifer STEWART
39 Dir of Student Housing .... Ms. Holly BINDER
40 Director Univ Bookstore .... Ms. Valerie RAINS
41 Director of Athletics .... Mr. Mark FISHER
42 Chaplain .... Dr. Peter BROWNING
04 Executive Asst to President .... Ms. Donna HANLEY
101 Administrative Asst to the Board ....Ms. Bonnie WILCOX
104 Associate Dean Study Abroad .... Dr. Thomas RUSSO
106 Dir Online Education .... Mr. Steve HYNDS
50 Dean School of Business .... Dr. Robin SRONCE
53 Dean School of Education .... Dr. Lauren EDMONDSON
102 Dir Foundation/Corporate Relations .... Ms. Emma RUZICKA
28 Director of Diversity .... Ms. Rosalyn THOMAS
29 Director Alumni Relations .... Ms. Andrea BATTAGLIA
90 Director Academic Computing .... Mr. Gary SWADLEY

Drury University Cabool Campus (H)

801 Walnut Ave., PO Box 526, Cabool MO 65689
Telephone: (417) 962-5314 Identification: 770318
Accreditation: &NH

Drury University Ft. Leonard Wood Campus (I)

6002 Cikiradi Ave., Ft. Leonard Wood MO 65473
Telephone: (573) 329-4400 Identification: 770319
Accreditation: &NH

Drury University Lebanon Campus (J)

PO Box 509, Lebanon MO 65536
Telephone: (417) 532-9828 Identification: 770320
Accreditation: &NH

Drury University Rolla Campus (K)

1034 S. Bishop Avenue, Rolla MO 65401
Telephone: (573) 368-4959 Identification: 770321
Accreditation: &NH

East Central College (L)

1964 Prairie Dell Road, Union MO 63084-0529
County: Franklin FICE Identification: 008862
Unit ID: 177250
Telephone: (636) 584-6500 Carnegie Class: Assoc/HT-High Trad
FAX Number: (636) 583-1897 Calendar System: Semester
URL: www.eastcentral.edu
Established: 1968 Annual Undergrad Tuition & Fees (In-District): $2,376
Enrollment: 3,222 Coed
Affiliation or Control: Local IRS Status: 501(c)3
Highest Offering: Associate Degree

Accreditation: NH, ACFEI, ART, CAHIIM, EMT, MAC, MUS, NAIT, OTA

01 President .... Dr. C. Jon BAUER
10 Vice Pres Finance/Administration .... Mr. Phil PENA
05 Vice President Academic Affairs .... Dr. Tia L. ROBINSON
32 Vice President Student Development .... Ms. Shelli R. ALLEN
26 VP External Relations .... Mr. Joel DOEPKER
12 Director ECC Rolla .... Ms. Christina M. AYRES
30 Dir of Institutional Development .... Ms. Shannon M. GRUS
18 Director Facilities & Grounds .... Vacant
08 Director of Library Services .... Ms. Lisa M. FARRELL
96 Purchasing Manager .... Ms. Melissa D. POPP
79 Dean of Instruction .... Ms. Ann BOEHMER
81 Div Chair Math/Engineering/Science .... Dr. Isaiah KELLOGG
75 Dean of Career & Technical Educ .... Mr. Richard HUDANICK
83 Division Chair Social Sciences .... Dr. William CUNNINGHAM
64 Division Chair Music .... Mr. Timothy SEXTON
15 Director Human Resources .... Ms. Wendy HARTMANN
76 Dean of Health Sciences .... Ms. Robyn C. WALTER
37 Director Financial Aid .... Ms. Karen GRIFFIN
06 Registrar .... Ms. Sarah SCROGGINS
21 Director Financial Svcs/Comptroller .... Ms. Annette MOORE
09 Director of Institutional Research .... Ms. Bethany L. LOHDEN
27 Director of Public Relations .... Mr. Jay SCHERDER
13 Director Information Technology .... Mr. Doug HOUSTON
40 Bookstore/Mail/Imaging Coordinator .... Mr. Doug A. AGEE
121 Coordinator Advisement Services .... Mr. Paul LAMPE
103 Executive Director Workforce Devel .... Mr. Mardy LEATHERS
51 Coordinator Adult Educ & Literacy .... Ms. Alice WHALEN
24 Coordinator Instructional Design .... Mr. R. Chad BALDWIN
35 Coordinator Student Activities .... Ms. Courtney HENRICHSEN
04 Executive Asst to President .... Ms. Bonnie S. GARDNER
41 Athletic Director .... Mr. Jay MEHRHOFF
101 Secretary of the Institution/Board .... Ms. Bonnie GARDNER

Eden Theological Seminary (A)

475 E Lockwood Avenue,
Webster Groves MO 63119-3192

County: Saint Louis FICE Identification: 002462
Unit ID: 177278
Telephone: (314) 961-3627 Carnegie Class: Spec-4-yr-Faith
FAX Number: (314) 918-2626 Calendar System: 4/1/4
URL: www.eden.edu
Established: 1850 Annual Graduate Tuition & Fees: N/A
Enrollment: 152 Coed
Affiliation or Control: United Church Of Christ IRS Status: 501(c)3
Highest Offering: Doctorate; No Undergraduates
Accreditation: NH, THEOL

01 President .... Dr. David M. GREENHAW
05 Academic Dean .... Dr. Deborah KRAUSE
06 Registrar .... Ms. Michelle WOBBE
07 Director of Admissions .... Rev. Tiffany PITTMAN
04 Admin Asst to the President .... Ms. Danita CARTER
20 Director of Academic Programs .... Ms. Denise STAUFFER
101 Secretary to Board of Trustees .... Ms. Denise STAUFFER
108 Director of Assessment .... Ms. Michelle WOBBE
32 Dean of Students .... Rev. Carol SHANKS
10 Chief Financial Officer .... Ms. Tammy CRAIG
30 Director of Development .... Ms. Sandi LAFATA

Evangel University (B)

1111 N Glenstone, Springfield MO 65802-2191

County: Greene FICE Identification: 002463
Unit ID: 177339
Telephone: (417) 865-2815 Carnegie Class: Masters/S
FAX Number: (417) 865-9599 Calendar System: Semester
URL: www.evangel.edu
Established: 1955 Annual Undergrad Tuition & Fees: $22,081
Enrollment: 1,958 Coed
Affiliation or Control: Assemblies Of God Church IRS Status: 501(c)3
Highest Offering: Doctorate
Accreditation: NH, ACBSP, CAATE, CAEPN, MUS, SW

01 President .... Dr. Carol A. TAYLOR
10 Vice Pres for Business/Finance .... Ms. Linda ALLEN
32 VP for Student Development .... Dr. Sheri PHILLIPS
30 VP for University Advancement .... Dr. Michael KOLSTAD
05 VP for Academic Affairs/Provost .... Dr. Michael MCCORCLE
84 Vice Pres Enrollment Management .... Mr. Chris BELCHER
18 Director of Physical Plant .... Mr. Brian HAUFF
41 Director of Athletics .... Dr. Dennis MCDONALD
06 Registrar .... Mrs. Cathy WILLIAMS
27 Chief Information Officer .... Mr. Gary BLACKARD
08 Librarian .... Mr. Dale JENSEN
19 Director of Public Safety .... Mr. Todd REVELL
38 Director of Counseling Services .... Mr. Brian UPTON
29 Director Alumni Relations .... Mr. Doug JENKINS
37 Dir of Student Financial Services .... Mrs. Valerie SHARP
36 Career Development/Placement .... Mrs. Tina MOORE
42 Campus Pastor .... Rev. Greg JOHNS
26 Director of Public Relations .... Mr. Paul LOGSDON
07 Executive Director of Admissions .... Ms. Patricia HANSEN
23 Director of Health Services .... Ms. Susan BRYAN
21 Controller .... Mr. Jeff HUINDA
35 Director Student Life .... Miss Gina RENTSCHLER
15 Supervisor Human Resources .... Mrs. Ocki HAAS
39 Housing Coordinator .... Mrs. Pamela SMALLWOOD
09 Director of Institutional Research .... Dr. Linda WELLBORN
04 Executive Asst to President .... Mrs. Angela DENSE
101 Secretary of the Institution/Board .... Mrs. Joanne STROM

Fontbonne University (C)

6800 Wydown Boulevard, Saint Louis MO 63105-3098

County: Saint Louis FICE Identification: 002464
Unit ID: 177418
Telephone: (314) 862-3456 Carnegie Class: Masters/L
FAX Number: (314) 889-1451 Calendar System: Semester
URL: www.fontbonne.edu
Established: 1923 Annual Undergrad Tuition & Fees: $24,610
Enrollment: 1,713 Coed
Affiliation or Control: Roman Catholic IRS Status: 501(c)3
Highest Offering: Master's
Accreditation: NH, ACBSP, CAEP, DIETD, SP, SW

01 President .... Dr. J. Michael PRESSIMONE
05 Vice President Academic Affairs .... Dr. Carey ADAMS
30 Vice President Advancement .... Mrs. Kitty LOHRUM
32 Vice President Student Affairs .... Mr. Joseph DEIGHTON
10 Vice President Finance & Admin/CFO .... Ms. Lisa VAN SICKEL
84 Vice President Enrollment Mgt .... Mr. Joseph HAVIS
13 Vice Pres Information Technology .... Mr. Mark FRANZ
35 Associate Vice Pres Student Affairs .... Mrs. Carla HICKMAN
20 Associate VP Acad Affairs .... Dr. Corinne WOHLFORD
53 Dean Education .... Dr. Adam WEYHAUPT
50 Dean Global Business/Prof Studies .... Dr. Jay JOHNSON
76 Dean Educ/Allied Health Prof .... Dr. Gale RICE
88 Asst to the Pres for Mission Integ .... Dr. Mary Beth GALLAGHER
06 Registrar .... Mr. Seth CARRUTHERS
15 Director Human Resources .... Mrs. Linda PIPITONE
08 University Librarian .... Dr. Sharon MCCASLIN
45 Director Academic Resources .... Dr. Kevin PELZEL
09 Director Inst Research & Assessment .... Mrs. Meaghan ONG
26 Director Communications/Marketing .... Mr. Mark JOHNSON
106 Director Online Programs .... Ms. Joanne MATTSON
37 Director Financial Aid .... Dr. Matthew KEARNEY
88 Director Academic Advising .... Ms. Lee DELAET
85 Director International Affairs .... Mrs. Rebecca GRANT BAHAN
29 Director Alumni Relations .... Ms. Kate FLATLEY
41 Director Athletics .... Mrs. Maria BUCKEL
28 Director Multicultural Affairs .... Ms. Leslie DOYLE
88 Dir Ldrshp Educ & Stdnt Activities .... Dr. Janelle JULIAN
42 Director Campus Ministry .... Mrs. Lori HELFRICH
19 Director Public Safety .... Mr. Larry VERTREES
07 Associate VP Admission .... Ms. Michelle PALUMBO
18 Director Physical Plant .... Mr. Brent SPIES
04 Exec Asst to Pres/Board .... Mrs. Patricia ETTER
88 Dir Student Success/Engagement .... Ms. Amy SIMONS
36 Director Career Development .... Ms. Christine KELLER
38 Director Counseling and Wellness .... Ms. Claudia CHARLES

Global University (D)

1211 South Glenstone Avenue,
Springfield MO 65804-1894

County: Greene Identification: 666687
Unit ID: 247296
Telephone: (800) 443-1083 Carnegie Class: Not Classified
FAX Number: (417) 865-7167 Calendar System: Other
URL: www.globaluniversity.edu
Established: 2000 Annual Undergrad Tuition & Fees: N/A
Enrollment: N/A Coed
Affiliation or Control: Assemblies Of God Church IRS Status: 501(c)3
Highest Offering: Doctorate
Accreditation: NH

01 President .... Dr. Gary SEEVERS, JR.
03 Executive Vice President .... Rev. Keith HEERMANN
05 Provost .... Dr. David L. DEGARMO
20 Vice Provost Academic Support .... Dr. John (Jack) NILL
58 Dean Graduate School/Theology .... Dr. Randy J. HEDLUN
73 UG School of Bible & Theology .... Dr. Kevin FOLK
13 VP Info Tech/Media Dept .... Mr. Wade W. PETTENGER
10 Vice President Finance .... Mr. Mark PERRY
111 Vice President Advancement .... Ms. Nicole VICARI
07 Director of Enrollment Services .... Rev. Todd WAGGONER
06 Registrar .... Mrs. Lynne KROH
15 Director of Human Resources .... Ms. Jami NEMETI
04 Administrative Asst to President .... Ms. Kristin DEGARMO
08 Head Librarian .... Rev. Russ LANGFORD
09 Director of Institutional Research .... Rev. Brad AUSBURY
18 Chief Facilities/Physical Plant .... Mr. Bruce HAVENS

Goldfarb School of Nursing at Barnes-Jewish College (E)

4483 Duncan Avenue, Stop: 90-36-697,
Saint Louis MO 63110-1111

County: Saint Louis FICE Identification: 006389
Unit ID: 177719
Telephone: (314) 454-7055 Carnegie Class: Spec-4-yr-Other Health
FAX Number: (314) 362-9250 Calendar System: Trimester
URL: www.barnesjewishcollege.edu
Established: 1902 Annual Undergrad Tuition & Fees: N/A
Enrollment: 654 Coed
Affiliation or Control: Independent Non-Profit IRS Status: 501(c)3
Highest Offering: Doctorate
Accreditation: NH, ANEST, NURSE

01 Interim Dean .... Dr. Gretchen DRINKARD
10 Vice Dean for Finance/Admin .... Mr. Djuan COLEMAN
32 Vice Dean Stdnt Affairs/Diversity .... Dr. Michael WARD
46 Associate Dean for Research .... Dr. Jean DAVIS
15 Vice Dean/HR .... Ms. Rosalynn BRYANT
08 Library & Info Services Director .... Ms. Renee GORRELL
13 Information System Director .... Mr. Carlos PARDO
06 Registrar .... Ms. Terri MONTGOMERY
84 Director Enrollment Mgmnt .... Mr. Jason CROWE
04 Administrative Asst to President .... Ms. Beth HOOK
29 Director Alumni Relations .... Dr. June COWELL-OATES

Graceland University (F)

1401 West Truman Road, Independence MO 64050-3434

Telephone: (816) 833-0524 Identification: 666262
Accreditation: &NH, NURSE

† Regional accreditation is carried under the parent institution in Lamoni, IA.

Hannibal-LaGrange University (G)

2800 Palmyra Road, Hannibal MO 63401-1999

County: Marion FICE Identification: 009089
Unit ID: 177542
Telephone: (573) 221-3675 Carnegie Class: Bac-Diverse
FAX Number: (573) 221-6594 Calendar System: Semester
URL: www.hlg.edu
Established: 1858 Annual Undergrad Tuition & Fees: $21,810
Enrollment: 1,167 Coed
Affiliation or Control: Southern Baptist IRS Status: 501(c)3
Highest Offering: Master's
Accreditation: NH, ADNUR, NURSE

01 President .... Dr. Anthony W. ALLEN
05 VP for Academic Administration .... Dr. Miles S. MULLIN, II
45 VP for Institutional Effectiveness .... Dr. Raymond W. CARTY
10 VP for Business & Finance .... Mrs. Betty L. ANDERSON
111 VP for Institutional Advancement .... Mr. Jason GEIKEN
32 Dean of Student Development .... Dr. Jeffery BROWN
26 Director Public Relations .... Mrs. Carolyn A. CARPENTER
06 Registrar/Director of Records .... Mrs. Natasha RUSHING
37 Director of Financial Aid .... Mr. Brice D. BAUMGARDNER
29 Director Alumni Services .... Ms. Lauren YOUSE
36 Director Student Placement .... Dr. Karry D. RICHARDSON
08 Library Director .... Mrs. Julie A. ANDRESEN
18 Chief Facilities/Physical Plant .... Mr. Kevin RUSHING
19 Director Public Safety .... Mr. Kyle BRENNEMANN
39 Director of Residential Life .... Mr. Joshua PIERCE
41 Athletic Director .... Mr. Jason D. NICHOLS
40 University Bookstore Manager .... Mrs. Susan A. BOOTH
07 Director of Admissions .... Mr. Sean C. FREEMAN
30 Director of Development .... Mr. David DEXHEIMER
106 Dir Graduate and Online Division .... Dr. Jill ARNOLD

Harris-Stowe State University (H)

3026 Laclede Avenue, Saint Louis MO 63103-2199

County: Independent City FICE Identification: 002466
Unit ID: 177551
Telephone: (314) 340-3366 Carnegie Class: Bac-Diverse
FAX Number: (314) 340-3399 Calendar System: Semester
URL: www.hssu.edu
Established: 1857 Annual Undergrad Tuition & Fees (In-State): $5,220
Enrollment: 1,390 Coed
Affiliation or Control: State IRS Status: 501(c)3
Highest Offering: Baccalaureate
Accreditation: NH, ACBSP, CAEPN, IACBE

01 President .... Dr. Dwaun WARMACK
05 Provost & VP Academic Affairs .... Dr. Dwayne SMITH
10 VP Administration & Finance Affs .... Mr. Brian HUGGINS
13 Vice President IT Services .... Mr. James FOGT
111 Exec Dir Inst Adv/Spec Asst to Pres .... Ms. Leslie HOLLOWAY
06 Registrar .... Ms. Chauvette MCELMURRY
07 Dir Admissions/Advise/Retention .... Ms. Loretta MCDONALD
08 Director Library Services .... Mrs. Barbara NOBLE
37 Director Financial Assistance .... Mr. James GREEN
15 Int Director Human Resources .... Mr. Rodney GEE
38 Director Counseling Services .... Mrs. Vicki BERNARD
25 Exec Dir Title III/Sponsored Pgms .... Mrs. Heather BOSTIC
20 Director of Academic Success .... Mr. Marion BERRY
41 Director of Athletics .... Mr. Jamaal MAYO
88 Director of Business Services .... Ms. Barbara A. MORROW
36 Director of Career Services .... Mrs. Wanda MCNEIL
21 Comptroller/Grants Officer .... Mr. Brian HUGGINS
53 Dean College of Education .... Dr. Lelia VICKERS
50 Dean Busch School of Business .... Ms. Fatemeh ZAKERY
49 Dean College of Arts & Sciences .... Dr. Sudarson KANT
101 Secretary of the Institution/Board .... Mrs. Lea SUTHERLIN
19 Director Security/Safety .... Vacant
111 Exec Dir Institutional Advancement .... Ms. Leslie HOLLOWAY
32 Chief Student Affairs/Student Life .... Mr. Emmanuel LALANDE

Heartland Christian College (I)

500 New Creation Rd, Newark MO 63458

County: Knox Identification: 667091
Telephone: (660) 284-4800 Carnegie Class: Not Classified
FAX Number: (680) 284-4098 Calendar System: Semester
URL: www.heartlandcollege.edu
Established: 1992 Annual Undergrad Tuition & Fees: N/A
Enrollment: N/A Coed
Affiliation or Control: Non-denominational IRS Status: 501(c)3
Highest Offering: Associate Degree

Accreditation: BI

01 President .... Kris R. PALMER
05 Chief Academic Officer .... Martha PALMER
10 CFO .... David BARTON
06 Registrar .... Judi BARTON
08 Head Librarian .... Molly NICKERSON

Hickey College (A)

2700 North Lindbergh Boulevard, Saint Louis MO 63114
County: Saint Louis FICE Identification: 010279
Unit ID: 177579
Telephone: (314) 434-2212 Carnegie Class: Bac/Assoc-Mixed
FAX Number: (314) 434-1974 Calendar System: Other
URL: www.hickeycollege.edu
Established: 1933 Annual Undergrad Tuition & Fees: $13,930
Enrollment: 391 Coed
Affiliation or Control: Proprietary IRS Status: Proprietary
Highest Offering: Baccalaureate
Accreditation: ACICS, ACFEI

01 President .... Mr. Christopher A. GEARIN
05 Director of Education .... Ms. Connie L. SCOTT
32 Director of Student Services .... Ms. Deanna L. PECORONI

† In teach-out mode.

Jefferson College (B)

1000 Viking Drive, Hillsboro MO 63050-2441
County: Jefferson FICE Identification: 002468
Unit ID: 177676
Telephone: (636) 797-3000 Carnegie Class: Assoc/MT-VT-High Trad
FAX Number: (636) 789-4012 Calendar System: Semester
URL: www.jeffco.edu
Established: 1963 Annual Undergrad Tuition & Fees (In-District): $2,400
Enrollment: 4,705 Coed
Affiliation or Control: State/Local IRS Status: 501(c)3
Highest Offering: Associate Degree
Accreditation: NH, CAHIIM, EMT, OTA, PTAA, RAD

01 President .... Dr. Raymond V. CUMMISKEY
05 VP Instruction .... Dr. Caron DAUGHERTY
10 VP Finance & Administration .... Mr. Daryl GEHBAUER
32 VP Student Services .... Dr. Kimberly HARVEY
49 Dean of Arts & Science Education .... Dr. Shirley DAVENPORT
75 Dean Career/Technical Education .... Dr. Dena MCCAFFREY
15 Director of Human Resources .... Ms. Tasha D. WELSH
30 Executive Director of Development .... Ms. Patricia CHRISTEN
26 Director of PR & Marketing .... Mr. Roger A. BARRENTINE
21 Controller .... Mr. Richard H. HARDIN
13 Director Information Technology .... Mr. Tracy JAMES
81 Division Chair Math & Science .... Dr. Robert BRIELER
83 Div Chair Social Sciences/Business .... Dr. Terry KITE
60 Division Chair Comm/Fine Arts .... Dr. Michael BOOKER
76 Div Chair Health Occupation Prog .... Mr. Kenny WILSON
75 Div Chair Business/Technical Educ .... Mr. Christopher DEGEARE
90 Sr Dir for Online Educ/Assessment .... Mr. Allan A. WAMSLEY
45 Dir Institutional Effec/Strat Plng .... Ms. Patricia AUMANN
41 Director Athletics .... Mr. Greg MCVEY
31 Director Business/Community Develop .... Mr. Bryan D. HERRICK
18 Director Buildings & Grounds .... Mr. Dale RICHARDSON
19 Director Public Safety Programs .... Ms. Diane SCANGA
66 Director of Nursing .... Ms. Kathleen HARRIS
06 Registrar .... Ms. Stacey WILSON
37 Director Student Financial Services .... Ms. Sarah BRIGHT
08 Director Library Services .... Ms. Lisa PRITCHARD
121 Director Advising & Retention .... Ms. Kathy JOHNSTON
124 Director Student Support Services .... Ms. Diane ARNZEN
74 Director Veterinary Technology .... Ms. Dana A. NEVOIS
84 Director Enrollment Services .... Ms. Holly LINCOLN
88 Director Child Care Center .... Ms. Stephanie CAGE
39 Director Residential & Student Life .... Ms. Kristen YELTON
96 Procurement Coordinator .... Ms. Sheree BELL
04 Admin Asst to the President & Board .... Ms. Lisa VINYARD

Kansas City Art Institute (C)

4415 Warwick Boulevard, Kansas City MO 64111-1874
County: Jackson FICE Identification: 002473
Unit ID: 177746
Telephone: (816) 472-4852 Carnegie Class: Spec-4-yr-Arts
FAX Number: (816) 472-3439 Calendar System: Semester
URL: www.kcai.edu
Established: 1885 Annual Undergrad Tuition & Fees: $36,450
Enrollment: 645 Coed
Affiliation or Control: Independent Non-Profit IRS Status: 501(c)3
Highest Offering: Baccalaureate
Accreditation: NH, ART

01 The Nerman Family President .... Mr. Tony JONES
10 EVP for Administration/CFO .... Ms. Laura SNOW
05 EVP for Academic Affairs .... Dr. Bambi BURGARD
111 Senior VP for Advancement .... Ms. Nicolle RATLIFF
20 VP for Academic Affairs .... Dr. Milton KATZ
15 Director of Human Resources .... Ms. Jennifer VARGO
13 Vice Pres/Chief Information Officer .... Mr. Larry DICKERSON
32 Dean of Student Affairs .... Ms. Gina GOLBA
84 VP for Enrollment .... Ms. Karen TOWNSEND
07 Director of Admissions .... Ms. Julia WELLES
26 Director of Communications and PR .... Ms. Dana SAWYER
51 Dir Continuing/Professional Studies .... Ms. Cambria POTTER
06 Registrar .... Ms. Nancy EASTMAN
35 Assistant Dean of Student Affairs .... Mr. Joe TIMSON
38 Psychologist and Counseling Coord .... Ms. Elisabeth SUNDERMEIER
18 Facilities Director/Plant Services .... Ms. Roxie CURTIS
29 Director of Alumni Relations .... Mr. Marcus CAIN
37 Director of Financial Aid .... Ms. Lori BAER
21 Controller .... Ms. Suzette NAYLOR
36 Dir of Acad Advising & Career Svcs .... Ms. Tori SINCLAIR
08 Director of Library .... Ms. M.J POEHLER
24 Director of Creative Media .... Mr. Aldo BACCHETTA
19 Director of Safety & Security .... Mr. LaVern FIELDS
109 Director of Auxiliary Services .... Mr. Ed RODRIGUEZ
88 Director of H&R Block Artspace .... Ms. Raechell SMITH
21 Director of Finance & Accounting .... Ms. Leah REICHERT
04 Administrative Asst to President .... Ms. Mauri FAYNE
39 Director Student Housing .... Mr. Thomas YU
102 Dir Foundation/Corporate Relations .... Mr. Randy WILLIAMS

Kansas City University of Medicine & Biosciences (D)

1750 East Independence Avenue, Kansas City MO 64119
County: Jackson FICE Identification: 002474
Unit ID: 179812
Telephone: (816) 654-7000 Carnegie Class: Spec-4-yr-Med
FAX Number: (816) 654-7101 Calendar System: Semester
URL: www.kcumb.edu
Established: 1916 Annual Graduate Tuition & Fees: N/A
Enrollment: 1,163 Coed
Affiliation or Control: Independent Non-Profit IRS Status: 501(c)3
Highest Offering: First Professional Degree; No Undergraduates
Accreditation: NH, OSTEO

01 President & CEO .... Dr. Marc B. HAHN
05 Provost/EVP Academic & Rsrch Affs .... Dr. Edward R. O'CONNOR
10 CFO/Chief Operating Officer .... Mr. Joseph MASSMAN
31 Sr VP of Community Engagement .... Dr. Marcia NIELSEN
30 VP for Institutional Advancement .... Dr. Jane LAMPO
32 Vice Prov Student/Enrollment Svcs .... Dr. Richard P. WINSLOW
45 Assoc Prov IE/Accred/Inclusion .... Mr. Adrian R. CLARK
17 Exec Dean Col of Osteopathic Med .... Dr. Darrin D'AGOSTINO
12 Dean Joplin Campus .... Dr. Paula GREGORY
76 Dean College of Biosciences .... Dr. Robert WHITE
20 Assistant Dean Academic Affairs .... Dr. Schoen KRUSE
35 Asst Director for Student Affairs .... Ms. LeAnn K. CARLTON
35 Asst Dean Student Svcs Joplin .... Dr. Catherine DOBSON
100 Chief of Staff/Dir Govt Relations .... Dr. Brooke YODER
26 Exec Dir Marketing and Comm .... Ms. Angie BLEDSOE
08 Director of Library .... Ms. Marilyn J. DEGEUS
88 Director of Strategic Initiatives .... Mr. Pete STOBIE
06 Registrar .... Ms. Freda STRACK
18 Facilities Manager .... Ms. Anna GRAETHER
13 Director of Information Technology .... Mr. Lance HUGGINS
37 Director of Financial Aid .... Ms. Kristi NICHOL
88 Associate Dean of Clinical Educ .... Dr. John GRANETO
88 Admin Dir Clinical Education .... Ms. Valorie MILLICAN
19 Director Campus Operations .... Mr. James HERRINGTON
38 Director Counseling and Support Svc .... Dr. James DUGAN
29 Sr Dir Institutional Advancement .... Ms. Kathryn HARVEL
35 Exec Dir Community/Student Activity .... Ms. Sara E. SELKIRK
07 Director of Admissions .... Ms. Patricia HARPER

Kenrick-Glennon Seminary, Kenrick School of Theology (E)

5200 Glennon Drive, Saint Louis MO 63119-4399
County: Saint Louis FICE Identification: 002476
Unit ID: 177816
Telephone: (314) 792-6100 Carnegie Class: Spec-4-yr-Faith
FAX Number: (314) 792-6500 Calendar System: Semester
URL: www.kenrick.edu
Established: 1893 Annual Undergrad Tuition & Fees: $20,750
Enrollment: 113 Male
Affiliation or Control: Roman Catholic IRS Status: 501(c)3
Highest Offering: Master's
Accreditation: NH, THEOL

01 President/Rector .... Rev. James MASON
03 Dir Pre-Theology/Vice Rector .... Msgr. Gregory MIKESCH
32 Dean of Seminarians .... Rev. Paul HOESING
08 Director of Library .... Ms. Mary Ann AUBIN
88 Director of Spiritual Formation .... Rev. Mark KRAMER, SJ
42 Director of Worship .... Rev. Jason SCHUMER
30 Director of Development .... Ms. Kate GUYOL
06 Registrar/Financial Aid .... Deacon Carl SOMMER
10 Chief Business Officer .... Mr. Greg NOVAK

L'Ecole Culinaire (F)

9811 South Forty Drive, Saint Louis MO 63124
Telephone: (314) 587-2433 Identification: 666275
Accreditation: ACCSC, ACFEI

† Branch campus of Vatterott College, Des Moines, IA.

L'Ecole Culinaire Kansas City (G)

310 Ward Parkway, Kansas City MO 64112
Telephone: (816) 627-0100 Identification: 770579
Accreditation: ACCSC

† Branch campus of Vatterott College-Des Moines, Des Moines, IA

Lincoln University (H)

820 Chestnut Street, Jefferson City MO 65101-3537
County: Cole FICE Identification: 002479
Unit ID: 177940
Telephone: (573) 681-5000 Carnegie Class: Masters/S
FAX Number: (573) 681-5566 Calendar System: Semester
URL: www.lincolnu.edu
Established: 1866 Annual Undergrad Tuition & Fees (In-State): $7,042
Enrollment: 2,944 Coed
Affiliation or Control: State IRS Status: 501(c)3
Highest Offering: Beyond Master's But Less Than Doctorate
Accreditation: NH, ACBSP, ADNUR, CAEPN, MUS, NUR, SW

01 Interim President .... Mr. Michael A. MIDDLETON
11 Dean Administration/Student Affairs .... Dr. Jerome OFFORD, JR.
05 Interim VP Academic Affairs/Provost .... Dr. Debra GREENE
30 Exec Director of Philanthropy .... Mr. Willie JUDE
83 Dean College of Arts & Sciences .... Dr. Jennifer BENNE
58 Dean Grad School/CDO/Asst Provost .... Dr. Rolundus RICE
47 Dean of Ag/Natural Sciences .... Dr. Albert ESSEL
08 Interim University Librarian .... Mr. Ethan CORDRAY
10 Chief Financial Officer .... Mrs. Sandy KOETTING
15 Director Human Resources .... Mr. James MARCANTONIO
18 Director of Facilities and Planning .... Mrs. Sheila GASSNER
19 Chief of Police .... Mr. Gary HILL
41 Director of Athletics .... Mr. John MOSELEY
29 Director Alumni Affairs .... Mrs. Sylvia WILSON
26 Director of University Relations .... Ms. Misty YOUNG
06 Asst Dean of Students/Registrar .... Ms. Liz MORROW
36 Director Career & Academic Support .... Mrs. Ruth CANADA
09 Director Ctr Assess/Inst Rsrch .... Mrs. Beth NOLTE
23 Director Student Health Services .... Mr. James SMITH
32 Exec Dir of Student Engagement .... Mrs. Tammy NOBLES
43 General Counsel .... Ms. Annie WILLIS
37 Dir Financial Aid/Stdnt Employment .... Mr. Alfred L. ROBINSON
96 Director of Purchasing .... Ms. Debra KIDWELL
13 Chief Information Officer .... Mr. John BAX
39 Asst Dean of Students/Campus Life .... Mr. Chio SHEPPARD
12 Director Fort Leonard Wood Site .... Mrs. Barbara LANE
24 Dir of Center Teaching/Learning .... Dr. Rachel SALE
40 Manager LU Bookstore .... Vacant
101 Exec Asst to President & Curators .... Ms. Rose Ann ORTMEYER
85 International Student Advisor .... Mr. Duwon CLARK
105 Web Content Manager .... Mr. Derek SCHWARTZE
22 Dir Affirmative Action/EEO .... Mr. James MARCANTONIO
100 Chief of Staff to the President .... Mr. Joseph WATKINS
66 Dean of the School of Nursing .... Dr. Ann MCSWAIN
50 Dean of the School of Business .... Dr. Eric BURGESS
53 Dean of the School of Education .... Dr. James KERN
86 Director of Campus/Cmty Relations .... Mr. Carlos GRAHAM

Lindenwood University (I)

209 S Kingshighway, Saint Charles MO 63301-1695
County: Saint Charles FICE Identification: 002480
Unit ID: 177968
Telephone: (636) 949-2000 Carnegie Class: DU-Mod
FAX Number: (636) 949-4910 Calendar System: Semester
URL: www.lindenwood.edu
Established: 1827 Annual Undergrad Tuition & Fees: $16,332
Enrollment: 11,620 Coed
Affiliation or Control: Independent Non-Profit IRS Status: 501(c)3
Highest Offering: Doctorate
Accreditation: NH, ACBSP, CAATE, CAEPT, NURSE, SW

01 President .... Dr. Michael SHONROCK
04 Exec Asst Pres & Asst Secy to BOD .... Mrs. Stefani SCHUETTE
05 Acting Provost .... Dr. Marilyn ABBOTT
30 Vice Pres Development .... Mr. Dan GRIGG
15 Vice Pres Human Resources .... Dr. Deb AYRES
84 Vice Pres for Enrollment Management .... Vacant
12 President Belleville Campus .... Mr. Brett BARGER
09 Asst VP Inst Effectiveness .... Dr. David WILSON
06 Registrar .... Ms. Christine HANNAR
10 Chief Financial Officer .... Mr. Greg PHELPS
29 Director Alumni Relations .... Ms. Michelle GIESSMAN
26 Dir Community & Public Relations .... Mr. Scott QUEEN
13 VP Information Technology .... Mr. TJ RAINS
08 Dean of Library Services .... Ms. Elizabeth MACDONALD
37 Director of Financial Aid .... Ms. Lori BODE
35 Dir of Student Life & Leadership .... Ms. Angela ROYAL
35 Dean of Students .... Ms. Shane WILLIAMSON
39 Director of Student Housing .... Mr. Terry RUSSELL
92 Director of Honors Program .... Dr. Michael WHALEY
43 General Counsel .... Mr. Grant SHOSTAK
86 Dir of Outreach & Govt Relations .... Vacant
22 Director of Compliance .... Ms. Anna GIRDWOOD
89 Director of First Year Programs .... Ms. Sarah TETLEY
20 Dean of Academic Services .... Mr. Barry FINNEGAN
36 Director of Career Placement .... Ms. Dana WEHRLI
41 VP Athletics .... Mr. Brad WACHLER
42 Chaplain .... Dr. Nicole TORBITZKY
79 School Dean Humanities .... Dr. Michael WHALEY
81 School Dean Sciences .... Dr. Ricardo DELGADO
53 Interim School Dean Education .... Dr. Joyce PIVERAL
57 Dean Fine & Performing Arts .... Mr. Joe ALSOBROOK
50 Sch Dean Business/Entrepreneurship .... Dr. Roger ELLIS
60 School Dean Communications .... Mr. Mike WALL
51 School Dean LCIE(Adult Learning) .... Dr. Gina GANAHL
68 Sch Dean Sport/Rec/Exercise Science .... Dr. Cynthia SCHROEDER
19 Director Security/Safety .... Mr. John BOWMANN
106 Dir Online Education/E-learning .... Dr. Joe ALSOBROOK

Logan University (A)

1851 Schoettler Road, Chesterfield MO 63017
County: Saint Louis FICE Identification: 004703
Unit ID: 177986
Telephone: (636) 227-2100 Carnegie Class: Spec-4-yr-Other Health
FAX Number: N/A Calendar System: Trimester
URL: www.logan.edu
Established: 1935 Annual Undergrad Tuition & Fees: N/A
Enrollment: 915 Coed
Affiliation or Control: Independent Non-Profit IRS Status: 501(c)3
Highest Offering: First Professional Degree
Accreditation: NH, CHIRO

01 President .... Dr. Clay MCDONALD
30 VP Chiropractic/Alumni Relations .... Dr. Ralph BARRALE
13 VP Information Technology .... Dr. Brad HOUGH
10 Chief Financial Officer .... Mr. Adil KHAN
05 Exec VP Academic Affairs .... Dr. Kimberly PADDOCK-O'REILLY

Maryville University of Saint Louis (B)

650 Maryville University Drive,
Saint Louis MO 63141-7299
County: Saint Louis FICE Identification: 002482
Unit ID: 178059
Telephone: (314) 529-9300 Carnegie Class: DU-Mod
FAX Number: (314) 529-9900 Calendar System: Semester
URL: www.maryville.edu
Established: 1872 Annual Undergrad Tuition & Fees: $27,958
Enrollment: 6,414 Coed
Affiliation or Control: Independent Non-Profit IRS Status: 501(c)3
Highest Offering: Doctorate
Accreditation: NH, ACBSP, ART, CACREP, CAEPN, CIDA, MUS, NURSE, OT, PTA, SP

01 President .... Dr. Mark LOMBARDI
05 Vice Pres Academic Affairs .... Dr. Mary Ellen FINCH
10 Vice Pres Finance & Facilities .... Dr. Steve MANDEVILLE
84 Vice President Enrollment .... Mr. Jeffrey MILLER
111 VP Inst Advancement/Chief Dev Ofcr .... Mr. Thomas ESCHEN
32 VP for Student Life .... Dr. Nina CALDWELL
121 VP for Student Success .... Dr. Jennifer MCCLUSKEY
26 VP Integrated Mktg & Communications .... Ms. Marcia SULLIVAN
41 VP for Athletics .... Mr. Marcus MANNING
20 Associate VP Academic Affairs .... Dr. Tammy GOCIAL
100 Chief of Staff .... Ms. Kathy LUNAN
50 Interim Dean School of Business .... Dr. Pam HORWITZ
53 Dean School of Education .... Dr. Mascheal SCHAPPE
76 Dean School Health Professions .... Dr. Charles GULAS
49 Dean College Arts & Sciences .... Ms. Cherie FISTER
08 Dean University Library .... Vacant
106 Dean Adult & Online Education .... Mr. Dan VIELE
88 Exec Dir Student Svcs Ctr .... Dr. Stephanie ELFRINK
88 Dir Acad Advising & Life Coaching .... Ms. Kelly MOCK
07 Assoc VP Enrollment .... Ms. Shani LENORE-JENKINS
29 Director of Alumni Affairs .... Mr. James PAGE
42 Dir Campus Ministry & Comm Service .... Mr. Stephen DISALVO
35 Dean of Students .... Dr. Kathy QUINN
36 Director Career & Prof Development .... Ms. Erin BOSWELL
35 Asst Dean/Dir Student Involvement .... Mr. Brian GARDNER
21 Controller/Dir Finance .... Ms. Nikki PAYNE
30 Director of Development .... Ms. Megan HOLMES
37 Director of Financial Aid .... Ms. Martha HARBAUGH
23 Director of Health & Wellness .... Ms. Pamela CULLITON
22 Asst Dean Diversity/Inclusion .... Mr. Turan MULLINS
13 Chief Technology Officer .... Mr. Doug GLAZE
09 Director Institutional Research .... Ms. Mary MERRIFIELD
90 Dir Learning Design & Technology .... Ms. Pamela BRYAN WILLIAMS
18 Director of Physical Plant .... Mr. Tom BENNING
112 Director of Planned Gifts .... Mr. Mark ROOCK
102 Dir Foundation/Corp Relations .... Ms. Peggy MICHELSON
19 Interim Director of Public Safety .... Mr. Sean KENNEDY
39 Director of Residential Life .... Mr. Ryan MCDONNELL
104 Assoc VP/Dir Ctr for Global Educ .... Dr. James HARF
88 Asst Athletic Dir-Communications .... Mr. Charles YAHNG
53 Assoc Dean & Dir Teacher Education .... Vacant
88 Director of Student Accts .... Ms. Elizabeth STACEY
88 Director Fresh Ideas Food Services .... Ms. Linda THACKER
38 Director Personal Counseling .... Ms. Jennifer HENRY
88 Inst Advancement Chief of Staff .... Ms. Fay FETICK
88 Assoc VP Ctr for Institution Values .... Dr. Alden CRADDOCK
04 Administrative Asst to President .... Ms. Jan JOHNSTON
109 Director of Auxiliary Operations .... Ms. Laura STEVENS
06 Registrar .... Mr. Matthew GERST
105 Director Web Services .... Ms. Kate BOELHAUF
91 Director Administrative Computing .... Mr. Doug GLAZE

Metro Business College (C)

1732 N Kingshighway, Cape Girardeau MO 63701-2122
County: Cape FICE Identification: 021802
Unit ID: 178110
Telephone: (573) 334-9181 Carnegie Class: Spec 2-yr-Health
FAX Number: (573) 334-0617 Calendar System: Other
URL: www.metrobusinesscollege.edu
Established: 1981 Annual Undergrad Tuition & Fees: $11,375
Enrollment: 92 Coed
Affiliation or Control: Proprietary IRS Status: Proprietary
Highest Offering: Associate Degree
Accreditation: ACICS

01 VP of Operations .... Ms. Mary BUCKLEY
12 Campus Director .... Mrs. Jan REIMANN
05 Education Director .... Mrs. Leslie WATKINS
37 Financial Aid Director .... Mrs. Janie WARNE
36 Career Services Coordinator .... Mrs. Diane JORDAN
07 Director of Admissions .... Mrs. Denise ACEY

Metro Business College (D)

210 El Mercado Plaza, Jefferson City MO 65109
Telephone: (573) 635-6600 Identification: 666454
Accreditation: ACICS

† Branch campus of Metro Business College, Cape Girardeau, MO.

Metro Business College (E)

1202 E Highway 72, Rolla MO 65401-3938
Telephone: (573) 364-8464 Identification: 666455
Accreditation: ACICS

† Branch campus of Metro Business College, Cape Girardeau, MO.

*Metropolitan Community College - Kansas City Administrative Center (F)

3200 Broadway, Kansas City MO 64111-2429
County: Jackson FICE Identification: 009137
Unit ID: 177995
Telephone: (816) 604-1000 Carnegie Class: N/A
FAX Number: (816) 759-1158
URL: www.mcckc.edu

01 Chancellor .... Dr. Kimberly BEATTY
101 Chancellor's Asst/Board Secretary .... Ms. Cindy K. JOHNSON
05 Vice Chanc of Academic Affairs .... Dr. Carlos PENALOZA
32 Vice Chanc Student Success/Engagmnt .... Dr. Kathrine SWANSON
10 Vice Chanc Financial & Admin Svcs .... Mrs. Shelley TEMPLE KNEUVEAN
100 Chief of Staff/Associate VC HR .... Ms. Kathy WALTER-MACK
88 Director of Resource Dev .... Ms. Kendra EDWARDS
114 Director Budget and Planning .... Ms. Deborah BALL
13 Director Information Technology .... Mr. Gary W. SCHIEBER
96 Manager Purchasing .... Ms. Amiee WENSON
18 Director Facility Services .... Mr. Jeffrey ULLMANN
103 Exec Dir Workforce Dev .... Ms. Nancy RUSSELL
88 Director Educational Services .... Ms. Fran A. PADOW
106 Director Distance Education .... Dr. Leo J. HIRNER
09 Director Inst Research/Assessment .... Mrs. Melissa GIESE
37 Director Student Financial Services .... Ms. Dena NORRIS
21 Assoc VC Fin Svcs & Admin Sys .... Ms. Patricia A. AMICK
88 Dir of Support Services PS .... Mr. Domenick R. BROUILLETTE
19 Chief of Campus Police .... Mr. Londell JAMERSON, JR.
88 Dir of CTE Accountability & Comp .... Ms. Teresa A. LONEY
109 Director Auxiliary Svcs & Bus Rels .... Mr. Scott GEORGE
36 Director Career Education .... Mr. Tristan LONDRE
111 Assoc VC of Advancement .... Ms. Jessica RAMIREZ
28 Executive Director Inclusion & Eng .... Mr. Robert PAGE
88 Director Student Disability Svcs .... Ms. Kim FERNANDES
90 Director Academic Sys & Instr Tech .... Mr. Thomas WHEELER

*Metropolitan Community College - Blue River (G)

20301 E 78 Highway, Independence MO 64057-2053
County: Jackson FICE Identification: 032613
Unit ID: 440305
Telephone: (816) 604-1000 Carnegie Class: Not Classified
FAX Number: N/A Calendar System: Semester
URL: www.mcckc.edu
Established: 1997 Annual Undergrad Tuition & Fees (In-District): N/A
Enrollment: N/A Coed
Affiliation or Control: State/Local IRS Status: 501(c)3
Highest Offering: Associate Degree
Accreditation: &NH

02 President .... Dr. Michael BANKS
04 Assistant to the President .... Mrs. Kimberly A. MORICONI
05 Dean of Instruction .... Dr. Todd MARTIN
32 Dean of Student Development .... Dr. Jonathan L. BURKE
20 Assoc Dean of Instruction .... Mr. Steven D. JOHNSON
35 Assoc Dean of Student Development .... Mr. Basil LISTER
19 Campus Police Sergeant .... Mr. Larry MCCREA
18 Facilities Superintendent .... Mr. Tom COOLEY
26 Marketing Coordinator .... Mr. Bob K. FLORENCE

† Regional accreditation is carried under the parent institution Metropolitan Community College-Kansas City Administrative Center in Kansas City, MO.

*Metropolitan Community College - Business and Technology (H)

1775 Universal Avenue, Kansas City MO 64120-2429
County: Jackson Identification: 666295
Unit ID: 442000
Telephone: (816) 604-1000 Carnegie Class: Not Classified
FAX Number: (816) 482-5256 Calendar System: Semester
URL: www.mcckc.edu/btc
Established: 1995 Annual Undergrad Tuition & Fees (In-District): N/A
Enrollment: N/A Coed
Affiliation or Control: Local IRS Status: 501(c)3
Highest Offering: Associate Degree
Accreditation: &NH

02 President .... Dr. Jackie GILL
05 Dean of Instruction .... Dr. Joe ROCHE
32 Dean Student Development/Enrollment .... Dr. Ryan MEADOR
20 Associate Dean .... Ms. Shawn SMITH
103 Exec Dir Workforce Development .... Vacant
04 Admin Assistant to the President .... Ms. Letonia (LT) TORRENCE

† Regional accreditation is carried under the parent institution Metropolitan Community College-Kansas City Administrative Center in Kansas City, MO.

*Metropolitan Community College - Longview (I)

500 SW Longview Road, Lee's Summit MO 64081-2105
County: Jackson FICE Identification: 009140
Telephone: (816) 604-1000 Carnegie Class: Not Classified
FAX Number: (816) 672-2025 Calendar System: Semester
URL: www.mcckc.edu
Established: 1969 Annual Undergrad Tuition & Fees (In-District): N/A
Enrollment: N/A Coed
Affiliation or Control: Local IRS Status: 501(c)3
Highest Offering: Associate Degree
Accreditation: &NH

02 President .... Dr. Kirk A. NOOKS
05 Dean of Instruction .... Dr. Arminda MCCALLUM
32 Dean Student Devel/Enrollment Mgmt .... Dr. Diana BOYD MCELROY
20 Associate Dean Instruction .... Vacant
35 Assoc Dean Student Dev/Enroll Mgmt .... Mrs. Linda NELSON
37 Manager of Student Financial Aid .... Ms. Lisa L. FANNAN
10 Business Office Supervisor .... Ms. Kimberly A. GREENE
18 Physical Facilities Superintendent .... Mr. Rick STANSBURY
36 Coordinator Student Employment Svcs .... Ms. Linda S. ANDERSON
38 Director Student Counseling .... Mrs. Gretchen S. BLYTHE

† Regional accreditation is carried under the parent institution Metropolitan Community College-Kansas City Administrative Center in Kansas City, MO.

*Metropolitan Community College - Maple Woods (J)

2601 NE Barry Road, Kansas City MO 64156-1299
County: Clay FICE Identification: 009139
Unit ID: 178022
Telephone: (816) 604-1000 Carnegie Class: Not Classified
FAX Number: (816) 437-3049 Calendar System: Semester
URL: www.mcckc.edu
Established: 1968 Annual Undergrad Tuition & Fees (In-District): N/A
Enrollment: N/A Coed
Affiliation or Control: Local IRS Status: 501(c)3
Highest Offering: Associate Degree
Accreditation: &NH

02 President .... Dr. Utpal K. GOSWAMI
05 Dean Instruction .... Mr. David OEHLER
32 Dean Student Devel/Enrollment .... Ms. Karen MOORE
35 Assoc Dean Student Development .... Ms. Mindy PETTEGREW
20 Associate Dean .... Dr. Brian BECHTEL
08 Librarian .... Mrs. Linda CARTER
41 Athletic Director .... Dr. Brian BECHTEL
37 Manager Student Financial Aid .... Mrs. Robin STIMAC
18 Physical Facilities Superintendent .... Mr. Tom HULETT
10 Business Office Supervisor .... Ms. Emily THOMPSON
31 Community Relations Coordinator .... Mrs. Heather K. PEREZ
36 Student Employment Service Coord .... Ms. Mary Lynn MUNGER

† Regional accreditation is carried under the parent institution Metropolitan Community College-Kansas City Administrative Center in Kansas City, MO.

*Metropolitan Community College - Penn Valley (K)

3201 Southwest Trafficway, Kansas City MO 64111-2764
County: Jackson FICE Identification: 002484
Unit ID: 178785
Telephone: (816) 604-1000 Carnegie Class: Not Classified
FAX Number: (816) 759-4161 Calendar System: Semester
URL: www.mcckc.edu
Established: 1915 Annual Undergrad Tuition & Fees (In-District): N/A
Enrollment: N/A Coed
Affiliation or Control: Local IRS Status: 501(c)3
Highest Offering: Associate Degree
Accreditation: &NH, ADNUR, CAHIIM, DA, EMT, OTA, PTAA, RAD, SURGT

02 President .... Dr. Tyjaun LEE
05 Dean of Instruction .... Dr. Cynthia CERRENTANO
32 Dean of Student Development .... Ms. Yvette SWEENEY
84 Dean of Enrollment Services .... Ms. Yvette SWEENEY
20 Assoc Dean Instruction .... Ms. Tarana CHAPPLE
35 Assoc Dean Student Development .... Mr. Terrell TIGNER
23 Director of Health Sciences .... Vacant
08 Librarian .... Mr. Michael KORKLAN
13 NUS Department Director .... Vacant
18 Facilities Services Superintendent .... Mr. Lloyd HALE
19 Campus Police Captain .... Cpt. Booker ARMSTRONG
84 Enrollment Manager .... Mr. Carlton FOWLER
41 Athletic Programs Manager .... Mr. Marcus HARVEY
37 Student Financial Aid Manager .... Ms. Rossann DOWNING
10 Business Office Supervisor .... Ms. Michele ALLEN

26 Community & Public Relations Coord ... Mr. Jordan WILLIAMS
36 Career Coordinator ... Ms. Margaret STEGMAN

† Regional accreditation is carried under the parent institution Metropolitan Community College-Kansas City Administrative Center in Kansas City, MO.

Midwest Institute (A)

964 S. Highway Drive, Fenton MO 63026
County: St. Louis FICE Identification: 021211
Unit ID: 178183
Telephone: (314) 965-8363 Carnegie Class: Spec 2-yr-Tech
FAX Number: (636) 326-1059 Calendar System: Other
URL: www.midwestinstitute.com
Established: 1965 Annual Undergrad Tuition & Fees: N/A
Enrollment: 202 Coed
Affiliation or Control: Proprietary IRS Status: Proprietary
Highest Offering: Associate Degree
Accreditation: **ABHES**

01 Director ... Dr. Adam EPSTEIN

Midwest Institute-Earth City (B)

4260 Shoreline Drive, Earth City MO 63045
County: Saint Louis Identification: 667074
Telephone: (314) 344-4440 Carnegie Class: Not Classified
FAX Number: (314) 344-0495 Calendar System: Other
URL: www.midwestinstitute.com
Established: 1970 Annual Undergrad Tuition & Fees: N/A
Enrollment: N/A Coed
Affiliation or Control: Proprietary IRS Status: Proprietary
Highest Offering: Associate Degree
Accreditation: **ABHES**, SURTEC

01 President ... Ms. Christine SHREFFLER

Midwest University (C)

851 Parr Road, Wentzville MO 63385-0365
County: Saint Charles FICE Identification: 035283
Unit ID: 440253
Telephone: (636) 327-4645 Carnegie Class: Not Classified
FAX Number: (636) 327-4715 Calendar System: Semester
URL: www.midwest.edu
Established: 1986 Annual Undergrad Tuition & Fees: N/A
Enrollment: N/A Coed
Affiliation or Control: Non-denominational IRS Status: 501(c)3
Highest Offering: Doctorate
Accreditation: **BI**

01 President ... Dr. James SONG
11 Executive Assistant to President ... Ms. Taylor J. BUMILLER
05 Academic Dean ... Dr. Myeong H. OH
09 Dir of Institutional Effectiveness ... Mr. Rolfe E. KIEHNE
32 Director of Student Affairs ... Mr. Kyong S. YEOM
42 Chaplain ... Dr. Dae G. KIM
06 Registrar/Admission ... Mr. Jeoung H. HAM
08 Director of Library Services ... Mrs. Hyun Shim JUNG
106 Director of E-Learning ... Dr. Hee C. LEE
10 Director of Finance ... Mr. Kyong S. YEOM
21 Business Office Manager ... Ms. Bok H. SONG
45 Director of Planning & Marketing ... Mr. Jae P. SONG
13 Director of Information Technology ... Dr. Hee C. LEE
12 Korea Office Regional Director ... Dr. Jae M. SONG
12 Washington DC Regional Director ... Dr. Yoo K. KO
07 Admission Counselor ... Mr. Sang Bae SEO
85 International Student Officer ... Mr. Kyong S. YEOM
85 International Student Officer ... Mr. Kyoo W. SEO
104 Director of International Devel ... Dr. Hee C. LEE
50 Director of Business School ... Dr. Young S. PARK
04 Administrative Asst to President ... Ms. Julia G. CHOO

Midwestern Baptist Theological Seminary (D)

5001 N Oak Trafficway, Kansas City MO 64118-4697
County: Clay FICE Identification: 002485
Unit ID: 178208
Telephone: (816) 414-3700 Carnegie Class: Spec-4-yr-Faith
FAX Number: (816) 414-3724 Calendar System: Semester
URL: www.mbts.edu
Established: 1957 Annual Undergrad Tuition & Fees: $6,925
Enrollment: 1,419 Coed
Affiliation or Control: Southern Baptist IRS Status: 501(c)3
Highest Offering: Doctorate
Accreditation: **NH**, THEOL

01 President ... Dr. Jason K. ALLEN
05 Provost ... Dr. Jason DUESING
10 VP for Inst Administration/Fin Svcs ... Mr. James KRAGENBRING
20 Undergraduate Dean ... Dr. John Mark YEATS
58 Graduate Dean ... Dr. Thor MADSEN
09 Dean of Institutional Effectiveness ... Dr. Rodney A. HARRISON
30 VP of Institutional Relations ... Mr. Charles SMITH
13 Director of Info Technology ... Mr. David MEYER
06 Registrar ... Dr. Mike HAWKINS
08 Librarian ... Ms. Kenette HARDER
73 Director of Postgraduate Studies ... Dr. Rodney A. HARRISON
04 Exec Assistant to the President ... Mr. Patrick HUDSON
18 Director of Campus Operations ... Mr. Merv CHAPMAN
84 Dir Student Recruitment & Admission ... Mr. Camden PULLIAM
20 Associate Dean ... Dr. Rustin UMSTATTD

Mineral Area College (E)

5270 Flat River Road, Park Hills MO 63601-2224
County: Saint Francois FICE Identification: 002486
Unit ID: 178217
Telephone: (573) 431-4593 Carnegie Class: Assoc/HT-High Trad
FAX Number: (573) 518-2164 Calendar System: Semester
URL: www.mineralarea.edu
Established: 1922 Annual Undergrad Tuition & Fees (In-District): $3,280
Enrollment: 4,388 Coed
Affiliation or Control: Local IRS Status: 501(c)3
Highest Offering: Associate Degree
Accreditation: **NH**, EMT, PTAA, RAD

01 President ... Dr. Steve KURTZ
03 Vice Pres/Dean Career/Tech Educ ... Mr. John (Gil) KENNON
49 Dean of Arts & Sciences ... Dr. Diana STUART
32 Dean Student Services ... Ms. Jean MERRILL-DOSS
10 Chief Financial Officer ... Ms. Shirley HOFSTETTER
13 Director of Computer Services ... Mr. Chad PIPKIN
06 Registrar ... Ms. Pam REEDER
07 Director of Admissions ... Ms. Julie SHEETS
09 Director of Institutional Research ... Ms. Lisa EDBURG
26 Chief Public Relations Officer ... Ms. Sarah HAAS
29 Director Alumni Relations ... Mr. Kevin THURMAN
15 Chief Human Resource Officer ... Ms. Kathryn NEFF
37 Director Student Financial Aid ... Ms. Denise SEBASTIAN
38 Director Student Counseling ... Mr. Michael EASTER
18 Facilities Manager ... Mr. Barry WILFONG
21 Director Payroll ... Ms. Sarah DEMENT
04 Administrative Asst to President ... Ms. Amy MCKENNA-JONES
08 Head Librarian ... Ms. Melissa HOPKINS
19 Director Security/Safety ... Mr. Jeff MCCREARY
39 Director Student Housing ... Ms. Debi BAYLESS
41 Athletic Director ... Mr. Chad MILLS

Missouri Baptist University (F)

One College Park Drive, Saint Louis MO 63141-8698
County: Saint Louis FICE Identification: 007540
Unit ID: 178244
Telephone: (314) 434-1115 Carnegie Class: Masters/L
FAX Number: (314) 434-7596 Calendar System: Semester
URL: www.mobap.edu
Established: 1964 Annual Undergrad Tuition & Fees: $24,924
Enrollment: 5,276 Coed
Affiliation or Control: Baptist IRS Status: 501(c)3
Highest Offering: Doctorate
Accreditation: **NH**, CAEPN, EXSC, MUS

01 President ... Dr. R. Alton LACEY
04 Assistant to the President ... Mrs. Janet MAYFIELD
05 Senior VP of Academic Affs/Provost ... Dr. Arlen R. DYKSTRA
111 Senior VP of Univ Advancement ... Dr. Keith ROSS
32 Senior VP of Student Development ... Dr. Andy CHAMBERS
10 Senior VP for Business Affairs ... Mr. Ken REVENAUGH
58 VP of Grad Stds/Academic Pgm Review ... Dr. Clark TRIPLETT
29 Director for Alumni Relations ... Mr. Brian KNAPP
85 Director of International Services ... Mrs. Jessica FITZGERALD
09 Director Institutional Research ... Mrs. Heather BRASE
08 Librarian ... Ms. Jeanna RYNER
37 Director Financial Services ... Mr. Zach GREENLEE
26 Assoc VP University Communications ... Mr. Bryce CHAPMAN
36 Dir Career Svcs/Assoc Dean Students ... Ms. Kimberly GREY
41 Assoc VP & Director of Athletics ... Dr. Thomas SMITH
18 Director Campus Operations ... Mr. Stu LINDLEY
06 Director of Records ... Mrs. Thea ABRAHAM
15 Director Personnel Services ... Mrs. Laurie WALLACE
13 Director of Information Systems ... Mr. Jerry MCKITTRICK
19 Director Public Safety ... Mr. Stephen HEIDKE
35 Director Student Activities ... Mrs. Lara HINES
21 Controller ... Mrs. Pam SAVAGE
30 Development Officer ... Mrs. Ashlee JOHNSON
07 Director of Admissions ... Mrs. Cynthia SUTTON
28 Diversity/Inclusion Initiative ... Mrs. Brenda BRADFORD

Missouri Southern State University (G)

3950 E Newman Road, Joplin MO 64801-1595
County: Jasper FICE Identification: 002488
Unit ID: 178341
Telephone: (417) 625-9300 Carnegie Class: Bac-Diverse
FAX Number: (417) 625-3121 Calendar System: Semester
URL: www.mssu.edu
Established: 1965 Annual Undergrad Tuition & Fees (In-State): $5,523
Enrollment: 5,783 Coed
Affiliation or Control: State IRS Status: 501(c)3
Highest Offering: Master's
Accreditation: **NH**, ACBSP, CAEP, COARC, DH, EMT, ENGT, NUR, RAD, @SW

01 President ... Dr. Alan MARBLE
05 Provost/Vice Pres Academic Affairs ... Dr. Paula CARSON
32 Vice Pres Stdnt Affs/Enrollment ... Mr. Darren S. FULLERTON
10 Vice President Business Affairs ... Mr. Rob YUST
30 Exec Vice Pres for Development ... Dr. Brad HODSON
20 Prov/Vice Pres Academic Affairs ... Dr. Wendy MCGRANE
35 Dean of Students ... Dr. Ronald S. MITCHELL
06 Registrar ... Ms. Cheryl DOBSON
08 Interim Library Director ... Mr. James CAPECI
37 Director Student Financial Aid ... Ms. Becca L. DISKIN
38 Director of ACTS ... Mrs. Kelly WILSON
21 Treasurer ... Mrs. Linda EIS
15 Director Human Resources ... Mr. Evan JEWSBURY
18 Director Facilities/Physical Plant ... Mr. Robert HARRINGTON
76 Dean School Health Sciences ... Dr. Richard SCHOOLER
49 Dean School of Arts & Sciences ... Dr. Richard B. MILLER
53 Dean School of Education ... Dr. Deborah BROWN
50 Int Dean Plaster School of Business ... Dr. Chris MOOS
04 Administrative Asst to President ... Ms. Sharon ODEM
07 Director of Admissions ... Mr. Derek S. SKAGGS
103 Dir Workforce/Career Development ... Ms. Nicole R. BROWN
104 Director Study Abroad ... Dr. Chad STEBBINS
106 Director Distance Learning ... Mr. Scott SNELL
108 Dir Institutional Effectiveness ... Dr. Josie WELSH
19 Chief of Campus Police ... Mr. Kenneth KENNEDY
41 Director of Athletics ... Mr. Jared BRUGGEMAN
44 Director of Annual Giving ... Ms. Elisa BRYANT
114 Dir Budget & Operations ... Mr. Jeff GIBSON
26 Dir University Relations/Marketing ... Ms. Cassie MATHES
29 Director Alumni Relations ... Ms. Lee ELLIFF POUND
28 Director of Diversity ... Ms. Faustina ABRAHAMS
105 Director Web Services ... Mr. Peter A. BLOMGREN
13 Chief Info Technology Officer (CIO) ... Mr. Albert E. STADLER
39 Director Student Housing ... Mr. Joshua M. DOAK

Missouri State University (H)

901 S National Avenue, Springfield MO 65897-0027
County: Greene FICE Identification: 002503
Unit ID: 179566
Telephone: (417) 836-8500 Carnegie Class: Masters/L
FAX Number: (417) 836-7669 Calendar System: Semester
URL: www.missouristate.edu
Established: 1905 Annual Undergrad Tuition & Fees (In-State): $7,060
Enrollment: 22,273 Coed
Affiliation or Control: State IRS Status: 501(c)3
Highest Offering: Doctorate
Accreditation: **NH**, ADNUR, ANEST, ARCPA, AUD, CAATE, CACREP, CAEPN, CEA, CONST, CS, DIETD, @DIETI, MUS, NRPA, NURSE, OT, PH, PLNG, PTA, SP, SPAA, SW, THEA

01 President ... Mr. Clifton M. SMART, III
05 Provost ... Dr. Frank E. EINHELLIG
12 Chancellor West Plains Campus ... Dr. Drew A. BENNETT
46 VP for Research/Economic Devel ... Dr. James P. BAKER
11 Vice Pres Administrative Services ... Mr. Matthew MORRIS
111 Vice Pres University Advancement ... Mr. W. Brent DUNN
32 VP Student Affairs & Dean of Stdts ... Dr. Dee SISCOE
26 VP Marketing and Communications ... Ms. Suzanne SHAW
20 Deputy Provost ... Dr. Christopher J. CRAIG
20 Associate Provost ... Dr. Rachelle DARABI
20 Associate Provost ... Dr. Joye NORRIS
58 Dean of Grad College ... Dr. Julie J. MASTERSON
10 Chief Financial Officer ... Mr. Steve FOUCART
84 Associate VP Enrollment Mgmt & Svcs ... Mr. Donald E. SIMPSON
08 Dean Library Services ... Mr. Thomas A. PETERS
28 Chief Diversity Officer ... Mr. H. Wes PRATT
09 Director of Institutional Research ... Dr. Michelle D. OLSEN
29 Exec Dir of Alumni Relations ... Ms. Lori FAN
15 Director of Human Resources ... Mr. Tamaria FEW
37 Director of Student Financial Aid ... Ms. Vicki S. MATTOCKS
19 Director of Safety & Transportation ... Mr. Thomas JOHNSON
36 Interim Dir of the Career Center ... Dr. Kelly E. RAPP
13 Chief Information Officer ... Mr. Jeff P. MORRISSEY
100 Chief of Staff ... Mr. Ryan DEBOEF
23 Director of Health & Wellness Svcs ... Dr. Dave MUEGGE
92 Director Honors College ... Dr. John F. CHUCHIAK
18 Director Facilities Management ... Mr. Brad B. KIELHOFNER
96 Director of Procurement ... Mr. Mike WILLS
07 Director of Admissions ... Ms. Nechell T. BONDS
06 Asst VP Enrollment Mgmt/Registrar ... Mr. Rob HORNBERGER
49 Dean College Arts & Letters ... Dr. Gloria GALANES
79 Dean Col Humanities/Public Affairs ... Dr. Victor MATTHEWS
76 Dean Col Health/Human Services ... Dr. Helen C. REID
81 Dean Col Natural/Applied Science ... Dr. Tamera S. JAHNKE
53 Dean College of Education ... Dr. David HOUGH
50 Dean College of Business ... Dr. Stephanie BRYANT
85 Associate VP International Program ... Mr. Stephen H. ROBINETTE
105 Director of Web and New Media ... Ms. Sara M. CLARK
41 Athletic Director ... Mr. Kyle MOATS
43 General Counsel ... Ms. Rachael M. DOCKERY

Missouri State University - West Plains (I)

128 Garfield, West Plains MO 65775-2715
County: Howell FICE Identification: 031060
Unit ID: 179344
Telephone: (417) 255-7255 Carnegie Class: Assoc/HT-High Trad
FAX Number: (417) 255-7962 Calendar System: Semester
URL: www.wp.missouristate.edu
Established: 1963 Annual Undergrad Tuition & Fees (In-State): $3,880
Enrollment: 1,961 Coed
Affiliation or Control: State IRS Status: 501(c)3
Highest Offering: Associate Degree
Accreditation: **NH**, #COARC

01 Chancellor ... Dr. Drew A. BENNETT
05 Dean of Academics ... Dr. Dennis LANCASTER

32 Dean of Student Services ... Dr. Angela TOTTY
20 Assistant Dean of Academic Affairs ... Dr. Michael ORF
10 Director of Business Services ... Mr. Scott SCHNEIDER
30 Director of Development ... Mr. Joe KAMMERER
27 Director of Univ Communications ... Mrs. Cheryl CALDWELL
31 Director of Univ/Community Pgms ... Ms. Brenda POLYARD
06 Registrar ... Mrs. Laurie WALL
07 Coord of Admissions ... Mrs. Melissa JETT
09 Coord of Institutional Research ... Mrs. Carrie STEEN
26 Chief Public Relations Officer ... Mrs. Cheryl CALDWELL
36 Coord of Career Services ... Vacant
18 Chief Facilities/Physical Plant ... Mr. Ron HENSLEY
04 Executive Asst to Chancellor ... Mrs. Debra MOSLEY
08 Head Librarian ... Mrs. Sylvia KUHLMEIER
15 Procurement/Human Resources Spec ... Mrs. Alyssa D. COLLINS
39 Coord Student Life and Development ... Mr. Jared CATES

Missouri Valley College (A)

500 E College, Marshall MO 65340-3197
County: Saline FICE Identification: 002489
Unit ID: 178369
Telephone: (660) 831-4000 Carnegie Class: Bac-Diverse
FAX Number: (660) 831-4039 Calendar System: Semester
URL: www.moval.edu
Established: 1889 Annual Undergrad Tuition & Fees: $19,750
Enrollment: 1,728 Coed
Affiliation or Control: Presbyterian Church (U.S.A.) IRS Status: 501(c)3
Highest Offering: Master's
Accreditation: NH, #CAATE, NURSE

01 President ... Dr. Bonnie HUMPHREY
00 Chancellor Emeritus ... Dr. Earl J. REEVES
10 Vice Pres Business/Finance ... Mr. Greg SILVEY
30 Vice Pres Institutional Advancement ... Mr. Eric SAPPINGTON
32 Vice Pres Student Affairs ... Mr. Heath MORGAN
05 VP Academic Affairs/Chief Acad Ofcr . Dr. Diane BARTHOLOMEW
18 Vice Pres of Operations ... Mr. Tim SCHULTE
07 Dean of Admissions ... Mr. Dillon HARP
06 Registrar ... Ms. Marsha LASHLEY
21 Business Officer ... Mrs. Tonia BARTEL
08 Head Librarian ... Mrs. Pamela K. REEDER
41 Athletic Director/Dir of Operations ... Mr. Tom FIFER
42 Director Campus Ministry ... Rev. Pam SEBASTIAN
09 Director of Institutional Research ... Dr. Tiffany NOLAN
37 Director Student Financial Aid ... Mr. Paul GORDON
38 Director Student Counseling ... Ms. Teresa CESELSKI
13 Director of Systems Administration ... Mr. Jason RINNE
26 Dir of Marketing & Media Relations ... Ms. Danielle DURHAM
04 Administrative Asst to President ... Ms. Brandy SCHULTE

Missouri Western State University (B)

4525 Downs Drive, Saint Joseph MO 64507-2294
County: Buchanan FICE Identification: 002490
Unit ID: 178387
Telephone: (816) 271-4200 Carnegie Class: Bac-Diverse
FAX Number: N/A Calendar System: Semester
URL: www.missouriwestern.edu
Established: 1915 Annual Undergrad Tuition & Fees (In-State): $7,330
Enrollment: 5,513 Coed
Affiliation or Control: State IRS Status: 501(c)3
Highest Offering: Master's
Accreditation: NH, CAEPN, CAHIIM, ENGT, MUS, NURSE, PTAA, SW

01 President ... Dr. Robert A. VARTABEDIAN
05 Provost/VP Academic Affairs ... Dr. Jeanne DAFFRON
111 Vice Pres University Advancement ... Mr. Jerry PICKMAN
10 VP Financial Planning and Admin ... Dr. Cale FESSLER
32 Vice Pres for Student Affairs ... Ms. Shana MEYER
20 Assoc Vice Pres Academic Affairs ... Dr. Doug DAVENPORT
21 Assoc VP Financial Plng/Admin ... Ms. Carey MCMILLIAN
84 AVP Enrollment Mgmt & Retention ... Mr. Paul ORSCHELN
107 Dean Professional Studies ... Dr. Kathleen O'CONNOR
57 Dean of Fine Arts ... Dr. Bob WILLENBRINK
49 Dean Liberal Arts & Science ... Dr. Murray NABORS
51 Dean of Western Institute ... Dr. Gordon MAPLEY
50 Dean of Business ... Dr. Mike LANE
35 Dean of Students ... Dr. Judith GRIMES
06 Registrar ... Ms. Susan BRACCIANO
08 Director of Library ... Ms. Sally GIBSON
37 Director Student Financial Aid ... Ms. Marilyn BAKER
13 Director of Information Technology ... Mr. Mark MABE
38 Director Student Counsel & Testing ... Mr. H. David BROWN
18 Director Physical Plant ... Mr. Jerry GENTRY
41 Director of Athletics ... Vacant
15 Director of Human Resources ... Ms. Sara FREEMYER
86 Director of External Relations ... Mr. Brandt SHIELDS
26 Dir of Public Relations & Marketing ... Ms. Jomel NICHOLS
29 Director of Alumni Services ... Ms. Colleen KOWICH
96 Director of Purchasing ... Ms. Letha NOLD
04 Executive Associate to President ... Ms. Kim SIGRIST
103 Dir Workforce/Career Development ... Vacant
39 Director Student Housing ... Mr. Nathan ROBERTS
19 Chief of University Police ... Ms. Yvonne MEYER

Moberly Area Community College (C)

101 College Avenue, Moberly MO 65270-1304
County: Randolph FICE Identification: 002491
Unit ID: 178448
Telephone: (660) 263-4100 Carnegie Class: Assoc/HT-Mix Trad/Non
FAX Number: (660) 263-6252 Calendar System: Semester
URL: www.macc.edu
Established: 1927 Annual Undergrad Tuition & Fees (In-District): $3,120
Enrollment: 4,863 Coed
Affiliation or Control: State/Local IRS Status: 501(c)3
Highest Offering: Associate Degree
Accreditation: NH, MLTAD, OTA

01 President ... Dr. Jeffery LASHLEY
10 Vice President for Finance ... Ms. Susan SPENCER
05 Vice President for Instruction ... Dr. Paula GLOVER
75 Dean of Career/Technical Educ ... Ms. Jo FEY
32 Dean of Student Affairs & Enroll ... Ms. Michele MCCALL
20 Dean of Academic Affairs ... Dr. Jacqueline FISCHER
09 Director Inst Effectiveness/Plng ... Ms. Meghan HOLLERAN
21 Director Business Services ... Ms. Sandra MAREK
26 Dir of Mktg and Public Relations ... Mr. Paul ZACHARIAS
18 Director of Plant Operations ... Mr. Eric ROSS
13 Chief Information Officer ... Mr. Lloyd MARCHANT
08 Director of Library & Academic Reso ... Ms. Valerie DARST
15 Director of Human Resources ... Mrs. Ann PARKS
40 Director of Inst Svcs/Bookstore Mgr ... Ms. Virginia GEBHARDT
37 Director of Financial Aid ... Ms. Amy HAGER
06 Registrar ... Ms. Julie PERKINS
29 Dir of Inst Develop & Alumni Svc ... Ms. Susan ARMENT
36 Dir of Career and Technical Pgms ... Ms. Suzi MCGARVEY
88 Dir of Academic Services ... Ms. Katelyn BRANDKAMP
04 Administrative Asst to President ... Ms. Cheryl SHOEMYER
103 Dir Workforce/Career Development ... Ms. Brandi GLOVER
19 Director Security/Safety ... Ms. Lori PERRY

National American University-Independence (D)

3620 Arrowhead Avenue, Independence MO 64057
Telephone: (816) 418-7700 Identification: 770402
Accreditation: &NH, MAC, #OTA

† Branch campus of National American University, Rapid City, SD

National American University-Lee's Summit (E)

401 NW Murray Road, Lee's Summit MO 64081
Telephone: (816) 600-3900 Identification: 770404
Accreditation: &NH

† Branch campus of National American University, Rapid City, SD

National American University-Zona Rosa (F)

7490 NW 87th Street, Kansas City MO 64153
Telephone: (816) 412-5500 Identification: 770403
Accreditation: &NH, ADNUR, MAC, MLTAD

† Branch campus of National American University, Rapid City, SD

Nazarene Theological Seminary (G)

1700 E Meyer Boulevard, Kansas City MO 64131-1263
County: Jackson FICE Identification: 002494
Unit ID: 178518
Telephone: (816) 268-5400 Carnegie Class: Spec-4-yr-Faith
FAX Number: (816) 268-5500 Calendar System: Semester
URL: www.nts.edu
Established: 1945 Annual Graduate Tuition & Fees: N/A
Enrollment: 269 Coed
Affiliation or Control: Church Of The Nazarene IRS Status: 501(c)3
Highest Offering: Doctorate; No Undergraduates
Accreditation: THEOL

01 President ... Dr. Carla SUNBERG
05 Dean of the Faculty ... Dr. Josh SWEEDEN
11 Dean for Administration ... Vacant
08 Director Library Service ... Mrs. Debra BRADSHAW
06 Registrar/Director of Admissions ... Mrs. Pamala ASHER
37 Financial Aid Coordinator ... Mr. Jeremy SHUNK
26 Director of Communications ... Ms. Marsha SAILORS

North Central Missouri College (H)

1301 Main Street, Trenton MO 64683-1824
County: Grundy FICE Identification: 002514
Unit ID: 179715
Telephone: (660) 359-3948 Carnegie Class: Assoc/MT-VT-Mix Trad/Non
FAX Number: (660) 359-2211 Calendar System: Semester
URL: www.ncmissouri.edu
Established: 1925 Annual Undergrad Tuition & Fees (In-District): $3,180
Enrollment: 1,708 Coed
Affiliation or Control: Local IRS Status: 501(c)3
Highest Offering: Associate Degree
Accreditation: NH, OTA

01 President ... Dr. Lenny KLAVER
10 Chief Financial Officer ... Mr. Tyson OTTO
32 Dean of Student Services ... Dr. Kristen ALLEY
05 Dean of Instruction ... Dr. Sharon WEISER
76 Dean Allied Health Sciences ... Ms. Brooke MCATEE
06 Registrar ... Ms. Linda BROWN
13 Chief Information Officer ... Mr. Alan BARNETT
08 Librarian ... Ms. Beth CALDARELLO
37 Director of Financial Aid ... Ms. Kimberly MEEKER
30 Director Development ... Ms. Teresa CROSS
40 Director Bookstore ... Ms. Cecilia MARSH
39 Director Student Housing ... Mr. Donnie HILLERMAN
41 Athletic Director ... Mr. Steve RICHMAN
18 Director of Facilities ... Mr. Randy YOUNG
105 Director Web Services ... Mr. Anthony ALEXANDER
09 Director of Institutional Research ... Ms. Tara NOAH
04 Administrative Asst to President ... Ms. Kristi HARRIS
07 Director of Admissions ... Ms. Kristie CROSS

Northwest Missouri State University (I)

800 University Drive, Maryville MO 64468-6015
County: Nodaway FICE Identification: 002496
Unit ID: 178624
Telephone: (660) 562-1212 Carnegie Class: Masters/L
FAX Number: (660) 562-1900 Calendar System: Trimester
URL: www.nwmissouri.edu
Established: 1905 Annual Undergrad Tuition & Fees (In-State): $7,343
Enrollment: 6,593 Coed
Affiliation or Control: State IRS Status: 501(c)3
Highest Offering: Beyond Master's But Less Than Doctorate
Accreditation: NH, ACBSP, CAEPN, DIETD, MUS, NRPA

01 President ... Dr. John JASINSKI
05 Interim Provost ... Dr. Jamie HOOYMAN
10 Vice Pres for Finance ... Ms. Stacy CARRICK
32 Vice Pres Student Affairs ... Dr. Matt BAKER
26 Vice Pres Marketing/Communications ... Mr. Brandon STANLEY
15 Vice Pres of Strategy and Operation ... Ms. Nola BOND
30 VP University Advancement ... Mr. Michael JOHNSON
28 VP Diversity/Equity/Inclusion ... Dr. Juanita SIMMONS
84 Assoc Provost Enroll/Retention Mgmt . Ms. Beverly S. SCHENKEL
09 Assoc Dir Institutional Research ... Ms. Mary Ann PENNISTON
08 Dir of Library Services and Opers ... Ms. Kathy HART
06 Registrar ... Ms. Terri VOGEL
37 Director Financial Assistance ... Mr. Charles MAYFIELD
36 Director of Career Services ... Ms. Joan SCHNEIDER
29 Director Alumni Relations ... Mr. Robert MACHOVSKY
19 Chief University Police Department ... Mr. Clarence GREEN
41 Director Athletics/HPERD ... Mr. Mel TJEERDSMA
23 Director Wellness Services ... Dr. Gerald WILMES
96 Director of Purchasing ... Ms. Ann MARTIN
18 Director Facility Services ... Mr. Allen MAYS
58 Assoc Prov for Grad Studies & Spec ... Dr. Gregory HADDOCK
53 Dean School of Education ... Dr. Timothy WALL
49 Dean Col of Arts & Sciences ... Dr. Michael STEINER
07 Associate Director of Admissions ... Ms. Tamara J. GROW
04 Admin Specialist to President ... Ms. Lynne GILBERT

Ozark Christian College (J)

1111 N Main Street, Joplin MO 64801-4804
County: Jasper FICE Identification: 022027
Unit ID: 178679
Telephone: (417) 626-1234 Carnegie Class: Spec-4-yr-Faith
FAX Number: (417) 624-0090 Calendar System: Semester
URL: www.occ.edu
Established: 1942 Annual Undergrad Tuition & Fees: $12,140
Enrollment: 681 Coed
Affiliation or Control: Independent Non-Profit IRS Status: 501(c)3
Highest Offering: Baccalaureate
Accreditation: BI

01 President ... Matt PROCTOR
03 Executive Vice President ... Damien SPIKEREIT
04 Executive Asst to the President ... Kathy BOWERS
05 Exec VP Academic Affairs/Dean ... Doug ALDRIDGE
06 Registrar ... Jennifer MCMILLIN
32 Vice Pres of Student Life ... Monte SHOEMAKE
10 Vice Pres of Campus Operations ... David MCMILLIN
84 Vice Pres of Enrollment Management ... Troy NELSON
26 Vice Pres of College Relations ... Jim DALRYMPLE
43 General Counsel ... Doug MILLER
30 Interim VP Development ... Sergio RIZO
09 VP Institution Research & Effective ... Teresa WELCH
20 Assistant Academic Dean ... Chad RAGSDALE
106 Dean of Online Learning ... Shawn LINDSAY
37 Director of Financial Aid ... Kim BALENTINE
121 Director of Student Success ... Andy STORMS
28 Assoc Director of Diversity ... Matthew MCBIRTH
90 LMS Administrator ... David FISH
07 Director of Enrollment Services ... Ashley NEGRON
08 Director of Library Services ... John HUNTER
64 Director of Worship Arts Dept ... Matt STAFFORD
64 Chapel Minister/Frontline Director ... Isaac SCHADE
42 Campus Minister ... Julie GARISS
42 Campus Minister ... Randy GARISS
23 Campus Nurse ... Sara WOOD
34 Dean of Women ... Lisa WHITE
27 Director Marketing & Communications ... Amy STORMS
88 Director Youth Ministry Relations ... Kevin GREER
88 Director of Ministry Center ... Bob WITTE
109 Director of Food Services ... Teresa BAKER
40 Director of Bookstore ... Bob HEATH
41 Director of Athletics ... Chris LAHM
18 Director Physical Plant ... Tim RUNYON
13 Director of IT Dept ... Mitchell PIERCY
105 Web Developer/Network Admin ... Matt DICKEY

Ozarks Technical Community College (K)

1001 E Chestnut Expressway, Springfield MO 65802-3625
County: Greene FICE Identification: 030830
Unit ID: 177472
Telephone: (417) 447-7500 Carnegie Class: Assoc/MT-VT-High Trad

FAX Number: N/A Calendar System: Semester
URL: www.otc.edu
Established: 1990 Annual Undergrad Tuition & Fees (In-District): $2,952
Enrollment: 13,614 Coed
Affiliation or Control: State/Local IRS Status: 501(c)3
Highest Offering: Associate Degree
Accreditation: NH, ACFEI, ADNUR, CAHIIM, COARC, DA, DH, EMT, IFSAC, MLTAD, OTA, PTAA, SURGT

01 Chancellor .... Dr. Hal L. HIGDON
100 Chief of Staff .... Ms. Stephanie SUMNERS
101 Secretary to the Chancellor .... Ms. Janel GRASSI
05 Vice Chancellor Academic Affairs .... Dr. Tracy MCGRADY
11 Vice Chancellor Admin Services .... Mr. Rob RECTOR
32 Vice Chancellor Student Affairs .... Ms. Joan BARRETT
10 Vice Chancellor Finance .... Ms. Marla MOODY
12 President Table Rock Campus .... Mr. Cliff DAVIS
12 President Richwood Valley Campus .... Dr. Jeff JOCHEMS
13 Chief Technology Officer .... Mr. David ESPING
15 Assoc VC Human Resources/Workforce .... Mr. Tim BALTES
20 Dean of Academic Services .... Dr. Vivian ELDER
76 Dean of Allied Health Programs .... Dr. Sherry TAYLOR
97 Dean of General Education .... Mr. Lance RENNER
72 Dean of Technical Education .... Dr. Matthew HUDSON
103 Exec Dir Workforce Development .... Mr. James ABRAMOVITZ
88 Director Business Development .... Ms. Sherry COKER
06 Asst Registrar Records/Registration .... Ms. Amy BERGANT
38 Director of Counseling Services .... Ms. Joyce BATEMAN
26 College Dir Comm & Marketing .... Mr. Mark MILLER
18 College Director Facilities/Grounds .... Mr. Rickie TAYLOR
28 College Dir Equity & Compliance .... Ms. Julia HOLMES
37 College Director of Financial Aid .... Ms. Kim CARY
08 Director College Library .... Ms. Sarah FANCHER
88 Director College Library RVC/TRC .... Ms. Angela SWIFT
36 Director of Career Employment Svcs .... Ms. Kathy CHRISTY
102 Exec Director of OTC Foundation .... Ms. Stephanie SUMNERS
30 College Director of Development .... Ms. Amy BACON
09 College Dir Research/Strategic Plng .... Mr. Matthew SIMPSON
19 College Director Safety & Security .... Mr. Scott LEVEN
35 Dean of Students .... Ms. Karla GREGG
88 Director Dual Credit/HS Admissions .... Ms. Piper WILSON
105 Director Web Services .... Mr. George LAMELZA
106 Dir Online Education/E-learning .... Mr. Matthew HARRIS
25 Director of Grant Development .... Dr. Abigail BENZ
96 Director of Procurement .... Ms. J'Neal MCCOY
07 Director of Admissions/Registrar .... Mr. Scott FIEDLER

Ozarks Technical Community College Richwood Valley (A)

3369 W Jackson Street, Nixa MO 65714
Telephone: (417) 447-7700 Identification: 770324
Accreditation: &NH

Ozarks Technical Community College Table Rock Campus (B)

10698 Historic Highway 165, Hollister MO 65672
Telephone: (417) 336-6239 Identification: 770325
Accreditation: &NH

Park University (C)

8700 River Park Drive, Parkville MO 64152-3795
County: Platte FICE Identification: 002498
Unit ID: 178721
Telephone: (816) 741-2000 Carnegie Class: Masters/M
FAX Number: (816) 746-6423 Calendar System: Semester
URL: www.park.edu
Established: 1875 Annual Undergrad Tuition & Fees: $12,130
Enrollment: 11,720 Coed
Affiliation or Control: Independent Non-Profit IRS Status: 501(c)3
Highest Offering: Master's
Accreditation: NH, ACBSP, SW

01 President .... Dr. Greg GUNDERSON
03 VP and Chief Operating Officer .... Mr. Shane SMEED
05 Interim Provost .... Dr. Michelle MYERS
10 Chief Financial Officer .... Mr. Brian BODE
111 Assoc VP of Advancement .... Mr. Nathan MARTICKE
43 Vice President & General Counsel .... Ms. Courtney GODDARD
20 Vice Provost .... Dr. Rebekkah STUTEVILLE
29 Assoc VP for External Relations .... Mr. Erik BERGRUD
32 Associate VP/Dean of Student Life .... Dr. Jayme UDEN
84 Associate VP Enrollment Services .... Mr. Eric BLAIR
20 Associate Provost .... Dr. Emily SALLEE
58 Director Graduate Student Success .... Ms. Joslyn CREIGHTON
06 Registrar .... Vacant
37 Director Student Financial Service .... Ms. Brynn BOLOGNA
08 Director of Library Systems .... Mr. Jon RITTERBUSH
44 Dir Advancement Svcs/Annual Fund .... Ms. Jessica GREASON
15 Chief Human Resources Officer .... Mr. Roger DUSING
41 Director of Athletics .... Mr. Claude ENGLISH
66 Director of Nursing Program .... Ms. Teresa CROWDER
85 Senior Dir Intl Students .... Mr. Kevin VICKER
13 Chief Information Officer .... Mr. David WHITTAKER
19 Director of Campus Safety .... Mr. William LONDON
50 MBA Gen Concentration Coordinator .... Dr. Nick KOUDOU
04 Executive Asst to the President .... Ms. Ami WISDOM
50 Dean College of Management .... Dr. Brad KLEINDL
106 Director of Online Operations .... Dr. Gregory ROSE
49 Int Dean Liberal Arts & Sciences .... Dr. James PASLEY
53 Dean School for Education .... Vacant
101 Asst Secretary to Board of Trustees .... Ms. Ami WISDOM
100 Chief of Staff .... Ms. Laure CHRISTENSEN
104 Director Global Educ/Study Abroad .... Ms. Angela PETERSON
105 Web Manager .... Ms. Gariela SA TELES
18 Manager Facilities Maintenance .... Mr. Kevin MARTINEAU
26 Dir of Comm & Public Relations .... Mr. Brad BILES
36 Director of Career Development .... Ms. Leah FLETCHER
38 Director of Counseling Center .... Mr. Dustin WALL
39 Director Student Housing .... Ms. Karie SCHAEFER
21 Senior Director Financial Report .... Ms. Donna BAKER
09 Director Institutional Effectivenes .... Ms. Fiorella PENALOZA

Pinnacle Career Institute (D)

10301 Hickman Mills Drive, Kansas City MO 64137
County: Jackson FICE Identification: 010405
Unit ID: 177302
Telephone: (816) 331-5700 Carnegie Class: Spec 2-yr-Health
FAX Number: (816) 331-2026 Calendar System: Quarter
URL: www.pcitraining.edu
Established: 1953 Annual Undergrad Tuition & Fees: N/A
Enrollment: 807 Coed
Affiliation or Control: Proprietary IRS Status: Proprietary
Highest Offering: Associate Degree
Accreditation: ACICS

01 Executive Director .... Matt KILLDAY
05 Chief Academic Officer .... Amanda EDWARDS
36 Director Student and Career Service .... Nick FOLEY

Pinnacle Career Institute (E)

11500 Ambassador Road, Suite 221, Kansas City MO 64153
Telephone: (816) 270-5300 Identification: 770737
Accreditation: ACICS

Ranken Technical College (F)

4431 Finney Avenue, Saint Louis MO 63113-2898
County: Saint Louis FICE Identification: 012500
Unit ID: 178891
Telephone: (314) 371-0236 Carnegie Class: Bac/Assoc-Mixed
FAX Number: (314) 371-0241 Calendar System: Semester
URL: ranken.edu/
Established: 1907 Annual Undergrad Tuition & Fees: $14,457
Enrollment: 1,923 Coed
Affiliation or Control: Independent Non-Profit IRS Status: 501(c)3
Highest Offering: Baccalaureate
Accreditation: NH

01 President .... Mr. Stan SHOUN
10 Vice President for Finance & Admin .... Mr. Peter T. MURTAUGH
03 Executive Vice President .... Mr. Don POHL
51 Dean of Continuing Education .... Mr. Keyvan GERAMI
05 Dean Academic Affairs .... Ms. Crystal HERRON
84 Dean of Enrollment Management .... Ms. Missy BORCHARDT
111 Dir Institutional Advancement .... Mr. Tony PISCIOTTA
07 Admissions Director .... Mr. Michael E. HAWLEY
06 Registrar .... Ms. Carol J. WINKLER
18 Director Buildings & Grounds .... Mr. David CADLE
29 Director of Alumni Relations .... Ms. Kathy T. FERN
37 Director Financial Aid .... Ms. Michelle L. WILLIAMS
21 Business Office Manager .... Ms. Sara M. DAMINSKI
36 Career Services Coordinator .... Ms. Janie K. SUMMERS
15 Human Resources Coordinator .... Ms. Janice A. BOLLMANN
04 Administrative Asst to President .... Ms. Patricia CAPPS

Research College of Nursing (G)

2525 E Meyer Boulevard, Kansas City MO 64132-1133
County: Jackson FICE Identification: 006392
Unit ID: 178989
Telephone: (816) 995-2800 Carnegie Class: Spec-4-yr-Other Health
FAX Number: (816) 995-2817 Calendar System: Semester
URL: www.researchcollege.edu
Established: 1980 Annual Undergrad Tuition & Fees: N/A
Enrollment: 385 Coed
Affiliation or Control: Proprietary IRS Status: Proprietary
Highest Offering: Master's
Accreditation: NH, NURSE

01 President .... Dr. Thad R. WILSON
05 Dean .... Dr. Julie NAUSER
07 Director Admissions .... Ms. Leslie BURRY
32 Director Student Affairs .... Ms. Amanda GRAY
37 Director Financial Aid .... Ms. Stacie WITHERS
24 Director LRC .... Ms. Tobey STOSBERG
09 Senior Technology Analyst .... Mr. Bill HAMPSON
04 Administrative Asst to President .... Mrs. Sherry L. OWEN
06 Registrar .... Ms. Camelia WILLIAMS
08 Head Librarian .... Ms. Kitty SERLING
106 Dir Online Education/E-learning .... Ms. Sheryl MAX

Rockbridge Seminary (H)

3111 East Battlefield Street, Springfield MO 65804
County: Greene Identification: 667151
Telephone: (866) 931-4300 Carnegie Class: Not Classified
FAX Number: (866) 931-4300 Calendar System: Semester
URL: www.rockbridge.edu
Established: 2002 Annual Graduate Tuition & Fees: N/A
Enrollment: N/A Coed
Affiliation or Control: Independent Non-Profit IRS Status: 501(c)3
Highest Offering: Doctorate; No Undergraduates
Accreditation: DEAC

01 President .... Dr. Daryl ELDRIDGE
05 Chief Academic Officer .... Dr. Mark SIMPSON
08 Head Librarian .... Seth ALLEN
04 Administrative Asst to President .... Heather WILLIAMSON
29 Director Alumni Relations .... Linda GRABER

Rockhurst University (I)

1100 Rockhurst Road, Kansas City MO 64110-2561
County: Jackson FICE Identification: 002499
Unit ID: 179043
Telephone: (816) 501-4000 Carnegie Class: Masters/L
FAX Number: (816) 501-4588 Calendar System: Semester
URL: www.rockhurst.edu
Established: 1910 Annual Undergrad Tuition & Fees: $35,670
Enrollment: 2,825 Coed
Affiliation or Control: Roman Catholic IRS Status: 501(c)3
Highest Offering: Doctorate
Accreditation: NH, CAEPT, OT, PTA, SP

01 President .... Rev. Thomas B. CURRAN
30 Vice President for Advancement .... Ms. Mary MOONEY BURNS
10 Chief Financial Officer .... Mr. Gerald MOENCH
05 Vice Pres for Academic Affairs .... Dr. Douglas N. DUNHAM
88 Asst to Pres for Mission & Ministry .... Dr. Ellen SPAKE
32 VP Student Development/Athletics .... Dr. Matthew D. QUICK
18 Assoc VP Facilities & Technology .... Mr. Matt W. HEINRICH
84 Associate Vice Pres Enrollment .... Mr. Matthew ELLIS
20 Assoc VP Academic Affairs/Planning .... Dr. Paula SHORTER
35 Director of Student Life .... Ms. Angie CARR ROBINETT
88 Assistant Dean of Students .... Mrs. Sandy WADDELL
39 Associate Dean of Students .... Mr. Mark HETZLER
04 Assistant to the President .... Ms. Decla TYLER-SIMPSON
50 Dean Helzberg Sch of Management .... Dr. Cheryl M. MCCONNELL
49 Dean Arts & Sciences .... Dr. Pedro MALIGO
58 Int Dean Col Health/Human Services .... Dr. Cheryl MCCONNELL
66 Pres Research College of Nursing .... Dr. Nancy DEBASIO
08 Director Library .... Ms. Laurie E. HATHMAN
06 Registrar .... Ms. Brenda LANEY
37 Director Student Financial Aid .... Ms. Maureen MCKINNON
41 Director of Athletics .... Mr. Gary BURNS
15 Director of Human Resources .... Ms. Barbra UPTON-GARVIN
13 Director of Infrastructure Services .... Mr. Michael CRAIG
36 Director of Career Center .... Mr. Michael J. THEOBALD
30 Director of Advancement .... Ms. Carrie MADDEN
26 Director of Public Relations .... Ms. Katherine FROHOFF
29 Director of University Engagement .... Ms. Mary MOONEY BURNS
88 Director of Marketing .... Ms. Jennifer KNOBEL
42 Director of Campus Ministry .... Ms. Cindy SCHMERSAL
19 Director Security/Safety .... Mr. Randy HOPKINS
38 Director of Student Counseling .... Dr. Elbert DARDEN
31 Director Community Relations .... Ms. Alicia R. DOUGLAS
07 Director of Operations-Admission .... Ms. Annie LEHWALD
40 Director Bookstore .... Ms. Jami CADE
108 Assessment Director .... Ms. Annalisa GRAMLICH
09 Institutional Research Director .... Ms. Wendy PICKEL
28 Area & Diversity Coordinator .... Ms. Emily J. KEMPF
14 Support Manager - Computer Services .... Mr. Darnell JONES
88 Controller .... Ms. Kris PACE
88 Dean Research College of Nursing .... Ms. Julie NAUSER
105 Web Development Director .... Mr. Jeremiah BARBER
104 Study Abroad Advisor .... Ms. Paivi GIANNIOS

St. Charles Community College (J)

4601 Mid Rivers Mall Drive, Cottleville MO 63376-2865
County: Saint Charles FICE Identification: 025306
Unit ID: 262031
Telephone: (636) 922-8000 Carnegie Class: Assoc/HT-High Trad
FAX Number: (636) 922-8352 Calendar System: Semester
URL: www.stchas.edu
Established: 1986 Annual Undergrad Tuition & Fees (In-District): $2,544
Enrollment: 6,865 Coed
Affiliation or Control: State/Local IRS Status: 501(c)3
Highest Offering: Associate Degree
Accreditation: NH, ADNUR, CAHIIM, CSHSE, EMT, OTA

01 President .... Dr. Barbara KAVALIER
04 Exec Assistant to the President .... Ms. Julie PARCEL
05 VP Academic/Student Affairs .... Dr. John BOOKSTAVER
30 VP College Advancement/Planning .... Ms. Kasey MCKEE
10 VP Administrative Services .... Mr. Todd GALBIERZ
15 VP Human Resources .... Ms. Donna DAVIS
26 VP Marketing/Enrollment Services .... Ms. Heather MCDORMAN
18 Director of Facilities .... Mr. Al KOEHLER
20 AVP for Academic/Student Affairs .... Dr. Michael B. DOMPIERRE
62 Dean Learning Resources & Acad Sup .... Dr. Stephanie TOLSON
09 Director Grants and Research .... Dr. Chris JACKSON
13 Chief Information Officer .... Mr. Chad SHEPHERD
84 Dean Enrollment Services .... Ms. Kathy BROCKGREITENS
19 Director Public Safety .... Mr. Bob RONKOSKI
90 Director Technology Support .... Ms. Lisa MOUSER
32 Dean of Student Success .... Mr. Boyd COPELAND
51 Assoc Dean Continuing Education .... Ms. Tina SIEKER
50 Dean Bus/Sci/Educ/Math & Comp Sci .... Vacant
57 Dean Arts/Humanities & Soc Sci .... Vacant
40 Director Bookstore and Food Service .... Ms. Patricia A. HAYNES
41 Athletic Director .... Mr. Chris G. GOBER

96 Director Purchasing ..... Ms. Christine E. ROMER
91 Director Administrative Computing ..... Vacant
06 Registrar ..... Ms. Kathy BROCKGREITENS
21 Director Financial Services ..... Ms. Susan RUBEMEYER
36 Job Placement Coordinator ..... Ms. Martha A. TOEBBEN
51 Dean Corporate & Community Dev ..... Ms. Amanda SIZEMORE
88 Assoc Dean Student Success ..... Ms. Kelley PFEIFFER

Saint Louis Christian College (A)

1360 Grandview Drive, Florissant MO 63033-6499
County: Saint Louis FICE Identification: 012580
Unit ID: 179256
Telephone: (314) 837-6777 Carnegie Class: Spec-4-yr-Faith
FAX Number: (314) 837-8291 Calendar System: Semester
URL: https://stlchristian.edu/
Established: 1956 Annual Undergrad Tuition & Fees: $11,240
Enrollment: 173 Coed
Affiliation or Control: Other Protestant IRS Status: 501(c)3
Highest Offering: Baccalaureate
Accreditation: BI

00 Chancellor ..... Mr. Thomas W. MCGEE
01 President ..... Dr. Terry STINE
05 Academic Dean ..... Dr. Eddy SANDERS
10 Vice Pres of Finance/Operations ..... Dr. Judy LINCOLN
32 Dean of Students ..... Ms. Christine CABLE
08 Library Manager ..... Dr. Michael PABARCUS
41 Athletic Director ..... Mr. Scott WOMBLE
06 Registrar ..... Ms. Cindy BINGAMON
37 Financial Aid Director ..... Ms. Pam RALLS
13 IT Tech Services Director ..... Ms. Norma BAKER
84 Director Enrollment Management ..... Mr. Bob FARRAR
40 Bookstore Manager ..... Ms. Jeri Ann JERALDS
07 Admissions Counselor ..... Ms. Haley WOMBLE

Saint Louis College of Health Careers-Fenton Campus (B)

1297 N Highway Drive, Fenton MO 63026-1909
Telephone: (636) 529-0000 Identification: 666274
Accreditation: ABHES, COARC, OTA, PTAA

† Branch campus of Saint Louis College of Health Careers-South Taylor, Saint Louis, MO.

Saint Louis College of Health Careers-South Taylor (C)

909 S Taylor Avenue, Saint Louis MO 63110-1511
County: Saint Louis FICE Identification: 023405
Unit ID: 179511
Telephone: (314) 652-0300 Carnegie Class: Spec 2-yr-Health
FAX Number: (314) 884-2838 Calendar System: Semester
URL: www.slchc.edu
Established: 1981 Annual Undergrad Tuition & Fees: N/A
Enrollment: 299 Coed
Affiliation or Control: Proprietary IRS Status: Proprietary
Highest Offering: Associate Degree
Accreditation: ABHES

11 Chief of Administration ..... Dr. Rush ROBINSON
06 Registrar ..... Ms. Teresa JACKSON
84 Director of Enrollment Management ..... Ms. Joanna FINCH
36 Director Student Placement ..... Ms. Hannah PFLANZ
53 Director of Education ..... Ms. Melissa BROWN

St. Louis College of Pharmacy (D)

4588 Parkview Place, Saint Louis MO 63110-1088
County: Independent City FICE Identification: 002504
Unit ID: 179265
Telephone: (314) 367-8700 Carnegie Class: Spec-4-yr-Other Health
FAX Number: (314) 446-8304 Calendar System: Semester
URL: www.stlcop.edu
Established: 1864 Annual Undergrad Tuition & Fees: $28,620
Enrollment: 1,389 Coed
Affiliation or Control: Independent Non-Profit IRS Status: 501(c)3
Highest Offering: First Professional Degree
Accreditation: NH, PHAR

01 President ..... Dr. John A. PIEPER
30 Vice Pres Devel/Alumni Relations ..... Vacant
10 VP Finance/Administration/CFO ..... Ms. Heather FLABIANO
84 VP Enrollment Services/Marketing ..... Ms. Beth KESERAUSKIS
13 Vice Pres Info Technology & CIO ..... Vacant
18 AVP College Services ..... Mr. Eric KNOLL
49 Dean Arts & Science/Student Affairs ..... Dr. Kimberly J. KILGORE
67 Dean of Pharmacy ..... Dr. Bruce CANADAY
15 Director of Human Resources ..... Mr. Daniel C. BAUER
30 Senior Development Officer ..... Ms. Colleen WATERMON
06 Registrar ..... Ms. Laura KLOS
08 Library Director ..... Ms. Jill NISSEN
37 Director of Financial Aid ..... Mr. Daniel J. STIFFLER
41 Director of Athletics ..... Ms. Jill HARTER
88 Special Assistant to the President ..... Sr. Mary Louise DEGENHART
88 Special Assistant to the President ..... Mr. Michael SASS
07 Director of Admissions ..... Mr. Chase DAVIS
108 AVP Institutional Effectiveness ..... Mr. George VINEYARD
19 Director Security/Safety ..... Mr. Scott PATTERSON
29 Director Alumni Relations ..... Ms. Stephanie HOFFMANN

38 Director Counseling Center ..... Ms. Michelle HASTINGS
43 General Counsel ..... Mr. Kenneth FLEISCHMANN
44 Annual Giving Officer ..... Mr. Kevin LISTER

*Saint Louis Community College - Cosand Center (E)

300 S Broadway, Saint Louis MO 63102-2820
County: Saint Louis FICE Identification: 002471
Unit ID: 179283
Telephone: (314) 539-5000 Carnegie Class: N/A
FAX Number: (314) 539-5170
URL: www.stlcc.edu

01 Chancellor ..... Dr. Jeff PITTMAN
05 Vice Chanc Academic Affairs ..... Dr. Andrew LANGREHR
10 Vice Chanc Finance/Administration ..... Mr. Paul ZINCK
32 Vice Chanc Student Affairs ..... Mr. Anthony CRUZ
103 Assoc VC Workforce & Cmty Develop ..... Mr. Stephen LONG
13 Chief Information Officer ..... Mr. Keith HACKE
15 Assoc Vice Chanc Human Resources ..... Mr. Bill MILLER
102 Executive Director STLCC Foundation ..... Ms. Jo-Ann DIGMAN
26 Exec Dir Marketing/Communication ..... Ms. Kendra TOLSON
09 Director of Institutional Research ..... Ms. Kelli BURNS
20 Associate Provost ..... Mr. Michael DREITH
112 Director of Grants ..... Ms. Gina BENESH
84 Sr Mgr Enrollment Processing ..... Ms. Karla GABLE
04 Administrative Asst to Chancellor ..... Ms. Yvonne BLOOM
101 Secretary of the Board ..... Ms. Rebecca GARRISON
106 Mgr Online Student Services ..... Ms. Stacey FOSTER
37 Dir Dist Financial Aid/Scholarships . Ms. Regina G. BLACKSHEAR
96 Assistant Controller ..... Ms. Cindy GREEN
19 Int Director Public Safety ..... LtCol. Alfred ADKINS
41 Director Athletics ..... Mr. Shawn SUMME
43 Dir Legal Services/General Counsel ..... Ms. Mary NELSON

**Saint Louis Community College at Florissant Valley* (F)

3400 Pershall Road, Saint Louis MO 63135-1499
Telephone: (314) 513-4200 FICE Identification: 002470
Accreditation: &NH, ADNUR, ART, DIETT, ENGT

**Saint Louis Community College at Forest Park* (G)

5600 Oakland Avenue, Saint Louis MO 63110-1393
Telephone: (314) 644-9100 Identification: 770946
Accreditation: NH, ACFEI, ADNUR, CAHIIM, COARC, DA, DH, DMS, EMT, FUSER, MLTAD, RAD, SURGT

**Saint Louis Community College at Meramec* (H)

11333 Big Bend Road, Kirkwood MO 63122-5799
Telephone: (314) 984-7500 FICE Identification: 002472
Accreditation: &NH, ADNUR, ART, OTA, PTAA

**Saint Louis Community College at Wildwood* (I)

2645 Generations Drive, Wildwood MO 63040-1168
Telephone: (636) 422-2000 Identification: 667084
Accreditation: &NH

Saint Louis University (J)

One Grand Boulevard, Saint Louis MO 63103-2097
County: Independent City FICE Identification: 002506
Unit ID: 179159
Telephone: (314) 977-2500 Carnegie Class: DU-Higher
FAX Number: (314) 977-3874 Calendar System: Semester
URL: www.slu.edu
Established: 1818 Annual Undergrad Tuition & Fees: $40,726
Enrollment: 17,047 Coed
Affiliation or Control: Roman Catholic IRS Status: 501(c)3
Highest Offering: Doctorate
Accreditation: NH, AAB, ARCPA, ART, CAATE, CAEPN, CAHIIM, CLPSY, DENT, DIETD, DIETI, ENG, HSA, LAW, #MED, MFCD, MT, NMT, NURSE, OT, PH, PTA, RADMAG, RTT, SP, SW

01 President ..... Dr. Fred P. PESTELLO
05 Provost ..... Dr. Nancy BRICKHOUSE
10 Vice Pres/Chief Financial Officer ..... Mr. David HEIMBURGER
18 Assoc VP Facilities Management ..... Mr. Michael LUCIDO
84 VP Enrollment & Ret Management ..... Mr. Jay GOFF
12 Director Madrid Campus ..... Dr. Paul VITA
15 VP Human Resources ..... Mr. Mickey LUNA
26 VP Marketing and Communications ..... Mr. Jeffrey FOWLER
43 Vice President/General Counsel ..... Mr. William R. KAUFFMAN
32 Vice President Student Development ..... Dr. Kent PORTERFIELD
30 VP Development ..... Ms. Sheila M. MANION
42 Spcl Asst to Pres Mission/Identity .. Fr. Christopher COLLINS, SJ
13 Vice Pres Information Tech Svcs/CIO ..... Mr. David HAKANSON
23 Vice President for Medical Affairs ..... Dr. Kevin BEHRNS
27 Asst VP for Marketing & Creat Svcs ..... Ms. Laura GEISER
29 Exec Development Director ..... Ms. Meg CONNOLLY
21 Assistant Controller ..... Mr. Fred R. WINKLER
35 Associate VP and Dean of Students ..... Dr. Ramona HICKS
54 Dean Parks Col Engr/Aviation ..... Dr. Michelle SABICK
76 Dean Doisy College of Health Scis ..... Dr. Mardell WILSON
49 Dean Arts & Sciences ..... Dr. Christopher DUNCAN
50 Dean Cook School of Business ..... Dr. Mark HIGGINS

61 Dean of Law ..... Mr. William P. JOHNSON
63 Dean of Medical School ..... Dr. Kevin BEHRNS
79 Dean Philosophy & Letters ..... Bro. William REHG, SJ
69 Dean Col Pub Health & Soc Justice ..... Dr. Collins AIRHIHENBUWA
53 Int Dean College of Education ..... Dr. Molly SCHALLER
08 University Librarian ..... Mr. David CASSENS
88 Exec Dir Ctr for Health Care Ethics ..... Dr. Jeffrey BISHOP
52 Exec Dir Ctr Advanced Dental Educ ..... Dr. John HATTON
46 Vice President for Research ..... Dr. Kenneth OLLIFF
19 Asst VP Pub Safety & Emergency Prep ..... Mr. James MORAN
06 University Registrar ..... Mr. Jay HAUGEN
07 Dean of Undergraduate Admission ..... Ms. Jean GILMAN
37 Director Financial Aid ..... Ms. Cari S. WICKLIFFE
39 Director Housing & Res Life ..... Ms. Melinda CARLSON
41 Athletics Director ..... Mr. Christopher V. MAY
36 Director Career Services ..... Ms. Kim REITTER
85 Director International Center ..... Vacant
92 Assistant Director Honors Program ..... Mr. Robert PAMPEL
23 Dir Student Health Ctr/Counseling ..... Dr. Steve BRYNES
31 Pgm Mgr Leadership Community Svcs ..... Dr. Bryan SOKOL
100 Chief of Staff ..... Mr. William KAUFFMAN
88 Director Univ Museums/Galleries ..... Dr. Petruta LIPAN
44 Exec Development Dir Planned Giving ..... Mr. Kent G. LEVAN
40 Manager Bookstore ..... Ms. Debbie SCHNEIDER
20 Asst Academic Vice President ..... Dr. Steven SANCHEZ
96 Director of Business Services ..... Mr. Jeff HOVEY
22 Dir Ofc of Inst Equity & Diversity ..... Ms. Michelle LEWIS
86 Director Government Relations ..... Mr. Marc SCHEESSELE
28 VP Diversity/Community Engagement ..... Dr. Jonathan C. SMITH
103 Executive Dir Workforce Development ..... Ms. Katherine CAIN
105 Director Web Services ..... Mr. Mark RIMAR
38 Director Student Counseling ..... Dr. Steve BYRNES

Saint Luke's College of Health Sciences (K)

624 Westport Road, Kansas City MO 64111
County: Jackson FICE Identification: 009782
Unit ID: 179450
Telephone: (816) 936-8700 Carnegie Class: Spec-4-yr-Other Health
FAX Number: N/A Calendar System: Semester
URL: www.saintlukescollege.edu
Established: 1903 Annual Undergrad Tuition & Fees: N/A
Enrollment: 516 Coed
Affiliation or Control: Independent Non-Profit IRS Status: 501(c)3
Highest Offering: Master's
Accreditation: NH, NURSE

01 President/CEO ..... Dr. Hubert BENITEZ
05 Academic Dean ..... Dr. Victoria GRANDO
10 Chief Financial Officer ..... Ms. Rebecca PECK
32 Dean of Students ..... Ms. Marcia LADAGE
88 Director Accreditation/Quality Mgmt ..... Ms. Tere NAYLOR
30 Chief Development Officer ..... Dr. Melody MESSNER
06 Registrar/Dir Records Management ..... Ms. Barbara NUTT
26 Communications/Alumni Rels Mgr ..... Ms. Laurie DELONG
84 Director Enrollment Management ..... Mr. Josh RICHARDS

Southeast Missouri Hospital College of Nursing and Health Sciences (L)

2001 William Street, 2nd Floor,
Cape Girardeau MO 63703-5815
County: Cape Girardeau FICE Identification: 030709
Unit ID: 417734
Telephone: (573) 334-6825 Carnegie Class: Spec 2-yr-Health
FAX Number: (573) 339-7805 Calendar System: Semester
URL: www.sehcollege.edu
Established: 1990 Annual Undergrad Tuition & Fees: $17,580
Enrollment: 243 Coed
Affiliation or Control: Independent Non-Profit IRS Status: 501(c)3
Highest Offering: Baccalaureate
Accreditation: NH, ADNUR, MT, NURSE, RAD, SURGT

01 President ..... Dr. Tonya BUTTRY
05 Dean for General Education ..... Dr. Lance RATCLIFF
66 Dean of Nursing ..... Dr. Donna SHIRRELL
06 Registrar ..... Ms. Debbie HOWEY
37 Financial Aid Coordinator ..... Ms. Margie SCHWENT
07 Admissions/Instl Research Officer ..... Ms. Rhonda VANDERGRIFF
10 Business Officer ..... Ms. Deanna SELLS

Southeast Missouri State University (M)

One University Plaza, Cape Girardeau MO 63701-4799
County: Cape Girardeau FICE Identification: 002501
Unit ID: 179557
Telephone: (573) 651-2000 Carnegie Class: Masters/L
FAX Number: (573) 651-2200 Calendar System: Semester
URL: www.semo.edu
Established: 1873 Annual Undergrad Tuition & Fees (In-State): $6,990
Enrollment: 11,987 Coed
Affiliation or Control: State IRS Status: 501(c)3
Highest Offering: Beyond Master's But Less Than Doctorate
Accreditation: NH, #CAATE, CACREP, CAEPN, CEA, CIDA, CS, DIETD, DIETI, ENG, ENGT, JOUR, MUS, NAIT, NRPA, NURSE, SP, SW, THEA

01 President ... Dr. Carlos VARGAS
05 Provost/Chief Academic Ofcr ... Dr. Karl KUNKEL
10 VP Finance & Administration ... Mrs. Kathy M. MANGELS
84 VP Enrollment Mgmt/Student Success ... Dr. Debbie BELOW
111 Vice Pres University Advancement ... Mr. Bill HOLLAND
20 Vice Provost ... Dr. Charles MCALLISTER
108 Assoc Prov for Acad Eff & Stdnt Suc ... Dr. Bethany ALDEN-RIVERS
09 Director of Institutional Research ... Mr. Eric CHAMBERS
100 Chief of Staff & Asst to the Pres ... Mr. Chris MARTIN
22 Coord of Inst Equity & Diversity ... Ms. Sonia RUCKER
13 Asst Vice Pres Information Tech ... Mr. Floyd DAVENPORT
58 Dean Sch of Grad Studies ... Dr. Charles MCALLISTER
50 Int Dean Harrison Col of Business ... Dr. Judy WILES
53 Dean College of Education ... Dr. Diana ROGERS-ADKINSON
76 Dean College Health & Human Svc ... Dr. Morris JENKINS
79 Dean College of Liberal Arts ... Dr. Francisco BARRIOS
72 Dean College of Science/Tech & Ag ... Dr. Chris MCGOWAN
32 Dean of Students ... Dr. Debbie BELOW
08 Dean of Kent Library ... Ms. Barbara GLACKIN
07 Director of Admissions ... Ms. Lenell HAHN
109 AVP Stdnt Success & Auxiliary Svcs ... Dr. Bruce SKINNER
35 Director of Campus Life & Event Svc ... Ms. Michele IRBY
26 Exec Dir Univ Comm & Mktg ... Mr. Jeff HARMON
41 Director of Athletics ... Mr. Brady L. BARKE
29 Director Alumni Services ... Mr. Jay WOLZ
85 Exec Dir Intl Education & Svcs ... Mr. Kevin TIMLIN
12 Director Malden Campus ... Dr. Nicholas THIELE
12 Director Kennett Campus ... Ms. Marsha L. BLANCHARD
12 Director Sikeston Campus ... Mr. Stephen BORGSMILLER
18 Director of Facilities Management ... Ms. Angela MEYER
37 Director of Financial Aid ... Ms. Karen WALKER
27 Director of News Bureau ... Ms. Ann K. HAYES
15 Director of Human Resources ... Ms. Alissa VANDEVEN
19 Dir of Public Safety/Trans ... Ms. Beth GLAUS
06 Registrar ... Ms. Sandy L. HINKLE
88 Director of Show Me Center ... Mr. Wil GORMAN
92 Int Dir Jane Stephens Honors Pgm ... Dr. Jim MCGILL
38 Dir Counseling & Disability Svcs ... Ms. Torie GROGRAN
21 Controller & Asst Treasurer ... Ms. Pam SANDER
39 Director of Residence Life ... Dr. Kendra SKINNER

Southwest Baptist University (A)

1600 University Avenue, Bolivar MO 65613-2597
County: Polk FICE Identification: 002502
Unit ID: 179326
Telephone: (417) 328-5281 Carnegie Class: Masters/M
FAX Number: (417) 328-1514 Calendar System: Semester
URL: www.sbuniv.edu
Established: 1878 Annual Undergrad Tuition & Fees: $22,508
Enrollment: 3,701 Coed
Affiliation or Control: Southern Baptist IRS Status: 501(c)3
Highest Offering: Doctorate
Accreditation: NH, ACBSP, ADNUR, CAATE, CS, MUS, NUR, PTA, RAD, SW

01 President ... Dr. Pat TAYLOR
05 Provost ... Dr. Lee SKINKLE
11 Vice President Administration ... Mrs. Tara PARSON
30 Vice President University Relations ... Dr. Brad JOHNSON
84 Dean of Enrollment Management ... Mr. Darren CROWDER
32 Vice Pres for Student Development ... Dr. Rob HARRIS
12 VP for Branch Campuses ... Dr. Robert MCGLASSON
20 Associate Provost ... Dr. Allison LANGFORD
10 Controller ... Ms. Terri ROGERS
29 Director of Alumni Engagement ... Mrs. Holly BRIDGE
07 Director Admissions ... Mrs. Becky VAN STAVERN
41 Athletic Director ... Mr. Mike PITTS
06 Registrar ... Mr. John CREDILLE
35 Director Student Activities ... Dr. Nathan PENLAND
39 Director Residence Life ... Ms. Landee NEVILLS
42 Director University Ministries ... Mr. Kurt CADDY
15 Director of Human Resources ... Mrs. Carolyn O'KELLEY
18 Director Physical Plant ... Mr. Bob GLIDWELL
19 Director Campus Security ... Mr. Mark GRABOWSKI
08 Director of Library Services ... Dr. Ed WALTON
50 Dean College Business/Computer Sci ... Dr. Troy BETHARDS
73 Dean College Theology/Ministry ... Dr. Rodney REEVES
53 Dean Education/Social Sciences ... Dr. Kevin SCHRIVER
57 Dean Music/Arts/Letters ... Dr. Jeff WATERS
81 Dean Science/Math ... Dr. Perry TOMPKINS
36 Director of Career Services ... Mrs. Suzanne POWERS
13 Network Administrator ... Mr. Kevin KELLEY
90 Director Instructional Technology ... Vacant
91 Chief Technology Officer ... Mr. David BOLTON
38 Director Counseling Services ... Mrs. Debbie WALKER
37 Director Student Financial Planning ... Mr. Brad GAMBLE
56 Director Extended Learning ... Mr. Scott MCNEAL
26 Chief Public Relations Officer ... Mrs. Charlotte MARSCH
09 Director of Institutional Research ... Vacant
96 Director of Purchasing ... Vacant
40 Book Store Manager ... Ms. Carol SHOEMAKER
04 Administrative Asst to President ... Mrs. Ashley DINWIDDIE

Southwest Baptist University Mountain View Center (B)

PO Box 489, Mountain View MO 65548
Telephone: (417) 934-2999 Identification: 770326
Accreditation: &NH

Southwest Baptist University Salem Center (C)

501 S Grand, Salem MO 65560
Telephone: (573) 729-7071 Identification: 770327
Accreditation: &NH

Southwest Baptist University Springfield Center (D)

4431 S Fremont, Springfield MO 65804
Telephone: (417) 820-5049 Identification: 770328
Accreditation: &NH

State Fair Community College (E)

3201 W 16th Street, Sedalia MO 65301-2199
County: Pettis FICE Identification: 008080
Unit ID: 179539
Telephone: (660) 596-7222 Carnegie Class: Assoc/HT-Mix Trad/Non
FAX Number: (660) 596-7335 Calendar System: Semester
URL: www.sfccmo.edu
Established: 1966 Annual Undergrad Tuition & Fees (In-District): $2,640
Enrollment: 4,934 Coed
Affiliation or Control: Local IRS Status: 501(c)3
Highest Offering: Associate Degree
Accreditation: NH, CAHIIM, CONST, DH, OTA, RAD

01 President ... Dr. Joanna ANDERSON
05 VP for Educ/Student Support Svcs ... Dr. Brent BATES
10 VP for Finance/Administration & HR ... Mr. Garry SORRELL
20 Dean of Academic Affairs ... Mr. Jim CUNNINGHAM
75 Dean Vocational/Technical Studies ... Mr. Mark KELCHNER
38 Dean Student/Academic Support ... Dr. Joe GILGOUR
13 Chief Information Officer ... Mr. Mark HAVERLY
102 Exec Director SFCC Foundation ... Ms. Mary TREVNER
06 Registrar ... Mrs. Jennifer WILBANKS
37 Director of Financial Aid ... Ms. Lana DEJAYNES
18 Chief Facilities/Physical Plant ... Mr. Justin O'NEAL
21 Controller Business Officer ... Mrs. Diane BROCKMAN
26 Exec Dir Marketing/Communication ... Mrs. Dana KELCHNER
07 Director of Admissions ... Vacant
04 Executive Asst to President ... Ms. Toni WALTER
41 Athletic Director ... Mr. Darren PANNIER
15 Director Human Resources ... Ms. Linda CHURCH

State Technical College of Missouri (F)

One Technology Drive, Linn MO 65051-0479
County: Osage FICE Identification: 004711
Unit ID: 177977
Telephone: (573) 897-5000 Carnegie Class: Assoc/HVT-High Trad
FAX Number: N/A Calendar System: Semester
URL: www.statetechmo.edu
Established: 1961 Annual Undergrad Tuition & Fees (In-State): $5,873
Enrollment: 1,274 Coed
Affiliation or Control: State IRS Status: 501(c)3
Highest Offering: Associate Degree
Accreditation: NH, DA, NAIT, PTAA, RAD

01 President ... Dr. Shawn D. STRONG
05 Dean Academic Affairs/Student Svcs ... Victoria SCHWINKE
13 Dean Information Technology ... Mike VANDELICHT
09 Dean Institutional Research/Plng ... Dr. Rick MIHALEVICH
30 Executive Director Development ... Vacant
08 Int College Librarian ... Christina PRUCHA
37 Director Student Financial Aid ... Becky WHITHAUS
06 Registrar ... Elaine BRANDT
07 Director Admissions ... Shelle JACOBS
10 Director of Finance ... Jennifer JACOBS
20 Associate Academic Officer ... Janet CLANTON
21 Controller ... Vacant
26 Director of Marketing ... Brandon MCELWAIN
32 Director Student Affairs ... Richard PEMBERTON
36 Director Student Placement ... Glenda WHITNEY
28 Director of Diversity ... Richard PEMBERTON
15 Director Personnel Services ... Jennifer JACOBS
84 Director Enrollment Management ... Shelle JACOBS
18 Chief Facilities/Physical Plant ... Brad CREDE
38 Student Counselor ... Rebecca MEHMERT
101 Secretary of the Institution/Board ... Amy AMES
86 Director Government Relations ... Becky DUNN

Stephens College (G)

1200 E Broadway, Columbia MO 65215-0001
County: Boone FICE Identification: 002512
Unit ID: 179548
Telephone: (573) 442-2211 Carnegie Class: Masters/S
FAX Number: (573) 876-7248 Calendar System: Semester
URL: www.stephens.edu
Established: 1833 Annual Undergrad Tuition & Fees: $29,754
Enrollment: 901 Female
Affiliation or Control: Independent Non-Profit IRS Status: 501(c)3
Highest Offering: Master's
Accreditation: NH, #ARCPA, CAHIIM

01 President ... Dr. Dianne LYNCH
10 Vice Pres Finance/Business/CFO ... Mr. Timothy KLOCKO
05 Vice Pres Academic Affairs ... Dr. Leslie WILLEY
111 Vice Pres Institutional Advancement ... Ms. Meichele FOSTER
32 Vice Pres Student Development ... Dr. Vicky OWLES
26 VP of Marketing/Public Relations ... Ms. Rebecca KLINE
84 Vice President Enrollment Mgmt ... Dr. Brian SAJKO
06 Registrar ... Ms. Linda SHARP
13 IT Director ... Mr. Mark BRUNNER
41 Athletic Director ... Mr. Adam SAMSON
21 Director of Accounting ... Vacant
37 Director of Financial Aid ... Ms. Kimberly STONECIPHER-FISHER
04 Executive Asst to President ... Ms. Lita PISTONO
07 Director of Admissions ... Ms. Tiffany GOALDER
08 Head Librarian ... Mr. Dan KAMMER
18 Director of Facilities Mgmt ... Mr. Ken ROBERTS
19 Director Security/Safety ... Mr. Ken HAMMOND
39 Director of Residence Life ... Ms. Alissa PEI

Stevens Institute of Business & Arts (H)

1521 Washington Avenue, Saint Louis MO 63103
County: Saint Louis FICE Identification: 008552
Unit ID: 178767
Telephone: (314) 421-0949 Carnegie Class: Spec-4-yr-Bus
FAX Number: (314) 421-0304 Calendar System: Quarter
URL: www.siba.edu
Established: 1947 Annual Undergrad Tuition & Fees: $14,310
Enrollment: 127 Coed
Affiliation or Control: Proprietary IRS Status: Proprietary
Highest Offering: Baccalaureate
Accreditation: ACICS

01 President ... Ms. Cynthia A. MUSTERMAN
05 Academic Dean & Registrar ... Ms. Emilee SCHNEFKE
37 Financial Aid Director ... Ms. Christa SIAMPOS
07 Director of Admissions ... Ms. Sara DORN
36 Career Services Director ... Ms. Emily HUEY

Texas County Technical College (I)

6915 S Highway 63 PO Box 314, Houston MO 65483
County: Texas FICE Identification: 035793
Unit ID: 441487
Telephone: (417) 967-5466 Carnegie Class: Spec 2-yr-Health
FAX Number: (417) 967-4604 Calendar System: Semester
URL: www.texascountytech.edu
Established: 1986 Annual Undergrad Tuition & Fees: $15,586
Enrollment: 106 Coed
Affiliation or Control: Independent Non-Profit IRS Status: 501(c)3
Highest Offering: Associate Degree
Accreditation: ACICS

01 President ... Ms. Charlotte GRAY
07 Director of Admissions/Registrar ... Ms. Clarice CASEBEER
37 Financial Aid Liaison ... Ms. Clarice CASEBEER

Three Rivers College (J)

2080 Three Rivers Boulevard,
Poplar Bluff MO 63901-2350
County: Butler FICE Identification: 004713
Unit ID: 179645
Telephone: (573) 840-9600 Carnegie Class: Assoc/HT-Mix Trad/Non
FAX Number: (573) 840-9604 Calendar System: Semester
URL: www.trcc.edu
Established: 1966 Annual Undergrad Tuition & Fees (In-State): $3,540
Enrollment: 3,856 Coed
Affiliation or Control: State IRS Status: 501(c)3
Highest Offering: Associate Degree
Accreditation: NH, ACBSP, ADNUR, EMT, MLTAD, OTA

01 President ... Dr. Wesley A. PAYNE
10 Chief Financial Officer ... Ms. Charlotte EUBANK
05 Chief Academic Officer ... Dr. Justin HOGGARD
08 Director Library Services ... Ms. Kathy SANDERS
37 Director Financial Aid ... Ms. Regina MORRIS
06 Registrar ... Ms. Melanie HAMANN
32 Dean of Student Services ... Ms. Ann MATTHEWS
09 Dean of Institutional Effectiveness ... Dr. Maribeth PAYNE
18 Chief Facilities/Physical Plant ... Mr. Rob TOMLINSON
15 Director Human Resources ... Ms. Kristina D. MCDANIEL
26 Chief Public Relations Officer ... Ms. Teresa JOHNSON
30 Chief Development/Dir Alumni Rels ... Ms. Michelle REYNOLDS
84 Director Enrollment Management ... Mr. Chris ADAMS
96 Dir Procurement/Risk Management ... Ms. Cambrea HALCUMB
04 Administrative Asst to President ... Ms. Janine HEATH
103 Dir Workforce/Career Development ... Mr. Kevin SWAN
13 Chief Info Technology Officer (CIO) ... Mr. Steve ATWOOD
22 Dir Affirmative Action/EEO ... Ms. Kristina D. MCDANIEL
39 Director Student Housing ... Ms. Laura MILLIGAN
19 Director Security/Safety ... Mr. Chuck STRATTON

Truman State University (K)

100 E Normal, Kirksville MO 63501-4221
County: Adair FICE Identification: 002495
Unit ID: 178615
Telephone: (660) 785-4000 Carnegie Class: Masters/M
FAX Number: (660) 785-4030 Calendar System: Semester
URL: www.truman.edu
Established: 1867 Annual Undergrad Tuition & Fees (In-State): $7,456
Enrollment: 6,208 Coed
Affiliation or Control: State IRS Status: 501(c)3
Highest Offering: Master's

Accreditation: NH, CAATE, CAEP, MUS, NURSE, SP

01 President .... Dr. Susan L. THOMAS
05 Exec VP Acad Affairs & Provost .... Dr. Janet GOOCH
30 Int Co-Director Univ Advancement .... Mr. Charles HUNSAKER
30 Int Co-Director Univ Advancement .... Mrs. Denise L. SMITH
10 VP for Admin Finance & Planning .... Mr. David RECTOR
84 VP for Enrollment Management .... Mrs. Regina MORIN
32 VP for Student Affairs .... Dr. Lou Ann GILCHRIST
43 General Counsel .... Mr. Warren WELLS
21 Comptroller .... Mrs. Judy MULLINS
41 Athletic Director .... Mr. Jerry WOLLMERING
15 Executive Dir of Human Resources .... Ms. Sally HERLETH
07 Director of Admissions .... Mrs. Melody CHAMBERS
37 Financial Aid Director .... Mrs. Kathy ELSEA
06 Registrar .... Mrs. Margaret HERRON
13 Director Information Technology .... Mrs. Donna LISS
26 Director of Public Relations .... Mrs. Heidi TEMPLETON
20 Assoc Prov UG Curricula & Outreach .... Dr. Kevin MINCH
38 Dir Student Health/Counseling Svcs .... Dr. Brenda HIGGINS
83 Dean Sch Social & Cultural Studies .... Dr. Elizabeth CLARK
49 Dean School of Arts & Letters .... Dr. James O'DONNELL
50 Dean School of Business .... Dr. Debra KERBY
53 Dean Sch of Health Sciences & Educ .... Dr. Janet GOOCH
81 Int Assoc Dean Sch Science & Math .... Dr. Timothy WALSTON

University of Central Missouri (A)

Administration Building, room 101,
Warrensburg MO 64093-5299

County: Johnson FICE Identification: 002454
Unit ID: 176965
Telephone: (660) 543-4255 Carnegie Class: Masters/L
FAX Number: (660) 543-4200 Calendar System: Semester
URL: www.ucmo.edu
Established: 1871 Annual Undergrad Tuition & Fees (In-State): $7,322
Enrollment: 14,395 Coed
Affiliation or Control: State IRS Status: 501(c)3
Highest Offering: Beyond Master's But Less Than Doctorate
Accreditation: NH, AAB, AAFCS, ART, CAATE, CACREP, CAEPN, CEA, CIDA, CONST, CS, DIETD, ENGR, MUS, NAIT, NURSE, SP, SW, THEA

01 President .... Dr. Charles M. AMBROSE
101 Exec Asst to Pres/Asst Sec to Board .... Ms. Monica R. HUFFMAN
05 Provost/Chief Learning Officer .... Dr. Deborah J. CURTIS
32 Vice Prov Student Experience/Engage .... Dr. Sharlene GARBER BAX
20 Vice Prov Academic Program/Services .... Dr. Kim ANDREWS
35 Assoc VP Student Services/Title IX .... Dr. Corey L. BOWMAN
84 Vice Provost Enrollment Management .... Dr. Mike GODARD
111 Vice Pres Univ Advancement .... Mr. Jason S. DRUMMOND
10 CFO/Univ Treasurer .... Ms. Toni L. KREKE
08 Dean of Library Services .... Dr. Gail STAINES
49 Dean College of Arts/Humanities/Sci .... Dr. Gersham NELSON
72 Dean College of Health/Science/Tech .... Dr. Alice L. GREIFE
50 Dean Harmon Col Business/Prof Stds .... Dr. Roger J. BEST
92 Dean Honors College & Intl Affairs .... Dr. Joseph D. LEWANDOWSKI
53 Dean of College of Education .... Dr. Michael D. WRIGHT
13 Vice Provost for Technology & CIO .... Dr. James F. GRAHAM
41 Athletic Director .... Mr. Jerry M. HUGHES
06 Director of Registrar .... Ms. Teri A. BOWMAN
26 Dir Marketing & Promotions .... Ms. Kelly WALDRAM CRAMER
88 Director Testing Services .... Ms. Carole NIMMER
36 Dir Career Development Services .... Mr. Kenneth SCHUELLER
37 Dir Student Financial Assistance .... Vacant
19 Director of Public Safety .... Mr. Scott RHOAD
109 AVP Student Auxiliary Services .... Mr. Patrick J. BRADLEY
18 Assoc VP Capital Plng/Fac Mgmt .... Mr. Timothy CASTILAW
96 Director Purchasing .... Ms. Lisa BUTLER
15 Assoc VP Human Resources .... Ms. Ranea TAYLOR
40 Director of Univ Store & Textbooks .... Mr. Charles D. RUTT
56 Vice Provost of Extended Studies .... Dr. Laurel HOGUE
07 Director Admissions .... Mr. J.D GRAGG
16 Asst Director of Human Resources .... Ms. Cheryl D. TRELOW
29 Asst VP Alumni & Development .... Ms. Jennifer L. VANDERBOUT
38 Director Counseling Center .... Dr. Paul D. POLYCHRONIS
24 Director CentralNET .... Mr. Michael JEFFRIES

*University of Missouri System Administration (B)

321 University Hall, Columbia MO 65211-3020

County: Boone FICE Identification: 002515
Unit ID: 178439
Telephone: (573) 882-2011 Carnegie Class: N/A
FAX Number: (573) 882-2721
URL: www.umsystem.edu

01 President .... Mr. Mun Y. CHOI
100 Interim Chief of Staff .... Mr. David RUSSEL
10 Vice President Finance/CFO .... Ryan RAPP
28 Chief Diversity/Equity/Incl Ofcr .... Dr. Kevin G. MCDONALD
05 Int VP Acad Affairs/Rsrch/Econ Dev .... Mark MCINTOSH
13 Vice President Info Technology .... Dr. Gary K. ALLEN
86 Vice President University Relations .... Mr. Stephen C. KNORR
15 Int Vice Pres Human Resource Svcs .... Ms. Jill POLLOCK
20 Sr Assoc Vice Pres Academic Affairs .... Dr. Steven W. GRAHAM
43 General Counsel .... Mr. Stephen J. OWENS
26 Chief Communications Officer .... Mr. John FOUGERE
17 Interim CEO/COO UM Health Care .... Mr. Jonathan CARTRIGHT
21 Treasurer .... Mr. Tom F. RICHARDS
21 Controller .... Mr. Eric VOGELWELD
04 Executive Asst to President .... Ms. Janet WAIBEL
101 Secretary of the Board of Curators .... Ms. Cindy S. HARMON

*University of Missouri - Columbia (C)

Columbia MO 65211-0001

County: Boone FICE Identification: 002516
Unit ID: 178396
Telephone: (573) 882-2121 Carnegie Class: DU-Highest
FAX Number: (573) 882-9907 Calendar System: Semester
URL: www.missouri.edu
Established: 1839 Annual Undergrad Tuition & Fees (In-State): $9,518
Enrollment: 35,424 Coed
Affiliation or Control: State IRS Status: 501(c)3
Highest Offering: Doctorate
Accreditation: NH, CAATE, CAEPT, CIDA, CLPSY, COARC, COPSY, CS, DIETC, DMS, ENG, HSA, IPSY, JOUR, LAW, LIB, MED, MUS, NMT, NRPA, NURSE, OT, PCSAS, PH, PHAR, PTA, RAD, SCPSY, SP, SPAA, SW, VET

02 Chancellor .... Dr. Alexander CARTWRIGHT
05 Exec Vice Chanc Acad Affs/Provost .... Dr. Garnett STOKES
20 Associate Provost .... Christine J. HOLT
32 Interim Vice Chanc Student Affairs .... Gary WARD
10 Vice Chancellor for Finance & CFO .... Ms. Rhonda GIBLER
28 Vice Chanc Inclusion/Diversity/Equ .... Dr. Kevin MCDONALD
58 Assc VC Advanced Studies .... Dr. Jeni HART
111 Vice Chancellor Univ Advancement .... Dr. Tom HILES
29 Assoc VC Alumni Relations .... Mr. Todd A. MCCUBBIN
17 Exec VC Health Affairs .... Dr. Jonathan W. CURTRIGHT
57 Director School of Music .... Dr. Robert SHAY
84 Vice Prov Enrollment Mgmt .... Dr. Pelema MORRICE
56 Vice Provost for Extension .... Dr. Marshall STEWART
85 Int Vice Prov International Pgms .... Mr. James SCOTT
46 VC Research & Grad Studies .... Dr. Mark MCINTOSH
13 Chief Information Officer .... Dr. Gary K. ALLEN
15 Interim AVP Human Resources .... Ms. Jatha SADOWSKI
88 Asst VC Diversity Engagement .... Ms. Noor AZIZAN-GARDNER
18 Chief Operations Officer .... Mr. Gary L. WARD
35 Asst Vice Chanc Student Affairs .... Dr. Jeffrey ZEILENGA
06 University Registrar .... Ms. Brenda V. SELMAN
09 VProv Inst Research & Quality Impr .... Dr. Mardy T. EIMERS
08 Dir of Libraries/Univ Librarian .... Ms. Ann C. RILEY
37 Director Student Financial Aid .... Mr. Nick PREWETT
47 Vice Chanc/Dean Agric/Food/Nat Res .... Dr. Christopher R. DAUBERT
49 Interim Dean Arts & Science .... Dr. Patricia OKKER
50 Dean of Business .... Dr. Ajay VINZE
88 Director School of Accountancy .... Dr. Vairam ARUNACHALAM
53 Dean of Education .... Dr. Kathryn B. CHVAL
54 Dean of Engineering .... Dr. Elizabeth G. LOBOA
65 Dir School of Natural Resources .... Dr. Mark R. RYAN
76 Dean School of Health Professions .... Dr. Kristofer HAGGLUND
59 Dean Human Environ Science .... Dr. James (Sandy) S. RIKOON
60 Dean of Journalism .... Dr. David D. KURPIUS
61 Dean of Law .... Lyrissa LIDSKY
63 Dean of Medicine .... Dr. Patrice DELAFONTAINE
66 Dean of Nursing .... Dr. Judith FITZGERALD MILLER
70 Director School of Social Work .... Dr. Marjorie SABLE
74 Interim Dean of Veterinary Medicine .... Dr. Carolyn J. HENRY
19 Director of University Police .... Mr. Doug SCHWANDT
26 Interim Exec Dir Strat Comm & Mktg .... Dr. Suzette T. HEIMAN
41 Athletic Director .... Mr. Jim STERK
39 Director Residential Life .... Vacant
25 Director Sponsored Program Admin .... Mr. David CRAIG
40 Regional Director Retail Operations .... Ms. Sherry POLLARD
38 Director Counseling Services .... Dr. David WALLACE
88 Director International Center .... Dr. James K. SCOTT
36 Director Career Center .... Dr. Rob MCDANIELS
23 Director Student Health Services .... Dr. Susan E. EVEN
92 Director Honors College .... Dr. J. D. BOWERS
94 Director Women's/Gender Studies .... Dr. Jacquelyn S. LITT
88 Director Info Science Learning Tech .... Dr. John WEDMAN
80 Director Truman Sch Public Affairs .... Vacant
07 Director of Admissions .... Mr. Charles A. MAY
104 Director Study Abroad .... Ms. Barbara LINDEMAN
105 Director Web Services .... Vacant
106 Dir Online Education/E-learning .... Ms. Kim SIEGENTHALER

*University of Missouri - Kansas City (D)

5100 Rockhill Road, Kansas City MO 64110-2499

County: Jackson FICE Identification: 002518
Unit ID: 178402
Telephone: (816) 235-1000 Carnegie Class: DU-Higher
FAX Number: (816) 235-1717 Calendar System: Semester
URL: www.umkc.edu
Established: 1929 Annual Undergrad Tuition & Fees (In-State): $7,846
Enrollment: 16,685 Coed
Affiliation or Control: State IRS Status: 501(c)3
Highest Offering: Doctorate
Accreditation: NH, AA, ANEST, #ARCPA, CAEPN, CEA, CLPSY, COPSY, CS, DANCE, DENT, DH, EMT, ENG, IPSY, LAW, MED, MUS, NURSE, OTA, PHAR, SPAA, SW, THEA

02 Interim Chancellor .... Dr. Barbara BICHELMEYER
28 Vice Chanc Diversity & Inclusion .... Dr. Susan WILSON
05 Provost .... Dr. Barbara BICHELMEYER
32 Vice Chanc Stdnt Affs/Enroll Mgmt .... Mr. Melvin C. TYLER
10 Vice Chanc Finance/Administration .... Ms. Sharon LINDENBAUM
114 Director Budgeting and Planning .... Ms. Karen D. WILKERSON
102 Pres UMKC Foundation .... Mr. Steven NORRIS
111 Vice Chanc for Univ Advancement .... Mr. Curt J. CRESPINO
41 Athletic Director .... Ms. Carla WILSON
13 CIO & Senior Vice Prov .... Dr. Mary Lou A. FRITTS
20 Deputy Prov for Academic Affairs .... Dr. Cynthia L. PEMBERTON
20 Vice Prov for Faculty Affairs .... Dr. Denis M. MEDEIROS
49 Dean College of Arts & Sciences .... Dr. Wayne VAUGHT
50 Dean Bloch School of Management .... Dr. Brian KLAAS
81 Dean Sch of Biological Sciences .... Dr. Theodore WHITE
64 Dean Conservatory of Music & Dance .... Mr. Peter T. WITTE
52 Dean School of Dentistry .... Dr. Marsha A. PYLE
53 Dean School of Education .... Dr. Justin PERRY
54 Dean Sch of Computing/Engineering .... Dr. Kevin Z. TRUMAN
61 Interim Dean School of Law .... Ms. Barbara GLESNER-FINES
63 Dean School of Medicine .... Dr. Steven KANTER
66 Dean Sch of Nursing & Health Stds .... Dr. Ann CARY
67 Dean School of Pharmacy .... Dr. Russell B. MELCHERT
62 Dean University Libraries .... Dr. Bonnie POSTLETHWAITE
58 Dean School of Graduate Studies .... Dr. Denis M. MEDEIROS
108 Director of Assessment .... Dr. Ruth CAIN
09 Int Dir Institutional Research .... Ms. Amy PRETTEJOHN
15 Vice Chanc Human Resources .... Ms. Carol HINTZ
84 Assoc Vice Chanc Enrollment Mgmt .... Ms. Jennifer DEHAEMERS
35 Assistant Vice Chanc Student Affs .... Dr. Jeff TRAIGER
35 Assistant Dean of Students .... Ms. Tiffany S. HAMILTON
88 Director Student Involvement .... Dr. Todd WELLS
26 Vice Chanc Strategic Market & Comm .... Ms. Anne SPENNER
27 Director Media Relations .... Mr. John MARTELLARO
29 Asst VC Alumni/Constituent Rels .... Ms. Lisen TAMMEUS
86 Asst Vice Chanc External Relations .... Mr. Troy LILLEBO
22 Title IX Coordinator .... Dr. Mikah THOMPSON
121 Int Dir Acad Support and Mentoring .... Dr. Rodney SMITH
07 Director of Admissions .... Ms. Tamara C. BYLAND
85 Director Internatl Student Affairs .... Ms. Tamara C. BYLAND
37 Director Student Financial Aid .... Mr. Scott YOUNG
06 Registrar .... Mr. Doug SWINK
19 Chief Campus Police .... Mr. Michael BONGARTZ
40 Director Bookstore .... Mr. Pete EISENTRAGER
38 Dir Counseling/Health/Disability .... Dr. Arnold ABELS
88 Director Women's Center .... Dr. Brenda BETHMAN
36 Director Career Services .... Vacant
39 Director Residential Life .... Mr. Sean GRUBE
88 Dir Multicultural Student Affairs .... Ms. Keichanda DEES-BURNETT
96 Manager Campus Procurement .... Ms. Catherine A. SIMONDS
25 Business Manager for Admin Services .... Mr. Jeffery ROSS
18 Assoc Vice Chanc Campus Facilities .... Mr. Robert A. SIMMONS
104 Director International Acad Pgms .... Dr. Linna F. PLACE
106 Vice Provost Online Education .... Dr. Devon CANCILLA

*University of Missouri - Saint Louis (E)

1 University Boulevard, Saint Louis MO 63121-4400

County: Saint Louis FICE Identification: 002519
Unit ID: 178420
Telephone: (314) 516-5000 Carnegie Class: DU-Higher
FAX Number: (314) 516-5378 Calendar System: Semester
URL: www.umsl.edu
Established: 1963 Annual Undergrad Tuition & Fees (In-State): $9,394
Enrollment: 16,738 Coed
Affiliation or Control: State IRS Status: 501(c)3
Highest Offering: Doctorate
Accreditation: NH, CACREP, CAEPN, CLPSY, ENG, IPSY, MUS, NURSE, OPT, OPTR, SPAA, SW

02 Chancellor .... Dr. Thomas F. GEORGE
05 Provost/Vice Chanc Acad Affairs .... Dr. Kristin SOBOLIK
10 Vice Chanc Finance/Admn & CFO .... Mr. Rick BANIAK
111 Vice Chancellor Univ Advancement .... Mr. Martin F. LEIFELD
26 Sr Assoc VC Univ Marketing/Comm .... Mr. Ronald H. GOSSEN
27 Assoc Vice Chanc Communications .... Mr. Robert D. SAMPLES
22 Dir of Equal Opportunity/Diversity .... Ms. Deborah J. BURRIS
46 Vice Provost Research Admin .... Dr. Christopher SPILLING
32 Vice Provost Student Affairs .... Dr. Curtis C. COONROD
58 Assoc Dean Graduate School .... Dr. Wesley HARRIS
13 Executive Director Info Technology .... Dr. Jane L. WILLIAMS
88 Dir Center for Teaching & Learning .... Dr. J. Andy GOODMAN
85 Director International Studies .... Dr. Joel N. GLASSMAN
49 Int Dean College Arts & Sciences .... Dr. Teresa THIEL
50 Interim Dean College Business Admin .... Mr. Charles E. HOFFMAN
53 Dean College of Education .... Dr. Ann TAYLOR
79 Assoc Dean Arts/Humanities .... Dr. Barbara HARBACH
66 Dean College of Nursing .... Dr. Susan DEAN-BAAR
92 Int Dean Honors College .... Dr. Daniel GERTH
88 Dean College of Optometry .... Dr. Larry J. DAVIS
08 Dean of Libraries .... Mr. Christopher DAMES
54 Dean Engineering Program .... Dr. Joseph O'SULLIVAN
88 Asst to the Chancellor .... Ms. Elizabeth VAN UUM
88 Asst Dean of Students/Stdnt Conduct .... Dr. D'Andre BRADDIX
93 Asst Dean of Stdnts/MultiCultural .... Dr. Natissia SMALL
35 Asst Dean of Students/Student Life .... Ms. Miriam I. ROCCIA
41 Director of Athletics .... Ms. Lori FLANAGAN
07 Dean of Enrollment .... Mr. Alan BYRD
40 Manager Bookstore .... Ms. Stephanie EATON
36 Director Career Services .... Ms. Teresa A. BALESTRERI
06 Registrar .... Ms. Theresa KEUSS
39 Director Residential Life .... Mr. Jonathan A. LIDGUS
37 Director Student Financial Aid .... Dr. Anthony C. GEORGES
88 Dir Scientific & Computing/ITE .... Dr. William J. LEMON
88 Dir MO Inst of Mental Health .... Dr. Robert H. PAUL
25 Manager Bus/Fiscal/Research Admin .... Ms. Karen O. BOYD
18 Assoc Vice Chanc Facilities Mgt .... Mr. Larry A. EISENBERG
114 Director Budget Services .... Ms. Joann F. WILLKINSON
88 Director of Finance & Accounting .... Mr. Randall VOGAN
113 Director Cashiers/Student Accounts .... Mr. Mitchell R. HESS
15 Executive Director Human Resources .... Mr. James W. HERTEL
19 Director Institutional Safety .... Mr. Forrest L. VAN NESS

09 Director Institutional Research .... Mr. Lawrence W. WESTERMEYER
102 Assoc VC Development .... Ms. Beth KRUMM
88 Director St Louis Public Radio .... Mr. Tim J. EBY
29 Assoc VC Engagement/Annual Giving .... Ms. Jennifer JEZEK-TAUSSIG
70 Dean Social Work .... Dr. Sharon JOHNSON
88 Dir Public Policy Administration .... Dr. Daniel M. SISE
88 Dir Sue Shear Institute for Women .... Ms. Vivian EVELOFF
31 Director Community College Relation .... Ms. Krystal P. LANG
88 Managing Dir Performing Arts Center ... Mr. John R. CATTANACH
88 Dir Des Lee Collaborative Vision .... Ms. Patricia ZAHN
108 Assoc Provost Planning/ Assessment .... Dr. Paulette E. ISAAC-SAVAGE

*Missouri University of Science & Technology (A)

300 W 13th Street, Rolla MO 65409-0001
County: Phelps — FICE Identification: 002517
Unit ID: 178411
Telephone: (573) 341-4111 — Carnegie Class: DU-Higher
FAX Number: (573) 341-4307 — Calendar System: Semester
URL: www.mst.edu
Established: 1870 — Annual Undergrad Tuition & Fees (In-State): $9,057
Enrollment: 8,886 — Coed
Affiliation or Control: State — IRS Status: 501(c)3
Highest Offering: Doctorate
Accreditation: NH, CEA, CS, ENG

02 Chancellor .... Dr. Christopher MAPLES
05 Provost/Exec Vice Chanc Acad Affs .... Dr. Robert MARLEY
10 Vice Chanc Finance and Operations .... Mr. Walter J. BRANSON
111 Vice Chanc University Advancement .... Ms. Joan M. NESBITT
32 Vice Chancellor Student Affairs .... Dr. Debra A G. ROBINSON
15 Vice Chanc HR/Equity & Inclusion .... Ms. Shenethia MANUEL
35 Assoc VC Student Affairs .... Dr. James H. MURPHY
46 Vice Provost Research Services .... Dr. Mariesa L. CROW
20 Vice Provost Academic Support .... Dr. Jeffrey CAWLFIELD
58 Vice Provost Graduate Studies .... Dr. Venkata ALLADA
56 Vice Provost Global Learning .... Dr. Anthony R. PETROY
84 Vice Prov & Dean Enrollment Mgmt .... Mr. Timothy L. ALBERS
54 VP/Dean Col Engr & Computing .... Dr. Richard WLEZIEN
49 VP/Dean Col of Arts/Sci & Business .... Dr. Stephen ROBERTS
45 Exec Dir Strategy/Planning/Assess .... Ms. Rose HORTON
08 Interim Director of Library .... Ms. Margaret TRISH
102 Executive Dir Corporate Relations .... Mr. John EASH
13 Chief Information Officer .... Mr. Dan UETRECHT
06 Registrar .... Ms. Deanne JACKSON
38 AVC Student Affairs/Support Svcs .... Dr. Edna GROVER-BISKER
41 Director of Athletics .... Mr. Mark E. MULLIN
23 Senior Dir Student Health Services .... Dr. Dennis S. GOODMAN
36 Dir Career Opportunities Center .... Ms. Julie PITTSER
85 AVC International/Cultural Affairs .... Dr. Jeanie H. HOFER
35 Director Student Life .... Mr. John GALLAGHER
39 Director Residential Life .... Dr. Dorie PAINE
09 Asst Vice Prov Inst Research/Assess .... Dr. Oyebanjo LAJUBUTU
07 Director of Admissions .... Ms. Lynn STICHNOTE
29 Asst Vice Chanc Advancement Svcs .... Ms. Darlene RAMSAY
37 Director Student Financial Aid .... Ms. Bridgette K. BETZ
26 Executive Director Communications .... Mr. Andrew P. CAREAGA
18 Director of Physical Facilities .... Mr. James PACKARD
93 Int Dir Student Div/Outreach/Women .... Ms. Cynthia GUESS
40 Manager of University Bookstore .... Mr. Mark GALLARDO
19 Director University Police .... Mr. Douglas P. ROBERTS
100 Chief of Staff .... Ms. Elizabeth SMITH
11 Associate Provost of Administration .... Dr. Caprice MOORE
88 Assoc Dir Stategic Communications .... Ms. Cheryl A. MCKAY
44 Director Planned Giving .... Mr. John HELD, II

*Missouri University of Science & Technology Engineering Education Center (B)

12837 Flushing Meadows Drive, St. Louis MO 63131
Telephone: (314) 835-9822 — Identification: 770323
Accreditation: &NH

University of Phoenix St. Louis Campus (C)

13801 Riverport Drive, St. Louis MO 63043
Telephone: (314) 298-9755 — Identification: 770214
Accreditation: &NH, ACBSP

† No longer accepting campus-based students.

Urshan Graduate School of Theology (D)

704 Howdershell Road, Florissant MO 63031-7526
County: St. Louis — FICE Identification: 041461
Unit ID: 455099
Telephone: (314) 921-9290 — Carnegie Class: Spec-4-yr-Faith
FAX Number: (314) 921-9203 — Calendar System: Semester
URL: www.ugst.edu
Established: 2001 — Annual Undergrad Tuition & Fees: N/A
Enrollment: 63 — Coed
Affiliation or Control: Other Protestant — IRS Status: 501(c)3
Highest Offering: Master's
Accreditation: THEOL

01 President .... Dr. David K. BERNARD
03 Executive Vice President .... Mrs. Jennie RUSSELL
05 Academic Dean .... Dr. Chris PARIS
32 Dean of Students .... Mr. David REID
10 CFO .... Mrs. Ashley CHANCELLOR
06 Registrar .... Dr. Jeanie BLAND
08 Head Librarian .... Dr. Gary ERICKSON
106 Dir Online Education/E-learning .... Ms. Vinessa D'SA
26 Chief Public Relations/Marketing .... Mr. David MOLINA

Vatterott College-Joplin (E)

809 Illinois Avenue, Joplin MO 64801-9538
Telephone: (417) 781-5633 — Identification: 666060
Accreditation: ACCSC

† Branch campus of Vatterott College-North Park, Berkeley, MO.

Vatterott College-Kansas City (F)

4131 N. Corrington Avenue, Kansas City MO 64117-1681
Telephone: (816) 861-1000 — Identification: 666519
Accreditation: ACCSC

† Branch campus of Vatterott College-North Park, Berkeley, MO.

Vatterott College-NorthPark (G)

8580 Evans Avenue, Berkeley MO 63134-2900
County: Saint Louis — FICE Identification: 025997
Unit ID: 245342
Telephone: (314) 264-1000 — Carnegie Class: Bac/Assoc-Assoc Dom
FAX Number: (314) 522-6174 — Calendar System: Other
URL: www.vatterott-college.edu
Established: 1969 — Annual Undergrad Tuition & Fees: $12,650
Enrollment: 1,141 — Coed
Affiliation or Control: Proprietary — IRS Status: Proprietary
Highest Offering: Baccalaureate
Accreditation: ACCSC

01 Campus Director .... Mr. Robert DONNELL
05 Co-Director of Education .... Ms. Brenetta UNDERWOOD
05 Co-Director of Education .... Mr. Greg SHEPHERD
06 Head Registrar .... Ms. Denise DAVIS
07 Director of Admissions .... Ms. Sherri MEDLIN

Vatterott College-St. Charles (H)

3550 West Clay Street, St. Charles MO 63301
Telephone: (636) 940-4100 — Identification: 666584
Accreditation: ACCSC

† Branch campus of Vatterott College-North Park, Berkeley, MO.

Vatterott College-Saint Joseph (I)

3709 N. Belt Highway, Saint Joseph MO 64506-1364
Telephone: (816) 558-7500 — Identification: 666520
Accreditation: ACCSC

† Branch campus of Vatterott College-Des Moines, Des Moines, IA.

Vatterott College-Springfield (J)

3850 S Campbell Avenue, Springfield MO 65807-5340
Telephone: (417) 831-8116 — Identification: 666521
Accreditation: ACCSC

† Branch campus of Vatterott College-North Park, Berkeley, MO.

Vatterott College-Sunset Hills (K)

12900 Maurer Industrial Drive, Sunset Hills MO 63127
Telephone: (314) 843-4200 — Identification: 666522
Accreditation: ACCSC

† Branch campus of Vatterott College-North Park, Berkeley, MO.

Washington University in St. Louis (L)

One Brookings Drive, Saint Louis MO 63130-4899
County: Saint Louis — FICE Identification: 002520
Unit ID: 179867
Telephone: (314) 935-5000 — Carnegie Class: DU-Highest
FAX Number: N/A — Calendar System: Semester
URL: www.wustl.edu
Established: 1853 — Annual Undergrad Tuition & Fees: $49,770
Enrollment: 14,688 — Coed
Affiliation or Control: Independent Non-Profit — IRS Status: 501(c)3
Highest Offering: Doctorate
Accreditation: NH, ACAE, ART, AUD, CLPSY, ENG, LAW, LSAR, MED, OT, PCSAS, PH, PTA, SW

01 Chancellor .... Dr. Mark S. WRIGHTON
05 Provost/Exec VC Academic Affairs .... Dr. Herbert Holden THORP
11 Exec VC Administration .... Mr. Henry S. WEBBER
63 Exec Vice Chanc/Dean of Medicine ... Dr. David H. PERLMUTTER
43 Vice Chanc/General Counsel .... Ms. Monica J. ALLEN
111 Exec VC Alumni & Development .... Mr. David T. BLASINGAME
10 Vice Chancellor for Finance/CFO .... Ms. Amy B. KWESKIN
46 Vice Chancellor for Research .... Dr. Jennifer K. LODGE
15 Vice Chanc for Human Resources .... Ms. Legail P. CHANDLER
13 Vice Chanc & Chief Info Officer .... Mr. John L. GOHSMAN, JR.
32 Vice Chancellor for Student Affairs .... Dr. Lori S. WHITE
26 Vice Chanc for Public Affairs .... Ms. Jill D. FRIEDMAN
86 VC Government & Community Relations . Ms. Pamela S. LOKKEN
115 Chief Investment Officer .... Vacant
21 Assoc VC for Finance and Treasurer .... Mr. Mark N. AMIRI
49 Dean Faculty of Arts & Sciences .... Dr. Barbara A. SCHAAL
61 Dean School of Law .... Dr. Nancy STAUDT
54 Dean Engineering & Applied Sciences .... Dr. Aaron F. BOBICK
57 Dean Sam Fox Sch Design/Visual Arts .... Prof. Carmon COLANGELO
58 Dir College & Grad Sch of Art .... Prof. Heather A. CORCORAN
50 Dean Olin School of Business .... Prof. Mark P. TAYLOR
58 Dean Graduate School of A & S .... Prof. William F. TATE
70 Dean Brown School of Social Work .... Prof. Mary M. MCKAY
55 Dean University College .... Prof. Mark ROLLINS
48 Dir College of Architecture & Grad .... Prof. Heather WOOFTER
100 Assoc Vice Chanc/Chief of Staff .... Mr. Steven J. GIVENS
101 Secretary to the Board of Trustees .... Ms. Ida H. EARLY
07 Vice Provost for Admissions & Fin .... Ms. Ronne P. TURNER
20 Vice Provost/Assoc VC Academic Affs .... Prof. Gerhild S. WILLIAMS
30 VC for Development .... Mr. William S. STOLL
29 VC Alumni & Development Pgm .... Ms. Pamella A. HENSON
26 Assoc VC Medical Public Affairs .... Ms. Joni L. WESTERHOUSE
28 Vice Provost .... Prof. Adrienne D. DAVIS
85 VC for International Affairs .... Prof. James V. WERTSCH
08 Vice Provost & University Librarian .... Ms. Denise STEPHENS
35 Assoc Vice Chanc for Students/Dean .... Dr. Robert M. WILD
92 Assoc VC & Dean Ervin Scholars Pgm .... Ms. Robyn S. HADLEY
14 Asst VC Information Tech .... Mr. Scott TAYLOR
27 Asst VC for Campus Communications .... Ms. Julie A. FLORY
85 Asst VC/Dir International Students .... Ms. Kathy STEINER-LANG
96 Assoc VC Resource Management .... Mr. Alan S. KUEBLER
36 Assoc VC/Director Career Center .... Mr. Mark W. SMITH
18 Assoc VC Facilities Planning/Mgmt .... Mr. JD LONG II
88 Asst VC Environ Health & Safety .... Mr. Bruce D. BACKUS
88 Assoc VC Real Estate .... Ms. Mary B. CAMPBELL
72 Managing Dir OTM .... Ms. Nichole R. MERCIER
90 Asst VC Univ Admin/Acad Computing .... Ms. Denise R. HIRSCHBECK
23 Asst VC/Dir Stdnt Hlth Counslng Svc .... Dr. Alan I. GLASS
37 Director Student Financial Services .... Mr. Michael J. RUNIEWICZ
41 Director of Athletics .... Mr. Anthony J. AZAMA
19 Chief of Police .... Mr. Mark R. GLENN
07 Director of Admissions .... Ms. Julie SHIMABUKURO
06 University Registrar .... Ms. Susan E. HOSACK
38 Director of Mental Health Services .... Dr. Thomas M. BROUNK
88 Assoc VC for Student Support & Well .... Ms. Tamara L. KING

Washington University in St. Louis-School of Medicine (M)

660 Euclid Avenue, Saint Louis MO 63110
Telephone: (314) 360-5000 — Identification: 770329
Accreditation: &NH

Webster University (N)

470 E Lockwood, Webster Groves MO 63119-3141
County: Saint Louis — FICE Identification: 002521
Unit ID: 179894
Telephone: (800) 981-9801 — Carnegie Class: Masters/L
FAX Number: N/A — Calendar System: Semester
URL: www.webster.edu
Established: 1915 — Annual Undergrad Tuition & Fees: $26,300
Enrollment: 15,256 — Coed
Affiliation or Control: Independent Non-Profit — IRS Status: 501(c)3
Highest Offering: Doctorate
Accreditation: NH, ACBSP, ANEST, CACREP, CAEPN, MUS, NUR

01 President .... Dr. Elizabeth J. STROBLE
05 Provost .... Dr. Julian Z. SCHUSTER
111 Vice Pres Advancement .... Ms. Patricia ARNOLD
84 Vice Pres Enrollment .... Mr. Robert PARRENT
10 VP & Chief Financial Officer .... Dr. Ana KARAMAN
13 Interim Chief Information Officer .... Ms. Margie MUTHUKUMARU
101 University Secretary .... Ms. Jeanelle WILEY
20 Vice Provost .... Ms. Nancy HELLERUD
58 Asst Provost for Graduate Studies .... Dr. Elizabeth RUSSELL
04 Executive Assistant to President .... Ms. Shari SKRABACZ
50 Dean School Business/Technology .... Dr. Simone CUMMINGS
53 Dean School of Education .... Dr. Brenda S. FYFE
57 Dean Leigh Gerdine Col of Fine Arts .... Dr. Peter E. SARGENT
49 Dean Col of Arts & Sciences .... Dr. Jennifer BROEDER
60 Dean School of Communications .... Dr. Eric ROTHENBUHLER
08 Dean of University Library .... Ms. Laura REIN
32 Associate VP/Dean of Students .... Dr. Ted HOEF
56 Dean of Extended Education .... Ms. Thao DANG-WILLIAMS
39 Assoc Dean Stdts/Housing/Res Life .... Dr. John BUCK
106 AVP/Dir OnLine Learning Center .... Dr. Michael COTTAM
82 AVP Academic Affairs Intl Pgms .... Dr. Peter MAHER
15 AVP & Chief Human Resources Officer .... Ms. Betsy SCHMUTZ
88 AVP Military & Government Programs .... Mr. Sean COLEMAN
27 AVP & Chief Comm Officer .... Mr. Rick ROCKWELL
12 AVP Extended US Campuses .... Dr. Donavan OUTTEN
37 AVP UG Admiss/Dir Financial Aid .... Mr. James MYERS
28 AVP Diversity & Inclusion .... Ms. Nicole ROACH
06 Registrar .... Mr. Don MORRIS
20 Director of Academic Advising .... Mr. Kim KLEINMAN
114 Dir Resource Plng & Budget .... Vacant
19 Director Public Safety .... Mr. Rick GERGER
26 Dir Public Relations/Global Mktg .... Mr. Patrick GIBLIN
24 Dir of Media & Acad Tech Services .... Mr. Dewey MARTIN
36 Dir Career Planning & Dev Center . Ms. Tamara GEGG-LAPLUME

29 Director of Alumni Programs .... Ms. Lara TUREK
41 Director Athletics .... Mr. Scott KILGALLON
23 Director Student Health Svcs .... Ms. Ann BROPHY
35 Director Student Engagement .... Ms. Jennifer STEWART
38 Director Counsel & Life Development .... Dr. Patrick STACK
96 Director of Procurement Services .... Vacant
09 Director of Inst Effectiveness .... Mr. Justin BITNER
18 Director Facilities Planning .... Mr. Craig MILLER
104 Int Dir Study Abrd & Intl Projects .... Ms. Hannah VERITY
44 Director Annual or Planned Giving .... Mr. Kenneth NICKLESS
07 Director of UG Admissions/Int GR .... Vacant

WellSpring School of Allied Health-Kansas City (A)

9140 Ward Pkwy Ste 100, Kansas City MO 64114

County: Jackson FICE Identification: 039704
Unit ID: 447999
Telephone: (816) 523-9140 Carnegie Class: Spec 2-yr-Health
FAX Number: (816) 523-0741 Calendar System: Other
URL: www.wellspring.edu
Established: 1988 Annual Undergrad Tuition & Fees: N/A
Enrollment: 241 Coed
Affiliation or Control: Proprietary IRS Status: Proprietary
Highest Offering: Associate Degree
Accreditation: ABHES

01 President .... Donald FARQUHARSON

Westminster College (B)

501 Westminster Avenue, Fulton MO 65251-1230

County: Callaway FICE Identification: 002523
Unit ID: 179946
Telephone: (573) 642-3361 Carnegie Class: Bac-A&S
FAX Number: (573) 592-5227 Calendar System: Semester
URL: www.westminster-mo.edu
Established: 1851 Annual Undergrad Tuition & Fees: $24,540
Enrollment: 951 Coed
Affiliation or Control: Independent Non-Profit IRS Status: 501(c)3
Highest Offering: Baccalaureate
Accreditation: NH, ACBSP

01 Acting President .... Dr. Carolyn J. PERRY
05 Sr Vice President/Dean of Faculty .... Dr. Carolyn J. PERRY
111 VP for Advancement .... Ms. Kelly DOPMAN
10 Chief Financial/Operating Officer .... Mr. Kenneth MAHER
84 Interim VP Enrollment Management .... Mr. Calvin SMITH
26 VP & Chief Communications Officer .... Ms. Lana POOLE
27 Director Media & Public Relations .... Mr. Robert CROUSE
32 Interim VP & Dean of Student Life .... Mr. Daniel HASLAG
20 Associate Academic Dean .... Dr. David JONES
08 Director of Library Services .... Ms. Angela GROGAN
06 Registrar .... Mrs. Phyllis J. MASEK
13 IT Technical Services Manager .... Mr. Glen KEHL
37 Director of Financial Aid .... Ms. Aimee BRISTOW
15 Interim Assoc VP/Chief HR Officer .... Ms. Jackie PLUNKETT
39 Director of Residential/Greek Life .... Ms. Jacqueline J. WEBER
41 Athletic Director .... Mr. Matt MITCHELL
23 Exec Director Wellness Center .... Dr. Kasi LACEY
29 Dir Alumni Engagement .... Ms. Sarah MUNNS
36 Director of Career Services .... Ms. Meg LANGLAND
18 Interim Exec Dir Plant Operations .... Mr. Jack BENKE
07 Director of Admissions .... Ms. Amy MAREK
09 Director of Institutional Research .... Dr. Sarah PARSONS
19 Dir Campus Safety & Security .... Vacant
42 Chaplain .... Rev. Jamie HASKINS
100 Chief of Staff .... Mr. Gary STOCKER

William Jewell College (C)

500 College Hill, Liberty MO 64068-1896

County: Clay FICE Identification: 002524
Unit ID: 179955
Telephone: (816) 781-7700 Carnegie Class: Bac-A&S
FAX Number: (816) 415-5027 Calendar System: Semester
URL: www.jewell.edu
Established: 1849 Annual Undergrad Tuition & Fees: $32,930
Enrollment: 1,063 Coed
Affiliation or Control: Independent Non-Profit IRS Status: 501(c)3
Highest Offering: Master's
Accreditation: NH, MUS, NURSE

01 President .... Dr. Elizabeth MACLEOD WALLS
05 Provost .... Dr. Anne C. DEMA
10 Vice Pres for Finance & Operations .... Mr. Brian CLEMONS
111 Vice Pres Institutional Advancement .... Mr. Clark MORRIS
88 Vice Pres for Social Responsibility .... Dr. Andrew L. PRATT
32 Dean of Student Life .... Ms. Shelly KING
07 Director of Admission Services .... Mr. Brian HAINES
06 Registrar .... Dr. Edwin H. LANE
08 Director of Library Services .... Ms. Rebecca HAMLETT
21 Controller .... Mr. Ron DEMPSEY
13 Director of Information Technology .... Ms. Lan GUO
97 Assoc Dean Core Curriculum .... Dr. Gary ARMSTRONG
37 Director of Financial Aid .... Mr. Daniel HOLT
15 Director of Human Resources .... Ms. Cherie SMITH
18 Director of Facilities Management .... Ms. Stephany GUEST
57 Executive Director Harriman-Jewell .... Mr. Clark W. MORRIS
41 Director of Athletics .... Mr. Thomas EISENHAUER
36 Director of Career Development .... Ms. Marissa BLAND
38 Director of Counseling Services .... Ms. Tricia HAGER
29 Director of Alumni Relations .... Ms. Andrea MELOAN
104 Director of Global Studies .... Ms. Sara ROUND
04 Executive Asst to President .... Ms. Dayna BEINKE
19 Director of Campus Safety .... Mr. Landon JONES
26 Director of Marketing .... Ms. Cara DAHLOR
39 Director of Residence Life .... Mr. Ernie STUFFLEBEAN
44 Director of Annual Giving .... Ms. Laura HANAVAN
90 Director of Teaching/Learning Tech .... Ms. Elise FISHER
101 Secretary of the Institution/Board .... Ms. Dayna BEINKE
50 Chair Comm in Business & Leadership .... Dr. Kelli SCHUTTE
53 Chair Education .... Dr. Donna GARDNER

William Woods University (D)

One University Avenue, Fulton MO 65251-1098

County: Callaway FICE Identification: 002525
Unit ID: 179964
Telephone: (800) 995-3159 Carnegie Class: Masters/L
FAX Number: (573) 592-1146 Calendar System: Semester
URL: www.williamwoods.edu
Established: 1870 Annual Undergrad Tuition & Fees: $23,040
Enrollment: 2,172 Coed
Affiliation or Control: Christian Church (Disciples Of Christ)
IRS Status: 501(c)3
Highest Offering: Doctorate
Accreditation: NH, ACBSP, #CAATE, CAEPT, SW

01 President .... Dr. Jahnae H. BARNETT
03 University Vice President .... Scott GALLAGHER
84 Vice President Enrollment & Mktg .... Kathy GROVES
32 Vice President/Dean of Student Life .... Dr. Venita MITCHELL
05 Executive Vice President Acad Affs .... Dr. Michael W. WESTERFIELD
04 Executive Assistant to President .... Kenda E G. SHINDLER
20 Academic Dean .... Dr. Aimee SAPP
58 Vice President of Graduate College .... Dr. Betsy TUTT
53 Dean of Education .... Dr. E. Douglas EBERSOLD
50 Dean of Business .... Lee BAILEY
41 Director of Athletics .... Jason VITTONE
20 Assoc Dean Academic Services .... Dr. Tom FRANKMAN
09 Director of Institutional Research .... Stacy MASKEY
111 Director of Advancement .... Dr. Shawn HULL
108 Assoc Dean Assessment .... Dr. Carrie MCCRAY
08 Director Libraries .... Erlene DUDLEY
26 Director of Content and Publicity .... Tiffany SMITH
18 Director of Physical Plant .... Mike DILLON
13 Director of Technology .... Jim LONG
06 Director of Records/Registrar .... Tara EMERSON
10 Chief Financial Officer .... Julie HOUSEWORTH
37 Director Student Financial Services .... Deana READY
36 Dir Career Svcs/Student Transition .... Amy DITTMER
39 Dir Residential Life/Campus Safety .... Mike WILLS
29 Director of Alumni Activities .... Becky STINSON
53 Chair of Education and Humanities .... Dr. Tim HANRAHAN
49 Chair Arts and Behavioral Sciences .Dr. Caroline BOYER FERHAT
88 Chair Equestrian Studies Division .... Jennifer PETTERSON
88 Chair Business/Law/Tech & Lang .... Dr. Linda DAVIS
88 Chair Mathematics and Science .... Raymond HUNE
35 Director of Student Involvement .... Lacy SWEETEN
42 Chaplain/Ethics/Global Student Dir .... Rev. Travis TAMERIUS
88 Director Student Disability Service .... Vacant
28 Coordinator Multicultural Affairs .... Cyndi KOONSE
38 Counselor .... Melinda MOTTER
15 Director Human Resources .... Margie BRAMON

MONTANA

Aaniiih Nakoda College (E)

PO Box 159, Harlem MT 59526-0159

County: Blaine FICE Identification: 025175
Unit ID: 180203
Telephone: (406) 353-2607 Carnegie Class: Tribal
FAX Number: (406) 353-2898 Calendar System: Semester
URL: www.ancollege.edu
Established: 1984 Annual Undergrad Tuition & Fees: $2,410
Enrollment: 219 Coed
Affiliation or Control: Tribal Control IRS Status: 501(c)3
Highest Offering: Associate Degree
Accreditation: NW

01 President .... Dr. Carole FALCON-CHANDLER
05 Int Dean of Academic Affairs .... Dr. Sean CHANDLER
32 Dean of Student Affairs .... Ms. Clarena BROCKIE
10 Comptroller .... Ms. Debra EVE
06 Registrar/Admissions Officer .... Mrs. Dixie BROCKIE
37 Financial Aid Director .... Ms. Toma CAMPBELL-HOOPS
08 Library Director .... Ms. Eva ENGLISH
25 Sponsored Programs Director .... Mr. Scott FRISKICS
13 Manager Information Systems .... Mr. Harold H. HEPPNER
40 Bookstore Manager .... Ms. Kimberly BROCKIE
04 Assistant to the President .... Ms. Michele BROCKIE
09 Institutional Research Assistant .... Ms. Danielle JACKSON

Apollos University (F)

600 Central Avenue, Ste 215, Great Falls MT 92647

County: Cascade Identification: 667096
Telephone: (406) 799-1515 Carnegie Class: Not Classified
FAX Number: (844) 476-5567 Calendar System: Quarter
URL: www.apollos-university.edu
Established: 2005 Annual Undergrad Tuition & Fees: N/A
Enrollment: N/A Coed
Affiliation or Control: Proprietary IRS Status: Proprietary
Highest Offering: Doctorate
Accreditation: DEAC

00 CEO .... Dr. Paul EIDSON
01 President/CAO .... Dr. Scott EIDSON
05 Executive Vice President/Provost .... Dr. Robin WESTERIK

Blackfeet Community College (G)

Box 819, Browning MT 59417-0819

County: Glacier FICE Identification: 025106
Unit ID: 180054
Telephone: (406) 338-5441 Carnegie Class: Tribal
FAX Number: (406) 338-3272 Calendar System: Semester
URL: www.bfcc.edu
Established: 1976 Annual Undergrad Tuition & Fees: $2,890
Enrollment: 442 Coed
Affiliation or Control: Independent Non-Profit IRS Status: 501(c)3
Highest Offering: Associate Degree
Accreditation: NW

01 President .... Dr. Billie Jo KIPP
05 Dean Academic Affairs .... Mrs. Carol MURRAY
32 Dean Student Services .... Mrs. Anne RACINE
10 Chief Financial Officer .... Mr. James LORAN
37 Director of Financial Aid .... Mrs. Gaylene DUCHARME
06 Registrar .... Ms. Deana M. MCNABB
07 Director of Admissions .... Ms. Deana M. MCNABB
09 Director of Institutional Research .... Mr. Brad R. HALL
18 Chief Facilities/Physical Plant .... Mr. Smokey HENRIKSEN
15 Human Resources Specialist .... Ms. Shannon CONNELLY

Carroll College (H)

1601 N Benton Avenue, Helena MT 59625-0002

County: Lewis And Clark FICE Identification: 002526
Unit ID: 180106
Telephone: (406) 447-4300 Carnegie Class: Bac-Diverse
FAX Number: (406) 447-4533 Calendar System: Semester
URL: www.carroll.edu
Established: 1909 Annual Undergrad Tuition & Fees: $33,192
Enrollment: 1,469 Coed
Affiliation or Control: Roman Catholic IRS Status: 501(c)3
Highest Offering: Baccalaureate
Accreditation: NW, ENG, IACBE, NURSE

01 President .... Dr. Thomas EVANS
05 Sr Vice President Academic Affairs .... Dr. Colin IRVINE
10 VP for Finance & Administration .... Ms. Lori PETERSON
31 VP Community Relations .... Mr. Thomas J. MCCARVEL
32 Vice President for Student Life .... Dr. James D. HARDWICK
30 Vice Pres Institutional Advancement .... Mr. Michael LARKIN
84 Assoc Vice Pres Enrollment Mgmt .... Ms. Antonina LOCOCO
42 Director Campus Ministry-Chaplain .... Rev. Marc LENNEMAN
26 Director of Public Relations .... Ms. Sarah LAWLOR
27 Director of Marketing .... Ms. Patty WHITE
06 Registrar .... Ms. Cassie HALL
08 Director of Library .... Mr. Christian FRAZZA
37 Financial Aid Director .... Ms. Janet RIIS
36 Dir of Career Services/Testing .... Ms. Rosalie K. WALSH
07 Director Admissions/Enrollment Ops .... Ms. Cynthia J. THORNQUIST
15 Dir Human Resources & Admin Svcs .... Ms. Renee M. MCMAHON
18 Director of Facilities .... Mr. Walter H. BISKUPIAK
39 Director of Community Living .... Ms. Maureen WARD
35 Dir Student Activities/Leadership .... Mr. Patrick HARRIS
21 Controller .... Ms. Kari BRUSTKERN
13 Campus Computing/Info Tech Director .... Ms. Loretta ANDREWS
29 Director Alumni Relations .... Ms. Kathy RAMIREZ
09 Dir Research/Planning/Assessment .... Dr. Dawn GALLINGER
41 Athletic Director .... Mr. Charles GROSS

Chief Dull Knife College (I)

One College Drive, PO Box 98, Lame Deer MT 59043

County: Rosebud FICE Identification: 025452
Unit ID: 180160
Telephone: (406) 477-6215 Carnegie Class: Tribal
FAX Number: (406) 477-6219 Calendar System: Semester
URL: www.cdkc.edu
Established: 1975 Annual Undergrad Tuition & Fees: $2,260
Enrollment: 218 Coed
Affiliation or Control: Independent Non-Profit IRS Status: 501(c)3
Highest Offering: Associate Degree
Accreditation: NW

01 President/Int Dean Cultural Affairs .... Dr. Richard LITTLEBEAR
03 Vice President .... Mr. William WERTMAN
05 Dean Academic Affairs .... Mr. William BRIGGS
32 Dean Student Affairs .... Mr. Zane SPANG
37 Director Financial Aid .... Mr. Jody JENSON
08 Head Librarian .... Mrs. Joan HANTZ

Dawson Community College (J)

P.O. Box 421, Glendive MT 59330-0421

County: Dawson FICE Identification: 002529
Unit ID: 180151
Telephone: (406) 377-3396 Carnegie Class: Assoc/HT-High Non
FAX Number: (406) 377-8132 Calendar System: Semester
URL: www.dawson.edu

Established: 1940 Annual Undergrad Tuition & Fees (In-District): $3,630
Enrollment: 305 Coed
Affiliation or Control: State/Local IRS Status: 501(c)3
Highest Offering: Associate Degree
Accreditation: NW

01 President .... Dr. Scott R. MICKELSEN
11 Vice President of Administration .... Ms. Kathleen ZANDER
05 VP Academic and Student Affairs .... Mr. Shawn HOLZ
06 Registrar .... Ms. Virginia BOYSUN
08 Library Director .... Vacant
37 Director of Financial Aid .... Ms. Danielle DINGES
13 Director of Information Technology .... Mr. Frank ROJAS
15 Human Resources Director .... Ms. Leslie WELDON
103 Dir Workforce/Career Development .... Ms. Traci MASAU
84 Director Enrollment Management .... Ms. Suela CELA

Flathead Valley Community College (A)

777 Grandview Drive, Kalispell MT 59901
County: Flathead FICE Identification: 006777
Unit ID: 180197
Telephone: (406) 756-3822 Carnegie Class: Assoc/MT-VT-High Non
FAX Number: (406) 756-3815 Calendar System: Semester
URL: www.fvcc.edu
Established: 1967 Annual Undergrad Tuition & Fees (In-District): $4,112
Enrollment: 2,169 Coed
Affiliation or Control: Local IRS Status: 501(c)3
Highest Offering: Associate Degree
Accreditation: NW, EMT, MAC, PTAA, SURGT

01 President .... Dr. Jane A. KARAS
05 Vice President Academic Affairs .... Dr. Chris CLOUSE
10 Vice Pres Administration & Finance .... Mr. Kirk ZANDER
12 Director Lincoln County Campus .... Mr. Chad SHILLING
32 Dean of Students .... Ms. Brenda HANSON
51 Exec Dir Economic Dev/Cont Educ .... Ms. Susan BURCH
30 Exec Dir Institutional Advancement .... Ms. Colleen UNTERREINER
13 Exec Dir Mgmt Information Services .... Mr. Bill E. BOND
15 Exec Director of Human Resources .... Ms. Karen GLASSER
06 Registrar/Coord/Admissions/Records .... Ms. Sharon NAU
37 Director Student Financial Aid .... Ms. Cindy KIEFER
88 Director of Adult Basic Education .... Ms. Margaret L. GIRKINS
18 Director Maintenance Service .... Mr. David EVANS
21 Controller .... Ms. Caroline HILL
26 Director Marketing & Communication .... Ms. Diane SKYLAND
96 Director of Purchasing .... Mr. Steve LARSON
24 Coord Instructional Media Services .... Ms. Malinda CRAWFORD
36 Career Advisor .... Ms. Cathy ALLARD
04 Administrative Asst to President .... Ms. Monica SETTLES

Fort Peck Community College (B)

PO Box 398, Poplar MT 59255-0398
County: Roosevelt FICE Identification: 023430
Unit ID: 180212
Telephone: (406) 768-6300 Carnegie Class: Tribal
FAX Number: (406) 768-6301 Calendar System: Semester
URL: www.fpcc.edu
Established: 1978 Annual Undergrad Tuition & Fees: $2,250
Enrollment: 321 Coed
Affiliation or Control: Tribal Control IRS Status: 501(c)3
Highest Offering: Associate Degree
Accreditation: NW

01 President .... Ms. Haven GOURNEAU
05 Vice President Academic Affairs .... Mr. Wayne TWO BULLS
32 Vice President Student Services .... Mr. Elijah HOPKINS
30 Director Institutional Development .... Mr. Craig SMITH
10 Business Manager .... Ms. Rose ATKINSON
06 Registrar .... Ms. Linda L. HANSEN
37 Financial Aid Officer .... Ms. Lanette CLARK
40 Bookstore Manager .... Ms. Jackie AZURE
08 Head Librarian .... Mrs. Anita A. SCHEETZ

Little Big Horn College (C)

PO Box 370, Crow Agency MT 59022-0370
County: Big Horn FICE Identification: 022866
Unit ID: 180328
Telephone: (406) 638-3104 Carnegie Class: Tribal
FAX Number: (406) 638-3169 Calendar System: Semester
URL: www.lbhc.edu
Established: 1980 Annual Undergrad Tuition & Fees: $3,200
Enrollment: 248 Coed
Affiliation or Control: Tribal Control IRS Status: 501(c)3
Highest Offering: Associate Degree
Accreditation: NW

01 President .... Dr. David YARLOTT, JR.
05 Dean of Academics .... Miss Frederica LEFTHAND
32 Dean of Student Affairs .... Miss Te-Atta OLD BEAR
11 Dean of Administration .... Mr. David SMALL
06 Registrar .... Mr. William OLD CROW
08 Director of Library .... Mr. Tim BERNARDIS
13 Chief Information Officer .... Mr. Franklin COOPER
10 Chief Finance Officer .... Ms. Aldean GOOD LUCK
15 Director Human Resources .... Ms. Shaleen OLD COYOTE
97 Dept Head/General Stds/Crow Stds .... Dr. Tim MCCLEARY
81 Dept Head/Math/Science/Technology .... Vacant
25 Chief Contracts/Grants Admin .... Mr. Curtis RIDES HORSE, JR.

Miles Community College (D)

2715 Dickinson, Miles City MT 59301-4799
County: Custer FICE Identification: 002528
Unit ID: 180373
Telephone: (406) 874-6100 Carnegie Class: Assoc/HT-Mix Trad/Non
FAX Number: (406) 874-6282 Calendar System: Semester
URL: www.milescc.edu
Established: 1939 Annual Undergrad Tuition & Fees (In-District): $3,990
Enrollment: 481 Coed
Affiliation or Control: State/Local IRS Status: 501(c)3
Highest Offering: Associate Degree
Accreditation: NW, ADNUR, PHLEB

01 President .... Dr. Stacy KLIPPENSTEIN
10 VP Administration & Finance .... Vacant
05 Vice Pres of Academic Affairs .... Dr. Rita KRATKY
07 VP Enrollment & Student Success .... Ms. Jessie DUFNER
08 Director of Library .... Mr. George DICKIE
13 Director Information Technology .... Mr. Donald D. WARNER
37 Director Student Financial Aid .... Mr. Loren LANCASTER
18 Chief Facilities/Physical Plant .... Mr. Ross LAWRENCE
21 Business Services Director .... Ms. Nancy AABERGE
06 Registrar .... Ms. Lisa BLUNT
15 Director Human Resources .... Ms. Kylene PHIPPS
66 Director Nursing .... Ms. Karla LUND
20 Associate Academic Officer .... Mr. Garth SLEIGHT
40 Manager Bookstore .... Ms. Michele TRIMBLE
04 Administrative Asst to President .... Ms. Candy LANEY

Montana Bible College (E)

3625 South 19th Avenue, Bozeman MT 59718-9108
County: Gallatin FICE Identification: 041403
Unit ID: 262165
Telephone: (406) 586-3585 Carnegie Class: Spec-4-yr-Faith
FAX Number: (406) 586-3585 Calendar System: Semester
URL: www.montanabiblecollege.edu
Established: 1987 Annual Undergrad Tuition & Fees: $7,540
Enrollment: N/A Coed
Affiliation or Control: Independent Non-Profit IRS Status: 501(c)3
Highest Offering: Baccalaureate
Accreditation: BI

01 President .... Mr. Ryan WARD
05 Academic Dean .... Dr. Gale HEIDE
06 Registrar .... Mrs. Louise TURNER
07 Admissions Director .... Ms. Susan JACKSON
08 Librarian .... Mrs. Jessica CARLSON
32 Dean of Students .... Mr. Danny JOHNSON
10 Business Manager .... Ms. Leota FRED
21 Office Manager .... Mrs. Tasha OARD
84 Director of Enrollment Management .... Mr. Dan HOVESTOL
30 Advance & Devel Dir/Dean of Women .... Ms. Jenni O'BRIAN
13 Information Technology Director .... Mr. Austin RUHL
88 Discipleship Director .... Mr. Micah FORSYTHE

*Montana University System Office (F)

2500 Broadway, Helena MT 59601-3201
County: Lewis And Clark FICE Identification: 029072
Unit ID: 180470
Telephone: (406) 444-6570 Carnegie Class: N/A
FAX Number: (406) 444-1469
URL: www.mus.edu

01 Commissioner Higher Education .... Mr. Clayton T. CHRISTIAN
05 Deputy Comm Academic/Student Affs .... Dr. John CECH
45 Deputy Comm for Plng/Public Policy .... Mr. Tyler TREVOR
15 Deputy Comm Communications/HR .... Mr. Kevin MCRAE
43 Chief Legal Counsel/Deputy Comm .... Ms. Viv HAMMILL
103 Deputy Comm Two-Year Educ .... Mr. John CECH
118 Director of Benefits .... Mrs. Mary LACHENBRUCH
21 Chief Financial Officer .... Ms. Robin GRAHAM
21 Director Accounting & Budget .... Ms. Frieda HOUSER
117 Director of Work Comp Risk Mgmt .... Ms. Leah Jo TIETZ
93 Dir Minority/Amer Ind Achievement .... Ms. Angela MCLEAN
13 OCHE IT Manager .... Ms. Edwina MORRISON

*University of Montana - Missoula (G)

32 Campus Drive, Missoula MT 59812-0001
County: Missoula FICE Identification: 002536
Unit ID: 180489
Telephone: (406) 243-2311 Carnegie Class: DU-Higher
FAX Number: (406) 243-2797 Calendar System: Semester
URL: www.umt.edu
Established: 1893 Annual Undergrad Tuition & Fees (In-State): $6,238
Enrollment: 13,044 Coed
Affiliation or Control: State IRS Status: 501(c)3
Highest Offering: Doctorate
Accreditation: NW, ART, CAATE, CACREP, CAEPN, CEA, CLPSY, COARC, CS, JOUR, LAW, MUS, PH, PHAR, PTA, SCPSY, SP, SW, THEA

02 President .... Dr. Sheila M. STEARNS
05 Interim Provost/VP Academic Affairs .... Dr. Beverly EDMOND
10 Vice President Finance/Admin .... Mr. Michael REID
84 VP for Enrollment/Student Affairs .... Dr. Thomas CRADY
46 Vice Pres Research/Development .... Dr. Scott WHITTENBURG
26 AVP for Integrated Communications .... Mr. Mario SCHULZKE
45 AVP for Plng/Budget Analysis .... Ms. Dawn RESSEL
15 AVP Human Resource Services .... Ms. Terri PHILLIPS
20 Associate Provost .... Dr. Nathan LINDSAY
32 Dean of Students .... Ms. Rhondie VOORHEES
43 Legal Counsel .... Ms. Lucy FRANCE
12 Director Mansfield Center .... Dr. Abraham KIM
104 Assoc Provost Global Engagement .... Ms. Effie KOEHN
88 Dir Broadcast Media Center .... Mr. Ray EKNESS
22 Dir Equal Opportunity/Affirm Action .... Ms. Jessica WELTMAN
06 Registrar .... Mr. Joseph HICKMAN
18 Director Facilities Svcs .... Mr. Kevin KREBSBACH
13 CIO .... Mr. Matt RILEY
38 Director Counseling .... Mr. Mike FROST
36 Director Career Services .... Ms. Laurie FISHER
37 Director of Financial Aid .... Mr. Kent MCGOWAN
29 Interim Director of Alumni Office .... Ms. Karen DYKSTRA
102 President & CEO/UM Foundation .... Ms. Cindy WILLIAMS
19 Director of Public Safety .... Mr. Martin LUDEMANN
23 Director Curry Health Center .... Dr. Rick CURTIS
39 Director Residence Life .... Ms. Sandra SCHOONOVER
41 Athletic Director .... Mr. Kent HASLAM
85 Dir Foreign Student & Scholar Svcs .... Ms. Effie KOEHN
21 Director Business Services .... Mr. John MCCORMICK
88 Exec Director Student Success .... Mr. Brian FRENCH
08 Dean Mansfield Library .... Dr. Sha Li ZHANG
51 Dean Continuing Education .... Dr. Roger MACLEAN
49 Dean College Humanities & Sciences .... Dr. Christopher COMER
61 Dean School of Law .... Mr. Paul KIRGIS
65 Dean College Forestry/Conservation .... Dr. Thomas DELUCA
50 Dean School of Business Admin .... Dr. Christopher SHOOK
76 Dean Col Health Prof & Biomed Sci .... Dr. Reed HUMPHREY
60 Dean School of Journalism .... Mr. Larry ABRAMSON
53 Dean College of Educ & Human Svcs .... Dr. Roberta EVANS
57 Dean College Visual/Performing Arts .... Mr. Stephen KALM
75 Dean Missoula College .... Dr. Shannon O'BRIEN
92 Dean Honors College .... Dr. Brock TESSMAN
04 Administrative Asst to President .... Ms. Rebecca C. POWER

*The University of Montana Western (H)

710 S Atlantic St, Dillon MT 59725-3598
County: Beaverhead FICE Identification: 002537
Unit ID: 180692
Telephone: (406) 683-7011 Carnegie Class: Bac-Diverse
FAX Number: (406) 683-7493 Calendar System: Other
URL: www.umwestern.edu
Established: 1893 Annual Undergrad Tuition & Fees (In-State): $4,893
Enrollment: 1,403 Coed
Affiliation or Control: State IRS Status: 501(c)3
Highest Offering: Baccalaureate
Accreditation: NW, CAEP, IACBE

02 Chancellor .... Dr. Beth WEATHERBY
05 Provost .... Dr. Deborah HEDEEN
10 Vice Chanc Administration/Finance .... Ms. Susan BRIGGS
26 Director Marketing/Univ Relations .... Vacant
20 Dean of Outreach .... Ms. Anneliese RIPLEY
06 Registrar .... Ms. Charity WALTERS
07 Director of Admissions .... Mr. Matt ALLEN
08 Interim Librarian .... Ms. Anne KISH
36 Director of Field Learning .... Mr. Adam MASTANDREA
41 Director of Athletics .... Mr. Russ RICHARDSON
13 Director of Information Technology .... Mr. Chad BAVER
32 Dean of Students .... Ms. Nicole HAZELBAKER
30 Director of Devel/Alumni Relations .... Ms. Roxanne ENGELLANT
37 Director of Student Financial Aid .... Vacant
38 Director Student Counseling .... Mr. Jerry GIRARD
15 Human Resources .... Ms. Patti LAKE
04 Administrative Asst to Chancellor .... Ms. Hillary LOWELL
22 Dir Affirmative Action/EEO .... Ms. Liane FORRESTER

*Helena College University of Montana (I)

1115 N Roberts, Helena MT 59601-3098
County: Lewis and Clark FICE Identification: 007570
Unit ID: 180276
Telephone: (406) 447-6900 Carnegie Class: Assoc/HVT-Mix Trad/Non
FAX Number: (406) 447-6397 Calendar System: Semester
URL: www.umhelena.edu
Established: 1939 Annual Undergrad Tuition & Fees (In-State): $3,109
Enrollment: 1,454 Coed
Affiliation or Control: State IRS Status: 501(c)3
Highest Offering: Associate Degree
Accreditation: NW, ADNUR, IFSAC

02 Interim Dean/CEO .... Ms. Jane G. BAKER
04 Administrative Assoc to Dean/CEO .... Ms. Summer S. MARSTON
05 Assoc Dean of Academic Affairs/VP .... Dr. Chad HICKOX
07 Director of Admissions and Records .... Ms. Sarah DELLWO
08 Director of Library Services .... Ms. Della DUBBE
51 Director of Continuing Education .... Ms. Mary LANNERT
18 Assistant Dean of Fiscal & Plant .... Mr. Russ FILLNER
13 Director of IT Services .... Mr. Jeff BLOCK
40 Bookstore Manager .... Mr. Josh BENNETT
32 Assistant Dean of Student Services .... Ms. Elizabeth STEARNS SIMS
26 Director of Marketing .... Ms. Barb MCALMOND
37 Director Financial Aid .... Ms. Valerie CURTIN
121 Director of Student Support Center .... Dr. Patrick TURNER
15 Director of Human Resources .... Mr. Matthew RICHARDS
09 Director of Institutional Research .... Mr. Michael BROWN

*Montana State University (A)

PO Box 172190, Bozeman MT 59717-2190
County: Gallatin FICE Identification: 002532
Unit ID: 180461
Telephone: (406) 994-2452 Carnegie Class: DU-Higher
FAX Number: (406) 994-1923 Calendar System: Semester
URL: www.montana.edu
Established: 1893 Annual Undergrad Tuition & Fees (In-State): $6,887
Enrollment: 15,236 Coed
Affiliation or Control: State IRS Status: 501(c)3
Highest Offering: Doctorate
Accreditation: NW, ART, CACREP, CAEP, CS, DIETD, DIETI, ENG, ENGT, IPSY, MT, MUS, NURSE

02 President .... Dr. Waded CRUZADO
05 Exec VP Acad Affs/Provost .... Dr. Robert MOKWA
20 Assoc Provost .... Dr. David SINGEL
88 Assoc Provost Accreditation .... Dr. Ron LARSEN
10 Vice Pres Admin/Finance .... Mr. Terry LEIST
32 Vice Pres Student Success .... Dr. Chris KEARNS
56 Exec Director Extension .... Dr. Jeff BADER
46 VP Research & Econ Development .... Dr. Renee REIJO PERA
04 Special Assistant to the President .... Vacant
18 Assoc Vice Pres University Services .... Mr. Daniel STEVENSON
88 Assoc VP Research & Econ Develop .... Dr. Mark YOUNG
15 Assoc VP HR/Chief HR Officer .... Ms. Cathy HASENPFLUG
21 Assoc Vice Pres Financial Services .... Ms. Laura HUMBERGER
102 President/CEO MSU Foundation .... Mr. Christopher D. MURRAY
104 Assoc Prov International Programs .... Dr. David DI MARIA
26 Exec Director Univ Communications .... Mr. Tracy ELLIG
88 Exec Director Museum of the Rockies .... Mr. Sheldon MCKAMEY
50 Dean Business .... Dr. Kregg AYTES
53 Dean Education/Health/Human Dev .... Dr. Alison HARMON
54 Dean Engineering .... Dr. Brett GUNNINK
49 Dean Letters & Science .... Dr. Nicol RAE
66 Dean Nursing .... Dr. Helen MELLAND
08 Dean Libraries .... Mr. Kenning ARLITSCH
35 Dean Students .... Dr. Matthew CAIRES
58 Dean Graduate School .... Dr. Karlene HOO
92 Dean Honors College .... Dr. Ilses-Mari LEE
47 VP and Dean Agriculture .... Dr. Charles BOYER
48 Dean Arts/Architecture .... Dr. Royce SMITH
70 Dean Gallatin College Programs .... Mr. Robert HIETALA
07 Director Admissions .... Ms. Ronda RUSSELL
22 Director Institutional Equity .... Ms. Jyl SHAFFER
29 Pres/CEO Alumni Foundation .... Mr. Christopher D. MURRAY
41 Director Athletics .... Mr. Leon COSTELLO
109 Assoc VP Auxiliary Services .... Mr. Tom STUMP
36 Dir Allen Yarnell Center .... Dr. Carina BECK
38 Dir Counseling/Psych Services .... Dr. Elizabeth ASSERSON
22 Dir Disability/Re-ent/Veteran Svcs .... Ms. Brenda YORK
56 Exec Director Extended University .... Dr. Kim OBBINK
37 Director Financial Aid .... Ms. Brandi PAYNE
43 Legal Counsel .... Ms. Kellie PETERSON
45 Director Planning & Analysis .... Dr. Chris FASTNOW
96 Director Procurement .... Mr. Brian O'CONNOR
06 Registrar .... Mr. Tony CAMPEAU
27 Director Marketing/Creative Service .... Ms. Julie KIPFER
19 Director University Police .... Mr. Robert PUTZKE
100 Asst to the President .... Ms. Maggie HAYES
105 Dir Web Communications .... Vacant
13 VP for Information Tech .... Mr. Jerry SHEEHAN
25 Asst Vice Pres for Research .... Ms. Leslie SCHMIDT
39 Director Housing/Res Life .... Mr. Jeff BONDY
14 Assoc Chief IT/CSO .... Mr. Adam EDELMAN
88 Dir Employee & Labor Relations .... Ms. Susan ALT
114 Dir University Budget Office .... Ms. Kathy ATTEBURY
88 Dir Women's Center .... Ms. Elizabeth DANFORTH
63 Dir WWAMI/Med Educ Program .... Dr. Martin TEINTZE
19 Chief of Campus Police .... Mr. Adam DAVIS
29 Director Alumni Relations .... Ms. Sarah BROCKEL
37 Director Student Financial Aid .... Ms. Emily WILLIAMSON
40 Director Bookstore .... Mr. Ed BROWN
39 Int Dean Student Life & Auxiliaries .... Ms. Kathy KOTECKI
31 Coordinator Community Involvement .... Ms. Shayla FOX
21 University Budget Director .... Ms. Trudy COLLINS
96 Director of Business Services .... Ms. Barb SHAFER
20 Dir Academic Support Center .... Mr. John GILLETTE
28 Dir Montana Ctr for Inclusive Educ .... Ms. Marsha SAMPSON
89 Dir New Student/Retention Services .... Ms. Tammi WATSON
88 Director American Indian Outreach .... Ms. Reno CHARETTE
85 Exec Dir Intl Studies/Outreach .... Dr. Paul FOSTER
106 Director e-Learning .... Dr. Susan BALTER-REITZ
92 Dir of University Honors Program .... Dr. David CRAIG
104 Specialist Intl Marketing/Outreach .... Mr. Neil BEYER
49 Dean of Arts & Sciences .... Dr. Christine SHEARER
53 Dean of Education .... Dr. Mary Susan FISHBAUGH
50 Interim Dean College of Business .... Dr. Diane DUIN
12 Dean City College MSU Billings .... Dr. Clifford COPPERSMITH
76 Dean College of Allied Health Prof .... Dr. Diane DUIN
88 Asc Dean City College MSU Billings .... Dr. Florence GARCIA

*Montana State University - Billings (B)

1500 University Drive, Billings MT 59101-0245
County: Yellowstone FICE Identification: 002530
Unit ID: 180179
Telephone: (406) 657-2011 Carnegie Class: Masters/M
FAX Number: (406) 657-2302 Calendar System: Semester
URL: www.msubillings.edu
Established: 1927 Annual Undergrad Tuition & Fees (In-State): $5,826
Enrollment: 4,425 Coed
Affiliation or Control: State IRS Status: 501(c)3
Highest Offering: Master's
Accreditation: NW, ART, CAATE, CACREP, CAEPN, EMT, MUS

02 Interim Chancellor .... Dr. Ron LARSEN
10 Administrative Vice Chancellor .... Ms. Terrie IVERSON
05 Academic Vice Chancellor & Provost .... Dr. Robert HOAR
32 Vice Chancellor for Student Affairs .... Dr. Joseph ORAVECZ
20 Vice Provost Academic Affairs .... Dr. Matthew REDINGER
102 President/CEO Foundation .... Mr. Bill KENNEDY
08 Director Library Services .... Ms. Darlene HERT
07 Director Admiss/Records/Registrar .... Dr. Cheri JOHANNES
15 Director Human Resources/EEO AA .... Ms. Janet SIMON
36 Director Advising/Career Services .... Dr. Becky LYONS
13 Chief Information Officer .... Dr. Michael J. BARBER
56 Director Extended Campus .... Mr. Kevin NEMETH
25 Dir Grants & Sponsored Pgms .... Ms. Cindy BELL
26 Int Director University Relations .... Ms. Sarah BROCKEL
09 Director Institutional Research .... Ms. Joann STRYKER
18 Director Facility Services .... Mr. Jason MCGIMPSEY
58 Int Director Graduate Programs .... Dr. Diane DUIN
41 Athletic Director .... Ms. Krista MONTAGUE

*Montana State University - Northern (C)

PO Box 7751, Havre MT 59501-7751
County: Hill FICE Identification: 002533
Unit ID: 180522
Telephone: (406) 265-3700 Carnegie Class: Bac-Diverse
FAX Number: N/A Calendar System: Semester
URL: www.msun.edu
Established: 1929 Annual Undergrad Tuition & Fees (In-State): $5,371
Enrollment: 1,234 Coed
Affiliation or Control: State IRS Status: 501(c)3
Highest Offering: Master's
Accreditation: NW, ADNUR, ENGT, NUR

02 Chancellor .... Mr. Gregory D. KEGEL
05 Interim Provost/VC Academic Affairs .... Dr. Lawrence STRIZICH
10 VC Finance & Administration .... Mr. Brian SIMONSON
102 Executive Director of Foundation .... Mr. Jim BENNETT
72 Dean College Technical Sciences .... Dr. Larry STRIZICH
32 Dean of Students .... Dr. Steven WISE
53 Dean Col Educ/Arts & Sci/Nursing .... Dr. Carol REIFSCHNEIDER
06 Registrar .... Ms. Alisha SCHROEDER
66 Director of Nursing .... Dr. Janice STARR
21 Controller .... Mr. Chris WENDLAND
41 Athletic Director .... Mr. Christian OBERQUELL
36 Director Career Center .... Ms. Mary HELLER
13 Interim Chief Info Tech Officer .... Ms. Marianne HOPPE
37 Director of Financial Aid .... Ms. Cindy SMALL
26 Director of University Relations .... Mr. James POTTER
08 Director of Library .... Ms. Vicki GIST
38 Director Student Support Services .... Mr. Brian HEUETT
07 Director of Admissions .... Ms. Maura GATCH
15 Human Resources Manager .... Ms. Suzanne HUNGER
121 Sr Director Student Success .... Ms. Tracey JETTE
18 Facilities Manager .... Mr. Dan ULMEN
29 Alumni Associate .... Ms. Becka STONE
100 Chief of Staff .... Ms. Rachel DEAN

*Great Falls College Montana State University (D)

2100 16th Avenue South, Great Falls MT 59405-4909
County: Cascade FICE Identification: 009314
Unit ID: 180249
Telephone: (406) 771-4300 Carnegie Class: Assoc/MT-VT-Mix Trad/Non
FAX Number: (406) 771-4317 Calendar System: Semester
URL: gfcmsu.edu
Established: 1969 Annual Undergrad Tuition & Fees (In-State): $3,130
Enrollment: 1,657 Coed
Affiliation or Control: State IRS Status: 501(c)3
Highest Offering: Associate Degree
Accreditation: NW, CAHIIM, COARC, DA, DH, EMT, MAC, PTAA, SURGT

02 CEO/Dean .... Dr. Susan J. WOLFF
10 Chief Financial Officer .... Dr. Darryl STEVENS
05 Chief Academic Officer .... Dr. Heidi PASEK
32 Chief Student Affairs & HR Officer .... Ms. Mary Kay BONILLA
26 Exec Dir Development/Comm & Mktg .... Mr. Lewis CARD
13 Interim Director IT Services .... Mr. David BONILLA
18 Director of Facilities Services .... Mr. Dennis DEVINE
36 Director Advising & Career Center .... Mr. Troy STODDARD
37 Director Student Financial Aid .... Ms. Leah HABEL
40 Bookstore Manager .... Mr. Steve HALSTED
96 Budget & Purchasing Analyst .... Ms. Carmen ROBERTS
09 Research Analyst .... Dr. Grace ANDERSON
08 Director of eLearning & Library .... Ms. Laura WIGHT
88 Trades Division Director .... Mr. Joel SIMS
97 Dir of Gen Educ/Bus/Tech & Transfer .... Ms. Leanne FROST
76 Director of Health Sciences .... Dr. Frankie LYONS
06 Registrar .... Ms. Dena WAGNER-FOSSEN
07 Director of Admissions .... Mr. Joe SIMONSEN

*Montana Tech of The University of Montana (E)

1300 W Park Street, Butte MT 59701-8997
County: Silver Bow FICE Identification: 002531
Unit ID: 180416
Telephone: (800) 445-8324 Carnegie Class: Bac-Diverse
FAX Number: (406) 496-4710 Calendar System: Semester
URL: www.mtech.edu
Established: 1893 Annual Undergrad Tuition & Fees (In-State): $6,561
Enrollment: 2,130 Coed
Affiliation or Control: State IRS Status: 501(c)3
Highest Offering: Doctorate
Accreditation: NW, CS, ENG, ENGR, NURSE

02 Chancellor .... Dr. Donald M. BLACKKETTER
05 Provost .... Dr. Douglas M. ABBOTT
10 Business Officer/Controller .... Ms. Carleen CASSIDY
11 VC for Administration & Finance .... Mr. Brandt WRIGHT
30 VC for Development & Univ Relations .... Mr. Joseph MCCLAFFERTY
84 Assoc VC for Enrollment Management .... Dr. Carrie VATH
46 VC Research & Dean Grad Sch .... Dr. Beverly HARTLINE
65 Director Bureau of Mines & Geology .... Dr. John J. METESH
88 Dir Inst of Educational Opportunity .... Ms. Amy VERLANIC
36 Director Career Services .... Ms. Sarah RAYMOND
08 Director Library .... Mr. Scott JUSKIEWICZ
37 Director of Financial Aid .... Mr. Michael W. RICHARDSON
18 Director of Physical Facilities .... Mr. Michael ALLEN
29 Director Alumni Affairs .... Ms. Peggy S. MCCOY
41 Athletic Director .... Mr. Chuck MORRELL
72 Dean College of Technology .... Dr. David GURCHIEK
81 Dean Col Letters/Sci/Prof Studies .... Dr. Douglas A. COE
54 Dean School of Mines & Engineering .... Dr. Dan TRUDNOWSKI
110 Director of Development .... Mr. Michael BARTH
39 Director Residence Life .... Mr. Scott FORTHOFER
26 Director Public Relations .... Ms. Amanda BADOVINAC
40 Bookstore Director .... Ms. Laurie VANDEL
09 Director Institutional Research .... Ms. Melissa KUMP
06 Registrar .... Ms. Leslie DICKERSON
07 Director of Recruiting .... Ms. Stephanie CROWE
105 Webmaster .... Mr. David NOLT
106 Director of Distance Learning .... Mr. David BENTZ
13 Director of Network Services .... Mr. Mike KUKAY
91 Director of Information Services .... Ms. Jennifer SIMON
96 Dir Purchasing & Budgets .... Ms. Marissa BENTLEY
15 Dir Human Resources .... Ms. Vanessa VAN DYK
04 Assistant to the Chancellor .... Ms. Victoria PAGAN
25 Dir of Sponsored Programs .... Vacant

*City College at Montana State University Billings (F)

3803 Central Avenue, Billings MT 59102-4398
Telephone: (406) 247-3000 FICE Identification: 010166
Accreditation: &NW

† Regional accreditation is carried under the parent institution Montana State University-Billings, Billings, MT.

*Highlands College of Montana Tech (G)

25 Basin Creek Road, Butte MT 59701-9704
Telephone: (406) 496-3701 FICE Identification: 009282
Accreditation: &NW

† Regional accreditation is carried under the parent institution Montana Tech of The University of Montanna, Butte, MT.

*Missoula College-University of Montana (H)

1205 East Broadway Street, Missoula MT 59802
Telephone: (406) 243-7811 FICE Identification: 007561
Accreditation: &NW, ACFEI, ADNUR, SURGT

† Regional accreditation is carried under the parent institution The University of Montana-Missoula, Missoula, MT.

Rocky Mountain College (I)

1511 Poly Drive, Billings MT 59102-1796
County: Yellowstone FICE Identification: 002534
Unit ID: 180595
Telephone: (406) 657-1000 Carnegie Class: Bac-Diverse
FAX Number: (406) 259-9751 Calendar System: Semester
URL: www.rocky.edu
Established: 1878 Annual Undergrad Tuition & Fees: $26,666
Enrollment: 1,035 Coed
Affiliation or Control: Interdenominational IRS Status: 501(c)3
Highest Offering: Master's
Accreditation: NW, AAB, ARCPA

01 President .... Dr. Robert WILMOUTH
05 Academic Vice President .... Dr. Stephen A. GERMIC
32 Vice President for Student Life .... Mr. Bradley A. NASON
111 Vice President of Advancement .... Vacant
10 Chief Financial Officer .... Ms. Melodie CHARETTE
88 Director of Educational Leadership .... Dr. Stevie SCHMITZ
08 Director of the Library .... Ms. Bobbi OTTE
112 Director of Major Gifts .... Mr. Peter BOLENBAUGH
26 Director of Communications .... Mr. Andrew KEATING
13 Director of Information Technology .... Mr. Daniel WOLTERS
18 Director of Campus Facilities .... Mr. Keith NORTH
41 Director of Athletics .... Mr. Bruce PARKER
44 Director of Annual Fund .... Ms. Della GARDNER
09 Institutional Research Analyst .... Miss Erica WALL
06 Registrar .... Dr. Jennifer BRATZ
37 Director of Financial Assistance .... Ms. Jessica FRANCISCHETTI
39 Director of Residence Life .... Ms. Shaydean SAYE
04 Executive Assistant to the Pres .... Ms. Tracy DAVIDSON

29 Director of Alumni Relations .... Ms. Sarah CLARK
84 Dean of Enrollment Services .... Mr. Austin MAPSTON
19 Director Security/Safety .... Ms. Amberly TANZOSH
91 Director Administrative Computing .... Ms. Kellee PIERCE

Salish Kootenai College (A)

PO Box 70, Pablo MT 59855-0070

County: Lake FICE Identification: 021434
Unit ID: 180647
Telephone: (406) 275-4800 Carnegie Class: Tribal
FAX Number: (406) 275-4801 Calendar System: Quarter
URL: www.skc.edu
Established: 1977 Annual Undergrad Tuition & Fees: $4,191
Enrollment: 784 Coed
Affiliation or Control: Independent Non-Profit IRS Status: 501(c)3
Highest Offering: Baccalaureate
Accreditation: NW, ADNUR, DA, NUR, SW

01 President .... Dr. Sandra BOHAM
05 Vice President of Academic Affairs .... Mr. Dan DURGLO
10 Vice Pres Business Affairs .... Ms. Audrey PLOUFFE
32 Vice Pres Student Affairs .... Vacant
06 Registrar .... Ms. Cleo KENMILLE
37 Financial Aid Director .... Ms. Jackie SWAIN
09 Dir Institutional Effectiveness .... Dr. Stacey SHERWIN
15 Human Resources/Inner Campus Dir .... Ms. Rachel ANDREWS-GOULD
30 Development Director .... Mr. Curtis COX
35 Dean of Students .... Ms. Tracie MCDONALD
13 Director of Information Technology .... Mr. Al ANDERSON
18 Facilities/Physical Plant Manager .... Mr. Michael BIGCRANE
04 Admin Assistant to President .... Ms. Anita BIG SPRING

Stone Child College (B)

8294 Upper Box Elder Road, Box Elder MT 59521-9796

County: Hill FICE Identification: 026109
Unit ID: 366340
Telephone: (406) 395-4875 Carnegie Class: Tribal
FAX Number: (406) 395-4836 Calendar System: Semester
URL: www.stonechild.edu/
Established: 1984 Annual Undergrad Tuition & Fees: $2,645
Enrollment: 540 Coed
Affiliation or Control: Tribal Control IRS Status: 501(c)3
Highest Offering: Associate Degree
Accreditation: NW

01 Interim President .... Ms. Cory SANGREY-BILLY
05 Dean of Academics .... Ms. Cory SANGREY-BILLY
32 Dean of Student Services .... Ms. Helen WINDY BOY
10 Chief Financial Officer .... Ms. Tiffany GALBARY
04 Admin Asst to the President .... Ms. Wanda ST. MARKS
06 Registrar .... Ms. Gaile TORRES
13 Network Administator .... Mr. Eli AQUINO
40 Bookstore Manager .... Ms. Jessie JONES
37 Financial Aid Officer .... Mr. Dennis SANGREY
18 Facilities/Maintenance Supervisor .... Mr. Gus BACON
08 Head Librarian .... Ms. Joy BRIDWELL

University of Providence (C)

1301 20th Street S, Great Falls MT 59405-4996

County: Cascade FICE Identification: 002527
Unit ID: 180258
Telephone: (800) 856-9544 Carnegie Class: Bac-Diverse
FAX Number: (406) 791-5209 Calendar System: Semester
URL: www.uprovidence.edu
Established: 1932 Annual Undergrad Tuition & Fees: $23,534
Enrollment: 1,134 Coed
Affiliation or Control: Roman Catholic IRS Status: 501(c)3
Highest Offering: Master's
Accreditation: NW, CACREP, NURSE

01 President .... Dr. Anthony ARETZ
05 VP for Academic Affairs .... Vacant
76 VP School of Health Professions .... Dr. Deborah BURTON
03 VP for Mission Integration .... Rev. Oliver J. DOYLE
84 VP for Enrollment Management .... Ms. Julie EDSTROM
15 VP for Finance & HR .... Ms. Stacey EVE
32 VP for Student Development .... Ms. Sherrie AREY
41 VP for Athletics .... Mr. Dave GANTT
20 Academic Dean .... Dr. Gregory MADSON
09 Director of Institutional Research .... Dr. Gregory MADSON
66 Dean Nursing and Clinical Programs .... Ms. Victoria HAYS
88 Senior Director Admin Programs .... Dr. Rob PACKER
88 Sr Proj Manager Nursing & Health .... Ms. Jamie OWENS
13 Chief Technology Officer .... Mr. John KOEHLER
121 Director Student Support Services .... Mr. Matthew HAUK
39 Director of Residential Life .... Mr. Aaron STUCKER
21 Director of the Business Office .... Ms. Amber HERIGON
37 Director Financial Aid .... Ms. Kelli ENGELHARDT
18 Director Physical Plant .... Mr. Chet PIETRYKOWSKI
106 Director of Distance Learning .... Mr. Jim GRETCH
06 Registrar .... Ms. Brittany BUDESKI
19 Director of Security .... Mr. Ross MURPHY
10 Controller .... Mr. Kris KESTER
111 Director of Advancement .... Ms. Kylie CARRANZA
16 Director of HR .... Mr. Jacob SUTTON
108 Director of Inst Effectiveness .... Ms. Leslie MILLS
36 Director of Career Services .... Ms. Leslie DAWSON
26 Exec Dir of Marketing & Comm .... Ms. Denise CZUPRYNSKI
91 Director Administrative Computing .... Ms. Kathryn CARBIS
04 Administrative Asst to President .... Ms. Trudi COLE

Yellowstone Christian College (D)

1515 S. Shiloh Road, Billings MT 59106

County: Yellowstone Identification: 667254
Telephone: (406) 656-9950 Carnegie Class: Not Classified
FAX Number: N/A Calendar System: Semester
URL: www.yellowstonechristian.edu
Established: 1880 Annual Undergrad Tuition & Fees: N/A
Enrollment: N/A Coed
Affiliation or Control: Independent Non-Profit IRS Status: 501(c)3
Highest Offering: Baccalaureate
Accreditation: @BI

01 President .... Bruce CANNON
03 Exec Vice Pres/Dean Chapel .... Darwin PAYTON
05 Dean of Academics .... Remigio RAMOS

NEBRASKA

Bellevue University (E)

1000 Galvin Road S, Bellevue NE 68005-3098

County: Sarpy FICE Identification: 009743
Unit ID: 180814
Telephone: (402) 293-2000 Carnegie Class: Masters/L
FAX Number: (402) 293-2020 Calendar System: Other
URL: www.bellevue.edu
Established: 1966 Annual Undergrad Tuition & Fees: $7,365
Enrollment: 9,760 Coed
Affiliation or Control: Independent Non-Profit IRS Status: 501(c)3
Highest Offering: Doctorate
Accreditation: NH, CACREP, IACBE

01 President .... Dr. Mary B. HAWKINS
03 Vice President Administration .... Mr. Jerry A. BLASIG
10 Exec VP University Affairs .... Ms. Donna BARNES
88 VP Strategic Partnerships .... Mr. Jim GROTRIAN
05 Chief Academic Officer .... Vacant
11 Chief Operating Officer .... Mr. Matthew DAVIS
72 Dean of College of Science & Tech .... Ms. Mary DOBRANSKY
50 Dean College of Business .... Dr. Rebecca MURDOCK
49 Dean College of Arts & Sciences .... Dr. Clif MASON
51 Dean of Continuing and Profess Educ .... Dr. Michelle EPPLER
13 Asst VP of Information Technology .... Mr. James S. VEREBELY
04 Exec Assistant to the President .... Ms. Christine HOW
32 AVP Community & Student Affairs .... Mr. Scott BIERMAN
37 Director Student Financial Aid .... Ms. Janet YALE
08 Sr Dir Library Services .... Ms. Robin BERNSTEIN
102 Foundation CEO .... Mr. Russ RUPIPER
41 Director of Athletics .... Mr. Ed LEHOTAK
40 Director Bookstore .... Mr. Mark RIGGERT
18 Director of Facilities .... Mr. Ralph (Sam) J. BORER
30 VP Development Programs .... Ms. Dorothy MORROW
21 Controller .... Ms. Lori PIRSCH
15 VP Performance Management .... Vacant
19 Director of Security/Safety .... Mr. Greg ALLEN
108 Quality Assurance Programs Director .... Mr. Pete HEINEMAN
26 Sr Dir Marketing Operations .... Ms. Geri MASON
06 Registrar .... Ms. Liz BRADLEY

Bryan College of Health Sciences (F)

5035 Everett Street, Lincoln NE 68506-1398

County: Lancaster FICE Identification: 006399
Unit ID: 180878
Telephone: (402) 481-3801 Carnegie Class: Spec-4-yr-Other Health
FAX Number: N/A Calendar System: Semester
URL: www.bryanhealthcollege.edu
Established: 2001 Annual Undergrad Tuition & Fees: $14,636
Enrollment: 704 Coed
Affiliation or Control: Independent Non-Profit IRS Status: 501(c)3
Highest Offering: Doctorate
Accreditation: NH, ANEST, CVT, DMS, NUR

01 President .... Dr. Richard LLOYD
05 Provost .... Dr. Kay MAIZE
97 Dean General Studies/Acad Advance .... Dr. Kristy PLANDER
11 Dean of Operations .... Dr. June SMITH
66 Dean of Undergraduate Nursing .... Dr. Theresa DELAHOYDE
76 Dean of Health Professions .... Dr. Kay CRABTREE
88 Dean of Nurse Anesthesia .... Dr. Sharon HADENFELDT
32 Dean of Students .... Ms. Debra BORDER
08 Director of Library Services .... Ms. Jan RICE
07 Director of Admissions .... Ms. Stacy DAM
06 Registrar .... Ms. Pam MCMASTER
29 Director of Student/Alumni Services .... Ms. Brenda NEEMANN
37 Director of Student Financial Aid .... Ms. Deborah WILKE
113 Bursar .... Mr. Larry MORRISON

Central Community College (G)

PO Box 4903, Grand Island NE 68802-4903

County: Hall FICE Identification: 020995
Unit ID: 180902
Telephone: (308) 398-4222 Carnegie Class: Assoc/HVT-High Non
FAX Number: (308) 398-7398 Calendar System: Semester
URL: www.cccneb.edu
Established: 1966 Annual Undergrad Tuition & Fees (In-District): $2,880
Enrollment: 6,227 Coed
Affiliation or Control: Local IRS Status: 501(c)3
Highest Offering: Associate Degree
Accreditation: NH, ADNUR, CAHIIM, DA, DH, EMT, MAC, MLTAD, OTA

01 College President .... Dr. Greg P. SMITH
03 Executive Vice President .... Dr. Deb BRENNAN
10 Vice President of Admin Services .... Mr. Joel KING
15 Vice President of Human Resources .... Dr. Chris WADDLE
12 Grand Island Campus President .... Dr. Marcie KEMNITZ
12 Columbus Campus President .... Dr. Matt GOTSCHALL
12 Hastings Campus President .... Mr. Bill HITESMAN
111 VP of Institutional Advancement .... Mr. Dean MOORS
106 Associate VP of Virtual Campus .... Dr. Candace WALTON
102 Foundation Director .... Mr. Dean MOORS
76 Dean of Health Sciences .... Ms. Paulette WOODS-RAMSEY
32 Dean of Student & Enrollment .... Dr. Jerry RACIOPPI
88 Dean of Skilled & Technical Science .... Dr. Nate ALLEN
50 Dean of Business .... Dr. Candace WALTON
56 Dean of Ext Learning & Training .... Mr. Ron KLUCK
05 Dean of Academic Education .... Dr. Kathy FUCHSER
13 Dir Information Technology Services .... Mr. Tom PETERS
06 Registrar .... Ms. Barb LARSON
29 Director Alumni Relations .... Ms. Cheri BEDA
37 Director Student Financial Aid .... Ms. Victoria KUCERA
41 Athletic Director .... Mr. Jack GUTIERREZ
09 Director Institutional Research .... Mr. Brian MCDERMOTT
28 Director Diversity .... Dr. Chris WADDLE
26 Public Relations/Marketing Director .... Mr. Scott MILLER
07 Director of Admissions Columbus .... Ms. Kristin HOESING
07 Director of Admissions Grand Island .... Ms. Erin LESIAK
07 Director of Admissions Hastings .... Mr. Robert GLENN
04 Administrative Asst to President .... Ms. Jessica WILLIAMS

Central Community College Columbus Campus (H)

PO Box 1027, 4500 63rd Street,
Columbus NE 68602-1027

Telephone: (402) 564-7132 Identification: 770331
Accreditation: &NH

Central Community College Hastings Campus (I)

550 S Technical Blvd, PO Box 1024,
Hastings NE 68902-1024

Telephone: (402) 463-9811 Identification: 770332
Accreditation: &NH

CHI Health School of Radiologic Technology (J)

6901 North 72nd Street, Omaha NE 68122

County: Douglas FICE Identification: 008492
Unit ID: 181145
Telephone: (402) 572-3650 Carnegie Class: Spec 2-yr-Health
FAX Number: (402) 398-6650 Calendar System: Semester
URL: www.chihealth.com/school-of-radiologic-technology
Established: 1953 Annual Undergrad Tuition & Fees: N/A
Enrollment: 19 Coed
Affiliation or Control: Independent Non-Profit IRS Status: 501(c)3
Highest Offering: Associate Degree
Accreditation: RAD

01 Program Director .... Robert A. HUGHES
10 Chief Financial Officer .... Jeanette WOJTALEWICZ
05 Chief Academic Officer .... Dr. Michael WHITE

Clarkson College (K)

101 S 42nd Street, Omaha NE 68131-2739

County: Douglas FICE Identification: 009862
Unit ID: 180832
Telephone: (402) 552-3100 Carnegie Class: Spec-4-yr-Other Health
FAX Number: (402) 552-3369 Calendar System: Semester
URL: www.clarksoncollege.edu
Established: 1888 Annual Undergrad Tuition & Fees: $15,780
Enrollment: 1,254 Coed
Affiliation or Control: Independent Non-Profit IRS Status: 501(c)3
Highest Offering: Doctorate
Accreditation: NH, ANEST, CAHIIM, NUR, PTAA, RAD

01 President .... Dr. Tony M. DAMEWOOD
00 President Emeritus .... Dr. Louis W. BURGHER
05 VP of Academic Affairs .... Dr. Andriea NEBEL
11 Vice Pres Operations .... Jina PAUL
10 Controller .... Megan WICKLESS
06 Registrar .... Michele D. STIRTZ
15 Director Human Resources .... Deb TOMEK
13 Director Technology .... Ryan SCHURMAN
28 Director Diversity Services .... Aubray D. ORDUNA
37 Director Student Financial Services .... Dale BROWN
08 Director Library Services .... Vacant
38 Director Success Center .... Chuck C. MACDONELL
97 Director General Education .... Lori BACHLE
66 Dean Nursing/Dir BS & Grad Nursing .... Dr. Aubrey ORDUNA
50 Dir of Business & HIM .... Carla DIRKSCHNEIDER
76 Dir Medical Imaging/Radiologic Tech .... Ellen COLLINS
76 Dir Physical Therapist Asst Pgm .... Dr. Michael WITTE
07 Director Admissions .... Denise WORK
51 Director of Professional Dev .... Judi B. DUNN
29 Coordinator Alumni Relations .... Rita VANFLEET

106 Coordinator Online Education Vacant
09 Coord Inst Effect/Quality Assurance Chris SWANSON

College of Saint Mary (A)

7000 Mercy Road, Omaha NE 68106-2606
County: Douglas FICE Identification: 002540
Unit ID: 181604
Telephone: (402) 399-2400 Carnegie Class: Masters/S
FAX Number: (402) 399-2647 Calendar System: Semester
URL: www.csm.edu
Established: 1923 Annual Undergrad Tuition & Fees: $29,954
Enrollment: 1,001 Female
Affiliation or Control: Roman Catholic IRS Status: 501(c)3
Highest Offering: Doctorate
Accreditation: NH, #ARCPA, NUR, OT

01 President Dr. Maryanne STEVENS, RSM
32 Vice President Student Development Dr. Tara KNUDSON-CARL
05 Vice Pres Academic Affairs Dr. William MANGAN
26 Vice President Marketing Mr. Nate NEUFIND
10 Vice Pres Financial Services/CFO Ms. Sarah KOTTICH
04 Executive Asst to the President Ms. Robyn KNIFFEN
84 Vice President Enrollment Ms. Sara HANSON
06 Registrar Mrs. Deb NUGEN
08 Director of Library Ms. Sara WILLIAMS
13 Vice President IT Mrs. Victoria HOSKOVEC
29 Vice Pres Alumnae/Donor Relations Ms. Terri CAMPBELL
37 Director Student Financial Aid Ms. Beth SISK
27 Public Relations Director Mr. Brittney LONG
35 Assoc Dean Student Affairs Mrs. Katty PETAK
39 Director Residence Life Ms. Christine SIMONE
40 Director Bookstore Mr. Steve WESTENBROEK
41 Athletic Director Mr. Peter HARING
42 Director Campus Ministry Ms. Carla GERRIETS
88 Director Mission Integration Ms. Marian STANDEVEN
18 Director Physical Plant Mr. Dan SPARGEN
44 Director Annual Giving Ms. Janelle DOMEYER
21 Controller Ms. Bridgette RENBARGER
15 Director Human Resources Ms. Jessica HOCHSTEIN
11 Chief of Administration Mrs. Kim SAVICKY
19 Director Security/Safety Mr. David FERBER

Concordia University (B)

800 N Columbia Avenue, Seward NE 68434-1599
County: Seward FICE Identification: 002541
Unit ID: 180984
Telephone: (402) 643-3651 Carnegie Class: Masters/L
FAX Number: (402) 643-4073 Calendar System: Other
URL: www.cune.edu
Established: 1894 Annual Undergrad Tuition & Fees: $28,480
Enrollment: 2,457 Coed
Affiliation or Control: Lutheran Church - Missouri Synod
IRS Status: 501(c)3
Highest Offering: Master's
Accreditation: NH, CAEPN, IACBE, MUS

01 President Rev Dr. Brian L. FRIEDRICH
05 Provost Dr. Jenny MUELLER-ROEBKE
111 Vice President Inst Advancement Mr. Kurth BRASHEAR
84 Sr VP Enrollment/Marketing Mr. Scott SEEVERS
32 VP for Student Affairs & Athletics Mr. Gene BROOKS
10 Chief Financial Officer Mr. David KUMM
53 Dean of Educ/Health & Human Svcs Dr. Nancy ELWELL
49 Dean of Arts & Sciences Dr. Brent ROYUK
13 Chief Information Officer Dr. Kent EINSPAHR
58 Dean College Grad Studies/Adult Ed Mr. Jonathon MOBERLY
08 Director of Library Services Mr. Philip HENDRICKSON
88 Dir of Education/Synodical Careers Mr. William SCHRANZ
29 Director Alumni/University Rels Mrs. Jennifer FURR
36 Dir Career Development & Retention Mr. Corey GRAY
41 Athletic Director Mr. Devin SMITH
42 Campus Pastor Rev. Ryan MATTHIAS
37 Assoc Director of Financial Aid Mr. Scott JENKINS
18 Chief Facilities/Physical Plant Mr. Rick IHDE
15 Director of Human Resources Mrs. Connie BUTLER
07 Director Undergraduate Admissions Mr. Aaron ROBERTS
26 Director of Marketing/Communication Mr. Seth MERANDA
21 Sr Dir Strategic Initiatives/Inves Mr. Curt SHERMAN
30 Director of Advancement Operations Mrs. Leigh LEWIS
106 Dir Classroom Innov & Online Educ Ms. Angie WASSENMILLER
06 Associate Registrar Undergraduate Mr. Brad WOODRUFF

Creative Center (C)

10850 Emmet Street, Omaha NE 68164-2911
County: Douglas FICE Identification: 031643
Unit ID: 430485
Telephone: (402) 898-1000 Carnegie Class: Spec-4-yr-Arts
FAX Number: (402) 898-1301 Calendar System: Semester
URL: www.creativecenter.edu
Established: 1993 Annual Undergrad Tuition & Fees: $27,700
Enrollment: 64 Coed
Affiliation or Control: Proprietary IRS Status: Proprietary
Highest Offering: Baccalaureate
Accreditation: ACCSC

01 President Mr. Ray DOTZLER
05 Director Ms. Kim GUYER
07 Director of Admissions Mr. Richard CALDWELL
10 Chief Business Officer Ms. Beth CONNOR
37 Director Student Financial Aid Ms. Sandy LAROCCA

Creighton University (D)

2500 California Plaza, Omaha NE 68178-0001
County: Douglas FICE Identification: 002542
Unit ID: 181002
Telephone: (402) 280-2700 Carnegie Class: Masters/L
FAX Number: N/A Calendar System: Semester
URL: www.creighton.edu
Established: 1878 Annual Undergrad Tuition & Fees: $37,606
Enrollment: 8,435 Coed
Affiliation or Control: Roman Catholic IRS Status: 501(c)3
Highest Offering: Doctorate
Accreditation: NH, CAEPN, CEA, DENT, EMT, LAW, MED, NURSE, OT, PHAR, PTA, SW

00 Chairman Creighton University Board Mr. Michael R. MCCARTHY
01 President Rev. Daniel S. HENDRICKSON, SJ
05 Provost Dr. Thomas F. MURRAY
100 Spec Asst to Pres & Board Liaison Mr. John W. DARWIN
04 Sr Exec Assistant President Office Ms. Lori L. VANDER MOLEN
04 Exec Assistant President Office Mr. David L. BARNUM
101 Corporate Secretary Mr. James S. JANSEN
11 Sr VP Operations and Treasurer Mr. Daniel E. BURKEY
42 Vice Provost Mission & Ministry Dr. Eileen C. BURKE-SULLIVAN
42 Director Campus Ministry Mr. Kyle C. LIERK
42 Director Ctr for Service & Justice Mr. Kenneth REED-BOULEY
42 Director Retreat Center Ms. Amy K. HOOVER
42 Director Ignatian Spirituality Rev. Lawrence GILLICK, SJ
42 Director Collaborative Ministry Rev. Andrew F. ALEXANDER, SJ
111 Vice President University Relations Mr. Matthew C. GERARD
30 Asst VP of Development Ms. Cortney A. BAUER
44 Director Creighton Fund Ms. Kathleen A. JACKSON
112 Sr Dir Estate and Gift Planning Mr. Robert J. SKRYDLAK
29 Asst VP Alumni Relations Vacant
102 Sr Dir Corp & Foundation Relations Mr. Andy A. KAMMERER
88 Sr Philanthropic Advisor Mr. Steven A. SCHOLER
45 Co-chair President's Plng Committee Dr. Mary E. CHASE
45 Co-chair President's Plng Committee Mr. Paul E. MCGREAL
108 Assoc VP Acad Excel & Assessment Dr. Mary Ann DANIELSON
08 University Librarian Mr. James BOTHMER
106 Exec Dir Ctr for Acad Innovation Vacant
09 Director Institutional Research Dr. Ying VUTHIPADADON
06 Registrar Ms. Melinda J. STONER
88 Dir Military/Veterans Liaison Svcs Mr. Mark P. TURNER
88 Director Disability Accommodations Ms. Denise Y. LE CLAIR
36 Director Career Center Mr. Jeremy M. FISHER
43 General Counsel Mr. James S. JANSEN
32 Vice Provost Student Life Dr. Tanya C. WINEGARD
39 Assoc VP Resident Life Vacant
35 Assoc VP Student Life Dr. Wayne YOUNG
35 Assoc VP Student Engagement Dr. Michele K. BOGARD
41 Athletic Director Mr. Bruce D. RASMUSSEN
84 VP Enrollment Mgmt & Univ Planning Dr. Mary E. CHASE
07 Director Admissions/Scholarships Ms. Sarah D. RICHARDSON
123 Dir Graduate and Adult Recruitment Ms. Linsay JOHNSON
124 Director Retention Ms. Katie CHRISTENSON
37 Director Student Financial Aid Ms. Paula S. KOHLES
121 Dir Acad Success & Edu Opportunity Dr. Joe ECKLUND
49 Dean College of Arts & Sciences Dr. Bridget M. KEEGAN
50 Dean Heider College of Business Dr. Anthony R. HENDRICKSON
107 Dean College of Prof Studies Dr. Gail M. JENSEN
52 Dean School of Dentistry Dr. Mark A. LATTA
58 Dean Graduate School Dr. Gail M. JENSEN
61 Dean School of Law Mr. Paul E. MCGREAL
63 Dean School of Medicine Dr. Robert W. DUNLAY
66 Dean College of Nursing Dr. Catherine M. TODERO
67 Dean School of Pharmacy & Hlth Prof Dr. J. Chris BRADBERRY
26 Chief Communications & Mktg Officer Mr. Jim P. BERSCHEIDT
27 Director Communication Mr. Rick C. DAVIS
11 Vice President Administration Mr. John L. WILHELM
18 Asst VP Facility Mgmt & Planning Mr. Louis M. MARCUCCIO
19 Director Public Safety Mr. Michael D. REINER
10 Vice President Finance Mr. John W. NISBET
21 Assoc VP Finance Mr. John J. JESSE, III
113 Dir Business Office Mr. Mark P. TURNER
114 Dir Budget/Planning & Analysis Ms. Tara S. MCGUIRE
116 Dir Internal Audit Mr. T. Paul TOMOSER
117 Risk Manager Ms. Katie BOOTON
88 Manager of Tax and GAAP Mr. Jason T. MCGILL
96 Sr Director Procurement Mr. Eric J. GILMORE
15 Assoc VP Human Resources Ms. Janel T. ALLEN
118 Sr Director Benefits & Compensation Ms. Molly BILLINGS
13 Vice President IT Mr. Tim L. BROOKS
90 Senior Director IT Mr. Ryan M. CAMERON
91 Director Information Technology Mr. J. D. RUMMEL
119 Information Security Officer Mr. Bryan S. MCLAUGHLIN
24 Director Learning Environment Vacant
22 Exec Director Equity & Inclusion Ms. Allison S. TAYLOR
23 Sr Director Student Health Services Ms. Debra C. SAURE
25 Director Sponsored Programs Admin Ms. Beth J. HERR
28 Director of Diversity Vacant
38 Sr Director Counseling Services Vacant
40 Bookstore Manager Ms. Melissa THOMPSON
85 VP Global Engagement Dr. Rene L. PADILLA
86 Director Comm & Govt Relationships Mr. Chris T. RODGERS
92 Director Honors Program Dr. Jeffrey P. HAUSE
104 Global Programs Coordinator Ms. Lizzy E. CURRAN
20 VP Academic Admin & Partnerships Ms. Tricia A. BRUNDO SHARRAR
20 VP Learning & Assessment Dr. Gail M. JENSEN
89 Dir Student Involvement & Formation Ms. Katie M. KELSEY

Doane University (E)

1014 Boswell Avenue, Crete NE 68333
County: Saline FICE Identification: 002544
Unit ID: 181020
Telephone: (402) 826-2161 Carnegie Class: Bac-A&S
FAX Number: (402) 826-8600 Calendar System: 4/1/4
URL: www.doane.edu
Established: 1872 Annual Undergrad Tuition & Fees: $30,434
Enrollment: 1,057 Coed
Affiliation or Control: United Church Of Christ IRS Status: 501(c)3
Highest Offering: Doctorate
Accreditation: NH, CAEPN, NURSE

01 President Dr. Jacque CARTER
05 Vice President Academic Affairs Dr. Paul SAVORY
10 Vice President Financial Affairs Ms. Julie SCHMIDT
111 Vice President for Advancement Mr. Marty FYE
32 Vice President Student Affairs Dr. Carrie LOVELACE PETR
13 VP for Information Technology Mr. Mike CARPENTER
07 VP for Enrollment Svcs & Marketing Mr. Joel WEYAND
53 Dean College of Education Dr. Lyn FORESTER
107 Dean College of Prof Studies Dr. Lorie COOK-BENJAMIN
49 Int Dean College of Arts/Sciences Dr. Jennifer BOSSARD
106 Assoc VP Online/Adult Educ Ms. Andrea BUTLER
06 Registrar Ms. Denise ELLIS
37 Director of Financial Aid Ms. Peggy TVRDY
08 Director of the Library Ms. Melissa GOMIS
21 Controller Mr. Ned TUCKER
36 Director College to Career Center Ms. Sarah COLLINS
26 Sr Director of Strategic Comm Mr. Mike LEFLER
29 Director of Alumni Relation Ms. Anne ZIOLA
15 Director of Human Resources Ms. Laura NORTHUP
18 Dir of Facilities & Constr Proj Mr. Brian FLESNER
12 Director of Lincoln Campus Ms. Angie KLASEK
12 Director of Omaha Campus Vacant
12 Director of Grand Island Campus Ms. Regina SOMER
41 Athletic Director Ms. Jill MCCARTNEY
42 Dir of Religious & Spiritual Life Dr. Leah REDIGER-SCHULTE
40 Bookstore Manager Ms. Lynette NEWTON
28 Director of Multicultural Pgm & Edu Ms. Wilma JACKSON
23 Director of Health and Wellness Ms. Kelly JIROVEC
35 Director of Student Support Service Ms. Anita HARKINS
09 Director of Institutional Research Dr. Raja TAYEH
19 Dir of Campus Safety/Assoc Dean Mr. Russ HEWITT

Doane University (F)

3180 W U.S. Highway 34, Grand Island NE 68801
Telephone: (308) 398-0800 Identification: 770333
Accreditation: &NH

Doane University (G)

303 North 52nd Street, Lincoln NE 68504
Telephone: (402) 466-4774 Identification: 770334
Accreditation: &NH

Grace University (H)

1311 S 9th Street, Omaha NE 68108-3629
County: Douglas FICE Identification: 002547
Unit ID: 181093
Telephone: (402) 449-2800 Carnegie Class: Bac-Diverse
FAX Number: (402) 449-2999 Calendar System: Semester
URL: www.graceuniversity.edu
Established: 1943 Annual Undergrad Tuition & Fees: $21,928
Enrollment: 471 Coed
Affiliation or Control: Independent Non-Profit IRS Status: 501(c)3
Highest Offering: Master's
Accreditation: #NH

01 CEO Mr. Bill BAUHARD
10 CFO Mr. Tom ROCHE
32 VP of Student Life and Donor Rel Dr. John D. HOLMES
05 VP of Academic Affairs Dr. Karl PAGENKEMPER
84 VP of Enrollment Mr. Chris PRUITT
30 VP of Advancement Vacant
21 Director of Finance Ms. Anita RODRIGUEZ
06 Registrar Dr. Kris J. UDD
58 Dean Professional & Graduate Stds Mr. C. James SANTORO
09 Dir of Assessment & Inst Research Vacant
37 Director of Financial Aid Mrs. Mackenzie DEHMER
15 Director Human Resources Ms. Deb OSMANSON
08 Librarian Vacant
04 Admin Assistant to the President Ms. Joanne R. FAST
33 Dean of Men Mr. Jeff BANKS
34 Dean of Women Dr. Tara RYE
41 Athletic Director Mr. Willie WILLIAMS
11 Asst VP Administration Ms. Deb OSMANSON

Hastings College (I)

710 N Turner Avenue, Box 269, Hastings NE 68902-0269
County: Adams FICE Identification: 002548
Unit ID: 181127
Telephone: (402) 463-2402 Carnegie Class: Bac-Diverse
FAX Number: (402) 461-7490 Calendar System: 4/1/4

URL: www.hastings.edu
Established: 1882 Annual Undergrad Tuition & Fees: $28,250
Enrollment: 1,219 Coed
Affiliation or Control: Presbyterian Church (U.S.A.) IRS Status: 501(c)3
Highest Offering: Master's
Accreditation: NH, CAEPN, MUS

01 President .... Dr. Travis FEEZELL
00 Chairman of the Board .... Mr. Glen MOSS
30 Exec VP for External Relations .... Mr. Gary FREEMAN
10 VP for Finance .... Mr. Tony BEATA
84 VP for Enrollment and Marketing .... Ms. Susan MEESKE
05 Exec VP of Acad Affairs and Provost .... Dr. Gary C. JOHNSON
20 Assoc VP for Academic Affairs .... Vacant
100 Chief of Staff .... Vacant
41 Athletic Director .... Ms. Patty SITORIUS
32 Assoc VP for Student Affairs .... Mr. Dan PETERS
112 Assoc VP for Planned & Major Gifts .... Mr. Michael KARLOFF
110 Assoc VP for Development .... Ms. Judee L. KONEN
06 Registrar .... Mr. Jim BOEVE
37 Director of Financial Aid .... Ms. Traci BOEVE
39 Director of Housing .... Mr. John MABUS
15 Director of Human Resources .... Ms. Kari FLUCKEY
26 Director of Marketing .... Mr. Michael HOWIE
08 Director of Libraries .... Ms. Susan FRANKLIN
29 Director of Alumni Relations .... Mr. Matt FONG
13 Interim Director of IT .... Ms. Patty KINGSLEY
14 Network Administrator .... Mr. Jim MACKIN
90 Acad Computer Support Specialist .... Mr. Erik NIELSEN
18 Director Physical Plant Services .... Mr. Ron GRIGGS
93 Minority Students .... Dr. Moses DOGBEVIA
28 International Studies/Diversity Pgm .... Dr. Rob BABCOCK
36 Director of Career Services .... Ms. Kimberly K. GRAVIETTE
23 Director Campus Health Services .... Ms. Beth LITTRELL
42 Chaplain .... Rev. Damen HEITMANN
21 Director of Accounting .... Ms. Susan TEUTSCHMANN
35 Director of Student Engagement .... Ms. Kara SIEDHOFF
19 Director of Security/Safety .... Mr. Dennis LEONARD
38 Director of Counseling Services .... Mr. Jon LOETTERLE
40 Bookstore Manager .... Ms. Nancy GLEASON
88 Graphic Designer/Publisher .... Mrs. Camille KASTL
85 Foreign Students/Student Life .... Dr. Antje ANDERSON
04 Executive Asst to President .... Ms. Marin SUHR
07 Director of Admissions .... Ms. Chris SCHUKEI

Kaplan University (A)

1821 K Street, PO Box 82826, Lincoln NE 68501-2826
Telephone: (402) 474-5315 FICE Identification: 004721
Accreditation: &NH, ACBSP, MAC

† Regional accreditation is carried under the parent institution in Davenport, IA.

Kaplan University (B)

5425 N. 103rd Street, Omaha NE 68134-1002
Telephone: (402) 431-6100 FICE Identification: 008491
Accreditation: &NH, ACBSP, DA

† Regional accreditation is carried under the parent institution in Davenport, IA.

Little Priest Tribal College (C)

601 East College Drive, PO Box 270,
Winnebago NE 68071-0270
County: Thurston FICE Identification: 033233
Unit ID: 434016
Telephone: (402) 878-2380 Carnegie Class: Tribal
FAX Number: (402) 878-2355 Calendar System: Semester
URL: www.littlepriest.edu
Established: 1996 Annual Undergrad Tuition & Fees: $5,290
Enrollment: 132 Coed
Affiliation or Control: Independent Non-Profit IRS Status: 501(c)3
Highest Offering: Associate Degree
Accreditation: NH

01 President .... Mr. Maunka MORGAN
05 Academic Dean .... Ms. Betty REDLEAF
10 Controller .... Vacant
37 Director of Financial Aid .... Ms. Yatty MOHAMMAD
13 IT Director .... Mr. Morrie CONWAY
09 Dir Inst Research/Stdnt Records .... Jeremy GONE
06 Registrar .... Jeremy GONE

Mary Lanning Healthcare School of Radiology (D)

715 North St. Joseph Avenue, Hastings NE 68901
County: Adams FICE Identification: 004431
Unit ID: 181251
Telephone: (402) 461-5177 Carnegie Class: Not Classified
FAX Number: (402) 460-5059 Calendar System: Other
URL: www.marylanning.org
Established: 1952 Annual Undergrad Tuition & Fees: N/A
Enrollment: N/A Coed
Affiliation or Control: Independent Non-Profit IRS Status: 501(c)3
Highest Offering: Associate Degree
Accreditation: RAD

01 Medical Director .... Eric BARBER
10 Chief Financial Officer .... Shawn NORDBY
26 Dir of Public Rels/Marketing Svcs .... Lisa BRANDT

McCook Community College (E)

1205 East Third Street, McCook NE 69001
Telephone: (308) 345-8100 Identification: 770337
Accreditation: &NH, EMT

Metropolitan Community College (F)

PO Box 3777, Omaha NE 68103-0777
County: Douglas FICE Identification: 012586
Unit ID: 181303
Telephone: (531) 622-2400 Carnegie Class: Assoc/MT-VT-High Non
FAX Number: (402) 457-2395 Calendar System: Quarter
URL: www.mccneb.edu
Established: 1974 Annual Undergrad Tuition & Fees (In-District): $2,880
Enrollment: 14,812 Coed
Affiliation or Control: Local IRS Status: 501(c)3
Highest Offering: Associate Degree
Accreditation: NH, ACBSP, ACFEI, ADNUR, CAHIIM, COARC, CSHSE, DA, EMT, MAC

01 President .... Mr. Randy SCHMAILZL
05 Vice President Academic Affairs .... Dr. Tom MCDONNELL
28 Assoc Vice Pres Equity/Diversity .... Dr. Cynthia GOOCH
15 Assoc Vice Pres of Human Resources .... Ms. Maureen MOEGLIN
20 Associate VP for Effect & Engag .... Mr. William OWEN
32 Asst Vice Pres for Student Affairs .... Ms. Marie VAZQUEZ
11 Vice President for Admin Services .... Mr. Dave KOEBEL
26 Assoc VP Marketing Brand & Commun .... Ms. Nannette RODRIGUEZ
18 Director Facilities Management .... Mr. Bernard SEDLACEK
37 Director of Financial Aid .... Ms. Wilma HJELLUM
96 Director Administrative Management .... Mr. Richard HANNEMAN
19 Chief of Police/Dir Emergency Mgmt .... Mr. Donald THORSON
84 Dean of Enrollment Management .... Ms. Ingrid BERLIN
27 Chief Information Officer .... Mr. Chad LYNCH
06 Registrar .... Ms. Albertha SCHMID
43 Dir Legal Services/General Counsel .... Mr. Jim THIBODEAU
30 Director of Development .... Dr. Jacqueline ALMQUIST
91 Director Administrative Computing .... Ms. Jodie SNIDER
04 Executive Assistant to President .... Ms. Rita EYERLY
100 Senior Aide to the President .... Ms. Patricia CRISLER

Metropolitan Community College Elkhorn Valley Campus (G)

204th & West Dodge Road, Omaha NE 68022
Telephone: (402) 289-1200 Identification: 770335
Accreditation: &NH

Metropolitan Community College South Omaha Campus (H)

2909 Edward Babe Gomez Avenue, Omaha NE 68107
Telephone: (531) 622-5231 Identification: 770336
Accreditation: &NH

Mid-Plains Community College (I)

601 W State Farm Road, North Platte NE 69101-9491
County: Lincoln FICE Identification: 002557
Unit ID: 181312
Telephone: (800) 658-4308 Carnegie Class: Assoc/MT-VT-High Non
FAX Number: (308) 535-3794 Calendar System: Semester
URL: www.mpcc.edu
Established: 1926 Annual Undergrad Tuition & Fees (In-District): $2,970
Enrollment: 2,235 Coed
Affiliation or Control: State/Local IRS Status: 501(c)3
Highest Offering: Associate Degree
Accreditation: NH, ADNUR, DA, EMT, MLTAD

01 President .... Mr. Ryan PURDY
12 VP North Platte Community College .... Dr. Jody TOMANEK
12 Vice Pres McCook Community College .... Mr. Andrew LONG
10 Area Business Officer .... Mr. Michael STEELE
05 Area VP for Academic Affairs .... Dr. Jody TOMANEK
09 Area Dir Instl Effectiveness .... Mr. Tad PFEIFER
32 Area Dean of Student Life .... Dr. Brian OBERT
56 Area Director of Outreach .... Ms. Gail KNOTT
36 Area Dean of Career Services .... Mr. Bill EAKINS
84 Area Dean of Enrollment Management .... Ms. Kelly RIPPEN
06 Area Registrar .... Ms. Mari Jo WIDGER
26 Area Dir Public Inform/Marketing .... Mr. Charles SALESTROM
15 Area Director of Human Resources .... Ms. Rebecca WRAGE
13 Area Director Information Services .... Mr. Tim HALL
37 Area Dir of Student Financial Aid .... Ms. Erinn BROWN

Midland University (J)

900 N Clarkson, Fremont NE 68025-4395
County: Dodge FICE Identification: 002553
Unit ID: 181330
Telephone: (402) 721-5480 Carnegie Class: Bac-Diverse
FAX Number: (402) 721-0250 Calendar System: 4/1/4
URL: www.midlandu.edu
Established: 1883 Annual Undergrad Tuition & Fees: $30,430
Enrollment: 1,646 Coed
Affiliation or Control: Evangelical Lutheran Church In America
IRS Status: 501(c)3
Highest Offering: Master's
Accreditation: NH, COARC, NUR

01 President .... Ms. Jody HORNER
05 Vice Pres Academic Affairs .... Ms. Susan KRUML
32 Vice Pres Student Affairs .... Mr. Merritt NELSON
10 Vice Pres Finance & Administration .... Ms. Jodi BENJAMIN
30 Vice Pres for Development .... Ms. Jessica JANSSEN
84 VP Admissions/Enrollment Management .... Ms. Eliza FERZELY
15 Vice Pres Human Resources .... Ms. Sharon ROBSON
06 Registrar .... Mr. Eric MACZKA
07 Director of Admissions .... Ms. Emily PACKARD
37 Director of Financial Aid .... Mr. Douglas WATSON
21 Controller .... Ms. Denise PRATT
41 Athletic Director .... Mr. Dave GILLESPIE
66 Director of Nursing .... Dr. Linda QUINN
13 Chief Information Officer .... Mr. Shane PERRIEN
18 Director Facilities Management .... Mr. Shawn NELSON
44 Director of Annual Giving .... Mr. Brad EBERSPACHER

Myotherapy Institute (K)

4001 Pioneer Woods Drive, Lincoln NE 68506-7547
County: Lancaster FICE Identification: 032793
Unit ID: 434432
Telephone: (402) 421-7410 Carnegie Class: Spec 2-yr-Health
FAX Number: (402) 421-6736 Calendar System: Other
URL: www.myotherapy.edu
Established: 1992 Annual Undergrad Tuition & Fees: $16,800
Enrollment: 20 Coed
Affiliation or Control: Proprietary IRS Status: Proprietary
Highest Offering: Associate Degree
Accreditation: ACCSC

01 Director .... Ms. Sue KOZISEK

National American University-Bellevue (L)

3604 Summit Plaza Drive, Bellevue NE 68123
Telephone: (402) 972-4250 Identification: 770406
Accreditation: &NH, MAC

† Branch campus of National American University, Rapid City, SD

Nebraska Indian Community College (M)

1111 Hwy 75 - PO Box 428, Macy NE 68039-0428
County: Thurston FICE Identification: 025508
Unit ID: 181419
Telephone: (402) 494-2311 Carnegie Class: Tribal
FAX Number: (402) 837-4183 Calendar System: Semester
URL: www.thenicc.edu
Established: 1973 Annual Undergrad Tuition & Fees: $4,080
Enrollment: 158 Coed
Affiliation or Control: Tribal Control IRS Status: Exempt
Highest Offering: Associate Degree
Accreditation: NH

01 President .... Dr. Michael OLTROGGE
05 Academic Dean .... Mary JOHNSON
32 Dean Student Services .... Dawne PRICE
13 Chief Information Officer .... Justin KOCIAN
06 Registrar .... Troy MUNHOFEN
15 Human Resource Director .... Cheryl HANSEN

Nebraska Indian Community College-Santee (N)

415 North River Road, Santee NE 68760
Telephone: (402) 494-2311 Identification: 770339
Accreditation: &NH

Nebraska Indian Community College-South Sioux City (O)

2605 1/2 Dakota Avenue, South Sioux City NE 68776
Telephone: (402) 494-2311 Identification: 770340
Accreditation: &NH

Nebraska Methodist College (P)

720 N 87th Street, Omaha NE 68114-2852
County: Douglas FICE Identification: 006404
Unit ID: 181297
Telephone: (402) 354-7000 Carnegie Class: Spec-4-yr-Other Health
FAX Number: (402) 354-7090 Calendar System: Semester
URL: www.methodistcollege.edu
Established: 1891 Annual Undergrad Tuition & Fees: $13,802
Enrollment: 1,000 Coed
Affiliation or Control: Independent Non-Profit IRS Status: 501(c)3
Highest Offering: Doctorate
Accreditation: NH, COARC, DMS, MAC, NURSE, PTAA, RAD, SURGT

01 President .... Dr. Dennis A. JOSLIN
03 Executive Vice President .... Dr. Deb CARLSON
05 Vice President Academic Affairs .... Dr. Jody WOODWORTH
10 VP Business & Operations .... Dr. Dean TICKLE
84 VP Enrollment & Student Success .... Dr. Lori GIGLIOTTI
66 Dean Nursing .... Dr. Linda HUGHES
58 Program Director Master's Nursing .... Dr. Linda FOLEY
66 Pgm Director Undergrad Nursing .... Dr. Karen JOHNSON

88 Director of Special Pgms Nursing ... Dr. Susie WARD
76 Dean Health Professions ... Dr. Stephanie LAPUMA
97 Dean General Education ... Dr. Dean MANTERNACH
76 Pgm Director Phys Therapist Asst ... Ms. Shannon STRUBY
76 Program Director Respiratory Care ... Ms. Lisa FUCHS
88 Program Director Radiography ... Ms. Kate ROLLINS
88 Program Director Sonography ... Ms. Jody BERG
88 Pgm Director Surgical Technology ... Ms. Christy GRANT
08 Director of Library Services ... Ms. Emily MCILLECE
42 Dir Spiritual Dev/Campus Ministry ... Vacant
29 Alumni Engagement Director ... Ms. Angela HEESACKER-SMITH
07 Director Enrollment Services ... Ms. Megan MARYOTT
06 Director Registration & Records ... Mr. Shawn BAKER
37 Director Financial Aid ... Ms. Penny JAMES
107 Exec Dir Professional Development ... Ms. Jillian SISSON
88 Educational Compliance Officer ... Ms. Lindsay SNIPES
04 Administrative Asst to President ... Ms. Cathy BECK
18 Chief Facilities/Physical Plant ... Dr. Dean TICKLE

*Nebraska State College System (A)

1327 H Street, Suite 200, Lincoln NE 68508
County: Lancaster FICE Identification: 033441
Telephone: (402) 471-2505 Carnegie Class: N/A
FAX Number: (402) 471-2669
URL: www.nscs.edu

01 Chancellor ... Mr. Stan CARPENTER
43 General Counsel & VC for Emp Rel ... Ms. Kristin PETERSEN
10 Vice Chancellor Finance/Admin ... Ms. Carolyn MURPHY
32 VC Student Affairs & Risk Mgmt ... Ms. Angela MELTON
18 Vice Chanc Facilities & Info Tech ... Mr. Steve HOTOVY
05 VC Acad Planning/Partnerships ... Dr. Jodi KUPPER
11 Operations Director ... Ms. Becky KOHRS
21 Director of Systemwide Accounting ... Ms. Amy HOCK
13 System Data Analyst/Reports Develop ... Mr. Mike DUNKLE
26 Sys Dir Mktg & Communications ... Ms. Rachel HENRY
22 System Director for Title IX ... Ms. Taylor SINCLAIR

*Chadron State College (B)

1000 Main Street, Chadron NE 69337-2690
County: Dawes FICE Identification: 002539
Unit ID: 180948
Telephone: (308) 432-6000 Carnegie Class: Masters/M
FAX Number: (308) 432-6464 Calendar System: Semester
URL: www.csc.edu
Established: 1911 Annual Undergrad Tuition & Fees (In-State): $6,510
Enrollment: 2,993 Coed
Affiliation or Control: State IRS Status: 501(c)3
Highest Offering: Master's
Accreditation: NH, ACBSP, CAEPN, MUS, SW

02 President ... Dr. Randy RHINE
05 Vice President Academic Affairs ... Dr. Charles SNARE
10 Vice Pres Administration & Finance ... Mr. Dale E. GRANT
84 Vice Pres Enrollment Mgmt & Mktg ... Mr. Jon HANSEN
20 Assoc VP Teaching & Learning Tech ... Vacant
13 Chief Information Officer ... Ms. Ann M. BURK
58 Dean Graduate Studies/BEAMS ... Dr. Joel HYER
49 Dean Essential Studies/Liberal Art ... Dr. James MARGETTS
108 Dean Assessment & Accreditation ... Dr. James POWELL
21 Comptroller ... Ms. Kari GASWICK
09 Director Institutional Research ... Ms. Malinda LINEGAR
102 Executive Director CS Foundation ... Ms. Connie A. RASMUSSEN
06 Director of Records ... Ms. Melissa MITCHELL
32 Sr Director Student Services ... Dr. Pat BEU
32 Assoc VP Student Services ... Ms. Sherry L. DOUGLAS
07 Director of Admissions ... Ms. Lisa STEIN
15 Assoc VP Human Resources ... Ms. Anne DEMERSSEMAN
39 Director of Housing ... Ms. Sherri J. SIMONS
41 Athletics Director ... Mr. Joel SMITH
36 Director of Internships/Career Svcs ... Ms. Deena KENNELL
21 Budget Director ... Ms. Melany HUGHES
26 Director College Relations ... Mr. Alex HELMBRECHT
18 Coordinator of Physical Facilities ... Mr. Blair BRENNAN
108 Director Inst Assessment ... Vacant

*Peru State College (C)

PO Box 10, Peru NE 68421-0010
County: Nemaha FICE Identification: 002559
Unit ID: 181534
Telephone: (402) 872-3815 Carnegie Class: Masters/S
FAX Number: (402) 872-2375 Calendar System: Semester
URL: www.peru.edu
Established: 1867 Annual Undergrad Tuition & Fees (In-State): $7,243
Enrollment: 2,506 Coed
Affiliation or Control: State IRS Status: 501(c)3
Highest Offering: Master's
Accreditation: NH, CAEPN

02 President ... Dr. Daniel HANSON
05 Vice Pres Academic Affairs ... Dr. Tim BORCHERS
10 Vice Pres Administration & Finance ... Ms. Kathy CARROLL
32 Vice Pres Enroll Mgmt & Stdnt Affs ... Dr. Jesse DORMAN
102 Exec Director PSC Foundations ... Mr. Todd SIMPSON
41 Director of Athletics ... Mr. Steve SCHNEIDER
26 Dir of Marketing & Communications ... Mr. Jason HOGUE
06 Dir Student Records/Coll Registrar ... Ms. Deann BAYNE
37 Director of Financial Aid ... Ms. Cheryl REID
08 Director of Library ... Ms. Veronica MEIER
15 Director of Human Resources ... Ms. Eulanda CADE
18 Director Campus Services ... Ms. Jill MCCORMICK
21 Director of Business Services ... Ms. Kathy TYNON
07 Director of Admissions ... Ms. Cindy CAMMACK
38 Licensed Student Counselor ... Ms. Jamie EBERLY
108 Director Institutional Assessment ... Ms. Kristin BUSCHER
13 Chief Info Technology Officer (CIO) ... Mr. Gene BEARDSLEE
19 Director Security/Safety ... Mr. Tim ROBERTSON

*Wayne State College (D)

1111 Main Street, Wayne NE 68787-1172
County: Wayne FICE Identification: 002566
Unit ID: 181783
Telephone: (402) 375-7000 Carnegie Class: Masters/M
FAX Number: (402) 375-7204 Calendar System: Semester
URL: www.wsc.edu
Established: 1909 Annual Undergrad Tuition & Fees (In-State): $6,462
Enrollment: 3,431 Coed
Affiliation or Control: State IRS Status: 501(c)3
Highest Offering: Beyond Master's But Less Than Doctorate
Accreditation: NH, ART, CACREP, CAEPN, CSHSE, IACBE, MUS

02 President ... Dr. Marysz RAMES
05 Vice President Academic Affairs ... Mr. Steven ELLIOTT
10 Vice Pres Admin/Finance ... Ms. Angela FREDRICKSON
102 CEO Foundation Office ... Mr. Kevin ARMSTRONG
32 Vice President & Dean Students ... Dr. Jeffrey CARSTENS
37 Director Financial Aid ... Ms. Annette KAUS
07 Director of Admissions ... Mr. Kevin HALLE
38 Director of Counseling ... Ms. Lin BRUMMELS
39 Director of Residence Life ... Ms. Quinneka LEE
36 Director of Career Services ... Mr. Jason BARELMAN
13 Chief Information Officer ... Mr. John DUNNING
26 Director College Relations ... Mr. Jay COLLIER
41 Director of Athletics ... Mr. Mike POWICKI
18 Director of Facility Services ... Mr. Chad ALTWINE
08 Director of Library Services ... Mr. David GRABER
06 Registrar ... Ms. Karla HIX
112 Director of Major Gifts ... Ms. Deb LUNDAHL
29 Director of Alumni Relations ... Ms. Laura ROBINETT
15 Director of Human Resources ... Ms. Candace TIMMERMAN
79 Dean School of Arts & Hum ... Dr. Yasuko TAOKA
50 Dean Sch of Business & Technology ... Dr. Vaughn BENSON
53 Dean Sch of Educ & Couns ... Dr. Nicholas SHUDAK
83 Dean Sch of Natural/Social Sci ... Dr. Tammy EVETOVICH
28 Director of Multicultural Affairs ... Dr. Leah KEINO
09 Research Analyst ... Ms. Jeannette BARRY
108 Director of Assessment ... Ms. Sue SYDOW
91 Director Administrative Computing ... Ms. Janell SCARDINO
04 Administrative Asst to President ... Ms. Joni BACKER
106 Extended Campus Program Coordinator ... Ms. Lisa REYNOLDS
19 Campus Security Manager ... Mr. Jason MRSNY

Nebraska Wesleyan University (E)

5000 St. Paul Avenue, Lincoln NE 68504-2794
County: Lancaster FICE Identification: 002555
Unit ID: 181446
Telephone: (402) 466-2371 Carnegie Class: Masters/M
FAX Number: (402) 465-2179 Calendar System: Semester
URL: www.nebrwesleyan.edu
Established: 1887 Annual Undergrad Tuition & Fees: $31,394
Enrollment: 2,049 Coed
Affiliation or Control: United Methodist IRS Status: 501(c)3
Highest Offering: Master's
Accreditation: NH, CAATE, CAEPN, MUS, NURSE, SW

01 President ... Dr. Frederik OHLES
05 Provost ... Dr. Graciela CANEIRO-LIVINGSTON
10 Vice Pres Finance/Administration ... Ms. Tish GADE-JONES
84 Vice President Enrollment Mgmt ... Mr. Bill MOTZER
111 Vice President Advancement ... Mr. John GREVING
28 Vice President Campus Community ... Mr. T. J. MCDOWELL, JR.
42 University Minister/Church Relation ... Rev. Eduardo BOUSSON
32 Dean of Students ... Mr. Peter ARMSTRONG
20 Dean of the Colleges ... Dr. Sarah A. KELEN
88 Asst Provost Integr/Exper Learning ... Dr. Patrick HAYDEN-ROY
21 Asst VP & Controller ... Mr. Greg D. MASCHMAN
41 Athletic Director ... Dr. Ira A. ZEFF
06 Vice Provost for Academic Systems ... Ms. Patty HALL
08 University Librarian ... Ms. Martha TANNER
09 Assoc Director Inst Research ... Ms. Brooke GLENN
38 Director Counseling Services ... Dr. Kimberly CORNER
07 Director of Admissions ... Mr. Benjamin SMITH
104 Director of Global Engagement ... Ms. Sarah BARR
102 Director of Foundation Relations ... Ms. Nancy WEHRBEIN
23 Director Student Health Services ... Ms. Nancy J. NEWMAN
24 Director Instructional Technology ... Mr. Jay L. KAHLER
14 Director Administrative Systems ... Mr. Mark MURPHY
92 Director Wesleyan Honors Academy ... Dr. Marian BORGMANN-INGWERSEN
44 Director Archway Fund ... Ms. Erika PASCHOLD
07 Director of Admissions ... Mr. Gordie COFFIN
36 Director Career Development ... Ms. Kim AFRANK
37 Director of Financial Aid ... Mr. Tom J. OCHSNER
13 Director of Computer Services ... Mr. Steven R. DOW
15 Director of Human Resources ... Ms. Maria HARDER
18 Director of Physical Plant ... Mr. Jim RUZICKA
26 Director of Marketing ... Ms. Peggy S. HAIN
27 Director of Public Relations ... Ms. Sara M. OLSON
29 Director of Alumni Relations ... Ms. Shelley MCHUGH
121 Asst Dean Stdnt Success/Engagement ... Ms. Karri SANDERSON
124 Asst Dean Stdnt Success/Persistence ... Ms. Candice HOWELL
39 Asst Dean Stdnt Success/Res Educ ... Ms. Brandi SESTAK
88 Asst Dean Stdnt Success/Campus Comm ... Ms. Janelle ANDREINI
04 Special Asst to President ... Ms. P. J. RABEL

North Platte Community College-North Campus (F)

1101 Halligan Drive, North Platte NE 69101
Telephone: (308) 535-3600 Identification: 770338
Accreditation: &NH

Northeast Community College (G)

801 E Benjamin, PO Box 469, Norfolk NE 68702-0469
County: Madison FICE Identification: 011667
Unit ID: 181491
Telephone: (402) 371-2020 Carnegie Class: Assoc/MT-VT-High Non
FAX Number: (402) 844-7400 Calendar System: Semester
URL: www.northeast.edu
Established: 1973 Annual Undergrad Tuition & Fees (In-District): $3,285
Enrollment: 5,051 Coed
Affiliation or Control: Local IRS Status: 501(c)3
Highest Offering: Associate Degree
Accreditation: NH, ADNUR, EMT, PTAA

01 President ... Dr. Michael R. CHIPPS
03 Executive Vice President ... Mr. John V. BLAYLOCK
05 Vice President Educational Services ... Mr. Lyle KATHOL
10 Vice Pres of Administrative Svcs ... Ms. Lynne D. KOSKI
32 Vice President of Student Services ... Mrs. Amanda NIPP
13 Vice President of Technology ... Mr. Derek BIERMAN
88 Associate VP of Ctr for Enterprise ... Mr. Eric JOHNSON
30 Assoc VP of Devel/External Affairs ... Dr. Tracy L. KRUSE
15 Associate VP of Human Resources ... Mr. Craig GARRETT
47 Dean Ag/Health/Sciences ... Mrs. Corinne MORRIS
49 Dean Humanities/Arts/Social Sci ... Mrs. Faye KILDAY
50 Dean of Business/Math/Tech ... Dr. Wade HERLEY
76 Dean of Health/Wellness ... Dr. Michele GILL
75 Assoc Dean of Applied Technology ... Mrs. Shanelle GRUDZINSKI
11 Dean of Administrative Services ... Mrs. Coleen BRESSLER
21 Exec Director of Business Services ... Mrs. Mary J. MEYER
45 Dean of Institutional Planning ... Mrs. Michela KEELER-STROM
84 Dean of Enrollment Management ... Ms. Lori VANDERHEIDEN
18 Exec Director of Physical Plant ... Mr. Brandon MCLEAN
06 Registrar ... Mrs. Makala MAPLE
37 Financial Aid Director ... Ms. Stacy DIECKMAN
36 Director of Career Services ... Mrs. Terri HEGGEMEYER
66 Director of Nursing Programs ... Mrs. Karen K. WEIDNER
21 Director of Accounting Services ... Mr. John ROBERTSON
16 Dir of Talent Acquisition/Retentio ... Mr. Marcus RIOS
96 Director of Purchasing ... Mr. Chris RUTTEN
41 Athletic Director ... Vacant
39 Director Residence Life ... Mr. Pete RIZZO
105 Director of Web and Enterprise Svc ... Mr. Mike AUTEN
08 Director of Library Services ... Mrs. Mary Louise FOSTER
26 Director of Public Relations ... Mr. James CURRY
40 College Store Manager ... Mrs. Julie CARLSON
35 Director of Student Conduct ... Mrs. Maureen BAKER
09 Director of Institutional Research ... Ms. Julie MELNICK
35 Director of Student Activities ... Ms. Carissa KOLLATH
27 Director of Marketing ... Mrs. Jennifer GREVE
07 Director of Admissions ... Mr. Bradley RANSLEM
104 Dir of Ctr for Global Engagement ... Ms. Pam SAALFELD
04 Executive Assistant to President ... Mrs. Diane REIKOFSKI

Omaha School of Massage and Healthcare of Herzing University (H)

9478 Park Drive, Omaha NE 68127
Telephone: (402) 331-3694 Identification: 770432
Accreditation: &NH

† Branch campus of Herzing University, Madison, WI

Saint Gregory the Great Seminary (I)

800 Fletcher Road, Seward NE 68434-8145
County: Seward Identification: 667027
Unit ID: 486114
Telephone: (402) 643-4052 Carnegie Class: Not Classified
FAX Number: (402) 643-6964 Calendar System: Semester
URL: www.sggs.edu
Established: 1998 Annual Undergrad Tuition & Fees: N/A
Enrollment: N/A Male
Affiliation or Control: Roman Catholic IRS Status: 501(c)3
Highest Offering: Baccalaureate
Accreditation: NH

01 Rector/President ... VRev. Jeffrey EICKHOFF

Southeast Community College (J)

4771 West Scott Road, Beatrice NE 68310-7042
Telephone: (402) 228-3468 Identification: 770341
Accreditation: &NH

Southeast Community College (K)

301 S 68 Street Place, Lincoln NE 68510-2449
County: Lancaster FICE Identification: 025083
Unit ID: 181640
Telephone: (402) 323-3400 Carnegie Class: Assoc/HVT-High Non

FAX Number: (402) 323-3420 Calendar System: Quarter
URL: www.southeast.edu
Established: 1973 Annual Undergrad Tuition & Fees (In-District): $3,214
Enrollment: 9,248 Coed
Affiliation or Control: State/Local IRS Status: 501(c)3
Highest Offering: Associate Degree
Accreditation: NH, ACBSP, ACFEI, ADNUR, COARC, CSHSE, DA, EMT, MAC, MLTAD, PNUR, POLYT, PTAA, RAD, SURGT

01 President .... Dr. Paul ILLICH
05 Vice President Instruction .... Dr. Dennis HEADRICK
22 Vice Pres Access/Equity/Diversity .... Mr. Jose SOTO
11 VP Administrative Svcs/Res Devel .... Ms. Amy G. JORGENS
12 VP Student Svcs/Campus Director .... Ms. Bev HARVEY
12 VP Technology/Campus Director .... Mr. Ed KOSTER
15 Vice Pres Human Resources .... Mr. Bruce TANGEMAN
12 Dean of Virtual Learning/Campus Dir .... Mr. Robert MORGAN
37 Director of Financial Aid .... Ms. Melissa TROYER
32 Dean Student Svcs/Dir Stdnt Support .... Dr. Thomas CARDWELL
84 Dean Student Enrollment .... Mr. Mike PEGRAM
26 Dir of Public Information/Marketing .... Mr. Stu OSTERTHUN
09 Director of Institutional Research .... Ms. Robin MOORE
90 Information Services Manager .... Mr. Alan BRUNKOW

Southeast Community College (A)

600 State Street, Milford NE 68405-8498
Telephone: (402) 761-2131 Identification: 770342
Accreditation: &NH

Summit Christian College (B)

2025 21st Street, Gering NE 69341
County: Scotts Bluff Identification: 667209
Unit ID: 181543
Telephone: (308) 632-6933 Carnegie Class: Not Classified
FAX Number: (308) 632-8599 Calendar System: Semester
URL: www.summitcc.net
Established: 1951 Annual Undergrad Tuition & Fees: $5,974
Enrollment: 36 Coed
Affiliation or Control: Independent Non-Profit IRS Status: 501(c)3
Highest Offering: Baccalaureate
Accreditation: @BI

01 President .... David K. PARRISH
05 Academic Dean .... Scott GRIBBLE
06 Registrar .... Andi GRANT

Union College (C)

3800 S 48th Street, Lincoln NE 68506-4300
County: Lancaster FICE Identification: 002563
Unit ID: 181738
Telephone: (402) 486-2600 Carnegie Class: Bac-Diverse
FAX Number: (402) 486-2895 Calendar System: Semester
URL: www.ucollege.edu
Established: 1891 Annual Undergrad Tuition & Fees: $22,538
Enrollment: 903 Coed
Affiliation or Control: Seventh-day Adventist IRS Status: 501(c)3
Highest Offering: Master's
Accreditation: NH, #ARCPA, CAEPN, NURSE, SW

01 President .... Dr. Vinita SAUDER
05 Vice President for Academic Admin .... Dr. Frankie ROSE
10 Vice President for Financial Admin .... Mr. Steve TRANA
32 Vice President Student Services .... Dr. Kim CANINE
30 Vice President for Advancement .... Ms. LuAnn DAVIS
42 Vice President for Spiritual Life .... Dr. Rich CARLSON
08 Library Director .... Ms. Kieren BAILEY
13 Director of Information Systems .... Mr. Richard HENRIQUES
33 Dean of Men .... Mr. Doug TALLMAN
06 Director Records/Registrar .... Ms. Salli JENKS
07 Director Enrollment & Admissions .... Mr. Kevin ERICKSON
26 Director of Public Relations .... Mr. Ryan TELLER
29 Director Alumni Relations .... Ms. Kenna Lee CARLSON
37 Director Student Financial Aid .... Ms. Taryn ROUSE
15 Human Resources Director .... Ms. Lisa R. FORBES
36 Career Center Coordinator .... Ms. Teresa EDGERTON

Universal College of Healing Arts (D)

8702 N 30th Street, Omaha NE 68112-1810
County: Douglas FICE Identification: 038214
Unit ID: 446598
Telephone: (402) 556-4456 Carnegie Class: Spec 2-yr-Health
FAX Number: (402) 561-0635 Calendar System: Semester
URL: www.ucha.edu
Established: 1995 Annual Undergrad Tuition & Fees: $15,440
Enrollment: 25 Coed
Affiliation or Control: Proprietary IRS Status: Proprietary
Highest Offering: Associate Degree
Accreditation: ABHES

01 Executive Director .... Ms. Paulette GENTHON

*University of Nebraska Central Administration (E)

3835 Holdrege, Lincoln NE 68583-0745
County: Lancaster FICE Identification: 008025
Unit ID: 181747
Telephone: (402) 472-8636 Carnegie Class: N/A
FAX Number: (402) 472-1237
URL: www.nebraska.edu

01 President .... Dr. Hank BOUNDS
05 Exec Vice President & Provost .... Dr. Susan M. FRITZ
10 Sr Vice Pres Business & Finance .... Mr. David E. LECHNER
43 Vice President & General Counsel .... Mr. Joel D. PEDERSEN
47 VP Agriculture/Natural Res .... Dr. Michael J. BOEHM
100 Chief of Staff .... Vacant
13 Vice Pres Info Technology/CIO .... Mr. Mark S. ASKREN
101 Corporation Secretary .... Ms. Carmen K. MAURER
86 Sr Assoc VP/Director Govt Relations .... Vacant
18 Asst VP/Dir Facility Plng/Mgmt .... Ms. Rebecca H. KOLLER
09 Asst VP/Dir Inst Research/Planning .... Dr. Kristin YATES
88 Asst VP P-16 Initiatives .... Dr. Gabrielle A. BANICK
88 Asst VP Global Strategy/Intl Init .... Dr. Steven T. DUKE
26 Asst VP Univ Affs/Dir Comm & Mktg .... Ms. Jacqueline M. OSTROWICKI
04 Special Assistant to the President .... Mr. Philip J. BAKKEN
53 Sr Assoc Dean Educ/Human Science .... Dr. Marjorie KOSTELNIK

*University of Nebraska at Kearney (F)

905 W 25th Street, Kearney NE 68849
County: Buffalo FICE Identification: 002551
Unit ID: 181215
Telephone: (308) 865-8208 Carnegie Class: Masters/L
FAX Number: (308) 865-8665 Calendar System: Semester
URL: www.unk.edu
Established: 1903 Annual Undergrad Tuition & Fees (In-State): $6,844
Enrollment: 6,747 Coed
Affiliation or Control: State IRS Status: 501(c)3
Highest Offering: Beyond Master's But Less Than Doctorate
Accreditation: NH, CAATE, CACREP, CAEPN, CIDA, MUS, NAIT, SP, SW

02 Chancellor .... Dr. Douglas A. KRISTENSEN
05 Sr VC Academic & Student Affairs .... Dr. Charles J. BICAK
10 Vice Chanc Business & Finance .... Mr. Jon C. WATTS
26 Asst VC Comm/Community Relations .... Ms. Kelly H. BARTLING
30 Vice President Development .... Mr. Lucas DART
13 Asst Vice Chanc Info Technology .... Ms. Debbie SCHROEDER
21 Asst Vice Chanc Business & Finance .... Ms. Jane SHELDON
49 Interim Dean Natural/Social Science .... Dr. Peter J. LONGO
50 Dean Business/Technology .... Dr. Timothy J. BURKINK
53 Dean of Education .... Dr. Sheryl J. FEINSTEIN
57 Dean Fine Arts & Humanities .... Dr. William JURMA
58 Dean Graduate Studies & Research .... Dr. Kenya S. TAYLOR
32 Dean of Student Affairs .... Dr. Gilbert HINGA
04 Exec Assistant to the Chancellor .... Mr. Neal H. SCHNOOR
06 Registrar .... Ms. Kim SCHIPPOREIT
08 Dean of the Library .... Ms. Janet S. WILKE
36 Director Academic & Career Services .... Ms. Amy L. RUNDSTROM
07 Dir UG Recruitment/Admissions .... Mr. Dusty NEWTON
18 Dir Facilities Mgmt & Planning .... Mr. Lee MCQUEEN
19 Director Police & Parking Services .... Mr. James F. DAVIS
22 Dir Affirm Action/Equal Opportunity .... Ms. Mary J. CHINNOCK PETROSKI
09 Director Institutional Research .... Ms. Kathy LIVINGSTON
27 Dir News/Internal Communication .... Mr. Todd GOTTULA
29 Director Alumni Services .... Mr. Lucas DART
35 Director Student Life .... Ms. Sharon PELC
23 Director Counseling & Health Care .... Ms. Wendy L. SCHARDT
39 Director Residence Life .... Mr. George HOLMAN
40 Director Bookstore .... Mr. Len J. FANGMEYER
41 Athletic Director .... Mr. Paul M. PLINSKE
88 Director Finance .... Ms. Jill PURDY
108 Director Assessment .... Dr. Beth D. HINGA
25 Director Sponsored Programs .... Mr. Richard A. MOCARSKI
85 Asst Vice Chanc for Intl Affairs .... Mr. Michael J. STOPFORD
114 Budget Director .... Ms. Jean MATTSON
96 Director Bus Svcs & Accts Payable .... Mr. Scott A. BENSON
37 Director Financial Aid .... Ms. Mary SOMMERS
93 Director Multicultural Affairs .... Mr. Juan GUZMAN
92 Director Honors Program .... Dr. John FALCONER
84 Assoc VC Acad Svcs/Enroll Mgmt .... Dr. Edgar (Ed) L. SCANTLING

*University of Nebraska - Lincoln (G)

14th and R Streets, Lincoln NE 68588-0002
County: Lancaster FICE Identification: 002565
Unit ID: 181464
Telephone: (402) 472-7211 Carnegie Class: DU-Highest
FAX Number: (402) 472-2410 Calendar System: Semester
URL: www.unl.edu
Established: 1869 Annual Undergrad Tuition & Fees (In-State): $8,537
Enrollment: 25,260 Coed
Affiliation or Control: State IRS Status: 501(c)3
Highest Offering: Doctorate
Accreditation: NH, ART, AUD, CAATE, CAEPT, CIDA, CLPSY, CONST, COPSY, CS, DANCE, DIETD, DIETI, ENG, IPSY, JOUR, LAW, LSAR, MFCD, MUS, PLNG, SCPSY, SP, THEA

02 Chancellor .... Dr. Ronnie D. GREEN
05 Exec Vice Chanc & Chief Acad Ofcr .... Dr. Donde PLOWMAN
10 Vice Chanc Business & Finance .... Ms. Christine JACKSON
32 Interim VC Student Affairs .... Dr. Laurie BELLOWS
65 Vice Chanc Agric/Nat Resources .... Dr. Michael BOEHM
46 Interim VC Research & Econ Dev .... Dr. Steve GODDARD
13 VC Information Technology & CIO .... Mr. Mark ASKREN
04 Associate to Chancellor .... Mr. William NUNEZ
31 Asst to Chanc Community Relations .... Ms. Michelle WAITE
15 Asst Vice Chanc for Human Resources .... Mr. Bruce A. CURRIN
20 Sr Assoc Vice Chanc & Dean .... Dr. Amy GOODBURN
18 Executive Director .... Mr. Mark MILLER
84 Asst VC for Enrollment Mgmt .... Ms. Amber S. WILLIAMS
08 Dean University Libraries .... Dr. Nancy BUSCH
58 Interim Assoc VC & Dean Grad Stds .... Dr. Timothy CARR
49 Dean Arts & Sciences .... Dr. Joseph FRANCISCO
54 Interim Dean Engineering .... Dr. Lance PEREZ
61 Dean of Law .... Dr. Richard MOBERLY
47 Dean Agric Scienc/Nat Resources .... Dr. Steven WALLER
50 Interim Dean Business .... Dr. Kathy FARRELL
60 Dean Journ/Mass Communications .... Dr. Maria MARRON
53 Dean Education & Human Sciences .... Dr. Marjorie KOSTELNIK
48 Dean College Architecture .... Dr. Katherine ANKERSON
47 Dean Agricultural Research Division .... Dr. Archie CLUTTER
56 Dean & Dir Cooperative Extens .... Dr. Charles HIBBERD
93 Director Educ Access & TRIO Pgms .... Ms. Catherine YAMAMOTO
57 Dean Fine & Performing Arts .... Dr. Charles D. O'CONNOR
37 Dir Scholarships/Financial Aid .... Mr. Justin C. BROWN
09 Interim Dir Research/Analytics .... Mr. Heath TUTTLE
88 Asst Dean Acad Svcs & Enrollment .... Mr. James VOLKMER
92 Director Honors Program .... Dr. Patrice BERGER
94 Director Women's Studies .... Dr. Marie-Chantal KALISA
06 University Registrar .... Dr. Richard MORRELL
36 Director Career Services Center .... Dr. Larry R. ROUTH
19 Chief University Police Services .... Mr. Owen YARDLEY
22 Director Inst Equity & Compliance .... Ms. Tamiko STRICKMAN
23 Director University Health Center .... Dr. James GUEST
39 Director Housing Office .... Ms. Susan M. GILDERSLEEVE
41 Director of Athletics .... Mr. Shawn EICHORST
100 Dir Distance Education Services .... Dr. Nancy ADEN-FOX
29 Exec Director Alumni Association .... Ms. Shelley ZABOROWSKI
26 Chief Communication/Marketing Ofcr .... Ms. Teresa PAULSEN
30 Chief Development .... Mr. Brian HASTINGS
38 Director Student Counseling .... Dr. Robert N. PORTNOY
96 Director of Purchasing .... Mr. Gary L. KRAFT
07 Interim Director of Admissions .... Ms. Abby FREEMAN
100 Chief of Staff .... Dr. William NUNEZ
28 Director Staff Diversity .... Ms. Karen KASSEBAUM

*University of Nebraska Medical Center (H)

987020 Nebraska Medical Center, Omaha NE 68198-7020
County: Douglas FICE Identification: 006895
Unit ID: 181428
Telephone: (402) 559-4000 Carnegie Class: Spec-4-yr-Med
FAX Number: (402) 559-4396 Calendar System: Semester
URL: www.unmc.edu
Established: 1869 Annual Undergrad Tuition & Fees (In-State): N/A
Enrollment: 3,790 Coed
Affiliation or Control: State IRS Status: 501(c)3
Highest Offering: Doctorate
Accreditation: NH, ARCPA, CYTO, DENT, DH, DIETI, DMS, MED, MT, NURSE, PERF, PH, PHAR, PTA, RAD, RADMAG, RTT

02 Chancellor .... Dr. Jeffery P. GOLD
05 Vice Chancellor Acad Affairs .... Dr. H. Dele O. DAVIES
10 Vice Chanc Business & Finance .... Ms. Deborah THOMAS
46 Vice Chancellor Research .... Dr. Jennifer LARSEN
86 Vice Chancellor External Affairs .... Mr. Robert BARTEE
20 Assoc Vice Chanc Academic Affairs .... Dr. James TURPEN
20 Asst Vice Chanc Acad Affairs .... Dr. Jilian ZHENG
20 Assoc Vice Chanc Acad Affs/Reg Comp .... Dr. Ernest D. PRENTICE
45 Assoc Vice Chanc Basic Sci Rsch .... Dr. Kenneth BAYLES
45 Assoc Vice Chancellor Clinical Rsch .... Dr. Christopher KRATOCHVIL
21 Sr Assoc Vice Chan Business/Finance .... Vacant
30 Assoc Vice Chanc Bus Development .... Dr. Rodney MARKIN
18 Asst Vice Chanc Facilities/Mgt/Plng .... Mr. Kenneth HANSEN
13 Asst Vice Chancellor ITS .... Vacant
15 Asst Vice Chanc for Human Resources .... Ms. Aileen WARREN
58 Dean Graduate Studies .... Dr. H. Dele O. DAVIES
52 Dean College of Dentistry .... Dr. Janet GUTHMILLER
63 Dean College of Medicine .... Dr. Bradley E. BRITIGAN
66 Dean College of Nursing .... Dr. Juliann SEBASTIAN
67 Dean College of Pharmacy .... Dr. Courtney FLETCHER
69 Dean College of Public Health .... Dr. Ali KHAN
76 Dean College of Allied Health Prof .... Dr. Kyle P. MEYER
88 Dir Eppley Cancer Research Inst .... Dr. Kenneth H. COWAN
88 Director Munroe-Meyer Institute .... Dr. Karoly MIRNICS
08 Director Library of Med .... Ms. Emily J. MCELROY
37 Dir Financial Aid Office .... Ms. Judith D. WALKER
26 Director of Public Relations .... Mr. William O'NEILL
29 Director Alumni Relations .... Ms. Catherine MELLO
38 Director Student Counseling .... Dr. David S. CARVER
28 Director of Diversity .... Ms. Linda CUNNINGHAM
96 Director Procurement & Mtrls Mgt .... Mr. Jeffrey ELLIOTT
09 Director Institutional Research .... Ms. Jeanne FERBRACHE
19 Director Campus Security .... Mr. Gary SVANDA

*University of Nebraska at Omaha (I)

6001 Dodge Street, Omaha NE 68182-0001
County: Douglas FICE Identification: 002554
Unit ID: 181394
Telephone: (402) 554-2200 Carnegie Class: DU-Mod
FAX Number: (402) 554-3555 Calendar System: Semester
URL: www.unomaha.edu
Established: 1908 Annual Undergrad Tuition & Fees (In-State): $7,204
Enrollment: 15,526 Coed
Affiliation or Control: State IRS Status: 501(c)3
Highest Offering: Doctorate
Accreditation: NH, AAB, ART, #CAATE, CACREP, CAEPN, CEA, CS, MUS, SP, SPAA, SW

02 Chancellor .... Dr. Jeffrey P. GOLD
05 Sr Vice Chanc Acad/Student Affs .... Dr. Burton J. REED
10 Vice Chanc Business & Finance .... Mr. Bill CONLEY
13 Chief Information Officer .... Mr. Bret BLACKMAN
21 Assoc Vice Chanc Business & Finance .... Ms. Carol KIRCHNER
32 Assoc Vice Chanc Student Affairs .... Dr. Daniel SHIPP
84 Assoc Vice Chanc Enroll Mgmt Svcs .... Mr. Omar CORREA
58 Dean Graduate Studies .... Dr. Deb SMITH-HOWELL
57 Dean Fine Arts/Communication/Media .... Dr. Michael HILT
53 Dean of Education .... Dr. Nancy EDICK
50 Dean of Business Administration .... Dr. Lou POL
49 Dean of Arts & Sciences .... Dr. David J. BOOCKER
82 Dean of International Studies/Pgms .... Mr. Patrick MCNAMARA
72 Dean Info Science/Technology .... Dr. Hesham ALI
80 Dean Public Affairs/Community .... Dr. John R. BARTLE
62 Dean of Library Services .... Mr. David E. RICHARDS
09 Dir Institutional Effectiveness .... Dr. T. Hank ROBINSON
35 Chief Student Life Officer .... Vacant
15 Director Human Resources .... Mr. Cecil HICKS, JR.
18 Director Facilities Mgmt/Planning .... Mr. John AMEND
06 Registrar .... Mr. Mark GOLDSBERRY
07 Director of Admissions .... Mr. Chris LIEWER
37 Director Financial Aid .... Mr. Marty HABROCK
88 Director Student Testing Center .... Ms. Marion FORTIN-WAVRA
41 Vice Chanc Athletic Leadership/Mgmt .... Mr. Trev ALBERTS
29 President/CEO Alumni Association .... Mr. Lee DENKER
26 Exec Dir University Communications .... Ms. Erin OWEN
96 Procurement Systems Coordinator .... Ms. Lynn MCALPINE
40 Manager Book Store .... Mr. Eric HAGER
19 Director of Public Safety .... Ms. Charlotte EVANS

*University of Nebraska - Nebraska College of Technical Agriculture (A)

404 E 7th Street, Curtis NE 69025-9502
County: Frontier — FICE Identification: 007358
Unit ID: 181765
Telephone: (308) 367-4124 — Carnegie Class: Spec 2-yr-Other
FAX Number: (308) 367-5203 — Calendar System: Semester
URL: www.ncta.unl.edu
Established: 1913 — Annual Undergrad Tuition & Fees (In-State): $4,710
Enrollment: 512 — Coed
Affiliation or Control: State — IRS Status: 501(c)3
Highest Offering: Associate Degree
Accreditation: NH

02 Dean .... Dr. Ron ROSATI
10 Assoc Dean Finance/Ops/Student Svcs .... Mrs. Jennifer A. MCCONVILLE
21 Business Manager/Human Resources .... Ms. Jan GILBERT
04 Administrative Asst to President .... Ms. Catherine M. HAUPTMAN
06 Registrar .... Mrs. Victoria LUKE
08 Head Librarian .... Mr. Mo KHAMOUNA
09 Director of Institutional Research .... Vacant
13 Chief Info Technology Officer (CIO) .... Mr. Justin BAUGHER
39 Director Student Housing .... Mr. Ryan BAUMAN
84 Director Enrollment Management .... Mrs. Tina SMITH

Western Nebraska Community College (B)

1601 E 27th Street, Scottsbluff NE 69361-1815
County: Scotts Bluff — FICE Identification: 002560
Unit ID: 181817
Telephone: (308) 635-3606 — Carnegie Class: Assoc/MT-VT-High Non
FAX Number: (308) 635-6100 — Calendar System: Semester
URL: www.wncc.edu
Established: 1926 — Annual Undergrad Tuition & Fees (In-District): $2,700
Enrollment: 1,534 — Coed
Affiliation or Control: State/Local — IRS Status: 501(c)3
Highest Offering: Associate Degree
Accreditation: NH, CA, CAHIIM, PHLEB, PNUR, SURGT

01 President .... Dr. Todd R. HOLCOMB
05 Executive Vice President .... Dr. Kim KUSTER-DALE
15 Executive Director of HR .... Ms. Kathy AULT
32 Vice President Student Services .... Ms. Nina GRANT
10 Vice Pres Administrative Services .... Mr. William D. KNAPPER
20 Dean of Instruction .... Ms. Hallie FEIL
50 Harms Adv Tech Ctr Exec Director .... Ms. Judith L. AMOO
35 Dean of Students .... Dr. Schvalla RIVERA
12 Sidney Campus Director .... Ms. Paula J. ABBOTT
88 Assoc Dean Instruct Support Svcs .... Ms. Ellen M. DILLON
102 Foundation Executive Director .... Ms. Jennifer ROGERS
06 Registrar .... Mr. Roger S. HOVEY
37 Financial Aid Director .... Ms. Sheila R. JOHNS
26 Public Relations & Marketing Dir .... Ms. Allison JUDY
38 Counseling Director .... Mr. Norman J. STEPHENSON
21 Accounting Services Director .... Mr. David KOEHLER
41 Athletic Director .... Mr. Ryan C. BURGNER
51 Lifelong Learning Director .... Ms. Lori S. STROMBERG
07 Admissions Director .... Ms. Gretchen K. FOSTER
39 Residence Life Director .... Mr. Norman COLEY
13 Information Technology Director .... Mr. Joe W. DEER
40 Bookstore Operations Director .... Mr. Rich RIDDICK
19 Safety/Environmental Mgmt Director .... Ms. Katrina TYLEE
09 Institutional Research Director .... Ms. Nino KALATOZI
88 Academic Testing & Tutoring Coord .... Ms. Tammie KLEICH
39 Student Life Assistant Director .... Ms. Megan WESCOAT
39 Student Life Assistant Director .... Ms. Molly A. BONUCHI
50 Div Chair Business/Applied Tech .... Ms. Aletia NORWOOD
79 Div Chair Acad Enrich/Lang/Fine Art .... Ms. Jennifer L. PEDERSEN
66 Nursing Program Director .... Ms. Rebecca KAUTZ
81 Division Chair Math & Science .... Ms. Laurie ALKIRE
88 Health Info Technology Program Dir .... Ms. Peg A. WOLFF
76 Division Chair Health Sciences .... Dr. Ronda KINSEY
29 Director Alumni Relations/Steward .... Ms. Jennifer R. SIBAL
106 Instructional Tech Coordinator .... Ms. Heidi JACKSON

Western Nebraska Community College Alliance Campus (C)

1750 Sweetwater Avenue, Alliance NE 69301
Telephone: (308) 763-2000 — Identification: 770343
Accreditation: &NH

Western Nebraska Community College Sidney Campus (D)

371 College Drive, Sidney NE 69162
Telephone: (308) 254-5450 — Identification: 770344
Accreditation: &NH

York College (E)

1125 E 8th Street, York NE 68467-2699
County: York — FICE Identification: 002567
Unit ID: 181853
Telephone: (402) 363-5600 — Carnegie Class: Bac-Diverse
FAX Number: (402) 363-5667 — Calendar System: Semester
URL: www.york.edu
Established: 1890 — Annual Undergrad Tuition & Fees: $17,700
Enrollment: 410 — Coed
Affiliation or Control: Churches Of Christ — IRS Status: 501(c)3
Highest Offering: Master's
Accreditation: NH, CAEPN

01 President .... Dr. Steven W. ECKMAN
05 Provost .... Dr. Shane MOUNTJOY
10 Vice President Finance & Operations .... Mr. Todd SHELDON
111 Vice Pres Advancement .... Mr. Brent MAGNER
41 VP for Athletics and Enrollment .... Mr. Jared STARK
32 Dean of Student Development .... Mrs. Catherine SEUFFERLEIN
21 Business Manager .... Mr. Dan COLE
06 Registrar .... Mr. Jared LEINEN
35 Dean of Students .... Mr. Stephen DETLEFS
08 Director of Library .... Mrs. Ruth CARLOCK
26 Director of Publications .... Mr. Steddon L. SIKES
37 Financial Aid Director .... Mr. Brien ALLEY
40 Campus Store Manager .... Mrs. Janet RUSH
18 Supervisor Buildings & Grounds .... Mr. Bob GAVER
42 Campus Minister .... Dr. Sam GARNER
73 Chair Bible .... Dr. Frank E. WHEELER
88 Chair History .... Mr. Tim D. MCNEESE
50 Chair English .... Dr. Jennifer DUTCH
81 Chair Math/Sciences .... Dr. Alex WILLIAMS
57 Chair Performing Arts/Communication .... Dr. Clark A. ROUSH
29 Dir Alumni & Community Relations .... Mrs. Chrystal HOUSTON
04 Executive Asst to President .... Mrs. Gayle A. GOOD
13 Chief Info Technology Officer (CIO) .... Mr. Joel COEHOORN
39 Director Student Housing .... Mr. Larry GOOD
106 Dir Online Education/E-learning .... Dr. Kirk MALLETTE
07 Director of Admissions .... Mr. David ODOM

NEVADA

Altierus Career College (F)

170 North Stephanie Street, Henderson NV 89074
County: Clark — FICE Identification: 022375
Unit ID: 182148
Telephone: (702) 567-1920 — Carnegie Class: Assoc/HVT-Mix Trad/Non
FAX Number: (702) 566-9725 — Calendar System: Semester
URL: www.altierus.org
Established: 2004 — Annual Undergrad Tuition & Fees: $12,510
Enrollment: 417 — Coed
Affiliation or Control: Independent Non-Profit — IRS Status: 501(c)3
Highest Offering: Associate Degree
Accreditation: #ACICS, ADNUR

01 President .... Dr. Peter PERHAC
32 Director of Student Success .... Mr. Ryan MILLER

The Art Institute of Las Vegas (G)

2350 Corporate Circle, Henderson NV 89074-7737
Telephone: (702) 369-9944 — FICE Identification: 030846
Accreditation: #ACICS, ACFEI, CIDA

† Branch campus of The Art Institute of Phoenix, AZ.

Brightwood College (H)

3535 West Sahara Avenue, Las Vegas NV 89102
County: Clark — FICE Identification: 030432
Unit ID: 374875
Telephone: (702) 368-2338 — Carnegie Class: Spec 2-yr-Health
FAX Number: (702) 368-3853 — Calendar System: Other
URL: www.brightwood.edu
Established: 1991 — Annual Undergrad Tuition & Fees: N/A
Enrollment: 833 — Coed
Affiliation or Control: Proprietary — IRS Status: Proprietary
Highest Offering: Associate Degree
Accreditation: ACICS, CAHIIM, PNUR

01 Campus President .... Ms. Lisia MOORE
05 Academic Dean .... Ms. Shanel HARRIS
07 Director of Admissions .... Ms. Kristie CHILES
10 Director of Finance .... Mr. Dean RILING
67 Dept Chair Pharmacy Technician .... Mr. Mark BRUNTON
36 Director of Career Services .... Ms. Hannah BARBOUR
66 Director of Nursing/PN .... Ms. Julia MILLARD

Career College of Northern Nevada (I)

1421 Pullman Drive, Sparks NV 89434
County: Washoe — FICE Identification: 026215
Unit ID: 181941
Telephone: (775) 856-2266 — Carnegie Class: Spec 2-yr-Health
FAX Number: (775) 856-0935 — Calendar System: Quarter
URL: www.ccnn.edu
Established: 1984 — Annual Undergrad Tuition & Fees: N/A
Enrollment: 541 — Coed
Affiliation or Control: Proprietary — IRS Status: Proprietary
Highest Offering: Associate Degree
Accreditation: ACCSC

01 President .... Mr. L. Nathan N. CLARK

Carrington College - Las Vegas (J)

5740 S Eastern Avenue, Suite 140, Las Vegas NV 89119
Telephone: (702) 688-4300 — Identification: 770742
Accreditation: &WJ, COARC, PTAA

† Regional accreditation is carried under the parent institution in Sacramento, CA.

Carrington College - Reno (K)

5580 Kietzke Lane, Reno NV 89511
Telephone: (775) 335-2900 — Identification: 770743
Accreditation: &WJ, ADNUR

† Regional accreditation is carried under the parent institution in Sacramento, CA.

Chamberlain University-Las Vegas (L)

9901 Covington Cross Dr, Las Vegas NV 89144
Telephone: (702) 786-1660 — Identification: 770852
Accreditation: &NH, NURSE

† Branch campus of Chamberlain University-Addison, Addison, IL

*Nevada System of Higher Education (M)

2601 Enterprise Road, Reno NV 89512-1666
County: Washoe — FICE Identification: 008026
Unit ID: 182519
Telephone: (775) 784-4901 — Carnegie Class: N/A
FAX Number: (775) 784-1127
URL: www.nevada.edu

01 Chancellor .... Mr. John WHITE
05 VC Academic & Student Affairs .... Ms. Crystal ABBA
10 Vice Chanc for Finance .... Mr. Vic REDDING
101 Chief Exec Ofcr Board of Regents .... Mr. Dean J. GOULD
43 Vice Chanc for Legal Affairs .... Mr. Nicholas VASKOV
86 VC Govt and Community Affairs .... Ms. Constance BROOKS
13 Vice Chanc for Info Tech .... Mr. Bob MOULTON

*College of Southern Nevada (N)

6375 W Charleston Boulevard, Las Vegas NV 89146-1139
County: Clark — FICE Identification: 010362
Unit ID: 182005
Telephone: (702) 651-5000 — Carnegie Class: Bac/Assoc-Assoc Dom
FAX Number: (702) 651-4835 — Calendar System: Semester
URL: www.csn.edu
Established: 1971 — Annual Undergrad Tuition & Fees (In-State): $2,910
Enrollment: 33,313 — Coed
Affiliation or Control: State — IRS Status: 501(c)3
Highest Offering: Baccalaureate
Accreditation: NW, ACBSP, ACFEI, ADNUR, CAHIIM, CEA, COARC, DA, DH, DMS, EMT, ENGT, MAC, MLTAD, OPD, PNUR, PTAA, SURGT

02 President .... Dr. Michael D. RICHARDS
04 Exec Assistant to the President .... Ms. Annette LORD
03 Sr VP Strategic Initiatives .... Ms. Patricia A. CHARLTON
05 Vice Pres Academic Affairs .... Dr. Margo MARTIN
32 Vice President of Student Affairs .... Ms. Juanita CHRYSANTHOU
10 Vice President of Finance .... Ms. Mary Kaye BAILEY
18 Assoc VP Facilities/Oper/Maint .... Ms. Sherri PAYNE
43 Legal Counsel .... Mr. Richard HINCKLEY
06 Registrar .... Ms. Pat ZOZAYA
88 Exec Director Foundation Ops .... Mr. Dan MORRIS
103 Exec Dir Workforce Education .... Dr. Ricardo VILLALOBOS
102 Exec Dir CSN Foundation .... Mr. Alan DISKIN
72 Dean Adv & Applied Technologies .... Dr. Michael SPANGLER
81 Dean Science & Mathematics .... Dr. John ADLISH
83 Dean Social Sciences & Education .... Dr. Charles OKEKE
88 Interim Dean Arts & Letters .... Mr. Lester TANAKA
76 Dean Health Sciences .... Dr. Josh HAMILTON

50 Dean of Business .... Dr. Marcus JOHNSON
96 Associate VP of Purchasing .... Mr. Rolando MOSQUEDA
41 Director of Athletics .... Mr. L. Dexter IRVIN
26 Director of Communications .... Ms. Kathryn C. BREKKEN
86 Director Government Relations .... Mr. Michael FLORES
88 Director of Budget Services .... Ms. Lisa BAKKE
09 Director of Institutional Research .... Mr. John BEARCE
62 Director Library Services .... Ms. Clarissa ERWIN
37 Director Student Financial Aid .... Ms. Victoria GOEKE
19 Chief of Police .... Mr. Darryl CARABALLO
85 Dir International Student Ctr .... Ms. Mary SASSO
13 Technology CIO .... Mr. Mugunth VAITHYLINGAM
15 Sr Director of Personnel Services .... Mr. John SCARBOROUGH
28 Executive Director of Diversity .... Ms. Maria MARINCH
106 Dir Online Education/E-learning .... Mr. Terry NORRIS
22 Dir Affirmative Action/EEO .... Vacant

*Great Basin College (A)

1500 College Parkway, Elko NV 89801-5032
County: Elko FICE Identification: 006977
Unit ID: 182306
Telephone: (775) 738-8493 Carnegie Class: Bac/Assoc-Mixed
FAX Number: (775) 738-8771 Calendar System: Semester
URL: www.gbcnv.edu
Established: 1967 Annual Undergrad Tuition & Fees (In-State): $2,910
Enrollment: 3,149 Coed
Affiliation or Control: State IRS Status: 501(c)3
Highest Offering: Baccalaureate
Accreditation: NW, ADNUR, CSHSE, NUR, RAD

02 President .... Ms. Joyce HELENS
05 Vice Pres Academic/Student Affairs .... Mrs. Lynn M. MAHLBERG
10 Vice President for Business Affairs .... Ms. Sonja SIBERT
106 Associate VP for Distance Education .... Ms. Lisa FRAZIER
04 Assistant to the President .... Ms. Mardell WILKINS
07 Director of Admissions .... Ms. Janice KING
09 Dir Institutional Rsrch/Effective .... Dr. Cathy FULKERSON
37 Dir Student Financial Svcs & VA .... Mr. Scott NIELSEN
84 Director Enrollment Management .... Ms. Julie BYRNES
49 Dean of Arts and Letters .... Mr. Thomas REAGAN
75 Dean of Applied Science .... Mr. Bret MURPHY
76 Dean of Health Sciences/Human Svcs .... Dr. Amber DONNELLI
12 Director Ely Center .... Ms. Veronica NELSON
12 Director Winnemucca Center .... Ms. Lisa CAMPBELL
12 Director Pahrump Valley Center .... Ms. Diane WRIGHTMAN
51 Director Continuing Education .... Mrs. Angie DEBRAGA
102 Director Foundation .... Mr. Gregory BRORBY
19 Director Safety and Security .... Ms. Patricia ANDERSON
25 Director Grants .... Ms. Jeannie BAILEY
43 General Counsel .... Mr. John ALBRECHT

*Nevada State College (B)

1300 Nevada State Drive, Henderson NV 89002-9455
County: Clark FICE Identification: 041143
Unit ID: 441900
Telephone: (702) 992-2000 Carnegie Class: Bac-Diverse
FAX Number: (702) 992-2226 Calendar System: Semester
URL: www.nsc.edu
Established: 2002 Annual Undergrad Tuition & Fees (In-District): $5,001
Enrollment: 3,534 Coed
Affiliation or Control: State/Local IRS Status: 501(c)3
Highest Offering: Baccalaureate
Accreditation: NW, NURSE

02 President .... Bart PATTERSON
05 Provost/Exec Vice President .... Dr. Vickie SHIELDS
10 Vice Pres Finance & Administration .... Kevin BUTLER
08 Head Librarian .... Nathaniel KING
09 Director of Institutional Research .... Dr. Sandip THANKI
28 AVP/Director of Diversity .... Dr. Edith FERNANDEZ
32 Chief Student Affairs/Student Life .... Dr. Richard YAO
37 Director Student Financial Aid .... Anthony MORRONE
53 Dean of Education .... Dr. Dennis POTTHOFF
06 Registrar .... Adelfa SULLIVAN

*Truckee Meadows Community College (C)

7000 Dandini Boulevard, Reno NV 89512-3999
County: Washoe FICE Identification: 021077
Unit ID: 182500
Telephone: (775) 673-7000 Carnegie Class: Assoc/MT-VT-Mix Trad/Non
FAX Number: (775) 673-7108 Calendar System: Semester
URL: www.tmcc.edu
Established: 1971 Annual Undergrad Tuition & Fees (In-State): $2,910
Enrollment: 11,085 Coed
Affiliation or Control: State IRS Status: 501(c)3
Highest Offering: Associate Degree
Accreditation: NW, ACFEI, ADNUR, DA, DH, DIETT, EMT

02 President .... Dr. Karin HILGERSOM
04 Executive Assistant to President .... Ms. Lisa D. FARMER
05 Vice President Academic Affairs .... Dr. Marie MURGOLO-POORER
10 Vice Pres Finance & Admin Services .... Jim NEW
32 VP of Student Services .... Ms. Estela LEVARIO GUTIERREZ
30 Exec Dir Institutional Advancement .... Mrs. Gretchen SAWYER
07 Director Admissions & Records .... Mr. Andrew HUGHES
21 Program Director Accounting Svcs .... Mr. Rich WILLIAMS
37 Director Financial Aid .... Ms. Sharon WURM

124 Exec Director Student Relations .... Ms. Joan STEINMAN
15 Chief Human Resources Officer .... Ms. Roni FOX
18 Exec Director Facilities Services .... Mr. Dave ROBERTS
103 Dir Workforce Devel/Cmty Education .... Ms. Nicole MCDOWELL
09 Assoc VP Institutional Research .... Ms. Elena BUBNOVA
08 Head Librarian .... Mr. Ken SULLIVAN

† Granted candidacy at the Baccalaureate level.

*University of Nevada, Las Vegas (D)

4505 S Maryland Parkway, Las Vegas NV 89154-1001
County: Clark FICE Identification: 002569
Unit ID: 182281
Telephone: (702) 895-3201 Carnegie Class: DU-Higher
FAX Number: (702) 895-1088 Calendar System: Semester
URL: www.unlv.edu
Established: 1957 Annual Undergrad Tuition & Fees (In-State): $7,183
Enrollment: 28,600 Coed
Affiliation or Control: State IRS Status: 501(c)3
Highest Offering: Doctorate
Accreditation: NW, ART, CAATE, CACREP, CIDA, CLPSY, CONST, CS, DENT, DIETD, DIETI, ENG, ENGR, IPSY, LAW, LSAR, #MED, MFCD, MUS, NURSE, PH, PTA, RAD, SPAA, SW

02 President .... Dr. Len JESSUP
100 Chief of Staff .... Dr. Fred TREDUP
05 Executive Vice President & Provost .... Dr. Diane CHASE
88 Special Counsel to the President .... Mrs. Nancy B. RAPOPORT
10 Vice Pres Finance & Business & CFO .... Mrs. Jean VOCK
41 Director of Athletics .... Mrs. Desiree REED-FRANCOIS
32 Vice President for Student Affairs .... Dr. Juanita FAIN
46 VP Research & Economic Development .... Dr. Mary S. CROUGHAN
30 VP Philanthropy & Alumni .... Mr. Scott ROBERTS
86 VP Government Affairs & Compliance .... Mr. Luis VALERA
26 VP Brand and Chief Marketing Offcr .... Mr. Vince ALBERTA
43 General Counsel .... Mrs. Elda SIDHU
07 AVP Enrollment & Student Services .... Dr. Mike SAUER
35 Assoc VP for Student Affairs .... Ms. Karen STRONG
29 Sr Assoc VP Alumni Relations .... Mr. Chad WARREN
31 Int Exec Dir of Community Relations .... Mrs. Sue DIBELLA
15 Chief Human Resources Officer .... Mr. Larry HAMILTON
87 Int Vice Prov Educational Outreach .... Dr. Margaret REES
13 Vice Provost Info Technology .... Dr. Lori TEMPLE
50 Dean Business .... Dr. Brent A. HATHAWAY
49 Dean Liberal Arts .... Dr. Chris HEAVEY
53 Dean of Education .... Dr. Kim K. METCALF
54 Dean of Engineering .... Dr. Rama VENKAT
63 Dean School of Medicine .... Dr. Barbara ATKINSON
52 Dean School of Dental Medicine .... Dr. Karen P. WEST
61 Dean School of Law .... Mr. Daniel W. HAMILTON
81 Dean of Sciences .... Dr. Eric CHRONISTER
88 Dean College of Hotel Admin .... Dr. Stowe SHOEMAKER
57 Dean Fine Arts .... Dr. Nancy USCHER
08 Dean of Libraries .... Ms. Patricia IANNUZZI
88 Dean Urban Affairs .... Dr. Robert R. ULMER
92 Dean Honors College .... Dr. Marta MEANA
121 Dean Academic Success Ctr .... Dr. Ann MCDONOUGH
88 Dean Community Health Sciences .... Dr. Shawn GERSTENBERGER
76 Dean Sch Allied Health Sciences .... Dr. Ronald T. BROWN
06 Registrar .... Ms. Katie HUMPHREYS
37 Dir Financial Aid & Scholarships .... Mr. Norm BEDFORD
27 Assoc VP Univ Communications .... Ms. Nikki TROXCLAIR
19 Director Public Safety .... Mr. Jose ELIQUE
09 Vice Provost Decision Support .... Dr. Brent DRAKE
39 Exec Dir Residential Life .... Mr. Richard CLARK
38 AVP Student Wellness .... Dr. Jamie DAVIDSON
23 Director Student Health .... Ms. Kathy A. UNDERWOOD
96 Director Purchasing .... Ms. Sharrie MAYDEN
85 Director Intl Students & Scholars .... Ms. Kristen YOUNG
25 Director Sponsored Programs .... Ms. Rochelle ATHEY

*University of Nevada, Reno (E)

1664 N. Virginia Street, Reno NV 89557
County: Washoe FICE Identification: 002568
Unit ID: 182290
Telephone: (775) 784-1110 Carnegie Class: DU-Higher
FAX Number: (775) 784-1300 Calendar System: Semester
URL: www.unr.edu
Established: 1874 Annual Undergrad Tuition & Fees (In-State): $7,142
Enrollment: 20,898 Coed
Affiliation or Control: State IRS Status: 501(c)3
Highest Offering: Doctorate
Accreditation: NW, CACREP, CAEPN, CEA, CLPSY, CS, DIETD, DIETI, ENG, JOUR, MED, MUS, NURSE, PH, SP, SW

02 President .... Dr. Marc JOHNSON
05 Exec Vice Pres & Provost .... Dr. Kevin CARMAN
11 Vice Pres Administration & Finance .... Mr. Ronald M. ZUREK
63 VP Health Sci/Dean Sch of Medicine .... Dr. Thomas L. SCHWENK
30 Vice President Devel/Alumni Rels .... Mr. John CAROTHERS
32 Vice President for Student Services .... Dr. Shannon ELLIS
46 Vice President for Research .... Dr. Mridul GAUTAM
08 Dean of Libraries .... Dr. Kathlin D. RAY
20 Vice Prov Instr/Undergrad Programs .... Dr. Joseph CLINE
20 Vice Provost Faculty Affairs .... Dr. Stacy BURTON
58 Vice Provost/Dean Grad School .... Dr. David ZEH
51 Vice Provost for Extended Studies .... Dr. Fred B. HOLMAN
10 Assoc VP Business & Finance .... Vacant
84 Assoc VP Enrollment Services .... Dr. Melisa N. CHOROSZY
38 Assoc VP Student Success Services .... Dr. Jerry MARCZYNSKI
45 Int Assoc VP Plng/Budget/Analysis .... Mr. Vince JOHNSON

18 Asst Vice Pres Facilities Svcs .... Mr. Sean MCGOLDRICK
21 Controller .... Ms. Sheri MENDEZ
41 Director Athletics .... Mr. Doug KNUTH
96 Director Purchasing .... Mr. Raymond MORAN
19 Director University Police Svcs .... Mr. Adam GARCIA
22 Dir Equal Opportunity & Title IX .... Ms. Denise CORDOVA
37 Director Student Financial Svcs .... Mr. Timothy WOLFE
39 Director Resident Life & Housing .... Mr. Rodney L. AESCHLIMANN
23 Director Student Health Svcs .... Dr. Cheryl HUG-ENGLISH
09 Director Institutional Analysis .... Dr. Serge HERZOG
86 Spec Asst to Pres External Affairs .... Ms. Heidi GANSERT
65 Dir Mackay Sch Mines/Earth Science .... Dr. Russell FIELDS
66 Dean of Nursing .... Dr. Patsy L. RUCHALA
57 Director School of the Arts .... Dr. Larry ENGSTROM
25 Director Sponsored Projects .... Ms. Charlene HART
40 Director Wolf Shop .... Mr. Steve DUBEY
49 Dean Liberal Arts .... Dr. Debra MODDELMOG
47 Dean Agriculture/Biotech/Nat Res .... Dr. William PAYNE
50 Dean Business Administration .... Dr. Gregory MOSIER
53 Dean of Education .... Dr. Kenneth COLL
54 Dean Engineering .... Dr. Emmanuel MARAGAKIS
60 Dean School of Journalism .... Mr. Alan STAVITSKY
81 Dean College of Science .... Dr. Jeffrey S. THOMPSON
07 Director of Admissions .... Dr. Stephen MAPLES
29 Director Alumni Relations .... Ms. Amy CAROTHERS
06 Associate Registrar .... Ms. Heather TURK FIECOAT
26 Exec Dir Marketing & Commun .... Mr. Thomas WHITE
04 Executive Asst to President .... Ms. Janet SANDERSON
100 Chief of Staff .... Ms. Patricia RICHARD
104 Dir/CEO Univ Study Abroad Consort .... Dr. Carmelo URZA
13 Chief Info Technology Officer (CIO) .... Mr. Steven SMITH
28 Dir Ctr for Student Cultural Dev .... Mr. Blane HARDING
43 General Counsel .... Ms. Mary DUGAN
44 Director of Planned Giving .... Ms. Lisa RILEY
67 Dean School of Public Health .... Dr. Trudy LARSON

*Western Nevada College (F)

2201 W College Parkway, Carson City NV 89703-7316
County: Carson FICE Identification: 010363
Unit ID: 182564
Telephone: (775) 445-3000 Carnegie Class: Bac/Assoc-Assoc Dom
FAX Number: (775) 445-3051 Calendar System: Semester
URL: www.wnc.edu
Established: 1971 Annual Undergrad Tuition & Fees (In-State): $2,910
Enrollment: 3,839 Coed
Affiliation or Control: State IRS Status: 501(c)3
Highest Offering: Baccalaureate
Accreditation: NW, ADNUR

02 President .... Mr. Chet BURTON
04 Assistant to the President .... Ms. Deb CONRAD
05 Vice Pres Academic/Student Affairs .... Mr. Scott MORRISON
11 Vice Pres Admin/Legal Svcs .... Mr. Mark GHAN
20 Dean of Instruction .... Vacant
32 Dean Student Services .... Mr. John KINKELLA
10 Controller .... Ms. Coral LOPEZ
88 Director Child Development Center .... Ms. Andrea DORAN
38 Director of Counseling/Advising .... Ms. Piper MCCARTHHY
18 Director Facilities Mgmt/Planning .... Mr. Kevin GAFFNEY
37 Director Financial Aid .... Mr. John (JW) LAZZARI
26 Director Information & Marketing .... Ms. Jamie MCNINCH
08 Director Library & Media Services .... Mr. Kenneth A. SULLIVAN
06 Registrar/Director of Admissions .... Ms. Dianne HILLIARD
30 Director of Development .... Ms. Niki GLADYS
09 Director of Institutional Research .... Ms. Cathy FULKERSON
13 Director of Computing Services .... Ms. Susan HOWLAND
21 Budget Officer .... Ms. Darla DODGE
15 Asst Director Human Resources .... Ms. Irene TUCKER
35 Student Life Coordinator .... Ms. Lilly LEON-VICKS
49 Academic Director Liberal Arts .... Mr. Scott MORRISON
72 Academic Director Career & Tech Div .... Dr. Georgia WHITE
66 Academic Dir Nursing/Allied Health .... Dr. Judith CORDIA
19 Director Security/Safety .... Mr. Jack PIIRAINEN
41 Athletic Director .... Mr. John KINKELLA

Northwest Career College (G)

7398 Smoke Ranch Road, Las Vegas NV 89128
County: Clark FICE Identification: 038385
Unit ID: 445948
Telephone: (702) 254-7577 Carnegie Class: Spec 2-yr-Other
FAX Number: (702) 256-9181 Calendar System: Other
URL: www.northwestcareercollege.edu
Established: 1997 Annual Undergrad Tuition & Fees: N/A
Enrollment: 321 Coed
Affiliation or Control: Proprietary IRS Status: Proprietary
Highest Offering: Associate Degree
Accreditation: ABHES

01 President/Founder .... Dr. John KENNY
05 Director of Education .... Dr. Thomas KENNY
11 COO .... Patrick KENNY
10 CFO .... Stephanie KENNY
37 Financial Aid Officer .... Guillermo BALDERAS
36 Director of Career Services .... Jilian LOPEZ
09 Director of Compliance .... Thomas KENNY
07 Asst Director of Admissions .... Grace PEREA
13 Director of Technology .... Michael KENNY
06 Registrar .... Cheryl DADEY

Pima Medical Institute-Las Vegas (A)

3333 E Flamingo Road, Las Vegas NV 89121-4329
Telephone: (702) 458-9650 Identification: 666273
Accreditation: ABHES, COARC, OTA, PTAA, RAD

† Branch campus of Pima Medical Institute, Tucson, AZ.

Roseman University of Health Sciences (B)

11 Sunset Way, Henderson NV 89014-2333
County: Clark FICE Identification: 040653
Unit ID: 445735
Telephone: (702) 990-4433 Carnegie Class: Spec-4-yr-Other Health
FAX Number: (702) 990-4435 Calendar System: Other
URL: www.roseman.edu
Established: 1999 Annual Undergrad Tuition & Fees: N/A
Enrollment: 1,447 Coed
Affiliation or Control: Independent Non-Profit IRS Status: 501(c)3
Highest Offering: Doctorate
Accreditation: NW, DENT, IACBE, NUR, PHAR

01 President .... Dr. Renee COFFMAN
12 Chancellor Summerlin Campus .... Dr. Mark A. PENN
05 Chancellor Henderson Campus .... Dr. Eucharia E. NNADI
10 VP Business & Finance .... Mr. Ken WILKINS
11 VP of Operations .... Mr. Terrell SPARKS
03 Vice President Executive Affairs .... Dr. Charles F. LACY
26 Vice President Communications & PR .... Mr. Jason ROTH
09 VP Qual Assurance/Intercampus Cons .... Dr. Thomas METZGER
32 VP for Student Services .... Dr. Michael DEYOUNG
67 Interim Dean College of Pharmacy .... Dr. Larry FANNIN
67 Campus Dean College of Pharmacy UT .... Dr. Larry FANNIN
66 Dean College of Nursing .... Dr. Mable H. SMITH
52 Dean College of Dental Medicine .... Dr. Frank LICARI
50 Director MBA Program .... Dr. Okeleke NZEOGWU
37 Director of Financial Aid .... Ms. Sally MICKELSON
88 Assoc Dean Clinical Affairs .... Dr. Kenneth KING
07 Assoc Dean Admissions/Student Svcs .... Dr. William HARMAN
15 Director of Human Resources .... Ms. Saralyn BARNES
62 Director of Library Services .... Ms. Karen CANEPI
06 Registrar/Director of Student Svcs .... Ms. Angela D. BIGBY

Sierra Nevada College (C)

999 Tahoe Boulevard, Incline Village NV 89451-9500
County: Washoe FICE Identification: 009192
Unit ID: 182458
Telephone: (775) 831-1314 Carnegie Class: Masters/M
FAX Number: (775) 832-1696 Calendar System: Semester
URL: www.sierranevada.edu
Established: 1969 Annual Undergrad Tuition & Fees: $31,150
Enrollment: 1,044 Coed
Affiliation or Control: Independent Non-Profit IRS Status: 501(c)3
Highest Offering: Master's
Accreditation: NW

00 Chairman Board of Trustees .... Dr. Atam LALCHANDANI
01 President .... Dr. Alan G. WALKER
05 Executive Vice President/Provost .... Ms. Shannon BEETS
111 Vice President for Advancement .... Ms. Rosanne NICHOLS
32 Dean of Students .... Mr. Will HOIDA
07 Director of UG Admissions .... Ms. Stacie LYANS
20 Associate Provost .... Dr. Dan O'BRYAN
10 Interim Chief Financial Officer .... Mr. Richard ANDERSON
37 Director of Financial Aid .... Ms. Nicole BURLEY
26 Director of Marketing .... Mr. Jim SCRIPPS
09 Director of Institutional Research .... Ms. Annamarie JONES
18 Chief Facilities/Physical Plant .... Mr. Layne SESSIONS
06 Registrar .... Ms. Rose WEHBY
53 Statewide Dir Teacher Education .... Ms. Beth TALIAFERRO
13 Director Information Technology .... Ms. Nicole BURLEY
15 Human Resources Coordinator .... Ms. Dana HOFFELT
21 Controller .... Vacant
04 Executive Asst to the President .... Ms. Kristine YOUNG
41 Athletic Director .... Branko ZAGAR

Touro University Nevada (D)

874 American Pacific Drive, Henderson NV 89014
Telephone: (702) 777-8687 Identification: 770966
Accreditation: &WC, ARCPA, NURSE, OSTEO, OT, PTA

† Branch campus of Touro University California, Vallejo, CA

University of Phoenix Las Vegas Campus (E)

3755 Breakthrough Way, Las Vegas NV 89135-3047
Telephone: (702) 638-7279 Identification: 770220
Accreditation: &NH, ACBSP

† Branch campus of University of Phoenix, Tempe, AZ

Wongu University of Oriental Medicine (F)

8620 S Eastern Avenue, Las Vegas NV 89123
County: Clark Identification: 667262
Unit ID: 488907
Telephone: (702) 463-2122 Carnegie Class: Not Classified
FAX Number: (702) 946-5050 Calendar System: Quarter
URL: www.wongu.org
Established: 2012 Annual Graduate Tuition & Fees: N/A
Enrollment: N/A Coed
Affiliation or Control: Independent Non-Profit IRS Status: 501(c)3
Highest Offering: Master's; No Undergraduates
Accreditation: @ACUP

01 President .... Dr. Daniel DAVIES
05 Chief Academic Officer .... Vacant
10 Chief Financial Officer .... Carolyn YANAI
20 Dean of Academic & Clinical Affs .... Dr. Nicholas POSSON
06 Registrar .... Chau NGUYEN
07 Admissions Coordinator .... Deborah FIALA

NEW HAMPSHIRE

Antioch University New England (G)

40 Avon Street, Keene NH 03431-3516
Telephone: (800) 553-8920 Identification: 666992
Accreditation: &NH, CACREP, CLPSY, MFCD

† Regional accreditation is carried under the parent institution in Yellow Springs, OH.

Colby-Sawyer College (H)

541 Main Street, New London NH 03257-7835
County: Merrimack FICE Identification: 002572
Unit ID: 182634
Telephone: (603) 526-3000 Carnegie Class: Bac-Diverse
FAX Number: (603) 526-2135 Calendar System: Semester
URL: www.colby-sawyer.edu
Established: 1837 Annual Undergrad Tuition & Fees: $39,450
Enrollment: 1,228 Coed
Affiliation or Control: Independent Non-Profit IRS Status: 501(c)3
Highest Offering: Master's
Accreditation: EH, ACBSP, CAATE, NURSE

01 President .... Dr. Susan D. STUEBNER
05 Academic Vice Pres/Dean of Faculty .... Dr. Laura A. ALEXANDER
10 Vice Pres for Finance/Adm & Treasur .... Mr. Robert J. CAMPE
32 Vice President and Dean of Students .... Ms. Robin BURROUGHS DAVIS
111 Vice President Advancement .... Mr. Daniel B. PARISH
07 Vice Pres Admissions/Financial Aid .... Ms. Anna D. MINER
101 Secretary of the College .... Ms. Rachel A. PARSONS
100 Chief of Staff .... Vacant
21 Controller/Treasurer .... Ms. Karen I. BONEWALD
09 Director Institutional Research .... Vacant
20 Academic Dean .... Dr. Lisa HAYWARD
39 Director Residential Education .... Ms. Mary MCLAUGHLIN
37 Director of Financial Aid .... Ms. Beth W. RENZULLI
08 Associate Director Library .... Ms. Sondra C. VANDERPLOEG
06 Registrar .... Ms. Diane H. DRISCOLL
13 Director Information Resources .... Vacant
41 Director of Athletics .... Mr. Bill FOTI
41 Director of Athletics .... Mr. George MARTIN
88 Dir Student Lrng Collaborative .... Ms. Caren BALDWIN-DIMEO
44 Dir Annual Giving .... Mr. Luke GORMAN
29 Dir Alumni Relations .... Ms. Tracey M. AUSTIN
19 Director of Campus Safety .... Mr. Peter L. BERTHIAUME
18 Senior Dir of Facilities .... Mr. Robert VACHON
40 Bookstore Manager .... Ms. Alison SEWARD
23 Dir of Baird Health & Counsel Ctr .... Ms. Pamela SPEAR
92 Coordinator of the Honors Program .... Ms. Ann Page STECKER

*Community College System of New Hampshire (I)

26 College Drive, Concord NH 03301-7407
County: Merrimack Identification: 666462
Telephone: (603) 230-3500 Carnegie Class: N/A
FAX Number: (603) 271-2725
URL: www.ccsnh.edu

01 Chancellor .... Dr. Ross GITTELL
03 Vice Chancellor .... Vacant
10 Assoc Vice Chanc Fin/Strategic Plng .... Charles ANSELL
15 Assoc Vice Chanc Human Res Plng/Dev .... Richard COLADARCI
26 Director of Communications .... Shannon REID
13 Chief Info Technology Officer (CIO) .... Susan BROUILLET

*Great Bay Community College (J)

320 Corporate Drive, Portsmouth NH 03801-2879
County: Rockingham FICE Identification: 002583
Unit ID: 183150
Telephone: (603) 427-7600 Carnegie Class: Assoc/HT-Mix Trad/Non
FAX Number: (603) 334-6308 Calendar System: Semester
URL: www.greatbay.edu
Established: 1945 Annual Undergrad Tuition & Fees (In-State): $7,104
Enrollment: 2,273 Coed
Affiliation or Control: State IRS Status: 501(c)3
Highest Offering: Associate Degree
Accreditation: EH, ACBSP, ADNUR, SURGT

02 President .... Mr. Wildolfo ARVELO
05 Vice President Academic Affairs .... Vacant
32 Vice Pres Student Affairs .... Dr. Sarah BEDINGFIELD
10 Chief Financial Officer .... Ms. Joanne BERRY
06 Registrar .... Ms. Sandra HO
07 Director Admissions .... Ms. Carey WALKER
09 Director Institutional Research .... Ms. Fran CHICKERING

*Lakes Region Community College (K)

379 Belmont Road, Laconia NH 03246-1364
County: Belknap FICE Identification: 007555
Unit ID: 183123
Telephone: (603) 524-3207 Carnegie Class: Assoc/MT-VT-High Non
FAX Number: (603) 527-2042 Calendar System: Semester
URL: www.lrcc.edu
Established: 1967 Annual Undergrad Tuition & Fees (In-District): $6,642
Enrollment: 1,170 Coed
Affiliation or Control: State/Local IRS Status: 501(c)3
Highest Offering: Associate Degree
Accreditation: EH, ADNUR

02 Interim President .... Dr. Larissa BAIA
05 VP of Academic & Community Affairs .... Dr. Alan PUNCHES
10 Chief Financial Officer .... Vacant
04 Administrative Asst to President .... Mrs. Julia L. VELIE
06 Registrar .... Ms. Laura LEMIEN
07 Director of Admissions .... Mr. Wayne FRASER
37 Director Student Financial Aid .... Ms. Kristen PURRINGTON
26 Public Information Officer .... Mr. Max BROWN

*Manchester Community College (L)

1066 Front Street, Manchester NH 03102-8518
County: Hillsborough FICE Identification: 002582
Unit ID: 183132
Telephone: (603) 206-8000 Carnegie Class: Assoc/MT-VT-Mix Trad/Non
FAX Number: (603) 668-5354 Calendar System: Semester
URL: www.mccnh.edu
Established: 1945 Annual Undergrad Tuition & Fees (In-State): $6,912
Enrollment: 2,968 Coed
Affiliation or Control: State IRS Status: 501(c)3
Highest Offering: Associate Degree
Accreditation: EH, ACBSP, ADNUR, CAHIIM, MAC

02 President .... Dr. Susan D. HUARD
05 Vice President Academic Affairs .... Dr. Brian BICKNELL
32 VP Students/Community Development .... Kim KEEGAN
07 Director of Admissions .... Miho BEAN
26 Director of Marketing .... Victoria JAFFE
37 Financial Aid Officer .... Stephanie J. WELDON
06 Registrar .... Evelyn R. PERRON
08 Library Director .... Vandana DHAKAR
09 Director Institutional Research .... Dr. Jere TURNER
10 Business Affairs Officer .... Kelly CHISHOLM
15 Human Resources Officer .... Jeannette DIBELLA
40 Bookstore Manager .... Vacant
66 Nursing Director .... Charlene WOLFE-STEPRO
21 Accountant I .... Carol DESPATHY
13 Director Information Technology .... George WAGGONER
35 Director Student Life .... Aileen CLAY
113 Bursar .... Amy WHEELER
04 Administrative Asst to President .... Karen KEELER
103 Dir Workforce/Career Development .... Kristine DUDLEY
106 Dir Online Education/E-learning .... Brian CHICK
18 Chief Facilities/Physical Plant .... Joshua MURPHY
19 Director Security/Safety .... Jeff NYHAN
29 Director Alumni Relations .... Vacant

*Nashua Community College (M)

505 Amherst Street, Nashua NH 03063-1092
County: Hillsborough FICE Identification: 009236
Unit ID: 183141
Telephone: (603) 578-8900 Carnegie Class: Assoc/HT-Mix Trad/Non
FAX Number: (603) 882-8690 Calendar System: Semester
URL: www.nashuacc.edu
Established: 1967 Annual Undergrad Tuition & Fees (In-State): $6,912
Enrollment: 2,056 Coed
Affiliation or Control: State IRS Status: 501(c)3
Highest Offering: Associate Degree
Accreditation: EH, ACBSP, ADNUR, ENGT

02 President .... Ms. Lucille A. JORDAN
05 Interim Vice Pres Academic Affairs .... Robyn GRISWOLD
32 Vice Pres Student & Community Affs .... Ms. Lizbeth GONZALEZ
10 Business Affairs Officer .... Vacant
09 Assoc VP Inst Research/Acad Affs .... Mr. Phil FRANKLAND
06 Registrar-Nashua .... Ms. Jennifer OLISZCZAK
37 Financial Aid Officer .... Ms. Ann EULE
15 Human Resources .... Ms. Catherine BARRY
18 Plant Maintenance Engineer .... Mr. Scott BIENVENUE
26 Director Marketing/Public Relations .... Mr. Barry MEEHAN
04 Administrative Asst to President .... Ms. Lucy JENKINS

*NHTI-Concord's Community College (N)

31 College Drive, Concord NH 03301-7412
County: Merrimack FICE Identification: 002581
Unit ID: 183099
Telephone: (603) 271-6484 Carnegie Class: Assoc/HT-High Trad
FAX Number: (603) 230-9311 Calendar System: Semester
URL: www.nhti.edu
Established: 1965 Annual Undergrad Tuition & Fees (In-State): $7,104
Enrollment: 4,349 Coed
Affiliation or Control: State IRS Status: 501(c)3

Highest Offering: Associate Degree
Accreditation: EH, ACBSP, ADNUR, DA, DH, DMS, EMT, ENGT, RAD, RTT

02 President ... Dr. Susan B. DUNTON
32 VP Student Affairs ... Mr. Stephen P. CACCIA
35 Associate VP Student Affairs ... Dr. Charles LLOYD
05 Vice President Academic Affairs ... Dr. Pamela LANGLEY
20 Assoc Vice Pres of Academic Affairs ... Dr. Denis NORMANDIN
10 Chief Financial Officer ... Ms. Melanie KIRBY
08 Director Learning Resources ... Mr. Stephen AMBRA
07 Director of Admissions ... Vacant
06 Registrar ... Ms. Michele KARWOCKI
13 Director of Computer Services ... Mr. Thomas TOWLE
18 Director of Facilities Maintenance ... Mr. Jonathan GARTHWAITE
26 Director of Communications ... Mr. Alan BLAKE
36 Dir Residence Life/Career Counsel ... Ms. Trish LORING
38 Director Student Counseling ... Ms. Donna DOOLEY
37 Financial Aid Director ... Ms. Sheri GONTHIER
19 Chief of Campus Safety ... Mr. Jason BISHOP
41 Athletic Director ... Mr. Paul HOGAN
15 Director Human Resources ... Ms. Susan MAKEE
28 Dir Cross-Cultural Education/ESOL ... Ms. Dawn HIGGINS
96 Director of Purchasing ... Ms. Barbara ANSTEY
105 Website Coordinator ... Ms. Christine METCALF
106 Dir Online Learning ... Ms. Trisha DIONNE
09 Director of Institutional Research ... Mr. Gary GONTHIER
29 Director Institutional & Alumni Dev ... Ms. Lee Ann LEWIS
39 Director Student Housing ... Ms. Trish LORING

*River Valley Community College (A)

1 College Place, Claremont NH 03743-9707
County: Sullivan FICE Identification: 007560
Unit ID: 183114
Telephone: (603) 542-7744 Carnegie Class: Assoc/HVT-High Non
FAX Number: (603) 543-1844 Calendar System: Semester
URL: www.rivervalley.edu
Established: 1968 Annual Undergrad Tuition & Fees (In-State): $6,855
Enrollment: 954 Coed
Affiliation or Control: State IRS Status: 501(c)3
Highest Offering: Associate Degree
Accreditation: EH, ACBSP, ADNUR, COARC, MAC, MLTAD, OTA, PTAA, RAD

02 Interim President ... Dr. Ali RAFIEYMEHR
05 Vice President of Academic Affairs ... Dr. Ali RAFIEYMEHR
12 Dir RVCC at Keene ... Ms. Linda RICHELSON
12 Dir RVCC at Lebanon ... Ms. Kristen MCKENNA
37 Financial Aid Officer ... Ms. Julia DOWER
06 Registrar ... Ms. Sharon GILBERT
10 Business Affairs Officer ... Ms. Andrea PINEAU ALLBEE
08 Director of Library Services ... Mr. James ALLEN
103 Coordinator Workforce & Cmty Educ ... Ms. Jessica O'CONNOR

*White Mountains Community College (B)

2020 Riverside Drive, Berlin NH 03570-3799
County: Coos FICE Identification: 005291
Unit ID: 183105
Telephone: (603) 752-1113 Carnegie Class: Assoc/MT-VT-High Non
FAX Number: (603) 752-6335 Calendar System: Semester
URL: www.wmcc.edu
Established: 1966 Annual Undergrad Tuition & Fees (In-State): $7,344
Enrollment: 1,001 Coed
Affiliation or Control: State IRS Status: 501(c)3
Highest Offering: Associate Degree
Accreditation: EH, MAC

02 Interim President ... Dr. Charles LLOYD
05 Vice Pres Academic Affairs ... Dr. Fran RANCOURT
32 Vice President Student Affairs ... Martha LAFLAMME
10 Chief Financial Officer ... Lynn MOORE
20 Associate VP of Academic Affairs ... Kristen MILLER
06 Interim Registrar ... Marie BLY
08 Director of Library Services ... Melissa LAPLANTE
18 Chief Facilities/Physical Plant ... Stephen DEROSIER
13 Director Computer Center ... Vacant
91 Director Administrative Computing ... Donald WEEKS
22 Dir Affirmative Action/Equal Oppty ... Julie COTE
40 Director Bookstore ... Karen SEVIER
07 Director of Admissions ... Vacant
09 Director of Institutional Research ... Suzanne WASILESKI
37 Asst Director Student Financial Aid ... Deborah BECK
105 Director Web Services ... Milton CAMILLE
15 Director Personnel Services ... Gretchen TAILLON

Dartmouth College (C)

Hanover NH 03755-4030
County: Grafton FICE Identification: 002573
Unit ID: 182670
Telephone: (603) 646-1110 Carnegie Class: DU-Higher
FAX Number: N/A Calendar System: Quarter
URL: www.dartmouth.edu
Established: 1769 Annual Undergrad Tuition & Fees: $51,438
Enrollment: 6,350 Coed
Affiliation or Control: Independent Non-Profit IRS Status: 501(c)3
Highest Offering: Doctorate
Accreditation: EH, ENG, IPSY, MED, PAST, PH

01 President ... Dr. Philip J. HANLON
03 Executive Vice President ... Mr. Richard G. MILLS
101 Secretary to Board of Trustees ... Ms. Laura H. HERCOD
05 Provost ... Dr. Carolyn M. DEVER
111 Sr Vice President for Advancement ... Mr. Robert W. LASHER
46 Vice Provost for Research ... Dr. Dean MADDEN
10 CFO and Vice Pres Finance ... Mr. Michael F. WAGNER
26 VP Communications ... Mr. Justin ANDERSON
28 Vice Pres for Inst Diversity/Equity ... Dr. Evelynn ELLIS
15 Chief Human Resources Officer ... Mr. Scot R. BEMIS
29 Vice President Alumni Relations ... Ms. Martha J. BEATTIE
63 Dean Geisel Sch of Med ... Dr. Duane A. COMPTON
18 Interim VP of Campus Services ... Mr. Steven C. MOORE
43 General Counsel ... Ms. Sandhya L. IYER
20 Dean of the College ... Dr. Rebecca E. BIRON
06 Registrar ... Ms. Meredith BRAZ
07 VProv Enroll/Dean Admiss & Fin Aid ... Mr. Lee COFFIN
37 Director of Financial Aid ... Mr. Gordon D. KOFF
13 VP and Chief Information Officer ... Mr. Mitchel W. DAVIS
08 Dean of Libraries ... Ms. Susanne MEHRER
49 Dean of Faculty of Arts & Sciences ... Dr. Elizabeth F. SMITH
50 Dean of Amos Tuck School ... Dr. Matthew J. SLAUGHTER
54 Dean of the Thayer School ... Dr. Joseph HELBLE
58 Dean of Graduate Studies ... Dr. F. Jon KULL
102 Dean of Tucker Foundation ... Rabbi Daveen H. LITWIN
41 Director of Athletics ... Mr. Harry SHEEHY
117 Dir Risk/Internal Control Svcs ... Ms. Catherine LARK
23 Director of the Health Services ... Dr. Mark REED
36 Director Center for Prof Dev ... Mr. Roger W. WOOLSEY
25 Dir Office of Sponsored Projects ... Ms. Jill M. MORTALI
32 Vice Provost for Student Affairs ... Vacant
19 Interim Director Safety & Security ... Mr. Keiselim C. MONTAS
09 Assoc Pro of Institutional Research ... Ms. Alicia M. BETSINGER
38 Dir Counseling/Human Development ... Dr. Heather A. EARLE
22 Dir Equal Opportunity/Affirm Action ... Ms. Theodosia COOK
96 Director of Procurement ... Ms. Tammy L. MOFFATT
115 Chief Investment Officer ... Ms. Alice A. RUTH
35 Sr Assoc Dean for Student Affairs ... Ms. Elilzabeth L. AGOSTO
21 Controller ... Ms. Gail C. GOODNESS
04 Senior Executive Asst to President ... Ms. Jennifer A. SHEPHERD
100 Chief of Staff ... Ms. Laura H. HERCOD
103 Dir Workforce/Career Development ... Mr. Roger W. WOOLSEY
104 Director Study Abroad ... Ms. John G. TANSEY
105 Director Web Services ... Mr. Jonathan CHIAPPA
106 Dir Online Education/E-learning ... Mr. Joshua M. KIM
39 Director Residential Life ... Mr. Michael W. WOOTEN
86 Director Government Relations ... Ms. Martha F. AUSTIN
90 Director Academic Computing ... Mr. Alan R. CATTIER

Franklin Pierce University (D)

40 University Drive, Rindge NH 03461-5046
County: Cheshire FICE Identification: 002575
Unit ID: 182795
Telephone: (603) 899-4000 Carnegie Class: Masters/M
FAX Number: (603) 899-6448 Calendar System: Semester
URL: www.franklinpierce.edu
Established: 1962 Annual Undergrad Tuition & Fees: $34,050
Enrollment: 2,273 Coed
Affiliation or Control: Independent Non-Profit IRS Status: 501(c)3
Highest Offering: Doctorate
Accreditation: EH, ARCPA, IACBE, NUR, PTA

01 President ... Dr. Kim MOONEY
05 VP Academic Affairs/Provost ... Vacant
11 VP & COO ... Dr. Nathaniel PEIRCE
10 Vice Pres Finance & Administration ... Ms. Sandra QUAYE
32 Vice President for Student Affairs ... Dr. James P. EARLE
30 Vice Pres for Institutional Advance ... Vacant
29 VP Alumni & Comm Rels ... Mr. Lawrence LEACH
84 Asst Vice Pres Enrollment Mgmt ... Ms. Linda QUIMBY
58 Dean Grad/Professional Studies ... Dr. Maria R. ALTOBELLO
35 Asst Dean Student Affairs ... Ms. Jill BASSETT
41 Athletic Director ... Mr. Bruce M. KIRSH
15 Director of Human Resources ... Ms. Roberta DELLHIME
06 Registrar ... Ms. Tonya B. LABROSSE
08 Director of Library Resource Center ... Vacant
37 Asst Vice Pres Financial Services ... Mr. Kenneth FERREIRA
29 Director of Alumni & Parent Rel ... Ms. Julie ZAHN
12 Academic Dean Rindge Campus ... Dr. Kerry MCKEEVER
26 Dir of Marketing & Communication ... Mr. James WOLKEN
36 Director of Career Development ... Ms. Rosemary NICHOLS
20 Dir Center for Academic Excellence ... Dr. Karen J. BROWN
42 Chaplain ... Vacant
19 Director Campus Safety ... Ms. Maureen STURGIS
39 Director Residential Life ... Ms. Kathleen DOUGHERTY
18 Chief Facilities/Physical Plant ... Mr. Doug LEAR
21 Accountant & Payroll Mgr ... Ms. Kathleen MAHONEY
96 Director of Purchasing ... Ms. Chere HALLETT-ADAMS
104 Director Study Abroad ... Ms. Patti VORFELD
13 Chief Info Technology Officer (CIO) ... Mr. Thomas MANLEY
04 Executive Asst to the President ... Ms. Heather RINGWALD

MCPHS-Manchester Campus (E)

1260 Elm Street, Manchester NH 03101
Telephone: (603) 314-0210 Identification: 770113
Accreditation: &EH, #ARCPA, PHAR

† Branch campus of MCPHS University, Boston, MA

New England College (F)

98 Bridge Street, Henniker NH 03242-3244
County: Merrimack FICE Identification: 002579
Unit ID: 182980
Telephone: (603) 428-2000 Carnegie Class: Masters/L
FAX Number: (603) 428-7230 Calendar System: Semester
URL: www.nec.edu
Established: 1946 Annual Undergrad Tuition & Fees: $35,952
Enrollment: 2,517 Coed
Affiliation or Control: Independent Non-Profit IRS Status: 501(c)3
Highest Offering: Doctorate
Accreditation: EH

01 President ... Dr. Michele D. PERKINS
05 VP of Academic Affairs ... Dr. Matt WOOD
84 VP of Enrollment ... Mr. Brad POZNANSKI
10 Sr Vice President/CFO ... Dr. Paula A. AMATO
08 Library Director ... Ms. Chelsea HANRAHAN
20 Assoc VP of Academic Effectiveness ... Dr. Nelly LEJTER
07 Director SGPS Admissions Operation ... Ms. Laura TREMBLAY
04 Admin Assistant to President ... Ms. Betsy MEDVETZ
13 VP for Information Technology ... Ms. Carol THOMAS
06 Registrar ... Ms. Beth DOWLING
37 Director Student Financial Svcs ... Ms. Kristen BLASE
21 Controller ... Ms. Carolyn MADDEN
36 Director Career/Life Planning ... Mr. Gene DURKEE
30 Associate VP of Development ... Ms. Meghan HALLOCK
26 Dir of Public Information ... Vacant
15 Human Resources Manager ... Ms. Julie GENDRON
102 Dir Corp & Foundation Relations ... Mr. Gregory PALMER
106 Exec Dir Enrollment SGPS ... Ms. Sarah WHITE
18 AVP of Capital and Facilities Mgmt ... Mr. Dan GEARAN
19 Director Campus Safety ... Mr. Scott LANE
28 Director of Diversity and Inclusion ... Mr. Lai-Monte HUNTER
39 Director Res Life & Student Housing ... Ms. Doreen LONG
41 Athletic Director ... Mr. Lou IZZI

New Hampshire Institute of Art (G)

148 Concord Street, Manchester NH 03104-4858
County: Hillsborough FICE Identification: 031823
Unit ID: 430810
Telephone: (603) 623-0313 Carnegie Class: Spec-4-yr-Arts
FAX Number: (603) 641-1832 Calendar System: Semester
URL: www.nhia.edu
Established: 1898 Annual Undergrad Tuition & Fees: $25,780
Enrollment: 452 Coed
Affiliation or Control: Independent Non-Profit IRS Status: 501(c)3
Highest Offering: Master's
Accreditation: EH, ART

01 President ... Mr. Kent DEVEREAUX
10 Vice President of Finance ... Ms. Leanna FLEMING
30 Vice President of Development ... Vacant
84 Vice President of Enrollment ... Mr. Jonathan LINDSAY
12 Sharon Arts Campus Director ... Ms. Camellia SOUSA
04 Executive Assistant to President ... Ms. Sara DADIAN PEREZ
05 Dean of Undergrad Studies ... Mr. Bill SCHAAF
58 Dean of Graduate Studies ... Ms. Lucinda BLISS
08 Library Director ... Ms. Betsy HOLMES
88 Director of Advising ... Ms. Tricia GIBBS
06 Registrar ... Ms. Karen GOSSELIN
20 Academic Affairs Administrator ... Ms. Claire SHEA
88 Bursar ... Vacant
32 Director of Student Affairs ... Ms. Michele TRACIA
37 Director Financial Aid ... Ms. Elayne PELOQUIN
31 Assoc Dean Community Education ... Mr. Chris ARCHER
15 Director of Human Resources ... Ms. Katrina KRAMER
21 Accounting Manager ... Ms. Nancy JORDAN
18 Facilities Director ... Mr. Paul GYMZIAK
13 Director Information Technologies ... Mr. John FALLAVOLLITA
38 Counselor ... Ms. Tanya POPOLOSKI
88 Academic Support Center Coordinator ... Ms. Kristen DRONEY

Northeast Catholic College (H)

511 Kearsarge Mountain Road, Warner NH 03278-4012
County: Merrimack FICE Identification: 022233
Unit ID: 182917
Telephone: (603) 456-2656 Carnegie Class: Bac/Assoc-Mixed
FAX Number: (603) 456-2660 Calendar System: Semester
URL: www.NortheastCatholic.edu
Established: 1973 Annual Undergrad Tuition & Fees: $22,000
Enrollment: 36 Coed
Affiliation or Control: Roman Catholic IRS Status: 501(c)3
Highest Offering: Baccalaureate
Accreditation: @EH

01 President ... Dr. George A. HARNE
05 Academic Dean ... Dr. Joe FORTE
10 Chief Operating Officer ... Mr. Daniel PETERSON
32 Dean of Students ... Ms. Maria JACOBS
07 Dir of Admissions/Communications ... Ms. Katie MOFFETT
37 Director Financial Aid/Librarian ... Mrs. Marie LASHER

Rivier University (I)

420 S Main Street, Nashua NH 03060-5086
County: Hillsborough FICE Identification: 002586
Unit ID: 183211
Telephone: (603) 888-1311 Carnegie Class: Masters/L
FAX Number: (603) 897-8811 Calendar System: Semester
URL: www.rivier.edu
Established: 1933 Annual Undergrad Tuition & Fees: $30,000
Enrollment: 2,599 Coed
Affiliation or Control: Roman Catholic IRS Status: 501(c)3
Highest Offering: Doctorate

Accreditation: EH, ADNUR, NUR

Code	Title	Name
01	President	Sr. Paula Marie BULEY
05	Vice President for Academic Affairs	Dr. Douglas HOWARD
10	Vice Pres Finance & Administration	Vacant
32	Vice President Student Affairs	Mr. Kurt STIMELING
84	Vice Pres Enrollment Management	Ms. Karen SCHEDIN
30	Vice Pres University Advancement	Ms. Karen COOPER
35	Asst Vice Pres Student Affairs	Ms. Paula RANDAZZA
13	Chief Information Officer	Ms. Heidi CROWELL
21	Controller	Ms. Jennifer YEOMANS
06	Registrar	Mr. Kevin GATELY
08	Library Director	Mr. Daniel SPEIDEL
36	Exec Dir Career Development Center	Ms. Patricia ANTONELLI
37	Director Student Financial Aid	Ms. Valerie PATNAUDE
15	Director Human Resources	Ms. Cheryl BAGTAZ
18	Director Facilities Management	Mr. Richard PERRINE
14	Director Instructional Computing	Sr. Martha VILLENEUVE
41	Athletic Director	Ms. Joanne MERRILL
42	Chaplain Campus Ministry	Bro. Paul DEMERS
28	Director Multicultural Affairs	Vacant
29	Dir Alumni Relations/Special Events	Ms. Joanne YOUNG
26	Director Marketing/Communication	Ms. Patricia GARRITY

Saint Anselm College (A)

100 Saint Anselm Drive, Manchester NH 03102-1310
County: Hillsborough
FICE Identification: 002587
Unit ID: 183239
Telephone: (603) 641-7000
Carnegie Class: Bac-A&S
FAX Number: (603) 641-7116
Calendar System: Semester
URL: www.anselm.edu
Established: 1889
Annual Undergrad Tuition & Fees: $39,036
Enrollment: 1,927
Coed
Affiliation or Control: Roman Catholic
IRS Status: 501(c)3
Highest Offering: Baccalaureate
Accreditation: EH, NURSE

Code	Title	Name
01	President	Dr. Steven R. DISALVO
05	Vice Pres Academic Affairs	Br. Isaac MURPHY, OSB
111	Sr VP College Advancement	Mr. James P. FLANAGAN
11	Vice President for Administration	Ms. Patricia SHUSTER
32	Vice President Student Affairs	Dr. Joseph M. HORTON
26	Exec Dir Col Comm & Mktg	Ms. Michelle ADAMS O'REGAN
10	Chief Financial Ofcr/Sr VP Finance	Vacant
06	Registrar	Fr. Benet PHILLIPS
07	Dean of Admissions/VP Enrollment	Mr. Eric NICHOLS
08	Librarian	Mr. Charles M. GETCHELL, JR.
37	Director of Financial Aid	Ms. Elizabeth KEUFFEL
35	Dean of Students	Dr. Alicia A. FINN
89	Dean of Freshmen	Dr. Anne E. HARRINGTON
66	Exec Director of Nursing	Dr. Maureen A. O'REILLY
04	Assistant to the President	Ms. Janet L. POIRIER
18	Director of Physical Plant	Mr. Donald MOREAU
23	Director of Health Services	Ms. Maura MARSHALL
29	Asst VP of Alum/Advanc Programming	Ms. Patrice RUSSELL
41	Director of Athletics	Mr. Daron MONTGOMERY
42	Director of Campus Ministry	Dr. Susan S. GABERT
09	Director of Institutional Research	Dr. Hui-Ling CHEN
13	Chief Information Officer	Mr. Adam R. ALBINA
15	Director Human Resources	Mr. David HARRINGTON
19	Director Security/Safety	Mr. Donald DAVIDSON
53	Director Education Planning	Dr. Laura WASIELEWSKI
28	Director Multicultural Center	Dr. Wayne CURRIE
39	Director Student Housing	Ms. Susan WEINTRAUB
96	Director of Purchasing	Mr. Jacques PLANTE
104	Assoc Dir Study Abroad	Ms. Sarah KEEFE
25	Dir Sponsored Programs & Research	Dr. William PLLOG
44	Asst VP Individual Giving	Mr. John DAVIS
86	Director Government Relations	Mr. Neil LEVESQUE
36	Director Student Placement	Mr. Samuel ALLEN

St. Joseph School of Nursing (B)

5 Woodward Avenue, Nashua NH 03060
County: Hillsborough
FICE Identification: 021404
Unit ID: 183248
Telephone: (603) 594-2567
Carnegie Class: Spec 2-yr-Health
FAX Number: (603) 578-5028
Calendar System: Semester
URL: www.sjson.edu
Established: 1908
Annual Undergrad Tuition & Fees: N/A
Enrollment: 123
Coed
Affiliation or Control: Independent Non-Profit
IRS Status: 501(c)3
Highest Offering: Associate Degree
Accreditation: ACCSC, ADNUR

Code	Title	Name
01	Dean	Vickie K. FIELER

Southern New Hampshire University (C)

2500 North River Road, Manchester NH 03106-1045
County: Hillsborough
FICE Identification: 002580
Unit ID: 183026
Telephone: (603) 626-9100
Carnegie Class: Masters/L
FAX Number: (603) 645-9665
Calendar System: Semester
URL: www.snhu.edu
Established: 1932
Annual Undergrad Tuition & Fees: $31,136
Enrollment: 61,285
Coed
Affiliation or Control: Independent Non-Profit
IRS Status: 501(c)3
Highest Offering: Doctorate
Accreditation: EH, ACBSP, CAEPT, NURSE

Code	Title	Name
00	Chairman Board of Trustees	Mr. Mark OUELLETTE
01	President	Dr. Paul LEBLANC
04	Director/Assistant to President	Ms. Lisa JENNINGS
03	EVP & Dean Engineering Tech	Mr. James SMITH
03	EVP University College Provost	Dr. Patricia LYNOTT
10	EVP & CFO Finance & Administration	Mr. Joseph SERGI
106	EVP Online	Ms. Amelia MANNING
111	SVP Institutional Advancement	Mr. Donald BREZINSKI
15	SVP Human Resources	Ms. Danielle STANTON
43	General Counsel/Secretary to Board	Ms. Yvette CLARK
13	SVP Technology & Transformation	Mr. Thomas DIONISIO
26	SVP External Affairs/Communications	Ms. Libby MAY
100	SVP/University Chief of Staff	Mr. William ZEMP
05	SVP & Chief Academic Officer	Dr. Kimberly BOGLE JUBINVILLE
103	SVP Workforce Partnerships	Mr. Scott DURAND
27	Chief Marketing Officer Online	Ms. Alana BURNS
28	Chief Diversity & Inclusion Officer	Ms. Jada HEBRA
46	Chief Innovation Officer	Dr. Michelle WEISE
05	Chief Academic Officer/VPAA Online	Dr. Gregory FOWLER
32	Chief Student Exp Officer Online	Ms. Jamie JAMES
14	Chief Operating Officer ITS	Mr. Daryl DREFFS
84	VP Enrollment Management	Mr. Gregg MAZZOLA
20	VP Academic Affairs	Mr. Michael EVANS
09	AVP Research & Planning	Mr. Thomas BERALDI, JR.
06	AVP & University Registrar	Ms. Deanna BECHARD
96	AVP Administration & Sourcing	Ms. Mary DUKAKIS
108	AVP Assessment	Mr. Alexandru MANUS
121	Dean of Student Success	Ms. Carey GLINES
32	Dean of Student Affairs	Ms. Heather LORENZ
49	Dean School of Arts & Sciences	Mr. Steven JOHNSON
53	Dean School of Education	Mr. Raymond MCNULTY
08	Dean of the Library	Mr. William MAYER
50	Dean School of Business	Vacant
88	Exec Director Online Business	Dr. Joseph CAPA
88	Exec Director Online Stem	Dr. Gwen BRITTON
88	Exec Director Online Business	Dr. Bruce STETAR
19	Assoc Dean/Dir of Public Safety	Mr. James WINN
29	Exec Director of Alumni Relations	Ms. Kristi DURETTE
36	Exec Dir Career Development Ctr	Ms. Beth PRIETO
85	Exec Dir Intl Student Services	Ms. Darbi ROBERTS
25	Director of Grants	Ms. Audrey MCLAUGHLIN
39	Director of Residence Life	Ms. Shannon BROWN
41	Director of Athletics	Mr. Anthony FALLACARO
42	Director of Campus Ministry	Rev. Bruce COLLARD
92	Director University Honors Program	Dr. Andrew MARTINO
31	Dir Community Engaged Learning	Ms. Elizabeth RICHARDS
07	Director of Transfer Admissions	Ms. Julie CALLAHAN
23	Director Wellness Center	Vacant
07	Director Freshman Admissions	Mr. Timothy WHITTUM
88	Director of Student Success Online	Ms. Theresa DIVER
88	Director of Learning Assessment	Dr. Randall CASE
88	Director of Academic Advising	Ms. Leah RICHARDS
88	Director of the Learning Center	Ms. Lori DECONINCK
22	Director of Disability Services	Mr. Dennis GREEN
104	Director Study Abroad	Mr. Stefano PARENTI
44	Director Annual Giving & Dev	Ms. Lisa ST. HILAIRE
86	Director Government Affairs	Ms. Lauren THOMPSON STARKS
37	Special Assistant Financial Aid	Mr. Michael MOORE

The Thomas More College of Liberal Arts (D)

6 Manchester Street, Merrimack NH 03054-4805
County: Hillsborough
FICE Identification: 030431
Unit ID: 183275
Telephone: (603) 880-8308
Carnegie Class: Bac-A&S
FAX Number: (603) 880-9280
Calendar System: Semester
URL: www.thomasmorecollege.edu
Established: 1978
Annual Undergrad Tuition & Fees: $20,400
Enrollment: 87
Coed
Affiliation or Control: Independent Non-Profit
IRS Status: 501(c)3
Highest Offering: Baccalaureate
Accreditation: EH

Code	Title	Name
01	President	Dr. William E. FAHEY
30	Vice Pres Institutional Advancement	Mr. Paul JACKSON
05	Academic Dean	Dr. Walter THOMPSON
32	Dean of Students	Mr. Denis KITZINGER
44	Director Institutional Advancement	Mr. Paul JACKSON
10	Director of Business	Ms. Pamela BERNSTEIN
35	Director of Student Life	Dr. Sara KITZINGER
04	Executive Asst President's Office	Ms. Valerie BURGESS
06	Registrar	Ms. Pamela BERNSTEIN
07	Director of Admissions	Mr. Jonathan RENSCH

*University System of New Hampshire (E)

5 Chenell Drive, Suite 301, Concord NH 03301
County: Merrimack
FICE Identification: 008027
Unit ID: 183327
Telephone: (603) 862-1800
Carnegie Class: N/A
FAX Number: (603) 862-0908
URL: usnh.edu

Code	Title	Name
01	Chancellor	Dr. Todd J. LEACH
10	Vice Chanc Fin Affs & Treasurer	Ms. Catherine A. PROVENCHER
43	General Counsel	Mr. Ronald F. RODGERS
09	Dir of Institutional Research	Ms. Heidi HEDEGARD
15	Chief Human Resource Officer	Mr. James MCGRAIL

*University of New Hampshire (F)

105 Main Street, Durham NH 03824
County: Strafford
FICE Identification: 002589
Unit ID: 183044
Telephone: (603) 862-1234
Carnegie Class: DU-Higher
FAX Number: N/A
Calendar System: Semester
URL: www.unh.edu
Established: 1866
Annual Undergrad Tuition & Fees (In-State): $17,624
Enrollment: 15,351
Coed
Affiliation or Control: State
IRS Status: 501(c)3
Highest Offering: Doctorate
Accreditation: EH, ACFEI, CAATE, CAEP, CAEPT, CARTE, CS, DIETD, DIETI, ENG, ENGT, IPSY, LAW, MFCD, MT, MUS, NRPA, NURSE, OT, PH, SP, SW

Code	Title	Name
02	President	Dr. Mark W. HUDDLESTON
100	Chief of Staff	Ms. Megan W. DAVIS
05	Prov & VP Academic Affairs	Dr. Nancy M. TARGETT
10	VP Finance/Administration	Mr. Christopher D. CLEMENT
84	VP Enrollment Management	Ms. Victoria J. DUTCHER
46	Sr Vice Provost Research	Dr. Jane A. NISBET
26	Assoc VP Univ Communications	Mr. Joel R. SELIGMAN
43	General Counsel	Mr. Ronald F. RODGERS
20	Assoc Prov Academic Administration	Ms. Leigh Anne MELANSON
28	Assoc VP Cmty/Equity/Diversity	Ms. Jamie NOLAN
20	Sr Vice Prov Academic Affairs	Dr. Palligarnai T. VASUDEVAN
15	Assoc VP/Chief HR Officer	Ms. Kathleen A. NEILS
20	Asst Prov Acad Adm/MPA Program Dir	Mr. James S. VARN
88	Sr VProv Engagement & Acad Outreach	Dr. Julie E. WILLIAMS
21	Assoc VP for Finance	Ms. Kerry SCALA
13	Asst VP Enterprise Computing	Mr. William HALL
40	Manager of UNH Bookstore	Ms. Karen MCLAUGHLIN
16	Asst VP Human Resources	Ms. Sari M. BENNETT
21	Assoc VP Business Affairs	Mr. David J. MAY
18	Assoc VP Facilities	Mr. William P. JANELLE
32	Dean of Students	Dr. John T. KIRKPATRICK
35	Int Director Residential Life	Ms. Ruth ABELMANN
23	Director Health Services	Dr. Kevin E. CHARLES
25	Dir Sponsored Programs	Mr. Victor SOSA
30	VP Advancement	Ms. Deborah DUTTON COX
47	Dean Life Sciences/Agriculture	Dr. Jon M. WRAITH
49	Dean Liberal Arts	Dr. Heidi L. BOSTIC
50	Dean Paul College of Business	Dr. Deborah MERRILL-SANDS
58	Int Dean Graduate School	Dr. Cari A. MOORHEAD
76	Dean Health & Human Services	Dr. Michael FERRARA
54	Dean Engineer/Physical Sci	Dr. Wayne JONES, JR.
61	Dean UNH School of Law	Ms. Megan CARPENTER
12	Dean UNH at Manchester	Dr. Michael P. DECELLE
08	Dean University Library	Dr. Tara Lynn FULTON
56	Dean/Dir Cooperative Extension	Dr. Ken LAVALLEY
88	Dir Thompson School Appl Science	Dr. Regina A. SMICK-ATTISANO
22	Dir Affirmative Action & Equity	Ms. Donna Marie SORRENTINO
07	Director Admissions	Mr. Robert P H. MCGANN
06	Registrar	Mr. Andrew COLBY
37	Dir Financial Aid	Mr. Joel B. CARSTENS
41	Dir Intercollegiate Athletics	Mr. Martin SCARANO
38	Dir Counseling Center	Dr. David CROSS
102	Dir Finance & Operations UNH Found	Mr. Erik GROSS
39	Dir Housing/Conf Services	Ms. Kathy IRLA-CHESNEY
19	Asst VP Public Safety & Risk Mgt	Chief Paul M. DEAN
85	Dir Intl Students & Scholars	Ms. Leila L. PAJE-MANALO
42	University Chaplain	Pastor Larry BRICKNER-WOOD
96	Dir Purchasing & Contract Svcs	Ms. Denise M. SMITH
92	Dir Honors Program	Dr. Jerry MARX
09	Dir Inst Research & Assessment	Dr. Yun XIANG
88	Dir Writing Program	Dr. Edward A. MUELLER
104	Dir Center International Education	Dr. Claire L. MALARTE-FELDMAN
94	Coord Women's Studies Program	Dr. Marla B. BRETTSCHNEIDER
27	Asst VP Public Relations	Mr. Mica STARK
90	Dir Academic Technology	Ms. Terri WINTERS
04	Sr Admin Asst to President	Ms. Annie JONES

*Granite State College (G)

25 Hall Street, Concord NH 03301-7317
County: Merrimack
FICE Identification: 031013
Unit ID: 183257
Telephone: (603) 228-3000
Carnegie Class: Bac-Diverse
FAX Number: (603) 513-1389
Calendar System: Quarter
URL: www.granite.edu
Established: 1972
Annual Undergrad Tuition & Fees (In-State): $7,425
Enrollment: 2,179
Coed
Affiliation or Control: State
IRS Status: 501(c)3
Highest Offering: Master's
Accreditation: EH, CAEPT, NURSE

Code	Title	Name
02	President	Dr. Mark RUBINSTEIN
05	Provost/VP Academic Affairs	Dr. Scott A. STANLEY
10	VP Finance & Administration	Ms. Lisa L. SHAWNEY
84	VP Enrollment Management	Ms. Tara PAYNE
53	Dean of School of Education	Mr. Nick MARKS
20	Vice Provost for Academic Affairs	Dr. Carole BEAUCHEMIN
20	Vice Provost for Academic Afairs	Dr. Johnna A. HERRICK-PHELPS
24	Director of Educational Technology	Ms. Reta CHAFFEE
08	Assistant Dean of Library Services	Ms. Patricia ERWIN-PLOOG
04	Administrative Asst to Provost	Ms. Susan L. ORR
13	Chief Information Officer	Mr. Kenneth WHITELAW
15	Director of Human Resources	Ms. Maggie HYNDMAN

21 Director of Financial Operations .... Mr. Steve PERROTTA
113 Bursar .... Ms. Jodi WOLBERT
18 Dir of Facilities/Safety/Sustain .... Mr. Peter CONKLIN
07 Director of Admissions Operations .... Ms. Christine WILLIAMS
121 Director of Advising .... Ms. Nicole HORNE
37 Director Student Financial Aid .... Mr. Mac BRODERICK
36 Director of Career Services .... Ms. Jan COVILLE
06 Registrar .... Ms. Kristin MULLANEY
09 Director of Institutional Research .... Mr. Jim MILLER
108 Dir Inst Effectiveness/Compliance .... Mr. Todd SLOVER
124 Director of Student Affairs .... Ms. Tiffany DOHERTY

*Keene State College (A)

229 Main Street, Keene NH 03435-0001

County: Cheshire | FICE Identification: 002590 | Unit ID: 183062

Telephone: (603) 352-1909 | Carnegie Class: Masters/S

FAX Number: (603) 358-2257 | Calendar System: Semester

URL: www.keene.edu

Established: 1909 | Annual Undergrad Tuition & Fees (In-State): $13,613

Enrollment: 4,383 | Coed

Affiliation or Control: State | IRS Status: 501(c)3

Highest Offering: Master's

Accreditation: EH, CAATE, CAEPN, DIETD, DIETI, MUS, NURSE

02 Interim President .... Dr. Melinda TREADWELL
05 Provost/VP Academic Affairs .... Mr. William SEIGH
32 VP Student Affairs & Enroll Mgmt .... Dr. Kemal ATKINS
10 VP Finance & Administration .... Vacant
100 Chief of Staff .... Ms. Kathleen WILLIAMS
04 Executive Assoc to the President .... Ms. Cindy KRAUTWURST
35 Dean of Students .... Dr. Gail ZIMMERMAN
08 Dean of Library .... Dr. Celia E. RABINOWITZ
07 Director of Admissions .... Ms. Margaret RICHMOND
06 Registrar .... Mr. Thomas RICHARD
13 Chief Information Officer .... Ms. Laura SERAICHICK
15 AVP Human Resources .... Vacant
26 AVP Marketing & Comm .... Ms. Kathleen WILLIAMS
111 AVP Constituent Relations .... Mr. Rod MILLER
84 AVP for Enrollment Management .... Mr. Steven A. GOETSCH
18 Director Physical Plant .... Mr. Frank MAZZOLA
39 Director of Residential Life .... Mr. Kent DRAKE-DEESE
21 AVP for Finance .... Vacant
09 AVP Inst Effectiveness & IR .... Vacant
29 Dir for Engagement of Alumni .... Ms. Sara BARRETT
38 Director Student Counseling .... Dr. Brian QUIGLEY
96 Campus Purchasing Director .... Ms. Renee HARLOW
81 Dean of Sciences .... Dr. Gordon LEVERSEE
58 Dean of Prof/Graduate Studies .... Dr. Karrie KALICH
58 Dean of Prof/Graduate Studies .... Ms. Anne MILLER
79 Interim Dean Arts & Humanities .... Dr. Kirsti SANDY
28 AVP Inst Diversity & Equity .... Dr. Dottie MORRIS

*Plymouth State University (B)

17 High Street, Plymouth NH 03264-1595

County: Grafton | FICE Identification: 002591 | Unit ID: 183080

Telephone: (603) 535-5000 | Carnegie Class: Masters/L

FAX Number: (603) 535-2654 | Calendar System: Semester

URL: www.plymouth.edu

Established: 1871 | Annual Undergrad Tuition & Fees (In-State): $13,472

Enrollment: 5,120 | Coed

Affiliation or Control: State | IRS Status: 501(c)3

Highest Offering: Doctorate

Accreditation: EH, ACBSP, ART, #CAATE, CACREP, CAEPN, NURSE, @PTA, SW

02 President .... Dr. Donald L. BIRX
10 VP for Finance & Administration .... Ms. Tracy L. CLAYBAUGH
32 Interim VP Student Affairs .... Mr. Mark J. FISCHLER
05 Assoc VP Undergraduate Studies .... Dr. David ZEHR
111 VP for University Advancement .... Ms. Paula L. HOBSON
13 Chief Info Ofcr .... Mr. Richard G. GROSSMAN
84 Dean Enroll Mgmt/Dir Admissions .... Mr. Jason MORAN
39 Dir Res Life/Housing/Conf Svcs .... Vacant
35 Dean of Students .... Mr. Jeffrey C. FURLONE
09 Dir Institutional Research .... Vacant
06 Interim Registrar .... Dr. Stacey L. CURDIE
08 Int Dean Library/Academic Support .... Ms. Elaine ALLARD
29 Director of Alumni Relations .... Mr. Rodney EKSTROM
37 Director of Financial Aid .... Ms. Crystal GAFF
15 Director of Human Resources .... Ms. Caryn L. INES
19 Dir Public Safety and Emer Planning . Mr. Steven H. TEMPERINO
41 Athletic Director .... Ms. Kim M. BOWNES
18 Director of Physical Plant .... Ms. Ellen SHIPPEE
38 Dir of Counseling/Human Rel Center .... Mr. Robert G. HLASNY
40 Bookstore Manager .... Mr. Steve RHEAUME
26 Interim Chief Public Rels/Marketing .. Mr. Marlin COLLINGWOOD

NEW JERSEY

Assumption College for Sisters (C)

200A Morris Avenue, Denville NJ 07834

County: Morris | FICE Identification: 002595 | Unit ID: 183600

Telephone: (973) 957-0188 | Carnegie Class: Assoc/HT-High Trad

FAX Number: (973) 957-0190 | Calendar System: Semester

URL: www.acs350.org

Established: 1953 | Annual Undergrad Tuition & Fees: $5,544

Enrollment: 31 | Female

Affiliation or Control: Roman Catholic | IRS Status: 501(c)3

Highest Offering: Associate Degree

Accreditation: M

01 President/Chief of Development .... Sr. Joseph SPRING, SCC
05 Academic Dean .... Sr. Teresa BRUNO, SC
10 Treasurer/Institutional Advancement .... Mrs. Patricia MCGRADY
32 Chief Student Life Officer .... Sr. Marie Cecelia LANDIS, SCC
06 Registrar .... Mrs. Barbara KELLY-VERGONA

Atlantic Cape Community College (D)

5100 Black Horse Pike, Mays Landing NJ 08330-2699

County: Atlantic | FICE Identification: 002596 | Unit ID: 183655

Telephone: (609) 343-4900 | Carnegie Class: Assoc/HT-High Trad

FAX Number: (609) 343-4917 | Calendar System: Semester

URL: www.atlantic.edu

Established: 1964 | Annual Undergrad Tuition & Fees (In-District): $4,407

Enrollment: 6,361 | Coed

Affiliation or Control: State/Local | IRS Status: 501(c)3

Highest Offering: Associate Degree

Accreditation: M, ACFEI, ADNUR

01 President .... Dr. Barbara GABA
03 Executive Vice President .... Dr. Richard PERNICIARO
15 Dean Human Resources & Compliance ... Ms. Eileen CURRISTINE
11 Dean Administration and Business .... Mr. August DAQUILA
100 Dean Res Dev/Pres & BOT Operations .... Ms. Jean MCALISTER
13 Dean Information Tech Services .... Mr. Douglas HEDGES
05 Vice President Academic Affairs .... Dr. Otto HERNANDEZ
10 Dean Finance .... Ms. Leslie JAMISON
32 Vice President Student Affairs .... Dr. Mitchell LEVY
08 Assoc Dean Academic Support Svcs .... Ms. Janet MARLER
49 Interim Dean Liberal Studies .... Dr. Denise COULTER
88 Dean Academy of Culinary Arts .... Ms. Kelly MCCLAY
75 Dean Career Education .... Ms. Donna VASSALLO
81 Dean STEM .... Mr. Ravi MANIMARAN
26 Director College Relations .... Ms. Stacey CLAPP
121 Director Counseling & Support Svcs .... Ms. Paula DAVIS
37 Director Financial Aid .... Ms. Linda DESANTIS
07 Director Admissions .... Ms. Kristin JACKSON
96 Director Business Services .... Ms. Dorie KEENER
30 Sr Director Res Dev/Alumni Outreach .... Ms. Maria KELLETT
09 Director Inst Research Plng/Assess .... Mr. Luis MONTEFUSCO
06 Registrar .... Ms. Heather PETERSON
35 Dir Student Dev & Judicial Officer .... Ms. Nancy PORFIDO
18 Director Facilities Management .... Mr. Russell WAUGH

Bais Medrash Mayan Hatorah (E)

101 Milton Street, Lakewood NJ 08701

County: Ocean | Identification: 667280

Telephone: (732) 367-9900 | Carnegie Class: Not Classified

FAX Number: N/A | Calendar System: Other

Established: | Annual Undergrad Tuition & Fees: N/A

Enrollment: N/A | Male

Affiliation or Control: Independent Non-Profit | IRS Status: 501(c)3

Highest Offering: First Talmudic Degree

Accreditation: AIJS

Bais Medrash Toras Chesed (F)

910 Monmouth Avenue, Lakewood NJ 08701-1921

County: Ocean | FICE Identification: 040813 | Unit ID: 449658

Telephone: (732) 364-1220 | Carnegie Class: Spec-4-yr-Faith

FAX Number: (732) 886-2323 | Calendar System: Semester

Established: 1999 | Annual Undergrad Tuition & Fees: $9,350

Enrollment: 104 | Male

Affiliation or Control: Independent Non-Profit | IRS Status: 501(c)3

Highest Offering: Baccalaureate

Accreditation: RABN

01 Dean .... Rabbi N. STEIN
37 Director of Financial Aid .... Mrs. H. WEISS

Bais Medrash Zicron Meir (G)

1500 Vermont Ave, Lakewood NJ 08701

County: Ocean | Identification: 667259

Telephone: (732) 370-1560 | Carnegie Class: Not Classified

FAX Number: (732) 363-7864 | Calendar System: Semester

Established: 2013 | Annual Undergrad Tuition & Fees: N/A

Enrollment: N/A | Male

Affiliation or Control: Independent Non-Profit | IRS Status: 501(c)3

Highest Offering: First Talmudic Degree

Accreditation: @RABN

01 CEO .... Zev MINTZ
10 CFO .... Nissim BASALA
37 Dir Student Financial Aid/Registrar .... Shimshon AMSEL

Bard High School Early College Newark (H)

321 Bergen Street, Newark NJ 07103

Telephone: (973) 733-8363 | Identification: 770980

Accreditation: &EH

† Branch campus of Bard College at Simon's Rock, Great Barrington, MA

Bergen Community College (I)

400 Paramus Road, Paramus NJ 07652-1595

County: Bergen | FICE Identification: 004736 | Unit ID: 183743

Telephone: (201) 447-7100 | Carnegie Class: Assoc/HT-High Trad

FAX Number: (201) 447-9042 | Calendar System: Semester

URL: www.bergen.edu

Established: 1965 | Annual Undergrad Tuition & Fees (In-District): $4,362

Enrollment: 14,585 | Coed

Affiliation or Control: State/Local | IRS Status: 501(c)3

Highest Offering: Associate Degree

Accreditation: M, ADNUR, COARC, DH, DMS, EMT, MAC, RAD, RTT, SURGT

01 Interim President .... Dr. Michael REDMOND
05 Vice President of Academic Affairs .... Dr. William MULLANEY
32 Vice President Student Services .... Dr. Waldon HAGAN
09 Vice Pres of Inst Effectiveness .... Dr. Yun KIM
50 Dean Business/Arts/Social Science .... Dr. Victor BROWN
79 Dean of Humanities .... Dr. Beatrice BRIDGLALL
76 Dean Health Professions .... Dr. Susan BARNARD
81 Dean Science/Math & Technology .... Dr. Pascal J. RICATTO
51 Dean of Continuing Education .... Ms. Christine GILLESPIE
08 Dean Library Services .... Mr. David MARKS
35 Dean of Student Affairs at Ciarco . Ms. Denise JERMAN LIGUORI
121 Dean of Student Support Services .... Ms. Jennifer REYES
15 Executive Director Human Resources .... Mr. James MILLER
18 Actg Mnging Director Physical Plant .... Mr. Samuel JOHN
19 VP Facil Opers/Plng & Pub Safety .... Mr. William CORCORAN
13 Executive Dir of Info Technology .... Mr. Stephen VALKENBURG
06 Mnging Dir Registration & Records .... Ms. Jacqueline OTTEY
31 Director of Community/Cultural Affs .... Mr. Peter LEDONNE
101 Exec Asst Board of Trustees/Pres .... Ms. Maria FERRARA
29 Managing Director of Alumni Affairs .... Vacant
37 Mnging Dir Fin Ops/Stdnt Assistance .... Ms. Caroline OFODILE
102 Exec Dir Foundation/Development .... Vacant
25 Dir Grants Admin/Inst Effectiveness .... Dr. William YAKOWICZ
96 Director of Purchasing & Services .... Ms. Barbara HAMILTON-GOLDEN
26 Managing Dir of Public Relations .... Mr. Lawrence HLAVENKA
04 Exec Assistant to the President .... Dr. Ursula DANIELS

Berkeley College (J)

44 Rifle Camp Road, Woodland Park NJ 07424-3367

County: Passaic | FICE Identification: 007502 | Unit ID: 183789

Telephone: (973) 278-5400 | Carnegie Class: Spec-4-yr-Bus

FAX Number: (973) 278-0282 | Calendar System: Semester

URL: www.berkeleycollege.edu

Established: 1931 | Annual Undergrad Tuition & Fees: $24,050

Enrollment: 3,842 | Coed

Affiliation or Control: Proprietary | IRS Status: Proprietary

Highest Offering: Master's

Accreditation: M, CIDA, IACBE, MAC, SURGT

00 Chairman of the Board .... Mr. Kevin L. LUING
01 President .... Mr. Michael J. SMITH
04 Special Assistant to the President .... Dr. Rose Mary HEALY
05 Provost .... Dr. Beth CASTIGLIA
84 Executive VP .... Mr. Tim LUING
10 VP Finance .... Mr. Dino KASAMIS
58 Dean School of Graduate Studies .... Dr. Chris GREVESEN
32 Senior VP Student Success .... Ms. Diane RECINOS
88 VP Information Analytics .... Mr. Brian MAHER
43 VP & Chief Compliance Officer .... Mr. William BRANDT
26 VP Marketing .... Mr. William DIMASI
13 Chief Information Officer .... Mr. Leonard DE BOTTON
86 Senior VP Government Relations NJ .... Ms. Teri DUDA
35 VP Student Development/Campus Life .... Dr. Dallas REED
08 VP Library Services .... Ms. Marlene DOTY
36 VP Career Services .... Ms. Amy SORICELLI
37 VP Financial Aid .... Mr. Howard LESLIE
114 VP Budget & Student Accounts .... Ms. Eileen LOFTUS-BERLIN
85 Senior VP International Division .... Ms. Cynthia C. MARCHESE
106 Dean Online .... Dr. Joseph SCURALLI
20 Associate Provost Faculty Affairs .... Dr. Judith KORNBERG
50 Dean School of Business .... Dr. Elana ZOLFO
76 Dean School Health Studies .... Dr. Eva SKUKA
49 Dean School of Liberal Arts .... Dr. Don KIEFFER
107 Dean School of Professional Studies .... Dr. Michael MCATEER
88 Dean Developmental Education .... Dr. Gerald IACULLO
121 Assistant VP Academic Advisement .... Mr. Joseph GIUFFRE
06 Registrar .... Ms. Deborah PALICIA
123 Director Graduate Admissions .... Mr. Michael LINCOLN
108 AVP Institutional Effectiveness .... Vacant
31 VP Communications & Ext Relations .. Ms. Angela HARRINGTON
19 AVP Public Safety .... Mr. Robert MAGUIRE
27 Director Media Relations .... Ms. Ilene GREENFIELD
119 Info Systems Security Manager .... Mr. Steven BECKER
41 Director Athletics .... Mr. Andrew DESTEPHANO
29 AVP Career Services Alumni Relation .... Mr. Michael IRIS
09 Director of Institutional Research .... Ms. Rebecca J. DRENNEN

Beth Medrash Govoha (K)

617 Sixth Street, Lakewood NJ 08701-2797

County: Ocean | FICE Identification: 007947 | Unit ID: 183804

Telephone: (732) 367-1060 | Carnegie Class: Spec-4-yr-Faith

FAX Number: (732) 367-7487 | Calendar System: Semester

URL: www.yeshivanotices.org

Established: 1943 | Annual Undergrad Tuition & Fees: N/A

Enrollment: 6,579 | Male

Affiliation or Control: Independent Non-Profit IRS Status: 501(c)3
Highest Offering: Beyond Master's But Less Than Doctorate
Accreditation: RABN

01 President/Chief Executive Officer ... Rabbi Aaron KOTLER
05 Chairman Academic Council ... Rabbi A. Malkiel KOTLER
10 Chief Financial Officer ... Mr. Isaac LEVINE
43 VP Finance/Corporate/Legal Affairs ... Rabbi Eli KUPERMAN
11 Vice President Admin/Campus Life ... Rabbi Yitzchok S. KOTLER
33 Dean of Students ... Rabbi Mattisyahu SALOMON
58 Dean of Graduate Studies ... Rabbi Yisroel NEUMAN
30 Vice President of Fundraising ... Rabbi Mordechai HERSKOWITZ
86 Director Government Affairs ... Mrs. Chanie JACOBOWITZ
06 Registrar ... Rabbi Jacob BURSZTYN
07 Director of Admissions ... Rabbi Avraham FEUER
08 Director Library/Research Programs ... Rabbi Benjamin SPIEGEL
36 Director of Placement ... Rabbi Moshe ROCKOVE
39 Director of Residence Halls ... Rabbi Avrohom COLMAN

Bloomfield College (A)

467 Franklin Street, Bloomfield NJ 07003-3425
County: Essex FICE Identification: 002597
Unit ID: 183822
Telephone: (973) 748-9000 Carnegie Class: Bac-A&S
FAX Number: (973) 743-3998 Calendar System: Semester
URL: www.bloomfield.edu
Established: 1868 Annual Undergrad Tuition & Fees: $28,600
Enrollment: 1,980 Coed
Affiliation or Control: Presbyterian Church (U.S.A.) IRS Status: 501(c)3
Highest Offering: Master's
Accreditation: M, CAEPT, NURSE

01 President ... Richard A. LEVAO
10 Vice Pres of Finance/Admin ... Howard BUXBAUM
04 Administrative Asst to President ... Christina NOLAN
05 Vice President Academic Affairs ... Tresmaine GRIMES
84 VP Enrollment Management/Admission ... Adam CASTRO
32 VP Student Affairs/Dean of Students ... Patrick J. LAMY
111 VP for Advancement ... Jacqueline BARTLEY
107 VP Inst Intl Training/Prof Studies ... Peter JEONG
21 AVP for Finance and Administration ... William A. MCDONALD
06 Registrar and Director of Advising ... Annette RAYMOND
09 Director Inst Research/Assessment ... Eugene W. MULLER
20 Associate Dean for Faculty ... Carolyn I. SPIES
79 Chair Div of Humanities ... Brandon FRALIX
83 Chair Div Social/Behavioral Science ... Daniel SKINNER
66 Chair Div of Nursing ... Neddie SERRA
81 Chair Div of Natural Science/Math ... Jim MURPHY
57 Chair Div Creative Arts Technology ... Yuichiro NISHIZAWA
50 Chair Div Accounting/Business/CIS ... Robert COLLMIER
53 Chair Div of Education ... Amy EGUCHI
08 Library Director ... Mark JACKSON
13 Director Enterprise Tech Services ... Andrew GERSTMAYR
36 Director of Career Services ... Rachel M. JACKIEWICZ
37 Director of Financial Aid ... Breanne SIMKIN
35 Associate Dean Student Development ... Rose MITCHELL
15 Assoc Director Human Resources ... Susan DACEY
18 Supervisor of Buildings & Grounds ... Jack V. MCGRANE
07 Coord Intl Admissions/Student Svcs ... Jamilah MOUDIAB
38 Director Personal Counseling ... Nicole PALAGANO
26 Director Public Rels/Advancemnt Mkt ... Alicia COOK
42 Int Dir Spirtual Life/Col Chaplain ... Rev. Terri OFORI
88 Director Teacher Education ... Mary PORCELLI
41 Director of Athletics ... Sheila WOOTEN
121 Director Center Academic Develop ... Heather SHPIRO
19 Director of Security ... Jack CORTEZ
39 Director Res Educ & Housing ... Nicole FAISON
105 Webmaster ... Miguel RODRIGUEZ
24 Director of Media Center ... Barbara ISACSON
14 Director Institutional Technology ... Yifeng BAI
40 Store Manager ... Elizabeth MCLEOD

Brookdale Community College (B)

Newman Springs Road, Lincroft NJ 07738-1597
County: Monmouth FICE Identification: 008404
Unit ID: 183859
Telephone: (732) 842-1900 Carnegie Class: Assoc/HT-Mix Trad/Non
FAX Number: (732) 224-2242 Calendar System: Other
URL: www.brookdalecc.edu
Established: 1967 Annual Undergrad Tuition & Fees (In-District): $3,861
Enrollment: 13,835 Coed
Affiliation or Control: State/Local IRS Status: 501(c)3
Highest Offering: Associate Degree
Accreditation: M, ACFEI, ADNUR, CAHIIM, COARC, CSHSE, #RAD

01 Interim President ... Dr. David STOUT
05 Vice President for Learning ... Dr. Matthew REED
10 Int Executive Director of Finance ... Mr. Joseph PINGITORE
46 Vice Pres Plng/Dev/Govt & Comm Rels ... Vacant
32 Int Vice Pres of Student Success ... Dr. Herbert COHEN
15 Dean Human Resources ... Ms. Patricia SENSI
08 Executive Director Library ... Dr. William BURNS
45 Dean Plng & Institutional Effective ... Dr. Nancy KEGELMAN
27 Dir Communications & Public Rels ... Ms. Avis MCMILLON
102 Exec Dir Foundation/Alumni Affs ... Mr. Timothy ZEISS
124 Dir of Student Engagement ... Mr. Robert QUINONES
37 Director of Financial Aid ... Ms. Stephanie FITZSIMMONS
25 Director Grants & Institutional Dev ... Ms. Laura V. QAISSAUNEE
38 Director Student Services ... Dr. Stephen A. CURTO
06 Registrar ... Ms. Kimberly HEUSER
09 Dir of Institutional Research/Evalu ... Dr. Laura LONGO
26 Dir of Marketing/Creative Services ... Ms. Laurie BENDER
28 Mgr Diversity/Inclusion/Compliance ... Ms. Sondra CANNON
103 Dir Workforce/Career Development ... Mr. Dominic LATORRACA
104 Director Study Abroad ... Ms. Janice THOMAS
13 Inter Chief Info Tech Officer (CIO) ... Mr. George SOTIRION
19 Director Security/Safety ... Mr. Robert KIMLER
41 Athletic Director ... Mr. Shawn NOEL
50 Dean Business & Social Science ... Ms. Patricia GALLO
81 Dean of STEM ... Dr. Anoop AHLUWALIA
04 Administrative Asst to President ... Ms. Cynthia GRUSKOS
11 Interim Dir of Operations ... Mr. Robert FRANCIS
18 Chief Facilities/Physical Plant ... Mr. Timothy DRURY
29 Exec Dir Foundation & Alumni Affair ... Mr. Timothy ZEISS

Brookdale Community College Western Monmouth Branch Campus (C)

3680 US Highway 9 South, Freehold NJ 07728
Telephone: (732) 780-0020 Identification: 770125
Accreditation: &M

Caldwell University (D)

120 Bloomfield Avenue, Caldwell NJ 07006-5310
County: Essex FICE Identification: 002598
Unit ID: 183910
Telephone: (973) 618-3000 Carnegie Class: Masters/M
FAX Number: (973) 618-3300 Calendar System: Semester
URL: www.caldwell.edu
Established: 1939 Annual Undergrad Tuition & Fees: $32,650
Enrollment: 2,138 Coed
Affiliation or Control: Roman Catholic IRS Status: 501(c)3
Highest Offering: Doctorate
Accreditation: M, ACBSP, CACREP, CAEPT, NURSE

01 President ... Dr. Nancy BLATTNER
05 Vice President for Academic Affairs ... Dr. Barbara CHESLER
15 VP Institutional Effectiveness ... Mrs. Sheila N. O'ROURKE
32 Vice President for Student Affairs ... Sr. Kathleen TUITE
84 Senior Vice President ... Mr. Joseph J. POSILLICO
30 Vice Pres Development/Alumni Affs ... Mr. Kevin BOYLE
50 Associate Dean Business Division ... Dr. Bernard C. O'ROURKE
53 Associate Dean Education Division ... Dr. Joan MORIARTY
85 Director International Student Svcs ... Mr. Maulin JOSHI
110 Director Development ... Ms. Beth GORAB
112 Director of Gift Planning ... Ms. Kathleen BUSE
06 University Registrar ... Mr. Ian K. WHITE
08 Head Librarian ... Ms. Ellen JOHNSTON
07 Asst Vice President Enrollment ... Mr. Stephen QUINN
58 Director Graduate Studies ... Dr. Ellina CHERNOBILSKY
38 Director of Counseling ... Ms. Robin DAVENPORT
39 Director Residence Llfe ... Ms. Crystal LOPEZ
13 Exec Director Information Tech ... Mr. Donald O'HAGAN
36 Dir Career Plng & Development ... Ms. Geraldine PERRET
37 Director Financial Aid ... Ms. Eileen FELSKE
41 Asst Vice Pres & Dir of Athletics ... Mr. Mark A. CORINO
26 Dir Media Relations and Advertising ... Ms. Colette LIDDY
19 Director Campus Safety ... Mr. Glenn GATES
91 Director Administrative Technology ... Mr. David BOHNY
16 Director of Human Resources ... Mrs. Michelle STAUSS
35 Director Student Engagement ... Mr. Timothy KESSLER-CLEARY
106 Dir Online Education/E-learning ... Ms. Soheila KOBLER
04 Administrative Asst to President ... Ms. Sharon KIEVIT
09 Director of Institutional Research ... Ms. Susan HAYES
121 Director of Advising ... Ms. Henrieta GENFI
102 Dir Foundation/Corporate Relations ... Ms. Pat LEVINS
105 Director Web Services ... Mr. Anthony YANG
42 Director of Campus Ministry ... Ms. Colleen O'BRIEN

Camden County College (E)

PO Box 200, Blackwood NJ 08012-0200
County: Camden FICE Identification: 006865
Unit ID: 183938
Telephone: (856) 227-7200 Carnegie Class: Assoc/HT-Mix Trad/Non
FAX Number: (856) 374-4894 Calendar System: Semester
URL: www.camdencc.edu
Established: 1967 Annual Undergrad Tuition & Fees (In-District): $4,320
Enrollment: 11,263 Coed
Affiliation or Control: State/Local IRS Status: 501(c)3
Highest Offering: Associate Degree
Accreditation: M, CAHIIM, DA, DH, DIETT, OPD

01 President ... Mr. Donald BORDEN
05 Interim Vice Pres Academic Affairs ... Dr. Arthur WEXLER
84 Exec Dean Enrollment/Student Svcs ... Dr. James CANONICA
10 Exec Dir Finance & Planning ... Ms. Helen ANTONAKAKIS
11 Exec Dir Financial Admin Svcs ... Mr. Maris KUKAINIS
15 Executive Director Human Resources ... Ms. Kathleen KANE
06 Dir Student System Records ... Ms. Bunny KOHL
08 Asst Director Library Services ... Ms. Isabel GRAY
37 Director of Financial Aid ... Ms. Felicia BRYANT
88 Director of Testing ... Mr. Daniel MCMASTERS
108 Ex Dir Institutional Effectiveness ... Dr. Vanessa O'BRIEN-MCMASTERS
09 Dean Inst Research/Plng/Grants ... Dr. Rebecca FIDLER-SHEPPARD
07 Dir Admissions/Registration Svcs ... Mr. Steve D'AMBROSIO
79 Dean Arts/Humanities/Soc Science ... Vacant
81 Dean Math/Science/Health Career ... Dr. Jacquelyn GALBIATI
51 Dean School & Comm Academic Pgm ... Ms. Margo VENABLE
12 Exec Dean Camden City Campus ... Mr. Gary DIVENS
41 Athletic Director ... Mr. William BANKS
13 Chief Info Technology Officer (CIO) ... Mr. John POST
19 Director Public Safety ... Mr. Stephen HETHERINGTON
29 External Resources Develop Assoc ... Ms. Melissa DALY
43 Dir Legal Services/General Counsel ... Mr. Karl MCCONNELL
26 Director of Communications ... Ms. Julie YANKANICH

Camden County College Camden City Campus (F)

200 N Broadway, Camden NJ 08102-1185
Telephone: (856) 338-1817 Identification: 770126
Accreditation: &M

Centenary University (G)

400 Jefferson Street, Hackettstown NJ 07840-2100
County: Warren FICE Identification: 002599
Unit ID: 183974
Telephone: (908) 852-1400 Carnegie Class: Masters/M
FAX Number: (908) 850-9508 Calendar System: Semester
URL: www.centenaryuniversity.edu
Established: 1867 Annual Undergrad Tuition & Fees: $32,098
Enrollment: 2,284 Coed
Affiliation or Control: Independent Non-Profit IRS Status: 501(c)3
Highest Offering: Doctorate
Accreditation: M, CAEPT, IACBE, SW

01 President ... Dr. David HANEY
05 VP for Academic Affairs ... Dr. Amy D'OLIVO
10 Interim CFO ... Mr. Frank WILLIAMS
111 Acting VP for Univ Advancement ... Ms. Kathy NAASZ
84 VP for Enrollment Mgmt & Mktg ... Dr. Robert L. MILLER, JR.
32 VP for Student Life Dean Students ... Ms. Kerry MULLINS
15 VP for Human Resources ... Ms. Virginia GALDIERI
18 Director of Facilities ... Mr. Roland JULIANO
26 Dean Community & College Affairs ... Ms. Nancy PAFFENDORF
09 Dean of Inst Research/Assessment ... Dr. Jeremy A. HOUSKA
35 Sr Dir Student Engagement ... Ms. Tiffany KUSHNER
06 Registrar ... Ms. Irma WILLIAMS
08 Director Taylor Memorial Library ... Mr. Timothy DOMICK
36 Director Career Development Center ... Mr. Joshua D. WALKER
41 Director of Athletics ... Mr. Keith O'CONNOR
19 Chief of Campus Safety ... Mr. Leonard KUNZ
38 Director of Counseling Center ... Ms. Lorna FARMER
13 Chief Information Officer ... Mr. Terry T. BAZYLEWICZ

Chamberlain University-North Brunswick (H)

630 US Highway One, North Brunswick NJ 08902
Telephone: (732) 875-1300 Identification: 770850
Accreditation: &NH, NURSE

† Branch campus of Chamberlain University-Addison, Addison, IL

The College of New Jersey (I)

2000 Pennington Road, Ewing NJ 08628-1104
County: Mercer FICE Identification: 002642
Unit ID: 187134
Telephone: (609) 771-1855 Carnegie Class: Masters/L
FAX Number: (609) 637-5191 Calendar System: Semester
URL: www.tcnj.edu
Established: 1855 Annual Undergrad Tuition & Fees (In-State): $15,794
Enrollment: 7,406 Coed
Affiliation or Control: State IRS Status: 501(c)3
Highest Offering: Master's
Accreditation: M, ART, CACREP, CAEPN, CS, ENG, MUS, NURSE

01 President ... Dr. R. Barbara GITENSTEIN
05 Provost/VP Academic Affairs ... Dr. Jacqueline TAYLOR
11 Vice Pres for Administration ... Mr. Curt HEURING
10 Treasurer ... Mr. Lloyd RICKETTS
43 General Counsel ... Mr. Thomas MAHONEY
111 Vice Pres Advancement ... Mr. John DONOHUE
32 Vice President Student Affairs ... Dr. Amy HECHT
15 Vice Pres Human Resources ... Dr. Gregory POGUE
84 Vice Pres Enrollment Management ... Ms. Lisa ANGELONI
13 CIO & VP for Info Technology ... Dr. Sharon BLANTON
100 Chief of Staff/Secy to Board ... Ms. Heather FEHN
18 Assoc VP Facilities & Admin Svcs ... Ms. Kathryn LEVERTON
30 Assoc Vice President of Development ... Mr. Charles WRIGHT
35 Asst VP for Student Affairs/Engage ... Ms. Elizabeth BAPASOLA
35 Asst Vice Pres Student Affairs ... Ms. Angela CHONG
86 Assoc VP for College Relations ... Ms. Stacy SCHUSTER
20 Vice Provost ... Dr. Ieva ZAKE
57 Dean School of The Arts & Comm ... Dr. James DAY
50 Dean School of Business ... Dr. William KEEP
79 Dean Sch Humanities/Soc Sci ... Dr. Jane WONG
53 Dean School of Education ... Dr. Jeffrey PASSE
54 Dean School of Engineering ... Dr. Steven SCHREINER
66 Dean Nursing/Health/Exercise Scienc ... Dr. Carole KENNER
81 Dean School of Science ... Dr. Jeffrey OSBORN
58 Dir Grad & Intersession Programs ... Dr. Susan HYDRO
37 Exec Dir of Student Fin Assistance ... Mr. Wil CASAINE
09 Asst Provost Ctr for Inst Effective ... Dr. Mosen AURYAN
41 Director of Athletics ... Vacant
29 Director Alumni Affairs ... Mr. John CASTALDO
26 Assoc VP Comm/Mktg/Brand Mgmt ... Mr. David MUHA
18 Director of Campus Construction ... Mr. William RUDEAU
23 Assoc Director for Health Services ... Ms. Janice VERMEYCHUK
06 Exec Director Records/Registration ... Mr. Frank COOPER

19 Interim Dir Campus Police .... Chief Timothy GRANT
96 Exec Dir Procurement Services .... Mr. Anup KAPUR
28 Assoc VP/Chief Diversity Officer .... Ms. Kerry TILLETT
07 Director of Admissions .... Ms. Grecia MONTERO
36 Director Career Center .... Ms. Debra KELLY
38 Director of Counseling & Psych Svcs .... Dr. Mark FOREST

College of Saint Elizabeth (A)

2 Convent Road, Morristown NJ 07960-6989
County: Morris FICE Identification: 002600
Unit ID: 186618
Telephone: (973) 290-4000 Carnegie Class: Masters/M
FAX Number: N/A Calendar System: Semester
URL: www.cse.edu
Established: 1899 Annual Undergrad Tuition & Fees: $32,282
Enrollment: 1,247 Coed
Affiliation or Control: Roman Catholic IRS Status: 501(c)3
Highest Offering: Doctorate
Accreditation: M, CAEPT, DIETD, DIETI, NUR, @SW

01 President .... Dr. Helen J. STREUBERT
05 VP for Academic Affairs .... Dr. Monique GUILLORY
32 VP Student Life .... Ms. Katherine BUCK
10 VP Finance Admin/Treasurer .... Mr. Michael FESCOE
111 Vice Pres Institutional Advancement .... Ms. Sally CLEARY
84 VP Enrollment Management .... Mr. Alexander SCOTT
21 Controller .... Vacant
06 Registrar .... Ms. Marybeth OBRYCKI
09 Dir Inst Research & Acad Assessment .... Dr. Michele YURECKO
08 Interim Dir Mahoney Library .... Mr. Mark FERGUSON
42 Campus Minister .... Ms. Clare ETTENSOHN
18 Director of Facilities & Security .... Mr. James GERRISH
37 Director of Financial Aid .... Ms. LaVerne O. WALKER
26 Director Marketing/Communications .... Ms. Maryann MATLOCK
22 Director EOF Program .... Mr. Clifford WOODWARD
36 Dir Experiential Lrng & Career Svcs .... Ms. Teri CORSO
38 Director of Counseling .... Ms. Zsuzsanna NAGY
88 Dir Volunteerism & Svc Learning .... Ms. Jayne I. MURPHY-MORRIS
35 Director of Student Engagement .... Ms. Naima K. RICKS
41 Director of Athletics .... Ms. Juliene SIMPSON
44 Director of Annual Fund .... Ms. Tanya SORCE
29 Dir Alumni Engage/Alum Assoc .... Ms. Carol Ann KOERT
15 Director Human Resources .... Ms. Rochelle DICKERSON
85 Director Intl/Multicultural Affairs .... Ms. Lenee WOODSON
40 C-Store/Dining Services .... Mr. Robert LOCONSOLE
30 Asst VP Inst Advancement .... Ms. Janice HILL
105 Director IT-Web .... Mr. David B. RABINOWITZ
04 Administrative Asst to President .... Ms. MaryAnn RICCIOTTI
13 Chief Info Technology Officer .... Ms. Margie ROHR
28 Dir Intl & Multicultural Affairs .... Ms. Lenee WOODSON
107 Dean of Professional Studies .... Dr. Patricia HEINDEL
49 Dean of Arts and Sciences .... Dr. Anthony SANTAMARIA
104 Coord Acad Internships & StudyAway .... Ms. Lindsey ROMES
19 Director Security/Safety .... Mr. Richard WALL
39 Director Residence Life .... Ms. Trisha D. FUENTES
04 Exec Asst to President .... Ms. Tracey O'CONNELL

County College of Morris (B)

214 Center Grove Road, Randolph NJ 07869-2086
County: Morris FICE Identification: 007729
Unit ID: 184180
Telephone: (973) 328-5000 Carnegie Class: Assoc/HT-High Trad
FAX Number: (973) 328-1282 Calendar System: Semester
URL: www.ccm.edu
Established: 1965 Annual Undergrad Tuition & Fees (In-District): $4,690
Enrollment: 8,026 Coed
Affiliation or Control: State/Local IRS Status: 501(c)3
Highest Offering: Associate Degree
Accreditation: M, ACBSP, ADNUR, COARC, ENGT, RAD

01 President .... Dr. Anthony J. IACONO
05 Vice President of Academic Affairs .... Dr. Dwight L. SMITH
10 Vice President of Business/Finance .... Ms. Karen VANDERHOOF
32 VP of Student Development .... Dr. Bette M. SIMMONS
111 Exec Dir College Advancement .... Mr. Joseph VITALE
15 VP Human Resources & Labor Rels .... Mr. Thomas BURK
09 Dean Inst Research .... Ms. Phebe SOLIMAN
114 Director Budget & Business Services .... Mr. John YOUNG
25 Director Resource Development .... Ms. Katrina BELL
07 Admissions Officer .... Mr. Eugene SOLTYS
37 Director Financial Aid .... Mr. Harvey WILLIS
06 Registrar .... Ms. Laura Lee BOWENS
26 Chief Public Relations Officer .... Ms. Kathleen BRUNET EAGAN
29 Director Alumni Office .... Ms. Barbara CAPSOURAS
13 VP Institutional Effectiveness/CIO .... Mr. E. Robert STIRTON
08 Dean Learning Resource Ctr .... Ms. Heather CRAVEN
36 Director Career Svcs/Coop Education .... Ms. Denise SCHMIDT
38 Counseling Services Coordinator .... Ms. Janique CAFFIE
79 Dean Liberal Arts .... Dr. Bruce DUTRA
76 Dean Health/Natural Sciences .... Ms. Monica MARASKA
103 AVP Workforce Dev/Dean Prof Studies .... Mr. Patrick ENRIGHT
19 Director Security & Safety .... Mr. Harvey JACKSON
41 Director Athletics .... Mr. Jack SULLIVAN
23 Health Services Coordinator .... Ms. Elizabeth HOBAN
18 Director of Plant & Maintenance .... Mr. Joseph PONTURO
96 Director of Purchasing .... Ms. Joanne KEARNS
40 Bookstore Manager .... Mr. Jeff LUBNOW

Cumberland County College (C)

3322 College Drive, PO Box 1500,
Vineland NJ 08362-1500
County: Cumberland FICE Identification: 002601
Unit ID: 184205
Telephone: (856) 691-8600 Carnegie Class: Assoc/HT-High Trad
FAX Number: (856) 690-0812 Calendar System: Semester
URL: www.cccnj.edu
Established: 1963 Annual Undergrad Tuition & Fees (In-District): $4,440
Enrollment: 3,453 Coed
Affiliation or Control: State/Local IRS Status: 501(c)3
Highest Offering: Associate Degree
Accreditation: M, ADNUR, RAD

01 President .... Dr. Yves SALOMON-FERNANDEZ
05 Vice Pres Academic/Student Affairs .... Mr. James PICCONE
10 Executive Director Finance/Budget .... Ms. Sherri L. WELCH
08 Director Library Services .... Ms. Patti A. SCHMID
20 Exec Dir Ctr Acad & Student Success .... Ms. Kellie W. SLADE
26 Director Communications & Marketing .... Vacant
29 Director Foundation & Alumni .... Ms. Alice WOODS
37 Director Student Financial Aid .... Mr. Maurice THOMAS
50 Dean Business/Educ/Soc Sci/Tech/Eng .... Dr. Lynn LICHTENBERGER
103 Dir Workforce/Cmty Tech Educ .... Dr. Terrence HARDEE
81 Dean STEM .... Vacant
15 Executive Director Human Resources .... Vacant
72 Executive Director IT Services .... Mr. Bernie CASTRO
18 Director Facilities & Grounds .... Mr. Brian EWAN
96 Purchasing Agent .... Ms. Melissa FALANCE
09 Exec Dir Plng/Research/Inst Effect .... Dr. Robert K. CLARK
19 Director Security/Safety .... Mr. Philip CECOLA
04 Asst to the President/BOT Liaison .... Ms. Pamela CARTY
32 Director Student Life & Athletics .... Mr. Keith GORMAN
07 Executive Director Enrollment Svcs .... Ms. Anne M. DALY EIMER

DeVry University - North Brunswick Campus (D)

630 US Highway One, North Brunswick NJ 08902-3362
Telephone: (732) 729-3960 FICE Identification: 009228
Accreditation: &NH, ENGT

† Regional accreditation is carried under the parent institution in Downers Grove, IL.

Drew University (E)

36 Madison Avenue, Madison NJ 07940-1493
County: Morris FICE Identification: 002603
Unit ID: 184348
Telephone: (973) 408-3000 Carnegie Class: DU-Mod
FAX Number: N/A Calendar System: 4/1/4
URL: www.drew.edu
Established: 1866 Annual Undergrad Tuition & Fees: $48,052
Enrollment: 2,082 Coed
Affiliation or Control: Independent Non-Profit IRS Status: 501(c)3
Highest Offering: Doctorate
Accreditation: M, CAEPT, THEOL

01 President .... Dr. MaryAnn BAENNINGER
05 Chief Academic Officer .... Dr. Christopher TAYLOR
30 Vice Pres Advanc/Alumni Affairs .... Dr. Kenneth ALEXO
10 Vice Pres Finance/Business Affairs .... Mr. John VITALI
49 Dean of College of Liberal Arts .... Dr. Christopher TAYLOR
73 Dean Theological School .... Dr. Javier VIERA
08 Associate Dean of Libraries .... Dr. Chris ANDERSON
32 Vice President Student Life .... Dr. Sara WALDRON
26 VP Communications & Marketing .... Ms. Kira POPLOWSKI
15 Director of Human Resources .... Vacant
22 Title IX Coordinator .... Ms. Emily RALPH
90 Dir Instructional Technology Svcs .... Dr. Gamin BARTLE
21 Controller .... Ms. Renee LISCHIN
96 Director Purchasing .... Mr. Mark MEHLER
18 Director Facilities Operations .... Mr. Michael KOPAS
37 Director Finan Assistance .... Ms. Colby MCCARTHY
19 Director Public Safety .... Mr. William ORTMAN
23 Director Health Services .... Ms. Joyce MAGLIONE
35 Director Student Activities .... Ms. Michelle BRISSON
38 Director Counseling Services .... Dr. Jim MANDALA
07 Director Theological Admissions .... Mr. Kevin D. MILLER
07 Director Graduate Admissions .... Ms. Corinn MCBRIDE
09 Dir Institutional Research .... Mr. Alex MCCLUNG
84 Director Enrollment Management .... Mr. Robert MASSA
41 Director Athletics .... Mr. Jason FEIN
06 Registrar .... Mr. Daniel OSTIN
40 Manager Bookstore .... Ms. Liz GALLO
04 Administrative Asst to President .... Ms. Kathleen SUTHERLAND
100 Chief of Staff .... Ms. Marti WINER
104 Director Study Abroad .... Ms. Stacy FISCHER
105 Webmaster .... Mr. Justin JACKSON
13 Chief Info Technology Officer (CIO) .... Mr. E. Axel LARSSON
25 Chief Contracts/Grants Admin .... Ms. Linda DETITTA
29 Director Alumni Relations .... Mr. John HOLDEN
36 Director Student Placement .... Ms. Suzanne CERAVOLO
43 Dir Legal Services/General Counsel .... Mr. William BROWN

Eastern International College (F)

684 Newark Avenue, Jersey City NJ 07306
County: Hudson FICE Identification: 031226
Unit ID: 421878
Telephone: (201) 216-9901 Carnegie Class: Spec-4-yr-Other Health
FAX Number: (201) 533-1027 Calendar System: Semester
URL: www.eicollege.edu
Established: 1990 Annual Undergrad Tuition & Fees: $21,225
Enrollment: 208 Coed
Affiliation or Control: Proprietary IRS Status: Proprietary
Highest Offering: Baccalaureate
Accreditation: ACCSC, CVT, DH

01 CEO .... Mr. Bashir MOHSEN
03 Executive Vice President .... Mr. Andrew S. ZINER
05 Vice President of Academic Affairs .... Dr. Mustafa MUSTAFA
06 Registrar .... Mrs. Soha ELSHICK
12 Campus Director .... Ms. Agnieszka DRUPKA
36 Corporate Director of Career Svcs .... Ms. Jennifer BATE
37 Director Student Financial Aid .... MS. Kinga GIZYNSKA
20 Dean of Education .... Mrs. Kimberly MCDONALD
04 Administrative Asst to President .... Ms. Soha ELSHICK
07 Director of Admissions .... Ms. Shirley BELL
13 Chief Info Technology Officer (CIO) .... Mr. Marc JEAN
32 Student Life Coordinator .... Mr. Joshua ZINER
38 Student Counseling Officer .... Ms. Maria BILLINGS
08 Head Librarian .... Ms. Lisa BOGART
22 Chief EEO Officer & Legal Liaison .... Mr. George CACERES

Eastern International College-Belleville Campus (G)

251 Washington Avenue, Belleville NJ 07109
Telephone: (973) 751-9051 Identification: 770580
Accreditation: ACCSC

Eastwick College (H)

250 Moore Street, Hackensack NJ 07601
County: Bergen Identification: 667131
Unit ID: 183488
Telephone: (201) 488-9400 Carnegie Class: Spec 2-yr-Health
FAX Number: (201) 488-1007 Calendar System: Quarter
URL: www.eastwick.edu
Established: 1985 Annual Undergrad Tuition & Fees: $15,428
Enrollment: 338 Coed
Affiliation or Control: Proprietary IRS Status: Proprietary
Highest Offering: Associate Degree
Accreditation: ACICS, FUSER

01 President .... Thomas M. EASTWICK

Eastwick College (I)

103 Park Avenue, Nutley NJ 07110
County: Essex FICE Identification: 020923
Unit ID: 185721
Telephone: (973) 661-0600 Carnegie Class: Not Classified
FAX Number: (973) 661-2954 Calendar System: Quarter
URL: www.eastwick.edu
Established: 2014 Annual Undergrad Tuition & Fees: $15,221
Enrollment: 324 Coed
Affiliation or Control: Proprietary IRS Status: Proprietary
Highest Offering: Associate Degree
Accreditation: ACICS

01 President .... Thomas EASTWICK
11 Vice Pres of Operations .... Bhavna TAILOR
05 Dean of Academics .... Sameh FARAGALLA

Eastwick College (J)

10 South Franklin Turnpike, Ramsey NJ 07446
County: Bergen FICE Identification: 020537
Unit ID: 184959
Telephone: (201) 327-8877 Carnegie Class: Spec 2-yr-Health
FAX Number: (201) 327-9054 Calendar System: Other
URL: www.eastwick.edu
Established: 1968 Annual Undergrad Tuition & Fees: $17,272
Enrollment: 710 Coed
Affiliation or Control: Proprietary IRS Status: Proprietary
Highest Offering: Associate Degree
Accreditation: ACICS, CVT, OTA, SURGT

01 President .... Thomas EASTWICK
03 Executive Vice President .... Rafael CASTILLA
05 Vice President Academic Affairs .... Joyce TRAINA
11 Vice Pres Operations .... Bhavna TAILOR
07 Director of Admissions .... Letitia BURKE
36 Director Career Development .... Allis WICKHAM
37 Corp Director of Financial Aid .... Christy DELAGUERRA

Essex County College (K)

303 University Avenue, Newark NJ 07102-1798
County: Essex FICE Identification: 007107
Unit ID: 184481
Telephone: (973) 877-3000 Carnegie Class: Assoc/HT-High Trad
FAX Number: (973) 877-3044 Calendar System: Other
URL: www.essex.edu
Established: 1966 Annual Undergrad Tuition & Fees (In-District): $4,546
Enrollment: 10,954 Coed
Affiliation or Control: State/Local IRS Status: 501(c)3
Highest Offering: Associate Degree
Accreditation: M, ACBSP, ADNUR, ENGT, OPD, PTAA, RAD

01 President Dr. Anthony MONROE
05 Vice Pres/Chief Academic Officer Dr. Jeffrey LEE
04 Admin Asst to the President Ms. Jonell CONGLETON
10 VP Administration & Finance Dr. Joyce W. HARLEY
49 Dean Liberal Arts Vacant
21 Comptroller/CFO Mr. Frank NOCELLA
43 General Counsel Ms. Joy TOLIVER
108 Exec Dir Instl Planning/Assessment Ms. Susan GAULDEN
13 Exec Dean/CIO Admin & Learning Tech Mr. Mohamed SEDDIKI
32 Dean Student Affairs Mr. Keith KIRKLAND
106 Assoc Dean Online Learning Resource Dr. Leigh BELLO-DECASTRO
25 Director Management Grant Funds Ms. Yvette JEFFERIES
09 Director Institutional Research Dr. Jinsoo PARK
51 Dean Comm & Continuing Educ/WEC Dr. Elvira VIEIRA
08 Director MLK Library Mrs. Gwendolyn SLATON
35 Assoc Dean Student Life/Development Ms. Patricia SLADE
18 Director Facilities Mgmt Mr. Jeff SHAPIRO
19 Director Public Safety Mr. Anthony CROMARTIE
96 Director Purchasing Mrs. Marylyn RUTHERFORD
37 Director Financial Aid Mrs. Mildred COFER
21 Director Bursar's Office Ms. Darlene MILLER
36 Director Student Development Dr. S. Aisha STEPLIGHT JOHNSON
88 Director Child Development Center Ms. Deloris GRIMSLEY
41 Director Athletics Mr. Melvin KNIGHT
24 Director Media Prod Tech Mrs. Nadine ABRAM
88 Director College Information Ctr Mr. Ronald ROSS
00 President Emeritus Dr. A. Zachary YAMBA

Essex County College-West Essex Branch Campus (A)

730 West Bloomfield Avenue, West Caldwell NJ 07006
Telephone: (973) 877-6590 Identification: 770127
Accreditation: &M

Fairleigh Dickinson University (B)

1000 River Road, Teaneck NJ 07666-1996
County: Bergen FICE Identification: 002607
Unit ID: 184603
Telephone: (201) 692-2000 Carnegie Class: DU-Mod
FAX Number: N/A Calendar System: Semester
URL: www.fdu.edu
Established: 1942 Annual Undergrad Tuition & Fees: $37,988
Enrollment: 8,652 Coed
Affiliation or Control: Independent Non-Profit IRS Status: 501(c)3
Highest Offering: Doctorate
Accreditation: M, CACREP, CAEPT, CLPSY, CS, ENG, ENGT, NURSE, PHAR

01 President Dr. Christopher CAPUANO
43 University Counsel/Secretary Mr. John CODD
05 University Provost/VPAA Dr. Gillian SMALL
111 Sr Vice Pres University Advancement Mr. Richard REISS
10 Senior VP for Finance & COO Ms. Hania FERRARA
18 VP for Facilities & Auxiliary Svcs Mr. Richard A. FRICK
84 AVP Admissions/Fin Aid/Enrollment Ms. Traci BANKS
13 VP/Chief Information Officer Mr. Neal M. STURM
26 Associate VP Communications Mr. Angelo CARFAGNA
15 Associate VP Human Resources Ms. Rose D'AMBROSIO
29 Director Alumni Affairs Vacant
51 Dean Petrocelli Col of Cont Stds Dr. Lisa BRAVERMAN
49 Dean Becton Col of Arts & Sci Dr. Geoffrey WEINMAN
50 Dean College Business Admin Dr. Andrew ROSMAN
20 Interim Dean University College Dr. Vicki COHEN
32 Dean of Students-Teaneck Campus Ms. Michelle MCCROY-HEINS
32 Dean of Students-Madison Campus Dr. Jas VEREM
08 Assoc University Librarian-Florham Vacant
08 Associate University Librarian-Met Ms. Kathy STEIN-SMITH
51 Director Continuing Education Dr. Thomas SWANZEY
88 Dir Public Administration Institute Dr. William ROBERTS
116 Director Internal Audit Ms. Agnes SCAGLIONE
53 Director School of Education Vacant
66 Director Sch of Nurs/Allied Health Dr. Minerva GUTTMAN
41 Director of Athletics-Teaneck Mr. David LANGFORD
41 Interim Dir Athletics-Florham Mr. Roger KINDEL
07 Univ Dir of Undergrad Admissions Mr. Andrew IPPOLITO
09 Director of Institutional Research Dr. Sam MICHALOWSKI
37 University Director Financial Aid Ms. Renee VOLAK
19 Florham Campus Dir Public Safety Ms. Willie THORNTON
12 Provost Metropolitan Campus Dr. Robert VODDE
12 Provost Florham Campus Dr. Peter WOOLLEY
19 Metro Campus Dir Public Safety Mr. David A. MILES
96 Director of Purchasing Ms. Juliette BROOKS
04 Assistant to the President Ms. Jeanne MAZZOLLA
25 Univ Dir Grants & Sponsored Proj Ms. Jane TSAMBIS
36 University Dir Career Development Ms. Donna ROBERTSON

Felician University (C)

262 S Main Street, Lodi NJ 07644-2198
County: Bergen FICE Identification: 002610
Unit ID: 184612
Telephone: (201) 559-6000 Carnegie Class: Masters/S
FAX Number: (201) 559-6188 Calendar System: Semester
URL: www.felician.edu
Established: 1942 Annual Undergrad Tuition & Fees: $32,990
Enrollment: 1,957 Coed
Affiliation or Control: Roman Catholic IRS Status: 501(c)3
Highest Offering: Doctorate
Accreditation: M, CAEPT, IACBE, NURSE

01 President Dr. Anne PRISCO
05 Provost/Vice Pres Acad Affairs Dr. Edward OGLE
20 Asst VP Academic Support Services Dr. Ann V. GUILLORY
111 Vice Pres Institutional Advancement Dr. John FARKAS
10 Int Vice Pres for Business/Finance Mr. Thomas TRUCHAN
84 VP Enroll Mgmt & Student Affairs Ms. Francine ANDREA
04 Admin Assistant to the President Ms. Meggan O'NEILL
06 Registrar Ms. Priscilla KLYMENKO
123 Assoc Vice Pres Grad & Intl Enroll Mr. Michael SZAREK
07 Director Undergraduate Admissions Ms. Colleen FULLER
08 Director of the Library Mr. Clevell ROSEBORO, II
09 Director Institutional Research Ms. Reema NEGI
15 Director of Human Resources Ms. Virginia TOPOLSKI
88 Director Conferences and Event Plng Ms. Maria MALLIA
37 Director Student Financial Aid Ms. Cynthia MONTALVO
29 Director of Alumni Relations Ms. Patricia MALIZIA
42 Director Campus Ministry/Chaplain Fr. Richard KELLY
39 Director of Residence Life Ms. Laura PIEROTTI
36 Director of Career Counseling Ms. Melissa FAULKNER
13 Asst VP of Information Technology Mr. Christopher FINCH
24 Director A-V Center Mr. Anthony KLYMENKO
88 Assoc Director Center for Learning Mr. Hamdi SHAHIN
26 Dir Inst Marketing & Publications Ms. Barbara PURDUE-LYNCH
40 Manager College Bookstore Ms. Beth LIGNOWSKI
76 Dean School of Nursing Dr. Muriel SHORE
53 Dean School of Education Dr. Stephanie MCGOWAN
49 Dean School of Arts/Science Dr. George E. ABAUNZA
50 Dean School of Business Dr. Beth CASTIGLIA
108 Dean Assessment/Fac Excellence Dr. Dolores HENCHY
88 Director EOF Program Ms. Dinelia GARDNER
104 Director Study Abroad Program Mr. Carlo COLECCHIA
51 Dir of Cont/Professional Studies Dr. Geraldine KOCH
23 Director Health Services Ms. Carolyn LEWIS
41 Director of Athletics Mr. Benjamin DINALLO, JR.
92 Director Honors Program Dr. Maria VECCHIO
91 Director Administrative Computing Mr. John PANNEGGIANTE
14 Director of Information Systems Mr. Wisam SHAHIN

Georgian Court University (D)

900 Lakewood Avenue, Lakewood NJ 08701-2697
County: Ocean FICE Identification: 002608
Unit ID: 184773
Telephone: (732) 987-2200 Carnegie Class: Masters/M
FAX Number: N/A Calendar System: Semester
URL: www.georgian.edu
Established: 1908 Annual Undergrad Tuition & Fees: $31,618
Enrollment: 2,122 Coed
Affiliation or Control: Roman Catholic IRS Status: 501(c)3
Highest Offering: Master's
Accreditation: M, ACBSP, CACREP, CAEPT, NURSE, SW

01 President Dr. Joseph R. MARBACH
05 Provost Dr. William BEHRE
10 Chief Financial Officer/VP Finance Mr. John SOMMER
111 Vice Pres Institutional Advancement Dr. Brian AGNEW
20 Assoc Provost Academic Pgm Devel Dr. Michael GROSS
07 Dean of Admissions Mr. Justin ROY
32 Dean of Students Dr. Amani JENNINGS
42 Director of Campus Ministry Mr. Jeff SCHAFFER
41 Director Athletics/Recreation Ms. Laura LIESMAN
50 Dean School of Business Dr. Janice WARNER
53 Dean of School of Education Dr. Lynn DECAPUA
49 Dean School of Arts & Sciences Dr. Mary CHINERY
09 Director of Institutional Research Mr. Wayne ARNDT
08 Director of Library Svcs Mr. Jeffrey DONNELLY
06 Registrar Ms. Christina REEVES
21 Controller Ms. Maureen RYAN-HOFFMAN
15 Director of Human Resources Ms. Tracey OWENS
13 Chief Information Officer Mr. Steve CAROL
07 Director Undergraduate Admissions Mr. Steven LAMBERT
37 Director of Financial Aid Mr. Randy BROWN
26 Exec Dir of Marketing & Comm Ms. Gail TOWNS
88 Dir Conferences & Special Events Ms. Mary CRANWELL
29 Director of Alumni Relations Ms. ToniAnn MCLAUGHLIN
36 Exec Dir of Career Svc & Corp Engag Ms. Kathleen BRADY
38 Director of Counseling Dr. Robin SOLBACH
23 Director of Health Services Ms. Cynthia MATTIA
22 Affirmative Action Officer Ms. Tracey OWENS
18 Director of Facilities Mr. Michael PUTNAM
19 Director of Security Mr. Thomas ZAMBRANO
07 Director Graduate Admissions Mr. Patrick GIVENS
39 Director of Residence Life Mr. Gary MILLER
04 Executive Asst to President Ms. Kathy SMITH
105 Web Administrator Mr. Richard BERARDI
108 Director of Assessment Sr. Janet THIEL
96 Purchasing Coordinator Ms. Julie PARLACOSKI
103 Exec Director Career Services Ms. Kathleen BRADY
30 Development Officer/Annual Giving Ms. Megan O'KEEFE

Hudson County Community College (E)

70 Sip Avenue, Jersey City NJ 07306
County: Hudson FICE Identification: 012954
Unit ID: 184995
Telephone: (201) 714-7100 Carnegie Class: Assoc/HT-High Trad
FAX Number: (201) 656-1799 Calendar System: Semester
URL: www.hccc.edu
Established: 1974 Annual Undergrad Tuition & Fees (In-District): $5,353
Enrollment: 9,051 Coed
Affiliation or Control: State/Local IRS Status: 501(c)3
Highest Offering: Associate Degree
Accreditation: M, ACFEI

01 President Dr. Glen E. GABERT
05 Senior Vice Pres Academic Affairs Dr. Eric FRIEDMAN
30 Vice Pres Development Mr. Joseph SANSONE
12 Senior VP North Hudson Campus Dr. Paula PANDO
88 Dean for Non Traditional Programs Vacant
32 Assoc Dean Student Services Mr. Michael REIMER
09 Assoc Dean Institutional Rsrch/Plng Dr. Jerry TROMBELLA
84 Assoc Dean Enrollment Services Mrs. Lisa DOUGHERTY
50 Assoc Dean Business and Science Ms. Catherine SIRANGELO-ELBADAWY
37 Executive Director Financial Aid Ms. Sylvia F. MENDOZA
88 Assoc Dean ESL/Bilingual & Dev Educ Mr. Chris WAHL
06 Registrar Ms. Victoria ORELLANA
13 Chief Information Officer Mr. Vincent SALAMONE
10 Chief Fiscal Officer Ms. Veronica ZEICHNER
07 Director of Admissions Mr. Matthew FESSLER
49 Dean of Arts and Sciences Mr. Chris WAHL
88 Director Testing & Assessment Ms. Darlery FRANCO
88 Director EOF Ms. Tieka HARRIS
88 Executive Director Culinary Arts Mr. Paul DILLON
88 Ex Dir Ctr Bus/Industry/Cntrct Trng Ms. Ana CHAPMAN
45 Director Academic Foundations Ms. Elizabeth NESIUS
21 Controller Mr. Geoffrey SIMS
25 Director of Grants Mr. Ryan MARTIN
08 Librarian Ms. Ellen RENAUD
35 Director Student Activities Ms. Veronica ZEROSIMO
26 Director of Communications Ms. Jennifer CHRISTOPHER
15 Executive Director Human Resources Ms. Vivyen RAY
38 Director Advisement & Counseling Ms. Sabrina MAGLIULO
40 Manager HCCC Bookstore Ms. Tom COLBAN
96 Manager Purchasing Mr. Marvin SMITH
36 Coordinator Career & Transfer Svc Ms. Jennie NESENJUK
19 Director Security/Safety Mr. Rafael NIVAR
04 Executive Admin Asst to President Ms. Jennifer OAKLEY
18 Exec Dir Engineering Operations Mr. Ilya ASHMYAN
08 Interim Dean of Libraries Mr. David HARDGROVE
106 Dir Online Education/E-learning Mr. Robert KHAN
108 Director Institutional Assessment Mr. Jerry TROMBELLA

Kean University (F)

1000 Morris Avenue, Union NJ 07083-0411
County: Union FICE Identification: 002622
Unit ID: 185262
Telephone: (908) 737-5326 Carnegie Class: Masters/L
FAX Number: (908) 737-4636 Calendar System: Semester
URL: www.kean.edu
Established: 1855 Annual Undergrad Tuition & Fees (In-State): $11,870
Enrollment: 14,112 Coed
Affiliation or Control: State IRS Status: 501(c)3
Highest Offering: Doctorate
Accreditation: M, ART, CAATE, CACREP, CAEPN, CIDA, CS, MUS, NUR, OT, PSPSY, @PTA, SP, SPAA, SW, THEA

01 President Dr. Dawood FARAHI
10 VP Administration & Finance Mr. Andrew BRANNEN
05 Provost/VP Academic Affairs Dr. Jeffrey TONEY
20 Associate Provost Dr. Suzanne BOUSQUET
111 Acting VP Institutional Advancement Ms. Audrey KELLY
32 VP for Student Affairs Ms. Janice MURRAY-LAURY
26 VP University Relations Vacant
100 Chief of Staff Ms. Audrey KELLY
45 Special Counsel & VP Planning Ms. Felice VAZQUEZ
12 Exec Vice Chancellor WKU Mr. Philip CONNELLY
43 Assoc VP/Chief University Counsel Ms. Geri BENEDETTO
84 Assoc VP Enrollment Management Ms. Marsha MCCARTHY
12 Assoc VP/Dean Kean Ocean Dr. Stephen KUBOW
12 Assoc VPAA Kean Wenzhou Dr. Holger HENKE
20 Asst VP Academic Affairs Ms. Joy MOSKOVITZ
39 Asst VP Residential Stdnt Services Ms. Maximina RIVERA
58 Dean Nathan Weiss Grad Col Dr. Jeffrey BECK
53 Dean Col Education Dr. Anthony PITTMAN
18 Asst VP for Operations Mr. Kevin GARVEY
79 Dean Col Humanities/Social Sci Vacant
50 Dean Col Business & Public Mgt Dr. Michael COOPER
81 Dean Col Nat & Appl Hlth Sci Dr. George CHANG
57 Dean Col Visual & Performing Arts Vacant
48 Dean Michael Graves Col Dr. David MOHNEY
15 Assoc Dir Human Resources Mrs. Laura BARKLEY-HAELIG
09 Dir Institutional Research Dr. Shiji SHEN
06 Registrar Mr. Adam STONE
108 Assoc Dir Accredit & Assessment Ms. Susan DEMATTEO
37 Dir Financial Aid Ms. Sherrell WATSON-HALL
07 Dir of Admissions Vacant
13 Dir Office for Computer/Inform Svcs Mr. Anthony SANTORA
21 Dir General Accounting Mr. Joseph ANTONOWICZ
08 Dir University Librarian Vacant
25 Dir Research & Sponsored Pgms Ms. Susan GANNON
84 Exec Dir Enroll Mgt Operations Mr. Chad AUSTEIN
106 Dir Online Learning Mr. Corey VIGDOR
27 Dir Media Relations Ms. Margaret MCCORRY
29 Dir Alumni Relations Ms. Stella MAHER
96 Interim Dir for Purchasing Mrs. Jennifer SOYKA
38 Dir Counseling & Disability Servs Mr. Vincent KIEFNER
65 Dir for Sustainability Dr. Feng QI
104 Dir Center International Studies Mrs. Rebeccah NEWMAN
41 Dir for Athletics Mr. Jack MCKIERNAN
35 Dir Ctr for Student Lead & Svcs Mr. Scott SNOWDEN
19 Acting Dir of Campus Police Ms. Ana ZSAK
23 Dir for Health Services Ms. Robin MANSFIELD
88 Veterans Affairs Mr. Vito ZAJDA
22 Dir Affirmative Action Dr. Charlie WILLIAMS
42 Chaplain for Campus Ministry Ms. Jackie OESMANN

Mercer County Community College (A)

1200 Old Trenton Road, PO Box 17202,
West Windsor NJ 08550
County: Mercer FICE Identification: 004740
Unit ID: 185509
Telephone: (609) 586-4800 Carnegie Class: Assoc/HT-High Trad
FAX Number: (609) 570-3870 Calendar System: Semester
URL: www.mccc.edu
Established: 1966 Annual Undergrad Tuition & Fees (In-District): $3,768
Enrollment: 7,979 Coed
Affiliation or Control: State/Local IRS Status: 501(c)3
Highest Offering: Associate Degree
Accreditation: M, AAB, ADNUR, FUSER, MACTE, MLTAD, PTAA, RAD

01 President ... Dr. Jianping WANG
111 Vice President College Advancement ... Mr. Edward GWAZDA
05 Vice President Academic Affairs ... Dr. David EDWARDS
10 Vice President for Admin & Finance ... Dr. Mark HARRIS
32 Vice President for Student Affairs ... Dr. Diane CAMPBELL
76 Dean Health Professions ... Dr. Robert SCHREYER
49 Dean Liberal Arts ... Dr. Robert KLEINSCHMIDT
50 Dean Business/Technology and STEM ... Dr. Winston MADDOX
12 Dean and Provost JKC ... Ms. Monica WEAVER
21 Exec Dir of Finance ... Mr. Brian MCCLOSKEY
26 Dir Marketing/Public Information ... Ms. Lynn HOLL
15 Exec Dir for Compliance & Human Res .. Ms. Monise PRINCILUS
06 Registrar ... Ms. Shannon KRAUSE
37 Director of Financial Aid ... Mr. Jason TAYLOR
09 Senior Dir Institutional Research ... Ms. Nina MAY
18 Chief Facilities/Physical Plant ... Mr. Bryon MARSHALL
96 Director of Purchasing ... Mr. Stephen GREGOROWICZ
84 Asst Dean Strategic Enrollment Svcs ... Ms. Savita BAMBHROLIA
08 Director of Library Services ... Ms. Pam PRICE
101 Exec Asst to the President/Board ... Ms. Beth BROWER
51 Dean Division of Lifelong Learning ... Ms. Leah PONTANI
104 Coord of Global Education ... Prof. Andrea LYNCH
106 Dean Innov/Online Educ/Stdnt Suc ... Dr. Alexandra SALAS
25 Chief Contracts/Grants Admin ... Ms. Kami ABDALA
36 Director Transfer & Career Services ... Ms. Laurene JONES
41 Athletic Director ... Mr. John SIMONE
108 Dean Inst Effectiveness ... Dr. Elizabeth ANDERSON
19 Director Security/Safety ... Mr. Bryon MARSHALL

Middlesex County College (B)

2600 Woodbridge Avenue, Edison NJ 08818-3050
County: Middlesex FICE Identification: 002615
Unit ID: 185536
Telephone: (732) 548-6000 Carnegie Class: Assoc/HT-Mix Trad/Non
FAX Number: (732) 494-8244 Calendar System: Semester
URL: www.middlesexcc.edu
Established: 1964 Annual Undergrad Tuition & Fees (In-District): $3,420
Enrollment: 11,662 Coed
Affiliation or Control: State/Local IRS Status: 501(c)3
Highest Offering: Associate Degree
Accreditation: M, ADNUR, DH, DIETT, ENGT, MLTAD, RAD

01 President ... Dr. Joann LA PERLA-MORALES
05 VP Academic & Student Affairs ... Dr. Mark MCCORMICK
10 VP Finance & Administration ... Ms. Maureen LAWRENCE
111 VP for Institutional Advancement ... Mr. Patrick MADAMA
32 Dean Student Affairs ... Ms. Marla BRINSON
84 Dean Enrollment Management ... Mr. Brian CLEMMONS
107 Dean Professional Studies ... Mr. Jeffrey HERRON
51 Dean Continuing Education ... Dr. Roseann BUCCIARELLI
18 Exec Director Facilities Management ... Mr. Donald DROST
13 Exec Director Information Tech ... Mr. Bradley MORTON
21 Controller ... Ms. Lori WILKIN
07 Director Admissions & Recruitment ... Ms. Lisa RODRIGUEZ-GREGORY
06 Registrar ... Mr. Richard COLE
37 Financial Aid Director ... Ms. Lujia ZHANG
26 Chief Public Relations Officer ... Mr. Thomas PETERSON
96 Director of Purchasing ... Mr. David FRICKE
09 Director of Institutional Research ... Ms. Meghan ALAI
25 Director Grants Development ... Mr. Til DALLAVALLE
29 Dir Development & Alumni Relations ... Ms. Veronica CLINTON
41 Athletic Director ... Mr. Robert WISNIEWSKI
04 Administrative Asst to President ... Ms. Sally D'ALOISIO

Monmouth University (C)

400 Cedar Avenue, West Long Branch NJ 07764-1898
County: Monmouth FICE Identification: 002616
Unit ID: 185572
Telephone: (732) 571-3400 Carnegie Class: Masters/L
FAX Number: (732) 571-3629 Calendar System: Semester
URL: www.monmouth.edu
Established: 1933 Annual Undergrad Tuition & Fees: $35,364
Enrollment: 6,394 Coed
Affiliation or Control: Independent Non-Profit IRS Status: 501(c)3
Highest Offering: Doctorate
Accreditation: M, #ARCPA, CACREP, CAEPN, CS, ENG, NURSE, @SP, SW

01 President ... Mr. Grey J. DIMENNA
04 Executive Assistant to President ... Ms. Annette GOUGH
101 Special Asst Board of Trustees ... Ms. Janet FELL
05 Provost/VP Academic Affairs ... Dr. Laura MORIARTY
58 Vice Provost for Graduate Studies ... Dr. Michael PALLADINO
20 Vice Provost for Global Educ ... Dr. Jon STAUFF
20 Vice Provost for Transform Lrng ... Dr. Kathryn KLOBY
20 Vice Provost for Plng & Dec Support ... Ms. Christine BENOL
20 Vice Provost for Acad & Fac Affs ... Dr. Nicolle PARSONS-POLLARD
06 Registrar ... Mrs. Lynn REYNOLDS
49 Dean Sch Humanities/Social Science ... Dr. Kenneth WOMACK
50 Dean Leon Hess Business Sch ... Dr. Donald MOLIVER
53 Dean School of Education ... Dr. John HENNING
81 Dean Sch of Science ... Dr. Steven BACHRACH
66 Dean School of Nursing/Health Stds ... Dr. Janet MAHONEY
70 Dean School of Social Work ... Dr. Robin MAMA
92 Dean Honors School ... Dr. Walter GREASON
08 University Librarian ... Mr. Kurt WAGNER
10 Vice President Finance ... Mr. William G. CRAIG
21 Assoc VP for Finance/Budgets ... Mr. Jack GAVIN
96 Director of Purchasing ... Mr. Mark MIRANDA
43 Vice President & General Counsel ... Mr. John J. CHRISTOPHER
88 Dir of Compliance/Risk Mgr ... Mr. Michael WUNSCH
22 Director Equity and Diversity ... Ms. Nina ANDERSON
11 Vice President Administrative Svcs ... Mrs. Patricia SWANNACK
18 Assoc VP Campus Plng/Construction ... Mr. Robert CORNERO
19 Director/Chief of Police ... Capt. William MCELRATH
15 Director of Human Resources ... Ms. Robyn SALVO
32 VP Student Life & Ldrshp Engagement ... Mrs. Mary Anne NAGY
35 Assoc VP for Student Life ... Mr. James PILLAR
35 Dir Student Activities/Student Ctr ... Ms. Amy BELLINA
27 Chief Univ Editor/Dir Exec Com ... Mr. Michael MAIDEN
30 Vice Pres External Affairs ... Mr. Jason KROLL
26 Assoc VP Univ Mktg/Communications ... Ms. Tara PETERS
29 Asst VP for University Engagement ... Vacant
84 Vice Pres Enrollment Management ... Dr. Robert MC CAIG
37 Assoc VP Enr Mgmt/Dir Fin Aid ... Ms. Claire ALASIO
07 Assoc VP for UG & GR Admission ... Ms. Lauren VENTO-CIFELLI
41 Vice Pres & Director of Athletics ... Dr. Marilyn MCNEIL
13 Vice Pres Information Management ... Dr. Edward CHRISTENSEN
97 Assoc Vice Prov/Acad Found/Gen Ed ... Dr. Judith NYE
09 Director of Institutional Research ... Vacant
36 Assistant Dean for Career Services ... Mr. William HILL
86 Dir of Government & Community Rels ... Mr. Paul DEMENT
25 Director of Grants & Contracts ... Mr. Tony LAZROE

Montclair State University (D)

1 Normal Avenue, Montclair NJ 07043-9987
County: Essex and Passaic FICE Identification: 002617
Unit ID: 185590
Telephone: (973) 655-4000 Carnegie Class: DU-Mod
FAX Number: N/A Calendar System: Semester
URL: www.montclair.edu
Established: 1908 Annual Undergrad Tuition & Fees (In-State): $12,116
Enrollment: 20,465 Coed
Affiliation or Control: State IRS Status: 501(c)3
Highest Offering: Doctorate
Accreditation: M, ART, AUD, CAATE, CACREP, CAEPN, CS, DANCE, DIETD, DIETI, MUS, PH, SP, THEA

01 President ... Dr. Susan A. COLE
05 Provost/Vice Pres Academic Affairs ... Dr. Willard P. GINGERICH
10 Vice Pres Finance & Treasurer ... Mr. Jonathan ROSENHEIN
32 Vice Pres Student Devel/Campus Life . Dr. Karen L. PENNINGTON
111 Vice Pres University Advancement ... Mr. John T. SHANNON
15 Vice Pres Human Resources ... Vacant
18 Vice Pres Univ Facilities ... Mr. Shawn M. CONNOLLY
13 Vice Pres Info Technology ... Ms. Candace C. FLEMING
88 Associate VP for Program Management ... Mr. Samir BAKANE
43 University Counsel ... Mr. Mark FLEMING
86 Director Government Relations ... Ms. Shivaun P. GAINES
114 Exec Director Budget and Planning ... Mr. David JOSEPHSON
79 Dean Col Humanities & Soc Sciences ... Dr. Robert S. FRIEDMAN
81 Dean Col Science & Mathematics ... Vacant
53 Dean Col Educ & Human Services ... Dr. Tamara F. LUCAS
57 Dean Col of the Arts ... Mr. Daniel A. GURSKIS
50 Dean School of Business ... Dr. Alan G. CANT
66 Dean School of Nursing ... Dr. Janice SMOLOWITZ
08 Dean Library Services ... Dr. Judith L. HUNT
58 Dean of the Graduate School ... Dr. Joan C. FICKE
35 Dean of Students ... Ms. Margaree COLEMAN-CARTER
108 Assoc Provost Acad Pgm/ Assessment ... Dr. Joanne F. COTE-BONANNO
43 Associate University Counsel ... Ms. Maria ANDERSON
20 Assoc Provost Undergrad Educ ... Dr. James D. GERMAN
21 Associate VP Finance ... Mr. Michael GALVIN
91 Assoc VP Enterprise App Services ... Ms. Donna SADLON
35 Assoc VP Student Dev/Campus Life ... Ms. Kathleen E. RAGAN
16 Director of Employee Relations ... Mr. Eric CARR
16 Asst VP Talent Management ... Ms. Keesha CHAVIS
64 Director School of Music ... Dr. J. Robert CART
09 Director Institutional Research ... Dr. Steven L. JOHNSON
06 Registrar ... Ms. Leslie SUTTON-SMITH
07 Director Undergraduate Admissions ... Mr. Jeffrey D. INDIVERI-GANT
26 Asst VP Communications & Marketing ... Ms. Ellen GRIFFIN
30 Associate VP for Development ... Ms. Lisa HOYT
19 Chief of University Police ... Mr. Paul M. CELL
22 Dir EO/Affirmative Action/Diversity ... Ms. Barbara J. MILTON
38 Dir Counseling & Psych Services ... Dr. Jaclyn J. FRIEDMAN-LOMBARDO
39 Exec Director Residence Life ... Mr. John DELATE
40 Gen Manager University Bookstore ... Ms. Diana PELLEGRINO
41 Dir Intercollegiate Athletics ... Ms. Holly P. GERA
37 Director Financial Aid ... Mr. James T. ANDERSON
96 Director Procurement/Goods Svcs ... Ms. Christine G. PALMA
121 Exec Dir Ctr Advising/Stdnt Trans ... Dr. Michele CAMPAGNA
92 Director Honors Program ... Vacant
88 Director of Student Accounts ... Ms. Marion CAGGIANO
23 Director University Health Center ... Vacant
28 Director Equity & Diversity ... Dr. Sidney GARDNER
25 Dir Research & Sponsored Programs ... Mr. Frederic J. RUSSO
88 Associate Dean of Students ... Ms. Fatima M. DECARVALHO
105 Director Web Services ... Ms. Katherine TASHEFF
04 Exec Assistant to the President ... Ms. Karen M. AIELLO
42 Chaplain ... Fr. James CHERN
88 Dir Construction Procurement/Acct ... Mr. Daniel ROCHE
88 Dir Tech Training and Integration ... Dr. Yanling SUN
88 Dir Environmental Health and Safety ... Dr. Amy V. JOHNSON-FERDINAND
27 Director Media Relations ... Ms. Erika BLEIBERG
100 Chief of Staff ... Mr. Keith D. BARRACK
106 Exec Dir Online Extended Learning ... Dr. Peter MCALINEY

New Brunswick Theological Seminary (E)

35 Seminary Place, New Brunswick NJ 08901
County: Middlesex FICE Identification: 002619
Unit ID: 185758
Telephone: (732) 247-5241 Carnegie Class: Spec-4-yr-Faith
FAX Number: (732) 249-5412 Calendar System: Semester
URL: www.nbts.edu
Established: 1784 Annual Graduate Tuition & Fees: N/A
Enrollment: 136 Coed
Affiliation or Control: Reformed Church In America IRS Status: 501(c)3
Highest Offering: Doctorate; No Undergraduates
Accreditation: THEOL

01 President ... Dr. Micah L. MCCREARY
04 Assistant to the President ... Ms. Michelle SANDERS
05 Dean of the Seminary ... Dr. Willard W.C ASHLEY, SR.
10 Chief Financial Officer ... Mr. Kenneth TERMOTT
21 Accounting Manager ... Ms. Tara HAMILL
30 Director of Development ... Vacant
08 Director of the Library ... Tracy HUNTER HAYES
06 Registrar ... Ms. Yasha PEOPLE
32 Dean of Students/Title IX Coord ... Ms. Joan MARSHALL
07 Admissions Committee Chair ... Dr. Beth L. TANNER
18 Facilities Manager ... Mr. Paul KUHN
13 Network Technician ... Vacant
108 Director of Assessment ... Dr. Terry SMITH
36 Director of Field Education ... Dr. Faye TAYLOR

New Jersey City University (F)

2039 Kennedy Boulevard, Jersey City NJ 07305-1597
County: Hudson FICE Identification: 002613
Unit ID: 185129
Telephone: (201) 200-2000 Carnegie Class: Masters/L
FAX Number: (201) 200-2352 Calendar System: Semester
URL: www.njcu.edu
Established: 1927 Annual Undergrad Tuition & Fees (In-State): $11,430
Enrollment: 8,237 Coed
Affiliation or Control: State IRS Status: 501(c)3
Highest Offering: Doctorate
Accreditation: M, ACBSP, ART, CACREP, CAEPT, MUS

01 President ... Dr. Sue HENDERSON
05 Provost/Sr VP Academic Affairs ... Dr. Daniel J. JULIUS
32 Vice Pres for Student Affairs ... Dr. Jimmy JUNG
10 Vice Pres Administration/Finance ... Dr. Aaron ASKA
111 Vice Pres University Advancement ... Vacant
21 Controller ... Vacant
13 Assoc VP Computer Info Systems ... Mr. Robert MCBRIDE
18 Interim AVP Facil/Construction Mgmt ... Mr. Michael D'AQUILA
07 Assoc VP Admissions/Enrollment Mgmt ... Mr. Benjamin ROHDIN
26 Assoc VP of Communications ... Dr. Sherrie MADIA
20 Assoc VP Academic Affairs ... Dr. Guillermo DE VEYGA
15 Assoc VP Human Resources ... Ms. Natalie THOMPSON
20 Interim Assistant Provost ... Dr. Nurdan AYDIN
20 Interim Assistant Provost ... Dr. Karen MORGAN
27 Asst VP Public Information ... Ms. Ellen WAYMAN-GORDON
14 Asst VP Information Technology ... Ms. Phyllis SZANI
30 Asst VP of Development ... Ms. Lori FUNICELLO
35 Asst Vice Pres Student Affairs ... Dr. Demond HARGROVE
88 Asst VP for Global Initiatives ... Ms. Tamara CUNNINGHAM
49 Dean Arts & Sciences ... Dr. Joao SEDYCIAS
53 Int Dean Education & Prof Studies ... Dr. Deborah WOO
50 Dean School of Business ... Dr. Bernard MCSHERRY
35 Dean of Students ... Dr. Lyn HAMLIN
108 Asst VP Institutional Effectivenes ... Dr. Sue GERBER
08 Director of the University Library ... Mr. Frederick SMITH
06 Registrar ... Vacant
36 Director Career Planning/Placement ... Dr. Jennifer JONES
16 Director Human Resources ... Mr. Robert PIASKOWSKY
19 Director Public Safety ... Dr. Ronald HURLEY
41 Director Athletics/Recreation ... Ms. Alice DE FAZIO
22 Dir Affirmative Action/Equal Oppty ... Ms. Lisa NORCIA
29 Director Alumni Relations ... Ms. Jane MCCLELLAN
38 Director Student Counseling ... Dr. Abisola GALLAGHER
96 Director of Purchasing ... Ms. Edie DELVECCHIO
43 University Counsel ... Mr. Alfred E. RAMEY, JR.
85 Director of International Programs ... Mr. Craig KATZ
37 Director Student Financial Aid ... Vacant
88 Director Student Fin Svcs/Risk Mgr ... Mr. Jeffrey BRUNETTO
16 Labor Relations Associate ... Mr. Matthew STIEGLITZ
39 Director Student Housing ... Ms. Jodi BAILEY

106 Acting Dir Online E-learning .... Ms. Jennifer FOX
25 Executive Director Grants Admin .... Dr. Ashok VASEASHTA
44 Director Annual Giving .... Ms. Andrea VELASCO
84 Associate VP Enrollment Management .... Mr. Benjamin ROHDIN

New Jersey Institute of Technology (A)

University Heights, Newark NJ 07102-1982
County: Essex FICE Identification: 002621
Unit ID: 185828
Telephone: (973) 596-3000 Carnegie Class: DU-Higher
FAX Number: (973) 642-4380 Calendar System: Semester
URL: www.njit.edu
Established: 1881 Annual Undergrad Tuition & Fees (In-State): $16,430
Enrollment: 11,325 Coed
Affiliation or Control: State IRS Status: 501(c)3
Highest Offering: Doctorate
Accreditation: M, ART, CIDA, CS, ENG, ENGT

01 President .... Dr. Joel S. BLOOM
05 Provost and Senior Executive VP .... Dr. Fadi P. DEEK
10 Sr Vice Pres Finance/CFO .... Mr. Edward J. BISHOF, SR.
30 Vice Pres University Advancement .... Dr. Charles DEES
46 Sr VP Tech & Bus Dev/Pres NJII .... Dr. Donald H. SEBASTIAN
88 VP for Real Estate & Capital Dev .... Mr. Andrew P. CHRIST
15 Vice President Human Resources .... Ms. Kay CLARKE-TURNER
32 VP Academic Support & Stdnt Affairs .... Dr. Charles J. FEY
43 General Counsel/VP Legal Affairs .... Ms. Holly C. STERN
20 Vice Provost for Academic Affairs .... Dr. Basil BALTZIS
54 Dean Newark College of Engineering .... Dr. Moshe KAM
48 Int Dean Col Arch & Design .... Mr. Anthony W. SCHUMAN
49 Dean Col Sci/Liberal Arts .... Dr. Kevin D. BELFIELD
50 Dean School of Management .... Dr. Reggie J. CAUDILL
92 Int Dean A Dorman Honors College .... Dr. John BECHTOLD
77 Dean Ying Wu College of Computing .... Dr. Craig GOTSMAN
88 Vice Provost for Research .... Dr. Atam P. DHAWAN
21 Assoc VP Finance & Controller .... Mr. William GARCIA
18 Assoc VP Design & Construction .... Mr. Joseph F. TARTAGLIA
58 Assoc Provost Grad Studies .... Dr. Sotirios G. ZIAVRAS
13 Assoc Provost Information Svcs Tech .... Mr. David F. ULLMAN
45 Assoc VP for Business & Econ Devel .... Dr. Timothy V. FRANKLIN
51 Assoc VP Cont/Distance Education .... Dr. Gale T. SPAK
84 Assoc VP Enroll Mgmt & Acad .... Dr. Wendy LIN-COOK
44 Assoc VP for Development .... Ms. Jacqueline G. RHODES
27 Asst VP for Communications .... Dr. Denise ANDERSON
41 Asst VP & Dir Athletics/Phys Educ .... Mr. Leonard I. KAPLAN
35 Assoc VP Stdnt Engag/Dean of Stdnts .... Dr. Laura VALENTE
89 Assoc Dean Ctr First Year Students .... Dr. Sharon E. MORGAN
26 Assoc VP Comm/Marketing & Branding .... Dr. Denise ANDERSON
29 Sr Exec Dir for Constituent Rels .... Mr. Michael A. WALL
04 Sr Assistant to President .... Ms. Mary Jane POHERO
88 Exec Dir Pre-College Program .... Dr. Jacqueline L. CUSACK
36 Exec Director Career Devel Svcs .... Mr. Gregory MASS
09 Director Inst Research/Planning .... Dr. Eugene P. DEESS
08 University Librarian .... Mr. Richard T. SWEENEY
06 Acting Registrar .... Dr. Charles J. FEY
37 Dir Student Financial Aid Services .... Ms. Ivon NUNEZ
88 Executive Director EOP .... Mr. Laurence A. HOWELL
38 Dir Counseling & Psych Services .... Dr. Phyllis BOLLING
19 Chief of Police .... Mr. Joseph S. MARSWILLO
24 Dir Instructional Tech/Media Svcs .... Mr. William F. REYNOLDS
85 Director International Students/Fac .... Mr. Jeffrey W. GRUNDY
88 Interim Director Campus Center .... Mr. Albert M. MARTINEZ
96 Director Purchasing .... Ms. Eugenia REGENCIO
100 Spec Asst to Pres Pol/Partnership .... Ms. Angela R. GARRETSON
105 Director Web Services .... Mr. Ersal ASLAM
108 Director Academic Assessment .... Dr. Charles R. BROOKS
07 Director of University Admissions .... Mr. Stephen M. ECK

Ocean County College (B)

PO Box 2001, Toms River NJ 08754-2001
County: Ocean FICE Identification: 002624
Unit ID: 185873
Telephone: (732) 255-0400 Carnegie Class: Assoc/HT-Mix Trad/Non
FAX Number: (732) 255-0444 Calendar System: Semester
URL: www.ocean.edu
Established: 1964 Annual Undergrad Tuition & Fees (In-District): $4,345
Enrollment: 8,663 Coed
Affiliation or Control: State/Local IRS Status: 501(c)3
Highest Offering: Associate Degree
Accreditation: M, ADNUR, EMT

01 President .... Dr. Jon H. LARSON
10 Exec VP of Finance & Administration .... Ms. Sara WINCHESTER
32 VP Student Affairs .... Vacant
05 Assoc VP of Academic Affairs .... Dr. Lisa DIBISCEGLIE
15 Asst VP Human Resources .... Ms. Tracey DONALDSON
20 Asst VP for Academic Affairs .... Dr. Antoinette M. CLAY
18 Asst VP Facilities .... Mr. Matthew KENNEDY
04 Senior Aide to the President .... Dr. Joseph KONOPKA
57 Dean Language and the Arts .... Ms. Heidi SHERIDAN
81 Dean Math/Science & Tech .... Mr. Paul SILBERQUIT
66 Dean of Nursing .... Ms. Teresa WALSH
83 Dean of Social Science .... Ms. Rosann BAR
88 Dean of Instructional Outreach .... Dr. Maysa HAYWARD
102 Exec Dir OCC Foundation .... Ms. Heather BARBERI
103 Asst VP CPE/Workforce Devel .... Ms. Patricia FENN
106 Assoc VP of e-Learning .... Mr. Jeff S. HARMON
106 Dean of e-Learning Faculty .... Mr. Jack KELNHOFER
08 Director of Library Services .... Ms. Donna ROSINSKI-KAUS
13 Chief Information Officer .... Mr. Hatem AKL
37 Interim Director of Financial Aid .... Ms. Yessica GARCIA-GUZMAN
06 Registrar .... Mr. Eric DANIELS
121 Dir of Academic Advising Services .... Ms. Anna REGAN
19 Director of College Security .... Mr. Frank IANNONE
26 Exec Director of College Relations .... Ms. Jan KIRSTEN
07 Director of Admissions .... Vacant
93 Director of EOF & OMS .... Ms. Laura RICKARDS
18 Director of Facilities .... Mr. James CALAMIA
41 Exec Dir of Judicial Aff & Athletic .... Ms. Ilene COHEN
45 Exec Dir of Institutional Planning .... Ms. Alexa BESHARA
21 Exec Dir of Strategic Projects .... Ms. Karen PAPAKONSTANTINOU
124 Dean of Academic Services .... Ms. Lori HARRIS-RANSOM
35 Director of Student Life .... Ms. Jennifer FAZIO
29 Director Alumni Relations .... Vacant

Passaic County Community College (C)

1 College Boulevard, Paterson NJ 07509-1179
County: Passaic FICE Identification: 009994
Unit ID: 186034
Telephone: (973) 684-6868 Carnegie Class: Assoc/HT-High Trad
FAX Number: (973) 684-5843 Calendar System: Semester
URL: www.pccc.edu
Established: 1968 Annual Undergrad Tuition & Fees (In-District): $4,553
Enrollment: 8,389 Coed
Affiliation or Control: State/Local IRS Status: 501(c)3
Highest Offering: Associate Degree
Accreditation: M, ADNUR, CAHIIM, ENGT, RAD

01 President .... Dr. Steven ROSE
05 Vice Pres Academic/Student Affairs .... Dr. Jacqueline KINEAVY
10 Vice Pres Finance/Administration .... Mr. Steven HARDY
12 Vice Pres Passaic Academic Center .... Ms. Josephine HERNANDEZ
13 Vice Pres Information Technology .... Mr. Robert MONDELLI
15 Associate Vice Pres Human Resources .... Mr. Jose FERNANDEZ
20 Dean Academic Affairs .... Dr. Bassel STASSIS
08 Associate Dean Learning Resources .... Mr. Greg FALLON
66 Assoc Dean Nurse Educ/Health Scis .... Ms. Donna STANKIEWICZ
88 Asst Dean for Testing & Tutoring .... Mr. Peter HYNES
09 Dir Institutional Research .... Mr. Justin HULL
88 Ex Dir Cultural Affs/The Poetry Ctr .... Ms. Maria GILLAN
30 Exec Dir of Institutional Devel .... Mr. Todd SORBER
84 Exec Dir of Enrollment Management .... Ms. Betsy MARINACE
18 Exec Dir Facilities Mgmt/Planning .... Mr. Brian EGAN
37 Director Financial Aid .... Ms. Linda GAYTON
06 Registrar .... Ms. Donna FISCHER
19 Director Security .... Mr. Glenn BROWN
35 Director Student Activities .... Ms. Maria MARTE
41 Athletic Director .... Mr. Wayne MARTIN
07 Director of Admissions .... Ms. Stephanie DECKER
29 Director Alumni Relations .... Mr. William MORRISON
32 Chief Student Life Officer .... Dr. Sharon GOLDSTEIN
26 Chief Public Relations Officer .... Ms. Betsy MARINACE
96 Director of Purchasing .... Mr. Michael D'AGATI
101 Dir Board Affairs/Asst to President .... Ms. Evelyn DEFEIS
103 Dir Workforce/Career Development .... Mr. Michael POWELL

Pillar College (D)

60 Park Place, Suite 701, Newark NJ 07102
County: Essex FICE Identification: 036663
Unit ID: 440794
Telephone: (973) 803-5000 Carnegie Class: Spec-4-yr-Faith
FAX Number: (973) 242-3282 Calendar System: Semester
URL: www.pillar.edu
Established: 1908 Annual Undergrad Tuition & Fees: $20,400
Enrollment: 421 Coed
Affiliation or Control: Other IRS Status: 501(c)3
Highest Offering: Master's
Accreditation: M, BI

01 President .... Dr. David E. SCHROEDER
05 Provost/Int Chief Academic Officer .... Mr. Daniel W. WRIGHT
20 VP Academic Affairs .... Dr. Alford H. OTTLEY
11 VP Operations/Public Affairs .... Dr. Ralph T. GRANT
32 VP Student Life .... Ms. Linda SCHMITT
100 Chief of Staff .... Mr. Kelvin THOMAS
51 VP Strategic Alliances .... Dr. Wayne R. DYER
10 Assistant VP of Financial Services .... Vacant
20 Assistant VP of Academics .... Mrs. Amy HUBER
06 Registrar .... Mr. Brian SCHROEDER
37 Assistant Director of Financial Aid .... Ms. Eboni CRAWFORD
07 Director of Admissions .... Mr. Dominic DIGIOACCHINO
42 Coordinator of Spiritual Formation .... Mr. Nishanth THOMAS
08 Director of Library .... Ms. Lorraine HODGES
26 Director of Marketing .... Mr. Kelvin THOMAS

Princeton Theological Seminary (E)

PO Box 821, Princeton NJ 08542-0803
County: Mercer FICE Identification: 002626
Unit ID: 186122
Telephone: (609) 921-8300 Carnegie Class: Spec-4-yr-Faith
FAX Number: (609) 924-2973 Calendar System: Semester
URL: www.ptsem.edu
Established: 1812 Annual Graduate Tuition & Fees: N/A
Enrollment: 556 Coed
Affiliation or Control: Presbyterian Church (U.S.A.) IRS Status: 501(c)3
Highest Offering: Doctorate; No Undergraduates
Accreditation: M, THEOL

01 President .... Dr. M. Craig BARNES
10 Sr Vice Pres/Chief Oper Ofcr/Treas .... Mr. John W. GILMORE
30 VP for Advancement .... Ms. Jaime ZAMPARELLI
26 VP for Communication & External Rel .... Dr. Shane A. BERG
05 Dean and VP of Academic Affairs .... Dr. James F. KAY
32 Dean Student Life & VP Stdnt Rels .... Rev. John E. WHITE
45 Assoc Dean of Planning & Assessment .... Dr. Shawn OLIVER
35 Assoc Dean Stdnt Life/Dir Sr Plcmnt .... RevDr. Catherine C. DAVIS
51 Assoc Dean of Continuing Educ .... Rev. Dayle G. ROUNDS
21 Assoc VP for Finance and Admin .... Mr. Kurt A. GABBARD
88 Director of Church Relations .... Rev. Larissa KWONG ABAZIA
06 Registrar .... Ms. Brenda D. WILLIAMS
07 Director Admissions/Financial Aid .... Mr. Matthew R. SPINA
08 Interim Librarian .... Ms. Melody MAZUK
88 Assoc VP for Advancement .... Rev. J. Thomas KORT
15 Director of Human Resources .... Ms. Barbara MECCIA
13 Chief Technology Officer .... Mr. Jeffrey SIEBEN
18 Director of Facilities .... Mr. German MARTINEZ
88 Director of Campus Relations .... Rev. Joicy BECKER-RICHARDS
39 Director of Housing/Auxiliary Svcs .... Mr. Stephen CARDONE
20 Assoc Dean for Academic Admin .... Dr. Rose Ellen DUNN
38 Director of Student Counseling .... Rev. Nancy L. SCHONGALLA-BOWMAN
42 Minister of the Chapel .... Rev. Janice S. AMMON
28 Director Multicultural Relations .... Rev. Victor ALOYO, JR.
04 Executive Asst to the President .... Ms. Catherine AHMAD
37 Assoc Director Financial Aid .... Mr. Michael D. LIVIO
44 Director of Annual Giving .... Ms. Cheryl ALI
44 Director of Planned Giving .... Mr. Murray LOPDELL-LAWRENCE
106 Director of Digital Learning .... Mr. Reno LAURO
29 Director Alumni/ae Relations .... Mr. Brian K. MCCOLLUM
27 Associate Vice Pres Communications .... Ms. Anne WHITAKER STEWART

Princeton University (F)

Princeton NJ 08544-1098
County: Mercer FICE Identification: 002627
Unit ID: 186131
Telephone: (609) 258-3000 Carnegie Class: DU-Highest
FAX Number: N/A Calendar System: Semester
URL: www.princeton.edu
Established: 1746 Annual Undergrad Tuition & Fees: $45,320
Enrollment: 8,138 Coed
Affiliation or Control: Independent Non-Profit IRS Status: 501(c)3
Highest Offering: Doctorate
Accreditation: M, CAEPT, ENG

01 President .... Cristopher L. EISGRUBER
03 Executive Vice President .... Treby WILLIAMS
05 Provost .... David S. LEE
04 Vice President & Secretary .... Robert K. DURKEE
10 Vice Pres for Finance & Treasurer .... Carolyn N. AINSLIE
111 Vice President for Advancement .... Kevin B. HEANEY
26 Vice President for Public Affairs .... Robert K. DURKEE
32 Vice President of Campus Life .... Rochelle CALHOUN
18 Vice President for Facilities .... KyuJung E. WHANG
13 Vice President Info Technology/CIO .... Jay DOMINICK
15 Vice President for Human Resources .... Lianne C. SULLIVAN-CROWLEY
109 VP for University Services .... Chad L. KLAUS
20 Vice Provost Academic Affairs .... Katherine ROHRER
22 Vice Provost Inst Equity/Diversity .... Michelle MINTER
09 Vice Provost Institutional Research .... Jed MARSH
88 Vice Prov Space Programming/Plan .... Paul LAMARCHE
114 Budget Dir/Vice Provost Finance .... Steven GILL
116 Chief Audit & Compliance Officer .... Nilufer K. SHROFF
20 Vice Provost Intl Initiatives .... Anastasia T. VRACHNOS
27 Asst Vice President Communications .... Daniel A. DAY
29 Asst Vice President Alumni Affairs .... Margaret M. MILLER
44 Asst Vice President Annual Giving .... William M. HARDT
88 Asst VP for University Services .... Amy CAMPBELL
88 AVP Facilities Design/Construction .... Anne ST. MAURO
88 Asst Vice Pres University Services .... Andrew KANE
46 Chair Univ Rsrch Bd/Dean Research .... Pablo DEBENEDETTI
43 General Counsel .... Ramona E. ROMERO
88 President PRINCO .... Andrew K. GOLDEN
88 Dean of the Faculty .... Deborah PRENTICE
58 Dean of Graduate School .... Sanjeev KULKARNI
49 Dean of the College .... Jill S. DOLAN
54 Dean of School of Engineering .... Emily CARTER
82 Dean of WW Sch of Public/Intl Affs .... Cecilia ROUSE
48 Dean of School of Architecture .... Monica PONCE DE LEON
42 Dean of Religious Life .... Alison BODEN
35 Dean of Undergraduate Students .... Kathleen DEIGNAN
07 Dean of Admission .... Janet L. RAPELYE
17 Exec Director Health Services .... John KOLLIGIAN
08 University Librarian .... Anne JARVIS
06 Registrar .... Polly WINFREY GRIFFIN
37 Dir Undergraduate Financial Aid .... Robin A. MOSCATO
86 Director Government Affairs .... Joyce A. RECHTSCHAFFEN
31 Dir Community & Regional Affairs .... Kristin APPELGET
41 Director of Athletics .... Mollie D. MARCOUX
96 Director of Purchasing .... Donald E. WESTON, JR.
38 Dir of Counseling & Psych Services .... Anita MCLEAN
16 Director Human Resources .... Claire JACOBS ELSON
85 Director Davis International Center .... Jackie LEIGHTON
36 Executive Director Career Services .... Pulin SANGHVI
90 Assoc CIO/Dir Academic Services OIT .... Serge J. GOLDSTEIN
14 Assoc CIO/Dir Support Services OIT .... Steven M. SATHER
91 Dir Enterprise Infrastructure OIT .... Donna E. TATRO
30 AVP for Development .... Kerstin LARSEN
104 Sr Asc Dn of Col/Dir Ofc Intl Pgms .... Nancy A. KANACH

39 Director Housing ... Andrew KANE
19 Executive Director Public Safety ... Paul OMINSKY

Rabbi Jacob Joseph School (A)

1 Plainfield Avenue, Edison NJ 08817-4494
County: Middlesex FICE Identification: 030775
Unit ID: 384421
Telephone: (732) 985-6533 Carnegie Class: Spec-4-yr-Faith
FAX Number: (732) 985-6553 Calendar System: Semester
Established: 1982 Annual Undergrad Tuition & Fees: $11,900
Enrollment: 98 Male
Affiliation or Control: Independent Non-Profit IRS Status: 501(c)3
Highest Offering: Baccalaureate
Accreditation: RABN

01 President ... Dr. Marvin SCHICK
03 Rosh Yeshiva ... Rabbi Yaakov BUSEL
05 Rosh Yeshiva ... Rabbi Joseph EICHENSTEIN
37 Financial Aid Director ... Rabbi Yitzchok WEINTRAUB

Rabbinical College of America (B)

226 Sussex Avenue, Morristown NJ 07960-3600
County: Morris FICE Identification: 008609
Unit ID: 186186
Telephone: (973) 267-9404 Carnegie Class: Spec-4-yr-Faith
FAX Number: (973) 267-5208 Calendar System: Trimester
URL: www.rca.edu
Established: 1956 Annual Undergrad Tuition & Fees: $11,100
Enrollment: 258 Male
Affiliation or Control: Independent Non-Profit IRS Status: 501(c)3
Highest Offering: Baccalaureate
Accreditation: RABN

01 Dean ... Rabbi Moshe HERSON
04 Admin Assistant to the Dean ... Rabbi Mendy HERSON
26 Public Relations Officer ... Rabbi Mendel SOLOMON
06 Registrar ... Mrs. Shoshana SOLOMON
88 Director New Direction Program ... Rabbi Zalman DUBINSKY
10 Chief Business Officer ... Vacant
37 Director Student Financial Aid ... Rabbi Yisroel GOLDBERG
08 Chief Librarian ... Rabbi Sholom SPALTER
51 Dir Continuing Educ/Alumni Rels ... Rabbi Boruch HECHT
88 Director Semicha Program ... Rabbi Chaim SCHAPIRO
18 Director Building and Grounds ... Rabbi Hershel LIPSKIER

Ramapo College of New Jersey (C)

505 Ramapo Valley Road, Mahwah NJ 07430-1680
County: Bergen FICE Identification: 009344
Unit ID: 186201
Telephone: (201) 684-7500 Carnegie Class: Masters/M
FAX Number: (201) 684-7508 Calendar System: Semester
URL: www.ramapo.edu
Established: 1969 Annual Undergrad Tuition & Fees (In-State): $13,870
Enrollment: 6,026 Coed
Affiliation or Control: State IRS Status: 501(c)3
Highest Offering: Master's
Accreditation: M, CAEPT, NUR, SW

01 President ... Dr. Peter P. MERCER
05 Provost/VP Academic Affairs ... Dr. Beth BARNETT
10 VP Administration & Finance ... Ms. Kirsten DASILVA
43 VP and General Counsel ... Mr. Michael A. TRIPODI
111 VP Inst Advance/Dir Fdtn/Chief Dev ... Ms. Cathleen DAVEY
84 Assoc VP of Enrollment Mgmt ... Mr. Christopher ROMANO
45 Chief Planning Officer ... Dr. Dorothy ECHOLS TOBE
100 Chief of Staff ... Ms. Brittany A. WILLIAMS-GOLDSTEIN
116 Director of Internal Audit ... Ms. Patricia CHAVEZ
20 Vice Prov Curriculum & Assessment ... Dr. Emily WILLIAMS
21 Assoc Vice Pres Admin/Finance ... Mr. Richard ROBERTS
13 Assoc VP/Chief Information Officer ... Mr. George TABBACK
86 Asst Vice Pres Government Rels ... Ms. Anna FARNESKI
105 Asst VP Mktg/Comm & Web Admin ... Ms. Melissa HORVATH-PLYMAN
08 College Librarian/Dean ... Ms. Elizabeth SIECKE
06 Registrar ... Ms. Michele DUNN
07 Director of Admissions ... Mr. Peter RICE
37 Director of Financial Aid ... Mr. F. Shawn O'NEILL
21 Controller ... Ms. Colleen O'KEEFE
15 Asst VP of HR & Benefits ... Mr. David VERNON
78 Dir Exper Learning/Career Svcs ... Ms. Beth RICCA
32 Dean of Students ... Ms. Melissa VAN DER WALL
41 Director of Athletics ... Mr. Harold CROCKER
18 Director of Facilities ... Mr. Michael CUNNINGHAM
19 Director Public Safety ... Mr. Vincent MARKOWSKI
88 Director Educ Opportunity Program ... Ms. Barbara HARMON-FRANCIS
50 Dean Anisfield School of Business ... Dr. Edward PETKUS
82 Interim Dean Salameno Sch Hum/Glob ... Dr. Susan HANGEN
57 Dean Sch of Contemporary Arts ... Mr. Steven PERRY
83 Dean Sch Soc Science & Human Svc ... Dr. Aaron R S. LORENZ
81 Dean Sch Theoretical/Applied Sci ... Dr. Edward SAIFF
53 Asst Dean for Teacher Education ... Dr. Rexton LYNN
38 Director Ctr for Health/Counseling ... Dr. Judith GREEN
29 Dir Alumni Relations ... Ms. Joanne FAVATA
24 Asst Manager Academic Media Svcs ... Mr. Michael SAVIANESO
04 Executive Assistant to President ... Ms. Sara GAZZILLO
23 Coordinator Health Services ... Ms. Debbie LUKACSKO
09 Director of Institutional Research ... Dr. Gurvinder KHANEJA
22 Dir Affirmative Action/EEO ... Ms. Helen HIGGINBOTHAM
40 Bookstore Manager ... Ms. Theresa KING
85 Director of Intl Education ... Mr. Ben LEVY
36 Asst Dir Career Dev & Placement ... Ms. Debra STARK
96 Director of Purchasing ... Mr. Stephen SONDEY
103 Manager of Learning/Devel & Perf ... Mr. Roger JANS
25 Asst VP of Grants/Sponsor Programs ... Ms. Angela CRISTINI
30 Asst VP for Inst Advancement ... Ms. Lisa JOHNSON
28 Chief Diversity & Equity Officer ... Ms. Nicole MORGAN AGARD
35 Director of Student Conduct ... Ms. Kathleen HALLISSEY
121 Asst VP of Student Success ... Mr. Joseph CONNELL
114 Director Budget/Fiscal Planning ... Ms. Beth WALKLEY
113 Director of Student Accounts ... Ms. Debra SCHULTES
118 Benefits Manager ... Ms. Valerie HUNTER
119 Network Administrator ... Ms. Joelisio DOSANJOS

Raritan Valley Community College (D)

118 Lamington Road, Branchburg NJ 08876
County: Somerset FICE Identification: 007731
Unit ID: 186645
Telephone: (908) 526-1200 Carnegie Class: Assoc/HT-Mix Trad/Non
FAX Number: (908) 526-0253 Calendar System: Semester
URL: www.raritanval.edu
Established: 1966 Annual Undergrad Tuition & Fees (In-District): $4,224
Enrollment: 8,099 Coed
Affiliation or Control: State/Local IRS Status: 501(c)3
Highest Offering: Associate Degree
Accreditation: M, ADNUR, CAHIIM, MAC, OPD

01 President ... Dr. Michael MCDONOUGH
05 Provost & VP Academic Affairs ... Dr. Deborah PRESTON
10 Vice President Finance/Facilities ... Mr. John TROJAN
13 Vice Pres Technology/Assess/Plng ... Mr. Charles E. CHULVICK
15 VP Human Resources/Labor Relations ... Ms. Nancy MOORE
30 VP of Strategic Programs & Develop ... Ms. Jacki BELIN
20 Dean of Liberal Arts ... Dr. Patrice MARKS
32 Dean Student Services ... Ms. Diane LEMCOE
85 Dean Multicultural Affairs ... Ms. Richeleen DASHIELD
18 Exec Director Facilities/Grounds ... Mr. Brian O'ROURKE
38 Dir of Student Advising & Couns ... Mr. Greg DESANCTIS
24 Director Media Relations ... Ms. Donna STOLZER
88 Conference Services Director ... Ms. Karen VAUGHAN
72 Executive Director Inst Technology ... Mr. Michael E. MACHNIK
102 Executive Director Foundation ... Ms. Ronnie WEYL
14 Exec Dir Technology Services ... Mr. Robert PESCINSKI
21 Controller/Exec Dir of Finance ... Ms. Violet J. WILLENSKY
57 Director of Theatre ... Mr. Alan C. LIDDELL
09 Dir of Inst Research/Assessment ... Ms. Sarah DONNELLY
88 Director of Planetarium ... Ms. Amie GALLAGHER
88 Director of Child Care Center ... Ms. Cathy GRIFFIN
37 Director of Financial Aid ... Mr. Lenny MESONAS
08 Library Director ... Vacant
06 Registrar ... Mr. Dan PALUBNIAK
96 Director of Purchasing ... Mr. Michael DEPINTO
35 Director of Student Life ... Mr. Russell BAREFOOT
36 Director Transfer/Career Services ... Mr. Paul MICHAUD
26 Executive Director Marketing ... Ms. Janet THOMPSON
07 Director Admissions & Recruitment ... Ms. Carolyn WHITE
103 Exec Dir Workforce Development ... Ms. Michele BORONKAS
19 Director Security/Safety ... Mr. Robert SZKODNEY
41 Athletic Director ... Ms. Amanda DEMARTINO

Rider University (E)

2083 Lawrenceville Road, Lawrenceville NJ 08648-3099
County: Mercer FICE Identification: 002628
Unit ID: 186283
Telephone: (609) 896-5000 Carnegie Class: Masters/L
FAX Number: (609) 896-8029 Calendar System: Semester
URL: www.rider.edu
Established: 1865 Annual Undergrad Tuition & Fees: $39,820
Enrollment: 5,069 Coed
Affiliation or Control: Independent Non-Profit IRS Status: 501(c)3
Highest Offering: Master's
Accreditation: M, CACREP, CAEPN, MUS, NURSE

01 President ... Dr. Gregory DELL'OMO
05 Provost/Vice Pres Academic Affairs ... Dr. DonnaJean A. FREDEEN
10 Vice President Finance/Treasurer ... Ms. Julie A. KARNS
111 Vice Pres University Advancement ... Mr. Jonathan D. MEER
32 VP Student Affairs/Dean of Students ... Vacant
84 Vice Pres Enrollment Management ... Mr. James P. O'HARA
13 Assoc VP Information Technology ... Ms. Carol S. KONDRACH
21 Associate Vice President/Controller ... Ms. Jennifer M. POTTER
09 Assoc Vice Pres Institutional Rsrch ... Vacant
18 VP Facilities/Auxiliary Services ... Mr. Michael F. RECA
45 Sr Assoc Vice President Planning ... Ms. Debbie STASOLLA
26 Asst VP for Univ Comm/Marketing ... Ms. Kristine A. BROWN
20 Associate Provost ... Dr. James O. CASTAGNERA
12 Dean Westminster ... Dr. Matthew R. SHAFTEL
07 Dean of Enrollment ... Ms. Susan C. CHRISTIAN
51 Dean College of Cont Studies ... Mr. Boris VILIC
49 Dean Liberal Arts & Science ... Dr. Jonathan MILLEN
53 Dean College of Education ... Dr. Sharon SHERMAN
50 Dean Business Administration ... Dr. Cynthia M. NEWMAN
06 Registrar ... Ms. Susan A. STEFANICK
08 Dean of Library Services ... Mr. F. William CHICKERING
15 Assoc VP HR/Affirm Action ... Mr. Robert STOTO
19 Director of Public Safety ... Ms. Vickie L. WEAVER
29 Director of Alumni Relations ... Ms. Natalie M. POLLARD
41 Director of Athletics ... Mr. Donald P. HARNUM
37 Exec Dir Student Financial Svcs ... Mr. Drew C. AROMANDO
40 Manager College Store ... Ms. Deana REED
04 Director of Office of the President ... Ms. Christine ZELENAK
36 Director of Career Placement ... Ms. Kim BARBERICH
28 Director of Multicultural Affairs ... Dr. Pamela PRUITT
35 Assoc VP for Student Affairs ... Ms. Cindy THREATT
38 Director of Counseling ... Dr. Nadine MARTY
96 Director of Procurement ... Ms. Ann Marie MEAD

Rowan College at Burlington County (F)

900 College Circle, Mt. Laurel NJ 08054
County: Burlington FICE Identification: 007730
Unit ID: 183877
Telephone: (856) 222-9311 Carnegie Class: Assoc/HT-High Non
FAX Number: (609) 894-0183 Calendar System: Semester
URL: www.rcbc.edu
Established: 1966 Annual Undergrad Tuition & Fees (In-District): $4,065
Enrollment: 8,762 Coed
Affiliation or Control: State/Local IRS Status: 501(c)3
Highest Offering: Associate Degree
Accreditation: M, ADNUR, CAHIIM, DH, DMS, ENGT, RAD

01 President ... Mr. Paul DRAYTON
04 Exec Asst to the President ... Ms. Lynne Marie DEVERICKS
05 Sr Vice President/Provost ... Dr. David SPANG
84 VP Enroll Mgmt and Student Success ... Mr. Michael CIOCE
103 VP WDI and Lifelong Learning ... Ms. Anna PAYANZO COTTON
13 Chief Information Officer ... Mr. Mark MEARA
10 Exec Dir Financial Services ... Ms. Jaclyn ANGERMEIER
11 Chief Operations Officer ... Mr. Matthew FARR
102 Exec Director Foundation ... Ms. Anika RAGINS-RILEY
26 Exec Dir Marketing/Communications ... Mr. Greg VOLPE
15 Exec Director of HR/Admin Svcs ... Vacant
49 Dean of Liberal Arts ... Ms. Donna VANDERGRIFT
81 Dean of STEM ... Dr. Edem TETTEH
66 Dean of Nursing/Allied Health ... Dr. Karen MONTALTO
106 Dean of Learning Resources ... Dr. Martin A. HOFFMAN, SR.
32 Dean of Student Success ... Dr. Catherine R. BRIGGS
07 Dean of Enrollment Management ... Dr. Karen L. ARCHAMBAULT
06 Registrar ... Ms. LacyJane RYMAN-MESCAL
41 Director of Athletics ... Ms. Heather CONGER
88 Director of Culinary Arts ... Mr. James BRUDNICKI
88 Director of EOF Program ... Ms. Edith CORBIN
25 Director of Educ Pgm & Grant Dev ... Dr. Nicole SCOTT
19 Director of Public Safety ... Ms. Linda SCHMIDT
88 Director of Transfer Center ... Ms. Anne EDWARDS

Rowan College at Gloucester County (G)

1400 Tanyard Road, Sewell NJ 08080-9518
County: Gloucester FICE Identification: 006901
Unit ID: 184791
Telephone: (856) 468-5000 Carnegie Class: Assoc/HT-High Trad
FAX Number: N/A Calendar System: 4/1/4
URL: www.rcgc.edu
Established: 1966 Annual Undergrad Tuition & Fees (In-District): $4,445
Enrollment: 6,836 Coed
Affiliation or Control: State/Local IRS Status: 501(c)3
Highest Offering: Associate Degree
Accreditation: M, ADNUR, DMS, NMT, @PTAA

01 President ... Dr. Frederick KEATING
05 VP Academic Services ... Dr. Linda HURLBURT
11 Vice President & COO ... Mr. Dominick BURZICHELLI
32 Vice President Student Svcs ... Ms. Judith ATKINSON
13 Vice President/CIO ... Mr. Josh R. PIDDINGTON
10 Exec Director Financial Services ... Mrs. Elizabeth HALL
15 Exec Director Human Resource ... Mrs. Marlene LOGLISCI
04 Sr Exec Assistant to the President ... Mrs. Karen SITARSKI
28 Exec Dir Diversity and Equity ... Mrs. Almarie JONES
09 Dean Inst Research & Assessment ... Ms. Karen DURKIN
66 Dean Nursing & Allied Health ... Dr. Susan HALL
49 Dean Liberal Arts ... Dr. Paul RUFINO
81 Dean STEM ... Dr. Brenden RICKARDS
20 Dean Academic Compliance ... Ms. Yvonne GREENBAUN
88 Dean Public Safety & Security ... Mr. Fred H. MADDEN
50 Dean Business Studies ... Ms. Patricia CLAGHORN
07 Exec Director Admissions/Registrar ... Ms. Sandra HOFFMAN
36 Director Career & Academic Planning ... Mr. John ORTIZ
35 Exec Director Student Engagement ... Ms. Samantha VAN KOOY
08 Director Library Services ... Mrs. Jane S. CROCKER
111 Exec Director Inst Advancement ... Ms. Randee DAVIDSON
19 Director Security/Safety ... Mr. Joseph GETSINGER
37 Exec Dir Financial Aid & Admission ... Mr. Michael CHANDO
96 Controller/Purchasing ... Mr. Mark ZORZI

Rowan University (H)

201 Mullica Hill Road, Glassboro NJ 08028-1700
County: Gloucester FICE Identification: 002609
Unit ID: 184782
Telephone: (856) 256-4000 Carnegie Class: Masters/L
FAX Number: (856) 256-4929 Calendar System: Semester
URL: www.rowan.edu
Established: 1923 Annual Undergrad Tuition & Fees (In-State): $13,108
Enrollment: 16,155 Coed
Affiliation or Control: State IRS Status: 501(c)3
Highest Offering: Doctorate
Accreditation: M, ART, CAATE, CACREP, CAEPN, CS, DIETC, ENG, MED, MUS, NURSE, OSTEO, THEA

01 President .... Dr. Ali A. HOUSHMAND
05 Provost .... Dr. James NEWELL
10 Senior Vice Pres of Finance/CFO .... Mr. Joseph F. SCULLY
111 Senior VP University Advancement .... Mr. John ZABINSKI
32 VP Student Life/Dean of Students .... Mr. Richard JONES
86 EVP Policy/External Relationships .... Mr. Steve WEINSTEIN
18 Senior VP for Facilities & Opers .... Mr. Donald MOORE
44 VP Advance/Deputy Exec Dir Fndn .... Mr. Ronald J. TALLARIDA
20 VP Academic Affairs .... Dr. Roberta HARVEY
103 SVP Cmty/Economic Development .... Mr. Robert ZAZZALI
46 VP Research .... Dr. Shreekanth MANDAYAM
13 VP Information Resources/CIO .... Dr. Mira LALOVIC-HAND
26 VP for University Relations .... Dr. Joe CARDONA
84 VP Strategic Enrollment Management .... Dr. Jeffrey HAND
88 Asst VP Campus Rec/Stdnt Ctr/CES .... Ms. Tina M. PINOCCI
19 Asst VP Public Safety/Emerg Mgmt .... Mr. Michael KANTNER
15 Asst VP Labor Relations .... Mr. Kenneth KUERZI
38 Sr Dir Counseling/Psych Services .... Dr. David RUBENSTEIN
91 Asst VP of EIS .... Mr. James HENDERSON
63 Dean of Cooper Medical School of RU .... Dr. Annette REBOLI
08 Assoc Provost Library Info Services .... Mr. Scott MUIR
50 Dean Rohrer College of Business .... Dr. Susan LEHRMAN
81 Dean College of Science/Mathematics .. Dr. Karen MAGEE-SAUER
53 Dean of Education .... Dr. Monika SHEALEY
57 Dean of Performing Arts .... Dr. Rick DAMMERS
58 VP Global Learning & Partnerships .... Dr. Horacio SOSA
54 Dean of Engineering .... Dr. Tony LOWMAN
60 Dean Communication & Creative Arts .... Dr. Sanford M. TWEEDIE
83 Dean Humanities & Social Sciences .... Dr. Nawal H. AMMAR
88 Dean School of Osteopathic Medicine .... Dr. Thomas CAVALIERI
88 AVP Global Learning & Partnerships .... Ms. Lorraine RICCHEZZA
16 Assoc VP Employment/Labor Relations .... Ms. Eileen SCOTT
22 Asst VP for Equity and Diversity .... Dr. Johanna VELEZ-YELIN
41 Director of Athletics .... Mr. Dan GILMORE
88 Dir Distinguished Events/Spec Proj .... Ms. Kathy ROZANSKI
07 Director of Admissions .... Dr. Albert BETTS
36 Asst Dir Ofc Career Advancement .... Dr. Alicia MONROE
96 Sr Dir Contracting & Procurement .... Ms. Christina BRASTETER
27 Asst VP University Relations .... Ms. Lori MARSHALL
105 Director University Web Services .... Ms. Jennifer BELL
85 Assoc Director International Center .... Ms. Ghina NAJJAR
28 Asst VP Acad Enrich/EOF/MAP Dir .... Dr. Penny MCPHERSON
100 Chief of Staff/BOT Liaison .... Dr. Joanne M. CONNOR

*Rutgers the State University of New Jersey Central Office (A)

83 Somerset Street, New Brunswick NJ 08901-1281

County: Middlesex FICE Identification: 002629

Unit ID: 186362

Telephone: (848) 445-4636 Carnegie Class: N/A

FAX Number: (732) 932-8060

URL: www.rutgers.edu

01 President .... Dr. Robert L. BARCHI
10 VP Finance & Assoc Treasurer .... Mr. Richard M. AKS
05 Sr VP Academic Affairs .... Dr. Barbara A. LEE
102 Pres Rutgers Found/EVP Dev & Alum .... Mr. Nevin E. KESSLER
11 Senior VP for Finance & Admin .... Mr. John M. GOWER
114 VP Financial Planning & Budgeting .... Dr. Kathy L. DETTLOFF
13 Vice President Info Tech .... Ms. Michele NORIN
26 VP Univ Communications & Mktg .... Ms. Kimberly M. MANNING
45 Vice Pres Inst Planning & Operation .... Mr. Antonio CALCADO
88 Vice Chanc Interprofessional Educ .... Dr. Denise RODGERS
43 Senior VP & General Counsel .... Mr. John J. HOFFMAN
30 Sr VP Campaign & Development Oper .... Ms. Julie SHADLE
04 Exec Assistant to the President .... Ms. Jessica OTERO
20 VP Academic Affairs & Admin .... Dr. Karen R. STUBAUS
15 VP HR and Org Effectiveness .... Ms. Vivian FERNANDEZ
08 VP Info Services & Univ Librarian .... Ms. Krisellen MALONEY
101 Secretary of the University .... Ms. Kimberlee M. PASTVA
19 Exec Director Police Services .... Mr. Kenneth B. COP
23 Asst Vice Chancellor Health Svcs .... Dr. Melodee S. LASKY
06 Executive University Registrar .... Mr. Kenneth J. IUSO
37 University Dir Financial Aid .... Ms. Jean MCDONALD-RASH
41 Director Intercollegiate Athletics .... Mr. Patrick HOBBS
22 Assoc VP Labor Relations .... Mr. Harry M. AGNOSTAK
36 Exec Director Career Services .... Mr. Rick HEARIN
09 VP Inst Research & Planning .... Dr. Robert J. HEFFERNAN
86 Senior VP External Affairs .... Mr. Peter J. MCDONOUGH, JR.
84 VP Enrollment Management .... Dr. Courtney MCANUFF
29 VP Alumni Relations & Annual Giving .... Ms. Donna THORNTON
86 Asst VP Federal Relations .... Ms. Francine PFEIFFER
86 VP State Government Affairs .... Mr. David A. WEINSTEIN
88 Assc VP Promtg Women Sci Eng Math .... Dr. Joan W. BENNETT
88 VP Health Science Partnerships .... Dr. Kenneth J. BRESLAUER
12 Chancellor Rutgers-New Brunswick .... Dr. Debasish DUTTA
12 Chancellor Rutgers-Camden .... Dr. Phoebe A. HADDON
12 Chancellor RU Newark .... Dr. Nancy E. CANTOR
88 Chancellor Biomed & Health Sci .... Dr. Brian L. STROM
88 Director Cancer Institute NJ .... Dr. Steven K. LIBUTTI
88 Senior VP Research & Econ Dev .... Dr. Christopher J. MOLLOY
88 VP Physical Sci & Eng Partnership .... Dr. Leonard C. FELDMAN
88 Sr Vice Chancellor Pub Affairs .... Dr. Peter T. ENGLOT
11 Vice Chancellor Admin & Finance .... Dr. Larry R. GAINES, JR.
20 Vice Chancellor Acad Pgms & Svcs .... Dr. John GUNKEL
88 University Controller .... Mr. Peter LARSON
21 VP Finance & Assoc Treasurer .... Ms. Delanie S. MOLER
88 VP International & Global Affairs .... Dr. Eric L. GARFUNKEL
106 VP Cont Stdnt & Dist Educ .... Dr. Richard J. NOVAK
28 VP Intl Diversity & Inclusion .... Dr. Jorge R. SCHEMENT
117 Sr VP/Chief Enterprise Risk Mgmt .... Dr. Timothy J. FOURNIER
18 VP University Facilities .... Mr. John SHULACK
88 Vice President Business Services .... Mr. Henry X. VELEZ
88 Vice Chancellor UG Academic Affairs .... Dr. Ben SIFUENTES-JAUREGUI
88 Senior Vice Chanc Clinic Affairs .... Dr. Vincente H. GRACIAS
88 Special Counsel to the President .... Mr. John J. FARMER
100 Chief of Staff .... Mr. Brian BALLENTINE
46 Vice President Research .... Dr. Terri GROSS-KINZY
86 VP Government & Fiscal Affairs .... Dr. George J. LEBLANC

*Rutgers University - Camden (B)

303 Cooper Street, Camden NJ 08102-1461

County: Camden FICE Identification: 004741

Unit ID: 186371

Telephone: (856) 225-6026 Carnegie Class: Masters/L

FAX Number: (856) 225-6495 Calendar System: Semester

URL: www.camden.rutgers.edu

Established: 1927 Annual Undergrad Tuition & Fees (In-State): $14,238

Enrollment: 6,408 Coed

Affiliation or Control: State IRS Status: 501(c)3

Highest Offering: Doctorate

Accreditation: &M, CAEPT, LAW, NURSE, PTA, SPAA

02 Chancellor .... Dr. Phoebe A. HADDON
05 Provost .... Dr. Michael PALIS
11 Sr Vice Chancellor Admin & Finance .... Dr. Larry R. GAINES, JR.
32 Vice Chancellor Student Affairs .... Dr. Mary Beth B. DAISEY
20 Vice Chancellor for UG Education .... Vacant
84 Vice Chancellor Enroll Mgmt .... Dr. Craig WESTMAN
88 Assoc Chancellor Civic Engage .... Ms. Nyemma WATSON
88 Director Economic Development .... Mr. Gregory GAMBLE
61 Co-Dean School of Law .... Dr. Michael T. CAHILL
58 Dean Grad School .... Dr. Kriste LINDENMEYER
50 Dean School of Business .... Dr. Jaishankar GANESH
49 Dean Fac Arts & Sci/Univ Col .... Dr. Kriste LINDENMEYER
66 Dean School of Nursing .... Dr. Joanne P. ROBINSON
26 Assoc Chancellor for Ext Relations .... Mr. Michael J. SEPANIC
06 Registrar .... Ms. Theresa R. CRISTOFARO
37 Executive Director Financial Aid .... Ms. Danielle BARBEE
10 Director Campus Financial Services .... Ms. Rosa M. RIVERA
19 Chief Campus Police .... Chief Richard DINAN
29 Director Alumni Relations .... Mr. Scott D. OWENS
15 Human Resources Manager .... Mr. Gregory M. O'SHEA
18 Assoc Director Facilities Services .... Ms. Rona LEHTONEN
21 Business Manager .... Ms. Marlene DRUDING
41 Dir Athletics & Rec Services .... Mr. Jeffrey L. DEAN
36 Asst Dean Career Center .... Ms. Cheryl A. HALLMAN
23 Health Center Director .... Dr. Neuza M. SERRA
30 Acting Assoc Chancellor Development .... Ms. Kate BRENNAN
08 Interim Dir Paul Robeson Library .... Katherine E. ANDERSON
39 Director Housing .... Mr. Brandon CHANDLER
87 Summer Coord/Sr Program Coordinator .... Dr. Paul C. BUTLER
25 Director Sponsored Research .... Ms. Carberta A. MORRISON
13 Director Information Technology .... Mr. Thomas J. RYAN
07 Director of Admissions .... Vacant
85 Asst Dean International Students .... Ms. Elizabeth A. ATKINS
35 Dean of Students .... Dr. Thomas J. DIVALERIO
96 Senior Buyer .... Mr. Christian AHA
100 Chief of Staff .... Dr. Loree D. JONES
46 Assoc Provost Research .... Dr. Beneditto PICCOLI
09 Director Inst Research Camden .... Dr. Jason C. SCHWEITZER

† Regional accreditation is carried under Rutgers the State University of New Jersey New Brunswick.

*Rutgers University - New Brunswick (C)

85 Somerset Street, New Brunswick NJ 08901-1281

County: Middlesex FICE Identification: 006964

Unit ID: 186380

Telephone: (848) 932-4636 Carnegie Class: DU-Highest

FAX Number: (732) 932-8060 Calendar System: Semester

URL: www.rutgers.edu

Established: 1766 Annual Undergrad Tuition & Fees (In-State): $14,372

Enrollment: 49,428 Coed

Affiliation or Control: State IRS Status: 501(c)3

Highest Offering: Doctorate

Accreditation: M, ART, CACREP, CAEPT, CEA, CLPSY, DANCE, DIETD, ENG, LIB, LSAR, MUS, PCSAS, PH, PHAR, PLNG, SCPSY, SPAA, SW

02 Chancellor Rutgers New Brunswick .... Dr. Debasish DUTTA
32 Vice Chancellor Student Affairs .... Ms. Felicia E. MCGINTY
10 Vice Chancellor Finance & Admin .... Ms. Mary Lou ORTIZ
05 Provost New Brunswick .... Dr. Lily Y. YOUNG
84 VP Enrollment Management .... Dr. Courtney O. MCANUFF
11 VP Acad Affairs & Administration .... Dr. Karen R. STUBAUS
28 VP Inst Diversity & Inclusion .... Dr. Jorge R. SCHEMENT
08 Interim VP Info Svcs/U Librarian .... Ms. Jeanne E. BOYLE
58 Dean Graduate School-NB .... Dr. Jerome J. KUKOR
80 Interim Dean EJB Plan/Public Policy .Dr. Michael R. GREENBERG
81 Exec Dean Sch Enviro/Biological Sci .... Dr. Robert M. GOODMAN
12 Dean Douglass Residential College .... Dr. Jacquelyn S. LITT
49 Executive Dean SAS .... Dr. Peter MARCH
92 Honors College Academic Dean .... Dr. Matt K. MATSUDA
54 Dean School of Engineering .... Dr. Thomas N. FARRIS
67 Dean Ernest Mario Sch Pharm .... Dr. Joseph BARONE
57 Dean Mason Gross School of Art .... Dr. George B. STAUFFER
62 Dean Sch Communication & Info .... Dr. Jonathan POTTER
83 Dean Grad School Applied/Prof Psych .... Dr. Francine CONWAY
53 Dean Grad School of Education .... Dr. Wanda J. BLANCHETT
66 Dean School of Nursing .... Dr. William L. HOLZEMER
70 Dean School of Social Work .... Dr. Cathryn C. POTTER
50 Dean Sch of Business Newark/NB .... Dr. Lei LEI
88 Dean Sch Mgmt Labor Relations .... Dr. James C. HAYTON
06 Executive University Registrar .... Mr. Kenneth J. IUSO
104 VP Internatl & Global Affairs .... Dr. Eric GARFUNKLE
123 Director Graduate Admissions .... Ms. Linda J. COSTA
37 University Dir Financial Aid .... Ms. Jean MCDONALD-RASH
36 Director Career Services .... Ms. Jennifer BROYLES
13 Sr VP & Chief Information Officer .... Ms. Michele NORIN
09 VP Institutional Rsrch & Plng .... Dr. Robert J. HEFFERNAN
39 Director Residence Life .... Mr. Michael TOLBERT
19 Exec Dir Police Services/Chief .... Mr. Kenneth B. COP
12 Director Rutgers China Office .... Dr. Jeff (Jianfeng) WANG
41 Director Intecollegiate Athletics .... Mr. Patrick E. HOBBS
26 Assoc V Chancellor Comm & Marketing .... Dr. Zachariah (Zach) HOSSEINI
88 Asst Vice Chancellor .... Dr. Paul D. HAMMOND

*Rutgers University - Newark (D)

249 University Avenue, Newark NJ 07102-1897

County: Essex FICE Identification: 002631

Unit ID: 186399

Telephone: (973) 353-5568 Carnegie Class: DU-Higher

FAX Number: (973) 353-1048 Calendar System: Semester

URL: www.newark.rutgers.edu

Established: 1892 Annual Undergrad Tuition & Fees (In-State): $13,829

Enrollment: 11,720 Coed

Affiliation or Control: State IRS Status: 501(c)3

Highest Offering: Doctorate

Accreditation: &M, ANEST, CAEPT, IPSY, LAW, NURSE, SPAA, SW

02 Chancellor .... Dr. Nancy E. CANTOR
05 Provost & Exec Vice Chancellor .... Dr. Jerome D. WILLIAMS
11 Exec Vice Chanc & Chief Oper Ofcr .... Dr. Shirley M. COLLADO
100 Senior Vice Chanc & Chief of Staff .... Dr. Peter T. ENGLOT
10 Vice Chancellor Admin & CFO .... Dr. Arcelio APONTE
86 Vice Chanc External & Govt Rels .... Dr. Marcia W. BROWN
15 Asst Vice Chanc Human Resources .... Dr. Bil LEIPOLD
18 Exec Director Facilities .... Dr. Christopher PYE
30 Vice Chancellor for Development .... Dr. Irene O'BRIEN
20 Vice Chancellor Acad Pgms & Svcs .... Dr. John GUNKEL
46 Vice Chancellor Research .... Dr. Nabil ADAM
84 Asst Chanc Enrollment Management .... Dr. Ben ROHDIN
114 Asst Provost for Budget .... Dr. Mary TAMASCO
32 Vice Chancellor for Student Affairs .... Dr. Corlisse THOMAS
31 Asst Chancellor Comm Partner .... Dr. Diane HILL
06 Registrar .... Dr. Marie DIAZ-TORRES
21 Exec Dir Business & Financial Svcs .... Vacant
13 Interim Dir Information Technology .... Mr. Galen J. WORK
07 Asst Prov & Dean of Admissions ... Ms. LaToya BATTLE-BROWN
19 Director Public Safety Newark .... Mr. Carmelo V. HUERTAS
26 Director Public Relations .... Ms. Kimberlee S. WILLIAMS
37 Director Financial Aid .... Ms. Natalie L. MORISSEAU
49 Dean Faculty Arts & Science .... Dr. Jan Ellen LEWIS
61 Co-Dean of School of Law .... Dr. Ronald K. CHEN, JR.
50 Dean Business Newark/New Bruns .... Dr. Lei LEI
66 Dean School of Nursing .... Dr. William L. HOLZEMER
88 Dean School Criminal Justice .... Dr. Rod BRUNSON
38 Director Student Counseling .... Dr. Anice THOMAS
96 Senior Buyer .... Ms. Ida ANGELONE
80 Interim Dean Sch Pub Aff & Admin .... Dr. Gregg G. VAN RYZIN
39 Director Housing & Residence Life .... Dr. Angelita BONILLA
23 Director Health Services .... Dr. Sandra SAMUELS
41 Director of Athletics & Recreation .... Mr. Mark GRIFFIN
82 Director of Global Affairs .... Dr. Richard O'MEARA
58 Dean Graduate School Newark .... Dr. Kyle W. FARMBRY
87 Manager Summer Session .... Ms. Carmen L. PARDO
88 Assoc Dean/Dir Robeson Campus Ctr .... Dr. Clayton WALTON
04 Sr Exec Assoc to the Chancellor .... Ms. Carla M. HAILEY PENN
45 Vice Chancellor Plng & Implement .... Dr. Bonita M. VEYSEY
29 Director Alumni Relations .... Vacant
08 Director Dana Library .... Ms. Consuella A. ASKEW
88 Director LGBTQ & Div Res Center .... Ms. Yoleidy ROSARIO

† Regional accreditation is carried under Rutgers the State University of New Jersey New Brunswick.

*Rutgers Graduate School of Biomedical Sciences (E)

185 South Orange Avenue, MSB C-696, Newark NJ 07107-1709

Telephone: (973) 972-4511 FICE Identification: 011174

Accreditation: &M

*Rutgers-New Jersey Medical School (F)

185 S Orange Avenue, Newark NJ 07101-1709

Telephone: (973) 972-4538 FICE Identification: 002620

Accreditation: &M, MED

*Rutgers - Robert Wood Johnson Medical School (G)

675 Hoes Lane, Piscataway NJ 08854-5635

Telephone: (732) 235-6300 FICE Identification: 024549

Accreditation: &M, IPSY, MED, PAST

*Rutgers School of Dental Medicine (H)

110 Bergen Street, Room B-830, Newark NJ 07101-1709

Telephone: (973) 972-4633 FICE Identification: 024635

Accreditation: &M, DENT

* Rutgers School of Health Professions (A)

65 Bergen Street, Room 149, Newark NJ 07101-1709
Telephone: (973) 972-5454 FICE Identification: 020668
Accreditation: &M, ARCPA, CACREP, CAHIIM, COARC, CVT, CYTO, DH, DIETC, DIETI, DMS, MT, NMT, OTA, PHLEB, PTA

* Rutgers School of Nursing (B)

180 University Avenue, Newark NJ 07102
Telephone: (973) 353-5293 Identification: 666970
Accreditation: &M, MIDWF, NURSE

* Rutgers School of Public Health (C)

683 Hoes Lane West, Room 235,
Piscataway NJ 08854-8021
Telephone: (732) 235-9700 Identification: 666991
Accreditation: &M, PH

Saint Peter's University (D)

2641 Kennedy Boulevard, Jersey City NJ 07306-5997
County: Hudson FICE Identification: 002638
Unit ID: 186432
Telephone: (201) 761-6000 Carnegie Class: Masters/L
FAX Number: (201) 761-7801 Calendar System: Semester
URL: www.saintpeters.edu
Established: 1872 Annual Undergrad Tuition & Fees: $35,192
Enrollment: 3,406 Coed
Affiliation or Control: Roman Catholic IRS Status: 501(c)3
Highest Offering: Doctorate
Accreditation: M, CAEPT, IACBE, NURSE

01 President ... Dr. Eugene J. CORNACCHIA
05 Provost/VP Academic Affairs ... Dr. Frederick BONATO
10 Interim VP of Finance & Business ... Mr. Hector O. PAREDES
111 Vice President Advancement ... Ms. Leah LETO
32 VP Stdnt Life & Dev/Dean Stdnt ... Mr. Anthony SKEVAKIS
42 Vice Pres for Mission & Ministry ... Fr. Rocco DANZI, SJ
84 VP Enrollment Mgmt & Marketing ... Mr. Jeffrey HANDLER
45 Spec Asst to President for Planning ... Dr. Virginia BENDER
51 Dean & Director of JC SPCS ... Ms. Elizabeth KANE
78 Exec Dir of Experiential Lrng ... Ms. Laura PAKHMANOV
26 Director University Communications ... Ms. Sarah MALINOWSKI-FERRARY
84 Director Enrollment/Research/Tech ... Mr. Ben SCHOLZ
07 Assoc VP and Dean of Admissions ... Ms. Elizabeth SULLIVAN
08 Director of the Libraries ... Ms. Daisy DECOSTER
37 Director of Student Fin Aid ... Ms. Jennifer RAGSDALE
06 Registrar ... Ms. Kamla SINGH
13 VP & Chief Information Officer ... Mr. Milos TOPIC
09 Director of Institutional Research ... Mr. Lamberto C. NIEVES
66 Dean of Nursing ... Dr. Lauren O'HARE
19 Director of Campus Safety ... Mr. Scott TORRE
15 Director of Human Resources ... Ms. Elena SERRA
29 Exec Director Alumni Engagement ... Ms. Gloria MERCURIO
44 Director of Annual Giving ... Ms. Ana M. CRAVO
38 Director Personal Development ... Mr. Ron BECKER
39 Director of Residence Life ... Mr. Travis WHISLER
41 Interim Director of Athletics ... Mr. Dave BRYNGIL
42 Director of Campus Ministry ... Ms. Christine BOYLE
14 Director of Network Services ... Mr. Bert VABRE
85 Foreign Studies Adviser ... Mr. Tushar TRIVEDI
18 Manager of College Services ... Ms. Anna DE PAULA
102 Dir Foundation/Corp & Govt Rels ... Mr. Emory EDWARDS
104 Director Study Abroad ... Mr. Scott KELLER
105 Director Web Services ... Mr. Kyle RIVERS
49 Dean College of Arts & Sciences ... Dr. Scott STODDART
50 Dean School of Business ... Mr. Bruce ROSENTHAL
53 Dean School of Education ... Dr. Joseph DORIA
96 Director of Purchasing ... Mr. John MATTHEWS
04 Administrative Asst to President ... Ms. Janice P. VIZZACCHERO
101 Secretary of the Institution/Board ... Dr. Virginia A. BENDER
28 Director of Diversity & Inclusion ... Ms. Marilu MARCILLO

Salem Community College (E)

460 Hollywood Avenue, Carneys Point NJ 08069-2799
County: Salem FICE Identification: 005461
Unit ID: 186469
Telephone: (856) 299-2100 Carnegie Class: Assoc/MT-VT-High Trad
FAX Number: (856) 351-2634 Calendar System: Semester
URL: www.salemcc.edu
Established: 1972 Annual Undergrad Tuition & Fees (In-District): $4,104
Enrollment: 1,140 Coed
Affiliation or Control: State/Local IRS Status: 501(c)3
Highest Offering: Associate Degree
Accreditation: M, ADNUR

01 President ... Dr. Michael GORMAN
05 VP of Academic Affairs/CAO ... Dr. Eric PELLEGRINO
04 Admin Asst Office to the President ... Ms. Maria FANTINI
20 Associate Dean of Academic Affairs ... Mr. John STEINER
88 Assistant Dean of Academic Affairs ... Mr. Kenneth ROBEL
07 Dean of Enrollment/Admissions ... Mr. Kevin CATALFAMO
10 Chief Financial/Business Ofcr ... Mr. Kevin KUTCHER
06 Registrar ... Ms. Jill JAMES
88 Dir of Institutional Effectiveness ... Mr. Marc ROY
19 Director of Security/Safety ... Mr. John MORRISON
88 Director of Retention & Admissions ... Ms. Jasmine LYNCH
09 Director Inst Rsrch/Planning/Devel ... Ms. Denise DERSCH
30 Dir of Inst Advancement/Alumni ... Mr. William CLARK
37 Dir Student Financial Services ... Mr. Ronald BURKHARDT
66 Director of Nursing ... Mr. Charles MCGLADE
88 Director of Academic & Info Svcs ... Ms. Jennifer PIERCE
13 Director of Information Technology ... Mr. Larry MCKEE
102 Chief Foundation Officer ... Ms. Ceil SMITH
21 Manager of Finance ... Ms. Catherine PRIEST
96 Manager of Purchasing ... Vacant
88 Accounts Manager ... Ms. Maureen DOUGHERTY

Seton Hall University (F)

400 S Orange Avenue, South Orange NJ 07079-2697
County: Essex FICE Identification: 002632
Unit ID: 186584
Telephone: (973) 761-9000 Carnegie Class: DU-Mod
FAX Number: N/A Calendar System: Semester
URL: www.shu.edu
Established: 1856 Annual Undergrad Tuition & Fees: $39,258
Enrollment: 9,824 Coed
Affiliation or Control: Roman Catholic IRS Status: 501(c)3
Highest Offering: Doctorate
Accreditation: M, ARCPA, CAATE, COPSY, HSA, LAW, MFCD, NURSE, OT, PTA, SP, SPAA, SW, THEOL

01 Interim President ... Dr. Mary MEEHAN
05 Interim Provost and Executive VP ... Dr. Karen A. BOROFF
20 Senior Associate Provost ... Dr. Joan GUETTI
20 Associate Vice Provost ... Msgr. Robert COLEMAN
10 Vice Pres for Finance/CFO ... Mr. Stephen A. GRAHAM
11 Vice President for Administration ... Mr. Dennis J. GARBINI
43 Vice President & General Counsel ... Ms. Catherine A. KIERNAN
111 Interim Vice Pres Univ Advancement ... Mr. Matthew BOROWICK
32 Vice President Student Affairs ... Dr. Tracy T. GOTTLIEB
84 Vice President of Enrollment Mgmt ... Dr. Alyssa MCCLOUD
42 Vice Pres for Mission & Ministry ... Msgr. C. Anthony ZICCARDI
15 Assoc Vice Pres Human Resources ... Mr. Michael SILVESTRO
29 Assoc VP Alumni/Government Rels ... Mr. Matthew BOROWICK
110 Assoc Vice Pres Univ Advance ... Mr. Joseph GUASCONI
26 Assoc VP Public Relations & Mktg ... Mr. Dan P. KALMANSON
18 Assoc VP for Facilities & Operation ... Mr. John SIGNORELLO
35 Assoc VP/Dean of Students ... Ms. Karen VAN NORMAN
21 Assoc Prov Finance/Administration ... Ms. Mary Ann HART
45 Assoc Provost ... Dr. Gregory A. BURTON
88 Assoc Provost for Academic Projects ... Mr. Erik LILLQUIST
19 Asst VP Security ... Mr. Patrick LINFANTE
49 Dean of Arts & Sciences ... Dr. Peter SHOEMAKER
50 Dean School of Business ... Dr. Joyce A. STRAWSER
60 Dean Communication & the Arts ... Ms. Deirdre YATES
66 Dean of Nursing ... Dr. Marie FOLEY
53 Dean College Education Svcs ... Dr. Maureen GILLETTE
73 Dean School of Theology ... Msgr. Joseph R. REILLY
63 Dean School of Health & Med Science ... Dr. Brian SHULMAN
82 Dean Diplomacy/Intl Relations ... Dr. Andrea BARTOLI
63 Dean Medical School ... Dr. Bonita STANTON
61 Dean of Law School ... Ms. Kathleen BOOZANG
08 Dean of University Libraries ... Dr. John E. BUSCHMAN
51 Dean Cont Educ/Professional Studies ... Ms. Karen PASSARO
88 Assoc Dean/Director of EOP ... Dr. Majid WHITNEY
88 Assoc Dean/Exec Dir of Special Pgms ... Ms. Cassandra E. DAVIS
21 Director of Business Affairs ... Mr. Michael GARCIA
13 Chief Information Officer ... Dr. Stephen LANDRY
28 Director Compliance & Risk Mgmt ... Ms. Lori A. BROWN
37 Director for Financial Aid ... Ms. Javonda ASANTE
39 Director of Housing/Residence Life ... Mr. Timothy MORAN
06 University Registrar ... Ms. Mary Ellen FARRELL
36 Director of the Career Center ... Ms. Reesa GREENWALD
41 Dir Athletics/Recreational Services ... Mr. Patrick G. LYONS
18 Director of Physical Plant ... Mr. Steve KURTYKA
38 Director of Counseling ... Dr. Katherine EVANS
42 Director of Campus Ministry ... Rev. Robert P. MCLAUGHLIN
88 Minister to Priest Community ... Msgr. Robert M. COLEMAN
09 Dir Plng Inst Research & Assessment ... Ms. Connie L. BEALE
07 Dir of Undergraduate Admissions ... Ms. Mary Clare CULLUM
96 Director of Procurement ... Mr. Martin E. KOELLER
23 Director Health Services ... Ms. Mary Elizabeth COSTELLO
88 Director Core Curriculum ... Dr. Anthony C. SCIGLITANO, JR.
102 Dir Foundation/Corporate Relations ... Ms. Lily M. CABRERA
104 Director Study Abroad ... Ms. Maria BOUZAS
108 Director Institutional Assessment ... Ms. Agata WOLFE
88 Asst Provost for Academic Affairs ... Dr. Christopher CUCCIA
86 Director Government Relations ... Mr. Matthew BOROWICK

Stevens Institute of Technology (G)

Castle Point on Hudson, Hoboken NJ 07030-5991
County: Hudson FICE Identification: 002639
Unit ID: 186867
Telephone: (201) 216-5000 Carnegie Class: DU-Higher
FAX Number: (201) 216-8341 Calendar System: Semester
URL: www.stevens.edu
Established: 1870 Annual Undergrad Tuition & Fees: $48,838
Enrollment: 6,359 Coed
Affiliation or Control: Independent Non-Profit IRS Status: 501(c)3
Highest Offering: Doctorate
Accreditation: M, CS, ENG

01 President ... Dr. Nariman FARVARDIN
04 Exec Assistant to the President ... Ms. Karen CUOZZO
05 Provost/University Vice President ... Dr. Christophe PIERRE
30 Vice President for Development ... Mr. Brodie REMINGTON
10 CFO/VP for Finance/Treasurer ... Dr. Louis MAYER
84 VP Enrollment Mgt/Student Affairs ... Ms. Marybeth MURPHY
15 Vice President Human Resources ... Mr. Warren PETTY
43 Vice President General Counsel ... Ms. Kathy L. SCHULZ
13 VP for Information Technology & CIO ... Mr. David DODD
26 VP Communications & Marketing ... Mr. Edward STUKANE
18 VP for Facilities/Campus Operations ... Mr. Robert MAFFIA
32 Assistant VP Student Affairs ... Ms. Sara KLEIN
21 AVP for Financial Planning/Budgets ... Mr. Justin OATES
20 Dean Undergraduate Academics ... Dr. Larry RUSS
35 Dean of Student Life ... Mr. Kenneth NILSEN
39 Dean for Residence Life ... Ms. Trina BALLANTYNE
20 Assoc Dean Undergraduate Academics ... Dr. Erol CESMEBASI
29 AVP Alumni Engagement & ED/SAA ... Ms. Melissa FUEST
36 Exec Director of Career Services ... Ms. Lynn INSLEY
19 Chief & Director of Campus Police ... Mr. Timothy GRIFFIN
41 Athletic Director ... Mr. Russell ROGERS
85 Assoc Dean/Intl Student & Scholars ... Ms. Doris CLAUSEN
38 Director of Student Counseling ... Dr. Eric D. ROSE
40 Manager Campus Bookstore ... Ms. Teresa TRIDENTE
25 Exec Director Sponsored Research ... Ms. Barbara DEHAVEN
54 Dean School of Engr & Science ... Dr. Jean ZU
50 Dean School of Business ... Dr. Gregory PRASTACOS
49 Dean College of Arts & Letters ... Dr. Kelland THOMAS
77 Int Dean School Systems/Enterprise ... Dr. Anthony BARRESE
09 Director of Institutional Research ... Ms. Minghui WANG
100 Chief of Staff/Dir Govt/Cmty Rels ... Ms. Beth MCGRATH
28 Exec Director Diversity & Inclusion ... Ms. Susan METZ
20 Vice Provost of Academics ... Dr. Constantin CHASSAPIS
46 Vice Provost of Research ... Dr. Mo DEHGHANI
06 Registrar ... Ms. Anna-Lize HARRIS
08 Director of Library & Info Svcs ... Ms. Linda BENINGHOVE
104 Director International Programs ... Ms. Susan RACHOUH
105 Director Enterprise Web Services ... Mr. Aaron GARY
106 Assistant Dean Web Campus ... Mr. Robert ZOTTI
37 Director of Financial Aid ... Ms. Susan GROSS
96 Director of Procurement ... Vacant

Stockton University (H)

101 Vera King Farris Drive, Galloway NJ 08205-9441
County: Atlantic FICE Identification: 009345
Unit ID: 186876
Telephone: (609) 652-1776 Carnegie Class: Masters/L
FAX Number: (609) 652-0275 Calendar System: Semester
URL: www.stockton.edu
Established: 1969 Annual Undergrad Tuition & Fees (In-State): $13,077
Enrollment: 8,674 Coed
Affiliation or Control: State IRS Status: 501(c)3
Highest Offering: Doctorate
Accreditation: M, CAEPT, NURSE, OT, PTA, SP, SW

01 President ... Dr. Harvey KESSELMAN
05 Provost & VP for Academic Affairs ... Dr. Lori VERMEULEN
100 Exec VP and Chief of Staff ... Dr. Susan C. DAVENPORT
10 Vice Pres Administration & Finance ... Mr. Charles E. INGRAM
32 Vice President Student Affairs ... Dr. Thomasa GONZALEZ
20 Asst Provost Programs & Planning ... Dr. Carra HOOD
20 Assistant Provost ... Dr. Michelle MCDONALD
96 Dir Procurement & Contracting ... Ms. Margaret QUINN
13 Chief Information Officer ... Mr. Robert R. HEINRICH
21 AVP Business Svcs/Chief Bdgt Ofcr ... Mr. James TIERNEY
18 Assoc VP Facilities/Construction ... Mr. Donald M. HUDSON
22 Chief Ofcr Inst Diversity/Equity ... Dr. Valerie HAYES
26 Ex Dir William J Hughes Ctr ... Ms. Sharon SCHULMAN
30 Chief Dev Ofcr/Exec Dir Foundation ... Dr. Philip T. ELLMORE
84 Dean of Enrollment Management ... Mr. John IACOVELLI
07 Assoc Dean Enrollment Mgmt ... Ms. Alison HENRY
35 Dean of Students ... Dr. Pedro SANTANA
06 Registrar ... Mr. Joseph LOSASSO
53 Dean School of Education ... Dr. Claudine KEENAN
97 Dean School of General Studies ... Dr. Robert S. GREGG
79 Dean School Arts & Humanities ... Dr. Lisa HONAKER
50 Dean School of Business ... Dr. Janet M. WAGNER
123 Dir of Graduate Enrollment Mgmt ... Ms. AmyBeth GLASS
81 Dean School of Natural Sci/Math ... Dr. Peter STRAUB
83 Dean Sch Social/Behavioral Sciences ... Dr. Cheryl KAUS
76 Dean School of Health Sciences ... Dr. Theresa BARTOLOTTA
15 Director of Human Resources ... Mr. Thomas P. CHESTER
09 Director Institutional Research ... Dr. Xiangping KONG
08 Director of Library Services ... Mr. Joseph TOTH
88 Director SRI & ETTC ... Ms. Patricia WEEKS
37 Director of Financial Aid ... Ms. Jeanne LEWIS
19 Interim Chief of Police ... Ms. Cynthia Ann PARKER
88 Manager Performing Arts Center ... Ms. Suze DIPIETRO-STEWART
88 Dir for Student Affairs Operations ... Mr. Lonnie FOLKS
41 Exec Dir Athletics & Recreation ... Mr. Kevin MCHUGH
39 Director for Residential Life ... Mr. Steven E. RADWANSKI
36 Director of Career Center ... Mr. Walter L. TARVER, III
43 Gen Counsel & Dir of Govt Relations ... Mr. Michael ANGULO
38 Director of Counseling ... Dr. Donald CASSIDY
121 Dir Center for Academic Advising ... Dr. Peter HAGEN
114 Director Budget & Fiscal Planning ... Mr. Michael WOOD
29 Director Alumni Relations ... Ms. Sara FAUROT
110 Assoc Chf Devel Ofcr/Campaign Mgr ... Ms. Cindy CRAGER
12 COO Atlantic City Campus ... Mr. Brian K. JACKSON

Sussex County Community College (I)

One College Hill Road, Newton NJ 07860-1146
County: Sussex FICE Identification: 025688
Unit ID: 247603

Telephone: (973) 300-2100 Carnegie Class: Assoc/HT-High Trad
FAX Number: (973) 579-9351 Calendar System: Semester
URL: www.sussex.edu
Established: 1982 Annual Undergrad Tuition & Fees (In-District): $6,750
Enrollment: 2,732 Coed
Affiliation or Control: State/Local IRS Status: 501(c)3
Highest Offering: Associate Degree
Accreditation: M, MAC, SURGT

01 President ... Dr. Jon H. CONNOLLY
04 Asst to President/Board of Trustees ... Wendy FULLEM
05 Int VP of Academic Affairs/CAO ... Dr. James BAKER
10 EVP of Finance/Operations/CFO ... Ketan GANDHI
49 Int Asst VP Acad Affs/Dean of Fac ... Dr. Kathleen OKAY
15 Exec Dir of Human Resources ... Michael GALLEGLY
26 Dir of Marketing/Public Info ... Kathleen PETERSON
24 Assoc Dean of Learning Resources ... Jan TENSEN
41 Dir of Athletics/Dean Student Affs ... John KUNTZ
21 Director of Accounting ... Manal MESCHA
19 Director Campus Safety & Security ... Fred MAMAY
88 Dir of Bursar/Financial Services ... Tatsiana SHUMSKAYA
08 Director of College Library ... Stephanie COOPER
07 Director of Admissions ... Todd POLTERSDORF
37 Director of Financial Aid ... Diane PIENTA-LETTA
09 Dir of Inst Research & Assessment ... Cory HOMER
06 Registrar ... Solweig DIMINO
108 Director Institutional Assessment ... Cory HOMER

Talmudical Academy of New Jersey (A)

Route 524, Adelphia NJ 07710-9999
County: Monmouth FICE Identification: 011989
Unit ID: 186900
Telephone: (732) 431-1600 Carnegie Class: Spec-4-yr-Faith
FAX Number: (732) 431-3951 Calendar System: Semester
URL: taofnj@gmail.com
Established: 1971 Annual Undergrad Tuition & Fees: $13,000
Enrollment: 66 Male
Affiliation or Control: Independent Non-Profit IRS Status: 501(c)3
Highest Offering: Baccalaureate
Accreditation: RABN

01 President ... Mr. Charles SEMAH
05 Dean ... Rabbi Yeruchim SHAIN

Thomas Edison State University (B)

111 W State Street, Trenton NJ 08608-1176
County: Mercer FICE Identification: 021922
Unit ID: 187046
Telephone: (609) 984-1100 Carnegie Class: Masters/M
FAX Number: (609) 292-9000 Calendar System: Other
URL: www.tesu.edu
Established: 1972 Annual Undergrad Tuition & Fees (In-State): $6,350
Enrollment: 13,093 Coed
Affiliation or Control: State IRS Status: 501(c)3
Highest Offering: Doctorate
Accreditation: M, ACBSP, CAEPT, ENGT, NURSE, POLYT

01 President ... Dr. George A. PRUITT
05 Vice President & Provost ... Mr. William J. SEATON
10 Vice Pres Administration & Finance ... Mr. Christopher STRINGER
26 Vice President Public Affairs ... Mr. John P. THURBER
31 Vice Pres Cmty & Govt Affairs ... Ms. Robin WALTON
45 VP Institutional Planning/Research ... Dr. Dennis DEVERY
84 VP Enrollment Mgmt/Learner Services ... Dr. Mary Ellen CARO
51 Vice Prov/Dean Watson Sch Cont Stds ... Dr. Joseph YOUNGBLOOD
88 Vice Prov Ctr Assessment of Lrng ... Mr. Marc SINGER
88 Assoc VP Enrollment Management ... Ms. Sylvia HAMILTON
88 Assoc VP Military/Veteran Education ... Mr. Louis MARTINI
09 Assoc VP for Planning & Research ... Dr. Ann Marie SENIOR
27 Assoc VP/Director of Communications ... Mr. Joseph GUZZARDO
88 Assoc Provost Learning Technology ... Mr. Matthew COOPER
21 Treasurer ... Mr. Stephen D. ALBANO
100 Chief of Staff ... Ms. Linda M. MEEHAN
27 Director Market Research/Assessment ... Ms. Marie R. POWER-BARNES
43 General Counsel ... Ms. Barbara KLEVA
66 Dean School of Nursing ... Dr. Phyllis MARSHALL
49 Dean Heavin Sch of Arts & Sciences ... Dr. John WOZNICKI
50 Dean School of Business & Mgmt ... Dr. Michael WILLIAMS
06 Assoc Vice Pres/Univ Registrar ... Ms. Catharine PUNCHELLO-COBOS
72 Dean School of Applied Sci/Tech ... Dr. John AJE
21 Controller ... Mr. John SCHAIBLE
13 Chief Information Officer ... Mr. Drew W. HOPKINS
88 Dir Office of Test Administration ... Mr. David HOFTIEZER
29 Director of Alumni Affairs ... Ms. Meg FRANTZ
37 Director of Financial Aid ... Mr. James OWENS
18 Director Facilities & Operations ... Ms. Mary C. HACK
30 Associate VP for Development ... Ms. Misty ISAK
102 Director Corporate Relations ... Mr. Frederick BRAND
08 State Librarian ... Ms. Mary CHUTE
105 Dir Website/Multimedia Productivity ... Mr. Jeffery LUSHBAUGH
88 Director of Advancement Services ... Ms. Erica SPIZZIRRRI
44 Dir Annual Fund/Donor Relations ... Ms. Jennifer GUERRERO
88 Executive Director Watson Institute ... Ms. Barbara JOHNSON
88 ADA Coordinator ... Ms. Laura BRENNER-SCOTTI
04 Assistant to the President ... Ms. Melissa A. MASZCZAK

† The Thomas Edison State University 12-month enrollment is 17,511.

Union County College (C)

1033 Springfield Avenue, Cranford NJ 07016-1598
County: Union FICE Identification: 002643
Unit ID: 187198
Telephone: (908) 709-7000 Carnegie Class: Assoc/HT-High Trad
FAX Number: (908) 709-0527 Calendar System: Semester
URL: www.ucc.edu
Established: 1933 Annual Undergrad Tuition & Fees (In-District): $4,620
Enrollment: 11,220 Coed
Affiliation or Control: State/Local IRS Status: 501(c)3
Highest Offering: Associate Degree
Accreditation: M, PNUR, PTAA

01 President ... Dr. Margaret M. MCMENAMIN
05 Vice President Academic Affairs ... Dr. Maris LOWN
10 Vice Pres Financial Affs/Treasurer ... Mr. Bernard LENIHAN
32 Vice President Student Development ... Vacant
11 Vice Pres Administrative Services ... Vacant
12 Provost Elizabeth Campus ... Dr. Lisa HISCANO
12 Dean Plainfield Campus ... Dr. Victoria UKACHUKWU
26 Exec Director College Relations ... Ms. Ellen DOTTO
13 Director of IT Operations ... Mr. Thomas CHERUBINO
06 Dir Admissions/Records/Registrar ... Ms. Nina HERNANDEZ
08 Director of Libraries ... Ms. Dena LEITER
38 Director of Counseling ... Ms. Heather KEITH
37 Director of Financial Aid ... Mr. Dayne CHANCE
21 Director of Student Accounts ... Mr. Larry GOLDMAN
51 Dean Continuing Educ & Prof Educ ... Dr. Lisa HISCANO
108 Exec Dir of Institutional Research ... Ms. Elizabeth COONER
15 Director of Human Resources ... Mr. Vincent LOTANO
18 Director Facilities ... Mr. Robert HOGAN
45 Director of Grants ... Ms. Cheryl SHIBER
102 Exec Director Foundation ... Mr. Douglas ROUSE
20 Director Student Assessment Center ... Vacant
28 Director EOF ... Mr. Ruben MELENDEZ
41 Dean of College Life ... Ms. Tamalea SMITH
19 Director Public Safety ... Mr. Joseph HINES
27 Director Media Services ... Mr. Patrick GALLAGHER
88 Asst Dir Acad Learning Center ... Mr. Jose PAEZ-FIGUEROA
21 Controller ... Ms. Lynne WELCH
96 Director of Purchasing ... Ms. Phyllis MIRABELLA
40 Manager Bookstore ... Ms. Christine SALZMAN
92 AVP/Dean of American Honors ... Dr. Bernard POLNARIEV
84 Director Enrollment Services ... Ms. Beatriz RODRIGUEZ

Union County College Elizabeth Campus (D)

40 W Jersey Street, Elizabeth NJ 07202-2314
Telephone: (908) 965-6000 Identification: 770134
Accreditation: &M, EMT

Union County College Plainfield Campus (E)

232 E 2nd Street, Plainfield NJ 07060
Telephone: (908) 412-3599 Identification: 770135
Accreditation: &M

University of Phoenix Jersey City Campus (F)

100 Town Square Place, Jersey City NJ 07310-1756
Telephone: (201) 610-1408 Identification: 770218
Accreditation: &NH, ACBSP

† No longer accepting campus-based students.

Warren County Community College (G)

475 Route 57 W, Washington NJ 07882-4343
County: Warren FICE Identification: 025039
Unit ID: 245625
Telephone: (908) 835-9222 Carnegie Class: Assoc/HT-High Trad
FAX Number: (908) 689-9262 Calendar System: Semester
URL: www.warren.edu
Established: 1981 Annual Undergrad Tuition & Fees (In-District): $4,590
Enrollment: 2,822 Coed
Affiliation or Control: State/Local IRS Status: 501(c)3
Highest Offering: Associate Degree
Accreditation: M, ADNUR, MAC

01 President ... Dr. William AUSTIN
10 Vice Pres Finance & Operations ... Ms. Barbara PRATT
51 Vice Pres Corporate/Continuing Educ ... Ms. Eve AZAR
11 Dean of Administration ... Mr. Dennis FLORENTINE
07 VP of Student Services ... Mr. Jeremy BEELER
05 Acting VP of Academics ... Ms. Marianne VANDEURSEN
37 Director of Financial Aid ... Ms. Jacqueline DALY
15 Director Human Resources ... Ms. Sharon HINTZ
21 Director Business Services ... Mr. Jay ALEXANDER
04 Administrative Asst to President ... Ms. Genevieve VASKO
08 Head Librarian ... Ms. Lisa STOLL
09 Director of Institutional Research ... Ms. Nikki DADARRIA
102 Dir Foundation/Corporate Relations ... Ms. Samir ELBASSIOUNY

Westminster Choir College (H)

101 Walnut Lane, Princeton NJ 08540
Telephone: (609) 921-7100 Identification: 770128
Accreditation: &M

William Paterson University of New Jersey (I)

300 Pompton Road, Wayne NJ 07470-2152
County: Passaic FICE Identification: 002625
Unit ID: 187444
Telephone: (973) 720-2000 Carnegie Class: Masters/L
FAX Number: N/A Calendar System: Semester
URL: www.wpunj.edu
Established: 1855 Annual Undergrad Tuition & Fees (In-State): $12,574
Enrollment: 10,862 Coed
Affiliation or Control: State IRS Status: 501(c)3
Highest Offering: Doctorate
Accreditation: M, ART, CAATE, CACREP, CAEPN, CS, MUS, NURSE, PH, SP

01 President ... Dr. Kathleen WALDRON
05 Senior Vice President/Provost ... Dr. Warren SANDMANN
100 Chf of Staff to Pres/Board of Trust ... Dr. Robert SEAL
10 Vice Pres Administration/Finance ... Mr. Stephen BOLYAI
111 Vice Pres Institutional Advancement ... Ms. Pamela FERGUSON
32 Vice President Student Development ... Dr. Miki CAMMARATA
84 VP of Enrollment Management ... Dr. Reginald ROSS
88 Assoc Provost Academic Development ... Ms. Danielle LIAUTAUD
114 Assoc VP Finance Budget/Fiscal Plng ... Ms. Pamela WINSLOW
11 Assoc VP for Administration ... Mr. Richard STOMBER
26 VP Mktg & Public Relations ... Mr. Stuart GOLDSTEIN
15 Associate Vice Pres Human Resources ... Mr. John POLDING
19 Dir Public Safety & Univ Police ... Vacant
35 Associate VP for Campus Life ... Mr. Francisco DIAZ
35 Assoc VP/Dean Student Development ... Dr. Glen SHERMAN
60 Dean Col Arts/Comm ... Mr. Daryl MOORE
53 Dean College of Education ... Dr. Candace BURNS
66 Dean College of Science & Health ... Dr. Kenneth WOLF
79 Dean Human & Social Science ... Dr. Kara M. RABBITT
50 Dean College of Business ... Dr. Siamack SHOJAI
08 Dean D & L Cheng Library ... Dr. Edward OWUSU-ANSAH
21 Assoc VP Finance & Comptroller ... Ms. Samantha GREEN
28 Dir Employment Equity & Diversity ... Ms. Michele JOHNSON
51 Exec Dir Cont Educ/Distance Lrng ... Dr. Bernadette TIERNAN
20 Associate Provost Academic Affairs ... Dr. Stephen HAHN
20 Assoc Prov for Curriculum & Intl Ed ... Dr. Jonathan LINCOLN
86 Assoc VP Govt & External Relations ... Mr. Patrick DEDEO
27 Director Public Information ... Ms. Mary Beth ZEMAN
29 Executive Director Alumni ... Ms. Janis SCHWARTZ
108 Director Inst Research & Assessment ... Dr. Jane ZEFF
13 Chief Information Officer ... Mr. Eric ROSENBERG
43 General Counsel ... Mr. Glenn JONES
16 Director of Human Resources ... Ms. Denise ROBINSON-LEWIS
07 Director of Undergrad Admissions ... Mr. Michael DIBARTOLOMEO
37 Director Financial Aid ... Mr. Michael CORSO
06 Registrar ... Ms. Nina TRELISKY
41 Director Athletics ... Ms. Sabrina GRANT
36 Director of Career Dev & Advisement ... Ms. Sharon ROSENGART
39 Director of Residence Life ... Mr. Joseph CAFFARELLI
23 Dir Counseling/Health & Wellness ... Dr. Eileen LUBECK
14 Deputy Chief CIO ... Dr. Sandra MILLER
09 Dir Institutional Research/Assess ... Dr. Jane ZEFF
40 Director Bookstore ... Mr. Scott DUNLAP
18 Director Capital Plng/Design/Constr ... Vacant
85 Director International Student Svcs ... Ms. Cinzia RICHARDSON
94 Director of Women's Center ... Ms. Librada SANCHEZ
96 Director of Purchasing ... Mr. Lirse JONES
89 Director of Freshmen Studies ... Dr. Kim DANIEL-ROBINSON
92 Director of Honors College ... Dr. Barbara ANDREW
35 Dir Campus Activ/Svc & Leadership ... Ms. Donna MINNICH SPUHLER
88 Assoc Dir Instruction/Research Tech ... Mr. Patrick RYAN
04 Administrative Asst to President ... Ms. Sherin FAVOCCI

Yeshiva Bais Aharon (J)

905 Park Avenue, Lakewood NJ 08701
County: Ocean Identification: 667291
Telephone: (732) 367-7604 Carnegie Class: Not Classified
FAX Number: (732) 367-1777 Calendar System: Semester
Established: 2012 Annual Undergrad Tuition & Fees: N/A
Enrollment: N/A Male
Affiliation or Control: Independent Non-Profit IRS Status: 501(c)3
Highest Offering: First Talmudic Degree
Accreditation: @RABN

01 CEO ... Binyomin SCHULGASSER
06 Registrar ... Nosson SCHULGASSER
36 Financial Aid Administrator ... Aharon FISCHER

Yeshiva Chemdas Hatorah (K)

950 Massachusetts Avenue, Lakewood NJ 08701
County: Ocean Identification: 667281
Telephone: N/A Carnegie Class: Not Classified
FAX Number: N/A Calendar System: Other
Established: Annual Undergrad Tuition & Fees: N/A
Enrollment: N/A Male
Affiliation or Control: Independent Non-Profit IRS Status: 501(c)3
Highest Offering: First Talmudic Degree
Accreditation: AIJS

Yeshiva Gedolah of Cliffwood (L)

200 Center Street, Keyport NJ 07735
County: Monmouth Identification: 667322
Telephone: (732) 765-9126 Carnegie Class: Not Classified
FAX Number: (732) 865-7247 Calendar System: Semester

Established: 2004 Annual Undergrad Tuition & Fees: N/A
Enrollment: N/A Male
Affiliation or Control: Independent Non-Profit IRS Status: 501(c)3
Highest Offering: First Talmudic Degree
Accreditation: RABN

01 CEO .... Samuel ALSTER
06 Registrar .... Baruch SEGEL
10 CFO .... Shimon ALSTER
37 Financial Aid Adminstrator .... Aryeh BRODSKY

Yeshiva Gedolah Keren Hatorah (A)

1083 Brook Road, Lakewood NJ 08701
County: Ocean Identification: 667282
Telephone: (732) 942-1811 Carnegie Class: Not Classified
FAX Number: (732) 994-4222 Calendar System: Other
URL: yeshivagedolahkerenhatorah.com
Established: 2009 Annual Undergrad Tuition & Fees: N/A
Enrollment: N/A Male
Affiliation or Control: Independent Non-Profit IRS Status: 501(c)3
Highest Offering: First Talmudic Degree
Accreditation: AIJS

01 CEO/Executive Director .... Rabbi Yehuda L. LANDAU

Yeshiva Gedolah Shaarei Schmuel (B)

511 Ocean Ave, Lakewood NJ 08701
County: Ocean Identification: 667260
Unit ID: 488350
Telephone: (732) 363-2164 Carnegie Class: Not Classified
FAX Number: (732) 364-3331 Calendar System: Other
Established: 2008 Annual Undergrad Tuition & Fees: $7,700
Enrollment: N/A Male
Affiliation or Control: Independent Non-Profit IRS Status: 501(c)3
Highest Offering: First Talmudic Degree
Accreditation: @RABN

Yeshiva Gedolah Tiferes Boruch (C)

21 Rockview Avenue, North Plainfield NJ 07060
County: Union Identification: 667283
Telephone: (908) 753-2600 Carnegie Class: Not Classified
FAX Number: (908) 753-4243 Calendar System: Semester
URL: yeshivagedolahtiferesboruch.com
Established: 1989 Annual Undergrad Tuition & Fees: N/A
Enrollment: N/A Male
Affiliation or Control: Independent Non-Profit IRS Status: 501(c)3
Highest Offering: First Talmudic Degree
Accreditation: AIJS

Yeshiva Gedolah Zichron Leyma (D)

2035 Vauxhall Road, Union NJ 07083
County: Union FICE Identification: 041924
Unit ID: 476692
Telephone: (908) 587-0502 Carnegie Class: Spec-4-yr-Faith
FAX Number: N/A Calendar System: Semester
Established: 1999 Annual Undergrad Tuition & Fees: $9,000
Enrollment: 21 Male
Affiliation or Control: Independent Non-Profit IRS Status: 501(c)3
Highest Offering: First Talmudic Degree
Accreditation: RABN

Yeshiva Toras Chaim (E)

999 Ridge Avenue, Lakewood NJ 08701-2120
County: Ocean FICE Identification: 041311
Unit ID: 451398
Telephone: (732) 414-2834 Carnegie Class: Spec-4-yr-Faith
FAX Number: (732) 414-2838 Calendar System: Semester
Established: 2000 Annual Undergrad Tuition & Fees: $12,100
Enrollment: 211 Male
Affiliation or Control: Independent Non-Profit IRS Status: 501(c)3
Highest Offering: Baccalaureate
Accreditation: RABN

05 Chief Academic Officer .... Rabbi Mendel SLOMOVITS
06 Registrar .... Mrs. Devoiry DURST
10 Bookkeeper .... Mrs. Michal GROSSMAN

Yeshiva Yesodei Hatorah (F)

2 Yesodei Court, Lakewood NJ 08701
County: Ocean Identification: 667109
Unit ID: 481438
Telephone: (732) 370-3360 Carnegie Class: Spec-4-yr-Faith
FAX Number: (732) 886-2659 Calendar System: Semester
Established: 1995 Annual Undergrad Tuition & Fees: $11,000
Enrollment: 56 Male
Affiliation or Control: Independent Non-Profit IRS Status: 501(c)3
Highest Offering: First Talmudic Degree
Accreditation: RABN

05 Dean .... Rabbi Shaya TREFF
10 Chief Financial/Business Officer .... Rabbi Shaya UNGAR
20 Associate Academic Officer .... Rabbi Yisroel Meir TREFF

Yeshivas Be'er Yitzchok (G)

1391 North Avenue, Elizabeth NJ 07208-2480
County: Union FICE Identification: 041234
Unit ID: 451370
Telephone: (908) 354-6057 Carnegie Class: Spec-4-yr-Faith
FAX Number: (908) 820-0431 Calendar System: Semester
Established: 1999 Annual Undergrad Tuition & Fees: $10,400
Enrollment: 49 Male
Affiliation or Control: Independent Non-Profit IRS Status: 501(c)3
Highest Offering: Baccalaureate
Accreditation: AIJS

01 Chief Executive Officer .... Rabbi Avrohom SCHULMAN
37 Director of Student Financial Aid .... Chani MILLER
11 Chief of Administration .... Chani MILLER

NEW MEXICO

Brookline College (H)

4201 Central Avenue NW Ste J,
Albuquerque NM 87105-1649
Telephone: (505) 880-2877 Identification: 666724
Accreditation: ACICS, NUR

† Branch campus of Brookline College, Phoenix, AZ

Brown Mackie College - Albuquerque (I)

10500 Cooper Avenue NE, Albuquerque NM 87123
Telephone: (505) 559-5200 Identification: 770741
Accreditation: ACICS, OTA, SURTEC

† In teach-out mode. Branch campus of The Art Institute of Phoenix, Phoenix, AZ

Burrell College of Osteopathic Medicine (J)

3501 Arrowhead Drive, Las Cruces NM 88001
County: Dona Ana Identification: 667248
Telephone: (575) 647-2266 Carnegie Class: Not Classified
FAX Number: (575) 647-2267 Calendar System: Semester
URL: www.bcomnm.org
Established: 2013 Annual Graduate Tuition & Fees: N/A
Enrollment: N/A Coed
Affiliation or Control: Independent Non-Profit IRS Status: 501(c)3
Highest Offering: Doctorate; No Undergraduates
Accreditation: @OSTEO

01 Executive Director/President .... Mr. John HUMMER
05 Dean/CAO .... Dr. George MYCHASKIW
10 Sr VP Admin & Finance/CFO .... Ms. Angela THRONEBERRY

Carrington College - Albuquerque (K)

1001 Menaul Boulevard NE, Albuquerque NM 87107-1642
Telephone: (505) 254-7777 Identification: 666014
Accreditation: &WJ

† Regional accreditation is carried under the parent institution in Sacramento, CA.

Central New Mexico Community College (L)

525 Buena Vista, SE, Albuquerque NM 87106-4096
County: Bernalillo FICE Identification: 004742
Unit ID: 187532
Telephone: (505) 224-4412 Carnegie Class: Assoc/MT-VT-Mix Trad/Non
FAX Number: (505) 224-4417 Calendar System: Semester
URL: www.cnm.edu
Established: 1965 Annual Undergrad Tuition & Fees (In-District): $1,472
Enrollment: 25,760 Coed
Affiliation or Control: State/Local IRS Status: 501(c)3
Highest Offering: Associate Degree
Accreditation: NH, ACBSP, ACFEI, ADNUR, CAHIIM, COARC, CONST, DA, DMS, EMT, MLTAD, @PTAA, SURGT

01 President .... Dr. Katharine W. WINOGRAD
05 Vice President for Academic Affairs .... Dr. Sydney D. GUNTHORPE
32 Vice President for Student Services .... Mr. Phillip BUSTOS
10 Vice Pres for Finance & Operations .... Mrs. Katherine ULIBARRI
84 Assoc Vice Pres Enrollment Mgmt .... Mr. Eugene PADILLA
08 Director Learning Resources .... Ms. Poppy JOHNSON RENVALL
13 Chief Information Officer .... Mr. Feng HOU
103 Assoc Dir Ingenuity .... Ms. Evelyn DOW
36 Academic Advisement Job Connection .... Ms. Stacey COOLEY
30 Exec Director of Development .... Mr. Clinton WELLS
07 Director Enrollment Services .... Mr. Glenn DAMIANI
26 Dir Marketing & Public Relations .... Mrs. Jennifer BROWER
27 Dir Communications/Media Relations .... Mr. Brad MOORE
37 Director Student Financial Aid .... Mr. Lee CARRILLO
15 Executive Director Human Resources .... Ms. Juliane ZITER
81 Dean Sch of Math/Sci/Engr .... Mr. John CORNISH
50 Dean School of Bus/Info Technology .... Ms. Donna DILLER
72 Dean School of Applied Technologies .... Mr. John BRONISZ
97 Dean Sch of Adult & Gen Educ .... Ms. LouAnne LUNDGREN
83 Dean Comm/Humanities/Soc Sci .... Ms. Erica VOLKERS
76 Dean Health/Well/Pub Safety .... Ms. Tamra MASON
06 Registrar .... Ms. Yvonne MARTINEZ
18 Exec Dir Physical Plant .... Mr. Marvin MARTINEZ
21 Exec Dir Fiscal Ops/Comptroller .... Ms. Wanda HELMS
35 Director of Student Life .... Mr. Christopher CAVAZOS
96 Director of Purchasing .... Ms. Gerrie BECKER
19 Chief of Safety & Security .... Mr. John CORVINO
04 Administrative Asst to President .... Ms. Erin BRADSHAW
09 Sr Dir Outcomes And Assessment .... Ms. Ursula WALN
29 Director Alumni Relations .... Mrs. Roberta RICCI

Clovis Community College (M)

417 Schepps Boulevard, Clovis NM 88101-8381
County: Curry FICE Identification: 004743
Unit ID: 187639
Telephone: (575) 769-2811 Carnegie Class: Assoc/HVT-High Non
FAX Number: (575) 769-4190 Calendar System: Semester
URL: www.clovis.edu
Established: 1971 Annual Undergrad Tuition & Fees (In-State): $1,176
Enrollment: 3,133 Coed
Affiliation or Control: State IRS Status: 501(c)3
Highest Offering: Associate Degree
Accreditation: NH, ADNUR, PTAA, RAD

01 President .... Dr. Becky ROWLEY
03 Executive Vice President .... Dr. Robin JONES
10 Chief Financial Officer .... Mr. Tom DRAKE
05 Chief Academic Officer .... Dr. Robin JONES
13 Chief Information Officer .... Mr. Norman KIA
11 VP Administration/Govt Relations .... Mr. Tom DRAKE
21 Director of Business Affairs .... Ms. Jayne CRAIG
07 Dir Admissions/Records/Registrar .... Ms. Kim TATE
37 Director of Financial Aid .... Ms. April CHAVEZ
08 Director Library/Learning Resources .... Ms. Kelly GRAY
121 Dir Center for Student Success .... Mrs. Mona Lee NORMAN-ARMSTRONG
38 Dir of Counseling/Testing/Advisemnt .... Mr. Marcus SMITH
15 Director of Human Resource Services .... Mrs. Gay GOETTSCH
88 Director Small Business Development .... Mrs. Sandra TAYLOR-SAWYER
91 Director of Administrative Info Sys .... Ms. Teresa WHITEHEAD
56 Director Extended Learning .... Ms. Robin KUYKENDALL
36 Director Student Placement .... Vacant
111 Dir of Institutional Advancement .... Ms. Natalie DAGGETT
18 Director of Physical Plant .... Mr. Paul ARAGON
26 Director of Marketing/Cmty Rels .... Ms. Natalie DAGGETT
76 Div Chair Allied Health Programs .... Ms. Shawna MCGILL
83 Div Chair Liberal Arts/Dev Studies .... Ms. Janett JOHNSON
50 Div Chair of Business Admin & Tech .... Mrs. Monica SANCHEZ
81 Division Chair of Math/Science .... Mr. Todd KUYKENDALL
04 Administrative Asst to President .... Ms. Beverly ARAGON
09 Director of Institutional Research .... Ms. Courtney TEMPEL
19 Director Security/Safety .... Mr. Freddie SALAZAR

Dine College Shiprock Branch (N)

1228 Yucca St., PO Box 580, Shiprock NM 87420
Telephone: (505) 368-3500 Identification: 770007
Accreditation: &NH

† Branch campus of Dine College, Tsaile, AZ

Eastern New Mexico University Main Campus (O)

1500 S Avenue K, Portales NM 88130-7400
County: Roosevelt FICE Identification: 002651
Unit ID: 187648
Telephone: (575) 562-1011 Carnegie Class: Masters/M
FAX Number: (575) 562-2980 Calendar System: Semester
URL: www.enmu.edu
Established: 1927 Annual Undergrad Tuition & Fees (In-State): $5,618
Enrollment: 5,725 Coed
Affiliation or Control: State IRS Status: 501(c)3
Highest Offering: Master's
Accreditation: NH, ACBSP, CAEPN, MUS, NUR, SP, SW

01 President .... Dr. Jeffery ELWELL
05 Vice President Academic Affairs .... Dr. Jamie LAURENZ
10 Vice President Business Affairs .... Mr. Scott SMART
32 Vice President for Student Affairs .... Dr. Jeff LONG
13 Vice President of Technology .... Mr. Clark ELSWICK
45 Exec Dir Planning/Analysis/Inst Ren .... Dr. Patrice CALDWELL
20 Asst Vice Pres for Academic Affairs .... Dr. Suzanne BALCH-LINDSAY
20 Asst Vice Pres Academic Affairs .... Dr. John MONTGOMERY
21 Comptroller .... Mrs. Carol FLETCHER
53 Dean Education/Technology .... Dr. Penny A. GARCIA
50 Interim Dean Business .... Dr. John LUHMAN
57 Dean Fine Arts .... Dr. Jeff GENTRY
49 Dean Liberal Arts & Science .... Dr. Mary AYALA
58 Dean Graduate School .... Dr. Linda WEEMS
22 Affirmative Action Officer .... Ms. Jessica SMALL
08 Director of Library .... Ms. Melveta WALKER
06 Interim Registrar .... Ms. DeLynn BARGAS
37 Director Student Financial Aid .... Mr. Brent SMALL
07 Director Enrollment Services .... Mr. Cody SPITZ
30 Director Development .... Ms. Noelle BARTL
15 Director of Human Resources .... Mr. Benito GONZALES
88 Director of Broadcasting .... Mr. Duane RYAN
18 Director Physical Plant .... Mr. Ted FARES

41 Athletic Director .... Dr. Greg WAGGONER
19 Chief of University Police .... Mr. Brad MAULDIN
36 Dir Counseling Ctr/Career Svcs .... Ms. Susan LARSEN
39 Director Student Housing .... Mr. Steven ESTOCK
09 Dir Institutional Research .... Mr. Brendan HENNESSEY
96 Director of Purchasing interim .... Ms. Jane BLAKELEY
26 Director of Publications .... Mr. John HOUSER
29 Coordinator of Alumni .... Vacant
106 Dir of Distance Learning/Outreach .... Mr. Ryan ROARK
35 Director Campus Life .... Vacant

Eastern New Mexico University-Roswell (A)

PO Box 6000, Roswell NM 88202-6000
County: Chaves FICE Identification: 002661
Unit ID: 187666
Telephone: (575) 624-7000 Carnegie Class: Assoc/HVT-High Non
FAX Number: (575) 624-7342 Calendar System: Semester
URL: www.roswell.enmu.edu
Established: 1958 Annual Undergrad Tuition & Fees (In-State): $1,944
Enrollment: 2,679 Coed
Affiliation or Control: State IRS Status: 501(c)3
Highest Offering: Associate Degree
Accreditation: NH, ADNUR, COARC, EMT, MAC, #OTA

01 President .... Dr. John MADDEN
05 VP for Acacdemic Affairs .... Dr. Ken MAGUIRE
10 VP for Business Affairs .... Mr. Eric JOHNSTON-ORTIZ
32 VP for Student Affairs .... Mr. Mike MARTINEZ
21 Controller .... Ms. Karen FRANKLIN
35 Asst VP for Student Affairs .... Vacant
08 Director Learning Resource Center .... Mr. Rollah ASTON
37 Director Financial Aid .... Ms. Analisa BHAKTA
30 Director College Development .... Ms. Donna ORACION
07 Director Admissions and Records .... Ms. Linda NEEL
13 Director of Computer Services .... Vacant
15 Director of Human Resources .... Vacant
18 Director of Physical Plant .... Mr. Derek DUBIEL
19 Director of Security .... Mr. Robert NEWBERRY
96 Director of Purchasing .... Mr. Cole COLLINS
09 Director Institutional Research .... Mr. Todd DEKAY
04 Administrative Asst to President .... Ms. Lorinda WILKINS
49 AVP of Arts & Science Education .... Ms. Annemarie OLDFIELD
76 AVP of Health Education .... Ms. Dyan ELLINGTON
72 AVP of Technical Education .... Mr. Chad SMITH

EC-Council University (B)

101C Sun Avenue NE, Albuquerque NM 87109
County: Bernalillo Identification: 667232
Telephone: (505) 922-2886 Carnegie Class: Not Classified
FAX Number: (505) 341-0050 Calendar System: Other
URL: www.eccu.edu
Established: 2003 Annual Undergrad Tuition & Fees: N/A
Enrollment: N/A Coed
Affiliation or Control: Proprietary IRS Status: Proprietary
Highest Offering: Master's
Accreditation: DEAC

01 CEO/President .... Sanjay BAVISI
03 Executive Vice President .... Lata BAVISI
05 Dean .... Drumm MCNAUGHTON

Institute of American Indian Arts (C)

83 Avan Nu Po Road, Santa Fe NM 87508-1300
County: Santa Fe FICE Identification: 021464
Unit ID: 187745
Telephone: (505) 424-2300 Carnegie Class: Tribal
FAX Number: (505) 424-4500 Calendar System: Semester
URL: www.iaia.edu
Established: 1962 Annual Undergrad Tuition & Fees: $4,700
Enrollment: 493 Coed
Affiliation or Control: Federal IRS Status: Exempt
Highest Offering: Master's
Accreditation: NH, ART

01 President .... Dr. Robert MARTIN
05 Academic Dean .... Ms. Charlene TETERS
10 Chief Financial Officer .... Mr. Larry MIRABAL
32 Dean of Student Life .... Ms. Carmen HENAN
84 Chief Enrollment & Retention Ofcr .... Ms. Nena ANAYA
111 Dir of Institutional Advancement .... Ms. Judith PEPPER
26 Dir of Marketing and Communication .... Mr. Eric DAVIS
88 Director of Land Grant Programs .... Ms. Charlene CARR
88 Dir of IAIA Museum .... Ms. Patsy PHILLIPS
102 Dir of Sponsored Programs .... Ms. Laurie BRAYSHAW
09 Dir of Institutional Research .... Dr. William SAYRE

Luna Community College (D)

366 Luna Drive, Las Vegas NM 87701-1510
County: San Miguel FICE Identification: 009962
Unit ID: 363633
Telephone: (505) 454-2500 Carnegie Class: Assoc/MT-VT-High Non
FAX Number: (505) 454-2519 Calendar System: Semester
URL: www.luna.edu
Established: 1970 Annual Undergrad Tuition & Fees (In-District): $962
Enrollment: 1,481 Coed
Affiliation or Control: State/Local IRS Status: 501(c)3
Highest Offering: Associate Degree
Accreditation: NH, ACBSP, ADNUR, DA

01 President .... Mr. Ricky SERNA
05 VP of Instruction/Student Services .... Dr. Vidal MARTINEZ
10 Vice Pres of Finance/Administration .... Ms. Donna FLORES-MEDINA
09 Director Institutional Research .... Mr. Abran ROMERO
07 Director of Admissions .... Mr. Moses MARQUEZ
06 Registrar .... Ms. Bernadette C. RAEL
18 Manager Physical Plant .... Mr. Matthew CORDOVA
37 Director Student Financial Aid .... Mr. Michael MONTOYA
15 Director Human Resources .... Ms. Leticia ARCHULETA
30 Director Development .... Ms. Elaina LUNA
13 Director of Computer Services .... Ms. Denise MONTOYA

Mesalands Community College (E)

911 S 10th Street, Tucumcari NM 88401-3352
County: Quay FICE Identification: 032063
Unit ID: 188261
Telephone: (505) 461-4413 Carnegie Class: Assoc/HVT-High Trad
FAX Number: (505) 461-1901 Calendar System: Semester
URL: www.mesalands.edu
Established: 1980 Annual Undergrad Tuition & Fees (In-District): $1,740
Enrollment: 796 Coed
Affiliation or Control: State/Local IRS Status: 501(c)3
Highest Offering: Associate Degree
Accreditation: NH

01 President .... Dr. Thomas W. NEWSOM
04 Executive Asst to President .... Ms. Consuelo E. CHAVEZ
32 Vice President Student Affairs .... Dr. Aaron KENNEDY
05 Vice President of Academic Affairs .... Ms. Natalie GILLARD
11 Vice President of Admin Affairs .... Ms. Amanda HAMMER
37 Director Financial Aid .... Ms. Jessica ELEBARIO
26 Director Public Relations .... Ms. Kimberly HANNA
72 Director of NAWRTC .... Mr. Jim MORGAN
84 Director of Enrollment Management .... Ms. Amber MCCLURE
13 Director of Inst Technology .... Mr. James JONES
09 Dir Inst Research and Development .... Dr. Forrest KAATZ
15 Director of HR and Accounting .... Ms. Kacee BENFORD
20 Director of Academic Affairs .... Ms. Donna GARCIA
102 Foundation Chair .... Ms. Laurie BIDEGAIN
08 Library Director .... Vacant

National American University-Albuquerque (F)

4775 Indian School Road NE, Ste 200,
Albuquerque NM 87110
Telephone: (505) 348-3700 Identification: 770407
Accreditation: &NH, MAC

† Branch campus of National American University, Rapid City, SD

National American University-Albuquerque West (G)

10131 Coors Blvd NW, Suite I-01, Albuquerque NM 87114
Telephone: (505) 348-3750 Identification: 770408
Accreditation: &NH

† Branch campus of National American University, Rapid City, SD

National College of Midwifery (H)

1041 Reed Street, Suite C, Taos NM 87571
County: Taos Identification: 666251
Telephone: (575) 758-8914 Carnegie Class: Not Classified
FAX Number: N/A Calendar System: Trimester
URL: www.midwiferycollege.edu
Established: 1989 Annual Undergrad Tuition & Fees: N/A
Enrollment: N/A Coed
Affiliation or Control: Independent Non-Profit IRS Status: 501(c)3
Highest Offering: Doctorate
Accreditation: #MEAC

01 CEO/President .... Marcy ANDREW
11 COO .... Anna KHAMSAMRAN
30 Chief Development Officer .... Cassaundra JAH

Navajo Technical University (I)

PO Box 849, Crownpoint NM 87313-0849
County: McKinley FICE Identification: 023576
Unit ID: 187596
Telephone: (505) 786-4100 Carnegie Class: Tribal
FAX Number: (505) 786-5644 Calendar System: Semester
URL: www.navajotech.edu
Established: 1979 Annual Undergrad Tuition & Fees: $4,070
Enrollment: 1,686 Coed
Affiliation or Control: Tribal Control IRS Status: 501(c)3
Highest Offering: Baccalaureate
Accreditation: NH, ACFEI

01 President .... Dr. Elmer GUY
32 Interim Dean of Student Services .... Mr. Wilson GILMORE
10 Interim Chief Financial Officer .... Ms. Geraldine GAMBLE
05 Dean of Undergraduate Studies .... Dr. Casmir AGBARAJI
06 Registrar/Director of Admissions .... Ms. Jerlynn HENRY
09 Data Assessment Director .... Ms. Shawnia GAMBLE
25 Contracts & Grant Officer .... Ms. Thomasina GREY
37 Student Financial Aid Officer .... Mr. Tyrrell HARDY
15 Director Human Resources .... Dr. Perphelia FOWLER
08 Head Librarian .... Mr. Darwin C. HENDERSON
04 Executive Assistant .... Ms. Tonilee BECENTI
13 IT Director .... Mr. Jason ARVISO
41 Athletic Director .... Mr. George LAFRANCE

† Tuition figure is for a student enrolled in a federally recognized Indian tribe.

New Mexico Highlands University (J)

PO Box 9000, Las Vegas NM 87701-9000
County: San Miguel FICE Identification: 002653
Unit ID: 187897
Telephone: (505) 425-7511 Carnegie Class: Masters/L
FAX Number: N/A Calendar System: Semester
URL: www.nmhu.edu
Established: 1893 Annual Undergrad Tuition & Fees (In-State): $5,550
Enrollment: 3,499 Coed
Affiliation or Control: State IRS Status: 501(c)3
Highest Offering: Master's
Accreditation: #NH, ACBSP, CACREP, CAEPN, NURSE, SW

01 President .... Dr. Sam MINNER
05 Provost/VP for Academic Affairs .... Dr. Roxanne GONZALES
10 Interim VP Finance & Admin .... Mr. Max BACA
84 VP for Strategic Enroll Mgmt .... Dr. Edward MARTINEZ
32 Dean of Students .... Ms. Kimberly BLEA
07 Dir of Student Recruitment/Admiss .... Ms. Jessica JARAMILLO
06 Interim Registrar .... Ms. Thomasinia ORTIZ-GALLEYOS
09 Dir Inst Effectiveness & Research .... Mr. Gilbert RIVERA
13 Director of Information Technology .... Mr. Joe GIERI
15 Director Human Resources .... Ms. Denise MONTOYA
18 Interim Dir of Facilities Mgmt .... Ms. Sylvia BACA
19 Chief Police/Security .... Mr. Clarence ROMERO
26 Director of University Relations .... Mr. Sean WEAVER
29 Coordinator of Alumni Affairs .... Ms. Juli SALMAN
30 Vice President for Advancement .... Ms. Theresa LAW
36 Director of Career Services .... Mr. Ron GARCIA
37 Director of Financial Aid .... Ms. Susan CHAVEZ
40 Bookstore Manager .... Mr. Justin RICE
50 Dean School of Business .... Dr. William TAYLOR
53 Dean School of Education .... Dr. Virginia PADILLA-VIGIL
39 Director Student Housing .... Ms. Yvette WILKES

New Mexico Institute of Mining and Technology (K)

801 Leroy Place, Socorro NM 87801-4796
County: Socorro FICE Identification: 002654
Unit ID: 187967
Telephone: (575) 835-5434 Carnegie Class: Masters/S
FAX Number: (575) 835-6329 Calendar System: Semester
URL: www.nmt.edu
Established: 1889 Annual Undergrad Tuition & Fees (In-State): $6,891
Enrollment: 2,150 Coed
Affiliation or Control: State IRS Status: 501(c)3
Highest Offering: Doctorate
Accreditation: NH, CS, ENG

01 President .... Dr. Stephen G. WELLS
10 Vice Pres Administration & Finance .... Mr. Cleve MCDANIEL
05 Vice President Academic Affairs .... Dr. Doug WELLS
32 VP Student & Univ Rels/Dean Stdnt .... Ms. Melissa JARAMILLO FLEMING
46 Vice Pres Research/Economic Devel .... Dr. Van D. ROMERO
20 Assoc Vice Pres Academic Affairs .... Dr. Peter MOZLEY
45 Assoc VP Research/Econ Development .... Mr. Carlos REY ROMERO
58 Dean of Graduate Studies .... Dr. Lorie LIEBROCK
08 Librarian .... Mr. David COX
15 Director of Human Resources .... Ms. Joann SALOME
06 Registrar .... Ms. Sara GRIJALVA
07 Director of Admission .... Mr. Anthony ORTIZ
37 Director of Financial Aid .... Mr. Kenneth AERTS
30 Director Office for Advancement .... Ms. Colleen FOSTER
22 Director Affirm Action & Compliance .... Mr. Randy SAAVEDRA
14 Director Computer Center .... Vacant
13 Director of Information Services .... Mr. Joseph FRANKLIN
65 Director Bur Geology & Mineral Res .... Dr. Nelia DUNBAR
12 Director Petro Recovery Res Ctr .... Dr. Robert BALCH
18 Director Facilities Management .... Ms. Yvonne MANZANO
21 Director of Finance .... Ms. Arleen VALLES
31 Dir Community Education/Outreach .... Ms. Lillian ARMIJO
38 Dir Counseling/Disabilities Svcs .... Vacant
96 Chief Procurement Officer .... Ms. Kimela MILLER
09 Institutional Researcher .... Ms. Stephany MOORE
26 Chief Public Relations Officer .... Mr. Dave LEPRE

New Mexico Junior College (L)

1 Thunderbird Circle, Hobbs NM 88240-9123
County: Lea FICE Identification: 002655
Unit ID: 187903
Telephone: (575) 392-4510 Carnegie Class: Assoc/HT-High Non
FAX Number: (575) 492-2732 Calendar System: Semester
URL: www.nmjc.edu
Established: 1965 Annual Undergrad Tuition & Fees (In-District): $1,248
Enrollment: 2,923 Coed
Affiliation or Control: Local IRS Status: 501(c)3
Highest Offering: Associate Degree
Accreditation: NH, ADNUR

01 President ... Dr. Kelvin SHARP
05 Vice President Instruction ... Dr. Dennis ATHERTON
10 Vice President Finance ... Dan HARDIN
32 Vice President Student Services ... Cathy MITCHELL
103 Vice President Training & Outreach ... Jeff MCCOOL
84 Dean Enrollment Management ... Vacant
13 Dir Computer Information System ... Bill KUNKO
26 Director of Communications ... Susan FINE
04 Executive Asst to the President ... Norma FAUGHT
37 Director Financial Aid ... Kerrie MITCHELL
09 Director of Inst Effectiveness ... Dr. Larry SANDERSON
66 Director of Nursing ... Misty STINE
18 Chief Facilities/Physical Plant ... Dr. Charley CARROLL
81 Dean Business/Math & Sciences ... Kelly HOLLADAY
79 Dean Arts & Humanities ... Dianne MARQUEZ
40 Director of Bookstore Services ... Robert ADAMS
75 Dean of Public Safety ... Dr. August FONS
08 Director of Library Services ... James BRITSCH
96 Coordinator of Purchasing ... Regina CHOATE
41 Director of Athletics ... Deron CLARK
102 Acct/Controller-NMJC Foundation ... Christina KUNKO
88 Controller ... Joshua MORGAN
39 Director Student Housing ... Sandy HARDIN
88 Executive Director WHM/LCCHF ... Dr. Darrell BEAUCHAMP
88 Exec Dir NMJC Research Foundation ... Dale GANNAWAY
06 Associate Registrar ... Rebecca WHITLEY
19 Director of Public Safety ... Dennis KELLEY

New Mexico Military Institute (A)

101 W College, Roswell NM 88201-5173
County: Chaves FICE Identification: 002656
Unit ID: 187912
Telephone: (575) 622-6250 Carnegie Class: Assoc/HT-High Trad
FAX Number: (575) 624-8058 Calendar System: Semester
URL: www.nmmi.edu
Established: 1891 Annual Undergrad Tuition & Fees (In-State): $5,141
Enrollment: 428 Coed
Affiliation or Control: State IRS Status: 501(c)3
Highest Offering: Associate Degree
Accreditation: NH

01 Superintendent/President ... MGen. Jerry W. GRIZZLE
32 Commandant ... LtCol. Jonathan K. GRAFF
100 Chief of Staff ... Col. David WEST
10 Chief Financial Officer ... Col. Judy SCHARMER
05 Dean ... BGen. Douglas J. MURRAY
41 Athletic Director/Dir Physical Educ ... Col. Jose BARRON
30 Development and Advancement Officer ... Maj. Kris WARD
116 Internal Auditor ... Col. David GRAY
88 Professor of Military Science ... LtCol. Hubert STEPHENS
20 Vice Dean & High School Princ ... Col. George BRICK
15 Assistant Human Resources Director ... Ms. Carmen BELL
50 Assoc Dean Social Science/Business ... LtCol. Philip BACA
81 Assoc Dean Science/Mathematics ... Col. John R. MCVAY
79 Associate Dean Humanities ... Maj. Joel DYKSTRA
64 Director of Music ... LtCol. Stephen M. THORP
08 Director of the Library ... Col. Jerome J. KLOPFER
26 Marketing & Communication Director ... LtCol. Colleen COLE-VELASQUEZ
18 Chief Facilities/Physical Plant ... Mr. Kent TAYLOR
06 Registrar ... Maj. Chris WRIGHT
37 Director of Financial Aid ... Maj. Sonya F. RODRIGUEZ
88 Mil Services Academies Prep Dir ... Shawn HEBERT
19 Chief of Campus Police ... Mr. Jerrold LONOWSKI
38 Director of Cadet Counseling Center ... Maj. Chance MACE
29 Director Alumni Association ... LtCol. Danny ARMIJO
04 Executive Secretary to President ... Ms. Bernadette BEATTY
09 Director of Institutional Research ... Ms. Michele BATES
102 Dir Foundation/Corporate Relations ... Mr. Jimmy BARNES
13 Chief Info Technology Officer ... Mr. Duane ELMS
07 Director of Admissions ... LtCol. Kalith SMITH

New Mexico State University Main Campus (B)

Box 30001, Las Cruces NM 88003-8001
County: Dona Ana FICE Identification: 002657
Unit ID: 188030
Telephone: (575) 646-2035 Carnegie Class: DU-Higher
FAX Number: (575) 646-6334 Calendar System: Semester
URL: www.nmsu.edu
Established: 1888 Annual Undergrad Tuition & Fees (In-State): $6,094
Enrollment: 15,490 Coed
Affiliation or Control: State IRS Status: 501(c)3
Highest Offering: Doctorate
Accreditation: NH, CAATE, CACREP, CAEPN, COPSY, CS, DIETD, DIETI, ENG, ENGT, IPSY, MUS, NURSE, PH, SP, SPAA, SW

01 President ... Dr. Garrey E. CARRUTHERS
05 Provost & Exec VP ... Dr. Dan HOWARD
10 Sr VP Administration/Finance ... Dr. Andrew BURKE
111 VP Univ Advance/Pres NMSU Found ... Ms. Andrea S. TAWNEY
32 VP Student Affairs/Enroll Mgmt ... Dr. Bernadette MONTOYA
85 Assoc Provost Intl & Border Program ... Dr. Cornell MENKING
26 Interim Assoc VP Marketing & Comm ... Mr. Justin BANNISTER
21 Assoc VP Admin & Finance ... Ms. D'Anne STUART
15 Assoc VP Human Resources Svcs ... Dr. Andrew M. PENA
20 Assoc VP/Deputy Provost ... Dr. Greg FANT
09 Asst VP Institutional Analysis ... Ms. Judy BOSLAND
86 Asst VP Government Relations ... Mr. Ricardo REL
49 Dean College of Arts & Sciences ... Dr. Enrico PONTELLI
50 Dean Business College ... Dr. James HOFFMAN
53 Dean College of Education ... Dr. Don POPE-DAVIS
54 Dean College of Engineering ... Dr. Lakshmi REDDI
58 Dean Graduate School ... Dr. Loui REYES
76 Dean Col Health & Social Svcs ... Dr. Donna WAGNER
35 Dean of Students ... Dr. Michael D. JASEK
13 Chief Information Officer ... Ms. Norma GRIJALVA
06 Interim University Registrar ... Ms. Dacia SEDILLO
43 General Counsel ... Ms. Liz ELLIS
08 Dean University Library ... Dr. Elizabeth TITUS
29 AVP Alumni Engagement/Participation ... Ms. Leslie CERVANTES
21 University Controller ... Ms. Norma NOEL
39 Director Student Housing ... Mr. Matt CROUSE
23 Director Student Health Center ... Ms. Lori MCKEE
38 Director Counseling Center ... Dr. Karen D. SCHAEFER
41 Director Athletics ... Mr. Mario MOCCIA
35 Director Student Affairs ... Dr. Anthony S. MARIN
96 Dir Procurement Services ... Ms. Kathy AGNEW
22 Dir Institutional Equity/EEO ... Ms. Lauri MILLOT
07 Director Admissions ... Ms. Delia DELEON
18 Assoc VP Facilities Services ... Mr. Glen HAUBOLD
27 Dir of Marketing/Creative Svcs ... Ms. Ellen J. CASTELLO
47 Dean College of Agric ... Dr. Rolando FLORES
92 Dean Honors College ... Dr. Miriam CHAIKEN
12 President NMSU-DACC ... Dr. Renay SCOTT
12 President NMSU Alamogordo ... Dr. Ken VAN WINKLE
12 President NMSU-Carlsbad ... Dr. John GRATTON
12 President NMSU-Grants ... Dr. Mickey BEST
100 Acting Chief of Staff ... Ms. Lydia DURAN
37 Director Student Financial Aid ... Dr. Vandeen MCKENZIE

New Mexico State University at Alamogordo (C)

2400 N Scenic Drive, Alamogordo NM 88310-4239
County: Otero FICE Identification: 002658
Unit ID: 187994
Telephone: (575) 439-3600 Carnegie Class: Assoc/HT-High Non
FAX Number: (575) 439-3643 Calendar System: Semester
URL: www.nmsua.edu
Established: 1958 Annual Undergrad Tuition & Fees (In-State): $1,968
Enrollment: 1,848 Coed
Affiliation or Control: State IRS Status: 501(c)3
Highest Offering: Associate Degree
Accreditation: NH

01 President ... Dr. Ken VAN WINKLE
05 Vice President for Academic Affairs ... Dr. Mark CAL
32 Vice President for Student Services ... Mrs. Kathy FULLER
10 Vice President for Business/Finance ... Mr. Antonio SALINAS
56 Assoc Vice Pres Extended Programs ... Mrs. Donna L. COOK
26 Marketing Representative ... Ms. Catherine PACELLI
13 Chief Info Technology Officer (CIO) ... Mr. David SANDERS
08 Librarian ... Dr. Sharon JENKINS
07 Director of Admissions/Registrar ... Mrs. Kathy FULLER
37 Financial Aid Representative ... Mr. Paul ARAGON
09 Director of Institutional Research ... Mr. Greg HILLIS
15 Director Human Resources ... Mrs. Brenda W. GARCIA
18 Director Facilities/Physical Plant ... Ms. Nancy WILKSON
96 Buyer Sr ... Mr. Lee M. KINNEY
04 Administrative Asst to President ... Ms. Mary FECHNER
106 Dir Online Education/E-learning ... Mrs. Sherrell WHEELER

New Mexico State University at Carlsbad (D)

1500 University Drive, Carlsbad NM 88220-3598
County: Eddy FICE Identification: 002659
Unit ID: 188003
Telephone: (575) 234-9200 Carnegie Class: Assoc/HT-High Non
FAX Number: (575) 885-4951 Calendar System: Semester
URL: www.carlsbad.nmsu.edu
Established: 1950 Annual Undergrad Tuition & Fees (In-State): $1,108
Enrollment: 1,931 Coed
Affiliation or Control: State IRS Status: 501(c)3
Highest Offering: Associate Degree
Accreditation: NH, ADNUR

01 Campus President ... Dr. John GRATTON
05 Chief Academic Officer/Provost ... Dr. Andrew I. NWANNE
32 Vice Pres Student Services ... Vacant
10 VP Business & Finance ... Ms. Karla VOLPI
37 Director Financial Aid ... Ms. Diana CAMPOS
15 Human Resources Specialist ... Ms. Judith COX TINDOL
26 Director Marketing & Publications ... Vacant
09 Director of Institutional Research ... Mr. William FINLEY
04 Administrative Asst to President ... Ms. Janice CARNATHAN
18 Chief Facilities/Physical Plant ... Mr. Jeff NEAL

New Mexico State University Dona Ana Community College (E)

Box 30001, MSC 3DA, Las Cruces NM 88003-8001
County: Dona Ana Identification: 666649
Unit ID: 187620
Telephone: (575) 527-7500 Carnegie Class: Assoc/HT-Mix Trad/Non
FAX Number: (575) 527-7515 Calendar System: Semester
URL: dacc.nmsu.edu
Established: 1973 Annual Undergrad Tuition & Fees (In-State): $1,632
Enrollment: 8,252 Coed
Affiliation or Control: State IRS Status: 501(c)3
Highest Offering: Associate Degree
Accreditation: NH, ACBSP, ADNUR, COARC, DA, DH, DMS, EMT, IFSAC, RAD

01 President/CEO ... Dr. Renay M. SCOTT
05 VP for Academic Affairs ... Dr. Monica TORRES
10 VP for Business & Finance ... Ms. Kelly BROOKS
32 VP for Student Services ... Mr. Amadeo LEDESMA
26 Vice Pres External Relations ... Mr. Arthur BINDER
20 Assoc VP for Academic Affairs ... Dr. Susan WOODS
49 Int Div Dean Arts/Hum/Social Sci ... Mr. David BURLESON
50 Division Dean Business/Public Svcs ... Ms. Lydia BAGWELL
97 Division Dean General Studies ... Dr. Bernard PINA
76 Div Dean Health/Public Services ... Mr. Douglas SCRIBNER
72 Division Dean Technical Studies ... Ms. Saundra CASTILLO
103 Exec Director Workforce Dev/Trng ... Mr. Fred OWENSKY
62 Director Library Services ... Ms. Tammy POWERS
36 Dir Career Development/Placement ... Vacant
09 Director Institutional Analysis ... Ms. Mary Beth WORLEY
27 Director of Marketing/Publications ... Mr. John PAULMAN
31 Director Community Education ... Ms. Mary ULRICH
21 Manager Business Office ... Ms. Diane PIERCE
15 Human Resources Operation Manager ... Mr. Mack ADAMS
90 Director Computer Support ... Ms. Lori ALLEN
18 Manager Facilities Services ... Ms. Kathleen REDDINGTON
07 Director Admissions ... Ms. Geraldine MARTINEZ
37 Director Financial Aid ... Ms. Michelle LUKESH
22 Director Disabled Student Services ... Mr. Jesse HAAS

New Mexico State University Dona Ana Community College East Mesa Campus (F)

2800 N Sonoma Ranch Boulevard, Las Cruses NM 88011
Telephone: (575) 528-7250 Identification: 770346
Accreditation: &NH

New Mexico State University Grants (G)

1500 Third Street, Grants NM 87020-2025
Telephone: (505) 287-6678 FICE Identification: 008854
Accreditation: &NH

† Regional accreditation is carried under the parent institution in Las Cruces, NM.

Northern New Mexico College (H)

921 N Paseo de Onate, Espanola NM 87532-2649
County: Rio Arriba FICE Identification: 020839
Unit ID: 188058
Telephone: (505) 747-2100 Carnegie Class: Bac/Assoc-Mixed
FAX Number: (505) 747-2170 Calendar System: Semester
URL: www.nnmc.edu
Established: 1909 Annual Undergrad Tuition & Fees (In-State): $4,560
Enrollment: 923 Coed
Affiliation or Control: State IRS Status: 501(c)3
Highest Offering: Baccalaureate
Accreditation: NH, ACBSP, ADNUR, CAEPN, ENGT, NURSE

01 President ... Dr. Richard J. BAILEY, JR.
10 Interim VP for Finance & Admin ... Mr. Ricky BEJARANO
05 Provost/VP Academic Affairs ... Dr. Ivan LOPEZ
32 Interim Dean of Students ... Mr. Frank ORONA
06 Interim Registrar ... Mr. Gerald WHEELER
08 Head Librarian ... Ms. Amy ORTIZ
84 Director of Recruitment ... Mr. Frank ORONA
37 Director of Financial Aid ... Mr. Jacob PACHECO
13 Director of IT ... Mr. Jimi MONTOYA
15 Director of Human Resources ... Ms. Donna CASTRO
18 Director of Facilities ... Mr. Andy ROMERO
09 Director of Institutional Research ... Ms. Carmella SANCHEZ
21 Director of Business Operations ... Vacant
121 Dir Inst Advise/Coord Stdnt Advise ... Mr. Tobe BOTT-LYONS
41 Athletic Director/Coach ... Mr. Ryan CORDOVA
51 Coordinator Continuing Education ... Ms. Cecilia ROMERO
53 Dean College of Teacher Education ... Dr. Joaquin VILA
49 Dean College of Arts and Sciences ... Mr. David F. GARCIA
76 Dean of College of Health Sciences ... Ms. Ellen TRABKA
04 Executive Asst to the Pres/Bd Sec ... Ms. Amy PENA
07 Director of Admissions ... Mr. Frank ORONA
102 Dir Foundation/Corporate Relations ... Mr. Terry MULERT
28 Director of Equity & Diversity ... Dr. Patricia TRUJILLO
50 Dean Business Administration ... Dr. Lori BACA
54 Dean Engineering & Technology ... Dr. Jorge CHRICHIGNO

Pima Medical Institute-Albuquerque (I)

4400 Cutler Avenue NE, Albuquerque NM 87110-3935
Telephone: (505) 881-1234 FICE Identification: 036783
Accreditation: ABHES, COARC, DH, PTAA, RAD

† Branch campus of Pima Medical Institute-Tucson, Tucson, AZ

Ruidoso Branch Community College (J)

709 Mechem Drive, Ruidoso NM 88345
Telephone: (575) 257-2120 Identification: 770345
Accreditation: &NH

St. John's College (K)

1160 Camino de la Cruz Blanca,
Santa Fe NM 87505-4599
County: Santa Fe FICE Identification: 002093
Unit ID: 245652
Telephone: (505) 984-6000 Carnegie Class: Bac-A&S

FAX Number: (505) 984-6003 Calendar System: Semester
URL: www.sjc.edu
Established: 1964 Annual Undergrad Tuition & Fees: $50,878
Enrollment: 390 Coed
Affiliation or Control: Independent Non-Profit IRS Status: 501(c)3
Highest Offering: Master's
Accreditation: NH

01 President ... Mr. Mark ROOSEVELT
05 Dean ... Mr. Matt DAVIS
30 Vice Pres for Dev/Alumni Affairs ... Ms. Phelosha COLLAROS
10 Treasurer/Financer Officer ... Mr. Michael DURAN
06 Registrar ... Mrs. Marline MARQUEZ-SCALLY
08 Library Director ... Ms. Jennifer SPRAGUE
07 Director of Admissions ... Mr. Yvette SHAFFER
58 Director of Graduate Institute ... Mr. David MCDONALD
09 Director of Institutional Research ... Vacant
15 Director of Human Resources ... Mr. Aaron YOUNG
18 Chief Facilities/Physical Plant ... Mr. Pat HOLMAN
26 Dir of Communications/External Rels ... Mr. Gabe GOMEZ
29 Assoc Dir of Alumni Relations ... Ms. Chris AAMOT
36 Director Career Services ... Ms. Margaret ODELL
37 Director Student Financial Aid ... Mr. Mike RODRIQUEZ

† Affiliated with St. John's College, Maryland.

San Juan College (A)

4601 College Boulevard, Farmington NM 87402-4699
County: San Juan FICE Identification: 002660
Unit ID: 188100
Telephone: (505) 326-3311 Carnegie Class: Assoc/MT-VT-Mix Trad/Non
FAX Number: (505) 566-3385 Calendar System: Semester
URL: www.sanjuancollege.edu
Established: 1956 Annual Undergrad Tuition & Fees (In-District): $1,474
Enrollment: 7,254 Coed
Affiliation or Control: Local IRS Status: 501(c)3
Highest Offering: Associate Degree
Accreditation: NH, ADNUR, CAHIIM, COARC, DH, EMT, MLTAD, OTA, PTAA, SURGT

01 President ... Dr. Toni PENDERGRASS
05 Vice Pres for Learning ... Dr. Barbara AKE
10 Vice Pres Administrative Services ... Mr. Edward DESPLAS
32 Vice Pres for Student Services ... Mr. David EPPICH
04 Executive Asst to President ... Ms. Jeanne NOTSON
20 Assoc VP Learning/Strategic Init ... Ms. Adrienne FORGETTE
102 Executive Director Foundation ... Ms. Gayle DEAN
21 Controller ... Mr. Kristie ELLIS
26 Director Marketing/Public Relations ... Ms. Rhonda SCHAEFER
121 Sr Dir Student Success Ctr ... Mr. John BOGGS
84 Sr Dir Enrollment Management ... Mr. Jon BETZ
50 Dean Sch Business & Workforce Dev ... Dr. Brad PURDY
79 Dean School of Humanities ... Mr. Allan NASS
76 Dean Sch of Health Sciences ... Dr. Virgil CALDWELL
65 Dean School of Energy ... Ms. Barbara WICKMAN
72 Dean School Trades & Technology ... Mr. Bill LEWIS
81 Dean Math/Science & Engineering ... Dr. Michael OTTINGER
22 Director Affirmative Action/EEO ... Ms. Stacey ALLEN
88 Director Native American Programs ... Mr. Byron TSABETSAYE
08 Director Library Services ... Mr. Chris SCHIPPER
37 Sr Director of Financial Aid ... Ms. Mindi-Kim SCHRUM
18 Director Physical Plant ... Mr. Chris HARRELSON
19 Director Security/Safety ... Mr. Kelly ANDERSON
35 Director Student Activities ... Ms. Marcia STERLING
96 Director Purchasing ... Mr. Frank COLE
38 Director Student Advising Center ... Ms. Christy FERRATO
74 Director Vet-Tech Program ... Dr. David WRIGHT
06 Registrar ... Ms. Sherri GAUGH
09 Dir of Institutional Research ... Mr. Ron JERNIGAN
15 AVP Human Resources and Legal Act ... Ms. Kerri LANGONI
13 Chief Info Technology Officer (CIO) ... Ms. Shelley AMATOR

Santa Fe Community College (B)

6401 Richards Avenue, Santa Fe NM 87508-4887
County: Santa Fe FICE Identification: 022781
Unit ID: 188137
Telephone: (505) 428-1000 Carnegie Class: Assoc/MT-VT-High Non
FAX Number: (505) 428-1296 Calendar System: Semester
URL: www.sfcc.edu
Established: 1983 Annual Undergrad Tuition & Fees (In-State): $1,695
Enrollment: 4,880 Coed
Affiliation or Control: State IRS Status: 501(c)3
Highest Offering: Associate Degree
Accreditation: NH, ADNUR, COARC, DA, MAC, RAD

01 President ... Mr. Randy W. GRISSOM
05 Vice Pres Academic Affairs ... Ms. Margaret PETERS
10 Vice Pres Finance ... Mr. Nick TELLES
09 VP Planning & Inst Effectiveness ... Mr. Yash MORIMOTO
84 Assoc VP Enrollment & Student Svcs ... Dr. Cheryl FIELDS
51 Director Cont Educ/Workforce Dev ... Ms. Kris SWEDIN
26 Exec Dir Marketing/Public Rels ... Mr. Todd LOVATO
102 Exec Dir SFCC Foundation ... Ms. Deborah BOLDT
06 Registrar ... Ms. Barbara TUCCI
13 Interim Chief Information Officer ... Mr. Jeremy LOVATO
37 Financial Aid Director ... Mr. Scott WHITAKER
66 Int Director of Nursing ... Ms. Terri TEWART
08 Library Director ... Ms. Peg JOHNSON
15 Exec Director of Human Resources ... Mr. Daniel GUTIERREZ
88 Director Small Business Development ... Mr. Brian DUBOFF
18 Director Plant & Operations Mgmt ... Mr. Henry MIGNARDOT
12 Executive Director HEC ... Ms. Rebecca ESTRADA
49 Dean School of Liberal Arts ... Dr. Bernadette JACOBS
54 Dean Sch Health/Engineering & Math ... Dr. Jenny LANDEN
76 Dean School of Fitness Education ... Dr. Jenny LANDEN
57 Dean Sch Arts/Design & Media Arts ... Dr. Bernadette JACOBS
75 Dean Trds/Tech/Sustn & Prof Stds ... Dr. Camilla BUSTAMANTE
50 Dean School of Business & Educ ... Dr. Camilla BUSTAMANTE
101 Executive Asst to the President ... Ms. Rosemarie M. GARCIA
96 Director of Purchasing ... Vacant
25 Chief Contracts/Grants Admin ... Ms. Ann BLACK

Santa Fe University of Art and Design (C)

1600 St. Michael's Drive, Santa Fe NM 87505-7634
County: Santa Fe FICE Identification: 002649
Unit ID: 188146
Telephone: (505) 473-6011 Carnegie Class: Spec-4-yr-Arts
FAX Number: (505) 473-6127 Calendar System: Semester
URL: www.santafeuniversity.edu
Established: 1947 Annual Undergrad Tuition & Fees: $32,346
Enrollment: 919 Coed
Affiliation or Control: Proprietary IRS Status: Proprietary
Highest Offering: Master's
Accreditation: NH

01 Interim President ... Dr. Maria PUZZIFERRO
03 Provost ... Ms. Debra TERVALA
32 Exec Dir Student Affairs/Operations ... Ms. Christine GUEVARA
35 Asst Dir Student Affs/Operations ... Mr. Jeremy HADLEY
84 VP Marketing & Enrollment ... Ms. Betty CESARANO
10 Finance Director ... Mr. Steven POSEY
18 Dir Facilities & Security ... Mr. Peter ROMERO
13 Dir Information Technology ... Mr. Jeff PEARCE
37 Int Director of Financial Aid ... Ms. Anita KEIM
36 Director of Career Services ... Ms. Deanne BROWN
06 Registrar ... Ms. Mary ANGELL
26 Manager External & Public Relations ... Ms. Rachael LIGHTLY
15 Manager of Human Resources ... Ms. Yolanda SMITH MORA

† In teach-out mode.

Southwest Acupuncture College (D)

1622 Galisteo Street, Santa Fe NM 87505-6351
County: Santa Fe FICE Identification: 026220
Unit ID: 366605
Telephone: (505) 438-8884 Carnegie Class: Spec-4-yr-Other Health
FAX Number: (505) 438-8883 Calendar System: Semester
URL: www.acupuncturecollege.edu
Established: 1980 Annual Undergrad Tuition & Fees: N/A
Enrollment: 72 Coed
Affiliation or Control: Proprietary IRS Status: Proprietary
Highest Offering: Master's; No Lower Division
Accreditation: ACUP

01 CEO ... Dr. Anthony ABBATE
03 Executive Director ... Dr. Skya ABBATE
10 Chief Fiscal Officer ... Mr. Jim KUTSKO
12 Campus Director Santa Fe ... Dr. Paul ROSSIGNOL
17 Clinical Director Santa Fe ... Dr. Melanie RICHARDSON
05 Academic Dean Santa Fe ... Ms. Susan CHANEY
37 Director of Financial Aid ... Ms. Angela ANAYA
07 Director of Admissions ... Ms. Sophia BUNGAY

Southwest University of Visual Arts (E)

5000 Marble Avenue, NE, Albuquerque NM 87110-6344
Telephone: (505) 254-7575 Identification: 666524
Accreditation: &NH, CIDA

† Regional accreditation is carried under the parent institution in Tucson, AZ.

Southwestern College (F)

3960 San Filipe Road, Santa Fe NM 87507
County: Santa Fe FICE Identification: 030761
Unit ID: 188207
Telephone: (505) 471-5756 Carnegie Class: Masters/S
FAX Number: (505) 471-4071 Calendar System: Quarter
URL: www.swc.edu
Established: 1979 Annual Graduate Tuition & Fees: N/A
Enrollment: 168 Coed
Affiliation or Control: Independent Non-Profit IRS Status: 501(c)3
Highest Offering: Master's; No Undergraduates
Accreditation: NH

01 President ... Dr. Jim NOLAN
03 Exec VP/Dir New Earth Institute SWC ... Ms. Katherine NINOS
05 Vice Pres Academic Affairs/Dean ... Dr. Ann FILEMYR
84 Director of Enrollment Svcs ... Ms. Dru PHOENIX
06 Registrar ... Ms. Andrea PACHECO
10 Chief Finance Officer ... Ms. Allison FRANK
13 Chief Technology Officer ... Ms. Donna HARRINGTON

Southwestern Indian Polytechnic Institute (G)

9169 Coors Boulevard, NW, Albuquerque NM 87120
County: Bernalillo FICE Identification: 025110
Unit ID: 188216
Telephone: (505) 346-2348 Carnegie Class: Tribal
FAX Number: (505) 346-2343 Calendar System: Trimester
URL: www.sipi.edu
Established: 1971 Annual Undergrad Tuition & Fees: $1,095
Enrollment: 402 Coed
Affiliation or Control: Federal IRS Status: 501(c)3
Highest Offering: Associate Degree
Accreditation: NH, OPD, OPLT

01 President ... Dr. Sherry ALLISON
10 Vice Pres College Operations ... Mr. Eric CHRISTENSEN
05 Vice President Academic Programs ... Ms. Valerie MONTOYA
09 Dir Institutional Rsch/Effect/Plng ... Mr. Edward HUMMINGBIRD
32 Director of Student Services ... Mr. Allen (Ray) GACHUPIN
07 Director Admissions/Registrar ... Mr. Joseph CARPIO
15 Human Resources Specialist ... Ms. Dawn AMI
18 Facilities Director ... Ms. Renee ALLEN
37 Director Student Financial Aid ... Mr. Joseph CARPIO

University of New Mexico Main Campus (H)

1 University of New Mexico, Albuquerque NM 87131-0001
County: Bernalillo FICE Identification: 002663
Unit ID: 187985
Telephone: (505) 277-0111 Carnegie Class: DU-Highest
FAX Number: (505) 277-6019 Calendar System: Semester
URL: www.unm.edu
Established: 1889 Annual Undergrad Tuition & Fees (In-State): $7,340
Enrollment: 27,285 Coed
Affiliation or Control: State IRS Status: 501(c)3
Highest Offering: Doctorate
Accreditation: NH, ARCPA, CAATE, CACREP, CAEPN, CLPSY, CONST, CS, DANCE, DENT, DH, DIETD, DIETI, EMT, ENG, IPSY, JOUR, LAW, LSAR, MED, MIDWF, MT, MUS, NMT, NURSE, OT, PH, PHAR, PLNG, PTA, SP, SPAA, THEA

01 Acting President ... Dr. Chaouki T. ABDALLAH
05 Acting Provost ... Dr. Craig WHITE
17 Chancellor of Health Sciences Ctr ... Dr. Paul B. ROTH
10 Exec Vice Pres Administration ... Dr. David W. HARRIS
100 Chief of Staff ... Dr. Amy WOHLERT
12 Special Asst for Branch Affairs ... Dr. Wynn M. GOERING
20 Int Sr Vice Prov for Acad Affairs ... Dr. Richard WOOD
46 Vice President Research ... Dr. Gabriel J. LOPEZ
25 AVP Research Administration ... Patricia HENNING
32 Vice President Student Affairs ... Dr. Eliseo S. TORRES
28 Vice Chancellor HSC Diversity ... Dr. Valerie ROMERO-LEGGOTT
84 Vice Provost of Enrl and Analytics ... Dr. Terry BABBITT
15 Vice President Human Resources ... Dorothy ANDERSON
21 University Controller ... Elizabeth METZGER
13 Interim Chief Information Officer ... Duane ARRUTTI
14 Int Deputy Chief Information Ofcr ... Brian PIETREWICZ
43 University Counsel ... Elsa KIRCHER COLE
29 AVP Alumni Relations ... Dana ALLEN
20 AVP Academic Administration ... Curtis R. PORTER
35 AVP Student Life ... Dr. Walter C. MILLER
35 AVP Student Services ... Dr. Tim GUTIERREZ
50 Int Dean Anderson School of Mgmt ... Shawn BERMAN
48 Dean Sch of Architecture & Planning ... Dr. Geraldine FORBES ISAIS
49 Dean College of Arts & Sciences ... Dr. Mark PECENY
53 Dean College of Education ... Dr. Hector OCHOA
54 Interim Dean School of Engineering ... Dr. Joseph CECCHI
57 Dean College of Fine Arts ... Dr. Kymberly PINDER
61 Dean School of Law ... Alfred MATHEWSON
63 Exec Vice Dean School of Medicine ... Dr. Martha MCGREW
66 Dean College of Nursing ... Dr. Nancy A. RIDENOUR
67 Dean College of Pharmacy ... Dr. Lynda S. WELAGE
80 Interim Dir School of Public Admin ... Dr. Philip GONZALES
92 Dean University College ... Dr. Kate KRAUSE
58 Dean Office of Graduate Studies ... Dr. Julie COONROD
51 Assoc Dean Continuing Education ... Joseph MIERA
08 Dean University Libraries ... Dr. Richard CLEMENT
26 Chief Univ Marketing & Comm Officer ... Cinnamon BLAIR
27 HSC Exec Dir Comm & Marketing ... William O. SPARKS
27 Director University Communications ... Dianne ANDERSON
105 Mgr University Web Communications ... Matt CARTER
86 Interim Director Government Affairs ... Connie BEIMER
09 Director Institutional Analytics ... Dr. Heather S. MECHLER
88 University Architect ... Amy COBURN
18 Director Physical Plant ... Jeff ZUMWALT
19 Chief of Police ... Kevin MCCABE
96 Chief Procurement Officer ... Bruce E. CHERRIN
23 Director Student Health Center ... Dr. Beverly KLOEPPEL
22 Director Equal Opportunity ... Francie CORDOVA
24 Dir New Media & Extended Learning ... Debby KNOTTS
35 Dean of Students ... Nasha TORREZ
07 Director Admissions and Recruitment ... Matt HULETT
06 Registrar ... Alex GONZALEZ
37 Director Student Financial Aid ... Brian MALONE
36 Director Career Services ... Dr. Jenna S. CRABB
39 Director Student Housing & Res Life ... Wayne SULLIVAN
40 Director Bookstore ... Carrie MITCHELL
108 Director of Assessment ... Vacant
102 UNM Foundation President and CEO ... Henry NEMCIK
30 VP University Development ... Larry RYAN
30 VP Development Health Sciences Ctr ... Bill UHER
88 CEO UNM Hospital ... Steve MCKERNAN
04 Administrative Asst to President ... Mitch GARRITY
101 Secretary of the Institution/Board ... Mallory REVIERE

University of New Mexico-Gallup (A)

705 Gurley Avenue, Gallup NM 87301
Telephone: (505) 863-7500 FICE Identification: 006881
Accreditation: &NH, ADNUR, CAHIIM, DA, MLTAD

† Regional accreditation is carried under the parent institution in Albuquerque, NM.

University of New Mexico-Los Alamos (B)

4000 University Drive, Los Alamos NM 87544-2233
Telephone: (505) 662-5919 Identification: 666742
Accreditation: &NH

† Regional accreditation is carried under the parent institution in Albuquerque, NM.

University of New Mexico-Taos (C)

1157 Country Road 110, Ranchos de Taos NM 87557
Telephone: (575) 737-6200 Identification: 666743
Accreditation: &NH, ADNUR

† Regional accreditation is carried under the parent institution in Albuquerque, NM.

University of New Mexico-Valencia (D)

280 La Entrada Road, Los Lunas NM 87031-7633
Telephone: (505) 925-8500 Identification: 666741
Accreditation: &NH, ADNUR

† Regional accreditation is carried under the parent institution in Albuquerque, NM.

University of Phoenix New Mexico Campus (E)

5700 Pasadena Avenue, NE,
Albuquerque NM 87113-1570
Telephone: (505) 821-4800 Identification: 770219
Accreditation: &NH, ACBSP

† No longer accepting campus-based students.

University of St. Francis (F)

1500 N. Renaissance Blvd, NE, Ste C,
Albuquerque NM 87107
Telephone: (505) 266-5565 Identification: 770099
Accreditation: &NH, ARCPA

† Branch campus of University of St. Francis, Joliet, IL

University of the Southwest (G)

6610 Lovington Highway, Hobbs NM 88240-9129
County: Lea FICE Identification: 002650
Unit ID: 188182
Telephone: (575) 392-6561 Carnegie Class: Masters/M
FAX Number: (575) 392-6006 Calendar System: Semester
URL: www.usw.edu
Established: 1962 Annual Undergrad Tuition & Fees: $15,456
Enrollment: 1,059 Coed
Affiliation or Control: Independent Non-Profit IRS Status: 501(c)3
Highest Offering: Master's
Accreditation: NH

01	President	Dr. Quint THURMAN
05	Provost	Dr. Larry GUERRERO
10	VP for Financial Services/CFO	Mr. Ronald MCBEE
37	Vice President of Student Finance	Mrs. Dawny KRINGEL
111	VP for Institutional Advancement	Mr. William J. WEIDNER
18	Campus Steward	Dr. David ARNOLD
15	Asst VP HR & Regulatory Compliance	Mrs. Veronica TORREZ
49	Dean School of Arts & Sciences	Dr. Elyn PALMER
50	Dean School of Business	Dr. Ryan TIPTON
53	Dean School of Education	Dr. Scarlet CLOUSE
08	Dean Library Services	Mr. John MCCANCE
84	Director Enrollment Management	Dr. Larry GUERRERO
41	Dir of Intercollegiate Athletics	Mr. William J. WEIDNER
06	University Registrar	Ms. Mary Ann BRADSHAW
38	University Counselor	Mr. Brian ARNOLD
42	Campus Pastor	Dr. Danny KIRKPATRICK
07	Director of Admissions	Ms. Lissete TERRAZAS
32	Director of Student Life	Vacant
39	Director Student Housing	Ms. Jessica BECKER
105	Director Web Services	Mr. Josh FORD
30	Development & External Relations	Ms. Kathryn EADES
04	Administrative Asst to President	Mrs. Linda WOODFIN
88	Maintenance Supervisor	Mr. Lonnie HARRISON

Western New Mexico University (H)

PO Box 680, Silver City NM 88062-0680
County: Grant FICE Identification: 002664
Unit ID: 188304
Telephone: (505) 538-6011 Carnegie Class: Masters/M
FAX Number: (505) 538-6364 Calendar System: Semester
URL: www.wnmu.edu
Established: 1893 Annual Undergrad Tuition & Fees (In-State): $5,906
Enrollment: 3,354 Coed
Affiliation or Control: State IRS Status: 501(c)3
Highest Offering: Beyond Master's But Less Than Doctorate
Accreditation: NH, ACBSP, ADNUR, CAEPN, NURSE, #OTA, SW

01	President	Dr. Joseph SHEPARD
05	Provost/Vice Pres Academic Affairs	Dr. Jack CROCKER
32	VP Student Affairs/Enrollment Mgmt	Dr. Isaac BRUNDAGE
10	Interim VP Business Affairs	Ms. Kelley RIDDLE
30	VP External Affairs	Dr. Magdaleno MANZANARES
20	Assoc Vice Pres Academic Affairs	Dr. Linda HOY
06	Registrar	Ms. Betsy MILLER
08	University Librarian	Ms. Gilda BAEZA-ORTEGO
37	Director Student Financial Aid	Ms. Cheryl HAIN
07	Int Director Admiss & Recruitment	Mr. Matthew LARA
09	Director of Institutional Research	Vacant
15	Director of Human Resources	Ms. Maura GONSIOR
18	Asst VP of Facilities	Mr. Ron JAMES
26	Chief Public Relations Officer	Mr. Abe VILLARREAL
29	Director of Alumni Affairs	Ms. Amanda MOFFETT LANE
36	Coord of Career/Student Svcs	Ms. Vanessa STROMAN
35	Director of Student Life	Ms. Jessica MORALES
96	Director Materials/Resources	Ms. Amy BACA
100	Chief of Staff	Ms. Julie MORALES
19	Director Campus Police	Mr. Eddie FLORES
41	Athletic Director	Mr. Mark COLEMAN
49	Dean of College of Arts and Science	Vacant
53	Interim Dean of Education	Dr. Barbara TAYLOR

NEW YORK

Adelphi University (I)

1 South Avenue, PO Box 701,
Garden City NY 11530-0701
County: Nassau FICE Identification: 002666
Unit ID: 188429
Telephone: (516) 877-3000 Carnegie Class: DU-Mod
FAX Number: (516) 877-3545 Calendar System: Semester
URL: www.adelphi.edu
Established: 1896 Annual Undergrad Tuition & Fees: $35,740
Enrollment: 7,256 Coed
Affiliation or Control: Independent Non-Profit IRS Status: 501(c)3
Highest Offering: Doctorate
Accreditation: M, CAEPN, CLPSY, IPSY, NURSE, SP, SW

01	President	Dr. Christine M. RIORDAN
05	Interim Provost/Exec VP	Dr. Sam L. GROGG
10	Executive VP of Finance & Admin	Mr. Timothy P. BURTON
28	VP of Diversity and Inclusion	Dr. Perry GREENE
30	VP of University Advancement	Mr. Brady CROOK
26	Assoc VP Branding & Communications	Ms. Joanna TEMPLETON
20	Deputy Provost	Dr. Audrey S. BLUMBERG
20	Sr Assoc Provost UG Programs	Dr. Lester B. BALTIMORE
20	Assoc Provost Fac Adv & Research	Dr. Chris K. STORM, JR.
07	Assoc VP of Admissions	Ms. Kristen CAPEZZA
32	Assoc VP of Student Affairs	Ms. Esther GOODCUFF
21	Assoc VP for Finance & Co-Treasurer	Mr. Robert L. DECARLO
15	Assoc VP Human Resource/Labor Rel	Ms. Lisa ARAUJO
19	Assoc VP for Public Safety	Mr. Eugene PALMA
09	Assistant Provost for IR	Dr. Nava LERER
18	Asst VP of Facilities	Mr. Robert J. SHIPLEY
37	Asst VP Student Financial Aid	Ms. Sheryl L. MIHOPULOS
49	Acting Dean of Arts & Sciences	Dr. Susan BRIZIARELLI
53	Dean RS Ammon School of Education	Dr. Jane ASHDOWN
66	Actg Dean Nursing & Public Health	Dr. Elaine L. SMITH
70	Dean School of Social Work	Dr. Andrew SAFYER
83	Dean GF Derner Sch of Psychology	Dr. Jacques BARBER
50	Dean RB Willumstad Sch of Business	Dr. Rajib N. SANYAL
92	Dean Honors College	Dr. Richard GARNER
107	Dean Col of Prof & Cont Studies	Dr. Shawn O'RILEY
08	Dean University Libraries	Mr. Brian LYM
35	Dean Student Affairs/Asst VP	Mr. Jeffrey A. KESSLER
13	Chief Information Officer/CIO	Mr. Jack CHEN
14	Deputy CIO	Ms. Carol Ann BOYLE
16	Director Employee & Labor Relations	Ms. Jane FISHER
41	Director of Athletics	Mr. Daniel MCCABE
36	Exec Dir Career Plng & Placement	Mr. Thomas J. WARD, JR.
06	Registrar	Mr. Steven E. SMITH
104	Director International Education	Ms. Shannon HARRISON
23	Director Health Services	Ms. Jacqueline CARTABUKE
38	Director Counseling & Support Svcs	Dr. Carol A. LUCAS
39	Director Residential Life/Housing	Mr. Guy SENEQUE
29	Exec Director Alumni Relations	Ms. Jodie SPERICO
21	Assoc Treasurer/Budget Director	Mr. Michael J. MCLEOD
21	Director Business Affairs	Mr. Russell A. PALMER
96	Purchasing Manager	Ms. Elizabeth F. KASH
108	Director Institutional Assessment	Dr. Lori HOEFFNER
100	Chief of Staff	Ms. Maggie GRAFER
105	Director Web Services	Ms. Erica KLEIN

Albany College of Pharmacy and Health Sciences (J)

106 New Scotland Avenue, Albany NY 12208-3492
County: Albany FICE Identification: 002885
Unit ID: 188526
Telephone: (518) 694-7200 Carnegie Class: Spec-4-yr-Other Health
FAX Number: (518) 694-7202 Calendar System: Semester
URL: www.acphs.edu
Established: 1881 Annual Undergrad Tuition & Fees: $31,981
Enrollment: 1,482 Coed
Affiliation or Control: Independent Non-Profit IRS Status: 501(c)3
Highest Offering: Doctorate
Accreditation: M, CYTO, MT, PHAR

01	President	Greg DEWEY
05	Provost	Tarun PATEL
46	Vice Provost for Research	Shaker MOUSA
88	Vice Provost Innovative Learning	Jennifer MCVAY-DYCHE
49	Dean School of Arts and Sciences	David CLARKE
67	Dean of the School of Pharmacy	Robert HAMILTON
45	Director of Inst Effectiveness	Vaishali JAHAGIRDAR
58	Dean School of Graduate Studies	Martha HASS
12	Associate Dean for Vermont Campus	Vacant
32	Dean of Students	Wendy NEIFELD WHEELER
10	VP of Finance	Michele VIEN
111	VP of Institutional Advancement	Vicki DILORENZO
84	VP of Enrollment Management	Tiffany GUTIERREZ
13	Chief Technology Officer	Joshua SINGLETARY
11	VP of Administrative Operations	Packy MCGRAW
07	Director of Admissions	Nicholas BALK
06	Registrar	Jeff DUFOUR
08	Director of Library Services	Sue IWANOWICZ
26	Exec Director of Marketing/Comm	Gil CHORBAJIAN
41	Director of Athletics & Rec	Christine KANAWADA
15	Director of Human Resources	Susan KARAVOLAS
110	Interim AVP of Development	Deanna ENNELLO-BUTLER

Albany Law School (K)

80 New Scotland Avenue, Albany NY 12208-3494
County: Albany FICE Identification: 002886
Unit ID: 188535
Telephone: (518) 445-2311 Carnegie Class: Spec-4-yr-Law
FAX Number: (518) 445-2315 Calendar System: Semester
URL: www.albanylaw.edu
Established: 1851 Annual Undergrad Tuition & Fees: N/A
Enrollment: 414 Coed
Affiliation or Control: Independent Non-Profit IRS Status: 501(c)3
Highest Offering: First Professional Degree
Accreditation: LAW

01	President & Dean	Dean Alicia OUELLETTE
05	Assoc Dean Acad Affairs	Dean Connie MAYER
10	Vice President Finance & Business	Mr. Victor E. RAUSCHER
08	Director of Library	Ms. Colleen SMITH
111	Asst Dean Inst Advancement	Ms. Anne Marie JUDGE
32	Associate Dean for Student Affairs	Prof. Rosemary QUEENAN
06	Assistant Dean and Registrar	Ms. Joanne FITZSIMMONS
36	Asst Dean Career Center	Ms. Mary WALSH FITZPATRICK
26	Director Communications	Mr. David SINGER
04	Executive Assistant to the Dean	Ms. Barbara JORDAN-SMITH
07	Assistant Dean of Admissions	Vacant
88	Director Clinical Program	Prof. Sarah ROGERSON
13	Assoc Dir Enterprise Info Systems	Ms. Geraldine ROHLING
29	Interim Director Alumni Affairs	Ms. Jordyn CONWAY
15	Director Human Resources	Ms. Sherri DONNELLY
37	Director Student Financial Aid	Ms. Andrea WEDLER
18	Director of Facilities & Admin Svcs	Mr. Brian LAPLANTE
36	Director of Career Services	Ms. Joanne CASEY
106	Assoc Dir Online Learning	Dr. Patricia BAIA

Albany Medical College (L)

47 New Scotland Avenue, Mail #34,
Albany NY 12208-3479
County: Albany FICE Identification: 002887
Unit ID: 188580
Telephone: (518) 262-6008 Carnegie Class: Spec-4-yr-Med
FAX Number: (518) 262-6515 Calendar System: Other
URL: www.amc.edu
Established: 1839 Annual Graduate Tuition & Fees: N/A
Enrollment: 822 Coed
Affiliation or Control: Independent Non-Profit IRS Status: 501(c)3
Highest Offering: Doctorate; No Undergraduates
Accreditation: M, ANEST, ARCPA, IPSY, MED, PAST

01	Dean/Exec VP Health Affairs	Dr. Vincent P. VERDILE
10	EVP/Chief Financial Officer	Ms. Frances SPREER-ALBERT
05	Vice Dean for Academic Admin	Dr. Henry S. POHL
17	Vice Dean Clinical Affairs	Dr. Ferdinand VENDITTI
32	Assoc Dean for Acad & Student Affs	Dr. Kimberly KILBY
63	Assoc Dean Graduate Medical Educ	Dr. Joel BARTFIELD
22	Assoc Dean Cmty Outreach/Medical Ed	Dr. Ingrid M. ALLARD
08	Asc Dn Info Resrcs/Tech/Dir Library	Ms. Enid GEYER
88	Asst Dean Medical Education	Dr. Rebecca KELLER
58	Assoc Dean for Graduate Studies	Dr. Richard KELLER
06	Registrar	Mr. Len SCHLEGEL
63	Director Graduate Medical Education	Ms. Catherine RIDDLE
76	Director Physician Asst Program	Dr. David IRVINE
07	Asst Dean Admiss & Student Records	Mr. Donald PRITCHETT
29	Executive Director Alumni Relations	Vacant
26	Director Public Relations	Mr. Jeffrey GORDON
30	Chief Development	Ms. Molly NICHOL
51	Director Cont Medical Education	Ms. Jennifer PRICE
15	Director Human Resources	Ms. Cathy HALAKAN
37	Director Student Financial Aid	Ms. Ann LOUGHMAN
96	Director of Purchasing	Ms. Ann CRISLIP
27	Marketing Specialist	Ms. Nicolette VISCUSI
03	Executive Assoc Dean	Mr. John DEPAOLA
09	Director of Institutional Research	Dr. Paul FEUSTEL
85	Director Foreign Students	Ms. Marianne R. WILLIAMS
13	Chief Info Technology Officer (CIO)	Mr. George HICKMAN
18	Chief Facilities Physical Plant	Mr. Donald STICHTER
19	Director Security/Safety	Mr. John HERRITAGE
38	Director Student Counseling	Dr. Jeffrey WINSEMAN

43 Dir Legal Services/General Counsel .... Mr. Lee HESSBERG
45 Chief Institutional Planning .... Ms. Courtney BURKE
88 Director Nurse Anesthesia Pgm ....Dr. Jodi DELLA ROCCA

Alfred University (A)

One Saxon Drive, Alfred NY 14802-1205
County: Allegany FICE Identification: 002668
Unit ID: 188641
Telephone: (607) 871-2111 Carnegie Class: Bac-A&S
FAX Number: (607) 871-2339 Calendar System: Semester
URL: www.alfred.edu
Established: 1836 Annual Undergrad Tuition & Fees: $27,078
Enrollment: 2,286 Coed
Affiliation or Control: Independent Non-Profit IRS Status: 501(c)3
Highest Offering: Doctorate
Accreditation: M, ART, #CAATE, CACREP, CAEPT, ENG, SCPSY

01 President .... Dr. Mark A. ZUPAN
05 Provost/VP for Academic Affairs .... Dr. Rick STEPHENS
10 VP for Business & Finance/Treasurer .... Ms. Giovina LLOYD
30 VP for University Relations .... Mr. Jason AMORE
84 VP for Enrollment Management ....Mr. Brian DALTON
32 VP for Student Affairs .... Mrs. Kathy WOUGHTER
57 Dean School of Art & Design .... Mr. Gerar EDIZEL
49 Dean Col of Lib Arts & Sciences .... Ms. Elizabeth A. DOBIE
107 Dean College of Prof Studies .... Dr. Nancy EVANGELISTA
54 Int Dean School of Engineering .... Dr. Alastair CORMACK
35 Dean of Students .... Mr. Norm POLLARD
29 Asst Dir Alumni Engagement .... Ms. Janet MARBLE
37 Director of Student Financial Aid .... Vacant
07 Director of Admissions .... Vacant
06 Registrar ....Mr. Lawrence J. CASEY
19 Chief of Public Safety ....Mr. John M. DOUGHERTY
26 Director of Communications .... Mrs. Susan GOETSCHIUS
39 Director of Residence Life ....Ms. Vicky GEBEL
13 Director Information Tech Svcs .... Mr. Gary O. ROBERTS
36 Director Career Development Ctr .... Ms. Amanda BAKER
41 Athletic Director .... Mr. Paul VECCHIO
23 Dir Counseling & Wellness Center .... Dr. Del Ray HONEYCUTT
18 Director of Physical Plant ....Mr. Brian R. DODGE
08 Dir Herrick Lib/Dean of Libraries .... Mr. Stephen S. CRANDALL
08 Director of Scholes Library ....Mr. Mark SMITH
15 Director of Human Resources ....Mr. Mark A. GUINAN
21 Controller ....Ms. Jodi L. HOWE
92 Director of the Honors Program .... Dr. Gordan ATLAS
94 Dir of Women's Leadership Center ....Ms. Abby GRIFFITH
43 Dir Capital Operations/Leg Affairs .... Vacant
101 Secretary to the Corporation .... Ms. Mary C. MCALLISTER
104 Dir Intl Programs/Writing Ctr .... Dr. Vicky WESTACOTT
40 Bookstore Manager .... Mrs. Marcy K. BRADLEY
87 Dir of Summer/Parent Programs ....Mrs. Bonnie J. DUNGAN
09 Director of Institutional Research .... Mr. Frederick B. RODGERS
28 Director of Diversity .... Mr. Daniel J. NAPOLITANO

AMDA College and Conservatory of the Performing Arts (B)

211 West 61st Street, New York NY 10023-7832
County: New York FICE Identification: 007572
Unit ID: 188854
Telephone: (212) 787-5300 Carnegie Class: Spec-4-yr-Arts
FAX Number: (212) 247-0488 Calendar System: Semester
URL: www.amda.edu
Established: 1964 Annual Undergrad Tuition & Fees: $35,900
Enrollment: 1,509 Coed
Affiliation or Control: Independent Non-Profit IRS Status: 501(c)3
Highest Offering: Baccalaureate
Accreditation: THEA

01 President/Artistic Director .... Mr. David MARTIN
03 President/Executive Director .... Ms. Jan MARTIN
32 Director of Student Affairs .... Mr. Robert MANGANARO
07 Director of Admissions .... Vacant
37 Assoc Dir Financial Aid/Cont Stdnt ....Ms. Gloria LITTLE

American Academy of Dramatic Arts (C)

120 Madison Avenue, New York NY 10016-7089
County: New York FICE Identification: 007465
Unit ID: 188678
Telephone: (212) 686-9244 Carnegie Class: Spec 2-yr-A&S
FAX Number: (212) 545-7934 Calendar System: Other
URL: www.aada.edu
Established: 1884 Annual Undergrad Tuition & Fees: $33,190
Enrollment: 261 Coed
Affiliation or Control: Independent Non-Profit IRS Status: 501(c)3
Highest Offering: Associate Degree
Accreditation: M, THEA

01 President .... Ms. Susan ZECH
10 Chief Financial Officer .... Mr. Joel BLOCK
05 Director of Instruction .... Mr. Constantine SCOPAS
07 Director of Admissions .... Ms. Kerin REILLY
27 Director of Marketing ....Mr. Lance STICKSEL
37 Director Financial Aid ....Mr. Roberto LOPEZ
08 Librarian .... Ms. Deborah PICONE
21 Controller .... Ms. Linda VIALA
11 Director of Operations .... Mr. Peter TUFEL
26 Director External Affairs ....Mrs. Elizabeth LAWSON
04 Assistant to the President .... Ms. Jackie REINKING

American Academy McAllister Institute of Funeral Service (D)

619 W 54th Street, 2nd Floor, New York NY 10019
County: New York FICE Identification: 010813
Unit ID: 188687
Telephone: (212) 757-1190 Carnegie Class: Spec 2-yr-A&S
FAX Number: (212) 765-5923 Calendar System: Semester
URL: www.funeraleducation.org
Established: 1926 Annual Undergrad Tuition & Fees: $16,568
Enrollment: 493 Coed
Affiliation or Control: Independent Non-Profit IRS Status: 501(c)3
Highest Offering: Associate Degree
Accreditation: FUSER

01 President/CEO ....Ms. Meg DUNN
03 Executive Vice President .... Dr. George CONNICK
10 Bursar .... Mr. Jay TSO
37 Financial Aid Officer .... Ms. Natalie GIVAN
05 Dir Student Svcs/CH General Educ ....Ms. Regina SMITH
69 Div Chair Public Health/Technical .... Dr. Elissa DEBENEDICTS
50 Division Chair Business/Law/Ethics .... Mr. Brian KASLER
06 Registrar ....Mr. Andre RAMPAUL
07 Dir of Admissions/Enrollment Mgmt ....Mr. Alan LOVEDER
08 Librarian .... Ms. Mary MOON
20 Academic Advisor .... Ms. Charlotte RERRICK
20 Academic Advisor .... Ms. Karen CARR
04 Exec Assistant to the President .... Ms. Stephanie HELSTON
43 Legal Counsel .... Mr. Charles MAURER

ASA College (E)

151 Lawrence Street, Brooklyn NY 11201
County: Kings FICE Identification: 030955
Unit ID: 404994
Telephone: (718) 522-9073 Carnegie Class: Assoc/MT-VT-Mix Trad/Non
FAX Number: (718) 532-1433 Calendar System: Semester
URL: www.asa.edu
Established: 1985 Annual Undergrad Tuition & Fees: $13,531
Enrollment: 4,541 Coed
Affiliation or Control: Proprietary IRS Status: Proprietary
Highest Offering: Baccalaureate
Accreditation: M, MAC

01 President ....Mr. Alex SHCHEGOL
05 Provost .... Dr. Shanthi KONKOTH
13 Vice President for Facilities & IT .... Ms. Alla SHCHEGOL
26 Vice President Marketing/Admissions .. Ms. Victoria KOSTYUKOV
36 Vice Pres Placement/Alumni Svcs ....Ms. Lesia WILLIS
86 Vice Pres Govt & Community Rels ....Mr. Roberto DUMAUAL
37 Vice President Financial Aid Svcs ....Ms. Victoriya SHTAMLER
06 Registrar ....Ms. Mariana ZINDER
08 Head Librarian .... Mr. Brook STOWE
10 Chief Business Officer ....Mr. Jose VALENCIA
14 IT Director .... Mr. David ESTRIN
04 Administrative Asst to President .... Ms. Ksenia KASIMOVA
09 Director of Institutional Research .... Ms. Anna BOUKHMAN
15 Director of Human Resources .. Ms. Austria Jazmin GREENBLATT
18 Chief Facilities/Physical Plant .... Mr. Walter KRUMER
32 Chief Student Affairs/Student Life .... Mr. Marcus BROWNE
41 Athletic Director .... Mr. Kenneth WILCOX
50 Dean of Business ....Dr. Edward KUFUOR
76 Dean of Health Disciplines .... Vacant
88 Dean of Legal Studies ....Dr. Oscar ODOM, III
49 Dean of Arts and Sciences .... Mr. Lizhi (Frank) ZHU
106 Dir Online Education/E-learning .... Vacant
108 Director Institutional Assessment .... Vacant
38 Director Student Counseling .....Ms. Tatyana KRYZHANOVSKAYA
39 Director Student Housing .... Vacant
20 Dean Academic & Program Development ... Ms. Deborah HUGHES
66 Dean of Nursing ....Ms. Donna M. REID
70 Coordinator for Language Studies .... Ms. Ludmilla DRAGUSHANSKAYA
75 Instructional Designer .... Mr. David F. SANCHEZ

Bais Binyomin Academy, Inc (F)

51 Carlton Road, Monsey NY 10952
County: Rockland FICE Identification: 029120
Unit ID: 414975
Telephone: (845) 207-0330 Carnegie Class: Not Classified
FAX Number: N/A Calendar System: Trimester
Established: 1976 Annual Undergrad Tuition & Fees: N/A
Enrollment: N/A Male
Affiliation or Control: Independent Non-Profit IRS Status: 501(c)3
Highest Offering: First Talmudic Degree
Accreditation: RABN

01 Rosh Hayeshiva ....Rabbi Meyer HERSHKOWITZ
04 Associate Rosh Hayeshiva .... Rabbi Yeruchom ZEILBERGER
05 Dean ....Rabbi Michael BENDER

Bais Medrash Ateres Shlomo (G)

220 Bennett Avenue, New York NY 2124195758
County: New York Identification: 667321
Telephone: (914) 736-1055 Carnegie Class: Not Classified
FAX Number: N/A Calendar System: Semester
URL: baismedrashateresshlomo.com
Established: 2016 Annual Undergrad Tuition & Fees: N/A
Enrollment: N/A Male
Affiliation or Control: Jewish IRS Status: 501(c)3
Highest Offering: First Talmudic Degree
Accreditation: AIJS

Bank Street College of Education (H)

610 W 112 Street, New York NY 10025-1898
County: New York FICE Identification: 002669
Unit ID: 189015
Telephone: (212) 875-4400 Carnegie Class: Spec-4-yr-Other
FAX Number: (212) 875-4759 Calendar System: Semester
URL: www.bankstreet.edu
Established: 1916 Annual Graduate Tuition & Fees: N/A
Enrollment: 650 Coed
Affiliation or Control: Independent Non-Profit IRS Status: 501(c)3
Highest Offering: Master's; No Undergraduates
Accreditation: M, CAEPN

01 President ....Shael POLAKOW-SURANSKY
100 Chief of Staff ....Katherine CONNELLY
10 Chief Financial Officer ....Marion KOWALSKI
11 Chief Operating Officer .... Justin TYACK
30 VP Development/External Relations ....Sonja CARTER
86 VP Governance/Community Engagement .... Akilah ROSADO
05 Dean of Innov/Policy & Research .... Josh THOMASES
58 Dean of the Graduate School ....Cecelia TRAUGH
88 Dean of Children's Programs ....Jed LIPPARD
88 Associate Dean of Administration .... Barbara COLEMAN
20 Associate Dean of Academic Affairs ....Wendi WILLIAMS
123 Director of Graduate Admissions .... Stephen OSTENDORFF
06 Registrar ....Ann COX
37 Director of Student Financial Aid ....Emmett COOPER
29 Director of Alumni Relations ....Linda REING
15 Chief Human Resources Officer ....Elyse MATTHEWS
13 Chief Information Officer ....Judith JOHNSON
18 Dir of Facilities/Security/Safety .... Carlos ESQUIVEL
08 Director of Library Services .... Kristin FREDA
36 Director of Student Placement ....Susan LEVINE
09 Director of Institutional Research .... Amy KLINE
04 Executive Assistant to President ....Regina WRIGHT

Bard College (I)

PO Box 5000, Annandale-On-Hudson NY 12504-5000
County: Dutchess FICE Identification: 002671
Unit ID: 189088
Telephone: (845) 758-6822 Carnegie Class: Bac-A&S
FAX Number: (845) 758-4294 Calendar System: Semester
URL: www.bard.edu
Established: 1860 Annual Undergrad Tuition & Fees: $51,384
Enrollment: 2,332 Coed
Affiliation or Control: Independent Non-Profit IRS Status: 501(c)3
Highest Offering: Doctorate
Accreditation: M

01 President .... Dr. Leon BOTSTEIN
03 Executive Vice President of College ....Dr. Dimitri B. PAPADIMITRIOU
45 Vice Pres for Strategic Initiatives .... Mr. Taun TOAY
30 Vice Pres Alumni/ae Affairs/Devel ....Ms. Debra PEMSTEIN
10 VP for Admin & Finance/CFO .... Dr. James BRUDVIG
11 Vice President for Administration ....Ms. Coleen MURPHY ALEXANDER
05 Vice President/Dean of the College .... Ms. Rebecca THOMAS
32 VP Student Affairs/Dir Admissions ....Ms. Mary I. BACKLUND
20 VP Acad Affairs/Dir Civic Engagmt ....Dr. Jonathan BECKER
20 Associate VP for Academic Affairs .... Dr. David SHEIN
08 VP/Dean Info Svcs/Dir Libraries .... Mr. Jeffrey KATZ
32 VP for Student Affairs ....Ms. Erin CANNAN
09 VP for Institutional Research ....Dr. Mark D. HALSEY
35 Dean of Student Affairs ....Ms. Bethany NOHLGREN
57 Dir Milton Avery Grad Sch of Arts .... Mr. Arthur GIBBONS
88 Dir Bard Grad Ctr Decorative Arts ....Dr. Susan WEBER
88 Exec Dir Ctr Curatorial Studies ....Mr. Tom ECCLES
110 Asst VP Dir of Inst Support .... Ms. Karen UNGER
88 Director Ctr Environmental Policy ....Dr. Eban GOODSTEIN
37 Director Financial Aid .... Ms. Denise ACKERMAN
06 Registrar .... Mr. Peter GADSBY
26 Associate VP of Communications .... Mr. Mark PRIMOFF
15 Director of Human Resources ....Ms. Kimberly ALEXANDER
21 Associate VP for Finance .... Mr. Kevin PARKER
88 Director Inst Writing/Thinking .... Ms. Peg PEOPLES
18 Director of Buildings & Grounds .... Mr. Randy CLUM
13 Director Mgmt Info Systems .... Mr. Michael TOMPKINS
29 Director Alumni/ae Affairs .... Ms. Jane BRIEN
36 Director Career Development ....Ms. Elizabeth GIGLIO
19 Director Safety & Security ....Mr. Kenneth COOPER
09 Director of Institutional Research .... Mr. Joseph F. AHERN
24 Director of Audio/Video Services ....Mr. Paul LABARBERA
28 Director of Multicultural Affairs ....Dr. Ann SEATON
41 Director of Athletics ....Ms. Kristin E. HALL
40 Bookstore Manager .... Ms. Merry MEYER
23 Director Student Health Services .... Ms. Marsha DAVIS
38 Director Student Counseling ....Ms. Tamara TELBERG
07 Director of Admission .... Ms. Mackie SIEBENS
39 Director of Housing ....Ms. Nancy W. SMITH
90 Chief Information Officer ....Mr. David BRANGAITIS

Bard High School Early College Manhattan (J)

525 East Houston Street, New York NY 10002
Telephone: (212) 995-8479 Identification: 770114
Accreditation: &EH

† Branch campus of Bard College at Simon's Rock, Great Barrington, MA

Bard High School Early College Queens (A)

30-20 Thomson Avenue, Long Island City NY 11101
Telephone: (718) 361-3133 Identification: 770115
Accreditation: &EH

† Branch campus of Bard College at Simon's Rock, Great Barrington, MA

Barnard College (B)

3009 Broadway, New York NY 10027-6598
County: New York FICE Identification: 002708
Unit ID: 189097
Telephone: (212) 854-5262 Carnegie Class: Bac-A&S
FAX Number: (212) 854-6220 Calendar System: Semester
URL: www.barnard.edu
Established: 1889 Annual Undergrad Tuition & Fees: $50,394
Enrollment: 2,548 Female
Affiliation or Control: Independent Non-Profit IRS Status: 501(c)3
Highest Offering: Baccalaureate
Accreditation: M, CAEPT, DANCE

01 President .... Sian L. BEILOCK
43 Chief of Staff to Pres/Gen Counsel .... Jomysha STEPHEN
05 Provost & Dean of Faculty .... Linda BELL
03 Chief Operating Officer .... Robert GOLDBERG
20 Dean of the College .... Avis HINKSON
30 Vice President for Development .... Vacant
26 Vice Pres Communications .... Justin HARMON
10 Vice President for Finance .... Eileen M. DIBENEDETTO
11 Vice Pres Campus Services .... Gail BELTRONE
13 Vice Pres Information Technology .... Carol KATZMAN
15 Vice President of Human Resources .... Catherine GEDDIS
88 Dean of Studies .... Natalie FRIEDMAN
84 Dean of Enrollment Management .... Jennifer FONDILLER
06 Registrar .... Jennifer SIMMONS
37 Director of Financial Aid .... Nanette DILAURO
32 Associate Dean for Student Life .... Alina WONG
39 Exec Dir Res Life and Housing .... Alicia LAWRENCE
23 Exec Director of Student Health Svc .... Mary Joan MURPHY
36 Director of Career Development .... Robert EARL
29 Exec Director of Alumnae Relations .... Caitlin TRAMEL
08 Dean of the Library .... Jennifer GREEN
101 Secretary to the Board of Trustees .... Alyssa SCHIFFMAN
19 Director of Safety/Security .... Antonio GONZALEZ
109 Director of Business Operations .... Douglas MAGET
18 Director Facilities Services .... Daniel DAVIS
09 Dir Institutional Research & Assess .... Rebecca FRIEDKIN

† Affiliated with Columbia University in the City of New York.

Be'er Yaakov Talmudic Seminary (C)

12 Jefferson Avenue, Spring Valley NY 10977
County: Rockland FICE Identification: 041928
Unit ID: 476717
Telephone: (845) 362-3053 Carnegie Class: Spec-4-yr-Faith
FAX Number: (845) 406-9699 Calendar System: Semester
Established: 1995 Annual Undergrad Tuition & Fees: $9,140
Enrollment: 469 Male
Affiliation or Control: Independent Non-Profit IRS Status: 501(c)3
Highest Offering: First Talmudic Degree
Accreditation: RABN

01 CEO .... Mr. Jacob UNGAR
05 Dean .... Rabbi Israel EISENBERGER
06 Registrar/Administrator .... Rabbi Yitzchok SOIFER
37 Financial Aid Administrator .... Mrs. Chana NOTIS

Beis Medrash Heichal Dovid (D)

211 Beach 17th Street, Far Rockaway NY 11691-4433
County: Queens FICE Identification: 037133
Unit ID: 444413
Telephone: (718) 868-2300 Carnegie Class: Spec-4-yr-Faith
FAX Number: (718) 868-0517 Calendar System: Semester
Established: 1999 Annual Undergrad Tuition & Fees: $9,200
Enrollment: 125 Male
Affiliation or Control: Independent Non-Profit IRS Status: 501(c)3
Highest Offering: Second Talmudic Degree
Accreditation: RABN

01 Dean .... Rabbi Yaakov BENDER
05 Rosh Yeshiva .... Rabbi Shlomo Avidgor ALTUSKY
37 Financial Aid Officer .... Rabbi Aaron STEINBERG

The Belanger School of Nursing (E)

650 McClellan Street, Schenectady NY 12304
County: Schenectady FICE Identification: 006448
Unit ID: 190956
Telephone: (518) 243-4471 Carnegie Class: Spec 2-yr-Health
FAX Number: (518) 243-4470 Calendar System: Other
URL: www.ellisbelangerschoolofnursing.org
Established: 1903 Annual Undergrad Tuition & Fees: $10,345
Enrollment: 127 Coed
Affiliation or Control: Independent Non-Profit IRS Status: 501(c)3
Highest Offering: Associate Degree
Accreditation: ADNUR

01 Director .... Dr. Marilyn STAPLETON
05 Chief Academic Officer .... Dr. Marilyn STAPLETON
37 Student Financial Aid Coordinator .... Mr. Michael DAGGETT
11 Associate Director .... Ms. Michele HEWITT
88 ADA Coordinator .... Ms. Amy TESSITORE
08 Head Librarian .... Ms. Emily HART

Berkeley College (F)

3 East 43rd Street, New York NY 10017-4604
County: New York FICE Identification: 007394
Unit ID: 189228
Telephone: (212) 986-4343 Carnegie Class: Spec-4-yr-Bus
FAX Number: (212) 818-1169 Calendar System: Semester
URL: www.berkeleycollege.edu
Established: 1931 Annual Undergrad Tuition & Fees: $24,050
Enrollment: 4,403 Coed
Affiliation or Control: Proprietary IRS Status: Proprietary
Highest Offering: Baccalaureate
Accreditation: M, IACBE

00 Chairman of the Board .... Mr. Kevin L. LUING
01 President .... Mr. Michael J. SMITH
04 Special Assistant to the President .... Dr. Rose Mary HEALY
05 Provost .... Dr. Beth CASTIGLIA
84 Executive VP .... Mr. Tim LUING
10 VP Finance .... Mr. Dino KASAMIS
32 Senior VP Student Success .... Ms. Diane RECINOS
88 VP Information Analytics .... Mr. Brian MAHER
43 VP & Chief Compliance Officer .... Mr. William BRANDT
26 VP Marketing .... Mr. William DIMASI
13 Chief Information Officer .... Mr. Leonard DE BOTTON
86 VP Government Relations NY .... Mr. Gbubemi OKOTIEURO
35 VP Student Development/Campus Life .... Dr. Dallas REED
08 VP Library Services .... Ms. Marlene DOTY
36 VP Career Services .... Ms. Amy SORICELLI
37 VP Financial Aid .... Mr. Howard LESLIE
114 VP Budget & Student Accounts .... Ms. Eileen LOFTUS-BERLIN
85 Senior VP International Division .... Ms. Cynthia C. MARCHESE
106 Dean Online .... Dr. Joseph SCURALLI
20 Associate Provost Faculty Affairs .... Dr. Judith KORNBERG
50 Dean School of Business .... Dr. Elana ZOLFO
76 Dean School Health Studies .... Dr. Eva SKUKA
49 Dean School of Liberal Arts .... Dr. Don KIEFFER
107 Dean School of Professional Studies .... Dr. Michael MCATEER
88 Dean Developmental Education .... Dr. Gerald IACULLO
121 Assistant VP Academic Advisement .... Mr. Joseph GIUFFRE
06 Registrar .... Ms. Deborah PALICIA
108 AVP Institutional Effectiveness .... Vacant
31 VP Communications & Ext Relations .. Ms. Angela HARRINGTON
19 AVP Public Safety .... Mr. Robert MAGUIRE
27 Director Media Relations .... Ms. Ilene GREENFIELD
119 Info Systems Security Manager .... Mr. Steven BECKER
41 Director Athletics .... Mr. Andrew DESTEPHANO
29 AVP Career Services Alumni Relation .... Mr. Michael IRIS
09 Director Institutional Research .... Ms. Rebecca J. DRENNEN

Bet Medrash Gadol Ateret Torah (G)

901 Quentin Road, Brooklyn NY 11223
County: Kings Identification: 667146
Unit ID: 485999
Telephone: (347) 394-1036 Carnegie Class: Not Classified
FAX Number: (347) 394-1096 Calendar System: Semester
Established: 1992 Annual Undergrad Tuition & Fees: $9,200
Enrollment: 124 Male
Affiliation or Control: Independent Non-Profit IRS Status: 501(c)3
Highest Offering: Second Talmudic Degree
Accreditation: @RABN

01 President/CEO .... Rabbi Joseph HARARI-RAFUL
10 Chief Financial/Business Officer .... Irwin SHAMAH
06 Registrar .... Mrs. Ruchana MANSOUR
11 Chief of Operations/Administration .... Zev KLEINER

Beth Hamedrash Shaarei Yosher Institute (H)

4102-10 16th Avenue, Brooklyn NY 11204-1099
County: Kings FICE Identification: 011192
Unit ID: 189273
Telephone: (718) 854-2290 Carnegie Class: Spec-4-yr-Faith
FAX Number: (718) 436-9045 Calendar System: Semester
Established: 1962 Annual Undergrad Tuition & Fees: $8,850
Enrollment: 44 Male
Affiliation or Control: Independent Non-Profit IRS Status: 501(c)3
Highest Offering: Second Talmudic Degree
Accreditation: RABN

05 Chief Academic Officer .... Rabbi Chaim ROSENBERG
10 Chief Business Officer .... Rabbi Pinches KAFF
29 Director Alumni Association .... Rabbi Eliyohu ROSENBLUM
15 Director Personnel Services .... Rabbi Mordechai MARGULIES
37 Director Student Financial Aid .... Rabbi Aaron ROTTENBERG
06 Registrar .... Rabbi Sol ROSENBERG

Beth Hatalmud Rabbinical College (I)

2127 82nd Street, Brooklyn NY 11214-2594
County: Kings FICE Identification: 011922
Unit ID: 189264
Telephone: (718) 259-2525 Carnegie Class: Spec-4-yr-Faith
FAX Number: (718) 256-5592 Calendar System: Semester
Established: 1950 Annual Undergrad Tuition & Fees: $7,750
Enrollment: 25 Male
Affiliation or Control: Independent Non-Profit IRS Status: 501(c)3
Highest Offering: Second Talmudic Degree
Accreditation: RABN

01 President .... Rabbi Chaim STEFANSKY
10 Fiscal Officer .... Rabbi C. L. PERKOWSKI
08 Librarian .... Mr. Shimon HESS
06 Registrar .... Mr. Naftoli BORCHARDT

Beth Medrash Meor Yitzchok (J)

65 Dykstra's Way East, Monsey NY 10952
County: Rockland Identification: 667111
Unit ID: 486196
Telephone: (845) 426-3488 Carnegie Class: Not Classified
FAX Number: (845) 425-5415 Calendar System: Semester
Established: 2007 Annual Undergrad Tuition & Fees: $8,100
Enrollment: 162 Male
Affiliation or Control: Independent Non-Profit IRS Status: 501(c)3
Highest Offering: First Talmudic Degree
Accreditation: RABN

Bill and Sandra Pomeroy College of Nursing at Crouse Hospital (K)

736 Irving Avenue, Syracuse NY 13210
County: Onondaga FICE Identification: 006445
Unit ID: 190451
Telephone: (315) 470-7481 Carnegie Class: Spec 2-yr-Health
FAX Number: (315) 470-5774 Calendar System: Semester
URL: www.crouse.org/nursing
Established: 1913 Annual Undergrad Tuition & Fees: $11,755
Enrollment: 299 Coed
Affiliation or Control: Independent Non-Profit IRS Status: 501(c)3
Highest Offering: Associate Degree
Accreditation: ADNUR

01 Dean .... Rhonda READER
06 Registrar .... Michele SPENARD
07 Assistant Dean for Enrollment .... Amy GRAHAM
08 Head Librarian .... Kristine DELANEY
37 Director Student Financial Aid .... Kenny KENDALL
05 Program Chair .... Patricia MORGAN
32 Assistant Dean for Students .... Ryan BARKER

Boricua College (L)

3755 Broadway, New York NY 10032-1599
County: New York FICE Identification: 013029
Unit ID: 189413
Telephone: (212) 694-1000 Carnegie Class: Bac/Assoc-Mixed
FAX Number: (212) 694-1015 Calendar System: Semester
URL: www.boricuacollege.edu
Established: 1974 Annual Undergrad Tuition & Fees: $10,625
Enrollment: 995 Coed
Affiliation or Control: Independent Non-Profit IRS Status: 501(c)3
Highest Offering: Master's
Accreditation: M, CAEPT

01 President .... Dr. Victor G. ALICEA
04 Exec Assistant to the President .... Ms. Sandra BELLAMY
03 Sr Vice President .... Dr. Maria MONTES-MORALES
05 VP Academic Affairs .... Dr. Shivaji SENGUPTA
13 VP Information & Tech/Facil Mgmt .... Mr. Irving RAMIREZ
20 VP Academic Planning & Programming .... Dr. John GUZMAN
43 Legal Counsel .... Mr. Jorge BATISTA
10 Director Finance .... Mr. Elias OYOLA
07 Director Admissions Bronx Campus .... Ms. Brenda RODRIGUEZ
07 Director Admissions Manhattan Ctr .... Mr. Ismael SANCHEZ
07 Director Admissions Graham Ctr .... Ms. Aurea MORALES
07 Director Admissions Northside Ctr .... Mr. Frank SERRANO
06 Director Registration & Assessments .... Ms. Beatriz AHORRIO
37 Director Financial Aid .... Ms. Rosalia CRUZ
15 Director Personnel/Human Resources .... Ms. Francia L. CASTRO
08 Director Library/Learning Resources .... Ms. Liza RIVERA
18 Director Environmental Services .... Mr. Elias RIVERA
41 Director of Athletics .... Vacant
30 Director of Development .... Vacant
20 Dean Academic Affairs Manhattan Ctr .... Mr. Moises PEREYRA
20 Dean of Academic Affairs Bronx Ctr .... Mr. Jose Israel LOPEZ

Briarcliffe College (M)

1055 Stewart Avenue, Bethpage NY 11714-3545
County: Nassau FICE Identification: 020757
Unit ID: 189459
Telephone: (516) 918-3600 Carnegie Class: Bac/Assoc-Mixed
FAX Number: (516) 470-6020 Calendar System: Semester
URL: www.briarcliffe.edu
Established: 1966 Annual Undergrad Tuition & Fees: N/A
Enrollment: 1,355 Coed
Affiliation or Control: Proprietary IRS Status: Proprietary
Highest Offering: Baccalaureate
Accreditation: M

01 President .... Dr. George SANTIAGO
12 Campus Dir/VP Operations .... Mr. Louis COMMISSO
07 Vice Pres Admissions .... Mr. C. Gabriel CASTANO
32 Vice President Student Affairs .... Ms. Kathy GENUA
10 VP Finance/CFO .... Mr. Louis COMMISSO

13 Director of Information Systems ..... Mr. Hoober ZULUAGA
21 Business Office Manager ..... Ms. Cindy ROYS
06 Registrar ..... Ms. Christy LAW
36 Director of Career Services ..... Mr. Tony EMERSON
08 Librarian ..... Mr. Jeremy LAUBER

† Currently in teach-out mode. Closing December 2018.

Brooklyn Law School (A)

250 Joralemon Street, Brooklyn NY 11201-3798
County: Kings FICE Identification: 002677
Unit ID: 189501
Telephone: (718) 625-2200 Carnegie Class: Spec-4-yr-Law
FAX Number: (718) 780-0393 Calendar System: Semester
URL: www.brooklaw.edu
Established: 1901 Annual Graduate Tuition & Fees: N/A
Enrollment: 1,175 Coed
Affiliation or Control: Independent Non-Profit IRS Status: 501(c)3
Highest Offering: First Professional Degree; No Undergraduates
Accreditation: LAW

00 Dean and President Emerita ..... Dean Joan G. WEXLER
01 President/Dean ..... Dean Nicholas W. ALLARD
05 Vice Dean of Academic Affairs ..... Dean William ARAIZA
20 Assoc Dean for Profess Legal Educ ..... Dean Stacy CAPLOW
20 Vice Dean ..... Dean Suzanne DENNIS
32 Dean of Students ..... Dean Jennifer R. LANG
10 Chief Financial Officer ..... Ms. Laurie H. NEWITZ
21 Treasurer ..... Ms. Shoshanna M. CAMPBELL
07 Dean of Admissions ..... Dean Eulas BOYD, JR.
36 Dean of Career Development ..... Ms. Karen EISEN
08 Director of Library & Assoc Prof ..... Prof. Janet SINDER
30 Director of Development ..... Ms. Kamille JAMES
29 Asst Director of Alumni Relations ..... Ms. Andrea POLCI
06 Registrar ..... Mr. Christian BESTER
37 Director of Financial Aid ..... Ms. Nancy L. ZAHZAM
11 Chief Operating Ofcr/Chief of Staff ..... Ms. Linda HARVEY
18 Facilities Manager ..... Mr. Salvatore DECANDIA
15 Human Resources Manager ..... Ms. Christina WALLACE
13 Chief Info Technology Officer (CIO) ..... Mr. Steven MARKS
19 Director of Public Safety ..... Ms. Mercedes RAVELO
43 Gen Counsel/Chf Compliance Officer ..... Ms. Stephanie VULLO

*Bryant & Stratton College System Office (B)

2410 N. Forest Road, Suite 101, Getzville NY 14068-1224
County: Erie Identification: 666828
Telephone: (716) 250-7500 Carnegie Class: N/A
FAX Number: (716) 250-7510
URL: www.bryantstratton.edu

01 President & CEO ..... Dr. Francis J. FELSER
11 VP/Chief Operating Officer ..... Mr. David VADEN
05 VP/Chief Academic Officer ..... Ms. Beth A. TARQUINO
10 VP/Chief Financial Officer ..... Mr. Christopher GERACE
13 VP/Online Division and CIO ..... Ms. Doreen JUSTINGER
07 VP/Marketing and Admissions ..... Ms. Tracy NANNERY
108 Exec Dir Strat Plng & Assessment ..... Ms. Anne LORIA

*Bryant & Stratton College (C)

465 Main Street, Suite 400, Buffalo NY 14203-1795
County: Erie FICE Identification: 002678
Unit ID: 189583
Telephone: (716) 884-9120 Carnegie Class: Bac/Assoc-Assoc Dom
FAX Number: (716) 884-0091 Calendar System: Semester
URL: www.bryantstratton.edu
Established: 1854 Annual Undergrad Tuition & Fees: $16,545
Enrollment: 600 Coed
Affiliation or Control: Proprietary IRS Status: Proprietary
Highest Offering: Baccalaureate
Accreditation: M, MAC

02 Campus Director ..... Dr. Marvel E. ROSS-JONES
05 Dean of Instruction ..... Dr. Adiam TSEGAI
07 Director of Admissions ..... Mr. Kevin MUSE
36 Director of Career Services ..... Ms. Kelly HENRY
10 WNY Business Office Director ..... Ms. Kathleen OWCZARCZAK

*Bryant & Stratton College (D)

1259 Central Avenue, Albany NY 12205-5230
Telephone: (518) 437-1802 FICE Identification: 004749
Accreditation: &M, MAC

*Bryant & Stratton College (E)

854 Long Pond Road, Rochester NY 14612-3049
Telephone: (585) 720-0660 FICE Identification: 012470
Accreditation: &M, MAC, OTA

*Bryant & Stratton College (F)

953 James Street, Syracuse NY 13203-2502
Telephone: (315) 472-6603 FICE Identification: 008276
Accreditation: &M, MAC, OTA, @PTAA

Canisius College (G)

2001 Main Street, Buffalo NY 14208-1098
County: Erie FICE Identification: 002681
Unit ID: 189705
Telephone: (716) 883-7000 Carnegie Class: Masters/L
FAX Number: (716) 888-2525 Calendar System: Semester
URL: www.canisius.edu
Established: 1870 Annual Undergrad Tuition & Fees: $35,424
Enrollment: 3,900 Coed
Affiliation or Control: Roman Catholic IRS Status: 501(c)3
Highest Offering: Master's
Accreditation: M, #CAATE, CACREP, CAEP

01 President ..... Mr. John J. HURLEY
05 VP Academic Affairs ..... Dr. Margaret MCCARTHY
10 Vice President Business & Finance ..... Mr. Marco F. BENEDETTI
32 VP Student Affs & Dean of Students ..... Dr. Terri L. MANGIONE
111 VP Institutional Advancement ..... Mr. William COLLINS, II
84 VP Enrollment Management ..... Ms. Kathleen B. DAVIS
20 Assoc VP for Academic Affairs ..... Dr. Sara MORRIS
113 Asst VP/Dir Stdnt Rec & Fin Svcs ..... Mr. Kevin M. SMITH
26 Asst VP Mktg & Communications ..... Mr. Matther Z. WOJICK
88 Asst VP/Director Griff Center ..... Ms. Anne Marie DOBIES
08 Director of Library ..... Ms. Kristine E. KASBOHM
07 Director Undergrad Admissions ..... Mr. Justin P. ROGERS
112 Director of Principal Gifts ..... Mr. J. Patrick GREENWALD
21 Controller ..... Mr. Ronald J. HABERER
49 Dean Col of Arts & Sciences ..... Dr. Elizabeth A. GILL
50 Dean School of Business ..... Dr. Daniel J. BORGIA
37 Assoc Dir of Stdnt Records/Fin Svcs ..... Ms. Mary A. KOEHNEKE
06 Registrar/Asst Dir Stdnt Rec & FA ..... Ms. Deborah W. PROHN
26 Director of Public Relations ..... Ms. Eileen C. HERBERT
15 Director of Human Resources ..... Ms. Linda M. WALLESHAUSER
102 Director of the Canisius Fund ..... Ms. Erin HARTNETT
53 Assc Dean School Ed/Human Svcs ..... Dr. Nancy WALLACE
25 Director of Sponsored Programs ..... Ms. Mary Ann LANGLOIS
18 Director Facilities Management ..... Mr. Thomas E. CIMINELLI
19 Director of Public Safety ..... Mr. H. Wilson JOHNSON
23 Director Student Health Center ..... Ms. Patricia H. CREAHAN
38 Director Counseling Center ..... Ms. Eileen A. NILAND
39 Assoc Dean of Stdnts/Dir Resid Life ..... Mr. Matthew H. MULVILLE
104 Director Study Abroad ..... Mr. Brian SMITH
40 Course Materials Manager/Bookstore ..... Mr. Andrew J. THOMAS
41 Director Athletics ..... Mr. William J. MAHER
42 Director Campus Ministry ..... Mr. Michael F. HAYES, JR.
90 Director of User Services ..... Mr. Scott D. CLARK
94 Dir of Women's Business Center ..... Ms. Sara L. VESCIO
92 Director of All College Honors Pgm ..... Dr. Bruce J. DIERENFIELD
09 Sr Analyst Inst & Research Effect ..... Mr. Michael W. TAMPIO
88 Director of Multi Cultural Programs ..... Mr. Sababu C. NORRIS
13 Interim Chief Information Officer ..... Mr. Lawrence DENI
24 Director Media Center ..... Mr. Daniel J. DREW
96 Director of Purchasing ..... Mr. Gary B. LEW
105 Web Devel Specialist/Mktg Comm ..... Mr. Kevin M. BLAKE
04 Assistant to the President ..... Ms. Erica C. SAMMARCO
91 Director Administrative Computing ..... Ms. Michele FOLSOM
108 Director Inst & Research Effectiv ..... Ms. Lauren YOUNG

Cayuga Community College (H)

197 Franklin Street, Auburn NY 13021-3099
County: Cayuga FICE Identification: 002861
Unit ID: 189839
Telephone: (315) 255-1743 Carnegie Class: Assoc/HT-High Non
FAX Number: (315) 255-2117 Calendar System: Semester
URL: www.cayuga-cc.edu
Established: 1953 Annual Undergrad Tuition & Fees (In-District): $5,043
Enrollment: 4,184 Coed
Affiliation or Control: State/Local IRS Status: 501(c)3
Highest Offering: Associate Degree
Accreditation: M, ADNUR

01 President ..... Mr. Brian M. DURANT
04 Assistant to President/Board ..... Ms. Carolyn L. GUARIGLIA
05 Provost/Vice Pres Academic Affairs ..... Dr. Anne J. HERRON
32 Vice President Student Affairs ..... Mr. Jeffrey E. ROSENTHAL
10 Vice Pres Administration/Treasurer ..... Mr. Dan DOBELL
102 Executive Director Foundation ..... Mr. Jeffrey L. HOFFMAN
84 Dean Enrollment Management ..... Ms. Cheryl A. LINDSAY
13 Dean Information Technology ..... Mr. John KAFTAN
07 Director of Admissions ..... Mr. Bruce M. BLODGETT
09 Director Institutional Research ..... Ms. Carol E. RUNGE
41 Director Athletics ..... Mr. Peter E. LIDDELL
15 Director HR & Affirmative Action ..... Vacant
35 Director Student Activities ..... Mr. Norman LEE

Cazenovia College (I)

22 Sullivan Street, Cazenovia NY 13035
County: Madison FICE Identification: 002685
Unit ID: 189848
Telephone: (800) 654-3210 Carnegie Class: Bac-Diverse
FAX Number: (315) 655-4143 Calendar System: Semester
URL: www.cazenovia.edu
Established: 1824 Annual Undergrad Tuition & Fees: $32,674
Enrollment: 1,072 Coed
Affiliation or Control: Independent Non-Profit IRS Status: 501(c)3
Highest Offering: Baccalaureate
Accreditation: M, CAEPT, IACBE

01 President ..... Dr. Ronald D. CHESBROUGH
05 VP Academic Affs/Dean of Faculty ..... Dr. Sharon A. DETTMER
10 VP Financial Affs/Chief Fin Officer ..... Mr. Mark H. EDWARDS
84 VP Enrol Mgmt/Dean Admiss/Fin Aid ..... Mr. Patrick QUINN
111 VP for Institutional Advancement ..... Vacant
32 Dean for Student Life ..... Ms. Katie O'BRIEN
89 Dean First Year Program ..... Mr. Jesse LOTT
08 Director of Library Services ..... Ms. Heather C. WHALEN-SMITH
37 Assoc Dean Financial Aid/Registrar ..... Ms. Christine MANDEL
26 Director Marketing/Communications ..... Mr. Timothy D. GREENE
15 Director Human Resources ..... Ms. Janice ROMAGNOLI
23 Director Health Services ..... Ms. Deborah FRANK
36 Dir Career/Extended Learning Svcs ..... Ms. Christine RICHARDSON
41 Director Intercollegiate Athletics ..... Mr. Pete WAY
13 Director of Technology Development ..... Mr. David PALMER
06 Registrar ..... Ms. Christine MANDEL
09 Dir Institutional Rsrch/Assessment ..... Dr. Sara S. PHILLIPS
18 Dir of Physical Plant Operations ..... Mr. Jeff SLOCUM
29 Director Alumni Relations ..... Ms. Shari WHITAKER
42 Chaplain ..... Vacant
07 Sr Assistant Director of Admissions ..... Mr. Brett M. CARGUELLO

Central Yeshiva Beth Joseph (J)

1502 Avenue N, Brooklyn NY 11230
County: Kings Identification: 667157
Unit ID: 488004
Telephone: (718) 269-4080 Carnegie Class: Not Classified
FAX Number: (718) 269-4080 Calendar System: Semester
Established: 1942 Annual Undergrad Tuition & Fees: $11,000
Enrollment: N/A Male
Affiliation or Control: Independent Non-Profit IRS Status: 501(c)3
Highest Offering: First Talmudic Degree
Accreditation: RABN

01 Chief Executive Officer ..... Rabbi Moshe JOFEN
37 Director Student Financial Aid ..... Rabbi Yechezkel MOSCOVITZ
06 Registrar ..... Rabbi Baruch MILLER

Central Yeshiva Tomchei Tmimim Lubavitch America (K)

841-853 Ocean Parkway, Brooklyn NY 11230-2798
County: Kings FICE Identification: 004776
Unit ID: 189857
Telephone: (718) 434-0784 Carnegie Class: Spec-4-yr-Faith
FAX Number: (718) 434-1519 Calendar System: Semester
Established: 1941 Annual Undergrad Tuition & Fees: $6,700
Enrollment: 641 Male
Affiliation or Control: Independent Non-Profit IRS Status: 501(c)3
Highest Offering: Second Talmudic Degree
Accreditation: RABN

01 President ..... Rabbi Shloime ZARCHI
05 Dean ..... Rabbi Zalman LABKOWSKI
06 Registrar ..... Rabbi Joseph WILMOWSKY
37 Financial Aid Director ..... Rabbi Moshe M. GLUCKOWSKY
26 Director Public Relations ..... Mr. Shaya BOYMELGREEN
10 Treasurer ..... Rabbi Moshe BOGOMILSKY

Christ the King Seminary (L)

711 Knox Road, P.O. Box 607,
East Aurora NY 14052-0607
County: Erie FICE Identification: 002822
Unit ID: 189981
Telephone: (716) 652-8900 Carnegie Class: Spec-4-yr-Faith
FAX Number: (716) 652-8903 Calendar System: Semester
URL: www.cks.edu
Established: 1974 Annual Graduate Tuition & Fees: N/A
Enrollment: 84 Coed
Affiliation or Control: Roman Catholic IRS Status: 501(c)3
Highest Offering: Master's; No Undergraduates
Accreditation: M, THEOL

01 Rector/President ..... Rev. Joseph C. GATTO
03 Vice Rector ..... Rev. Robert A. WOZNIAK
05 Academic Dean ..... Mr. Michael SHERRY
10 Comptroller ..... Mrs. Nancy M. EHLERS
111 Director Institutional Advancement ..... Mrs. Susan LANKES
18 Director of Facilities ..... Rev. John M. STAAK, OMI
08 Library Director ..... Ms. Teresa LUBIENECKI
06 Registrar ..... Mrs. Julie GALEY
04 Administrative Asst to President ..... Ms. Nadine OATES
15 Director Personnel Svcs/Fin Aid ..... Mrs. Nancy M. EHLERS

Christie's Education, New York (M)

1230 Avenue of the Americas, Fl 20, New York NY 10020
County: New York FICE Identification: 036654
Unit ID: 475510
Telephone: (212) 355-1501 Carnegie Class: Spec-4-yr-Arts
FAX Number: (212) 355-7370 Calendar System: Quarter
URL: www.christies.edu
Established: 1993 Annual Graduate Tuition & Fees: N/A
Enrollment: 61 Coed
Affiliation or Control: Proprietary IRS Status: Proprietary
Highest Offering: Master's; No Undergraduates
Accreditation: NY

01 Academic Director ..... Dr. Veronique CHAGNON-BURKE
08 Learning Resources Manager ..... Ms. Karen MAGUIRE

07 Recruitment and Admissions Officer .... Ms. Hilary SMITH
10 Business Manager .... Ms. Margaret CONKLIN
37 Academic/Financial Aid Administator .... Ms. Catherine WARDEN
21 Admissions and Business Coordinator ... Ms. Lindsay SCHWARTZ

*City University of New York (A)

205 E. 42nd Street, New York NY 10017
County: New York　FICE Identification: 025061
Unit ID: 190035
Telephone: (646) 664-9100　Carnegie Class: N/A
FAX Number: (646) 664-3868
URL: www2.cuny.edu

01 Chancellor .... Mr. James B. MILLIKEN
05 Exec VC/University Provost .... Dr. Vita RABINOWITZ
10 Sr Vice Chancellor Budget/Finance .... Mr. Matthew SAPIENZA
101 Secretary of the Board of Trustees .... Ms. Gayle HORWITZ
43 Interim General Counsel .... Ms. Jane P. SOVERN
88 Sr Advisor for Fiscal Policy .... Mr. Marc SHAW
18 VC Facility Plng/Constr Mgt .... Ms. Judy BERGTRAUM
13 VC/Chief Information Officer .... Mr. Brian COHEN
32 Interim VC Student Affairs .... Dr. Chris ROSA
88 Vice Chancellor for Labor Relations .... Ms. Pamela S. SILVERBLATT
09 Interim Vice Provost for Research .... Mr. Mark E. HAUBER
15 Vice Chanc for Human Resources Mgmt ... Ms. Gloriana WATERS
102 Ass VC for Corporate Foundation ... Ms. Andrea SHAPIRO DAVIS
20 Sr Dean for Academic Affairs .... Mr. John MOGULESCU
06 Registrar .... Vacant
09 Dean Institutional Research .... Mr. David CROOK
26 Senior Advisor for Communications .... Mr. James STERNGOLD
07 Director of Admissions .... Ms. Clare NORTON
100 Chief of Staff .... Ms. Doris L. SUAREZ

*Baruch College/City University of New York (B)

One Bernard Baruch Way, New York NY 10010-5526
County: New York　FICE Identification: 007273
Unit ID: 190512
Telephone: (646) 312-1000　Carnegie Class: Masters/L
FAX Number: N/A　Calendar System: Semester
URL: www.baruch.cuny.edu
Established: 1968　Annual Undergrad Tuition & Fees (In-District): $6,810
Enrollment: 18,433　Coed
Affiliation or Control: State/Local　IRS Status: 501(c)3
Highest Offering: Doctorate
Accreditation: M, HSA, IPSY, SPAA

02 President .... Dr. Mitchel B. WALLERSTEIN
05 Provost/SVP Academic Affairs .... Dr. David CHRISTY
20 Sr VP Academic Affs/Assoc Provost .... Dr. Dennis SLAVIN
10 Vice Pres Administration/Finance .... Ms. Katharine COBB
84 VP Enroll Mgmt/Strategic Init .... Ms. Mary GORMAN
30 VP for College Advancement .... Mr. David SHANTON
13 VP for Information Services .... Mr. Arthur DOWNING
26 VP for Comm/Ext Rels & Econ Dev .... Ms. Christina LATOUF
32 VP Student Affairs/Dean of Students .... Dr. Art KING
18 Asst VP Campus Facilities .... Ms. Lisa EDWARDS
21 Asst Vice President Finance .... Ms. Mary FINNEN
43 Asst VP Legal Counsel .... Ms. Olga DAIS
102 President Baruch College Fund .... Vacant
50 Dean Zicklin School of Business .... Dr. Fenwick HUSS
49 Dean Weissman School Arts & Science .... Dr. Aldemaro ROMEO, JR.
80 Dean School Public/Intl Affairs .... Dr. David BIRDSELL
08 Dean of Library .... Mr. Arthur DOWNING
58 Executive Officer Doctoral Program .... Dr. Joseph WEINTROP
100 Chief of Staff .... Ms. Kenya N. LEE
25 Director of Sponsored Programs .... Mr. Dominic ESPOSITO
15 Exec Dir of Human Resources .... Ms. Monique GEORGE
36 Director Career Development Center .... Dr. Patricia IMBIMBO
90 Asst Dir Client Svcs/Fac Liaison .... Mr. Frank WERBER
85 Director Intl Student Office .... Ms. Rosa KELLEY
19 Director Public Safety .... Mr. Henry J. MCLAUGHLIN
09 Dir Institutional Rsrch/Pgm Assess .... Mr. John CHOONOO
29 Director Alumni Relations .... Ms. Janet ROSSBACH
96 Director of Purchasing .... Dr. Diane OQUENDO
22 Chief Diversity Officer .... Ms. Mona JHA
41 Athletic Director .... Ms. Heather MACCULLOCH
86 Dir of Govt and Community Relations .... Mr. Eric LUGO
06 Senior Registrar .... Mr. Edward ADAMS
104 Director Study Abroad .... Dr. Richard MITTEN
37 Director of Financial Aid Services .... Ms. Elizabeth RIQUEZ
07 Dir of Undergraduate Admissions .... Ms. Marisa DELACRUZ

*City University of New York Borough of Manhattan Community College (C)

199 Chambers Street, New York NY 10007-1047
County: New York　FICE Identification: 002691
Unit ID: 190521
Telephone: (212) 220-1230　Carnegie Class: Assoc/HT-High Trad
FAX Number: (212) 220-1244　Calendar System: Semester
URL: www.bmcc.cuny.edu
Established: 1963　Annual Undergrad Tuition & Fees (In-District): $5,250
Enrollment: 27,309　Coed
Affiliation or Control: State/Local　IRS Status: 501(c)3
Highest Offering: Associate Degree
Accreditation: M, ADNUR, CAHIIM, COARC, EMT

02 President .... Dr. Antonio PEREZ
05 Provost/Senior VP Academic Affairs .... Dr. Karrin WILKS
11 Vice President Administration/Plng .... Mr. G. Scott ANDERSON
43 VP Legal Affs/Faculty & Staff Rels .... Mr. Robert DIAZ
32 Vice President of Student Affairs .... Dr. Marva CRAIG
30 Vice Pres of Development .... Ms. Doris HOLZ
10 Asst Vice Pres of Finance .... Ms. Elena SAMUELS
51 Dean Ctr for Cont Ed/Workforce Dev .... Mr. Sunil GUPTA
25 Dean Grants & Development .... Mr. John MONTANEZ
20 Dean for Instruction/Curriculum .... Dr. Erwin WONG
88 Assoc Dean Academic Support Svcs .... Dr. James BERG
37 Director Financial Aid .... Mr. Ralph W. BUXTON
15 Deputy Director Human Resources .... Ms. Gloria CHAO
07 Director of Admissions & Outreach .... Ms. Lisa KASPER
84 Vice Pres Enrollment Management .... Dr. Diane WALLESER
06 Senior Registrar .... Mr. Mohammad ALAM
08 Act Dir Learning Resource Center .... Mr. Gregory FARRELL
09 Dean Institutional Research .... Dr. Christopher SHULTS
28 Chief Diversity Officer .... Ms. Odelia LEVY
18 Campus Facilities Officer .... Vacant
26 Public Relations Officer .... Mr. Manuel ROMERO
41 Director of Athletics .... Mr. Stephen KELLY
102 Dir Foundation/Corporate Relations .... Mr. Bryan HALLER
36 Act Dir Acad Advise/Transfer Ctr .... Ms. Carei THOMAS
38 Director Counseling Center ..... Dr. Cicely Horsham BRATHWAITE
96 Director of Procurement .... Mr. Robert COX

*City University of New York Bronx Community College (D)

2155 University Avenue, Bronx NY 10453-2895
County: Bronx　FICE Identification: 002692
Unit ID: 190530
Telephone: (718) 289-5100　Carnegie Class: Assoc/HT-High Trad
FAX Number: (718) 289-6011　Calendar System: Semester
URL: www.bcc.cuny.edu
Established: 1957　Annual Undergrad Tuition & Fees (In-District): $5,206
Enrollment: 11,434　Coed
Affiliation or Control: State/Local　IRS Status: 501(c)3
Highest Offering: Associate Degree
Accreditation: M, ACBSP, ADNUR, ENGT, NMT, RAD

02 President .... Dr. Thomas ISEKENEGBE
05 VP of Academic Affairs & Provost .... Dr. Claudia V. SCHRADER
86 Government Rels and Ext Affairs Dir .... Mr. David W. LEVERS
32 VP for Student Affairs .... Ms. Irene R. DELGADO
111 VP for Advance/Comm & Ext Rels .... Dr. Eddy BAYARDELLE
26 Asst VP Comm & Marketing .... Ms. Diane WEATHERS
35 Dean of Student Services .... Mr. Bernard GANTT
11 AVP for Administrative Affairs .... Mr. David A. TAYLOR
30 Asst VP for Development .... Ms. Angela WAMBUGU COBB
103 Dean for Workforce & Econ Develop .... Mr. Kenneth ADAMS
45 Dean for Research/Plng & Assessment .... Dr. Nancy RITZE
20 Assoc Dean AA for Curr & Fac Dev .... Dr. Alexander OTT
10 Dir for Financial & Business Svcs .... Ms. Gina GALLIGAN
06 Registrar/Dir Enrollment .... Mr. Sanjay RAMDATH
13 Chief Information Officer .... Mr. Lonc AUDUSSEAU
37 Financial Aid Director .... Vacant
07 Admissions Officer .... Ms. Patricia A. RAMOS
15 Human Resources Director .... Vacant
08 Chief Librarian .... Prof. Michael J. MILLER
19 Public Safety Director .... Mr. James VERDICCHIO
41 Student Athletics Director .... Mr. Ryan MCCARTHY
18 Chief Super Phys Plant Svcs .... Mr. Lamont WATSON
29 Alum Rel/Plan Giv/Indiv Donors Mgr .... Mr. Robert WHELAN
35 Assoc Dean Stdnt Engagement/Success .... Vacant
88 Mgr of College Discovery .... Ms. Cynthia SUAREZ-ESPINAL
43 Exe Counsel & Deputy to President .... Ms. Karla R. WILLIAMS
96 Director of Purchasing .... Ms. Anjanette ANTONIO
28 Chief Diversity/Affirm Act Ofcr .... Ms. Jessenia PAOLI
14 Deputy Chief Technology Officer .... Ms. Luisa MARTICH
108 Academic Assessment Manager .... Dr. Richard LAMANNA
20 Dean for Academic Affairs .... Dr. Luis MONTENEGRO
90 Dir for Academic Comp Svcs Desk .... Ms. Wanda SANTIAGO
91 Manager of Admin Systems & Svcs .... Mr. Rolly WILTSHIRE
51 Mgr Continuing/Prof Education .... Mr. Wendell JOYNER
25 Dir of Grants Development .... Vacant
22 Affirmative Action Specialist .... Mr. Raymond GONZALEZ
102 Dev Corp and Foundation Rel Mgmt .... Ms. Julia OLIVA
104 Dir Intl Educ and Study Aboard Pgm .... Vacant
09 OIR Inst Research Specialist .... Mrs. Chelsea RAMOS
46 Director of Research & Testing .... Mr. Chris EFTHIMIOU
106 Dir IT Academic App/CTLT .... Mr. Mark LENNERTON
36 Dir Transfer and Job Placement .... Mr. Alán FUENTES
04 Administrative Asst to President .... Ms. Amirah COUSINS
100 Chief of Staff .... Ms. Karla Renee WILLIAMS
38 Director Student Counseling .... Ms. Vasiliki TORRES

*City University of New York Brooklyn College (E)

2900 Bedford Avenue, Brooklyn NY 11210-2889
County: Kings　FICE Identification: 002687
Unit ID: 190549
Telephone: (718) 951-5000　Carnegie Class: Masters/L
FAX Number: N/A　Calendar System: Semester
URL: www.brooklyn.cuny.edu
Established: 1930　Annual Undergrad Tuition & Fees (In-District): $6,838
Enrollment: 17,410　Coed
Affiliation or Control: State/Local　IRS Status: 501(c)3
Highest Offering: Master's
Accreditation: M, AUD, CACREP, CAEPN, DIETD, DIETI, SP

02 President .... Dr. Michelle J. ANDERSON
05 Provost/Sr Vice Pres Acad Affairs . Dr. William A. TRAMONTANO
11 Sr VP for Finance & Administration .... Mr. Joseph GIOVANNELLI
111 Vice Pres Institutional Advancement .... Vacant
32 Vice President for Student Affairs .... Mr. Ronald JACKSON
26 AVP Communications and Marketing .... Mr. Jason CAREY
84 VP Enroll Management and Retention .... Dr. Lillian O'REILLY
100 Chief of Staff to President .... Ms. Nicole HAAS
86 Exec Dir Govt & External Affairs .... Mr. Steven SCHECHTER
20 Assoc Provost for Faculty & Admin .... Dr. Matthew MOORE
108 Assoc Prov Inst Planning/Assessment .... Dr. Jo-Ellen ASBURY
53 Dean School of Education .... Dr. April BEDFORD
57 Dean Schl Visual Media & Perf Arts .... Dr. Maria A. CONELLI
83 Act Dean Schl Humanities & Soc Sci .... Dr. Kenneth GOULD
50 Dean School of Business .... Dr. Wille HOPKINS
81 Dean Schl Natural & Behav Sciences .... Dr. Kleanthis PSARRIS
114 Assoc VP Budget & Planning/CFO .... Mr. Alan GILBERT
18 Asst VP Facilities Plng/Operations .... Mr. Francis X. FITZGERALD
13 Asst VP Info Technology Svcs/CIO .... Mr. Mark GOLD
43 Int AVP Legl Affairs & Lab Relation .... Mr. Michael HEWITT
50 Asst Dean School of Bussiness .... Dr. Susanne G. SCOTT
20 Asst Dean Academic Affairs .... Dr. Geraldine FARIA
35 Dean for Student Affairs .... Ms. Vannessa GREEN
58 Asst Dean Grad Center for Worker Ed .... Dr. Lucas RUBIN
08 Assoc Dean Libr/Ex Dir Acd Inf Tech .... Ms. Mary MALLERY
09 Sr Dir Inst Plng/Rsrch/Assessment .... Dr. Michael AYERS
25 Dir Research & Sponsored Programs .... Ms. Sabrina CERERZO
108 Director Academic Assessment .... Dr. Fredrik DEBOER
29 Director of Alumni Affairs .... Ms. Lisa DICCE
06 Registrar .... Mr. Richard FELTMAN
41 Dir Rec Intramurals/Intercol Athl .... Mr. Bruce FILOSA
36 Dir Magner Career Ctr/Internships ..... Ms. Natalia GUARIN-KLEIN
102 Assoc Exec Director of Foundation .... Ms. Beth F. LEVINE
37 Assoc Dir Fin Aid/Title IV Com Mang ...... Mr. Antonio MARRERO
37 Assoc Dir Fin Aid/Syst & Operations .. Mr. Marcus RICHARDSON
92 Dir Scholars Pgm & Honors Academy .... Dr. Lisa SCHWEBEL
07 Senior Dir Admissions & Recruitment .... Ms. Penelope TERRY
22 Exc Chf Diversit & Spc Asst to Pres .... Tony THOMAS
88 Dir Feirstein Grad School of Cinema .... Mr. Jonathan WACKS
19 Director Safety & Security .... Mr. Donald A. WENZ
15 Exc Dir Human Resources Services .... Ms. Renita WHITE SIMMONS
104 Senr Dir Intnation Ed & Global Eng .... Dr. Alice G. BIER
38 Director Personal Counseling .... Dr. Gregory KUHLMAN
90 Dir Acad Information Technologies .... Mr. Howard SPIVAK
96 Dir Procurement & Support Services ...... Ms. Madonna CHARLES

*City University of New York The City College (F)

160 Convent Avenue, New York NY 10031-9198
County: New York　FICE Identification: 002688
Unit ID: 190567
Telephone: (212) 650-7000　Carnegie Class: Masters/L
FAX Number: (212) 650-7680　Calendar System: Semester
URL: www.ccny.cuny.edu
Established: 1847　Annual Undergrad Tuition & Fees (In-District): $6,689
Enrollment: 15,778　Coed
Affiliation or Control: State/Local　IRS Status: 501(c)3
Highest Offering: Doctorate
Accreditation: M, ARCPA, CAEPN, CLPSY, CS, ENG, LSAR, #MED

02 Interim President .... Dr. Vincent G. BOUDREAU
05 Int Provost/Sr VP Academic Affairs .... Dr. Mary E. DRISCOLL
30 Int Dir Develop & Inst Advancement .... Ms. Dee Dee MOZELESKI
29 Executive Director Alumni Affairs .... Mr. Donald K. JORDAN
10 Vice Pres Finance & CFO .... Mr. Felix LAM
84 Assistant Vice President CUNYfirst .... Ms. Celia P. LLOYD
18 AVP Facilities Mgmt .... Mr. David ROBINSON
86 VP Governmental/Community Affairs .. Ms. Karen WITHERSPOON
32 Dean of Student Development .... Ms. Wendy J. THORNTON
13 AVP Information Technology/CIO .... Mr. Kenneth IHRER
26 Sr Advisor to Pres for External Aff .... Ms. Dee Dee MOZELESKI
63 Dean Sophie Davis Sch of BioMed Ed ..... Dr. Maurizio TREVISAN
54 Dean of Engineering .... Dr. Gilda BARABINO
53 Acting Dean School of Education .... Ms. Gretchen JOHNSON
47 Acting Dean School of Architecture .... Mr. Gordon GEBERT
88 Dean of CWE-Div of Interdiscip Stds . Dr. Juan Carlos MERCADO
81 Dean of Science .... Dr. Tony LISS
82 Acting Dean Colin Powell School .... Dr. Kevin FOSTER
79 Dean of Humanities & The Arts .... Mr. Erec KOCH
43 Executive Counsel to the President .... Mr. Paul F. OCCHIOGROSSO
15 Asst Vice Pres of Human Resources .... Mr. John SIDERAKIS
23 Exec Director Health and Wellness .... Ms. Teresa WALKER
06 Senior Registrar .... Vacant
35 Exec Dir of Student Affairs at CWE .... Ms. Sophia DEMETRIOU
08 Acting Chief Librarian .... Dr. Charles STEWART
25 Dir for Grants & Sponsored Pgms .... Dr. Alan SHIH
09 Director of Institutional Research .... Mr. Edward SILVERMAN
37 Director of Financial Aid .... Ms. Arshaw RAMKARAN
27 Public Relations Coordinator .... Ms. Ashley AROCHO
28 Chf Diversity Ofcr/Dean Faculty Rel .... Ms. Michele BAPTISTE
90 Computer Systems Manager Level IV .... Mr. Curtis RIAS
36 Director of Career Services .... Ms. Katie NAILLER
19 Exec Dir Public Safety/Security .... Mr. Pat MORENA
24 Director of Instructional Media .... Mr. Nana ABEYIE
07 Exec Director of Admissions .... Mr. Joseph FANTOZZI
96 Director of Business Services .... Ms. Sharon RUSSELL

*College of Staten Island CUNY (A)

2800 Victory Boulevard, Staten Island NY 10314-6600
County: Richmond FICE Identification: 002698
Unit ID: 190558
Telephone: (718) 982-2000 Carnegie Class: Masters/L
FAX Number: N/A Calendar System: Semester
URL: www.csi.cuny.edu
Established: 1976 Annual Undergrad Tuition & Fees (In-District): $6,890
Enrollment: 13,701 Coed
Affiliation or Control: State/Local IRS Status: 501(c)3
Highest Offering: Doctorate
Accreditation: M, ADNUR, CAEPN, CS, ENG, ENGT, MT, NUR, PTA, SW

02 President .... Dr. William J. FRITZ
05 Sr VP Acad Affairs/Provost .... Dr. Gary W. REICHARD
10 VP for Finance and Administration .... Mr. Ira PERSKY
32 VP Student & Enrollment Services .... Ms. Jennifer S. BORRERO
111 VP Inst Advance/External Affairs .... Ms. Khatmeh OSSEIRAN-HANNA
21 AVP for Finance & Budget .... Mr. Carlos A. SERRANO
86 VP Econ Dev/Cont Stds/Govt Rels .... Mr. Kenichi IWAMA
35 AVP Student Services/Dean Students . Dr. Christopher GIORDANO
20 Int Assoc Provost Undergrad Studies .... Dr. Ralf PEETZ
18 AVP Campus Planning/Facilities Mgmt .... Mr. Cameron CHRISTENSEN
13 AVP & CIO Info Technology Services .... Dr. Patricia KAHN
26 AVP Inst Advance/External Affairs .... Vacant
81 Dean of Science & Technology .... Dr. Vivian INCERA
79 Dean Humanities & Social Sci .... Dr. Nan M. SUSSMAN
08 Assoc Dean/Chief Librarian .... Dr. Wilma JONES
43 Interim Legal Counsel to President .... Ms. Meryl KAYNARD
28 Director of Diversity & Compliance ..... Ms. Danielle E. DIMITROV
50 Dean of School of Business .... Dr. Susan L. HOLAK
76 Interim Dean School of Health Sci .... Dr. Maureen BECKER
53 Dean School of Education .... Dr. Kenneth GOLD
58 Assoc Provost Grad Studies/Research .... Dr. Margaret-Ellen (Mel) PIPE
15 Exec Dir Human Resource/Labor Des .... Ms. Hope BERTE

*City University of New York Graduate Center (B)

365 Fifth Avenue, New York NY 10016-4309
County: New York FICE Identification: 004765
Unit ID: 190576
Telephone: (212) 817-7000 Carnegie Class: DU-Highest
FAX Number: N/A Calendar System: Semester
URL: www.gc.cuny.edu
Established: 1961 Annual Undergrad Tuition & Fees (In-District): N/A
Enrollment: 6,954 Coed
Affiliation or Control: State/Local IRS Status: 501(c)3
Highest Offering: Doctorate
Accreditation: M, AUD, CAHIIM, CLPSY, @DIETI, JOUR, NURSE, PH, SCPSY

02 President .... Dr. Chase F. ROBINSON
05 Provost and Sr VP .... Dr. Joy CONNOLLY
10 Sr VP Finance and Administration .... Dr. Sebastian T. PERSICO
13 VP Information Technology .... Mr. Robert D. CAMPBELL
30 VP Institutional Advancement .... Mr. Jay GOLAN
26 VP Communications .... Ms. Lori DUGGAN GOLD
32 VP Student Affairs .... Mr. Matthew G. SCHOENGOOD
21 Asst Vice President Finance .... Mr. Stuart B. SHOR
81 Dean for Science .... Dr. Joshua BRUMBERG
20 Assoc Provost & Dean Academic Affs .... Dr. David OLAN
08 Chief Librarian .... Ms. Polly THISTLETHWAITE
100 Chief of Staff .... Ms. Jane HERBERT
19 Exec Dir Security & Public Safety .... Mr. John FLAHERTY
15 Exec Director of Human Resources .... Ms. Ella KISELYUK
46 Exec Dir Research & Sponsored Pgm .... Dr. Edith GONZALEZ
37 Exec Dir Fellowships/Financial Aid .... Ms. Phyllis SCHULZ
20 Exec Director of Academic Affairs .... Ms. Stacie TIONGSON
06 Dir Stdnt Services/Senior Registrar .... Mr. Vincent J. DELUCA
88 Director of Special Events .... Ms. Harlisha HAMM
85 Director International Students .... Ms. Linda ASARO
09 Dir Institutional Research & Effect .... Ms. Jennifer KOBRIN
43 Legal Counsel & Labor Designee .... Ms. Lynette M. PHILLIPS
18 Director Facilities .... Mr. Charles SCOTT
22 Chief Diversity Officer .... Ms. Edith RIVERA
07 Director Admissions .... Mr. Les GRIBBEN
25 Director Sponsored Research .... Ms. Hilry FISHER
88 Director Building Design/Exhibits .... Mr. Ray RING
28 Executive Officer Educ Opp/Div Pgm .... Dr. Herman BENNETT
38 Dir Well Ctr/Psy Coun Svc/Adult Dev .... Dr. Robert HATCHER
35 Director Student Affairs .... Ms. Sharon LERNER
23 Director Student Health Services .... Ms. Adraenne BOWE
96 Director of Purchasing .... Mr. Ronald PAYNTER
04 Administrative Asst to President .... Ms. Alexandra ROBINSON

*City University of New York Herbert H. Lehman College (C)

250 Bedford Park Boulevard W, Bronx NY 10468-1589
County: Bronx FICE Identification: 007022
Unit ID: 190637
Telephone: (718) 960-8000 Carnegie Class: Masters/L
FAX Number: N/A Calendar System: Semester
URL: www.lehman.cuny.edu
Established: 1968 Annual Undergrad Tuition & Fees (In-District): $6,812
Enrollment: 12,807 Coed
Affiliation or Control: State/Local IRS Status: 501(c)3
Highest Offering: Master's
Accreditation: M, CACREP, CAEPN, DIETD, DIETI, NURSE, SP, SW

02 President .... Dr. Jose L. CRUZ
100 Deputy to President Strategic Init .... Ms. Gladys MALDOON
05 Int Provost/SVP Academic Affairs .... Dr. Harriet FAYNE
84 Assoc Provost/VP Enroll Mgmt .... Dr. Reine SARMIENTO
10 Vice Pres Administration/Finance .... Mr. Vincent W. CLARK
111 Vice Pres Institutional Advancement .... Vacant
32 Vice President Student Affairs .... Mr. Jose MAGDALENO
13 Vice Pres/Chief Info Officer .... Mr. Ronald BERGMANN
79 Dean School of Arts/Humanities .... Dr. Deirdre PETTIPIECE
83 Dean School of Nat & Soc Sci .... Dr. Gautam SEN
20 Vice Provost Academic Programs .... Dr. Stefan BECKER
76 Dean Sch Health Sci/Hum Svc & Nurs .... Dr. William LATIMER
51 Int Dean School of Cont Ed/Prof St .... Dr. Jane MACKILLOP
53 Int Dean School of Education .... Dr. Deborah SHANLEY
08 Chief Librarian .... Dr. Kenneth SCHLESINGER
43 Counsel to Pres/Labor Designee .... Mr. Dennis DACOSTA
28 Chief Diversity Officer .... Ms. Dawn EWING-MORGAN
18 Asst VP Campus Planning/Facilities .... Ms. Rene M. ROTOLO
35 Dean of Student Affairs .... Dr. Stanley BAZILE
21 Asst VP for Financial Operations .... Ms. Gina HARWOOD
14 Asst VP Information Technology .... Ms. Ediltrudys RUIZ
06 Senior Registrar .... Ms. Yvette ROSARIO
07 Director of Admissions .... Ms. Laurie AUSTIN
29 Director of Alumni Relations .... Ms. Maria-Cristina NECULA
88 Director of the Art Gallery .... Mr. Bartholomew F. BLAND
36 Director Career Services .... Ms. Nancy A. CINTRON
38 Director Counseling Center .... Vacant
37 Director Financial Aid .... Ms. Alvira SENESE
89 Director Freshman Year Initiative .... Dr. Steven WYCKOFF
46 Dir Research & Sponsored Programs .... Ms. Saeedah HICKMAN
92 Director of Honors College Program .... Dr. Gary SCHWARTZ
15 Director of Human Resources .... Mr. Eric WASHINGTON
09 Director of Institutional Research .... Vacant
121 Dir Instruct Support Services Pgm .... Ms. Althea FORDE
27 Dir Media Relations & Publications .... Mr. Joseph TIRELLA
88 Director Performing Arts Center .... Ms. Eva BORNSTEIN
19 Director of Public Safety .... Mr. Fausto RAMIREZ
96 Director of Purchasing .... Ms. Andrea PINNOCK
41 Athletic Director .... Dr. Martin ZWIREN
40 Bookstore Manager .... Ms. Caitlin NEWSOME
120 Dir Online Education/E-learning .... Dr. Olena ZHADKO

*Hostos Community College-City University of New York (D)

500 Grand Concourse, Bronx NY 10451-5323
County: Bronx FICE Identification: 008611
Unit ID: 190585
Telephone: (718) 518-4300 Carnegie Class: Assoc/HT-High Trad
FAX Number: (718) 518-4294 Calendar System: Semester
URL: www.hostos.cuny.edu
Established: 1970 Annual Undergrad Tuition & Fees (In-District): $5,208
Enrollment: 7,371 Coed
Affiliation or Control: State/Local IRS Status: 501(c)3
Highest Offering: Associate Degree
Accreditation: M, DH, RAD

02 President .... Dr. David GOMEZ
05 Provost/VP for Academic Affairs .... Dr. Christine MANGINO
10 Senior Vice Pres for Admin/Finance .... Ms. Esther RODRIGUEZ-CHARDAVOYNE
32 VP Student Development/Enroll Mgmt .... Mr. Nathaniel CRUZ
100 Deputy to President .... Ms. Dolly MARTINEZ
111 Vice Pres Institutional Advancement .... Ms. Ana MARTINEZ
103 VP for Cont Educ & Workforce Dev .... Dr. Carlos MOLINA
13 Asst Vice Pres Info Technology .... Mr. Varun SEHGAL
114 Finance/Budget Director .... Ms. Fanny DUMANCELA
18 Exec Dir Facil Plng Des Mgmt .... Ms. Elizabeth FRIEDMAN
04 Associate Dean for Community Rels .. Ms. Ana I. GARCIA-REYES
20 Asst Dean of Academic Affairs .... Mr. Felix CARDONA
35 Assistant Dean of Student Life .... Ms. Johanna GOMEZ
43 Exec Counsel & Labor Designee .... Mr. Eugene SOHN
26 Dir of Publications Development .... Vacant
38 Director of Counseling .... Ms. Linda ALEXANDER-WALLACE
15 Director Human Resources .... Ms. Shirley SHEVACH
86 Dir Government/External Affairs .... Mr. Joshua RIVERA
06 Registrar .... Ms. Nelida PASTORIZA
07 Director of Admissions .... Mr. Roland VELEZ
37 Director of Financial Aid .... Ms. Leslie KING
19 Director of Campus Security .... Mr. Arnaldo BERNABE
25 Director Grants & Contracts .... Ms. Lourdes TORRES
09 Director Institutional Research .... Mr. Piotr KOCIK
08 Head Librarian .... Ms. Madeline FORD
22 Chief Diversity Officer .... Ms. Lauren GRETINA
29 Dir Development/Alumni Relations .... Ms. Nydia EDGECOMBE
36 Director Student Career Programs .... Ms. Lisanette ROSARIO
35 Director Student Activities .... Mr. Jerry ROSA
96 Director of Procurement .... Mr. Kevin CARMINE
28 Director of Diversity .... Vacant

*City University of New York Hunter College (E)

695 Park Avenue, New York NY 10065
County: New York FICE Identification: 002689
Unit ID: 190594
Telephone: (212) 772-4000 Carnegie Class: Masters/L
FAX Number: N/A Calendar System: Semester
URL: www.hunter.cuny.edu
Established: 1870 Annual Undergrad Tuition & Fees (In-District): $6,782
Enrollment: 22,918 Coed
Affiliation or Control: State/Local IRS Status: 501(c)3
Highest Offering: Doctorate
Accreditation: M, AUD, CACREP, CAEPN, CYTO, DIETD, DIETI, ENGR, NURSE, PLNG, PTA, SP, SW

02 President .... Ms. Jennifer J. RAAB
100 Chief of Staff/Exec Asst to Pres .... Ms. Anne LYTLE
10 Vice Pres/Chief Operating Officer .... Mr. Robert PIGNATELLO
05 Provost/Vice Pres Academic Affairs .... Mr. Lon KAUFMAN
32 VP Student Affs/Dean of Stdnts .... Ms. Eija AYRAVAINEN
43 Counsel to the President .... Ms. Laura HERTZOG
30 Asst VP Institutional Advancement .... Ms. Barbara GUNN
26 Asst VP & Dir Communication .... Vacant
13 Asst Vice Pres Information Tech .... Mr. Mitch AHLBAUM
21 Executive Director Business Svcs .... Ms. Livia CANGEMI
21 Asst Vice Pres Business Services .... Ms. Patricia KETTERER
35 Asst Vice Pres of Student Affairs .... Vacant
18 Asst Vice Pres of Facilities .... Mr. James GLEBA
28 Dean Diversity and Compliance .... Mr. John ROSE
49 Dean School of Arts & Sciences .... Dr. Andrew POLSKY
70 Acting Dean School of Social Work .... Ms. Mary CAVANAUGH
53 Dean School of Education .... Mr. Michael MIDDLETON
66 Dean School of Nursing .... Dr. Gail C. MCCAIN
08 Acting Chief Librarian .... Mr. Clay WILLIAMS
06 Registrar .... Vacant
09 Director of Institutional Research .... Ms. Joan LAMBE
15 Director of Human Resources .... Ms. Galia GALANSKY
35 Director Student Advising .... Mr. Bryan MAASJO
36 Director Student Placement .... Ms. Susan MCCARTY
37 Director Student Financial Aid .... Ms. Delika DANIELS
29 Director Alumni Relations .... Mr. Jorge DEJESUS
19 College Security Director .... Mr. Joseph FOELSCH
07 Director of Admissions .... Ms. Lori JANOWSKI
104 Director Study Abroad .... Ms. Elizabeth SACHS
108 Dir Institutional Assessment .... Ms. Maureen ERICKSON
41 Athletic Director .... Ms. Terry WANSART
84 Dir Enrollment Mgmt/Recruit .... Ms. Sarah FARSAD

*City University of New York John Jay College of Criminal Justice (F)

524 West 59th Street, New York NY 10019-1093
County: New York FICE Identification: 002693
Unit ID: 190600
Telephone: (212) 237-8000 Carnegie Class: Masters/L
FAX Number: (212) 237-8607 Calendar System: Semester
URL: www.jjay.cuny.edu
Established: 1964 Annual Undergrad Tuition & Fees (In-District): $6,810
Enrollment: 14,732 Coed
Affiliation or Control: State/Local IRS Status: 501(c)3
Highest Offering: Master's
Accreditation: M, CLPSY, FEPAC, SPAA

02 President .... Mr. Jeremy TRAVIS
05 Prov/Sr Vice Pres Academic Affairs .... Dr. Jane BOWERS
32 Vice Pres Student Affairs .... Ms. Lynette COOK-FRANCIS
26 Vice Pres Marketing/Dev .... Ms. Jayne ROSENGARTEN
84 Interim VP Enrollment Management .... Ms. Dana DAVIES
04 Executive Assoc to President .... Ms. Raeanne DAVIS
100 Chief of Staff .... Ms. Rulisa GALLOWAY-PERRY
58 Assoc Prov & Dean of Grad Studies .... Dr. Anne LOPES
46 Associate Provost/Dean of Research .... Dr. Anthony CARPI
32 Asst VP and Dean of Students ... Dr. Michael MARTINEZ-SACHS
11 Assistant VP for Administration .... Mr. Raj SINGH
20 Assoc Prov & Dean of Undergrad Stds .... Dr. Dara BRYNE
10 Assistant VP for Finance .... Mr. Mark FLOWER
08 Chief Librarian .... Dr. Lawrence SULLIVAN
37 Director of Financial Aid .... Ms. Sylvia CRESPO-LOPEZ
30 Director of Development .... Ms. Kathryn COUSINS
35 Director Student Activities .... Ms. Danielle OFFICER
25 Director of Funded Research .... Ms. Susy MENDES
09 Director of Institutional Research .... Mr. Ricardo ANZALDUA
89 Director of First Year Experience .... Ms. Katalin SZUR
06 Registrar .... Mr. Daniel MATOS
88 Director of CRJ Research & Eval .... Dr. Jeffrey BUTTS
07 Director of Admissions .... Mr. Vincent PAPANDREA
13 Chief Information Officer .... Mr. Joe LAUB
19 Director of Public Safety .... Vacant
24 Director of Media Services .... Vacant
27 Chief Communications Officer .... Ms. Rama SUDHAKAR
36 Director of Career Development Svcs .... Mr. Will SIMPKINS
38 Director of Counseling .... Dr. Gerard BRYANT
41 Athletic Director .... Ms. Carol KASHOW
21 Associate Business Officer .... Ms. Emily KARP
29 Director Alumni Relations .... Ms. Jerylle KEMP
96 Director of Purchasing .... Mr. Daniel DOLAN
88 Senior International Officer .... Ms. Mayra NIEVES
18 Director Facilities/Physical Plant .... Mr. Anthony BRACCO
43 Assistant Vice President & Counsel .... Ms. Marjorie SINGER
86 Exec Dir of External Relations .... Ms. Mindy BOCKSTEIN
121 Director of Academic Advisement .... Dr. Sumaya VILLANUEVA
22 Int Dir of Accessibility Services .... Ms. Malanie CLARKE
104 Director Study Abroad .... Mr. Kenneth YANES
28 Director of Diversity .... Ms. Silvia MONTALBAN
39 Director Student Housing .... Ms. Jessica CARSON
102 Dir Foundation/Corporate Relations .... Ms. Kathryn COUSINS
106 Dir Online Education/E-learning .... Ms. Judith CAHN
15 Director Personnel Services .... Vacant

† The Clinical Psychology PhD is awarded through the CUNY Graduate Center.

*City University of New York Kingsborough Community College (A)

2001 Oriental Boulevard, Brooklyn NY 11235-2333
County: Kings FICE Identification: 002694
Unit ID: 190619
Telephone: (718) 368-5109 Carnegie Class: Assoc/HT-Mix Trad/Non
FAX Number: (718) 368-5003 Calendar System: Other
URL: www.kbcc.cuny.edu
Established: 1963 Annual Undergrad Tuition & Fees (In-District): $5,256
Enrollment: 17,032 Coed
Affiliation or Control: State/Local IRS Status: 501(c)3
Highest Offering: Associate Degree
Accreditation: M, ADNUR, EMT, PTAA, SURGT

02 President ... Mr. Farley HERZEK
05 Vice Pres Academic Affs/Provost ... Dr. Joanne RUSSELL
10 Vice Pres Finance/Administration ... Mr. Eduardo RIOS
100 Executive Chief of Staff ... Dr. Tasheka SUTTON-YOUNG
32 Vice Pres of Student Affairs ... Mr. Peter COHEN
51 Dean Continuing Education ... Ms. Christine BECKNER
35 Director of Student Life ... Ms. Maria PATESTAS
20 Vice Pres Academic Administration ... Vacant
84 Vice Pres Enrollment Management ... Mr. Thomas FRIEBEL
09 Vice Pres Inst Effectiveness ... Dr. Richard FOX
30 Vice Pres Institutional Advancement ... Dr. Elizabeth BASILE
15 Director of Human Resources ... Ms. Micheline DRISCOLL
22 Dir Affirmative Action/EO Officer ... Ms. Victoria AJIBADE
19 Director of Security & Safety ... Vacant
08 Chief Librarian ... Ms. Josephine MURPHY
06 Registrar ... Mr. Michael KLEIN
18 Campus Facilities Officer ... Mr. Anthony CORAZZA
37 Financial Aid Officer ... Mr. Wayne H. HAREWOOD
13 Chief Information Officer ... Mr. Asif HUSSAIN
36 Dir Career Couns/Placement/Transfer ... Vacant
24 Director of Educational Media ... Mr. Michael ROSSON
41 Director of Athletics ... Mr. Damani THOMAS
96 Director of Purchasing ... Ms. Lynn RELAY
29 Director Alumni Relations ... Ms. Laura GLAZIER-SMITH
38 Director Student Counseling ... Ms. Dasha GORINSHTEYN
21 Business Manager ... Vacant

*LaGuardia Community College/ City University of New York (B)

31-10 Thomson Avenue, Long Island City NY 11101-3083
County: Queens FICE Identification: 010051
Unit ID: 190628
Telephone: (718) 482-7200 Carnegie Class: Assoc/HT-High Trad
FAX Number: (718) 609-2000 Calendar System: Semester
URL: www.lagcc.cuny.edu
Established: 1971 Annual Undergrad Tuition & Fees (In-District): $5,218
Enrollment: 19,582 Coed
Affiliation or Control: State/Local IRS Status: 501(c)3
Highest Offering: Associate Degree
Accreditation: M, ADNUR, DIETT, EMT, OTA, PTAA

02 President ... Dr. Gail O. MELLOW
05 Provost and Senior Vice President ... Dr. Paul ARCARIO
04 Executive Associate to President ... Ms. Rosemary TALMADGE
11 Vice President of Administration ... Mr. Shahir ERFAN
30 VP of Institutional Advancement ... Ms. Susan LYDDON
13 Vice Pres Information Technology ... Mr. Henry SALTIEL
51 Vice Pres Adult/Continuing Educ ... Ms. Jane SCHULMAN
20 Assoc Dean for Academic Affairs ... Mr. Bret EYNON
84 Asst Dean Enrollment Services ... Ms. Nireata SEALS
18 Exec Dir Facilities Mgmt/Planning ... Mr. Kenneth CAMPANELLI
15 Exec Director of Human Resources ... Vacant
10 Exec Director Finance & Business ... Mr. Thomas HLADEK
86 Government Relations Manager ... Ms. Claudia CHAN
08 Chief Librarian ... Ms. Scott WHITE
37 Director Student Financial Services ... Ms. Gail BAKSH-JARRETT
103 Asst Dean of Workforce Development ... Ms. Francesca FIORE
07 Director of Admissions ... Ms. LaVora DESVIGNE
26 Dir Marketing/Communications ... Mr. Charles ELIAS
21 Associate Business Manager ... Ms. Carmen LUONG
36 Director Employment/Career Svc Ctr ... Ms. Claudia BALDONEDO
96 Director Procurement & Contracts ... Mr. Mitchell HENDERSON
20 Assoc Dean for Academic Affairs ... Ms. Ann FEIBEL

*City University of New York Medgar Evers College (C)

1650 Bedford Avenue, Brooklyn NY 11225-2010
County: Kings FICE Identification: 010097
Unit ID: 190646
Telephone: (718) 270-4900 Carnegie Class: Bac-Diverse
FAX Number: (718) 270-5126 Calendar System: Semester
URL: www.mec.cuny.edu
Established: 1970 Annual Undergrad Tuition & Fees (In-District): $6,756
Enrollment: 6,765 Coed
Affiliation or Control: State/Local IRS Status: 501(c)3
Highest Offering: Baccalaureate
Accreditation: M, ACBSP, ADNUR, CAEPN, NUR, SW

02 President ... Dr. Rudolph F. CREW
11 Chief Operating Officer ... Mr. Jerald POSMAN
05 Provost/Senior Vice President ... Dr. Augustine OKEREKE
10 VP Finance & Administration ... Ms. Jacqueline CLARK
51 Interim Dean Sch Prof & Comm Dev ... Dr. Evelyn CASTRO
50 Dean of the School of Business ... Dr. Jo-Ann ROLLE
49 Interim Dean Sch of Lib Arts & Educ ... Dr. Sheilah PAUL
72 Dean School of Science/Health/Tech ... Dr. Terrance BLACKMAN
100 Chief of Staff ... Ms. Lakisha MURRAY
43 Counsel to President ... Ms. Vanessa VAZQUEZ-FRANK
04 Exec Assistant to the President ... Mrs. Lisa ANDERSON
22 Director of Affirmative Action ... Ms. Sylvia KINARD
06 Registrar ... Ms. Tatiana MEJIC
13 Interim Asst VP/CIO ... Mr. Troy HAHN
37 Director of Financial Aid ... Mr. Nigel THOMPSON
38 Director of Counseling ... Dr. JoAnn JOYNER-GRAHAM
19 Director of Security ... Mr. Victor STEVENS
41 Director of Athletics ... Ms. Renee BOSTIC
25 Grants Officer ... Mr. Chi KOON
89 Dir Freshman Year Program ... Ms. Nicole BERRY
55 Director Evening/Weekend Programs ... Ms. Yvette WALL
36 Sr Director of Career Development ... Vacant
30 Vice Pres Inst Advancement ... Mr. Jonathan SANDVILLE
18 Supt of Buildings & Grounds ... Mr. Dave ADEBANJO
84 Exec Dir Enrollment Management ... Mrs. Shannon CLARKE-ANDERSON
29 Director of Alumni Relations ... Mrs. Tara REGIST-TOMLINSON
07 Director Admissions ... Ms. Jo-Ann JACOBS
09 Director of Institutional Research ... Dr. Eva CHAN
08 Chief Librarian ... Dr. Alexei OULANOV
66 Chair Dept of Nursing ... Dr. Hazel SANDERSON
50 Chair Dept of Business Admin ... Ms. Sambhavi LAKSHMINARAYANAN
53 Chair Department of Education ... Dr. Rupam SARAN
60 Interim Chair Dept of Mass Comm ... Dr. Clinton CRAWFORD
88 Chair Department Accounting ... Dr. Rosemary WILLIAMS
81 Chair Department of Mathematics ... Dr. Jean JEAN - MICHEL
77 Chair Dept Physical/Computer Sci ... Dr. Leon JOHNSON
81 Chair Department of Biology ... Dr. Carolle BOLNET
83 Chair Dept of Social/Behavioral Sci ... Dr. Owen BROWN
88 Chair Department of Psychology ... Dr. Hollie JONES
88 Chair Dept of Public Administration ... Dr. Wallace FORD
13 Chair Computer Info Systems ... Dr. Orandel ROBOTHAM
88 Chair Department Economics/Finance ... Dr. Emmanuel EGBE
88 Chair Department of English ... Ms. Brenda GREENE
88 Chair Dept of Philosophy & Religion ... Dr. Vivaldi JEAN MARIE
88 Chair Dept of Foreign Languages ... Dr. Maria-Luisa RUIZ
35 Director of Student Life ... Mr. Larry MARTIN
15 Executive Dir of Human Resources ... Ms. Tanya ISAACS
88 Director of Bursar ... Ms. Thais PILIERI
28 Chief Diversity Officer ... Dr. Sylvia G. KINARD
104 Director Study Abroad ... Mr. Eugene PURSOO
86 Director Government Relations ... Ms. Jennifer JAMES

*New York City College of Technology/City University of New York (D)

300 Jay Street, Brooklyn NY 11201-1909
County: Kings FICE Identification: 002696
Unit ID: 190655
Telephone: (718) 260-5000 Carnegie Class: Bac-Diverse
FAX Number: (718) 260-5198 Calendar System: Semester
URL: www.citytech.cuny.edu
Established: 1946 Annual Undergrad Tuition & Fees (In-District): $6,669
Enrollment: 17,424 Coed
Affiliation or Control: State/Local IRS Status: 501(c)3
Highest Offering: Baccalaureate
Accreditation: M, ADNUR, CAEPN, CSHSE, DH, DT, ENGT, NUR, OPD, RAD

02 President ... Dr. Russell K. HOTZLER
05 Provost ... Dr. Bonne AUGUST
10 Vice Pres Finance/Administration ... Dr. Miguel CAIROL
84 VP Enrollment/Student Affairs ... Dr. Marcela ARMOZA
20 Associate Provost Academic Affairs ... Dr. Pamela BROWN
22 Counsel/Affirmative Action Officer ... Ms. Gilen CHAN
07 Director of Admissions ... Ms. Alexis CHACONIS
06 Registrar ... Ms. Tasha RHODES
37 Director of Financial Aid ... Ms. Sandra HIGGINS
08 Librarian ... Ms. Maura SMALE
13 Director of Computer Center ... Ms. Rita UDDIN
107 Dean of Professional Studies ... Mr. David SMITH
72 Dean of Technology ... Mr. Kevin HOM
49 Dean of Arts & Science ... Mr. Justin VASQUEZ-PORITZ
51 Dean Continuing Education ... Dr. Carol SONNENBLICK
55 Director Evening Session ... Mr. James LAP
15 Director of Human Resources ... Ms. Sandra GORDON
25 Grants Officer ... Ms. Barbara BURKE
24 Director of Inst Tech/Media Svcs ... Ms. Karen LUNDSTREM
09 Director of Assessment ... Dr. Tammie CUMMING
26 Exec Dir Public Relations ... Ms. Faith CORBETT
29 Director Alumni Relations ... Vacant
38 Director Student Counseling ... Ms. Cynthia BINK
96 Director of Purchasing ... Mr. Wayne ROBINSON
18 Chief Facilities/Physical Plant ... Mr. James VASQUEZ
30 Chief Development/Spec Asst to Pres ... Dr. Stephen SOIFFER
21 Executive Dir of Business Mgmt ... Mr. Wayne ROBINSON

*City University of New York Queens College (E)

65-30 Kissena Boulevard, Flushing NY 11367-1597
County: Queens FICE Identification: 002690
Unit ID: 190664
Telephone: (718) 997-5000 Carnegie Class: Masters/L
FAX Number: (718) 997-5598 Calendar System: Semester
URL: www.qc.cuny.edu
Established: 1937 Annual Undergrad Tuition & Fees (In-District): $6,938
Enrollment: 19,520 Coed
Affiliation or Control: State/Local IRS Status: 501(c)3
Highest Offering: Master's
Accreditation: M, AAFCS, CAEP, CAEPN, CLPSY, DIETD, DIETI, LAW, LIB, SP

02 President ... Dr. Felix V. MATOS RODRIGUEZ
05 Provost ... Dr. Elizabeth HENDREY
10 Vice Pres Finance/Administration ... Mr. William KELLER
32 Vice President for Student Affairs ... Dr. Adam ROCKMAN
26 VP Communications ... Mr. Jay HERSHENSON
84 VP Enrollment & Retention ... Mr. Richard ALVAREZ
111 VP Institutional Advancement ... Ms. Laurie DORF
43 AVP General Counsel/Chief of Staff ... Ms. Glenda GRACE
27 Director of Communications ... Vacant
91 AVP Information Tech ... Ms. Claudia COLBERT
20 Assoc Provost Academic Plng/Pgms ... Dr. Steven SCHWARZ
21 AVP Finance ... Ms. Jeanne DEMASTERS
88 Assistant Provost ... Dr. Eva FERNANDEZ
57 Dean Arts & Humanities ... Dr. William MCCLURE
81 Dean Math & Natural Sciences ... Dr. Susan A. ROTENBERG
53 Dean Education ... Dr. Craig MICHAELS
58 Dean of Research/Grad Studies ... Vacant
83 Dean Social Sciences ... Dr. Michael WOLFE
15 AVP Human Resources ... Ms. Lee KELLY
41 AVP Athletics ... Ms. China JUDE
88 Director of Events ... Ms. Sylvia HERNANDEZ
18 AVP Facilities ... Mr. Zeco KRCIC
07 Executive Director Admissions ... Mr. Vincent ANGRISANI
38 Dir of Counseling and Advisement ... Dr. Barbara MOORE
06 Director Registrar's Office ... Mr. Matthew CASANOVA
09 Dean of Inst Effectiveness ... Dr. Cheryl LITTMAN
08 Chief Librarian ... Mr. Manuel SANUDO
37 Director Financial Aid Services ... Mr. Clifford COULOTTE
29 Manager Alumni Affairs ... Ms. Kami CRARY
19 Director Security/Safety ... Mr. Pedro PINEIRO
22 Dir Affirmative Action/Diversity ... Ms. Cynthia ROUNTREE
96 Director of Purchasing ... Mr. Surinder VIRK
86 AVP Ext Affairs & Govt Relations ... Mr. Jeffrey ROSENSTOCK
26 Director of Marketing ... Vacant
100 Deputy Chief of Staff ... Dr. Odalys DIAZPINEIRO

† The Clinical Psychology PhD is awarded through the CUNY Graduate Center.

*City University of New York Queensborough Community College (F)

222-05 56th Avenue, Bayside NY 11364-1497
County: Queens FICE Identification: 002697
Unit ID: 190673
Telephone: (718) 631-6262 Carnegie Class: Assoc/HT-High Trad
FAX Number: N/A Calendar System: Semester
URL: www.qcc.cuny.edu
Established: 1958 Annual Undergrad Tuition & Fees (In-District): $5,210
Enrollment: 15,493 Coed
Affiliation or Control: State/Local IRS Status: 501(c)3
Highest Offering: Associate Degree
Accreditation: M, ACBSP, ADNUR, ART, ENGT, THEA

02 President ... Dr. Diane CALL
11 Sr Vice Pres/Chief Operating Ofcr ... Ms. Sherri NEWCOMB
05 Vice Pres Academic Affairs ... Dr. Timothy LYNCH
10 Vice Pres Finance & Admin ... Mr. William FAULKNER
30 Vice Pres Institutional Advancement ... Ms. Rosemary S. ZINS
32 Vice President Student Affairs ... Mr. Michel HODGE
15 Dean Human Resource/Labor Rels ... Ms. Liza LARIOS
51 VP Continuing Ed/Workforce Dev ... Ms. Denise WARD
108 VP Strategic Plng/Assessment ... Dr. Karen B. STEELE
88 Dean Accred Assessment ... Dr. Arthur CORRADETTI
13 Chief Information Technology Ofcr ... Mr. George SHERMAN
08 Chief Librarian ... Ms. Jeanne GALVIN
06 Registrar ... Ms. Ann TULLIO
37 Financial Aid Exec Director ... Ms. Veronica LUKAS
07 Assoc Dean Admissions/Recruitment ... Ms. Laura BRUNO
09 Director of Institutional Research ... Ms. Elisabeth LACKNER
16 Personnel Officer ... Ms. Ellen ADAMS
26 VP/Chief Communications/Mktg Ofcr ... Mr. Stephen DI DIO
19 Director of Safety & Security ... Mr. John TRIOLO
22 Chief Diversity Officer ... Ms. Josephine PANTALEO
04 Executive Assistant to President ... Ms. Millie CONTE
104 Dir Ctr for Intl Stds/Study Abroad ... Ms. Lampeto (Betty) EFTHYMIOU
18 Chief Admin Superintendent ... Mr. Joseph CARTOLANO
36 Director of Career Services ... Ms. Constance PELUSO
44 Development Officer ... Ms. Saji SHEERAZI
21 Exec Dir Finance & Admin Services ... Mr. David WASSERMAN
45 Exec Dir Budget/Resource Planning ... Mr. Mark CARPENTIER
20 Dean of Faculty ... Dr. Sandra PALMER
35 Assoc Dean of Student Development ... Dr. Brian KERR

*City University of New York Stella and Charles Guttman Community College (G)

50 West 40th Street, New York NY 10018
County: New York Identification: 667126
Unit ID: 475565
Telephone: (646) 313-8000 Carnegie Class: Not Classified
FAX Number: N/A Calendar System: Semester
URL: www.guttman.cuny.edu
Established: 2011 Annual Undergrad Tuition & Fees (In-District): $5,194
Enrollment: 824 Coed

Affiliation or Control: State/Local IRS Status: 501(c)3
Highest Offering: Associate Degree
Accreditation: M, NY

02 President Scott EVENBECK
05 Provost and Vice President Howard M. WACH
10 Vice Pres Admin & Finance Mary COLEMAN
45 Dean Strategic Plng & Effectiveness Stuart COCHRAN
09 Director of Institutional Research Elisa HERTZ
100 Chief of Staff Linda MERIANS
13 Chief Info Technology Officer (CIO) John STROUD
15 Director Human Resources Nila BHAUMIK
18 Director Facilities Planning Shirley LAW
19 Director Public Safety Anastasia KOUTSIDIS
37 Director Student Financial Aid Cristina ORTIZ-HARVEY
06 Registrar Cortes MARISOL
07 Director of Admissions So SOPHEA
86 Director Government Relations Lavita MCMATH-TURNER
04 Administrative Asst to President Nina CONROY
102 Dir Foundation/Corporate Relations Bruce LYONS
29 Director Alumni Relations LaToya JACKSON
32 Dean of Student Engagement Charles PRYOR

*City University of New York York College (A)

94-20 Guy Brewer Boulevard, Jamaica NY 11451-0001
County: Queens FICE Identification: 004759
Unit ID: 190691
Telephone: (718) 262-2000 Carnegie Class: Bac-Diverse
FAX Number: (718) 262-2352 Calendar System: Semester
URL: www.york.cuny.edu
Established: 1966 Annual Undergrad Tuition & Fees (In-District): $6,748
Enrollment: 8,511 Coed
Affiliation or Control: State/Local IRS Status: 501(c)3
Highest Offering: Master's
Accreditation: M, ARCPA, CAEPN, EXSC, MT, NUR, OT, SW

02 President Dr. Marcia V. KEIZS
05 Provost/Sr VP for Academic Affs Dr. Panayiotis MELETIES
10 VP of Administration & Finance/COO Mr. Ronald C. THOMAS
32 Vice Pres for Student Development Dr. Vincent BANREY
49 Dean School of Arts & Sciences Dr. Donna CHIRICO
83 Dean Sch of Health & Behavioral Sci Vacant
50 Dean Sch of Business & Info Systems Dr. Charles GENGLER
43 Labor & Legal Affairs Mr. Russell PLATZEK
15 Interim Assoc Exec Director HR Ms. Gwendolyn HAREWOOD
13 Chief Information Officer Mr. Peter TIGHE
09 Exec Dir Inst Effec/Strategic Plng Dr. Mary OSBORNE
06 Registrar Ms. Sharon DAVIDSON
08 Chief Librarian Ms. Njoki KINYATTI
90 Director of Academic Computing Dr. Che-Tsao HUANG
86 Dir of Govt and Community Relations Dr. Earl G. SIMONS
19 Director of Security Chief Rufus MASSIAH
37 Director of Financial Aid Ms. Beverly BROWN
18 Director Campus Planning Mr. Noel GAMBOA
35 Director Student Activities Dr. Jean PHELPS
36 Director Career Services Ms. Linda H. CHESNEY
25 Dir Research/Sponsored Programs Ms. Dawn HEWITT
38 Interim Director of Counseling Dr. Jayoung CHOI
41 Director of Athletics & Recreation Vacant
04 Executive Assoc to the President Ms. Sandra BELL ADAMS
84 Exec Dir Enrollment Mgmt Dr. Latoro YATES
29 Director Alumni Relations Ms. Mondell SEALY
111 VP Institutional Advancement Mr. Shereitte STOKES
28 Director of Diversity Ms. Alicia FRANQUI
96 Director of Purchasing Ms. Rashmi MALESH

Clarkson University (B)

8 Clarkson Ave, Potsdam NY 13699
County: St. Lawrence FICE Identification: 002699
Unit ID: 190044
Telephone: (315) 268-6400 Carnegie Class: DU-Mod
FAX Number: (315) 268-7647 Calendar System: Semester
URL: www.clarkson.edu
Established: 1896 Annual Undergrad Tuition & Fees: $46,132
Enrollment: 3,910 Coed
Affiliation or Control: Independent Non-Profit IRS Status: 501(c)3
Highest Offering: Doctorate
Accreditation: M, ARCPA, CAEPT, ENG, HSA, OT, PTA

01 President Dr. Anthony G. COLLINS
26 Vice Pres External Relations Mrs. Kelly O. CHEZUM
88 Vice Pres International Relations Ms. Kathryn B. JOHNSON
30 Vice Pres Devel & Alumni Relations Mr. Patrick ROCHE
84 VP Enrol Mgmt & Stdnt Advancement Mr. Brian T. GRANT
32 AVP Student Affairs Mr. Jeffrey D. TAYLOR
28 AVP Stdnt Success/Diversity/Incl Mrs. Catherine MCNAMARA
10 Chief Financial Officer Mr. James D. FISH
15 Chief Inclusion & Human Res Officer Ms. Suong IVES
13 Chief Information Officer Mr. Joshua A. FISKE
58 Dean of Graduate School Dr. Kerop JANOYAN
49 Interim Dean of Arts & Sciences Dr. Charles E. THORPE
50 Dean of Business School Dr. Dayle M. SMITH
54 Dean of Engineering Dr. William JEMISON
35 Dean of Students Mr. James PITTMAN
53 Education Chair Dr. Catherine SNYDER
21 Controller Mr. Christopher ALGER
110 Sr Dir Devel & Alumni Relations Mr. Andrew BREWER
20 Dir Academic Policies & Practices Mrs. Amanda PICKERING
91 Director Administrative Computing Mr. Chris CUTLER
07 Director Admissions Ms. Trish DOBBS
29 Director Alumni Relations Ms. Teresa PLANTY
41 Director Athletics & Recreation Mr. Steven J. YIANOUKOS
45 Director Budget & Planning Mrs. Allison S. ALDRICH
19 Director Campus Safety & Security Mr. David W. DELISLE
36 Director Career Center Mr. Jeffrey D. TAYLOR
102 Dir Corp & Foundation Rels Mrs. Elizabeth COLELLO
38 Acting Dir Counseling Services Ms. Theresa SAMWAYS
18 Director Facilities & Services Mr. Ian HAZEN
37 Director Financial Aid Mrs. Pamela NICHOLS
92 Director Honors Program Mr. Jonathan D. GOSS
15 Director Human Resources Operations Mrs. Amy MCGAHERAN
45 Dir Inst Planning Assess & Effectiv Mrs. Shannon ROBINSON
85 Director Intl Students & Scholars Mrs. Tess C. CASLER
86 Director Government Relations Mrs. Kelly O. CHEZUM
08 Director Libraries Ms. Michelle L. YOUNG
96 Dir Payroll/Purchasing/Risk Mgmt Mr. George GIORDANO
46 Director Research & Tech Transfer Mr. Gregory C. SLACK
88 Dir Student Administrative Services Mrs. Suzanne E. DAVIS
23 Director Student Health Services Mrs. Susan KNOWLES
104 Director Study Abroad Ms. Kathryn B. JOHNSON
105 Director Web Development Mrs. Julie DAVIS
06 Registrar Mrs. Karen J. BURKUM
09 Assoc Director Institutional Rsrch Mrs. Jenna STONE
90 Academic Technology Manager Mrs. Laura PERRY
40 Bookstore Manager Ms. Sara JOHNSON
25 Contract & Grant Administrator Ms. Anna Marie DAWLEY
04 Assistant to the President Mrs. Barbara PARKER

Clinton Community College (C)

136 Clinton Point Drive, Plattsburgh NY 12901-9573
County: Clinton FICE Identification: 006787
Unit ID: 190053
Telephone: (518) 562-4200 Carnegie Class: Assoc/HT-High Trad
FAX Number: (518) 561-4890 Calendar System: Semester
URL: www.clinton.edu
Established: 1966 Annual Undergrad Tuition & Fees (In-District): $5,347
Enrollment: 1,813 Coed
Affiliation or Control: State/Local IRS Status: 501(c)3
Highest Offering: Associate Degree
Accreditation: M, ADNUR

01 President Mr. Ray DI PASQUALE
05 Vice President for Academic Affairs Dr. Cheryl A. LESSER
10 Vice Pres for Admin/Business Affs Mrs. Lisa SHOVAN
32 Dean of Student Affairs Mr. John BORNER
111 Vice Pres InstitutionalAdvancement Mr. Steven G. FREDERICK
20 Assoc Vice Pres Academic Affairs Ms. Michele SNYDER
37 Director of Financial Aid Ms. Mary LA PIERRE
84 Dean of Enrollment Management Mrs. Anna MIARKA-GRZELAK
06 Registrar Ms. Lauren CURRIE
13 Mgmt Information Systems Director Mr. Rick BATCHELDER
15 Human Resource/Affirm Act Officer Ms. Sarah POTTER
18 Chief Facilities/Physical Plant Vacant
04 Administrative Asst to President Mrs. Tammy M. VILLANUEVA

Cochran School of Nursing (D)

967 North Broadway, Yonkers NY 10701-1399
County: Westchester FICE Identification: 006443
Unit ID: 190071
Telephone: (914) 964-4282 Carnegie Class: Spec 2-yr-Health
FAX Number: (914) 964-4266 Calendar System: Semester
URL: www.cochranschoolofnursing.us
Established: 1894 Annual Undergrad Tuition & Fees: N/A
Enrollment: 89 Coed
Affiliation or Control: Independent Non-Profit IRS Status: 501(c)3
Highest Offering: Associate Degree
Accreditation: ADNUR

01 Dean Dr. Annemarie MCALLISTER
08 Learning Resources Director Ms. Paula GRAHAM
32 Dir Student Services/Finances Mr. Drew THOMPSON

Cold Spring Harbor Laboratory/ Watson School of Biological Sciences (E)

PO Box 100, One Bungtown Road,
Cold Spring Harbor NY 11724-0100
County: Suffolk FICE Identification: 034563
Unit ID: 436377
Telephone: (516) 367-6890 Carnegie Class: Not Classified
FAX Number: (516) 367-6919 Calendar System: Other
URL: www.cshl.edu
Established: 1890 Annual Graduate Tuition & Fees: N/A
Enrollment: N/A Coed
Affiliation or Control: Independent Non-Profit IRS Status: 501(c)3
Highest Offering: Doctorate; No Undergraduates
Accreditation: NY

125 Chancellor Emeritus Dr. James D. WATSON
01 President Dr. Bruce STILLMAN
05 Dean Dr. Alexander GANN

Colgate Rochester Crozer Divinity School (F)

1100 S Goodman Street, Rochester NY 14620-2589
County: Monroe FICE Identification: 002700
Unit ID: 190080
Telephone: (585) 271-1320 Carnegie Class: Spec-4-yr-Faith
FAX Number: (585) 271-8013 Calendar System: Semester
URL: www.crcds.edu
Established: 1817 Annual Graduate Tuition & Fees: N/A
Enrollment: 84 Coed
Affiliation or Control: Independent Non-Profit IRS Status: 501(c)3
Highest Offering: Doctorate; No Undergraduates
Accreditation: THEOL

01 President Dr. Marvin A. MCMICKLE
05 VP Academic Life & Dean of Faculty Prof. Stephanie L. SAUVE
10 Chief Financial Officer Mr. Gerald E. VANSTRYDONCK
84 Vice Pres of Enrollment Services Ms. Melissa MORRAL
30 VP Institutional Advancement Mr. W. Thomas MCDADE-CLAY
94 Dean of Women & Gender Studies Vacant
06 Registrar Ms. Andrea MASON
18 Director of Facilities Mr. Mark DEVINCENTIS
08 Director of Library Services Ms. Margaret A. NEAD
40 Director Bookstore Ms. Margaret A. NEAD
37 Director of Financial Aid Ms. Andrea MASON
26 Communications Coordinator Ms. Michele KAIDER-KOROL
07 Admissions Coordinator Ms. Polly BUSH
29 Director of Alumni Relations Mr. W. Thomas MCDADE-CLAY
60 Dir of Learning Comm/Online Pgms Dr. Rachel A. MCGUIRE

Colgate University (G)

13 Oak Drive, Hamilton NY 13346-1386
County: Madison FICE Identification: 002701
Unit ID: 190099
Telephone: (315) 228-1000 Carnegie Class: Bac-A&S
FAX Number: (315) 228-7798 Calendar System: Semester
URL: www.colgate.edu
Established: 1819 Annual Undergrad Tuition & Fees: $51,955
Enrollment: 2,861 Coed
Affiliation or Control: Independent Non-Profit IRS Status: 501(c)3
Highest Offering: Master's
Accreditation: M, CAEPT

01 President Brian W. CASEY
101 VP/Sr Advisor/Sec Board of Trustees Robert L. TYBURSKI
05 Dean of Faculty & Provost Tracey E. HUCKS
10 Sr VP for Finance & Admin Joseph S. HOPE
111 Sr VP External Rels/Advancement Murray L. DECOCK
07 VP & Dean of Admiss/Financial Aid Gary L. ROSS
32 VP & Dean of the College Paul J. MCLOUGHLIN, II
21 Associate Vice Pres/Controller Thomas O'NEILL
18 Assoc VP for Buildings Stephen HUGHES
11 Assoc VP for Administration Kim WALDRON
20 Associate Dean of the Faculty Kenneth BELANGER
28 Assoc Provost Equity & Diversity Marilyn RUGG
06 Interim Registrar Tori CARHART
08 University Librarian Joanne SCHNEIDER
13 VP & Chief Information Officer Steve FABIANI
29 AVP Inst Advancement/Alumni Affairs Tim MANSFIELD
37 Director of Financial Aid Gina M. SOLIZ
109 AVP Cmty Affairs/Auxiliary Services Joanne BORFITZ
19 Interim Director of Campus Safety Gert NEUBAUER
36 AVP of Adv & Dir Career Initiatives Michael SCIOLA
41 VP & Director of Athletics Victoria CHUN
40 Dir Off-Campus Retail Operations Leslie PASCO
42 University Chaplain Mark SHINER
112 AVP Inst Advancement/Planned Giving Andrew CODDINGTON
38 Director Counseling/Psych Services Dawn LAFRANCE
96 Director of Purchasing Alan LEONARD
23 Director Student Health Services Merrill MILLER
94 Director Women's Studies Susan THOMSON
44 Director Annual Fund Operations Sara GROH
39 Director of Residential Housing Stacey MILLARD
09 Dir Institutional Planning/Research Neil ALBERT
04 Assistant to the President Claudia CARAHER
22 Dir EEO & Affirmative Action Tamala FLACK
102 Dir of Corp Foundation & Govt Rels Helen KEBABIAN
104 Director of Off-Campus Study Joanna HOLVEY BOWLES
88 Sr Advisor to the President Christopher WELLS

College of Mount Saint Vincent (H)

6301 Riverdale Avenue, Riverdale NY 10471-1093
County: Bronx FICE Identification: 002703
Unit ID: 193399
Telephone: (718) 405-3200 Carnegie Class: Masters/S
FAX Number: (718) 601-6392 Calendar System: Semester
URL: www.mountsaintvincent.edu
Established: 1847 Annual Undergrad Tuition & Fees: $35,130
Enrollment: 1,807 Coed
Affiliation or Control: Independent Non-Profit IRS Status: 501(c)3
Highest Offering: Master's
Accreditation: M, ACBSP, CAEPT, NURSE

01 President Dr. Charles L. FLYNN, JR.
05 Provost/Dean of Faculty Dr. Sarah STEVENSON
20 Dean Undergraduate College Dr. Lynne BONGIOVANNI
07 Sr VP for Admission/External Rels Ms. Madeleine MELKONIAN
10 Executive VP/Treasurer/CFO Mr. Abed ELKESHK
11 VP for Operations Mr. Kevin DEGROAT
13 VP Information Technology/CIO Mr. Adam WICHERN
32 Dean of Students Ms. Kelli BODRATO
88 Director Mission Integration Mr. Matthew SHIELDS
51 Dean School Professional/Cont Stds Dr. Mitchell SAKOFS
06 Registrar Mrs. Jeannette PICHARDO
08 Director of Library Mr. Joseph LEVIS

09 Director of Institutional Research .... Sr. Carol M. FINEGAN, SC
36 Director Career Education .... Mr. Robson CHERETTA
37 Director of Financial Aid .... Vacant
42 Dir Campus Ministry/Act Dir Mission .... Mr. Mathew SHIELDS
35 Dir of Student Affairs/Assoc Dean .... Dr. Gabrielle OCCHIOGROSSO
41 Dir Athletics & Recreation .... Mr. Barima YEBOAH
38 Director Counseling Services .... Ms. Rebecca HALPERIN
23 Director of Health Services .... Mrs. Eileen MCCABE
29 Dir Alumnae Relations/Annual Giving .... Mr. Michael QUINN
26 Assoc Director of College Relations .... Ms. Leah MUNCH
19 Dir Campus Safety/Security .... Mr. Thomas VASSALLO
66 Director of Nursing .... Dr. Judith ERICKSON
44 Assoc Dir Alumnae Rels/Annual Giv .... Ms. Kristin YANNIELLO
15 Director of Human Resources .... Ms. Melissa SAMUELS
21 Controller .... Mr. Shin MOON
04 Assistant to the President .... Ms. Mary BAUER
18 Director of Facilities .... Mr. Ryan ANDERSON
07 Director of Admissions .... Ms. Curt DIRCKS
92 Director of Honors Program .... Dr. Rosita VILLAGOMEZ
97 Director of Core Curriculum .... Dr. Robert JACKLOSKY

The College of New Rochelle (A)

29 Castle Place, New Rochelle NY 10805-2338
County: Westchester FICE Identification: 002704
Unit ID: 193645
Telephone: (914) 654-5000 Carnegie Class: Masters/L
FAX Number: (914) 654-5554 Calendar System: Semester
URL: www.cnr.edu
Established: 1904 Annual Undergrad Tuition & Fees: $34,960
Enrollment: 3,593 Coed
Affiliation or Control: Independent Non-Profit IRS Status: 501(c)3
Highest Offering: Master's
Accreditation: M, CAEPT, NURSE, SW

01 Interim President .... Dr. Dorothy A. ESCRIBANO
45 Exec Vice Pres Strategy & Planning .... Mr. Kevin CAVANAGH
05 Sr Vice Pres Acad Affairs & Provost .. Dr. Dorothy A. ESCRIBANO
10 Vice President Financial Affairs .... Mr. Thomas CUNNINGHAM
30 Vice President College Advancement .... Ms. Brenna S. MAYER
84 Asst Vice Pres of Enrollment Mgmt .... Ms. Michelle NOVOTNY
49 Interim Dean School of Arts & Sci .... Dr. David DONNELLY
58 Dean of the Graduate School .... Dr. David DONNELLY
51 Dean School of New Resources .... Dr. Kristine SOUTHARD
66 Int Dean Sch of Nursing/Healthcare .... Dr. Debra SIMONS
06 Associate Registrar .... Ms. Carmen ROSA
08 Dean of the Library .... Ms. Ana FONTOURA
32 Dean of Students .... Ms. Tiffani BLAKE
37 Director of Financial Aid .... Ms. Anne C. PELAK
36 Director of Career Development .... Ms. Mariela TORRES
19 Director Security/Safety .... Mr. Rodney SAMUELS
18 Asst Director Facilities Management .... Mr. Alfred CHRISTIAN
21 Controller .... Mr. Michael O'DONNELL

The College of Saint Rose (B)

432 Western Avenue, Albany NY 12203-1490
County: Albany FICE Identification: 002705
Unit ID: 195234
Telephone: (518) 454-5111 Carnegie Class: Masters/L
FAX Number: (518) 438-3293 Calendar System: Semester
URL: www.strose.edu
Established: 1920 Annual Undergrad Tuition & Fees: $30,692
Enrollment: 4,345 Coed
Affiliation or Control: Independent Non-Profit IRS Status: 501(c)3
Highest Offering: Master's
Accreditation: M, ACBSP, ART, CAEPN, MUS, SP, SW

01 President .... Dr. Carolyn J. STEFANCO
100 Chief of Staff .... Ms. Lisa HALEY-THOMSON
05 Int Provost/VP Academic Affairs .... Dr. Margaret MCLANE
32 Vice President of Student Affairs .... Dr. Dennis MCDONALD
84 Vice Pres of Enrollment Mgmt & Mktg .... Mrs. Mary M. GRONDAHL
111 Vice Pres Institutional Advancement .... Mr. Ian FARRELL
15 Assoc Vice Pres Human Res/Risk Mgt .... Mr. Jeffrey KNAPP
10 Assoc VP Financial Planning and Aux .... Ms. Valerie MYERS
07 Asst VP Undergraduate Recruitment .... Ms. Kathleen LESKO
123 Asst VP of Graduate Recruitment .... Ms. Cris MURRAY
37 Asst VP of Financial Aid .... Mr. Steven W. DWIRE
110 Asst VP for Advancement Operations .... Ms. Lisa MCKENZIE
35 Asst VP Student Affairs .... Ms. Mary R. MCLAUGHLIN
42 Dean of Spiritual Life/Pfaff Endow .... Dr. Michael BRANNIGAN
86 Exec Dir of Govt Community Affairs .... Mr. Michael D'ATTILIO
11 Interim Assoc VP for Operations .... Mr. John ELLIS
29 Director of Alumni Relations .... Ms. Whitney PAGANO
21 Assoc VP Financial Reporting/Comptr .... Ms. Beatrice DIEHL
06 Registrar .... Mr. Craig TYNAN
08 Director of Library .... Mr. Andrew URBANEK
39 Director Residence Life .... Ms. Jennifer RICHARDSON
36 Director of the Career Center .... Ms. Michelle OSBORNE
38 Clinical Dir Counseling/Psych Svcs .... Mr. Ronald J. HAMER
41 Director Athletics & Recreation .... Ms. Catherine A. HAKER
91 Director Infrastructure & Programs .... Mr. William TRAVER
31 Director Community Services .... Mr. Kenneth SCOTT
42 Director of Campus Ministry .... Ms. Joan HORGAN
23 Director of Health Services .... Ms. Sandra FRESE
19 Director of Safety/Security .... Mr. Steven STELLA
121 VP for Student Success & Engagement .... Ms. Shai BUTLER
88 Director of Advisement .... Dr. Kelly MEYER
23 Director of Clinical Services .... Ms. Jacqueline KLEIN
96 Director Purchasing/Auxiliary Svcs .... Ms. Patricia BUCKLEY

18 Dir Facilities Planning & SpaceMgmt ... Ms. Nancy MACDONALD
09 Assoc VP of Institutional Effective .... Mrs. Lisa KEATING
40 Manager of Campus Store .... Ms. Emily IVES
24 Dir of Computer/Media Services .... Mr. Michael STRATTON
04 Exec Admin Asst to the President .... Mrs. Julie KOCHAN
101 Board Liaison/General Counsel Asst .... Ms. Maria RUSSO
102 Dir Corporate & Foundation Relation .... Ms. Devon STEIN
105 Web Programmer .... Mr. Bryan BURNS
106 Dir Online Learning Services .... Mr. Thomas ROSENBERGER
43 General Counsel .... Ms. Nancy WILLIAMSON
50 Interim Dean School of Business .... Dr. K. Michael MATHEWS
79 Interim Dean Arts & Humanities .... Dr. Jeffrey MARLETT
81 Interim Dean Math & Sciences .... Dr. Ian MACDONALD
112 Director of Principal & Major Gifts .... Ms. Therese STILLMAN
26 Dir of Marketing & Communications .... Ms. Jennifer GISH
104 Int Dir Center International Pgms .... Ms. Colleen THAPALIA

The College of Westchester (C)

325 Central Avenue, White Plains NY 10606
County: Westchester FICE Identification: 005208
Unit ID: 197285
Telephone: (914) 948-4442 Carnegie Class: Bac/Assoc-Mixed
FAX Number: (914) 948-5441 Calendar System: Semester
URL: www.cw.edu
Established: 1915 Annual Undergrad Tuition & Fees: $21,015
Enrollment: 1,067 Coed
Affiliation or Control: Proprietary IRS Status: Proprietary
Highest Offering: Baccalaureate
Accreditation: M

00 Chairman Emeritus .... Mr. Ernest H. SUTKOWSKI
01 President & CEO .... Mrs. Mary Beth DEL BALZO
05 Provost/VP Academic Affairs .... Dr. Warren ROSENBERG
88 Vice President Special Projects .... Mr. Dale T. SMITH
20 Dean Academic Services .... Dr. Daphne GALKIN
84 VP of Enrollment Management .... Mr. Matt CURTIS
36 Director of Career Services .... Ms. Joann SONDEY
121 Associate Dean of Student Success .... Dr. Judith LILLESTON
124 Dir of Retention & Enrollment .... Mrs. Maria GANGI
37 Dir of Student Financial Services .... Mrs. Dianne PEPITONE

Columbia-Greene Community College (D)

4400 Route 23, Hudson NY 12534-9543
County: Columbia FICE Identification: 006789
Unit ID: 190169
Telephone: (518) 828-4181 Carnegie Class: Assoc/HT-Mix Trad/Non
FAX Number: (518) 822-2015 Calendar System: Semester
URL: www.sunycgcc.edu
Established: 1966 Annual Undergrad Tuition & Fees (In-District): $4,744
Enrollment: 1,777 Coed
Affiliation or Control: State/Local IRS Status: 501(c)3
Highest Offering: Associate Degree
Accreditation: M, ADNUR

01 President .... Mr. James R. CAMPION
05 VP & Dean of Academic Affairs .... Ms. Phyllis CARITO
10 VP/Dean of Administration .... Ms. Dianne TOPPLE
32 VP/Dean of Students/Enrollment Mgmt .... Dr. Joseph WATSON
38 Counselor .... Ms. Diane JOHNSON
18 Director Building & Grounds .... Mr. James FOLZ
26 Director Public Information .... Ms. Jaclyn STEVENSON
37 Dir Stndt Fin Aid/Asst Dean Stdnts .... Mr. Joel PHELPS
06 Registrar .... Ms. Gail SHADER
13 Director Information Systems .... Mr. Gino RIZZI
15 Director of Human Resources .... Ms. Melissa FANDOZZI
22 Affirmative Action Officer .... Ms. Melissa FANDOZZI
09 Dir of Institutional Effectiveness .... Mr. Casey O'BRIEN
31 Director of Community Services .... Mr. Robert BODRATTI
41 Athletic Director .... Ms. Richanna LINDO
121 Director Academic Support Center .... Dr. Mary-Teresa HEATH
103 Director of Workforce Development .... Ms. Mary Alane WILTSE
07 Acting Director of Admissions .... Ms. Rachel KAPPEL
30 Dir of Development & Alumni Svcs .... Ms. Joan KOWEEK
20 Assistant Dean of Academic Affairs .... Ms. Carol DOERFER
113 Bursar .... Ms. Christy DECKER
19 Director of Security .... Mr. John LEONE
96 Purchasing Officer .... Ms. Patricia DAY
62 Department Chair Library Services .... Ms. Geralynn DEMAREST
83 Div Chair Behavioral/Social Science .... Mr. William DELUCA
81 Div Chair Math & Science .... Ms. Dawn HOLSAPPLE
57 Division Chair Arts & Humanities .... Ms. Siri CARLISEL
66 Division Chair Nursing .... Ms. Dawn WRIGLEY
72 Division Chair Technology .... Ms. Marcia FITZGERALD
88 Division Chair of Automotive .... Mr. Michael ALLARD

Columbia University in the City of New York (E)

615 West 131st Street, New York NY 10027-6902
County: New York FICE Identification: 002707
Unit ID: 190150
Telephone: (212) 854-1754 Carnegie Class: DU-Highest
FAX Number: (212) 851-7022 Calendar System: Semester
URL: www.columbia.edu
Established: 1754 Annual Undergrad Tuition & Fees: $55,056
Enrollment: 28,086 Coed
Affiliation or Control: Independent Non-Profit IRS Status: 501(c)3
Highest Offering: Doctorate
Accreditation: M, ANEST, CEA, DENT, ENG, HSA, IPSY, JOUR, LAW, MED, MIDWF, NURSE, OT, PH, PLNG, PTA, SPAA, SW

01 President .... Mr. Lee C. BOLLINGER
05 Provost .... Dr. John COATSWORTH
03 Senior Exec Vice President .... Mr. Gerald M. ROSBERG
49 Exec Vice Pres Arts & Sciences .... Mr. David MADIGAN
76 Exec VP Health/Biomed Sciences .... Dr. Lee GOLDMAN
09 Exec Vice President Research .... Dr. G. Michael PURDY
86 Exec Vice Pres Govt & Cmty Affairs .... Ms. Maxine F. GRIFFITH
43 General Counsel .... Ms. Jane E. BOOTH
26 Exec Vice Pres Communications .... Mr. David M. STONE
101 Secretary of the University .... Mr. Jerome DAVIS
10 Exec Vice President for Finance .... Ms. Anne R. SULLIVAN
18 Exec Vice President Facilities .... Mr. David GREENBERG
88 Exec Vice President Global .... Mr. Safwan M. MASRI
30 Exec Vice Pres Development & Alumni .... Ms. Amelia J. ALVERSON
88 Special Advisor to the President .... Ms. Susan K. FEAGIN
32 Exec Vice President University Life ... Ms. Suzanne B. GOLDBERG
41 Athletic Director .... Mr. Peter E. PILLING
88 Ombuds Officer .... Ms. Joan WATERS
100 Chief of Staff to President .... Ms. Susan K. GLANCY
115 CEO IMC Ofc of Univ Investments .... Mr. Peter HOLLAND
20 Vice Provost Academic Programs .... Dr. Melissa D. BEGG
20 Vice Provost Faculty Affairs .... Mr. Christopher L. BROWN
11 Vice Provost Administration .... Mr. Troy EGGERS
88 Vice Provost Teaching & Learning .... Soulaymane KACHANI
28 Vice Provost Diversity & Inclusion .... Dr. Dennis MITCHELL
08 Vice Provost & Univ Librarian .... Ms. Ann D. THORNTON
48 Dean Grad School Arch/Plng/Preserv .... Ms. Amale ANDRAOS
57 Dean School of the Arts .... Dr. Carol BECKER
58 Dean Grad School of Arts & Science .... Dr. Carlos J. ALONSO
50 Dean Graduate School of Business .... Dr. R. Glenn HUBBARD
49 Dean Columbia College .... Dr. James J. VALENTINI
51 Dean School Continuing Education .... Mr. Jason M. WINGARD
54 Dean Sch Engr/Applied Science .... Dr. Mary C. BOYCE
82 Dean School Intl/Public Affairs .... Ms. Merit E. JANOW
97 Dean School General Studies .... Dr. Peter AWN
60 Dean Graduate School Journalism .... Mr. Stephen W. COLL
61 Dean School of Law .... Ms. Gillian LESTER
70 Dean School of Social Work .... Dr. Jeanette C. TAKAMURA
63 Dean Faculty of Medicine .... Dr. Lee GOLDMAN
52 Dean Sch Dental & Oral Surgery .... Dr. Christian S. STOHLER
66 Dean School of Nursing .... Dr. Bobbie BERKOWITZ
69 Dean School of Public Health .... Dr. Linda P. FRIED
38 Exec Director Student Counseling .... Dr. Richard EICHLER
37 Assoc VP Student Financial Svcs .... Ms. Jane HOJAN-CLARK
06 Assoc Vice Pres & Registrar .... Mr. Barry S. KANE
07 Dean of Undergraduate Admissions ...... Ms. Jessica MARINACCIO

† Parent institution of Barnard College and Teachers College, Columbia University.

Concordia College (F)

171 White Plains Road, Bronxville NY 10708-1923
County: Westchester FICE Identification: 002709
Unit ID: 190248
Telephone: (914) 337-9300 Carnegie Class: Bac-Diverse
FAX Number: (914) 395-4500 Calendar System: Semester
URL: www.concordia-ny.edu
Established: 1881 Annual Undergrad Tuition & Fees: $30,530
Enrollment: 1,156 Coed
Affiliation or Control: Lutheran Church - Missouri Synod
IRS Status: 501(c)3
Highest Offering: Master's
Accreditation: M, CAEPN, IACBE, NURSE, SW

01 President .... Rev.Dr. John A. NUNES
05 Provost .... Dr. Sherry J. FRASER
10 Chief Financial Officer & COO .... Mr. Harry WALPOLE
111 Vice President Advancement .... Ms. Heather MCGINNESS
45 VP Strategic Planning & Management .... Mr. Theodore FRANCAVILLA
42 VP Leadership/Campus Pastor .... Rev Dr. Victor BELTON
43 General Counsel .... Ms. Arlene TORRES
20 Vice Prov Undergraduate Acad Affs .... Dr. Mandana NAKHAI
106 Vice Prov Graduate/Online Educ .... Dr. James BURKEE
84 Sr Director of Enrollment .... Mr. John MCLOUGHLIN
66 Dean Division of Nursing .... Dr. Kathleen FLAHERTY
88 Dean of Adult Education & Business .... Dr. William M. SALVA
32 Dir Academic/Student Services .... Ms. Patrice SULLIVAN
06 Registrar Coordinator .... Ms. Kasona HEWITT
08 Library Director .... Mr. William L. PERRENOD
41 Athletic Director .... Ms. Kathy LAOUTARIS
23 Director Student Health Services .... Ms. Susan CRANE
88 Assoc Dean Academic Operations . Mr. Christopher D'AMBROSIO
18 Director Support Services .... Mr. Paul A. SCHULZ
26 Director of Marketing/Webmaster .... Ms. Holly MAGNANI
42 Director of Church Relations .... Ms. Kathy DRESSER
31 Sr Director Community Relations .... Ms. Joyce KENNEDY
92 Director of Fellows Program .... Dr. Kate E. BEHR
15 Director of Human Resources .... Ms. Terry VIDAL
13 Dir Information Technology Services .... Mr. Gary GOLLENBERG
21 Controller .... Mr. Edward J. MCPARTLAN
35 Director of Student Success .... Ms. Johanna L. PERRY
36 Director of Career Development .... Ms. Laura GREVI
88 Dean of Teacher Education .... Dr. Stephanie SQUIRES
29 Dir of Alumni/Donor Relations .... Ms. Lois MONTORIO
09 Dir Institutional Effect/Research .... Ms. Kimberly GARGIULO
102 Dir Foundation/Corporate Relations .... Ms. Joyce KENNEDY
103 Director Career Development .... Ms. Laura GREVI
19 Director of Campus Safety .... Mr. Stephen BONURA

106 Dean Online Education/E-learning .... Ms. Susan KRAUSS
108 Director Institutional Assessment .... Ms. Kimberly GARGIULO

Cooper Union (A)

30 Cooper Square, New York NY 10003-7120
County: New York FICE Identification: 002710
Unit ID: 190372
Telephone: (212) 353-4100 Carnegie Class: Bac-Diverse
FAX Number: (212) 353-4244 Calendar System: Semester
URL: www.cooper.edu
Established: 1859 Annual Undergrad Tuition & Fees: $43,850
Enrollment: 972 Coed
Affiliation or Control: Independent Non-Profit IRS Status: 501(c)3
Highest Offering: Master's
Accreditation: M, ART, ENG

01 President .... Laura SPARKS
10 Vice President Finance and Admin .... William E. MEA
21 Controller .... Keith STOKELD
07 VP Enrollment Svcs/Dean Admissions .... Mitchell LIPTON
57 Acting Dean School of Art .... Mike ESSL
48 Dean School of Architecture .... Nader TEHRANI
79 Actg Dean Humanities/Social Sci .... Peter BUCKLEY
54 Acting Dean School of Engineering .... Richard STOCK
08 Director of the Library .... Carol SALOMON
114 Dir Budget/Personnel/Inst Research .... Steven GLEIMER
44 Director of Gift Planning .... Peter CONGLETON
13 Chief Technology Officer .... Robert P. HOPKINS
88 Director of Off Campus Programming .... Margaret MORTON
18 Director of Facilities Mgmt .... Carmelo PIZZUTO
36 Director of Career Services .... Robert THILL
24 Director of Audiovisual/Media .... Paul TUMMOLO
35 Dean of Students .... Christopher CHAMBERLIN
91 Director of Administrative Database .... Dominic MATAR
88 Creative Director .... Mindy LANG
27 Media Relations Manager .... Kim NEWMAN
11 Administrative Manager .... Lauren DESIDERIO

† Every student receives a full-tuition scholarship.

Cornell University (B)

Day Hall Lobby, Ithaca NY 14850
County: Tompkins FICE Identification: 002711
Unit ID: 190415
Telephone: (607) 255-2000 Carnegie Class: DU-Highest
FAX Number: (607) 255-5396 Calendar System: Semester
URL: www.cornell.edu
Established: 1865 Annual Undergrad Tuition & Fees: $50,953
Enrollment: 21,904 Coed
Affiliation or Control: Independent Non-Profit IRS Status: 501(c)3
Highest Offering: Doctorate
Accreditation: M, CIDA, DIETD, DIETI, ENG, HSA, LAW, LSAR, PLNG, VET

01 President .... Martha E. POLLACK
05 Provost .... Michael I. KOTLIKOFF
63 Prov Medical Affairs/Dean Med Col .... Augustine M.K CHOI
20 Deputy Provost .... John A. SILICIANO
10 Executive VP Financial Affairs/CFO .... Joanne M. DESTEFANO
46 Vice Provost Research/Tech Transfer ... Emmanuel P. GIANNELLIS
58 Senior Vice Prov & Dean Grad School .... Barbara A. KNUTH
88 Vice Prov for International Affairs .... Laura M. SPITZ
20 Vice Provost .... Judith A. APPLETON
114 Vice Pres Budget & Planning .... Paul STREETER
30 VP Alumni Affairs/Development .... Fred VAN SICKLE
15 VP and Chief Human Resources .... Mary George G. OPPERMAN
32 VP Student & Campus Life .... Ryan T. LOMBARDI
26 Vice Pres for University Relations .... Joel M. MALINA
86 Associate VP for Govt Relations .... Charles KRUZANSKY
72 Dean/Vice Prov Cornell NYC Tech ..... Daniel S. HUTTENLOCHER
43 University Counsel & Secretary Corp .... Madelyn F. WESSEL
21 Vice President Financial Affairs .... Gerald HECTOR
13 VP & CIO for Info Technology .... David LIFKA
115 Chief Investment Officer .... Kenneth M. MIRANDA
18 Vice Pres Infrastructure/Property .... Frederick BURGESS
97 Int Vice Provost Undergrad Educ .... John A. SILICIANO
84 Assoc Vice Provost Enrollment .... Jason LOCKE
21 Interim University Controller .... Kim YEOH
21 Assoc Vice President/Treasurer .... Harper WATTERS
116 University Auditor .... Glen C. MUELLER
20 Dean of Faculty .... Charles VAN LOAN
47 Dean Col Agriculture/Life Sciences .... Kathryn J. BOOR
48 Dean College Arch/Art/Planning .... Kent KLEINMAN
49 Dean College Arts & Science .... Gretchen RITTER
54 Dean College of Engineering .... Lance R. COLLINS
88 Interim Dean School Hotel Admin .... Kate D. WALSH
59 Dean College Human Ecology .... Alan D. MATHIOS
50 Dean SC Johnson College of Business .... Soumitra DUTTA
88 Dean Dyson School Applied Economics ... Lynn PERRY WOOTEN
50 Dean Industrial/Labor Rels .... Kevin F. HALLOCK
61 Dean Law School .... Eduardo M. PEÑALVER
74 Dean College Veterinary Medicine .... Lorin D. WARNICK
77 Dean of Computing and Info Science .... Gregory J. MORRISETT
51 Dean Cont Education/Summer Session ..... Glenn C. ALTSCHULER
50 Dean of the Weill Graduate School .... Gary KORETZKY
08 University Librarian .... Anne R. KENNEY
88 Interim Dir Africana Stds/Research .... Noliwe L. ROOKS
07 Dir Undergraduate Admissions .... Shawn FELTON
37 Director Financial Aid .... Susan HITCHCOCK
35 Dean of Students .... Vijay PENDAKUR
06 University Registrar .... Cassandra C. DEMBOSKY
41 Director Athletics/Physical Educ .... J. Andrew NOEL, JR.
36 Director of Cornell Career Services .... Rebecca M. SPARROW
22 Assoc VP Wrkfrce Dvrsty & Inclusion .... Lynette CHAPPELL-WILLIAMS
23 Assoc Vice Pres Campus Health .... Janet L. CORSON-RIKERT
28 Assoc Vice Provost Acad Diversity .... Andrew T. MILLER
28 Assoc Vice Prov Faculty Diversity .... Yael LEVITTE
42 Dir Cornell United Religious Works .... Rev. Kenneth I. CLARKE
88 Assoc Vice Pres Research Admin .... Catherine E. LONG
25 Sr Director Sponsored Fin Svcs .... Jeffrey A. SILBER
19 Chief Cornell Police .... Kathy R. ZONER
96 Sr Dir Procurement and Bus Svcs .... Thomas W. ROMANTIC
29 Assoc Vice Pres Alumni Affairs .... James A. MAZZA
09 Assc Vice Provost Inst Res/Planning .... Marin E. CLARKBERG
80 Dean Johnson Grad School of Mgmt .... Mark W. NELSON
08 Carl A. Kroch University Librarian .... Gerald R. BEASLEY

† Parent institution of Weill Medical College of Cornell University.

Corning Community College (C)

One Academic Drive, Corning NY 14830-3297
County: Steuben FICE Identification: 002863
Unit ID: 190442
Telephone: (607) 962-9011 Carnegie Class: Assoc/HT-Mix Trad/Non
FAX Number: (607) 962-9456 Calendar System: Semester
URL: www.corning-cc.edu
Established: 1956 Annual Undergrad Tuition & Fees (In-District): $4,872
Enrollment: 3,972 Coed
Affiliation or Control: State/Local IRS Status: 501(c)3
Highest Offering: Associate Degree
Accreditation: M, ADNUR

01 President .... Dr. Katherine P. DOUGLAS
05 VP & Dean Academic Affairs .... Dr. Marian EBERLY
11 Vice President Administrative Svcs .... Dr. Kenneth ENGLAND
32 VP & Dean Stdnt Dev & Enroll Mgmt .... Dr. L. Dean FISHER
30 Exec Dir Institutional Advancement .... Mr. William LITTLE
08 Asst Dean Learning Resources ... Dr. Sabrina JOHNSON-TAYLOR
06 Registrar .... Ms. Karen BOULAS
07 Director of Admissions .... Ms. Tyre BUSH
15 Director Human Resources .... Ms. Nannette NICHOLAS
10 Chief Business Officer .... Dr. Kenneth ENGLAND
18 Chief Facilities/Physical Plant .... Mr. Calvin WILLIAMS
37 Director Student Financial Aid .... Ms. Nancy JOHNSON
09 Research Analyst .... Mr. Paul ANDREWS

The Culinary Institute of America (D)

1946 Campus Drive, Hyde Park NY 12538-1499
County: Dutchess FICE Identification: 007304
Unit ID: 190503
Telephone: (845) 905-4288 Carnegie Class: Spec-4-yr-Other
FAX Number: (845) 452-0165 Calendar System: Semester
URL: www.ciachef.edu
Established: 1946 Annual Undergrad Tuition & Fees: $30,730
Enrollment: 2,859 Coed
Affiliation or Control: Independent Non-Profit IRS Status: 501(c)3
Highest Offering: Baccalaureate
Accreditation: M

01 President .... Dr. Tim RYAN
10 VP Finance and Administration .... Ms. Maria KRUPIN
111 VP Advancement .... Mr. Kevin ALLAN
05 Provost .... Mr. Mark ERICKSON
20 VP Academic Affairs .... Dr. Michael SPERLING
84 VP Enrollment Management .... Dr. Jackie NEALON
45 VP Strategic Init & Industry Ldrsp .... Mr. Greg DRESCHER
32 AVP & Dean of Student Affairs .... Dr. Kathleen MERGET
35 Assistant Director Student Life .... Mr. Nathan FLINTJER
38 Director Counseling Services .... Dr. Daria PAPALIA
09 Director Assessment & Inst Research .... Ms. Betsy CARROLL
23 Director Health Services .... Ms. Katherine MILLER
21 Director Finance & Accounting .... Mr. Steven STROM
96 Director Purchasing & Storeroom .... Mr. Brad MATTHEWS
18 Director Facilities .... Mr. Evin LEDERMAN
19 Director Safety .... Mr. William CAREY
37 Director Student Financial Planning .... Ms. Kathleen GAILOR
110 Senior Advancement Officer .... Ms. Denise ZANCHELLI
88 Dean Academic Engagement & Admin .... Ms. Carolyn TRAGNI
12 AVP Branch Campuses .... Ms. Susan CUSSEN
88 Dean School of Culinary Arts .... Mr. Brendan WALSH
88 Dean Baking & Pastry Arts .... Mr. Thomas VACCARO
49 Dean School of Lib Arts & Food Std .... Ms. Denise BAUER
108 Dir Inst Liaison & Accreditation .... Ms. Sharon ZRALY
06 Registrar .... Mr. Chet KOULIK
36 Director Career & Academic Advising ..... Ms. Crystal DECAROLIS
08 Director Library & Information Sys .... Mr. Jon GRENNAN
100 AVP/Chief of Staff .... Mr. Rick TIETJEN
15 Senior Director Human Resources .... Ms. Shay GARRIOCH
04 Executive Asst to President .... Ms. Shannon CAMPER
102 Senior Advancement Officer .... Ms. Elly ERICKSON
50 Dean School of Bus & Mgmt Studies .... Ms. Annette GRAHAM
88 Acting Dean School of Cul Science .... Mr. Ted RUSSIN
88 Senior Director Faculty Relations .... Mr. Joe MORANO
07 Sr Dir Admissions & Enrollment .... Ms. Rachel BIRCHWOOD
88 Director Creative Services .... Ms. Terri TOTTEN

Daemen College (E)

4380 Main Street, Amherst NY 14226-3592
County: Erie FICE Identification: 002808
Unit ID: 190725
Telephone: (716) 839-3600 Carnegie Class: Masters/L
FAX Number: (716) 839-8516 Calendar System: Semester
URL: www.daemen.edu
Established: 1947 Annual Undergrad Tuition & Fees: $26,940
Enrollment: 2,767 Coed
Affiliation or Control: Independent Non-Profit IRS Status: 501(c)3
Highest Offering: Doctorate
Accreditation: M, ARCPA, CAATE, CAEPT, CYTO, @DIETI, IACBE, NUR, PTA, SW

01 President .... Dr. Gary A. OLSON
05 VP Academic Affairs/Dean .... Dr. Michael S. BROGAN
10 VP for Business Affairs & Treasurer .... Mr. Richard G. SCHOTT
30 VP Institutional Advancement .... Mr. Craig HARRIS
84 Int VP for Enrollment Management .... Mr. Frank WILLIAMS
32 VP Student Affairs .... Dr. Greg J. NAYOR
20 Assoc VP Academic Affairs .... Dr. Kathleen C. BOONE
07 Dean of Admissions/Assoc VP Enroll ...... Mr. Frank S. WILLIAMS
21 Controller & VP for Business Affs .... Ms. Lisa A. ARIDA
13 Chief Information Technology Ofcr .... Ms. Kelly DURAN
09 Director of Institutional Research .... Dr. Patricia L. BEAMAN
108 Assoc VP of Inst Effectiveness .... Dr. Mimi H. STEADMAN
08 Director of RIC and Library Service .... Ms. Melissa PETERSON
06 Registrar .... Ms. Irene HOLOHAN-MOYER
100 Exec Director President's Office .... Ms. Sherrie A. GUSTAS
88 Dir for Academic Advisement .... Ms. Sabrina FENNELL
37 Director of Financial Aid .... Mr. Jeffrey M. PAGANO
15 Director of Human Resources .... Ms. Marissa PACE
26 Dir of Institutional Communication .... Ms. Paula WITHERELL
44 Director of Development and Gifts .... Mr. Justin JOHNSTON
78 Director of Career Services .... Dr. Maureen MILLANE
39 Dir of Housing & Residence Life .... Ms. Danielle WEAVER
35 Director of Student Activities .... Mr. Christopher P. MALIK
18 Director of Facilities .... Mr. Don PHILLIPS
19 Director Security & Fire Safety .... Mr. Ken BAKER
42 Director Campus Ministry ...... Rev. Cassandra L. SALTER-SMITH
41 Director of Athletics .... Ms. Bridget NILAND
96 Dir of Purchasing/Central Services .... Ms. Annette BITTERMAN
92 Director of Honors Program .... Dr. Matthew WARD
29 Director Alumni Relations .... Ms. Katie M. GRAF
40 Bookstore Manager .... Ms. Jaclyn HERNE
88 Dir of New Program Development ..... Ms. Susan M. MARCHIONE
04 Admin Assoc Office of the President .... Ms. Deborah GIANTURCO
104 Director Study Abroad .... Ms. Ann ROBINSON
106 Dir Online Education/E-learning ... Mr. Thomas WOJCIECHOWSKI
28 Director of Diversity .... Mr. Alvin ROBERTS, III
38 Director Student Counseling .... Ms. Shannon RADDER

Davis College (F)

400 Riverside Drive, Johnson City NY 13790-2714
County: Broome FICE Identification: 021691
Unit ID: 194569
Telephone: (607) 729-1581 Carnegie Class: Spec-4-yr-Faith
FAX Number: (607) 729-2962 Calendar System: Semester
URL: www.davisny.edu
Established: 1900 Annual Undergrad Tuition & Fees: $16,400
Enrollment: 390 Coed
Affiliation or Control: Independent Non-Profit IRS Status: 501(c)3
Highest Offering: Baccalaureate
Accreditation: M, BI

01 Chief Executive Officer .... Dr. Dino J. PEDRONE
05 Provost .... Vacant
32 Student Development Officer .... Mrs. Nichole POST
11 Operating Officer .... Vacant
10 Financial Officer .... Mr. Larry ELLIS
04 Assistant to the President .... Mr. Corey ADAMS
06 Registrar .... Mrs. Susan VANDEVENTER
08 Library Manager .... Mrs. Shelley BYRON
37 Director Financial Aid .... Mrs. Sandra CONKLIN
88 Assistant to the Provost .... Miss Naomi SARAVANAPAVAN
07 Director of Admissions .... Mr. Charles DRESSER
108 Director Institutional Assessment .... Dr. George SNYDER
18 Chief Facilities/Physical Plant .... Mr. James GATES
41 Athletic Director .... Mr. Dan J. RATHMELL
106 Dir Online Education/E-learning .... Mrs. JoAnna OSTER

Dominican College of Blauvelt (G)

470 Western Highway, Orangeburg NY 10962-1210
County: Rockland FICE Identification: 002713
Unit ID: 190761
Telephone: (845) 848-7800 Carnegie Class: Masters/S
FAX Number: (845) 359-2313 Calendar System: Semester
URL: www.dc.edu
Established: 1952 Annual Undergrad Tuition & Fees: $27,438
Enrollment: 2,061 Coed
Affiliation or Control: Independent Non-Profit IRS Status: 501(c)3
Highest Offering: Doctorate
Accreditation: M, #CAATE, CAEPT, IACBE, NURSE, OT, PTA, SW

01 President .... Sr Dr. Mary Eileen O'BRIEN
00 Chancellor .... Sr. Kathleen SULLIVAN
05 Vice Pres/Dean Academic Affairs .... Dr. Thomas S. NOWAK
84 Vice Pres of Enrollment Management .... Mr. Brian FERNANDES
32 Dean of Students .... Mr. John BURKE
10 Director of Fiscal Affairs .... Mr. Anthony CIPOLLA
06 Registrar .... Ms. Mary MCFADDEN
07 Director of Admissions .... Mr. Joseph AHLSTRIN
08 Librarian .... Ms. Jennifer SHELTON
30 Director of Inst Advancement .... Ms. Dorothy FILORAMO
15 Director Human Resources .... Ms. Marybeth BRODERICK
26 Chief Public Relations Officer .... Ms. Susan CERRA

29 Director Alumni Relations .... Ms. Mary MCHUGH
35 Director Student Activities .... Ms. Katrina REDMOND
09 Inst Research/Plng/Assessment Ofcr .... Dr. Shao-Wei WU
37 Director Student Financial Aid .... Ms. Stacy SALINAS
36 Director Student Placement .... Ms. Evelyn FISKAA
38 Director Student Counseling .... Ms. Alise COHEN
21 Controller .... Ms. Roxanne DROWN
13 Director Information Technology .... Mr. Russell DIAZ
18 Chief Facilities/Physical Plant .... Mr. Michael DEMPSEY
20 Associate Academic Officer .... Ms. Ann VAVOLIZZA
39 Director Student Housing .... Mr. Ryan O'GORMAN
41 Athletic Director .... Mr. Joseph CLINTON
42 Director Campus Ministry .... Sr. Barbara MCENEANY
96 Director of Purchasing .... Ms. Amy BIANCO
28 Director of Diversity .... Vacant
19 Director of Security/Safety .... Mr. John LENNON
42 Chaplain .... Vacant
31 Dir Cmty Engagemt/Ldrship Develop .... Ms. Melissa GRAU

Dutchess Community College (A)

53 Pendell Road, Poughkeepsie NY 12601-1595
County: Dutchess FICE Identification: 002864
Unit ID: 190840
Telephone: (845) 431-8000 Carnegie Class: Assoc/HT-Mix Trad/Non
FAX Number: (845) 431-8984 Calendar System: Semester
URL: www.sunydutchess.edu
Established: 1957 Annual Undergrad Tuition & Fees (In-District): $4,034
Enrollment: 9,546 Coed
Affiliation or Control: State/Local IRS Status: 501(c)3
Highest Offering: Associate Degree
Accreditation: M, ADNUR, EMT, MLTAD

01 President .... Dr. Pamela R. EDINGTON
05 VP of Academic Affairs & Stdnt Svcs .... Dr. Ellen M. GAMBINO
32 Dean of Student Services .... Dr. Melvin ADAMS
10 VP & Dean of Administration .... Vacant
20 Associate Dean of Academic Affairs .... Ms. Colleen TROGISCH
20 Associate Dean of Academic Affairs .... Dr. Kristel KEMMERER
20 Dean of Academic Affairs .... Dr. Holly MOLELLA
31 Dean Community Svcs/Special Pgms .... Ms. Virginia STOEFFEL
21 Associate Dean Administration .... Ms. Donna ROCAP
06 Registrar .... Ms. Angela ROMANO
84 Assoc Dean Stdnt Svcs/Enrollment .... Mr. Michael ROE
08 Director of the Library .... Ms. Cathy CARL
14 Director Information Systems .... Mr. Patrick GRIFFIN
111 Director Institutional Advancement .... Ms. Diana POLLARD
09 Director Planning/Inst Research .... Mr. Scott SCHNACKENBERG
37 Director Financial Aid .... Ms. Susan MEAD
36 Director Counseling/Career Svcs .... Mr. Mark BALABAN
15 Director Human Resources Mgmt .... Ms. Esther COURET
18 Assoc Dean of Admin Facilities Mgmt . Ms. Bridgette ANDERSON
19 Director Campus Security .... Mr. Ed COX
13 Assoc Dean Admin Info Technology .... Mr. Klaus GESSLER
35 Director of Student Activities .... Vacant
26 Chief Public Relations Officer .... Ms. Judi STOKES
88 Assoc Dir Teaching Learning Center .... Ms. Chrisie MITCHELL
88 Director of Scheduling .... Ms. Virginia POZNACK
12 Director DCC South Branch .... Mr. Timothy DECKER
04 Exec Assistant to the President .... Ms. AnneMarie ANDREWS
101 Secretary to the Board of Trustees .... Ms. Linda M. BEASIMER
22 Dir Affirmative Action/EEO .... Ms. Esther COURET
39 Director Residence Life .... Ms. Adrianna GRECO

D'Youville College (B)

320 Porter Avenue, Buffalo NY 14201-1084
County: Erie FICE Identification: 002712
Unit ID: 190716
Telephone: (716) 829-8000 Carnegie Class: Masters/L
FAX Number: (716) 829-7820 Calendar System: Semester
URL: www.dyc.edu
Established: 1908 Annual Undergrad Tuition & Fees: $25,210
Enrollment: 2,909 Coed
Affiliation or Control: Independent Non-Profit IRS Status: 501(c)3
Highest Offering: Doctorate
Accreditation: M, ARCPA, CAEPN, CHIRO, DIETC, IACBE, NURSE, OT, PHAR, PTA

01 President .... Dr. Lorrie CLEMO
11 Exec VP of Administrative Affairs .... Dr. William MARIANI
05 VP for Academic Affairs .... Dr. Arup SEN
10 VP for Financial Affairs .... Mr. John GARFOOT
32 VP Student Life & Enrollment Mgmt .... Mr. Randyll BOWEN
18 VP of Operations .... Mr. Nathan MARTON
111 VP of Institutional Advancement .... Ms. Kathleen CHRISTY
88 VP for Mission Integration .... Dr. Robert PERELLI
66 Dean School of Nursing .... Dr. Judith LEWIS
49 Dean Sch of Arts/Sciences & Educ .... Dr. Jason ADSIT
67 Dean School of Pharmacy .... Dr. Canio MARASCO
76 Dean School of Health Professions .... Dr. Maureen FINNEY
35 Assoc VP for Student Life .... Mr. Jeffrey PLATT
85 Assoc VP for Global Education .... Ms. Laryssa PETRYSHYN
07 Assoc VP Global Admiss & Partner .... Mr. Ronald DANNECKER
29 Assoc VP for Alumni Engagement .... Ms. Meg RITTLING
25 Assoc VP Grants & Spec Developments .... Ms. Molly FLYNN
30 Assoc VP for Advancement Svcs .... Ms. Aimee PEARSON
35 Assistant VP for Student Life .... Mr. Anthony SPINA
21 Assistant VP of Finance .... Mr. Timothy KORN
88 Artistic Director Kavinoky Theater .... Mr. David LAMB
13 Chief Information Officer .... Mr. Roozbeh TAVAKOLI
06 Registrar .... Mr. Daryl SMITH
113 Bursar .... Ms. Andrea ADDISON
09 Director Inst Rsrch/Assess Support .... Mr. Mark ECKSTEIN
108 Assistant Dean of Assessment .... Mr. Salvatore D'AMATO
91 Director Administrative Computing .... Mr. Robert HALL
44 Director Annual Giving .... Ms. Kelly BIEHLS
41 Director Athletics .... Mr. Brian CAVANAUGH
42 Director Campus Ministry .... Fr. Patrick O'KEEFE
36 Director Career Services Center .... Vacant
88 Director College Center .... Ms. Deborah E. OWENS
14 Director Computer & Network Svcs .... Ms. Mary SPENCE
102 Director Foundation Relations .... Mr. William P. MCKEEVER
23 Director Health Center .... Ms. Nicole CONROE
15 Director Human Resources .... Ms. Linda MORETTI
88 Director Learning Center .... Ms. Christina SPINK-FORMANSKI
08 Director Library Services .... Mr. Rand BELLAVIA
28 Director Multicultural Affairs .... Ms. Yolanda WOOD
38 Director Personal Counseling .... Ms. Kimberly ZITTEL
26 Director Marketing & Communications .... Mr. Colin NEKRITZ
19 Director Security .... Mr. Keith BOVA
37 Director Student Financial Aid .... Mr. Matthew METZ
07 Director Undergraduate Admissions .... Dr. Steve SMITH
124 Director Retention Services .... Ms. Amy YODER
123 Director Graduate Admissions .... Mr. Mark PAVONE
88 Director Veterans Affairs Office .... Mr. Benjamin RANDLE
120 Director E-Learning Services .... Ms. Kristen HORTMAN-FOWLER
88 Director CRPASH .... Dr. Renee CADZOW
88 Director Ctr Health Behav Rsrch .... Dr. Brian WROTNIAK
88 Dir of Int Aff VA & Mil Rsrch Ctr .... Dr. Bonnie FOX-GARRITY
88 Dir of Ext Aff VA & Mil Rsrch Ctr .... Dr. Dion DALY

Elim Bible Institute and College (C)

7245 College Street, Lima NY 14485
County: Livingston Identification: 667245
Unit ID: 488305
Telephone: (800) 670-3546 Carnegie Class: Not Classified
FAX Number: (585) 582-8130 Calendar System: Semester
URL: www.elim.edu
Established: 1924 Annual Undergrad Tuition & Fees: $7,968
Enrollment: N/A Coed
Affiliation or Control: Independent Non-Profit IRS Status: 501(c)3
Highest Offering: Associate Degree
Accreditation: @TRACS

01 President .... Michael CAVANAUGH
05 Vice President of Academic Affairs .... Danuta CASE
32 Dean of Students .... Stacy CLINE
10 Chief Financial Officer .... Mary Lynne KNILEY
07 Director of Admissions .... Wayne HEDLUND
73 Program Chair .... John MILLER
35 Campus Life Director .... Emily SANDERS
18 Facilities Director .... James BERCEL
06 Registrar .... Meredith ADER

The Elmezzi Graduate School of Molecular Medicine (D)

350 Community Drive, Manhasset NY 11030-3828
County: Nassau Identification: 666671
Unit ID: 486080
Telephone: (516) 562-3405 Carnegie Class: Not Classified
FAX Number: (516) 562-1022 Calendar System: Other
URL: www.elmezzigraduateschool.org
Established: 1999 Annual Graduate Tuition & Fees: N/A
Enrollment: 9 Coed
Affiliation or Control: Independent Non-Profit IRS Status: 501(c)3
Highest Offering: Doctorate; No Undergraduates
Accreditation: NY

01 President .... Dr. Kevin J. TRACEY
03 Provost .... Dr. Bettie M. STEINBERG
05 Dean .... Dr. Annette LEE
20 Associate Dean .... Dr. Christine METZ
10 Chief Business Officer .... Ms. Cynthia HAHN
101 Secretary of the Institution/Board .... Mr. Laurence KRAEMER
11 Chief of Administration .... Ms. Emilia HRISTIS
19 Director Security/Safety .... Mr. Robert KIKEL
25 Director Contracts/Grants Admin .... Ms. Diane MARBURY

Elmira Business Institute (E)

Langdon Plaza, 303 N Main Street, Elmira NY 14901-3086
County: Chemung FICE Identification: 009043
Unit ID: 190974
Telephone: (607) 733-7177 Carnegie Class: Spec 2-yr-Health
FAX Number: (607) 733-7178 Calendar System: Semester
URL: www.ebi-college.com
Established: 1858 Annual Undergrad Tuition & Fees: $21,700
Enrollment: 327 Coed
Affiliation or Control: Proprietary IRS Status: Proprietary
Highest Offering: Associate Degree
Accreditation: ACICS, MAC

01 President .... Mr. Brad C. PHILLIPS
11 Vice President of Administration .... Vacant
05 Chief Academic Officer .... Vacant
32 Dean of Students .... Vacant
07 Regional Director of Admissions .... Mr. Scott GALELEI

Elmira Business Institute (F)

4100 Old Vestal Road, Vestal NY 13850
Telephone: (607) 729-8915 Identification: 770745
Accreditation: ACICS

Elmira College (G)

One Park Place, Elmira NY 14901-2099
County: Chemung FICE Identification: 002718
Unit ID: 190983
Telephone: (607) 735-1800 Carnegie Class: Bac-A&S
FAX Number: (607) 735-1758 Calendar System: Other
URL: www.elmira.edu
Established: 1855 Annual Undergrad Tuition & Fees: $41,900
Enrollment: 1,376 Coed
Affiliation or Control: Independent Non-Profit IRS Status: 501(c)3
Highest Offering: Master's
Accreditation: M, CAEPT, NUR

01 President .... Dr. Charles W. LINDSAY
10 VP of Finance and Administration .... Mr. John C. ADAMS
05 Provost .... Dr. Charles E. MITCHELL
30 Vice Pres of External Relations .... Mr. Michael B. ROGERS
84 Vice Pres of Enrollment Management ... Mr. Christopher R. COONS
41 Vice President of Athletics .... Ms. Patricia A. THOMPSON
09 VP of Inst Assessment/Compliance .... Ms. Karen L. JOHNSON
20 Dean of Academic Affairs .... Dr. Lynn L. GILLIE
32 Dean of Students .... Mr. Brandon T. DAWSON
37 Dean of Financial Aid .... Ms. Kathleen L. COHEN
06 Registrar .... Mr. Michael HALPERIN
51 Director Cont Educ & Grad Studies .... Ms. Joann KOWALSKI
08 Dir of the Gannett-Tripp Library .... Ms. Margaret KAPPANADZE
36 Director of Career Development .... Ms. Julie FIELDING
50 Dept Chair of Business/Economics .... Dr. Mariam KHAWAR
57 Dept Chair of Creative Arts .... Prof. George H. DE FALUSSY
79 Dept Chair of Humanities .... Dr. Mitchell R. LEWIS
81 Dept Chair of Math/Natural Sciences .... Dr. Corey E. STILTS
83 Dept Chair of Soc/Behavior Science .... Dr. Jim TWOMBLY
53 Dept Chair of Teacher Education .... Dr. Deborah D. OWENS
107 Dept Chair of Speech & Hearing .... Prof. Cathy M. THORNTON
66 Dept Chair of Nursing .... Dr. Milissa VOLINO
29 Director of Alumni Relations .... Ms. Ellen HIMMELREICH
26 Dir of Communications & Marketing .... Ms. Jennifer L. SWAIN
39 Director of Residence Life .... Mr. Nathan FRIESEMA
40 Dir of Bookstore & Special Projects .... Ms. Shannon MOYLAN
15 Director of Human Resources .... Ms. Jessica CARPENTER
13 Chief Information Officer .... Mr. Brian CORNELL
19 Director of Campus Security .... Mr. Gary D. MILLER
44 Director of Annual Giving .... Vacant
102 Director of Grants .... Mrs. Valerie R. ROSPLOCK
23 Director of Health Services .... Mrs. Wendy FISCUS
04 Exec Assistant to the President .... Mrs. Mary C. BARRETT
38 Director of Counseling .... Dr. Kevin MURPHY
90 Dir Acad Technology/User Services .... Mr. Joseph C. FAHS

Elyon College (H)

1400 West 6th Street, Brooklyn NY 11204
County: Kings Identification: 667290
Telephone: (718) 259-5600 Carnegie Class: Not Classified
FAX Number: (218) 259-8024 Calendar System: Trimester
URL: elyoncollege.org
Established: Annual Undergrad Tuition & Fees: N/A
Enrollment: N/A Coed
Affiliation or Control: Independent Non-Profit IRS Status: 501(c)3
Highest Offering: Associate Degree
Accreditation: CNCE

01 President .... Chaim A. WALDMAN

Erie Community College (I)

121 Ellicott Street, Buffalo NY 14203-2698
County: Erie FICE Identification: 010684
Unit ID: 191083
Telephone: (716) 842-2770 Carnegie Class: Assoc/HT-Mix Trad/Non
FAX Number: (716) 851-1129 Calendar System: Semester
URL: www.ecc.edu
Established: 1971 Annual Undergrad Tuition & Fees (In-District): $5,408
Enrollment: 12,022 Coed
Affiliation or Control: State/Local IRS Status: 501(c)3
Highest Offering: Associate Degree
Accreditation: M, ACFEI, ADNUR, CAHIIM, COARC, DH, DIETT, DT, EMT, ENGT, MAC, MLTAD, OPD, OTA, #RTT

01 President .... Dr. Dan HOCOY
111 EVP Inst Advancement & Efficiency .... Mr. Michael PIETKIEWICZ
05 Provost Academic Affairs .... Mr. Richard C. WASHOUSKY
20 Vice Provost Academic Affairs .... Dr. Edward J. HOLMES
84 Vice President Enrollment Mgmt .... Dr. Erik D'AQUINO
32 VP Student Affairs .... Dr. Nuriyah CLARK
35 Dean of Students City .... Ms. Petrina HILL-CHEATOM
35 Dean of Students North .... Mr. Jason PERRI
35 Dean of Students South .... Ms. Heather A. CRUZ
13 Chief Information Officer .... Ms. F. Meena LAKHAVANI
23 Vice Provost Health Sciences .... Mr. Patrick J. WILES
88 AVP Data Analytics/Sys Integration .... Mr. Rob ELNICKY
14 Director of ERP Sys & Info Svcs .... Mr. David L. ARLINGTON
19 Assoc Vice President Security .... Mr. Tracy GAST
102 Vice Pres Foundation .... Mr. Jeffrey BAGEL
10 Chief Admin & Financial Officer .... Vacant

109 Coordinator Institutional Services ... Mr. Joel J. DAMIANI
15 Associate Vice Pres Human Resources ... Ms. Tracey CLEVELAND
16 Director Talent Mgmt & Empl Engmt ... Ms. Maria CARROLL
103 Exec Dean Workforce Dev/Cmty Svcs ... Ms. Carrie W. KAHN
49 Dean Liberal Arts & Science North ... Ms. Jamie SMITH
49 Dean Liberal Arts & Science South ... Ms. Joanne COLMERAUER
50 Dean Business/Public Service ... Dr. Kenneth J. BARNES
56 Director Dist Learning/Altern Pgm ... Mr. Patrick RYAN
72 Dean Engineering/Technology ... Mr. Mark S. HOEBER
28 Interim Chief Diversity Officer ... Mr. Lydell FORTUNE
06 Director of Registration ... Mr. Paul A. LAMANNA
07 Director of Admissions ... Mr. Philip STRUEBEL
08 Librarian City ... Ms. Kathleen POWERS
08 Librarian North ... Mr. Matthew BEST
08 Librarian South ... Ms. Taheera SHAHEED-SONUBI
40 Bookstore Manager City ... Ms. Susan SCHMITTENDORF
40 Bookstore Manager North ... Ms. Teresa KALINOWSKI
40 Bookstore Manager South ... Mr. Michael FOX
88 Health Services Nurse South ... Ms. Frances WILLIAMS
88 Health Services Nurse North ... Ms. Lisa GRAZIANO
88 Health Services Nurse City ... Ms. Kelly ROCKWELL
36 Career Resource Center Director ... Ms. Katherine MARSHALL
26 Director Marketing & Communications ... Vacant
09 Director Institutional Research ... Ms. Marlene ARNO
45 Vice Provost IRAAP ... Dr. Fabio ESCOBAR
27 Public Information Officer ... Mr. Michael FARRELL
41 Director of Athletics ... Mr. Peter J. JEREBKO
88 Assistant Director Athletics ... Mr. Steve L. MULLEN
18 Director Buildings & Grounds ... Vacant
37 Director of Financial Aid ... Mr. Scott WELTJEN
21 Business Manager ... Mr. Paul F. DANIEU
24 Audio Visual Coordinator City ... Mr. Mark DZIELSKI
24 Audio Visual Coordinator North ... Mr. Ryan NOGLE
24 Audio Visual Coordinator North ... Mr. Nicholas SONRICKER
24 Audio Visual Coordinator South ... Mr. David SEIFERT
88 Coordinator of Corporate Training ... Mr. John P. SLISZ
25 Grants Coordinator ... Mr. Michael J. BIGGANE
29 Director of Alumni Relations ... Ms. Stephanie KING
85 Foreign Student Advisor ... Mr. John DANNA
88 Dir of Student Access/Veteran Affs ... Mr. Daniel FRONTERA
88 Advanced Studies Coordinator ... Ms. Deborah F. SCHMITT

Excelsior College (A)

7 Columbia Circle, Albany NY 12203-5156

County: Albany FICE Identification: 002834
Unit ID: 196680
Telephone: (518) 464-8500 Carnegie Class: Masters/L
FAX Number: (518) 464-8777 Calendar System: Other
URL: www.excelsior.edu
Established: 1971 Annual Undergrad Tuition & Fees: N/A
Enrollment: 43,123 Coed
Affiliation or Control: Independent Non-Profit IRS Status: 501(c)3
Highest Offering: Master's
Accreditation: M, ADNUR, CS, ENGT, IACBE, NUR

01 President ... Dr. James BALDWIN
43 General Counsel ... Ms. Karen HALACO
05 Chief Academic Officer/Provost ... Dr. Debbie SOPCZYK
11 Chief Operating Officer ... Mr. James LETTKO
32 Assoc Provost Student & Fac Svcs ... Dr. Joan MIKALSON
13 VP Information Technology/CIO ... Dr. Wayne BROWN
15 VP Human Resources ... Mr. Mark HOWE
10 CFO/VP Finance ... Dr. Karl LAWRENCE
111 VP Institutional Advancement ... Mr. Keith BARROWS
108 AVP Analytics/Decision Support ... Dr. Lisa DANIELS
20 AVP for Academic Operations ... Ms. Emilsen HOLGUIN
86 AVP for Government Relations ... Dr. Paul SHIFFMAN
84 AVP for Enrollment Management ... Mr. Thomas DALTON
14 Deputy CIO ... Mr. Ron MARZITELLI
16 Exec Dir for Human Resources ... Ms. Anita BURNS
88 AVP Center for Military & Veteran ... Ms. Susan DEWAN
56 COO Extended Education ... Dr. Susan KRYCZKA
21 Controller ... Ms. Hillary KOLDIN
49 Dean of Liberal Arts ... Dr. George TIMMONS
50 Dean of Business & Technology ... Dr. Li-Fang SHIH
66 Dean of Nursing ... Dr. Mary Lee POLLARD
76 Dean of Health Sciences ... Dr. Laurie CARBO-PORTER
97 Dean of Public Service ... Dr. Robert WATERS
88 Ombudsperson ... Ms. Kathy MORAN
06 Registrar ... Ms. Lori MORANO
88 Exec Director of Strategic Partners ... Ms. Lisa LAVIGNA
88 General Manager CEM ... Ms. Nurit SONNENSCHEIN
26 Chief Marketing Officer ... Ms. Dawn GERRAIN
25 Exec Dir of Grants and Research ... Ms. Patricia CROOP
88 Deputy CIO of Enterprise Systems ... Mr. Donn AIKEN
88 Exec Dir Enrollment Mgmt Ops ... Mr. Dan MERKT
88 Director of Creative Services ... Ms. Maria SPARKS
29 Director of Alumni Affairs ... Ms. Renee KELLY
18 Facilities Manager ... Mr. Robert RANALLI
27 Chief Communications Officer ... Mr. Michael LESCZINSKI
28 Diversity Coordinator ... Ms. Toby HAMLIN
37 Exec Dir Financial Aid ... Ms. Susan MERCHANT
14 Chief Operations Officer for IT ... Ms. Andrea LALA
88 Exec Dir Center for Learning Design ... Ms. Wendy TREVOR
88 Exec Dir of Enterprise Apps Support ... Mr. Jim WALL
119 Exec Director of Info Security ... Mr. Kevin REEDY
121 Exec Dir Student Success Center ... Mr. Glenn BRADDOCK
88 Exec Director Transcript Analysis ... Ms. Kat MCGRATH
07 Director of Admissions ... Ms. Diane NASS
09 AVP of Analytics ... Dr. Lisa DANIELS
101 Asst to Pres for Trustee ... Ms. Laurie KEENAN

Fashion Institute of Technology (B)

Seventh Avenue at 27 Street, New York NY 10001-5992

County: New York FICE Identification: 002866
Unit ID: 191126
Telephone: (212) 217-7999 Carnegie Class: Bac/Assoc-Mixed
FAX Number: N/A Calendar System: Semester
URL: www.fitnyc.edu
Established: 1944 Annual Undergrad Tuition & Fees (In-District): $5,335
Enrollment: 9,565 Coed
Affiliation or Control: State/Local IRS Status: 501(c)3
Highest Offering: Master's
Accreditation: M, ART, CIDA

01 President ... Dr. Joyce F. BROWN
10 Treasurer/VP Finance/Administration ... Ms. Sherry F. BRABHAM
101 Secy of College/General Counsel ... Dr. Stephen TUTTLE
05 Vice President Academic Affairs ... Dr. Giacomo OLIVA
26 Vice Pres Comm/External Rels ... Ms. Loretta LAWRENCE KEANE
84 Vice Pres Enrollment Mgmt/Student ... Dr. Kelly BRENNAN
15 Int VP Human Res Mgmt/Labor Rels ... Ms. Brenda J. SMITH
13 VP for Information Technology/CIO ... Mr. Gregg CHOTTINER
30 VP Devel & Exec Dir Foundation ... Vacant
20 Assoc Vice Pres Academic Affairs ... Mr. Sidney GRIMES
16 Asst Vice Pres Human Res/Labor Rels ... Vacant
21 Actg Asst Vice Pres Finance ... Mr. Bayard KING
11 Actg Assistant VP of Administration ... Ms. Natalie POLVERE
88 Asst VP Enterprise Application Svcs ... Mr. Van Buren WINSTON
27 Asst Vice Pres for Communications ... Ms. Carol LEVEN
32 Asst VP Student Success/Dean Stdnts ... Ms. Shadia SACHEDINA
88 Asst VP Enrollment Management ... Mr. Terence PEAVY
20 Assoc VP Academic Affairs ... Dr. Yasemin JONES
51 Dean Continuing & Prof Studies ... Mr. Daniel GERGER
57 Dean Art & Design ... Mr. Troy RICHARDS
58 Dean School of Graduate Studies ... Dr. Mary DAVIS
49 Dean Liberal Arts ... Dr. Patrick KNISLEY
50 Dean Business & Technology ... Mr. Steven FRUMKIN
121 Assoc Dean Academic Advisement ... Mr. Tardis JOHNSON
07 Dir of Admissions/Strat Recruiting ... Ms. Magda FRANCOIS
88 Director Special Events ... Ms. Victoria GURANOWSKI
11 Director Operational Services ... Mr. John WILSON
18 Executive Director of Facilities ... Mr. George JEFREMOW
22 Affirm Action Ofcr/Dir Compliance ... Ms. Griselda GONZALEZ
38 Director of the Counseling Center ... Ms. Terry GINDER
37 Director of Financial Aid ... Ms. Mina FRIEDMANN
08 Dir of the Gladys Marcus Library ... Mr. NJ BRADEEN
06 Director of Registration & Records ... Ms. Rita CAMMARATA
39 Director of Residential Life ... Ms. Ann Marie GRAPPO
36 Director Career & Internship ... Vacant
35 Director of Student Life ... Ms. Michelle VAN-ESS
23 Director of Health Services ... Ms. Anne MILLER
19 Director of Campus Safety ... Mr. Mario CABRERA
88 Director of The Museum at FIT ... Dr. Valerie STEELE
09 Asst Dean Inst Research & Effect ... Mr. Darrell GLENN
86 Dir Government/Community Relations ... Ms. Lisa WAGER
27 Exec Director of Public & Media Rel ... Ms. Cheryl FEIN
104 Dean of International Programs ... Dr. Deirdre SATO
41 Director of Athletics & Recreation ... Mr. Keith HERON
96 Director of Budget ... Ms. Nancy SU
88 Dir of Education Opportunity Pgms ... Ms. Taur D. ORANGE
21 Controller/Assistant Treas ... Ms. Shelci GRAHAM
88 Director Env Health/Sfty Compliance ... Mr. Paul DEBIASE
92 Coord Presidential Scholars Pgm ... Ms. Yasemin LEVINE
105 Manager Digital Strategies ... Ms. Taryn REJHOLEC
55 Dir Evening/Weekend/Pre-College ... Ms. Michele NAGEL
29 Manager Alumni Engagement & Giving ... Mr. Kenneth LAM
28 Chair of Diversity Council ... Mr. Michael COKKINOS
119 Chief Information Security Officer ... Mr. Walter KERNER
96 Director Purchasing ... Mr. Walter WINTER
39 Director of Residential Life ... Ms. Christina DIGGS
85 Asst Dir International Student Svcs ... Ms. Erika ROHRBACK

Fei Tian College (C)

140 Galley Hill Road, Cuddebackville NY 12729

County: Orange Identification: 667205
Telephone: (845) 672-0550 Carnegie Class: Not Classified
FAX Number: (845) 977-0481 Calendar System: Semester
URL: www.feitian.edu
Established: Annual Undergrad Tuition & Fees: N/A
Enrollment: N/A Coed
Affiliation or Control: Independent Non-Profit IRS Status: 501(c)3
Highest Offering: Master's
Accreditation: NY

01 President ... Ms. Vina LEE

Finger Lakes Community College (D)

3325 Marvin Sands Drive, Canandaigua NY 14424-8405

County: Ontario FICE Identification: 007532
Unit ID: 191199
Telephone: (585) 394-3522 Carnegie Class: Assoc/HT-High Non
FAX Number: (585) 394-5005 Calendar System: Semester
URL: www.flcc.edu
Established: 1965 Annual Undergrad Tuition & Fees (In-District): $4,952
Enrollment: 6,755 Coed
Affiliation or Control: State/Local IRS Status: 501(c)3
Highest Offering: Associate Degree
Accreditation: M, ADNUR

01 President ... Dr. Robert NYE
05 Provost ... Ms. Kristen M. FRAGNOLI
10 Sr Vice President of Admin/Finance ... Mr. James R. FISHER
84 Vice Pres Enrollment Management ... Ms. Carol S. URBAITIS
32 Assoc Vice Pres of Student Affairs ... Mr. Jacob AMIDON
20 Assoc VP Instruction & Assessment ... Dr. Cassy KENT
20 Assoc VP Academic Affairs ... Mr. Jacob E. AMIDON
15 Director of Human Resources ... Ms. Grace H. LOOMIS
30 Chief Advancement Officer ... Mr. Joseph NAIRN
19 Dir of Campus Security Operations ... Mr. Jason R. MAITLAND
21 Controller ... Mr. Joseph L. DELFORTE
18 Director of Facilities & Grounds ... Ms. Catherine AHERN
07 Director of Admissions ... Ms. Bonnie B. RITTS
06 Registrar ... Mr. Michael FISHER
25 Director of Grants Development ... Ms. Karen A. VAN KEUREN
37 Director of Financial Aid ... Ms. Dawn LANGDON
35 Director of Student Life ... Ms. Jennie ERDLE
13 Chief Information Officer ... Mr. John TAYLOR
38 Dir Educ Planning/Career Services ... Ms. Corrine M. CANOUGH
36 Career Services Coordinator ... Ms. Tammie WOODY
08 Director Library Learning Resources ... Ms. Sarah MOON
26 Director of Marketing ... Ms. Heidi C. MARCIN
23 Director of Student Health Services ... Ms. Janette ARUK
24 Dir Instructional Technology ... Mr. Daniel P. FARSACI
09 Director Institutional Effectivenes .. Ms. Mary MCLEAN-SCANLON
29 Director of Alumni Relations ... Ms. Lisa L. SCOTT
96 Director of Business Services ... Ms. Andrea BARBER
72 Chair Science & Technology ... Mr. Clinton KRAGER
50 Interim Chair Business ... Mr. Gary SLOAN
65 Chair Environment Conservation Hort ... Mr. John FOUST
57 Chair Visual/Performing Arts ... Ms. Catherine JOHNSON
66 Chair Nursing ... Ms. Mary CORIALE
68 Chair Physical Education ... Mr. Eric MARSH
81 Chair Computer Science ... Ms. April A. DEVAUX
79 Chair Humanities ... Ms. Charlotte CLINE
83 Chair Social Science ... Mr. Joshua W. HELLER
81 Chair Mathematics ... Ms. Theresa GAUTHIER

Finger Lakes Health College of Nursing (E)

196 North Street, Geneva NY 14456

County: Ontario Identification: 667154
Unit ID: 475422
Telephone: (315) 787-4005 Carnegie Class: Spec 2-yr-Health
FAX Number: (313) 787-4275 Calendar System: Semester
URL: www.flhealth.org/fornurses
Established: 2008 Annual Undergrad Tuition & Fees: $11,540
Enrollment: 124 Coed
Affiliation or Control: Independent Non-Profit IRS Status: 501(c)3
Highest Offering: Associate Degree
Accreditation: ABHES, ADNUR, SURGT, SURTEC

01 Dean ... Victoria RECORD
32 Student Services Coordinator ... Ann SPAYD

Five Towns College (F)

305 North Service Road, Dix Hills NY 11746-6055

County: Suffolk FICE Identification: 012561
Unit ID: 191205
Telephone: (631) 656-2157 Carnegie Class: Bac-Diverse
FAX Number: (631) 656-2172 Calendar System: Semester
URL: www.ftc.edu
Established: 1972 Annual Undergrad Tuition & Fees: $19,380
Enrollment: 653 Coed
Affiliation or Control: Proprietary IRS Status: Proprietary
Highest Offering: Doctorate
Accreditation: M, CAEPN

01 President ... Mr. David COHEN
05 Provost ... Ms. Carolann MILLER
10 Vice Pres Finance/Administration ... Mr. Hubert STACHURA
32 Dean of Students ... Dr. Jennifer ALBERT
06 Senior Registrar ... Ms. Deborah EBBERT
106 Director of Online Education ... Vacant
37 Director of Financial Aid ... Mr. Jason LABONTE
08 Library Director ... Mr. John VANSTEEN
38 College Counselor ... Ms. Carolyn NEWMAN
64 Chair of Music Division ... Prof. Jill MILLER-THORN
50 Deputy Chair of Business Division ... Vacant
49 Chair of Liberal Arts Division ... Vacant
53 Chair of Education Division ... Mr. William FORTGANG
88 Chair of Film/Video ... Mr. James BOCK
88 Chair of Theatre Arts ... Mr. Jared HERSHKOWITZ
36 Director Student Placement ... Ms. Krysti O'ROURKE
18 Chief Facilities/Physical Plant ... Mr. Mark SHAUGHNESSY
19 Director of Public Safety ... Mr. William JANSSEN
39 Director of Residential Life ... Mr. Thomas O'BOYLE
07 Director of Admissions ... Ms. Terry DONOHUE
09 Director of Institutional Research ... Vacant

Fordham University (G)

441 East Fordham Road, Bronx NY 10458-9993

County: Bronx FICE Identification: 002722
Unit ID: 191241
Telephone: (718) 817-1000 Carnegie Class: DU-Higher
FAX Number: (718) 817-4925 Calendar System: Semester
URL: www.fordham.edu
Established: 1841 Annual Undergrad Tuition & Fees: $49,073
Enrollment: 15,286 Coed
Affiliation or Control: Independent Non-Profit IRS Status: 501(c)3
Highest Offering: Doctorate

Accreditation: M, CAEPN, CLPSY, COPSY, LAW, SCPSY, SW

01 President .... Rev. Joseph M. MCSHANE, SJ
100 Assoc VP Pres Operations .... Mrs. Dorothy MARINUCCI
04 Asst Univ Sec/Spec Asst to Pres .... Mr. Michael R. TREROTOLA
05 Provost .... Dr. Stephen FREEDMAN
10 SVP/CFO and Treasurer .... Ms. Martha K. HIRST
32 Sr Vice President Student Affairs .... Mr. Jeffrey L. GRAY
21 Vice President for Finance .... Mr. Nicholas B. MILOWSKI
13 VP for Information Technology/CIO .... Dr. Frank SIRIANNI
84 Vice President for Enrollment .... Dr. Peter A. STACE
12 Vice President for Lincoln Center .... Dr. Brian J. BYRNE
30 Vice President for Development .... Mr. Roger A. MILICI, JR.
88 Vice President for Mission .... Rev. Michael C. MCCARTHY, SJ
18 VP for Facilities Management .... Mr. Marco VALERA
11 Vice President for Administration .... Mr. Thomas A. DUNNE
101 Secretary of the University .... Ms. Margaret T. BALL
20 Assoc Vice Pres Academic Affairs .... Dr. Benjamin CROOKER
20 Assoc Vice Pres Academic Affairs .... Dr. Jonathan CRYSTAL
20 Assoc Vice Pres Academic Affairs .... Dr. Ron JACOBSON
29 AVP/Director of Alumni Relations .... Mr. Michael GRIFFIN
07 Assoc Vice Pres Undgrad Enrollment .... Mr. John W. BUCKLEY
06 Asst Vice Pres Enrollment/Registrar .... Dr. Gene FEIN
37 Assoc VP Student Financial Services .... Ms. Angela VAN DEKKER
86 Assoc Vice Pres for Government Rels .... Mr. Joseph P. MURIANA
86 Assoc Vice Pres for Government Rels .... Ms. Lesley A. MASSIAH-ARTHUR
43 General Counsel .... Ms. Elaine CROSSON
35 Asst VP and Dean of Students .... Mr. Christopher RODGERS
35 Asst VP & Dean of Student Services .... Mr. Gregory J. PAPPAS
12 Dean Fordham College at Rose Hill .... Dr. Maura B. MAST
58 Dean Graduate Arts & Science .... Dr. Eva BADOWSKA
73 Dean Graduate Religious Education .... Dr. C. Colt ANDERSON
50 Dean Gabelli School of Business .... Dr. Donna RAPACCIOLI
107 Dean Sch of Prof and Cont Studies .... Dr. Anthony R. DAVIDSON
12 Dean Fordham College Lincoln Center .... Rev. Robert GRIMES, SJ
53 Dean Graduate Education LC .... Dr. Virginia ROACH
61 Dean School of Law LC .... Mr. Matthew DILLER
70 Dean Graduate Social Service LC .... Dr. Debra MCPHEE
15 Exec Director of Human Resources .... Mr. Michael MINEO
09 Director Institutional Research .... Dr. Peter FEIGENBAUM
42 Executive Director Campus Ministry .... Rev. Jose-Luis SALAZAR, SJ
21 Controller .... Mr. Anthony GRONO
19 AVP Public Safety .... Mr. John CARROLL
22 Director of Institutional Equity .... Ms. Anastasia COLEMAN
46 Chief Research Officer/AVP .... Dr. Z. George HONG
08 Director of University Libraries .... Ms. Linda LOSCHIAVO
24 Director Media Center .... Mr. Jerry GREEN
23 Director of Health Center .... Ms. Kathleen MALARA
35 Asst Dean Student Involvement .... Mr. Cody ARCURI
88 AVP of Athletic Alumni Relations .... Mr. Francis X. MCLAUGHLIN
96 Director of Procurement .... Mr. Frank A. DEORIO
38 Director of Psychological Svcs .... Dr. Jeffrey NG
28 Asst Dean/Dir Multicultural Affairs .... Mr. Juan Carlos MATOS
36 Director Career Services .... Vacant
39 Asst Dean/Dir of Residential Life .... Ms. Kimberly RUSSELL

Fulton-Montgomery Community College (A)

2805 State Highway 67, Johnstown NY 12095-3790
County: Montgomery FICE Identification: 002867
Unit ID: 191302
Telephone: (518) 736-3622 Carnegie Class: Assoc/HT-High Trad
FAX Number: (518) 762-5693 Calendar System: Semester
URL: www.fmcc.edu
Established: 1963 Annual Undergrad Tuition & Fees (In-District): $4,770
Enrollment: 2,551 Coed
Affiliation or Control: State/Local IRS Status: 501(c)3
Highest Offering: Associate Degree
Accreditation: M, ADNUR, RAD

01 President .... Dr. Dustin SWANGER
05 Provost/Vice Pres Academic Affairs .... Dr. Greg TRUCKENMILLER
10 Vice Pres Finance & Administration .... Mr. David M. MORROW
32 Vice President of Student Affairs .... Ms. Jane KELLEY
20 Dean of Academic Affairs .... Ms. Diana PUTNAM
20 Assistant Dean of Academic Affairs .... Ms. Ronalyn WILSON
21 Director of Business Affairs .... Mr. Gregg WILBUR
13 Director of Information Technology .... Mr. Gregg ROTH
18 Director of Facilities .... Mr. Joshua FLEMING
07 Director of Admissions .... Ms. Laura LAPORTE
06 Registrar .... Mr. Scott COLLINS
08 Librarian .... Ms. Mary DONOHUE
36 Director of Career Planning .... Ms. Andrea SCRIBNER
121 Director Advisement/Counseling/Test .... Ms. Mary-Jo FERRAUILO-DAVIS
30 Chief Development .... Ms. Lesley LANZI
09 Director of Institutional Research .... Mr. Eric KIMMELMAN
37 Coordinator Financial Aid .... Ms. Rebecca COZZOCREA
04 Administrative Asst to President .... Ms. Paula WEAVER
108 Director Institutional Assessment .... Ms. Jacqueline SNYDER
15 Director of Human Resources .... Mr. Jason RAUCH
19 Director of Public Safety .... Mr. Mark PIERCE
25 Director of Grants .... Ms. Jean KARUTIS
26 Coordinator Public Relations .... Ms. Amy RADIK
39 Director Student Housing .... Ms. Christine SMITH
41 Athletic Director .... Mr. Kevin JONES
90 IT Infrastructure Administrator .... Mr. William BONNER
91 Associate Director of IT .... Mr. Paul PUTMAN

General Theological Seminary (B)

440 West 21st Street, New York NY 10011-2981
County: New York FICE Identification: 002726
Unit ID: 191320
Telephone: (212) 243-5150 Carnegie Class: Spec-4-yr-Faith
FAX Number: (212) 727-3907 Calendar System: Semester
URL: www.gts.edu
Established: 1817 Annual Graduate Tuition & Fees: N/A
Enrollment: 46 Coed
Affiliation or Control: Protestant Episcopal IRS Status: 501(c)3
Highest Offering: Master's; No Undergraduates
Accreditation: THEOL

01 President and Dean .... Rev. Kurt DUNKLE
11 Vice President of Operations .... Mr. Anthony KHANI
111 VP for Institutional Advancement .... Ms. Donna ASHLEY
05 VP & Dean of Academic Affairs .... Dr. Michael DELASHMUTT
10 VP & Controller .... Mr. Robert ELLIOT
26 Director of Communications .... Mr. Joshua BRUNER
06 Director of Acad Mgmt & Registrar .... Ms. Stacie WARING
15 Director of HR & Financial Aid .... Ms. Trecia O'SULLIVAN
30 Director of Development .... Mr. Jonathan SILVER
04 Exec Asst to the President & Dean .... Ms. Tracey PITTS
08 Head Librarian .... Vacant

Genesee Community College (C)

One College Road, Batavia NY 14020-9704
County: Genesee FICE Identification: 006782
Unit ID: 191339
Telephone: (585) 343-0055 Carnegie Class: Assoc/HT-Mix Trad/Non
FAX Number: (585) 343-4541 Calendar System: Semester
URL: www.genesee.edu
Established: 1966 Annual Undergrad Tuition & Fees (In-District): $4,460
Enrollment: 6,507 Coed
Affiliation or Control: State/Local IRS Status: 501(c)3
Highest Offering: Associate Degree
Accreditation: M, ADNUR, COARC, POLYT, PTAA

01 President .... Dr. James SUNSER
05 Provost/Exec VP Academic Affairs .... Dr. Kathleen SCHIEFEN
81 Dean Math/Science/Career Education .... Dr. Rafael ALICEA-MALDONADO
83 Dean Human Communication/Behavior .... Dr. Katharina E. KOVACH-ALLEN
56 Dean of Distributed Learning .... Dr. Craig LAMB
20 Asc Dean Accelerated Col Enrol Pgms .... Mr. Edward LEVINSTEIN
06 Registrar .... Mr. Terrence REDING
57 Director Fine & Performing Arts .... Ms. Maryanne ARENA
68 Director of Health & Physical Educ .... Ms. Rebecca DZIEKAN
45 Exec VP for Planning/Inst Effectiv .... Mr. William T. EMM
09 Assoc VP Inst Rsrch & Assessment .... Ms. Carol MARRIOTT
15 Assoc VP for Human Resources .... Ms. Gina WEAVER
25 Director of Grants Services .... Mr. James DONSBACH
103 Exec Dir for Workforce Development .... Mr. Reid SMALLEY
88 Director Business Skills Training .... Mr. John MCGOWAN
10 Vice Pres for Finance & Operations .... Mr. Kevin HAMILTON
21 Controller .... Ms. Kristin L. YUNKER
13 Director of Computer Services .... Ms. Cindy DELMAR
18 Director of Buildings & Grounds .... Mr. Timothy M. LANDERS
32 VP for Student & Enrollment Svcs .... Dr. Virginia TAYLOR
35 Dean of Students .... Ms. Patricia CHAYA
07 Director of Admissions .... Ms. Tanya LANE-MARTIN
37 Director of Financial Aid .... Mr. Joseph A. BAILEY
88 Director of Student Activities .... Mr. Clifford M. SCUTELLA
41 Director of Athletics .... Ms. Kristen SCHUTH
30 Director Devel & External Affairs .... Mr. Richard G. ENSMAN, JR.
90 Manager of Academic Computing .... Mrs. Mary Jane HEIDER
04 Administrative Asst to President .... Ms. Cathy COSTELLO
102 Dir Foundation/Corporate Relations .... Mr. Richard ENSMAN
19 Director Security/Safety .... Mr. Stephen WISE

Hamilton College (D)

198 College Hill Road, Clinton NY 13323-1218
County: Oneida FICE Identification: 002728
Unit ID: 191515
Telephone: (315) 859-4011 Carnegie Class: Bac-A&S
FAX Number: (315) 859-4991 Calendar System: Semester
URL: www.hamilton.edu
Established: 1812 Annual Undergrad Tuition & Fees: $51,240
Enrollment: 1,877 Coed
Affiliation or Control: Independent Non-Profit IRS Status: 501(c)3
Highest Offering: Baccalaureate
Accreditation: M

01 President .... David WIPPMAN
05 VPAA/Dean of Faculty .... Margaret GENTRY
11 Vice Pres Administration/Finance .... Karen L. LEACH
30 Vice Pres Communication/Development .... Lori R. DENNISON
13 Vice Pres Information Technology .... David L. SMALLEN
07 VP/Dean Admission & Financial Aid .... Monica C. INZER
32 Vice Pres/Dean of Students .... Terry MARTINEZ
20 Associate Dean of Faculty .... Samuel PELLMAN
41 Athletic Director .... Jonathan T. HIND
39 Director Residential Life .... Travis R. HILL
10 Controller .... Shari K. WHITING
08 Dir of Library/Info Technology .... Joe SHELLLEY
27 Director Strategic Communications .... Stacey J. HIMMELBERGER
37 Director of Financial Aid .... K. Cameron FEIST
36 Int Exec Director Career Center .... Sam WELCH

06 Registrar .... Kristin M. FRIEDEL
15 Director of Human Resources .... Stephen STEMKOSKI
18 Director Physical Plant .... Steven J. BELLONA
19 Director of Campus Safety .... Francis A. MANFREDO
38 Director Counseling/Psych Services .... David WALDEN
42 Newman Chaplain .... John CROGHAN
24 Director Audiovisual Services .... Timothy J. HICKS
09 Director of Institutional Research .... Gordon J. HEWITT
26 Exec Director of Communications .... Michael J. DEBRAGGIO
28 Chief Diversity Officer .... Phyllis BRELAND
29 Director Alumni Relations .... Sharon T. RIPPEY
96 Director of Purchasing .... Irene K. CORNISH
40 Manager College Store .... Jennifer PHILLIPS

Hartwick College (E)

One Hartwick Drive, Oneonta NY 13820-1790
County: Otsego FICE Identification: 002729
Unit ID: 191533
Telephone: (607) 431-4000 Carnegie Class: Bac-A&S
FAX Number: (607) 431-4206 Calendar System: 4/1/4
URL: www.hartwick.edu
Established: 1797 Annual Undergrad Tuition & Fees: $42,860
Enrollment: 1,393 Coed
Affiliation or Control: Independent Non-Profit IRS Status: 501(c)3
Highest Offering: Master's
Accreditation: M, ART, CAEPT, MUS, NURSE

01 President .... Dr. Margaret L. DRUGOVICH
05 Executive Vice President & Provost .... Dr. Michael TANNENBAUM
10 Vice President Finance/CFO .... Ms. Sydney R. LEO
111 Vice Pres Institutional Advancement .... Mr. Gregg FORT
32 Vice President for Student Life .... Dr. Meg NOWAK
84 Vice Pres for Enrollment Management .... Ms. Karen MCGRATH
04 Senior Assistant to the President .... Ms. Kerri GREEN
15 Director Human Resources .... Ms. Suzanne JANITZ
39 Director Residence Life .... Mr. Zachary BROWN
06 Registrar .... Mr. Matthew SANFORD
20 Dean of Academic Affairs .... Dr. Kellie BEAN
37 Director of Financial Aid .... Ms. Melissa ALLEN
08 Interim Director of Libraries .... Mr. David HEYDUK
85 Director International Pgms .... Dr. Godlove FONJWENG
13 Director Inst Info Systems Services .... Ms. Deb B. HILTS
91 Director Technologies Services .... Ms. Suzanne GAYNOR
18 Director of Facilities Services .... Mr. Joseph MACK
41 Director of Athletics .... Dr. Kimberly FIERKE
38 Director of Counseling Services .... Mr. Gary ROBINSON
23 Director of Student Health Center .... Ms. Amy GARDNER, FNP
27 Marketing Communications Manager .... Mr. Christopher LOTT
26 Exec Dir of Donor & Alumni Rels .... Ms. Alicia FISH
07 Director Admissions .... Ms. Lisa STARKEY-WOODS
12 Director Pine Lake Campus .... Ms. Erin TOAL
21 Director Financial Svcs/Controller .... Ms. Karen ZUILL
09 Director of Institutional Research .... Dr. Amanda Kay MOSKE
29 Director of Alumni Engagement .... Vacant
19 Director of Campus Safety .... Mr. Thomas KELLY
40 Manager of B&N Bookstore .... Mr. Frank WERDANN
96 Manager of Purchasing .... Vacant
102 Dir Foundation/Corporate Relations .... Ms. Lisa IANNELLO
105 Director Web Services .... Ms. Stephanie BRUNETTA
108 Dean of Assessment .... Dr. Kimberly YOUSNEY-ELSENER

Hebrew Union College-Jewish Institute of Religion (F)

1 West 4th Street, New York NY 10012-1186
County: New York FICE Identification: 004054
Unit ID: 203067
Telephone: (212) 674-5300 Carnegie Class: Spec-4-yr-Faith
FAX Number: (212) 388-1720 Calendar System: Semester
URL: www.huc.edu
Established: 1875 Annual Graduate Tuition & Fees: N/A
Enrollment: 326 Coed
Affiliation or Control: Jewish IRS Status: 501(c)3
Highest Offering: Doctorate; No Undergraduates
Accreditation: M, PAST

01 President .... Rabbi Aaron PANKEN
05 Vice Pres Academic Affairs/Provost .... Rabbi Michael MARMUR
30 Vice President Inst Advancement .... Dr. Lissie DIRINGER
10 Chief Financial Officer .... Ms. Sandra M. MILLS
101 Exec Sec to Board of Governors .... Ms. Andrea KANN
26 AVP National Dir Public Affs/Comm .... Ms. Jean B. ROSENSAFT
44 Natl Dir of Institutional Giving .... Dr. Andrew GRANT
08 Librarian .... Mr. Yoram BITTON
79 Director American Jewish Archives .... Dr. Gary ZOLA
09 Manager Institutional Research .... Mr. Bobby COVITZ
07 Asst Director Recruitment/Admission .... Rabbi Andrew GOODMAN
13 Director of Information Systems .... Mr. John H. BRUGGEMAN
15 Director of Legal Affairs & HR .... Mr. Jeremy PERLIN
37 Director of Financial Aid .... Ms. Roseanne ACKERLEY

Helene Fuld College of Nursing (G)

24 East 120th Street, New York NY 10035
County: New York FICE Identification: 010153
Unit ID: 191597
Telephone: (212) 616-7200 Carnegie Class: Spec-4-yr-Other Health
FAX Number: (212) 616-7299 Calendar System: Quarter
URL: www.helenefuld.edu
Established: 1945 Annual Undergrad Tuition & Fees: N/A
Enrollment: 459 Coed
Affiliation or Control: Independent Non-Profit IRS Status: 501(c)3

Highest Offering: Baccalaureate
Accreditation: M, ADNUR, NURSE

01 President .... Dr. Wendy ROBINSON
05 Vice President for Academic Affairs .... Dr. Cynthia HUGHES
10 Head of Finance .... Mrs. Galina VILKINA
11 Director of Administration .... Ms. Celeste WALLIN
32 Director of Student Services .... Mrs. Sandra SENIOR
08 Director of Library & IT .... Mr. Indrajeet SINGH CHAUHAN
35 Assoc Director of Student Services .... Ms. Gladys PINEDA
26 Director of External Affairs .... Ms. Michelle HERNANDEZ
88 Director of BSN program .... Dr. Wendy ROBINSON
20 Director of Associate Program .... Ms. Heather LASHLEY
37 Financial Aid Counselor .... Ms. Andrine THOMAS
15 Human Resources Generalist .... Ms. Alysha WILLIS
09 Institutional Researcher .... Vacant
38 College Counselor .... Ms. Dana GOLIN
04 Executive Assistant .... Ms. Kadia DARBY
13 Information Technology/Library Asst .... Mr. Eickel ORTIZ
07 College Recruiter .... Ms. Alphonsa ITTOOP
29 Director Alumni Relations .... Vacant

Herkimer County Community College (A)

100 Reservoir Road, Herkimer NY 13350-1598
County: Herkimer FICE Identification: 004788
Unit ID: 191612
Telephone: (315) 574-3997 Carnegie Class: Assoc/HT-High Non
FAX Number: (315) 866-5539 Calendar System: Semester
URL: www.herkimer.edu
Established: 1966 Annual Undergrad Tuition & Fees (In-District): $4,980
Enrollment: 3,019 Coed
Affiliation or Control: State/Local IRS Status: 501(c)3
Highest Offering: Associate Degree
Accreditation: M, EMT, PTAA

01 President .... Dr. Cathleen C. MCCOLGIN
10 Sr VP for Admin & Finance .... Mr. Nicholas LAINO
05 Provost .... Mr. Michael ORIOLO
32 Dean of Students .... Dr. Matthew HAWES
20 Associate Dean Academic Affairs BH .... Mr. William MCDONALD
13 Exec Director Information Services .... Mrs. AnneMarie AMBROSE
83 Assoc Dean Academic Affairs Soc Sci .... Dr. Robin VOETTERL RIECKER
20 Assoc Dean of Academic Affairs .... Mrs. Linda LAMB
15 Director of Human Resources .... Mr. James SALAMY
41 Director of Athletics .... Mr. Donald DUTCHER
08 Director of Library Services .... Mr. Alfred BEROWSKI
09 Director Institutional Research .... Ms. Karen AYOUCH
100 Assistant to the President .... Mr. Daniel SARGENT
18 Director Facilities Operations .... Mr. Robert WOUDENBERG
37 Director Student Financial Aid .... Mrs. Susan TRIPP
26 Director of Public Relations .... Ms. Rebecca RUFFING
06 Asst Dean of Academic Affairs .... Mr. Eric VERNOLD
36 Career Services Counselor .... Mrs. Suzanne PADDOCK
96 Purchasing Agent .... Mr. Robert NEARY
102 Dir Foundation/Corporate Relations .... Mr. Robert FOWLER
19 Director of Campus Safety .... Mr. Timothy ROGERS
39 Director Residence Life .... Mr. Jason RATHBUN
84 Dean of Enrollment Management .... Ms. Erin CRAIG

Hilbert College (B)

5200 S Park Avenue, Hamburg NY 14075-1597
County: Erie FICE Identification: 002735
Unit ID: 191621
Telephone: (716) 649-7900 Carnegie Class: Bac-Diverse
FAX Number: (716) 649-0702 Calendar System: Semester
URL: www.hilbert.edu
Established: 1957 Annual Undergrad Tuition & Fees: $21,300
Enrollment: 946 Coed
Affiliation or Control: Independent Non-Profit IRS Status: 501(c)3
Highest Offering: Master's
Accreditation: M

01 President .... Dr. Cynthia A. ZANE
05 Provost/Vice Pres Academic Affs .... Dr. Kristina LANTZKY-EATON
30 Vice Pres Inst Advancement .... Ms. Kelly SMITH
10 Vice President Business/ Finance .... Mr. Richard J. PINKOWSKI, JR.
27 Vice President Information Services .... Mr. Michael MURRIN
84 VP Enrollment Management .... Mr. David RHODES
88 Vice Prov for Student Engagement .... Ms. Denise HARRIS
32 VProv Leadership Dev/Dean of Stdnts .... Mr. James P. STURM
26 Dir Marketing & Communications .... Mr. Matthew HEIDT
92 Director Honors Program .... Dr. Amy E. SMITH
39 Dir Residence Life/Judicial Affairs .... Ms. Jill COLE
41 Athletic Director .... Mr. John CZARNECKI
19 Director Security/Safety .... Mr. Matthew SCHAMANN
29 Asst Dir Annual Giving/Alum Engage .... Mr. Matthew GORCZYCA
42 Dir Mission Intgrtn/Campus Ministry .... Mr. Jeffrey PAPIA
08 Director of McGrath Library .... Vacant
07 Director of Admissions .... Mr. Jacob YALE
36 Director Placement/Career Services .... Ms. Katie MARTOCHE
37 Director Financial Aid .... Ms. Beverly CHUDY-SZCZUR
06 Director of Student Records .... Ms. Katelyn LETIZIA
38 Director Student Counseling .... Ms. Phyllis K. DEWEY
09 Director of Institutional Research .... Dr. Ron ESKEW
15 Director of Human Resources .... Ms. Maura FLYNN
28 Director of Multicultural Affairs .... Ms. Ahyana KING
35 Director of Student Activities .... Vacant

96 Director of Purchasing .... Mr. Gary DILLSWORTH
21 Asst Vice Pres Business/Finance .... Mr. Anthony WIERTEL
18 Chief Facilities/Physical Plant .... Mr. Gary DILLSWORTH
04 Administrative Asst to President .... Ms. Kathleen FAIRBANKS
102 Dir Corp Foundation/Govt Relations .... Ms. Elizabeth SIMONS

Hobart and William Smith Colleges (C)

300 Pulteney Street, Geneva NY 14456-3397
County: Ontario FICE Identification: 002731
Unit ID: 191630
Telephone: (315) 781-3000 Carnegie Class: Bac-A&S
FAX Number: (315) 781-3654 Calendar System: Semester
URL: www.hws.edu
Established: 1822 Annual Undergrad Tuition & Fees: $51,559
Enrollment: 2,351 Coordinate
Affiliation or Control: Independent Non-Profit IRS Status: 501(c)3
Highest Offering: Master's
Accreditation: M, CAEPT

01 President .... Mr. Gregory J. VINCENT
04 Exec Assistant to the President .... Ms. Valerie VISTOCCO
03 Vice President and General Counsel .... Mr. Louis GUARD
15 Associate VP for Human Resources .... Ms. Sonya WILLIAMS
100 Assistant VP/Chief of Staff .... Ms. Marylyn UHNAK
16 Associate Director Human Resources .... Ms. Peggy FERRAN
05 Interim Provost .... Dr. Dwayne LUCAS
20 Sr Dean of Faculty .... Dr. Nan Crystal ARENS
84 VP for Enrollment/Dean of Admission .... Mr. Robert MURPHY
103 Director Center for Career Services .... Ms. Brandi FERRARA
07 Director of Admissions .... Mr. John YOUNG
37 Director of Financial Aid .... Ms. Beth NEPA
32 Vice President for Campus Life .... Mr. Robert FLOWERS
35 Associate VP/Dean of Students .... Dr. Montrose STREETER
35 Asst VP/Dean Campus Operations .... Ms. Stacey PIERCE
39 Director of Residential Education .... Ms. Shelle BASILIO
88 Director of Intercultural Affairs .... Dr. Alejandra MOLINA
88 Director Conferences/Events .... Ms. Erica COONEY-CONNOR
40 Director of the College Store .... Ms. Lucille SMART
23 Coordinator Health Services/NP .... Vacant
19 Director of Campus Safety .... Mr. Martin CORBETT
38 Dir Counseling Ctr/Student Wellness .... Dr. Shelly LEAR
85 Director of International Students .... Mr. David GAGE
111 Vice President for Advancement .... Mr. Robert O'CONNOR
110 Associate VP for Advancement .... Ms. Leila RICE
29 Assistant VP for Alumni Relations .... Mr. Jared WEEDEN
29 Assistant VP for Alumnae Relations .... Ms. Kathleen REGAN
44 Sr Director of Annual giving .... Mr. Joshua FOLADARE
102 Dir Corp/Foundation Rels/Legal Affs .... Mr. Gerard BUCKLEY
88 Director Advancement Services .... Ms. Karen REUSCHER
10 Vice President for Finance/CFO .... Ms. Carolee WHITE
21 Controller .... Ms. Angela FREEMAN
113 Assoc Controller/Student Accounts .... Ms. Rebecca BARNES
13 VP for Strategic Initiatives/CIO .... Mr. Fred DAMIANO
14 Deputy CIO/Dir Enterprise Solutions .... Mr. Jeremy TRUMBLE
88 Dir Network/Systems Infrastructure .... Mr. Derek LUSTIG
106 Director of Digital Learning .... Ms. Juliet BOISSELLE
88 Director Operations & Tech Services .... Ms. Kelly Anne MCLAUGHLIN
26 VP for Marketing & Communications .... Ms. Cathy WILLIAMS
27 Director of Communications .... Ms. Mary LECLAIR
88 Director of Publications .... Ms. Margaret KOWALIK
105 Director Web Development .... Mr. Michael DIMAURO
88 Director Athletic Communications .... Mr. Ken DEBOLT
33 Dean of Hobart College .... Dr. Eugen BAER
34 Dean of William Smith College .... Ms. Lisa KAENZIG
42 Chaplain .... Rev. D. Maurice CHARLES
104 Associate Dean Global Education .... Dr. Thomas D'AGOSTINO
108 Assoc Dean Teach/Learn & Assessment .... Dr. Susan PLINER
88 Director Finger Lakes Institute .... Dr. Lisa CLECKNER
08 Director of the Library .... Mr. Vincent BOISSELLE
06 Registrar .... Mr. Peter SARRATORI
09 Assoc Dean Inst Research/Retent .... Mr. Don EMMONS
31 Dir Community Engagement .... Ms. Kathleen FLOWERS
88 Director Academic Opportunity Pgm .... Mr. James BURRUTO
41 Director of William Smith Athletics .... Ms. Deborah STEWARD
41 Director of Hobart Athletics .... Mr. Michael HANNA

Hofstra University (D)

100 Hofstra University, Hempstead NY 11549-1000
County: Nassau FICE Identification: 002732
Unit ID: 191649
Telephone: (516) 463-6600 Carnegie Class: DU-Mod
FAX Number: (516) 463-4848 Calendar System: Semester
URL: www.hofstra.edu
Established: 1935 Annual Undergrad Tuition & Fees: $42,160
Enrollment: 10,814 Coed
Affiliation or Control: Independent Non-Profit IRS Status: 501(c)3
Highest Offering: Doctorate
Accreditation: M, ARCPA, AUD, CAATE, CACREP, CAEPT, CLPSY, ENG, JOUR, LAW, MED, OT, PH, SCPSY, SP

01 President .... Mr. Stuart RABINOWITZ
05 Provost/Sr VP for Academic Affairs .... Dr. Gail M. SIMMONS
45 Sr VP for Planning and Admin .... Ms. M. Patricia ADAMSKI
10 VP Financial Affairs/Treasurer .... Ms. Catherine HENNESSY
32 Vice President for Student Affairs .... Mr. W. Houston DOUGHARTY
30 Vice President for Development .... Mr. Alan J. KELLY
26 Vice President University Relations .... Ms. Melissa A. CONNOLLY
43 VP Legal Affairs & General Counsel .... Ms. Dolores FREDRICH
13 Vice Pres Information Technology .... Mr. Robert W. JUCKIEWICZ

18 VP for Facilities and Operations .... Mr. Joseph BARKWILL
84 Vice Pres Enrollment Management .... Ms. Jessica L. EADS
91 Asst VP for Information Technology .... Ms. Linda J. HANTZSCHEL
09 VP Inst Research/Admin Assess .... Dr. Stephanie BUSHEY
20 Vice Provost for Undergrad Affairs .... Dr. Neil DONAHUE
114 Assoc Provost Budget & Planning .... Mr. Richard M. APOLLO
25 Assoc Provost Rsrch/Sponsored Pgms .... Ms. Sofia KAKOULIDIS
07 VP Admissions & Financial Aid .... Ms. Jessica L. EADS
50 Dean Zarb Sch of Business .... Dr. Herman A. BERLINER
54 Dean School of Engineering .... Dr. Sina Y. RABBANY
60 Dean School of Communication .... Dr. Evan W. CORNOG
49 Dean College Liberal Arts/Science .... Dr. Benjamin RIFKIN
08 Director Library & Info Services .... Mr. Howard E. GRAVES
121 Dean for University Advisement .... Ms. Anne M. MONGILLO
61 Dean Law School .... Hon. A. Gail PRUDENTI
63 Dean Medical School .... Dr. Lawrence SMITH
66 Dean Sch/Grad Nursing & Health Prof .... Dr. Kathleen GALLO
35 Dean of Students .... Ms. Sofia B. PERTUZ
29 Senior Director Alumni Affairs .... Ms. Amy R. REICH
39 Assoc Director Residential Programs .... Ms. Novia P. WHYTE
38 Dir Student Counseling Services .... Dr. John C. GUTHMAN
22 Equal Rights/Opportunity Ofcr .... Ms. Jennifer MONE
23 Asst Dir Health & Wellness Center .... Ms. Maryann WALSH
41 Director Intercollegiate Athletics .... Mr. Jeffrey HATHAWAY
15 Director of Human Resources .... Ms. Evelyn V. MILLER-SUBER
90 Director Faculty Computing Services .... Ms. Judith L. TABRON
40 Manager Bookstore .... Mr. Steven BABBITT
19 Director Public Safety .... Ms. Karen O'CALLAGHAN
96 Director of Procurement Services .... Mr. John JAGARD
92 Dean Honors College .... Dr. Warren FRISINA
06 Registrar .... Ms. Lynne DOUGHERTY
04 Admin Assistant to the President .... Ms. Isabel D. FREY
37 Director Student Financial Aid .... Ms. Sandra MERVIUS
36 Exec Dir Career Center .... Ms. Michelle KYRIAKIDES
44 Director Annual Giving .... Ms. Julia C. PALMEDO

Holy Trinity Orthodox Seminary (E)

PO Box 36, Jordanville NY 13361-0036
County: Herkimer FICE Identification: 002733
Unit ID: 191658
Telephone: (315) 858-0945 Carnegie Class: Not Classified
FAX Number: (315) 858-0945 Calendar System: Semester
URL: www.hts.edu
Established: 1948 Annual Undergrad Tuition & Fees: N/A
Enrollment: N/A Male
Affiliation or Control: Russian Orthodox IRS Status: 501(c)3
Highest Offering: Baccalaureate
Accreditation: NY

01 Rector .... V.Rev. Luke MURIANKA
05 Dean .... V.Rev. Alexander WEBSTER
20 Assistant Dean .... Rev. Ephraim WILLMARTH
32 Dean of Students .... Rev. Cyprian ALEXANDROU
06 Registrar .... V.Rev. Theophylact CLAPPER-DEWELL
07 Director of Admissions .... Rev. Ephraim WILLMARTH
08 Librarian .... Mr. Michael PEREKRESTOV

Houghton College (F)

One Willard Avenue, Houghton NY 14744-0128
County: Allegany FICE Identification: 002734
Unit ID: 191676
Telephone: (585) 567-9200 Carnegie Class: Bac-A&S
FAX Number: (585) 567-9572 Calendar System: Semester
URL: www.houghton.edu
Established: 1883 Annual Undergrad Tuition & Fees: $30,336
Enrollment: 1,084 Coed
Affiliation or Control: Wesleyan Church IRS Status: 501(c)3
Highest Offering: Master's
Accreditation: M, CAEPT, MUS

01 President .... Dr. Shirley A. MULLEN
05 Provost and Dean of the Faculty .... Dr. Jack CONNELL
32 Vice President for Student Life .... Mr. Robert POOL
10 Vice President for Finance and Plng .... Mr. Vince MORRIS
30 Vice President for Advancement .... Mr. Karl SISSON
84 Vice President for Enrollment .... Vacant
04 Dir of Operations Ofc of the Pres .... Ms. Cindy LASTORIA
06 Registrar .... Mr. Kevin KETTINGER
37 Director of Financial Aid .... Ms. Marianne LOPER
08 Director of the Library .... Mr. David STEVICK
29 Dir Alumni & Community Relations .... Ms. Phyllis GAERTE
42 Dean of the Chapel .... Dr. Michael JORDAN
09 Assoc Dean Institutional Research .... Dr. John WISE
36 Director of VOCA .... Ms. Kim POOL
15 Director of Human Resources .... Mr. Dale F. WRIGHT
26 Dir Marketing & Communications .... Mr. Jeff BABBITT
13 Director of Technology .... Mr. Donald HAINGRAY
18 Director of Facilities .... Mr. Chad PLYMALE
19 Chief Security Officer .... Mr. Ray M. PARLETT
23 Director of Health Services .... Dr. David BRUBAKER
41 Executive Director of Athletics .... Mr. Harold W. LORD
21 Controller .... Ms. Danae FORREST
39 Director Residence Life .... Mr. Marc SMITHERS
38 Director Counseling Services .... Dr. William BURRICHTER
92 Director of Honors Program .... Dr. Benjamin LIPSCOMB

Hudson Valley Community College (G)

80 Vandenburgh Avenue, Troy NY 12180-6096
County: Rensselaer FICE Identification: 002868
Unit ID: 191719

Telephone: (518) 629-4822 Carnegie Class: Assoc/MT-VT-Mix Trad/Non
FAX Number: (518) 629-4576 Calendar System: Semester
URL: www.hvcc.edu
Established: 1953 Annual Undergrad Tuition & Fees (In-District): $5,426
Enrollment: 11,796 Coed
Affiliation or Control: State/Local IRS Status: 501(c)3
Highest Offering: Associate Degree
Accreditation: M, ADNUR, COARC, DH, DMS, EMT, ENGT, FUSER, POLYT, SURGT

01 President ...... Dr. Andrew J. MATONAK
14 VP Technology/Inst Assess/Planning ...... Dr. Michael S. GREEN
04 Assistant to the President ...... Ms. Suzanne K. KALKBRENNER
11 VP for Administration and Finance ...... Mr. William D. REUTER
05 Vice President for Academic Affairs ...... Dr. Carolyn G. CURTIS
32 VP Enroll Mgmt/Student Development ...... Dr. Alexander J. POPOVICS
10 Chief Fiscal Officer ...... Vacant
49 Dean School of Liberal Arts ...... Dr. Fabian VEGA
72 Dean Engr/Indus Tech/Business ...... Mr. P. Phillip WHITE
107 Dean Cmty/Professional Pgms ...... Ms. Christine A. HELWIG
76 Dean School of Health Sciences ...... Dr. Carol BOSCO
08 Dir of Learning Resources Center ...... Vacant
07 Director of Admissions ...... Ms. Mary Claire BAUER
06 Registrar ...... Ms. Kathleen PETLEY
13 Chief Information Officer ...... Mr. Jonathan BRENNAN
18 Director Physical Plant ...... Mr. Richard EDWARDS
38 Exec Dir Student Development ...... Dr. Kathleen SWEENER
37 Director of Financial Aid ...... Ms. Lisa VAN WIE
36 Dir Center For Careers & Transfer ...... Ms. Gayle HEALY
15 Director of Human Resources ...... Ms. Karen PAQUETTE
19 Director of Public Safety ...... Mr. Fred ALIBERTI
23 Coordinator Health Services ...... Ms. Claudine POTVIN-GIORDANO
22 Director of Disability Resources ...... Ms. Deanne MARTOCCI
09 Director Planning & Research ...... Mr. James F. MACKLIN
35 Director of Student Life ...... Mr. Louis COPLIN
85 International Student Advisor ...... Dr. Jay DEITCHMAN
40 Bookstore Manager ...... Ms. Sandra DOWLING
41 Director of Athletics ...... Mr. Justin HOYT
72 Interim Asst to VP of Academics ...... Dr. David C. CLICKNER
124 Assoc Dean Instruct SuppSvcs/Reten ...... Ms. Karen FERRER-MUNIZ
96 Dir Business Services/Purchasing ...... Ms. Patricia GASTON
21 Comptroller ...... Mr. John BRAUNGARD
26 Exec Dir Communications/Marketing ...... Mr. Dennis KENNEDY
102 Interim Exec Director Foundation ...... Ms. Regina LAGATTA
103 Assoc Dean Workforce Development ...... Mr. Richard E. BENNETT, II
25 Director of Grants ...... Ms. Cheryl L. BEAUCHAMP
29 Alumni Relations/Annual Givings ...... Vacant
88 Scholarship & Operations Coord ...... Ms. Kimberly G. BERRY
106 Director of Distance Learning ...... Ms. Susan P. GALLAGHER
108 Dean Institutional Assessment ...... Dr. Margaret GEEHAN
105 Web Coordinator ...... Ms. Sandra EYERMAN
28 Chief Diversity Officer ...... Mr. Ainsley THOMAS

Icahn School of Medicine at Mount Sinai (A)

One Gustave L. Levy Place, New York NY 10029-6500
County: New York FICE Identification: 007026
Unit ID: 193405
Telephone: (212) 241-6500 Carnegie Class: Spec-4-yr-Med
FAX Number: (212) 241-7146 Calendar System: Other
URL: www.icahn.mssm.edu
Established: 1963 Annual Graduate Tuition & Fees: N/A
Enrollment: 1,150 Coed
Affiliation or Control: Independent Non-Profit IRS Status: 501(c)3
Highest Offering: Doctorate; No Undergraduates
Accreditation: M, DENT, IPSY, MED, PH

01 President & CEO ...... Dr. Kenneth L. DAVIS
05 Exec Vice Pres/Dean Sch of Medicine ...... Dr. Dennis S. CHARNEY
63 Dean for Medical Education ...... Dr. David MULLER
11 Dean for Operations ...... Mr. Jeffrey SILBERSTEIN
04 Administrative Asst to President ...... Ms. JoAnn L. FINK
10 Chief Business Officer ...... Mr. Stephen HARVEY
28 Director of Diversity ...... Dr. Gary BUTTS
90 Director Academic Computing ...... Mr. Paul LAWRENCE

Iona College (B)

715 North Avenue, New Rochelle NY 10801-1890
County: Westchester FICE Identification: 002737
Unit ID: 191931
Telephone: (914) 633-2000 Carnegie Class: Masters/L
FAX Number: (914) 633-2642 Calendar System: Semester
URL: www.iona.edu
Established: 1940 Annual Undergrad Tuition & Fees: $36,584
Enrollment: 3,977 Coed
Affiliation or Control: Independent Non-Profit IRS Status: 501(c)3
Highest Offering: Master's
Accreditation: M, CAEPN, CS, JOUR, MFCD, @SP, SW

01 President ...... Dr. Joseph E. NYRE
05 Provost/Sr VP Academic Affairs ...... Dr. Vincent CALLUZZO
10 Sr Vice President Finance & Admin ...... Ms. Anne Marie SCHETTINI-LYNCH
30 Sr VP Advance/External Affairs ...... Mr. Paul J. SUTERA
100 Chief of Staff and Board Secretary ...... Ms. MaryEllen CALLAGHAN
84 VP Enrollment Management ...... Dr. Lauren MOUNTY
13 Vice Provost Info Technology/CIO ...... Ms. Joanne STEELE
32 Vice Provost Student Life ...... Ms. Denise HOPKINS-POSELLE
37 Asst VP Student Financial Services ...... Ms. Eileen DOYLE
91 Asst Vice Provost for Info Tech ...... Mr. Dimitris HALARIS
20 Associate VP Academic Affairs ...... Dr. Michael JORDAN
35 Asst Vice Prov Student Development ...... Ms. Elizabeth OLIVIERI-LENAHAN
49 Dean School Arts & Sciences ...... Dr. Sibdas GHOSH
50 Dean School of Business ...... Dr. William B. LAMB
43 General Counsel ...... Ms. Kathleen MCELROY
18 Director of Facilities Management ...... Mr. Richard MURRAY
39 Director Residential Life ...... Ms. Courtney FERRICK
15 Director of Human Resources ...... Ms. Tracey WILMOT
38 Director of Counseling Center ...... Dr. Brielle STARK-ADLER
36 Director of Career Development ...... Ms. F. Phyllis BLAKE
08 Director of Libraries ...... Mr. Richard PALLADINO
42 Director of Campus Ministries ...... Mr. Carl PROCARIO-FOLEY
06 Registrar ...... Mr. Thomas MURASSO
41 Director of Athletics ...... Mr. Richard COLE, JR.
86 Director of Govt Relations/Grants ...... Mr. Daniel KONOPKA
12 Co-Director of Rockland Campus ...... Vacant
12 Co-Director of Rockland Campus ...... Dr. Vincent CALLUZZO
09 Dir of Inst Effectiveness/Planning ...... Mr. Jason DIFFENDERFER
21 Director of Business Services ...... Ms. Nancy MORANO
26 Director of Public Relations ...... Mr. Todd WILSON
19 Dir Campus Safety and Security ...... Mr. Dominic LOCATELLI
23 Director of Health Services ...... Ms. Robin SCHAFER
44 Director of Annual Giving ...... Ms. Jill KRUEGER
96 Purchasing Coordinator ...... Ms. Carol Ann KENNY
92 Director of Honors Program ...... Dr. Kim PAFFENROTH
07 Director of Graduate Admissions ...... Vacant
04 Executive Asst to President ...... Ms. Laura PROSTANO
105 Director Web Services ...... Mr. Peter MACELI
29 Director Alumni Relations ...... Ms. Elizabeth FAIA ORGERA

Island Drafting and Technical Institute (C)

128 Broadway, Amityville NY 11701-2704
County: Suffolk FICE Identification: 007375
Unit ID: 191959
Telephone: (631) 691-8733 Carnegie Class: Spec 2-yr-Tech
FAX Number: (631) 691-8738 Calendar System: Semester
URL: www.idti.edu
Established: 1957 Annual Undergrad Tuition & Fees: $16,200
Enrollment: 112 Coed
Affiliation or Control: Proprietary IRS Status: Proprietary
Highest Offering: Associate Degree
Accreditation: ACCSC

01 President ...... Mr. James G. DI LIBERTO
03 Vice President ...... Mr. John G. DI LIBERTO
05 Dean ...... Ms. Patricia HAUSFELD

Ithaca College (D)

953 Danby Road, Ithaca NY 14850-7001
County: Tompkins FICE Identification: 002739
Unit ID: 191968
Telephone: (607) 274-3011 Carnegie Class: Masters/L
FAX Number: N/A Calendar System: Semester
URL: www.ithaca.edu
Established: 1892 Annual Undergrad Tuition & Fees: $41,776
Enrollment: 6,769 Coed
Affiliation or Control: Independent Non-Profit IRS Status: 501(c)3
Highest Offering: Doctorate
Accreditation: M, CAATE, CAEPN, MUS, NRPA, OT, PTA, SP, THEA

01 President ...... Dr. Shirley M. COLLADO
100 Chief of Staff ...... Vacant
04 Assistant to the President ...... Ms. Minnie LAUZON
05 Provost/Vice Pres Education Affairs ...... Dr. Linda PETROSINO
10 Interim VP of Finance & Admin ...... Ms. Janet WILLIAMS
43 Senior VP & General Counsel ...... Ms. Nancy E. PRINGLE
84 VP Enrollment Management ...... Mr. Gerard TURBIDE
111 VP College Relations & Advancement ...... Mr. Christopher BIEHN
15 VP for Human Resources ...... Dr. Brian DICKENS
20 Asst Prov/Dean Interdis/Intl Stds ...... Dr. Tanya R. SAUNDERS
26 Assoc VP Marketing/Communications ...... Ms. Jennifer CAMPBELL
13 Assoc VP Information Technology ...... Mr. David WEIL
18 Assoc VP for Facilities Management ...... Mr. Tim CAREY
32 Assoc Prov Diversity/Inclusion/Eng ...... Dr. Roger RICHARDSON
20 Vice Provost ...... Dr. Danette JOHNSON
49 Dean School Humanities/Sci ...... Dr. Vincent WANG
64 Dean of School of Music ...... Dr. Karl PAULNACK
76 Dean Sch Health Sciences/Human Perf ...... Ms. Linda PETROSINO
50 Dean School of Business ...... Mr. Sean REID
60 Dean School of Communications ...... Ms. Diane GAYESKI
29 Executive Director Alumni Relations ...... Ms. Carrie BROWN
06 Registrar ...... Ms. Vikki LEVINE
09 Chief Analytics Officer ...... Dr. Yuko MULUGETTA
07 Director of Admission ...... Ms. Nicole EVERSLEY BRADWELL
12 Director London Center ...... Ms. Thorunn LONSDALE
36 Director Career Services ...... Dr. Daniel PASCOE-AGUILAR
38 Director Counseling/Health/Wellness ...... Dr. Deborah HARPER
37 Dir of Student Financial Services ...... Mrs. Lisa HOSKEY
39 Dir Res Life/Judicial Affairs ...... Ms. Bonnie S. PRUNTY
08 College Librarian ...... Ms. Lisabeth CHABOT
41 Dir Intercol Athletics/Rec Sports ...... Ms. Susan BASSETT
114 Director of Budget ...... Ms. Sally DIETZ
19 Director Public Safety ...... Ms. Terri STEWART
27 Senior Assoc Dir for Campus Comm ...... Mr. David C. MALEY
40 Manager of College Stores ...... Mr. Rick WATSON
42 Coordinator of Chaplains ...... Fr. Carsten P. MARTENSEN
89 Director of First Year Experience ...... Ms. Erica SHOCKLEY
28 Director of Mulitcultural Affairs ...... Ms. Malinda SMITH
85 Dir International Student Services ...... Ms. Diana DIMITROVA
104 Director of Study Abroad ...... Ms. Rachel CULLENEN
88 Dir Center for Faculty Excellence ...... Mr. Wade PICKREN

Jamestown Business College (E)

7 Fairmount Avenue, Box 429, Jamestown NY 14702-0429
County: Chautauqua FICE Identification: 008495
Unit ID: 192004
Telephone: (716) 664-5100 Carnegie Class: Spec-4-yr-Bus
FAX Number: (716) 664-3144 Calendar System: Quarter
URL: www.jamestownbusinesscollege.edu
Established: 1886 Annual Undergrad Tuition & Fees: $12,600
Enrollment: 296 Coed
Affiliation or Control: Proprietary IRS Status: Proprietary
Highest Offering: Baccalaureate
Accreditation: M

01 President ...... Mr. David CONKLIN
05 Dean ...... Ms. Pamela REESE
07 Director Admissions ...... Ms. Brenda SALEMME
37 Director of Financial Aid ...... Mrs. Diane STURZENBECKER
26 Communications ...... Ms. Emily BUTCHER

Jamestown Community College (F)

525 Falconer Street, Jamestown NY 14701
County: Chautauqua FICE Identification: 002869
Unit ID: 191986
Telephone: (716) 338-1000 Carnegie Class: Assoc/HT-Mix Trad/Non
FAX Number: (716) 338-1466 Calendar System: Semester
URL: www.sunyjcc.edu
Established: 1950 Annual Undergrad Tuition & Fees (In-District): $5,500
Enrollment: 4,826 Coed
Affiliation or Control: State/Local IRS Status: 501(c)3
Highest Offering: Associate Degree
Accreditation: M, ADNUR, OTA

01 President ...... Dr. Cory L. DUCKWORTH
05 Vice Pres of Academic Affairs ...... Dr. Marilyn A. ZAGORA
32 Vice Pres of Student Development ...... Dr. Eileen J. GOODLING
84 VP Enrollment Mgmt/Advancement ...... Mr. Kirk YOUNG
12 VP of Catt County Campus/Cont Educ ...... Mr. John J. SAYEGH
11 Vice Pres of Administration ...... Mr. Michael MARTELLO
09 Dean Research & Planning ...... Ms. Barbara RUSSELL
06 Registrar ...... Ms. Tracy KELLY
07 Director Admission ...... Ms. Wendy PRESENT
08 Library Director ...... Mr. Timothy ARNOLD
37 Exec Dir Student Finance/Records ...... Ms. Jill COLBURN
15 Director Human Resources ...... Ms. Nicolette RICZKER
41 Athletic Director ...... Mr. Keith MARTIN
43 Legal Counsel ...... Mr. Stephen ABDELLA
18 Director Facilities/Physical Plant ...... Mr. David JOHNSON
04 Administrative Asst to President ...... Ms. Marsha L. HERN
19 Director Security/Safety ...... Mr. Barry SWANSON
30 Chief Development/Advancement ...... Mr. Tim SMEAL
39 Director Student Housing ...... Ms. Amy HADLEY
105 Director Web Services ...... Mr. Vincent PEZZIMENTI
13 Chief Info Technology Officer (CIO) ...... Ms. Denise BURBEY
25 Chief Contracts/Grants Admin ...... Ms. Judy YONKERS
29 Director Alumni Relations ...... Ms. Amanda GESING
21 Director Administrative Services ...... Ms. Karen FULLER
96 Financial Analyst/Business Office ...... Ms. Roxanne MONROE

Jamestown Community College Cattaraugus County Campus (G)

260 North Union Street, PO Box 5901, Olean NY 14760-5901
Telephone: (716) 376-7500 Identification: 770138
Accreditation: &M

Jefferson Community College (H)

1220 Coffeen Street, Watertown NY 13601-1897
County: Jefferson FICE Identification: 002870
Unit ID: 192022
Telephone: (315) 786-2200 Carnegie Class: Assoc/HT-Mix Trad/Non
FAX Number: (315) 786-0158 Calendar System: Semester
URL: www.sunyjefferson.edu
Established: 1961 Annual Undergrad Tuition & Fees (In-District): $5,067
Enrollment: 3,748 Coed
Affiliation or Control: State/Local IRS Status: 501(c)3
Highest Offering: Associate Degree
Accreditation: M, ADNUR

01 President ...... Dr. Ty A. STONE
05 Vice President Academic Affairs ...... Mr. Thomas FINCH
10 Vice President Admin/Finance ...... Mr. Daniel DUPEE
32 Vice Pres of Students/Enrollment ...... Ms. Betsy PENROSE
49 Associate VP for Liberal Arts ...... Ms. Jerilyn FAIRMAN
81 Associate VP for Math/Science ...... Ms. Linda DITTRICH
121 Dean of Student Success ...... Ms. Rebecca SMALL KELLOGG
51 Dean for Continuing Education ...... Mr. Terrence HARRIS
32 Dean of Students ...... Mr. Rocco CAPPELLOO
04 Assistant to the President ...... Ms. Karen FREEMAN
08 Library Director ...... Ms. Connie HOLBERG
07 Dean of Enrollment Services ...... Ms. Sandra SPADONI
37 Director Financial Aid ...... Mr. James AMBROSE
06 Registrar ...... Ms. Deborah M. ELLIOTT

88 Director Small Business Center Mr. Eric F. CONSTANCE
09 Director of Planning/IR/Grants Ms. Megan STADLER
18 Chief Facilities/Physical Plant Mr. Bruce ALEXANDER
29 Alumni Development Officer Ms. Edie ROGGIE
35 Director Student Devel/Activities Vacant
36 Director Career Planning/Placement Ms. Michele D. GEFELL
88 Director of Advising Mr. Michael BURNS
26 Chief Public Relations Officer Ms. Leslie DISTEFANO
15 Exec Dir Finance/Human Resources Ms. Kerry A. YOUNG
30 College Development Officer Mr. Greg GRIFFIN
31 Director Community Services Ms. Kathleen MORRIS
13 Chief Information Officer Mr. James BUYEA
19 Director Security/Safety Mr. Wesley HISSONG
41 Athletic Director Mr. Jeffrey WILEY

Jewish Theological Seminary of America (A)

3080 Broadway, New York NY 10027-4649
County: New York FICE Identification: 002740
Unit ID: 192040
Telephone: (212) 678-8023 Carnegie Class: Spec-4-yr-Faith
FAX Number: (212) 678-8947 Calendar System: Semester
URL: www.jtsa.edu
Established: 1886 Annual Undergrad Tuition & Fees: $52,660
Enrollment: 359 Coed
Affiliation or Control: Independent Non-Profit IRS Status: 501(c)3
Highest Offering: Doctorate
Accreditation: M, PAST

01 Chancellor Dr. Arnold M. EISEN
03 Exec VC/Chief Operating Officer Mr. Marc GARY
30 Vice Chanc/Chief Development Office Ms. Bonnie EPSTEIN
05 Provost Dr. Alan COOPER
10 Chief Financial Officer Mr. Fred SCHNUR
43 General Counsel Mr. Martin OPPENHEIMER
49 Dean List College Jewish Studies Dr. Shuly SCHWARTZ
53 Dean Davidson School of Education Dr. Bill ROBINSON
58 Dean The Graduate School Dr. Shuly SCHWARTZ
64 Director Miller Cantorial School Cantor Nancy ABRAMSON
73 Dean of Religious Leadership Rabbi Daniel NEVINS
32 Dean of Student Life Ms. Sara HOROWITZ
08 Librarian Dr. David KRAEMER
15 Director of Human Resources Ms. Diana TORRES-PETRILLI
18 Director of Operations Mr. James ESPOSITO
13 Director Information Technology Mr. Ray MORALES
26 Chief Communications Officer Ms. Elise DOWELL
06 Registrar/Director Financial Aid Ms. Amy HERSH
39 Director of Residence Life Mr. Bradley MOOT
84 Director of Enrollment Management Ms. Melissa PRESENT
35 Director of Student Life Ms. Ruth DECALO
38 Director Student Counseling Dr. David DAVAR
29 Director of Alumni Affairs Mrs. Melissa FRIEDMAN
20 Associate Provost Dr. Stephen GARFINKEL
37 Director of Financial Aid Ms. Amy HERSH
88 Director of Community Engagement Rabbi Julia ANDELMAN
04 Executive Asst to Chancellor Ms. Michelle MEHRING
19 Director Security/Safety Chief Anthony VAUGHAN

The Juilliard School (B)

60 Lincoln Center Plaza, New York NY 10023-6588
County: New York FICE Identification: 002742
Unit ID: 192110
Telephone: (212) 799-5000 Carnegie Class: Spec-4-yr-Arts
FAX Number: (212) 724-0263 Calendar System: Semester
URL: www.juilliard.edu
Established: 1905 Annual Undergrad Tuition & Fees: $41,310
Enrollment: 894 Coed
Affiliation or Control: Independent Non-Profit IRS Status: 501(c)3
Highest Offering: Doctorate
Accreditation: M

01 President Dr. Joseph W. POLISI
05 Provost & Dean Mr. Ara GUZELIMIAN
10 Vice Pres/Chief Financial Officer Ms. Christine TODD
30 Vice Pres for Dev/Public Affairs Ms. Elizabeth HURLEY
08 VP for Library/Info Resources Ms. Jane GOTTLIEB
18 Vice Pres for Facilities Management Mr. Joseph MASTRANGELO
84 Vice Pres for Enroll Mgmt/Stdnt Dev Ms. Joan D. WARREN
43 Vice Pres Admin/General Counsel Mr. Maurice F. EDELSON
100 Chief of Staff Ms. Jacqueline SCHMIDT
26 Assoc VP Marketing/Communications Ms. Alexandra DAY
88 Assoc VP for Special Projects Ms. Tricia ROSS
32 Dean of Student Affairs Ms. Jennifer AWE
20 Associate Dean Academic Affairs Mr. Jose GARCIA-LEON
64 Assoc Dean/Director Music Division Mr. Adam MEYER
64 Asst Dean/Dir of Chamber Music Ms. Barli NUGENT
35 Asst Dean for Student Affairs Ms. Sabrina TANBARA
20 Sr Mng Dir Educ/Artistic Affairs Mr. Christopher MOSSEY
57 Actg Dir Richard Rodgers Drama Div Mr. Richard FELDMAN
57 Artistic Director of Dance Division Mr. Lawrence RHODES
88 Artistic Director of Vocal Arts Mr. Brian ZEGER
88 Artist in Residence/Artistic Advise Ms. Monica HUGGETT
88 Director of Performance Activities Ms. Monica THAKKAR
88 Artistic Dir Pre-College Division Ms. Yoheved KAPLINSKY
06 Registrar Ms. Katherine GERTSON
07 Director Admissions/Academic Affs Ms. Ekaterina LAWSON
15 Director of Human Resources Ms. Caryn G. DOKTOR
38 Director of Counseling Services Mr. William BUSE
37 Director Student Financial Aid Ms. Tina GONZALEZ

88 Director of Juilliard Jazz Mr. Wynton MARSALIS
96 Director of Office Services Mr. Scott A. HOLDEN
36 Director Career Services Mr. Barrett HIPES
13 Chief Technology Officer Mr. Tunde GIWA

Kehilath Yakov Rabbinical Seminary (C)

638 Bedford Avenue, Brooklyn NY 11211-8007
County: Kings FICE Identification: 010549
Unit ID: 192165
Telephone: (718) 963-1212 Carnegie Class: Spec-4-yr-Faith
FAX Number: (718) 387-8586 Calendar System: Semester
Established: 1948 Annual Undergrad Tuition & Fees: $9,600
Enrollment: 147 Male
Affiliation or Control: Independent Non-Profit IRS Status: 501(c)3
Highest Offering: First Talmudic Degree
Accreditation: RABN

01 President Mr. Sandor SCHWARTZ

Keuka College (D)

141 Central Avenue, Keuka Park NY 14478
County: Yates FICE Identification: 002744
Unit ID: 192192
Telephone: (315) 279-5000 Carnegie Class: Masters/M
FAX Number: (315) 279-5216 Calendar System: Semester
URL: www.keuka.edu
Established: 1890 Annual Undergrad Tuition & Fees: $29,451
Enrollment: 1,932 Coed
Affiliation or Control: Independent Non-Profit IRS Status: 501(c)3
Highest Offering: Master's
Accreditation: M, CAEPT, IACBE, NURSE, OT, SW

01 President Dr. Jorge L. DIAZ-HERRERA
05 Provost/VP for Academic Affairs Dr. Paul FORESTELL
10 VP for Finance/Administration Vacant
30 VP for Advancement/External Affs Ms. Amy STOREY
84 VP for Enroll Mgmt/Student Devel Mr. Mark PETRIE
20 Assoc Provost for Acad Innovation Dr. Timothy SELLERS
36 Dean Student Engagement/Success Ms. Elizabeth LAMBERT
08 Director of Library Ms. Linda PARK
29 Dir Alumni Relations/Development Ms. Brittany CHAMBERS
20 AVP for Program Development Dr. Vicki SMITH
37 Director Financial Aid Ms. Catherine BUZANSKI
108 Dir of Institutional Assessment Mr. Matthew DREITLEIN
13 Chief Information Officer Ms. Andrea CAMPBELL
18 Interim Director of Facilities Mr. Glenn DIKES
21 Controller Ms. Carol N. GROVER
19 Director of Campus Safety Mr. James CUNNINGHAM
23 Coordinator of Health Services Ms. Cindy CHRISTIE
38 Director of Counseling Services Ms. Mary MARTINI-HAUSNER
32 AVP for Student Affairs/Dean Stdnts Dr. Tracy MCFARLAND
07 Director of Admissions on Campus Ms. Megan PERKINS
41 Director of Athletics Mr. David M. SWEET
107 AVP Center for Professional Studies Dr. Anne KILLEN
42 College Chaplain Mr. Eric DETAR
06 Registrar Ms. Jill BIRD
44 Sr Director of Advancement Ms. Ann TURNER
26 Sr Dir of Marketing/Communications Mr. Pete BEKISZ
96 Purchasing Liaison Ms. Brenda DEUCK
15 AVP HR/Equity/Organizational Dev Ms. Michelle POLOWCHAK
76 Div Chair Occupational Therapy Dr. Christopher ALTERIO
83 Div Chair Basic Soc & Applied Sci Dr. Tom TREMER
50 Div Chair Business & Management Ms. Ann TUTTLE
53 Div Chair Ed & Dir Ed Grad Studies Dr. Patricia PULVER
79 Div Chair Humanities/Fine Arts Dr. Jennie JOINER
81 Div Chair Natural Sciences/Math Dr. Mark SUGALSKI
66 Div Chair Nursing Dr. Debra GATES
70 Div Chair Social Work Dr. Ed SILVERMAN
28 Director of Diversity Vacant
35 Associate Student Affairs Officer Vacant
21 Budget Director Mr. Jeffrey HECKMAN

The King's College (E)

56 Broadway, New York NY 10004-1613
County: New York FICE Identification: 040953
Unit ID: 454184
Telephone: (212) 659-7200 Carnegie Class: Bac-A&S
FAX Number: (212) 659-7210 Calendar System: Semester
URL: www.tkc.edu
Established: 1938 Annual Undergrad Tuition & Fees: $34,320
Enrollment: 513 Coed
Affiliation or Control: Independent Non-Profit IRS Status: 501(c)3
Highest Offering: Baccalaureate
Accreditation: M

00 Chairman of the Board of Trustees Mr. William Lee HANLEY
01 President Dr. Gregory A. THORNBURY
07 Vice Pres Admissions/Advancement Dr. Kimberly THORNBURY
32 Vice President Student Development Mr. Eric BENNETT
05 Vice President for Academic Affairs Dr. Mark HIJLEH
35 Dean of Students Mr. David LEEDY
10 Vice President Finance/CFO Mr. Frank TORINO
21 Controller Ms. Judy BARRINGER
06 Registrar Mr. Paul MIDDLEKAUFF
37 Director of Financial Aid Ms. Anna PETERS
04 Executive Asst to President Ms. Hannah GRUBB
09 Director of Institutional Research Dr. Kimberly THORNBURY

11 Administrative Director Ms. Laura MERRITT
18 Chief Facilities/Physical Plant Mr. Rich SWITZER
26 Chief Public Relations Officer Ms. Natalie NAKAMURA
30 Director Development Services Ms. Tonnie CHEN
36 Dir Vocational/Career Development Ms. Bethany JENKINS
38 Director Student Counseling Ms. Eileen HAWKINS
84 Director Enrollment Management Mr. Luke SMITH
08 Director Library Services Ms. Christina ROGERS
39 Director Student Housing Mr. Nick SWEDICK
41 Athletic Director Mr. Bryan FINLEY
15 Manager Human Resources Ms. Melody GARCIA

Le Moyne College (F)

1419 Salt Springs Road, Syracuse NY 13214-1301
County: Onondaga FICE Identification: 002748
Unit ID: 192323
Telephone: (315) 445-4100 Carnegie Class: Masters/L
FAX Number: (315) 445-4540 Calendar System: Semester
URL: www.lemoyne.edu
Established: 1946 Annual Undergrad Tuition & Fees: $33,030
Enrollment: 3,478 Coed
Affiliation or Control: Independent Non-Profit IRS Status: 501(c)3
Highest Offering: Master's
Accreditation: M, ARCPA, CAEPT, NURSE, OT

01 President Dr. Linda M. LEMURA
05 Provost & VP Acad Affairs Rev. Joseph G. MARINA
10 Senior VP Fin & Admin & Treasurer Mr. Roger W. STACKPOOLE
111 Vice Pres Comm & Advancement Mr. Bill BROWER
32 Vice Pres Student Development Dr. Deborah M. CADY MELZER
88 Vice Pres Mission Integration & Dev Rev. David C. MCCALLUM, SJ
88 Rector of the Jesuit Community Rev. John P. BUCKI, SJ
49 Dean of Arts & Sciences Dr. Kathleen P. COSTELLO-SULLIVAN
50 Dean School of Business Mr. James E. JOSEPH
58 Dean of Graduate & Prof Studies Dr. Dennis R. DEPERRO
20 Assoc Provost Dr. Mary K. COLLINS
21 Assoc VP for Finance & Controller Mr. Brian M. LOUCY
15 Asst VP for HR and Org Dev Ms. Karin BOTTO
41 Asst VP & Director of Athletics Mr. Matthew D. BASSETT
18 Asst VP Facilities Mgmt & Planning Mr. Jed S. SCHNEIDER
26 Assoc VP for Marketing Mr. Peter S. KILLIAN
84 Asst VP for Enrollment Mgmt Mr. William C. CHEETHAM
35 Dean of Students Ms. Anne E. KEARNEY
35 Asst Dean for Student Development Mr. Mark G. GODLESKI
121 Asst Dean for Academic Advising Ms. Allison FARRELL
88 Asst Dean/Dir CSTEP & STEP Ms. Darshini ROOPNARINE
88 Sr Dir Enrollment Management Ms. Kristen P. TRAPASSO
07 Senior Director of Admission Ms. Mary CHANDLER
51 Director of Continuing Education Ms. Patricia J. BLISS
88 Dir of Transfer Admission Mr. Scott SETEK
13 Director of Info Technology Mr. Shaun C. BLACK
09 Director of Institutional Research Dr. Daniel L. SKIDMORE
22 EEO/Affirmative Action Officer Ms. Karin BOTTO
06 Registrar/Sr Director Enrollment Ms. Cynthia A. ALIBRANDI
08 Director of the Library Dr. Robert C. JOHNSTON
42 Int Director of Campus Ministry Mr. Thomas ANDINO
27 Director of Communications Mr. Joseph B. DELLA POSTA
88 Director Campus Life & Leadership Mr. John R. HALEY
19 Director of Security Mr. Mark J. PETTERELLI
112 Senior Dir Leadership Giving Ms. Kimberly B. MCAULIFF
39 Dir of Campus Life & Leadership Mr. John HALEY
36 Director Career Advising/Devpment Ms. Meredith TORNABENE
04 Assistant to the President Ms. Carly J. COLBERT
28 Asst to the Provost for Diversity Mr. Ludger VIEFHUES-BAILEY
44 Sr Dir Annual Giving/Stewardship Ms. Katherine COGSWELL
86 Director Govt/Foundation Relations Mr. Steven W. KULICK
88 Director of Advancement Services Mr. Paul F. LYNCH
29 Director of Alumni Engagement Ms. Kasha GODLESKI
23 Dir Wellness Ctr for Health & Couns Ms. Maria RANDAZZO
88 Int Director of HEOP and AHANA Ms. Lynnell CABEZAS
40 Bookstore Manager Ms. Jessica L. MANNINO

LIM College (G)

12 E 53rd Street, New York NY 10022-5268
County: New York FICE Identification: 007466
Unit ID: 192271
Telephone: (212) 752-1530 Carnegie Class: Spec-4-yr-Bus
FAX Number: (212) 832-6109 Calendar System: Semester
URL: www.limcollege.edu
Established: 1939 Annual Undergrad Tuition & Fees: $25,725
Enrollment: 1,700 Coed
Affiliation or Control: Proprietary IRS Status: Proprietary
Highest Offering: Master's
Accreditation: M, ACBSP

01 President Elizabeth S. MARCUSE
05 Provost Vacant
10 Exec VP Finance & Operations/Treas Michael T. DONOHUE
00 President Emeritus Adrian G. MARCUSE
04 Special Assistant to the President Linda HARRIS PAOLILLO
11 VP Admin/Chief Accountability Ofcr Thomas MCDONALD
04 Assistant to the President Ann M. GONG
20 Vice Pres for Academic Affairs Michael P. LONDRIGAN
26 VP for Marketing and Communications Vacant
58 Dean of Graduate Studies Jacqueline M. JENKINS
20 Assoc Dean of Academic Affairs Patricia FITZMAURICE
08 Director of Library Services Lou ACIERNO
06 College Registrar Carolyn DISNEW
36 Sr Dir Exper Educ & Career Mgmt Vacant

32 VP for Student Development .... Michael H. FERRY
35 Dean of Student Affairs .... Michael RICHARDS
35 Assistant Dean of Student Life .... Christopher CONZEN
38 Sr Dir Counseling & Wellness Svcs .... Jodi N. LICHT
39 Dir of Housing & Residence Life .... Jennifer K. LUCIANO
07 Dean of Admissions .... Kristina ORTIZ
07 Director of Admissions .... Adeline AFFONSO
88 Director of Online Admissions .... Michael VILLANELLA
88 Asst VP for Student Success .... William IMBRIALE
09 Director of Institutional Research .... Nikisha WILLIAMS
21 Accounting Manager .... Svetlana KANEVSKAYA
96 Purchasing Director .... Eric MARTIN
113 VP Student Finance .... Christopher E. BARTO
37 Sr Dir of Student Financial Svcs .... Vacant
30 VP for Institutional Advancement .... Gail NARDIN
88 VP for Strategic Initiatives .... Pamela LINTON
26 Director of Communications .... Meredith FINNIN
88 Director of College Marketing .... Laura CIOFFI
105 Web Application Developer .... Joshua J. HELLER
13 Chief Technology Officer .... Maurice MORENCY
14 Director of Information Technology .... Nelson LEON
90 Director of Instructional Tech .... Joseph THOMAS
15 Dir of HR & Title IX Coordinator .... Andrea L. GRANVILLE
18 Manager of Facilities .... Jonathan ABREU
108 VP for Planning & Assessment .... Jacqueline LEBLANC

Long Island Business Institute (A)

6500 Jericho Turnpike, Commack NY 11725
Telephone: (631) 499-7100 Identification: 770746
Accreditation: ACICS

Long Island Business Institute (B)

136-18 39th Avenue, 5th Floor, Flushing NY 11354
County: Queens FICE Identification: 020937
Unit ID: 192509
Telephone: (718) 939-5100 Carnegie Class: Spec 2-yr-Other
FAX Number: (718) 939-9235 Calendar System: Semester
URL: www.libi.edu
Established: 1968 Annual Undergrad Tuition & Fees: $14,475
Enrollment: 583 Coed
Affiliation or Control: Proprietary IRS Status: Proprietary
Highest Offering: Associate Degree
Accreditation: ACICS

01 President .... Ms. Monica W. FOOTE
05 Provost .... Ms. Stacey JOHNSON
12 Asst Campus Program Director .... Ms. Michelle HOUSTON
11 Assoc Director of Administration .... Mr. Li ZHU
37 Financial Aid Director .... Ms. Cynthia YUN LIN
08 Librarian Commack Campus .... Ms. Terry CANAVAN
08 Sr Librarian Flushing Campus .... Ms. Adrianna ARGUELLES

*Long Island University (C)

700 Northern Boulevard, Brookville NY 11548-1327
County: Nassau FICE Identification: 002751
Unit ID: 192457
Telephone: (516) 299-2501 Carnegie Class: N/A
FAX Number: N/A
URL: www.liu.edu

01 President .... Dr. Kimberly R. CLINE
09 Chief of IR & Effectiveness .... Mr. Andy PERSON
45 Chief Strategy and Planning Officer .... Dr. Edward SUMMERS
43 University Counsel .... Mr. Michael BEST
37 Assoc VP Financial Svcs/Compliance .... Mr. David MAINENTI
84 Assoc Dean Enrollment/Registrar .... Ms. Beth WILKOW
108 Sr Dir of Accred & Assessment .... Dr. Joel BLOOM
88 Chief Talent Officer .... Ms. Denise DICK
15 Executive Director Human Resources .... Ms. Pamela DUFFY
25 Executive Director of Grants .... Mr. Alan EVELYN
102 Dir Foundation Relations .... Ms. Suzanne FARRELL
96 Dir Sourcing/Procurement Svcs .... Mr. Allan HOWELL
11 Chief Operating Officer .... Ms. Gale STEVENS HAYNES
05 Senior VP for Academic Affairs .... Vacant
10 Vice President Finance & Treasurer ... Mr. Christopher N. FEVOLA
88 Sr Advisor & Treasurer Emerita .... Mrs. Mary M. LAI
13 VP for Information Technology & CIO .... Mr. George BAROUDI
21 Assoc Vice Pres/Controller .... Mr. Mark SCHMOTZER
111 Vice President of Univ Advancement .... Mr. Charles RASBERRY
07 Chief of Admissions & Enr Strategy .... Dr. William MARTINOV
32 Chief of Admin & Student Affairs .... Mr. Joseph SCHAEFER
26 Chief Communications Officer .... Mr. Jim CONENELLO

*LIU Post (D)

720 Northern Boulevard, Brookville NY 11548-1300
County: Nassau FICE Identification: 002754
Unit ID: 192448
Telephone: (516) 299-2900 Carnegie Class: Masters/L
FAX Number: (516) 299-2137 Calendar System: Semester
URL: www.liu.edu/post
Established: 1954 Annual Undergrad Tuition & Fees: $36,256
Enrollment: 8,623 Coed
Affiliation or Control: Independent Non-Profit IRS Status: 501(c)3
Highest Offering: Doctorate
Accreditation: M, CACR

02 President .... Dr. Kimberly R. CLINE
11 Exec Dir Operations/Partnerships .... Ms. Rita LANGDON
07 Chief of Admissions & Enr Strategy .... Mr. William MARTINOV
37 Exec Dir of Student Financial Svcs .... Ms. Joanne GRAZIANO
49 Dean College Lib Arts/Science .... Dr. Nathaniel BOWDITCH
66 Dean Sch Health Prof/Nursing .... Dr. Stacy GROPACK
50 Dean College of Management .... Dr. Robert VALLI
53 Dean College of Educ/Info & Tech .... Dr. Albert INSERRA
57 Dean Col Arts/Comm & Design .... Mr. Steven BREESE
51 Dir Hutton House Continuing Educ .... Dr. Kay SATO
32 Dean of Students/LIU Promise .... Ms. Abagail VAN VLERAH
41 Director of Athletics .... Ms. Debbie DEJONG
18 Director of Facilities .... Mr. Roy FERGUS
05 Vice President for Academic Affairs .... Dr. Lori KNAPP
19 Director of Public Safety .... Mr. Paul RAPESS

**LIU Brentwood* (E)

Grant Campus, 1001 Crooked Hill Rd.,
Brentwood NY 11717
Telephone: (631) 287-8500 Identification: 666076
Accreditation: &M

**LIU Brooklyn* (F)

1 University Plaza, Brooklyn NY 11201-5372
Telephone: (718) 488-1011 FICE Identification: 004779
Accreditation: &M, ARCPA, CAATE, CAEPT, CLPSY, COARC, DMS, NURSE, OT, PHAR, PTA, SP, SPAA, SURGT, SW

**LIU Hudson at Westchester* (G)

735 Anderson Hill Road, Purchase NY 10577
Telephone: (914) 831-2700 Identification: 666078
Accreditation: &M, CAEPT

**LIU Riverhead* (H)

121 Speonk-Riverhead Road - LIU Bld,
Riverhead NY 11901-3499
Telephone: (631) 287-8010 Identification: 666174
Accreditation: &M, CAEPT

Louis V. Gerstner Jr. Graduate School of Biomedical Sciences, Memorial Sloan Kettering Cancer Center (I)

1275 York Avenue, P.O. Box 441, New York NY 10065
County: New York Identification: 666643
Unit ID: 458511
Telephone: (646) 888-6639 Carnegie Class: Not Classified
FAX Number: N/A Calendar System: Semester
URL: www.sloankettering.edu
Established: 2004 Annual Graduate Tuition & Fees: N/A
Enrollment: N/A Coed
Affiliation or Control: Independent Non-Profit IRS Status: 501(c)3
Highest Offering: Doctorate; No Undergraduates
Accreditation: NY

01 President .... Dr. Craig B. THOMPSON
05 Provost .... Dr. Joan MASSAGUE
20 Dean .... Dr. Kenneth J. MARIANS
88 Associate Dean .... Mrs. Linda BURNLEY
06 Registrar .... Mr. David L. MCDONAGH
08 Director of Library Services .... Ms. Donna S. GIBSON

Machzikei Hadath Rabbinical College (J)

5407 16th Avenue, Brooklyn NY 11204-1805
County: Kings FICE Identification: 013026
Unit ID: 192624
Telephone: (718) 854-8777 Carnegie Class: Spec-4-yr-Faith
FAX Number: (718) 851-1265 Calendar System: Semester
Established: 1956 Annual Undergrad Tuition & Fees: $11,200
Enrollment: 153 Male
Affiliation or Control: Independent Non-Profit IRS Status: 501(c)3
Highest Offering: First Talmudic Degree
Accreditation: RABN

01 President .... Mr. Alexander SCHAECHTER

Mandl School - The College of Allied Health (K)

254 W 54th Street, 9th Floor, New York NY 10019
County: New York FICE Identification: 007401
Unit ID: 192688
Telephone: (212) 247-3434 Carnegie Class: Spec 2-yr-Health
FAX Number: (212) 247-3617 Calendar System: Semester
URL: www.mandl.edu
Established: 1924 Annual Undergrad Tuition & Fees: $14,070
Enrollment: 830 Coed
Affiliation or Control: Proprietary IRS Status: Proprietary
Highest Offering: Associate Degree
Accreditation: ABHES, #COARC, SURTEC

01 President .... Mr. Melvyn P. WEINER
05 Vice President of Academic Affairs .... Dr. Orsete DIAS
37 EVP/Director of Financial Aid .... Mr. Stuart WEINER
36 Vice President of Career Services .... Mr. James FLANAGAN
06 Dean of Records & Registration .... Mr. Marc WEINER
84 Director of Enrollment Management .... Ms. Randie SENSER
06 Registrar .... Ms. Tina PAPULI
07 Director of Recruitment .... Ms. Racquel GARCIA
08 Head Librarian .... Ms. Clover STEELE
32 Assistant Dean Student Support Svcs .. Dr. Karlene RICHARDSON
10 Chief Business Officer .... Mrs. Nettie WEINER

Manhattan College (L)

Manhattan College Parkway, Bronx NY 10471-4099
County: Bronx FICE Identification: 002758
Unit ID: 192703
Telephone: (718) 862-8000 Carnegie Class: Masters/M
FAX Number: (718) 862-8014 Calendar System: Semester
URL: www.manhattan.edu
Established: 1853 Annual Undergrad Tuition & Fees: $40,004
Enrollment: 4,071 Coed
Affiliation or Control: Independent Non-Profit IRS Status: 501(c)3
Highest Offering: Master's
Accreditation: M, CAEPT, ENG, NMT

01 President .... Dr. Brennan O'DONNELL
05 Executive Vice President & Provost .... Dr. William CLYDE
10 VP for Finance & CFO .... Mr. Matthew S. MCMANNESS
32 Vice President Student Life .... Dr. Richard SATTERLEE
111 Vice President College Advancement ..... Mr. Thomas MAURIELLO
15 Vice President for Human Resources .... Ms. Barbara A. FABE
18 Vice President for Facilities .... Mr. Andrew RYAN
84 Vice President Enrollment Mgmt .... Dr. William J. BISSET
88 Vice President for Mission .... Br. Jack CURRAN
20 Assoc Prov Res/Fac/Computer System .. Mr. Walter F. MATYSTIK
35 Assistant VP of Student Life .... Dr. Emmanuel AGO
35 Dean of Students .... Dr. Michael CAREY
06 Registrar .... Ms. Susan ASTARITA
07 Director of Admissions .... Ms. Caitlin READ
08 Director of Libraries .... Dr. William WALTERS
13 Director of Information Tech Svcs .... Mr. Jake HOLMQUIST
19 Director of Public Safety .... Mr. Juan E. CEREZO
29 Director of Alumni Relations .... Mr. Louis CALVELLI
26 Director of Mktg & Communications .... Mrs. Lydia E. GRAY
36 Director Ctr Career Development .... Ms. Rachel CIRELLI
38 Dir of Counseling & Health Services .... Ms. Jennifer MCARDLE
39 Director of Residence Life .... Mr. Andrew WEINGARTEN
41 Director of Athletics .... Ms. Marianne REILLY
42 Director of Campus Ministry .... Ms. Lois HARR
30 Director of Development/Advancement .... Mr. Stephen WHITE
78 Director Academic Support Services .... Ms. Marilyn CARTER-STEVENS
40 Director of Campus Bookstore .... Mr. Henry CASTILLO
22 Dir of Personnel/Affirm Action Ofcr .... Ms. Vickie M. COWAN
09 Dir Inst Research/Assessment .... Dr. Ellen BOYLAN
21 Controller .... Mr. Dennis LONERGAN
21 Business Manager .... Mr. Kenneth WALDHOF
85 International Student Advisor .... Ms. Debra L. DAMICO
37 Director of Student Financial Svcs .... Vacant
49 Dean of Liberal Arts .... Dr. Keith BROWER
50 Interim Dean of Business .... Dr. Janet ROVENPOR
53 Dean of Education & Health .... Dr. Karen NICHOLSON
54 Dean of Engineering .... Dr. Tim WARD
51 Exec Dir Sch Cont & Prof Studies .... Dr. Cheryl HARRISON
121 Director Ctr for Academic Success ...... Ms. Marisa PASSAFIUME
81 Dean of Science .... Dr. Constantine THEODOSIOU
88 Dir of Specialized Resource Center .... Ms. Anne VACCARO
88 Dir Grad & Fellowship Advisement .... Dr. Rani R. ROY

Manhattan School of Music (M)

120 Claremont Avenue, New York NY 10027-4698
County: New York FICE Identification: 002759
Unit ID: 192712
Telephone: (212) 749-2802 Carnegie Class: Spec-4-yr-Arts
FAX Number: (212) 749-5471 Calendar System: Semester
URL: www.msmnyc.edu
Established: 1917 Annual Undergrad Tuition & Fees: $44,600
Enrollment: 998 Coed
Affiliation or Control: Independent Non-Profit IRS Status: 501(c)3
Highest Offering: Doctorate
Accreditation: M

01 President .... Dr. James GANDRE
05 Interim Provost and Sr VP .... Ms. Joan GORDON
10 VP for Business and Finance .... Mr. Gary MEYER
111 VP for Advancement .... Mr. Stephen JACOBSOHN
26 VP for Media and Communications .... Mr. Jeff BREITHAUPT
84 Dean of Enrollment Management .... Ms. Amy A. ANDERSON
32 Dean of Students .... Dr. Monica CHRISTENSEN
15 VP for Human Relations & Admin .... Ms. Carol MATOS
106 Dean of Dist Learning & Rec Arts .... Ms. Christianne ORTO
100 Chief of Staff .... Mr. Bryan GREANEY
101 Liaison to the Board of Trustees .... Mr. Bryan GREANEY
20 Associate Dean in Office of Provost .... Ms. Lianna PORTNOY
06 Registrar .... Mr. Jeffrey NAMIAN
13 Chief Information Officer .... Mr. Ray MORALES
14 Assistant IT Director .... Mr. Luis MOREL
37 Director of Financial Aid .... Mr. Thomas ZARKOS
35 Director of Student Engagement .... Ms. Melanie DORSEY
39 Director of Residence Life .... Mr. Jim LOVE
31 Director of Educational Outreach .... Ms. Rebecca CHARNOW
29 Alumni Engagement Officer .... Ms. Lauren FRANKOVICH
08 Director of Library Services .... Mr. Peter CALEB

102 Director of Institutional Giving .... Ms. Ronnie BORISKIN
40 Campus Store Manager .... Ms. Katherine COPLAND
85 Director Intl Student Services .... Mr. Michael LOCKHART
88 Dir Ctr for Music Entrepreneurship .... Mr. Casey MOLIN-DUNN
88 Dean of Instrumental Performance .... Mr. David GEBER
21 Director of Accounting & Controller .... Ms. Susan FINK
18 Dir of Facilities & Campus Safety .... Mr. Luis PLAZA
07 Director of Admissions .... Ms. Christan CASSIDY
04 Admin Asst to the President .... Mr. Robert SMITH

Manhattanville College (A)

2900 Purchase Street, Purchase NY 10577-2132
County: Westchester FICE Identification: 002760
Unit ID: 192749
Telephone: (914) 694-2200 Carnegie Class: Bac-A&S
FAX Number: (914) 694-2386 Calendar System: Semester
URL: www.mville.edu
Established: 1841 Annual Undergrad Tuition & Fees: $36,920
Enrollment: 2,921 Coed
Affiliation or Control: Independent Non-Profit IRS Status: 501(c)3
Highest Offering: Doctorate
Accreditation: M, CAEPN, IACBE

01 President .... Dr. Michael E. GEISLER
04 Exec Admin Asst to the President .... Ms. Deborah A. FALLONE
05 Provost/VP of Academic Affairs .... Dr. Lisa DOLLING
10 VP Finance/Administration .... Mr. Erik PAULSON
84 Vice Pres Enrollment Management .... Mr. Nikhil KUMAR
30 Vice Pres Inst Advance/Alum Rels .... Ms. Teresa WEBER
11 Vice President of Operations .... Mr. Gregory PALMER
32 Vice Pres of Student Affairs .... Vacant
58 Interim Dean School of Business .... Mr. Steve ALBANESE
53 Dean School of Education .... Dr. Shelley WEPNER
26 Managing Director Media/PR/Comm .... Vacant
06 Registrar .... Ms. Jeneen KELLY
85 Director of English Lang Institute .... Ms. Marisa ANNUNZIATA
08 Director of the Library .... Mr. Jeff ROSEDALE
37 Director of Financial Aid .... Mr. Robert GILMORE
38 Director of Counseling Center .... Ms. Melissa BOSTON
35 Dean of Students .... Ms. Sharlise SMITH-RODRIGUEZ
41 Director of Athletics .... Vacant
42 Int Catholic Chpln/Interfaith Coord .... Fr. Wil TYRRELL
36 Director Center for Career Devel .... Ms. Tiffany AUSTIN
19 Director of Security .... Mr. Anthony HERRMANN
07 Director of Admissions .... Mr. Joseph COSENTINO
15 Director of Human Resources .... Mr. Don DEAN
35 Asst Director of Student Activities .... Mr. Andrew FULTON
96 Director of Purchasing .... Ms. Cheryl DOBSON
104 Director Study Abroad .... Mr. Wil TYRRELL
22 Dir Affirmative Action/EEO .... Mr. Donald DEAN
23 Director Health Center .... Ms. Kristen DONOHUE-GONZALEZ

Maria College of Albany (B)

700 New Scotland Avenue, Albany NY 12208-1798
County: Albany FICE Identification: 002763
Unit ID: 192785
Telephone: (518) 438-3111 Carnegie Class: Spec-4-yr-Other Health
FAX Number: (518) 438-7170 Calendar System: 4/1/4
URL: www.mariacollege.edu
Established: 1958 Annual Undergrad Tuition & Fees: $14,210
Enrollment: 824 Coed
Affiliation or Control: Independent Non-Profit IRS Status: 501(c)3
Highest Offering: Baccalaureate
Accreditation: M, ADNUR, NUR, OTA

01 President .... Dr. Thomas J. GAMBLE
05 Dean/Vice Pres Academic Affairs .... Dr. John KOWAL
10 VP for Finance & Administration .... Mr. Joel NUDI
32 VP Student Life/Mission Integr .... Ms. Victoria L. BATTELL
30 Dir Development/Alumni Engagement . Ms. Helen ADAMS-KEANE
37 Director Financial Aid .... Ms. Donna MYERS
25 AVP Grants/Spons Rsch/Strat Plng .... Mr. Thomas IWANKOW
21 Director of Business Affairs .... Mrs. Frances BERNARD
06 Registrar .... Ms. Kari BENNETT
07 Director of Admissions .... Mr. John RAMOSKA
08 Librarian .... Ms. Marisa GITTO
13 Director of Information Technology .... Vacant
18 Superintendent Physical Plant .... Mr. Andrew PEREZ
26 Director Marketing/Communications .... Ms. Beth WALES
42 Campus Minister .... Mrs. Michelle THIVIERGE
36 Director Career Services .... Mr. David COVEY

Marist College (C)

3399 North Road, Poughkeepsie NY 12601-1387
County: Dutchess FICE Identification: 002765
Unit ID: 192819
Telephone: (845) 575-3000 Carnegie Class: Masters/L
FAX Number: (845) 471-6213 Calendar System: Semester
URL: www.marist.edu
Established: 1929 Annual Undergrad Tuition & Fees: $35,210
Enrollment: 6,474 Coed
Affiliation or Control: Independent Non-Profit IRS Status: 501(c)3
Highest Offering: Doctorate
Accreditation: M, #ARCPA, CAATE, CAEPN, MT, SPAA, SW

01 President .... Dr. David YELLEN
03 Executive Vice President .... Dr. Geoffrey L. BRACKETT
05 Vice President for Academic Affairs ...... Dr. Thomas S. WERMUTH
84 VP Admission & Enrollment Planning .... Mr. Sean P. KAYLOR
111 Vice President College Advancement .... Mr. Christopher M. DELGIORNO
13 VP Information Technology/CIO .... Mr. William T. THIRSK
32 VP/Dean of Student Affairs .... Mrs. Deborah A. DICAPRIO
10 Vice President Business Affairs/CFO .... Mr. John P. PECCHIA
20 Assoc VP/Dean Academic Affairs .... Dr. John RITSCHDORFF
07 Asst VP Enroll Mgmt/Dean UG Admiss ... Mr. Kent W. RINEHART
35 Assoc Dean of Student Affairs .... Mr. Steve SANSOLA
29 Executive Director Alumni Relations .... Ms. Amy K. WOODS
09 Director Inst Research & Planning .... Dr. Judith STODDARD
20 Assoc Dean of Academic Affairs .... Mrs. Judith IVANKOVIC
37 Exec Dir Student Financial Services .... Mr. Joseph R. WEGLARZ
08 Director Library .... Ms. Becky ALBITZ
90 Director Academic Technology .... Vacant
18 Director of Physical Plant .... Mr. Justin BUTWELL
26 Chief Public Affairs Officer .... Mr. Gregory CANNON
15 Assoc VP for Human Resources .... Mrs. Deborah RAIKES-COLBERT
96 Director of Purchasing .... Mr. Stephen J. KOCHIS
36 Director Career Services .... Ms. Mary O. JONES
19 Director of Safety & Security .... Mr. John BLAISDELL
39 Director of Housing & Resident Life .... Mrs. Sarah H. ENGLISH
41 Director of Athletics .... Mr. Timothy S. MURRAY
04 Exec Assistant to the President .... Ms. Eileen SICO
24 Director of Media & Instruct Tech .... Ms. Joey WALL
23 Director of Health Services .... Dr. Melissa SCHISKIE
38 Director of Counseling .... Dr. Naomi A. FERLEGER
43 Director Campus Ministry .... Bro. Francis E. KELLY
44 Director of Annual Giving .... Vacant
105 Director Web Services .... Mr. Antoni SOUSA
50 Dean School of Management .... Mr. Larry G. SINGLETON
104 Dean International Programs .... Mr. John PETERS

Marymount Manhattan College (D)

221 E 71st Street, New York NY 10021-4597
County: New York FICE Identification: 002769
Unit ID: 192864
Telephone: (212) 517-0400 Carnegie Class: Bac-A&S
FAX Number: (212) 517-0541 Calendar System: Semester
URL: www.mmm.edu
Established: 1936 Annual Undergrad Tuition & Fees: $30,290
Enrollment: 1,928 Coed
Affiliation or Control: Independent Non-Profit IRS Status: 501(c)3
Highest Offering: Baccalaureate
Accreditation: M

01 President .... Dr. Kerry WALK
05 VP for Acad Aff/Dean of Faculty .... Dr. Sharon MEAGHER
10 Exec Vice Pres Admin & Finance .... Mr. Paul CIRAULO
111 VP Institutional Advancement .... Ms. Marilyn L. WILKIE
32 VP Student Affairs/Dean of Students .... Dr. Carol JACKSON
21 Associate VP Admin & Controller .... Mr. Wayne SANTUCCI
07 Dean of Admissions .... Mr. James ROGERS
20 Sr Assoc Dean for Acad Affairs .... Dr. Kathleen LEBESCO
06 Registrar .... Ms. Regina CHAN
15 Assistant VP of Human Resources .... Ms. Bree BULLINGHAM
08 Librarian .... Mr. Brian ROCCO
13 Chief Information Officer .... Ms. Dale HOCHSTEIN
37 Asst VP of Fin & Registration Svcs .. Ms. Maria DEINNOCENTIIS
38 Dir Counseling & Psychological Svcs .... Vacant
18 Director of Facilities .... Mr. Pete ROMAIN
36 Exec Dir of Career Svcs .... Ms. Robin E. NACKMAN
96 Director of Administrative Services .... Ms. Maria MARZANO
88 Asst Controller .... Ms. Cassie GOULD
30 Director of Development .... Vacant
09 Dir Institutional Research .... Ms. Cheryl GOLDSTEIN
19 Director of Campus Safety .... Mr. James CAMBRIA
26 Dir Public Relations/ Communications .... Ms. Stephanie POLICASTRO
28 Asst VP Str Init/Diversity/Title IX .... Ms. Christine GREGORY
39 Asst Dean Stdnt Aff/Dir of Res Life .... Ms. Emmalyn YAMRICK
102 Dir Foundation/Corporate Relations .... Ms. Kayla MCCAFFREY
29 Director Alumni Relations .... Ms. Kristen ANDERSON

Mechon L'Hoyroa (E)

168 Maple Avenue, Monsey NY 10952
County: Rockland FICE Identification: 042615
Telephone: (845) 425-9565 Carnegie Class: Not Classified
FAX Number: (845) 425-2094 Calendar System: Other
Established: 1990 Annual Undergrad Tuition & Fees: N/A
Enrollment: N/A Male
Affiliation or Control: Jewish IRS Status: 501(c)3
Highest Offering: First Talmudic Degree
Accreditation: AIJS

Medaille College (F)

18 Agassiz Circle, Buffalo NY 14214-2695
County: Erie FICE Identification: 002777
Unit ID: 192925
Telephone: (716) 880-2000 Carnegie Class: Masters/L
FAX Number: (716) 884-0291 Calendar System: Semester
URL: www.medaille.edu
Established: 1875 Annual Undergrad Tuition & Fees: $27,276
Enrollment: 2,112 Coed
Affiliation or Control: Independent Non-Profit IRS Status: 501(c)3
Highest Offering: Doctorate
Accreditation: M, CACREP, CAEPT, CAHIIM, IACBE

01 President .... Dr. Kenneth M. MACUR
05 Vice President Academic Affairs .... Dr. Lori QUIGLEY
10 Vice President Business/Finance .... Mr. Matthew J. CARVER
30 Vice Pres for College Relations .... Mr. John P. CRAWFORD
07 VP Enroll Mgmt/Marketing/Admiss . Mr. Christopher P. LARUSSO
09 Director of Institutional Research .... Dr. Mary M. TODD
32 VP for Student Development .... Ms. Amy M. DEKAY
44 Dir of Major Gifts & Planned Giving .... Ms. Jeanine PURCELL
41 Athletic Director .... Ms. Amy DEKAY
36 Director Career Planning/Placement .... Ms. Carol CULLINAN
13 Chief Information Officer .... Mr. Robert D. CHYKA
06 Registrar .... Mrs. Kathleen LAZAR
08 Library Director .... Mr. Andrew YEAGER
37 Director Financial Aid .... Mr. James P. AYERS
15 Director of Human Resources .... Ms. Barbara J. BILOTTA
35 Director of Student Involvement .... Ms. Kayla A. BETACCHINI
38 Director Counseling Services .... Ms. Rosalina B. RIZZO
19 Director of Campus Public Safety .... Mr. Earl WELLS
29 Coordinator of Alumni Relations .... Mr. Nicholas J. KOZIOL
26 Director of Marketing .... Ms. Melissa D. HARRIS

Medaille College Rochester Branch Campus (G)

1880 S Winston Road, Rochester NY 14618
Telephone: (585) 272-0030 Identification: 770140
Accreditation: &M

Memorial School of Nursing (H)

600 Northern Boulevard, Albany NY 12204-1004
County: Albany FICE Identification: 012203
Unit ID: 192961
Telephone: (518) 471-3260 Carnegie Class: Spec 2-yr-Health
FAX Number: (518) 447-3559 Calendar System: Semester
URL: www.nehealth.com
Established: 1901 Annual Undergrad Tuition & Fees: $12,674
Enrollment: 119 Coed
Affiliation or Control: Independent Non-Profit IRS Status: 501(c)3
Highest Offering: Associate Degree
Accreditation: NY, ADNUR

01 Director .... Ms. Mary-Jane S. ARALDI

Mercy College (I)

555 Broadway, Dobbs Ferry NY 10522-1189
County: Westchester FICE Identification: 002772
Unit ID: 193016
Telephone: (800) 637-2969 Carnegie Class: Masters/L
FAX Number: (914) 674-5978 Calendar System: Semester
URL: www.mercy.edu
Established: 1950 Annual Undergrad Tuition & Fees: $18,392
Enrollment: 11,295 Coed
Affiliation or Control: Independent Non-Profit IRS Status: 501(c)3
Highest Offering: Doctorate
Accreditation: M, ARCPA, CAEP, CAEPN, EXSC, NURSE, OT, #OTA, PTA, SP, SW

01 President .... Mr. Timothy HALL
05 Provost & Vice Pres Acad Affairs .... Dr. Jose HERRERA
20 Associate Provost for Acad Affairs .... Dr. Lucretia MANN
32 Vice President of Student Affairs .... Mr. Kevin JOYCE
50 Dean School of Business .... Dr. Ed WEIS
53 Dean School of Education .... Dr. Rose RUDNITSKI
83 Dean School Soc/Behavioral Sci .... Dr. Karol DEAN
76 Dean School Health/Natural Sci .... Dr. Joan TOGLIA
49 Dean School Liberal Arts .... Dr. Tamara JHASHI
15 Exec Dir of Human Resources/Safety .... Ms. Anne GILMARTIN
11 VP Operations & Facilities .... Mr. Thomas SIMMONDS
84 Vice Pres for Enrollment Management ...... Ms. Deirdre WHITMAN
10 VP & Chief Financial/Plng Officer .... Mr. Donald AUNGST
88 VP Enrollment Services .... Ms. Margaret MCGRAIL
111 Chief Advancement Officer .... Ms. Bernadette WADE
100 Chief of Staff .... Ms. Irene BUCKLEY
04 Exec Assistant Office of President .... Ms. Grace CREIGHTON
88 Director of Learning Assessment .... Ms. Victoria FERRARA
43 General Counsel .... Ms. Kristen BOWES
07 Executive Director of Admissions .... Ms. Tara FAY-REILLY
09 Dir Institutional Research/Planning .... Mrs. Victoria TYLER
39 Assistant Dean of Student Affairs .... Mr. Jason ALT
13 Director of Information Technology .... Mr. Todd PRATTELLA
06 Exec Director of Registrar .... Ms. Debra KENNEY
45 Asst VP of Inst Assess/Plng/Analy .... Ms. Jessica HABER
88 Sr Director of Student Accounts .... Ms. Felicia BRANDON
21 Controller .... Ms. Narda ROMERO
114 Director of Budgets & Planning .... Mr. Bernard COSTELLO
96 Director of Purchasing .... Ms. Patricia SABATINO
08 Director of Mercy College Libraries .... Mr. Mustafa SAKARYA
41 Director of Athletics .... Mr. Matt KILCULLEN
27 Director of Communications .... Ms. Jessica BAILY
29 Director of Alumni Relations .... Ms. Alexis MCGRATH-ROTHENBERG
25 Dir Sponsored Programs .... Ms. Janet PARTENZA
104 Director Center Global Engagement .... Dr. Sheila GERSH
106 Director Online Learning .... Dr. Mary LOZINA
103 Senior Director of Career Services .... Ms. Jill HART
101 Secretary of the Institution/Board .... Ms. Irene BUCKLEY
26 Asst VP Marketing & Analytics .... Ms. Alexa D'AGOSTINO
112 Director Major Gifts/Planned Giving .... Mr. Phil KEEFE
105 Director Marketing Communications .... Mr. Alfonso ANTONAGLIA
38 Director Student Counseling Center .... Ms. Ori SHINAR

Mesivta of Eastern Parkway Rabbinical Seminary (A)

510 Dahill Road, Brooklyn NY 11218-5559
County: Kings FICE Identification: 009335
Unit ID: 193061
Telephone: (718) 438-1002 Carnegie Class: Spec-4-yr-Faith
FAX Number: (718) 438-2591 Calendar System: Semester
Established: 1947 Annual Undergrad Tuition & Fees: $8,600
Enrollment: 26 Male
Affiliation or Control: Independent Non-Profit IRS Status: 501(c)3
Highest Offering: Second Talmudic Degree
Accreditation: RABN

01 President ....Rabbi Issac HEIMOVITZ
32 Dean of Students ....Rabbi Shlomo Z. EPSTEIN
37 Director of Student Financial Aid ....Rabbi Ira LIBERMAN
46 Director of Research ....Rabbi Hersch BASCH
10 Chief Fiscal Officer ....Rabbi Joseph HALBERSTADT

Mesivta Tifereth Jerusalem of America (B)

145 E Broadway, New York NY 10002-6301
County: New York FICE Identification: 003974
Unit ID: 193070
Telephone: (212) 964-2830 Carnegie Class: Spec-4-yr-Faith
FAX Number: (212) 349-5213 Calendar System: Semester
Established: 1907 Annual Undergrad Tuition & Fees: $10,750
Enrollment: 72 Male
Affiliation or Control: Independent Non-Profit IRS Status: 501(c)3
Highest Offering: Second Talmudic Degree
Accreditation: RABN

01 President & Dean Faculties ....Rabbi David FEINSTEIN
06 Registrar ....Chana YAMPOLSKY
37 Director Student Financial Aid ....E. GOLD

Mesivta Torah Vodaath Seminary (C)

425 E Ninth Street, Brooklyn NY 11218-5299
County: Kings FICE Identification: 007264
Unit ID: 193052
Telephone: (718) 941-8000 Carnegie Class: Spec-4-yr-Faith
FAX Number: (718) 941-8032 Calendar System: Semester
Established: 1918 Annual Undergrad Tuition & Fees: $11,310
Enrollment: 324 Male
Affiliation or Control: Independent Non-Profit IRS Status: 501(c)3
Highest Offering: Second Talmudic Degree
Accreditation: RABN

01 Dean ....Rabbi Yisroel BELSKY
03 Executive Director ....Rabbi Yitzchok GOTTDIENER
06 Registrar ....Rabbi Yaakov EHRENREICH
33 Dean of Men ....Rabbi Elya KATZ
31 Director Community Services ....Mr. Shraga WERNER

Metropolitan College of New York (D)

60 West Street, New York NY 10006
County: New York FICE Identification: 009769
Unit ID: 190114
Telephone: (212) 343-1234 Carnegie Class: Masters/L
FAX Number: (212) 343-7399 Calendar System: Semester
URL: www.metropolitan.edu
Established: 1964 Annual Undergrad Tuition & Fees: $18,730
Enrollment: 1,195 Coed
Affiliation or Control: Independent Non-Profit IRS Status: 501(c)3
Highest Offering: Master's
Accreditation: M, ACBSP, CAEPN

01 President ....Dr. Vinton THOMPSON
10 VP Finance & Administration/CFO ....Vacant
05 Chief Academic Officer ....Dr. Tilokie DEPOO
84 Vice Pres for Enrollment Management ....Dr. Collette GARRITY
07 Director of Admissions ....Ms. Erica SILBIGER
58 Dean School Public Affairs & Admin ....Dr. Humphrey CROOKENDALE
50 Dean School for Business ....Dr. Tilokie DEPOO
88 Dean ACSHSE ....Dr. Adele WEINER
32 Dean of Students ....Ms. Dona SOSA
37 Director of Financial Aid ....Mr. Douane CAMPBELL
06 Registrar ....Ms. Noreen SMITH
08 Director of Library Services ....Ms. Kate ADLER
09 Dir Institutional Rsrch/Assessment ....Mr. Anthony WILLIAMS
15 Director Human Resources ....Ms. Judith SANTIAGO
30 Chief Development Officer ....Ms. Beth DUNPHE
26 Chief Public Relations Officer ....Ms. Tina GEORGIOU
13 Director of Technology ....Mr. Adrian SMITH
21 Bursar ....Mr. Taurean KENNEDY
04 Exec Assistant to the President ....Ms. Isabel CABRERA
29 Director Alumni Relations ....Ms. Tina GEORGIOU
36 Director Career Development ....Mr. John EDWARDS

Mildred Elley (E)

855 Central Avenue, Albany NY 12206
County: Albany FICE Identification: 022195
Unit ID: 193201
Telephone: (518) 786-0855 Carnegie Class: Assoc/HVT-High Non
FAX Number: (518) 786-0898 Calendar System: Other
URL: www.mildred-elley.edu
Established: 1917 Annual Undergrad Tuition & Fees: $11,205
Enrollment: 731 Coed
Affiliation or Control: Proprietary IRS Status: Proprietary
Highest Offering: Associate Degree
Accreditation: ACICS

01 President ....Ms. Faith A. TAKES

Mildred Elley-New York City (F)

25 Broadway, 16th Floor, New York NY 10004
Telephone: (212) 380-9004 Identification: 770747
Accreditation: ACICS

Mirrer Yeshiva Central Institute (G)

1795 Ocean Parkway, Brooklyn NY 11223-2010
County: Kings FICE Identification: 004798
Unit ID: 193247
Telephone: (718) 645-0536 Carnegie Class: Spec-4-yr-Faith
FAX Number: (718) 645-9251 Calendar System: Semester
Established: 1947 Annual Undergrad Tuition & Fees: $6,980
Enrollment: 203 Male
Affiliation or Control: Independent Non-Profit IRS Status: 501(c)3
Highest Offering: Second Talmudic Degree
Accreditation: RABN

00 Chancellor ....Rabbi Avrohom Yaakov NELKENBAUM
01 President and Dean ....Rabbi Osher KALMANOWITZ
05 Vice President & Dean ....Rabbi Asher BERENBAUM
33 Dean of Men ....Rabbi Esrael ERLANGER
03 Executive Director ....Rabbi Pinchas HECHT
06 Registrar-Administrator ....Mrs. Devorah BERENBAUM
08 Director of the Library ....Rabbi Aaron SAPOZNICK
38 Director of Guidance ....Rabbi Yisroel FISHMAN
37 Financial Aid Director ....Mrs. Rachel BERENBAUM

Mohawk Valley Community College (H)

1101 Floyd Avenue, Rome NY 13440
Telephone: (315) 339-3470 Identification: 770141
Accreditation: &M

Mohawk Valley Community College (I)

1101 Sherman Drive, Utica NY 13501-5394
County: Oneida FICE Identification: 002871
Unit ID: 193283
Telephone: (315) 792-5400 Carnegie Class: Assoc/HT-Mix Trad/Non
FAX Number: (315) 792-5666 Calendar System: Semester
URL: www.mvcc.edu
Established: 1946 Annual Undergrad Tuition & Fees (In-District): $4,860
Enrollment: 6,675 Coed
Affiliation or Control: State/Local IRS Status: 501(c)3
Highest Offering: Associate Degree
Accreditation: M, ADNUR, CAHIIM, COARC, ENGT, RAD, SURTEC

01 President ....Dr. Randall J. VAN WAGONER
04 Assistant to the President ....Ms. Jill HEINTZ
88 Exec Dir Organizational Development ....Mr. David KATZ
09 Dir Institutional Research/Analysis ....Ms. Marie MIKNAVICH
05 Vice Pres Learning/Academic Affairs ....Dr. Maryrose EANNACE
88 Asst Vice Pres Bus/Educ/Lib Arts ....Mr. Lewis KAHLER
53 Assoc Dean Educ & Lang Studies ....Ms. Julie DEWAN
88 Asst Vice Pres STEM/Health/Soc Sci ....Dr. Kathleen LINAKER
54 Assoc Dean Phys Sci/Engr/App Tech ....Mr. Timothy THOMAS
57 Assoc Dean Art ....Mr. Todd BEHRENDT
77 Assoc Dean Bus/Cyber/Comp Sci ....Mr. Jake MIHEVC
81 Assoc Dean Math & Natural Sci ....Dr. Robert WOODROW
79 Assoc Dean Humanities ....Ms. Deb BOGAN
76 Assoc Dean Health Professions ....Ms. Lisa COOLEY
83 Assoc Dean Soc Sci & Public Svc ....Mr. Mark MONTGOMERY
88 Dean of Emer Prep & Public Svc ..Ms. Marianne BUTTENSCHON
08 Director College Libraries ....Mr. Stephen FRISBEE
88 Exec Dean Academic Dev & Innovation ....Mr. James LYNCH
10 Vice Pres Administrative Services ....Mr. Thomas SQUIRES
32 Vice Pres Student Affairs ....Ms. Stephanie C. REYNOLDS
84 Assoc Dean Enrollment & Advisement ..Mrs. Jennifer DEWEERTH
36 Assoc Dean Development & Transition ....Mr. James MAIO
39 Assoc Dean Student & Residence Life ....Mr. Dennis GIBBONS
103 Assoc VP of Workforce Development ... Ms. Franca ARMSTRONG
111 Exec Dir Institutional Advancement ....Mr. Frank DUROSS
44 Dir of Donor & Resource Development ....Ms. Deanna FERRO
96 Coord Expend/Fixed Asset Procure ....Ms. Joyce PALMER
13 Exec Dir of Information Technology ....Mr. Paul KATCHMAR
88 Dir Ctr Community/Economic Dev ....Ms. Kristen SKOBLA
15 Exec Director of Human Resources . Mrs. Kimberly EVANS-DAME
26 Director Marketing/Communications ....Mr. Alen SMAJIC
07 Director of Admissions ....Mr. Daniel IANNO
37 Director of Financial Aid ....Mr. Michael PEDE
06 Dir of Student Records/Registrar ....Mrs. Rosemary V. SPETKA
18 Dir of Facilities and Operations ....Mr. Michael MCHARRIS
19 Exec Dir Public Safety & Emerg Mgmt ....Mr. David AMICO
21 Business Office Controller ....Mr. Brian MOLINARO
29 Coord Annual Funds/Alumni Relations ....Ms. Marie KOHL
41 Athletic Director ....Mr. Gary BROADHURST

Molloy College (J)

1000 Hempstead Avenue, PO Box 5002, Rockville Centre NY 11571-5002
County: Nassau FICE Identification: 002775
Unit ID: 193292
Telephone: (516) 323-3000 Carnegie Class: Masters/L
FAX Number: N/A Calendar System: 4/1/4
URL: www.molloy.edu
Established: 1955 Annual Undergrad Tuition & Fees: $29,100
Enrollment: 4,894 Coed
Affiliation or Control: Independent Non-Profit IRS Status: 501(c)3
Highest Offering: Doctorate
Accreditation: M, CAEPN, COARC, CVT, MUS, NMT, NURSE, SP, SW

01 President ....Dr. Drew BOGNER
05 VP Academic Affairs/Dean of Faculty ....Dr. Ann Z. BRANCHINI
10 Vice Pres for Finance & Treasurer ....Mr. Michael MC GOVERN
84 Vice Pres Enrollment Management ....Ms. Linda ALBANESE
111 VP for Mission & Advancement ....Mr. Edward J. THOMPSON
32 Vice President Student Affairs ....Mr. Robert HOULIHAN
45 VP Tech & Inst Effectiveness ....Mr. Michael TORRES
42 Director of Campus Ministries ....Mr. Scott SALVATO
37 Director Student Financial Services ....Ms. Debra OCONNOR
36 Director of Career Development ....Ms. Mary BROSNAN
41 Director of Athletics ....Ms. Susan CASSIDY
07 Asst VP for Enrollment Management ....Ms. Marguerite LANE
37 Director of Financial Aid ....Mrs. Ana C. LOCKWARD
21 Asst VP for Finance ....Ms. Barbara CALISSI
30 Asst VP Mission Int & Development ....Ms. Catherine MUSCENTE
06 Registrar ....Ms. Susan FORTMAN
09 Dir of Institutional Effectiveness ....Ms. Christina D'AMATO
15 Asst VP for HR & Title IX Coord ....Ms. Lisa MILLER
18 Director of Facilities ....Mr. James MULTARI
26 Asst VP of Marketing & PR ....Mr. Ken YOUNG
35 Interim VP for Student Affairs ....Dr. Janine PAYTON
29 Director of Alumni Relations ....Ms. Mary Jane REILLY
19 Director of Public Safety ....Mr. Harry HERMAN
85 Director of International Education ....Ms. Kathleen REBA
105 Director Web Technologies ....Vacant
121 Assoc Dean Acad Support Svcs ....Vacant
13 Sr Director of IT ....Mr. Michael OLIVO
88 Director of Networking & Infra ....Mr. Sean LAURIE
08 Head Librarian ....Ms. Judith BRINK-DRESCHER
100 Chief of Staff ....Ms. Diane K. FORNIERI
106 Dean Innovative Delivery Methods ....Ms. Amy GAIMARO

Monroe College (K)

2501 Jerome Avenue, Bronx NY 10468-5407
County: Bronx FICE Identification: 004799
Unit ID: 193308
Telephone: (718) 933-6700 Carnegie Class: Bac/Assoc-Mixed
FAX Number: (718) 295-5861 Calendar System: Semester
URL: www.monroecollege.edu
Established: 1933 Annual Undergrad Tuition & Fees: $14,460
Enrollment: 6,858 Coed
Affiliation or Control: Proprietary IRS Status: Proprietary
Highest Offering: Master's
Accreditation: M, ACBSP, ACFEI, PNUR

01 President ....Marc M. JEROME
03 Exec VP/Director of Branch Campus ....David DIMOND
05 Vice President for Academics ....Dr. Karenann CARTY
11 Vice President Administration ....David DIMOND
10 Vice President for Finance ....Michael ANASTASIO
84 Vice Pres Enroll Mgmt/Campus Dean ....Anthony ALLEN
32 Vice President Student Affairs ....Roberta GREENBERG
58 Dean of Graduate Programs ....Alex CANALS
12 Assoc Vice Pres New Rochelle Camp ....Carol GENESE
86 Asst Vice Pres Governmental Affairs ....Dr. Donald E. SIMON
108 Asst VP Institutional Effectiveness ....Dr. Edward S. SCHNEIDERMAN
55 Director of Evening Division ....Allen JENKINS
26 Director of Marketing ....Shane SEAMAN
06 Registrar ....Abigail THORPE
09 Dir Institutional Research ....Peter NWAKEZE
113 Bursar/Branch Campus ....Michael NIEDZWIECKI
21 Director Student Financial Services ....Daniel SHARON
113 Bursar ....Villan CRUZ
35 Dean for Student Services ....Mark SONNENSTEIN
109 Director Auxiliary Services ....Nivia CAMARA
07 Dean of Admissions Branch ....Gersom LOPEZ
07 Vice President Admissions ....Craig PATRICK
37 Dir Student Financial Aid Services ....Vacant
36 Exec Dir Ofc of Career Services ....Pamela DELLAPORTA
08 Director of Library Services ....Christine ARTIS
08 Director of Library Services/Branch ....Tom GORDON
39 Exec Director of Residential Life ....Marcus JOHNSON
29 Director of Alumni Relations ....Leslie JEROME
13 Chief Info Technology Officer (CIO) ....Terrance MCGOWAN

Monroe Community College (L)

1000 E Henrietta Road, Rochester NY 14623-5780
County: Monroe FICE Identification: 002872
Unit ID: 193326
Telephone: (585) 292-2000 Carnegie Class: Assoc/HT-High Non
FAX Number: (585) 427-2749 Calendar System: Semester
URL: www.monroecc.edu
Established: 1961 Annual Undergrad Tuition & Fees (In-District): $4,959
Enrollment: 14,586 Coed
Affiliation or Control: State/Local IRS Status: 501(c)3
Highest Offering: Associate Degree
Accreditation: M, ADNUR, CAHIIM, DA, DH, EMT, ENGT, MLTAD, RAD

01 President ....Dr. Anne M. KRESS
05 Provost & VP Academic Svcs ....Dr. Andrea C. WADE

84 Assoc VP Enrollment Mgmt .... Ms. Christine CASALINUOVO-ADAMS
32 Vice President Student Services .... Dr. Lloyd A. HOLMES
10 CFO and VP Administrative Svcs .... Mr. Hezekiah N. SIMMONS
103 VP Econ Dev/Workforce Svc .... Mr. Todd M. OLDHAM
102 Exec Director MCC Foundation .... Vacant
12 Exec Dean Damon City Campus .... Dr. Joel L. FRATER
26 Asst to the Pres Mktg & Comm Rels .... Ms. Cynthia L. MAPES
35 Asst Vice Pres Student Services .... Vacant
13 Asst VP/CIO Educational Tech Svcs .... Ms. Eileen M. WIRLEY
18 Assistant Vice President Facilities .... Mr. Paul E. WURSTER
88 Asst Vice Pres ETS .... Mr. Terrance KEYS
20 Asst Vice Pres Academic Services .... Ms. Kimberley COLLINS
37 Director Financial Aid Compliance .... Mr. Jerome S. ST. CROIX
09 Director Institutional Research .... Vacant
08 Interim Director ETS Libraries .... Ms. Katherine E. DERUSSO
36 Director Career & Veteran Services .... Ms. Michelle P. MAYO
21 Asst Vice President Admin Svcs .. Mr. Darrell K. JACHIM-MOORE
06 Director Registrar & Records .... Ms. Elizabeth R. RIPTON
30 Director of Development .... Mr. Mark J. PASTORELLA
38 Dir Counseling & Disability Svcs .... Ms. Aubrey ZAMIARA
19 Interim Director Public Safety .... Mr. Kevin A. HALL
41 Director Athletics .... Vacant
25 Director Grants .... Ms. Remegia A. MITCHELL
35 Director of Student Life .... Ms. Elizabeth J. STEWART
23 Director of Health Services .... Ms. Donna G. MUELLER
21 Controller .... Mr. Michael G. QUINN
79 Dean Humanities & Social Services .... Mr. Michael JACOBS
81 Dean STEM and Health .... Mr. Daniel E. ROBINSON
88 Dean Academic Foundations .... Ms. Medea RAMBISH
19 Dean Public Safety Training Ctr .... Mr. Michael S. KARNES
32 Dean Student Services-DCC .... Dr. Ann V. TOPPING
35 Director Student Svcs-DCC .... Ms. Kimberly F. DELARGE
20 Dean Acad Svcs DCC .... Dr. Kimberly MCKINSEY-MABRY
15 Asst to President HR/Affirm Act Ofc .... Ms. Melissa A. FINGAR
40 Manager Bookstore .... Ms. Charlene SUTER
22 Director Educ Opportunity Program .... Ms. Brenda A. SMITH
88 Director Advis & Transfer Services .... Ms. Marlene A. FINE
43 Legal Counsel .... Vacant
88 Interim Dir Financial Aid Opers .... Ms. Melissa M. JARKOWSKI
96 Director of Purchasing .... Mr. Patrick M. BATES
39 Director Housing/Residence Life .... Ms. Jamia DANZY
28 Chief Diversity Officer .... Dr. Lloyd A. HOLMES
04 Executive Asst to President .... Ms. Sheila M. STRONG
07 Interim Director of Admissions .... Ms. Sarah HAGREEN
101 Secy to the Board of Trustees/Pres .... Ms. Linda M. HALL
108 Asst Director Assess and Curriculum .... Mr. Michael A. HEEL
29 Coord Alumni & Annual Giving .... Ms. Karen A. SHAW
45 Director Planning .... Ms. Valarie L. AVALONE
90 Director Comm and Network Services .... Ms. Donna J. POGROSZEWSKI

Montefiore School of Nursing (A)

53 Valentine Street, Mount Vernon NY 10550

County: Westchester FICE Identification: 022178
Unit ID: 193380
Telephone: (914) 361-6221 Carnegie Class: Not Classified
FAX Number: (914) 665-7047 Calendar System: Semester
URL: www.montefioreschoolofnursing.org
Established: 2014 Annual Undergrad Tuition & Fees: N/A
Enrollment: N/A Coed
Affiliation or Control: Independent Non-Profit IRS Status: 501(c)3
Highest Offering: Associate Degree
Accreditation: ADNUR

01 Dean .... Rebecca GREER
06 Registrar .... Sandra FARRIOR
07 Director of Admissions .... Sandra FARRIOR

Mount Saint Mary College (B)

330 Powell Avenue, Newburgh NY 12550-3412

County: Orange FICE Identification: 002778
Unit ID: 193353
Telephone: (845) 561-0800 Carnegie Class: Masters/M
FAX Number: (845) 562-6762 Calendar System: Semester
URL: www.msmc.edu
Established: 1959 Annual Undergrad Tuition & Fees: $29,048
Enrollment: 2,508 Coed
Affiliation or Control: Independent Non-Profit IRS Status: 501(c)3
Highest Offering: Master's
Accreditation: M, CAEPN, IACBE, NURSE

01 Interim President .... Dr. David KENNETT
05 Interim VP for Academic Affairs .... Dr. Michael OLIVETTE
10 Vice Pres Finance & Admin/Treasurer .... Mr. Art GLASS
111 Vice Pres for College Advancement .... Mr. Joseph VALENTI
32 Vice President for Students .... Mrs. Elaine O'GRADY
18 Vice Pres Facilities & Operations .... Mr. James RAIMO
07 Interim Dean of Admissions .... Mr. John MAHON
35 Dean of Students .... Ms. Kelly YOUGH
38 Asst Dean of Support Services .... Dr. Orin STRAUCHLER
20 Asst Vice Pres Academic Affairs .... Vacant
06 Registrar .... Mr. Carlos TONCHE, JR.
07 Director of Admissions .... Mrs. Nancy SCAFFIDI CLARKE
08 Director of the Library .... Mrs. Barbara W. PETRUZZELLI
37 Director of Financial Aid .... Mr. Jason FRANKY
09 Director of Planning and Research .... Mr. Ryan WILLIAMS
15 Director of Human Resources .... Mrs. Sharnie CANARY
42 Chaplain .... Fr. Gregoire J. FLUET
35 Director of Student Activities .... Ms. Barbara MULLIGAN
39 Exec Dir of Operations and Housing .... Mr. Michael O'KEEFE
29 Director of Alumni Affairs .... Ms. Michelle A. IACUESSA
41 Director of Athletics & Recreation .... Ms. Jessica MUSHEL
36 Director of the Career Center .... Mrs. Kathleen O'KEEFE
13 Chief Information Officer .... Mr. Dennis RUSH
96 Purchasing Manager .... Mr. Brian MOORE
106 Director of Online Learning .... Ms. Kristen DELLASALA
39 Director of Residence Life .... Ms. Maxine MONROE
18 Exec Director of Facilities & Space .... Ms. Maryann PILON
26 Director of Marketing & Advertising .... Mr. Dean DIMARZO
04 Administrative Asst to President .... Ms. Barbara CONNOLLY
104 Director Study Abroad .... Ms. Ashley KNOX
19 Director Security/Safety .... Mr. Matthew BYRNE
44 Director Annual Giving .... Ms. Natalie MCKINSTRIE

Nassau Community College (C)

1 Education Drive, Garden City NY 11530-6793

County: Nassau FICE Identification: 002873
Unit ID: 193478
Telephone: (516) 572-7501 Carnegie Class: Assoc/HT-High Trad
FAX Number: (516) 572-7750 Calendar System: Semester
URL: www.ncc.edu
Established: 1959 Annual Undergrad Tuition & Fees (In-District): $5,248
Enrollment: 21,558 Coed
Affiliation or Control: State/Local IRS Status: 501(c)3
Highest Offering: Associate Degree
Accreditation: #M, ADNUR, COARC, ENGT, FUSER, MLTAD, MUS, PTAA, RTT, SURGT

01 President .... Dr. W. Hubert KEEN
05 Interim Vice Pres Academic Affairs .... Dr. Valerie H. COLLINS
18 Vice Pres Facilities Management .... Dr. Joseph V. MUSCARELLA
10 Vice President Finance .... Ms. Inna REZNIK
32 Vice Pres Academic/Student Svcs .... Ms. Maria P. CONZATTI
22 AVP Equity & Inclusion/AA Officer .... Dr. Craig J. WRIGHT
43 Spec Asst to Pres/College Counsel .... Ms. Donna M. HAUGEN
103 Asst Vice Pres Workforce Devel .... Dr. Janet CARUSO
21 Treasurer .... Ms. Lisa HAHN
88 Asst VP Maintenance/Operations .... Mr. Robert FOLEY
15 Assoc Vice Pres Human Resources .... Ms. Dorlena DUNBAR
96 Director Procurement .... Mr. Phillip CAPPELLO
35 Dean of Students .... Ms. Charmian SMITH
09 Dean Institutional Effectiveness .... Vacant
37 Dean Financial Aid .... Ms. Patricia NOREN
07 Dean of Admissions .... Mr. David FOLLICK
25 Resource Devel/Grants Fiscal Mgr .... Mr. Edmund KOEPPEL
86 Asst to Pres/Media & Govt Relations .... Ms. Kate MURRAY
26 Director Marketing/Communications .... Ms. Alicia STEGER
08 Director of Library .... Ms. Nancy WILLIAMSON
41 Director Special Pgm Athletics/PED ... Ms. Kerri-Ann MCTIERNAN
06 Registrar .... Mr. Chester BARKAN
19 Director of Public Safety .... Mr. Martin RODDINI
23 Director Health Services .... Ms. Margaret MCGOVERN
36 Director of Placement Testing .... Ms. Noreen WADE
121 Director Academic Advisement .... Ms. Amanda FOX
13 Chief Information Officer .... Mr. Richard LAWLESS
102 Exec Dir Nassau CC Foundation .... Ms. Joy DEDONATO
04 Administrative Asst to President .... Ms. Anne E. BRANDI

Nazareth College of Rochester (D)

4245 East Avenue, Rochester NY 14618-3790

County: Monroe FICE Identification: 002779
Unit ID: 193584
Telephone: (585) 389-2525 Carnegie Class: Masters/L
FAX Number: (585) 586-2452 Calendar System: Semester
URL: www.naz.edu
Established: 1924 Annual Undergrad Tuition & Fees: $32,649
Enrollment: 2,871 Coed
Affiliation or Control: Independent Non-Profit IRS Status: 501(c)3
Highest Offering: Doctorate
Accreditation: M, CAEPT, IACBE, MUS, NURSE, OT, PTA, SP, SW

01 President .... Mr. Daan BRAVEMAN
04 Assistant to President .... Ms. Patricia GENTHNER
04 Executive Assistant to President .... Ms. Cathleen M. STEVENS
05 Vice President Academic Affairs .... Dr. Andrea TALENTINO
111 Vice Pres Institutional Advancement .... Ms. Kelly GAGAN
10 Vice President Finance & Admin .... Mr. Patrick RICHEY
32 Vice President Student Development .... Mr. Kevin WORTHEN
84 Vice Pres Enrollment Management .... Mr. Ian MORTIMER
29 Director of Alumni Relations .... Ms. Donna BORGUS
15 Assoc VP Human Resources .... Mrs. JoEllen PINKHAM
20 Asst VP Academic Affairs .... Dr. Lisa DURANT JONES
06 Registrar .... Ms. Alison TEETER
37 Director Student Financial Aid .... Ms. Janice SCHEUTZOW
26 Director Marketing & Communications .... Ms. Elizabeth ZAPATA
13 Director Information Tech Svcs .... Ms. Karen KUPPINGER
08 Director of Library .... Ms. Catherine DOYLE
19 Director of Security .... Ms. Terri STEWART
39 Director of Campus Life .... Ms. Carey BACKMAN
41 Director of Athletics .... Mr. Peter G. BOTHNER
42 Director Center for Spirituality .... Mr. Jamie FAZIO
36 Director of Career Services .... Mr. Michael D. KAHL
18 Director Buildings/Grounds .... Mr. Peter LANA
09 Director of Institutional Research .... Mr. Nicholas LAMENDOLA
23 Director of Health Services .... Ms. Susan QUINN
121 Director of Academic Advisement .... Ms. Linda SEARING
88 Director of the Arts Center .... Ms. Rita J. MANNELLI
113 Bursar .... Mr. John GARBE
92 Director Honors Program .... Dr. Marjorie ROTH
49 Dean of Col of Arts and Sciences .... Dr. Diane OLIVER
76 Dean School of Health & Human Svcs .... Dr. Brigid NOONAN
53 Dean School of Education .... Dr. Kathleen DABOLL-LAVOIE
88 Dean School of Management .... Mr. Gerard ZAPPIA
88 Exec Dir of Ctr International Educ .... Dr. Nevan FISHER
88 Dir of Center for Service Learning .... Dr. David STEITZ
89 Dir Stdnt Transition/First Year Ctr .... Mr. Andrew MORRIS
96 Director of Purchasing .... Ms. Joanne FITZGERALD
88 Dir Center for Civic Engagement .... Ms. Nuala BOYLE
07 Dir Graduate Admissions/Transfer .... Ms. Judith G. BAKER
86 Director Government Relations .... Ms. Mary Kay BISHOP

The New School (E)

66 W 12th Street, New York NY 10011-8603

County: New York FICE Identification: 020662
Unit ID: 193654
Telephone: (212) 229-5600 Carnegie Class: DU-Higher
FAX Number: N/A Calendar System: Semester
URL: www.newschool.edu
Established: 1919 Annual Undergrad Tuition & Fees: $45,440
Enrollment: 10,344 Coed
Affiliation or Control: Independent Non-Profit IRS Status: 501(c)3
Highest Offering: Doctorate
Accreditation: M, ART, CLPSY, SPAA

01 President .... Dr. David VAN ZANDT
04 Executive Assistant to President .... Ms. Lindsey WARFORD
05 Provost and Chief Academic Officer .... Mr. Tim MARSHALL
88 Exec Asst and Comm Mgr to Prov .... Ms. Heather O'BRIEN
48 Exec Dean Parsons School for Design .... Mr. Joel TOWERS
82 Exec Dean School for Public Engage .... Dr. Mary WATSON
64 Exec Dean Perf Arts and Dean Mannes .... Mr. Richard KESSLER
83 Dean New School for Social Research .... Dr. William MILBERG
49 Dean Eugene Lang College .... Ms. Stephanie BROWNER
12 Dean Parsons Paris .... Ms. Florence LECLERC-DICKLER
84 Chief Enrollment & Success Officer .... Mr. Donald RESNICK
88 VP Corporate Partnerships .... Ms. Deborah GIBB
11 Chief Operating Officer .... Mr. Tokumbo SHOBOWALE
30 Chief Development Officer .... Mr. Mark GIBBEL
26 Chief Marketing Officer .... Ms. Anne ADRIANCE
43 Chief Legal Officer & Sec of Corp .... Mr. Roy P. MOSKOWITZ
28 Sr VP for Social Justice .... Ms. Maya WILEY
13 Sr VP & Chief Information Officer .... Mr. Anand PADMANABHAN
15 Chief Human Resources Officer .... Mr. Jerry CUTLER
10 VP Finance/Business & Treasurer .... Mr. Steve STABILE
32 VP for Student Success .... Ms. Michelle RELYEA
88 VP Buildings .... Ms. Lia GARTNER
100 Chief of Staff .... Ms. Deborah BOGOSIAN
20 Dep Provost & Sr VP Academic Affs .... Dr. Bryna SANGER
20 Vice Provost Acad Planning Admin .... Ms. Pat BAXTER
20 Vice Provost Curriculum & Learning .... Dr. Laura AURICCHIO
88 Vice Prov Transdisciplinary Initiat .... Dr. Jamer HUNT
46 Vice Provost Research .... Dr. Michael SCHOBER
07 VP Strat Enrollment Mgmt .... Ms. Carol KIM
88 Assoc Dean/Dean Fashion .... Mr. Burak CAKMAK
88 Assc Dean/Dean Milano School .... Ms. Michelle DEPASS
88 Assc Dn/Dean Art/Design Hist/Theory .... Dr. Sarah LAWRENCE
88 Assoc Dean/Dean Art/Media & Tech .... Ms. Anne GAINES
48 Assoc Dean/Dean Constructed Envir .... Mr. Robert KIRKBRIDE
88 Assoc Dean/Dean Media Studies .... Dr. Carol WILDER
48 Assoc Dean/Dean Design Strategies .... Ms. Jane PIRONE
88 Assoc Dean/Dean Undergrad Stds .... Dr. Melissa FRIEDLING
88 Assoc Dean/Dean School of Drama .... Mr. Pippin PARKER
64 Assoc Dean/Dean School of Jazz .... Mr. Keller COKER
88 Director Creative Writing .... Mr. Luis JARAMILLO
20 Assoc Provost Faculty Affairs .... Dr. Eleni LITT
09 Assoc Provost Inst Rsrch .... Dr. Paula MAAS
108 Assoc Provost for Assessment .... Dr. Michaela ROME
88 Asst Provost Curriculum .... Dr. Larry JACKSON
25 Assoc Provost Research .... Mr. David NGO
27 Assoc VP Strategic Marketing .... Ms. Lisa PRESTON
35 Asst VP Campus & Stdnt Engage .... Ms. Maureen SHERIDAN
121 Asst VP Advising & Success .... Dr. Monique RINERE
124 Sr Dir Retention/Data/Commun .... Ms. Rachael RITCHIE
21 Asst VP & Controller .... Ms. Natalie PRESSEY
114 Asst VP Budget & Planning .... Ms. Loretta FERRARI
06 Assoc VP & Registrar .... Ms. Rebecca HUNTER
16 Asst VP Human Resources .... Mr. Irwin KROOT
91 Asst VP IT Enterprise Applications .... Mr. Chris BREZIL
90 Asst VP IT Educational Services .... Ms. Lillian SARTORI
91 Assoc VP IT Enterprise Apps & BI .... Mr. Daniel O'CONNELL
110 VP Development .... Ms. Marie-Noel APPEL
88 Asst VP Design & Construction .... Ms. Jo GOLDBERGER
88 Asst VP Capital Infrastructure .... Mr. Silviu HERSCHER
88 Asst VP Process Improvement .... Ms. Lisa BONNER
08 University Librarian .... Mr. Ed SCARCELLE
23 Asst VP Student Health .... Ms. Tracy ROBIN
19 Director Security .... Mr. Thomas ILICETO
37 Senior Director Financial Aid .... Vacant
18 Asst VP Facilities Management .... Mr. Thomas WHALEN
96 Sr Director of Business Operations .... Mr. Ed VERDI
38 Director Counseling Services .... Dr. Jerry FINKELSTEIN
29 Sr Director Alumni Relations .... Ms. Amy GARAWITZ
22 Director Student Disability Svcs .... Mr. Nicholas FARANDA
24 Director Media Services .... Mr. Mark FITZPATRICK
41 Director Athletics and Recreation .... Ms. Diane YEE
101 Asst Secretary to the Corporation .... Ms. Lori SINGER

New York Academy of Art (F)

111 Franklin Street, New York NY 10013

County: New York FICE Identification: 026001
Unit ID: 366368
Telephone: (212) 966-0300 Carnegie Class: Spec-4-yr-Arts
FAX Number: N/A Calendar System: Semester

URL: www.nyaa.edu
Established: 1982 Annual Graduate Tuition & Fees: N/A
Enrollment: 119 Coed
Affiliation or Control: Independent Non-Profit IRS Status: 501(c)3
Highest Offering: Master's; No Undergraduates
Accreditation: M, NY, ART

01 President ....Mr. David KRATZ
05 Dean of Academic Affairs ....Mr. Peter DRAKE
10 Chief Financial Officer ....Mr. Stephan KORSAKOV
11 Director of Operations ....Mr. Michael SMITH
06 Registrar ....Ms. Katie HEMMER
30 Director of Development ....Ms. Lisa KIRK

New York Chiropractic College (A)

2360 State Route 89, Seneca Falls NY 13148-0800
County: Seneca FICE Identification: 012277
Unit ID: 193751
Telephone: (315) 568-3000 Carnegie Class: Spec-4-yr-Other Health
FAX Number: (315) 568-3012 Calendar System: Trimester
URL: www.nycc.edu
Established: 1919 Annual Undergrad Tuition & Fees: N/A
Enrollment: 942 Coed
Affiliation or Control: Independent Non-Profit IRS Status: 501(c)3
Highest Offering: First Professional Degree
Accreditation: M, ACUP, CHIRO

01 President ....Dr. Michael A. MESTAN
05 Vice President of Academic Affairs ....Dr. Anne KILLEN
10 Vice Pres of Finance/Admin Svcs ....Mr. Sean ANGLIM
111 VP Inst Advance & Special Proj ....Dr. J. Todd KNUDSEN
84 Vice Pres Enrollment Management ....Ms. Magdalen KELLOGG
96 Assoc VP Admin Svcs/Dir Purchasing ....Mr. Richard B. WORDEN
108 AVP Inst Effectiveness & Planning ....Dr. Jennifer SESSLER
13 Assoc VP Informational Tech ....Mr. Christophe MCQUEENEY
76 Dean School of Health Sciences & Ed ....Dr. J. Nicolas POIRIER
88 Dean of Chiropractic ....Dr. Karen A. BOBAK
06 Registrar ....Mr. Kevin MCCARTHY
07 Director of Admissions ....Mr. Michael LYNCH
37 Director Financial Aid ....Mr. Darrin ROOKER
88 Director of Bachelor Prof Studies ....Dr. John DEMETROS
46 Dean of Research ....Dr. Jeanmarie R. BURKE
12 Depew Health Center Administrator ....Dr. Michael FLYNN
12 Levittown Health Ctr Chief of Staff ....Ms. Melissa MURPHY
17 Assoc Dean for Chiro Clinical Educ ....Dr. Wendy L. MANERI
51 Dean Post Grad & Cont Educ ....Dr. Thomas VENTIMIGLIA
08 Director of the Library ....Ms. Bethyn BONI
88 Dir Academy Admc Excl Stdnt Success ....Mr. Peter THOMPSON
39 Secretary Housing ....Ms. Janette ELSTER
41 Dir Health & Fitness Education ....Mr. Rhett TICCONI
32 Director Student Life ....Ms. Holly Anne WAYE
36 Dir Ctr Career Dev Prof Success ....Ms. Susan D. PITTENGER
29 Director of Alumni Relations ....Ms. Diane ZINK
45 Director Accreditation ....Dr. Beth DONOHUE
09 Quality Engineer ....Ms. Patricia MERKLE
15 Human Resources Manager ....Ms. Christine MCDERMOTT
14 Information Tech Administrator ....Mr. Shane SHOWERS
19 Director Facilities/Security ....Mr. William WAYNE
40 Bookstore Manager ....Ms. Helen STUCK
76 Dir Applied Clinical Nutrition Pgm ....Dr. Peter NICKLESS
88 Dean of FL Sch Acup/Oriental Med ....Dr. Phil GARRISON
88 Dir MS Diagnostic Imaging Program ....Dr. Chad WARSHEL
12 Campus Health Ctr Chief of Staff ....Dr. Lisa BARWINCZAK
12 Rochester Hlth Ctr Chf of Staff ....Dr. Ryan NADEAU
90 Systems Administrator ....Ms. Shelly STUCK
24 Educational Tech Administrator ....Mr. Bernard CECCHINI
23 Director Health Center Operations ....Mrs. Melissa BAXTER
21 Controller ....Ms. Karen QUEST
88 Dir MS Hum Anat Phys Instructn Pgm ....Dr. William GERMANO

New York College of Health Professions (B)

6801 Jericho Turnpike, Syosset NY 11791-4413
County: Nassau FICE Identification: 025994
Unit ID: 418126
Telephone: (516) 364-0808 Carnegie Class: Spec-4-yr-Other Health
FAX Number: (516) 364-6645 Calendar System: Trimester
URL: www.nycollege.edu
Established: 1981 Annual Undergrad Tuition & Fees: $14,226
Enrollment: 602 Coed
Affiliation or Control: Independent Non-Profit IRS Status: 501(c)3
Highest Offering: Master's
Accreditation: NY, ACUP

01 President ....Ms. Lisa PAMINTUAN
10 Chief Financial Officer ....Mr. Errol VIRASAWMI
63 Dean Grad Sch Oriental Medicine ....Dr. A. Li SONG
05 Dean of Academic Affairs ....Vacant
06 Registrar ....Mr. Timothy BOUDREAU
07 Senior Admissions Counselor ....Ms. Mary RODAS
08 Dir Library/Information Services ....Ms. Cynthia CAYEA
09 Director of Institutional Research ....Mr. Ross GRIFFITH
113 Bursar ....Ms. Jacqueline MCINTYRE
13 Manager Information Technology ....Mr. Brian ALVAREZ
32 Director of Student Services ....Ms. Mary RODAS
88 Dean Sch of Massage Therapy NYC ....Dr. Serge NERLI

New York College of Podiatric Medicine (C)

53 E 124th Street, New York NY 10035-1815
County: New York FICE Identification: 002749
Unit ID: 194073
Telephone: (212) 410-8000 Carnegie Class: Spec-4-yr-Other Health
FAX Number: (212) 876-7670 Calendar System: Semester
URL: www.nycpm.edu
Established: 1911 Annual Undergrad Tuition & Fees: N/A
Enrollment: 389 Coed
Affiliation or Control: Independent Non-Profit IRS Status: 501(c)3
Highest Offering: First Professional Degree
Accreditation: POD

01 President ....Mr. Louis L. LEVINE
05 Vice Pres Academic Affairs/Dean ....Dr. Michael J. TREPAL
11 Chief Operating Ofcr/VP Admin ....Mr. Joel STURM
10 Chief Financial Officer ....Mr. Greg ONAIFO
13 Vice Pres Info Systems & Technology ....Mr. Aman SAFAEI
63 VP Medical Education/Medical Dir ....Dr. Mark SWARTZ
30 VP of Development & Operations ....Mr. Desander MAS
32 Dean Student Affairs ....Ms. Lisa LEE
20 Dean Clinical Educ/Dir Res Pgms ....Dr. Robert ECKLES
09 Dean Institutional Research ....Dr. Eileen CHUSID
07 Assoc Dean Admissions/Student Svcs ....Vacant
26 Director Public Affairs/Development ....Ms. Ellen LUBELL
08 Director of Library ....Mr. Paul TREMBLAY
37 Director Financial Aid ....Ms. Eve TRAUBE
06 Registrar ....Ms. Doreen D'AMICO
19 Director Security/Safety ....Mr. James WARREN, JR.
39 Director Student Housing ....Mr. Lee BLACKWELL

New York College of Traditional Chinese Medicine (D)

200 Old Country Road, Suite 500, Mineola NY 11501-4204
County: Nassau FICE Identification: 034433
Unit ID: 439783
Telephone: (516) 739-1545 Carnegie Class: Spec-4-yr-Other Health
FAX Number: (516) 873-9622 Calendar System: Trimester
URL: www.nyctcm.edu
Established: 1996 Annual Undergrad Tuition & Fees: N/A
Enrollment: 178 Coed
Affiliation or Control: Independent Non-Profit IRS Status: 501(c)3
Highest Offering: Master's
Accreditation: ACUP

01 President ....Dr. Yemeng CHEN
10 Administrative Dean ....Dr. James S. BARE
05 Academic Dean ....Dr. Sunny SHEN
07 Admissions Manager ....Ms. Lynn BAI
23 Clinic Director ....Ms. Mona LEE-YUAN
88 Clinic Manager ....Ms. Yiping ZHAO
06 Records Manager ....Ms. Susan SU
37 Financial Aid/Admin Coordinator ....Ms. Elise MA
21 Financial Manager ....Ms. Lily ZOU
08 Operations Manager ....Ms. Ling Ling CHANG

The New York Conservatory for Dramatic Arts (E)

39 West 19th Street, New York NY 10011
County: New York FICE Identification: 031207
Unit ID: 421841
Telephone: (212) 645-0030 Carnegie Class: Spec 2-yr-A&S
FAX Number: (212) 645-0039 .Calendar System: Semester
URL: www.nycda.edu
Established: 1980 Annual Undergrad Tuition & Fees: $31,200
Enrollment: 286 Coed
Affiliation or Control: Proprietary IRS Status: Proprietary
Highest Offering: Associate Degree
Accreditation: THEA

00 CEO ....Mike DABIDAT
01 President ....Richard OMAR
05 Director of Education ....Jay GOLDENBERG
20 Assoc Director of Education ....Sara BUFFAMANTI
06 Registrar ....Stefon SIMMONS
08 Head Librarian ....Martha REPETTO
07 Director of Admissions ....Lisa HILDEBRAND
10 Chief Business Officer ....Emily CHOU
37 Director Student Financial Aid ....Eva OGIRRI
39 Director Student Housing ....Danelle NOLT

New York Graduate School of Psychoanalysis (F)

16 West Tenth Street, New York NY 10011
Telephone: (212) 260-7050 Identification: 770116
Accreditation: &EH

† Branch campus of Boston Graduate School of Psychoanalysis, Brookline, MA

New York Institute of Technology (G)

Northern Boulevard, Old Westbury NY 11568-8000
County: Nassau FICE Identification: 004804
Unit ID: 194091
Telephone: (516) 686-7516 Carnegie Class: Masters/L
FAX Number: (516) 686-7613 Calendar System: Semester
URL: www.nyit.edu
Established: 1955 Annual Undergrad Tuition & Fees: $35,160
Enrollment: 8,064 Coed
Affiliation or Control: Independent Non-Profit IRS Status: 501(c)3
Highest Offering: Doctorate
Accreditation: M, ARCPA, CACREP, CAEPN, CIDA, ENG, ENGT, NURSE, OSTEO, OT, PTA

01 President ....Dr. Hank FOLEY
05 Provost/Vice Pres Academic Affairs ....Dr. Rahmat SHOURESHI
20 Associate Provost ....Dr. Lou REINISCH
45 Vice Pres for Planning Analytics DS ....Dr. Mark HAMPTON
30 Vice President for Development ....Mr. John ELIZANDRO
32 Vice Pres Student Affairs ....Dr. Patrick LOVE
13 Vice Pres of IT & Infrastructure ....Dr. Niyazi BODUR
84 Interim VP Enrollment ....Mr. Mark HAMPTON
26 Vice Pres Comm & Mktg ....Ms. Nancy DONNER
10 CFO & Treasurer ....Mr. Leonard AUBREY
21 Controller ....Ms. Barbara HOLAHAN
43 General Counsel ....Ms. Catherine FLICKINGER
06 Registrar ....Ms. Kristen SMITH
76 Dean School of Health Professions ....Dr. Sheldon FIELDS
48 Dean Sch Architecture & Design ....Ms. Maria PERBELLINI
53 Int Dn Sch of Interdisciplinary Ed ....Mr. Christian PONGRATZ
54 Dean School of Engr & Comp Sciences ....Dr. Nada ANID
49 Dean School Arts & Sciences ....Vacant
50 Dean School of Management ....Dr. Jess BORONICO
108 Dean Operations/Assessments & Acc ....Dr. Patricia BURLAUD
35 Dean for Campus Life ....Ms. Gabrielle ST. LEGER
36 Dean of Career Services ....Mr. John HYDE
75 Sr Dr Vocational Independence Pgm ....Mr. Paul CAVANAGH
88 Exec Director Office Global Engage ....Ms. Emily RUKOBO
09 Director Inst Research & Assessment ....Mr. Michael LANE
88 Director Environmental Health/Safe ....Mr. Kristen PANELLA
22 Director Compliance Title IX Coord ....Ms. Cheryl MONTICCIOLO
07 Dean Admissions & Financial Aid ....Ms. Karen VAHEY
88 Director Marketing & Promotions ....Mr. Alex WANG
27 Director of Communications ....Ms. Bobbie DELL'AQUILO
29 Asst Director of Alumni Relations ....Ms. Sabrina POLIDORO
18 Director of Facilities Operations ....Mr. William MARCHAND
37 Associate Dean of Financial Aid ....Ms. Rosemary FERRUCCI
19 Director Security ....Mr. Anthony REPALONE
41 Director Athletics & Recreation ....Mr. Duane BAILEY
25 Asst Provost Spnsrd Pgms & Research ....Dr. Allison ANDORS
88 Director Plng & Business Affairs ....Ms. Ajisa DERVISEVIC
96 Director Procurement Services ....Ms. Gina ARMS
116 Director of Internal Audit ....Ms. Rachel BERTHOUMIEUX
38 Director Counseling & Wellness Svcs ..Ms. Alice HERON-BURKE
121 Asst Dean Advising & Enrichment ....Ms. Monika ROHDE
15 Director of Human Resources ....Ms. Carol JABLONSKY
90 Director Client Services ....Ms. Laurie HARVEY
91 Director Systems & Network ....Mr. Brian MAROLDO
35 Sr Director Campus Life ....Ms. Zennabelle SEWELL
88 Dir Events & Conferences ....Mr. Jerry LIMONCELLI
63 Vice President Med Affs/Global Hlth ....Dr. Jerry BALENTINE
04 Administrative Asst to President ....Ms. Anne COOLEY

New York Law School (H)

185 West Broadway, New York NY 10013-2959
County: New York FICE Identification: 002783
Unit ID: 193821
Telephone: (212) 431-2100 Carnegie Class: Spec-4-yr-Law
FAX Number: (212) 965-8838 Calendar System: Semester
URL: www.nyls.edu
Established: 1891 Annual Graduate Tuition & Fees: N/A
Enrollment: 931 Coed
Affiliation or Control: Independent Non-Profit IRS Status: 501(c)3
Highest Offering: Doctorate; No Undergraduates
Accreditation: LAW

01 Dean and President ....Dean Anthony CROWELL
05 Assoc Dean Academic & Student Engag ....Dean William P. LAPIANA
10 Executive Vice President & CFO ....Mr. Stuart KLEIN
11 Assoc Dean for Inst Accountability ....Dean Joan R. FISHMAN
26 VP of Marketing & Communications ....Ms. Silvia ALVAREZ
111 VP of Institutional Advancement ....Mr. Elliot BERGER
08 Director of Law Library/Assoc Dean ... Prof. Camille BROUSSARD
84 Assoc Dean Admissions & Prof Dev ....Mr. Jeffery BECHERER
07 Asst Dean of Admissions & Finan Aid ....Ms. Ella Mae ESTRADA
36 Asst Dean of Advising & Prof Dev ... Ms. Courtney FITZGIBBONS
21 Sr Asst VP Financial Plng & Mgmt ....Ms. Susan REDLER
18 Chief Maintenance/Operations/Secur ....Mr. Paul REPETTO
15 Asst Vice President Human Resources ....Ms. Jody PARIANTE
09 Asst VP Institutional Research ....Dr. Joanne INGHAM
32 Assistant Dean for Student Life ....Ms. Sally HARDING
88 Senor Asst VP Project Management ....Mr. George HAYES
30 Director of Development ....Ms. Anna FERBER
20 Asst Dean Academic Program Develop ....Ms. Erin BOND
06 Assistant Dean and Registrar ....Mr. Oral HOPE
13 Chief Information Officer ....Mr. Thomas SOCASH
35 Sr Director of Student Life ....Ms. Shani DARBY
96 Purchasing Coordinator ....Mr. Norman DAWKINS
39 Asst Dir Admissions/Housing Coord ....Ms. Lauren MAJCHROWSKI
104 Director Study Abroad ....Mr. Michael RHEE
86 Director Government Relations ....Mr. Ariel DVORKIN
101 Secretary of the Institution/Board ....Ms. Joan FISHMAN
28 Director of Diversity & Inclusion ....Ms. EllaMae ESTRADA
37 Director Student Financial Aid ....Mr. Christopher CLARKE

New York Medical College (A)

40 Sunshine Cottage Road, Valhalla NY 10595-1690

County: Westchester | FICE Identification: 002784 | Unit ID: 193830
Telephone: (914) 594-4900 | Carnegie Class: Spec-4-yr-Med
FAX Number: (914) 594-4145 | Calendar System: Other
URL: www.nymc.edu
Established: 1860 | Annual Graduate Tuition & Fees: N/A
Enrollment: 1,426 | Coed
Affiliation or Control: Jewish | IRS Status: 501(c)3
Highest Offering: Doctorate; No Undergraduates
Accreditation: M, DENT, MED, PAST, PH, PTA, SP

Code	Title	Name
01	President	Dr. Alan H. KADISH
00	Chancellor and CEO	Dr. Edward C. HALPERIN
100	Chief of Staff	Ms. Vilma BORDONARO
05	Vice Prov/Sr Assoc Dean Acad Admin	Mr. William A. STEADMAN, II
10	Vice Pres Financial Operations	Mr. Adam D. HAMMERMAN
11	Vice President Operations	Mr. Michael ROGOVIN
26	Vice Pres Communications	Ms. Jennifer RIEKERT
63	Dean School of Medicine	Dr. D. Douglas MILLER
58	Dean Grad Sch Basic Medical Science	Dr. Francis L. BELLONI
76	Dean Sch Health Sciences & Practice	Dr. Robert W. AMLER
43	General Counsel/Chf Compliance Ofcr	Mr. Michael NEWMAN
30	Vice Pres Devel/Alumni Affairs	Ms. Amy S. KAHN
86	Vice President Government Affairs	Dr. Robert W. AMLER
21	Assoc Vice Pres/Controller	Mr. George NESTLER
20	Assoc Dean Academic Administration	Mr. Randi D. SCHWARTZ
13	Sr Dir Information Tech Services	Mr. Luis MONTES
63	Vice Dean Grad Med Ed/Affiliations	Dr. Richard G. MCCARRICK
09	Asst Dean Research Administration	Mr. Charles B. HATHAWAY
32	Sr Assoc Dean Student Affairs	Dr. Gladys M. AYALA
37	Asc Dn Stdnt Affs/Dir Finan Plng	Mr. Anthony M. SOZZO
07	Sr Associate Dean Admissions	Dr. Fern R. JUSTER
51	Assoc Dean Continuing Med Education	Dr. Joseph F. DURSI
08	Assoc Dean/Dir Health Sci Library	Ms. Marie ASCHER
07	Director of Admissions	Ms. Robin BAUM
06	Int University Registrar	Ms. Eileen ROMERO
39	Director Student Housing	Ms. Katherine E. DILLON
18	Dir Capital Planning/Facilities	Mr. Thomas ALLEN
19	Director of Security	Mr. William ALLISON
85	Intl Student/Scholar Advisor	Ms. Elizabeth WARD
51	Director of Continuing Medical Educ	Ms. Kathy J. KAVANAGH
23	Director Health Services	Dr. Joseph F. DURSI
38	Director Student Counseling	Dr. Mark SINGER
105	Director Web Communications	Mr. Kevin R. CUMMINGS
40	Director Bookstore	Ms. Liz REYNOLDS
24	Head Educational Media	Mr. Michael COTTER
14	Coord of Instruct Computing Tech	Mr. Jason DI NARDI
04	Administrative Asst to President	Ms. Vera ROSARIO

New York School of Interior Design (B)

170 East 70th Street, New York NY 10021-5110

County: New York | FICE Identification: 020690 | Unit ID: 194116
Telephone: (212) 472-1500 | Carnegie Class: Spec-4-yr-Arts
FAX Number: (212) 472-3800 | Calendar System: 4/1/4
URL: www.nysid.edu
Established: 1916 | Annual Undergrad Tuition & Fees: $22,710
Enrollment: 538 | Coed
Affiliation or Control: Independent Non-Profit | IRS Status: 501(c)3
Highest Offering: Master's
Accreditation: M, ART, CIDA

Code	Title	Name
01	President	Mr. David SPROULS
05	VP Academic Affairs/Dean	Dr. Ellen FISHER
10	VP for Finance & Administration	Ms. Jane CHEN
32	Dean of Students	Ms. Karen HIGGINBOTHAM
04	Assistant to the President	Ms. Jeanne KO
06	Registrar	Ms. Jennifer MELENDEZ
08	Director of the Library	Mr. Billy KWAN
07	Director of Admissions	Ms. Celeste COLLINS
37	Financial Aid Coordinator	Mr. Nicholas SCOTT
15	Director of Personnel Services	Ms. Yvonne MORAY
18	Chief Facilities/Physical Plant	Mr. Zeke KOLENOVIC
26	Director of External Relations	Mr. David OWENS-HILL
20	Associate Dean	Ms. Barbara LOWENTHAL
13	Dir Computing/Information Mgmt	Mr. Tomasz SOWINSKI
90	Director Academic Computing	Mr. Richard T. CLASS
38	Director Student Counseling	Dr. Penny MORGANSTEIN
09	Director of Institutional Research	Mr. Christopher VINGER
30	Director Development	Ms. Elizabeth GRAY KOGEN

New York Theological Seminary (C)

475 Riverside Drive, Suite 500, New York NY 10115-0083

County: New York | FICE Identification: 002674 | Unit ID: 193894
Telephone: (212) 870-1211 | Carnegie Class: Spec-4-yr-Faith
FAX Number: (212) 870-1236 | Calendar System: Semester
URL: www.nyts.edu
Established: 1900 | Annual Graduate Tuition & Fees: N/A
Enrollment: 336 | Coed
Affiliation or Control: Independent Non-Profit | IRS Status: 501(c)3
Highest Offering: Doctorate; No Undergraduates
Accreditation: THEOL

Code	Title	Name
01	President	Dr. Dale T. IRVIN
30	VP Development/Inst Advancement	Dr. Courtney WILEY-HARRIS
05	Academic Dean	Dr. Kirkpatrick G. COHALL
10	Chief Financial Officer/Controller	Mr. Craig KING
08	Librarian	Dr. Jerry REISIG
06	Registrar	Ms. Lydia R. BUMGARDNER
37	Director Financial Aid	Ms. Tamisia WHITE
26	Coordinator Publications/Marketing	Ms. Cathy A. MORALES
105	Director Web Services	Ms. Angelica C. MORALES
106	Dir Online Education/E-learning	Ms. Ava CARROLL
108	Director Institutional Assessment	Dr. Elaine PADILLA
29	Director Alumni Relations	Ms. Cynthia GARDNER-BRIM
38	Director Student Counseling	Dr. Edward L. HUNT

New York University (D)

70 Washington Square S, New York NY 10012-1092

County: New York | FICE Identification: 002785 | Unit ID: 193900
Telephone: (212) 998-1212 | Carnegie Class: DU-Highest
FAX Number: N/A | Calendar System: Semester
URL: www.nyu.edu
Established: 1831 | Annual Undergrad Tuition & Fees: $49,062
Enrollment: 50,027 | Coed
Affiliation or Control: Independent Non-Profit | IRS Status: 501(c)3
Highest Offering: Doctorate
Accreditation: M, CAEPT, COPSY, DENT, DH, DIETD, DIETI, ENG, HSA, IPSY, JOUR, LAW, MED, MIDWF, NURSE, OT, PAST, PH, PLNG, PTA, SP, SPAA, SURGT, SW

Code	Title	Name
01	President	Dr. Andrew HAMILTON
05	Provost	Dr. Katherine FLEMING
10	Executive VP for Finance/IT	Dr. Martin DORPH
17	Executive VP for Health	Dr. Robert BERNE
100	Chief of Staff to the President	Mr. Richard BAUM
26	Sr VP for Univ Rels/Pub Affairs	Dr. Lynne BROWN
30	Sr VP Development/Alumni Relations	Ms. Debra A. LAMORTE
32	Sr Vice Pres for Student Affairs	Dr. Marc L. WAIS
43	General Counsel & Secretary	Mr. Terrance NOLAN
28	VProv Faculty/Arts/Human/Diversity	Dr. Ulrich C. BAER
46	Sr Vice Provost for Research	Dr. Paul M. HORN
03	Senior Presidential Fellow	Ms. Ellen SCHALL
88	Sr VProv Global Fac Dev NYUAD/NYUSH	Vacant
20	Sr Vice Provost Academic Affairs	Dr. Matthew S. SANTIROCCO
35	VC Global Pgms/Univ Life at NYU	Dr. Linda G. MILLS
54	Exec VProv Engineering/Applied Sci	Dr. Katepalli R. SREENIVASAN
18	VP Facilities & Construction Mgmt	Mr. David ALONSO
26	Sr Vice Pres for Public Affairs	Mr. John H. BECKMAN
88	VP Public Resource Admin & Develop	Dr. Richard N. BING
84	Vice Pres Enrollment	Ms. MJ KNOLL-FINN
110	Deputy VP Development and Campaigns	Mr. David C. KOEHLER
15	Vice Pres Human Resources	Ms. Sabrina ELLIS
13	VP for Global Technology & CGTO	Mr. Len PETERS
86	VP Govt Affs/Community Engagement	Vacant
114	VP Budget & Planning	Mr. Anthony JIGA
88	Asst VP of Global Campus Services	Mr. Owen MOORE
21	Sr VP Finance Operations/Treasurer	Ms. Stephanie PIANKA
19	VP Global Campus Safety	Mr. Marlon LYNCH
06	University Registrar	Ms. Elizabeth A. KIENLE-GRANZO
54	Vice Prov Science/Engineering Devel	Mr. Gerard A. BEN AROUS
45	VProv & Assoc VC Strategic Planning	Mr. Joseph P. JULIANO
88	Vice Prov Research/Faculty Affairs	Dr. C. Cybele RAVER
88	Vice Prov Global Stdnt Ldrshp Init	Ms. Melody C. BARNES
21	Assoc VP Facilities Finance & Tech	Mr. Chris TANG
27	Assoc VP for Univ Rels & Pub Affs	Ms. Deborah BRODERICK
29	Assoc VP for Alumni Relations	Mr. Brian PERILLO
88	Assoc VProv Rsrch Compliance/Admin	Dr. Martha L. DUNNE
96	Assoc VP Purchasing & Logistics	Vacant
88	Asst VP Fac Housing/Resid Svcs	Ms. Erin J. LYNCH
88	VP for Global Programs	Dr. Nancy J. MORRISON
20	Vice Prov/Chf of Staff to Prov	Dr. Carol K. MORROW
07	Asst VP for Undergrad Admissions	Mr. Shawn L. ABBOTT
20	Asst Provost Academic Pgm Review	Dr. Diana L. KARAFIN
31	Asst VP Cmty Outreach/Engagement	Mr. Allen M. MCFARLANE
21	Assoc Vice Pres Fin Ops/Controller	Ms. Kerri J. TRICARICO
41	Asst VP Stdnt Affairs/Dir Athletics	Mr. Christopher BLEDSOE
23	Assoc VP Stdnt Hlth/Exec Dir SHC	Dr. Carlo CIOTOLI
37	Asst VP Financial Aid	Ms. Lynn E. HIGINBOTHAM
102	Dir Office of Sponsored Programs	Ms. Nancy S. DANEAU
116	Asst VP Internal Audit	Ms. Jasmine A. DE NULLY
22	Exec Dir Ofc of Equal Opportunity	Ms. Mary SIGNOR
36	Asst VP Student Affairs	Ms. Trudy G. STEINFELD
08	Dean of Libraries	Ms. Carol A. MANDEL
38	Sr Director SHC	Ms. Patricia DELORENZO
39	Sr Director Housing Services	Mr. Neil S. HANRAHAN
50	Dean Business	Dr. Peter B. HENRY
53	Dean Education	Dr. Dominic BREWER
04	Counselor to the President	Vacant
104	Vice Chancellor for Global Programs	Dr. Linda MILLS
108	Asst V Prov Acad Pgm Review/Assess	Dr. Diana KARAFIN
09	Director of Institutional Research	Mr. David P. VINTINNER

Niagara County Community College (E)

3111 Saunders Settlement Road, Sanborn NY 14132-9460

County: Niagara | FICE Identification: 002874 | Unit ID: 193946
Telephone: (716) 614-6200 | Carnegie Class: Assoc/MT-VT-High Trad
FAX Number: (716) 614-6700 | Calendar System: Semester
URL: www.niagaracc.suny.edu
Established: 1962 | Annual Undergrad Tuition & Fees (In-District): $4,518
Enrollment: 6,116 | Coed
Affiliation or Control: State/Local | IRS Status: 501(c)3
Highest Offering: Associate Degree
Accreditation: M, ACFEI, ADNUR, MAC, PTAA, RAD, SURGT

Code	Title	Name
01	Officer in Charge	Dr. Luba CHLIWNIAK
05	Vice President Academic Affairs	Dr. Luba CHLIWNIAK
103	Asst VP Workforce Development	Ms. Phyllis ULETT
10	Vice President of Finance/Info Tech	Mr. William SCHICKLING
32	Vice President of Student Services	Mrs. Julia PITMAN
11	Vice President of Operations	Mr. Michael DOMBROWSKI
09	Director Planning and Research	Dr. Mary Jane FELDMAN
15	Director of Human Resources	Ms. Catherine BROWN
07	Director of Admissions	Vacant
21	Director of Business Services	Mr. John EICHNER
04	Assistant to President	Ms. Barbara WALCK
06	Registrar	Ms. Julie SCHUCKER
35	Director of Student Development	Mrs. Allison ARMUSEWICZ
30	Chief Development Officer	Ms. Deborah BREWER
37	Director of Financial Aid	Mr. James TRIMBOLI
26	Interim Director Public Relations	Ms. Barbara DESIMONE
18	Assistant Director of Facilities	Mr. Dennis GASBARRO
16	Asst Director of HR/Compliance	Ms. Jennifer CAWLEY
08	Head Librarian	Ms. Nancy KENNEDY
105	Director Web Services	Mr. Cory WRIGHT
106	Dir Online Education/E-learning	Ms. Lisa DUBUC
13	Chief Info Technology Officer	Mr. Dennis MICHAELS
19	Director Security/Safety	Mr. Francis GILES
102	Foundation Director	Ms. Deborah BREWER
39	Director Student Housing	Ms. Kristen BECK
41	Athletic Director	Mr. Robert MCKEOWN
91	Dir User & Administrative Tech	Vacant
29	Alumni Development Specialist	Ms. Allison KORTA

Niagara University (F)

5795 Lewiston Road, Niagara University NY 14109

County: Niagara | FICE Identification: 002788 | Unit ID: 193973
Telephone: (716) 285-1212 | Carnegie Class: Masters/L
FAX Number: (716) 286-8710 | Calendar System: Semester
URL: www.niagara.edu
Established: 1856 | Annual Undergrad Tuition & Fees: $30,950
Enrollment: 4,128 | Coed
Affiliation or Control: Independent Non-Profit | IRS Status: 501(c)3
Highest Offering: Doctorate
Accreditation: M, CACREP, CAEPN, NURSE, SW

Code	Title	Name
01	President	Rev. James MAHER, CM
03	Executive Vice President	Dr. Debra COLLEY
05	Provost/VP for Academic Affairs	Dr. Timothy IRELAND
10	Senior VP Operations & Finance	Ms. Mary E. BORGOGNONI
11	VP for Administration	Mr. Michael S. JASZKA
32	Asst VP for Inst Eff & Student Affs	Mr. Christopher R. SHEFFIELD
88	VP for International Relations	Rev. Kevin CREAGH, CM
111	VP for Institutional Advancement	Dr. Derek M. WESLEY
42	VP Univ Mission and Ministry	Rev. Kevin CREAGH, CM
20	Associate Provost	Dr. Henrik C. BORGSTROM
26	Assoc VP of Comm/Public Relations	Mr. Thomas BURNS
84	Asst VP Enrollment Management	Ms. Cathleen ANDERSON
43	General Counsel	Vacant
35	Dean of Student Affairs	Mr. Jason JAKUBOWSKI
49	Interim Dean Col of Arts & Sci	Dr. Peter BUTERA
50	Interim Dean Col of Business Admin	Dr. Tenpao LEE
53	Dean Col of Education	Dr. Chandra FOOTE
88	Dean Col Hospitality/Tourism Mgt	Dr. Kurt A. STAHURA
09	Director of Institutional Research	Dr. Vennessa L. WALKER
88	Facility Planner	Mr. Daniel MCMANN
07	Director of Admissions Operations	Mr. Harry S. GONG
07	Director of Admissions	Mr. Mark E. WOJNOWSKI
08	Director of Libraries	Mr. David SCHOEN
19	Director of Campus Safety	Mr. John F. BARKER
37	Director of Financial Aid	Ms. Katie L. KOCSIS
39	Director of Residence Life	Ms. Kimberly FENTON
35	Director of Campus Activities	Mrs. Mati ORTIZ
29	Exec Director Alumni Engagement	Ms. Christine S. O'HARA
13	Director Information Technology	Mr. Richard P. KERNIN
88	Director of Art Museum	Ms. Kate KOPERSKI
15	Director of Human Resources	Ms. Donna MOSTILLER
23	Director of Health Services	Ms. Adrienne KASBAUM
41	Director of Athletics	Mr. Simon GRAY
18	Director of Facility Services	Mr. Daniel M. GUARIGLIA
88	Exec Dir Division of Academic Svcs	Ms. Antonia KNIGHT
121	Director of Academic Support	Mrs. Diane STOELTING
51	Dir Continuing/Community Education	Mr. Jon Jay STOCKSLADER
88	Exec Dir Inst for Civic Engagement	Mrs. Patricia WROBEL
88	Dir Rec & Intramurals/Kiernan Ctr	Mr. Derek PUFF
38	Director Counseling Services	Ms. Jeannine D. SUK
21	Controller	Mr. Donald E. SMITH
117	Dir of Contract Services & Risk Mgt	Ms. Christy FERGUSON
88	Assoc Dean for Graduate Recruitment	Mr. Evan F. PIERCE
92	Honors Program Coordinator	Dr. Michael BARNWELL
85	Dir Multicultural & Intl Stdnt Affs	Ms. Averl HARBIN
06	University Registrar	Mr. R. Ryan KENDRICK
88	Director of Student Accounts	Ms. Martie HOWELL
25	Director Grants & Sponsored Program	Ms. Valerie NOLAN
36	Director of Career Services	Mr. Robert P. SWANSON
104	Exec Dir Brennan Ctr & Intl Rels	Dr. Deborah CURTIS
88	Director of IMPACT	Mr. Thomas LOWE
88	Veterans Services Coordinator	Mr. Robert HEALY
112	Director of Planned Giving	Vacant
04	Administrative Asst to President	Ms. Jesenia RIVERA

North Country Community College (A)

23 Santanoni Avenue, PO Box 89,
Saranac Lake NY 12983-0089
County: Essex FICE Identification: 007111
Unit ID: 194028
Telephone: (518) 891-2915 Carnegie Class: Assoc/MT-VT-Mix Trad/Non
FAX Number: (518) 891-2915 Calendar System: Semester
URL: www.nccc.edu
Established: 1967 Annual Undergrad Tuition & Fees (In-District): $5,551
Enrollment: 1,883 Coed
Affiliation or Control: State/Local IRS Status: 501(c)3
Highest Offering: Associate Degree
Accreditation: M

01 President .... Dr. Steve J. TYRELL
05 Vice Pres of Academic Affairs .... Mr. Joe KEEGAN
10 Vice Pres for Administration/CFO .... Mr. Robert FARMER
07 Dean of Admissions .... Mr. Christopher TACEA
06 Int Registrar/Records Officer .... Ms. Shelly ST. LOUIS
09 Asst Dean Inst Research/Support .... Mr. Scott HARWOOD
32 Dean of Campus & Student Life .... Ms. Kim IRLAND
29 Director Alumni Relations .... Ms. Diana FORTUNE
04 Executive Asst to the President .... Ms. Stacie HURWITCH
37 Director Student Financial Aid .... Mr. Matthew SANCHEZ
41 Athletic Director .... Mr. Chad LADUE

Northeastern Seminary (B)

2265 Westside Drive, Rochester NY 14624-1932
County: Monroe FICE Identification: 034194
Unit ID: 439817
Telephone: (585) 594-6800 Carnegie Class: Spec-4-yr-Faith
FAX Number: (585) 594-6801 Calendar System: Semester
URL: www.nes.edu
Established: 1998 Annual Graduate Tuition & Fees: N/A
Enrollment: 148 Coed
Affiliation or Control: Independent Non-Profit IRS Status: 501(c)3
Highest Offering: Doctorate; No Undergraduates
Accreditation: M, THEOL

01 President .... Dr. Deana L. PORTERFIELD
05 Academic Vice President and Dean .... Dr. Douglas CULLUM
26 AVP for Communications/Enrollment .... Ms. Lisa BENNETT
32 VP for Student and Organ Dev .... Mrs. Ruth LOGAN
07 Director of Admissions .... Mr. Caleb MATTHEWS
04 Administrative Asst to President .... Mrs. Patti RADEL
06 Registrar .... Ms. Lesa KOHR
10 Chief Business Officer .... Mrs. Laurie LEO
111 VP for Institutional Advancement .... Mr. Darrell BELL
13 AVP Information Technology .... Mr. Peter SAXENA

† The Seminary is affiliated with Roberts Wesleyan College.

Nyack College (C)

1 South Boulevard, Nyack NY 10960-3698
County: Rockland FICE Identification: 002790
Unit ID: 194161
Telephone: (845) 675-4400 Carnegie Class: Masters/L
FAX Number: (845) 358-1751 Calendar System: Semester
URL: www.nyack.edu
Established: 1882 Annual Undergrad Tuition & Fees: $24,850
Enrollment: 2,664 Coed
Affiliation or Control: The Christian And Missionary Alliance
IRS Status: 501(c)3
Highest Offering: Doctorate
Accreditation: M, CAEPN, MFCD, MUS, NURSE, SW, THEOL

01 President .... Dr. Michael G. SCALES
04 Assistant to the President .... Mrs. Carol Ann FREEMAN
10 Exec Vice President & Treasurer .... Mr. David C. JENNINGS
05 Provost/VP for Academic Affairs .... Dr. David F. TURK
84 Vice President for Enrollment .... Mr. Bill VOLTMER
30 Vice President of Advancement .... Rev. Jeffery QUINN
20 Assistant Provost .... Dr. Bennett SCHEPENS
20 Assoc Dean Faculty Development .... Dr. Leonard KAGELER
73 Dean Seminary .... Dr. Ronald WALBORN
50 Dean School of Business & Ldrshp .... Dr. Anita UNDERWOOD
64 Dean School of Music .... Dr. Glenn KOPONEN
53 Dean School of Education .... Dr. JoAnn LOONEY
66 Dean School of Nursing .... Mrs. Elizabeth SIMON
08 Dean of Library Services .... Mrs. Linda K. POSTON
89 Assoc Dean Student Success .... Dr. Gwen PARKER AMES
73 ATS Director NYC .... Dr. Louis DECARO
73 Asst Dean Seminary (Puerto Rico) .... Dr. Julio APONTE
32 Assoc Dean of Students .... Mrs. Wanda VELEZ
32 Assoc Dean of Students (NYC) .... Mr. Charles HAMMOND
06 Undergraduate Registrar .... Ms. Evangeline COUCHEY
06 Graduate Registrar .... Ms. Rebecca NOSS
07 Dir of Admissions Undergrad .... Mr. Dan BAILEY
07 Dir of Graduate Admissions .... Vacant
37 Dir of Fin Svcs Undergrad .... Mr. Steve PHILLIPS
37 Dir of Fin Svcs Undergrad (NYC) .... Mr. Isaac FOSTER
41 Director of Athletics .... Mr. Keith A. DAVIE
15 Director of Human Resources .... Mrs. Karen DAVIE
13 Director of Information Technology .... Mr. Kevin A. BUEL
09 Director of Institutional Research .... Mr. Greg BEEMAN
18 Director of Operations/Aramark .... Mr. Doug WALKER
26 Dir of Public & Media Relations .... Mrs. Deborah WALKER
42 Director of Spiritual Formation .... Mrs. Wanda F. WALBORN
38 Director of Wellness Services .... Ms. Jacqueline LOPEZ
29 Coordinator of Alumni Services .... Mrs. Melissa HICKEY
105 Webmaster .... Mr. Joshua WAY

Nyack College Manhattan Center (D)

2 Washington Street, New York NY 10004
Telephone: (212) 625-0500 Identification: 770143
Accreditation: &M

Ohr Hameir Theological Seminary (E)

141 Furnace Woods Road,
Cortlandt Manor NY 10567-6112
County: Westchester FICE Identification: 011984
Unit ID: 194189
Telephone: (914) 736-1500 Carnegie Class: Spec-4-yr-Faith
FAX Number: (914) 736-1055 Calendar System: Semester
Established: 1962 Annual Undergrad Tuition & Fees: $10,500
Enrollment: 126 Male
Affiliation or Control: Independent Non-Profit IRS Status: 501(c)3
Highest Offering: Second Talmudic Degree
Accreditation: RABN

01 President .... Rabbi E. KANAREK
30 Chief Devel Ofcr/Dir Financial Aid .... Rabbi Jacob ROTHBERG
06 Registrar .... Rabbi Berel KANAREK

Ohr Somayach Tanenbaum Educational Center (F)

244 Route 306, Monsey NY 10952-0334
County: Rockland FICE Identification: 023201
Unit ID: 243805
Telephone: (845) 425-1370 Carnegie Class: Not Classified
FAX Number: (845) 425-8865 Calendar System: Trimester
URL: www.os.edu
Established: 1979 Annual Undergrad Tuition & Fees: N/A
Enrollment: N/A Coordinate
Affiliation or Control: Independent Non-Profit IRS Status: 501(c)3
Highest Offering: First Professional Degree
Accreditation: RABN

01 Director .... Rabbi Abraham BRAUN
05 Dean .... Rabbi Israel ROKOWSKY
06 Registrar .... Mrs. Miriam GROSSMAN
10 Chief Business Officer .... Rabbi Moshe HASS

Onondaga Community College (G)

4585 West Seneca Turnpike, Syracuse NY 13215-4585
County: Onondaga FICE Identification: 002875
Unit ID: 194222
Telephone: (315) 498-2622 Carnegie Class: Assoc/HT-High Non
FAX Number: (315) 492-9208 Calendar System: Semester
URL: www.sunyocc.edu
Established: 1962 Annual Undergrad Tuition & Fees (In-District): $5,154
Enrollment: 11,886 Coed
Affiliation or Control: State/Local IRS Status: 501(c)3
Highest Offering: Associate Degree
Accreditation: M, ADNUR, CAHIIM, PTAA, SURGT

01 President .... Dr. Casey CRABILL
05 Provost and SVP Educational Svcs .... Dr. Daria WILLIS
124 SVP Student Engage & Learning Supp .... Dr. Julie WHITE
03 VP Governance and Compliance .... Ms. Anastasia URTZ
30 Vice President Development .... Ms. Lisa MOORE
84 VP Enrollment Development & Comm .... Ms. Amy KREMENEK
09 VP Inst Planning/Assess/Research .... Dr. Agatha AWUAH
13 Chief Information Officer .... Ms. Andrea VENUTI
21 SVP & Chief Financial Officer .... Mr. Mark MANNING
124 AVP Student Engagement .... Ms. Rebecca HODA-KEARSE
20 Asst VP Academic & Support Svcs .... Ms. Kathleen D'APRIX
28 VP/Chief Diversity Officer .... Ms. Eunice WILLIAMS
18 VP Property Management .... Mr. John PADDOCK
37 Director Financial Aid .... Ms. Rebecca ROSE
41 Athletic Director .... Mr. Michael BORSZ
08 Chair Library .... Ms. Pauline SHOSTACK
38 Chair Counseling Department .... Mr. Timothy SINGER
19 VP Campus Safety & Security .... Mr. David WALL
22 Director Disability Services .... Ms. Nancy CARR
06 Registrar .... Dr. Chris HOCKEY
113 Assistant Director Student Accounts .... Ms. Sally LUTON
96 Assistant VP Management Services .... Mr. Michael MCMULLEN
38 Director Advising & Counseling .... Ms. Jeanine ECKENRODE
18 Director of Sustainability .... Mr. Sean VORMWALD
04 Assistant to the President .... Ms. Julie HART
103 AVP Economic & Workforce Dev .... Mr. Michael METZGAR
25 AVP Research & Grants .... Ms. Nicole SCHLATER
29 Assistant Director Alumni Comm .... Mr. Russ CORBIN
45 AVP Inst Effectiveness & Planning .... Ms. Wendy TARBY
26 AVP Advancement Communications .... Ms. Susan TORMEY
43 Interim General Counsel .... Dr. Kevin MOORE

Orange County Community College (H)

115 South Street, Middletown NY 10940-6437
County: Orange FICE Identification: 002876
Unit ID: 194240
Telephone: (845) 344-6222 Carnegie Class: Assoc/HT-High Trad
FAX Number: (845) 343-1228 Calendar System: Semester
URL: www.sunyorange.edu
Established: 1950 Annual Undergrad Tuition & Fees (In-District): $5,278
Enrollment: 6,982 Coed
Affiliation or Control: State/Local IRS Status: 501(c)3
Highest Offering: Associate Degree
Accreditation: M, ACBSP, ADNUR, DH, MLTAD, OTA, PHLEB, PTAA, RAD

01 President .... Dr. Kristine M. YOUNG
05 Vice Pres Academic Affairs .... Ms. Erika HACKMAN
32 Vice Pres Student Services .... Ms. Gerianne BRUSATI
10 VP Administration/Finance .... Ms. Linda DAUER
30 Vice Pres Institutional Advancement .... Mr. Vinnie CAZZETTA
13 Chief Information Ofcr .... Vacant
20 Sr Assoc Vice Pres Newburgh Campus .... Dr. Peter SOSCIA
84 Assoc VP for Enrollment Management .... Vacant
76 Assoc VP Health Professions .... Dr. Michael GAWRONSKI, JR.
88 Assoc Vice Pres Resource Devel .... Dr. Russell HAMMOND
50 Int Assoc VP Business/Math/Sci/Tech .... Ms. Anne PRIAL
35 Assoc Vice Pres Stdnt Engagemt/ Comp .... Ms. Madeline TORRES-DIAZ
15 Assoc Vice Pres Human Resources .... Ms. Wendy HOLMES
08 Director Learning Resource .... Ms. Susan PARRY
51 Dir Continuing/Professional Educ .... Mr. David KOHN
19 Director Campus Security/Safety .... Mr. Ed KIELY
09 Inst Plng/Assessment/Research Ofcr .... Ms. Christine WORK
18 Director Administrative Services .... Mr. Michael WORDEN
37 Director of Financial Aid .... Mr. John IVANKOVIC
06 Registrar .... Vacant
26 Communications Officer .... Mr. Mike ALBRIGHT
88 Director Academic Advising .... Ms. Talia LLOSA
07 Director of Admissions .... Mr. Maynard SCHMIDT
35 Director Student Activities .... Mr. Steve HARPST
37 Assoc Director of Financial Aid .... Ms. Rosemary BARRETT
04 Administrative Asst to President .... Ms. Carol MURRAY
41 Athletic Director .... Mr. Wayne SMITH

Orange County Community College Newburgh Branch Campus (I)

1 Washington Center, Newburgh NY 12550
Telephone: (845) 562-2454 Identification: 770144
Accreditation: &M

Pace University (J)

1 Pace Plaza, New York NY 10038-1598
County: New York FICE Identification: 002791
Unit ID: 194310
Telephone: (212) 346-1200 Carnegie Class: DU-Mod
FAX Number: (212) 346-1933 Calendar System: Semester
URL: www.pace.edu
Established: 1906 Annual Undergrad Tuition & Fees: $42,772
Enrollment: 12,843 Coed
Affiliation or Control: Independent Non-Profit IRS Status: 501(c)3
Highest Offering: Doctorate
Accreditation: M, ARCPA, CAEPN, CS, IPSY, LAW, NURSE, PSPSY

01 President .... Mr. Stephen J. FRIEDMAN
10 Exec Vice President/CFO .... Mr. Robert C. ALMON
05 Int Provost/Exec VP Academic Affrs .... Dr. Nira HERRMANN
84 Vice Pres Enrollment/Placement .... Ms. Robina C. SCHEPP
30 Int VP Development/Alumni Relations .... Ms. Nina RESTUCCIA
13 VP Information Tech/CIO .... Mr. Paul DAMPIER
26 VP/Chief Marketing Ofcr Univ Rels .... Ms. Frederica N. WALD
15 Assoc Vice Pres Human Resources .... Ms. Elizabeth GARTI
09 Asst Vice Pres Plng/Assess/Inst Res .... Ms. Nancy DERIGGI
86 Asst Vice Pres Govt/Community Rels .... Ms. Vanessa J. HERMAN
32 AVP Ofc Student Assistance .... Mr. James CURRY
19 Associate VP General Services .... Mr. Frank MCDONALD
50 Dean Lubin School of Business .... Mr. Neil S. BRAUN
49 Acting Dean Dyson College Arts/Sci .... Dr. Richard SCHLESINGER
53 Acting Dean School of Education .... Dr. Xiao-lei WANG
76 Dean College Health Professions .... Dr. Harriet R. FELDMAN
77 Dean School of CSIS .... Dr. Jonathan H. HILL
32 Dean of Students New York .... Dr. Marijo RUSSELL-OÆGRADY
32 Dean of Students Westchester .... Dr. Lisa BARDILL MOSCARITOLO
61 Dean School of Law .... Mr. David YASSKY
06 Assoc VP Stdnt Svcs/Univ Registrar .... Vacant
107 Assit VP Continuing/Professional Ed .... Dr. Christine SHAKESPEARE
06 Graduate Registrar .... Ms. Margaret JONES
06 Law School Registrar .... Ms. Nilda RODRIGUEZ
88 Associate University Registrar .... Ms. Barbara MCCARTHY
88 Asst Director Adult Education NY .... Ms. Nicola FOSTER
21 Interim Comptroller .... Mr. William VOLL
43 University Counsel .... Mr. Stephen BRODSKY
21 University Bursar .... Ms. Susan WEYGANT
07 Dean of Admissions .... Mr. Todd E. HEILMAN
07 Dir of Admissions NY/Westchester .... Ms. Joanna BRODA
22 Affirmative Action Officer .... Ms. Arletha MILES
14 Assit VP Information Technology Svs .... Mr. Chris ELARDE
84 Director Adult Enroll Svcs/New York .... Ms. Janet KIRTMAN
38 Director Counseling Services .... Dr. Richard SHADICK
39 Director of Residential Life .... Mr. A. Patrick ROGER-GORDON
40 Executive Director Bookstore .... Ms. Mary LIETO
85 Assoc Dir Intl Pgms & Services .... Mr. Kraig WALKUP
96 Director of Purchasing - Contracts .... Ms. Alice SEIFERT
18 Director Facilities/Physical Plant .... Mr. Abdul JABAR
28 Director of Diversity .... Ms. Shanelle HENRY ROBINSON

Pacific College of Oriental Medicine (K)

110 William Street, 19th Floor, New York NY 10038
Telephone: (212) 982-3456 Identification: 666139

Accreditation: &WC, ACUP, NUR

† Branch campus of Pacific College of Oriental Medicine, San Diego CA.

Paul Smith's College (A)

PO Box 265, Paul Smiths NY 12970-0265
County: Franklin FICE Identification: 002795
Unit ID: 194392
Telephone: (518) 327-6000 Carnegie Class: Bac-Diverse
FAX Number: N/A Calendar System: Trimester
URL: www.paulsmiths.edu
Established: 1937 Annual Undergrad Tuition & Fees: $27,103
Enrollment: 885 Coed
Affiliation or Control: Independent Non-Profit IRS Status: 501(c)3
Highest Offering: Baccalaureate
Accreditation: M, ACFEI, ENGT

01 President .... Dr. Cathy S. DOVE
04 Assistant to the President .... Ms. Kathleen A. KECK
05 Provost .... Dr. Nicholas HUNT-BULL
10 Vice Pres Finance/Administration .... Mr. Martin HANIFIN
30 Vice President Inst Advancement .... Mr. F. Raymond AGNEW
84 Vice Pres Enrollment Management .... Mr. Peter BURNS
18 VP Facilities Mgmt/Capital Project ... Mr. Steven W. MCFARLAND
13 Director Information Services .... Mr. Jeffrey WALTON
29 Director of Alumni Relations .... Ms. Heather TUTTLE
38 Director of Student Development .... Ms. Ellen GOOCH
37 Director of Financial Aid .... Ms. Mary Ellen M. CHAMBERLAIN
23 Director of Health Services .... Ms. Reiko REXILIUS-TUTHILL
24 Director Education Support Services .... Mr. Michael BECCARIA
26 Director of Communications .... Mr. Robert BENNETT
06 Registrar .... Dr. Jeffrey WALTON
07 Director of Admissions .... Mr. Keith BRAUN
19 Lead Campus Safety Officer .... Ms. Holly PARKER
09 Director Institutional Research .... Dr. Jeffrey WALTON
22 Director HEOP .... Ms. Kate MULLEN
41 Dir of Athletics/Physical Educ .... Mr. James TUCKER
21 Comptroller .... Ms. Laura ROZELL
32 VP Student Affairs/Campus Life .... Mr. Terry LINDSAY
40 Manager of College Store .... Ms. Diana L. LYNG-GLIDDI
15 Human Resources Director .... Ms. Sharon VAN AUKEN
96 Purchasing Coordinator .... Ms. Cynthia LEMERY
36 Career Coordinator .... Ms. Debra DUTCHER
20 Assoc Academic Officer/Provost .... Vacant

Phillips School of Nursing at Mount Sinai Beth Israel (B)

776 Sixth Avenue, 4th Floor, New York NY 10001-6354
County: New York FICE Identification: 006438
Unit ID: 189282
Telephone: (212) 614-6110 Carnegie Class: Spec-4-yr-Other Health
FAX Number: (212) 614-6109 Calendar System: Semester
URL: www.pson.edu
Established: 1904 Annual Undergrad Tuition & Fees: $27,765
Enrollment: 254 Coed
Affiliation or Control: Independent Non-Profit IRS Status: 501(c)3
Highest Offering: Baccalaureate
Accreditation: NY, ADNUR, NURSE

01 Dean .... Dr. Todd AMBROSIA
05 Assistant Dean .... Mrs. Bernice PASS-STERN
30 Dir Development/Communications .... Ms. Linda FABRIZIO

Plaza College (C)

118-33 Queens Boulevard, Forest Hills NY 11375
County: Queens FICE Identification: 012358
Unit ID: 194499
Telephone: (718) 779-1430 Carnegie Class: Bac/Assoc-Mixed
FAX Number: (718) 779-7423 Calendar System: Semester
URL: www.plazacollege.edu
Established: 1916 Annual Undergrad Tuition & Fees: $12,450
Enrollment: 732 Coed
Affiliation or Control: Proprietary IRS Status: Proprietary
Highest Offering: Baccalaureate
Accreditation: M, CAHIIM, MAC

01 President .... Charles E. CALLAHAN, III
05 Provost .... Vacant
10 Vice Pres of Financial Services .... Vacant
11 Chief Operating Officer .... Charles E. CALLAHAN, IV
20 Dean of Academic Affairs .... Marie DOLLA
06 Registrar .... Carol GARCIA
21 Comptroller .... Linda ROCKHILL
07 Dean of Admissions .... Vanessa LOPEZ
20 Dean Curriculum Development .... Marianne C. ZIPF
08 College Librarian .... Eva BABALIS
23 Director Health Services .... Candice CALLAHAN
37 Director Financial Aid .... Peggy CHUNG
35 Dean Student Activities .... Jonathan HOWLE
100 Chief of Staff/HR Officer/Placement .... Correne CAVALIERI
09 Assoc Dean Institutional Research .... Edward DEE
13 Director Information Technology .... David COLUCCI
32 Dean of Students .... Dawn VETRANO
88 Director of ARC/Library .... Michelle RULLO
14 Manager Information Technology .... Norman ALVARADO
76 Program Director Medical Assisting .... Daryl ANDERSON
26 Director of Communications .... Brittany TRAVIS
38 Freshman Counseling .... Caroline CALLAHAN
103 Dir Career Services & Alumni Dev .... Anita LUCKETT

Pratt Institute (D)

200 Willoughby Avenue, Brooklyn NY 11205-3899
County: Kings FICE Identification: 002798
Unit ID: 194578
Telephone: (718) 636-3600 Carnegie Class: Spec-4-yr-Arts
FAX Number: (718) 636-3670 Calendar System: Semester
URL: www.pratt.edu
Established: 1887 Annual Undergrad Tuition & Fees: $48,154
Enrollment: 4,784 Coed
Affiliation or Control: Independent Non-Profit IRS Status: 501(c)3
Highest Offering: Master's
Accreditation: M, ART, CAEPT, CIDA, LIB, PLNG

01 Interim President .... Dr. Kirk E. PILLOW
00 President Emeritus .... Dr. Thomas F. SCHUTTE
05 Acting Provost .... Dr. Donna HEILAND
32 Vice President for Student Life .... Dr. Helen MATUSOW-AYRES
10 Vice Pres Finance/Administration .... Ms. Cathleen KENNY
111 VP Institutional Advancement .... Ms. Joan BARRY MCCORMICK
84 Vice President for Enrollment .... Ms. Judith AARON
20 Associate Provost Academic Affairs .... Dr. Donna HEILAND
88 Assoc Provost Strat Partnerships .... Dr. Allison DRUIN
11 Assistant to Pres Administration .... Ms. Josie CAPORUSCIO
06 Registrar .... Mr. Lisle HENDERSON
08 Director of the Library .... Mr. Russ ABELL
15 Director Human Resources .... Mr. Steve RICCOBONO
51 Dean Continuing Education .... Ms. Maira SEARA
26 Acting Exec Director Communications .... Ms. Jolene TRAVIS
36 Director of Career Services .... Ms. Rhonda SCHALLER
37 Director Student Financial Aid .... Mr. Nedzad GOGA
09 Exec Dir Strat Planning & Inst Eff .... Dr. Vladimir BRILLER
88 Director of Legal Affairs .... Mr. Thomas GREENE
96 Director of Purchasing .... Ms. Mitzi BRYAN
57 Dean of Art .... Mr. Gerry SNYDER
49 Dean Liberal Arts/Science .... Dr. Andrew BARNES
48 Dean School of Architecture .... Mr. Thomas HANRAHAN
62 Dean Information/Library Sci .... Dr. Tula GIANNINI
88 Dean of Design .... Ms. Anita COONEY
13 Chief Info Technology Officer (CIO) .... Mr. Joseph HEMWAY
18 Chief Facilities Officer .... Mr. Christopher GAVLICK
19 Director Security/Safety .... Mr. William SCHMITZ
39 Director Student Housing .... Mr. Christopher KASIK
41 Athletic Director .... Mr. Walter RICKARD

Rabbinical Academy Mesivta Rabbi Chaim Berlin (E)

1605 Coney Island Avenue, Brooklyn NY 11230-4715
County: Kings FICE Identification: 003976
Unit ID: 194657
Telephone: (718) 377-0777 Carnegie Class: Spec-4-yr-Faith
FAX Number: (718) 338-5578 Calendar System: Semester
Established: 1939 Annual Undergrad Tuition & Fees: $12,450
Enrollment: 262 Male
Affiliation or Control: Independent Non-Profit IRS Status: 501(c)3
Highest Offering: Second Talmudic Degree
Accreditation: RABN

01 Provost .... Rabbi Abraham H. FRUCHTHANDLER
05 President of the Faculty .... Rabbi Aaron M. SCHECHTER
03 Executive Director .... Rabbi Y. Mayer LASKER
29 Director of Alumni Association .... Mendel SCHECHTER
45 Chief Planning Officer .... Rabbi Tuvia M. OBERMEISTER
20 Associate Director .... Eli RABINOWITZ
37 Financial Aid Administrator .... Michael A. REISS

Rabbinical College Beth Shraga (F)

28 Saddle River Road, Monsey NY 10952-3035
County: Rockland FICE Identification: 010943
Unit ID: 194693
Telephone: (845) 356-1980 Carnegie Class: Spec-4-yr-Faith
FAX Number: (845) 425-2604 Calendar System: Semester
Established: 1965 Annual Undergrad Tuition & Fees: $12,450
Enrollment: 43 Male
Affiliation or Control: Independent Non-Profit IRS Status: 501(c)3
Highest Offering: Second Talmudic Degree
Accreditation: RABN

01 President .... Rabbi Emanuel SCHIFF

Rabbinical College Bobover Yeshiva B'nei Zion (G)

1577 48th Street, Brooklyn NY 11219-3293
County: Kings FICE Identification: 008614
Unit ID: 194666
Telephone: (718) 438-2018 Carnegie Class: Spec-4-yr-Faith
FAX Number: (718) 871-9031 Calendar System: Semester
Established: 1947 Annual Undergrad Tuition & Fees: $7,750
Enrollment: 335 Male
Affiliation or Control: Independent Non-Profit IRS Status: 501(c)3
Highest Offering: Second Talmudic Degree
Accreditation: RABN

01 President .... Rabbi Boruch Avrohom HOROWITZ

Rabbinical College of Long Island (H)

205 W Beech Street, Long Beach NY 11561-0630
County: Nassau FICE Identification: 010378
Unit ID: 194736
Telephone: (516) 255-4700 Carnegie Class: Spec-4-yr-Faith
FAX Number: (516) 255-4701 Calendar System: Semester
Established: 1965 Annual Undergrad Tuition & Fees: $8,800
Enrollment: 152 Male
Affiliation or Control: Independent Non-Profit IRS Status: 501(c)3
Highest Offering: First Talmudic Degree
Accreditation: RABN

01 President .... Rabbi Yitzchok FEIGELSTOCK
06 Registrar .... Rabbi Dovid N. ROTHSCHILD
32 Dean of Students .... Rabbi Yeruchem PITTER
07 CEO and Director of Admissions .... Rabbi Chaim HOBERMAN
37 Financial Aid Administrator .... Rabbi Shlomo TEICHMAN

Rabbinical College Ohr Shimon Yisroel (I)

215-217 Hewes Street, Brooklyn NY 11211-8102
County: Kings FICE Identification: 031292
Unit ID: 405854
Telephone: (718) 855-4092 Carnegie Class: Spec-4-yr-Faith
FAX Number: (718) 855-8479 Calendar System: Semester
Established: Annual Undergrad Tuition & Fees: $12,100
Enrollment: 194 Male
Affiliation or Control: Independent Non-Profit IRS Status: 501(c)3
Highest Offering: First Talmudic Degree
Accreditation: RABN

01 President .... Rabbi Shulem WALTER

Rabbinical College Ohr Yisroel (J)

8800 Seaview Avenue, Brooklyn NY 11236
County: Kings Identification: 667145
Unit ID: 484871
Telephone: (718) 633-4715 Carnegie Class: Not Classified
FAX Number: (347) 702-5436 Calendar System: Semester
Established: 2009 Annual Undergrad Tuition & Fees: $9,000
Enrollment: 104 Male
Affiliation or Control: Independent Non-Profit IRS Status: 501(c)3
Highest Offering: First Talmudic Degree
Accreditation: @RABN

01 President .... Rabbi Daniel GELDZAHLER

Rabbinical Seminary of America (K)

76-01 147th Street, Flushing NY 11367-3148
County: Queens FICE Identification: 003978
Unit ID: 194763
Telephone: (718) 268-4700 Carnegie Class: Spec-4-yr-Faith
FAX Number: (718) 268-4684 Calendar System: Semester
Established: 1933 Annual Undergrad Tuition & Fees: $10,300
Enrollment: 448 Male
Affiliation or Control: Independent Non-Profit IRS Status: 501(c)3
Highest Offering: Second Talmudic Degree
Accreditation: RABN

01 President .... Rabbi David HARRIS
01 President .... Rabbi Akiva GRUNBLATT
03 Executive Vice President .... Rabbi Hayim SCHWARTZ
11 Director of Operation .... Rabbi Meir GLAZER
06 Registrar .... Rabbi Abraham SEMMEL
30 Director Development .... Rabbi Yossi SINGER
37 Director of Financial Aid .... Mrs. Laya EISENSTEIN
18 Chief Physical Plant .... Mr. Ariel WOLFARTH
88 Director of Special Projects .... Vacant
91 Director of Admin Computing .... Mr. Jonathan PLATOVSKY
39 Director Student Housing .... Rabbi Elisha FEINBERG
46 Director Research & Development .... Vacant

Relay Graduate School of Education (L)

40 West 20th Street, 7th Floor, New York NY 10011
County: New York Identification: 667117
Unit ID: 475033
Telephone: (212) 228-1888 Carnegie Class: Spec-4-yr-Other
FAX Number: (212) 228-1855 Calendar System: Other
URL: www.relayschool.org
Established: 2011 Annual Graduate Tuition & Fees: N/A
Enrollment: 1,695 Coed
Affiliation or Control: Independent Non-Profit IRS Status: 501(c)3
Highest Offering: Master's; No Undergraduates
Accreditation: M, CAEPN

01 Co-Founder/President .... Mr. Norman ATKINS
05 Provost .... Dr. Brent MADDIN
10 Chief Financial Officer .... Ms. Piper EVANS
11 Chief Operating Officer .... Ms. Pamela INBASEKARAM
32 Chief Student Services Officer .... Ms. Kelly BOUCHER MORRIS
20 Dean .... Ms. Jennifer RAMOS

Rensselaer Polytechnic Institute (A)

110 8th Street, Troy NY 12180-3590
County: Rensselaer FICE Identification: 002803
Unit ID: 194824
Telephone: (518) 276-6000 Carnegie Class: DU-Higher
FAX Number: N/A Calendar System: Semester
URL: www.rpi.edu
Established: 1824 Annual Undergrad Tuition & Fees: $50,797
Enrollment: 6,982 Coed
Affiliation or Control: Independent Non-Profit IRS Status: 501(c)3
Highest Offering: Doctorate
Accreditation: M, ENG

01 President .... Dr. Shirley Ann JACKSON
05 Provost .... Dr. Prabhat HAJELA
11 Vice President for Administration .... Mr. Claude ROUNDS
26 VP Strategic Comm/External Rels .... Ms. Richie C. HUNTER
10 Vice President for Finance/CFO .... Ms. Virginia GREGG
45 Vice Pres for Research .... Mr. Jonathan S. DORDICK
111 Vice Pres Institutional Advancement .... Mr. Graig R. EASTIN
32 Interim Vice President Student Life .... Dr. LeNorman STRONG
15 Vice Pres Human Resources .... Mr. Curtis N. POWELL
13 Vice Pres for Info Services & CIO .... Mr. John E. KOLB
84 Vice Pres Enrollment Management .... Dr. Jonathan D. WEXLER
43 Secretary of Inst/General Counsel .... Mr. Craig A. COOK
27 Assoc VP Marketing/Communications .... Ms. Pamela S. SMITH
41 Assoc Vice Pres/Director Athletics .... Dr. Lee MCELROY
21 Asst Vice Pres for Administration .... Mr. Paul W. MARTIN
29 Asst Vice Pres Alumni Relations .... Mr. Jeff SCHANZ
35 Asst Vice Pres & Dean of Students .... Mr. Travis APGAR
121 Asst Vice Pres of Student Success .... Ms. Lisa TRAHAN
54 Dean School of Engineering .... Dr. Shekhar GARDE
81 Dean School of Science .... Dr. Curt BRENEMAN
79 Dean Sch of Humanities/Arts/Soc Sci .... Dr. Mary SIMONI
50 Dean Lally School of Management .... Dr. Thomas BEGLEY
48 Dean School of Architecture .... Mr. Evan DOUGLIS
20 Vice Provost/Dean Graduate Educ .... Dr. Stanley DUNN
20 Vice Provost/Dean Undergrad Educ .... Dr. Linda SCHADLER
06 Registrar .... Vacant
37 Director Financial Aid .... Mr. Martin C. DANIELS
09 Director of Institutional Research .... Vacant
08 Director of Libraries .... Mr. Andrew C. WHITE
25 Director of Contracts .... Mr. Richard E. SCAMMELL
36 Director Career Development Center .... Vacant
07 Director Undergrad Admissions .... Ms. Karen S. LONG
123 Director Graduate Admissions .... Mr. Jarron P. DECKER
18 Director Physical Plant .... Mr. Ernest J. KATZWINKEL
86 Director of Federal Relations .... Ms. Deborah E. ALTENBURG
23 Exec Director Student Health Center .... Dr. Leslie LAWRENCE
38 Director Student Counseling .... Dr. Benjamin MARTE
19 Director Public Safety/EmergencyMgt .... Mr. Jerry MATTHEWS
96 Director Procurement Services .... Mr. Ron MORASKI

Richard Gilder Graduate School at the American Museum of Natural History (B)

Central Park West at 79th Street, New York NY 10024
County: New York Identification: 667003
Unit ID: 458548
Telephone: (212) 769-5055 Carnegie Class: Not Classified
FAX Number: (212) 769-5257 Calendar System: Other
URL: www.amnh.org/our-research/richard-gilder-graduate-school
Established: 2006 Annual Graduate Tuition & Fees: N/A
Enrollment: N/A Coed
Affiliation or Control: Independent Non-Profit IRS Status: 501(c)3
Highest Offering: Doctorate; No Undergraduates
Accreditation: NY

01 Dean .... Dr. John J. FLYNN

Roberts Wesleyan College (C)

2301 Westside Drive, Rochester NY 14624-1997
County: Monroe FICE Identification: 002805
Unit ID: 194958
Telephone: (585) 594-6000 Carnegie Class: Masters/L
FAX Number: (585) 594-6371 Calendar System: Semester
URL: www.roberts.edu
Established: 1866 Annual Undergrad Tuition & Fees: $29,540
Enrollment: 1,712 Coed
Affiliation or Control: Independent Non-Profit IRS Status: 501(c)3
Highest Offering: Doctorate
Accreditation: M, ART, CAEPT, IACBE, MUS, NURSE, SW

01 President .... Dr. Deana L. PORTERFIELD
05 Sr VP & Chief Academic Officer .... Dr. David BASINGER
10 Sr Vice President & Treasurer .... Ms. Laurie LEO
32 VP for Student Development .... Mrs. Ruth LOGAN
111 VP Institutional Advancement .... Mr. Darrell BELL
84 VP for Enrollment Management .... Mrs. Kimberley WIEDEFELD
07 Assoc VP for UG Admissions .... Mr. JP ANDERSON
112 Assoc VP for Major Gifts .... Mr. Maurice (Max) MCGINNIS
26 AVP for Brand/Marketing Comm .... Ms. Donna MCLAREN
13 Assoc VP for Information Technology .... Mr. Pradeep SAXENA
40 Director of Bookstore Services .... Mr. Darren WALTON
41 Director of Athletics .... Mr. Robert SEGAVE
37 Director of Student Financial Svcs .... Mr. Stephen G. FIELD
09 Dir Institutional Research/Assess .... Dr. Paul W. KENNEDY
42 Chaplain .... Rev. Jonathan BRATT
06 Registrar .... Mrs. Lesa J. KOHR
04 Administrative Asst to President .... Mrs. Patti RADEL
15 Director Personnel Services .... Mrs. Amy PORPILIA
18 Chief Facilities/Physical Plant .... Mr. T. Richard GREER
19 Director Security/Safety .... Mr. Rick BILLITIER
25 Chief Contracts/Grants Admin .... Mrs. Lisa TIFFIN
29 Director Alumni Relations .... Mr. Kirk KETTINGER
103 Dir Workforce/Career Development .... Ms. Mary FLAHERTY
104 Director International Engagement .... Ms. Julie RUSHIK

† Parent institution of Northeastern Seminary.

Rochester Institute of Technology (D)

1 Lomb Memorial Drive, Rochester NY 14623-5604
County: Monroe FICE Identification: 002806
Unit ID: 195003
Telephone: (585) 475-2411 Carnegie Class: DU-Mod
FAX Number: (585) 475-7049 Calendar System: Quarter
URL: www.rit.edu
Established: 1829 Annual Undergrad Tuition & Fees: $38,568
Enrollment: 16,639 Coed
Affiliation or Control: Independent Non-Profit IRS Status: 501(c)3
Highest Offering: Doctorate
Accreditation: M, ARCPA, ART, CAEPT, CEA, CIDA, CS, DIETD, DMS, ENG, ENGT

01 President .... Dr. David C. MUNSON, JR.
05 Provost & Sr VP for Acad Affs .... Dr. Jeremy A. HAEFNER
100 Chief of Staff .... Mrs. Karen A. BARROWS
10 Sr Vice Pres Finance/Administration .... Dr. James H. WATTERS
84 Sr VP Enroll Mgmt/Career Svcs .... Dr. James G. MILLER
32 Sr Vice President Student Affairs .... Dr. Sandra S. JOHNSON
46 President NTID/RIT Vice Pres & Dean .... Dr. Gerard J. BUCKLEY
12 President RIT Dubai .... Dr. Yousef AL-ASSAF
30 VP for Development & Alumni Rels .... Dr. Lisa CAUDA
86 Vice President Govt/Cmty Relations .... Ms. Deborah M. STENDARDI
46 Vice President Research .... Dr. Ryne RAFFAELLE
28 Interim VP Diversity & Inclusion .... Dr. Keith JENKINS
12 VP AUK/Academic Dir RIT Pgms Kosovo .... Dr. Daniel COSENTINO
76 VP/Dean Coll Health Sciences/Tech .... Dr. Daniel B. ORNT
46 Senior Assoc Provost .... Dr. Christine M. LICATA
36 Sr AVP/Dir Coop Educ/Career Svcs .... Dr. Emanuel CONTOMANOLIS
26 Chief Communications Officer .... Mr. Robert FINNERTY
20 Assoc Provost and Director CIMS .... Dr. Nabil NASR
08 Director of RIT Libraries .... Ms. Marcia TRAVERNICHT
88 Assoc Provost Fac Dev Wallace Ctr .... Dr. Lynn A. WILD
12 President-RIT Croatia .... Mr. Donald HUDSPETH
29 Assoc VP Alumni/Parent & Annual Giv .... Ms. Kimberly SLUSSER
21 Asst VP/Controller/Asst Treasurer .... Ms. Lyn KELLY
18 Asst VP Facilities Management Svs .... Mr. John MOORE
06 Assoc VP/Registrar .... Mr. Joe LOFFREDO
07 Assoc VP/Exec Dir of Admissions .... Dr. Daniel SHELLEY
37 Asst VP & Dir Fin Aid & Scholarship .... Mr. Larry CHAMBERS
84 Assoc VP & Dir Grad/PT Enroll Svc .... Ms. Diane ELLISON
44 Assoc VP for Campaigns & Const Dev .... Ms. Heather ENGEL
09 Asst VP Inst Rsrch/Policy Studies .... Dr. Joan E. GRAHAM
15 Asst VP/Director Human Resources .... Ms. Judy BENDER
44 Exec Dir Fund for RIT .... Ms. Marisa PSAILA
35 Assoc VP Student Development .... Dr. Heath BOICE-PARDEE
85 Director International Student Svcs .... Mr. Jeffrey W. COX
96 Exec Director Procurement Services .... Ms. Debra KUSSE
102 Sr Director Foundation Relations .... Ms. Bonnie BUTKUS
102 Exec Dir Corp/Foundation Relations .... Mr. Paul HARRIS
101 Secretary of the Institute .... Mrs. Karen A. BARROWS
50 Dean of Business .... Dr. Jacqueline MOZRALL
54 Dean of Engineering .... Dr. Doreen EDWARDS
72 Dean Applied Science/Technology .... Dr. S. Manian RAMKUMAR
49 Dean of Liberal Arts .... Dr. James J. WINEBRAKE
81 Dean of Science .... Dr. Sophia MAGGELAKIS
57 Int Dean College Imaging Arts/Sci .... Dr. Robin CASS
77 Dean Col Computer/Info Science .... Dr. Anne HAAKE
58 Dean Graduate Education .... Dr. Twyla CUMMINGS
04 Exec Admin Asst to President .... Ms. Sonia RODRIGUEZ
11 Chief of Administration .... Ms. Karen A. BARROWS
13 Chief Info Technology Officer (CIO) .... Ms. Jeanne CASARES
41 Exec Dir Intercollegiate Athletics .... Mr. Louis SPIOTTI
26 Chief Marketing Officer .... Mr. John K. TRIERWEILER

Rockefeller University (E)

1230 York Avenue, New York NY 10065-6399
County: New York FICE Identification: 002807
Unit ID: 195049
Telephone: (212) 327-8000 Carnegie Class: DU-Higher
FAX Number: (212) 327-8699 Calendar System: Trimester
URL: www.rockefeller.edu
Established: 1901 Annual Graduate Tuition & Fees: N/A
Enrollment: 209 Coed
Affiliation or Control: Independent Non-Profit IRS Status: 501(c)3
Highest Offering: Doctorate; No Undergraduates
Accreditation: NY

01 President .... Dr. Richard P. LIFTON
03 Executive Vice President .... Dr. Timothy O'CONNOR
43 Vice President & General Counsel .... Ms. Harriet RABB
05 Vice President Academic Affairs .... Mr. Michael W. YOUNG
10 Vice President Finance .... Mr. James H. LAPPLE
30 Sr Vice President Development .... Ms. Maren E. IMHOFF
17 Vice President for Medical Affairs .... Dr. Barry S. COLLER
20 Dean & Vice Pres of Educ Affairs .... Dr. Sidney STRICKLAND
15 Vice President Human Resources .... Ms. Virginia A. HUFFMAN
18 Assoc Vice Pres Plant Operations .... Mr. Alexander KOGAN
45 Assoc Vice Pres Plng & Constr .... Mr. George B. CANDLER
13 Chief Information Officer .... Mr. Anthony CARVALLOZA
25 Dir Pgm Dev & Sponsored Research .... Ms. Collette L. RYDER
08 University Librarian .... Ms. Carol FELTES
19 Director Security .... Mr. James ROGERS

Rockland Community College (F)

145 College Road, Suffern NY 10901-3699
County: Rockland FICE Identification: 002877
Unit ID: 195058
Telephone: (845) 574-4000 Carnegie Class: Assoc/HT-High Trad
FAX Number: (845) 574-4463 Calendar System: Semester
URL: www.sunyrockland.edu
Established: 1959 Annual Undergrad Tuition & Fees (In-District): $4,815
Enrollment: 7,180 Coed
Affiliation or Control: State/Local IRS Status: 501(c)3
Highest Offering: Associate Degree
Accreditation: M, ADNUR, OTA

01 President .... Dr. Michael A. BASTON
10 VP Finance/Administration .... Dr. Nayyer HUSSAIN
05 Provost/VP Academic & Student Affs .... Dr. Susan DEER
21 Assoc VP Finance/Administration .... Mr. Joseph MARRA
88 AVP Academic/Community Partnershp .... Mr. Thomas DELLA TORRE
32 AVP Student Development .... Vacant
84 AVP of Enrollment Management .... Ms. Dana STILLEY
37 Director Financial Aid .... Ms. Debra BOUABIDI
06 Registrar .... Ms. Robin CONKLIN
13 Director of Information Services .... Dr. Steven FERRES
18 Chief Facilities/Physical Plant .... Mr. Douglas SCHMIDT
28 Dir Equity/Compliance/Affirm Act .... Ms. Melissa ROY
09 Director of Institutional Research .... Dr. Jim ROBERTSON
20 Asst to Vice Pres Academic Affairs .... Ms. Patricia KOBES
26 Chief Public Relations Officer .... Ms. Tzipora REITMAN
04 Administrative Asst to President .... Mr. Ben NAYLOR
07 Director of Admissions .... Mr. Jude FLEURISMOND
101 Secretary of the Board .... Mr. Ben NAYLOR
106 Dir Online Education/E-learning .... Ms. Lilia JUELE
11 Chief of Administration .... Mr. Dennis CALLINAN
15 Director Human Resources .... Vacant
19 Director Public Safety .... Mr. William MURPHY
25 Assoc VP for Resource Development .... Ms. Elizabeth KENDALL
41 Athletic Director .... Mr. Dan KEELEY
90 Director Academic Computing .... Ms. Lilia JUELE

The Sage Colleges (G)

65 First Street, Troy NY 12180-4199
County: Rensselaer FICE Identification: 002810
Unit ID: 195128
Telephone: (518) 244-2000 Carnegie Class: Masters/L
FAX Number: (518) 244-2460 Calendar System: Semester
URL: www.sage.edu
Established: 1916 Annual Undergrad Tuition & Fees: $28,805
Enrollment: 2,897 Coed
Affiliation or Control: Independent Non-Profit IRS Status: 501(c)3
Highest Offering: Doctorate
Accreditation: M, ART, CAEPN, DIETD, DIETI, IACBE, NURSE, OT, PTA

01 President .... Dr. Christopher AMES
05 Provost .... Dr. Susan W. BEATTY
111 VP for Institutional Advancement .... Ms. Melissa KOMORA
84 VP Marketing/Enrollment Management .... Ms. Lizzie WAHAB
12 Dean Sage College of Albany .... Ms. Jean DAHLGREN
12 Dean Russell Sage College .... Dr. Deborah LAWRENCE
10 VP for Finance & Treasurer .... Mr. Rick BARTHELMAS
32 Vice Pres for Campus Life .... Ms. Patricia CELLEMME
11 VP Administration & Planning .... Ms. Deirdre ZARRILLO
20 Associate Provost .... Vacant
35 Dean of Students-RSC .... Ms. Stacy GONZALEZ
35 Dean of Students-SCA .... Ms. Sharon MURRAY
76 Dean of Health Sciences .... Dr. Theresa HAND
06 Interim Registrar .... Ms. Kathy SCOVILLE
07 Senior Director of UG Admission .... Mr. Thomas BREEN
88 Assoc Dean School of Management .... Dr. Kimberly FREDERICKS
53 Interim Dean School of Education .... Dr. John PELIZZA
29 Dir of Alumni Relations SCA/SGS .... Vacant
29 Director Alumnae Relations RSC .... Ms. Joan CLIFFORD
123 Dir of Graduate & Adult Admissions .... Ms. Wendy DIEFENDORF
37 Director of Financial Aid .... Ms. Kelley ROBINSON
15 Director of Human Resources .... Ms. Laura D'AGOSTINO
09 Director of Institutional Research .... Ms. Lori PIZER
18 Director Facilities Management .... Mr. John ZAJACESKOWSKI
36 Dir of Academic Advisement-SCA .... Ms. Karen SCHELL
36 Dir of Academic Advisement-RSC .... Ms. Beth MANEY
26 Dir of Communications & Marketing .... Vacant
92 Director of Honors Programs .... Dr. Tonya MOUTRAY
21 Director of Finance .... Ms. Kristina L. PRILL
96 Dir of Purchasing/Accts Payable .... Ms. Paula SELMER
04 Administrative Asst to President .... Ms. Rose L. GRIGNON
08 Head Librarian .... Ms. Lisa C. BRAINARD
105 Webmaster .... Mr. Kurt EYE
108 Director Institutional Assessment .... Vacant
19 Director Security/Safety .... Mr. Michael TREMBLAY
39 Director of Residence Life .... Ms. Shylah ADDANTE
41 Athletic Director .... Ms. Sandy AUGESTINE-COLLINS
44 Sr Director of Annual Giving .... Ms. Kathleen DANICA
86 Assoc Director Government Relations .... Mr. Nicholas DECAPRIO
91 Director of IT/Network Services .... Mr. John HARRIS
106 Director of Online Education .... Ms. Kimberly TAYLOR

Saint Bernard's School of Theology & Ministry (A)

120 French Road, Rochester NY 14618-3822
County: Monroe FICE Identification: 002815
Unit ID: 195155
Telephone: (585) 271-3657 Carnegie Class: Spec-4-yr-Faith
FAX Number: (585) 271-2045 Calendar System: Semester
URL: www.stbernards.edu
Established: 1893 Annual Graduate Tuition & Fees: N/A
Enrollment: 82 Coed
Affiliation or Control: Roman Catholic IRS Status: 501(c)3
Highest Offering: Master's; No Undergraduates
Accreditation: THEOL

01 President ... Rev. George P. HEYMAN
05 Academic Dean ... Dr. Devadasan N. PREMNATH
06 Registrar ... Vacant
10 Controller ... Ms. Mary MUGGLETON
07 Admiss Director/Dir Stdnt Fin Aid ... Mr. Mark CAPELLAZZI
08 Librarian ... Vacant

St. Bonaventure University (B)

P.O. Box 2450, St. Bonaventure NY 14778
County: Cattaraugus FICE Identification: 002817
Unit ID: 195164
Telephone: (716) 375-2000 Carnegie Class: Masters/M
FAX Number: N/A Calendar System: Semester
URL: www.sbu.edu
Established: 1858 Annual Undergrad Tuition & Fees: $32,331
Enrollment: 1,992 Coed
Affiliation or Control: Roman Catholic IRS Status: 501(c)3
Highest Offering: Master's
Accreditation: M, CACREP, CAEPN, JOUR

01 President ... Dr. Dennis R. DEPERRO
05 Provost and VP for Academic Affairs ... Dr. Joseph ZIMMER
32 Int Vice Pres for Student Affairs ... Ms. Nichole GONZALEZ
10 Acting Chief Financial Officer ... Ms. Nancy K. TAYLOR
26 Int Vice Pres University Relations ... Mr. Thomas MISSEL
42 Exec Dir University Ministries ... Fr. Francis J. DISPIGNO, OFM
111 Vice Pres for Advancement ... Mr. Robert VAN WICKLIN
84 Vice President for Enrollment ... Mr. Bernard VALENTO
57 Exec Dir of Q Arts Center ... Mr. Ludwig BRUNNER
20 Assoc Vice Pres Academic Affairs ... Ms. Ann LEHMAN
11 Exec Assistant to the President ... Ms. Sarah STANGLE
15 Director Human Resources ... Mr. Erik SEASTEDT
07 Director of Recruitment ... Mr. Douglas BRADY
37 Director of Financial Aid ... Mr. Troy MARTIN
06 Registrar ... Mr. George B. SWINDOLL
39 Int Exec Dir Res Living/Conduct ... Mr. Robert DEFAZIO
13 Assoc Provost/Chief Info Officer ... Dr. Michael HOFFMAN
08 Director of Friedsam Mem Library ... Mr. Paul J. SPAETH
101 Director of Board/Govt/Cmty Rels ... Mr. Thomas BUTTAFARRO, JR.
41 Director of Athletics ... Mr. Tim KENNEY
09 Director of Institutional Research ... Ms. Ann LEHMAN
29 Director of Alumni Services ... Mr. Joseph FLANAGAN
36 Director of Career Services ... Ms. Connie F. WHITCOMB
43 University Counsel ... Mr. Jeff REISNER
23 Director Wellness Center ... Mr. Christopher ANDERSON
18 Director of Facilities Operations ... Mr. Rob HURLBURT
21 Controller ... Mr. Karl STRAUSS
19 Director of Safety and Security ... Mr. Gary SEGRUE
40 Manager Bookstore ... Ms. Annette DONAVON
44 Director Annual Giving Program ... Ms. Karen HEITZINGER
92 Director of Honors Program ... Dr. Darryl MAYEAUX
96 Director of Budget & Purchasing ... Ms. Lorraine SMITH
73 Dean SFS/Dir Franciscan Institute ... Fr. David COUTURIER, OFM
49 Dean School of Arts & Sci ... Dr. David HILMEY
50 Dean School of Business ... Dr. Matricia JAMES
58 Dean School of Graduate Studies ... Dr. Pauline HOFFMANN
53 Dean School of Education ... Dr. Lisa BUENAVENTURA
60 Dean Jandoli Sch of Communications ... Dr. Pauline HOFFMANN
76 Dean School of Allied Health ... Dr. Douglas PISANO
104 Director of International Studies ... Vacant
26 Director Marketing and Promotions ... Mr. Seth JOHNSON

St. Elizabeth College of Nursing (C)

2215 Genesee Street, Utica NY 13501-5998
County: Oneida FICE Identification: 006461
Unit ID: 195702
Telephone: (315) 798-8144 Carnegie Class: Not Classified
FAX Number: (315) 798-8271 Calendar System: Semester
URL: www.secon.edu
Established: 1904 Annual Undergrad Tuition & Fees: $15,570
Enrollment: 206 Coed
Affiliation or Control: Independent Non-Profit IRS Status: 501(c)3
Highest Offering: Associate Degree
Accreditation: M, ADNUR

01 President ... Dr. Varinya SHEPPARD
32 Dean of Students/Faculty Devel ... Mrs. Beverly PLANTE
32 Dean of Students/Faculty Devel ... Mrs. Shannon HOLTSLAG
06 Registrar & Bursar ... Mrs. Samantha ERNST
10 Director of Finance & Enrollment ... Ms. Sherry WOJNAS

St. Francis College (D)

180 Remsen Street, Brooklyn NY 11201-4398
County: Kings FICE Identification: 002820
Unit ID: 195173
Telephone: (718) 522-2300 Carnegie Class: Bac-Diverse
FAX Number: (718) 522-1274 Calendar System: Semester
URL: www.sfc.edu
Established: 1859 Annual Undergrad Tuition & Fees: $25,300
Enrollment: 2,672 Coed
Affiliation or Control: Independent Non-Profit IRS Status: 501(c)3
Highest Offering: Master's
Accreditation: M, CAEPT, NURSE

01 President ... Dr. Miguel MARTINEZ-SAENZ
10 Vice President of Financial Affairs ... Mr. John RAGNO
05 Provost/Vice Pres for Academic Affs ... Dr. Timothy J. HOULIHAN
26 Vice Pres Govt/Community Relations ... Ms. Linda WERBEL DASHEFSKY
30 Vice President of Development ... Mr. Thomas FLOOD
84 Vice Pres Enrollment Mgmt Svcs ... Mr. Joseph CUMMINGS
18 VP Facilities Mgmt/Capital Projects ... Mr. Kevin O'ROURKE
20 Vice President Academic Affairs ... Dr. Jennifer LANCASTER
20 Academic Dean ... Dr. Kathleen GRAY
58 Assoc Dean Grad Pgms/Adult Educ ... Dr. Danielle BUDENZ
121 Assoc Dean for Student Success ... Ms. Monica MICHALSKI
15 Director of Human Resources ... Mr. Richard GRASSO
13 Chief Information Officer ... Ms. Madalyn HANLEY
06 Registrar ... Ms. Susan E. WEISMAN
32 Dean of Students ... Dr. Jose RODRIGUEZ
08 Director Library Services ... Dr. James SMITH
36 Director of Career Development ... Ms. Naomi KINLEY
29 Director of Alumni Relations ... Mr. Dennis MCDERMOTT
41 Director of Athletics ... Ms. Irma GARCIA
42 Director Campus Ministry ... Fr. Brian JORDAN
09 Director of Institutional Research ... Mr. Steven CATALANO
07 Director Admissions ... Ms. Lisa RANDAZZO

St. John Fisher College (E)

3690 East Avenue, Rochester NY 14618-3597
County: Monroe FICE Identification: 002821
Unit ID: 195720
Telephone: (585) 385-8000 Carnegie Class: DU-Mod
FAX Number: (585) 899-3870 Calendar System: Semester
URL: www.sjfc.edu
Established: 1948 Annual Undergrad Tuition & Fees: $31,880
Enrollment: 3,823 Coed
Affiliation or Control: Independent Non-Profit IRS Status: 501(c)3
Highest Offering: Doctorate
Accreditation: M, CACREP, CAEPN, NURSE, PHAR

01 President ... Dr. Gerard J. ROONEY
04 Exec Asst to Pres/Secy to Board ... Ms. Joan R. BENULIS
05 Provost ... Dr. Kevin RAILEY
84 VP Enrollment Management ... Mr. Jose J. PERALES
10 Vice President for Finance/CFO ... Ms. Linda M. STEINKIRCHNER
32 VP Student Affairs & Diversity ... Dr. Richard DEJESUS-RUEFF
49 Int Dean School of Arts/Sciences ... Dr. James R. BOWERS
50 Dean School of Business ... Dr. Rama YELKUR
53 Dean School of Education ... Dr. Michael WISCHNOWSKI
66 Dean School of Nursing ... Dr. Dianne C. COONEY MINER
67 Dean School of Pharmacy ... Dr. Christine R. BIRNIE
28 Director Multicultural Affairs ... Mr. Yantee SLOBERT
06 Registrar ... Ms. Julia M. THOMAS
15 Asst Vice Pres Human Resources ... Ms. Elizabeth SKRAINER
26 Director Marketing & Communications ... Ms. Kate M. TOROK
06 Associate Registrar ... Ms. Cheryl O. EVANS
08 Director of the Library ... Ms. Melissa JADLOS
13 Chief Information/Computing Officer ... Mr. Stacy S. SLOCUM
16 Director of Payroll & Benefits ... Ms. Mary R. POWLEY
29 Sr Director of Alumni Relations ... Mr. Joshua FOLDARE
37 Director Student Financial Aid ... Mrs. Angela B. MONNAT
42 Director Campus Ministry ... Vacant
19 Director of Safety & Security ... Mr. David DICARO
41 Athletic Director ... Mr. Robert A. WARD
18 Director of Physical Plant ... Mr. Kenneth J. WIDANKA
21 Controller ... Vacant
23 Dir of Health & Wellness Center ... Ms. Rebecca KIEFFER
31 Director of Community Service ... Mrs. Sally J. VAUGHAN
07 Director of Freshman Admissions ... Ms. Stacy A. LEDERMANN
07 Assoc Dir of Transfer/Grad Admiss ... Ms. Michelle GOSIER
09 Dir Inst Research/Assessment ... Ms. Elizabeth A. LACHANCE
35 Director Student Affairs ... Ms. Teah M. TERRANCE
36 Director Career Services ... Mr. Matt CARDIN
105 Webmaster ... Ms. Jody C. BENEDICT

St. John's University (F)

8000 Utopia Parkway, Queens NY 11439-0001
County: Queens FICE Identification: 002823
Unit ID: 195809
Telephone: (718) 990-6161 Carnegie Class: DU-Mod
FAX Number: (718) 990-5723 Calendar System: Semester
URL: www.stjohns.edu
Established: 1870 Annual Undergrad Tuition & Fees: $39,460
Enrollment: 20,877 Coed
Affiliation or Control: Roman Catholic IRS Status: 501(c)3
Highest Offering: Doctorate
Accreditation: M, ARCPA, ART, AUD, CACREP, CAEPT, CLPSY, EMT, LAW, LIB, MT, PHAR, RAD, SCPSY, SP

01 President ... Dr. Conrado M. GEMPESAW
03 Executive VP Mission ... Rev. Bernard M. TRACEY, CM
05 Provost & VP For Academic Affairs ... Dr. Robert A. MANGIONE
10 VP Business Affairs/CFO/Treasurer ... Ms. Sharon HEWITT WATKINS
43 VP Admin/Secretary & Gen Counsel ... Mr. Joseph E. OLIVA
32 VP Student Affairs ... Dr. Kathryn T. HUTCHINSON
84 Vice Provost & Chief Enroll Officer ... Mr. Jorge RODRIGUEZ
111 VP University Advancement/Relations ... Dr. Christian P. VAUPEL
15 Assoc VP HR/Chief Diversity Officer ... Ms. Nada` M. LLEWELLYN
20 Senior Vice Provost ... Dr. Simon MOLLER
13 VP Information Technology/CIO ... Mr. Joseph J. TUFANO
41 Director of Athletics ... Mr. Anton GOFF
49 Dean St John's College ... Dr. Jeffrey W. FAGEN
53 Dean The School of Education ... Dr. Michael SAMPSON
61 Dean School of Law ... Mr. Michael A. SIMONS
50 Dean Tobin College of Business ... Dr. Norean R. SHARPE
67 Dean Pharmacy/Health Sciences ... Dr. Russell J. DIGATE
107 Dean College Prof Studies ... Dr. Katia PASSERINI
08 Dean University Libraries ... Dr. Valeda F. DENT
12 Vice Provost - SI ... Dr. James O'KEEFE
31 VP Community Relations ... Mr. Joseph A. SCIAME
20 Vice Provost Acad Support Services ... Dr. Andre A. MCKENZIE
106 Vice Provost Digital Learning ... Dr. Elizabeth CIABOCCHI
110 Assoc VP University Advancement ... Ms. Jeanne M. UMLAND
41 Assoc VP Athletics ... Ms. Kathleen F. MEEHAN
21 Assoc VP Business Affairs ... Mr. Anthony MACALUSO
18 Assoc VP Campus Facilities/Services ... Mr. Brian BAUMER
26 Assoc VP External Relations ... Mr. Dominic P. SCIANNA
91 Assoc VP Information Technology ... Ms. Maura A. WOODS
42 Assoc VP University Ministry ... Ms. Victoria R. SANTANGELO
27 Assoc VP Marketing & Communications ... Ms. Caren BATZER
11 Assoc Provost Admin/Inst Accred ... Ms. Linda A. SHANNON
104 Assoc Provost Global Studies ... Mr. Matthew PUCCIARELLI
121 Assoc Provost Student Success ... Dr. Jacqueline H. GROGAN
20 Assoc Provost Acad Res & Mgmt Plng ... Ms. Judy CHEN
20 Assoc Provost Academic - SI ... Dr. Robert FANUZZI
86 Asst VP Gov Rel/Exec Dir Univ Rel ... Mr. Brian BROWNE
88 Asst VP University Events ... Ms. Nunziatina A. MANULI
06 University Registrar ... Ms. Joanne A. LLERANDI
19 Exec Dir Public Safety/Risk Mgt ... Ms. Denise VENCAK-TONER
88 Exec Director Vincentian Center ... Rev. Patrick J. GRIFFIN, CM
14 Exec Dir Enterprise Infrastructure ... Ms. Anne L. ROCCO PACIONE
90 Exec Director User Services ... Mr. Kenneth J. MAHLMEISTER
36 Exec Dir University Career Services ... Ms. Paulette B. GONZALEZ
29 Director Alumni Relations ... Mr. Mark A. ANDREWS
88 Director Ctr for Teaching/Learning ... Dr. Cynthia R. PHILLIPS
07 Director Admissions ... Mrs. Samantha R. WRIGHT
105 Director Digital Communications ... Ms. Linda ROMANO
92 Director Honors Program ... Dr. Robert J. FORMAN
16 Director Human Resources Services ... Ms. Cynthia F. SIMPSON
25 Dir Grants & Sponsored Research ... Mr. Jared E. LITTMAN
116 Director Internal Audit ... Mr. Alex J. HOEHN
37 Director Int Financial Aid/Research ... Ms. Maryanne H. TWOMEY
112 Director Planned Giving ... Ms. Susan M. DAMIANI
88 Dir Pre-Admin/Asst to VP S&O P ... Mrs. Cecelia M. RUSSO
96 Director Purchasing ... Mr. Jeffery I. WEISS
39 Director Residence Life ... Mr. Eric M. FINKELSTEIN
23 Director Queens Health Services ... Mrs. Pauline TUMMINO
09 Acting Dir Institutional Research ... Ms. Christine M. GOODWIN
38 Assoc Director Counseling Center ... Ms. Dorothy M. SCHMITT
38 Associate Dir Counseling Ctr - SI ... Dr. Erin RYAN
07 Sr Asst Director Admissions - SI ... Mr. David A. PIERRE
37 Asst Director Financial Aid - SI ... Mr. Thomas J. MARLOW
85 Asst Dir Int Students/Scholar Svcs ... Ms. Amy R. HARVEY
39 Asst Dir of Res Life-SI ... Mr. Jason T. BARTLETT
40 Manager of Bookstore ... Mrs. Denise SERVIDIO

Saint Joseph's College, New York (G)

245 Clinton Avenue, Brooklyn NY 11205-3688
County: Kings FICE Identification: 002825
Unit ID: 195544
Telephone: (718) 940-5300 Carnegie Class: Masters/L
FAX Number: (718) 636-7245 Calendar System: Semester
URL: www.sjcny.edu
Established: 1916 Annual Undergrad Tuition & Fees: $25,114
Enrollment: 4,749 Coed
Affiliation or Control: Independent Non-Profit IRS Status: 501(c)3
Highest Offering: Master's
Accreditation: M, ADNUR, CAEPT, NRPA, NUR

01 President ... Dr. Donald R. BOOMGAARDEN
05 Interim Provost ... Dr. Thomas TRAVIS
26 VP of Marketing and Communications ... Ms. Jessica MCALEER
10 Chief Financial Officer ... Mr. John C. ROTH
20 VP for Academic Affairs - BK ... Dr. Barb GARII
13 VP IT and Chief Information Officer ... Ms. Michelle PAPAJOHN
32 VP for Student Life - BK ... Ms. Sherrie VAN ARNAM
111 VP for Institutional Advancement ... Vacant
84 VP for Enrollment Management - BK ... Ms. Christine MURPHY
41 AVP and Senior Athletics Director ... Ms. Shantey HILL
19 Director Security/Safety ... Mr. Michael MCGRANN
88 Director of Child Study Center ... Dr. Susan SHAPIRO
90 Exec Director Client Services ... Ms. Lichele ABEAR
37 Director of Financial Aid ... Ms. Amy THOMPSON
36 Exec Director Career Development ... Ms. Ellen BURTI
15 Exec Director of Human Resources ... Ms. D'adra CRUMP
18 Director Physical Plant ... Mr. Fred FORAN
21 Controller ... Mr. Matthew BRELLIS
14 Exec Director Network Operations ... Mr. Ted DEC
06 College Registrar ... Mr. Robert PERGOLIS
08 Director of Library ... Dr. Elizabeth POLLICINO MURPHY

88 Director of Public Affairs ... Mr. Michael BANACH
28 Coordinator of Diversity ... Ms. Christy BANKS
112 Planned Giving Officer ... Ms. Susan LOUCKS
38 Director Student Counseling ... Dr. Anissa MOODY
29 Associate Director Alumni Relations ... Ms. Dee KAYALAR
09 Director of Institutional Research ... Ms. Allison LIST
102 Director Foundation Relations ... Ms. Amy ENGEL
86 Director Government Relations ... Mr. Michael BANACH
04 Executive Admin Asst to President ... Ms. Ann PAIVA

Saint Joseph's College, New York - Suffolk Campus (A)

155 W Roe Boulevard, Patchogue NY 11772-2399
Telephone: (631) 687-5100 FICE Identification: 029081
Accreditation: &M

† Regional accreditation is carried under the parent institution in Brooklyn, NY.

St. Joseph's College of Nursing (B)

206 Prospect Avenue, Syracuse NY 13203-1806
County: Onondaga FICE Identification: 006467
Unit ID: 195191
Telephone: (315) 448-5040 Carnegie Class: Spec 2-yr-Health
FAX Number: (315) 448-5745 Calendar System: Semester
URL: www.sjhcon.org
Established: 1898 Annual Undergrad Tuition & Fees: $19,360
Enrollment: 287 Coed
Affiliation or Control: Independent Non-Profit IRS Status: 501(c)3
Highest Offering: Associate Degree
Accreditation: M

01 Dean ... Mrs. Marianne MARKOWITZ

Saint Joseph's Seminary (C)

Dunwoodie, #201 Seminary Avenue, Yonkers NY 10704-1852
County: Westchester FICE Identification: 002826
Unit ID: 195571
Telephone: (914) 968-6200 Carnegie Class: Not Classified
FAX Number: (914) 376-2019 Calendar System: Semester
URL: www.dunwoodie.edu
Established: 1896 Annual Graduate Tuition & Fees: N/A
Enrollment: N/A Coed
Affiliation or Control: Roman Catholic IRS Status: 501(c)3
Highest Offering: Master's; No Undergraduates
Accreditation: M, THEOL

01 Rector ... Msgr. Peter I. VACCARI
05 Academic Dean ... Rev. Kevin P. O'REILLY
32 Dean of Students/Admissions ... Rev. Nicholas A. ZIENTARSKI
08 Director Library Services ... Mr. Connor FLATZ
06 Registrar ... Ms. Kathleen M. RUSSELL
38 Director of Psychological Services ... Dr. Richard GALLAGHER
18 Director of Buildings & Grounds ... Mr. Joseph DI LELLO
26 Director of Communications ... Ms. Cynthia F. HARRISON
07 Director of Admissions ... Fr. Thomas BERG
108 Director Institutional Assessment ... Msgr. Michael CURRAN

St. Lawrence University (D)

23 Romoda Drive, Canton NY 13617-1423
County: St. Lawrence FICE Identification: 002829
Unit ID: 195216
Telephone: (315) 229-5011 Carnegie Class: Bac-A&S
FAX Number: (315) 229-5502 Calendar System: Other
URL: www.stlawu.edu
Established: 1856 Annual Undergrad Tuition & Fees: $51,200
Enrollment: 2,472 Coed
Affiliation or Control: Independent Non-Profit IRS Status: 501(c)3
Highest Offering: Master's
Accreditation: M, CAEPT

01 President ... Dr. William L. FOX
05 Vice Pres/Dean Academic Affairs ... Dr. Karl K. SCHONBERG
111 Vice Pres University Advancement ... Mr. Thomas PYNCHON
10 Vice President Finance & Treasurer ... Mr. Joseph MANORY
32 Vice Pres/Dean Student Life ... Dr. Joseph TOLLIVER
07 VP & Dean for Admissions/Fin Aid ... Vacant
26 VP for Employee/Community Relations ... Mrs. Lisa M. CANIA
21 Assoc Vice President for Finance ... Ms. Carol GABLE
89 Associate Dean of the First-Year ... Dr. Jennifer HANSEN
35 Associate Dean of Student Life ... Mr. Rance DAVIS
06 Registrar ... Ms. Lorie MACKENZIE
37 Director of Financial Aid ... Mrs. Patricia J B. FARMER
08 VP Libraries & Information Tech ... Mr. Justin SIPHER
36 Director of Career Services ... Mr. Ronald G. ALBERTSON
09 Director of Institutional Research ... Ms. Christine ZIMMERMAN
18 Chief Facilities/Physical Plant ... Mr. Daniel B. SEAMAN
20 Assoc Dean of Academic Admin ... Ms. Lorie R. MACKENZIE
29 Director Alumni Relations ... Mr. Joseph C. KENISTON
39 Director Residence Life ... Mr. Christopher MARQUARDT
23 Director of Health & Counseling ... Mr. Timothy CORBITT
84 Director Enrollment Management ... Mr. Jeremy FREEMAN
96 Director of Purchasing ... Ms. Ruta OZOLS
15 Director Personnel Services ... Mrs. Colleen MANLEY
38 Director Student Counseling ... Mr. Timothy CORBITT

St. Paul's School of Nursing (E)

97-77 Queens Blvd, Queens NY 11374
County: Queens FICE Identification: 012364
Unit ID: 189811
Telephone: (718) 357-0500 Carnegie Class: Spec 2-yr-Health
FAX Number: (718) 357-4683 Calendar System: Semester
URL: www.stpaulsschoolofnursing.edu
Established: 1969 Annual Undergrad Tuition & Fees: $30,944
Enrollment: 517 Coed
Affiliation or Control: Proprietary IRS Status: Proprietary
Highest Offering: Associate Degree
Accreditation: ABHES

01 President ... Dr. Eric RICIOPPO

Saint Paul's School of Nursing-Staten Island (F)

2 Teleport Dr Ste 203, Corp Comm 2, Staten Island NY 10311
County: Richmond FICE Identification: 009479
Unit ID: 195784
Telephone: (718) 818-6470 Carnegie Class: Spec 2-yr-Health
FAX Number: (718) 818-6020 Calendar System: Semester
URL: www.stpaulsschoolofnursing.edu
Established: 1904 Annual Undergrad Tuition & Fees: $16,828
Enrollment: 546 Coed
Affiliation or Control: Proprietary IRS Status: Proprietary
Highest Offering: Associate Degree
Accreditation: ABHES

01 President ... Mr. David SMITH
05 Director of Education ... Dr. Ann LUBRANO
66 Dean of Nursing ... Dr. Coleen KUMAR
06 Registrar ... Ms. Maria HOFFMANN
10 Business Office Manager ... Ms. Olga FORINA
07 Director of Admissions ... Ms. Nickeshia BULLOCK
32 Director of Career Services ... Ms. Lynn SALVAGE
37 Director of Financial Aid ... Ms. Nayamka WARD
08 LRC Manager ... Ms. Judy LEE

St. Thomas Aquinas College (G)

125 Route 340, Sparkill NY 10976-1050
County: Rockland FICE Identification: 002832
Unit ID: 195243
Telephone: (845) 398-4000 Carnegie Class: Masters/S
FAX Number: (845) 359-8136 Calendar System: 4/1/4
URL: www.stac.edu
Established: 1952 Annual Undergrad Tuition & Fees: $29,600
Enrollment: 1,836 Coed
Affiliation or Control: Independent Non-Profit IRS Status: 501(c)3
Highest Offering: Master's
Accreditation: M, CAEPN, IACBE

01 President ... Dr. Margaret M. FITZPATRICK, SC
03 Senior Vice President ... Mr. Vincent CRAPANZANO
10 Vice Pres Administration & Finance ... Mr. Joseph DONINI
05 Provost/Vice Pres Academic Affairs ... Dr. Robert MURRAY
32 Vice Pres/Dean Student Development ... Dr. Kirk MANNING
30 Vice Pres Institutional Advancement ... Mrs. Karen WRIGHT
15 Director Human Resources ... Mrs. Maria COUPE
07 Director Admissions ... Ms. Samantha BAZILE
09 Dir Inst Research/Program Develop ... Dr. Renee QUINTYNE
21 Controller ... Ms. Jennifer MAZZA
44 Dir Annual Giving & Alumni Affairs ... Mrs. Jennifer TANIS
35 Director Student Activities ... Mr. Dave ENG
38 Director Student Counseling ... Dr. Louis MUGGEO
06 Registrar ... Ms. Eileen MURPHY
36 Director Career Development ... Mrs. Maureen MULHERN
37 Director Financial Aid ... Mrs. Jean Marie MOHR
13 Director of Computing Services ... Mr. Sunny ANTHWAL
18 Dir Facilities & Construction ... Mr. Patrick LAMBERT
26 Dir Campus Communications/Enr Mktg ... Mrs. Danielle KOBRYN
50 Dean School of Business ... Mr. Michael MURPHY
53 Dean School of Education ... Dr. Meenakshi GAJRIA
49 Dean School of Arts & Sciences ... Dr. Steven BURNS
04 Executive Asst to President ... Ms. Lee TAUSSI

Saint Vladimir's Orthodox Theological Seminary (H)

575 Scarsdale Road, Yonkers NY 10707
County: Westchester FICE Identification: 002833
Unit ID: 195580
Telephone: (914) 961-8313 Carnegie Class: Spec-4-yr-Faith
FAX Number: (914) 961-4507 Calendar System: Semester
URL: www.svots.edu
Established: 1938 Annual Graduate Tuition & Fees: N/A
Enrollment: 77 Coed
Affiliation or Control: Independent Non-Profit IRS Status: 501(c)3
Highest Offering: Doctorate; No Undergraduates
Accreditation: THEOL

01 President ... V.Rev. Chad HATFIELD
05 Dean ... Vacant
10 Chief Financial Officer ... Ms. Melanie RINGA
13 Chief Technology Officer ... Mr. Georgios KOKONAS
20 Assoc Dean Academic Affairs ... Dr. John BARNET
32 Assoc Dean for Student Affairs ... RevDr. David MEZYNSKI
06 Registrar ... Dr. John BARNET
08 Librarian ... Ms. Eleana SILK
35 Student Affairs Administrator ... Ms. Gabrielle RUSSIN
108 Dir Institutional Assessment ... Dr. Peter BOUTENEFF
111 Sr Advisor Advancement ... Mr. Ted BAZIL
26 Director Marketing/Operations ... Rev Dn. Gregory HATRAK

Salvation Army College for Officer Training (I)

201 Lafayette Avenue, Suffern NY 10901-4707
County: Rockland Identification: 666020
Telephone: (845) 368-7200 Carnegie Class: Not Classified
FAX Number: (845) 357-6644 Calendar System: Other
URL: www.use.salvationarmy.org
Established: 1905 Annual Undergrad Tuition & Fees: N/A
Enrollment: N/A Coed
Affiliation or Control: Independent Non-Profit IRS Status: 501(c)3
Highest Offering: Associate Degree
Accreditation: NY

01 Principal ... Col. Janet A. MUNN
03 Associate Principal ... Major William F. FURMAN
11 Asst Principal for Administration ... Major Jongwoo KIM
05 Director of Curriculum ... Major Alberto SUAREZ
06 Registrar ... Ms. Allyssa COMPTON
09 Coord Inst Research/Accred Liaison . Dr. Dennis VANDER WEELE
10 Chief Business Officer ... Major Ronald STARNES
15 Director Personnel Services ... Major Sherry PELLETIER
20 Associate Academic Officer ... Major Heather GARRETT
21 Associate Business Officer ... Mrs. Robin FRASER
32 Director Student Affairs ... Vacant

Samaritan Hospital School of Nursing (J)

1300 Massachusetts Avenue, Troy NY 12180
County: Rensselaer FICE Identification: 009248
Unit ID: 195289
Telephone: (518) 268-5010 Carnegie Class: Spec 2-yr-Health
FAX Number: (518) 268-5040 Calendar System: Semester
URL: www.nehealth.com
Established: 1903 Annual Undergrad Tuition & Fees: $13,331
Enrollment: 147 Coed
Affiliation or Control: Independent Non-Profit IRS Status: 501(c)3
Highest Offering: Associate Degree
Accreditation: NY, ADNUR, PNUR

01 Director ... Ms. Susan BIRKHEAD

Sarah Lawrence College (K)

1 Meadway, Bronxville NY 10708-5999
County: Westchester FICE Identification: 002813
Unit ID: 195304
Telephone: (914) 337-0700 Carnegie Class: Bac-A&S
FAX Number: N/A Calendar System: Semester
URL: www.slc.edu
Established: 1926 Annual Undergrad Tuition & Fees: $52,550
Enrollment: 1,643 Coed
Affiliation or Control: Independent Non-Profit IRS Status: 501(c)3
Highest Offering: Master's
Accreditation: M, CAEPT

01 President ... Dr. Cristle COLLINS JUDD
05 Dean of the College ... Dr. Kanwal SINGH
10 Vice Pres Finance/Operations ... Stephen SCHAFER
111 Interim VP for Advancement ... Ellen REYNOLDS
26 Vice Pres Communication & Marketing ... Vacant
11 Vice President for Administration ... Thomas L. BLUM
20 Associate Dean of the College ... Melissa FRAZIER
32 Dean of Studies & Student Life ... Daniel TRUJILLO
22 Dean of Equity and Inclusion ... Dr. Allen GREEN
35 Dean of Student Affairs ... Dr. Paige CRANDALL
07 Dean of Enrollment ... Kevin MCKENNA
58 Dean Graduate/Professional Studies ... Dr. Judith BABBITTS
06 Registrar ... Daniel LICHT
08 Director of Libraries ... Bobbie SMOLOW
13 Chief Technology Officer ... Sean JAMESON
29 Director of Alumni ... Dania ABU-SHAHEEN
36 Director Career Counseling ... Angela CHERUBINI
44 Individual Giving Officer ... Elisa BALESTRA
28 Director of Diversity ... Natalie GROSS
18 Asst Vice President of Facilities ... Maureen GALLAGHER
19 AVP of Public Safety/Purchasing ... Larry HOFFMAN
04 Executive Asst to President ... Rosemary DAHILL
100 Chief of Staff ... Thomas BLUM
104 Asst Dean Study Abroad ... Prema SAMUEL
37 Director Student Financial Aid ... Nick SALINAS

Schenectady County Community College (L)

78 Washington Avenue, Schenectady NY 12305
County: Schenectady FICE Identification: 006785
Unit ID: 195322
Telephone: (518) 381-1200 Carnegie Class: Assoc/HT-Mix Trad/Non
FAX Number: (518) 346-0379 Calendar System: Semester
URL: www.sunysccc.edu
Established: 1967 Annual Undergrad Tuition & Fees (In-District): $4,368
Enrollment: 6,126 Coed

Affiliation or Control: State/Local IRS Status: 501(c)3
Highest Offering: Associate Degree
Accreditation: M, ACFEI, MUS

01 President Dr. Steady MOONO
05 VP for Acad/Student Affs & Provost Dr. Penny A. HAYNES
10 Vice President of Administration Mr. Charles J. RICHARDSON
30 VP Development/External Affairs Ms. Marcia STEINER
103 VP Workforce Development/Cmty Educ Ms. Denise ZIESKE
13 Chief Information Officer Mr. Antione HARRISON
20 Assistant VP Academic Affairs Vacant
11 Assistant VP of Administration Ms. Susan BEAUDOIN
32 Dean of Students Mr. Stephen FRAGALE
37 Director of Financial Aid Mr. Mark BESSETTE
06 Registrar Ms. Cynthia ZIELASKOWSKI
07 Dir Admiss/Matriculated Enrollment Mr. David G. SAMPSON
08 Director Library Services Ms. Jacqueline KELEHER-HUGHES
90 Director of Academic Computing Vacant
18 Director of Facilities Mr. Anthony SCHWARTZ
91 Manager of Administrative Computing Vacant
36 Exec Dir SUNY Col/Career Coun Ctr Dr. DeShawn MCGARRITY
15 Human Resources Specialist Ms. Carianne TROTTA
88 Recruitment Specialist Ms. Sandra TROIANO
09 Coordinator Institutional Research Mr. Dale MILLER
28 Dir Educ Opportunity Pgms/Access Ms. Angela WEST-DAVIS
21 Controller Ms. Aimee S. WARFIELD
100 Chief of Staff Ms. Paula OHLHOUS
26 Director Marketing/Public Relations Mr. David REGAN WHITE
27 Public Rels/Publications Specialist Ms. Heather L. MEANEY

School of Visual Arts (A)

209 E 23rd Street, New York NY 10010-3994
County: New York FICE Identification: 007468
Unit ID: 197151
Telephone: (212) 592-2000 Carnegie Class: Spec-4-yr-Arts
FAX Number: (212) 725-3587 Calendar System: Semester
URL: www.sva.edu
Established: 1947 Annual Undergrad Tuition & Fees: $36,500
Enrollment: 4,408 Coed
Affiliation or Control: Proprietary IRS Status: Proprietary
Highest Offering: Master's
Accreditation: M, ART, CAEPN, CIDA

01 President David J. RHODES
03 Executive Vice President Anthony P. RHODES
05 Provost Jeffrey NESIN
10 Chief Financial Officer Gary SHILLET
32 Exec Dir of Student Affairs/Admiss Javier VEGA
26 Exec Director of External Relations Susan MODENSTEIN
13 Chief Information Officer Cosmin TOMESCU
06 Registrar Jason KOTH
07 Director Admission Matthew R. FARINA
35 Director of Student Affairs Bill MARTINO
08 Director Visual Arts Library Caitlin KILGALLEN
37 Director Financial Aid William BERRIOS
36 Director Career Development Angie WOJAK
30 Director Development/Alumni Affairs Jane NUZZO
19 Director Security Nick AGJMURATI
15 Exec Director of Human Resources Frank AGOSTA
09 Director of Institutional Research Jerold DAVIS
26 Director of Communications Joyce KAYE

Sh'or Yoshuv Rabbinical College (B)

1 Cedar Lawn Avenue, Lawrence NY 11559-1714
County: Nassau FICE Identification: 025059
Unit ID: 195438
Telephone: (516) 239-9002 Carnegie Class: Spec-4-yr-Faith
FAX Number: (516) 239-9003 Calendar System: Semester
URL: www.shoryoshuv.org
Established: 1963 Annual Undergrad Tuition & Fees: $9,460
Enrollment: 152 Male
Affiliation or Control: Independent Non-Profit IRS Status: 501(c)3
Highest Offering: Second Talmudic Degree
Accreditation: RABN

01 Dean Rabbi Naftalie JAEGER
05 Executive Director Mr. Moshe RUBIN
32 Director of Student Affairs Rabbi Elysha SANDLER
06 Registrar Mrs. Sheila FLEISCHER
37 Director SFA Rabbi Chaim MAJEROVIC

Siena College (C)

515 Loudon Road, Loudonville NY 12211-1462
County: Albany FICE Identification: 002816
Unit ID: 195474
Telephone: (518) 783-2300 Carnegie Class: Bac-A&S
FAX Number: (518) 783-4293 Calendar System: Semester
URL: www.siena.edu
Established: 1937 Annual Undergrad Tuition & Fees: $34,611
Enrollment: 3,176 Coed
Affiliation or Control: Independent Non-Profit IRS Status: 501(c)3
Highest Offering: Master's
Accreditation: M, CAEPN, SW

01 President Bro. F. Edward COUGHLIN, OFM
05 Vice President for Academic Affairs Dr. Margaret MADDEN
32 Vice President for Student Life Dr. Maryellen GILROY
10 Vice President for Finance & Admin Mr. Paul T. STEC
84 VP for Enrollment Management Mr. Ned J. JONES
30 VP for Development & Ext Affairs Mr. David B. SMITH
100 VP & Chief of Staff Mr. Michael J. HICKEY
41 VP & Director of Athletics Mr. John D'ARGENIO
13 Chief Information Officer Mr. Mark A. BERMAN
49 Dean of Liberal Arts Dr. Lara WHELAN
50 Dean of Business Dr. Charles SEIFERT
81 Dean of Science Dr. John CUMMINGS
124 Assoc VP Stdnt Retention & Success Dr. Tamara DURANT
37 Assoc Vice Pres Financial Aid Ms. Mary K. LAWYER
35 Assoc VP Student Life Mr. John R. FELIO
15 Asst VP for Human Resources Ms. Cynthia B. KING-LEROY
21 Asst VP for Finance & Admin Ms. Mary C. STRUNK
18 Asst VP for Facilities Management Mr. Mark FROST
19 Asst VP Stdnt Life/Dir Public Safe Mr. Michael PAPADOPOULOS
20 Asst VP Academic Affairs Ms. Laurie FAY
06 Registrar Mr. James SERBALIK
07 Director of Admissions Ms. Katie SZALDA
08 Dir of Library/Audio Visual Svcs Ms. Loretta EBERT
92 Director of Honors Program Dr. Lois K. DALY
35 Dean of Students Ms. Jabrina ROBINSON
39 Director of Community Living Mr. Adam CASLER
36 Director of Career Center Ms. Debra DELBELSO
26 Deputy Chief Information Officer Ms. Mary W. PARLETT-SWEENEY
42 Chaplain of the College Fr. Lawrence ANDERSON, OFM
38 Director of Counseling Center Dr. Nathan PRUITT
29 Director of Alumni Relations Ms. Mary Beth FINNERTY
09 Dir of Institutional Research Dr. Lee ALLARD
117 Dir of Risk Analysis/Project Mgmt Ms. Sandy SERBALIK
94 Dir Sr Thea Bowman Ctr for Women Ms. Beth DEANGELIS
23 Director of Health Services Ms. Carrie HOGAN
40 Bookstore Manager Mr. Richard IVES
110 Director of Development Mr. Brad R. BODMER
28 Dir of Damietta Cross-Cultural Ctr Ms. Christa J. GRANT
104 Director of Study Abroad/Intl Pgms Bro. Brian C. BELANGER, OFM
96 Dir of Auxiliary Svcs & Procurement Ms. Laura S. PARRY
43 Legal Services/General Counsel Ms. Rose SEGGOS
35 Director of Student Activities Ms. Karen KEIS
20 Director of Academic Programs Ms. Lynn ROGERS
121 Dir Student Success & Advising Ms. Holly CHEVERTON
20 Director HEOP Ms. Carol SANDOVAL
25 Dir Grants & Sponsored Pgms Ms. Sally SOUTHWICK
22 Title IX Coord/EEO Specialist Ms. Lois GOLAND
88 Dir Svcs/Students w Disabilities Mr. Robert BAHNY

Skidmore College (D)

815 N Broadway, Saratoga Springs NY 12866-1632
County: Saratoga FICE Identification: 002814
Unit ID: 195526
Telephone: (518) 580-5000 Carnegie Class: Bac-A&S
FAX Number: (518) 580-5936 Calendar System: Semester
URL: www.skidmore.edu
Established: 1911 Annual Undergrad Tuition & Fees: $50,834
Enrollment: 2,642 Coed
Affiliation or Control: Independent Non-Profit IRS Status: 501(c)3
Highest Offering: Master's
Accreditation: M, ART, CAEPT, SW

01 President Dr. Philip A. GLOTZBACH
05 VP Academic Affairs/Dean of Faculty Dr. Beau BRESLIN
10 Vice President Finance/Treasurer Mr. Michael D. WEST
111 Vice President for Advancement Vacant
15 Assoc VP Fin & Admin/Dir of HR Ms. Barbara E. BECK
32 Dean of Students and Vice President Ms. Cerri A. BANKS
07 VP & Dean of Admiss & Fin Aid Ms. Mary Lou W. BATES
71 Dean of Special Programs Mr. Paul CALHOUN
06 Registrar Mr. David DECONNO
20 Assoc Dean for Student Academics Dr. Ronald SEYB
28 Assoc Dn for Diversity/Faculty Affs Dr. Crystal D. MOORE
89 Dir of First Year Experience Ms. Janet CASEY
35 Assoc Dean Student Affs/Campus Life Ms. Mariel MARTIN
39 Director of Residential Life Ms. Ann Marie PRZYWARA
45 VP Strategic Plng & Inst Diversity Dr. Joshua C. WOODFORK
26 VP Communications & Mktg Vacant
09 Director of Institutional Research Mr. Joseph STANKOVICH
102 Dir Foundation & Corporate Rels Mr. Barry PRITZKER
46 Director of Sponsored Research Mr. Bill TOMLINSON
13 Dir Network & Technical Services Mr. Mark BAUER
105 Director Web Communications Mr. Andy CAMP
88 Dir Acad Pgm/Resid/Inst & Cmty Pgms Dr. Auden THOMAS
88 Dir Ctr for Leadership/Teach/Lrng Dr. Kristie A. FORD
22 Asst Dir EEO & Workforce Diversity Ms. Saytra GREEN
91 Director IT-Enterprise Systems Mr. Kevin L. CRIDER
104 Dir of Off-Campus Study & Exchanges Ms. Cori FILSON
44 Senior Director Donor Relations Ms. Mary L. SOLOMONS
30 Executive Director of Development Ms. Lori EASTMAN
29 Executive Dir Alumni Aff & Col Eve Mr. Michael SPOSILI
36 Exec Dir Career Development Center Ms. Kim CRABBE
37 Director of Financial Aid Ms. Beth POST-LUNDQUIST
38 Assoc Dean Stdnt Affs/Health & Well Dr. Julia C. ROUTBORT
21 Director of Business Services Ms. Christine KACZMAREK
23 Director of Health Services Ms. Patricia BOSEN
18 Director of Facilities Services Mr. Daniel RODECKER
19 Director of Campus Safety Mr. Timothy J. MUNRO
08 College Librarian Ms. Marta BRUNNER
96 Director of Purchasing Mrs. Carol N. SCHNITZER
42 Dir Religious & Spiritual Life Ms. Parker DIGGORY
24 Director of Media Services Mr. Michael G. FORBES
40 Assc Dir of Bus Svc & Dir Skid Shop Mr. Jon NEIL
88 Special Assistant to the President Ms. Jeanne M. SISSON
101 Board Coordinator Ms. Susan W. KOPPI

Sotheby's Institute of Art (E)

570 Lexington Ave, 15th Floor, New York NY 10022
County: New York Identification: 667007
Unit ID: 481094
Telephone: (212) 517-3929 Carnegie Class: Spec-4-yr-Arts
FAX Number: (212) 517-6568 Calendar System: Semester
URL: www.sothebysinstitute.com
Established: 2006 Annual Graduate Tuition & Fees: N/A
Enrollment: 173 Coed
Affiliation or Control: Proprietary IRS Status: Proprietary
Highest Offering: First Professional Degree; No Undergraduates
Accreditation: ART

01 Director Ms. Christine KUAN
06 Registrar Mr. David GASTON
08 Head Librarian Ms. Erin ELLIOTT
10 Chief Business Officer Ms. Lilly KOGAN
15 Director Personnel Services Ms. Christine KUAN
32 Chief Student Affairs/Student Life Ms. Sara MOORE

*State University of New York System Office (F)

State University Plaza, Albany NY 12246-0001
County: Albany FICE Identification: 008788
Unit ID: 195827
Telephone: (518) 320-1100 Carnegie Class: N/A
FAX Number: (518) 320-1561
URL: www.suny.edu

01 Chancellor Dr. Kristina JOHNSON
03 Provost & Executive Vice Chancellor Vacant
10 Vice Chancellor for Finance and CFO Ms. Eileen MCLOUGHLIN
05 Vice Provost & VC for Acad Affairs Dr. Elizabeth BRINGSJORD
46 Vice Chanc Research & Econ Devel Dr. Grace WANG
43 VC for Legal Affairs & General Coun Mr. Joseph PORTER
100 Chief of Staff Ms. Stacey HENGSTERMAN
17 Chief Ofcr Acad Health & Univ Hosp Dr. Ricardo AZZIZ
26 Asst VC for Communications Ms. Casey VATTIMO
88 Sr VC for Cmty Col & Educ Pipeline Ms. Johanna DUNCAN-POITIER
11 Assistant VC for Operations Ms. Kellie J. DUPUIS
88 Pres Faculty Council of Cmty Col Ms. Nina TAMROWSKI
18 VC for Cap Facil/GM Constr Fund Mr. Robert HAELEN
88 University Faculty Senate President Ms. Gwen KAY
20 Sr Assoc VC and Vice Prov Acad Affs Vacant
15 Vice Chancellor for Human Resources Mr. Curtis LLOYD
84 Assoc VC for Enrollment Management Vacant

*University at Albany, SUNY (G)

1400 Washington Avenue, Albany NY 12222-1000
County: Albany FICE Identification: 002835
Unit ID: 196060
Telephone: (518) 442-3300 Carnegie Class: DU-Highest
FAX Number: N/A Calendar System: Semester
URL: www.albany.edu
Established: 1844 Annual Undergrad Tuition & Fees (In-State): $9,223
Enrollment: 17,178 Coed
Affiliation or Control: State IRS Status: 501(c)3
Highest Offering: Doctorate
Accreditation: M, CAEPT, CLPSY, COPSY, IPSY, LIB, PH, PLNG, SCPSY, SPAA, SW

02 President Havidan RODRIGUEZ
05 Provost & Sr VP Academic Affairs James R. STELLAR
46 Vice President for Research James DIAS
10 Vice Pres Finance & Administration James VAN VOORST
30 VP Univ Dev & Exec Dir UA Found Fardin SANAI
26 VP Communications and Marketing Joseph A. BRENNAN
32 Vice President Student Affairs Michael N. CHRISTAKIS
41 Director of Athletics Mark BENSON
21 Assoc Vice President & Controller Kevin WILCOX
35 Assoc VP Student Affairs Ed ENGELBRIDE
11 Chief of Staff & Vice Prov Admin Bruce SZELEST
18 Associate VP Facilities John GIARRUSSO
84 VP & Assoc VP for Enrollment Mgmt Sandra STARKE
88 Vice Provost Acad Resource Plng Jack D. MAHONEY
28 Asst VP Diversity/Inclusion Tamra MINOR
88 AVP for Enrollment Management Robert K. ANDREA, JR.
20 Vice Prov & Dean Undergrad Educ Jeanette ALTARRIBA
49 Dean of College of Arts & Sciences Edelgard WULFERT
53 Dean School of Education Robert L. BANGERT-DROWNS
50 Dean School of Business Hany A. SHAWKY
69 Dean School of Public Health Philip C. NASCA
61 Dean of Criminal Justice William A. PRIDEMORE
80 Dean Rockefeller Col of Pub Affs R. Karl RETHEMEYER
70 Dean of School of Social Welfare Darrell P. WHEELER
54 Dean Engineering & Applied Sci Kim L. BOYER
58 Vice Provost & Dean Grad Studies Kevin WILLIAMS
08 Dean/Director of Libraries Mary F. CASSERLY
13 VP Chief Information Officer Simeon ANANOU
06 College Registrar Karen CHICO HURST
29 Exec Director Alumni Association Lee SERRAVILLO, JR.
45 VP Planning/Policy & Compliance Leanne WIRKKULA
88 Asst Vice Prov/Dir Advisement Ctr Suzanne K. FREED
43 Senior Counsel John H. REILLY
38 Director of Counseling & Psych Svcs Estela RIVERO
36 Director Career Services Philippe ABRAHAM
07 Director of Undergrad Admissions Timothy LEE
105 Director Web Services Fred DOYLE

40 VP Health Sci & Biomed Initiatives ... Laura SCHWEITZER
20 Sr Vice Prov/Assoc VP Acad Affs ... William B. HEDBERG
104 VP Ctr for Intl Educ/Global Strat ... Harvey CHARLES
88 Asst Vice Prov Faculty & Acad Affrs ... Benjamin WEAVER
106 Assoc Provost for Online Education ... Peter J. SHEA
88 Assoc Provost Program Development ... Ann Marie MURRAY

*State University of New York at Binghamton (A)

Vestal Parkway E, Box 6000, Binghamton NY 13902-6000
County: Broome — FICE Identification: 002836
Unit ID: 196079
Telephone: (607) 777-2000 — Carnegie Class: DU-Higher
FAX Number: (607) 777-4000 — Calendar System: Semester
URL: www.binghamton.edu
Established: 1946 — Annual Undergrad Tuition & Fees (In-State): $9,271
Enrollment: 16,913 — Coed
Affiliation or Control: State — IRS Status: 501(c)3
Highest Offering: Doctorate
Accreditation: M, CAEPT, CLPSY, CS, ENG, MUS, NURSE, @PHAR, SPAA, SW

02 President ... Dr. Harvey G. STENGER, JR.
100 Chief of Staff ... Mr. Terrence KANE
05 Exec VP for Academic Affs/Provost ... Dr. Donald NIEMAN
10 Vice President Operations ... Ms. JoAnn NAVARRO
32 Vice Pres Student Affairs ... Mr. Brian T. ROSE
46 Vice President for Research ... Dr. Bahgat SAMMAKIA
104 Exec Vice Prov Intl Initiatives ... Dr. Hari SRIHARI
45 Senior Vice Provost ... Dr. Michael F. MCGOFF
58 Vice Prov/Dean of Graduate School ... Dr. Susan STREHLE
18 Assoc VP Facilities Management ... Mr. Lawrence J. ROMA
35 Dean of Students ... Dr. April THOMPSON
102 Exec Dir of Bing Foundation ... Ms. Sheila DOYLE
26 Assoc Vice Pres Univ Comm/Mktg ... Mr. Gregory DELVISCIO
27 Chief Information Officer ... Ms. Sharon PITT
04 Exec Assistant to the President ... Ms. Laura L. O'NEIL
15 Asst Vice Pres for Human Resources ... Mr. Joseph P. SCHULTZ
07 Int Asst Vice Prov & Dir of Admiss ... Ms. Krista MEDIONTE-PHILIPS
08 Dean of Libraries ... Dr. Curtis KENDRICK
85 Director Intl Students/Scholar Svcs ... Ms. Patricia MARRAPESE
86 Director of State Relations ... Mr. Terrence KANE
37 Dir Financial Aid/Stdnt Records ... Mr. Dennis J. CHAVEZ
06 University Registrar ... Vacant
38 Director Health & Counseling ... Ms. Johann FIORE CONTE
36 Director Career Development Center ... Ms. Kelli SMITH
19 Director Public Safety ... Mr. Timothy FAUGHANAN
41 Director Athletics ... Mr. Patrick ELLIOTT
71 Director Educ Opportunities Prog ... Mr. Calvin GANTT
22 Dir Diversity/Equity & Inclusive ... Ms. Valerie J. HAMPTON
28 Director Multi-Cultural Res Ctr ... Ms. Nicole SIRJU-JOHNSON
92 Director Binghamton Univ Scholars ... Dr. William ZIEGLER
94 Exec Director of Women's Studies ... Ms. Dara J. SILBERSTEIN
96 Director of Purchasing ... Mr. Kenneth G. WASKIE
09 Asst Provost Institutional Research ... Ms. Nasrin FATIMA
49 Dean Arts & Science Harpur Col ... Dr. Elizabeth CHILTON
53 Dean School of Education ... Vacant
50 Dean School of Management ... Dr. Upinder S. DHILLON
54 Dn Watson Sch Engr/Applied Science ... Dr. Hari SRIHARI
66 Dean Decker School of Nursing ... Dr. Mario ORTIZ
31 Dean Community & Public Affairs ... Dr. Laura BRONSTEIN
106 Dir Center for Innov/Cont Educ ... Mr. Thomas KOWALIK
29 Sr Director Alumni Relations ... Vacant
43 Campus Atty/General Counsel ... Ms. Barbara SCARLETT

*University at Buffalo-SUNY (B)

3435 Main Street, Buffalo NY 14214
County: Erie — FICE Identification: 002837
Unit ID: 196088
Telephone: (716) 645-2000 — Carnegie Class: DU-Highest
FAX Number: N/A — Calendar System: Semester
URL: www.buffalo.edu
Established: 1846 — Annual Undergrad Tuition & Fees (In-State): $9,574
Enrollment: 29,796 — Coed
Affiliation or Control: State — IRS Status: 501(c)3
Highest Offering: Doctorate
Accreditation: M, ANEST, AUD, CACREP, CAEPT, CEA, CLPSY, CS, DA, DENT, DIETI, ENG, IPSY, LAW, LIB, MED, MT, NMT, NURSE, OT, PCSAS, PH, PHAR, PLNG, PSPSY, PTA, SP, SW

02 President ... Dr. Satish K. TRIPATHI
05 Provost/Exec VP Academic Affs ... Dr. Charles F. ZUKOSKI
10 Vice Pres Finance & Administration ... Ms. Laura E. HUBBARD
32 Vice President Student Affairs ... Dr. A. Scott WEBER
17 Vice President Health Sciences ... Dr. Michael CAIN
30 Vice Pres Philanthropy & Alumni Eng ... Vacant
46 Vice Pres for Research/Econ Develop ... Dr. Venu GOVINDARAJU
84 Vice Provost of Enrollment ... Dr. Lee H. MELVIN
15 Assoc VP Human Resources ... Mr. Mark COLDREN
58 Vice Provost Graduate Education ... Dr. Graham L. HAMMILL
20 Sr Vice Provost Acad Affairs ... Vacant
20 Vice Provost for Faculty Affairs ... Prof. Robert GRANFIELD
104 Vice Provost for International Educ ... Dr. Stephen C. DUNNETT
08 Assoc VP for Univ Libraries ... Mr. H. Austin BOOTH
13 VP & Chief Information Officer ... Mr. Brice BIBLE
37 Director Financial Aid ... Mr. John GOTTARDY
09 Assoc V Provost/Dir Inst Research ... Mr. Craig W. ABBEY
96 Asst Vice Pres Procurement Services ... Mr. Daniel VIVIAN
26 VP Univ Communications ... Ms. Nancy E. PATON
22 Vice Provost Equity & Inclusion ... Ms. Teresa A. MILLER
28 Dir Equity/Diversity/Inclusion ... Ms. Sharon E. NOLAN-WEISS
41 Director of Athletics ... Mr. Allen GREENE
91 Director Enterprise Application Svc ... Ms. Susan A. HUSTON
07 Director of UG Admissions ... Vacant
19 Chief of Police ... Mr. Gerald W. SCHOENLE, JR.
39 Director of Campus Living ... Ms. Andrea COSTANTINO
38 Director of Counseling Services ... Dr. Sharon L. MITCHELL
23 Director Health Services ... Ms. Susan M. SNYDER
36 Director Career Services ... Ms. Arlene F. KAUKUS
85 Director Intl Students/Scholar Svc ... Ms. Ellen A. DUSSOURD
40 Director University Bookstores ... Mr. Gregory NEUMANN
92 Admin Dir Univ Honors College ... Ms. Krista L. HANYPSIAK
29 Sr Director Dev & Alumni Events ... Mr. Jay R. FRIEDMAN
27 Director of Marketing ... Mr. David WEDEKINDT
20 Dean of Undergraduate Educ ... Vacant
48 Dean School Arch & Planning ... Dr. Robert SHIBLEY
49 Dean College of Arts/Sciences ... Dr. Robin G. SCHULZE
52 Dean School Dental Medicine ... Dr. Joseph ZAMBON
53 Dean Graduate Sch of Education ... Dr. Suzane ROSENBLITH
54 Dean School Engr/Applied Sci ... Dr. Liesl FOLKS
61 Dean School of Law ... Prof. Aviva ABRAMOVSKY
50 Dean School of Management ... Prof. Paul E. TESLUK
63 Dean School Medicine/Biomed Sci ... Dr. Michael E. CAIN
66 Dean School of Nursing ... Dr. Marsha L. LEWIS
67 Dean School Pharmacy/Pharm Sciences ... Dr. James O'DONNELL
76 Dean Sch Public Hlth/Hlth Prof ... Dr. Jean WACTAWSKI-WENDE
70 Dean School of Social Work ... Dr. Nancy J. SMYTH
06 Registrar ... Dr. Kara C. SAUNDERS

*State University of New York at Fredonia (C)

280 Central Avenue, Fredonia NY 14063-1136
County: Chautauqua — FICE Identification: 002844
Unit ID: 196158
Telephone: (716) 673-3111 — Carnegie Class: Masters/M
FAX Number: N/A — Calendar System: Semester
URL: www.fredonia.edu
Established: 1826 — Annual Undergrad Tuition & Fees (In-State): $8,089
Enrollment: 4,842 — Coed
Affiliation or Control: State — IRS Status: 501(c)3
Highest Offering: Master's
Accreditation: M, ART, CAEP, MUS, SP, SW, THEA

02 President ... Dr. Virginia S. HORVATH
05 Provost & VP for Acad Affairs ... Dr. Terry BROWN
10 VP for Finance and Admin ... Mr. Michael D. METZGER
32 Vice President for Student Affairs ... Dr. Cedric B. HOWARD
35 Assoc Vice Pres for Student Affairs ... Ms. Monica J. WHITE
111 Interim VP for Univ Advancement ... Ms. Betty GOSSETT
20 Assoc VP Curriculum/Assessment/Ac ... Dr. Lisa HUNTER
49 Dean College of Liberal Arts & Sci ... Dr. Andy KARAFA
88 VP Engagement & Economic Dev ... Dr. Kevin KEARNS
57 Dean College of Visual & Perf Arts ... Dr. Ralph BLASTING
58 Assoc Provost for Graduate Studies ... Dr. Judy HOROWITZ
50 Dean School of Business ... Vacant
53 Dean College of Education ... Dr. Christine E. GIVNER
102 Interim Director Corp/Univ Advance ... Ms. Betty GOSSETT
18 Director Facilities Services ... Mr. Kevin P. CLOOS
06 Registrar ... Mr. Scott D. SAUNDERS
07 Director of Admissions ... Mr. Cory M. BEZEK
37 Director Financial Aid ... Mr. Daniel M. TRAMUTA
08 Director Library Services ... Mr. Randolph Lee GADIKIAN
09 Dir Institutional Research/Planning ... Dr. Xiao Y. ZHANG
36 Director of Career Development ... Ms. Tracy COLLINGWOOD
84 Assoc Vice Pres for Enrollment Mgmt ... Mr. Daniel M. TRAMUTA
19 Chief University Police ... Ms. Ann K. BURNS
39 Director Residence Life ... Mrs. Kathy FORSTER
41 Athletic Director ... Vacant
23 Director of Health Services ... Ms. Deborah A. DIBBLE
38 Director Counseling Center ... Dr. Tracy L. STENGER
90 Academic Information Technology ... Mr. Stephen J. RIEKS
15 Director of Human Resources ... Mr. Michael D. DALEY
26 Director of Public Relations ... Vacant
85 Director of Intercultural Center ... Dr. Khristian J. KING
92 Director of Honors Program ... Dr. David KINKELA
94 Coordinator of Women's Studies ... Mr. Jeffry J. IOVANNONE
96 Director of Purchasing ... Mrs. Shari K. MILLER
28 Chief Diversity Officer ... Dr. William BOERNER
29 Director Alumni Affairs ... Ms. Patricia A. FERALDI
04 Administrative Asst to President ... Mrs. Denise M. SZALKOWSKI
104 Director Office International Educ ... Ms. Naomi BALDWIN
105 Web Content Manager ... Mr. Jonathan WOOLSON
106 Online Learning Coordinator ... Ms. Lisa MELOHUSKY
13 Chief Info Technology Officer (CIO) ... Mr. Stephen RIEKS

*State University of New York at New Paltz (D)

1 Hawk Drive, New Paltz NY 12561-2443
County: Ulster — FICE Identification: 002846
Unit ID: 196176
Telephone: (845) 257-7869 — Carnegie Class: Masters/L
FAX Number: (845) 257-3009 — Calendar System: Semester
URL: www.newpaltz.edu
Established: 1823 — Annual Undergrad Tuition & Fees (In-State): $7,754
Enrollment: 7,751 — Coed
Affiliation or Control: State — IRS Status: 501(c)3
Highest Offering: Beyond Master's But Less Than Doctorate
Accreditation: M, ART, CAEPN, ENG, MUS, SP, THEA

02 President ... Dr. Donald P. CHRISTIAN
100 Chief of Staff/VP Communication ... Ms. Shelly A. WRIGHT
05 Provost ... Dr. Lorin Basden ARNOLD
10 Vice Pres Administration & Finance ... Ms. Michele HALSTEAD
30 VP Development/Alumni Relations ... Ms. Erica MARKS
32 Student Affairs Vice President ... Dr. Stephanie BLAISDELL
84 Vice Pres Enrollment Management ... Mr. L. David EATON
58 Assoc Provost/Dean Graduate School ... Dr. Laurel GARRICK DUHANEY
13 Asst Vice Pres Tech/Info Systems ... Mr. John REINA
21 Asst Vice President Administration ... Ms. Julieta MAJAK
114 Asst VP Budget ... Ms. Julie WALSH
09 Asst VP Inst Research/Planning ... Ms. Lucy WALKER
18 Asst VP Facilities Management ... Mr. John SHUPE
53 Dean of Education ... Dr. Michael ROSENBERG
57 Dean Fine & Performing Arts ... Dr. Jennifer MOKREN
49 Dean Liberal Arts & Sciences ... Dr. Laura BARRETT
50 Dean School of Business ... Dr. Kristin BACKHAUS
54 Dean Science and Engineering ... Dr. Daniel FREEDMAN
07 Dean of Admissions ... Ms. Lisa JONES
08 Dean Sojourner Truth Library ... Mr. W. Mark COLVSON
86 Ex Dir Compliance/Camp Clm/Title IX ... Ms. Tanhena PACHECO DUNN
07 Assoc Dean/Dir Freshmen Admissions ... Ms. Kimberly STRANO
15 Director Human Resources ... Ms. Tanhena PACHECO DUNN
37 Director of Financial Aid ... Ms. Maureen LOHAN-BREMER
06 Registrar ... Ms. Laura SCHULTZ
29 Director Alumni Relations ... Ms. Shana CIRCE
38 Director Student Counseling ... Dr. Gweneth LLOYD
26 Media Relations Manager ... Ms. Melissa KACZMAREK
96 Director of Purchasing/Procurement ... Mr. David FARBANIEC
19 Director Security/Safety ... Mr. David DUGATKIN
41 Athletic Director ... Mr. Stuart ROBINSON

*State University of New York at Oneonta (E)

108 Ravine Parkway, Oneonta NY 13820-4015
County: Otsego — FICE Identification: 002847
Unit ID: 196185
Telephone: (607) 436-3500 — Carnegie Class: Masters/S
FAX Number: N/A — Calendar System: Semester
URL: www.oneonta.edu
Established: 1889 — Annual Undergrad Tuition & Fees (In-State): $7,932
Enrollment: 6,119 — Coed
Affiliation or Control: State — IRS Status: 501(c)3
Highest Offering: Master's
Accreditation: M, AAFCS, CAEPN, DIETD, DIETI, IPSY, MUS, THEA

02 President ... Dr. Nancy KLENIEWSKI
04 Exec Assistant to the President ... Ms. Colleen E. BRANNAN
05 Provost/Vice Pres Academic Affairs ... Dr. James MACKIN
10 Vice Pres Finance/Administration ... Mr. Todd D. FOREMAN
32 Vice President Student Development ... Dr. Franklin D. CHAMBERS
30 Vice President College Advancement ... Mr. Paul J. ADAMO
09 Assoc Prov Inst Assessment & Eff ... Vacant
20 Assoc Provost Academic Programs ... Dr. Eileen MORGAN-ZAYACHEK
83 Interim Dean of Arts and Humanities ... Dr. Richard LEE
50 Dean School of Econ & Business ... Dr. Wade THOMAS
53 Dean School of Educ & Human Ecology ... Dr. Jan BOWERS
81 Dean School of Nat/Math Sciences ... Dr. Venkat SHARMA
83 Interim Dean of Social Science ... Dr. Tracy ALLEN
58 Director of Graduate Studies ... Mr. Patrick J. MENTE
84 Chief Enrollment Services Officer ... Mr. Kevin JENSEN
35 Assoc Vice Pres Student Development ... Ms. Amanda FINCH
18 Assoc Vice Pres Facilities/Safety ... Mr. Thomas M. RATHBONE
19 Chief of Police ... Mr. Daniel P. CHAMBERS
15 Sr Exec Employee Services Officer ... Ms. Lisa M. WENCK
26 Exec Director of Communications ... Mr. Hal S. LEGG
07 Director of Admissions ... Ms. Karen A. BROWN
29 Director of Alumni Engagement ... Ms. Laura MADELONE LINCOLN
88 Director Advancement Services ... Mr. Michael SULLIVAN
44 Director Fund for Oneonta ... Ms. Kim NOSTROM
41 Athletic Director ... Ms. Tracey M. RANIERI
21 Budget Control Officer/Budget Dir ... Ms. Julie PISCITELLO
25 Director Business Services ... Ms. Betty M. TIRADO
36 Dir Career Dev/Student Emp Svcs ... Dr. Amy BENEDICT
13 Dir Computing Ctr/Chief Info Ofcr ... Dr. Karlis KAUGARS
90 Director IT Customer Support ... Mr. Steven J. MANISCALCO
23 Dir Health & Counseling Services . Dr. Melissa A. FALLON-KORB
24 Director Creative Media Services ... Mr. David W. GEASEY
37 Associate Director Financial Aid ... Ms. Barbara PLEDGER
09 Dir Institutional Research ... Mr. Ernesto HENRIQUEZ
85 Director of International Education ... Dr. Vernon C. LARSON
89 Director Orientation/First Year Exp ... Ms. Monica C. GRAU
96 Procurement/Travel Office Manager ... Ms. Terri THOMAS
06 College Registrar ... Ms. Maureen P. ARTALE
39 Director Residential Community Life ... Ms. Michele LUETTGER
93 Director Special Programs/EOP ... Ms. Lynda D. BASSETTE-FARONE
28 Chief Diversity Officer ... Mr. Terrence MITCHELL
22 Affirmative Action Officer ... Mr. Andrew STAMMEL

*Stony Brook University (F)

310 Administration Building, Stony Brook NY 11794-0701
County: Suffolk — FICE Identification: 002838
Unit ID: 196097
Telephone: (631) 632-6265 — Carnegie Class: DU-Highest
FAX Number: (631) 632-6621 — Calendar System: Semester
URL: www.stonybrook.edu
Established: 1957 — Annual Undergrad Tuition & Fees (In-State): $8,999
Enrollment: 25,272 — Coed

Affiliation or Control: State IRS Status: 501(c)3
Highest Offering: Doctorate
Accreditation: M, ARCPA, CAATE, CAEPN, CLPSY, COARC, COARCP, CS, DENT, DIETI, ENG, IPSY, JOUR, MED, MIDWF, MT, NMT, NURSE, OT, PCSAS, PH, POLYT, PTA, RADDOS, SW

02 President/CEO Dr. Samuel L. STANLEY
05 Provost Dr. Michael BERNSTEIN
63 Sr VP HSC/Dean School of Medicine Dr. Kenneth KAUSHANSKY
46 Vice President Research Dr. Richard REEDER
32 Vice President Student Affairs Dr. Peter M. BAIGENT
10 VP Finance Mr. Lyle GOMES
30 Sr VP University Advancement Mr. Dexter BAILEY
54 VP Econ Dev/Dean Engr/Applied Sci Dr. Yacov SHAMASH
100 SVP Govt & Community Relations Ms. Judith GREIMAN
21 Associate VP for Budget Mr. Mark MACIULAITIS
11 Sr VP for Administration Mr. Robert MEGNA
26 VP Comm & Mktg/Chief Comm Officer Mr. Nicholas SCIBETTA
39 Asst Vice Pres Campus Residences Dr. Dallas BAUMAN
17 CEO University Hospital Dr. Reuven PASTERNAK
84 Assoc Prov Enrollment/Retent Mgmt Mr. Rodney MORRISON
13 CIO Ms. Melissa WOO
45 Vice President Strategic Initiative Dr. Matthew WHELAN
43 Senior Counsel in Charge Ms. Susan BLUM
49 Dean College Arts & Sciences Dr. Sacha KOPP
88 Dean School of Marine & Atmos Sci Dr. Lawrence SWANSON
52 Dean School of Dental Medicine Dr. Mary R. TRUHLAR
68 Dean Div Physical Educ & Athletics Mr. Shawn R. HEILBRON
58 Dean Grad Sch & Sch of Prof Develop Dr. Charles TABER
76 Dean School Health Technology Mgmt Dr. Craig LEHMANN
35 Interim Dean of Students Dr. Jerrold STEIN
66 Dean School of Nursing Dr. Lee XIPPOLITOS
70 Dean School of Social Welfare Dr. Jacqueline MONDROS
08 Dean of Libraries Dr. Constantia CONSTANINOU
86 VP Government & Community Relations Ms. Judith GREIMAN
88 Exec Dir LI State Vets Home Mr. Fred SGANGA
19 Chief of Police Mr. Robert LENAHAN
15 VP Human Resource Svcs Ms. Lynn JOHNSON
28 Dir Diversity/AA/Equal Employ Oppty Ms. Marjolie LEONARD
09 AVP Inst Rsrch/Plng/Effectiveness Dr. Braden J. HOSCH
85 Dean International Programs Dr. Jun LIU
102 Exec Dir of Stony Brook Foundation Mr. Dexter A. BAILEY
29 Director Alumni Relations Mr. Matthew COLSON
23 Director University Health Services Dr. Rachel BERGESON
38 Int Dir Counseling/Psych Services Dr. Julian PESSIER
36 Director Career Placement Center Ms. Marianna SAVOCA
06 Registrar Ms. Diane BELLO
37 Financial Aid/Scholarships Ms. Jacqueline PASCARIELLO
50 Dean College of Business Dr. Manuel LONDON
27 University Media Relations Officer Ms. Lauren SHEPROW
96 Director of Purchasing/Procurement Mr. James FABIAN
60 Dean School of Journalism Mr. Howard SCHNEIDER
04 Executive Asst to President Ms. Carol LONDOIRO

*SUNY Downstate Medical Center (A)

450 Clarkson Avenue, Brooklyn NY 11203-2098
County: Kings FICE Identification: 002839
Unit ID: 196255
Telephone: (718) 270-1000 Carnegie Class: Spec-4-yr-Med
FAX Number: (718) 270-4092 Calendar System: Semester
URL: www.downstate.edu
Established: 1860 Annual Undergrad Tuition & Fees (In-State): N/A
Enrollment: 1,858 Coed
Affiliation or Control: State IRS Status: 501(c)3
Highest Offering: Doctorate
Accreditation: M, ANEST, ARCPA, DMS, MED, MIDWF, NURSE, OT, PH, PTA

02 President Dr. Wayne J. RILEY
10 Chief Financial Officer Mr. Thomas J. GRAY
11 COO/Exec VP Administration Vacant
05 Senior Vice President for Academic Dr. Pascal IMPERATO
32 VP Student Affairs/Dean of Students Dr. Jeffrey PUTMAN
30 AVP Institutional Advancement Ms. Ellen WATSON
13 Chief Information Officer Mr. Roy SOOKHOO
07 Director of Admissions Dr. Shushawna DEOLIVEIRA
06 Registrar Ms. Anne SHONBRUN
37 Director Student Financial Aid Ms. Farah BURNETT
26 Chief Public Relations Officer Ms. Ellen WATSON
04 Executive Asst to President Ms. Yesenia PEREZ
08 Head Librarian Dr. Richard WINANT
09 Director of Institutional Research Ms. Charis NG
15 Director Personnel Services Ms. Judith DORSEY
18 Chief Facilities/Physical Plant Ms. Yvonne KIELB
19 Director Security/Safety Mr. Vincent CARDOZO
22 Dir Affirm Action/EEO/Diversity Mr. Kevin ANTOINE
25 Chief Contracts/Grants Admin Ms. Maureen CRYSTAL
29 Director Alumni Relations Mr. Eric SHOEN
39 Director Student Housing Ms. Margaret O'SULLIVAN
43 Dir Legal Services/General Counsel Mr. Kevin O'MARA
45 Chief Institutional Planning Ms. Dorothy FYFE
53 Dean College of Nursing Dr. Lori A. ESCALLIER
86 Director Government Relations Mr. Michael HARRELL
90 Director Academic Computing Mr. Gregory CONYERS
96 Director of Purchasing Mr. Martin DEANE
113 Bursar Mr. Peter LJUTIC
100 Chief of Staff Dr. Keydron GUINN
108 Director Institutional Assessment Dr. Bonnie GRANAT
36 Director Student Placement Vacant

*State University of New York Upstate Medical University (B)

750 E Adams Street, Syracuse NY 13210-2375
County: Onondaga FICE Identification: 002840
Unit ID: 196307
Telephone: (315) 464-5540 Carnegie Class: Spec-4-yr-Med
FAX Number: (315) 464-8823 Calendar System: Semester
URL: www.upstate.edu
Established: 1834 Annual Undergrad Tuition & Fees (In-State): N/A
Enrollment: 1,480 Coed
Affiliation or Control: State IRS Status: 501(c)3
Highest Offering: Doctorate
Accreditation: M, ARCPA, COARC, DENT, DMOLS, IPSY, MED, MT, NURSE, PAST, PERF, PH, PTA, RAD, RTT

02 President Dr. Danielle L. LARAQUE-ARENA
63 Dean College of Medicine Dr. Julio LICINIO
17 Interim CEO University Hospital Mr. Steven SCOTT
10 Vice President Finance & Management Mr. Eric SMITH
05 Vice President Academic Affairs Dr. Lynn CLEARY
46 Dean College Graduate Studies Dr. Mark SCHMITT
32 Dean Student Affairs Dr. Julie R. WHITE
102 Exec Director HSC Foundation Ms. Eileen PEZZI
66 Interim Dean College of Nursing Dr. Lynn CLEARY
76 Int Dean College Health Profession Dr. Katherine BEISSNER
06 Registrar/Dir Inst Research Ms. Jennifer MARTIN TSE
25 Vice President for Research Dr. David AMBERG
29 Director of Medical Alumni Affairs Mr. Paul W. NORCROSS
15 Assoc VP Human Resources Mr. Eric FROST
13 Chief Information Officer Ms. Teresa J. WAGNER
08 Director of Libraries Ms. Christina POPE
28 Dir Diversity & Affirmative Action Vacant
07 Assoc Dean Admissions/Financial Aid Ms. Jennifer C. WELCH
18 Chief Facilities/Physical Plant Mr. Bob LOTKOWICTZ
21 Assistant Vice President Finance Mr. David ANTHONY
37 Director Student Financial Aid Mr. Michael ALSHEIMER

*SUNY Broome Community College (C)

PO Box 1017, Binghamton NY 13902-1017
County: Broome FICE Identification: 002862
Unit ID: 189547
Telephone: (607) 778-5000 Carnegie Class: Assoc/HT-High Trad
FAX Number: (607) 778-5310 Calendar System: Semester
URL: www.sunybroome.edu
Established: 1946 Annual Undergrad Tuition & Fees (In-District): $4,951
Enrollment: 5,926 Coed
Affiliation or Control: State/Local IRS Status: 501(c)3
Highest Offering: Associate Degree
Accreditation: M, ADNUR, CAHIIM, DH, ENGT, MAC, MLTAD, PTAA, RAD

02 President Dr. Kevin DRUMM
05 Exec VP/Chief Academic Officer Dr. Francis BATTISTI
11 Vice Pres Admin/Financial Affairs Mr. Michael SULLIVAN
32 VP Student Development & CDO Dr. Carol ROSS
10 Associate Vice Pres & Controller Ms. Jeanette TILLOTSON
50 Assoc VP & Dean Bus/Public Svcs Ms. Elizabeth MOLLEN
76 Assoc VP & Dean of Health Sciences Dr. Amy BRANDT
49 Assoc VP & Dean of Liberal Arts Dr. Michael KINNEY
51 Dir Continuing Educ & Workforce Dev Ms. Janet HERTZOG
81 Interim Assoc Vice Pres & Dean STEM Mr. Kenneth MANSFIELD
35 Dean of Students Mr. Scott SCHUHERT
102 Executive Director BCC Foundation Ms. Catherine R. WILLIAMS
08 Director Learning Resource Center Ms. Robin PETRUS
07 Director of Admissions Mr. Jesse WELLS
15 Human Resources Officer Ms. Lynn FEDORCHAK
06 Registrar Mr. Martin GUZZI
36 Director of Placement Services Vacant
108 Dean Institutional Effectiveness Dr. Sesime ADANU
18 Interim Campus Operations Director Mr. David LIGEIKIS
37 Director of Financial Aid Ms. Laura HODEL
13 Dir Information Technology Services Mr. John PETKASH
23 Director of Health Services Mr. Joseph O'CONNOR
25 Director of Sponsored Programs Ms. Shelli CORDISCO
41 Director of Athletics Mr. Brett CARTER
19 Dir of Campus Safety & Security Mr. Joseph O'CONNOR
29 Director Alumni Affairs Ms. Regina ALFIERI
40 Bookstore Manager Mr. Joseph KOPYAR
88 Dir Educational Opportunity Pgm Ms. Venessa RODRIGUEZ
96 Director of Purchasing Mr. Randy CAMPBELL
26 Dir of Marketing/Communications Mr. Jesse WELLS
85 Ast Dir Intl Admiss/Intl Stdnt Stds Ms. Susan WELLINGTON
104 Coordinator Study Abroad Program Ms. Maria BASUALDO
38 Student Counseling Ms. Mary MCCARTHY
101 Secretary of the Institution/Board Ms. Patricia G. O'DAY
22 Dir Affirmative Action/EEO Ms. Paige SEDLACEK
39 Director Student Housing Ms. Amy ZIEZIULA
04 Administrative Asst to President Ms. Patricia O'DAY
84 Exec Enrollment Management Officer Mr. Jesse WELLS

*State University of New York, The College at Brockport (D)

350 New Campus Drive, Brockport NY 14420-2914
County: Monroe FICE Identification: 002841
Unit ID: 196121
Telephone: (585) 395-2211 Carnegie Class: Masters/L
FAX Number: (585) 395-2401 Calendar System: Semester
URL: www.brockport.edu
Established: 1835 Annual Undergrad Tuition & Fees (In-State): $7,928
Enrollment: 8,161 Coed
Affiliation or Control: State IRS Status: 501(c)3
Highest Offering: Master's
Accreditation: M, CAATE, CACREP, CAEP, CS, DANCE, EXSC, NRPA, NURSE, SPAA, SW, THEA

02 President Dr. Heidi R. MACPHERSON
05 Int Provost & VP Academic Affairs Dr. James HAYNES
10 VP Administration & Finance Dr. James A. WILLIS
32 VP Enrollment Mgmt/Student Affairs Dr. Kathryn WILSON
111 VP Advancement Mr. Michael ANDRIATCH
20 Vice Provost Dr. Eileen DANIEL
28 Chief Diversity Officer Dr. Cephas ARCHIE
18 Director of Physical Plant Mr. Kevin RICE
21 Asst VP Finance & Management Ms. Karen M. RIOTTO
13 CIO Mr. Robert CUSHMAN
49 Dean Arts and Sciences Dr. Jose MALIEKAL
50 Dean Business and Management Dr. Joyendu BHADURY
53 Dean Educ/Health & Hum Svcs Dr. Thomas J. HERNANDEZ
14 Director of Info Tech System Mr. David R. STRASENBURGH
07 Dir of Undergrad Admissions Mr. Robert WYANT
56 Exec Dir Brockport Metro Center Dr. Celia WATT
58 Dir Center for Grad Studies Ms. Kathleen H. GROVES
104 Dir International Education Dr. George SIPOS
26 Chief Communications Officer Mr. David MIHALYOV
37 Dir Financial Aid & Enrollment Svcs Mr. J. Scott ATKINSON
36 Director of Career Services Ms. Jill WESLEY
19 Int Chief of University Police Mr. John ARMITAGE
06 College Registrar Mr. Peter DOWE
15 Director of Human Resources Ms. Wendy CRANMER
22 Affirmative Action Officer Mr. Ryan REYNOLDS
23 Director Student Health/Counseling Ms. Elizabeth S. CARUSO
39 Dir Res Life/Assoc Dean of Students Dr. Sara KELLY
41 Director of Athletics Mr. Erick HART
25 Director of Grants Development Ms. Patricia WILLIAMS
92 Director of Honors Program Dr. Donna M. KOWAL
09 Dir Inst Research & Analysis Dr. Jeffrey T. LASHBROOK
96 Director of Procurement & Payment Mr. Mark W. STACY
94 Dir of Women and Gender Studies Dr. Barbara LESAVOY
29 Director Alumni Relations Mr. Kerry GOTHAM
04 Assistant to the President Ms. Julie A. PRUSS
08 Directory of Library Services Dr. Mary Jo ORZECH
86 Director Government Relations Mr. David MIHALYOV
88 Title IX & College Compliance Ofcr Ms. Denine CARR

*State University of New York College at Buffalo (E)

1300 Elmwood Avenue, Buffalo NY 14222-1091
County: Erie FICE Identification: 002842
Unit ID: 196130
Telephone: (716) 878-4000 Carnegie Class: Masters/L
FAX Number: (716) 878-3039 Calendar System: Semester
URL: www.buffalostate.edu
Established: 1871 Annual Undergrad Tuition & Fees (In-State): $7,701
Enrollment: 10,330 Coed
Affiliation or Control: State IRS Status: 501(c)3
Highest Offering: Master's
Accreditation: M, ART, CAEPN, CIDA, DIETC, DIETD, ENGT, FEPAC, JOUR, MUS, NAIT, SP, SW, THEA

02 President Dr. Katherine S. CONWAY-TURNER
100 Chief of Staff/Secretary to Board Dr. Bonita R. DURAND
05 Provost Dr. Melanie L. PERREAULT
10 Vice President Finance & Management Mr. Michael F. LEVINE
32 Interim Vice Pres Student Affairs Dr. Daniel C. VELEZ
111 VP Inst Advance & Found Exec Dir Dr. Susanne P. BAIR
28 Chief Diversity Officer Dr. Karen A. CLINTON JONES
13 VP and Chief Information Officer Dr. David M. DEMERS
19 Chief University Police Mr. Peter M. CAREY
84 Associate Vice Pres Enrollment Mgmt Ms. Erin R. ALONZO
21 Assoc Vice President & Comptroller Mr. James A. THOR
15 Assoc VP Human Resource Management Ms. Susan J. EARSHEN
20 Special Adv to Provost for Educ Dr. John F. SISKAR
88 Asst to the Provost/Inst Effect Mr. Bradley J. FUSTER
35 Assoc VP Student Affs/Dean of Stdnt Dr. Charles B. KENYON
14 Assoc Vice Pres Computing Services Ms. Judith B. BASINSKI
108 Interim Associate Provost Dr. Amitra WALL
26 Assoc VP College Relations Mr. Timothy J. WALSH
08 Assoc VP RITE Ms. Maryruth F. GLOGOWSKI
30 Assoc VP Development Mr. R. Scott BURNS
86 AVP Govt Relations/Alumni Director Mr. William J. BENFANTI
51 Assoc VP Continuing Prof Studies Dr. Margaret A. SHAW-BURNETT
53 Dean School of Education Dr. Wendy A. PATERSON
49 Dean School of Arts & Humanities Mr. Benjamin C. CHRISTY
83 Dean Natural & Social Sciences Dr. Mark W. SEVERSON
107 Dean School of the Professions Dr. James MAYROSE
58 Interim Dean Graduate School Dr. Kevin J. MILLER
88 Resident Manager Chartwells Mr. Glenn R. BUCELLO
88 Director Liberty Partnership Ms. Patrice A. CATHEY
88 Director STEP Mr. Darryl CARTER
88 Director Upward Bound Mr. Donald A. PATTERSON
36 Director of Career Development Ms. Stephanie B. ZUCKERMAN-AVILES
27 Director Public Relations Mr. Jerod T. DAHLGREN
07 Interim Director Admissions Vacant
06 Registrar Dr. Nigel R. MARRINER
37 Director of Financial Aid Ms. Connie F. COOKE
39 Director Residence Life Mr. Michael A. HEFLIN
113 Director of Student Accounts Ms. Susan F. WRIGHT
38 Director Counseling Center Dr. Joan L. MCCOOL
41 Director Intercollegiate Athletics Mr. Jerry S. BOYES
88 Director New Student/Family Program Mr. David W. COX

23 Director Student Health Center .... Vacant
35 Director Student Life .... Ms. Sarah M. YOUNG
85 Director Intl Student Affairs .... Dr. Jean F. GOUNARD
88 Director Accounts Payable & Travel .... Mr. Robert L. BAUMET
25 AVP for Sponsored Program Operation .... Mrs. Donna L. SCUTO
88 Director Special Events & Protocol .... Ms. Kathyrn C. NEESON
18 Director Campus Services .... Mr. Terry M. HARDING
114 Director Budget & Internal Controls .... Ms. Rebecca J. SCHENK
09 Director Institutional Research .... Mr. Yves M. GACHETTE
29 Director of Alumni Affairs .... Ms. Mary-Jo JAGORD
88 Director Parking Services .... Ms. Jayme S. RITER
96 Asst to Comptroller for Procurement .... Mr. Steven M. OLSEN
40 Manager BSC Bookstore .... Ms. Lynn M. PUMA
88 Director Campbell Student Union .... Mrs. Sarah M. VELEZ
22 Director Assessibility Service .... Ms. Lisa T. MORRISON-FRONCKOWIAK
88 Director Judicial Affairs .... Dr. Latonia D. MARSH
88 Manager Design & Construction .... Mr. Steven E. SHAFFER

*State University of New York College at Cortland (A)

PO Box 2000, Cortland NY 13045-0900
County: Cortland
FICE Identification: 002843
Unit ID: 196149
Telephone: (607) 753-2011
Carnegie Class: Masters/L
FAX Number: (607) 753-5999
Calendar System: Semester
URL: www.cortland.edu
Established: 1868
Annual Undergrad Tuition & Fees (In-State): $8,106
Enrollment: 6,926
Coed
Affiliation or Control: State
IRS Status: 501(c)3
Highest Offering: Master's
Accreditation: M, CAATE, CAEPN, NRPA, PH, @SP

02 President .... Dr. Erik J. BITTERBAUM
05 Provost .... Dr. Mark PRUS
32 Vice Pres Student Affairs .... Mr. C. Gregory SHARER
111 Vice Pres Inst Advancement .... Mr. Peter PERKINS
10 Vice Pres for Finance & Admin .... Mr. David DURYEA
21 Assoc VP for Finance .... Vacant
13 Assoc Provost for Info Resources .... Ms. Amy BERG
18 Assoc VP Facilities Management .... Ms. Nasrin PARVIZI
20 Assoc Prov for Academic Affairs .... Dr. Carol VAN DER KARR
84 Asst Vice Pres Enrollment Mgmt .... Mr. Mark YACAVONE
04 Exec Assistant to the President .... Dr. Virginia LEVINE
09 Director Inst Rsrch/Assessment .... Mr. Stephen CUNNINGHAM
08 Director of Libraries .... Vacant
06 Registrar .... Mr. Thomas HANFORD
36 Director of Career Services .... Mr. John SHIRLEY
15 Asst VP Human Resources .... Mr. Gary EVANS
29 Int Director Alumni Engagement .... Ms. Erin BOYLAN
38 Dir Counseling/Student Devel .... Dr. Carolyn BERSHAD
37 Dir of Student Financial Aid .... Ms. Karen GALLAGHER
19 Chief of University Police .... Mr. Mark DEPAULL
91 Director Admin Computing Svcs .... Mr. Daniel SIDEBOTTOM
90 Director Campus Technology Services .... Ms. Lisa KAHLE
107 Dean Professional Studies .... Dr. John COTTONE
49 Dean Arts & Sciences .... Dr. Bruce MATTINGLY
26 Director of Communications .... Mr. Frederic PIERCE
53 Dean of Education .... Dr. Andrea LACHANCE
93 Director Educational Oppty Program .... Dr. Lewis ROSENGARTEN
92 Director of Honors Program .... Dr. Frank ROSSI
94 Coordinator of Women's Studies .... Dr. Jena CURTIS
96 Director of Purchasing .... Ms. Melissa FOX
22 Affirmative Action Officer .... Ms. Dawn NORCROSS
28 Director Multicult Life/Diversity .... Ms. AnnaMaria CIRRINCIONE
41 Athletic Director .... Mr. Mike URTZ
104 Director International Programs .... Dr. Mary SCHLARB
25 Assoc Dir Research & Sponsored Pgms .... Mr. Thomas FRANK
39 Director Student Housing .... Mr. Ralph CARRASQUILLO
07 Director of Admissions .... Mr. Mark YACAVONE

*State University of New York College at Geneseo (B)

1 College Circle, Geneseo NY 14454-1401
County: Livingston
FICE Identification: 002845
Unit ID: 196167
Telephone: (585) 245-5000
Carnegie Class: Masters/S
FAX Number: (585) 245-5005
Calendar System: Semester
URL: www.geneseo.edu
Established: 1871
Annual Undergrad Tuition & Fees (In-State): $8,176
Enrollment: 5,699
Coed
Affiliation or Control: State
IRS Status: 501(c)3
Highest Offering: Master's
Accreditation: M, CAEPN

02 President .... Dr. Denise A. BATTLES
05 Provost .... Dr. Stacey ROBERTSON
20 Interim Associate Provost .... Dr. Kenneth KALLIO
11 Vice President Administration .... Dr. James B. MILROY
32 Vice Pres for Student & Campus Life .... Dr. Robert A. BONFIGLIO
111 VP of College Advancement .... Ms. K. Johnson BOWLES
84 Vice Pres Enrollment Mgmt .... Dr. Meaghan ARENA
10 Assoc VP Administration/Controller .... Mr. Brice M. WEIGMAN
26 Chief Comm & Marketing Officer .... Ms. Gail GLOVER
15 Asst Vice Pres Human Resources .... Ms. Julie A. BRIGGS
29 Director of Alumni & Parent Rels .... Ms. Ronna BOSKO
20 Asst Provost Curriculum & Assess .... Dr. Savitri V. IYER
35 Dean of Students .... Dr. Leonard SANCILIO
07 Director of Admissions .... Ms. Kimberly HARVEY
08 Library Director .... Mr. Benjamin RAWLINS
13 Director Computing/Info Technology .... Ms. Susan E. CHICHESTER
37 Director of Financial Aid .... Ms. Susan ROMANO
25 Director of Sponsored Research .... Dr. Anne E. BALDWIN
09 Director of Institutional Research .... Dr. Julie M. RAO
06 Registrar .... Ms. Kimberley WILLIS
36 Director of Career Development .... Ms. Stacey WILEY
22 Affirmative Action Officer .... Ms. Robbie ROUTENBERG
88 Asst Dean of Stdnt for Multicul Pgm .... Ms. Fatima R. JOHNSON
19 Chief of University Police .... Mr. Thomas KILCULLEN
18 Chief Facilities/Physical Plant .... Mr. George F. STOOKS
114 Dir of Acct & Budgeting Services .... Mr. Jeffrey NORDLAND
38 Clinical Dir Counseling Services .... Dr. Beth K. CHOLETTE
96 Director of Purchasing .... Ms. Rebecca E. ANCHOR
04 Asst to President .... Ms. Gayle DYCKMAN
121 Dean of Acad Planning & Advising .... Dr. Celia A. EASTON
41 Dir of Intercollegiate Athletics .... Mr. Michael C. MOONEY
50 Dean of School of Business .... Dr. Denise ROTONDO
53 Dean of the School of Education .... Dr. Anjoo SIKKA
88 Dir Research Tech & Strategic Proj .... Mr. Kirk ANNE
14 Assoc Director & Manager Info Sys .... Mr. Paul JACKSON

*State University of New York College at Old Westbury (C)

P.O. Box 210, 223 Store Hill Road, Old Westbury NY 11568-0210
County: Nassau
FICE Identification: 007109
Unit ID: 196237
Telephone: (516) 876-3000
Carnegie Class: Masters/S
FAX Number: (516) 876-3209
Calendar System: Semester
URL: www.oldwestbury.edu
Established: 1965
Annual Undergrad Tuition & Fees (In-State): $7,683
Enrollment: 4,353
Coed
Affiliation or Control: State
IRS Status: 501(c)3
Highest Offering: Master's
Accreditation: M, CAEPN

02 President .... Dr. Calvin O. BUTTS, III
100 Chief of Staff .... Ms. Mona G. RANKIN
05 Provost/Sr VP Academic Affairs .... Dr. Patrick O'SULLIVAN
84 VP for Enrollment Services .... Ms. Mary MARQUEZ BELL
32 VP Student Affs/Chf Diversity Ofcr .... Dr. Wayne EDWARDS
10 Sr VP Div Business & Finance/CFO .... Mr. Len L. DAVIS
15 Asst to Pres for Admin/Dir HR .... Mr. William P. KIMMINS
30 Asst to President for Advancement .... Mr. Michael G. KINANE
21 Assoc VP Bus Affairs/Controller .... Mr. Pat LETTINI
21 Assoc VP of Business Compliance .... Mr. Arthur H. ANGST, JR.
20 Asst Vice Pres Academic Affairs .... Mr. Anthony BARBERA
09 Asst VP Inst Research & Assessment .... Mr. Kuldeep PUPPALA
35 Asst Vice Pres Student Affairs .... Mr. Usama SHAIKH
49 Dean School of Arts & Sciences .... Dr. Barbara HILLERY
50 Interim Dean School of Business .... Dr. Jishan ZHU
53 Dean School of Education .... Dr. Nancy BROWN
35 Dean of Students .... Mr. Omar ESTRADA TORRES
19 Chief of Police .... Mr. Steven SIENA
26 Director Public & Media Relations .... Mr. Michael G. KINANE
13 Chief Information Officer .... Mr. Evan KOBOLAKIS
06 Registrar .... Ms. Patricia A. SMITH
96 Director of Purchasing .... Mr. Patrick ADAMS
89 Director First-Year Experience .... Dr. Laura M. ANKER
31 Director of Community Relations .... Ms. Carolyn BENNETT
38 Dir Counseling/Psych Wellness Svcs .... Dr. Trisha BILLARD
88 Environmental Health & Safety Ofcr .... Mr. Douglas BRODMERKEL
29 Director of Alumni Affairs .... Ms. Penny J. CHIN
71 Dir Special Student Programs .... Ms. Stacey DEFELICE
92 Director Honors College .... Dr. Anthony L. DELUCA
08 Acting Library Director .... Ms. Antonia DIGREGORIO
88 Coordinator of Scholarships .... Ms. Pritpal KAINTH
108 Dir Inst Research & Assessment .... Ms. Sandra KAUFMANN
109 Exec Dir Auxiliary Svc Corp .... Ms. Carol KAUNITZ
88 Director of Capital Planning .... Mr. Ray MAGGIORE
71 Dir Spec Programs Acad Affairs .... Mr. Yves M. MAGLOIRE
36 Dir Career Plng & Development .... Ms. Jerilyn MARINAN
88 Dir Educational Opportunity Program .... Mr. Alonzo L. MCCOLLUM
18 Director of Facilities .... Mr. Timothy MCGARRY
35 Director of Student Activities .... Ms. Suzanne MCLOUGHLIN
25 Director of Sponsored Programs .... Mr. Thomas MURPHY
37 Director Financial Aid .... Ms. Mildred O'KEEFE
07 Director of Admissions .... Mr. Frank PIZZARDI
88 Dir Ofc of Student Conduct .... Mr. Brian SCHWIRZBIN
39 Director Residential Life .... Mr. Gareth SHUMACK
23 Interim Dir Student Health Svcs .... Ms. Christine TESORIERO
88 Dir Commuter Program & Svcs .... Ms. Nicole M. THOMAS
88 Dir Orientation & Special Events .... Ms. Jaclyn VENTO
41 Director of Athletics .... Ms. Lenore J. WALSH

*State University of New York College at Oswego (D)

7060 State Route 104, Oswego NY 13126-3501
County: Oswego
FICE Identification: 002848
Unit ID: 196194
Telephone: (315) 312-2500
Carnegie Class: Masters/L
FAX Number: (315) 312-5799
Calendar System: Semester
URL: www.oswego.edu
Established: 1861
Annual Undergrad Tuition & Fees (In-State): $7,961
Enrollment: 7,937
Coed
Affiliation or Control: State
IRS Status: 501(c)3
Highest Offering: Master's
Accreditation: M, ART, CACREP, CAEPN, MUS, THEA

02 President .... Dr. Deborah F. STANLEY
05 VP Academic Affairs/Provost .... Dr. Scott R. FURLONG
10 Vice President Admin/Finance .... Mr. Nicholas A. LYONS
84 Vice Pres Student Affs/Enroll Mgmt .... Dr. Jerald WOOLFOLK
30 Interim VP Devel/Alumni Relations .... Ms. Mary CANALE
100 Chief of Staff .... Ms. Kristi ECK
88 Dep to the Pres Ext Prtnr Econ Dev .... Ms. Pamela CARACCIOLI
32 Assoc VP/Dean of Students Affs .... Dr. Jerri HOWLAND
18 Asst VP for Facilities Services .... Mr. Mitch FIELDS
21 Actg Asst VP for Finance & Budget .... Ms. Vicki FURLONG
20 Associate Provost .... Dr. Rameen MOHAMMADI
04 Ex Asst to Pres/Int Affrm Act Ofcr .... Mr. Howard GORDON
26 Chief Communication Officer .... Mr. Wayne WESTERVELT
25 Dir Research/Sponsored Pgms .... Mr. William BOWERS
94 Director Gender & Women's Studies .... Dr. Joanna GOPLEN
06 Registrar .... Mr. Jerret LEMAY
08 Director of Libraries .... Ms. Sarah CONRAD WEISMAN
91 Assoc Dir Campus Tech Services .... Mr. Michael C. PISA
37 Director of Financial Aid .... Mr. Mark HUMBERT
09 Director Inst Research & Assessment .... Dr. Mehran NOJAN
36 Director Career Services .... Mr. Gary MORRIS
38 Director Counseling Services Center .... Ms. Katherine WOLFE-LYGA
15 Director Human Resources .... Ms. Amy PLOTNER
19 University Police Chief .... Mr. John ROSSI
23 Director of Student Health Center .... Ms. Angela BROWN
28 Assoc Prov Multicltrl Pgms & Opps .... Ms. Catherine SANTOS
39 Dir Residence Life/Housing .... Dr. Richard KOLENDA
41 Director of Athletics .... Ms. Susan VISCOMI
96 Director Purchasing .... Mr. Mark COLE
13 Chief Technology Officer .... Mr. Sean MORIARTY
29 Director Alumni Relations .... Ms. Laura KELLY
07 Director of Admissions .... Mr. Daniel GRIFFIN
40 College Store Manager .... Ms. Susan RABY
49 Dean Col Lib Arts & Science .... Dr. Adrienne MCCORMICK
53 Dean School of Education .... Dr. Pamela MICHEL
58 Dean Grad Studies .... Dr. Kristen C. EICHHORN
50 Dean School of Business .... Dr. Richard J. SKOLNIK
51 Dean of Extended Learning .... Ms. Jill PIPPIN
88 Dean of Comm/Media & the Arts .... Dr. Julie PRETZAT
35 Asst VP Student Affairs .... Ms. Kathleen EVANS
109 Director of Auxiliary Services .... Mr. Michael FLAHERTY
104 Dir International Educ & Programs .... Dr. Joshua S. MCKEOWN

*State University of New York College at Plattsburgh (E)

101 Broad Street, Plattsburgh NY 12901-2637
County: Clinton
FICE Identification: 002849
Unit ID: 196246
Telephone: (518) 564-2000
Carnegie Class: Masters/L
FAX Number: (518) 564-3932
Calendar System: Semester
URL: www.plattsburgh.edu
Established: 1889
Annual Undergrad Tuition & Fees (In-State): $7,866
Enrollment: 5,718
Coed
Affiliation or Control: State
IRS Status: 501(c)3
Highest Offering: Master's
Accreditation: M, CACREP, CAEPT, DIETD, NURSE, SP, SW

02 President .... Dr. John ETTLING
05 Interim Provost/VP Acad Affairs .... Dr. Michael D. MORGAN
10 Vice President for Administration .... Ms. Josee LAROCHELLE
111 Vice Pres Institutional Advancement .... Ms. Anne W. HANSEN
32 Vice President for Student Affairs .... Mr. Bryan G. HARTMAN
49 Dean of Arts & Sciences .... Dr. Andrew S. BUCKSER
53 Int Dean Educ/Health/Human Svcs .... Dr. Denise SIMARD
50 Dean of Business/Economics .... Dr. Rowena ORTIZ-WALTERS
12 Dean Branch Campus at Queensbury .... Mr. Stephen DANNA
08 Dean Library/Info Services .... Ms. Holly B. HELLER-ROSS
22 Director of Affirmative Action .... Dr. Lynda J. AMES
88 Title IX Coordinator .... Ms. Butterfly L. BLAISE
20 Assistant Provost .... Ms. Diane K. MERKEL
11 Asst to Vice Pres Administration .... Mr. Sean B. DERMODY
15 Asst VP for Human Resources .... Ms. Susan T. WELCH
110 Asst VP for Institutional Advanc .... Mr. David P. GREGOIRE
06 Registrar .... Ms. Denise M. PHILO
11 Assoc VP for Admin & Finance .... Mr. Clark M. FOSTER
114 Budget Officer .... Ms. Magen M. RENADETTE
19 Chief University Police .... Mr. Jerry W. LOTTIE
109 Exec Dir College Auxiliary Services .... Mr. Wayne A. DUPREY
26 Exec Dir Marketing & Comm .... Mr. Kennith KNELLY
121 Director of Academic Advising .... Ms. Suzanne L. DALEY
29 Director of Alumni Relations .... Vacant
41 Director of Athletics .... Mr. Michael P. HOWARD
36 Director of Career Development Ctr .... Ms. Julia OVERTON-HEALY
40 Director of College Store .... Mr. Jerry L. DECELLE
30 Director of Development .... Ms. Faith M. LONG
18 Director of Facilities .... Mr. William A. CIRCELLI
37 Director of Financial Aid .... Mr. Todd A. MORAVEC
39 Director of Housing .... Mr. Stephen P. MATTHEWS
09 Dir of Institutional Effectiveness .... Mr. Robert M. KARP
96 Director of Purchasing .... Mr. Christopher J. JACKSON
46 Dir Sponsored Research/Programs .... Mr. Michael E. SIMPSON
88 Director of Student Conduct .... Mr. Larry K. ALLEN
23 Dir Ctr for Stdnt Hlth & Psych Svcs .... Dr. Kathleen M. CAMELO
91 Programming Manager .... Mr. Thomas J. HIGGINS
100 Chief of Staff .... Mr. Keith D. TYO
13 Chief Info Technology Officer (CIO) .... Ms. Holly B. HELLER ROSS

*State University of New York College at Potsdam (A)

44 Pierrepont Avenue, Potsdam NY 13676-2294
County: Saint Lawrence FICE Identification: 002850
Unit ID: 196200
Telephone: (315) 267-2000 Carnegie Class: Bac-A&S
FAX Number: (315) 267-2496 Calendar System: Semester
URL: www.potsdam.edu
Established: 1816 Annual Undergrad Tuition & Fees (In-State): $7,964
Enrollment: 3,904 Coed
Affiliation or Control: State IRS Status: 501(c)3
Highest Offering: Master's
Accreditation: M, CAEPN, IACBE, MUS, THEA

02 President Dr. Kristin G. ESTERBERG
03 Executive Vice President Dr. Enrico A. MILLER
05 Provost Dr. Bette S. BERGERON
10 Vice President for Business Affairs Vacant
32 Vice President for Student Affairs Vacant
111 Vice President College Advancement Ms. Vicki L. TEMPLETON-CORNELL
84 Assoc VP Enroll Mgmt/Inst Effect Vacant
04 Assistant to the President Ms. Carol M. ROURKE
20 Associate Provost Dr. Jill R. PEARON
18 Asst Vice Pres for Facilities Vacant
26 Chief Information Officer Mr. Kyle A. BROWN
53 Interim Dean Educ & Prof Studies Dr. Walter J. CONLEY
49 Dean of Arts and Sciences Dr. Steven J. MARQUSEE
64 Dean of Music Dr. Michael R. SITTON
15 Assoc VP for Human Resources Ms. Mary K. DOLAN
08 Director of Libraries Ms. Jenica P. ROGERS
06 Registrar Ms. Stephanie L. CLAXTON
07 Director of Admissions Mr. Thomas W. NESBITT
37 Director of Financial Aid Ms. Susan E. GODREAU
36 Director of Career Planning Vacant
38 Director of Counseling Center Mrs. Gena C. NELSON
19 Chief of University Police Mr. Tim M. ASHLEY
29 Director of Alumni Relations Ms. Mona O. VROMAN
109 Executive Dir of Auxiliary Corp Mr. Daniel J. HAYES
23 Director of Health Services Mrs. Gena C. NELSON
39 Interim Assoc Dean Students Mr. Eric D. DUCHSCHERER
40 Director of College Bookstore Mr. Lyndon J. LAKE
41 Athletic Director Mr. James A. ZALACCA
25 Director Research & Sponsored Pgms Dr. Nancy M. DODGE-REYOME
92 Director of Honors Program Dr. Thomas N. BAKER
94 Director of Women's Studies Dr. Christine M. DORAN
27 Asst VP Marketing/Communications Mrs. Mindy E. THOMPSON
86 Community/Govt Rels Associate Mrs. Alexandra M. JACOBS-WILKE
58 Director of Graduate and Cont Educ Mr. Joshua J. LAFAVE
28 Chief Diversity Officer Dr. Bernadette S. TIAPO
09 Director of Institutional Research Mrs. Judith R. SINGH
104 Director Study Abroad Mrs. Krista M. LAVACK
96 Director of Purchasing Mr. Mark E. MARTINCHEK

*Purchase College, State University of New York (B)

735 Anderson Hill Road, Purchase NY 10577-1402
County: Westchester FICE Identification: 006791
Unit ID: 196219
Telephone: (914) 251-6000 Carnegie Class: Bac-A&S
FAX Number: (914) 251-6014 Calendar System: Semester
URL: www.purchase.edu
Established: 1967 Annual Undergrad Tuition & Fees (In-State): $8,298
Enrollment: 4,169 Coed
Affiliation or Control: State IRS Status: 501(c)3
Highest Offering: Master's
Accreditation: M, ART

02 President Mr. Thomas J. SCHWARZ
19 Chief of University Police Mr. Dayton TUCKER
10 CFO/VP Operations Ms. Judy NOLAN
05 Provost/VP Academic Affairs Dr. Barry PEARSON
32 Vice Pres Student Affs & Enroll Mgt Mr. Dennis CRAIG
111 VP of Institutional Advancement Ms. Catherine BROD
57 Director Conservatory Theatre Arts Dr. Rebecca RUGG
51 Exec Dir Liberal Stds/Cont Educ Ms. Trudy MILBURN
81 Dean Sch Natural/Social Sciences Dr. Suzanne KESSLER
79 Chair School of Humanities Dr. Ross DALY
20 Assoc Prov Academic Affairs Dr. Peggy DECOOKE
88 Interim Dir Performing Arts Center Mr. Seth SOLOWAY
88 Director Neuberger Museum of Art Dr. Tracy FITZPATRICK
08 Director of the Library Mr. Patrick F. CALLAHAN
64 Dir Conservatory of Music Dr. Jennifer UNDERCOFLER
57 Interim Dean School of Arts Dr. Peggy DECOOKE
13 Director Campus Technology Services Mr. Bill JUNOR
37 Director Student Financial Services Corey YORK
38 Director of Counseling Center Dr. Cathie CHESTER
36 Director Career Development Ms. Wendy MOROSOFF
15 Director of Human Resources Ms. Kathleen FARRELL
41 Athletic Director Mr. Chris BISIGNANO
39 Director Community Engagement Mr. Mario RAPETTI
96 Director of Purchasing Mr. Edward HERRAN
35 Dean of Student Affairs Ms. Patricia BICE
09 Director of Institutional Research Ms. Barbara MOORE
18 Sr Dir Capital Facilities Planning Mr. Michael KOPAS
22 Title IX Officer & Asst Affirm Act Mr. Jeremy DELICH
88 Environmental Health/Safety Officer Mr. Edward MUSAL
44 Director Annual Giving Ms. Carla WEILAND-ZALEZNAK
26 Dir Communications/Creative Svcs Ms. Sandy DYLAK
86 Director of Govt Relations/Sp Proj Ms. Elizabeth C. ROBERTSON
04 Assistant to President Ms. Carrie K. BIANCHI
104 Director Study Abroad Ms. Suzanne NEARY
29 Director Alumni Relations Ms. Nadege ROC

*State University of New York College of Agriculture and Technology at Cobleskill (C)

Route 7, Knapp Hall, Cobleskill NY 12043
County: Schoharie FICE Identification: 002856
Unit ID: 196033
Telephone: (518) 255-5011 Carnegie Class: Bac/Assoc-Mixed
FAX Number: (518) 255-5333 Calendar System: Semester
URL: www.cobleskill.edu
Established: 1911 Annual Undergrad Tuition & Fees (In-State): $7,929
Enrollment: 2,441 Coed
Affiliation or Control: State IRS Status: 501(c)3
Highest Offering: Baccalaureate
Accreditation: M, ACFEI, EMT, HT

02 President Dr. Marion TERENZIO
05 Provost & Vice Pres Academic Affs Dr. Susan ZIMMERMANN
100 Chief of Staff Ms. Amy HEALY
32 VP for Student Affairs Dr. Anne HOPKINS-GROSS
10 Vice Pres Business & Finance Ms. Wendy GILMAN
11 Vice Pres Operations Ms. Bonnie MARTIN
30 Chief Advancement Officer Ms. Lois GOBLET
47 Dean Agriculture/Natural Res Mr. Timothy MOORE
49 Dean Liberal Arts & Sciences Dr. Jeffrey ANDERSON
08 Dean Library/Information Svcs Ms. Elizabeth ORGERON
26 Director of Communications Mr. James FELDMAN
16 Director Employee Relations Ms. Lynn BERGER
06 Registrar Ms. Christine JOHANNESEN
21 Chief Business Officer Ms. Carol VOSATKA
84 Chief Enrollment Officer Dr. Tara WINTER
29 Director Alumni Relations Mr. Matthew S. BARNEY
07 Assistant Director of Admissions Mr. Caleb GRANT
39 Director of Residential Life Mr. Edward E. ASSELIN
36 Director of Student Success Ctr Ms. Donna PESTA
23 Co-Director Wellness Center Ms. Mary RADLIFF
23 Co-Director Wellness Center Ms. Lynn ONTL
37 Director of Financial Aid Ms. Louise BIRON
35 Director Student Life Center Mr. Jeffrey C. FOOTE
41 Director of Athletics Vacant
13 Director Information Tech Services Mr. James DUTCHER
19 Chief University Police Dept Mr. Frank LAWRENCE
09 Director of Institutional Research Vacant
15 Director of Human Resources Ms. Lynn BERGER
18 Director Facilities/Physical Plant Mr. Joseph BATCHELDER
40 Manager Bookstore Ms. Jeri USATCH
85 Director of International Programs Dr. Susan JAGENDORF
96 Director of Purchasing Ms. Laura GROSS
25 Dir of Grants and Sponsored Program Mr. Barry GELL
22 Director of EOP Mr. Derwin BENNETT
88 Dir of Student Accounts Ms. Sarah LEDERMANN
105 Webmaster Ms. Naomi MEKEEL

*State University of New York College of Environmental Science and Forestry (D)

1 Forestry Drive, Syracuse NY 13210-2778
County: Onondaga FICE Identification: 002851
Unit ID: 196103
Telephone: (315) 470-6500 Carnegie Class: DU-Mod
FAX Number: (315) 470-6779 Calendar System: Semester
URL: www.esf.edu
Established: 1911 Annual Undergrad Tuition & Fees (In-State): $8,103
Enrollment: 2,222 Coed
Affiliation or Control: State IRS Status: 501(c)3
Highest Offering: Doctorate
Accreditation: M, ENG, ENGT, LSAR

02 President Dr. Quentin D. WHEELER
05 Provost/Exec Vice President Dr. Nosa EGIEBOR
11 Vice President for Administration Mr. Joseph RUFO
100 Chief of Staff Mr. Mark LICHTENSTEIN
04 Asst to the President Ms. Ragan A. SQUIER
86 VP for Govt & External Relations Dr. Maureen O. FELLOWS
30 Asst VP for Development Ms. Brenda T. GREENFIELD
46 Vice Provost for Research Dr. Christopher T. NOMURA
58 Assoc Prov & Dean Grad School Mr. Scott S. SHANNON
84 Chief Enrollment Officer Vacant
32 Vice Provost/Dean Student Affairs Dr. Anne E. LOMBARD
10 Director Business Affairs Mr. David R. DZWONKOWSKI
13 Chief Information Officer Vacant
15 Director Human Resources Ms. Marcia A. BARBER
26 Director of Communications Mrs. Claire B. DUNN
19 Chief of University Police Mr. Thomas LEROY
28 Chief Diversity Officer Vacant
08 Director of College Libraries Mr. Matthew R. SMITH
07 Director of Admissions Mrs. Susan H. SANFORD
06 Registrar Ms. Leslie RUTKOWSI
37 Director of Financial Aid Mr. Mark J. HILL
29 Director of Alumni Affairs Ms. Debbie J. CAVINESS
28 Director of Multicultural Affairs Vacant
18 Dir of Facilities/Physical Plant Mr. Gary S. PEDEN
36 Dir of Career Services Mr. John TURBEVILLE
38 Dir of Counseling Services Ms. Ruth LARSON
35 Director Student Activities Mrs. Laura CRANDALL
51 Dean ESF Open Academy Dr. Charles M. SPUCHES
41 Coordinator of College Athletics Mr. Daniel RAMIN
43 Associate Counsel Mr. Kevin HAYDEN
104 Coordinator International Education Mr. Thomas E. CARTER
101 Secretary of the Institution/Board Mr. Joseph L. RUFO

*State University of New York College of Optometry (E)

33 W 42nd Street, New York NY 10036-8003
County: New York FICE Identification: 009929
Unit ID: 196228
Telephone: (212) 938-4000 Carnegie Class: Spec-4-yr-Other Health
FAX Number: (212) 938-5696 Calendar System: Semester
URL: www.sunyopt.edu
Established: 1971 Annual Graduate Tuition & Fees: N/A
Enrollment: 381 Coed
Affiliation or Control: State IRS Status: 501(c)3
Highest Offering: Doctorate; No Undergraduates
Accreditation: M, OPT, OPTR

02 President Dr. David A. HEATH
05 Dean/VP Academic Affairs Dr. David TROILO
10 VP For Administration and Finance Mr. David A. BOWERS
32 Vice Pres Student Affairs Dr. Guilherme ALBIERI
17 Vice Pres for Clinical Admin Ms. Liduvina MARTINEZ-GONZALEZ
111 Vice Pres Institutional Advancement Ms. Ann WARWICK
04 Assistant to the President Ms. Karen DEGAZON
09 Dir Institutional Research/Planning Dr. Steven SCHWARTZ
08 Director Library Services Ms. Elaine WELLS
15 Director of Human Resources Mr. Douglas SCHADING
37 Financial Aid Officer Mr. Vito CAVALLARO
06 Registrar Ms. Jacqueline MARTINEZ
58 Assoc Dean Rsrch/Graduate Studies Dr. Stewart BLOOMFIELD
26 Director of Communications Ms. Amber HOPKINS-JENKINS
13 Chief Info Technology Officer (CIO) Mr. Robert PELLOT
84 Director Enrollment Management Dr. Guilherme ALBIERI
96 Director of Purchasing Ms. Maureen MORLEY

*Alfred State College (F)

10 Upper College Drive, Alfred NY 14802-1196
County: Allegany FICE Identification: 002854
Unit ID: 196006
Telephone: (607) 587-4010 Carnegie Class: Bac/Assoc-Mixed
FAX Number: N/A Calendar System: Semester
URL: www.alfredstate.edu
Established: 1908 Annual Undergrad Tuition & Fees (In-State): $8,075
Enrollment: 3,699 Coed
Affiliation or Control: State IRS Status: 501(c)3
Highest Offering: Baccalaureate
Accreditation: M, ADNUR, CAHIIM, CONST, ENGT, FEPAC, NURSE

02 President Dr. Irby (Skip) SULLIVAN
05 Provost Ms. Kristin POPPO
32 Vice President Student Affairs Mr. Gregory S. SAMMONS
11 Exec Vice President Ms. Valerie NIXON
111 Sr Dir Institutional Advancement Ms. Danielle M. WHITE
20 Assoc Vice Pres Academic Affairs Mr. Charles V. NEAL
09 Institutional Research Analyst Mr. Daniel D. JARDINE
84 Assoc VP for Enrollment Mgmt Ms. Deborah J. GOODRICH
13 Director Computer Services Mr. Michael A. CASE
15 Director Human Res/Affirm Action Ms. Wendy DRESSER-RECKTENWALD
37 Sr Dir Student Financial Services Mrs. Jane A. GILLILAND
29 Director Alumni Relations Ms. Colleen ARGENTIERI
18 Director of Physical Plant Mr. Glenn R. BRUBAKER
14 Asst Director of Computing Services Mr. Carl H. RAHR, JR.
23 Sr Director Health Svcs/Wellness Ms. Hollie M. HALL
121 Assoc VP of Academic Services Ms. Kathleen EBERT
19 Chief of University Police Mr. Matthew D. HELLER
96 Director of Purchasing Mr. Glen E. CLINE
10 Controller Mr. Joseph T. GREENTHAL
36 Director of Career Services Ms. Elaine MORSMAN
49 Int Dean School of Arts & Sciences Dr. Ingrid JOHNSTON
54 Dean School of Mgmt & Engr Tech Dr. John WILLIAMS
75 Int Dean Sch Applied Technology Mr. Jeff STEVENS

*SUNY Adirondack (G)

640 Bay Road, Queensbury NY 12804-1498
County: Warren FICE Identification: 002860
Unit ID: 188438
Telephone: (518) 743-2200 Carnegie Class: Assoc/HT-High Trad
FAX Number: (518) 745-1433 Calendar System: Semester
URL: www.sunyacc.edu
Established: 1960 Annual Undergrad Tuition & Fees (In-District): $4,693
Enrollment: 3,993 Coed
Affiliation or Control: State/Local IRS Status: 501(c)3
Highest Offering: Associate Degree
Accreditation: M, ADNUR

02 President Dr. Kristine DUFFY
05 Vice Pres Academic Affairs Mr. John JABLONSKI
10 Vice Pres Admin Services/Treasurer Ms. Ann Marie SOMMA
30 Exec Dir Dev/Alumni Rels/ACC Fndtn Ms. Rachael HUNSINGER PATTEN
20 Dean for Academic Initiatives Ms. Diane WILDEY

32 Dean for Student Affairs .... Mr. Jason ENSER
84 Dean of Enrollment Mgt and Mktg .... Mr. Rob PALMIERI
09 Director of Inst Research/Planning .... Ms. Carol RUNGE
13 Chief Information Officer .... Ms. Mary HAND
15 Director of Human Resources .... Ms. Mindy WILSON
51 Asst Dean Cont Educ & Workforce .... Mrs. Caelynn PRYLO
40 Director Bookstore .... Mr. Tom KENT
21 Director of Business Affairs .... Ms. Lisa DESTER
18 Director Facilities .... Mr. Anthony PALANGI
37 Director Financial Aid .... Ms. Colleen WISE
06 Registrar .... Ms. Mary ALDOUS
07 Director of Admissions .... Ms. Sarah J. LINEHAN
90 Director of Educational Technology .... Ms. Roseann ANZALONE
08 Director of Library Services .... Ms. Teresa RONNING
35 Dir of Student Life & Diversity .... Matthew MCKAY
41 Athletic Director .... Mr. John QUATTROCCHI
101 Secretary to the Board of Trustees .... Ms. Kathy DRISLANE
102 Dir Foundation/Corporate Relations .... Ms. Rachael HUNSINGER PATTEN
19 Asst Director of Public Safety .... Mr. Richard CONINE
39 Director of Residence Life .... Ms. Phylicia COLEY

*SUNY Canton-College of Technology (A)

34 Cornell Drive, Canton NY 13617-1098
County: Saint Lawrence FICE Identification: 002855
Unit ID: 196015
Telephone: (315) 386-7011 Carnegie Class: Bac/Assoc-Mixed
FAX Number: (315) 386-7930 Calendar System: Semester
URL: www.canton.edu
Established: 1906 Annual Undergrad Tuition & Fees (In-State): $7,881
Enrollment: 3,140 Coed
Affiliation or Control: State IRS Status: 501(c)3
Highest Offering: Baccalaureate
Accreditation: M, ADNUR, DH, ENGT, #FUSER, NUR, PNUR, PTAA

02 President .... Dr. Zvi SZAFRAN
05 Provost .... Dr. Douglas SCHEIDT
11 Vice Pres for Administration .... Ms. Shawn MILLER
10 Chief Financial Officer .... Ms. Shawn MILLER
111 Vice Pres for Advancement .... Ms. Anne SIBLEY
32 Vice President for Student Affairs .... Ms. Courtney D. BISH
35 Dean of Students .... Ms. Courtney D. BISH
72 Dean Canino Sch Eng Tech .... Mr. Michael J. NEWTOWN
76 Dean Sch Sci/Health/Crim Justice .... Dr. Kenneth M. ERICKSON
50 Dean Sch Business/Liberal Arts .... Mr. Jondavid S. DELONG
20 Associate Provost .... Dr. Molly MOTT
88 Dean Acad Support Svcs/Instr Tech .... Dr. Molly A. MOTT
41 Director of Athletics .... Mr. Randy B. SIEMINSKI
100 Exec Dir for University Relations .... Dr. Lenore VANDERZEE
101 College Council Secretary .... Ms. Michaela J. YOUNG
04 Exec Assistant to the President .... Ms. Michaela J. YOUNG
35 Director Student Activities .... Ms. Priscilla LEGGETTE
28 Co-Chief Diversity Officer/AAO .... Ms. Lashawanda T. INGRAM
28 Co-Chief Diversity Officer/AAO .... Mr. William T. JONES
96 Director of Purchasing .... Ms. Bethany A. MARTIN
37 Director of Financial Aid .... Ms. Kerrie L. COOPER
21 College Accountant .... Ms. Terry WALDRUFF
15 Director of Human Resources .... Mr. David M. ROURKE
36 Director of Career Services .... Ms. Julie PARKMAN
06 Registrar .... Ms. Memorie L. SHAMPINE
08 Interim Dir of Library Services .... Ms. Cori WILHELM
18 Director of Physical Plant .... Mr. Patrick G. HANSS
18 Plant Superintendent .... Mr. Martin D. AVERY
19 Chief of University Police .... Mr. Alan MULKIN
23 Director of Health Services .... Ms. Patricia A. TODD
26 Dir Public Rels/Web Coord .... Mr. Travis SMITH
40 Manager Campus Store .... Mr. Corey JORDAN
39 Director of Residence Life .... Mr. John M. KENNEDY
09 Dir of Inst Research/Assessment .... Ms. Sarah E. TODD
13 Assistant VP IT/CIO .... Mr. Kyle BROWN
29 Director of Alumni Affairs .... Ms. Peggy S. LEVATO
38 Director of Counseling .... Ms. Melinda A. MILLER
07 Director of Admissions .... Ms. Melissa EVANS
88 Director of Facilities .... Mr. Michael R. MCCORMICK
30 Director of Development .... Ms. Peggy S. LEVATO
90 Int Help Desk Coordinator .... Mr. Benjamin MATOTT
104 Coord Intl Student Initiatives .... Ms. Erin LASSIAL
103 Dir of Workforce Development .... Mr. Art GARNO
25 Grants Coordinator .... Ms. JoAnne M. FASSINGER

*State University of New York College of Technology at Delhi (B)

454 Delhi Drive, Delhi NY 13753-4454
County: Delaware FICE Identification: 002857
Unit ID: 196024
Telephone: (607) 746-4000 Carnegie Class: Bac/Assoc-Mixed
FAX Number: (607) 746-4208 Calendar System: Semester
URL: www.delhi.edu
Established: 1913 Annual Undergrad Tuition & Fees (In-State): $7,875
Enrollment: 3,457 Coed
Affiliation or Control: State IRS Status: 501(c)3
Highest Offering: Master's
Accreditation: M, ACFEI, ADNUR, CONST, NUR, NURSE

02 President .... Dr. Michael R. LALIBERTE
05 Provost .... Dr. Kelli H. LIGEIKIS
32 VP for Student Life .... Mr. Tomas A. AGUIRRE
10 VP for Business & Finance .... Ms. Carol M. BISHOP
30 VP for College Relations & Advance .... Mr. Joel M. SMITH
36 Coordinator Career & Transfer Svcs .... Ms. Kristin A. DEFOREST
07 Director of Admissions .... Mr. Robert C. PIUROWSKI
13 Chief Information Officer .... Mr. Shawn P. BRISLIN
19 Chief of University Police .... Mr. Martin A. PETTIT
39 Director of Residence Life .... Mr. John J. PADOVANI
08 Director of the Resnick Library .... Ms. Carrie J. FISHNER
36 Dir Career & Business Development .... Ms. Glenda V. ROBERTS
28 VP Diversity/Equity/Inclusion .... Ms. Michele T. DEFREECE
18 Director of Physical Plant .... Mr. David A. LOVELAND
41 Director of Athletics .... Mr. Robert H. BACKUS
06 Registrar .... Ms. Nancy L. SMITH
37 Director of Financial Aid .... Ms. Elizabeth D. BERRY
38 Director Counseling & Health Svcs .... Ms. Lori B. OSTERHOUDT
29 Alumni/Annual Giving Coordinator .... Ms. Lucinda C. BRYDON
21 Controller .... Ms. Amy L. BROWN
26 Dir of Communications & News Media .... Ms. Kimberly M. MACLEOD
09 Asst for Institutional Research .... Ms. JoAnna M. BROSNAN
04 Administrative Asst to President .... Mr. George L. SPIELMAN
102 Exec Dir College Foundation .... Mr. Joel M. SMITH
15 Mgr of Human Resource Operations .... Ms. Jan A. ELWELL
22 Dir Human Resources/Affirm Action .... Ms. Mary B. MORTON
25 Grants Specialist .... Ms. Ellen A. LIBERATORI
96 Accts Payable/Purchasing Manager .... Ms. Cheryl L. DIETZMAN

*State University of New York Empire State College (C)

2 Union Avenue, Saratoga Springs NY 12866-4390
County: Saratoga FICE Identification: 010286
Unit ID: 196264
Telephone: (518) 587-2100 Carnegie Class: Masters/M
FAX Number: (518) 587-2886 Calendar System: Other
URL: www.esc.edu
Established: 1971 Annual Undergrad Tuition & Fees (In-State): $6,985
Enrollment: 11,878 Coed
Affiliation or Control: State IRS Status: 501(c)3
Highest Offering: Master's
Accreditation: M, CAEPT, IACBE, NURSE

02 President .... Dr. Merodie HANCOCK
100 Chief of Staff .... Mr. Michael MANCINI
05 Provost/Vice Pres AA .... Dr. David BEJOU
86 VP for Communications & Govt Rels .... Ms. Mary Caroline VAN DER VEER
111 VP of Advancement .... Mr. Walter WILLIAMS
13 Executive VP for ITS & Admin .... Mr. Joseph GARCIA
84 VP for Enrollment Management .... Dr. Clayton STEEN
09 VP for Decision Support .... Dr. Mitchell S. NESLER
20 Interim VP Academic Administration .... Dr. Tai ARNOLD
10 Assoc Vice Pres for Administration .... Vacant
97 Dean Undergrad Studies .... Dr. Nikki SHRIMPTON
20 Dean Academic/Instructional Svcs .... Dr. Lisa D'ADAMO-WEINSTEIN
16 Associate Dean Human Services .... Dr. John LAWLESS
70 Associate Dean Social Science .... Dr. Frank VANDER VALK
81 Assoc Dean Science/Math/Technology .... Dr. Brian HAGENBUCH
50 Associate Dean Business .... Dr. Julie GEDRO
79 Associate Dean Humanities .... Dr. Megan MULLEN
58 Assoc Dean School for Grad Studies .... Dr. Nathan GONYEA
66 Dean School of Nursing .... Dr. Bridget NETTLETON
20 Vice Provost for Academic Affairs .... Dr. Thomas MACKEY
14 Executive Director ITT .... Mr. AJ LACOMBA
12 Executive Director Western Region .... Ms. Cathleen SHEILS
12 Co-Int Exec Director Metro Center .... Dr. Christopher WHANN
12 Co-Int Exec Director Metro Center .... Dr. Catherine LEAKER
91 Director Admin Applications .... Mr. Mark CLAVERIE
110 Director Advancement Services .... Ms. Vicki SCHAAKE
29 Dir Alumni and Student Relations .... Ms. Maureen WINNEY
44 Director of the Fund .... Ms. Stephanie CORP
21 Director Business Office .... Ms. Becky PALMIERI
20 Dir Collegewide Academic Review .... Dr. Nan TRAVERS
32 Dir Collegewide Student Services .... Ms. Patricia MYERS
26 Director of Communications .... Mr. David HENAHAN
88 Director of Academic Development .... Mr. Brian GOODALE
88 Dir Compliance/Environment Sustain .... Ms. Sadie ROSS
18 Senior Director of Operations .... Mr. Rick REIMANN
37 Director Financial Aid .... Ms. Kristina DELBRIDGE
30 Director of Development .... Mr. Toby TOBROCKE
15 Assoc VP for Human Resources .... Ms. Mary Ellen R. KEENEY
88 Director College Project Management .... Mr. Walter LEWIS
96 Director Procurement .... Mr. Charley SUMMERSELL
24 Director Publications .... Mr. Kirk STARCZEWSKI
19 Director of Safety & Security .... Mr. Mark JANKOWSKI
21 Director Student Accounts .... Ms. Pamela MALONE
88 Int Dir Veteran & Military Educ .... Ms. Desiree DRINDAK
22 Affirmative Action Officer .... Mr. Michael MANCINI
06 Registrar .... Vacant
07 Director Admissions .... Ms. Jennifer D'AGOSTINO

*Farmingdale State College (D)

2350 Broadhollow Road, Farmingdale NY 11735-1021
County: Suffolk FICE Identification: 002858
Unit ID: 196042
Telephone: (631) 420-2000 Carnegie Class: Bac-Diverse
FAX Number: N/A Calendar System: Semester
URL: www.farmingdale.edu
Established: 1912 Annual Undergrad Tuition & Fees (In-State): $7,860
Enrollment: 8,648 Coed
Affiliation or Control: State IRS Status: 501(c)3
Highest Offering: Master's
Accreditation: M, DH, ENGT, MLTAD, MT, NAIT, NURSE

02 President .... Dr. John S. NADER
05 Provost/Vice Pres for Academic Affs .... Dr. Laura JOSEPH
10 Vice Pres Admin/Finance and CFO .... Mr. Gregory O'CONNOR
32 Vice Pres Student Affairs .... Dr. Tom CORTI
84 VP Inst Advancement/Enrollment Mgmt .... Mr. Patrick CALABRIA
30 VP for Development/Philanthropy .... Ms. Nancy CONNORS
20 Acting Associate Provost .... Dr. Michael GOODSTONE
11 Director of Admin Services .... Ms. Dorothy HUGHES
35 Dean of Students .... Ms. Terry ESNES-JOHNSON
07 Dir Admissions/Enrollment Planning .... Mr. Jim HALL
19 Chief University Police .... Mr. Marvin J. FISCHER
18 Director of Physical Plant .... Mr. John S. DZINANKA
26 Sr Director of Communications .... Ms. Kathryn S. COLEY
06 Registrar .... Ms. Cindy MCCUE
08 Head Librarian .... Ms. Karen GELLES
15 Director Human Resources .... Ms. Marybeth INCANDELA
90 Director of Admin Technology .... Mr. Jeffrey BORAH
36 Director Career Development .... Ms. Dolores CIACCIO
37 Director Student Financial Services .... Ms. Diane KAZANECKI-KEMPTER
09 Chief Inst Research Officer .... Ms. Patricia LIND-GONZALEZ
23 Director Student Health Services .... Mr. Kevin MURPHY
41 Dir Athletics Admin & Ext Affairs .... Mr. Michael HARRINGTON
41 Dir of Athletics Comp & Operations .... Mr. Tom AZZARA
39 Director of Residence Life .... Ms. Angela JASUR
102 President Farmingdale Foundation .... Mr. John MOLLOY
24 Director Media Resources .... Mr. Martin BRANDT
29 Director Alumni Relations .... Ms. Michelle JOHNSON
28 Chief Diversity Officer .... Dr. Veronica HENRY
40 Manager Bookstore .... Ms. Roberta MIRRO
21 Controller .... Ms. Ellen WEBER
96 Purchasing Associate .... Ms. Lisa BRUNS
75 Exec Dir LI Educ Opportunity Center .... Dr. Elsa-Sofia MOROTE
50 Dean School of Business .... Dr. Richard VOGEL
76 Dean School Health Sciences .... Dr. Denny RYMAN
49 Acting Dean Sch of Arts & Sciences .... Dr. Charles ADAIR
104 Study Abroad Advisor .... Ms. Agata ADAMCZUK
105 Director Web Services .... Ms. Sylvia NAVARRO-NICOSIA
53 Dean International Education .... Dr. Lorraine GREENWALD
04 Administrative Asst to President .... Ms. Claire LISI

*State University of New York Maritime College (E)

6 Pennyfield Avenue, Throggs Neck NY 10465-4198
County: Bronx FICE Identification: 002853
Unit ID: 196291
Telephone: (718) 409-7200 Carnegie Class: Masters/S
FAX Number: (718) 409-7392 Calendar System: Semester
URL: www.sunymaritime.edu
Established: 1874 Annual Undergrad Tuition & Fees (In-State): $7,834
Enrollment: 1,860 Coed
Affiliation or Control: State IRS Status: 501(c)3
Highest Offering: Master's
Accreditation: M, ENG

02 President .... RADM. Michael A. ALFULTIS
04 Executive Assistant to President .... Ms. Claudine TAVIN-WARKENTHIEN
05 Provost/Vice Pres Academic Affairs .... Dr. Joeseph HOFFMAN
10 Vice Pres Finance/Admin .... Mr. Scott DIETERICH
26 Vice President University Relations .... Ms. Aimee BERNSTEIN
32 Commandant of Cadets/Master TSES .... CAPT. Richard S. SMITH
20 Academic Dean .... Dr. Gilbert TRAUB
100 Chief of Staff .... CAPT. Mark WOOLLEY
07 Dean of Admissions .... Mr. Rohan HOWELL
35 Assoc Provost/Dean of Students .... Mr. William IMBRIALE
27 Exec Director of External Affairs .... Ms. Mary MUECKE
15 Director Human Resources .... Ms. LuAnn AUGUSTINE-PLAISANCE
19 University Police Chief .... Mr. Myron PRYJMAK
84 Exec Dir Enroll Svcs/Financial Aid .... Mr. Paul BAMONTE
41 Director of Athletics .... Mr. Kristofer SCHNATZ
06 Registrar .... Ms. Sarah GRADY
09 Dir Inst Research/Assessment .... CAPT. Mark WOOLLEY
08 Library Director .... Ms. Kristin HART
88 Dean of Maritime Educ/Training .... CAPT. Ernest FINK

*Morrisville State College (F)

PO Box 901, Morrisville NY 13408-0901
County: Madison FICE Identification: 002859
Unit ID: 196051
Telephone: (315) 684-6000 Carnegie Class: Bac/Assoc-Mixed
FAX Number: (315) 684-6116 Calendar System: Semester
URL: www.morrisville.edu
Established: 1908 Annual Undergrad Tuition & Fees (In-State): $8,023
Enrollment: 2,940 Coed
Affiliation or Control: State IRS Status: 501(c)3
Highest Offering: Baccalaureate
Accreditation: M, ACBSP, ADNUR, DIETT, ENGT

02 President .... Dr. David E. ROGERS
05 Provost .... Dr. Barry A. SPRIGGS
10 Vice Pres for Administration .... Ms. Mary Ellen BURDICK
32 Dean of Students .... Mr. Geoffrey S. ISABELLE
47 Dean School Ag & Natural Resources .... Dr. Christopher L. NYBERG
81 Dean School Sci/Tech & Health .... Dr. Joseph H. BULARZIK
49 Dean School of Liberal Arts .... Dr. Paul F. GRIFFIN
50 Dean Sch Business & Hospitality .... Ms. Jeannette H. EVANS
111 Exec Dir Advancement & PR .... Ms. Lisa A. IANELLO

07 Dean of Admission ... Mr. Robert C. BLANCHET
37 Director of Financial Aid ... Ms. Dacia L. BANKS
09 Director of Institutional Research ... Ms. Marian D. WHITNEY
08 Director of Library ... Ms. Christine A. RUDECOFF
23 Director Student Health Center ... Ms. Debra P. BABOWICZ
15 Dir HR/Affirmative Action ... Ms. Sarah G. STEELE
29 Coordinator of Alumni Relations ... Ms. Anastasia BRENCHER
26 Exec Director Communication Mktg ... Mr. Graham GARNER
06 Associate Registrar ... Ms. Tashana M. CURTIS
13 Chief Info Technology Officer (CIO) ... Dr. Roberta H. SLOAN
18 Chief Facilities/Physical Plant ... Mr. Mark P. GRISI
19 Director Security/Safety ... Mr. Enrico L. D'ALESSANDRO
36 Career Planning/Development Ofcr ... Ms. Barbara A. ROBACK
39 Director Student Housing ... Ms. Elizabeth R. ACKMAN
41 Athletic Director ... Mr. Gregory M. CARROLL
14 Asst Dir of Technology Services ... Mr. Jeff GAY
04 Administrative Asst to President ... Ms. JoAnn GODFREY
100 Chief of Staff ... Ms. Cydney M. JOHNSON
28 Director of Diversity ... Ms. Mary H. BONDEROFF

*SUNY Polytechnic Institute (A)

100 Seymour Road, Utica NY 13502
County: Oneida FICE Identification: 011678
Unit ID: 196112
Telephone: (315) 792-7100 Carnegie Class: Masters/M
FAX Number: (315) 792-7222 Calendar System: Semester
URL: www.sunypoly.edu
Established: 1966 Annual Undergrad Tuition & Fees (In-State): $7,777
Enrollment: 2,779 Coed
Affiliation or Control: State IRS Status: 501(c)3
Highest Offering: Master's
Accreditation: M, CAHIIM, ENG, ENGT, NURSE

02 President ... Dr. Bahgat SAMMAKIA
86 VP External Rels & Chief of Staff ... Mr. Michael FRAME
04 Executive Assistant ... Ms. Laurie HARTMAN
46 VP for Research ... Dr. Michael LIEHR
15 VP for Human Resources ... Ms. Rhonda HAINES
32 VP for Student Affairs ... Ms. Marybeth LYONS
111 VP for Advancement ... Vacant
58 Dean Graduate Studies ... Dr. Shadi SHAHEDIPOUR-SANDVIK
05 Provost/Vice Pres Academic Affairs ... Dr. William DURGIN
20 Associate Provost ... Dr. Michael MANNING
84 Assoc Provost Enrollment Mgmt ... Vacant
49 Dean Arts & Sciences ... Dr. Andrew RUSSELL
50 Dean Business Management ... Dr. Robert EDGELL
54 Dean Engineering ... Dr. Andrew WOLFE
72 Dean NanoEngr & Tech Innovation ... Dr. Michael CARPENTER
81 Dean Nanoscale Science ... Dr. Alain DIEBOLD
66 Dean Health Professions ... Dr. Kathleen ROURKE
19 VP for Security & Safety Mgmt ... Mr. Tom LOUIS
44 Director Annual Giving ... Ms. Amanda SAGENDORF
18 Vice President of Facilities ... Vacant
26 Director University Communications ... Mr. Steve FERRENCE
41 Director Athletics ... Mr. Kevin M. GRIMMER
10 Associate VP for Finance ... Mr. Scott BATEMAN
21 Associate VP of Business Affairs ... Ms. Susan HEAD
88 Director of Student Conduct ... Ms. Megan WYETT
36 Director Career Services ... Mr. Sim COVINGTON
23 Director Health & Wellness Center ... Ms. Jo RUFFRAGE
09 Assistant VP Institutional Research ... Ms. Valerie FUSCO
35 AVP Student Affairs ... Mrs. Jennifer ADAMS
37 Director Student Financial Aid ... Ms. Melissa ROSE
06 Registrar ... Mrs. Meghan GETMAN
123 Coordinator Graduate Center ... Ms. Maryrose RAAB
43 Associate Counsel ... Mr. Mark LEMIRE
108 Director Institutional Assessment ... Dr. Joanne JOSEPH
13 Chief Information Officer ... Mr. Andrew BELLINGER
07 Director of Admissions ... Ms. Gina LISCIO
08 Director of Library Services ... Mr. Shannon PRITTING
120 Dir Online Education/E-learning ... Mr. Rick SHELTON
29 Director Alumni Relations ... Ms. Courtney KERWIN
96 Director of Purchasing ... Mr. David MANORE

*Suffolk County Community College Central Administration (B)

533 College Road, Selden NY 11784-2899
County: Suffolk Identification: 666658
Unit ID: 366395
Telephone: (631) 451-4000 Carnegie Class: N/A
FAX Number: (631) 451-4715
URL: www.sunysuffolk.edu

01 President ... Dr. Shaun L. MCKAY
27 College Communications Director ... Mr. Drew BIONDO
43 College General Counsel ... Mr. Louis S. PETRIZZO
05 VP Academic Affairs ... Vacant
10 VP Business Financial Affairs ... Ms. Gail VIZZINI
30 Vice Pres Institutional Advancement ... Ms. Mary Lou ARANEO
45 VP Planning/Inst Effectiveness ... Dr. Jeffrey M. PEDERSEN
20 Assoc VP Academic Affairs ... Dr. Paul BEAUDIN
32 VP of Student Affairs ... Dr. Christopher J. ADAMS
13 VP Computer Information Systems ... Mr. Shady AZZAM-GOMEZ
103 Assoc VP Workforce/Econ Development ... Mr. John LOMBARDO
15 Assistant VP Human Resources ... Mr. Jeffrey L. TEMPERA
84 College Dean Enrollment Management ... Ms. Joanne E. BRAXTON
06 Assoc Dean Master Sched/Registrar ... Ms. Anna FLACK
35 Campus Assoc Dean Student Serv ... Mr. Charles BARTOLOTTA
37 College Director of Financial Aid ... Ms. Nancy A. BREWER
28 Col Coord Multicultural Affairs ... Mr. James W. BANKS
100 Assistant to the President ... Ms. Sandra O'HARA
102 Executive Director Foundation ... Dr. Sylvia DIAZ
30 Col Assoc Dean Inst Advancement ... Mr. Andrew FAWCETT
104 Col Assoc Dean Spec Prog & Ext Part ... Dr. Iaroslava BABENCHUK
106 Asst Dean Instructional Technology ... Mr. Douglas KAHN
14 Assoc Dean Computer Info Systems ... Mr. Gary RIS
19 Director Fire/Public Safety ... Mr. Baycan FIDELI
22 Chief Diversity Officer/Title IX ... Ms. Christina VARGAS
25 Col Asst Dean Grants Development ... Dr. William T. TUCKER
26 Dir College Relations/Publications ... Ms. Mary M. FEDER
29 Director Alumni Relations ... Mr. Russell MALBROUGH
41 College Director of Athletics ... Mr. Kevin FOLEY
86 Col Director Legislative Affairs ... Mr. Benjamin ZWIRN
96 Admin Director Business Operations ... Ms. Beatriz CASTANO
36 Director Career Services ... Ms. Tania VELAZQUEZ
100 Chief of Staff ... Ms. Carol WICKLIFFE-CAMPBELL
18 Executive Director Facilities ... Mr. Paul COOPER

*Suffolk County Community College Ammerman Campus (C)

533 College Road, Selden NY 11784-2899
County: Suffolk FICE Identification: 002878
Unit ID: 195951
Telephone: (631) 451-4000 Carnegie Class: Not Classified
FAX Number: (631) 451-4015 Calendar System: Semester
URL: www.sunysuffolk.edu
Established: 1959 Annual Undergrad Tuition & Fees (In-District): N/A
Enrollment: N/A Coed
Affiliation or Control: State/Local IRS Status: 501(c)3
Highest Offering: Associate Degree
Accreditation: M, ADNUR, EMT, PTAA

02 Executive Dean/Campus CEO ... Mr. P. Wesley LUNDBURG
05 Assoc Dean of Academic Affairs ... Dr. Sandra SPROWS
32 Assoc Dean of Student Services ... Mr. Charles BARTOLOTTA
37 Director of Financial Aid ... Vacant
07 Director of Admissions ... Dr. Katherine AGUIRRE
08 Head Librarian ... Ms. Susan LIEBERTHAL
13 Asst Dir of Application Development ... Mr. Christopher T. BLAKE
18 Director Facilities/Physical Plant ... Mr. Edward BENZ
36 Dir Career Svcs/Cooperative Educ ... Ms. Tania VELAZQUEZ
92 Coordinator Honors Program ... Mr. Albin COFONE
10 Admin Director of Business Affairs ... Mr. John P. CIENSKI
90 Coord of Instructional Technology ... Mr. Paul BASILEO
91 Data Control Supervisor ... Mr. Paul MATUS

*Suffolk County Community College Eastern Campus (D)

121 Speonk-Riverhead Road, Riverhead NY 11901-3499
Telephone: (631) 548-2500 FICE Identification: 004816
Accreditation: &M, DIETT, PNUR

*Suffolk County Community College Grant Campus (E)

1001 Crooked Hill Road, Brentwood NY 11717-1091
Telephone: (631) 851-6700 FICE Identification: 013204
Accreditation: &M, ADNUR, CAHIIM, OTA

Sullivan County Community College (F)

112 College Road, Loch Sheldrake NY 12759-5721
County: Sullivan FICE Identification: 002879
Unit ID: 195988
Telephone: (845) 434-5750 Carnegie Class: Assoc/HT-Mix Trad/Non
FAX Number: (845) 434-4806 Calendar System: Semester
URL: www.sunysullivan.edu
Established: 1962 Annual Undergrad Tuition & Fees (In-District): $5,550
Enrollment: 1,595 Coed
Affiliation or Control: State/Local IRS Status: 501(c)3
Highest Offering: Associate Degree
Accreditation: M, ACBSP, #COARC

01 President ... Mr. John (Jay) QUAINTANCE
05 Vice Pres Academic & Student Affs ... Dr. Keith POMAKOY
10 Chief Financial Officer/Controller ... Ms. Susan HORTON
45 Assoc VP for Planning/HR & Facil ... Mr. Stephen MITCHELL
20 Asst VP Academic/Student Affairs ... Vacant
32 Dean Student Development Services ... Mr. Chris DEPEW
45 Dean of Community Outreach ... Ms. Cindy KASHAN
39 Residence Director ... Ms. Jaycee DE GROAT
04 Exec Assistant to the President ... Ms. Linda ROFFEL
18 Director Facilities/Physical Plant ... Mr. Darren STEELE
07 Director Admissions/Registration ... Vacant
37 Director of Financial Aid ... Mr. Brandon GILLILAND
08 Director of Library Services ... Ms. Evangela OATES
35 Director Student Activities ... Mr. Frank SINIGAGLIA
41 Director of Athletics ... Mr. Chris DEPEW
15 Asst Director of Human Resources ... Ms. Stephanie SMART
09 Director Institutional Research ... Ms. Janet HALPRIN
38 Director Student Counseling ... Ms. Rose HANOFEE
13 Director Information Technology ... Mr. James SAMMANN
19 Director Security/Safety ... Mr. David SEIGERMAN
06 Dir Registration Services/Registrar ... Ms. Anne MARCHAL
26 Coord of Public & Alumni Relations ... Vacant
96 Purchasing Agent ... Ms. Lorry IRWIN
50 Chair Business/Information Tech ... Ms. Mary SUDOL
79 Chair Liberal Arts & Humanities ... Dr. Paul REIFENHEISER
83 Chair Health/Social/Behavioral Sci ... Dr. Susan ROGERS
81 Chair Mathematics/Natural Sciences ... Ms. Debra LEWKIEWICZ

Swedish Institute-College of Health Sciences (G)

226 W 26th Street, New York NY 10001-6700
County: New York FICE Identification: 021700
Unit ID: 196389
Telephone: (212) 924-5900 Carnegie Class: Spec 2-yr-Health
FAX Number: (212) 924-7600 Calendar System: Semester
URL: www.swedishinstitute.edu
Established: 1916 Annual Undergrad Tuition & Fees: $19,000
Enrollment: 888 Coed
Affiliation or Control: Proprietary IRS Status: Proprietary
Highest Offering: Associate Degree
Accreditation: ACCSC, ADNUR, SURGT

01 President ... Mr. Peter NEIGLER
03 Executive Vice President ... Ms. Stacey JAMESON
05 Director of Education ... Dr. Joseph BALATBAT
10 Chief Financial Officer ... Mr. Bill BERNARD
07 Director of Admissions ... Vacant
88 VP for Program Development ... Mr. John KATOMSKI
88 Dean of Advanced Personal Training ... Mr. Vincent METZO
88 Dean for Massage Therapy ... Ms. Ericka CLINTON
66 Dean of Nursing ... Dr. Maxinee BLACK-ARIAS
13 Director of Information Technology ... Mr. Rob SIEFKEN
32 Director of Student Services ... Ms. Theresa ROBBINSON
26 Director of Public Relations ... Vacant
37 Financial Aid Director ... Ms. Desire DEJESUS-AVILES
08 Director of Library Services ... Mr. Matthew FORTINO
06 Registrar ... Ms. Karen HOLDER
113 Bursar ... Ms. Beatriz ACEVEDO
51 Director of Continuing Education ... Ms. Tania OGULLUKIAN
40 Bookstore Manager ... Mr. Dan YUEN
36 Director of Career Services ... Mr. Richard GARDNER

Syracuse University (H)

900 South Crouse Avenue, Syracuse NY 13244
County: Onondaga FICE Identification: 002882
Unit ID: 196413
Telephone: (315) 443-1870 Carnegie Class: DU-Highest
FAX Number: (315) 443-3503 Calendar System: Semester
URL: www.syr.edu
Established: 1870 Annual Undergrad Tuition & Fees: $45,022
Enrollment: 21,789 Coed
Affiliation or Control: Independent Non-Profit IRS Status: 501(c)3
Highest Offering: Doctorate
Accreditation: M, ART, AUD, CACREP, CAEPN, CIDA, CLPSY, CS, DIETD, DIETI, ENG, JOUR, LAW, LIB, MFCD, MUS, PH, SCPSY, SP, SPAA, SW

01 Chancellor & President ... Mr. Kent SYVERUD
05 Vice Chanc/Prov Academic Affs ... Dr. Michele WHEATLY
10 Executive Vice President & CFO ... Dr. Amir RAHNAMAY-AZAR
43 Sr VP and General Counsel ... Mr. Daniel J. FRENCH
111 Chief Advancement Ofcr/Sr VP ... Mr. Matthew TER MOLEN
32 Sr VP/Enroll and the Student Exp ... Mr. Dolan EVANOVICH
41 Athletic Director ... Mr. John WILDHACK
26 Sr Vice Pres Public Affairs ... Mr. Kevin C. QUINN
21 Comptroller ... Ms. Jean B. GALLIPEAU
104 Assoc Prov International Education ... Dr. Margaret R. HIMLEY
15 Sr VP/Chief Human Resources Officer ... Mr. Andrew GORDON
20 Assoc Provost Faculty Affairs ... Ms. LaVonda REED
13 VP Information Technology/CIO ... Mr. Samuel SCOZZAFAVA
101 Secretary Board of Trustees ... Ms. Lisa A. DOLAK
48 Dean School of Architecture ... Dr. Michael A. SPEAKS
49 Dean College of Arts & Sciences ... Dr. Karin RUHLANDT
58 Dean of Graduate School ... Dr. Peter VANABLE
08 Dean of University Libraries ... Mr. David SEAMAN
53 Dean School of Education ... Dr. Joanna O. MASINGILA
76 Dean Col of Sport & Human Dynamics ... Dr. Diane Lyden MURPHY
54 Dean Col Engineering/Computer Sci ... Dr. Teresa DAHLBERG
62 Dean School of Info Studies ... Dr. Elizabeth D. LIDDY
61 Dean College of Law ... Dr. Craig M. BOISE
50 Dean Whitman School of Management ... Dr. Eugene ANDERSON
80 Dean Maxwell Sch of Citizenship ... Dr. David VAN SLYKE
60 Dean Newhouse School of Public Comm ... Dr. Lorraine BRANHAM
57 Dean Col Visual & Performing Arts ... Dr. Michael TICK
51 Interim Dean University College ... Dr. Michael FRASCIELLO
07 Dean of Admissions ... Dr. Maurice A. HARRIS
100 Sr VP and Chief of Staff ... Dr. Candace CAMPBELL JACKSON
88 Vice Chancellor Strat Init & Innov ... Mr. Michael HAYNIE
18 VP and Chief Facilities Officer ... Mr. Pete SALA
19 Sr VP Safety/Chief Law Enforc Ofc ... Mr. Anthony CALLISTO

Talmudical Institute of Upstate New York (I)

769 Park Avenue, Rochester NY 14607-3046
County: Monroe FICE Identification: 025506
Unit ID: 196440
Telephone: (585) 473-2810 Carnegie Class: Spec-4-yr-Faith
FAX Number: (585) 442-0417 Calendar System: Semester
Established: 1974 Annual Undergrad Tuition & Fees: $5,300
Enrollment: 17 Male
Affiliation or Control: Independent Non-Profit IRS Status: 501(c)3
Highest Offering: Second Talmudic Degree

Accreditation: RABN

01 Dean .... Rabbi Menachem DAVIDOWITZ
03 Executive Vice President .... Rabbi Shlomo NOBLE

Talmudical Seminary of Bobov (A)

5120 New Utrecht Avenue, Brooklyn NY 11204-1108
County: Kings FICE Identification: 041155
Unit ID: 451404
Telephone: (718) 854-8700 Carnegie Class: Spec-4-yr-Faith
FAX Number: (718) 854-8707 Calendar System: Semester
Established: 2005 Annual Undergrad Tuition & Fees: $7,600
Enrollment: 362 Male
Affiliation or Control: Independent Non-Profit IRS Status: 501(c)3
Highest Offering: First Talmudic Degree
Accreditation: RABN

01 Dean .... Rabbi Joshua RUBIN
37 Director Student Financial Aid .... Josef DEUTSCH
06 Registrar .... Mendel GROSS

Talmudical Seminary Oholei Torah (B)

667 Eastern Parkway, Brooklyn NY 11213-3397
County: Kings FICE Identification: 012011
Unit ID: 196431
Telephone: (718) 774-5050 Carnegie Class: Spec-4-yr-Faith
FAX Number: (718) 778-0784 Calendar System: Semester
Established: 1956 Annual Undergrad Tuition & Fees: $9,300
Enrollment: 349 Male
Affiliation or Control: Independent Non-Profit IRS Status: 501(c)3
Highest Offering: First Talmudic Degree
Accreditation: RABN

01 Chief Executive Officer .... Mr. Zalman CHEIN
05 Dean .... Elchonon LESCHES
10 Business Officer .... Gary SUSSKIND
37 Financial Aid Officer .... Sholom ROSENFELD

Teachers College, Columbia University (C)

525 West 120th Street, New York NY 10027
County: New York FICE Identification: 003979
Unit ID: 196468
Telephone: (212) 678-3000 Carnegie Class: DU-Higher
FAX Number: (212) 678-4048 Calendar System: Semester
URL: www.tc.columbia.edu
Established: 1887 Annual Graduate Tuition & Fees: N/A
Enrollment: 4,984 Coed
Affiliation or Control: Independent Non-Profit IRS Status: 501(c)3
Highest Offering: Doctorate; No Undergraduates
Accreditation: M, CAEPN, CLPSY, COPSY, DIETI, SCPSY, SP

01 President .... Dr. Susan H. FUHRMAN
05 Provost & VP for Academic Affairs .... Dr. Thomas JAMES
100 Secretary to College/Chief of Staff .... Dr. Katie CONWAY
10 Vice Pres Finance & Administration .... Mr. Harvey SPECTOR
30 Vice Pres Devel/External Affairs .... Ms. Suzanne MURPHY
22 Vice Pres for Diversity/Cmty Affs .... Ms. Janice S. ROBINSON
88 VP Sch/Cmty Partnshp/Spec Advis .... Dr. Nancy STREIM
21 Assoc Vice Pres/Controller .... Mr. Henry PERKOWSKI
18 Asst VP Facilities .... Mr. Suzanne JABLONSKI
84 Vice Provost Enrollment Services .... Dr. Thomas ROCK
06 Registrar .... Mr. Sam FUGAZZOTTO
13 Chief Information Officer .... Mr. Naveed HUSAIN
08 Library Director .... Dr. Gary NATRIELLO
15 Director Human Resources .... Mr. Randy GLAZER
19 Director Public Safety .... Mr. John DE ANGELIS
43 General Counsel .... Mr. Michael FEIERMAN
09 Director of Institutional Research .... Ms. Haley ROSENFELD
29 Director Alumni Relations .... Ms. Rosella GARCIA
39 Director Student Housing .... Mr. Dewayne WHITE

† Affiliated with Columbia University in the City of New York.

Tompkins Cortland Community College (D)

170 North Street, PO Box 139, Dryden NY 13053-8504
County: Tompkins FICE Identification: 006788
Unit ID: 196565
Telephone: (607) 844-8211 Carnegie Class: Assoc/HT-High Non
FAX Number: (607) 844-9665 Calendar System: Semester
URL: www.TompkinsCortland.edu
Established: 1968 Annual Undergrad Tuition & Fees (In-District): $5,832
Enrollment: 3,083 Coed
Affiliation or Control: State/Local IRS Status: 501(c)3
Highest Offering: Associate Degree
Accreditation: M, ADNUR

01 President .... Dr. Orinthia T. MONTAGUE
05 Provost and VP of College .... Dr. John R. CONNERS
32 Dean of Student Life .... Mr. John BRADAC
20 Dean of Instruction .... Mr. Carl PENZIUL
08 Library Director .... Mr. Gregg KIEHL
84 Dean Operations & Enrollment Mgmt .... Ms. Blixy K. TAETZSCH
14 Director of Technology Support .... Mr. Brian ACKLEY
88 Dean Org Success & Learning .... Ms. Kathryn WUNDERLICH
09 Assoc Dean IR and Org Learning .... Dr. Kristine ALTUCHER
37 Director of Financial Aid .... Ms. LaSonya GRIGGS
26 Dean of External Relations .... Dr. Bruce RYAN
15 Human Resources Administrator .... Ms. Sharon DOVI
07 Director of Admissions .... Mr. Sandy DRUMLUK
10 Director of Budget & Finance .... Ms. Susan DEWEY
13 Chief Information Officer .... Mr. Timothy DENSMORE
19 Director of Safety & Security .... Mr. J. Beau SAUL
41 Athletic Director .... Mr. Mick R. MCDANIEL
39 Director Residence Life .... Ms. Darese DOSKAL
36 Coordinator Counseling/Career Svcs .... Ms. Joan DONOVAN
18 Director of Facilities .... Mr. James TURNER
23 Director of Health Services .... Ms. Shari SHAPLEIGH
28 Director of Multicultural Services .... Mr. Seth THOMPSON
101 Asst to President/Clerk of Board .... Ms. Cathy NORTHROP

Torah Temimah Talmudical Seminary (E)

507 Ocean Parkway, Brooklyn NY 11218-5913
County: Kings FICE Identification: 021916
Unit ID: 196583
Telephone: (718) 853-8500 Carnegie Class: Spec-4-yr-Faith
FAX Number: (718) 438-5779 Calendar System: Semester
Established: 1978 Annual Undergrad Tuition & Fees: $10,750
Enrollment: 89 Male
Affiliation or Control: Independent Non-Profit IRS Status: 501(c)3
Highest Offering: Second Talmudic Degree
Accreditation: RABN

01 President & Dean .... Rabbi L. MARGULIES
03 Executive Director .... Rabbi L. MARGULIES
05 Chief Academic Officer .... Rabbi Lipa GELDWORTH
37 Financial Aid Administrator .... Mr. Mendel ROCHLITZ
38 Director of Guidance .... Rabbi Yirmiya GUGENHEIMER
11 Administrator .... Rabbi Yisroel KLEINMAN

Touro College (F)

500 7th Avenue, New York NY 10018
County: New York FICE Identification: 010142
Unit ID: 196592
Telephone: (646) 565-6000 Carnegie Class: Masters/L
FAX Number: N/A Calendar System: Semester
URL: www.touro.edu
Established: 1970 Annual Undergrad Tuition & Fees: $16,880
Enrollment: 13,033 Coordinate
Affiliation or Control: Independent Non-Profit IRS Status: 501(c)3
Highest Offering: Doctorate
Accreditation: M, ARCPA, CAEPT, LAW, NURSE, OSTEO, OT, #PHAR, PTA, SP, SW

01 President/Chief Executive Officer .... Dr. Alan KADISH
03 Executive Vice President .... Mr. David RAAB
03 Executive Vice President .... Mr. Moshe KRUPKA
10 Senior Vice President & CFO .... Mr. Melvin M. NESS
11 Sr Vice Pres/Chief Admin Officer .... Mr. Jeffrey ROSENGARDEN
30 Vice Pres Institutional Advancement .... Mr. Henry RUBIN
05 VP Undergrad Acad Affs/Dean of Fac .... Dr. Stanley L. BOYLAN
58 Vice Pres of Grad Studies .... Dr. Nadja GRAFF
45 VP Plng & Assessment/Dean of Stdnts .... Dr. Robert GOLDSCHMIDT
13 VP of Operations & Info Systems .... Dr. Franklin STEEN
84 VP Student Administrative Services .... Mr. Matthew BONILLA
53 Dean Grad School Education .... Dean Arnold SPINNER
56 Vice President Com Ed/Ex Dn NYSCAS .... Ms. Eva SPINELLI-SEXTER
106 VP Online Edu/Dean Women's Division .... Dr. Marian STOLTZ-LOIKE
09 Director Institutional Research .... Mr. Michael LIPKIN
43 Senior VP of Legal Affairs .... Mr. Michael NEWMAN
58 Provost Graduate/Professional Div .... Dr. Patricia SALKIN
63 Dean Col of Osteopathic Medicine .... Dr. Kenneth STEIER
67 Dean College of Pharmacy .... Dr. Henry COHEN
70 Dean School of Social Work .... Dr. Steven HUBERMAN
76 Dean of School of Health Sciences .... Dr. Louis H. PRIMAVERA
58 Dean Grad School Jewish Studies .... Dr. Michael A. SHMIDMAN
90 Dn Grad Sch of Tech/Dir Acad Comp .... Dr. Issac HERSKOWITZ
12 Dean Lander College for Men .... Dr. Moshe Z. SOKOL
50 Acting Dean Grad School of Business .... Dr. Sabra BROCK
38 Dean of Advising & Counseling .... Dr. Avery HOROWITZ
51 Asst Dean School Lifelong Education .... Dr. Briendy STERN
06 University Registrar .... Ms. Lidia MEINDL
37 Int Dir Financial Aid/Compliance .... Ms. Margherite POWELL
08 Director of Libraries .... Ms. Bashe SIMON
07 Director of Admissions .... Mr. Benjamin ENOMA
76 Director Physician Asst Program .... Dr. Joseph TOMMASINO
75 Director of Occupational Therapy .... Dr. Stephanie DAPICE-WONG
76 Director of Physical Therapy .... Ms. Jill HORBACEWICZ
88 Pgm Dir Speech Lang Path/Grad Pgm .... Ms. Hindy LUBINSKY
44 Director Advancement .... Mr. Henry RUBIN
91 Chief Info Security Officer .... Ms. Patricia CIUFFO
19 Director of Security .... Ms. Lydia PEREZ
19 Dir of Emergency Preparedness .... Ms. Shoshana YEHUDAH
15 Director of Human Resources .... Mr. Matthew BONNILLA
96 Director of Purchasing .... Ms. Wanda HERNANDEZ
18 Dir of Facilities/Real Estate .... Mr. Mark GOODMAN
21 Controller .... Mr. Stuart LIPPMAN
26 Dir of Communication/External Rels .... Ms. Elisheva SCHLAM
29 Director Alumni Relations .... Vacant
36 Director Student Placement .... Mr. Stuart ANSEL
108 Director of Assessment & Evaluation .... Dr. Eric LINDEN
25 Director Office Sponsored Pgm .... Mr. Glenn DAVIS
04 Administrative Asst to President .... Ms. Elaine GOLDBERG
104 Director Study Abroad .... Dr. Chana SOSEVSKY
105 Director Web Services .... Ms. Lisa HALBERSTAM
41 Athletic Director .... Mr. Irv BADER
45 Director of Budget & Planning .... Mr. David BELL

Touro College Bay Shore (G)

1700 Union Boulevard, Bay Shore NY 11706
Telephone: (631) 665-1600 Identification: 770145
Accreditation: &M, ARCPA, OT

Touro College Flatbush (H)

1602 Avenue J, Brooklyn NY 11230
Telephone: (718) 252-7800 Identification: 770146
Accreditation: &M

Touro Law School (I)

225 Eastview Drive, Central Islip NY 11722
Telephone: (631) 761-7000 Identification: 770148
Accreditation: &M

Tri-State College of Acupuncture (J)

80 Eighth Avenue, #400, New York NY 10011-0890
County: New York FICE Identification: 025460
Unit ID: 130581
Telephone: (212) 242-2255 Carnegie Class: Spec-4-yr-Other Health
FAX Number: (212) 242-2920 Calendar System: Semester
URL: www.tsca.edu
Established: 1982 Annual Graduate Tuition & Fees: N/A
Enrollment: 112 Coed
Affiliation or Control: Proprietary IRS Status: Proprietary
Highest Offering: Master's; No Undergraduates
Accreditation: ACUP

01 President .... Dr. Dennis MOSEMAN
06 Registrar .... Sandra TURNER

Trocaire College (K)

360 Choate Avenue, Buffalo NY 14220-2094
County: Erie FICE Identification: 002812
Unit ID: 196653
Telephone: (716) 826-1200 Carnegie Class: Spec-4-yr-Other Health
FAX Number: (716) 828-6107 Calendar System: Semester
URL: www.trocaire.edu
Established: 1958 Annual Undergrad Tuition & Fees: $16,770
Enrollment: 1,369 Coed
Affiliation or Control: Independent Non-Profit IRS Status: 501(c)3
Highest Offering: Baccalaureate
Accreditation: M, ADNUR, CAHIIM, DIETT, MAC, NUR, PHLEB, PNUR, RAD, SURGT

01 President .... Dr. Bassam M. DEEB
03 Senior Vice President .... Dr. Richard T. LINN
10 VP for Finance .... Mr. John J. HUDACK
05 Chief Academic Officer .... Dr. Theresa KNOTT
32 Chief Student Affairs Officer .... Ms. Kathleen SAUNDERS
30 VP Development & Cmty Engagement .... Ms. Pamela WITTER
21 Associate VP for Finance .... Mr. Edward JOHNSON
13 AVP Technology/Information Svcs .... Mr. Jim POULOS
121 Dean Student Success .... Mr. Tony FUNIGIELLO
84 Chief Enrollment Officer .... Ms. Jacqueline MATHENY
66 Dean Catherine McAuley Sch Nursing .... Dr. Catherine GRISWOLD
15 Chief Human Resources Officer .... Ms. Janet PETERS
37 Director of Financial Aid .... Mr. Jeffrey LUCAS
25 Grant Coordinator .... Ms. Rachel FLAMMER
26 Director of Public Relations .... Ms. Emily Burns PERRYMAN
06 Registrar .... Mrs. Theresa HORNER
121 Dir Advisement & Student Support .... Dr. Christine RYAN
88 Director Learning Center .... Ms. Bridget HODGES
124 Director of Student Engagement .... Mr. Thomas VANE
88 Director Wellness Center .... Ms. Lauren ELLIS
08 Director Library Services .... Ms. Elise TORRE
18 Facilities Director .... Mr. Richard MCGILVRAY
110 Director of Development .... Ms. Lindsey DOTSON
07 Dean of Admissions & Workforce Dev .... Mrs. Mollie A. BALLARO
40 Manager Bookstore .... Mr. Shawn HENRIS
49 Dean of Arts/Sciences & Prof Stds .... Dr. Jennifer Higgins MCCORMICK
76 Dean Division of Health Prof .... Dr. Linda KERWIN
108 Director of Assessment & Research .... Dr. Nicole TOMASELLO
88 Director of Mission & Service .... Mr. Robert SHEARN

Ulster County Community College (L)

491 Cottekill Road, PO Box 557, Stone Ridge NY 12484
County: Ulster FICE Identification: 002880
Unit ID: 196699
Telephone: (845) 687-5000 Carnegie Class: Assoc/HT-High Non
FAX Number: (845) 687-5083 Calendar System: Semester
URL: www.sunyulster.edu
Established: 1961 Annual Undergrad Tuition & Fees (In-District): $5,156
Enrollment: 3,468 Coed
Affiliation or Control: State/Local IRS Status: 501(c)3
Highest Offering: Associate Degree
Accreditation: M, ADNUR

01 President ... Dr. Alan P. ROBERTS
84 Sr Vice Pres Enrollment Mgmt ... Ms. Ann MARROTT
05 VP for Academic Affairs ... Mr. Kevin STONER
51 Dean of Continuing & Prof Educ ... Mr. Christopher MARX
10 VP Admin Svcs/Chief Business Ofcr ... Mr. Christopher NGUYEN
30 Exec Dir of Inst Advance & Ext Rels ... Ms. Lorraine SALMON
04 Assistant to President ... Ms. Jennifer ZELL
08 Director of Library Services ... Ms. Kari MACK
37 Director of Financial Aid ... Mr. Christopher CHANG
06 Registrar ... Ms. Debra MILLER
41 Athletic Director ... Mr. Matthew BRENNIE
19 Director of Safety & Security ... Mr. Wayne FREER
07 Asst Dean Enrollment & Dir Admiss ... Mr. Matthew GREEN
26 Chief Public Relations Officer ... Ms. Ann MARROTT
36 Dir Student Place/Acad Support Svcs ... Ms. Jane KITHCART
32 Director Student Affairs ... Ms. Ann MARROTT
18 Director of Plant Operations ... Vacant
09 Director of Institutional Research ... Mr. Clarence (Hank) MILLER
103 Workforce Development ... Mr. Christopher MARX
15 Coordinator of Personnel Services ... Mrs. Debra DELANOY
21 Asst Dean of Admin Services ... Ms. Amy WINTERS
96 Coord Procurement/General Services ... Mr. Stephen GALLART
101 Secretary of the Institution/Board ... Ms. Jennifer ZELL
38 Assistant Dean of Student Success ... Ms. Wendy MCCORRY

Unification Theological Seminary (A)

30 Seminary Drive, Barrytown NY 12507-5021
County: Dutchess FICE Identification: 032163
Unit ID: 246789
Telephone: (845) 752-3000 Carnegie Class: Spec-4-yr-Faith
FAX Number: (845) 758-2156 Calendar System: Semester
URL: www.uts.edu
Established: 1975 Annual Undergrad Tuition & Fees: N/A
Enrollment: 82 Coed
Affiliation or Control: Unification Church IRS Status: 501(c)3
Highest Offering: Doctorate
Accreditation: M

01 President ... Dr. Hugh SPURGIN
05 Vice President for Academic Affairs ... Dr. Kathy WININGS
11 VP for Administration ... Dr. Michael MICKLER
88 Director of Field Education ... Dr. Jacob DAVID
10 Director of Finances ... Mr. Frank ZOCHOL
06 Registrar ... Mrs. Ute DELANEY
08 Library Technician ... Mr. Robert WAGNER
37 Student Financial Aid Director ... Mr. Henry CHRISTOPHER
18 Plant Director ... Mr. Carl VERDERBER
07 Director of Admissions ... Mr. Henry CHRISTOPHER
30 Dir for Development & Alumni Rels ... Mr. Robin GRAHAM
108 Director Institutional Assessment ... Dr. Keisuke NODA
32 Chief Student Affairs/Student Life ... Dr. Drissa KONE

Union College (B)

807 Union Street, Schenectady NY 12308-3181
County: Schenectady FICE Identification: 002889
Unit ID: 196866
Telephone: (518) 388-6000 Carnegie Class: Bac-A&S
FAX Number: (518) 388-6800 Calendar System: Trimester
URL: www.union.edu
Established: 1795 Annual Undergrad Tuition & Fees: $51,696
Enrollment: 2,269 Coed
Affiliation or Control: Independent Non-Profit IRS Status: 501(c)3
Highest Offering: Baccalaureate
Accreditation: M, ENG

01 President ... Dr. Stephen C. AINLAY
05 VP Academic Affs/Dean Faculty ... Dr. Strom THACKER
111 Vice President College Relations ... Ms. Terri A. CERVENY
10 Vice President for Finance & Admin ... Ms. Diane T. BLAKE
07 VP Admissions/Fin Aid/Enrollment ... Mr. Matthew J. MALATESTA
100 Chief of Staff ... Ms. Darcy CZAJKA
22 Chief Diversity Officer ... Dr. Gretchel L. HATHAWAY
32 VP Student Affairs/Dean of Students ... Dr. Stephen C. LEAVITT
20 Dean of Studies ... Dr. Mark E. WUNDERLICH
13 Chief Information Officer ... Ms. Ellen Y. BORKOWSKI
06 Registrar ... Ms. Penelope S. ADEY
30 Sr Director of Development ... Mr. Nick FAMULARE
08 College Librarian ... Ms. Frances J. MALOY
26 Director of Media and Public Rels ... Mr. Phillip J. WAJDA
37 Director of Financial Aid ... Ms. Linda M. PARKER
38 Director of Student Counseling ... Mr. Marcus S. HOTALING
36 Director of Career Center ... Mr. Robert C. SOULES
15 Director of Human Resources ... Mr. Eric NOLL
41 Director of Athletics ... Mr. James MCLAUGHLIN
19 Director Campus Safety ... Mr. Christopher M. HAYEN
39 Director Residence Life ... Ms. Amanda J. BINGEL

† Tuition figure is a comprehensive fees figure.

Union Theological Seminary (C)

3041 Broadway, New York NY 10027-5792
County: New York FICE Identification: 002890
Unit ID: 196884
Telephone: (212) 662-7100 Carnegie Class: Spec-4-yr-Faith
FAX Number: (212) 280-1416 Calendar System: Semester
URL: www.utsnyc.edu
Established: 1836 Annual Graduate Tuition & Fees: N/A
Enrollment: 220 Coed
Affiliation or Control: Independent Non-Profit IRS Status: 501(c)3
Highest Offering: Doctorate; No Undergraduates
Accreditation: M, THEOL

01 President ... Dr. Serene JONES
03 Executive Vice President ... Mr. Fred DAVIE
10 Int VP Finance & Operations ... Mr. Brent DICKMAN
30 VP for Development ... Mr. Martin DUUS
05 Dean of Academic Affairs ... Dr. Mary C. BOYS
32 Associate Dean Student Affairs ... Dr. Yvette WILSON-BARNES
20 Associate Academic Dean ... Dr. Beth BIDLACK
88 Senior Director of Integrative Educ ... Dr. Su Y. PAK
06 Registrar/Asst Dir Financial Aid ... Mr. Rafael ORTIZ
18 Deputy Vice Pres Building/Grounds ... Mr. Michael MALONEY
88 Sr Director Special Initiatives ... Rev. Richard LANDERS
39 Director Housing/Campus Services ... Mr. Michael ORZECHOWSKI
07 Assoc Dean Admissions/Financial Aid ... Ms. Nichelle JENKINS
15 Director Personnel Services ... Ms. Diana TORRES-PETRILLI

United Talmudical Seminary (D)

191 Rodney Street, Brooklyn NY 11211-7900
County: Kings FICE Identification: 011189
Unit ID: 197018
Telephone: (718) 963-9770 Carnegie Class: Spec-4-yr-Faith
FAX Number: (718) 963-9775 Calendar System: Semester
Established: 1949 Annual Undergrad Tuition & Fees: $13,620
Enrollment: 2,447 Male
Affiliation or Control: Independent Non-Profit IRS Status: 501(c)3
Highest Offering: Second Talmudic Degree
Accreditation: RABN

01 Dean ... Rabbi Zalman TEITLBAUM
05 Assoc Dean Scholastic Services ... Rabbi Yeruchem DEUTSCH
37 Financial Aid Administrator ... Mr. Bernard KATZ
10 Business Officer ... Mr. Solomon GREENFELD

University of Rochester (E)

500 Joseph C. Wilson Boulevard, Rochester NY 14627
County: Monroe FICE Identification: 002894
Unit ID: 195030
Telephone: (585) 275-2121 Carnegie Class: DU-Highest
FAX Number: (585) 275-0359 Calendar System: Semester
URL: www.rochester.edu
Established: 1850 Annual Undergrad Tuition & Fees: $50,142
Enrollment: 11,105 Coed
Affiliation or Control: Independent Non-Profit IRS Status: 501(c)3
Highest Offering: Doctorate
Accreditation: M, CACREP, CAEPN, CLPSY, DENT, ENG, IPSY, MED, MFCD, MUS, NURSE, PAST, PDPSY, PH

01 President and CEO ... Mr. Joel SELIGMAN
05 Provost and Sr VP for Research ... Mr. Rob CLARK
49 Int Dean of Arts/Sci & Engr Faculty ... Mr. Rick WAUGH
10 Sr VP Administration & Fin/CFO ... Ms. Holly CRAWFORD
88 VP and University Dean ... Mr. Paul J. BURGETT
17 Sr VP Health Sciences/Med Ctr CEO ... Dr. Mark B. TAUBMAN
45 Sr VP for Institutional Resources ... Mr. Douglas PHILLIPS
111 Sr VP and Chief Advanc Officer ... Mr. Thomas FARRELL
43 VP and General Counsel ... Ms. Gail NORRIS
26 VP for Communications ... Ms. Elizabeth STAUDERMAN
13 VP and CIO for the University ... Mr. David E. LEWIS
15 Assoc VP Human Resources ... Mr. Tony KINSLOW
58 Vice Provost/Univ Dean Grad Studies ... Ms. Margaret KEARNEY
100 General Secy/Pres Chief of Staff ... Ms. Lamar R. MURPHY
28 Vice Provost Fac Devel & Diversity ... Dr. Vivian LEWIS
08 Dean River Campus Libraries ... Ms. Mary Ann MAVRINAC
88 Vice President/Laser Lab Director ... Mr. Robert L. MCCRORY
49 Dean of School of Arts & Sciences ... Ms. Gloria CULVER
54 Dean of Hajim Engineering School ... Ms. Wendi HEINZELMAN
84 Dean AS&E Undergrad Admis & Fin Aid ... Mr. Jonathan BURDICK
37 Director of Financial Aid ... Ms. Samantha VEEDER
108 Asst Provost for Academic Admin ... Ms. Jane Marie SOUZA
114 Sr Assoc VP for Budgets & Planning ... Mr. Michael ANDREWS
32 Dean of Students Arts/Sci & Engr ... Mr. Matthew BURNS
63 Dean of School of Medicine & Dent ... Dr. Mark B. TAUBMAN
64 Dean of Eastman School of Music ... Mr. Jamal ROSSI
66 Dean of School of Nursing ... Ms. Kathy RIDEOUT
50 Dean of Simon Business School ... Mr. Andrew AINSLIE
53 Dean Warner Grad Sch Educ & Hum Dev ... Ms. Raffaella BORASI
89 Dean of Freshmen Arts/Sci & Engr ... Ms. Marcy KRAUS
88 Dean of Sophmores Arts/Sci & Engr ... Mr. Sean HANNA
35 Assoc Dean Students Arts/Sci & Engr ... Ms. Anne-Marie ALGIER
23 Strong Health Chief Medical Officer ... Dr. Raymond MAYEWSKI
52 Dir Eastman Institute Oral Health ... Dr. Eli ELIAV
25 Assoc VP Research & Project Admin ... Ms. Gunta LIDERS
18 Assoc VP Facilities & Services ... Mr. Bruce BASHWINER
86 Executive Director Govt Relations ... Mr. Peter J. ROBINSON
96 Assoc VP Purchasing & Supply ... Mr. Carl TIETJEN
04 Executive Asst to the President ... Ms. Susan NIGGLI
06 University Registrar ... Ms. Nancy SPECHT
19 Director of Public Safety ... Mr. Mark T. FISCHER
57 Dir of the Memorial Art Gallery ... Mr. Jonathan BINSTOCK
41 Director of Athletics & Recreation ... Mr. George VANDERZWAAG
39 Exec Dir Res Life & Housing Svcs ... Ms. Laurel CONTOMANOLIS
36 Exec Dir Career & Internship Center ... Mr. Joe TESTANI
101 Administrator to Board of Trustees ... Ms. Jackie E. KING
42 Director Religious & Spiritual Life ... Rev. Denise YARBROUGH
104 Director Study Abroad ... Ms. Tynelle STEWART
22 Equal Opp Dir and Title IX Coord ... Ms. Morgan LEVY

USC The Business College (F)

201 Bleecker Street, Utica NY 13501-2200
County: Oneida FICE Identification: 009077
Unit ID: 197081
Telephone: (315) 733-2307 Carnegie Class: Spec 2-yr-Other
FAX Number: (315) 733-9281 Calendar System: Semester
URL: www.uscny.edu
Established: 1896 Annual Undergrad Tuition & Fees: $14,040
Enrollment: 148 Coed
Affiliation or Control: Proprietary IRS Status: Proprietary
Highest Offering: Associate Degree
Accreditation: NY

01 President & Treasurer ... Mr. Philip M. WILLIAMS
05 Exec Vice President for Academics ... Vacant
32 Exec Vice Pres Student Affairs ... Mr. Scott K. WILLIAMS
11 Exec Vice President Administration ... Mr. John L. CROSSLEY
103 VP Corp/Workforce Develop ... Mr. Donald G. REESE
10 Vice President of Finance ... Mr. Richard H. HILTON
43 General Counsel ... Mr. John H. STORY, JR.
12 Director Canastota Branch ... Mrs. Wendy M. CARY
12 Director Oneonta Campus ... Ms. Deborah E. HADDOW
06 Registrar/Bursar ... Mrs. Marian J. NIELSON
29 Director Alumni/Public Relations ... Mr. William H. RANDALL
08 Head Librarian ... Ms. Anne K. NASSAR
37 Financial Aid Consultant ... Mr. Fred P. ZUCALLA
07 Dir of Admissions/Enrollment Mgmt ... Mr. Tom VERDOW
13 Director Information Technology ... Mr. Joseph M. CHEVRETTE, II
36 Dir of Career Svc/Human Resources ... Ms. Emily TRACY
18 Facilities Manager Physical Plant ... Ms. Camilo JIMENEZ

U.T.A. Mesivta of Kiryas Joel (G)

PO Box 2009, Monroe NY 10949-8509
County: Orange FICE Identification: 038023
Unit ID: 446604
Telephone: (845) 783-9901 Carnegie Class: Spec-4-yr-Faith
FAX Number: (845) 782-3620 Calendar System: Semester
Established: 1999 Annual Undergrad Tuition & Fees: $10,500
Enrollment: 1,688 Male
Affiliation or Control: Independent Non-Profit IRS Status: 501(c)3
Highest Offering: First Talmudic Degree
Accreditation: RABN

00 Chief Executive Officer ... David GOLDBERGER
01 President ... Elias HOROWITZ
05 Rosh Yeshiva ... Rabbi Aharon TEITELBAUM
37 Financial Aid Director ... David SCHWARTZ

Utica College (H)

1600 Burrstone Road, Utica NY 13502-4892
County: Oneida FICE Identification: 002883
Unit ID: 197045
Telephone: (315) 792-3111 Carnegie Class: Masters/L
FAX Number: (315) 792-3292 Calendar System: Semester
URL: www.utica.edu
Established: 1946 Annual Undergrad Tuition & Fees: $19,996
Enrollment: 4,463 Coed
Affiliation or Control: Independent Non-Profit IRS Status: 501(c)3
Highest Offering: Doctorate
Accreditation: M, CAEPT, CONST, NURSE, OT, PTA

01 President ... Dr. Laura CASAMENTO
05 Provost & Vice Pres Academic Aff ... Dr. John JOHNSEN
10 Vice Pres Financial Affs/Treasurer ... Ms. Pamela SALMON
32 Vice Pres Student Affairs ... Mr. Jeffrey GATES
04 Executive Assistant to President ... Ms. Kim D. LAMBERT
111 VP of Advancement ... Mr. George NEHME
84 Vice President for Enrollment Mgmt ... Mr. Jeffrey GATES
20 Associate Provost ... Dr. Robert M. HALLIDAY
26 Asst VP Marketing/Communication ... Mr. Kelly L. ADAMS
76 Dean for Health Professions/Educ ... Dr. Harry SLIFE
49 Dean for Arts & Sciences ... Dr. Sharon H. WISE
50 Dean for Business & Justice Studies ... Dr. Richard FENNER
53 Dean for Education ... Dr. Patrice HALLOCK
35 Dean of Students ... Ms. Alane P. VARGA
21 Director of Student Acct Operation ... Ms. Rosanna FALCHER
29 Director Alumni & Parent Relations ... Mr. Mark C. KOVACS
36 Director Career Services ... Ms. Halina LOTYCZEWSKI
37 Exec Dir of Student Financial Svcs ... Ms. Laura BEDFORD
06 Registrar ... Mr. Craig DEWAN
30 Director of Development ... Mr. Athony VILLANTI
41 Director of Physical Educ/Athletics ... Mr. David FONTAINE
39 Director of Residence Life ... Mr. Scott NONEMAKER
13 Dir College Info & Application Svcs ... Mr. Scott HUMPHREY
15 Director of Human Resources ... Ms. Lisa GREEN
24 Dir Computer User Svcs ... Mr. Daniel SLOAN
107 Exec Dir Corp/Professional Pgms ... Ms. Joni L. PULLIAM
51 Director of Credit Programs ... Ms. Evelyn FAZEKAS
85 Dean of International Education ... Mr. Christopher JOHNSON
18 Director Facilities Management ... Mr. Donald L. HARTER
19 Director of Campus Safety ... Mr. Wayne SULLIVAN
92 Director Honors Program ... Dr. Lawrence DAY
28 Dir Office of Opportunity Programs ... Ms. Johnni F. MAHDI
96 Manager of Purchasing ... Ms. Bobbie H. SMOROL
09 Assoc VP IT & Inst Research ... Mr. Matthew S. CARR
101 Secretary of the Institution/Board ... Ms. Jacqueline LYNCH
108 Director Institutional Assessment ... Vacant
38 Director Student Counseling ... Ms. Alison FRANKLIN
07 Asst VP UG Admissions ... Ms. Donna SHAFFNER
08 Head Librarian ... Mr. James K. TELIHA
106 Assoc Prov/VP E-learning ... Dr. Polly SMITH
43 Dir Legal Services/General Counsel ... Mr. Andrew W. BEAKMAN

† Utica College maintains an academic tie with Syracuse University that allows undergraduates to receive a Syracuse University degree.

Vassar College (A)

124 Raymond Avenue, Poughkeepsie NY 12604-0001
County: Dutchess FICE Identification: 002895
Unit ID: 197133
Telephone: (845) 437-7000 Carnegie Class: Bac-A&S
FAX Number: (845) 437-7187 Calendar System: Semester
URL: www.vassar.edu
Established: 1861 Annual Undergrad Tuition & Fees: $53,090
Enrollment: 2,435 Coed
Affiliation or Control: Independent Non-Profit IRS Status: 501(c)3
Highest Offering: Master's
Accreditation: M, CAEPT

01 President — Dr. Elizabeth BRADLEY
05 Dean of the Faculty — Dr. Jonathan CHENETTE
20 Dean of the College — Dr. Christopher ROELLKE
10 Actg Vice Pres for Finance & Admin — Mr. Stephen DAHNERT
30 VP Alumnae/i Affairs/Development — Ms. Catherine E. BAER
26 Vice Pres for Communications — Ms. Susan DEKREY
13 Chief Information Officer — Mr. Michael CATO
32 Dean of Students — Dr. Adraina DIBARTOLO
07 Dean Admission/Financial Aid — Mr. Art D. RODRIGUEZ
49 Dean of Studies — Dr. Benjamin LOTTO
20 Associate Dean College — Mr. Edward L. PITTMAN
35 Assoc Dean Col/Dir Campus Activit — Ms. Teresa QUINN
06 Registrar — Ms. Colleen MALLET
08 Director of the Libraries — Mr. Andrew ASHTON
37 Director of Financial Aid — Ms. Jessica BERNIER
36 Director Career Development Center — Ms. Stacy Lee SCHNEIDER BINGHAM
39 Director Residential Life — Mr. Luis INOA
09 Director of Institutional Research — Mr. David DAVIS-VAN ATTA
15 Director Human Resources — Ms. Ruth SPENCER
18 Exec Dir of Facilities Operations — Mr. William PEABODY
38 Director of Psychological Services — Dr. Wendy A. FREEDMAN
96 Director of Purchasing — Ms. Rosaleen CARDILLO
04 Administrative Asst to President — Ms. Ilene COOKE
101 Secretary of the Institution/Board — Dr. John FEROE
104 Director Study Abroad — Dr. Tracey HOLLAND
108 Director Institutional Assessment — Dr. David DAVIS-VAN ATTA
19 Director Security/Safety — Ms. Arlene SABO
29 Director Alumni Relations — Ms. Lisa TESSLER
41 Athletic Director — Ms. Michelle WALSH

Vaughn College of Aeronautics and Technology (B)

86-01 23rd Avenue, Flushing NY 11369
County: Queens FICE Identification: 002665
Unit ID: 188340
Telephone: (718) 429-6600 Carnegie Class: Bac/Assoc-Mixed
FAX Number: (718) 429-0671 Calendar System: Semester
URL: www.vaughn.edu
Established: 1932 Annual Undergrad Tuition & Fees: $23,540
Enrollment: 1,541 Coed
Affiliation or Control: Independent Non-Profit IRS Status: 501(c)3
Highest Offering: Master's
Accreditation: M, ENG, ENGT, IACBE

01 President — Dr. Sharon B. DEVIVO
05 Sr Vice Pres Academic/Student Affs — Vacant
10 Vice Pres for Business & Finance — Mr. Robert G. WALDMANN
84 Vice President Enrollment Services — Mr. Ernie SHEPELSKY
15 Assoc VP College Services/Human Res — Ms. Mary DURKIN
20 Vice Pres of Academic Affairs — Dr. Paul LAVERGNE
32 Interim VP Student Affairs — Ms. Kathy DEANER
35 Assoc VP/Dean Student Affairs — Vacant
30 Asst VP Development/Alumni Affair — Mr. Michael BRADY
37 Director of Financial Aid — Ms. Tameika BENNETT
06 Registrar/Assoc VP Enrollment — Mrs. Beatriz CRUZ
08 Librarian — Ms. Joann JAYNE
26 Director of Public Affairs — Ms. Maureen KIGGINS
96 Coordinator of Purchasing — Mr. Manuel ADRIANZEN
09 Manager of Inst Effectiveness — Ms. Rebekah CHOW
07 Assoc VP Enrollment — Mr. Celso ALVAREZ
18 Director of Facilities — Mr. Justin BURMEISTER
38 Dir Student Counseling/Wellness — Dr. Dinelly HOLDER
13 Asst Director Computer Operations — Mr. Hamwant (Neil) SINGH
88 Vice Pres Training — Mr. Domenic PROSCIA
04 Administrative Asst to President — Ms. Barbara LOCKE
103 Dir Workforce/Career Development — Mr. Phil MEADE
106 Dir Online Education/E-learning — Mr. Ray AXMACHER
41 Athletic Director — Mr. Ricky MCCOLLUM
101 Secretary of the Institution/Board — Ms. Barbara LOCKE
29 Director Alumni Relations — Mr. Neil GOUVEIA

Villa Maria College of Buffalo (C)

240 Pine Ridge Road, Buffalo NY 14225-3999
County: Erie FICE Identification: 002896
Unit ID: 197142
Telephone: (716) 896-0700 Carnegie Class: Bac/Assoc-Mixed
FAX Number: (716) 896-0705 Calendar System: Semester
URL: www.villa.edu
Established: 1960 Annual Undergrad Tuition & Fees: $21,080
Enrollment: 543 Coed
Affiliation or Control: Independent Non-Profit IRS Status: 501(c)3
Highest Offering: Baccalaureate
Accreditation: M, CIDA, MUS, OTA, PTAA

01 President — Sr. Marcella Marie GARUS
05 Vice President for Academic Affairs — Dr. Matthew GIORDANO
10 Vice President for Business Affairs — Mr. John IVES
30 Vice President for Development — Mrs. Mary ROBINSON
32 VP for Enroll Mgmt & Student Svcs — Mr. Brian EMERSON
06 Registrar — Mrs. Melany SHIELDS
07 Director of Admissions — Mr. Kevin DONOVAN
08 Director of Library — Ms. Lucy BUNGO
37 Director of Financial Aid — Ms. Aimee MURCH
09 Director of Institutional Research — Sr. Mary Albertine STACHOWSKI
38 Director Student Counseling — Ms. Palma M. ZANGHI
13 Director of Computer Services — Ms. Christine E. PALCZEWSKI
14 Systems Analyst — Ms. Francis MONTGOMERY
18 Plant & Grounds Manager — Mr. David WISNER
23 Director of Health Services — Mrs. Minerva MONTIJO
25 Director of Grants — Mr. Spencer MORGAN
88 Instructional Design & Program Dev — Dr. Ryan HARTNETT
36 Director of Career Services — Ms. Blythe KACZMARCZYK
42 Director of Campus Ministry — Ms. Joan MULLIN
85 Director of Foreign Students — Ms. Palma ZANGHI
26 Communications Specialist — Ms. Kristen SCHOBER
35 Director of Student Life — Mr. DJ SCHIER
88 Archivist — Sr. Mary Mark JANIK
22 Affirmative Action Officer — Ms. Diane M. HANDZLIK
29 Director of Alumni Relations — Ms. Katheryn ROSS-WINNIE
121 Director Student Success Center — Ms. Agnes ZAK-MOSKAL
57 Art Department Chair — Mr. Robert GRIZANTI
64 Music Department Chair — Mr. Anthony CASUCCIO
49 LiberalArts/Prof Studies Chair — Ms. Joyce KESSEL
108 Director Institutional Assessment — Vacant
04 Administrative Asst to President — Mrs. Kathy IVES
103 Dir Workforce/Career Development — Dr. Ryan HARTNETT
41 Athletic Director — Mr. Don SILVERI

Wagner College (D)

1 Campus Road, Staten Island NY 10301-4479
County: Richmond FICE Identification: 002899
Unit ID: 197197
Telephone: (718) 390-3100 Carnegie Class: Masters/M
FAX Number: (718) 390-3467 Calendar System: Semester
URL: www.wagner.edu
Established: 1883 Annual Undergrad Tuition & Fees: $43,980
Enrollment: 2,213 Coed
Affiliation or Control: Independent Non-Profit IRS Status: 501(c)3
Highest Offering: Doctorate
Accreditation: M, ACBSP, ARCPA, CAEPN, NUR

01 President — Dr. Richard GUARASCI
05 Provost/SVP Academic Affairs — Dr. Lily D. MCNAIR
84 Sr VP for Planning & Enrollment — Mr. Angelo G. ARAIMO
11 VP Administration — Vacant
04 Assistant to the President — Ms. Pat FITZPATRICK
88 VP Internationalization — Ms. Ruta SHAH-GORDON
10 CFO and VP for Finance & Business — Mr. John CARRESCIA
108 Assoc Provost for Assessment — Dr. Anne LOVE
20 Vice Provost for Academic Affairs — Dr. Jeffrey KRAUS
06 Registrar — Ms. Athena TURNER-FREDERICK
13 Chief Information Officer — Mr. Frank CAFASSO
42 Chaplain — Rev. Martin MALZAHN
29 Director Alumni Relations — Vacant
39 Director Residential Educ — Ms. Angelica CONCEPCION
30 Chief Development Officer — Mr. Patrick MINSON
18 Director of Campus Operations — Mr. Christian MILLER
41 Director of Athletics — Mr. Walter HAMELINE
23 Assistant Dean Health & Wellness — Ms. Kathleen OBERFELDT
19 Director of Public Safety — Mr. Edwin MOSS
15 Director of Human Resources — Ms. Jazzmine CLARKE-GLOVER
37 Director of Financial Aid — Ms. Theresa WEIMER
58 Dean of Graduate Studies — Dr. Jeffrey KRAUS
07 Dean of Enrollment — Mr. Robert HERR
88 Asst Dean of Enrollment — Ms. Patricia CLANCY
32 Dean of Campus Life and Leadership — Mr. Curtis WRIGHT
35 Dean of Campus Life and Engagement — Vacant
36 Senior Assoc Dean & Director CACE — Mr. Geoffrey HEMPILL
08 Head Librarian — Ms. Dorothy DAVISON
101 Secretary to the Board of Trustees — Mr. David MARTIN

Webb Institute (E)

298 Crescent Beach Road, Glen Cove NY 11542-1398
County: Nassau FICE Identification: 002900
Unit ID: 197221
Telephone: (516) 671-2213 Carnegie Class: Spec-4-yr-Eng
FAX Number: (516) 674-9838 Calendar System: Semester
URL: www.webb.edu
Established: 1889 Annual Undergrad Tuition & Fees: $47,400
Enrollment: 91 Coed
Affiliation or Control: Independent Non-Profit IRS Status: 501(c)3
Highest Offering: Baccalaureate
Accreditation: M, ENG

01 President — Mr. R. Keith MICHEL
05 Dean — Prof. Matthew R. WERNER
20 Assistant Dean — Prof. Richard C. HARRIS
08 Librarian — Ms. Patricia M. PRESCOTT
30 Chief Development — Mr. Anthony ZIC
10 Director of Financial Affairs — Ms. Rhonda LIGHTCAP
09 Director of Institutional Research — Prof. Richard A. ROYCE
32 Director of Student Affairs — Mr. Michael MALINOWSKI
18 Director of Facilities — Mr. John FERRANTE
84 Director of Enrollment Management — Ms. Lauren CARBALLO
29 Director of Alumni Relations — Ms. Gailmarie SUJECKI
26 Chief Public Relations Officer — Ms. Kerri ALLEGRETTA
13 Director of Communications and IT — Mr. Peter MILLER
06 Registrar — Ms. Jocelyn M. WILSON
37 Director of Financial Aid — Ms. Jocelyn M. WILSON
04 Administrative Asst to President — Ms. Gailmarie SUJECKI
15 Director Personnel Services — Ms. Svetlana MILLER

Weill Cornell Medical College (F)

1300 York Avenue, F-113, New York NY 10065-4805
Telephone: (212) 746-5900 FICE Identification: 004762
Accreditation: &M, ARCPA, DENT, IPSY, MED

† Regional accreditation is carried under the parent institution Cornell University, Ithaca, NY.

Wells College (G)

170 Main Street, Aurora NY 13026-0500
County: Cayuga FICE Identification: 002901
Unit ID: 197230
Telephone: (315) 364-3266 Carnegie Class: Bac-A&S
FAX Number: (315) 364-3227 Calendar System: Semester
URL: www.wells.edu
Established: 1868 Annual Undergrad Tuition & Fees: $38,530
Enrollment: 555 Coed
Affiliation or Control: Independent Non-Profit IRS Status: 501(c)3
Highest Offering: Baccalaureate
Accreditation: M, CAEPT

01 President — Dr. Jonathan GIBRALTER
05 Provost and Dean of the College — Dr. Cindy SPEAKER
10 Vice President and CFO — Mr. Robert A. CREE
21 Treasurer and Controller — Ms. Susan WEATHERBY
111 Vice President for Advancement — Dr. Craig S. EVANS
32 Dean of Students — Ms. Jennifer MICHAEL
84 Vice President for Enrollment Svcs — Ms. Kishan ZUBER
06 Registrar — Ms. Nicole PELLEGRINO
08 Library Director — Ms. Carol HENDERSON
37 Director Financial Aid — Ms. Laura BURNS
44 Director of Annual Giving — Ms. Pamela SHERADIN
26 Dir of Communications/Marketing — Ms. Ann ROLLO
29 Dir Alumnae & Alumni Engagement — Ms. Jennifer JANES
19 Director of Campus Safety — Mr. Anthony PLURETTI
18 Dir of Facilities/Physical Plant — Mr. Brian BROWN
15 Manager of Human Resources — Ms. Kit VAN ORMAN

Westchester Community College (H)

75 Grasslands Road, Valhalla NY 10595-1636
County: Westchester FICE Identification: 002881
Unit ID: 197294
Telephone: (914) 606-6600 Carnegie Class: Assoc/HT-Mix Trad/Non
FAX Number: (914) 606-6780 Calendar System: Semester
URL: www.sunywcc.edu
Established: 1946 Annual Undergrad Tuition & Fees (In-District): $4,723
Enrollment: 12,966 Coed
Affiliation or Control: State/Local IRS Status: 501(c)3
Highest Offering: Associate Degree
Accreditation: M, COARC, DIETT, RAD

01 President — Dr. Belinda S. MILES
05 Provost & VP Academic Affairs — Dr. Vanessa MOREST
32 VP Stdnt Access/Involve/Success — Ms. Sara THOMPSON-TWEEDY
10 Vice Pres Administrative Services — Vacant
102 VP Ext Affs/Exec Dir Found for WCC — Mrs. Eve LARNER
51 VP & Dean Community/Adult/Cont Educ — Ms. Teresita WISELL
81 Assoc Dean Math/Phys Engr/Tech — Dr. Kwesi AMOA
76 Assoc Dean Natural/Health Sciences — Dr. Ronald BLOOM
83 Assoc Dean Bus/Behav/Soc Sci Svcs — Dr. Carmen Leonor MARTINEZ-LOPEZ
79 Assoc Dean Arts/Humanities/Lrng Res — Dr. Karen TAYLOR
22 Associate Dean & Director of EOC — Ms. Gina GAINES
35 Assoc Dean Student Personnel Svcs — Ms. Ellen ZENDMAN
08 Asc Dn Lrng Res/Dist Lrng/Inst Tech — Ms. Pamela POLLARD
26 Director of College/Cmty Relations — Mr. Patrick HENNESSEY
06 Registrar — Vacant
37 Dir of Student Financial Assistance — Ms. Anita COOK
13 Vice President of IT — Mr. Anthony SCORDINO
07 Director of Admissions — Ms. Gloria DE LA PAZ
38 Acting Director of Counseling — Mr. Ruben BARATO
15 Director Human Resources — Ms. Sabrina J. CHANDLER
88 Director Faculty Student Assoc — Mr. David SKLAR
09 Director Inst Research & Planning — Vacant
19 Director of Security — Vacant
24 Director Media Services — Mr. Gennaro MASELLI
41 Athletic Director — Mr. Michael BELFIORE
21 Assoc Business Officer/Controller — Ms. Dawn GILLIS
18 Director Physical Plant — Mr. Robert CIRILLO
96 Deputy Purchasing Agent — Mr. John-Paul IANNACE
27 Publications Manager — Mr. Craig FISCHER
23 Coordinator Student Health Services — Ms. Janice GILROY
88 Coord of Transfer & Career Service — Dr. Gwen D. ROUNDTREE

Wood Tobé-Coburn School (I)

Eight E 40th Street, New York NY 10016
County: New York FICE Identification: 007405
Unit ID: 197522
Telephone: (212) 686-9040 Carnegie Class: Assoc/MT-VT-High Trad
FAX Number: (212) 686-9171 Calendar System: Semester
URL: www.woodtobecoburn.edu

Established: 1879 Annual Undergrad Tuition & Fees: $16,920
Enrollment: 296 Coed
Affiliation or Control: Proprietary IRS Status: Proprietary
Highest Offering: Associate Degree
Accreditation: NY, MAC

01 President .... Ms. Sandra GRUNINGER
05 Director of Education .... Mr. James INDELICATO
07 Director of Admissions .... Ms. Sandra ANDUJAR-WENDLAND
32 Student Services Director .... Ms. Celeste GRIFFITH
37 Financial Aid Administrator .... Ms. Celeste GRIFFITH
36 Placement Director .... Mr. Christopher MASSEY

Yeshiva Derech Chaim (A)

1573 39th Street, Brooklyn NY 11218-4413
County: Kings FICE Identification: 022651
Unit ID: 197647
Telephone: (718) 438-5476 Carnegie Class: Spec-4-yr-Faith
FAX Number: (718) 435-9285 Calendar System: Semester
Established: 1975 Annual Undergrad Tuition & Fees: $11,800
Enrollment: 145 Male
Affiliation or Control: Independent Non-Profit IRS Status: 501(c)3
Highest Offering: Second Talmudic Degree
Accreditation: RABN

01 President .... Rabbi Chaim RENNERT
01 President .... Rabbi Yisroel PLUTCHOK

Yeshiva D'Monsey Rabbinical College (B)

2 Roman Boulevard, Monsey NY 10952-3106
County: Rockland FICE Identification: 031473
Unit ID: 420325
Telephone: (845) 426-3276 Carnegie Class: Spec-4-yr-Faith
FAX Number: (845) 352-1119 Calendar System: Semester
Established: 1984 Annual Undergrad Tuition & Fees: $6,500
Enrollment: 61 Male
Affiliation or Control: Independent Non-Profit IRS Status: 501(c)3
Highest Offering: Second Talmudic Degree
Accreditation: RABN

01 Rosh Yeshiva .... Rabbi Moishe GREEN
05 Rosh Yeshiva .... Rabbi Ruvain GREEN
37 Financial Aid Director .... Rabbi Aron BERGER

Yeshiva of Far Rockaway (C)

802 Hicksville Road, Far Rockaway NY 11691-5219
County: Queens FICE Identification: 041196
Unit ID: 190752
Telephone: (718) 327-7600 Carnegie Class: Spec-4-yr-Faith
FAX Number: (718) 327-1430 Calendar System: Semester
Established: 1969 Annual Undergrad Tuition & Fees: $11,750
Enrollment: 34 Male
Affiliation or Control: Independent Non-Profit IRS Status: 501(c)3
Highest Offering: First Talmudic Degree
Accreditation: RABN

01 President .... Rabbi Yechiel I. PERR
03 Executive Director .... Rabbi Shayeh KOHN
32 Dean of Students .... Rabbi Dovid KLEINKAUFMAN
06 Registrar .... Mrs. Tamara MASLOW

Yeshiva Gedolah Imrei Yosef D'Spinka (D)

1466 56th Street, Brooklyn NY 11219-4696
County: Kings FICE Identification: 030001
Unit ID: 375230
Telephone: (718) 851-8721 Carnegie Class: Spec-4-yr-Faith
FAX Number: (718) 686-8849 Calendar System: Semester
Established: 1987 Annual Undergrad Tuition & Fees: $8,000
Enrollment: 109 Male
Affiliation or Control: Independent Non-Profit IRS Status: 501(c)3
Highest Offering: First Talmudic Degree
Accreditation: RABN

01 President .... Joseph SOLOMON

Yeshiva Gedolah Kesser Torah (E)

50 Cedar Lane, Monsey NY 10952
County: Rockland Identification: 667112
Unit ID: 481410
Telephone: (845) 406-4308 Carnegie Class: Spec-4-yr-Faith
FAX Number: (845) 406-4199 Calendar System: Semester
Established: 2004 Annual Undergrad Tuition & Fees: $10,200
Enrollment: 70 Male
Affiliation or Control: Independent Non-Profit IRS Status: 501(c)3
Highest Offering: First Talmudic Degree
Accreditation: RABN

00 CEO .... Rabbi David FISHMAN
01 President .... David BERNSTEIN
06 Registrar .... Rabbi Ephraim SALB
37 Director Student Financial Aid .... Yaakov BERGER

Yeshiva Gedolah Ohr Yisrael (F)

2899 Nostrand Avenue, Brooklyn NY 11229
County: Kings Identification: 667077
Unit ID: 486017
Telephone: (718) 382-8702 Carnegie Class: Not Classified
FAX Number: (718) 382-8703 Calendar System: Semester
Established: 1999 Annual Undergrad Tuition & Fees: $7,050
Enrollment: 40 Male
Affiliation or Control: Independent Non-Profit IRS Status: 501(c)3
Highest Offering: First Talmudic Degree
Accreditation: RABN

01 Rosh Yeshiva .... Avraham ZUCKER
10 Treasurer .... Avi KAHN

Yeshiva Karlin Stolin Beth Aaron V'Israel Rabbinical Institute (G)

1818 54th Street, Brooklyn NY 11204-1545
County: Kings FICE Identification: 025058
Unit ID: 197601
Telephone: (718) 232-7800 Carnegie Class: Spec-4-yr-Faith
FAX Number: (718) 331-4833 Calendar System: Semester
Established: 1948 Annual Undergrad Tuition & Fees: $11,500
Enrollment: 136 Male
Affiliation or Control: Independent Non-Profit IRS Status: 501(c)3
Highest Offering: First Talmudic Degree
Accreditation: RABN

01 Chief Executive Officer .... Rabbi Yochanan PILCHICK
05 Dean Theology/Chief Acad Officer .... Rabbi Chaim WOLPIN
06 Registrar .... Rabbi Aryeh WOLPIN
08 Librarian .... Rabbi Yochanan GOLDHABER
10 Fiscal Officer .... Rabbi Irving PERRES
37 Financial Aid Director .... Rabbi David STEIN
33 Dean of Men .... Rabbi Gedelyah MACHLIS

Yeshiva and Kolel Bais Medrash Elyon (H)

73 Main Street, Monsey NY 10952-3013
County: Rockland Identification: 666707
Unit ID: 245777
Telephone: (845) 371-2481 Carnegie Class: Spec-4-yr-Faith
FAX Number: (845) 356-7065 Calendar System: Semester
Established: 1945 Annual Undergrad Tuition & Fees: $8,600
Enrollment: 98 Male
Affiliation or Control: Independent Non-Profit IRS Status: 501(c)3
Highest Offering: Second Talmudic Degree
Accreditation: @RABN

01 President .... Rabbi Yerachmiel CENSOR
05 Dean .... Rabbi Israel FALK

Yeshiva of Machzikai Hadas (I)

1301 47th Street, Brooklyn NY 11219
County: Kings FICE Identification: 041381
Unit ID: 455257
Telephone: (718) 853-2442 Carnegie Class: Spec-4-yr-Faith
FAX Number: (718) 853-2504 Calendar System: Semester
Established: 2001 Annual Undergrad Tuition & Fees: $8,400
Enrollment: 410 Male
Affiliation or Control: Independent Non-Profit IRS Status: 501(c)3
Highest Offering: First Talmudic Degree
Accreditation: RABN

01 Rosh Yeshiva .... Rabbi Yidel MONHEIT

Yeshiva of Nitra Rabbinical College (J)

194 Division Avenue, Brooklyn NY 11211-7199
County: Kings FICE Identification: 011670
Unit ID: 197674
Telephone: (718) 387-0422 Carnegie Class: Spec-4-yr-Faith
FAX Number: (718) 387-9400 Calendar System: Semester
Established: 1946 Annual Undergrad Tuition & Fees: $8,400
Enrollment: 245 Male
Affiliation or Control: Independent Non-Profit IRS Status: 501(c)3
Highest Offering: Second Talmudic Degree
Accreditation: RABN

01 President .... Mr. Alfred SCHOENBERGER
03 Vice President .... Mr. Mendel KLEIN
05 Dean .... Rabbi Samuel D. UNGAR
11 Administrative Officer .... Mr. Ernest SCHWARTZ

Yeshiva Ohr Naftoli (K)

701 Blooming Grove Turnpike, New Windsor NY 12553
County: Orange Identification: 667284
Telephone: (845) 784-4020 Carnegie Class: Not Classified
FAX Number: N/A Calendar System: Other
Established: Annual Undergrad Tuition & Fees: N/A
Enrollment: N/A Male
Affiliation or Control: Independent Non-Profit IRS Status: 501(c)3
Highest Offering: First Talmudic Degree
Accreditation: AIJS

Yeshiva Shaar HaTorah-Grodno (L)

83-96 117th Street, Kew Gardens NY 11415
County: Queens FICE Identification: 021520
Unit ID: 197692
Telephone: (718) 846-1940 Carnegie Class: Spec-4-yr-Faith
FAX Number: (718) 850-7916 Calendar System: Semester
Established: 1976 Annual Undergrad Tuition & Fees: $15,110
Enrollment: 86 Male
Affiliation or Control: Independent Non-Profit IRS Status: 501(c)3
Highest Offering: Second Talmudic Degree
Accreditation: RABN

01 Administrator .... Rabbi Yoel YANKELEWITZ

Yeshiva Shaarei Torah of Rockland (M)

91 W Carlton Road, Suffern NY 10901-4013
County: Rockland FICE Identification: 034963
Unit ID: 441609
Telephone: (845) 352-3431 Carnegie Class: Spec-4-yr-Faith
FAX Number: (845) 352-3433 Calendar System: Semester
Established: 1977 Annual Undergrad Tuition & Fees: $11,750
Enrollment: 91 Male
Affiliation or Control: Independent Non-Profit IRS Status: 501(c)3
Highest Offering: First Talmudic Degree
Accreditation: RABN

01 President .... Rabbi Eli ABRAHAM
37 Financial Aid Administrator .... Mrs. Teri SCHILLER
06 Registrar .... Mrs. Rachel CELNIK

Yeshiva Sholom Shachna (N)

401 Elmwood Avenue, Brooklyn NY 11230
County: Kings Identification: 667147
Unit ID: 486026
Telephone: (718) 252-6333 Carnegie Class: Not Classified
FAX Number: (718) 338-2536 Calendar System: Semester
URL: yeshivasholomshachna.com
Established: 2005 Annual Undergrad Tuition & Fees: $9,750
Enrollment: 73 Male
Affiliation or Control: Independent Non-Profit IRS Status: 501(c)3
Highest Offering: First Talmudic Degree
Accreditation: @RABN

01 Chief Executive Officer .... Rabbi Meir Chaim GUTFREUND
10 Chief Financial/Business Officer .... Mrs. Dina GUTFREUND
05 Chief Academic Officer/Registrar .... Rabbi Simcha OLEN
37 Director Student Financial Aid .... Mrs. Malka Bracha KRUPNIK

Yeshiva of the Telshe Alumni (O)

4904 Independence Avenue, Riverdale NY 10471
County: Bronx FICE Identification: 025463
Unit ID: 431983
Telephone: (718) 601-3523 Carnegie Class: Spec-4-yr-Faith
FAX Number: (718) 601-2141 Calendar System: Semester
Established: 1981 Annual Undergrad Tuition & Fees: $9,500
Enrollment: 112 Male
Affiliation or Control: Independent Non-Profit IRS Status: 501(c)3
Highest Offering: First Talmudic Degree
Accreditation: RABN

01 President .... Rabbi Avrohom AUSBAND
03 Executive Director .... Rabbi Noson JOSEPH
29 Director Alumni Relations .... Rabbi Moshe FERBER

Yeshiva University (P)

500 W 185th Street, New York NY 10033-3201
County: New York FICE Identification: 002903
Unit ID: 197708
Telephone: (212) 960-5400 Carnegie Class: DU-Higher
FAX Number: (212) 960-0055 Calendar System: Semester
URL: www.yu.edu
Established: 1886 Annual Undergrad Tuition & Fees: $40,670
Enrollment: 6,194 Coordinate
Affiliation or Control: Independent Non-Profit IRS Status: 501(c)3
Highest Offering: Doctorate
Accreditation: M, CAEPT, CLPSY, DENT, IPSY, LAW, MED, PSPSY, @SP, SW

01 President .... Dr. Ari BERMAN
05 Provost/Sr VP Academic Affairs .... Dr. Selma BOTMAN
100 Sr Vice Pres/Chief of Staff .... Mr. Josh JOSEPH
17 Vice President Medical Affairs .... Dr. Allen M. SPIEGEL
10 Vice Pres/Chief Financial Officer .... Mr. Jacob HARMAN
111 Vice Pres Institutional Advancement .... Ms. Alyssa HERMAN
11 Vice President University Affairs .... Dr. Herbert C. DOBRINSKY
13 Chief Information Officer .... Mr. Jim VASQUEZ
43 VP Legal Affs/Secretary/Gen Counsel .... Mr. Andrew J. LAUER
32 Vice Pres Univ & Cmty Life .... Rabbi Kenneth BRANDER
26 Exec Dir Communications/Public Affs .... Vacant
04 Exec Assistant to President .... Ms. Linda DOS SANTOS
08 Director of University Libraries .... Mr. Paul GLASSMAN
35 Dean of Students .... Dr. Chaim NISSEL
88 Dn Undergrad Torah Stds/REITS .... Rabbi Menachem PENNER

49 Dean YU Undergrad Fac Arts Sci ....Dr. Karen BACON
50 Dean Sy Syms School of Business ....Vacant
63 Dean Albert Einstein Col Medicine ....Dr. Allen M. SPIEGEL
58 Dean Ferkauf Graduate School Psych ....Dr. Lawrence J. SIEGEL
58 Dean Bernard Revel Graduate School ....Dr. David BERGER
58 Dean Azrieli Grad Sch Jewish Educ ....Dr. Rona NOVICK
70 Dean Wurzweiler School Social Work ....Dr. Danielle WOZNIAK
58 Director Sue Golding Grad Program ....Dr. Victoria FREEDMAN
37 Director of Student Finances ....Mr. Robert FRIEDMAN
07 Director Undergraduate Admissions ....Ms. Geri MANSDORF
29 Director University Alumni Affairs ....Ms. Dina BURCAT
06 University Registrar ....Ms. Jeannine ENGLERT
09 Director of Institutional Research ....Mr. Yuxiang LIU
96 Director of Procurement ....Mr. Thomas CANNON
15 Chief Human Resources Officer ....Ms. Julie AUSTER
38 Director Student Counseling ....Dr. Yael MUSKAT
22 Dir Affirmative Action/EEO ....Ms. Renee COKER
41 Athletic Director ....Mr. Joe BENDARSH

Yeshiva Zichron Aryeh (A)

1213 Bay 25th Street, Far Rockaway NY 11691
County: Queens　Identification: 667110
Unit ID: 487746
Telephone: (347) 619-9074　Carnegie Class: Not Classified
FAX Number: (516) 295-5737　Calendar System: Semester
Established: 1992　Annual Undergrad Tuition & Fees: $8,750
Enrollment: N/A　Male
Affiliation or Control: Independent Non-Profit　IRS Status: 501(c)3
Highest Offering: Second Talmudic Degree
Accreditation: RABN

03 Executive Vice President ....Rabbi Shaya COHEN
06 Registrar ....Rabbi Yosef AMSTER
07 Director of Admissions ....Rabbi Yehuda COHEN
10 Controller/Financial Aid Admin ....Mr. Yaakov JAFFE
18 Chief Facilities ....Mr. Danny SCHUSTER
08 Head Librarian ....Mr. Yechezkel MOSKOWITZ

Yeshivas Maharit Dsatmar (B)

475 County Rt. 105, Monroe NY 10950
County: Orange　Identification: 667204
Unit ID: 488101
Telephone: (845) 782-1380　Carnegie Class: Not Classified
FAX Number: (845) 782-5169　Calendar System: Semester
Established: 2011　Annual Undergrad Tuition & Fees: $11,500
Enrollment: N/A　Male
Affiliation or Control: Independent Non-Profit　IRS Status: 501(c)3
Highest Offering: First Talmudic Degree
Accreditation: @RABN

01 CEO ....Yitzchok TYRNAUER
06 Registrar ....Joel BRAVER
10 Associate Business Officer ....Moses JACOBOWITZ
37 Director of Financial Aid ....Yoel KESTENBAUM

Yeshivas Novominsk (C)

1690 60th Street, Brooklyn NY 11204-2138
County: Kings　FICE Identification: 031271
Unit ID: 405058
Telephone: (718) 438-2727　Carnegie Class: Spec-4-yr-Faith
FAX Number: (718) 438-2472　Calendar System: Semester
Established: 1988　Annual Undergrad Tuition & Fees: $9,700
Enrollment: 144　Male
Affiliation or Control: Independent Non-Profit　IRS Status: 501(c)3
Highest Offering: First Talmudic Degree
Accreditation: RABN

01 Executive Director ....Rabbi Lipa BRENNAN
32 Dean of Students ....Rabbi Yaakov PERLOW
11 Administrator ....Rabbi Boruch TWERSKI

Yeshivath Viznitz (D)

PO Box 446, Monsey NY 10952-0446
County: Rockland　FICE Identification: 013027
Unit ID: 197735
Telephone: (845) 731-3700　Carnegie Class: Spec-4-yr-Faith
FAX Number: (845) 356-7359　Calendar System: Semester
Established: 1946　Annual Undergrad Tuition & Fees: $9,300
Enrollment: 651　Male
Affiliation or Control: Independent Non-Profit　IRS Status: 501(c)3
Highest Offering: Second Talmudic Degree
Accreditation: RABN

01 President ....Gershon NEIMAN
10 Chief Fiscal Officer ....Rabbi Berel ROSENFELD

Yeshivath Zichron Moshe (E)

PO Box 580, South Fallsburg NY 12779-0580
County: Sullivan　FICE Identification: 011821
Unit ID: 197744
Telephone: (845) 434-5240　Carnegie Class: Spec-4-yr-Faith
FAX Number: (845) 434-1009　Calendar System: Semester
Established: 1969　Annual Undergrad Tuition & Fees: $11,600
Enrollment: 178　Male
Affiliation or Control: Independent Non-Profit　IRS Status: 501(c)3
Highest Offering: Second Talmudic Degree
Accreditation: AIJS

01 President ....Rabbi Ephraim Y. SHER
37 Director Student Financial Aid ....Rabbi Dov PERECMAN
06 Registrar ....Mrs. Miryom R. MILLER

NORTH CAROLINA

Apex School of Theology (F)

1701 T. W. Alexander Drive, Durham NC 27703-8024
County: Durham　FICE Identification: 035134
Unit ID: 441511
Telephone: (919) 572-1625　Carnegie Class: Spec-4-yr-Faith
FAX Number: (919) 572-1762　Calendar System: Other
URL: www.apexsot.edu
Established: 1995　Annual Undergrad Tuition & Fees: $5,100
Enrollment: 1,151　Coed
Affiliation or Control: Independent Non-Profit　IRS Status: 501(c)3
Highest Offering: Doctorate
Accreditation: TRACS

01 President ....Dr. Joseph E. PERKINS
03 Executive Vice President ....Dr. Herbert R. DAVIS
05 Academic Dean/Graduate Dean ....Dr. Lafayette MAXWELL
06 Registrar ....Mr. Joseph A. PERKINS
08 Head Librarian ....Ms. Cynthia RUFFIN
10 Director of Finance ....Mrs. Carolyn PEEBLES
20 Undergraduate Dean ....Dr. Gladys LONG
88 Dean Master of Arts Christian Couns ......Dr. Tonya ARMSTRONG
73 Dean Doctor of Ministry ....Dr. Lafayette MAXWELL
32 Director Student Affairs ....Rev. George T. DANIELS
45 Dir of Institutional Effectiveness ....Dr. Henry D. WELLS, JR.
04 Executive Admin Asst to President ....Ms. Rolanda J. HOLLAND
07 Admissions Coordinator ....Ms. Sandra J. MANNING
13 Dir of Educational Technology ....Dr. Clarence BURKE
18 Chief Facilities/Physical Plant ....Mr. Anthony PATTERSON
26 Director of Recruiting ....Dr. M. Andrew DAVIS
37 Director Student Financial Aid ....Ms. Floya COTTEN-BROWN

The Art Institute of Charlotte (G)

2110 Water Ridge Parkway, Charlotte NC 28217-4536
Telephone: (704) 357-8020　FICE Identification: 021105
Accreditation: &SC, ACFEI

† Regional accreditation is carried under the parent institution in Miami, FL.

The Art Institute of Raleigh-Durham (H)

410 Blackwell Street, Suite 200, Durham NC 27701
Telephone: (919) 317-3050　Identification: 770843
Accreditation: &SC, ACFEI

† Branch campus of Miami International University of Art & Design, Miami, FL

Barton College (I)

704-A College Street, PO Box 5000, Wilson NC 27893
County: Wilson　FICE Identification: 002908
Unit ID: 197911
Telephone: (252) 399-6300　Carnegie Class: Bac-Diverse
FAX Number: (252) 399-6374　Calendar System: Semester
URL: www.barton.edu
Established: 1902　Annual Undergrad Tuition & Fees: $29,052
Enrollment: 1,047　Coed
Affiliation or Control: Christian Church (Disciples Of Christ)
IRS Status: 501(c)3
Highest Offering: Master's
Accreditation: SC, CAEPN, NURSE, SW

01 President ....Dr. Douglas N. SEARCY
05 Vice President Academic Affairs ....Dr. Gary DAYNES
10 Vice Pres Finance & Administration ....Mr. David A. BROWNING
111 Vice President Inst Advancement ....Ms. Jan Y. MERIWETHER
32 Vice President Student Life ....Mr. George SOLAN
100 Senior Advisor to President ....Mrs. Carolyn L. HARMON
84 Vice President for Enrollment Mgmt ....Mr. Dennis T. MATTHEWS
07 Asst VP of Admissions ....Ms. Amanda METTS
30 Asst VP for Development ....Mr. Tom MAZE
50 Dean School of Business ....Mr. Ron EGGERS
66 Dean School of Nursing ....Dr. Sharon SARVEY
53 Dean School of Education ....Dr. Jackie ENNIS
79 Dean School of Humanities ....Dr. James CLARK
81 Dean School of Sciences ....Dr. Kevin PENNINGTON
76 Dean Allied Health & Sport Studies ....Dr. Claudia DUNCAN
88 Dean School of Social Work ....Dr. Barbara CONKLIN
57 Dean Visual/Performing & Comm Arts ....Ms. Susan FECHO
58 Dean Graduate/Professional Studies ....Dr. Susan BANE
41 Athletic Director ....Mr. Todd WILKINSON
106 Dir Online Education/E-learning ....Mrs. Lorraine RAPER
121 Asst Dean of Student Success ....Ms. Angie WALSTON
06 Registrar ....Ms. Sheila MILNE
21 Controller ....Mr. Larry GRIFFIN
37 Director Student Financial Aid ....Mr. Thomas WELCH
26 Director of Public Relations ....Mrs. Kathy DAUGHETY
08 Director of the Library ....Vacant
15 Director Human Resources ....Mrs. Linda TYSON
23 Director of Health Services ....Mrs. Jennifer HIGH
29 Director of Alumni Affairs ....Ms. Summer BROCK
14 Director Technology ....Vacant
13 AVP of Information Resources ....Mr. Daniel MURPHY
35 Dean of Students ....Mr. Jared TICE
28 Director of Diversity and Inclusion ....Ms. Holly ZACHARIAS
18 Director of Physical Plant ....Mr. Sean WOODARD
42 Chaplain ....Rev. Jamie EUBANKS
40 Bookstore Manager ....Ms. Candice MOORE
04 Executive Asst to President ....Mrs. Sheila WILSON
39 Director of Housing/Res Life ....Mr. Joseph DLUGOS
88 Director of Publications ....Mr. Keith TEW
105 Director Web Services ....Mr. Ken DOZIER
44 Director Annual Giving ....Mr. Bryan FEGLEY
91 Director Administrative Computing ....Ms. Linda MERCER

Belmont Abbey College (J)

100 Belmont Mount Holly Road, Belmont NC 28012-1802
County: Gaston　FICE Identification: 002910
Unit ID: 197984
Telephone: (704) 461-6701　Carnegie Class: Bac-Diverse
FAX Number: (704) 461-6670　Calendar System: Semester
URL: belmontabbeycollege.edu/
Established: 1876　Annual Undergrad Tuition & Fees: $18,500
Enrollment: 1,495　Coed
Affiliation or Control: Roman Catholic　IRS Status: 501(c)3
Highest Offering: Baccalaureate
Accreditation: SC

01 President ....Dr. William K. THIERFELDER
10 Chief Financial Officer ....Mr. Allan MARK
05 VP for Academic Affairs ....Dr. David WILLIAMS
26 VP College Relations ....Mr. Gregory SWANSON
20 Assoc Dean for Academic Affairs ....Dr. Joseph WYSOCKI
30 Development Officer ....Ms. Chris Goff PEELER
29 Director of Alumni Relations ....Ms. Bridget CONBOY
08 Director of the Library ....Mr. Donald BEAGLE
06 Registrar ....Ms. Margot RHOADES
09 Director of Institutional Research ....Mr. Stephen CHEMASK
36 Director Career Counseling/Placemnt ....Ms. Stephannie MILES
27 Director Marketing ....Mr. Rolando RIVAS
37 Director of Financial Aid ....Mrs. Anne A. STEVENS
38 Wellness Center Counselor ....Mrs. Melanie ECKSTEIN
41 Athletic Director ....Mr. Stephen MISS
21 Staff Accountant ....Ms. Patti PIZZANO
19 Chief of Campus Police ....Mr. Andy LEONARD
42 Director of Campus Ministry ....Mr. Patrick FORD
15 Director of Human Resources ....Ms. Cheryl TROTTER
18 Chief Facilities/Physical Plant ....Vacant
07 Executive Director of Admissions ....Ms. Nicole FOCARETO
13 Chief Info Technology Officer (CIO) ....Mr. Nash HASAN
32 Dean of Student Life ....Mr. Tom MACALESTER
04 Sr Executive Assistant ....Ms. Ashley MCCALLISTER

Bennett College (K)

900 E Washington Street, Greensboro NC 27401-3239
County: Guilford　FICE Identification: 002911
Unit ID: 197993
Telephone: (336) 273-4431　Carnegie Class: Bac-Diverse
FAX Number: (336) 370-8688　Calendar System: Semester
URL: www.bennett.edu
Established: 1873　Annual Undergrad Tuition & Fees: $18,513
Enrollment: 583　Female
Affiliation or Control: United Methodist　IRS Status: 501(c)3
Highest Offering: Baccalaureate
Accreditation: #SC, CAEPN, SW

01 President ....Dr. Phyllis W. DAWKINS
05 Interim Provost/Academic VP ....Mr. Steve WILLIS
10 Interim VP Admin & Finance ....Mr. Leroy SUMMERS, JR.
111 Vice Pres Inst Advancement ....Ms. Evelyn LEATHERS
26 Dir Public Relations & Publication ....Ms. Laurie WILLIS
09 Dir Institutional Rsrch & Testing ....Ms. Karen JAMES
06 Registrar ....Ms. Gisele ABRON
08 Director of Holgate Library ....Ms. Joan WILLIAMS
07 Interim Director of Admissions ....Mr. James CRAWFORD
37 Director of Financial Aid ....Mr. Shawn GUY
29 Director Alumnae Affairs ....Ms. Audrey FRANKLIN
36 Director Career Services ....Mr. Darryl JOHNSON
38 Dir Coun Svcs/Supervisor Health Svc ....Ms. Robin CAMPBELL
15 Director of Human Resources ....Ms. Linda DIAMOND
42 Chaplain/Director Campus Ministry ....Rev Dr. Natalie MCLEAN
88 Chair Curriculum & Instruction ....Dr. Henry JOHNSON
79 Int Chair Humanities ....Ms. Keri PETERSEN
81 Chair Natural & Behavioral Sciences ....Dr. Michael COTTON
19 Director Security/Safety ....Mr. Keifer BRADSHAW
32 Chief Student Affairs/Student Life ....Ms. Kimberly DRYE

Brevard College (L)

One Brevard College Drive, Brevard NC 28712-3306
County: Transylvania　FICE Identification: 002912
Unit ID: 198066
Telephone: (828) 883-8292　Carnegie Class: Bac-Diverse
FAX Number: (828) 884-3790　Calendar System: Semester
URL: www.brevard.edu
Established: 1853　Annual Undergrad Tuition & Fees: $27,790
Enrollment: 729　Coed
Affiliation or Control: United Methodist　IRS Status: 501(c)3
Highest Offering: Baccalaureate
Accreditation: SC, MUS

01 President ....Dr. David C. JOYCE
05 VP Academic Affairs/Dean of Faculty ....Dr. Roy S. SHEFFIELD
10 Vice President for Business/Finance ....Ms. Deborah P. HALL
111 Vice Pres Institutional Advancement ....Ms. Kathryn HOLTEN
84 Vice Pres Admissions/Financial Aid ....Mr. Ryan C. HOLT
04 Executive Asst to the President ....Ms. Julia S. GRAY
32 Dean of Students ....Mrs. Debora D'ANNA
13 Int Dir of Information Technology ....Mr. Jay TRUSSELL
06 Registrar ....Mrs. Amy HERTZ
37 Director of Financial Aid ....Mrs. Caron SURRETT
08 Director of Library ....Dr. Marie JONES
29 Director of Alumni Affairs ....Mr. Jeff JOYCE
19 Dir of Safety/Security/Risk Mgmt ....Mr. Stan JACOBSEN
41 Director of Athletics ....Mr. Juan MASCARO
18 Director of Facilities/Grounds ....Mr. Burke ULREY
24 Director Academic Enrichment Ctr ....Ms. Shirley E. ARNOLD
36 Director of Career Exploration/Dev ....Ms. Nacole POTTS
92 Director of Honors Program ....Dr. Robert J. CABIN
21 Controller ....Mr. Thomas Ove ANDERSEN
38 Assoc Dean/Dir of Counseling ....Ms. Deanne DASBURG
57 Chair Division of Fine Arts ....Dr. Kathryn GRESHAM
79 Chair Division of Humanities ....Dr. Tom J. BELL
83 Chair Div of Social Sciences ....Dr. Barbara B. BOERNER
81 Chair Div Env Stds/Math/Nat Science ....Dr. Jennifer E. FRICK-RUPPERT
88 Chair Division of WLEE ....Dr. Jennifer L. KAFSKY
09 Director of Institutional Research ....Ms. Sherry DOWNING
102 Director of Development/Foundation ....Mrs. Mary WALDROFF
26 Asst Director of Communications ....Ms. Christie CAUBLE
39 Director Student Housing ....Ms. Beth ABRAMS
07 Director of Admissions ....Mr. David VOLRATH

Brightwood College (A)

6070 East Independence Boulevard, Charlotte NC 28212
Telephone: (704) 567-3700 Identification: 770543
Accreditation: **ACICS**, DA

† Branch campus of Brightwood College, Nashville, TN

Cabarrus College of Health Sciences (B)

401 Medical Park Drive, Concord NC 28025-3959
County: Cabarrus FICE Identification: 006477
Unit ID: 198109
Telephone: (704) 403-1555 Carnegie Class: Spec-4-yr-Other Health
FAX Number: (704) 403-1764 Calendar System: Semester
URL: www.cabarruscollege.edu
Established: 1942 Annual Undergrad Tuition & Fees: $12,268
Enrollment: 452 Coed
Affiliation or Control: Independent Non-Profit IRS Status: 501(c)3
Highest Offering: Master's
Accreditation: **SC**, ADNUR, MAC, NURSE, OT, OTA, SURGT

01 President ....Dr. Dianne O. SNYDER
05 Provost ....Dr. Margaret B. PATCHETT
32 Dean of Student Aff/Enrollment Mgt ....Ms. Christine L. CORSELLO
10 Chief Financial Officer ....Mrs. Kim BRADSHAW
66 ADN Program Chair ....Mrs. Kim PLEMMONS
88 OT Assistant Program Chair ....Ms. Nancy GREEN
88 Master OT Program Chair ....Dr. Carol FAIN
88 Medical Assisting Program Chair ....Ms. Rachel HOUSTON
88 Surgical Technology Program Chair ....Mrs. Michelle GAY
88 Medical Imagining Program Chair ....Mrs. Rhonda WEAVER
88 Associate in Science Program Chair ....Mrs. Zinat HASSANPOUR
88 Pharmacy Technology Program Chair ....Mrs. Annette SIMMONS
97 General Education Program Chair ....Mrs. Stacey WILSON
66 Dean of Nursing ....Dr. Delores BENN
88 Coord Campus & Community Outreach ....Mrs. Cara LURSEN
26 Coord of Marketing & Graduate Educ ....Mrs. Melanie GASS
37 Director of Financial Aid ....Mrs. Valerie RICHARD
06 Dir Student Records & Info Mgmt ....Mrs. Mary ELMORE
07 Director of Recruitment & Retention ....Mrs. Lorri B. CONNOR
04 Administrative Asst to President ....Mrs. Donna HARLESS
08 Head Librarian ....Mrs. Cassie DIXON

Campbell University (C)

PO Box 97, Buies Creek NC 27506-0097
County: Harnett FICE Identification: 002913
Unit ID: 198136
Telephone: (910) 893-1200 Carnegie Class: Masters/L
FAX Number: (910) 893-1424 Calendar System: Semester
URL: www.campbell.edu
Established: 1887 Annual Undergrad Tuition & Fees: $30,050
Enrollment: 6,484 Coed
Affiliation or Control: Baptist IRS Status: 501(c)3
Highest Offering: Doctorate
Accreditation: **SC**, ACBSP, ARCPA, CAATE, CAEP, LAW, OSTEO, PHAR, PTA, SW, THEOL

00 Chancellor ....Dr. Jerry WALLACE
01 President ....Dr. J. Bradley CREED
05 Vice Pres Academic Affs & Provost ....Dr. Mark HAMMOND
10 Vice President Business/Treasurer ....Mr. Jim O. ROBERTS
30 Vice President for Advancement ....Mr. Britt DAVIS
32 Vice President for Student Life ....Dr. Dennis BAZEMORE
84 Vice Pres Enrollment Management ....Vacant
07 Asst Vice Pres of Admissions ....Mr. Jason HALL
49 Dean of College of Arts & Science ....Dr. Michael WELLS
61 Dean of the Law School ....Mr. J. Rich LEONARD
50 Dean Lundy-Fetterman Sch Business ....Mr. Kevin O'MARA
53 Dean School of Education ....Dr. Karen NERY
67 Acting VP of Health Sciences & Dean ....Dr. Michael ADAMS
63 Dean of Osteopathic Medical School ....Dr. John M. KAUFFMAN, JR.
35 Dean of Students ....Vacant
06 Registrar ....Ms. Karen PORE
21 Assistant VP for Business ....Mr. Al HARDISON
29 AVP of Alumni Engagement ....Ms. Sarah SWAIN
89 Director of Freshman Experience ....Ms. Shari MCGUIRE
08 Dean of Library ....Mrs. Borree KWOK
37 Director of Financial Aid ....Ms. Mary OTTO
13 Int Director of Computing Services ....Mr. John R. SKUCE
26 AVP Communications/Marketing ....Ms. Haven HOTTEL
15 Director Human Resources ....Ms. Traci M. ANTER
18 Chief Facilities/Physical Plant ....Mr. J. Scot PHILLIPS
38 Director Student Counseling ....Mrs. Laura RICH
96 Director of Purchasing ....Mr. Win QUAKENBUSH
92 Director of Honors Program ....Dr. Ann ORTIZ
09 Asst Provost for Inst Effectiveness ....Mrs. Maren HESS
106 Dean of Adult & Online Education ....Dr. Beth RUBIN
04 Executive Asst to the President ....Dr. John ROBERSON
108 Director of Assessment ....Ms. Jessica KING BLANCK
41 Athletic Director ....Mr. Robert ROLLER
43 Dir Legal Services/General Counsel ....Mr. Bob COGSWELL

Carolina Christian College (D)

PO Box 777, Winston-Salem NC 27102
County: Forsyth FICE Identification: 035703
Unit ID: 199971
Telephone: (336) 744-0900 Carnegie Class: Spec-4-yr-Faith
FAX Number: (336) 744-0901 Calendar System: Semester
URL: www.carolina.edu
Established: 1945 Annual Undergrad Tuition & Fees: $4,075
Enrollment: 45 Coed
Affiliation or Control: Independent Non-Profit IRS Status: 501(c)3
Highest Offering: Master's
Accreditation: **BI**

01 President ....Ms. LaTanya V. TYSON
05 VP of Academics ....Ms. Derrick THORPE
32 Dean of Students ....Mr. Thayer TYSON
10 Chief Business Officer ....Ms. Amy BARNHART
08 Library Director ....Ms. Meredith ADER
37 Financial Aid Director ....Ms. LaJada CREWS
06 Registrar ....Ms. Debra BRADSHAW
26 Chief Public Relations Officer ....Mr. MacArthur DAVIS
09 Director of Institutional Research ....Vacant

Carolina College of Biblical Studies (E)

817 S. McPherson Church Road, Fayetteville NC 28303
County: Cumberland FICE Identification: 041542
Unit ID: 461032
Telephone: (910) 323-5614 Carnegie Class: Spec-4-yr-Faith
FAX Number: (910) 323-0425 Calendar System: Quarter
URL: www.ccbs.edu
Established: 1973 Annual Undergrad Tuition & Fees: $5,325
Enrollment: 117 Coed
Affiliation or Control: Non-denominational IRS Status: 501(c)3
Highest Offering: Baccalaureate
Accreditation: **BI**

01 President ....Dr. Bill KORVER
05 Academic Dean ....Dr. Harry GHEE
30 Vice Pres Strategic Development ....Dr. Bill BOYD
06 Financial Aid Officer/Registrar ....Ms. Aby CURLEY
07 Admissions Director ....Dr. Rodney PHILLIPS

Carolinas College of Health Sciences (F)

1200 Blythe Boulevard, Charlotte NC 28203
County: Mecklenburg FICE Identification: 031042
Unit ID: 433174
Telephone: (704) 355-5043 Carnegie Class: Spec 2-yr-Health
FAX Number: (704) 355-9336 Calendar System: Semester
URL: www.CarolinasCollege.edu
Established: 1990 Annual Undergrad Tuition & Fees (In-District): $12,192
Enrollment: 474 Coed
Affiliation or Control: State/Local IRS Status: 501(c)3
Highest Offering: Associate Degree
Accreditation: **SC**, ADNUR, HT, MT, PHLEB, RAD, RTT, SURGT

01 President ....Dr. T. Hampton HOPKINS
05 Provost ....Dr. Lori BEQUETTE
10 Dean Administrative/Financial Svcs ....Ms. Kim BRADSHAW
32 Dean Student Affair/Enrollment Mgmt ....Dr. Karen LEWIS
66 Program Chair Nursing ....Ms. Cathy BORYSEWICZ
06 Director Student Records & Informat ....Ms. Chrisanne RANCATI
51 Director Continuing Education ....Ms. Susan THOMASSON
29 Manager Alumni Relations ....Ms. Ruthie MIHAL
07 Director Recruitment & Retention ....Ms. Kenielle MORRRIS
37 Director Financial Aid ....Ms. Kirstie CLARK
90 Manager Instructional Technology ....Mr. Larry TURNER
09 Institutional Research Coordinator ....Ms. Cheryl PULLIAM
04 Administrative Asst to President ....Ms. Pat LEWIS

Catawba College (G)

2300 W Innes Street, Salisbury NC 28144-2488
County: Rowan FICE Identification: 002914
Unit ID: 198215
Telephone: (704) 637-4111 Carnegie Class: Bac-Diverse
FAX Number: (704) 637-4444 Calendar System: Semester
URL: www.catawba.edu
Established: 1851 Annual Undergrad Tuition & Fees: $29,333
Enrollment: 1,275 Coed
Affiliation or Control: United Church Of Christ IRS Status: 501(c)3
Highest Offering: Master's
Accreditation: **SC**, #CAATE, CAEPN

01 President ....Mr. Brien LEWIS
03 Senior Vice President/Chaplain ....Dr. Kenneth W. CLAPP
05 Provost ....Dr. Michael BITZER
30 Vice President of Development ....Vacant
84 Vice Pres of Enrollment Management ....Mrs. Cindy BARR
04 Assistant to President ....Mrs. Amy H. WILLIAMS
09 Dir Institutional Research ....Mr. Timothy KENNEDY
10 Chief Financial Officer ....Mr. Nelson MURPHY
15 Chief Human Resources Officer ....Mr. Larry G. FARMER
26 Chief Public Relations Officer ....Mrs. Tonia BLACK-GOLD
32 Interim Dean of Students ....Dr. Michael BITZER
39 Director of Student Conduct ....Ms. Laura GILLAND
08 Acting Library Director ....Mr. Earl GIVENS
06 Registrar ....Ms. Susan AGNER
07 Sr Director of Admissions ....Ms. Elaine P. HOLDEN
37 Director of Financial Assistance ....Ms. Kelli HAND
36 Director of Placement ....Ms. Robin PERRY
88 Director Sports Info & Promotion ....Mr. Jim D. LEWIS
40 Director Bookstore ....Mrs. Stephanie TAYLOR
41 Athletic Director ....Mr. Larry W. LECKONBY
18 Chief Facilities/Physical Plant ....Vacant
29 Director Alumni Relations ....Vacant
38 Director Student Counseling ....Dr. Nancy ZIMMERMAN

Chamberlain University-Charlotte (H)

2015 Ayrsley Town Blvd, Ste 204, Charlotte NC 28273
Telephone: (980) 939-6241 Identification: 770979
Accreditation: **&NH**, NURSE

† Branch campus of Chamberlain University-Addison, Addison, IL

Charlotte Christian College and Theological Seminary (I)

PO Box 790106, Charlotte NC 28206-7901
County: Mecklenburg FICE Identification: 038273
Unit ID: 444778
Telephone: (704) 334-6882 Carnegie Class: Spec-4-yr-Faith
FAX Number: (704) 334-6885 Calendar System: Semester
URL: www.charlottechristian.edu
Established: 1996 Annual Undergrad Tuition & Fees: $9,680
Enrollment: 122 Coed
Affiliation or Control: Independent Non-Profit IRS Status: 501(c)3
Highest Offering: Doctorate
Accreditation: **TRACS**

01 President ....Dr. Eddie G. GRIGG
04 Executive Asst to the President ....Vacant
05 Vice President of Academic Affairs ....Dr. Kenneth BANDY
32 Vice President of Student Affairs ....Vacant
30 Director of Advancement ....Vacant
06 Registrar/Dir International Student ....Ms. Nancy MCNAMARA
08 Head Librarian ....Mr. Robert MCINNES
07 Director of Admissions ....Mr. George SHEARS, III
10 Business Office Manager ....Mr. Heith PICKLESIMER
37 Financial Aid Officer ....Mr. Kenneth ROACH

The Chef's Academy (J)

2001 Carrington Mill Boulevard, Morrisville NC 27560
Telephone: (919) 246-9394 Identification: 770101
Accreditation: **ABHES**

† Branch campus of Harrison College - Indianapolis Downtown Campus, Indianapolis, IN

Chowan University (K)

One University Place, Murfreesboro NC 27855-1844
County: Hertford FICE Identification: 002916
Unit ID: 198303
Telephone: (252) 398-6500 Carnegie Class: Bac-Diverse
FAX Number: (252) 398-1190 Calendar System: Semester
URL: www.chowan.edu
Established: 1848 Annual Undergrad Tuition & Fees: $23,930
Enrollment: 1,532 Coed
Affiliation or Control: Baptist IRS Status: 501(c)3
Highest Offering: Master's
Accreditation: **SC**, CAEPN, MUS

01 President ....Dr. M. Chrisopher WHITE
05 Vice President Academic Affairs ....Dr. Danny B. MOORE
10 Vice President Business Affairs ....Mr. Donnie O. CLARY
32 Vice President Student Affairs ....Mr. P. Randy HARRELL
111 Vice President Advancement ....Mr. John TAYLOE
15 Vice President Human Resources ....Mr. John A. HINTON

07 Vice President Admissions .... Mr. P. Randy HARRELL
13 Exec Dir Info Tech/Network Svcs .... Mr. James R. HOWELL
06 Registrar .... Ms. Donna ROBBINS
26 Director of Public Relations .... Mrs. Brooke REICH
08 Head Librarian .... Mrs. Georgia E. WILLIAMS
37 Director of Financial Aid .... Mrs. Sharon ROSE
42 Campus Minister .... Ms. Mari E. WILES
18 Director Physical Plant .... Mr. Rex HARRELL
19 Chief of Security .... Mr. Derek A. BURKE
35 Director Student Life .... Ms. Leah LAMBSON
36 Director Counseling/Career Services .... Ms. Yolanda MAJETTE
39 Director Housing & Residence Life .... Ms. Danielle COLEMAN
41 Athletics Director .... Mr. F. Ozzie MCFARLAND
09 Director Institutional Research .... Mrs. Mitch KELLY
88 Director Upward Bound .... Mr. E. Frank STEPHENSON
21 Director Business Services .... Mrs. Julie W. EMORY
29 Director Alumni Services .... Mrs. Kay M. THOMAS
49 Dean Liberal Arts .... Dr. John DILUSTRO
50 Dean Business .... Dr. Linda MILES
53 Dean Education .... Dr. Ella BENSON
40 Bookstore Manager .... Vacant

Daoist Traditions College of Chinese Medical Arts (A)

382 Montford Avenue, Asheville NC 28801

County: Buncombe FICE Identification: 041464
Unit ID: 455178
Telephone: (828) 225-3993 Carnegie Class: Spec-4-yr-Other Health
FAX Number: (828) 255-3306 Calendar System: Semester
URL: www.daoisttraditions.edu
Established: 2003 Annual Graduate Tuition & Fees: N/A
Enrollment: 78 Coed
Affiliation or Control: Proprietary IRS Status: Proprietary
Highest Offering: Master's; No Undergraduates
Accreditation: **ACUP**

07 Director of Admissions .... Juliet DANIEL
01 President .... Dr. Mary Cissy MAJEBE
04 Administrative Asst to President .... Matthew NANNIS

Davidson College (B)

PO Box 5000, Davidson NC 28035-5000

County: Mecklenburg FICE Identification: 002918
Unit ID: 198385
Telephone: (704) 894-2000 Carnegie Class: Bac-A&S
FAX Number: (704) 894-2005 Calendar System: Semester
URL: www.davidson.edu
Established: 1837 Annual Undergrad Tuition & Fees: $48,376
Enrollment: 1,784 Coed
Affiliation or Control: Presbyterian Church (U.S.A.) IRS Status: 501(c)3
Highest Offering: Baccalaureate
Accreditation: **SC**

01 President .... Dr. Carol E. QUILLEN
05 Vice Pres Acad Affs/Dean of Faculty ...... Dr. Wendy E. RAYMOND
26 Vice President College Relations .... Ms. Eileen M. KEELEY
10 Vice Pres Finance & Administration .... Mr. Edward A. KANIA
32 VP Student Life/Dean of Students .... Dr. Thomas C. SHANDLEY
07 VP & Dean Admissions/Financial Aid .... Mr. Christopher J. GRUBER
09 VP Planning/Institutional Research .... Ms. Linda M. LEFAUVE
43 VP and General Counsel .... Mrs. Sarah L. PHILLIPS
111 Assoc VP of Advancement Operations .... Ms. Cat S. NIEKRO
20 Assoc Dean Academic Administration .... Ms. Leslie M. MARSICANO
45 VP for Strategic Initiatives .... Dr. Patrick J. SELLERS
20 Assoc Dean Teaching/Lrng/Rsrch .... Dr. Verna M. CASE
06 Registrar .... Ms. Angela B. DEWBERRY
13 Chief Information Officer .... Ms. Raechelle CLEMMONS
37 Director Financial Aid .... Mr. David GELINAS
15 Director of Human Resources .... Dr. Kim BALL
41 Director of Athletics .... Mr. James E. MURPHY, III
08 Director of the Library .... Ms. Gillian (Jill) S. GREMMELS
29 Director Alumni Relations .... Ms. Marya L. HOWELL
21 Controller/Director Business Svcs .... Ms. Lori GASTON
18 Director Facilities & Engineering ...... Mr. David M. HOLTHOUSER
19 Chief of Campus Police .... Mr. Todd D. SIGLER
36 Executive Director Career Services .... Mrs. Jeanne-Marie C. RYAN
35 Director of College Union .... Mr. William H. BROWN
39 Dir Resid Life/Assoc Dean Students .... Mr. Jason S. SHAFFER
42 College Chaplain .... Dr. Robert C. SPACH
88 Dir Ctr for Interdisciplinary Stds .... Dr. Peter M. KRENTZ
82 Assoc Dean Intl Programs/Studies .... Dr. M. Christopher ALEXANDER
25 Director of Grants & Contracts .... Dr. Mary W. MUCHANE
24 Director Instructional Support .... Ms. Diane S. STIRLING
38 Director Student Counseling Center .... Dr. Trish MURRAY
44 Director of Annual Giving .... Ms. Lisa H. COMBS
96 Director of Purchasing .... Ms. Elizabeth S. CHRISTENBURY
40 College Store General Manager .... Mr. William T. REILLY
04 Executive Asst to President .... Mrs. Traci L. RUSS-WILSON

Duke University (C)

Durham NC 27706-8001

County: Durham FICE Identification: 002920
Unit ID: 198419
Telephone: (919) 684-8111 Carnegie Class: DU-Highest
FAX Number: (919) 684-3200 Calendar System: Semester
URL: www.duke.edu
Established: 1838 Annual Undergrad Tuition & Fees: $51,265
Enrollment: 15,984 Coed
Affiliation or Control: Independent Non-Profit IRS Status: 501(c)3
Highest Offering: Doctorate
Accreditation: **SC**, ANEST, ARCPA, CAEPN, CLPSY, DIETI, ENG, IPSY, LAW, MED, NURSE, PA, PAST, PCSAS, PTA, THEOL

01 President .... Vincent PRICE
05 Provost .... Sally KORNBLUTH
17 Chancellor for Health Affairs .... A. Eugene WASHINGTON
03 Exec Vice Pres for Administration .... Tallman TRASK, III
10 Vice President Financial Services .... Timothy WALSH
15 Vice President for Administration .... Kyle CAVANAUGH
07 Dean Undergraduate Admissions .... Christoph O. GUTTENTAG
21 Exec Vice Provost Finance & Admin .... James S. ROBERTS
13 Vice Prov Information Technology .... Tracy FUTHEY
88 Vice Provost Interdisciplin Studies .... Edward BALLEISEN
20 Vice Provost for Academic Affairs .... Jennifer FRANCIS
88 Vice Provost for Faculty Advancemnt .... Abbas BENMAMOUN
88 Vice Provost for the Arts .... Scott A. LINDTORTH
46 Vice Provost for Research .... Lawrence CARIN
88 Vice Prov Innov/Entrepreneurship .... Eric TOONE
08 Librarian/Vice Prov Library Affairs .... Deborah JAKUBS
37 Asst Vice Provost/Dir Financial Aid .... Alison RABIL
65 Dean Sch of the Environment .... Jeffrey R. VINCENT
61 Dean of Law School .... David F. LEVI
63 Dn Sch Med/Sr Vice Chanc Acad Affs .... Mary E. KLOTMAN
50 Dean Fuqua School of Business .... William BOULDING
73 Dean of the Divinity School .... Elaine HEATH
58 Dean Grad Sch/Vice Prov Grad Educ .... Paula D. MCCLAIN
49 Dean Faculty Arts/Science .... Valerie ASHBY
66 Dean School of Nursing .... Marion BROOME
54 Dean of Engineering .... Ravi BELLAMKONDA
88 Dean Sanford Sch of Public Policy .... Kelly D. BROWNELL
88 Director Duke University Press .... Stephen A. COHN
18 Vice President for Facilities .... John NOONAN
88 Vice Pres/Vice Prov Global Strategy .... Michael H. MERSON
06 Registrar .... Frank BLALARK
09 Director of Institutional Research .... David JAMIESON-DRAKE
04 Executive Asst to the President .... Lisa JORDAN
101 VP and University Secretary .... Richard RIDDELL
102 Asst VP Foundation Relations .... Beth EASTLICK
104 Director Study Abroad .... Amanda KELSOE
105 Senior Manager Web Services .... Ryn NASSER
22 Vice President Institutional Equity .... Benjamin REESE, JR.
26 Chief Public Relations/Marketing .... Michael SCHOENFELD
29 Director Alumni Relations .... Sterly WILDER
30 Vice President Development .... Robert SHEPARD
32 Vice President Student Affairs .... Larry MONETA
36 Director Career Center .... William WRIGHT-SWADEL
38 Director Student Counseling .... Wanda COLLINS
39 Director Student Housing .... Rick JOHNSON
41 VP and Director Athletics .... Kevin WHITE
43 Vice President and General Counsel .... Pamela BERNARD
44 Asst VP Annual Giving .... Jennifer SPISAK-CAMERON
53 Vice Provost Undergraduate Educ .... Stephen NOWICKI
86 Assoc VP Federal Relations .... Christopher SIMMONS
96 Assoc VP Procurement .... Jane PLEASANTS

ECPI University-Charlotte (D)

4800 Airport Center Pkwy #100, Charlotte NC 28208

Telephone: (704) 399-1010 Identification: 770951
Accreditation: **&SC**, MAAB

† Branch campus of ECPI University, Virginia Beach, VA

ECPI University-Greensboro (E)

7802 Airport Center Drive, Greensboro NC 27409

Telephone: (336) 665-1400 Identification: 770952
Accreditation: **&SC**, MAAB

† Branch campus of ECPI University, Virginia Beach, VA

ECPI University-Raleigh (F)

4101 Doie Cope Road, Raleigh NC 27613

Telephone: (919) 283-5748 Identification: 770953
Accreditation: **&SC**, MAAB

† Branch campus of ECPI University, Virginia Beach, VA

Elon University (G)

2700 Campus Box, Elon NC 27244-2010

County: Alamance FICE Identification: 002927
Unit ID: 198516
Telephone: (336) 278-2000 Carnegie Class: Masters/M
FAX Number: N/A Calendar System: 4/1/4
URL: www.elon.edu
Established: 1889 Annual Undergrad Tuition & Fees: $33,104
Enrollment: 6,631 Coed
Affiliation or Control: Independent Non-Profit IRS Status: 501(c)3
Highest Offering: Doctorate
Accreditation: **SC**, ARCPA, CAEPN, JOUR, LAW, PTA

01 President .... Dr. Leo M. LAMBERT
05 Provost/Exec VP Academic Affairs .... Dr. Steven D. HOUSE
100 Chief of Staff/Sec to the Board .... Mr. Jeff STEIN
07 VP of Admissions/Financial Planning .... Mr. Greg ZAISER
10 Senior VP for Business/Finance/Tech .... Mr. Gerald O. WHITTINGTON
111 Vice Pres Institutional Advancement .... Mr. James B. PIATT
32 Vice Pres/Dean of Student Life .... Dr. Jon DOOLEY
26 Vice Pres University Communications ... Mr. Daniel J. ANDERSON
108 Associate Provost for Assessment .... Dr. Maurice LEVESQUE
27 Asst Provost for Comm & Operations .... Dr. Paul MILLER
22 Assoc Provost for Inclusive Excel .... Dr. Brooke BARNETT
88 Associate Provost for Faculty Affs .... Dr. Tim PEEPLES
21 Asst VP for Business and Finance .... Ms. Susan M. KIRKLAND
49 Dean College of Arts & Sci .... Dr. Gabie SMITH
50 Dean Love School of Business .... Dr. Raghu TADEPALLI
60 Dean of School of Communications .... Dr. Paul F. PARSONS
53 Dean of School of Education .... Dr. Ann BULLOCK
61 Dean of School of Law .... Mr. Luke BIERMAN
76 Dean of School of Health Sciences .... Dr. Becky NEIDUSKI
85 Dean of Global Studies .... Mr. Woody PELTON
35 Associate VP of Student Life .... Mrs. Jana Lynn F. PATTERSON
08 Dean and University Librarian .... Ms. Joan RUELLE
41 Director of Athletics .... Mr. Dave L. BLANK
06 Registrar .... Dr. Rodney PARKS
42 University Chaplain .... Dr. Janet FULLER
37 Director of Financial Planning .... Dr. M. Patrick MURPHY
29 Dir of Alumni Engagement .... Mr. Brian FEELEY
121 Assoc Dean of Academic Support .... Dr. Becky OLIVE-TAYLOR
36 Exec Director of Std Prof Dev Ctr .... Mr. Tom BRINKLEY
88 Dir of Planning/Design/Construction .... Mr. Brad D. MOORE
18 Assoc VP for Facilities Management .... Mr. Robert BUCHHOLZ
15 Exec Director of Human Resources .... Mr. John LEW
109 Director of Auxiliary Services .... Ms. Carrie RYAN
19 Director of Campus Safety & Police .... Mr. Dennis FRANKS
23 Director of Health Services .... Dr. Ginette ARCHINAL
38 Director Counseling Services .... Mr. Bruce F. NELSON
11 Assistant VP for Admin Svcs ...... Mr. Christopher D. FULKERSON
09 Exec Director Institutional Rsch .... Dr. Robert I. SPRINGER
13 Assistant VP for Technology and CIO .... Mr. Christopher C. WATERS
25 Director of Sponsored Programs .... Ms. Bonnie BRUNO
124 Associate VP for Campus Engagement .... Dr. Randy WILLIAMS
92 Director of Honors Program .... Dr. Tom MOULD
94 Director Women's Stds/Gender Stds .... Dr. Sarah GLASCO
96 Director of Purchasing .... Mr. Jeff HENDRICKS
88 Director of Sustainability .... Ms. Elaine DURR
21 Assoc VP for Business/Finance/Tech .... Mr. Bob SHEA

Gardner-Webb University (H)

PO Box 897 (110 South Main Street), Boiling Springs NC 28017-0897

County: Cleveland FICE Identification: 002929
Unit ID: 198561
Telephone: (704) 406-2361 Carnegie Class: DU-Mod
FAX Number: (704) 406-4329 Calendar System: Semester
URL: www.gardner-webb.edu
Established: 1905 Annual Undergrad Tuition & Fees: $29,810
Enrollment: 4,329 Coed
Affiliation or Control: Baptist IRS Status: 501(c)3
Highest Offering: Doctorate
Accreditation: **SC**, ACBSP, ADNUR, #ARCPA, CAATE, CACREP, CAEPN, MUS, NUR, THEOL

01 President .... Dr. A. Frank BONNER
05 Provost & Executive Vice President .... Dr. Benjamin C. LESLIE
04 Sr Assistant to the President .... Mrs. Stephanie L. STEARNS
11 Vice President for Administration .... Mr. Mike W. HARDIN
26 VP of Marketing .... Mr. Richard K. MCDEVITT
111 VP for External Affairs/Advancement .... Mr. H. Woodrow FISH
32 Vice Pres Student Development .... Ms. Sarah CURRIE
84 Vice Pres Enrollment Management .... Ms. Kristen SETZER
41 Vice President for Athletics .... Mr. Chuck S. BURCH
45 VP Planning & Inst Effectiveness .... Dr. Jeffrey L. TUBBS
18 Assoc Vice Pres for Operations .... Mr. Wayne E. JOHNSON
13 Assoc VP for Technology Services .. Mr. Gregory G. HUMPHRIES
20 Assoc Provost Prof/Graduate Studies .... Dr. Franki BURCH
49 Assoc Provost for Arts & Sciences .... Dr. David YELTON
21 Assoc VP for Business & Finance .... Ms. Robin G. HAMRICK
106 Asst Provost for Digital Learning .... Dr. Jeff ROGERS
07 Assoc VP for Undergrad Admissions .... Ms. Annie FREEMAN
37 Asst VP for Financial Planning .... Ms. Summer NANCE
06 Registrar .... Mrs. LouAnn P. SCATES
20 Assoc Provost Academic Development .... Dr. Doug BRYAN
19 Chief of University Police .... Mr. Barry JOHNSON
27 Assoc VP for Marketing/Comm .... Mr. Noel T. MANNING
08 Director of the Library .... Ms. Mary ROBY
38 Director of Counseling Services .... Ms. Cindy WALLACE
89 Director of Freshmen Programs .... Ms. Jessica HERRNDON
58 Dean of Graduate School .... Dr. Jeffrey ROGERS
73 Dean of Divinity School .... Dr. Robert W. CANOY
66 Dean of Nursing School .... Dr. Nicole WATERS
50 Director of School Management .... Dr. Sue C. CAMP
92 Director of Honors Program .... Dr. Thomas H. JONES
88 Director Program for Blind/Deaf .... Mrs. Cheryl J. POTTER
21 Comptroller .... Ms. Haley KENDRICK
35 Director Student Activities .... Mr. Brian ARNOLD
42 Minister to the University .... Dr. Tracy C. JESSUP
39 Director of Residence Life .... Mr. John R. JOHNSON, JR.
50 Dean of Business School .... Ms. Mischia TAYLOR
15 Director Human Resources .... Mr. W. Scott WHITE
09 Director of Institutional Research .... Ms. Lisa KINDLER
29 Director Alumni Relations .... Mrs. Leah CLEVENGER
44 Director of Annual Campaign .... Ms. Sara MCCALL
27 Asst Dir University Media Relations .... Ms. Kathy MARTIN
40 Bookstore Manager .... Ms. Cary CALDWELL
109 Director of Operations Support .... Mr. Brian SPEER

Grace College of Divinity (A)

5117 Cliffdale Road, Fayetteville NC 28314
County: Cumberland FICE Identification: 041737
Unit ID: 461528
Telephone: (910) 221-2224 Carnegie Class: Spec-4-yr-Faith
FAX Number: (910) 221-2226 Calendar System: Semester
URL: www.gcd.edu
Established: 2000 Annual Undergrad Tuition & Fees: $4,240
Enrollment: 164 Coed
Affiliation or Control: Other Protestant IRS Status: 501(c)3
Highest Offering: Baccalaureate
Accreditation: BI

01 President Dr. Steven CROWTHER
11 Vice President of Administration Ms. Cathy LUCAS
05 Academic Dean Mr. Ron MCBRIDE
84 Dean of Enrollment Management Mr. John MCINTYRE
32 Dean of Students Mrs. Stefanie ERTEL
106 Dean of Online Education/E-Learning Mr. Tom JOHNSON
10 Chief Financial Officer Ms. Omayra COON
30 Director of Development Ms. Diane SHARP
08 Librarian Mr. David ASPINALL
108 Director of Assessment & Planning Ms. Sharyn J. TEAGUE
06 Registrar Ms. Nakiya SMITH

Greensboro College (B)

815 W Market Street, Greensboro NC 27401-1875
County: Guilford FICE Identification: 002930
Unit ID: 198598
Telephone: (336) 272-7102 Carnegie Class: Bac-Diverse
FAX Number: (336) 217-6634 Calendar System: Semester
URL: www.greensboro.edu
Established: 1838 Annual Undergrad Tuition & Fees: $28,000
Enrollment: 978 Coed
Affiliation or Control: United Methodist IRS Status: 501(c)3
Highest Offering: Master's
Accreditation: SC, ACBSP, CAATE, MUS

01 President Dr. Lawrence D. CZARDA
04 Exec Asst to President/Clerk to BoT Ms. Susan J. BARRINGER
101 Exec Asst to President/Clerk to BoT Ms. Susan J. BARRINGER
05 Senior VP Chief Academic Officer Dr. Paul L. LESLIE
11 Exec VP Chief Operating Officer Dr. Robin L. DANIEL
10 VP Chief Financial Officer Mr. Chris ELMORE
111 VP Chief Advancement Officer Ms. Anne J. HURD
20 Assoc VP Academic Admin Ms. Martha M. BUNCH
20 Dean of the Faculty Dr. Richard A. MAYES
57 Dean School of Arts Dr. David SCHRAM
50 Dean School of Business Dr. William K. MACREYNOLDS
53 Dean School of Soc Sci & Education Dr. Rebecca BLOMGREN
79 Dean School of Humanities Dr. Daniel MALOTKY
81 Dean School of Science & Mathematic Dr. Jessica G. SHARPE
07 Dean of Admissions Ms. Julianne SCHATZ
13 Asst VP Information Technology Dr. Larry BURTON
37 Financial Aid Director Ms. Lindsay S. LATHEM
26 Communications Director Mr. Lex ALEXANDER
27 Marketing Director Mr. Tom SAITTA
06 Registrar Mr. Travis MICKEY
32 Dean of Students Dr. Matthew LONG
39 Residence Life Director Ms. Shana PLASTERS
36 Career Services Director Ms. Caryn ATWATER
104 Study Abroad Director Ms. Georgiann BOGDAN
09 Institutional Research Director Ms. Patricia ALBERT
108 Director Institutional Assessment Ms. Patricia ALBERT
121 Academic Success Director Ms. Tica D. GREEN
15 Human Resources Director Ms. Sonia HOFFMAN
18 Facilities Director Mr. Justin LISZKA
19 Security Director Mr. Calvin L. GILMORE
23 Student Health Director Ms. Lauren T. CHILDREY
38 Counseling Services Director Ms. Emily HOLMES
92 George Ctr/Honors Studies Director Mr. Neill CLEGG
30 Asst VP Development Ms. Ellie YEARNS
29 Alumni Engagement Director Ms. Kristen C. BROWN
85 International Programs Director Ms. Cathryn BENNETT
08 Library Director Mr. Will RITTER
41 Athletic Director Mr. Bryan GALUSKI
42 Campus Chaplain Rev. Robert W. BREWER
40 Bookstore Manager Mr. Cliff BRALY, JR.
21 Controller Vacant

Guilford College (C)

5800 W Friendly Avenue, Greensboro NC 27410-4173
County: Guilford FICE Identification: 002931
Unit ID: 198613
Telephone: (336) 316-2000 Carnegie Class: Bac-A&S
FAX Number: (336) 316-2950 Calendar System: Semester
URL: www.guilford.edu
Established: 1837 Annual Undergrad Tuition & Fees: $34,090
Enrollment: 1,917 Coed
Affiliation or Control: Friends IRS Status: 501(c)3
Highest Offering: Master's
Accreditation: SC, ACBSP

01 President Dr. Jane K. FERNANDES
05 VP Academic Affairs/Academic Dean Dr. Frank BOYD
04 Admin Asst to the President Mrs. Angela DUNCAN
10 Vice Pres Finance/Administration Mr. Len SIPPEL
26 Vice President for Marketing Mr. Roger DEGERMAN
30 Vice Pres Advancement Mr. Ara SERJOIE
32 VP Student Affairs/Dean of Students Dr. Todd A. CLARK
84 Vice Pres of Enrollment Management Dr. Arlene W. CASH
22 VP Diversity/Equity/Inclusion Dr. Barbara LAWRENCE
29 Assoc VP Alumni/Constituent Rels Mr. R. Ty BUCKNER
51 Asst Dean Continuing Education Mr. Martee HOLT
31 Asst Dean of Career/Community Lrng Mr. Alan C. MUELLER
20 Assistant Academic Dean Dr. Barbara G. BOYETTE
37 Director Student Financial Svcs Mr. Brian DE YOUNG
06 Registrar Mr. Alfred MOORE
08 Director of the Library Ms. Suzanne M. BARTELS
41 Director of Athletics Mr. Tom J. PALOMBO
19 Director of Public Safety Mr. William ANDERSON
15 Director Human Resources Ms. Alisa QUICK
09 Dir Institutional Research/Assess Ms. Stephanie HARGRAVE
90 Director Info Technology & Services Mr. Chuck CURRY, JR.
42 WR Rogers Dir of Friends Center Rev. C. Wess DANIELS
38 Director Student Counseling Ms. Gaither M. TERRELL
92 Director Honors Program Dr. Heather HAYTON
89 Director of First Year Program Dr. Barbara G. BOYETTE
96 Director of Purchasing Ms. Tracy A. HALL
104 Interim Director Study Abroad Mr. Daniel DIAZ

Heritage Bible College (D)

PO Box 1628, Dunn NC 28335-1628
County: Harnett FICE Identification: 030893
Unit ID: 198677
Telephone: (910) 892-3178 Carnegie Class: Spec-4-yr-Faith
FAX Number: (910) 891-1809 Calendar System: Semester
URL: www.heritagebiblecollege.edu
Established: 1971 Annual Undergrad Tuition & Fees: $9,170
Enrollment: 65 Coed
Affiliation or Control: Other IRS Status: 501(c)3
Highest Offering: Baccalaureate
Accreditation: TRACS

01 President Mr. Randy BARKER
05 Academic Dean Mr. Stephen RZONCA
32 Dean Student Services Vacant
06 Registrar/Director of Financial Aid Mrs. Kayla BULLARD
07 Admissions Mrs. Kayla BULLARD
10 Business Administrator Mrs. LeAnne PAGE
29 Director Alumni Rels/Inst Effectiv Mr. Sterling THARRINGTON
111 Director of Advancement Ms. Iris PRINCE
13 Chief Info Technology Officer (CIO) Mr. James SHEARON
26 Chief Public Relations/Marketing Ms. Iris PRINCE

High Point University (E)

One University Parkway, High Point NC 27268-0001
County: Guilford FICE Identification: 002933
Unit ID: 198695
Telephone: (336) 841-9000 Carnegie Class: Bac-Diverse
FAX Number: (336) 841-4599 Calendar System: Semester
URL: www.highpoint.edu
Established: 1924 Annual Undergrad Tuition & Fees: $33,405
Enrollment: 4,573 Coed
Affiliation or Control: United Methodist IRS Status: 501(c)3
Highest Offering: Doctorate
Accreditation: SC, #ARCPA, CAATE, CAEP, CIDA, @PHAR, @PTA

01 President Dr. Nido R. QUBEIN
05 Provost Dr. Dennis G. CARROLL
46 VP for Research and Planning Dr. Jeffrey M. ADAMS
84 Sr VP for Enrollment Mr. Andy BILLS
26 Sr VP for Communications Mr. Roger D. CLODFELTER, JR.
32 Sr VP for Student Life Mrs. Gail C. TUTTLE
30 Sr VP for Development Mr. Christopher H. DUDLEY
18 VP for Facilities & Auxiliary Svcs Mr. Stephen L. POTTER
10 VP for Financial Affairs Ms. Debi S. BUTT
88 VP for Exp Learning & Career Dev Dr. Stephanie O. CROFTON
41 Athletic Director Mr. Dan HAUSER
07 Assoc VP of Graduate Admissions Mr. Andrew S. MODLIN
07 Assoc VP of Undergrad Admissions Mr. Kerr C. RAMSAY
35 Asst VP for Student Life & Dean Dr. Paul KITTLE
123 Asst VP for Graduate Admissions Mr. Lars C. FARABEE
76 Dean of School of Health Sciences Dr. Daniel E. ERB
49 Dean of College of Arts & Science Dr. Carole B. STONEKING
57 Dean of School of Art and Design Dr. John C. TURPIN
50 Dean of School of Business Dr. James B. WEHRLEY
60 Int Dean of School of Communication Dr. Virginia M. MCDERMOTT
53 Dean of School of Education Dr. Mariann W. TILLERY
67 Dean of School of Pharmacy Dr. Ronald E. RAGAN
121 Assoc Dean of Student Success Dr. Beth HOLDER
20 Assistant Dean Academic Services Ms. Karen C. NAYLON
08 Director of Library Services Mr. David L. BRYDEN
23 Medical Director Dr. Marnie S. MARLETTE
19 Chief of Security Mr. Jeff A. KARPOVICH
06 Registrar Mr. Danny K. BROOKS
13 Chief Information Officer Vacant
29 Director of Alumni Engagement Ms. Kim M. BLAIR
37 Dir of Student Financial Planning Mr. Ronald ELMORE
25 Director of Sponsored Programs Mr. Timothy L. LINKER
15 Director of Human Resources Mrs. Kathy S. SMITH
113 Director of Student Accounts Ms. Janice A. FOLEY
38 Director of Counseling Services Dr. M.J RALEIGH
31 Director of Community Relations Mr. Barry S. KITLEY
24 Sr Director of Interactive Media Ms. Hillary C. KOKAJKO
88 Director of University Events Ms. Melissa L. ANDERSON
09 Dir of Inst Research & Assessment Ms. Andrea KENNEDY
88 Director of Facility Operations Mr. Troy J. THOMPSON
96 Mgr Contracts & Procurement Mr. Gene BUNTING
40 Manager Bookstore Mr. William HOLSTON
85 Director of International Students Ms. Marjorie R. CHURCH
36 Director of Career Services Dr. Douglas L. HALL
104 Director of Study Abroad Ms. Heidi FISCHER
88 Director of Service Learning Dr. Joseph D. BLOSSER
88 Director of Undergraduate Research Dr. Joanne D. ALTMAN
27 Media Relations Coordinator Ms. Pamela J. HAYNES
04 Admin Assistant to President Ms. Judy K. RAY
88 Manager of University Mail Center Mr. Michael R. HALL

Hood Theological Seminary (F)

1810 Lutheran Synod Drive, Salisbury NC 28144-5768
County: Rowan FICE Identification: 036633
Unit ID: 443076
Telephone: (704) 636-7611 Carnegie Class: Spec-4-yr-Faith
FAX Number: (704) 636-7699 Calendar System: Semester
URL: www.hoodseminary.edu
Established: 1904 Annual Undergrad Tuition & Fees: N/A
Enrollment: 156 Coed
Affiliation or Control: African Methodist Episcopal Zion Church
IRS Status: 501(c)3
Highest Offering: Doctorate
Accreditation: THEOL

01 President-Elect Dr. Vergel L. LATTIMORE
05 Academic Dean Dr. Trevor EPPEHIMER
32 Dean of Students Dr. Dora R. MBUWAYESANGO
10 Chief Financial Ofcr/Dir Human Res Rev.Dr. Regina M. DANCY
26 Dir Communication/Info/Pub Ms. Carol PALMER
30 Institutional Advancement Officer Mr. John C. EVERETT
06 Registrar Ms. Nancy BAKER

John Wesley University (G)

1215 Eastchester Drive, High Point NC 27265-3115
County: Guilford FICE Identification: 002935
Unit ID: 198747
Telephone: (336) 887-3000 Carnegie Class: Spec-4-yr-Faith
FAX Number: (336) 889-2261 Calendar System: Semester
URL: www.johnwesley.edu
Established: 1903 Annual Undergrad Tuition & Fees: $11,230
Enrollment: 158 Coed
Affiliation or Control: Independent Non-Profit IRS Status: 501(c)3
Highest Offering: Doctorate
Accreditation: BI

01 President Dr. Stephen M. CONDON
10 Vice Pres for Finance & Instruction Vacant
05 Academic Dean Dr. Ron SELLECK
73 Dean School of Ministry Dr. John LINDSEY
06 Registrar Mr. Greg WORKMAN
32 Exec Dir Stdt Svcs/Spiritual Life Mr. Jake SMITH
08 Director of Library Services Mrs. April LINDSEY
15 Exec Director of Human Resources Mrs. Kathy CUTRELL
21 Director of Business Services Mrs. Mary Emily KENNON
50 Director School of Management Dr. Caldwell JASON
29 Alumni Coordinator Ms. Kathy CUTRELL

Johnson & Wales University-Charlotte (H)

801 W Trade Street, Charlotte NC 28202-1122
Telephone: (980) 598-1000 Identification: 666375
Accreditation: &EH

† Regional accreditation is carried under the parent institution in Providence, RI.

Johnson C. Smith University (I)

100 Beatties Ford Road, Charlotte NC 28216-5398
County: Mecklenburg FICE Identification: 002936
Unit ID: 198756
Telephone: (704) 378-1000 Carnegie Class: Bac-A&S
FAX Number: (704) 372-1242 Calendar System: Semester
URL: www.jcsu.edu
Established: 1867 Annual Undergrad Tuition & Fees: $18,236
Enrollment: 1,438 Coed
Affiliation or Control: Independent Non-Profit IRS Status: 501(c)3
Highest Offering: Master's
Accreditation: SC, SW

01 President Dr. Ronald L. CARTER
05 VP for Academic/Student Services Dr. Kelli RAINEY
10 Vice Pres for Finance Mr. Greg PETZKE
111 Vice President for Inst Advancement Ms. Tami SIMMONS
86 VP Government Sponsored Pgms Dr. Diane BOWLES
15 VP Administrative Services/CHRO Ms. Latrelle P. MCALLISTER
81 Dean of STEM Dr. Hang CHEN
49 Dean of Arts and Letters Dr. Brian JONES
70 Dean of School of Social Work Dr. Helen CALDWELL
32 Dean of Students Mr. Takeem DEAN
89 Associate Dean of First-Year Exper Dr. Cathy JONES
88 Dean of the University College Dr. Antonio HENLEY
107 Dean Metro College Prof Studies Dr. Laura MCLEAN
121 Dean of Academic Support Services Mr. John NORRIS
08 Director of the Library Ms. Monika RHUE
07 Director of Admissions Mr. James BURRELL
13 Director Information Technology Mr. John NORRIS
09 Dir Plng/Assess/Effect/Rsrch Mrs. Sharell CANNADY
26 Director of Comm and Marketing Ms. Sherri BELFIELD
29 Director Alumni Affairs Mrs. Wanda FOY-BURROUGHS

37 Director Financial Aid ... Ms. Shelline WARREN
41 Athletic Director ... Mr. Stephen JOYNER, SR.
06 Registrar ... Mrs. Keisha WILSON
39 Coordinator of Housing Services ... Ms. Ashley SMITH
40 Manager of Bookstore ... Ms. Robin SORENSEN
117 Manager Risk Management ... Mrs. Debra HOLLIS
23 Health Center Coordinator ... Ms. Marian JONES

King's College (A)

322 Lamar Avenue, Charlotte NC 28204-2493
County: Mecklenburg FICE Identification: 002937
Unit ID: 382504
Telephone: (704) 372-0266 Carnegie Class: Assoc/HVT-High Trad
FAX Number: (704) 348-2029 Calendar System: Semester
URL: www.kingscollegecharlotte.edu
Established: 1901 Annual Undergrad Tuition & Fees: $14,320
Enrollment: 380 Coed
Affiliation or Control: Proprietary IRS Status: Proprietary
Highest Offering: Associate Degree
Accreditation: ACICS, MAC

01 School Director ... Mrs. Diane RYON
05 Chief Academic Officer ... Ms. Barbara ROCKECHARLIE

Lees-McRae College (B)

191 Main Street, Banner Elk NC 28604-0128
County: Avery FICE Identification: 002939
Unit ID: 198808
Telephone: (828) 898-5241 Carnegie Class: Bac-Diverse
FAX Number: (828) 898-8814 Calendar System: Semester
URL: www.lmc.edu
Established: 1900 Annual Undergrad Tuition & Fees: $25,648
Enrollment: 1,033 Coed
Affiliation or Control: Presbyterian Church (U.S.A.) IRS Status: 501(c)3
Highest Offering: Baccalaureate
Accreditation: SC, #CAATE, CAEPT, NURSE

01 President ... Dr. Barry M. BUXTON
04 Secretary to the President ... Ms. Vicki FOSTER
05 Provost & Dean of Faculty ... Dr. Todd LIDH
10 VP Finance/Business Affairs ... Ms. Suzette FRONK
32 VP Stdnt Dev & Dean of Students ... Mr. Jon DRIGGERS
45 VP Strategic Planning/Effectiveness ... Mr. Blaine J. HANSEN
111 VP Advancement ... Mr. Brent THOMAS
41 VP Athletics/Club Sports ... Mr. Craig MCPHAIL
84 VP Enrollment Management ... Ms. Erin HEALEY
20 Associate Provost ... Dr. Bo BENNETT
66 Dean Nursing/Health Sciences ... Dr. Laura FERO
79 Dean Arts/Humanities/Education ... Dr. Pamela VESELY
81 Dean Natural & Behavioral Sciences ... Dr. Billy CARVER
50 Dean Business & Management ... Ms. Amy ANDERSON
66 Assistant Dean Nursing ... Dr. Teresa DARNALL
57 Assistant Dean Arts/Humanities ... Ms. Danielle CURTIS
81 Assistant Dean Natural & Behavioral ... Dr. Sean COLLINS
71 Director Burton Center ... Ms. Keri MAGANA
08 Director Libraries ... Ms. Jess BELLEMER
06 Registrar ... Ms. Lynn HINSHAW
19 Director Security/Safety ... Mr. H.D STEWART
18 Director Facilities ... Mr. David PHILYAW
13 Director Technology ... Mr. Ben HOLTSCLAW
15 Director Human Resources ... Ms. Carolyn WARD
21 Controller ... Ms. Susan STEPHENSON
35 Assistant Dean of Students ... Mr. Josh GAISSER
26 Director Marketing & Design ... Ms. Lauren FOSTER
120 Learning Systems Analyst ... Ms. Melissa MERCER
29 Director Alumni Relations ... Ms. Jillian ROSATO
07 Director Admissions ... Ms. Candace SILVER
37 Director Financial Aid ... Ms. Cathy SHELL

Lenoir-Rhyne University (C)

625 7th Avenue NE, Hickory NC 28601-3984
County: Catawba FICE Identification: 002941
Unit ID: 198835
Telephone: (828) 328-1741 Carnegie Class: Masters/S
FAX Number: (828) 328-7368 Calendar System: Semester
URL: www.lr.edu
Established: 1891 Annual Undergrad Tuition & Fees: $33,730
Enrollment: 2,221 Coed
Affiliation or Control: Evangelical Lutheran Church In America
IRS Status: 501(c)3
Highest Offering: Master's
Accreditation: SC, ACBSP, #ARCPA, CAATE, CACREP, CAEPN, DIETI, NURSE, OT, PH, THEOL

01 President ... Dr. Fred WHITT
05 Provost ... Dr. Larry HALL
10 Sr Vice President Finance/Admin ... Mr. Peter KENDALL
111 Vice Pres Institutional Advancement ... Vacant
84 Vice President for Enrollment Mgmt ... Ms. Rachel NICHOLS
32 Asst Provost/Dean of Students ... Dr. Katie FISHER
104 Assoc Dean Global Learning ... Ms. Charlotte WILLIAMS
58 Dean Grad Studies/Lifelong Learning ... Dr. Amy WOOD
06 Registrar ... Mr. Stacey BRACKETT
08 Librarian ... Ms. Rita JOHNSON
15 Director of Human Resources ... Mr. Rick NICHOLS
40 Director of Bookstore ... Ms. Lucy MANZANARES
18 Director of Facilities/Plant ... Mr. Otis PITTS
41 Athletic Director ... Ms. Kim PATE
42 Campus Pastor ... Rev. Andrew WEISNER
19 Director of Security ... Mr. Norris YODER
92 Director of Honors Program ... Dr. Joshua RING
13 CIO ... Mr. John ROSEBROCK
26 Dir of Marketing/Communication ... Ms. Angela REITER
88 Director of Conferences & Events ... Ms. Janet MATTHEWS
29 Director of Alumni Relations ... Ms. Cheryl ABEE
07 Director of Enrollment Services ... Mr. Eric BRANDON
09 Dir of Inst Research/Assess ... Dr. Debra TEMPLETON
37 Director Student Financial Aid ... Mr. Nick JENKINS
38 Dir Student Counseling/Placement ... Ms. Jenny SMITH
88 Dir Liberal Arts/Visiting Writers ... Dr. Rand BRANDES
28 Director Multicultural Affairs ... Ms. Emma SELLERS
88 Institute on Obesity ... Ms. Kimberly PENNINGTON
65 Institute on Conservation ... Dr. John BRZORAD
85 Dir of International Programs ... Dr. Laura DOBSON
53 College of Education/Human Services ... Dr. Hank WEDDINGTON
73 College of Theology ... Dr. David RATKE
76 College of Health Sciences ... Dr. Michael MCGEE
49 College of Arts & Sciences ... Dr. Dan KISER
81 Col of Professional/Math Studies ... Dr. Mary LESSER
04 Administrative Asst to President ... Ms. Sherry ERIKSON
36 Director Student Placement ... Ms. Katie WOHLMAN
39 Director Student Housing ... Mr. Jonathan RINK
43 Dir of Compliance/Title IX ... Ms. Dawn FLOYD

Living Arts College @ School of Communication Arts (D)

3000 Wakefield Crossing Drive, Raleigh NC 27614-7076
County: Wake FICE Identification: 031090
Unit ID: 421832
Telephone: (919) 488-8500 Carnegie Class: Bac-Diverse
FAX Number: (919) 488-8490 Calendar System: Quarter
URL: www.living-arts-college.edu
Established: 1992 Annual Undergrad Tuition & Fees: $16,940
Enrollment: 362 Coed
Affiliation or Control: Proprietary IRS Status: Proprietary
Highest Offering: Baccalaureate
Accreditation: ACICS, MAC

01 Director ... Ms. Debra A. HOOPER

Livingstone College (E)

701 W Monroe Street, Salisbury NC 28144-5298
County: Rowan FICE Identification: 002942
Unit ID: 198862
Telephone: (704) 216-6000 Carnegie Class: Bac-Diverse
FAX Number: (704) 216-6217 Calendar System: Semester
URL: www.livingstone.edu
Established: 1879 Annual Undergrad Tuition & Fees: $17,764
Enrollment: 1,262 Coed
Affiliation or Control: African Methodist Episcopal Zion Church
IRS Status: 501(c)3
Highest Offering: Baccalaureate
Accreditation: SC, CAEPN, SW

01 President ... Dr. Jimmy R. JENKINS, SR.
04 Exec Asst to the President ... Dr. State W. ALEXANDER
05 Vice Pres Academic Affairs ... Dr. Carolyn W. DUNCAN
10 Vice Pres Business & Finance/Ops ... Mr. Reginald DICKENS
32 Vice President Student Affairs ... Dr. Orlando LEWIS
30 Vice Pres Inst Advance/College Rels ... Vacant
35 Assoc Vice Pres of Student Affairs ... Mr. Tony BALDWIN
20 Asst Vice Pres Academic Affairs ... Dr. Alexander ERWIN
38 Dean of Counseling Services . Mrs. Elizabeth ALSTON-PINCKNEY
06 Registrar ... Mrs. Wendy JACKSON
08 Director Library Services ... Ms. Laura JOHNSON
26 Vice Pres Communications & PR ... Dr. State W. ALEXANDER
37 Director of Financial Aid ... Ms. Stephanie MCNEIL
36 Director of Career Services ... Ms. Sereyna WALLACE
13 Director of Computer Info Systems ... Mr. Chong DAN
15 Director of Human Resources ... Mr. Mark SANDERS
29 Director Alumni Affairs ... Ms. Vincia MILLER
09 Director of Institutional Research ... Mr. Robert L. MCINNIS
84 Director of Enrollment Management ... Vacant
07 Director of Admissions ... Vacant
40 Bookstore Director ... Mr. Keith ANDERSON
41 Athletic Director ... Mr. Andre SPRINGS
96 Director of Purchasing ... Ms. Debra WOOD
18 Director of Physical Plant ... Mr. Weldon SPENCER
23 Health Services Manager ... Ms. Sarah GAITHER
27 Asst Director Public Relations ... Ms. Kimberly HARRINGTON

Louisburg College (F)

501 N. Main Street, Louisburg NC 27549-7705
County: Franklin FICE Identification: 002943
Unit ID: 198871
Telephone: (919) 496-2521 Carnegie Class: Assoc/HT-High Trad
FAX Number: (919) 496-7141 Calendar System: Semester
URL: www.louisburg.edu
Established: 1787 Annual Undergrad Tuition & Fees: $18,007
Enrollment: 705 Coed
Affiliation or Control: United Methodist IRS Status: 501(c)3
Highest Offering: Associate Degree
Accreditation: SC

01 Interim President ... Ms. Stephanie TOLBERT
05 Interim Dean of Academic Affairs ... Ms. Emily ZANK
111 VP of Institutional Advancement ... Mr. Chad BAREFOOT
32 VP of Student Life ... Mr. Jason E. MODLIN
10 VP of Finance ... Vacant
84 Senior VP of Enrollment Management ... Ms. Stephanie B. TOLBERT
29 Alumni Director ... Ms. Jamie PATRICK
06 Registrar ... Dr. Michelle AHERON
08 Librarian ... Ms. Pat HINTON
38 Director of Counseling Services ... Ms. Fonda PORTER
37 Director of Financial Aid ... Ms. Tracy POTTER
26 Director of College Communications ... Vacant
18 Associate VP of Facilities ... Mr. Nathan BIEGENZAHN
04 Executive Asst to President ... Ms. Jennifer MITCHELL WHEELER
07 Director of Admissions ... Ms. Maura BUDUSKY
09 Director of Institutional Research ... Ms. Brittany HUNT
19 Campus Police Chief ... Mr. Jermaine THOMAS
39 Director of Housing ... Mr. Christopher REID
41 Athletic Director ... Mr. Mike HOLLOMAN
13 Chief Technology Officer ... Mr. Mark JOYNER
15 Director of Human Resources ... Ms. Terry WRIGHT

Mars Hill University (G)

PO Box 370, Mars Hill NC 28754-0370
County: Madison FICE Identification: 002944
Unit ID: 198899
Telephone: (828) 689-1307 Carnegie Class: Bac-Diverse
FAX Number: (828) 689-1478 Calendar System: Semester
URL: www.mhu.edu
Established: 1856 Annual Undergrad Tuition & Fees: $30,534
Enrollment: 1,410 Coed
Affiliation or Control: Independent Non-Profit IRS Status: 501(c)3
Highest Offering: Master's
Accreditation: SC, #CAATE, CAEPN, MUS, NURSE, SW, THEA

01 President ... Dr. Dan G. LUNSFORD
30 Vice President for Inst Advancement ... Mr. Harold (Bud) G. CHRISTMAN
05 Int Vice Pres for Academic Affairs ... Dr. Carol BOGGESS
10 Vice Pres Finance/Facilities Mgmt ... Mr. Neil TILLEY
32 Assoc Vice Pres for Student Devel ... Dr. Laura WHITAKER-LEA
20 Asst Vice Pres for Academic Admin ... Dr. Jim BROWN
07 Director of Admissions ... Ms. Kristie VANCE
06 Dean Academic Records/Registrar ... Ms. Marie NICHOLSON
08 Director of Library Services ... Ms. Beverly ROBERTSON
26 Sr Director of Marketing ... Ms. Samantha FENDER
42 Campus Chaplain ... Rev. Stephanie MCLESKEY
41 Director of Athletics ... Mr. David W. RIGGINS
37 Director of Financial Aid ... Ms. Nichole BUCKNER
29 Director of Alumni & Donor Rels ... Ms. Amy GARRISON
85 Director International Education ... Mr. Gordon HINNERS
09 Director Institutional Research ... Ms. Jennifer RHINEHART
38 Director Student Counseling ... Ms. Cassandra PAVONE
15 AVP Human Resources/Strategic Init ... Dr. Joy KISH
13 Director Information Technology Svc ... Mr. Ted BRUNER
18 Director of Facilities ... Mr. Donald EDWARDS
40 Director of Bookstore ... Mr. Darryl R. NORTON
51 Dean of Adult & Graduate Studies ... Vacant
97 Chair of General Studies ... Ms. Cathy L. ADKINS

Meredith College (H)

3800 Hillsborough Street, Raleigh NC 27607-5298
County: Wake FICE Identification: 002945
Unit ID: 198950
Telephone: (919) 760-8600 Carnegie Class: Bac-A&S
FAX Number: (919) 760-2828 Calendar System: Semester
URL: www.meredith.edu
Established: 1891 Annual Undergrad Tuition & Fees: $34,907
Enrollment: 1,949 Female
Affiliation or Control: Independent Non-Profit IRS Status: 501(c)3
Highest Offering: Master's
Accreditation: SC, CAEPN, CIDA, DIETD, DIETI, MUS, SW

01 President ... Dr. Jo ALLEN
05 Sr Vice Pres and Provost ... Dr. Matthew POSLUSNY
30 Vice Pres Institutional Advancement ... Dr. Charles (Lennie) BARTON
10 Vice Pres for Business & Finance ... Mr. Craig BARFIELD
32 Vice President for College Programs ... Dr. Jean JACKSON
26 Vice President of Marketing ... Ms. Kristi EAVES-MCLENNAN
35 Dean of Students ... Ms. Ann C. GLEASON
58 Director of Graduate Programs ... Dr. Monica MCKINNEY
06 Registrar ... Ms. Evie ODOM
09 Dir Research/Planning & Assessment ... Dr. C. Dianne RAUBENHEIMER
08 Director Library Info Services ... Ms. Laura DAVIDSON
07 Director of Admissions ... Ms. Shery BOYLES
37 Director of Financial Assistance ... Mr. Kevin MICHAELSEN
35 Dir Student Activ/Leadership Devel ... Ms. Cheryl S. JENKINS
28 Assistant Dean of Students ... Ms. Tomecca SLOANE
36 Director Office of Career Planning ... Ms. Dana SUMNER
29 Dir of Alumnae & Parent Relations ... Ms. Hilary ALLEN
38 Director of Counseling Center ... Ms. Beth A. MEIER
39 Director Resident Life/Housing ... Ms. Heidi LECOUNT
20 Director of Academic Advising ... Mr. Alex DAVIS
31 Director Campus Events ... Mr. Bill BROWN
23 Director Health Services ... Dr. Mary JOHNSON
42 Campus Minister ... Rev. Donna BATTLE
13 Chief Information Officer ... Mr. Jeffrey HOWLETT
19 Chief Campus Police ... Mr. Al WHITE
15 Director of Human Resources ... Ms. Pamela GALLOWAY
18 Chief Facilities/Physical Plant ... Ms. Sharon CAMPBELL
21 Director of Accounting ... Ms. Susan WILLIAMS

88 Director of Learning Center .... Dr. Carmen CHRISTOPHER
104 Director of International Programs .... Dr. Brooke SHURER
88 Dir Retention & Student Success .... Mr. Brandon STOKES
88 Director of Strong Points .... Ms. Candice WEBB

Methodist University (A)

5400 Ramsey Street, Fayetteville NC 28311-1498
County: Cumberland FICE Identification: 002946
Unit ID: 198969
Telephone: (910) 630-7000 Carnegie Class: Masters/S
FAX Number: (910) 630-7317 Calendar System: Semester
URL: www.methodist.edu
Established: 1956 Annual Undergrad Tuition & Fees: $31,980
Enrollment: 2,474 Coed
Affiliation or Control: United Methodist IRS Status: 501(c)3
Highest Offering: Doctorate
Accreditation: SC, ACBSP, ARCPA, CAATE, NURSE, @PTA, SW

01 President .... Dr. Ben E. HANCOCK, JR.
05 Exec Vice Pres & Academic Dean .... Dr. Delmas S. CRISP, JR.
10 VP Business Affairs/Controller .... Ms. Dawn AUSBORN
32 Vice President for Student Affairs .... Mr. William WALKER
30 VP Univ Relations & Advancement .... Ms. Sandy AMMONS
09 VP Planning & Evaluation .... Dr. Donald L. LASSITER
84 Vice Pres Enrollment Management .... Mr. Rick D. LOWE
42 VP Campus Ministry/Cmty Engagement .... Rev. Kelli TAYLOR
26 VP University Relations/Advancement .... Mrs. Sandy AMMONS
41 VP/Director of Athletics .... Mr. Dave EAVENSON
20 Associate VP for Academic Affairs .... Ms. Beth CARTER
35 Assoc Dean Student Services .... Mr. Todd D. HARRIS
36 Assoc Dean Student/Career Services . Ms. Antoinette P. BELLAMY
29 Director of Alumni Affairs .... Ms. Kirbie DOCKERY
07 Dean of Admissions .... Mr. Jamie W. LEGG
37 Director of Financial Aid .... Ms. Bonnie J. ADAMSON
06 Registrar .... Ms. Jasmin K. BROWN
08 Head Librarian .... Ms. Tracey PEARSON
104 Dir Intl Programs/Study Abroad .... Mr. Lyle SHEPPARD
19 Director Police/Public Safety .... Mr. Mark BREWINGTON
15 Director Personnel Services .... Mrs. Debra YEATTS
18 Director of Facilities .... Mr. Charles GOURLAY
38 Director Student Counseling .... Ms. Darlene HOPKINS
96 Director of Purchasing .... Ms. Deborah DEMBOSKY

Mid-Atlantic Christian University (B)

715 N Poindexter, Elizabeth City NC 27909-4054
County: Pasquotank FICE Identification: 022809
Unit ID: 199458
Telephone: (252) 334-2000 Carnegie Class: Spec-4-yr-Faith
FAX Number: (252) 334-2071 Calendar System: Semester
URL: www.macuniversity.edu
Established: 1948 Annual Undergrad Tuition & Fees: $13,600
Enrollment: 204 Coed
Affiliation or Control: Churches Of Christ IRS Status: 501(c)3
Highest Offering: Baccalaureate
Accreditation: SC

01 Interim President .... Mr. John W. MAURICE, JR.
05 Vice President Academic Affairs .... Dr. Kevin W. LARSEN
32 Vice President Student Services .... Dr. Ken S. GREENE
111 Vice President Institutional Advanc .... Vacant
10 Vice President Finance .... Mrs. Carol M. STUART
09 Director of Institutional Research .... Dr. Kevin W. LARSEN
06 Registrar .... Miss Yolanda K. TESKE
08 Director of Library .... Mr. Ken D. GUNSELMAN
38 Counselor .... Mr. Donald W. MCKINNEY
37 Financial Aid Administrator .... Mrs. Jenny ROWLAND
35 Student Life Administrator .... Mr. Drew BROMM
49 Chair of Arts and Sciences .... Dr. Robert W. SMITH
73 Chair of Biblical Studies .... Dr. Lee M. FIELDS
42 Chair of Christian Ministry .... Dr. Claudio F. DIVINO
88 Chair of Marketplace Ministry .... Mr. Donald W. MCKINNEY
07 Enrollment Director .... Mr. Daniel C. SMITH

Miller-Motte College (C)

2205 Walnut Street, Cary NC 27518
Telephone: (919) 532-7171 Identification: 770726
Accreditation: ACICS, MAC, SURGT

† Branch campus of Miller-Motte Technical College, Lynchburg, VA

Miller-Motte College (D)

3725 Ramsey Street, Fayetteville NC 28311
Telephone: (910) 354-1900 Identification: 770728
Accreditation: ACICS

† Branch campus of Miller-Motte Technical College, Lynchburg, VA

Miller-Motte College (E)

1021 W.H. Smith Blvd, Suite 102, Greenville NC 27834
Telephone: (252) 215-2000 Identification: 770730
Accreditation: ACICS

† Branch campus of Miller-Motte Technical College, Clarksville, TN. No longer accepting campus-based students

Miller-Motte College (F)

1291 Hargett Street, Jacksonville NC 28540
Telephone: (910) 478-4300 Identification: 770729
Accreditation: ACICS

† Branch campus of Miller-Motte Technical College, Lynchburg, VA

Miller-Motte College (G)

3901 Capital Boulevard, Suite 151, Raleigh NC 27604
Telephone: (919) 723-2820 Identification: 770727
Accreditation: ACICS, DA, MAC

† Branch campus of Miller-Motte Technical College, Lynchburg, VA

Miller-Motte Technical College (H)

5000 Market Street, Wilmington NC 28405-3430
Telephone: (910) 392-4660 FICE Identification: 030632
Accreditation: ACICS, DA, MAC, SURGT

† Branch campus of Miller-Motte Technical College, TN.

Montreat College (I)

PO Box 1267, 310 Gaither Circle,
Montreat NC 28757-1267
County: Buncombe FICE Identification: 002948
Unit ID: 199032
Telephone: (828) 669-8012 Carnegie Class: Masters/S
FAX Number: (828) 669-9554 Calendar System: Semester
URL: www.montreat.edu
Established: 1916 Annual Undergrad Tuition & Fees: $24,940
Enrollment: 1,008 Coed
Affiliation or Control: Non-denominational IRS Status: 501(c)3
Highest Offering: Master's
Accreditation: SC

01 President .... Dr. Paul J. MAURER
10 VP for Finance and Administration .... Mr. Jack HEINEN
30 VP of Advancement .... Vacant
58 VP and Dean for Adult/Grad Studies .... Vacant
05 VP and Dean for Academic Affairs .... Dr. Greg KERR
84 VP for Enrollment and Management .... Ms. Kristin JANES
32 VP and Dean for Student Services .... Dr. Daniel BENNETT
88 Counselor to the President .... Mr. Joe KIRKLAND
26 Exec Dir Marketing/Communications .... Vacant
09 Assoc Dean of Academics & Inst Eff .... Vacant
20 Associate Dean of Academic Affairs .... Vacant
108 Director of Assessment .... Mr. Brad FAIRCLOTH
41 Athletic Director .... Mr. Jose LARIOS
29 Director Alumni Relations .... Vacant
37 Director of Financial Aid .... Ms. Beth POCOCK
38 Director of Counseling .... Mrs. Holleigh WOODWARD
88 Director for Advancement Services .... Ms. Kristine BUCKWALTER
08 Library Director .... Ms. Elizabeth R. PEARSON
21 Controller .... Mrs. Patti GUFFEY
04 Executive Assistant to President .... Ms. Hope DEIFELL
42 Dean of Spiritual Formation .... Rev. David TAYLOR
06 Registrar .... Ms. Keri BOER
40 Bookstore Manager .... Ms. Carly BRAENDEL
19 Interim Chief of Campus Police .... Ms. Phyllis COMRIE
18 Chief Facilities/Physical Plant .... Mr. Mike SHOAF

Native American Bible College (J)

PO Box 248, Shannon NC 28386
County: Robeson Identification: 667092
Telephone: (910) 843-5304 Carnegie Class: Not Classified
FAX Number: N/A Calendar System: Semester
URL: nabc.edu
Established: 1968 Annual Undergrad Tuition & Fees: N/A
Enrollment: N/A Coed
Affiliation or Control: Assemblies Of God Church IRS Status: 501(c)3
Highest Offering: Baccalaureate
Accreditation: BI

01 President .... James A. KEYS
05 Chief Academic Officer .... Vacant
32 Chief Student Development Officer .... John DAVIS
08 Chief Librarian .... T. Liisa KELLY
04 Administrative Asst to President .... Misa D. LOWERY
06 Registrar .... Isabel LOPEZ

*North Carolina Community College System (K)

200 W Jones Street, 5001 MSC, Raleigh NC 27699-5001
County: Wake FICE Identification: 033445
Unit ID: 199166
Telephone: (919) 807-7100 Carnegie Class: N/A
FAX Number: (919) 807-7166
URL: www.nccommunitycolleges.edu

01 Acting President .... Ms. Jennifer HAYGOOD
05 Senior VP Programs/Chief Acad Ofcr .... Dr. Lisa CHAPMAN
100 Chief of Staff .... Ms. Jennifer HAYGOOD
10 Vice Pres/Chief Financial Officer ..... Ms. Elizabeth GROVENSTEIN
13 VP Technology Solutions .... Mr. Jim PARKER
46 Assoc VP for STEM Innovation .... Dr. Matthew MEYER
101 Exec Director State Board Affairs .... Mr. Bryan JENKINS
04 Special Assistant to the President .... Ms. Pia MCKENZIE

*Alamance Community College (L)

1247 Jimmie Kerr Road/PO Box 8000,
Graham NC 27253-8000
County: Alamance FICE Identification: 005463
Unit ID: 199786
Telephone: (336) 578-2002 Carnegie Class: Assoc/MT-VT-Mix Trad/Non
FAX Number: (336) 578-1987 Calendar System: Semester
URL: www.alamancecc.edu
Established: 1958 Annual Undergrad Tuition & Fees (In-District): $2,190
Enrollment: 4,531 Coed
Affiliation or Control: State/Local IRS Status: 501(c)3
Highest Offering: Associate Degree
Accreditation: SC, ACFEI, DA, MAC, MLTAD

02 President .... Dr. Algie C. GATEWOOD
03 Executive Vice President .... Mr. Scott QUEEN
10 VP Admin & Fiscal Svcs .... Ms. Cynthia COLLIE
111 VP Institutional Advancement .... Ms. Carolyn RHODE
05 VP of Instruction .... Ms. Catherine W. JOHNSON
103 VP Workforce Development .... Mr. Gary SAUNDERS
32 VP Student Success .... Dr. Carol DISQUE
50 Dean Business/Arts & Sciences .... Ms. Sonya MCCOOK
72 Dean Industrial Technologies .... Mr. Justin SNYDER
69 Dean Health & Public Svcs .... Mr. David FRAZEE
21 Controller .... Mr. Matthew BANKO
06 Registrar .... Mr. Kenneth DOBBINS
11 Director Administrative Services .... Mr. Thomas HARTMAN
15 Director Human Resources .... Ms. Lorri ALLISON
13 Director Information Services .... Mr. Winfield HENRY
08 Director Learning Resources Center .... Ms. Sheila STREET
26 Director Public Information/Mktg .... Mr. Edward WILLIAMS
56 Director Occupational Ext Program .... Vacant
84 Director Enrollment Management .... Ms. Elizabeth BREHLER
37 Director Financial Aid .... Ms. Sabrina DEGAIN
36 Director Counseling & Career Svcs .... Ms. Ilona OWENS
38 Special Needs/Counseling Svcs Coord .... Ms. Monica ISBELL
121 Academic Support Specialist .... Ms. Jennifer BROWNELL
09 Institutional Researcher .... Dr. Jessica HARRELL
19 Director Security/Safety .... Mr. David PREVATTE

*Asheville - Buncombe Technical Community College (M)

340 Victoria Road, Asheville NC 28801-4897
County: Buncombe FICE Identification: 004033
Unit ID: 197887
Telephone: (828) 254-1921 Carnegie Class: Assoc/MT-VT-Mix Trad/Non
FAX Number: (828) 251-6355 Calendar System: Semester
URL: www.abtech.edu
Established: 1959 Annual Undergrad Tuition & Fees (In-District): $2,547
Enrollment: 7,233 Coed
Affiliation or Control: State/Local IRS Status: 501(c)3
Highest Offering: Associate Degree
Accreditation: SC, ACFEI, DA, DH, DMS, EMT, MAC, MLTAD, PHLEB, RAD, SURGT

02 President .... Dr. Dennis KING
10 VP Business & Finance/CFO .... Dr. Dirk WILMOTH
13 Vice Pres Information Technology .... Mr. Brian WILLIS
05 VP Instructional Services .... Dr. Beth STEWART
20 Associate VP Instructional Services .... Dr. Gene LOFLIN
32 VP Student Services .... Dr. Terry BRASIER
15 Vice President Human Resources & OD .... Ms. Kaye SCHMIDT
103 VP Econ Workforce Dev/Cont Educ .... Dr. Shelley WHITE
04 Executive Administrative Assistant .... Ms. Carolyn RICE
111 Exec Director College Advancement .... Ms. Amanda EDWARDS
49 Dean Arts & Sciences .... Mr. Kenet ADAMSON
50 Dean Business & Hospitality Educ .... Mr. RJ CORMAN
54 Dean Engineering & Applied Tech ..... Mr. Vernon D. DAUGHERTY
91 Director Info Systems Technology .... Mr. David C. MCKINNEY
30 Development/Events Coordinator .... Ms. Susan HALDANE
35 Director Student Life/Development .... Ms. Michele HATHCOCK
61 Director Law Enforcement Academy .... Vacant
21 Director Business Services .... Ms. Lisa LANKFORD
37 Director of Financial Aid .... Ms. Cynthia ANDERSON
06 Registrar .... Mr. Aaron RICHMAN
84 Director Enrollment Services .... Ms. Lisa F. BUSH
24 Director Library Services .... Mr. Russell TAYLOR
12 Director Madison County Campus .... Ms. Sherri DAVIS
18 Director Plant Operations .... Mr. Benny R. SMITH
19 Chief of Police/Security .... Ms. Kara WALKER
31 Director Community Services Program .... Ms. Brinda W. CALDWELL
08 Librarian .... Mr. Russell TAYLOR
09 Exec Director Research & Planning .... Mr. David B. WHITE
26 Exec Dir Community Rels/Marketing .... Ms. Kerri GLOVER
28 Director of Diversity .... Vacant
40 Bookstore Manager .... Mr. Kevin MILLS
96 Purchasing Agent .... Ms. Rebecca R. WATKINS
72 Dir Cust Rels/Technology Services .... Mr. Cris HARSHMAN

*Beaufort County Community College (N)

5337 US Hwy 264 East, Washington NC 27889-7889
County: Beaufort FICE Identification: 008558
Unit ID: 197966
Telephone: (252) 946-6194 Carnegie Class: Assoc/MT-VT-Mix Trad/Non
FAX Number: (252) 946-0271 Calendar System: Semester
URL: www.beaufortccc.edu
Established: 1967 Annual Undergrad Tuition & Fees (In-District): $2,504
Enrollment: 1,820 Coed

Affiliation or Control: State/Local IRS Status: 501(c)3
Highest Offering: Associate Degree
Accreditation: SC, MLTAD

02 President ... Dr. David LOOPE
05 VP of Academics ... Dr. Crystal ANGE
10 VP of Administrative Services ... Mr. Mark NELSON
32 VP of Student Services ... Mr. Rick ANDERSON
51 VP of Continuing Education ... Mrs. Stacey GERARD
09 VP of Research & Inst Effectiveness ... Dr. Jay SULLIVAN
26 Public Relations Coordinator ... Mr. Attila NEMECZ
31 Dir of Community Partnerships ... Mr. Clay CARTER
76 Dean Allied Health/Profess Services .. Mrs. Erica S. CARACOGLIA
49 Dean Arts & Sciences ... Mrs. Lisa HILL
50 Dean of Business & Industrial Tech ... Mr. Ben MORRIS
08 Dir Learning Resources Center ... Vacant
14 Network Administrator ... Mr. Whiting TOLER
91 System Administrator ... Mr. Randy BURNETTE
15 Director of Human Resources ... Mrs. Emily WOOLARD
19 Chief of Campus Police ... Mr. Christopher HARRISON
88 Systems Administrator Assistant ... Mr. Brandon BUNCH
37 Director of Financial Aid ... Ms. Jo WOOLARD
06 Registrar ... Ms. Melissa A. FRANCIS
07 Director of Admissions ... Mrs. Michele MAYO
103 Dir of Business & Industry Svcs ... Mr. Lentz STOWE
04 Administrative Asst to President ... Mrs. Jennie SINGLETON
96 Purchasing Coordinator ... Ms. Rebecca ADAMS
38 Director of Counseling ... Mrs. Kimberly JACKSON
102 Executive Dir of Foundation ... Ms. Serena SULLIVAN
105 Webmaster ... Mr. Keith SULLIVAN
18 Dir Campus Operations ... Mr. Wesley ADAMS
13 Director of Information Technology ... Mr. Arthur RICHARD
21 Director of Accounting ... Ms. Cecelia SCOTT

*Bladen Community College (A)

PO Box 266, Dublin NC 28332-0266
County: Bladen FICE Identification: 007987
Unit ID: 198011
Telephone: (910) 879-5500 Carnegie Class: Assoc/MT-VT-High Non
FAX Number: (910) 879-5564 Calendar System: Semester
URL: www.bladencc.edu
Established: 1967 Annual Undergrad Tuition & Fees (In-State): $2,528
Enrollment: 1,378 Coed
Affiliation or Control: State IRS Status: 501(c)3
Highest Offering: Associate Degree
Accreditation: SC

02 President ... Dr. William FINDT
04 Exec Admin Asst to the President ... Ms. Melissa HESTER
05 Executive VP and Chief Acad Officer ... Mr. Jeffrey KORNEGAY
51 VP for Continuing Education ... Ms. Sondra GUYTON
20 Assoc VP for Academic Services ... Ms. Cynthia MCKOY
32 Vice President for Student Services ... Mr. Barry PRIEST
10 Vice President for Finance ... Mr. Jay STANLEY
88 Assoc VP for Program Services ... Mr. Lynn KING
21 Controller ... Ms. Lacie JACOBS
08 Director Student Resource Center ... Ms. Sherwin RICE
09 Dir Institutional Effect & Planning ... Ms. Twyla DAVIS
37 Director of Financial Aid ... Ms. Samantha BENSON
106 Director of Distance Learning ... Mr. Ray SHEPPARD
15 Director of Human Resources ... Ms. Tiina MUNDY
18 Director of Facilities ... Mr. Junior RIDEOUT
26 Public Information Specialist ... Ms. Cathy KINLAW
102 Foundation Director ... Ms. Linda BURNEY

*Blue Ridge Community College (B)

180 W Campus Drive, Flat Rock NC 28731-4728
County: Henderson FICE Identification: 009684
Unit ID: 198039
Telephone: (828) 694-1700 Carnegie Class: Assoc/MT-VT-High Trad
FAX Number: (828) 694-1690 Calendar System: Semester
URL: www.blueridge.edu
Established: 1969 Annual Undergrad Tuition & Fees (In-District): $2,601
Enrollment: 2,118 Coed
Affiliation or Control: State/Local IRS Status: 501(c)3
Highest Offering: Associate Degree
Accreditation: SC, EMT, SURGT

02 President ... Dr. Laura B. LEATHERWOOD
05 VP for Instruction ... Vacant
32 Interim VP for Student Services ... Ms. Kirsten BUNCH
103 VP Workforce Dev/Cont Education ... Ms. Julie G. THOMPSON
10 AVP for Finance/CFO ... Ms. Carolyn W. ALLEY
11 Vice Pres General Administration ... Dr. Chad MERRILL
49 Dean for Arts and Sciences ... Mr. David H. DAVIS
72 Dean for Advanced Technology ... Mr. Chris ENGLISH
76 Dean for Allied Health & Emerg Svc ... Mr. Jay ALLEY
97 Dean for Basic Skills ... Ms. Robin NORRIS-PAULISON
50 Dean for Business/Service Careers ... Ms. Kathy ALLEN
102 Executive Director Foundation ... Ms. Ann F. GREEN
44 Institutional Advance/Rsrch Coord ... Ms. Carol Ann LYDON
06 Registrar ... Ms. Kirsten H. BUNCH
08 Director for Library Services ... Ms. Ali NORVELL
37 Director Financial Aid ... Ms. Lisanne MASTERSON
14 Assoc VP for Technologies/CIO ... Mr. Steve YOUNG
18 Director of Facilities ... Mr. Peter HEMANS
26 Dir of Marketing & Communications ... Ms. Lee Anna HANEY
84 Director of Enrollment Management ... Vacant
15 Director of Human Resources ... Mr. Tommy OAKMAN
19 Chief of Police/Dir Public Safety ... Mr. Daran DODD

*Brunswick Community College (C)

50 College Road, Bolivia NC 28422
County: Brunswick FICE Identification: 021707
Unit ID: 198084
Telephone: (910) 755-7300 Carnegie Class: Assoc/HT-High Trad
FAX Number: (910) 754-9609 Calendar System: Semester
URL: www.brunswickcc.edu
Established: 1979 Annual Undergrad Tuition & Fees (In-State): $2,532
Enrollment: 1,651 Coed
Affiliation or Control: State IRS Status: 501(c)3
Highest Offering: Associate Degree
Accreditation: SC, CAHIIM, PHLEB

02 President ... Dr. Susanne H. ADAMS
05 VP Academic & Student Affairs ... Dr. Lois SMITH
10 Vice President Budget and Finance ... Ms. Sheila GALLOWAY
32 Dean Student Services/Enroll Mgmt ... Ms. Lori GRAHAM
09 Director of Institutional Planning ... Mr. Michael COBB
08 Director Library ... Ms. Carmen BLANTON
06 Registrar ... Ms. Christine DYE
15 Director Human Resources ... Ms. Nicole WILLIAMS
19 Public Safety/Police Director ... Mr. Lindsay WALTON
18 Physical Plant Director ... Mr. Jack LUCIANO
102 Director Resource Development ... Ms. Elina DICOSTANZO
26 Director of Marketing & Public Info ... Ms. London SCHMIDT
37 Financial Aid/Veterans Affs Coord ... Ms. Tracy SOMERLAD
72 Dean Professional Technical Service ... Ms. Gina ROBINSON
49 Dean Arts & Sciences ... Dr. John GRAY
04 Sr Executive Asst to President ... Ms. Bea PALAZZI
13 Chief Info Officer ... Mr. Ronnie BRYANT
41 Athletic Director ... Mr. Robert ALLEN
36 Director Student Placement ... Mrs. Christen COX

*Caldwell Community College and Technical Institute (D)

2855 Hickory Boulevard, Hudson NC 28638-1399
County: Caldwell FICE Identification: 004835
Unit ID: 198118
Telephone: (828) 726-2200 Carnegie Class: Assoc/HT-High Trad
FAX Number: (828) 726-2216 Calendar System: Semester
URL: www.cccti.edu
Established: 1964 Annual Undergrad Tuition & Fees (In-District): $2,508
Enrollment: 3,251 Coed
Affiliation or Control: State/Local IRS Status: 501(c)3
Highest Offering: Associate Degree
Accreditation: SC, DMS, EMT, NMT, PTAA, RAD

02 President ... Dr. Mark POARCH
32 Vice President Student Services ... Mrs. Dena HOLMAN
103 VP Continuing Educ/Workforce Dev ... Mrs. Elaine LOCKHART
11 Chief of Administration ... Mr. Dennis SEAGLE
12 Executive Director Watauga Campus ... Mr. Steve MELTON
05 Director Academic Support ... Vacant
84 Dir Enrollment Mgmt Services ... Mr. Dennis SEAGLE
08 Director Learning Resources Center ... Ms. Alison BEARD
37 Director Financial Aid/Veterans Aff ... Ms. Juli9e AHOUSE
36 Dir Career Planning/Job Placement ... Mr. Rick SHEW
15 Director Human Resources ... Mrs. Kathy SEITZ
26 Director Marketing & Communications ... Mrs. Sherry WILSON
10 Controller ... Mr. Scott ROGERS
09 Dir Inst Effectiveness/Research ... Mrs. Liz SILVERS
27 Public Relations Officer ... Mr. Edward TERRY
102 Director Foundation Office ... Ms. Marla CHRISTIE
28 Director of Diversity ... Mr. Jimmie GRIFFITH
38 Director Student Counseling ... Mr. Shannon BROWN
96 Director of Purchasing ... Mr. Vincent LINNEY
40 Manager Bookstore ... Mrs. Trina CURTIS
04 Executive Assistant ... Mrs. Donna CHURCH
19 Director Security/Safety ... Mr. Dennis HOPKINS
18 Director Facility Services ... Mr. Jeff HERMAN
06 Registrar ... Mrs. Debra YOUNT
13 Chief Info Technology Officer (CIO) ... Ms. Susan WOOTEN

*Cape Fear Community College (E)

411 N Front Street, Wilmington NC 28401-3993
County: New Hanover FICE Identification: 005320
Unit ID: 198154
Telephone: (910) 362-7000 Carnegie Class: Assoc/MT-VT-Mix Trad/Non
FAX Number: (910) 763-2279 Calendar System: Semester
URL: www.cfcc.edu
Established: 1958 Annual Undergrad Tuition & Fees (In-District): $2,748
Enrollment: 8,851 Coed
Affiliation or Control: State/Local IRS Status: 501(c)3
Highest Offering: Associate Degree
Accreditation: SC, ADNUR, DA, DH, DMS, OTA, PHLEB, RAD, SURGT

02 President ... Dr. Amanda LEE
05 VP Academic Affairs & Workforce Dev ... Ms. Melissa SINGLER
03 Executive Vice President ... Mr. Jim MORTON
32 VP Student Svcs & Enrollment Mgmt ... Mr. Daryl MINUS
20 Asst Vice Pres Instructional Opers ... Dr. Jason CHAFFIN
09 Exec Dir Inst Effective/Planning ... Mr. Pat HOGAN
06 Registrar ... Ms. Angela MURPHY
102 Exec Dir of the Foundation ... Mr. Marty RICHARDS
31 Exec Dir Community Relations ... Ms. Rachel NADEAU
84 Dean of Enrollment Management ... Ms. Jackie FOSTER
08 Dean Learning Resources Center ... Ms. Catherine LEE
37 Director of Financial Aid ... Ms. Rachel CAVANUAGH

26 Director of Creative Services ... Mr. David M. HARDIN
15 Exec Dir Human Resources ... Ms. Sharon SMITH
35 Dean of Student Affairs ... Mr. Robby MCGEE
96 Director of Purchasing & Inventory ... Mr. Wade QUINN
10 Controller ... Ms. Christina GREENE
51 Dean of Continuing Education ... Mr. Robert TURNER
75 Dean Vocational/Technical Education ... Mr. Mark COUNCIL
49 Dean Arts & Sciences ... Ms. Orangel J. DANIELS
105 Web Services Analyst ... Ms. Christina HEIKKILA
04 Sr Exec Assistant to the President ... Ms. Michelle LEE
19 Director Security/Safety ... Chief Dan WILCOX
89 First Year Student Success Init ... Dr. Jennifer MCBRIDE
79 Dir Humanities & Fine Arts Center ... Mr. Shane FERNANDO
25 Director of Grant Development ... Ms. Val CLEMMONS
22 Dir of Disability Support Services ... Ms. Aimee HELMUS
41 Dir Student Activities/Athletics ... Mr. Ryan MANTLO
88 Dir of Capital Projects Mgmt/Reno ... Mr. David KANOY
106 Online Learning Coordinator ... Dr. Chantae CALHOUN
13 Interim Director Info Technology ... Mr. Jakim FRIANT

*Carteret Community College (F)

3505 Arendell Street, Morehead City NC 28557-2989
County: Carteret FICE Identification: 008081
Unit ID: 198206
Telephone: (252) 222-6000 Carnegie Class: Assoc/MT-VT-High Trad
FAX Number: (252) 222-2514 Calendar System: Semester
URL: www.carteret.edu
Established: 1963 Annual Undergrad Tuition & Fees (In-District): $2,847
Enrollment: 1,363 Coed
Affiliation or Control: State/Local IRS Status: 501(c)3
Highest Offering: Associate Degree
Accreditation: SC, ADNUR, COARC, MAC, RAD

02 President ... Dr. John D. HAUSER
05 VP for Instruction/Student Support ... Dr. Tracy MANCINI
10 VP Finance/Administrative Services ... Mr. Steven DAVIS
31 Vice Pres Corp/Community Education ... Mr. Perry L. HARKER
04 Exec Dir Office of the President ... Ms. Logan L. OKUN
08 Director of Library Resources ... Ms. Elizabeth BAKER
32 Dean of Student Services ... Mr. Dana MERCK
35 Director of Student Success ... Mr. Rick HILL
13 Director Information Technology ... Mr. John GREEN
15 Director of Human Resources ... Ms. Amanda BRYANT
30 Director of Development ... Ms. Brenda REASH
49 Dean Arts & Sciences ... Ms. Doree HILL
76 Dean of Health Sciences ... Ms. Laurie A. FRESHWATER
88 Dean of Applied Science ... Ms. Catherine LASSITER
37 Dir Financial Aid & Veteran Svcs ... Ms. Brenda J. LONG
06 Registrar ... Ms. Tammi COBLE
09 Dir of Institutional Effectiveness ... Ms. Mary CLARK
18 Dir Operations/Facil Maintenance ... Mr. Steve SPARKS
26 Director of Public Affairs ... Ms. Alize PROISY
96 Director of Business Operations ... Ms. Donna L. CUMBIE
106 Director Distance Learning ... Mr. Ed LADENBURGER

*Catawba Valley Community College (G)

2550 Highway 70, SE, Hickory NC 28602-9699
County: Catawba FICE Identification: 005318
Unit ID: 198233
Telephone: (828) 327-7000 Carnegie Class: Assoc/HT-Mix Trad/Non
FAX Number: (828) 327-7276 Calendar System: Semester
URL: www.cvcc.edu
Established: 1960 Annual Undergrad Tuition & Fees (In-District): $2,251
Enrollment: 4,571 Coed
Affiliation or Control: State/Local IRS Status: 501(c)3
Highest Offering: Associate Degree
Accreditation: SC, ADNUR, CAHIIM, COARC, DH, EMT, IFSAC, NDT, POLYT, RAD, SURGT

02 President ... Dr. Garrett D. HINSHAW
05 Exec Vice President of Instruction ... Dr. Keith MACKIE
10 Sr VP Business Affairs-Operations ... Mr. Wes BUNCH
32 Dean of Student Access/Development ... Mrs. Cindy COULTER
15 Director Human Resources ... Mr. Roger IRVIN
07 Director of Admissions/Records ... Ms. Kelly PLUMLEY
21 Controller ... Ms. Jennifer HAMM
37 Director Scholarships/Financial Aid ... Ms. RaChele SUMMERS
09 Ofc Accountability/Efficienc/Effect ... Mr. Kevin ROUSE
88 Director Industrial Training ... Ms. Crystal GLENN
88 Director Small Business Center ... Mr. Jeff NEUVILLE
50 Director Business/Technology Ext ... Ms. Susan KILLIAN
88 Director Hosiery Technology Center ... Mr. Daniel C. ST. LOUIS
13 Director Information Technologies ... Mr. Ken ELLIOTT
19 Director Campus Safety/Security ... Mr. Steve HUNT
31 Director Community Education ... Ms. Chanell MORELLO
36 Counselor/Job Placement Svcs Coord ... Ms. Teresa RAY
16 Coordinator Health/Human Services ... Ms. Robin ROSS
04 Administrative Asst to President ... Ms. Sherry WILLIAMS
29 Director Alumni Relations ... Ms. Mary REYNOLDS
41 Athletic Director ... Mr. Nick SCHROEDER

*Central Carolina Community College (H)

1105 Kelly Drive, Sanford NC 27330-9000
County: Lee FICE Identification: 005449
Unit ID: 198251
Telephone: (919) 775-5401 Carnegie Class: Assoc/MT-VT-Mix Trad/Non
FAX Number: (919) 718-7380 Calendar System: Semester
URL: www.cccc.edu

Established: 1958 Annual Undergrad Tuition & Fees (In-District): $2,544
Enrollment: 4,977 Coed
Affiliation or Control: State/Local IRS Status: 501(c)3
Highest Offering: Associate Degree
Accreditation: SC, DA, DH, MAC, POLYT

02 President .... Dr. T. Eston MARCHANT
05 Vice President of Student Learning .... Dr. Brian MERRITT
11 Vice Pres of Administrative Svcs .... Mr. Philip PRICE
32 Vice President Student Services .... Mr. Ken R. HOYLE
26 Assoc VP of Marketing/HR .... Ms. Marcie DISHMAN
12 Provost Chatham Campus .... Mr. Mark HALL
12 Provost Harnett Campus .... Dr. Jon MATTHEWS
20 Dean of Student Learning .... Mr. Mike BECK
08 Director of Library Services .... Ms. Tara LUCAS
15 Assoc Director of Human Resources .... Ms. Valerie BENN
102 Exec Director of CCCC Foundation .... Ms. Emily HARE
06 Dean of Enrollment/Registrar .... Ms. Jamie CHILDRESS
07 Director of Admissions .... Mr. Adam WADE
37 Director Financial Aid .... Ms. Zilma LOPES
96 Purchasing Director .... Mrs. Starlene JACKSON
18 Physical Plant Manager .... Mr. Ronnie MEASAMER
75 Dean Vocational/Technical Programs .... Mr. Drew GOODSON
36 Dean of College & Career Readiness .... Ms. Dawn TUCKER
76 Dean of Health Sciences .... Ms. Lisa GODFREY

*Central Piedmont Community College (A)

PO Box 35009, Charlotte NC 28235-5009
County: Mecklenburg FICE Identification: 002915
Unit ID: 198260
Telephone: (704) 330-2722 Carnegie Class: Assoc/HT-Mix Trad/Non
FAX Number: (704) 330-5045 Calendar System: Semester
URL: www.cpcc.edu
Established: 1963 Annual Undergrad Tuition & Fees (In-District): $2,792
Enrollment: 19,394 Coed
Affiliation or Control: State/Local IRS Status: 501(c)3
Highest Offering: Associate Degree
Accreditation: SC, ACFEI, ADNUR, CAHIIM, COARC, CSHSE, CVT, CYTO, DA, DH, EMT, ENGT, MAC, MLTAD, OTA, PTAA, SURGT

02 President .... Dr. Kandi W. DEITEMEYER
05 VP for Learning and Workforce Devel .... Mr. Richard ZOLLINGER
32 VP Student and Enrollment Services .... Dr. Marcia CONSTON
11 VP Finance/Administrative Services .... Mr. Michael MOSS
13 VP for Technology and CIO .... Mr. David KIM
111 VP for Institutional Advancement .... Dr. Kevin MCCARTHY
04 Exec Assistant to the President .... Dr. Tracie CLARK
26 PIO & Asst to Pres Cmty Rels/Mktg .... Mr. Jeffrey LOWRANCE
103 Assoc VP Learning and Workforce Dev .... Dr. Deborah BOUTON
10 Assoc VP Financial Services .... Mr. Michael WHITEMAN
18 Assoc VP Facilities & Construction .... Ms. Vicki SAVILLE
09 Assoc VP Institutional Research .... Dr. Terri MANNING
88 Assoc VP Compliance and Audit .... Dr. Brenda LEONARD
15 Assoc VP of Human Resources .... Mr. Paul SANTOS
25 Assoc VP Government Rels & Grants .... Mr. Michael HORN
88 Assoc VP Services Corporation .... Ms. Quincy FOIL WHITE
121 Assoc VP Student Success .... Ms. Rita DAWKINS
12 Dean Levine Campus .... Dr. Edith MCELROY
12 Dean Merancas Campus .... Ms. Tamara WILLIAMS
12 Dean Central Campus .... Dr. Paul KOEHNKE
12 Dean Cato Campus .... Mr. George HENDERSON
12 Dean Harris Campus/AVP Corp Dev ... Ms. Mary VICKERS-KOCH
12 Dean Harper Campus .... Dr. Kelly TRAINOR
54 Dean STEM-S .... Mr. Chris PAYNTER
124 Dean Retention Services .... Dr. Clint MCELROY
35 Dean Student Life/Service Learning .... Mr. Mark HELMS
84 Dean Enrollment Management .... Dr. Daniel (JJ) MCEACHERN
08 Dean Libraries .... Ms. Gloria KELLEY
88 Dean College & Career Readiness .... Ms. Kathi MCLENDON
07 Dean Enrollment Services .... Dr. April JONES
106 Dean Profess Development/eLearning .... Ms. Karen MERRIMAN
22 Dir Affirmative Action/EEO .... Mr. Leon MATTHEWS
88 Dean Center for Global Engagement .... Ms. Janet MALKEMES
06 Dean Admissions & Registration .... Mr. Greg STANLEY
102 AVP Foundation/Inst Advancement .... Ms. Vivian HAILEY
19 Exec Dir College Security .... Mr. Charles WRIGHT
21 AVP Finance/Admin Services .... Mr. Ian BRICE
76 Dean Health Sciences .... Dr. Ruth HEDGPETH

*Cleveland Community College (B)

137 S Post Road, Shelby NC 28152-6296
County: Cleveland FICE Identification: 008082
Unit ID: 198321
Telephone: (704) 669-6000 Carnegie Class: Assoc/MT-VT-Mix Trad/Non
FAX Number: (704) 669-4202 Calendar System: Semester
URL: www.clevelandcc.edu
Established: 1965 Annual Undergrad Tuition & Fees (In-District): $2,526
Enrollment: 2,666 Coed
Affiliation or Control: State/Local IRS Status: 501(c)3
Highest Offering: Associate Degree
Accreditation: SC, EMT, MAC, RAD, SURGT

02 Interim President .... Dr. William C. AIKEN
05 Vice President of Academic Programs .... Dr. Becky SAIN
32 Vice President of Student Services .... Dr. Andy GARDNER
03 Executive Vice President .... Dr. Shannon KENNEDY
51 Vice Pres of Continuing Education .... Mr. Ken MOONEY
30 Sr Dean Devel/Governmental Rels .... Mr. Eddie HOLBROOK
102 Executive Director CCC Foundation .... Mr. U. L. PATTERSON, III
09 Dean of Plng & Institutional Effect .... Mrs. Laura BOWEN
88 Director CECHS Relations .... Ms. Nedra MADDOX
84 Director of Enrollment Services .... Ms. Emily HURDT
08 Dean of Learning Resources .... Mrs. Barbara MCKIBBIN
96 Purchasing Officer .... Mr. Lance ASHLEY
18 Director of Physical Plant .... Mr. Mark FOX
19 Director of Security .... Mr. Richard FIELDS
15 Human Resources & Safety Manager .... Mr. Allen KNICELEY
13 Chief Information Officer .... Mr. Jonathan DAVIS
14 Network Administrator .... Mr. Robin DYER
24 Audiovisual Coordinator .... Mr. Rodger PERRY
26 Public Info/Marketing Coordinator .... Mrs. Paula VESS
07 Admissions/Records Coordinator .... Ms. Emily AREY
49 Dean Arts & Sciences .... Ms. Betty STACK
50 Dean Business & Allied Health .... Dr. John LATTIMORE
75 Dean Vocational/Engrng/Public Svcs .... Mr. Bruce MACK
88 Dean Learning Center .... Dr. Chris NANNEY

*Coastal Carolina Community College (C)

444 Western Boulevard, Jacksonville NC 28546-6816
County: Onslow FICE Identification: 005316
Unit ID: 198330
Telephone: (910) 455-1221 Carnegie Class: Assoc/HVT-Mix Trad/Non
FAX Number: (910) 455-7027 Calendar System: Semester
URL: www.coastalcarolina.edu
Established: 1963 Annual Undergrad Tuition & Fees (In-District): $2,462
Enrollment: 4,186 Coed
Affiliation or Control: State/Local IRS Status: 501(c)3
Highest Offering: Associate Degree
Accreditation: SC, DA, DH, EMT, MLTAD, SURGT

02 President .... Mr. David L. HEATHERLY
05 VP for Instruction .... Ms. Ginger TUTON
09 VP Inst Eff/Research/Innovation .... Ms. Sharon R. MCGINNIS
11 VP for Administrative Supp Svcs .... Dr. Annette HARPINE
32 Division Chair for Student Services .... Dr. Donald R. HERRING
15 Personnel Officer .... Ms. Cindy BURKHART
26 Pub Info Ofcr/Ex Dir Col Foundation .... Ms. Krystal PHILLIPS
07 Director of Admissions .... Dr. Jessica RANERO-RAMIREZ
18 Dir Physical Plant/Auxiliary Svcs .... Ms. Carol LURZ
37 Director for Financial Aid Services .... Ms. Tammy LYON
88 Director for Veterans Services .... Mr. Christopher P. SABIN
88 Director Economic Development .... Ms. Anne C. SHAW
04 Assistant to the President and BOT .... Ms. Tonya L. MORTON
06 Registrar .... Ms. Mishelle DUPUIS

*College of the Albemarle (D)

1208 North Road Street, Elizabeth City NC 27906-2327
County: Pasquotank FICE Identification: 002917
Unit ID: 197814
Telephone: (252) 335-0821 Carnegie Class: Assoc/HT-Mix Trad/Non
FAX Number: (252) 335-2011 Calendar System: Semester
URL: www.albemarle.edu
Established: 1960 Annual Undergrad Tuition & Fees (In-District): $2,227
Enrollment: 2,141 Coed
Affiliation or Control: State/Local IRS Status: 501(c)3
Highest Offering: Associate Degree
Accreditation: SC, ADNUR, MAC, MLTAD, SURGT

02 President .... Dr. Robert WYNEGAR
10 Chief Financial Officer .... Mrs. Susan GENTRY
05 Vice President for Learning .... Dr. Evonne CARTER
32 VP for Student Suc & Enr Mgmt .. Ms. Lynn HURDLE-WINSLOW
12 Dean Dare County Campus .... Mr. Timothy SWEENEY
30 Executive Director Foundation & Dev .... Mrs. Lisa A. JOHNSON
37 Director Admissions & Financial Aid .... Ms. Angela R. GODFREY-DAWSON
88 Coord Student Life & Leadership .... Ms. Alicia STOKLEY
06 Registrar .... Ms. Andrea DANCE
88 Director Small Business Center .... Ms. Ginger H. O'NEAL
78 Work-Based Learning Liaison .... Mrs. Lynn JENNINGS
04 Exec Assistant to the President .... Mrs. Jenna HATFIELD
08 Director Library .... Mr. Rodney WOOTEN
12 Dean Edenton-Chowan Campus .... Mr. Charles PURSER
13 Director Mgmt Information Services .... Mr. Wayman WHITE
15 Director Human Resources .... Ms. Wendy W. BRICKHOUSE
18 Director Physical Facilities .... Mr. Patrick CUTHRELL
11 Chief Operations Officer .... Mr. Joseph TURNER
40 Administrative Services Manager .... Ms. Lisa JONES
09 Director of Inst Effectiveness .... Ms. Pamela FEDERLINE
88 Coord Prison Education Programs .... Mr. Andre WILLIAMS
88 Coordinator Secondary Education .... Mr. Derek MEREDITH
49 Dean Arts and Sciences .... Mr. Dean ROUGHTON
50 Dean Business & Applied Tech .... Mrs. Michelle WATERS
76 Dean Health & Wellness .... Ms. Robin HARRIS
81 Dept Chair Sciences .... Mr. Bobby ADAMS
83 Department Chair Social Sciences .... Mr. Brian EDWARDS
60 Dept Chair English & Comm .... Mrs. Laura MORRISON
81 Dept Chair Math and Engineering .... Ms. Rhonda WATTS
75 Dept Chair Design Manuf & Ind Tech .... Mr. Charles PURSER
76 Interim Dept Chair Allied Health .... Mr. Jeffrey CARTER
77 Dept Chair Bus & Computer Sys Tech .... Ms. Sharon BROWN
57 Department Chair Human & Fine Arts .... Ms. Ekaterina YOUNGER
66 Dept Chair ADN .... Mrs. Katie MILLER
19 Director Public Safety & Preparedns .... Mr. Dennis SMITH
88 Dir Basic Skills/Workforce Reading .... Mrs. Wanda FLETCHER
121 Director Advising & Student Success .... Mr. Kelvin BROWN
103 Dean Workforce Dev/Pub Svc/Career .. Mrs. Robin ZINSMEISTER
106 Coordinator Distance Education .... Dr. Susan PECK

*Craven Community College (E)

800 College Court, New Bern NC 28562-4984
County: Craven FICE Identification: 006799
Unit ID: 198367
Telephone: (252) 638-7200 Carnegie Class: Assoc/HT-Mix Trad/Non
FAX Number: (252) 638-4232 Calendar System: Semester
URL: www.cravencc.edu
Established: 1965 Annual Undergrad Tuition & Fees (In-District): $2,053
Enrollment: 3,012 Coed
Affiliation or Control: State/Local IRS Status: 501(c)3
Highest Offering: Associate Degree
Accreditation: SC, ACBSP, CAHIIM, MAC, PTAA

02 President .... Dr. Ray STAATS
05 VP for Instruction .... Ms. Kathleen GALLMAN
11 Vice Pres of Administrative Svcs .... Dr. Karla (Page) JONES-VARNELL
32 VP for Students .... Mr. Gery BAUCHER
49 Dean Liberal Arts & Univ Transfer .... Dr. Betty K. HATCHER
36 Dean Career Programs .... Mr. James R. MILLARD
09 Exec Dir of Institutional Effective .... Dr. Cynthia M. BELLACERO
06 Registrar .... Mr. John A. FONVILLE
111 Int Exec Dir Inst Advancement .... Mr. Charles WETHINGTON
12 Dean Havelock-Cherry Point Campus .... Mr. Walter CALABRESE
37 Director Financial Aid .... Ms. Kathryn M. BANKS
103 Dir Workforce Readiness & Spec Pgms .... Mr. Greg SINGLETON
88 Director Basic Skills Programs .... Vacant
08 Director Library Services .... Mrs. Catherine C. CAMPBELL
10 Exec Dir Financial Svcs/Purchasing .... Mrs. Cynthia A. PATTERSON
88 Director TRIO Student Support Svcs .... Ms. Donna MARSHALL
15 Exec Dir HR/Chief Diversity Officer .... Mrs. Vickie MOSELEY-JONES
103 Dean Workforce Development .... Mr. Robin MATTHEWS
18 Director of Facilities .... Mr. John MELVILLE
13 Dean Technology Services/Facilities .... Ms. Bambi EDWARDS
96 Procurement & Fixed Assets Officer .... Mr. Hiram Todd MURPHREY
84 Dean Enrollment Management .... Ms. Zomar PETER
25 Dir Strategic Partnerships/Grants .... Ms. Monica MINUS
04 Exec Asst to Pres/Board of Trustees .... Ms. Cynthia ENSLEY
19 Dir of Security & Emergency Mgmt .... Mr. Paul DAMICO
121 Executive Director of Academic Supp . Ms. Jennifer BUMGARNER

*Davidson County Community College (F)

PO Box 1287, Lexington NC 27293-1287
County: Davidson FICE Identification: 002919
Unit ID: 198376
Telephone: (336) 249-8186 Carnegie Class: Assoc/MT-VT-High Trad
FAX Number: (336) 249-0379 Calendar System: Semester
URL: www.davidsonccc.edu
Established: 1958 Annual Undergrad Tuition & Fees (In-District): $2,588
Enrollment: 3,797 Coed
Affiliation or Control: State/Local IRS Status: 501(c)3
Highest Offering: Associate Degree
Accreditation: SC, ADNUR, CAHIIM, MAC, MLTAD, SURGT

02 President .... Dr. Mary E. RITTLING
05 VP Academic Programs & Services .... Ms. Margaret H. ANNUNZIATA
32 VP Student Affairs .... Dr. Rhonda Q. COATS
10 VP Financial/Administrative Svcs .... Ms. Laura L. YARBROUGH
102 VP Ext Affairs/Exec Dir Foundation .... Ms. Jenny M. VARNER
76 Dean Health/Wellness/Pub Safety .... Ms. Rose MCDANIEL
97 Dean Gen Studies & Acad Support .... Dr. Christy FORREST
50 Dean Business Engineering Technical .... Mr. Rodney JACKSON
12 Dean Davie Campus .... Ms. Teresa KINES
35 Dean Student Services .... Mr. Kevin LINEBERRY
121 VP Student Success & Communications .... Ms. Susan BURLESON
26 Director Marketing & Communications .... Ms. DeeDe PINCKNEY
06 Dir Student Records/Registration .... Mr. Bryan MCCULLOUGH
36 Director Career Development .... Mr. Charles MAYER
18 Director Physical Plant Services .... Mr. Keith RAKER
15 Director Personnel Services .... Ms. Denise BARNHARDT
04 Administrative Asst to President .... Ms. Carleen TERRELL
08 Head Librarian .... Mr. Jason SETZER
37 Director Student Financial Aid .... Ms. Lori BLEVINS
41 Athletic Director .... Mr. Kenneth KIRK
07 Director of Admissions .... Mr. Antonio JORDAN
09 Director of Institutional Research .... Mr. Mark PUTERBAUGH
19 Director Security/Safety .... Ms. Rita MATHEWS
111 Chief Development/Advancement .... Ms. Kristin BRIGGS
124 Dean Student Engagement/Completion .... Ms. Keisha JONES

*Durham Technical Community College (G)

1637 Lawson Street, Durham NC 27703-5023
County: Durham FICE Identification: 005448
Unit ID: 198455
Telephone: (919) 536-7200 Carnegie Class: Assoc/HT-Mix Trad/Non
FAX Number: (919) 686-3601 Calendar System: Semester
URL: www.durhamtech.edu
Established: 1961 Annual Undergrad Tuition & Fees (In-District): $1,840
Enrollment: 5,118 Coed
Affiliation or Control: State/Local IRS Status: 501(c)3
Highest Offering: Associate Degree

Accreditation: SC, ADNUR, CAHIIM, COARC, DT, EMT, MAC, OPD, OTA, PNUR, SURGT

02 President ... Dr. William G. INGRAM
30 Sr Vice Pres Institutional Advance ... Mr. Tom JAYNES
05 VP Stdnt Learning/Instruction Svcs ... Ms. Susan PARIS
10 VP Finance and Administration ... Mr. Matt WILLIAMS
51 VP Corp/Continuing Education ... Dr. Peter WOOLDRIDGE
32 VP Student Engage Dev Support ... Dr. Christine KELLY KLEESE
04 Executive Secy to the President ... Ms. Gloria GAY
09 Director Institutional Research ... Dr. Melanie RIESTER
35 Dean Student Services ... Ms. Lisa INMAN
13 Executive Director Info Tech Svcs ... Mr. Patrick HINES
15 Director Human Resources ... Ms. Kathy MCKINLEY
08 Interim Director Library ... Ms. Julie HUMPHREY
37 Director Financial Aid ... Ms. Nadine FORD
109 Director Auxiliary Services ... Ms. Yolanda V. MOORE-JONES
06 Asst Dean Student Records/Registrar ... Mr. Abraham DONES
07 Director Admissions ... Mr. Jairo S. MCMICAN

*Edgecombe Community College (A)

2009 W Wilson Street, Tarboro NC 27886-9399
County: Edgecombe FICE Identification: 008855
Unit ID: 198491
Telephone: (252) 823-5166 Carnegie Class: Assoc/HVT-Mix Trad/Non
FAX Number: (252) 823-6817 Calendar System: Semester
URL: www.edgecombe.edu
Established: 1967 Annual Undergrad Tuition & Fees (In-District): $2,504
Enrollment: 2,322 Coed
Affiliation or Control: State/Local IRS Status: 501(c)3
Highest Offering: Associate Degree
Accreditation: SC, ADNUR, CAHIIM, COARC, MAC, PNUR, RAD, SURGT

02 President ... Dr. Deborah L. LAMM
05 Vice President of Instruction ... Dr. Harry STARNES
11 Vice Pres Administrative Services ... Ms. Stephanie FISHER
32 Vice President Student Services ... Mr. Michael J. JORDAN
84 Dean Enrollment Management ... Mr. Tony ROOK
35 Dean of Students ... Ms. Samanthia PHILLIPS
108 Director of Inst Effectiveness ... Ms. Sheila HOSKINS
26 Director of Public Information ... Ms. Mary T. BASS
08 Director of Library Services ... Ms. Deborah PARISHER
06 Registrar ... Ms. Cathy P. DUPREE
15 Director Personnel Services ... Ms. Susan BARKALOW
18 Chief Facilities/Physical Plant ... Mr. John BUTZ
37 Director Student Financial Aid ... Mr. Sherlock MCDOUGALD
04 Administrative Asst to President ... Ms. Julie B. THOMAS
13 Chief Info Technology Officer ... Mr. Neil BAKER
43 Dir Legal Services/General Counsel ... Mr. Mark S. LORENCE

*Fayetteville Technical Community College (B)

PO Box 35236, 2201 Hull Road,
Fayetteville NC 28303-0236
County: Cumberland FICE Identification: 007640
Unit ID: 198534
Telephone: (910) 678-8400 Carnegie Class: Assoc/HT-Mix Trad/Non
FAX Number: (910) 678-8269 Calendar System: Semester
URL: www.faytechcc.edu
Established: 1961 Annual Undergrad Tuition & Fees (In-State): $2,528
Enrollment: 11,546 Coed
Affiliation or Control: State IRS Status: 501(c)3
Highest Offering: Associate Degree
Accreditation: SC, ADNUR, COARC, DA, DH, EMT, FUSER, PTAA, RAD, SURGT

02 President ... Dr. Larry KEEN
05 Sr Vice Pres Academic/Student Svcs ... Dr. David BRAND
10 Sr Vice Pres Business and Finance ... Mrs. Betty J. SMITH
15 VP Human Res/Inst Effect/Assessment ... Mr. Carl MITCHELL
11 Vice Pres for Administrative Svcs .. Mr. Joseph W. LEVISTER, JR.
13 Vice Pres Learning Technologies ... Mr. Bob J. ERVIN
43 Vice President for Legal Services ... Mr. David SULLIVAN
26 Exec Dir Marketing/Public Relations ... Mr. Brent MICHAELS
112 Executive Director of Foundation ... Ms. Lorna RICOTTA
84 Dean Enrollment Mgmt/Financial Aid . Mr. Harper SHACKELFORD
51 Assoc Vice Pres for Cont Educ ... Dr. Jolee MARSH
32 Assoc Vice Pres Student Services ... Dr. Rosemary KELLY
06 Registrar ... Ms. Melissa A. JONES
21 Assoc Vice Pres Business & Finance ... Mrs. Robin DEAVER
07 Director of Admissions ... Dr. Louanna CASTLEMAN
20 Assoc Vice Pres of Academic Support ... Ms. DeSandra WASHINGTON
14 Director Management Information Svc ... Mrs. Pamela SCULLY
18 Director of Facility Services ... Mr. Harold WYCKOFF
96 Procurement Manager Business/Financ ... Ms. Amy SAMPERTON
50 Dean of Business Programs ... Mrs. Cindy BURNS
49 Dean of Arts/Humanities ... Mr. Antonio JACKSON
76 Dean of Health Programs ... Mrs. Susan ELLIS
54 Dean Engr/Applied Tech Pgms ... Mrs. Pamela GIBSON
81 Dean of Sciences & Mathematics ... Mr. Chris DIORIETES
88 Dean of Public Service ... Mrs. Linda NOVAK
77 Dean of Computer Technologies ... Mrs. Darlene WOOD

*Forsyth Technical Community College (C)

2100 Silas Creek Parkway,
Winston-Salem NC 27103-5197
County: Forsyth FICE Identification: 005317
Unit ID: 198552
Telephone: (336) 723-0371 Carnegie Class: Assoc/MT-VT-High Trad
FAX Number: (336) 761-2399 Calendar System: Semester
URL: www.forsythtech.edu
Established: 1960 Annual Undergrad Tuition & Fees (In-State): $2,056
Enrollment: 8,396 Coed
Affiliation or Control: State IRS Status: 501(c)3
Highest Offering: Associate Degree
Accreditation: SC, COARC, CVT, DA, DH, DMS, ENGT, MAC, NMT, RAD, RTT

02 President ... Dr. Gary M. GREEN
03 Executive Vice President ... Dr. Rachel M. DESMARAIS
05 Vice Pres Instructional Svcs ... Dr. Joel WELCH
32 Vice President Student Services ... Dr. Jewel B. CHERRY
102 Executive Director FT Foundation ... Dr. Corey MILLER
10 Vice President Business Services ... Ms. Wendy R. EMERSON
103 Vice Pres Economic & Workforce Dev ... Mr. Alan K. MURDOCK
15 Associate VP/Chief Human Resources ... Ms. Anna Marie SMITH
13 Associate VP/Chief Information Ofc ... Mr. Chris PEARCE
100 Director Office of the President ... Ms. Sherri W. BOWEN
50 Dean Business Info Tech Div ... Ms. Pamela SHORTT
79 Dean of Humanities/Social Sci Div ... Ms. Anu WILLIAMS
81 Dean Math/Science & Technologies ... Mr. Michael V. AYERS
54 Dean of Engineering Tech Div ... Mr. Todd BISHOP
17 Dean of Health Technologies ... Ms. Linda LATHAM
31 Dean Community/Economic Development ... Ms. Sharon D. ANDERSON
08 Dean Learning Resources ... Mr. J. Randel CANDELARIA
88 Dean Adult Literacy ... Vacant
66 Director Nursing ... Ms. Linda H. LATHAM
76 Director Imaging ... Ms. Tamara BECK
76 Director Health Services ... Ms. Jean E. MIDDLESWARTH
21 Dean Financial Services ... Ms. Melanie L. NUCKOLS
38 Dir Student Success Ctr/Counseling ... Vacant
15 Director Human Resources ... Mr. Gregory M. CHASE
09 Exec Dir Institutional Research ... Mr. Kevin OSBORNE
88 Dir Recruiting/Student Support Svcs ... Mr. Edwin B. WADDELL
37 Director Student Financial Services ... Mr. Ricky C. HODGES
06 Director Records/Registrar ... Ms. Gwen D. WHITAKER
07 Director of Admissions ... Ms. Jean M. GROOME
18 Director Physical Plant Services ... Mr. Scott BOOTH
19 Director Campus Police ... Vacant
88 Director Small Business Center ... Mr. Allan YOUNGER
35 Director Student Activities ... Ms. Beverly N. LEWIS
96 Director Purchasing/Equipment ... Mr. Philip L. MCCLUNG
109 Director Auxiliary Services ... Mr. Brian A. HICKS
12 Director Grady Swisher Center ... Ms. Mary B. KING
12 Director Mazie Woodruff Center ... Mr. TerCraig D. EDWARDS
12 Director Northwest Forsyth Center ... Ms. Kristie F. HENDRIX
12 Director Stokes County Center ... Ms. Sally ELLIOTT
88 Director Educational Partnerships ... Ms. Kimberly BRYANT
88 Dean Business and Industry ... Ms. Jennifer B. COULOMBE
88 Dean Health and Emergency Programs ... Mr. Wesley D. HUTCHINS
88 Dir Transportation Technology Ctr ... Ms. Kristen BATES
88 Dean Transformative Learning Center ... Mr. James COOK
112 Dir Major Gifts & Planned Giving ... Ms. Edyce ELWORTH
44 Director Donor Relations ... Ms. Angela COOK
04 Senior Administrative Associate ... Ms. Dawn P. MITCHELL
25 Director Grants and Contracts ... Mr. Mike MASSOGLIA

*Gaston College (D)

201 Highway 321 South, Dallas NC 28034-1499
County: Gaston FICE Identification: 002973
Unit ID: 198570
Telephone: (704) 922-6200 Carnegie Class: Assoc/MT-VT-High Trad
FAX Number: (704) 922-2323 Calendar System: Semester
URL: www.gaston.edu
Established: 1964 Annual Undergrad Tuition & Fees (In-District): $2,562
Enrollment: 5,582 Coed
Affiliation or Control: State/Local IRS Status: 501(c)3
Highest Offering: Associate Degree
Accreditation: SC, ACBSP, ADNUR, DIETT, EMT, ENGT, IFSAC, MAC, PNUR

02 President ... Dr. Patricia A. SKINNER
05 VP Academic Affairs ... Dr. Dewey DELLINGER
103 VP Economic & Workforce Develop ... Dr. Dennis MCELHOE
10 VP Finance/Facilities/Operations ... Ms. Cynthia MCCRORY
32 VP Student Affairs/Enrollment Mgmt ... Dr. Silvia Patricia RIOS-HUSAIN
11 Chief Administrative Officer ... Mr. Todd BANEY
102 Chief Develop Ofcr/Dir Foundation ... Ms. Julia ALLEN
04 Exec Admin Assistant to Pres ... Ms. Mary Ellen DILLON
20 Assoc VP Academic Affairs ... Vacant
21 Assoc VP Fin/Oper/Fac & Controller ... Mr. Bruce COLE
88 Assoc VP Economic/Workforce Develop ... Ms. Jill LUTZ
35 Asst VP Student Affairs ... Ms. Audrey SHERRILL
12 Dean Kimbrell Campus/Textile Ctr ... Dr. Joe KEITH
12 Dean Lincoln Campus ... Dr. John MCHUGH
50 Dean Business & Information Tech ... Vacant
72 Dean Engr/Industrial Technologies ... Mr. Virgil COX
66 Dean Health & Human Services ... Vacant
49 Dean Liberal Arts & Sciences ... Dr. Heather WOODSON
07 Dir Admissions/Counseling ... Ms. Jennifer NICHOLS
40 Dir Bookstore/Vending Services ... Mr. Charles WILSON
78 Dir Educational Partnerships ... Ms. Kimberly WYONT
18 Dir Facilities Management ... Mr. Russell SMYRE
37 Dir Financial Aid/Veteran Affs ... Mr. Everett JETER
25 Dir Grants/Special Projects ... Mr. Luke UPCHURCH
09 Dir Institutional Effectiveness ... Dr. Rex CLAY
88 Dir Learn/Persist/Completion Ctr ... Mr. John ERICKSON
08 Dir Libraries ... Dr. Harry COOKE
26 Dir Marketing/PR ... Ms. Stephanie MICHAEL-PICKETT
96 Interim Dir Purch/Receive/Shipping ... Mr. Bruce COLE

06 Dir Registration/Records ... Vacant
75 Dir Textile Technology Ctr ... Mr. Sam BUFF
19 Chief Campus Police & Security ... Mr. Billy LYTTON
13 Chief Technology Services Officer ... Ms. Savonne MCNEILL
15 Mgr HR/Envir/Health/Safety/Prof Dev ... Ms. Carol DENTON

*Guilford Technical Community College (E)

PO Box 309, Jamestown NC 27282-0309
County: Guilford FICE Identification: 004838
Unit ID: 198622
Telephone: (336) 334-4822 Carnegie Class: Assoc/HVT-High Trad
FAX Number: (336) 454-2745 Calendar System: Semester
URL: www.gtcc.edu
Established: 1958 Annual Undergrad Tuition & Fees (In-State): $2,176
Enrollment: 11,518 Coed
Affiliation or Control: State IRS Status: 501(c)3
Highest Offering: Associate Degree
Accreditation: SC, ACFEI, DA, DH, EMT, MAC, PTAA, RAD, SURGT

02 President ... Dr. Randy PARKER
05 Vice President of Instruction ... Dr. Beth PITONZO
32 Vice Pres Student Support Services ... Dr. Quentin JOHNSON
11 AVP Facility Operations & Safety ... Mr. Mitchell JOHNSON
10 Assoc VP of Business & Finance ... Ms. Nancy B. SOLLOSI
20 Assoc VP Student Support Services ... Dr. Alison WIERS
51 VP Corp & Continuing Educ ... Dr. Ralph SONEY
12 Dean Greensboro Campus ... Dr. Manuel DUDLEY
12 Dean High Point Campus ... Mr. Mark HARRIS
50 Dir Business & Industry Training ... Mr. Stephen CASTELLOE
30 Director of Development ... Vacant
15 Director of Human Resources ... Vacant
13 Chief Information Officer ... Mr. Rob RAMEY
18 Director of Construction ... Mr. Charles YOUNG
09 Director of Institutional Research ... Mr. Rod FOTH
07 Director of Admissions ... Mr. Jesse CROSS
35 Director of Student Life ... Ms. Berri V. CROSS
37 Director Financial Aid ... Ms. Lisa A. KORETOFF
19 Chief of Campus Police ... Mr. James PHILLIPS
06 Registrar ... Mr. Kirby MOORE
21 Controller ... Ms. Angela M. CARTER
40 Bookstore Manager ... Mr. Shawn G. DEE
36 Coordinator Career Services ... Vacant
38 Director Counseling & Assessment ... Mr. Chris CHAFIN
29 Asst Director of Development ... Ms. Nancy GRIFFIN CALKINS
08 Dir of Library Services ... Ms. Monica YOUNG
41 Athletic Director ... Mr. Kirk CHANDLER
96 Director of Purchasing ... Mr. Michael STOUT

*Halifax Community College (F)

PO Drawer 809, Weldon NC 27890-0809
County: Halifax FICE Identification: 007986
Unit ID: 198640
Telephone: (252) 536-4221 Carnegie Class: Assoc/HVT-Mix Trad/Non
FAX Number: (252) 536-4144 Calendar System: Semester
URL: www.halifaxcc.edu
Established: 1967 Annual Undergrad Tuition & Fees (In-District): $2,564
Enrollment: 1,154 Coed
Affiliation or Control: State/Local IRS Status: 501(c)3
Highest Offering: Associate Degree
Accreditation: SC, DH, MLTAD, PHLEB

02 President ... Dr. Michael A. ELAM
04 Exec Assistant to the President ... Ms. Kimberly J. MACK
05 Vice Pres Academic Affairs ... Dr. Deryl FULMER
10 Vice President Admin Services ... Ms. Debra SMITH
30 VP Institutional Effective/Advance ... Dr. Edwin IMASUEN
32 VP Student Svcs & Enrollment Mgmt ... Dr. Barbara BRADLEY-HASTY
20 Dean of Curriculum Programs ... Ms. B. T. BROWN
06 Registrar ... Ms. Dawn VELIKY
07 Director of Admissions/Enrol Mgmt ... Ms. Chalisa HARRELL
08 Director Learning Resources ... Ms. Lynn ALLEN
09 Dir of Institutional Effectiveness ... Dr. Adriane LECHE
26 Dir Public Relations & Marketing ... Ms. Molly WALLACE
38 Director Counseling Services ... Ms. Charice ROSSER
18 Facilities/Physical Plant ... Ms. Debra SMITH
36 Director Career/College Promise ... Ms. Jennifer JONES
37 Director of Financial Aid ... Mrs. Tara KEETER
96 Purchasing Agent ... Ms. Darlene PERRY
15 Human Resources Manager ... Mrs. Margaret MURGA
13 Information Systems Manager ... Mr. Jerry THOMPSON
49 Div Chair Arts & Sciences/Business ... Mr. Calvin STANSBURY
76 Div Chair Health Sciences & Humanit ... Ms. Sheril ROBERTS
75 Div Chair Vocation/Industrial Tech ... Mr. Hunter TAYLOR
106 Dir Online Education/E-learning ... Ms. Ellen GRANT
19 Chief Campus Security ... Mr. Emmett SMITH
25 Chief Contracts/Grants Admin ... Mr. Daniel LOVETT
44 Director Annual or Planned Giving ... Dr. Dianne BARNES-RHOADES

*Haywood Community College (G)

185 Freedlander Drive, Clyde NC 28721-9453
County: Haywood FICE Identification: 008083
Unit ID: 198668
Telephone: (828) 627-2821 Carnegie Class: Assoc/MT-VT-High Trad
FAX Number: (828) 627-3606 Calendar System: Semester
URL: www.haywood.edu
Established: 1965 Annual Undergrad Tuition & Fees (In-State): $2,538
Enrollment: 1,803 Coed

Affiliation or Control: State IRS Status: 501(c)3
Highest Offering: Associate Degree
Accreditation: SC, MAC

02 President .... Dr. Barbara PARKER
05 Vice President of Instruction .... Mrs. Wendy HINES
32 Vice President Student Services .... Vacant
10 Vice President Business Operations .... Mrs. Karen DENNEY
18 Director of Campus Development .... Mr. Brek LANNING
111 Dir Institutional Advancement .... Mrs. Pam HARDIN
26 Director Marketing & Communications .... Ms. Jessica DUQUE
15 Director of Human Resources .... Mrs. Marsha STINES
84 Director of Enrollment Management . Mrs. Kimberly MOREHOUSE
37 Director of Financial Aid .... Mrs. Tracy RAPP
09 Data Analyst/SACSCOC Liaison .... Mr. David ONDER
103 Dean of Workforce Dev/Cont Educ .... Mr. Doug BURCHFIELD

*Isothermal Community College (A)

PO Box 804, Spindale NC 28160-0804
County: Rutherford FICE Identification: 002934
Unit ID: 198710
Telephone: (828) 286-3636 Carnegie Class: Assoc/HVT-High Non
FAX Number: (828) 286-1120 Calendar System: Semester
URL: www.isothermal.edu
Established: 1964 Annual Undergrad Tuition & Fees (In-District): $2,542
Enrollment: 2,018 Coed
Affiliation or Control: State/Local IRS Status: 501(c)3
Highest Offering: Associate Degree
Accreditation: SC

02 President .... Mr. Walter H. DALTON
11 Vice Pres Administrative Services .... Mr. Stephen MATHENY
05 Vice Pres Academic & Student Svcs .... Dr. Dolly HORTON
103 Vice Pres Cmty/Workforce Educ .... Mr. Thad HARRILL
32 Dean of Student Affairs .... Ms. Sandra LACKNER
50 Dean of Business Sciences .... Ms. Kim ALEXANDER
49 Dean of Arts & Sciences .... Dr. Kathy ACKERMAN
75 Dean of Applied Science & Engr .... Mr. Joe LOONEY
51 Dean of Continuing Education .... Mrs. Donna HOOD
12 Director of Polk Campus .... Mrs. Kate BARKSCHAT
20 Director Academic Development .... Mrs. Debbie PUETT
08 Director Library Services .... Mr. Charles WIGGINS
10 Controller .... Mrs. Amy M. PENSON
37 Financial Aid Officer .... Mrs. Pamela ELLIS
26 Dir Marketing/Community Relations .... Mr. Mike GAVIN
18 Dir Plant Operations/Maintenance .... Mr. Rick EDWARDS
121 Director Advising & Success Center .... Mrs. Kimberly SNYDER
84 Director of Enrollment Management .... Ms. Alice MCCLUNEY
06 Registrar .... Ms. Vanessa CAPPS
96 Director of Purchasing .... Ms. Trish HUNTSINGER
13 Director of Information Technology .... Mr. Robby WALTERS
40 Bookstore Manager .... Mrs. Danielle ALEY
04 Administrative Asst to President .... Mrs. DeeDee BARNARD
15 Director Personnel Services .... Mrs. Amy HARPER

*James Sprunt Community College (B)

PO Box 398, Kenansville NC 28349-0398
County: Duplin FICE Identification: 007687
Unit ID: 198729
Telephone: (910) 296-2400 Carnegie Class: Assoc/HT-High Non
FAX Number: (910) 296-1636 Calendar System: Semester
URL: www.jamessprunt.edu
Established: 1964 Annual Undergrad Tuition & Fees (In-State): $2,502
Enrollment: 1,195 Coed
Affiliation or Control: State IRS Status: 501(c)3
Highest Offering: Associate Degree
Accreditation: SC

02 Chief Executive Officer/President .... Dr. Lawrence L. ROUSE
05 VP of Curriculum Services .... Ms. June DAVIS
51 VP of Continuing Education .... Vacant
10 VP of Admin & Fiscal Services .... Mr. John HARDISON
32 VP of Student Services .... Vacant
111 VP Col Advance/Inst Effectiveness .... Mr. Stanley TURBEVILLE
06 Registrar .... Ms. Kelly MICAL
07 Admissions Specialist .... Ms. Wanda EDWARDS
37 Director Financial Aid/Vet Affairs .... Ms. Tracy WARD
38 Director of Student Counseling .... Ms. Amber FERRELL
08 Director Library Services .... Ms. Christine VASICA
15 Dir Human Resources/Campus Safety .... Ms. Debbie MARTIN
97 Director of General Education .... Mr. Andy CAVENAUGH
09 Dir Research/Plng/Instl Effective .... Vacant
26 Dir of Public Info/Print Media .... Ms. Cheryl HEMRIC
18 Chief Facilities/Physical Plant .... Mr. Dennis SUTTON
96 Director of Purchasing .... Ms. Toni HENDERSON
55 Instr/Coord Evening/Weekend Svcs .... Mr. James THOMAS
13 Chief Info Technology Officer (CIO) .... Vacant
19 Director Security/Safety .... Mr. Richard WHITMAN

*Johnston Community College (C)

PO Box 2350, 245 College Road,
Smithfield NC 27577-2350
County: Johnston FICE Identification: 009336
Unit ID: 198774
Telephone: (919) 934-3051 Carnegie Class: Assoc/HVT-High Trad
FAX Number: (919) 209-2142 Calendar System: Semester
URL: www.johnstoncc.edu
Established: 1969 Annual Undergrad Tuition & Fees (In-District): $2,529
Enrollment: 3,969 Coed
Affiliation or Control: State/Local IRS Status: 501(c)3
Highest Offering: Associate Degree
Accreditation: SC, ADNUR, DMS, MAC, RAD

02 President .... Dr. David N. JOHNSON
10 VP Admin/Financial & IT Resourc .... Dr. Darryl MCGRAW
05 Vice Pres of Instruction .... Mrs. Dee Dee D. DAUGHTRY
32 Vice Pres of Student Services .... Dr. Pamela J. HARRELL
09 Dir of Research and IE .... Dr. Terri S. LEE
102 Executive Director of Foundation .... Dr. Twyla C. WELLS
13 Chief Information Officer .... Mr. Jeff PICKERING
08 Lead Librarian .... Ms. Jennifer SEAGRAVES
105 Internet Info Systems Coordinator .... Ms. Lisa H. MCLAURIN
06 Registrar .... Ms. Deena H. HENRY
37 Director Financial Aid .... Mrs. Betty C. WOODALL
109 Assoc VP of Auxiliary Enterprises .... Mr. Ken H. MITCHELL
15 Director of Human Resources .... Ms. Bernadette CARTER-DOVE
07 Dir of Enrollment & Student Success .... Mrs. Megan L. SHANER
103 Dean of Economic and Community Dev ... Mrs. Joy T. CALLAHAN
76 Dean Health/Wellness & Human Svcs .... Dr. Linda D. SMITH
49 Dean Arts/Sciences & Learning Res .... Mrs. Dawn S. DIXON
50 Dean Business and Advanced Tech .... Dr. Deborah PORTO
26 Senior Director of Communications .... Mrs. Traci D. ASHLEY
18 Maintenance Director .... Mr. Michael MASSEY
96 Purchasing and Equipment Director .... Ms. Cassandra HAIRE
88 Secy and Emer Preparedness Coord .... Ms. Sarah GIBBS
04 Exec Asst to the President .... Ms. Sandy MILLARD

*Lenoir Community College (D)

231 Highway 58 South, Kinston NC 28502-0188
County: Lenoir FICE Identification: 002940
Unit ID: 198817
Telephone: (252) 527-6223 Carnegie Class: Assoc/MT-VT-High Non
FAX Number: (252) 233-6879 Calendar System: Semester
URL: www.lenoircc.edu
Established: 1958 Annual Undergrad Tuition & Fees (In-District): $2,551
Enrollment: 2,757 Coed
Affiliation or Control: State/Local IRS Status: 501(c)3
Highest Offering: Associate Degree
Accreditation: SC, ACFEI, EMT, MAC, POLYT, RAD, SURGT

02 President .... Dr. Rusty HUNT
51 VP Continuing Education .... Dr. Jay CARRAWAY
11 Senior VP Administrative Services .... Ms. Deborah SUTTON
05 Sr VP Instruc & Student Services .... Dr. Deborah GRIMES
10 Chief Financial Officer .... Ms. Deborah S. SUTTON
06 Registrar .... Ms. Shelia WIGGINS
84 Director Enrollment Mgmt/Admissions .... Vacant
32 Dean of Student Services .... Dr. John Paul BLACK
37 Director of Student Financial Aid .... Mr. J. D GIBBS
13 Chief Information Officer .... Mr. Lee WETHERINGTON
09 Director Inst Effectiveness .... Mrs. Jo WILSON
15 Director Human Resources .... Mrs. Tasha JOHNSON
18 Director of Maintenance .... Mr. Reed LOVICK
41 Athletic Director .... Mrs. Shelly BARNES
21 Director of Financial Services .... Ms. Jessica MCMAHON
96 Purchasing Agent .... Ms. Rhonda DEAVER
26 Director of Mktg/Recruiting/Comm .... Mrs. Richy HUNEYCUTT
30 Director Institutional Advancement .... Mrs. Jeanne KENNEDY
103 Work-Based Lrng Coord .... Mrs. Sherry IRSIK
08 Director of Learning Resources .... Mr. Rich GARAFOLO
50 Dean of Business/Industrial/Technol .... Mr. Gary CLEMENTS
49 Dean of Arts & Sciences .... Dr. Levy BROWN
76 Dean of Health Sciences & Nursing .... Dr. Alexis WELCH
92 Dean/Director of Honors Program .... Dr. John Paul BLACK
94 Dean/Director of Women's Studies .... Dr. Deborah GRIMES
35 Director Student Activities .... Mrs. Shelly BARNES
07 Director of Admissions .... Ms. Kimberly HILL

*Martin Community College (E)

1161 Kehukee Park Road, Williamston NC 27892-9988
County: Martin FICE Identification: 007988
Unit ID: 198905
Telephone: (252) 792-1521 Carnegie Class: Assoc/HVT-Mix Trad/Non
FAX Number: (252) 792-0826 Calendar System: Semester
URL: www.martincc.edu
Established: 1967 Annual Undergrad Tuition & Fees (In-State): $1,862
Enrollment: 870 Coed
Affiliation or Control: State IRS Status: 501(c)3
Highest Offering: Associate Degree
Accreditation: SC, DA, MAC, PTAA

02 President .... Dr. Kenneth A. BOHAM
05 Dean Academic Affairs/Student Svcs .... Vacant
11 Dean of Administrative Services .... Mr. Steve TAYLOR
10 Financial Services Director .... Ms. Tammy BAILEY
20 Assoc Dean Acad Affs/Student Svcs .... Dr. Brian BUSCH
04 Asst to Pres for Business/Industry .... Mr. Billy BARBER
37 Financial Aid Director .... Ms. Terri LEGGETT
38 Counselor and Admissions .... Ms. Crystal PUGH
06 Registrar .... Ms. Eileen JARMUL
51 Exec Dir Continuing Education .... Vacant
13 Systems Administrator .... Ms. Donna ROGERS
18 Director of Facilities .... Mr. Walter WHEELER
15 Human Resource Director .... Mr. Harland FRYE
14 Director of IT .... Mr. Elijah T. FREEMAN
09 Director of Institutional Research .... Ms. Maureen GREEN
96 Director of Purchasing .... Ms. Jennifer CHERRY
12 Director of Bertie Campus .... Mr. Norman CHERRY
08 Library Director .... Ms. Mary Anne CAUDLE
101 Exec Asst to President and BOT .... Ms. Kismet MATTHEWS
26 Dir Public Affairs/Inst Advancement .... Ms. Judy JENNETTE

*Mayland Community College (F)

PO Box 547, Spruce Pine NC 28777-0547
County: Avery FICE Identification: 011197
Unit ID: 198914
Telephone: (828) 765-7351 Carnegie Class: Assoc/MT-VT-High Non
FAX Number: (828) 765-0728 Calendar System: Semester
URL: www.mayland.edu
Established: 1971 Annual Undergrad Tuition & Fees (In-District): $2,430
Enrollment: 1,156 Coed
Affiliation or Control: State/Local IRS Status: 501(c)3
Highest Offering: Associate Degree
Accreditation: SC, MAC

02 President .... Dr. John C. BOYD
04 Assistant to the President .... Ms. Brooke BURLESON
05 VP Academics & Student Development .... Mr. Randy LEDFORD
10 Vice President Administrative Svcs .... Mr. Tim GREENE
103 Vice Pres Economic/Workforce Devel .... Mrs. Rita EARLEY
32 Dean of Students .... Ms. Michelle MUSICH
76 Dean of Health Sciences Programs .... Mrs. Kim BURR
49 Dean of Arts & Sciences .... Ms. Sherry SHERMAN
72 Dean of Career Technologies .... Ms. Brenda MCFEE
08 Director Learning Resources Center .... Mr. Jon WILMESHERR
09 Dir Institutional Effectiveness .... Mr. Ryan RAY
06 Registrar .... Vacant
88 Dean of Basic Skills Programs .... Mr. Steve GUNTER
12 Dean Avery County EWD .... Mrs. Melissa C. PHILLIPS
12 Dean Mitchell County EWD .... Mr. Chris HELMS
12 Dean Yancey County EWD .... Dr. Monica S. CARPENTER
37 Director Student Financial Aid .... Mrs. Cassie FORBES
18 Director Facilities/Physical Plant .... Mr. Lee WHITTINGTON
13 Dir Management Information Systems .... Mr. Tommy R. LEDFORD
15 Director Personnel Services .... Mr. Judy MCCLURE
26 Chief Public Relations Officer .... Mrs. Beth MORRIS
96 Coordinator of Purchasing/Equipment .... Mr. Eddie BUCHANAN

*McDowell Technical Community College (G)

54 College Drive, Marion NC 28752-8728
County: McDowell FICE Identification: 008085
Unit ID: 198923
Telephone: (828) 652-6021 Carnegie Class: Assoc/MT-VT-High Non
FAX Number: (828) 652-1014 Calendar System: Semester
URL: www.mcdowelltech.edu
Established: 1964 Annual Undergrad Tuition & Fees (In-District): $1,900
Enrollment: 1,106 Coed
Affiliation or Control: State/Local IRS Status: 501(c)3
Highest Offering: Associate Degree
Accreditation: SC, CAHIIM

02 President .... Dr. Bryan WILSON
05 Vice Pres for Learning/Student Svcs .... Dr. John GOSSETT
10 Vice Pres Finance/Administration .... Mr. Ryan GARRISON
20 Dean Academic Programs .... Dr. James BENTON
09 Director of Inst Effectiveness .... Mr. Ladelle HARMON
26 Director of External Relations .... Mr. Michael K. LAVENDER
13 Director of Technology/Info Systems .... Mr. Elmer R. MACOPSON
08 Director of Library Services .... Ms. Sharon P. SMITH
88 Director of Industrial Training .... Mr. Eddie SHUFORD
76 Director of Health Sciences .... Mrs. Penny CROSS
06 Registrar .... Ms. Kelly HAMLIN
37 Director Student Financial Aid .... Ms. Kim M. LEDBETTER
36 Director of Student Enrichment Ctr .... Mrs. Donna SHORT
88 Director Adult Basic Skills .... Mrs. Teresa VALENTINO
88 Counselor/VA Director .... Mrs. Donna SHORT
51 Director of Continuing Education .... Mr. Brad LEDBETTER
88 Director Basic Law Enforcement Trng .... Mr. Stacy BUFF
07 Director of Admissions .... Mr. Wingate CAIN
15 Director of Human Resources Devel ..... Mrs. Mary L. LEDBETTER
30 Foundation Resource Devel Officer .... Ms. Susan BERLEY
106 Coordinator of Distance Education .... Mrs. Joan WEILER
18 Coord Maintenance/Custodial Svcs .... Mr. Carl COSTNER
88 Coord of Small Business Center .... Mr. Frank SILVER
04 Exec Assistant to the President .... Ms. Madalyn GAITO

*Mitchell Community College (H)

500 W Broad Street, Statesville NC 28677-5293
County: Iredell FICE Identification: 002947
Unit ID: 198987
Telephone: (704) 878-3200 Carnegie Class: Assoc/HT-High Trad
FAX Number: (704) 878-0872 Calendar System: Semester
URL: www.mitchellcc.edu
Established: 1852 Annual Undergrad Tuition & Fees (In-State): $2,631
Enrollment: 3,024 Coed
Affiliation or Control: State IRS Status: 501(c)3
Highest Offering: Associate Degree
Accreditation: SC, ADNUR, MAC

02 President .... Dr. Tim BREWER
05 Vice President of Instruction .... Dr. Camille REESE
10 Vice Pres of Finance/Administration .... Mr. Gerald HYDE
11 Vice President for Administration .... Mr. John WILKINSON
103 Vice Pres Workforce Development/CEC .... Ms. Carol JOHNSON
111 Vice President for Advancement .... Mr. James HOGAN
32 Vice Pres Student Services .... Dr. Porter BRANNON
09 Director of Research & Planning .... Ms. Eva EISNAUGLE
121 Director Student Academic Success .... Dr. Sandra LANDRY
37 Director of Financial Aid .... Ms. Candace COOPER

18 Facilities Supervisor II .... Mr. Chad LACKEY
88 Director of Educational Partnership .... Ms. Amanda RHEA
07 Director of Admissions .... Ms. Elizabeth PATTERSON
19 Director of Public Safety .... Mr. David BULLINS

*Montgomery Community College (A)

1011 Page Street, Troy NC 27371-0787
County: Montgomery FICE Identification: 008087
Unit ID: 199023
Telephone: (910) 898-9600 Carnegie Class: Assoc/HVT-Mix Trad/Non
FAX Number: (910) 576-2176 Calendar System: Semester
URL: www.montgomery.edu
Established: 1967 Annual Undergrad Tuition & Fees (In-District): $2,537
Enrollment: 818 Coed
Affiliation or Control: State/Local IRS Status: 501(c)3
Highest Offering: Associate Degree
Accreditation: SC, CSHSE, DA, MAC

02 President .... Dr. Chad A. BLEDSOE
05 Vice Pres of Instruction .... Lee PROCTOR
11 VP of Administrative Services .... Jeanette MCBRIDE
32 VP of Student Services .... Beth SMITH
51 Dean of Continuing Education .... Jonathan THILL
102 Executive Director Foundation/Grant .... Lynn EPPS
26 Public Information Officer .... Michele HAYWOOD
09 Dir Institutional Effectiveness .... Carol HOLTON
13 Dir of Information Technology .... Cindy ELLISON
04 Assistant to the President .... Korrie ERVIN
38 Counseling Services .... Natalie WINFREE
07 Admissions Officer .... Karen FRYE
37 Director of Financial Aid .... Doni S. HATCHEL
15 Coordinator Of Human Resources .... Melisa BOND
10 Accountant .... Tonya LUCK
18 Director of Facilities .... Wanda FRICK
35 Student Activities Coordinator .... Savannah HEATH
08 Head Librarian .... Deborah ASHBY

*Nash Community College (B)

522 N Old Carriage Road, Rocky Mount NC 27804-0488
County: Nash FICE Identification: 008557
Unit ID: 199087
Telephone: (252) 443-4011 Carnegie Class: Assoc/MT-VT-Mix Trad/Non
FAX Number: (252) 451-8201 Calendar System: Semester
URL: www.nashcc.edu
Established: 1967 Annual Undergrad Tuition & Fees (In-District): $2,632
Enrollment: 3,116 Coed
Affiliation or Control: State/Local IRS Status: 501(c)3
Highest Offering: Associate Degree
Accreditation: SC, MAC, PHLEB, PTAA

02 President .... Dr. William S. CARVER, II
04 Admin Asst to President/Board .... Ms. Donna L. BATCHELOR
103 VP Corporate/Economic Dev .... Ms. Wendy C. MARLOWE
111 VP Institutional Advancement .... Ms. Pamela H. BALLEW
05 Vice President for Instruction .... Dr. Trent L. MOHRBUTTER
10 Vice President of Finance .... Ms. Adrienne S. COVINGTON
13 Vice President Technology & CIO .... Dr. Jonathan S. VESTER
32 Assoc VP Student & Enrollment Svcs . Mr. Michael W. COLEMAN
86 Assoc VP Community & Govt Affairs .... Dr. Keith SMITH
20 Assoc VP Curriculum .... Mr. Mike LATHAM
26 Dean of Marketing .... Mrs. Kelley P. DEAL
88 Dean of Transfer/Learning Resources .... Ms. Deana L. GUIDO
09 Assoc Dean Institutional Effective .... Ms. Farley A. PHILLIPS
88 Director Small Business Center .... Ms. Theresa R. PEADEN
07 Director of Admissions/Recruitment .... Mrs. Stephanie B. GEANES
24 Dir Instructional Publ/Printing .... Mr. James M. QUIGLEY
37 Director of Financial Aid .... Ms. Tammy LESTER
15 Director Human Resources .... Ms. Morgan R. BLAND
18 Director of Facilities .... Mr. Greg DEANS
06 Registrar/Director of Records .... Mrs. Kathy S. ADCOX

*Pamlico Community College (C)

PO Box 185, Grantsboro NC 28529-0185
County: Pamlico FICE Identification: 007031
Unit ID: 199263
Telephone: (252) 249-1851 Carnegie Class: Assoc/HVT-High Non
FAX Number: (252) 249-2377 Calendar System: Semester
URL: www.pamlicocc.edu
Established: 1962 Annual Undergrad Tuition & Fees (In-District): $1,867
Enrollment: 494 Coed
Affiliation or Control: State/Local IRS Status: 501(c)3
Highest Offering: Associate Degree
Accreditation: SC, MAC, NDT

02 President .... Dr. Jim ROSS
11 Vice Pres Administrative Svcs .... Mr. Mark PULLIAM
05 Vice Pres Instructional Svcs .... Ms. Michelle WILLIS
32 Vice Pres of Student Services .... Mr. Jamie GIBBS
09 Director of Planning & Research .... Ms. Sherry RABY
06 Registrar .... Ms. Tammy SPAIN
37 Director of Financial Aid .... Ms. Melissa WHITMAN
10 Controller .... Vacant
26 Director of Public Affairs .... Mr. Sandy WALL
04 Administrative Asst to President .... Ms. Michelle NOEVERE
106 Dir Online Education/E-learning .... Ms. Kathy MAYO

*Piedmont Community College (D)

1715 College Dr, Roxboro NC 27573-1197
County: Person FICE Identification: 009646
Unit ID: 199324
Telephone: (336) 599-1181 Carnegie Class: Assoc/MT-VT-Mix Trad/Non
FAX Number: (336) 597-3817 Calendar System: Semester
URL: www.piedmontcc.edu
Established: 1970 Annual Undergrad Tuition & Fees (In-District): $2,547
Enrollment: 1,321 Coed
Affiliation or Control: State/Local IRS Status: 501(c)3
Highest Offering: Associate Degree
Accreditation: SC, EMT, MAC

02 President .... Dr. Pamela G. SENEGAL
05 Interim VP Instruction/Student Dev .... Ms. Shelly STONE
51 Vice Pres Continuing Education .... Dr. Doris W. CARVER
11 Vice Pres Administrative Services .... Mr. Richard B. SELF
12 Provost Caswell County Campus .... Ms. Shelly T. STONE
106 Spec Asst to VP/Distance Educ .... Dr. Libbie M. MOORE
88 Dean Adult Basic Skills .... Ms. Debra B. HARLOW
103 Dean Occupational Ext & Corr Ed .... Ms. Tracey P. BRANDON
76 Dean Health Sciences and Human Svcs .... Ms. Alisa L. MONTGOMERY
08 Dean LRC .... Ms. Vanessa L. BASS
72 Dean Tech/Occup & Early Col Liaison .... Mr. Walter C. MONTGOMERY
105 Webmaster/Graphics Designer .... Mr. Kevin R. TYBURSKI
88 Director TRiO Programs .... Ms. Carolyn W. FUNDERBURK
103 Dean Workforce Development .... Ms. Angela P. WEBB
06 Registrar .... Ms. Susan L. GREINER
37 Dir Financial Aid/Veterans Affairs .... Ms. Paulita N. WILLIAMS
18 Director Buildings and Grounds .... Mr. Bruce T. CHISHOLM
25 Director Grants .... Mr. Ricky FARMER
15 Director Personnel/Payroll .... Ms. Pamelia C. HOBBS
88 Director QEP .... Ms. Lisa K. COOLEY
26 Director Public Information .... Ms. Elizabeth R. TOWNSEND
09 Dir Research/Inst Effectiveness .... Dr. Jeff PATON
13 Chief Information Officer .... Mr. Kumar LAKHAVANI
19 Deputy Director College Safety .... Mr. Adam W. IRBY
29 Fin Coord Foundation/Alumni Rels .... Ms. Patricia I. CLAYTON
96 Purchasing Officer/Accountant .... Ms. Jovana AMARO
40 Manager Bookstore .... Ms. Tammy H. MORRIS
04 Administrative Asst to President .... Ms. Cindy W. FOX
10 Controller .... Ms. Beverly J. MURPHY
102 Executive Director PCC Foundation .Ms. Allison D. SATTERFIELD
49 Dean Arts/Sciences Univ Trsf .... Ms. Karen SANDERS
32 Dean Student Development .... Dr. Joelle D. CARTER

*Pitt Community College (E)

PO Drawer 7007, Greenville NC 27835-7007
County: Pitt FICE Identification: 004062
Unit ID: 199333
Telephone: (252) 493-7200 Carnegie Class: Assoc/MT-VT-Mix Trad/Non
FAX Number: (252) 321-4458 Calendar System: Semester
URL: www.pittcc.edu
Established: 1961 Annual Undergrad Tuition & Fees (In-State): $1,929
Enrollment: 8,574 Coed
Affiliation or Control: State IRS Status: 501(c)3
Highest Offering: Associate Degree
Accreditation: SC, ADNUR, CAHIIM, COARC, CSHSE, DMS, MAC, OTA, POLYT, RAD, RADDOS, RTT

02 President .... Dr. Dennis MASSEY
05 Vice President Academic Affairs .... Dr. Thomas GOULD
11 Vice Pres Administrative Services .... Mr. Rick OWENS
32 Vice President Student Development .... Dr. Donald R. SPELL
30 Vice Pres Institutional Advancement .... Mrs. Susan Q. NOBLES
20 Asst Vice Pres Academic Affairs .... Ms. Lori PREAST
13 AVP Information Technology/Services .... Mr. Ernest SIMONS
10 Chief Financial Officer .... Mr. Ricky BROWN
04 Administrative Asst to President .... Mrs. Kathy M. CARNES
31 Dean Economic & Cmty Development .... Vacant
08 Director Library .... Ms. Leigh RUSSELL
09 Dean of Planning & Research .... Vacant
46 Resource Development Director .... Vacant
15 Director of Human Resources .... Vacant
91 Director of Admin Computing .... Mrs. Janet MINTERN
06 Registrar .... Ms. Angela CLINE
38 Director of Counseling .... Dr. Kimberly WILLIAMSON
88 Director Basic Skills Program .... Vacant
18 Director of Facilities .... Mr. Timothy STRICKLAND
103 Director of JobLink Career Center .... Vacant
84 Dean Student Svcs/Enrollment Mgmt .... Ms. Joanne T. CERES
41 Athletic Director .... Vacant
29 Director of Alumni Relations .... Mrs. Ashley SMITH
36 Director of Student Placement .... Mrs. Sharon CERES
96 Director of Purchasing .... Ms. Jane ALLIGOOD
19 Chief Public Safety/Campus Police .... Mr. Jay SHINGLETON
88 Director Business & Industry Svcs .... Vacant
104 Director Study Abroad .... Vacant
09 Director Planning & Analysis .... Dr. Brian MILLER
37 Director Financial Aid .... Ms. Tamara GLASPIE
40 Manager of College Store .... Ms. Holly EDWARDS
106 Coord Instructional Tech/Dist Educ .... Mr. Mike CLENDENEN
55 Coord/Counselor Evening Programs .... Mr. Kendrick PRICE
50 Division Dean of Business .... Ms. Katherine CLYDE
76 Division Dean Health Sciences .... Ms. Donna V. NEAL
49 Division Dean of Art & Sciences ... Dr. Stephanie MANLEY-ROOK
75 Div Dean Construct/Indus Tech .... Mr. Mark FAITHFUL
61 Div Dean Legal Sci/Public Svc .... Dr. Dan MAYO

*Randolph Community College (F)

629 Industrial Park Avenue, Asheboro NC 27205
County: Randolph FICE Identification: 005447
Unit ID: 199421
Telephone: (336) 633-0200 Carnegie Class: Assoc/MT-VT-High Trad
FAX Number: (336) 629-4695 Calendar System: Semester
URL: www.randolph.edu
Established: 1962 Annual Undergrad Tuition & Fees (In-District): $1,912
Enrollment: 2,670 Coed
Affiliation or Control: State/Local IRS Status: 501(c)3
Highest Offering: Associate Degree
Accreditation: SC, MAC, RAD

02 President .... Dr. Robert S. SHACKLEFORD, JR.
10 Vice Pres Administrative Services .... Ms. Daffie H. GARRIS
05 Vice Pres Instructional Services ..... Ms. Suzanne Y. ROHRBAUGH
32 Vice President Student Services .... Mr. Chad WILLIAMS
103 VP Workforce Development/Cont Educ .... Mr. Elbert J. LASSITER
111 Assoc VP Institutional Advancement .... Ms. Shelley W. GREENE
62 Dean Library Services .... Ms. Deborah S. LUCK
12 Director Archdale Center .... Ms. Tonya C. MONROE
21 Dir Financial Svcs/Controller .... Ms. Susan I. RICE
26 Director Marketing .... Mr. Kris N. JULIAN
18 Director Facilities Operations .... Ms. Cindi J. GOODWIN
13 Director Information Tech Svcs .... Ms. Tara A. WILLIAMS
09 Planning & Assessment Specialist .... Ms. Stacy C. SCHMITT
15 Director of Human Resources .... Ms. Melanie AVELINO
37 Director Financial Aid & Veteran Af .... Mr. Joel TROGDON
06 Director Enrollment Mgmt/Registrar .... Ms. Brandi F. HAGERMAN
106 Director Distance Education .... Mr. Devin A. SOVA
88 Director of ABE and AHS .... Vacant
88 Director Public Safety Programs .... Ms. Regina L. BREWER
96 Purchasing Agent .... Ms. Sharon P. REYNOLDS
27 Asst Dir Public Information .... Ms. Cathy D. HEFFERIN
04 Exec Asst to Pres/Board of Trustees .. Ms. Heather O. CLOUSTON
102 Dir Foundation/Corporate Relations ..... Ms. Lorie L. MCCROSKEY
19 Dir Safety/Emergency Preparedness .... Mr. Matthew R. NEEDHAM

*Richmond Community College (G)

Box 1189, Hamlet NC 28345-1189
County: Richmond FICE Identification: 005464
Unit ID: 199449
Telephone: (910) 410-1700 Carnegie Class: Assoc/MT-VT-High Trad
FAX Number: (910) 582-7028 Calendar System: Semester
URL: www.richmondcc.edu
Established: 1964 Annual Undergrad Tuition & Fees (In-District): $2,510
Enrollment: 2,550 Coed
Affiliation or Control: State/Local IRS Status: 501(c)3
Highest Offering: Associate Degree
Accreditation: SC, CAHIIM, MAC

02 President .... Dr. W. Dale MCINNIS
32 Vice President for Student Services .... Ms. Sharon GOODMAN
05 Vice President for Instruction/CAO .... Mr. Kevin PARSONS
10 Executive VP and CFO .... Mr. Brent BARBEE
103 VP for Workforce & Economic Develop .... Dr. Robbie TAYLOR
08 Dean of Learning Resources .... Ms. Carolyn BITTLE
88 Director of Basic Skills .... Mr. John KESTER
108 Dean of Inst Effectiveness & Improv .. Ms. Sheri DUNN-RAMSAY
09 Director of Institutional Research .... Ms. Chihoko TERRY
15 Director of Human Resources .... Ms. Gaye CLARK
26 Dir of Marketing & Communications .... Ms. Wylie BELL
21 Controller .... Ms. Debbie CASHWELL
36 Director of Career and Transfer Ser .... Ms. Patsy STANLEY
37 Director Student Financial Aid .... Ms. Andrea DANIELS
96 Purchasing Officer .... Mr. Martin BRIDGES
18 Director of Facility Services .... Mr. Scotty MABE
38 Director Student Counseling .... Mr. Chris GARDNER
04 Executive Asst to President .... Ms. Teena PARSONS
06 Registrar .... Ms. Cayce HOLMES
106 Director of Distance Learning .... Mr. Alan QUESTELL
13 Chief Information Officer .... Mr. Lee MONTROSE

*Roanoke-Chowan Community College (H)

109 Community College Road, Ahoskie NC 27910
County: Hertford FICE Identification: 008613
Unit ID: 199467
Telephone: (252) 862-1200 Carnegie Class: Assoc/MT-VT-High Trad
FAX Number: (252) 862-1358 Calendar System: Semester
URL: www.roanokechowan.edu
Established: 1967 Annual Undergrad Tuition & Fees (In-District): $2,642
Enrollment: 899 Coed
Affiliation or Control: State/Local IRS Status: 501(c)3
Highest Offering: Associate Degree
Accreditation: SC

02 President .... Dr. Jimmy T. TATE
05 Dean of Academic Affairs .... Mrs. Deborah DICKINSON
76 Director Allied Health Programs .... Ms. Jamie BURNS
32 Dean of Student Services .... Mr. Anthony THOMAS
10 Controller .... Ms. Belinda SMITH
18 Director Facilities .... Mr. Timothy LASSITER
106 Director Distance Learning .... Ms. Melanie TEMPLE
37 Director Financial Aid .... Mrs. Ruchelle RICKS
13 Director of Information Systems .... Dr. Mary LEARY
84 Director Enrollment Svcs/Curric Reg .... Mrs. Amy F. WIGGINS
121 Director Student Support Services .... Dr. Tanya OLIVER
15 Director Human Resources .... Mr. Bryan HOWARD
06 Registrar/Continuing Educ/Workforce .... Ms. Shirley GAY
102 Director R-CCC Foundation .... Ms. Tarsha DUDLEY
09 Director of Institutional Research .... Mrs. Jaime P. HECKSTALL
50 Dean of Administrative Fiscal Ser .... Mr. David L. FORESTER

*Robeson Community College (A)

PO Box 1420, Lumberton NC 28359-1420
County: Robeson FICE Identification: 008612
Unit ID: 199476
Telephone: (910) 272-3700 Carnegie Class: Assoc/MT-VT-Mix Trad/Non
FAX Number: (910) 272-3328 Calendar System: Semester
URL: www.robeson.edu
Established: 1965 Annual Undergrad Tuition & Fees (In-District): $2,540
Enrollment: 1,936 Coed
Affiliation or Control: State/Local IRS Status: 501(c)3
Highest Offering: Associate Degree
Accreditation: SC, COARC, RAD, SURGT

02 President ... Dr. Kimberly GOLD
05 VP Instruction/Sppt Svcs/CAO ... Mr. Bill MAUNEY
51 Vice Pres Adult & Continuing Educ ... Mr. R. Channing JONES
10 Vice President Business Services ... Mrs. Tami B. GEORGE
55 Asst VP Public Svc/Appl Tech Pgms ... Mr. William L. LOCKLEAR
88 Asst VP Univ Transfer/Bus/Hlth Pgms ... Ms. Connie IVEY
32 Asst Vice Pres Student Services ... Mr. Billy L. MAUNEY
13 Asst VP/Chief Information Officer ... Mr. Dustin LONG
07 Director of Admissions/Enroll Svcs ... Mr. Ronnie LOCKLEAR
22 Director Affirm Action/Equal Oppty ... Mr. Alphonzo MCRAE
08 Director of Learning Resource Svcs ... Mrs. Maryellen O'BRIEN
38 Director Counseling & Testing ... Vacant
06 Dir Records/Registration/Registrar ... Mrs. Beth CARMICAL
37 Financial Aid Director ... Ms. Teresa TUBBS
25 Director of Grants and Sponsored ... Vacant
18 Directors of Facilities ... Mr. Kenny DAVIS
102 Director Foundation/Development ... Ms. Rebekah R. LOWRY
29 Director Alumni Relations ... Ms. Rebekah LOWRY
36 Counseling & Career Services ... Mr. Ronnie SAMPSON
15 Personnel Services Specialist ... Ms. Pam ROMANO
96 Purchasing Officer ... Ms. Christy MUSSELWHITE
04 Administrative Asst to President ... Ms. Regina L. BRANCH
09 Director of Institutional Effective ... Ms. Toni SACRY
19 Director Security ... Ms. Patricia CLARK

*Rockingham Community College (B)

PO Box 38, Wentworth NC 27375-0038
County: Rockingham FICE Identification: 002958
Unit ID: 199485
Telephone: (336) 342-4261 Carnegie Class: Assoc/MT-VT-Mix Trad/Non
FAX Number: (336) 349-9986 Calendar System: Semester
URL: www.rockinghamcc.edu
Established: 1963 Annual Undergrad Tuition & Fees (In-District): $1,940
Enrollment: 1,866 Coed
Affiliation or Control: State/Local IRS Status: 501(c)3
Highest Offering: Associate Degree
Accreditation: SC, COARC, PHLEB, SURGT

02 President ... Dr. Mark O. KINLAW
05 Vice President for Academic Affairs ... Ms. Sheila REGAN
11 VP of Administrative Services ... Mr. Steven W. WOODRUFF
32 Vice Pres for Student Development ... Dr. Robert S. LOWDERMILK
88 Assoc VP Administrative Services ... Dr. E. Anthony GUNN
103 Dean of Workforce Development & CE ... Ms. Laura F. COFFEE
49 Dean of Arts & Sciences ... Ms. Celeste H. ALLIS
76 Dean of Health & Public Services ... Dr. Kimberly M. CLARK
25 Director Testing Services & Grants ... Ms. Kimberly SHIREMAN
45 Assoc VP Inst Effectiveness ... Mr. Kevin OSBORNE
06 Registrar ... Ms. Carla MOORE
08 Director Library Services/Archivist ... Ms. Mary GOMEZ
30 Director Development/Foundation ... Ms. Cindy SARWI
13 Dir Technology Support Services ... Ms. Gretchen PARRISH
37 Director of Financial Aid ... Ms. Sarah EVANS
84 Director of Enrollment Services ... Mr. Derick SATTERFIELD
35 Director Student Life ... Mr. Stewart MCCLINTOCK
40 Bookstore Manager ... Ms. Della J. GASTON
15 Director Human Resources ... Ms. Joy G. CHAPPELL
26 Director Public Information ... Ms. Kim A. PRYOR
96 Purchasing Officer/Equip Coord ... Mr. Caleb RORRER

*Rowan-Cabarrus Community College (C)

1333 Jake Alexander Blvd., South, Salisbury NC 28145
County: Rowan FICE Identification: 005754
Unit ID: 199494
Telephone: (704) 216-7222 Carnegie Class: Assoc/HVT-Mix Trad/Non
FAX Number: N/A Calendar System: Semester
URL: www.rccc.edu
Established: 1963 Annual Undergrad Tuition & Fees (In-State): $2,626
Enrollment: 5,180 Coed
Affiliation or Control: State IRS Status: 501(c)3
Highest Offering: Associate Degree
Accreditation: SC, ADNUR, DA, PNUR, RAD

02 President ... Dr. Carol SPALDING
05 Academic Vice President ... Dr. Michael D. QUILLEN
11 Chief Operating Officer ... Ms. Janet SPRIGGS
51 Vice President of Corp & Cont Educ ... Mr. Craig LAMB
13 Chief Officer Info Services & CIO ... Mr. Kenneth G. INGLE, III
18 Chief Facilities & Ofc of Civility ... Mr. Jonathan CHAMBERLAIN
20 Assoc Academic Vice President ... Mr. Angelo MARKANTONAKIS
21 Assoc Chief Financial Officer ... Ms. Kizzy LEA
88 Assoc Officer of Civility ... Mr. Mark EBERSOLE
103 Assoc VP Corporate/Continuing Educ ... Mrs. Ann MORRIS
76 Dean Health Programs ... Mrs. Wendy BARNHARDT
50 Dean Arts and Sciences ... Ms. Carol SCHERCZINGER
49 Dean Liberal Arts & General Educ ... Vacant
71 Dean Public Services ... Vacant
54 Dean Engineering Tech & Pub Svcs ... Mr. Van MADRAY
106 Dean Distance Educ & Learn Supp ... Ms. Debra NEESMITH
88 Exec Dir Pre-College Studies ... Mr. Gary CONNOR
08 Director Learning Resource Ctr ... Vacant
25 Director Grants Development ... Ms. Rebecca HOOKS
37 Exec Dir Students Operations ... Mrs. Lisa LEDBETTER
96 Director of Purchasing ... Ms. Kathy PIPER
07 Director Admissions & Recruitment ... Vacant
06 Director Enrollment & Records ... Mrs. Joan CREEGER
35 Director Student Life & Leadership ... Ms. Natasha LIPSCOMB
36 Director Academic & Career Svcs ... Ms. Marcia MILLER
16 Assoc Chief Human Resources ... Mrs. Nekita EUBANKS
09 Dir Research/Plng/Inst Effectiv ... Vacant
19 Director Campus Safety & Security ... Mr. Tim BOST
102 Director of Development ... Vacant
26 Exec Dir Marketing & Recruiting ... Ms. Paula DIBLEY

*Sampson Community College (D)

PO Box 318, Clinton NC 28329-0318
County: Sampson FICE Identification: 007892
Unit ID: 199625
Telephone: (910) 592-8081 Carnegie Class: Assoc/MT-VT-High Trad
FAX Number: (910) 592-8048 Calendar System: Semester
URL: www.sampsoncc.edu
Established: 1967 Annual Undergrad Tuition & Fees (In-District): $2,509
Enrollment: 1,384 Coed
Affiliation or Control: State/Local IRS Status: 501(c)3
Highest Offering: Associate Degree
Accreditation: SC, ADNUR, PNUR

02 President ... Dr. Paul C. HUTCHINS
05 Vice Pres Academic Affairs/Admin ... Dr. William STARLING
10 Vice Pres Finance/Auxiliary Svcs ... Mrs. Kelly JACKSON
32 Dean of Student Services ... Ms. Blair HAIRR
51 Dean of Continuing Education ... Mrs. Amanda BRADSHAW
07 Director of Admissions ... Ms. Holly BREWINGTON
09 Director of Institutional Research ... Mr. Marvin RONDON
06 Registrar ... Mrs. Betsy LLOYD
26 Public Information Office ... Mr. Dan GRUBB
37 Dir Financial Aid/Veteran Services ... Ms. Marleen POWELL
08 Director Library Services ... Ms. Donna ODOM
102 Foundation Director ... Mrs. Lisa TURLINGTON
15 Personnel Ofcr/Exec Asst to Pres ... Mrs. Frankie K. SUTTER

*Sandhills Community College (E)

3395 Airport Road, Pinehurst NC 28374-8283
County: Moore FICE Identification: 002961
Unit ID: 199634
Telephone: (910) 692-6185 Carnegie Class: Assoc/MT-VT-Mix Trad/Non
FAX Number: (910) 695-1823 Calendar System: Semester
URL: www.sandhills.edu
Established: 1963 Annual Undergrad Tuition & Fees (In-State): $2,598
Enrollment: 3,853 Coed
Affiliation or Control: State IRS Status: 501(c)3
Highest Offering: Associate Degree
Accreditation: SC, COARC, EMT, MLTAD, POLYT, RAD, SURGT

02 President ... Dr. John R. DEMPSEY
03 Executive Vice President ... Ms. Brenda JACKSON
05 VP of Academic Affairs ... Dr. Rebecca ROUSH
32 VP of Student Services ... Mrs. Kellie SHOEMAKE
51 VP of Continuing Education ... Ms. Andrea KORTE
88 VP College Initiatives ... Mr. Ron LANE
15 Assoc VP Human Resources ... Ms. Wendy B. DODSON
35 Dean of Student Services ... Mr. David FARMER
04 Exec Assistant to the President ... Ms. Heather LYONS
10 Chief Financial Officer ... Ms. Elizabeth THOMAS
20 Dean of Instruction ... Ms. Linda CHANDLER
09 Dean of Institutional Plng/Rsrch ... Dr. Kristie SULLIVAN
102 Exec Director of SCC Foundation ... Ms. Germaine ELKINS
08 Dean of Learning Resources ... Vacant
06 Director of Records & Registration ... Ms. Jean BLUE
37 Financial Aid Officer ... Ms. Lindsey FARMER
106 Director of Distance Learning ... Ms. Wendy KAUFFMAN
13 Chief Information Officer ... Mr. Roderick BROWER
19 Director of Security/Safety ... Mr. Dwight THREET
18 Director of Facilities ... Mr. Doug SMITH
21 Dir Finance & Student Accounts ... Mr. Joseph BROWN
26 Director of Marketing and PR ... Ms. Karen MANNING
40 Bookstore Manager ... Ms. Sandra DALES
07 Director of Admissions ... Ms. Cary GREENE

*South Piedmont Community College (F)

PO Box 126, Polkton NC 28135-0126
County: Anson/Union FICE Identification: 007985
Unit ID: 197850
Telephone: (704) 272-5300 Carnegie Class: Assoc/MT-VT-High Non
FAX Number: (704) 272-5350 Calendar System: Semester
URL: www.spcc.edu
Established: 1999 Annual Undergrad Tuition & Fees (In-District): $1,873
Enrollment: 2,608 Coed
Affiliation or Control: State/Local IRS Status: 501(c)3
Highest Offering: Associate Degree
Accreditation: SC, DMS, EMT, MAC

02 President ... Dr. Maria PHARR
05 Vice Pres Academic Affairs/CAO ... Vacant
10 VP Finance/Administrative Svcs/CFO ... Ms. Michelle BROCK
32 Vice Pres Student Services ... Mrs. Elaine CLODFELTER
31 Vice Pres Community/Corporate Rels ... Mr. Dan MERLE
30 VP Inst Advancement/SPCC Foundation ... Vacant
04 Exec Assistant to President ... Ms. Sarah NICHOLS
15 Assoc VP Human Res/Payroll/Org Dev ... Ms. Lauren SELLERS
21 Asst Vice Pres Finance/Admin Svcs ... Mr. Richard ASHLEY
13 Int Asst VP Info Tech Svcs/CIO ... Ms. Natisha GIVENS
18 Asst VP of Facilities ... Mr. William M. TRUETT
108 Assoc VP Planning/IE ... Ms. Jill MILLARD
49 Dean School of Arts & Science ... Mr. Carl BISHOP
76 Dean Allied Health ... Ms. Alice BRADLEY
66 Dean Nursing ... Ms. Alice BRADLEY
72 Dean Applied Science & Technology ... Dr. Maria LANDER
84 Dean of Enrollment Services ... Mr. John RATLIFF
35 Dean of Student Development ... Ms. Makena STEWART
06 Registrar ... Ms. Cathy HORNE
08 Director Library Services ... Mr. Grant LEFOE
88 Director of Basic Skills ... Ms. Kelly STEGALL
16 Director Human Resources ... Ms. Linda KAPPAUF
38 Director of Counseling ... Vacant
36 Director of Advising/QEP ... Ms. Jessica YOUNG
35 Director Student Engagement ... Mr. Michael MAFFUCCI
44 Development Officer ... Ms. Gina RHODES
25 Dir Corporate/Community Development ... Mr. Scott COLLIER
26 Dir Marketing/Public Info Ofcr ... Mr. Michael MCALLISTER
09 Dir Institutional Research/Analyst ... Ms. Christine TEACH

*Southeastern Community College (G)

4564 Chadbourn Highway, PO Box 151, Whiteville NC 28472-0151
County: Columbus FICE Identification: 002964
Unit ID: 199722
Telephone: (910) 642-7141 Carnegie Class: Assoc/HVT-High Non
FAX Number: (910) 642-5658 Calendar System: Semester
URL: www.sccnc.edu
Established: 1964 Annual Undergrad Tuition & Fees (In-State): $2,589
Enrollment: 1,348 Coed
Affiliation or Control: State IRS Status: 501(c)3
Highest Offering: Associate Degree
Accreditation: SC, MLTAD

02 President ... Dr. Anthony CLARKE
10 Vice President Administrative Svcs ... Mr. Daniel FIGLER
05 Vice Pres Academic Affairs ... Ms. Lauren G. COLE
103 VP Workforce & Cmty Development ... Ms. Beverlee S. NANCE
32 Exec Dean Stdnt Svcs/Title IX Dpty ... Ms. Sylvia COX
76 Dean Allied Hlth/Sci/Fine Arts/Math ... Dr. James HUTCHERSON
08 Librarian ... Ms. Kay HOUSER
30 Director Institutional Advancement ... Ms. Lisa CLARK
15 Director Human Resources ... Mr. Bill MAULTSBY
21 Controller ... Ms. Donna TURBEVILLE
26 Director Marketing & Outreach ... Ms. Liz MCLEAN
13 Director of Information Technology ... Mr. Jason STRICKLAND
51 Director of Continuing Education ... Ms. Brenda ORDERS
37 Director of Financial Aid ... Vacant
06 Dir of Student Records/Registrar ... Ms. Sylvia MCQUEEN
36 Director of Counseling ... Ms. Julia ROBERTS
09 Research & Reporting Coordinator ... Mr. Don WHITE

*Southwestern Community College (H)

447 College Drive, Sylva NC 28779-8581
County: Jackson FICE Identification: 008466
Unit ID: 199731
Telephone: (828) 339-4000 Carnegie Class: Assoc/MT-VT-High Non
FAX Number: (828) 586-3129 Calendar System: Semester
URL: www.southwesterncc.edu
Established: 1964 Annual Undergrad Tuition & Fees (In-District): $2,213
Enrollment: 2,469 Coed
Affiliation or Control: State/Local IRS Status: 501(c)3
Highest Offering: Associate Degree
Accreditation: SC, CAHIIM, COARC, DMS, EMT, MAC, MLTAD, OTA, PHLEB, PTAA, RAD

02 President ... Dr. Don L. TOMAS
05 Exec VP Instructional/Student Svcs ... Dr. Thom R. BROOKS
10 VP for Financial & Admin Services ... Mr. William BROTHERS
13 VP Information Technology ... Mr. Scott BAKER
30 Exec Dir Institutional Development ... Ms. Lynda W. PARLETT
103 Dean of Workforce/Economic Devel ... Mr. Jason LAMBERT
12 Dean Macon Campus ... Dr. Cheryl DAVIDS
32 Dean of Students ... Ms. Cheryl CONTINO-CONNER
06 Dir Student Records/Registrar ... Ms. Clyanne HYDE
08 Library Director ... Mrs. Dianne LINDGREN
09 Director Inst Research & Planning ... Mr. Jonathan E. DEAN
37 Financial Aid Director ... Ms. Melody L. LAWRENCE
26 Director of Public Relations ... Mr. Tyler GOODE
102 Director of SCC Foundation ... Mr. Brett WOODS
84 Director of Enrollment Management ... Mr. Martin AUCOIN
18 Chief Facilities/Physical Plant ... Ms. Lisa SIZEMORE

*Stanly Community College (I)

141 College Drive, Albemarle NC 28001-7458
County: Stanly FICE Identification: 011194
Unit ID: 199740
Telephone: (704) 982-0121 Carnegie Class: Assoc/MT-VT-High Non
FAX Number: (704) 982-0819 Calendar System: Semester
URL: www.stanly.edu
Established: 1971 Annual Undergrad Tuition & Fees (In-District): $2,661

Enrollment: 2,644 Coed
Affiliation or Control: State/Local IRS Status: 501(c)3
Highest Offering: Associate Degree
Accreditation: SC, COARC, MAC, MLTAD, RAD

02 President .... Dr. John ENAMAIT
05 Exec VP of Educational Services .... Mrs. Robin MCCREE
32 VP Student Success/Dean of Students .... Dr. Myra FURR
10 VP Administrative Services/CFO .... Vacant
76 Assoc VP Health & Public Svcs .... Dr. Tammy CRUMP
50 Assoc VP Business & Technology .... Mrs. Merlin AMIRTHARAJ
04 Exec Aide to Pres/Governmental Affs .... Mrs. Ashley SMITH
37 Dean Financial Aid Management .... Ms. Petra FIELDS
84 Dean of Enrollment Management .... Mr. Patrick HOLYFIELD
36 Asst Dean Students/Career Placement .... Mr. Marcus PRYOR
06 Dir Registration/Stdnt Information .... Ms. Michelle POPLIN
26 Director Marketing & Communication .... Mrs. Michelle PEIFER
07 Director of Admissions .... Ms. Jeania MARTIN
21 Controller .... Mrs. Catherine BIBY
18 Director of Facilities Services .... Mr. Blake BOSTIC
102 Exec Director of SCC Foundation .... Ms. Christy BOGLE
15 Human Resources Officer .... Mrs. Lori POPLIN
08 Director Library Services .... Mrs. Erin ALLEN
24 Media Specialist Services .... Mr. Mark SAMPLE
96 Purchasing Agent .... Mrs. Shelley OSBORNE

*Surry Community College (A)

630 S Main Street, Dobson NC 27017-0304
County: Surry FICE Identification: 002970
Unit ID: 199768
Telephone: (336) 386-8121 Carnegie Class: Assoc/MT-VT-Mix Trad/Non
FAX Number: (336) 386-8951 Calendar System: Semester
URL: www.surry.edu
Established: 1964 Annual Undergrad Tuition & Fees (In-State): $2,540
Enrollment: 3,385 Coed
Affiliation or Control: State IRS Status: 501(c)3
Highest Offering: Associate Degree
Accreditation: SC, MAC, PTAA

02 President .... Dr. David R. SHOCKLEY
05 Vice Pres Curriculum Programs .... Dr. Jami WOODS
10 Vice President for Finance .... Mr. Tony L. MARTIN
45 Vice Pres Institutional Effective .... Dr. Anne R. HENNIS
51 VP Corporate & Cont Education .... Dr. George O. SAPPENFIELD
13 Vice President Technology Services .... Dr. Candace HOLDER
15 Director Personnel Services .... Ms. Melonie WEATHERS
18 Chief Facilities/Physical Plant .... Mr. Randy ROGERS
19 Director Security/Safety .... Mr. Marty SHROPSHIRE
26 Chief Public Relations/Marketing .... Ms. Julie PHARR
41 Athletic Director .... Mr. Mark TUCKER

*Tri-County Community College (B)

21 Campus Circle, Murphy NC 28906-7919
County: Cherokee FICE Identification: 009430
Unit ID: 199795
Telephone: (828) 837-6810 Carnegie Class: Assoc/HT-High Non
FAX Number: (828) 837-0028 Calendar System: Semester
URL: www.tricountycc.edu
Established: 1964 Annual Undergrad Tuition & Fees (In-State): $2,363
Enrollment: 1,082 Coed
Affiliation or Control: State IRS Status: 501(c)3
Highest Offering: Associate Degree
Accreditation: SC, EMT

02 President .... Dr. Donna TIPTON-ROGERS
05 VP Instruction/Institution Effect .... Dr. Steve WOOD
10 VP for Business & Finance .... Mr. Bill VESPASIAN
45 VP College & Community Initiatives .... Mr. Bo GRAY
13 Dir of Computing & Information Mgt .... Mr. Jason OUTEN
88 Coordinator Recruitment/Retention .... Ms. Samantha Major JONES
103 Dir of Economic & Workforce Develop .... Mr. Paul WORLEY
12 Asst to Pres Graham Cty Operations .... Ms. Charlene WOOD
88 Dean Research & Planning/EC Liaison .... Dr. Jason CHAMBERS
15 Director of Human Resources .... Ms. Sallie BAKER
91 Systems Administrator/Data Base Mgr .... Mr. Randy GUYETTE
08 Dean Learning Resources .... Ms. Linda KRESSAL
106 Learning Mgt Systems Administrator .... Mr. Donnie MORROW
30 Dir Foundation/Coord Instl Advance .... Mr. Roarke ARROWOOD
06 Registrar Curriculum .... Ms. Holly HYDE
37 Director of Financial Aid .... Ms. Diane OWL
96 Purchasing Agent .... Ms. Judy OWENBY
84 Director of Enrollment Management .... Ms. Lee BEAL
18 Coordinator of Facility Services .... Mr. Tim NICHOLSON

*Vance-Granville Community College (C)

PO Box 917, Henderson NC 27536-0917
County: Vance FICE Identification: 009903
Unit ID: 199838
Telephone: (252) 492-2061 Carnegie Class: Assoc/MT-VT-High Trad
FAX Number: (252) 430-0460 Calendar System: Semester
URL: www.vgcc.edu
Established: 1969 Annual Undergrad Tuition & Fees (In-State): $1,944
Enrollment: 3,257 Coed
Affiliation or Control: State Related IRS Status: 501(c)3
Highest Offering: Associate Degree
Accreditation: SC, CSHSE, MAC, RAD

02 President .... Dr. Stelfanie WILLIAMS
05 Vice Pres of Academic Affairs .... Dr. Angela BALLENTINE
32 Vice Pres of Student Services .... Dr. Levy BROWN
26 VP of Employee & Public Relations .... Ms. Stacey CARTER-COLEY
10 Vice Pres for Finance & Operations .... Mr. Steve GRAHAM
09 VP of Institutional Research & Tech .... Dr. Kenneth A. LEWIS, JR.
12 Dean Franklin County Campus .... Ms. Bobbie Jo C. MAY
12 Dean South Campus .... Ms. Cecilia B. WHEELER
12 Dean Warren County Campus .... Mr. Lyndon HALL
84 Dean of Enrollment and Outreach .... Mr. Jeff ALLEN
27 Director of Communications .... Mr. James EDWARDS
37 Director of Financial Aid .... Ms. Kali BROWN
15 Director of Human Resources .... Ms. Audrey PARKER
08 Director Learning Resources Center .... Ms. Elaine STEM
09 Director of Planning & Research .... Ms. Julie HICKS
18 Director of Plant Operations .... Mr. Jack PUCKETT
121 Director of Student Success .... Ms. Amy O'GEARY
06 Registrar .... Ms. Kathy KTUL
40 Bookstore Manager .... Ms. Sandra NEWTON

*Wake Technical Community College (D)

9101 Fayetteville Road, Raleigh NC 27603-5696
County: Wake FICE Identification: 004844
Unit ID: 199856
Telephone: (919) 866-5000 Carnegie Class: Assoc/HT-Mix Trad/Non
FAX Number: (919) 779-3360 Calendar System: Semester
URL: www.waketech.edu
Established: 1958 Annual Undergrad Tuition & Fees (In-District): $2,768
Enrollment: 21,003 Coed
Affiliation or Control: State/Local IRS Status: 501(c)3
Highest Offering: Associate Degree
Accreditation: SC, ACFEI, ADNUR, DA, DH, MAC, MLTAD, PHLEB, RAD, SURGT

02 President .... Dr. Stephen C. SCOTT
03 Executive Vice President .... Mrs. Gayle GREENE
102 Executive Director of Foundation .... Mr. Matthew B. SMITH
05 VP Curriculum Education Svcs .... Mrs. Sandra L. DIETRICH
32 SVP Enrollment & Student Services .... Mrs. Willa H. JERMAN
103 VP Workforce Continuing Education .... Mr. Anthony CAISON
10 AVP of Financial & Business Svcs .... Mrs. Marla L. TART
18 Facility Engineering Officer .... Mr. Wendell B. GOODWIN
26 VP Communications/Public Relations .... Mrs. Laurie C. CLOWERS
84 AVP Enrollment Services .... Mr. John W. SAPARILAS
15 AVP Human Res and Title IX Coord .... Ms. Benita I. CLARK
19 Chief of Police .... Mr. Michael A. PENRY
10 VP Finance/Business Services .... Ms. Marla TART
46 Dean IE/Accreditation & Research .... Dr. John B. BOONE
30 Sr Dir Foundation Rels/Admin .... Mrs. Stephanie S. LAKE
25 Dean Sponsored Programs .... Mr. Richard W. SULLINS
06 Dean/Curriculum Registrar .... Ms. Holly Elaine SWART
35 Dean Student Dev/Stdnt Conduct Ofcr .... Mr. Mark T. GIBSON
72 Dean Educ Svcs & Technology .... Mr. Ray L. TIMS
37 Dean Financial Aid/Veterans Affairs .... Mrs. Regina M. HUGGINS
35 Sr Dean Strat Innovations Sp Proj .... Mrs. Karen B. PHINAZEE
20 AVP Student Services .... Mr. Kevin A. BROWN
07 Associate Dean Admissions .... Ms. Tina P. CARTER
12 Dean Public Safety Education Campus .... Ms. Angela J. MIZELLE
27 Dir Communications Ops/Brand Mgmt .... Mrs. Francie W. SANDERSON
36 Assoc Dean Career & Empl Resources .... Mrs. Lynn E. KAVCSAK
76 Dean Health Sciences Campus .... Dr. Molly CURRY
81 Dean Mathematics/Sciences Div .... Ms. Sharon L. WELKER
79 Dean Arts/Humanities/Soc Sci Div .... Dr. Rebecca NEAGLE
50 Dean Business & Public Svcs Tech .... Mr. Walter MARTIN
75 Dean Applied Engr & Technologies .... Ms. Patricia A. GODIN
88 Sr Dean Instructional Support .... Mr. James A. ROBERSON
77 Dean Computer Technologies .... Ms. Angela L. BEQUETTE
88 AVP CE Open Enrollment .... Mrs. Monica P. GEMPERLEIN

*Wayne Community College (E)

3000 Wayne Memorial Drive Box 8002, Goldsboro NC 27533-8002
County: Wayne FICE Identification: 002980
Unit ID: 199892
Telephone: (919) 735-5151 Carnegie Class: Assoc/MT-VT-Mix Trad/Non
FAX Number: (919) 739-7137 Calendar System: Semester
URL: www.waynecc.edu
Established: 1957 Annual Undergrad Tuition & Fees (In-District): $2,524
Enrollment: 3,363 Coed
Affiliation or Control: State/Local IRS Status: 501(c)3
Highest Offering: Associate Degree
Accreditation: SC, ADNUR, DA, DH, MAC, MLTAD, PNUR

02 President .... Dr. Thomas A. WALKER, JR.
05 VP Academic and Student Services .... Dr. Gene SMITH
10 VP Finance/Chief Financial Officer .... Mrs. Joy KORNEGAY
11 Vice Pres Administrative Services .... Mr. Don MAGOON
45 VP Inst Effectiveness/Innovation .... Dr. Tracey IVEY
32 AVP Academic and Student Services .... Ms. Joanna MORRISETTE
51 AVP Continuing Education Services .... Ms. Renita DAWSON
15 AVP Human Res/Safety/Compliance .... Mr. Charles GAYLOR, IV
72 Division Dean Applied Technologies .... Dr. Ernie WHITE
49 Division Dean Arts & Sciences .... Dr. Brandon JENKINS
101 Asst Sec to the Board of Trustees .... Mrs. Leasa O. HOLMES
50 Div Dean Business & Computer Tech .... Ms. Tracy SCHMELTZER
76 Div Dean Allied Health/Public Svc .... Dr. Pattie PFEIFFER
88 Division Dean Public Safety .... Ms. Beverly DEANS
08 Director Library Services .... Dr. Ruth Aletha ANDREW
12 Coordinator Seymour Johnson AFB .... Mrs. Dori FRASER
92 Honors Program Coordinator .... Mr. Brandon JENKINS
106 Distance Education Specialist .... Mr. Randall SHEARON
26 Director Office of Communications .... Mr. Brent HOOD
13 Director Information Technology .... Mr. Matt BAUER
18 Facility Operations Superintendent .... Mr. Edward E. FARRIS
19 Chief Campus Police & Security .... Chief Willie L. BRINSON
40 Manager Bookstore .... Mrs. Trellie HERRING
103 Ex Dir Wayne Bus/Indus Ctr & WORKS .... Mr. Craig FOUCHT
07 Director Admissions & Records .... Ms. Jennifer MAYO
37 Director Student Financial Aid .... Mrs. Brenda D. MERCER
36 Director College & Career Promise .... Mrs. Lorie WALLER
78 Director Cooperative Programs .... Ms. Lorie WALLER
35 Student Activities Coordinator .... Ms. Paige HAM
96 Director Purchasing & Equipment .... Mr. Mark R. JOHNSON
102 Executive Director of Foundation .... Mrs. Adrienne NORTHINGTON
26 Public Information Officer .... Ms. Tara HUMPHRIES
15 Director Human Resources .... Ms. Melanie BELL
04 Senior Executive Asst to President .... Mrs. Leasa O. HOLMES

*Western Piedmont Community College (F)

1001 Burkemont Avenue, Morganton NC 28655-4504
County: Burke FICE Identification: 002982
Unit ID: 199908
Telephone: (828) 438-3500 Carnegie Class: Assoc/MT-VT-Mix Trad/Non
FAX Number: (828) 438-6015 Calendar System: Semester
URL: www.wpcc.edu
Established: 1964 Annual Undergrad Tuition & Fees (In-State): $2,577
Enrollment: 1,950 Coed
Affiliation or Control: State IRS Status: 501(c)3
Highest Offering: Associate Degree
Accreditation: SC, ADNUR, DA, MAC, MLTAD

02 President .... Dr. Michael S. HELMICK
05 VP Academic & Student Success .... Ms. Rhia M. CRAWFORD
10 VP Admin Svcs/Chief Financial Ofcr .... Ms. Sandra K. HOILMAN
26 VP External Affairs & Workforce Dev .... Mr. Atticus J. SIMPSON
103 Dean Workforce Dev & Cont Educ .... Mr. Lee KISER
32 Dean of Student Services .... Ms. Susan WILLIAMS
08 Library Director .... Ms. Nancy DANIEL
54 Dean HEAT .... Mr. Michael DANIELS
49 Dean Arts & Sciences .... Ms. Ann Marie MCNEELY
50 Dean Business/PS/Academic Support .... Ms. Leslie MCKESSON
21 Controller .... Vacant
06 Director Records & Registration .... Mrs. Joan P. HOGAN
15 Director Human Resources .... Ms. Lisa H. SESSIONS
84 Director Enrollment Management .... Mrs. Jennifer PROPST
37 Director Student Financial Aid .... Ms. Dori BARRON
13 Director Management Info Systems .... Ms. Nancy E. NORRIS
09 Director Inst Research/Eval .... Ms. Susan A. BERLEY
96 Director of Purchasing .... Ms. Linda CARSWELL
18 Director of Maintenance .... Vacant
04 Exec Admin Asst to President .... Ms. Kathy F. DURHAM

*Wilkes Community College (G)

1328 S Collegiate Drive, Wilkesboro NC 28697-0120
County: Wilkes FICE Identification: 002983
Unit ID: 199926
Telephone: (336) 838-6100 Carnegie Class: Assoc/HT-Mix Trad/Non
FAX Number: (336) 903-3219 Calendar System: Semester
URL: www.wilkescc.edu
Established: 1965 Annual Undergrad Tuition & Fees (In-State): $2,572
Enrollment: 2,636 Coed
Affiliation or Control: State IRS Status: 501(c)3
Highest Offering: Associate Degree
Accreditation: SC, COARC, DA, MAC, RAD

02 President .... Dr. Jeff A. COX
05 VP of Instruction .... Ms. Blair HANCOCK
10 Senior VP of Administration .... Mr. D. Morgan FRANCIS, JR.
32 VP of Instr Support/Student Svcs .... Ms. Kim E. FAW
103 Applied Career Technologies .... Mr. Ronald DOLLYHITE
13 Assoc VP Information Technology .... Mr. Mike WINGLER
51 VP WDCE/Ashe Campus .... Mr. Christopher D. ROBINSON
12 Director Alleghany Center .... Ms. Susan NILO
09 Inst Effectiveness Exec Director .... Mr. J. Kelly PIPES, III
50 Dean Business/Public Svc Tech Div .... Mrs. Kristen MACEMORE
76 Dean Health Sciences Division .... Mr. Billy WOODS
18 Exec Director/Facilities Services .... Mr. Morgan FRANCIS
30 Exec Director Development .... Ms. Allison PHILLIPS
15 Director of Human Resources .... Ms. Sherry P. COX
06 Registrar .... Mr. Michael WARD
35 Dean of Student Services .... Mr. Scott JOHNSON
37 Director of Financial Aid .... Ms. Roberta HARLESS
38 Director Counseling & Career Svcs .... Dr. Lynda K. BLACK
16 Director Career & Talent Develop .... Mr. Curt MILLER
08 Director Learning Resources .... Ms. Christy EARP
38 Director SAGE .... Mr. John CANTY
40 Bookstore Manager .... Ms. Kelly CHURCH
26 Public Info & Relations Officer .... Ms. Amber HERMAN
19 Chief of Police/Campus Police Dept .... Mr. Jamie MCGUIRE
04 Executive Asst to President .... Ms. Cynthia ALFORD
96 Purchasing Agent .... Ms. Kim BARFIELD
07 Director of Admissions .... Ms. Elisabeth BLEVINS

*Wilson Community College (H)

PO Box 4305, Wilson NC 27893-0305
County: Wilson FICE Identification: 004845
Unit ID: 199953
Telephone: (252) 291-1195 Carnegie Class: Assoc/MT-VT-High Non
FAX Number: (252) 243-7148 Calendar System: Semester

URL: www.wilsoncc.edu
Established: 1958 Annual Undergrad Tuition & Fees (In-State): $2,552
Enrollment: 1,786 Coed
Affiliation or Control: State IRS Status: 501(c)3
Highest Offering: Associate Degree
Accreditation: SC, SURGT

02 President .... Dr. Tim WRIGHT
05 Vice Pres for Academic Affairs .... Mr. Robert HOLSTEN
10 Vice Pres for Finance & Admin Svcs .... Mr. Hadie C. HORNE
09 Director of Institutional Effective .... Mr. Andrew WALKER
51 Exec Dean of Cont Educ .... Ms. Kim GAMLIN
32 Exec Dean of Student Development .... Ms. Amy NOEL
76 Dean of Allied Health & Sciences .... Ms. Glenda P. BONDURANT
50 Dean of Business & Applied Tech .... Mr. Wes HILL
72 Dean of Industrial Technologies .... Ms. Margie NORFLEET
15 Director of Human Resources .... Ms. Kathy WILLIAMSON
08 Head Librarian .... Mr. Gerry J. O'NEILL
21 Controller .... Ms. Jessica S. JONES
06 Dir of Enrollment Svcs/Registrar .... Ms. Jennifer GONYEA
07 Director of Admissions .... Mr. Joshua HARRIS
18 Director of Facilities .... Mr. Ray OWENS
37 Dir of Financial Aid/Vet Affairs .... Ms. Lisa BAKER
111 Director of Institutional Advance .... Ms. Renee WATKEVICH
13 Director of IT .... Ms. Susan WEEKLEY
96 Purchasing & Capital Projects Mgr .... Ms. Donna A. TURNER
40 Bookstore Manager .... Ms. Kaschia SPELLS

North Carolina Wesleyan College (A)

3400 N Wesleyan Boulevard,
Rocky Mount NC 27804-8630
County: Nash FICE Identification: 002951
Unit ID: 199209
Telephone: (252) 985-5100 Carnegie Class: Bac-Diverse
FAX Number: (252) 985-5231 Calendar System: 4/1/4
URL: www.ncwc.edu
Established: 1956 Annual Undergrad Tuition & Fees: $29,150
Enrollment: 2,119 Coed
Affiliation or Control: United Methodist IRS Status: 501(c)3
Highest Offering: Baccalaureate
Accreditation: SC, CAEPN

01 President .... Dr. Dewey CLARK
05 Interim Provost/VP Academic Affairs .... Dr. Evan DUFF
10 Vice President of Finance .... Mr. Jason EDWARDS
111 Vice President of Advancement .... Mr. Eddie COATS
84 Vice President of Enrollment .... Mrs. Judy ROLLINS
32 VP Student Affairs/Dean of Students .... Mr. Edward NAYLOR
15 Vice President of Human Services .... Mr. Tim OZMENT
09 Chief Planning & Research Officer .... Dr. Larry H. KELLEY
06 Registrar .... Mrs. Candace CASHWELL
08 Director of Library .... Ms. Esther BURGESS
26 Director of Communications .... Vacant
23 Director Health Services .... Ms. Jessica BRYS-WILSON
36 Director of Career Services .... Mr. Kenny DICKERSON
19 Director of Campus Security .... Mr. J. W. SEARS
41 Director of Athletics .... Mr. John THOMPSON
29 Director Alumni Rels/Annual Fund .... Ms. Rebekah CAIN
21 Controller .... Ms. Suzanne BRACKETT
37 Director of Financial Aid .... Ms. Elena KOUTOUZOS
16 Director of Human Resources .... Mr. Darrell S. WHITLEY
18 Director of Facilities .... Mr. Raymond THOMPSON
07 Assistant Director of Admissions .... Mr. Ben LILLEY
38 Director of Counseling and DSS .... Ms. Lindy KITCHIN
40 Manager College Store .... Mr. Marcus RICH
20 Associate Academic Officer .... Dr. Molly WYATT
108 Director Institutional Assessment .... Dr. Larry H. KELLEY
13 Chief Info Technology Officer (CIO) .... Mr. Gregory BOYKIN
39 Director Student Housing .... Ms. Jesse LANGLEY
50 Chair Business .... Dr. Jackie LEWIS

Pfeiffer University (B)

48380 US Highway 52 N / PO Box 960,
Misenheimer NC 28109-0960
County: Stanly FICE Identification: 002955
Unit ID: 199306
Telephone: (704) 463-1360 Carnegie Class: Masters/L
FAX Number: (704) 463-1363 Calendar System: Semester
URL: www.pfeiffer.edu
Established: 1885 Annual Undergrad Tuition & Fees: $28,995
Enrollment: 1,624 Coed
Affiliation or Control: United Methodist IRS Status: 501(c)3
Highest Offering: Master's
Accreditation: SC, ACBSP, CAEPN, MFCD, MUS, NURSE

01 President .... Dr. Colleen PERRY KEITH
04 Executive Assistant to President .... Ms. Teena P. MAULDIN
13 CIO .... Dr. Kenneth RUSSELL
10 Vice President for Finance/CFO .... Mr. Jeffrey B. PLYLER
05 Provost/VP Academic Affairs .... Dr. Tracy Y. ESPY
32 VP Student Affairs/Dean of Students .... Mr. Ron LAFFITTE
111 Vice Pres Inst Advancement .... Mr. Robert FUZY
84 Vice Pres for Enrollment .... Ms. Catherine HURD
41 Vice Pres Athletics .... Mr. Bob REASSO
06 Registrar .... Ms. Lourdes SILVA
84 Director of Enrollment Operations .... Vacant
15 Director of Human Resources .... Ms. Twyla KIDD
09 Exec Director IR/Plng & Research ..... Ms. Mary Ellen GOLDSTEIN
26 Director of Inst Communications .... Ms. Susan G. MESSINA
38 Director of Counseling .... Mr. Barry KEITH
08 Director of the Library .... Ms. Lara LITTLE
37 Exec Director of Financial Aid .... Ms. Frances KING
14 Director Information Technology .... Ms. Julie KENNERLY
07 Director of Undergrad Admissions .... Ms. Emily CARELLA
121 Dir of Academic Support Services .... Dr. Jim E. GULLEDGE
19 Dir of Campus Safety & Security .... Mr. Erik MCGINNIS
18 Director of Facilities .... Ms. Sharon K. BARD
42 University Chaplain .... Rev. Maegan HABICH
36 Director of Career Development .... Ms. Caroline SAWYER
39 Director of Residence Life .... Ms. Regina SIMMONS
58 Director of MCE Program .... Rev. Kathleen KILBOURNE
30 Exec Dir of Institutional Advance .... Ms. JoEllen NEWSOME
29 Director of Alumni Affairs .... Ms. Amy BUNTING
112 Advisor Planned Giving .... Mr. John LELFER
39 Asst Director of Residence Life .... Ms. Jill ROGERS
40 Bookstore Manager .... Ms. Dechelle ELLIS
104 Coord of Intl Studies/Study Abroad .... Ms. Rebecca HRACZO
50 Int Dean Division of Business .... Dr. Dawn LUCAS
53 Dean Division of Education .... Dr. Dawn LUCAS
49 Dean Division of Arts & Sciences .... Dr. Marilyn SUTTON-HAYWOOD
76 Dean Div of Applied Health Science .... Ms. Vernease MILLER

Piedmont International University (C)

420 S Broad Street, Winston-Salem NC 27101-5197
County: Forsyth FICE Identification: 002956
Unit ID: 489937
Telephone: (336) 725-8344 Carnegie Class: Spec-4-yr-Faith
FAX Number: (336) 725-5522 Calendar System: Semester
URL: www.piedmontu.edu
Established: 1945 Annual Undergrad Tuition & Fees: $9,650
Enrollment: N/A Coed
Affiliation or Control: Independent Non-Profit IRS Status: 501(c)3
Highest Offering: Doctorate
Accreditation: TRACS

00 Chancellor .... Dr. Howard L. WILBURN
01 President .... Dr. Charles W. PETITT
05 Provost .... Dr. Beth D. ASHBURN
11 Vice President of Operations .... Mr. Chris RONK
73 Vice Pres Temple Baptist Seminary .... Dr. Barkev TRACHIAN
20 VP of Academic Initiatives .... Dr. Byron EDENS
06 Registrar .... Mr. Jeremy BONTRAGER
08 Librarian .... Dr. Catherine CHATMON
32 Director of Student Services .... Mr. Paul SMELTZER
34 Dean of Women .... Mrs. Rebecca BOTTOMS
42 Director of Church Relations .... Mr. Tony WILSON
04 Administrative Asst to President .... Ms. Stephanie MCKAY
07 Director of Admissions .... Ms. Angela HOOVER
37 Financial Aid Director .... Mrs. Mandy MCLAIN
45 Institutional Effectiveness Dir .... Mr. Jeremy PATTISALL

Queens University of Charlotte (D)

1900 Selwyn Avenue, Charlotte NC 28274-0001
County: Mecklenburg FICE Identification: 002957
Unit ID: 199412
Telephone: (704) 337-2200 Carnegie Class: Masters/M
FAX Number: (704) 337-2517 Calendar System: Semester
URL: www.queens.edu
Established: 1857 Annual Undergrad Tuition & Fees: $32,560
Enrollment: 2,286 Coed
Affiliation or Control: Presbyterian Church (U.S.A.) IRS Status: 501(c)3
Highest Offering: Master's
Accreditation: SC, CAEPN, MUS, NURSE

01 President .... Dr. Pamela L. DAVIES
05 VP Academic Affairs & Provost .... Dr. Sarah FATHERLY
30 VP University Advancement .... Mr. James BULLOCK
26 VP Strategy & HR/Title IX Coord .... Ms. Rebecca ANDERSON
45 VP Campus Planning .... Mr. Bill NICHOLS
10 CFO & VP for Administration .... Mr. Matthew PACKEY
49 Dean Col Arts & Sci & Cato Sch Educ .... Dr. John SISKO
50 Dean of McColl School of Business .... Dr. Richard MATHIEU
60 Dean Knight School of Communication .... Vacant
76 Dean Blair College of Health .... Dr. Tama MORRIS
06 Registrar .... Ms. Linda FLEISCHMAN
15 Director of Human Resources .... Ms. Teri ORSINI, SPHR

Reformed Theological Seminary (E)

2101 Carmel Road, Charlotte NC 28226-6399
Telephone: (704) 366-5066 Identification: 666785
Accreditation: &SC, THEOL

† Regional accreditation is carried under the parent institution in Jackson, MS.

St. Andrews University (F)

1700 Dogwood Mile, Laurinburg NC 28352-5598
Telephone: (910) 277-5000 FICE Identification: 002967
Accreditation: &SC

† Regional accreditation is carried under the parent institution, Webber International University, Babson Park, FL.

Saint Augustine's University (G)

1315 Oakwood Avenue, Raleigh NC 27610-2298
County: Wake FICE Identification: 002968
Unit ID: 199582
Telephone: (919) 516-4000 Carnegie Class: Bac-Diverse
FAX Number: (919) 828-0817 Calendar System: Semester
URL: www.st-aug.edu
Established: 1867 Annual Undergrad Tuition & Fees: $17,890
Enrollment: 810 Coed
Affiliation or Control: Protestant Episcopal IRS Status: 501(c)3
Highest Offering: Baccalaureate
Accreditation: #SC

01 President .... Dr. Everett B. WARD
04 Exec Assistant to the President .... Ms. Audrey IVORY
111 VP Inst Advance & Chief Oper Ofcr .... Dr. Steven E. HAIRSTON
05 Provost and VP of Academic Affairs .... Dr. Yvonne COSTON
10 VP for Business & Finance .... Mr. Walter C. DAVENPORT
32 VP Enrollment Mgmt & Student Svcs .... Dr. Gaddis J. FAULCON
11 VP for Administration .... Ms. Sharon M. CHAVIS
09 Assoc Provost/Inst Eff & Planning .... Dr. Orlando E. HANKINS
21 Assoc VP/Comptroller .... Ms. Pamela E. TWITTY
20 Assoc Provost/ADA Coordinator .... Dr. Linda H. CURTIS
15 Acting Director Human Resources .... Ms. Lottie FERRELL
89 Dean of First Year Experience .... Mr. Paul A. NORMAN
34 Dean of Women/Director Student Act .... Ms. Ann BROWN
42 Chaplain .... Rev. Nita BYRD
13 Chief Information Officer .... Mr. Harod C. DEMBY
41 Director Athletics .... Mr. George D. WILLIAMS
06 Registrar .... Ms. Martarash M. TORAIN
50 Dean Business/Mgmt & Technology .... Dr. Kanton REYNOLDS
83 Dean Social and Behavioral Sciences .... Dr. Zaphon WILSON
81 Dean Sciences/Math/Public Health .... Dr. Mark A. MELTON
49 Dean Liberal Arts & Educ .... Vacant
97 Executive Director General College .... Dr. Sevealyn V. SMITH
07 Dean of Enrollment .... Mr. Christopher J. WITHERS
37 Director Financial Aid/Scholarships .... Ms. Barbara M. GRIMM
08 Director of Library Service .... Ms. Tiawanna S. NEVELS
36 Director of Professional Management .... Dr. Cindy LOVE
19 Chief of Police .... Mr. Randy D. NELSON
18 Director Physical Plant .... Mr. Hector F. GALLEGO
29 Director Alumni Affairs .... Ms. Sheryl H. XIMINES
88 Dir of Cmty Develop/Corp Program .... Ms. Bernadine WALDEN
22 Dir Affirmative Action/EEO .... Ms. Jamila A. ORMOND

Salem College (H)

601 South Church Street, Winston-Salem NC 27101
County: Forsyth FICE Identification: 002960
Unit ID: 199607
Telephone: (336) 721-2600 Carnegie Class: Bac-A&S
FAX Number: (336) 917-5339 Calendar System: 4/1/4
URL: www.salem.edu
Established: 1772 Annual Undergrad Tuition & Fees: $27,406
Enrollment: 1,087 Female
Affiliation or Control: Moravian Church IRS Status: 501(c)3
Highest Offering: Master's
Accreditation: SC, CAEPN, MUS

01 President .... Dr. D. E. Lorraine STERRITT
05 VP Acad & Stdnt Affs/Dn of College .... Dr. Susan CALOVINI
111 VP for Institutional Advancement .... Ms. Jennifer L. LYNCH
07 VP for Enrollment/Fin Aid/Comm .... Ms. Katherine K. WATTS
32 Dean of Students .... Ms. Krispin W. BARR
58 Dean of Graduate Studies .... Dr. Sheryl LONG
51 Dean of Continuing Studies .... Dr. Sydney RICHARDSON
20 Dean Undergraduate Studies .... Dr. Richard VINSON
11 VP for Admin/Special Asst to Pres .... Ms. Anna GALLIMORE
08 Director of Libraries .... Ms. Elizabeth NOVICKI
44 Director Annual Giving .... Ms. Felicia CAREY
13 Director Information Technology .... Mr. Kris KELLEY
15 Director of Payroll & Benefits .... Ms. Cheryl HAMILTON
10 Chief Financial Officer .... Mr. Jeremy SHREVE
38 Director Counseling Services .... Dr. Jack LOCICERO
37 Director Student Financial Aid .... Mr. Paul COSCIA
36 Director Career Devel/Internships .... Ms. Monica BOYD
06 Registrar/Dir Inst Research .... Ms. Jeannette RORK
18 Chief Facilities/Physical Plant .... Vacant
29 Director Alumnae Relations .... Ms. Jenny STOKES
21 Accounts Receivable Manager .... Ms. Nikki BROCK
21 Accounts Payable Manager .... Ms. Judy SIGMON
19 Coordinator Institutional Services .... Mr. Tommy WILLIAMSON
04 Executive Asst to President .... Ms. Rosemary L. WHEELER
102 Dir Foundation/Corporate Relations .... Ms. Jennifer MORGAN
41 Athletic Director .... Ms. Melissa BARRETT

Shaw University (I)

118 E South Street, Raleigh NC 27601
County: Wake FICE Identification: 002962
Unit ID: 199643
Telephone: (919) 546-8300 Carnegie Class: Bac-Diverse
FAX Number: (919) 546-8301 Calendar System: Semester
URL: www.shawu.edu
Established: 1865 Annual Undergrad Tuition & Fees: $16,580
Enrollment: 1,646 Coed
Affiliation or Control: Baptist IRS Status: 501(c)3
Highest Offering: Master's
Accreditation: SC, CAEPN, KIN, SW, THEOL

01 Interim President .... Dr. Paulette DILLARD
05 Interim VP for Academic Affairs .... Dr. Renata DUSENBURY
10 Vice Pres for Finance & Admin .... Ms. Gwen KEA
111 Vice Pres Institutional Advancement .... Vacant
32 Vice Pres for Student Affairs .... Dr. Stanley ELLIOTT
84 Chief Enrollment Management Officer .... Mr. Anthony BROOKS
20 Interim Assoc VP Academic Affairs .... Dr. Pamela DENNING

35 Asst VP for Student Affairs ..... Dr. Keith POWELL
15 Director of Human Resources ..... Mr. Lee WOOD
13 Director Information Technology ... Mr. Hooshang FOROUDASTAN
07 Director of Admissions/Recruitment ..... Ms. Stacey SOWELL
06 Registrar ..... Ms. Jody HAMILTON
88 Executive Director of CAPE ..... Dr. Michael WEST
26 Dir Memberships(WSHA) & Public Rel ..... Vacant
08 Int Director of Library Services ..... Mr. Thomas CLARK
45 Director of OSPIRE ..... Vacant
41 Director of Athletics ..... Dr. Alfonza CARTER
38 Director of Counseling Center ..... Ms. Jerelene CARVER
88 Director of Judicial Affairs ..... Ms. Agnes BAXTER
121 Director of Academic Success ..... Ms. Rishard WEDDERBURN
36 Dir Exper Learning/Career Develop ..... Ms. Nikesha ROLLACK
50 Div Head Business & Prof Studies ..... Dr. Mma KALU
53 Div Head Education & Social Work .... Dr. Paula MOTEN-TOLSON
81 Div Head Science & Technology ..... Dr. Doreen CUNNINGHAM
76 Div Head Health & Human Sciences ..... Dr. Vanessa RAYNOR
60 Div Head Communications/Humanities . Dr. Cassandra MITCHELL
83 Interim Div Head Social Sciences ..... Dr. Cynthia GRAHAM
79 Div Head Humanities/Religion & Phil ..... Dr. James KIRKLEY
19 Interim Chief of Police & Security ..... Ms. Sharon HERMAN
18 Manager of Procurement & Contracts ..... Mr. Donald PEARSALL
101 Special Asst to Pres/Board Liaison ..... Dr. Kandace HARRIS
04 Administrative Asst to President ..... Ms. Kendra MOODY
09 Sr Data Analyst/Inst Research Coor ..... Mr. Brian CUMBERBATCH
105 Digital Media Manager ..... Ms. Renee SADDLER
25 Director of Grants ..... Dr. Jared DAUGHERTY
124 Director of Student Retention ..... Mr. Kenneth FRIERSON
29 Director Alumni Relations ..... Mr. Valentino BRYANT
37 Director Student Financial Aid ..... Ms. Russelle KEESE

Shepherds Theological Seminary (A)

6051 Tryon Road, Cary NC 27518-9316
County: Wake FICE Identification: 041730
Unit ID: 461485
Telephone: (919) 573-5350 Carnegie Class: Spec-4-yr-Faith
FAX Number: (919) 573-1438 Calendar System: Semester
URL: www.shepherds.edu
Established: 2003 Annual Graduate Tuition & Fees: N/A
Enrollment: 68 Coed
Affiliation or Control: Independent Non-Profit IRS Status: 501(c)3
Highest Offering: Master's; No Undergraduates
Accreditation: THEOL

01 President ..... Dr. Stephen DAVEY
05 Provost/Dean ..... Dr. Larry PETTEGREW
20 Vice President of Academic Affairs ..... Mr. Edward HERRELKO
111 Vice President of Advancement ..... Dr. Alan POTTER
10 Chief Financial Officer ..... Mr. Ewart HODGINS
07 Director of Recruitment ..... Dr. Douglas BOOKMAN
18 Chief Facilities/Physical Plant ..... Dr. Samuel WINCHESTER
06 Registrar/Financial Aid Officer ..... Mrs. Lucy BURGGRAFF
08 Head Librarian ..... Mr. William COBERLY
19 Director Security/Safety ..... Mr. Ed MANESS

South University (B)

3975 Premier Drive, High Point NC 27265
Telephone: (336) 812-7200 Identification: 770915
Accreditation: &SC, ACBSP, NURSE, PTAA

† Branch campus of South University, Savannah, GA

Southeastern Baptist Theological Seminary (C)

Box 1889, Wake Forest NC 27588-1889
County: Wake FICE Identification: 002963
Unit ID: 199759
Telephone: (919) 761-2100 Carnegie Class: Masters/L
FAX Number: N/A Calendar System: Semester
URL: www.sebts.edu
Established: 1950 Annual Undergrad Tuition & Fees: $10,500
Enrollment: 2,742 Coed
Affiliation or Control: Southern Baptist IRS Status: 501(c)3
Highest Offering: Doctorate
Accreditation: SC, THEOL

01 President ..... Dr. Daniel L. AKIN
05 Provost/Dean of Faculty ..... Dr. Bruce R. ASHFORD
10 Executive VP for Operations ..... Mr. Ryan HUTCHINSON
20 VP Academic Administration ..... Dr. Keith WHITFIELD
111 Vice Pres Institutional Advancement ..... Mr. Art RAINER
32 VP Student Services/Dean Students ..... Dr. Mark LIEDERBACH
04 Administrative Asst to President ..... Mrs. Kim HUMPHREY
06 Registrar ..... Mr. Cody OLDARCE
07 Director of Admissions ..... Dr. Larry LYON
29 Dir Financial/Alumni Development ..... Mr. Jonathan SIX
37 Director of Financial Aid ..... Mr. Jesse PARKER
08 Director Library Services ..... Mr. Jason FOWLER
106 Dir Online Education ..... Mr. Jerry LASSETTER
09 Coord Institutional Research ..... Mr. John STICKLES
13 Director Information Technologies ..... Mr. Wayne JENKS
15 Director Human Resources ..... Mrs. Dawn SATTERWHITE
28 Spec Asst Pres for Diversity ..... Mr. Walter STRICKLAND
39 Director Student Housing ..... Mr. Doug NALLEY
43 General Counsel ..... Mr. George HARVEY

Southeastern Free Will Baptist College (D)

532 Eagle Rock Rd, Box 1960, Wendell NC 27591
County: Wake Identification: 667309
Telephone: (919) 365-7711 Carnegie Class: Not Classified
FAX Number: (919) 365-4940 Calendar System: Semester
URL: sfwbc.edu
Established: 1983 Annual Undergrad Tuition & Fees: N/A
Enrollment: N/A Coed
Affiliation or Control: Free Will Baptist IRS Status: 501(c)3
Highest Offering: Baccalaureate
Accreditation: @TRACS

01 President ..... Rev. Jim MARCUM
05 Academic Dean ..... Dr. Danny BAER
30 Director of Development ..... Rev. Steve BERRY
32 Director of Student Affairs ..... Rev. Ronald DAVIS

Southern Evangelical Seminary (E)

3000 Tilley Morris Road, Matthews NC 28105-8635
County: Union FICE Identification: 036115
Unit ID: 438522
Telephone: (704) 847-5600 Carnegie Class: Not Classified
FAX Number: (704) 845-1747 Calendar System: Semester
URL: www.ses.edu
Established: 1992 Annual Undergrad Tuition & Fees: N/A
Enrollment: N/A Coed
Affiliation or Control: Independent Non-Profit IRS Status: 501(c)3
Highest Offering: Doctorate
Accreditation: TRACS

01 President & COO ..... Dr. Richard D. LAND
05 Academic Dean ..... Dr. J. Thomas BRIDGES
07 Director of Admissions ..... Ms. Dianna NEWMAN
10 Business Manager ..... Mrs. Jennifer DRAKE
08 Librarian ..... Mr. Ronald I. JORDAHL
06 Registrar ..... Dr. Douglas E. POTTER
32 Director Student Services ..... Mrs. Jill JOYNER
13 Dir of Information Technology ..... Mr. Timothy BURKETT
26 Director Communications ..... Mr. Jeff LENHART
04 Executive Asst to President ..... Mrs. Christina S. WOODSIDE
33 Dean of Men ..... Dr. Mel WINSTEAD
88 Director Missions ..... Mr. Adam TUCKER
106 Dir Online Education/E-learning ..... Mr. Jeff LENHART
30 Dir of Institutional Advancement ..... Mr. Eric GUSTAFSON
12 Director of Bible College ..... Dr. Floyd ELMORE

University of Mount Olive (F)

634 Henderson Street, Mount Olive NC 28365-1263
County: Wayne FICE Identification: 002949
Unit ID: 199069
Telephone: (919) 658-2502 Carnegie Class: Bac-Diverse
FAX Number: (919) 658-7180 Calendar System: Semester
URL: www.umo.edu
Established: 1951 Annual Undergrad Tuition & Fees: $19,000
Enrollment: 3,371 Coed
Affiliation or Control: Original Free Will Baptist Church IRS Status: 501(c)3
Highest Offering: Master's
Accreditation: SC, ACBSP, NURSE

01 President ..... Dr. Philip P. KERSTETTER
03 Executive Vice President ..... Dr. Carol G. CARRERE
05 VP for Academic Affairs ..... Dr. Kenneth D. HINES
10 VP for Finance & Administration ..... Mr. John KUNST
84 VP for Enrollment ..... Dr. Barbara R. KORNEGAY
32 VP for Student Affairs ..... Dr. Dan SULLIVAN
111 VP for Institutional Advancement ..... Ms. Teresa HINES
49 Dean School of Arts and Sciences ..... Dr. Burt LEWIS
50 Dean Tillman School of Business ..... Dr. Kathy BEST
56 Dean of Extended Education ..... Dr. Lisa M. NUESELL
08 Director of Library Services ..... Ms. Pamela R. WOOD
12 Director of UMO New Bern ..... Ms. Christy COX
12 Director of UMO Jacksonville ..... Ms. Debbie GASKELL
12 Director of UMO Goldsboro ..... Dr. John P. RUTTER
12 Director of UMO Evening College ..... Dr. John P. RUTTER
12 Director of UMO Wilmington ..... Dr. Marna R. MCMURRY
12 Director UMO Research Triangle Park ..... Mr. Oscar RODRIGUEZ
09 Director Inst Research & Planning ..... Dr. Juliane SANTIAGO
108 Director of Assessment ..... Dr. Ron STEVENS
07 Director of Admissions ..... Mr. Timothy E. WOODARD
06 Registrar ..... Mr. David L. BOURGEOIS
35 Director of Campus Life ..... Ms. Nicole L. GARRETT
36 Director of Career Center ..... Ms. Laurica YANCEY
39 Director of Housing/Resident Life ..... Vacant
26 Director of Public Relations ..... Ms. Rhonda E. JESSUP
102 Dir Foundations & Sponsored Program ..... Ms. Kari SANDER
29 Director of Alumni Relations . Ms. Hope S. MCPHERSON FIELDS
44 Director of Annual Fund ..... Ms. Melinda HOLLAND
37 Director of Financial Aid ..... Ms. Katrina K. LEE
15 Director of Human Resources ..... Ms. Cordelia A. WILCOX
23 Student Health Services ..... Ms. Joanne L. MORGAN
42 Campus Chaplain ..... Ms. Carla WILLIAMSON
04 Assistant to the President ..... Ms. Katherine B. GARDNER
18 Director Building & Grounds ..... Mr. Jeff D. BROGDEN
13 Director Technology Services ..... Mr. Kenneth M. DAVIS, JR.
14 Director Technology Support ..... Mr. Robert R. PRUETT
92 Director Honors Program ..... Dr. Brenda B. CATES
41 VP for Athletics ..... Mr. Jeffrey M. EISEN
20 AVP Acad Affairs/Dean Grad Studies ..... Dr. David DOMMER

*University of North Carolina General Administration (G)

Box 2688, 910 Raleigh Road, Chapel Hill NC 27515-2688
County: Orange FICE Identification: 002971
Unit ID: 199175
Telephone: (919) 962-1000 Carnegie Class: N/A
FAX Number: (919) 962-2751
URL: www.northcarolina.edu

01 President ..... Dr. Margaret SPELLINGS
11 Sr Vice Pres/Chief Operating Ofcr ..... Vacant
100 Chief of Staff ..... Ms. Meredith DIDIER
05 Sr Vice Pres Academic Affairs ..... Dr. Junius GONZALES
10 Sr Vice President Finance/Budget ..... Mr. Jonathan PRUITT
20 VP Academic/Student Affairs ..... Ms. Karrie DIXON
13 Vice Pres Data & Analytics ..... Mr. John LEYDON
43 Sr VP Govt/Legal/Risk/Gen Counsel ..... Mr. Thomas SHANAHAN
46 VP Academic Pgms/Faculty/Research ..... Ms. Kim VAN NOORT
101 Sr Assoc VP/Sec of the University ..... Ms. Andrea POOLE
86 Vice Pres State Govt Relations ..... Mr. Drew MORETZ
86 Vice Pres Federal Relations ..... Ms. Kimrey RHINEHARDT
26 Vice President for Communications ..... Vacant
15 Vice Pres for Human Resources ..... Mr. Matthew BRODY
88 Int VP Intl/Community/Econ Engagmnt ..... Mr. Scott DAUGHERTY

*Appalachian State University (H)

287 Rivers Street, Boone NC 28608-0001
County: Watauga FICE Identification: 002906
Unit ID: 197869
Telephone: (828) 262-2000 Carnegie Class: Masters/L
FAX Number: (828) 262-2347 Calendar System: Semester
URL: www.appstate.edu
Established: 1899 Annual Undergrad Tuition & Fees (In-State): $7,136
Enrollment: 17,932 Coed
Affiliation or Control: State IRS Status: 501(c)3
Highest Offering: Doctorate
Accreditation: SC, ART, CAATE, CACREP, CAEPN, CIDA, CS, DANCE, DIETD, DIETI, IPSY, MFCD, MUS, NRPA, NURSE, SP, SPAA, SW, THEA

02 Chancellor ..... Dr. Sheri N. EVERTS
100 Interim Chief of Staff ..... Mr. Hank T. FOREMAN
05 Provost/Exec Vice Chancellor ..... Dr. Darrell P. KRUGER
10 Vice Chanc Business Affairs ..... Mr. Paul D. FORTE
32 Vice Chanc Student Development ..... Mr. J.J BROWN
30 Vice Chanc Univ Advancement ..... Dr. Randy EDWARDS
20 Vice Provost for Undergrad Educ ..... Dr. Mike W. MAYFIELD
46 Vice Provost for Research ..... Dr. Alan UTTER
26 Sr Assc VC Advance/Chief Comm Ofcr ..... Mr. Hank T. FOREMAN
84 Assoc VC for Enrollment Services ..... Mrs. Susan DAVIES
29 Exec Director of Alumni Affairs ..... Mr. Patrick K. SETZER
43 General Counsel ..... Mr. Dayton T. COLE
13 Chief Information Officer ..... Mr. David E. HAYLER
06 University Registrar ..... Ms. Debbie RACE
38 Dir Counseling/Psychological Svcs ..... Dr. Dan L. JONES
37 Director of Financial Aid ..... Ms. Lori A. TOWNSEND
15 Director of Human Resources ..... Mr. Mark BACHMEIER
09 Int Director Inst Research/Planning ..... Mrs. Heather H. LANGDON
51 Exec Director of Distance Education ..... Dr. Terry RAWLS
41 Director of Athletics ..... Mr. Douglas P. GILLIN
49 Dean for College of Arts & Sciences ..... Dr. Anthony G. CALAMAI
50 Dean for College of Business ..... Dr. Heather NORRIS
53 Dean for College of Education ..... Dr. Melba C. SPOONER
57 Dean for College Fine/Applied Arts .... Dr. Glenda J. TREADAWAY
64 Dean for the School of Music ..... Dr. William L. PELTO
58 Dean of Research/Graduate Studies ..... Dr. Max C. POOLE
08 Interim Dean of Libraries ..... Dr. Mary REICHEL
18 Director of the Physical Plant ..... Mr. Mike J. O'CONNOR
21 Budget Director ..... Mr. Ken W. SMITH
96 Director of Materials Management ..... Mr. Dwayne E. ODVODY
28 Dir Multicultural Student Devel ..... Ms. Traci D. ROYSTER

*East Carolina University (I)

1000 East Fifth Street, Greenville NC 27858-4353
County: Pitt FICE Identification: 002923
Unit ID: 198464
Telephone: (252) 328-6212 Carnegie Class: DU-Higher
FAX Number: (252) 328-4155 Calendar System: Semester
URL: www.ecu.edu
Established: 1907 Annual Undergrad Tuition & Fees (In-State): $6,997
Enrollment: 28,289 Coed
Affiliation or Control: State IRS Status: 501(c)3
Highest Offering: Doctorate
Accreditation: SC, AAFCS, ANEST, ARCPA, ART, AUD, CAATE, CACREP, CAEPN, CAHIIM, CARTE, CEA, CIDA, CLPSY, CONST, DENT, DIETD, DIETI, ENG, ENGR, LIB, MED, MFCD, MIDWF, MT, MUS, NAIT, NRPA, NURSE, OT, PH, PLNG, PTA, SCPSY, SP, SPAA, SW, THEA

02 Chancellor ..... Dr. Cecil P. STATON
100 Chief of Staff ..... Mr. Jim HOPF
05 Provost & Sr VC Academic Affairs ..... Dr. Ron MITCHELSON
32 Vice Chancellor for Student Affairs ..... Dr. Virginia HARDY
17 Vice Chanc Health Sciences ..... Dr. Phyllis N. HORNS
10 Vice Chanc Administration & Finance . Dr. Frederick NISWANDER
111 Vice Chanc Univ Advancement ..... Mr. Christopher DYBA
46 VC Research/Econ Dev/Engagement ..... Dr. Jay GOLDEN
29 VC for Alumni Relations ..... Mr. Heath BOWMAN
39 Assoc VC Camp Liv/Dining ..... Mr. William L. MCCARTNEY, JR.
35 Assoc Vice Chanc & Dean of Stdnts ..... Dr. Lynn M. ROEDER

22 Assoc Provost Equity/Diversity ... Ms. Lakesha ALSTON FORBES
43 Vice Chancellor for Legal Affairs ... Ms. Donna G. PAYNE
09 Associate Provost IPAR ... Dr. Ying ZHOU
41 Athletic Director ... Mr. Jeff COMPHER
13 CIO and Assoc Vice Chanc ITCS ... Mr. Don SWEET
15 Assoc Vice Chanc Human Resources ... Ms. Melissa BARD
18 Assoc VC for Campus Opers ... Mr. William BAGNELL
21 Assoc VC for Business Services ... Mr. A. Scott BUCK
88 Assoc VC Environ Health & Safety ... Mr. Bill KOCH
88 Exec Dir of Global Affairs ... Dr. Jon REZEK
88 Assoc VC for Emerging Acad Init ... Dr. Elmer POE
20 Int Dir Acad Pgm Planning & Develop ... Ms. Rita REAVES
88 Dir of Campus Rec & Wellness ... Mr. William EHLING
84 Assoc Provost for Enrollment Svcs ... Dr. John FLETCHER
26 Ex Dir Communication/Pub Affs/Mktg ... Mr. Tom EPPES
07 Director of Admissions ... Dr. Dave MEREDITH
06 Registrar ... Ms. Angela R. ANDERSON
08 Director JY Joyner Library ... Ms. Jan LEWIS
88 Int Dir Health Sciences Library ... Ms. Beth KETTERMAN
101 Asst Secretary to Board of Trustees ... Dr. Steve DUNCAN
37 Director of Financial Aid ... Ms. Julie POORMAN
19 Interim Chief of Police ... Mr. Jason SUGG
51 Director of Continuing Studies ... Mr. Anthony BRITT
27 Director of University Marketing ... Mr. Clint BAILEY
27 Director of Publications ... Mr. Jimmy ROSTAR
88 Director of Military Programs ... Mr. Tim WISEMAN
96 Director of Purchasing ... Mr. Kevin CARRAWAY
36 Director Career Center ... Ms. Leslie ROGERS
116 Director of Internal Audit ... Ms. Stacie TRONTO
21 Interim AVC for Financial Services ... Ms. Dee BOWLING
49 Dean College of Arts & Sciences ... Dr. William DOWNS
76 Dean College of Allied Health ... Dr. Robert ORLIKOFF
68 Dean Col Health/Human Performance ... Dr. Glen G. GILBERT
59 Dean College of Human Ecology ... Dr. Judy SIGUAW
66 Dean College of Nursing ... Dr. Sylvia BROWN
50 Dean College of Business ... Dr. Stanley G. EAKINS
57 Dean Col Fine Arts/Comm ... Dr. Christopher BUDDO
53 Dean College of Education ... Dr. B. Grant HAYES
72 Dean Col of Engineering and Tech ... Dr. David WHITE
58 Dean Graduate School ... Dr. Paul GEMPERLINE
92 Dean Honors College ... Dr. David WHITE
63 Dean Brody School of Medicine ... Dr. Paul R G. CUNNINGHAM
52 Dean School of Dental Medicine ... Dr. Gregory CHADWICK
04 Assistant to Chancellor ... Ms. Christy DANIELS
25 Dir of Grants and Contracts ... Mr. Steve AYERS
86 Director of Strategic Initiatives ... Ms. Michelle BROOKS
102 President/CEO ECU Foundation ... Mr. Chris DYBA
54 Chairperson Engineering ... Dr. Hayden GRIFFIN

*Elizabeth City State University (A)

1704 Weeksville Road, Elizabeth City NC 27909-7806
County: Pasquotank FICE Identification: 002926
Unit ID: 198507
Telephone: (252) 335-3400 Carnegie Class: Masters/S
FAX Number: (252) 335-3731 Calendar System: Semester
URL: www.ecsu.edu
Established: 1891 Annual Undergrad Tuition & Fees (In-State): $4,889
Enrollment: 1,585 Coed
Affiliation or Control: State IRS Status: 501(c)3
Highest Offering: Master's
Accreditation: SC, CAEPN, ENGT, MUS, SW

02 Chancellor ... Dr. Thomas CONWAY, JR.
05 VC Academic Affairs ... Dr. Vann NEWKIRK
20 Assoc VC Academic Affairs ... Dr. Derrick WILKINS
10 VC for Business & Finance/CFO ... Mr. Joshua LASSITER
111 VC for University Advancement ... Dr. John M. LEE, JR.
43 General Counsel ... Mr. Alyn GOODSON
32 Chief Student Affairs Officer ... Mr. Nolan DAVIS
13 Chief Information Officer ... Mr. Suresh MURUGAN
15 Director Human Resources ... Mr. Rafael BONES
41 Athletic Director ... Mr. Derrick JOHNSON
84 Asst VC Enrollment Mgmt ... Vacant
09 Dir Institutional Effectiveness ... Dr. Fred OKANDA
06 Registrar ... Dr. Althea L. RIDDICK
35 Asst VC/Dean of Students ... Ms. Valerie HOLMES
08 Director of Library Services ... Dr. Juanita MIDGETTE
07 Interim Director of Admissions ... Mr. Darius EURE
38 Dir Counsel/Test Student Affairs ... Dr. Jacqueline HUFF
36 Director of Career Services ... Ms. Makitta WHITEHURST-MCLEAN
37 Director Student Financial Aid ... Ms. Jill GABLE
29 Director of Alumni Relations ... Ms. Barbara B. SUTTON
18 Director of Facilities/Planning ... Mr. Charles HALL
26 Director of Marketing ... Ms. Rhonda HAYES
92 Dir of Honors Pgm/Summer School ... Dr. Kenneth E. JONES
96 Director of Purchasing ... Ms. Rachel HAINES
58 Director of Graduate Education ... Dr. Sharon D. RAYNOR
04 Executive Asst to President ... Ms. Lucretia BANKS
101 Secretary of the Institution/Board ... Ms. Gwendolyn SANDERS
104 Director Study Abroad ... Dr. Glen BOWMAN
105 Director Web Services ... Vacant
106 Dir Online Education/E-learning ... Dr. Kim STEVENSON
100 Chief of Staff ... Vacant
19 Director Security/Safety ... Mr. John MANLEY
39 Director Student Housing ... Ms. Tamnekia GRANT
86 Director Government Relations ... Mrs. Kathryn UNDERWOOD

*Fayetteville State University (B)

1200 Murchison Road, Fayetteville NC 28301-4298
County: Cumberland FICE Identification: 002928
Unit ID: 198543
Telephone: (910) 672-1111 Carnegie Class: Masters/M
FAX Number: (910) 672-1769 Calendar System: Semester
URL: www.uncfsu.edu
Established: 1867 Annual Undergrad Tuition & Fees (In-State): $5,085
Enrollment: 6,104 Coed
Affiliation or Control: State IRS Status: 501(c)3
Highest Offering: Doctorate
Accreditation: SC, ART, CAEPN, CS, FEPAC, MUS, NURSE, SW

02 Chancellor ... Dr. James A. ANDERSON
100 Vice Chancellor and Chief of Staff ... Vacant
05 Provost & Vice Chanc Academic Affs ... Dr. Jon YOUNG
10 Vice Chancellor Business/Finance ... Mr. Carlton SPELLMAN
32 Vice Chancellor Student Affairs ... Dr. Janice HAYNIE
111 Vice Chancellor Inst Advancement ... Mr. Getchel CALDWELL
13 Vice Chanc Info Technology/CIO ... Mr. Arasu GANESAN
30 Interim Vice Chanc for Advancement ... Mr. J. Lea CALLAWAY
35 Assoc Vice Chanc Student Affairs ... Dr. Juanette COUNCIL
18 Assoc Vice Chanc Facilities Mgmt ... Mr. Jon PARSONS
21 Asst VC Business/Financ/Controller ... Ms. Christine M. JUMALON
15 Assoc Vice Chanc Human Resources ... Ms. Terri TIBBS
85 Asst VC Acad Affs/Interntl Studies ... Dr. Chen YUNKAI
88 Senior Assoc Vice Chancellor ... Dr. Perry A. MASSEY
45 Assoc VC Pgms/Plng/Assessment ... Vacant
36 Director Career Svcs & Bus Mgr SA ... Dr. Curtis STREET
92 Acting Program Director Honors ... Dr. Erin WHITE
06 Registrar ... Ms. Sarah BAKER
29 Director of Alumni Affairs ... Ms. YaKima RHINEHART
26 Director Public Relations ... Mr. Jeff WOMBLE
08 Director of Library Services ... Mr. Bobby C. WYNN
07 Director of Admissions ... Ms. Ulisa BOWLES
90 Director of IT Operations ... Ms. Michelle WHITAKER
09 Director Institutional Research ... Dr. Dana DALTON
39 Director of Residence Life ... Mr. Courtney THOMPSON
37 Director Student Financial Aid ... Mrs. Kamesia HOUSE
43 General Counsel ... Mrs. Wanda LESSANE JENKINS
41 Athletic Director ... Mr. Anthony T. BENNETT
96 Director of Purchasing ... Ms. Willie MCINTYRE
38 Dir Center Personal Development ... Mr. Fred SAPP
28 Director of Diversity ... Vacant
88 Dean University College ... Dr. John I. BROOKS
66 Department Chair Nursing ... Dr. Afua ARHIN
50 Dean School Business/Economics ... Dr. Pamela JACKSON
53 Dean School of Education ... Dr. Marion GILLIS-OLION
49 Dean College Arts and Sciences ... Dr. Samuel ADU-MIREKU
101 Secretary of Univ/Board Liaison ... Ms. Suzetta M. PERKINS
19 Acting VC Police & Public Safety ... Capt. Leroy WILLIAMS, JR.
04 Administrative Asst to President ... Mrs. Ann ZOMERFELD
86 Director Government Relations ... Mr. Wesley FOUNTAIN
25 Chief Contracts/Grants Admin ... Ms. Chrystal COOPER

*North Carolina Agricultural and Technical State University (C)

1601 East Market Street, Greensboro NC 27411-0001
County: Guilford FICE Identification: 002905
Unit ID: 199102
Telephone: (336) 334-7500 Carnegie Class: DU-Higher
FAX Number: (336) 334-7136 Calendar System: Semester
URL: www.ncat.edu
Established: 1891 Annual Undergrad Tuition & Fees (In-State): $6,372
Enrollment: 10,852 Coed
Affiliation or Control: State IRS Status: 501(c)3
Highest Offering: Doctorate
Accreditation: SC, AAFCS, CACREP, CAEPN, CONST, CS, ENG, #JOUR, LSAR, MUS, NAIT, NUR, SW, THEA

02 Chancellor ... Dr. Harold L. MARTIN, SR.
05 Provost/Vice Chanc Academic Affairs ... Dr. Joe B. WHITEHEAD, JR.
10 Vice Chanc Business & Finance ... Mr. Robert POMPEY, JR.
100 Chief of Staff ... Ms. Nicole PRIDE
46 Vice Chanc Research/Economic Dev ... Dr. Barry L. BURKS
32 Vice Chancellor of Student Affairs ... Dr. Melody C. PIERCE
15 Vice Chancellor for Human Resources ... Dr. Ericka M. SMITH
13 VC Info Tech Services/CIO ... Mr. H. Thomas JACKSON
43 General Counsel for Legal Affairs ... Dr. J. Charles WALDRUP
111 VC of University Advancement ... Mr. Kenneth E. SIGMON, JR.
20 Vice Prov for Acad Affs/UG Programs ... Dr. G. Scott JENKINS
26 Associate VC University Relations ... Mr. Todd H. SIMMONS
45 Asst VC for Budget & Planning ... Mrs. Chartarra JOYNER
88 Vice Prov Rsrch Grad Pgm/Extnd Lrng ... Dr. Sanjiv SARIN
18 Asst VC for Bus/Finance/Facilities ... Mr. Andrew M. PERKINS, JR.
19 Asst VC Police/Public Safety ... Mr. Charles E. WILSON, JR.
08 Dean of Library Services ... Ms. Vicki COLEMAN
47 Int Dean Agric/Environmental Sci ... Dr. Shirley HYMON-PARKER
49 Int Dean Arts/Human/Soc Sciences ... Dr. Craig RHODES
53 Dean College of Education ... Dr. Anthony GRAHAM
54 Dean College of Engineering ... Dr. Robin N. COGER
58 Dean The Graduate College ... Dr. Sanjiv SARIN
66 Int Dean College Health & Hum Sci ... Dr. Lenora CAMPBELL
50 Dean Col of Business & Economics ... Dr. Beryl MCEWEN
72 Dean Col Science and Technology ... Dr. Abdellah AHMIDOUCH
88 Dean Joint Sch Nanoscience/Nanoengr ... Dr. James G. RYAN
09 Vice Prov Strag Plng & Inst Effect ... Dr. Muktha B. JOST
06 University Registrar ... Mrs. Kelly A. ROWETT JAMES
84 AVC for Enroll Management ... Mrs. Erin HILL HART
37 Director Financial Aid ... Mrs. Sherri M. AVENT
36 Director Career Services ... Ms. Joyce P. EDWARDS
29 Interim Assoc VC for Alumni Affairs ... Ms. Teresa DAVIS
85 Dir International Student Affairs ... Ms. Loreatha D. GRAVES
88 Dir Multicultural Student Center ... Mr. Gerald SPATES
41 Director of Athletics ... Mr. Earl M. HILTON, III
39 Dir Student Housing/Residence Life ... Ms. Linda D. INMAN
23 Phys/Dir Student Health Services ... Dr. David H. WAGNER
38 Director of Counseling Service ... Dr. Vivian D. BARNETTE
25 Director of Contracts/Grants ... Ms. Natalie TEAGLE
92 Director of Honors Program ... Dr. Michael CUNDALL, JR.
96 Interim Director of Purchasing ... Ms. Martinique WILLIAMS
27 Director of Media Relations ... Ms. Tiffany S. JONES
40 Bookstore Manager ... Ms. Michaele WIGGINS
88 Dir Ctr Leadership & Org Excellence ... Ms. Ericka GONZALEZ SMITH
104 Asst Director for Study Abroad ... Mr. Christopher M. BROWN
106 Dir of ITS/Distance Education ... Dr. Tracie O. LEWIS
108 Director Institutional Research ... Dr. Khoi D. TO
22 Dir Affirmative Action/EEO ... Ms. Linda MANGUM
30 Senior Director of Development ... Ms. Carletta SIMMONS
86 Director External Affairs ... Mr. Michael A. BROWN, II

*North Carolina Central University (D)

1801 Fayetteville Street, Durham NC 27707-3129
County: Durham FICE Identification: 002950
Unit ID: 199157
Telephone: (919) 530-6100 Carnegie Class: Masters/L
FAX Number: (919) 530-5014 Calendar System: Semester
URL: www.nccu.edu
Established: 1910 Annual Undergrad Tuition & Fees (In-State): $6,132
Enrollment: 8,011 Coed
Affiliation or Control: State IRS Status: 501(c)3
Highest Offering: Doctorate
Accreditation: SC, #CAATE, CACREP, CAEPN, DIETD, DIETI, LAW, LIB, NRPA, NUR, SP, SW, THEA

02 Chancellor ... Dr. Johnson O. AKINLEYE
05 Interim Provost/VC Academic Affairs ... Dr. Carlton E. WILSON
100 Chief of Staff ... Mr. Wendell F. PHILLIPS
43 General Counsel ... Ms. Hope TYEHIMBA
11 Vice Chanc Admin & Finance ... Mr. Benjamin DURANT
32 Interim VC for Student Affairs ... Dr. Gary L. BROWN
111 Vice Chanc Inst Advancement ... Dr. Harriet F. DAVIS
20 Assoc Provost for Academic Programs ... Dr. Michelle L. MAYO
10 Assoc VC Administration/Finance ... Ms. Yolanda E. BANKS-DEAVER
20 Assoc VC Faculty Develop ... Dr. Yolanda B. ANDERSON
15 Chief Human Resources ... Ms. Sylvia ANDERSON
88 Assoc VC Innovat/Engaged & Global ... Dr. Ontario S. WOODEN
88 Director Student Union ... Mr. Orok OROK
45 Director Strategic Planning ... Mr. Johnnie SOUTHERLAND
35 Assistant VC of Student Affairs ... Mr. Tierney J. BATES
13 Chief Information Officer ... Ms. Leah KRAUS
07 Director Undgraduate Admissions ... Dr. Nicole GIBBS
88 Director of External Affairs ... Ms. Pamela THORPE-YOUNG
06 Registrar ... Dr. Jerome GOODWIN
91 Student Systems Manager ... Ms. Billie HANES
29 Director of Alumni Relations ... Ms. Chatonda COVINGTON
26 Assoc VC for Public Relations ... Ms. Ayana D. HERNANDEZ
37 Director of Financial Aid ... Ms. Sharon J. OLIVER
08 Director Library Services ... Dr. Theodosia T. SHIELDS
19 Interim Chief of University Police ... Mr. Connie M. BULLOCK
121 Assoc Dean Univ Col/Acad Advising ... Dr. Jennifer SCHUM
88 Director Art Museum ... Dr. Kenneth G. RODGERS
39 Director Residential Life ... Mr. James B. LEACH
41 Director Athletics ... Dr. Ingrid L. WICKER-MCCREE
09 Assoc VC Inst Research/Eval/Plng ... Dr. Jeanette BARKER
96 Director of Purchasing ... Ms. Lucy P. GODWIN-HANSON
92 Director of Honors Program ... Dr. Ansel E. BROWN
38 Exec Director of Counseling Center . Dr. Ruth GILLIAM PHILLIPS
22 Director of EEO & Employee Relation ... Ms. Ann PENN
84 Assoc VC Enrollment Management ... Dr. Monica T. LEACH
109 Dir Auxiliaries/Business Services ... Mr. Timothy J. MOORE
40 Manager Bookstore ... Ms. Stephanie L. GETCHELL
58 Dean Sch Grad Stds/Asc VC Grad Rsch ... Dr. Jaleh REZAIE
61 Dean of the Law School ... Ms. Phyliss V. CRAIG-TAYLOR
62 Dean School of Library/Info Science ... Dr. Jon P. GANT
50 Interim Dean School of Business ... Dr. Wanda LESTER
124 Dean of University College ... Dr. David S. HOOD
49 Dean College of Arts and Sciences ... Dr. Veronica C. NWOSU
83 Dean College Behavioral/Social Scis ... Dr. Debra O. PARKER
53 Dean School of Education ... Dr. Audrey W. BEARD
04 Executive Asst to Chancellor ... Ms. Zelda STANFIELD
101 Secretary of the Board of Trustees ... Mr. Wendell F. PHILLIPS
102 Executive Director NCCU Foundation ... Mr. Antonio L. MCDANIEL
104 Asst Director International Affairs ... Dr. Olivia JONES
105 Director Web Services ... Mr. Damond NOLLAN
106 Director Division Extended Studies ... Ms. Kimberly C. PHIFER-MCGHEE
108 Director of Assessment ... Ms. Tia M. DOXEY
25 Director Contracts/Grants Admin ... Ms. Denise Y. WYNN
36 Director Career Services ... Ms. Catrina S. DOSREIS
44 Director Annual Giving ... Ms. Kara ENDSLEY

*North Carolina State University (E)

20 Watauga Club Drive, Raleigh NC 27695-0001
County: Wake FICE Identification: 002972
Unit ID: 199193
Telephone: (919) 515-2191 Carnegie Class: DU-Highest
FAX Number: (919) 515-7740 Calendar System: Semester
URL: www.ncsu.edu
Established: 1887 Annual Undergrad Tuition & Fees (In-State): $8,880
Enrollment: 34,015 Coed
Affiliation or Control: State IRS Status: 501(c)3
Highest Offering: Doctorate
Accreditation: SC, ART, CACREP, CAEP, CS, ENG, IPSY, LSAR, NRPA, SCPSY, SPAA, SW, VET

02 Chancellor Dr. William Randy WOODSON
05 Provost/Exec Vice Chancellor Dr. Warwick A. ARDEN
43 Vice Chanc & General Counsel Ms. Eileen GOLDGEIER
10 Vice Chanc Finance & Admin Mr. Scott R. DOUGLASS
46 Vice Chanc Research & Innovation Dr. Alan REBAR
32 Vice Chan/Dean Div Acad & Stdnt Aff Dr. Michael D. MULLEN
111 Vice Chanc Univ Advancement Mr. Brian C. SISCHO
13 Vice Chanc Information Technology Dr. Marc I. HOIT
101 Secretary of the University Ms. P. J. TEAL
86 Asst to Chanc External Affairs Ms. Sarah STONE
88 Sr Vice Provost for Acad Strategy Dr. Duane K. LARICK
106 Sr Vice Prov Acad Outreach/Entrepre Dr. Thomas K. MILLER
08 Vice Provost/Director of Libraries Ms. Susan K. NUTTER
22 Vice Pres Inst Equity & Diversity Ms. Linda MCCABE SMITH
18 Assoc Vice Chanc Facilities Mr. Doug MORTON
39 Assoc Vice Chanc Housing and Living Dr. Barry OLSON
26 Assoc Vice Chanc Univ Communication Mr. Brad BOHLANDER
29 Assoc Vice Chanc Alumni Relations Mr. Benny SUGGS
15 Assoc Vice Chanc Human Resources Ms. Marie WILLIAMS
19 Chief of Public Safety Mr. Jack W. MOORMAN
09 Sr Vice Prov Inst Rsrch & Planning Ms. Mary K. LELIK
07 AVP & Director of UG Admissions Mr. Thomas H. GRIFFIN
06 Sr Vice Provost & Univ Registrar Dr. Louis D. HUNT
25 Director Contracts & Grants Mr. Justo TORRES
37 Director of Financial Aid Ms. Krista RINGLER
38 Director of Counseling Center Dr. Monica OSBURN
41 Director Athletics Ms. Deborah YOW
21 Assoc Vice Chancellor & Treasurer Ms. Mary T. PELOQUIN-DODD
88 Director of Materials Management Mrs. Sharon LOOSMAN
79 Dean Humanities/Social Sciences Dr. Jeffery P. BRADEN
48 Dean of Design Dr. Mark HOVERSTEN
54 Dean of Engineering Dr. Louis A. MARTIN-VEGA
47 Dean Agriculture/Life Sciences Dr. Richard H. LINTON
65 Dean of Natural Resources Dr. Mary WATZIN
53 Dean of Education Dr. Mary Ann DANOWITZ
50 Dean of Poole College of Management Dr. Annette RANFT
81 Dean College of Sciences Dr. William DITTO
88 Dean of Textiles Dr. David HINKS
74 Dean of Veterinary Medicine Dr. D. Paul LUNN
58 Interim Dean of Graduate School Dr. Peter J. HARRIES

*University of North Carolina at Asheville (A)

1 University Heights, Asheville NC 28804-8503

County: Buncombe FICE Identification: 002907
Unit ID: 199111
Telephone: (828) 251-6600 Carnegie Class: Bac-A&S
FAX Number: (828) 251-6495 Calendar System: Semester
URL: www.unca.edu
Established: 1927 Annual Undergrad Tuition & Fees (In-State): $6,977
Enrollment: 3,891 Coed
Affiliation or Control: State IRS Status: 501(c)3
Highest Offering: Master's
Accreditation: SC, CAEPN, ENG

02 Chancellor Dr. Mary K. GRANT
100 Chief of Staff Ms. Shannon C. EARLE
05 Provost/VC Academic Affairs Dr. Joseph URGO
10 Vice Chancellor Admin & Finance Mr. John PIERCE
30 Vice Chancellor Advancement Ms. Carla WILLIS
32 Vice Chanc for Student Affairs Dr. Bill HAGGARD
41 Director of Athletics Ms. Janet R. CONE
43 University General Counsel Mr. Clifton WILLIAMS
15 Dir Human Res/Affirmative Action Ms. Nicole NORIAN
09 Dir Inst Research/Effect/Plng Dr. Michael GASS
20 Asst Provost Academic Admin Ms. Patricia MCCLELLAN
81 Dean Natural Science Dr. Keith KRUMPE
79 Dean Humanities Dr. Wiebke STREHL
83 Dean Social Science Dr. Jeff KONZ
88 Asst Provost/Dean Univ Programs Dr. Edward J. KATZ
08 University Librarian Ms. Leah DUNN
13 Chief Information Officer Mr. Jeff BROWN
07 Sr Dir Admissions/Financial Aid Mr. Steve MCKELLIPS
58 Dir Graduate Studies/Continuing Ed Dr. Gerard VOOS
06 Registrar Ms. Lynne HORGAN
21 Assoc Vice Chancellor of Finance Ms. Suzanne BRYSON
21 Controller Ms. Mary HALL
19 Asst VC for Public Safety Mr. Eric BOYCE
96 Purchasing Officer Ms. Darlene BERGER
26 Chief Communication & Mktg Ofc Vacant
27 Public Communication Spec Mr. Steve PLEVER
23 Dir Student Health/Counseling Mr. John CUTSPEC
88 Assoc Dean of Students Ms. Melanie FOX
39 Dir of Housing/Student Life Opers Mr. Vollie BARNWELL
36 Dir Ctr for Career Development Vacant
35 Dean of Students Ms. Jackie MCHARGUE
04 Exec Asst to Chancellor Ms. Chelsey BURKE

*University of North Carolina at Chapel Hill (B)

Chapel Hill NC 27599-0001

County: Orange FICE Identification: 002974
Unit ID: 199120
Telephone: (919) 962-2211 Carnegie Class: DU-Highest
FAX Number: (919) 962-5604 Calendar System: Semester
URL: www.unc.edu
Established: 1789 Annual Undergrad Tuition & Fees (In-State): $8,834
Enrollment: 29,084 Coed
Affiliation or Control: State IRS Status: 501(c)3
Highest Offering: Doctorate
Accreditation: SC, ACAE, #ARCPA, AUD, CAATE, CACREP, CAEPN, CLPSY, DA, DENT, DH, DIETC, DMOLS, HSA, IPSY, JOUR, LAW, LIB, MED, MT, NMT, NURSE, OT, PAST, PCSAS, PH, PHAR, PLNG, PTA, #RAD, RADDOS, RTT, SCPSY, SP, SPAA, SW

02 Chancellor Dr. Carol L. FOLT
05 Exec Vice Provost/Chief Intl Ofcr Dr. Ronald STRAUSS
10 Vice Chancellor Finance & Admin Mr. Matthew W. FAJACK
32 Vice Chancellor Student Affairs Mr. Winston B. CRISP
13 VC Info Technology/Chief Info Ofcr Mr. Chris KIELT
46 Vice Chancellor for Research Dr. Terry MAGNUSON
26 Assoc VC University Communications Mr. Rick WHITE
90 Asst VC Rsch Computing/Learng Tech Dr. Michael BARKER
08 Assoc Prov/University Librarian Ms. Sarah MICHALAK
21 Senior Assoc Vice Chancellor & CFO Dr. Dwayne PINKNEY
20 Vice Provost Academic Initiatives Dr. Carol TRESOLINI
18 Assoc Vice Chanc Facilities Plng Ms. Anna WU
31 Director Community Relations Ms. Linda DOUGLAS
28 Vice Prov Diversity/Multicultural Vacant
11 Provost Administration Dr. Lynn E. WILLIFORD
39 Dir Housing & Residential Education Mr. Alan BLATTNER
41 Director of Athletics Mr. Lawrence (Bubba) R. CUNNINGHAM
06 Int Asst Vice Prov/Univ Registrar Ms. Allison LEGGE
07 Vice Prov Enrollment & Undgrad Admiss Dr. Stephen M. FARMER
29 Pres/Director General Alumni Assoc Mr. Douglas S. DIBBERT
37 Assoc Prov/Dir Scholar/Student Aid Ms. Shirley A. ORT
36 Director University Career Services Mr. Gary Alan MILLER
38 Dir Counseling & Psychological Svcs Dr. Allen H. O'BARR
44 Exec Director of Annual Giving Ms. Darlene GOOCH
19 Dir Public Safety/Chief of Police Chief Jeff B. MCCRACKEN
51 Director Center for Cont Education Mr. Rob BRUCE
27 Director University Relations Mr. Mike MCFARLAND
96 Director Procurement Services Ms. Martha PENDERGRASS
35 Assoc Vice Chanc Student Affairs Dr. Bettina SHUFORD
87 Dean of the Summer School Ms. Jan YOPP
49 Dean College Arts & Sciences Dr. Kevin GUSKIEWICZ
61 Dean School of Law Mr. Martin BRINKLEY
17 V Chanc Med Affs/CEO UNC HlthCare Dr. William L. ROPER
52 Dean School of Dentistry Dr. Scott S. DE ROSSI
58 Dean of Graduate School Dr. Steven W. MATSON
50 Dean Kenan-Flagler Business School Mr. Douglas SHACKLEFORD
70 Dean School of Social Work Dr. Gary L. BOWEN
67 Dean School of Pharmacy Dr. Robert A. BLOUIN
60 Dean School of Journalism/Mass Comm Ms. Susan R. KING
62 Dean School of Info/Library Science Dr. Gary MARCHIONINI
69 Dean School of Public Health Dr. Barbara K. RIMER
53 Dean School of Education Dr. Fouad ABD-EL-KHALICK
80 Dean School of Government Dr. Michael R. SMITH
23 Exec Dir Campus Health Services Dr. Mary COVINGTON
92 Associate Dean for Honors Dr. James L. LELOUDIS

*University of North Carolina at Charlotte (C)

9201 University City Boulevard, Charlotte NC 28223-0001

County: Mecklenburg FICE Identification: 002975
Unit ID: 199139
Telephone: (704) 687-8622 Carnegie Class: DU-Higher
FAX Number: N/A Calendar System: Semester
URL: www.uncc.edu
Established: 1946 Annual Undergrad Tuition & Fees (In-State): $6,763
Enrollment: 27,983 Coed
Affiliation or Control: State IRS Status: 501(c)3
Highest Offering: Doctorate
Accreditation: SC, ANEST, CAATE, CACREP, CAEPN, CLPSY, #COARC, DANCE, ENG, ENGT, EXSC, HSA, IPSY, MUS, NURSE, PH, POLYT, SPAA, SW

02 Chancellor Dr. Philip L. DUBOIS
100 Chief of Staff Ms. Kim S. BRADLEY
05 Provost/Vice Chanc Acad Affairs Dr. Joan F. LORDEN
20 Senior Associate Provost Dr. Jay RAJA
88 Int Assc Prov Met Stds/Ext Acad Pgm Mr. Curt WALTON
10 Vice Chancellor Business Affairs Ms. Elizabeth A. HARDIN
30 Vice Chancellor Univ Advancement Mr. Niles F. SORENSEN
86 Spec Asst for Constituent Relations Ms. Betty DOSTER
32 Vice Chancellor Student Affairs Dr. Kevin BAILEY
46 Vice Chanc Research/Econ Dev Dr. Robert W. WILHELM
13 Vice Chanc Info Tech Svcs/CIO Dr. Michael CARLIN
18 Assoc Vice Chanc Facilities Mgmt Mr. Philip M. JONES, JR.
08 Dean Atkins Library Dr. Anne C. MOORE
88 Assoc Prov Budget & Personnel Ms. Lori MCMAHON
82 Asst Provost for Intl Programs Mr. Joel A. GALLEGOS
88 Assistant Provost Dr. Leslie ZENK
26 Exec Dir Univ Communications Mr. Stephen P. WARD
106 Dir Distance Educ/Summer School Mr. Jody CEBINA
51 Dir Continuing Education Mr. Asher HAINES
27 Senior Dir Public Relations & News Mr. John D. BLAND
31 Director Community Relations Ms. Jeanette SIMS
39 Assoc Vice Chanc/Dir Residence Life Ms. Jacklyn A. SIMPSON
21 Assoc Vice Chancellor for Finance Ms. Anne BROWN
21 Assoc Vice Chanc Business Svcs Mr. Keith N. WASSUM
58 Assoc Provost/Dean Graduate School Dr. Thomas L. REYNOLDS
84 Assoc Provost for Enrollment Mgmt Ms. Tina M. MCENTIRE
43 General Counsel Mr. James E. HUMPHREY, IV
07 Director Undergraduate Admissions Ms. Claire J. KIRBY
35 Dean of Students/Assoc VC Stdnt Aff Ms. Christine REED DAVIS
37 Director of Financial Aid Mr. Bruce BLACKMON
38 Assoc VC Health Programs & Services Dr. David B. SPANO
36 Director University Career Center Dr. Patrick MADSEN
40 Bookstore Manager Ms. Cheryl GRIFFITH-KLINE
29 Exec Director Alumni Affairs Ms. Sallie HUTTON SISTARE
88 Assoc VC Risk Mgmt/Safety/Security Mr. Henry D. JAMES
19 Chief/Dir Police & Public Safety Mr. Jeffrey A. BAKER
09 Asst Provost Institutional Research Mr. Stephen A. COPPOLA
41 Director of Athletics Ms. Judy W. ROSE
96 Director of Purchasing Mr. Randy DUNCAN
93 Int Dir Multicultural Academic Svcs Ms. Jodi TURNER
23 Admin Director Student Health Svcs Mr. David ROUSMANIERE
15 Assoc Vice Chanc Human Res/Aff Act Mr. Gary W. STINNETT
16 Exec Dir HR/EPA/Emp Rel/Compliance Ms. Jeanne L. MADORIN
85 Dir Intl Student/Scholar Svcs Mr. Tarek A. ELSHAYEB
104 Director Study Abroad Mr. Brad SEKULICH
48 Dean College of Arts/Architecture Mr. Kenneth A. LAMBLA
50 Dean College of Business Dr. Steven H. OTT
54 Dean College of Engineering Dr. Robert E. JOHNSON
53 Dean College of Education Dr. Ellen C. MCINTYRE
49 Dean Col of Liberal Arts & Sciences Dr. Nancy A. GUTIERREZ
88 Dean College Health & Human Svcs Dr. Nancy FEY-YENSAN
72 Dean College Computing/Informatics Dr. Fatma MILI
97 Dean University College Dr. John SMAIL
92 Exec Director of Honors College Dr. Malin PEREIRA
06 University Registrar Mr. Christopher B. KNAUER
44 Director of Planning Giving Mr. John W. CULLUM
44 Director of Annual Giving Ms. Stacie G. YOUNG
04 Executive Asst to President Ms. Shari DUNN
108 Exec Dir Assessment & Accreditation Dr. Christine ROBINSON
25 Int Exec Dir Contracts/Grants Admin Ms. Valerie CRICKARD
28 Director Faculty Affairs/Diversity Dr. Yvette HUET

*University of North Carolina at Greensboro (D)

PO Box 26170,1000 Spring Garden St, Greensboro NC 27402-6170

County: Guilford FICE Identification: 002976
Unit ID: 199148
Telephone: (336) 334-5000 Carnegie Class: DU-Higher
FAX Number: (336) 256-0408 Calendar System: Semester
URL: www.uncg.edu
Established: 1891 Annual Undergrad Tuition & Fees (In-State): $6,971
Enrollment: 19,393 Coed
Affiliation or Control: State IRS Status: 501(c)3
Highest Offering: Doctorate
Accreditation: SC, ANEST, CAATE, CACREP, CAEPN, CIDA, CLPSY, CS, DANCE, DIETD, DIETI, LIB, MUS, NRPA, NURSE, PH, SP, SPAA, SW, THEA

02 Chancellor Dr. Franklin D. GILLIAM
100 Chief of Staff Ms. Waiyi TSE
05 Provost/Exec VC Academic Affairs Dr. Dana L. DUNN
10 Vice Chancellor Business Affairs Mr. Charles A. MAIMONE
11 Int Vice Chanc Info Tech Services Ms. Donna R. HEATH
32 Vice Chanc for Student Affairs Dr. Cheryl M. CALLAHAN
84 Vice Chancellor Enrollment Mgmt Dr. Bryan J. TERRY
111 VC University Advancement Ms. Janis I. ZINK
43 University General Counsel Mr. Jerry D. BLAKEMORE
20 Senior Vice Provost Dr. Alan J. BOYETTE
97 Dir Univ Teaching/Learning Commons Dr. David J. TEACHOUT
46 Vice Chanc Research & Econ Devel Dr. Terri L. SHELTON
104 Assoc Provost Intl Programs Dr. Penelope J. PYNES
15 Assoc VC Human Resources Ms. Michelle L. MOONE
21 Associate VC Financial Services Mr. Steven W. RHEW
18 Associate Vice Chanc for Facilities Mr. Jorge QUINTAL
09 Assoc Vice Prov/Director Research Dr. Larry D. MAYES
88 Assoc Dir for Data Analytics Dr. Sarah D. CARRIGAN
88 Assoc Dir Opers & Ext Reporting Dr. William B. ZHANG
26 Assoc VC/Chief Comm Officer Mr. Jeff S. SHAFER
35 Associate VC for Student Affairs Dr. Jim S. SETTLE
91 Assoc VC for Admin Systems Mr. Lee NORRIS
58 Vice Provost Graduate Education Dr. Kelly J. BURKE
49 Dean of Arts & Sciences Dr. John Z. KISS
50 Dean of Business & Economics Dr. McRae BANKS
53 Dean of Education Dr. Randall D. PENFIELD
68 Dean of Health & Human Sciences Dr. Celia R. HOOPER
64 Dean of Visual & Performing Arts Dr. Peter ALEXANDER
66 Dean of Nursing Dr. Robin E. REMSBURG
54 Dean Joint Sch NanoScience/Engineer Dr. James G. RYAN
08 Int Dean of University Libraries Ms. Kathryn M. CROWE
06 Dir of Registration & Records/URO Mr. Michael GAINES
108 Dir Assessment and Accreditation Dr. Jodi E. PETTAZZONI
07 Director of Admissions Mr. Christopher J. KELLER
29 Dir Alumni Assn & Annual Giving Ms. Mary G. LANDERS
88 Director of Recreation and Wellness Dr. Jill BEVILLE
23 Interim Dir Student Health Services Ms. Kathy BABER
36 Director Career Services Ctr Ms. Nicole HALL
106 Dean Division of Online Learning Dr. James M. EDDY
25 Dir Contracts and Grants Mr. William D. WALTERS
37 Director of Financial Aid Ms. Deborah TOLLEFSON
39 Director Housing & Residence Life Mr. Timothy JOHNSON
41 Director Intercollegiate Athletics Ms. Kim RECORD
89 Dir New Student Transitions & FYE Dr. Kim SOUSA-PEOPLES
19 Assoc VC for Safety/Emergency Mgmt Mr. Rollin DONELSON
28 Director Multicultural Affairs Vacant
96 Director Purchasing Mr. Michael F. LOGAN
40 University Bookstore Manager Mr. Brad LIGHT

*University of North Carolina at Pembroke (E)

One University Drive, PO Box 1510, Pembroke NC 28372-1510

County: Robeson FICE Identification: 002954
Unit ID: 199281
Telephone: (910) 521-6000 Carnegie Class: Masters/L
FAX Number: (910) 521-6176 Calendar System: Semester

URL: www.uncp.edu
Established: 1887 Annual Undergrad Tuition & Fees (In-State): $5,816
Enrollment: 6,441 Coed
Affiliation or Control: State IRS Status: 501(c)3
Highest Offering: Master's
Accreditation: SC, ART, #CAATE, CACREP, CAEPN, MUS, NURSE, SW

02 Chancellor .... Dr. Robin G. CUMMINGS
43 General Counsel .... Mr. Joshua MALCOLM
100 Chief of Staff .... Mr. Daniel KENNEY
26 Dir University Communications/Mktg .... Ms. Jodi PHELPS
03 Assoc Vice Chancellor .... Dr. Scott BILLINGSLEY
116 Chief Audit Officer .... Ms. Kelley R. HORTON
10 Interim Vice Chanc Finance .... Mr. Kenneth SPAYD
41 Director of Athletics .... Mr. Dick CHRISTY
111 Vice Chancellor for Advancement .... Ms. Wendy LOWERY
32 Vice Chanc Student Affairs .... Dr. Lisa L. SCHAEFFER
88 Director Title IX and Clery Act Co .... Ms. Ronette SUTTON GERBER
46 Asst to the Chancellor Rsrch/Comm .... Mr. Justin S. SMITH
04 Executive Asst to the Chancellor .... Ms. Marla LOCKLEAR
05 Provost/VC Academic Affairs .... Dr. David WARD
20 Assoc Vice Chanc Planning and Acred .... Dr. Elizabeth NORMANDY
84 Assoc Vice Chanc for Enrollment Mgt .... Ms. Lois H. WILLIAMS
09 Director Inst Research .... Dr. Chunmei YAO
58 Dean of The Graduate School .... Dr. Irene AIKEN
92 Dean of Honors College .... Dr. Mark MILEWICZ
53 Dean of School of Education .... Dr. Alfred BRYANT, JR.
49 Dean of Arts & Sciences .... Dr. Jeff FREDERICK
50 Dean of School of Business .... Dr. Barry O'BRIEN
45 Assoc Vice Chanc for Startegic Plng .... Vacant
25 Assoc VC Research and Sponsored .... Dr. Rebecca BULLARD-DILLARD
08 Dean of Library Services .... Dr. Dennis SWANSON
88 Assoc Vice Chancellor for Outreach .... Dr. Cammie HUNT
88 Director for Academic Resources .... Ms. Leslie T. BELL
21 Asst Vice Chancellor for Finance .... Vacant
35 Assoc Vice Chanc Student Affairs .... Ms. Cynthia OXENDINE
13 Assoc VC Information Resources/CIO .... Ms. Nancy CROUCH
15 Asst Vice Chanc for Human Resources .... Ms. Angela REVELS-BULLARD
88 Faculty Senate Chair .... Dr. Sara SIMMONS
06 Registrar .... Ms. Lourdes SILVA
85 Interim Dir of International Pgm .... Mr. Alexander BRANDT
07 Director of Admissions .... Vacant
37 Director Financial Aid .... Ms. Jenelle HANDCOX
121 Dir Center for Student Success .... Dr. Derek OXENDINE
106 Dir Online/Distance Education .... Ms. Joy FUQUA
39 Director Housing and Resident Life .... Mr. R. Preston SWINEY
38 Director Counseling/Testing Center .... Ms. LynnDee HORNE
36 Director Career Services Center .... Ms. Dawn A. WHEELER
29 Director Alumni Relations .... Ms. Morgan HUNT
40 Interim Director of Bookstore .... Mr. Keats L. ELLIS
28 Dir Multicultural/Minority Affairs .... Mr. Robert L. CANIDA, II
22 Director Accessibility Resource .... Dr. Nicolette CAMPOS
96 Director of Business Services .... Ms. Karen SWINEY
104 Director Study Abroad .... Mr. Alexander BRANDT
23 Director of Student Health Services .... Ms. Cora BULLARD
88 Director Public Administration Pgm .... Dr. Joe F. WEST
44 Assistant Director of Annual Fund .... Mr. David HIBBARD
88 Sports Information Director .... Mr. Todd ANDERSON
88 Dir Fac Plng/Construction/Univ Engr .... Mr. Michael CLARK
19 Director Security/Safety .... Mr. McDuffie CUMMINGS, JR.
18 Director of Facilities Management .... Mr. David HATCH

*University of North Carolina Wilmington (A)

601 S College Road, Wilmington NC 28403-5931
County: New Hanover FICE Identification: 002984
Unit ID: 199218
Telephone: (910) 962-3030 Carnegie Class: Masters/L
FAX Number: (910) 962-4050 Calendar System: Semester
URL: www.uncw.edu
Established: 1947 Annual Undergrad Tuition & Fees (In-State): $6,951
Enrollment: 14,918 Coed
Affiliation or Control: State IRS Status: 501(c)3
Highest Offering: Doctorate
Accreditation: SC, CAATE, CAEPN, CEA, CS, MUS, NURSE, PH, SPAA, SW

02 Chancellor .... Dr. Jose V. SARTARELLI
05 Provost/Vice Chanc Academic Affairs .... Dr. Marilyn SHEERER
10 Vice Chancellor Business Affairs .... Dr. Rick WHITFIELD
32 Vice Chanc for Student Affairs .... Ms. Patricia L. LEONARD
111 Vice Chanc University Advancement .... Mr. Eddie STUART
110 Assoc Vice Chanc Univ Advancement .... Ms. Missy KENNEDY
21 Assoc Vice Chanc Business Services .... Ms. Sharon H. BOYD
21 Assoc VC Business Affs/Facilities .... Mr. Mark D. MORGAN
28 Chief Diversity Officer .... Dr. Kent GUION
26 Chief Communications Officer .... Ms. Janine IAMUNNO
09 Assoc Provost Inst Research/Plng .... Dr. Andy MAUK
35 Assoc VC/Dean of Students .... Dr. Michael A. WALKER
84 Dir Admissions/Enrollment Mgmt .... Mr. Marcio MORENO
85 Assoc VC International Programs .... Dr. Michael WILHELM
15 Assoc VC Human Resources .... Ms. Elizabeth GRIMES
100 Chief of Staff .... Mr. Bradley BALLOU
06 Registrar .... Mr. Jonathan REECE
08 Interim University Librarian .... Ms. Laura WIEGAND
37 Director Financial Aid/Scholarships .... Mr. Frederick HOLDING
18 Director of Physical Plant .... Mr. Stanley OLSON
19 Director Envir Health & Safety .... Mr. Stanley H. HARTS
23 Dir Student Health/Wellness Center .... Ms. Katrin WESNER
109 Director of Auxiliary Services .... Mr. Brian DAILEY
41 Director of Athletics .... Mr. Jimmy BASS
36 Director Career Services/Asst to VC .... Mr. Thomas D. RAKES
29 Director of Alumni Relations .... Mrs. Lindsay LEROY
96 Director of Purchasing .... Mr. John ROBINSON
38 Dir Counseling Center/Univ Testing .... Dr. Bonita REEDER
40 Manager Bookstore .... Mr. Nick CARROLL
49 Dean Col Arts & Sciences .... Dr. Aswani VOLETY
50 Dean Cameron School of Business .... Dr. Robert BURRUS
53 Dean Watson School of Education .... Dr. Van O. DEMPSEY
66 Director School of Nursing .... Dr. Laurie BADZEK
58 Assoc Prov/Dean of Graduate School .... Dr. Ron VETTER
76 Dean Col Health & Human Svcs .... Dr. Charles HARDY
04 Executive Assistant to the Chanc .... Ms. Carolyn S. GAVIT
07 Dir Admissions/Enrollment Managem .... Mr. Marcio MORENO
13 Chief Info Technology Officer (CIO) .... Ms. Sharyne MILLER
25 Dir of Sponsored Programs/Research .... Ms. Panda POWELL
43 General Counsel .... Mr. John SCHERER
54 Director Engineering .... Dr. Amy REAMER
90 Consulting Services Support Dir .... Ms. Beverly VAGNERINI
101 Asst to the Chancellor/Trustees .... Mr. Mark LANIER
39 Director Housing/Residence Life .... Mr. Peter GROENENDYK

*University of North Carolina School of the Arts (B)

1533 S Main Street, Winston-Salem NC 27127-2738
County: Forsyth FICE Identification: 003981
Unit ID: 199184
Telephone: (336) 770-3399 Carnegie Class: Spec-4-yr-Arts
FAX Number: (336) 770-3375 Calendar System: Semester
URL: www.uncsa.edu
Established: 1963 Annual Undergrad Tuition & Fees (In-State): $9,139
Enrollment: 970 Coed
Affiliation or Control: State IRS Status: 501(c)3
Highest Offering: Master's
Accreditation: SC

02 Chancellor .... Mr. Lindsay BIERMAN
05 Provost & Exec Vice Chancellor .... Dr. David ENGLISH
10 Vice Chanc for Business Affairs .... Ms. Carin IOANNOU
111 Vice Chanc for Advancement .... Mr. Edward LEWIS
18 Assoc VC Facilities/Services .... Mr. Chrispher BOYD
26 Chief Marketing Officer .... Ms. Katharine LAIDLAW
09 Director of Institutional Research .... Mr. Jeff PATON
07 Director of Admissions .... Ms. Sheeler LAWSON
08 Librarian .... Ms. Vicki WEAVIL
27 Director of Communications .... Ms. Marla CARPENTER
06 Registrar .... Ms. Erin MORIN
15 Director of Human Resources .... Mr. James LUCAS
37 Director of Financial Aid .... Mrs. Jane KAMIAB
49 Dean of Liberal Arts .... Mr. Dean WILCOX
64 Dean School of Music .... Mr. Brian COLE
57 Dean School of Dance .... Ms. Susan JAFFE
48 Dean Sch of Design/Production .... Mr. Michael KELLEY
88 Dean School of Drama .... Mr. Scott ZIGLER
13 Chief Technology Officer .... Ms. Claire MACHAMER
19 Chief of Police .... Mr. Thomas YOUNCE
38 Dir of Counseling & Testing Svcs .... Dr. Thomas MURRAY
32 Vice Provost & Dean Student Affairs .... Mr. Ward CALDWELL
96 Director of Purchasing .... Mr. Allen CARNES
88 Dir Ctr for Design Innovation .... Ms. Betsy TOWNS
88 Exec Dir Kenan Inst for the Arts .... Ms. Corey MADDEN
88 Dean School of Filmmaking .... Ms. Susan RUSKIN
88 Headmaster/Dean HS Academic Program .... Mr. Martin FERRELL
35 Director of Student Engagement .... Mr. Steve GALLAGHER
87 Dir Educ Outreach & Summer Programs .... Ms. Suzanna WATKINS
39 Assistant Dean & Dir of RLPH .... Mr. Joseph RICK
23 Director of Health Services .... Ms. Sharon SUMMER
100 Chief of Staff .... Mr. James DECRISTO
43 General Counsel .... Mr. David HARRISON
102 Foundation Director .... Ms. Cynthia LIBERTY
108 Director of Inst Effectiveness .... Mr. Jeff PATON

*Western Carolina University (C)

65 West University Way, HFR 501,
Cullowhee NC 28723-9646
County: Jackson FICE Identification: 002981
Unit ID: 200004
Telephone: (828) 227-7211 Carnegie Class: Masters/L
FAX Number: (828) 227-7202 Calendar System: Semester
URL: www.wcu.edu
Established: 1889 Annual Undergrad Tuition & Fees (In-State): $6,737
Enrollment: 10,340 Coed
Affiliation or Control: State IRS Status: 501(c)3
Highest Offering: Doctorate
Accreditation: SC, ANEST, ART, CAATE, CACREP, CAEPN, CARTE, CIDA, CONST, DIETD, DIETI, EMT, ENG, ENGT, IPSY, MUS, NURSE, PTA, SP, SPAA, SW, THEA

02 Chancellor .... Dr. David O. BELCHER
05 Provost .... Dr. Alison MORRISON-SHETLAR
10 Vice Chanc Admin & Finance .... Mr. Mike BYERS
32 Vice Chancellor/Student Affairs .... Dr. H. Samuel MILLER
35 Asst Vice Chanc Student Affairs .... Mrs. Jane ADAMS-DUNFORD
35 Asst Vice Chanc Student Success .... Dr. Lowell K. DAVIS
35 Asst Vice Chanc/Student Affairs .... Ms. Kellie MONTEITH
30 Assoc Vice Chancellor Development .... Mrs. Lori LEWIS
44 Assoc Provost Academic Affairs .... Dr. Brandon SCHWAB
20 Assoc Provost Undergraduate Studies .... Dr. Carol BURTON
18 Assoc VC for Facilities Management .... Mr. Joe WALKER
100 Chief of Staff .... Dr. Melissa WARGO
04 Assistant to the Chancellor .... Ms. Claire COLLINS
43 Legal Counsel .... Mr. Shea BROWNING
38 Director of Counseling Services .... Dr. Kimberly GORMAN
06 Registrar .... Mr. Larry HAMMER
07 Director of Student Recruitment .... Mr. Phil CAULEY
09 Asst Vice Chancellor of OIPE .... Mr. Tim METZ
37 Director of Financial Aid .... Ms. Trina ORR
15 Assoc VC of Human Resources .... Dr. Cory CAUSBY
13 Chief Information Officer .... Mr. Craig FOWLER
29 Director of Alumni Affairs .... Mr. Marty RAMSEY
08 Dean of Library Services .... Dr. Farzaneh RAZZAGHI
19 Director University Police .... Mr. Earnest HUDSON
88 Exec Director Education Outreach .... Dr. Susan FOUTS
31 Director Campus Services .... Mr. Bryant BARNETT
41 Athletic Director .... Mr. Randy EATON
23 Director University Health Services .... Ms. Pamela BUCHANAN
28 Asst Director Intercultural Affairs .... Ms. Niki PAGANELLI
96 Director of Purchasing .... Ms. Cindy NICHOLSON
40 Director Book & Supply Store .... Ms. Pamela DEGRAFFENREID
88 Director of Orientation .... Ms. Tammy HASKETT
38 Director of Advising Center .... Mr. Travis BULLUCK
36 Director of Career Services .... Ms. Theresa CRUZ PAUL
26 Sr Director Comm & Public Relations .... Mr. Bill STUDENC
57 Dean of Fine & Performing Arts .... Mr. George H. BROWN
58 Dean Grad School & Research .... Dr. Brian KLOEPPEL
49 Dean Arts & Sciences .... Dr. Richard STARNES
72 Dean Kimmel School Constr Mgmt/Tech .... Dr. Jeffrey RAY
50 Dean College of Business .... Dr. Darrell PARKER
53 Dean Educ & Allied Professions .... Dr. Kim WINTER
76 Dean Health & Human Sciences .... Dr. Douglas R. KESKULA
92 Dean of Honors College .... Dr. Jill GRANGER
88 Director of Marketing .... Ms. Robin C. OLIVER
86 Director of External Relations .... Ms. Meredith WHITFIELD
25 Director of Sponsored Research .... Ms. Andrea MOSHIER
39 Director of Residence Life .... Ms. Mistie BIBBEE

*Winston-Salem State University (D)

601 MLK Jr. Drive, 200 Blair Hall,
Winston-Salem NC 27110-0001
County: Forsyth FICE Identification: 002986
Unit ID: 199999
Telephone: (336) 750-2000 Carnegie Class: Masters/M
FAX Number: (336) 750-2049 Calendar System: Semester
URL: www.wssu.edu
Established: 1892 Annual Undergrad Tuition & Fees (In-State): $5,804
Enrollment: 5,107 Coed
Affiliation or Control: State IRS Status: 501(c)3
Highest Offering: Doctorate
Accreditation: SC, CACREP, CAEPN, CS, MT, MUS, NRPA, NURSE, OT, PTA, SW

02 Chancellor .... Dr. Elwood L. ROBINSON
05 Provost/VC Academic Affairs .... Dr. Brenda ALLEN
32 Vice Chancellor Student Affairs .... Dr. Trae COTTON
09 Associate Provost .... Dr. Carolynn BERRY
45 Asst Prov Administration/Plng .... Mrs. Letitia C. WALL
10 Vice Chanc Finance & Admin .... Dr. Randy W. MILLS
30 Vice Chanc University Advance .... Mrs. Michelle COOK
18 Assoc Vice Chanc Facilities Mgmt .... Ms. Rosabla LEDEZMA
13 Assoc Prov/Chief Information Ofcr .... Dr. Derrick MURRAY
88 Director Internal Audit/Compliance .... Ms. Shannon B. HENRY
19 Chief of Campus Police .... Mrs. Patricia D. NORRIS
08 Director of Library Services .... Ms. Wanda BROWN
39 Director Hous/Residence Life .... Ms. Chantal BOUCHEREAU
37 Director of Financial Aid .... Mr. Robert MUHAMMED
15 Asst Vice Chanc Human Resources .... Mr. Lester ARNOLD
26 Director Marketing/Communications .... Ms. Jamie HUNT
88 Dir Enrollment Communications .... Ms. Cathy HOOTS
44 Director Annual Fund .... Mrs. Kimberly REESE
35 Assoc Director Student Activities .... Ms. Heather DAVIS
23 Dir of Student Health Center .... Dr. Anthony PHILADELPHIA
41 Athletic Director .... Mrs. Tonia WALKER
101 Vice Chancellor/Sec of Univ .... Mrs. Camille KLUTTZ-LEACH
07 Director of Admissions .... Dr. Kerwin GRAHAM
43 Int General Legal Counsel .... Mr. Ivey BROWN
96 Director Purchasing .... Mr. Alan IRELAND
90 Director Academic Computer Center .... Mr. Cuthrell JOHNSON
88 Dean University College LLL .... Dr. Doria K. STITTS
76 Dean School of Health Sciences .... Dr. Peggy VALENTINE
88 Director of Title III .... Dr. Everette L. WITHERSPOON
06 Registrar .... Ms. Sharon STODDARD
108 Director Institutional Assessment . Dr. Becky MUSSAT-WHITLOW

University of Phoenix Charlotte Campus (E)

3800 Arco Corporate Drive, Charlotte NC 28273-3409
Telephone: (704) 504-5409 Identification: 770216
Accreditation: &NH, ACBSP

† No longer accepting campus-based students.

Virginia College (F)

3740 South Holden Road, Greensboro NC 27406
Telephone: (336) 398-5400 Identification: 770619
Accreditation: ACICS, ACFEI, MAAB

† Branch campus of Virginia College, Birmingham, AL

Wake Forest University (A)

1834 Wake Forest Road, Winston-Salem NC 27109-8758
County: Forsyth FICE Identification: 002978
Unit ID: 199847
Telephone: (336) 758-5000 Carnegie Class: DU-Higher
FAX Number: (336) 758-6074 Calendar System: Semester
URL: www.wfu.edu
Established: 1834 Annual Undergrad Tuition & Fees: $49,308
Enrollment: 7,837 Coed
Affiliation or Control: Independent Non-Profit IRS Status: 501(c)3
Highest Offering: Doctorate
Accreditation: SC, ANEST, ARCPA, CACREP, CAEP, DENT, LAW, MED, THEOL

01 President .... Dr. Nathan O. HATCH
43 SVP Gen Counsel/Sec Board of Trust .... Mr. J. Reid MORGAN
10 Exec Vice Pres/Chief Financial Ofcr .... Mr. B. Hofler MILAM
05 Provost .... Mr. Rogan KERSH
17 CEO Wake Forest Baptist Med Ctr .... Dr. John D. MCCONNELL
11 Vice President for Administration .... Vacant
30 Vice Pres University Advancement .... Mr. Mark A. PETERSEN
32 Vice Pres Campus Life .... Dr. Penny RUE
115 Vice Pres/Chief Investment Officer .... Mr. James J. DUNN
100 Chief of Staff .... Ms. Mary E. PUGEL
35 Assoc VP/Dean of Student Services .... Mr. Adam GOLDSTEIN
44 Ast VP/Dir Parent/Donor Relations .... Ms. Minta A. MCNALLY
30 Asst VP/Director of Development .... Mr. Robert T. BAKER
13 CIO/Assoc Provost for Tech/IS .... Mr. Mur MUCHANE
46 Assoc Provost for Research .... Dr. S. Bruce KING
49 Dean of the College .... Dr. Michele K. GILLESPIE
63 Dean School Med/Int Health Sci Pres .... Dr. Edward ABRAHAM
61 Dean School of Law .... Mr. Suzanne REYNOLDS
50 Dean of Business .... Mr. Charles IACOVOU
73 Dean of Divinity .... Dr. Gail R. O'DAY
09 Dir Inst Research/Academic Admin .... Mr. Phil HANDWERK
08 Dir of the Z Smith Reynolds Library .... Dr. Lynn SUTTON
85 Director of International Studies .... Mr. Steven DUKE
07 Director of Admissions .... Ms. Martha B. ALLMAN
37 Director of Financial Aid .... Mr. William T. WELLS
36 VP/Office of Personal & Career Dev .... Mr. Andy CHAN
06 Registrar .... Mr. Harold PACE
41 Director of Athletics .... Mr. Ronald D. WELLMAN
15 Chief Human Resources Officer .... Ms. Carmen I. CANALES
18 Director Facilities Management .... Mr. John SHENETTE
38 Dir University Counseling Center .... Dr. Marianne A. SCHUBERT
23 Director Student Health Service .... Dr. Cecil D. PRICE
39 Dean Residence Life & Housing .... Ms. Donna MCGALLIARD
42 Chaplain .... Rev. Timothy L. AUMAN
19 Chief University Police .... Ms. Regina G. LAWSON
22 EEO Mgr/Diversity & Compliance Dir .... Ms. Angela CULLER
94 Director Women's & Gender Studies .... Dr. Wanda BALZANO
26 Chief Public Relations Officer .... Mr. Brett EATON
28 Director of Diversity & Inclusion .... Dr. Barbee OAKES
102 Dir Foundation/Corporate Relations .... Ms. Linda LUVAAS
104 Director Study Abroad .... Mr. David F. TAYLOR
29 Director Alumni Engagement .... Mrs. Kelly MCCONNICO

Warren Wilson College (B)

PO Box 9000, Asheville NC 28815-9000
County: Buncombe FICE Identification: 002979
Unit ID: 199865
Telephone: (828) 298-3325 Carnegie Class: Bac-A&S
FAX Number: (828) 771-7097 Calendar System: Semester
URL: www.warren-wilson.edu
Established: 1894 Annual Undergrad Tuition & Fees: $33,970
Enrollment: 812 Coed
Affiliation or Control: Presbyterian Church (U.S.A.) IRS Status: 501(c)3
Highest Offering: Master's
Accreditation: SC, SW

01 President .... Dr. Lynn M. MORTON
05 VP Academic Affairs/Dean of College .... Dr. Paula K. GARRETT
10 VP for Administration & Finance .... Mr. Scott MCKINNEY
30 Int Vice Pres for Advancement .... Mr. Zanne GARLAND
84 VP Enrollment Management/Marketing .... Ms. Janelle HOLMBOE
32 Vice Pres Student Life .... Mr. Paul C. PERRINE
88 Vice Pres Applied Learning .... Ms. Cathy KRAMER
06 Registrar .... Miss Christa L. BRIDGMAN
09 Director Institutional Research .... Ms. Allyson HETTRICK
37 Director Financial Aid .... Ms. Lori LEWIS
21 Controller .... Ms. Mary DAVIS
44 Director Annual Fund .... Ms. Mary HAY
26 Director of Media Relations .... Mr. Kyle MCCURRY
20 Director Academic Support Service .... Ms. Lyn O'HARE
31 Assoc Director Community Engagement .... Ms. Brooke MILLSAPS
35 Director of Student Activities .... Ms. Tacci SMITH
38 Director of Counseling .... Mr. Arthur SHUSTER
36 Director Career Services .... Ms. Wendy SELIGMANN
42 Dir of Spiritual Life & Chaplain .... Rev. Brian AMMONS
91 Dir Admin Data Processing .... Ms. Omega HODGES
15 Director Human Resources .... Ms. Mandy KUTSHIED
18 Acting Dir Facil Mgmt/Tech Svcs .... Mr. Scott MCKINNEY
19 Director Public Safety .... Mr. Justin GILDNER
104 Director of International Studies .... Ms. Anna WELTON
28 Inclusion/Diversity/Equity Director .... Ms. Clarissa HARRIS
96 Purchasing Supervisor .... Mr. Bobby FREEMAN

William Peace University (C)

15 E Peace Street, Raleigh NC 27604-1194
County: Wake FICE Identification: 002953
Unit ID: 199272
Telephone: (919) 508-2000 Carnegie Class: Bac-A&S
FAX Number: (919) 508-2326 Calendar System: Semester
URL: www.peace.edu
Established: 1857 Annual Undergrad Tuition & Fees: $27,080
Enrollment: 1,038 Coed
Affiliation or Control: Presbyterian Church (U.S.A.) IRS Status: 501(c)3
Highest Offering: Baccalaureate
Accreditation: SC

01 President .... Dr. Brian C. RALPH
100 Dir of Presidential Operations .... Ms. Kelley DIETZ
05 Vice President for Academic Affairs .... Dr. Charles DUNCAN
32 Vice President for Student Services .... Mr. Frank RIZZO
30 Vice President for Advancement .... Ms. Jodi STAMEY
06 Registrar .... Ms. Sharon KISSICK
09 Director of Institutional Research .... Ms. Carolyn BLATTNER
10 Vice Pres Finance & Administration .... Mr. George A. YEARWOOD
84 Vice Pres Enrollment Mgmt/Marketing .... Dr. Kristin E. COHEN
15 Assoc Vice Pres for Human Resources .... Ms. Amber M. KIMBALL
13 Chief Information Technology Office .... Mr. Josh FRANK
18 Asst VP for Buildings and Grounds .... Mr. John B. CRANHAM
37 Director of Financial Aid .... Ms. Michelle HEMMER
41 Director of Athletics .... Mr. Philip ROWE

Wingate University (D)

220 N. Camden Road, Wingate NC 28174-0159
County: Union FICE Identification: 002985
Unit ID: 199962
Telephone: (704) 233-8000 Carnegie Class: Masters/M
FAX Number: (704) 233-8014 Calendar System: Semester
URL: www.wingate.edu
Established: 1896 Annual Undergrad Tuition & Fees: $29,170
Enrollment: 3,149 Coed
Affiliation or Control: Southern Baptist IRS Status: 501(c)3
Highest Offering: Doctorate
Accreditation: SC, ACBSP, ARCPA, CAATE, MUS, NUR, PHAR, PTA

01 President .... Dr. T. Rhett BROWN
05 Provost .... Dr. Helen TATE
10 VP Business/Chief Financial Ofcr .... Mr. William H. DURHAM
30 VP Resource Development .... Ms. Hannah DICKERSON
41 VP & Director of Athletics .... Mr. R. Stephen POSTON
84 VP for Enrollment/Marketing & Comm .... Dr. Heather C. MILLER
76 Vice Provost Health Sciences .... Dr. Robert B. SUPERNAW
11 VP for Business Operations .... Mr. Scott E. HUNSUCKER
110 Assoc VP Resource Development .... Mr. Roy Lee RAGSDALE, JR.
88 AVP for Proj Mgmt & Sustainability .... Mr. Cameron JACKSON
121 Dean of Academic Support Programs .... Mrs. Glenda H. BEBBER
49 Dean School Arts & Sciences .... Dr. H. Donald MERRILL
50 Dean School of Business .... Dr. Peter FRANK
53 Dean School of Education .... Dr. Annette DIGBY
08 Director of Library .... Mrs. Amee M. ODOM
39 Assoc Dean Res Life & Involvement .... Ms. Brandy SHOTT
37 Director Student Financial Planning .... Ms. Teresa G. WILLIAMS
12 Asst VP Ballantyne Campus .... Mr. Jeffrey ATKINSON
91 Director Administrative Computing .... Mr. Timothy D. HERRIN
29 Director of Alumni Development .... Ms. Brittany BUMGARNER
42 Minister to Stdnts/Sr Dir CVICS .... Rev. A. Dane JORDAN
40 Director of Campus Store .... Mrs. Sherri SHANK
19 Campus Safety Chief .... Mr. Mike EASLEY
44 Director of Annual Giving .... Ms. Candice KANE
112 Director of Gift Planning .... Vacant
38 Director of Counseling Services .... Ms. Lori HINNANT
13 Director of Information Technology .... Ms. Jeanette K. BUJAK
36 Dir of Internships and Career Svcs .... Ms. Sharon ROBINSON
15 Human Resources Coordinator .... Mrs. Lisa B. RAGSDALE
32 Dean of Campus LIfe/Student Life .... Mr. Michael REYNOLDS
06 Registrar .... Ms. Maria TAYLOR
07 Director of Admissions .... Mr. Gabe HOLLINGSWORTH
04 Executive Assistant to President .... Ms. Tammy T. BRITT
13 CIO .... Mr. Steve SHANK
88 VP Strategic Partnerships .... Mr. Vincent TILSON
20 Vice Provost Student Engagement .... Dr. Nancy RANDALL

NORTH DAKOTA

Cankdeska Cikana Community College (E)

PO Box 269, 214 First Avenue,
Fort Totten ND 58335-0269
County: Benson FICE Identification: 022365
Unit ID: 200208
Telephone: (701) 766-4415 Carnegie Class: Tribal
FAX Number: (701) 766-4077 Calendar System: Semester
URL: www.littlehoop.edu
Established: 1974 Annual Undergrad Tuition & Fees: $3,300
Enrollment: 188 Coed
Affiliation or Control: Independent Non-Profit IRS Status: 501(c)3
Highest Offering: Associate Degree
Accreditation: #NH

01 President .... Dr. Cynthia A. LINDQUIST
05 Academic Dean .... Mrs. Teresa HARDING
10 CFO .... Mrs. Chelly VEER
11 Dean of Administration .... Mr. Stuart YOUNG
06 Registrar .... Mr. Ermen BROWN, JR.

*North Dakota University System Office (F)

600 E Boulevard Avenue, Dept 215,
Bismarck ND 58505-0230
County: Burleigh FICE Identification: 033434
Telephone: (701) 328-2960 Carnegie Class: N/A
FAX Number: (701) 328-2961
URL: www.ndus.edu

01 Chancellor .... Mark HAGEROTT
05 Vice Chanc Acad/Student Affairs .... Richard ROTHAUS
10 Chief Financial Officer .... Tammy DOLAN
13 VC for IT & Institutional Research .... Lisa FELDNER
45 VC of Strategic Engagement .... Vacant
37 Director Financial Aid .... Brenda ZASTOUPIL
21 Director of Finance .... David KREBSBACH
88 Research Analyst .... Jennifer WEBER
26 Dir of Communications & Media Rels .... Billie Jo LORIUS
88 Director Financial Reporting .... Robin PUTNAM
124 Dir Student Entry Trans & Retention .... Lisa JOHNSON
32 Director of Student Affairs .... Katie FITZSIMMONS
18 Director Facility Planning .... Rick TONDER

*University of North Dakota (G)

264 Centennial Drive, Grand Forks ND 58202
County: Grand Forks FICE Identification: 003005
Unit ID: 200280
Telephone: (701) 777-2011 Carnegie Class: DU-Higher
FAX Number: (701) 777-2696 Calendar System: Semester
URL: www.und.edu
Established: 1883 Annual Undergrad Tuition & Fees (In-State): $8,136
Enrollment: 14,951 Coed
Affiliation or Control: State IRS Status: 501(c)3
Highest Offering: Doctorate
Accreditation: NH, AAB, ANEST, ARCPA, ART, CAATE, CAEPN, CLPSY, COPSY, CS, DIETC, ENG, HT, IPSY, LAW, MED, MT, MUS, NAIT, NURSE, OT, PH, PTA, #SP, SPAA, SW, THEA

02 President .... Mr. Mark KENNEDY
29 CEO Alumni Assoc & Foundation .... Ms. Deanna CARLSON ZINK
05 Vice Pres Academic Affairs/Provost .... Dr. Thomas DILORENZO
10 Vice President Operations/Finance .... Ms. Alice BREKKE
32 Int Vice Pres Stdnt Affs/Diversity .... Dr. Cara HALGREN
17 Vice President Health Affairs .... Dr. Joshua WYNNE
46 VP Research/Economic Devel .... Dr. Grant MCGIMPSEY
26 VP for University Relations .... Vacant
30 Chief Development Officer .... Mr. Dan MUUS
35 Associate Dean of Students .... Dr. Cassie GERHARDT
21 Assoc VP Finance .... Ms. Karla MONGEON-STEWART
18 Assoc VP Facilities .... Mr. Michael PIEPER
45 AVP Research & Economic Dev/RDC .... Dr. Barry MILAVETZ
88 AVP Rsrch & Econ Dev/Capacity Bldg .... Dr. Mark HOFFMANN
25 AVP Corp Engage/Commercialization .... Mr. Michael MOORE
20 Asst VP Student Academic Services .... Ms. Lisa BURGER
07 Asst VP Enrollment Services .... Vacant
13 Chief Information Officer .... Dr. Madhavi MARASINGHE
20 Senior Vice Provost .... Dr. Hesham EL-REWINI
20 Senior Vice Provost .... Dr. Debbie STORRS
28 Assoc VP Diversity & Inclusion .... Vacant
27 Assoc Director Government Affairs .... Ms. Susan CARAHER
08 Dean of Libraries & Info Res .... Ms. Stephanie WALKER
06 Registrar .... Mr. Scott CORRELL
15 Dir Human Resources/Payroll Svcs .... Ms. Patricia HANSON
19 AVP Public Safety/Police Chief .... Mr. Eric PLUMMER
38 Director Counseling Center .... Dr. Kenneth CARLSON
36 Director Career Services .... Ms. Ilene ODEGARD
20 Director Instructional Development .... Dr. Anne KELSCH
22 Director EEO/Affirmative Action .... Ms. Donna SMITH
37 Director Student Financial Aid .... Ms. Janelle KILGORE
39 Exec Director Housing & Dining .... Ms. Connie FRAZIER
23 Interim Director of Student Health .... Ms. Rosy DUB
43 General Counsel .... Ms. Heather WAGES
41 Director Athletics .... Mr. Brian FAISON
85 Director International Programs .... Ms. Katie DAVIDSON
21 Controller .... Ms. Sharon LOILAND
88 Dir Student Rights/Responsibilities .... Mr. Alex POKORNOWSKI
94 Director Women's Center .... Vacant
96 Director Purchasing .... Ms. Jana THOMPSON
92 Director Honors Program .... Dr. Amanda BOYD
28 Dir Multicultural Student Services .... Dr. Stacey BORBOA-PETERSON
21 Budget Manager .... Ms. Cindy FETSCH
40 Manager University Bookstore .... Mr. Griffin GILLESPIE
49 Dean of Arts & Sciences .... Dr. Debbie STORRS
58 Dean School of Graduate Studies .... Dr. Grant MCGIMPSEY
61 Dean School of Law .... Ms. Kathryn RAND
66 Dean Col Nursing/Profess Discip .... Dr. Gayle ROUX
50 Int Dean Business/Public Admin .... Dr. Steve LIGHT
54 Dean College of Engr/Mines .... Dr. Hesham EL-REWINI
53 Dean Col Education/Human Devel .... Dr. Cindy JUNTUNEN
88 Dean of Aerospace Sciences .... Dr. Paul LINDSETH
63 Dean Sch Medicine/Health Science .... Dr. Joshua WYNNE
88 Dir American Indian Student Svcs .... Vacant
35 Assoc Dean of Students .... Dr. Cassie GERHARDT
88 Executive Director Memorial Union .... Ms. Cheryl GREW-GILLEN
88 Director Wellness Center .... Vacant
88 Dir Health & Wellness Promotions .... Vacant
109 Director Dining Services .... Mr. Orlynn ROSAASEN
88 Dir Children's Learning Center .... Ms. Dawnita NILLES
13 Dir Admin Service Technology .... Ms. Sherry LAWDERMILT

22 Dir Disability Svcs for Students .... Ms. Debrah GLENNEN
88 Director TRIO Programs .... Mr. Derek SPORBERT
27 Director Student Affairs Marketing .... Ms. Sarah NISSEN
88 Dir One Stop Student Serv .... Mr. Matt LUKACH
07 Director Admissions .... Mr. Jason TRAINER

*Dickinson State University (A)

291 Campus Drive, Dickinson ND 58601-4896
County: Stark FICE Identification: 002989
Unit ID: 200059
Telephone: (701) 483-2507 Carnegie Class: Bac-Diverse
FAX Number: (701) 483-2006 Calendar System: Semester
URL: www.dickinsonstate.edu
Established: 1918 Annual Undergrad Tuition & Fees (In-State): $6,348
Enrollment: 1,317 Coed
Affiliation or Control: State IRS Status: 501(c)3
Highest Offering: Master's
Accreditation: NH, CAEPN, IACBE, MUS, NUR, PNUR

02 President .... Dr. Thomas MITZEL
05 Provost/Vice Pres Academic Affairs .... Dr. Carmen WILSON
10 VP for Finance & Administration .... Mr. Marty PARSONS
20 Dean of Instruction .... Dr. Kenneth HAUGHT
29 Exec Dir Alumni Assoc/Foundation .... Mr. Ty ORTON
84 Exec Dir Communications/Public Aff .... Ms. Marie MOE
41 Director of Intercollege Athletics .... Mr. Pete STANTON
56 Asst Director of Extended Learning .... Mr. Anthony WILLER
12 Director of DSU Bismarck/Williston .... Ms. Annette MARTEL
06 Director of Academic Records .... Ms. Kathy MEYER
08 Head of Library Services .... Ms. Staci GREEN
13 Director of Information Technology .... Mr. Todd HAUF
37 Director of Financial Aid .... Mr. Christopher MEEK
121 Asst Director Academic Success Ctr .... Ms. Jennifer WITHERS
109 Director of Food Service .... Mr. Jason BENSON
40 Manager University Store .... Ms. Loretta A. HEIDT
21 Controller .... Ms. Laura NELSON
36 Director of Career Services .... Vacant
85 Assoc Dir International Program .... Ms. Perzen POLISHWALLA
39 Housing Coordinator .... Ms. Jennifer WITHERS
15 Int Coordinator of Human Resources .... Ms. Krissy KILWEIN
04 Executive Asst to President .... Ms. Kari HANSTAD
18 Chief Facilities/Physical Plant .... Mr. Mick RIESINGER
19 Director Security/Safety .... Mr. Jack SCHULZ
22 Affirmative Action Officer/Title IX .... Mr. Michael DENIS
26 Chief Public Relations/Marketing .... Ms. Marie MOE

*Mayville State University (B)

330 3rd Street, NE, Mayville ND 58257-1299
County: Traill FICE Identification: 002993
Unit ID: 200226
Telephone: (701) 788-2301 Carnegie Class: Bac-Diverse
FAX Number: (701) 788-4748 Calendar System: Semester
URL: www.mayvillestate.edu
Established: 1889 Annual Undergrad Tuition & Fees (In-State): $6,254
Enrollment: 1,110 Coed
Affiliation or Control: State IRS Status: 501(c)3
Highest Offering: Master's
Accreditation: NH, CAEPN, NURSE

02 President .... Dr. Gary D. HAGEN
05 Vice President for Academic Affairs .... Dr. Keith A. STENEHJEM
10 Vice President for Business Affairs .... Ms. Jami HOVET
32 Vice President for Student Affairs .... Dr. Andrew J. PFLIPSEN
102 Executive Foundation Director .... Vacant
09 Exec Dir Institution Effectiveness .... Ms. Maren A. JOHNSON
41 Athletic Director .... Mr. Mike K. MOORE
04 Exec Assistant to the President .... Ms. Mary L. TRUDEAU
26 Assoc Dir Found/Dir Marketing .... Ms. Beth I. SWENSON
07 Director of Admissions .... Mr. James R. MOROWSKI
06 Dir Academic Records/Registrar .... Ms. Pamela K. BRAATEN
106 Director of Extended Learning .... Ms. Misti L. WUORI
37 Director of Financial Aid .... Ms. Shirley M. HANSON
08 Director of Library Services .... Ms. Kelly J. KORNKVEN
35 Director of Student Life .... Dr. Jeffrey A. POWELL
40 Director of Bookstore .... Ms. Pam B. SOHOLT
18 Director of Physical Plant .... Mr. Dan P. LORENZ
18 Director of Facilities Services .... Mr. Bob J. KOZOJED
15 Director of Human Resources .... Ms. Crystal BEGGS
13 Chief Information Officer .... Mr. Patrick W. STEELE
21 Controller .... Mr. Ian BJERKE
38 Dir Counseling/Freshmen Retention .... Ms. Kristi L. LENTZ
121 Dir Student Success/Disability Svc .... Ms. Katie J. RICHARDS
108 Dir Acad Assess/Instruct Design .... Ms. Chris GONNELLA
28 Dir Cultural Diversity/ Inclusion .... Ms. Dina ZAVALA-PETHERBRIDGE
36 Director of Career Services .... Mr. Jay A. HENRICKSON
27 Dir Strategic Student Communication .... Mr. Catlin E. SOLUM
50 Director of Business .... Ms. Rhonda L. NELSON
53 Dean of Education .... Dr. Andi L. DULSKI-BUCHOLZ
88 Director of Physical Education .... Dr. Jeremiah T. MOEN
81 Director of Mathematics/Science .... Dr. Bob D. MIESS
66 Director of RN to BSN Nursing .... Ms. Tami L. SUCH
83 Dir of Social/Behavioral Science .... Dr. Dalton MCMAHON

*Minot State University (C)

500 University Avenue W, Minot ND 58707-0001
County: Ward FICE Identification: 002994
Unit ID: 200253
Telephone: (701) 858-3000 Carnegie Class: Masters/M
FAX Number: (701) 839-6933 Calendar System: Semester
URL: www.minotstateu.edu
Established: 1913 Annual Undergrad Tuition & Fees (In-State): $6,568
Enrollment: 3,354 Coed
Affiliation or Control: State IRS Status: 501(c)3
Highest Offering: Beyond Master's But Less Than Doctorate
Accreditation: NH, CAATE, CAEPN, IACBE, MUS, NUR, SP, SW

02 President .... Dr. Steven SHIRLEY
05 VP for Academic Affairs .... Dr. Laurie GELLER
10 Vice President for Finance/Admin .... Mr. Brent WINIGER
111 Vice President for Advancement .... Mr. Rick HEDBERG
32 Vice President for Student Affairs .... Mr. Kevin HARMON
21 AVP Business Services/Controller .... Ms. Jonelle WATSON
07 Admissions .... Ms. Katie TYLER
18 Facilities Management .... Mr. Brian SMITH
06 Registrar .... Ms. Rebecca RINGHAM
08 Director of the Library .... Mr. Stephen BANISTER
88 Director of Student Wellness .... Mr. Paul BREKKE
37 Director of Financial Aid .... Ms. Laurie WEBER
50 AVP CEL/Graduate .... Dr. Jacek MROZIK
29 Director Alumni Relations .... Ms. Janna MCKECHNIE
13 Director Computer Services .... Mr. George WITHUS
40 Director Bookstore .... Ms. Gerri KUNA
41 Athletic Director .... Mr. Andy CARTER
26 Director of Public Information .... Mr. Michael LINNELL
15 Director of Human Resources .... Dr. Marc WACHTFOGEL
12 Dean of Dakota College at Bottineau .... Dr. Jerry MIGLER
36 Director of Campus Career Services .... Ms. Lynda BERTSCH
25 Grants & Contracts Accountant .... Ms. Sheila LATHAM
09 Director of Institutional Research .... Ms. Cari OLSON
04 Administrative Asst to President .... Ms. Deb WENTZ
39 Director Student Housing .... Mr. Devin MCCALL
27 Director of Marketing .... Ms. Teresa LOFTESNES
104 Director International Programs .... Ms. Libby CLAERBOUT
19 Director Security/Safety .... Mr. Gary ORLUCK
88 Director of Veterans Services .... Mr. Andrew HEITKAMP
88 Title IX Coordinator .... Ms. Lisa DOOLEY

*North Dakota State University Main Campus (D)

P.O. Box 6050, Fargo ND 58108-6050
County: Cass FICE Identification: 002997
Unit ID: 200332
Telephone: (701) 231-8011 Carnegie Class: DU-Higher
FAX Number: (701) 231-8722 Calendar System: Semester
URL: www.ndsu.edu
Established: 1890 Annual Undergrad Tuition & Fees (In-State): $8,327
Enrollment: 14,516 Coed
Affiliation or Control: State IRS Status: 501(c)3
Highest Offering: Doctorate
Accreditation: NH, ART, CAATE, CACREP, CAEPN, CIDA, COARC, CONST, DIETC, DIETD, ENG, EXSC, LSAR, MUS, NURSE, PH, PHAR, THEA

02 President .... Dr. Dean BRESCIANI
05 Provost/Vice Pres Academic Affairs .... Dr. Beth INGRAM
10 Vice President Business & Finance .... Mr. Bruce BOLLINGER
32 Vice President for Student Affairs .... Dr. Timothy ALVAREZ
46 Vice Pres Research Crea Act & Tech .... Dr. Kelly RUSCH
88 Vice President Ag/Univ Extension .... Dr. Ken GRAFTON
30 Int Pres/CEO Dev/Fdn/Alum Assn .... Mr. Keith BJERKE
13 Chief Information Officer .... Mr. Marc WALLMAN
22 VP Equity/Diversity/Global Outreach .... Mrs. Eveadean MYERS
84 Assoc VP Enrollment Management .... Ms. Laura OSTER-AALAND
88 Assoc VP Sponsored Programs Admin .... Ms. Valrey V. KETTNER
88 Assoc VP University Relations .... Ms. Laura MCDANIEL
06 University Registrar .... Ms. Rhonda KITCH
88 Director Administrative Systems .... Mr. Viet DOAN
08 Dean of Libraries .... Mr. Joe MOCNIK
35 Dean Student Life .... Ms. Janna M. STOSKOPF
51 Int Dir Distance/Continuing Educ .... Mr. Paul KELTER
37 Director Student Financial Services .... Mr. Jeff JACOBS
36 Director Career Center .... Mr. Mark MATTHES
26 Communication Coordinator .... Ms. Ann ROBINSON-PAUL
56 Director Extension Service .... Mr. Chris BOERBOOM
50 Dean Business .... Dr. Scott BEAULIER
54 Dean Engineering/Architecture .... Dr. Gary R. SMITH
53 Dean Human Development & Education .... Dr. Margaret FITZGERALD
49 Dean Arts/Humanities/Social Science .... Dr. Kent SANDSTROM
81 Dean of Science & Math .... Dr. Scott WOOD
67 Dean of Pharmacy/Nursing/Allied Sci ... Dr. Charles D. PETERSON
58 Dean Graduate School .... Dr. David A. WITTROCK
89 Assoc Dean University Studies .... Dr. Carolyn A. SCHNELL
21 Director of Budget .... Ms. Cynthia ROTT
18 Director Facilities Management .... Mr. Mike ELLINGSON
19 Dir of Univ Police/Safety Officer .... Mr. Mike BORR
38 Director Counseling/Disability Svcs .... Dr. William BURNS
23 Director Wellness Center .... Mr. Jobey LICHTBLAU
39 Director of Residence Life .... Mr. Rian NOSTRUM
40 Director Bookstore .... Ms. Carol J. MILLER
41 Director of Athletics .... Mr. Matt LARSEN
57 Director Fine Arts .... Dr. E. John MILLER
09 Dir Institutional Research/Analysis .... Ms. Emily BERG
96 Director of Purchasing .... Ms. Stacey O. WINTER
07 Director of Admissions .... Ms. Merideth SHERLIN
04 Executive Asst to President .... Ms. Barb PEDERSON
108 Dir Accred/Assessment/Acad Advising .... Dr. Larry PETERSON
15 Director HR/Payroll .... Ms. Colette ERICKSON
25 Manager Grant & Contract Accounting .... Ms. Karen HENDRICKSON

*Valley City State University (E)

101 College Street, SW, Valley City ND 58072-4098
County: Barnes FICE Identification: 003008
Unit ID: 200572
Telephone: (701) 845-7122 Carnegie Class: Bac-Diverse
FAX Number: (701) 845-7104 Calendar System: Semester
URL: www.vcsu.edu
Established: 1889 Annual Undergrad Tuition & Fees (In-State): $7,196
Enrollment: 1,422 Coed
Affiliation or Control: State IRS Status: 501(c)3
Highest Offering: Master's
Accreditation: NH, CAATE, CAEPN, MUS

02 President .... Dr. Tisa MASON
05 Vice Pres Academic Affairs .... Dr. Margaret DAHLBERG
10 Vice President Business Affairs .... Mr. Wesley WINTCH
32 Vice President Student Affairs .... Mr. Pete SMITHHISLER
53 Dean Sch of Educ/Graduate Stds .... Dr. Gary THOMPSON
08 Library Director .... Ms. Donna JAMES
20 Director Student Academic Services .... Mr. Cory BURGER
37 Director Student Financial Aid .... Ms. Marcia PRITCHERT
13 Chief Information Officer .... Mr. Joseph TYKWINSKI
41 Athletic Director .... Ms. Jill DEVRIES
84 Director of Enrollment Services .... Ms. Charlene STENSON
30 Director of University Advancement .... Mr. Larry J. ROBINSON
18 Asst Director Facilities Services .... Mr. Pat HORNER
15 Human Resources Director .... Ms. Jennifer LARSON
44 Asst Dir Univ Advance/Alumni Rels .... Ms. Kim HESCH
38 Director of Student Counseling .... Ms. Erin KLINGENBERG
26 Director Marketing/Communications .... Mr. Greg VANNEY
40 Director Bookstore .... Mr. Todd ROGELSTAD
06 Registrar .... Ms. Jody KLIER
09 Dir Institutional Rsch/Assessment .... Ms. Kerry GREGORYK
36 Career Services Coordinator .... Ms. Kari BODINE
28 Learning Ctr Coord/Disability Svcs .... Ms. Monica MOORE

*Bismarck State College (F)

PO Box 5587, Bismarck ND 58506-5587
County: Burleigh FICE Identification: 002988
Unit ID: 200022
Telephone: (701) 224-5400 Carnegie Class: Bac/Assoc-Assoc Dom
FAX Number: (701) 224-5550 Calendar System: Semester
URL: bismarckstate.edu
Established: 1939 Annual Undergrad Tuition & Fees (In-State): $3,659
Enrollment: 4,078 Coed
Affiliation or Control: State IRS Status: 501(c)3
Highest Offering: Baccalaureate
Accreditation: NH, ADNUR, EMT, ENGT, MLTAD, PHLEB, SURGT

02 President .... Dr. Larry C. SKOGEN
03 Executive Vice President .... Mr. Dave CLARK
05 VP Academic Affairs .... Mr. Dan LEINGANG
111 VP College Advance/Exec Dir Found .... Ms. Kari KNUDSON
10 Assoc VP Finance/Operations .... Ms. Tamara BARBER
32 VP Student Affairs .... Dr. Donna FISHBECK
88 Dean Nat Energy Ctr of Excell .... Mr. Bruce EMMIL
88 Dean Current & Emerging Technology .... Ms. Carla HIXON
13 Chief Information Officer .... Ms. Carol FLAA
15 Chief Human Resources Officer .... Ms. Rita LINDGREN
106 Chief Dist Learning/Military Affs .... Mr. Lane HUBER
51 Director Continuing Education .... Ms. Sara VOLLMER
08 Director of Library Services .... Ms. Marlene ANDERSON
26 Director of College Relations .... Ms. Marnie PIEHL
18 Chief Buildings/Grounds Officer .... Mr. Don ROETHLER
41 Director of Athletics .... Mr. Buster GILLISS
37 Director of Financial Aid .... Mr. Scott LINGEN
07 Dir Admissions/Enrollment Services .... Ms. Karen ERICKSON
88 Dir Great Plains Energy Corridor .... Ms. Emily CASH
35 Director Student & Residence Life .... Ms. Heather SHEEHAN
06 Director Academic Records/Registrar .... Mr. Tom LENO
35 Associate Dean of Student Affairs .... Mr. Jay MEIER
36 Dir Counseling & Advising Services .... Ms. Kate MILLNER
88 Program Manager NECE .... Mr. Dan SCHMIDT
88 Project Manager NECE .... Mr. Zachery ALLEN
88 Program Manager NECE .... Mr. Kyren MILLER
88 Training & Program Manager NECE .... Ms. Alicia UHDE
30 Resource Development Manager .... Ms. Janet DIXON
29 Alumni Coordinator .... Ms. Rita NODLAND
40 Bookstore Manager/Purchasing Coord .... Ms. Debra SANDNESS
04 Executive Assistant to President .... Ms. Janell CAMPBELL
19 Campus Safety & Security Manager .... Mr. Duane JOHNSON

*Dakota College at Bottineau (G)

105 Simrall Boulevard, Bottineau ND 58318-1198
County: Bottineau FICE Identification: 002995
Unit ID: 200314
Telephone: (701) 228-2277 Carnegie Class: Assoc/MT-VT-Mix Trad/Non
FAX Number: (701) 228-5468 Calendar System: Semester
URL: www.dakotacollege.edu
Established: 1906 Annual Undergrad Tuition & Fees (In-State): $4,281
Enrollment: 692 Coed
Affiliation or Control: State IRS Status: 501(c)3
Highest Offering: Associate Degree
Accreditation: NH, EMT

02 Campus Dean .... Dr. Jerry MIGLER
10 Director of Business Affairs .... Ms. Lisa MOCK
32 Assoc Dean for Student Affairs .... Mr. Larry BROOKS
05 Assoc Dean for Academic Affairs .... Mr. Larry BROOKS

08 Librarian .... Ms. Hattie ALBERTSON
06 Registrar .... Ms. April ABRAHAMSON
37 Director Financial Aid .... Ms. Valerie HEILMAN
41 Athletic Director .... Mr. Dan DAVIS
29 Director Alumni Relations .... Ms. Courtney VANDAL
39 Housing Director .... Ms. Michelle DAVIS
28 Director of Diversity .... Mr. James HOLLOWELL
40 Bookstore Manager .... Ms. Janeen POLLMAN
18 Chief Facilities/Physical Plant .... Mr. Darrell WATERS
38 Director Student Counseling .... Ms. Corey GORDER
04 Administrative Asst to President .... Ms. Sandy HAGENESS
106 Dir Online Education/E-learning .... Ms. Kayla O'TOOLE
25 Chief Contracts/Grants Admin .... Ms. Stephanie BLUMHAGEN

*Lake Region State College (A)

1801 College Drive N, Devils Lake ND 58301-1598
County: Ramsey FICE Identification: 002991
Unit ID: 200192
Telephone: (701) 662-1600 Carnegie Class: Assoc/HT-High Non
FAX Number: (701) 662-1570 Calendar System: Semester
URL: www.lrsc.edu
Established: 1941 Annual Undergrad Tuition & Fees (In-State): $4,203
Enrollment: 1,918 Coed
Affiliation or Control: State IRS Status: 501(c)3
Highest Offering: Associate Degree
Accreditation: NH, ADNUR

02 President .... Dr. Douglas D. DARLING
05 VP Academic/Student Affairs .... Mr. Lloyd HALVORSON
10 VP Administrative Affairs .... Mr. Corry G. KENNER
12 Director of Branch Campus .... Mr. John COWGER
30 Vice Pres Advancement/Foundation .... Ms. Laurel GOULDING
84 Director of Enrollment Management .... Ms. Stephanie SHOCK
37 Dir Student Finan Aid/Placemnt Svcs .... Ms. Katie NETTELL
109 Director Food Service .... Ms. Rosalie SEIBEL
18 Director Physical Plant .... Mr. Chad ESTENSON
08 Librarian .... Ms. Elonda NORD
41 Director Athletics .... Mr. Daniel MERTENS
13 Chief Information Officer .... Ms. Toofawn SIMHAI
15 HR Risk Mgmt/Placement Svcs .... Mrs. Sandi LILLEHAUGEN
40 Director of Bookstore .... Ms. Melissa STOTTS
06 Registrar .... Mr. Daniel JOHNSON
26 Director of Public Relations/Mktg .... Ms. Erin WOOD
31 Director Community Education .... Mr. Daniel DRIESSEN
09 Director of Institutional Research .... Ms. Brandi NELSON
28 Director of Diversity .... Mrs. Kristi HERNANDEZ
38 Director Counseling Services .... Mrs. Brigitte GREYWATER
07 Director of Admissions .... Ms. Stephanie SHOCK
21 Controller .... Ms. Joann KITCHENS
04 Administrative Asst to President .... Ms. Bobbi J. LUNDAY
29 Director Alumni Relations .... Ms. Elonda NORD
39 Director Student Housing .... Dr. Randall FIXEN

*North Dakota State College of Science (B)

800 N Sixth Street, Wahpeton ND 58076-0002
County: Richland FICE Identification: 002996
Unit ID: 200305
Telephone: (800) 342-4325 Carnegie Class: Assoc/HVT-High Trad
FAX Number: (701) 671-2145 Calendar System: Semester
URL: www.ndscs.edu
Established: 1903 Annual Undergrad Tuition & Fees (In-State): $4,697
Enrollment: 3,123 Coed
Affiliation or Control: State IRS Status: 501(c)3
Highest Offering: Associate Degree
Accreditation: NH, CAHIIM, DA, DH, EMT, OTA, PNUR

02 President .... Dr. John RICHMAN
05 VP Academic & Student Affairs .... Mr. Harvey LINK
11 Vice Pres Administrative Affairs .... Mr. Dennis GLADEN
32 Vice Pres Student Affairs .... Dr. Jane VANGSNESS FRISCH
103 Vice Pres Workforce Development .... Mr. Tony GRINDBERG
37 Director Financial Aid .... Mrs. Shelley BLOME
08 Director Library .... Ms. Tina GRENIER
26 Dir Marketing/Communications/PR .. Mrs. Barbara SPAETH-BAUM
29 Exec Dir of Alumni Foundation .... Mrs. Kim NELSON
41 Athletic Director .... Mr. Stuart ENGEN
15 Exec Dir Human Resources .... Mrs. Sandi GILBERTSON
18 Director Facilities/Physical Plant .... Mr. Dallas FOSSUM
20 Academic Services Chair .... Ms. Maria KADUC
39 Exec Director of Residence Life .... Mrs. Melissa JOHNSON
07 Director of Admissions & Records .... Mrs. Barb MUND
10 Chief Financial Officer .... Mr. Keith JOHNSON
24 Instructional Technology Coord .... Mr. Tom HICKMAN
06 Asst Director Admissions & Records .... Mr. Justin GRAMS
38 Counseling Center .... Mr. Vince PLUMMER
49 Dean Arts Sciences/Business .... Mr. Ken KOMPELIEN
64 Director of Music .... Mr. Bryan POYZER

*Williston State College (C)

1410 University Avenue, Williston ND 58801-1326
County: Williams FICE Identification: 003007
Unit ID: 200341
Telephone: (701) 774-4200 Carnegie Class: Assoc/HT-Mix Trad/Non
FAX Number: (701) 774-4211 Calendar System: Semester
URL: www.willistonstate.edu
Established: 1961 Annual Undergrad Tuition & Fees (In-State): $5,027
Enrollment: 1,038 Coed
Affiliation or Control: State IRS Status: 501(c)3
Highest Offering: Associate Degree
Accreditation: NH

02 Acting President .... Dr. John MILLER
05 Vice President Academic Affairs .... Dr. John MILLER
30 VP College Advancement .... Vacant
32 Vice President Student Affairs .... Kaylyn BONDY
10 Chief Financial Officer .... Vincent PACHUILO
103 CEO of Workforce Education Train .... Deanette PIESIK
37 Director Student Financial Aid .... Heather FINK

Nueta Hidatsa Sahnish College (D)

PO Box 490, New Town ND 58763-0490
County: Mountrail FICE Identification: 025537
Unit ID: 200086
Telephone: (701) 627-4738 Carnegie Class: Tribal
FAX Number: (701) 627-3609 Calendar System: Semester
URL: www.nhsc.edu
Established: 1973 Annual Undergrad Tuition & Fees: $3,870
Enrollment: 229 Coed
Affiliation or Control: Independent Non-Profit IRS Status: 501(c)3
Highest Offering: Baccalaureate
Accreditation: NH

01 President .... Dr. Twyla BAKER-DEMARAY
05 Vice President of Academics .... Dr. Waylon BAKER
32 Vice Pres Student Services .... Dr. Constance FRANKBERRY
10 Chief Finance Ofcr/VP Support Svcs .... Mr. Philip LEWIS
37 Financial Aid Assistant .... Mr. Tim OLSON
06 Registrar .... Ms. Alicia REED
08 Director Library Services .... Ms. Amy SOLIS
38 Guidance Counselor .... Ms. Deanna RAINBOW
40 Bookstore Manager .... Ms. Iona LITTLE WHITEMAN

Rasmussen College - Fargo/Moorhead (E)

4012 19th Avenue, SW, Fargo ND 58103-7196
Telephone: (701) 277-3889 FICE Identification: 004846
Accreditation: &NH

† Regional acrreditation is carried under parent institution in Saint Cloud, MN. The tuition figure is an average, actual tuition may vary.

Sitting Bull College (F)

9299 Highway 24, Fort Yates ND 58538-9706
County: Sioux FICE Identification: 021882
Unit ID: 200466
Telephone: (701) 854-8000 Carnegie Class: Tribal
FAX Number: (701) 854-8197 Calendar System: Semester
URL: www.sittingbull.edu
Established: 1971 Annual Undergrad Tuition & Fees: $3,910
Enrollment: 261 Coed
Affiliation or Control: Tribal Control IRS Status: 501(c)3
Highest Offering: Master's
Accreditation: NH

01 President .... Dr. Laurel VERMILLION
11 Vice President of Operations .... Dr. Koreen RESSLER
37 Director Financial Student Aid .... Ms. Donna SEABOY
06 Registrar .... Ms. Melody AZURE
08 Head Librarian .... Mr. Mark HOLMAN
40 Director of Bookstore .... Mrs. Tracy MAHER

Trinity Bible College & Graduate School (G)

50 S 6th Avenue, Ellendale ND 58436-7150
County: Dickey FICE Identification: 012059
Unit ID: 200484
Telephone: (701) 349-3621 Carnegie Class: Spec-4-yr-Faith
FAX Number: (701) 349-5786 Calendar System: Semester
URL: www.trinitybiblecollege.edu
Established: 1948 Annual Undergrad Tuition & Fees: $15,912
Enrollment: 217 Coed
Affiliation or Control: Assemblies Of God Church IRS Status: 501(c)3
Highest Offering: Master's
Accreditation: BI

01 President .... Dr. Paul ALEXANDER
03 Executive Vice President .... Rev. Ian O'BRIEN
05 Vice President of Academic Affairs .... Rev. Rick WADHOLM
32 Vice President of Student Affairs .... Ms. Twyla KUNTZ
07 Director Enrollment Management .... Rev. Jordy H. NUNEZ
58 Director of Graduate School .... Dr. Carol ALEXANDER
106 Director of Distance Education .... Mr. Daryel ERICKSON
06 Academic Registrar .... Ms. Sara BEST
08 Librarian .... Mrs. Phyllis KUNO
18 Director of Facility Services .... Mr. Bryan JACOBSON
41 Athletic Director .... Mr. Jordan NOWELL

Turtle Mountain Community College (H)

Box 340, Belcourt ND 58316-0340
County: Rolette FICE Identification: 023011
Unit ID: 200527
Telephone: (701) 477-7862 Carnegie Class: Tribal
FAX Number: (701) 477-7870 Calendar System: Semester
URL: www.tm.edu
Established: 1972 Annual Undergrad Tuition & Fees: $2,250
Enrollment: 555 Coed
Affiliation or Control: Independent Non-Profit IRS Status: 501(c)3
Highest Offering: Baccalaureate
Accreditation: NH, MLTAD, PHLEB

01 President .... Dr. Jim L. DAVIS
02 Vice President .... Kellie HALL
05 Academic Dean .... Dr. Terri MARTIN-PARISIEN
32 Dean of Student Affairs .... Wanda LADUCER
10 Comptroller .... Tracy AZURE
75 Director Vocational/Education .... Sheila TROTTIER
06 Registrar .... Angel GLADUE
31 Dir of Community/Adult Education .... Sandra LAROCQUE
07 Director of Admissions .... Joni LAFONTAINE
15 Director Personnel Services .... Holly CAHILL
37 Financial Aid Officer .... Alexsis MARCELLAIS
40 Director of Bookstore .... Shirley MORIN
18 Chief Facilities/Physical Plant .... Wesley DAVIS
30 Chief Development .... Dave RIPLEY
04 Administrative Asst to President .... Nicole GAGNON
101 Secretary of the Institution/Board .... Candace LONGIE
38 Director Student Counseling .... Dr. Andrea LAVERDURE
41 Athletic Director .... Dr. Eugene MONETTE
09 Director of Institutional Research .... Ace CHARETTE
19 Director Security/Safety .... Wes DAVIS
08 Head Librarian .... Laisee ALLERY
13 IT Director .... Chad DAVIS
36 Placement Center Coordinator .... Denise MARCELLAIS
53 Director of Teacher Education .... Dr. Teresa DELORME

United Tribes Technical College (I)

3315 University Drive, Bismarck ND 58504-7596
County: Burleigh FICE Identification: 022429
Unit ID: 200554
Telephone: (701) 255-3285 Carnegie Class: Tribal
FAX Number: (701) 530-0605 Calendar System: Semester
URL: www.uttc.edu
Established: 1969 Annual Undergrad Tuition & Fees: $5,757
Enrollment: 391 Coed
Affiliation or Control: Independent Non-Profit IRS Status: 501(c)3
Highest Offering: Baccalaureate
Accreditation: NH, PNUR

01 President .... Dr. Leander MCDONALD
05 Vice Pres Academic Affairs .... Dr. Lisa AZURE
11 Vice Pres Campus Services .... Dr. William GOURNEAU
10 Finance Director .... Mrs. Katina DECOTEAU
07 Admissions Director .... Mrs. Camille MARTELL
06 Registrar .... Vacant
15 Human Resources Director .... Mrs. Rae GUNN
41 Athletic Director .... Mr. Pete CONWAY
13 IT Director .... Mr. Christopher BAILLIE
19 Safety and Security Director .... Mr. Joely HEAVY RUNNER
04 Exec Assistant to the President .... Ms. Melissa BUFFALO
08 Librarian .... Mrs. Charlene WEIS
30 Institutional Resources Director .... Mrs. Larretta HALL
37 Financial Aid Director .... Mr. Scott SKARRO
106 Dir Online Education/E-learning .... Mr. Leah HAMANN
108 Director Institutional Assessment .... Mr. Monte SCHAFF
39 Director Student Housing .... Ms. Jolene DECOUTEAU

University of Jamestown (J)

6000 College Lane, Jamestown ND 58405-0001
County: Stutsman FICE Identification: 002990
Unit ID: 200156
Telephone: (701) 252-3467 Carnegie Class: Bac-Diverse
FAX Number: (701) 253-4318 Calendar System: Semester
URL: www.uj.edu
Established: 1883 Annual Undergrad Tuition & Fees: $20,480
Enrollment: 1,005 Coed
Affiliation or Control: Presbyterian Church (U.S.A.) IRS Status: 501(c)3
Highest Offering: Doctorate
Accreditation: NH, IACBE, NUR, PTA

01 President .... Dr. Robert S. BADAL
05 Vice Pres/Dean Academic Affairs .... Dr. Paul OLSON
32 Dean of Students .... Vacant
11 VP Planning/Administrative Services .... Mr. Thomas R. HECK
03 Executive Vice President .... Ms. Polly J. PETERSON
84 Vice President of Enrollment Mgmt .... Mr. Mike HEITKAMP
26 VP for Marketing/Public Relations .... Ms. Tena LAWRENCE
101 Asst to Pres/Secy to Bd of Trustees .... Ms. Erin KLEIN
06 Registrar .... Mr. Michael P. WOODLEY
37 Director of Financial Aid .... Ms. Judy HAGER
08 Librarian .... Mrs. Phyllis K. BRATTON
36 Director Experiential Education .... Ms. Heidi LARSON
27 Director Information Office .... Ms. Donna SCHMITZ
41 Athletic Director .... Mr. Sean JOHNSON
13 Director Computer Center .... Mr. Chris HOKE
18 Chief Facilities/Physical Plant .... Mr. Mark KOEPKE
105 Director Web Services .... Mr. Dallas ROSIN
19 Director Security/Safety .... Ms. Elizabeth KAPP
22 Dir Affirmative Action/EEO .... Ms. Becky KNODEL
39 Director Student Housing .... Mr. Eric THORSON

University of Mary (K)

7500 University Drive, Bismarck ND 58504-9652
County: Burleigh FICE Identification: 002992
Unit ID: 200217
Telephone: (701) 255-7500 Carnegie Class: Masters/L
FAX Number: (701) 255-7687 Calendar System: Other
URL: www.umary.edu

Established: 1959 Annual Undergrad Tuition & Fees: $17,445
Enrollment: 2,872 Coed
Affiliation or Control: Roman Catholic IRS Status: 501(c)3
Highest Offering: Doctorate
Accreditation: NH, CAATE, COARC, EXSC, IACBE, MUS, NURSE, OT, PTA, SW

01 President ... Msgr. James P. SHEA
03 Executive Vice President ... Mr. Gregory A. VETTER
05 Vice President for Academic Affairs ... Dr. Diane FLADELAND
10 Vice President Financial Affairs ... Vacant
32 Vice President Student Development ... Dr. Timothy SEAWORTH
84 Vice President Enrollment Services ... Mr. Michael MCMAHON
26 Vice President for Public Affairs ... Mr. Jerome J. RICHTER
30 Director of Mission Advancement ... Vacant
06 Registrar ... Ms. Melissa MCDOWALL
08 Librarian ... Mr. David GRAY
37 Director of Financial Aid ... Mrs. Karrie K. HUBER
07 Director of Admissions ... Mr. Richard HINTON
09 Director of Institutional Research ... Mr. Phil REESE
15 Director Human Resources ... Mrs. Bonnie L. DAHL
18 Chief Facilities/Physical Plant ... Mr. Mark R. STEPHENS
20 Associate Academic Officer ... Dr. Alyssa MARTIN
35 Associate Student Affairs Officer ... Mrs. Sarah D. EBERLE

OHIO

AIC College of Design (A)

1171 East Kemper Road, Cincinnati OH 45246-3322
County: Hamilton FICE Identification: 021286
Unit ID: 200624
Telephone: (513) 751-1206 Carnegie Class: Spec-4-yr-Arts
FAX Number: (513) 751-1209 Calendar System: Semester
URL: www.aic-arts.edu
Established: 1976 Annual Undergrad Tuition & Fees: $23,341
Enrollment: 35 Coed
Affiliation or Control: Proprietary IRS Status: Proprietary
Highest Offering: Baccalaureate
Accreditation: ACCSC

00 CEO ... Ms. Marion K. ALLMAN
01 President ... Mr. Sean M. MENDELL
07 Vice Pres of Admissions ... Ms. Cyndi MENDELL
08 Head Librarian ... Ms. Donna WAKEFIELD
10 Chief Business Officer ... Ms. Laura LEWIS
36 Director Career Services ... Mr. Dennis GATES
37 Director Student Financial Aid ... Ms. Rita SCHRAND

Allegheny Wesleyan College (B)

2161 Woodsdale Road, Salem OH 44460-8920
County: Columbiana FICE Identification: 034573
Unit ID: 200873
Telephone: (330) 337-6403 Carnegie Class: Spec-4-yr-Faith
FAX Number: (424) 228-3006 Calendar System: Semester
URL: www.awc.edu
Established: 1956 Annual Undergrad Tuition & Fees: $5,000
Enrollment: 63 Coed
Affiliation or Control: Wesleyan Church IRS Status: 501(c)3
Highest Offering: Baccalaureate
Accreditation: BI

01 President ... Rev. Daniel R. HARDY, SR.
05 Academic Dean ... Mrs. Jeanne W. ZVARITCH
10 Business Manager ... Miss Katrina KAUFMAN
32 Dean of Students ... Rev. Timothy FORRIDER
30 Director of Development ... Mr. Tom SANDERS
06 Registrar & Director Admissions ... Mrs. Jeanne ZVARITCH
08 Head Librarian ... Mrs. Crystal WHITHAM
37 Financial Aid Administrator ... Mrs. Esther PHELPS
09 Dir of Institutional Effectiveness ... Mrs. Jeanne ZVARITCH
40 Bookstore Manager ... Rev. Daniel GILES
33 Dean of Men ... Mr. Stefan LETONEK
34 Dean of Women ... Miss Heidi MCINTIRE
07 Director of Admissions ... Mr. James DENTLER
18 Chief Facilities/Physical Plant ... Mr. Darrin PATTERSON
29 Director Alumni Relations ... Rev. John DYE
35 Director Student Affairs ... Rev. Timothy FORRIDER
38 Director Student Counseling ... Mrs. Kimberly FORD
19 Director Security/Safety ... Mr. Darrin PATTERSON

American Institute of Alternative Medicine (C)

6685 Doubletree Avenue, Columbus OH 43229-1113
County: Franklin FICE Identification: 035344
Unit ID: 441636
Telephone: (614) 825-6255 Carnegie Class: Spec 2-yr-Health
FAX Number: (614) 825-6279 Calendar System: Quarter
URL: www.aiam.edu
Established: 1994 Annual Undergrad Tuition & Fees: N/A
Enrollment: 386 Coed
Affiliation or Control: Proprietary IRS Status: Proprietary
Highest Offering: Master's
Accreditation: ACCSC, ACUP

01 Campus President ... Mark SULLIVAN
05 Academic Dean ... Dr. Elaine HIATT
10 Chief Financial Officer ... Helen YEE
32 Dir of Student & Graduate Services ... Linda FLEMING-WILLIS
06 Registrar ... Emily MINNEMA
37 Financial Aid Officer ... Ulrike ROSSER
66 Director of Nursing ... Pamela FROST

American National University (D)

1837 Woodman Center Drive, Kettering OH 45420
Telephone: (937) 299-9450 Identification: 770697
Accreditation: ACICS, CAHIIM, MAC, SURGT

† Branch campus of American National University, Salem, VA

American National University (E)

3487 Belmont Avenue, Youngstown OH 44505
Telephone: (330) 759-0205 Identification: 770701
Accreditation: ACICS, CAHIIM, MAC, SURGT

† Branch campus of American National University, Salem, VA

Antioch College (F)

One Morgan Place, Yellow Springs OH 45387
County: Greene Identification: 667214
Unit ID: 483018
Telephone: (937) 767-1286 Carnegie Class: Not Classified
FAX Number: N/A Calendar System: Quarter
URL: www.antiochcollege.org
Established: 1853 Annual Undergrad Tuition & Fees: $35,568
Enrollment: 266 Coed
Affiliation or Control: Independent Non-Profit IRS Status: 501(c)3
Highest Offering: Baccalaureate
Accreditation: NH

01 President ... Dr. Thomas MANLEY
05 Provost/Vice Pres Acad Affairs ... Dr. Lori COLLINS-HALL
111 Vice Pres Advancement ... Ms. Susanne HASHIM
28 Vice Pres Diversity & Inclusion ... Ms. Mila COOPER
07 Dean of Admission ... Vacant
06 Registrar ... Mr. Ron NAPOLI
09 Dir Innovation & Inst Effectiveness ... Ms. Hannah SPIRRISON
13 Dir Information Technology ... Mr. Kevin STOKES
04 Administrative Asst to President ... Ms. Nancy WUEBBEN

*Antioch University (G)

900 Dayton Street, Yellow Springs OH 45387-1635
County: Greene FICE Identification: 003010
Unit ID: 442392
Telephone: (937) 769-1800 Carnegie Class: N/A
FAX Number: (937) 769-1806
URL: www.antioch.edu

01 Interim Chancellor ... Mr. William GROVES
10 Vice Chancellor/CFO ... Dr. Allan GOZUM
05 Vice Chancellor Academic Affairs ... Dr. Iris WEISMAN
30 Vice Chancellor Inst Advancement ... Mr. Tim FORBESS
26 Vice Chancellor for Marketing ... Dr. MB LUFKIN
15 Chief Human Resources Officer ... Ms. Suzette CASTONGUAY
88 Chief Global Officer ... Ms. Felice NUDELMAN
91 Dir Administrative Info Systems ... Ms. Candice SANTELL
04 Executive Asst Chancellor's Office ... Ms. Judy OWENS
06 Registrar ... Ms. Maureen HEACOCK
08 Head Librarian ... Mr. Steve SHAW
101 Secretary to the Board ... Ms. Leslie JOHNSON
29 Director Alumni Relations ... Mr. Brice THOMAS
37 Director Student Financial Aid ... Ms. Susan HOWARD
86 Director Government Relations ... Mr. Paul BRADLEY

† Parent institution of Antioch University Midwest in OH; Antioch University Seattle in WA; Antioch University New England in NH; and Antioch University Los Angeles and Antioch University Santa Barbara in CA.

**Antioch University Midwest* (H)

900 Dayton Street, Yellow Springs OH 45387-1745
Telephone: (937) 769-1800 Identification: 666811
Accreditation: NH, CAEPN

Antonelli College (I)

124 E Seventh Street, Cincinnati OH 45202-2592
County: Hamilton FICE Identification: 012891
Unit ID: 201016
Telephone: (800) 505-4338 Carnegie Class: Assoc/HT-High Non
FAX Number: (513) 241-9396 Calendar System: Semester
URL: www.antonellicollege.edu
Established: 1947 Annual Undergrad Tuition & Fees: $15,980
Enrollment: 147 Coed
Affiliation or Control: Proprietary IRS Status: Proprietary
Highest Offering: Associate Degree
Accreditation: ACCSC

01 Campus President ... Ms. Yvonne SILVA
05 Director Of Education ... Ms. Andrea MILLETTE
32 Associate Campus Director ... Mr. Corey BJARNSON
06 Registrar ... Vacant
36 Career Services Coordinator ... Ms. Charlene SMITH
07 Director of Admissions ... Ms. Yolanda STEWARD
37 Director Student Financial Aid ... Ms. Leah C. ELKINS

Art Academy of Cincinnati (J)

1212 Jackson Street, Cincinnati OH 45202-7106
County: Hamilton FICE Identification: 003011
Unit ID: 201061
Telephone: (513) 562-6262 Carnegie Class: Spec-4-yr-Arts
FAX Number: (513) 562-8778 Calendar System: Semester
URL: www.artacademy.edu
Established: 1869 Annual Undergrad Tuition & Fees: $29,752
Enrollment: 207 Coed
Affiliation or Control: Independent Non-Profit IRS Status: 501(c)3
Highest Offering: Master's
Accreditation: NH, ART

01 President ... Mr. John M. SULLIVAN
05 VP for Academic Affairs/CAO ... Mr. Kimberly G. KRAUSE
10 VP for Finance & Operations/CFO ... Mr. Thomas J. PACK
30 VP of Institutional Advancement ... Ms. Joan M. KAUP
37 Director of Financial Aid ... Ms. Jean SPOHR
06 Director of Registrar Services ... Mr. Alex SIEBERT
21 Interim Director of Finance ... Ms. Madonna DUVAL
84 Dir of Enrollment Management ... Ms. Jamie OWENS
15 Director of Human Resources ... Ms. Chris ROEDIGER
32 Director of Student Services ... Mr. Mack MAYNARD
18 Director of Facilities and Security ... Mr. Frank VONDER MEULEN
31 Director of Community Education ... Ms. Jennifer SPURLOCK
04 Executive Assistant to President ... Ms. Kelly ENWRIGHT
105 Digital Media Specialist ... Mr. Jimmy BAKER
13 Lead Systems Engineer ... Mr. Kyle GRIZZELL
26 Marketing/Communications Specialist ... Ms. Amanda PARKER-WOLERY

The Art Institute of Ohio-Cincinnati (K)

8845 Governors Hill Drive, Cincinnati OH 45249
Telephone: (513) 833-2400 Identification: 666693
Accreditation: &NH, ACFEI

† In teach-out mode. Regional accreditation is carried under the parent institution The Illinois Institute of Art, Chicago, IL. School is in teach-out plan.

Ashland University (L)

401 College Avenue, Ashland OH 44805
County: Ashland FICE Identification: 003012
Unit ID: 201104
Telephone: (800) 882-1548 Carnegie Class: DU-Mod
FAX Number: N/A Calendar System: Semester
URL: www.ashland.edu
Established: 1878 Annual Undergrad Tuition & Fees: $20,392
Enrollment: 5,677 Coed
Affiliation or Control: Brethren Church IRS Status: 501(c)3
Highest Offering: Doctorate
Accreditation: NH, ACBSP, #CAATE, CACREP, CAEPN, CEA, DIETD, MUS, NURSE, SW, THEOL

01 President ... Dr. Carlos CAMPO
73 President Theological Seminary ... Dr. Mark HARDEN
05 Provost ... Dr. Eun-Woo CHANG
32 Vice President Student Affairs ... Dr. Hannah CLAYBORNE
111 Vice Pres Development & Inst Advanc ... Ms. Margaret POMFRET
18 Vice Pres Facilities/Mgmt & Plng ... Mr. Rick M. EWING, II
10 Interim VP/CFO ... Mr. Randall PATTERSON
13 Chief Tech & Info Officer ... Dr. Donald THARP
42 Director of Religious Life ... Mr. Glenn BLACK
06 Interim Registrar ... Mrs. Vicki YOHO
37 Director Student Financial Aid ... Mr. Stephen C. HOWELL
29 Director Alumni/Parent Relations ... Mr. Jeff ALIX
15 Director of Human Resources/Legal ... Mr. Joshua A. HUGHES
36 Executive Director Career Services ... Mr. Lenroy JONES
26 Director of Public Relations ... Mr. Steven M. HANNAN
41 Director of Athletics ... Mr. Albert KING
88 Exec Dir Ashbrook Ctr ... Mr. Roger BECKETT
09 Director Inst Research & Assessment ... Dr. Larry BUNCE
07 Director of Admissions ... Mr. W.C VANCE
49 Dean College of Arts & Sciences ... Dr. Dawn WEBER
50 Dean College Business/Econ ... Dr. Elad GRANOT
53 Dean College of Education ... Dr. Donna BREAULT
66 Dean Col Nursing & Health Sci ... Dr. Faye GRUND
51 Dean Founders School of Cont Educ ... Dr. Eugene LINTON
28 Dir Multicultural Stdnt Svcs & Stds ... Mr. Jonathan E. LOCUST, JR.
19 Director Security/Safety ... Mr. David B. MCLAUGHLIN
38 Director of Counseling ... Dr. Oscar MCKNIGHT
112 Director Planned Giving ... Ms. Frances REDDICK
39 Director Student Housing ... Ms. Kimberly LAMMERS
102 Dir Foundation/Corporate Relations ... Dr. Dan LAWSON
104 Director Study Abroad ... Ms. Rebecca PARILLO
25 Chief Contracts/Grants Admin ... Mr. Scott SAVAGE

Athenaeum of Ohio (M)

6616 Beechmont Avenue, Cincinnati OH 45230-5900
County: Hamilton FICE Identification: 003013
Unit ID: 201140
Telephone: (513) 231-2223 Carnegie Class: Spec-4-yr-Faith
FAX Number: (513) 231-3254 Calendar System: Semester
URL: www.athenaeum.edu
Established: 1829 Annual Graduate Tuition & Fees: N/A
Enrollment: 209 Coed
Affiliation or Control: Roman Catholic IRS Status: 501(c)3
Highest Offering: Master's; No Undergraduates

Accreditation: NH, THEOL

01 President & Rector .... Rev. Benedict O'CINNSEALAIGH
10 Vice President for Finance ....Mr. Dennis K. EAGAN
111 Vice President for Advancement .... Mr. Kyle ISAACK
05 Dean of Athenaeum .... Rev. David ENDRES
08 Librarian ....Mrs. Connie SONG
06 Registrar ....Mr. Nicholas JOBE
42 Dir Lay Pastoral Ministry Program ....Dr. Susan MCGURGAN
108 Director of Assessment ....Mr. Nicholas JOBE

Aultman College of Nursing and Health Sciences (A)

2600 Sixth Street SW, Canton OH 44710-1799

County: Stark FICE Identification: 006487

Unit ID: 201177

Telephone: (330) 363-6347 Carnegie Class: Spec-4-yr-Other Health

FAX Number: (330) 580-6654 Calendar System: Semester

URL: www.aultmancollege.edu

Established: 2004 Annual Undergrad Tuition & Fees: $17,370

Enrollment: 372 Coed

Affiliation or Control: Independent Non-Profit IRS Status: 501(c)3

Highest Offering: Baccalaureate

Accreditation: NH, ADNUR, NURSE, RAD

01 President ....Ms. Rebecca R. CROWL
10 VP Business & Student Affairs ....Ms. Jeannine SHAMBAUGH
05 VP Academic Affairs .... Dr. Jean PADDOCK
30 VP Community Engagement ....Ms. Vi LEGGETT
09 Director IE and Compliance ....Ms. Lyn SABINO

Baldwin Wallace University (B)

275 Eastland Road, Berea OH 44017-2088

County: Cuyahoga FICE Identification: 003014

Unit ID: 201195

Telephone: (440) 826-2900 Carnegie Class: Masters/L

FAX Number: (440) 826-3777 Calendar System: Semester

URL: www.bw.edu/

Established: 1845 Annual Undergrad Tuition & Fees: $30,776

Enrollment: 3,996 Coed

Affiliation or Control: United Methodist IRS Status: 501(c)3

Highest Offering: Master's

Accreditation: NH, #ARCPA, CAATE, CAEPN, EXSC, MUS, NURSE, @SP

01 President ....Dr. Robert C. HELMER
03 Senior Vice President ....Mr. Richard L. FLETCHER
05 Provost ....Dr. Stephen D. STAHL
10 Vice President for Finance & Admin .... Mr. William M. RENIFF
32 VP Student Affairs/Dean of Students ...... Dr. Trina DOBBERSTEIN
84 Vice Pres of Enrollment Management ....Dr. Scott SCHULZ
111 Vice Pres for Advancement .... Mr. Patrick DUNLAVEY
26 Asst VP/Director College Relations ....Mr. Dan KARP
20 Associate Provost .... Dr. Guy E. FARISH
89 Dean of First Year Students .... Mr. Marc WEST
51 Director of Adult Learning ....Ms. Nancy JIROUSEK
08 Director of Ritter Library ....Mr. John DIGENNARO
13 Chief Information Officer .... Mr. Greg G. FLANIK
44 Director Annual Giving .... Ms. Ann MILLER
29 Director Alumni Relations .... Mr. Terry J. KURTZ
30 Senior Advancement Officer .... Ms. Deborah S. MILLER
37 Director of Financial Aid ....Dr. George ROLLESTON
15 Asst VP for Human Resources ....Mr. Sam RAMIREZ
38 Director of Counseling Services ....Ms. Sophia D. KALLERGIS
121 Coordinator of Academic Advising ....Ms. Dianna SPYCHER
06 Registrar ....Mr. Tim SEITZ
07 Dir Undergraduate Admission ....Dr. Scott A. SCHULZ
123 Dir of Tr/Adult & Grad Admission .... Ms. Winifred GERHARDT
18 Director of Buildings & Grounds .... Mr. William KERBUSCH
88 Director of Intercultural Education ....Dr. Judith B. KRUTKY
96 Director of Purchasing .... Ms. Karen STENGER
28 Director Campus Diversity Affairs .... Mr. Charles HARKNESS
04 Administrative Asst to President .... Ms. Kimberlee A. KUHAJDA
09 Director of Institutional Research ....Ms. Susan T. WARNER
104 Director Study Abroad ....Ms. Christy L. SHREFLER
39 Director Student Housing ....Mr. Robin W. GAGNOW
102 Dir Foundation/Corporate Relations ......Ms. Annie HEIDERSBACH
19 Director Security/Safety .... Mr. Gary BLACK
41 Athletic Director ....Mr. Kris DIAZ
50 Dean of School of Business ....Mr. John LANIGAN
53 Dean of School of Education ....Dr. Karen KAYE

Beckfield College (C)

225 Pictoria Drive Suite 200, Cincinnati OH 45246

Telephone: (513) 671-1920 Identification: 666673

Accreditation: ACICS

† Branch campus of Beckfield College, Florence, KY.

Belmont College (D)

68094 Hammond Road, Saint Clairsville OH 43950-9766

County: Belmont FICE Identification: 009941

Unit ID: 201283

Telephone: (740) 695-9500 Carnegie Class: Assoc/HVT-Mix Trad/Non

FAX Number: (740) 695-2247 Calendar System: Semester

URL: www.belmontcollege.edu

Established: 1969 Annual Undergrad Tuition & Fees (In-State): $3,541

Enrollment: 1,082 Coed

Affiliation or Control: State IRS Status: 501(c)3

Highest Offering: Associate Degree

Accreditation: NH, MAC

01 President ....Dr. Paul GASPARRO
05 VP of Learning & Student Success .... Dr. Rebecca KURTZ
11 Vice Pres of Administrative Affairs .. Mr. John S. KOUCOUMARIS
32 Dean of Stdnt Affs/Enrollment Mgmt ....Mr. Tim HOUSTON
20 Dean of Instruction .... Dr. Jeremy VITTEK
09 Dir of Institutional Research/Plng .... Mr. Steven HOAGLAND
06 Registrar ....Ms. Jennifer NIPPERT
15 Vice President of HR & Org Dev ....Mr. Matt KENDALL
37 Assoc Dean of Financial Aid .... Ms. Alicia FREY
88 Dir Teaching and Learning ....Mrs. Amy LEONI
121 Transfer/Articulat/Academic Advisor .... Ms. Jane BLACK
13 Exec Dir of Information Services .... Mr. Troy CALDWELL
111 Vice President of Advancement & Mkt .... Mr. RJ KONKOLESKI
04 Asst to President ....Ms. Kristy KOSKY
19 Director Security/Safety ....Mr. Glenn TRUDO
26 Public Relations Coordinator .... Ms. Julie MAMIE

Bluffton University (E)

1 University Drive, Bluffton OH 45817-2104

County: Allen FICE Identification: 003016

Unit ID: 201371

Telephone: (419) 358-3000 Carnegie Class: Bac-Diverse

FAX Number: (419) 358-3323 Calendar System: Semester

URL: www.bluffton.edu

Established: 1899 Annual Undergrad Tuition & Fees: $30,762

Enrollment: 1,011 Coed

Affiliation or Control: Mennonite Church IRS Status: 501(c)3

Highest Offering: Master's

Accreditation: NH, CAEPN, DIETD, MUS, SW

01 President .... Dr. James M. HARDER
10 Vice President for Fiscal Affairs .... Mr. Kevin A. NICKEL
111 Vice President for Inst Advancement ....Dr. Hans HOUSHOWER
05 Vice Pres & Dean Academic Affairs ....Dr. Lamar NISLY
84 VP for Enrollment Management/Mktg ....Vacant
32 VP for Student Life/Dean of Stdnts ....Dr. Julie DEGRAW
21 Chief Business Officer ....Mr. David BRUNS
08 Director of Libraries ....Ms. Mary Jean JOHNSON
06 Registrar ....Ms. Iris NEUFELD
26 Chief Public Relations Officer ....Mrs. Robin BOWLUS
29 Dir of Alumni Relations/Annual Giv .... Mrs. Julia SZABO
07 Director of UG Admissions ....Vacant
18 Director Building/Grounds ....Mr. Mustaq AHMED
15 Director Human Resources .... Mr. Scott A. SHARIK
04 Administrative Asst to President .... Ms. Jane PAHL
13 Chief Info Technology Officer (CIO) ....Ms. Deb TURNER
36 Director Student Placement ....Ms. Shari AYERS
38 Director Student Counseling ....Ms. Rae STATON
39 Director Student Housing ....Mr. Kevin WILLIAMS
41 Athletic Director ....Mr. Phillip TALAVINIA
44 Director Annual or Planned Giving ....Ms. Julia SZABO
105 Director Web Services ....Ms. Sara KISSEBERTH
37 Director of Financial Aid ....Mr. Christopher FOWLER

Bowling Green State University (F)

220 McFall Center, Bowling Green OH 43403-0001

County: Wood FICE Identification: 003018

Unit ID: 201441

Telephone: (419) 372-2211 Carnegie Class: DU-Higher

FAX Number: (419) 372-8446 Calendar System: Semester

URL: www.bgsu.edu

Established: 1910 Annual Undergrad Tuition & Fees (In-State): $11,057

Enrollment: 16,908 Coed

Affiliation or Control: State IRS Status: 501(c)3

Highest Offering: Doctorate

Accreditation: NH, ART, #CAATE, CACREP, CAEPN, CLPSY, CONST, DIETD, DIETI, ENGT, EXSC, IPSY, #JOUR, MT, MUS, NAIT, NRPA, NURSE, PH, SP, SPAA, SW, THEA

01 President ....Dr. Mary Ellen MAZEY
05 Sr VP Academic Affairs/Provost ....Dr. Rodney K. ROGERS
10 CFO/VP Finance & Admin ....Ms. Sherideen S. STOLL
100 Chief of Staff ....Ms. Lisa C. MATTIACE
32 Vice President Student Affairs .... Dr. Tom GIBSON
04 Asst to President ....Ms. Laurel E. ZAWODNY
111 VP Univ Advancement ....Mr. Shea MCGREW
84 VP Strategic Enrollment Planning .... Ms. Cecilia CASTELLANO
20 Vice Provost Undergraduate Educ ....Dr. John FISCHER
35 Dean of Students ....Ms. Jodi WEBB
11 Assoc VP for Campus Operations ....Mr. Bruce MEYER
26 Chief Marketing & Comm Officer .... Mr. David KIELMEYER
29 Assoc VP Alum/Dev/Annual Giv ....Ms. Becky KOCHER
46 VP Research & Econ Engagement .... Dr. Michael Y. OGAWA
88 Asst VP Student Affs/Dir Rec Sports .... Dr. Stephen KAMPF
41 Director of Athletics ....Mr. Bob MOOSBRUGGER
15 Chief Human Resources Officer .... Ms. Viva MCCARVER
39 Director of Residence Life ....Ms. Sarah WATERS
45 VP Capital Planning & Design ....Mr. Steve P. KRAKOFF
13 Chief Information Officer ....Mr. John M. ELLINGER
43 Vice President & General Counsel ....Mr. Sean P. FITZGERALD
58 Interim Dean Graduate College ....Dr. Margaret BOOTH
49 Dean College Arts/Sciences ....Dr. Raymond CRAIG
50 Dean College Business Admin .... Mr. Raymond BRAUN
88 Director Service Learning ....Dr. Virginia J. ROSSER
53 Dean Col of Educ & Human Dev ....Dr. Dawn SHINEW
12 Dean Firelands College .... Dr. Andrew KURTZ
69 Dean College Hlth/Human Svcs ....Dr. Marie HUFF
08 Dean University Libraries ....Ms. Sara BUSHONG
64 Dean College of Musical Arts .... Dr. William MATHIS
72 Interim Dean College of TAAE ....Dr. Venu DASIGI
57 Director of School of Art ....Dr. Katerina RUEDI RAY
60 Dir Sch of Media & Communication .... Dr. Laura STAFFORD
88 Dir Sch Human Move/Sport/ Leisure .... Dr. Stephen J. LANGENDORGER
88 Dir Sch Family & Consumer Sciences .... Dr. Deborah G. WOOLDRIDGE
53 Dir Sch Educ Fnds/Leadership/Policy ....Dr. Patrick PAUKEN
53 Int Dir Sch of Teaching & Learning ....Dr. Tim MURNEN
92 Dean Honors College ....Dr. Simon MORGAN-RUSSELL
106 Assoc Director eCampus .... Dr. Sheri ORWICK OGDEN
85 Exec Dir International Student Svcs .... Dr. Marcia SALAZAR-VALENTINE
21 Exec Dir of Business Operations .... Mr. Bradley K. LEIGH
07 Director Admissions .... Ms. Adrea SPOON
21 Dir Budgeting & Resource Planning .... Ms. Sharon SWARTZ
06 University Registrar ....Mr. Christopher P. COX
40 Director Bookstore ....Mr. Jeffrey D. NELSON
19 Director Public Safety ....Mr. Timothy JAMES
36 Director Career Center .... Mr. Jeff JACKSON
23 Exec Director Center for Health ....Vacant
38 Director Counseling Center .... Dr. Garrett GILMER
37 Dir Student Financial Aid .... Dr. Betsy JOHNSON
23 Asst Director Center for Health .... Ms. Marlene REYNOLDS
44 Director of Annual Giving .... Ms. Jenny WENSINK
101 Secretary to the Board ....Dr. Patrick PAUKEN
88 Co-Gen Manager WBGU Public Media ......Mr. Anthony E. SHORT
88 Co-Gen Manager WBGU Public Media ....Ms. Tina L. SIMON
35 Interim Dir Trio Programs ....Dr. Emily MONAGO
21 Internal Auditing & Adv Svcs ....Mr. James LAMBERT
88 Director Women's Center ....Dr. Mary M. KRUEGER
22 Disability Svcs/Int Title IX Coord ....Ms. Peggy DENNIS
88 President's Leadership Acad ....Dr. Jacob E. CLEMENS
109 Director Dining Services ....Mr. Michael L. PAULUS
96 Director of Business Operations .... Mr. Andrew D. GRANT
88 Director Student Employment .... Ms. Dawn CHONG
88 Director Learning Commons ....Mr. Mark NELSON
121 Director Advising Services .... Mr. Dermot M. FORDE
88 Asst VP Non-Trad & Transfer Svcs .... Dr. Barbara L. HENRY
09 Assoc VP for Inst Effectiveness ....Dr. Julia MATUGA
65 Dir Sch Earth/Environ & Society ....Dr. Jeffrey SNYDER
102 Dir Foundation/Corporate Relations ....Vacant
28 Asst to Pres Diversity & Incl ....Dr. Christina LUNCEFORD

Bowling Green State University Firelands College (G)

One University Drive, Huron OH 44839-9719

Telephone: (419) 433-5560 FICE Identification: 007856

Accreditation: &NH, CAHIIM, COARC, DMS

† Regional accreditation is carried under the parent institution in Bowling Green, OH.

Bradford School (H)

2469 Stelzer Road, Columbus OH 43219-3129

County: Franklin FICE Identification: 004853

Unit ID: 202161

Telephone: (614) 416-6200 Carnegie Class: Assoc/HVT-Mix Trad/Non

FAX Number: (614) 416-6210 Calendar System: Semester

URL: www.bradfordschoolcolumbus.edu

Established: 1985 Annual Undergrad Tuition & Fees: $13,980

Enrollment: 410 Coed

Affiliation or Control: Proprietary IRS Status: Proprietary

Highest Offering: Associate Degree

Accreditation: ACICS, ACFEI, MAC, PTAA

01 President ....Mr. Dennis BARTELS
05 Director of Education ....Ms. Beth WOOD
07 Director of Admissions .... Ms. Raeann LEE

Brightwood College (I)

2800 East River Road, Dayton OH 45439

County: Montgomery FICE Identification: 020520

Unit ID: 204626

Telephone: (937) 294-6155 Carnegie Class: Spec 2-yr-Health

FAX Number: (937) 294-2259 Calendar System: Quarter

URL: brightwood.edu

Established: 1971 Annual Undergrad Tuition & Fees: N/A

Enrollment: 326 Coed

Affiliation or Control: Proprietary IRS Status: Proprietary

Highest Offering: Associate Degree

Accreditation: ACICS, MAC

01 President ....Mr. Sean KUHN
05 Director of Education ....Ms. Melissa CURRY

Brown Mackie College-Akron (J)

755 White Pond Drive, Suite 101, Akron OH 44320-4221

Telephone: (330) 869-3600 Identification: 666470

Accreditation: ACICS, OTA

† In teach-out mode. Branch campus of Brown Mackie College-Cincinnati, Cincinnati, OH.

Bryant & Stratton College (K)

12955 Snow Road, Parma OH 44130-1013

Telephone: (216) 265-3151 FICE Identification: 022744

Accreditation: &M, ADNUR, MAC, NURSE, @PTAA

† Regional accreditation is carried under the parent institution (corporate office) in Buffalo, NY.

Capital University (A)

1 College and Main Street, Columbus OH 43209-2394
County: Franklin FICE Identification: 003023
Unit ID: 201548
Telephone: (614) 236-6011 Carnegie Class: Masters/M
FAX Number: (614) 236-6820 Calendar System: Semester
URL: www.capital.edu
Established: 1850 Annual Undergrad Tuition & Fees: $33,492
Enrollment: 3,465 Coed
Affiliation or Control: Evangelical Lutheran Church In America
IRS Status: 501(c)3
Highest Offering: First Professional Degree
Accreditation: NH, ACBSP, CAATE, CAEPN, LAW, MUS, NURSE, SW

01 President .... Dr. Elizabeth L. PAUL
05 Provost & VP for Learning .... Dr. Jody FOURNIER
10 Vice President Business & Finance .... Vacant
43 University Counsel .... Dr. Tanya J. POTEET
26 VP Integrated Marketing & Comm .... Ms. Tina GUEGOLD
84 VP Strategic Enrollment Mgmt .... Mr. Jean-Paul SPAGNOLO
111 Vice Pres Inst Advancement .... Ms. Jennifer PATTERSON
100 Exec Asst to Pres/Board Liaison .... Ms. Nona S. MCGUIRE
20 Sr Assoc Provost .... Dr. Terry D. LAHM
21 Asst VP Business & Finance .... Ms. Mary Ellen BORCHERS
27 Asst VP IMC .... Ms. D. Nichole JOHNSON
07 Asst VP Enrollment Services .... Ms. Susan E. KANNENWISCHER
30 Asst Vice President Development .... Ms. April NOVOTNY
88 Director Public Relations & Mktg .... Ms. Denise RUSSELL
09 Director of Institutional Research .... Dr. Larry T. HUNTER
06 Registrar .... Mr. Brent KOERBER
07 Interim Director of Admissions .... Ms. Sara THOMPSON
29 Director Alumni Relations .... Vacant
36 Director of Career Services .... Mr. Eric R. ANDERSON
08 University Librarian/Director IMC .... Ms. Rachel RUBIN
121 Director Academic Success .... Mr. Bruce EPPS
41 Athletic Director .... Mr. Roger INGLES
13 Director Information Technology .... Mr. Steve TERRY
85 Director Intl Education & ESL .... Ms. Jennifer ADAMS
32 Dean Engagement & Services .... Ms. Deanna WAGNER
18 Director Facilities Management .... Mr. Paul MATTHEWS
15 Interim Director Human Resources .... Mr. Mark PRINGLE
38 Dir Univ Counseling/Health Svcs .... Dr. Cathy MCDANIELS WILSON
28 Director Diversity and Inclusion .... Mr. Almar WALTER
92 Honors Program .... Dr. Stephanie GRAY WILSON
40 Manager Bookstore .... Mr. Joseph AMBUSKE
42 University Pastor .... Vacant
61 Dean of Law School .... Ms. Rachel JANUTIS
64 Dean of the Conservatory .... Dr. Lynn ROSEBERRY
53 Chair Department of Education .... Dr. James WIGHTMAN
66 Dean School of Nursing .... Dr. Ann PEDEN
102 Dir Foundation/Corporate Relations .... Mr. Gregory WINSLOW
108 Assoc Provost Accred & Analytics .... Dr. Jens HEMMINGSEN
22 Asst Provost/Title IX Coordinator .... Ms. Jennifer SPEAKMAN
04 Administrative Asst to President .... Ms. Emma MULVANEY
19 Director Security/Safety .... Mr. Frank FERNANDEZ
105 Assoc Director Web & Digital Svcs .... Mr. Russel PEPPER
39 Director Residential & Comm Life .... Mr. Jon GEYER
50 Dean School of Management & Ldrshp .... Mr. John GENTNER

Capital University Law School (B)

303 East Broad Street, Columbus OH 43215
Telephone: (614) 236-6500 Identification: 770347
Accreditation: &NH

Case Western Reserve University (C)

10900 Euclid Avenue, Cleveland OH 44106-7001
County: Cuyahoga FICE Identification: 003024
Unit ID: 201645
Telephone: (216) 368-2000 Carnegie Class: DU-Highest
FAX Number: N/A Calendar System: Semester
URL: www.case.edu
Established: 1826 Annual Undergrad Tuition & Fees: $46,006
Enrollment: 11,340 Coed
Affiliation or Control: Independent Non-Profit IRS Status: 501(c)3
Highest Offering: Doctorate
Accreditation: NH, AA, ANEST, #ARCPA, CAEPT, CLPSY, CS, DENT, DIETD, DIETI, ENG, LAW, MED, MIDWF, MUS, NURSE, PH, SP, SW

01 President .... Ms. Barbara R. SNYDER
100 Chief of Staff .... Katie M. BRANCATO
05 Provost/Executive Vice President .... Dr. William A. BAESLACK, III
20 Deputy Provost/VP Academic Affairs .... Dr. Lynn T. SINGER
10 Senior Vice Pres for Finance & CFO .... Mr. John F. SIDERAS
11 Senior Vice Pres for Administration .... Ms. Elizabeth J. KEEFER
30 Sr VP Univ Relations & Development .... Mr. Bruce A. LOESSIN
17 Sr VP Medical Affairs/Dean Medicine .... Dr. Pamela B. DAVIS
46 Vice President for Research .... Dr. Suzanne M. RIVERA
13 VP for Information Services/CIO .... Ms. Sue B. WORKMAN
32 Vice President for Student Affairs .... Mr. Louis W. STARK
18 VP Campus Planning/Facilities Mgmt .... Mr. Stephen M. CAMPBELL
15 Vice President for Human Resources .... Ms. Carolyn GREGORY
43 Sr Vice Pres/Gen Counsel/Secretary .... Ms. Elizabeth J. KEEFER
19 Vice President for Campus Services .... Mr. Richard J. JAMIESON
26 VP Univ Marketing & Communications .... Ms. Chris SHERIDAN
86 VP Government/Foundation Relations .... Dr. Julie M. REHM
88 Exec Director Government Relations .... Ms. Jennifer RUGGLES
31 Exec Dir Local Govt & Community Rel .... Ms. Dionne C. BROADUS
29 Sr Exec Director Alumni Relations .... Mr. Bradford CREWS
45 Assoc VP Univ Plng & Administration .... Ms. Victoria WRIGHT
84 Vice Pres for Enrollment Management .... Mr. Richard W. BISCHOFF
28 VP Inclusion/Diversity/Equal Opptny .... Dr. Marilyn S. MOBLEY
27 Dir Media Relations/Communications .... Mr. Bill LUBINGER
88 Treasurer .... Mr. Robert C. BROWN
115 Interim Chief Investment Officer .... Mr. Timothy R. MILANICH
20 Vice Provost Undergrad Education .... Dr. Donald L. FEKE
82 Vice Prov International Affairs .... Mr. David FLESHLER
88 Dean of Undergraduate Studies .... Dr. Jeffrey WOLCOWITZ
21 Controller .... Ms. Patricia L. KOST
06 Registrar .... Ms. Amy S. HAMMETT
37 Director of Financial Aid .... Ms. Venus PULIAFICO
07 Director Undergraduate Admissions .... Mr. Robert R. MCCULLOUGH
08 University Librarian & Assoc Prov .... Mr. Arnold HIRSHON
36 Director Career Center .... Dr. Thomas MATTHEWS
85 Dir International Student Svcs .... Ms. Marielena MAGGIO
38 Exec Dir Univ Health & Counsel Svcs .... Jenna MCCARTHY
09 Director of Institutional Research .... Ms. Jean E. GUBBINS
96 Int Dir Procurement/Distrib Svcs .... Ms. Mandy CARTE
41 Athletic Director .... Ms. Amy BACKUS
61 Co-Dean of Law .... Mr. Michael P. SCHARF
61 Co-Dean of Law .... Ms. Jessica W. BERG
49 Dean of Arts & Sciences .... Dr. Cyrus C. TAYLOR
63 Dean of Medicine .... Dr. Pamela B. DAVIS
66 Dean of Nursing .... Dr. Mary E. KERR
52 Dean of Dental Medicine .... Dr. Kenneth B. CHANCE
50 Dean of Management .... Dr. Manoj MALHOTRA
70 Dean Applied Social Science .... Dr. Grover C. GILMORE
54 Interim Dean of Engineering .... Dr. James D. MCGUFFIN-CAWLEY
58 Dean of Graduate Studies .... Dr. Charles E. ROZEK
04 Executive Asst to President .... Ms. Jane M. VONDRAK
102 Asst VP Corporate Rels .... Ms. Anne M. BORCHERT

Cedarville University (D)

251 N Main Street, Cedarville OH 45314-0601
County: Greene FICE Identification: 003025
Unit ID: 201654
Telephone: (937) 766-2211 Carnegie Class: Bac-Diverse
FAX Number: (937) 766-2760 Calendar System: Semester
URL: www.cedarville.edu
Established: 1887 Annual Undergrad Tuition & Fees: $28,110
Enrollment: 3,654 Coed
Affiliation or Control: Baptist IRS Status: 501(c)3
Highest Offering: Doctorate
Accreditation: NH, ACBSP, CAATE, CAEPN, CS, ENG, MUS, NURSE, PHAR, SW

01 President .... Dr. Jerry T. WHITE
05 Vice President for Academics .... Dr. Thomas MACH
10 Vice President for Business .... Mr. Christopher SOHN
111 Vice President for Advancement .... Dr. Rick MELSON
32 VP Stdt Life/Christian Ministries .... Dr. Jon WOOD
26 VP for Marketing and Communications .... Dr. Janice SUPPLEE
84 Vice President for Enrollment Mgmt .... Dr. Scott VAN LOO
41 Athletic Director .... Dr. Alan GEIST
43 General Counsel .... Mr. John HART
20 Assistant VP for Academics .... Dr. Randall MCKINION
15 Associate VP for Human Resources .... Mrs. Lydia GADDIS
21 Associate VP for Finance/Controller .... Mr. Phillip GRAFTON
18 Associate VP for Operations .... Mr. Rodney JOHNSON
13 Associate VP for Technology/CIO .... Mr. Micah COOPER
110 Associate VP for Advancement .... Vacant
42 Associate VP Christian Ministries .... Mr. Jim CATO
06 University Registrar .... Mrs. Fran CAMPBELL
97 Dean Undergraduate Programs .... Dr. Pamela D. JOHNSON
08 Dean Library Services .... Mr. Lynn A. BROCK
73 Dean School of Biblical/Theological .... Dr. Jason LEE
53 Dean School of Education .... Dr. Jeremy ERVIN
50 Dean School of Business .... Dr. Jeffrey HAYMOND
67 Dean School of Pharmacy .... Dr. Marc SWEENEY
66 Dean School of Nursing .... Mrs. Angela MICKLE
54 Dean School Engineering/Comp Sci .... Dr. Robert CHASNOV
34 Director Stdt Dvlpmnt/Dean of Women .... Miss Mindy MAY
33 Assc Dean Stdnt Dvlpmt/Dean of Men .... Mr. Brad D. SMITH
26 Exec Director of Public Relations .... Mr. Mark WEINSTEIN
37 Exec Director of Financial Aid .... Mr. Kim JENERETTE
44 Director of Alumni & Annual Giving .... Mrs. Stephanie CARROLL
19 Director of Campus Safety .... Mr. Douglas W. CHISHOLM
105 Director Web Services .... Mr. Mark MAZELIN
108 Director Assessment & Accreditation .... Mr. Tom BETCHER
36 Director Career Services .... Mr. Jeff REEP
28 Director Intercultural Leadership .... Mr. Greg DYSON
40 Manager of Retail Services .... Mrs. Tammy L. SLONE
04 Executive Asst to the President .... Mr. Zach BOWDEN
101 Admin Assoc to Pres/Asst Secy BOT .... Mrs. Angela MCINTOSH

Central Ohio Technical College (E)

1179 University Drive, Newark OH 43055-1767
County: Licking FICE Identification: 011046
Unit ID: 201672
Telephone: (740) 366-1351 Carnegie Class: Assoc/HT-High Non
FAX Number: (740) 366-5047 Calendar System: Semester
URL: www.cotc.edu
Established: 1971 Annual Undergrad Tuition & Fees (In-State): $4,296
Enrollment: 3,566 Coed
Affiliation or Control: State IRS Status: 501(c)3
Highest Offering: Associate Degree
Accreditation: NH, ACBSP, ADNUR, CSHSE, DMS, EMT, ENGT, IFSAC, RAD, SURGT

01 President .... Dr. Bonnie L. COE
10 Vice President Business & Finance .... Mr. David BRILLHART
32 Director of Student Life .... Ms. Holly MASON
15 VP for Inst Planning & HR Develop .... Dr. Jacqueline PARRILL
08 Director of Library .... Ms. Katie BLOCKSIDGE
06 Records Manager/Registrar .... Ms. Veronica RINE
84 Director of Enrollment Management .... Ms. Robin WASHINGTON
26 Director Marketing/Public Relations .... Vacant
37 Director Financial Aid/Veteran Affs .... Ms. Faith PHILLIPS
19 Director Public Safety .... Mr. Denny HOLLERN
29 Dir Alumni Rels/Development Officer .... Mr. Matthew KELLY
35 Asst Director of Student Affairs .... Vacant
13 Chief Information Officer .... Mr. Howard IMHOF
22 Program Mgr Learn Asst Ctr Disabled .... Ms. Connie ZANG
05 Director of Academic Operations .... Mr. Chad WEIRICK
96 Manager of Purchasing .... Ms. Kimberley SIBERT
18 Manager Facilities .... Mr. Brian BOEHMER
51 Coord of Community Svc/Learning .... Ms. Vorley TAYLOR
36 Dir Career Dev & Experiential Lrng .... Mr. Derek THATCHER
04 Assistant to the President .... Ms. Jan TOMLINSON
09 Director of Institutional Research .... Mr. Christopher DOLL
50 Dean for Business/Engineering/IT .... Vacant
07 Gateway Manager/Admission .... Mr. Dustin DUNLAVY
101 Secretary of the Institution/Board .... Ms. Jan TOMLINSON
103 VP for Workforce Development .... Ms. Vicki MAPLE

Central Ohio Technical College Coshocton Campus (F)

200 North Whitewoman Street, Coshocton OH 43812
Telephone: (740) 622-1408 Identification: 770348
Accreditation: &NH

Central Ohio Technical College Knox Campus (G)

236 South Main Street, Mount Vernon OH 43050
Telephone: (740) 392-2526 Identification: 770350
Accreditation: &NH

Central Ohio Technical College Pataskala Campus (H)

8660 East Broad Street, Reynoldsburg OH 43068
Telephone: (740) 755-7090 Identification: 770351
Accreditation: &NH

Central State University (I)

PO Box 1004, 1400 Brush Row Road, Wilberforce OH 45384-1004
County: Greene FICE Identification: 003026
Unit ID: 201690
Telephone: (937) 376-6332 Carnegie Class: Bac-Diverse
FAX Number: (937) 376-6138 Calendar System: Semester
URL: www.centralstate.edu
Established: 1887 Annual Undergrad Tuition & Fees (In-State): $6,246
Enrollment: 1,804 Coed
Affiliation or Control: State IRS Status: 501(c)3
Highest Offering: Master's
Accreditation: NH, ART, ENG, MUS, SW

01 President .... Dr. Cynthia JACKSON-HAMMOND
100 Chief of Staff .... Mrs. Wendy HAYES
05 Provost/VP Academic Affairs .... Dr. Pedro L. MARTINEZ
10 Vice President Admin & Finance .... Mr. Curtis PETTIS
111 Vice Pres Institutional Advancement .... Mr. Jahan CULBREATH
32 Vice President Student Affairs .... Dr. Stephanie KRAH
13 Director/Chief Information Officer .... Dr. Tonjia DELAVALLADE
20 Assoc Vice Pres Academic Affairs .... Dr. Lovette CHINWAH
06 University Registrar .... Ms. Felicia HARRIS
08 Director of Hallie Q Brown Library .... Ms. Carolin STERLING
89 Exec Director of University College .... Dr. Gene MOORE
12 Director of CSU Dayton .... Dr. Michael GAINES
09 Director Assessment/Inst Research .... Mr. Mohammad ALI
19 Chief of Police .... Capt. Stephanie HILL
26 Director Public Relations .... Dr. Edwina BLACKWELL-CLARK
23 Medical Director .... Dr. Karen MATHEWS
29 Director Alumni Relations .... Mr. Keith PERKINS
36 Director Career Services .... Ms. Karla HARPER
37 Director Student Financial Aid .... Ms. Sonia SLOMBIA
39 Interim Director of Residence Life .... Mr. Corey OWENS
41 Associate Athletic Director .... Mr. Harry STINSON
42 Director Campus Ministry .... Rev. Kima CUNNINGHAM
46 Director Sponsored Pgms/Research .... Mr. Morakinyo KUTI
49 Dean Coll Humanities/Arts & Sci .... Dr. George ARASIMOWICZ
50 Dean College of Business .... Dr. Fidelis M. IKEM
53 Interim Dean College of Education .... Dr. Zaki SHARIF
15 Int Director of Human Resources .... Mr. Gayle BERRY
21 Director Business Svcs/Capital Dev .... Ms. Cynthia MICHAEL
25 Director Grants Accounting .... Vacant
92 Director Honors Program .... Dr. Geoffrey J. GIDDINGS
21 Controller .... Ms. Candy CARR
114 Budget Director .... Ms. Sheila BROWN
38 Director Student Counseling .... Mr. NseAbasi EKPO
07 Enrollment Specialist .... Mr. William RANDOLPH
104 Director of Global Education .... Dr. Fahmi ABBOUSHI
106 Dir Online Learning .... Dr. Jean-Jacques MEDASTIN
18 Director Facilities/Physical Plant .... Mr. Milton THOMPSON
43 General Counsel .... Ms. Laura WILSON
54 Dean Col of Science and Engineering .... Dr. Alton JOHNSON
86 Chief Ofcr of Government Relations .... Mr. Charles SHAHID

Chamberlain University-Cleveland (A)
6700 Euclid Avenue, Suite 201, Cleveland OH 44103
Telephone: (216) 361-6005 Identification: 770505
Accreditation: &NH, NURSE

† Branch campus of Chamberlain University-Addison, Addison, IL

Chamberlain University-Columbus (B)
1350 Alum Creek Drive, Columbus OH 43209
Telephone: (614) 252-8890 Identification: 770499
Accreditation: &NH, NURSE

† Branch campus of Chamberlain University-Addison, Addison, IL

Chatfield College (C)
20918 State Route 251, Saint Martin OH 45118-9059
County: Brown FICE Identification: 010880
Unit ID: 201751
Telephone: (513) 875-3344 Carnegie Class: Assoc/HT-High Trad
FAX Number: (513) 875-3912 Calendar System: Semester
URL: www.chatfield.edu
Established: 1971 Annual Undergrad Tuition & Fees: $10,523
Enrollment: 396 Coed
Affiliation or Control: Independent Non-Profit IRS Status: 501(c)3
Highest Offering: Associate Degree
Accreditation: #NH

01 President ....Mr. John P. TAFARO
11 Vice President/COO ....Mr. Robert ELMORE
05 Chief Academic Officer/Dean ....Mr. Peter HANSON
10 Director of Finance ....Ms. Mary R. JACOBS
111 Director of Advancement ....Mr. James LUDWIG
07 Director of Admissions ....Mr. John PENROSE
20 Associate Dean/Site Director ....Sr. Patricia HOMAN
20 Associate Dean/Site Director ....Mr. Ryan HALL
26 Director of Marketing Communication ....Ms. Pamela SPENCER
04 Administrative Asst to President ....Ms. Cheryl A. KERN
06 Registrar ....Mr. Gordon GILES
08 Head Librarian ....Ms. Dolores BERISH
37 Financial Aid Counselor ....Mr. Brad JONES
37 Financial Aid Counselor ....Ms. Becki BROWN

The Christ College of Nursing and Health Sciences (D)
2139 Auburn Avenue, Cincinnati OH 45219
County: Hamilton FICE Identification: 006489
Unit ID: 201821
Telephone: (513) 585-2401 Carnegie Class: Spec-4-yr-Other Health
FAX Number: (513) 585-3540 Calendar System: Semester
URL: www.thechristcollege.edu
Established: 2006 Annual Undergrad Tuition & Fees: $15,882
Enrollment: 737 Coed
Affiliation or Control: Independent Non-Profit IRS Status: 501(c)3
Highest Offering: Baccalaureate
Accreditation: NH, ADNUR, NURSE

01 President ....Dr. W. Gary PACK
05 Dean of Academics ....Dr. Kelly M. SIMMONS
121 Dean of College Support Services ....Dr. Meghan E. HOLLOWELL
11 Dn Operations/Presidential Liaison ....Ms. Carolyn A. HUNTER
84 Dean of Enrollment Management ....Mr. Bradley A. JACKSON
04 Assistant to the President ....Ms. Cheryl A. BOONE

Cincinnati Christian University (E)
2700 Glenway Avenue, Cincinnati OH 45204-3200
County: Hamilton FICE Identification: 003029
Unit ID: 201858
Telephone: (513) 244-8100 Carnegie Class: Spec-4-yr-Faith
FAX Number: (513) 244-8140 Calendar System: Semester
URL: www.ccuniversity.edu
Established: 1924 Annual Undergrad Tuition & Fees: $16,414
Enrollment: 883 Coed
Affiliation or Control: Christian Churches And Churches of Christ
IRS Status: 501(c)3
Highest Offering: First Professional Degree
Accreditation: NH, CACREP, CAEPT, MUS, THEOL

01 Interim President ....Dr. David H. RAY
05 Chief Academic Officer ....Dr. Tom THATCHER
10 Director of Financial Services ....Mr. Randy KOEHLER
111 Dir of Advancement & Development ....Vacant
51 Dir of College of Adult Learning ....Mr. Aaron BURGESS
84 Director of Adult Enrollment ....Mr. Mark TUCKER
73 Dean of Russell School of Ministry ....Dr. David H. RAY
49 Dean Biblical Studies/Arts & Sci ....Mr. Paul FRISKNEY
83 Dean Education/Behavioral Sciences ....Dr. Marlene ESTENSON
50 Dean of School of Business ....Dr. Daryl SMITH
108 Dean of Institutional Effectiveness ....Dr. Sara FUDGE
20 Director of Faculty Development ....Dr. James A. SMITH
113 Bursar ....Mrs. Linda WAUGH
06 Registrar ....Mrs. Amanda DERICO
08 Director of Library Services ....Mr. James LLOYD
32 Director of Student Life ....Mr. Ray HORTON
37 Associate Director of Financial Aid ....Ms. Marcella FARMER
07 Director of Undergrad Admissions ....Ms. Tracy VEITH
41 Director of Athletics ....Mr. John TAYLOR
18 Director of Operations ....Mr. Rich ELLISON
15 Director of Human Resources ....Mr. Randy KOEHLER
13 Director of Information Technology ....Vacant
19 Director of Security ....Mr. John TAYLOR
04 Exec Assistant to the President ....Mrs. Wendy SPALDING
104 Director Study Abroad ....Vacant
89 First Year Experience Coordinator ....Ms. Karin ADMIRAAL
28 Director of Diversity ....Mr. Jonathan GARRETT
39 Director Student Housing ....Mr. Ray HORTON
96 Director of Purchasing ....Mrs. Sharon KNISLEY

Cincinnati College of Mortuary Science (F)
645 W North Bend Road, Cincinnati OH 45224-1462
County: Hamilton FICE Identification: 010906
Unit ID: 201867
Telephone: (513) 761-2020 Carnegie Class: Spec-4-yr-Other
FAX Number: (513) 761-3333 Calendar System: Semester
URL: www.ccms.edu
Established: 1882 Annual Undergrad Tuition & Fees: $20,025
Enrollment: 100 Coed
Affiliation or Control: Independent Non-Profit IRS Status: 501(c)3
Highest Offering: Baccalaureate
Accreditation: NH, FUSER

01 President ....Mr. Jack E. LECHNER, JR.
07 Admissions Director ....Dr. Pam DONLON
37 Financial Aid Director ....Mr. Russ ROMANDINI
04 Administrative Asst to President ....Mrs. Beth WILLIAMS
05 Chief Academic Officer ....Ms. Teresa DUTKO
08 Head Librarian ....Ms. Molly JONES
10 Chief Business Officer ....Mrs. Leslie BOEHM

Cincinnati State Technical and Community College (G)
3520 Central Parkway, Cincinnati OH 45223-2690
County: Hamilton FICE Identification: 010345
Unit ID: 201928
Telephone: (513) 569-1500 Carnegie Class: Assoc/MT-VT-Mix Trad/Non
FAX Number: (513) 569-1495 Calendar System: Other
URL: www.cincinnatistate.edu
Established: 1966 Annual Undergrad Tuition & Fees (In-State): $3,825
Enrollment: 9,630 Coed
Affiliation or Control: State IRS Status: 501(c)3
Highest Offering: Associate Degree
Accreditation: NH, ACFEI, ADNUR, CAHIIM, COARC, CONST, DIETT, DMS, EMT, ENGT, IFSAC, MAC, MLTAD, OTA, SURGT

01 President ....Dr. Monica POSEY
05 Provost ....Mr. Robbin HOOPES
13 Vice President for Technology ....Mr. Frankie BAKER
10 Vice President Finance/CFO ....Mr. Michael GEOGHEGAN
103 Vice Pres Workforce Development ....Ms. Amy WALDBILLIG
84 VP Enrollment/Student Development ....Dr. Soni HILL
72 Dean of Innovative Technology ....Mr. Doug BOWLING
50 Dean of Business Technologies ....Dr. Linda SCHAFFELD
76 Interim Dean Health/Public Safety ....Ms. Denise ROHR
81 Dean Humanities/Sciences ....Ms. Angela HAENSEL
06 Registrar ....Mr. Jason A. MOORE
08 Library Director ....Mrs. Cindy SEFTON
35 Director Student Activities ....Ms. Andrea MILANI
18 Director of Physical Facilities ....Mr. Michael SCHWEINFEST
09 Director of Institutional Research ....Ms. Anne FOSTER
07 Director Office of Admissions ....Mr. Keith GRANT
15 Director of Human Resources ....Ms. Lawra BAUMANN
30 Executive Director Development ....Ms. Casondra COOPER
102 Executive Director CS Foundation ....Mr. Elliot RUTHER
96 Director of Purchasing ....Mr. Jeffrey COOK
04 Executive Administrative Associate ....Mrs. Lachanna JACKSON
19 Director of Public Safety ....Mr. Michael WYLIE
37 Director of Financial Aid ....Mrs. La Saundra CRAIG
101 Secretary to the Board of Trustees ....Mrs. Nancy STUBBEMAN
88 Director Pathways to Employment ....Ms. Regina LIVERS

Clark State Community College (H)
570 E Leffel Lane, PO Box 570,
Springfield OH 45501-0570
County: Clark FICE Identification: 004852
Unit ID: 201973
Telephone: (937) 325-0691 Carnegie Class: Assoc/MT-VT-Mix Trad/Non
FAX Number: (937) 328-6142 Calendar System: Semester
URL: www.clarkstate.edu
Established: 1966 Annual Undergrad Tuition & Fees (In-State): $3,359
Enrollment: 5,619 Coed
Affiliation or Control: State IRS Status: 501(c)3
Highest Offering: Associate Degree
Accreditation: NH, ADNUR, EMT, MAC, MLTAD, PTAA

01 President ....Dr. Jo A. BLONDIN
05 Provost/Vice Pres Academic Affairs ....Dr. Amit SINGH
10 Vice President Business Affairs ....John DEVILLIER
32 VP Student Affairs and GC Operation ....Felder THERESA
102 Foundation Director ....Catie STIPE
21 Controller ....Kyle FUCHS
124 Dean Student Support Services ....Ronald GORDON
84 Dean Enrollment Services ....Nina WILEY
49 Dean Arts & Sciences ....Naomi LOUIS
50 Dean Business/Applied Technologies ....Aimee BELANGER-HAAS
76 Dean Health and Human Services ....Kathleen J. WILCOX
37 Financial Aid Director ....Kathy A. KLAY
06 Registrar ....Diane SEAMAN
13 Chief Information Officer ....Matt FRANZ
15 Chief Human Resources Officer ....Marvin NEPHEW
57 Exec Dir Performing Arts Center ....Adele ADKINS
08 Director Library Services ....Dr. Sterling J. COLEMAN, JR.
18 Dir Facilities/Oper/Maint ....Daniel AYARS
41 Dir Athletics and Student Life ....Justin MCCULLA
103 Dir Workforce & Business Solutions ....Toni OVERHOLSER
88 Dir Commercial Trans Train Center ....Duane HODGE
106 Dir Center for Teaching & Learning ....Cindra PHILLIPS
26 Director Marketing ....Laurie MEANS
04 Assistant to the President ....Mellanie TOLES
09 Institutional Research Technician ....Kelly NERIANI

Clark State Community College Greene Center (I)
3775 Pentagon Boulevard, Beavercreek OH 45431
Telephone: (937) 429-8819 Identification: 770352
Accreditation: &NH

Cleveland Institute of Art (J)
11610 Euclid Avenue, Cleveland OH 44106-1710
County: Cuyahoga FICE Identification: 003982
Unit ID: 202046
Telephone: (216) 421-7000 Carnegie Class: Spec-4-yr-Arts
FAX Number: (216) 421-7438 Calendar System: Semester
URL: www.cia.edu
Established: 1882 Annual Undergrad Tuition & Fees: $39,585
Enrollment: 606 Coed
Affiliation or Control: Independent Non-Profit IRS Status: 501(c)3
Highest Offering: Baccalaureate
Accreditation: NH, ART

01 President & CEO ....Mr. Grafton J. NUNES
05 Sr VP Faculty Affairs & CAO ....Mr. Chris WHITTEY
30 Vice President Inst Advancement ....Ms. Malou MONAGO
10 Sr VP Business Affairs/CFO ....Mrs. Almut ZVOSEC
26 Vice President Mktg & Communication ....Mr. Mark INGLIS
84 VP Enrollment/Dean Admissions & Fin ....Mr. Jonathan WEHNER
37 Assoc Director of Financial Aid ....Ms. Delores HALL
06 Registrar ....Mrs. Karen HUDY
08 Library Director ....Ms. Laura PONIKVAR
07 Assoc Director of Admissions ....Mr. Tom GREEN
13 VP Support Service & CIO ....Mr. Mat FELTHOUSEN
29 Director Annual Giving/Alumni Rels ....Ms. Kylie EYRE
20 Director of Academic Services ....Vacant
44 Dir Leadership/Giving/Corp Rels ....Ms. Lesley HOOVER
15 Vice Pres of HR & Inclusion ....Mr. Raymond SCRAGG
32 Dean of Student Affairs ....Ms. Nancy NEVILLE
37 Director of Financial Aid ....Mr. Martin CARNEY
27 Director of Mktg & Communications ....Ms. Karen SANDSTROM
57 Art Director ....Mr. Richard SARIAN
21 Assoc VP of Business Affairs ....Ms. Julie MELVIN
25 Director of Grants/Special Projects ....Ms. Jennifer GRASSO

Cleveland Institute of Music (K)
11021 East Boulevard, Cleveland OH 44106-1776
County: Cuyahoga FICE Identification: 003031
Unit ID: 202073
Telephone: (216) 791-5000 Carnegie Class: Spec-4-yr-Arts
FAX Number: (216) 791-3063 Calendar System: Semester
URL: www.cim.edu
Established: 1920 Annual Undergrad Tuition & Fees: $49,106
Enrollment: 432 Coed
Affiliation or Control: Independent Non-Profit IRS Status: 501(c)3
Highest Offering: Doctorate
Accreditation: NH, MUS

01 President/CEO ....Mr. Paul HOGLE
11 Vice President/COO ....Mr. Eric BOWER
05 Chief Academic Officer ....Dr. Judy BUNDRA
10 CFO ....Ms. Kristen KOLLAR
05 Sr Assoc Dean ....Mr. Brian SWEIGART
13 Director Systems Management ....Mr. Daniel BETTING
07 Asst Dean of Admissions ....Vacant
32 Associate Dean of Student Affairs ....Mr. David GILSON
37 Director Financial Aid ....Ms. Kristine GRIPP
10 Chief Financial Officer ....Ms. Kristen KOLLAR
06 Assoc Dean Acad Affs/Registrar ....Mrs. Hallie MOORE
15 Director Human Resources ....Mrs. Megan SWERBINSKY
08 Director of the Library ....Dr. Kevin MCLAUGHLIN
04 Executive Admin Asst to President ....Ms. Nancy SNELL
09 Institutional Research Analyst ....Mrs. Caryn REYNOLDS

Cleveland State University (L)
2121 Euclid Avenue, Cleveland OH 44115-2214
County: Cuyahoga FICE Identification: 003032
Unit ID: 202134
Telephone: (216) 687-2000 Carnegie Class: DU-Higher
FAX Number: (216) 687-9366 Calendar System: Semester
URL: www.csuohio.edu
Established: 1964 Annual Undergrad Tuition & Fees (In-State): $9,768
Enrollment: 16,915 Coed
Affiliation or Control: State IRS Status: 501(c)3
Highest Offering: Doctorate

Accreditation: NH, ARCPA, CACREP, CAEP, CEA, COPSY, ENG, ENGT, LAW, MUS, NURSE, OT, PH, PLNG, PTA, SP, SPAA, SW

01 President .... Dr. Ronald M. BERKMAN
05 Provost/Sr VP Academic Affairs .... Dr. Jianping ZHU
10 VP Business Affairs/Finance .... Ms. Stephanie MCHENRY
84 VP Enrollment Services .... Dr. Cindy SKARUPPA
46 VP Research .... Dr. Jerzy SAWICKI
111 VP Univ Advancement/Exec Dir Found .... Ms. Berinthia LEVINE
32 VP Student Affairs .... Dr. Ernest YARBROUGH
20 Vice Provost for Academic Planning .... Dr. Teresa LAGRANGE
20 Vice Provost Academic Programs .... Dr. Peter MEIKSINS
26 Assoc VP University Mktg .... Mr. Robert SPADEMAN
15 Asst VP Human Resources .... Mr. Jesse DRUCKER
35 Assoc VP Student Affairs .... Ms. Clare RAHM
21 Controller/Asst VP Finance .... Ms. Kathleen MURPHY
49 Dean Col Liberal Arts/Soc Sci .... Dr. Gregory M. SADLEK
81 Dean College of Science .... Dr. Meredith R. BOND
50 Dean College of Business .... Dr. Sanjay PUTREVU
53 Dean College Education & Human Svcs .... Dr. Sajit ZACHARIAH
54 Dean Fenn College of Engineering .... Dr. Anette KARLSSON
58 Dean College Graduate Studies .... Dr. Nigamanth SRIDHAR
61 Dean of College of Law .... Mr. Lee FISHER
80 Dean College Urban Affairs .... Dr. Roland ANGLIN
92 Dean Honors College .... Dr. Elizabeth LEHFELDT
43 General Counsel .... Ms. Sonali B. WILSON
101 Sr Advisor to Pres/Sec Bd Trustees .... Dr. William NAPIER
08 Director of Libraries .... Dr. Glenda THORNTON
22 Dir Office of Institutional Equity .... Ms. Rachel LUTNER
07 Director Undergraduate Admissions .... Ms. Lee FURBECK
09 Director Institutional Research .... Mr. Tom GEAGHAN
85 Director International Programs .... Mr. Harlan SMITH
38 Director Counseling Center .... Dr. Katharine HAHN
19 Assoc VP Administration/Operations .... Dr. Joseph HAN
37 Director Student Financial Aid .... Ms. Rachel SCHMIDT
06 Asst Vice President/Registrar .... Ms. Janet STIMPLE
41 Director of Athletics .... Mr. Michael THOMAS
29 Asst VP Alumni Relations .... Mr. Brian BREITHOLZ
18 Director Facilities Management .... Mr. Shehadeh ABDELKARIM
96 Assoc Director Purchasing .... Ms. Laurie WOLOHAN
04 Executive Asst to President .... Ms. Shane CONNOR
114 Sr Dir Budget & Operations .... Mr. William WILSON

The College of Wooster (A)

1189 Beall Avenue, Wooster OH 44691-2363
County: Wayne FICE Identification: 003037
Unit ID: 206589
Telephone: (330) 263-2000 Carnegie Class: Bac-A&S
FAX Number: (330) 263-2427 Calendar System: Semester
URL: www.wooster.edu
Established: 1866 Annual Undergrad Tuition & Fees: $46,860
Enrollment: 2,050 Coed
Affiliation or Control: Independent Non-Profit IRS Status: 501(c)3
Highest Offering: Baccalaureate
Accreditation: NH, CAEPN, MUS

01 President .... Dr. Sarah BOLTON
05 Provost .... Dr. Carolyn NEWTON
10 Vice Pres Finance/Bus/Treasurer .... Ms. Dee MCCORMICK
111 Vice President for Advancement .... Mr. Wayne WEBSTER
84 Vice Pres Enrollment/College Rels .... Dr. Scott FRIEDHOFF
32 VP Stdnt Affairs/Dean of Students .... Mr. Scott C. BROWN
04 Administrative Asst to President .... Mrs. Lynette ARNER
26 Assoc VP College Rels & Marketing .... Mr. John HOPKINS
109 Assoc VP Facilities & Auxiliaries .... Ms. Jacqueline MIDDLETON
15 Assoc VP of Human Resources .... Ms. Marcia BEASLEY
20 Dean Curriculum/Academic Engagement .... Bryan KARAZSIA
20 Dean for Faculty Development .... Dr. Peter MOWREY
07 Dean of Admissions .... Ms. Jennifer D. WINGE
13 Chief Information Planning Officer .... Dr. Ellen FALDUTO
06 Registrar .... Ms. Suzanne BATES
08 Librarian of the College .... Irene HEROLD
37 Director of Financial Aid .... Ms. Dana KENNEDY
27 Director Communications .... Mr. Hugh HOWARD
29 Dir of Alumni Rels & Wooster Fund .... Mr. Thomas MCARTHUR
36 Director Career Services .... Ms. Lisa KASTOR
41 Dir Phys Educ/Athletics/Recreat .... Dr. Keith BECKETT
18 Director Physical Plant Operations .... Mr. Doug LADITKA
19 Director Security/Protective Svcs .... Mr. Steven GLICK
42 Chaplain .... Rev. Alexander SERNA-WALLENDER
101 Secretary of College/Chief Staff .... Ms. Angela JOHNSTON

Columbus College of Art & Design (B)

60 Cleveland Avenue, Columbus OH 43215-1758
County: Franklin FICE Identification: 003039
Unit ID: 202170
Telephone: (614) 224-9101 Carnegie Class: Spec-4-yr-Arts
FAX Number: (614) 222-4040 Calendar System: Semester
URL: www.ccad.edu
Established: 1879 Annual Undergrad Tuition & Fees: $32,880
Enrollment: 1,140 Coed
Affiliation or Control: Independent Non-Profit IRS Status: 501(c)3
Highest Offering: Master's
Accreditation: NH, ART

01 President .... Dr. Melanie CORN
04 Exec Assistant to the President .... Ms. Sheri LUCAS
05 Provost .... Ms. Dona LANTZ
10 Senior Vice President/CFO .... Mr. Jeffrey FISHER
30 Vice President for Advancement .... Ms. Lindsey DUNLEAVY
26 Exec Dir Mktg & Commincations .... Ms. Jill MOORHEAD
84 Assoc VP for Enrollment Management .... Ms. Jean HESTER
32 VP Student Affairs/Dean Students .... Mr. Chris MUNDELL
60 Dean School of Design Arts .... Mr. Tom GATTIS
57 Dean School of Studio Arts .... Ms. Julie TAGGART
58 Director Graduate Studies .... Mr. Ric PETRY
06 Registrar .... Ms. Michele KIBLER
13 Chief Information Officer .... Mr. Jeffrey BROTHERTON
15 Director of Human Resources .... Vacant
08 Director of Library Services .... Ms. Leslie JANKOWSKI NIEMCZURA
19 Director of Safety & Security .... Mr. Wallace TANKSLEY
18 Director of Facilities .... Mr. Joseph SPYBEY
38 Director of Counseling & Wellness .... Ms. Erin VLACH
37 Director Student Financial Aid .... Ms. Anna SCHOFIELD
36 Director Career Resources .... Ms. Tiffany SPERRING
21 Controller .... Mr. Roger ESCOLAS
35 Dir of Student Engagement .... Ms. Maria D'APOLITO
51 Community Education Program Coord .... Ms. Christine HILL
39 Director of Residence Life .... Mr. Mickey HART
88 Director of Special Projects .... Mr. Dave STOCKWELL
40 Supply Store Manager .... Mr. Danny HINTY

Columbus State Community College (C)

Box 1609, Columbus OH 43216-1609
County: Franklin FICE Identification: 006867
Unit ID: 202222
Telephone: (614) 287-5353 Carnegie Class: Assoc/MT-VT-High Non
FAX Number: (614) 287-5113 Calendar System: Semester
URL: www.cscc.edu
Established: 1963 Annual Undergrad Tuition & Fees (In-State): $3,808
Enrollment: 25,983 Coed
Affiliation or Control: State IRS Status: 501(c)3
Highest Offering: Associate Degree
Accreditation: NH, ACBSP, ACFEI, ADNUR, CAHIIM, COARC, CONST, CSHSE, DH, DIETT, EMT, ENGT, MAC, MLTAD, PHLEB, RAD, SURGT

01 President .... Dr. David T. HARRISON
05 Senior Vice Pres Academic Affairs .... Dr. John COOLEY
10 VP Business Svcs/CFO/Treasurer .... Ms. Aletha SHIPLEY
26 VP Marketing and Communications .... Mr. Allen KRAUS
13 Vice Pres Information Technology .... Dr. Michael BABB
11 Senior VP Admin & General Counsel .... Ms. Kimberly HALL
84 Vice Pres Enroll Mgmt/Student Svcs .... Dr. Rebecca BUTLER
12 Dean of Delaware Campus .... Dr. Stacia EDWARDS
49 Dean of Arts & Sciences .... Dr. Allysen TODD
76 Dean Health and Human Services .... Dr. Thomas HABEGGER
50 Dean Business & Engineering Tech .... Mr. Angelo FROLE
32 Dean Student Life .... Ms. Renee HILL
102 Executive Director Foundation .... Ms. Pamela BISHOP
91 Director IT Budget/Planning .... Mr. Etienne MARTIN
21 Director II Controller .... Ms. Jan ELLIS
06 Director Office of the Registrar .... Dr. Regina RANDALL
37 Director Financial Aid .... Mr. David METZ
19 Chief of Police .... Chief Sean ASBURY
18 Director II Facilities Management .... Mr. Mark FRENCH
28 Dir of Global Diversity/Inclusion .... Mr. Brett WELSH
09 Director II Inst Effectiveness .... Dr. Jennifer ANDERSON
08 Director Library .... Mr. Bruce MASSIS
07 Director of Admissions .... Vacant
40 Director Operations/Bookstore .... Ms. Stacey MULINEX
96 Director Procurement/College Svcs .... Mr. Bradley FARMER
14 Chief Technology Officer IT .... Mr. James BEIDLER
20 Associate VP Academic Affairs .... Dr. Martin MALIWESKY
35 Exec Dean Advis & Student Support .... Ms. Desiree POLK-BLAND

Columbus State Community College-Delaware (D)

5100 Cornerstone Drive, Delaware OH 43015
Telephone: (740) 203-8345 Identification: 770353
Accreditation: &NH

Cuyahoga Community College (E)

700 Carnegie Avenue, Cleveland OH 44115-2878
County: Cuyahoga FICE Identification: 003040
Unit ID: 202356
Telephone: (216) 987-4000 Carnegie Class: Assoc/HT-High Non
FAX Number: (216) 566-5977 Calendar System: Semester
URL: www.tri-c.edu
Established: 1963 Annual Undergrad Tuition & Fees (In-District): $3,136
Enrollment: 25,449 Coed
Affiliation or Control: State/Local IRS Status: 501(c)3
Highest Offering: Associate Degree
Accreditation: NH, ACFEI, ADNUR, ARCPA, CAHIIM, COARC, DH, DIETT, DMS, EMT, ENGT, MAC, MLTAD, NDT, NMT, OTA, POLYT, PTAA, RAD, SURGT

01 President .... Dr. Alex JOHNSON
05 Exec VP & Provost .... Dr. Karen MILLER
10 Exec VP Admin & Finance .... Mr. David KUNTZ
103 Exec VP Workforce/Comm & Econ Dev .... Mr. William GARY
12 Campus President East Campus .... Dr. J. Michael THOMSON
12 President/CEO Corporate College .... Mr. Robert PETERSON
12 Campus President Metro Campus .... Dr. Michael SCHOOP
12 Campus President Westshore Campus .... Dr. Terri POPE
12 Campus President West Campus .... Dr. Donna IMHOFF
21 Vice Pres Finance & Business Svcs .... Ms. Jennifer DEMMERLE
15 Vice Pres/Chief Human Res Officer .... Ms. Judith MCMULLEN
30 Vice Pres Development/Foundation .... Ms. Megan O'BRYAN
27 Vice Pres/Chief Information Officer .... Mr. Gerard HOURIGAN
86 Vice Pres Govt Affair/Comm Outreach .... Ms. Claire ROSACCO
84 VP Inst Research/Enroll Mgmt .... Ms. Angela JOHNSON
26 Vice Pres Integrated Communications .... Mr. David HOOVLER
43 Vice Pres Legal Services .... Ms. Renee RICHARD
20 Vice Pres Learning & Engagement .... Ms. Lisa WILLIAMS
88 VP Accreditation/Health Initiatives .... Ms. Diana DEL ROSARIO
88 VP & Dean Public Safety & Crim Just .... Chief Clayton HARRIS
88 Vice Pres Manufacturing .... Ms. Alicia BOOKER
32 Assoc VP Access & Comm Engagement .... Dr. JaNice MARSHALL
88 Exec Dir Access Learning & Success .... Dr. Sandra MCKNIGHT
88 Deputy Gen Counsel & Exec Dir .... Mr. Marvin RICHARDS
88 Exec Director Media Engineering .... Mr. Robert BRYAN
13 Exec Director EIS .... Mr. Jon DOLINAR
88 Exec Director Plant Operations .... Mr. Blair BOSWORTH
88 Exec Dir Veteran Services/Programs .... Mr. Richard DE CHANT
88 Exec Dir College Svcs & Retail .... Mr. Chris MOIR
88 Exec Dir Supplier Managed Svcs .... Mr. Stephen HILBERT
96 VP Capital Const & Supply Mgmt .... Ms. Cynthia LEITSON
88 Dean GM Hospitality Mgmt .... Mr. Michael HUFF
88 Exec Dir Organizational Development .... Mr. Barry ROYKO
20 Dean Learning & Engagement East .... Ms. Denise MCCORY
20 Dean Learning & Engagement West .... Dr. Janice TAYLOR HEARD
20 Dean Learning & Engagement Metro .... Ms. Delia BOBER
20 Dean Lrng & Engagement Westshore .... Mr. Robert SEARSON
35 Int Dean Access & Completion Metro .... Ms. Ralonda ELLIS-HILL
35 Dean Access & Completion West .... Dr. Tim DORSEY
35 Dean Access & Completion East .... Mr. Andrew CRAWFORD
35 Dean Access & Completion Westshore .... Dr. Ann PROUDFIT
66 Dean Nursing .... Dr. Vivian YATES
79 Dean for Humanities .... Dr. Lauren ONKEY
76 Assoc Dean Health Careers & Science .... Ms. Judith KAPLAN
76 Assoc Dean Health Careers & Science .... Mr. Gregory MALONE
81 Assoc Dean STEM West .... Mr. Ormond BRATHWAITE
83 Assoc Dean Social Sciences West .... Ms. Courtney CLARK
49 Assoc Dean Liberal Arts East .... Dr. William CUNION
49 Int Assoc Dean Liberal Arts Metro .... Ms. Amy PARKS
49 Assoc Dean Liberal Arts West .... Dr. Felisa EAFFORD
50 Assoc Dean Bus/Math & Tech Metro .... Dr. Pamela ELLISON
50 Assoc Dean Bus/Math & Tech East .... Dr. Lorraine HARTLEY
72 Assoc Dean Bus IT Applied Tech West .... Mr. Scott HALM
54 Assoc Dean Engineering .... Mr. Lam WONG
88 Assoc Dean Hospitality Mgmt .... Ms. Karen MONATH
76 Assoc Dean Health Careers West .... Mr. Daniel MCDERMOTT
66 Assoc Dean Nursing .... Ms. Ebony DRUMMER
100 Chief of Staff/Exec Asst to Pres .... Ms. Ronna MCNAIR
23 Assoc Dean Public Safety & EMT .... Dr. James PLOSKONKA
28 Director of Diversity & Inclusion .... Ms. Magda GOMEZ
37 District Dir Student Financial Aid .... Ms. Kimberly NASH
110 Exec Director Development .... Ms. Sharon COON
09 Exec Dir Institutional Research .... Mr. G. Rob STUART
38 Assistant Dean Counseling-Metro .... Mrs. Ralonda ELLIS-HILL
38 Assistant Dean Counseling-East .... Ms. Johanna BACIK
38 Assistant Dean Counseling-West .... Mr. Marcos RIVERA
04 Admin Associate to President .... Ms. Barbara BELL
102 Exec Dir Foundation/Corporate Rel .... Ms. Kate MCDADE
41 Athletic Director West .... Mr. Mark RODRIGUEZ
41 Athletic Director East .... Ms. Melissa SWAFFORD
41 Athletic Director Metro .... Ms. Jennifer DAVIS
108 Assoc VP Acad Prof Dev & Assessment .... Dr. Lindsay ENGLISH
88 Dean Creative Arts .... Dr. G. Paul COX
14 Exec Dir/Dep CIO/Ent App Svcs .... Ms. Standish STEWART
88 Director Network Services .... Mr. Peter ANDERSON

Cuyahoga Community College Eastern Campus (F)

4250 Richmond Road, Highland Hills OH 44122
Telephone: (800) 954-8742 Identification: 770355
Accreditation: &NH

Cuyahoga Community College Metropolitan Campus (G)

2900 Community College Avenue, Cleveland OH 44115
Telephone: (800) 954-8742 Identification: 770354
Accreditation: &NH, PHLEB

Cuyahoga Community College Western Campus (H)

11000 Pleasant Valley Road, Parma OH 44130
Telephone: (800) 954-8742 Identification: 770356
Accreditation: &NH

Cuyahoga Community College Westshore (I)

31001 Clemens Road, Westlake OH 44145
Telephone: (800) 954-8742 Identification: 770357
Accreditation: &NH

Davis College (J)

4747 Monroe Street, Toledo OH 43623-4389
County: Lucas FICE Identification: 004855
Unit ID: 202435
Telephone: (419) 473-2700 Carnegie Class: Assoc/HVT-High Non
FAX Number: (419) 473-2472 Calendar System: Quarter
URL: www.daviscollege.edu
Established: 1858 Annual Undergrad Tuition & Fees: $14,130
Enrollment: 159 Coed
Affiliation or Control: Proprietary IRS Status: Proprietary
Highest Offering: Associate Degree

Accreditation: NH, MAC

01 President .... Diane BRUNNER
05 Dean of Faculty .... Mary DELOE
32 VP of Student & Academic Services .... Mary RYAN BULONE
37 Director Student Financial Aid .... Marilyn BOVIA
07 Director of Admissions .... Timothy BRUNNER
36 Director of Student Placement .... Nick NIGRO
30 VP of Institutional Advancement .... Tim BRUNNER
08 Librarian .... Peggy PETERSON-SENIUK

The Defiance College (A)

701 N Clinton Street, Defiance OH 43512-1695
County: Defiance FICE Identification: 003041
Unit ID: 202514
Telephone: (419) 784-4010 Carnegie Class: Bac-Diverse
FAX Number: (419) 784-4101 Calendar System: Semester
URL: www.defiance.edu
Established: 1850 Annual Undergrad Tuition & Fees: $31,680
Enrollment: 751 Coed
Affiliation or Control: United Church Of Christ IRS Status: 501(c)3
Highest Offering: Master's
Accreditation: NH, #CAATE, CAEPN, IACBE, NURSE, SW

01 President .... Dr. Richanne C. MANKEY
05 VP for Academic Affairs .... Dr. Agnes CALDWELL
10 Vice Pres for Finance & Management .... Mrs. Lois N. MCCULLOUGH
84 VP Enrollment Mgmt/Dean of Stdnts .... Mrs. Lisa MARSALEK
88 Dean McMaster Sch Adv Hum .... Mrs. Mary Ann STUDER
07 Director of Admissions & Fin Aid .... Mrs. Brenda AVERESCH
15 Director of Human Resources .... Mrs. Mary E. BURKHOLDER
08 Dir of Library and Instr Resource .. Mrs. Lisa CRUMIT-HANCOCK
26 Director Public Relations/Marketing .... Mrs. Kathy M. PUNCHES
13 Director of Computer Services .... Mr. Jeremy KENNEDY
06 Registrar .... Mrs. Mariah ORZOLEK
37 Director of Financial Aid .... Mrs. Amy FRANCIS
41 Athletic Director .... Mr. Rudy YOVICH
28 Director Intercultural Relations .... Ms. Mercedes CLAY
39 Director of Residence Life .... Ms. Jennifer WALTON
18 Director of Physical Plant .... Mr. Cliff BRADY
21 Director of Accounting .... Mrs. Kristine BOLAND
04 Administrative Asst to President .... Mrs. Judy LYMANSTALL
103 Dir Workforce/Career Development .... Ms. Sally BISSELL
50 Dean of Business .... Vacant
53 Dean of Education .... Dr. Carla HIGGINS
38 Director Student Counseling .... Ms. Lynn BRAUN
44 Director of Annual Giving .... Ms. Michele TINKER

Denison University (B)

100 W College Street, Granville OH 43023-1359
County: Licking FICE Identification: 003042
Unit ID: 202523
Telephone: (740) 587-0810 Carnegie Class: Bac-A&S
FAX Number: (740) 587-6417 Calendar System: Semester
URL: www.denison.edu
Established: 1831 Annual Undergrad Tuition & Fees: $48,960
Enrollment: 2,254 Coed
Affiliation or Control: Independent Non-Profit IRS Status: 501(c)3
Highest Offering: Baccalaureate
Accreditation: NH, #CAATE

01 President .... Dr. Adam S. WEINBERG
05 Provost .... Dr. Kimberly A. COPLIN
20 Associate Provost Academic Admin .... Dr. Catherine L. DOLLARD
100 Chief of Staff .... Dr. Rajesh BELLANI
28 Associate Provost Diversity .... Dr. Alison P. WILLIAMS
10 VP Finance & Management .... Mr. David A. ENGLISH
111 VP Institutional Advancement .... Ms. Julia BEYER HOUPT
32 VP Student Development .... Dr. Laurel B. KENNEDY
84 VP Enrollment Management .... Mr. Gregory W. SNEED
07 Director of Admissions .... Mr. Michael S. HILLS
89 Dean of First-Year Students .... Dr. Mark MOLLER
35 Dean of Students .... Mr. William A. FOX
06 Registrar .... Ms. Yadigar COLLINS
08 Director of Libraries .... Ms. BethAnn ZAMBELLA
37 Dir of Financial Aid & Student Empl .... Ms. Laura E. MEEK
13 Dir Information Technology Services .... Ms. Dena L. SPERANZA
15 Director of Human Resources .... Mr. Jim ABLES
18 Director of Facilities Services .... Mr. Arthur J. CHONKO
19 Director of Campus Safety .... Mr. Daniel HECT
26 Assoc VP for Univ Communications ... Ms. Barbara STAMBAUGH
27 Asst VP for Univ Communications .... Mr. Scott TRIBBLE
29 Dir of Alumni & Family Engagement .... Ms. Mary FRAZELL
36 Dir Career Exploration & Dev .... Mr. Hank MALIN
38 Dir of Health & Counseling Svc .... Ms. Amanda L. LEFELD
42 Chaplain/Director of Religious Life .... Ms. Phoebe MYHRUM
88 Special Asst to Pres & Provost .... Dr. Joyce MEREDITH
88 Dean of Student Leadership .... Mr. Erik S. FARLEY
11 Director of Administrative Services .... Ms. Jenna MCDEVITT
09 Director of Institutional Research .... Dr. Todd M. JAMISON
41 Director of Athletics .... Ms. Nan CARNEY-DEBORD
115 Chief Investment Officer .... Ms. Kathleen BROWNE
04 Executive Asst to President .... Vacant
102 Dir Foundation/Corporate Relations .... Ms. Margaret GALIPAULT
104 Director Study Abroad .... Dr. Sue F. DAVIS
39 Director Student Housing .... Ms. Kristan R. HAUSMAN
110 Assoc VP Inst Advancement .... Mr. Greg R. BADER
22 Dir Affirmative Action/EEO .... Ms. Barbara A. LAY

DeVry University - Columbus Campus (C)

1350 Alum Creek Drive, Columbus OH 43209-2705
Telephone: (614) 253-1525 FICE Identification: 003099
Accreditation: &NH, ENGT

† Regional accreditation is carried under the parent institution in Downers Grove, IL.

Eastern Gateway Community College - Jefferson County Campus (D)

4000 Sunset Boulevard, Steubenville OH 43952-3594
County: Jefferson FICE Identification: 007275
Unit ID: 203331
Telephone: (740) 264-5591 Carnegie Class: Assoc/MT-VT-Mix Trad/Non
FAX Number: (740) 264-1338 Calendar System: Semester
URL: www.egcc.edu
Established: 1966 Annual Undergrad Tuition & Fees (In-District): $3,395
Enrollment: 3,024 Coed
Affiliation or Control: State/Local IRS Status: 501(c)3
Highest Offering: Associate Degree
Accreditation: NH, CAHIIM, COARC, DA, EMT, MAC, RAD

01 President .... Dr. Jimmie D. BRUCE
05 Provost .... Dr. Anne LOOCHTAN
10 Vice Pres Business Services .... Mr. James J. MCGRAIL, III
11 Vice Pres Administrative Services .... Ms. Sherri VAN TASSEL
32 VP for Employee/Student Development .... Ms. Christina WANAT
46 Vice Pres Strategic Initiatives .... Vacant
84 Dean Enrollment Management .... Ms. Patty J. STURCH
76 Dean Health & Biological Sciences .... Dr. Robin FLOHR
81 Dean Student Learning/Humanities .... Ms. Christina WANAT
35 Dean TRIO/Student Svcs & Retention .... Dr. Dorothy COLLINS
50 Dean Business/Engineering & Info .... Mr. Jerry KLINESMITH
21 Controller .... Ms. Joanna FLANIGAN
07 Dean of Admissions .... Mr. Ryan OGRODNIK
26 Dir Public Information/Web Coord .... Vacant
37 Exec Director Student/Financial Aid .... Ms. Kelly WILSON
102 Exec Director EGCC Foundation .... Dr. James BABER
103 Workforce/Community Outreach Coord .... Mr. Jerry KLINESMITH
13 Int Director Technology Services .... Mr. David SMITH
36 Director Career Services/Alumni .... Vacant
40 Director of Bookstore .... Mrs. Judith LUDE
21 Director Student Billing/Payroll .... Ms. Tonya LOGAN
18 Director Building & Grounds .... Mr. Julius J. DZIEWATKOSKI
08 Director of Library Services .... Mrs. Lois T. REKOWSKI
06 Registrar .... Ms. Patty J. STURCH
29 Director of Alumni Relations .... Vacant

Edison State Community College (E)

1973 Edison Drive, Piqua OH 45356-9239
County: Miami FICE Identification: 012750
Unit ID: 202648
Telephone: (937) 778-8600 Carnegie Class: Assoc/MT-VT-Mix Trad/Non
FAX Number: (937) 778-1920 Calendar System: Semester
URL: www.edisonohio.edu
Established: 1973 Annual Undergrad Tuition & Fees (In-State): $4,219
Enrollment: 3,122 Coed
Affiliation or Control: State IRS Status: 501(c)3
Highest Offering: Associate Degree
Accreditation: NH, ADNUR, MLTAD, PHLEB, PTAA

01 President .... Dr. Doreen LARSON
04 Executive Asst to the President .... Ms. Heather LANHAM
05 Provost .... Mr. Chris SPRADLIN
10 VP of Administration & Finance .... Mr. John W. SHISHOFF
30 VP for Institutional Advancement .... Ms. Kimberly HORTON
32 Vice President of Student Affairs .... Mr. Scott M. BURNAM
31 VP Business/Cmty Partnerships .... Mr. Rick HANES
13 Chief Information Officer .... Mr. Harry LAWHORN
15 Exec Director Human Resources .... Mrs. Linda M. PELTIER
35 Director of Student Services .... Mr. Nathan COLE
49 Dean of Arts and Science .... Ms. Naomi LOUIS
50 Dean of Business/IT & Engineering .... Ms. Shirley MOORE
66 Dean of Nursing & Health Sciences .... Ms. Gwendolyn A. STEVENSON
09 Assoc Prov Planning/Effectiveness .... Ms. Mona WALTERS
88 Director of Student Success .... Ms. Pamela GIBELLINO
21 Controller .... Mr. James LEHMKKUHL
41 Director Athletics .... Mr. Nathan COLE
37 Director of Financial Aid .... Ms. Kathi S. RICHARDS
26 Dir of Marketing & Communications .... Mr. Bruce MCKENZIE
84 Enrollment Manager .... Ms. Stacey BEAN
06 Registrar .... Ms. Mary BORNHORST
08 Director of Library/Learning Center .... Ms. Lisa HOOPS
18 Dir of Physical Plant/Facilities .... Mr. Douglas RIEHLE

Edison State Community College Darke County Campus (F)

601 Wagner Avenue, Greenville OH 45331
Telephone: (937) 548-5546 Identification: 770358
Accreditation: &NH

ETI Technical College of Niles (G)

2076-86 Youngstown-Warren Road, Niles OH 44446-4398
County: Trumbull FICE Identification: 030790
Unit ID: 200590
Telephone: (330) 652-9919 Carnegie Class: Assoc/HVT-High Non
FAX Number: (330) 652-4399 Calendar System: Semester
URL: www.eticollege.edu
Established: 1989 Annual Undergrad Tuition & Fees: $10,920
Enrollment: 124 Coed
Affiliation or Control: Proprietary IRS Status: Proprietary
Highest Offering: Associate Degree
Accreditation: ACCSC

01 Director .... Mrs. Renee ZUZOLO
07 Director of Admissions .... Mrs. Diane MARSTELLER
37 Director Financial Aid .... Ms. Kay MADIGAN

Fortis College (H)

555 E Alex-Bell Road, Centerville OH 45459-6120
County: Montgomery FICE Identification: 021907
Unit ID: 205179
Telephone: (937) 433-3410 Carnegie Class: Bac/Assoc-Assoc Dom
FAX Number: (937) 435-6516 Calendar System: Semester
URL: www.fortiscollege.edu
Established: 1970 Annual Undergrad Tuition & Fees: $18,046
Enrollment: 1,006 Coed
Affiliation or Control: Proprietary IRS Status: Proprietary
Highest Offering: Baccalaureate
Accreditation: ACCSC, ADNUR

01 President .... Wayne KORTICS
05 VP/Chief Academic Officer .... Lisa NAYS
09 Dir Inst Effectiveness/Compliance .... LaRee PINGATORE
20 Director Education .... Lisa NAYS
07 Director Admissions .... Angela COOPER
37 Director Financial Aid .... Rachel KARMON

Fortis College (I)

2545 Bailey Road, Cuyahoga Falls OH 44221-2949
County: Summit FICE Identification: 009412
Unit ID: 204307
Telephone: (330) 923-9959 Carnegie Class: Spec 2-yr-Health
FAX Number: (330) 923-0886 Calendar System: Other
URL: www.fortis.edu
Established: 1922 Annual Undergrad Tuition & Fees: N/A
Enrollment: N/A Coed
Affiliation or Control: Proprietary IRS Status: Proprietary
Highest Offering: Associate Degree
Accreditation: ACCSC, DA

01 President .... Ms. Carson BURKE

Fortis College (J)

653 Enterprise Parkway, Ravenna OH 44266-8058
Telephone: (330) 297-7319 FICE Identification: 023036
Accreditation: ACCSC, ACICS, CAHIIM

† Branch campus of Fortis College, Norfolk, VA

Fortis College (K)

4151 Executive Parkway, Suite 120, Westerville OH 43081-3860
County: Franklin Identification: 666602
Unit ID: 450058
Telephone: (614) 882-2551 Carnegie Class: Spec 2-yr-Health
FAX Number: (614) 882-2914 Calendar System: Quarter
URL: www.fortis.edu
Established: 2010 Annual Undergrad Tuition & Fees: $14,900
Enrollment: 661 Coed
Affiliation or Control: Proprietary IRS Status: Proprietary
Highest Offering: Associate Degree
Accreditation: ABHES, #RAD, SURGT, SURTEC

01 President .... Mr. Peter MARTINELLO
06 Registrar .... Ms. Eva REDA
07 Director of Admissions .... Mr. Josh WHITE
32 Chief Student Affairs/Student Life .... Ms. Jackie CRANDELL
36 Director Student Placement .... Ms. Marlene TEED
37 Director Student Financial Aid .... Ms. Deidre VANCE
05 Dean of Education .... Ms. Nikki PAPPAS

Franciscan University of Steubenville (L)

1235 University Boulevard, Steubenville OH 43952-1763
County: Jefferson FICE Identification: 003036
Unit ID: 205957
Telephone: (740) 283-3771 Carnegie Class: Masters/M
FAX Number: (740) 283-6472 Calendar System: Semester
URL: www.franciscan.edu
Established: 1946 Annual Undergrad Tuition & Fees: $25,680
Enrollment: 2,716 Coed
Affiliation or Control: Roman Catholic IRS Status: 501(c)3
Highest Offering: Master's
Accreditation: NH, CACREP, CAEPN, NURSE, SW

01 President .... Rev. Sean SHERIDAN, TOR
88 Vice Pres of Pastoral Care & Evange .... Rev. Nathan MALAVOLTI, TOR
10 VP of Finance & Admin Operations .... Mr. David M. SKIVIAT
05 Vice President of Academic Affairs .... Dr. Daniel KEMPTON

30 Vice President of Advancement ..... Mr. Michael HERNON
31 Vice Pres of Community Relations ..... Vacant
45 Vice Pres Institutional Effect ..... Dr. James MELLO
15 Vice Pres of Human Resources ..... Mr. Brenan PERGI
32 Vice President of Student Life ..... Mr. David A. SCHMIESING
84 Vice Pres of Enrollment Management ..... Mr. Joel S. RECZNIK
35 Asst Vice Pres of Student Life ..... Ms. Catherine J. HECK
88 Religious Administrator ..... Rev. John SHANAHAN, TOR
42 University Chaplain ..... Rev. Dominic SCOTTO, TOR
20 Dir of Advising & Acad Operations ..... Ms. Ann DULANY
105 Dir Telecommunications & Networks ..... Mr. Dennis BREEN
08 Int Director of Library ..... Ms. LuAnn BORIS
88 Exec Director Christian Outreach ..... Mr. Mark JOSEPH
44 Director of Planned Giving ..... Dr. Mark E. RECZNIK
30 Director of Development ..... Mr. Mark NEHRBAS
29 Director of Alumni Relations ..... Mr. Timothy J. DELANEY
26 Dir Marketing & Communications ..... Miss Lisa M. FERGUSON
07 Asst Director of Admissions ..... Ms. Vicky KUBICZ
07 Director of Graduate Enrollment ..... Mr. Mark T. MCGUIRE
06 Registrar ..... Mr. Cody SCHMITZ
84 Exec Dir of Enrollment Services ..... Mr. John L. HERRMANN
09 Director of Institutional Research ..... Dcn. Mark A. ERSTE, SR.
21 Controller ..... Mr. John A. STEITZ
96 Director of Business Services ..... Ms. Marlene K. TERPENNING
40 Bookstore Manager ..... Mr. John RECZNIK
91 Director Administrative Computing ..... Mrs. Pam SHANE
18 Director Physical Plant Services ..... Mr. Joseph P. MCGURN
88 Director of Missionary Outreach ..... Mr. Rhett YOUNG
88 Director of Chapel Ministries ..... Mr. Robert PALLADINO
88 Director of JCW Center/Planning ..... Mrs. Kathy L. MATTIOLI
104 Director of Study Abroad ..... Mr. Mark HANRAHAN
38 Director of Counseling ..... Mr. Joseph A. LOIZZO
41 Int Director of Athletics ..... Mr. Mike FLORAK
36 Director Career Services ..... Mrs. Nancy S. RONEVICH
73 Director MA Theology Program ..... Dr. Michael SIRILLA
50 Director MBA Program ..... Mr. Joseph ZORIC
83 Director MA Counseling Program ..... Dr. Christin JUNGERS
53 Director MS Education Program ..... Dr. Mark FURDA
88 Director MA Philosophy Program ..... Dr. John CROSBY
90 Coord Academic Computer Services ..... Ms. Sandy M. RADVANSKY
28 Director of Diversity ..... Vacant
66 Director MS Nursing ..... Dr. Carolyn MILLER
19 Director Security/Safety ..... Mr. Michael CONN
106 Dir Online Education/E-learning ..... Dr. Cory MALONEY
108 Director Institutional Assessment ..... Vacant
04 Executive Asst to President ..... Mr. Daniel MILES
37 Director Student Financial Aid ..... Ms. Jody PEELER
26 Exec Dir Marketing & Communication ..... Ms. Kimberly SPONSELLER

Franklin University (A)

201 S Grant Avenue, Columbus OH 43215-5399
County: Franklin — FICE Identification: 003046
Unit ID: 202806
Telephone: (614) 797-4700 — Carnegie Class: Spec-4-yr-Bus
FAX Number: N/A — Calendar System: Trimester
URL: www.franklin.edu
Established: 1902 — Annual Undergrad Tuition & Fees: $11,881
Enrollment: 5,102 — Coed
Affiliation or Control: Independent Non-Profit — IRS Status: 501(c)3
Highest Offering: Doctorate
Accreditation: NH, IACBE, NURSE

01 President ..... Dr. David R. DECKER
11 Sr VP Administration/Chief of Staff ..... Ms. Christi L. CABUNGCAL
05 Provost/Exec VP ..... Dr. Christopher L. WASHINGTON
07 VP Enrollment & Student Affairs ..... Ms. Linda M. STEELE
111 VP University Advancement ..... Ms. Bonnie SMITH QUIST
15 VP of Human Resources & Campus Svcs ..... Vacant
108 SVP Accred/Institutional Effective ..... Dr. Pamela SHAY
45 VP Planning & University Services ..... Ms. Evelyn LEVINO
20 Associate Provost Academic Quality ..... Vacant
04 Executive Assistant to President ..... Ms. Bonnie MCCANN
32 Dean of Students & Enrollment Mgmt ..... Dr. Lynne HULL
10 Chief Financial Officer ..... Dr. Marvin BRISKEY
13 Chief Information Officer ..... Mr. Rick SUNDERMAN
88 Dir of Accreditation & Inst Effect ..... Ms. Susanne SMITH
06 Registrar ..... Mr. Frank YANCHAK
08 Director of Library Services ..... Ms. Alyssa DARDEN
37 Director of Financial Aid ..... Ms. Goldie LANGLEY
46 Director of Strategic Relations ..... Ms. Jody NOREEN
121 Dir Academic Advising ..... Ms. Wendi ROBINSON
88 VP Institute & Global Operations ..... Mr. Patrick BENNETT
84 Exec Director of Marketing & Enroll ..... Vacant
12 Exec Dir Domestic Partnership Dev ..... Mr. Bill CHAN
18 Director of Facilities ..... Mr. Carl BROWN
26 Director of Public Relations ..... Ms. Sherry MERCURIO
29 Director of Alumni Engagement & Dev ..... Mr. Kevin GREENWOOD
96 Director of Purchasing ..... Mr. Bob DONAHUE
118 Director of Benefits ..... Ms. Brenda LISTON
88 Director Instructor Effectiveness ..... Dr. Meghan RAEHLL
49 Dean Arts/Science & Technology ..... Dr. Kody KUEHNL
50 Dean College of Business ..... Dr. Andy IGONOR
69 Dean College of Health & Public Adm ..... Dr. Jonathan MCCOMBS
88 SVP Global Programs ..... Dr. Godfrey MENDES
16 Director of Human Resources ..... Ms. Randi QUINN
88 Director of Accounting ..... Mr. Jeffrey GERBERRY
88 Exec Dir of Financial Services ..... Mr. Randolph SNYDER
19 Director Security/Safety ..... Mr. Clifton SPINNER

Galen College of Nursing (B)

100 E Business Way, Suite 200, Cincinnati OH 45241
Telephone: (513) 475-3600 — Identification: 770537
Accreditation: &SC, ADNUR

† Branch campus of Galen College of Nursing, Louisville, KY

Gallipolis Career College (C)

1176 Jackson Pike, Suite 312, Gallipolis OH 45631-2600
County: Gallia — FICE Identification: 030079
Unit ID: 205513
Telephone: (740) 446-4367 — Carnegie Class: Assoc/MT-VT-Mix Trad/Non
FAX Number: (740) 446-4124 — Calendar System: Quarter
URL: www.gallipoliscareercollege.edu
Established: 1962 — Annual Undergrad Tuition & Fees: $12,530
Enrollment: 84 — Coed
Affiliation or Control: Proprietary — IRS Status: Proprietary
Highest Offering: Associate Degree
Accreditation: ACICS

01 President ..... Mr. Robert L. SHIREY, JR.
05 Director of Education ..... Mrs. Karen D. SHAW
07 Director of Admissions ..... Vacant
10 Director of Finance ..... Mrs. Jeanette SHIREY
37 Director Student Financial Aid ..... Ms. Christina SHOCKEY

God's Bible School and College (D)

1810 Young Street, Cincinnati OH 45202-6838
County: Hamilton — FICE Identification: 022205
Unit ID: 202903
Telephone: (513) 721-7944 — Carnegie Class: Spec-4-yr-Faith
FAX Number: (513) 763-6649 — Calendar System: Semester
URL: www.gbs.edu
Established: 1900 — Annual Undergrad Tuition & Fees: $7,040
Enrollment: 280 — Coed
Affiliation or Control: Interdenominational — IRS Status: 501(c)3
Highest Offering: Master's
Accreditation: NH, BI

01 President ..... Rodney S. LOPER
05 Vice President Academic Affairs ..... Aaron PROFITT
32 Vice President Student Development ..... Richard MILES
26 VP for Constituent Relations ..... Marc SANKEY
06 Registrar ..... Kent STETLER
08 Head Librarian ..... Stephanie HOFFPAUIR
10 Director of Finance ..... David FREDERICK
13 Dir of UX and Digital Strategies ..... Jason WEED
07 Student Recruiter ..... Joshua CRAVENS
37 Financial Aid Coordinator ..... Sharree POUZAR
84 Director Enrollment Services ..... Nathan DAHLER

Good Samaritan College of Nursing and Health Science (E)

375 Dixmyth Avenue, Cincinnati OH 45220-2489
County: Hamilton — FICE Identification: 006494
Unit ID: 202912
Telephone: (513) 862-2743 — Carnegie Class: Spec-4-yr-Other Health
FAX Number: (513) 862-3572 — Calendar System: Semester
URL: www.gscollege.edu
Established: 2001 — Annual Undergrad Tuition & Fees: $15,530
Enrollment: 398 — Coed
Affiliation or Control: Independent Non-Profit — IRS Status: 501(c)3
Highest Offering: Baccalaureate
Accreditation: NH, ADNUR, NUR

01 President ..... Dr. James HAUSCHILDT
05 Dean Academic Affairs/Allied Health ..... Dr. Adam KALLMEYER
10 Chief Financial Officer ..... Mr. Michael CROFTON
11 Dean of Campus Operations ..... Dr. Beth MOORE
09 Dir of Inst Assessment/Planning ..... Dr. Terri PULLEN
84 Dean of Enrollment Management ..... Dr. Linda HAYES
06 Registrar ..... Ms. Leah BOERGER

Harrison College-Columbus Ohio Campus (F)

3880 Jackpot Road, Grove City OH 43123
Telephone: (614) 539-8800 — Identification: 770748
Accreditation: ACICS, MAC

† Branch campus of Harrison College - Indianapolis Downtown Campus, Indianapolis, IN

Heidelberg University (G)

310 E Market Street, Tiffin OH 44883-2462
County: Seneca — FICE Identification: 003048
Unit ID: 203085
Telephone: (419) 448-2000 — Carnegie Class: Bac-A&S
FAX Number: (419) 448-2124 — Calendar System: Semester
URL: www.heidelberg.edu
Established: 1850 — Annual Undergrad Tuition & Fees: $29,200
Enrollment: 1,197 — Coed
Affiliation or Control: United Church Of Christ — IRS Status: 501(c)3
Highest Offering: Master's
Accreditation: NH, ACBSP, CAATE, CACREP, CAEPN, MUS

01 President ..... Dr. Robert HUNTINGTON
05 VP for Academic Affairs & Provost ..... Dr. Beth SCHWARTZ
10 VP for Admin & Business Affairs ..... Mr. Hoa NGUYEN
84 VP for Enrollment Mgmt ..... Mr. Doug KELLAR
111 VP Univ Advancement & Marketing ..... Mr. Phil NESS
20 Assoc VP Acad Affs/Dean Undergr Fac ..... Dr. Vicki OHL
29 Exec Dir of Alumni Eng & Major Gift ..... Ms. Ashley HELMSTETTER
13 Assoc VP for Information Resources ..... Mr. Kurt HUENEMANN
18 Assoc VP for Facilities & Engr ..... Mr. Rodney MORRISON
50 Dean of the School of Business ..... Dr. Haseeb AHMED
06 Registrar ..... Ms. Cindy SUTER
88 Director MA in Counseling Pgm ..... Dr. Jo-Ann SANDERS
53 Director of School of Education ..... Dr. Karen JONES
64 Director of School of Music ..... Dr. Carol DUSDIEKER
92 Assoc Dean for Honors Program ..... Dr. Emily ISAACSON
104 Director Intl Affairs & Studies ..... Ms. Julie ARNOLD
26 Dir of Marketing & Communications ..... Ms. Audrey BURKHOLDER
36 Dir of Career Develop & Placement ..... Mr. Mark MCKEE
58 Dir Graduate Studies in Business ..... Vacant
88 Dir of Graduation Support Services ..... Dr. Ellen NAGY
08 Director of Library ..... Vacant
41 Athletic Director ..... Mr. Matt PALM
21 Business Officer ..... Ms. Barb GABEL
37 Director Student Financial Aid ..... Mrs. Juli WEININGER
30 Exec Dir for Development ..... Mr. James MINEHART
32 Dean of Student Affairs ..... Vacant
39 Asst Dn Stdnt Affs for Campus Life ..... Mr. Mark ZENO
124 Dir Student Engagement ..... Ms. Jacqueline SIRONEN
15 Director of Human Resources ..... Ms. Margaret RUDOLPH
21 Controller ..... Ms. Kelly WARNKE
04 Exec Assistant to President ..... Ms. Monica VERHOFF
40 Director of University Bookstore ..... Ms. Gail ROBERTS
42 Director of Campus Ministry ..... Rev. Paul STARK
19 Director Security/Safety ..... Mr. Jeff RHOADES

Herzing University-Akron (H)

1600 S Arlington Street, Akron OH 44306-3958
Telephone: (330) 724-1600 — FICE Identification: 020695
Accreditation: &NH, ADNUR, DA, MAC

† Regional accreditation is carried under the parent institution in Madison, WI.

Herzing University Toledo Campus (I)

5212 Hill Avenue, Toledo OH 43615
Telephone: (419) 776-0030 — Identification: 770434
Accreditation: &NH, MAAB, SURTEC

† Branch campus of Herzing University, Madison, WI

Hiram College (J)

Box 67, Hiram OH 44234-0067
County: Portage — FICE Identification: 003049
Unit ID: 203128
Telephone: (330) 569-3211 — Carnegie Class: Bac-A&S
FAX Number: (330) 569-5494 — Calendar System: Other
URL: www.hiram.edu
Established: 1850 — Annual Undergrad Tuition & Fees: $33,040
Enrollment: 1,122 — Coed
Affiliation or Control: Independent Non-Profit — IRS Status: 501(c)3
Highest Offering: Master's
Accreditation: NH, CAEPN, MUS, NURSE

01 President ..... Dr. Lori E. VARLOTTA
05 Interim VPAA & Dean of College ..... Dr. Judy MUYSKENS
10 CFO/VP Business and Finance ..... Mr. Dexter ODOM
30 Chief Development Officer ..... Ms. Jennifer SCHULLER
32 Vice President & Dean of Students ..... Dr. Elizabeth M. OKUMA
07 VP of Enrollment ..... Ms. Lindajean H. WESTERN
20 Associate Dean of the College ..... Ms. Ellen L. WALKER
107 Director Professional/Grad Studies ..... Ms. Jennifer L. MILLER
06 Interim Registrar ..... Ms. Christie BORKAN
08 Head Librarian ..... Mr. David D. EVERETT
29 Director Alumni Relations ..... Mr. John B. COYNE
37 Interim Director Financial Services ..... Ms. Linda SHIREY NELSON
36 Director of Career Services ..... Ms. Heather M. BALAS
13 Director of Computer Center ..... Mr. Frank J. VENTURA
09 Director of Institutional Research ..... Ms. Maria A. O'CONNOR
41 Director of Athletics ..... Ms. Ellen E. DEMPSEY
15 Director of Human Resources ..... Mr. Jeff FARLEY
18 Director of the Physical Plant ..... Mr. John SIBILIA
21 Controller ..... Mr. Brett RIEBAU
35 Int Director of Campus Involvement ..... Ms. Sarah DOWD
38 Director Student Counseling ..... Dr. Kevin P. FEISTHAMEL
28 Director Ethnic Diversity Affairs ..... Ms. Detra E. WEST
96 Director of Purchasing ..... Ms. Martha A. SCHETTLER
26 Exec Dir Marketing/Communications ..... Mr. Scott DUNNELL
04 Executive Asst to President ..... Mr. Phil J. EAVES
25 Dir Institutional Grants ..... Ms. Jenna CARIGLIO-DORRIS
104 Study Away Coordinator ..... Ms. Brittany JACKSON
19 Director Security/Safety ..... Mr. Daniel FYNES
39 Interim Director Student Housing ..... Mr. Ed FRATO-SWEENEY
44 Exec Dir Annual Giving ..... Ms. Aimee BELL

Hocking College (K)

3301 Hocking Parkway, Nelsonville OH 45764-9704
County: Athens — FICE Identification: 007598
Unit ID: 203155
Telephone: (740) 753-3591 — Carnegie Class: Assoc/HVT-Mix Trad/Non
FAX Number: (740) 753-7005 — Calendar System: Semester
URL: www.hocking.edu

Established: 1968 Annual Undergrad Tuition & Fees (In-State): $4,390
Enrollment: 3,243 Coed
Affiliation or Control: State IRS Status: 501(c)3
Highest Offering: Associate Degree
Accreditation: NH, ACBSP, ACFEI, ADNUR, CAHIIM, MAC, PNUR, PTAA

01 President Dr. Betty YOUNG
10 Vice President & Treasurer Vacant
05 Provost/VP Academic Affairs Dr. Myriah DAVIS
32 VP Student Affairs/Community Rels Ms. Jacqueline HAGEROTT
15 AVP HR/Diversity/Campus Relations Mr. Jeffrey WHITE
04 Executive Assistant to President Ms. Sheree CUNNINGHAM
66 Dean School Nursing/Allied Health Vacant
37 Exec Director Financial Aid Ms. Deneene MERCHANT
19 Commander Public Safety Services Dr. Penny PAYNE
08 Dir Learning Resource Ctr/Librarian Mr. Jeff GRAFFIUS
26 Exec Dir Mktg/Public & Cmty Rels Mr. Tim BRUNICORDI
19 Director Campus Safety Mr. Al MATTHEWS
06 Registrar Ms. Kensey LOVE
18 Exec Dir Physical Plant/Land Mgmt Mr. Andrew FREEMAN
102 Director Foundation Mr. Christopher BOOKMAN
21 Controller/Assistant Treasurer Mrs. Anna JOHNSON
101 Development Coordinator Foundation Ms. Jestinah MCDONALD
100 Chief of Staff Mr. Jeff DAUBENMIRE

Hocking College Perry Campus (A)

5454 State Route 37, New Lexington OH 43764
Telephone: (740) 342-3337 Identification: 770359
Accreditation: &NH

Hondros College (B)

1810 Successful Drive, Fairborn OH 45324
Telephone: (937) 879-1940 Identification: 770751
Accreditation: ACICS

Hondros College (C)

4100 Rockside Road, Second Floor, Independence OH 44131
Telephone: (216) 524-1143 Identification: 770750
Accreditation: ACICS

Hondros College (D)

7600 Tyler's Place Boulevard, West Chester OH 45069
Telephone: (513) 508-3005 Identification: 770749
Accreditation: ACICS

Hondros College (E)

4140 Executive Parkway, Westerville OH 43081-3855
County: Franklin FICE Identification: 040743
Unit ID: 203386
Telephone: (614) 508-7277 Carnegie Class: Spec-4-yr-Other Health
FAX Number: (614) 508-7280 Calendar System: Quarter
URL: www.hondros.edu
Established: 1981 Annual Undergrad Tuition & Fees: $18,235
Enrollment: 1,963 Coed
Affiliation or Control: Proprietary IRS Status: Proprietary
Highest Offering: Baccalaureate
Accreditation: ACICS, NURSE

01 CEO Mr. Harry T. WILKINS
12 Campus Executive Director Ms. Kelly CAVANAGH
66 President Nursing Programs Ms. Debra PIZZUTI
07 Director of Admission Mr. Scott SHELTON
06 Registrar Ms. Michelle HARDEN

International College of Broadcasting (F)

6 S Smithville Road, Dayton OH 45431-1898
County: Montgomery FICE Identification: 013132
Unit ID: 203289
Telephone: (937) 258-8251 Carnegie Class: Spec 2-yr-A&S
FAX Number: (937) 258-8714 Calendar System: Semester
URL: www.icb.edu
Established: 1968 Annual Undergrad Tuition & Fees: $12,569
Enrollment: 62 Coed
Affiliation or Control: Proprietary IRS Status: Proprietary
Highest Offering: Associate Degree
Accreditation: ACCSC

01 President J. Michael LEMASTER
05 School Director Eric CLARK
07 Director of Admissions John CHAFFIN

James A. Rhodes State College (G)

4240 Campus Drive, Lima OH 45804-3597
County: Allen FICE Identification: 010027
Unit ID: 203678
Telephone: (419) 995-8200 Carnegie Class: Assoc/MT-VT-Mix Trad/Non
FAX Number: (419) 221-0450 Calendar System: Semester
URL: www.rhodesstate.edu
Established: 1971 Annual Undergrad Tuition & Fees (In-State): $3,845
Enrollment: 4,368 Coed
Affiliation or Control: State IRS Status: 501(c)3
Highest Offering: Associate Degree
Accreditation: NH, ACBSP, ADNUR, COARC, COARCP, CSHSE, DH, EMT, ENGT, MAC, OTA, PTAA, RAD

01 President Dr. Debra L. MCCURDY
10 Vice President Business & Finance Mr. Russ LITKE
05 VP Academic Affairs Dr. Chris BOYETT
32 Vice President for Student Affairs Dr. Rose REINHART
45 VP Institutional Effect/Planning Ms. Becky BURRELL
30 Executive Director of Development Mr. Kevin L. REEKS
20 Associate VP for Academic Affairs Dr. Cherilee WALKER
37 Director Student Financial Aid Ms. Cathy L. KOHLI
09 Director Institutional Research Vacant
36 Director of Career Services Ms. Krista RICHARDSON
08 Head Librarian Ms. Tina SCHNEIDER
103 Exec Dir for Workforce & Econ Dev Mr. Kent KAHN
15 Director Human Resources Mr. Robert CARSON
54 Dean Business/Tech & Public Svcs Mr. Ken BAKER
49 Dean Div of Arts & Sciences Vacant
76 Dean of Health Sciences Dr. Paula BOLEY
18 Chief Facilities/Physical Plant Vacant
21 Assoc VP Fin/Controller/Asst Treas Ms. Beverly REX-COOK
26 Assoc Dir Mktg & College Relations Ms. Sandy PIEHL
38 Director Advising & Counseling Ms. Andrea ANDERSON

John Carroll University (H)

1 John Carroll Boulevard, Cleveland OH 44118
County: Cuyahoga FICE Identification: 003050
Unit ID: 203368
Telephone: (216) 397-1886 Carnegie Class: Masters/L
FAX Number: (216) 397-4256 Calendar System: Semester
URL: www.jcu.edu
Established: 1886 Annual Undergrad Tuition & Fees: $38,490
Enrollment: 3,673 Coed
Affiliation or Control: Roman Catholic IRS Status: 501(c)3
Highest Offering: Beyond Master's But Less Than Doctorate
Accreditation: NH, CACREP, CAEPN

01 Interim President Dr. Jeanne L. COLLERAN
88 Title IX Investigator Ms. Kendra E. SVILAR
04 Assistant to the President Ms. Bridget RINI
11 Vice President for Administration Mr. Richard F. MAUSSER
43 General Counsel Ms. Colleen TREML
88 VP for Univ Mission & Identity Dr. Edward J. PECK
05 Interim Provost & AVP Dr. Nicholas R. SANTILLI
111 Vice Pres University Advancement Ms. Doreen K. RILEY
84 VP for Enrollment Vacant
10 Chief Financial Officer Mr. Dennis F. HAREZA
32 Vice President for Student Affairs Dr. Mark D. MCCARTHY
20 Assoc Academic Vice President Dr. James H. KRUKONES
108 Assistant Provost Assessment & IE Dr. Robert (Todd) BRUCE
49 Dean College of Arts & Sciences Dr. Margaret E. FARRAR
50 Dean Boler School of Business Dr. Alan R. MICIAK
79 Assoc Dean Humanities/GR Programs Dr. Anne KUGLER
81 Assoc Dean Science and Health Dr. Graciela LACUEVA
83 Assoc Dean Soc Sci/Global/Ed Dr. Pamela MASON
35 Dean of Students Dr. Sherri A. CRAHEN
13 Interim Chief Information Officer Mr. James BURKE
18 Assoc Vice Pres for Facilities Ms. Carol P. DIETZ
26 Int Exec Director of Communications Ms. Tonya STRONG CHARLES
15 Asst Vice Pres Human Resources Mr. Alex J. TEODOSIO
08 Director of the Library Ms. Michelle MILLET
86 Assoc VP & Dir of Govt & Cmty Rels Vacant
36 AVP & Ed Center for Career Svcs Mr. Patrick MULLANE
22 Affirmative Action Officer/EEO Dr. James H. KRUKONES
06 Registrar Ms. Martha C. MONDELLO-HENDREN
21 Controller Mr. John P. CLIFFORD
113 Bursar & Dir of Student Accounts Vacant
39 Director of Residence Life Ms. Lisa M. BROWN
92 Director Honors Program Dr. Angela C. JONES
112 Sr Dir Major Gifts/Liaison to A&S Ms. Mary RYCYNA
37 Director of Financial Aid Ms. Claudia A. WENZEL
113 Director Budget/Financial Analysis Ms. Jennifer A. DILLON
88 Dir Ctr Service and Social Action Ms. Katherine FEELY, SND
42 Director of Campus Ministry Mr. John B. SCARANO
38 Director Univ Counseling Center Dr. Mark ONUSKO
23 Director Student Health Center Ms. Janet M. KREVH
41 Sr Director Athletics & Recreation Ms. Laurie J. MASSA
29 Director Alumni Relations Mr. David A. VITATOE
44 Sr Director Philanthropic Relations Mr. Peter R. BERNARDO
88 Dir Corporate Giving/Liaison Bus Ms. Christina BEG
102 Director Foundation Relations/Grant Ms. Pamela L. GEORGE
96 Director Purchasing/Auxiliary Svcs Mr. Andrew F. FRONCZEK
25 Director Sponsored Research Vacant
19 Director & Chief JCUPD Mr. Brian K. HURD
91 Director Enterprise Applications Mr. John M. SULLY
88 Center Digital Media Fac Liaison Dr. Jay TARBY
104 Asst Dir Center for Global Studies Vacant

Kent State University Kent Campus (I)

PO Box 5190, Kent OH 44242-0001
County: Portage FICE Identification: 003051
Unit ID: 203517
Telephone: (330) 672-3000 Carnegie Class: DU-Higher
FAX Number: (330) 672-2190 Calendar System: Semester
URL: www.kent.edu
Established: 1910 Annual Undergrad Tuition & Fees (In-State): $10,012
Enrollment: 30,067 Coed
Affiliation or Control: State IRS Status: 501(c)3
Highest Offering: Doctorate
Accreditation: NH, AAB, ART, CAATE, CACREP, CAEPN, CIDA, CLPSY, DANCE, DIETD, DIETI, ENGT, EXSC, JOUR, LIB, MUS, NAIT, NRPA, NURSE, PH, POD, SCPSY, SP, SPAA, THEA

01 President Dr. Beverly J. WARREN
05 Provost/Sr VP Academic Affairs Dr. Todd DIACON
10 Senior Vice Pres Finance & Admin Dr. Mark M. POLATAJKO
15 Vice Pres Human Resources Mr. Jack WITT
30 Vice Pres Institutional Advancement Mr. Stephen SOKANY
32 Vice Pres Student Affairs Dr. Shay DAVIS LITTLE
26 Senior VP Strategic Communications Ms. Karen CLARKE
46 Vice President Research Dr. Paul E. DICORLETO
13 Vice President Information Services Vacant
22 VP Diversity/Equity/Inclusion Dr. Alfreda BROWN
20 Dean Undergraduate Studies Dr. Eboni PRINGLE
35 Student Ombuds Ms. Amy QUILLIN
45 Sr Assoc Provost Dr. Melody TANKERSLEY
20 Assoc Provost Faculty Affairs Ms. Sue AVERILL
84 Sr Assoc Vice Pres Enrollment Svcs Mr. David GARCIA
29 Asst Vice Pres Alumni Affairs Mrs. Lori RANDORF
07 Director of Admissions Ms. Nancy J. DELLAVECCHIA
16 Human Resources Director-CPM Mr. David DIXON
06 Registrar Ms. Gail REBETA
43 Vice Pres University Counsel Mr. Willis WALKER
100 VP and University Secretary Ms. Charlene K. REED
41 Director Intercollegiate Athletics Mr. Joel NIELSON
22 Director of Compliance & Benefits Vacant
37 Director Student Financial Aid Mr. Mark EVANS
19 Director of Public Safety Mr. Dean TONDIGLIA
12 Dean Trumbull Campus Dr. Lance GRAHN
96 Director of Procurement Mr. Timothy J. KONCZAL
49 Dean Arts & Sciences Dr. James BLANK
50 Dean of Business Administration Dr. Deborah F. SPAKE
53 Interim Dean EHHS Dr. Mark KRETOVICS
57 Dean of the Arts Dr. John CRAWFORD
66 Dean College of Nursing Dr. Barbara BROOME
51 Exec Director Continuing Studies Ms. Deborah C. HUNTSMAN
92 Interim Dean Honors College Dr. Donald F. PALMER
08 Dean Library & Media Services Dr. James BRACKEN
48 Dean Architect/Environ Design Mr. Mark MISTUR
60 Dean Col of Comm & Information Dr. Amy REYNOLDS
72 Interim Dean Applied Engr/Sust/Tech Dr. Robert G. SINES
58 Interim Dean of Graduate Studies Dr. Melody TANKERSLEY
88 Dean College of Podiatric Medicine Dr. Allan BOIKE
20 Sr Assoc Dean-CPM Dr. Vincent J. HETHERINGTON
21 Sr Business Manager-CPM Mr. Mark M. MATEJCIK
08 Librarian-CPM Mrs. Donna M. PERZESKI
18 Director of Facilities Planning-CPM Mr. Dan RIDGWAY
84 Director of Enrollment Mgmt-CPM Vacant

Kent State University at Ashtabula (J)

3300 Lake Road W, Ashtabula OH 44004-2299
Telephone: (440) 964-3322 FICE Identification: 003052
Accreditation: &NH, ADNUR, COARC, OTA, PTAA, RAD

† Regional accreditation is carried under the parent institution in Kent, OH.

Kent State University East Liverpool Campus (K)

400 E Fourth Street, East Liverpool OH 43920-3497
Telephone: (330) 385-3805 FICE Identification: 003056
Accreditation: &NH, ADNUR, OTA

† Regional accreditation is carried under the parent institution in Kent, OH.

Kent State University Geauga Campus (L)

14111 Claridon-Troy Road, Burton Township OH 44021-9500
Telephone: (440) 834-4187 FICE Identification: 003059
Accreditation: &NH, ADNUR

† Regional accreditation is carried under the parent institution in Kent, OH.

Kent State University Salem Campus (M)

2491 State Road 45 South, Salem OH 44460-9412
Telephone: (330) 332-0361 FICE Identification: 003061
Accreditation: &NH, RAD, RTT

† Regional accreditation is carried under the parent institution in Kent, OH.

Kent State University Stark Campus (N)

6000 Frank Avenue NW, North Canton OH 44720-9988
Telephone: (330) 499-9600 FICE Identification: 003054
Accreditation: &NH

† Regional accreditation is carried under the parent institution in Kent, OH.

Kent State University Trumbull Campus (O)

4314 Mahoning Avenue, NW, Warren OH 44483-1998
Telephone: (330) 847-0571 FICE Identification: 003064
Accreditation: &NH

† Regional accreditation is carried under the parent institution in Kent, OH.

Kent State University Tuscarawas Campus (P)

330 University Drive, NE, New Philadelphia OH 44663-9403
Telephone: (330) 339-3391 FICE Identification: 003062

Accreditation: &NH, ADNUR, ENGT

† Regional accreditation is carried under the parent institution in Kent, OH.

Kenyon College (A)

106 College-Park Street, Gambier OH 43022-9623
County: Knox FICE Identification: 003065
Unit ID: 203535
Telephone: (740) 427-5000 Carnegie Class: Bac-A&S
FAX Number: (740) 427-3077 Calendar System: Semester
URL: www.kenyon.edu
Established: 1824 Annual Undergrad Tuition & Fees: $51,200
Enrollment: 1,711 Coed
Affiliation or Control: Independent Non-Profit IRS Status: 501(c)3
Highest Offering: Baccalaureate
Accreditation: NH

01 President ... Dr. Sean DECATUR
05 Provost ... Dr. Joe L. KLESNER
30 Vice President College Relations ... Ms. Heidi H. MCCRORY
10 Vice President for Finance ... Mr. Todd E. BURSON
08 Vice Pres Library & Info Svcs ... Mr. Ronald K. GRIGGS
100 Chief of Staff ... Ms. Susan MORSE
21 Assoc Vice President for Finance ... Vacant
112 Assoc VP for Planned Giving ... Mr. Kyle W. HENDERSON
32 Dean of Students ... Ms. Robin HART RUTHENBECK
07 Dean of Admissions/Fin Aid ... Ms. Diane ANCI
20 Associate Provost ... Dr. Jan THOMAS
20 Associate Provost ... Dr. Jeff BOWMAN
06 Registrar/Dean Academic Support ... Ms. Ellen K. HARBOURT
26 Assoc VP for Communications ... Ms. Janet MARSDEN
29 Dir Alumni/Parent Rels ... Mr. Scott R. BAKER
37 Director of Financial Aid ... Mr. Craig SLAUGHTER
38 Director of Counseling Services ... Vacant
15 Director of Human Resources ... Ms. Jennifer G. CABRAL
42 Director of Religious/Spiritual ... Rabbi Marc BRAGIN
21 Chief Business Officer ... Mr. Mark KOHLMAN
22 Civil Rights/Title IX Coordinator ... Ms. Samantha HUGHES
19 Director of Campus Safety ... Mr. Robert D. HOOPER
09 Director of Institutional Research ... Ms. Erika M. FARFAN
21 Manager of Business Services ... Mr. Frederick S. LINGER
28 Director of Multicultural Affairs ... Mr. A. Chris KENNERLY
101 Director of Board Relations ... Ms. Kathryn LAKE
04 Executive Asst to President ... Ms. Mary Ellen O'MEARA

Kettering College (B)

3737 Southern Boulevard, Kettering OH 45429-1299
County: Montgomery FICE Identification: 007035
Unit ID: 203544
Telephone: (937) 395-8601 Carnegie Class: Spec-4-yr-Other Health
FAX Number: (937) 395-8106 Calendar System: Semester
URL: www.kc.edu
Established: 1967 Annual Undergrad Tuition & Fees: $11,808
Enrollment: 732 Coed
Affiliation or Control: Seventh-day Adventist IRS Status: 501(c)3
Highest Offering: Doctorate
Accreditation: NH, ADNUR, ARCPA, COARC, DMS, NUR, PAST, RAD

00 Chairman of the Board ... Mr. Jarrod MCNAUGHTON
01 President ... Dr. Nate BRANDSTATER
15 Vice President Human Resources ... Mr. Timothy DUTTON
05 Dean for Academic Affairs ... Dr. Ruth ABBOTT
05 Dean for Academic Affairs ... Dr. Josefer MONTES
102 President Foundation ... Mrs. Susan BARCUS
84 Dean Enrollment Mgmt/Student Affs ... Mr. Victor BROWN
10 Chief Business Officer ... Mr. Terry BURNS
21 Director of Finance/Administration ... Mr. Nicholas HENSON
06 Registrar ... Mrs. Robin VANDERBILT
37 Director Student Financial Aid ... Mrs. Kim SNELL
40 Manager Bookstore ... Mrs. Jessica HILL
42 Chaplain Director Campus Ministry ... Mr. Steve CARLSON
32 Director Student Life ... Mr. Kris HARTER
26 Public Relations Officer ... Ms. Jessica BEANS
08 Director of Library ... Mr. John KISSINGER
29 Director Alumni Relations ... Mrs. Teresa SIMMONS
07 Director of Admissions ... Mrs. Katrina HILL
13 Senior Information Officer ... Mr. Jim NESBIT

Lake Erie College (C)

391 W Washington Street, Painesville OH 44077-3389
County: Lake FICE Identification: 003066
Unit ID: 203580
Telephone: (440) 375-7000 Carnegie Class: Masters/S
FAX Number: (440) 375-7005 Calendar System: Semester
URL: www.lec.edu
Established: 1856 Annual Undergrad Tuition & Fees: $29,960
Enrollment: 1,243 Coed
Affiliation or Control: Independent Non-Profit IRS Status: 501(c)3
Highest Offering: Master's
Accreditation: NH, #ARCPA, CAEPT, IACBE

01 President ... Dr. Brian POSLER
05 Vice Pres for Academic Affairs/CAO ... Bryan DEPOY
10 Vice Pres Administration & Finance ... Brian DIRK
30 VP for Institutional Advancement ... Scott EVANS
20 Assoc VP for Academic Admin ... Dr. Jennifer COLLIS
53 Dean School of Educ & Prof Studies ... Dr. Katharine DELAVAN
50 Dean School of Business ... Dr. Robert TREBAR
88 Dean School of Equine Studies ... Dr. Pam HESS
88 Interim Dean Sch of Arts/Human & SS ... Dr. Jennifer SWARTZ-LEVINE
81 Dean School of Nat Sci & Math ... Dr. Jonathan TEDESCO
06 Registrar ... Barbara ARILSON
107 Director Prof Development ... Lisa STRAUSBAUGH
88 Director Physician Assistant Pgm ... Sean KRAMER
36 Director Career Services ... Eric EVANS
13 Director of Information Technology ... Brad LUHTA
38 Director Student Success Center ... Dr. John SPIESMAN
15 Director Human Resources ... Andrea MYERS
32 VP Student Affairs ... Billie DUNN
84 VP for Enrollment & Fin Aid ... Terry FINEFROCK
18 Director Physical Plant ... Herb DILL
29 Director Alumni & Community Rels ... Debra REMINGTON
41 Director Athletics ... Billie DUNN
08 Director Lincoln Library ... Christopher BENNETT
19 Director Security ... Richard KLINE
40 Bookstore Manager ... Natalie SCALA
04 Executive Asst to President & BOD ... Julie HERBERT
26 Director of PR/Mktg and Comm Relati ... Leah JACKSON
44 Director of Development ... Pamela PALERMO
07 Director of Admissions ... Marlo YANDIO
37 Director Student Financial Aid ... Tricia PANGONIS

Lakeland Community College (D)

7700 Clocktower Drive, Kirtland OH 44094-5198
County: Lake FICE Identification: 006804
Unit ID: 203599
Telephone: (440) 525-7000 Carnegie Class: Assoc/HT-Mix Trad/Non
FAX Number: (440) 525-7651 Calendar System: Semester
URL: www.lakelandcc.edu
Established: 1967 Annual Undergrad Tuition & Fees (In-District): $3,316
Enrollment: 7,941 Coed
Affiliation or Control: State/Local IRS Status: 501(c)3
Highest Offering: Associate Degree
Accreditation: NH, ADNUR, CAHIIM, COARC, DH, EMT, ENGT, HT, IFSAC, MAC, MLTAD, RAD, SURGT

01 President ... Dr. Morris W. BEVERAGE, JR.
05 Exec VP & Provost ... Dr. Laura BARNARD
10 Exec Vice Pres Admin Svcs/Treasurer ... Mr. Michael E. MAYHER
100 Chief of Staff/Sr VP Inst Effectiv ... Ms. Catherine BUSH
26 Chief Commun Ofcr/VP College Rels ... Ms. Dawn M. PLANTE
20 Assoc Provost Teach & Learn ... Dr. Deborah L. HARDY
84 Assoc Provost for Enrollment Mgmt ... Mr. William KRAUS
32 Assoc VP Student Dev/Dean of Stdnts ... Mr. Richard J. NOVOTNY
81 Dean of Arts and Sciences ... Dr. Steven OLUIC
76 Dean of Health Technologies ... Dr. Deborah L. HARDY
88 Dean of Applied Studies ... Mr. Brian COOK
21 Assoc VP Bus Svcs/Deputy Treasurer ... Ms. Andrea AUSPERK
13 CIO Administrative Technologies ... Mr. Rick PENNY
21 Controller ... Mr. Michael GRAFF
15 Director Human Resources ... Ms. Cathy BUSH
18 Director for Facilities Management ... Mr. Bert DIEHL
19 Chief of Police/Director of Safety ... Mr. Ronald MORENZ
07 Director for Admissions/Registrar ... Ms. Tracey L. COOPER
37 Dir Financial Aid/Enroll Support ... Ms. Melissa A. AMSPAUGH
35 Director of Student Activities ... Mr. Mario PETITTI
30 Dir Development/Alumni Relations ... Dr. Robert CAHEN
96 Director of Purchasing ... Mr. Tom A. KIRCHNER
09 Director of Institutional Research ... Mrs. Lisa DURST

Lakewood College (E)

2231 North Taylor Road, Cleveland Heights OH 44112
County: Cuyahoga Identification: 666715
Telephone: (800) 517-0857 Carnegie Class: Not Classified
FAX Number: (216) 803-9899 Calendar System: Other
URL: www.lakewoodcollege.edu
Established: 1998 Annual Undergrad Tuition & Fees: N/A
Enrollment: N/A Coed
Affiliation or Control: Independent Non-Profit IRS Status: 501(c)3
Highest Offering: Associate Degree
Accreditation: DEAC

01 CEO and Founder ... Ms. Tanya HAGGINS
21 Success Coach Director ... Mr. Anthony NATHAL
05 Academic Dean ... Mr. James GEPPERTH
30 Vice President of Business Devel ... Mr. Isaac HAGGINS

Lorain County Community College (F)

1005 N Abbe Road, Elyria OH 44035-1691
County: Lorain FICE Identification: 003068
Unit ID: 203748
Telephone: (440) 365-5222 Carnegie Class: Assoc/HT-High Trad
FAX Number: (440) 365-6519 Calendar System: Semester
URL: www.lorainccc.edu
Established: 1963 Annual Undergrad Tuition & Fees (In-District): $3,077
Enrollment: 11,520 Coed
Affiliation or Control: State/Local IRS Status: 501(c)3
Highest Offering: Associate Degree
Accreditation: NH, ADNUR, ART, DH, DMS, EMT, ENGT, MAC, MLTAD, OTA, PHLEB, PNUR, PTAA, RAD, SURGT

01 President ... Dr. Marcia J. BALLINGER
46 VP Strategic & Institutional Devel ... Ms. Tracy A. GREEN
05 Int Provost/VP Acad & Learner Svcs ... Dr. Jonathan N. DRYDEN
10 Vice President Admin Svcs/Treasurer ... Mr. Jonathan VOLPE
88 Assoc Prov University Partnership ... Dr. John R. CROOKS
08 Dean Library/Instruction Media ... Ms. Karla ALEMAN
84 Assoc Prov Enroll/Fin Career Svcs ... Dr. Stephanie SUTTON
09 Dir Inst Research & Planning ... Ms. Cynthia APPLIN
13 Chief Information Tech Officer ... Mr. Donald HUFFMAN
15 Director Human Resources/Campus Sec ... Mr. Keith BROWN
88 Dir Talent and Business Innovation ... Ms. Terri B. SANDU
18 Int Manager of Physical Plant ... Mr. Ken COLLINS
57 Dir Stocker Humanit/Fine Arts Ctr ... Ms. Janet HERMAN-BARLOW
96 Dir Purchasing/Facilities Planning ... Ms. Laura K. CARISSIMI
54 Dean Engr/Business & Info Tech ... Ms. Kelly ZELESNIK
76 Int Dean Allied Health & Nursing ... Dr. Hope MOON
79 Int Dean Arts/Humanities ... Dr. Karin HOOKS
81 Int Dean Science/Mathematics ... Mr. Aaron WEISS
83 Int Dean Social Science/Human Svc ... Dr. Steven HUBBARD
06 Registrar ... Ms. Sun Kyong JAMERSON
101 Executive Assoc Board Liaison ... Ms. Karen BUESCHER
19 Manager Security/Safety ... Mr. Ken COLLINS
26 Dir Marketing & Outreach Initiative ... Ms. Cynthia KUSHNER
102 LCC Foundation Director ... Mr. Charles WIERSMA

Lourdes University (G)

6832 Convent Boulevard, Sylvania OH 43560-2898
County: Lucas FICE Identification: 003069
Unit ID: 203757
Telephone: (419) 885-3211 Carnegie Class: Masters/M
FAX Number: (419) 882-3987 Calendar System: Semester
URL: www.lourdes.edu
Established: 1958 Annual Undergrad Tuition & Fees: $20,620
Enrollment: 1,530 Coed
Affiliation or Control: Roman Catholic IRS Status: 501(c)3
Highest Offering: Master's
Accreditation: NH, ANEST, CAEPT, IACBE, NURSE, SW

01 President ... Dr. Mary Ann GAWELEK
00 President Emerita ... Sr. Ann Francis KLIMKOWSKI
05 Provost ... Dr. Geoffrey J. GRUBB
10 Vice Pres Finance & Administration ... Dr. Robert ROOD
42 Vice Pres for Mission & Ministry ... Sr. Ann Carmen BARONE, OSF
111 Vice President for Inst Advancement ... Ms. Mary ARQUETTE
45 Asst Vice Pres for Inst Planning ... Ms. Michelle RABLE
49 Int Dean College of Arts & Sciences ... Dr. Kate BEUTEL
53 Int Dean Col of Social Services ... Mr. Terry KELLER
66 Int Dean College of Nursing ... Dr. Hollis HAMILTON
50 Dean Col Business & Leadership ... Vacant
32 Dean of Student Life ... Ms. Rachel DUFF-ANDERSON
39 Director of Residence Life ... Mr. Andy HAM
37 Dir of Student Financial Services ... Ms. Deb LAJEUNESSE
26 Director of University Relations ... Ms. Helene SHEETS
08 Director of Library Services ... Sr. Sandra RUTKOWSKI
06 Registrar ... Ms. Michelle A. RABLE
13 Asst VP for Technology & CIO ... Mr. Scott CROW
15 Int Director of Human Resources ... Ms. Chanie REINHART
36 Director of Career Counseling ... Ms. Andrea DOMACHOWSKI
21 Director of Finance ... Ms. Kimberly MCGILL
30 Director of Development ... Ms. Brittanie KUHR
18 Director of Facilities & Grounds ... Mr. Michael CRAVENS
19 Title IX Coord & Dir Public Safety ... Ms. Michelle MCDEVITT
07 Director of Admissions ... Mr. Shawn BUSSELL
123 Director of Graduate Admissions ... Ms. Tara HANNA
88 Dir Campus Ministry/Svc Learning ... Sr. Barbara VANO, OSF
40 Manager of Bookstore ... Ms. Ann MORRIS
121 Director of Student Success ... Ms. Alisa SMITH

Malone University (H)

2600 Cleveland Avenue NW, Canton OH 44709-3308
County: Stark FICE Identification: 003072
Unit ID: 203775
Telephone: (330) 471-8100 Carnegie Class: Masters/M
FAX Number: (330) 471-8478 Calendar System: Semester
URL: www.malone.edu
Established: 1892 Annual Undergrad Tuition & Fees: $29,422
Enrollment: 1,722 Coed
Affiliation or Control: Friends IRS Status: 501(c)3
Highest Offering: Master's
Accreditation: NH, ACBSP, CACREP, CAEPN, MUS, NURSE, SW

01 President ... Dr. David A. KING
10 Vice Pres for Finance/CFO ... Mrs. Elaine C. ARICK
05 Provost ... Dr. D. Nathan PHINNEY
32 Vice Pres for Student Development ... Dr. Christopher T. ABRAMS
111 Vice Pres for Univ Advancement ... Mr. Stephen T. WEINGART
26 Vice Pres for Marketing & Comm ... Mr. Timothy A. BRYAN
84 Vice Pres for Enrollment Management ... Mr. Mark SEYMOUR
49 Int Dean Col of Theol/Arts & Sci ... Dr. James H. BROWNLEE
53 Int Dean Sch of Educ & Human Dev ... Dr. Debra A. LEE
66 Dean Sch of Nursing & Health Sci ... Dr. Debra A. LEE
30 Associate VP for Development ... Ms. Sharon L. SIRPILLA
21 Controller ... Mr. Tracy L. MILLER
06 Registrar ... Mr. Gary L. PHELPS
07 Director of Admissions ... Mrs. Linda A. KURTZ HOFFMAN
29 Dir of Alumni & Parent Relations ... Mrs. Deborah M. ROBINSON
44 Director of Annual Giving ... Mrs. Paula M. CALHOUN
108 Dir Inst Effectiveness/Assessment ... Dr. Charles R. LARTEY
37 Director of Financial Aid ... Mrs. Pamela S. PUSTAY
15 Assoc VP Human Res/Facilities Mgmt ... Mr. Michael J. FAIRLESS
41 Athletic Director ... Mr. Charles R. GRIMES
08 Director of Library ... Ms. Rebecca L. FORT
106 Dir Online Education/E-learning ... Mr. John W. KOSHMIDER, III
93 Director of Multicultural Services ... Mrs. Brenda D. STEVENS
104 Dir Ctr/Cross-Cultural Engagement ... Mr. Ryan J. DONALD
19 Director Security/Safety ... Mr. David W. BURNIP
13 Chief Information Officer ... Mr. M. Adam KLEMANN

90 Senior Network Engineer ... Mr. James M. SHAFFER
42 Director of Spiritual Formation ... Rev Dr. Linda J. LEON
105 Content Mgr for Publications/Web ... Mrs. Amber L. BALASH
40 Bookstore Manager ... Mrs. Kathy L. SECREST
04 Exec Asst to Pres/Asst to Board ... Mrs. Teresa L. PITTINGER
88 Assistant to the Provost ... Ms. Karen R. WARNER
92 Director of Honors Program ... Dr. Steven M. JENSEN
89 Dir of the College Experience Pgm ... Dr. Marcia K. EVERETT
38 Director of Counseling Center ... Mr. Timothy T. MORBER
23 Health Center Director ... Ms. Rebecca K. RODAK

Marietta College (A)

215 Fifth Street, Marietta OH 45750-4033

County: Washington FICE Identification: 003073

Unit ID: 203845

Telephone: (740) 376-4000 Carnegie Class: Bac-Diverse

FAX Number: (740) 376-4896 Calendar System: Semester

URL: www.marietta.edu

Established: 1835 Annual Undergrad Tuition & Fees: $35,330

Enrollment: 1,331 Coed

Affiliation or Control: Independent Non-Profit IRS Status: 501(c)3

Highest Offering: Master's

Accreditation: NH, ARCPA, CAATE, ENG, MUS

01 President ... Dr. William N. RUUD
05 Provost/Dean of Faculty ... Dr. Janet L. BLAND
10 VP for Administration & Finance ... Ms. Michele L. MARRA
111 VP for Advancement ... Ms. Angela B. ANDERSON
32 VP Student Life/Chf Diversity Ofcr ... Dr. Richard K. DANFORD
84 VP for Enrollment Mgmt ... Mr. Stephen LAZOWSKI
88 Dean McDonough Ctr for Leadership ... Dr. Gamaliel (Gama) PERRUCI
101 Secretary to the Board of Trustees ... Dr. Mark MILLER
08 Director of Library ... Dr. N. Douglas ANDERSON
07 Assistant VP for Enrollment Mgmt ... Ms. Emily G. SCHUCK
18 Director of Physical Plant ... Mr. Fred R. SMITH
06 Registrar ... Ms. Tina K. PERDUE
15 Director of Human Resources ... Ms. Debra C. WAYLAND
19 Chief of Campus Police ... Mr. James S. WEAVER
26 Exec Dir of Strategic Comm & Mktg ... Mr. Thomas D. PERRY
09 Institutional Researcher ... Mr. William (Bill) CLARK
36 Career Center Director ... Ms. B. Hilles HUGHES
41 Director of Athletics ... Mr. Larry R. HISER
13 Director of Information Technology ... Mr. Aaron COWDERY
63 PA Program Director ... Ms. Miranda COLLINS
104 Director of Education Abroad ... Ms. Christy BURKE
25 Grants Officer ... Ms. Robin STEWART
51 Continuing Education ... Ms. Tina K. PERDUE
35 Dean of Students ... Dr. Lisa PHILLIPS
04 Administrative Asst to President ... Paula LEWIS
29 Director Alumni Relations ... Brandee NORRIS

Marion Technical College (B)

1467 Mount Vernon Avenue, Marion OH 43302-5694

County: Marion FICE Identification: 010736

Unit ID: 203881

Telephone: (740) 389-4636 Carnegie Class: Assoc/HT-Mix Trad/Non

FAX Number: (740) 389-6136 Calendar System: Semester

URL: www.mtc.edu

Established: 1971 Annual Undergrad Tuition & Fees (In-State): $4,480

Enrollment: 2,441 Coed

Affiliation or Control: State IRS Status: 501(c)3

Highest Offering: Associate Degree

Accreditation: NH, ADNUR, CAHIIM, DMS, MAC, MLTAD, OTA, PTAA, RAD

01 President ... Dr. Ryan MCCALL
05 Chief Academic Officer ... Vacant
32 Dean of Student Services ... Mr. Mike STUCKEY
111 Vice Pres Planning & Advancement ... Dr. Amy ADAMS
06 Registrar ... Ms. Kristy TAYLOR
13 Executive Director IT Operations ... Mr. Steve DUVALL
26 Director of Marketing ... Mr. Justin DEAN
66 Director of Nursing Technology ... Ms. Cynthia HARTMAN
103 Director Ctr Workforce Development ... Ms. Tami GALLOWAY
15 Director Human Resources ... Ms. Brenda FEASEL
88 Dir Physical Therapist Asst Pgm ... Mr. Chad HENSEL
88 Dir Occupational Therapy ... Mr. Josh LINE
100 Chief of Staff ... Ms. Teresa PARKER
18 Coord Facil Improvements/Operations ... Ms. Leeann GRAU
37 Director Student Financial Aid ... Ms. Deb LANGDON
54 Director of Engineering Technology ... Mr. Matthew FARSON
50 Dean of Business/Tech/Public Serv ... Ms. Debbie STARK
49 Dean of Arts and Sciences ... Dr. Chad SCHNEIDER
76 Dean of Allied Health ... Mr. Chris GASE
10 Chief Financial Officer ... Mr. Jeff NUTTER
108 Chief Strategy Officer ... Dr. Bob HAAS
07 Director of Admissions ... Mr. Brandon MOONEY

Mercy College of Ohio (C)

2221 Madison Avenue, Toledo OH 43604

County: Lucas FICE Identification: 030970

Unit ID: 203960

Telephone: (419) 251-1313 Carnegie Class: Spec-4-yr-Other Health

FAX Number: (419) 251-1570 Calendar System: Semester

URL: www.mercycollege.edu

Established: 1993 Annual Undergrad Tuition & Fees: $13,430

Enrollment: 1,243 Coed

Affiliation or Control: Roman Catholic IRS Status: 501(c)3

Highest Offering: Master's

Accreditation: NH, ADNUR, CAHIIM, EMT, NURSE, POLYT, RAD

01 President ... Dr. Susan WAJERT
05 VP Acad Affs/Dean of Faculty ... Dr. Trevor BATES
32 VP Student Affs/Dean of Student ... Mr. Marc ADKINS
66 Dean Nursing and Allied Hlth ... Dr. Elizabeth SPRUNK
76 Dean of Arts and Sciences ... Dr. Barbara STOOS
117 Dir of Compliance/Risk Mgmt ... Ms. Leslie ERWIN
13 Dir of College Info Tech Services ... Mr. David BURGIN
10 Director College Finances/Res Plng ... Ms. Joan M. RUTHERFORD
30 Director College Advancement ... Mr. Michael WHALEN
84 VP of Strategic Plng & Enroll Mgmt ... Ms. Lori EDGEWORTH
08 Director Library/Resource Services ... Ms. Deborah JOHNSON
09 Dir Inst Research/Registrar ... Mr. Mark MCKELLIP
37 Financial Aid Director ... Ms. Julie LESLIE
26 Director of Communication ... Ms. Denise HUDGIN
42 Dir Campus Ministry & Svcs Learning ... Sr. Sally BOHNETT
21 Business Manager ... Ms. Diane RAHN
18 Manager of Operations ... Ms. Sherri BOGGS
29 Director Alumni Relations ... Vacant
121 Director of Student Success Center ... Ms. Lisa SANCRANT
36 Dir of Career/Prof Dev & Retention ... Ms. Kristen PORTER
106 Interim Dir of Distance Education ... Dr. Dan FRENCH
28 Dir of Diversity & Inclusion ... Mr. Quatez SCOTT
04 Administrative Asst to President ... Ms. Jane STUNTZ
07 Director of Admissions ... Ms. Amy MERGEN

Methodist Theological School in Ohio (D)

3081 Columbus Pike, Delaware OH 43015-3211

County: Delaware FICE Identification: 003075

Unit ID: 203997

Telephone: (740) 363-1146 Carnegie Class: Spec-4-yr-Faith

FAX Number: (740) 362-3135 Calendar System: 4/1/4

URL: www.mtso.edu

Established: 1958 Annual Graduate Tuition & Fees: N/A

Enrollment: 148 Coed

Affiliation or Control: United Methodist IRS Status: 501(c)3

Highest Offering: Doctorate; No Undergraduates

Accreditation: NH, THEOL

01 President ... Rev. Jay A. RUNDELL
05 Interim Dean ... Dr. Valerie BRIDGEMAN
111 VP of Institutional Advancement ... Ms. April CASPERSON
04 Executive Asst to the President ... Ms. Leigh PRECISE
26 Director of Communications ... Mr. Danny RUSSELL
07 Director of Admissions ... Rev. Benjamin HALL
06 Registrar ... Mr. Lee RICHARDS
08 Director of the Library ... Mr. Paul BURNAM
10 Controller ... Rev. Jim SUMMERS
18 Facilities Manager ... Mr. Keith HUFFMAN
32 Director of Student Services ... Ms. Kristin LOFRUMENTO
13 Director Information Technology ... Mr. Matthew REHM
37 Director of Financial Aid ... Ms. Molly HOFFMAN
44 Director of Annual Giving ... Rev. Claudine LEARY
117 Dir of Human Resources & Compliance ... Ms. Grace WELCH

Miami-Jacobs Career College (E)

150 E Gay Street, 1st Floor, Columbus OH 43215-3227

Telephone: (614) 221-7770 Identification: 666465

Accreditation: ACICS, MAC

† Branch campus of McCann School of Business & Technology, Pottsville, PA

Miami-Jacobs Career College (F)

401 E. Third Street, Dayton OH 45402

Telephone: (937) 552-4006 FICE Identification: 003076

Accreditation: ACICS, MAC, #SURGT

† Branch campus of McCann School of Business & Technology, Pottsville, PA

Miami-Jacobs Career College (G)

6400 Rockside Road, Independence OH 44131

Telephone: (216) 430-0348 FICE Identification: 021521

Accreditation: ACICS

† Branch campus of McCann School of Business & Technology, Pottsville, PA

Miami-Jacobs Career College (H)

865 West Market Street, Troy OH 45373

Telephone: (937) 332-8585 Identification: 770756

Accreditation: ACICS

† Branch campus of McCann School of Business & Technology, Pottsville, PA

Miami University (I)

501 E High Street, Oxford OH 45056-1846

County: Butler FICE Identification: 003077

Unit ID: 204024

Telephone: (513) 529-1809 Carnegie Class: DU-Higher

FAX Number: (513) 529-3841 Calendar System: Semester

URL: www.miamioh.edu

Established: 1809 Annual Undergrad Tuition & Fees (In-State): $14,736

Enrollment: 19,076 Coed

Affiliation or Control: State IRS Status: 501(c)3

Highest Offering: Doctorate

Accreditation: NH, ART, #CAATE, CAEP, CIDA, CLPSY, CS, DIETD, @DIETI, ENG, ENGT, IPSY, MUS, NURSE, SP, SW, THEA

01 President ... Dr. Gregory CRAWFORD
05 Provost ... Dr. Phyllis CALLAHAN
10 Sr VP Finance & Bus Svcs/Treasurer ... Dr. David CREAMER
32 Vice President Student Affairs ... Dr. Jayne E. BROWNELL
30 VP University Advancement ... Mr. Tom HERBERT
13 VP Information Technology ... Mr. J. Peter NATALE
15 Asst Prov Acad Personnel ... Ms. Ruth GROOM
21 Assoc VP Finance/Business Svcs ... Dr. David A. ELLIS
20 Assoc Provost for Undergrad Studies ... Dr. Carolyn A. HAYNES
35 Dean of Students ... Dr. Michael A. CURME
26 Assoc VP Comm/Marketing ... Ms. Deedie Kay DOWDLE
18 Assoc VP Facilities Planning & Op ... Mr. Cody J. POWELL
84 Sr VP Enroll Mgmt & Student Success ... Mr. Michael S. KABBAZ
28 Assoc VP Inst Diversity ... Dr. Ronald B. SCOTT
29 Asst Vice Pres Alumni Relations ... Vacant
27 Director Institutional Relations ... Mr. Randi Malcolm THOMAS
27 Assoc Dir Univ Communications ... Ms. Claire M. WAGNER
100 Secy Board/Exec Asst to President ... Mr. Ted O. PICKERILL
49 Dean College Arts & Science ... Dr. Christopher A. MAKAROFF, JR.
53 Dean Education/Health & Society ... Dr. Michael DANTLEY
50 Interim Dean Farmer Sch of Business ... Dr. Marc A. RUBIN
57 Dean College of Creative Arts ... Dr. Elizabeth R. MULLENIX
54 Dean College of Engr & Computing ... Dr. Marek DOLLAR
08 Dean University Libraries ... Mr. Jerome CONLEY
58 Dean Graduate School ... Dr. James T. ORIS
49 Int Dean Col of Liberal Art & Sci ... Dr. Catherine U. BISHOP-CLARK
07 Director of Admissions ... Ms. Susan SCHAURER
88 Asst Provost Global Initiatives ... Ms. Cheryl D. YOUNG
108 Univ Dir Ctr for Teaching Excellenc ... Dr. Rose Marie WARD
88 Univ Dir Liberal Educ/Assessment ... Dr. Shelly JARRETT BROMBERG
92 Univ Dir Honors & Scholars Program ... Dr. Linda MARCHANT
16 Int Assoc VP Human Resources ... Ms. Dawn FAHNER
23 Medical Director Student Health Svc ... Dr. Gregory CALKINS
104 Assoc Dir Intl Student & Scholar ... Ms. Molly HEIDEMANN
06 University Registrar ... Mr. David M. SAUTER
36 Asst VP Career Exploration/Success ... Ms. Jen FRANCHAK
38 Director Student Counseling Service ... Dr. Kip C. ALISHIO
09 Director Institutional Research ... Ms. Denise A. KRALLMAN
19 Chief of Police/Dir Public Safety ... Mr. John MCCANDLESS
96 Sr Director Purchasing/Central Svcs ... Mr. William G. SHAWVER
43 University General Counsel ... Ms. Robin L. PARKER
22 Director Equity & Equal Opportunity ... Ms. Kenya D. ASH
41 Director Intercollegiate Athletics ... Mr. David A. SAYLER
17 Director Student Wellness ... Ms. Rebecca BAUDRY YOUNG
04 Assistant to the President ... Ms. Dawn TSIRELIS
106 Asst Provost for E-learning ... Vacant
37 Director Student Financial Aid ... Mr. Brent L. SHOCK
102 Asst Dir Corporate/Found Relations ... Mr. Ryan GILLEY
109 Assoc VP Auxiliaries ... Mrs. Kim K. KINSEL
44 Sr Director Annual Giving ... Ms. Emily BERRY
45 Assoc VP Budgeting & Analysis ... Dr. David A. ELLIS
105 Univ Web Content Manager ... Ms. Jeri MOORE
25 Dir Research & Sponsored Pgms ... Ms. Anne P. SCHAUER
39 Exec Mgr Residential Services ... Ms. Stacy GEORGE
86 Director Government Relations ... Mr. Randi THOMAS

Miami University Hamilton Campus (J)

1601 University Boulevard, Hamilton OH 45011-3399

Telephone: (513) 785-3000 FICE Identification: 003079

Accreditation: &NH

† Regional accreditation is carried under the parent institution in Oxford, OH.

Miami University Middletown (K)

4200 N University Boulevard, Middletown OH 45042-3497

Telephone: (513) 727-3200 FICE Identification: 003080

Accreditation: &NH

† Regional accreditation is carried under the parent institution in Oxford, OH.

Mount Carmel College of Nursing (L)

127 S Davis Avenue, Columbus OH 43222-1504

County: Franklin FICE Identification: 030719

Unit ID: 204176

Telephone: (614) 234-5800 Carnegie Class: Spec-4-yr-Other Health

FAX Number: (614) 234-2875 Calendar System: Semester

URL: www.mccn.edu

Established: 1990 Annual Undergrad Tuition & Fees: $12,673

Enrollment: 1,063 Coed

Affiliation or Control: Roman Catholic IRS Status: 501(c)3

Highest Offering: Doctorate

Accreditation: NH, NURSE

01 Interim President ... Dr. Ann Marie BROOKS
05 Asst Academic Dean ... Ms. Jami NININGER
66 Assoc Dean Undergrad Nursing Pgm ... Dr. Scott DOLAN
58 Associate Dean Graduate Nursing Pgm ... Dr. Jill KILANOWSKI
106 Asst Dean Distance Education ... Ms. Jami NININGER
06 Director of Records & Registration ... Ms. Karen L. GREENE
10 Director Business Affairs ... Ms. Kathy SMITH
84 Director Enrollment Management ... Dr. Kim CAMPBELL

13 Systems Administrator ... Mr. John SMITH
37 Director Financial Aid ... Dr. Todd EVERETT
32 Director Student Life ... Ms. Colleen CIPRIANI
29 Director Alumni Relations ... Ms. Debbie DUNN BOGGS
26 Dir Marketing/College Relations .. Ms. Robin HUTCHINSON BELL
08 Regional Director Library Services ... Mr. Stevo ROKSANDIC

Mount St. Joseph University (A)

5701 Delhi Road, Cincinnati OH 45233-1670

County: Hamilton FICE Identification: 003033
Unit ID: 204200
Telephone: (513) 244-4200 Carnegie Class: Masters/M
FAX Number: (513) 244-4654 Calendar System: Semester
URL: www.msj.edu
Established: 1920 Annual Undergrad Tuition & Fees: $28,300
Enrollment: 2,073 Coed
Affiliation or Control: Roman Catholic IRS Status: 501(c)3
Highest Offering: Doctorate
Accreditation: NH, #ARCPA, CAATE, CAEPT, NURSE, PTA, SW

01 President ... Dr. H. James WILLIAMS
111 Vice Pres Institutional Advancement ... Ms. Raye ALLEN
26 Vice Pres University Communications ... Mr. Zachary SILKA
05 Provost ... Dr. Diana DAVIS
10 Chief Financial Officer ... Ms. Anne Marie WAGNER
117 Chief Compliance and Risk Officer ... Ms. Linda PANZECA
20 Associate Academic Dean ... Ms. Maggie DAVIS
15 Director of Human Resources ... Ms. Lisa KOBMAN
32 Dean of Students ... Ms. Janet COX
06 Registrar ... Ms. Irene RICHARDSON
29 Director of Alumni Relations ... Ms. Mark OSBORNE
37 Director Student Admin Services ... Ms. Kathy KELLY
36 Director Career/Exper Educ ... Ms. Linda POHLGEERS
102 Director Corporate & Found Rels ... Ms. Linda B. LIEBAU
18 Director Buildings & Grounds ... Mr. Michael DITTMER
09 Director Institutional Rsrch ... Ms. Erin MULLIGAN-NGUYEN
07 Director of Admission ... Ms. Peggy MINNICH
21 Controller Fiscal Operations ... Mr. Ronald KUKER
38 Director Wellness Center ... Ms. Patsy SCHWAIGER
08 Director Library ... Mr. Scott LLOYD
13 Director Instructional Technology ... Ms. Kim HUNTER
19 Director of Campus Police ... Mr. John KRAFT
41 Director of Athletics ... Mr. Steve RADCLIFFE
88 Director Learning Center ... Ms. Meghann LITTRELL
42 Director of Campus Ministry ... Sr. Karen ELLIOTT, SC
30 Director of Development ... Ms. Michelle OLMSTED
40 Manager of Bookstore ... Ms. Lori HATTENDORF
76 Dean Div of Health Sciences ... Dr. Darla VALE
79 Dean of Div of Arts & Hum ... Dr. Michael SONTAG
50 Acting Dean of Business ... Dr. Anna GOLDHAHN
53 Dean of Education ... Dr. Laura SAYLOR
83 Dean Behav/Natural Sci ... Dr. Gene KRITSKY
27 Director of Marketing ... Mr. Trevor GRIFFITH
91 Director Administrative Computing ... Mr. Dan LUKAC
105 Webmaster ... Ms. Carolyn BOLAND
44 Director Individual & Campaign Giv ... Mr. Joe CORNELY
88 Exec Dir Ethical Leadership Devel ... Dr. Tim BRYANT
23 Coordinator Health Services ... Ms. Amy DEMKO
39 Coordinator of Residence Life ... Ms. Tina HOESL
04 Admin Asst to the President ... Ms. Tina MERSMANN
28 Director of Diversity ... Dr. Terri HURDLE

Mount Vernon Nazarene University (B)

800 Martinsburg Road, Mount Vernon OH 43050-9500

County: Knox FICE Identification: 007085
Unit ID: 204194
Telephone: (740) 392-6868 Carnegie Class: Masters/L
FAX Number: (740) 397-2769 Calendar System: Semester
URL: www.mvnu.edu
Established: 1968 Annual Undergrad Tuition & Fees: $26,950
Enrollment: 2,131 Coed
Affiliation or Control: Church Of The Nazarene IRS Status: 501(c)3
Highest Offering: Master's
Accreditation: NH, ACBSP, CAEPN, MUS, NURSE, SW

01 President/CEO ... Dr. Henry W. SPAULDING, II
10 Vice Pres for Finance/CFO ... Dr. Robert P. HAMILL
05 Vice Pres for Academic Affairs/CAO ... Dr. B. Barnett COCHRAN
32 Vice President Student Life ... Rev. Joe NOONEN
42 University Chaplain ... Rev. Joe NOONEN
26 VP for University Relations ... Vacant
111 Managing Dir of Advancement ... Vacant
21 Director of Business Services ... Mr. Steven JENKINS
84 Vice President for Enrollment Mgmt ... Mr. James SMITH
58 Director of Faculty Services GPS ... Mr. Kevin CHANEY
06 University Registrar ... Mr. Mel SEVERNS
15 Director of Human Resources ... Mr. Alan SHAFFER
38 Director Counseling and Wellness ... Dr. Eric BROWNING
13 Director of Information Tech ... Mr. John WALCHLE
29 Director of Alumni Relations ... Mr. Travis KELLER
40 Director of the Bookstore ... Mrs. Gina A. BLANCHARD
27 Coord Communications & Pub Rels ... Ms. Emily ROGERS
53 Dir Teacher Education/Certification ... Dr. Sharon METCALFE
37 Dir of Student Fin Services ... Mr. Jared SPONSELLER
18 Director of Facilities Operations ... Mr. Russell BRAY
21 Controller ... Ms. Debra DEVORE
35 Director of Campus Life ... Ms. Rochel FURNISS
28 Director Intercultural Affairs ... Mr. James M. SINGLETARY
108 Director University Assessment ... Mrs. Kathy GRIFFITH
04 Assistant to President ... Mrs. Pamela K. SNOW
08 Director of the Library ... Mr. Paul NIXON

105 Director Web Services ... Mr. Carlos SERRAO
106 Dir Online Education/E-learning ... Dr. Dean GOON
50 Dean of the School of Business ... Dr. Melanie TIMMERMAN
81 Dean School of Natural & Social Sci ... Dr. LeeAnn COUTS
09 Director of Institutional Research ... Dr. Randie L. TIMPE
07 Director of Admissions ... Mr. Tracy WAAL
104 Director Study Abroad ... Mrs. Krissta HADSELL
41 Athletic Director ... Mr. Aaron M. QUINN
54 Dept Chair Engineering ... Dr. David WINYARD

Muskingum University (C)

163 Stormont Street, New Concord OH 43762-1199

County: Muskingum FICE Identification: 003084
Unit ID: 204264
Telephone: (740) 826-8211 Carnegie Class: Masters/M
FAX Number: (740) 826-8404 Calendar System: Semester
URL: www.muskingum.edu
Established: 1837 Annual Undergrad Tuition & Fees: $26,928
Enrollment: 2,427 Coed
Affiliation or Control: Presbyterian Church (U.S.A.) IRS Status: 501(c)3
Highest Offering: Beyond Master's But Less Than Doctorate
Accreditation: NH, CAATE, CAEPN, ENG, MUS, NURSE

01 President ... Dr. Susan SCHNEIDER HASSELER
05 Interim Provost ... Dr. Rick NUTT
10 Vice President Business & Finance ... Mr. Philip LAUBE
30 Vice Pres of Inst Advancement ... Ms. Janet HEETER-BASS
32 Dean of Students ... Mrs. Susan WARYCK
84 Vice Pres of Enrollment/Marketing ... Mr. Steve SOBA
08 Director of Library ... Dr. Nainsi HOUSTON
06 Registrar ... Mr. Daniel B. WILSON
36 Assistant Director Career Services ... Mrs. Jacquelyn L. VASCURA
13 Director of Computing Services ... Mr. Ryan D. HARVEY
26 Dir Communications/Media Relations ... Mr. Josh CHANEY
29 Director Alumni Relations ... Ms. Jennifer L. BRONNER
07 Director of Admissions ... Mrs. Beth A. DALONZO
19 Director of Public Safety ... Mr. Danny E. VINCENT
42 College Minister ... Rev. William E. MULLINS
18 Supt of Building & Grounds ... Mr. Kevin J. WAGNER
41 Director of Athletics ... Mr. Larry L. SHANK
21 Associate Business Officer ... Mr. Timothy CROSS
35 Director of Student Affairs ... Ms. Susan H. WARYCK
37 Director of Student Financial Aid ... Mrs. Beth A. DALONZO
38 Director of Student Counseling ... Mrs. Tracy F. BUGGLIN
40 Manager of Bookstore ... Ms. Jessica M. MILLER
15 Coordinator of Human Resources ... Ms. Kathy J. MOORE

National Institute of Massotherapy (D)

3681 Manchester Road, Suite 304, Akron OH 44319

County: Summit FICE Identification: 034684
Unit ID: 412003
Telephone: (330) 867-1996 Carnegie Class: Spec 2-yr-Health
FAX Number: (330) 867-6422 Calendar System: Other
URL: www.nim.edu
Established: 1991 Annual Undergrad Tuition & Fees: N/A
Enrollment: 36 Coed
Affiliation or Control: Proprietary IRS Status: Proprietary
Highest Offering: Associate Degree
Accreditation: CNCE

01 President ... Mr. Stephen PERKINSON
32 Dean of Students ... Ms. Ewa PERKINSON
37 Director Financial Aid ... Mr. Dan BILICH

North Central State College (E)

2441 Kenwood Circle, Mansfield OH 44906

County: Richland FICE Identification: 005313
Unit ID: 204422
Telephone: (419) 755-4800 Carnegie Class: Assoc/MT-VT-High Trad
FAX Number: (419) 755-4750 Calendar System: Semester
URL: www.ncstatecollege.edu
Established: 1961 Annual Undergrad Tuition & Fees (In-State): $3,591
Enrollment: 2,939 Coed
Affiliation or Control: State IRS Status: 501(c)3
Highest Offering: Associate Degree
Accreditation: NH, ACBSP, ADNUR, COARC, OTA, PTAA, RAD

01 President ... Dr. Dorey DIAB
04 Exec Assistant to the President ... Mr. Stephen R. WILLIAMS
10 VP Business & Student Services ... Mr. Koffi AKAKPO
05 Vice President Academic Services ... Dr. Karen A. REED
26 Exec Dir Marketing & Public Rels ... Mr. Keith STONER
32 Dean Student Services & Enroll Mgmt ... Mr. Thomas MANSPERGER
15 Director of Human Resources ... Mr. R. Douglas HANUSCIN
37 Director of Financial Aid ... Mr. James PHINNEY
08 Head Librarian ... Ms. Vanessa KRAPS
22 Coord Disability Services ... Mr. Doug HESTAND
49 Dean of Liberal Arts ... Mr. David MURRAY
88 Asst Dean Liberal Arts ... Ms. Deborah HYSELL
50 Dean of Business Ind & Technology ... Dr. Gregory TIMBERLAKE
88 Asst Dean Business Ind & Technology ... Mr. Daniel WAGNER
76 Dean Health Sciences ... Dr. Kelly GRAY
66 Asst Dean Health Sci/Dir Nursing ... Ms. Melinda ROEPKE
13 Director of IT ... Mr. Major PRICE, JR.
06 Registrar ... Mr. Mark J. MONNES
18 Chief Facilities/Physical Plant ... Mr. Dean SCHAAD
96 Purchasing Specialist ... Ms. Renee NUSSBAUM
102 Foundation Director ... Ms. Christine COPPER

09 Director of Institutional Research ... Mr. Thomas M. PRENDERGAST
121 Dir of Student Success & Transition ... Ms. Monica DURHAM
88 Director of Title III ... Ms. Beverly WALKER
88 Phi Theta Kappa Advisor ... Ms. Barb KEENER
40 Campus Bookstore Manager ... Ms. Carla BUTDORFF
21 Controller ... Ms. Lori MCKEE
105 Web Master ... Mr. Mark HUPP
88 Director of Tech Prep ... Mr. Tom KLUDING
88 Director Academic Services ... Ms. Gina KAMWITHI
35 Coordinator of Student Engagement ... Mr. Andy SOKOLICH
41 Dir Athletics & Student Engagement ... Mr. Mike LACROIX
29 Coord of Alumni/Employer Relations ... Ms. Mary J. RODRIGUEZ
36 Career Development Counselor ... Ms. Caitlyn RETHORST

Northeast Ohio Medical University (F)

4209 State Route 44, PO Box 95,
Rootstown OH 44272-0095

County: Portage FICE Identification: 024544
Unit ID: 204477
Telephone: (330) 325-2511 Carnegie Class: Spec-4-yr-Med
FAX Number: (330) 325-7943 Calendar System: Other
URL: www.neomed.edu
Established: 1973 Annual Graduate Tuition & Fees: N/A
Enrollment: 922 Coed
Affiliation or Control: State IRS Status: 501(c)3
Highest Offering: First Professional Degree; No Undergraduates
Accreditation: NH, MED, PH, PHAR

01 President ... Dr. Jay A. GERSHEN
100 Chief of Staff/VP Div Equity & Incl ... Ms. Carolyn D. LANIER
26 VP External Affairs ... Mr. Richard W. LEWIS
46 VP Research ... Dr. Steven P. SCHMIDT
05 VP for Academic Affairs ... Vacant
17 Int VP Health Affairs & Cmty Health ... Dr. Elisabeth H. YOUNG
10 VP Administration/Finance ... Mr. John W. WRAY
111 VP Advancement ... Mr. Daniel S. BLAIN
63 Interim Dean College of Medicine ... Dr. Elisabeth H. YOUNG
58 Dean College of Graduate Studies ... Dr. Steven P. SCHMIDT
67 Dean College of Pharmacy ... Vacant
43 General Counsel ... Ms. Maria R. SCHIMER
04 Exec Assistant to the President ... Ms. Michelle M. MULHERN
32 Chief Student Affairs Officer ... Ms. Sandra M. EMERICK
88 Exec Dir Interprofess Education ... Ms. Holly A. GERZINA
88 Executive Director Research ... Ms. Rebecca L. HAYES
09 Exec Dir Institutional Research ... Dr. Margarita D. KOKINOVA
84 Exec Dir Enrollment Services ... Ms. Heidi L. TERRY
88 Exec Dir Academic Services ... Ms. Penny R. SMITH
88 Director Comparative Medicine Unit ... Dr. Stanley D. DANNEMILLER
29 Dir Alumni Rels & Annual Giving ... Mr. Craig S. EYNON
38 Director Counseling Services ... Vacant
11 Chief Operating Officer ... Ms. Carrie L. BAST
109 Dir Operations & Auxiliary Services ... Mr. Chris J. METTEE
13 Director Information Technology ... Mr. Ronald L. MCGRADY
15 Director Human Resources ... Ms. Barbara A. TOBIAS
18 Director Campus Operations ... Mr. Dale A. HLUCH
24 Dir Academic Technology Services ... Mr. Rey T. NOTARESCHI
26 Director Public Relations ... Mr. Roderick L. INGRAM, SR.
88 Director Learning Center ... Mr. Craig THEISSEN
19 Director Public Safety/Police Chief ... Ms. Kali A. MEONSKE
35 Dir Career Development & Advising ... Ms. Anita R. POKORNY
07 Director of Admissions ... Mr. James F. BARRETT
96 Accounting Purchasing Controller ... Ms. Kathy L. CHUDAKOFF
40 Supervisor Bookstore ... Ms. Christine L. KOVACICH
06 Registrar ... Ms. Susan M. LAMPHERE
37 Dir Financial Aid ... Mr. Michael A. KEMPE
08 Chief Medical Librarian ... Mr. Thomas G. KLINGLER
28 Exec Dir Div Equity/Inclusion ... Mr. Andre L. BURTON

Northwest State Community College (G)

22-600 State Route 34, Archbold OH 43502-9542

County: Henry FICE Identification: 008677
Unit ID: 204440
Telephone: (419) 267-5511 Carnegie Class: Assoc/HVT-High Non
FAX Number: (419) 267-3688 Calendar System: Semester
URL: www.northweststate.edu
Established: 1968 Annual Undergrad Tuition & Fees (In-State): $3,858
Enrollment: 3,630 Coed
Affiliation or Control: State IRS Status: 501(c)3
Highest Offering: Associate Degree
Accreditation: NH, ACBSP, ADNUR, MAC

01 President ... Dr. Thomas L. STUCKEY
05 VP for Academics ... Ms. Lori ROBISON
88 VP for Innovation ... Mr. Todd HERNANDEZ
86 Assoc VP for Strategic Iniatives ... Mr. James HOOPS
32 Dean of Student Services ... Mr. Michael BLACK
69 Dean of AHPS & Business Tech ... Ms. Janet KOEPPLINGER
49 Dean of Arts & Science ... Ms. Lana SNIDER
66 Dean of Nursing ... Ms. Patti ALTMAN
06 Registrar ... Ms. Connie KLINGSHIRN
18 Director of Plant Operations ... Mr. Timothy NELSON
15 Human Resource Officer ... Ms. Kathryn MCKELVEY
21 Director of Business Services ... Ms. Lynn SPEISER
07 Director of Admissions ... Vacant
10 Chief Fiscal Officer ... Ms. Kathy SOARDS
30 Chief Development ... Ms. Robbin WILCOX
37 Director Student Financial Aid ... Ms. Amber YOCOM

35 Coordinator Student Activities .... Mr. Michael JACOBS
26 Coordinator PR & Marketing .... Mr. James BELLAMY
40 Bookstore Manager .... Mr. Kemp STAPLETON
08 Head Librarian .... Ms. Kristi ROTROFF
103 Dean of Industrial Tech .... Mr. Ron SCOZZARI
54 Dean of STEM .... Dr. Daniel BURKLO

Notre Dame College (A)

4545 College Road, South Euclid OH 44121-4293
County: Cuyahoga FICE Identification: 003085
Unit ID: 204468
Telephone: (216) 381-1680 Carnegie Class: Masters/S
FAX Number: (216) 381-3802 Calendar System: Semester
URL: www.notredamecollege.edu
Established: 1922 Annual Undergrad Tuition & Fees: $28,300
Enrollment: 2,094 Coed
Affiliation or Control: Roman Catholic IRS Status: 501(c)3
Highest Offering: Master's
Accreditation: NH, CAEPN, NURSE

01 President .... Mr. Thomas KRUCZEK
32 Vice Pres Student/Academic Affs .... Dr. Vincent PALOMBO
10 Sr Vice Pres Finance/Administration .... Mr. John TORTELLI
111 Vice Pres College Advancement .... Ms. Shawna WHITLOCK
26 Vice Pres for Board/Community Rels .... Ms. Karen L. POELKING
20 Assoc Dean of Academic Affairs .... Dr. Ronald E. MATTHEWS
66 Nursing Division Chair .... Dr. Patrice MCCARTHY
53 Education Division Chair .... Dr. Yvonne ALLEN
81 Math & Science Division Chair .... Dr. Sharon BALCHAK
50 Business Division Chair .... Ms. Natalie STROUSE
57 Fine Arts Division Chair .... Ms. Lynn ZIMMERMAN
84 Dean of Enrollment .... Ms. Beth FORD
07 Director of Admissions .... Mr. David HILBORN
88 Int Dir of the Finn Center (Adult) .... Dr. Joyce BANJAC
06 Registrar .... Ms. Jameka WINDHAM
37 Dir Student Financial Assistance .... Ms. Allison MCBRADY
88 Director of Student Accounts .... Ms. Annette SZALAY
19 Director Security/Safety .... Mr. Jeff SCOTT
18 Director Physical Plant .... Mr. Tom MEEKS
13 Director Information Technology .... Mr. Michael KIEC
15 Director Personnel Services .... Ms. Susan ANDERSON
08 Director of Library .... Ms. Karen ZOLLER
42 Director Ctr Campus Theol/Ministry .... Mr. Ted STEINER
78 Director Coop Educ & Career Devel .... Mr. George PHILLIPS
38 Director of Counseling Center .... Mr. Jerry HAYES
39 Director of Residence Life .... Mr. Nick AYLWARD
29 Dir Alumni Rels/Asc Dir Development .... Ms. Heather COONTZ
04 Exec Assistant to the President .... Ms. Angel JAMES
27 Chief Communications Officer .... Mr. Brian JOHNSTON
106 Online Education/E-learning .... Dr. Carol ZIEGLER

Oberlin College (B)

173 West Lorain Street, Oberlin OH 44074-1057
County: Lorain FICE Identification: 003086
Unit ID: 204501
Telephone: (440) 775-8121 Carnegie Class: Bac-A&S
FAX Number: (440) 775-8886 Calendar System: 4/1/4
URL: www.oberlin.edu
Established: 1833 Annual Undergrad Tuition & Fees: $52,002
Enrollment: 2,929 Coed
Affiliation or Control: Independent Non-Profit IRS Status: 501(c)3
Highest Offering: Master's
Accreditation: NH

01 President .... Mrs. Carmen T. AMBAR
10 Interim VP for Finance & Admin .... Mr. Alan NORTON
30 VP Development/Alumni Affair .... Mr. William BARLOW
26 Vice President College Relations .... Mr. Ben JONES
49 Dean of Arts & Sciences .... Dr. Timothy ELGREN
64 Dean Conservatory Music .... Ms. Andrea KALYN
32 VP and Dean of Students .... Dr. Meredith RAIMONDO
07 Dean Admissions/Financial Aid .... Dr. Manuel CARBALLO
43 Interim VP/GC and Secretary .... Ms. Donica VARNER
86 Spec Asst Community/Govt Relations .... Ms. Tita REED
21 Associate Vice President Finance .... Ms. Mary Jo DIEKMAN
29 Exec Director Alumni Assoc .... Ms. Danielle YOUNG
88 Sr Assoc Dean of College Arts & Sci .... Dr. David KAMITSUKA
88 Assoc Dean of College of Arts & Sci .... Dr. Daphne JOHN
13 Chief Information Tech Officer .... Mr. Ben HOCKENHULL
08 Azariah Smith Root Dir of Libraries .... Dr. Alexia HUDSON-WARD
07 Director Admissions Conservatory .... Mr. Michael C. MANDEREN
38 Director of Counseling Center .... Dr. John HARSHBARGER
57 Director of Allen Art Museums .... Dr. Andria DERSTINE
06 Registrar .... Ms. Elizabeth CLERKIN
37 Director of Financial Aid .... Mr. Robert A. REDDY, JR.
09 Director of Institutional Research .... Mr. Ross PEACOCK
18 Assistant VP of Facility Operations .... Mr. James S. KLAIBER
36 Director Career Devel/Placement .... Dr. Gayle BOYER
42 Director Religious and Spiritual Li .... Rev. David F. DORSEY
39 Asst VP/Strategic Initiatives .... Mr. Adrian BATISTA
41 Director of Physical Educ/Athletics .... Ms. Natalie WINKELFOOS
19 Director of Safety & Security .... Mr. Michael MARTINSEN
28 Director Multicultural Affairs .... Ms. Antoinette MYERS
96 Institutional Buyer .... Mr. Rick SNODGRASS
15 Chief Human Resources Officer .... Mr. Joseph VITALE, JR.
04 Assistant to President .... Mrs. Jennifer S. BRADFIELD
104 Interim Dean & Dir of Intl Studies .... Ms. Linda ARBOGAST
100 Chief of Staff .... Mr. Ferdinand PROTZMAN
102 Exec Dir Office of Foundations .... Ms. Pamela SNYDER
44 Sr Philanthropic Advisor .... Ms. Catherine GLETHEROW

Ohio Business College (C)

5202 Timber Commons Drive, Sandusky OH 44870-5894
Telephone: (419) 627-8345 Identification: 666467
Accreditation: ACICS

† Branch campus of Ohio Business College, Sheffield Village, OH.

Ohio Business College (D)

5095 Waterford Drive, Sheffield Village OH 44035-0701
County: Lorain FICE Identification: 021585
Unit ID: 203720
Telephone: (440) 934-3101 Carnegie Class: Assoc/HVT-High Non
FAX Number: (440) 934-3105 Calendar System: Quarter
URL: www.ohiobusinesscollege.edu
Established: 1903 Annual Undergrad Tuition & Fees: $9,025
Enrollment: 392 Coed
Affiliation or Control: Proprietary IRS Status: Proprietary
Highest Offering: Associate Degree
Accreditation: ACICS, MAC

01 Executive Director .... Mrs. Rosanne CATELLA
07 Admissions Director .... Ms. Rosemerry NICKELS
10 Financial Manager .... Mrs. Victoria DONLEY
36 Career Services .... Ms. Cheryl JANKOWSKI

Ohio Christian University (E)

1476 Lancaster Pike, Circleville OH 43113-0458
County: Pickaway FICE Identification: 003030
Unit ID: 201964
Telephone: (740) 474-8896 Carnegie Class: Bac-Diverse
FAX Number: (740) 477-7755 Calendar System: Semester
URL: www.ohiochristian.edu
Established: 1948 Annual Undergrad Tuition & Fees: $19,540
Enrollment: 4,290 Coed
Affiliation or Control: Other Protestant IRS Status: 501(c)3
Highest Offering: Master's
Accreditation: NH, BI, CAEPT, NURSE

01 President .... Dr. Jon KULAGA
05 Provost .... Dr. Hank KELLY
10 Vice President of Finance .... Mr. Ted PERRY
111 Vice President for Advancement .... Mr. Mark TAYLOR
32 Vice President Student Development .... Vacant
11 Vice President of Operations .... Vacant
13 Vice President for IT .... Mr. Ryan WHISLER
09 Asst VP for Institutional Research .... Dr. Cynthia TWEEDELL
06 Registrar .... Mr. Dustin EPPERLY
55 VP College of Adult & Graduate Stds .... Dr. Bradford SAMPLE
84 Assistant VP of AGS Enrollment Mgmt .... Mr. Joshua MOORE
08 Director of Library Services .... Mrs. Barbara MEISTER
37 Director Student Financial Services .... Mr. Brandon RITCHEY
41 Athletic Director .... Mr. David BIRELINE
29 Alumni Relations Coordinator .... Vacant
50 Dean/Director of Business .... Mr. Monty LOBB
53 Director of Education .... Ms. Valerie JONES
04 Administrative Asst to President .... Mrs. Lois TAYLOR
07 Director of Admissions .... Mr. Kevin EDWARDS
106 PSEO Director .... Mrs. Beth ASH
19 Director of Security .... Mr. Tyler PAYNE
26 Marketing Content Manager .... Mr. Dave HIRSHLER
15 Asst Director of HR .... Mr. Zach STEPHENS

Ohio Dominican University (F)

1216 Sunbury Road, Columbus OH 43219-2099
County: Franklin FICE Identification: 003035
Unit ID: 204617
Telephone: (614) 251-4500 Carnegie Class: Masters/M
FAX Number: (614) 251-4634 Calendar System: Semester
URL: www.ohiodominican.edu
Established: 1911 Annual Undergrad Tuition & Fees: $31,080
Enrollment: 2,534 Coed
Affiliation or Control: Roman Catholic IRS Status: 501(c)3
Highest Offering: Master's
Accreditation: NH, ACBSP, #ARCPA, CAEPN, SW

01 President .... Dr. Robert GERVASI
05 Vice President Academic Affairs .... Dr. Theresa HOLLERAN
10 Vice Pres Finance & Admin/CFO .... Mr. Alvin RODACK
84 Vice Pres Enrollment Management .... Ms. Julie BURDICK
111 Vice President for Advancement .... Mr. Adam NEAL
26 Vice Pres Marketing & Public Rels .... Mr. Mark COOPER
04 Executive Asst to the President .... Ms. Amy THOMAS
32 Asst Vice Pres Student Development .... Ms. Sharon REED
20 Assoc Vice Pres Academic Affairs .... Dr. Linda WOLF
58 Dean Graduate/Professional Studies .... Dr. James STRODE
97 Dean Undergraduate Studies .... Dr. Manuel MARTINEZ
103 Exec Dir of Academic Partnerships .... Ms. Karen GRAY
11 Assoc Vice Pres Administration .... Ms. Donna PICKLESIMER
121 Asst Dean Student Success .... Mr. Torrance POWELL
07 Director of Admissions .... Mr. Michael HALLIGAN
123 Director of Graduate Admissions .... Mr. John NAUGHTON
114 Controller .... Ms. Vicki STEELE
13 Chief Information Officer .... Ms. Christine KURTH
37 Director of Financial Aid .... Ms. Tara SCHNEIDER
08 Director of the Library .... Ms. Michelle SARFF
36 Director Career Services .... Ms. Jessica HALL
15 Director of Human Resources .... Vacant
42 Director of Campus Ministry .... Sr. Margie DAVIS

29 Dir of Alumni Rels/Annual Giving .... Ms. Christie FLOOD-WEINER
39 Director of Resident Life .... Ms. Lara CONRAD
41 Athletic Director .... Mr. Jeff BLAIR
92 Director of Honors Program .... Mr. John MARAZITA
19 Director of Safety .... Mr. Robin OLSON
25 Dir of Sponsored Research .... Ms. Sarah ELVEY

Ohio Northern University (G)

525 S Main Street, Ada OH 45810-1599
County: Hardin FICE Identification: 003089
Unit ID: 204635
Telephone: (419) 772-2000 Carnegie Class: Bac-Diverse
FAX Number: (419) 772-1932 Calendar System: Semester
URL: www.onu.edu
Established: 1871 Annual Undergrad Tuition & Fees: $29,820
Enrollment: 3,238 Coed
Affiliation or Control: United Methodist IRS Status: 501(c)3
Highest Offering: First Professional Degree
Accreditation: NH, CAATE, CAEPN, CEA, CS, ENG, EXSC, LAW, MT, MUS, NAIT, NURSE, PHAR

01 President .... Dr. Daniel A. DIBIASIO
05 Provost/Vice Pres Academic Affairs .... Dr. Maria L. CRONLEY
10 Vice President Financial Affairs .... Mr. William H. BALLARD
111 Vice Pres of University Advancement .... Ms. Shannon M. SPENCER
84 Vice Pres Enrollment Management .... Dr. William T. EIOLA
32 VP Student Affairs/Dean of Students .... Dr. Adriane THOMPSON-BRADSHAW
49 Dean of Arts & Sciences .... Ms. Holly L. BAUMGARTNER
54 Dean of Engineering .... Dr. John-David YODER
67 Dean of Pharmacy .... Dr. Steven J. MARTIN
50 Dean Business Administration .... Dr. John C. NAVIN
61 Dean of Law .... Dr. David C. CRAGO
30 Senior Director of Development .... Mr. Scott D. WILLS
08 Director of Heterick Library .... Ms. Kathleen T. BARIL
39 Dir of Res Life/Int Dir Career Svcs .... Mr. Justin F. COURTNEY
38 Director of Counseling .... Dr. Michael D. SCHAFER
29 Int Director of Alumni Relations .... Mrs. Annmarie BAUMGARTNER
08 Law Librarian .... Dr. Nancy A. ARMSTRONG
42 University Chaplain .... Dr Rev. David MACDONALD
18 Director of Physical Plant .... Mr. Marc STALEY
13 Director of Technology .... Mr. Jeff RIEMAN
09 Director of Institutional Research .... Dr. Omer MINHAS
15 Director of Human Resources .... Ms. Tonya PAUL
20 Associate Academic Officer .... Dr. Juliet K. HURTIG
37 Director of Student Financial Aid .... Mrs. Melanie WEAVER
92 Director of Honors Program .... Dr. Patrick T. CROSKERY
21 Controller .... Mr. Mark RUSSELL
26 Dir of Communications & Marketing .... Mrs. Amy PRIGGE
07 Director of Admissions .... Ms. Deborah MILLER
06 Registrar .... Ms. Melanie HOUGH
28 Director Multicultural Development .... Ms. LaShonda GURLEY
41 Athletic Director .... Mr. Thomas SIMMONS
44 Director of Annual Giving .... Ms. Kelly ANDERSON
96 Manager of Purchasing .... Ms. Vicki J. NIESE
04 Executive Assistant to President .... Ms. Ann E. DONNELLY HAMILTON
101 Secretary of the Institution/Board .... Ms. Sharon A. STECHSCHULTE
19 Director of Public Safety .... Mr. Greg HORNE
25 Chief Contracts/Grants Admin .... Ms. Beckie WATERCUTTER

The Ohio State University Main Campus (H)

281 W. Lane Ave., Columbus OH 43210-1358
County: Franklin FICE Identification: 003090
Unit ID: 204796
Telephone: (614) 292-6446 Carnegie Class: DU-Highest
FAX Number: (614) 292-9180 Calendar System: Semester
URL: www.osu.edu
Established: 1870 Annual Undergrad Tuition & Fees (In-State): $10,037
Enrollment: 58,663 Coed
Affiliation or Control: State IRS Status: 501(c)3
Highest Offering: Doctorate
Accreditation: NH, AAB, ACAE, ART, AUD, CAATE, CACREP, CAEPN, CAHIIM, CIDA, CLPSY, COARC, CONST, CS, DANCE, DENT, DH, DIETC, DIETD, DIETI, DMS, ENG, HSA, IPSY, LAW, LSAR, MED, MFCD, MIDWF, MT, MUS, NMT, NURSE, OPT, OPTR, OT, PCSAS, PH, PHAR, PLNG, PTA, RTT, SCPSY, SP, SPAA, SW, THEA, VET

01 President .... Dr. Michael V. DRAKE
05 Executive Vice Pres/Provost .... Dr. Bruce MCPHERON
10 Senior VP Business & Finance/CFO .... Mr. Geoffrey CHATAS
43 Sr VP & General Counsel .... Mr. Christopher M. CULLEY
32 Sr Vice President for Student Life .... Dr. Javaune ADAMS-GASTON
20 Vice Provost for Academic Programs .... Mr. W. Randy SMITH
26 VP University Communications .... Ms. Ann HAMILTON
46 Sr Vice Pres for Research .... Dr. Caroline WHITACRE
86 Vice Pres of Govt Affairs .... Mr. Blake THOMPSON
23 Exec VP Health Sciences .... Vacant
47 Vice Pres Ag Admin & Dean FAES .... Dr. Cathann KRESS
111 Sr VP for Advance/Pres OSU Found .... Mr. Michael EICHER
28 Int Vice Prov Diversity & Inclusion .... Dr. James L. MOORE
58 Int Vice Provost/Dean Grad School .... Dr. Scott HERNESS
41 Sr VP/Director Athletics .... Mr. Gene D. SMITH
18 Assoc VP Facilities Op/Dev .... Ms. Mary L. READEY
07 Int VP Enrol Strategic Planning .... Mr. Vern GRANGER
13 Vice President and CIO .... Mr. Michael HOFHERR
08 Vice Provost/Director of Libraries .... Mr. Damon E. JAGGARS
100 Chief of Staff .... Ms. Katie HALL

101 Secretary Board of Trustees ....Mr. Blake THOMPSON
17 COO Medical Center ....Mr. David P. MCQUAID
85 Asst Vice Prov Glob Strat/Intl Affs ....Dr. Gifty AKO-ADOUNVO
90 Int Exec Dir Ohio Supercomp Ctr ....Mr. David HUDAK
29 SVP Alumni Rels/CEO Alumni Assoc ....Mr. James E. SMITH
12 Exec Dean of Reg Campuses ....Dr. William L. MACDONALD
49 Vice Prov & Exec Dean Arts & Sci ....Dr. David C. MANDERSCHEID
50 Dean Fisher Col of Business ....Dr. Anil K. MAKHIJA
52 Dean College of Dentistry ....Dr. Patrick M. LLOYD
53 Dean College of Educ & Hum Ecology ....Dr. Cheryl L. ACHTERBERG
54 Dean College of Engineering ....Dr. David B. WILLIAMS
61 Dean College of Law ....Dr. Alan C. MICHAELS
63 Dean College of Medicine ....Dr. K. Craig KENT
88 Dean College of Optometry ....Dr. Karla S. ZADNIK
67 Dean College of Pharmacy ....Dr. Henry J. MANN
69 Dean College of Public Health ....Dr. William J. MARTIN
70 Dean College of Social Work ....Dr. Tom GREGOIRE
74 Dean Col Veterinary Medicine ....Dr. Rustin MOORE
66 Dean College of Nursing ....Dr. Bernadette MELNYK
09 Asst VP Inst Research/Planning ....Ms. Julie CARPENTER-HUBIN
37 Exec Dir Student Financial Aid ....Ms. Diane CORBETT
06 University Registrar ....Mr. Jack MINER
88 Director of OES Analysis & Reportng ...Ms. Gail C. STEPHENOFF
35 Sr Assoc VP Student Life ....Dr. Gretchen METZELAARS
96 Director of Purchasing ....Mr. Russell CHUNG
11 Sr Vice Pres Admin & Planning ....Mr. Jay D. KASEY
40 General Manager OSU Bookstores ....Ms. Kathy SMITH
19 Asst VP Public Safety ....Ms. Monica MOLL
39 Director Housing Administration .Ms. Toni GREENSLADE-SMITH
88 Dean JG College of Public Affairs ....Dr. Trevor L. BROWN

The Ohio State University Agricultural Technical Institute (A)

1328 Dover Road, Wooster OH 44691-4000
Telephone: (330) 264-3911 FICE Identification: 010687
Accreditation: NH

† Regional accreditation is carried under the parent institution in Columbus, OH.

The Ohio State University at Lima Campus (B)

4240 Campus Drive, Lima OH 45804-3597
Telephone: (419) 995-8600 FICE Identification: 003092
Accreditation: &NH

† Regional accreditation is carried under the parent institution in Columbus, OH.

The Ohio State University Mansfield Campus (C)

1760 University Drive, Mansfield OH 44906-1599
Telephone: (419) 755-4011 FICE Identification: 003093
Accreditation: &NH

† Regional accreditation is carried under the parent institution in Columbus, OH.

The Ohio State University at Marion (D)

1465 Mount Vernon Avenue, Marion OH 43302-5628
Telephone: (740) 389-6786 FICE Identification: 003094
Accreditation: &NH

† Regional accreditation is carried under the parent institution in Columbus, OH.

The Ohio State University Newark Campus (E)

1179 University Drive, Newark OH 43055-9990
Telephone: (740) 366-3321 FICE Identification: 003095
Accreditation: &NH

† Regional accreditation is carried under the parent institution in Columbus, OH.

Ohio Technical College (F)

1374 E 51st Street, Cleveland OH 44103-1269
County: Cuyahoga FICE Identification: 011745
Unit ID: 204608
Telephone: (216) 881-1700 Carnegie Class: Spec 2-yr-Tech
FAX Number: (216) 881-9145 Calendar System: Quarter
URL: www.ohiotech.edu
Established: 1969 Annual Undergrad Tuition & Fees: N/A
Enrollment: 1,072 Coed
Affiliation or Control: Proprietary IRS Status: Proprietary
Highest Offering: Associate Degree
Accreditation: ACCSC

01 President ....Mr. Bill HANTL
07 Director of Admissions ....Mr. Greg KOZARIK

Ohio University Main Campus (G)

1 Ohio University, Athens OH 45701-2979
County: Athens FICE Identification: 003100
Unit ID: 204857
Telephone: (740) 593-1000 Carnegie Class: DU-Higher
FAX Number: N/A Calendar System: Semester
URL: www.ohio.edu
Established: 1804 Annual Undergrad Tuition & Fees (In-State): $11,744
Enrollment: 29,157 Coed
Affiliation or Control: State IRS Status: 501(c)3
Highest Offering: Doctorate
Accreditation: NH, AAFCS, ADNUR, #ARCPA, AUD, CAATE, CACREP, CAEPN, CIDA, CLPSY, CS, DANCE, DIETD, @DIETI, ENG, #FEPAC, IPSY, JOUR, MUS, NAIT, NRPA, NURSE, OSTEO, PH, PTA, SP, SW, THEA

01 President ....Dr. Duane NELLIS
100 Chief of Staff President's Ofc ....Ms. Jennifer KIRKSEY
05 Interim Executive VP & Provost ....Dr. David DESCUTNER
10 VP for Finance & Administration ....Ms. Deborah SHAFFER
32 VP for Student Affairs ....Dr. Jason PINA
111 Interim VP for Advancement ....Dr. Tom DAVIS
13 Chief Information Officer ....Mr. Craig BANTZ
46 VP Research & Dean Grad College ....Dr. Joseph SHIELDS
84 Vice Provost Enrollment Management ....Mr. Craig CORNELL
43 General Counsel ....Mr. John J. BIANCAMANO
26 Exec Dir Comm/Marketing ....Ms. Renea MORRIS
88 Dean University College ....Dr. Elizabeth SAYRS
45 Sr Vice Pres Strategic Initiatives ....Mr. Stephen GOLDING
49 Dean College of Arts & Sciences ....Dr. Robert FRANK
50 Dean College of Business ....Dr. Hugh SHERMAN
60 Dean Scripps Col Communication ....Dr. Scott TITSWORTH
53 Dean Patton College of Education ....Dr. Renee A. MIDDLETON
54 Dean Russ Col Engineering/Tech ....Dr. Dennis IRWIN
57 Dean College of Fine Arts ....Dr. Matthew SHAFTEL
69 Dean Col Health/Human Services ....Dr. Randy LEITE
92 Interim Dean Honors Tutorial Col ....Dr. Cary FRITH
63 Dean Heritage Col Osteopathic Med ....Dr. Kenneth JOHNSON
62 Dean University Libraries ....Mr. Scott H. SEAMAN
35 Dean of Students ....Dr. Jenny HALL-JONES
12 Exec Dean Regional Campuses ....Dr. William WILLAN
12 Dean Eastern Campus ....Dr. Paul ABRAHAM
12 Dean Southern Campus ....Dr. Nicole PENNINGTON
12 Dean Chillicothe Campus ....Dr. Martin TUCK
12 Dean Lancaster Campus ....Dr. James SMITH
12 Dean Zanesville Campus ....Dr. Jeremy WEBSTER
20 Associate Provost Academic Affairs ....Dr. Howard DEWALD
58 Director Graduate Student Services ....Dr. Katherine TADLOCK
88 Vice Provost Global Affairs ....Dr. Lorna Jean EDMONDS
09 Assoc Prov Inst Rsrch/Effectiveness ....Dr. Barbara WHARTON
41 Director of Athletics ....Mr. Jim SCHAUS
06 University Registrar ....Mrs. Debra M. BENTON
15 Chief Human Resources Officer ....Ms. Colleen BENDEL
29 Asst Vice Pres Alumni Relations ....Ms. Jennifer NEUBAUER
36 Asst Dean for Career Services ....Mr. Imants JAUNARAJS
07 Asst Vice Provost/Dir Ungrad Admiss ..Ms. Candace BOENINGER
38 Director Counseling Services ....Dr. Alfred B. WEINER
112 Exec Dir of Develop Planned Giving ....Ms. Kelli KOTOWSKI
37 Director Student Financial Aid ....Ms. Valerie MILLER
23 Medical Dir of Campus Care ....Dr. John J. KEMERER
106 Senior Vice Provost for Instruction ....Mr. Brad COHEN
19 Chief of Police/Dir Campus Safety ....Chief Andrew POWERS
85 Interim Dir Intl Students/Fac Svcs ....Dr. Diane CAHILL
39 Exec Director of Residential Hous ....Mr. Peter TRENTACOSTE
109 Asst Vice Pres Auxiliary Services ....Ms. Christine SHEETS
24 Media Library Manager ....Ms. Robin KRIVESTI
113 Bursar ....Ms. Sherry ROSSITER
101 Secretary to Board of Trustees ....Dr. David MOORE
86 Director of Government Relations ....Mr. Eric BURCHARD
88 Ombudsman ....Mr. Mac STRICKLEN
04 Administrative Asst to President ....Ms. Kelli TACKETT

Ohio University Chillicothe Campus (H)

PO Box 629, 101 University Drive,
Chillicothe OH 45601-0629
Telephone: (740) 774-7200 FICE Identification: 003102
Accreditation: &NH

† Regional accreditation is carried under the parent institution in Athens, OH.

Ohio University Eastern Campus (I)

45425 National Road, Saint Clairsville OH 43950-9724
Telephone: (740) 695-1720 FICE Identification: 003101
Accreditation: &NH

† Regional accreditation is carried under the parent institution in Athens, OH.

Ohio University Lancaster Campus (J)

1570 Granville Pike, Lancaster OH 43130-1097
Telephone: (740) 654-6711 FICE Identification: 003104
Accreditation: &NH, MAC

† Regional accreditation is carried under the parent institution in Athens, OH.

Ohio University Southern Campus (K)

1804 Liberty Avenue, Ironton OH 45638-2279
Telephone: (740) 533-4600 Identification: 666000
Accreditation: &NH

† Regional accreditation is carried under the parent institution in Athens, OH.

Ohio University Zanesville Branch (L)

1425 Newark Road, Zanesville OH 43701-2695
Telephone: (740) 453-0762 FICE Identification: 003108
Accreditation: &NH

† Regional accreditation is carried under the parent institution in Athens, OH.

Ohio Valley College of Technology (M)

15258 State Route 170, East Liverpool OH 43920
County: Columbiana FICE Identification: 023014
Unit ID: 204884
Telephone: (330) 385-1070 Carnegie Class: Spec 2-yr-Health
FAX Number: (330) 385-4606 Calendar System: Semester
URL: www.ovct.edu
Established: 1886 Annual Undergrad Tuition & Fees: $11,698
Enrollment: 173 Coed
Affiliation or Control: Proprietary IRS Status: Proprietary
Highest Offering: Associate Degree
Accreditation: ABHES, ACICS, MAAB

01 President ....Mr. Scott S. ROGERS
37 Director of Financial Aid ....Ms. Rebecca STECKMAN

Ohio Wesleyan University (N)

61 S Sandusky Street, Delaware OH 43015-2398
County: Delaware FICE Identification: 003109
Unit ID: 204909
Telephone: (740) 368-2000 Carnegie Class: Bac-A&S
FAX Number: (740) 368-3299 Calendar System: Semester
URL: www.owu.edu
Established: 1842 Annual Undergrad Tuition & Fees: $44,090
Enrollment: 1,671 Coed
Affiliation or Control: United Methodist IRS Status: 501(c)3
Highest Offering: Baccalaureate
Accreditation: NH, CAEPN, MUS

01 President ....Dr. Rockwell F. JONES
05 Provost ....Dr. Charles L. STINEMETZ
10 VP for Finance/Admin/Treasurer ....Ms. Lauri STRIMKOVSKY
111 VP for University Advancement ....Ms. Colleen C. GARLAND
84 Vice President for Enrollment ....Ms. Susan R. DILENO
32 Vice President for Student Affairs ....Dr. Dwayne K. TODD
110 Asst VP for University Advancement ....Ms. Jodi L. BOPP
26 Chief Communications Officer ....Mr. Will E. KOPP
09 Assoc Provost for Inst Research ....Dr. Dale E. SWARTZENTRUBER
108 Asst Provost Assmt/Accreditation ....Dr. Barbara S. ANDERECK
37 Director Student Financial Aid ....Mr. Kevin F. PASKVAN
36 Director of Career Services ....Ms. Leslie J. MELTON
06 Registrar ....Ms. Shelly A. MCMAHON
13 Chief Information Officer ....Dr. Brian RELLINGER
19 Director of Public Safety ....Mr. Robert A. WOOD
29 Director Alumni Relations ....Ms. Katie P. WEBSTER
85 Director International Student Svcs ....Mr. Darrell J. ALBON
18 Director Physical Plant ....Vacant
15 Director Human Resources ....Mr. Scott L. SIMON
31 Director Community Svc Learning ....Ms. Sally S. LEBER
04 Asst to President/Board Secy ....Ms. Janet L. LEWIS
23 Director Wellness Center ....Ms. Marsha A. TILDEN
35 Dean of Students ....Dr. Dwayne K. TODD
39 Director Residential Life ....Vacant
41 Director of Athletics ....Mr. Doug W. ZIPP
42 Chaplain ....Rev. Jon R. POWERS
89 Director First Year Experience ....Mr. Brad T. PULCINI
92 Honors Program Director ....Dr. Amy MCCLURE
102 Foundation Relations Manager ....Ms. Sue E. HAIDLE
07 Dir Transfer & Operations Recruit ....Ms. Alisha M. COUCH
40 Bookstore Manager ....Ms. Lisa K. TACKETT
38 Coord Counseling/Mental Health Svcs ....Dr. Doug L. BENNETT
96 Director of Purchasing ....Ms. Melanie T. KALB

Otterbein University (O)

1 South Grove Street, Westerville OH 43081-2006
County: Franklin FICE Identification: 003110
Unit ID: 204936
Telephone: (614) 890-3000 Carnegie Class: Masters/M
FAX Number: (614) 823-3114 Calendar System: Semester
URL: www.otterbein.edu
Established: 1847 Annual Undergrad Tuition & Fees: $31,874
Enrollment: 2,808 Coed
Affiliation or Control: United Methodist IRS Status: 501(c)3
Highest Offering: Doctorate
Accreditation: NH, ANEST, CAATE, CAEPN, MUS, NURSE, THEA

01 President ....Dr. Kathy A. KRENDL
100 Chief of Staff ....Ms. Kristine ROBBINS
05 Provost/VPAA ....Vacant
32 Vice President Student Affairs ....Mr. Robert M. GATTI
10 Vice President for Business Affairs ....Mrs. Rebecca D. VAZQUEZ-SKILLINGS
111 VP Institutional Advancement ....Mr. Michael MCGREEVEY
84 Vice President for Enrollment ....Mr. Jefferson BLACKBURN-SMITH
20 Assoc VP AA/Dean Academic Services ....Dr. Wendy SHERMAN-HECKLER
91 Exec Director of Information Tech ....Mr. Dave BENDER
08 Director of the Library ....Ms. Tiffany LIPSTREU
06 Registrar ....Mr. David SCHNEIDER
26 Exec Dir Marketing/Communications ....Mrs. Jennifer PEARCE
36 Director Career Planning/Placement ....Mr. Ryan BRECHBILL
37 Director of Financial Aid ....Mr. Thomas V. YARNELL

41 Athletic Director ... Ms. Dawn STEWART
42 Chaplain ... Dr. Judy GUION-UTSLER
107 Dean School of Prof Studies ... Dr. Barbara H. SCHAFFNER
49 Dean School of Arts/Sciences ... Dr. Paul EISENSTEIN
07 Director of Admissions ... Mr. Mark MOFFETT
15 Director Human Resources ... Mr. Scott FITZGERALD
18 Director/Physical Plant ... Mr. David D. BELL
29 Director Alumni Relations ... Ms. Rebecca F. SMITH
28 Director of Diversity ... Mr. James PRYSOCK
21 Assistant Controller ... Mr. Christopher A. HAYTER
09 Director of Institutional Research ... Dr. Sean M. MCLAUGHLIN
19 Director of Security ... Mr. Larry BANASZAK
04 Executive Assistant to President ... Mrs. Tamara LOWKS
39 Director Student Housing ... Ms. Tracy BENNER
38 Director Student Counseling ... Dr. Kathleen RYAN
44 Director Annual Giving ... Mr. Matthew D'OYLY

Owens Community College (A)

30335 Oregon, PO Box 10000, Toledo OH 43699-1947
County: Wood FICE Identification: 005753
Unit ID: 204945
Telephone: (567) 661-7000 Carnegie Class: Assoc/MT-VT-Mix Trad/Non
FAX Number: N/A Calendar System: Semester
URL: www.owens.edu
Established: 1965 Annual Undergrad Tuition & Fees (In-State): $4,643
Enrollment: 11,531 Coed
Affiliation or Control: State IRS Status: 501(c)3
Highest Offering: Associate Degree
Accreditation: NH, ACBSP, ACFEI, ADNUR, CAHIIM, DH, DIETT, DMS, EMT, MAC, NAIT, OTA, PTAA, RAD, RADMAG, SURGT

01 Interim President ... Dr. Steve ROBINSON
101 Secretary to the Board of Trustees ... Ms. Patricia JEZAK
04 Executive Assistant to President ... Ms. Kristine HOLLAND
05 Int VP Academic Affairs/Provost ... Ms. Denise SMITH
10 Treasurer ... Mr. Jeff GANUES
15 VP Human Resources ... Ms. Lisa NAGEL
84 VP Enrollment Mgmt/Student Svcs ... Ms. Amy GIORDANO
20 Assoc VP Academic Services ... Ms. Denise SMITH
103 Exec Dir Workforce/Comm Service ... Mr. Robert KRAUS
12 Associate VP Findlay Campus ... Ms. Julie BAKER
21 Controller ... Ms. Kimberly (Jean) THOMAS
13 Chief Information Officer ... Ms. Laurie ORZECHOWSKI
19 Chief of Police ... Mr. Scott STEINKE
37 Director Financial Aid ... Ms. Andrea MORROW
26 Director Mktg & Communications ... Mr. Jason GRIFFIN
18 Executive Director Operations ... Mr. Michael MCDONALD
09 Director Inst Research ... Ms. Debra RATHKE
81 Dean School of STEM ... Mr. Glenn RETTIG
66 Dean School of Nursing/Health Prof ... Ms. Cathy FORD
50 Dean Sch Business/Info/Public Svc ... Dr. Ann THEIS
57 Int Dean School of Liberal Arts ... Mr. Michael SANDER
62 Dean Library ... Mr. Tom SINK
106 Director eLearning ... Mr. Mark KARAMOL
43 Legal Services Coordinator ... Ms. Linda WIRICK
06 Registrar ... Mr. David SHAFFER
86 Exec Dir Govt/Comm Relations ... Ms. Jennifer FEHNRICH
29 Director Alumni Affairs ... Ms. Jennifer FEHNRICH
32 Director Student Life/Stdnt Conduct ... Ms. Danielle FILIPCHUK
109 Director Auxiliary Services ... Ms. Danielle TRACY
85 Manager Intl Stdnt Services ... Ms. Annette SWANSON
41 Director Athletics ... Mr. JD ETTORE

Owens Community College Findlay Campus (B)

3200 Bright Road, Findlay OH 45840
Telephone: (567) 429-3500 Identification: 770360
Accreditation: &NH

Payne Theological Seminary (C)

PO Box 474, Wilberforce OH 45384-0474
County: Greene FICE Identification: 010017
Unit ID: 204990
Telephone: (937) 376-2946 Carnegie Class: Spec-4-yr-Faith
FAX Number: (937) 376-3330 Calendar System: 4/1/4
URL: www.payne.edu
Established: 1844 Annual Graduate Tuition & Fees: N/A
Enrollment: 174 Coed
Affiliation or Control: African Methodist Episcopal IRS Status: 501(c)3
Highest Offering: Doctorate; No Undergraduates
Accreditation: THEOL

01 President ... Dr. Michael BROWN
05 Academic Dean ... Dr. Michael MILLER
100 Chief of Staff ... Rev. Brandon STEWART
20 Associate Dean ... Dr. Michael MILLER
30 Director of Development ... Rev. Jules DUNHAM HOWIE
10 Director of Finance ... Ms. Elise PEYROUX
37 Financial Aid Officer ... Ms. Pat COPELY
06 Registrar ... Ms. Maryjo LEWIS

Pontifical College Josephinum (D)

7625 N High Street, Columbus OH 43235-1498
County: Franklin FICE Identification: 003113
Unit ID: 205027
Telephone: (614) 885-5585 Carnegie Class: Spec-4-yr-Faith
FAX Number: (614) 885-2307 Calendar System: Semester
URL: www.pcj.edu
Established: 1888 Annual Undergrad Tuition & Fees: $22,092
Enrollment: 223 Male
Affiliation or Control: Roman Catholic IRS Status: 501(c)3
Highest Offering: Beyond Master's But Less Than Doctorate
Accreditation: NH, THEOL

01 Rector/President ... R.Msgr. Christopher J. SCHRECK
11 Vice Rector Administration ... Msgr. Kevin T. MCMAHON
10 VP for Administration/Treasurer ... Mr. John O. ERWIN
05 Vice Rec Sch Theology/Dn Cmty Life ... Rev. Raymond N. ENZWEILER
30 Vice President for Advancement ... Rev. John A. ALLEN
49 Vice Rector College Liberal Arts ... Rev. John ROZEMBAJGIER
73 Academic Dean School of Theology ... Dr. Perry J. CAHALL
49 Academic Dean College Liberal Arts ... Dr. David J. DE LEONARDIS
06 Registrar ... Mr. Samuel J. DEAN
08 Librarian ... Mr. Peter G. VERACKA
31 Dean of Community Life ... Rev. John S. BAKER
37 Director Financial Aid ... Mrs. Marky LEICHTNAM
108 Dir of Inst Plng/Assessment/Accred ... Mr. Eric S. GRAFF
26 Director of Communications ... Ms. Carolyn DINOVO
07 Admissions Coordinator ... Ms. Arminda CRAWFORD
105 Web Developer ... Ms. Tracy BROCKMAN

PowerSport Institute (E)

21210 Emery Road, North Randall OH 44128
Telephone: (216) 587-5000 Identification: 770582
Accreditation: ACCSC

Professional Skills Institute (F)

1505 Holland Road, Maumee OH 43537
County: Lucas FICE Identification: 023377
Unit ID: 205054
Telephone: (419) 720-6670 Carnegie Class: Spec 2-yr-Health
FAX Number: (419) 720-6674 Calendar System: Quarter
URL: www.proskills.edu
Established: 1984 Annual Undergrad Tuition & Fees: $14,611
Enrollment: 289 Coed
Affiliation or Control: Proprietary IRS Status: Proprietary
Highest Offering: Associate Degree
Accreditation: ABHES, PTAA

01 CEO/Campus Director ... Mr. Michael MARINO
07 Asst Campus Director Admissions ... Mr. Joe GRAHAM
05 Dean of Education ... Ms. Kimberly OSBURN

Rabbinical College of Telshe (G)

28400 Euclid Avenue, Wickliffe OH 44092-2584
County: Lake FICE Identification: 003115
Unit ID: 205124
Telephone: (440) 943-5300 Carnegie Class: Spec-4-yr-Faith
FAX Number: (440) 943-5303 Calendar System: Quarter
Established: 1941 Annual Undergrad Tuition & Fees: $10,500
Enrollment: 65 Male
Affiliation or Control: Independent Non-Profit IRS Status: 501(c)3
Highest Offering: Doctorate
Accreditation: RABN

01 President ... Rabbi David GOLDBERG
06 Registrar ... Rabbi Abraham MATITIA

Remington College Cleveland Campus (H)

14445 Broadway Avenue, Cleveland OH 44125-1900
County: Cuyahoga FICE Identification: 007777
Unit ID: 375416
Telephone: (216) 475-7520 Carnegie Class: Spec 2-yr-Other
FAX Number: (216) 475-6055 Calendar System: Other
URL: www.remingtoncollege.edu
Established: 1990 Annual Undergrad Tuition & Fees: $14,953
Enrollment: 548 Coed
Affiliation or Control: Independent Non-Profit IRS Status: 501(c)3
Highest Offering: Associate Degree
Accreditation: ACCSC, PTAA

01 Campus President ... Mr. Terhan FREEMAN

Rosedale Bible College (I)

2270 Rosedale Road, Irwin OH 43029-9517
County: Madison FICE Identification: 034253
Unit ID: 439899
Telephone: (740) 857-1311 Carnegie Class: Spec 2-yr-Other
FAX Number: (877) 857-1312 Calendar System: Semester
URL: www.rosedale.edu
Established: 1952 Annual Undergrad Tuition & Fees: $8,336
Enrollment: 56 Coed
Affiliation or Control: Mennonite Church IRS Status: 501(c)3
Highest Offering: Associate Degree
Accreditation: BI

01 President ... Mr. Jonathan SHOWALTER
05 Academic Dean ... Mr. Phil WEBER
32 Dean of Students ... Mr. Matthew SHOWALTER
84 Director of Enrollment Services ... Mr. Hans SHENK
08 Director of Library Services ... Mr. Reuben SAIRS
06 Registrar ... Ms. Bethany GEIB
10 Chief Financial Officer ... Mr. Lynford SCHROCK
26 Chief Public Relations Officer ... Mr. Kenneth MILLER
04 Administrative Asst to President ... Mrs. Twila WEBER
18 Chief Facilities/Physical Plant ... Mr. Darnell BRENNEMAN

Saint Mary Seminary and Graduate School of Theology (J)

28700 Euclid Avenue, Wickliffe OH 44092-2585
County: Lake FICE Identification: 004061
Unit ID: 205319
Telephone: (440) 943-7600 Carnegie Class: Not Classified
FAX Number: (440) 943-7577 Calendar System: Semester
URL: www.stmarysem.edu
Established: 1848 Annual Graduate Tuition & Fees: N/A
Enrollment: N/A Coed
Affiliation or Control: Roman Catholic IRS Status: 501(c)3
Highest Offering: Doctorate; No Undergraduates
Accreditation: NH, THEOL

01 President/Rector ... Rev. Mark A. LATCOVICH
03 Vice President/Vice Rector ... Rev. Gerald J. BEDNAR
05 Academic Dean ... Sr. Mary MCCORMICK, OSU
33 Student Dean ... Rev. Michael G. WOOST
42 Spiritual Director ... Rev. Mark HOLLIS
06 Registrar/Assistant Dean ... Sr. Brendon ZAJAC, SND
08 Librarian ... Mr. Alan K. ROME
10 CFO/Treasurer ... Mr. Philip GUBAN
04 Administrative Asst to President ... Vacant
90 Director Academic Computing ... Sr. Brendon ZAJAC
18 Chief Facilities/Physical Plant ... Mr. Philip GUBAN
108 Director Institutional Assessment ... Dr. Edward KACZUK
13 Chief Info Technology Officer (CIO) ... Mr. Alan K. ROME
19 Director Security/Safety ... Mr. Philip GUBAN

School of Advertising Art (K)

1725 E David Road, Dayton OH 45440-1612
County: Montgomery FICE Identification: 025530
Unit ID: 205391
Telephone: (877) 300-9866 Carnegie Class: Spec 2-yr-A&S
FAX Number: (937) 294-5869 Calendar System: Semester
URL: www.saa.edu
Established: 1983 Annual Undergrad Tuition & Fees: $26,181
Enrollment: 172 Coed
Affiliation or Control: Proprietary IRS Status: Proprietary
Highest Offering: Associate Degree
Accreditation: ACCSC

01 Owner/President/Creative Director ... Ms. Jessica BARRY
03 Vice President ... Mr. Matt FLICK
06 Vice President/HR/Registrar ... Mr. Nathan SUMMERS
05 Director of Education ... Ms. Karen ABNEY KORN
36 Director of Career Services ... Ms. Sara FARR
37 Director of Financial Aid ... Ms. Tracy GARDNER
07 Director of Admissions ... Ms. Mariesa BLOOM

Shawnee State University (L)

940 Second Street, Portsmouth OH 45662-4344
County: Scioto FICE Identification: 009942
Unit ID: 205443
Telephone: (740) 351-3205 Carnegie Class: Bac-Diverse
FAX Number: (740) 351-3470 Calendar System: Semester
URL: www.shawnee.edu
Established: 1975 Annual Undergrad Tuition & Fees (In-State): $7,365
Enrollment: 3,881 Coed
Affiliation or Control: State IRS Status: 501(c)3
Highest Offering: Master's
Accreditation: NH, ADNUR, #CAATE, CAEPN, COARC, DH, EMT, MLTAD, NUR, OT, OTA, PTAA, RAD

01 President ... Dr. Rick KURTZ
05 Provost/VP Academic Affairs ... Dr. Jeff BAUER
10 Vice President for Finance & Admin ... Dr. Elinda BOYLES
111 VP for Advancement & External Affs ... Mr. Eric BRAUN
84 VP for Enrollment Mgmt & Stdnt Affs . Dr. Anne Marie GILLESPIE
43 General Counsel/Asst to the Pres ... Ms. Cheryl HACKER
26 Director Communications ... Ms. Elizabeth BLEVINS
107 Dean College Professional Studies ... Dr. Paul MADDEN
49 Dean College Arts & Sciences ... Dr. Roberta MILLIKEN
62 Dean Library Services ... Ms. Janet STEWART
13 Director Univ Information Systems ... Mr. Charles WARNER
30 Executive Director of Development ... Mr. Eric BRAUN
07 Director of Admission ... Ms. Amanda MEANS
06 Registrar ... Ms. Jennifer HAMMONDS
32 Dean of Students ... Ms. Marcie SIMMS
15 Director of Human Resources ... Ms. Malonda JOHNSON
41 Athletic Director ... Mr. Jeff HAMILTON
37 Director of Financial Aid ... Dr. Nicole NEAL
36 Director Student Career Development ... Vacant
38 Director of Counseling & Psych Svcs ... Dr. Linda KOENIG
88 Dean University College ... Dr. Chris KACIR
85 Director for International Pgms ... Mr. Ryan WARNER
18 Director of Facilities ... Mr. Butch KOTCAMP
97 Director General Education Program ... Dr. Phil BLAU
09 Dir of Institutional Research ... Mr. Christopher SHAFFER
21 Controller ... Mr. Greg BALLENGEE
19 Chief of Police ... Mr. David THOROUGHMAN
04 Administrative Asst to President ... Ms. Sandra DUDUIT
39 Director Housing & Residence Life ... Ms. Monique HARMON

Sinclair Community College (A)

444 W Third Street, Dayton OH 45402-1460
County: Montgomery FICE Identification: 003119
Unit ID: 205470
Telephone: (937) 512-3000 Carnegie Class: Assoc/MT-VT-High Non
FAX Number: (937) 512-4596 Calendar System: Semester
URL: www.sinclair.edu
Established: 1887 Annual Undergrad Tuition & Fees (In-District): $2,476
Enrollment: 18,136 Coed
Affiliation or Control: State/Local IRS Status: 501(c)3
Highest Offering: Associate Degree
Accreditation: NH, ACBSP, ACFEI, ADNUR, ART, CAHIIM, COARC, CSHSE, DH, DIETT, EMT, ENGT, MAC, MLTAD, MUS, OTA, PTAA, RAD, SURGT, THEA

00 President Emeritus .... Dr. Ned J. SIFFERLEN
01 President .... Dr. Steven L. JOHNSON
05 Provost .... Dr. Dave COLLINS
103 VP for Workforce Development .... Ms. Deb NORRIS
100 Chief of Staff .... Ms. Laura MERCER
111 VP for Advancement .... Ms. Madeline ISELI
10 Sr VP and CFO .... Mr. Jeff BOUDOURIS
21 VP for Business Operations .... Dr. Ty STONE
88 VP for School & Community Partners .... Dr. Annesa CHEEK
45 VP for Organizational Development .... Dr. Mary GAIER
84 VP Enroll Mgmt & Student Affairs .... Dr. Scott MARKLAND
12 VP for Regional Centers .... Dr. Scott MARKLAND
20 Associate Provost Stdnt Completion .... Dr. Kathleen CLEARY
81 Dean of Science/Math/Engineering .... Mr. Anthony PONDER
76 Dean Health Sciences .... Ms. Rena SHUCHAT
105 Dean Distance Learning/Inst Support .... Dr. Nancy THIBEAULT
20 Associate Provost .... Dr. Lori ZAKEL
50 Dean Business & Public Services .... Dr. Sue MERRELL
26 Director of Public Affairs .... Mr. Adam MURKA
83 Dean Arts/Commun & Social Science .... Ms. Shari RETHMAN
13 Chief Information Officer .... Mr. Scott MCCOLLUM
43 General Counsel .... Ms. Lauren ROSS
06 Registrar .... Ms. Tina HUMMONS
37 Director Financial Aid .... Mr. Matthew MOORE
104 Director International Education .... Ms. Deborah GAVLIK
121 Chief Academic Advising Officer .... Mr. Andy RUNYAN

South University (B)

4743 Richmond Road, Cleveland OH 44128
Telephone: (216) 755-5000 Identification: 770916
Accreditation: &SC, ACBSP, CACREP, NURSE, PTAA

† Branch campus of South University, Savannah, GA

Southern State Community College (C)

100 Hobart Drive, Hillsboro OH 45133-9488
County: Highland FICE Identification: 012870
Unit ID: 205966
Telephone: (937) 393-3431 Carnegie Class: Assoc/MT-VT-High Trad
FAX Number: (937) 393-9370 Calendar System: Semester
URL: www.sscc.edu
Established: 1975 Annual Undergrad Tuition & Fees (In-State): $4,412
Enrollment: 2,408 Coed
Affiliation or Control: State IRS Status: 501(c)3
Highest Offering: Associate Degree
Accreditation: NH, ADNUR, MAC

01 President .... Dr. Kevin S. BOYS
05 Vice President Academic Affairs .... Dr. Nicole ROADES
10 Vice President Business & Finance .... Mr. James E. BUCK
32 Vice Pres Student Svcs/Enroll Mgmt .... Mr. James BLAND
12 Director of Fayette Campus .... Dr. Jessica WISE
12 Director of Brown Co Campus .... Dr. J.R ROUSH
12 Director of Central Campus .... Mr. Jeff MONTGOMERY
103 Dean Workforce Dev/Community Svcs .... Mr. John JOY
15 Director of Human Resources .... Ms. Mindy MARKEY-GRABILL
88 Dean of Adult Opportunity Center .... Ms. Karyn EVANS
91 Computer System/Communication Mgr .... Ms. Shirley A. CORNWELL
26 Director of Public Relations .... Ms. Kris CROSS
06 Registrar .... Ms. Amanda THOMPSON
66 Director of Nursing .... Dr. Julianne KREBS
08 Librarian .... Ms. Angel MOOTISPAW
37 Director Financial Aid .... Ms. Linda MYERS
07 Director of Admissions .... Ms. Lisa HORD
41 Athletic Director .... Mr. Matt WELLS
13 Executive Director of IT Services .... Mr. Brian RICE
04 Executive Asst to President .... Ms. Robin THOLEN
09 Director of Institutional Research .... Mr. Pierre LUCIEN

† Enrollment figure emcompasses all 4 campuses.

Southern State Community College Brown County Campus (D)

351 Brooks-Malott Rd, Mt Orab OH 45154
Telephone: (937) 444-7722 Identification: 770361
Accreditation: &NH

Southern State Community College Fayette Campus (E)

1270 US Route 62 SW,
Washington Court House OH 43160
Telephone: (740) 333-5115 Identification: 770362
Accreditation: &NH, COARC

Southern State Community College North Campus (F)

1850 Davids Drive, Wilmington OH 45177
Telephone: (937) 382-6645 Identification: 770363
Accreditation: &NH

Stark State College (G)

6200 Frank Avenue, NW, North Canton OH 44720-7299
County: Stark FICE Identification: 010881
Unit ID: 205841
Telephone: (330) 494-6170 Carnegie Class: Assoc/MT-VT-High Trad
FAX Number: (330) 497-6313 Calendar System: Semester
URL: www.starkstate.edu
Established: 1960 Annual Undergrad Tuition & Fees (In-District): $3,686
Enrollment: 12,645 Coed
Affiliation or Control: State/Local IRS Status: 501(c)3
Highest Offering: Associate Degree
Accreditation: NH, ACBSP, ADNUR, CAHIIM, COARC, DH, DIETT, EMT, ENGT, MAC, MLTAD, OTA, PTAA

01 President .... Dr. Para M. JONES
05 Provost and Chief Academic Officer .... Dr. Lada GIBSON-SHREVE
10 VP for Business and Finance .... Mr. Thomas A. CHIAPPINI
11 VP for EM/SS and Administration .... Mr. Michael DRONEY
15 Director of Human Resources .... Ms. Melissa A. GLANZ
53 Dean Ed/Liberal Arts/Math/Science .... Mr. Andrew STEPHAN
76 Dean Health and Human Services .... Dr. Kathleen SOMMERS
21 Controller .... Mr. Scott ANDREANI
37 Exec Dir Fin Aid & Registration .... Ms. Amy WELTY
18 Director of Physical Plant and Cons .... Mr. Steve SPRADLING
40 Bookstore Manager .... Ms. Kathryn FEICHTER
06 Registrar .... Ms. Pam ARRINGTON
111 Exec Dir Advance & SSC Foundation .... Ms. Marisa ROHN
114 Director of Budget .... Mr. Bruce WYDER
09 Director of Institutional Research .... Mr. Peter TRUMPOWER
54 Dean Engineering Technologies .... Dr. Don BALL
106 Director eStarkState .... Ms. Linda MOROSKO
08 Head Librarian .... Ms. Marcia ADDISON
04 Exec Admin Asst to President .... Ms. Catherine D. SPINO
103 Exec Dir Workforce and Econ Devel .... Dr. Daryl REVOLDT
07 Exec Director of Admissions .... Mr. J.P COONEY
50 Dean Business and IT .... Dr. James FALTER

Stautzenberger College (H)

8001 Katherine Boulevard, Brecksville OH 44141
Telephone: (440) 838-1999 Identification: 770760
Accreditation: ACICS, CVT, DMS

Stautzenberger College (I)

1796 Indian Wood Circle, Maumee OH 43537-4007
County: Lucas FICE Identification: 004866
Unit ID: 205887
Telephone: (419) 866-0261 Carnegie Class: Assoc/HVT-Mix Trad/Non
FAX Number: (419) 867-9821 Calendar System: Other
URL: www.sctoday.edu
Established: 1926 Annual Undergrad Tuition & Fees: $12,090
Enrollment: 650 Coed
Affiliation or Control: Proprietary IRS Status: Proprietary
Highest Offering: Associate Degree
Accreditation: ACICS

01 Campus President .... Mr. Steven R. ALLEN
09 Compliance Officer .... Mr. Brian E. NIEDZWIECKI
07 Director of Admissions .... Mr. Brandon L. PAUL
05 Dean of Academics .... Mr. Michael L. CARR
37 Financial Aid Director .... Mrs. Mari L. HUFFMAN
36 Career Services Director .... Mr. Robert A. GARVER
06 Registrar .... Ms. Debbie BRUNK
08 Head Librarian .... Ms. Lori VAN LIERE

Terra State Community College (J)

2830 Napoleon Road, Fremont OH 43420-9670
County: Sandusky FICE Identification: 008278
Unit ID: 206011
Telephone: (419) 334-8400 Carnegie Class: Assoc/MT-VT-High Trad
FAX Number: (419) 334-3719 Calendar System: Semester
URL: www.terra.edu
Established: 1968 Annual Undergrad Tuition & Fees (In-State): $4,284
Enrollment: 2,652 Coed
Affiliation or Control: State IRS Status: 501(c)3
Highest Offering: Associate Degree
Accreditation: NH, ADNUR, CAHIIM, MAC, PTAA

01 President .... Dr. Jerome WEBSTER
10 VP for Financial Affairs .... Mr. Randy MCCULLOUGH
30 VP Inst Advancement .... Dr. Cory STINE
05 Interim Vice Pres Academic Affairs .... Dr. Jennifer SPIELVOGEL
84 AVP Student & Enrollment Services .... Mr. Heath MARTIN
15 AVP of Administrative Services .... Ms. Nanci KOSANKA
50 Dean Business/Comm/Industrial Tech .... Ms. Jolene CHAPMAN
76 Dean Allied Hlth/Nursing/Human Svcs .... Ms. Amy ANWAY
09 Dean Planning & Inst Effect .... Vacant
06 Registrar .... Mr. Eric STEINBERGER
19 Exec Director of Campus Services .... Mr. Jeffery HUFFMAN
21 Coordinator of Financial Services .... Ms. Renee D. BROWN
13 Manager Information Technology .... Mr. Wayne YERDON
08 Librarian .... Vacant
88 Coordinator of Global Partnerships .... Dr. Julianna G. BORDERS
04 Executive Assistant to President .... Ms. Jessica HUFFMAN
106 Instructional Technologist .... Ms. Melinda YERDON
32 Associate Dean of Students .... Ms. Elizabeth SABEL
38 Director ASC & Student Counseling .... Ms. Dori DALTON

Tiffin University (K)

155 Miami Street, Tiffin OH 44883-2161
County: Seneca FICE Identification: 003121
Unit ID: 206048
Telephone: (419) 447-6442 Carnegie Class: Masters/L
FAX Number: N/A Calendar System: Semester
URL: www.tiffin.edu
Established: 1888 Annual Undergrad Tuition & Fees: $23,125
Enrollment: 3,496 Coed
Affiliation or Control: Independent Non-Profit IRS Status: 501(c)3
Highest Offering: Master's
Accreditation: NH, ACBSP

01 President .... Dr. Lillian SCHUMACHER
05 Provost .... Dr. Peter HOLBROOK
84 EVP Enrollment Mgmt/Student Affairs .... Dr. Jeremy MARINIS
30 VP University Advancement .... Mr. Mitchell BLONDE
10 VP Finance/Administration .... Ms. Donna FRANK
15 AVP Human Resources/Campus Services .... Ms. Nadia LEWIS
108 VP Inst Planning & Effectiveness .... Dr. Teresa SHAFER
26 AVP Marketing/Communications .... Ms. Kathleen LAWRY
84 Asst VP for Enrollment Management .... Dr. Amy WOOD
21 Assistant VP for Finance .... Mr. Charles ARDNER
04 Exec Assistant to the President .... Ms. Nancy GILBERT
32 Dean of Students .... Mr. Mike HERDLICK
13 Chief Information Officer .... Mr. Scott FERGUSON
07 Director Undergrad Admissions .... Ms. Sarah JOHNSON
27 Exec Dir Media Rels/Publications .... Ms. Lisa WILLIAMS
06 Registrar .... Ms. Melissa WEININGER
41 Director Athletics .... Mr. Lonny ALLEN
21 Asst VP & Controller .... Mr. Robert WATSON
08 Head Librarian .... Ms. Catherine CARLSON
29 Director Alumni Relations .... Ms. Vickie WILKINS
36 Exec Director of Career Services .... Ms. Amanda HUMMEL
18 Director of Physical Plant .... Mr. Orion JONES
39 Director of Residence Life .... Mr. Jacob SIMON
44 Director of Annual Fund .... Vacant
28 AVP Equity/Access/Opp/Title IX .... Dr. Sharon PERRY-FANTINI
37 Director Student Financial Aid .... Ms. Andrea FABER
49 Dean of Arts & Sciences .... Dr. Joyce HALL-YATES
50 Dean of Business .... Dr. Terry SULLIVAN
83 Dean Criminal Justice/Social Sci .... Mr. Kevin CASHEN
09 Director of Institutional Research .... Mr. Mondrail MYRICK
104 Director Study Abroad .... Ms. Tiffanie GOFF
106 Exec Dir Distance Educ/Innov Lrng .... Mr. Nathan TREADWAY
19 Director Security/Safety .... Ms. Jennifer BOUCHER

Tri-State Bible College (L)

506 Margaret Street, PO Box 445,
South Point OH 45680-8402
County: Lawrence FICE Identification: 034754
Unit ID: 206154
Telephone: (740) 377-2520 Carnegie Class: Spec-4-yr-Faith
FAX Number: (740) 377-0001 Calendar System: Semester
URL: www.tsbc.edu
Established: 1970 Annual Undergrad Tuition & Fees: $9,100
Enrollment: 52 Coed
Affiliation or Control: Independent Non-Profit IRS Status: 501(c)3
Highest Offering: Baccalaureate
Accreditation: BI

00 Chancellor .... Dr. Clifford L. MARQUARDT
01 Interim President .... Dr. Kevin BLOOMFIELD
05 Vice President Academic Affairs .... Mr. John DUNCAN
10 Vice President Finance .... Mr. Brian TRIPPETT
11 Vice President Administrative Affs .... Ms. Roberta (Bobby) MERCER
32 Vice Pres Student Affairs .... Mr. Leroy FULFORD
18 Vice President Operations .... Mr. Manfred LANGER
20 Academic Dean Online Programs .... Mr. David LAMBERT

Trinity Lutheran Seminary (M)

2199 E Main Street, Columbus OH 43209-2334
County: Franklin FICE Identification: 003044
Unit ID: 206215
Telephone: (614) 235-4136 Carnegie Class: Spec-4-yr-Faith
FAX Number: (614) 238-0263 Calendar System: Semester
URL: www.TLSohio.edu
Established: 1830 Annual Graduate Tuition & Fees: N/A
Enrollment: 93 Coed
Affiliation or Control: Evangelical Lutheran Church In America
IRS Status: 501(c)3
Highest Offering: Doctorate; No Undergraduates
Accreditation: NH, THEOL

01 President ... Rev. Robert C. BARGER
11 Vice President for Operations ... Mr. Ronald W. BENEDICK
88 Vice Pres Leadership Formation ... Ms. Denise SAGER
05 Academic Dean ... Dr. Brad A. BINAU
20 Associate Academic Dean ... Dr. Diane J. HYMANS
88 Dean of Leadership Formation ... Rev. Emlyn A. OTT
30 Director of Development ... Mr. Chris NORMAN
07 Director of National Recruiting ... Ms. Kayla ASPESLAGH
06 Registrar ... Vacant
08 Int Asst Director Hamma Library ... Ms. Elli CUCKSEY
26 Director Communications/Marketing ... Ms. Margaret L. FARNHAM
37 Director Financial Aid ... Mrs. Melissa CURTIS POWELL
88 Director MA in Church Music Program ... Ms. May L. SCHWARZ
58 Director Graduate Studies ... Dr. Walter F. TAYLOR, JR.
88 Director MACE/MAYFM Programs ... Dr. Diane J. HYMANS
10 Controller ... Mrs. Patricia A. FORK
18 Director Facilities Management ... Ms. Laura K. STARKEY
88 Contextual Education Administrator ... Ms. Penny THOMAS

Union Institute & University (A)

440 E McMillan Street, Cincinnati OH 45206-1947
County: Hamilton FICE Identification: 010923
Unit ID: 206279
Telephone: (513) 861-6400 Carnegie Class: DU-Mod
FAX Number: (513) 861-0779 Calendar System: Semester
URL: www.myunion.edu
Established: 1964 Annual Undergrad Tuition & Fees: $12,416
Enrollment: 1,396 Coed
Affiliation or Control: Independent Non-Profit IRS Status: 501(c)3
Highest Offering: Doctorate
Accreditation: NH, SW

01 President ... Dr. Roger H. SUBLETT
05 VP Academic Affairs ... Dr. Nelson SOTO
04 Executive Assistant to President ... Ms. Carolyn KRAUSE
10 Chief Fiscal Officer ... Mr. Tom CUNNINGHAM
15 Vice President Human Resources ... Ms. Deborah EAMOE
84 VP Enrollment Management ... Ms. Kimbrea BROWNING
30 Vice President Advancement ... Ms. Carolyn KRAUSE
51 Dean of Education ... Dr. Arlene SACKS
58 Dean PsyD Program ... Dr. William LAX
06 Registrar ... Ms. Lew Rita MOORE
13 Director Information Technology ... Dr. Bob COTTER
18 Director Facilities Management ... Mr. Ken LAMB
12 Regional Dean Florida Center ... Vacant
12 Regional Dean LA Center ... Dr. Elizabeth PASTORRES-PALFFY
12 National Dean Undergrad Programs ... Dr. Peter CACCAVERI
12 Regional Dean Sacramento Center ... Ms. Julie CRANDALL
08 Library Director ... Mr. Matthew PAPPATHAN
37 Interim Director Financial Aid ... Ms. Jean POHLMAN
29 Director Alumni Relations ... Dr. Neal MEIER
32 Director Student Success ... Dr. Jay KEEHN
106 Dir Center for Teaching & Learning ... Dr. Bob COTTER

United Theological Seminary (B)

4501 Denlinger Road, Dayton OH 45426-2308
County: Montgomery FICE Identification: 003122
Unit ID: 206288
Telephone: (937) 529-2201 Carnegie Class: Spec-4-yr-Faith
FAX Number: (866) 433-8235 Calendar System: Semester
URL: www.united.edu
Established: 1871 Annual Graduate Tuition & Fees: N/A
Enrollment: 542 Coed
Affiliation or Control: United Methodist IRS Status: 501(c)3
Highest Offering: Doctorate; No Undergraduates
Accreditation: NH, THEOL

01 President ... Dr. Kent MILLARD
05 Vice Pres Academic Affairs & Dean ... Dr. David WATSON
10 Vice Pres Finance/Treasurer ... Mr. Steven SWALLOW
07 Vice Pres Enrollmnt/Assoc Dean DMin ... Dr. Harold HUDSON
30 Vice Pres Development ... Ms. Calle PICARDO
101 Sr Asst to the President/Corp Secy ... Ms. Laura WEBER
20 Assoc Dean Academic Affairs ... Dr. Vivian JOHNSON
06 Registrar ... Ms. Courtney WARD
13 Director of Information Technology ... Mr. Rick MOHR
106 Dir Distance Learning/Educ Tech ... Ms. Phyllis ENNIST
08 Librarian ... Ms. Sarah D. BROOKS BLAIR
42 Dean of the Chapel/Dir of Cntxl Ed ... Rev. Dan GILDNER
26 Coordinator of Communications ... Ms. Rachel HURLEY
37 Director Financial Aid ... Ms. Marcia BYRD
29 Coordinator of Alumni/ae Relations ... Rev. Tesia MALLORY
18 Facility Manager ... Mr. Max FULLER
108 Chf Strategy/Admin/Assessment Ofcr ... Ms. Karen E. PAYNE
84 Senior Dir Enrollment Mgmt ... Rev. Trent HAYES
32 Director of Student Services ... Rev. R. Dean BLIMLINE

The University of Akron, Main Campus (C)

302 Buchtel Common, Akron OH 44325
County: Summit FICE Identification: 003123
Unit ID: 200800
Telephone: (330) 972-7111 Carnegie Class: DU-Higher
FAX Number: (330) 972-6990 Calendar System: Semester
URL: www.uakron.edu
Established: 1870 Annual Undergrad Tuition & Fees (In-State): $10,270
Enrollment: 23,101 Coed
Affiliation or Control: State IRS Status: 501(c)3
Highest Offering: Doctorate
Accreditation: NH, ACBSP, ANEST, ART, CAATE, CACREP, CAEPN, CIDA, COARC, COPSY, DANCE, DIETC, DIETD, ENG, ENGR, ENGT, IFSAC, IPSY, LAW, MAC, MFCD, MUS, NURSE, PH, RAD, SP, SURGT, SW

01 President ... Mr. Matthew J. WILSON
05 Senior Vice Pres & Provost ... Dr. Rex RAMSIER
45 VP Innovation & Economic Dev ... Vacant
10 VP Finance & Administration/CFO ... Mr. Nathan J. MORTIMER
43 Vice President & General Counsel ... Ms. M. Celeste COOK
13 Chief Information Officer ... Vacant
18 Vice Pres Capital Plng/Facil Mgmt ... Vacant
32 Dean of Students ... Mr. Mike STRONG
30 Vice President of Development ... Mrs. Kimberly M. COLE
88 Dir of Presidential Communication ... Mr. David NYPAVER
21 Assc VP Treasury/Financial Planning ... Mr. Brian E. DAVIS
46 Assoc Vice President for Research ... Mr. Kenneth G. PRESTON
22 VP Inclusion and Equity ... Ms. Jolene A. LANE
15 Assoc VP Talent Dev/Human Resources ... Mr. Bill J. VIAU
26 VP/Chief Comm and Marketing Officer ... Mr. Wayne R. HILL
35 VP for Student Affairs ... Dr. John A. MESSINA
19 Asst VP Camp Safety/Chief of Police ... Major Jim P. WEBER
43 Asst VP & Assoc General Counsel ... Vacant
06 Registrar ... Mr. Ronald L. BOWMAN, JR.
07 Director of Admissions ... Ms. Diane R. RAYBUCK
09 Asst Dir Institutional Research ... Ms. Lynn LUCAS
14 Director Technology Transfer ... Mr. Kenneth G. PRESTON
08 Dean University Libraries ... Dr. Aimee L. DECHAMBEAU
49 Dean Buchtel College Arts & Sci ... Dr. John C. GREEN
54 Dean College of Engineering ... Dr. Donald P. VISCO, JR.
53 Acting Dean College of Education ... Dr. Jarrod TUDOR
50 Dean College of Business Admin ... Dr. Ravi KROVI
76 Act Dean College Health Professions ... Dr. Elizabeth A. KENNEDY
72 Int Dean Col of Appl Sci & Tech ... Dr. Elizabeth A. KENNEDY
61 Dean School of Law ... Mr. Christopher PETERS
54 Dean of Polymer Science/Engineering ... Dr. Eric J. AMIS
12 Dean Wayne College ... Dr. Jarrod TUDOR
37 Director Student Financial Aid ... Mrs. Jennifer E. HARPHAM
29 Director of Alumni Relations ... Mr. Willy KOLLMAN
96 Director of Purchasing ... Mr. Andrew W. ROTH
88 Senior Director Integrated Comm ... Mr. Robert KROPFF
105 Director of Web Services ... Mr. Eric W. KRIEDER
92 Dean Honors College ... Dr. Lakeesha K. RANSOM
88 Director UA Adult Focus ... Mrs. Laura H. CONLEY
41 Director Athletics ... Mr. Lawrence R. WILLIAMS
36 Ex Dir Counseling/Test/Career Ctr ... Dr. Juanita K. MARTIN
39 Dir of Residence Life and Housing ... Dr. Melinda GROVE
25 Asst VP Office Research Admin .. Ms. Katie WATKINS-WENDELL
85 Director International Programs ... Vacant
23 Director Health Services ... Ms. Alma E. OLSON
86 Dir Government Relations ... Dr. Matthew P. AKERS
88 Asst VP Computer Operations ... Mrs. Deborah WHITE
88 Director of Media Relations ... Mr. Dan MINNICH
102 Asst VP Corp Fund Relations ... Mrs. Ellen PERDUYN
84 Assoc VP Enrollment Management ... Ms. Lauri S. THORPE
100 Chief of Staff ... Ms. Barbara C. WEINZIERL

The University of Akron-Wayne College (D)

1901 Smucker Road, Orrville OH 44667-9758
County: Wayne FICE Identification: 010818
Unit ID: 200846
Telephone: (330) 683-2010 Carnegie Class: Assoc/HT-High Non
FAX Number: (330) 684-8989 Calendar System: Semester
URL: www.wayne.uakron.edu
Established: 1972 Annual Undergrad Tuition & Fees (In-State): $6,116
Enrollment: 1,992 Coed
Affiliation or Control: State IRS Status: 501(c)3
Highest Offering: Associate Degree
Accreditation: NH

01 Dean ... Dr. Jarrod TUDOR
04 Senior Admin Assistant to Dean ... Ms. Ann MARTIN
05 Associate Dean of Instruction ... Dr. Timothy VIERHELLER
10 Director Business/Finance ... Vacant
32 Asst Dean Student Success ... Mr. Gordon K. HOLLY
18 Facilities/Physical Plant Manager ... Mr. Roy (Alan) DARR
26 Chief Public Relations Officer ... Mrs. Debby MUNIAK
08 Manager Library Services ... Mrs. Maureen T. LERCH
06 Registrar/Manager Student Services ... Mrs. Barb CAILLET
07 Manager of Admissions/Recruitment ... Mrs. Alicia BROADUS
09 Director of Institutional Research ... Mr. William CLARK
15 Director Personnel Services ... Ms. Kathy BATCHELDER
20 Dir Instruction/Program Development .. Mr. Garth D. SCHOFFMAN
30 Director of Development ... Mr. Kevin E. ENGLE
35 Student Activities Coordinator ... Ms. Jackie E. ASHBAUGH
36 Coord Career and Assessment Svcs ... Ms. Carol J. PLEUSS
37 Manager Student Svcs/Financial Aid ... Ms. Barb CAILLET
38 Academic Advisor ... Ms. Wendy CUNDIFF
96 Assistant Director Business/Finance ... Ms. Amy M. HAYNES
13 Manager Technical Support Services ... Ms. Cher DEEDS
19 University Police ... Lt. Chad CUNNINGHAM
40 Director Bookstore ... Ms. Pat PAXTON
41 Athletic Director ... Mr. Dave RUBENS

University of Cincinnati Main Campus (E)

2624 Clifton Avenue, Cincinnati OH 45221-0001
County: Hamilton FICE Identification: 003125
Unit ID: 201885
Telephone: (513) 556-6000 Carnegie Class: DU-Highest
FAX Number: (513) 556-3237 Calendar System: Quarter
URL: www.uc.edu
Established: 1819 Annual Undergrad Tuition & Fees (In-State): $11,000
Enrollment: 36,042 Coed
Affiliation or Control: State IRS Status: 501(c)3
Highest Offering: Doctorate
Accreditation: NH, ANEST, ART, AUD, CAATE, CACREP, CAEP, CAEPN, CAHIIM, CIDA, CLPSY, CONST, CS, DANCE, DENT, DIETC, DIETD, ENG, ENGR, ENGT, LAW, MED, MIDWF, MT, MUS, NMT, NURSE, PH, PHAR, PLNG, PTA, RADMAG, SCPSY, SP, SW, THEA

01 President ... Dr. Neville G. PINTO
05 Sr VP/Provost Academic Affairs ... Mr. Peter E. LANDGREN
11 Sr VP for Administration & Finance ... Mr. Robert AMBACH
03 Executive VP ... Dr. Ryan HAYS
46 Vice President for Research ... Dr. Patrick A. LIMBACH
63 Dean Medicine/Sr VP Health Affairs ... Dr. Williams S. BALL
30 VP Development/Alumni Rels ... Mr. Robert FEALY
86 Vice Pres Govt Rels/University Comm ... Mr. Gregory J. VEHR
32 Vice Pres Student Affairs & Svcs ... Ms. Debra S. MERCHANT
10 Vice President for Finance ... Mr. Patrick A. KOWALSKI
13 VP & CIO for Information Technology ... Dr. Nelson C. VINCENT
20 Sr Vice Provost Academic Affairs ... Dr. Eileen L. STREMPEL
43 General Counsel ... Ms. Lori A. ROSS
15 Sr Assoc VP/Chief HR Officer ... Ms. Tamie L. GRUNOW
84 Sr Assoc Vice President Enrollment ... Dr. Caroline B. MILLER
88 Director of Community Dev ... Mr. William S. FISCHER
26 Director Media Relations ... Ms. MB REILLY
07 Assoc Vice Pres for Admissions ... Dr. Thomas CANEPA
112 Assoc Vice Pres for Principal Gifts ... Mr. E.R. (Jay) BROWNING
76 Dean Allied Health Sciences ... Dr. Tina WHALEN
49 Dean Arts & Sciences ... Dr. Kenneth PETREN
50 Dean Business Administration ... Dr. David M. SZYMANSKI
64 Int Dean Col-Conservatory of Music ... Dr. Bruce D. MCCLUNG
48 Dean Design/Architecture/Art & Plng ... Dr. Robert PROBST
53 Dean Education/Crim Justice & HS ... Dr. Lawrence J. JOHNSON
54 Int Dean Engineering & Applied Sci ... Dr. Paul D. ORKWIS
61 Int Dean Law ... Ms. Verna L. WILLIAMS
66 Dean Nursing ... Dr. Greer L. GLAZER
67 Dean Pharmacy ... Dr. Neil J. MACKINNON
70 Director School Social Work ... Mr. James CLARK
08 Dean Library ... Mr. Xuemao WANG
29 VP Alumni Affairs ... Ms. Jennifer HEISEY
28 VP Equity & Inclusion ... Dr. Bleuzette MARSHALL
41 Director Athletics ... Mr. Michael BOHN
40 Director Bookstore ... Mr. Kevin EAST
36 Int Director Career Development ... Dr. Gisela ESCOE
38 Director Counseling Center ... Dr. Tara H. SCARBOROUGH
22 Exec Director Equal Opportunity ... Mr. Matthew J. OLOVSON
39 Asst VP Housing/Food Service ... Mr. Todd DUNCAN
37 Director Student Financial Aid ... Mr. Randy ULSES
09 Director Institutional Research ... Mrs. Suzana H. LUZURIAGA
19 Director Public Safety ... Mr. James L. WHALEN
06 Registrar ... Dr. Douglas BURGESS
96 Assoc VP Purchasing ... Mr. Thomas B. GUERIN
45 Co-Dir Institute for Policy Rsrch ... Dr. Eric RADEMACHER
45 Co-Dir Institute for Policy Rsrch ... Dr. Kimberly DOWNING
104 Vice Provost International Programs ... Dr. Raj MEHTA
18 Chief Facilities/Physical Plant ... Mr. Joseph H. HARRELL
101 Secretary of the Institution/Board ... Ms. Nicole BLOUNT
102 Dir Foundation/Corporate Relations ... Ms. Dee ROBINSON
105 Asst VP Digital Comm ... Ms. Nicola ZIADY
25 Assoc VP Sponsored Research ... Ms. Deborah J. GALLOWAY
90 Int Director Academic Computing ... Mr. Paul C. FOSTER
04 Administrative Asst to President ... Mr. Lawrence P. LAMPE
100 Chief of Staff ... Dr. Ryan HAYS
106 Dir Distance Learning/E-Learning ... Dr. Melody A. CLARK

University of Cincinnati Blue Ash College (F)

9555 Plainfield Road, Blue Ash OH 45236-1096
County: Hamilton FICE Identification: 004868
Unit ID: 201955
Telephone: (513) 745-5600 Carnegie Class: Bac/Assoc-Assoc Dom
FAX Number: (513) 745-5780 Calendar System: Semester
URL: www.ucblueash.edu
Established: 1967 Annual Undergrad Tuition & Fees (In-State): $6,010
Enrollment: 5,065 Coed
Affiliation or Control: State IRS Status: 501(c)3
Highest Offering: Baccalaureate
Accreditation: NH, ADNUR, ART, DH, MAC, RAD

01 Interim Dean ... Dr. Robin LIGHTNER
05 Interim Assoc Dean Academic Affairs ... Dr. Charlotte SKINNER
10 Director Business Affairs ... Mr. Marc WATSON
20 Asst Dean Academic Affairs ... Dr. Gregory METZ
18 Director Facilities & Campus Plan ... Mr. Rob KNARR
13 Director Information Technology ... Mr. Dale HOFSTETTER
07 Director Admissions ... Mr. Brad TATE
09 Director Institutional Research ... Mr. Steve MILLER
30 Senior Director Development ... Ms. Meredith DELANEY
08 Library Director ... Ms. Heather MALONEY
26 Director Communication ... Mr. Pete GEMMER
32 Director Student Engagement ... Vacant
121 Director Acad/Student Advising ... Mr. Mark MILLER
35 Director One Stop Student Service ... Ms. Martha GEIGER
15 HR Manager ... Ms. Amy OWENS SMITH

University of Cincinnati-Clermont College (G)

4200 Clermont College Drive, Batavia OH 45103-1785
County: Clermont FICE Identification: 010805
Unit ID: 201946
Telephone: (513) 732-5200 Carnegie Class: Bac/Assoc-Mixed

FAX Number: (513) 732-5275 Calendar System: Quarter
URL: www.ucclermont.edu
Established: 1972 Annual Undergrad Tuition & Fees (In-State): $5,316
Enrollment: 3,099 Coed
Affiliation or Control: State IRS Status: 501(c)3
Highest Offering: Baccalaureate
Accreditation: NH, CAHIIM, COARC, PTAA, SURGA, SURGT

01 Dean Dr. Jeffrey C. BAUER
05 Int Assoc Dean Academic Affairs Ms. Kim JACOBS-BECK
20 Sr Assistant Dean Academic Affairs Ms. Mary F. STEARNS
18 Asst Dean Facilities & Tech Svcs Mr. Stephen W. YOUNG
26 Sr Asst Dean Student Services Ms. Mae HANNA
08 Director Library Ms. Katie FORHAN-MULCAHY
24 Director Learning Center Ms. Amy ABAFO
09 Dir Institutional Effectiveness Ms. Susan RILEY
10 Director Business Affairs Ms. Maria KERI
32 Sr Dir Retention & Student Success Ms. Jennifer RADT
07 Assoc Director Recruitment Mr. Blaine KELLY
06 Asst Dir Registration & Records Ms. Kristine LOUGHRAN
88 Director Disability Services Ms. Jennifer RADT
35 Director of Student Life Ms. Kimberly ELLISON
41 Athletic Director Mr. Brian SULLIVAN
30 Director of Development Mr. Denny SKETCH

University of Dayton (A)

300 College Park, Dayton OH 45469-0001
County: Montgomery FICE Identification: 003127
Unit ID: 202480
Telephone: (937) 229-1000 Carnegie Class: DU-Higher
FAX Number: (937) 229-4000 Calendar System: Semester
URL: www.udayton.edu
Established: 1850 Annual Undergrad Tuition & Fees: $40,940
Enrollment: 11,250 Coed
Affiliation or Control: Roman Catholic IRS Status: 501(c)3
Highest Offering: Doctorate
Accreditation: NH, #ARCPA, ART, CACREP, CAEP, CEA, CS, DIETD, ENG, ENGT, LAW, MUS, PTA, SPAA

01 President Dr. Eric F. SPINA
05 Provost Dr. Paul H. BENSON
32 VP Student Development Mr. William M. FISCHER
10 VP Finance & Admin Services Mr. Andrew E. HORNER
111 VP Univ Advancement Ms. Jennifer L. HOWE
41 VP/Director of Athletics Mr. Neil G. SULLIVAN
15 VP Human Resources Mr. Troy W. WASHINGTON
84 VP for Strategic Enrollment Mgmt Dr. Jason K. REINOEHL
46 VP of Research/Exec Dir UDRI Dr. John E. LELAND
30 Sr Dir Development/Principal Gifts Mr. James F. BROTHERS
42 Exec Director Campus Ministry Ms. Crystal C. SULLIVAN
88 VP for Mission and Rector Rev. James F. FITZ, SM
31 Dir Ctr for Ldrshp in Cmty Ms. Hunter P. GOODMAN
20 Assoc Provost Faculty & Admin Affs Dr. Carolyn ROECKER-PHELPS
88 Asc Prov Lrng Spprt/Dir Rch Tch Ctr Dr. Deborah J. BICKFORD
06 Registrar Ms. Jennifer M. CREECH
07 Asst VP/Dean of Admission & Fin Aid Mr. Robert F. DURKLE
19 Exec Director/Chief of Police Mr. Rodney CHATMAN
09 Director Institutional Studies Ms. Susan K. SEXTON
21 Comptroller Ms. Angela K. BUECHELE
35 Assoc VP/Dean of Students Ms. Christine M. SCHRAMM
36 Director Career Services Mr. Jason C. ECKERT
38 Asst VP Student Dev/Dir Counseling Dr. Steven D. MUELLER
18 VP for Facilities/Campus Opers Ms. Beth H. KEYES
23 Medical Director Univ Health Ctr Dr. Mary P. BUCHWALDER
08 Dean University Libraries Ms. Kathleen M. WEBB
49 Dean College A&S Dr. Jason L. PIERCE
61 Dean School of Law Mr. Andrew L. STRAUSS
50 Dean Sch of Business Admin Dr. John MITTELSTAEDT
58 Assoc Prov Graduate Acad Affairs Dr. Paul M. VANDERBURGH
13 Assoc Provost & Chief Info Officer Dr. Thomas D. SKILL
53 Dean School of Educ & Health Sci Dr. Kevin R. KELLY
54 Dean School of Engineering Dr. Eddy M. ROJAS
29 Sr Development Officer Mr. Todd W. IMWALLE
35 Dir Student Life & Kennedy Union Ms. Amy L. LOPEZ-MATTHEWS
37 Exec Dir Flyers First/Dir Fin Aid Ms. Catherine MIX
39 Asst Dean Students & Dir Res Life Mr. Steven T. HERNDON
40 Manager UD Bookstore Ms. Julie M. BANKS
43 Univ Counsel/Dir Legal Affairs Ms. Mary A. RECKER
96 Dir Univ Purchases/Business Service Ms. Sara HARRISON
92 Dir University Honors/Scholars Pgm Dr. John P. MCCOMBE
94 Women's and Gender Studies Program Dr. Rebecca S. WHISNANT
22 Dir Affirmative Action & Compliance Ms. Patricia BERNAL-OLSON
86 Exec Dir Govt/Regional Relations Mr. S. Ted BUCARO
28 VP Diversity & Inclusion Dr. Lawrence A. BURNLEY
26 Dir Marketing & Creative Services Ms. Kim B. LALLY
04 Exec Asst to President Ms. Jane PERRICH
100 Executive Director/Chief of Staff Mr. Thomas U. WECKESSER
101 Secretary of the Board of Trustees Ms. Lisa S. RISMILLER

The University of Findlay (B)

1000 North Main Street, Findlay OH 45840-3653
County: Hancock FICE Identification: 003045
Unit ID: 202763
Telephone: (419) 422-8313 Carnegie Class: Masters/L
FAX Number: (419) 434-4822 Calendar System: Semester
URL: www.findlay.edu
Established: 1882 Annual Undergrad Tuition & Fees: $32,402
Enrollment: 5,031 Coed
Affiliation or Control: Church Of God IRS Status: 501(c)3
Highest Offering: Doctorate
Accreditation: NH, ACBSP, ARCPA, CAATE, CAEPN, CEA, DMS, ENGR, NMT, OT, PHAR, PTA, SW

01 President Dr. Katherine R. FELL
05 Vice President for Academic Affairs Dr. Darin FIELDS
10 Vice President for Business Affairs Mr. Leon WYDEN, JR.
84 VP Enrollment Mgmt Mr. Edward RECKER
20 Assoc VPAA/Inst Effectiveness Dr. John OSAE-KWAPONG
111 Vice Pres University Advancement Dr. Marcia SLOAN LATTA
32 Vice President for Student Affairs Mr. David W. EMSWELLER
04 Assistant to the President Ms. Liz DITTO
81 Dean College of Sciences Dr. Jeffrey FRYE
50 Dean College of Business Dr. E. Kevin RENSHLER
49 Dean College of Liberal Art Dr. Ronald TULLEY
76 Int Dean College Health Professions Dr. Richard STATES
67 Dean College of Pharmacy Dr. Debra PARKER
53 Dean College of Education Dr. Julie MCINTOSH
18 Director of Physical Plant Mr. Myreon K. COBB
06 Registrar/Dir of Inst Research Mr. Tony G. GOEDDE
41 Athletic Director Ms. Brandi LAURITA
08 Director of Shafer Library Mr. Andrew WHITIS
37 Director of Financial Aid Mr. Joseph F. SPENCER
13 Chief Information Officer Dr. Raymond MCCANDLESS
29 Director of Alumni Affairs Ms. Deanna SPRAW
26 Dir Public Relations/Media Rels Ms. Rebecca JENKINS
36 Director of Career/Prof Development Mr. Bradley C. HAMMER
15 Director of Human Resources Mr. Robert LINK
23 Director of Health Services Ms. Julie R. YINGLING
38 Director Counseling Services Ms. Karyn J. WESTRICK
40 Manager of Bookstore Mr. Jay CANTERBURY
42 Director Christian Ministries Mr. Matthew GINTER
19 Chief of Police/Dir of Security Mr. William SPRAW
88 Asst Dean International Education Mr. Christopher SIPPEL
85 Int Dir Intl Student Admiss & Svcs Ms. Kelli WAGES
101 Secretary to the Board of Trustees Ms. Liz DITTO
25 Grants Manager Ms. Tricia VALASEK
07 Director of Admissions Mr. Christopher HARRIS
21 Associate Business Officer Mr. Dane ERFORD
35 Asst Dean of Students Ms. Rachel WALTER
39 Director Residence Life Mr. Johnathan FERRARO
44 Director Annual Giving Ms. Kelly M. ANDERSON

University of Mount Union (C)

1972 Clark Avenue, Alliance OH 44601-3993
County: Stark FICE Identification: 003083
Unit ID: 204185
Telephone: (330) 821-5320 Carnegie Class: Bac-Diverse
FAX Number: (330) 823-3457 Calendar System: Semester
URL: www.mountunion.edu
Established: 1846 Annual Undergrad Tuition & Fees: $29,120
Enrollment: 2,191 Coed
Affiliation or Control: United Methodist IRS Status: 501(c)3
Highest Offering: Doctorate
Accreditation: NH, ARCPA, #CAATE, CAEP, ENG, MUS, NURSE, @PTA

01 President Dr. W. R. MERRIMAN, JR.
05 Vice Pres Acad Affs/Dean of Univ Dr. Jeffrey R. BREESE
10 Vice Pres Business Affs/Treasurer Mr. Patrick D. HEDDLESTON
111 Vice President Univ Advancement Mr. Gregory KING
32 Vice Pres Student Affs/Dean Stdnts Mr. John FRAZIER
84 Vice President for Enrollment Mgmt Ms. Michelle SUNDSTROM
26 Vice President for Marketing Ms. Melissa GARDNER
08 Librarian Mr. Robert R. GARLAND
06 University Registrar Mr. Bryan BOATRIGHT
07 Director of Admission Ms. Jessie CANAVAN
112 Director of Planned Giving Ms. Sherrie WALLACE
13 Director of Information Technology Ms. Tina STUCHELL
30 Director of Advancement Mr. Joseph D. MONTGOMERY
29 Director Alumni/College Activities Ms. Tiffany HOGYA
85 Director Center for Global Educ Dr. Jennifer HALL
18 Director of Physical Plant Mr. Blaine D. LEWIS
15 Director of Human Resources Ms. Kristin HANNON
39 Director of Residence Life Ms. Sara SHERER
42 Chaplain Rev. Martha D. CASHBURLESS
36 Exec Director of Career Services Ms. Jessica CUNION
40 Manager of College Bookstore Ms. Aimee SCHULLER
41 Athletic Director Mr. Larry T. KEHRES
04 Exec Assistant to the President Ms. Audra YOUNGEN
21 Assoc VP for Business Affairs Mr. Ronald CROWL
35 Associate Dean of Students Ms. Michelle GAFFNEY
96 Purchasing Agent Mr. Shawn BAGLEY
19 Director Security/Safety Mr. William KETJEN
28 Director of Diversity Mr. Ronald HOLDEN
38 Director Student Counseling Ms. Shannon ORTIZ

University of Northwestern Ohio (D)

1441 N Cable Road, Lima OH 45805-1498
County: Allen FICE Identification: 004861
Unit ID: 204486
Telephone: (419) 227-3141 Carnegie Class: Bac/Assoc-Mixed
FAX Number: (419) 229-6926 Calendar System: Quarter
URL: www.unoh.edu
Established: 1920 Annual Undergrad Tuition & Fees: $10,440
Enrollment: 3,996 Coed
Affiliation or Control: Independent Non-Profit IRS Status: 501(c)3
Highest Offering: Master's
Accreditation: NH, ACBSP, CAHIIM, MAC

01 President Dr. Jeffrey A. JARVIS
05 Vice Provost/Dean Col Business Dr. Dean HOBLER
10 Vice President Finance Mrs. Marcia EICKHOLT
84 Vice Pres Enrollment Management Mr. Tony AZZARELLO
18 Vice Pres of Property Management Mr. Don RICKER
26 VP Public Rels/Mktg/Special Events Mrs. Cheryl STEINWEDEL
30 Vice President Development Mr. Steve FARMER
15 Exec Director of Human Resources Ms. Geri MORRIS
21 Controller Mr. James S. BRONDER
37 Director of Financial Aid Mr. Wendell SCHICK
04 Executive Assistant to President Mrs. Jennifer BENDELE
72 Dean College of Technologies Mr. Andy O'NEAL

University of Rio Grande (E)

218 N College Avenue, PO BOX 500, Rio Grande OH 45674-3100
County: Gallia FICE Identification: 003116
Unit ID: 205203
Telephone: (740) 245-5353 Carnegie Class: Bac/Assoc-Mixed
FAX Number: (740) 245-5266 Calendar System: Semester
URL: www.rio.edu
Established: 1876 Annual Undergrad Tuition & Fees: $23,860
Enrollment: 2,077 Coed
Affiliation or Control: Independent Non-Profit IRS Status: 501(c)3
Highest Offering: Master's
Accreditation: NH, ADNUR, CAEPN, COARC, DMS, IACBE, NUR, RAD, SW

01 President Dr. Michelle R. JOHNSTON
05 Provost/VP of Academic Affairs Dr. Richard SAX
84 VP Enrollment Mgmt & Marketing Mr. James BESSETTE
10 Chief Financial Officer/VP Finance Mr. Tim PRUETT
32 VP Student & Administrative Affairs Mrs. Rebecca LONG
15 Director of Human Resources Mr. Chris NOURSE
21 Controller Mr. Russell HENCHEY
49 Dean Col of Arts & Sciences Dr. Heather DUDA
107 Dean College Prof/Tech Studies Dr. Donna MITCHELL
06 Registrar Mrs. Tami SHEETS
07 Director Recruitment Ms. Kristie RUSSELL
88 Director of Admissions Operations Mrs. Amanda EHMAN
30 Director of Development Mrs. Kara WILLIS
32 Dean of Students Ms. Dena WARREN
41 Athletics Director Mr. Jeff LANHAM
08 Director of the Library Ms. Amy R. WILSON
14 Dir Campus Computing & Networking Mr. Kingsley MEYER
13 Management Information Systems Adm Mr. Eric LOLLATHIN
29 Director of Alumni Relations Mrs. Delyssa EDWARDS
04 Executive to the President Ms. Annette WARD
88 Chief Financial Officer RGCC Mr. Kent HALEY
19 Director Security/Safety Mr. Scott BORDEN

University of Toledo (F)

2801 W Bancroft, Toledo OH 43606-3390
County: Lucas FICE Identification: 003131
Unit ID: 206084
Telephone: (419) 530-4636 Carnegie Class: DU-Higher
FAX Number: (419) 530-4984 Calendar System: Semester
URL: www.utoledo.edu
Established: 1872 Annual Undergrad Tuition & Fees (In-State): $9,547
Enrollment: 20,377 Coed
Affiliation or Control: State IRS Status: 501(c)3
Highest Offering: Doctorate
Accreditation: NH, #ARCPA, ART, CAATE, CACREP, CAEP, CAEPN, CAHIIM, CLPSY, COARC, CS, DENT, ENG, ENGR, ENGT, LAW, MED, MT, MUS, NRPA, NURSE, OT, PH, PHAR, PTA, SP, SW

01 President Dr. Sharon L. GABER
100 Chief of Staff Mr. Matt J. SCHROEDER
05 EVP Academic Affairs/Provost Dr. Andrew HSU
63 EVP for Clin Affs/Dean COMLS Dr. Christopher COOPER
10 EVP Finance & Admin/CFO Mr. Lawrence KELLEY
43 Vice President/General Counsel Mr. Peter J. PAPADIMOS
32 Int VP for Student Affairs Dr. Phillip COCKRELL
111 Vice President for Advancement Mr. Michael HARDERS
84 Int VP Enrollment Management Ms. Stephanie SANDERS
46 Vice President Research Dr. Frank J. CALZONETTI
13 Vice President CIO/CTO Mr. William MCCREARY
41 Vice Pres and Director of Athletics Mr. Michael E. O'BRIEN
17 Int CEO Univ Toledo Med Ctr Mr. Dan BARBEE
09 Exec Dir Inst Research Mr. Ying LIU
86 AVP Government Relations Ms. Diane MILLER
06 Interim University Registrar Ms. Julie R. QUINONEZ
58 Dean College of Graduate Studies Dr. Amanda BRYANT-FRIEDRICH
50 Dean Business & Innovation Dr. Gary INSCH
53 Int Dean J Herb College of Educ Dr. Virginia KEIL
54 Dean Engineering Dr. Michael TOOLE
76 Dean Health & Human Services Dr. Christopher INGERSOLL
83 Dean Arts & Letters Dr. Charlene GILBERT
61 Dean Law Mr. Ben BARROSS
81 Dean Natural Sciences & Mathematics Dr. Karen BJORKMAN
66 Dean Nursing Dr. Linda LEWANDOWSKI
67 Dean Pharmacy & Pharm Sciences Dr. Johnnie EARLY
92 Dean Jesup Scott Honors College Dr. Heidi APPEL
88 Dean University College Dr. Barbara KOPP-MILLER
35 Dean of Students Vacant
39 AVP Residence Life Ms. Valerie WALSTON
37 AVP Financial Aid/Enrollment Svcs Mr. Gina ROBERTS
15 Sr Director Faculty Labor Relations Mr. Kevin WEST
102 President Foundation Ms. Brenda LEE
29 Assoc Vice Pres Alumni Relations Mr. Daniel J. SAEVIG
36 Dir Exp Lrng and Career Svcs Ms. Shelly DROUILLARD

Code	Title	Name
85	Asst Provost Ctr for Intl Studies	Mr. Sammy SPANN
21	Director Internal Audit	Mr. David CUTRI
19	Chief of Police	Mr. Jeff NEWTON
40	General Manager Bookstore SU	Ms. Colleen STRAYER
18	AVP Facilities/Physical Plant	Mr. Jason TOTH
08	Int Director University Libraries	Ms. Barbara FLOYD
04	Administrative Asst to President	Ms. Katie DEBENEDICTIS
07	Director of Admissions	Mr. Billie PIERCE
101	Secretary of the Institution/Board	Ms. Joan STASA
28	VP for Diversity and Inclusion	Dr. Willie MCKETHER
96	Director of Supply Chain Management	Ms. Jennifer PASTOREK

Urbana University (A)

579 College Way, Urbana OH 43078-2091
Telephone: (937) 772-9200 FICE Identification: 003133
Accreditation: NH, IACBE, NURSE

† Branch campus of Franklin University, Columbus, OH

Ursuline College (B)

2550 Lander Road, Cleveland OH 44124-4398
County: Cuyahoga FICE Identification: 003134
Unit ID: 206349
Telephone: (440) 449-4200 Carnegie Class: Masters/L
FAX Number: (440) 646-8318 Calendar System: Semester
URL: www.ursuline.edu
Established: 1871 Annual Undergrad Tuition & Fees: $29,940
Enrollment: 1,178 Female
Affiliation or Control: Roman Catholic IRS Status: 501(c)3
Highest Offering: Doctorate
Accreditation: NH, CACREP, CAEP, CAEPN, IACBE, NURSE, SW

Code	Title	Name
01	President	Sr. Christine DEVINNE
05	Vice President Academic Affairs	Dr. Kathryn LAFONTANA
10	Vice Pres & Chief Financial Officer	Mr. Timothy REARDON
111	Vice Pres Institutional Advancement	Mr. Richard KONISIEWICZ
18	Vice Pres of Facility Management	Ms. June GRACYK
32	Vice President of Student Affairs	Ms. Deanne HURLEY
84	Vice Pres of Enrollment Management	Ms. Deanne HURLEY
58	Interim Dean of Graduate Studies	Dr. James CONNELL
49	Dean Arts & Sciences	Dr. Elizabeth KAVRAN
66	Dean College of Nursing	Dr. Patricia SHARPNACK
88	Exec Director Accelerated Program	Ms. Brooke SCHARLOTT
08	Director of Library	Vacant
06	Registrar	Ms. Leah SULLIVAN
21	Accounting Manager	Ms. Susan VALITSKY
30	Director of Development	Dr. Patrick RILEY
07	Director of Admissions	Ms. Carolyn NOLL SORG
37	Director of Financial Aid	Ms. Mary Lynn PERRI
29	Dir Alumae Relations & Annual Fund	Ms. Lynne DEWYRE
26	Dir of Marketing/Communications	Ms. Ann MCGUIRE
38	Director Counseling & Career Svcs	Ms. Geraldine M. JENKINS
15	Director of Personnel	Ms. Kelli KNAUS
13	Dir of Information Technology	Mr. Richard MCCOURT
09	Director of Institutional Research	Vacant
102	Dir of Corp & Foundation Relations	Vacant
39	Director of Residence Life	Ms. Gina DEMART-KRAUS
42	Director Campus Ministry	Dr. Joann PIOTRKOWSKI
28	Asst Dean of Inclusion	Ms. Tina LINING
93	Director of Wellness Program	Vacant
24	Library Electronic & Media Services	Ms. Marylouise DEEHR
40	Manager Bookstore	Ms. Kendra CORENO
41	Athletic Director	Ms. Cynthia MCKNIGHT
43	Dir Legal Services/General Counsel	Mr. Terry BILLUPS
09	Institutional Research Analyst	Ms. Marilyn VALENCIA
04	Administrative Asst to President	Ms. Kathleen ALLEN
108	Interim Director Inst Assessment	Dr. Mary Jo CHERRY
19	Director Security/Safety	Mr. James KRZYWICKI
22	Dir Compliance/Title IX/Disability	Ms. Deborah KAMAT

Valor Christian College (C)

PO Box 800, Columbus OH 43216
County: Franklin Identification: 667093
Unit ID: 486257
Telephone: (614) 837-4088 Carnegie Class: Not Classified
FAX Number: (614) 837-6904 Calendar System: Semester
URL: www.valorcollege.com
Established: 1990 Annual Undergrad Tuition & Fees: $4,490
Enrollment: 255 Coed
Affiliation or Control: Independent Non-Profit IRS Status: 501(c)3
Highest Offering: Associate Degree
Accreditation: BI

Code	Title	Name
01	President	Randy TURPIN
05	Vice Pres Academic Affairs	Laquetta CORTNER
32	Dean of Students	Cherisse CONLEY
35	Director of Student Life	Ashton PARSLEY
04	Admin Asst to Pres/Office Mgr	Holly BARNETT
37	Director of Financial Aid	Norm STOPPENBRINK

Vatterott College-Cleveland (D)

5025 E Royalton Road,
Broadview Heights OH 44147-3502
Telephone: (440) 526-1660 Identification: 666156
Accreditation: ACCSC, MAAB

† Branch campus of Vatterott College-North Park, Berkeley, MO.

Virginia Marti College of Art & Design (E)

11724 Detroit Avenue, Lakewood OH 44107-3002
County: Cuyahoga FICE Identification: 012896
Unit ID: 206394
Telephone: (216) 221-8584 Carnegie Class: Assoc/HT-High Trad
FAX Number: (216) 221-2311 Calendar System: Quarter
URL: www.vmcad.edu
Established: 1966 Annual Undergrad Tuition & Fees: $17,980
Enrollment: 135 Coed
Affiliation or Control: Proprietary IRS Status: Proprietary
Highest Offering: Associate Degree
Accreditation: ACCSC

Code	Title	Name
01	President	Dr. Milan MILASINOVIC
05	Dean of Academic Affairs	Mr. Patrick MELNICK
37	Financial Aid Administrator	Ms. Martha SNODGRASS
07	Director of Enrollment	Mr. Matt MILLER

Walsh University (F)

2020 East Maple Street, North Canton OH 44720
County: Stark FICE Identification: 003135
Unit ID: 206437
Telephone: (330) 490-7090 Carnegie Class: Masters/M
FAX Number: (330) 499-7165 Calendar System: Semester
URL: www.walsh.edu
Established: 1958 Annual Undergrad Tuition & Fees: $28,720
Enrollment: 2,860 Coed
Affiliation or Control: Roman Catholic IRS Status: 501(c)3
Highest Offering: Doctorate
Accreditation: NH, CACREP, CAEPN, NURSE, PTA

Code	Title	Name
01	President	Mr. Richard JUSSEAUME
10	Vice Pres Finance/Business Affairs	Ms. Shelley BROWN
32	VP Student Affairs/Dean of Students	Ms. Amy MALASKA
05	Provost/Vice Pres Academic Affairs	Dr. Douglas PALMER
111	Vice Pres of Advancement/Univ Rels	Mr. Eric BELDEN
41	Vice Pres for Athletics	Mr. Dale S. HOWARD
88	Academic Projects	Ms. Nancy BLACKFORD
26	VP for Marketing/Communications	Ms. Teresa FOX
13	VP of Administration/CIO	Mr. Brian GREENWELL
20	Dean for Academic Services	Ms. Edna MCCULLOH
09	Dean Inst Effectiveness	Dr. Ute LAHAIE
18	Director of Facilities & Grounds	Mr. John SCHISSLER
91	Database Administrator	Ms. Hope STANCIU
22	Director of Compliance	Mr. Jason FAUTAS
36	Director of Career Services	Mr. Andy WEYAND
42	Chaplain	Fr. Thomas CEBULA
38	Director Counseling Services	Ms. Frances MORROW
42	Director of Campus Ministry	Mr. Miguel CHAVEZ
31	Dir Campus & Community Programs	Ms. Jacqueline M. MANSER
37	Director Financial Aid	Mrs. Holly VAN GILDER
15	Director of Human Resources	Mr. Frank MCKNIGHT
29	Director of Alumni Relations	Ms. Sarah TRESCOTT
25	Director of Grants	Ms. Rachel HAMMEL
19	Chief of Campus Police	Mr. Louis DARROW
08	Director of Library Services	Ms. Heidi BEKE-HARRIGAN
83	Dean School of Behav/Health Science	Dr. Pamela RITZLINE
49	Dean School of Arts & Sciences	Dr. Michael DUNPHY
66	Dean Byers School of Nursing	Dr. Linda LINC
79	Chair Div of Humanities	Dr. Bradley BEACH
81	Chair Division of Math & Sciences	Dr. Jackie NOVAK
92	Director Honors Program	Dr. Hawkins TY
04	Administrative Asst to President	Ms. Christine SCHEETZ
06	Registrar	Ms. Stacie HERMAN
50	Dean DeVille School of Business	Dr. Carole MOUNT
53	Chair Div of Education	Dr. Jeannie DEFAZIO
101	Secretary of the Institution/Board	Ms. Christine SCHEETZ
104	Director Study Abroad	Mr. Michael CINSON
39	Director Student Housing	Ms. Tiffany KINNARD-PAYTON
86	Director Government Relations	Mr. Derrick WYMAN
96	Director of Purchasing	Ms. Rebecca MIMA
07	Assoc Dean of Undergrad Admissions	Ms. Rebecca CONEGLIO
28	Chief Diversity Officer	Mr. Michael DOUGLAS

Washington State Community College (G)

710 Colegate Drive, Marietta OH 45750-9225
County: Washington FICE Identification: 010453
Unit ID: 206446
Telephone: (740) 374-8716 Carnegie Class: Assoc/MT-VT-High Non
FAX Number: (740) 374-9562 Calendar System: Semester
URL: www.wscc.edu
Established: 1971 Annual Undergrad Tuition & Fees (In-State): $4,500
Enrollment: 1,477 Coed
Affiliation or Control: State IRS Status: 501(c)3
Highest Offering: Associate Degree
Accreditation: NH, COARC, MLTAD, PTAA

Code	Title	Name
01	President	Dr. Vicky WOOD
10	VP of Finance and Operations/Treas	Mr. Jess N. RAINES
84	VP of Enrollment & Student Success	Ms. Amanda K. HERB
05	Vice President for Academic Affairs	Dr. Mark NUTTER
13	Chief Information Officer	Mr. Terry RATAICZAK
15	Executive Director Human Resources	Mr. Jess N. RAINES
102	Exec Dir Foundation & Grants Dev	Ms. Anna RITTENHOUSE
76	Dean of Health Sciences	Dr. Heather KINCAID
49	Dean of Arts and Sciences	Vacant
50	Dean of Bus/Engr/Industrial Tech	Ms. Brenda L. KORNMILLER
06	Registrar	Ms. Sarah ALLAN
07	Director of Admissions	Ms. Carrie THRASH
26	Dir of Marketing & Communications	Ms. Amanda HERB
37	Director of Financial Aid	Ms. Reba BARTRUG
08	Director Library Services	Ms. Mary Lou MOEGLING
37	Assistant Director of Financial Aid	Vacant
88	Director of College Access and ETS	Ms. Donna MUNTZ

Wilberforce University (H)

PO Box 1001, Wilberforce OH 45384-1001
County: Greene FICE Identification: 003141
Unit ID: 206491
Telephone: (937) 376-2911 Carnegie Class: Bac-Diverse
FAX Number: (937) 376-2627 Calendar System: Semester
URL: www.wilberforce.edu
Established: 1856 Annual Undergrad Tuition & Fees: $13,250
Enrollment: 646 Coed
Affiliation or Control: African Methodist Episcopal IRS Status: 501(c)3
Highest Offering: Master's
Accreditation: NH, CACREP

Code	Title	Name
01	President	Dr. Herman J. FELTON
05	Provost/Executive Vice President	Dr. Elfred A. PINKARD
10	Sr VP of Administration & Finance	Mr. William WOODSON
32	Sr VP of Student Engagement	Dr. Tashia BRADLEY
15	VP of Administration and HR	Mrs. Anita R. JEFFERSON-GOMEZ
108	Assoc Provost Institutional Effect	Dr. Pamela RICHARDSON-WILKS
20	Asst Provost for Faculty Affairs	Dr. Michael LUKE-ROBINSON
49	Dean of Arts & Sciences	Dr. Kizito NAKIZITO
107	Dean of Professional Studies	Mr. Michael SIMMONS
07	Director of Admissions	Ms. Katrina JARRETT
06	Registrar	Mrs. Rudell MOORE
100	Chief of Staff	Ms. Genevieve HALL
113	Assistant Bursar	Ms. Debra OLIVER
41	Athletic Director	Ms. Dorianne JOHNSON
51	Director of CLIMB Program	Mr. Javan REED
25	Director Title III/Sponsored Pgms	Ms. Veronica WELLS
19	Safety and Security Administrator	Mr. Lawrence MACK

Wilmington College (I)

1870 Quaker Way, Wilmington OH 45177-2499
County: Clinton FICE Identification: 003142
Unit ID: 206507
Telephone: (937) 382-6661 Carnegie Class: Bac-Diverse
FAX Number: (937) 383-8574 Calendar System: Semester
URL: www.wilmington.edu
Established: 1870 Annual Undergrad Tuition & Fees: $25,000
Enrollment: 1,112 Coed
Affiliation or Control: Friends IRS Status: 501(c)3
Highest Offering: Master's
Accreditation: NH, CAATE, CAEPT

Code	Title	Name
01	President	Dr. James M. REYNOLDS
04	Assistant to the President	Mrs. Leslie A. NICHOLS
05	Vice President Academic Affairs	Dr. Erika A. GOODWIN
10	Vice President Business/Finance	Mr. Bradley J. MITCHELL
30	Vice President College Advancement	Mr. Matt WAHRHAFTIG
88	Vice President External Programs	Ms. Sylvia STEVENS
32	Vice Pres Student Affs/Stdnt Life	Ms. Sigrid B. SOLOMON
41	Vice President Athletic Admin	Dr. Terry A. RUPERT
84	Chief Enrollment Officer/Admissions	Mr. Dennis KELLY
20	Assoc Vice Pres Academic Affairs	Dr. Mei Mei BURR
35	Assoc Vice Pres Student Activities	Mr. Kenneth A. LYDY
09	AVP Acad Affs/Institutional Effect	Ms. Katie BONTRAGER
26	Director of Public Relations	Mr. Randall F. SARVIS
06	Registrar/Academic Records	Ms. Sue HUTCHENS
08	Director of Watson Library	Ms. Lucinda CHANDLER
15	Director of Human Resources	Ms. Libby HAYES
36	Director of Career Services	Ms. Nina TALLEY
18	Director of Physical Plant	Mr. Terry L. JOHNSON
29	Dir Alumni/Parent Rels/Advancement	Ms. Kathy L. MILAM
37	Dir Financial Aid/One Stop Center	Ms. Cheryl LOUALLEN
07	Director of Admission	Mr. Adam LOHREY
96	Purchasing Manager	Ms. Laura BAESSLER

Wilmington College Blue Ash Branch (J)

9987 Carver Road, Blue Ash OH 45242
Telephone: (513) 793-1337 Identification: 770364
Accreditation: &NH

Winebrenner Theological Seminary (K)

950 N Main Street, Findlay OH 45840-3652
County: Hancock FICE Identification: 004060
Unit ID: 206516
Telephone: (419) 434-4200 Carnegie Class: Spec-4-yr-Faith
FAX Number: (419) 434-4267 Calendar System: Trimester
URL: www.winebrenner.edu
Established: 1942 Annual Graduate Tuition & Fees: N/A
Enrollment: 74 Coed
Affiliation or Control: Independent Non-Profit IRS Status: 501(c)3
Highest Offering: Doctorate; No Undergraduates
Accreditation: NH, THEOL

01 President/CEO Dr. Brent C. SLEASMAN
111 VP Institutional Advance/Dir Dev Dr. Gregory GUZMAN
05 VP of Academic Advancement Dr. Joel COCKLIN
10 Director of Finance Mr. Tom WEAVER
84 Director of Enrollment Management Mr. James SMARKEL
08 College Librarian Mrs. Margaret HIRSCHY
06 Registrar Ms. Shari BUIS
04 Assistant to the President Vacant
108 Director Institutional Assessment Dr. Kathryn HELLEMAN

Wittenberg University (A)

PO Box 720, Springfield OH 45501-0720
County: Clark FICE Identification: 003143
Unit ID: 206525
Telephone: (937) 327-6231 Carnegie Class: Bac-A&S
FAX Number: (937) 327-6340 Calendar System: Semester
URL: www.wittenberg.edu
Established: 1845 Annual Undergrad Tuition & Fees: $38,090
Enrollment: 1,876 Coed
Affiliation or Control: Evangelical Lutheran Church In America
IRS Status: 501(c)3
Highest Offering: Master's
Accreditation: NH, CAEPN, MUS, NURSE

01 President Dr. Michael FRANDSEN
05 Interim Provost Dr. Mary Jo ZEMBAR
10 Vice Pres Finance/Administration Mr. Randal FREEBOURN
32 Vice Pres Student Development Vacant
46 Vice Pres Strategic Initiatives Dr. Ty BUCKMAN
30 Vice Pres Advancement Ms. Wendy KOBLER
26 Vice Pres Marketing/Communications Ms. Karen GERBOTH
20 Asst Provost Academic Services Dr. Mary Jo ZEMBAR
31 Dean School Community Education Dr. Thomas KAPLAN
35 Dean of Students Ms. Casey GILL
88 Assoc Dean Student Success/Retent Mr. Jonathan DURAJ
85 Director International Education Ms. JoAnn BENNETT
42 Pastor to the University Rev. Rachel SANDUM TUNE
08 Director of the Library Mr. Douglas K. LEHMAN
13 Chief Information Officer Mr. Richard MICKOOL
31 Director Community Service Ms. Kristen L. COLLIER
06 Registrar Ms. Debra LOVELESS
41 Director Athletics/Recreation Dr. Gary WILLIAMS
58 Director Graduate Studies in Educ Dr. Roberta LINDER
94 Director of Women's Studies Dr. Heather H. WRIGHT
09 Asst Prov Acad Affs/Inst Research Dr. Darby L. HILLER-FREUND
29 Director of Alumni Relations Ms. Linda M. BEALS
27 Sports Information Director Mr. Kuris DUGGAN
105 Webmaster Mr. Ryan MAURER
39 Associate Dean for Residence Life Ms. Sherri SADOWSKI
38 Director Student Counseling Ms. Amanda ADDY
88 Director Fraternity & Sorority Life Ms. Carol NICKOSON
28 Assoc Dean Multicultural Affairs Mr. John YOUNG
07 Exec Director of Admission Ms. Karen HUNT
37 Exec Director of Financial Aid Mr. Jonathan RANDY GREEN
18 Asst VP Plant/Safety & Environment Vacant
15 Director Human Resources Ms. Mary Beth WALTER
19 Chief of Police Mr. Jim HUTCHINS
40 Manager of Bookstore Ms. Amy DALTON

Wright State University Main Campus (B)

3640 Colonel Glenn Highway, Dayton OH 45435-0001
County: Greene FICE Identification: 003078
Unit ID: 206604
Telephone: (937) 775-3333 Carnegie Class: DU-Mod
FAX Number: (937) 775-3301 Calendar System: Semester
URL: www.wright.edu
Established: 1964 Annual Undergrad Tuition & Fees (In-State): $8,730
Enrollment: 17,070 Coed
Affiliation or Control: State IRS Status: 501(c)3
Highest Offering: Doctorate
Accreditation: NH, CAATE, CACREP, CAEPN, CEA, CLPSY, CS, ENG, EXSC, IPSY, MED, MT, MUS, NURSE, PH, SPAA, SW

01 President Dr. Cheryl B. SCHRADER
05 Provost Dr. Thomas A. SUDKAMP
10 Vice Pres Business and Finance Mr. Jeff ULLIMAN
32 Interim VP Student Affairs Dr. Gary DICKSTEIN
46 Vice Pres Research/Graduate Studies Dr. Robert FYFFE
111 Vice Pres University Advancement Ms. Rebecca S. COLE
84 Vice Pres Enrollment Management Ms. Mary Ellen ASHLEY
20 VP Instruction & Curriculum Dr. Thomas A. SUDKAMP
58 Dean Sch Graduate Studies Dr. Robert FYFFE
08 University Librarian Mrs. Sheila G. SHELLABARGER
15 Assoc Vice Pres for Human Resources Ms. Shari MICKEY-BOGGS
50 Int Dean Raj Soin Col of Business Dr. Thomas L. TRAYNOR
53 Dean Education/Human Services Dr. Joseph E. KEFERL
54 Dean Engineering/Computer Science Dr. Nathan W. KLINGBEIL
12 Dean WSU Lake Campus Dr. Jay ALBAYYARI
49 Dean Liberal Arts Dr. Linda CARON
66 Int Dean College Nursing & Health Dr. Deborah L. ULRICH
63 Dean Boonshaft School of Medicine Dr. Margaret DUNN
83 Dean Sch of Prof Psychology Dr. LaPearl Logan WINFREY
81 Dean Science/Mathematics Dr. Douglas W. LEAMAN
06 Registrar Ms. Amanda STEELE-MIDDLETON
13 Chief Information Officer Mr. Craig WOOLLEY
46 Asst VP Research/Sponsored Pgms Ms. Ellen REINSCH FRIESE
36 Director Career Services Ms. Cheryl STUART
37 Director of Financial Aid Ms. Amy BARNHART
38 Director Counsel/Wellness Svcs Dr. Robert A. RANDO
29 Exec Director Alumni Relations Mr. Gregory SCHARER
22 Chief Diversity Officer Mr. Matt BOAZ
22 Director Disability Services Mr. Tom WEBB
86 Assoc VP Public Affairs Mr. Robert E. HICKEY, JR.
41 Director of Athletics Mr. Bob GRANT
43 General Counsel Mr. Larry CHAN
40 Store Manager Ms. Jennifer L. GEBHART
85 Director Intl Student/Scholar Svcs Mr. Steven J. LYONS
39 Director Residence Services Mr. Daniel BERTSOS
19 Chief Police Department Mr. David A. FINNIE
92 Director Honors Program Dr. Susan CARRAFIELLO
94 Director Womens Studies Program Dr. Hope JENNINGS
09 Asst VP Institutional Research Mr. Craig THIS
04 Executive Asst to President Ms. Teresa M. BEDWELL
102 CFO WSU Foundation Mr. Robert BATSON
44 Director Annual Giving Ms. Amy N. SHOPE JONES
101 Secretary of the Board Mr. Larry CHAN
26 Director Communications Mr. Seth BAUGUESS

Wright State University Lake Campus (C)

7600 Lake Campus Drive, Celina OH 45822-2952
Telephone: (419) 586-0300 FICE Identification: 009169
Accreditation: &NH

† Regional accreditation is carried under the parent institution in Dayton, OH.

Xavier University (D)

3800 Victory Parkway, Cincinnati OH 45207-1096
County: Hamilton FICE Identification: 003144
Unit ID: 206622
Telephone: (513) 745-3000 Carnegie Class: Masters/L
FAX Number: (513) 745-4223 Calendar System: Semester
URL: www.xavier.edu
Established: 1831 Annual Undergrad Tuition & Fees: $36,150
Enrollment: 6,260 Coed
Affiliation or Control: Roman Catholic IRS Status: 501(c)3
Highest Offering: Doctorate
Accreditation: NH, CAATE, CACREP, CAEPT, CEA, CLPSY, HSA, MACTE, MUS, NURSE, OT, RAD, SW

01 President Rev. Michael J. GRAHAM, SJ
11 Administrative Vice President Dr. John F. KUCIA
05 Provost/Chief Academic Officer Dr. Melissa J. BAUMANN
10 Exec VP Financial Admin/CFO Ms. Maribeth AMYOT
26 Vice Pres for University Relations Mr. Gary R. MASSA
88 Asst to Pres for Mission & Identity Dr. Debra MOONEY
13 Exec Dir Information Technologies Mr. Mark BROCKMAN
28 Chief Diversity/Inclusion Officer Dr. Janice B. WALKER
27 Director Strategic Communications Ms. Kelly LEON
30 Assoc VP for University Relations Ms. Susan ABEL
32 Assoc Provost for Student Affairs Dr. David J. JOHNSON
18 Vice President for Facilities Mr. Robert M. SHEERAN
41 Director Athletics Mr. Greg CHRISTOPHER
15 Assoc Vice Pres for Human Resources Mrs. Connie PERME
84 Vice Pres Enrollment Management Mr. Aaron MEIS
44 Exec Dir Gifts & Estate Planning Mr. Mark MCLAUGHLIN
42 Dir Center for Mission/Identity Mr. Joseph P. SHADLE
06 Registrar Dr. Andrea WAWRZUSIN
85 Exec Dir Center for Intl Education Ms. Lea MINNITI
27 AVP Marketing & Communications Mr. Doug RUSCHMAN
39 Sr Dir Student Affairs/Ofc Res Life Ms. Lori A. LAMBERT
40 Director of Bookstore Mr. Michael HUBBARD
86 Director of Government Relations Mr. Sean COMER
83 Dean Col of Professional Sciences Dr. Paul GORE
07 Dir Enrol Events/Campaign/Ext Rels Ms. Lauren COBBLE
35 Senior Director Student Affairs Ms. Leah BUSAM KLENOWSKI
49 Dean College Arts & Sciences Dr. David MENGEL
19 Dir Public Safety/Chief of Police Chief Joseph MILEK
37 Director of Financial Aid Ms. Donna SALAK
43 General Counsel/Sec of the Board Joseph H. FELDHAUS, ESQ
29 Dir Alumni Rels/Ex Dir Athletic Dev Mr. Brian MALEY
09 Dir Office Institutional Research Mrs. Emily SHIPLEY
50 Dean Williams College of Business Dr. Thomas HAYES
51 Director Weekend Degree Program Ms. Patricia MEYER
96 Dir Purchasing & Supply Management Mr. John MERCER
88 Dir TRIO Student Support Services Dr. Daniel MCSPADDEN

Youngstown State University (E)

One University Plaza, Youngstown OH 44555-0001
County: Mahoning FICE Identification: 003145
Unit ID: 206695
Telephone: (330) 941-3001 Carnegie Class: Masters/L
FAX Number: (330) 941-7169 Calendar System: Semester
URL: www.ysu.edu
Established: 1908 Annual Undergrad Tuition & Fees (In-State): $8,317
Enrollment: 12,442 Coed
Affiliation or Control: State IRS Status: 501(c)3
Highest Offering: Doctorate
Accreditation: NH, AAFCS, ANEST, ART, CACREP, CAEPN, COARC, COARCP, DH, DIETC, DIETD, DIETT, EMT, ENG, ENGT, MAC, MLTAD, MUS, NUR, PH, PTA, SW, THEA

01 President Mr. James P. TRESSEL
05 Provost & VP for Academic Affairs Dr. Martin ABRAHAM
10 Vice Pres Finance & Business Op Mr. Neal P. MCNALLY
26 Assoc VP for University Relations Mrs. Shannon TIRONE
32 Assoc VP for Student Experience Dr. Eddie HOWARD, JR.
84 Assoc Vice Pres Enrollment Mgmt Mr. Gary D. SWEGAN
43 Vice President and General Counsel Ms. Holly A. JACOBS
49 Dean Liberal Arts/Soc Science Dr. Kristine BLAIR
50 Dean of Business Administration Dr. Betty Jo LICATA
53 Dean of Education Dr. Charles HOWELL
81 Dean of Science/Tech/Eng/Math Dr. Wim F. STEELANT
57 Dean Creative Arts & Communication Dr. Phyllis M. PAUL
76 Dean Health & Human Services Dr. Joseph L. MOSCA
58 Dean College of Graduate Studies Dr. Salvatore A. SANDERS
45 Assoc Provost Acad Pgms/Planning Dr. Kevin BALL
15 Chief Human Resources Officer Mr. Kevin W. REYNOLDS
13 Director Computer Services Mr. Richard J. MARSICO
41 Exec Director of Athletics Mr. Ronald A. STROLLO
121 Int Assoc VP for Student Success Dr. Mike CRIST
08 Manager Library Operations Ms. Anna TORRES
29 Dir University Events & Protocol Ms. Jacquelyn LEVISEUR
28 AVP Multicultural Affairs Dr. Sylvia J. IMLER
07 Director Undergrad Recruit/Admiss Ms. Sue E. DAVIS
06 Registrar Ms. Jeanne HERMAN
19 Chief of University Police Mr. Shawn V. VARSO
18 Executive Director Facilities Mr. John P. HYDEN
21 Director Student Accts/Receivables Ms. Gloria KOBUS
23 Dir Environ/Occup Health & Safety Mr. Daniel SAHLI
37 Director Financial/Scholarships Ms. Elaine RUSE
21 Director General Accounting Ms. Katrena J. DAVIDSON
21 Cash Management Officer Mr. David EDWARDS
25 Director Grants & Sponsored Pgms Mr. Andrew P. SHEPARD-SMITH
39 Director Housing Services Ms. Kate FITZGERALD
85 AVP for International & Global Init Dr. Nathan R. MYERS
30 Director of Development Ms. Catherine CALA
28 Director Student Diversity Programs Mr. William J. BLAKE
88 Dir Assoc Degree/Tech Prep Pgms Ms. Arlene FLOYD
88 Director Support Services Mr. Danny J. O'CONNELL
88 Dir Electronic Maintenance Svcs Mr. Michael REPETSKI
90 Director Media/Acad Computing Mr. Michael S. HRISHENKO
92 Director Univ Scholars/Honors Pgm Dr. Ronald SHAKLEE
91 IT Operations Mr. James YUKECH
35 Dir Campus Rec/Intramural Sports Ms. Joy POLKABLA-BYERS
88 Director WYSU-FM Mr. Gary SEXTON
04 Exec Assistant to President Ms. Cynthia M. BELL
106 Dir Online Education/E-learning Ms. Millie RODRIGUEZ
86 Director Government Relations Dr. William C. BINNING
81 Dean of STEM Dr. Wim STEELANT
103 Dir Career and Academic Advising Ms. Christina HARDY
104 Assoc Provost Intl Programs Dr. Nathan MYERS
108 Director Institutional Assessment Ms. Hillary FUHRMAN
22 Dir Affirmative Action/EEO Ms. Cynthia KRAVITZ
38 Director Student Counseling Dr. Ann JARANSKI

Zane State College (F)

9900 Brick Church Road, Cambridge OH 43725
Telephone: (740) 432-6568 Identification: 770365
Accreditation: &NH

Zane State College (G)

1555 Newark Road, Zanesville OH 43701-2626
County: Muskingum FICE Identification: 008133
Unit ID: 204255
Telephone: (740) 454-2501 Carnegie Class: Assoc/MT-VT-Mix Trad/Non
FAX Number: (740) 454-0035 Calendar System: Semester
URL: www.zanestate.edu
Established: 1969 Annual Undergrad Tuition & Fees (In-State): $4,646
Enrollment: 3,362 Coed
Affiliation or Control: State IRS Status: 501(c)3
Highest Offering: Associate Degree
Accreditation: NH, ACBSP, ACFEI, CAHIIM, ENGT, MAC, MLTAD, OTA, PTAA, RAD

01 President Dr. Chad M. BROWN
111 Exec Dir Inst Advancemnt/Foundation Mr. Anthony ADORNETTO
05 Provost/Chief Academic Officer Dr. Richard WOODFIELD
10 Chief Financial Officer Ms. Terri M. BALDWIN
84 Chief Enrollment Officer Mr. Nick WELCH
54 Acad Dean Business & Engineering Mr. Randy WHARTON
103 Assoc Dean Workforce Development Ms. Tracey TONNOUS
15 Chief Human Resources Officer Dr. James KEMPER
13 Exec Dir of ITS Mr. Joseph KEATING
08 Library Director Ms. Janelle HUBBLE
09 Dir of Inst Effectiveness & Plng Mr. Andrew MORRISON
25 Director of Grants & Contracts Vacant
07 Dir of Admissions & Recruitment Mrs. Jody BURCHETT
37 Director Student Financial Aid Ms. Amanda B. REISINGER
36 Director Career/Employment Services Ms. Jamie K. CLARK
26 Director Marketing & Communications Mr. Nick WELCH
38 Dir of One Stop Mr. Kevin HURST
21 Comptroller Ms. Tammy S. HUFFMAN
40 Director of Bookstore Operations Ms. Vicki MITCHELL
76 Dean Health/Liberal Arts/Public Svc Dr. Barbara SHELBY
06 Asst Dean Curriculum/Registrar Ms. Theresa KOLK-CONNER
18 Director Facilities Management Mr. Todd TACKER
04 Administrative Asst to President Mrs. Julie A. MACLAINE
106 Dir Online Education/E-learning Mr. Phil WENTWORTH

OKLAHOMA

Bacone College (H)

2299 Old Bacone Road, Muskogee OK 74403-1568
County: Muskogee FICE Identification: 003147
Unit ID: 206817
Telephone: (918) 683-4581 Carnegie Class: Bac/Assoc-Mixed

FAX Number: (918) 781-7422 Calendar System: Semester
URL: www.bacone.edu
Established: 1880 Annual Undergrad Tuition & Fees: $14,850
Enrollment: 839 Coed
Affiliation or Control: American Baptist IRS Status: 501(c)3
Highest Offering: Baccalaureate
Accreditation: NH, IACBE, NURSE, RAD

01 President ... Mr. Franklin K. WILLIS
05 Provost ... Vacant
20 Interim VP of Academic Affairs ... Dr. Jeffrey DUPREE
32 VP of Student Affairs ... Mr. Kindle HOLDERBY
10 VP Finance ... Mr. Mustafa YUNDEM
88 Director Center for American Indian ... Dr. Patricia J. KING
30 Director of Development ... Vacant
42 Chair Christian Ministry ... Rev Dr. Leroy THOMPSON
32 Director of Student Life/Housing ... Vacant
06 Registrar ... Mrs. Virginia THOMPSON
40 Bookstore Manager ... Ms. Dawn OSBORNE
41 Asst VP Athletics ... Mr. Alan FOSTER
37 Interim Director Financial Aid ... Ms. Marcia CHEERS
15 Director Human Resources ... Ms. Jeanetta RAINWATER
07 Director of Admissions ... Vacant
108 Coord Institutional Assessment Data ... Ms. Linda MILAM
08 Dir Betts Library/Head Librarian ... Vacant
13 Director of Network Systems ... Mr. Chris EHLERS
04 Assistant to President ... Ms. Marcia TAYLOR
19 Chief of Campus Police ... Mr. Brad BEESLEY

Cameron University (A)

2800 W Gore Boulevard, Lawton OK 73505-6377
County: Comanche FICE Identification: 003150
Unit ID: 206914
Telephone: (580) 581-2200 Carnegie Class: Masters/M
FAX Number: (580) 581-2867 Calendar System: Semester
URL: www.cameron.edu
Established: 1908 Annual Undergrad Tuition & Fees (In-State): $5,970
Enrollment: 5,177 Coed
Affiliation or Control: State IRS Status: 501(c)3
Highest Offering: Master's
Accreditation: NH, ACBSP, CAEPN, COARC, MUS, RAD

01 President ... Dr. John M. MCARTHUR
05 Vice President for Academic Affairs .. Dr. Ronna J. VANDERSLICE
10 Vice Pres for Business & Finance ... Ms. Ninette CARTER
30 Vice Pres University Advancement ... Mr. Albert D. JOHNSON, JR.
84 VP for Enroll Mgmt & Stdnt Success ... Mr. Jerrett PHILLIPS
20 Assoc Vice Pres Academic Affairs ... Dr. Sylvia BURGESS
20 Asst Vice Pres Academic Affairs ... Dr. Margery KINGSLEY
49 Dean School of Arts and Sciences ... Dr. Von E. UNDERWOOD
58 Dean Sch of Grad and Prof Studies ... Dr. Lisa HUFFMAN
12 Director Duncan Campus ... Ms. Susan CAMP
21 Controller ... Ms. Lindsey BILLEN
26 Senior Director of Public Affairs ... Mr. Keith MITCHELL
29 Director Develop & Alumni Relations ... Ms. Lorie GARRISON
41 Director Athletic Administration ... Mr. Jim C. JACKSON
07 Director of Admissions ... Ms. Brenda DALLY
06 Registrar ... Mrs. Linda PHILLIPS
09 Dir Inst Rsrch/Assess/Accountabity ... Dr. Karla OTY
37 Director of Financial Assistance ... Mr. Gary GAROFFOLO
13 Director Information Tech Services ... Mr. Kelly MCCLURE
15 Director of Human Resources ... Mr. Gordon SHAW
36 Director of Student Development ... Dr. Jennifer PRUCHNICKI
32 Dean of Students ... Mr. Zeak NAIFEH
19 Director Public Safety ... Mr. John DEBOARD
18 Director Physical Facilities ... Mr. Robert HANEFIELD
96 Purchasing Agent ... Mr. Richard MCCOMAS
22 EEO Officer/Title IX Coordinator ... Mr. Thomas RUSSELL

Carl Albert State College (B)

1507 S McKenna, Poteau OK 74953-5208
County: Le Flore FICE Identification: 003176
Unit ID: 206923
Telephone: (918) 647-1200 Carnegie Class: Assoc/HT-High Trad
FAX Number: (918) 647-1201 Calendar System: Semester
URL: www.carlalbert.edu
Established: 1933 Annual Undergrad Tuition & Fees (In-State): $3,160
Enrollment: 2,276 Coed
Affiliation or Control: State IRS Status: 501(c)3
Highest Offering: Associate Degree
Accreditation: NH, ACBSP, ADNUR, PTAA

01 President ... Mr. Jay FALKNER
32 VP for Student Affairs/Athletic Dir ... Mr. Randy GRAVES
05 Vice President of Academic Affairs ... Mr. Marc WILLIS
10 Chief Financial Officer ... Mr. Brian ROBERTS
84 VP of Enrollment Mgmt ... Ms. Jennifer HUMPHREYS
13 Director Information Technology ... Mr. Michael MARTIN
101 Secy of the Board/Exec Asst to Pres ... Ms. Jean Ann BARLOW
26 Dir Public Relations/Marketing ... Ms. Judi WHITE
06 Registrar/VA Coordinator ... Ms. Dee Ann DICKERSON
37 Director of Financial Aid ... Ms. Robin BENSON
88 TRIO Director ... Ms. Michelle WHITE
08 Director of Libraries ... Ms. Terri CARROLL
18 Director of Physical Plant ... Mr. Chuck LEWIS
15 Human Resources Dir/Title IX Coord ... Ms. Vicki SULLIVAN
21 Business Office Manager ... Ms. Amanda WILSON
108 Inst Effectiv Off/Assmt Out Spec ... Ms. Kelly KELLOG
102 Exec Dir of CASC Dev Foundation ... Ms. Mandy ROBERTS
106 Dev English Instr/Coord Vir Campus ... Ms. Sarah BROWN
19 Instructor/Campus Police Coord ... Mr. Chad BROWN

Carl Albert State College (C)

1507 S. McKenna, Poteau OK 74953
Telephone: (918) 647-1473 Identification: 770366
Accreditation: &NH

Clary Sage College (D)

3131 South Sheridan Road, Tulsa OK 74145-1102
Telephone: (918) 298-8200 Identification: 666368
Accreditation: ACICS

† Branch campus of Community Care College, Tulsa, OK.

College of the Muscogee Nation (E)

PO Box 917, 2170 Raven Circle, Okmulgee OK 74447
County: Okmulgee Identification: 667122
Unit ID: 480967
Telephone: (918) 549-2800 Carnegie Class: Tribal
FAX Number: (918) 759-6930 Calendar System: Semester
URL: www.cmn.edu
Established: 1994 Annual Undergrad Tuition & Fees: $6,600
Enrollment: 202 Coed
Affiliation or Control: Tribal Control IRS Status: 501(c)3
Highest Offering: Associate Degree
Accreditation: NH

01 President ... Mr. Robert BIBLE
05 Dean of Academic Affairs ... Mr. Monte RANDALL

Community Care College (F)

4242 S Sheridan Road, Tulsa OK 74145-1119
County: Tulsa FICE Identification: 033674
Unit ID: 439570
Telephone: (918) 610-0027 Carnegie Class: Spec 2-yr-Health
FAX Number: (918) 610-0029 Calendar System: Other
URL: www.communitycarecollege.edu
Established: 1995 Annual Undergrad Tuition & Fees: N/A
Enrollment: 633 Coed
Affiliation or Control: Independent Non-Profit IRS Status: 501(c)3
Highest Offering: Associate Degree
Accreditation: ACICS, MAAB, SURGT

01 President ... Dr. Kelly BAILEY

Connors State College (G)

700 College Road, Warner OK 74469-9700
County: Muskogee FICE Identification: 003153
Unit ID: 206996
Telephone: (918) 463-2931 Carnegie Class: Assoc/HT-High Trad
FAX Number: (918) 463-2233 Calendar System: Semester
URL: www.connorsstate.edu
Established: 1908 Annual Undergrad Tuition & Fees (In-State): $3,210
Enrollment: 2,303 Coed
Affiliation or Control: State IRS Status: 501(c)3
Highest Offering: Associate Degree
Accreditation: NH, ADNUR

01 President ... Dr. Ron RAMMING
05 VP for Academic Affairs ... Vacant
10 VP for Fiscal Services ... Mr. Mike LEWIS
30 Assoc VP for External Affairs ... Vacant
37 Director of Financial Aid ... Ms. Mattie ENGLISH
08 Director of Learning Center ... Ms. Ona BRITTON-SPEARS
13 Director of Information Technology ... Vacant
06 Registrar ... Ms. Kwanna KING
07 Director of Recruitment ... Ms. Logan KNAPPER
26 Director of Public Information ... Vacant
15 Director of Human Resources ... Mr. Nate WALKER
09 Director of Institutional Research ... Vacant
41 Athletic Director ... Mr. Bill MUSE
32 Dean of Students ... Mr. Mike JACKSON
19 Chief of Police ... Mr. James MENDENHALL
04 Executive Asst to the President ... Ms. Cindy ANDERSON
108 Asst VP Acad/Stdt Affs/Assessment ... Vacant
20 Asst VP Acad/Stdt Affs/Acad Support ... Ms. Robin O'QUINN

Connors State College Muskogee Port Branch Campus (H)

2501 N 41st Street East, Muskogee OK 74403
Telephone: (918) 687-6747 Identification: 770367
Accreditation: &NH, @PTAA

East Central University (I)

1100 E 14th Street, Ada OK 74820-6899
County: Pontotoc FICE Identification: 003154
Unit ID: 207041
Telephone: (580) 332-8000 Carnegie Class: Masters/L
FAX Number: (580) 332-1623 Calendar System: Semester
URL: www.ecok.edu
Established: 1909 Annual Undergrad Tuition & Fees (In-State): $6,279
Enrollment: 4,444 Coed
Affiliation or Control: State IRS Status: 501(c)3
Highest Offering: Master's
Accreditation: NH, ACBSP, #CAATE, CACREP, CAEPN, MUS, NUR, SW

01 President ... Dr. Katricia PIERSON
05 Acting Provost/VP Academic Affairs ... Dr. Adrianna LANCASTER
10 Exec VP Administration/Finance ... Ms. Jessica KILBY
32 VP Student Development ... Dr. Gerald FORBES
20 Asst VP Academic Affairs ... Dr. Adrianna LANCASTER
35 AVP Student Devel/Dean of Students ... Dr. Boomer APPLEMAN
53 Dean College of Educ & Psych ... Dr. Brenda SHERBOURNE
50 Dean School of Business ... Mr. Wendell GODWIN
81 Dean College of Health & Sciences ... Dr. Carl GILBERT
49 Dean College of Lib Arts & Soc Sci ... Dr. Katherine LANG
58 Dean College of Grad Studies ... Dr. Brenda SHERBOURNE
06 Registrar ... Ms. Adeidra SIMMONS
13 Director Information Technology ... Mr. Jeremy BENNETT
09 Director Institutional Research ... Ms. Meredith JONES
26 Director Mktg & Communication ... Ms. Amy FORD
41 Director Athletics ... Dr. Jeff WILLIAMS
18 Director Facilities Mgmt ... Mr. Darryl OVERSTREET
15 Director Employment Services ... Mr. Ty ANDERSON
29 Director Alumni Relations ... Ms. Ashia HILLMAN
07 Director Admissions ... Mr. Sheppard MCCONNELL
96 Director Purchasing ... Ms. Jo Ann JOHNSON
37 Director Financial Aid ... Ms. Becky ISAACS
08 Director Library ... Ms. Dana BELCHER
23 Director Stdnt Health Services ... Ms. Lisa YOUNG
39 Director Housing & Resid Life ... Ms. Debbie CHALMERS
38 Director Stdnt Counseling Ctr ... Ms. Jennifer COX
85 Director Intl Student Pgms & Svcs ... Ms. Jessika BAILEY
108 Director Assessment ... Dr. Robin ROBERSON
25 Director Grants & Research ... Ms. Leah LYON
20 Director Academic Services ... Ms. Holly SEWELL
22 Director Testing & Accssbility Svcs ... Ms. Kim ROGERS
21 Controller ... Ms. Susie SHOCKEY
113 Bursar ... Mr. Brian HAMPTON
19 Chief of University Police ... Mr. Bert MILLER

Eastern Oklahoma State College (J)

1301 W Main Street, Wilburton OK 74578-4999
County: Latimer FICE Identification: 003155
Unit ID: 207050
Telephone: (918) 465-2361 Carnegie Class: Assoc/HT-High Trad
FAX Number: (918) 465-2431 Calendar System: Semester
URL: www.eosc.edu
Established: 1909 Annual Undergrad Tuition & Fees (In-State): $4,224
Enrollment: 1,608 Coed
Affiliation or Control: State IRS Status: 501(c)3
Highest Offering: Associate Degree
Accreditation: NH, ADNUR, MLTAD

01 President ... Dr. Stephen E. SMITH
05 Vice President of Academic Affairs ... Dr. Janet WANSICK
10 Vice Pres of Business Affairs ... Ms. La Donna HOWELL
32 Vice Pres for Student Affairs ... Dr. Steve G. GLAZIER
12 Dean of McAlester Campus ... Ms. Ann BROOKS
35 Director of Student Life ... Mr. Bryan DENNY
41 Athletic Director ... Mr. Kirk KELLEY
30 Exec Dir Development/Alumni Rels ... Mrs. Treva KENNEDY
26 Dir Marketing/Communications ... Mrs. Trish MCBEATH
09 Director of Institutional Research ... Dr. Janet WANSICK
20 Associate Academic Officer ... Dr. Janet WANSICK
84 Dir Enrollment Mgmt/Financial Aid ... Dr. Steve GLAZIER
13 Chief Technical Officer ... Mr. Jeff WEEMS
08 Director Library & Media Services ... Ms. Maria MARTINEZ
15 Director Human Resources ... Mrs. Joyce BILLS
06 Registrar/Admissions ... Mrs. Jennifer LABOR
18 Int Dir Physical Plant Operations ... Mr. Alan MOSS
44 Dir of Institutional Advancement ... Mrs. Treva KENNEDY
37 Financial Aid Director ... Ms. Mimi KELLEY
19 Campus Police Chief ... Mr. Bryan DENNY

Family of Faith Christian University (K)

PO Box 1805, Shawnee OK 74802-1805
County: Pottawatomie FICE Identification: 036763
Unit ID: 443058
Telephone: (405) 695-5533 Carnegie Class: Spec-4-yr-Faith
FAX Number: (405) 273-8535 Calendar System: Semester
URL: www.familyoffaith.edu
Established: 1992 Annual Undergrad Tuition & Fees: $6,220
Enrollment: 32 Coed
Affiliation or Control: Independent Non-Profit IRS Status: 501(c)3
Highest Offering: Baccalaureate
Accreditation: BI

01 President ... Dr. Samuel W. MATTHEWS
05 Provost ... Mrs. Elaine W. PHILLIPS
10 Vice Pres Operations/Finance ... Mr. Daniel MATTHEWS
32 Vice Pres Student Affs/Dir Fin Aid ... Mrs. Dara GILLIAM
20 Vice President Academic Affairs ... Ms. Bonnie CARRERA
46 Director of Resource Development ... Vacant
42 Director of Spiritual Life ... Mr. Daniel J. MATTHEWS
108 Dir of Accreditation/Assessment ... Mrs. Elaine W. PHILLIPS
104 Director of International Studies ... Mrs. Dara GILLIAM

Langston University (L)

PO Box 1500, Langston OK 73050
County: Logan FICE Identification: 003157
Unit ID: 207209
Telephone: (405) 466-2231 Carnegie Class: Masters/M
FAX Number: N/A Calendar System: Semester
URL: www.langston.edu

Established: 1897 Annual Undergrad Tuition & Fees (In-State): $5,734
Enrollment: 2,543 Coed
Affiliation or Control: State IRS Status: 501(c)3
Highest Offering: Doctorate
Accreditation: NH, ACBSP, CACREP, CAEPN, NUR, PTA

01 President Dr. Kent J. SMITH, JR.
05 Vice President Academic Affairs Dr. Clyde MONTGOMERY, JR.
10 VP Fiscal/Admin Affairs Helen RAMBO
32 VP Student Affairs Vacant
30 VP Inst Development/External Affs Mrs. Mautra JONES
100 Chief of Staff Ms. Theresa D. GRAVES
13 Chief Information Officer Mr. Pritchard MONCRIFFE
20 Assoc VP Academic Affairs LU/ OKC Mrs. Alice STRONG-SIMMONS
20 Assoc VP Academic Affs LU/Tulsa Dr. Lisa K. WEIS
114 Asst VP of Accounting/Budgeting Ms. Nykkia HARRIS
35 Interim Dean of Students Mr. Joshua BUSBY
29 Director Alumni Affairs Mrs. Vonnie W. ROBERTS
36 Director of Career & Prof Develop Ms. Bianca BRYANT
26 Director Public Relations Mrs. Mautra JONES
07 Director of Admissions Mr. Jeremy LANE
37 Director Financial Aid Ms. Shelia R. MCGILL
15 Director of Human Resources Mrs. Cynthia S. BUCKLEY
18 Director Facilities Vacant
38 Director of Counseling Services Dr. Jason K. WHITE
09 Director Inst Research & Planning Dr. Carol S. CAWYER
08 Director of Libraries Ms. Bettye R. BLACK
06 Registrar Ms. Deleanor A. KIRKPATRICK
41 Athletic Director Mrs. Donnita ROGERS
58 Director of Graduate Programs Dr. Marsha HERRON
19 Chief of Police Mr. Demario HOLLAND
96 Purchasing Manager Mrs. Charlotte BROWN
49 Dean School of Arts & Sciences Dr. Alonzo PETERSON
50 Dean School of Business Dr. Joshua M. SNAVELY
46 Dean School Agric/Applied Science Dr. Wesley WHITTAKER
66 Dean School of Nursing/Hlth Profess Dr. Teressa HUNTER
53 Dean School of Education/Behav Sci Dr. Ruth R. JACKSON
88 Dean School of Physical Therapy Dr. Aliya CHAUDRY
88 Director Entrepreneurial Studies Dr. Sharron HUNTER-RAINEY
84 Exec Director Enrollment Mgmt Mr. Chauncey J. JACKSON
04 Executive Asst to President Ms. Elaine C. PRESTON
39 Director Student Housing Mr. Ricky JENKINS
44 Annual Giving Officer Ms. Jillian WHITAKER

Langston University Oklahoma City Campus (A)

6700 Martin Luther King Ave, Oklahoma City OK 73111
Telephone: (405) 962-1620 Identification: 770370
Accreditation: &NH

Langston University Tulsa Campus (B)

914 North Greenwood, Tulsa OK 74106
Telephone: (918) 877-8100 Identification: 770371
Accreditation: &NH

Mid-America Christian University (C)

3500 SW 119th Street, Oklahoma City OK 73170-4500
County: Cleveland FICE Identification: 006942
Unit ID: 245953
Telephone: (405) 691-3800 Carnegie Class: Masters/M
FAX Number: (405) 692-3165 Calendar System: Semester
URL: www.macu.edu
Established: 1953 Annual Undergrad Tuition & Fees: $17,132
Enrollment: 2,540 Coed
Affiliation or Control: Church Of God IRS Status: 501(c)3
Highest Offering: Master's
Accreditation: NH

01 President Dr. John D. FOZARD
03 Executive Vice President Dr. Bill MCDOWELL
05 Vice Pres for Academic Affairs Dr. Sharon LEASE
32 VP Student Engagement/Success Mrs. Jessica RIMMER
45 Vice Pres Strategic Initiatives Dr. Eric JOSEPH
13 Chief Information Officer Mr. Jody ALLEN
15 Chief Administration Officer (HR) Mrs. Darwina MARSHALL
108 Dir Institutional Effectiveness Mr. Ray DILLMAN
42 Exec Director of Church Relations Rev. Morgan ALSIP
06 Registrar Ms. Stephanie DAVIDSON
37 Director Office of Financial Aid Ms. Deaun MAAS-STEED
07 Asst VP of Enrollment Services Mr. Mike WILKINSON
18 Director of Facilities Ms. Connie GALL
29 Director Alumni Relations Vacant
04 Administrative Asst to President Mrs. Tamra COSSEY
08 Head Librarian Mr. Michael FOOTE
10 Chief Business Officer Mrs. Mici SARTEN
19 Director Security/Safety Chief Jacob POOL
41 Athletic Director Mr. Marcus MOELLER

Murray State College (D)

One Murray Campus, Tishomingo OK 73460-3130
County: Johnston FICE Identification: 003158
Unit ID: 207236
Telephone: (580) 387-7000 Carnegie Class: Assoc/HT-High Trad
FAX Number: (580) 371-9844 Calendar System: Semester
URL: www.mscok.edu
Established: 1908 Annual Undergrad Tuition & Fees (In-State): $4,638
Enrollment: 2,373 Coed
Affiliation or Control: State IRS Status: 501(c)3
Highest Offering: Associate Degree
Accreditation: NH, ADNUR, OTA, PTAA

01 President Ms. Joy MCDANIEL
05 VP Acad Affs/Institutional Effect Ms. Becky HENTHORN
04 Exec Assistant to President/Board Mrs. Malynda COBB
10 VP Finance/Administration/CFO Mr. Dennis WESTMAN
32 Vice Pres for Student Affairs Ms. Michaelle GRAY
20 Dean of Instruction Ms. Ginger COTHRAN
18 Exec Director Campus Facilities Mr. Sam HOLT
102 Exec Director MSC Foundation Ms. Malynda COBB
84 Exec Dir Enrollment Services Ms. Marilyn SCHWARZ
37 Dir Financial Aid/Acad Advisement Ms. Machelle ELLIS
08 Director of Library Ms. Mary RIXEN
74 Veterinary Tech Program Director Ms. Debbie REED
66 Director of Nursing Ms. Robin COPPEDGE
121 Director of Academic Advisement Ms. Amanda BALDRIDGE
07 Registrar Ms. Pam WARD
15 Director of Human Resources Ms. Michaelle GRAY
35 Director Student Support Services Ms. Linda TAYLOR
21 Comptroller Ms. Sherry GRAY-DEVINE

National American University-Tulsa (E)

8040 S Sheridan Road, Tulsa OK 74133
Telephone: (918) 879-8400 Identification: 770409
Accreditation: &NH, MAC, SURTEC

† Branch campus of National American University, Rapid City, SD

Northeastern Oklahoma Agricultural and Mechanical College (F)

200 I Street, NE, Miami OK 74354-6434
County: Ottawa FICE Identification: 003160
Unit ID: 207290
Telephone: (918) 542-8441 Carnegie Class: Assoc/HT-High Trad
FAX Number: (918) 542-9759 Calendar System: Semester
URL: www.neo.edu
Established: 1919 Annual Undergrad Tuition & Fees (In-State): $4,178
Enrollment: 2,107 Coed
Affiliation or Control: State IRS Status: 501(c)3
Highest Offering: Associate Degree
Accreditation: NH, ADNUR, MLTAD, PTAA

01 President Dr. Jeffery L. HALE
05 Vice President Academic Affairs Dr. Bethene FAHNESTOCK
10 Vice President for Fiscal Affairs Mr. Mark RASOR
32 VP Student Affairs/Enrollment Svcs Mrs. Amy ISHMAEL
20 Asst VP for Academic Affairs Vacant
37 Director of Financial Aid Mr. David FISHER
26 Chief Public Relations Officer Mr. Jordan ADAMS
15 Director Human Resources Vacant
18 Director Facilities/Physical Plant Mr. Steve GRIMES
13 Coord InstructionalTechnology Mr. Matt WESTPHAL
30 Exec Dir Development Foundation Ms. Jennifer WALKER
38 Director Academic Advising Center Mrs. Rachel LLOYD
41 Athletic Director Mr. Dale PATTERSON
88 Economic Development Coordinator Vacant
105 Webmaster Mr. David FRAZIER
06 Registrar Mrs. Shay CLAPP
21 AVP for Fiscal Affairs/Controller Mr. Michael ALLGOOD
40 Bookstore Manager Mrs. Kathryn VANOVER
36 Dir Ctr for Academic Success & Adv Ms. Rachel LLOYD
08 Director Library Services Ms. Sloane ARANA
47 Department Chair Agriculture Ms. McKenzie NYGREN
83 Department Chair Social Science Dr. Jeff BIRDSONG
57 Dept Chair Commun/Performing Arts Vacant
81 Dept Chair Mathematics/Science Dr. Mark GRIGSBY
66 Dept Chr Nurs/Allied Hlth/Phys Educ Mrs. Deborah MORGAN
50 Dept Chair Business and Technology Mrs. Pat CREECH
04 Executive Asst to President Ms. Cindy BIGBY
19 Director Security/Safety Mr. Mark WALL
39 Director Student Housing Mr. Jim ROWLAND
90 Coordinator IT/Technical Services Mr. Matt WESTPHAL
96 Coordinator of Purchasing Ms. Kendra CUMMINS

Northeastern State University (G)

600 N Grand Avenue, Tahlequah OK 74464-2399
County: Cherokee FICE Identification: 003161
Unit ID: 207263
Telephone: (918) 456-5511 Carnegie Class: Masters/L
FAX Number: (918) 458-2015 Calendar System: Semester
URL: www.nsuok.edu
Established: 1909 Annual Undergrad Tuition & Fees (In-State): $6,207
Enrollment: 8,251 Coed
Affiliation or Control: State IRS Status: 501(c)3
Highest Offering: First Professional Degree
Accreditation: NH, ACBSP, CACREP, CAEPN, DIETD, MT, MUS, NUR, OPT, OPTR, SP, SW

01 President Dr. Steve TURNER
05 Interim Provost & VP Academic Affs Dr. Debbrah LANDRY
11 VP for Administration/Finance Ms. Christy LANDSAW
86 Dir Community/Government Relations Ms. Mary BOWER
26 VP University Relations Mr. Ben HARDCASTLE
32 Vice President Student Affairs Dr. Jerrid FREEMAN
20 Asst VP Acad Affs Admin Dr. Tom JACKSON
20 Asst VP Acad Affs Admin Dr. Pam FLY
12 Dean Broken Arrow Campus Dr. Roy WOOD
12 Dean Muskogee Campus Dr. Tim MCELROY
49 Dean College of Liberal Arts Dr. Phillip BRIDGMON
50 Dean College of Business/Technology Dr. Roger COLLIER
53 Dean College of Education Dr. Debbie LANDRY
81 Dean Science & Health Professions Dr. Pamela HATHORN
88 Dean Optometry Dr. Douglas PENISTEN
08 Exec Director of NSU Libraries Mr. Steven EDSCORN
108 Exec Dir Inst Effectiveness Dr. Julie SAWYER
30 Director of Development Ms. Peggy GLENN-SUMMITT
15 Director of Human Resources Ms. Monica BARNETT
37 Director Student Financial Services Dr. Teri COCHRAN
06 Registrar Ms. Janet KELLEY
07 Director Admissions/Recruitment Ms. Jennifer MCCLENDON
84 Asst VP Enrollment Management Mr. Dan MABERRY
18 Assistant VP Facilities Mr. Jonathan ASBILL
41 Director of Athletics Mr. Tony DUCKWORTH
27 Director of Communications Mr. David JOPLIN
19 Director of Campus Police Ms. Patti BUHL
29 Director Alumni Services Mr. Daniel JOHNSON
07 Asst Director of Admission/Rec Ms. Damita CUNNINGHAM
109 Director of Auxiliary Services Mr. Chris ADNEY
39 Director of Housing Mr. Craig REINEHR
35 Asst VP Student Affairs Admin Ms. Sheila SELF
96 Director Purchasing Contr Payments Mr. Thad TURMAN
44 Stewards/Annual Giving Coordinator Ms. Cami HIGHERS
04 Administrative Asst to President Ms. Robin HUTCHINS
13 Chief Info Tech Officer/Director IT Dr. Richard REIF

Northeastern State University (H)

3100 East New Orleans St, Broken Arrow OK 74014
Telephone: (918) 449-6000 Identification: 770372
Accreditation: &NH

Northeastern State University at Muskogee (I)

2400 W Shawnee, Muskogee OK 74401
Telephone: (918) 683-0040 Identification: 770373
Accreditation: &NH, OT

Northern Oklahoma College (J)

1220 E Grand Avenue, PO Box 310, Tonkawa OK 74653-0310
County: Kay FICE Identification: 003162
Unit ID: 207281
Telephone: (580) 628-6200 Carnegie Class: Assoc/HT-Mix Trad/Non
FAX Number: (580) 628-6209 Calendar System: Semester
URL: www.noc.edu
Established: 1901 Annual Undergrad Tuition & Fees (In-State): $3,675
Enrollment: 4,642 Coed
Affiliation or Control: State IRS Status: 501(c)3
Highest Offering: Associate Degree
Accreditation: NH, ACBSP, ADNUR, COARC

01 President Dr. Cheryl EVANS
05 Vice President for Academic Affairs Dr. Pam STINSON
10 Vice President Financial Affairs Mrs. Anita SIMPSON
12 Vice President for NOC Enid Dr. Ed VINEYARD
12 Vice President for NOC Stillwater Dr. Shannon CUNNINGHAM
32 Vice President for Student Affairs Mr. Jason JOHNSON
30 Vice President for Devel/Cmty Rels Mrs. Sheri SNYDER
13 Director Information Technology Mr. Michael MACHIA
15 Director Human Resources Ms. Shannon CRANFORD
84 Vice Pres Enroll Mgmt/Registrar Dr. Rick EDGINGTON
08 Director of Library Services Mr. Benjamin HAINLINE
18 Assoc Vice Pres of Physical Plant Mr. Larry DYE
41 Athletic Director Mr. Jeremy HISE
37 Director Student Financial Aid Ms. Holly LEE
40 Manager Student Bookstore Mrs. Jimilea JANSSON

Northwestern Oklahoma State University (K)

709 Oklahoma Boulevard, Alva OK 73717-2799
County: Woods FICE Identification: 003163
Unit ID: 207306
Telephone: (580) 327-1700 Carnegie Class: Masters/S
FAX Number: (580) 327-1881 Calendar System: Semester
URL: www.nwosu.edu
Established: 1897 Annual Undergrad Tuition & Fees (In-State): $6,690
Enrollment: 2,136 Coed
Affiliation or Control: State IRS Status: 501(c)3
Highest Offering: Doctorate
Accreditation: NH, ACBSP, CAEPN, NUR, SW

01 President Dr. Janet L. CUNNINGHAM
11 Vice President for Administration Dr. David M. PECHA
05 Vice President for Academics Dr. Bo S. HANNAFORD
20 Assoc VP for Academics Dr. James L. BELL
26 Assoc VP for University Relations Mr. Steven J. VALENCIA
32 Dean of Student Affairs Mr. Calleb N. MOSBURG
41 Athletic Director Mr. Brad FRANZ
06 Registrar Mrs. Sheri K. LAHR
37 Director Financial Aid Mrs. Rita J. CASTLEBERRY
113 Bursar Mrs. Fawn M. KINGCADE
07 Director of Recruitment Ms. Paige L. FISCHER
18 Chief Facilities/Physical Plant Mr. Jim DETGEN
15 Human Resource Director Mrs. Cheryl ELLIS
39 Director of Students/Housing Mrs. Kaylyn L. HANSEN
29 Director Alumni Relations Mr. John W. ALLEN
58 Assoc Dean of Graduate Studies Dr. Shawn P. HOLLIDAY

08 Director of Libraries ....Mrs. Susan K. JEFFRIES
09 Institutional Research Specialist ....Ms. Kylea C. AMERIN

Oklahoma Baptist University (A)

500 W University, Shawnee OK 74804-2590
County: Pottawatomie FICE Identification: 003164
Unit ID: 207403
Telephone: (405) 585-4000 Carnegie Class: Bac-Diverse
FAX Number: N/A Calendar System: Semester
URL: www.okbu.edu
Established: 1910 Annual Undergrad Tuition & Fees: $25,310
Enrollment: 1,986 Coed
Affiliation or Control: Southern Baptist IRS Status: 501(c)3
Highest Offering: Master's
Accreditation: **NH**, ACBSP, CAEPN, MUS, NURSE

01 President ....Dr. David W. WHITLOCK
05 Provost/Exec Vice Pres Campus Life ....Dr. Robert S. NORMAN
10 Exec VP Business Affs/Admin Svcs ....Mr. Randy L. SMITH
111 Sr VP for Advancement & Univ Rels ....Mr. Will SMALLWOOD
13 VP Info Integra & CIO/Dean Library ....Mr. Paul ROBERTS
42 Dean of Spiritual Life ....Mr. Dale M. GRIFFIN
26 Assoc VP Marketing & Communication ....Mrs. Paula GOWER
79 Assc Provost/Dn Humanities/Soc Sci ....Dr. Pam ROBINSON
14 Asst Vice Pres Info Sys/Services ....Mr. Gary NICKERSON
32 Dean of Students ....Mr. Odus COMPTON
29 Exec Director OBU Alumni Assn ....Mrs. Lori R. HAGANS
11 Director of Executive Offices ....Mrs. Tonia KELLOGG
37 Director Student Financial Services ....Mrs. Jonna G. RANEY
88 Dir of Events/Conf & Camps ....Ms. Cynthia K. GATES
06 Dir Academic Records/Registrar ....Ms. Marcia MCQUERRY
21 Asst VP Finance/Admin Svcs ....Mrs. Lauri A. FLUKE
21 Controller ....Mr. Steven FLOYD
15 Director of Human Resources ....Mr. Mike JOHNSON
35 Director of Campus Services ....Mr. Larry A. WALKER
19 Chief of University Police ....Mr. David SHANNON
41 Athletic Director ....Mr. Robert DAVENPORT
18 Dir Facilities Mgmt & Services ....Mr. George HAINES
96 Director of Purchasing ....Mr. Larry WALKER
84 Assoc VP for Enrollment Management ....Mr. Bruce PERKINS
58 Dean College of Grad & Prof Stds ....Dr. Heath THOMAS
36 Director of Career Development ....Vacant
57 Dean College of Fine Arts ....Dr. Chris MATHEWS
81 Dean College of Math and Science ....Dr. Chris JONES
73 Dir School of Christian Service ....Dr. Tony HIGGINS
50 Dean College of Business ....Dr. David C. HOUGHTON
66 Dean College of Nursing ....Dr. Lepaine MCHENRY
108 AVP of Institutional Effectiveness ....Dr. Andrew SPENCER
07 Director of Admissions ....Mr. Will BRANTLEY
04 Exec Secretary to the President ....Mrs. Angela WILLIAMS
39 Director Student Housing ....Vacant

Oklahoma Christian University (B)

PO Box 11000, Oklahoma City OK 73136-1100
County: Oklahoma FICE Identification: 003165
Unit ID: 207324
Telephone: (405) 425-5000 Carnegie Class: Masters/L
FAX Number: (405) 425-5090 Calendar System: Semester
URL: www.oc.edu
Established: 1950 Annual Undergrad Tuition & Fees: $20,840
Enrollment: 2,570 Coed
Affiliation or Control: Independent Non-Profit IRS Status: 501(c)3
Highest Offering: Master's
Accreditation: **NH**, ACBSP, CAEPN, CIDA, ENG, MT, MUS, NURSE

01 President ....Mr. John DESTEIGUER
03 Executive Vice President ....Dr. William GOAD
05 Vice Pres for Academic Affairs ....Dr. Scott LAMASCUS
11 Exec Dir of University Services ....Mr. Kinney BRYANT
26 Vice Pres for Marketing ....Mrs. Risa FORRESTER
29 Exec Dir for Alumni Relations ....Mr. Bob LASHLEY
112 Vice Pres Estate/Planned Giving ....Mr. Stephen ECK
32 Vice Pres and Dean of Student Life ....Mr. Neil ARTER
07 Vice President for Admissions ....Mrs. Risa FORRESTER
13 Vice President for Information Tech ....Mr. John HERMES
43 Vice President & General Counsel ....Mr. Stephen ECK
111 Vice President for Advancement ....Mr. Kent ALLEN
50 Dean Col of Business Administration ....Dr. Jeff SIMMONS
73 Dean College of Biblical Studies ....Dr. Charles RIX
49 Dean College of Liberal Arts ....Dr. John FLETCHER
54 Dean Col of Engineering & Comp Sci ....Dr. Byron NEWBERRY
81 Dean Col of Nat & Health Sciences ....Dr. Jeff MCCORMACK
06 Registrar ....Dr. Stephanie BAIRD
08 Library Director ....Mrs. Tamie L. WILLIS
19 Chief of Police Dept ....Mr. Greg GILTNER
41 Athletic Director ....Mr. David LYNN
18 Director of Physical Plant Services ....Mr. Cary FALLING
27 Director Communications Marketing ....Mr. Wes MCKINZIE
37 Exec Dir Financial Svcs & Budgets ....Mr. Clint LARUE
104 Director of International Programs ....Mr. John OSBORNE
15 Vice Pres and Chief HR Officer ....Mr. Terry WINN
42 Dean for Spiritual Life ....Mr. Jeff MCMILLON
89 Dir of Freshman Experience ....Ms. Kirby KILLEN
88 Director of Creative Services ....Mr. Judson COPELAND
36 Director of Career Services ....Mrs. Candace OWENS
85 International Student Adviser ....Mrs. Joslyn HILL
38 Director of Counseling Services ....Mr. Sheldon ADKINS
35 Director of Student Services ....Mrs. Amy JANZEN
28 Multicultural & Service Learning ....Mr. Gary JONES
04 Administrative Asst to President ....Mrs. Teri MUELLER
09 Institutional Effectiveness Analyst ....Mr. Phil DREW
39 Director Student Housing ....Vacant

Oklahoma City Community College (C)

7777 S May Avenue, Oklahoma City OK 73159-4444
County: Oklahoma FICE Identification: 010391
Unit ID: 207449
Telephone: (405) 682-1611 Carnegie Class: Assoc/HT-Mix Trad/Non
FAX Number: (405) 682-7585 Calendar System: Other
URL: www.occc.edu
Established: 1972 Annual Undergrad Tuition & Fees (In-District): $3,727
Enrollment: 13,072 Coed
Affiliation or Control: State/Local IRS Status: 501(c)3
Highest Offering: Associate Degree
Accreditation: **NH**, ACBSP, ADNUR, COARC, EMT, OTA, PTAA

01 President ....Dr. Jerry L. STEWARD
100 Chief of Staff ....Dr. Marlene SHUGART
04 Exec Assistant to the President ....Ms. Roshell ROBERTS
101 Exec Asst to the Board of Regents ....Ms. Paige LANDRETH
03 Executive Vice President ....Mr. Steven BLOOMBERG
05 VP for Academic Affairs ....Mr. Greg GARDNER
45 Executive Dir Planning & Research ....Mr. Stu HARVEY
84 VP Enrollment/Student Svcs ....Vacant
10 Chief Financial Officer ....Dr. John BOYD
103 VP Community/Workforce Development .Mr. Lemuel BARDEGUEZ
15 Vice Pres Human Resources ....Mr. Danny HENDERSON
13 VP for Info/Instructional Tech Svcs ....Mr. David ANDERSON
20 Associate VP Academic Affairs ....Ms. Kim JAMESON
18 Exec Dir of Facilities Management ....Mr. Chris SNOW
79 Dean of Arts English/Humanities ....Vacant
76 Dean of Health Professions ....Ms. Debbie MYERS
81 Dean Math/Engineering/Phys Science ....Dr. Max SIMMONS
83 Dean of Social Sciences ....Dr. Susan TABOR
50 Dean of Bus & Information Tech ....Mr. John CLAYBON
30 Actg Director of Development ....Mr. Randy CASSIMUS
26 Exec Director of Marketing & PR ....Mr. Cordell JORDAN
25 Director of Grants & Contracts ....Vacant
09 Dir Institutional Effectiveness ....Dr. Janet PERRY
37 Director of Student Financial Aid ....Ms. Sonya GORE
32 Director of Student Life ....Vacant
88 Dir Child Development/Lab School ....Ms. Bonita SPINNER
106 Director of E-Student Services ....Ms. E.J WARREN
21 Director of Financial Accounting ....Ms. Brenda CARPENTER
114 Dir of Budgeting/Fiscal Planning ....Mr. David CHURCHILL
19 Chief of Police ....Mr. Daniel PIAZZA
113 Bursar ....Ms. Cynthia GARY
40 Director of Bookstore ....Ms. Brenda REINKE
88 Emergency Manager ....Mr. Jeremy BOHANNON
96 Director of Purchasing ....Mr. Craig SISCO
88 Director of Cultural Programs ....Mr. Richard CHARNAY
88 Dir Recreation and Fitness ....Mr. Michael SHUGART
31 Dir Community Outreach & Educ ....Mr. Alan DALE
103 Director Career Transitions Program ....Ms. Lisa BROWN
16 Dir of Human Resources Services ....Ms. Denise STEWART
22 Director of Equal Opportunity ....Dr. Regina SWITZER
14 Dir Enterprise Resource Planning ....Ms. Connie DRUMMOND
14 Dir Info Technology Infrastructure ....Mr. Rob GREGGS
14 Dir of Info Systems and Services ....Mr. Tim WHISENHUNT
08 Director of Library Services ....Vacant
88 Dir of Ctr for Learning/Teaching ....Dr. Glenne WHISENHUNT
07 Dir of Recruitment & Admissions .Ms. Mary BODINE AL-SHARIF
121 Director of Academic Advising ....Ms. Stephanie MILLER
06 Registrar ....Mr. Alan STRINGFELLOW

Oklahoma City University (D)

2501 N Blackwelder, Oklahoma City OK 73106-1493
County: Oklahoma FICE Identification: 003166
Unit ID: 207458
Telephone: (405) 208-5000 Carnegie Class: Masters/L
FAX Number: (405) 208-5916 Calendar System: Semester
URL: www.okcu.edu
Established: 1904 Annual Undergrad Tuition & Fees: $30,726
Enrollment: 2,991 Coed
Affiliation or Control: United Methodist IRS Status: 501(c)3
Highest Offering: First Professional Degree
Accreditation: **NH**, #ARCPA, CAEPN, LAW, MACTE, MUS, NUR

01 President ....Mr. Robert H. HENRY
05 Provost/VPAA ....Dr. Kent L. BUCHANAN
111 Vice Pres University Advancement ....Mr. Marty O'GWYNN
26 Vice Pres Univ/Church Relations ....Rev. Charles NEFF
10 CFO/VP Finance & Business Opers .....Ms. Catherine MANINGER
32 VP Student Affairs/Dean of Students ....Dr. Amy AYRES
84 Asst VP/Dean Enrollment Services ....Mr. Kevin WINDHOLZ
06 Registrar ....Mr. Charles MONNOT
09 Director of Institutional Research ....Dr. Kelly WILLIAMS
08 Director Dulaney-Browne Library ....Dr. Victoria SWINNEY
37 Director of Financial Aid ....Ms. Denise FLIS
27 Director of Communications ....Ms. Leslie BERGER
15 Chief Human Resources Officer ....Ms. Joey CROSLIN
92 Director of Honors Program ....Dr. Karen YOUMANS
07 Director of Undergrad Admissions ....Ms. Michelle COOK
18 Chief Facilities/Physical Plant ....Mr. Mark CLOUSE
29 Director Alumni Relations ....Mr. Cary PIRRONG
36 Director of Career Services ....Ms. Amelia HURT
49 Dean of Arts & Sciences ....Dr. Amy E. CATALDI
50 Dean School of Business ....Dr. Steve AGEE
61 Dean School of Law ....Dr. Valerie COUCH
64 Dean School of Music ....Mr. Mark PARKER
66 Dean of School of Nursing ....Dr. Lois SALMERON
73 Dean School of Religion ....Dr. Mark DAVIES
88 Dean School of Amer Dance/Arts Mgt ....Mr. John BEDFORD
88 Associate Dean School of Theatre ....Mr. Brian PARSONS
104 Director Study Abroad ....Ms. Mary BENNER
108 Director Institutional Assessment ....Dr. Jo Lynn DIGRANES
13 Chief Info Officer (CIO) ....Mr. Gerry HUNT
19 Chief of Police ....Mr. Bradd BROWN
38 Director of Counseling Services ....Ms. Mindy WINDHOLZ
39 Director University Housing ....Mr. Michael BURNS
41 Director of Athletics ....Mr. Jim ABBOTT
43 University General Counsel ....Ms. Casey ROSS
44 Assistant Director Annual Giving ....Ms. Carrie SAUER
106 Instructional Technologist ....Ms. Amanda DILLS
04 Administrative Asst to President ....Ms. Sarah POWERS
28 Dir Stdnt Engage/Incl/Multicult Pgm ....Mr. Russ TALL CHIEF

Oklahoma Panhandle State University (E)

Box 430, Goodwell OK 73939-0430
County: Texas FICE Identification: 003174
Unit ID: 207351
Telephone: (580) 349-2611 Carnegie Class: Bac-Diverse
FAX Number: (580) 349-2302 Calendar System: Semester
URL: www.opsu.edu
Established: 1909 Annual Undergrad Tuition & Fees (In-State): $7,294
Enrollment: 1,232 Coed
Affiliation or Control: State IRS Status: 501(c)3
Highest Offering: Baccalaureate
Accreditation: **NH**, CAEP, NUR

01 President ....Dr. Tim FALTYN
05 Vice Pres Academic Affairs ....Dr. Julie DINGER
10 Vice Pres Business & Fiscal Affairs ....Mr. Benny DAIN
111 Vice President of Outreach ....Dr. Ryan BLANTON
47 Dean Agriculture ....Dr. Peter CAMFIELD
50 Dean Business & Technology ....Mr. Davin WINGER
53 Dean Education ....Mr. Jerry MIHELIC
57 Dean Liberal Arts ....Dr. Sara RICHTER
66 Dean Science/Mathematics/Nursing ....Dr. Justin COLLINS
32 Director of Student Services ....Mr. Rantz TRAYLER
06 Registrar/Director of Admissions ....Ms. Amber GLASS
37 Director Student Financial Aid ....Ms. Lori FERGUSON
09 Director Institutional Research ....Mr. Dillon SCHOENHALS
13 Director of Technology ....Mr. Howard HENDERSON
15 Director Personnel Services ....Ms. Dana COLLINS
08 Director of Library ....Ms. Alton (Tony) HARDMAN
21 Comptroller ....Ms. Elizabeth MCMURPHY
38 Director Counseling/Career Services .... Ms. Deanna Rene RAMON
26 Campus Communications Director ....Ms. Danae MOORE
41 Athletic Officer ....Ms. Meghan MULCAHY
40 Bookstore Manager ....Mr. Eric BEGLEY
18 Director Physical Plant ....Ms. Laura DURAN
29 Director Alumni Relations ....Mr. Nick TUTTLE
96 Director of Purchasing ....Ms. Elizabeth MCMURPHY
04 Administrative Asst to President ....Ms. Jill OLSON

Oklahoma State University (F)

Stillwater OK 74078
County: Payne FICE Identification: 003170
Unit ID: 207388
Telephone: (405) 744-5000 Carnegie Class: DU-Higher
FAX Number: N/A Calendar System: Semester
URL: osu.okstate.edu/
Established: 1890 Annual Undergrad Tuition & Fees (In-State): $8,321
Enrollment: 25,930 Coed
Affiliation or Control: State IRS Status: 501(c)3
Highest Offering: Doctorate
Accreditation: **NH**, AAB, CAATE, CACREP, CAEPN, CARTE, CIDA, CLPSY, COPSY, DIETD, DIETI, ENG, ENGT, JOUR, LSAR, MFCD, MUS, SCPSY, SP, THEA, VET

01 President ....Dr. V. Burns HARGIS
04 Exec Assistant to the President ....Ms. Deborah LANE
29 President & CEO OSU Alumni Assoc ......Mr. Chris BATCHELDER
102 President & CEO OSU Foundation ....Mr. Kirk JEWELL
88 President OSU Research Foundation ....Dr. David WAITS
03 Sr Vice President & General Counsel ....Mr. Gary C. CLARK
05 Provost & Sr Vice President ....Dr. Gary SANDEFUR
10 Sr Vice Pres Admin & Finance ....Mr. Joseph B. WEAVER, JR.
47 VP/Dean/Director Ag Sci & Nat Res ....Dr. Thomas COON
41 Vice President Athletic Programs ....Mr. Mike HOLDER
26 Vice Pres Enroll Mgmt/Univ Mktg ....Mr. Kyle WRAY
46 Vice President for Research ....Dr. Kenneth SEWELL
32 Vice President Student Affairs ....Dr. Lee E. BIRD
09 Assoc VP/Dir Inst Res/Info Mgmt .... Dr. Christie HAWKINS
20 Prov/Sr VP Academic Affairs ....Dr. Pamela FRY
58 Assoc Provost/Dean Graduate College ....Dr. Sheryl TUCKER
21 Assoc Vice President & Controller ....Ms. Kathy ELLIOTT
28 Assoc VP Institutional Diversity ....Dr. Jason KIRKSEY
15 Asst Vice Pres Human Resources ....Ms. Jamie A. PAYNE
24 Asst Prov/Dir Inst Tch/Lrng Excel ....Dr. Christine ORMSBEE
88 Asst VP/Director Student Union ....Mr. Mitch KILCREASE
13 Chief Information Officer ....Ms. Darlene HIGHTOWER
18 Chief Facilities Officer ....Mr. Ron TARBUTTON
96 Chief Procurement Officer ....Mr. Scott SCHLOTTHAUER
19 Chief Public Safety Officer ....Mr. Michael ROBINSON
36 Director Career Services ....Dr. Pam EHLERS
27 Director Communication Services ....Mr. Gary SHUTT
22 Director EEO/Title IX/ADA ....Dr. Rosalyn GREEN
25 Dir Grants/Contracts/Financial Admn ....Dr. Robert DIXON
37 Director Scholarships/Financial Aid ....Mr. Chad BLEW

39 Director of University Housing .... Dr. Leon MCCLINTON
07 Director Undergraduate Admissions .... Ms. Christine CRENSHAW
108 Director Univ Assessment & Testing ....Mr. James KNECHT
38 Director University Counseling Svcs ..... Dr. Trevor RICHARDSON
23 Director University Health Services .... Mr. Christopher BARLOW
88 Assoc Dir Institutional Research ....Mr. Doug REED
40 Dir Student Union Bookstore .... Mr. Lance HINKLE
39 Asst Director Resident Life .... Ms. Tanya MASSEY
85 Asst Dir Intl Students & Scholars ....Mr. Tim T. HUFF
49 Dean Arts & Sciences .... Dr. Bret DANILOWICZ
53 Dean College of Education .... Dr. John ROMANS
54 Dean Engineering .... Dr. Paul J. TIKALSKY
92 Dean Honors College .... Dr. Keith GARBUTT
59 Dean Human Sciences .... Dr. Stephan M. WILSON
08 Dean Library ....Dr. Sheila G. JOHNSON
50 Dean Spears School of Business .... Dr. Ken EASTMAN
74 Dean Veterinary Medicine .... Dr. Christopher R. ROSS
43 Board of Regents General Counsel ....Mr. Steve STEPHENS
06 Registrar .... Dr. K. Celeste TABER

Oklahoma State University Center for Health Sciences College of Osteopathic Medicine (A)

1111 W 17th Street, Tulsa OK 74107-1898
Telephone: (918) 582-1972 FICE Identification: 011282
Accreditation: &NH, FEPAC, OSTEO

† Regional accreditation is carried under the parent institution in Stillwater, OK.

Oklahoma State University Institute of Technology-Okmulgee (B)

1801 E Fourth Street, Okmulgee OK 74447-3901
County: Okmulgee FICE Identification: 003172
Unit ID: 207564
Telephone: (918) 293-4678 Carnegie Class: Bac/Assoc-Mixed
FAX Number: (918) 293-4644 Calendar System: Trimester
URL: www.osuit.edu
Established: 1946 Annual Undergrad Tuition & Fees (In-State): $5,100
Enrollment: 2,617 Coed
Affiliation or Control: State IRS Status: 501(c)3
Highest Offering: Baccalaureate
Accreditation: NH, ADNUR, ENGT

01 President ....Dr. Bill PATH
10 VP Fiscal Services .... Mr. Jim SMITH
05 VP Academic Affairs .... Dr. Scott NEWMAN
32 VP Student Services .... Dr. Ina AGNEW
20 Associate VP Academic Affairs .... Ms. Jody GRAMMER
66 Nursing & Health Sciences .... Ms. Jana MARTIN
49 Arts & Sciences ....Dr. Mark ALLEN
72 Automotive Technologies ....Mr. Leo VAN DELFT
72 Construction Technologies ....Mr. Steve OLMSTEAD
88 Culinary Arts .... Mr. Gene LEITERMAN
54 Engineering Technologies ....Dr. Abul HASAN
88 Diesel & Heavy Equipment Tech ....Mr. Terryl LINDSEY
88 Energy Technologies .... Mr. Roy ACHEMIRE
77 Information Technologies .... Mr. Randy RITCHEY
88 Watchmaking .... Mr. Jason CHAMPION
57 Visual Communications .... Mr. James MCCULLOUGH
37 Dir Student Financial Services ....Mr. Matt SHORT
13 Associate VP Technology Services ....Mr. Kevin HULETT
06 Registrar .... Ms. Crystal BOWLES
07 Director of Admissions .... Mr. Kyle GREGORIO
106 Director of Distance Learning .... Mr. David FILES
103 Associate VP Workforce & Econ Dev ....Ms. Sheryl HALE
15 Director of Human Resources ....Ms. Paula NORTH
09 Director of Institutional Research .... Ms. Michelle CANAN
18 Dir Physical Plant Services ....Mr. Mark PITCHER
35 Dean of Students ....Mr. Devin DEBOCK
109 Dir Student Union & Auxiliary Svcs .... Mr. James BYRD
35 Director of Student Life ....Mr. Bruce FORCE
39 Director of Residential Life ....Mr. Bo HUDSON
08 Director of Library .... Ms. Jenny DUNCAN
96 Director of Purchasing ....Mrs. Chandra MILLER
12 Dir MAIP-Pryor Campus ....Mr. Charles HARRISON
38 Counselor .... Ms. Kathy AVERY
40 Manager Bookstore ....Ms. Alison WARD
26 Director of Marketing ....Ms. Shari ERWIN
19 Campus Police Chief ....Mr. Matt WOOLIVER
04 Admin Asst to President .... Ms. Claudette BUTCHER
88 Dir Tutoring Ctr/Acad Accommodation .... Mr. Chad SPURLOCK
29 Director Alumni Relations ....Mr. Bruce FORCE
30 Director Development ....Mr. Glenn ZANNOTTI

Oklahoma State University - Oklahoma City (C)

900 N Portland Ave, Oklahoma City OK 73107-6195
County: Oklahoma FICE Identification: 009647
Unit ID: 207397
Telephone: (405) 947-4421 Carnegie Class: Bac/Assoc-Assoc Dom
FAX Number: (405) 945-3289 Calendar System: Semester
URL: www.osuokc.edu
Established: 1961 Annual Undergrad Tuition & Fees (In-State): $3,634
Enrollment: 5,963 Coed
Affiliation or Control: State IRS Status: 501(c)3
Highest Offering: Baccalaureate
Accreditation: NH, ADNUR, DIETT, DMS, EMT, IFSAC

01 President .... Ms. Natalie SHIRLEY
05 Vice President Academic Affairs .... Dr. Joey FRONHEISER
10 Vice President Budget & Finance ....Ms. Ronda REECE
32 Vice President Student Services .... Mr. Brad WILLIAMS
50 Vice Pres for Business and Industry ....Ms. Robin ROBERTS KRIEGER
20 Associate VP Academic Affairs .... Mr. Tracy EDWARDS
84 Sr Dir Enrollment Management .... Mr. Kyle WILLIAMS
30 Associate Dir Development ....Mr. Donovan WOODS
11 Vice Pres of Operations ....Mr. Mike WIDELL
08 Director Library Services .... Ms. Elaine REGIER
37 Director Financial Aid .... Ms. Bessie CARTER
15 Director Human Resources ....Ms. Melissa HERREN
18 Dir of Building Maint/Energy Mgr ....Mr. Mickey FULLER
26 Sr Dir Marketing/Communications ....Ms. Sandy PANTLIK
07 Dir of Recruitment & Admissions .... Mr. Kyle WILLIAMS
96 Director of Purchasing .... Ms. Sharon FITZPATRICK
06 Registrar .... Ms. Lyndsay PITTMAN
25 Sr Dir Institutional Grants .... Ms. Jackie WESTON
19 Director Security/Safety .... Mr. Sam COX
108 Sr Dir Institutional Effectiveness .... Ms. Lisa DILLON

Oklahoma State University - Tulsa (D)

700 N Greenwood Avenue, Tulsa OK 74106-0702
Telephone: (918) 594-8000 Identification: 666053
Accreditation: &NH

† Regional accreditation is carried under the parent institution in Stillwater, OK.

Oklahoma Technical College (E)

4444 South Sheridan, Tulsa OK 74145-1122
Telephone: (918) 895-7500 Identification: 666718
Accreditation: ACICS

Oklahoma Wesleyan University (F)

2201 Silver Lake Road, Bartlesville OK 74006-6299
County: Washington FICE Identification: 003151
Unit ID: 206835
Telephone: (918) 333-6151 Carnegie Class: Masters/S
FAX Number: (918) 335-6228 Calendar System: Semester
URL: www.okwu.edu
Established: 1910 Annual Undergrad Tuition & Fees: $25,070
Enrollment: 1,527 Coed
Affiliation or Control: Wesleyan Church IRS Status: 501(c)3
Highest Offering: Master's
Accreditation: NH, CAEPN, IACBE, NURSE

01 President ....Dr. Everett G. PIPER
05 Acting Provost/VP for Acad Affairs .... Dr. Gentry SUTTON
07 Executive Vice President ....Mr. John MEANS
10 Vice President for Business Affairs ....Mrs. Andrea ZEPEDA
32 Vice President for Student Life ....Mr. Kyle WHITE
20 Assoc VP for Academic Affairs .... Dr. Mark WEETER
35 Assoc VP for Student Dev ....Rev. Ben ROTZ
07 VP for Enroll Svcs and Annual Fund ..Mrs. Samantha PETERSON
53 Dean of School of Education .... Dr. Jeffrey KEENEY
73 Dean of School of Min and Christ Th .... Dr. Mark WEETER
49 Dean of School of Arts & Sciences .... Dr. Gentry SUTTON
50 Dean of School of Business .... Dr. Brian EPPERSON
66 Dean School of Nursing .... Mrs. Jessica JOHNSON
106 Dean of Online Learning .... Dr. Devon SMITH
108 Dir Academic Effectiveness .... Dr. Danielle VALLE
21 Director of Accounting .... Mrs. Betty-Jo ANDERSON
06 Registrar .... Mr. Jeff LEBERT
13 Director of Computer Services .... Mr. Eric GOINGS
08 Head Librarian .... Mrs. Stephanie LEUPP
37 Director of Financial Aid .... Mrs. Kandi MOLDER
15 Exec Dir Human Resources .... Ms. Julia CROUCH
41 Athletic Director .... Mr. Mark MOLDER
26 Director of University Relations .... Mrs. Marci PIPER
04 Executive Assistant to President .... Mrs. Kathy LINDQUIST
39 Dir of Residential Life .... Mr. Chris BREILAND
34 Women's RD/Campus Care .... Mrs. Whitney BREILAND
88 FYE/SYE Director .... Mr. Aaron BUNKER
23 Director Student Health .... Mrs. Debra COOK
18 Director of Buildings and Grounds ....Mr. Dalton HIGGINS
19 Dir of Security/Educ Counselor .... Mr. Stevan DJUKIC
101 Secretary of the Institution/Board .... Mr. Francisco GONZALEZ
40 Bookstore Manager .... Mrs. Melissa HECK

Oklahoma Wesleyan University Tulsa Campus (G)

10810 E 45th Street, Tulsa OK 74146
Telephone: (918) 728-6143 Identification: 770378
Accreditation: &NH

Oral Roberts University (H)

7777 S Lewis Avenue, Tulsa OK 74171-0003
County: Tulsa FICE Identification: 003985
Unit ID: 207582
Telephone: (918) 495-6161 Carnegie Class: Masters/M
FAX Number: (918) 495-6033 Calendar System: Semester
URL: www.oru.edu
Established: 1965 Annual Undergrad Tuition & Fees: $25,676
Enrollment: 3,611 Coed
Affiliation or Control: Independent Non-Profit IRS Status: 501(c)3
Highest Offering: Doctorate
Accreditation: NH, ACBSP, CAEPN, ENG, MUS, NURSE, SW, THEOL

01 President .... Dr. William M. WILSON
05 Provost .... Dr. Kathaleen REID-MARTINEZ
10 Chief Financial Officer .... Mr. Neal STENZEL
11 Chief Operations Officer .... Mr. Tim PHILLEY
30 VP for Development/Alumni Relations .... Mrs. Laura BISHOP
84 VP for Enrollment Management .... Dr. Nancy BRAINARD
43 University Counsel .... Mr. Terry KOLLMORGEN
32 Vice President Student Life ....Vacant
26 VP Comm/Mktg/Exec Dir Empowered .... Mr. Ossie MILLS
13 AVP of Technology & Innovation ....Mr. Michael MATHEWS
21 Controller .... Ms. Michelle MCMILLAN
42 Dean of Spiritual Formation .... Dr. Clarence BOYD
08 Dean of the University Library ....Dr. Mark ROBERTS
54 Dean Col of Science & Engineering .... Dr. Kenneth WEED
49 Dean Col of Arts & Cultural Studies ....Dr. Mark HALL
73 Int Dean College Theology/Ministry ....Dr. Samuel THORPE
50 Dean College of Business ....Dr. Julie HUNTLEY
66 Dean & Chairman College of Nursing ....Dr. Kenda JEZEK
53 Dean College of Education .... Dr. Kim BOYD
32 Dean of Student Development ....Ms. Lori COOK
88 Assoc Vice Pres of Student Services .... Dr. Sergio MATVIUK
09 Dir of Institutional Effectiveness .... Dr. Connie SJOBERG
41 Director for Athletics .... Mr. Mike CARTER
25 Director of Sponsored Programs ....Ms. Kim FALCON
38 Director of Student Counseling .... Ms. Michelle TAYLOR
35 Director of Student Resources ....Vacant
92 Director of Honors Program ....Dr. John KORSTAD
88 Director Student Accounts .... Ms. Karen JOHNSON
96 Director of Purchasing ....Mr. Mark PEPIN
06 Registrar ....Mr. David FULMER
07 Director of Admissions Operations ....Mr. Jordan CRANDALL
84 Director International Enrollment .... Ms. Wendy MORTON
106 AVP of Online/Lifelong Learning .... Dr. Kim NUGENT
37 Director of Financial Aid .... Mr. William WOMACK
29 Director of Alumni Relations .... Mr. Robert BEARD
19 Director of Security/Safety .... Mr. Bill (William) HUNT
15 Human Resources Manager ....Ms. Marleen JONES
04 Executive Asst to President ....Mrs. Lisa BOWMAN
101 Secretary of the Institution/Board ....Vacant

Phillips Theological Seminary (I)

901 N Mingo Road, Tulsa OK 74116-5612
County: Tulsa FICE Identification: 025602
Unit ID: 414966
Telephone: (918) 610-8303 Carnegie Class: Spec-4-yr-Faith
FAX Number: (918) 610-8404 Calendar System: Semester
URL: www.ptstulsa.edu
Established: 1906 Annual Graduate Tuition & Fees: N/A
Enrollment: 97 Coed
Affiliation or Control: Christian Church (Disciples Of Christ)
IRS Status: 501(c)3
Highest Offering: Doctorate; No Undergraduates
Accreditation: NH, THEOL

01 President .... Gary PELUSO-VERDEND
05 Vice Pres Academic Affairs & Dean .... Nancy Claire PITTMAN
10 Vice Pres Finance & Admin .... Karen MCMILLAN
108 Assoc Dn Assessment & Faculty .... Joseph A. BESSLER
20 Assoc Dn Contextual Ed/Church Rels ....John THOMAS, JR.
73 Doctor of Ministry Program Director .... Kathleen D. MCCALLIE
37 Financial Aid Officer ....John FOREST
08 Library Director .... Sandy SHAPOVAL
29 Sr Director Stewardship ....Geoffrey BREWSTER
44 Stewardship Director .... Malisa PIERCE
26 Sr Director Seminary Relations .... Kurt GWARTNEY
06 Registrar .... Toni WINE IMBLER
15 Human Resources Manager .... Gwen DERRICK
04 Executive Assistant to President ....Vacant

Platt College (J)

201 N Eastern Avenue, Moore OK 73160
Telephone: (405) 912-3260 Identification: 770585
Accreditation: ACCSC, COARC

Platt College (K)

3801 S Sheridan, Tulsa OK 74145-1132
County: Tulsa FICE Identification: 023068
Unit ID: 245962
Telephone: (918) 663-9000 Carnegie Class: Bac/Assoc-Assoc Dom
FAX Number: (918) 622-1240 Calendar System: Other
URL: www.plattcolleges.edu
Established: 1979 Annual Undergrad Tuition & Fees: N/A
Enrollment: 200 Coed
Affiliation or Control: Proprietary IRS Status: Proprietary
Highest Offering: Associate Degree
Accreditation: ACCSC

01 Director of Campus .... Mr. John PAPPAS
07 Director of Admission & Marketing ....Mr. John ROBERTS

Platt College-OKC Central (L)

309 South Ann Arbor Avenue,
Oklahoma City OK 73128-1112
Telephone: (405) 946-7799 Identification: 666341
Accreditation: ACCSC, SURGT

† Branch campus of Platt College, Tulsa, OK.

Randall University (A)

7301 S. I-35 Service Road, Moore OK 73160
County: Cleveland FICE Identification: 010266
Unit ID: 207157
Telephone: (405) 912-9000 Carnegie Class: Spec-4-yr-Faith
FAX Number: (405) 912-9050 Calendar System: Semester
URL: www.ru.edu
Established: 1959 Annual Undergrad Tuition & Fees: $13,040
Enrollment: 329 Coed
Affiliation or Control: Free Will Baptist IRS Status: 501(c)3
Highest Offering: Master's
Accreditation: TRACS

01 President ....Dr. Timothy W. EATON
05 Chief Academic Officer ....Dr. Mark H. BRAISHER
10 Chief Business Officer ....Ms. Pat MILLER
111 Director Institutional Advancement ....Mr. Bob THOMPSON
07 Admissions Coordinator ....Ms. Lyndsey BRAISHER
37 Financial Aid Coordinator ....Mr. Cliff BRISTOW
08 LRC Director ....Ms. Nancy J. DRAPER
13 Director of MIS ....Mr. Quentin C. LOOP
06 Registrar ....Ms. Patti ASHBY
58 Dean of Graduate Studies ....Dr. Mark H. BRAISHER
39 Resident Life Coordinator ....Ms. Jody BLACKWELL
41 Athletic Director ....Mr. Mark BEROKOFF
32 Dean of Students ....Ms. Jody BLACKWELL
40 Bookstore Manager ....Mr. Greg MCALLISTER
106 Director of Online Learning ....Dr. Paulette JONES

Redlands Community College (B)

1300 S Country Club Road, El Reno OK 73036-5304
County: Canadian FICE Identification: 003156
Unit ID: 207069
Telephone: (405) 262-2552 Carnegie Class: Assoc/HT-High Non
FAX Number: (405) 422-1200 Calendar System: Semester
URL: www.redlandscc.edu
Established: 1938 Annual Undergrad Tuition & Fees (In-District): $4,154
Enrollment: 2,690 Coed
Affiliation or Control: State/Local IRS Status: 501(c)3
Highest Offering: Associate Degree
Accreditation: NH, ADNUR, EMT

01 President ....Mr. Jack BRYANT
10 Exec Vice Pres of Admin & Finance ....Ms. Jena MARR
32 Executive Dean of Student Success ....Mr. Brennan APOSTOLO
05 Dean of Agriculture & Academics ....Ms. Reonna SLAGELL-GOSSEN
18 Director Physical Plant ....Mr. Richard BUCHHOLZ
66 Dean of Nursing/Allied Health ....Ms. Rose Marie SMITH
08 Director Learning Resource Center ....Mrs. Rebecca RATTERMAN
06 Registrar/Director Student Records ....Mr. Dennis HARRIS
37 Director Financial Aid ....Ms. Paris PRZEKURAT
41 Athletic Director ....Mr. Eli ZUCKSWORTH
13 Chief Tech Ofcr/Campus & Info Sec ....Mr. Curtis BRABHAM
22 Director of Upward Bound ....Mrs. Linda MCDOWN
09 Director of Institutional Research ....Mr. Troy MILLIGAN
84 Dean of Enrollment Management ....Mrs. Tricia HOBSON
21 Associate Business Officer ....Mrs. Maxine CALVERT
36 Coordinator Career Services ....Vacant
15 Coordinator Personnel/Payroll ....Mrs. Kim ANDRADE
26 Director of Communication/Marketing ....Mrs. Dayna ROWE
29 Coord Alumni Rels/Alternative Educ ....Vacant
39 Coordinator of Resident Life ....Ms. Tina JACOBS
96 Director of Purchasing ....Ms. Brenda HARKINS

Rogers State University (C)

1701 W Will Rogers Boulevard,
Claremore OK 74017-3252
County: Rogers FICE Identification: 003168
Unit ID: 207661
Telephone: (918) 343-7777 Carnegie Class: Bac-Diverse
FAX Number: (918) 343-7898 Calendar System: Semester
URL: www.rsu.edu
Established: 1909 Annual Undergrad Tuition & Fees (In-State): $6,540
Enrollment: 4,081 Coed
Affiliation or Control: State IRS Status: 501(c)3
Highest Offering: Master's
Accreditation: NH, ADNUR, EMT, NUR

01 President ....Dr. Larry RICE
05 Vice President for Academic Affairs ....Dr. Richard BECK
10 Exec VP for Admin & Finance ....Mr. Tom VOLTURO
30 Vice President for Development ....Dr. Maynard PHILLIPS
32 Vice Pres for Student Affairs ....Dr. Brent MARSH
84 Vice President Enrollment Mgmt ....Ms. Heidi HOSKINSON
12 Assoc VP Bartlesville Campus ....Dr. Bruce MCGOWAN
108 Asst VP Accountability & Academics ....Dr. Mary MILLIKIN
21 Comptroller/Asst Vice Pres Bus Affs ....Mr. Mark MEADORS
12 Director Pryor Campus ....Ms. Sherry ALEXANDER
107 Dean School of Professional Studies ....Dr. Susan WILLIS
49 Dean School of Arts and Sciences ....Dr. Keith MARTIN
35 Director of Student Development ....Ms. Katy LAUNIUS
08 Director of the Library ....Mr. J. Alan LAWLESS
07 Director of Admissions ....Ms. Joy Lin HALL
29 Director of Alumni ....Ms. Katelyn TITTLE
04 Exec Assistant to the President ....Ms. Rhonda SPURLOCK
18 Director Physical Plant ....Mr. Karl REYNOLDS
19 Director Campus Police ....Mr. Gary BOERGERMANN
26 Director Public Relations ....Mr. David HAMBY
37 Director of Financial Aid ....Ms. Kelly HICKS
91 Director Administrative Computing ....Ms. Cathy BURNS
13 Director Information Technology ....Mr. Brian REEVES
15 Director Employment & Benefits ....Ms. Alisa HAMETT
41 Director of Athletics ....Mr. Chris RATCLIFF
39 Director Residential Life ....Ms. Kyla SHORT
23 Director Student Health Clinic ....Ms. Lisa MARTIN
25 Director Research & Sponsored Pgm ....Mr. Daniel MARANGONI

Rogers State University-Bartlesville (D)

401 South Dewey Avenue, Bartlesville OK 74003
Telephone: (918) 338-8000 Identification: 770379
Accreditation: &NH

Rogers State University-Pryor (E)

2155 Highway 69A, Pryor Creek OK 74361
Telephone: (918) 825-6117 Identification: 770380
Accreditation: &NH

Rose State College (F)

6420 SE 15th, Midwest City OK 73110-2799
County: Oklahoma FICE Identification: 009185
Unit ID: 207670
Telephone: (405) 733-7311 Carnegie Class: Assoc/HT-Mix Trad/Non
FAX Number: (405) 733-7399 Calendar System: Semester
URL: www.rose.edu
Established: 1970 Annual Undergrad Tuition & Fees (In-District): $3,808
Enrollment: 6,612 Coed
Affiliation or Control: State/Local IRS Status: 501(c)3
Highest Offering: Associate Degree
Accreditation: NH, ADNUR, CAHIIM, COARC, DA, DH, MLTAD, RAD

01 President ....Dr. Jeanie WEBB
10 Exec Vice President and CFO ....Dr. Kent LASHLEY
05 Vice President for Academic Affairs ....Dr. Frances HENDRIX
32 Vice President for Student Affairs ....Mr. Lance NEWBOLD
26 VP for External Affairs & Marketing ....Ms. Tamara PRATT
13 Vice President for Info Technology ....Mr. John PRIMO
103 Vice President for Workforce Devel ....Mr. Stan GREIL
41 Exec Dir Athletic Programs ....Mr. Joey DAVAULT
102 Exec Dir Foundation & Resource Dev ....Ms. Cindy MIKEMAN
20 Associate VP Academic Affairs ....Dr. Jeff CALDWELL
09 Assoc VP Inst Effectiveness ....Ms. Isabelle BILLEN
103 Assoc VP Workforce and Comm Dev ....Dr. Bret WOOD
21 Sr Dir Fiscal Operations ....Mr. Raymond BLANKE
15 Sr Dir Human Res/Affirm Act Ofcr ....Ms. Alberta NUTTER
109 Sr Dir Campus Operatation ....Mr. Richard ANDREWS
84 Assoc VP Enrollment Mgmt/ Registrar ....Ms. Mechelle AITSON-ROESSLER
37 Director Financial Aid ....Mr. Steve DAFFER
26 Director Marketing ....Mr. Daniel BECK
18 Director Operations ....Mr. Ardie RODGERS
41 Dir Health & Wellness Activities ....Mr. Chris LELAND
36 Director Spec Svcs/Student Outreach ....Dr. Joanne STAFFORD
08 Dean Learning Resources Center ....Mr. Chris MEYER
50 Dean Business & Info Tech Division ....Dr. Mark TIPPIN
54 Dean Engineering & Science Division ....Dr. Wayne JONES
79 Dean Humanities Division ....Ms. Claudia BUCKMASTER
76 Dean Health Sciences Division ....Mr. Dan POINTS
83 Dean Social Sciences Division ....Dr. Juanita ORTIZ
101 Exec Asst to the President & Board ....Ms. Michelle NUTTER
19 Coord of Safety/Security/Risk Mgmt ..Dr. Anita POOLE-ENDSLEY
39 Director of Residence Life ....Ms. Alyssa LOVELESS

St. Gregory's University (G)

1900 W MacArthur, Shawnee OK 74804-2499
County: Pottawatomie FICE Identification: 003183
Unit ID: 207689
Telephone: (405) 878-5100 Carnegie Class: Bac-Diverse
FAX Number: (405) 878-5198 Calendar System: Semester
URL: www.stgregorys.edu
Established: 1875 Annual Undergrad Tuition & Fees: $21,300
Enrollment: 650 Coed
Affiliation or Control: Roman Catholic IRS Status: 501(c)3
Highest Offering: Master's
Accreditation: NH, ACBSP, NURSE

01 President ....Dr. Michael SCAPERLANDA
04 Executive Asst to President ....Dr. Theresa BRAGG
11 VP Finance & Administration ....Dr. Ron DIGGS
05 VP Academic Affairs ....Dr. Richard MELOCHE
66 Dean of Nursing ....Dr. Susan BARNES
10 Chief Financial Officer ....Ms. April DUNSWORTH
30 Executive Director of Development ....Mr. Sean DUPRE
108 Director of Compliance & Accred ....Dr. Ron DIGGS
32 Dean of Students ....Ms. Emilia (Lilly) BERMUDEZ
06 Registrar ....Mrs. Ramah NATION
84 Vice President of Enrollment Mgmt ....Dr. Paul CARNEY
08 Library Director ....Mrs. Anita SEMTNER
37 Associate Director Financial Aid ....Mrs. Lori DEARDORFF
26 Asst Director of Marketing ....Ms. Jessica ESTES
41 Athletic Director ....Mr. John MARTIN
15 Director of Human Resources ....Ms. Marria BRYDON
18 Director of Operations ....Mr. Mark SAUNDERS
13 Director of Information Systems ....Mr. Chris FLY

St. Gregory's University Tulsa Campus (H)

5801 E 41st Street, Suite 900, Tulsa OK 74135
Telephone: (405) 878-5200 Identification: 770381
Accreditation: &NH

Seminole State College (I)

PO Box 351, Seminole OK 74818-0351
County: Seminole FICE Identification: 003178
Unit ID: 207740
Telephone: (405) 382-9950 Carnegie Class: Assoc/HT-Mix Trad/Non
FAX Number: (405) 382-3122 Calendar System: Semester
URL: www.sscok.edu
Established: 1931 Annual Undergrad Tuition & Fees (In-District): $4,140
Enrollment: 1,839 Coed
Affiliation or Control: State/Local IRS Status: 501(c)3
Highest Offering: Associate Degree
Accreditation: NH, ADNUR, MLTAD

01 President ....Dr. Jim W. UTTERBACK
05 Vice President Academic Affairs ....Dr. Tom MILLS
10 Vice President Fiscal Affairs ....Mr. Braden BROWN
32 Vice President of Student Affairs ....Mr. Bill KNOWLES
13 Director Mgmt Information Systems ....Mr. Marc HUNTER
66 Director of Nursing ....Ms. Valarie WATTS
06 Registrar ....Mrs. Corey QUIETT
15 Director Personnel Services ....Mrs. Courtney JONES
26 Director of Public Relations ....Ms. Kristin DUNN
04 Administrative Asst to President ....Ms. Mechell DOWNEY
22 Dir Affirmative Action/EEO ....Vacant
37 Director Student Financial Aid ....Ms. Melanie RINEHART
39 Director Student Housing ....Ms. Melinda SIMS
41 Athletic Director ....Mr. Mike ST. JOHN

Southeastern Oklahoma State University (J)

1405 N 4th Avenue, Durant OK 74701-3330
County: Bryan FICE Identification: 003179
Unit ID: 207847
Telephone: (580) 745-2000 Carnegie Class: Masters/M
FAX Number: N/A Calendar System: Semester
URL: www.se.edu
Established: 1909 Annual Undergrad Tuition & Fees (In-State): $6,450
Enrollment: 3,754 Coed
Affiliation or Control: State IRS Status: 501(c)3
Highest Offering: Master's
Accreditation: NH, AAB, CACREP, CAEPN, MUS

01 President ....Mr. Sean BURRAGE
05 Vice Pres Acad Affairs ....Dr. Bryon CLARK
10 Vice President Business Affairs ....Mr. Dennis WESTMAN
32 Dean of Student Affairs ....Ms. Liz MCCRAW
07 Assoc Dean Admissions/Registrar ....Ms. Kristie LUKE
58 Dean Graduate School ....Mr. Tim BOATMUN
13 Exec Dir of Information Technology ....Mr. Dan MOORE
111 Vice President of Univ Advancement ....Mr. Kyle STAFFORD
37 Director Student Financial Aid ....Mr. Tony LEHRLING
08 Library Director ....Ms. Sandra THOMAS
41 Director of Athletics ....Mr. Keith BAXTER
26 Dir Univ Comm/Spec Asst Pres ....Mr. Alan BURTON
21 Director Finance/Controller ....Ms. Kay Lynn ROBERTS
18 Director Facilities/Physical Plant ....Mr. Dan SIMMONS
28 Director of Compliance and Safety ....Mr. Mike DAVIS
96 Purchasing Agent ....Ms. Dana BELL
40 Book Store Manager ....Ms. Jackie CODNER
29 Director Alumni Relations ....Ms. Stephanie SHADE-DAVISON
106 Dir Online Education/E-learning ....Ms. Christala SMITH
19 Interim Chief of Police ....Mr. Jody HALL
39 Director Student Housing ....Dr. Kelly D'ARCY
04 Exec Admin Asst to President ....Ms. Terri ROGERS

Southern Nazarene University (K)

6729 NW 39 Expressway, Bethany OK 73008-2694
County: Oklahoma FICE Identification: 003149
Unit ID: 206862
Telephone: (405) 789-6400 Carnegie Class: Masters/L
FAX Number: (405) 491-6381 Calendar System: Semester
URL: www.snu.edu
Established: 1899 Annual Undergrad Tuition & Fees: $24,468
Enrollment: 2,252 Coed
Affiliation or Control: Church Of The Nazarene IRS Status: 501(c)3
Highest Offering: Master's
Accreditation: NH, ACBSP, #CAATE, CAEPN, MUS, NURSE

01 President ....Dr. J. Keith NEWMAN
05 Provost & VP Academic Affairs ....Dr. Melany KYZER
10 Vice President Financial Affairs ....Dr. Scott STRAWN
88 VP of Church Relations ....Dr. Terry TOLER
32 Vice President Student Development ....Dr. Mike REDWINE
42 University Pastor ....Dr. Blair SPINDLE
84 Vice Pres of Enrollment Management ....Dr. Linda CANTWELL
79 Dean College of Humanities ....Dr. Steve BETTS
81 Dean College of Sci & Health ....Dr. Mark WINSLOW
06 Registrar ....Mr. Charles CHITWOOD
37 Director Student Financial Aid ....Mr. Perry DIEHM
35 Director Student Affairs ....Mrs. Marian REDWINE
38 Director Student Counseling ....Mrs. Kimberly CAMPBELL
36 Director Career Planning/Placement ....Mrs. Angela RHODES

08 Director Learning Resources Center ..... Prof. Katie KING
29 Director Alumni Relations ..... Mrs. Marcia MOSSHART
13 Director Information Technology ..... Vacant
20 Director Academic Services ..... Mr. Wes LEE
09 Director Institutional Research ..... Dr. Randy ZABEL
58 Dean Col of Grad & Prof Study ..... Vacant
66 Director of Nursing ..... Dr. Mary HIBBERT
15 Director Human Resources ..... Vacant
18 Director of Physical Plant ..... Mr. Ron LESTER
24 Director Network ..... Mrs. Chichi FREELANDER
26 Director Communications & Marketing ..... Mr. Bill MCCLOUD
40 Bookstore Manager ..... Mr. Keith PIERCE
41 Athletic Director ..... Mr. Bobby MARTIN
53 Vice Prov/Dean Col Teach/Learn ..... Dr. Dennis WILLIAMS
04 Executive Asst to President ..... Mrs. Tollya SPINDLE
19 Director Security/Safety ..... Mr. Glen HOLCOMB
25 Chief Contracts/Grants Admin ..... Dr. Gwen HACKLER
39 Director Student Housing ..... Mrs. Katy BRADLEY
111 Exec Director Univ Advancement ..... Mr. Todd BRANT

Southwestern Christian University (A)

PO Box 340, 7210 NW 39th Expressway, Bethany OK 73008-0340

County: Oklahoma FICE Identification: 003180
Unit ID: 207856
Telephone: (405) 789-7661 Carnegie Class: Bac-Diverse
FAX Number: (405) 495-0078 Calendar System: Semester
URL: www.swcu.edu
Established: 1946 Annual Undergrad Tuition & Fees: $13,080
Enrollment: 746 Coed
Affiliation or Control: Pentecostal Holiness Church IRS Status: 501(c)3
Highest Offering: Master's
Accreditation: NH

01 President ..... Dr. Reggies WENYIKA
10 Vice President Business & Finance ..... Mr. Tony CROUCH
10 VP Academic Affairs ..... Dr. Dana DELONG
32 Vice President for Student Services ..... Mr. Brad DAVIS
11 Vice President of Operations & Athl ..... Mr. Mark ARTHUR
41 Associate VP Operations & Athletics ..... Mr. Joe BLACKWELL
37 Director of Financial Aid ..... Mrs. Kellye JOHNSON
07 Director of Admissions ..... Mrs. Jesse BURPO
08 Director of Library Services ..... Mr. Michael LOWDER
06 Registrar ..... Mr. Robert LENK
107 Dean of Professional Studies & Grad ..... Dr. Adrian HINKLE
49 Dean of Arts & Sciences ..... Dr. Gayle KEARNS
18 Director of Plant/Property Mgmt ..... Mr. Robert PALMER
26 Director of Sports Information/PR ..... Mr. Matthew STEPHENS
13 Director of Information Technology ..... Mr. Scott KLEPPER
106 Dean of Online Education ..... Mr. Zach DICKSON
108 Dean of Institutional Effectiveness ..... Vacant
15 Director of Employee Relations ..... Ms. Rita PALMER
30 Chief Development Officer ..... Ms. April BLACK
84 Director Enrollment Services ..... Mr. George WASHINGTON
04 Executive Asst to President ..... Ms. Erin BROWN
09 Director of Institutional Research ..... Vacant
19 Director Security/Safety ..... Vacant
39 Director of Housing ..... Mr. Zach SHERRILL
39 Director Student Life/Resident Dir ..... Ms. Kaylee BISHOP

Southwestern Oklahoma State University (B)

100 Campus Drive, Weatherford OK 73096-3098

County: Custer FICE Identification: 003181
Unit ID: 207865
Telephone: (580) 772-6611 Carnegie Class: Masters/L
FAX Number: (580) 774-3795 Calendar System: Semester
URL: www.swosu.edu
Established: 1901 Annual Undergrad Tuition & Fees (In-State): $6,690
Enrollment: 5,113 Coed
Affiliation or Control: State IRS Status: 501(c)3
Highest Offering: First Professional Degree
Accreditation: NH, #CAATE, CAEPN, CAHIIM, ENGT, IACBE, MLTAB, MUS, NAIT, NUR, OTA, PHAR, PTAA, RAD

01 President ..... Dr. Randy L. BEUTLER
10 VP Business and Finance ..... Ms. Brenda K. BURGESS
05 VP for Academic Affairs/Provost ..... Dr. James D. SOUTH
32 VP Student Affairs/Assoc Provost ..... Dr. Ruth BOYD
20 Assoc Provost Acad Affairs ..... Dr. Monica VARNER
26 VP for Marketing/Public Relations ..... Mr. Brian D. ADLER
30 Asst to Pres for Inst Advancement ..... Mr. Garrett KING
96 Dir Business Affairs/Comptroller ..... Ms. Patricia GARCIA
35 Dean of Students/Dir Student Act ..... Ms. Cynthia R. DOUGHERTY
13 Dir Information Technology Services ..... Ms. Karen KLEIN
06 Registrar ..... Mr. Shamus MOORE
08 Library Director ..... Mr. Jason M. DUPREE
37 Director Student Financial Services ..... Mr. Jerome L. WICHERT
15 Dir Human Resources/Affirm Action ..... Mr. David MISAK
84 Dir Enrollment Mgmt/Career Svcs ..... Mr. Todd T. BOYD
41 Athletic Director ..... Mr. Todd A. THURMAN
06 Registrar Sayre Campus ..... Ms. Terry L. BILLEY
38 Director Counseling Services ..... Ms. Kim K. LIEBSCHER
18 Director Physical Plant ..... Mr. James SKINNER
57 Director of Facilities FAC & PCEC ..... Mr. Nate DOWNS
36 Career Services Coordinator ..... Ms. Heather HUMMEL
58 Dean College of Prof/Grad Studies ..... Dr. Chad L. KINDER
49 Dean College of Arts/Sciences ..... Dr. Peter GRANT
67 Dean College of Pharmacy ..... Dr. David RALPH
12 Dean College of Assoc/Applied Prog ..... Ms. Sherron K. MANNING
53 Assoc Dean Sch of Behavioral Sci ..... Dr. Randy BARNETT
50 Assoc Dean School of Business/Tech ..... Dr. Patsy PARKER
66 Assoc Dn Sch Nursing/Allied Health ..... Dr. Marcy TANNER

† Campus at Sayre offers a two-year degree and is regionally accredited (NH) under parent institution.

Spartan College of Aeronautics and Technology (C)

8820 E Pine Street, Tulsa OK 74115

County: Tulsa FICE Identification: 007678
Unit ID: 207254
Telephone: (918) 836-6886 Carnegie Class: Spec-4-yr-Other Tech
FAX Number: (918) 831-5287 Calendar System: Other
URL: www.spartan.edu
Established: 1928 Annual Undergrad Tuition & Fees: $16,395
Enrollment: 759 Coed
Affiliation or Control: Proprietary IRS Status: Proprietary
Highest Offering: Baccalaureate
Accreditation: ACCSC

00 CEO ..... Mr. Dan PETERSON
01 President ..... Mr. Lamar HAYNES
10 CFO ..... Mr. Neil D. AMARI
32 VP Student Services ..... Mr. Damon BOWLING
04 Administrative Asst to President ..... Ms. Rasha MOSABEH

Tulsa Community College (D)

6111 E Skelly Drive, Tulsa OK 74135-6198

County: Tulsa FICE Identification: 009763
Unit ID: 207935
Telephone: (918) 595-7000 Carnegie Class: Assoc/HT-Mix Trad/Non
FAX Number: (918) 595-7910 Calendar System: Semester
URL: www.tulsacc.edu
Established: 1968 Annual Undergrad Tuition & Fees (In-State): $3,071
Enrollment: 17,160 Coed
Affiliation or Control: State IRS Status: 501(c)3
Highest Offering: Associate Degree
Accreditation: NH, ADNUR, CAHIIM, COARC, CVT, DH, MLTAD, OTA, PHLEB, PTAA, RAD

01 President/CEO ..... Dr. Leigh GOODSON
05 Sr VP and Chief Academic Officer ..... Dr. Cynthia HESS
100 Sr Advisor to the President ..... Dr. Bill IVY
102 VP Ext Affairs & Foundation Pres ..... Ms. Lauren F. BROOKEY
11 VP Administration ..... Mr. Sean A. WEINS
10 Chief Financial Officer ..... Mr. Mark MCMULLEN
32 Sr Student Affairs Officer ..... Dr. Jan L. CLAYTON
12 Interim Provost Northeast Campus ..... Dr. Eunice TARVER
12 Provost West Campus & Assoc VP IE ..... Dr. Kevin M. DAVID
12 Provost Metro Campus ..... Dr. Greg STONE
12 Provost Southeast Campus ..... Dr. John GIBSON
84 Asst VP Enrollment Mgmt ..... Ms. Eileen KENNEY
28 Asst VP Diversity/Inclusion ..... Ms. Eunice TARVER
13 Chief Technology Officer ..... Mr. Michael SIFTAR
15 Chief Human Resources Officer ..... Ms. Sandy COOPER
88 Dean Community Campuses ..... Dr. Paula WILLYARD
08 Dean Libraries ..... Ms. Paula SETTOON
51 Director Continuing Education ..... Ms. Beth WILD
06 Dir Compl Reporting/Col Registrar ..... Ms. Traci HECK
26 Sr Dir Marketing/Communications ..... Ms. Kari SHULTS
18 Dir Physical Facilities ..... Mr. Steven COX
88 Dir Emergency Ops/Title IX ..... Ms. Heather HANCOCK
37 Dir Financial Aid ..... Ms. Karen JEFFERS
96 Dir Purch & Inventory Control ..... Mr. Bill CREECH
09 Dir Institutional Research/Assess ..... Dr. Jennifer IVIE
19 Dir Campus Public Safety ..... Mr. Gene WIDEMAN
92 Honors Program Coord ..... Ms. Susan ONEAL
25 Dir Sponsored Programs ..... Dr. Barbara WAXMAN
104 Dir Global Learning ..... Dr. Douglas PRICE
106 Dir Online Learning ..... Mr. Randy G. DOMINGUEZ
105 Web Manager ..... Vacant
04 Exec Asst to President ..... Ms. Carrie BATESON
07 Dir Admissions/Prosp Stdnt Svcs ..... Vacant
30 Director of Development ..... Ms. Rachel HUTCHINGS
36 Dir Career and Retention ..... Ms. Kristie COLEMAN
54 Dean Engineering/Applied Tech ..... Mr. Patrick GREEN
112 Director of Major Gifts ..... Ms. Monica CHAMP

Tulsa Community College Metro Campus (E)

909 South Boston Avenue, Tulsa OK 74119

Telephone: (918) 595-7224 Identification: 770383
Accreditation: &NH, DMS

Tulsa Community College Northeast Campus (F)

3727 East Apache Street, Tulsa OK 74115

Telephone: (918) 595-7524 Identification: 770384
Accreditation: &NH

Tulsa Community College Southeast Campus (G)

10300 East 81st Street, Tulsa OK 74133

Telephone: (918) 595-7724 Identification: 770385
Accreditation: &NH

Tulsa Community College West Campus (H)

7505 W 41st Street South, Tulsa OK 74107-8633

Telephone: (918) 595-8100 Identification: 770386
Accreditation: &NH

Tulsa Welding School (I)

2545 E 11th Street, Tulsa OK 74104-3909

County: Tulsa FICE Identification: 009618
Unit ID: 207962
Telephone: (918) 587-6789 Carnegie Class: Spec 2-yr-Tech
FAX Number: (918) 587-8170 Calendar System: Other
URL: www.weldingschool.com
Established: 1949 Annual Undergrad Tuition & Fees: N/A
Enrollment: 1,055 Coed
Affiliation or Control: Proprietary IRS Status: Proprietary
Highest Offering: Associate Degree
Accreditation: ACCSC

01 Campus President ..... Ms. Susan KUHL
05 Academic Dean ..... Mr. Michael BARRETT
07 Director of Adult Admissions ..... Mr. Monte SCHAICH
37 Director of Financial Aid ..... Vacant
36 Director of Career Services ..... Mr. Darin MCDUGLE

University of Central Oklahoma (J)

100 N University Drive, Edmond OK 73034-5209

County: Oklahoma FICE Identification: 003152
Unit ID: 206941
Telephone: (405) 974-2000 Carnegie Class: Masters/L
FAX Number: (405) 359-5841 Calendar System: Semester
URL: www.uco.edu
Established: 1890 Annual Undergrad Tuition & Fees (In-State): $6,699
Enrollment: 16,910 Coed
Affiliation or Control: State IRS Status: 501(c)3
Highest Offering: Master's
Accreditation: NH, ACBSP, ART, CAATE, CAEPN, CIDA, CS, DIETD, DIETI, ENG, EXSC, FEPAC, FUSER, MUS, NURSE, SP

01 President ..... Dr. Don BETZ
05 Provost/Vice Pres Academic Affairs ..... Dr. John BARTHELL
11 Vice Pres for Operations ..... Mr. Kevin FREEMAN
32 Vice President Student Affairs ..... Dr. Myron POPE
13 Chief Information Officer ..... Ms. Sonya WATKINS
26 Vice Pres University Relations ..... Mr. Charlie JOHNSON
86 Vice Pres Public Affairs ..... Dr. Mark KINDERS
30 Vice Pres Development ..... Mrs. Anne HOLZBERLEIN
10 Vice Pres Finance ..... Ms. Patti NEUHOLD
06 Associate Vice President/Registrar ..... Dr. Adam JOHNSON
20 Assoc VP Academic Affairs ..... Dr. Charlotte SIMMONS
108 Assoc VP Inst Effectiveness ..... Dr. Gary STEWARD
21 Asst VP Financial Operations ..... Ms. Lisa HARPER
18 Asst Vice Pres Facilities Mgt ..... Mr. Mark RODOLF
35 Asst Vice Pres Student Affairs ..... Mr. Cole STANLEY
88 Asst Vice Pres Operations ..... Dr. Josh OVEROCKER
41 Athletic Director ..... Mr. Joe MULLER
09 Exec Dir Institutional Research ..... Ms. Cindy BOLING
08 Exec Director University Libraries ..... Dr. Habib TABATABAI
37 Director Student Financial Services ..... Ms. Deanna BRANDT
29 Director Alumni Relations ..... Mr. David LEWIS
85 Exec Dir Global Affairs ..... Dr. Dennis DUNHAM
19 Exec Dir Public Safety/Trans ..... Mr. Jeff HARP
15 Asst VP Human Resources ..... Ms. Diane FEINBERG
88 Exec Director Leadership Central ..... Dr. Jarrett JOBE
07 Dir of Undergraduate Admissions ..... Mr. Dallas CALDWELL
28 Director of Diversity & Inclusion ..... Ms. MeShawn CONLEY
96 Director of Purchasing ..... Mr. David YOUNG
43 Senior Legal Counsel ..... Dr. Brad MORELLI
50 Dean of Business Administration ..... Vacant
53 Dean College Education ..... Dr. James MACHELL
49 Dean College of Liberal Arts ..... Dr. Catherine WEBSTER
81 Dean College Math/Science ..... Dr. Wei CHEN
58 Dean Graduate Studies ..... Dr. Richard BERNARD
57 Dean College Fine Arts & Design ..... Dr. Steven HANSEN

University of Oklahoma Health Sciences Center (K)

1100 N. Lindsay, Oklahoma City OK 73104

Telephone: (405) 271-4000 FICE Identification: 005889
Accreditation: &NH, ARCPA, AUD, DENT, DH, DIETC, DIETI, DMS, ENGR, HSA, IPSY, MED, NMT, NURSE, OT, PDPSY, PH, PHAR, PTA, RAD, #RADDOS, RTT, SP

† Regional accreditation is carried under the parent institution in Norman, OK.

University of Oklahoma Norman Campus (L)

660 Parrington Oval, Norman OK 73019-3070

County: Cleveland FICE Identification: 003184
Unit ID: 207500
Telephone: (405) 325-0311 Carnegie Class: DU-Highest
FAX Number: (405) 325-7605 Calendar System: Semester
URL: www.ou.edu
Established: 1890 Annual Undergrad Tuition & Fees (In-State): $10,881
Enrollment: 27,428 Coed
Affiliation or Control: State IRS Status: 501(c)3
Highest Offering: Doctorate

Accreditation: NH, AAB, CAEPN, CIDA, CONST, COPSY, CS, ENG, JOUR, LAW, LIB, LSAR, MUS, PLNG, SW

01 President .... Mr. David L. BOREN
10 VP Administration & Finance .... Mr. Nicholas S. HATHAWAY
88 VP for Univ Governance .... Dr. Chris A. PURCELL
05 Senior Vice President/Provost .... Dr. Kyle HARPER
43 VP of Univ/General Counsel .... Mr. Anil V. GOLLAHALLI
32 Vice President for Student Affairs .... Mr. Clarke A. STROUD
30 Vice Pres for University Devel .... Mr. Jim HALL, III
51 Interim VP for Univ Outreach .... Dr. Belinda P. BISCOE
58 Interim Dean Graduate College .... Dr. Randy HEWES
46 Vice President for Research .... Dr. Kelvin K. DROEGEMEIER
26 Assoc VP for Public Affairs .... Mr. Rowdy C. GILBERT
13 VP/Chief Information Ofcr .... Ms. Loretta M. EARLY
86 Vice Pres for Governmental Relation .... Mr. W. Scott MASON, IV
20 Associate Provost/Dir of Acad Integ .... Dr. Gregory M. HEISER
121 Assoc Prov for Acad Advising .... Dr. Kathleen S. SMITH
09 Assoc Provost/Dir Inst Research .... Ms. Susannah B. LIVINGOOD
06 Registrar/VP Enroll/Stdnt Fin Svcs .... Mr. Matthew W. HAMILTON
35 Assoc VP for Student Affairs .... Ms. Kristen N. PARTRIDGE
21 Assoc VP Administration & Finance .... Mr. B. Burr MILLSAP
21 Assoc VP Admin & Finance/CFO .... Mr. Chris KUWITZKY
29 Assoc VP Alum & Dev/Ex Dir Alum Asn .... Mr. Jean Paul AUDAS
18 Director Facilities Management .... Mr. Brian F. ELLIS
39 Director of Housing & Food Services .... Mr. David L. ANNIS
41 VP for Intercollegiate Athl Pgms .... Mr. Joseph R. CASTIGLIONE
21 Asst VP for Admin & Fin/Controller .... Ms. Terri B. PINKSTON
23 Assoc VP for Stdnt Affs/Health Svs .... Dr. William R. WAYNE
36 Director Career Services .... Ms. Robin E. HUSTON
19 Chief of Police .... Ms. Elizabeth G. WOOLLEN
15 Human Resources Director .... Ms. Marcella B. FLEMING
22 Equal Opportunity Officer .... Mr. Bobby J. MASON
07 Exec Dir of Admissions/Recruitment .... Mr. Jeffrey J. BLAHNIK
25 Assoc VP for Research Services .... Ms. Andrea D. DEATON
85 Dir International Student Services .... Ms. Robyn D. ROJAS
104 Director Education Abroad .... Ms. Whitney R. FRANCA
37 Director of Financial Aid .... Ms. Caryn L. PACHECO
48 Dean Col of Architecture .... Mr. Hans W. BUTZER
49 Interim Dean Col of Arts & Sciences .... Dr. David R. WROBEL
53 Dean Jeannine Rainbolt Col of Educ .... Dr. Gregg A. GARN
54 Dean Gallogly Col of Engineering .... Dr. Thomas L. LANDERS
57 Dean Weitzenhoffer Col Fine Arts .... Ms. Mary Margaret HOLT
61 VP/Dean College of Law .... Mr. Joseph HARROZ, JR.
62 Assoc VP/Dean Univ Libraries .... Mr. Richard E. LUCE
65 VP/Dn Col Atmospheric/Geographic Sc .... Dr. Berrien MOORE, III
50 VP/Dean Price Col of Business .... Mr. Daniel W. PULLIN
92 Dean Honors College .... Dr. David H. RAY
60 Dean Gaylord Col Journ/Mass Comm .... Mr. Ed KELLEY
89 Dean University College .... Dr. Nicole J. CAMPBELL
65 Dean Mewborne Col of Earth & Energy .... Dr. J. Michael STICE
82 Vice Provost/Dean Col Intl Studies .... Dr. Suzette R. GRILLOT
28 VP for the University Community .... Mr. Jabar SHUMATE
84 Assoc VP Enrollment/Stdnt Fin Svcs .... Mr. Bradley T. BURNETT
04 Administrative Asst to President .... Ms. Sherry L. EVANS
102 Dir Foundation/Corporate Relations .... Mr. Guy L. PATTON
103 Dir Workforce/Career Development .... Ms. Cynthia B. CLEGG
105 Assoc VP/Director Web Services .... Ms. Erin A. YARBROUGH
106 Dir Ctr for Indep & Distant Learing .... Mr. Randy B. DOERNEMAN
38 Director Student Counseling .... Dr. William R. WAYNE
96 Director of Purchasing .... Mr. Matthew W. ROBERTS
112 Director Planned Giving & Develop .... Mr. Eric MELTON

† Tuition is based on 30 credit hour per year.

University of Oklahoma Schusterman Center (A)

4502 E 41st Street, Tulsa OK 74135-2512
Telephone: (918) 660-3000 Identification: 770387
Accreditation: &NH, ARCPA, OT

University of Science and Arts of Oklahoma (B)

1727 W Alabama, Chickasha OK 73018-5322
County: Grady FICE Identification: 003167
Unit ID: 207722
Telephone: (405) 224-3140 Carnegie Class: Bac-A&S
FAX Number: (405) 574-1220 Calendar System: Trimester
URL: www.usao.edu
Established: 1908 Annual Undergrad Tuition & Fees (In-State): $7,200
Enrollment: 873 Coed
Affiliation or Control: State IRS Status: 501(c)3
Highest Offering: Baccalaureate
Accreditation: NH, CAEP, MUS

01 President .... Dr. John H. FEAVER
05 VP for Academic Affairs .... Dr. Krista MAXSON
10 Vice Pres for Business & Finance .... Mr. Mike D. COPONITI
84 Vice Pres for Enrollment Management .... Ms. Monica TREVINO
30 Vice Pres University Advancement .... Mr. Sid HUDSON
13 VP for Library/Information Services .... Ms. Kelly BROWN
06 Registrar/Dir of Enrollment/Records .... Ms. Chelsea PHILLIPS
08 Director of Nash Library .... Ms. Kelly BROWN
26 Dir of Communications/Marketing .... Ms. Amy GODDARD
37 Director of Financial Aid .... Ms. Laura I. COPONITI
32 Dean of Students/Dir Student Svcs .... Ms. Nancy HUGHES
29 Director of Alumni Development .... Mr. Eric FEUERBORN
18 Director of Physical Plant .... Mr. Mike COPONITI
09 Director of Institutional Research .... Ms. Kristi JOHN
15 Director Personnel Services .... Mr. Mike COPONITI
07 Acting Director of Admissions .... Ms. Monica TREVINO
38 Director Student Counseling .... Ms. Misty STEELE
49 Chair Div of Arts & Humanities .... Dr. Stephen WEBER
50 Chair Div of Business & Social Sci .... Dr. James WELCH
53 Chair Division of Education .... Dr. Donna GOWER
81 Chair Div of Science/Physical Educ .... Dr. J.C SANDERS
88 Chair Interdisciplinary Studies .... Dr. Jennifer LONG
19 Director Security/Safety .... Mr. Chris BASCO
41 Athletic Director .... Mr. Brisco MCPHERSON

University of Tulsa (C)

800 S Tucker, Tulsa OK 74104
County: Tulsa FICE Identification: 003185
Unit ID: 207971
Telephone: (918) 631-2000 Carnegie Class: DU-Higher
FAX Number: (918) 631-2033 Calendar System: Semester
URL: www.utulsa.edu
Established: 1894 Annual Undergrad Tuition & Fees: $41,509
Enrollment: 4,671 Coed
Affiliation or Control: Independent Non-Profit IRS Status: 501(c)3
Highest Offering: Doctorate
Accreditation: NH, CAATE, CAEPT, CEA, CLPSY, CS, ENG, LAW, MUS, NUR, SP

01 President .... Dr. Gerard CLANCY
10 Exec Vice President & Treasurer .... Mr. Kevan C. BUCK
05 Provost/Vice Pres Academic Affairs .... Dr. Roger N. BLAIS
45 Vice Pres Institutional Advancement .... Dr. Kayla HALE
84 VP Enrollment Mgmt/Student Services .... Mr. Earl JOHNSON
41 VP & Athletic Director .... Dr. Derrick GRAGG
13 VP Info Services & CIO .... Mr. Richard KEARNS
28 VP Diversity & Engagement .... Ms. Jacqueline H. CALDWELL
86 VP Public Affairs/COO Gilcrease .... Ms. Susan NEAL
20 Sr Vice Provost/Assoc VP Acad Affs .... Ms. Winona M. TANAKA
46 Vice Prov Research/Dean Grad School .... Dr. Janet A. HAGGERTY
104 Vice Provost Global Education .... Dr. Jane KUCKO
09 Assoc VP Institutional Research .... Mr. John BURY
42 University Chaplain .... Dr. Jeffrey FRANCIS
49 Dean Arts & Sciences .... Dr. Kalpana MISRA
50 Dean Business Administration .... Dr. A. Gale SULLENBERGER
54 Dean Engineering/Natural Sciences .... Dr. James R. SOREM, JR.
61 Dean Law .... Ms. Lyn ENTZEROTH
08 RM & Ida McFarlin Dean of Library .... Mr. Adrian W. ALEXANDER
111 Assoc VP Institutional Advancement .... Ms. Amy ENGLAND
06 Registrar .... Ms. Ginna V. LANGSTON
15 Associate VP Human Resources .... Mr. Wayne PAULISON
22 Dir Acad Support/504 Coordinator .... Dr. Tawny RIGSBY
18 Assoc VP Operations/Physical Plant .... Mr. Robert SHIPLEY
21 Assoc VP & Controller .... Mr. Michael D. THESENVITZ
07 Assoc VP Enrollment Dean Admission .... Ms. Casey REED
32 Assoc VP Enrollment Dean Students .... Mr. Michael MILLS
39 Assoc VP Director Housing .... Ms. Melissa H. FRANCE
85 Dean International Students .... Ms. Pamela A. SMITH
51 Dean Lifelong Learning .... Dr. J. Phillip APPLEGATE
62 Assoc Dean McFarlin Library .... Ms. Francine J. FISK
88 Director Helmerich Center .... Dr. Duane KING
38 Director Counseling & Psych Svcs .... Dr. Thomas J. BRIAN
19 Director Campus Security .... Mr. Joseph F. TIMMONS
29 Exec Director Alumni Relations .... Ms. Amy M. FREIBERGER
36 Director Career Services .... Ms. Shelly HOLLY
37 Director Student Financial Svcs .... Ms. Vicki A. HENDRICKSON
96 Director Purchasing .... Mr. Jerry R. HOLLOWAY
90 Dir Academic Tech Services .... Ms. Janet CAIRNS
91 Dir ERP Operations .... Mr. Martin PAGE
31 Assoc Dean Community Relations .... Mr. Michael MILLS
26 Dir Marketing & Communications .... Ms. Mona CHAMBERLIN
105 Exec Dir Digital Communication .... Mr. Matt CASTEEL
101 Secretary Board of Trustees .... Ms. June E. BROWN
04 Sr Admin Associate to President .... Ms. Susan LAYMAN

Vatterott College-Oklahoma City (D)

5537 NW Expressway, Warr Acres OK 73132-5230
Telephone: (405) 945-0088 Identification: 666061
Accreditation: ACCSC

† Branch campus of Vatterott College, Quincy, IL.

Vatterott College-Tulsa (E)

4343 S 118th E Avenue, Ste A, Tulsa OK 74146-4406
Telephone: (918) 835-8288 Identification: 666102
Accreditation: ACCSC

† Branch campus of Vatterott College-NorthPark, Berkeley, MO.

Virginia College (F)

5124 South Peoria Avenue, Tulsa OK 74105
Telephone: (918) 960-5400 Identification: 770825
Accreditation: ACICS

† Branch campus of Virginia College, Birmingham, AL

Western Oklahoma State College (G)

2801 N Main Street, Altus OK 73521-1397
County: Jackson FICE Identification: 003146
Unit ID: 208035
Telephone: (580) 477-2000 Carnegie Class: Assoc/HT-Mix Trad/Non
FAX Number: (580) 477-7777 Calendar System: Semester
URL: www.wosc.edu
Established: 1926 Annual Undergrad Tuition & Fees (In-State): $3,561
Enrollment: 1,424 Coed
Affiliation or Control: State IRS Status: 501(c)3
Highest Offering: Associate Degree
Accreditation: NH, ADNUR, RAD

01 President .... Dr. Phil BIRDINE
04 Admin Secretary to the President .... Ms. Briar JENKINS
05 VP for Academic Affairs .... Ms. Lisa GREENLEE
10 Vice President for Business Affairs .... Ms. Tricia LATHAM
32 Vice Pres Student Support Services .... Mr. Chad WIGINTON
49 Dean Arts & Sciences .... Vacant
20 Academic Dean .... Ms. Chrystal OVERTON
09 Dir of Institutional Effectiveness .... Mr. Justin SMITH
13 Chief Tech Ofcr/Dean Lrng Supp Sys .... Mr. Steve PRATER
26 Dir Public Information/Marketing .... Vacant
07 Director of Admissions & Registrar .... Ms. Lana SCOTT
37 Director of Financial Aid .... Ms. Myrna J. CROSS
30 Dir Development/Alumni Relations .... Ms. Whitney GRAHAM
41 Director Athletics .... Mr. Bob PEARSON
08 Director of Learning Resources .... Ms. Suzanne ROOKER
15 Director Personnel Services .... Ms. April NELSON
18 Director Physical Plant .... Mr. Doyle JENCKS
40 Bookstore Manager .... Ms. Kass DEWEESE
38 Counselor .... Ms. Cheryl ORR

OREGON

American College of Healthcare Sciences (H)

5005 SW Macadam, Portland OR 97239
County: Multnomah FICE Identification: 041944
Unit ID: 443599
Telephone: (503) 244-0726 Carnegie Class: Spec-4-yr-Other Health
FAX Number: (503) 244-0727 Calendar System: Semester
URL: www.achs.edu
Established: 1978 Annual Undergrad Tuition & Fees: $10,800
Enrollment: 689 Coed
Affiliation or Control: Proprietary IRS Status: Proprietary
Highest Offering: Master's
Accreditation: DEAC

01 President/CEO .... Dorene PETERSEN
11 Chief Operating Officer .... Tracey ABELL
45 Chief Strategy Officer .... Erika YIGZAW
10 Chief Financial Officer .... Debbie PARIGIAN
88 Director of Operations .... Heather BALEY
07 Dean of Admissions .... Amy SWINEHART
06 Registrar .... Jennifer MORRISON
26 Chief Marketing Officer .... Kate HARMON

The Art Institute of Portland (I)

1122 NW Davis Street, Portland OR 97209-2911
County: Multnomah FICE Identification: 007819
Unit ID: 208239
Telephone: (503) 228-6528 Carnegie Class: Spec-4-yr-Arts
FAX Number: (503) 228-4227 Calendar System: Quarter
URL: www.artinstitutes.edu/portland
Established: 1963 Annual Undergrad Tuition & Fees: $17,412
Enrollment: 899 Coed
Affiliation or Control: Proprietary IRS Status: Proprietary
Highest Offering: Baccalaureate
Accreditation: NW, CIDA

01 President .... Dr. Gregg CROWE
05 Dean of Academic Affairs .... Dr. Robert RIDEL
32 Director of Student Services .... Mr. Jonathan SCRIMENTI
06 Registrar .... Ms. Yvonne PETERSON
07 Senior Director of Admissions .... Ms. Tami BELLENGHI
08 Head Librarian .... Ms. Jennifer COX
37 Director of Financial Services .... Ms. Lauren PATTERSON

† Granted candidacy at the Master's level.

Birthingway College of Midwifery (J)

12113 SE Foster Road, Portland OR 97266-4042
County: Multnomah FICE Identification: 036683
Unit ID: 442949
Telephone: (503) 760-3131 Carnegie Class: Spec-4-yr-Other Health
FAX Number: (503) 760-3332 Calendar System: Quarter
URL: www.birthingway.edu
Established: 1993 Annual Undergrad Tuition & Fees: N/A
Enrollment: 81 Coed
Affiliation or Control: Independent Non-Profit IRS Status: 501(c)3
Highest Offering: Baccalaureate
Accreditation: MEAC

01 President .... Ms. Holly SCHOLLES
05 Academic Coordinator .... Ms. Nicholc REDING
10 Finance Coordinator .... Ms. Elizabeth BRAGG
20 Faculty Coordinator .... Ms. Natalie HUTCHINSON
37 Financial Aid Officer .... Ms. Stace MAURER
06 Registrar .... Ms. Sadie JULIN
88 Midwifery Program Coordinator .... Ms. Rhonda RAY
88 Lactation Program Coordinator .... Ms. Sarah LONGWELL
88 Administrative Programs Coordinator .... Ms. Tiffany HARRISON-TAYLOR
08 Head Librarian .... Ms. Daina DICKMAN
30 Outreach/Development Coordinator .... Ms. Elaura DUNNING

Blue Mountain Community College (A)

PO Box 100, Pendleton OR 97801-0100
County: Umatilla/Morrow/Baker FICE Identification: 003186
Unit ID: 208275
Telephone: (541) 276-1260 Carnegie Class: Assoc/HT-High Non
FAX Number: (541) 278-5886 Calendar System: Quarter
URL: www.bluecc.edu
Established: 1962 Annual Undergrad Tuition & Fees (In-District): $4,925
Enrollment: 1,686 Coed
Affiliation or Control: State/Local IRS Status: 501(c)3
Highest Offering: Associate Degree
Accreditation: NW, DA

01 President ..... Ms. Camille PREUS
05 Vice President of Instruction ..... Ms. MJ KUHAR
32 Vice Pres Student Affairs ..... Ms. Diane DREBIN
11 Vice Pres Admin Services ..... Ms. Tammie PARKER
08 Director of Library & Media Svcs ..... Ms. Jacqueline RAY
102 Executive Director Foundation ..... Ms. Margaret GIANOTTI
37 Director of Student Financial Aid ..... Ms. Yadira GONZALEZ
04 Administrative Asst to President ..... Ms. Shannon FRANKLIN
10 AVP Finance & Business Operations ..... Ms. Celeste INSKO
106 Dir Online Education/E-learning ..... Mr. Bruce KAUSS
13 Chief Info Technology Officer (CIO) ..... Mr. Brad HOLDEN
38 Director Student Counseling ..... Vacant
15 Director Human Resources ..... Ms. Kelli BULLINGTON
41 Athletic Director ..... Mr. Brett BRYAN
09 Director of Institutional Research ..... Mr. Timothy WILSON
26 Chief Public Relations/Marketing ..... Ms. Casey WHITE-ZOLLMAN
75 Dean CTE/Community Educ ..... Mr. Carl MELLE
121 Dean Student Success & Retention ..... Mr. Ralph MURPHY, II
84 Director Enrollment Svcs/Registrar ..... Ms. Theresa BOSWORTH
18 Chief Facilities/Physical Plant ..... Mr. Dwayne WILLIAMS
102 Exec Director BMCC Foundation ..... Ms. Margaret GIANETTI

Central Oregon Community College (B)

2600 NW College Way, Bend OR 97703
County: Deschutes FICE Identification: 003188
Unit ID: 208318
Telephone: (541) 383-7700 Carnegie Class: Assoc/MT-VT-Mix Trad/Non
FAX Number: (541) 383-7506 Calendar System: Quarter
URL: www.cocc.edu
Established: 1949 Annual Undergrad Tuition & Fees (In-District): $3,627
Enrollment: 6,073 Coed
Affiliation or Control: Local IRS Status: 501(c)3
Highest Offering: Associate Degree
Accreditation: NW, ACFEI, CAHIIM, COMTA, DA, EMT, IFSAC, MAC

01 President ..... Dr. Shirley I. METCALF
05 Vice President for Instruction ..... Dr. Betsy JULIAN
11 Vice Pres for Administration ..... Mr. Matthew J. MCCOY
10 Chief Financial Officer ..... Mr. David DONA
51 Dean of Extended Learning ..... Mr. Jerry SCHULZ
20 Instructional Dean ..... Dr. Michael FISHER
20 Instructional Dean ..... Dr. Jennifer NEWBY
84 Dean of Student/Enrollment Svcs ..... Dr. Alicia MOORE
07 Director of Admissions & Records ..... Ms. Courtney WHETSTINE
08 Director of Library Services ..... Dr. Tina HOVEKAMP
26 Director College Relations ..... Mr. Ronald S. PARADIS
13 Director Information Technology ..... Mr. Dan CECCHINI
18 Director Campus Services ..... Mr. Joe VIOLA
15 Director Human Resources ..... Ms. Danielle FEGLEY
22 Affirmative Action Officer ..... Ms. Diane ROSS
37 Director Student Financial Aid ..... Mr. Kevin MULTOP
28 Dir of Multicultural Activities ..... Ms. Karen ROTH
32 Director of Student and Campus Life ..... Mr. Andrew DAVIS
09 Dir Institutional Effectiveness ..... Ms. Brynn PIERCE
38 Director Student Counseling ..... Ms. Seana BARRY
40 Director Bookstore/Auxiliary Svcs ..... Ms. Lori BENEFIEL
108 Director Curriculum & Assessment ..... Ms. Vickery VILES
19 Interim Director Security/Safety ..... Mr. Don DOUGHTY
25 Director Contracts/Risk Management ..... Ms. Sharla ANDRESEN
102 Director Foundation ..... Mr. Zak BOONE
51 Director of Continuing Education ..... Ms. Glenda LANTIS

Chemeketa Community College (C)

PO Box 14007, Salem OR 97309-7070
County: Marion FICE Identification: 003218
Unit ID: 208390
Telephone: (503) 399-5000 Carnegie Class: Assoc/HT-High Non
FAX Number: (503) 399-5214 Calendar System: Quarter
URL: www.chemeketa.edu
Established: 1962 Annual Undergrad Tuition & Fees (In-District): $4,230
Enrollment: 11,454 Coed
Affiliation or Control: Local IRS Status: 501(c)3
Highest Offering: Associate Degree
Accreditation: NW, ADNUR, DA, EMT, IFSAC

01 President/Chief Executive Officer ..... Ms. Julie HUCKESTEIN
05 VP/Chief Academic Officer ..... Mr. Jim EUSTROM
03 VP Governance & Administration ..... Mr. Andrew BONE
12 Campus President Yamhill Valley ..... Mr. Jim EUSTROM
20 Exec Dean Career/Tech Education ..... Mr. Johnny MACK
32 Exec Dean Student Dev/Learning Res ..... Mr. Manuel GUERRA
88 Exec Dean Acad Progress/Reg Ed Svcs ..... Ms. Holly NELSON
88 Dean Emergency Services ..... Mr. Marshall ROACHE
83 Dean Liberal Arts & Social Sciences ..... Mr. Don BRASE
76 Dean Health Services ..... Ms. Sandi KELLOGG
37 Dean Financial Aid/Enrollment Svcs ..... Mr. Ryan WEST
38 Dean Counseling/Career Services ..... Mr. Jon MATHIS
72 Dean Applied Technologies ..... Mr. Larry CHEYNE
81 Dean Science/Engineering/Math ..... Mr. Michael MILHAUSEN
50 Dean Bus/Tech/Early Childhood Educ ..... Ms. R. TAYLOR
84 Dir Marketing/Student Recruitment ..... Mr. Greg HARRIS
53 Dean Teaching and Learning ..... Vacant
47 Director Wine Studies ..... Ms. Jessica SANDROCK
08 Director Learning Resource Center ..... Ms. Natalie BEACH
88 Director Enterprise Services ..... Mr. Brian RADER
10 Assoc VP Financial Management ..... Ms. Miriam SCHARER
18 Director Facilities & Operations ..... Mr. Phil WRIGHT
15 Director Human Resources ..... Ms. Alice SPRAGUE
19 Director Public Safety ..... Mr. Bill KOHLMEYER
109 Director Auxiliary Services ..... Ms. Meredith SCHREIBER
41 Athletic Director ..... Ms. Cassie BELMODIS
50 Dir Chemeketa Ctr for Bus/Industry ..... Ms. Diane MCLARAN
88 Coordinator Prof Tech Educ ..... Mr. Ed WOODS
28 Diversity & Equity Officer ..... Ms. Linda HERRERA
35 Director Student Life/Retention ..... Vacant
07 Registrar/Director of Admissions ..... Ms. Melissa FREY
26 Assoc VP/Chief Information Officer ..... Mr. Tim ROGERS
102 Executive Director Foundation ..... Ms. Nancy DUNCAN
25 Grants Coordinator ..... Ms. Peggy GREENE
09 Director of Institutional Research ..... Mr. Fauzi NAAS
43 General Counsel ..... Ms. Rebecca HILLYER
12 Dean Woodburn Center ..... Mr. Elias VILLEGAS
12 Director Polk Center ..... Mr. Glen MILLER

Clackamas Community College (D)

19600 Molalla Avenue, Oregon City OR 97045-7998
County: Clackamas FICE Identification: 004878
Unit ID: 208406
Telephone: (503) 594-6000 Carnegie Class: Assoc/HT-High Non
FAX Number: N/A Calendar System: Quarter
URL: www.clackamas.edu
Established: 1966 Annual Undergrad Tuition & Fees (In-District): $4,412
Enrollment: 6,407 Coed
Affiliation or Control: Local IRS Status: 501(c)3
Highest Offering: Associate Degree
Accreditation: NW, CA, MAC

01 President ..... Dr. Joanne TRUESDELL
05 VP Instruct & Stdnt Svcs/Provost ..... Dr. David PLOTKIN
11 Vice Pres College Services ..... Ms. Alissa MAHAR
04 Executive Asst to the President ..... Ms. Denice BAILEY
102 Executive Director Foundation ..... Mr. Paul MOREDOCK
26 Public Information Officer ..... Ms. Lori HALL
06 Registrar/Enrol Svcs/Operations Mgr ..... Mr. Chris SWEET
32 Assoc Dean Acad Found/Connect Div ..... Ms. Darlene GEIGER
13 Dean/CIO Information Technology ..... Mr. Dion BAIRD
49 Dean Arts & Sciences ..... Ms. Sue GOFF
46 Dean Curriculum/Planning/Research ..... Mr. Bill WATERS
72 Assoc Dn Tech/Hlth Occup/Wrkfc Div ..... Ms. Donna LARSON
15 Dean Human Resources ..... Ms. Patricia ANDERSON WIECK
88 Dir Office Education Partnerships ..... Ms. Jaime CLARKE
10 Director Business Services ..... Ms. Chris ROBUCK
11 Dean Campus Services ..... Mr. Bob COCHRAN
18 Director Campus Services ..... Mr. Lloyd HELM
41 Director Health/PE/Athletics ..... Mr. Jim MARTINEAU
13 Director IT Operations ..... Mr. David GATES

Clatsop Community College (E)

1651 Lexington Avenue, Astoria OR 97103
County: Clatsop FICE Identification: 003189
Unit ID: 208415
Telephone: (503) 325-0910 Carnegie Class: Assoc/MT-VT-High Non
FAX Number: (503) 325-5738 Calendar System: Quarter
URL: www.clatsopcc.edu
Established: 1958 Annual Undergrad Tuition & Fees (In-District): $4,014
Enrollment: 833 Coed
Affiliation or Control: State/Local IRS Status: 501(c)3
Highest Offering: Associate Degree
Accreditation: NW

01 President ..... Mr. Chris BREITMEYER
05 VP Academic & Student Affairs ..... Vacant
10 Vice President Finance & Operations ..... Ms. JoAnn ZAHN
32 Dean Students & Enrollment Mngt ..... Dr. Chris OUSLEY
06 Registrar ..... Dr. Chris OUSLEY
26 Director Marketing & Communication ..... Ms. Julie KOVATCH
13 Director Computer Services ..... Ms. Christine RIEHL
15 Director Human Resources ..... Ms. Leslie HALL
37 Director Student Financial Aid ..... Mr. Lloyd MUELLER
09 Director of Institutional Research ..... Vacant
18 Director Physical Plant ..... Mr. Greg DORCHEUS
21 Director Accounting Services ..... Ms. Margaret ANTILLA
102 Director College Foundation ..... Ms. Sunny KLEVER
04 Asst to President/Board Secretary ..... Ms. Stephanie DORCHEUS
51 Distance Education Coordinator ..... Mrs. Kirsten HORNING

College of Emergency Services (F)

9800 SE McBrod Ave, Ste 200, Milwaukie OR 97222
County: Clackamas Identification: 667128
Telephone: (971) 236-9231 Carnegie Class: Not Classified
FAX Number: (971) 653-9239 Calendar System: Semester
URL: www.collegeofems.com
Established: 1995 Annual Undergrad Tuition & Fees: N/A
Enrollment: N/A Coed
Affiliation or Control: Proprietary IRS Status: Proprietary
Highest Offering: Associate Degree
Accreditation: ABHES, EMT

01 Program Director ..... Mr. William THRASHER

Columbia Gorge Community College (G)

400 East Scenic Drive, The Dalles OR 97058
County: Wasco FICE Identification: 041519
Unit ID: 420556
Telephone: (541) 506-6000 Carnegie Class: Assoc/MT-VT-High Non
FAX Number: N/A Calendar System: Quarter
URL: www.cgcc.edu
Established: 1977 Annual Undergrad Tuition & Fees (In-District): $4,068
Enrollment: 895 Coed
Affiliation or Control: State/Local IRS Status: 501(c)3
Highest Offering: Associate Degree
Accreditation: NW, MAC

01 President ..... Dr. Frank TODA
05 Chief Academic Officer ..... Lori UFFORD
11 Chief Operating Officer ..... Robb VAN CLEAVE
32 Chief Student Services Officer ..... Eric STUDEBAKER
30 Chief Inst Advancement Officer ..... Dan SPATZ
13 Chief Technology/Planning Officer ..... Bill BOHN
10 Controller ..... Lisa DESWERT
101 Dir of Board/Executive Services ..... Tria BULLARD
06 Registrar ..... Dawn SALLEE-JUSTESEN
07 Director of Admissions ..... Vacant
08 Director of Library Services ..... John SCHOPPERT
108 Dir Curriculum & Assessment ..... Susan LEWIS
15 Director Human Resources ..... Vacant
18 Director of Facilities Services ..... Jim AUSTIN
37 Director Financial Aid ..... Sara VIEMEISTER

Concorde Career College (H)

1425 NE Irving Street, Suite 300, Portland OR 97232
County: Multnomah FICE Identification: 008887
Unit ID: 208479
Telephone: (503) 281-4181 Carnegie Class: Spec 2-yr-Health
FAX Number: (503) 281-6739 Calendar System: Other
URL: www.concorde.edu/campus/portland
Established: 1996 Annual Undergrad Tuition & Fees: N/A
Enrollment: 585 Coed
Affiliation or Control: Proprietary IRS Status: Proprietary
Highest Offering: Associate Degree
Accreditation: ACCSC, COARC, MAC, POLYT, SURGT

01 Campus President ..... Kim IERIEN

Concordia University (I)

2811 NE Holman Ave, Portland OR 97211-6099
County: Multnomah FICE Identification: 003191
Unit ID: 208488
Telephone: (503) 288-9371 Carnegie Class: Spec-4-yr-Other
FAX Number: (503) 280-8518 Calendar System: Semester
URL: www.cu-portland.edu
Established: 1905 Annual Undergrad Tuition & Fees: $29,390
Enrollment: 7,182 Coed
Affiliation or Control: Lutheran Church - Missouri Synod
IRS Status: 501(c)3
Highest Offering: Doctorate
Accreditation: NW, ACBSP, #LAW, NURSE, SW

01 President ..... Dr. Charles E. SCHLIMPERT
26 Exec Vice Pres External Affairs ..... Dr. Gary WITHERS
102 Exec Vice Pres Strategic Planning ..... Mr. Johnnie DRIESSNER
05 Provost/Chief Academic Officer ..... Dr. Joe MANNION
10 Chief Financial Officer ..... Mr. Dennis J. STOECKLIN
11 Chf Operating Ofcr/Chf Gen Counsel ..... Ms. Jilma MENESES
32 Int Vice Pres Student Affairs ..... Ms. Megan BOUSLAUGH
07 Vice President Enrollment ..... Ms. Bobi SWAN
15 Vice President of Human Resources ..... Ms. Heyke KIRKENDALL-BAKER
41 Vice Pres & Athletic Director ..... Mr. Brian JAMROS
13 VP Info Systems/Chief Info Officer ..... Mr. Jason NAIRN
04 Executive Administrator ..... Ms. Brenna THOMAS
30 Chief Development Officer ..... Mr. Kevin MATHENY
06 Registrar ..... Ms. Danielle AMBROSE
09 Director of Institutional Research ..... Mr. Ron FONGER
18 Chief Facilities/Physical Plant ..... Mr. Doug MEYER
88 Chief Public Relations Officer ..... Ms. Madeline TURNOCK
29 Director Alumni & Parent Engagement ..... Ms. Becky SPRECHER
35 Dean of Students ..... Mr. Steve DEKLOTZ
08 Librarian ..... Mr. Brent MAI
37 Senior Director of Financial Aid ..... Mr. Robert CLARKE
19 Director of Campus Safety ..... Mr. John HROMCO
38 Director Student Counseling ..... Ms. Rae CHRESFIELD
85 Director of International Studies ..... Ms. Linda ROUNTREE
42 Director of Campus Ministries ..... Rev. Bo BAUMEISTER
50 Dean School of Management ..... Dr. Michelle COWING
53 Dean College of Education ..... Dr. Sheryl REINISCH
49 Dean College of Arts & Sciences ..... Dr. David KLUTH
76 Dean Col of Health/Human Service ..... Dr. Sarah SWEITZER
61 Dean School of Law ..... Ms. Cathy SILAK

Corban University (A)

5000 Deer Park Drive SE, Salem OR 97317
County: Marion FICE Identification: 001339
Unit ID: 210331
Telephone: (503) 581-8600 Carnegie Class: Masters/S
FAX Number: (503) 585-4316 Calendar System: Semester
URL: www.corban.edu
Established: 1935 Annual Undergrad Tuition & Fees: $30,640
Enrollment: 1,232 Coed
Affiliation or Control: Independent Non-Profit IRS Status: 501(c)3
Highest Offering: Master's
Accreditation: NW, CACREP

01 President ....Dr. Sheldon NORD
05 Provost/Executive Vice President ....Dr. Matthew LUCAS
10 Vice President For Business ....Mr. Kevin BRUBAKER
32 Vice President For Student Life ....Dr. Brenda ROTH
111 Vice Pres of Advancement & Comm ....Mr. Steve SAMMONS
35 Dean of Students ....Mr. Nathan GEER
88 Director of DMin Program ....Dr. Leroy GOERTZEN
88 Associate Provost Global Engagement ....Dr. Janine ALLEN
20 Associate Provost for Academics ....Dr. Pam TESCHNER
50 Dean Hoff School of Business ....Mr. P. Griffith LINDELL
53 Dean of Education and Counseling ....Dr. Kristin DIXON
13 Chief Information Officer ....Mr. Brian SCHMIDT
18 Campus Care Project Manager ....Mr. Troy CROFF
84 Assoc Provost Enrollment Management ....Dr. Chris VETTER
08 Librarian ....Mr. Garrett TROTT
06 University Registrar ....Mrs. Rebecka VESSEY
39 Director of Community Life ....Mr. Eugene EDWARDS
42 Dean School of Ministry ....Dr. Gregory TRULL
41 Athletic Director ....Mr. Greg EIDE
26 Directory of Marketing/Comm ....Mr. Chris HOLDREN
29 Director of Alumni ....Ms. Hope NAKAGAWA
121 Director of Student Support ....Mr. Daren MILIONIS
37 Director of Financial Aid ....Mrs. Ellen ZARFAS
21 Associate Business Officer ....Mr. Brian ELLIOTT
40 Bookstore Manager ....Mr. Larry HULTBERG
123 Asst Dir Grad/Online Admissions ....Ms. Allison SMALL
04 Executive Asst to President ....Ms. Kathy MARTENS
09 Director of Assessment & Inst Rsrch ....Dr. Felicia SQUIRES
104 Director Study Abroad ....Mr. Sam PEARSON
106 Coordinator Undergrad Online Educ ....Mr. Dan CHRISTENSEN
15 Director of Human Resources ....Ms. Nancy MARSHALL
19 Chief of Security ....Mr. Mike ROTH
38 Clinical Director ....Dr. Mary AGUILERA
45 Assoc Dir of Strategic Intiatives ....Mr. Steve HUNT
07 Asst Director of UG Admissions ....Mr. Jordan LINDSEY

Eastern Oregon University (B)

One University Boulevard, La Grande OR 97850-2807
County: Union FICE Identification: 003193
Unit ID: 208646
Telephone: (541) 962-3672 Carnegie Class: Masters/S
FAX Number: (541) 962-3493 Calendar System: Quarter
URL: www.eou.edu
Established: 1929 Annual Undergrad Tuition & Fees (In-State): $8,004
Enrollment: 3,488 Coed
Affiliation or Control: State IRS Status: 501(c)3
Highest Offering: Master's
Accreditation: NW, IACBE

01 President ....Mr. Thomas INSKO
05 Provost/Sr VP Academic Affairs ....Dr. Sarah WITTE
32 Vice President for Student Affairs ....Dr. Lacy KARPILO
10 Vice President Finance & Admin ....Ms. Lara MOORE
30 Vice Pres UA ....Mr. Tim SEYDEL
49 Int Dean College Arts & Science ....Dr. Regina BRAKER
50 Int Dean College of Business & Educ ....Dr. Dan MIELKE
37 Director of Financial Aid ....Ms. Lara MOORE
08 Director of Pierce Library ....Ms. Karen CLAY
07 Director of Admissions ....Ms. Gina GALAVIZ
06 Registrar ....Ms. Emily SHARRATT
15 Director of Human Resources ....Mr. Chris MCLAUGHLIN
29 Dir of Alumni Relations ....Ms. Jessie BRETT
41 Director of Athletics ....Ms. Anji WEISSENFLUH
39 Director of Residence Life ....Mr. Jeremy JONES
18 Director of Facilities & Planning ....Mr. David LAGESON
38 Director Counseling Center ....Dr. Marianne WEAVER
04 Exec Assistant to the President ....Ms. Heather CASHELL
21 Director of Business Affairs ....Ms. Cora BEACH
20 Int Vice Provost Academic Affairs ....Dr. Donald WOLFF
88 Learning Center Operations Manager ....Ms. Kathryn SHORTS
35 Dir of Student Relations/Title IX ....Ms. Colleen DUNNE-CASCIO
19 Campus Security/Public Safety Ofcr ....Mr. Bill BENSON

George Fox University (C)

414 N Meridian, Newberg OR 97132-2697
County: Yamhill FICE Identification: 003194
Unit ID: 208822
Telephone: (503) 538-8383 Carnegie Class: Masters/L
FAX Number: (503) 554-3834 Calendar System: Semester
URL: www.georgefox.edu
Established: 1891 Annual Undergrad Tuition & Fees: $33,730
Enrollment: 3,925 Coed
Affiliation or Control: Friends IRS Status: 501(c)3
Highest Offering: Doctorate
Accreditation: NW, ACBSP, CAATE, CACREP, CAEPN, CLPSY, ENG, IPSY, MUS, NURSE, PTA, SW, THEOL

01 President ....Dr. Robin E. BAKER
03 Vice President/Dean of Seminary ....Dr. Charles J. CONNIRY, JR.
05 Provost ....Dr. Linda SAMEK
10 Exec VP Finance/Business Operations ....Ms. Vicki PIERSALL
111 Vice President Advancement ....Dr. Lynn ANDREWS
32 Vice President Student Life ....Dr. Bradley A. LAU
84 VP Enrollment & Marketing ....Mr. Ryan DOUGHERTY
88 VP for Innovation and Empowerment ....Mr. Rob WESTERVELT
28 AVP Intercultural Engagement ....Dr. Rebecca HERNANDEZ
21 Asst VP of Finance/Controller ....Ms. Cris BANTON
100 Chief of Staff ....Ms. Missy D. TERRY
08 Dean of Libraries ....Mr. Ryan INGERSOLL
07 Director of Undergrad Admissions ....Ms. Lindsay KNOX
06 Registrar ....Ms. Melissa THOMAS
36 Dir of Career Services/IDEA Center ....Ms. Wendy FLINT
18 Director of Plant Services ....Mr. Clyde G. THOMAS
37 Director of Financial Aid ....Ms. Johanna KAYE
96 Director Purchasing/Admin Services ....Mr. Matt HAMMAR
41 Director of Athletics ....Mr. Adam PUCKETT
105 Director of Web Development ....Mr. Peter CRACKENBERG
15 Director Employee Empowerment (HR) ....Vacant
42 Univ Pastor/Dean of Spiritual Life ....Ms. Jamie NOLING-AUTH
26 Exec Dir Mktg Communications ....Mr. Rob FELTON
13 Chief Information Officer ....Mr. Tim GOODFELLOW
19 Director Security Services ....Mr. Ed GIEROK
35 Dean Stdnt Svcs/Dir Hlth/Counseling ....Dr. William C. BUHROW
49 Dean School of Arts & Sciences ....Ms. Laura HARTLEY
83 Dean Sch Behavioral/Health Sci ....Dr. James E. FOSTER
53 Dean School of Education ....Dr. Scot HEADLEY
50 Dean School of Business ....Dr. Jekabs BIKIS
09 Director of Data Analytics ....Mr. Doug BEATTY

Gutenberg College (D)

1883 University Street, Eugene OR 97403-1368
County: Lane FICE Identification: 039324
Unit ID: 420510
Telephone: (541) 683-5141 Carnegie Class: Not Classified
FAX Number: (541) 683-6997 Calendar System: Quarter
URL: www.gutenberg.edu
Established: 1994 Annual Undergrad Tuition & Fees: N/A
Enrollment: N/A Coed
Affiliation or Control: Independent Non-Profit IRS Status: 501(c)3
Highest Offering: Baccalaureate
Accreditation: TRACS

01 President ....Chris SWANSON
03 Vice President ....Moctar ZIBARE
05 Dean ....Thomas DEWBERRY
07 Admissions Director ....Tim MCINTOSH
06 Registrar ....Chris SWANSON

Klamath Community College (E)

7390 S 6th Street, Klamath Falls OR 97603-7121
County: Klamath FICE Identification: 034283
Unit ID: 428392
Telephone: (541) 882-3521 Carnegie Class: Assoc/MT-VT-High Non
FAX Number: (541) 885-7758 Calendar System: Quarter
URL: www.klamathcc.edu
Established: 1996 Annual Undergrad Tuition & Fees (In-District): $3,687
Enrollment: 1,224 Coed
Affiliation or Control: State/Local IRS Status: 501(c)3
Highest Offering: Associate Degree
Accreditation: NW

01 President ....Dr. Roberto GUTIERREZ
11 Vice Pres Administrative Svcs ....Ms. Allison BRYSON
05 Vice Pres Academic Affairs ....Ms. Jamie JENNINGS
07 Vice Pres Enroll & External Affairs ..Ms. Julie MURRAY-JENSEN
15 VP Stdnt & Pers Svcs/Legal Counsel ....Dr. Anthony ROSILEZ
20 Dean of Instruction ....Dr. Ronda WERY
20 Dean of Instruction ....Mr. Christopher STICKLES
103 Director of Workforce ....Mr. Charles MASSIE
13 Director Information Services ....Mr. Paul BREEDLOVE
06 Registrar/Dean of Enrollment ....Dr. Elizabeth WHITE-HURST
26 Chief Public Information Officer ....Ms. Lacey JARRELL
18 Facilities Director ....Mr. Mike HOMFELDT
10 Director Business Services ....Ms. Melissa LINDSAY
37 Financial Aid Director ....Ms. Robin SUNDSETH
04 Executive Admin Asst to President ....Ms. Shannon CHILDS
09 Institutional Researcher ....Mr. Bill JENNINGS
25 Grants Program Manager ....Ms. Paula PENCE

Lane Community College (F)

4000 E 30th Avenue, Eugene OR 97405-0640
County: Lane FICE Identification: 003196
Unit ID: 209038
Telephone: (541) 463-3000 Carnegie Class: Assoc/MT-VT-Mix Trad/Non
FAX Number: (541) 463-5201 Calendar System: Quarter
URL: www.lanecc.edu
Established: 1964 Annual Undergrad Tuition & Fees (In-District): $4,155
Enrollment: 8,583 Coed
Affiliation or Control: Local IRS Status: 501(c)3
Highest Offering: Associate Degree
Accreditation: NW, ACFEI, COARC, DA, DH, EMT, MAC, PTAA

01 President ....Dr. Margaret HAMILTON
05 Int Exec Vice President/CAO ....Ms. Dawn DEWOLF
11 Vice President College Operations ....Mr. Brian KELLY
32 Exec Dean Student/Academic Affairs ....Ms. Kerry LEVETT
72 Exec Dean School Prof & Tech Career ....Ms. Vicki TRIER
49 Exec Dean School Arts & Science ....Dr. Jennifer FREI
35 Int Dean Student Engagement ....Ms. Christina WALSH
68 Int Dean Health/PE/Athletics ....Ms. Julie GOOD
28 Chief Diversity Officer ....Vacant
13 Chief Information Officer ....Mr. Bill SCHUETZ
10 Chief Financial Officer ....Mr. Greg HOLMES
15 Chief Human Resources Officer ....Mr. Dennis CARR
09 Dir Inst Research/Assess/Planning ....Dr. Craig TAYLOR
18 Director Facilities & PM ....Ms. Jennifer HAYWARD
19 Director Public Safety ....Mr. Jace SMITH
08 Interim Library Director ....Ms. Lori WAMSLEY
121 Int Dean Student Success ....Ms. Lida HERBURGER
88 Dean of New Student Transitions ....Ms. Helen FAITH
113 Director Student Financial Svs ....Ms. Rose ELLIS
26 Public Information Officer ....Ms. Joan ASCHIM
102 Foundation Director ....Ms. Wendy JETT
04 Administrative Asst to President ....Ms. Donna ZMOLEK
30 Development Director ....Ms. Tiana MARRONE-CREECH
44 Annual Gifts Officer ....Mr. Philip HUDSPETH
104 Director International Programs ....Ms. Jennifer FALZERANO

Lewis and Clark College (G)

0615 SW Palatine Hill, Portland OR 97219-7899
County: Multnomah FICE Identification: 003197
Unit ID: 209056
Telephone: (503) 768-7000 Carnegie Class: Bac-A&S
FAX Number: (503) 768-7055 Calendar System: Semester
URL: www.lclark.edu
Established: 1867 Annual Undergrad Tuition & Fees: $46,894
Enrollment: 3,526 Coed
Affiliation or Control: Independent Non-Profit IRS Status: 501(c)3
Highest Offering: Doctorate
Accreditation: NW, CACREP, CAEPN, LAW, MFCD

01 Interim President ....Mr. David ELLIS
05 Vice President & Provost ....Dr. Jane M. ATKINSON
58 Dean Grad Sch Education/Counseling ....Dr. Scott FLETCHER
49 Interim Dean of Arts & Sciences ....Dr. Bruce SUTTMEIER
28 Dean of Diversity and Inclusion ....Ms. Janet STEVERSON
61 Dean of the Law School ....Ms. Jennifer JOHNSON
10 Vice Pres Business/Finance/Treas ....Mr. Alan FINN
111 Vice Pres Institutional Advancement ....Mr. Josh WALTER
32 Dean of Students ....Dr. Anna GONZALEZ
09 Assoc Provost Research & Planning ....Dr. Mark FIGUEROA
26 Exec Dir of Public Affairs & Comm ....Mr. Joe BECKER
07 Dean for Enrollment & Communication ....Ms. Lisa MEYER
13 Assoc VP & Chief Information Ofcr ....Mr. Adam BUCHWALD
15 Assoc VP/Director Human Resources ....Mrs. Heyke KIRKENDALL-BAKER
18 Assoc Vice Pres Facilities ....Mr. Michel GEORGE
06 Registrar College of Arts/Sciences ....Ms. Judy FINCH
06 Registrar Law School ....Mr. Seneca GRAY
06 Registrar Graduate School ....Ms. River MONTIJO
37 Director of Financial Aid ....Ms. Anastacia DILLON
08 Director of Watzek Library ....Mr. Mark DAHL
85 Assoc Dean Intl Stdnts & Scholars ....Mr. Brian WHITE
30 Assoc VP & Director of Development ....Mr. Aaron WHITEFORD
29 Senior Director Alumni/Parent Pgms ....Mr. Andrew MCPHEETERS
19 Director of Campus Safety ....Mr. Timothy O'DWYER
42 Dean of Religious & Spiritual Life ....Dr. Mark DUNTLEY
41 Director of Athletics ....Ms. Shana LEVINE
39 Director of Housing & Orientation ....Ms. Sandi BOTTEMILLER
14 Director of IT Operations ....Mr. Patrick RYALL
17 Assoc Dean Stdnt Health & Wellness ....Dr. John HANCOCK
101 Executive Asst Board Relations ....Ms. Moira DOMANN
04 Executive Asst to the President ....Ms. Annette LANIER
102 Int Dir Corp/Foundation Relations ....Mr. Zach LYNOTT
104 Director Overseas & Off Campus Pgms ....Ms. Blythe KNOTT

Linfield College (H)

900 SE Baker Street, McMinnville OR 97128-6894
County: Yamhill FICE Identification: 003198
Unit ID: 209065
Telephone: (503) 883-2200 Carnegie Class: Bac-A&S
FAX Number: (503) 883-2472 Calendar System: 4/1/4
URL: www.linfield.edu
Established: 1858 Annual Undergrad Tuition & Fees: $40,175
Enrollment: 1,700 Coed
Affiliation or Control: American Baptist IRS Status: 501(c)3
Highest Offering: Baccalaureate
Accreditation: NW, CAATE, MUS, NURSE

01 President ....Dr. Thomas HELLIE
05 Vice Pres Acad Affs/Dean of Faculty ....Ms. Susan AGRE-KIPPENHAN
10 Vice Pres Finance/Admin/CFO ....Ms. Mary Ann RODRIGUEZ
30 VP Inst Advancement/General Counsel ....Mr. John MCKEEGAN
84 Vice Pres for Enrollment Management ....Mr. Daniel PRESTON
32 VP Student Affairs/Dean of Students ....Ms. Susan HOPP
66 Int Dean of Nursing ....Dr. Donna POTTS
20 Associate Dean of Faculty ....Dr. J. Christopher GAISER
35 Associate Dean of Students ....Mr. Jeff MACKAY
15 Director of Human Resources ....Ms. Betty HENNINGER
18 Director Facilities & Auxiliary Svc ....Ms. Allison HORN
28 Director Multicultural Programs ....Mr. Jason RODRIQUEZ
06 Registrar ....Ms. Diane CRABTREE
07 Director of Admission ....Ms. Lisa KNODLE-BRAGIEL
08 Library Director ....Ms. Susan BARNES WHYTE
09 Director of Institutional Research ....Ms. Jennifer BALLARD
37 Director of Financial Aid ....Ms. Keri BURKE

13 Chief Technology Officer .... Ms. Virginia TOMLINSON
105 Webmaster .... Mr. Jonathan PIERCE
85 Director of International Programs .... Dr. Shaik ISMAIL
51 Director of Continuing Education .... Dr. Laura BRENER
19 Director of Security .... Mr. Ronald NOBLE
38 Director of Counseling Services .... Ms. Patricia HADDELAND
26 Director Communications/Marketing .... Mr. Scott Bernard NELSON
44 Director of Annual Giving .... Ms. Lisa GOODWIN
30 Director of Development .... Mr. Craig HAISCH
102 Dir Corp & Foundation Relations .... Ms. Catherine JARMIN MILLER
29 Director of Alumni/Parent Relations .... Ms. Debbie HARMON FERRY
36 Director of Careers .... Mr. Michael HAMPTON
42 Chaplain .... Dr. David MASSEY
41 Athletic Director .... Mr. Scott CARNAHAN
40 Bookstore Manager .... Mr. Chad COTTRILL
04 Exec Assistant to the President .... Ms. Kathy COOK

Linn-Benton Community College (A)

6500 Pacific Boulevard, SW, Albany OR 97321-3774
County: Linn FICE Identification: 006938
Unit ID: 209074
Telephone: (541) 917-4999 Carnegie Class: Assoc/MT-VT-High Non
FAX Number: (541) 917-4445 Calendar System: Quarter
URL: www.linnbenton.edu
Established: 1966 Annual Undergrad Tuition & Fees (In-District): $4,512
Enrollment: 5,721 Coed
Affiliation or Control: State/Local IRS Status: 501(c)3
Highest Offering: Associate Degree
Accreditation: NW, DA, MAC, OTA, POLYT

01 President .... Dr. Gregory J. HAMANN
05 Vice Pres Academic Affs/Wrkfce Dev .... Dr. Ann BUCHELE
10 Vice Pres Finance & Operations .... Mr. Dave HENDERSON
32 Vice President Student Affairs .... Dr. Bruce CLEMETSEN
35 Assoc Dean Student Affairs .... Vacant
12 Regional Director Linn County .... Mr. Gary PRICE
12 Regional Director Benton County .... Mr. Jeff DAVIS
15 Dir Human Resources/Affirm Act Ofcr .... Mr. Scott ROLEN
41 Director of Athletics .... Mr. Randy FALK
81 Dean Science/Engr & Tech .... Vacant
49 Dean Arts/Soc Sci/Humanities Div .... Ms. Katie WINDER
20 Dean Instruction .... Dr. Sally WIDENMANN
111 Exec Dir Institutional Advancement .... Mr. Dale STOWELL
04 Executive Asst to President .... Ms. Amanda KLIEVER
06 Registrar .... Mr. Danny AYNES
13 Chief Info Technology Officer (CIO) .... Mr. Michael QUINER
18 Chief Facilities/Physical Plant .... Mr. Scott KRAMBUHL
19 Director Security/Safety .... Ms. Marcene OLSON
28 Director of Diversity .... Mr. Javier CERVANTES

Marylhurst University (B)

PO Box 261, 17600 Pacific Highway,
Marylhurst OR 97036-0261
County: Clackamas FICE Identification: 003199
Unit ID: 209108
Telephone: (503) 636-8141 Carnegie Class: Masters/L
FAX Number: (503) 636-9526 Calendar System: Quarter
URL: www.marylhurst.edu
Established: 1893 Annual Undergrad Tuition & Fees: $20,835
Enrollment: 982 Coed
Affiliation or Control: Independent Non-Profit IRS Status: 501(c)3
Highest Offering: Master's
Accreditation: NW, CIDA, IACBE, MUS

01 President .... Dr. Melody ROSE
05 Interim Provost/VP Academic Affairs .... Dr. Carol MACK
10 VP Finance/Administration .... Ms. Jennifer CHAMBERS
111 Vice Pres University Advancement .... Ms. Nicola SYSYN
88 Vice Pres Mission Integration .... Ms. Joan SAALFELD
84 VP Enrollment Mgmt/Student Services .... Ms. Robyn JONES
100 Chief of Staff .... Mr. Rod JOHNSON
84 Director Enrollment Services .... Mr. Ryan CLARK
06 Registrar .... Mr. Ryan CLARK
08 University Librarian .... Ms. Nancy HOOVER
26 Director Marketing & Communications .... Ms. Simona BEATTIE
37 Director of Financial Aid .... Ms. Tracy REISINGER
88 Director Art Therapy Graduate Pgm .... Ms. Christine TURNER
72 Director Center for Learning Tech .... Mr. Nathan PHILLIPS
13 Director of Infrastructure Services .... Mr. Keelan CLEARY
18 Director of Facilities .... Mr. Mark STRULOEFF
49 Chair Sci/Religion/Interdisc Stds .... Dr. Jan DABROWSKI
88 Chair Art/Music/Creative Therapies .... Dr. Laura BEER
64 Director of Choral Activities .... Dr. Justin SMITH
50 Director School of Business .... Dr. Stuart NOBLE-GOODMAN
57 Art Dept/Dir Interior Design Dept .... Ms. Nancy HISS
73 Religious Studies & Philosophy .... Dr. Jeroid ROUSSELL
88 Interdisciplinary Studies .... Mr. Simeon DREYFUSS
79 Chrpsn Culture & Media .... Dr. David DENNY
81 Science & Math .... Mr. Greg DARDIS
83 Chairperson Human Sciences .... Dr. Jennifer SASSER
88 Chrpsn English Literature/Writing .... Dr. Meg ROLAND
109 Chair Food Systems & Society .... Dr. Patricia ALLEN

Mount Angel Seminary (C)

1 Abbey Drive, St. Benedict OR 97373-0505
County: Marion FICE Identification: 003203
Unit ID: 209241
Telephone: (503) 845-3951 Carnegie Class: Spec-4-yr-Faith
FAX Number: (503) 845-3128 Calendar System: Semester
URL: www.mountangelabbey.org
Established: 1889 Annual Undergrad Tuition & Fees: $20,784
Enrollment: 162 Coed
Affiliation or Control: Roman Catholic IRS Status: 501(c)3
Highest Offering: Master's
Accreditation: NW, THEOL

01 President-Rector .... Msgr. Joseph V. BETSCHART
05 Vice President/Academic Dean .... Dr. Owen CUMMINGS
11 VP of Admin/Dir Pastoral Formation .... Rev. Stephen CLOVIS
20 Associate Academic Dean College .... Dr. Andrew CUMMINGS
73 Associate Academic Dean Theology .... Dr. Seymour HOUSE
06 Registrar .... Ms. Marina KEYS
07 Director of Admissions .... Fr. Teresio CALDWELL, OSB
04 Admin Asst to the President-Rector .... Mrs. Carol MARTIN
37 Student Financial Aid .... Ms. Marina KEYS
10 Business Manager .... Fr. Martin GRASSEL, OSB
30 Director of Development .... Ms. Jodi KILCUP
26 Communications Manager .... Ms. Theresa MYERS
08 Librarian .... Ms. Victoria ERTELT
29 Alumni Relations .... Ms. Sharley LAMORA
112 Director of Planned Giving .... Ms. Susan GALLAGHER
44 Director of Annual Giving .... Ms. Maurissa FISHER

† Granted candidacy at the Doctorate level.

Mt. Hood Community College (D)

26000 SE Stark, Gresham OR 97030-3300
County: Multnomah FICE Identification: 003204
Unit ID: 209250
Telephone: (503) 491-6422 Carnegie Class: Assoc/HT-High Non
FAX Number: (503) 491-7389 Calendar System: Quarter
URL: www.mhcc.edu
Established: 1965 Annual Undergrad Tuition & Fees (In-District): $5,313
Enrollment: 8,758 Coed
Affiliation or Control: Local IRS Status: 501(c)3
Highest Offering: Associate Degree
Accreditation: NW, COARC, DH, FUSER, PTAA, SURGT

01 President .... Dr. Debra DERR
15 Director Human Resources .... Mr. Travis BROWN
88 Dir Child Dev/Family Support Pgms .... Ms. Jean WAGNER
18 Director Facilities Management .... Mr. Charles GEORGE
10 Chief Operations Officer .... Ms. Jennifer DEMENT
09 Director of Institutional Research .... Mr. Sergey SHEPELOV
37 Director Student Financial Aid .... Ms. Christi HART
32 Director of Student Services .... Mr. John HAMBLIN
13 Chief Information Officer .... Ms. Linda VIGESAA
28 Director of Diversity .... Vacant
29 Exec Dir Foundation/Alumni Rels .... Mr. Al SIGALA
76 Dean Allied Health & Nursing .... Ms. Janie GRIFFIN
81 Dean Visual Arts/Integ Media/Sci .... Ms. Janet MCINTYRE
79 Dean Humanities/Math/Social Science .... Ms. Sara RIVARA
72 Dean Sciences .... Vacant
50 Dean Business and Info Systems .... Mr. Rod BARKER
103 Exec Dean WF Dev & Industrial Tech .... Mr. Jarrod HOGUE
26 Chief Public Relations Officer .... Mr. Bruce BATTLE
84 Director Enrollment Management .... Mr. John HAMBLIN

Multnomah University (E)

8435 NE Glisan Street, Portland OR 97220-5898
County: Multnomah FICE Identification: 003206
Unit ID: 209287
Telephone: (503) 255-0332 Carnegie Class: Spec-4-yr-Faith
FAX Number: (503) 254-1268 Calendar System: Semester
URL: www.multnomah.edu
Established: 1936 Annual Undergrad Tuition & Fees: $23,680
Enrollment: 737 Coed
Affiliation or Control: Independent Non-Profit IRS Status: 501(c)3
Highest Offering: Doctorate
Accreditation: NW, THEOL

01 President .... Dr. G. Craig WILLIFORD
84 VP Enrollment Management/IT .... Ms. Gina BERQUIST
10 CFO and VP Administration .... Mr. W. Chandler WILSON
49 Dean School of Arts and Sciences .... Dr. Daniel SCALBERG
73 Dean School of Bible & Theology .... Dr. Derek CHINN
107 Dean Adult & Professional Studies .... Dr. Steve HOLLER
32 Director/Dean of Students .... Ms. Kim STAVE
42 Assoc Dean Spiritual Life/Calling .... Mr. Richard WARD
35 Associate Dean of Students .... Dr. Karen FANCHER
12 Executive Director of MU Reno .... Mr. John MCKENDRICKS
108 Dir of Institutional Effectiveness .... Dr. David FUNK
06 Registrar .... Ms. Amy M. STEPHENS
21 Controller .... Mrs. Debbie WHITEHEAD
08 Librarian .... Dr. Philip M. JOHNSON
37 Director Student Financial Aid .... Mrs. Stephanie POLLARD
36 Seminary Director of Placement .... Vacant
13 Director Information Technology .... Mrs. Brenda GIBSON
15 Director of Human Resources .... Ms. Tracy L. MORESCHI
41 Athletic Director .... Ms. Lois VOS
26 Director of Marketing .... Mr. Tom MORLAN
07 Director of Admissions .... Mrs. Mindy-Kate HASENKAMP
18 Director of Campus Facilities .... Mr. Eric LINMAN
29 Director Alumni Relations .... Mrs. Natalie CORRELL
04 Assistant to the President .... Mrs. Denise STONE
19 Director of Campus Safety .... Mr. Josh HARPER
38 Director Student Counseling .... Vacant
121 Associate Dean of Student Success .... Mrs. Christy MARTIN
106 Dir Online Education/E-learning .... Mr. Levi MARTIN
30 Vice President of Advancement .... Vacant

50 Dean of Business .... Mr. Lee SELLERS
53 Dean of Education .... Ms. Susan BOE

National University of Natural Medicine (F)

049 SW Porter Street, Portland OR 97201-4878
County: Multnomah FICE Identification: 025340
Unit ID: 209296
Telephone: (503) 552-1555 Carnegie Class: Spec-4-yr-Other Health
FAX Number: (503) 499-0022 Calendar System: Quarter
URL: nunm.edu
Established: 1956 Annual Undergrad Tuition & Fees: N/A
Enrollment: 631 Coed
Affiliation or Control: Independent Non-Profit IRS Status: 501(c)3
Highest Offering: Doctorate
Accreditation: NW, ACUP, NATUR

01 President .... Dr. David J. SCHLEICH
05 Provost/VP Academic Affairs .... Dr. Sandra SNYDER
10 EVP/Chief Finance Officer .... Mr. Gerald BORES
111 VP of Advancement .... Vacant
09 VP of Inst Research & Compliance .... Dr. Andrea C. SMITH
15 VP of Human Resources .... Ms. Kathy STANFORD
32 AVP of Student Affairs .... Ms. Cheryl MILLER
84 AVP of Enrollment Management .... Mr. Brandon HAMILTON
04 Executive Asst to the President .... Ms. Colleen CORDER
63 Dean of Naturopathic Medicine .... Dr. Melanie HENRIKSEN
63 Dean Classical Chinese Medicine .... Dr. Laurie REGAN
46 Dean of Research & Graduate Studies .... Dr. Heather ZWICKEY
20 Dean of Undergraduate Studies .... Dr. Tim IRVING
17 Dean of Clinics/Chief Medical Offic .... Dr. Regina DEHEN
06 Registrar .... Ms. Kelly GAREY
26 Director PR & Communications .... Ms. Marilynn S. CONSIDINE
07 Assoc Director of Admissions .... Ms. Danielle LAW
37 Director of Financial Aid .... Ms. Laurie RADFORD
13 Manager of IT .... Mr. Steve FONG
08 College Librarian .... Ms. Noelle STELLO
19 Director of Campus Security .... Mr. Spencer BRAZES
36 Manager of Career Services .... Ms. Tafflyn WILLIAMS-THOMAS
51 Assoc Director Continuing Education .... Mr. Justin FOWLER
105 Webmaster .... Ms. Ellen YARNELL
38 Director Student Counseling .... Dr. Adrienne WOLMARK
28 Manager of Intercultural Engagement .... Ms. Ayasha SAHMSUD-DIN

New Hope Christian College (G)

2155 Bailey Hill Road, Eugene OR 97405-1194
County: Lane FICE Identification: 021597
Unit ID: 208725
Telephone: (541) 485-1780 Carnegie Class: Spec-4-yr-Faith
FAX Number: (541) 343-5801 Calendar System: Semester
URL: www.newhope.edu
Established: 1925 Annual Undergrad Tuition & Fees: $14,230
Enrollment: 140 Coed
Affiliation or Control: Other IRS Status: 501(c)3
Highest Offering: Baccalaureate
Accreditation: BI

01 President .... Dr. Wayne CORDEIRO
05 Academic Dean .... Dr. Mark KELLEY
04 Executive Assistant to President .... Mrs. Lori HIGASHI
32 Dean of Student Services .... Mr. Paul WRIGHT
29 Director of Alumni Relations .... Ms. Karen BOBST
06 Registrar .... Ms. Donald GRAFTON
84 Enrollment Management .... Mr. Josiah LYNCH
37 Director of Financial Aid .... Mr. Victor HUX
08 Head Librarian .... Ms. Janet L. KELLEY

Northwest Christian University (H)

828 E. 11th Ave., Eugene OR 97401-3745
County: Lane FICE Identification: 003208
Unit ID: 209409
Telephone: (541) 343-1641 Carnegie Class: Masters/S
FAX Number: (541) 343-9159 Calendar System: Semester
URL: www.nwcu.edu
Established: 1895 Annual Undergrad Tuition & Fees: $27,930
Enrollment: 740 Coed
Affiliation or Control: Christian Church (Disciples Of Christ)
IRS Status: 501(c)3
Highest Offering: Master's
Accreditation: NW, CACREP, IACBE, NURSE

01 President .... Dr. Joseph WOMACK
05 VP Academic Affairs/Dean of Faculty .... Dr. Dennis LINDSAY
10 Vice Pres Finance/Administration .... Mr. Gene DE YOUNG
111 Vice President Advancement .... Mr. Keith POTTER
32 VP Student Development/Enrollment .... Mr. Michael FULLER
26 Director Marketing & Communication .... Mr. Patrick WALSH
39 Dir Residence Life & Student Svcs .... Mr. Greg BROCK
08 Director Kellenberger Library .... Mr. Steve SILVER
06 Registrar .... Mr. Aaron PRUITT
42 Campus Pastor Dir Church Relations .... Mr. Troy DEAN
37 Director Financial Aid .... Ms. Jocelyn HUBBS
07 Executive Director Admissions .... Ms. Kacie GERDRUM
35 Director Student Programs .... Ms. Princess FOX
18 Plant Manager .... Mr. Oskar BUCHER
41 Athletic Director .... Mr. Corey ANDERSON
36 Dir Academic Svc & Career Develop .... Ms. Angela DOTY

04	Exec Admin Asst to President	Ms. Jennifer BOX
44	Director of Annual Fund	Ms. Glenda GORDON
108	Director of Assessment	Mr. Brian MILLS
29	Director of Alumni Relations	Ms. Corynn GILBERT
107	Assoc Dean of Professional Studies	Ms. Melanie TOWNE
88	Asst Dean Business	Mr. Pete DIFFENDERFER
88	Program Director for CMHC	Ms. Marilyn MONTGOMERY
13	Director of Information Technology	Mr. Stead HALSTEAD

Oregon College of Art and Craft (A)

8245 SW Barnes Road, Portland OR 97225-6349

County: Washington FICE Identification: 030073
Unit ID: 209533

Telephone: (503) 297-5554 Carnegie Class: Spec-4-yr-Arts
FAX Number: (503) 297-3155 Calendar System: Semester
URL: www.ocac.edu
Established: 1907 Annual Undergrad Tuition & Fees: $32,130
Enrollment: 151 Coed
Affiliation or Control: Independent Non-Profit IRS Status: 501(c)3
Highest Offering: Master's
Accreditation: NW, ART

01	President	Ms. Denise MULLEN
10	Controller	Ms. Christie LOK
05	CAO/Dean of Academic Affairs	Ms. Jiseon LEE ISBARA
30	Chief Advancement Officer	Mr. Joe PEACOCK
07	Chief Enroll Officer/Dir of Admiss	Mr. Mark TAKIGUCHI
06	Registrar	Ms. Anna VARGAS
08	Head of Library Services	Ms. Elsa LOFTIS
32	Director of Student Services	Mr. Eric GOODWIN
31	Community Programs Coordinator	Ms. Katie WISDOM WEINSTEIN
37	Director of Financial Aid	Ms. Linda ANDERSON
04	Exec Assistant to the President	Ms. Kris KEBISEK

Oregon College of Oriental Medicine (B)

75 NW Couch Street, Portland OR 97209-4018

County: Multnomah FICE Identification: 026037
Unit ID: 369659

Telephone: (503) 253-3443 Carnegie Class: Spec-4-yr-Other Health
FAX Number: (503) 253-2701 Calendar System: Quarter
URL: www.ocom.edu
Established: 1983 Annual Graduate Tuition & Fees: N/A
Enrollment: 258 Coed
Affiliation or Control: Independent Non-Profit IRS Status: 501(c)3
Highest Offering: Doctorate; No Undergraduates
Accreditation: ACUP

01	President	Dr. Deborah HOWE
10	Chief Finance Officer	Karen RASMUSSEN
11	Vice Pres Planning & Operations	Phil LUNDBERG
05	Vice Pres Comm & Academic Services	Beth HOWLETT
58	Dean of Master's Studies	Dr. Martin KIDWELL
30	Chief Development Officer	Dave ESHBAUGH
88	Dean of Doctoral Studies	Dr. Beth BURCH
32	Dean of Students	Nancy GROTTON
17	Assoc Dean of Clinical Education	Dr. Debra MULROONEY
46	Interim Director of Research	Ben MARX
15	Human Resources Generalist	Amber APPLETON
06	Registrar	Carol ACHESON
07	Director of Admissions	Anna GRACE
37	Director Student Financial Aid	Judy GJESDAL
44	Director of Annual Giving	Mike PAULSEN

Oregon Culinary Institute (C)

1701 SW Jefferson Street, Portland OR 97201-2571

Telephone: (503) 961-6200 Identification: 666177
Accreditation: PPPA

† Branch campus of Pioneer Pacific College, Wilsonville, OR.

Oregon Health & Science University (D)

3181 SW Sam Jackson Park Road, Portland OR 97239-3098

County: Multnomah FICE Identification: 004882
Unit ID: 209490

Telephone: (503) 494-8311 Carnegie Class: Spec-4-yr-Med
FAX Number: (503) 494-5738 Calendar System: Quarter
URL: www.ohsu.edu
Established: 1974 Annual Undergrad Tuition & Fees (In-State): N/A
Enrollment: 2,895 Coed
Affiliation or Control: State IRS Status: 501(c)3
Highest Offering: Doctorate
Accreditation: NW, ANEST, ARCPA, CAHIIM, DENT, DIETI, EMT, IPSY, MED, MIDWF, MT, NURSE, PH, RTT

01	President	Dr. Joseph E. ROBERTSON
03	Executive Vice Provost	Dr. David W. ROBINSON
05	Provost Education & Research	Dr. Elena ANDRESEN
18	Assoc VP Facilities/Physical Plant	Mr. Scott PAGE
84	Vice Prov Enroll & Academic Program	Ms. Cherie HONNELL
63	Dean School of Medicine	Dr. John G. HUNTER
52	Dean School of Dentistry	Dr. Phillip T. MARUCHA
69	Dean Joint School of Public Health	Dr. David BANGSBERG
66	Dean School of Nursing	Dr. Susan BAKEWELL-SACHS
06	Registrar	Mrs. Mickie BUSH
17	Director University Hospital	Mr. Peter RAPP
88	Director Vollum Inst Adv Biomed Res	Dr. Richard H. GOODMAN
15	Vice Provost of Human Resources	Mr. Dan FORBES
08	Director Health Sciences Libraries	Mr. Chris SHAFFER
46	Senior Vice Pres for Research	Dr. Daniel DORSA
26	VP and Chief Marketing Officer	Ms. Kimberly OVITT
88	Director Child Devel/Rehab Center	Dr. Brian ROGERS
37	Director Student Financial Aid	Ms. Rachel DURBIN
28	Vice Pres for Equity & Inclusion	Dr. Brian GIBBS

Oregon Institute of Technology (E)

3201 Campus Drive, Klamath Falls OR 97601-8801

County: Klamath FICE Identification: 003211
Unit ID: 209506

Telephone: (541) 885-1000 Carnegie Class: Bac-Diverse
FAX Number: (541) 885-1101 Calendar System: Quarter
URL: www.oit.edu
Established: 1947 Annual Undergrad Tuition & Fees (In-State): $9,625
Enrollment: 4,777 Coed
Affiliation or Control: State IRS Status: 501(c)3
Highest Offering: Master's
Accreditation: NW, COARC, DH, DMS, ENG, ENGR, ENGT, IACBE, MT, POLYT

01	President	Dr. Nagi G. NAGANATHAN
05	Provost/Vice Pres Academic Affairs	Dr. Gary KULECK
10	VP Finance/Administration	Mr. Brian FOX
32	VP Student Affairs/Dean of Students	Dr. Erin FOLEY
35	Dean of Students	Dr. Erin FOLEY
37	Director of Financial Aid	Ms. Tracey A. LEHMAN
15	Director of Human Resources	Mrs. Suzette YAEZENKO
07	Director of Admissions	Mr. Carl THOMAS
06	Registrar	Ms. Wendy IVIE
21	Director of Business Affairs	Ms. Michelle MEYER
13	Assoc VP/Chief Information Officer	Mr. Jim JOMES
23	Director Student Health Services	Mrs. Gaylyn MAURER
18	Interim Director Facilities Svcs	Mr. Thom DARRAH
41	Interim Athletic Director	Mr. Greg STEWART
35	Director Campus Life	Ms. Holly ANDERSON
88	Assoc Director Campus Life	Ms. Josie HUDSPETH
36	Director of Career Services	Ms. Jennifer KASS
09	Institutional Research Analyst	Mr. Farooq SULTAN
30	Assoc VP Devel/Alumni Relations	Mrs. Tracy RICKETTS

Oregon State University (F)

1500 SW Jefferson Avenue, Corvallis OR 97331-8507

County: Benton FICE Identification: 003210
Unit ID: 209542

Telephone: (541) 737-0123 Carnegie Class: DU-Highest
FAX Number: N/A Calendar System: Quarter
URL: www.oregonstate.edu
Established: 1868 Annual Undergrad Tuition & Fees (In-State): $10,366
Enrollment: 29,576 Coed
Affiliation or Control: State IRS Status: 501(c)3
Highest Offering: Doctorate
Accreditation: NW, CAATE, CACREP, CAEPN, CEA, CONST, CS, DIETD, DIETI, ENG, ENGR, IPSY, PH, PHAR, SPAA, VET

01	President	Dr. Edward J. RAY
05	Provost/Exec Vice President	Dr. Ed FESER
10	Int Vice Pres Finance/Admin	Mr. Mike GREEN
111	Vice Pres University Advancement	Mr. Steve CLARK
46	Vice President for Research	Ms. Cynthia SAGERS
20	Vice Prov Academic Affs/Intl Pgms	Ms. Susan CAPALBO
13	Vice Prov for Information Svcs/CIO	Ms. Lois BROOKS
32	Vice Prov for Student Affairs	Dr. Susie BRUBAKER-COLE
56	Vice Prov Univ Outreach/Engagement	Dr. Scott REED
12	V Prov/Campus Ex Ofcr OSU-Cascades	Dr. Rebecca JOHNSON
84	Asst Provost Enrollment Management	Ms. Kate M. PETERSON
102	President & CEO OSU Foundation	Mr. Mike GOODWIN
47	Dean of Agricultural Sciences	Dr. Dan ARP
50	Dean of Business	Dr. Mitzi MONTOYA
54	Dean of Engineering	Dr. Scott ASHFORD
65	Dean of Forestry	Dr. Thomas MANESS
68	Dean of Health & Human Sciences	Dr. Javier NIETO
49	Dean of Liberal Arts	Dr. Larry RODGERS
65	Dean of Earth/Ocean & Atmos Science	Dr. Roberta MARINELLI
67	Dean of Pharmacy	Dr. Mark ZABRISKIE
81	Dean of Science	Dr. Roy HAGGERTY
74	Interim Dean of Veterinary Medicine	Dr. Susan TORNQUIST
51	Assoc Provost Extended Campus	Dr. David A. KING
58	Dean of Graduate School	Dr. Jennifer DENNIS
35	Interim Dean of Student Life	Mr. Dan LARSON
92	Dean University Honors College	Dr. Toni DOOLEN
53	Dean of Education	Dr. Toni DOOLEN
08	University Librarian	Ms. Faye CHADWELL
22	Director Equity and Inclusion	Dr. Allison DAVIS-WHITE EYES
43	General Counsel	Ms. Becca GOSE
41	Director Intercollegiate Athletics	Mr. Scott BARNES
36	Director of Career Services	Mr. Douglas COCHRAN
37	Dir of Financial Aid/Scholarship	Mr. Doug SEVERS
23	Dir Student Health Services	Ms. Jenny HAUBENREISER
38	Dir Univ Counseling/Psych Svcs	Dr. Jackie ALVAREZ
39	Director Univ Housing/Dining Svcs	Mr. Dan LARSON
06	Registrar	Ms. Rebecca MATHERN
07	Director of Admissions	Mr. Noah BUCKLEY
24	Director Media & Outreach Services	Mr. John GREYDANUS
14	Dir of Enterprise Computing Service	Mr. Kent KUO
21	AVP Finance & Administration	Mr. Mike GREEN
15	Director of Human Resources	Ms. Donna CHASTAIN
18	Assoc Vice Pres Facilities	Ms. Anita AZAREKNO
19	Director Public Safety	Ms. Suzy TANNENBAUM
29	Exec Dir of Alumni Association	Ms. Kathy BICKEL
86	Director Government Relations	Mr. Jock S. MILLS
44	Director of Annual Giving	Ms. Lacie LA RUE
27	Dir News/Comm Svcs/Asst Vice Pres	Ms. Annie HECK
26	Director of University Marketing	Ms. Melody K. OLDFIELD
105	Asst Director Web Communications	Mr. David A. BAKER
28	Chief Diversity Officer	Ms. Charlene ALEXANDER
09	Director of Institutional Research	Mr. Salvador CASTILLO
40	General Mgr & CEO OSU Bookstores	Mr. Steve E. ECKRICH
96	Manager Procurement/Contract Svcs	Ms. Kelly L. KOZISEK
101	Secretary of the Institution/Board	Ms. Debbie COLBERT

Pacific Bible College (G)

28 S. Fir St., Suite 212, Medford OR 97501

County: Jackson Identification: 667252
Unit ID: 407610

Telephone: (541) 776-9942 Carnegie Class: Not Classified
FAX Number: (541) 770-9065 Calendar System: Semester
URL: www.pacificbible.com
Established: 1991 Annual Undergrad Tuition & Fees: $3,650
Enrollment: 30 Coed
Affiliation or Control: Non-denominational IRS Status: 501(c)3
Highest Offering: Associate Degree
Accreditation: @BI

01	President	Mr. Mike ROBINSON
05	Chief Academic Officer	Mr. John OSBOURN
32	Dean of Men & Women	Mr. Kevin MONK

Pacific Northwest College of Art (H)

511 NW Broadway, Portland OR 97209-3023

County: Multnomah FICE Identification: 003207
Unit ID: 209603

Telephone: (503) 226-4391 Carnegie Class: Spec-4-yr-Arts
FAX Number: (503) 226-3587 Calendar System: Semester
URL: www.pnca.edu
Established: 1909 Annual Undergrad Tuition & Fees: $34,500
Enrollment: 501 Coed
Affiliation or Control: Independent Non-Profit IRS Status: 501(c)3
Highest Offering: Master's
Accreditation: NW, ART

01	President	Mr. Don TUSKI
10	Chief Financial Officer/HR Director	Mr. Mark MORELAND
04	Executive Administrative Assistant	Vacant
51	Interim Dir of Continuing Education	Ms. Kate COPELAND
37	Director Financial Aid	Ms. Heidi LOCKE
06	Registrar	Mr. Ron RUTTER
08	Dir of Library Services	Ms. Serenity IBSEN
07	Director of Admissions	Ms. Anna MILTENBERGER
18	Facilities Manager	Mr. Charles VAWTER
32	Director of Student Services	Ms. Rachael ALLEN
39	Director of Residence Life	Mr. Jordan BERMINGHAM
13	Chief Info Technology Officer (CIO)	Mr. Jason REDCEDER
111	Chief Development/Advancement	Ms. Darby KNOX
43	Dir Legal Services/General Counsel	Ms. Cordelia DANIELS

Pacific University (I)

2043 College Way, Forest Grove OR 97116-1797

County: Washington FICE Identification: 003212
Unit ID: 209612

Telephone: (503) 357-6151 Carnegie Class: Masters/L
FAX Number: (503) 352-2242 Calendar System: Semester
URL: www.pacificu.edu
Established: 1849 Annual Undergrad Tuition & Fees: $41,054
Enrollment: 3,810 Coed
Affiliation or Control: Independent Non-Profit IRS Status: 501(c)3
Highest Offering: Doctorate
Accreditation: NW, ARCPA, @AUD, CAATE, CAEPN, CLPSY, DH, IPSY, MUS, OPT, OPTR, OT, PHAR, PTA, @SP, SW

01	President	Dr. Lesley M. HALLICK
05	Vice Pres Academic Affairs/Provost	Dr. John MILLER
10	Vice Pres Finance & Administration	Mr. Mike MALLERY
111	Vice Pres University Advancement	Ms. Cassie WARMAN
32	Vice Pres Enrollment/Student Affs	Dr. Mark ANKENY
35	Assoc Vice Pres Student Affairs	Mr. Will PERKINS
26	Interim Assoc VP of Marketing/Comm	Ms. Jenni LUCKETT
110	Assoc VP for University Advancement	Ms. Jan STRICKLIN
21	Assistant Vice Pres for Finance	Mr. William RAY
20	Vice Provost Academic Affairs	Dr. Lisa CARSTENS
18	Director of Facilities	Ms. Cindy SCHUPPERT
07	Executive Director of Admissions	Ms. Karen DUNSTON
06	Registrar	Ms. Anne HERMAN
37	Director Financial Aid	Ms. Leslie LIMPER
13	Chief Information Officer	Mr. James FLEMING
88	Director of Conference Services	Ms. Lois HORNBERGER
88	Director University Events	Ms. Paula THATCHER
76	Exec Dean Col of Health Professions	Dr. Ann BARR-GILLESPIE
49	Interim Dean of Arts & Sciences	Dr. Sarah PHILLIPS
63	Dean of Optometry	Dr. Jennifer COYLE
67	Dean of Pharmacy	Dr. Reza KARIMIGEVARI
53	Dean College of Education	Dr. Leif GUSTAVSON
83	Dean Sch Professional Psychology	Dr. Christiane BREMS
41	Athletic Director	Mr. Kenneth SCHUMANN
76	Director School Physical Therapy	Dr. Kevin CHUI
76	Dir School Occupational Therapy	Dr. Gregory WINTZ

15 Director of Human Resources .... Vacant
23 Director of Health Services .... Ms. Kathryn L. EISENBARTH
88 Acad Coord/English Language Inst .... Ms. Monique GRINDELL
44 Director Leadership Annual Giving .... Ms. Karine KADYAN
123 Exec Director of Grad/Prof Admiss .... Mr. Jon-Erik LARSEN
76 Director Physician Asst Studies .... Dr. Mary VON
29 Director Alumni Relations .... Ms. Martha CALUS-MCLAIN
88 Dir External Relations Optometry .... Ms. Jeanne OLIVER
08 Director of University Libraries .... Mr. Isaac GILMAN
32 Dir Univ Center/Student Activities .... Mr. Steve KLEIN
36 Director Career Development .... Mr. Brian O'DRISCOLL
52 Program Director-Dental .... Ms. Lisa ROWLEY
40 Manager Bookstore .... Ms. Stacie BLANKENHORN
38 Director Counseling Center .... Ms. Robin KEILLOR
09 Director of Institutional Research .... Mr. William O'SHEA
04 Executive Asst to President .... Ms. Sue WEINBENDER
100 Chief of Staff .... Ms. Mic HOWE
112 Major Gift Ofcr Found/Corp Rels .... Ms. Amy CALLAHAN
104 Director International Programs .... Dr. Stephen PRAG
28 Director Equity/Diversity/Inclusion .... Ms. Narcedalia RODRIGUEZ
50 Dean of College of Business .... Dr. James GOODRICH

Pioneer Pacific College (A)

27501 SW Parkway Avenue, Wilsonville OR 97070-9296
County: Clackamas FICE Identification: 023301
Unit ID: 210076
Telephone: (503) 682-3903 Carnegie Class: Bac/Assoc-Assoc Dom
FAX Number: (503) 682-1514 Calendar System: Other
URL: www.pioneerpacific.edu
Established: 1981 Annual Undergrad Tuition & Fees: $14,649
Enrollment: 1,170 Coed
Affiliation or Control: Proprietary IRS Status: Proprietary
Highest Offering: Baccalaureate
Accreditation: **PPPA**, MAAB, RAD

01 President .... Mr. Don MOUTOS
05 Vice President of Academic Affairs .... Mr. Fred OSBORN
10 Controller .... Ms. Wendy HUTCHISONS

Pioneer Pacific College-Eugene Branch (B)

3800 Sports way, Springfield OR 97447
Telephone: (541) 684-4644 Identification: 770764
Accreditation: **PPPA**, MAAB

Portland Community College (C)

PO Box 19000, Portland OR 97280-0990
County: Multnomah FICE Identification: 003213
Unit ID: 209746
Telephone: (971) 722-6111 Carnegie Class: Assoc/MT-VT-Mix Trad/Non
FAX Number: (971) 722-4960 Calendar System: Quarter
URL: www.pcc.edu/
Established: 1961 Annual Undergrad Tuition & Fees (In-District): $3,802
Enrollment: 29,003 Coed
Affiliation or Control: Local IRS Status: 501(c)3
Highest Offering: Associate Degree
Accreditation: **NW**, ADNUR, CAHIIM, DA, DH, DT, EMT, IFSAC, MAC, MLTAD, RAD

01 College President .... Mr. Mark MITSUI
100 Program Administrator .... Dr. Traci FORDHAM
05 VP Academic Affairs .... Ms. Katy W. HO
32 VP Student Affairs .... Mr. Rob STEINMETZ
11 Vice Pres Finance/Administration .... Mr. Jim LANGSTRAAT
10 Assoc VP Financial Services .... Mr. Eric BLUMENTHAL
13 Chief Information Officer .... Mr. Michael NORTHOVER
44 Assoc VP College Advancement .... Mr. Robert A. WAGNER
12 Campus President Sylvania .... Dr. Lisa AVERY
12 Campus President Cascade .... Dr. Karin EDWARDS
12 Campus President Rock Creek .... Dr. Sandra FOWLER-HILL
12 Campus President Southeast .... Dr. Jessica HOWARD
20 Int Dean Instruction Sylvania .... Dr. Karen PAEZ
20 Dean Instruction Cascade Campus .... Mr. Kurt SIMONDS
20 Int Dean Instr Rock Creek Campus .... Dr. Cheryl SCOTT
20 Dean Instruction Southeast Campus .... Mr. Al D. MCQUARTERS
32 Dean Student Dev Sylvania Campus .... Ms. Heather LANG
32 Dean Stdnt Dev Rock Creek Campus .... Mr. Ryan A. AIELLO
32 Dean Student Dev Cascade Campus .... Ms. Michele CRUSE
35 Dean Student Affairs .... Ms. Tammy N. BILLICK
15 Associate VP Human Resources .... Ms. Lisa BLEDSOE
18 Director Facilities Management .... Mr. Tony ICHSAN
08 Dean Library Services .... Ms. Michelle M. BAGLEY
09 Dir Institutional Effectiveness .... Ms. Laura MASSEY
19 Director Public Safety .... Mr. Derrick FOXWORTH
37 Director Financial Aid .... Mr. Peter GOSS
22 Chief Diversity Officer .... Ms. Kim BAKER-FLOWERS
30 Director of Development .... Ms. Ann PRATER
84 Dir of Enrollment Services .... Ms. Darilis GARCIA-MCMILLIAN
06 Registrar .... Ms. Kristin R. BENSON
31 Director of Community Engagement .... Ms. Kate CHESTER
96 Interim Manager Purchasing .... Ms. Karen PRESTON

Portland State University (D)

PO Box 751, Portland OR 97207-0751
County: Multnomah FICE Identification: 003216
Unit ID: 209807
Telephone: (503) 725-3000 Carnegie Class: DU-Higher
FAX Number: (503) 725-4882 Calendar System: Quarter
URL: www.pdx.edu
Established: 1946 Annual Undergrad Tuition & Fees (In-State): $8,337
Enrollment: 27,488 Coed
Affiliation or Control: State IRS Status: 501(c)3
Highest Offering: Doctorate
Accreditation: **NW**, CACREP, CAEP, CEA, CS, ENG, HSA, MUS, PH, PLNG, SP, SPAA, SW, THEA

01 President .... Dr. Rahmat SHOURESHI
43 General Counsel .... Mr. David REESE
05 Provost & VP Academic Affairs .... Dr. Sona ANDREWS
10 Vice President Finance/Admin .... Dr. Kevin REYNOLDS
102 CEO PSU Foundation .... Mr. Bill BOLDT
100 Chief of Staff & VP Public Affairs .... Ms. Lois DAVIS
32 VP Enroll Mgmt & Student Affairs .... Dr. John FRAIRE
46 VP Rsrch & Strategic Partnerships .... Vacant
22 VP Global Diversity & Inclusion .... Dr. Carmen SUAREZ
45 Vice Prov Academic/Fiscal Planning .... Mr. Scott MARSHALL
20 Vice Provost Acad Pers Ldrshp & Dev .... Dr. Shelly CHABON
26 Assoc VP Communications .... Mr. Christopher BRODERICK
09 Director Inst Research/Planning .... Dr. Kathi A. KETCHESON
19 Director Campus Public Safety .... Mr. Phil ZERZAN
14 AVP Strategic Plng/Prtnrshps/Tech .... Mr. Erin FLYNN
08 Dean University Librarian .... Dr. Marilyn MOODY
41 Athletics Director .... Ms. Valerie CLEARY
121 Vice Prov Acad Innov/Stdnt Success .... Mr. Sukhwant S. JHAJ
49 Dean of CLAS .... Dr. Karen MARRONGELLE
50 Dean of SBA .... Mr. Clifford ALLEN
53 Dean Graduate Sch of Education .... Dr. Marvin LYNN
54 Dean Col Engr/Computer Science .... Dr. Ren Jeng SU
57 Dean College of the Arts .... Dr. Leroy BYNUM
70 Dean School of Social Work .... Dr. Laura NISSEN
80 Dean College Urban/Public Affairs .... Dr. Stephen PERCY
35 Dean Student Life .... Ms. Michele TOPPE
13 AVP/Chief Information Officer .... Mr. Kirk KELLY
85 Dir Diversity & Mult Student Svcs .... Ms. Cece RIDDER
06 AVP & University Registrar .... Ms. Cindy BACCAR
86 Asst Director Government Relations .... Ms. Alyson KRAUS
86 Dir State Govt Relations .... Vacant
23 Exec Dir Stdnt Health & Counseling .... Dr. Dana TASSON
58 AVP & Dean Graduate Studies .... Ms. Margaret EVERETT
46 AVP Research .... Ms. Lisa ZURK

Process Work Institute (E)

2049 NW Hoyt Street, Portland OR 97209
County: Multnomah Identification: 667297
Telephone: (503) 223-8188 Carnegie Class: Not Classified
FAX Number: (503) 227-7003 Calendar System: Quarter
URL: www.processwork.org
Established: Annual Graduate Tuition & Fees: N/A
Enrollment: N/A Coed
Affiliation or Control: Independent Non-Profit IRS Status: 501(c)3
Highest Offering: Master's; No Undergraduates
Accreditation: **ACICS**

01 President .... Dr. Chris ALLEN

Reed College (F)

3203 SE Woodstock Boulevard, Portland OR 97202-8199
County: Multnomah FICE Identification: 003217
Unit ID: 209922
Telephone: (503) 771-1112 Carnegie Class: Bac-A&S
FAX Number: (503) 777-7769 Calendar System: Semester
URL: www.reed.edu
Established: 1908 Annual Undergrad Tuition & Fees: $52,150
Enrollment: 1,453 Coed
Affiliation or Control: Independent Non-Profit IRS Status: 501(c)3
Highest Offering: Master's
Accreditation: **NW**

01 President .... Mr. John KROGER
05 Dean of the Faculty .... Dr. Nigel J. NICHOLSON
26 Vice President College Relations .... Mr. Hugh E. PORTER
10 Vice President & Treasurer .... Dr. Lorraine ARVIN
32 Vice President for Student Services .... Dr. Michael BRODY
04 Exec Asst to the President .... Ms. Dawn G. THOMPSON
28 Dean for Institutional Diversity .... Dr. Mary B. JAMES
35 Dean of Students .... Dr. Bruce SMITH
23 Director Health & Counseling .... Ms. Kathryn A. SMITH
07 Vice Pres/Dean Admission & Fin Aid .... Mr. Milyon TRULOVE
06 Registrar .... Ms. Nora MCLAUGHLIN
08 College Librarian .... Ms. Dena HUTTO
30 Director of Development .... Vacant
37 Director of Financial Aid .... Ms. Sandy SUNDSTROM
09 Director of Institutional Research .... Mr. Mike TAMADA
27 Exec Dir Comm & Public Affairs .... Ms. Mandy HEATON
29 Director of Alumni Programs .... Ms. Katie RAMSEY
13 Chief Information Officer .... Dr. Martin D. RINGLE
105 Director of Web Support Services .... Ms. Marianne M. COLGROVE
91 Director Administrative Computing .... Mr. Gabriel LEAVITT
21 Controller .... Mr. Rob TUST
15 Director of Human Resources .... Ms. Michelle VALINTIS
29 Dir Alumni Programs & Annual Fund .... Ms. Mary M. ASKELSON
102 Dir Corporate/Foundation Support .... Ms. Diane B. GUMZ
104 Director International Programs .... Dr. Paul D. DEYOUNG
36 Dean of Stdnts/Dir Life Beyond Reed .... Ms. Alice HARRA
88 Director of Special Programs .... Ms. Barbara A. AMEN
18 Director Facilities Operations .... Mr. Townsend ANGELL
19 Director Community Safety .... Mr. Gary GRANGER
68 Director of Physical Education .... Mr. Michael LOMBARDO
40 Director Bookstore & Auxiliary Svcs .... Ms. Jessica VALESKE
39 Asst Dean of Students for Res Life .... Ms. Amy SCHUCKMAN

Rogue Community College (G)

3345 Redwood Highway, Grants Pass OR 97527-9298
County: Josephine FICE Identification: 010182
Unit ID: 209940
Telephone: (541) 956-7500 Carnegie Class: Assoc/MT-VT-High Non
FAX Number: (541) 471-3591 Calendar System: Quarter
URL: www.roguecc.edu
Established: 1970 Annual Undergrad Tuition & Fees (In-District): $4,164
Enrollment: 4,954 Coed
Affiliation or Control: Local IRS Status: 501(c)3
Highest Offering: Associate Degree
Accreditation: **NW**, EMT

01 College President .... Dr. Cathy KEMPER-PELLE
05 VP of Instruction/CAO .... Mr. Kirk GIBSON
13 VP of College Services/CIO .... Mr. Curtis SOMMERFELD
32 VP Student Serv/CSSO/Dir Athletics .... Ms. Kori EBENHACK
103 Dean School of Workforce/Col Prep .... Ms. Theresa RIVENES
72 Dean Sch Arts/Tech/Health/Pub Svc .... Mr. Kevin HOFF
88 Director Small Bus Dev Center .... Mr. Ronald GOSS
81 Dean School of Science and Tech .... Mr. Steve SCHILLING
08 Head Librarian .... Mr. Robert FELTHOUSEN
102 Executive Director Foundation .... Ms. Judy BASKER
15 Director HR and Risk Mgmt .... Ms. Sara MOYE
24 Director Instructional Media .... Mr. Josh OGLE
109 Director Auxiliary Services .... Ms. Laura HAGA-DUFFY
26 Dir Marketing & Recruitment .... Mr. Grant WALKER
37 Director Student Financial Aid .... Ms. Anna MANLEY
14 Director IT Network & User Support .... Mr. Mike MCCLURE
71 Director TRiO-EOC .... Ms. Janet BASNEY
71 Director TRiO-SSS .... Ms. Colletta YOUNG
09 Director of Institutional Research .... Vacant
51 Apprenticeship Coordinator .... Ms. Cathy PIERSON
96 Contract and Procurement Manager .... Ms. Jodie FULTON
04 Admin Coord/Accreditation Liaison .... Ms. Denise SWAFFORD
91 Director of IT Programming .... Mr. Al SHELDON
18 Director of Facilities/Operations .... Mr. Grant LAGORIO
20 Dir Curriculum and Scheduling .... Ms. Laura BENNETT
88 Director of Student Programs .... Ms. Rene MCKENZIE
07 Director Enrollment Services .... Mr. John DUARTE
04 Assistant to Board of Education .... Ms. Denise NELSON
04 Assistant to the President .... Vacant
35 Dean of Student Success .... Ms. Brooke MCDERMID
10 Chief Financial Officer .... Ms. Lisa STANTON
108 Outcomes & Assessment Strategist .... Ms. Lori SOURS
28 Diversity Programming Coordinator .... Ms. Sharon SMITH
38 Faculty/Chair Student Counseling .... Ms. Gaia LAYSER
50 Faculty/Dept Chair Bus Tech .... Dr. Randy WADE
06 Registrar .... Mr. John DUARTE
88 Director Educational Partnerships .... Ms. Danielle BIVENS
88 Director of WF Training and Comm Ed .... Mr. Bill JIRON
88 Director Adult Basic Skills .... Ms. Julie ROSSI
76 Director Allied Health Occupations .... Ms. Teri SMITH

Southern Oregon University (H)

1250 Siskiyou Boulevard, Ashland OR 97520-5001
County: Jackson FICE Identification: 003219
Unit ID: 210146
Telephone: (541) 552-7672 Carnegie Class: Masters/L
FAX Number: (541) 552-6329 Calendar System: Quarter
URL: www.sou.edu
Established: 1872 Annual Undergrad Tuition & Fees (In-State): $8,523
Enrollment: 6,088 Coed
Affiliation or Control: State IRS Status: 501(c)3
Highest Offering: Master's
Accreditation: **NW**, ACBSP, CACREP, MUS

01 President .... Dr. Linda SCHOTT
05 Prov/VP Acad & Student Affairs .... Dr. Susan WALSH
10 VP for Finance & Administration .... Mr. Craig MORRIS
30 Vice President Development .... Ms. Janet FRATELLA
15 Director for Human Resource Svcs .... Ms. Alana LARDIZABAL
100 Chief of Staff/Dir Government Rels .... Vacant
84 Assoc VP Enrollment & Retention .... Vacant
26 Ex Dir Interactive Mktg/Media Rels .... Ms. Nicolle ALEMAN
18 Dir for Facilities Mgmt & Planning .... Mr. Drew GILLILAND
58 Assoc Provost/Director Grad Stds .... Dr. Jody WATERS
21 Director of Business Services .... Mr. Steve LARVICK
08 University Librarian .... Mr. Jeffrey GAYTON
32 Director for Student Life .... Ms. Jennifer FOUNTAIN
51 Exec Dir Division of Continuing Edu .... Ms. Jeanne STALLMAN
19 Director of Campus Public Safety .... Mr. Frederick CREEK
13 Director of Information Technology .... Mr. Brad CHRIST
29 Director of Alumni Affairs .... Mr. Mike BEAGLE
21 Assoc Director of Business Services .... Ms. Debbie MICHAELS
106 Director of the Center for Instruct .... Dr. Vicki SUTER
88 Director of Schneider Museum of Art .... Mr. Scott MALBAURN
88 Dir of Accelerated Baccalaureate Pgm .... Mr. Curt BACON
28 Director of Diversity and Inclusion .... Ms. Marjorie TRUEBLOOD-GAMBLE
44 Annual Fund Coordinator .... Ms. Chava FLORENDO
57 Director Performing Arts .... Dr. David HUMPHREY
83 Director Social Sciences .... Dr. Dan DENEUI
97 Director Undergraduate Studies .... Dr. Lee AYERS
81 Director STEM .... Dr. Sherry ETTLICH
50 Director Business Comm & Environmt .... Ms. Katie PITTMAN
79 Director Humanities & Culture .... Dr. Scott REX
88 Director Educ Health & Leadership .... Dr. John KING
06 Registrar .... Dr. Matt STILLMAN
07 Director of Admissions .... Ms. Kelly MOUTSATSON
37 Director of Financial Aid .... Ms. Kristen DUNCAN

09 Director of Institutional Research ....Mr. Chris STANEK
25 Chief Contracts/Grants Admin .... Ms. Joanne PRESTON
41 Athletic Director ....Mr. Matt SAYRE
04 Administrative Asst to President .... Ms. Jennifer ATHANAS
101 University Board Secretary ....Ms. Sabrina PRUD'HOMME
39 Director Student Housing .... Ms. Staci BUCHWALD
43 General Counsel .... Mr. Jason CATZ

Southwestern Oregon Community College (A)

1988 Newmark Avenue, Coos Bay OR 97420-2911
County: Coos FICE Identification: 003220
Unit ID: 210155
Telephone: (541) 888-2525 Carnegie Class: Assoc/MT-VT-High Trad
FAX Number: (541) 888-7285 Calendar System: Quarter
URL: www.socc.edu
Established: 1961 Annual Undergrad Tuition & Fees (In-District): $5,847
Enrollment: 2,338 Coed
Affiliation or Control: Local IRS Status: 501(c)3
Highest Offering: Associate Degree
Accreditation: NW, ACFEI, EMT, MAAB

01 President ....Dr. Patty SCOTT
11 VP Administrative Services ....Mr. Jeff WHITEY
05 VP Instructional Services ....Dr. Ali MAGEEHON
12 Dean Curry County ....Mr. Leslie BALSIGER
72 Dean of Career and Technical Educ .... Ms. Cody YEAGER
56 Dean of Extended Learning .... Ms. Karen DOMINE
32 Dean of Student Services ....Mr. Tim DAILEY
84 Exec Director Enrollment Management ....Mr. Tom NICHOLLS
13 Director Integrated Technology ....Mr. Carl GERISCH
88 Exec Director OCCI (Culinary) .... Mr. Shawn HANLIN
20 Assoc Dean of LDC & Devel Education ....Mr. Rod KELLER
41 Director Athletics .... Dr. Mike HERBERT
07 Director of Admissions ....Mr. Tom NICHOLLS
19 Director Campus Safety .... Mr. Joe THOMAS
30 Dir College Advancement/Alumni Rels ....Ms. Elise HAMNER
18 Director Facilities Services .... Ms. Emerald BRUNETT
06 Registrar .... Ms. Jennifer SILVA
37 Director Financial Aid ....Ms. Avena SINGH
15 Exec Director Human Resources ....Mr. Matt GILROY
08 Manager of Learning Resources ....Ms. Alicia MUELLER
66 Director Nursing ....Ms. Susan WALKER
39 Director Residence Life .... Mr. Joe BELTER
88 Director SOCC Business Dev Center .... Ms. Arlene SOTO
38 Director Student Support Srvcs .... Ms. Michele BENOIT
40 Manager Bookstore .... Ms. Shawna STEPHENS
09 Institutional Researcher ....Ms. Robin BUNNELL
35 Coordinator Student Life and Events ....Mr. Kyle CROY
04 Exec Asst to the Pres/Board of Educ .... Ms. Deb NICHOLLS
10 Chief Business Officer ....Ms. Kathy DIXON
26 Chief Public Relations/Marketing ....Ms. Anne MATTHEWS

Sumner College (B)

8338 NE Alderwood Rd., Ste 100, Portland OR 97220
County: Multnomah FICE Identification: 021049
Unit ID: 208512
Telephone: (503) 972-6230 Carnegie Class: Spec 2-yr-Other
FAX Number: (503) 972-0781 Calendar System: Other
URL: www.sumnercollege.edu
Established: 1974 Annual Undergrad Tuition & Fees: N/A
Enrollment: 287 Coed
Affiliation or Control: Proprietary IRS Status: Proprietary
Highest Offering: Associate Degree
Accreditation: ABHES

01 President ....Joanna S. RUSSELL

Tillamook Bay Community College (C)

4301 3rd Street, Tillamook OR 97141
County: Tillamook Identification: 666647
Unit ID: 420723
Telephone: (503) 842-8222 Carnegie Class: Assoc/HT-High Non
FAX Number: (503) 842-8336 Calendar System: Quarter
URL: www.tillamookbaycc.edu
Established: 1981 Annual Undergrad Tuition & Fees (In-District): $3,816
Enrollment: 295 Coed
Affiliation or Control: State/Local IRS Status: 501(c)3
Highest Offering: Associate Degree
Accreditation: NW

01 President ....Dr. Constance C. GREEN
05 Chief Academic Officer ....Dr. Ann HOVEY
10 Comptroller/Budget Officer .... Ms. Kyra WILLIAMS
30 Chief Development .... Mrs. Heidi LUQUETTE
32 Dir Student Services & Registrar .... Mrs. Rhoda HANSON
15 Dir Human Resources/Facilities ....Mr. Pat RYAN
09 Coordinator Institutional Research ....Vacant

Treasure Valley Community College (D)

650 College Boulevard, Ontario OR 97914-3423
County: Malheur FICE Identification: 003221
Unit ID: 210234
Telephone: (541) 881-8822 Carnegie Class: Assoc/MT-VT-High Non
FAX Number: (541) 881-2753 Calendar System: Quarter
URL: www.tvcc.cc
Established: 1961 Annual Undergrad Tuition & Fees (In-District): $5,400
Enrollment: 2,170 Coed
Affiliation or Control: Local IRS Status: 501(c)3
Highest Offering: Associate Degree
Accreditation: NW, ADNUR

01 President ....Ms. Dana YOUNG
05 Vice President of Academic Affairs .... Mr. Eddie ALVES
11 Vice Pres Admin Services .... Mr. Kevin KIMBALL
08 Librarian ....Mr. Dennis GILL
26 Assoc VP College/Public Relations ....Ms. Abby LEE
10 Comptroller ....Ms. Shirley HAIDLE
37 Financial Aid Director ....Ms. Diahann DERRICK
13 Director Information Technology .... Mr. Scott CARPENTER
07 Director of Admissions .... Ms. Stephanie OESTER
15 Director of Human Resources ....Ms. Anne-Marie KELSO
51 Director of Continuing Education .... Ms. Andrea TESTI
18 Dir of Housing/Building & Grounds .... Mr. Bernie BABCOCK
41 Athletic Director .... Mr. Ed ARONSON
88 Corrections Education Director .... Mr. Jeremy YRAGUEN
06 Registrar ....Vacant
09 Director of Institutional Effective .... Mr. David KOEHLER
102 TVCC Foundation Exec Dir ....Ms. Cathy YASUDA
40 Bookstore Manager .... Mr. Kjetil ROM
04 Executive Asst to President .... Ms. Gina ROPER
84 Director Enrollment Management .... Mr. Sage MWIINGA
19 Director Security/Safety .... Ms. Michelle POTTER
39 Director Student Housing ....Ms. Tasha WIXOM

Umpqua Community College (E)

1140 Umpqua College Road, Roseburg OR 97470
County: Douglas FICE Identification: 003222
Unit ID: 210270
Telephone: (541) 440-4600 Carnegie Class: Assoc/MT-VT-High Non
FAX Number: (541) 440-4637 Calendar System: Quarter
URL: www.umpqua.edu
Established: 1964 Annual Undergrad Tuition & Fees (In-District): $4,417
Enrollment: 2,246 Coed
Affiliation or Control: Local IRS Status: 501(c)3
Highest Offering: Associate Degree
Accreditation: NW, ADNUR, DA, EMT

01 President .... Dr. Debra THATCHER
05 Provost .... Dr. Kacy CRABTREE
10 CFO ....Ms. Rebecca REDELL
37 Director of Financial Aid .... Ms. Michelle BERGMANN
13 Director Informational Technology ....Mr. Dan YODER
08 Director of Library Services .... Ms. Carol MCGEEHON
103 Director of Community/Workforce .... Ms. Robin VAN WINKLE
09 Director Institutional Research .... Ms. Xiana SMITHHART
15 Director of Human Resources ....Ms. Lynn JOHNSON
04 Executive Asst to President & Board ....Ms. Robynne WILGUS
06 Registrar .... Mr. David FARRINGTON
111 Executive Director of Advancement ....Ms. Susan TAYLOR
18 Director of Facilities ....Mr. Jess MILLER
19 Director of Security ....Mr. Kelly RIGSBY
26 Director of Communications & Market .... Ms. Tiffany COLEMAN
41 Athletic Director ....Mr. Craig JACKSON
96 Purchasing Manager ....Mr. Jules DEGIULIO

University of Oregon (F)

1585 E. 13th Avenue, Eugene OR 97403
County: Lane FICE Identification: 003223
Unit ID: 209551
Telephone: (541) 346-1000 Carnegie Class: DU-Highest
FAX Number: N/A Calendar System: Quarter
URL: www.uoregon.edu
Established: 1876 Annual Undergrad Tuition & Fees (In-State): $10,761
Enrollment: 24,032 Coed
Affiliation or Control: State IRS Status: 501(c)3
Highest Offering: Doctorate
Accreditation: NW, ART, CAATE, CEA, CIDA, CLPSY, COPSY, CSHSE, IPSY, JOUR, LAW, LSAR, MFCD, MUS, PCSAS, PLNG, SCPSY, SP, SPAA

01 President ....Mr. Michael H. SCHILL
100 Senior Advisor/Chief of Staff ....Mr. Greg J. STRIPP
05 Senior Vice President & Provost ....Dr. Jayanth BANAVAR
10 VP Finance & Admin & CFO .... Ms. Jamie H. MOFFITT
32 Interim Vice Pres Student Life ....Dr. Kevin MARBURY
111 Vice Pres University Advancement ... Mr. Michael C. ANDREASEN
46 VP Research & Innovation .... Dr. David CONOVER
26 VP University Communications ....Mr. Kyle HENLEY
43 Vice President and General Counsel .... Mr. Kevin REED
20 Vice Provost Undergraduate Studies .... Dr. Lisa FREINKEL
28 Vice Pres Equity & Inclusion ....Dr. Yvette M. ALEX-ASSENSOH
13 Vice Prov Information Services/CIO .... Ms. Jessie MINTON
85 Vice Provost International Affairs ....Dr. Dennis C. GALVAN
86 Assoc Vice Pres Federal Affairs ....Ms. Betsy A. BOYD
29 AVP Alumni Affairs/Exec Dir UOAA ....Ms. Kelly MENACHEMSON
102 Chief Investment Officer Foundation .... Mr. Jay NAMYET
06 University Registrar ....Ms. Susan M. EVELAND
07 Director of Admissions ....Mr. Jim H. RAWLINS
08 Philip H Knight Dean of Libraries .... Dr. Adriene I. LIM
21 Dir Business Affairs and Controller ....Mr. Kelly B. WOLF
37 Director Student Financial Aid .... Mr. Jim J. BROOKS
36 Director of Career Center ....Vacant
15 Chief Human Resources Officer ....Ms. Nancy E. RESNICK
18 Assoc VP Planning & Facilities Mgmt .... Mr. Mike HARWOOD
22 Interim Director Affirmative Action .... Ms. Nancy RESNICK
41 Director Intercollegiate Athletics ....Mr. Rob A. MULLENS
56 Executive Dir UO Academic Extension .... Ms. Sandra K. GLADNEY
49 Dean College Arts & Sciences ....Dr. W. Andrew MARCUS
48 Dean Architecture/Allied Arts .... Dr. Christoph LINDER
50 Dean College of Business ....Dr. Sarah NUTTER
53 Dean College of Education ....Dr. Randy W. KAMPHAUS
60 Dean School of Journ & Comm .... Dr. Juan-Carlos MOLLEDA
58 Dean of Graduate School .... Dr. Scott L. PRATT
61 Dean School of Law ....Ms. Marcilynn BURKE
64 Dean School of Music & Dance ....Dr. Brad FOLEY
92 Dean Clark Honors College ....Dr. Terry L. HUNT
09 Director of Institutional Research ....Dr. JP MONROE
38 Dir Counseling & Testing Center .... Dr. Shelly K. KERR
84 VP Enrollment Mgmt & Student Svc ....Mr. Roger J. THOMPSON
96 Dir Purchasing & Contracting Svcs .... Mr. Craig ASHFORD
101 Secretary of the University/Board .... Ms. Angela WILHELMS
19 Chief of Police ....Mr. Matthew CARMICHAEL
39 Director Student Housing ....Mr. Michael M. GRIFFEL
114 Vice Provost Budget & Planning .... Dr. Brad SHELTON
90 Director Academic Technology ....Ms. Helen Y. CHU

University of Phoenix Oregon Campus (G)

13221 SW 68th Parkway, Tigard OR 97223-8328
Telephone: (503) 403-2900 Identification: 770222
Accreditation: &NH, ACBSP

† No longer accepting campus-based students.

University of Portland (H)

5000 N Willamette Boulevard, Portland OR 97203-5798
County: Multnomah FICE Identification: 003224
Unit ID: 209825
Telephone: (503) 943-8000 Carnegie Class: Masters/M
FAX Number: (503) 943-7491 Calendar System: Semester
URL: www.up.edu
Established: 1901 Annual Undergrad Tuition & Fees: $44,104
Enrollment: 4,338 Coed
Affiliation or Control: Independent Non-Profit IRS Status: 501(c)3
Highest Offering: Doctorate
Accreditation: NW, CAEPN, CS, ENG, MUS, NURSE, SW, THEA

01 President ....Rev. Mark L. POORMAN, CSC
05 Provost .... Dr. Thomas G. GREENE
26 Vice Pres for University Relations . Rev. Gerard J. OLINGER, CSC
11 Vice Pres for University Operations ....Mr. James B. RAVELLI
10 Vice Pres for Financial Affairs .... Mr. Alan P. TIMMINS
32 Vice President for Student Affairs ....Rev. John J. DONATO, CSC
43 Gen Counsel/Specia Asst to the Pres .... Ms. Andrea M. BARTON
07 Dean of Admissions .... Mr. Jason S. MCDONALD
21 Assoc Vice Pres & Controller ....Mr. Eric C. BARGER
06 Registrar ....Ms. Roberta D. LINDAHL
08 Dean of Library ....Ms. Xan ARCH
30 Sr Assoc Vice President Development ....Mr. Bryce B. STRANG
36 Director Career Services ....Ms. Amy CAVANAUGH
15 Director of Human Resources ....Ms. Sandy S. CHUNG
37 Director Student Financial Aid ....Ms. Janet K. TURNER
27 Director of Marketing ....Ms. Rachel E. BARRY-ARQUIT
49 Dean of Arts & Sciences ....Dr. Gary L. MALECHA
50 Dean of the Business School ....Dr. Robin D. ANDERSON
66 Dean of Nursing ....Dr. Joane T. MOCERI
54 Dean of Engineering ....Dr. Sharon A. JONES
53 Dean of Education ....Dr. John L. WATZKE
23 Director University Health Center .... Ms. Margaret A. TROUT
19 Director of Public Safety ....Mr. Gerald A. GREGG
29 Director Alumni Relations ....Mr. Craig SWINYARD
39 Director Residence Life .... Mr. Christopher T. HAUG
41 Athletic Director ....Mr. Scott R. LEYKAM
42 Director Campus Ministry .... Rev. James T. GALLAGHER, CSC
102 Director Foundation Relations .... Ms. Dawn M. GEOPPINGER
18 Director Facilities Planning Constr ....Mr. Paul J. LUTY
18 Director Physical Plant ....Mr. Andre HUTCHINSON
40 Director Bookstore ....Ms. Erin L. CAVE
88 Director University Events .... Mr. William O. REED
09 Director of Institutional Research ....Ms. Elizabeth LEE
35 Director Student Activities .... Mr. Jeromy A. KOFFLER
04 Administrative Asst to President .... Ms. Kathy M. SIMEK
104 Director Study Abroad .... Mr. Eduardo R. CONTRERAS
13 Chief Info Technology Officer .... Mr. Curtis R. PEDERSON
44 Director Annual or Planned Giving ....Ms. Sharon HOGAN

University of Western States (I)

2900 NE 132nd Avenue, Portland OR 97230-3099
County: Multnomah FICE Identification: 012309
Unit ID: 210438
Telephone: (503) 256-3180 Carnegie Class: Spec-4-yr-Other Health
FAX Number: (503) 251-5723 Calendar System: Quarter
URL: www.uws.edu
Established: 1904 Annual Undergrad Tuition & Fees: N/A
Enrollment: 839 Coed
Affiliation or Control: Independent Non-Profit IRS Status: 501(c)3
Highest Offering: Doctorate
Accreditation: NW, CHIRO, COMTA

01 President ....Dr. Joseph BRIMHALL
10 Chief Business Officer ....Ms. Lisa LOPEZ
05 Provost/VP Academic Affairs ....Dr. Bernadette HOWLETT
88 Special Assistant to the President .... Dr. Patrick BROWNE
23 Vice President of Clinic Affairs ....Dr. Joseph PFEIFER
09 Ex Dir Institutional Effectiveness .... Dr. Rebekah ANDERSON
86 VP for University Affairs ....Ms. Rosalia MESSINA
109 Assoc VP for University Operations .... Ms. Sara MATHOV
46 Assoc Vice President of Research ....Dr. Mitch HAAS
23 Assoc VP of Clinical Internships ....Dr. Stanley EWALD

13 Director of Information Technology .... Vacant
84 Dean of Enrollment & Student Svcs .... Dr. Colman JOYCE
26 Dir of PR/Marketing/Communications .... Ms. Megan NUGENT
15 Director Human Resources .... Ms. Kathleen CANNON
06 Registrar .... Ms. Michelle DODGE
08 University Librarian .... Ms. Janet TAPPER
108 Exec Director Academic Assessment .... Mr. Jim MASCENIK
07 Director of Admissions .... Ms. Mary STAFFORD
18 Director Campus Facilities .... Mr. Terry COWDIN
37 Director Financial Aid .... Vacant
31 Director of Community Relations/CE ..... Ms. Alisa FAIRWEATHER
21 Controller .... Ms. Olga KLOCHKOVA
30 Development Officer .... Ms. Kelli RULE
106 Dir of Academic Support/Training .... Mr. Jim FRISCIA
29 Alumni Relations Manager .... Ms. Erika STANLEY

Warner Pacific College (A)

2219 SE 68th Avenue, Portland OR 97215
County: Multnomah FICE Identification: 003225
Unit ID: 210304
Telephone: (503) 517-1000 Carnegie Class: Bac-Diverse
FAX Number: (503) 517-1350 Calendar System: Semester
URL: www.warnerpacific.edu
Established: 1937 Annual Undergrad Tuition & Fees: $23,370
Enrollment: 523 Coed
Affiliation or Control: Church Of God IRS Status: 501(c)3
Highest Offering: Master's
Accreditation: NW, SW

01 President .... Dr. Andrea P. COOK
05 Vice Pres Acad Affs/Dean of Faculty .... Dr. Reginald NICHOLS
10 VP Finance/Chief Financial Officer .... Mr. Doug WADE
111 VP Inst Advancement/External Rels .... Mr. Mike GIERING
32 Vice Pres Student Life/Dean .... Mr. Jon SAMPSON
84 VP for Enrollment and Marketing .... Mr. Dale SEIPP
20 Assoc VP for Academic Affairs .... Dr. Lori K. JASS
37 Dir of Stdnt Financial Svcs/Fin Aid .... Mrs. Cindy POLLARD
07 Director of Admissions .... Ms. Kidesti TADESSE
41 Interim Director of Athletics .... Mr. Frank JOHNSON
08 Director of Library Services .... Dr. Lishi KWASITSU
06 Registrar .... Ms. Victoria R. CUMINGS
13 Dir Technology/Information Svcs .... Ms. Linda RUDAWITZ
29 Director of Alumni/Church Relations .... Ms. Serena CLINE
88 Dir of Contextualized Ministries .... Dr. Jess BIELMAN
42 Associate Dir Campus Ministries .... Ms. Michelle LANG
35 Director of Student Life .... Mr. Jared VALENTINE
18 Director of Facilities .... Mr. Dean JENKS
15 Director of Human Resources .... Mrs. Bev FITTS
09 Dir of Assessment/Inst Research .... Ms. Aundrea SNITKER
26 Mgr Marketing/Communications .... Ms. Melody BURTON
38 Director Student Counseling .... Dr. Carol DELLOLIVER
21 Associate Business Officer .... Mr. Nathan DUNBAR
36 Director of Academic Support .... Mr. Rod JOHANSON

Western Oregon University (B)

345 N Monmouth Avenue, Monmouth OR 97361-1394
County: Polk FICE Identification: 003209
Unit ID: 210429
Telephone: (503) 838-8000 Carnegie Class: Masters/M
FAX Number: (503) 838-8474 Calendar System: Quarter
URL: www.wou.edu
Established: 1856 Annual Undergrad Tuition & Fees (In-State): $9,285
Enrollment: 5,445 Coed
Affiliation or Control: State IRS Status: 501(c)3
Highest Offering: Beyond Master's But Less Than Doctorate
Accreditation: NW, CACREP, CAEPN, MUS

01 President .... Dr. Rex FULLER
03 Vice President & General Counsel .... Mr. Ryan HAGEMANN
05 Provost/Vice Pres Academic Affairs .... Dr. Stephen SCHECK
32 Vice President Student Affairs .... Dr. Gary DUKES
10 Vice Pres Finance & Administration .... Mr. Eric YAHNKE
35 Dean of Students .... Ms. Tina M. FUCHS
49 Dean Col Liberal Arts & Sciences .... Dr. Kathy CASSITY
53 Dean College of Education .... Dr. Mark GIROD
20 Associate Provost .... Mr. David MCDONALD
56 Director Division Extended Progams .... Mr. Dan CLARK
06 Registrar .... Ms. Amy CLARK
30 Director of Development .... Ms. Erin MCDONOUGH
08 Dean Hamersly Library .... Dr. Allen MCKIEL
13 Director University Computing Svcs .... Mr. William KERNAN
15 Director Human Resources .... Ms. Judy J. VANDERBURG
18 Director Physical Plant .... Mr. Michael SMITH
19 Director University Public Safety .... Ms. Rebecca CHILES
23 Dir Student Health/Counseling Ctr .... Mr. Jaime SILVA
26 Dir Public Relations/Communications .... Ms. Denise VISUANO
32 Dir Student Leadership & Activities .... Mr. Patrick MOSER
37 Director Financial Aid .... Ms. Kella HELYER
41 Athletic Director .... Mr. Curtis CAMPBELL
46 Dir of Teaching Research Institute .... Vacant
85 Dir Intl Students/Scholars Affairs .... Mr. Neng YANG
28 Dir Multicultural Student Svcs/ Pgms .... Ms. Anna HERNANDEZ-HUNTER
22 Director AAEO .... Ms. Judy J. VANDERBURG
29 Dir Leadership Giving/Athletic Dev .... Mr. Michael FEULING
04 Executive Asst to President .... Mrs. LouAnn VICKERS
21 Director of Business Services .... Mr. Darin SILBERNAGEL
07 Director of Admissions .... Mr. Rob FINDTNER
09 Director of Institutional Research .... Abdus SHAHID

Western Seminary (C)

5511 SE Hawthorne Boulevard, Portland OR 97215-3399
County: Multnomah FICE Identification: 007178
Unit ID: 210368
Telephone: (503) 517-1800 Carnegie Class: Spec-4-yr-Faith
FAX Number: (503) 517-1801 Calendar System: Semester
URL: www.westernseminary.edu
Established: 1927 Annual Graduate Tuition & Fees: N/A
Enrollment: 726 Coed
Affiliation or Control: Independent Non-Profit IRS Status: 501(c)3
Highest Offering: Doctorate; No Undergraduates
Accreditation: NW, CACREP, THEOL

01 President .... Dr. Randal R. ROBERTS
10 Administrative Vice President/CFO .... Mr. Wing-Kit CHUNG
05 Academic Dean .... Dr. Rob WIGGINS
88 VP of Educ Innovation/Global Outrea .... Andy PETERSON
111 VP for Advancement/Dir Alumni Rels .... Mr. Greg MOON
20 Associate Academic Dean .... Dr. Patrick SCHREINER
06 Dean Student Devel/Registrar .... Dr. Reid KISLING
21 Controller .... Ms. Patricia A. PRICHARD
32 Dean of Students .... Mr. Andy PELOQUIN
36 Director of Student Placement .... Dr. Larry MCCRACKEN
13 Director of Information Services .... Mr. Doug MABRY
37 Financial Aid Director .... Ms. Shelle RIEHL
106 Asst Director of Distance Education .... Mr. Jon RAIBLEY
88 Assistant Registrar .... Ms. Hannah HAYES
15 Human Resources Director .... Ms. Julia EIDENBERG
08 Library Director .... Dr. Robert A. KRUPP
84 Director Enrollment Services/Mktg .... Mr. P.J OSWALD
18 Chief Facilities/Physical Plant .... Mr. Cliff STEIN
106 Director of Distance Education .... Mr. James STEWART
07 Director of Admissions .... Mr. Demetrius ROGERS

Willamette University (D)

900 State Street, Salem OR 97301-3930
County: Marion FICE Identification: 003227
Unit ID: 210401
Telephone: (503) 370-6300 Carnegie Class: Bac-A&S
FAX Number: (503) 370-6148 Calendar System: Semester
URL: www.willamette.edu
Established: 1842 Annual Undergrad Tuition & Fees: $47,217
Enrollment: 2,746 Coed
Affiliation or Control: Independent Non-Profit IRS Status: 501(c)3
Highest Offering: Doctorate
Accreditation: NW, CEA, LAW, MUS, SPAA

01 President .... Dr. Stephen THORSETT
10 Senior VP Finance & Administration .... Ms. Monica RIMAI
05 Senior VP Academic & Student Affair .... Dr. Carol LONG
111 Vice President for Advancement .... Ms. Shelby RADCLIFFE
07 Assoc VP & Dean of Admission .... Mr. Jeremy BOGAN
13 Chief Information Officer .... Ms. Jacqueline BARRETTA
18 VP Capital Planning & Facilities .... Mr. James R. BAUER
32 VP for Student Affairs .... Dr. Edward G. WHIPPLE
49 Dean of the College Liberal Arts .... Dr. Ruth P. FEINGOLD
61 Dean of the College of Law .... Mr. Curtis BRIDGEMAN
50 Dean Graduate School Management .... Ms. Debra RINGOLD
42 Chaplain .... Dr. Karen WOOD
23 Director of Bishop Wellness Center .... Mr. Donald A. THOMSON
88 Director Center Dispute Resolution .... Dr. Richard BIRKE
91 Director Administrative Computing .. Mr. Harvey J. PRUDHOMME
37 Director Student Financial Aid .... Ms. Patricia K. HOBAN
09 Director of Institutional Research .... Dr. Michael J. MOON
06 University Registrar .... Ms. Laura JACOBS ANDERSON
08 University Librarian .... Mr. Craig MILBERG
21 Controller .... Mr. Kenneth PIFER
40 Bookstore Manager .... Mr. Dan C. VALLES
104 Director of International Education .... Mr. Kris LOU
41 Athletic Director .... Mr. Rob PASSAGE
29 Assoc VP Alumni & Parent Relations .... Mr. Tyler REICH
112 Senior Director Gift Planning & Dev .... Ms. Lori L. HOBY
15 Associate VP Human Resources .... Ms. Shana SECHRIST
35 Director of Student Activities .... Ms. Lisa C. HOLLIDAY
36 Director Career Development .... Ms. Mandy DEVEREUX
28 Director of Multicultural Affairs .... Mr. Gordon K. TOYAMA
18 Manager Operations/Energy .... Mr. Gary GRIMM
96 Purchasing Coordinator .... Ms. Kindra K. JORDAN
26 Chief Communications Officer .... Mr. Russ YOST
19 Director Security/Safety .... Mr. Ross STOUT
04 Administrative Asst to President .... Ms. Elizabeth GARLAND
100 Director of the President's Office .... Ms. Colleen KAWAHARA
22 VP for Equity/Diversity/Inclusion .... Ms. Jade AGUILAR
39 Director of Housing & Conferences .... Mr. Scott ETHERTON
43 General Counsel .... Ms. Yvonne TAMAYO

PENNSYLVANIA

Albright College (E)

13th & Bern Streets, PO Box 15234,
Reading PA 19612-5234
County: Berks FICE Identification: 003229
Unit ID: 210571
Telephone: (610) 921-2381 Carnegie Class: Bac-A&S
FAX Number: (610) 921-7530 Calendar System: 4/1/4
URL: www.albright.edu
Established: 1856 Annual Undergrad Tuition & Fees: $41,544
Enrollment: 2,267 Coed
Affiliation or Control: United Methodist IRS Status: 501(c)3
Highest Offering: Master's
Accreditation: M

01 President .... Dr. Jacquelyn S. FETROW
05 Provost & VP Academic Affairs .... Dr. Mary MCGEE
10 Vice President Finance & Admin .... Mr. Gregory L. FULMER
111 Vice President Advancement .... Ms. Deborah M. MCCREERY
84 VP Enrollment Mgt/Dean Admission .... Mr. Paul CRAMER
32 VP Student Affairs/Dean of Students .... Dr. Gina-Lyn CRANCE
26 Assoc VP College Relations/Mktg .... Mr. Thomas W. DURSO
13 Chief Information Officer .... Ms. Rashmi RADHAKRISHNAN
04 Executive Assistant to President .... Mrs. Kathy L. CAFONCELLI
20 Dean of Undergraduate Studies .... Dr. Joseph THOMAS
08 Interim Library Director .... Ms. Sandra STUMP
30 Asst VP for Development .... Vacant
14 Sr Dir of Information Tech Svcs .... Mr. Hoerr U. JASON
21 Controller .... Mr. Rick W. MELCHER
37 Director of Financial Aid .... Mr. Christopher HANLON
58 Chair of Education Graduate Program .... Mr. Kevin EZZELL
35 Assistant Dean of Students .... Ms. Amanda HANINCIK
06 Registrar .... Mr. David C. BALLABAN
36 Director Career Development Center .... Ms. Karen V. EVANS
39 Acting Director of Residential Life . Ms. Amanda HIGGINBOTHAM
38 Director of Counseling Center .... Dr. Brenda J. INGRAM-WALLACE
29 Dir of Alumni Relations .... Vacant
18 Director Facilities/Operations/Svcs .... Mr. Timothy RISSEL
41 Co-Athletic Director .... Mr. Richard E. FERRY
41 Co-Athletic Director .... Ms. Janice J. LUCK
19 Director of Safety & Security .... Mr. Michael L. GROSS
40 Book Store Manager .... Ms. Coreen MCCAFFERTY
23 Director of Gable Health Center .... Ms. Samantha WESNER
42 Chaplain .... Rev. Paul E. CLARK
22 Affirmative Action Coord/Dir HR .... Ms. Kimberly A. HUBRIC
85 Dir Multi-Ethnic Student Affs .... Ms. Tiffany CLAYTON
88 Dir of Accelerated & Grad Program .... Mr. Kevin EZZELL
09 Director of Institutional Research .... Mr. Jack LAFAYETTE
35 Director of Student Involvement .... Ms. Tiffany CLAYTON
25 Dir of Corp & Foundation Relations .... Ms. Charlene WYSOCKI
92 Director Honors Program .... Dr. Julia F. HEBERLE
07 Director of Admission .... Ms. Jennifer WILLIAMSON
88 Director of Conferences .... Ms. Lois A. KUBINAK
100 Chief of Staff .... Ms. Kathy L. CAFONCELLI

Allegheny College (F)

520 N Main Street, Meadville PA 16335-3902
County: Crawford FICE Identification: 003230
Unit ID: 210669
Telephone: (814) 332-3100 Carnegie Class: Bac-A&S
FAX Number: (814) 332-2796 Calendar System: Semester
URL: www.allegheny.edu
Established: 1815 Annual Undergrad Tuition & Fees: $44,250
Enrollment: 1,931 Coed
Affiliation or Control: United Methodist IRS Status: 501(c)3
Highest Offering: Baccalaureate
Accreditation: M

01 President .... Dr. James H. MULLEN
03 Exec Vice President and COO .... Ms. Eileen E. PETULA
30 Vice Pres Devel & Alumni Affairs .... Ms. Marjorie S. KLEIN
84 VP for Enrollment & Dean of Admiss .... Mr. Cornell LESANE, II
04 Assistant to the President .... Ms. Pamela S. HIGHAM
110 AVP Development & Alumni Affairs .... Mr. Philip R. FOXMAN
26 Vice President College Relations .... Ms. Susan SALTON
05 Provost & Dean of the College .... Dr. Ronald B. COLE
32 VP & Dean of Students .... Dr. Kimberly FERGUSON
28 Assoc Dean IDEAS Center .... Mr. Justin ADKINS
20 Associate Provost .... Dr. Terry BENSEL
37 Director Financial Aid .... Mr. Jonathan BOLERATZ
108 VP for Info Svcs & Assessment .... Dr. Richard A. HOLMGREN
06 Registrar .... Dr. Ian BINNINGTON
08 Director of the Library .... Dr. Richard A. HOLMGREN
15 Director of Human Resources .... Ms. Jennifer MANGUS
19 Director of Public Safety .... Dr. Ali AWADI
44 Director of Annual Giving .... Ms. Sara PINEO
18 Director Physical Plant .... Mr. Cliff K. WILLIS
91 Associate Director of Info Tech Svc .... Mr. Jason M. RAMSEY
41 Director of Athletics .... Ms. Portia HOEG
31 Director of Civic Engagement .... Dr. David RONCOLATO
13 Dir Tech Computer & Networking Svcs .... Mr. Tim W. HUNTER
38 Director of Counseling Center .... Ms. Pamela JACKSON
09 Director of Institutional Research .... Ms. Marian D. SHERWOOD
36 Director Career Education .... Mr. James FITCH
35 Associate Dean of Students .... Ms. Jacquelyn KONDROT
10 CFO & Treasurer .... Ms. Linda S. WETSELL
42 Chaplain .... Dr. Jane Ellen NICKELL
88 Dir Center Political Participation .... Dr. Brian HARWARD
22 Director of Disability Services .... Mr. John J. MANGINE
57 Director of Art & Publications .... Ms. Penny M. DREXEL
27 Associate Dir of Marketing & Commun .... Mr. Jason ANDRACKI
40 Manager of Bookstore .... Mr. Peter M. LEBAR
96 Purchasing & Student Services Coord .... Ms. Kathleen M. CONAWAY
88 Asst Dir of Leadership & Involvem .... Ms. Brittany MARTIN

Allegany College of Maryland Bedford County Campus (G)

18 North River Lane, Everett PA 15337-1410
Telephone: (814) 652-9528 Identification: 770124
Accreditation: &M

† Branch campus of Allegany College of Maryland, Cumberland, MD

Alvernia University (A)

400 Saint Bernardine Street, Reading PA 19607-1799
County: Berks FICE Identification: 003233
Unit ID: 210775
Telephone: (610) 796-8200 Carnegie Class: Masters/M
FAX Number: (610) 777-6632 Calendar System: Semester
URL: www.alvernia.edu
Established: 1958 Annual Undergrad Tuition & Fees: $32,270
Enrollment: 2,856 Coed
Affiliation or Control: Roman Catholic IRS Status: 501(c)3
Highest Offering: Doctorate
Accreditation: M, ACBSP, CAATE, CACREP, NURSE, OT, @PTA, SW

01 President ....Dr. Thomas F. FLYNN
05 Provost ....Dr. Shirley J. WILLIAMS
10 VP for Finance & Administration ....Mr. Douglas F. SMITH
111 Vice Pres for Advancement ....Mr. Tony DEMARCO
32 Vice Pres Univ Life/Dean of Stdnts .. Dr. Joseph J. CICALA, RSM
84 Vice Pres for Enrollment Management ....Mr. John R. MCCLOSKEY, JR.
42 Asst to the President For Mission .... Sr. Roberta MCKELVIE, OSF
26 VP Mktg & Comms/Chief PR Ofcr ....Dr. Deidra HILL
35 Director of Student Activities ....Ms. Abby SWATCHICK
39 Director Residence Life ....Ms. Karolina DREHER
06 Registrar ....Ms. Beki STEIN
21 Controller ....Mr. Larry SHAUB
30 Assoc VP of Advancement ....Mr. Thomas MINICK
92 Director Honors Program ....Dr. Victoria WILLIAMS
41 Director Athletics & Recreation ....Mr. Bill STILES
07 Dean of UG Admissions ....Ms. Rebecca FINNKENNEY
09 Director of Institutional Research ....Dr. Evelina PANAYOTOVA
15 Director Human Resources ....Ms. Laurel CLINE
18 Dir of Facilities Planning ....Mr. David REPPERT
36 Director of Career Services ....Mrs. Megan ADUKAITIS
37 Dir of Student Financial Planning ....Ms. Christine SAADI
96 Procurement Manager ....Ms. Ann NAWROCKI
28 Dir of Multicultural Initiatives ....Ms. Wanda COPELAND
113 Director of Student Billing ....Ms. Gwynne KOLODZIEJSKI
31 Dir Ctr for Community Engagement ....Mr. Jay WORRALL
58 Dean of Graduate & Cont Studies ....Ms. Daria LATORRE
49 Dean of Arts & Sciences ....Dr. Beth ROTH
107 Dean of Professional Programs ....Ms. Karen S. THACKER
04 Assistant to the President ....Ms. Karen SCHRODER
13 Chief Info Technology Officer (CIO) ....Ms. Robin ALLEN
19 Director of Public Safety ....Mr. Edward HEIM
08 Director of Library ....Ms. Sharon NEAL
25 Director of Grants ....Ms. Mary RIZZO

The American College of Financial Services (B)

270 S Bryn Mawr Avenue, Bryn Mawr PA 19010-2196
County: Delaware FICE Identification: 033173
Unit ID: 210809
Telephone: (610) 526-1000 Carnegie Class: Spec-4-yr-Bus
FAX Number: (610) 526-1310 Calendar System: Quarter
URL: www.theamericancollege.edu
Established: 1927 Annual Graduate Tuition & Fees: N/A
Enrollment: 16,764 Coed
Affiliation or Control: Independent Non-Profit IRS Status: 501(c)3
Highest Offering: Doctorate; No Undergraduates
Accreditation: M

01 President & CEO ....Dr. Robert R. JOHNSON
11 Executive Vice President & COO ....Mr. Keith E. HICKERSON
05 Dean & Chief Academic Office ....Dr. Michael FINKE
111 Sr Vice President Advancement ....Mr. Charles CRONIN
15 VP Admin & Chief HR Officer ....Ms. Debra GLENN
45 VP Organizational Effectiveness ....Mr. Bryan JOHNSON
32 VP Student Experience ....Mr. Brian KAIN
04 Assistant to the President ....Ms. Mary C. VARNER
117 Chief Financial and Risk Officer ....Mr. Gary TANG
26 Chief Marketing Officer ....Mr. Jack HONDROS
13 Chief Technology Officer ....Mr. Ed M. MCEVOY
108 AVP Institutional Assessment ....Mr. Thomas ARMINGTON
06 Registrar ....Ms. Antoinette CHRISTALDI
08 Head of Library Services ....Mr. John H. WHITHAM
88 Director Exam Systems ....Ms. Diane M. HAMMONDS
88 Chief Product & Innovation Officer ....Mr. David EURICH

Antonelli Institute (C)

300 Montgomery Avenue, Erdenheim PA 19038-8242
County: Montgomery FICE Identification: 007430
Unit ID: 210890
Telephone: (215) 836-2222 Carnegie Class: Spec 2-yr-A&S
FAX Number: (215) 836-2794 Calendar System: Semester
URL: www.antonelli.edu
Established: 1938 Annual Undergrad Tuition & Fees: $19,870
Enrollment: 177 Coed
Affiliation or Control: Proprietary IRS Status: Proprietary
Highest Offering: Associate Degree
Accreditation: ACCSC

01 President ....Mr. John D. HAYDEN
05 Director of Education/Student Svcs ....Ms. Trish FLEMING
37 Financial Aid Officer ....Ms. Stephanie BROCKLEHURST

Arcadia University (D)

450 S Easton Road, Glenside PA 19038-3295
County: Montgomery FICE Identification: 003235
Unit ID: 211088
Telephone: (215) 572-2900 Carnegie Class: Bac-A&S
FAX Number: (215) 572-0240 Calendar System: Semester
URL: www.arcadia.edu
Established: 1853 Annual Undergrad Tuition & Fees: $40,920
Enrollment: 3,984 Coed
Affiliation or Control: Independent Non-Profit IRS Status: 501(c)3
Highest Offering: Doctorate
Accreditation: M, ACBSP, ARCPA, ART, FEPAC, PH, PTA

01 Interim President ....Mr. George H. BROWN
05 Provost & VP Academic Affairs ....Dr. John HOFFMAN
84 VP Enrollment Management ....Mr. Mark LAPREZIOSA
10 VP Finance & Treasurer ....Mr. Eric R. NELSON
43 General Counsel ....Mr. Michael KOROLISHIN
13 Chief Information Officer ....Vacant
30 VP University Advancement ....Ms. Mary MCRAE
32 Dean of Students ....Mr. Andrew GORETSKY
18 Assoc VP Facilities/Capital Plng ....Mr. Thomas J. MACCHI
88 VP/Exec Dir Col of Global Studies ....Ms. Lorna STERN
21 Assoc VP Finance & COO TCGS ....Ms. Colleen BURKE
15 Assoc VP Human Resources ....Ms. Rhonda HOSPEDALES
20 Deputy Provost ....Dr. Thomas EGAN
06 Registrar ....Mr. William ELNICK
06 Associate Registrar ....Mrs. Nicole M. ZUCKER
49 Dean College Arts & Sciences ....Dr. Rebecca KOHN
76 Dean College of Health Sciences ....Dr. Rebecca L. CRAIK
51 Coord Office of Continuing Studies ....Ms. Kathryn PHILLIPS
50 Dean School of Global Business ....Dr. Alla WILSON
58 Dean Graduate & Undergrad Studies ....Dr. Nancy ROSOFF
82 Dean International Affairs ....Dr. Warren HAFFAR
53 Interim Dean of Education ....Dr. John GROVES
28 Assoc Dean Institutional Diversity ....Ms. Judith DALTON
35 Dean of Students ....Dr. Andrew GORETZKY
20 Assoc Dean Undergraduate Studies ....Mr. Bruce KELLER
88 Asst Dean Graduate Studies ....Ms. Mary Kate MCNULTY
37 Exec Dir Federal Aid Pgms & FA ....Ms. Elizabeth RIHL-LEWINSKY
109 Director Auxiliary Services ....Ms. Mimi BASSETTI
29 Director Alumni Relations ....Mr. Jeffery SPENCE
88 Director University Art Gallery ....Mr. Richard TORCHIA
41 Director Athletics & Recreation ....Mr. Brian GRANATA
88 Director Campus Visits and EM ....Ms. Kathleen BEARDSLEY
36 Director Career Education ....Ms. Marissa DEITCH
38 Director Counseling Services ....Ms. Amy HENNING
37 Exec Director EM & Financial Aid ....Ms. Holly R. KIRKPATRICK
25 Director Sponsored Research ....Ms. Nataliia SHABLIA
09 Director Institutional Research ....Mr. Will PADDOCK
88 Director of Academic Administration ....Ms. Kristin O. JUDGE
96 Purchasing Coordinator ....Ms. Jennifer SUDLOW
88 Payroll Manager ....Ms. Sharon ANTHONY
19 Director of Public Safety ....Ms. Joanna GALLAGHER
88 Title IX Coordinator ....Ms. Nora NELLE
101 Executive Dir Board of Trustees ....Mr. Kevin MULDOON
88 Assoc Dean International Affairs ....Ms. Janice FINN
04 Admin Director Office of the Pres ....Ms. Joemille SANTIAGO
07 Director of Admissions ....Ms. Collene PERNICELLO
26 Chief Public Relations/Marketing ....Ms. Laura BALDWIN

Art Institute of Philadelphia (E)

1622 Chestnut Street, Philadelphia PA 19103-5198
County: Philadelphia FICE Identification: 008350
Unit ID: 210942
Telephone: (215) 567-7080 Carnegie Class: Spec-4-yr-Arts
FAX Number: (215) 405-6398 Calendar System: Quarter
URL: www.artinstitutes.edu/philadelphia
Established: 1971 Annual Undergrad Tuition & Fees: $17,916
Enrollment: 1,536 Coed
Affiliation or Control: Proprietary IRS Status: Proprietary
Highest Offering: Baccalaureate
Accreditation: M, ACFEI, CIDA

01 President ....Mr. Robert KANE
05 Dean of Academic Affairs ....Dr. Harry COSTIGAN
10 Regional Director of Finance ....Mr. Mubashar SYED
09 Dir Institutional Effectiveness ....Dr. Anita RUDMAN
07 Sr Director of Admissions ....Ms. Amanda HOSKING
36 Director of Career Services ....Ms. Kimberly BURNS
20 Assoc Dean of Academic Affairs ....Mr. Harry COSTIGAN
32 Dean of Student Affairs ....Mr. John ROBINSON
37 Director Financial Services ....Ms. Fatisha STRICKLAND
06 Registrar ....Ms. Adriane MEDFORD
08 Library Director ....Ms. Marie DENNIS
38 Counselor/Disability Coordinator ....Ms. Lisa STANKIEWICZ

Art Institute of Pittsburgh (F)

1400 Penn Avenue, Pittsburgh PA 15222
County: Allegheny FICE Identification: 007470
Unit ID: 210960
Telephone: (412) 263-6600 Carnegie Class: Spec-4-yr-Arts
FAX Number: (412) 263-3715 Calendar System: Quarter
URL: www.artinstitutes.edu/pittsburgh
Established: 1921 Annual Undergrad Tuition & Fees: $17,628
Enrollment: 919 Coed
Affiliation or Control: Proprietary IRS Status: Proprietary
Highest Offering: Baccalaureate
Accreditation: M, ACFEI, CIDA

01 President ....Mr. George W. SEBOLT
10 Vice Pres/Dir Admin/Financial Svcs ....Mr. Parker CHARLTON
05 VP/Dean Academic Affairs ....Mr. Daniel GARLAND
32 Vice Pres/Director Student Affairs ....Ms. Dana MELVIN
36 VP/Director Career Services ....Ms. Dana MELVIN
07 Director of Admissions ....Ms. Jennifer O'BRIEN
37 Director Student Financial Aid ....Mr. Parker CHARLTON
15 Director Human Resources ....Mr. Daniel KLAAS
97 Director General Education ....Ms. Katie TALERICO
105 Dir Graphic/Dig Design/Web Design ....Ms. Kelly SPEWOCK
72 Director of Technology ....Mr. Ryan SLATER
88 Dir Indust Dsgn Tech/Entertnmt Dsgn ....Ms. Kelly SPEWOCK
88 Dir Media Anim/Game Des/Photo/Video .. Mr. Anderson ENGLISH
06 Registrar ....Ms. Diane E. CARNEY
84 Enrollment Management Supervisor ....Ms. Marissa KLASS
88 Director Culinary ....Ms. Rachel HOMAN
88 Dir Fashion/Retail Mktng/Fashn Dsgn ....Ms. Kelly SPEWOCK
88 College Affiliate/HS Articulation ....Mr. Daniel GARLAND
29 Director Alumni Relations ....Mr. Justin SHOOK

Berks Technical Institute (G)

2205 Ridgewood Road, Wyomissing PA 19610-1168
County: Berks FICE Identification: 022539
Unit ID: 213534
Telephone: (610) 372-1722 Carnegie Class: Assoc/HVT-Mix Trad/Non
FAX Number: (610) 376-4684 Calendar System: Other
URL: www.berks.edu
Established: 1974 Annual Undergrad Tuition & Fees: $10,240
Enrollment: 938 Coed
Affiliation or Control: Proprietary IRS Status: Proprietary
Highest Offering: Associate Degree
Accreditation: ACICS, MAC

01 Campus Director ....Ms. Elizabeth VLASTOS
05 Dean ....Vacant

Biblical Theological Seminary (H)

200 N Main Street, Hatfield PA 19440-2499
County: Montgomery FICE Identification: 023230
Unit ID: 211130
Telephone: (215) 368-5000 Carnegie Class: Spec-4-yr-Faith
FAX Number: (215) 368-2301 Calendar System: Semester
URL: www.biblical.edu
Established: 1971 Annual Graduate Tuition & Fees: N/A
Enrollment: 258 Coed
Affiliation or Control: Independent Non-Profit IRS Status: 501(c)3
Highest Offering: Doctorate; No Undergraduates
Accreditation: M, THEOL

01 President ....Dr. Frank JAMES, III
111 VP for Advancement ....Mr. Thomas SKINNER
05 Dean of the Faculty ....Dr. David LAMB
04 Executive Assistant to the Pres ....Mrs. Beatrice L. BARKLEY
10 Controller ....Ms. Cynthia DAYMON
88 Director of DMin Program ....Dr. Kyuboem LEE
88 Director of Urban Initiatives ....Dr. Dan WILLIAMS
20 Director of Academic Services ....Mr. Rick HOUSEKNECHT
13 Director of Information Technology ....Mr. Gregg ALDERFER
18 Director of Physical Plant ....Mr. Anthony W. PLETSCHER
06 Registrar ....Mr. Rick HOUSEKNECHT
101 Secretary of the Institution/Board ....Mrs. Patricia MILLEN
37 Director Student Financial Aid ....Mrs. Virginia HARTMAN
44 Director Annual Giving ....Mr. Thomas CAULEY
08 Director of Library Services ....Ms. Lydia PUTNAM
15 Director Personnel Services ....Mrs. Beatrice BARKLEY
39 Director Student Housing ....Mrs. Virginia HARTMAN
29 Director Alumni Relations ....Mr. Paul ZAZZO
38 Director Student Counseling ....Ms. Lisa MUTCH
45 Chief Institutional Planning ....Mr. David VIEHMAN
84 Director Enrollment Mgmt & Mktg ....Mr. Ryan EGLI

Bidwell Training Center (I)

1815 Metropolitan Street, Pittsburgh PA 15233-2200
County: Allegheny FICE Identification: 031015
Unit ID: 211149
Telephone: (412) 323-4000 Carnegie Class: Spec 2-yr-Tech
FAX Number: (412) 325-7378 Calendar System: Quarter
URL: bidwelltraining.edu
Established: 1968 Annual Undergrad Tuition & Fees: N/A
Enrollment: 180 Coed
Affiliation or Control: Independent Non-Profit IRS Status: 501(c)3
Highest Offering: Associate Degree
Accreditation: ACCSC, MAC

01 Exec Director/Sr Vice President ....Ms. Valerie NJIE
11 Senior Director/Operations ....Mr. Ken HUSELTON
05 Academic Associate Director ....Ms. Susan COOPER

Bradford School (J)

125 W Station Square Drive, Ste 129, Pittsburgh PA 15219-2602
County: Allegheny FICE Identification: 009721
Unit ID: 211200
Telephone: (412) 391-6710 Carnegie Class: Assoc/HVT-High Trad
FAX Number: (412) 471-6714 Calendar System: Semester
URL: www.bradfordpittsburgh.edu
Established: 1968 Annual Undergrad Tuition & Fees: $15,380
Enrollment: 400 Coed
Affiliation or Control: Proprietary IRS Status: Proprietary

Highest Offering: Associate Degree
Accreditation: **ACICS**, DA, MAC

01 President .... Mr. Vincent S. GRAZIANO

Brightwood Career Institute (A)

5650 Derry Street, Harrisburg PA 17111-4112
County: Dauphin FICE Identification: 004910
Unit ID: 251075
Telephone: (717) 564-4112 Carnegie Class: Assoc/HVT-High Non
FAX Number: (717) 564-3779 Calendar System: Quarter
URL: www.brightwoodcareer.edu
Established: 1918 Annual Undergrad Tuition & Fees: N/A
Enrollment: 206 Coed
Affiliation or Control: Proprietary IRS Status: Proprietary
Highest Offering: Associate Degree
Accreditation: **ACICS**

01 Executive Director .... Susan LYNCH
07 Director Admissions .... Greta NORTH
36 Director Student Placement .... Jennifer ZECHMAN
05 Director of Education .... Jenny PIPER
37 Director Student Financial Aid .... Sarah BROOKER

Brightwood Career Institute (B)

177 Franklin Mills Boulevard, Philadelphia PA 19154-3140
County: Bucks FICE Identification: 022898
Unit ID: 211617
Telephone: (215) 612-6600 Carnegie Class: Assoc/HVT-Mix Trad/Non
FAX Number: (215) 612-6695 Calendar System: Quarter
URL: www.brightwoodcareer.edu
Established: 1982 Annual Undergrad Tuition & Fees: N/A
Enrollment: 665 Coed
Affiliation or Control: Proprietary IRS Status: Proprietary
Highest Offering: Associate Degree
Accreditation: **ACICS**, COARC

01 President .... Ms. Karen SPRINGER
07 Director of Admissions .... Mr. Dan WATKINS
05 Education Department Head .... Mrs. Diane DARLING
36 Director of Placement .... Ms. Cheryl BRAIDES
37 Director Financial Aid .... Ms. India FLOYD

Brightwood Career Institute (C)

3010 Market Street, Philadelphia PA 19104
Telephone: (215) 594-4000 Identification: 770766
Accreditation: **ACICS**

Brightwood Career Institute (D)

933 Penn Avenue, Pittsburgh PA 15222-3802
County: Allegheny FICE Identification: 007436
Unit ID: 213002
Telephone: (412) 338-4770 Carnegie Class: Assoc/HVT-Mix Trad/Non
FAX Number: (412) 261-0998 Calendar System: Quarter
URL: www.brightwoodcareer.edu
Established: 1963 Annual Undergrad Tuition & Fees: N/A
Enrollment: 512 Coed
Affiliation or Control: Proprietary IRS Status: Proprietary
Highest Offering: Associate Degree
Accreditation: **ACICS**, OTA

01 President .... Mr. Jay CLAYTON
05 Academic Dean .... Mr. John FLINTER
37 Director of Financial Aid .... Mr. Chris FOX
07 Director of Admissions .... Mr. Justin PAPARIELLA
36 Director of Career Services .... Ms. Jennifer KELLY

Brightwood Career Institute - Broomall Campus (E)

1991 Sproul Road, Suite 42, Broomall PA 19008-3516
County: Delaware FICE Identification: 007781
Unit ID: 215646
Telephone: (610) 353-7630 Carnegie Class: Spec 2-yr-Health
FAX Number: (610) 359-1370 Calendar System: Quarter
URL: www.brightwoodcareer.edu
Established: 1958 Annual Undergrad Tuition & Fees: N/A
Enrollment: 326 Coed
Affiliation or Control: Proprietary IRS Status: Proprietary
Highest Offering: Associate Degree
Accreditation: **ACICS**

01 President .... Mr. William SCHNELL
05 Academic Dean .... Ms. Amy BERRIOS
36 Career Development Director .... Mr. James LINCKE
07 Director of Admissions .... Mr. Mark GARNER

Bryn Athyn College of the New Church (F)

PO Box 717, Bryn Athyn PA 19009-0717
County: Montgomery FICE Identification: 003228
Unit ID: 210492
Telephone: (267) 502-2400 Carnegie Class: Bac-A&S
FAX Number: (215) 938-2658 Calendar System: Trimester
URL: www.brynathyn.edu
Established: 1876 Annual Undergrad Tuition & Fees: $19,932
Enrollment: 278 Coed
Affiliation or Control: Church of New Jerusalem IRS Status: 501(c)3
Highest Offering: Master's
Accreditation: **M**

01 President .... Mr. Brian BLAIR
10 Chief Finance Officer .... Mr. Daniel T. ALLEN
05 Dean of Academic Affairs .... Rev Dr. Thane GLENN
73 Dean of Theological School .... Rev. Andrew M T. DIBB
32 Dean of Student Affairs .... Dr. Suzanne NELSON
07 Dean of Admissions & Enroll Mgmt .... Dr. Roberta NOLAN
08 Director of Swedenborg Library .... Mrs. Carol TRAVENY
41 Director of Athletics .... Mr. Matthew KENNEDY
13 Chief Information Officer .... Ms. Lelia HOWARD
15 Director of Human Resources .... Ms. Renee ROSENFELD
19 Director of Security & Safety .... Mr. R. Scott COOPER
42 Chaplain .... Rev. Grant SCHNARR
04 Executive Asst to President .... Ms. Melodie GREER
37 Director of Financial Aid .... Mr. Brian KEISTER
14 Director Information Technology .... Mr. Richard DAUM

Bryn Mawr College (G)

101 N Merion Avenue, Bryn Mawr PA 19010-2899
County: Montgomery FICE Identification: 003237
Unit ID: 211273
Telephone: (610) 526-5000 Carnegie Class: Bac-A&S
FAX Number: (610) 526-7450 Calendar System: Semester
URL: www.brynmawr.edu
Established: 1885 Annual Undergrad Tuition & Fees: $48,790
Enrollment: 1,692 Female
Affiliation or Control: Independent Non-Profit IRS Status: 501(c)3
Highest Offering: Doctorate
Accreditation: **M**, SW

01 President .... Kimberly CASSIDY
05 Provost .... Mary J. OSIRIM
49 Dean Undergraduate College .... Jennifer WALTERS
10 Chief Financial Officer .... Kari FAZIO
30 Chief Development Officer .... Bob MILLER
08 Director Libraries/Chief Info Ofcr .... Gina SIESING
58 Dean of Graduate Studies .... Sharon BURGMAYER
28 Asst Dean Col of Access/Cmty Devel .... Vanessa CHRISTMAN
06 Registrar .... Kirsten O'BEIRNE
37 Director of Financial Aid .... Ethel M. DESMARAIS
19 Director of Public Safety .... Tom KING
68 Dir Athletics & Physical Education .... Kathleen TIERNEY
21 Controller .... Betsy STEWART
09 Director of Institutional Research .... Richard BARRY
18 Director of Facilities .... Nina BISBEE

Bucknell University (H)

1 Dent Drive, Lewisburg PA 17837
County: Union FICE Identification: 003238
Unit ID: 211291
Telephone: (570) 577-2000 Carnegie Class: Bac-A&S
FAX Number: (570) 577-3760 Calendar System: Semester
URL: www.bucknell.edu
Established: 1846 Annual Undergrad Tuition & Fees: $51,960
Enrollment: 3,625 Coed
Affiliation or Control: Independent Non-Profit IRS Status: 501(c)3
Highest Offering: Master's
Accreditation: **M**, CS, ENG, MUS

01 President .... Dr. John C. BRAVMAN
05 Provost .... Dr. Barbara ALTMAN
10 VP Finance & Administration .... Mr. David J. SURGALA
30 VP Development & Alumni Rels .... Dr. Scott G. ROSEVEAR
43 General Counsel .... Ms. Amy C. FOERSTER
84 VP Enrollment Management .... Mr. William T. CONLEY
41 Director Athletics & Recreation .... Mr. John P. HARDT
13 VP Library & Information Technology .... Mr. Param S. BEDI
26 VP Communications & Cmty Rels .... Mr. Andrew HIRSCH
49 Dean of Arts & Sciences .... Dr. Karl VOSS
54 Dean of Engineering .... Dr. Patrick MATHER
15 Assoc VP Human Resources .... Mr. Pierre D. JOANIS
32 Acting Dean of Students .... Ms. Amy A. BADAL
21 Associate VP Finance .... Mr. Dennis W. SWANK
21 Treasurer and Controller .... Mr. Michael S. COVER
110 Assoc VP Development & Alumni Rels .... Ms. Kathleen GRAHAM
06 AProv/Regis/Dn Grad Std & Summ Sess .... Dr. Robert M. MIDKIFF, JR.
20 Assoc Provost .... Dr. Karen M. MORIN
50 Director School of Management .... Dr. Michael E. JOHNSON-CRAMER
18 Associate VP Facilities .... Mr. Kenneth OGAWA
45 Director Business Planning .... Mr. Edward J. LOFTUS
28 Assoc Provost for Diversity .... Ms. Georgina DODGE
04 Dir President Ofc & Univ Secretary .... Ms. Carol M. KENNEDY
46 Assistant Provost for Research .... Vacant
116 Director of Internal Audit .... Mr. Robert L. HOSTER
88 Executive Dir Leadership Gifts .... Mr. Mark SHARER
29 Exec Dir Alumni Relations .... Mr. Joshua L. GRILL
88 Exec Dir Advancement Services .... Ms. Cindy BELKNAP
44 Executive Director of Annual Fund .... Ms. Lucille M. TARIN
102 Dir Corporate & Foundation Rels .... Mr. Edmond CLARK
88 Director Parents Fund .... Ms. Ann L. DISTEFANO
112 Director of Gift Planning .... Ms. Melissa M. DIEHL
14 Asst Chief Info Tech Officer .... Mr. Mark E. YERGER
14 Director of Enterprise Systems .... Mr. Kevin WILLEY
119 Chief Info Sec Officer .... Mr. Christopher BERNARD
27 Asst VP of Communications .... Vacant
88 Dir of Construction & Design .... Ms. Kathy MONTEIRO
88 Dir of Facility Services .... Mr. Michael J. PATTERSON
84 Asst VP Enroll Mgmt/Dir Partnerships .... Mr. Mark D. DAVIES
07 Dean of Admissions .... Mr. Robert G. SPRINGALL
37 Director Financial Aid .... Ms. Andrea C. LEITHNER STAUFFER
38 Dir Counseling & Stdnt Dev Ctr .... Dr. Kelly KETTLEWELL
115 Dir of Investments .... Mr. John R. LUTHI
36 Exec Director Career Services .... Ms. Pamela G. KEISER
16 Dir of Recruitment & Compensation .... Ms. Marcia J. COONEY
118 Director of HRIS & Benefits .... Ms. Cindy L. BILGER
09 Asst Provost Inst Research/Assess .... Mr. Kevork T. HORISSIAN
109 Director of Business Services .... Ms. Lori J. WILSON
88 Exec Dir Events Management Office .... Ms. Dana M. MIMS
88 Assoc Controller Financial Services . Mr. Ronald E. STAUFFER, II
88 Assoc Controller Accounting Svcs .... Mr. William D. GEORGE
88 Asst Controller .... Ms. Michelle M. HENDRICKS
104 Dir Global & Off-Campus Education .... Mr. Stephen K. APPIAH-PADI
117 Dir Risk Management & Insurance .... Mr. Clint D. WEVODAU
19 Chief of Public Safety .... Mr. Stephen J. BARILAR
35 Associate Dean of Students .... Ms. Kari M. CONRAD
35 Associate Dean of Students .... Mr. Daniel C. REMLEY
88 Exec Dir Weis Center Perform Arts .... Ms. Kathryn L. MAGUET
88 Title IX Coord Clery Act Comp .... Ms. Kathleen GRIMES
88 Dir of Instructional Technology .... Mr. Matthew K. GARDZINA
88 Dir Advancement Campaign Mgmt .... Ms. Barbara A. HARTMAN
88 Dir Dev Research & Prospect Mgmt .... Ms. Cynthia D. JANESCH
42 University Chaplain .... Mr. John P. COLATCH
88 Dir Publications/Print & Mail .... Ms. Lisa D. HOOVER
105 Interim Dir Digital Communications .... Mr. Ryan LEBRETON
88 Dir Provost Business Operations .... Ms. Pamela A. BENFER
88 Director of Disbursement Services .... Mr. Jody D. GRAYBILL
105 Dir University Marketing & Web .... Ms. Molly E. O'BRIEN-FOELSCH
88 Dir Small Business Development Ctr .... Mr. Steven V. STUMBRIS
88 Dir Card Svcs & Student Transit .... Mr. Glenn R. FISHER
88 Dir of Civic Engagement .... Ms. Janice R. BUTLER
96 Director of Procurement Services .... Mr. Donald A. KRECH
88 Dir Financial Information Systems .... Ms. Pamela K. NOONE
22 Dir of Disability Services .... Ms. Heather L. FOWLER
85 Dir International Student Services .... Ms. Jennifer E. FIGUEROA
88 Director Office of LGBTQ Resources .... Mr. William K. MCCOY
92 Honors Council Chair .... Vacant
88 Director of Writing Center .... Ms. Deirdre M. O'CONNOR
39 Dir of Housing Services .... Mr. Stephen J. APANEL
100 Chief of Staff .... Ms. Amy FOERSTER

Bucks County Community College (I)

275 Swamp Road, Newtown PA 18940-4106
County: Bucks FICE Identification: 003239
Unit ID: 211307
Telephone: (215) 968-8000 Carnegie Class: Assoc/HT-Mix Trad/Non
FAX Number: (215) 968-8129 Calendar System: Semester
URL: www.bucks.edu
Established: 1964 Annual Undergrad Tuition & Fees (In-District): $4,298
Enrollment: 8,611 Coed
Affiliation or Control: Local IRS Status: 501(c)3
Highest Offering: Associate Degree
Accreditation: **M**, ACBSP, ADNUR, ART, MUS, RAD

01 President .... Dr. Stephanie SHANBLATT
05 Provost .... Ms. Lisa ANGELO
10 VP for Administrative Affairs & CFO ..Mr. Dennis W. MATTHEWS
32 VP Student Affairs/Dean of Students .... Vacant
13 Vice Pres Technology & Innovation .... Mr. Jason MAYLAND
111 Vice Pres Advancement .... Dr. Tobias BRUHN
20 Assoc Provost Academic Svcs .... Vacant
21 Controller .... Mr. David JERDAN
114 Exec Dir Budget & Internal Audit .... Ms. Loren HERBERT
09 Exec Dir Inst Research & Assessment .... Dr. Jenell BRAMLAGE
12 Exec Dir Upper Bucks Campus .... Dr. Rodney H. ALTEMOSE
88 Exec Dir Public Safety Training .... Mr. Rob FREESE
103 Exec Dir Workforce Development .... Ms. Lauren LOEFFLER
18 Exec Director Physical Plant .... Mr. Martin SNYDER
26 Director Marketing .... Ms. Megan SMITH
04 Exec Assistant to President .... Ms. Kathleen C. FEDORKO
15 Exec Director Human Resources .... Dr. Patricia BRINING
96 Director of Purchasing .... Mr. James F. LOUGHERY
106 Director Online Learning .... Ms. Georglyn L. DAVIDSON
37 Director Financial Aid .... Ms. Donna M. WILKOSKI
36 Director Career Services .... Ms. Sharon STEPHENS
35 Director Student Life & Athletics .... Mr. Matt J. CIPRIANO
19 Exec Dir Security & Safety .... Mr. Dennis MCCAULEY
08 Director Library Services .... Ms. Linda MCCANN
07 Director of Admissions .... Ms. Marlene T. BARLOW
06 Registrar .... Ms. Rebecca BREUNINGER
29 Alumni Relations Manager .... Ms. Jackie GEAR
68 Dean Kinesiology & Sport Studies .... Dr. Priscilla RICE
81 Interim Dean STEM .... Ms. Debra GEOGHAN
50 Dean Business Studies .... Ms. Tracy TIMBY
57 Dean Arts .... Mr. John MATHEWS
88 Dean Language & Literature .... Dr. Kelly KELLEWAY
83 Dean Social & Behavioral Sci .... Dr. Lynn DELLAPIETRA
107 Interim Dean Professional Studies .... Ms. Mariann KERR
102 Dir Foundation/Alumni .... Ms. Jennifer SALISBURY

Butler County Community College (J)

107 College Drive, Butler PA 16002
County: Butler FICE Identification: 003240
Unit ID: 211343
Telephone: (724) 287-8711 Carnegie Class: Assoc/HT-High Trad
FAX Number: (724) 285-6047 Calendar System: Semester
URL: www.bc3.edu

Established: 1965 Annual Undergrad Tuition & Fees (In-District): $4,590
Enrollment: 3,573 Coed
Affiliation or Control: Local IRS Status: 501(c)3
Highest Offering: Associate Degree
Accreditation: M, ACBSP, ADNUR, MAC, PTAA

01 President ... Dr. Nicholas C. NEUPAUER
05 VP for Academic Affairs ... Dr. Belinda M. RICHARDSON
11 VP for Administration & Finance ... Mr. James A. HRABOSKY
32 VP Student Affairs/Enrollment Mgt ... Dr. G. Case WILLOUGHBY
10 Chief Business Officer ... Mr. Wm. Jake FRIEL
50 Dean of Business ... Dr. J. Christian OLA
83 Interim Dean Social Science/Hum ... Mr. Stephen M. JOSEPH
66 Dean of Nursing/Allied Health ... Ms. Patricia T. ANNEAR
72 Dean of Nat Science/Tech ... Mr. Matt KOVAC
106 Dean of Education Technology ... Ms. Ann MCCANDLESS
08 Interim Dean of Library Services ... Mr. Martin J. MILLER
35 Dean of Students ... Dr. Joshua NOVAK
103 Interim Dir Workforce Development ... Ms. Lisa M. CAMPBELL
15 Int Exec Director Human Resources ... Ms. Christina M. FLEEGER
26 Exec Director of Comm & Marketing .. Ms. Jessica M. MATONAK
51 Director of Lifelong Learning ... Mr. Paul M. LUCAS
06 Director of Records & Registration ... Ms. Amy DOUBLE PIGNATORE
13 Director of Information Technology ... Ms. Kathleen C. SOMMERS
32 Director of Student Life ... Mr. Rob A. SNYDER
09 Coordinator of Inst Research ... Ms. Sharla M. ANKE
18 Exec Director of Operations ... Mr. Brian R. OPITZ
07 Director of Admissions ... Mr. Robert G. MORRIS
12 Director of BC3 @ Lawrence Crossing ... Mr. Sean M. CARROLL
12 Director of BC3 @ Cranberry ... Ms. Lauren A. BUCHANAN
12 Director of BC3 @ LindenPointe ... Mr. John P. SUESSER
12 Director of BC3 @ Brockway ... Ms. Jill MARTIN-REND
37 Director of Financial Aid ... Ms. Julianne E. LOUTTIT
41 Athletic Director ... Mr. Rob A. SNYDER
50 Director of Business/Industry Trng ... Ms. Lisa M. CAMPBELL
38 Director Student Counseling ... Vacant
102 Exec Director of the Foundation ... Ms. Ruth PURCELL
19 Director of Campus Police/Security ... Mr. K. Scott RICHARDSON
88 Director of Cultural Center ... Mr. Lawrence E. STOCK
88 Director of Children's Center ... Ms. Judith A. ZUZACK
88 Associate Director Admissions ... Ms. Morgan M. RIZZARDI
40 Interim Bookstore Manager ... Mr. Richard A. BENKO
96 Director of Purchasing ... Ms. Nicole BARNES
105 Web Manager ... Mr. R. Dennis BIRKES
44 Director Annual or Planned Giving ... Ms. Michelle E. JAMIESON
04 Administrative Asst to President ... Ms. Juliann SHEPTAK
22 Dir Affirmative Action/EEO ... Ms. Linda M. DODD

Byzantine Catholic Seminary of Ss. Cyril and Methodius (A)

3605 Perrysville Avenue, Pittsburgh PA 15214-2229
County: Allegheny FICE Identification: 041180
Unit ID: 444103
Telephone: (412) 321-8383 Carnegie Class: Spec-4-yr-Faith
FAX Number: (412) 321-9936 Calendar System: Semester
URL: www.bcs.edu
Established: 1950 Annual Graduate Tuition & Fees: N/A
Enrollment: 17 Coed
Affiliation or Control: Other IRS Status: 501(c)3
Highest Offering: Master's; No Undergraduates
Accreditation: THEOL

01 Rector ... V.Rev. Robert M. PIPTA
05 Academic Dean ... Rev. Christiaan KAPPES
06 Registrar/Director of Seminary ... Ms. Carol PRZYBOROKI

Cabrini University (B)

610 King of Prussia Road, Radnor PA 19087-3698
County: Delaware FICE Identification: 003241
Unit ID: 211352
Telephone: (610) 902-8200 Carnegie Class: Masters/L
FAX Number: (610) 902-8204 Calendar System: Semester
URL: www.cabrini.edu
Established: 1957 Annual Undergrad Tuition & Fees: $30,588
Enrollment: 2,428 Coed
Affiliation or Control: Roman Catholic IRS Status: 501(c)3
Highest Offering: Doctorate
Accreditation: M, SW

01 President ... Dr. Donald TAYLOR
05 Provost/VP Academic Affairs ... Dr. Jeffrey GINGERICH
10 VP Finance & Treasurer ... Mr. Eric OLSON
30 VP Institutional Advancement ... Mr. Stephen HIGHSMITH
32 VP of Student Life ... Dr. Christine LYSIONEK
84 VP of Enrollment Management ... Mr. Robert REESE
26 VP Marketing & Communication ... Ms. Celia CAMERON
35 Asst VP Student Life/Dean of Studen ... Dr. George STROUD
50 Dean School Business/Arts & Media ... Dr. Mary VAN BRUNT
53 Dean School of Education ... Dr. Beverly BRYDE
04 Executive Asst to the President ... Ms. Joan KLECKNER
06 Registrar ... Ms. M. Frances HARKNESS
08 Interim Library Director ... Ms. Anne SCHWELM
91 Director Administrative Computing ... Mr. Rob GETZ
19 Director Public Safety ... Mr. Joseph FUSCO
18 Director of Facilities ... Ms. Dawn BARNETT
29 Dir Alumni Engagement/Annual Giving ... Ms. Jackie MARCIANO
37 Director of Financial Aid ... Mr. Thor KRESS
36 Dir of Career & Professional Dev ... Ms. Shakeyia KERSEY
41 Director of Athletics & Recreation ... Mr. Bradley KOCH
15 Director of Human Resources ... Ms. Susan ROHANNA
21 Controller ... Ms. Diane SCUTTI
24 Coord of Education Resources Center ... Ms. Mary BUDZILOWICZ
40 Bookstore Manager ... Mr. Bill BRIDDES
105 Director of Content Marketing ... Ms. Linda BOYK
09 Asst Provost Instl Effectiveness ... Dr. Maliha ZAMAN
35 Exec Dir Student Engage/Leadership ... Ms. Anne FILIPPONE
92 Asst Prov Intl Affs/Dir Honors Pgm ... Dr. Paul WRIGHT
92 Asst Director of the Honors Program ... Dr. Jennifer BULCOCK
28 Dir Student Diversity Initiatives ... Vacant
38 Director Counseling/Psych Service ... Dr. Sara MAGGITTI
39 Director of Residence Life ... Ms. Sue KRAMER
07 Asst VP Enrol/Dir UG Admissions ... Ms. Shannon ZOTTOLA
101 Exec Governance Admin Sec Board ... Mrs. Nancy OLLINGER
102 Dir Sponsored Pgms & Foundation Rel ... Ms. Jean JACOBSON
88 Creative Director ... Mr. Kevin HAUGH
86 Chief of Staff/VP External Rels ... Mr. Brian EURY
91 Director Administrative Computing ... Mr. Rob GETZ
96 Procurement Manager ... Ms. Elizabeth KANARAS

Cairn University (C)

200 Manor Avenue, Langhorne Manor PA 19047-2990
County: Bucks FICE Identification: 003351
Unit ID: 215114
Telephone: (215) 752-5800 Carnegie Class: Masters/S
FAX Number: (215) 702-4341 Calendar System: Semester
URL: www.cairn.edu
Established: 1913 Annual Undergrad Tuition & Fees: $25,246
Enrollment: 1,043 Coed
Affiliation or Control: Independent Non-Profit IRS Status: 501(c)3
Highest Offering: Master's
Accreditation: M, BI, IACBE, MUS, SW

01 President ... Dr. Todd J. WILLIAMS
05 Provost ... Dr. Brian G. TOEWS
32 Sr VP Student Affairs ... Mr. J. Scott CAWOOD
10 Sr VP Finance & Administration ... Vacant
30 Sr VP Univ Advancement ... Mr. Russell T. NIXON
26 Sr VP Marketing & Enrollment ... Mr. Paul NEAL
15 VP Human Resources ... Ms. Mary BOYER
108 Vice Provost ... Dr. Jean MINTO
06 Registrar ... Dr. Steven SCHLENKER
08 Dean Educational Resources ... Dr. Timothy K. HUI
35 Dean Student Life ... Mr. Tom SHERF
73 Dean School of Divinity ... Dr. Jonathan L. MASTER
49 Dean School of Liberal Arts & Sci ... Dr. Brenda EBERSOLE
50 Dean School of Business ... Mr. Evan CURRY
53 Dean School of Education ... Mr. Joseph BEESON
64 Dean School of Music ... Dr. Benjamin HARDING
70 Dean School of Social Work ... Dr. Lloyd GESTOSO
07 Director Admissions ... Ms. Rebecca LIPPERT
29 Director Alumni Relations ... Mr. Nathan WAMBOLD
18 Director Campus Services ... Mr. Andrew NORTON
40 Campus Store Manager ... Mr. Daniel MUNOZ
36 Director Career Center ... Ms. Teri T. CANTANIO
37 Director Financial Aid ... Mr. Stephen CASSEL
23 Director Health Services ... Ms. Alison KIKENDALL
09 Director Institutional Research ... Dr. Lynn WALLACE
39 Director Resident Life ... Mr. Nick COATES
19 Director Safety & Security ... Mr. Chris LLOYD
38 Director Student Counseling ... Vacant
13 Director Technology Services ... Mr. Curt D. WINTERS
106 Dir Online Education/E-learning ... Mr. Sali KACELI
11 Controller ... Mr. Jeff EUBANK
21 Asst Director Business Services ... Dr. Andrew HUI
04 Administrative Asst to President ... Ms. Lori MILLER
41 Athletic Director ... Ms. Laura BEHNKE

Career Training Academy (D)

179 Hillcrest Shopping Center, Lower Burrell PA 15068
County: Westmoreland FICE Identification: 026095
Unit ID: 210951
Telephone: (724) 337-1000 Carnegie Class: Spec 2-yr-Health
FAX Number: N/A Calendar System: Other
URL: www.careerta.edu
Established: 1986 Annual Undergrad Tuition & Fees: N/A
Enrollment: 123 Coed
Affiliation or Control: Proprietary IRS Status: Proprietary
Highest Offering: Associate Degree
Accreditation: ACCSC

01 Campus Director ... Mr. Michael DISCELLO

Career Training Academy (E)

4314 Old William Penn Hwy, Ste 103,
Monroeville PA 15146-1455
Telephone: (412) 372-3900 Identification: 666051
Accreditation: ACCSC

† Branch campus of Career Training Academy, New Kensington, PA.

Career Training Academy (F)

1014 West View Park Drive, Pittsburgh PA 15229
Telephone: (412) 367-4000 Identification: 666100
Accreditation: ACCSC

† Branch campus of Career Training Academy, New Kensington, PA.

Carlow University (G)

3333 Fifth Avenue, Pittsburgh PA 15213-3165
County: Allegheny FICE Identification: 003303
Unit ID: 211431
Telephone: (800) 333-2275 Carnegie Class: Masters/L
FAX Number: (412) 578-6668 Calendar System: Semester
URL: www.carlow.edu
Established: 1929 Annual Undergrad Tuition & Fees: $27,764
Enrollment: 2,272 Coed
Affiliation or Control: Roman Catholic IRS Status: 501(c)3
Highest Offering: Doctorate
Accreditation: M, #COARC, COPSY, NURSE, SW

01 President ... Dr. Suzanne K. MELLON
05 Interim Provost/VP Academic Affairs ... Mr. Russ PINIZZOTTO
10 CFO/VP Finance ... Mr. David J. MEADOWS
111 VP Advancement ... Ms. Kimberley A. HAMMER
13 Chief Information Officer ... Mr. Jeffrey P. DEVLIN
88 Special Asst to Pres/Mercy Heritage ... Sr. Sheila A. CARNEY
32 VP Student Engagement ... Dr. Jennifer A. CARLO
09 AVP Inst Rsrch/Effect & Planning ... Ms. Anne M. CANDREVA
66 Dean Health and Wellness ... Dr. Lynn E. GEORGE
83 Dean Leadership & Social Change ... Dr. Allyson M. LOWE
49 Dean Learning & Innovation ... Dr. Matthew E. GORDLEY
106 Dean Online/Digital Learning ... Dr. Rachael O. AFOLABI ROYES
04 Exec Asst to the President ... Ms. Barbara L. GILLES
25 Dir Sponsored Programs & Research ... Dr. Michael E. AYEWHO
15 Director Human Resources ... Ms. Bridgette N. COFIELD
06 Registrar ... Mr. Jason KRALL
88 Exec Dir & Principal Campus School ... Vacant
07 Director Undergraduate Admissions ... Ms. Wivinia A. CHMURA
123 Director Graduate Admissions ... Ms. Wendy S. PHILLIPS
36 Director Career Development ... Ms. Jennifer A. HOLBERT
88 Dir Student Accounts ... Mr. James V. SHANKEL
08 Exec Dir Library & Lrng Commons ... Dr. Michael JONES
85 Director Center for Global Lrng ... Mr. Benjamin J. PILCHER
35 Director Campus Life ... Mr. Charlie N. JUDGE
39 Asst Director Campus Life ... Ms. Gwendolyn M. STEVENS
23 Director Health Services ... Ms. Carla R. BERGAMASCO
41 Director Athletics ... Mr. George S. SLIMAN
88 Director Wellness & Fitness Svcs ... Ms. Julie M. GAUL
21 Controller ... Ms. Deanna J. SIEBERKROB
18 Director Facilities ... Mr. Timothy D. CARNEY
19 Chief of Police ... Mr. Martin M. WHITE
37 Director Financial Aid ... Ms. Natalie L. WILSON
30 Exec Director Advancement ... Ms. Anita S. DACAL
29 Director Alumni Engagement ... Ms. Lachelle N. BINION
102 Director of Corp & Found Relations ... Ms. Patricia L. BEAUMONT
27 Director Media & Public Rels ... Mr. Andrew G. WILSON
105 Director Digital Communication ... Mr. Carl R. ZAPPA
108 Director of Assessment ... Mr. August C. DELBERT
42 Campus Minister ... Ms. Siobhan K. DEWITT

Carnegie Mellon University (H)

5000 Forbes Avenue, Pittsburgh PA 15213-3890
County: Allegheny FICE Identification: 003242
Unit ID: 211440
Telephone: (412) 268-2000 Carnegie Class: DU-Highest
FAX Number: (412) 268-2330 Calendar System: Semester
URL: www.cmu.edu
Established: 1900 Annual Undergrad Tuition & Fees: $52,310
Enrollment: 12,963 Coed
Affiliation or Control: Independent Non-Profit IRS Status: 501(c)3
Highest Offering: Doctorate
Accreditation: M, ENG, MUS, SPAA

01 Interim President ... Dr. Farnam JAHANIAN
05 Interim Provost ... Dr. Laurie WEINGART
10 Vice President and CFO ... Ms. Angela BLANTON
111 VP for University Advancement ... Mr. Scott MORY
46 Interim Vice Provost for Research ... Dr. Vijayakumar (Kumar) BHAGAVATULA
43 Vice President/General Counsel ... Ms. Mary Jo DIVELY
26 VP Marketing & Communications ... Mr. Steven KLOEHN
101 Secretary of the Corporation ... Ms. Cathy A. LIGHT
04 Interim Exec Asst to President ... Ms. Kelly ELDER
20 Vice Provost for Education ... Dr. Amy L. BURKERT
11 Vice President for Operations ... Dr. Rodney P. MCCLENDON
13 Interim Chief Information Officer ... Mr. David M. BAISLEY
15 Interim VP HR & Chief HR Officer ... Mr. Dan MCNULTY
29 Asst VP Alumni Relations ... Ms. Nancy MERRITT
18 Asc VP Campus Design/Facility Devel ... Mr. Ralph R. HORGAN
27 Exec Dir For Media Relations ... Mr. Kenneth WALTERS
28 Asst Vice Pres for Diversity & EOS ... Mr. Everett L. TADAMY
41 Dir Athletics & Physical Education ... Mr. Josh CENTOR
19 Director Security/Chief Univ Police ... Mr. Thomas A. OGDEN
32 VP Student Affairs/Dean of Students ... Ms. Gina CASALEGNO
84 AVP & Dir of Enrollment Services ... Ms. Lisa M. KRIEG
14 Director Software Engr Inst ... Dr. Paul D. NIELSEN
07 Director of Admission ... Mr. Michael STEIDEL
08 Dean of University Libraries ... Mr. Keith WEBSTER
06 Registrar ... Mr. John R. PAPINCHAK
09 Director of Institutional Research ... Ms. Janel SUTKUS
36 Assoc Dean for Career/Prof Dev ... Mr. Kevin MONAHAN
38 Dir Counseling & Psychological Svcs ... Dr. Kurt KUMLER
54 Dean Carnegie Inst of Technology ... Dr. James GARRETT
57 Dean College Fine Arts ... Dr. Dan J. MARTIN
49 Dean Dietrich College ... Dr. Richard SCHEINES
50 Dean Tepper School of Business ... Dr. Robert DAMMON
81 Dean Mellon College of Science ... Dr. Rebecca w. DOERGE
80 Dean Heinz Sch Publ Policy/Mgmt ... Dr. Ramayya KRISHNAN

77 Dean School of Computer Science ... Dr. Andrew MOORE
35 Asst Dean of Student Affairs ... Ms. Renee CAMERLENGO
100 Chief of Staff Office of President ... Ms. Cathy LIGHT
102 Dir Foundation Relations ... Ms. Jennifer SOBOL
104 Director of International Education ... Ms. Linda GENTILE
25 Chief Contracts/Grants Admin ... Mr. Matthew D'EMILIO
37 Director Student Financial Aid ... Mr. Brian HILL
39 Director Housing Services ... Mr. Thomas COOLEY
30 Sr Assoc Vice Pres for Development ... Ms. Pamela EAGER
86 Assoc VP Government Relations ... Mr. Timothy MCNULTY

Cedar Crest College (A)

100 College Drive, Allentown PA 18104-6196

County: Lehigh FICE Identification: 003243
Unit ID: 211468
Telephone: (610) 437-4471 Carnegie Class: Bac-Diverse
FAX Number: (610) 437-5955 Calendar System: Semester
URL: www.cedarcrest.edu
Established: 1867 Annual Undergrad Tuition & Fees: $36,825
Enrollment: 1,591 Female
Affiliation or Control: Non-denominational IRS Status: 501(c)3
Highest Offering: Doctorate
Accreditation: M, ACBSP, DIETD, DIETI, FEPAC, NUR, SW

01 Interim President ... Dr. Elizabeth MEADE
05 Provost ... Dr. Robert A. WILSON
10 Chief Financial Officer/Treasurer ... Ms. Audra J. KAHR
30 VP of Institutional Advancement ... Ms. Susan ARNOLD
32 VP Student Affairs/Trad Enrollment ... Ms. Mary-Alice OZECHOSKI
06 Registrar ... Ms. Janet BAKER
29 Exec Director for Alumnae Affairs ... Mrs. Susan S. COX
19 Chief of Campus Safety and Security ... Mr. Mark VITALOS
18 Director of Facilities ... Mr. Matthew YENCHA
08 Library Director ... Ms. Mary Beth FREEH
13 Director Information Technology ... Mr. Bruce SARTE
09 Dir of Institutional Research ... Ms. Lyn WILLIAMS
04 Assistant to the President ... Ms. Meghan GRADY
37 Dir Student Financial Services ... Ms. Valerie KREISER
22 Director Health/Counseling Services ... Ms. Nancy ROBERTS
26 Chief Marketing Officer ... Mr. Gaetan GIANNINI
40 Manager Bookstore ... Ms. Maureen YOACHIM

Central Penn College (B)

College Hill Road, Summerdale PA 17093-0309

County: Cumberland FICE Identification: 004890
Unit ID: 211477
Telephone: (800) 759-2727 Carnegie Class: Bac-Diverse
FAX Number: (717) 732-5254 Calendar System: Quarter
URL: www.centralpenn.edu
Established: 1881 Annual Undergrad Tuition & Fees: $17,646
Enrollment: 1,385 Coed
Affiliation or Control: Proprietary IRS Status: Proprietary
Highest Offering: Master's
Accreditation: M, MAC, OTA, PTAA

01 President ... Dr. Karen SCOLFORO
05 VP of Academic Affairs & Provost ... Dr. Linda FEDRIZZI-WILLIAMS
07 VP Enrollment Mgmt & Marketing ... Ms. Stacey OBI
10 Chief Financial Officer ... Mr. Richard VARMECKY
29 Director Alumni Relations ... Ms. Sarah BLUMENSCHEIN
06 Director Records & Registration ... Mr. Jen CORRELL
108 Assessment and Compliance Officer ... Mr. Shawn HUMPHREY
18 Facilities Director ... Mr. Robert WHITCOMB III
26 Director of Marketing & Comm ... Mrs. Mary E. WETZEL
37 Financial Aid Director ... Ms. Kathy J. SHEPARD
41 Retention Officer/Athletic Director ... Mr. Dave BAKER
36 Career Services Director ... Mr. Steven HASSINGER
15 Exec Director of Human Resources ... Ms. Maggie LEBO
39 Residence Life Director ... Ms. Lindsay GARBER

Chatham University (C)

Woodland Road, Pittsburgh PA 15232-2826

County: Allegheny FICE Identification: 003244
Unit ID: 211556
Telephone: (412) 365-1100 Carnegie Class: Masters/L
FAX Number: (412) 365-1505 Calendar System: Other
URL: www.chatham.edu
Established: 1869 Annual Undergrad Tuition & Fees: $35,475
Enrollment: 2,224 Coed
Affiliation or Control: Independent Non-Profit IRS Status: 501(c)3
Highest Offering: Doctorate
Accreditation: M, ARCPA, CIDA, COPSY, IACBE, NURSE, OT, PTA, SW

01 President ... Dr. David FINEGOLD
10 Vice Pres Finance/Administration ... Mr. Walter B. FOWLER
05 Vice President Academic Affairs ... Dr. Jenna TEMPLETON
84 Vice Pres Enrollment Management ... Ms. Amy BECHER
32 VP Student Affairs/Dean of Stdnts ... Dr. Zauyah WAITE
26 Vice Pres for Mktg & Communications ... Mr. Bill CAMPBELL
111 Vice Pres University Advancement ... Ms. Carey MILLER
106 Director Chatham Online ... Mr. Mark KASSEL
88 Dn Falk Sch Sustainability/Environ ... Dr. Peter WALKER
21 Asst VP Finance/Administration ... Ms. Jennifer LUNDY
45 VP of Planning/Sec to the Board ... Mr. Sean COLEMAN
09 Director of Institutional Research ... Dr. Robert ZHANG
06 Registrar ... Ms. Maria KRONISER
37 Director of Financial Aid ... Ms. Jennifer A. BURNS
08 Director of Library ... Ms. Jill AUSEL

29 Exec Director Alumni Relations ... Ms. Catherine LUNN
44 Director of Annual Giving ... Mr. Dominick OLIVER
102 Director of Foundation/Corp Support ... Vacant
15 Director of Human Resources ... Mr. Frank M. GRECO
18 Director of Facilities Management ... Mr. Robert R. DUBRAY
19 Director of Safety & Security ... Vacant
41 Director of Athletics ... Mr. Leonard TREVINO
36 Asst Dean of Students/Career Devel ... Mr. Mary UTTER
38 Director of Student Counseling ... Dr. Elsa M. ARCE
39 Dir Student Affs/Residence Life ... Ms. Heather BLACK
49 Dean School Arts/Science/Business ... Dr. Darlene MOTLEY
76 Dean School of Health Sciences ... Dr. Patricia DOWNEY

Chestnut Hill College (D)

9601 Germantown Avenue, Philadelphia PA 19118-2693

County: Philadelphia FICE Identification: 003245
Unit ID: 211583
Telephone: (215) 248-7000 Carnegie Class: Masters/L
FAX Number: (215) 248-7155 Calendar System: Semester
URL: www.chc.edu
Established: 1924 Annual Undergrad Tuition & Fees: $34,140
Enrollment: 1,951 Coed
Affiliation or Control: Roman Catholic IRS Status: 501(c)3
Highest Offering: Doctorate
Accreditation: M, CLPSY, IPSY, MACTE

01 President ... Sr. Carol Jean VALE, SSJ
05 Vice Pres for Academic Affairs ... Dr. Christopher DOUGHERTY
10 Sr Vice Pres for Financial Affairs ... Ms. Lauri STRIMKOVSKY
30 Vice President for Inst Advancement ... Ms. Susannah COLEMAN
32 Vice President for Student Life ... Dr. Lynn ORTALE
07 Vice President for Admissions ... Ms. Jodie KING
11 Asst to Pres for Administration ... Sr. Kathryn MILLER, SSJ
42 Asst to Pres for Mission & Ministry ... Sr. Roseann QUINN, SSJ
58 Dean School of Graduate Studies ... Dr. Barbara HOGAN
97 Dean School of Undergrad Studies ... Sr. Cecelia CAVANAUGH, SSJ
51 Dean of Continuing Studies ... Dr. Elaine GREEN
08 Dean Library/Information Resources ... Sr. Mary Josephine LARKIN, SSJ
20 Director Student Success ... Ms. Kim COONEY
06 Registrar ... Mr. Michael REIG
35 Director of Student Activities ... Ms. Emily SCHADEMAN
38 Director Counseling Center ... Sr. Sheila KENNEDY, SSJ
85 Foreign Student Advisor ... Ms. Trachanda BROWN
28 Dir Cultural Diversity Initiatives ... Vacant
92 Director of Honors Programs ... Vacant
23 Director Health Services ... Ms. Barbara DOUGHERTY
36 Director of Career Services ... Ms. Nancy DACHILLE
07 Dir Admission/Sch Graduate Studies .. Ms. Denise SAURENNANN
07 Director Accelerated Admissions ... Sr. Mary Esther LEE, SSJ
21 Controller ... Ms. Ellen MCGUINN
37 Int Director Financial Aid ... Ms. Toshia WILLIAMS
09 Director of Institutional Research ... Sr. Patricia O'DONNELL, SSJ
102 Dir Corporate/Found/Govt Relations ... Ms. Charles BLACHFORD
29 Director of Alumnae/i Affairs ... Ms. Maureen MCLAUGHLIN
41 Director of Athletics ... Ms. Lynn TUBMAN
15 Director Human Resources ... Ms. Sharon DOUGHERTY
19 Dir Security/Safety/Bldgs/Grounds ... Ms. Polly TETI
18 Director of Physical Plant ... Mr. Mark MCGRATH
91 Administrative Software Manager ... Ms. Darlene BROWN
26 Director of Communications ... Ms. Kathleen SPIGELMYER
40 Manager of Campus Store ... Ms. Christina WEBSTER
04 Administrative Asst to President ... Ms. Regina BERNHARDT
39 Director Student Housing ... Ms. Jenn THORPE

Clarks Summit University (E)

538 Venard Road, S. Abington Twp. PA 18411-1297

County: Lackawanna FICE Identification: 002670
Unit ID: 211024
Telephone: (570) 586-2400 Carnegie Class: Spec-4-yr-Faith
FAX Number: (570) 585-9226 Calendar System: Semester
URL: www.clarkssummitu.edu
Established: 1932 Annual Undergrad Tuition & Fees: $22,510
Enrollment: 804 Coed
Affiliation or Control: Baptist IRS Status: 501(c)3
Highest Offering: Doctorate
Accreditation: M, BI

01 President ... Dr. James R. LYTLE
05 VP of Academics ... Dr. William J. HIGLEY
10 VP of Business and Finance ... Mr. Thomas BEVAN
20 Associate Seminary Dean ... Dr. Wayne SLUSSER
32 Dean of Students ... Mr. Frank JUDSON
33 Associate Dean of Men ... Mr. Ted BOYKIN
34 Associate Dean of Women ... Mrs. Faye MOORE
04 Exec Dir of President's Office ... Mr. Paul GOLDEN
11 Exec Dir of Administrative Svcs ... Mr. Allen R. DREYER
08 Interim Library Director ... Mrs. Sharon GARDOSKI
37 Director of Financial Aid ... Mrs. Deb CRAGLE
26 Director Communications/Marketing ... Ms. Dena CAMBRA
19 Special Consultant-Safety/Security ... Mr. Ken MORRIS
84 VP for Enrollment Management ... Mr. Andrew WHIPPLE
18 Interim Director of Facilities ... Mr. Devin RAVEN
13 Director of Information Technology ... Mr. David BOSKET
73 Dean of School of Theology ... Dr. David A. LACKEY
53 Dean of School of Education ... Dr. Ritch KELLEY
49 Dean of School of Arts & Sciences ... Dr. Janet K. HICKS
15 Human Resources Coordinator ... Ms. Marilyn LUSTER
106 Tech Director of Distance Education ... Mr. Chris WELMAN
41 Interim Athletic Director ... Ms. Lori HUCKABY

06 Registrar ... Mr. Howard HICKS
07 Director of Enrollment Management ... Mr. Nick CHARLTON
09 Director of Institutional Research ... Mr. Robert PLANTZ
29 Director of Alumni Services ... Mr. Paul GOLDEN

Commonwealth Technical Institute at the Hiram G. Andrews Center (F)

727 Goucher Street, Johnstown PA 15905-3092

County: Cambria FICE Identification: 025366
Unit ID: 212975
Telephone: (814) 255-8200 Carnegie Class: Assoc/HVT-High Non
FAX Number: (814) 255-5709 Calendar System: Semester
URL: www.dli.pa.gov/Individuals/Disability-Services/hgac/
Established: 1959 Annual Undergrad Tuition & Fees: $16,836
Enrollment: 177 Coed
Affiliation or Control: Proprietary IRS Status: Proprietary
Highest Offering: Associate Degree
Accreditation: ACCSC

01 President ... Vacant
12 Center Director ... Jill MORICONI
88 Center Deputy Director ... James MARKER
05 Director of Education ... Karen BILCHAK
07 Director of Admissions ... Jason GIES
32 Chief Student Life Officer ... Stacie ANDREWS
37 Director Student Financial Aid ... Vacant

Community College of Allegheny County (G)

800 Allegheny Avenue, Pittsburgh PA 15233-1895

County: Allegheny FICE Identification: 003231
Unit ID: 210605
Telephone: (412) 323-2323 Carnegie Class: Assoc/MT-VT-Mix Trad/Non
FAX Number: (412) 237-4420 Calendar System: Semester
URL: www.ccac.edu
Established: 1966 Annual Undergrad Tuition & Fees (In-District): $4,131
Enrollment: 16,737 Coed
Affiliation or Control: State/Local IRS Status: 501(c)3
Highest Offering: Associate Degree
Accreditation: M, ADNUR, CA, CAHIIM, COARC, DIETT, DMS, EMT, MAC, MLTAD, NMT, OTA, PTAA, RAD, RTT, SURGT

01 President ... Dr. Quintin B. BULLOCK
05 Provost/Exec Vice Pres Acad Affairs ... Dr. Stuart BLACKLAW
10 Vice President Finance ... Ms. Joyce BRECKENRIDGE
43 Vice President and General Counsel ... Mr. Anthony DITOMMSO
12 Campus President Allegheny ... Dr. Evon WALTERS
12 Campus President Boyce ... Hon. Charles MARTONI
12 Campus President North ... Dr. Gretchen SAWICKI
12 Campus President South ... Dr. Charlene NEWKIRK
86 Executive Director Govt Affairs ... Ms. Nancilee BURZACHECHI
103 VP Workforce Development ... Ms. Theresa BRYANT
15 VP Human Resources ... Ms. Kimberly MANIGAULT
102 CEO Educational Foundation ... Ms. Rose Ann DICOLA
13 Interim Chief Information Officer ... Dr. Diane JACOBS
06 Registrar ... Dr. Diane JACOBS
51 Dir Center Professional Dev ... Mr. Reginald OVERTON
45 AVP Strategic Plng/Inst Research ... Mr. Kevin SMAY
18 Director of Facilities Management ... Mr. James MESSER
21 Controller ... Vacant
25 Director Contracts & Grants ... Dr. Carol YOANNONE
96 Director Purchasing/Contracts Admin ... Mr. Mike CVETIC
28 Special Asst to Pres for Diversity ... Dr. Clyde PICKETT
100 Assistant to the President ... Ms. Bonita L. RICHARDSON
29 Dir Alumni Affairs ... Mr. Rocco PALELLA
26 Executive Director Public Relations ... Ms. Elizabeth JOHNSTON

Community College of Allegheny County Boyce Campus (H)

595 Beatty Road, Monroeville PA 15146-1396

Telephone: (724) 327-1327 Identification: 770150
Accreditation: &M

Community College of Allegheny County North Campus (I)

8701 Perry Highway, Pittsburgh PA 15237-5353

Telephone: (412) 366-7000 Identification: 770151
Accreditation: &M

Community College of Allegheny County, South Campus (J)

1750 Clairton Road, West Mifflin PA 15122-3029

Telephone: (412) 469-1100 Identification: 770152
Accreditation: &M

Community College of Beaver County (K)

1 Campus Drive, Monaca PA 15061-2588

County: Beaver FICE Identification: 006807
Unit ID: 211079
Telephone: (724) 480-2222 Carnegie Class: Assoc/MT-VT-High Trad
FAX Number: (724) 480-3573 Calendar System: Semester
URL: www.ccbc.edu
Established: 1966 Annual Undergrad Tuition & Fees (In-District): $5,790
Enrollment: 2,303 Coed

Affiliation or Control: State/Local IRS Status: 501(c)3
Highest Offering: Associate Degree
Accreditation: M, ADNUR, PHLEB

01 President .... Dr. Christopher M. REBER
03 Executive Vice President .... Dr. Roger W. DAVIS
05 Executive Vice President & Provost .... Dr. Roger W. DAVIS
10 VP Finance/Operations and IT .... Mr. Glenn NATALI
15 VP Human Resources .... Ms. Sally MERCER
26 Exec Dir Public Relations & Mktg .... Ms. Leslie A. TENNANT
38 VP Student Affairs & Enrollment .... Ms. Janice M. KAMINSKI
18 Assoc VP & Dir Facilities & Ground .... Mr. Scott MONIT
84 Director Enrollment Services .... Ms. Angela M. HAMILTON
103 Dean Workforce & Continuing Educ .... Mr. John S. GOBERISH
37 Director Student Financial Services .... Ms. Janet DAVIDSON
04 Assistant to the President & Board .... Ms. Leanne CONDRON
76 Dean Nursing & Allied Health .... Dr. Shelly MOORE
49 Dean Business/Arts/Sciences & Tech .... Dr. John HIGGS
88 Dean Aviation Sciences .... Ms. Dana DONATI
41 Athletic Director .... Mr. John ASHAOLU
88 Dean HS Academies & Dual Enroll .... Ms. Joyce CIRELLI
111 Exec Dir Advance & Sponsored Pgms .... Mr. Kolton CODNER
45 Exec Dir Plng/Assess & Improv .... Ms. Katie THOMAS
08 Head Librarian .... Ms. Terri GALLAGHER

Community College of Philadelphia (A)

1700 Spring Garden Street, Philadelphia PA 19130-3991
County: Philadelphia FICE Identification: 003249
Unit ID: 215239
Telephone: (215) 751-8000 Carnegie Class: Assoc/HT-High Trad
FAX Number: (215) 751-8762 Calendar System: Semester
URL: www.ccp.edu
Established: 1965 Annual Undergrad Tuition & Fees (In-District): $4,920
Enrollment: 18,966 Coed
Affiliation or Control: State/Local IRS Status: 501(c)3
Highest Offering: Associate Degree
Accreditation: M, ACFEI, ADNUR, COARC, DH, MLTAD, PHLEB, RAD

01 President .... Dr. Donald GENERALS
10 Vice President Business & Finance .... Mr. Jacob EAPEN
45 VP Strategic Initiatives and COS .... Dr. Judith GAY
111 Vice Pres Institutional Advancement .... Mr. Gregory MURPHY
05 VP Academic and Student Success .... Dr. Samuel HIRSCH
86 Vice Pres Marketing/Government Rels .... Ms. Lynette BROWN-SOW
103 VP Workforce Dev & Economic Innova .... Ms. Carol DE FRIES
43 General Counsel .... Ms. Victoria ZELLERS
13 Chief Information Officer .... Ms. Jody BAUER
32 Dean of Students .... Dr. Donovan MCCARGO
84 Dean of Enrollment Services .... Dr. Donna RICHEMOND
49 Dean Liberal Studies .... Dr. Chae SWEET
51 Dean Div Adult/Community Education .... Dr. David E. THOMAS
72 Div Dean of Business/Technology .... Dr. Pam CARTER
09 Director Institutional Research .... Dr. Dawn SINNOT
06 Director Stdnt Records/Registration .... Ms. Bonnie HARRINGTON
18 Chief Facilities/Physical Plant .... Mr. Gary BIXBY
28 Affirmative Action Director .... Mr. Simon BROWN
07 Director of Recruitment/Admissions .... Ms. Jeri DRAPER
37 Director Financial Aid .... Mr. Gim LIM
96 Director of Purchasing .... Ms. Marsia HENLEY
38 Dept Head Student Counseling .... Mr. Todd JONES
36 Coord Career Info/Placement Svcs .... Ms. Tarsha SCOVENS
29 Coord Alumni Rels/Annual Giving .... Ms. Lyvette BROOKS
25 Coord Grants/Prospect Research .... Ms. Anne GRECO

Consolidated School of Business (B)

1605 Clugston Road, York PA 17404-1798
County: York FICE Identification: 022896
Unit ID: 211820
Telephone: (717) 764-9550 Carnegie Class: Assoc/HVT-High Trad
FAX Number: (717) 764-9469 Calendar System: Other
URL: www.csb.edu
Established: 1981 Annual Undergrad Tuition & Fees: N/A
Enrollment: 130 Coed
Affiliation or Control: Proprietary IRS Status: Proprietary
Highest Offering: Associate Degree
Accreditation: ACICS

01 CEO/President .... Mr. Robert L. SAFRAN
11 Vice President .... Mr. Bill HOYT
37 Financial Aid Director .... Mrs. Gail E. DOUGHERTY
05 School Director .... Ms. Debra MARTINEZ

Curtis Institute of Music (C)

1726 Locust Street, Philadelphia PA 19103-6187
County: Philadelphia FICE Identification: 003251
Unit ID: 211893
Telephone: (215) 893-5252 Carnegie Class: Spec-4-yr-Arts
FAX Number: (215) 893-9065 Calendar System: Semester
URL: www.curtis.edu
Established: 1924 Annual Undergrad Tuition & Fees: $2,525
Enrollment: 174 Coed
Affiliation or Control: Independent Non-Profit IRS Status: 501(c)3
Highest Offering: Master's
Accreditation: M, MUS

01 President & Chief Executive Officer .... Mr. Roberto DIAZ
10 Sr VP Admin/Chief Financial Officer .... Mr. Larry BOMBACK
30 Sr VP Advancement .... Ms. Kristin B. LODEN
05 Dean of Faculty/Students .... Mr. Paul BRYAN
06 Registrar .... Mr. Darin KELLY
07 Admissions Officer .... Mr. Christopher HODGES
08 Library Director .... Ms. Michelle OSWELL

Dean Institute of Technology (D)

1501 W Liberty Avenue, Pittsburgh PA 15226-1197
County: Allegheny FICE Identification: 009186
Unit ID: 211909
Telephone: (412) 531-4433 Carnegie Class: Assoc/HVT-High Trad
FAX Number: (412) 531-4435 Calendar System: Quarter
URL: www.deantech.edu
Established: 1947 Annual Undergrad Tuition & Fees: $14,050
Enrollment: 158 Coed
Affiliation or Control: Proprietary IRS Status: Proprietary
Highest Offering: Associate Degree
Accreditation: ACCSC

01 President/Director .... Mr. James S. DEAN
05 Director of Education/Asst Director .... Mr. Richard D. ALI
07 Director of Admissions .... Mr. Nicholas D. ALI
37 Director Student Financial Aid .... Ms. Valerie L. VELTRI
36 Placement Director .... Ms. Valerie A. HAGEDORN
26 Director Information Office .... Mr. Stephen FALAVOLITO

Delaware County Community College (E)

901 S Media Line Road, Media PA 19063-1094
County: Delaware FICE Identification: 007110
Unit ID: 211927
Telephone: (610) 359-5000 Carnegie Class: Assoc/HT-High Trad
FAX Number: (610) 359-5343 Calendar System: Semester
URL: www.dccc.edu
Established: 1967 Annual Undergrad Tuition & Fees (In-District): $4,960
Enrollment: 11,742 Coed
Affiliation or Control: State/Local IRS Status: 501(c)3
Highest Offering: Associate Degree
Accreditation: M, ADNUR, ART, COARC, EMT, MAC, SURGT

01 President .... Dr. L. Joy GATES BLACK
10 Vice Pres Administration/Treasurer .... Mr. John A. GLAVIN, JR.
05 Acting Provost .... Dr. Mary Jo BOYER
111 Vice President for Advancement .... Ms. Kathleen A. BRESLIN
12 Vice Provost & Vice Pres Chester Co .... Dr. Mary Jo BOYER
84 Vice President of Enrollment Mgmt .... Ms. Frances M. CUBBERLEY
13 VP & CIO Information Technology .... Mr. George J. SULLIVAN
32 Vice Provost Student/Instr Support .... Dr. Grant S. SNYDER
11 Assoc VP Admin & Facilities Plng .... Mr. Jeffrey S. BAUN
88 Director Municipal Police Academy .... Mr. William DAVIS
106 Director Distance Learning Services .... Mr. Alexander PLUCHUTA
37 Director of Financial Aid .... Mr. Raymond L. TOOLE
07 Asst VP Enrollment Svcs & Registrar .... Ms. Hope L. DIEHL
36 Dean Career/Counseling Center .... Dr. Mitchell MURTHA
108 Assoc Vice Prov Inst Effectiveness .... Dr. Christopher TOKPAH
21 Associate VP Finance .... Mr. Carlos GARCIA
103 Director Workforce Entry Center .... Ms. Susan E. BOND
85 Director International Student Svcs .... Ms. Kathryn A. LOZIER
16 Director Human Resources .... Ms. Sara EVANS
14 Assoc CIO OIT/Technical Services .... Ms. Bianca VALENTE
91 Director Admin Computing .... Mr. Bob HARDCASTLE
29 Director Alumni Programs .... Mr. Douglas J. FERGUSON
25 Director Grants Management .... Ms. Susan M. SHISLER-RAPP
31 Director Community Education .... Ms. Patricia S. SCEPANSKY
35 Director Campus Life .... Ms. Allison GLEESON
19 Director Safety & Security .... Mr. Raymond VISCUSI
88 Dir Dual Enrollment HS Initiatives .... Ms. Patricia SHANNON
12 Director Southeast & UD Centers .... Ms. Jane SCHURMAN
89 Director First Year Experiences .... Dr. Kendrick MICKENS
88 Director Assessment Center .... Ms. Carol MULLIN
96 Director Purchasing .... Vacant
18 Dir Plant Oper/Construction Svcs .... Mr. Tony DELUCA
103 Dean Workforce Dev & Cmty Educ .... Ms. Karen KOZACHYN
81 Dean STEM .... Dr. Mark SCHWARTZ
88 Dean Educational Support Svcs .... Ms. Tonya M. BRIGGS
50 Dean Business & Social Science .... Dr. Marian MCGORRY
79 Dean Comm/Arts & Humanities .... Dr. Nicholas WERNICKI
76 Dean Health/Nursing/EMS .... Dr. Faye A. MELOY
40 Manager Bookstore .... Mr. Kris STACHOWIAK
04 Executive Assistant to President .... Ms. Diane FOSTER
26 Director of Marketing .... Mr. Daniel KANAK
45 Asst to President for Planning .... Mr. Craig R. FITZ
88 Asst to President for Communication .... Mr. Anthony TWYMAN

Delaware Valley University (F)

700 E Butler Avenue, Doylestown PA 18901-2697
County: Bucks FICE Identification: 003252
Unit ID: 211981
Telephone: (215) 345-1500 Carnegie Class: Masters/S
FAX Number: (215) 345-5277 Calendar System: Semester
URL: www.delval.edu
Established: 1896 Annual Undergrad Tuition & Fees: $36,750
Enrollment: 2,266 Coed
Affiliation or Control: Independent Non-Profit IRS Status: 501(c)3
Highest Offering: Doctorate
Accreditation: M, LSAR

01 President .... Dr. Maria GALLO
100 Administrative Director .... Ms. Angela T. RECKNER
05 Int VP Acad Affs/Dean of Faculty .... Dr. Benjamin RUSILOSKI
32 VP Student Affairs/Dean of Students .... Dr. April VARI
10 VP for Finance & Administration .... Ms. Jenni SAUER
111 Vice President for Inst Advancement .... Mr. Joseph ERCKERT
09 AVP Rsrch/Plng/Accr & Dir I&R .... Ms. Deborah DAILEY
84 VP for Enrollment Mgmt .... Mr. Arthur GOON
81 Dean of Life & Physical Sciences .... Dr. Benjamin RUSILOSKI
47 Interim Dean of Agric & Environ Sci .... Dr. Christopher TIPPING
50 Interim Dean Business & Humanities .... Dr. Tanya CASAS
58 Dean of Graduate & Prof Studies .... Dr. James MORYAN
06 Registrar .... Mr. James SLIZEWSKI
41 Athletic Director .... Mr. Steve CANTRELL
26 Interim Chief Marketing Officer .... Ms. Sarah BOYLE
07 Director of Admissions .... Mr. Dwayne WALKER
13 Exec Dir of Technology Services .... Mr. Mike DAVIS
36 Exec Dir Ctr for Student Prof Dev .... Dr. Benjamin RUSILOSKI
08 Librarian .... Mr. Peter A. KUPERSMITH
37 Director Student Financial Aid .... Mrs. Joan HOCK
58 Director Graduate & Prof Studies .... Ms. Yolonda UDVARDY
38 Director Counseling/Learn Support .... Ms. Sharon DONNELLY
23 Director Health Services .... Ms. Miriam TORRES
14 Assoc Dir of Help Desk Operations .... Mr. Darren MOSES
39 Director of Student Affs Operations .... Mr. Derek SMITH
19 Director Security/Public Safety .... Ms. Cynthia TRANSUE
15 Interim Director Human Resources .... Ms. Theresa TAVERNIER
18 Director Physical Plant .... Mr. Joseph GUCKAVAN
44 Director Annual Giving & Adv Svcs .... Mr. Kevin LADDEN
96 Director of Purchasing .... Mr. William LYLE
102 Dir Foundation/Corporate Relations .... Ms. Wendy CONNUCK
103 Dir Workforce/Career Development .... Ms. Deanna PARKTON
104 Director Study Abroad .... Ms. Stephanie WOBENSMITH
106 Dir Online Education/E-learning .... Ms. Cynthia RENNER
29 Director Alumni Engagement .... Ms. Amanda GOODWIN
04 Admin Asst to the President .... Ms. Kristen OLSZEWSKI

DeSales University (G)

2755 Station Avenue, Center Valley PA 18034-9568
County: Lehigh FICE Identification: 003986
Unit ID: 210739
Telephone: (610) 282-1100 Carnegie Class: Masters/L
FAX Number: (610) 282-2254 Calendar System: Semester
URL: www.desales.edu
Established: 1965 Annual Undergrad Tuition & Fees: $34,850
Enrollment: 3,136 Coed
Affiliation or Control: Roman Catholic IRS Status: 501(c)3
Highest Offering: Doctorate
Accreditation: M, ACBSP, ARCPA, NURSE, PTA

01 President .... V.Rev. James J. GREENFIELD, OSFS
04 Admin Assistant to the President .... Ms. Mary A. GOTZON
05 Provost/Vice Pres Academic Affairs .... Dr. Karen WALTON
06 Registrar .... Mr. Thomas MANTONI
08 Librarian .... Ms. Deborah MALONE
51 Dean of Lifelong Learning .... Ms. Deborah BOOROS
20 Dean of Undergraduate Education .... Dr. Robert BLUMENSTEIN
36 Director of Career Development .... Ms. Kristin EICHOLTZ
111 Vice Pres Institutional Advancement .... Mr. Thomas L. CAMPBELL
86 Director of Government Relations .... Vacant
102 Director Corp/Foundation Relations .... Mrs. Kathy DIAMANDOPOULOS
26 Executive Director of Communication .... Mr. Thomas MCNAMARA
44 Executive Director of Annual Giving .... Ms. Lina BARBIERI
29 Director of Alumni Relations .... Ms. Nicole GINGRICH
10 VP for Admin/Finance & Campus Env .... Mr. Robert J. SNYDER
45 Assoc VP for Admin & Planning .... Mr. Peter RAUTZHAN
21 Director of Finance/Treasurer .... Mr. Michael SWEETANA
19 Chief of Police .... Chief Steven MARSHALL
09 Dir of Institutional Rsrch/Analysis .... Ms. Lisa PLUMMER
88 Assoc VP of Campus Environment .... Mr. Marc ALBANESE
18 Director of Facilities .... Mr. Jim MOLCHANY
40 Campus Store Manager .... Ms. Bridget SCOGNA
15 Director of Human Resources .... Ms. Margie GRANDINETTI
16 Employment Benefits Coord/HR Gen .... Ms. Lisa LIGHTCAP
13 Director of Information Technology .... Ms. Patricia CLAY
32 Vice President Student Life .... Dr. Gerard JOYCE
84 Dean of Enrollment Mgmt .... Mrs. Mary BIRKHEAD
35 Dean of Students .... Mrs. Linda ZERBE
39 Director of Residence Life .... Ms. Melinda QUINONES
07 Director of Admissions .... Mr. Derrick WETZEL
37 Director of Student Financial Aid .... Mrs. Joyce FARMER
42 Chaplain .... Fr. Timothy MCINTIRE, OSFS
38 Director of Counseling Center .... Ms. Wendy KRISAK
41 Athletic Director .... Mr. Scott COVAL
28 Director Multicultural/Intl Affairs .... Vacant
58 Dean of Graduate Education .... Vacant
96 Campus Environment/Dir Purchasing .... Mr. Michael DUFFY
103 Dir Workforce/Career Development .... Ms. Kristin EICHOLTZ
104 Director of International Learning .... Mr. Brian MACDONALD
50 Division Head of Business .... Mr. Christopher R. COCOZZA
53 Dean of Education .... Dr. Judith RANCE-RONEY
105 Director Web Communications .... Ms. Kristin LAUDENSLAGER
106 Dir Online Education/E-learning .... Dr. Eric HAGAN

† Dr. Gerard Joyce, Vice President of Student life, will be the Interim President from July 1, to December 31, 2017.

DeVry University - Fort Washington Campus (H)

1140 Virginia Drive, Fort Washington PA 19034-3204
Telephone: (215) 591-5700 Identification: 666218
Accreditation: &NH, ENGT

† Regional accreditation is carried under the parent institution in Downers Grove, IL.

Dickinson College (A)

Box 1773, College & Louther Street,
Carlisle PA 17013-2896

County: Cumberland FICE Identification: 003253
Unit ID: 212009
Telephone: (717) 243-5121 Carnegie Class: Bac-A&S
FAX Number: N/A Calendar System: Semester
URL: www.dickinson.edu
Established: 1783 Annual Undergrad Tuition & Fees: $51,205
Enrollment: 2,420 Coed
Affiliation or Control: Independent Non-Profit IRS Status: 501(c)3
Highest Offering: Baccalaureate
Accreditation: M

01 President Dr. Margee M. ENSIGN
05 Provost/Dean of the College Dr. Neil B. WEISSMAN
84 VP Enrollment Marketing and Comm Dr. Stefanie D. NILES
10 VP Finance & Administration Dr. Bronté BURLEIGH-JONES
111 VP College Advancement Mr. Kirk I. SWENSON
32 VP Student Life Ms. Joyce A. BYLANDER
13 VP & Chief Information Officer Mr. Robert E. RENAUD
09 VP Institutional Initiatives Mr. Michael E. REED
07 Dean of Admissions Ms. Catherine M. DAVENPORT
15 Assoc VP Human Resource Services Ms. Debra HARGROVE
43 General Counsel Ms. Dana E. SCADUTO
100 Chief of Staff/Secretary of College Ms. Karen N. FARYNIAK
18 Assoc VP Sustain & Facilities Plng Mr. Kenneth E. SHULTES
20 Sr Assoc Provost Academic Affairs Dr. John H. HENSON
20 Sr Assoc Provost Academic Affairs Dr. Brenda K. BRETZ
110 Assoc VP College Advance Mr. Brian G. FALCK
109 Assoc VP Auxil Svcs & Budget Mgmt Mr. Stephen C. HIETSCH
26 Exec Dir Marketing & Communications Ms. Connie MCNAMARA
06 Registrar Ms. Karen A. WEIKEL
41 Director Athletics Mr. Joe GIUNTA
09 Director Institutional Research Dr. Jason E. RIVERA
37 Director of Financial Aid Mr. Richard A. HECKMAN
104 Exec Dir Ctr Global Stdy & Engagmnt Ms. Samantha C. BRANDAUER
36 Dean Career Dev/Asst VP Studnt Life Mr. Philip JONES
88 Executive Director Wellness Center Dr. Alecia D. SUNDSMO
35 Assoc VP Stdnt Ldrshp/Campus Engmnt Ms. Rebecca J. HAMMELL
90 Director Academic Computing Ms. Patricia A. PEHLMAN
27 Director of Media Relations Ms. Christine BAKSI
29 Director of Alumni Relations Ms. Liz GLYNN TOTH
08 Director Library Services Ms. Eleanor MITCHELL
40 Dir College Bookstore/Central Svcs Mr. David A. NELSON
19 Asst VP Compliance/Campus Safety Ms. Dolores A. DANSER
91 Assoc VP Enterprise Systems Ms. Jill M. FORRESTER
102 Dir Academic & Foundation Relations Ms. Cheryl E. KREMER
39 Assoc Dean Stdnts/Dir Res Life Ms. Angie HARRIS
88 Executive Director Donor Relations Ms. Tara C. RENAULT
105 Director Online Marketing Ms. Sarah M. SHERIFF
42 Director Cmty Svcs/Religious Life Rev. Donna D. HUGHES

Douglas Education Center (B)

130 Seventh Street, Monessen PA 15062-1097

County: Westmoreland FICE Identification: 020683
Unit ID: 212045
Telephone: (724) 684-3684 Carnegie Class: Spec 2-yr-A&S
FAX Number: (724) 684-7463 Calendar System: Semester
URL: www.dec.edu
Established: 1904 Annual Undergrad Tuition & Fees: $17,717
Enrollment: 254 Coed
Affiliation or Control: Proprietary IRS Status: Proprietary
Highest Offering: Associate Degree
Accreditation: ACICS

01 President Mr. Jeffrey D. IMBRESCIA
05 Executive Director of Education Mr. Julian IMBRESCIA
10 Director of Financial Services Mr. Debra B. WISE
20 Senior Academic Affairs Coordinator Ms. N. Renee MCDOWELL
07 Director of Admissions Mr. Tony BAEZ MILAN
11 Executive Director of Operations Ms. Amanda PHILLIPS
26 Chief Marketing Officer Mr. Kevin G. FEAR
88 Supervisor of Cosmetology Mr. Gary NESTER
36 Director of Career Services Ms. Lauri ASTON
32 Student Life/Social Media Ms. Janelle IMBRESCIA
13 Director of Information Technology Mr. John SECHRIST

Drexel University (C)

3141 Chestnut Street, Philadelphia PA 19104-2875

County: Philadelphia FICE Identification: 003256
Unit ID: 212054
Telephone: (215) 895-2000 Carnegie Class: DU-Higher
FAX Number: (215) 895-1414 Calendar System: Quarter
URL: www.drexel.edu
Established: 1891 Annual Undergrad Tuition & Fees: $51,030
Enrollment: 25,595 Coed
Affiliation or Control: Independent Non-Profit IRS Status: 501(c)3
Highest Offering: Doctorate
Accreditation: M, ANEST, ARCPA, ART, CEA, CIDA, CLPSY, CONST, CS, DENT, DIETD, ENG, ENGT, HT, IPSY, LAW, LIB, MED, MFCD, NURSE, PA, PH, PTA

01 President Mr. John A. FRY
05 Provost/Executive Vice President Dr. Brian BLAKE
111 SVP Inst Advancement Mr. David L. UNRUH
11 Exec Vice Pres/Treasurer/COO Mrs. Helen Y. BOWMAN
84 SVP Enrollment Mgmt/Student Success Dr. Randall C. DEIKE
26 Sr VP University Communications Ms. Lori N. DOYLE
43 Sr VP & General Counsel Mr. Michael J. EXLER
86 Sr VP Govt & Community Relations Mr. Brian T. KEECH
20 Vice Provost Dr. Koren A. BEDEAU
13 Vice Pres IRT & CIO Mr. Thomas DECHIARO
88 Exec Dir & Vice Prov Cultural Partn Dr. Rosalind REMER
07 Vice Pres/Dean of Admissions Ms. Evelyn THIMBA
102 Sr VP Corp Relations & Economic Dev Mr. Keith A. ORRIS
46 Sr Vice Provost for Research Dr. Aleister SAUNDERS
32 Vice Pres and Dean of Student Life Dr. Subir SAHU
09 Vice Provost Institutional Research Dr. Mark FREEMAN
100 VP & Exec Dir Office of President Mr. Gregory P. MONTANARO
108 VP Compliance/Privacy & IA Mr. Edward G. LONGAZEL
115 Vice President Investments Ms. Catherine B. ULOZAS
88 Sr Vice Provost Partnerships Dr. Lucy E. KERMAN
15 Vice Pres Human Resources & PMOE Ms. Megan E. WEYLER
49 Dean College Arts & Sciences Dr. Donna MURASKO
50 Int Dean LeBow College of Business Dr. Paul E. JENSEN
54 Int Dean College of Engineering Dr. Giuseppe R. PALMESE
77 Dean Col of Computing & Informatics Dr. Yi DENG
92 Dean of Pennoni Honors College Dr. Paula COHEN
88 Dean Grad Sch of Biomed Science Dr. Elisabeth VANBOCKSTAELE
62 Dean of Libraries Dr. Danuta A. NITECKI
88 Dean of Close School Dr. Donna M. DECAROLIS
61 Dean Kline School of Law Mr. Roger J. DENNIS
60 Dean Col of Media Arts & Design Mr. Allen C. SABINSON
53 Dean School of Education Dr. Nancy B. SONGER
63 Sr VP & Dean College of Medicine Dr. Daniel V. SCHIDLOW
66 Int Dean Col Nursing/Health Prof Dr. Susan S. SMITH
69 Dean Urban Health Collaborative Dr. Ana V. DIEZ ROUX
88 Dean School Biomed Engineering Dr. Paul BRANDT-RAUF
19 Vice President Public Safety Ms. Eileen W. BEHR
109 Vice President Campus Services Ms. Rita E. LARUE
41 Athletic Director Dr. Eric A. ZILLMER
36 Vice Prov Career Development Ctr Vacant
22 Assoc VP Equality & Diversity Ms. Michele M. ROVINSKY-MAYER
106 SVP of Drexel & President of DEL Dr. Susan C. ALDRIDGE
85 Assoc Vice Provost Intl Programs Ms. Daniela E. ASCARELLI
88 Vice Chair Faculty Senate Dr. Michael KENNEDY
88 Director AJ Drexel Autism Institute Dr. Craig J. NEWSCHAFFER
96 Assoc Vice Pres Procurement Svcs Vacant
04 Administrative Asst to President Ms. Kiera MURASKO-BLANK

Duquesne University (D)

600 Forbes Avenue, Pittsburgh PA 15282-0001

County: Allegheny FICE Identification: 003258
Unit ID: 212106
Telephone: (412) 396-6000 Carnegie Class: DU-Higher
FAX Number: (412) 396-4186 Calendar System: Semester
URL: www.duq.edu
Established: 1878 Annual Undergrad Tuition & Fees: $35,062
Enrollment: 9,404 Coed
Affiliation or Control: Roman Catholic IRS Status: 501(c)3
Highest Offering: Doctorate
Accreditation: M, #ARCPA, CAATE, CACREP, CAEPN, CEA, CLPSY, FEPAC, LAW, MUS, NURSE, OT, PHAR, PTA, SCPSY, SP

01 President Mr. Kenneth G. GORMLEY
04 Assistant to the President Ms. Margaret EISEMAN
05 Provost/Academic Vice President Dr. Timothy R. AUSTIN
10 Vice Pres for Management Business Dr. Matthew J. FRIST
32 Vice Pres for Student Life Dr. Douglas FRIZZELL
111 VP for University Advancement Mr. John J. PLANTE
88 Vice President Mission & Identity Rev. Raymond FRENCH, CSSP
43 VP Legal Affairs & General Counsel Ms. Madelyn REILLY
20 Assoc Academic Vice Pres Research Dr. Alan W. SEADLER
20 Assoc Academic Vice President Dr. Jeffrey A. MILLER
13 Asst Vice President/CIO Dr. Charles R. BARTEL
109 Director Auxiliary Services Mr. Scott RICHARDS
85 Exec Dir International Programs Dr. Roberta C. ARONSON
84 Assoc Vice Pres Enrollment Mgmt Mr. Paul-James CUKANNA
06 Registrar Ms. Kim HOERITZ
08 Librarian Dr. Sara BARON
29 Director Alumni Relations Ms. Sarah SPERRY
09 Director of Institutional Research Mr. Matthew NORTH
37 Director Financial Aid Mr. Richard C. ESPOSITO
15 Asst Vice Pres/CHRO Mr. John G. GREENO
19 Director of Security Mr. Thomas HART
88 Dir Environmental Health/Safety Ms. Paula D. SWEITZER
18 Asst VP/Chief Facilities Officer Mr. Rodney W. DOBISH
36 Director of Career Services Ms. Nicole FELDHUES
41 Director of Athletics Mr. David HARPER
26 Assoc Vice Pres of Public Affairs Ms. Bridget M. FARE
22 Director of Anti-discrimination Mr. Sean F. WEAVER
23 Director Health Service Ms. Dessa MRVOS
38 Dir University Counseling Center Dr. Ian C. EDWARDS
39 Director Residence Life Mrs. Sharon G. OELSCHLAGER
42 Director Campus Ministry Rev. Daniel WALSH, CSSP
28 Director of Multicultural Affairs Mr. Jeff MALLORY
50 Dean Business & Administration Dr. Dean B. MCFARLIN
66 Dean of Nursing Dr. Mary Ellen S. GLASGOW
67 Dean of Pharmacy Dr. J. Douglas BRICKER
64 Dean of Music Dr. Seth BECKMAN
53 Dean of Education Dr. Cindy M. WALKER
76 Interim Dean of Health Sciences Dr. Paula S. TUROCY
61 Dean of Law Ms. Maureen LALLY-GREEN
49 Dean of Liberal Arts/Graduate Dr. James SWINDAL
65 Dean of Natural/Environment Sci Dr. Philip P. REEDER
40 Bookstore Manager Mr. John KACHUR
07 Director of Admissions Ms. Debra A. ZUGATES
88 Asst VP for Executive Affairs Ms. Mary Ellen SOLOMON
88 Asst VP for External Relations Ms. Mary Beth FORD
106 Dir Online Education/E-learning Dr. Michael W. BRIDGES

Eastern University (E)

1300 Eagle Road, Saint Davids PA 19087-3696

County: Delaware FICE Identification: 003259
Unit ID: 212133
Telephone: (610) 341-5800 Carnegie Class: Masters/L
FAX Number: (610) 341-1377 Calendar System: Semester
URL: www.eastern.edu
Established: 1925 Annual Undergrad Tuition & Fees: $31,140
Enrollment: 3,505 Coed
Affiliation or Control: American Baptist IRS Status: 501(c)3
Highest Offering: Doctorate
Accreditation: M, CAATE, EXSC, NURSE, SW, THEOL

01 President Dr. Robert DUFFETT
10 Vice Pres for Finance/Operations Mr. J. Pernell JONES
21 Associate VP Finance/Operations Ms. Polly BEROL
03 Executive Vice President Dr. M. Thomas RIDINGTON
05 Provost Dr. Kenton SPARKS
06 Registrar Ms. Sarah ROCHE
32 Vice Provost Student Development Dr. Bettie Ann BRIGHAM
45 Vice Pres Inst Plng Research Assess Dr. Christine P. MAHAN
111 Vice President Advancement Ms. Lisa TITUS
110 Assoc Vice Pres Advancement Mr. James ROGERS
84 Vice Pres Enrollment/Marketing Dr. Kenton SPARKS
07 Exec Director Enrollment Mr. Michael DZIEDZIAK
15 Senior Director of Human Resources Ms. Kacey BERNARD
04 Exec Asst to the President Ms. Heather NORCINI
35 Dean of Students Mr. Daryl HAWKINS
49 Vice Provost Acad Oper/Dean CAS Dr. John PAULEY, II
12 Dean/VP Educ Esperanza College Dr. Elizabeth CONDE-FRAZIER
11 Dean Admin/Pgm Esperanza College Dr. David HURTADO
83 Dean College of Health/Soc Sciences Dr. Patricia REGER
73 Dean Palmer Theological Seminary Dr. F. David BRONKEMA
50 Dean College of Business/Leadership Dr. Douglas CLARK
92 Dean Templeton Honors College Dr. Brian WILLIAMS
53 Dean College of Education Dr. Susan EDGAR-SMITH
66 Chair Department of Nursing Dr. Dianne DELONG
18 Exec Dir Facilities/Campus Svcs Mr. Jeffrey GROMIS
105 Dir Web and User Services Mr. Mark HOFFMAN
09 Director Institutional Research Mr. Thomas A. DAHLSTROM
108 Director of Assessment Dr. Shantelle JENKINS
26 Director of Communications Ms. Denise MCMILLAN
113 Senior Director Student Accounts Ms. Lisa WELLER
08 Library Director Dr. James L. SAUER
42 University Chaplain Rev Dr. Joseph B. MODICA
37 Director of Financial Aid Ms. Christal JENNINGS
13 Chief Information Officer Mr. Eric MCCLOY
36 Director of Talent & Career Dev Ms. Sarah TODD
29 Dir Alumni/Parent Relations Ms. Mary GARDNER
25 Dir Foundations/Grants/Govt Rel Ms. Ingrid COOPER
41 Interim Director of Athletics Ms. Heidi BIRTWISTLE
19 Director of Public Safety Vacant
88 Director of Conferences/Spec Events Ms. Meggin CAPERS
38 Dir Counseling/Academic Support Dr. Lisa M. HEMLICK
85 Dir Intl Student & Scholar Services Ms. Augusta ALLEN
39 Housing Coordinator Ms. Courtney JOHNSON
40 Follett Bookstore Manager Ms. Helen RICOTTA
88 Chair Urban Studies Dr. Kimberlee JOHNSON
93 Asst Dean Stdnts for Multicultural Ms. Jacqueline IRVING
121 Asst Dean Students/Dir of Advising Mr. David SCHLOSSER
109 Director Auxiliary Services Mr. Byron MCMILLAN
88 Dir Faculty Development Dr. Sherry KULL
101 Assistant to the President/Board Ms. Beth RUTLEDGE
44 Director Annual Giving Mr. Joseph TREMOGLIE

† Parent institution of Palmer Theological Seminary.

Elizabethtown College (F)

1 Alpha Drive, Elizabethtown PA 17022-2298

County: Lancaster FICE Identification: 003262
Unit ID: 212197
Telephone: (717) 361-1000 Carnegie Class: Bac-A&S
FAX Number: (717) 361-1207 Calendar System: Semester
URL: www.etown.edu
Established: 1899 Annual Undergrad Tuition & Fees: $43,490
Enrollment: 1,820 Coed
Affiliation or Control: Church Of The Brethren IRS Status: 501(c)3
Highest Offering: Master's
Accreditation: M, ACBSP, ENG, MUS, OT, SW

01 President Dr. Carl J. STRIKWERDA
05 Sr Vice Pres Acad Affs/Dn Faculty Dr. Elizabeth (Betty) RIDER
10 Vice Pres Administration/Finance Mr. Robert M. WALLET
30 Vice President Advancement/Cmty Rel Mr. David C. BEIDLEMAN
84 Int Vice Pres Enrollment Management Mr. George WALTER
32 VP Student Affairs/Dean of Students Ms. Marianne CALENDA
51 Dean Ctr Continuing Educ/Dist Lrng Mr. John KOKOLUS
07 Director Admissions Ms. Lauren C. DEIBLER
35 Asst Dean of Students & Dir of CSS Ms. Stephanie A. RANKIN
26 Exec Dir Marketing/ Communications Ms. Elizabeth (Liz) A. BRAUNGARD
13 Exec Director Information/Tech Svcs Mr. Todd SPAHR
102 Exec Dir Foundation/Govt Relations Ms. Lesley M. FINNEY
46 Director Research & Planning Dr. Richard BASOM
37 Director of Financial Aid Ms. Melodie R. JACKSON
08 Director The High Library Ms. Sarah PENNIMAN

29 Director Alumni Devel & Programs .... Mr. Mark A. CLAPPER
19 Director of Campus Security .... Mr. Andrew L. POWELL
41 Director of Athletics .... Mr. Chris MORGAN
42 Chaplain/Director Religious Life ....Dr. Tracy SADD

Erie Institute of Technology (A)

940 Millcreek Mall, Erie PA 16565-1002
County: Erie FICE Identification: 022039
Unit ID: 212434
Telephone: (814) 868-9900 Carnegie Class: Spec 2-yr-Tech
FAX Number: (814) 868-9977 Calendar System: Semester
URL: www.erieit.edu
Established: 1958 Annual Undergrad Tuition & Fees: $13,770
Enrollment: 259 Coed
Affiliation or Control: Proprietary IRS Status: Proprietary
Highest Offering: Associate Degree
Accreditation: ACCSC

01 Director .... Mr. Paul FITZGERALD
05 Director of Education ....Ms. Kate HUSHON
37 Financial Aid Officer .... Ms. Kelly SCHULTZ
07 Admissions Director ....Ms. Barb BOLT
36 Career Services Director .... Ms. Tara YOCHIN

Esperanza College (B)

4261 North 5th Street, Philadelphia PA 19140
Telephone: (215) 324-0746 Identification: 770153
Accreditation: &M

† Branch campus of Eastern University, Saint Davids, PA

Evangelical Theological Seminary (C)

121 S College Street, Myerstown PA 17067-1222
County: Lebanon FICE Identification: 003263
Unit ID: 212443
Telephone: (717) 866-5775 Carnegie Class: Spec-4-yr-Faith
FAX Number: (717) 866-4667 Calendar System: 4/1/4
URL: www.evangelical.edu
Established: 1953 Annual Graduate Tuition & Fees: N/A
Enrollment: 124 Coed
Affiliation or Control: Evangelical Congregational Church
IRS Status: 501(c)3
Highest Offering: Master's; No Undergraduates
Accreditation: M, MFCD, THEOL

01 President ....Dr. Anthony L. BLAIR
111 Vice Pres Institutional Advancement ....Rev. Ann E. STEEL
10 Vice President Finance & Operations .... Mr. Kevin C. HENRY
26 VP of Marketing/Communications .... Mr. George DAVIS
05 Dean of Academic Programs .... Mr. James E. EHRMAN
08 Head Librarian .... Dr. Mark DRAPER
18 Director of Buildings & Grounds ....Mr. William J. ROBERTSON
88 Database Manager ....Mrs. Marsha A. CONLEY
06 Registrar/Financial Aid Admin ....Mr. Ellis I. KIRK
07 Director of Admissions ....Ms. Gwen SCHEIRER
04 Executive Asst to President ....Mrs. Deanna M. VAN ELSWYK

Fortis Institute (D)

5757 West Ridge Road, Erie PA 16506-1013
County: Erie FICE Identification: 030108
Unit ID: 216418
Telephone: (814) 838-7673 Carnegie Class: Assoc/HVT-High Trad
FAX Number: (814) 838-8642 Calendar System: Quarter
URL: www.fortis.edu
Established: 1984 Annual Undergrad Tuition & Fees: $15,306
Enrollment: 548 Coed
Affiliation or Control: Proprietary IRS Status: Proprietary
Highest Offering: Associate Degree
Accreditation: ACICS, DH

01 Campus President & Academic Dean .... Mr. Peter CORREA
10 Business Officer ....Ms. Shelley FAYTAK
07 Admissions .... Ms. Barbara BORGESON
06 Registrar .... Ms. Margo DEVERS
37 Financial Aid .... Mr. Marc GRUTKOWSKI
36 Placement ....Mr. John ZACZYK

Fortis Institute (E)

166 Slocum Street, Forty Fort PA 18704-2347
County: Luzerne FICE Identification: 030115
Unit ID: 249609
Telephone: (570) 288-8400 Carnegie Class: Spec 2-yr-Health
FAX Number: (570) 287-7936 Calendar System: Other
URL: www.fortis.edu
Established: 1984 Annual Undergrad Tuition & Fees: $15,214
Enrollment: 166 Coed
Affiliation or Control: Proprietary IRS Status: Proprietary
Highest Offering: Associate Degree
Accreditation: ACCSC

01 Campus President ....Ruth BRUMAGIN
05 Director of Education ....Ruth BRUMAGIN
07 Director of Admissions ....Jane AUSTIN

Fortis Institute (F)

517 Ash Street, Scranton PA 18509
County: Lackawanna FICE Identification: 030116
Unit ID: 385503
Telephone: (570) 558-1818 Carnegie Class: Spec 2-yr-Health
FAX Number: (570) 342-4537 Calendar System: Other
URL: www.fortis.edu/scranton-pennsylvania.php
Established: 1986 Annual Undergrad Tuition & Fees: $25,963
Enrollment: 373 Coed
Affiliation or Control: Proprietary IRS Status: Proprietary
Highest Offering: Associate Degree
Accreditation: ACCSC, DH

01 Campus President ....Ms. Madeline LEVY CRUZ
06 Registrar .... Mr. Art BOBBOUINE
07 Director of Admissions .... Mr. Timothy PARSONS
36 Director Student Placement .... Ms. Heather CONTARDI
37 Director Student Financial Aid .... Ms. Stacie TAROLI

† Tuition varies by degree program.

Franklin & Marshall College (G)

PO Box 3003, Lancaster PA 17604-3003
County: Lancaster FICE Identification: 003265
Unit ID: 212577
Telephone: (717) 358-3971 Carnegie Class: Bac-A&S
FAX Number: (717) 358-4183 Calendar System: Semester
URL: www.fandm.edu
Established: 1787 Annual Undergrad Tuition & Fees: $52,290
Enrollment: 2,249 Coed
Affiliation or Control: Independent Non-Profit IRS Status: 501(c)3
Highest Offering: Baccalaureate
Accreditation: M

01 President .... Dr. Daniel R. PORTERFIELD
10 Vice Pres for Finance and Treasurer ....Mr. David R. PROULX
111 Vice Pres for College Advancement ....Mr. Matthew EYNON
84 VP/Dean of Admission/Financial Aid .... Mr. Eric G. MAGUIRE
26 Vice Pres for College Communication ....Mr. Kevin BURKE
05 Provost/Dean of Faculty ....Dr. Joel MARTIN
20 Dean of the College .... Ms. Margaret HAZLETT
88 Assoc Dean of Col & Dir Klehr Ctr ....Dr. Ralph TABER
21 Assoc Vice President for Finance .... Ms. Wendy S. STARNER
11 Associate VP for Administration .... Mr. Barry BOSLEY
45 VP for Planning .... Dr. Alan S. CANIGLIA
100 Chief of Staff .... Ms. Robyn PIGGOTT
08 College Librarian .... Mr. Scott VINE
112 Major Gifts Officer ....Ms. Catherine T. FERRY
85 Assoc Dean International Programs ....Ms. Sue MENNICKE
20 Associate Dean of Faculty .... Dr. Ken KREBS
20 Associate Dean of Faculty .... Dr. Kimberly ARMSTRONG
28 Assoc Dean of Multicultural Affairs .... Dr. Marion A. COLEMAN
88 Assistant Dean/College House Dean .... Ms. Katharine J. SNIDER
88 Assistant Dean/College House Dean ....Dr. Suzanna L. RICHTER
88 Assistant Dean/College House Dean ....Dr. Beth PROFFITT
88 Assistant Dean/College House Dean .... Todd DEKAY
88 Assistant Dean/College House Dean .... Dr. Brian W. SAMBLE
21 Controller .... Mr. Sean GALLOWAY
15 Associate VP Human Resources ....Ms. Laura FIORE
18 Associate VP/Facilities Management .... Mr. Mike WETZEL
19 Assoc VP Public Safety ....Mr. William MCHALE, JR.
23 Managing Physician Student Wellness ....Dr. Amy A. MYERS
13 Assoc VP/Chief Information Officer .... Ms. Carrie RAMPP
37 Director Financial Aid ....Mr. Clarke C. PAINE
38 Head of Counseling Services ....Dr. Lauren A. FIRESTONE
90 Dir Instruct/Emerging Technology ....Mr. Teb LOCKE
06 Registrar & Assoc Director Inst Res ....Ms. Christine D. ALEXANDER
29 Executive Dir of Alumni Relations .... Ms. Mary MAZZUCA
07 Director of Admission .... Ms. Julie A. KERICH
41 Athletic Director ....Ms. Patricia EPPS
43 General Counsel .... Mr. Pierce BULLER
101 Secretary of the Institution/Board .... Ms. Robyn PIGGOTT
102 Sr Dir Col Grants/Found & Corp ....Mr. Ryan SAUDER

Gannon University (H)

University Square, Erie PA 16541-0001
County: Erie FICE Identification: 003266
Unit ID: 212601
Telephone: (814) 871-7000 Carnegie Class: Masters/L
FAX Number: (814) 871-7338 Calendar System: Other
URL: www.gannon.edu
Established: 1925 Annual Undergrad Tuition & Fees: $30,042
Enrollment: 4,416 Coed
Affiliation or Control: Roman Catholic IRS Status: 501(c)3
Highest Offering: Doctorate
Accreditation: M, ACBSP, ANEST, ARCPA, CAATE, CACREP, COARC, COARCP, CS, ENG, NURSE, OT, PTA, RAD, SW

01 President ....Dr. Keith TAYLOR
05 VP Academic Affairs ....Dr. Walter IWANENKO, JR.
10 Vice President Finance/Admin .... Mrs. Linda L. WAGNER
30 Vice Pres University Advancement .... Mr. R. Scott RASH
88 Assoc Vice President for Mission .... Rev. Michael KESICKI
84 Vice President for Enrollment .... Mr. William EDMONDSON
32 VP Student Development & Engagement .... Mr. Brian NICHOLS
20 VP Academic Administration .... Dr. Steven A. MAURO
04 Assistant to the President ....Mrs. Darlene A. THEISEN
79 Dean Col Humanities/Educ/Soc Sci .... Dr. Linda FLEMING
54 Dean College Engineering/Business ......Dr. William L. SCHELLER
76 Int Dn Morosky Col Health Prof/Sci ....Dr. Sarah EWING
49 Director of Liberal Studies .... Dr. Penny L. SMITH
08 Director Nash Library ....Mr. Ken BRUNDAGE
37 Director of Financial Aid ....Ms. Sharon A. KRAHE
06 Registrar ....Ms. Kara A. MORGAN
36 Dir Career Develop/Employment Svcs . Mr. Brian COLLINGWOOD
39 Director of Residence Life .... Ms. Denise GOLDEN
23 Head Nurse ....Vacant
88 Dir Student Organiz/Leadership Dev ....Ms. Beth Ann SCHICK
44 Director Development ....Ms. Cathy FRESCH
26 Chief Marketing/Communications Ofcr ... Ms. Melanie A. WHALEY
102 Dir of Research/Foundation Rels ....Ms. Anita L. MILLER
21 Controller .... Mr. Jeffrey S. TAYLOR
45 Director of Budgeting ....Ms. Mary Kathleen LEONARD
15 Director of Human Resources ....Mr. Robert J. CLINE
41 Director of Athletics ....Ms. Lisa GODDARD MCGUIRK
19 Director Campus Police & Safety .... Mr. Les FETTERMAN
13 Director of Computing/Telecomm ....Mr. Mark JORDANO
42 University Chaplain ....Vacant
07 Director of Admissions ....Mr. Thomas P. CAMILLO
09 Director of Institutional Research ....Mr. Dana BAGWELL
18 Chief Facilities/Physical Plant .... Mr. Josh EBERLE
27 Chief Media Relations Officer ....Vacant
38 Director Student Counseling .... Mr. Brian COLLINGWOOD
86 Dir Community/Government Relations ...... Ms. Erika A. RAMALHO
96 Director of Purchasing ....Mr. Andrew TEETS
40 Bookstore Manager ....Ms. Amber COOK

Geisinger Commonwealth School of Medicine (I)

525 Pine Street, Scranton PA 18509
County: Lackawanna FICE Identification: 041672
Unit ID: 456542
Telephone: (570) 504-7000 Carnegie Class: Masters/S
FAX Number: (570) 504-9660 Calendar System: Semester
URL: www.tcmc.edu
Established: 2009 Annual Graduate Tuition & Fees: N/A
Enrollment: 442 Coed
Affiliation or Control: Independent Non-Profit IRS Status: 501(c)3
Highest Offering: Doctorate; No Undergraduates
Accreditation: M, MED

01 President and Dean .... Dr. Steven J. SCHEINMAN
10 VP for Finance & Admin/CFO .... Ms. Anna RUSNAK NOON
30 VP Institutional Advancement .... Ms. Marise GAROFALO
31 VP Cmty & Government Relations ....Ms. Ida L. CASTRO
05 VP Acad & Clin Affairs/Vice Dean .... Dr. William IOBST
45 VP Strategic Initiatives/Planning .... Mr. V. Scott KOERWER
32 Director of Student Affairs .... Ms. Julia KOLCHARNO
20 Assoc Dean of Fac Affairs/Fac Devel .... Ms. Andrea DIMATTIA
07 Assoc Dean Admission/Enrol/Fin Aid ......Ms. Michelle SCHMUDE
20 Assoc Dean of Curriculum ....Ms. Carien WILLIAMS
21 Dir Budgeting & Financial Services .... Mr. Sam DIAZ
13 Chief Information Technology Ofcr .... Mr. James MICHAELS
35 Asst Dean of Students .... Ms. Jacquelyn GHORMOZ
06 Registrar .... Mr. Edward LAHART
37 Director of Financial Aid ....Vacant
29 Dir Alumni Relations/Annual Giving .... Mr. Anthony CERNERA

Geneva College (J)

3200 College Avenue, Beaver Falls PA 15010-3557
County: Beaver FICE Identification: 003267
Unit ID: 212656
Telephone: (724) 846-5100 Carnegie Class: Masters/M
FAX Number: (724) 847-6687 Calendar System: Semester
URL: www.geneva.edu
Established: 1848 Annual Undergrad Tuition & Fees: $25,680
Enrollment: 1,714 Coed
Affiliation or Control: Reformed Presbyterian Church IRS Status: 501(c)3
Highest Offering: Master's
Accreditation: M, ACBSP, CACREP, ENG

01 President .... Dr. Calvin L. TROUP
03 Executive Vice President .... Mr. Larry K. GRIFFITH
05 Chief Academic Officer ....Dr. Melinda R. STEPHENS
30 Vice Pres of Advancement ....Vacant
10 Assoc Vice Pres & Controller ....Mr. Stephen C. ROSS
15 AVP Operations & Human Recources ....Mr. Timothy R. BAIRD
32 Dean of Students .... Mr. Brian C. JENSEN
20 Dean of Undergraduate Programs ....Dr. Melinda R. STEPHENS
84 Assoc VP for Enrollment .... Mr. David B. LAYTON
35 Director of Student Programs ....Mr. Ryan J. HOLT
58 Dean Grad/Adult & Online Programs ....Mr. John D. GALLO
06 Registrar .... Mrs. Jennifer L. CARTER
37 Director of Financial Aid ....Ms. Allyson BENTZ
08 Librarian ....Dr. John G. DONCEVIC
26 Director Public Relations ....Mrs. Cheryl L. JOHNSTON
29 Director of Alumni Relations .... Ms. Laura A. DEPIETRO
13 CIO & AVP Information Technology .... Mr. Scott F. BARNES
41 Director of Athletics .... Mr. Van G. ZANIC
18 Director of Physical Plant .... Mr. Robert M. SKOFF
36 Director of Career Development ....Mrs. Joy E. DOYLE
85 International Admissions Counselor .... Ms. Jillian MOOMAW
40 Campus Store Manager .... Ms. Rachael E. VAN DERVEER
19 Director of Security .... Mr. Dennis E. DAMAZO
93 Interim Coordinator of Diversity .... Mrs. Kristie A. MARTEL
92 Director of Honors Program ....Dr. Eric MILLER
39 Director of Residence Life ....Mr. Neil A. BEST
23 Health Services Director ....Mrs. Connie I. ERWIN

96 Director of Purchasing .... Mr. Joseph ANDINO
21 Accounting and Payroll Manager .... Ms. Ruth Ann HARTZEL
38 ACCESS Director .... Mr. Thomas C. PYLE
04 Administrative Asst to President .... Ms. Anfrea KAMICKER
09 Director of Institutional Research .... Mr. Jordan BOUSCHER
50 Business Dept Chair .... Dr. Gordon RICHARDS
53 Education Dept Chair .... Mrs. Adel G. AIKEN
54 Engineering Dept Chair .... Dr. James S. GIDLEY
90 Director of Technology Services .... Dr. Joseph D. HINES
07 Assoc Director of Admissions .... Mr. Joel A. BRUBAKER
104 Dir Crossroads/Ctr Special Progrm .... Dr. Jeffrey S. COLE
105 Online Marketing/Webmaster .... Mr. Michael W. DUNCAN

Gettysburg College (A)

300 N Washington Street, Gettysburg PA 17325-1486
County: Adams FICE Identification: 003268
Unit ID: 212674
Telephone: (717) 337-6000 Carnegie Class: Bac-A&S
FAX Number: (717) 337-6008 Calendar System: Semester
URL: www.gettysburg.edu
Established: 1832 Annual Undergrad Tuition & Fees: $50,860
Enrollment: 2,447 Coed
Affiliation or Control: Evangelical Lutheran Church In America
IRS Status: 501(c)3
Highest Offering: Baccalaureate
Accreditation: M, MUS

01 President .... Dr. Janet MORGAN RIGGS
03 Executive Vice President .... Ms. Jane D. NORTH
05 Provost .... Dr. Christopher ZAPPE
30 Vice Pres Dev & Alumni/Parent Rels .... Mr. Robert KALLIN
10 Vice President Finance/Treasurer .... Mr. Daniel T. KONSTALID
32 Vice President for College Life .... Dr. Julie L. RAMSEY
84 Vice Pres Enrollment/Education Svcs .... Ms. Barbara B. FRITZE
13 Vice President Information Tech .... Dr. Rod TOSTEN
45 Assoc Provost for Planning .... Mrs. Rhonda GOOD
28 Chief Diversity Officer .... Ms. Jeanne ARNOLD
21 Associate Vice President/Treasurer .... Mr. Christopher DELANEY
26 Exec Dir of Comm & Marketing .... Mr. Paul W. REDFERN
35 Associate Dean of College Life .... Mr. James P. DUFFY
110 Associate Vice Pres for Development .... Ms. Susan PYRON
85 Dir Intl Student Svcs/Multicul Eng .... Mr. Brad LANCASTER
06 Registrar .... Mr. Brian REESE
37 Director of Financial Aid .... Ms. Christina L. GORMLEY
07 Director Admissions .... Ms. Gail M. SWEEZEY
42 Chaplain .... Rev. Kristin LARGEN
09 Director for Institutional Analysis .... Ms. Suhua DONG
38 Exec Dir of Health & Counseling .... Ms. Kathy BRADLEY
36 Assoc Director of Career Services .... Mr. Manuel RUIZ
08 Dean of the Library .... Ms. Robin WAGNER
29 Exec Director of Alumni Relations .... Mr. Joe LYNCH
41 Asst VP for Athletics .... Mr. David W. WRIGHT
19 Exec Dir of Campus Safety/Security .... Mr. William J. LAFFERTY
18 Director Facilities Planning & Mgmt .... Mr. James BIESECKER
21 Dir of Financial Svs/Controller .... Ms. Sharon S. DAYHOFF
80 Director Center for Public Service .... Ms. Gretchen NATTER
39 Director Residence Life .... Ms. Danielle PHILLIPS
20 Dean of Academic Advising .... Ms. Gail Ann RICKERT
23 Director Health Services .... Ms. Susan S. REYNOLDS
35 Director Student Activities .... Mr. Joseph GURRERI
40 Director of College Bookstore .... Mr. Michael J. KOTLINSKI
94 Dir Women's Center .... Ms. Jennifer Q. MCCARY
96 Asst Director of Procurement .... Ms. Patricia K. VERDEROSA
15 Co-Director Human Resources .... Ms. Jennifer R. LUCAS
15 Co-Director Human Resources .... Ms. Regina Z. CAMPO
102 Asst Dir of Found/Govt Grants .... Ms. Laura RUNYAN
27 Dir of Comm & Media Relations .... Ms. Jamie YATES
104 Director of Off-Campus Studies .... Ms. Rebecca A. BERGREN
04 Administrative Asst to President .... Ms. Pamela EISENHART
109 Dir of Auxiliary Services .... Mr. Peter C. NORTH

Gratz College (B)

7605 Old York Road, Melrose Park PA 19027-3010
County: Montgomery FICE Identification: 004058
Unit ID: 212771
Telephone: (215) 635-7300 Carnegie Class: Spec-4-yr-Other
FAX Number: (215) 635-1046 Calendar System: Trimester
URL: www.gratz.edu
Established: 1895 Annual Undergrad Tuition & Fees: $19,772
Enrollment: 292 Coed
Affiliation or Control: Independent Non-Profit IRS Status: 501(c)3
Highest Offering: Doctorate
Accreditation: M

01 Interim President .... Rabbi Erin HIRSH
05 Dean and Vice Pres for Acad Affairs .... Dr. Rosalie GUZOFSKY
26 Chief Public Relations Officer .... Ms. Dodi KLIMOFF
08 Librarian .... Ms. Nancy NITZBERG
84 Director of Enrollment Management .... Ms. Ann PERAZZELLI
06 Director of Student Records .... Ms. Lovisa WOODSON
15 Director Personnel Services .... Ms. Yaffa HOWARD
09 Director of Institutional Research .... Vacant
07 Assistant Director of Admissions .... Ms. Mindy BLECHMAN
88 Dir Jewish Community High Sch .... Rabbi Erin HIRSH
37 Student Financial Services Advisor .... Ms. Michelle TAYLOR
105 Director Web Services .... Ms. Rose ACTOR-ENGEL
106 Dir Online Education/E-learning .... Ms. Deborah ARON
13 Chief Info Technology Officer .... Ms. Suzette MARTINEZ-QUILES
53 Director of Jewish Education Prog .... Dr. Saul WACHS
03 Executive Vice President .... Dr. Rosalie GUZOFSKY

18 Chief Facilities/Physical Plant .... Ernest COLLINS
04 Administrative Asst to President .... Ms. Dodi KLIMOFF

Great Lakes Institute of Technology (C)

5100 Peach Street, Erie PA 16509
County: Erie FICE Identification: 021122
Unit ID: 213181
Telephone: (814) 864-6666 Carnegie Class: Spec 2-yr-Health
FAX Number: (814) 868-1717 Calendar System: Other
URL: www.glit.edu
Established: 1965 Annual Undergrad Tuition & Fees: N/A
Enrollment: 381 Coed
Affiliation or Control: Proprietary IRS Status: Proprietary
Highest Offering: Associate Degree
Accreditation: ACCSC, DMS, SURGT

01 Executive Director .... Tony PICCIRILLO
07 Director of Admissions .... Barbara BOLT
37 Director Student Financial Aid .... Erin POULLIOTT
05 Director of Education .... Vickie CLEMENTS

Grove City College (D)

100 Campus Drive, Grove City PA 16127-2104
County: Mercer FICE Identification: 003269
Unit ID: 212805
Telephone: (724) 458-2000 Carnegie Class: Bac-A&S
FAX Number: (724) 458-2190 Calendar System: Semester
URL: www.gcc.edu
Established: 1876 Annual Undergrad Tuition & Fees: $16,630
Enrollment: 2,444 Coed
Affiliation or Control: Non-denominational IRS Status: 501(c)3
Highest Offering: Baccalaureate
Accreditation: M, ACBSP, CS, ENG, EXSC

01 President .... Mr. Paul J. MCNULTY
05 Provost & VP for Academic Affairs .... Dr. Robert J. GRAHAM
10 Vice Pres for Business & Finance .... Mr. Michael R. BUCKMAN
32 Vice Pres For Student Life/Learning .... Mr. Larry E. HARDESTY
111 Vice President for Inst Advancement .... Mr. Jeffrey D. PROKOVICH
11 Vice President for Operations .... Mr. James M. LOPRESTI
13 Vice Pres/Chief Information Officer .... Dr. Vincent F. DISTASI
84 VP of Enrollment Svcs & Registrar .... Dr. John G. INMAN
88 Vice Pres for Student Recruitment .... Mr. Lee S. WISHING, III
20 Assistant Provost .... Dr. P. Jesse RINE
100 Assistant to the President .... Ms. Betty L. TALLERICO
49 Dean of School of Arts/Letters .... Dr. David J. AYERS
81 Dean of School of Sci/Engr/Math .... Dr. Stacy G. BIRMINGHAM
21 Director of Financial Services .... Mrs. Michelle M. WILLIAMS
15 Director of Human Resources .... Mrs. Marci K. WAGNER
35 Assistant Dean of Students .... Mr. John M. COYNE
07 Director of Admissions .... Mrs. Sarah E. GIBBS
36 Director of Career Services .... Mrs. Amanda L. SPOSATO
08 Librarian .... Mrs. Barbra M. MUNNELL
37 Director of Financial Aid .... Mr. Thomas G. BALL
88 Dir Std Rec/Club Sports/Frat Life .... Mr. Andrew A. TONCIC, JR.
35 Director Stdnt Activities/Programs .... Mr. T. Scott GORDON
19 Director of Campus Safety .... Mr. Seth J. VAN TIL
23 Director of Health & Wellness Ctr .... Mrs. Amy E. PAGANO
40 Bookstore Manager .... Mrs. Carrie J. ROSE
41 Athletic Director .... Mr. Todd D. GIBSON
42 Dean of the Chapel .... Rev. F. Stanley KEEHLWETTER
29 Sr Dir Alumni & College Relations .... Mrs. Melissa A. MACLEOD
30 Sr Director of Development .... Mr. Brian M. POWELL
26 Sr Dir Marketing & Communications .... Mrs. Jacquelyn P. MULLER
38 Director of College Counseling .... Dr. Suzanne N. HOUK
39 Director of Residence Life .... Mrs. Lyndsay L. GRIMM

Gwynedd Mercy University (E)

1325 Sumneytown Pike, PO Box 901,
Gwynedd Valley PA 19437-0901
County: Montgomery FICE Identification: 003270
Unit ID: 212832
Telephone: (215) 646-7300 Carnegie Class: Masters/M
FAX Number: (215) 641-5596 Calendar System: Semester
URL: www.gmercyu.edu
Established: 1948 Annual Undergrad Tuition & Fees: $32,480
Enrollment: 2,582 Coed
Affiliation or Control: Roman Catholic IRS Status: 501(c)3
Highest Offering: Doctorate
Accreditation: M, COARC, IACBE, NURSE, RTT

01 President .... Ms. Deanne H. D'EMILIO
05 VP Academic Affairs .... Dr. Frank E. SCULLY, JR.
10 Vice President Finance & Admin .... Mr. Kevin O'FLAHERTY
111 Vice Pres Institutional Advancement .... Mr. Gerald MCLAUGHLIN
32 Interim VP for Student Services .... Sr. Catherine MCMAHON, RSM
42 VP Mission & Ministry .... Sr. Catherine MCMAHON, RSM
26 Chief Communications Officer .... Ms. Kelly STATMORE
84 Interim VP for Mktg & Enroll Mgmt .... Ms. Kelly STATMORE
101 Secretary of the Institution/Board .... Ms. Barbara MCHALE
108 AVP for Assessment & Compliance .... Dr. Dawn HAYWARD
06 Registrar .... Ms. Joanna VACCHIANO
08 Director of Library .... Mr. Daniel SCHABERT
37 Director of Student Financial Aid .... Ms. Elizabeth HOWARD
13 Chief Information Officer .... Mr. Joseph PUPPO
35 Dean of Students .... Dr. Carol GRUBER
29 Director Alumni Relations .... Ms. Gianna QUINN

35 Director Student Activities .... Dr. Rouseline EMMANUEL-FRENEL
09 Director of Institutional Research .... Dr. Jing GAO
15 Director Human Resources .... Ms. Rosina DEVER
18 Director of Physical Plant .... Mr. Kevin WALDRON
21 Controller .... Ms. Jennifer GINNETTI
38 Director Counseling .... Ms. Pamela MOORE
07 Director of Undergrad Admissions .... Ms. Michele DIEHL
96 Director of Purchasing/Payables .... Ms. Joyce SCHARLE
102 Dir Foundation/Corporate Relations .... Vacant
19 Director Campus Safety/Security .... Mr. James MCNESBY
41 Athletic Director .... Mr. Keith MONDILLO
39 Director Student Housing .... Mr. Bryan DUNPHY-CULP

Gwynedd Mercy University at East Norriton (F)

480 East Germantown Pike, East Norriton PA 19401
Telephone: (215) 643-8458 Identification: 770155
Accreditation: &M

† Tuition varies by degree program. Additional sites include Gwynedd Mercy University Philadelphia and Gwynedd Mercy University Bensalem.

HACC, Central Pennsylvania's Community College (G)

1 HACC Drive, Harrisburg PA 17110-2999
County: Dauphin FICE Identification: 003273
Unit ID: 212878
Telephone: (800) 222-4222 Carnegie Class: Assoc/HT-High Trad
FAX Number: (717) 909-1491 Calendar System: Semester
URL: www.hacc.edu
Established: 1964 Annual Undergrad Tuition & Fees (In-District): $6,525
Enrollment: 19,121 Coed
Affiliation or Control: State/Local IRS Status: 501(c)3
Highest Offering: Associate Degree
Accreditation: M, ACBSP, ACFEI, ADNUR, ART, COARC, CSHSE, CVT, DA, DH, DMS, EMT, MAC, MLTAD, PNUR, RAD, SURGT

01 President/CEO .... Dr. John J. SYGIELSKI
05 Provost/VP Academic Affairs .... Dr. Cynthia A. DOHERTY
32 VP Student Affairs/Enrollment Mgmt .... Vacant
10 Vice Pres Finance/CFO .... Mr. Timothy SANDOE
111 VP College Advancement .... Dr. Linnie S. CARTER
20 Assoc Provost Academic Affairs .... Dr. Kathleen T. DOHERTY
103 Assoc Provost Workforce Development .... Mr. Victor RODGERS
15 Chief HR Officer .... Ms. Aimee B. BROUGH
28 Chief Inclusion/Diversity Officer .... Dr. Warren R. ANDERSON
12 Campus VP Harrisburg Campus .... Vacant
12 Campus VP Lancaster/Lebanon .... Mr. Victor E. RAMOS
12 Exec Dir Lebanon Campus .... Ms. Laurie A. BOWERSOX
12 Campus VP Gettysburg .... Ms. Shannon S. HARVEY
12 Campus VP York .... Dr. Darryl E. JONES
106 Exec Dir Virtual Learning Outreach .... Ms. Amy S. WITHROW
08 Executive Director HACC Libraries .... Ms. Beth A. EVITTS
121 Dean Student/Acad Success .... Vacant
06 Registrar .... Ms. Genita D. MANGUM
26 VP Information Technology/CIO .... Mr. Robert H. MESSNER
96 Director Procurement .... Mr. William W. BYRNES
19 Director Safety and Security .... Mr. Ivan A. QUINONES
30 Dir Develop and Alumni Relations .... Ms. Hope A. HARRISON
40 Director College Bookstores .... Mr. Kyle J. DIBRITO
21 Controller .... Mr. Sanjiv NAYYAR
09 Exec Dir Inst Effectiveness .... Mr. Lynold K. MCGHEE
37 Director Financial Aid .... Mr. Andrew E. MARAH
84 Dean Enrollment Management .... Vacant
102 Executive Director HACC Foundation .... Dr. Linnie S. CARTER

Harcum College (H)

750 Montgomery Avenue, Bryn Mawr PA 19010-3476
County: Montgomery FICE Identification: 003272
Unit ID: 212869
Telephone: (610) 525-4100 Carnegie Class: Assoc/MT-VT-High Trad
FAX Number: (610) 526-6009 Calendar System: Semester
URL: www.harcum.edu
Established: 1915 Annual Undergrad Tuition & Fees: $22,760
Enrollment: 1,636 Coed
Affiliation or Control: Independent Non-Profit IRS Status: 501(c)3
Highest Offering: Associate Degree
Accreditation: M, ADNUR, DA, DH, HT, MLTAD, OTA, PHLEB, PTAA, #RAD

01 President .... Dr. Jon Jay DETEMPLE
05 VP of Academic & Legal Affairs .... Ms. Julia INGERSOLL
10 Vice Pres of Finance & Operations .... Dr. Patricia BENSON
32 Dean of Student Life .... Mr. Urick LEWIS
84 Exec Dir Enrollment Management .... Ms. Rachel BOWEN
111 VP of College Advancement .... Vacant
20 Asst VP Academic Support Services .... Ms. Koyuki YIP
51 Exec Dir of Partnership Sites .... Ms. Evelyn SANTANA
18 Facilities Manager .... Mr. Nikolay KARPALO
15 Exec Dir of HR & Compliance Officer .... Ms. Claudine VITA
06 Registrar .... Ms. Karen GREEN
08 Director of Library Services .... Ms. Katie MCGOWAN
85 Director of International Programs .... Mr. Daniel STABB
26 Dir of Communications & Marketing .... Ms. Gale MARTIN
29 Director of Alumni Relations .... Ms. Melissa SAMANGO
38 Director of Counseling Services .... Ms. Kathy ANTHONY
36 Dir of Career & Transfer Services .... Ms. Danyele DOVE
37 Director of Financial Aid .... Ms. Melissa WALSH
39 Director of Residence Life .... Mr. Jameel TUCKER
35 Director of Campus Activities .... Ms. Laurie PLAZA
21 Director of Business Services .... Mr. Stephen KLEPONIS

19 Director of Campus Safety ... Mr. Rick SANFILIPPO
41 Director of Athletics ... Mr. Drew KELLY
04 Executive Assistant to President ... Ms. Margaret WALLACE
13 Director of IT Services ... Mr. Joseph DONAHUE
09 Director of Institutional Research ... Mr. Tim ELY
101 Secretary of the Institution/Board ... Ms. Margaret T. WALLACE
106 Dir Online Education/E-learning ... Mr. Stephen PIPITONE
108 Director Institutional Assessment ... Mr. Tim ELY
50 Director of Business Mgmt Program ... Mr. Mike PRUSHAN
86 External Affairs ... Dr. Jon Jay DETEMPLE
102 Dir Foundation/Corporate Relations ... Ms. Bernadette WALSH

Harrisburg Area Community College Gettysburg Campus (A)

731 Old Harrisburg Road, Gettysburg PA 17325
Telephone: (717) 337-3855 Identification: 770156
Accreditation: &M

Harrisburg Area Community College Lancaster Campus (B)

1641 Old Philadelphia Pike, Lancaster PA 17602
Telephone: (717) 293-5000 Identification: 770157
Accreditation: &M

Harrisburg Area Community College Lebanon Campus (C)

735 Cumberland Street, Lebanon PA 17042
Telephone: (717) 270-4222 Identification: 770158
Accreditation: &M

Harrisburg Area Community College York Campus (D)

2010 Pennsylvania Avenue, York PA 17404
Telephone: (717) 718-0328 Identification: 770159
Accreditation: &M

Harrisburg University of Science and Technology (E)

326 Market Street, Harrisburg PA 17101-2116
County: Dauphin FICE Identification: 039483
Unit ID: 446640
Telephone: (717) 901-5100 Carnegie Class: Masters/S
FAX Number: (717) 901-3152 Calendar System: Trimester
URL: www.harrisburgu.edu
Established: 2001 Annual Undergrad Tuition & Fees: $23,900
Enrollment: 2,099 Coed
Affiliation or Control: Independent Non-Profit IRS Status: 501(c)3
Highest Offering: Doctorate
Accreditation: M

01 President ... Dr. Eric D. DARR
05 Provost/Chief Academic Officer ... Dr. Bili S. MATTES
10 Vice Pres Finance & Chief Fin Ofcr ... Mr. Duane F. MAUN
103 VP Strategic Workforce Devel ... Ms. Kelly POWELL LOGAN
26 Assoc VP Comm/Marketing/Alum Rels ... Mr. Steven M. INFANTI
88 Assoc VP for University Centers ... Ms. Kelly POWELL LOGAN
15 Assoc VP Human Resources ... Mr. Ben ALLATT
13 Assoc VP/Chief Technology Officer ... Mr. Alex C. PITZNER
108 Director of Assessment ... Ms. Penny L. WEIDNER
30 Director of Advancement ... Ms. Amy SCHREIBER
37 Director Financial Aid ... Mr. Vincent P. FRANK
06 Associate Registrar ... Ms. Debra ALTHOFF
07 Director Undergraduate Admission ... Ms. Laurie BARROW
08 University Librarian ... Mr. David RUNYON
32 Asst Director of Student Affairs ... Ms. Kimberly BOWMAN

Haverford College (F)

370 Lancaster Avenue, Haverford PA 19041-1392
County: Delaware & Montgomery FICE Identification: 003274
Unit ID: 212911
Telephone: (610) 896-1000 Carnegie Class: Bac-A&S
FAX Number: (610) 896-4202 Calendar System: Semester
URL: www.haverford.edu
Established: 1833 Annual Undergrad Tuition & Fees: $51,259
Enrollment: 1,233 Coed
Affiliation or Control: Independent Non-Profit IRS Status: 501(c)3
Highest Offering: Master's
Accreditation: M

01 President ... Dr. Kimberly W. BENSTON
05 Provost ... Dr. Frances R. BLASE
10 SVP Finance/Chief Admin Officer ... Mitchell L. WEIN
30 VP for Institutional Advancement ... Ann W. FIGUEREDO
20 Dean of the College ... Dr. Martha DENNEY
07 VP & Dean of Admission ... Jess LORD
104 Dean of Intl Academic Programs ... Dr. Donna MANCINI
89 Dean of First Year Students ... Michael MARTINEZ
115 Chief Investment Officer ... Michael CASEL
88 Asst VP Institutional Advancement ... Diane WILDER
100 VP & Chief of Staff ... Dr. Jesse LYTLE
41 Director of Athletics ... Wendall SMITH
26 Asst VP College Communications ... Chris MILLS
09 Director of Institutional Research ... Catherine FENNELL
08 Librarian ... Dr. Terry SNYDER
15 Director of Human Resources ... T. Muriel BRISBON
21 Assoc VP & Controller ... Deborah FULLAM
96 Director of Purchasing ... Nikoletta MILLAS
18 Director of Physical Plant ... Donald CAMPBELL
19 Director of Safety & Security ... Thomas KING
88 Director Conferences/Dir Campus Ctr ... Geoffey LABE
109 Assoc Director of Dining Services ... Joseph BINOTTO
40 Bookstore Manager ... Lydia WHITELAW
39 Director of Student Housing ... Marianne SMITH
34 Director of Women's Center ... Vacant
23 Director of Health Services ... Catherine SHARBAUGH
38 Director Counseling/Disability Svcs ... Dr. Philip ROSENBAUM
36 Dean of Career & Prof Advising ... Kelly CLEARY
06 Registrar ... James KEANE
37 Director of Financial Aid ... Michael COLAHAN
29 Director of Alumni & Parent Rels ... Lauren PORTNOY
44 Director of Individual Giving ... Deborah STRECKER
112 Director of Gift Planning ... Steven KAVANAUGH
20 AVP for Academic Resources ... Dr. John MOSTELLER
28 Assoc Dean Diversity/Access/Engage ... Dr. Theresa TENSUAN
32 Asst Dean of Student Activities ... Michael ELIAS
13 Chief Information Officer ... Megan FITCH
04 Administrative Asst to President ... Joan WANKMILLER

Holy Family University (G)

9801 Frankford Avenue, Philadelphia PA 19114-2009
County: Philadelphia FICE Identification: 003275
Unit ID: 212984
Telephone: (215) 637-7700 Carnegie Class: Masters/L
FAX Number: (215) 637-3787 Calendar System: Semester
URL: www.holyfamily.edu
Established: 1954 Annual Undergrad Tuition & Fees: $29,750
Enrollment: 2,711 Coed
Affiliation or Control: Roman Catholic IRS Status: 501(c)3
Highest Offering: Doctorate
Accreditation: M, ACBSP, IFSAC, NURSE, RAD

01 President ... Sr. Maureen MCGARRITY
10 Vice Pres Finance & Administration ... Mr. James TRUSDELL
05 VP for Academic Affairs ... Dr. Michael MARKOWITZ
42 Vice President for Mission ... Ms. Margaret S. KELLY
13 Vice Pres Information Technology ... Mr. Eugene KOVALCHICK
32 Dean of Students ... Sr. Marcella BINKOWSKI
111 VP for University Advancement ... Dr. James GARVEY
32 VP for Student Affairs ... Dr. Alexandra ADAMS
06 Assoc VP Academic Svcs/Registrar ... Dr. Ann Marie VICKERY
51 Assoc VP Academic Ops & Cont Ed ... Dr. Karen GALARDI
35 Assoc VP for Student Life ... Mr. Michael MCNULTY
28 Assoc VP Inst Effective/Diversity ... Dr. Nicole STOKES-DUPASS
37 Director Student Financial Aid ... Ms. Janice HETRICK
21 Associate VP/Controller & Treas ... Ms. Judy KLEIN
15 Asst VP for Human Resources ... Ms. Jennifer LULING
08 Exec Director Library Services ... Ms. Shannon BROWN
36 Director of Careers Center ... Mr. Don BROM
26 Exec Dir Marketing/Communications ... Ms. Heather DOTCHEL
38 Director Counseling Center ... Mr. John WATSON
42 Chaplain/Dir Campus Ministry ... Rev. James MACNEW
07 Executive Director of Admissions ... Ms. Lauren CAMPBELL
41 Assoc VP/Dir Athletics ... Ms. Sandra MICHAEL
53 Dean of the School of Education ... Dr. Kevin ZOOK
66 Dean Nursing/Allied Health Prof ... Dr. Cynthia RUSSELL
49 Dean of School of Arts & Sciences ... Dr. Rochelle ROBBINS
50 Dean of School of Business Admin ... Dr. J. Barry DICKINSON
29 Asst Dir Alumni & Parent Giving ... Ms. Julie REMPFER
09 Director of Institutional Research ... Mr. Chad L. MAY
18 Director Campus Operations ... Mr. Ralph CARP
28 Coordinator Diversity ... Vacant
39 Assoc Director Residence Life ... Ms. Kim MAGUIRE
102 Dir Foundation/Corporate Relations ... Vacant
100 Special Asst to the President ... Ms. Kate BRESLIN
105 Web Specialist ... Mr. Robert TOEPPNER
19 Director Security/Safety-Allied ... Mr. Dave NEUMAN
85 Dir International Student Affairs ... Sr. Josita CHURLA
23 Director of Health Services ... Ms. Julie SCHERPENBERG
108 Dir Inst Assessment and Accred ... Dr. Lisa BELFIELD
30 Asst VP for Development ... Mr. Josha LISS

Hussian College (H)

1500 Spring Garden Street, Philadelphia PA 19130
County: Philadelphia FICE Identification: 007469
Unit ID: 212993
Telephone: (215) 574-9600 Carnegie Class: Spec-4-yr-Arts
FAX Number: (215) 574-9800 Calendar System: Semester
URL: www.hussiancikkege.edu
Established: 1946 Annual Undergrad Tuition & Fees: $19,650
Enrollment: 73 Coed
Affiliation or Control: Proprietary IRS Status: Proprietary
Highest Offering: Baccalaureate
Accreditation: ACCSC

01 President ... Dr. Jeremiah STAROPOLI
32 Dir of Student Services/Registrar ... Ms. Maureen P. FLANAGAN
37 Director Financial Aid ... Ms. Susan J. COHEN
07 Director of Admissions ... Mr. Peter BROOKS
10 Director of Finance ... Mr. Eric STRUBEL
11 Administrative Services Coordinator ... Ms. Jodi BRABAZON

Immaculata University (I)

1145 King Road, Immaculata PA 19345-0654
County: Chester FICE Identification: 003276
Unit ID: 213011
Telephone: (610) 647-4400 Carnegie Class: DU-Mod
FAX Number: (610) 251-1668 Calendar System: Semester
URL: www.immaculata.edu
Established: 1920 Annual Undergrad Tuition & Fees: $35,210
Enrollment: 2,961 Coed
Affiliation or Control: Roman Catholic IRS Status: 501(c)3
Highest Offering: Doctorate
Accreditation: M, ACBSP, #CAATE, CACREP, CLPSY, DIETD, DIETI, IPSY, MUS, NURSE

01 President ... Ms. Barbara LETTIERE
05 Vice President Academic Affairs ... Dr. Maria GREEN COWLES
10 Vice Pres Finance/Administration ... Ms. Janet GARRITY
111 Vice Pres Advancement/Communication ... Vacant
32 Vice Pres Student Development ... Ms. Patti CANTERINO
84 Vice President Enrollment Mgmt ... Mr. Gerald WARGO
42 Vice Pres of Mission and Ministry ... Sr. Mary HENRICH, IHM
20 Assistant VP of Academic Affairs ... Dr. Angela TEKELY
06 Acting Registrar ... Dr. Angela TEKELY
26 Exec Director of Communications ... Ms. Melissa KUSHNER
15 Exec Director of Human Res/Title IX ... Ms. Geri LARSEN
08 Executive Director of Library ... Dr. Jeffrey ROLLISON
90 Director Academic Technology ... Ms. Sharon AINSLEY
14 Director of Technology Services ... Mr. Robert IANNELLI
37 Director Student Financial Aid ... Mr. Robert FOREST
112 Director Planned Giving ... Sr. Rita O'LEARY, IHM
91 Director Administrative Computing ... Mr. Grant DAVIS
102 Dir Corp/Foundation and Government ... Ms. Laura CHISHOLM
29 Director Alumni Relations ... Ms. Karen MATWEYCHUK
36 Director Career Development ... Ms. Kathleen MCCAULEY
41 Athletic Director ... Ms. Janelle CRONMILLER
104 Director Study Abroad ... Sr. Elaine GLANZ, IHM
85 International Student Advisor ... Sr. Catarin CONJAR, IHM
42 Chaplain ... Fr. Samuel VERRUNI
20 Dean of Academic Affairs ... Ms. Mary Kate BOLAND
58 Dean College of Graduate Studies ... Dr. Thomas O'BRIEN
34 Dean College of Undergrad Studies ... Dr. Jean SHINGLE
51 Acting Dean Lifelong Learning ... Ms. Kate KEARNEY
19 Director Campus Safety & Protection ... Mr. Dennis DOUGHERTY
88 Director of Business Systems Analys ... Ms. June GORMAN
38 Director Counseling Services ... Vacant
18 Director of Facilities ... Mr. Jeff BROWN
25 Director of Sponsored Research ... Ms. Kathryn DUMAS
39 Director Res Life & Student Housing ... Ms. Rhonda FIORESI
108 Assoc Director Academic Assessment ... Ms. Bobbijo PINNELLI
13 Chief Info Technology Officer (CIO) ... Mr. Mike SALEM
09 Office Inst Research/Effectiveness ... Ms. Cecelia OSWALD
04 Administrative Asst to President ... Ms. Leslie BOKOSKI
106 Online Education/E-learning ... Dr. Angela TEKELY
121 Exec Director of Academic Success ... Sr. Joseph Marie CARTER, IHM
07 Exec Director of Admissions ... Vacant

Institute of Medical and Business Careers (J)

133 Jefferson Rd, Ste 101, Pittsburgh PA 15235
County: Allegheny FICE Identification: 041551
Telephone: (412) 244-3240 Carnegie Class: Not Classified
FAX Number: (412) 244-3241 Calendar System: Other
URL: www.imbc.edu
Established: Annual Undergrad Tuition & Fees: N/A
Enrollment: N/A Coed
Affiliation or Control: Proprietary IRS Status: Proprietary
Highest Offering: Associate Degree
Accreditation: ABHES

01 Director ... Ms. Jennifer SMITH

International Institute for Restorative Practices (K)

P.O. Box 229, Bethlehem PA 18016-0229
County: Northampton FICE Identification: 042061
Unit ID: 448691
Telephone: (610) 807-9221 Carnegie Class: Spec-4-yr-Other
FAX Number: (610) 807-0423 Calendar System: Trimester
URL: www.iirp.edu
Established: 2005 Annual Graduate Tuition & Fees: N/A
Enrollment: 67 Coed
Affiliation or Control: Independent Non-Profit IRS Status: 501(c)3
Highest Offering: Master's; No Undergraduates
Accreditation: M

01 President ... Dr. John BAILIE
05 Provost ... Dr. Craig ADAMSON
11 Vice President for Administration ... Ms. Linda B. KLIGMAN

JNA Institute of Culinary Arts (L)

1212 S Broad Street, Philadelphia PA 19146-3119
County: Philadelphia FICE Identification: 031033
Unit ID: 419341
Telephone: (215) 468-8800 Carnegie Class: Spec 2-yr-A&S
FAX Number: (215) 468-8838 Calendar System: Quarter
URL: www.culinaryarts.edu
Established: 1988 Annual Undergrad Tuition & Fees: $12,725
Enrollment: 43 Coed
Affiliation or Control: Proprietary IRS Status: Proprietary
Highest Offering: Associate Degree
Accreditation: ACCSC

01 Director Mr. Joseph DIGIRONIMO
07 Director of Admission Ms. Cheryl FREEDMAN

Johnson College (A)

3427 North Main Avenue, Scranton PA 18508-1495
County: Lackawanna
FICE Identification: 021142
Unit ID: 213233
Telephone: (570) 702-8900
Carnegie Class: Assoc/HVT-High Trad
FAX Number: (570) 348-2181
Calendar System: Semester
URL: www.johnson.edu
Established: 1912
Annual Undergrad Tuition & Fees: $18,235
Enrollment: 469
Coed
Affiliation or Control: Independent Non-Profit
IRS Status: 501(c)3
Highest Offering: Associate Degree
Accreditation: @M, ACCSC, PTAA, RAD

01 President & CEO Dr. Ann L. PIPINSKI
10 Chief Financial Officer Mr. Jeffrey NOVAK
09 Sr Director of Inst Effectiveness Ms. Sue PHILLIPS
03 Executive Vice President Ms. Katie LEONARD
04 Assistant to the President Ms. Julia JACIEN
07 Sr Dir Strategic Enroll Mgmt Ms. Rita LAPERA
08 Librarian Mr. Ron KRYSIEWSKI
32 Manager of Student Engagement Ms. Tara KARMOL
38 Counselor/Manager Disability Svcs Ms. Emily HOLMES
06 Assistant Registrar Ms. Aubree ARMEZZANI
11 Chief Administrative Officer Mr. Mike NOVAK
13 Director of Network & Systems Admin Mr. Wil ESBRANDT
15 Sr Director Org Development Ms. Stephenie VERGNETTI
18 Facilities & Planning Manager Mr. Joseph MUSHENO
26 Assoc Director of Communications Ms. Sean Ann KELLY
30 Manager of Development Ms. Tracey PRATT
36 Director of Career Services Ms. Roseann MARTINETTI
37 Sr Dir Financial Aid & Stdnt Care Ms. Liz RENDA
39 Coord Student Conduct & Housing Mr. Nolan RENZ

Juniata College (B)

1700 Moore Street, Huntingdon PA 16652-2119
County: Huntingdon
FICE Identification: 003279
Unit ID: 213251
Telephone: (814) 641-3000
Carnegie Class: Bac-A&S
FAX Number: (814) 641-3199
Calendar System: Semester
URL: www.juniata.edu
Established: 1876
Annual Undergrad Tuition & Fees: $42,170
Enrollment: 1,583
Coed
Affiliation or Control: Independent Non-Profit
IRS Status: 501(c)3
Highest Offering: Master's
Accreditation: M, IACBE, SW

01 President Dr. James A. TROHA
05 Provost Dr. Lauren BOWEN
84 VP Enrollment and Retention Mr. Robert E. YELNOSKY
10 Vice President Finance/Operations Ms. Christine GIBSON
111 Vice President Advancement/Mktg Mr. Gabriel WELSCH
32 VP Student Life & Dean of Students Dr. Matthew DAMSCHRODER
13 Asst VP/Chief Information Officer Ms. Anne WOOD
27 Exec Director of Marketing Ms. Rosann BROWN
07 Dean of Enrollment Ms. Michelle M. BARTOL
85 Dean of International Education Ms. Kati R. CSOMAN
06 Registrar Ms. Lucille CONDRON
36 Director Career Services Dr. Darwin V. KYSOR
37 Dir Student Financial Plng Ms. Tracie M. PATRICK
08 Dean of the Library Ms. Lisa MCDANIELS
91 Director Admin Information Svcs Mr. Rick BROWN
15 Director of Human Resources Ms. Gail L. ULRICH
09 Dir Institutional Planning/Research Ms. Carlee K. RANALLI
18 Director of Facilities Services Mr. Tristan S. DEL GIUDICE
19 Director Public Safety Mr. Jesse W. LEONARD
41 Athletic Director Mr. Greg M. CURLEY
90 Dir Technology Solutions Center Mr. Joel C. PHEASANT
113 Bursar Ms. Lauren A. PEROW
114 Budget Director Ms. Susan F. SHONTZ
21 Controller Ms. Karla D. WISER
30 Executive Director of Development Mr. Joseph M. SCIALABBA
35 Assistant Dean of Students Ms. Ellen CAMPBELL
42 College Chaplain Mr. Lowell D. WITKOVSKY
124 Director of Student Engagement Ms. Erin PASCHAL
88 Director of Conferences & Events Ms. Lorri P. SHIDELER
07 Senior Associate Dean of Admission Ms. Terri L. BOLLMAN-DALANSKY
38 College Counselor Ms. Kerry HARPER
28 Asst to Pres Diversity & Inclusion Vacant
29 Director Alumni Relations Mr. David D. MEADOWS
39 Director of Residential Life Ms. Tasia Y. WHITE
04 Executive Asst to President Mrs. Bethany D. SHEFFIELD

Keystone College (C)

One College Green, P.O. Box 50,
La Plume PA 18440-0200
County: Lackawanna
FICE Identification: 003280
Unit ID: 213303
Telephone: (570) 945-8000
Carnegie Class: Bac-Diverse
FAX Number: (570) 945-8962
Calendar System: Semester
URL: www.keystone.edu
Established: 1868
Annual Undergrad Tuition & Fees: $25,798
Enrollment: 1,459
Coed
Affiliation or Control: Independent Non-Profit
IRS Status: 501(c)3
Highest Offering: Master's
Accreditation: M, IACBE

01 President Dr. David L. COPPOLA
05 Provost & VP Academic Affairs Dr. Tracy BRUNDAGE
10 Vice Pres Finance & Administration Mr. Stuart RENDA
111 Vice President for Advancement Ms. Heather SCHIELD
84 Vice Pres Enrollment & Marketing Dr. Janine BECKER
32 Dean of Student Life Ms. Nicole LANGAN
08 Associate Dean of Miller Library Ms. Mari FLYNN
07 Director of Admissions Ms. Jennifer SEKOL
06 Registrar Ms. Kate OWENS
37 Dir Financial Assistance & Planning Ms. Delaina JAYNE
13 Chief Information Officer Mr. Charles L. PROTHERO
15 Director of Human Resources Ms. Alberta GRUSHINSKI
26 Senior Director College Relations Mr. Fran CALPIN
29 Director of Alumni Engagement Ms. Ehrin CLARK
36 Director Career Development Ms. Kourtney SHICK
09 Director Institutional Research Mr. Curtis BAUMAN
41 Director of Athletics Dr. Matthew GRIMALDI

King's College (D)

133 N River Street, Wilkes-Barre PA 18711-0801
County: Luzerne
FICE Identification: 003282
Unit ID: 213321
Telephone: (570) 208-5900
Carnegie Class: Masters/S
FAX Number: (570) 825-9049
Calendar System: Semester
URL: www.kings.edu
Established: 1946
Annual Undergrad Tuition & Fees: $34,720
Enrollment: 2,310
Coed
Affiliation or Control: Roman Catholic
IRS Status: 501(c)3
Highest Offering: Master's
Accreditation: M, ARCPA, CAATE, CAEPN

01 President Rev. John RYAN, CSC
05 Provost & VP for Academic Affairs Dr. Joseph EVAN
10 Executive VP for Business Affairs Mr. John LOYACK
111 Vice President for Inst Advancement Mr. Frederick PETTIT
32 Vice President for Student Affairs Ms. Janet E. MERCINCAVAGE
84 Vice President for Enrollment Mgmt Mr. Corry UNIS
04 Exec Assistant to the President Mrs. Anne NOONE
13 Associate VP/Chief Info Officer Mr. Paul J. MORAN
08 Director of Library Dr. Terrence F. MECH
35 Assoc Vice Pres Student Affairs Mr. Robert B. MCGONIGLE
50 Dean Wm G McGowan Sch Business Dr. Barry WILLIAMS
06 Registrar Mr. Daniel T. CEBRICK
37 Director of Financial Aid Ms. Donna CERZA
42 Chaplain/Director Campus Ministry Rev. Thomas LOONEY, CSC
36 Director Career Planning & Placemnt Mr. Christopher SUTZKO
15 Associate VP Human Resources Ms. Kristin FINO
26 Director of Public Relations Mr. John MCANDREW
29 Director of Alumni Relations Ms. Patrice PERSICO
18 Executive Director of Facilities Mr. Thomas BUTCHKO
19 Director of Security/Safety Mr. James GILGALLON
41 Dir of Intercollegiate Athletics Ms. Cheryl J. ISH
21 Controller Mr. Thomas GRABER
39 Director of Residence Life Ms. Megan SELLICK
09 Director of Institutional Research Ms. Marian K. PALMERI
28 Director of College Diversity Ms. Jasmine TABRON
90 Managing Dir of User Services Mr. Raymond G. PRYOR
91 Managing Director for MIS Mr. William M. CORCORAN
112 Major Gifts Officer Mr. Richard LANAHAN
104 Director Study Abroad Ms. Margaret KOWALSKY

La Roche College (E)

9000 Babcock Boulevard, Pittsburgh PA 15237-5898
County: Allegheny
FICE Identification: 003987
Unit ID: 213358
Telephone: (412) 367-9300
Carnegie Class: Bac-Diverse
FAX Number: (412) 536-1062
Calendar System: Semester
URL: www.laroche.edu
Established: 1963
Annual Undergrad Tuition & Fees: $27,000
Enrollment: 1,523
Coed
Affiliation or Control: Roman Catholic
IRS Status: 501(c)3
Highest Offering: Doctorate
Accreditation: M, ACBSP, ADNUR, ANEST, ART, CIDA, NUR

01 President Sr. Candace INTROCASO, CDP
04 Exec Asst to the President Ms. Karen P. WILLOUGHBY
05 VP for Acad Affairs & Acad Dean Dr. Howard J. ISHIYAMA
84 VP for Enrollment Mgmt Dr. James (Chip) E. WEISGERBER
10 VP for Business & Finance Mr. Robert VOGEL
32 VP for Student Life/Dean Stdnts Ms. Colleen RUEFLE
111 VP for Institutional Advancement Mr. Michael ANDREOLA
20 Assoc VP Academic Affairs Dr. Rosemary MCCARTHY
20 Assoc VP Academic Affairs Dr. Thomas G. SCHAEFER
121 Assoc Dean Academic/Student Support Ms. Marie DEEM
35 Director of Student Development Mr. David DAY
83 Div Chair Natural & Behavioral Sci Ms. Jane ARNOLD
79 Div Chair Humanities Dr. Jeff RITTER
50 Div Co-Chair Business Dr. Lynn ARCHER
50 Div Co-Chair Business Ms. Shelia MUELLER
57 Div Chair Design Ms. Lisa KAMPHAUS
53 Div Co-Chair Education & Nursing Dr. Kathryn SILVIS
53 Div Co-Chair Education & Nursing Dr. Terri LIBERTO
06 Registrar Ms. Joan CUTONE
08 Director Library/Learning Center Ms. Laverne COLLINS
07 Executive Director for Enrollment Ms. Hope SCHIFFGENS
26 Assoc VP Mktg & Media Relations Mr. Brady BUTLER
37 Director of Financial Aid Ms. Sharon PLATT
41 Director of Athletics Mr. Jim TINKEY
42 Director of Mission & Ministry Sr. Elena ALMENDAREZ
39 Director Residence Life Vacant
13 Director Information Technology Ms. Terri BALLARD
85 Director International Student Svcs Dr. Natasha GARRETT
29 Director Alumni Relations Ms. Gina MILLER
21 Director of Finance Ms. Cathleen JACOBS
09 Director of Institutional Research Ms. Patricia A. CONNOLLY
18 Assoc VP of Facilities Management Mr. J.R YOUNG
38 Director Counseling Services Ms. Lori AREND
19 Director Public Safety Mr. Mark WILCOX
15 Assoc VP of Human Resources Ms. Eileen PETRONE
40 Bookstore Manager Ms. Michelle JAMES
113 Director of Student Accounts Ms. Danya TINKEY
101 Secretary of the Institution/Board Ms. Kathy KOZDEMBA
104 Coordinator Study Abroad Ms. Nicole GABLE
44 Director Annual Giving & Advance Sv Mr. Craig BRUNO
86 Director Government Relations Mr. Michael ANDREOLA
102 Dir Foundation/Corporate Relations Ms. Janet DENNIS
28 Director of Diversity and Inclusion Ms. Candace OKELLO

La Salle University (F)

1900 W Olney Avenue, Philadelphia PA 19141-1199
County: Philadelphia
FICE Identification: 003287
Unit ID: 213367
Telephone: (215) 951-1000
Carnegie Class: Masters/L
FAX Number: N/A
Calendar System: Semester
URL: www.lasalle.edu
Established: 1863
Annual Undergrad Tuition & Fees: $41,100
Enrollment: 5,683
Coed
Affiliation or Control: Roman Catholic
IRS Status: 501(c)3
Highest Offering: Doctorate
Accreditation: M, ANEST, CACREP, CLPSY, DIETC, DIETD, MFCD, NURSE, PH, SP, SW

01 President Dr. Colleen M. HANYCZ
05 Provost/VP Academic Affairs Dr. Brian A. GOLDSTEIN
04 Exec Assistant to the President Bro. Joseph WILLARD
111 VP University Advancement Ms. Cathleen PARSONS-NIKOLIC
10 VP Finance and Administration Mrs. Stephanie PRICKEN
32 VP Student Affairs Dr. Dawn M. SOUFLERIS
84 VP for Enrollment Mr. Thomas F. DELAHUNT, III
43 Vice President and General Counsel Mr. Kevin DOLAN
20 Assistant Provost Bro. John MCGOLDRICK
07 Asst VP Enrollment Services Ms. Kathryn PAYNE
30 Asst VP Development Mr. Richard VAN FOSSEN, JR.
49 Int Dean School of Arts & Sciences Dr. Lynn A. TEXTER
50 Int Dean School of Business Admin Ms. MarySheila A. MCDONALD
66 Dean School of Nursing/Health Sci Dr. Kathleen CZEKANSKI
22 Affirmative Action Officer/Title IX Ms. Rose Lee PAULINE
26 Chief Mktg and Chief Comm Officer Ms. Jaine LUCAS
29 Asst VP Alumni Relations Mr. Trey P. ULRICH
88 Exec Dir Advancement Operations Mr. Melissa SLY
82 Dir Grad Ctr/East Eur Studies Vacant
77 Director Grad Computer Info Science Ms. Margaret MCCOEY
53 Director Grad Education Program Dr. Greer RICHARDSON
83 Dir Grad Counseling & Family Therap Dr. Donna A. TONREY
73 Director Grad Pgms of Theology Fr. Francis J. BERNA
60 Dir Grad Communication Dr. Michael SMITH
66 Director Undergraduate Nursing Dr. Jane KURZ
66 Dir Grad Nursing RN-MSN Pgm Dr. Patricia DILLON
69 Dir Master Public Health Program Dr. Candace ROBERTSON-JAMES
88 Dir Grad Econ Crime Forensics Ms. Margaret MCCOEY
88 Dir Grad Pgm Human Capital Develop Ms. Lynnette CLEMENT
58 Dir Grad Pgm Nonprofit Leadership Dr. Laura OTTEN
39 Asst VP Res Life Community Dev Mr. Alan B. WENDELL
35 Asst VP for Campus Life Ms. Anna M. ALLEN
42 Director Univ Ministry & Service Bro. Robert J. KINZLER
92 Dir University Honors Program Bro. Michael MCGINNISS
13 Chief Information Officer Mr. Karl HORVATH
08 Interim Director of the Library Ms. Carol A. BRIGHAM
18 Asst VP Facilities Mgmt Mr. Dennis SHORES, JR.
19 Asst VP Public Safety Ms. Amanda GUTHORN
15 Asst VP Human Resources Ms. Kristin HEASLEY
41 Dir Intercollegiate Athletics Mr. William BRADSHAW
112 Director of Major Gifts Mr. Daniel JOYCE
102 Director of The La Salle Fund Mr. Brian FRANKOWSKI
88 Assc Dir Prospect Research/Strategy Ms. Karen MCNAMARA
07 Executive Director of Admission Mr. James C. PLUNKETT
37 Director Financial Aid Mr. Joseph ALAIMO
06 Registrar Ms. Jean W. LANDIS
09 Exec Dir Inst Eff and Spons Rsrch Mr. Eric DAVENPORT
88 Dir Doctorate in Psych Program Dr. Randy FINGERHUT
88 Dir Academic Partnerships Dr. Elizabeth LANGEMAK
88 Grad Director Instr Tech Mgt Ms. Margaret MCCOEY
88 Director Part-time MBA Program Mr. John FARRELL
88 Director Full-time MBA Program Ms. Elizabeth SCOFIELD
40 Manager Campus Store Mr. Mark ALLAN
28 Multicultural Education Coordinator Ms. Cherylyn L. RUSH
105 Director of Web Communication Mr. Gregory FALA
88 Dir Doctor of Nursing Practice Pgm Vacant
88 Director Graduate History Dr. George B. STOW
58 Associate Provost Dr. Holly HARNER
88 Dir Prof Clinical Counseling Psych Dr. John J. ROONEY
88 Sr Dir Development for Athletics Mr. Brian QUINN
88 Sr Dir of Brand Marketing Ms. Amy CRANSTON
100 Chief of Staff/Dir of Gov Affairs Mr. Joseph MEADE
104 Director Study Abroad Ms. Melinda INGERSOLL
96 Director of Procurement Mr. Christopher KANE

Lackawanna College (A)

501 Vine Street, Scranton PA 18509-3206
County: Lackawanna FICE Identification: 003283
Unit ID: 213376
Telephone: (570) 961-7810 Carnegie Class: Assoc/HT-High Non
FAX Number: (570) 961-7858 Calendar System: 4/1/4
URL: www.lackawanna.edu
Established: 1894 Annual Undergrad Tuition & Fees: $14,580
Enrollment: 1,629 Coed
Affiliation or Control: Independent Non-Profit IRS Status: 501(c)3
Highest Offering: Baccalaureate
Accreditation: M, DMS, EMT, PTAA, SURGT

01 President .... Mr. Mark VOLK
03 Exec Vice Pres/Chief Innovation Ofc .... Dr. Jill MURRAY
10 Vice Pres Finance/Administration .... Ms. Alycia SCHWARTZ
05 Vice President Academic Affairs .... Dr. Erica PRICCI
32 VP for Student Affairs .... Mrs. Suellen MUSEWICZ
84 VP for Enrollment Management .... Mr. T.J ELTRINGHAM
111 Vice Pres for College Advancement .... Mr. Brian COSTANZO
15 VP for Human Resources .... Ms. Renee MUNDY
35 Dean of Students .... Mr. Dan LAMAGNA
20 Dean of Faculty .... Mrs. Suzanne CERCONE
29 Director Alumni Relations .... Vacant
88 Dir Programming & Special Events .... Mr. Jim CULLEN
26 Director of External Relations .... Ms. Wendy HINTON
41 Director of Athletics .... Ms. Joya WHITTINGTON
88 Director of Advising & Transfer Svc .Mrs. Barbara NOWOGORSKI
06 Registrar .... Mrs. Theresa SCOPELLITI
19 Director of Public Safety .... Mr. Gary SHOENER
12 Director of Hazleton Center .... Mrs. April HARRIS-SNYDER
07 Director of Admissions .... Mr. Jeffery GREGORY
12 Exec Director School of PNGT .... Mr. Richard MARQUARDT
08 Library Director .... Mrs. Mary Beth ROCHE
102 Director of Grant Support Services .... Ms. Michelle MCGLOIN
39 Director Housing & Residence Life .... Mr. Stephen DUDA
18 Director of Facilities .... Mr. Derek GREGORY
37 Director of Financial Aid .... Mr. Matthew PETERS
12 Director Towanda Center .... Ms. Kim MAPES
13 Director of MIS .... Mrs. Melanie KOWALSKI
35 Director of Student Life .... Ms. Karen LEGGE
07 Assistant Director of Admissions .... Mrs. Michelle KETTEN
88 Service Learning Coordinator .... Ms. Jo-Ann ORCUTT
04 Administrative Asst to President .... Ms. Mary A. OLIVERI
09 Director of Institutional Research .... Mrs. Michelle MCGLOIN
106 Dir Online Education/E-learning .... Mrs. Katherine FISNE

Lafayette College (B)

730 High Street, Markle Hall Suite, Easton PA 18042-1798
County: Northampton FICE Identification: 003284
Unit ID: 213385
Telephone: (610) 330-5000 Carnegie Class: Bac-A&S
FAX Number: (610) 330-5127 Calendar System: Semester
URL: www.lafayette.edu
Established: 1826 Annual Undergrad Tuition & Fees: $49,635
Enrollment: 2,533 Coed
Affiliation or Control: Independent Non-Profit IRS Status: 501(c)3
Highest Offering: Baccalaureate
Accreditation: M, CS, ENG

01 President .... Dr. Alison R. BYERLY
05 Provost .... Dr. S. Abu Turab RIZVI
30 Vice Pres Dev/College Relations .... Ms. Kimberly SPANG
32 VP Campus Life .... Dr. Annette DIORIO
15 Vice President Human Resources .... Ms. Leslie F. MUHLFELDER
26 VP Marketing/Communications .... Mr. Mark EYERLY
13 VP and Chief Information Officer .... Mr. John L. O'KEEFE
10 VP Finance & Administration .... Mr. Roger DEMARESKI
54 Director of Engineering .... Dr. Scott R. HUMMEL
100 VP & Liaison to Board of Trustees .... Dr. James F. KRIVOSKI
84 Vice Pres for Enrollment Management .... Mr. Gregory MACDONALD
121 Dean Advising & Co-Curricular Pgms .... Dr. Erica D'AGOSTINO
08 Dean of Libraries .... Ms. Anne HOUSTON
35 Dean of Students .... Vacant
07 Dean of Admissions .... Mr. Matthew HYDE
37 Director of Student Financial Aid .... Ms. Ashley BIANCHI
09 Director of Institutional Research .... Dr. Simon T. TONEV
06 Registrar .... Mr. Francis A. BENGINIA
41 Director of Athletics .... Dr. Bruce E. MCCUTCHEON
36 Exec Director Career Services .... Vacant
23 Director Health Services .... Dr. Jeffrey E. GOLDSTEIN
38 Director Counseling Center .... Dr. Karen J. FORBES
19 Director of Public Safety .... Mr. Jeffrey E. TROXELL
18 Dir Physical Planning & Plant Oper .... Mr. Bruce S. FERRETTI
29 Executive Director Alumni Relations .... Ms. Rachel NELSON MOELLER
16 Director of HR/Employment .... Ms. Lisa Youngkin REX
96 Manager of Procurement .... Ms. Linda L. JROSKI
88 Interim Title IX Coordinator .... Ms. Lisa Youngkin REX
20 Dean of Faculty/Chf Diversity Ofcr .... Dr. Robin C. RINEHART
115 Chief Investment Officer .... Mr. Joseph S. BOHRER
04 Executive Assistant to President .... Ms. Marie L. ENEA

Lake Erie College of Osteopathic Medicine (C)

1858 W Grandview Boulevard, Erie PA 16509-1025
County: Erie FICE Identification: 030908
Unit ID: 407629
Telephone: (814) 866-6641 Carnegie Class: Spec-4-yr-Med
FAX Number: (814) 866-8123 Calendar System: Semester
URL: www.lecom.edu
Established: 1993 Annual Graduate Tuition & Fees: N/A
Enrollment: 3,968 Coed
Affiliation or Control: Independent Non-Profit IRS Status: 501(c)3
Highest Offering: First Professional Degree; No Undergraduates
Accreditation: M, DENT, OSTEO, PHAR

01 President/CEO .... Dr. John M. FERRETTI
05 Provost/Sr Vice Pres/Dean Acad Affs .... Dr. Silvia M. FERRETTI
10 Vice Pres of Fiscal Affairs/CFO .... Mr. Richard P. OLINGER
20 VP Acad Affs/Dn LECOM Sch Pharmacy .... Dr. Hershey BELL
12 Vice Pres for LECOM at Seton Hill .... Dr. Irving FREEMAN
52 Dean School of Dental Medicine .... Dr. Mathew BATEMAN
58 Assoc Dean Students/Grad Studies .... Dr. Mark KAUFFMAN
20 Assoc Dean Acad Affairs Bradenton .... Dr. Robert GEORGE
63 Assoc Dean Clinical Educ Bradenton .... Dr. Anthony J. FERRETTI
63 Assoc Dean of Preclinical Educ .... Dr. Christine KELL
63 Assoc Dean of Clinical Education .... Dr. Michael ROWANE
63 Asst Dean of Clinical Education .... Dr. Regan SHABLOSKI
63 Asst Dean Preclinical Ed Bradenton .... Dr. Mark COTY
63 Asst Dean Preclinical Educ Erie .... Dr. Jon KALMEY
63 Asst Dean of Post Bac/MS Programs .... Dr. Randy KULESZA
20 Asst Dean Acad Affairs Bradenton .... Dr. Ronald BEREZNIAK
67 Assoc Dean of Accelerated Pathway .... Dr. Rachel OGDEN
67 Assoc Dean for Florida Pathway .... Dr. Julie WILKINSON
108 Assistant Dean for Assessment .... Dr. Nina PAVULURI
52 Asst Dean Preclinial Dental .... Vacant
88 Asst Dean Clinical Dental Med .... Dr. Francis CURD
32 Director of Student Affairs .... Dr. David FRIED
09 Inst Dir Plng/Assess/Accred/Rsrch .... Dr. Mathew BATEMAN
43 Dir Legal Services/General Counsel .... Mr. Richard FERRETTI
26 Inst Dir Communications/Marketing .... Mr. Pierre A. BELLICINI
27 Asst Inst Dir Comm/Marketing .... Mr. Eric NICASTRO
08 Inst Dir of Learning Resources .... Mr. Dan WELCH
88 Director of Behavioral Health .... Dr. Melanie DUNBAR
13 Director of Information Technology .... Mr. Randy HARRIS
46 Director of Research .... Dr. Bertalan DUDAS
15 Inst Dir of Human Resources .... Mr. Aaron SUSMARSKI
28 Director of Diversity .... Dr. Sonia DILLION
19 Inst Dir of Police & Security .... Mr. Kevin GOODE
88 Asst Dean Med Educ/Fac Dev .... Dr. Mark TERRELL
18 Facilities Director .... Mr. Brian KING
37 Inst Director of Financial Aid .... Ms. Bonnie CRILLEY
06 Institutional Registrar .... Mr. Jeremy SIVILLO
07 Admissions Coordinator .... Ms. Amy W. ROWE
96 Director of Purchasing .... Ms. Naz KROL

Lancaster Bible College (D)

901 Eden Road, Lancaster PA 17601-5036
County: Lancaster FICE Identification: 003285
Unit ID: 213400
Telephone: (717) 569-7071 Carnegie Class: Spec-4-yr-Faith
FAX Number: (717) 560-8260 Calendar System: Semester
URL: www.lbc.edu
Established: 1933 Annual Undergrad Tuition & Fees: $21,500
Enrollment: 1,913 Coed
Affiliation or Control: Independent Non-Profit IRS Status: 501(c)3
Highest Offering: Doctorate
Accreditation: M, BI, MUS, SW

01 President .... Dr. Peter W. TEAGUE
04 Assistant to the President .... Mrs. Judith M. HECKAMAN
03 Executive Vice President .... Mr. John ZESWITZ
05 Provost .... Dr. Philip E. DEARBORN
84 VP for Student Experience .... Mr. Josh BEERS
30 VP of Advancement .... Mr. Ron KUBEK

Lancaster County Career and Technology Center (E)

1730 Hans Herr Drive, P.O. Box 527,
Willow Street PA 17584
County: Lancaster FICE Identification: 023108
Unit ID: 418533
Telephone: (717) 464-7050 Carnegie Class: Spec 2-yr-Health
FAX Number: (717) 464-9518 Calendar System: Semester
URL: www.lancasterctc.edu
Established: 1970 Annual Undergrad Tuition & Fees (In-District): N/A
Enrollment: 467 Coed
Affiliation or Control: State/Local IRS Status: 501(c)3
Highest Offering: Associate Degree
Accreditation: COE

01 Director .... Michael DELPRIORE

Lancaster Theological Seminary (F)

555 W James Street, Lancaster PA 17603-2812
County: Lancaster FICE Identification: 003286
Unit ID: 213446
Telephone: (717) 393-0654 Carnegie Class: Spec-4-yr-Faith
FAX Number: (717) 393-4254 Calendar System: Trimester
URL: www.lancasterseminary.edu
Established: 1825 Annual Graduate Tuition & Fees: N/A
Enrollment: 94 Coed
Affiliation or Control: United Church Of Christ IRS Status: 501(c)3
Highest Offering: Doctorate; No Undergraduates
Accreditation: M, THEOL

01 President .... Dr. Carol E. LYTCH
10 Vice President Business & Finance .... Ms. Elizabeth P. BENNETT
05 Vice Pres Academic Affairs & Dean .... Dr. David M. MELLOTT
07 Dean of Admissions .... Rev. Ruth-Aimée BELONNI-ROSARIO
08 Seminary Librarian .... Mrs. Myka K. STEPHENS
06 Registrar .... Mrs. Teresa BENNEIAN
29 Director Alumni/ae Relations .... Rev. Paul EYER
13 Director Computing/Information Mgmt .... Mr. Augustine APPREY
30 Executive Director of Development .... Rev. Carolyne CALL
04 Exec Assistant to the President .... Ms. Carter FARMER

Lansdale School of Business (G)

290 Wissahickon Ave, North Wales PA 19454-4114
County: Montgomery FICE Identification: 007779
Unit ID: 213473
Telephone: (215) 699-5700 Carnegie Class: Assoc/HVT-Mix Trad/Non
FAX Number: (215) 699-8770 Calendar System: Semester
URL: www.LSB.edu
Established: 1918 Annual Undergrad Tuition & Fees: $10,500
Enrollment: 244 Coed
Affiliation or Control: Proprietary IRS Status: Proprietary
Highest Offering: Associate Degree
Accreditation: ACICS

01 President .... Mr. Marlon D. KELLER
03 Executive Director .... Mrs. Marianne H. JOHNSON
05 Academic Dean .... Ms. Janine L. DILLARD
32 Student Services Coordinator .... Ms. Jacklyn G. WHEELER
08 Librarian .... Mrs. Marie B. WALCROFT
37 Financial Aid Coordinator .... Mr. David E. SOUZA
36 Career Services Coordinator .... Ms. Kellyann R. GERIA

Laurel Business Institute (H)

11 East Penn Street, Uniontown PA 15401-3453
County: Fayette FICE Identification: 025462
Unit ID: 250027
Telephone: (724) 439-4900 Carnegie Class: Assoc/HVT-Mix Trad/Non
FAX Number: (724) 439-3607 Calendar System: Semester
URL: www.laurel.edu
Established: 1985 Annual Undergrad Tuition & Fees: $9,744
Enrollment: 206 Coed
Affiliation or Control: Proprietary IRS Status: Proprietary
Highest Offering: Associate Degree
Accreditation: ACICS, COARC

01 President .... Mrs. Nancy M. DECKER
11 Executive Director .... Mrs. Bonnie MARSH
10 Vice President of Finance .... Ms. Vicki M. JOLLIFFE
15 Vice President of Human Resources .... Mr. Chuck SANTORE, JR.
05 Director of Education .... Mrs. Toni R. HARTLEY
13 Director of IT .... Mr. Ken LAPIKAS
37 Vice President of Financial Aid .... Ms. Stephanie M. MIGYANKO
07 Director of Admission .... Mr. Douglas S. DECKER

Laurel Technical Institute (I)

200 Sterling Avenue, Sharon PA 16146
County: Mercer FICE Identification: 020925
Unit ID: 215992
Telephone: (724) 983-0700 Carnegie Class: Assoc/HVT-High Trad
FAX Number: (724) 983-8355 Calendar System: Semester
URL: www.laurel.edu
Established: 1925 Annual Undergrad Tuition & Fees: $9,744
Enrollment: 145 Coed
Affiliation or Control: Proprietary IRS Status: Proprietary
Highest Offering: Associate Degree
Accreditation: ACICS, COARC, MLTAD

01 President .... Ms. Nancy DECKER
05 Director/Exec VP of Operations .... Mr. Douglas DECKER
07 Director of Admission .... Mr. Douglas DECKER

Lebanon Valley College (J)

101 N College Avenue, Annville PA 17003-1400
County: Lebanon FICE Identification: 003288
Unit ID: 213507
Telephone: (717) 867-6161 Carnegie Class: Masters/S
FAX Number: (717) 867-6124 Calendar System: Semester
URL: www.lvc.edu
Established: 1866 Annual Undergrad Tuition & Fees: $40,550
Enrollment: 1,918 Coed
Affiliation or Control: United Methodist IRS Status: 501(c)3
Highest Offering: Doctorate
Accreditation: M, ACBSP, MUS, PTA

01 President .... Dr. Lewis E. THAYNE
05 Vice Pres Acad Affs/Dean of Faculty .... Dr. Michael R. GREEN
111 Vice President of Advancement .... Mr. Daniel HELWIG
10 Vice Pres Finance/Administration .... Mr. Shawn P. CURTIN
84 Vice President of Enrollment .... Mr. Edwin R. WRIGHT
32 VP Student Affairs/Dean of Students . Mr. Gregory H. KRIKORIAN
45 VP for Strategic Initiatives & Secy .... Mr. Steven P. O'DAY
26 Chief Communications Officer .... Mrs. Molly O'BRIEN-FOELSCH
13 Senior Director of Information Tech .... Mr. David W. SHAPIRO
15 Director of HR/Title IX Coordinator .... Mrs. Ann C. HAYES
20 Associate Dean of Academic Affairs .... Dr. Marc HARRIS
09 Director of Institutional Research .... Mrs. Jessica L. ICKES
58 Assoc Dean of Grad Stds/Cont Educ .... Vacant
06 Assistant Dean and Registrar .... Mr. Jeremy A. MAISTO

41 Director of Athletics ... Mr. Richard L. BEARD
114 Dir of Finance and Budget ... Ms. Wendy ALBERT
21 Controller ... Mr. Gabriel PAZ
37 Director of Financial Aid ... Mrs. Kendra M. FEIGERT
36 Director of Career Development ... Vacant
28 Director of Intercultural Affairs ... Mrs. Renata WILLIAMS
19 Director of Public Safety ... Mr. Brent OBERHOLTZER
104 Director of Global Education ... Mrs. Jill T. RUSSELL
39 Director of Residential Life ... Dr. Michael R. DIESNER
22 Director of Disability Services ... Ms. Dawn R. SHOWERS
50 Director of the MBA Program ... Dr. David M. SETLEY
107 Director of Professional Studies ... Ms. Beth E. ROMANSKI
08 Director of the Bishop Library ... Ms. Sarah E. GREENE
105 Director of Communications ... Mrs. Jasmine A. BUCHER
30 Director of Development ... Mr. Matthew WEAVER
18 Sr Director Facilities Management ... Mr. Donald SANTOSTEFANO
35 Assoc Dean Student Affairs ... Dr. Robert L. MIKUS
42 Chaplain ... Vacant
27 Dir Editorial Standards/Brand Msgng ... Dr. Thomas M. HANRAHAN
91 Dir Enterprise Information Systems ... Mr. Robert J. DILLANE
90 Director of Client Services ... Mr. Michael C. ZEIGLER
24 Director of Audiovisual Technology ... Mr. Andrew S. GREENE
38 Director of Counseling ... Dr. Stephanie A. FALK
88 Director of Student Activities ... Mrs. Jennifer M. EVANS
23 Director of Health Services ... Vacant
88 Assistant Controller ... Mr. Todd M. LATSHAW
04 Executive Asst to President ... Ms. Amy LINTZ
29 Director Alumni & Parent Engagement ... Mrs. Susan SARISKY JONES

Lehigh Carbon Community College (A)

4525 Education Park Drive, Schnecksville PA 18078-2598
County: Lehigh FICE Identification: 006810
Unit ID: 213525
Telephone: (610) 799-2121 Carnegie Class: Assoc/MT-VT-Mix Trad/Non
FAX Number: (610) 799-1527 Calendar System: Semester
URL: www.lccc.edu
Established: 1966 Annual Undergrad Tuition & Fees (In-District): $3,900
Enrollment: 6,738 Coed
Affiliation or Control: Local IRS Status: 501(c)3
Highest Offering: Associate Degree
Accreditation: M, ACBSP, ADNUR, CAHIIM, CSHSE, MAC, OTA, PNUR, PTAA

01 President ... Dr. Ann D. BIEBER
05 VP Academic/Student Development ... Dr. Thomas W. MEYER
10 VP Finance & Admin Svcs ... Mr. Brian KAHLER
84 VP Enrollment Management ... Ms. Cindy M. HANEY
04 Exec Asst to President and Board ... Mrs. Cindy L. BROOKS
32 Dean of Student Development ... Ms. Peggy M. HEIM
72 Dean Commun Arts/Computers/Tech ... Dr. Richard W. WILT
81 Dean Science/Eng/Math ... Ms. Larissa M. VERTA
13 Chief Information Officer ... Mr. Irving BRUCKSTEIN
106 Assoc Dean Distance Education ... Mr. Dominic CHRISTISON
79 Dean Humanities & Soc Sci ... Dr. Andra M. BASU
76 Dean Healthcare Sciences ... Mr. Craig A. KOLLER
103 Dean Employer Engage & Cmty Educ ... Ms. Terri K. KEEFE
26 Exec Dir College Relations ... Ms. Linda BAKER
09 Exec Dir Inst Research & Effectiv ... Vacant
50 Dean Bus/Educ/Legal/Soc Svc ... Dr. Cecelia A. CONNELLY-WEIDA
114 Dir Budgets & Purchasing ... Ms. Shannon HELMER
102 Executive Director Foundation ... Vacant
07 Exec Director of Enrollment ... Ms. Ellia SABLAN-ZEBEDY
36 Dir Career Development ... Ms. Christina L. MOYER
88 Assoc Dean Prof Accred/Curriculum ... Mr. Scott W. AQUILA
88 Dir High School Connections ... Ms. Jennifer K. AQUILA
15 Dir HR/Title IX/Equity Coord ... Ms. Donna M. WILLIAMS
88 Dir Fac Dev/Student Retention ... Ms. Cheryl A. DOLL
66 Director Nursing Programs ... Ms. Barbara H. LUPOLE
35 Dir Student Life ... Ms. Gene F. EDEN
14 Asst Dir IT Support Services ... Mr. Ervin J. MEASE
18 Dir Facilities Management ... Mr. Carl S. PECKITT, JR.
37 Dir of Financial Aid ... Ms. Marian L. SNYDER
88 Dir Academic Grants ... Ms. Linda L. MESICS
41 Director Athletics ... Mr. Andrew JOHNSON
88 Dir Early Learning Center ... Ms. Elizabeth D. LIPMAN
88 Dir of Literacy and Job Training ... Ms. Mary KOVALCHICK
88 Dir Audits & Reporting ... Ms. Stefanie E. NESTER
25 Dir Institutional Advance Grants ... Mr. Thomas J. MULDERICK
74 Co-Dir Veterinary Tech Program ... Ms. Lisa A. MARTINI-JOHNSON
27 Dir Marketing and Publications ... Ms. Leanne R. RECLA
06 Dir Registration/Student Records ... Mr. Gregory J. GOLETZ, JR.
40 Bookstore Manager ... Ms. Jennifer L. ERB
121 Assoc Dean Student Success ... Mr. Brian C. DELONG
19 Dir Public Safety ... Mr. James W. SURGEONER
113 Dir Student Accounts ... Ms. Stacey A. BETZ

Lehigh University (B)

27 Memorial Drive W, Bethlehem PA 18015-3094
County: Northampton FICE Identification: 003289
Unit ID: 213543
Telephone: (610) 758-3000 Carnegie Class: DU-Higher
FAX Number: (610) 691-5420 Calendar System: Semester
URL: www.lehigh.edu
Established: 1865 Annual Undergrad Tuition & Fees: $48,320
Enrollment: 7,054 Coed
Affiliation or Control: Independent Non-Profit IRS Status: 501(c)3
Highest Offering: Doctorate
Accreditation: M, COPSY, CS, ENG, IPSY, SCPSY, THEA

01 President ... Dr. John D. SIMON
05 Provost & VP for Academic Affairs ... Dr. Patrick V. FARRELL
10 Vice Pres Finance & Administration ... Ms. Patricia A. JOHNSON
88 VP for International Affairs ... Dr. Cheryl A. MATHERLY
30 VP Development and Alumni Relations ... Mr. Joseph E. BUCK
46 VP & Assoc Prov Research/Graduate ... Dr. Alan J. SNYDER
26 VP Communications & Public Affairs ... Mr. Frederick J. MCGRAIL
28 VP Diversity/Inclusion & Equity ... Dr. Donald A. OUTING
115 Chief Investment Officer ... Vacant
09 Vice Provost Institutional Research ... Dr. Henry Y. ZHENG
32 Vice Provost Student Affairs ... Dr. Ricardo HALL
13 Vice Provost Library & Tech Svcs ... Dr. Bruce M. TAGGART
88 Vice Provost for Academic Diversity ... Mr. Henry U. ODI
86 Assoc VP for Govt Relations ... Mr. William D. MICHALERYA
21 Assoc VP Finance/Asst Secy Board ... Ms. Denise M. BLEW
15 Assoc VP for Human Resource ... Mr. Chris HALLADAY
18 Assoc Vice Pres Facilities Services ... Vacant
20 Deputy Provost Academic Affairs ... Ms. Jennifer M. JENSEN
35 Dean of Students ... Ms. Katherine W. LAVINDER
29 Asst VP of Alumni Engagement ... Ms. Jennifer L. CUNNINGHAM
31 Asst VP Community & Regional Affs ... Ms. Adrienne J. WASHINGTON
54 Dean Engr & Applied Science ... Dr. Stephen P. DEWEERTH
49 Dean Arts & Sciences ... Dr. Donald E. HALL
50 Dean of Business/Economics ... Dr. Georgette C. PHILLIPS
53 Dean of Education ... Dr. Gary M. SASSO
07 Interim Dean Admiss/Financial Aid ... Mr. Bruce R. BUNNICK
41 Murray H Goodman Dean of Athletics ... Mr. Joseph D. STERRETT
06 Registrar ... Mr. Steven H. WILSON
37 Director Financial Aid ... Ms. Jennifer L. MERTZ
106 Director Distance Education ... Ms. Margaret A. PORTZ
36 Director Career Services ... Ms. Lori B. KENNEDY
23 Director Health Center ... Dr. Susan C. KITEI
39 Director Residential Services ... Mr. Ozzie BREINER
40 Director Bookstore ... Mr. Brian ADLER
19 Chief University Police ... Mr. Edward K. SHUPP
38 Director of Counseling Services ... Dr. Ian T. BIRKY
42 Chaplain ... Rev. Lloyd H. STEFFEN
43 General Counsel ... Mr. Frank A. ROTH
114 Director of Budget ... Mr. Stephen J. GUTTMAN
96 Manager Strategic Sourcing ... Ms. Jane ALTEMOSE
84 Director Enrollment Management ... Ms. Jennifer E. O'BRIEN-KNOTTS
100 Chief of Staff ... Mr. Erik J. WALKER

Lincoln Technical Institute (C)

5151 Tilghman Street, Allentown PA 18104-3298
County: Lehigh FICE Identification: 007759
Unit ID: 213570
Telephone: (610) 398-5300 Carnegie Class: Assoc/HVT-High Non
FAX Number: (610) 395-2706 Calendar System: Semester
URL: www.lincolnedu.com
Established: 1946 Annual Undergrad Tuition & Fees: N/A
Enrollment: 495 Coed
Affiliation or Control: Proprietary IRS Status: Proprietary
Highest Offering: Associate Degree
Accreditation: ACCSC

01 Campus President ... Mrs. Lisa M. KUNTZ
05 Director of Education ... Ms. Anne CONNELY
11 Director of Administration ... Mrs. Angela REPPERT
07 Director of Admissions ... Mr. Vincent SALVANTORIELLO
36 Director of Career Services ... Mrs. Charmain BRODY
37 Financial Aid Manager ... Ms. Erica BRANDI

Lincoln Technical Institute (D)

9191 Torresdale Avenue, Philadelphia PA 19136-1595
County: Philadelphia FICE Identification: 007832
Unit ID: 213589
Telephone: (215) 335-0800 Carnegie Class: Spec 2-yr-Tech
FAX Number: (215) 335-1443 Calendar System: Other
URL: www.lincolntech.com
Established: 1946 Annual Undergrad Tuition & Fees: N/A
Enrollment: 319 Coed
Affiliation or Control: Proprietary IRS Status: Proprietary
Highest Offering: Associate Degree
Accreditation: ACCSC

01 Campus President ... Mr. John WILLIE
07 Dir Admiss High School/Adult Educ ... Mr. Dave BARAN
32 Student Services Coordinator ... Ms. Mijana KONA
05 Director of Education ... Mrs. Jennifer MCLAUGHLIN
11 Director Administration ... Ms. Gina ALTSHULER
36 Director of Career Services ... Mr. John FALLOWS

Lincoln University (E)

PO Box 179, 1570 Baltimore Pike,
Lincoln University PA 19352-0999
County: Chester FICE Identification: 003290
Unit ID: 213598
Telephone: (484) 365-8000 Carnegie Class: Masters/M
FAX Number: (484) 365-7316 Calendar System: Semester
URL: www.lincoln.edu
Established: 1854 Annual Undergrad Tuition & Fees (In-State): $11,102
Enrollment: 1,904 Coed
Affiliation or Control: State Related IRS Status: 501(c)3
Highest Offering: Master's
Accreditation: M, NURSE

01 President ... Dr. Brenda A. ALLEN
111 Interim VP for Institutional Advanc ... Mr. Stephen MCDANIEL
100 Chief of Staff/Mgr Board Trustees ... Ms. Diane M. BROWN
05 Provost and VP for Academic Affairs ... Dr. Patricia RAMSEY
10 Vice Pres Fiscal Affairs/Treasurer ... Mr. Charles GRADOWSKI
32 Interim VP for Student Affairs ... Dr. Roselle WILSON
13 Asst VP for Information Technology ... Mr. Andre WARNER
09 Dir of Inst Effectiv/Research/Plng ... Ms. Tiffany LEE
39 Dean Students and Campus Life ... Dr. Lenetta LEE
84 Assoc VP of Enrollment Management ... Ms. Kimberly TAYLOR-BENNS
26 Assoc VP External Relations/Mktg ... Ms. Maureen STOKES
27 Director of Communications ... Ms. Shelley MIX
29 Director of Alumni Relations ... Ms. Deborah JOHNSON
06 Registrar ... Ms. Catherine RUTLEDGE
36 Director Career Svcs Ctr ... Mr. Ralph SIMPSON
41 Director of Athletics ... Mr. Harry STINSON
42 Chaplain ... Mr. Frederick FAISON
21 Controller ... Mr. Jay SIMMONS
85 Director International Services ... Vacant
23 Director Health Services ... Ms. Velva GREENE-RAINEY
123 Dir Graduate Student Svcs/Admission ... Ms. Jernice LEA
35 Director of Student Life & Develop ... Ms. Ihsan R. MUJAHID
37 Director Financial Aid ... Ms. Kim ANDERSON
96 Director of Purchasing ... Ms. Sue REED
81 Dean College of Science & Tech ... Dr. Larry SHANNON
83 Dean Col Professional/Grad/Ext Stds ... Dr. Patricia JOSEPH
79 Actg Dean Col Arts/Humanit/Soc Sci ... Dr. Patricia JOSEPH

Luzerne County Community College (F)

1333 S Prospect Street, Nanticoke PA 18634-3899
County: Luzerne FICE Identification: 006811
Unit ID: 213659
Telephone: (570) 740-0200 Carnegie Class: Assoc/MT-VT-High Trad
FAX Number: (570) 740-0386 Calendar System: Semester
URL: www.luzerne.edu
Established: 1966 Annual Undergrad Tuition & Fees (In-District): $5,040
Enrollment: 5,788 Coed
Affiliation or Control: Local IRS Status: 501(c)3
Highest Offering: Associate Degree
Accreditation: M, ACBSP, ADNUR, COARC, DA, DH, EMT, SURGT

01 President ... Mr. Thomas P. LEARY
101 Executive Asst to President/BOT ... Ms. Paula LABENSKI
05 Vice Pres Academic Affairs ... Vacant
32 VP of Enrollment Mgmt/Student Dev ... Ms. Rosana REYES
103 VP of Applied Tech/Workforce Devel ... Ms. Susan SPRY
15 Dean Human Resources ... Mr. John SEDLAK
66 Dean of Nursing/Health Sciences ... Ms. Deborah VILEGI PAYNE
49 Dean of Arts & Sciences ... Vacant
10 Dean Finance ... Mr. Joseph GASPER
13 Vice President of Operations & CTO ... Mr. Don NELSON
07 Assistant Director Admissions ... Mr. Ed HENNIGAN
37 Director of Student Financial Aid ... Mr. Mark CARPENTIER
08 Director of Library ... Mrs. Mia W. BASSHAM
38 Dir Counseling/Stdnt Support Svcs ... Mrs. Janine KELLEY
35 Dir Student Life/Athletics ... Ms. Mary SULLIVAN
09 Director Inst Research/Planning ... Ms. Graceann PLATUKUS
36 Director Career Services ... Ms. Mary GHILANI
18 Director of Physical Plant ... Mr. Keith GRAHAM
30 Exec Dir of Institutional Advance ... Ms. Sandra NICHOLAS
84 Director Enrollment Management ... Mr. Jim DOMZALSKI
26 Director of College Relations ... Ms. Lisa NELSON
29 Director Alumni Relations ... Ms. Bonnie LAUER
96 Director of Purchasing ... Mr. Len OLZINSKI
28 Diversity Coordinator ... Ms. Judi MYERS
19 Director of Safety/Security ... Mr. William BARRETT

Lycoming College (G)

700 College Place, Williamsport PA 17701-5192
County: Lycoming FICE Identification: 003293
Unit ID: 213668
Telephone: (570) 321-4000 Carnegie Class: Bac-A&S
FAX Number: (570) 321-4337 Calendar System: Semester
URL: www.lycoming.edu
Established: 1812 Annual Undergrad Tuition & Fees: $37,162
Enrollment: 1,285 Coed
Affiliation or Control: United Methodist IRS Status: 501(c)3
Highest Offering: Baccalaureate
Accreditation: M

01 President ... Dr. Kent C. TRACHTE
05 Provost and Dean of the College ... Dr. Philip W. SPRUNGER
10 VP for Finance and Admin/Treasurer ... Mr. Jeffrey L. BENNETT
111 Vice President for Advancement ... Mr. Charles W. EDMONDS
84 VP for Enrollment Management ... Mr. Michael J. KONOPSKI
21 Controller ... Ms. Dawn HENDRICKS
32 Vice President for Student Life ... Dr. Daniel P. MILLER
30 Associate VP for Development ... Vacant
20 Assoc Provost for Experiential Lrng ... Dr. Susan ROSS
89 Dean for First Year Students ... Mr. Andrew W. KILPATRICK
08 Director of Snowden Library ... Ms. Alison GREGORY
06 Registrar ... Ms. Whitney A. MERINAR
37 Director of Financial Aid ... Mr. James LAKIS
13 Chief Information Officer ... Mr. Robert L. DUNKLEBERGER
29 Director Alumni Relations ... Ms. Amy S. REYES
112 Director of Planned Giving ... Mr. Robb DIETRICH
39 Director Residence Life ... Ms. Kate HUMMEL
41 Director of Athletics ... Mr. Michael CLARK

110	Assoc Dir of Major Gifts	Mr. Gregory J. BELL
44	Director of Annual Giving	Ms. Lesley LARSON
42	Campus Minister	Rev. Jeffrey L. LECRONE
15	Director of Human Resources	Ms. Jackie BILGER
18	Chief Facilities/Physical Plant	Mr. F. Douglas KUNTZ
23	Director of Health Services	Ms. Sondra L. STIPCAK
38	Director Student Counseling	Mr. Townsend VELKOFF
40	Campus Store Manager	Ms. Patricia E. BAUSINGER
92	Lycoming Scholars	Dr. Cullen J. CHANDLER
94	Women's Studies	Dr. Kerry RICHMOND
16	Human Resources Coordinator	Mrs. Cathleen A. LUTZ
04	Assistant to the President	Ms. Diane CARL
09	Director of Institutional Research	Dr. Chiaki KOTORI
108	Associate Provost	Dr. Eileen PELUSO
90	Dir Instructional & Emerging Tech	Mr. Steve CARAVAGGIO
91	Director Administrative Computing	Ms. Janet PAYNE
07	Director of Admissions	Ms. Jessica A. QUINTANA HESS
102	Foundations Relations Officer	Ms. Melanie TAORMINA
104	Coordinator of Study Abroad	Ms. Allison HOLLADAY
105	Director Web Services	Mr. Robert BROWN

Manor College (A)

700 Fox Chase Road, Jenkintown PA 19046-3399

County: Montgomery
FICE Identification: 003294
Unit ID: 213774
Telephone: (215) 885-2360
Carnegie Class: Assoc/MT-VT-High Trad
FAX Number: (215) 576-6564
Calendar System: Semester
URL: www.manor.edu
Established: 1947
Annual Undergrad Tuition & Fees: $16,550
Enrollment: 696
Coed
Affiliation or Control: Independent Non-Profit
IRS Status: 501(c)3
Highest Offering: Associate Degree
Accreditation: M, ACBSP, DA, DH

01	President	Dr. Jonathan PERI
05	Exec VP/Dean of Academic Affairs	Dr. Stephen GRIECO
06	Registrar	Ms. Dianne I. SARIDAKIS
10	Director Finance & Physical Plant	Mr. John W. WINICKI
13	Director Information Technology	Mr. Paul VAN RIJN
15	Human Resource Generalist	Ms. Christine COLELLA
18	Director Finance & Physical Plant	Mr. John W. WINICKI
19	Manager of Security Information	Ofcr. William PEPITONE
30	Interim Director of Development	Ms. Christine LINVILL
26	Director of Marketing Communication	Ms. Kelly PEIFFER
32	Dean of Students	Ms. Allison C. MOOTZ
37	Director Financial Aid	Mr. Chris T. HARTMAN
38	Director Counseling	Ms. Christine B. PRINCE
39	Residence Hall Coordinator	Ms. Lynn WALES
41	Director Athletics	Mr. John DEMPSTER
49	Lib Arts Chair/Dir of Psychology	Ms. Christine ERDNER
08	Head Librarian	Ms. Donna GUERIN
09	Director of Institutional Research	Mr. John T. KREBS
07	Director of Admissions	Ms. Stephanie WALKER

Marywood University (B)

2300 Adams Avenue, Scranton PA 18509-1598

County: Lackawanna
FICE Identification: 003296
Unit ID: 213826
Telephone: (570) 348-6211
Carnegie Class: Masters/L
FAX Number: (570) 961-4769
Calendar System: Semester
URL: www.marywood.edu
Established: 1915
Annual Undergrad Tuition & Fees: $33,000
Enrollment: 3,010
Coed
Affiliation or Control: Roman Catholic
IRS Status: 501(c)3
Highest Offering: Doctorate
Accreditation: M, ACBSP, ARCPA, ART, #CAATE, CACREP, CAEPN, CLPSY, DIETC, DIETD, DIETI, MUS, NUR, NURSE, SP, SW

01	President	Sr. Mary PERSICO, IHM
05	Provost/Vice Pres Academic Affairs	Dr. Susan C. TURELL
10	VP Business Affairs/Treasurer	Ms. Tammy J. MCHALE
111	Vice Pres University Advancement	Dr. Renee G. ZEHEL
84	VP Enrollment Svcs/Student Success	Ms. Ann BOLAND-CHASE
101	Secretary Univ & General Counsel	Atty. Mary T. GARDIER PATERSON
15	Assoc Vice Pres for Human Resources	Dr. Patricia E. DUNLEAVY
26	Assoc VP Marketing/Communication	Vacant
18	Asst VP for Buildings & Grounds	Mrs. Wendy YANKELITIS
49	Dean College Liberal Arts/Sci	Dr. Frances M. ZAUHAR
76	Dean Col of Health/Human Svcs	Dr. Mark E. RODGERS
107	Dean Col of Prof Studies	Mr. James J. SULLIVAN
90	Director User Support Services	Dr. Michael MIRABITO
70	Director School of Social Work	Dr. Stephen BURKE
08	Director of Library Services	Mr. David G. SCHAPPERT
06	Registrar	Ms. Rosemary BURGER
07	Sr Dir of University Admissions	Mr. Christian M. DIGREGORIO
21	Controller/Asst Treasurer	Mr. Patrick E. CASTELLANI
21	Asst Controller	Ms. Melissa A. SADDLEMIRE
88	Asst Director Buildings & Grounds	Mr. Myron MARCINEK
37	Director of Financial Aid	Ms. Barbara L. SCHMITT
44	Annual Giving Officer	Ms. Patricia H. ROSETTI
112	Director of Planned Giving	Ms. Elizabeth A. CONNERY
27	Public Relations Director	Ms. Juneann GRECO
42	Chaplain/Asst Dir Campus Ministry	Rev. Joseph P. ELSTON
39	Dean of Students	Mr. Ross NOVAK
41	Director Athletics/Recreation	Dr. Mary Jo GUNNING
36	Asst Dir of Advising & Career Dev	Ms. Christina BRUNDAGE
42	Dir of Mission & Campus Ministry	Sr. Catherine LUXNER
88	Dir of Dining Services	Mr. Jon BARZENSKY
13	Chief Information Officer	Vacant
19	Chief Campus Safety	Mr. Michael J. FINEGAN
23	Director of Student Health Services	Ms. Linda MCDADE
38	Director Counseling & Student Devel	Dr. Robert S. SHAW
40	Bookstore Manager	Ms. Joan DIEHL
104	Assoc Dir Intl & Multicultl Affairs	Ms. Anne O. MALONEY
14	Director of Operations	Mr. John B. PORTER
30	Dir Advancement Services	Ms. Elizabeth M. STIRES
29	Director of Alumni Engagement	Vacant
35	Dir of Student Act/Leadership Devel	Ms. Kimberly E. COLEMAN
28	Director of Diversity	Dr. Lia Richards PALMITER
09	Asst Dir for Res & Spons Programs	Dr. Diane KELLER
45	Assoc VP Plng/Inst Effectiveness	Dr. Kathleen O. RUTHKOSKY
90	Asst Director of User Support	Ms. Katherine P. LEWIS

McCann School of Business & Technology (C)

2200 North Irving Street, Allentown PA 18109

Telephone: (484) 223-4601
Identification: 770768
Accreditation: ACICS, MAC, MLTAD

McCann School of Business & Technology (D)

346 York Road, Carlisle PA 17013

Telephone: (714) 218-3400
Identification: 770767
Accreditation: ACICS, SURGT

McCann School of Business & Technology (E)

2227 Scranton Carbondale Highway,
Dickson City PA 18519

Telephone: (570) 969-4330
Identification: 770769
Accreditation: ACICS, MAC

† Branch campus of McCann School of Business & Technology, Pottsville, PA. No longer accepting campus-based students.

McCann School of Business & Technology (F)

370 Maplewood Drive, Humbolt Ind Pk,
Hazleton PA 18202-9790

Telephone: (570) 454-6172
Identification: 666484
Accreditation: ACICS, EMT, MAC, SURGT

† Branch campus of McCann School of Business & Technology, Pottsville, PA. No longer accepting campus-based students.

McCann School of Business & Technology (G)

7495 Westbranch Highway, Lewisburg PA 17837

Telephone: (570) 497-8014
Identification: 666485
Accreditation: ACICS, MAC, MLTAD, SURGT

† Branch campus of McCann School of Business & Technology, Pottsville, PA.

McCann School of Business & Technology (H)

2650 Woodglen Road, Pottsville PA 17901-1335

County: Schuylkill
FICE Identification: 004898
Unit ID: 438212
Telephone: (570) 622-7622
Carnegie Class: Assoc/HVT-Mix Trad/Non
FAX Number: (570) 622-7770
Calendar System: Quarter
URL: www.mccann.edu
Established: 1897
Annual Undergrad Tuition & Fees: $10,135
Enrollment: 1,812
Coed
Affiliation or Control: Proprietary
IRS Status: Proprietary
Highest Offering: Associate Degree
Accreditation: ACICS, MAC

01	Campus Director	Ms. Shanon BRENNAN
05	Director of Education	Ms. Jo Ann BARTUSIK
36	Director of Career Services	Ms. Michelle SCRIBBICK

McCann School of Business & Technology (I)

264 Highland Park Boulevard, Wilkes Barre PA 18702

Telephone: (570) 235-2200
Identification: 770770
Accreditation: ACICS

† Branch campus of McCann School of Business & Technology, Pottsville, PA. No longer accepting campus-based students.

Mercyhurst University (J)

501 E 38th Street, Erie PA 16546-0001

County: Erie
FICE Identification: 003297
Unit ID: 213987
Telephone: (814) 824-2000
Carnegie Class: Masters/M
FAX Number: (814) 824-2438
Calendar System: Semester
URL: www.mercyhurst.edu
Established: 1926
Annual Undergrad Tuition & Fees: $34,580
Enrollment: 2,828
Coed
Affiliation or Control: Roman Catholic
IRS Status: 501(c)3
Highest Offering: Doctorate
Accreditation: M, #ARCPA, CAATE, DANCE, IACBE, MUS, NUR, PTAA, SW

01	President	Mr. Michael T. VICTOR
05	Provost & VP Academic Affairs	Dr. David DAUSEY
10	Vice Pres Finance & Administration	Mr. David P. MYRON
12	Exec VP Mercyhurst - NE	Dr. David HYLAND
30	Vice Pres University Development	Mr. Caleb M. PIFER
32	Vice Pres of Student Life	Dr. Laura ZIRKEL
84	VP for Enrollment	Mr. Joe HOWARD
13	Chief Information Officer	Ms. Jeanette BRITT
18	Director Facilities/Physical Plant	Mr. David MYRON
38	Director Student Counseling Service	Ms. Judy SMITH
07	Director Undergraduate Admissions	Mr. Christian BEYER
06	Registrar	Ms. Michele WHEATON
08	Dir Univ Libraries/Online Learning	Ms. Darci JONES
39	Dir Residential Life/Stdnt Conduct	Ms. Megan MCKENNA
19	Director of Public Safety Programs	Mr. Donald J. FUHRMANN
29	Dir Alumni Rels & Annual Giving	Ms. Courtney OLEVNIK
42	Director of Campus Ministry	Fr. James PISZKER
37	Director of Student Financial Svcs	Ms. Carrie NEWMAN
41	Director of Athletics	Mr. Joseph KIMBALL
09	Director of Institutional Research	Mrs. Sheila W. RICHTER
15	Director Human Resources	Mr. Jim TOMETSKO
28	Coordinator Multicultural Affairs	Mr. Tyler BRENTLEY
04	Administrative Asst to President	Ms. Stacey WILEY
104	Director Study Abroad	Dr. Heidi HOSEY
26	Chief Public Relations/Marketing	Mrs. Dionne VEITCH
43	Dir Legal Services/General Counsel	Mrs. Meredith BOLLHEIMER

Mercyhurst University Northeast (K)

16 W Division Street, North East PA 16428

Telephone: (814) 725-6100
Identification: 770161
Accreditation: &M, ADNUR, COARC, MLTAD, OTA

Messiah College (L)

One College Avenue, Mechanicsburg PA 17055

County: Cumberland
FICE Identification: 003298
Unit ID: 213996
Telephone: (717) 766-2511
Carnegie Class: Bac-Diverse
FAX Number: (717) 691-6025
Calendar System: Semester
URL: www.messiah.edu
Established: 1909
Annual Undergrad Tuition & Fees: $33,180
Enrollment: 3,302
Coed
Affiliation or Control: Interdenominational
IRS Status: 501(c)3
Highest Offering: Doctorate
Accreditation: M, ACBSP, ART, CAATE, CACREP, DIETD, @DIETI, ENG, MUS, NURSE, SW, THEA

01	President	Dr. Kim S. PHIPPS
05	Provost	Dr. Randall G. BASINGER
10	Vice Pres for Finance & Planning	Mr. David S. WALKER
11	Vice President for Operations	Mrs. Kathrynne G. SHAFER
30	Vice President for Advancement	Mr. Barry G. GOODLING
84	Vice Pres for Enrollment Management	Mr. John A. CHOPKA
15	VP for Human Res & Compliance	Ms. Amanda A. COFFEY
13	VP Info Technology/Assoc Provost	Dr. William G. STRAUSBAUGH
32	Vice Provost & Dean of Students	Dr. Kristin M. HANSEN-KIEFFER
58	Asst Provost Grad & Nontrad Pgms	Dr. Robert PEPPER
57	Dean School of the Arts	Dr. Richard E. ROBERSON
53	Dean School of Bus/Educ/Soc Sci	Dr. Carolyn MAURER
79	Dean School of Humanities	Dr. Peter K. POWERS
81	Dean School of Science/Engr/Health	Dr. Angela HARE
35	Associate Dean of Students	Mr. Douglas M. WOOD
88	Dir of Intercultural Office	Mrs. Faith MINNICH KJESBO
07	Director of Admissions	Mrs. Dana J. BRITTON
37	Director of Financial Aid	Mr. Gregory L. GEARHART
39	Asst Dir of Residence Life/Housing	Mrs. Rhonda KING
21	Dir Financial Operations/Controller	Mrs. Christine HARTMAN
06	Registrar	Mr. James J. SOTHERDEN
08	Director of the Murray Library	Mr. Jonathan D. LAUER
91	Director Information Services	Mr. John P. LUFT
90	Dir Learning Technology Services	Mrs. Susan K. SHANNON
09	Director of Institutional Research	Ms. Laura M. MILLER
42	College Pastor	Dr. Donald OPITZ
30	Director of Development	Dr. Jon C. STUCKEY
26	Exec Director Communications	Ms. Carla E. GROSS
29	Director Alumni & Parent Relations	Mr. Jay W. MCCLYMONT
44	Director of Annual Giving	Ms. Beth TROTT CLARK
38	Director of the Engle Center	Ms. Eleanor M. ADDLEMAN
41	Exec Dir of Athletics/Fundraising	Mr. Jack T. COLE
92	Dir of the College Honors Program	Dr. Dean C. CURRY
18	Director of Facility Services	Mr. Bradley A. MARKLEY
36	Dir Career/Profess Development	Mrs. Christina R. HANSON
40	Campus Store Manager	Ms. Candice TRITLE
19	Director Safety/Dispatch Services	Ms. Cindy L. BURGER
04	Executive Asst to President	Ms. Melissa COHEN
96	Purchasing Manager	Mrs. Daisy ANDERSON
23	Coordinator of Health Services	Mrs. Michelle LUCAS

Misericordia University (M)

301 Lake Street, Dallas PA 18612-1098

County: Luzerne
FICE Identification: 003247
Unit ID: 214069
Telephone: (570) 674-6400
Carnegie Class: Masters/M
FAX Number: (570) 675-2441
Calendar System: Semester
URL: www.misericordia.edu
Established: 1924
Annual Undergrad Tuition & Fees: $30,740
Enrollment: 2,963
Coed
Affiliation or Control: Roman Catholic
IRS Status: 501(c)3
Highest Offering: Doctorate
Accreditation: M, #ARCPA, DMS, IACBE, NURSE, OT, PTA, RAD, SP, SW

01 President Dr. Thomas J. BOTZMAN
10 Vice Pres Finance & Administration Mr. Mark VAN ETTEN, JR.
05 Vice President Academic Affairs Dr. David REHM
111 VP of Institutional Advancement Ms. Susan M. HELWIG
88 Vice Pres of Mission Integration Sr. Jean MESSAROS
45 Sec to BOT/VP Plng/External Rels Dr. Barbara SAMUEL LOFTUS
32 Vice President of Student Life Ms. Kathleen FOLEY
84 Vice President of Enrollment Mgmt Mr. Glenn BOZINSKI
21 Controller Mr. Ronald S. HROMISIN
06 Registrar Mr. Joseph REDINGTON
29 Director Alumni Relations Vacant
08 Librarian Ms. Jennifer LUKSA
04 Exec Assistant to the President Ms. Nancy ALLAN
96 Director of Purchasing Mr. Thomas F. KANE
38 Exec Dir Learning Resource Ctr Ms. Jessica RANDALL
42 Director Campus Ministry Ms. Christine SOMERS
41 Director of Athletics Mr. Charles EDKINS
39 Director of Residents Ms. Donna ELLIS
13 Manager Applications Development Mr. Matt MIHAL
14 Director of Information Technology Mr. Val APANOVICH
35 Director of Student Life Ms. Darcy BRODMERKEL
36 Dir Insalaco Ctr Career Development Ms. Bernadette RUSHMER
102 Dir Foundation/Government Relations Mr. Larry PELLEGRINI
51 Director of Adult Education/CACE Mr. Paul NARDONE
15 Director of Human Resources Ms. Pamela PARSNIK
04 Special Assistant to President Mr. James ROBERTS
37 Director of Financial Aid Ms. Susan FRONZONI
28 Dir Multicultural/Student Outreach Ms. Charmaine AGUILAR
19 Assoc Director Security/Safety Mr. Robert ZAVADA
18 Director of Facilities Vacant
09 Asst Dir of Institutional Research Ms. Sharon HUDAK
90 Manager of User Services Mr. David A. JOHNDROW

Montgomery County Community College (A)

340 Dekalb Pike, Blue Bell PA 19422-1400

County: Montgomery FICE Identification: 004452
Unit ID: 214111
Telephone: (215) 641-6300 Carnegie Class: Assoc/HT-Mix Trad/Non
FAX Number: (215) 461-1460 Calendar System: Semester
URL: www.mc3.edu
Established: 1964 Annual Undergrad Tuition & Fees (In-District): $5,610
Enrollment: 12,372 Coed
Affiliation or Control: State/Local IRS Status: 501(c)3
Highest Offering: Associate Degree
Accreditation: M, ADNUR, CSHSE, DH, IFSAC, MAC, MLTAD, PHLEB, RAD, SURGT

01 President Dr. Kevin POLLOCK
04 Exec Assistant to the President Mrs. Lynn KUSH
101 Exec Asst to the Board of Trustees Ms. Deborah A. ROGERS
05 VP for Academic Affairs & Provost Dr. Victoria BASTECKI-PEREZ
12 VP of the West Campus Dr. David DIMATTIO
13 VP for Information Technology Ms. Celeste M. SCHWARTZ
10 VP for Finance & Administration Mr. Charles SOMERS
30 Vice Pres of Devel & External Rels Ms. Arline STEPHAN
84 VP for Stdnt Affs & Enroll Mgmt Mr. Philip NEEDLES
06 Registrar Ms. Sherry PHILLIPS
15 Executive Director Human Resources Ms. Diane O'CONNOR
21 Controller Ms. Heather MEIER
110 Senior Director of Development Ms. Leslie BLUESTONE
19 Director of Campus Safety Mr. Joseph MCGURIMAN
37 Director of Financial Aid Ms. Tracey RICHARDS
09 Exec Dir of Inst Research Mr. David KOWALSKI
28 Dir Equity & Diversity Initiatives Ms. Rose MAKOFSKE
29 Dir of Alumni Rel & Major Gifts Mr. Bradley SMITH
26 Director of Strategic Communication Mr. Daniel HANSON
41 Dir of Athletics & Campus Rec Mr. Bruce BACH
07 Exec Dir of Recruitment & Partner Ms. Joyce WHEATLEY
08 Dean of Libraries & Acad Support Ms. Jenifer BLADWIN
18 Director of Facilities Mgmt Mr. Charles SCANDONE
102 Dir of Corp & Found Rels & Grants Ms. Susan FRIEDLAND
32 Dean of Student Affairs Ms. Nicole HENDERSON
96 Director of Procurement Ms. Jenny RARIG
103 Executive Director of Workforce Dev Mr. Jim FOX
50 Dean of Business & Entepreneurial Mr. Gaetan GIANNINI

Montgomery County Community College West Campus (B)

101 College Drive, Pottstown PA 19464
Telephone: (610) 718-1800 Identification: 770162
Accreditation: &M

Moore College of Art and Design (C)

20th and The Parkway, Philadelphia PA 19103-1179

County: Philadelphia FICE Identification: 003300
Unit ID: 214148
Telephone: (215) 965-4000 Carnegie Class: Spec-4-yr-Arts
FAX Number: (215) 568-8017 Calendar System: Semester
URL: www.moore.edu
Established: 1848 Annual Undergrad Tuition & Fees: $38,301
Enrollment: 439 Female
Affiliation or Control: Independent Non-Profit IRS Status: 501(c)3
Highest Offering: Master's
Accreditation: M, ART, CIDA

01 President Ms. Cecelia FITZGIBBON
10 SVP Finance & Administration Mr. William L. HILL, II
05 Academic Dean Ms. Patti PHILLIPS
32 Dean of Students Mr. Joshua WILKIN
20 Assoc Dean Educational Support Svcs Ms. Claudine THOMAS
39 Director Residence Life/Housing Mr. Matthew POINT
88 Director of Galleries Ms. Gabrielle LAVIN
51 Director of Continuing Education Ms. Judith WOODWORTH
26 Chief Communications Officer Mr. Roy A. WILBUR
30 Director of Development Ms. Elizabeth CAHILL
110 Assoc Director of Development Ms. Patricia MA
29 Dir Alumnae Affairs/Annual Fund Ms. Claire WILSON
08 Library Director Ms. Kimberly LESLEY
07 Dean of Admissions Mr. Jonathan SQUIRE
37 Director of Financial Aid Ms. Devon WEAVER
06 Registrar Ms. Brooke TOBEY
18 Director of Operations Mr. Kenneth M. FERRETTI
15 Director Human Resources Ms. Rachel PHILLIPS
36 Director Career Center Ms. Belena CHAPP
58 Graduate Studies Coordinator Ms. Alison GIANTISCO
38 Director Student Counseling Ms. Ruth R. GAYLE
90 Academic Computing Manager Mr. Dennis DAWTON
04 Executive Asst to President Ms. Alysson CWYK

Moravian College (D)

1200 Main St., Bethlehem PA 18018-6650

County: Northampton FICE Identification: 003301
Unit ID: 214157
Telephone: (610) 861-1300 Carnegie Class: Bac-A&S
FAX Number: (610) 625-7918 Calendar System: Semester
URL: www.moravian.edu
Established: 1742 Annual Undergrad Tuition & Fees: $40,287
Enrollment: 2,261 Coed
Affiliation or Control: Moravian Church IRS Status: 501(c)3
Highest Offering: Master's
Accreditation: M, ACBSP, MUS, NURSE, THEOL

01 President Dr. Bryon L. GRIGSBY
05 Provost Dr. Cynthia KOSSO
10 Vice President Finance & Admin Mr. Mark F. REED
111 Vice Pres Institutional Advancement Mr. Gary CARNEY
32 Vice President Student Affairs Dr. Nicole L. LOYD
73 Vice Pres/Dean of the Seminary Dr. Frank CROUCH
84 Dean of Enrollment Mr. William SLIWA
13 Interim Chief Information Officer Mr. David BRANDES
09 VP Planning and Research Ms. Carole A. REESE
15 VP Resources Officer Mr. Jon B. CONRAD
35 VP Student Affairs Dean of Students Dr. Nicole L. LOYD
36 Assoc Dean of Career Ms. Amy SAUL
20 Assoc Provost Dr. Carol TRAUPMAN-CARR
39 Asst Dean for Residence Life Ms. Liz YATES
121 Asst Dean for Academic Advising Vacant
21 Treasurer Ms. Anne M. REID
88 Director of Student Accounts Ms. Dawn SNOOK
06 Institutional Registrar Ms. Monique DAVIS
21 Dir Business/Financial Operations Ms. Rachel LYALL
44 Director of Leadership Giving Ms. Bertie KNISELY
18 Dir Facilities Mgt Plng/Construct Mr. Douglas J. PLOTTS
19 Director of Campus Safety Mr. George BOKSAN
26 Dir of Marketing & Communications Mr. Michael CORR
08 Library Director Ms. Janet OHLES
37 Director of Financial Aid Dr. Dennis P. LEVY
38 Director of Counseling Dr. Ronald J. KLINE
40 Bookstore Manager Mr. Robert RUSH, III
41 Director of Athletics Ms. Mary Beth SPIRK
42 Chaplain Rev. Jennika BORGER
88 Director of the Payne Gallery Dr. Diane RADYCKI
101 Asst to Pres Projects & Board Suppt Mrs. Elaine C. DEITCH
23 Nurse Coordinator Mrs. Stephanie C. DILLMAN
104 Director of International Studies Mr. Christian SINCLAIR
24 Media Center Manager Mr. Craig UNDERWOOD
123 Executive Dir Grad Admissions Mr. Scott DAMS
29 Director Alumni Relations Ms. Patricia HANNA
105 Webmaster Ms. Christie JACOBSEN
28 Assoc Dir of Intercultural Advance Ms. Liliana MADRID

Mount Aloysius College (E)

7373 Admiral Peary Highway, Cresson PA 16630-1999

County: Cambria FICE Identification: 003302
Unit ID: 214166
Telephone: (814) 886-6383 Carnegie Class: Bac/Assoc-Mixed
FAX Number: (814) 886-2978 Calendar System: Semester
URL: www.mtaloy.edu
Established: 1853 Annual Undergrad Tuition & Fees: $21,850
Enrollment: 1,877 Coed
Affiliation or Control: Independent Non-Profit IRS Status: 501(c)3
Highest Offering: Master's
Accreditation: M, ADNUR, DMS, MAC, MLTAD, NUR, PTAA, SURGT

01 President Dr. Thomas P. FOLEY
05 Sr VP Academic Affs/Dean of Faculty Vacant
32 VP Student Affs/Dean Students Dr. Jane M. GRASSADONIA
84 VP Enrollment Mgmt/Dean Admissions Mr. Francis C. CROUSE, JR.
07 Director of Freshmen Admissions Mr. Andrew D. CLOUSE
07 Director of Transfer Admissions Mr. Richard MISHLER
111 VP Institutional Advancement Ms. Jennifer DUBUQUE
10 VP Finance & Administration Mr. Michael BAKER
06 Registrar Dr. Christopher M. LOVETT
08 Director of Library Vacant
37 Director of Financial Aid Ms. Stacy L. SCHENK
15 Director of Human Resources Ms. Tonia J. GORDON
26 Director of Communications Mr. John COYLE
13 Director of Information Technology Mr. Rich J. SHEA
23 Director of Health Services Ms. Shannon D. GROVE
40 Director of Bookstore Ms. Christine M. CLINTON
41 Director of Athletics Mr. Ryan M. SMITH
19 Director of Safety & Security Mr. William H. TREXLER
18 Director of Physical Plant Mr. Gerald RUBRITZ
09 Institutional Researcher Mr. Bryan J. PEARSON
36 Career Development Coordinator Ms. Kristy MAGEE
38 Dir Student Counseling/Disabilities Ms. Marisa L. EVANS
39 Director of Residence Life Mr. Matthew LOVELL
88 Exec Dir of Mission Integration Ms. Christina KOREN
42 Director Campus Ministry Ms. Amy KANICH
44 Manager of Annual Giving Ms. Sally GORDON
04 Administrative Asst to President Ms. Carla NELEN

Muhlenberg College (F)

2400 West Chew Street, Allentown PA 18104-5586

County: Lehigh FICE Identification: 003304
Unit ID: 214175
Telephone: (484) 664-3100 Carnegie Class: Bac-A&S
FAX Number: (484) 664-3234 Calendar System: Semester
URL: www.muhlenberg.edu
Established: 1848 Annual Undergrad Tuition & Fees: $48,310
Enrollment: 2,397 Coed
Affiliation or Control: Evangelical Lutheran Church In America
IRS Status: 501(c)3
Highest Offering: Baccalaureate
Accreditation: M

01 President Mr. John I. WILLIAMS, JR.
05 Provost Dr. Kathleen HARRING
10 Treasurer & Chief Finance Officer Mr. Kent DYER
26 Executive Director of Communication Mr. William KELLER
111 Vice President of Advancement Ms. Rebekkah L. BROWN
15 Vice President of Human Resources Ms. Anne SPECK
32 Vice President of Student Affairs Ms. Allison GULATI
04 Exec Asst to the President & BoT Mr. Ken BUTLER
30 Senior Assoc VP for Development Ms. Deborah J. KIPP
35 Dean of Students Ms. Allison GULATI
20 Dean of Academic Life Dr. Bruce ANDERSON
86 Dean of Global Education Dr. Donna M. KISH-GOODLING
06 Assoc Dean Admission/Dir Finan Aid Mr. Gregory S. MITTON
22 Asst Dean Acad Res/Disability Svcs Mr. David HALLOWELL
29 Asst VP Alumni Affairs/Career Svc Ms. Natalie HAND
51 Dean Wescoe Sch of Continuing Educ Ms. Jane E. HUDAK
84 VP of Enrollment Management Mr. Robert SPRINGALL
08 Director of Trexler Library Ms. Tina L. HERTEL
06 Registrar Ms. Deborah TAMTE-HORAN
13 Chief Information Officer Mr. Allan CHEN
19 Dir/Chief of Campus Safety/Security Mr. Brian FIDATI
124 Assoc Dean Students/Dir Stu Engage Ms. Janette SCHUMACHER
36 Executive Director Career Svcs Mr. Tom DOWD
21 Assistant Treasurer Mr. Jason FEIERTAG
23 Exec Dir Health/Counseling Svcs Ms. Brynnmarie DORSEY
38 Director Counseling Services Dr. Timothy SILVESTRI
42 Chaplain Rev. Callista S. ISABELLE
09 Dir Institutional Research/Records Ms. Nicole HAMMEL
18 Director Plant Operations Mr. James BOLTON
96 Director of Purchasing Mr. Brian BLENIS
40 Bookstore Manager Ms. Karen R. NORMANN

Neumann University (G)

One Neumann Drive, Aston PA 19014-1298

County: Delaware FICE Identification: 003988
Unit ID: 214272
Telephone: (610) 459-0905 Carnegie Class: Masters/M
FAX Number: (610) 459-1370 Calendar System: Semester
URL: www.neumann.edu
Established: 1965 Annual Undergrad Tuition & Fees: $28,580
Enrollment: 2,901 Coed
Affiliation or Control: Roman Catholic IRS Status: 501(c)3
Highest Offering: Doctorate
Accreditation: M, ACBSP, CAATE, CACREP, MT, NUR, PTA, @SW

01 President Dr. Chris E. DOMES
05 Vice President Academic Affairs Dr. Lawrence DIPAOLO
43 General Counsel Ms. Danielle MCNICHOL
10 Vice Pres Finance/Administration Mr. Gene MCWILLIAMS
42 Vice President Mission/Ministry Sr. Marguerite O'BEIRNE, OSF
111 Vice Pres Inst Advance/Univ Rels Mr. Henry A. SUMNER
32 Vice Pres Student Affairs & Enroll Dr. Dianna C. DALE
15 Vice President HR & Risk Management Mr. David W. BROWNLEE
49 Dean Division of Arts & Science Dr. Alfred G. MUELLER, II
50 Dean Div of Business/Info Mgmt Dr. Eric R. WELLINGTON
53 Dean Div of Educ/Human Svcs Dr. Barbara HANES
51 Dean Cont Adult/Prof Stds Dr. Jilian DONNELLY
66 Dean Div Nursing/Health Sciences Dr. Kathleen HOOVER
04 Assistant to President Ms. Danielle WAGNER
06 Registrar Mr. Joel A. NATALE
18 Facilities Director Mr. William LEONARD
19 Director Safety & Security Mr. Leon FRANCIS
08 Director Library Ms. Tiffany MCGREGOR
26 Exec Director Mktg/Communications Mr. Stephen BELL
09 Dir of IR and Assessment Ms. Melissa THORPE
42 Chaplain Fr. Stephen D. THORNE
44 Director Annual Giving/Prospect Mgt Ms. Christina FARRELL
29 Dir Alumni Rels/Special Programs Ms. Judi STANAITIS
38 Director Counseling Vacant

39 Director Housing & Residence Life .... Mr. Michael WEBSTER
13 Exec Director University Computing .... Mr. David O'LEARY
24 Director Academic Resource Center .... Ms. Theresa HUKE
41 Director Athletics .... Mr. Chuck SACK
36 Dir Career & Personal Development .... Ms. Mary MCCAFFREY
88 Dean Academic Support Services .... Mr. Michael MULLEN
88 Director Child Development Center .... Ms. Mary Ann MELISI
21 Controller .... Mr. John YOUHOUSE
37 Director Financial Assistance .... Ms. Andrea DEL VACCHIO
23 Director Health Services .... Ms. Janet GEDDIS
96 Coordinator for Purchasing .... Ms. Elena BARRAR
88 Director Physical Therapy Program .... Dr. Robert POST
07 Dir of Undergraduate Admissions .... Vacant
88 Dir Ctr for Sprt/Spir/Char Dev .... Ms. Lee M. DELLEMONACHE
90 Director Instructional Technology .... Vacant
88 Director Conference/Scheduling Svcs .... Ms. Melissa HAINES
40 Director University Bookstore .... Ms. Natalie VAN WYK
88 Director Transitional Education .... Ms. Lori BLOUNT
104 Coord International Studies Educ .... Ms. Jen MINTZER
121 Director of Student Success .... Ms. Coleen NEDBALSKI
105 Director Web Services .... Vacant
106 Dir Online Education/E-learning .... Dr. Jilian DONNELLY
84 Dean of Enrollment Management .... Ms. Susan P. KASSAB
88 Program Director Athletic Training .... Dr. Hubert LEE
123 Dir of Adult & Graduate Admissions .... Dr. Erika DAVIS

New Castle School of Trades (A)

4117 Pulaski Road, New Castle PA 16101
County: Lawrence FICE Identification: 007780
Unit ID: 214290
Telephone: (724) 964-8811 Carnegie Class: Assoc/HVT-Mix Trad/Non
FAX Number: (724) 202-6147 Calendar System: Other
URL: www.ncstrades.edu
Established: 1945 Annual Undergrad Tuition & Fees: N/A
Enrollment: 759 Coed
Affiliation or Control: Proprietary IRS Status: Proprietary
Highest Offering: Associate Degree
Accreditation: ACCSC

01 Director .... Mr. Jim BUTTERMORE
05 Director of Education .... Mr. Tony GIOVANNELLI
07 Director of Admissions .... Mr. Joe BLAZAK
88 Veteran Affairs Director .... Mr. Jim CATHELINE
10 Fiscal Director .... Mrs. JoAnn MELNIK
36 Director Student Placement .... Mrs. Carrie KRAYNAK
37 Director Student Financial Aid .... Mrs. Trudy SOTTER

Northampton Community College (B)

3835 Green Pond Road, Bethlehem PA 18020-7599
County: Northampton FICE Identification: 007191
Unit ID: 214379
Telephone: (610) 861-5300 Carnegie Class: Assoc/MT-VT-High Trad
FAX Number: (610) 861-5070 Calendar System: Semester
URL: www.northampton.edu
Established: 1967 Annual Undergrad Tuition & Fees (In-District): $4,110
Enrollment: 10,269 Coed
Affiliation or Control: State/Local IRS Status: 170(c)1
Highest Offering: Associate Degree
Accreditation: M, ACBSP, ADNUR, DH, DMS, FUSER, PNUR, RAD

01 President .... Dr. Mark H. ERICKSON
05 Vice President Academic Affairs .... Dr. Carolyn BORTZ
100 Chief of Staff .... Dr. David RUTH
10 Vice President Finance & Operations .... Mr. James F. DUNLEAVY
30 Vice Pres Institutional Advancement .... Ms. Sharon BEALES
32 Vice Pres Enroll/Student Affairs .... Mr. Sedwick HARRIS
31 Vice President Community Education .... Dr. Paul E. PIERPOINT
12 Dean Monroe Campus .... Dr. Matthew J. CONNELL
79 Dean Humanities & Social Sciences .... Dr. Christine PENSE
53 Dean Education/Academic Success .... Dr. Elizabeth BUGAIGHIS
50 Dean Business & Technology .... Dr. Denise FRANCOIS-SEENY
76 Dean Allied Health & Sciences .... Dr. Judith REX
13 Assoc VP/Chief Information Officer .... Dr. Deborah BURAK
26 Exec Dir Marketing & Communications .... Mr. Brad DREXLER
06 Interim Registrar .... Ms. Ginger YAVORSKI
07 Director Admissions .... Mr. James MCCARTHY
37 Director Financial Aid .... Ms. Cynthia L. KING
108 Dir of Institutional Effectiveness .... Ms. Dorothy SCHRAMM
15 Exec Director of Human Resources .... Mr. Brett I. LAST
09 Director of Institutional Research .... Ms. Kathy KAPCSOS
18 Director Buildings & Grounds .... Mr. Mark K. CULP
29 Dir Alumni Engagement/Annual Fund .... Ms. Karen GLOSE
36 Director Career Services .... Ms. Karen VERES
35 Dean of Students .... Mr. Eric ROSENTHAL
84 Senior Assoc Dir of Enrollment Svcs .... Ms. Mary S. MANCINO

Northampton Community College Monroe County Branch Campus (C)

205 Old Mill Road, Tannersville PA 18372
Telephone: (570) 620-9221 Identification: 770164
Accreditation: &M

Peirce College (D)

1420 Pine Street, Philadelphia PA 19102-4699
County: Philadelphia FICE Identification: 003309
Unit ID: 214883
Telephone: (215) 545-6400 Carnegie Class: Bac-Diverse
FAX Number: (215) 670-9366 Calendar System: Semester
URL: www.peirce.edu
Established: 1865 Annual Undergrad Tuition & Fees: $14,472
Enrollment: 1,708 Coed
Affiliation or Control: Independent Non-Profit IRS Status: 501(c)3
Highest Offering: Master's
Accreditation: M, ACBSP, CAHIIM

01 President & CEO .... Mr. James J. MERGIOTTI
10 VP Finance/Administration .... Ms. Elizabeth M. KRAPP
05 VP Academic Advancement .... Dr. Rita J. TOLIVER-ROBERTS
111 VP Institutional Advancement .... Ms. Uva C. COLES
26 VP Marketing & Admissions .... Ms. Lisa PARIS
32 VP Student Services/Retention Mgmt .... Mr. Brad K. HODGE
15 VP Human Res/Chief Diversity Ofcr .... Ms. Harriet S. GOLEN
108 Asst VP Institutional Assessment .... Ms. Debra S. SCHRAMMEL
13 Chief Information Officer .... Mr. James T. BURNS
109 Chief Auxiliary Services Officer .... Mr. Vito R. CHIMENTI
20 Assoc Dean Academic Ops/Faculty Sup .... Mr. Jon LENROW
04 Administrative Asst to President .... Ms. Tara E. MCBRIDE

Penn Commercial Business/ Technical School (E)

242 Oak Spring Road, Washington PA 15301-6822
County: Washington FICE Identification: 004902
Unit ID: 214892
Telephone: (724) 222-5330 Carnegie Class: Assoc/HVT-High Trad
FAX Number: (724) 222-4722 Calendar System: Quarter
URL: www.penncommercial.edu
Established: 1929 Annual Undergrad Tuition & Fees: $25,000
Enrollment: 294 Coed
Affiliation or Control: Proprietary IRS Status: Proprietary
Highest Offering: Associate Degree
Accreditation: ACICS

01 Director .... Mr. Robert S. BAZANT
11 Vice President of Operations .... Ms. Marianne ALBERT
04 Assistant to the President .... Ms. Barbara KENNEDY
07 Director of Admissions .... Mr. Ron ZUBATY
32 Director of Student Affairs .... Mr. Brian CHIODO
37 Director of Financial Aid .... Ms. Jayne TUITE
88 Director of Education .... Ms. Pat DECONCILLIS
05 Director of Academic Affairs .... Ms. Anita ROSELL
09 Director of Reports & Statistics .... Mrs. Melissa PAPSON
36 Director of Career Services .... Mrs. Kristin WISSINGER

Penn State University Park (F)

201 Old Main, University Park PA 16802-1503
County: Centre FICE Identification: 003329
Unit ID: 214777
Telephone: (814) 865-4700 Carnegie Class: DU-Highest
FAX Number: (814) 863-7590 Calendar System: Semester
URL: www.psu.edu
Established: 1855 Annual Undergrad Tuition & Fees (In-State): $17,900
Enrollment: 47,307 Coed
Affiliation or Control: State Related IRS Status: 501(c)3
Highest Offering: Doctorate
Accreditation: M, ART, CAATE, CACREP, CAEPN, CEA, CLPSY, COPSY, DIETD, DIETI, ENG, FEPAC, HSA, IPSY, JOUR, LAW, LSAR, MUS, NURSE, PCSAS, SCPSY, SP, THEA

01 President .... Dr. Eric J. BARRON
05 Executive Vice President & Provost .... Dr. Nicholas P. JONES
46 Vice President Research .... Dr. Neil A. SHARKEY
32 Vice President Student Affairs .... Dr. Damon R. SIMS
26 Vice Pres Strategic Communications .... Mr. Lawrence H. LOKMAN
30 Vice Pres Develop/Alumni Relations .... Mr. O. Richard BUNDY, III
10 Sr Vice Pres Finance & Bus/Treas .... Mr. David J. GRAY
106 Interim Vice President for Outreach .... Ms. Tracey D. HUSTON
11 Vice President for Administration .... Dr. Thomas G. POOLE
104 Vice Provost for Global Programs .... Dr. Michael A. ADEWUMI
43 Vice President & General Counsel .... Dr. Stephen S. DUNHAM
49 Vice Pres & Dean Undergrad Educ ...... Dr. Robert N. PANGBORN
20 Vice Provost Faculty Affairs .... Dr. Kathleen BIESCHKE
28 Vice Provost Educ Equity .... Dr. Marcus A. WHITEHURST
12 Vice Pres Commonwealth Campuses .... Dr. Madlyn L. HANES
13 Vice Pres Info Technology/CIO .... Mr. Michael J. KUBIT
45 Vice Provost Plng and Assessment .... Dr. Lance C. KENNEDY-PHILLIPS
09 Assoc VP Plng/Inst Research .... Dr. Betty J. HARPER
108 Assoc VP Lng Outcomes Assessment .... Dr. Barbara A. MASI
22 Interim Vice Provost Affirm Action .... Ms. Carmen B. BORGES
114 Interim University Budget Officer .... Mr. Andrew G. REISINGER
21 Assoc Vice Pres Finance/Corp Cont .... Mr. Joseph J. DONCSECZ
21 Associate VP Finance/Business .... Mr. Kurt A. KISSINGER
15 Interim Vice Pres Human Resources .... Ms. Mary G. BEAHM
18 Assoc Vice President Physical Plant ...... Mr. William E. SITZABEE
109 Assoc VP Auxiliary & Business Svcs ...... Mr. John PAPAZOGLOU
106 Interim Vice Prov Online Education .... Dr. Renata S. ENGEL
27 Director News/Media Relations .... Ms. Lisa M. POWERS
39 Asst VP HFS & Residence Life .... Ms. Diane L. ANDREWS
37 Asst VP UG Ed/Exec Dir Stdnt Aid .... Ms. Anna M. GRISWOLD
29 Assoc VP Alum Rel/CEO PS Alum Assoc ... Mr. Paul J. CLIFFORD
115 Exec Director Office of Investment .... Mr. David E. BRANIGAN
07 Exec Director Undergrad Admissions .... Mr. Clark V. BRIGGER
38 Director Counseling/Psych Services .... Dr. Benjamin D. LOCKE
41 Athletic Director .... Ms. A. Sandy BARBOUR
86 Vice President for Govt Affairs .... Mr. Zachery MOORE
06 University Registrar .... Mr. Robert A. KUBAT
36 Senior Director Career Services .... Dr. Robert M. ORNDORFF
17 Sr Vice Pres Hlth Affs/CEO & Dean ...... Dr. A. Craig HILLEMEIER
08 Dean Univ Libraries/Scholar Comm .... Ms. Barbara I. DEWEY
47 Dean Agricultural Sciences .... Dr. Richard T. ROUSH
48 Dean Arts & Architecture .... Dr. Barbara O. KORNER
50 Dean Business .... Dr. Charles H. WHITEMAN
60 Dean Communications .... Dr. Marie HARDIN
65 Dean Earth & Mineral Sciences .... Dr. Lee KUMP
53 Dean Education .... Dr. David H. MONK
54 Dean Engineering .... Dr. Justin SCHWARTZ
58 V Prov Grad Educ/Dean Grad School .... Dr. Regina VASILATOS-YOUNKEN
76 Dean Health & Human Development .... Dr. Ann C. CROUTER
66 Interim Dean School of Nursing .... Dr. Janice L. PENROD
56 Assoc Dean/Dir Cooperative Exten .... Dr. Dennis D. CALVIN
83 Dean Liberal Arts .... Dr. Susan WELCH
81 Dean Science .... Dr. Douglas R. CAVENER
72 Dean Info Sciences and Technology .... Dr. Andrew L. SEARS
92 Dean Honors College .... Dr. Peggy A. JOHNSON
61 Interim Dean Penn State Law .... Dr. James W. HOUCK
63 Dean College of Medicine .... Dr. A. Craig HILLEMEIER
75 Chief Penn College of Technology .... Dr. Davie J. GILMOUR
44 Executive Director Annual Giving .... Ms. Jennifer D. BENOIT
88 Assoc Vice President for Research .... Dr. John W. HANOLD
19 Asst VP Univ Police/Public Safety .... Mr. Charles A. NOFFSINGER
23 Director University Health Services .... Dr. Robin E. OLIVER-VERONESI
96 Director Procurement Services .... Mr. R. Duane ELMORE
31 Director Campus & Cmty Affairs .... Ms. Barbara ETTARO
102 Exec Dir Corp/Foundation Relations .... Mr. Mark S. ARMAGOST
04 Exec Admin Assistant to President .... Ms. Carmella MULROY-DEGENHART
40 General Manager Bookstore .... Mr. Steve J. FALKE
25 Contract Coordinator .... Ms. Cristene N. BOOB
16 Senior Director Employee Relations .... Ms. Susan RUTAN
116 Director of Internal Audit .... Mr. Daniel P. HEIST
119 Chief Information Security Officer .... Mr. Donald J. WELCH, JR.

† The legal name of Penn State and all its campuses is The Pennsylvania State University. For communication purposes, the name is shortened to Penn State followed by the name of the campus.

Penn State Abington (G)

1600 Woodland Road, Abington PA 19001-3918
Telephone: (215) 881-7300 FICE Identification: 003342
Accreditation: &M, ENG

† Regional accreditation is carried under the parent institution in University Park, PA.

Penn State Altoona (H)

3000 Ivyside Park, Altoona PA 16601-3777
Telephone: (814) 949-5000 FICE Identification: 003331
Accreditation: &M, ENGT

† Regional accreditation is carried under the parent institution in University Park, PA.

Penn State Beaver (I)

100 University Drive, Monaca PA 15061-2764
Telephone: (724) 773-3800 FICE Identification: 003332
Accreditation: &M

† Regional accreditation is carried under the parent institution in University Park, PA.

Penn State Berks (J)

Tulpehocken Road, PO Box 7009, Reading PA 19610-1016
Telephone: (610) 396-6000 FICE Identification: 003334
Accreditation: &M, ENG, ENGT, OTA

† Regional accreditation is carried under the parent institution in University Park, PA.

Penn State Brandywine (K)

25 Yearsley Mill Road, Media PA 19063-5522
Telephone: (610) 892-1200 FICE Identification: 006922
Accreditation: &M, ENG

† Regional accreditation is carried under the parent institution in University Park, PA.

Penn State Dickinson Law (L)

150 South College Street, Carlisle PA 17013-2861
Telephone: (717) 240-5000 FICE Identification: 003254
Accreditation: &M, LAW

† Part of Penn State University. Regional accreditation is carried under the parent institution in University Park, PA.

Penn State DuBois (M)

One College Place, DuBois PA 15801-2549
Telephone: (814) 375-4700 FICE Identification: 003335
Accreditation: &M, ENG, ENGT, OTA, PTAA

† Regional accreditation is carried under the parent institution in University Park, PA.

Penn State Erie, The Behrend College (A)

4701 College Drive, Erie PA 16563-0001
Telephone: (814) 898-6000 FICE Identification: 003333
Accreditation: &M, ENG, ENGT

† Regional accreditation is carried under the parent institution in University Park, PA.

Penn State Fayette, The Eberly Campus (B)

2201 University Drive, Lemont Furnace PA 15456-1025
Telephone: (724) 430-4100 FICE Identification: 003336
Accreditation: &M, EMT, ENGT, PTAA

† Regional accreditation is carried under the parent institution in University Park, PA.

Penn State Great Valley School of Graduate Professional Studies (C)

30 E Swedesford Road, Malvern PA 19355-1488
Telephone: (610) 648-3200 FICE Identification: 003348
Accreditation: &M

† Regional accreditation is carried under the parent institution in University Park, PA.

Penn State Greater Allegheny (D)

4000 University Drive, McKeesport PA 15132-7644
Telephone: (412) 675-9000 FICE Identification: 003339
Accreditation: &M

† Regional accreditation is carried under the parent institution in University Park, PA.

Penn State Harrisburg (E)

777 West Harrisburg Pike, Middletown PA 17057-4846
Telephone: (717) 948-6250 FICE Identification: 006814
Accreditation: &M, CAEPN, ENG, ENGT, SPAA

† Regional accreditation is carried under the parent institution in University Park, PA.

Penn State Hazleton (F)

76 University Drive, Hazleton PA 18202-8025
Telephone: (570) 450-3000 FICE Identification: 003338
Accreditation: &M, ENG, MLTAD, PTAA

† Regional accreditation is carried under the parent institution in University Park, PA.

Penn State Lehigh Valley (G)

2809 Saucon Valley Road, Center Valley PA 18034-8447
Telephone: (610) 285-5000 FICE Identification: 003330
Accreditation: &M

† Regional accreditation is carried under the parent institution in University Park, PA.

Penn State Milton S. Hershey Medical Center College of Medicine (H)

500 University Drive, Hershey PA 17033-2360
Telephone: (717) 531-8563 FICE Identification: 006813
Accreditation: &M, #ARCPA, IPSY, MED, PAST, PH

† Regional accreditation is carried under the parent institution in University Park, PA.

Penn State Mont Alto (I)

One Campus Drive, Mont Alto PA 17237-9700
Telephone: (717) 749-6000 FICE Identification: 003340
Accreditation: &M, OTA, PTAA

† Regional accreditation is carried under the parent institution in University Park, PA.

Penn State New Kensington (J)

3550 Seventh Street Road, Route 780,
New Kensington PA 15068-1765
Telephone: (724) 334-5466 FICE Identification: 003341
Accreditation: &M, ENGT, RAD

† Regional accreditation is carried under the parent institution in University Park, PA.

Penn State Schuylkill (K)

200 University Drive, Schuylkill Haven PA 17972-2202
Telephone: (570) 385-6000 FICE Identification: 003343
Accreditation: &M, RAD

† Regional accreditation is carried under the parent institution in University Park, PA.

Penn State Shenango (L)

147 Shenango Avenue, Sharon PA 16146-1537
Telephone: (724) 983-2803 FICE Identification: 003345
Accreditation: &M, OTA, PTAA

† Regional accreditation is carried under the parent institution in University Park, PA.

Penn State Wilkes-Barre (M)

Old Route 115, PO Box PSU, Lehman PA 18627-0217
Telephone: (570) 675-2171 FICE Identification: 003346
Accreditation: &M, ENG, ENGT

† Regional accreditation is carried under the parent institution in University Park, PA.

Penn State Worthington-Scranton (N)

120 Ridge View Drive, Dunmore PA 18512-1602
Telephone: (570) 963-2500 FICE Identification: 003344
Accreditation: &M

† Regional accreditation is carried under the parent institution in University Park, PA.

Penn State York (O)

1031 Edgecomb Avenue, York PA 17403-3326
Telephone: (717) 771-4000 FICE Identification: 003347
Accreditation: &M, ENGT

† Regional accreditation is carried under the parent institution in University Park, PA.

Pennco Tech (P)

3815 Otter Street, Bristol PA 19007-3696
County: Bucks FICE Identification: 009449
Unit ID: 214944
Telephone: (215) 785-0111 Carnegie Class: Spec 2-yr-Tech
FAX Number: (215) 785-1945 Calendar System: Other
URL: www.penncotech.edu
Established: 1973 Annual Undergrad Tuition & Fees: N/A
Enrollment: 413 Coed
Affiliation or Control: Proprietary IRS Status: Proprietary
Highest Offering: Associate Degree
Accreditation: ACCSC

01 CEO .... Michael S. HOBYAK
03 School Director .... Fred PARCELLS
05 Director of Education .... Fred PARCELLS
07 Director of Admissions .... Vacant
06 Registrar .... Sondra KOOB
32 Director Student Services .... Hakien COLES
37 Director Student Financial Aid .... Keena FITZHUGH
36 Director Student Placement .... Teresa SCHEERER

Pennsylvania Academy of the Fine Arts (Q)

128 N Broad St, Philadelphia PA 19102-1424
County: Philadelphia FICE Identification: 021073
Unit ID: 214971
Telephone: (215) 972-7600 Carnegie Class: Spec-4-yr-Arts
FAX Number: (215) 569-0153 Calendar System: Semester
URL: www.pafa.edu
Established: 1805 Annual Undergrad Tuition & Fees: $36,058
Enrollment: 300 Coed
Affiliation or Control: Independent Non-Profit IRS Status: 501(c)3
Highest Offering: Master's
Accreditation: M, ART

01 President & CEO .... Dr. David R. BRIGHAM
30 Exec Vice President Development .... Ms. Melissa D. KAISER
26 Exec Vice President of Marketing .... Ms. Heike RASS
10 Chief Financial Officer .... Mr. Anthony DECOCINIS
07 Dean of Enrollment .... Ms. Casey TURNER
57 Dean of the School of Fine Arts .... Mr. Clint A. JUKKALA
32 Dean of Students .... Ms. Anne K. STASSEN
37 Director of Financial Aid .... Ms. Celeste FRANKLIN
36 Director of Career Services .... Mr. Gregory MARTINO
08 Director of Library Services .... Mr. Brian DUFFY
06 Registrar .... Mr. Peter MEDWICK
18 Director of Facilities Management .... Mr. Ed POLETTI
19 Director of Security and Safety .... Mr. Jimmie GREENO
13 Director of Information Technology .... Mr. Kevin MARTIN
05 Director of Academic Affairs .... Mr. Nathanael T. BROUHARD
04 Exec Assistant to President and CEO .... Ms. Sheryl KESSLER
58 Director of Grad Program Services .... Mr. Steven CONNELL
20 Academic Services Coordinator .... Mr. C.J STAHL

Pennsylvania College of Art & Design (R)

204 N Prince Street, Box 59, Lancaster PA 17608-0059
County: Lancaster FICE Identification: 022600
Unit ID: 215053
Telephone: (717) 396-7833 Carnegie Class: Spec-4-yr-Arts
FAX Number: (717) 396-1339 Calendar System: Semester
URL: www.pcad.edu
Established: 1982 Annual Undergrad Tuition & Fees: $23,800
Enrollment: 223 Coed
Affiliation or Control: Independent Non-Profit IRS Status: 501(c)3
Highest Offering: Baccalaureate
Accreditation: M, ART

01 President .... Ms. Mary Colleen HEIL
05 Academic Dean .... Mr. Marc TORICK
32 Dean of Student Services .... Ms. Jessica EDONICK
26 Director of Communications .... Ms. Kathleen TROY SMYSER
10 VP for Finance .... Ms. Jonelle MATTHEWS
07 Dir of Admiss/Mktg & Recruitment .... Ms. Natalie LASCEK
84 Director of Enrollment Planning .... Ms. Barbara ELLIOTT
37 Director Financial Aid .... Mr. J. David HERSHEY
08 Library Director .... Ms. Karen HUTCHISON
30 Director of Development .... Ms. Megan GALLAGHER
51 Director of Continuing Education .... Mr. Nick MOHLER
18 Director of Facilities .... Mr. Dan FREILER
06 Registrar .... Ms. Katie MYERS
13 Director of Information Technology .... Mr. Derrick GUTIERREZ

Pennsylvania College of Health Sciences (S)

850 Greenfield Road, Lancaster PA 17601
County: Lancaster FICE Identification: 009863
Unit ID: 442356
Telephone: (800) 622-5443 Carnegie Class: Spec-4-yr-Other Health
FAX Number: (717) 947-6250 Calendar System: Semester
URL: www.pacollege.edu
Established: 1903 Annual Undergrad Tuition & Fees: $25,510
Enrollment: 1,377 Coed
Affiliation or Control: Independent Non-Profit IRS Status: 501(c)3
Highest Offering: Master's
Accreditation: M, ADNUR, COARC, CVT, DMS, EMT, MT, NMT, NURSE, RAD, SURGT

01 President .... Dr. Mary Grace SIMCOX
05 VP Academic Affairs .... Mr. Jim SIBURT
45 VP Institutional Effectiveness .... Dr. Penni LONGENECKER
10 VP Finance & Administration .... Mr. Thomas HULSTINE
30 VP Advancement .... Ms. Ellen WILEY
84 VP Strategic Enrollment Mgmt .... Ms. Anne HAMILL
15 VP Human Resources .... Ms. Nancy FLOREY
13 AVP Information Technology .... Mr. Kevin BALSBAUGH
07 AVP Admissions and Strategic Mktg .... Ms. Michelle MEISER
88 AVP Enrollment Management .... Mr. Matthew SWATCHICK
04 Administrative Asst to President .... Ms. Susan GARDINA
06 Registrar .... Mr. Edwin ADDIS
32 Manager Student Services .... Mr. Bill RHINIER
29 Director Alumni Relations .... Mr. John ENDERLE

Pennsylvania College of Technology (T)

One College Avenue, Williamsport PA 17701-5799
County: Lycoming FICE Identification: 003395
Unit ID: 366252
Telephone: (570) 326-3761 Carnegie Class: Bac/Assoc-Mixed
FAX Number: (570) 327-4503 Calendar System: Semester
URL: www.pct.edu
Established: 1989 Annual Undergrad Tuition & Fees (In-State): $16,080
Enrollment: 5,514 Coed
Affiliation or Control: State IRS Status: 501(c)3
Highest Offering: Master's
Accreditation: M, ACBSP, ACFEI, ADNUR, ARCPA, CAHIIM, CONST, DH, EMT, ENGT, NAIT, NUR, OTA, PNUR, @PTAA, RAD, SURGT

01 President .... Dr. Davie Jane GILMOUR
05 VP for Academic Affairs/Provost .... Dr. Paul L. STARKEY
10 VP for Finance/CFO .... Ms. Suzanne T. STOPPER
111 Vice Pres Institutional Advancement .... Ms. Loni N. KLINE
13 Vice Pres for Info Tech/CIO .... Mr. A.J LACOMBA
84 VP Enrollment Mgmt & Assoc Provost .... Dr. Carolyn R. STRICKLAND
32 VP for Student Affairs .... Mr. Elliott STRICKLAND, JR.
26 VP for College Relations .... Mr. Patrick MARTY
103 VP for Workforce Development .... Ms. Shannon M. MUNRO
20 Associate VP for Instruction .... Mr. Tom F. GREGORY
15 Assoc VP for Human Resources .... Ms. Hillary E. HOFSTROM
04 Administrative Asst to President .... Mrs. Valerie A. BAIER
76 Dean of Health Sciences .... Dr. Edward A. HENNINGER
88 Dean Construction & Design Tech .... Mr. Marc E. BRIDGENS
54 Dean Industrial/Comp/Engineering .... Mr. Dave R. COTNER
81 Dean of Sciences/Human/Visual Comm .... Dr. Michael J. REED
65 Dean Transportation/Natl Resources .... Mr. Brett A. REASNER
50 Dean of Business/Hospitality .... Dr. Gerri F. LUKE
37 Assoc Dean of Admissions & Fin Aid .... Mr. Dennis L. CORRELL
102 Exec Dir of Penn College Foundation .... Mr. Kyle A. SMITH
88 Director for Academic Services .... Ms. Wendy A. MILLER
08 Director of the Madigan Library .... Ms. Tracey AMEY
88 Director Instructional Technology .... Mr. Walter J. SHULTZ, JR.
18 Director of Facilities Operations .... Mr. Don J. LUKE
09 Exec Dir Assessment/Research/Plng .... Dr. Brian L. CYGAN
06 Registrar .... Ms. Heather A. SWIMLEY
35 Associate Dean of Student Affairs .... Dr. Jennifer MCLEAN
39 Dir Residence Life/Student Conduct .... Mr. Jon D. WESCOTT
19 Chief of Police .... Mr. Chris E. MILLER
26 Assoc VP Public Rels & Marketing .... Mr. Joseph S. YODER
29 Director Alumni Relations .... Ms. Kimberly R. CASSEL
88 Director of Corporate Relations .... Ms. Elizabeth A. BIDDLE
88 Director Children Learning Center .... Ms. Barbara J. ALBERT

40 Interim Director of College Store ..... Ms. Jennifer L. MCCRACKEN
41 Director of Athletics ..... Mr. John D. VANDEVERE
90 Director Network Services ..... Mr. Mike E. RAE
91 Director Administrative Info Sys ..... Mr. Randall L. MONROE
23 Director College Health Services ..... Mr. Carl L. SHANER
28 Coord Diversity & Cultural Life ..... Ms. Sammie L. DAVIS
22 Director of Disability Services ..... Ms. Kay E. DUNKLEBERGER
85 Coord International Programs ..... Ms. Shanin L. DOUGHERTY
96 Director/Procurement Services ..... Ms. Karen P. FESSLER
07 Director of Admissions ..... Ms. Ashley R. MURPHY
124 Dir Campus & Community Engagement ..... Ms. Katie L. MACKEY
89 Dean Acad Svcs/College Transitions ..... Mr. Paul R. WATSON, II

† Affiliate of Pennsylvania State University.

Pennsylvania Highlands Community College (A)

101 Community College Way, Johnstown PA 15904-2949
County: Cambria FICE Identification: 031804
Unit ID: 414911
Telephone: (814) 262-6400 Carnegie Class: Assoc/MT-VT-High Non
FAX Number: (814) 269-9700 Calendar System: Semester
URL: www.pennhighlands.edu
Established: 1994 Annual Undergrad Tuition & Fees (In-District): $5,790
Enrollment: 2,456 Coed
Affiliation or Control: State/Local IRS Status: 501(c)3
Highest Offering: Associate Degree
Accreditation: M, MAC

01 President ..... Dr. Walter J. ASONEVICH
05 VP of Academic Affairs ..... Dr. Edward NICHOLS
32 VP of Student Services ..... Trish CORLE
10 VP of Finance/Administration ..... Lorraine DONAHUE
30 Assoc VP of External Affairs ..... Dr. Melissa MURRAY
15 Assistant VP of Human Resources ..... Susan FISHER
13 Assistant VP Information Technology ..... Matthew HOFFMAN
09 Assistant VP Institutional Research ..... Gary BOAST
12 Director Blair Center ..... Julie PATOSKY
12 Director Huntingdon Center ..... Marissa DAVIS
12 Director Somerset Center ..... Adam BOWSER
12 Director Ebensburg Center ..... Robert SEKERAK
84 Dean Enrollment Services/Registrar ..... Michelle STUMPF
20 Dean of Faculty ..... Erica REIGHARD
08 Dean for Learning Resources ..... Dr. Barbara ZABOROWSKI
51 Dean of Curriculum/Cont Educ ..... Cynthia MCCABE
88 Dean of Adjunct Faculty ..... Christine ZERNICK
103 Assoc Dean Career Svcs/Workforce Ed ..... Larry BRUGH
07 Director of Admissions ..... Jeffrey MAUL
18 Director of Facilities Operation ..... Reb BROWNLEE
21 Director of Finance/Administration ..... Christopher PRIBULSKY
37 Director of Financial Aid ..... Judy EBBERTS
26 Director of Marketing ..... Raymond WEIBLE, JR.
19 Director of Security and Safety ..... Cregg DIBERT
35 Dir of Student Activities/Athletics ..... Suzanne BRUGH
121 Director of Student Success Center ..... Mindy NITCH
113 Bursar ..... Matthew SNYDER
04 Exec Asst to the President's Office ..... Michelle MAKSYMIK

Pennsylvania Institute of Health and Technology (B)

PO Box 278 1015 Mount Braddock Road,
Mount Braddock PA 15465-0278
Telephone: (724) 437-4600 Identification: 666035
Accreditation: ABHES

† Branch campus of West Virginia Junior College, Morgantown, WV.

Pennsylvania Institute of Technology (C)

800 Manchester Avenue, Media PA 19063-4098
County: Delaware FICE Identification: 010998
Unit ID: 214582
Telephone: (610) 892-1500 Carnegie Class: Assoc/HVT-High Non
FAX Number: (610) 892-1510 Calendar System: Semester
URL: www.pit.edu
Established: 1953 Annual Undergrad Tuition & Fees: $16,380
Enrollment: 596 Coed
Affiliation or Control: Independent Non-Profit IRS Status: 501(c)3
Highest Offering: Associate Degree
Accreditation: #M, PTAA

01 President/CEO ..... Mr. William B. ROBINSON
11 Vice President/COO ..... Mr. Jack BACON
05 Provost ..... Dr. Robert E. HANCOX
10 Chief Financial Officer ..... Ms. Annamarie CASSIDY
32 Director of Student Services ..... Ms. Kamira EVANS
06 Dir of Inst Research/Registrar ..... Mr. Craig M. JACOBS
07 Director of Admissions ..... Mr. Matthew MEYERS
37 Financial Aid Director ..... Ms. Laura BLOMGREN
18 Director of Facilities ..... Mr. Frederick FIVECOAT
13 Dir of Information Technology ..... Mr. Michael TESTA
08 Director of the Library ..... Ms. Lynea ANDERMAN
20 Asst Dean of Academic Affairs ..... Ms. Rachelle CHAYKIN
04 Executive Asst to President ..... Ms. Kathryn DIGIORGIO

*Pennsylvania State System of Higher Education, Office of the Chancellor (D)

Dixon University Ctr, 2986 N 2nd St,
Harrisburg PA 17110-1201
County: Dauphin FICE Identification: 029371
Unit ID: 214661
Telephone: (717) 720-4000 Carnegie Class: N/A
FAX Number: (717) 720-4011
URL: www.passhe.edu

01 Interim Chancellor ..... Dr. Karen M. WHITNEY
03 Executive Vice Chancellor ..... Dr. Peter H. GARLAND
10 Vice Chancellor Admin/Finance ..... Mr. James S. DILLON
05 Dpty Vice Chanc Acad/Stdnt Affairs ..... Dr. Kathleen HOWLEY
21 Assoc Vice Chancellor Admin/Finance ..... Ms. Lois M. JOHNSON
100 Chief of Staff ..... Mr. Randy GOIN, JR.
18 Asst Vice Chancellor Facilities ..... Mr. Steven DUPES
43 Chief Legal Counsel ..... Mr. Andrew LEHMAN

*Bloomsburg University of Pennsylvania (E)

400 E Second Street, Bloomsburg PA 17815-1399
County: Columbia FICE Identification: 003315
Unit ID: 211158
Telephone: (570) 389-4000 Carnegie Class: Masters/L
FAX Number: (570) 389-3700 Calendar System: Semester
URL: www.bloomu.edu
Established: 1839 Annual Undergrad Tuition & Fees (In-State): $10,154
Enrollment: 9,737 Coed
Affiliation or Control: State IRS Status: 501(c)3
Highest Offering: Doctorate
Accreditation: M, ANEST, ART, AUD, CAATE, CAEPN, CS, ENGT, EXSC, MUS, NURSE, SP, SW, THEA

02 President ..... Dr. Bashar W. HANNA
05 Sr VP/Provost Academic Affairs ..... Vacant
10 Vice Pres Finance/Administration ..... Mr. John F. LOONAN
32 Vice Pres Student Affairs ..... Dr. Dionne D. SOMERVILLE
111 Vice Pres University Advancement ..... Mr. Erik EVANS
84 VP Strategic Enrol Mgt/Dean Ext Pgm ..... Mr. Thomas FLETCHER
22 Deputy to Pres for Equity ..... Dr. Robert WISLOCK
86 Director External & Govt Relations ..... Mr. Dan KNORR
04 Exec Asst to the President ..... Ms. Brenda CROMLEY
58 Interim Asst VP/Dean Grad Studies ..... Dr. Mark TAPSAK
13 Assoc VP Technology & Library Svcs ..... Mr. Wayne C. MOHR
108 Asst VP Planning & Assessment ..... Dr. Sheila Dove JONES
18 Asst VP for Facilities Management ..... Mr. Eric NESS
21 Asst VP Finance/Budget & Bus Svcs ..... Ms. Claudia THRUSH
35 Asst VP Student Affairs ..... Mr. Thomas KRESCH
26 AVP Marketing/Communications ..... Vacant
29 AVP Alumni/Professional Engagement ..... Ms. Lynda MICHAELS
49 Dean College of Liberal Arts ..... Dr. James BROWN
50 Dean College of Business ..... Dr. Jeffrey KRUG
81 Dean College of Science/Tech ..... Dr. Robert S. ARONSTAM
53 Interim Dean College of Education ..... Dr. James KRAUSE
20 Int Assoc Dean Academic Achievement ..... Dr. Scott RICHARDSON
15 Director Human Resources/Labor Rel ..... Mr. Jerry REED
46 Dir Research Programs ..... Ms. Sadie HAUCK
06 Registrar/Dir Enroll Services ..... Mr. Joseph KISSELL
07 Director of Admissions ..... Mr. Christopher LAPOS
09 Director of Institutional Research ..... Ms. Karen L. SLUSSER
104 Director Global & Multicultural Ed ..... Ms. Nawal BONOMO
37 Interim Director Financial Aid ..... Ms. Amanda KISHBAUGH
36 Dir Career/Professional Development ..... Dr. Wren FRITSKY
38 Director of Counsel & Human Devel ..... Dr. Shell E. LUNDAHL
90 Manager Technology Support Services ..... Mr. David S. CELLI
40 Interim Manager University Store ..... Ms. Laura HEGER
41 Director of Athletics ..... Mr. Michael S. MCFARLAND
85 Director International Educ Svcs ..... Dr. Madhav P. SHARMA
42 Director Protestant Campus Ministry ..... Rev. Jill YOUNG
42 Director Catholic Campus Ministry ..... Fr. David HERESHKO
19 Dir Univ Safety & Police ..... Mr. Tom PHILLIPS
92 Director Univ Honors Pgm ..... Dr. Julie VANDIVERE
96 Director Procurement & Operations ..... Mr. Jeffrey MANDEL
08 Director Library Services ..... Ms. Charlotte DROLL
91 Interim Dir Applications Develop ..... Ms. Frances DONAHOE
102 Exec Dir BU Foundation ..... Mr. Jerome DVORAK

*California University of Pennsylvania (F)

250 University Avenue, California PA 15419-1394
County: Washington FICE Identification: 003316
Unit ID: 211361
Telephone: (724) 938-4000 Carnegie Class: Masters/L
FAX Number: (724) 938-4138 Calendar System: Semester
URL: www.calu.edu
Established: 1852 Annual Undergrad Tuition & Fees (In-State): $10,339
Enrollment: 7,854 Coed
Affiliation or Control: State IRS Status: 501(c)3
Highest Offering: Doctorate
Accreditation: M, ART, #CAATE, CACREP, CAEPN, CS, ENGT, NAIT, NRPA, NURSE, PTAA, SP, SW, THEA

02 President ..... Ms. Geraldine JONES
100 Chief of Staff to the President ..... Ms. Kelly MORAN
05 Provost/Vice Pres Academic Affairs ..... Dr. Bruce BARNHART
10 VP Administration & Finance ..... Mr. Robert THORN
09 Director Institutional Research ..... Dr. Wei ZHOU
58 Dean of Graduate Studies ..... Dr. Stan KOMACEK
84 Director Enrollment Management ..... Dr. Stan KOMACEK
20 Assoc Provost/Student Retent Ofcr ..... Dr. Dan M. ENGSTROM
30 Assoc VP for Development & Alumni ..... Mr. Anthony F. MAURO
72 Dean of Science/Technology ..... Vacant
49 Dean of Liberal Arts ..... Dr. Mohamed YAMBA
53 Dean Col Education/Human Svcs ..... Dr. Kevin A. KOURY
62 Dean of Library Services ..... Mr. Douglas HOOVER
07 Dean of Admissions ..... Ms. Tracey SHEETZ
106 Dir Online Education/E-learning ..... Ms. Stephanie L. FRANKS-HELWICH
37 Sr Assoc Director of Financial Aid ..... Mr. Jeff DERUBBO
06 Registrar ..... Ms. Heidi WILLIAMS
36 Director of Career Services ..... Ms. Rhonda GIFFORD
92 Director Honors Program ..... Mr. Mark AUNE
29 Director of Alumni Relations ..... Ms. Leslie FLEENOR
38 Assoc VP Student Development & Svcs ..... Dr. Timothy SUSICK
13 Assoc VP for University Technology ..... Mr. Brian KRAUS
39 Director of University Housing ..... Ms. Jackie THORN
94 Director Women's Studies ..... Dr. Marta MCCLINTOCK
85 International Student Advisor ..... Mr. John WATKINS
41 Athletic Director ..... Dr. Karen HJERPE
15 Interim Director of Personnel ..... Mr. Eric GUISER
22 Director of Social Equity ..... Dr. John BURNETT
19 Chief of Police ..... Mr. Ed MCSHEFFERY
18 Interim Dir of Facilities Mgmt ..... Mr. Mike KANALIS
26 Director of Communications & PR ..... Mrs. Christine KINDL
27 Director of Marketing ..... Ms. Keli HENDERSON
88 Director of Creative Services ..... Mr. Greg SOFRANKO
40 Book Store Manager ..... Ms. Amy NASH
96 Director of Purchasing ..... Ms. Joyce SHEPPICK
51 Dir Continuing Education ..... Vacant

*Cheyney University of Pennsylvania (G)

1837 University Circle PO Box 200,
Cheyney PA 19319-0200
County: Delaware FICE Identification: 003317
Unit ID: 211608
Telephone: (610) 399-2000 Carnegie Class: Bac-A&S
FAX Number: (610) 399-2415 Calendar System: Semester
URL: www.cheyney.edu
Established: 1837 Annual Undergrad Tuition & Fees (In-State): $11,356
Enrollment: 711 Coed
Affiliation or Control: State IRS Status: 501(c)3
Highest Offering: Master's
Accreditation: M

02 Interim President ..... Mr. Aaron A. WALTON
05 Interim Provost ..... Dr. Tara KENT
10 Vice Pres Finance & Administration ..... Vacant
21 Asst VP of Finance/Controller ..... Ms. Layna HOLMES-BUTLER
38 Chairperson Guidance & Counseling ..... Ms. Jolly RAMAKRISHNAN
06 Registrar ..... Ms. Susan CHESTERTON
37 Director Financial Aid ..... Ms. Charlene ERVIN
09 Director Institutional Research ..... Dr. Erika SHEHATA
18 Facilities Manager ..... Mr. Eric ERLE
19 Chief of Police ..... Mr. Lawrence RICHARDS
41 Interim Athletic Director ..... Ms. Sue KILIAN
17 College Physician ..... Dr. Pamela HADLEY
43 University Legal Counsel ..... Ms. Cathleen MCCORMICK
32 Director Student Affairs ..... Ms. Elisabeth BURTON
39 Manager Housing Ops/Auxiliary Svcs ..... Ms. Elizabeth BURTON
103 Dir Economic/Workforce Devel ..... Ms. Sharon CANNON
113 Bursar ..... Ms. Lauronda FLETCHER
92 Dean of Keystone Honors Academy ..... Ms. Nicole RAYFIELD
84 Interim Dir of Enrollment Mgmt ..... Ms. Christina M. DENNIS
04 Administrative Asst to President ..... Ms. Ramona DIXON

*Clarion University of Pennsylvania (H)

840 Wood Street, Clarion PA 16214-1232
County: Clarion FICE Identification: 003318
Unit ID: 211644
Telephone: (814) 393-2000 Carnegie Class: Masters/L
FAX Number: (814) 393-1826 Calendar System: Semester
URL: www.clarion.edu
Established: 1867 Annual Undergrad Tuition & Fees (In-State): $10,287
Enrollment: 5,368 Coed
Affiliation or Control: State IRS Status: 501(c)3
Highest Offering: Master's
Accreditation: M, ART, CAEPN, CSHSE, LIB, SP

02 Acting President ..... Dr. Todd PFANNESTIEL
05 Provost/AVP ..... Dr. Todd PFANNESTIEL
32 Vice Pres Student & University Affs ..... Dr. Susanne FENSKE
10 Vice Pres Finance/Administration ..... Mr. Lenoard CULLO
102 Chief Exec Officer Foundation ..... Mr. Michael R. KEEFER
111 Vice President Univ Advancement ..... Mr. James GEIGER
21 Assoc VP for Administration ..... Mr. Timothy P. FOGARTY
22 Int Director of Social Equity ..... Ms. Amy SALSGIVER
84 AVP of Enrollment Management ..... Mr. David DOLLINS
08 Dean of Libraries ..... Dr. Terry S. LATOUR
49 Int Dean of Arts & Sciences ..... Dr. Steven HARRIS
50 Dean of Business Administration ..... Dr. Philip FRESE
06 Registrar ..... Ms. Lisa L. HEPLER
21 Assoc VP for Finance ..... Ms. Tamara B. VARSEK
13 Assoc VP for Information Technology ..... Mr. Samuel T. PULEIO

46 Director Faculty Research Ms. Amy ESTERHUIZEN
26 Dir of Marketing & Communications Mr. David LOVE
37 Director of Student Financial Svcs Ms. Sue BLOOM
18 Director of Facilities Mgmt Mr. Eric MARTIN
29 Director of Alumni Relations Ms. Ann THOMPSON
36 Director Career & Profess Develop Mr. William BAILEY
39 Director of Residence Life Ms. Jennifer DUTKIEWICZ
19 Director of Public Safety Mr. Jason HENDERSHOT
41 Athletic Director Ms. Wendy SNODGRASS
96 Director of Purchasing Mr. Rein A. POLD
04 Executive Staff Asst to President Ms. Ann M. JAMISON
09 Inst Research Business Analysrt Mr. Robert GATESMAN
112 Director of Planned Giving Mr. Larry W. JAMISON

*East Stroudsburg University of Pennsylvania (A)

200 Prospect Street, East Stroudsburg PA 18301-2999

County: Monroe FICE Identification: 003320
Unit ID: 212115
Telephone: (570) 422-3211 Carnegie Class: Masters/M
FAX Number: (570) 422-3777 Calendar System: Semester
URL: www.esu.edu
Established: 1893 Annual Undergrad Tuition & Fees (In-State): $9,968
Enrollment: 6,828 Coed
Affiliation or Control: State IRS Status: 501(c)3
Highest Offering: Doctorate
Accreditation: M, CAATE, CAEPN, CS, EXSC, NRPA, NUR, PH, SP, SW

02 President Dr. Marcia G. WELSH
05 Provost & Vice Pres Academic Affair Ms. Joanne Z. BRUNO
32 Vice President Student Affairs Dr. Doreen M. TOBIN
10 Vice Pres Administration & Finance Mr. Kenneth A. LONG
46 VP Economic Devel/ Entrepreneurship Ms. Mary Frances POSTUPACK
84 Vice Pres Enrollment Management Mr. David BOUSQUET
58 Dir Graduate/Extended Studies Dr. William BAJOR
49 Dean of Arts & Sciences Dr. Peter HAWKES
76 Dean of Health Sciences Vacant
53 Dean of Education Dr. Terry BARRY
50 Dean of Business & Management Dr. Tribhuvan PURI
08 Dean of Library & Univ Collections Dr. Jingfeng XIA
20 Assoc Provost & Dean Univ College Dr. Thomas TAUER
35 Dean of Student Life Ms. Cornelia SEWELL-ALLEN
100 Chief of Staff Mr. Miguel BARBOSA
07 Director of Admissions Vacant
06 Registrar/Dir Enrollment Services Ms. Kizzy MORRIS
37 Sr Assoc Director Financial Aid Vacant
36 Director of Career Services Ms. Daria WIELEBINSKI
38 Director Counseling Center Dr. Linda L. VAN METER
41 Director Intercollegiate Athletics Mr. Joshua LOONEY
39 Director of Residence Life Mr. Robert M. MOSES
88 Dir of Student Activity Association Mr. Joe AKOB
21 Controller Ms. Donna R. BULZONI
13 Chief Information Officer Mr. Robert D'AVERSA
15 Director of Human Resources Ms. Teresa FRITSCHE
18 Int Director Facilities Management Mr. John BLOSHINSKI
96 Director of Procurement/Contracting Ms. Patricia REICH
29 Director of Alumni Engagement Mr. Leon S. JOHN, JR.
26 Director University Relations Dr. Brenda FRIDAY
09 Director Inst Research & Assessment Vacant
28 Director of Multicultural Affairs Ms. Juanita M. JENKINS

*Edinboro University (B)

219 Meadville Street, Edinboro PA 16444-0001

County: Erie FICE Identification: 003321
Unit ID: 212160
Telephone: (814) 732-2000 Carnegie Class: Masters/L
FAX Number: (814) 732-2880 Calendar System: Semester
URL: www.edinboro.edu
Established: 1857 Annual Undergrad Tuition & Fees (In-State): $9,984
Enrollment: 6,548 Coed
Affiliation or Control: State IRS Status: 501(c)3
Highest Offering: Doctorate
Accreditation: M, ART, ACBSP, CACREP, CAEPN, CS, MUS, NUR, NURSE, SP, SW

02 President Dr. H. Fred WALKER
05 Provost/VP Academic Affairs Dr. Michael HANNAN
10 VP Finance & Administration Mr. Guilbert BROWN
32 Int Dean of Stdnts & Campus Life Dr. Mary Beth MERCATORIS
30 Assistant VP University Advancement Ms. Marilyn GOELLNER
15 Director of Human Resources/Faculty Mr. Wayne PATTERSON
08 Assoc VP University Libraries Dr. Donald H. DILMORE
84 VP for Enrollment Management Mr. William EDMONDS
09 Dir Inst Research & Assessment Mr. Matthew CETTIN
20 Sr Exec Associate to the Provost Ms. Judy KUBEJA
18 Dir Facilities Management/Planning Vacant
27 Director of Communications Mr. Jeffrey HILEMAN
26 Director of Marketing Mr. William BERGER
37 Director of Student Financial Aid Ms. Kelly VITELLI
92 Director Honors Program Dr. Roger SOLBERG
22 Dir of Social Equity/Title IX Coord Mr. Ronald O. WILSON
79 Int Dn Col Arts/Humanities/Soc Sci Dr. Scott MILLER
81 Interim Dean Col Science & Health Dr. Denise OHLER
58 Exec Director of Graduate Studies Dr. Erinn LAKE
53 Interim Dean School of Education Dr. Erinn LAKE
50 Dean School of Business Dr. Scott MILLER
06 Registrar Mr. Tim W. PILEWSKI
36 Dir Office of Career Development Ms. Monica CLEM
29 Dir Alumni Relations/Fund Devel Mr. Jon PULICE
41 Athletic Director Mr. Bruce BAUMGARTNER
38 Dir Counseling/Psychological Svcs Dr. Michael BUCELL
19 Chief of Police Ms. Angela VINCENT
22 Dir Ofc Students with Disabilities Ms. Kim KENNEDY
12 Dir & Outreach Coord EUP in Erie Ms. Janet L. BOWKER
23 Medical Dir Student Health Services Dr. Thomas MITCHELL
109 Director Auxiliary Operations Vacant
85 Dir Global Education Office Ms. Linda KIGHTLINGER
25 Dir Grant & Sponsored Programs Ms. Rosmari GRAHAM
14 Dir Networks & Telecommunications Ms. Karen MURDZAK
90 Director Client Support Services Mr. Dennis J. BRADLEY
13 Director of Information Services Ms. Sallie A. TERPACK
96 Director Purchasing & Contracts Ms. Darla SPAID
30 Director of Development Ms. Julie A. CHACONA
44 Assistant VP for Advancement Ms. Marilyn GOELLNER
114 Director of Budget and Payroll Ms. Theresa VILLELLA
21 Controller Mr. Wayne T. OCHS
113 Bursar Ms. Shari GOULD
35 Dir Campus Life/Leadership Dev Ms. Michelle BARBICH
17 Director of Health & Wellness Ctr Ms. Darla ELDER
106 Manager of Online Programs Dr. James BOULDER
24 Learning Technology Specialist Ms. Jill LINTON
88 Coordinator Non-Credit Programs Ms. Beth ZEWE

*Indiana University of Pennsylvania (C)

1011 South Drive, Indiana PA 15705-0001

County: Indiana FICE Identification: 003277
Unit ID: 213020
Telephone: (724) 357-2100 Carnegie Class: DU-Mod
FAX Number: (724) 357-6213 Calendar System: Semester
URL: www.iup.edu
Established: 1875 Annual Undergrad Tuition & Fees (In-State): $11,368
Enrollment: 13,835 Coed
Affiliation or Control: State IRS Status: 501(c)3
Highest Offering: Doctorate
Accreditation: M, ACFEI, ART, #CAATE, CACREP, CAEPN, CLPSY, COARC, CS, DIETD, DIETI, ENGR, EXSC, MUS, NURSE, PLNG, SP, THEA

02 President Dr. Michael A. DRISCOLL
05 Provost & VP Academic Affairs Dr. Timothy S. MOERLAND
11 Vice Pres Administration/Finance Dr. Cornelius WOOTEN
32 Vice President Student Affairs Dr. Rhonda H. LUCKEY
111 Vice Pres University Advancement Mr. William SPEIDEL, III
20 Assoc VP Academic Administration Dr. John N. KILMARX
58 Dean Graduate Studies & Research Dr. Randy L. MARTIN
15 Assoc Vice Pres Human Resources Mr. Craig BICKLEY
79 Dean College Humanities & Soc Sci Dr. Yaw A. ASAMOAH
50 Dean Eberly Col Bus/Inform Tech Dr. Robert C. CAMP
53 Dean College Educ/Educ Tech Dr. Lara M. LUETKEHANS
81 Dean Col Natural Science & Math Dr. Deanne SNAVELY
57 Dean College of Fine Arts Mr. Michael J. HOOD
66 Dean College Health & Human Svcs Dr. Mary E. WILLIAMS
84 VP Enrollment Mgmt & Communications Ms. Patricia MCCARTHY
08 Dean of Libraries Dr. Luis J. GONZALEZ
06 Registrar Mrs. Jennifer J. FEDELE
13 Chief Information Officer Mr. William S. BALINT
45 Director of Planning & Assessment Mrs. Barbra MOORE
14 Exec Dir of Technology Services Ctr Mr. Todd D. CUNNINGHAM
28 Asst to the Pres for Social Equity Dr. Pablo MENDOZA
19 Director of Public Safety & Police Mr. Kevin THELEN
36 Director Career Development Ctr Dr. Tammy P. MANKO
29 Exec Director Alumni Relations Mrs. Mary MORGAN
44 Director Annual Giving Ms. Emily SMELTZ
85 Asst VP Intl Education & Global Dr. Michele L. PETRUCCI
46 Assistant Dean for Research Dr. Hilliary E. CREELY
39 Exec Director Housing/Resid Living Dr. Sondra R. DENNISON
40 Co-op Store Director Mr. Tim L. SHARBAUGH
41 Athletic Director Mr. Steve ROACH
23 Nurse Director Ms. Melissa L. DICK
12 Director of Regional Campuses Mr. Richard J. MUTH
12 Director of Regional Campuses Mr. Richard J. MUTH
43 Staff Attorney Ms. Suzanne WILLIAMSON
26 Exec Dir Commun & Media Relations Ms. Michelle S. FRYLING
96 Procurement Services & Central Stor Mr. Terry BRESLAWSKI
10 Assoc Vice President for Finance Mrs. Susanna C. SINK
86 Exec Asst to Pres for Govt Relation Ms. Robin A. GORMAN
37 Director of Financial Aid Ms. Ragan K. GRIFFIN
35 Assoc VP Student Affairs/Well-Being Mr. Michael W. LEMASTERS
88 Dir Admin Services Culinary Arts Ms. Enid E. RESENIC
07 Executive Director of Admissions Ms. Stacy HOPKINS
105 Dir of Electronic Communication Dr. Michael POWERS
18 Assoc VP for Facilities Management Mr. R. Michael BROWN
31 Assoc VP Univ & Community Rels Dr. Kathleen R. LINDER

*Kutztown University of Pennsylvania (D)

15200 Kutztown Road, Kutztown PA 19530-0730

County: Berks FICE Identification: 003322
Unit ID: 213349
Telephone: (610) 683-4000 Carnegie Class: Masters/L
FAX Number: (610) 683-4693 Calendar System: Semester
URL: www.kutztown.edu
Established: 1866 Annual Undergrad Tuition & Fees (In-State): $9,618
Enrollment: 8,995 Coed
Affiliation or Control: State IRS Status: 501(c)3
Highest Offering: Doctorate
Accreditation: M, ART, CACREP, CAEPN, MUS, SW

02 President Dr. Kenneth S. HAWKINSON
05 Provost/VP Academic Affairs Dr. Anne ZAYAITZ
10 VP Administration & Finance Mr. Gerald L. SILBERMAN
84 VP Enrollment Management Dr. Warren HILTON
22 Deputy to Pres Compliance/Equity Mr. Jesus PENA
102 Executive Director KU Foundation Ms. Tracey THOMPSON
26 Interim AVP Comm/Mktg & Ext Aff Mr. Matt SANTOS
20 Vice Prov Acad Affs/Dean Grad Stds Dr. Carole WELLS
21 Asst VP Finance & Business Services Mr. Matthew DELANEY
32 Asst VP/Dean of Students Vacant
13 Asst Vice Pres/Info Technology Vacant
15 Asst VP for Human Resources Ms. Sharon M. PICUS
18 Asst Vice President for Facilities Mr. Terry BROWN
88 Interim Dean College Vis/Per Arts Dr. Michele KIEC
49 Dean College Liberal Arts/Sci Dr. David BEOUGHER
50 Dean College of Business Dr. Anne CARROLL
53 Dean College Education Vacant
62 Director of Library Services Ms. Martha STEVENSON
09 Director Institutional Research Ms. Natalie SNOW
06 Registrar Mr. Ted WITRYK
37 Director of Financial Aid Mr. Bernard L. MCCREE
39 Director Housing/Residential Svcs Mr. Kent R. DAHLQUIST
41 Director of Athletics Mr. Gregory BAMBERGER
38 Director Counseling & Psych Svcs Dr. Lisa COULTER
96 Purchasing Manager Ms. Barbara REITZ
07 Spec Asst Enrl Mgmt/Div Recr Admis Mr. Jeffrey JONES
19 Chief of Police Mr. John DILLON
36 Director Career/Community Services Ms. Kerri GARDI
30 Dir Develop & Alumni Engagement Mr. Alex OGEKA
04 Sr Executive Assoc to President Ms. Toyia HEYWARD
108 Asst Vice Provost/Assessment Mr. Ernest CLARY
106 Dir Online Education/E-learning Mr. Douglas SCOTT

*Lock Haven University (E)

401 N Fairview Street, Lock Haven PA 17745-2390

County: Clinton FICE Identification: 003323
Unit ID: 213613
Telephone: (570) 484-2001 Carnegie Class: Masters/M
FAX Number: (570) 484-2432 Calendar System: Semester
URL: www.lockhaven.edu
Established: 1870 Annual Undergrad Tuition & Fees (In-State): $10,229
Enrollment: 4,607 Coed
Affiliation or Control: State IRS Status: 170(c)1
Highest Offering: Master's
Accreditation: M, ACBSP, ADNUR, ARCPA, CAATE, CACREP, CAEPN, NRPA, NUR, SW

02 President Dr. Michael FIORENTINO, JR.
05 Provost & Executive Vice President Dr. Donna WILSON
11 COO & Senior Vice President Mr. William HANELLY
32 Dean of Student Affairs Dr. Dwayne ALLISON
84 Vice President for Enrollment Mgmt Dr. Tyana LANGE
49 Dean of Liberal Arts & Education Dr. Koyoko AMANO
83 Dean Natural/Behavioral/Health Sci Dr. Scott CARNICOM
50 Dean Business/Info Sys/Human Svcs Dr. Stephen NEUN
12 Director Clearfield Branch Campus Dr. William CURLEY
85 Director of International Studies Ms. Rosana CAMPBELL
09 Director Institutional Research Mr. Mike ABPLANALP
15 Associate VP of Human Resources Ms. Deana HILL
07 Interim Director of Admissions Ms. Angelic HARDY
06 Registrar Ms. Jill MITCHLEY
22 Dir Affirm Action/Equal Opportunity Mr. Lucas FANNING
37 Director of Financial Aid Mr. Robert FRYER
36 Director of Career Services Ms. Maryjo CAMPANA
26 Exec Director of Communications Ms. Elizabeth ARNOLD
19 Director of Public Safety Mr. Paul ALTIERI
18 Director of Facilities Mr. Keith ROUSH
41 Director of Athletics Dr. Tom GIOGLIO
66 Director of Nursing Program Vacant
38 Director of Counseling Dr. Dan TESS
90 Dir Computing/Instructional Tech Mr. Boise MILLER
88 Director of Physician Asst Program Mr. Walt EISENHAUER
92 Director Honors Program Dr. Elizabeth GRUBER
94 Director Women's Studies Dr. Holle CANATELLA
93 Director Minority Students Mr. Kenneth HALL
40 Manager University Bookstore Mr. James KOWNACKI
29 Director Alumni Relations Ms. Ashley KOSER
102 Dir Foundation/Corporate Relations Mr. Carl POFF
103 Dir Workforce Development & CE Ms. Shannon TYSON

*Mansfield University of Pennsylvania (F)

Academy Street, Mansfield PA 16933-1697

County: Tioga FICE Identification: 003324
Unit ID: 213783
Telephone: (570) 662-4000 Carnegie Class: Masters/S
FAX Number: (570) 662-4995 Calendar System: Semester
URL: www.mansfield.edu
Established: 1857 Annual Undergrad Tuition & Fees (In-State): $11,908
Enrollment: 2,352 Coed
Affiliation or Control: State IRS Status: 501(c)3
Highest Offering: Master's
Accreditation: M, ACBSP, COARC, DIETD, MUS, NUR, RAD, SW

02 President Gen. Francis L. HENDRICKS
10 VP Finance/Administration Mr. Scott W. BARTON
30 AVP for University Advancement Vacant
32 VP for Student Affairs Vacant
39 Assoc Vice Pres Residence Life Vacant
05 Provost/Sr Vice Pres Acad Affs Dr. Steven SICONOLFI

15 Exec Dir Employee & Leadership Svcs ... Ms. Kacy HAGAN
08 Director Library/Info Resource Svcs ... Mr. Scott R. DIMARCO
18 Director Facilities ... Mr. Kenneth B. LAWTON
84 Exec Director Enrollment Management ... Vacant
35 Dean of Students ... Mr. Frank CROFCHICK
26 Assoc Dir Public & Media Relations ... Mr. Terry DAY
27 Director of Marketing ... Ms. Casey WOOD
37 Director of Student Financial Aid ... Ms. Pamela KATHCART
19 Int Dir University Police & Safety ... Mr. Paul DELOSA
41 Director of Athletics ... Mr. Ryan EHRIE
85 Social Equity/Multicultural Affairs ... Vacant
09 Dir Institutional Rsrch/Assess Data ... Dr. John COSGROVE
29 Director of Alumni/Govt Relations ... Ms. Lindsey SIKORSKI
06 Registrar ... Ms. Lori CASS
38 Director Counseling Center ... Ms. Jolene MEISNER
07 Dir of Admissions Tactical/Enroll ... Ms. Rachel GREEN
13 Chief Info Technology Officer ... Mr. Nicholas ANDRE

*Millersville University of Pennsylvania (A)

PO Box 1002, Millersville PA 17551-0302
County: Lancaster FICE Identification: 003325
Unit ID: 214041
Telephone: (717) 871-4636 Carnegie Class: Masters/L
FAX Number: (717) 871-7930 Calendar System: 4/1/4
URL: www.millersville.edu
Established: 1855 Annual Undergrad Tuition & Fees (In-State): $11,494
Enrollment: 7,959 Coed
Affiliation or Control: State IRS Status: 501(c)3
Highest Offering: Doctorate
Accreditation: M, ACBSP, ART, CAEPN, COARC, CS, ENGR, MUS, NAIT, NUR, SW

02 President ... Dr. John M. ANDERSON
05 Vice Pres Academic Affs/Provost ... Dr. Vilas A. PRABHU
10 Vice Pres Finance & Administration ... Mr. Roger BRUSZEWSKI
111 Interim Vice Pres for Advancement ... Ms. Alice MCMURRY
32 VP Student Affs & Enrollment Mgmt ... Mr. Brian HAZLETT
28 Dir Diversity & Social Justice ... Vacant
20 Associate Provost Academic Admin ... Dr. Jeffrey R. ADAMS
121 Asst VP for Student Success and Ret ... Vacant
108 Asst VP Inst Assessment & Planning ... Dr. Lisa R. SHIBLEY
13 Associate VP for Info Tech/CIO ... Ms. Nancy PRUSKOWSKI
15 Exec Director of Human Resources ... Mrs. Melanie A. DESANTIS
37 Executive Director of Financial Aid ... Mr. Dwight G. HORSEY
35 Assoc VP/Dean of Students ... Mr. Thomas J. RICHARDSON
88 Corporate Gift Officer ... Mr. Gregory FREEDLAND
18 Asst VP Facilities ... Mr. Thomas A. WALTZ, JR.
53 Dean Education & Human Services ... Dr. George DRAKE
79 Dean Arts/Human & Social Sci ... Dr. Diane UMBLE
81 Dean Science & Technology ... Dr. Michael JACKSON
58 Dean Grad Studies & Adult Lrng ... Dr. Victor DESANTIS
06 Registrar ... Ms. Alison HUTCHINSON
07 Director of Admissions ... Ms. Katy FERRIER
36 Assoc Director Career Management ... Ms. Margo J. SASSAMAN
38 Director Counseling/Human Devel ... Dr. Kelsey K. BACKELS
19 Chief of University Police ... Mr. Peter J. ANDERS
41 Director of Intercollegiate Ath ... Mr. Miles GALLAGHER
40 Manager University Bookstore ... Ms. Audrey HERR
42 Campus Minister ... Ms. Yvonne DEBLOIS
30 AVP Advancement & Dir External Rels ... Mr. Steven A. DIGUISEPPE
110 Assoc VP for Advancement ... Ms. Alice MCMURRY
09 Director Institutional Research ... Dr. Kyle W. VERBOSH
112 Senior Major Gift Officer ... Ms. Amy C. SPELLMAN
102 Dir Sponsored Pgms & Research Admin ... Dr. Rene MUNOZ
96 Interim Dir of Purch/Campus Svcs ... Ms. Lauren N. WEITZEL
57 Int Dir Visual & Performing Arts ... Ms. Robin D. ZAREMSKI
26 Director of Communications ... Ms. Janet KACSKOS
106 Interim Director of Online Programs ... Ms. Janice MOORE
29 Director Alumni Engagement ... Ms. Denise BERG
43 Dir Legal Services/General Counsel ... Mr. Jeffrey HAWKINS
101 Executive Secretary ... Ms. Jennifer L. HART

*Shippensburg University of Pennsylvania (B)

1871 Old Main Drive, Shippensburg PA 17257-2200
County: Cumberland FICE Identification: 003326
Unit ID: 216010
Telephone: (717) 477-7447 Carnegie Class: Masters/L
FAX Number: (717) 477-1273 Calendar System: Semester
URL: www.ship.edu
Established: 1871 Annual Undergrad Tuition & Fees (In-State): $11,452
Enrollment: 7,048 Coed
Affiliation or Control: State IRS Status: 501(c)3
Highest Offering: Doctorate
Accreditation: M, CACREP, CAEPN, CS, ENG, JOUR, SW

02 President ... Dr. Laurie A. CARTER
05 Provost & Executive Vice President ... Dr. Barbara G. LYMAN
84 VP Enroll Mgmt/Tech/Library Svcs ... Dr. Rick RUTH
10 Vice Pres Administration/Finance ... Vacant
32 VP for Student Affairs ... Dr. Roger L. SERR
26 VP External & Univ Relations ... Vacant
15 Assoc VP for A&F/CHRO ... Dr. David TOPPER
102 Pres Shippensburg Univ Foundation ... Dr. Leslie CLINTON
21 Assoc VP for A&F/CFO ... Ms. Melinda D. FAWKS
13 AVP Technology/Library Svcs ... Ms. Amy DIEHL
58 Dean of Graduate School ... Dr. Tracy SCHOOLCRAFT
51 Int Dean of Prof/Cont/Distance Educ ... Dr. Carolyn CALLAGHAN
35 Dean of Students ... Dr. David L. LOVETT
06 Registrar ... Ms. Cathy J. SPRENGER
36 Director Career Development ... Ms. Victoria KERR BUCHBAUER
37 Director Financial Aid ... Ms. Trina SNYDER
29 Exec Dir University/Alumni Rels ... Vacant
27 Director Communications & Marketing ... Ms. Laura LUDLAM
08 Dean Library & Multi-Media Services ... Dr. Dennis MATHES
22 Executive Director Social Equity ... Ms. Carlesha HALKIAS
88 Director Womens Center ... Ms. Stephanie ERDICE
09 Director Inst Research & Planning ... Mr. Mark PILGRIM
25 Dir Sponsored Pgms/Inst Public Svc ... Mr. Christopher WONDERS
38 Int Director Counseling Services ... Dr. Christopher CARLTON
88 Director of Conferences ... Mr. Randy HAMMOND
53 Dean College Education & Human Svcs ... Dr. Nicole R. HILL
49 Dean College Arts & Science ... Dr. James MIKE
50 Dean College of Business ... Dr. John KOOTI
121 Dean Acad Engage/Student Support ... Dr. Sarah STOKELY
18 Chief Facilities/Physical Plant ... Mr. Lance BRYSON
96 Director of Purchasing/Contracting ... Mr. Wesley LIGHT
07 AVP Enrollment Mgt/Dean Admissions ... Dr. Jennifer A. HAUGHIE
19 Director Public Safety ... Ms. Cytha D. GRISSOM
41 Athletic Director ... Mr. Jeff A. MICHAELS
04 Exec Asst to the President ... Ms. Robin MAUN
101 Secretary of the Institution/Board ... Ms. Robin MAUN
104 Director Study Abroad ... Ms. Mary BURNETT
39 Director Student Housing ... Mr. Barry MCCLANAHAN

*Slippery Rock University of Pennsylvania (C)

1 Morrow Way, Slippery Rock PA 16057-1326
County: Butler FICE Identification: 003327
Unit ID: 216038
Telephone: (724) 738-9000 Carnegie Class: Masters/L
FAX Number: (724) 738-2169 Calendar System: Semester
URL: www.sru.edu
Established: 1889 Annual Undergrad Tuition & Fees (In-State): $9,862
Enrollment: 8,611 Coed
Affiliation or Control: State IRS Status: 501(c)3
Highest Offering: Doctorate
Accreditation: M, ART, ACBSP, #ARCPA, CAATE, CACREP, CAEPN, CARTE, CS, DANCE, EXSC, MUS, NUR, PTA, SW, THEA

02 Interim President ... Dr. Philip WAY
05 Provost/Vice Pres Acad & Stdnt Affs ... Dr. Philip WAY
10 Vice Pres Finance/Administration ... Dr. Amir MOHAMMADI
111 Vice President for Univ Advancement ... Vacant
21 Asst Vice Pres for Finance ... Ms. Molly MERCER
18 Asst Vice Pres for Facilities/Plng ... Mr. Scott ALBERT
23 Exec Dir Student Health & Wellness ... Vacant
32 Exec Dir for Student Services ... Ms. Debra PINCEK
15 Asst Vice Pres Human Resources ... Ms. Lynne M. MOTYL
28 Asst VP Diversity & Equal Oppty ... Ms. Holly M. MCCOY
100 Chief of Staff ... Ms. Tina L. MOSER
84 Assoc Provost Enrollment Services ... Dr. Amanda A. YALE
13 Assoc Provost Info Technology ... Dr. John ZIEGLER
102 Exec Director Univ Foundation ... Dr. Edward R. BUCHA
26 Exec Director Public Relations ... Ms. Rita E. ABENT
37 Director Student Financial Aid ... Ms. Alyssa DOBSON
19 Director Public Safety ... Mr. Paul NOVAK
19 Director University Police ... Mr. Michael SIMMONS
09 Assoc Prov Inst Rsrch/Acad Fin Mgmt ... Ms. Carrie J. BIRCKBICHLER
08 Manager of Library Operations ... Ms. Jennifer J. BARTEK
14 Director of Info & Adm Tech Svcs ... Mr. Henry MAGUSIAK
06 Director Acad Records & Registr ... Ms. Connie EDWARDS
07 Director Undergraduate Admissions ... Mr. Michael MAY
23 Director Health Services ... Ms. Kristina BENKESER
36 Associate Director Career Services ... Mr. John F. SNYDER
29 Director Alumni Affairs ... Ms. Kelly BAILEY
76 Dean Col Health Environ/Sci ... Dr. Jerry CHMIELEWSKI
07 Director Graduate Admissions ... Ms. Brandi WEBER-MORTIMER
41 Athletic Director ... Mr. Paul A. LUEKEN
39 Director of Residence Life ... Mr. Patrick T. BESWICK
25 Director Grants & Sponsored Rsrch ... Ms. Nancy L. CRUIKSHANK
38 Director of Student Counseling ... Dr. Chris CUBERO
93 Director of Minority Students ... Ms. Corinne J. GIBSON
96 Director of Contracts & Purchasing ... Mr. James REVESZ
88 Assoc Provost Trans Exper ... Dr. Bradley WILSON
49 Dean College Liberal Arts ... Dr. Danny BAUER
50 Dean College of Business ... Dr. Lawrence SHAO
53 Dean College of Education ... Dr. Keith DILS
88 Assoc Provost Student Success ... Mr. David WILMES

*West Chester University of Pennsylvania (D)

University & High Street, West Chester PA 19383-0001
County: Chester FICE Identification: 003328
Unit ID: 216764
Telephone: (610) 436-1000 Carnegie Class: Masters/L
FAX Number: (610) 436-3115 Calendar System: Semester
URL: www.wcupa.edu
Established: 1871 Annual Undergrad Tuition & Fees (In-State): $9,720
Enrollment: 16,597 Coed
Affiliation or Control: State IRS Status: 501(c)3
Highest Offering: Doctorate
Accreditation: M, ART, CAATE, CACREP, CAEPN, COARC, CS, DIETD, EXSC, FEPAC, MUS, NURSE, PH, SP, SPAA, SW, THEA

02 President ... Dr. Chris FIORENTINO
100 COS and Exec Deputy to President ... Dr. John VILLELLA
04 Sr Assoc to the President ... Ms. Rebecca HOOK
22 Director Social Equity ... Ms. Lynn KLINGENSMITH
05 Provost & VP for Academic Affairs ... Dr. R. Lorraine BERNOTSKY
10 Vice President Admin/Finance ... Dr. Janice ORLOV
13 Vice President Info Services ... Dr. Dikran KASSABIAN
111 Vice President Advancement ... Dr. Mark G. PAVLOVICH
32 Vice President Student Affairs ... Dr. Zebulun DAVENPORT
49 Int Dean College Arts & Humanities ... Dr. Jen BACON
20 Int Assoc Provost Acad Budget/Plng ... Dr. Corrine MURPHY
20 Int Assoc Prov Curriculum Plng/Dev ... Dr. Loretta RIESER-DANNER
58 Senior Vice Provost ... Dr. Jeffery OSGOOD
07 Director Admissions ... Ms. Marsha L. HAUG
53 Dean College Education/Social Work ... Dr. Kenneth D. WITMER
50 Dean College of BPM ... Dr. Anthony WHEELER
81 Interim Dean College Science & Math ... Dr. Jack WABER
76 Interim Dean College Health Science ... Dr. Scott HEINERICHS
88 AVP Cultural Engagement ... Dr. Timothy V. BLAIR
64 Interim Dean School of Music ... Dr. Chris HANNING
25 Assoc VP Sponsored Research ... Dr. Gautam PILLAY
23 Director Health Center ... Ms. Robyn SPRAGINS
15 Assoc Vice Pres Human Resources ... Mr. Michael T. MALOY
35 Asst Vice Pres Student Affairs ... Ms. Sara HINKLE
35 Int Asst VP Student Affairs ... Mr. Peter GALLOWAY
21 AVP Finance/Business Svcs ... Mr. Todd MURPHY
84 Asst Prov & Asst VP Enrollment Mgmt ... Mr. Joseph SANTIVASCI
85 Interim Dir International Programs ... Dr. Peter LOEDEL
102 Exec Director WCU Foundation ... Mr. Richard T. PRZYWARA
18 Assoc VP for Facilities ... Mr. Jim LEWIS
88 Dir Facilities Finance/Support Svcs ... Ms. Susan MILLER
21 Dir Accounting/Financial Reporting ... Mr. Kevin MCCADDEN
09 AVP Institutional Research ... Ms. Lisa YANNICK
113 Bursar/Director Student Finan Svcs ... Vacant
114 Director Budget ... Ms. Ilene MATES
26 Executive Director Communications ... Ms. Nancy GAINER
88 Director Publications/Printing Svcs ... Mr. Matthew BORN
31 Director Cultural/Community Affairs ... Mr. John RHEIN
88 Director Conference Services ... Ms. Mary Beth KURIMAY
08 University Librarian ... Ms. Mary PAGE
88 Director Teacher Education Center ... Dr. James B. PRICE
36 Director Career Devel Center ... Ms. Rebecca ROSS
88 Dir Acad Development Pgm ... Dr. John CRAIG
88 Dir Learning Asst/Resource ... Ms. Gerardina MARTIN
37 Director Financial Aid ... Mr. Dana C. PARKER
38 Director Counseling Center ... Dr. Julie PERONE
29 Director Alumni Relations ... Ms. Debbie NAUGHTON
41 Interim Director Athletics ... Dr. Terry BEATTIE
88 Director Sports Information ... Mr. James ZUHLKE
28 Director Multicultural Affairs ... Mr. Jerome HUTSON
88 Director Women & Gender Equity ... Ms. Alicia HAHN-MURPHY
19 Director Public Safety ... Mr. Michael D. BICKING
96 Director Business Services ... Ms. Marianne PEFFALL
88 Dir Environmental Health/Safety ... Ms. Gail FELLOWS
14 Director Network & Telecom ... Mr. Joseph SINCAVAGE
91 Enterprise Architect ... Mr. Patrick LENZI
88 Asst Dir Sourcing/Planning/Project ... Ms. Chaw-ye CHANG
105 Sr Dir Enterprise Services ... Ms. Kimberly SLATTERY
90 Spec Asst to VP Information Svcs ... Dr. James FABREY
89 Director New Student Programs ... Mr. Jared BROWN
88 Asst Dean Student Dev & Involvmnt ... Mr. Peter GALLOWAY
39 Director Residence Life ... Ms. Marion MCKINNEY
88 Director Student Conduct ... Ms. Christina BRENNER
88 Dir Student Leadership/Involve ... Mr. Charles WARNER
109 Director Sykes Student Union ... Mr. David TIMMANN
88 Dir Fraternity & Sorority Life ... Ms. Cara JENKINS
88 Dir Service Lrng & Volunteer Pgm ... Ms. Jodi ROTH-SAKS
121 Interim AVP Student Success ... Dr. Francis ATUAHENE
88 Dir Pre-major Academic Advising ... Dr. Ann COLGAN
92 Director Honors College ... Dr. Kevin DEAN
104 Asst VP for International Programs ... Vacant
106 Exec Director Distance Education ... Dr. Rui LI
88 Exec Dir Student Service Inc ... Ms. Donna SNYDER
40 Student Svcs Inc Bookstore Manager ... Mr. Stephen MANNELLA
06 Registrar ... Ms. Megan JERABEK

*Clarion University, Venango (E)

1801 W First Street, Oil City PA 16301-3297
Telephone: (814) 676-6591 FICE Identification: 003319
Accreditation: &M, ADNUR, COARC, NAIT, NUR

*Lock Haven University Clearfield Branch Campus (F)

201 University Drive, Clearfield PA 16830
Telephone: (814) 768-3405 Identification: 770186
Accreditation: &M

Philadelphia College of Osteopathic Medicine (G)

4170 City Avenue, Philadelphia PA 19131-1694
County: Philadelphia FICE Identification: 003352
Unit ID: 215123
Telephone: (215) 871-6100 Carnegie Class: Spec-4-yr-Med
FAX Number: (215) 871-6719 Calendar System: Trimester
URL: www.pcom.edu
Established: 1899 Annual Graduate Tuition & Fees: N/A
Enrollment: 2,789 Coed
Affiliation or Control: Independent Non-Profit IRS Status: 501(c)3
Highest Offering: Doctorate; No Undergraduates
Accreditation: M, ARCPA, CLPSY, IPSY, OSTEO

01 President & CEO ... Dr. Jay S. FELDSTEIN
05 Provost/Senior VP Acad Affairs/Dean ... Dr. Kenneth J. VEIT
10 Vice Pres Finance/Treasurer/CFO ... Mr. Peter DOULIS
58 Vice Pres Grad Pgms/Academic Plng ... Dr. Robert G. CUZZOLINO
17 Chief Acad Ofcr-PCOM Mednet-Opti ... Dr. David KUO
43 Chief Legal Affairs Officer ... Mr. David F. SIMON
63 Dean Osteopathic Med Pgm-GA Campus ... Dr. William CRAVER, III
67 Interim Dean School of Pharmacy ... Dr. Michael LEE
20 Assoc Dean Graduate Medical Educ ... Dr. David KUO
20 Assoc Dean Clinical Education ... Dr. Joseph KACZMARCZYK
20 Assoc Dean Curriculum ... Dr. Kerin FRESA
20 Assoc Dean Curriculum ... Dr. Bonnie BUXTON
12 Chief Campus Officer-Georgia Campus ... Mr. Bryan GINN
46 Chief Science Officer ... Dr. Mindy GEORGE-WEINSTEIN
32 Chief Student Affair Officer ... Dr. Tina WOODRUFF
26 Chief Marketing/Communications Ofcr ... Ms. Wendy W. ROMANO
37 Chief Student Financial Aid Officer ... Mr. Michael WISNIEWSKI
15 Chief Human Resources Officer ... Ms. Christina MAZZELLA
07 Chief Admissions Officer ... Ms. Deborah A. BENVENGER
28 Chief Diversity Officer ... Dr. Marcine PICKRON-DAVIS
13 Chief Technology Officer ... Mr. James A. WILLIAMS
88 Chief Compliance Officer ... Ms. Margaret MCKEON
88 Chief Risk Management Officer ... Ms. Laura G. BELL
18 Chief Facilities/Plant Operations ... Mr. Frank H. WINDLE
30 Chief Advancement Officer ... Ms. Carrie COLLINS
08 Chair of Library/Exec Director ... Ms. Stephanie FERRETTI
06 Registrar ... Ms. Deborah A. CASTELLANO
96 Director of Purchasing ... Vacant
19 Director Security/Safety ... Mr. Richard KRALLE

Pittsburgh Career Institute (A)

421 Seventh Avenue, Pittsburgh PA 15219-1907
County: Allegheny FICE Identification: 022023
Unit ID: 216782
Telephone: (412) 281-2600 Carnegie Class: Spec 2-yr-Health
FAX Number: (412) 227-0807 Calendar System: Other
URL: www.pci.edu
Established: 2014 Annual Undergrad Tuition & Fees: $24,919
Enrollment: 171 Coed
Affiliation or Control: Proprietary IRS Status: Proprietary
Highest Offering: Associate Degree
Accreditation: ACICS, COARC, DMS, SURTEC

01 Campus President ... Patti L. YAKSHE

Pittsburgh Institute of Aeronautics (B)

5 Allegheny County Airport, West Mifflin PA 15122-2674
County: Allegheny FICE Identification: 005310
Unit ID: 215381
Telephone: (412) 346-2100 Carnegie Class: Spec 2-yr-Tech
FAX Number: (412) 466-0513 Calendar System: Quarter
URL: www.pia.edu
Established: 1929 Annual Undergrad Tuition & Fees: $20,438
Enrollment: 370 Coed
Affiliation or Control: Independent Non-Profit IRS Status: 501(c)3
Highest Offering: Associate Degree
Accreditation: ACCSC

01 President/CEO ... Ms. Suzanne MARKLE
05 Director of Education ... Mr. Jason MONGAN
37 Director of Financial Aid ... Mr. Jonathan VUKMANIC
26 Director of Marketing/IT ... Mr. Steven SABOLD
07 Director of Admissions ... Ms. Roxanne OBER
18 Director of Campus Operations ... Mr. Gary HOYLE

Pittsburgh Institute of Mortuary Science (C)

5808 Baum Boulevard, Pittsburgh PA 15206-3706
County: Allegheny FICE Identification: 010814
Unit ID: 215390
Telephone: (412) 362-8500 Carnegie Class: Spec 2-yr-A&S
FAX Number: (412) 362-1684 Calendar System: Trimester
URL: www.pims.edu
Established: 1939 Annual Undergrad Tuition & Fees: N/A
Enrollment: 214 Coed
Affiliation or Control: Independent Non-Profit IRS Status: 501(c)3
Highest Offering: Associate Degree
Accreditation: FUSER

01 President & CEO ... Eugene C. OGRODNIK
06 Registrar ... Karen S. ROCCO

Pittsburgh Technical College (D)

1111 McKee Road, Oakdale PA 15071-3205
County: Allegheny FICE Identification: 007437
Unit ID: 215415
Telephone: (412) 809-5100 Carnegie Class: Assoc/MT-VT-High Trad
FAX Number: (412) 809-5320 Calendar System: Quarter
URL: www.ptcollege.edu
Established: 1946 Annual Undergrad Tuition & Fees: $16,415
Enrollment: 1,936 Coed
Affiliation or Control: Proprietary IRS Status: Proprietary
Highest Offering: Associate Degree
Accreditation: M, ACFEI, MAC, PNUR, SURGT

01 President ... Mr. Gregory DEFEO
03 Executive Vice President ... Mr. George PRY
05 Sr Vice Pres Academic Affairs ... Mr. Mark SCOTT
10 Sr Vice Pres Financial Affairs/IT ... Mr. Terry FARRELL
26 Vice Pres Marketing/Communication ... Mr. Bart LEVITT
10 Vice President of Business Affairs ... Mr. Chuck CUBELIC
21 Vice President Financial Services ... Mrs. Connie VANCAMP
32 Vice President Student Services ... Mr. Keith MERLINO
20 Vice President Education ... Ms. Eileen STEFFAN
30 Vice President of Inst Advancement ... Mrs. Ruth DELACH
09 Vice Pres of Strategic Initiatives ... Mr. Jeff BELSKY
43 General Counsel ... Mr. William KIEFER
06 Registrar ... Mrs. Patricia TARVIN
36 Director of Career Services ... Mrs. Josephine SMITH
27 Director of Public Relations ... Mrs. Linda ALLAN
15 Director of Human Resources ... Ms. Nancy SHEPPARD
13 Director Information Technology ... Mr. Bill SHOWERS
19 Director of Security ... Dr. James LAURIA
39 Director of Resident Life ... Ms. Gloria RITCHIE
105 Digital Marketing Director ... Mr. Tom ESTLACK
18 Director of Facilities Services ... Mr. Tom VUCELICH
37 Assoc Dir Student Financial Aid ... Ms. Teresa BARGER
88 Manager of Compliance ... Ms. Melissa BROWN
40 Campus Store Manager ... Mrs. Cynthia KLEIN
29 Alumni Coordinator ... Mrs. Christine IOLI

Pittsburgh Theological Seminary (E)

616 N. Highland Avenue, Pittsburgh PA 15206-2596
County: Allegheny FICE Identification: 003356
Unit ID: 215424
Telephone: (412) 362-5610 Carnegie Class: Spec-4-yr-Faith
FAX Number: (412) 363-3260 Calendar System: Quarter
URL: www.pts.edu
Established: 1794 Annual Graduate Tuition & Fees: N/A
Enrollment: 249 Coed
Affiliation or Control: Presbyterian Church (U.S.A.) IRS Status: 501(c)3
Highest Offering: Doctorate; No Undergraduates
Accreditation: M, THEOL

01 President ... Dr. David V. ESTERLINE
05 VP Academic Affs/Dean of Faculty ... Dr. Heather H. VACEK
111 VP Institutional Advancement ... Vacant
32 VP Student Svcs/Dean of Students ... Mr. John WELCH
45 VP Planning/Inst Effectiveness ... Dr. James DOWNEY
10 Vice Pres Finance & Administration ... Mr. Thomas HINDS
06 Registrar ... Ms. Anne B. MALONE
08 Director of the Library ... Ms. Michelle SPOMER
88 Director of Field Education ... Dr. Catherine M. BRALL
29 Director of Alumni/ae Services ... Ms. Carolyn CRANSTON
88 Director Doctor of Ministry Program ... Dr. Brian WELLS
51 Director Continuing Education ... Dr. Helen BLIER
37 Director of Financial Aid ... Ms. Cheryl DEPAOLIS
84 Director of Enrollment Mgmt ... Rev. Derek DAVENPORT
07 Director of Admissions ... Rev. Anthony RIVERA
04 Administrative Asst to President ... Ms. Linda SMITH
13 Director of Information Technology ... Mr. David MIDDLETON
15 Human Resources Manager ... Ms. Karen MCMANON
18 Facilities Director ... Mr. Tom FULTON

Point Park University (F)

201 Wood Street, Pittsburgh PA 15222-1984
County: Allegheny FICE Identification: 003357
Unit ID: 215442
Telephone: (412) 391-4100 Carnegie Class: Masters/L
FAX Number: (412) 392-3998 Calendar System: Semester
URL: www.pointpark.edu
Established: 1960 Annual Undergrad Tuition & Fees: $29,030
Enrollment: 3,844 Coed
Affiliation or Control: Independent Non-Profit IRS Status: 501(c)3
Highest Offering: Doctorate
Accreditation: M, DANCE, ENGT, IACBE

01 President ... Dr. Paul HENNIGAN
05 Provost ... Dr. John PEARSON
20 Assistant Provost ... Dr. Jonas PRIDA
10 Sr VP Finance and Operations ... Ms. Bridget MANCOSH
43 Sr VP and General Counsel ... Ms. Amy Elizabeth MCCALL
26 VP of External Affairs ... Ms. Mariann K. GEYER
84 Acting VP Enrollment Management ... Ms. Trudy WILLIAMS
30 Vice Pres Development/Alumni Rels ... Ms. Sharon M. NAVONEY
32 VP of Student Affairs ... Mr. Keith PAYLO
15 VP of Human Resources ... Ms. Lisa STEFANKO
07 Asst Vice Pres for Admissions ... Vacant
96 Asst VP Procurement/Business Svcs ... Ms. Ruth RAULUK
18 Vice President of Operations ... Mr. Christopher J. HILL
19 AVP Public Safety/Chief Police ... Mr. Jeffrey D. BESONG
09 AVP Institutional Research ... Mr. Christopher E. CHONCEK
21 AVP of Finance ... Mr. Jim HARDT
20 Asst VP Academic Affairs ... Mr. George KIERSCH
13 Asst Vice Pres Info Technology ... Mr. Tim WILSON
50 Dean Rowand School of Business ... Dr. Steve TANZILLI
53 Chair Education ... Dr. Darlene MARNICH
79 Chair Psychology ... Dr. Brent ROBBINS
54 Chair Natural Science/Engr Tech ... Dr. Gregg JOHNSON
88 Chair Criminal Justice/Intell Stds ... Mr. Michael BOTTA
88 Chair Business Management ... Mr. Soren HOGSGAARD
88 Chair Acctg Econ & Fin/IT ... Ms. Margaret GILFILLAN
88 Chair Theatre ... Mr. Aaron BOLLINGER
88 Chair Dance ... Mr. Garfield LEMONIUS
88 Chair Cinema ... Vacant
88 Chair Literary Arts ... Dr. Sarah PERRIER
60 Chair School of Communication ... Dr. Thom BAGGERMAN
88 Chair Sport Art Entertain Mgt ... Ms. Paige BEAL
83 Chair Humanities/Social Science ... Dr. Channa NEWMAN
88 Chair Community Engagement ... Dr. Heather STARR FIEDLER
04 Exec Assistant to the President ... Ms. Margaret SMITH
06 University Registrar ... Vacant
08 Director/Librarian/Academic Svcs ... Ms. Liz EVANS
27 Mng Dir Marketing/Public Relations ... Mr. Louis CORSARO
39 Director of Campus Life ... Ms. Janet D. EVANS
07 Director of Admissions ... Ms. Joell MINFORD
41 Director of Athletics ... Mr. Dan SWALGA
88 Dir Conference & Event Services ... Ms. Christina MORTON
38 Student Counseling ... Ms. Taffie BUCCI
106 Dir Online Education/E-learning ... Mr. Nelson CHIPMAN
29 Director Alumni Relations ... Vacant
37 Director Student Financial Aid ... Mr. George SANTUCCI
44 Director Annual Fund Pgms/Indiv Giv ... Ms. Sarah GEORGE
88 Dir Center for Media Innovation ... Mr. Andrew CONTE

Reading Area Community College (G)

PO Box 1706, Reading PA 19603-1706
County: Berks FICE Identification: 010388
Unit ID: 215585
Telephone: (610) 372-4721 Carnegie Class: Assoc/HT-Mix Trad/Non
FAX Number: (610) 372-4264 Calendar System: Semester
URL: www.racc.edu
Established: 1971 Annual Undergrad Tuition & Fees (In-District): $5,310
Enrollment: 4,090 Coed
Affiliation or Control: State/Local IRS Status: 501(c)3
Highest Offering: Associate Degree
Accreditation: M, ADNUR, COARC, MLTAD, PNUR

01 President ... Dr. Anna D. WEITZ
05 Sr VP of Academic Affairs/Provost ... Dr. Susan D. LOONEY
10 Sr VP Fin & Admin Svcs/Treasurer ... Mr. Kenneth DEARSTYNE
30 VP External Aff/Exec Dir Foundation ... Mr. Michael NAGEL
32 Dean of Student Affairs ... Ms. Maria MITCHELL
21 Assoc VP for Bus Svcs/Controller ... Ms. Dolores PETERSON
84 Dean of Enrollment Management ... Ms. Kay LITMAN
09 Dean Assessment/Research/Planning ... Ms. Mary FLAGG
81 Assoc Dean of Science/Math ... Dr. Gloria OIKELOME
62 Asst Dean Library Svcs/Learning Res ... Ms. Mary Ellen HECKMAN
50 Asst Dean of Business Division ... Ms. Linda BELL
76 Asst Dean of Health Professions ... Dr. Amelia CAPOTOSTA
79 Asst Dean of Comm/Arts/Humanities ... Mr. Kevin COOTS
83 Asst Dean of Social Sci/Human Svc ... Dr. Robin ECKERT
15 Director Human Resources ... Vacant
103 Exec Dir Workforce Dev/Cmty Educ ... Ms. Bonnie SPAYD
26 Director Marketing/Communications ... Mr. David HESSEN
13 Director Information Technology ... Mr. Chet WINTERS
37 Director Financial Aid/Registrar ... Mr. Benjamin ROSENBERGER
57 Dir of Miller Center for the Arts ... Ms. Cathleen STEPHEN
96 Director of Purchasing ... Mr. Michael HODOWANEC
18 Director of Facilities ... Mr. Kevin MACKLEN
04 Exec Admin Asst to the President ... Ms. Sandra STRAUSE
20 Dean of Instruction ... Ms. Cynthia SEAMAN
07 Dir Admiss & Enrollment Svcs ... Dr. Agibail WERNICKI
35 Coordinator of Student Life ... Ms. Kimberly UPHOLD

Reconstructionist Rabbinical College (H)

1299 Church Road, Wyncote PA 19095-1898
County: Montgomery FICE Identification: 022734
Unit ID: 215619
Telephone: (215) 576-0800 Carnegie Class: Spec-4-yr-Faith
FAX Number: (215) 576-6143 Calendar System: Semester
URL: www.rrc.edu
Established: 1968 Annual Graduate Tuition & Fees: N/A
Enrollment: 44 Coed
Affiliation or Control: Jewish IRS Status: 501(c)3
Highest Offering: Doctorate; No Undergraduates
Accreditation: M

01 President ... Rabbi Deborah WAXMAN
05 Vice Pres Academic Affairs ... Dr. Elsie STERN
88 Director Center for Jewish Ethics ... Rabbi David TEUTSCH
45 VP Strategic Advancement ... Dr. Josh PESKIN
03 Executive Vice President ... Rabbi Amber POWERS
30 Asst Vice Pres Development ... Ms. Barbara G. LISSY
11 Director of Operations ... Mr. Robert CHAVEZ
08 Library Director ... Mr. Alan LAPAYOVER

Reformed Episcopal Seminary (I)

826 Second Avenue, Blue Bell PA 19422-1257
County: Montgomery Identification: 667050
Unit ID: 216348
Telephone: (610) 292-9852 Carnegie Class: Not Classified
FAX Number: (610) 292-9853 Calendar System: Quarter
URL: www.reseminary.edu
Established: 1887 Annual Graduate Tuition & Fees: N/A
Enrollment: 28 Coed
Affiliation or Control: Reformed Episcopal Church IRS Status: 501(c)3
Highest Offering: Master's; No Undergraduates
Accreditation: THEOL

01 Chancellor and President ... Rt Rev. David L. HICKS
05 Dean and Vice President ... Rev Dr. Jonathan S. RICHES
13 IT Director & Asst Librarian ... Rev. Russell BUCHANAN
07 Director of Admissions & Recruiting ... Rev. David A. FRANCE

30 Director of Development .... Mr. Mark CERNERO
13 Director Information & Technology .... Vacant
108 Director Institutional Assessment .... Dr. Robert ARNER

Reformed Presbyterian Theological Seminary (A)

7418 Penn Avenue, Pittsburgh PA 15208-2594
County: Allegheny FICE Identification: 003358
Unit ID: 215628
Telephone: (412) 731-6000 Carnegie Class: Spec-4-yr-Faith
FAX Number: (412) 731-4834 Calendar System: Quarter
URL: www.rpts.edu
Established: 1810 Annual Graduate Tuition & Fees: N/A
Enrollment: 86 Coed
Affiliation or Control: Reformed Presbyterian Church IRS Status: 501(c)3
Highest Offering: Doctorate; No Undergraduates
Accreditation: THEOL

01 President .... Dr. Jerry F. O'NEILL
05 Dean of the Faculty .... Mr. Barry YORK
06 Registrar/Head Librarian .... Mr. Thomas G. REID, JR.
40 Bookstore Manager .... Mrs. Vicki SMITH
10 Treasurer .... Mr. James MCFARLAND
07 Director of Admissions .... Mr. Edwin BLACKWOOD
37 Director of Financial Aid .... Mrs. Sharon SAMPSON
111 Dir of Institutional Advancement .... Mr. Mark SAMPSON
04 Administrative Asst to President .... Mrs. Vicki SMITH
18 Chief Facilities/Physical Plant .... Rev. Andrew JACKSON
32 Chief Student Affairs/Student Life .... Rev. Edwin BLACKWOOD

The Restaurant School at Walnut Hill College (B)

4207 Walnut Street, Philadelphia PA 19104-3518
County: Philadelphia FICE Identification: 021928
Unit ID: 215637
Telephone: (215) 222-4200 Carnegie Class: Spec-4-yr-Other
FAX Number: (215) 222-4219 Calendar System: Other
URL: www.walnuthillcollege.edu
Established: 1974 Annual Undergrad Tuition & Fees: $23,550
Enrollment: 407 Coed
Affiliation or Control: Proprietary IRS Status: Proprietary
Highest Offering: Baccalaureate
Accreditation: ACCSC

01 President .... Mr. Daniel LIBERATOSCIOLI
03 Executive Vice President .... Mr. Karl D. BECKER
11 Vice President Administrative Svcs .. Ms. Peggy LIBERATOSCIOLI
10 Vice President of Operations .... Mr. Dennis LIBERATI
88 Vice President of Culinary Arts .... Chef Gary TREVISANI
05 Chief Academic Officer .... Mr. David MORROW
07 Director of Admissions .... Ms. Caitlin SNEDEKER
21 Controller .... Mr. Chris MOLZ
32 Dir Student/Community Engagement .... Ms. Meghan BLOOME
37 Director Financial Aid .... Ms. Caitlin SNEDEKER
50 Director School of Management .... Mr. David MORROW

Robert Morris University (C)

6001 University Boulevard,
Moon Township PA 15108-1189
County: Allegheny FICE Identification: 003359
Unit ID: 215655
Telephone: (412) 397-6400 Carnegie Class: DU-Mod
FAX Number: (412) 397-5958 Calendar System: Semester
URL: www.rmu.edu
Established: 1921 Annual Undergrad Tuition & Fees: $28,250
Enrollment: 5,377 Coed
Affiliation or Control: Independent Non-Profit IRS Status: 501(c)3
Highest Offering: Doctorate
Accreditation: M, CAEPT, CS, ENG, NMT, NURSE

01 President .... Dr. Christopher HOWARD
10 Sr Vice Pres for Business Affairs .... Mr. Dan W. KIENER
05 Provost/Sr VP Academic Affairs .... Mr. David L. JAMISON
30 Sr VP Institutional Advancement .... Mr. Jay T. CARSON
43 Vice President & General Counsel .. Ms. Renee T. CAVALOVITCH
21 Vice President Financial Operations .... Mr. Jeffrey A. LISTWAK
15 Vice President of Human Resources ... Ms. Ellen G. WIECKOWSKI
106 VP Corporate Rels/SVP Academic Affs .... Dr. Derya A. JACOBS
84 VP Enrollment Management .... Ms. Wendy C. BECKEMEYER
32 Vice President for Student Life .... Mr. John MICHALENKO
30 Vice President for Development .... Ms. Kimberley A. HAMMER
13 Vice Pres Information Technology ...... Ms. Ellen G. WIECKOWSKI
18 Vice Pres for Facilities .... Mr. Perry F. ROOFNER
26 Vice Pres Public Rels/Marketing .... Mr. Jonathan POTTS
20 Vice Provost for Academic Affairs .... Dr. Lawrence A. TOMEI
09 VP Planning & Administration .... Dr. David R. MAJKA
60 Dean School Comm/Info Systems .... Dr. AnnMarie M. LEBLANC
50 Dean School of Business .... Dr. Michelle PATRICK
54 Dean School of Engr/Math/Science .... Dr. Maria V. KALEVITCH
53 Dean Sch Education/Social Sciences .... Dr. Mary Ann RAFOTH
66 Dean School Nursing/Health .... Dr. Valerie M. HOWARD
88 Dir Univ Sponsorships/Athletic Fund .... Mr. Matthew B. MILLET
07 Dean of Admissions .... Ms. Kellie L. LAURENZI
88 Exec Dir Bayer Ctr Nonprofit Mgmt .... Ms. Peggy M. OUTON
35 Assistant Dean of Students .... Mrs. Maureen H. KEEFER
41 Director of Athletics .... Dr. Craig S. COLEMAN
08 Director University Library .... Dr. Timothy M. SCHLAK
21 Chief Accounting Officer/Controller .... Ms. Melissa A. MICCO

06 Registrar/Exec Dir of Academic Svcs .... Mr. Frank E. PERRY
19 Director Public Safety .... Mr. Randy L. MINK
36 Director Career Center .... Ms. Kishma DECASTRO-SALLIS
39 Director Residence Life .... Mrs. Anne L. LAHODA
38 Director Center for Student Success .... Mr. Paul D. SPRADLEY
28 Chief Diversity/Inclusion Officer .... Dr. Yasmin S. PUROHIT
27 Senior Director Public Relations .... Mr. Jonathan POTTS
109 Sr Director Financial Operations .... Anita NILKANT
37 Director Student Financial Aid ... Ms. Stephanie N. HENDERSHOT
29 Asst Dir Alumni Relations .... Mary C. GERAD

Rosedale Technical College (D)

215 Beecham Drive, Suite 2, Pittsburgh PA 15205-9791
County: Allegheny FICE Identification: 012050
Unit ID: 215682
Telephone: (412) 521-6200 Carnegie Class: Spec 2-yr-Tech
FAX Number: (412) 521-2520 Calendar System: Semester
URL: www.rosedaletech.org
Established: 1949 Annual Undergrad Tuition & Fees: $12,980
Enrollment: 419 Coed
Affiliation or Control: Independent Non-Profit IRS Status: 501(c)3
Highest Offering: Associate Degree
Accreditation: ACCSC

01 President .... Dennis F. WILKE
05 Director of Education .... Kara CHAN
30 VP College Development/Comm .... Debbie BIER
07 Director of Admissions .... Dave DETAR

Rosemont College (E)

1400 Montgomery Avenue, Rosemont PA 19010-1699
County: Montgomery FICE Identification: 003360
Unit ID: 215691
Telephone: (610) 527-0200 Carnegie Class: Masters/M
FAX Number: (610) 527-0341 Calendar System: Semester
URL: www.rosemont.edu
Established: 1921 Annual Undergrad Tuition & Fees: $19,480
Enrollment: 887 Coed
Affiliation or Control: Roman Catholic IRS Status: 501(c)3
Highest Offering: Master's
Accreditation: M

01 President .... Dr. Sharon LATCHAW HIRSH
05 Provost/VP Academic/Student Affairs .... Dr. B. Christopher DOUGHERTY
10 VP for Finance & Administration .... Dr. Randy ELDRIDGE
37 Dir Enrollment Svcs/Fin Compliance .... Ms. Deborah CAWLEY
30 Vice Pres College Relations .... Ms. Christyn MORAN
32 Dean of Students .... Mr. Troy CHIDDICK
84 Vice President for Enrollment Mgmt .... Vacant
88 Vice President for Mission .... Sr. Jeanne Marie HATCH, SHCJ
08 Exec Director of Library Services .... Mrs. Catherine FENNELL
58 Dean Schools Graduate/Prof Studies .. Dr. Dennis R. DOUGHERTY
20 Academic Dean Undergrad College ... Mrs. Paulette HUTCHINSON
29 Director of Alumni Relations .... Mr. Kevin GARY
26 Managing Director of Communications .... Ms. Antoinette MACDONALD
06 Registrar/Dir of Inst Research .... Ms. Jennifer HAWKES
41 Director of Athletics .... Ms. Lynn S. ROTHENHOEFER
15 Asst VP Human Resources .... Ms. Jane FEDEROWICZ
42 Director of Campus Ministry .... Mr. Jay VERZOSA
18 Director of Operations .... Mr. Raymond A. BROWN
38 Director Student Counseling .... Ms. Kruti QUAZI
39 Director of Residence Life .... Mr. Benjamin HUELSKAMP
19 Director of Public Safety .... Mr. Matthew BAKER
21 Controller .... Ms. Faith BYRNE
07 Associate Director of Admissions .... Ms. Bettsy MCKLAINE

Saint Charles Borromeo Seminary (F)

100 E Wynnewood Road, Wynnewood PA 19096-3099
County: Montgomery FICE Identification: 003364
Unit ID: 216047
Telephone: (610) 667-3394 Carnegie Class: Spec-4-yr-Faith
FAX Number: (610) 667-7635 Calendar System: Semester
URL: www.scs.edu
Established: 1832 Annual Undergrad Tuition & Fees: $20,655
Enrollment: 211 Male
Affiliation or Control: Roman Catholic IRS Status: 501(c)3
Highest Offering: Master's
Accreditation: M, THEOL

01 Rector & President .... M.Rev. Timothy C. SENIOR
05 Vice President for Academic Affairs .. Rev. Robert A. PESARCHICK
03 Vice Rector Theology/Dir of Liturgy .... Rev. Patrick J. WELSH
03 Vice Rector of the College .... Rev. Joseph SHENOSKY
10 Chief Financial Officer .... Mr. Stephen DOLAN
108 VP Info Services & Assessment .... Mrs. Cait KOKOLUS
33 Dean of Men Theology .... Rev. Brian KANE
33 Dean of Men College .... Rev. George SZPARAGOWSKI
08 Director of Library Services .... Mr. James HUMBLE
06 Registrar .... Mrs. Shura SULLIVAN
42 Dir Spiritual Formation College .... Fr. Herb SPERGER
42 Dir Spiritual Formation Theology .... Fr. Ned SHLESINGER
88 Director Pastoral/Apostolic Form .... Rev. Augustine ESPOSITO
73 Dean School of Theological Studies .... Rev. John AMES
21 Director of Financial Services .... Ms. Barbara COADY
37 Director Student Financial Aid .... Ms. Nora DOWNEY
19 Director of Safety and Security .... Mr. Nicholas MANCINI

Saint Francis University (G)

PO Box 600, Loretto PA 15940-0600
County: Cambria FICE Identification: 003366
Unit ID: 215743
Telephone: (814) 472-3000 Carnegie Class: Masters/L
FAX Number: (814) 472-3003 Calendar System: Semester
URL: www.francis.edu
Established: 1847 Annual Undergrad Tuition & Fees: $33,344
Enrollment: 2,664 Coed
Affiliation or Control: Roman Catholic IRS Status: 501(c)3
Highest Offering: Doctorate
Accreditation: M, ARCPA, ENG, EXSC, IACBE, NURSE, OT, PTA, SW

01 President .... Rev. Malachi VAN TASSELL, TOR
05 Provost .... Dr. Wayne POWEL
10 Vice President for Finance .... Mr. Jeffrey SAVINO
32 Vice Pres for Student Development .... Dr. Frank MONTECALVO
42 Director of Mission Integration .... Rev. Joseph LEHMAN
30 Vice President for Advancement .... Mr. Robert CRUSCIEL
84 Vice Pres for Enrollment Management ... Ms. Erin E. MCCLOSKEY
08 Dean of Library Services .... Ms. Sandra A. BALOUGH
97 Assoc Dean of General Education .... Ms. Martha O'BRIEN
06 Registrar .... Dr. Stephen R. ROMBOUTS
09 Director of Institutional Research .... Ms. Kate DEATER
37 Financial Aid Director .... Mr. Jamie KOSH
26 Director Marketing & Public Affairs .... Ms. Marie YOUNG
44 Director of Development .... Ms. Marie B. MELUSKY
38 Director of Counseling Center .... Mr. David P. WILSON
13 Director Computer Services .... Mr. George F. PYO
29 Director of Alumni Relations .... Mr. Eric HORELL
51 Director Continuing Education .... Ms. Julie BARRIS
18 Director of Physical Plant .... Vacant
21 Controller .... Mr. Thomas R. FRITZ
41 Director of Athletics .... Ms. Susan ROBINSON-FRUCHTL
88 Dir Small Business Devel Center .... Mr. Barry SURMA
19 University Police .... Capt. Christopher LYTLE
39 Director of Residence Life .... Mr. Donald MILES
42 Director of Campus Ministry .... Rev. Christopher DOBSON
121 Dir Center for Academic Success .... Ms. Renee BERNARD
35 Dir of Student Engagement .... Mr. Bobby ANDERSON
15 Director of Human Resources .... Ms. Marian BENDER
28 Director of Multicultural Affairs .... Ms. Lynne BANKS
96 Director of Purchasing .... Mr. Caleb DRENNING
20 Associate Provost .... Dr. Peter R. SKONER
40 Manager of Bookstore .... Ms. Barbara SHINGLE

Saint Joseph's University (H)

5600 City Avenue, Philadelphia PA 19131-1376
County: Philadelphia FICE Identification: 003367
Unit ID: 215770
Telephone: (610) 660-1000 Carnegie Class: Masters/L
FAX Number: (610) 660-1201 Calendar System: Semester
URL: www.sju.edu
Established: 1851 Annual Undergrad Tuition & Fees: $43,020
Enrollment: 8,625 Coed
Affiliation or Control: Roman Catholic IRS Status: 501(c)3
Highest Offering: Doctorate
Accreditation: M, CS

01 President .... Dr. Mark C. REED
05 Provost .... Dr. Jeanne F. BRADY
88 Executive Director of Mission .... Mr. Dan JOYCE
32 VP Student Life/Assoc Provost .... Dr. Cary M. ANDERSON
11 Vice Pres Administrative Services .... Mr. Timothy MCGURIMAN
111 VP University Advancement .... Mr. Martin F. FARRELL
10 Vice President Financial Affairs .... Mr. David R. BEAUPRE
15 VP Human Resources .... Ms. Sharon O'GRADY EISENMANN
27 VP Marketing & Communications .... Mr. Joseph M. LUNARDI
39 VP Campus Life .... Dr. John A. JEFFERY
43 General Counsel .... Ms. Marianne SCHIMELFINIG
100 Assistant Vice President .... Ms. Sarah F. QUINN
20 Associate Provost Academic Support .... Dr. Paul ASPAN
49 Dean Col Arts & Sciences .... Dr. Shaily A. MENON
50 Dean Haub School of Business ..... Dr. Joseph A. DIANGELO, JR.
41 Vice Pres/Director Athletics .... Mr. Dominick J. DIJULIA
84 Assoc Provost Enrollment Mgmt .... Mr. Robert J. MCBRIDE
06 University Registrar .... Mr. Scott J. SPENCER
08 Director Drexel Library .... Ms. Anne Z. KRAKOW
21 Controller .... Ms. April LEE
86 Asst VP Govt & Community Rels .... Mr. Wadell RIDLEY, JR.
35 Asst VP Student Educ Support Svcs .... Dr. Kimberly M. ALLEN-STUCK
29 Asst Vice Pres Alumni Relations .... Mr. Thomas MONAGHAN
13 Chief Information Officer .... Mr. Francis J. DISANTI
88 Asst Provost for Business and Analy .... Ms. Dawn M. BURDSALL
88 Asst VP Student Development .... Dr. Mary Elaine PERRY
24 Asst Provost Online Education .... Dr. Peter MCLALLEN
07 Asst Prov Undergrad Admiss/Enroll .... Ms. Maureen MATHIS
42 Director Campus Ministry .... Mr. Thomas J. SHEIBLEY
36 Exec Director Career Dev Center .... Ms. Trish SHAFER
38 Director Counseling/Pers Dev Ctr .... Dr. Gregory NICHOLLS
18 Director Facilities Management .... Mr. Kevin M. KANE
19 Director Public Safety & Security .... Mr. Arthur GROVER
96 Director Purchasing .... Mr. William O. ANDERSON
23 Director Student Health Service .... Ms. Laura HURST
35 Dir Student Leadership/Activities .... Dr. Beth HAGOVSKY
09 Director Institutional Effectivenes .... Ms. Wenjun CHI
102 Dir Foundation/Corporate Relations .... Ms. Georgette HAMATY
104 Director International Programs .... Mr. Thomas L. KESARIS
25 Director Academic Research Svcs .... Mr. Thomas J. KAEO
112 Director Planned Giving .... Ms. Anat BECKER

St. Tikhon's Orthodox Theological Seminary (A)

PO Box 130, South Canaan PA 18459-0130
County: Wayne FICE Identification: 039193
Unit ID: 216180
Telephone: (570) 561-1818 Carnegie Class: Not Classified
FAX Number: N/A Calendar System: Semester
URL: www.stots.edu
Established: 1938 Annual Undergrad Tuition & Fees: N/A
Enrollment: N/A Coed
Affiliation or Control: Other IRS Status: 501(c)3
Highest Offering: First Professional Degree
Accreditation: THEOL

01 President .... Metr. Tikhon MOLLARD
03 Rector/CEO .... Abp. Michael DAHULICH
05 Dean/COO .... V.Rev. Steven A. VOYTOVICH
10 Chief Financial Officer .... V.Rev. Dennis SWENCKI
04 Administrative Asst to Dean/COO .... Mr. Marshall M. GOODGE
08 Librarian .... Prof. Sergei D. ARHIPOV
06 Registrar .... Dr. Paul J. WITEK
30 Dir Office of Mission Development .... Mr. Seraphim DANCKAERT

Saint Vincent College (B)

300 Fraser Purchase Road, Latrobe PA 15650-2690
County: Westmoreland FICE Identification: 003368
Unit ID: 215798
Telephone: (724) 805-2500 Carnegie Class: Bac-A&S
FAX Number: (724) 805-2019 Calendar System: Semester
URL: www.stvincent.edu
Established: 1846 Annual Undergrad Tuition & Fees: $33,426
Enrollment: 1,857 Coed
Affiliation or Control: Roman Catholic IRS Status: 501(c)3
Highest Offering: Doctorate
Accreditation: M, ACBSP, ANEST

01 President .... Br. Norman W. HIPPS, OSB
03 Executive Vice President .... Rev. Paul TAYLOR, OSB
05 VP Academic Affairs .... Dr. John SMETANKA
10 VP/Chief Finance/Admin Officer .... Mr. Richard WILLIAMS
32 VP Student Affairs .... Ms. Mary COLLINS
26 VP Marketing and Communication .... Ms. Suzanne ENGLISH
07 Dean of Admissions .... Mr. Stephen NEITZ
13 Chief Information Officer .... Mr. Peter E. MAHONEY
20 Dean of Studies .... Ms. Alice J. KAYLOR
50 Dean McKenna Sch Bus/Econ/Govt .... Dr. Gary QUINLIVAN
60 Dean Sch Soc Sci/Communication/Educ .... Dr. MaryBeth SPORE
79 Dean Humanities & Fine Arts .... Rev. Rene KOLLAR, OSB
81 Dean Science/Math & Computing .... Dr. Stephen M. JODIS
06 Registrar .... Ms. Celine R. BRUDNOK
08 Librarian .... Bro. David KELLY, OSB
29 Director of Alumni Affairs .... Mr. Shawn GOUCH
27 Director of Public Relations .... Mr. Donald A. ORLANDO
36 Director Career Services .... Ms. Courtney BAUM
15 Director of Human Resources .... Ms. Judith MAHER
42 Director of Campus Ministry .... Rev. Killian LOCH, OSB
23 Director Wellness Center .... Ms. Gretchen FLOCK
19 Director Public Safety .... Mr. Steve BROWN
41 Athletic Director .... Rev. Myron KIRSCH, OSB
39 Director Resident Life .... Mr. Robert BAUM
96 Director of Purchasing .... Mr. Terry NOEL
09 Director of Institutional Research .... Ms. Julia CAVALLO
18 Director of Facility Management .... Mr. Douglas EPPLEY
40 Manager Book Center .... Rev. Anthony GROSSI, OSB
88 Exec Dir Fred Rogers Center .... Mr. Rick FERNANDES
58 Coord of Graduate Studies .... Ms. Amanda GUNTHER
04 Administrative Asst to President .... Ms. Patricia OWENS
104 Director Study Abroad .... Ms. Sara HART
37 Director Student Financial Aid .... Ms. Mary GAZAL
102 Dir Foundation/Govt/Corporate Rels .... Ms. Christine FOSCHIA
43 Dir Legal Services/General Counsel .... Mr. Bruce ANTKOWIAK

Saint Vincent Seminary (C)

300 Fraser Purchase Road, Latrobe PA 15650-2690
County: Westmoreland Identification: 666018
Unit ID: 215813
Telephone: (724) 805-2592 Carnegie Class: Spec-4-yr-Faith
FAX Number: (724) 532-5052 Calendar System: Semester
URL: www.saintvincentseminary.edu
Established: 1846 Annual Undergrad Tuition & Fees: N/A
Enrollment: 49 Coed
Affiliation or Control: Roman Catholic IRS Status: 501(c)3
Highest Offering: Master's
Accreditation: THEOL

01 Rector .... V.Rev. Edward M. MAZICH, OSB
88 Director of Spiritual Formation .... Rev. Boniface N. HICKS, OSB
05 Academic Dean .... Rev. Patrick T. CRONAUER, OSB
03 Vice-Rector .... Rev. John-Mary TOMPKINS, OSB
42 Director of Liturgy .... Rev. Cyprian G. CONSTANTINE, OSB
88 Director of Pastoral Formation .... Rev. Nathan MUNSCH, OSB
32 Dean of Students .... Rev. Emmanuel O. AFUNUGO
38 Dir of Pre-Theologian Formation .... Dr. Lawrence SUTTON
04 Administrative Asst to President .... Ms. Patricia OWENS
06 Registrar .... Ms. Celine BRUDNOK
07 Director of Admissions .... Mr. Stephen NEITZ
08 Head Librarian .... Br. David KELLY, OSB
09 Director of Institutional Research .... Ms. Julia CAVALLO
10 Chief Business Officer .... Mr. Richard WILLIAMS
100 Chief of Staff .... Rev. Paul R. TAYLOR, OSB
101 Secretary of the Institution/Board .... Rev. Jeffrey S. NYARDY, OSB
105 Director Web Services .... Ms. Cindy HOFFMAN
11 Chief of Administration .... Rt Rev. Douglas R. NOWICKI, OSB
13 Chief Info Technology Officer (CIO) .... Mr. Peter MAHONEY
15 Director Personnel Services .... Mrs. Judith MAHER
18 Chief Facilities/Physical Plant .... Mr. Douglas EPPLEY
19 Director Security/Safety .... Fr. Joseph ADAMS, OSB
22 Dir Affirmative Action/EEO .... Miss Eileen FLINN
25 Chief Contracts/Grants Admin .... Ms. Christine L. FOSCHIA
26 Chief Public Relations/Marketing .... Ms. Suzanne ENGLISH
28 Director of Diversity .... Dr. Nancy ROTTLER
29 Director Alumni Relations .... Mr. Shawn GOUCH
30 Chief Development/Advancement .... Mr. Shannon JORDAN
37 Director Student Financial Aid .... Ms. Mary GAZAL
41 Athletic Director .... Rev. Myron KIRSCH, OSB
43 Dir Legal Services/General Counsel .... Mr. Bruce ANTKOWIAK
44 Director Annual or Planned Giving .... Mr. David HOLLENBAUGH
96 Director of Purchasing .... Mr. Terry NOEL

Salus University (D)

8360 Old York Road, Elkins Park PA 19027-1516
County: Philadelphia FICE Identification: 003311
Unit ID: 214564
Telephone: (215) 780-1400 Carnegie Class: Spec-4-yr-Other Health
FAX Number: (215) 780-1325 Calendar System: Quarter
URL: www.salus.edu
Established: 1919 Annual Undergrad Tuition & Fees: N/A
Enrollment: 1,121 Coed
Affiliation or Control: Independent Non-Profit IRS Status: 501(c)3
Highest Offering: Doctorate
Accreditation: M, ARCPA, AUD, OPT, OPTR, OT, @SP

01 President .... Dr. Michael H. MITTLEMAN
05 Vice President Faculty Affairs .... Dr. Janice SCHARRE
10 Vice Pres Finance/Business Affairs .... Mr. Donald KATES
17 Vice Pres Clinical Services .... Dr. John GAAL
45 Vice President for Inst Planning .... Mr. Brian ZUCKERMAN
32 Dean Student Affairs .... Dr. James CALDWELL
20 Exec Assistant to the Provost .... Ms. Karen BOYKIN
09 Asst Dir Research Admin .... Ms. Lydia PARKE
06 Registrar .... Ms. Shannon BOSS
13 Chief Information Officer .... Mr. William BRICHTA
38 Director Personal/Prof Development .... Dr. James CALDWELL
37 Assoc Dean Student Financial Affs .... Ms. Jamie SCHLANG
18 Director Physical Plant .... Mr. Richard ECHEVARRI
30 Director of Development .... Dr. Susan OLESZEWSKI
26 Director Publications/Communication .... Ms. Alexis ABATE
29 Director Alumni Relations/Giving .... Ms. Jamie LEMISCH
51 Coord Continuing/Post-Graduate Educ .... Mrs. Melissa VITEK
58 Chairperson Graduate Studies .... Vacant
40 Bookstore Manager .... Mr. Joe NOCE
24 Director Instructional Media .... Mr. Glenn ROEDEL
36 Dir Student Placement/Student Affs .... Mr. Ryan HOLLISTER
84 Director Enrollment Management .... Dr. Jim CALDWELL
88 Exec Dir Inst Visually Impaired .... Dr. Brooke KRUEMMLING
08 Head Librarian .... Ms. Marietta DOOLEY
19 Director of Security .... Mr. Gary HUGHES
15 Dir Human Res/Affirm Action/Facil .... Ms. Maura KEENAN
96 Director of Purchasing .... Ms. Lydia FRIEL

Seton Hill University (E)

1 Seton Hill Drive, Greensburg PA 15601-1599
County: Westmoreland FICE Identification: 003362
Unit ID: 215947
Telephone: (724) 834-2200 Carnegie Class: Masters/M
FAX Number: (724) 830-4611 Calendar System: Semester
URL: www.setonhill.edu
Established: 1883 Annual Undergrad Tuition & Fees: $33,520
Enrollment: 2,359 Coed
Affiliation or Control: Roman Catholic IRS Status: 501(c)3
Highest Offering: Master's
Accreditation: M, ARCPA, DENT, DIETC, IACBE, MFCD, MUS, SW

01 President .... Dr. Mary FINGER
32 VP Mission .... Sr. Vivien LINKHAUER, SC
05 Provost .... Sr. Susan YOCHUM
10 Vice Pres Finance & Business .... Mr. Paul EDSALL
11 Vice Pres Administration/Registrar .... Mrs. Barbara C. HINKLE
111 Vice Pres Institutional Advancement .... Mrs. Christine MUESELER
13 Chief Information Officer .... Ms. Melissa ALSING
84 Vice Pres Enrollment Management .... Mr. Brett FRESHOUR
21 Controller .... Ms. Rebecca DUXBURY
35 Dean of Student Services .... Dr. Charmaine R. STRONG
07 Director Admissions .... Ms. Ashley JOSAY ZULLO
08 Director of Library .... Mr. David STANLEY
30 Director Development .... Ms. Molly ROBB SHIMKO
29 Director of Alumni Relations .... Ms. Mary COX
37 Director of Financial Aid .... Ms. Tracey DE BAEZ SNYDER
36 Director of Career Development .... Ms. Renee STAREK
15 Director Personnel Services .... Mrs. Darlene SAUERS
18 Director Facilities .... Mr. Bill VOKES
41 Executive Athletic Director .... Mr. Chris SNYDER
42 Director Campus Ministry .... Sr. Maureen O'BRIEN
04 Assistant to the President .... Mrs. Carol BILLMAN
06 Registrar .... Ms. Barbara HINKLE
38 Director Student Counseling .... Ms. Teresa BASSI-COOK
09 Director of Institutional Research .... Mrs. Edith COOK
26 Chief Public Relations Officer .... Ms. Jennifer REEGER
96 Director of Purchasing .... Mr. Charles O'NEILL
19 Director Security/Safety .... Vacant
22 Dir Affirmative Action/EEO .... Ms. Darlene SAUERS
25 Chief Contracts/Grants Admin .... Ms. Cynthia FERRARI
39 Director Student Housing .... Mr. Cory CAMPBELL
86 Director Government Relations .... Mrs. Carol BILLMAN

South Hills School of Business and Technology (F)

541 58th Street, Altoona PA 16602
Telephone: (814) 944-6134 Identification: 770772
Accreditation: ACICS, CAHIIM, MAAB

South Hills School of Business and Technology (G)

480 Waupelani Drive, State College PA 16801-4516
County: Centre FICE Identification: 013263
Unit ID: 216083
Telephone: (814) 234-7755 Carnegie Class: Assoc/MT-VT-High Trad
FAX Number: (814) 234-0926 Calendar System: Quarter
URL: www.southhills.edu
Established: 1970 Annual Undergrad Tuition & Fees: $16,612
Enrollment: 491 Coed
Affiliation or Control: Proprietary IRS Status: Proprietary
Highest Offering: Associate Degree
Accreditation: ACICS, CAHIIM, DMS, MAAB

00 Owner .... Mrs. Maralyn MAZZA
01 President .... Mr. S. Paul MAZZA, III
05 Director .... Mr. Mark MAGGS
06 Registrar .... Ms. Ingrid THOMPSON
07 Director of Admissions .... Ms. Holly EMERICK
26 Chief Public Relations/Marketing .... Ms. Misty FREDERICK-RITZ
29 Director Alumni Relations .... Ms. Maryann LINGENFELTER
37 Director Student Financial Aid .... Ms. Anne FALK
20 Director of Education .... Mr. David SCHAITKIN

Susquehanna University (H)

514 University Avenue, Selinsgrove PA 17870-1025
County: Snyder FICE Identification: 003369
Unit ID: 216278
Telephone: (570) 374-0101 Carnegie Class: Bac-A&S
FAX Number: (570) 372-4040 Calendar System: Semester
URL: www.susqu.edu
Established: 1858 Annual Undergrad Tuition & Fees: $43,720
Enrollment: 2,199 Coed
Affiliation or Control: Evangelical Lutheran Church In America
IRS Status: 501(c)3
Highest Offering: Baccalaureate
Accreditation: M, MUS

01 President .... Dr. Jonathan GREEN
100 VP & Chief of Staff .... Dr. Philip E. WINGER
05 Co-COO & Provost/Dean of Faculty .... Dr. Linda A. MCMILLIN
10 Co-COO & VP for Finance & Admin .... Mr. Michael COYNE
26 Vice President for Univ Relations .... Mr. Ronald A. COHEN
84 VP for Enrollment & Marketing .... Ms. Madeleine E. RHYNEER
32 VP Student Engagement & Success .... Dr. Susan LANTZ
20 Assoc Provost/Dean A&S .... Dr. Valerie G. MARTIN
50 Int Dean Weis School of Business .... Dr. Matthew ROUSU
27 Chief Communications Officer .... Vacant
112 Interim Asst VP Gift Planning .... Ms. Kim ANDRETTA
04 Assistant to the President .... Ms. Joann B. MIERES
04 Senior Admin Asst to the President .... Ms. Sharon POPE
38 Asst Dean & Director of Counseling .... Dr. Stacey PEARSON-WHARTON
89 Director of First Year Experience .... Ms. Katherine BURR
28 Asst Dean Intercultural/Cmty Engage .... Ms. Dena SALERNO
07 Director of Admissions .... Mr. Philip BETZ
08 Director of the Library .... Ms. Katherine FURLONG
37 Director of Student Financial Svcs .... Ms. Erin M. WOLFE
06 Registrar .... Ms. Alison A. RICHARD
42 University Chaplain .... Rev. Scott M. KERSHNER
13 Chief Information Officer .... Mr. Mark D. HUBER
41 Director of Athletics .... Dr. Pamela SAMUELSON
18 Director of Facilities Management .... Mr. Chris C. BAILEY
36 Asst Provost Post-Graduate Outcomes .... Ms. Michaeline SHUMAN
88 Director of Event Management .... Ms. Brenda MULL
29 Asst VP Alumni/Parent & Donor .... Ms. Becky DEITRICK
09 Dir Institute Research/Asst Provost .... Vacant
25 Grants Coordinator .... Mr. Malcolm DERK
104 Dean of Global Programs .... Dr. Scott MANNING
15 Director Human Resources .... Ms. Jennifer BUCHER
19 Director Public Safety .... Mr. Angelo MARTIN
92 Director of Honors Program .... Dr. Dave RAMSARAN
22 Dir of Workforce Div & Inclusion .... Ms. Barbara JOHNSON

Swarthmore College (I)

500 College Avenue, Swarthmore PA 19081-1390
County: Delaware FICE Identification: 003370
Unit ID: 216287
Telephone: (610) 328-8000 Carnegie Class: Bac-A&S
FAX Number: (610) 328-8000 Calendar System: Semester
URL: www.swarthmore.edu
Established: 1864 Annual Undergrad Tuition & Fees: $49,104
Enrollment: 1,581 Coed
Affiliation or Control: Independent Non-Profit IRS Status: 501(c)3
Highest Offering: Baccalaureate

Accreditation: **M**, ENG

01 President .... Valerie A. SMITH
05 Provost .... Thomas STEPHENSON
10 Vice President Finance & Admin .... Gregory N. BROWN
111 Vice President for Advancement .... Karl CLAUSS
18 Vice Pres Facilities & Services .... C. Stuart HAIN
15 Vice Pres for Human Resources .... Pamela PRESCOD-CAESAR
26 VP/Communications & Secretary/Col .... Nancy NICELY
07 Vice Pres & Dean of Admissions .... Jim BOCK
21 Asst Vice Pres Finance & Controller .... Alice TURBIVILLE
32 Dean of Students .... H. Elizabeth BRAUN
28 Assoc Dean of Diversity/Inclusion .... Sha Duncan SMITH
06 Registrar .... Martin O. WARNER
08 College Librarian .... Peggy SEIDEN
09 Director Institutional Research .... Robin H. SHORES
29 Director Alumni & Parent Engagement .... Lisa SHAFER
37 Director of Financial Aid .... Varo L. DUFFINS
36 Director Career Services .... Nancy BURKETT
19 Director of Public Safety .... Michael HILL
43 General Counsel/Asst Sec of College .... Sharmaine LAMAR
23 Director Worth Health Center .... Alice HOLLAND
38 Director Psychological Services .... David RAMIREZ
41 Director Physical Educ/Athletics .... Adam HERTZ
13 Chief Info Technology Officer .... Joel COOPER
35 Director Student Engagement .... Rachel HEAD
104 Director Off-Campus Study .... Pat MARTIN
39 Asst Dir Residential Communities .... Isaiah THOMAS
04 Special Assistant to the President .... Susan EAGAR
105 Web Developer .... Les LEACH
22 Dir Equal Opportunity & Engagement .... Zenobia HARGUST
96 Director of Purchasing .... Cindy URICK

Talmudical Yeshiva of Philadelphia (A)

6063 Drexel Road, Philadelphia PA 19131-1296
County: Philadelphia FICE Identification: 012523
Unit ID: 216311
Telephone: (215) 477-1000 Carnegie Class: Spec-4-yr-Faith
FAX Number: (215) 477-5065 Calendar System: Semester
Established: 1953 Annual Undergrad Tuition & Fees: $8,600
Enrollment: 115 Male
Affiliation or Control: Independent Non-Profit IRS Status: 501(c)3
Highest Offering: First Talmudic Degree
Accreditation: **RABN**

01 Chief Executive Officer (President) .... Mr. Alexander TAUB
05 Dean .... Rabbi Shmuel KAMENETSKY
05 Dean .... Rabbi Yehuda SVEI
05 Dean .... Rabbi Sholom KAMENETSKY

Temple University (B)

1801 N. Broad Street, Philadelphia PA 19122-6072
County: Philadelphia FICE Identification: 003371
Unit ID: 216339
Telephone: (215) 204-7000 Carnegie Class: DU-Highest
FAX Number: (215) 204-5694 Calendar System: Semester
URL: www.temple.edu
Established: 1884 Annual Undergrad Tuition & Fees (In-State): $16,274
Enrollment: 38,007 Coed
Affiliation or Control: State Related IRS Status: 501(c)3
Highest Offering: Doctorate
Accreditation: **M**, #ARCPA, ART, CAATE, CAHIIM, CARTE, CLPSY, DANCE, DENT, ENG, ENGT, HSA, IPSY, JOUR, LAW, LSAR, MED, MUS, NRPA, NURSE, OT, PCSAS, PH, PHAR, PLNG, POD, PTA, SCPSY, SP, SW, THEA

01 President .... Dr. Richard M. ENGLERT
03 VP for Public Affairs .... Mr. William T. BERGMAN, JR.
05 Exec VP and Provost .... Ms. JoAnne A. EPPS
43 VP & University Counsel .... Mr. Michael B. GEBHARDT
32 VP for Student Affairs .... Dr. Theresa A. POWELL
13 VP Computer/CIO .... Ms. Cindy LEAVITT
17 Sr EVP for Health Affairs .... Dr. Larry R. KAISER
26 Sr Vice Provost Strategic Comm .... Dr. Elizabeth LEEBRON TUTELMAN
10 VP/CFO & Treasurer .... Mr. Kenneth H. KAISER
29 VP Alumni Relations .... Vacant
88 VP International Affairs .... Dr. Hai-Lung DAI
35 Assoc VP/Dean of Students .... Dr. Stephanie IVES
111 Int VP Institutional Advancement .... Ms. Meaghan HOGAN
46 VP for Research Administration .... Dr. Michele M. MASUCCI
18 VP Planning & Capital Projects .... Mr. Gennaro J. LEVA
21 Sr Assoc VP Finance .... Mr. William J. WILKINSON
88 Assoc VP Business Services .... Mr. Michael D. SCALES
15 Assoc VP Human Resources .... Ms. Sharon I. BOYLE
21 Assoc VP/Controller .... Mr. David MARINO
22 Asst VP Inst Diversity .... Dr. Tiffenia D. ARCHIE
11 Asst VP Fin/Admin & VP-CFO & Treas .... Ms. Kathryn P. D'ANGELO
88 Vice Provost for Faculty Affairs .... Dr. Kevin J. DELANEY
20 Sr Vice Provost Undergrad Studies .... Dr. David BERMAN
20 Vice Provost .... Dr. Jodi LEVINE LAUFGRABEN
08 Dean for University Libraries .... Mr. Joseph P. LUCIA
06 Registrar .... Mr. Bhavesh BAMBHROLIA
41 Director of Athletics .... Mr. Patrick KRAFT
38 Director Tuttleman Counseling Svcs .... Dr. John L. DIMINO
36 Sr Director Career Services .... Ms. Rosalie SHEMMER
09 Director IR/Assessment .... Ms. Sally M. FRAZEE
104 Asst VP Study Abroad .... Ms. Denise A. CONNERTY
23 Sr Admin Student & Employee Health .... Dr. Mark DENYS
37 Interim Director Student Fin Svcs .... Ms. Emilie VANTRIESTE
88 Vice Provost .... Dr. Vicki Lewis MCGARVEY
96 Sr Director Purchasing .... Mr. Alvin COOLEY
113 Assistant VP/Bursar .... Mr. David R. GLEZERMAN
97 Asst Director General Education .... Ms. Dana G. DAWSON
12 Director TU Center City .... Mr. William PARSHALL
84 Assoc Director Enrollment Mgmt .... Ms. Laura S. REDDICK
40 Bookstore Manager .... Ms. Amanda HOWE
49 Dean Liberal Arts .... Dr. Richard DEEG
53 Dean of Education .... Dr. Greg ANDERSON
61 Dean Law School .... Mr. Gregory M. MANDEL
64 Dean Boyer College of Music .... Dr. Robert T. STROKER
57 Dean Tyler School of Art .... Ms. Susan CAHAN
50 Dean Tourism/Hospitality Mgmt .... Dr. Moshe PORAT
52 Dean of Dentistry .... Dr. Amid ISMAIL
63 Sr Exec VP Health Dean of Medicine .... Dr. Larry KAISER
67 Dean of Pharmacy .... Dr. Peter H. DOUKAS
54 Dean Engineering .... Dr. Keya SADEGHIPOUR
88 Dean Podiatric Medicine .... Dr. John A. MATTIACCI
72 Dean Science & Technology .... Dr. Michael KLEIN
60 Dean Media & Communication .... Mr. David BOARDMAN
76 Dean Health Prof & Social Work .... Dr. Laura SIMINOFF
88 Dean of Tourism/Hospitality Mgmt .... Dr. Moshe PORAT
88 Dean Temple Japan .... Dr. Bruce STRONACH
88 Dean Temple Rome .... Dr. Hilary L. LINK
07 Director of Admissions .... Ms. Karin W. MORMANDO
101 VP & Secretary of Board of Trustees .... Ms. Anne K. NADOL
19 Executive Director Public Safety .... Mr. Charles LEONE

Thaddeus Stevens College of Technology (C)

750 E King Street, Lancaster PA 17602-3198
County: Lancaster FICE Identification: 007912
Unit ID: 216296
Telephone: (717) 299-7731 Carnegie Class: Assoc/HVT-High Trad
FAX Number: (717) 299-7748 Calendar System: Semester
URL: www.stevenscollege.edu
Established: 1905 Annual Undergrad Tuition & Fees (In-State): $7,630
Enrollment: 1,023 Coed
Affiliation or Control: State IRS Status: 501(c)3
Highest Offering: Associate Degree
Accreditation: **M**

01 President .... Dr. William E. GRISCOM
05 Vice President Academic Affairs .... Dr. Zoann PARKER
10 Vice President Finance and Admin .... Mrs. Betty TOMPOS
32 Dean for Student Services .... Dr. Christopher METZLER
84 Dean of Enrollment Svcs/Admissions .... Mr. Michael DEGROFT
08 Learning Resources Center Director .... Ms. Sharon MCILHENNEY
108 Director Assessment/Accountability .... Ms. Cheryl LUTZ
15 Human Resource Specialist .... Ms. Sue EMSWILER
26 Dir of Marketing/Public Information .... Mr. Adam AURAND
38 Director of Student Counseling .... Ms. Debra SCHUCH
29 Alumni Foundation Exec Director .... Mr. Alex MUNRO
37 Director Financial Aid/Registrar .... Ms. Melissa WISNIEWSKI
41 Athletic Director .... Dr. Christopher METZLER
30 Director of Development .... Mr. Allen TATE
36 Director of Career Services .... Ms. Laurie GROVE
39 Director Residence Life/Registrar .... Mr. Jason KUNTZ
18 Facilities Maintenance Manager .... Mr. Eugene DUNCAN, JR.

† Qualified individuals are eligible for full scholarships based on family/financial status.

Thiel College (D)

75 College Avenue, Greenville PA 16125-2181
County: Mercer FICE Identification: 003376
Unit ID: 216357
Telephone: (724) 589-2000 Carnegie Class: Bac-A&S
FAX Number: (724) 589-2850 Calendar System: Semester
URL: www.thiel.edu
Established: 1866 Annual Undergrad Tuition & Fees: $29,740
Enrollment: 926 Coed
Affiliation or Control: Evangelical Lutheran Church In America
IRS Status: 501(c)3
Highest Offering: Baccalaureate
Accreditation: **M**

01 President .... Dr. Susan TRAVERSO
05 VP Academic Affairs/Dean of College .... Dr. Elizabeth FROMBGEN
30 Vice Pres for College Advancement .... Ms. Roberta LEONARD
10 Vice President Finance/Management .... Mr. Robert SCHMOLL
13 Dir IT Support/Instructional Tech .... Mr. Eric ULRICH
04 Administrative Asst to President .... Mrs. Linda NOCHTA
32 VP of Student Life .... Mr. Michael MCKINNEY
84 Interim VP Enrollment Management .... Ms. Amy SCHAFER
20 Assoc Academic Dean .... Ms. Mary Theresa HALL
26 Exec Dir Communications/Marketing .... Mr. Richard ORR
41 Director of Athletics .... Ms. Amy SCHAFER
44 Dir of Special & Planned Giving .... Mr. Mario MARINI
29 Director of Alumni Development .... Vacant
44 Director of Alumni Relations .... Ms. Kelly SANZARI
18 Director of Facilities .... Mr. Michael SHULTZ
08 Director Library .... Mr. Allen MORRILL
15 Director Human Resources .... Mrs. Jennifer CLARK
36 Assoc Dean of Career Development .... Mr. Martin BLACK
19 Chief of Police/Dir Public Safety .... Mr. Eric ALLEN
06 Registrar .... Ms. Denise UREY
42 Campus Pastor .... Rev. Jayne M. THOMPSON
07 Director of Admissions .... Mrs. Sonya L. LAPIKAS
37 Exec Director Financial Aid .... Ms. Cynthia H. FARRELL
23 Director Student Health Services .... Ms. Christine CIANCI

Thomas Jefferson University (E)

1020 Walnut Street, Philadelphia PA 19107
County: Philadelphia FICE Identification: 012393
Unit ID: 216366
Telephone: (215) 955-6000 Carnegie Class: Spec-4-yr-Med
FAX Number: (215) 955-3739 Calendar System: Quarter
URL: www.jefferson.edu
Established: 1824 Annual Undergrad Tuition & Fees: N/A
Enrollment: 3,717 Coed
Affiliation or Control: Independent Non-Profit IRS Status: 501(c)3
Highest Offering: Doctorate
Accreditation: **M**, ANEST, #ARCPA, CYTO, DENT, DMS, MED, MFCD, MT, NMT, NURSE, OT, PAST, PH, PHAR, PTA, RAD, RADDOS, RADMAG, RTT

01 President & CEO .... Dr. Stephen K. KLASKO
03 EVP & Chief Operating Officer .... Ms. Kathleen GALLAGHER
05 Provost .... Dr. Mark L. TYKOCINSKI
26 Senior VP Univ Marketing/Relations .... Mr. Charles LEWIS
10 Exec VP and CFO .... Mr. Peter DEANGELIS
111 Sr VP Institutional Advancement .... Dr. Elizabeth DALE
43 Sr VP & University Counsel .... Ms. Cristina G. CAVALIERI
46 Assoc Provost Clinical Research .... Dr. David WHELLAN
18 Sr Vice Pres for Facilities Mgmt .... Mr. Ronald E. BOWLAN
15 SVP Human Resources .... Mr. Jeffrey STEVENS
11 Vice President University Affairs .... Ms. Janice MARINI
58 Dean Jeff College of Biomed Science .... Dr. Gerald GRUNWALD
63 Dean Sidney Kimmel Medical College .. Dr. Mark L. TYKOCINSKI
66 Int Dean Jeff Coll of Nursing .... Dr. Ann PHALEN
67 Dean Jefferson College of Pharmacy .... Dr. Rebecca FINLEY
76 Interim Dean Jeff Coll Health Prof .... Dr. Debra ZELNICK
69 Dean Jefferson Sch of Pop Health .... Dr. David NASH
32 Dean of Student & Admissions SKMC .... Dr. Clara A. CALLAHAN
07 Director of Admissions .... Ms. Erin FINN
06 University Registrar .... Mr. David CLAWSON
29 Exec Director of Alumni Assoc SKMC .... Ms. Cristina GESO
08 University Librarian .... Mr. Anthony FRISBY
23 Medical Director Univ Health Svcs .... Dr. Ellen M. O'CONNOR
24 Director Medical Media Services .... Mr. Pejman MAKARECHI
35 Assoc VP Student Affairs .... Ms. Jennifer FOGERTY
39 Manager Housing/Residence Life .... Ms. Laurie YUNKE
37 Univ Director Student Financial Aid .... Ms. Susan MCFADDEN
40 Director Bookstore .... Mr. Christopher HOAGLAND
91 Chief Information Officer .... Vacant
19 Director of Security .... Mr. Joseph BYHAM
85 Dir International Exchange Services .... Ms. Janice M. BOGEN
07 Dir Admission/Recruitment/Grad Stds .... Mr. Marc STEARNS
28 Assoc Dean Diversity/Minority Affs .... Dr. Bernard LOPEZ
96 Director of Purchasing .... Mr. Robert C. BURKHOLDER
35 Associate Provost Student Affairs .... Dr. Charles A. POHL
04 Executive Associate to President .... Ms. Grace L. HARDESKI
09 Director of Institutional Research .... Vacant
101 Secretary of the Institution/Board .... Ms. Michele R. DOUGHERTY
102 Dir Foundation/Corporate Relations .... Ms. Molly GERBER
103 Dir Workforce/Career Development .... Ms. Jennifer M. GRONSKY
105 Director Web Services .... Ms. Chris MCNAMEE-SMITH
25 Chief Contracts/Grants Admin .... Mr. Timothy SHAILEY
36 Director Student Placement .... Ms. Jennifer GRONSKY
38 Director Student Counseling .... Dr. Deanna NOBLEZA
44 Director Annual or Planned Giving .... Ms. Lisa REPKO
45 Chief Institutional Planning .... Mr. John EKARIUS
84 Director Enrollment Management .... Ms. Erin M. FINN
86 Director Government Relations .... Mr. Hugh J. LAVERY
90 Director Academic Computing .... Mr. Kenneth M. OEFFLER
22 Dir Affirmative Action/EEO .... Mr. Joseph HILL
100 Chief of Staff .... Mr. John EKARIUS
104 Director Study Abroad .... Ms. Janice BOGEN

Triangle Tech (F)

191 Performance Road, Sunbury PA 17801
Telephone: (570) 988-0700 Identification: 770586
Accreditation: **ACCSC**

Triangle Tech, Bethlehem (G)

3184 Airport Road, Bethlehem PA 18017
Telephone: (610) 691-1300 Identification: 770587
Accreditation: **ACCSC**

Triangle Tech, Dubois (H)

225 Tannery Row Rd, Falls Creek PA 15840
County: Clearfield FICE Identification: 021744
Unit ID: 216454
Telephone: (814) 371-2090 Carnegie Class: Assoc/HVT-Mix Trad/Non
FAX Number: (814) 371-9227 Calendar System: Semester
URL: www.triangle-tech.edu
Established: 1982 Annual Undergrad Tuition & Fees: $16,629
Enrollment: 133 Coed
Affiliation or Control: Proprietary IRS Status: Proprietary
Highest Offering: Associate Degree
Accreditation: **ACCSC**

01 Director .... Mrs. Stephanie A. CRAIG
03 Assistant Director .... Mr. Steve CURLL
05 Academic Affairs Advisor .... Mrs. Joan HOCKMAN
07 Admiss/Recruiting/Training Coord .... Mrs. Joy BURKE
36 Career Advisor .... Mr. Jarred HETRICK
37 Financial Aid Administrator .... Ms. Michelle L. JASHINSKI

Triangle Tech, Erie (A)

2000 Liberty Street, Erie PA 16502-2594
County: Erie FICE Identification: 020902
Unit ID: 216427
Telephone: (814) 453-6016 Carnegie Class: Spec 2-yr-Tech
FAX Number: (814) 454-2818 Calendar System: Semester
URL: www.triangle-tech.edu
Established: 1976 Annual Undergrad Tuition & Fees: $16,383
Enrollment: 30 Coed
Affiliation or Control: Proprietary IRS Status: Proprietary
Highest Offering: Associate Degree
Accreditation: ACCSC

00 CEO .... Mr. James R. AGRAS
01 Campus Director .... Mr. Ken ADAMS
07 Vice President of Admissions .... Vacant

Triangle Tech, Greensburg (B)

222 E Pittsburgh Street, Suite A,
Greensburg PA 15601-3304
County: Westmoreland FICE Identification: 021290
Unit ID: 216445
Telephone: (724) 832-1050 Carnegie Class: Spec 2-yr-Tech
FAX Number: (724) 834-0325 Calendar System: Semester
URL: www.triangle-tech.edu
Established: 1944 Annual Undergrad Tuition & Fees: $16,594
Enrollment: 163 Coed
Affiliation or Control: Proprietary IRS Status: Proprietary
Highest Offering: Associate Degree
Accreditation: ACCSC

00 Chairman/CEO .... James R. AGRAS
01 President .... Timothy J. MCMAHON
11 Dir School Compliance/Operations .... Deborah G. HEPBURN
12 Director of Branch Campus/CEO .... George THIELER

Triangle Tech, Pittsburgh (C)

1940 Perrysville Avenue, Pittsburgh PA 15214-3897
County: Allegheny FICE Identification: 007839
Unit ID: 216436
Telephone: (412) 359-1000 Carnegie Class: Assoc/HVT-High Non
FAX Number: (412) 359-1012 Calendar System: Semester
URL: www.triangle-tech.edu
Established: 1944 Annual Undergrad Tuition & Fees: $16,632
Enrollment: 170 Coed
Affiliation or Control: Proprietary IRS Status: Proprietary
Highest Offering: Associate Degree
Accreditation: ACCSC

00 Chairman/CEO .... James R. AGRAS
01 President .... Timothy J. MCMAHON
03 Executive Vice President .... Rudy J. AGRAS
15 Vice President of Human Resources .... Sofia A. JANIS
05 Dir School Operations & Compliance .... Deborah G. HEPBURN
07 Director of Admissions .... Terry KUCIC
21 Controller .... Sharon GRASWICK
12 Acting School Director .... Deborah G. HEPBURN

Trinity Episcopal School for Ministry (D)

311 11th Street, Ambridge PA 15003-2397
County: Beaver FICE Identification: 022993
Unit ID: 216463
Telephone: (724) 266-3838 Carnegie Class: Spec-4-yr-Faith
FAX Number: (724) 266-4617 Calendar System: Semester
URL: www.tsm.edu
Established: 1976 Annual Graduate Tuition & Fees: N/A
Enrollment: 173 Coed
Affiliation or Control: Protestant Episcopal IRS Status: 501(c)3
Highest Offering: Doctorate; No Undergraduates
Accreditation: THEOL

01 Dean/President .... Rev. Henry L. THOMPSON
05 Academic Dean .... Dr. Erika MOORE
111 Dean of Advancement .... Rev. Aidan SMITH
32 Director of Student Life .... Mr. Geoffrey MACKEY
06 Registrar/Financial Aid Director .... Ms. Stacey WILLIARD
07 Director of Recruitment .... Rev. Aidan SMITH
11 Dean of Administration .... Mrs. Karen GETZ
30 Director of Development .... Mr. Jerry MOTE
04 Administrative Asst to President .... Ms. Lee-Anna UPPERMAN
26 Director of Communications .... Rev. Christopher M. KLUKAS
15 Human Resources Administrator .... Ms. Elaine LUCCI
13 Information Technology Manager .... Mr. Steve SIMS

United Lutheran Seminary (E)

61 Seminary Ridge, Gettysburg PA 17325-1795
County: Adams FICE Identification: 003291
Unit ID: 213631
Telephone: (717) 334-6286 Carnegie Class: Spec-4-yr-Faith
FAX Number: (717) 334-3469 Calendar System: 4/1/4
URL: www.unitedlutheranseminary.edu
Established: 1826 Annual Graduate Tuition & Fees: N/A
Enrollment: 138 Coed
Affiliation or Control: Evangelical Lutheran Church In America
IRS Status: 501(c)3
Highest Offering: Doctorate; No Undergraduates
Accreditation: M, THEOL

01 President .... RevDr. Theresa F. LATINI
11 Sr Vice Pres for Administration .... Rev. John R. SPANGLER
111 Vice Pres Advancement .... Ms. Angela ZIMMERMAN
10 Chief Financial Officer .... Mr. Scott GANLEY
05 Co-Dean of the Seminary .... Dr. Kristin LARGEN
05 Co-Dean of the Seminary .... Dr. J. Jayakiran SEBASTIAN
08 Library Director and Archivist .... Mr. Evan E. BOYD
37 Director of Financial Aid .... Ms. Kimberley CLARK
06 Registrar .... Ms. Julie RITTER
13 Director of Info Systems/Ed Tech .... Mr. Donald L. REDMAN
15 Human Resources Director .... Mrs. Elizabeth A. MEIGHAN
07 Director of Admissions .... Mr. Nathaniel PREISINGER

The University of the Arts (F)

320 S Broad Street, Philadelphia PA 19102-4944
County: Philadelphia FICE Identification: 003350
Unit ID: 215105
Telephone: (215) 717-6000 Carnegie Class: Spec-4-yr-Arts
FAX Number: (215) 717-6045 Calendar System: Semester
URL: www.uarts.edu
Established: 1876 Annual Undergrad Tuition & Fees: $41,464
Enrollment: 1,876 Coed
Affiliation or Control: Independent Non-Profit IRS Status: 501(c)3
Highest Offering: Master's
Accreditation: M, ART, MUS

01 President .... Dr. David YAGER
05 Provost .... Dr. Patricia KUCKER
100 Chief of Staff .... Vacant
10 Vice Pres Finance/Administration .... Mr. Stephen LIGHTCAP
13 Vice Pres Technology & Info Svcs .... Vacant
84 VP Enroll Mgmt/Retention/Stdnt Affs .... Mr. Rick LONGO
30 Asst Vice Pres Advancement/Devel .... Mr. Andrew PACK
06 Registrar .... Mr. Jeffrey KISLER
04 Administrative Assistant .... Ms. Carley JOHNSON

University of Pennsylvania (G)

1 College Hall, Room 100, Philadelphia PA 19104-6830
County: Philadelphia FICE Identification: 003378
Unit ID: 215062
Telephone: (215) 898-5000 Carnegie Class: DU-Highest
FAX Number: (215) 898-5756 Calendar System: Semester
URL: www.upenn.edu
Established: 1740 Annual Undergrad Tuition & Fees: $51,464
Enrollment: 24,876 Coed
Affiliation or Control: Independent Non-Profit IRS Status: 501(c)3
Highest Offering: Doctorate
Accreditation: M, ANEST, CEA, CLPSY, CS, DENT, ENG, IPSY, LAW, LSAR, MED, MIDWF, NURSE, PAST, PCSAS, PH, PLNG, SW, #VET

01 President .... Dr. Amy GUTMANN
03 Executive Vice President .... Mr. Craig CARNAROLI
05 Provost .... Dr. Wendell E. PRITCHETT
06 Registrar .... Mr. Adam B. SHERR
07 Dean of Admissions .... Mr. Eric J. FURDA
32 Vice Provost University Life .... Dr. Valarie S. MCCOULLUM
10 Vice Pres Finance & Treasurer .... Ms. MaryFrances MCCOURT
18 Vice Pres Facil/Real Est Svcs .... Ms. Anne PAPAGEORGE
17 CEO Univ of PA Health System .... Dr. Ralph W. MULLER
08 Vice Provost/Dir of Libraries .... Mr. Harry C. ROGERS
13 Vice Pres Info Technology/CIO .... Mr. Thomas H. MURPHY
100 Vice Pres & Chief of Staff .... Mr. Gregory S. ROST
09 Sr VP Inst Rsrch/Chf Diversity Ofc .... Ms. Joann MITCHELL
30 Vice Pres Dev/Alumni Relations .... Mr. John H. ZELLER
15 Vice Pres Human Resources .... Dr. John J. HEUER
86 Vice Pres Govt & Cmty Relations .... Mr. Jeffrey COOPER
19 Vice President Public Safety .... Ms. Maureen RUSH
26 Vice Pres for Univ Communications .... Mr. Stephen J. MACCARTHY
21 Vice Pres Business Services .... Ms. Marie D. WITT
114 Vice Pres Budget Mgmt Analysis .... Mr. Trevor C. LEWIS
43 Senior Vice Pres/General Counsel .... Ms. Wendy S. WHITE
101 VP & Secretary of the University .... Ms. Leslie L. KRUHLY
20 Vice Provost for Education .... Dr. Beth A. WINKELSTEIN
20 Vice Provost Faculty Affairs .... Dr. Anita L. ALLEN
29 Asst Vice Pres Alumni Relations .... Mr. Fredrick H. WAMPLER
46 Vice Provost for Research .... Dr. Dawn A. BONNELL
88 Assoc Vice Pres Rsrch Svcs .... Ms. Elizabeth D. PELOSO
116 Assoc VP Audit Compl & Privacy .... Mr. Gregory J. PELLICANO
31 Assoc VP/Dir Ctr Cmty Partnerships .... Dr. Ira HARKAVY
28 Assoc Vice Prov Equity & Access .... Rev. William GIPSON
21 Comptroller .... Mr. John F. HORN
63 Exec Vice Pres/Dean Sch of Medicine .... Dr. J. L. JAMESON
49 Dean School Arts & Sciences .... Dr. Steven J. FLUHARTY
54 Dean School of Engr/Applied Science .... Dr. Vijay KUMAR
66 Dean School of Nursing .... Dr. Antonia VILLARRUEL
50 Dean Wharton School .... Dr. Geoffrey GARRETT
60 Dean Annenberg Sch Communications .... Dr. Michael X. DELLI CARPINI
52 Dean School of Dental Medicine .... Dr. Denis F. KINANE
48 Dean School of Design .... Dr. Frederick STEINER
53 Dean Graduate School Education .... Dr. Pam GROSSMAN
61 Dean School of Law .... Dr. Theodore W. RUGER
70 Dean School Social Policy/Practice .... Dr. John L. JACKSON
74 Dean School of Veterinary Medicine .... Dr. Joan C. HENDRICKS
107 Vice Dean Liberal & Prof Studies .... Ms. Nora E. LEWIS
88 Assoc VP Inst Rsrch/Sr Adv to Pres .... Ms. Stacey J. LOPEZ
85 Dir Intl Student & Scholar Svcs .... Dr. Rodolfo R. ALTAMIRANO
36 Dir of Career Services .... Ms. Patricia L. ROSE
37 Dir Student Financial Aid .... Ms. Elaine P. VARAS
35 Assoc Vice Prov for Student Affairs .... Ms. Hikaru KOZUMA
38 Dir Counseling/Psych Services .... Dr. William B. ALEXANDER
102 Exec Dir Corp & Found Rels .... Dr. Diana B. ALTEGOER
22 Exec Dir Affirm Action & Equal Op .... Mr. Sam B. STARKS
23 Exec Dir Student Health Services .... Dr. Giang T. NGUYEN
88 Mgng Dir Annenberg Cr/Penn Presents .... Dr. Michael J. ROSE
88 Exec Dir Morris Arboretum .... Mr. Paul W. MEYER
88 Dir Institute of Contemporary Art .... Ms. Amy SADAO
88 Dir Museum of Archlgy/Anthrplgy .... Mr. Julian F. SIGGERS
41 Dir Intercollegiate Athletics .... Ms. M. Grace CALHOUN
14 IT Director .... Mr. James F. JOHNSON
91 IT Exec Dir Admin Info Tech .... Ms. Jeanne F. CURTIS
39 Exec Dir Col Houses & Acad Svcs .... Mr. Martin REDMAN
42 University Chaplain .... Rev. Charles L. HOWARD
104 Director Study Abroad .... Mr. Nigel COSSAR
106 Exec Director Online Learning Init .... Dr. Rebecca STEIN
04 Administrative Asst to President .... Ms. Jodi SARKISIAN
105 Dir Web Strategy & Visual Comm .... Mr. Steven MINICOLA
44 Exec Dir Gift Plng/Assoc Gen Couns .... Ms. Marcie L. MERZ
96 Director of Purchasing .... Mr. Mark MILLS

University of Phoenix Philadelphia Campus (H)

30 South 17th Street, 2nd Floor, Philadelphia PA 19103
Telephone: (267) 234-2000 Identification: 770933
Accreditation: &NH, ACBSP

† No longer accepting campus-based students.

University of Pittsburgh (I)

4200 Fifth Avenue, Pittsburgh PA 15260-3583
County: Allegheny FICE Identification: 003379
Unit ID: 215293
Telephone: (412) 624-4141 Carnegie Class: DU-Highest
FAX Number: N/A Calendar System: Semester
URL: www.pitt.edu
Established: 1787 Annual Undergrad Tuition & Fees (In-State): $18,618
Enrollment: 28,649 Coed
Affiliation or Control: State Related IRS Status: 501(c)3
Highest Offering: Doctorate
Accreditation: M, ANEST, ARCPA, AUD, CAATE, CACREP, CAHIIM, CEA, CLPSY, DENT, DH, DIETC, DIETD, ENG, HSA, IPSY, LAW, LIB, MED, @MIDWF, NURSE, OPE, OT, PCSAS, PH, PHAR, PTA, SP, SPAA, SW, THEA

01 Chancellor and Chief Exec Officer .... Dr. Patrick GALLAGHER
05 Sr Vice Chancellor & Provost .... Dr. Patricia E. BEESON
63 Sr VC Health Sci/Dean Sch of Med .... Dr. Arthur S. LEVINE
101 Secy of Board of Trustees .... Dr. Kathy W. HUMPHREY
10 Senior Vice Chancellor and CFO .... Mr. Arthur G. RAMICONE
111 Int Vice Chan Inst Advancement .... Mr. O'Neil A. OUTAR
43 Sr Vice Chanc & Chief Legal Officer .... Ms. Geovette E. WASHINGTON
26 Vice Chanc for Communications .... Ms. Susan ROGERS
100 Sr VC for Engmnt and Chief of Staff .... Dr. Kathy W. HUMPHREY
11 Sr VC Business and Operations .... Mr. Gregory A. SCOTT
86 Vice Chanc Community & Govt Rels .... Mr. Paul A. SUPOWITZ
15 Vice Chanc Human Resources .... Ms. Cheryl L. JOHNSON
27 Interim Director University News .... Mr. Joseph T. MIKSCH
20 Vice Provost Undergraduate Studies .... Dr. Joseph J. MCCARTHY
58 Vice Provost Graduate Studies .... Dr. Nathan N. URBAN
45 Executive Vice Provost .... Dr. David N. DEJONG
29 Assoc Vice Chanc Alumni Relations .... Mr. Jeffery T. GLEIM
39 Associate Vice Chancellor Business .... Mr. Eli SHORAK
102 Assoc VC Corp & Found Rel & Operat .... Mr. Thomas P. CRAWFORD
19 Assoc VC Public Safety & Emer Mngmt .... Mr. Ted P. FRITZ
18 Assoc VC Facilities Mgmt .... Mr. Scott C. BERNOTAS
16 Asst VC Human Resources .... Mr. Stephen M. FERBER
06 University Registrar .... Ms. Patti J. MATHAY
41 Athletic Director .... Ms. Heather R. LYKE
07 Chief Enrollment Officer .... Mr. Marc L. HARDING
32 Vice Prov & Dean of Students .... Mr. Kenyon R. BONNER
46 Vice Provost Research .... Dr. Mark S. REDFERN
49 Dean Deitrich Sch Arts & Sci/CGS .... Dr. Kathleen M. BLEE
92 Dean University Honors College .... Dr. Brian A. PRIMACK
50 Dean Jos M Katz Gr Sch Bus .... Dr. Arjang A. ASSAD
53 Dean of School of Education .... Dr. Valerie KINLOCH
54 Dean Swanson School of Engineering .... Dr. Gerald D. HOLDER
61 Dean of School of Law .... Mr. William M. CARTER
80 Dean Grad Sch Public/Intl Affs .... Dr. John T. KEELER
70 Dean School of Social Work .... Dr. Larry E. DAVIS
62 Dean School of Computing and Inform .... Dr. Paul R. COHEN
52 Dean School of Dental Medicine .... Dr. Thomas W. BRAUN
66 Dean of School of Nursing .... Dr. Jacqueline DUNBAR-JACOB
67 Dean School of Pharmacy .... Dr. Patricia D. KROBOTH
69 Dean Grad School Public Health .... Dr. Donald S. BURKE
76 Dean Sch of Health & Rehabilitation .... Dr. Anthony DELITTO
12 President Johnstown Campus .... Dr. Jem M. SPECTAR
12 President Greensburg Campus .... Dr. Sharon P. SMITH
12 President Bradford and Titusville .... Dr. Livingston ALEXANDER
104 Sr Dir Intl Pgms & Dir UCIS .... Dr. Ariel ARMONY
40 Director Book Centers .... Ms. Debra R. FYOCK
24 Dir Univ Ctr for Teach & Learning .... Ms. Cynthia GOLDEN
13 Chief Info Office and Dir CSSD .... Ms. Jinx P. WALTON
09 Director Institutional Research .... Mr. Robert D. GOGA
116 Director Internal Audit .... Mr. John P. ELLIOTT
36 Assoc Dean & Dir Career Dev .... Ms. Cheryl S. FINLAY
08 Dir Univ Library System .... Ms. Kornelia TANCHEVA
19 Chief University Police .... Mr. James K. LOFTUS
23 Director Student Health Svcs .... Ms. Marian S. VANEK

96 Manager Purchasing Services .... Mr. Thomas E. YOUNGS, JR.
112 Sr Exec Director Planned Giving .... Mr. Walter E. BROWN, JR.
04 Exec Asst to the Chancellor .... Ms. Mary Jo RACE
106 Dir Online Programs .... Ms. Lorna R. KEARNS
37 Director Financial Aid .... Dr. Randall MCCREADY
38 Director Counseling Center .... Vacant
28 Vice Chanc Diversity & Inclusion .... Ms. Pamela W. CONNELLY
88 Vice Chanc Economic Partnerships .... Ms. Rebecca BAGLEY

University of Pittsburgh at Bradford (A)

300 Campus Drive, Bradford PA 16701-2812
Telephone: (814) 362-7500 FICE Identification: 003380
Accreditation: &M, ADNUR, CAATE, NUR

† Regional accreditation is carried under the parent institution in Pittsburgh, PA.

University of Pittsburgh at Greensburg (B)

150 Finoli Drive, Greensburg PA 15601-5898
Telephone: (724) 837-7040 FICE Identification: 003381
Accreditation: &M

† Regional accreditation is carried under the parent institution in Pittsburgh, PA.

University of Pittsburgh at Johnstown (C)

450 Schoolhouse Road, Johnstown PA 15904-2990
Telephone: (814) 269-7000 FICE Identification: 003382
Accreditation: &M, COARC, ENGT

† Regional accreditation is carried under the parent institution in Pittsburgh, PA.

University of Pittsburgh at Titusville (D)

504 E Main, Titusville PA 16354-2097
Telephone: (814) 827-4400 FICE Identification: 003383
Accreditation: &M, ADNUR, PTAA

† Regional accreditation is carried under the parent institution in Pittsburgh, PA.

University of the Sciences in Philadelphia (E)

600 S 43rd Street, Philadelphia PA 19104-4495
County: Philadelphia FICE Identification: 003353
Unit ID: 215132
Telephone: (215) 596-8800 Carnegie Class: Spec-4-yr-Other Health
FAX Number: (215) 895-1100 Calendar System: Semester
URL: www.usciences.edu
Established: 1821 Annual Undergrad Tuition & Fees: $38,850
Enrollment: 2,664 Coed
Affiliation or Control: Independent Non-Profit IRS Status: 501(c)3
Highest Offering: Doctorate
Accreditation: M, ACBSP, #ARCPA, OT, PHAR, PTA

01 President .... Dr. Paul KATZ
05 Provost .... Dr. Peter J. MILLER
10 Chief Financial/Operating Officer .... Dr. Valerie WEIL
111 Int VP Institutional Advancement .... Ms. Patricia VANSTON
26 Exec Dir Marketing/ Communications .... Mr. Michael SCHWARTZMAN
102 Dir of Corporate & Foundation Rels .... Ms. Rebecca POWERS
13 Exec Dir Information Technology .... Mr. John MASCIANTONIO
14 Associate Provost/CIO .... Dr. Mark NESTOR
37 Director of Financial Aid .... Ms. Pamela RAMANATHAN
06 Registrar .... Ms. Therese ANDERSON
29 Director of Alumni Relations .... Mr. Casey RYAN
32 Interim Dean of Students .... Mr. Ross RADISH
67 Interim Dean of Pharmacy .... Dr. Patricia R. AUDET
49 Dean Misher College Arts & Sci .... Dr. Suzanne K. MURPHY
76 Dean Samson College of Health Sci .... Dr. Michelle E. COHEN
69 Dean of Mayes College .... Dr. Andrew PETERSON
15 Director Human Resources .... Mr. Michael G. JANES
19 Director Public Safety/Security .... Mr. Michael STITLEY
41 Athletic Director .... Dr. Mark CASERIO
39 Associate Director Residence Life .... Mr. Anthony FLORENDO
21 Controller/Asst VP Finance .... Ms. Brigid K. ISACKMAN
36 Director Career Services .... Ms. Kimberly BRYANT
38 Director Student Counseling .... Dr. Karen LEVINSON
96 Manager University Purchasing .... Mr. Vincent HORN
20 Associate Provost Academic Affairs .... Dr. John CONNORS
121 Exec Director Student Success .... Mr. Joseph CANADAY
18 Director of Facilities .... Mr. Dan SEVERINO
04 Executive Asst to President .... Ms. Beth PILIPZECK
104 Director Study Abroad .... Mr. James YARRISH
106 Exec Director Academic Technology .... Dr. Rodney B. MURRAY
84 Int Asst VP Enrollment Management .... Mr. Peter NACY
07 Executive Director of Admissions .... Mr. Augustine DISTEFANO
123 Assoc Director Graduate Admissions .... Ms. Sally REDMAN
30 Senior Director of Development .... Ms. Kim BARKHAMER

The University of Scranton (F)

800 Linden St, Scranton PA 18510-4622
County: Lackawanna FICE Identification: 003384
Unit ID: 215929
Telephone: (570) 941-7400 Carnegie Class: Masters/L
FAX Number: (570) 941-6369 Calendar System: Semester
URL: www.scranton.edu
Established: 1888 Annual Undergrad Tuition & Fees: $42,162
Enrollment: 5,422 Coed
Affiliation or Control: Roman Catholic IRS Status: 501(c)3
Highest Offering: Doctorate
Accreditation: M, ANEST, CACREP, CAEPT, CS, CSHSE, ENG, HSA, NURSE, OT, PTA

01 President .... Rev. Herbert R. KELLER, SJ
05 Int Sr VP Acad Affairs & Provost .... Dr. Joseph H. DREISBACH
10 Sr VP Finance & Administration .... Mr. Edward J. STEINMETZ, JR.
111 Int VP for University Advancement .... Ms. Melissa D. STARACE
26 VP Enroll Mgmt/External Affairs .... Mr. Gerald C. ZABOSKI
114 Asst VP Budget/Financial Planning .... Mr. Patrick R. DONOHUE
13 CIO .... Ms. Susan G. BOWEN
15 Assoc Vice Pres Human Resources .... Ms. Patricia L. TETREAULT
42 Exec Dir of the Jesuit Center .... Rev. Patrick RODGERS, SJ
43 General Counsel .... Mr. Robert B. FARRELL
100 Chief of Staff .... Mr. Robert W. DAVIS, JR.
49 Dean Arts & Sciences .... Dr. Brian P. CONNIFF
50 Dean Kania School Management .... Dr. Michael O. MENSAH
107 Dean Panuska Col of Prof Studies .... Dr. Debra A. PELLEGRINO
08 Dean of the Library/Info Fluency .... Mr. Charles E. KRATZ, JR.
51 Asst Dir for OL/Off Campus-Programs .... Mrs. Lisa M. LOBASSO
32 Vice Prov Std Formation/Campus Life .... Dr. Anitra M. MCSHEA
20 Assoc Provost Academic Affairs .... Dr. Sunil AHUJA
07 Assoc VP Admiss & Undergrad Enroll .... Mr. Joseph M. ROBACK
07 Asst VP Admissions & Enrollment .... Ms. Mary Kay ASTON
18 Assoc VP Facilities Operations .... Mr. James DEVERS
29 Assoc VP Annual Fund/Alumni Rels .... Ms. Melissa D. STARACE
06 Registrar .... Ms. Julie FERGUSON
37 Director of Financial Aid .... Mr. William R. BURKE
36 Director of Career Services .... Ms. Chris WHITNEY
28 Director of Equity/Diversity Office .... Ms. Jennifer LAPORTA
09 Director of Institutional Research .... Ms. Robyn DICKINSON
38 Director of Counseling Center .... Mr. Thomas P. SMITH
96 Director of Purchasing .... Mr. Gary S. ZAMPANO

University of Valley Forge (G)

1401 Charlestown Road, Phoenixville PA 19460-2399
County: Chester FICE Identification: 003306
Unit ID: 216542
Telephone: (610) 935-0450 Carnegie Class: Bac-Diverse
FAX Number: (610) 935-9353 Calendar System: Semester
URL: www.valleyforge.edu
Established: 1939 Annual Undergrad Tuition & Fees: $20,694
Enrollment: 919 Coed
Affiliation or Control: Assemblies Of God Church IRS Status: 501(c)3
Highest Offering: Master's
Accreditation: M, SW

01 Interim President .... Dr. Ron MCMANUS
32 VP of Student Life .... Rev. Jennifer GALE
05 VP of Academic Affairs .... Dr. Jerome DOUGLAS
10 Adjunct Chief Financial Officer .... Mr. Dave DALLENBACH
09 VP of Institutional Effectiveness .... Dr. Todd GUEVIN
11 Chief Operating Officer .... Rev. David KIM
21 Controller .... Mrs. Myra OCASIO
49 Arts & Sciences Dept Chair .... Mrs. Laura BROOKINS
83 Behavioral Sciences Dept Chair .... Dr. Debra BROWN
50 Business Dept Chair .... Dr. William CLARKSON
88 Church Ministry Dept Chair .... Dr. David DIPPOLD
73 Dean Pastoral Ministries Dept Chair .... Dr. JoAnn SMITH
24 Digital Media/Cmty Dept Chair .... Mr. Leone BILOTTA
53 Education Dept Chair .... Dr. A. Glenn MCCLURE
88 Intercultural Studies Dept Chair .... Mr. Troy TABOR
64 Music Dept Chair .... Dr. William DESANTO
88 Director of Accounting .... Mrs. Betty SMITH
07 Director of Admissions .... Mr. Mark CERNERO
30 Coordinator of Development .... Mrs. Darlene GRUBER
41 Director of Athletics .... Ms. Gretchen LEVAN
37 Director of Financial Aid .... Mrs. Linda STEIN
15 Director Human Resources .... Mrs. Veronica BIRD
08 Librarian/Dir Storms Research Ctr .... Mrs. Deborah HIRNEISEN
26 Director of Marketing .... Mr. Dominick GARCIA
06 Registrar .... Mr. Craig MILLER
23 Nurse .... Mrs. Lauren BORN
39 Residence Director .... Mrs. Katharyn MCLELLAN
39 Residence Director .... Mr. Yung Won PARK
04 Administrative Asst to President .... Ms. Chrysta M. ARCHER

Ursinus College (H)

PO Box 1000, 601 East Main Street, Collegeville PA 19426-1000
County: Montgomery FICE Identification: 003385
Unit ID: 216524
Telephone: (610) 409-3000 Carnegie Class: Bac-A&S
FAX Number: (610) 489-0627 Calendar System: Semester
URL: www.ursinus.edu
Established: 1869 Annual Undergrad Tuition & Fees: $49,370
Enrollment: 1,643 Coed
Affiliation or Control: Independent Non-Profit IRS Status: 501(c)3
Highest Offering: Baccalaureate
Accreditation: M

01 President .... Dr. Brock BLOMBERG
05 Vice Pres Academic Affairs/Dean .... Dr. Mark SCHNEIDER
10 Vice Pres Finance & Administration .... Ms. Annette PARKER
111 Senior Vice Pres for Advancement .... Ms. Jill A. MARSTELLER
84 Vice President for Enrollment .... Mr. David TOBIAS
32 Vice Pres of Student Affairs/Dean .... Ms. Deborah O. NOLAN
21 Associate Vice Pres/Controller .... Ms. Andrea BOHN
112 Exec Director of Planned Giving .... Mr. Mark P. GADSON
08 Special Library Collections .... Mr. Charles JAMISON
36 Director of Career Services .... Mrs. Carla M. RINDE
18 Facilities Operations Manager .... Mr. Steve GEHRINGER
41 Director of Athletics .... Mrs. Laura MOLIKEN
26 Chief Communications Officer .... Mr. Thomas YENCHO
37 Director Student Financial Services .... Mrs. Suzanne SPARROW
06 Registrar .... Ms. Barbara A. BORIS
29 Director of Alumni Relations .... Ms. Pamela PANARELLA
15 Director Human Resources .... Ms. Kelley WILLIAMS
09 Director of Institutional Research .... Ms. Annemarie BARTLETT
102 Dir Foundation/Corporate Relations .... Mr. Edmond CLARKE
13 Chief Info Technology Officer (CIO) .... Mr. Eugene SPENCER
28 Coord of Diversity/Inclusion .... Mr. Terrence WILLIAMS
04 Exec Ast to Pres/Conf & Spec Events .... Ms. Teri A. LOBO

Valley Forge Military College (I)

1001 Eagle Road, Wayne PA 19087-3695
County: Delaware FICE Identification: 003386
Unit ID: 216551
Telephone: (610) 989-1200 Carnegie Class: Not Classified
FAX Number: (610) 975-9642 Calendar System: Semester
URL: www.vfmac.edu
Established: 1935 Annual Undergrad Tuition & Fees: $29,975
Enrollment: 334 Coed
Affiliation or Control: Independent Non-Profit IRS Status: 501(c)3
Highest Offering: Associate Degree
Accreditation: M

01 President Military Academy/College .... Col. John C. CHURCH
05 Head of School Academy .... Ms. Sandra YOUNG
10 Chief Financial Officer/COO .... Mr. Vincent VUONO
32 Commandant of Cadets .... Col. Stuart HELGESON
30 Vice Pres of Development .... Mr. Greg BRINN
84 VP Enrollment Mgmt .... Mr. James DUNN
20 Dean of the College .... Mrs. Maureen MALONE
18 Director of Facilities .... Mr. Bryan K. GEILING
07 Director College Admissions .... Ms. Dawn DREESE
08 Director of Library Services .... Ms. Dana KERRIGAN
15 Director of Human Resources .... Ms. Marianne MEADE
13 Director Information Technology .... Mr. Michael G. BROCK
41 Director of Athletics .... Mr. Richard CASEY
35 Dean Student Activities .... Ms. Elizabeth WAHLBERG
06 Registrar .... Ms. Patty VOIGHT
88 Transfer Advisor .... Ms. Marisa BRNARDIC
04 Administrative Asst to President .... Mrs. Patricia TOLVAISA
26 Chief Public Relations/Marketing .... Ms. Mary HELLER
29 Director Alumni Relations .... Mr. Tom GOLDBLUM
110 Director of Development .... Ms. Pamela JOHNSON

Vet Tech Institute (J)

125 Seventh Street, Pittsburgh PA 15222-3400
County: Allegheny FICE Identification: 008568
Unit ID: 213914
Telephone: (412) 391-7021 Carnegie Class: Spec 2-yr-Health
FAX Number: (412) 232-4348 Calendar System: Semester
URL: www.vettechinstitute.edu
Established: 1958 Annual Undergrad Tuition & Fees: $14,860
Enrollment: 345 Coed
Affiliation or Control: Proprietary IRS Status: Proprietary
Highest Offering: Associate Degree
Accreditation: ACCSC

01 Director .... Mrs. Jackie FLYNN

Villanova University (K)

800 Lancaster Avenue, Villanova PA 19085-1699
County: Delaware FICE Identification: 003388
Unit ID: 216597
Telephone: (610) 519-4500 Carnegie Class: DU-Mod
FAX Number: (610) 519-5000 Calendar System: Semester
URL: www.villanova.edu
Established: 1842 Annual Undergrad Tuition & Fees: $49,280
Enrollment: 10,711 Coed
Affiliation or Control: Roman Catholic IRS Status: 501(c)3
Highest Offering: Doctorate
Accreditation: M, ANEST, CACREP, CS, ENG, LAW, NURSE, SPAA

01 President .... Rev. Peter M. DONOHUE, OSA
43 Vice President & General Counsel .... Ms. Debra FICKLER
05 Provost .... Dr. Patrick G. MAGGITTI
30 Sr Vice Pres University Advancement .... Mr. Michael O'NEILL
10 Exec VP Administration/Finance .... Mr. Kenneth G. VALOSKY
13 Vice Pres/Chief Information Officer .... Mr. Stephen FUGALE
32 Vice President for Student Life .... Rev. John P. STACK, OSA
26 Vice Pres University Communication .... Ms. Ann DIEBOLD
42 Vice Pres for Mission & Ministry .... Dr. Barbara E. WALL
20 Vice Provost for Academics .... Dr. Craig WHEELAND
35 Assoc Vice Pres for Student Life .... Ms. Kathleen J. BYRNES
15 AVP Human Res/Affirm Action Ofcr .... Ms. Ellen KRUTZ
109 Assoc Vice Pres for Auxiliary Svcs .... Mr. Anthony ALFANO
29 Assoc Vice Pres Alumni Relations .... Mr. George R. KOLB
46 Assoc Vice Provost for Research .... Dr. Amanda GRANNAS
28 Assoc Vice Prov Diversity/Inclusion .... Dr. Teresa A. NANCE
84 Dean Enrollment Management .... Mr. Stephen R. MERRITT
09 Exec Dir Planning/Inst Research .... Dr. James F. TRAINER
18 Vice Pres Facilities Management .... Mr. Robert MORRO
07 Director University Admission .... Mr. Michael M. GAYNOR

08	Librarian & Dir of Falvey Library	Ms. Millicent GASKELL
35	Dean of Students	Mr. Paul F. PUGH
49	Dean Liberal Arts & Sciences	Dr. Adele LINDENMEYR
50	Dean Villanova Sch of Business	Dr. Joyce RUSSELL
58	Dean Graduate Studies LA&S	Dr. Christine PALUS
61	Dean Widger School of Law	Mr. Mark ALEXANDER
66	Dean of Nursing	Dr. M. Louise FITZPATRICK
54	Dean of Engineering	Dr. Gary A. GABRIELE
88	Dir Ctr Worship/Spirituality	Ms. Linda JACZYNSKI
88	Dir Ctr Service/Social Justice	Ms. Irene KING
88	Director Center for Worship	Rev. Joseph MOSTARDI, OSA
88	Dir Ctr Grad Pastoral Ministry Educ	Ms. Joyce ZAVARICH
107	Dean Col of Professional Studies	Dr. Deborah J. TYKSINSKI
85	Dir Intl Students & Human Services	Mr. Stephen T. MCWILLIAMS
37	Director Financial Assistance	Ms. Bonnie Lee BEHM
19	Director of Public Safety	Mr. David TEDJESKE
36	Executive Director Career Services	Mr. Kevin GRUBB
92	Director of the Honors Program	Dr. Thomas W. SMITH
38	Director of Univ Counseling Center	Dr. Joan G. WHITNEY
94	Dir Gender & Women's Studies	Dr. Lisa SEWELL
39	Director Office of Residence Life	Mr. Thomas DE MARCO
96	Director of Procurement	Mr. John R. DURHAM
27	Director of Media Relations	Mr. Jonathan GUST
41	Director of Athletics	Mr. Mark JACKSON
23	Director Student Health Center	Dr. Mary MCGONIGLE
23	Medical Director Student Health Ctr	Dr. Brian BULLOCK
06	Registrar	Ms. Pamela BRAXTON
88	University Compliance Officer	Ms. Leyda L. BENITEZ
100	Executive Assistant to President	Ms. Teisa BROWN
106	Exec Dir Online Programs	Ms. Kristy IRWIN
53	Assoc Vice Prov Teach/Learning	Dr. Randy WEINSTEIN
86	AVP Government Relations	Mr. Chris KOVOLSKI

Washington & Jefferson College (A)

60 S Lincoln Street, Washington PA 15301-4801

County: Washington — FICE Identification: 003389 — Unit ID: 216667

Telephone: (724) 503-1001 — Carnegie Class: Bac-A&S

FAX Number: (724) 223-6534 — Calendar System: 4/1/4

URL: www.washjeff.edu

Established: 1781 — Annual Undergrad Tuition & Fees: $44,900

Enrollment: 1,350 — Coed

Affiliation or Control: Independent Non-Profit — IRS Status: 501(c)3

Highest Offering: Master's

Accreditation: M

01	President	Dr. John KNAPP
05	VP Academic Affairs/Dean of Faculty	Dr. Judy KIRKPATRICK
10	CFO/VP Business/Finance	Mr. Dennis MCMASTER
30	VP Development/Alumni Relations	Mr. Michael P. GRZESIAK
84	Vice President for Enrollment	Mr. Robert J. GOULD
21	Assoc VP for Business & Finance	Mr. Thomas SZEJKO
32	VP and Dean of Student Life	Ms. Eva CHATTERJEE-SUTTON
112	Dir of Campaigns & Advancement Ops	Ms. Lori WEAVER
20	Associate Dean of the Faculty	Dr. Sharon TAYLOR
58	Assoc Dean Grad/Continuing Studies	Dr. Michael SHAUGHNESSY
28	Asst Dean Stdnt Life/Dir Diver Pgm	Ms. Ketwana SCHOOS
20	Asst Dean for Academic Affairs	Dr. Steven MALINAK
18	Dir of Campus Operations & Planning	Mr. Jim MILLER
26	Dir Marketing/Communications	Mr. Erik RUETER
06	Registrar	Ms. Leslie MAXIN
29	Assoc VP Alumni Relations & Dev	Ms. Michele HUFNAGEL
07	Director of Admission	Mr. Robert ADKINS
07	Associate VP of Enrollment	Ms. Michelle DUFFY
13	Dir of Information/Technology Svcs	Mr. Daniel FAULK
15	Director Human Resources	Mr. Robert ALLISON
19	Director Protection Services	Mr. Robert COCCO
36	Director Career Services	Ms. Roberta CROSS
40	Bookstore Manager	Ms. Cynthia BRICELAND
41	Director of Athletics	Mr. Scott MCGUINNESS
08	Director of Library Services	Ms. Ronalee CIOCCO
102	Foundation & Corp Relations Officer	Vacant
91	Assoc Director for Admin Computing	Mr. Michael A. TIMKO
104	Director of Study Abroad	Ms. Sara KOCHUBA
108	Dir of Assessment & Inst Research	Ms. Lindsey GUINN
121	Director of Academic Advising	Ms. Elizabeth MCCLINTOCK
88	Director Conferences and Events	Ms. Maureen VALENTINE
38	Director of Counseling Services	Ms. Lisa HAMILTON
39	Director of Residence Life	Mr. Tyler KOWCHECK

Waynesburg University (B)

51 W College Street, Waynesburg PA 15370-1222

County: Greene — FICE Identification: 003391 — Unit ID: 216694

Telephone: (724) 627-8191 — Carnegie Class: Masters/L

FAX Number: N/A — Calendar System: Semester

URL: www.waynesburg.edu

Established: 1849 — Annual Undergrad Tuition & Fees: $22,800

Enrollment: 1,869 — Coed

Affiliation or Control: Presbyterian Church (U.S.A.) — IRS Status: 501(c)3

Highest Offering: Doctorate

Accreditation: M, CAATE, CACREP, IACBE, NURSE

00	Chancellor	Dr. Timothy R. THYREEN
01	President	Mr. Doug LEE
05	Provost	Dr. Dana BAER
10	Chief Financial Officer	Mr. John OLON
32	VP of Student Services	Rev. James TINNEMEYER
06	Registrar	Mrs. Vicki WILSON
41	Athletic Director	Mr. Larry MARSHALL
13	VP Information Technology Services	Mr. William DUMIRE
08	Director Eberly Library	Mr. Rea REDD
26	Communication Specialist	Ms. Ashley WISE
36	Director of Placement	Mrs. Marie E. COFFMAN
38	Student Counselor	Mrs. Jane S. OWEN
21	Business Ofc Supervisor/Controller	Mr. Dave MARTIN
23	Director of Health Services	Ms. Jennifer SHIRING
15	Director Human Resources	Mr. Tom HELMICK
37	Director Student Financial Aid	Mr. Matthew STOKAN

Westminster College (C)

319 South Market Street, New Wilmington PA 16172-0001

County: Lawrence — FICE Identification: 003392 — Unit ID: 216807

Telephone: (724) 946-8761 — Carnegie Class: Bac-A&S

FAX Number: (724) 946-7132 — Calendar System: Semester

URL: www.westminster.edu

Established: 1852 — Annual Undergrad Tuition & Fees: $35,210

Enrollment: 1,310 — Coed

Affiliation or Control: Presbyterian Church (U.S.A.) — IRS Status: 501(c)3

Highest Offering: Master's

Accreditation: M, MUS

01	President	Dr. Kathy B. RICHARDSON
05	Vice Pres Academic Affairs	Mr. Jeffrey S. COKER
30	VP Institutional Advancement	Mr. Matthew P. STINSON
10	Vice Pres Finance/Mgmt Services	Mr. Kenneth J. ROMIG
84	Vice President for Enrollment	Dr. Thomas H. STEIN
32	VP Student Affs/Dean Student Affs	Dr. Neal A. EDMAN
42	College Chaplain	Rev. James R. MOHR
35	Assoc Dean of Student Affairs	Ms. Gina M. VANCE
08	Assoc Dean Library/Info Service	Ms. Erin T. SMITH
20	Assoc Dean Academic Affairs	Dr. Jamie G. MCMINN
37	Director Student Financial Aid	Ms. Cheryl GERBER
06	Registrar	Mr. Scott D. WIGNALL
36	Director of Career Center	Ms. Kathryn K. DEMEDAL
29	Director of Alumni Relations	Ms. Kara H. MONTGOMERY
26	Sr Dir Marketing/Communications	Mr. Richard A. SHERLOCK
58	Dir Graduate School/Adult Studies	Dr. Robert L. ZORN
41	Athletic Director	Mr. James E. DAFLER
18	Director of Physical Plant	Mr. Ronald J. PENNINGTON
21	Business Manager	Ms. Janet M. SMITH
19	Director of Public Safety	Mr. James D. WALKER
09	Director of Institutional Research	Dr. Jamie G. MCMINN
23	Health Center Director	Ms. Melissa M. BARON
40	Bookstore Manager	Ms. Kay A. GALANSKI
21	Controller	Ms. Christine A. MILLER
15	Director of Human Resources	Ms. Kimberlee K. CHRISTOFFERSON
38	Counselor	Ms. Barbara I. QUINCY
28	Director of Diversity Services	Ms. Jeannette HUBBARD

Westminster Theological Seminary (D)

2960 Church Road, Glenside PA 19038

County: Montgomery — FICE Identification: 003393 — Unit ID: 216816

Telephone: (215) 887-5511 — Carnegie Class: Spec-4-yr-Faith

FAX Number: (215) 887-5404 — Calendar System: Semester

URL: www.wts.edu

Established: 1929 — Annual Graduate Tuition & Fees: N/A

Enrollment: 535 — Coed

Affiliation or Control: Independent Non-Profit — IRS Status: 501(c)3

Highest Offering: Doctorate; No Undergraduates

Accreditation: M, THEOL

01	President	Dr. Peter A. LILLBACK
05	Academic Dean	Dr. Carl TRUEMAN
43	General Counsel/Vice President	Mr. James M. SWEET
32	VP for Campus Life/Dean of Students	Mr. Steven J. CARTER
111	Vice Pres Advancement	Mr. David GARNER
11	Vice President Operations	Mr. Chun LAI
106	Dean of Distance Education	Mr. Iain DUGUID
20	Associate Dean for Academic Affairs	Mr. John KIM
06	Registrar	Ms. Melinda E. DUGAN
07	Director of Admissions	Mr. Jonathan M. BRACK
08	Director of Library Services	Mr. Alexander (Sandy) FINLAYSON
73	Director DMin/Supervised Ministry	Mr. Timothy Z. WITMER
40	Director Bookstore	Mr. Chun LAI
37	Financial Aid Officer	Ms. Fiona E. DAVENPORT
13	Information Systems Director	Mr. Mike HALPIN
18	Physical Plant Manager	Mr. Richard W. MAIENSHEIN
04	Administrative Asst to President	Ms. Lauren BEINING

Westmoreland County Community College (E)

145 Pavilion Lane, Youngwood PA 15697-1895

County: Westmoreland — FICE Identification: 010176 — Unit ID: 216825

Telephone: (724) 925-4000 — Carnegie Class: Assoc/MT-VT-Mix Trad/Non

FAX Number: (724) 925-1150 — Calendar System: Semester

URL: www.wccc.edu

Established: 1970 — Annual Undergrad Tuition & Fees (In-District): $5,070

Enrollment: 5,517 — Coed

Affiliation or Control: Local — IRS Status: 501(c)3

Highest Offering: Associate Degree

Accreditation: M, ACFEI, ADNUR, DA, DH, DMS, MAC

01	President	Dr. Tuesday STANLEY
05	Vice Pres Acad Affs/Stdnt Svcs	Dr. Kristy BISHOP
11	Vice Pres Administrative Services	Mr. Steve LIPPIELLO
51	VP Cont Educ/Workforce & Cmty Devel	Dr. Patrick E. GERITY
25	Director of Grants	Ms. Debra J. WILLIAMS
15	Director Human Resources	Ms. Lauren M. FARRELL
106	Dir Distance Edu/Learning Resources	Ms. Annette BOYER
50	Dean Business/Math/Science/Engineer	Ms. Cynthia PROCTOR
76	Dean Health Profess/Culinary Arts	Dr. Cindy KOMARINSKI
72	Dean Technology	Vacant
79	Dean Public Svc/Human/Soc Science	Dr. Andrew BARNETTE
88	Dean Dist Educ & Educ Centers	Ms. Tara ZIRKEL
84	Vice Pres Enrollment Mgmt	Ms. Sydney BEELER
102	Exec Director Education Foundation	Ms. Debra D. WOODS
37	Director Financial Aid	Ms. Darylann THOMAS
18	Director Facilities	Mr. Jeff MARTINEC
13	Director Information Technology	Mr. Steve BUDNY
26	Director Communications	Vacant
07	Director Admissions	Ms. Janice T. GRABOWSKI
41	Director Student Life/Athletics	Mr. Richard G. HOLLER
09	Dir Institutional Research/Data Svc	Vacant
96	Director of Purchasing	Vacant

Widener University (F)

One University Place, Chester PA 19013-5792

County: Delaware — FICE Identification: 003313 — Unit ID: 216852

Telephone: (610) 499-4000 — Carnegie Class: DU-Mod

FAX Number: N/A — Calendar System: Semester

URL: www.widener.edu

Established: 1821 — Annual Undergrad Tuition & Fees: $42,870

Enrollment: 5,303 — Coed

Affiliation or Control: Independent Non-Profit — IRS Status: 501(c)3

Highest Offering: Doctorate

Accreditation: M, CAEPN, CLPSY, ENG, HSA, IPSY, LAW, NURSE, PTA, SW

01	President	Dr. Julie E. WOLLMAN
05	Sr Vice President/Provost	Dr. Dale SCALISE-SMITH
10	Sr Vice Pres Administration/Finance	Mr. Joseph J. BAKER
111	Vice Pres University Advancement	Ms. Linda S. DURANT
13	Chief Information Officer	Mr. Eric BEHRENS
21	Associate VP & Controller	Ms. Catherine MCGEEHAN
11	Associate VP of Administration	Mr. George E. HASSEL
18	Director of Operations	Mr. Carl G. PIERCE
58	Assoc Provost Grad Studies	Dr. Kimberly C. O'HALLORAN
20	Associate Provost Undergraduate	Dr. Geraldine A. BLOEMKER
32	Assoc Provost/Dean of Students	Dr. Denise D. GIFFORD
54	Dean School of Engineering	Dr. Fred A. AKL
49	Dean College Arts & Sciences	Dr. Sharon M. MEAGHER
50	Dean School of Business Admin	Dr. Jayati GHOSH
66	Dean School of Nursing	Dr. Laura C. DZUREC
88	Dean Sch Human Svc Professions	Dr. Paula SILVER
21	Bursar	Ms. Diana BARRACLOUGH
08	Director Wolfgram Library	Mr. Oscar LANZA-GALINDO
84	Assoc VP for Enrollment Services	Mr. Thomas K. MALLOY
06	Director of Records/Registration	Ms. Kristen CHANDO
09	Dir of Inst Res & Effectiveness	Dr. Stephen W. THORPE
36	Placement Director	Ms. Janet R. LONG
41	Director of Athletics	Mr. Jack L. SHAFER
85	Director International Student Svcs	Ms. Kandy TURNER
19	Director of Campus Safety	Mr. Patrick SULLIVAN
23	Director of Health Services	Vacant
40	Manager Campus Bookstore	Vacant
91	Director Information Systems	Mrs. Linda TAYLOR
88	Director Technical Resources	Mr. Perry M. DRAYFAHL
15	Director of Human Resources	Ms. Beth GLASSMAN
96	Director of Purchasing	Ms. Michelle SHELTON
121	Dir Student Success/Retention	Mr. Timothy J. CAIRY
97	Dir Honors Program in General Educ	Dr. Ilene LIEBERMAN
94	Director of Women's Studies	Dr. Annalisa CASTALDO
86	Director Government Relations	Ms. Julie DIETRICH
100	Chief of Staff	Dr. Kathryn J. HERSCHEDE

† See Delaware listing of Widener University School of Law.

Widener University Commonwealth Law School (G)

3800 Vartan Way, PO Box 69380,
Harrisburg PA 17106-9380

Telephone: (717) 541-3900 — Identification: 667244

Accreditation: &M, LAW

† Branch campus of Widener University, Chester, PA.

Wilkes University (H)

84 W South Street, Wilkes-Barre PA 18766-0001

County: Luzerne — FICE Identification: 003394 — Unit ID: 216931

Telephone: (570) 408-5000 — Carnegie Class: Masters/L

FAX Number: (570) 408-2934 — Calendar System: Semester

URL: www.wilkes.edu

Established: 1933 — Annual Undergrad Tuition & Fees: $33,568

Enrollment: 5,053 — Coed

Affiliation or Control: Independent Non-Profit — IRS Status: 501(c)3

Highest Offering: Doctorate

Accreditation: M, ACBSP, CEA, ENG, NURSE, PHAR

01	President	Dr. Patrick F. LEAHY
05	Provost & Sr Vice President	Dr. Anne SKLEDER
111	Vice Pres University Advancement	Mr. Thomas MACKINNON

10 Vice Pres Finance & General Counsel ... Mr. Loren D. PRESCOTT
21 Controller ... Ms. Janet KOBYLSKI
84 Associate Provost Enrollment Mgmt ... Dr. Terese WIGNOT
32 Vice President Student Affairs ... Dr. Paul S. ADAMS
15 Chief Human Resource Officer ... Mr. Joseph HOUSENICK
35 Dean of Students ... Mr. Mark R. ALLEN
54 Dean of Science & Engineering ... Dr. William HUDSON
49 Dean College Arts & Humanities ... Dr. Paul RIGGS
67 Dean Nesbitt Col Pharmacy ... Dr. Scott STOLTE
86 Asst to Pres External Affairs ... Mr. Michael WOOD
50 Dean Sidhu School of Business ... Dr. Abel ADEKOLA
62 Dean Library ... Mr. John STACHACZ
09 Exec Director Info/Analysis/Plng ... Mr. Brian BOGERT
29 Director Alumni Relations ... Vacant
41 Director of Athletics ... Ms. Addy MALATESTA
23 Director Health Services ... Ms. Diane E. O'BRIEN
36 Director Career Services ... Mrs. Carol A. BOSACK-KOSEK
39 Director Residence Life ... Vacant
58 Director Graduate Teach Education ... Ms. Grace SURDOVEL
06 Registrar ... Mrs. Susan A. HRITZAK
37 Executive Director of Financial Aid ... Ms. Chanel GREENE POROCHNIAK
26 Executive Director of Marketing ... Ms. Kimberly BOWER SPENCE
18 Director Facilities Services ... Mr. Charles CARY
07 Exec Dir Undergraduate Enrollment ... Mr. John BAUM
28 Exec Director of Diversity ... Ms. Georgia COSTALAS
96 Dir Procurement & Financial Svcs ... Ms. Alicia BOND
25 Director of Sponsored Programs ... Ms. Amanda MODROVSKY
27 Director of Communications ... Ms. Gabrielle D'AMICO
04 Executive Assistant to President ... Ms. Bridget GIUNTA

Williamson College of the Trades (A)

106 S New Middletown Road, Media PA 19063-5299
County: Delaware FICE Identification: 041238
Unit ID: 216940
Telephone: (610) 566-1776 Carnegie Class: Not Classified
FAX Number: (610) 566-6502 Calendar System: Semester
URL: www.williamson.edu
Established: 1888 Annual Undergrad Tuition & Fees: N/A
Enrollment: N/A Male
Affiliation or Control: Independent Non-Profit IRS Status: 501(c)3
Highest Offering: Associate Degree
Accreditation: **ACCSC**

01 President ... Mr. Michael J. ROUNDS
03 Senior VP/Chief of Staff ... Dr. Todd M. ZACHARY
05 VP and Dean of Education/CAO ... Dr. Samuel H. WRIGHTSON, JR.
10 VP Resource Management/CFO ... Mr. Gregory L. LINDEMUTH
30 VP Institutional Advancement ... Ms. Arlene A. SNYDER
11 VP Plans and Operations ... Mr. Daniel J. WAWRZYNIAK
09 VP Research and Assessment ... Mr. Thomas E. WISNESKI
32 Dean of Students ... Mr. Thomas J. MOFFITT
07 Dean of Admissions ... Mr. Jason C. MERILLAT
41 Athletic Director/Sports Center Mgr ... Mr. Dale H. PLUMMER
38 Chaplain/Counselor ... Rev. Mark A. SPECHT
06 Registrar ... Ms. Olivia MARTINEZ
36 Director of Placement ... Ms. Margaret T. KINGHAM
26 Director Public & Alumni Relations ... Mr. Carl A. VAIRO
102 Director of Grants and Research ... Ms. Michele MINICOZZI
44 Director of Annual Giving/Events ... Ms. Michelle MARTELLA
105 Creative Director ... Mr. Ross D. DEITRICH
04 Exec Assistant to the President ... Ms. Joan E. BERRY
39 Director of Residence Life ... Mr. John J. TULLY
08 Library Supervisor ... Ms. Gena M. KERRIGAN
100 Chief of Staff ... Dr. Todd M. ZACHARY
101 Secretary of the Institution/Board ... Ms. Joan E. BERRY
108 Director Institutional Assessment ... Mr. Thomas E. WISNESKI
13 Chief Information Technology Office ... Dr. Todd A. ZACGARY
19 Director Security/Safety ... Mr. Daniel J. WAWRZYNIAK
29 Director Alumni Affairs ... Mr. Carl A. VAIRO
18 Director of Facilities and Grounds ... Mr. Corey A. JACKSON

Wilson College (B)

1015 Philadelphia Avenue, Chambersburg PA 17201-1285
County: Franklin FICE Identification: 003396
Unit ID: 217013
Telephone: (717) 264-4141 Carnegie Class: Bac-Diverse
FAX Number: (717) 264-1578 Calendar System: 4/1/4
URL: www.wilson.edu
Established: 1869 Annual Undergrad Tuition & Fees: $24,430
Enrollment: 923 Coed
Affiliation or Control: Presbyterian Church (U.S.A.) IRS Status: 501(c)3
Highest Offering: Master's
Accreditation: **M**

01 President ... Dr. Barbara K. MISTICK
05 VP for Academic Affairs/Dean of Fac ... Dr. Elissa HEIL
111 VP for Institutional Advancement ... Ms. Camilla B. RAWLEIGH
10 Vice Pres Finance & Administration ... Mr. Brian ECKER
84 Interim VP for Enrollment ... Mr. David BOISVERT
32 Vice President for Student Dev/Dean ... Dr. Mary Beth WILLIAMS
26 VP for Marketing and Communications ... Mr. Brian SPEER
100 Chief of Staff ... Ms. Melissa J. IMES
06 Registrar ... Ms. Jean B. HOOVER
37 Dean of Financial Aid ... Ms. Linda D. BRITTAIN
09 Director of Institutional Effective ... Mr. Andrew S. ABEL
08 AVP for Technology and Library Svcs ... Mr. Jose DIEUDONNE
18 Director of Physical Plant ... Mr. Jack KELLY
27 Manager of Media Relations ... Ms. Cathy MENTZER
40 College Store Coordinator ... Ms. Robin HERRING
41 Athletic Director ... Ms. Lori FREY
88 Director of Conferences ... Mr. Joel PAGLIARO
29 Director of Alumnae Programs ... Ms. Marybeth FAMULARE
44 Director of Annual Fund ... Ms. Carolyn WOODS
15 Director Human Resources ... Ms. Bonnie COURTNEY
121 Assoc Dean of Academic Advising ... Dr. Deborah AUSTIN
21 Assoc VP for Finance/Admin ... Ms. Lori TOSTEN
36 Director of Career Development ... Ms. Linda A. BOECKMAN
38 Director of Student Counseling ... Ms. Cindy SHOEMAKER
88 Dir of Single Parent Scholars Pgm ... Ms. Katherine KOUGH
37 Coordinator of Financial Aid ... Ms. Christine KNOUSE
28 Coordinator of Diversity ... Vacant
42 Chaplain ... Rev. Derek WADLINGTON
39 Director of Residence Life ... Mr. Jared HIRTZ
102 Dir Foundation/Corporate Relations ... Ms. Margaret LIGHT
07 Director of Admissions ... Mr. Michael MONTANA

Won Institute of Graduate Studies (C)

137 S Easton Road, Glenside PA 19038
County: Montgomery FICE Identification: 039493
Unit ID: 442064
Telephone: (215) 884-8942 Carnegie Class: Spec-4-yr-Other Health
FAX Number: (215) 884-9002 Calendar System: Trimester
URL: www.woninstitute.edu
Established: 2002 Annual Graduate Tuition & Fees: N/A
Enrollment: 85 Coed
Affiliation or Control: Independent Non-Profit IRS Status: 501(c)3
Highest Offering: Master's; No Undergraduates
Accreditation: **M**, ACUP

01 President ... Dr. Bokin KIM
11 Chief Administrative Officer ... Ms. Colleen O'CONNELL
10 Chief Financial Officer ... Ms. Maria PERRY
05 Chief Academic Officer ... Mr. Gerry O'SULLIVAN
06 Registrar ... Mrs. Debbie LYND
08 Librarian ... Mrs. Amy CZOP-BARTLEY
85 International Student Advisor ... Rev. Hojin PARK
13 Chief Info Technology Officer (CIO) ... Ms. Elizabeth REED
26 Chief Public Relations/Marketing ... Mr. James WALKER

The Workforce Institute's City College (D)

1231 North Broad Street, Philadelphia PA 19122
County: Philadelphia FICE Identification: 031091
Unit ID: 214023
Telephone: (215) 568-9215 Carnegie Class: Spec 2-yr-Tech
FAX Number: (215) 568-3511 Calendar System: Semester
URL: www.citycollege-careers.org
Established: 1974 Annual Undergrad Tuition & Fees: $12,097
Enrollment: 52 Coed
Affiliation or Control: Independent Non-Profit IRS Status: 501(c)3
Highest Offering: Associate Degree
Accreditation: **ACCSC**

01 President ... Dr. Richard COHEN
11 Executive Director ... Ms. Wendy-Anne ROBERTS-JOHNSON
10 Controller ... Ms. Mary DURSO
05 Director of Education ... Mr. Robert PHILLIPS
37 Financial Aid Director ... Ms. Madeline SARGENT
07 Admissions Representative ... Mr. Eric MAISTER
36 Career Manager ... Mr. Eric MAISTER

WyoTech-Blairsville (E)

500 Innovation Drive, Blairsville PA 15717-8060
Telephone: (724) 459-9500 Identification: 666305
Accreditation: **ACCSC**

† Branch campus of Wyoming Technical Institute, Laramie, WY.

Yeshiva Beth Moshe (F)

930 Hickory Street, Scranton PA 18505-2196
County: Lackawanna FICE Identification: 013134
Unit ID: 217040
Telephone: (570) 346-1747 Carnegie Class: Spec-4-yr-Faith
FAX Number: (570) 346-2251 Calendar System: Semester
Established: 1965 Annual Undergrad Tuition & Fees: $8,950
Enrollment: 56 Male
Affiliation or Control: Independent Non-Profit IRS Status: 501(c)3
Highest Offering: Second Talmudic Degree
Accreditation: **RABN**

01 Chief Executive Officer ... Rabbi Yaakov SCHNAIDMAN
03 Executive Director ... Rabbi Avraham PRESSMAN

York College of Pennsylvania (G)

Country Club Road, York PA 17403-3651
County: York FICE Identification: 003399
Unit ID: 217059
Telephone: (717) 846-7788 Carnegie Class: Masters/S
FAX Number: (717) 849-1607 Calendar System: Semester
URL: www.ycp.edu
Established: 1787 Annual Undergrad Tuition & Fees: $18,780
Enrollment: 4,739 Coed
Affiliation or Control: Independent Non-Profit IRS Status: 501(c)3
Highest Offering: Doctorate
Accreditation: **M**, ACBSP, ANEST, COARC, CS, ENG, MUS, NRPA, NURSE

01 President ... Dr. Pamela J. GUNTER-SMITH
05 Provost & Dean Academic Affairs ... Dr. Laura NIESEN DE ABRUNA
10 Chief Financial Officer ... Mr. Matthew SMITH
20 Assoc Dean Academic Affairs ... Dr. Carl SEAQUIST
121 Associate Provost ... Dr. Joshua LANDAU
32 Dean of Student Affairs ... Mr. Joseph F. MERKLE
18 Dean of Campus Operations ... Dr. Kenneth M. MARTIN
111 Dean of College Advancement ... Dr. Jane HOGGE
50 Associate Dean Business ... Dr. James NORRIE
41 Asst Dean Athletics & Recreation ... Mr. Paul SAIKIA
84 Dean of Enrollment Management ... Dr. Danny GREEN
26 Asst Dean Office of Communication ... Ms. Mary E. DOLHEIMER
07 Director of Admissions ... Vacant
06 Registrar ... Mr. William BENTON
08 Librarian ... Mr. Jim KAPOUN
37 Director of Financial Aid ... Mr. Calvin H. WILLIAMS
13 CIO ... Dr. Ilya YAKOVLEV
29 Director Alumni Relations ... Ms. Kristin SCHAB
36 Asst Dean Career Development ... Ms. Beverly A. EVANS
06 Assistant Registrar ... Mr. Matthew ROSS
19 Director of Public Safety ... Mr. Edward C. BRUDER
39 Director of Residence Life ... Mr. Robbie BACON
15 Director Human Resources ... Mrs. Vicki L. STEWART
38 Director Counseling Services ... Mr. Darrell WILT
91 Dir Administrative Computer Center ... Mr. Brian K. SMELTZER
23 Director Health Services ... Mrs. Amy DOWNS
40 Director Bookstore ... Mrs. Lynn P. FERRO
88 Director Campus & Special Events ... Ms. Sherry HEFLIN
102 Dir Corporate/Foundation/Govt Rels ... Mr. Jeffrey VERMEULEN
27 College Editor ... Mrs. Gail HUGANIR
42 Coordinator Religious Activities ... Mrs. Louise WORLEY
31 Dean Ctr for Community Engagement ... Dr. Dominic F. DELLICARPINI
09 Director of Institutional Research ... Dr. Sarah GALLIMORE
24 Dir Center for Teaching & Learning ... Mrs. Cindy CRIMMINS
112 Sr Dir Principal & Planned Gifts ... Mr. Mark RANK
04 Executive Asst to President ... Mrs. Cynthia E. REISINGER

YTI Career Institute (H)

2900 Fairway Drive, Altoona PA 16602
County: Blair FICE Identification: 030819
Unit ID: 375939
Telephone: (814) 944-5643 Carnegie Class: Assoc/HVT-High Trad
FAX Number: (814) 944-5309 Calendar System: Quarter
URL: www.yti.edu
Established: 2006 Annual Undergrad Tuition & Fees: N/A
Enrollment: 296 Coed
Affiliation or Control: Proprietary IRS Status: Proprietary
Highest Offering: Associate Degree
Accreditation: **ACCSC**, #COARC, MAC

01 Campus President ... Ms. Natalie LOMBARDO
05 Assoc Director of Education ... Ms. Vicki KANE

YTI Career Institute (I)

3050 Hempland Road, Lancaster PA 17601
Telephone: (717) 295-1100 Identification: 770588
Accreditation: **ACCSC**, CAHIIM, MAC

YTI Career Institute (J)

1405 Williams Road, York PA 17402-9017
County: York FICE Identification: 021274
Unit ID: 217077
Telephone: (717) 757-1100 Carnegie Class: Assoc/HVT-High Trad
FAX Number: (717) 757-4964 Calendar System: Quarter
URL: www.yti.edu
Established: 1967 Annual Undergrad Tuition & Fees: N/A
Enrollment: 1,421 Coed
Affiliation or Control: Proprietary IRS Status: Proprietary
Highest Offering: Associate Degree
Accreditation: **ACCSC**, ACFEI, MAC

01 Chairman and CEO ... Mr. Timothy FOSTER
12 President - York ... Ms. Adrienne SCOTT
12 President - Lancaster ... Ms. Sherry ERNEY
12 President - Altoona ... Mrs. Natalie LOMBARDO
12 President - MTC ... Ms. Adrienne SCOTT
05 Sr VP Education & Regulatory ... Vacant

RHODE ISLAND

Brown University (K)

One Prospect Street, Providence RI 02912
County: Providence FICE Identification: 003401
Unit ID: 217156
Telephone: (401) 863-1000 Carnegie Class: DU-Highest
FAX Number: (401) 863-3700 Calendar System: Semester
URL: www.brown.edu
Established: 1764 Annual Undergrad Tuition & Fees: $51,366
Enrollment: 9,458 Coed
Affiliation or Control: Independent Non-Profit IRS Status: 501(c)3
Highest Offering: Doctorate
Accreditation: **EH**, ENG, IPSY, MED, PDPSY, PH

01 President ... Christina H. PAXSON
05 Provost ... Richard M. LOCKE

45 Exec Vice Pres Planning & Policy ... Russell C. CAREY
43 Vice President/General Counsel ... Beverly E. LEDBETTER
10 Exec VP Finance/Administration ... Barbara D. CHERNOW
26 VP for Communications ... Cass CLIATT
15 Vice Pres for Human Resources ... Vacant
111 VP Strategic Advancement Initiative ... Patricia WATSON
30 Senior VP for Advancement ... Sergio GONZALEZ
32 Vice Pres Campus Life/Student Svcs ... Eric S. ESTES
28 VP Acad Dev/Diversity & Inclusion ... Vacant
13 Vice Pres Computing/Info Services ... Ravindra PENDSE
100 Assistant to the President ... Kimberly O. ROSKIEWICZ
20 Dean of the Faculty ... Kevin MCLAUGHLIN
63 Dean Medicine & Biological Sciences ... Jack ELIAS
58 Dean of Graduate School ... Andrew G. CAMPBELL
20 Dean of the College ... Maud MANDEL
54 Dean of Engineering ... Lawrence E. LARSON
69 Dean School of Public Health ... Bess MARCUS
107 Dean School Professional Studies ... Karen H. SIBLEY
46 Vice President for Research ... Jill PIPHER
20 Deputy Provost ... Joseph S. MEISEL
08 University Librarian ... Harriette HEMMASI
07 Dean of Admission ... Logan POWELL
37 Director of Financial Aid ... James TILTON
06 Registrar ... Robert F. FITZGERALD
41 Director of Athletics ... Jack HAYES
18 VP for Facilities Management ... Vacant
86 Asst VP Govt & Community Relations ... Albert A. DAHLBERG
21 Controller/Exec VP of Fin & Admin ... Charlene M. SWEENEY
29 Vice President Alumni Relations ... Todd G. ANDREWS
23 Exec Dir of Health & Wellness ... Unab I. KHAN
38 Dir Counseling & Psychological Svcs ... William D. MEEK
19 Exec Dir & Chief of Public Safety ... Mark J. PORTER
09 Director of Institutional Research ... Katharine T. BARNES

Bryant University (A)

1150 Douglas Pike, Smithfield RI 02917-1291
County: Providence
FICE Identification: 003402
Unit ID: 217165
Telephone: (401) 232-6000
Carnegie Class: Masters/M
FAX Number: (401) 232-6319
Calendar System: Semester
URL: www.bryant.edu
Established: 1863
Annual Undergrad Tuition & Fees: $40,962
Enrollment: 3,670
Coed
Affiliation or Control: Independent Non-Profit
IRS Status: 501(c)3
Highest Offering: Beyond Master's But Less Than Doctorate
Accreditation: EH, #ARCPA

00 Chairman Board of Trustees ... Mr. William CONATY
01 President ... Mr. Ronald K. MACHTLEY
04 Exec Asst to the President ... Dr. Roger ANDERSON
05 Provost ... Mr. Glenn SULMASY
32 VP Student Affairs/Dean of Students ... Dr. John SADDLEMIRE
82 VP International Affairs ... Dr. Hong YANG
10 VP Business Affairs ... Mr. Barry F. MORRISON
111 VP University Advancement ... Mr. David WEGRZYN
13 VP Information Services/CIO ... Mr. Chuck LOCURTO
84 VP Enrollment Management ... Ms. Michelle CLOUTIER
15 Assoc VP Human Resources ... Mr. Timothy PAIGE
18 Assoc VP Campus Management ... Mr. Brian J. BRITTON
26 Assoc VP University Relations ... Ms. Ellizabeth O'NEILL
21 Assoc VP Business & Controller ... Mr. Farokh BHADA
20 Associate Provost ... Dr. Carol DEMORANVILLE
49 Dean College of Arts & Sciences ... Dr. Wendy SAMTER
50 Dean College of Business ... Dr. Madan ANNAVARJULA
58 Asst Dean Graduate School ... Mr. Tony WHEELER
51 Dir Exec Development Center ... Ms. Annette CERILLI
88 Exec Dir Inst for Family Enterprise ... Dr. William T. O'HARA
88 Dir RI Export Assistance Center ... Mr. Raymond FOGARTY
89 Dir Academic Center for Excellence ... Dr. Laurie L. HAZARD
20 Dir Faculty Dev and Innovation ... Dr. Edward KAIRISS
06 Registrar ... Ms. Susan MCLACKEN
35 Assoc Dean of Student Affairs ... Mr. John DENIO
39 Assoc Dean of Students ... Mr. Robert SLOSS
88 Dir Bryant Center Operations ... Mr. Richard DANKEL
36 Dir Career Services ... Dr. Kevin GAW
42 Chaplain Campus Ministry ... Rev. Philip DEVENS
38 Dir Counseling Services ... Mr. William PHILLIPS
23 Dir Health Services ... Ms. Susan CURRAN
28 Dir PwC Ctr Diversity & Inclusion ... Dr. Mailee KUE
19 Dir Public Safety ... Mr. Stephen BANNON
31 Dir Student Involvement Center ... Mr. John LINDSAY
88 Asst Dir Women's Center ... Ms. Kelly BOUTIN
07 Dir Transfer Admission ... Ms. Brenda DORAN
07 Sr Assoc Dir Mulitcult Admission ... Ms. Priscilla ALICEA
07 Assoc Dir International Admission ... Mr. John ERIKSEN
37 Dir Financial Aid ... Mr. John B. CANNING
88 Dir Conferences & Special Events ... Ms. Sheila GUAY
96 Dir Purchasing & Support Services ... Mr. Edward COOK
30 Exec Dir Development ... Mr. Edward MAGRO
29 Dir Alumni Relations ... Ms. Robin T. WARDE
90 Dir Acad Computing & Media Svcs ... Mr. Phillip LOMBARDI
91 Dir Admin Systems ... Ms. Christine BIGWOOD
14 Dir Computer & Telecomm Svcs ... Mr. Richard SIEDZIK
08 Dir Library Services ... Ms. Mary F. MORONEY
16 Assoc Dir Human Resources ... Ms. Catherine CURRIE
41 Dir Athletics ... Mr. Bill SMITH
09 Dir Planning & Inst Research ... Mr. Robert JONES
88 Exec Dir US-China Institute ... Dr. Hong YANG
40 Manager Bookstore ... Mr. Stanley STOWIK
104 Director Study Abroad ... Ms. Cyndi LEWIS
102 Dir Foundation/Corporate Relations ... Ms. Robin RICHARDSON

Community College of Rhode Island (B)

400 East Avenue, Warwick RI 02886-1807
County: Kent
FICE Identification: 003408
Unit ID: 217475
Telephone: (401) 825-1000
Carnegie Class: Assoc/HT-High Trad
FAX Number: (401) 825-2166
Calendar System: Semester
URL: www.ccri.edu
Established: 1964
Annual Undergrad Tuition & Fees (In-State): $4,266
Enrollment: 16,195
Coed
Affiliation or Control: State
IRS Status: 501(c)3
Highest Offering: Associate Degree
Accreditation: EH, ACBSP, ADNUR, ART, COARC, COMTA, DA, DH, DMS, HT, MLTAD, MUS, OTA, PNUR, PTAA, RAD

01 President ... Dr. Meghan HUGHES
05 Vice President for Academic Affairs ... Dr. Rosemary COSTIGAN
10 Vice President for Business Affairs ... Mr. David B. PATTEN
32 VP Stdnt Affs & Chf Outcomes Ofcr ... Ms. Sara ENRIGHT
111 Assoc VP Institutional Advancement ... Ms. Izabel D. DEARAUJO-RIVERA
32 Assoc VP for Student Services ... Dr. Ronald L. SCHERTZ
18 Director of Physical Plant ... Mr. Kenneth F. MCCABE
49 Int Dean Arts/Humanities/Soc Sci ... Mr. John W. COLE
76 Interim Dean Health & Rehab Service ... Dr. Hilary JANSSON
50 Dean Business/Science/Technology ... Dr. Thomas M. SABBAGH
103 Vice President of Workforce Develop ... Mr. Julian ALSSID
08 Dean of Learning Resources ... Ms. Ruth D. SULLIVAN
35 Dean of Students ... Mr. Michael J. CUNNINGHAM, II
21 Controller ... Ms. Sharon A. PICARD
35 Assoc Dean Student Life/Svc Lrng ... Dr. Rebecca H. YOUNT
15 Director of Human Resources ... Ms. Sheri L. NORTON
13 Chief Information Officer ... Mr. Anthony J. PARZIALE
19 Director of Safety & Security ... Mr. Dale R. WETHERELL
26 Director Marketing & Communications ... Mr. Patrick A. STONE
41 Interim Director of Athletics ... Mr. Kevin S. SALISBURY
09 Director Inst Research/Planning ... Vacant
113 Bursar ... Mr. Dennis J. GRASSINI
88 Director Access to Opportunity ... Ms. Tracy KARASINSKI
40 Director Bookstore Operations ... Ms. Colleen D. TURCOTTE
29 Director of Alumni Affairs ... Ms. Marisa ALBINI
22 Dir AA/EEO/Div/Incl/Title IX Coord ... Ms. Elizabeth CANNING
96 Director of Purchasing ... Ms. Lisa M. CONSIDINE-FONTES
21 Business Manager ... Ms. Ruth A. BARRINGTON
36 Coordinator Career Services ... Ms. Camille NUMRICH
37 Interim Director of Financial Aid ... Ms. Andrea M. LACHAPELLE
04 Administrative Asst to President ... Ms. Deborah M. ZIELINSKI
06 Registrar ... Ms. Cathy L. PICARD-TESSIER
07 Director of Admissions ... Ms. Teresa M. KLESS
100 Chief of Staff ... Ms. Alix R. OGDEN
11 Chief of Administration ... Mr. William R. FERLAND
38 Director Student Counseling ... Mr. Robert D. CIPOLLA
43 Dir Legal Services/General Counsel ... Mr. Ronald A. CAVALLARO

Johnson & Wales University (C)

8 Abbott Park Place, Providence RI 02903-3703
County: Providence
FICE Identification: 003404
Unit ID: 217235
Telephone: (401) 598-1000
Carnegie Class: Masters/L
FAX Number: (401) 598-2880
Calendar System: Quarter
URL: https://www1.jwu.edu/
Established: 1914
Annual Undergrad Tuition & Fees: $30,746
Enrollment: 9,454
Coed
Affiliation or Control: Independent Non-Profit
IRS Status: 501(c)3
Highest Offering: Doctorate
Accreditation: EH, #ARCPA, DIETD

01 Chancellor ... Mr. John J. BOWEN
03 Vice Chancellor and Executive Vice ... Mr. Thomas L. DWYER
12 COO/Providence Campus President ... Ms. Mim L. RUNEY
00 Chairman of the Board ... Mr. James H. HANCE, JR.
20 Vice Provost ... Ms. Billye AUCLAIR
84 Sr VP of Enrollment Management ... Vacant
08 Dean of Libraries ... Ms. Rosita HOPPER
76 Dean College of Health & Wellness ... Mr. George BOTTOMLEY
49 Dean of Arts & Sciences ... Ms. Angela RENAUD
50 Dean of College of Business ... Mr. Lou D'ABROSCO
106 Dean School Online & Cont Educ ... Ms. Cynthia L. PARKER
88 Assoc Dean Col of Culinary Arts ... Ms. Susan MARSHALL
72 Dean of the School of Engr & Design ... Mr. Frank TWEEDIE
88 Dean College of Hospitality ... Mr. Paul J. MCVETY
111 Vice Chancellor Resource Develop ... Mr. Joseph STALEY
30 Vice President ofResource Develop ... Ms. Page C. SCIOTTO
29 Exec Dir of Alumni Relations ... Mr. Kevin WESLEY
112 Exec Dir of Major Gifts ... Mr. Michael EATOUGH
96 Director of Procurement ... Mr. Michael GILLARDI
26 SVP of Communication ... Mr. Doug WHITING
10 Treasurer and CFO ... Mr. Joseph J. GREENE
45 Dir of Fin Planning & Analysis ... Ms. Danielle SANTAMARIA
88 Director of Student Communications ... Ms. Kristine E. MCNAMARA
109 Vice President of Auxiliary Service ... Mr. Michael DOWNING
114 University Budget Director ... Ms. Eileen T. HASKINS
86 Director of Acctng Services ... Ms. Laurie O'KEEFE
116 Director of Internal Audit ... Ms. Michele VON HEIN
121 Director Center for Acad Support ... Vacant
11 SVP of Admin & Enrollment Mgmt ... Ms. Marie BERNARDO-SOUSA
15 Vice President of Human Resources ... Ms. Diane D'AMBRA
16 Director of Human Resources ... Ms. Rebecca TONDREAU
88 Director of Payroll ... Ms. Christine WOOD
118 Director of Benefits ... Ms. Christine OLIVER
09 Director of Institutional Research ... Mr. George REZENDES
108 Director Institutional Assessment ... Ms. Eileen DEMAGISTRIS
43 General Counsel ... Mr. Bud REMILLARD
19 Director Safety & Security ... Mr. LeRoy ROSE, JR.
18 VP of Facilities and Const Mgmt ... Mr. Robert TAYLOR
86 VP Comm/Government Relations ... Ms. Lisa PELOSI
13 Chief Information Officer ... Mr. Akhi GUPTA
14 Exec Dir of IT Operations ... Mr. Wayne ROBIN
119 Director of Information Security ... Mr. Nicholas TELLA
120 Director Online Education ... Ms. Amy RICCI
32 Vice President of Student Affairs ... Mr. Ronald MARTEL
38 Assoc Dean Counsel/Health/Wellness ... Mr. Joseph BARRESI, JR.
88 Assoc Dean of Athletics ... Ms. Mel GRAF
35 Assoc Dean of Student Development ... Mr. Dameian SLOCUM
101 Chief of Staff & Univ Secretary ... Ms. Emily GILCREAST
07 Director of Undergraduate Admission ... Ms. Amy PODBELSKI
123 Director of Grad Admissions ... Ms. Teresa MAUK
06 University Registrar ... Ms. Tammy HARRIGAN
37 Vice Pres of Student Acad Fin Svcs ... Ms. Lynn ROBINSON
39 Director Residential Life ... Mr. Nev KRAGULJEVIC
36 VP of Experiential Educ/Career Svcs ... Ms. Maureen DUMAS
88 Dean of Exp Educ & Career Svcs ... Ms. Sheri YOUNG
85 Dir International Student Services ... Mr. Wesley ROY
104 Dir Study Abroad Programs ... Ms. Lisa MCADAM DONEGAN
41 Director of Athletics ... Ms. Jamie MARCOUX
05 Provost ... Ms. Lily HSU

New England Institute of Technology (D)

One New England Tech Blvd., East Greenwich RI 02818
County: Kent
FICE Identification: 007845
Unit ID: 217305
Telephone: (800) 736-7744
Carnegie Class: Bac/Assoc-Mixed
FAX Number: (401) 886-0859
Calendar System: Quarter
URL: www.neit.edu
Established: 1940
Annual Undergrad Tuition & Fees: $26,151
Enrollment: 2,919
Coed
Affiliation or Control: Independent Non-Profit
IRS Status: 501(c)3
Highest Offering: Master's
Accreditation: EH, ADNUR, COARC, ENGT, MLTAD, NUR, OT, OTA, PTAA, SURGT

01 President ... Mr. Richard I. GOUSE
03 Executive Vice President ... Mr. Seth KURN
05 Senior Vice President and Provost ... Dr. Douglas H. SHERMAN
10 Sr VP Financial Affs & Endowment ... Ms. Cheryl C. CONNORS
32 Vice Pres Student Support Services ... Ms. Catherine B. KENNEDY
21 VP of Finance & Business Admin ... Mr. Robert R. THEROUX
20 Associate Provost ... Dr. Henry YOUNG
07 Director of Admissions ... Mr. Michael CARUSO
37 Director Financial Aid ... Ms. Anna KELLY
08 Director Library ... Ms. Susan WARTHMAN
36 Director of Career Services ... Ms. Patricia BLAKEMORE
109 Director Auxiliary Services ... Mr. Patrick TRACEY
06 Registrar ... Ms. Doreen LASIEWSKI
35 Director Student Affairs ... Ms. Lee PEEBLES
30 Director of Dev & Alumni Engagement ... Ms. Liz SCANLON
13 Chief Info Technology Officer (CIO) ... Mr. Jacques LAFLAMME
18 Chief Facilities/Physical Plant ... Mr. Patrick TRACEY
26 Chief Public Relations/Marketing ... Mr. Steven H. KITCHIN
84 Director Enrollment Management ... Ms. Lynn FAWTHROP
103 Dir Workforce/Career Development ... Mr. Steven H. KITCHIN
19 Director Security/Safety ... Ms. Pamela MOFFATT-LIMOGES
43 Dir Legal Services/General Counsel ... Mr. Philip PARSONS
96 Director of Purchasing ... Mr. William MENARD
108 Director Institutional Assessment ... Dr. Douglas SHERMAN
39 Director Student Housing ... Ms. Danielly JAMOUS
44 Director Annual or Planned Giving ... Ms. Nancy CARRIUOLO

Providence College (E)

1 Cunningham Square, Providence RI 02918-0001
County: Providence
FICE Identification: 003406
Unit ID: 217402
Telephone: (401) 865-1000
Carnegie Class: Masters/L
FAX Number: (401) 865-2057
Calendar System: Semester
URL: www.providence.edu
Established: 1917
Annual Undergrad Tuition & Fees: $46,970
Enrollment: 4,562
Coed
Affiliation or Control: Roman Catholic
IRS Status: 501(c)3
Highest Offering: Master's
Accreditation: EH, SW

01 President ... Rev. Brian J. SHANLEY, OP
03 Executive Vice President/Treasurer ... Rev. Kenneth R. SICARD, OP
04 Asst to Pres & Exec Vice President ... Ms. Ann MANCHESTER-MOLAK
05 Sr VP Academic Affairs/Provost ... Dr. Hugh F. LENA, III
10 Sr VP for Finance & Business/CFO ... Mr. John M. SWEENEY
30 Sr VP for Institutional Advancement ... Mr. Gregory T. WALDRON
32 Vice Pres Student Affairs ... Ms. Kristine C. GOODWIN
43 Vice President/General Counsel ... Ms. Marifrances MCGINN
42 Vice Pres for Mission & Ministry ... Rev. R. Gabriel PIVARNIK, OP
21 Assoc VP for Finance/Asst Treasurer ... Ms. Jacqueline M. WHITE
35 Assoc VP for Student Affairs ... Dr. Steven A. SEARS
20 Assoc VP for Academic Affairs ... Dr. Brian J. BARTOLINI
41 Assoc VP for Athletics/Athletic Dir ... Mr. Robert G. DRISCOLL
15 Assoc Vice Pres for Human Resources ... Ms. Kathleen M. ALVINO
28 Assoc VP/Chief Diversity Officer ... Mr. Rafael A. ZAPATA

26 Assoc VP Public Affairs/Cmty Rels ....Mr. Steven J. MAURANO
20 Asst Vice Pres for Academic Affairs ....Mr. Charles J. HABERLE
21 Asst Vice Pres for Business Svcs ....Mr. Warren S. GRAY
29 Asst Vice Pres for Alumni Relations .... Mr. Robert FERREIRA
44 Asst Vice Pres for Development .... Ms. Lynne FRASER
45 Asst VP Capital Projects & Fac Plng .... Mr. Mark F. RAPOZA
58 Dean of Undergrad & Grad Studies ...... Rev. Mark D. NOWEL, OP
49 Dean School of Arts & Sciences ....Dr. Sheila A. LIOTTA
107 Dean School of Professional Studies .... Dr. Brian M. MCCADDEN
07 Assoc VP Admissions/Financial Aid ....Mr. Raul A. FONTS
50 Dean School of Business ....Dr. Sylvia MAXFIELD
51 Dean School of Continuing Education ...Dr. Janet L. CASTLEMAN
35 AVP Stdnt Affs/Asst Dean of Stdnts .... Ms. Tiffany D. GAFFNEY
84 Dean of Enrollment Services ....Ms. Yvonne D. ARRUDA
104 Dean of International Studies .... Mr. Adrian G. BEAULIEU
35 Director of Student Activities ....Ms. Sharon L. HAY
84 Associate Dean of Enrollment Svcs .... Ms. Ann E. BARONE
37 Exec Director of Financial Aid ....Ms. Sandra J. OLIVEIRA
19 Exec Director Safety & Security .... Mr. John J. LEYDEN
88 Asst VP Integrated Learning & Admin ....Ms. Patricia A. GOFF
18 Exec Director of Physical Plant .... Mr. William J. HARTIGAN
08 Director of Library ....Dr. Donald R. BAILEY
09 Director of Institutional Research ....Ms. Melanie R. SULLIVAN
90 Dir Enterprise Infrastructure & Ops .... Mr. Carmine R. PISCOPO
92 Director Liberal Arts Honors ....Dr. Stephen J. LYNCH
96 Director Central Purch/Receiving ....Mr. Mark S. MCGOVERN
88 Director of Academic Svcs/Wrt Ctr .... Mr. Bryan D. MARINELLI
38 VP Student Development & Compliance ....Dr. James F. CAMPBELL
13 Chief Info Technology Officer (CIO) ....Mr. Paul V. FONTAINE

Rhode Island College (A)

600 Mount Pleasant Avenue, Providence RI 02908-1991
County: Providence FICE Identification: 003407
Unit ID: 217420
Telephone: (401) 456-8000 Carnegie Class: Masters/L
FAX Number: (401) 456-8379 Calendar System: Semester
URL: www.ric.edu
Established: 1854 Annual Undergrad Tuition & Fees (In-State): $8,206
Enrollment: 8,512 Coed
Affiliation or Control: State IRS Status: 501(c)3
Highest Offering: Doctorate
Accreditation: EH, ANEST, ART, CACREP, CAEPN, MUS, NURSE, SW

01 President ....Dr. Frank A. SANCHEZ
05 Provost/VP Academic Affairs ....Dr. Joshua W. HAMILTON
10 Vice Pres Administration & Finance ....Mr. David A. GINGERELLA
32 Vice President for Student Success ... Dr. Jason L. MERIWETHER
111 Int VP College Advance & Col Rels .... Mr. Edwin R. PACHECO
45 Executive Director Strategic Int .... Mr. Clark M. GREENE
107 Assoc VP Prof Studies & Cont Educ .... Ms. Jenifer GIROUX
28 Assoc VP Comm/Equity & Diversity ....Ms. Anna M. CANO-MORALES
30 Assc VP for Develop & External Rels .... Mr. Edwin R. PACHECO
102 Executive Director RIC Foundation .... Mr. Edwin R. PACHECO
20 Asst VP Acad Affairs/Enroll Mgmt .... Dr. Holly L. SHADOIAN
58 Int Dean of Graduate Studies .... Dr. Leslie SCHUSTER
49 Dean Faculty Arts & Sciences ....Dr. Earl L. SIMSON
53 Int Dean Sch Education & Human Dev ....Dr. Gerri S. AUGUST
53 Int Dean Sch Education & Human Dev ....Dr. Julie R. HORWITZ
50 Dean School of Management .... Dr. Jeffrey MELLO
66 Dean School of Nursing .... Dr. Jane WILLIAMS
70 Dean School of Social Work .... Dr. Roberta S. PEARLMUTTER
11 Asst VP Administration .... Mr. Jeffrey L. MARTIN
21 Controller ....Mr. Stephen J. NEDDER
13 Asst VP Information Services .... Ms. Pamela CHRISTMAN
32 Dean of Students ....Dr. Scott KANE
15 Director of Human Resources .... Ms. Maggie SULLIVAN
09 Dir Inst Research & Planning .... Dr. Christopher P. HOURIGAN
08 Director of the Library .... Ms. Carissa DELIZIO
07 Director of Admissions ....Mr. Jason S. ANTHONY
06 Director of Records .... Ms. Tamecka C. HARDMON
37 Director Student Financial Aid .... Mr. Kenneth S. FERUS
25 Director of Research & Creative Act ....Ms. Lisa SMOLSKI
18 Director Facilities & Operations .... Mr. James M. JERUE
90 Director User Support Services ....Mr. David E. TOMS
91 Director Management Info Sys .... Dr. Bin YU
14 Director Network/Telecommunications .... Mr. Henk E. SONDER
19 Director of Security & Safety .... Mr. Frederick W. GHIO
96 Director of Purchasing ....Ms. Jessica L. SILVA
41 Dir of Athletics ....Mr. Donald E. TENCHER
39 Director Residential Life/Housing ....Vacant
36 Director Career Dev Center .... Ms. Demetria MORAN
23 Director College Health Services ....Ms. Lynn A. WACHTEL
38 Director Counseling Center ....Dr. A. Chantelle PSEEKOS
29 Director Alumni Affairs ....Ms. Suzanna ALBA
104 Director of Study Abroad .... Dr. Olga JUZYN
114 Director of Budget .... Mr. Robert EATON
28 Director of Unity Center ....Ms. Antoinette GOMES
22 Dir Institutional Equity ....Ms. Margaret A. LYNCH GADALETA
51 Director Continuing Education .... Mr. Dante T. DEL GIUDICE
113 Bursar .... Ms. Charlene L. SZCZEPANEK
18 Director Capital Projects ....Mr. Kevin J. FITTA
105 Director Web Services .... Ms. Karen M. RUBINO
26 Dir of College Comm & Marketing .... Mr. Chad A. MINNICH
121 Director Academic Support .... Dr. Patrice METTAUER
26 Assoc Dir Comm Office of Pres ....Ms. Kristy DOSREIS

Rhode Island School of Design (B)

2 College Street, Providence RI 02903-2784
County: Providence FICE Identification: 003409
Unit ID: 217493
Telephone: (401) 454-6100 Carnegie Class: Spec-4-yr-Arts
FAX Number: (401) 454-6320 Calendar System: 4/1/4
URL: www.risd.edu
Established: 1877 Annual Undergrad Tuition & Fees: $47,110
Enrollment: 2,481 Coed
Affiliation or Control: Independent Non-Profit IRS Status: 501(c)3
Highest Offering: Master's
Accreditation: EH, ART, LSAR

01 President .... Ms. Rosanne SOMERSON
04 Executive Assistant to President .... Ms. Jessica HODGDEN
05 Provost .... Dr. Pradeep SHARMA
111 Vice Pres Institutional Engagement ....Vacant
15 Vice Pres Human Resources .... Ms. Candace BAER
26 Exec Dir Marketing & Communications ..... Ms. Kerci M. STROUD
88 Director RISD Museum of Art .... Mr. John W. SMITH
45 VP Integrated Planning .... Ms. Mara HERMANO
10 Chief Financial Officer ....Vacant
20 Assoc Provost Academic Affairs ....Ms. Tracie COSTANTINO
88 Assoc Provost Rsrch/Global/Practice ....Dr. Daniel CAVICCHI
48 Dean Architecture & Design ....Ms. Scheri FULTINEER
57 Dean of Fine Arts .... Mr. Robert BRINKERHOFF
89 Dean of Foundation Studies ....Ms. Joanne STRYKER
49 Dean of Liberal Arts .... Dr. Damian WHITE
51 Exec Dir Continuing Education ....Ms. Sarah CAGGIANO
08 Dean of Libraries ....Ms. Lareese HALL
07 Assoc VP Enrollment ....Mr. Edward NEWHALL, JR.
37 Asst VP for Enrollment Services ....Mr. Anthony GALLONIO
13 CIO ....Mr. Rick MICKOOL
18 VP Facilities & EHS .... Mr. Jack SILVA
32 Dean of Students ....Ms. Margaret BALCH
105 Sr Dir Digital Media Communication .... Mr. Brian CLARK
43 General Counsel ....Mr. Steven MCDONALD
27 Director of Media Relations .... Ms. Jaime MARLAND
19 Director Public Safety ....Mr. Normand GAMACHE
09 Director Institutional Research .... Mr. Yi NI
108 Director Institutional Assessment ....Vacant
21 Director Budget .... Mr. Robert HANKE
21 Controller ....Mr. Thomas MATTOS
86 Director Government Relations .... Ms. Babette ALLINA
29 Director of Alumni Relations .... Ms. Christina HARTLEY
88 AVP Strategic Initiatives .... Mr. Brian GOLDBERG
44 Director Annual Fund ....Ms. Sarah SLIGO
06 Registrar .... Ms. Alison SHERMAN
96 Director Procurement Services ....Mr. Christopher SWEZEY
14 Director Network Services .... Mr. Steven BOUDREAU
27 Director Editorial Services/Media ....Ms. Liisa SILANDER
23 Director Health Services ....Ms. Mary Jo MACKINNON
39 Director of Residence Life .... Mr. Kevin FORTI
38 Dir Student Development/Counseling .... Ms. Shauna SUMMERS
102 Dir Corp/Found & Govt Partnerships ....Ms. Sara SULLIVAN
109 Dir of Auxiliary Services .... Ms. Ginnie DUNLEAVY
35 Assistant Dean Student Affairs ....Mr. Anthony JOHNSON
104 Director RISD Global .... Ms. Gwen FARRELLY
40 Director RISD Store ....Ms. Tila ADAMS

Roger Williams University (C)

One Old Ferry Road, Bristol RI 02809-2921
County: Bristol FICE Identification: 003410
Unit ID: 217518
Telephone: (401) 253-1040 Carnegie Class: Masters/M
FAX Number: N/A Calendar System: Semester
URL: www.rwu.edu
Established: 1956 Annual Undergrad Tuition & Fees: $32,100
Enrollment: 4,801 Coed
Affiliation or Control: Independent Non-Profit IRS Status: 501(c)3
Highest Offering: First Professional Degree
Accreditation: EH, CONST, ENG, LAW

01 President ....Dr. Donald J. FARISH
05 Provost/Sr VP Academic Affairs ....Dr. Andrew A. WORKMAN
10 EVP Finance/Administration .... Mr. Jerome WILLIAMS
84 VP Enrollment Mgmt & Marketing .... Mr. Brian WILLIAMS
21 VP for Accounting/Treasury Mgmt .... Mr. Marc LEONETTI
32 Vice President for Student Life ....Mr. John J. KING
30 VP Institutional Advancement .... Ms. Lisa RAIOLA
45 Chief of Staff/VP Community Rels .... Mr. Peter B. WILBUR
08 Dean University Library ....Ms. Betsy P. LEARNED
35 Asst VP & Dean of Student Life .... Ms. Lisa LANDREMAN
88 Assoc VP Enrollment Mgmt/Marketing .....Ms. Tracy M. DACOSTA
15 Asst Vice Pres of Human Resources .. Mr. Thomas MCDONOUGH
28 Director Intercultural Center ....Mr. Don MAYS
61 Dean RWU School of Law .... Mr. Michael J. YELNOSKY
48 Dean Sch Arch/Art & Hist Preserv ....Mr. Stephen E. WHITE
50 Dean Gabelli School of Business .... Dr. Susan MCTIERNAN
54 Dean Sch Engrng/Comput/Constr Mgmt ..... Dr. Robert A. POTTER
61 Dean School of Justice Studies ....Dr. Eric BRONSON
20 Vice Provost Academic Affairs .... Dr. Robert A. COLE
07 Director Graduate Admissions ....Mr. Marcus HANSCOM
49 Dean Sch Social/Natural Sciences ...... Dr. Benjamin GREENSTEIN
07 Dir Admissions Operations/Outreach ....Ms. Amanda MARSILI
26 Chief Advance Ofcr/Comm/Stewardship .... Ms. Lori COCHRANE
37 Director Student Financial Aid ....Ms. Diane USHER
96 Director of Purchasing ....Vacant
29 Dir Conferences/Spec Asst Advance ....Mr. David KEMMY
06 Registrar .... Mr. Daniel O'DRISCOLL
19 Director of Public Safety .... Mr. Steven MELARAGNO
41 Director of Athletics ....Vacant
18 Director of Facilities Management .... Mr. John TAMEO
36 Assoc Dean/Dir Ctr Career/Prof Dev ....Mr. Stephen CANTINE
38 Int Dir Counseling/Student Devel .... Mr. Christopher BAILEY
23 Director Health Services ....Ms. Anne M. MITCHELL
39 Director of Housing ....Mr. Anthony MONTEFUSCO
46 Director of Prospect Research .... Ms. Nancy L. RAMOS
39 Title IX Coord/Dir Gndr & Sxlty Ctr .... Ms. Jennifer STANLEY
09 Director Institutional Research .... Ms. Jennifer DUNSEATH
40 Manager Bookstore ....Vacant

Salve Regina University (D)

100 Ochre Point Avenue, Newport RI 02840-4192
County: Newport FICE Identification: 003411
Unit ID: 217536
Telephone: (401) 847-6650 Carnegie Class: Masters/M
FAX Number: (401) 341-2925 Calendar System: Semester
URL: www.salve.edu
Established: 1947 Annual Undergrad Tuition & Fees: $37,820
Enrollment: 2,757 Coed
Affiliation or Control: Roman Catholic IRS Status: 501(c)3
Highest Offering: Doctorate
Accreditation: EH, ART, CACREP, IACBE, NURSE, SW

01 President .... Dr. Jane GERETY, RSM
05 Vice President Academic Affairs ....Vacant
32 Vice President Student Affairs ....Dr. Barbara LOMONACO
30 VP University Rels/Advancement .... Mr. Michael L. SEMENZA
10 Vice President Administration & CFO ....Mr. William B. HALL
84 Vice Pres Enrollment Management ....Mr. James R. FOWLER
26 Assoc Vice Pres Univ Rels/CCO ....Ms. Kristine HENDRICKSON
21 Assoc Vice Pres Finance/ Controller .... Mr. Michael N. GRANDCHAMP
13 Sr Director Info Technology .... Mr. Glenn CLARK
15 Director Human Resources .... Ms. Cynthia DONNELLY
20 Associate Provost .... Dr. Donna M. COOK
09 Asst VP for Research & Compliance ....Dr. Frederick C. PROMADES
07 Dean of Undergraduate Admissions ....Ms. Colleen EMERSON
35 Assoc VP and Dean of Students ....Mr. J. Malcolm SMITH
06 Registrar ....Ms. Louise MONAST
37 Director of Financial Aid ....Ms. Anne MCDERMOTT
29 Director Alumni & Parent Pgms ....Dr. Gerry WILLIS
41 Athletic Director .... Ms. Jody MOORADIAN
08 Director of Library Services ....Ms. Kathleen BOYD
39 Director of Campus Life .... Dr. Jim MOURNIGHAN
90 Director Academic Computing .... Mr. Brian A. MCDONNELL
18 Director of Facilities .... Mr. Eric MILNER
19 Director of Security/Safety .... Mr. Michael CARUOLO
40 Director of Bookstore .... Mr. Michael LEDDY
44 Sr Dir Advancement Operations/ Pgms .... Ms. Victoria DUCLOS-BARRETT
23 Manager of Health Services ....Ms. Sharon Q. CAPUANO
35 Director of Student Activities .... Ms. Chiquita BAYLOR
36 Director of Career Development ....Mr. Michael WISNEWSKI
96 Director of Purchasing ....Ms. Francine LUNN
104 Director of International Programs .... Ms. Erin FITZGERALD
38 Dir of Student Counseling Services .... Ms. Meghan M. DECARVALHO

University of Rhode Island (E)

45 Upper College Road, Kingston RI 02881
County: Washington FICE Identification: 003414
Unit ID: 217484
Telephone: (401) 874-1000 Carnegie Class: DU-Higher
FAX Number: (401) 874-7149 Calendar System: Semester
URL: www.uri.edu
Established: 1892 Annual Undergrad Tuition & Fees (In-State): $12,884
Enrollment: 16,613 Coed
Affiliation or Control: State IRS Status: 501(c)3
Highest Offering: Doctorate
Accreditation: EH, CAEPN, CLPSY, CYTO, DIETD, DIETI, ENG, EXSC, LIB, LSAR, MFCD, MUS, NURSE, PHAR, PTA, SCPSY, SP

01 President ....Dr. David M. DOOLEY
100 Chief of Staff ....Ms. Michelle CURRERI
05 Provost/Vice Pres Academic Affairs ....Dr. Donald H. DEHAYES
46 Vice Pres Research/Economic Devel ..... Dr. Gerald SONNENFELD
10 Vice Pres for Admin & Finance ....Ms. Abigail RIDER
88 Assoc VP Res/Int Prop Mgmt/Comm ....Mr. Michael KATZ
88 Dir Univ Res External Relations ....Ms. Melissa MCCARTHY
88 Dir Research Development .... Ms. Karen MARKIN
25 Director Sponsored Projects .... Ms. Winifred NWANGWU
29 Exec Dir Alumni Relations/Secy Assn .... Ms. Michele NOTA
26 Exec Dir Ext Rels & Communications ....Ms. Kelly MAHONEY
27 Exec Dir Communications & Mktg ....Ms. Linda A. ACCIARDO
88 Dir Publications and Creative Svcs ....Vacant
114 Dir Budget & Financial Planning ....Ms. Linda BARRETT
21 Int Controller .... Ms. Tricia CASEY
15 Asst Vice Pres Human Resource Admin ....Ms. Anne Marie COLEMAN
16 Director Personnel Services .... Ms. Laura KENERSON
18 Asst Vice Pres Business Services ....Mr. J. Vernon WYMAN
19 Director Public Safety ....Mr. Stephen N. BAKER
12 Dir W.A. Jones Campus ....Ms. Maria DISANO
88 Assoc Dean Business Administration .... Dr. Deborah ROSEN
88 Dir Capital Projects .... Mr. Paul DEPACE
88 Dir Campus Planning and Design ..... Mr. Christopher MCMAHAN
88 Dir Facility Services .... Mr. Jerome SIDIO
88 Dir Property & Support Svc ....Mr. Bill MATTESON
96 Director Purchasing & Univ Stores ....Ms. Betty GIL
28 Assoc VP Comm/Equity/Diversity .... Ms. Naomi THOMPSON
43 General Counsel .... Mr. Louis J. SACCOCCIO
32 Vice President Student Affairs ....Ms. Kathy M. COLLINS
109 Dir Dining Services/Auxiliary ....Mr. Steven MELLO
41 Director of Athletics ....Mr. Thorr D. BJORN

103 Dir Career and Experiential Edu .... Ms. Kim STACK
38 Director Counseling Center .... Dr. Robert SAMUELS
88 Dir Recreational Services .... Ms. Jodi HAWKINS
35 Asst VP Stdnt Affs & Dean of Stdnts .... Vacant
88 Dir Special Pgms/Talent Devel .... Mr. Gerald WILLIAMS
88 Mgr Conf & Spec Pgm Dev .... Mr. Joseph PITTLE
35 Asst VP Student Affs & Dir HRL .... Vacant
39 Assoc Dir Housing & Res Life .... Dr. Jeffrey PLOUFFE
23 Director Health Services .... Ms. Ellen REYNOLDS
40 Administrator Bookstore .... Mr. Paul WHITNEY
88 Spec Asst to the Prov for Acad Plng ....Ms. Ann M. MORRISSEY
88 Int Vice Prov Acad Finan/Personnel .... Dr. Matthew H. BODAH
09 Director of Institutional Research .... Vacant
84 Vice Provost Enrollment Management .... Mr. Dean LIBUTTI
07 Dean of Admissions .... Ms. Cynthia L. BONN
06 Dir Enrollment Services .... Dr. Carnell JONES
101 Vice Provost Faculty Affairs .... Dr. Laura BEAUVAIS
13 Int Chief Information Officer .... Mr. Richard KUBICA
90 Dir Media & Technology Services .... Mr. David S. PORTER
91 Dir University Computing Systems .... Mr. Charlie SCHIFINO
51 A S Feinstein Col Educ & Prof Stds .... Dr. Anthony ROLLE
49 Dean of Arts & Sciences .... Dr. Jeanette E. RILEY
50 Dean Business Administration .... Dr. Maling EBRAHIMPOUR
54 Dean of Engineering .... Dr. Raymond M. WRIGHT
88 Dean Univ Col & Spec Acad Pgms .... Dr. Jayne E. RICHMOND
58 Dean of Graduate School .... Dr. Nasser H. ZAWIA
66 Dean of Nursing .... Dr. Barbara E. WOLFE
67 Dean of Pharmacy .... Dr. Paul LARRAT
69 Dean Col of Health Sciences .... Dr. Gary LIQUORI
53 Director School of Education .... Dr. David BYRD
88 Dean Grad School Oceanography .... Dr. Bruce CORLISS
88 Dean of Environment & Life Sciences .... Dr. John KIRBY
08 Dean University Libraries .... Mr. Karim B. BOUGHIDA
22 Director Affirm Act/Equal Oppty/Div .... Ms. Roxanne GOMES
37 Sr Assoc Dir Enrol Svcs/Fin Aid .... Mr. Paul LANGHAMMER
92 Director Honors Program .... Dr. Lynne DERBYSHIRE
102 President URI Foundation .... Ms. Elizabeth O'ROURKE
85 Dir Intl Students and Scholars .... Dr. Dania BRANDFORD-CALVO
106 Dir Learning/Assessment & Online .... Dr. Diane GOLDSMITH
94 Dir Gender and Women Studies .... Dr. Rosaria PISA
105 Manager Web Services .... Ms. Lisa CHEN
30 Dir Advancement Services .... Mr. John PELTIER
44 Director of Annual Giving .... Ms. Bernadine SADWIN

University of Rhode Island Feinstein Providence Campus (A)

80 Washington Street, Providence RI 02903
Telephone: (401) 277-5000 Identification: 770118
Accreditation: &EH

University of Rhode Island Narragansett Bay Campus (B)

215 South Ferry Road, Narragansett RI 02882-1197
Telephone: (401) 874-6222 Identification: 770129
Accreditation: &EH

SOUTH CAROLINA

Aiken Technical College (C)

PO Drawer 696, Aiken SC 29802-0696
County: Aiken FICE Identification: 010056
Unit ID: 217615
Telephone: (803) 508-7263 Carnegie Class: Assoc/MT-VT-High Trad
FAX Number: (803) 593-6641 Calendar System: Semester
URL: www.atc.edu
Established: 1972 Annual Undergrad Tuition & Fees (In-District): $4,348
Enrollment: 2,359 Coed
Affiliation or Control: State/Local IRS Status: 501(c)3
Highest Offering: Associate Degree
Accreditation: SC, ACBSP, ADNUR, DA, MAC, PNUR, RAD, SURGT

01 President .... Dr. Forest E. MAHAN
04 Executive Assistant to President .... Ms. Jill UHLER
30 Director Foundation & Alumni .... Ms. Mary COMMONS
05 Vice President Education & Training .... Dr. Gemma FROCK
76 Dean of Health Sciences .... Vacant
72 Dean of Technical Education .... Vacant
97 Dean of General Education .... Fr. Frederick ROGERS
51 Dean Business/Computer Technolog .... Dr. Steven SIMMONS
10 Vice Pres Administrative Services .... Mr. Andy JORDAN
37 Director of Financial Aid .... Ms. Sue SIMS
13 Director of Info Systems Mgmt .... Mr. Walter BUSBEE
15 Director of Human Resources .... Ms. Sylvia BYRD
21 Director of Financial Accounting .... Mr. Don TRUE
96 Director of Purchasing .... Ms. Toni MARSHALL
18 Director Facilities & Operations .... Ms. Dorenda SPROWL
84 Vice President Enrollment Mgmt .... Dr. Vinson BURDETTE
07 Director of Intake Services .... Mrs. Jessica MOON
06 Registrar .... Mrs. Dawn BUTTS
38 Director Counseling/Disabilities .... Mr. Rich WELDON
26 Int Dir Marketing & Publications .... Ms. Nikasha DICKS

Allen University (D)

1530 Harden Street, Columbia SC 29204-1085
County: Richland FICE Identification: 003417
Unit ID: 217624
Telephone: (803) 376-5700 Carnegie Class: Bac-A&S
FAX Number: N/A Calendar System: Semester
URL: www.allenuniversity.edu
Established: 1870 Annual Undergrad Tuition & Fees: $13,140
Enrollment: 625 Coed
Affiliation or Control: African Methodist Episcopal IRS Status: 501(c)3
Highest Offering: Baccalaureate
Accreditation: SC

01 President .... Dr. Ernest MCNEALEY
05 VP Academic Affairs .... Dr. Charlene SPEAREN
32 VP Student Affairs .... Dr. Cynthia SELLERS-SIMON
10 VP Fiscal Affairs .... Ms. Ruby FIELDING
111 VP Institutional Advancement .... Mr. William ROBINSON
41 Athletic Director .... Mr. Chad WASHINGTON
08 Library Director .... Ms. Carol BOWERS
09 Director Institutional Research .... Dr. Kimberly LEBBY
36 Director Counseling/Placement .... Dr. Flavia ELDEMIRE
39 Director Residential Life & Health .... Ms. Oveta GLOVER
19 Chief of Police .... Chief Kelvin DAVIS
84 Dean Enrollment Mgmt/Registrar .... Ms. Marilyn DEBERRY
07 Director of Admissions .... Mr. Charles SINGLEY
37 Director of Financial Aid .... Ms. Lola KENNEDY
113 Bursar .... Ms. Sharon DAVIS
18 Director of Operations .... Mr. Vincent NORTHINGTON
15 Chief Human Resources Officer .... Ms. Paige MOORE
29 Director of Alumni Affairs .... Mr. G. Nimai GARRETT
25 Director of Grants .... Ms. S. Michelle YOUNG

Anderson University (E)

316 Boulevard, Anderson SC 29621-4035
County: Anderson FICE Identification: 003418
Unit ID: 217633
Telephone: (864) 231-2000 Carnegie Class: Masters/M
FAX Number: (864) 231-2004 Calendar System: Semester
URL: www.andersonuniversity.edu
Established: 1911 Annual Undergrad Tuition & Fees: $25,880
Enrollment: 3,212 Coed
Affiliation or Control: Other IRS Status: 501(c)3
Highest Offering: Doctorate
Accreditation: SC, ACBSP, ART, CAEPN, MUS, NURSE

01 President .... Dr. Evans P. WHITAKER
05 Exec Vice Pres/Provost & CFO .... Dr. Danny PARKER
10 Sr VP Administration & Brand .... Mr. David RASHED
20 Sr VP Inst Eff/Vice Provost .... Mrs. Susan WOOTEN
30 SVP Development/Pres Affairs .... Mr. James LANDRITH
32 Sr VP Student Development .... Dr. James FEREIRA
13 VP Information Technology .... Mr. Peter HARVIN
28 VP Diversity and Inclusion .... Mr. Beverly MCADAMS
42 VP Church Rel/Sr Campus Pastor .... Dr. James CLINE
42 VP Christian Life/Campus Min .... Rev. Samuel BRASHIER
84 VP Enrollment Management .... Ms. Pam ROSS
26 Dir Marketing & Communications .... Mr. Barry RAY
27 Assoc VP Mktg/Comm/Post-Tr .... Mr. James DUGUID
20 Asst Provost .... Mr. Nathan COX
20 Asst Provost .... Dr. Ryan NEAL
29 Assoc VP for Alumni and Parent Rel .... Mr. Jason RUTLAND
73 Dean COCS & Clamp Div Sch .... Mr. James DUDUIT
66 Dean School of Nursing .... Dr. Carol ARCHULETA
49 Dean College of Arts/Sciences .... Dr. Wayne COX
57 Dean SC School of the Arts .... Dr. David LARSON
88 Dean School Int Design .... Ms. Emily MARTIN
50 Dean College of Business .... Mr. Steven NAIL
76 Dean College of Health Profess .... Dr. Donald PEACE
82 Dean School Pub Svc/Admin .... Dr. Timothy TURNER
88 Assoc Dean College of Business .... Dr. John DUNCAN
88 Dean Student Success .... Dr. Linda KING
06 Dean Enroll Serv & Univ Registrar .... Mrs. Carol PARKER
14 Dean Ctr for Innovation/Digi .... Dr. Benjamin DEATON
88 Dean Student Life .... Mr. Jonathan GROPP
88 Dean Student Development .... Ms. Robyn SANDERSON
41 Dir Athletics .... Mr. William D'ANDREA
88 Exec Dir Conf Svcs/Univ Events .... Mrs. Jody BRYANT
39 Assoc Dean of Residence Life .... Ms. Melissa JONES
07 Dir Admission .... Mr. Jacob QUEEN
08 Dir Thrift Library .... Mr. Kent MILLWOOD
09 Dir External Reporting .... Mr. Daryl A. IVERSON
15 Dir Human Resources .... Mrs. Rose Mariee ALLISON
18 Dir Facilities .... Mr. Charles DICKERSON
19 Dir Campus Safety .... Mr. James KINES
21 Controller .... Ms. Kristie COLE
88 Dir Sports Med/Asst Dir Ath .... Mr. William DUVALL
23 Dir Heath Services/Nurse .... Mrs. Debbie TAYLOR
35 Dir Student Activities .... Ms. Bethany TURNER
36 Dir Career Services .... Ms. Kelly BELL
37 Dir Financial Services .... Mrs. Nancy TATE
38 Dir Counseling .... Ms. Erin MAURER
104 Dir International Programs .... Dr. Ann-Margaret THEMISTOCLEOUS
04 Exec Assistant to the President .... Mrs. Diane SUTHERLAND

The Art Institute of Charleston (F)

24 North Market Street, Charleston SC 29401-2623
Telephone: (843) 727-3500 Identification: 770976
Accreditation: &SC

† Branch campus of The Art Institute of Atlanta, Atlanta, GA

Benedict College (G)

Harden and Bland Streets, Columbia SC 29204-1086
County: Richland FICE Identification: 003420
Unit ID: 217721
Telephone: (803) 253-5000 Carnegie Class: Bac-Diverse
FAX Number: (803) 253-5059 Calendar System: Semester
URL: www.benedict.edu
Established: 1870 Annual Undergrad Tuition & Fees: $19,566
Enrollment: 2,465 Coed
Affiliation or Control: Independent Non-Profit IRS Status: 501(c)3
Highest Offering: Baccalaureate
Accreditation: SC, ACBSP, ART, CAEPN, NRPA, SW

01 President .... Dr. Roslyn C. ARTIS
05 Senior Vice Pres Academic Affairs .... Dr. Janeen WITTY
03 Executive Vice President .... Dr. Ruby W. WATTS
10 Vice President Business/Finance .... Ms. Brenda WALKER
32 Vice President Student Affairs .... Mr. Gary E. KNIGHT
30 Vice Pres Institutional Advancement .... Mrs. Barbara C. MOORE
20 Assoc Vice Pres Academic Affairs .... Dr. George A. DEVLIN
21 Asst VP for Business & Finance .... Ms. Jackie BROWN
26 Asst VP for Comm & Marketing .... Ms. Kymm HUNTER
07 Asst VP for Admissions/Student Mktg ...Mrs. Phyllis THOMPSON
29 Assistant VP for Alumni Relations .... Mrs. Ada A. BELTON
13 Dir Information Technology .... Mr. Dave MEDEIROS
27 Chief Information Officer .... Vacant
15 Director of Human Resources .... Mrs. Betty A. JENKINS
06 Registrar/Director Student Records .... Mrs. Wanda A. SCOTT-KINNEY
41 Athletics Director .... Mr. Willie WASHINGTON
38 Director Service Learning & Leaders .... Ms. Tondaleya JACKSON
42 Dir Campus Ministry/Dean of Chapel .... Mr. Thomas DAVIS
19 Director Campus Safety .... Mr. Haywood M. BAZEMORE
36 Director Career Services .... Ms. Karen W. RUTHERFORD
37 Director Financial Aid .... Ms. Sul BLACK
19 Director Physical Plant .... Mr. Todd FOSTER
08 Director of Library .... Mrs. Darlene ZINNERMAN-BETHEA
09 Director Institutional Research .... Mr. Jesse BELLINGER
108 Director Institutional Assessment .... Vacant
25 Coordinator Title III .... Vacant
96 Manager Procurement Services .... Ms. Sharling THOMPSON
49 Dean Sch Human/Arts/Soc Sci .... Dr. Charles AUSTIN
50 Dean School of Business/Econ .... Mr. Gerald SMALLS
88 Dean School of Health Human Service .... Dr. Tanya BRICE
53 Dean School of Education .... Dr. Damara HIGHTOWER
72 Dean Sch Science/Tech/Engrng/Math .... Dr. Samir S. RAYCHOUDHURY
92 Dean School of Honors .... Dr. Warren ROBINSON
57 Chair Fine Arts .... Ms. Gina MOORE
50 Chair Business Admin/Mgmt/Mktg .... Dr. Melvin MILLER
88 Chair Education and Family Studies .... Dr. Tracy MIDDLETON
70 Int Chair Social Work .... Dr. Tanya BRICE
88 Chair English/Foreign Language Dept .... Ms. Faye B. HARDY
88 Chair Bio/Chem/Enviroment Hlth Sci .... Dr. Larry LOWE
81 Chair Math/Computer Science .... Dr. Negash BEGASHAW
54 Chair Physics/Engineering .... Dr. Fouzi H. ARAMMASH
88 Int Chair Economics/Finance/Acctg .... Ms. Cathy FRANKLIN

Bob Jones University (H)

1700 Wade Hampton Boulevard, Greenville SC 29614-0001
County: Greenville FICE Identification: 003421
Unit ID: 217749
Telephone: (864) 242-5100 Carnegie Class: Masters/M
FAX Number: (864) 235-6661 Calendar System: Semester
URL: www.bju.edu
Established: 1927 Annual Undergrad Tuition & Fees: $15,550
Enrollment: 3,005 Coed
Affiliation or Control: Independent Non-Profit IRS Status: 501(c)3
Highest Offering: Doctorate
Accreditation: SC, TRACS, ENG

00 Chancellor .... Dr. Bob JONES, III
01 President .... Dr. Stephen D. PETTIT
05 Exec Vice Pres for Academic Affairs .... Dr. Gary M. WEIER
11 Executive Vice Pres for Operations .... Mr. Marshall E. FRANKLIN
88 Exec VP for Enrollment & Min Advanc .... Dr. Samuel E. HORN
111 VP Advancement & Alumni Relations .... Mr. John D. MATTHEWS
26 Chief Communication Officer .... Ms. Carol A. KEIRSTEAD
88 Vice Provost/Chief Admin Officer .... Dr. David A. FISHER
20 Vice Provost Strategic Initiatives .... Dr. Beverly CORMICAN
10 Chief Financial Officer .... Mr. Kennie M. STILL
32 Dean of Students/Chief SLO .... Dr. Eric D. NEWTON
84 Chief Enrollment Officer .... Dr. Bobby WOOD
15 Chief Human Resources Officer .... Mr. Kevin TAYLOR
18 Chief Facilities Management Officer .... Mr. Steve L. HENSLEY
13 Chief Information Officer .... Mr. Marvin P. REEM
49 Dean College of Arts and Science .... Dr. Renae WENTWORTH
73 Dean School of Religion & Seminary .... Dr. Samuel E. HORN
57 Dean Sch Fine Arts & Communication .... Dr. Darren P. LAWSON
53 Dean School of Education .... Dr. Brian A. CARRUTHERS
50 Dean School of Business .... Mr. Mike BUITER
73 Dean School of Religion .... Dr. Samuel E. HORN
73 Dean Seminary/GrdSch Religion .... Dr. Samuel E. HORN
06 Registrar .... Dr. Daniel SMITH
33 Dean of Men .... Mr. Jonathan G. DAULTON
34 Dean of Women .... Ms. Deneen LAWSON
07 Director of Admission .... Mr. Gary A. DEEDRICK
88 Director of Ministry Training .... Dr. Nathan CROCKETT
41 Athletic Director .... Dr. Neal RING
37 Director of Financial Aid .... Mrs. Susan YOUNG
08 Dean of Libraries .... Vacant
09 Sr Dir Planning/Rsrch/Assessment .... Rev. Phil GERARD

Brown Mackie College-Greenville (I)

75 Beattie Place, Ste. 100, Greenville SC 29601-2155
Telephone: (864) 239-5301 Identification: 666781
Accreditation: ACICS, OTA

† In teach-out mode. Branch campus of Brown Mackie College, Tucson, AZ.

Central Carolina Technical College (A)

506 N Guignard Drive, Sumter SC 29150-2499
County: Sumter FICE Identification: 003995
Unit ID: 218858
Telephone: (803) 778-1961 Carnegie Class: Assoc/HVT-Mix Trad/Non
FAX Number: (803) 778-7880 Calendar System: Semester
URL: www.cctech.edu
Established: 1962 Annual Undergrad Tuition & Fees (In-State): $4,639
Enrollment: 3,662 Coed
Affiliation or Control: State IRS Status: 501(c)3
Highest Offering: Associate Degree
Accreditation: **SC**, ADNUR, MAC, SURGT

01 Interim President .... Ms. Terry L. BOOTH
05 Interim Vice Pres Academic Affairs .... Ms. Ann COOPER
10 Vice President for Business Affairs .... Ms. Terry L. BOOTH
32 Vice President for Student Affairs .... Ms. Lisa BRACKEN
04 Assistant to the President .... Ms. Diana REARDON
51 Director Cont Educ/Workforce Devel .... Ms. Elizabeth WILLIAMS
08 Dean of Learning Resources .... Ms. Nancy BISHOP
102 Director Foundation .... Ms. Meree MCALISTER
26 Director Public Relations .... Ms. Catherine WOOD
15 Director of Personnel .... Mrs. Ronalda S. STOVER
13 Director Information Systems .... Mr. Brian DAVIS
06 Registrar .... Ms. Jennifer SZUPKA
37 Director Student Financial Aid .... Ms. Tiffany WILSON
09 Dir Research/Institutional Effect .... Mr. Bryan MAY
07 Director of Admissions & Counseling .... Mrs. Barbara WRIGHT
54 Dean of Industrial and Engineering .... Mr. Brent RUSSELL
76 Dean of Health Sciences .... Dr. Karen COWELL
53 Dean of General Education .... Mr. Myles WILLIAMS

Charleston School of Law (B)

81 Mary Street, PO Box 535, Charleston SC 29402
County: Charleston FICE Identification: 040963
Unit ID: 451510
Telephone: (843) 329-1000 Carnegie Class: Spec-4-yr-Law
FAX Number: (843) 720-7899 Calendar System: Semester
URL: www.charlestonlaw.edu
Established: 2003 Annual Graduate Tuition & Fees: N/A
Enrollment: 358 Coed
Affiliation or Control: Proprietary IRS Status: Proprietary
Highest Offering: First Professional Degree; No Undergraduates
Accreditation: **LAW**

01 President .... Mr. J. Edward BELL, III
05 Dean .... Mr. Andrew L. ABRAMS
20 Associate Dean Academic Affairs .... Ms. Margaret M. LAWTON
07 Associate Dean Admission .... Ms. Jacqueline B. BELL
32 Assoc Dean of Students .... Mr. Brett BARKER
13 Assoc Dean of Info Services .... Ms. Lisa SMITH-BUTLER
10 Chief Financial Officer .... Ms. Wende WOOD
06 Registrar .... Ms. Jennifer SUMMERS

Charleston Southern University (C)

PO Box 118087, Charleston SC 29423-8087
County: Charleston FICE Identification: 003419
Unit ID: 217688
Telephone: (843) 863-7000 Carnegie Class: Masters/M
FAX Number: (843) 863-8074 Calendar System: Semester
URL: www.csuniv.edu
Established: 1964 Annual Undergrad Tuition & Fees: $24,140
Enrollment: 3,621 Coed
Affiliation or Control: Southern Baptist IRS Status: 501(c)3
Highest Offering: Master's
Accreditation: **SC**, CAATE, CAEPN, CS, IACBE, MUS, NUR

01 President .... Dr. Jairy C. HUNTER, JR.
03 Executive Vice President .... Dr. Michael BRYANT
05 Vice President Academic Affairs .... Dr. Jacqueline FISH
10 Vice President for Business Affairs .... Mr. Luke BLACKMON
04 Exec Assistant to the President .... Mrs. Faye WOOD
84 Vice Pres Enrollment Management .... Dr. George METZ
26 Vice Pres Advancement & Marketing .... Mr. David BAGGS
20 Asst VP for Academic Affairs .... Dr. Scott YARBROUGH
30 Executive Director of Development .... Mr. Bill WARD
32 Dean of Students .... Mr. Clark CARTER
91 Director of Administrative Services .... Mr. Shannon PHILLIPS
08 Director of the Library .... Mrs. Sandra HUGHES
06 Registrar .... Mrs. Amanda SISSION
29 Director of BUC Club .... Mr. Tyler DAVIS
21 Associate Business Officer .... Mrs. Janet MIMS
27 Director of Integrated Marketing .... Mr. John STRUBEL
09 Dir of Institutional Effectiveness .... Mr. Jeffrey BABETZ
58 Dir of Graduate Business Program .... Dr. David PALMER
41 Athletic Director .... Mr. Hank SMALL
42 Director Campus Ministry .... Mr. Jon DAVIS
19 Director Security .... Mr. John WILSON
90 Director of Computer Science .... Dr. Valerie SESSIONS
18 Director Physical & Auxiliary Svcs .... Mr. Nick CIMORELLI
29 Director of Alumni Relations .... Mrs. Brittani WATKINS
07 Director of Admission .... Mr. James M. RHOTON
15 Director of Personnel Services .... Mrs. Lindsey WALKE
36 Director Career Planning .... Vacant
38 Director Student Counseling .... Ms. Katie BRAUER
96 Director of Purchasing .... Mrs. Lisa OROZCO
37 Director Student Financial Aid .... Mrs. Teri KARGES
39 Director Residence Life .... Mr. Tim GRANT
50 Interim Dean of Business .... Dr. David PALMER
83 Dean Humanities/Social Sciences .... Vacant
81 Dean Science & Mathematics .... Dr. Todd ASHBY
66 Dean of Nursing/Health Sciences .... Dr. Andreea MEIER
53 Dean of Education .... Dr. Melanie MURPHY
107 Asst VP for Academic Affairs .... Dr. Marc EMBLER

The Citadel, The Military College of South Carolina (D)

171 Moultrie Street, Charleston SC 29409-0001
County: Charleston FICE Identification: 003423
Unit ID: 217864
Telephone: (843) 225-3294 Carnegie Class: Masters/L
FAX Number: (843) 953-5287 Calendar System: Semester
URL: www.citadel.edu
Established: 1842 Annual Undergrad Tuition & Fees (In-State): $11,734
Enrollment: 3,506 Coed
Affiliation or Control: State IRS Status: 501(c)3
Highest Offering: Beyond Master's But Less Than Doctorate
Accreditation: **SC**, CACREP, CAEP, CAEPN, CS, ENG

01 President .... LtGen. John W. ROSA
05 Provost/Dean of College .... BGen. Connie L. BOOK
11 Senior Vice Pres for Operations .... Col. Thomas G. PHILIPKOSKY
10 Vice President of Finance .... Vacant
32 Commandant of Cadets .... Capt. Eugene PALUSO
26 Vice President for Comm & Marketing .... Col. John DORRIAN
41 Director Intercollegiate Athletics .... Mr. James E. SENTER
30 VP Inst Advanc/Citadel Fndtn Ex Dir .... Mr. Jay DOWD
04 Executive Assistant to President .... Cdr. William LIND
18 Assoc VP/Facilities & Engr .... Col. Jay BEAM
43 General Counsel .... Mr. Mark C. BRANDENBURG
20 Assoc Provost Academic Affairs .... Col. Mark A. BEBENSEE
20 Assoc Prov Plng/Assess/Evaluation .... Col. Tara F. HORNOR
07 Director of Admissions .... LtCol. John W. POWELL, JR.
06 Registrar .... Col. Sylvia L. NESMITH
21 Treasurer .... Ms. Julie WELCH
29 Director Alumni Affairs/Placement .... Col. J. Laurence HUTTO
08 Director of Library .... LtCol. David S. GOBLE
13 Dir Info Technology Services .... Mr. Kyle HERRON
37 Director Financial Aid/ Scholarships .... LtCol. Henry M. FULLER, JR.
15 Director of Human Resources .... Maj. Leah S. SCHONFELD
36 Director of Career Services .... Vacant
38 Director of Student Counseling .... Dr. Suzanne BUFANO
09 Institutional Research Director .... Ms. Lisa L. PACE
19 Director Security/Safety .... Col. William A. FLETCHER
23 College Physician .... Dr. Carey M. CAPELL
40 Director of the Cadet Store .... Mr. Kenneth A. WOODRUFF
42 Chaplain/Dir Religious Activities .... Cdr. Joe MOLINA
92 Director Honors Program .... Col. Jack W. RHODES
86 Director Govt & Community Affairs .... Col. Cardon B. CRAWFORD
96 Director of Purchasing .... LtCol. James P. DE LUCA
28 Chief Diversity Officer .... Ms. Shawn EDWARDS
50 Dean of the School of Bus Admin .... Col. William N. TRUMBULL
53 Dean of the School of Education .... Col. Larry DANIEL
54 Dean of the School of Engineering .... Col. Ronald W. WELCH
81 Int Dean School of Science/Math .... Col. John WEINSTEIN
79 Dean Sch Humanities/Social Sciences .... Col. Winifred B. MOORE
101 Spec Asst to President/Brd Matters .... Ms. Ashley WITHERSPOON
85 Director Multicultural Affairs .... LtCol. Robert P. PICKERING
16 Human Resources Deputy Director .... Mr. Wesley S. SAMS
25 Grants Writer .... Ms. Sylvia R. WILLIAMS
00 Chairman of the Board .... Col. Fred L. PRICE
114 Interim Chief Budget Administrator .... Mr. James OPENSHAW
121 Director of Student Success .... LtCol. Jane WARNER

Claflin University (E)

400 Magnolia Street, Orangeburg SC 29115-4477
County: Orangeburg FICE Identification: 003424
Unit ID: 217873
Telephone: (800) 922-1276 Carnegie Class: Bac-A&S
FAX Number: (803) 531-2860 Calendar System: Semester
URL: www.claflin.edu
Established: 1869 Annual Undergrad Tuition & Fees: $16,158
Enrollment: 1,925 Coed
Affiliation or Control: United Methodist IRS Status: 501(c)3
Highest Offering: Master's
Accreditation: **SC**, ACBSP, CAEPN, MUS

01 President .... Dr. Henry N. TISDALE
11 Vice President for Administration .... Mr. Drexel B. BALL
05 Provost/Chief Academic Officer .... Dr. Karl S. WRIGHT
10 Vice President for Fiscal Affairs .... Mrs. Tijuana R. HUDSON
111 Vice Pres Institutional Advancement .... Rev. Whittaker V. MIDDLETON
32 Vice Pres Student Devel & Services .... Dr. Leroy A. DURANT
45 VP Plng/Assessment/Information Svcs .... Dr. Zia HASAN
20 Vice Provost for Academic Programs .... Dr. Angela W. PETERS
26 Assistant VP Comm & Marketing .... Mr. George W. JOHNSON
35 Asst VP Student Devel & Services .... Mr. Devin L. RANDOLPH
108 AVP Institutional Effectiveness .... Dr. Bridget P. DEWEES
07 Director of Admissions .... Mr. Michael ZEIGLER
79 Dean Sch Humanities & Soc Science .... Dr. Isaiah R. MCGEE
50 Dean School of Business .... Dr. Charles W. RICHARDSON, JR.
53 Dean School of Education .... Dr. Nicole Y. STRANGE-MARTIN
81 Dean Sch Natural Sciences & Math .... Dr. Verlie A. TISDALE
13 Asst VP Information Tech Svcs .... Mr. James E. BRENN
51 Int Exec Dir for Prof/Cont Studies .... Mr. Mark A. ROBERTS
08 Library Director .... Mrs. Marilyn GIBBS DRAYTON
37 Director of Financial Aid .... Ms. Terria C. WILLIAMS
36 Director of Career Development .... Mrs. Carolyn R. SNELL
41 Athletic Director .... Dr. Jerome H. FITCH
15 Senior Director of Human Resources .... Ms. Shirley A. BIGGS
06 Registrar .... Mrs. Roe B. HUNT
29 Director Alumni Affairs/Annual Fund .... Mrs. Zelda LEE
19 Chief of Campus Public Safety .... Mr. Steven A. PEARSON
109 Director of Auxiliary Services .... Mr. Rodeny B. HUDSON
46 Interim Vice Provost for Research .... Dr. Muthukrishna RAJA
04 Executive Admin Asst to President .... Ms. Melvenia WILLIAMS
09 Director of Institutional Research .... Dr. Corey L. AMAKER
84 Director Enrollment Management .... Dr. Leroy A. DURANT

Clemson University (F)

201 Sikes Hall, Clemson SC 29634-0001
County: Pickens FICE Identification: 003425
Unit ID: 217882
Telephone: (864) 656-3311 Carnegie Class: DU-Highest
FAX Number: (864) 656-4040 Calendar System: Semester
URL: www.clemson.edu
Established: 1889 Annual Undergrad Tuition & Fees (In-State): $14,708
Enrollment: 22,698 Coed
Affiliation or Control: State IRS Status: 501(c)3
Highest Offering: Doctorate
Accreditation: **SC**, ART, CACREP, CAEPN, CONST, CS, CVT, DIETD, ENG, ENGR, IPSY, LSAR, NRPA, NURSE, PH, PLNG

01 President .... Dr. James P. CLEMENTS
05 Provost .... Dr. Robert H. JONES
43 General Counsel .... Mr. W.C. (Chip) HOOD
10 Chief Financial Officer .... Mr. Brett A. DALTON
32 Interim VP Student Affairs .... Dr. Almeda JACKS
101 Executive Secretary to the Board .... Ms. Angie LEIDINGER
111 Vice President for Advancement .... Mr. A. Neill CAMERON, JR.
103 Vice Pres Public Svc .... Dr. George R. ASKEW
46 Vice President for Research .... Dr. Larry DOOLEY
88 Vice President for Economic Develop .... Dr. John M. BALLATO
13 Vice Prov Computer/Info Technology .... Mr. Russell KAURLOTO
88 Vice Provost for International Affs .... Ms. Sharon NAGY
100 Chief of Staff .... Mr. Max ALLEN
29 Chief Alumni Officer .... Mr. Brian J. O'ROURKE
18 Interim Chief Facilities Officer .... Mr. Todd BARNETTE
35 Associate VP/Dean of Students .... Dr. Joy S. SMITH
88 Associate Provost for Faculty Devel .... Dr. Nadim AZIZ
26 Chief Public Affairs Officer .... Mr. Mark D. LAND
08 Dean of Libraries .... Ms. Mary M. FARRELL
07 Director of Admissions .... Mr. David KUSKOWSKI
06 Registrar .... Mrs. Debra SPARACINO
37 Director of Financial Aid .... Mrs. Elizabeth MILAM
36 Director of Career Center .... Mr. Burton O'NEIL
38 Director Counseling/Psych Services .... Dr. Raquel J. CONTRERAS
47 Dean Col Agric/Forestry/Life Sci .... Dr. Thomas R. SCOTT
58 Dean Graduate School/Vice Provost .... Dr. Jason W. OSBORN
48 Dean Col Arch/Arts/Humanities .... Dr. Richard E. GOODSTEIN
54 Dean Col Engr/Sciences .... Dr. Anand GRAMOPADHYE
83 Dean Col of Behavioral/Social Sci .... Dr. Brett WRIGHT
09 Director Institutional Research .... Vacant
39 Executive Director of Housing .... Ms. Verna G. HOWELL
41 Director of Athletics .... Mr. Dan RADAKOVICH
112 Director of Estate & Planned Giving .... Ms. Jovanna J. KING
22 Director Access & Equity .... Mr. Byron A. WILEY
28 Director of Diversity .... Mr. Lee A. GILL
23 Director Student Health Services .... Mr. George W. CLAY
15 Chief Human Resources .... Vacant
91 Executive Director Enterprise Appl .... Mr. Barrett KENDJORIA
25 Director Sponsored Programs .... Ms. Sheila T. LISCHWE
19 Director Law Enforcement & Safety .... Chief Johnson LINK
96 Director of Purchasing .... Mr. Michael NEBESKY
04 Int Asst to the President/Vice Prov .... Dr. Jeremy R. KING
88 Dir Teaching Effectiveness & Innova .... Ms. Linda TILSON
88 Director of Bridge to Clemson Pgm .... Ms. Susan WHORTON
104 Director Study Abroad .... Dr. Uttiyo RAYCHAUDHURI

Clinton College (G)

1029 Crawford Road, Rock Hill SC 29730-5152
County: York FICE Identification: 004923
Unit ID: 217891
Telephone: (803) 327-7402 Carnegie Class: Bac/Assoc-Mixed
FAX Number: (803) 327-3261 Calendar System: Semester
URL: www.clintoncollege.edu
Established: 1894 Annual Undergrad Tuition & Fees: $7,894
Enrollment: 161 Coed
Affiliation or Control: African Methodist Episcopal Zion Church
IRS Status: 501(c)3
Highest Offering: Baccalaureate
Accreditation: **TRACS**

01 Acting President .... Dr. Lester A. MCCORN
04 Assistant to the President .... Ms. Cheryl A. WEBB
05 VP for Academic Affairs/Dean .... Ms. Janis S. PENDLETON
30 VP for Development .... Mr. Raymond CORLEY
32 VP for Student Affairs .... Dr. Robert M. COPELAND, JR.
10 VP for Business & Finance .... Ms. Archinya INGRAM
06 Registrar .... Vacant
37 Financial Aid .... Ms. Pamela WHITE
08 Librarian .... Ms. Minora HICKS
41 Athletic Director .... Mr. Larry MULLINS
18 Director Facilities/Bldgs/Grounds .... Rev. Lloyd SNIPES
07 Admissions .... Ms. Kim SHEPARD
35 Director Student Support Services .... Ms. Judith COWAN

Coastal Carolina University (A)

PO Box 261954, Conway SC 29528-6054
County: Horry FICE Identification: 003451
Unit ID: 218724
Telephone: (843) 347-3161 Carnegie Class: Masters/L
FAX Number: (843) 349-2990 Calendar System: Semester
URL: www.coastal.edu
Established: 1954 Annual Undergrad Tuition & Fees (In-State): $10,876
Enrollment: 10,263 Coed
Affiliation or Control: State IRS Status: 501(c)3
Highest Offering: Doctorate
Accreditation: SC, ART, CAEPN, CS, MUS, NUR, THEA

01 President ....Dr. David A. DECENZO
05 Provost and Executive VP ....Dr. J. Ralph BYINGTON
10 Vice Pres Finance/Administration ....Ms. Jane JOHANSEN
30 Vice Pres Philanthropy ....Mr. Mark ROACH
32 VP Campus Life & Student Engagement ....Dr. Deborah CONNER
88 VP Stdnt Rights & Responsibilities ....Mr. Travis E. OVERTON
26 Vice Pres Univ Communications ....Mr. William PLATE
50 Dean Business Administration ....Dr. Barbara RITTER
53 Dean of Education ....Dr. Edward JADALLAH
79 Dean of Humanities & Fine Arts ....Dr. Daniel ENNIS
81 Dean of Science ....Dr. Michael H. ROBERTS
97 Dean of University College ....Dr. Sara HOTTINGER
13 Chief Information & Technology Ofcr ....Mr. Abdallah HADDAD
20 Assoc Provost Admin/Academic ....Ms. Sallie CLARKSON
108 Assoc Prov Assessment/Accreditation ....Dr. James SOLAZZO
58 Assoc Prov Grad Pgm/Vice Dean CENV ....Dr. James O. LUKEN
104 Assoc Provost Global Initiatives . Dr. Darla J. DOMKE-DAMONTE
09 Exec Dir of Planning and Research ....Ms. Christine L. MEE
06 University Registrar ....Mr. Daniel M. LAWLESS
19 Director Public Safety ....Mr. David ROPER
21 Controller ....Vacant
28 Dir Multicultural Student Services ....Ms. Patricia SINGLETON-YOUNG
41 Director of Athletics ....Mr. Matthew L. HOGUE
38 Asst VP Campus Life/Stdt Engagement ....Dr. Jennie M. CASSIDY
85 Director of International Programs ....Mr. Geoffrey J. PARSONS
39 Sr Dir of Housing/Residence Life ....Mr. Steve HARRISON
37 Dir Financial Aid & Scholarship ....Ms. Wendy WATTS
92 Director Honors Program ....Dr. Michael RUSE
36 Director Career Services ....Dr. Tom WOODLE
96 Dir Procurement/Business Services ....Mr. Dean P. HUDSON
18 Director of Facilities ....Mr. T. Rein MUNGO
27 Assoc VP for Univ Communications ....Ms. Martha S. HUNN
29 Director Alumni Relations ....Ms. Jean Ann BRAKEFIELD
07 Asst Provost Admiss & Merit Award . Ms. Amanda E. CRADDOCK
15 Vice Pres Human Resources ....Ms. Beverly J. LANDRUM
22 Director Human Resources/EEO Office . Ms. Kimberly SHERFESEE
43 Dir Legal Services/General Counsel ....Mr. Timothy E. MEACHAM
90 Director Academic Computing ....Mr. Fadi N. BAROODY
08 Head Librarian ....Vacant

Coker College (B)

300 E College Avenue, Hartsville SC 29550-3797
County: Darlington FICE Identification: 003427
Unit ID: 217907
Telephone: (843) 383-8000 Carnegie Class: Bac-Diverse
FAX Number: (843) 383-8048 Calendar System: Semester
URL: www.coker.edu
Established: 1908 Annual Undergrad Tuition & Fees: $27,624
Enrollment: 1,282 Coed
Affiliation or Control: Independent Non-Profit IRS Status: 501(c)3
Highest Offering: Master's
Accreditation: SC, ART, CAEPN, MUS, SW

01 President ....Dr. Robert L. WYATT
05 Provost & Dean of the College ....Dr. Tracy PARKINSON
03 Executive Vice President ....Mr. Tony FLOYD
104 Asst Dean/Dir of Transformations ....Ms. Darlene SMALL
26 VP Institutional Identity & IT ....Mr. R. Kyle SAVERANCE
41 VP Athletics & Athletic Facilities ....Dr. Lynn GRIFFIN
20 Assoc Provost/Dean of Faculty ....Dr. Susan HENDERSON
84 Assoc VP for Enrollment Management ....Mr. Adam CONNOLLY
11 VP for Administration ....Ms. Brianna DOUGLAS
06 Dir Academic Records/Inst Research ....Ms. Marcy KERSHNER
18 Director of Facilities ....Mr. Hayden HUTCHINGS
21 Director of Accounting & Reporting ....Ms. Robin A. PERDUE
37 Director of Financial Aid ....Mrs. Betty B. WILLIAMS
111 VP for Institutional Advancement ....Dr. William CARSWELL
29 Director of Alumni Engagement ....Ms. Shelli WILSON
07 Director of Admissions ....Vacant
08 Director of Library ....Mr. Todd RIX
19 Director of Campus Safety ....Mr. George MITCHELL
09 Assoc Prov of Inst Effectiveness ....Dr. Kathryn FLAHERTY
04 Executive Asst to President ....Ms. Johnna SHIRLEY
15 Director Personnel Services ....Ms. Ella MARSHALL
28 Director of Diversity ....Rev. John FOSTER

College of Charleston (C)

66 George Street, Charleston SC 29424-0100
County: Charleston FICE Identification: 003428
Unit ID: 217819
Telephone: (843) 953-5507 Carnegie Class: Masters/L
FAX Number: (843) 953-5811 Calendar System: Semester
URL: www.cofc.edu
Established: 1770 Annual Undergrad Tuition & Fees (In-State): $11,805
Enrollment: 11,531 Coed
Affiliation or Control: State IRS Status: 501(c)3
Highest Offering: Master's
Accreditation: SC, CAATE, CAEPN, CS, MUS, SPAA, THEA

01 President ....Mr. Glenn F. MCCONNELL
101 Vice Pres Col Events/Exec Sec BOT ....Ms. Elizabeth W. KASSEBAUM
05 Provost & Exec Vice Pres Admin ....Dr. Brian MCGEE
10 Exec VP Business Affairs ....Mr. Steven C. OSBORNE
11 VP for Admin & Planning ....Mr. Paul D. PATRICK
100 Sr Exec Admin for the Pres ....Ms. Debbie HAMMOND
26 Dir of College Mktg & Comm ....Mr. Mark E. BERRY
111 Exec VP Institutional Advancement ....Mr. George P. WATT, JR.
32 Dean of Students ....Dr. Jeri O. CABOT
43 General Counsel Legal Affairs ....Ms. Angela B. MULHOLLAND
19 Chief of Police/Dir Public Saf ....Chief Robert S. REESE
20 Associate Provost ....Dr. Deanna M. CAVENY-NOECKER
20 Associate Vice Pres ....Dr. Lynne E. FORD
104 Assoc Provost International Educ ....Dr. Andrew M. SOBIESUO
13 Senior VP/Chief Information Officer ....Mark STAPLES
30 Senior VP Economic Development ....Vacant
18 VP Facilities Planning ....Ms. Monica R. SCOTT
21 Dir of Financial Srvcs ....Ms. Debye B. ALDERMAN
109 Dir Business & Auxiliary Services ....Vacant
96 Procurement Director ....Ms. Wendy E. WILLIAMS
30 Vice President Development ....Mr. Christopher TOBIN
15 VP of Human Resources ....Mr. Edward POPE
22 Dir Equal Opportunity Programs ....Ms. Kimberly A. GERTNER
84 Assoc Vice Pres Enrollment Planning ....Vacant
09 Assoc VP Institutional Research ....Dr. James T. POSEY
28 Associate VP Diversity ....Dr. Renard HARRIS
88 Asst VP New Student Programs ....Ms. Melinda MILEY
06 Registrar ....Ms. Mary C. BERGSTROM
21 Controller ....Ms. Dawn E. WILLAN
21 Treasurer ....Mr. David G. KATZ
58 Dean Graduate School ....Dr. Brian MCGEE
57 Dean School of the Arts ....Ms. Valerie B. MORRIS
50 Dean School of Business ....Dr. Alan T. SHAO
53 Dean School of Education ....Dr. Frances C. WELCH
82 Dean School of Languages ....Dr. Antonio D. TILLIS
81 Dean School of Science & Math ....Dr. Michael AUERBACH
79 Dean Sch of Humanities/Social Sci ....Dr. Jerold L. HALE
107 Dean College of Charleston North ....Dr. Godfrey GIBBISON
51 Director CCEPD ....Dr. Alice M. HAMILTON
92 Dean Honors College ....Dr. Trisha H. FOLDS-BENNETT
41 Director Athletics ....Mr. Matt ROBERTS
25 Director Research and Grants ....Ms. Susan A. RIVALEAU
37 Dir Financial Asst/Veteran Affairs ....Mr. Donald R. GRIGGS
07 Exec Dir of Admissions ....Ms. Suzette STILLE
121 Dir Center for Academic Advising ....Ms. Karen HAUSCHILD
88 Dir Center for Student Learning ....Ms. Melissa M. THOMAS
108 Dir Academic Assessment & Planning ....Dr. Karin ROOF
88 Ombudsperson ....Ms. Denise MITCHELL
22 Dir Ctr for Disabilities Services ....Ms. Deborah F. MIHAL
35 Director Student Life ....Ms. Susan PAYMENT
36 Director Career Services ....Vacant
38 Dir Counseling & Substance Abuse ....Mr. Frank C. BUDD
23 Director Health Services ....Ms. Jane RENO-MUNRO
39 Director Residence Life ....Ms. Melantha ARDREY
19 Dir of Fire and Life Safety ....Mr. Richard N. KRANTZ
88 Dir Enviro Health and Safety ....Mr. Randy L. BEAVER
21 Associate Vice President ....Mr. Samuel B. JONES
88 Director of ECDC ....Ms. Candace L. JARUSZEWICZ
35 AVP Student Affairs/Dir HSLC ....Mr. K. Michael DUNCAN
18 Director of Sustainability ....Mr. P. Brian FISHER
88 Director Avery Research Center ....Ms. Patricia WILLIAMS LESSANE
31 Sr Dir of Community Relations ....Ms. Evelyn H. NADEL
88 Dir Undergrad Academic Services ....Ms. Michelle G. FUTRELL

Columbia College (D)

1301 Columbia College Drive, Columbia SC 29203-5998
County: Richland FICE Identification: 003430
Unit ID: 217934
Telephone: (803) 786-3178 Carnegie Class: Masters/M
FAX Number: (803) 786-3752 Calendar System: Semester
URL: www.columbiasc.edu
Established: 1854 Annual Undergrad Tuition & Fees: $28,900
Enrollment: 1,484 Female
Affiliation or Control: United Methodist IRS Status: 501(c)3
Highest Offering: Master's
Accreditation: SC, ART, CAEPN, DANCE, MUS, SW

01 President ....Dr. Carol A. MOORE
05 Provost/VP for Academic Affairs ....Dr. Robin ROSENTHAL
10 Vice President for Finance ....Mr. Mark HILTON
84 Vice Pres for Enrollment Management ....Vacant
88 Ex Dir Inst Lship & Prof Excellence ....Ms. Chris LACOLA
30 VP for Advancement ....Mr. Francis G. SCHODOWSKI
32 Dean Student Affairs ....Ms. LaNae R. BRIGGS
29 Exec Director of Alumnae Relations ....Vacant
09 Director Institutional Research ....Dr. Scott A. SMITH
08 Director of Library ....Ms. Jane TUTTLE
19 Chief of Police ....Chief Wayne JAMISON
37 Director of Financial Aid ....Ms. Constance M. DRAKEFORD
36 Director of Ctr for Career Coaching ....Vacant
13 Dir of Info Technology Services ....Mr. Floyd STAYNER
18 Director of Facilities Management ....Ms. Gaby HICKMAN
26 Exec Director Mktg & Communications ....Vacant
41 Director of Athletics ....Ms. Kellyanne STUBBLEFIELD
40 Director Bookstore ....Ms. Cory CORP
38 Director Counseling Services ....Ms. Mimi MERIWETHER
04 Executive Assistant to President ....Ms. Joye G. HIPP
07 Director of Admissions ....Ms. Julie A. KING
92 Director Honors Program/Faculty Dev ....Dr. John ZUBIZARRETA
06 Registrar ....Ms. Nicole SPENSLEY

Columbia International University (E)

7435 Monticello Road, Columbia SC 29203
County: Richland FICE Identification: 003429
Unit ID: 217925
Telephone: (803) 754-4100 Carnegie Class: Masters/M
FAX Number: (803) 786-4209 Calendar System: Semester
URL: www.ciu.edu
Established: 1923 Annual Undergrad Tuition & Fees: $21,490
Enrollment: 1,001 Coed
Affiliation or Control: Independent Non-Profit IRS Status: 501(c)3
Highest Offering: Doctorate
Accreditation: SC, BI, CACREP, THEOL

01 President ....Dr. Mark A. SMITH
00 Chancellor ....Dr. Bill H. JONES
05 Senior Vice President/Provost ....Dr. Jim LANPHER
112 Sr VP Estate & Gift Planning ....Mr. D. Keith MARION
111 Int VP of Institutional Advancement ....Mrs. Diane MULL
73 Dean Seminary & School of Ministry ....Dr. John HARVEY
49 Dean College of Arts and Sciences ....Dr. Bryan BEYER
53 Dean College of Education ....Dr. Connie MITCHELL
104 Dean College Intercultural Studies ....Dr. Edward SMITHER
09 Dir Institutional Research/Assess ....Dr. Ben BRYAN
101 Assoc Provost Online Studies ....Dr. Brian SIMMONS
08 Director of Library ....Mrs. Cynthia SNELL
06 University Registrar ....Mrs. Jennifer BOOTH
15 Director Human Resources ....Mr. Donald E. JONES
32 Dean of Students ....Mr. Rick SWIFT
07 VP Enrollment & Marketing ....Mrs. Silvia LUCASCHI-DECKER
13 Int Corporate IT Coordinator ....Ms. Dianne BRITTON
18 Director Physical Plant ....Mr. Dave MAGNUSON
10 Chief Financial Officer ....Mr. Rob HARTMAN
37 Director Financial Aid ....Mrs. Patty HIX
04 Administrative Asst to President ....Mrs. Debbie GERMANY
19 Director Security/Safety ....Mr. Bob REGISTER
41 Athletic Director ....Mr. James WHITAKER

Converse College (F)

580 E Main, Spartanburg SC 29302-0006
County: Spartanburg FICE Identification: 003431
Unit ID: 217961
Telephone: (864) 596-9000 Carnegie Class: Masters/M
FAX Number: (864) 596-9158 Calendar System: 4/1/4
URL: www.converse.edu
Established: 1889 Annual Undergrad Tuition & Fees: $17,000
Enrollment: 1,148 Female
Affiliation or Control: Independent Non-Profit IRS Status: 501(c)3
Highest Offering: Beyond Master's But Less Than Doctorate
Accreditation: SC, ART, CAEPN, CIDA, MFCD, MUS

01 President ....Ms. Krista L. NEWKIRK
05 Provost ....Dr. Jeffrey H. BARKER
10 Vice Pres Finance/Administration ....Mrs. Robin LESLIE
111 VP Institutional Advancement ....Mrs. Krista BOFILL
79 Dean Humanities/Sciences/Education ....Mrs. Ann PLETCHER
57 Dean School of the Arts ....Dr. Boone HOPKINS
32 Dean of Community Life ....Ms. Rhonda MINGO
08 Librarian ....Mr. Wade WOODWARD
37 Director of Financial Planning ....Mr. James KELLAM
06 Registrar ....Mrs. Mary L. BROWN
15 Human Resources Director ....Ms. Keshia GILLIAM
13 Chief Information Officer ....Mr. Zach CORBITT
36 Dean of Professional Development ....Ms. Witney FISHER
26 Director of Media/Communications ....Mrs. Beth LANCASTER
04 Assistant to the President ....Mrs. Stacey BREWER
38 Director of Counseling Services ....Ms. Bethany GARR
09 Director Institutional Research ....Dr. Yongmei LI
84 Assoc Vice Pres of Enrollment Mgmt ....Mr. Trevor PITTMAN
18 Chief Facilities/Physical Plant ....Mr. Robert BROWN
109 Facilities Planner ....Mr. Rick JOLLEY

Denmark Technical College (G)

PO Box 327, Denmark SC 29042-0327
County: Bamberg FICE Identification: 005363
Unit ID: 217989
Telephone: (803) 793-5176 Carnegie Class: Assoc/HVT-High Trad
FAX Number: (803) 793-5942 Calendar System: Semester
URL: www.denmarktech.edu
Established: 1948 Annual Undergrad Tuition & Fees (In-State): $4,456
Enrollment: 1,043 Coed
Affiliation or Control: State IRS Status: 501(c)3
Highest Offering: Associate Degree
Accreditation: SC, ACBSP, ENGT

01 Interim President ....Dr. Christopher HALL
09 VP for Inst Research/Plng/Dev ....Vacant
05 Interim VP for Academic Affairs ....Mrs. Tia WRIGHT-RICHARDS
10 Interim VP for Fiscal Affairs ....Ms. Shatika SPEARMAN
84 VP for Enrollment Management ....Mr. Marcus CORBETT
15 Director of Human Resources ....Vacant
32 Associate VP for Student Services ....Ms. Avis GATHERS
08 Dean of Learning Resources Ctr ....Ms. Carolyn FORTSON
13 Director of Information Technology ....Vacant
19 Chief of Public Safety ....Mr. Elton SHULER
25 Director of Grants & Contracts ....Vacant
36 Director Career Plng/Placement ....Mrs. Leslie HOLMAN-BROOKS
37 Director of Financial Aid ....Mrs. Laura FOGLE
88 Interim Dean of Public Service ....Mrs. Rosaland KENNER
49 Interim Dean of Arts & Sciences ....Ms. Mennu SHUKLA

66 Dean of Nursing ... Vacant
54 Dean of Industrial/Related Tech ... Mr. Stephen MANSON
50 Dean Business/Computer/Related Tech ... Mrs. Tia WRIGHT-RICHARDS
07 Interim Director of Recruitment ... Ms. Crystal BRAILEY
103 AVP Economic/Workforce Development ... Mr. Stephen MASON
39 Director Student Housing ... Ms. Charlene DICKERSON
06 Registrar ... Ms. Carolyn GRIMES
04 Administrative Asst to President ... Mrs. Gwendolyn BAMBERG

ECPI University-Charleston (A)

7410 Northside Drive, Ste 100,
North Charleston SC 29420
Telephone: (843) 606-5902 Identification: 770955
Accreditation: &SC, MAAB

† Branch campus of ECPI University, Virginia Beach, VA

ECPI University-Columbia (B)

250 Berryhill Road, Ste 300, Columbia SC 29210-6467
Telephone: (803) 772-3333 Identification: 770956
Accreditation: &SC, MAAB

† Branch campus of ECPI University, Virginia Beach, VA

ECPI University-Greenville (C)

1001 Keys Drive, Ste 100, Greenville SC 29615
Telephone: (864) 288-2828 Identification: 770954
Accreditation: &SC, MAAB

† Branch campus of ECPI University, Virginia Beach, VA

Edward Via College of Osteopathic Medicine-Carolinas Campus (D)

350 Howard Street, Sparntanburg SC 29303
Telephone: (864) 327-9800 Identification: 770941
Accreditation: OSTEO

† Branch campus of Edward Via College of Osteopathic Medicine, Blacksburg, VA.

Erskine College (E)

PO Box 338, 2 Washington Street,
Due West SC 29639-0338
County: Abbeville FICE Identification: 003432
Unit ID: 217998
Telephone: (864) 379-2131 Carnegie Class: Bac-A&S
FAX Number: (864) 379-2167 Calendar System: 4/1/4
URL: www.erskine.edu
Established: 1837 Annual Undergrad Tuition & Fees: $34,560
Enrollment: 761 Coed
Affiliation or Control: Other IRS Status: 501(c)3
Highest Offering: Doctorate
Accreditation: SC, #CAATE, CAEPN, THEOL

01 President ... Dr. Robert E. GUSTAFSON
05 Provost Erskine College ... Dr. John D. BASIE
10 Sr VP for Finance & Operations ... Mr. Gregory W. HASELDEN
30 Vice Pres Alumni/Advancement ... Mr. Buddy FERGUSON
41 Vice Pres for Athletics ... Mr. Mark L. PEELER
73 Provost Theological Seminary ... Dr. Leslie HOLMES
32 Dean Student Development ... Ms. Wendi SANTEE
108 Assoc Dean of Inst Effectiveness ... Mr. John F. KENNERLY, JR.
08 Assoc Dean of McCain Library ... Mr. John F. KENNERLY, JR.
06 Registrar ... Mrs. Tracy M. SPIRES
26 Director Communications/Marketing ... Mr. Brian SMITH
37 Director of Student Financial Aid ... Mrs. A. Michelle LODATO
13 Director of Information Technology ... Mr. Matt COCKRELL
09 Director of Institutional Research ... Mr. Buck F. BROWN, JR.
42 Chaplain ... Mr. Paul G. PATRICK
21 Controller ... Mr. Christian M. HABEGER
15 Director Human Resources ... Mrs. Barbara PECK
19 Chief of Erskine Police ... Mr. Randy ESTEP
29 Director of Alumni Affairs ... Mr. William L. FERGUSON
04 Administrative Asst to President ... Mrs. Dena S. HODGE
07 Director of Admissions ... Ms. Tobe R. FRIERSON
105 Director of Comm Technology ... Mr. Brian K. SMITH
36 Coordinator for Student Transitions ... Mr. Trent D. PAYNE

Florence - Darlington Technical College (F)

PO Box 100548, Florence SC 29502-0548
County: Florence FICE Identification: 003990
Unit ID: 218025
Telephone: (843) 661-8324 Carnegie Class: Assoc/MT-VT-High Trad
FAX Number: (843) 661-8011 Calendar System: Semester
URL: www.fdtc.edu
Established: 1964 Annual Undergrad Tuition & Fees (In-District): $4,174
Enrollment: 6,007 Coed
Affiliation or Control: State/Local IRS Status: 501(c)3
Highest Offering: Associate Degree
Accreditation: SC, ADNUR, CAHIIM, COARC, CSHSE, DA, DH, MLTAD, RAD, SURGT

01 President ... Dr. Ben P. DILLARD, III
05 Vice President Academic Affairs ... Dr. Suresh TIWARI
10 Vice Pres Business Affairs ... Dr. Douglas LANGE
30 Vice Pres Institutional Advancement ... Ms. Jill LEWIS
26 Vice Pres Marketing/Public Affs ... Mr. Edward BETHEA
10 Assoc Vice Pres Business Office ... Ms. Connie MORRIS
76 Assoc VP Allied Health ... Dr. Maureen DEVER-BUMBA
13 Assoc Vice Pres Info Tech/CIO ... Mr. Tyron JONES
15 Assoc VP Internal Relations/EEO ... Ms. Terry DINGLE
09 Director Institutional Research ... Ms. Melissa MILLER
06 Registrar ... Ms. Genell GAUSE
37 Director Financial Aid ... Ms. Monica STARR
96 Director of Purchasing ... Ms. Toni RICHARDSON

Forrest College (G)

601 E River Street, Anderson SC 29624-2405
County: Anderson FICE Identification: 004924
Unit ID: 218043
Telephone: (864) 225-7653 Carnegie Class: Assoc/HVT-Mix Trad/Non
FAX Number: (864) 261-7471 Calendar System: 4/1/4
URL: www.forrestcollege.edu
Established: 1946 Annual Undergrad Tuition & Fees: $8,428
Enrollment: 113 Coed
Affiliation or Control: Proprietary IRS Status: Proprietary
Highest Offering: Associate Degree
Accreditation: ACICS, MAC

00 Chairman Board of Directors ... Dr. John RE
01 President ... Dr. C. John RE
05 Academic Dean ... Jesse HARRIS
11 Administrative Dean/Mgr IT Services ... Scott PETERSON
101 Secy/Treasurer Board of Directors ... Charles PALMER
06 Registrar ... June PETERSON
08 Librarian ... Brandy ROSCOE
76 Medical Assisting Program Coord ... Celina CHASTAIN
07 Admissions Rep ... Jennifer ROGERS
07 Admissions Rep ... Stephanie GARRETT
37 Financial Aid Clerk ... Sharon ALEWINE

Francis Marion University (H)

PO Box 100547, Florence SC 29501-0547
County: Florence FICE Identification: 009226
Unit ID: 218061
Telephone: (843) 661-1362 Carnegie Class: Masters/S
FAX Number: (843) 661-1202 Calendar System: Semester
URL: www.fmarion.edu
Established: 1970 Annual Undergrad Tuition & Fees (In-State): $10,428
Enrollment: 3,947 Coed
Affiliation or Control: State IRS Status: Exempt
Highest Offering: Master's
Accreditation: SC, #ARCPA, ART, CAEPN, NUR, THEA

01 President ... Dr. Luther F. CARTER
05 Provost/Dean Col of Liberal Arts ... Dr. Peter D. KING
10 Vice President Business Affairs ... Mr. John J. KISPERT
11 Vice President Administration ... Dr. Charlene WAGES
30 Vice President Devel/Exec Dir ... Mr. Darryl BRIDGES
26 VP Public & Community Affairs ... Mr. Tucker MITCHELL
32 Vice President for Student Affairs ... Mrs. Teresa RAMEY
41 Athletic Director ... Mr. Murray G. HARTZLER
20 Assoc Provost For Academic Affairs ... Dr. Christopher KENNEDY
84 Assoc Provost of Enrollment Mgmt ... Dr. Alissa WARTERS
121 Assoc Provost for Advising ... Dr. Jennifer KUNKA
21 Asst Vice Pres for Accounting ... Mrs. Cathy SWARTZ
88 Asst Vice Pres Financial Services ... Mr. Thomas WELCH
50 Dean School of Business ... Dr. Hari K. RAJAGOPALAN
53 Dean School of Education ... Dr. Shirley BAUSMITH
76 Dean School of Health Sciences .. Dr. Ruth A. WITTMANN-PRICE
08 Dean of the Library ... Mrs. Joyce M. DURANT
37 Financial Assistance Director ... Ms. Kimberly M. ELLISOR
06 Registrar ... Ms. Dollie NEWHOUSE
38 Director Counseling and Testing ... Dr. Rebecca L. LAWSON
18 Director of Facilities Management ... Mr. Ralph U. DAVIS
36 Director Career Development ... Dr. Ronald E. MILLER, JR.
07 Director of Admissions ... Mrs. Perry T. WILSON
35 Asst Dean of Students ... Ms. R. Daphne CARTER
29 Director of Alumni Affairs ... Mr. Julian M. YOUNG
96 Director of Purchasing ... Mr. Eric L. GARRIS
92 Director of Honors Program ... Dr. Jon W. TUTTLE
13 Chief Information Officer ... Mr. John DIXON
04 Administrative Asst to President ... Mrs. Kim DAVIS
105 Media Production/Web Design Coord ... Mr. Larry B. FALCK
19 Chief of Campus Police ... Mr. Donald R. TARBELL
39 Director Student Housing ... Mrs. Cheryl R. TUTTLE
43 Dir Legal Services/General Counsel ... Mr. Jonathan P. EDWARDS

Furman University (I)

3300 Poinsett Highway, Greenville SC 29613-0001
County: Greenville FICE Identification: 003434
Unit ID: 218070
Telephone: (864) 294-2000 Carnegie Class: Bac-A&S
FAX Number: (864) 294-3001 Calendar System: Semester
URL: www.furman.edu
Established: 1826 Annual Undergrad Tuition & Fees: $47,164
Enrollment: 2,884 Coed
Affiliation or Control: Independent Non-Profit IRS Status: 501(c)3
Highest Offering: Master's
Accreditation: SC, CAEPN, MUS

01 President ... Dr. Elizabeth DAVIS
05 VP Academic Affairs & Provost ... Dr. George S. SHIELDS
10 VP for Finance & Administration ... Ms. Mary Lou MERKT
07 Vice President for Enrollment ... Dr. Michael HENDRICKS
32 Vice President for Student Life ... Ms. Connie L. CARSON
30 Vice President for Development ... Mr. Michael D. GATCHELL
26 VP University Communications ... Mr. Tom EVELYN
20 Int Dean of Faculty ... Dr. Ken PETERSON
20 Associate Academic Dean ... Dr. Beth PONTARI
06 University Registrar ... Mr. Brad E. BARRON
58 Director Graduate Studies ... Dr. Troy M. TERRY
08 Director Libraries ... Dr. Janis M. BANDELIN
19 Chief of Police ... Mr. Tom SACCENTI
108 Asst Vice President Assessment ... Dr. David EUBANKS
09 Director Inst Assessment & Research ... Ms. Chris GOFORTH
37 Assoc Vice Pres of Financial Aid ... Dr. Forrest M. STUART
29 Director of Alumni Association ... Mr. Mike WILSON
07 Assoc Vice President of Admissions ... Mr. Brad POCHARD
44 Director of Annual Giving ... Mr. John KEMP
112 Director of Planned Giving ... Mr. Steve PERRY
25 Grants Administrator ... Ms. Judith J. ROMANO
94 Dir Women's/Gender/Sexuality Study ... Dr. Karni BHATI
15 Asst VP Human Resources/AAO ... Mr. Robert BIERLY
13 Chief Information Officer ... Mr. David STEINOUR
36 Director Career Services ... Dr. John D. BARKER
109 Auxiliary Services Director ... Ms. Rebecca VUKSTA
18 Asst VP for Facilities Services ... Mr. Jeff P. REDDERSON
51 Director Continuing Education ... Dr. Brad BECHTOLD
41 Director of Athletics ... Mr. Mike BUDDIE
46 Director UG Research ... Dr. Eric CHING
88 Director CTL ... Dr. Min-Ken LIAO
17 Director Student Health Services ... Dr. Jill GOLDEN
38 Director Counseling Center ... Dr. Laura CREEL
39 Director University Housing ... Mr. Ronald C. THOMPSON
88 Director Accessibility Resources ... Ms. Judy BAGLEY
42 Chaplain ... Dr. Vaughn CROWETIPTON
40 Director Bookstore ... Ms. K. C ROBINSON
04 Assistant to President ... Ms. Cindy ALEXANDER
114 Assoc VP Finance Budget Director ... Ms. Amy BLACKWELL
96 Director of Purchasing ... Mr. Clay WOODY
35 Director Student Activities ... Ms. Jessica BERKEY
104 Director Study Abroad ... Ms. Nancy GEORGIEV
43 Dir Legal Services/General Counsel ... Vacant

Golf Academy of America (J)

1900 Mr. Joe White Ave., Myrtle Beach SC 29577
Telephone: (800) 342-7342 Identification: 666490
Accreditation: ACICS

† Branch campus of Virginia College, Birmingham, AL.

Greenville Technical College (K)

PO Box 5616, Greenville SC 29606-5616
County: Greenville FICE Identification: 003991
Unit ID: 218113
Telephone: (864) 250-8000 Carnegie Class: Assoc/HVT-High Trad
FAX Number: (864) 250-8507 Calendar System: Semester
URL: www.gvltec.edu
Established: 1962 Annual Undergrad Tuition & Fees (In-State): $4,326
Enrollment: 12,280 Coed
Affiliation or Control: State IRS Status: 501(c)3
Highest Offering: Associate Degree
Accreditation: SC, ACBSP, ACFEI, ADNUR, CAHIIM, COARC, DA, DH, DMS, EMT, ENGT, MAC, MLTAD, OTA, PTAA, RAD, SURGT

01 President ... Dr. Keith MILLER
05 Vice President for Academic Affairs ... Dr. Lenna YOUNG
10 Vice President for Finance ... Mrs. Jacqueline R. DIMAGGIO
32 Vice President Student Services ... Dr. Matteel JONES
51 VP Econ Dev/Corp Training ... Dr. Jermaine WHIRL
45 VP Institutional Effectiveness ... Mrs. Lauren SIMER
04 Administrative Asst to President ... Ms. Rita SNYDER
06 Registrar ... Ms. Mamie BOYD
07 Director Enrollment Services ... Ms. Tanisha LATIMER
15 AVP Human Resources ... Ms. Susan M. JONES
18 Director Facilities ... Mr. Scott WILBANKS
19 Chief of Police ... Mr. Terence BROOKS
25 Director Research and Grants ... Ms. Elizabeth VARGA
26 Director Marketing/Communications ... Mr. Joshua FRIESEN
28 AVP Executive Affairs ... Ms. Wendy WALDEN
111 VP for Advancement ... Ms. Ann WRIGHT
37 Director Financial Aid ... Mr. Jeff DENNIS
50 Dean Business and Technology ... Ms. Michelle E. BYRD

Horry-Georgetown Technical College (L)

2050 Highway 501 E, Conway SC 29526-9521
County: Horry FICE Identification: 004925
Unit ID: 218140
Telephone: (843) 347-3186 Carnegie Class: Assoc/MT-VT-High Trad
FAX Number: (843) 347-4207 Calendar System: Semester
URL: www.hgtc.edu
Established: 1966 Annual Undergrad Tuition & Fees (In-District): $4,978
Enrollment: 7,097 Coed
Affiliation or Control: State/Local IRS Status: 501(c)3
Highest Offering: Associate Degree
Accreditation: SC, ACBSP, ACFEI, ADNUR, #COARC, DA, DH, DMS, EMT, PNUR, PTAA, RAD, SURGT

01 President ... Dr. Marilyn J. FORE
05 VP Academic Affairs ... Dr. Jennifer WILBANKS

10 Vice President for Business/Finance .... Mr. Harold HAWLEY
13 Vice Pres of Technology .... Mr. John DOVE
103 VP Wrkfc Dev/Prov GS/Georgetwn Camp . Mr. Gregory MITCHELL
84 Registrar .... Mrs. Heather HOPPE
32 Asc VP Student Affs/Campus Life .... Dr. Melissa BATTEN
20 AVP for Institutional Support .... Dr. Becky BOONE
20 AVP Acad Affs/Den Univ Transf & Bus .....Mrs. Candace HOWELL
20 AVP Acad Affs/Dn of Health Sciences .... Dr. Christy BAILEY
15 Assoc VP Human Res/Employee Rels ... Mrs. Jacquelyne SNYDER
08 AVP for Library & Learning Supp Svc .... Ms. Peggy SAYLOR
21 AVP/Controller .... Ms. Ellen BLACK
84 AVP Student Enrollment Services .... Ms. Cynthia JOHNSTON
18 Superintendent Buildings & Grounds .... Mr. Kevin BROWN
37 Dir of Financial Aid/Veterans Affs .... Ms. Susan THOMPSON
36 Career Resource Ctr Coordinator .... Ms. April GARNER
09 AVP Inst Planning/Research/Grant .... Ms. Lori HEAFNER
96 Procurement Manager .... Ms. Dianna CECALA
105 Web Services Coordinator .... Ms. Melissa MONOLO
19 Director Security/Safety .... Mr. Barry MARSH
106 Director of Distance Learning .... Mr. Daniel HOPPE

Lander University (A)

320 Stanley Avenue, Greenwood SC 29649-2099
County: Greenwood FICE Identification: 003435
Unit ID: 218229
Telephone: (864) 388-8000 Carnegie Class: Bac-Diverse
FAX Number: (864) 388-8890 Calendar System: Semester
URL: www.lander.edu
Established: 1872 Annual Undergrad Tuition & Fees (In-State): $11,200
Enrollment: 2,701 Coed
Affiliation or Control: State IRS Status: 501(c)3
Highest Offering: Master's
Accreditation: SC, ART, CAEPN, MACTE, MUS, NURSE

01 President .... Dr. Richard E. COSENTINO
05 Provost/Vice Pres Academic Affairs .... Dr. Suzanne OZMENT
10 Vice Pres Business/Administration .... Mr. Greg LOVINS
32 Vice President for Student Affairs ...... Mr. H. Randall BOUKNIGHT
111 Vice President for Univ Advancement .... Ms. Kim ENGLISH
86 VP for Governmental Relations .... Mr. Adam TAYLOR
84 VP for Enrollment & Access Mgmt .... Mr. Andy BENOIT
08 Librarian .... Ms. Lisa WIECKI
38 Director Counseling .... Ms. Debra J. FRANKS
41 Vice President/Athletic Director .... Mr. Brian REESE
15 Director Human Resources .... Ms. Jeannie MCCALLUM
19 Director University Police .... Mr. Eddie BRIGGS
26 Director of Public Information .... Mrs. Megan PRICE
37 Director of Financial Aid .... Mr. Fred HARDIN
36 Director of Career Services .... Mrs. Amanda MORGAN
21 Controller .... Mr. Tom COVAR
40 Dir Bookstore/Procurement/Print Svc .... Mrs. Mary W. MCDANIEL
13 Dir Office Info Tech Services .... Ms. Robin P. LAWRENCE
07 Director of Admissions .... Ms. Jennifer M. MATHIS
18 Director Physical Plant/Engr Svcs .... Mr. Jeff S. BEAVER
06 Registrar .... Ms. Kelly PROCTOR
29 Director Alumni Relations .... Vacant
09 Director of Institutional Research .... Mr. Mac KIRKPATRICK

Limestone College (B)

1115 College Drive, Gaffney SC 29340-3799
County: Cherokee FICE Identification: 003436
Unit ID: 218238
Telephone: (864) 489-7151 Carnegie Class: Bac-Diverse
FAX Number: (864) 487-8706 Calendar System: Semester
URL: www.limestone.edu
Established: 1845 Annual Undergrad Tuition & Fees: $23,900
Enrollment: 3,139 Coed
Affiliation or Control: Independent Non-Profit IRS Status: 501(c)3
Highest Offering: Master's
Accreditation: SC, ACBSP, CAATE, CAEPN, MUS, SW

01 President .... Dr. Walt R. GRIFFIN
05 Exec Vice Pres/VP Academic Affairs .... Dr. Karen W. GAINEY
10 Vice President Financial Affairs .... Mr. L. Wayde DAWSON
30 VP Institutional Advancement .... Ms. Kelly T. CURTIS
84 Vice President Enrollment Services . Mr. Christopher N. PHENICIE
32 Vice President Student Services .... Mr. Robert A. OVERTON
13 Vice Pres Information Technology .... Mr. C. R. HORTON
41 Vice Pres Intercollegiate Athletics .... Mr. Michael H. CERINO
14 Assoc VP Information Technology .... Vacant
20 Assoc Vice Pres Academic Affairs .... Dr. Mark A. REGER
45 Assoc Vice Pres Planning/Assessment ......Dr. Bonnie M. WRIGHT
88 Dean Academic Support .... Vacant
106 Dean Extended Campus Program .... Dr. Mark A. REGER
04 Administrative Asst to President .... Mrs. Nani Lou S. COOPER
56 Dir Extended Campus Classroom Pgm ... Mrs. Donna P. HUDSON
06 Registrar .... Ms. Pennie D. HUGHES
37 Director Financial Aid .... Mr. Bobby T. GREER
44 Director Development .... Vacant
08 Director Library .... Ms. Lizah ISMAIL
26 Director Communications .... Mr. Charles W. WYATT
35 Director Student Services .... Ms. Jessica D. GOINS
36 Director Career Services .... Ms. Ileka L. LEAKS
90 Director Server Services .... Dr. Scott D. BERRY
18 Director Physical Plant .... Mr. Logan RICHARDSON
92 Director Academic Honors Program .... Ms. Carol R. TAYLOR
83 Assoc Dean/Director Social Work .... Mr. Jackie A. PUCKETT
19 Interim Chief Campus Security .... Mr. Howard M. COOK
21 Controller .... Ms. Iuliana A. WATSON
23 Campus Nurse .... Mrs. Sandy B. GREEN
44 Director Advancement Services .... Mrs. Brandi P. HARTMAN

20 Director Academic Advising .... Ms. Pennie D. HUGHES
29 Director Development & Alumni .... Ms. Candace R. WATERS
88 Dir Christian Ed/Leadership Program ......Rev. J. Ron SINGLETON
109 Director Food Services .... Mr. Joe FIELDS
42 College Chaplain ....Rev. J. Ron SINGLETON
88 Dir Accessibility Services/PALS .... Ms. Andrea L. ALLISON
15 Dir Human Resources/AAEEO Officer ......Ms. Brenda F. WATKINS
50 Director MBA Program .... Mr. Shannon B. CREIGHTON
88 Sr Assoc Athletics Dir Compliance .... Mr. Dennis L. BLOOMER
88 Asst Athletics Dir Media Relations .... Mr. Ernest G. MEYERS
88 Asst Athletics Dir Sports Perform .... Mr. Curtis S. LAMB
88 Assoc Dir Athletic Facilities .... Vacant
88 Assoc Athletics Dir External Rels .... Mr. C. Mike SMITH
88 Assc Dir Extend Campus Internet Pgm ....Mrs. Katie P. JONES
105 Dir Extended Campus Internet Pgm .... Vacant
07 Director Admissions .... Mr. Travis W. MCDOWELL
40 Campus Store Manager .... Mrs. Patti H. MCCRAW
38 College Counselor .... Mrs. Mary B. CAMPBELL
107 Chair Div Professional Studies .... Dr. Paul R. LEFRANCOIS
65 Chair Div Natural Sciences .... Mr. Brian F. AMELING
49 Chair Div Arts & Letters .... Dr. Gena E. POOVEY
83 Chair Div Social & Behav Sciences .... Dr. Betsy A. WITT
53 Chair Div Educ/Phys Ed/Teacher Educ ....Dr. Shelly A. MEYERS

Medical University of South Carolina (C)

179 Ashley Avenue, Charleston SC 29425
County: Charleston FICE Identification: 003438
Unit ID: 218335
Telephone: (843) 792-2300 Carnegie Class: Spec-4-yr-Med
FAX Number: N/A Calendar System: Semester
URL: www.musc.edu
Established: 1824 Annual Undergrad Tuition & Fees (In-State): N/A
Enrollment: 2,992 Coed
Affiliation or Control: State IRS Status: Exempt
Highest Offering: Doctorate
Accreditation: SC, ANEST, ARCPA, DENT, DIETI, HSA, HT, IPSY, MED, NURSE, OT, PERF, PHAR, PTA

01 President .... Dr. David J. COLE
100 Chief of Staff .... Dr. Sabra C. SLAUGHTER
05 EVP Academic Affairs & Provost .... Dr. Lisa SALADIN
17 Dean Col of Medicine .... Dr. Raymond DUBOIS
10 Exec Vice President Finance & Admin .... Ms. Lisa P. MONTGOMERY
30 Vice President Development .... Mr. Jim J. FISHER
17 VP Clinical Operations .... Dr. Patrick J. CAWLEY
13 VP Information Technology/CIO .... Mr. Michael P. CAPUTO
20 Assoc Prov Education/Student Life .... Dr. Darlene L. SHAW
46 VP Research .... Dr. Kathleen T. BRADY
108 Assoc Provost Institutional Effectv .... Dr. Suzanne THOMAS
52 Interim Dean of Dental Medicine .... Dr. Patricia L. BLANTON
76 Interim Dean of Health Professions .... Dr. James ZOLLER
58 Dean of Graduate Studies .... Dr. Paula TRAKTMAN
66 Dean of Nursing .... Dr. Gail W. STUART
67 Int Campus Dean SC Col of Pharmacy .... Dr. Philip D. HALL
08 Director of Libraries .... Ms. Shannon JONES
84 Director Enrollment Management .... Mr. George W. OHLANDT
28 Director Student Programs .... Mr. Kevin SMUNIEWSKI
43 General Counsel .... Ms. Annette R. DRACHMAN
26 Chief Communication & Marketing Ofc ...... Ms. Sheila CHAMPLIN
22 Dir Affirm Act/Equal Opportunity ..... Mr. Michael VANDERHURST
07 Director of Admissions .... Ms. Lyla HUDSON
18 Chief Facilities/Physical Plant .... Mr. Greg WEIGLE
06 Registrar .... Ms. Melissa A. FREELAND
15 Director Personnel Services .... Ms. Susan H. CARULLO
45 Dir Integrated Planning & Space Mgm .... Dr. Andrew GELASCO
38 Director Student Counseling .... Dr. Alice Q. LIBET
29 Director Alumni Affairs .... Ms. Sallie HUTTON SISTARE
37 Director Student Financial Aid .... Mr. Joseph M. DURANT
96 Director of Purchasing .... Ms. Velma STAMP

† Tuition varies by degree program.

Midlands Technical College (D)

PO Box 2408, Columbia SC 29202-2408
County: Richland FICE Identification: 003993
Unit ID: 218353
Telephone: (803) 738-8324 Carnegie Class: Assoc/MT-VT-High Trad
FAX Number: (803) 738-7784 Calendar System: Semester
URL: www.midlandstech.edu
Established: 1974 Annual Undergrad Tuition & Fees (In-District): $4,064
Enrollment: 10,946 Coed
Affiliation or Control: State/Local IRS Status: 501(c)3
Highest Offering: Associate Degree
Accreditation: SC, ACBSP, ADNUR, CAHIIM, COARC, DA, DH, ENGT, MAC, MLTAD, NMT, PNUR, PTAA, RAD, SURGT

01 President .... Dr. Ronald RHAMES
05 Vice President Academic Affairs .... Dr. Ronald DRAYTON
10 Vice President for Business Affairs .... Mrs. Debbie WALKER
32 Vice Pres Student Development Svcs .... Ms. Sandra OLIVER
30 VP for Institutional Support .... Ms. Starnell BATES
51 VP Corporate/Continuing Educ/Comm .... Dr. Barrie KIRK
43 General Counsel .... Ms. Crystal ROOKARD
102 Associate VP of Foundation .... Mr. Jack HOEKSTRA
06 Registrar .... Ms. Carla KAISER
13 Director Information Resource Mgmt .... Mr. Tony HOUGH
37 Director of Student Financial Aid .... Mrs. Angela WILLIAMS
84 Director of Enrollment Services .... Ms. Sylvia LITTLEJOHN

26 Director of Public Affairs .... Ms. Ann POULOS
15 Human Resource Director .... Ms. Faye GOWANS
07 Director of Admissions .... Mr. Derrah CASSIDY

Miller-Motte Technical College (E)

2451 Highway 501 East, Conway SC 29526
Telephone: (843) 591-1101 Identification: 770778
Accreditation: ACICS, MAC

† Branch campus of Miller-Motte Technical College, Lynchburg, VA

Miller-Motte Technical College (F)

8085 Rivers Avenue, Suite E, North Charleston SC 29406
Telephone: (843) 574-0101 Identification: 666256
Accreditation: ACICS, MAC, SURGT

† Branch campus of Miller-Motte Technical College, Clarksville, TN.

Morris College (G)

100 W College Street, Sumter SC 29150-3599
County: Sumter FICE Identification: 003439
Unit ID: 218399
Telephone: (803) 934-3200 Carnegie Class: Bac-Diverse
FAX Number: (803) 773-3687 Calendar System: Semester
URL: www.morris.edu
Established: 1908 Annual Undergrad Tuition & Fees: $13,045
Enrollment: 774 Coed
Affiliation or Control: Baptist IRS Status: 501(c)3
Highest Offering: Baccalaureate
Accreditation: SC, ACBSP, CAEPN

01 Interim President .... Dr. Leroy STAGGERS
125 President Emeritus .... Dr. Luns C. RICHARDSON
05 Academic Dean .... Dr. Leroy STAGGERS
10 Director of Business Affairs .... Mr. Robert EAVES
45 Dir Planning/Govt Relations/IR .... Ms. Dorothy S. CHEAGLE
32 Dean Student Affairs .... Dr. Juana DAVIS-FREEMAN
15 Dir Business Supp Svcs/Personnel .... Mr. Roy GRAHAM
111 Director Inst Advanc/Church Rels .... Rev. Melvin MACK
42 College Minister .... Dr. Charles M. PEE
07 Dir Admissions & Records/Registrar ... Ms. Deborah C. CALHOUN
37 Director of Financial Aid .... Mrs. Sandra S. GIBSON
108 Director of Assessment .... Dr. Lewis P. GRAHAM, JR.
13 Director MIS/Computer Center .... Vacant
21 Chief Accountant .... Mrs. Bernice IRBY
29 Director Alumni Affairs .... Mrs. Altoya A. FELDER-DEAS
26 Director Public Relations .... Ms. Anika V. COBB
88 Director Learning Resources Ctr .... Ms. Janet S. CLAYTON
08 Head Librarian .... Ms. Margaret N. MUKOOZA
36 Director Career Services Center .. Dr. Gloria SEABROOK WRIGHT
20 Dir Academic Administrative Svcs .... Dr. Kay M. RHOADS
38 Director Counseling .... Dr. Quanda D. SIMS
39 Director Residential Life .... Mrs. Venessa F. JEFFERSON
41 Director of Athletics .... Mr. Clarence M. HOUCK
23 Director of Health Services .... Mrs. Johnell ROGERS
89 Director of Freshmen Studies .... Dr. Lynette RICHARDSON
40 Bookstore Manager .... Ms. Jeanette MOSES-HOLMES
35 Coordinator Student Activities .... Mr. Alston FREEMAN
19 Coordinator Campus Safety Services .... Ms. Lucille W. WILLIAMS

Newberry College (H)

2100 College, Newberry SC 29108-2126
County: Newberry FICE Identification: 003440
Unit ID: 218414
Telephone: (800) 845-4955 Carnegie Class: Bac-Diverse
FAX Number: (803) 321-5627 Calendar System: Semester
URL: www.newberry.edu
Established: 1856 Annual Undergrad Tuition & Fees: $25,600
Enrollment: 1,064 Coed
Affiliation or Control: Evangelical Lutheran Church In America
IRS Status: 501(c)3
Highest Offering: Baccalaureate
Accreditation: SC, CAEPN, MUS, NURSE

01 President .... Dr. Maurice W. SCHERRENS
05 VP Academic Affairs & Dean .... Dr. Timothy G. ELSTON
10 VP for Admin Affairs & CFO .... Ms. Kathy WORSTER
111 VP for Institutional Advancement .... Mr. Scott JOYNER
84 Dean of Enrollment Management .... Mr. Joel VANDER HORST
32 Dean of Student Affairs .... Dr. Sandra ROUSE
41 Director of Athletics .... Mr. Ralph PATTERSON
15 Director of Human Resources .... Mrs. Peggy SHULER
09 VP for Institutional Effectiveness .... Dr. Sid PARRISH
06 Registrar .... Mrs. Carol A. BICKLEY
29 Assoc Dir of Alumni Relations .... Mr. Jeff WICKER
08 Librarian .... Ms. Nancy ROSENWALD
18 Director of Facilities .... Mr. Fred ERRIGO
42 Chaplain .... Rev. Ernie WORMAN
21 Director of Accounting .... Mrs. Landee BUZHARDT
38 Dir Health & Counselling Services .... Mrs. Martha DORRELL
37 Assoc Dir of Financial Aid .... Ms. Danielle BELL
26 Director of Marketing & PR .... Ms. Jill JOHNSON
19 Director Security/Safety .... Mr. Paul WHITMAN
37 Interim Dir of Financial Aid .... Ms. Holly WOOD

North Greenville University (I)

PO Box 1892, Tigerville SC 29688-1892
County: Greenville FICE Identification: 003441
Unit ID: 218441

Telephone: (864) 977-7000 Carnegie Class: Masters/S
FAX Number: (864) 977-7021 Calendar System: Semester
URL: www.ngu.edu
Established: 1892 Annual Undergrad Tuition & Fees: $17,594
Enrollment: 2,689 Coed
Affiliation or Control: Southern Baptist IRS Status: 501(c)3
Highest Offering: Doctorate
Accreditation: SC, #ARCPA, CAEPN, MUS

01 President/CEO .... Dr. Gene C. FANT, JR.
04 Admin Assistant for President .... Ms. Angie WATSON
05 Vice President Academics .... Dr. Randall PANNELL
32 Vice President Student Services .... Dr. Tony BEAM
20 Asst VP Acads/Dean Communication .... Dr. Linwood HAGIN
10 Vice President Business Affairs .... Ms. Michelle L. SABOU
07 VP Enrollment Services .... Ms. Keli SEWELL
111 Vice President Advancement .... Vacant
88 Exec Dir of Church Relations .... Rev. Mayson EASTERLING
42 Vice President Campus Ministries .... Dr. Steve CROUSE
102 Director of Foundation Giving .... Dr. Phil GARDNER
35 Asst VP for Student Services .... Mr. Billy WATSON
09 Director of Institutional Research .... Dr. George A. HOPSON, JR.
06 Registrar .... Ms. Pam FARMER
18 Asst VP Campus Enhancement Service .... Mr. Mick DANIEL
41 Athletic Director .... Ms. Jan MCDONALD
34 Director Residential Living Women .... Ms. Lorry GREEN
33 Director Residential Living Men .... Mr. Dillon KEY
08 Director of Hester Library .... Ms. Carla MCMAHAN
19 Director Campus Security .... Mr. Rick MORRIS
58 AVP of Graduate Studies .... Dr. Tawana SCOTT
26 Director of Communications .... Mr. LaVerne B. HOWELL
29 Dir Alumni Affairs/Planned Giving .... Mrs. Julie STYLES
15 Human Resource Manager .... Mrs. Beth HOUCK
40 Bookstore Manager .... Mrs. Cindy COWAN
38 Personal Counselor Men .... Mr. Steve BIELBY
38 Personal Counselor Women .... Vacant
36 Career Services Coordinator .... Mr. Stuart FLOYD
23 Director Health Services .... Vacant
44 Director of Corporate Giving .... Mr. Jason ROSS
13 Asst VP Information Tech Services .... Mr. Paul GARRETT
37 Director Financial Planning .... Mrs. Brenda BURNEY
53 Dean Education .... Dr. Constance WRIGHT
79 Dean Humanities .... Dr. H. Paul THOMPSON
57 Dean Fine Arts .... Dr. Jacquelyn H. GRIFFIN
81 Dean Science & Mathematics .... Dr. Tom ALLEN
73 Dean Christian Studies .... Dr. Walter JOHNSON
50 Dean Business & Sport Professions .... Dr. Ralph JOHNSON
106 Asst VP for Online Education .... Dr. Lena MASLENNIKOVA

Northeastern Technical College (A)

1201 Chesterfield Hwy, Cheraw SC 29520
County: Chesterfield FICE Identification: 007602
Unit ID: 217837
Telephone: (843) 921-6900 Carnegie Class: Assoc/HVT-High Trad
FAX Number: (843) 537-6148 Calendar System: Semester
URL: www.netc.edu
Established: 1969 Annual Undergrad Tuition & Fees (In-State): $4,090
Enrollment: 1,054 Coed
Affiliation or Control: State IRS Status: 501(c)3
Highest Offering: Associate Degree
Accreditation: SC

01 President .... Dr. Kyle WAGNER
05 Vice Pres Instruction/Student Svcs .... Mr. Heath MILLIGAN
10 Vice Pres Administration & Finance .... Mrs. Debbie Q. CHEEK
30 Director for Inst Advancement .... Mrs. Erin FANN
15 Director for Human Resources .... Mrs. Donna CHAVIS
06 Coordinator for Student Records .... Ms. Anne JONES
26 Coordinator for Public Relations .... Ms. Shannon JUSTICE
84 Director of Enrollment Services .... Mr. Darin COLEMAN
08 Head Librarian .... Mrs. Kulcey STAFFORD
09 Director of Institutional Research .... Vacant

Orangeburg-Calhoun Technical College (B)

3250 Saint Matthews Road, Orangeburg SC 29118-8299
County: Orangeburg FICE Identification: 006815
Unit ID: 218487
Telephone: (803) 536-0311 Carnegie Class: Assoc/HVT-High Trad
FAX Number: (803) 535-1388 Calendar System: Semester
URL: www.octech.edu
Established: 1966 Annual Undergrad Tuition & Fees (In-State): $4,130
Enrollment: 2,774 Coed
Affiliation or Control: State IRS Status: 501(c)3
Highest Offering: Associate Degree
Accreditation: SC, ACBSP, ADNUR, COARC, ENGT, MAC, PNUR, PTAA, RAD

01 President .... Dr. Walt TOBIN, JR.
05 Vice Pres Academic Affairs .... Mrs. Donna ELMORE
10 Vice President Business Affairs .... Mr. Kim HUFF
32 Vice President of Student Services .... Mrs. Sandra S. DAVIS
11 Dean of Administration .... Mr. Mike HAMMOND
36 Training/Econ Development Director .... Mrs. Sandra MOORE
06 Registrar .... Ms. Amy OTT
30 Dean Development/Marketing .... Ms. Faith MCCURRY
46 Dean Planning/Research/Development .... Ms. Faith MCCURRY
13 Director Information Technology .... Mr. John MCCASKILL
08 Dean Learning Resource Ctr/Library .... Mr. Haley HALL
18 Physical Plant Director .... Mr. James S. BRYANT, III
37 Director Student Financial Aid .... Ms. Bichevia GREEN

07 Director of Admissions .... Vacant
19 Chief of Safety/Security .... Mr. Douglas STOKES
09 Dir Acad Support/Inst Effectiveness .... Mr. Cleveland WILSON
15 Human Resource Director .... Ms. Marie HOWELL
96 Procurement Manager .... Mrs. Scarlet GEDDINGS
84 Enrollment/Records Mgmt Specialist .... Ms. Phyllis STOUDENMIRE

Piedmont Technical College (C)

620 N. Emerald Road, Greenwood SC 29646
County: Greenwood FICE Identification: 003992
Unit ID: 218520
Telephone: (864) 941-8324 Carnegie Class: Assoc/HVT-High Trad
FAX Number: (864) 941-8555 Calendar System: Semester
URL: www.ptc.edu
Established: 1966 Annual Undergrad Tuition & Fees (In-District): $4,193
Enrollment: 5,216 Coed
Affiliation or Control: State/Local IRS Status: 501(c)3
Highest Offering: Associate Degree
Accreditation: SC, ADNUR, COARC, CVT, ENGT, FUSER, MAC, OTA, RAD, SURGT

01 President .... Dr. L. Rayburn BROOKS
10 Vice Pres Business & Finance .... Ms. K. Paige CHILDS
05 Vice President Academic Affairs .... Dr. Jack BAGWELL
102 Asst VP Development/PTC Foundation .... Ms. Fran K. WILEY
32 Assoc Vice Pres Student Affairs .... Mr. Andy OMUNDSON
51 Assoc Vice Pres Cont Educ/Econ Dev .... Mr. Rusty DENNING
108 Assoc VP Assessment/Compliance .... Ms. Donna FOSTER
84 Assoc VP Enrollment/Communications .... Mr. Joshua BLACK
15 Assoc VP Human Resources .... Ms. Alesia BROWN
12 Dean County Centers .... Dr. Jennifer WILBANKS
76 Dean Health Sciences .... Mr. Jerry ALEWINE
54 Dean Engr/Indust Technologies .... Mr. David KIBLER
66 Dean Nursing .... Ms. Tara HARRIS
35 Dean of Students .... Mr. David R. ROSENBAUM
07 Dean of Admissions .... Ms. Renae FRAZIER
09 Director Institutional Reporting .... Ms. Zeolean F. KINARD
26 Director Marketing/Public Relations .... Mr. Russell MARTIN
88 Director Genesis Initiatives .... Mr. Steve B. COLEMAN
18 Director Facilities Management .... Mr. J. Chad TEAGUE
08 Head Librarian .... Ms. Meredith DANIEL
19 Director Campus Police/Security .... Mr. Terry LEDFORD
37 Director of Financial Aid .... Ms. Missy PERRY
06 Registrar .... Ms. Tamatha SELLS
21 Controller .... Ms. Wendy HUGHES
21 Manager Business Office .... Ms. Crystal PITTMAN

Presbyterian College (D)

503 S Broad Street, Clinton SC 29325-2865
County: Laurens FICE Identification: 003445
Unit ID: 218539
Telephone: (864) 833-2820 Carnegie Class: Bac-A&S
FAX Number: (864) 833-8481 Calendar System: Semester
URL: www.presby.edu
Established: 1880 Annual Undergrad Tuition & Fees: $37,142
Enrollment: 1,379 Coed
Affiliation or Control: Presbyterian Church (U.S.A.) IRS Status: 501(c)3
Highest Offering: Doctorate
Accreditation: SC, CAEPN, MUS, PHAR

01 President .... Mr. Robert E. STATON
101 Executive Asst to the President .... Ms. Christie L. MUELLER
04 Sr Admin Asst to the President .... Mrs. Jenny G. BOGAN
84 Dean of Enrollment Management .... Mr. Brian J. FORTMAN
07 Director of Admissions .... Mr. Mark O. FOX, II
05 Provost .... Dr. Donald R. RABER, II
20 Dean of Academic Programs .... Dr. J. Alicia ASKEW
37 VP for Enrollment & Financial Aid .... Mrs. Suzanne M. PETRUSCH
09 Director of Institutional Research .... Dr. Norman B. BRYAN, JR.
08 Director of Thomason Library .... Mr. David W. CHATHAM
24 Director of Media Services .... Mr. Douglas J. WALLACE
104 Director of International Programs .... Mr. Viet X. HA
85 Asst Dir of International Programs .... Ms. Adriana K. SMITH
06 Registrar & Director of Records .... Ms. Kendra B. WOODSON
67 Dean School of Pharmacy .... Dr. L. Clifton FUHRMAN, JR.
07 Dir of Admissions Pharmacy School .... Ms. Katherine J. KANE
10 VP Finance/Administration .... Ms. Susan A. MADDUX
21 Controller .... Ms. Dawn W. DURHAM
18 Exec Director of Campus Services .... Mr. Michael D. CRISP
37 Director of Financial Aid .... Ms. Linda J. MCANNALLY
13 Director of Information Technology .... Mr. H. William ROACH
90 Academic Computing Services Coord .... Dr. Robert W. HOWILER
91 Desktop Support/Aux Systems Sr Tech .... Ms. Nellie R. SHELTON
109 Manager of Auxiliary Services .... Mr. Jason T. KOENIG
32 VP for Campus Life/Dean of Students .... Dr. Joy S. SMITH
39 Assoc Dean Students/Residence Life .... Mr. Andrew T. PETERSON
36 Assoc Dean Students/Career Dev .... Ms. Kimberly A. LANE
42 Director of Campus Ministries .... Ms. Rachel E. PARSONS-WELLS
19 Director of Safety & Risk Mgmt .... Mr. Lawrence P. MULHALL
38 Director Counseling Services .... Ms. Susan C. GENTRY-WRIGHT
28 Asst Dir of Multicultural Programs .... Ms. Brittney SMITH
111 VP for Advancement .... Vacant
30 Director of College Development .... Mr. Alex K. SCULL
88 Director of Athletic Major Gifts .... Mr. Harold E. NICHOLS, JR.
29 Director Alumni Relations .... Ms. Leni N. PATTERSON
41 Director of Athletics .... Mr. Danny L. STERLING
15 VP of Human Resources .... Ms. Barbara H. FAYAD

Professional Golfers Career College (E)

4454 Bluffton Pk Crescent, Ste 200, Bluffton SC 29910
Telephone: (843) 759-9611 Identification: 770779
Accreditation: ACICS

† Branch campus of Professional Golfers Career College, Temecula, CA

Sherman College of Chiropractic (F)

PO Box 1452, Spartanburg SC 29304-1452
County: Spartanburg FICE Identification: 020637
Unit ID: 218751
Telephone: (864) 578-8770 Carnegie Class: Spec-4-yr-Other Health
FAX Number: (864) 599-4860 Calendar System: Quarter
URL: www.sherman.edu
Established: 1973 Annual Graduate Tuition & Fees: N/A
Enrollment: 391 Coed
Affiliation or Control: Independent Non-Profit IRS Status: 501(c)3
Highest Offering: Doctorate; No Undergraduates
Accreditation: SC, CHIRO

01 President .... Dr. Edwin CORDERO
03 Executive Vice President .... Dr. Neil COHEN
05 Provost .... Dr. Robert IRWIN
20 Vice Pres of Academic Affairs .... Dr. Joseph DONOFRIO
84 Director of Enrollment Services .... Ms. Vicky PEPPIN
10 Vice Pres for Business & Finance .... Mrs. Karen CANUP
32 Dean of Student Affairs .... Mrs. LaShanda HUTTO-HARRIS
29 Dir Alumni Rels/Instl Advancement .... Ms. Marggi ROLDAN
06 Registrar .... Ms. Melody SABIN
08 Librarian .... Mrs. Chandra PLACER
37 Director of Financial Aid .... Ms. Kendra STRANGE
45 Dir Institutional Effectiveness .... Mrs. Crissy LEWIS
04 Admin Asst to President/EVP .... Ms. Roberta THOMAS
26 Director of Public Relations .... Ms. Karen RHODES
09 Director of Institutional Research .... Dr. Pengju George LUO
106 Dir Online Education/E-learning .... Dr. Billie HARRINGTON
15 Director Personnel Services .... Mrs. Mandy SMITH
19 Director Security/Safety .... Mr. Patrick LAUSIER

South Carolina State University (G)

300 College Street, NE, Orangeburg SC 29117-0001
County: Orangeburg FICE Identification: 003446
Unit ID: 218733
Telephone: (803) 536-7000 Carnegie Class: Masters/M
FAX Number: (803) 533-3622 Calendar System: Semester
URL: www.scsu.edu
Established: 1896 Annual Undergrad Tuition & Fees (In-State): $10,420
Enrollment: 3,054 Coed
Affiliation or Control: State IRS Status: 501(c)3
Highest Offering: Doctorate
Accreditation: SC, AAFCS, ART, CACREP, CAEPN, CS, DIETD, ENG, ENGT, MUS, SP, SW

01 President .... Mr. James E. CLARK
04 Exec Asst to the President .... Ms. Shondra F. ABRAHAM
05 Provost .... Dr. Learie B. LUKE
10 Vice Pres for Finance/Mgmt .... Ms. Teare BREWINGTON
32 Vice Pres for Student Affairs .... Dr. Tamara JEFFERIES-JACKSON
111 AVP Institutional Advancement .... Vacant
88 Executive Dir 1890 Programs .... Mr. Delbert T. FOSTER
43 General Counsel .... Ms. Mercedes P. FABERS
20 Acting Associate Provost .... Dr. Matthew GUAH
26 VP External Affairs/Communications .... Vacant
46 Assoc Provost/Sponsored Program .... Mr. Elbert R. MALONE
07 Int Asst Director of Admissions .... Mrs. LaSandra ROBINSON
72 Dean Col Sci/Math/Engineering Tech .... Dr. Stanley N. IHEKWEAZU
53 Dean Col Educ/Humanities/Soc Sci .... Dr. Albert G. HAYWARD
58 Dean Col of Graduate Studies .... Dr. Frederick M G. EVANS
50 Dean School of Business .... Dr. Barbara L. ADAMS
08 Interim Dean Library Services .... Ms. Ruth A. HODGES
124 Dir Student Success Retention .... Mr. Frederick GOLDEN
06 Registrar/Director Veterans Affairs .... Ms. Ann BELTON
07 Asst Dir Admissions/Recruitment .... Vacant
13 Dir Univ Computing/Info Tech Svcs .... Dr. Damian A. CLARKE
37 Director of Financial Aid .... Ms. Tangar YOUNG
38 Director Counseling/Student Dev .... Dr. Cherilyn Y. TAYLOR-MINNIFIELD
21 Controller .... Vacant
27 Director of Public Relations .... Mrs. Elizabeth MOSELY-HAWKINS
36 Int Director of Career Placement .... Mr. Joseph THOMAS
15 Director Human Resource Mgmt .... Mr. Ronald S. YORK
41 Director Athletics .... Mr. Stacy DANLEY
18 Director of Facilities Mgmt .... Mr. Ken DAVIS
96 Director Procurement Services .... Ms. Jessica FAVOR
39 Director of Residential Life .... Ms. Cammy GRATE
19 Chief of Campus Police .... Mr. Joseph B. NELSON
92 Dean Honors College .... Dr. Harriet A. ROLAND
88 Director Sports Information .... Mr. Kendrick D. LEWIS
35 Asst Director of Student Life .... Vacant
25 Dir Grants & Contract .... Ms. Gwendolyn F. MITCHELL
88 Director of Title III .... Ms. Gloria D. PYLES
28 Director of Multicultural Affairs .... Ms. Carolyn G. FREE
88 Station Manager WSSB-FM .... Mr. Carlito D. A'SEE
88 Athletics Compliance Coordinator .... Mr. Eric M. SEIFARTH
101 Secretary/Board of Trustees .... Ms. Eartha J. MOSLEY
104 Dir International/National Exchange .... Dr. Learie B. LUKE
105 Web Services .... Mr. Jason BARR
29 Director Alumni Relations .... Ms. Iva L. GARDNER

South University Columbia Campus (A)

9 Science Court, Columbia SC 29203-6400
Telephone: (803) 799-9082 FICE Identification: 004922
Accreditation: &SC, ACBSP, CACREP, MAC, NURSE, OT, PHAR, @PTAA

† Regional accreditation is carried under the parent institution in Savannah, GA.

Southern Wesleyan University (B)

907 Wesleyan Drive, PO Box 1020,
Central SC 29630-1020
County: Pickens FICE Identification: 003422
Unit ID: 217776
Telephone: (864) 644-5556 Carnegie Class: Masters/L
FAX Number: N/A Calendar System: Semester
URL: www.swu.edu
Established: 1906 Annual Undergrad Tuition & Fees: $24,110
Enrollment: 1,736 Coed
Affiliation or Control: Wesleyan Church IRS Status: 501(c)3
Highest Offering: Master's
Accreditation: SC, CAEPN, MUS

01 President .... Dr. Todd S. VOSS
05 Provost .... Dr. Tonya STRICKLAND
10 VP for Finance & Auxiliary Services .... Mr. Mark T. REEVES
30 Vice President for Development .... Dr. Lisa MCWHERTER
32 Vice President for Student Life .... Dr. W. Joseph BROCKINTON
84 VP for Enrollment Management .... Mr. Chad PETERS
42 AVP Spiritual Life/Univ Chaplain .... Rev. Ken DILL
18 Director of Physical Plant .... Mr. Jonathan CATRON
13 Director Information Technology .... Mr. Mike PREUSZ
07 Dir of Admissions & Enrollment Mgmt .... Mr. David SLABAUGH
20 Dean of Institutional Effectiveness .... Mr. Robert HUDSON
66 Dean RN to BSN Program .... Dr. Beth FEZIO
49 Dean College of Arts & Sciences .... Dr. Randolph JOHNSON
41 Athletic Director .... Mr. Chris WILLIAMS
50 Dean of the School of Business .... Dr. Stephen PREACHER
53 Dean of the School of Education .... Dr. Sandra MCLENDON
106 Dir Center for Teaching Excellence .... Dr. Ted LONG
37 Director of Financial Aid .... Mrs. Melanie GILLESPIE
15 Director of Human Resources .... Mrs. Dana L. FROST
08 Director of Library Services .... Mrs. Shannon BROOKS
06 Registrar .... Ms. Janice HARTSOE
29 Exec Dir of Alumni/Constituent Rels .... Mrs. Joy L. BRYANT
38 Director Student Counseling .... Ms. Monica PEREZ
04 Administrative Asst to President .... Ms. Amy JARRETT
19 Director Security/Safety .... Mr. Brad BOWEN

Spartanburg Community College (C)

107 Community College Drive, Spartanburg SC 29303
County: Spartanburg FICE Identification: 003994
Unit ID: 218830
Telephone: (864) 592-4600 Carnegie Class: Assoc/HVT-High Trad
FAX Number: (864) 592-4642 Calendar System: Semester
URL: www.sccsc.edu
Established: 1963 Annual Undergrad Tuition & Fees (In-State): $4,300
Enrollment: 4,928 Coed
Affiliation or Control: State IRS Status: 501(c)3
Highest Offering: Associate Degree
Accreditation: SC, ACBSP, ACFEI, ADNUR, COARC, DA, EMT, ENGT, MAC, MLTAD, RAD, SURGT

01 President .... Mr. Henry C. GILES, JR.
05 Sr Vice President Academic Affairs .... Dr. Cheryl COX
10 Vice Pres for Business Affairs .... Mr. Ray SWITZER
111 Exec Dir Advancement/SCC Foundation .... Mrs. Bea SMITH
32 Vice President for Student Affairs .... Mr. Ron JACKSON
84 Assc Vice Pres Enroll Mgt/Retention .... Mrs. Lynn F. DALE
20 Assoc Vice Pres of Instruction .... Mrs. Patricia JONES
51 Exec Asst to Pres/Dir Economic Dev . Mr. Michael P. FORRESTER
12 Executive Director Cherokee Campus .... Mr. Daryl SMITH
12 Exec Director Tyger River Campus .... Dr. Anya SEBASTIEN
12 Exec Director Downtown Campus .... Mrs. Judy SIEG
12 Site Coord Union County Campus .... Mr. Issac MCKISSICK
108 Director Eval/Accreditation/Plng .... Mr. Jay JACKSON
88 Dean of CCE .... Mr. Robert LESLIE
08 Dean of Learning Resources .... Mr. Mark ROSEVEARE
76 Dean Health & Human Services .... Dr. Berta HOPKINS
49 Dean of Arts & Sciences .... Mrs. Kem HARVEY
07 Director of Admissions .... Ms. Alison CANN
15 Director of Human Resources .... Mr. Rick TEAL
13 Director Information Technologies .... Mr. Peter C. GALLEN
09 Director of Institutional Research .... Mr. Jack R. BOURGEOIS
26 Chief Public Relations Officer .... Mrs. Cheri A. HUCKS
29 Alumni Relations Coordinator .... Ms. Kim FOGEL
38 Director Student Counseling .... Vacant
14 Director Computer Center .... Mrs. Tina S. REID
18 Chief Facilities/Physical Plant .... Mr. Gladden SMOKE
19 Director Security/Safety .... Vacant
06 Registrar .... Ms. Celia N. BAUSS
96 Director Purchasing Office .... Mr. Cecil L. HUTCHERSON
21 Director of Finance .... Mr. Reggie BROWNING
37 Director of Financial Aid .... Mr. Jeffery BOYLE
106 Dir Online Education/E-learning .... Mr. Neil GRIFFIN
25 Chief Contracts/Grants Admin .... Mrs. Rebecca PARRISH
54 Dean of Engineering .... Mr. Jeff HUNT
04 Administrative Asst to President .... Ms. Betty HALL
36 Director Student Placement .... Ms. Jennifer LITTLE
90 Director Academic Computing .... Mr. Roy SMITH

Spartanburg Methodist College (D)

1000 Powell Mill Road, Spartanburg SC 29301-5899
County: Spartanburg FICE Identification: 003447
Unit ID: 218821
Telephone: (864) 587-4000 Carnegie Class: Assoc/HT-High Trad
FAX Number: (864) 587-4355 Calendar System: Semester
URL: www.smcsc.edu
Established: 1911 Annual Undergrad Tuition & Fees: $16,700
Enrollment: 771 Coed
Affiliation or Control: United Methodist IRS Status: 501(c)3
Highest Offering: Associate Degree
Accreditation: SC

01 President .... Mr. W. Scott COCHRAN
05 Exec VP Acad Affairs/Student Dev .... Dr. Anita K. BOWLES
10 Executive VP for Business Affairs .... Mr. Eric MCDONALD
30 Vice Pres Institutional Advancement .... Mrs. Jennifer DILLENGER
84 Vice President of Enrollment .... Mr. Wells SHEPARD
26 Vice President for Marketing .... Mrs. Lisa WARE
88 Vice President for Prof Development .... Ms. Courtney SHELTON
32 Dean of Students .... Ms. Teresa FERGUSON
06 Registrar .... Ms. Jill R. JOHNSON
08 Library Director .... Ms. Lori HETRICK
04 Admin Assistant to the President .... Mrs. Cheryl SOMERSET
13 Chief Information Officer .... Mr. Trey ARRINGTON
44 Director of Planned Giving .... Mr. Don TATE
37 Director of Financial Aid .... Mr. Christopher ROBERSON
38 Director of Student Counseling .... Mr. Pete AYLOR
42 Chaplain/Director Church Relations .... Rev. Tim DRUM
41 Director of Athletics .... Mr. Tim WALLACE
18 Director Facilities Management .... Mr. Marty WOODS
29 Director of Alumni Relations .... Mrs. Leah L. PRUITT
15 Exec Director of Human Resources .... Mrs. Jeanette R. DUNN
44 Director of Church Funding .... Rev. Michael E. BOWERS
19 Chief of Campus Safety .... Ms. Teresa D. FERGUSON
09 Director of Assessment Activities .... Mr. Jason WOMICK
39 Director Student Housing .... Ms. Trina WILLIAM

Technical College of the Lowcountry (E)

921 S Ribaut Road, PO Box 1288,
Beaufort SC 29901-1288
County: Beaufort FICE Identification: 009910
Unit ID: 217712
Telephone: (843) 525-8211 Carnegie Class: Assoc/MT-VT-High Trad
FAX Number: (843) 525-8330 Calendar System: Semester
URL: www.tcl.edu
Established: 1969 Annual Undergrad Tuition & Fees (In-State): $4,276
Enrollment: 2,332 Coed
Affiliation or Control: State IRS Status: 501(c)3
Highest Offering: Associate Degree
Accreditation: SC, ACBSP, ADNUR, COMTA, PNUR, PTAA, RAD, SURGT

01 President .... Dr. Richard J. GOUGH
11 Vice Pres Administrative Services .... Mr. Andrew SMITH
05 Vice President for Academic Affairs .... Dr. Gina MOUNFIELD
32 Vice President for Student Affairs .... Ms. Nancy WEBER
35 AVP for Student Affairs .... Mr. Rodney ADAMS
09 Director for Research/Planning .... Ms. Camille MYERS
15 Human Resources Director .... Ms. Sonya LYTTLE
20 Director for Learning Resources .... Ms. Sasha BISHOP
50 Div Dean Business Technologies .... Dr. Kenneth FLICK
49 Div Dean Arts & Sciences .... Dr. Gayle TREMBLE
76 Dean Health Sciences .... Dr. Glenn LEVICKI
13 Director of Information Technology .... Mr. Hayes WISER
37 Director Financial Aid .... Ms. Georgeann WILLIAMS
111 VP for Inst Advancement .... Ms. Mary Lee CARNS
26 AVP for Public Relations .... Ms. Leigh COPELAND
40 Bookstore Director .... Ms. Louise RENNIX
18 Director of Facility Management .... Mr. Larry BECKLER
96 Director of Purchasing .... Ms. Carol MACK
06 Registrar .... Ms. Allison CANNING
36 Career & Transfer Services Manager .... Ms. Melanie GALLION
04 Administrative Asst to President .... Ms. Ann CULLEN

Tri-County Technical College (F)

PO Box 587, Pendleton SC 29670-0587
County: Anderson FICE Identification: 004926
Unit ID: 218885
Telephone: (864) 646-8361 Carnegie Class: Assoc/HT-High Trad
FAX Number: (864) 646-1895 Calendar System: Semester
URL: www.tctc.edu
Established: 1962 Annual Undergrad Tuition & Fees (In-District): $4,050
Enrollment: 6,128 Coed
Affiliation or Control: State/Local IRS Status: 501(c)3
Highest Offering: Associate Degree
Accreditation: SC, ACBSP, ADNUR, DA, MAC, MLTAD, PNUR, SURGT

01 President .... Dr. Ronnie L. BOOTH
05 Senior Vice President .... Mr. Galen DEHAY
10 Vice Pres Business Affairs .... Ms. Cara HAMILTON
102 Executive Director Foundation .... Mr. Grayson KELLY
20 AVP Instruction & Effectiveness .... Vacant
51 Dean of Continuing Education .... Mr. Rick COTHRAN
84 Dean of Transition to College .... Ms. Jenni CREAMER
32 Dean of Student Development .... Mr. Mark DOUGHERTY
49 Dean Arts & Sciences Division .... Vacant
72 Dean Engineering Technology Div .... Ms. Amanda ORZECHOWSKI
50 Dean Business/Human Services Div .... Mrs. Jackie BLAKLEY
76 Dean Health Education Division .... Dr. Cindy LEWIS
37 Student Financial Aid Director .... Mr. Adam GHILONI
13 CIO/Information Technology Dir .... Mr. Matthew EDWARDS
26 Dir Public Relations/Communication .... Mrs. Rebecca W. EIDSON
30 Director of Development .... Mrs. Courtney WHITE
15 Asst VP Human Resources .... Mrs. Sharon COLCOLOUGH
07 Director of Admissions .... Ms. Tiffiny BLACKWELL
06 Registrar .... Mr. Scott HARVEY
09 Director of Institutional Research .... Mr. Chris MARINO
18 Chief Facilities/Physical Plant .... Mr. Ken KOPERA
21 Director of Fiscal Affairs .... Ms. Tracy WACTOR
96 Director of Purchasing .... Ms. Kristal DOHERTY
38 Director of Student Life/Counseling .... Ms. Croslena JOHNSON
25 Chief Contracts/Grants Admin .... Ms. Laneika MUSALINI
86 Dir Econ Dev/Government Relations .... Mr. Dan COOPER

Trident Technical College (G)

PO Box 118067, Charleston SC 29423-8067
County: Charleston FICE Identification: 004920
Unit ID: 218894
Telephone: (843) 574-6111 Carnegie Class: Assoc/MT-VT-High Trad
FAX Number: (843) 574-6541 Calendar System: Semester
URL: www.tridenttech.edu
Established: 1964 Annual Undergrad Tuition & Fees (In-District): $4,155
Enrollment: 15,043 Coed
Affiliation or Control: State/Local IRS Status: 501(c)3
Highest Offering: Associate Degree
Accreditation: SC, ACBSP, ACFEI, ADNUR, COARC, CSHSE, DA, DH, EMT, MAC, MLTAD, OTA, PNUR, PTAA, RAD

01 President .... Dr. Mary THORNLEY
10 Vice Pres Finance & Administration .... Mr. Scott POELKER
05 Vice President Academic Affairs .... Dr. Cathy AMQUIST
32 Vice President Student Services .... Dr. Patrice MITCHELL
111 Vice President Advancement .... Ms. Meg HOWLE
51 Vice Pres Continuing Educ/Econ Dev .... Mr. Robert WALKER
13 Vice Pres Information Technology .... Dr. Patricia ROBERTSON
45 Assoc VP Planning/Accreditation .... Mr. James "Dub" GREEN
20 Asst Vice Pres Academic Programs .... Ms. Susan NORTON
35 Asst Vice Pres for Student Svcs .... Ms. Lynne ANKERSEN
15 Associate VP Human Resources .... Ms. DeVetta HUGHES
96 Dir Procurement/Risk Management .... Ms. Carol BELCHER
109 Dir Auxiliary Enterprises/Bookstore .... Ms. Jloundia PINCKNEY
18 Director Facilities .... Mr. Eric HAMILTON
21 Director Finance .... Ms. Melody TAYLOR
26 Director Marketing .... Ms. Tina AHLEMANN
27 Director Public Info .... Mr. David HANSEN
88 Dean School & Community Initiatives . Ms. Melissa STOWASSER
30 Vice President Development .... Vacant
14 Dir Information Technology Training .... Mr. Joseph GIBSON
124 Dean of Student Engagement .... Mr. Brian ALMQUIST
81 Dean Science & Mathematics .... Mr. Bill LANDRY
79 Dean Humanities & Social Sciences .... Dr. Tim BROWN
88 Dean of The Learning Center .... Mr. David HARRIS
50 AVP Educ Tech/The Online College .... Ms. Connie JOLLY
76 Dean Allied Health Sciences .... Vacant
57 Dean Film Media and Visual Arts .... Vacant
54 Dean Industrial/Engineering Tech .... Ms. Christine LANG
88 Dean Culinary Inst of Charleston .... Mr. Mike SABOE
61 Dean Law-Related Studies .... Ms. Jan UTSEY
66 Dean Nursing .... Ms. Marilyn BRADY
38 Dean Student Development .... Ms. Pamela BROWN
88 Dean Comm/Family/Child Studies .... Ms. Stephany HEWITT
75 Dean Aeronautical Studies .... Dr. Barry FRANCO
12 Dean Berkeley Campus .... Ms. Karen WRIGHTEN
12 Dean Mount Pleasant Campus .... Dr. Darren FELTY
12 Dean Palmer Campus .... Dr. Louester ROBINSON
19 Director Public Safety .... Mr. Lawrence SAVIDGE
06 Registrar .... Vacant
07 Director of Admissions .... Ms. Clara MARTIN
09 Director of Institutional Research .... Ms. Samantha RICHARDS
37 Director Student Financial Aid .... Ms. Charlotte SORG
04 Administrative Asst to President .... Ms. Helen SUGHRUE

University of Phoenix Columbia SC Campus (H)

1001 Pinnacle Point Drive, Columbia SC 29223-5727
Telephone: (803) 699-5096 Identification: 770223
Accreditation: &NH, ACBSP

† No longer accepting campus-based students.

University of South Carolina Columbia (I)

Columbia SC 29208-0001
County: Richland FICE Identification: 003448
Unit ID: 218663
Telephone: (803) 777-7000 Carnegie Class: DU-Highest
FAX Number: (803) 777-0101 Calendar System: Semester
URL: www.sc.edu
Established: 1801 Annual Undergrad Tuition & Fees (In-State): $11,454
Enrollment: 33,724 Coed
Affiliation or Control: State IRS Status: 501(c)3
Highest Offering: Doctorate
Accreditation: SC, ANEST, #ARCPA, ART, CAATE, CACREP, CAEPN, CAHIIM, CEA, CLPSY, CS, DANCE, ENG, HSA, IPSY, JOUR, LAW, LIB, MED, MUS, NURSE, PH, PHAR, PTA, SCPSY, SP, SPAA, SW, THEA

01 President .... Dr. Harris PASTIDES

13 Vice President for IT & CIO ... Mr. Doug FOSTER
88 University Treasurer ... Mr. Patrick LARDNER
116 Exec Dir of Audit & Advisory Svcs ... Ms. Pam DORAN
05 Exec VP Acad Affairs and Provost ... Dr. Joan T. GABEL
05 Deputy Provost ... Dr. Helen DOERPINGHAUS
20 V Prov & Dean for U Grad Studies ... Dr. Sandra KELLY
11 Sr VP for Admininistration & COO ... Mr. Edward I. WALTON
10 CFO & VP for Finance ... Mrs. Leslie G. BRUNELLI
32 V Prov Acad Supp & Dean of Students ... Dr. Dennis A. PRUITT
15 Vice President Human Resources ... Mr. Christopher D. BYRD
30 VP Development & Alumni Relations ... Ms. Jancy HOUCK
46 Vice President for Research ... Dr. Prakash NAGARKATTI
26 Chief Communications Officer ... Mr. Wesley HICKMAN
21 Assoc VP Business Affairs ... Dr. Helen T. ZEIGLER
101 Uni Secretary and Sec to Board ... Mr. Cantey HEATH
58 Sr Vice Prov & Dean Grad Studies ... Dr. Cheryl ADDY
85 Vice Provost & Dir Global Carolina ... Dr. Allen MILLER
84 Asst V Prov Enrl Mgmt & Dean UG Adm ... Mr. Scott VERZYL
63 Exec Dean School of Medicine ... Dr. Les HALL
08 Dean of University Libraries ... Dr. Tom MCNALLY
43 Gen Counsel & Exec Dir Compliance ... Mr. Walter H. PARHAM
09 Exec Dir Inst Rsch/Assess/Analytics ... Ms. Sabrina ANDREWS
18 VP for Facilities & Transportation ... Mr. Derrick E. HUGGINS
19 Assoc VP Law Enfr & Chief of Police ... Mr. Christopher L. WUCHENICH
37 Dir Student Fin Aid & Scholarship ... Mr. Joey DERRICK
36 Director Career Center ... Mr. Thomas HALASZ
06 University Registrar ... Mr. Aaron C. MARTERER
22 Exec Asst to Pres Equal Oppty Pgm ... Mr. Clifford SCOTT
88 NCAA Compliance Coord ... Mr. Christopher ROGERS
07 Director of Admissions ... Dr. Mary WAGNER
39 Director Housing ... Ms. Kristen KENNEDY
23 Exec Director Student Health Svcs ... Dr. Deborah C. BECK
41 Athletic Director ... Mr. Ray TANNER
35 Assoc VP for Student Life ... Mr. Jerry T. BREWER
27 Director News & Internal Relations ... Mr. Wesley T. HICKMAN
96 Director of Purchasing ... Mrs. Venis MANIGO
29 Exec Director Alumni Association ... Mr. Jack CLAYPOOLE
88 VP for System Planning ... Dr. Mary Anne FITZPATRICK
12 Chancellor Palmetto College ... Dr. Susan ELKINS
88 Dean Hospitality/Retail/Sport HMgt ... Dr. Haemoon OH
50 Dean Moore School of Business ... Dr. Peter J. BREWS
53 Dean College of Education ... Dr. Jon E. PEDERSEN
54 Dean Col Engineering & Computing ... Dr. Hossein HAJ-HARIRI
69 Dean Arnold School of Public Health .. Dr. G. Thomas CHANDLER
60 Dean Col of Info & Communications ... Mr. Charles BIERBAUER
61 Dean School of Law ... Dr. Robert M. WILCOX
63 Sr Assoc Dean School of Medicine ... Dr. Caughman TAYLOR
63 Dean Greenville School of Medicine ... Dr. Jerry R. YOUKEY
64 Dean College of Pharmacy ... Dr. Stephen J. CUTLER
49 Dean Col of Arts & Sciences ... Dr. Lacy FORD
64 Dean School of Music ... Dr. Tayloe HARDING, JR.
92 Dean SC Honors College ... Dr. Steve LYNN
66 Dean College of Nursing ... Dr. Jeannette ANDREWS
70 Dean College of Social Work ... Dr. Sarah GEHLERT
92 Dir Fellowships & Scholar Programs ... Ms. Novella BESKID
88 Asst Provost Academic Programs ... Dr. Tena CREWS
88 Executive Director USC Connect ... Dr. Irma J. VANSCOY
28 Chief Diversity Officer ... Mr. John DOZIER
86 Director Govt & Community Relations ... Ms. Shirley D. MILLS
88 Director of Economic Engagement ... Mr. William B. KIRKLAND

University of South Carolina Aiken (A)

471 University Parkway, Aiken SC 29801-6399

County: Aiken — FICE Identification: 003449 — Unit ID: 218645

Telephone: (803) 648-6851 — Carnegie Class: Bac-Diverse

FAX Number: (803) 641-3362 — Calendar System: Semester

URL: www.usca.edu

Established: 1961 — Annual Undergrad Tuition & Fees (In-State): $10,196

Enrollment: 3,448 — Coed

Affiliation or Control: State — IRS Status: 501(c)3

Highest Offering: Master's

Accreditation: SC, CAEPN, MUS, NURSE

01 Chancellor ... Dr. Sandra JORDAN
05 Exec Vice Chanc Academic Affairs ... Dr. Jeff M. PRIEST
111 Vice Chanc Advance & External Rels ... Ms. Mary DRISCOLL
32 Vice Chancellor Student Life & Svcs ... Dr. Deborah KLADIVKO
13 Vice Chancellor Information Tech ... Mr. Ernest PRINGLE
10 VC for Admin and Finance/CFO ... Mr. Cam REAGIN
20 Asst Vice Chanc Academic Affairs ... Dr. Tim LINTNER
84 Assoc Vice Chanc Enrollment Svcs ... Mr. Daniel J. ROBB
79 Col Coord Humanitie & Soc Science ... Vacant
50 Dean School of Business Admin ... Dr. Michael FEKULA
53 Dean of the School of Education ... Dr. Judy BECK
66 Dean of the School of Nursing ... Dr. Thayer MCGAHEE
09 Dir Inst Effect/Research/Compliance ... Dr. Lloyd A. DAWE
08 Library Director ... Rodney LIPPARD
25 Director Sponsored Research ... Dr. Bill PIRKLE
40 Director of Pacer Shoppe ... Ms. Heidi DIFRANCO
109 Dir Campus Auxil & Support Services ... Mr. Jeff JENIK
88 Director Children's Center ... Ms. Lynn WILLIAMS
88 Dir USCA Convocation Center ... Mr. Josh SMALL
12 Exec Dir of Etherredge Center ... Mr. Jack BENJAMIN
21 Controller ... Mr. Kevin CRAWFORD
15 Dir Human Resources & Affirm Action ... Ms. Maria CHANDLER
88 Dir Campus Recreation & Wellness ... Ms. Mila PADGETT
07 Director of Admissions ... Mr. Andrew HENDRIX
36 Director of Career Services ... Mr. Corey FERALDI
37 Director Financial Aid ... Linda A. HIGGINS
06 Registrar ... Ms. Vivian D. GRICE

14 Director of Client Services ... Mr. Chris SPIRES
90 Dir Communications & Hardware ... Vacant
105 Dir Network Systems/Arch & Infra ... Ms. Joann WILLIAMSON
41 Director of Athletics ... Mr. Jim HERLIHY
38 Director Counseling & Disabilities ... Ms. Cynthia B. GELINAS
23 Director Student Health Center ... Ms. Cynthia B. GELINAS
39 Director of Housing ... Mr. Deri WILLS
28 Dir Global Stds/Multicult Engagemnt ... Mr. Mutombo KABASELE
35 Asst Vice Chanc Student Life ... Mr. Ahmed SAMAHA
19 Chief of Police ... Mr. Kevin LILES
29 Dir Alumni Rels/Cmty Partnerships ... Mr. Randy DUCKETT
51 Dir Office of Ext Pgms & Life Lrng ... Vacant
112 Director of Major Gifts ... Ms. Robin CALLICOTT
26 Dir Marketing & Community Relations ... Mr. James RABY
105 Web Specialist ... Ms. Lauren COULS
88 Director Instructional Services ... Mr. Keith PIERCE

University of South Carolina Beaufort (B)

1 University Boulevard, Bluffton SC 29909-6085

County: Beaufort — FICE Identification: 003450 — Unit ID: 218654

Telephone: (843) 208-8000 — Carnegie Class: Bac-Diverse

FAX Number: (843) 208-8299 — Calendar System: Semester

URL: www.uscb.edu

Established: 1959 — Annual Undergrad Tuition & Fees (In-State): $10,166

Enrollment: 1,980 — Coed

Affiliation or Control: State — IRS Status: 501(c)3

Highest Offering: Baccalaureate

Accreditation: SC, CAEPN, NURSE

01 Chancellor ... Dr. Al M. PANU
05 Exec VC for Acad Affairs ... Dr. Eric SKIPPER
10 Vice Chanc Finance/Operations ... Mr. Earle HOLLEY
111 Vice Chanc University Advancement ... Dr. Lynn MCGEE
32 Vice Chanc for Student Development ... Dr. Douglas OBLANDER
84 Vice Chanc for Enrollment Mgmt ... Mr. Mack PALMOUR
41 Athletic Director ... Mr. Quin MONAHAN
13 Chief Information Officer ... Mr. Eddie KING
20 Assoc Vice Chanc for Acad Affairs ... Dr. Martha MORIARTY
30 Asst Vice Chanc for Development ... Vacant
08 Interim Director of Libraries ... Ms. Geni FLOWERS
19 Director Public Safety ... Mr. Henry GARBADE
15 Director of Human Resources ... Dr. Sue GOLABEK
37 Director of Financial Aid ... Ms. Patricia GREENE
09 Dir Inst Effectiveness/Research ... Mr. Brian MALLORY
18 Director of Facilities ... Mr. Mike PARROTT
36 Director of Career Services ... Ms. Leta SALAZAR
06 Registrar ... Mr. Gary SUTTON
35 Director of Student Life ... Ms. Kate VERMILYEA
39 Director Housing and Judicial ... Ms. Deonne WHALEY
88 Director of Military Program ... Mr. Les BREDIGER
114 Budget Director ... Ms. Mary CORDRAY

University of South Carolina Lancaster (C)

PO Box 889, Lancaster SC 29721-0889

Telephone: (803) 313-7000 — FICE Identification: 003453

Accreditation: &SC, ACBSP, ADNUR, PNUR

† Regional accreditation is carried under University of South Carolina - Columbia.

University of South Carolina Salkehatchie (D)

PO Box 617, Allendale SC 29810-0617

County: Allendale — FICE Identification: 003454 — Unit ID: 218681

Telephone: (803) 584-3446 — Carnegie Class: Assoc/HT-High Trad

FAX Number: (803) 584-5038 — Calendar System: Semester

URL: uscsalkehatchie.sc.edu

Established: 1965 — Annual Undergrad Tuition & Fees (In-State): $6,702

Enrollment: 1,109 — Coed

Affiliation or Control: State — IRS Status: 501(c)3

Highest Offering: Associate Degree

Accreditation: &SC

01 Dean ... Dr. Ann C. CARMICHAEL
05 Interim Academic Dean ... Dr. Aaron ARD
32 Asc Dean Student Svcs/Dir Athletics ... Ms. Jane T. BREWER
08 Head Librarian ... Mr. Daniel JOHNSON
11 Director of Finance ... Ms. Jessica ALL
37 Director Financial Aid ... Ms. Julie HADWIN
18 Dir Facilities/Safety/HR Director ... Dr. William A. SANDIFER
40 Bookstore Manager ... Mr. Lamar HEWETT
07 Director of Admissions ... Ms. Carmen BROWN
30 Chief Development ... Dr. Ann C. CARMICHAEL
84 Director Enrollment Mgmt Svcs ... Mr. Mike SMITH
88 Asst Director Leadership Institute ... Ms. Terri BOONE
88 Dir Ctr Leadership Development ... Mr. Warren CHAVOUS
88 Sports Information Director ... Mr. Trent KINARD

† Regional accreditation is carried under University of South Carolina - Columbia.

University of South Carolina School of Medicine Greenville (E)

607 Grove Road, Greenville SC 29605

County: Greenville — Identification: 667114

Telephone: (864) 455-7992 — Carnegie Class: Not Classified

FAX Number: (864) 455-8404 — Calendar System: Semester

URL: greenvillemed.sc.edu

Established: 2010 — Annual Graduate Tuition & Fees: N/A

Enrollment: N/A — Coed

Affiliation or Control: State — IRS Status: 501(c)3

Highest Offering: Doctorate; No Undergraduates

Accreditation: MED

01 Dean ... Dr. Jerry R. YOUKEY
05 Associate Dean for Faculty Affairs ... Dr. Robert BEST
32 Associate Dean for Student Affairs ... Dr. Paul CATALANA
20 Asst Dean Academic Affairs ... Dr. April BUCHANAN
10 Exec Dir Business Opers & Finance ... Kristin LACEY
30 Director of Development ... Susan WARD
13 Director of IT and Facilities ... Ron KNAPPENBERGER
15 Director of HR and Faculty Affairs ... Claire GREGG
06 Registrar & Financial Aid Director ... Casey WILEY

University of South Carolina Sumter (F)

200 Miller Road, Sumter SC 29150-2498

County: Sumter — FICE Identification: 003426 — Unit ID: 218690

Telephone: (803) 775-8727 — Carnegie Class: Assoc/HT-High Trad

FAX Number: (803) 775-2180 — Calendar System: Semester

URL: www.uscsumter.edu

Established: 1966 — Annual Undergrad Tuition & Fees (In-State): $6,702

Enrollment: 901 — Coed

Affiliation or Control: State — IRS Status: 501(c)3

Highest Offering: Associate Degree

Accreditation: &SC

01 Regional Campus Dean ... Mr. Michael SONNTAG
05 Exec Assoc Dean Acad/Stdnt Affairs ... Mr. Eric REISENAUER
32 Dir of Student Life and eSports ... Mr. Kristopher E. WEISSMANN
10 Assoc Dean for Admin/Financial Svcs ... Mr. Bruce K. BLUMBERG
09 Institutional Research Analyst ... Mr. Chuck W. WRIGHT
08 Head Librarian ... Ms. Sharon H. CHAPMAN
07 Director of Admissions Services ... Mr. Keith E. BRITTON
51 Director of Continuing Education ... Ms. Susan S. BRABHAM
26 Dir of Public Relations/Marketing ... Ms. Misty HATFIELD
40 Bookstore Manager ... Ms. Julie MCCOY
15 Human Resources Officer ... Ms. Marchetta L. WILLIAMS
88 Program Dir Opportunity Scholars ... Ms. Lisa ROSDAIL
87 Director Shaw AFB Programs ... Mr. Rick BOYD
18 Superintendent Buildings & Grounds ... Mr. Jeff LINGEFELT
20 Academic Affairs Assistant ... Ms. Carol REYNOLDS
41 Athletic Director ... Ms. Adrienne CATALDO
13 Director of Info Technology ... Mr. Rodney CLAY
37 Director of Financial Aid ... Mr. Kenneth BERNARD
84 Exec Dir Enrollment Mgmt Svcs ... Mr. Joseph MEWS

† Regional accreditation is carried under University of South Carolina - Columbia.

University of South Carolina Union (G)

PO Drawer 729, Union SC 29379-0729

County: Union — FICE Identification: 004927 — Unit ID: 218706

Telephone: (864) 429-8728 — Carnegie Class: Assoc/HT-High Non

FAX Number: (864) 427-3682 — Calendar System: Semester

URL: uscunion.sc.edu

Established: 1965 — Annual Undergrad Tuition & Fees (In-State): $6,702

Enrollment: 569 — Coed

Affiliation or Control: State — IRS Status: 501(c)3

Highest Offering: Associate Degree

Accreditation: &SC

01 Dean/Distinguished Prof Emeritus ... Dr. John CATALANO
05 Acting Associate Dean Acad Affairs ... Dr. Randy LOWELL
84 Enrollment Director ... Mr. M. Bradley GREER
37 Director Financial Aid ... Mr. Robert HOLCOMBE
15 Human Resources ... Ms. Susan P. JETT
40 Bookstore Manager ... Ms. Tanja BLACK
13 Director of Information Technology ... Mr. Keith CAMP
30 Director of Marketing & Development ... Ms. Annie SMITH
08 Library Manager ... Ms. Sharon L. RUPP
121 Coord Academic Success Center ... Ms. Tammy WARR
10 Director of Budget and Business Ops ... Ms. Michele LEE
12 USC Laurens Location Director ... Mr. Matt DEAN
19 Health and Safety/Security Director ... Mr. Tony GREGORY
18 Maintenance Director ... Mr. Donald LAWSON
06 Registrar ... Mr. Blake WILSON

† Regional accreditation is carried under University of South Carolina - Columbia.

University of South Carolina Upstate (H)

800 University Way, Spartanburg SC 29303-4996

County: Spartanburg — FICE Identification: 006951 — Unit ID: 218742

Telephone: (864) 503-5000 — Carnegie Class: Bac-Diverse

FAX Number: (864) 503-5375 — Calendar System: Semester

URL: www.uscupstate.edu

Established: 1967 — Annual Undergrad Tuition & Fees (In-State): $11,190

Enrollment: 5,996 — Coed

Affiliation or Control: State — IRS Status: 501(c)3

Highest Offering: Master's

Accreditation: **SC**, ART, CAEPN, CAHIIM, CS, ENGT, NURSE

01 Chancellor ... Dr. Brendan KELLY
05 Interim Sr Vice Chanc Acad Affair ... Dr. Clif FLYNN
13 Int Vice Chanc Information Tech ... Mr. Luke VANWINGERDEN
10 Vice Chanc for Finance and Admin . Ms. Sheryl TURNER-WATTS
111 VC Advance Upstate Foundation ... Dr. Meredith BRUNEN
45 VC Cmty-based Res/Engagement/Plng ... Ms. Kathleen BRADY
12 Dir Acad Engagement Greenville Ctr ... Dr. Judith PRINCE
20 Assoc VC Academic Affairs ... Dr. Warren CARSON
32 VC Student Affs/Dean of Students ... Ms. Laura PUCKETT-BOLER
06 Registrar ... Ms. Mary David FOX
84 Vice Chanc Enrollment Services ... Ms. Donette STEWART
38 Director Counseling Services ... Dr. Elizabeth JODOIN
08 Dean Library ... Ms. Frieda M. DAVISON
37 Director Financial Aid ... Ms. Bonnie C. CARSON
49 Dean Arts & Sciences ... Dr. Dirk SCHLINGMANN
50 Dean Johnson Col Business & Econ ... Dr. Frank RUDISILL
53 Interim Dean Education ... Dr. Charles LOVE
66 Dean Nursing ... Dr. Katharine GIBB
58 Director Graduate Education ... Dr. Tina HERZBERG
29 Director of Alumni Relations ... Mr. Joshua JONES
102 Director Dev & Found Scholarships ... Vacant
40 Director Bookstore ... Mr. Jerry CARROLL
41 Athletic Director ... Mr. Lee FOWLER
18 Director Custodial Services ... Mr. Paul SCHMIDT
19 Dir Public Safety & Chief of Police ... Mr. Klay PETERSON
35 Asst Dean/Director Student Life ... Ms. Khrystal SMITH
39 Dir Housing Residential Life ... Ms. Mandy WHITTEN
23 Director Health Services ... Ms. Mary BUCHER
26 Exec Dir Univ Boards & Public Affs ... Mr. John F. PERRY
09 Dir Inst Effectiveness & Compliance ... Dr. Sam COOPER
88 Dir for Fitness and Campus Rec ... Mr. Mark RITTER
22 Dir Disability Services ... Ms. Wendy WOODSBY
51 Dir Continuing Education ... Dr. Faruk TANYEL
114 Budget Manager ... Ms. Vintress BROWN
22 Dir Equal Opp & Employee Relations ... Ms. Sharon WOODS
104 Dir Intl Studies & Language Svcs ... Dr. Deryle HOPE
25 Dir Sponsored Awards ... Ms. Elaine MARSHALL
106 Dir Distance Education ... Dr. David MCCURRY
92 Director Honors Program ... Dr. Cathy CANINO
88 Dir Ctr Teaching Excellence ... Dr. June CARTER

Virginia College (A)

7201 Two Notch Road, Columbia SC 29223
Telephone: (803) 509-7100 Identification: 770829
Accreditation: **ACICS**, SURGT

† Branch campus of Virginia College, Birmingham, AL

Virginia College (B)

2400 David H. McLeod Blvd, Suite F, Florence SC 29501
Telephone: (843) 407-2200 Identification: 770832
Accreditation: **ACICS**

† Branch campus of Virginia College, Birmingham, AL

Virginia College (C)

78 Global Drive, Greenville SC 29607
Telephone: (864) 679-4900 Identification: 770838
Accreditation: **ACICS**, ACFEI, SURGT

† Branch campus of Virginia College, Birmingham, AL

Virginia College (D)

6185 Rivers Avenue, North Charleston SC 29406-4999
Telephone: (843) 614-4300 Identification: 770830
Accreditation: **ACICS**

† Branch campus of Virginia College, Birmingham, AL

Virginia College (E)

8150 Warren H. Abernathy Highway,
Spartanburg SC 29301-2450
Telephone: (864) 504-3200 Identification: 770831
Accreditation: **ACICS**

† Branch campus of Virginia College, Birmingham, AL

Voorhees College (F)

PO Box 678, Denmark SC 29042-0678
County: Bamberg FICE Identification: 003455
Unit ID: 218919
Telephone: (803) 780-1234 Carnegie Class: Bac-Diverse
FAX Number: (803) 780-1015 Calendar System: Semester
URL: www.voorhees.edu
Established: 1897 Annual Undergrad Tuition & Fees: $12,630
Enrollment: 434 Coed
Affiliation or Control: Protestant Episcopal IRS Status: 501(c)3
Highest Offering: Baccalaureate
Accreditation: **SC**, ACBSP

01 President ... Dr. W. Franklin EVANS
05 Exec VP Academic Affairs ... Dr. Ronnie HOPKINS
10 VP Fiscal/Admin Affairs/CFO ... Mrs. V. Diane O'BERRY
30 VP Inst Advancement & Development ... Mrs. Sonia KING GASS
32 AVP Student Affairs/Dean Students ... Mr. Adrian WEST
20 AVP Academic Affairs/Registrar ... Mrs. Melika JACKSON
21 Director of Financial Aid ... Mr. Augusta KITCHEN
35 Director Student Support Services ... Ms. Lynda JEFFERSON
08 Director of Library Services ... Dr. Marie MARTIN
18 Director of Physical Plant ... Mr. Eddie PATTERSON
29 Director Alumni Affairs ... Mr. Ulysses WILLIAMS
36 Director Career Planning & Outreach ... Ms. Latasha SALLEY
42 Chaplain ... Rev. James YARSIAH
41 Director of Athletics ... Mr. Willie JEFFERSON
19 Director of Safety/Security ... Vacant
23 Director of Health Services ... Ms. Kimberly SOLOMON
07 Int Dir of Admissions/Recruitment ... Ms. Barbara MOORE
15 Director of Human Resources ... Mrs. Constance COLTER-BRABHAM
13 Chief Technology Officer ... Mr. Monterrio JONES
40 Bookstore Manager ... Mrs. Shanda FOGLE
04 Exec Assistant to the President ... Ms. Jade JENKINS

Williamsburg Technical College (G)

601 Martin Luther King, Jr. Avenue,
Kingstree SC 29556-4103
County: Williamsburg FICE Identification: 009322
Unit ID: 218955
Telephone: (843) 355-4110 Carnegie Class: Assoc/HVT-High Trad
FAX Number: (843) 355-4296 Calendar System: Semester
URL: www.wiltech.edu
Established: 1969 Annual Undergrad Tuition & Fees (In-District): $4,080
Enrollment: 693 Coed
Affiliation or Control: State/Local IRS Status: 501(c)3
Highest Offering: Associate Degree
Accreditation: **SC**, ACBSP

01 President ... Dr. Patricia A. LEE
05 VP for Academic/Student Affairs ... Dr. Clifton R. ELLIOTT
10 VP Administration & Finance ... Ms. Melissa A. COKER
30 Assoc VP for Inst Advancement ... Mr. Andrew MULLER
32 Assoc VP for Student Affairs ... Dr. Alexis W. DUBOSE
18 Asst VP for Facilities Management ... Mr. Tyrone THOMAS
20 Dean of Instruction ... Mrs. Margaret CHANDLER
08 Library Director ... Dr. Brandolyn LOVE
07 Director of Admissions/Advisement ... Ms. Cheryl DUBOSE
26 Director of Public Relations ... Ms. Sydney C. BERKELEY
37 Director of Financial Aid ... Mrs. Jean BOOS
13 Director MIS ... Mr. J. Brent LEE
15 Human Resources Manager ... Mrs. Jennifer STRONG
103 Dean Cont Education/Workforce Dev ... Mr. James BOSTIC

Winthrop University (H)

Oakland Avenue, Rock Hill SC 29733-0001
County: York FICE Identification: 003456
Unit ID: 218964
Telephone: (803) 323-2211 Carnegie Class: Masters/L
FAX Number: (803) 323-3001 Calendar System: Semester
URL: www.winthrop.edu
Established: 1886 Annual Undergrad Tuition & Fees (In-State): $14,810
Enrollment: 6,031 Coed
Affiliation or Control: State IRS Status: 501(c)3
Highest Offering: Beyond Master's But Less Than Doctorate
Accreditation: **SC**, ART, CAATE, CACREP, CAEPN, CIDA, CS, DANCE, DIETD, DIETI, JOUR, MUS, SW, THEA

01 President ... Dr. Daniel F. MAHONY
05 Provost/Exec VP Academic Affairs ... Dr. Debra C. BOYD
10 Vice President Finance & Business ... Mr. John P. MCKEE
111 Vice Pres Institutional Advancement ... Mr. Evan BOHNEN
32 Vice President of Student Life ... Dr. Frank P. ARDAIOLO
84 VP Access & Enrollment Management ... Mr. Eduardo PRIETO
100 Chief of Staff ... Dr. Kimberly A. FAUST
26 Vice President University Relations ... Dr. Jeffrey PEREZ
19 Asst VP/Chief Campus Police ... Chief Frank J. ZEBEDIS
20 Vice Prov Acad Quality/Innovation ... Dr. Meg WEBBER
88 Asst VP Curriculum/Program Support ... Mr. Tim DRUEKE
13 Asst Vice Pres Comp & Info Tech ... Mr. Patrice BRUNEAU
21 Associate VP Finance/Business ... Ms. Amanda F. MAGHSOUD
18 Assoc VP Facilities Management ... Mr. Walter A. HARDIN
15 VP Human Res/Empl Div & Wellness ... Ms. Lisa COWART
110 Assoc VP Institutional Advancement ... Mr. Ken SHEETZ
11 Vice Provost for Administration ... Ms. Karen JONES
27 Assoc VP/Exec Dir University Rels .. Ms. Ellen M. WILDER-BYRD
58 Dean of Graduate School ... Dr. Jack DEROCHI
49 Dean College Arts & Science ... Dr. Karen M. KEDROWSKI
50 Dean Col of Business Administration ... Dr. P.N SAKSENA
53 Dean College of Education ... Dr. Jennie RAKESTRAW
64 Dean College of Visual/Perf ... Dr. Jeffrey BELLANTONI
08 Dean Library Services ... Dr. Mark Y. HERRING
97 Dean University College ... Dr. Gloria JONES
35 Dean of Students ... Ms. Bethany MARLOWE
41 Athletic Director ... Mr. Ken HALPIN
06 Registrar ... Ms. Gina G. JONES
07 Director of Admissions ... Ms. Deborah G. BARBER
37 Director of Financial Aid ... Ms. Michelle HARE
39 Asst VP for Student Life ... Ms. Cynthia A. CASSENS
36 Director Career Development/Svcs ... Ms. Ellin MCDONOUGH
96 Director Procurement/Risk Mgmt ... Mr. JP MCKEE
53 Director Teaching/Learning Ctr ... Vacant
23 Dir Health/Counseling Services ... Ms. Jackie CONCODORA
85 Director-International Center ... Dr. Leigh POOLE
29 Exec Dir Alumni Rels/Annual Giving ... Ms. Lori TUTTLE
88 Director Advancement Services ... Mr. Ryan SHEEHAN
105 Director Web Development ... Ms. Kimberly BYRD
106 Director of Online Learning ... Dr. Kimarie WHETSTONE
104 Study Abroad Coordinator ... Ms. Chelsi COLLETON
108 Director of Assessment ... Dr. Noreen GAUBATZ
28 Assoc VP HR & Director of Diversity ... Ms. Zantrell Y. JONES
04 Administrative Asst to President ... Ms. Tammie C. PHILLIPS
102 Dir Foundation/Corporate Relations ... Ms. Robin EMBRY

Wofford College (I)

429 N Church Street, Spartanburg SC 29303-3663
County: Spartanburg FICE Identification: 003457
Unit ID: 218973
Telephone: (864) 597-4000 Carnegie Class: Bac-A&S
FAX Number: (864) 597-4018 Calendar System: 4/1/4
URL: www.wofford.edu
Established: 1854 Annual Undergrad Tuition & Fees: $40,245
Enrollment: 1,660 Coed
Affiliation or Control: United Methodist IRS Status: 501(c)3
Highest Offering: Baccalaureate
Accreditation: **SC**

01 President ... Dr. Nayef H. SAMHAT
10 Chief Financial Officer ... Ms. Barbie F. JEFFERSON
05 Provost ... Dr. Michael J. SOSULSKI
30 Sr Vice Pres for Advancement ... Dr. David S. WOOD
11 Sr Vice Pres for Administration ... Mr. David M. BEACHAM
32 Vice President for Student Affairs ... Ms. Roberta H. BIGGER
13 VP for Information Technology ... Mr. Jason H. WOMICK
84 Vice President for Enrollment ... Mr. Brand R. STILLE
26 VP for Marketing and Communications ... Ms. Annie S. MITCHELL
18 Assoc VP Facilities/Cap Projects ... Mr. Jason H. BURR
21 Assoc VP for Finance and Controller ... Mr. Chris L. GARDNER
08 Dean of Library ... Mr. Kevin J. REYNOLDS
82 Dean of International Programs ... Ms. Amy E. LANCASTER
23 Assoc Dean Students/Dir Health Svcs ... Ms. Beth D. WALLACE
20 Associate Academic Officer ... Ms. Stacey HETTES
04 Exec Admin Asst to President ... Ms. Crystal M. HOLMES
41 Director of Athletics ... Mr. Richard A. JOHNSON
06 College Registrar ... Ms. Jennifer R. ALLISON
42 Chaplain ... Dr. Ronald R. ROBINSON
15 Human Resources Director ... Vacant
07 Director of Admissions ... Mr. John W. BIRNEY
09 Director of Institutional Research ... Mr. Raymond H. RUFF
101 Secretary to the Board of Trustees ... Mr. David M. BEACHAM
108 Dir Institutional Effectiveness ... Dr. John D. MILES
38 Director Student Counseling ... Mr. Perry HENSON
19 Director Campus Safety ... Col. James R. HALL
102 Dir Found/Corp & Govt Relations ... Ms. Mary Beth KNIGHT
28 Director of Diversity/Inclusion ... Vacant
29 Director Alumni & Parents ... Ms. Debbi N. THOMPSON
36 Exec Director The Space ... Mr. P. Curtis MCPHAIL
37 Director Financial Aid ... Ms. Carolyn B. SPARKS
39 Asst Dean of Students for Res Life ... Mr. Brian J. LEMERE
44 Director Gift Planning ... Ms. Lisa H. DE FREITAS
96 Director Purchasing/Risk Management ... Mr. Daniel P. DEETER

York Technical College (J)

452 S Anderson Road, Rock Hill SC 29730-3395
County: York FICE Identification: 003996
Unit ID: 218991
Telephone: (803) 327-8000 Carnegie Class: Assoc/HVT-High Trad
FAX Number: (803) 327-8059 Calendar System: Semester
URL: www.yorktech.edu
Established: 1964 Annual Undergrad Tuition & Fees (In-State): $4,464
Enrollment: 4,753 Coed
Affiliation or Control: State IRS Status: 501(c)3
Highest Offering: Associate Degree
Accreditation: **SC**, ACBSP, ADNUR, DA, DH, ENGT, MLTAD, PNUR, RAD, SURGT

01 President ... Dr. Greg F. RUTHERFORD
05 Exec Vice Pres Acad/Student Affs ... Dr. Stacey MOORE
10 VP Business Services ... Dr. Marc TARPLEE
32 Assoc VP Academic/Student Affairs ... Vacant
30 Vice President for Advancement ... Ms. Melanie E. JONES
50 Assoc VP Business/Computer/AA/AS ... Ms. Yolanda WILSON
76 Assoc VP Health & Human Services ... Ms. Linda WEAVER-GRIGGS
54 Assoc VP Industry/Engineering Tech ... Ms. Susan SHERLOCK
103 Assoc VP Economic/Workforce Dev ... Vacant
15 Asst Vice Pres of Human Resources ... Ms. Edwina ROSEBORO-BARNES
08 Librarian ... Ms. Erinnae BAKER
84 Dean of Enrollment Services ... Ms. Monique PERRY
35 Dean for Student Engagement ... Mr. James B. ROBSON
88 Dean Center for Teaching/Learning ... Ms. Kathy L. HOELLEN
71 ReadySC Area Director ... Ms. Marianne BORDERS
09 Director of Institutional Research ... Ms. Mary Beth SCHWARTZ
37 Director Compliance/Financial Aid ... Ms. Elizabeth J. ROLLINS
13 Information Services Director ... Mr. Richard PARTRIDGE
19 Chief Campus Security ... Mr. Bryan L. MCDOUGALD
18 Facilities Management Director ... Mr. Robert L. BROWN
06 Registrar ... Vacant
26 Director of Strategic Communication ... Vacant
04 Administrative Asst to President ... Mrs. Jennifer GAMMON

SOUTH DAKOTA

Augustana University (K)

2001 S Summit, Sioux Falls SD 57197-0001
County: Minnehaha FICE Identification: 003458
Unit ID: 219000

Telephone: (605) 274-0770 Carnegie Class: Bac-Diverse
FAX Number: (605) 274-5299 Calendar System: 4/1/4
URL: www.augie.edu
Established: 1860 Annual Undergrad Tuition & Fees: $30,944
Enrollment: 1,837 Coed
Affiliation or Control: Evangelical Lutheran Church In America IRS Status: 501(c)3
Highest Offering: Master's
Accreditation: NH, CAATE, CAEPN, MUS, NURSE

01 President Ms. Stephanie HERSETH SANDLIN
05 Interim Sr VP Academic Affairs Dr. Jerry JORGENSEN
32 Vice President Student Services Dr. James B. BIES
10 Vice Pres Finance/Administration Mr. Thomas MEYER
111 Vice President for Advancement Mr. Robert PRELOGER
07 Vice President for Admission Ms. Nancy DAVIDSON
11 Assoc VP Admin/Chief Info Officer Mr. Daniel D. DRENKOW
21 Assoc Vice President for Finance Ms. Carol SPILLUM
20 Assoc VP for Academic Affairs Dr. Mitchell G. KINSINGER
51 Assoc VP of Grad and Cont Educ Dr. Jerry JORGENSEN
35 Asst Dean of Students & Dir of Div Mr. Mark BLACKBURN
15 Director of Human Resources Ms. Deanna VERSTEEG
37 Director of Financial Aid Ms. Tresse EVENSON
08 Director of Library Ms. Ronelle THOMPSON
36 Director Career Center Vacant
13 Director Mgmt Information Systems Ms. Debra FREDERICK
18 Chief Facilities/Physical Plant Mr. Frank HUGHES
29 Director of Alumni Relations Ms. Adrienne MCKEOWN
41 Athletic Director Mr. Slade LARSCHEID
06 Registrar/Asst Dean of Instr Data Ms. Joni KRUEGER
36 Exec Director of Career/Success Ctr Ms. Billie STREUFERT
121 Dir of Student Acad Support Service Ms. Susan BIES
104 Director of International Prgrams Mr. Donn GRINNAGER
108 Director of Assessment Dr. Mitchell KINSINGER
19 Director of Campus Safety Mr. Rick TUPPER
09 Director of Institutional Research Vacant

Dakota Wesleyan University (A)

1200 W University, Mitchell SD 57301-4398
County: Davison FICE Identification: 003461
Unit ID: 219091
Telephone: (605) 995-2600 Carnegie Class: Bac-Diverse
FAX Number: (605) 995-2699 Calendar System: Semester
URL: www.dwu.edu
Established: 1885 Annual Undergrad Tuition & Fees: $26,050
Enrollment: 991 Coed
Affiliation or Control: United Methodist IRS Status: 501(c)3
Highest Offering: Master's
Accreditation: NH, CAATE, IACBE, NURSE

01 President Dr. Amy C. NOVAK
10 Executive Vice President Ms. Theresa KRIESE
05 Provost Dr. Joseph ROIDT
26 Dir of Marketing & Communications Ms. Tawni BUHLER
111 VP for Institutional Advancement Ms. Kitty ALLEN
07 Dean of Admissions Ms. Fredel THOMAS
06 Registrar Ms. Karen KNOELL
88 Dir Kelley Ctr for Entrepreneurship Dr. Ryan VAN ZEE
88 Executive Director McGovern Center Dr. Alisha VINCENT
08 Chief Info Ofcr/Dir Lrng Resources Mr. Kevin KENKEL
29 Director of Alumni Relations Mr. Jory HANSEN
37 Director of Financial Aid Ms. Mary ALEXANDER
15 Director of Human Resources Ms. Janet HAYEN
42 Campus Pastor Rev. Eric VAN METER
41 Athletic Director Mr. Jon HART
18 Director of Physical Plant Mr. Louis SCHOENFELDER
32 Director of Student Life Dr. Diana GOLDAMMER
35 Director Student Support Services Ms. Laurie JOHNSON
38 Student Support Services Counselor Ms. Linda CIMPL
40 Director of University Services Ms. Lori SOLBERG
88 Dean Col Ldrshp & Pub Service Dr. W. Jesse WEINS
88 Dean Col Adult and Prof Studies Dr. Derek DRIEDGER
79 Dean College Arts & Humanities Dr. Vince REDDER
81 Dean Col Health/Fitness & Science Dr. Mike CATALANO
04 Exec Admin Asst to President Ms. Emily GEORGE
66 Chair of Nursing Ms. Diane SANDHOFF
50 Chair of Business Dr. Monty BOHRER
53 Chair of Education Dr. Ashley DIGMANN
13 Chief Info Technology Officer (CIO) Mr. Chad HARVEY

Institute of Lutheran Theology (B)

928 4th Street, Brookings SD 57006
County: Brookings Identification: 667318
Telephone: (605) 692-9337 Carnegie Class: Not Classified
FAX Number: N/A Calendar System: Semester
URL: www.ilt.org
Established: 2009 Annual Graduate Tuition & Fees: N/A
Enrollment: N/A Coed
Affiliation or Control: Proprietary IRS Status: Proprietary
Highest Offering: Doctorate; No Undergraduates
Accreditation: @BI

01 President Dr. Dennis BIELFELDT

John Witherspoon College (C)

4021 Range Road, Rapid City SD 57702
County: Pennington Identification: 667246
Telephone: (605) 342-0317 Carnegie Class: Not Classified
FAX Number: N/A Calendar System: Semester
URL: www.johnwitherspooncollege.org
Established: 2004 Annual Undergrad Tuition & Fees: N/A
Enrollment: N/A Coed
Affiliation or Control: Independent Non-Profit IRS Status: 501(c)3
Highest Offering: Baccalaureate
Accreditation: TRACS

01 President Dr. C. Richard WELLS
03 Provost and Director of Leadership Dr. Debra SHATTUCK
05 Vice President of Academic Affairs Dr. Ronald LEWIS
08 Director of Learning Resources Dr. Bret SAUNDERS
10 Director of Business Affairs Carol HARRIS
108 Director Institutional Assessment Dr. Jamin HUBNER
26 Marketing Officer Sandy BROCKHOUSE
32 Director of Student Services Alesha LIMBO

Lake Area Technical Institute (D)

1201 Arrow Avenue, PO Box 730,
Watertown SD 57201-2869
County: Codington FICE Identification: 005309
Unit ID: 219143
Telephone: (605) 882-5284 Carnegie Class: Assoc/HVT-High Trad
FAX Number: (605) 882-6299 Calendar System: Semester
URL: www.lakeareatech.edu
Established: 1965 Annual Undergrad Tuition & Fees (In-District): $5,076
Enrollment: 1,846 Coed
Affiliation or Control: Local IRS Status: 501(c)3
Highest Offering: Associate Degree
Accreditation: NH, DA, EMT, MAC, MLTAD, OTA, PNUR, PTAA

01 President Mr. Michael D. CARTNEY
03 Executive Vice President Ms. Diane STILES
84 Director of Enrollment Mr. Eric SCHULTZ
05 Dean of Academics Ms. Kim BELLUM
32 Director of Student Services Ms. LuAnn STRAIT
88 Corporate Education Coordinator Mr. Steven HAUCK
32 Director of Support Services Mr. Shane ORTMEIER
37 Director of Financial Aid Ms. Marlene SEEKLANDER
121 Academic Counselor Mrs. Megan LYNDE
18 Chief Facilities/Physical Plant Mr. Doug BUTALA

Mitchell Technical Institute (E)

1800 E Spruce, Mitchell SD 57301-2002
County: Davison FICE Identification: 008284
Unit ID: 219189
Telephone: (605) 995-3025 Carnegie Class: Assoc/HVT-High Trad
FAX Number: (605) 995-3083 Calendar System: Semester
URL: www.mitchelltech.edu
Established: 1968 Annual Undergrad Tuition & Fees (In-District): $6,432
Enrollment: 1,261 Coed
Affiliation or Control: Local IRS Status: 501(c)3
Highest Offering: Associate Degree
Accreditation: NH, ACFEI, MAC, MLTAD, RAD, RTT

01 President Mr. Mark WILSON
03 Vice President Mr. John HEEMSTRA
04 Associate to the President Ms. Julie BROOKBANK
05 Dean of Academics Dr. Carol GRODE-HANKS
103 Director of Advanced Technical Educ Mr. Doug GREENWAY
90 Director of Technology Mr. David BOOS
10 Financial Comptroller Mr. Jared HOFER
84 Dean of Enrollment Services Mr. Clayton DEUTER
32 Dean of Student Success Mr. Scott FOSSUM
09 Accred & Inst Effectiveness Dir Ms. Marla SMITH
18 Buildings & Grounds Director Mr. John SIEVERDING
15 Human Resources Manager Ms. Elizabeth KITCHENS
102 Foundation Director Ms. Heather LENTZ
36 Career Svcs & Advising Dir Ms. Janet GREENWAY
06 Registrar Ms. Darla KOTRBA
37 Director Student Financial Aid Ms. Morgan HUBER
105 Marketing Director Mr. Bob KOBERNUSZ

Mount Marty College (F)

1105 W 8th, Yankton SD 57078-3724
County: Yankton FICE Identification: 003465
Unit ID: 219198
Telephone: (605) 668-1011 Carnegie Class: Masters/S
FAX Number: (605) 668-1607 Calendar System: Semester
URL: www.mtmc.edu
Established: 1936 Annual Undergrad Tuition & Fees: $25,380
Enrollment: 1,190 Coed
Affiliation or Control: Roman Catholic IRS Status: 501(c)3
Highest Offering: Master's
Accreditation: NH, ANEST, NURSE

01 President Dr. Marcus LONG
101 Assistant to the President Ms. Joanna MUELLER
05 VP for Academic Affairs Dr. Jane WOOD
10 VP for Finance Ms. Tabitha LIKNESS
32 VP & Dean for Student Affairs Ms. Sarah CARDA
111 VP for Advancement Ms. Barb REZAC
11 Chief Operations Officer Mr. Greg HEINE
09 Director of Inst Effectiveness Ms. Kristen WELKER
66 Director of Nurse Anesthesia Dr. Mary Anne KROGH
42 Director of Campus Ministry Mr. Jordan FOOS
12 Director of Watertown Location Vacant
37 Director Student Financial Aid Mr. Ken KOCER
06 Registrar Ms. Jonna SUPURGECI
13 Chief Information Officer Mr. Christian HUNHOFF
08 Director of Library Ms. Sandra BROWN
40 Dir Bookstore/Central Scheduling Ms. Mary ABBOTT
36 Dir Career Planning Ms. Keley SMITH-KELLER
41 Athletic Director Mr. Chris KASSIN
15 Director of Human Resources Ms. Julie DATHER
26 Dir of Marketing & Communications Ms. Kristen HICKS
44 Director of Annual/Planned Giving Ms. Shannon VIERECK
19 Director Security/Safety Vacant
29 Director Alumni Relations Mr. David DICKES

National American University (G)

5301 Mt. Rushmore Road, Rapid City SD 57701-8932
County: Pennington FICE Identification: 004057
Unit ID: 219204
Telephone: (605) 394-4800 Carnegie Class: Bac-Diverse
FAX Number: (605) 721-5241 Calendar System: Quarter
URL: www.national.edu
Established: 1941 Annual Undergrad Tuition & Fees: $13,989
Enrollment: 1,298 Coed
Affiliation or Control: Proprietary IRS Status: Proprietary
Highest Offering: Doctorate
Accreditation: NH, CAHIIM, IACBE, MAC, NURSE

00 University President Dr. Jerry L. GALLENTINE
01 Senior Campus Director Ms. Holly HOEBELHEINRICH
11 COO Dr. Ronald SHAPE

National American University-Sioux Falls (H)

5801 S Corporate Place, Sioux Falls SD 57108
Telephone: (605) 336-4600 Identification: 770388
Accreditation: &NH

Oglala Lakota College (I)

Box 490, Kyle SD 57752-0490
County: Shannon FICE Identification: 014659
Unit ID: 219277
Telephone: (605) 455-6000 Carnegie Class: Tribal
FAX Number: (605) 455-2787 Calendar System: Semester
URL: www.olc.edu
Established: 1971 Annual Undergrad Tuition & Fees: $2,684
Enrollment: 1,366 Coed
Affiliation or Control: Tribal Control IRS Status: 501(c)3
Highest Offering: Master's
Accreditation: NH, SW

01 President Mr. Thomas H. SHORTBULL
05 Vice President for Instruction Dr. Dawn FRANK
10 Vice President for Business Ms. Julie JOHNSON
06 Registrar Ms. Leslie MESTETH
08 Director Learning Resources Ms. Michelle MAY
15 Personnel Director Ms. Faith RICHARDS
37 Financial Aid Director Ms. Billi HORNBECK
84 Director Enrollment Management Ms. Lynn CUNY
07 Director of Admissions Ms. Leslie MESTETH
09 Director of Institutional Research Mr. Theodore HAMILTON
96 Assoc Business Ofcr/Dir Purchasing Ms. Arlis POURIER
29 Director Alumni Relations Ms. Marilyn POURIER
89 Director of Freshman Studies Ms. Susanne AUER
13 MIS Director Mr. Cliff DELONG
32 Director Student Affairs Mr. Lance CHRISTENSEN
30 Inst Development Coordinator Ms. Marilyn POURIER
51 Community/Cont Education Coord Ms. Kateri MONTILEAUX
88 Applied Science Department Chair Mr. David WHITE BULL
81 Math & Science Department Chair Ms. Karla WITT
49 Art & History Department Chair Ms. Kim BETTELYOUN
53 Education Department Chair Ms. Shannon AMIOTTE
66 Nursing Department Chair Ms. Jessica ZEPHIER
83 Human Services Department Chair Ms. Monique APPLE
88 LAKOTA Studies Department Chair Ms. Karen LONE HILL
18 Chief Facilities/Physical Plant Mr. Leonard FERGUSON

Presentation College (J)

1500 N Main Street, Aberdeen SD 57401-1280
County: Brown FICE Identification: 003467
Unit ID: 219295
Telephone: (605) 225-1634 Carnegie Class: Spec-4-yr-Other Health
FAX Number: (605) 229-8330 Calendar System: Semester
URL: www.presentation.edu
Established: 1951 Annual Undergrad Tuition & Fees: $19,090
Enrollment: 769 Coed
Affiliation or Control: Roman Catholic IRS Status: 501(c)3
Highest Offering: Master's
Accreditation: NH, CAATE, IACBE, MAC, NUR, NURSE, RAD, SURGT, SW

01 President Dr. Margaret HUBER
05 Interim Vice Pres for Academics Dr. Parris WATTS
10 Vice Pres for Finance Ms. Cathy HALL
84 Vice Pres for Enrollment Mr. Michael MATTISON
32 Vice Pres for Student Services Mr. Bob SCHUCHARDT
111 Vice President for Advancement Vacant
88 Executive Director for Mission Sr. Pam DONELAN
06 Registrar Ms. Tennille BIBLE
37 Director Student Financial Aid Ms. Maureen SCHUCHARDT
108 Assessment Coordinator Dr. Nancy VANDER HOEK
15 Director of Human Resources Mr. Jason PETTIGREW
04 Administrative Asst to President Ms. Stacy BAUER
26 Dir of Marketing/Public Relations Mr. Tim BECKHAM
07 Director of Admissions Ms. Molly HILL
09 Director of Institutional Research Dr. Shuqi WU

29 Director Alumni Relations .... Ms. Teresa GAROFALO
39 Director Student Housing .... Mr. DJ MOUNGA
41 Athletic Director .... Mr. Greg HEIER

Sinte Gleska University (A)

PO Box 105, Mission SD 57555-0105
County: Todd FICE Identification: 021437
Unit ID: 219374
Telephone: (605) 856-5880 Carnegie Class: Tribal
FAX Number: (605) 856-5401 Calendar System: Semester
URL: www.sintegleska.edu
Established: 1970 Annual Undergrad Tuition & Fees: $3,154
Enrollment: 581 Coed
Affiliation or Control: Independent Non-Profit IRS Status: 501(c)3
Highest Offering: Master's
Accreditation: NH

01 President .... Mr. Lionel BORDEAUX
05 Provost/COO .... Mr. Phil BAIRD
32 Vice Pres Student Services .... Ms. Debra BORDEAUX
10 Vice Pres of Finance/CFO .... Ms. Leshia POIGNEE
31 VP Community Education .... Ms. Sherry RED OWL
20 Vice Pres Academic Affairs .... Ms. Cheryl MEDEARIS
06 Registrar .... Mr. Jack HERMAN
08 Int Library Director .... Ms. Diana DILLION
20 Chief Finance Officer .... Ms. Sarah AROBBA
37 Director Financial Aid .... Mr. Midas GUNHAMMER
55 Director Adult Education .... Mr. James SHERMAN, III
15 Interim Personnel Director .... Ms. Stephanie WHITE EYES

Sioux Falls Seminary (B)

2100 S Summit Ave, Sioux Falls SD 57105-2729
County: Minnehaha FICE Identification: 004056
Unit ID: 219240
Telephone: (605) 336-6588 Carnegie Class: Spec-4-yr-Faith
FAX Number: (605) 335-9090 Calendar System: 4/1/4
URL: www.sfseminary.edu
Established: 1858 Annual Graduate Tuition & Fees: N/A
Enrollment: 201 Coed
Affiliation or Control: North American Baptist IRS Status: 501(c)3
Highest Offering: Doctorate; No Undergraduates
Accreditation: NH, THEOL

01 President .... Mr. Gregory J. HENSON
05 Chief Academic Officer & Dean .... Dr. Larry W. CALDWELL
10 CFO and VP of Operations .... Mr. Nathan M. HELLING
07 Director of Enrollment Management .... Mr. Dustin J. BROUWER
06 Assoc Dir of Enrollment Mgmt .... Ms. Tracy A. JONES
26 Chief Creative Ofcr/VP Proj Design .... Ms. Shanda L. STRICHERZ
88 Director of Clinical Services .... Dr. Douglas ANDERSON
09 Vice President of Special Projects .... Mr. Josiah BLACK
30 Dir of Church & Alumni Relations .... Dr. Randall C. TSCHETTER
04 Exec Assistant to the President .... Ms. Thea RISA
21 Office Manager .... Ms. Sheryl L. SLETTEN
88 Director of Doctoral Studies .... Dr. Gary E. STRICKLAND
88 Director of Counseling Programs .... Dr. Gretchen L. HARTMANN
88 Dir of Luther House of Study .... Dr. Chris M. CROGHAN
88 Dir of Wesley House of Study .... Dr. Steve A. TREFZ

Sisseton-Wahpeton College (C)

PO Box 689, Sisseton SD 57262-0689
County: Roberts FICE Identification: 022773
Unit ID: 219408
Telephone: (605) 698-3966 Carnegie Class: Tribal
FAX Number: (605) 698-3132 Calendar System: Semester
URL: www.swc.tc
Established: 1979 Annual Undergrad Tuition & Fees (In-District): $4,410
Enrollment: 132 Coed
Affiliation or Control: Local IRS Status: 501(c)3
Highest Offering: Associate Degree
Accreditation: NH

01 President .... Dr. Randy SMITH
05 Vice President of Academic Affairs .... Dr. Jeanette GRAVDAHL
10 Chief Financial Officer .... Ms. Tanya LAFROMEOISE
37 Financial Aid Director .... Ms. Donnette RED BEAR
07 Registrar .... Mrs. Darlene REDDAY
66 Director Nursing .... Ms. Nola RAGAN
29 Alumni Director .... Mr. Tyler BIRNEY
13 Director Information Technology .... Mr. Derrick LAWRENCE
18 Facilities Manager .... Mr. Russell EBERHARDT

*South Dakota State Board of Regents System Office (D)

306 E Capitol Avenue, Suite 200, Pierre SD 57501-2545
County: Hughes FICE Identification: 033438
Telephone: (605) 773-3455 Carnegie Class: N/A
FAX Number: (605) 773-5320
URL: www.sdbor.edu

01 Executive Director & CEO .... Dr. Mike G. RUSH
10 System VP Finance & Administration .... Dr. Monte KRAMER
05 System VP Academic Affairs .... Dr. Paul TURMAN
46 Asst VP Research & Economic Dev .... Mr. Nathan LUKKES
43 General Counsel .... Mr. Guilherme COSTA
15 Director of Human Resources .... Ms. Kayla BASTIAN
26 Director of Communications .... Dr. Janelle TOMAN
32 System Director of Student Affairs .... Ms. Molly WEISGRAM
09 Director of Institutional Research .... Dr. Daniel PALMER
13 System CIO .... Mr. David HANSEN
20 Associate Academic Officer .... Dr. Jay PERRY

*The University of South Dakota (E)

414 E Clark, Vermillion SD 57069-2390
County: Clay FICE Identification: 003474
Unit ID: 219471
Telephone: (605) 677-5011 Carnegie Class: DU-Higher
FAX Number: (605) 677-5073 Calendar System: Semester
URL: www.usd.edu
Established: 1862 Annual Undergrad Tuition & Fees (In-State): $8,457
Enrollment: 9,971 Coed
Affiliation or Control: State IRS Status: 501(c)3
Highest Offering: Doctorate
Accreditation: NH, ADNUR, ARCPA, ART, AUD, CACREP, CAEPN, CLPSY, DH, JOUR, LAW, MED, MUS, NURSE, OT, PTA, SP, SPAA, SW, THEA

02 President .... Mr. James W. ABBOTT
05 Provost/VP Academic Affairs .... Dr. James D. MORAN, III
17 Vice President Health Affairs/Dean .... Dr. Mary DEKKER NETTLEMAN
10 Vice Pres Finance - CFO .... Ms. Sheila GESTRING
46 VP Research/Sponsored Programs .... Dr. Mary BERRY
26 VP Marketing/Enroll Svcs/Univ Rels .... Mr. Scott POHLSON
32 VP Student Svcs & Dean of Students .... Dr. Kimberly GRIEVE
15 Vice President Human Resources .... Mr. E. Lee FELDER, JR.
11 Vice Pres Admin/Technology .... Ms. Roberta S. AMBUR
28 Associate VP of Diversity .... Mr. Lamont SELLERS
18 Asst VP Facilities Management .... Mr. Bob OEHLER
09 AVP Inst Research/Plng/Assessment .... Mr. Daniel PALMER
51 Assoc Provost/Cont & Distance Educ .... Dr. Michael CARD
08 Dean of Libraries .... Mr. Daniel R. DAILY
96 Director of Auxiliary Services .... Mr. Darby GANSCHOW
37 Director of Financial Aid .... Ms. Julie H. PIER
36 Dir Ctr for Academic & Career Plng .... Mr. Steve WARD
06 Registrar .... Ms. Jennifer M. THOMPSON
41 Athletic Director .... Mr. David HERBSTER
19 Dir University Police Department .... Mr. Peter E. JENSEN
84 Dean of Enrollment .... Mr. Mark PETTY
49 Act Dean College Arts & Sciences .... Dr. Kurt HACKEMER
50 Dean School of Business .... Dr. Venky VENKATACHALAM
53 Dean School of Education .... Dr. Donald EASTON-BROOKS
57 Dean College Fine Arts .... Dr. Larry SCHOU
63 Dean Sanford School of Medicine .... Dr. Mary DEKKER NETTLEMAN
61 Dean School of Law .... Mr. Thomas GEU
04 Exec Admin Asst to the President .... Ms. Laura MCNAUGHTON

*Black Hills State University (F)

1200 University Street, Spearfish SD 57799-9500
County: Lawrence FICE Identification: 003459
Unit ID: 219046
Telephone: (605) 642-6111 Carnegie Class: Masters/S
FAX Number: (605) 642-6763 Calendar System: Semester
URL: www.bhsu.edu
Established: 1883 Annual Undergrad Tuition & Fees (In-State): $8,004
Enrollment: 4,395 Coed
Affiliation or Control: State IRS Status: 501(c)3
Highest Offering: Master's
Accreditation: NH, CAEPN, MUS

02 President .... Dr. Tom JACKSON, JR.
05 Provost/Vice Pres Academic Affairs .... Dr. Chris CRAWFORD
10 Vice President Finance/Admin .... Ms. Kathy J. JOHNSON
111 Vice Pres University Advancement .... Mr. Steve L. MEEKER
32 VP for Enrollment & Student Affairs .... Dr. Lois FLAGSTAD
26 Director Univ & Community Relations .... Ms. Corinne HANSEN
13 Chief Info Technology Officer .... Dr. Warren WILSON
37 Director Student Financial Aid .... Ms. Deb HENRIKSEN
38 Director Counseling Center .... Dr. Lois FLAGSTAD
22 Title IX Coordinator .... Dr. Michael L. ISAACSON
35 Dean of Students .... Dr. Jane KLUG
15 Director of Human Resources .... Mr. Nick OAKS
06 Registrar .... Ms. April M. MEEKER
07 Director of Admissions .... Ms. Beth OAKS
21 Director of Business Services .... Mr. Rob HOUDEK
18 Director Facilities/Physical Plant .... Mr. Randy CULVER
29 Director Alumni Relations .... Mr. Tom WHEATON
09 Director of Institutional Research .... Mr. Rich LOOSE
08 Director Library Operations .... Mr. Scott AHOLA
104 Director International Studies .... Ms. Katie WILDMAN
30 Director of Development .... Ms. Shauna JUNEK
19 Director Security/Safety .... Mr. Philip PESHECK
40 Director University Bookstore .... Mr. Michael JASTORFF
41 Director of Athletics .... Mr. Jhett ALBERS
14 Director Network & Computer Svcs .... Mr. Fred NELSON
49 Dean College of Liberal Arts .... Dr. Amy FUQUA
50 Dean Col of Business & Natural Sci .... Dr. Eileen HOGAN
53 Dean Col of Educ & Behavioral Sci .... Dr. Sharman ADAMS
04 Administrative Asst to President .... Ms. Judy A. BAUER
25 Chief Contracts/Grants Admin .... Mr. William KELLY

*Dakota State University (G)

820 N Washington Avenue, Madison SD 57042-1799
County: Lake FICE Identification: 003463
Unit ID: 219082
Telephone: (605) 256-5111 Carnegie Class: Masters/S
FAX Number: (605) 256-5316 Calendar System: Semester
URL: www.dsu.edu
Established: 1881 Annual Undergrad Tuition & Fees (In-State): $8,927
Enrollment: 3,145 Coed
Affiliation or Control: State IRS Status: 501(c)3
Highest Offering: Doctorate
Accreditation: NH, ACBSP, CAEP, CAHIIM, COARC

02 President .... Dr. José -Marie GRIFFITHS
04 Executive Assistant to President .... Ms. Kelli WHITEING
05 Provost & VP Academic Affairs .... Dr. Scott MCKAY
20 Assoc VP Academic Affairs .... Dr. Judy DITTMAN
10 Vice Pres for Business & Admin Svcs .... Mr. Stacy L. KRUSEMARK
32 Vice Pres/Dean Student Affairs .... Mr. Marcus GARSTECKI
13 CIO & VP for Technology .... Mr. David B. OVERBY
111 Vice Pres Institutional Advancement .... Mr. Mark JOHNSTON
41 Director of Athletics .... Mr. Jeff L. DITTMAN
26 Dir Communications & Marketing .... Ms. Starla STENSAAS
49 Dean College of Arts and Sciences .... Dr. Benjamin F. JONES
50 Dean Col Business/Info Systems .... Dr. Dorine BENNETT
77 Dean College of Computing .... Dr. Richard HANSON
53 Dean College of Education .... Dr. Crystal PAULI
58 Dean of Graduate Studies/Research .... Dr. Mark HAWKES
108 Director of Assessment .... Dr. Jay KAHL
09 Dir Institutional Research .... Ms. Kristy ULLOM
08 Director of Library .... Ms. Jan BRUE ENRIGHT
106 Director Online Education .... Ms. Sarah RASMUSSEN
25 Director of Sponsored Programs .... Vacant
06 Registrar .... Ms. Kathryn CALLIES
21 Controller .... Ms. Amy L. DOCKENDORF
18 Director Facilities Management .... Mr. Corey BRASKAMP
25 Director of Budget & Grants Admin .... Ms. Sara HARE
25 Director CAHIT .... Mr. Dan FRIEDRICH
36 Asst VP Stdnt Affs/Dir Career Svcs .... Dr. Marie A. LOHSANDT
124 Dir Activity/Learning Support .... Ms. Kacie FODNESS
121 Dir Student Development .... Ms. Michelle RUESINK
84 Assoc VP of Enrollment .... Ms. Amy S. CRISSINGER
35 Asst Dean for Student Affairs .... Mr. Steven J. BARTEL
38 Student Support/Wellness Counselor .... Ms. Nicole BOWEN
40 Director of Bookstore .... Vacant
28 Coordinator Diversity & Inclusion .... Mr. Mark EDWARDS
37 Director Financial Aid .... Ms. Denise R. GRAYSON
07 Asst Director of Admissions .... Ms. Amber SCHMIDT
85 Dir International Programs .... Ms. Nicole CLAUSSEN
88 Dir Technical Ops & Development .... Mr. Brent VANAARTSEN
91 Dir Admin Computing Services .... Ms. Marilyn HALGERSON
119 Security Engineer .... Mr. David MILLER
24 Multimedia Specialist .... Mr. Tyler EDWARDS
29 Director of Alumni Affairs .... Ms. Jona M. SCHMIDT
30 Development Officer .... Ms. Jill RUHD
30 Development Officer .... Mr. Mark GERHARDT
44 Annual Fund Manager .... Ms. Carrie SLAATHAUG
15 Director Human Resources/Title IX .... Ms. Angi KAPPENMAN

*Northern State University (H)

1200 S Jay Street, Aberdeen SD 57401-7198
County: Brown FICE Identification: 003466
Unit ID: 219259
Telephone: (605) 626-3011 Carnegie Class: Masters/S
FAX Number: (605) 626-3022 Calendar System: Semester
URL: www.northern.edu
Established: 1901 Annual Undergrad Tuition & Fees (In-State): $7,887
Enrollment: 3,449 Coed
Affiliation or Control: State IRS Status: 501(c)3
Highest Offering: Master's
Accreditation: NH, ACBSP, ART, CACREP, CAEPN, MUS

02 President .... Dr. Timothy DOWNS
05 Provost/VP Academic Affairs .... Dr. Alan LAFAVE
10 VP for Finance/Administration .... Ms. Veronica PAULSON
32 VP for Student Affairs/Enroll Mgmt .... Dr. Jeremy REED
20 Associate VP for Academic Affairs .... Dr. Joelle LIEN
35 Associate VP for Student Affairs .... Dr. Checka LEINWALL
13 VP for Information Technologies .... Dr. Debbi BUMPOUS
102 President/CEO of Foundation .... Mr. Todd JORDRE
06 Registrar .... Ms. Peggy HALLSTROM
08 Director of Library .... Mr. Robert RUSSELL
38 Director of Counseling Center .... Vacant
09 Dir Institutional Research/Assmnt .... Ms. Brenda MAMMENGA
25 Director Grants Sponsored Research .... Ms. Karen MARCHANT
37 Director of Financial Aid .... Ms. Sharon KIENOW
39 Director of Residence Life .... Mr. Martin SABOLO
21 Controller .... Ms. Kay FREDRICK
15 Director of Human Resources .... Ms. Susan BOSTIAN
26 Director of Communications/Mrktg .... Mr. Justin FRAASE
43 General Counsel .... Mr. John MEYER
18 Director of Facilities Management .... Mr. Monte MEHLHOFF
49 Dean College of Arts & Science .... Dr. Joshua HAGEN
50 Dean School of Business .... Dr. Timothy MANTZ
53 Dean School of Education .... Dr. Kelly DUNCAN
57 Dean School of Fine Arts .... Dr. Kenneth BOULTON
58 Director of Graduate Studies .... Dr. Joelle LIEN
41 Director of Athletics .... Mr. Joshua MOON
40 Director of Bookstore .... Ms. Beth RASMUSSON
96 Director of Purchasing .... Mr. Earl WEISENBURGER
92 Director of Honors Program .... Dr. Erin FOUBERG
88 Director of International Programs .... Dr. Leigh NEYS
28 Interim Multicultural Advisor .... Ms. Sarah BOTKIN
35 Director of Student Activities .... Ms. Sarah BOTKIN
04 Administrative Asst to President .... Ms. Lisa GROTE
104 Study Abroad Coordinator .... Mr. Nathan ROBERTS
106 Director Online Education .... Mr. Ronald BROWNIE
88 Director University College .... Mr. Steve RASMUSSEN

36 Director Student Placement .... Ms. Britt LORENZ
29 Coordinator of Alumni Operations .... Ms. Heather JORDAN
30 VP of Development .... Mr. Jon OLSON
110 Director Development .... Ms. Kelli Jo KRAUSE

*South Dakota School of Mines and Technology (A)

501 E Saint Joseph, Rapid City SD 57701-3995
County: Pennington | FICE Identification: 003470 | Unit ID: 219347
Telephone: (605) 394-2511 | Carnegie Class: Spec-4-yr-Eng
FAX Number: (605) 394-6131 | Calendar System: Semester
URL: www.sdsmt.edu
Established: 1885 | Annual Undergrad Tuition & Fees (In-State): $11,160
Enrollment: 3,230 | Coed
Affiliation or Control: State | IRS Status: 501(c)3
Highest Offering: Doctorate
Accreditation: NH, CS, ENG

02 Interim President .... Dr. Jan A. PUSZYNSKI
05 Provost/VP Academic Affairs .... Dr. Demitris KOURIS
10 Vice Pres Finance/Administration .... Mr. Stephen MALOTT
46 Vice President of Research .... Dr. Jan A. PUSZYNSKI
32 VP Student Affs/Dean of Students .... Dr. Patricia G. MAHON
15 Vice President Human Resources .... Ms. Kelli R. SHUMAN
20 Associate Provost Academic Affairs .... Dr. Kathryn E. ALLEY
07 Assoc Provost Acad Administration .... Ms. Molly MOORE
96 Purchasing Manager .... Ms. Barbara MUSTARD
26 Dir of Marketing & Communications . Ms. Ann M. BRENTLINGER
29 Director of Alumni Association .... Dr. Larry SIMONSON
90 Director Information Tech Svcs .... Mr. Bryan J. SCHUMACHER
08 Director Devereaux Library .... Ms. Patricia M. ANDERSEN
36 Director Career Services .... Dr. Darrell R. SAWYER
37 Director of Financial Aid .... Mr. David W. MARTIN
41 Director of Athletics .... Mr. Joel LEUKEN
102 President SDSM&T Foundation .... Mr. Joel KINCART
18 Director of Facilities Services .... Ms. Jerilyn C. ROBERTS
21 Director of Finance/Controller .... Ms. Heather FORNEY
39 Asst Dean of Students/Dir of Res .... Dr. Daniel SEPION
85 Director Ivanhoe International Ctr .... Ms. Susan R. AADLAND
58 Dean of Graduate Education .... Dr. Maribeth H. PRICE
38 Director Counseling/ADA Svcs .... Ms. Megan REDER-SCHOPP
06 Registrar .... Mr. Philip HUNT
40 Director of University Bookstore .... Mr. Marlin L. KINZER
35 Dir of Student Act/Leadership Ctr .... Mr. Cory L. HEADLEY
28 Director of Multicultural Affairs .... Mr. Jesse HERRERA

*South Dakota State University (B)

Campanile Avenue, Brookings SD 57007-2298
County: Brookings | FICE Identification: 003471 | Unit ID: 219356
Telephone: (605) 688-4151 | Carnegie Class: DU-Higher
FAX Number: (605) 688-5822 | Calendar System: Semester
URL: www.sdstate.edu
Established: 1881 | Annual Undergrad Tuition & Fees (In-State): $8,172
Enrollment: 12,576 | Coed
Affiliation or Control: State | IRS Status: 501(c)3
Highest Offering: Doctorate
Accreditation: NH, AAB, CAATE, CACREP, CAEPN, CIDA, CS, DIETD, @DIETI, ENG, EXSC, JOUR, MT, MUS, NURSE, PHAR

02 President .... Dr. Barry H. DUNN
05 Provost/Vice Pres Acad Affairs .... Dr. Dennis HEDGE
32 Vice President Student Affairs .... Dr. Michaela WILLIS
46 Int VP for Research/Economic Dev .... Dr. Kinchel DOERNER
13 VP for Tech/Security .... Dr. Michael ADELAINE
10 Vice Pres Finance & Business/CFO ... Mr. Wesley G. TSCHETTER
20 Assoc Vice Pres for Academic Affs .... Dr. Mary Kay HELLING
18 Asst Vice Pres Facilities Services .... Mr. Dean KATTELMANN
88 Asst VP AA Intl Affairs/Outreach .... Dr. Kathleen FAIRFAX
15 Asst Vice Pres Human Resources .... Mr. Marc SERRETT
100 Chief of Staff .... Ms. Karyn WEBER
08 Dean of the Library .... Dr. Kristi TORNQUIST
97 Interim Dean of University College .... Dr. Mary Kay HELLING
07 Director of Admissions .... Ms. Tracy WELSH
06 Registrar .... Ms. Joyce KEPFORD
38 Director Wellness .... Mr. Jeffrey HUSKEY
37 Financial Aid Officer .... Ms. Carolyn HALGERSON
102 President & CEO of Foundation .... Mr. Steve ERPENBACH
29 President & CEO Alumni Affairs .... Ms. Andi FOUBERG
14 Mgr Admin Information Svcs .... Mr. William (Joe) MOORE
19 Chief Security/Safety .... Mr. Tim HEATON
39 Director of Residential Life .... Mr. Jeffrey HALE
40 Director of Bookstore .... Mr. Derek PETERSON
41 Director of Athletics .... Mr. Justin SELL
28 Dir of Diversity/Equity/Inclus & Ac .... Dr. Nathan ZIEGLER
56 Interim Director of Extension .... Dr. Karla TRAUTMAN
26 Dir Marketing & Communications .... Mr. Michael LOCKREM
96 Purchasing Director .... Ms. Vicki SOREN
43 General Counsel .... Dr. Tracy GREENE
25 Director of Grants/Contracts .... Ms. Jackie NELSON
24 Mgr Instructional Design Services .... Dr. Shouhong ZHANG
85 Mgr International Students/Scholars .... Mr. Greg WYMER
47 Int Dean Agriculture/Biological Sci .... Dr. Daniel SCHOLL
49 Interim Dean of Arts & Sciences .... Dr. Jason ZIMMERMAN
54 Dean of Engineering .... Dr. Lewis BROWN
53 Dean Education & Human Science .... Dr. Jill THORNGREN
66 Dean of Nursing .... Dr. Nancy FAHRENWALD
67 Acting Dean of Pharmacy .... Dr. Jane MORT
58 Dean of Graduate School .... Dr. Kinchel DOERNER
92 Dean Honors College .... Dr. Rebecca BOTT
51 Dir Continuing & Distance Educ .... Ms. Lindsey HAMLIN
09 Coordinator Institutional Research .... Ms. Jennifer VANDER WAL
100 Chief of Staff .... Ms. Karyn WEBER
104 Director Study Abroad .... Ms. Sally GILLMAN
108 Director Institutional Assessment .... Dr. Janna HANSON
22 Title IX Coord/EEO .... Ms. Michelle JOHNSON
90 Director Academic Computing .... Mr. Ryan KNUTSON

Southeast Technical Institute (C)

2320 N Career Avenue, Sioux Falls SD 57107-1302
County: Minnehaha | FICE Identification: 007764 | Unit ID: 219426
Telephone: (605) 367-7624 | Carnegie Class: Assoc/HVT-High Trad
FAX Number: (605) 367-8305 | Calendar System: Semester
URL: www.southeasttech.edu
Established: 1968 | Annual Undergrad Tuition & Fees (In-District): $5,980
Enrollment: 2,047 | Coed
Affiliation or Control: Local | IRS Status: 501(c)3
Highest Offering: Associate Degree
Accreditation: NH, ADNUR, CVT, DMS, NDT, NMT, SURGT

01 President .... Mr. Robert J. GRIGGS
05 Vice President of Academics .... Mr. James JACOBSEN
10 Vice President Finance & Operations .... Mr. Richard KLUIN
32 Vice Pres Student Affs/Inst Rsrch .... Mr. Tracy NOLDNER
35 Director of Students .... Mr. Erik MERTEN
50 Training Solutions Institute .... Mr. Lon HIRD
06 Registrar .... Ms. Kristie VORTHERMS
15 Human Resources Specialist .... Ms. Kathy STRUCK
20 Director of Academic Support .... Dr. Craig PETERS
26 Marketing Coordinator .... Ms. Margaret PENNOCK
37 Financial Aid Director .... Ms. Lynette GRABOWSKA
102 Foundation Associate .... Ms. Chellee NEMEC
21 Business Manager .... Mr. James WESTCOTT
38 Student Personal Counselor .... Ms. Nicole MCMILLIN

University of Sioux Falls (D)

1101 W 22nd Street, Sioux Falls SD 57105-1699
County: Minnehaha | FICE Identification: 003469 | Unit ID: 219383
Telephone: (605) 331-5000 | Carnegie Class: Masters/M
FAX Number: (605) 331-6615 | Calendar System: 4/1/4
URL: www.usiouxfalls.edu
Established: 1883 | Annual Undergrad Tuition & Fees: $27,160
Enrollment: 1,482 | Coed
Affiliation or Control: American Baptist | IRS Status: 501(c)3
Highest Offering: Beyond Master's But Less Than Doctorate
Accreditation: NH, CAEP, IACBE, NURSE, SW

01 President .... Dr. Brett BRADFIELD
100 Dir Presidential and Bd Operations .... Ms. Karen BANGASSER
05 VP for Academic Affairs .... Ms. Joy LIND
50 Chair School of Business .... Dr. Tricia COLE
53 Chair School of Education .... Ms. Beth JERNBERG
57 Chair Visual & Performing Arts .... Mr. Jonathan NEIDERHISER
65 Chair of Natural Sciences .... Dr. William SOEFFING
79 Chair of Humanities .... Ms. Jenny BANGSUND
83 Chair of Social Sciences .... Ms. Beth O'TOOLE
66 Director School of Nursing .... Ms. Jessica CHERENEGAR
88 Director of Degree Comp Program .... Ms. LuAnn GROSSMAN
06 Registrar .... Ms. Anna HECKENLAIBLE
10 VP for Business and Finance .... Ms. Marsha DENNISTON
21 Controller .... Ms. Susan THIE
111 VP for Institutional Advancement .... Mr. Todd KNUTSON
112 VP for Principal Gifts .... Mr. Jon HIATT
29 Director Annual Giving & Alumni Rel .... Ms. Kelsey FREIDEL-NELSON
26 Dir of Marketing and Communications .... Ms. Sarah STRASBURG
84 VP for Enrollment Management .... Ms. Aimee VANDER FEEN
07 Director of Enrollment Management .... Mr. Ben WEINS
37 Director of Financial Aid .... Ms. Karrie MORGAN
15 VP of Human Resources .... Ms. Julie GEDNALSKE
09 AVP of Institutional Research .... Dr. Jason DOUMA
32 VP Student Dev/Dean of Students .... Mr. Corey ROSS
39 Asst Dean of Stdnts/Dir Res Life .... Ms. Ashley MATURAN
42 Dean of the Chapel .... Rev. Dennis L. THUM
38 University Counselor .... Ms. Michelle DEHOOGH-KLIEWER
104 Director of International Education .... Mr. Randy NELSON
13 VP Info Technology and CIO .... Mr. William BARTELL
105 Dir Web Services .... Mr. David CONE
91 Dir Administrative Applications .... Ms. Brenda THOMAS
106 Director of Online Education .... Ms. Veda IVERSON
08 Director of Library Services .... Ms. Rachel CROWLEY
41 Director Intercollegiate Athletics .... Mr. Josh SNYDER
18 Director of Facilities Services .... Mr. Jeff WENDT
19 Director of Campus Safety .... Mr. Kevin GREBIN
40 Dir of Cougar Central Bookstore .... Ms. Jennifer KNUTSON

Western Dakota Technical Institute (E)

800 Mickelson Drive, Rapid City SD 57703-4018
County: Pennington | FICE Identification: 010170 | Unit ID: 219480
Telephone: (605) 394-4034 | Carnegie Class: Assoc/HVT-High Trad
FAX Number: (605) 394-1789 | Calendar System: Semester
URL: www.wdt.edu
Established: 1968 | Annual Undergrad Tuition & Fees (In-District): $6,560
Enrollment: 836 | Coed
Affiliation or Control: Local | IRS Status: 501(c)3
Highest Offering: Associate Degree
Accreditation: #NH, EMT, SURGT

01 President .... Dr. Ann BOLMAN
05 VP for Teaching and Learning .... Ms. Tiffany HOWE
10 VP for Finance and Operations .... Mr. Brian WATLAND
108 VP for Institutional Effectiveness .... Ms. Kelly OEHLERKING
20 Associate Dean of Academics .... Vacant
37 Manager of Financial Aid .... Ms. Jill ELDER
15 Human Resources Manager .... Ms. Theresa SCHARN
07 Admissions Director .... Ms. Jill ELDER
08 Registrar .... Ms. Debbie TOMS
18 Chief Facilities/Physical Plant .... Mr. Daryl LEMME
26 Chief Public Relations Officer .... Ms. Megan NICOLAISEN
36 Director of Student Placement .... Ms. Chandra CALVERT
84 Director Enrollment Management .... Ms. Jill ELDER
96 Director of Purchasing .... Mr. Brian WATLAND
04 Administrative Asst to President .... Ms. JoLynn FLETCHER
06 Registrar .... Ms. Debbie TOMS
09 Director of Institutional Research .... Mr. Mark MCGRATH
28 Director of Diversity .... Ms. Theresa SCHARN
29 Director Alumni Relations .... Mr. Aaron JACOBS

TENNESSEE

American Baptist College (F)

1800 Baptist World Center Drive, Nashville TN 37207
County: Davidson | FICE Identification: 010460 | Unit ID: 219505
Telephone: (615) 256-1463 | Carnegie Class: Spec-4-yr-Faith
FAX Number: (615) 226-7855 | Calendar System: Semester
URL: www.abcnash.edu
Established: 1924 | Annual Undergrad Tuition & Fees: $10,074
Enrollment: 157 | Coed
Affiliation or Control: Baptist | IRS Status: 501(c)3
Highest Offering: Baccalaureate
Accreditation: BI

01 President .... Dr. Forrest E. HARRIS, SR.
05 Vice Pres Academic Affairs .... Dr. Renita WEEMS
10 VP Administration/Finance .... Atty. Richard JACKSON
32 Vice Pres Campus Life .... Mr. Martin ESPINOSA
06 Registrar .... Mr. Cedric AARON
10 Controller .... Ms. Brooke BELL
08 Director Library Services .... Ms. Nicole WHITE
04 Executive Assistant to President .... Ms. Mary CARPENTER
20 Assoc Dean Academic Affairs .... Ms. LaShante WALKER
09 Director of Institutional Research .... Dr. Regina PRUDE
07 Dir Admissions/Public Relations .... Ms. Dee BOMER

American National University (G)

1328 Highway 11 W, Bristol TN 37620-8530
Telephone: (423) 878-4440 | Identification: 666500
Accreditation: ACICS, MAC

† Branch campus of American National University, Salem, VA

Aquinas College (H)

4210 Harding Pike, Nashville TN 37205-2005
County: Davidson | FICE Identification: 003477 | Unit ID: 219578
Telephone: (615) 297-7545 | Carnegie Class: Spec-4-yr-Other Health
FAX Number: (615) 279-3898 | Calendar System: Semester
URL: www.aquinascollege.edu
Established: 1961 | Annual Undergrad Tuition & Fees: $21,950
Enrollment: 384 | Coed
Affiliation or Control: Roman Catholic | IRS Status: 501(c)3
Highest Offering: Master's
Accreditation: SC

01 President .... Sr. Mary Agnes GREIFFENDORF, OP
10 Vice Pres of Finance .... Mr. Keith GIGER
05 Provost and Vice Pres for Academics .... Sr. Thomas More STEPNOWSKI, OP
32 Director of Student Activities .... Vacant
20 Associate Provost .... Dr. William SMART
26 Dir of Communications/Marketing .... Vacant
07 Dir of Admiss & Fin Aid & Registrar .... Mrs. Michele WATSON
08 Librarian .... Mr. Mark HALL
30 Director of Development .... Vacant
40 Bookstore Manager .... Mrs. Kari BYARD
53 Dean School of Education ..... Sr. Mary Anne ZUBERBUELER, OP
21 Business Manager .... Mrs. Monica WARREN
09 Director of Institutional Research .... Dr. William SMART
29 Director of Alumni Relations .... Vacant
18 Chief of Facilities/Physical Plant .... Mr. John WALL
121 Director of Student Learning Svcs ...... Sr. Mary Esther POTTS, OP
88 Director of Catechetics .... Mr. Jason GALE
88 Dir Center for Catholic Education ... Sr. Elizabeth Anne ALLEN, OP
19 Director Security/Safety .... Mr. Anthony ATWOOD
04 Administrative Asst to President .... Mrs. Brenda L. KINCAID
101 Secretary of the Institution/Board ... Sr. Ann Hyacinth GENOW, OP
13 Chief Info Technology Officer (CIO) .... Mrs. Joyce WALL

Argosy University, Nashville (I)

100 Centerview Drive, Suite 225, Nashville TN 37214-3438
Telephone: (615) 525-2800 | Identification: 666668
Accreditation: &WC, ACBSP, CACREP

† Regional accreditation is carried under the parent institution in Orange, CA.

The Art Institute of Tennessee-Nashville (A)

100 Centerview Dr., Ste 250, Nashville TN 37214-3439
Telephone: (615) 874-1067 Identification: 770975
Accreditation: &SC

† Branch campus of The Art Institute of Atlanta, Atlanta, GA

Austin Peay State University (B)

601 College Street, Clarksville TN 37044-0002
County: Montgomery FICE Identification: 003478
Unit ID: 219602
Telephone: (931) 221-7011 Carnegie Class: Masters/L
FAX Number: (931) 221-7475 Calendar System: Semester
URL: www.apsu.edu
Established: 1927 Annual Undergrad Tuition & Fees (In-State): $7,689
Enrollment: 10,099 Coed
Affiliation or Control: State IRS Status: 501(c)3
Highest Offering: Beyond Master's But Less Than Doctorate
Accreditation: SC, ART, CAEPN, ENGT, MT, MUS, NUR, RAD, RTT, SW

Code	Title	Name
02	President	Dr. Alisa WHITE
04	Exec Asst to the President	Ms. Carol D. CLARK
05	Provost/VP Academic Affairs	Dr. Rex GANDY
10	Vice President for Finance & Admin	Mr. Mitch ROBINSON
43	General Counsel	Ms. Dannelle WHITESIDE
32	VP for Student Affairs	Dr. Sherryl BYRD
46	VP Advancement/Comm/Strategic Init	Mr. Derek VAN DER MERWE
21	Assoc VP for Finance	Ms. Sherry DEMARAY
20	Vice Provost/Assoc VP Acad Affairs	Dr. Lynne CROSBY
84	Assoc Provost for Enrollment Mgmt	Dr. Beverly BOGGS
111	Exec Director Univ Advancement	Mr. Kristopher PHILLIPS
86	Dir Community/Government Rels	Ms. Carol CLARK
26	Exec Dir Marketing/Public Rels	Mr. Bill PERSINGER
12	Exec Dir APSU Fort Campbell	Dr. Kristine NAKUTIS
29	Director of Alumni Relations	Ms. Nicole PETERSON
114	Director Budgets	Ms. Sonja STEWART
08	Director Library	Mr. Joe WEBER
13	Assoc VP & Chief Info Officer	Ms. Judith MOLNAR
09	Dir Inst Research & Effectiveness	Ms. Melissa HUNTER
07	Director of Admissions	Ms. Amy CORLEW
06	Registrar	Ms. Telaina WRIGLEY
18	Director of Plant Administration	Mr. Thomas HUTCHINS
45	Dir University Design/Construction	Mr. Marc BRUNNER
41	Athletic Director	Mr. Ryan IVEY
88	Athletics Communication Manager	Mr. Cody BUSH
37	Director of Student Financial Aid	Ms. Donna PRICE
121	Assoc Prov Student Success	Dr. Loretta GRIFFY
38	Dir of Student Counseling Services	Dr. Jeff RUTTER
35	Assoc Vice Pres & Dean of Students	Mr. Gregory SINGLETON
88	Dir African Amer Cultural Ctr	Mr. Marcelius BRAXTON
15	Asst VP & Chief HR Officer	Mr. Michael HAMLET
16	Director of Human Resources	Ms. Fonda FIELDS
19	Director Public Safety	Mr. Michael KASITZ
39	Asst Vice President Student Affairs	Mr. F. Joe MILLS
116	Director Internal Audit	Mr. Blayne CLEMENTS
25	Dir Research & Sponsored Pgms	Ms. Brandi CLEMENTS
96	Director of Purchasing	Ms. Judy BLAIN
22	Dir Equal Opport & Affirm Action	Ms. Sheila M. BRYANT
36	Director of Career Services	Ms. Amanda WALKER
49	Dean College Arts & Letters	Dr. Dixie WEBB
81	Dean Col Science & Math	Dr. Jaime TAYLOR
83	Dean Col Behav Health Science	Dr. David DENTON
58	Int Assoc Prov/Dean Col Grad Stds	Dr. Chad BROOKS
56	Int Exec Dir Extend/Intl Educ	Dr. Tim HUDSON
106	Director of Distance Education	Dr. Denise ROBLEDO
104	Dir Study Abroad/Intl Exchange	Dr. Marissa CHANDLER
50	Interim Dean Col of Business	Dr. Charles MOSES
53	Dean College of Education	Dr. Prentice CHANDLER

Baptist College of Health Sciences (C)

1003 Monroe Avenue, Memphis TN 38104-3199
County: Shelby FICE Identification: 034403
Unit ID: 219639
Telephone: (901) 575-2247 Carnegie Class: Spec-4-yr-Other Health
FAX Number: (901) 572-2461 Calendar System: Trimester
URL: www.bchs.edu
Established: 1994 Annual Undergrad Tuition & Fees: $11,204
Enrollment: 1,079 Coed
Affiliation or Control: Independent Non-Profit IRS Status: 501(c)3
Highest Offering: Baccalaureate
Accreditation: SC, COARC, DMS, MT, NMT, NURSE, RAD, RTT

Code	Title	Name
01	President	Dr. Betty S. MCGARVEY
04	Administrative Asst to President	Ms. Joyce J. PERKINS
10	Vice President Financial & Business	Ms. Leanne SMITH
11	Vice President Admin Svcs/HR	Dr. Adonna CALDWELL
05	Chief Academic Officer/Provost	Dr. Loredana C. HAEGER
97	Dean General Educ & Health Studies	Dr. Barry SCHULTZ
66	Dean Nursing	Dr. Anne M. PLUMB
76	Dean Allied Health	Dr. Carol WARREN
32	Dean Student Services	Ms. Nancy REED
06	Registrar	Mr. John BERGER
07	Director of Admissions	Ms. Lissa MORGAN
09	Dir of Institutional Effectiveness	Dr. Mitzi C. ROBERTS
29	Director Alumni Relations	Ms. Megan M. BURSI
35	Director Student Services & Housing	Mr. Jeremy WILKES
37	Director Financial Aid	Ms. Joanna DARDEN
84	Dean Enrollment Management	Dr. Arnold ARREDONDO

Belmont University (D)

1900 Belmont Boulevard, Nashville TN 37212-3757
County: Davidson FICE Identification: 003479
Unit ID: 219709
Telephone: (615) 460-6000 Carnegie Class: Masters/L
FAX Number: (615) 460-6446 Calendar System: Semester
URL: www.belmont.edu
Established: 1890 Annual Undergrad Tuition & Fees: $31,390
Enrollment: 7,350 Coed
Affiliation or Control: Christian Churches And Churches of Christ
IRS Status: 501(c)3
Highest Offering: Doctorate
Accreditation: SC, ART, CAEPN, ENGT, LAW, MUS, NURSE, OT, PHAR, PTA, SW, THEA

Code	Title	Name
01	President	Dr. Robert C. FISHER
05	Provost	Dr. Thomas D. BURNS
100	Vice President/Chief of Staff	Dr. Susan H. WEST
11	Vice Pres for Admin & Univ Counsel	Dr. Jason ROGERS
108	VP for Institutional Effectiveness	Dr. Paula GILL
30	VP Development/External Relations	Dr. Perry MOULDS
10	Vice President Finance & Operations	Mr. Steven T. LASLEY
42	VP Spiritual Development	Dr. Todd LAKE
13	Assoc VP/Chief Information Officer	Mr. William INGRAM
32	Assoc Provost/Dean of Students	Dr. Jeffery BURGIN
20	Assoc Provost for Academic Affairs	Dr. Beverly SCHNELLER
84	Assoc Provost/Dean Enrollment Svcs	Dr. David MEE
09	Assoc Provost/Assess/Inst Research	Ms. Mary LUCAS
88	Assoc Provost ISGE	Dr. Mimi BARNARD
50	Dean College of Business	Dr. Patrick RAINES
57	Dean College Visual/Performing Arts	Dr. Stephen EAVES
88	Dean College of Ent & Music Bus	Mr. Doug HOWARD
49	Dean Col of Lib Arts & Soc Sci	Dr. Bryce SULLIVAN
81	Dean Col of Sciences & Mathematics	Dr. Thomas SPENCE
76	Dean Col Health Sciences/Nursing	Dr. Cathy TAYLOR
73	Dean of Col Theol & Christian Min	Dr. Darrell GWALTNEY
61	Dean College of Law	Dr. Alberto GONZALES
67	Dean College of Pharmacy	Dr. Phil JOHNSTON
06	University Registrar	Mr. Steven REED
35	Asst Dean of Students	Dr. Molly ZLOCK
35	Asst Dean of Students	Ms. Angie BRYANT
39	Assistant Dean of Students	Mr. Anthony DONOVAN
07	Director of University Admissions	Ms. Brooke BRANNIN
15	Sr Director of Human Resources	Mrs. Leslie A. LENSER
37	Director of Financial Aid	Mrs. Patricia SMEDLEY
29	Director of Alumni Relations	Ms. Suzanne THIGPEN
18	Director of Facilities Management	Mr. Robert CHAVEZ
19	Chief of Campus Security	Mr. Pat CUNNINGHAM
90	Director Technology Services	Mr. Randall REYNOLDS
08	Director of Library Services	Ms. Sue MASZAROS
41	Athletics Director	Mr. Scott CORLEY
40	Manager Bookstore	Mrs. Catherine MURPHY
36	Dir Career & Professional Develop	Vacant
26	Dir Marketing & Public Relations	Mr. John CARNEY
27	Director of Communications	Mr. Greg S. PILLON
38	Director Student Counseling	Ms. Peg LEONARD-MARTIN
104	Director Study Abroad	Ms. Shelley JEWELL
85	Director of International Education	Ms. Katherine SKINNER
43	Dir Legal Services/General Counsel	Dr. Jason ROGERS

Bethel University (E)

325 Cherry Avenue, McKenzie TN 38201-1705
County: Carroll FICE Identification: 003480
Unit ID: 219718
Telephone: (731) 352-4000 Carnegie Class: Masters/L
FAX Number: (731) 352-4069 Calendar System: Semester
URL: www.bethelu.edu
Established: 1842 Annual Undergrad Tuition & Fees: $15,764
Enrollment: 5,951 Coed
Affiliation or Control: Cumberland Presbyterian IRS Status: 501(c)3
Highest Offering: Master's
Accreditation: SC, ARCPA, CAATE, CAEPN, NURSE

Code	Title	Name
01	President	Dr. Walter BUTLER
05	Chief Academic Officer	Dr. Phyllis CAMPBELL
49	VP College of Arts and Sciences	Ms. Cindy MALLARD
10	VP of Finance	Mr. David HUSS
30	Vice President for Development	Dr. Dale HENRY
06	University Registrar	Ms. Becky HAMES
84	Dean of Enrollment CLA	Mrs. Tina HODGES
32	Dean of Student Affairs	Mr. James STEWART
26	Director of Public Relations	Ms. Jennifer GLASS
88	Director of College Orientation	Mrs. Sandy LOUDEN
42	Chaplain	Rev. Anne HAMES
08	Library Director	Ms. Jill WHITFILL
15	Human Resource Director	Ms. Carolyn DOTSON
41	Athletic Director	Mr. Dale KELLEY
09	Director of Institutional Effective	Dr. Lisa NORRIS
29	Director Alumni Relations	Mrs. Myra CARLOCK
76	Director of Col of Health Sciences	Dr. Joe HAMES
07	Assoc Dean of Enrollment Services	Ms. Kim HOUSTON
18	Chief Facilities/Physical Plant	Mr. Randy TANAKA
04	Administrative Asst to President	Ms. Vicky WILLIAMS
105	Director Web Services	Ms. Jennifer GLASS
13	Chief Info Technology Officer (CIO)	Mr. Jimmy BOMAR
19	Director Security/Safety	Mr. James HARRIS
22	Dir Affirmative Action/EEO	Dr. Jacqueline DEBERRY
39	Director Student Housing	Ms. Peggy CARTER

Brightwood College (F)

750 Envious Lane, Nashville TN 37217-1342
County: Davidson FICE Identification: 023262
Unit ID: 246202
Telephone: (615) 279-8300 Carnegie Class: Spec 2-yr-Other
FAX Number: (615) 297-6678 Calendar System: Other
URL: www.brightwood.edu
Established: 1981 Annual Undergrad Tuition & Fees: N/A
Enrollment: 398 Coed
Affiliation or Control: Proprietary IRS Status: Proprietary
Highest Offering: Associate Degree
Accreditation: ACICS

Code	Title	Name
01	Executive Director	Ms. Haley JOHNSON

Bryan College (G)

721 Bryan Drive, Dayton TN 37321-6275
County: Rhea FICE Identification: 003536
Unit ID: 219790
Telephone: (423) 775-2041 Carnegie Class: Masters/S
FAX Number: (423) 775-7330 Calendar System: Semester
URL: www.bryan.edu
Established: 1930 Annual Undergrad Tuition & Fees: $24,450
Enrollment: 1,489 Coed
Affiliation or Control: Independent Non-Profit IRS Status: 501(c)3
Highest Offering: Master's
Accreditation: SC, IACBE

Code	Title	Name
01	President	Dr. Stephen D. LIVESAY
04	Exec Assistant to the President	Ms. Margaret A. LEGG
05	Academic Vice President	Dr. Kevin L. CLAUSON
10	VP of Finance and Enrollment	Mr. Rick J. TAPHORN
30	Vice Pres of College Advancement	Mr. Chuck S. BAKER
32	VP Student Services/Ministries	Mr. Timothy J. HOSTETLER
13	Vice Pres Information Systems	Vacant
58	Dean Sch of Adult & Graduate Stds	Dr. Adina SCRUGGS
35	Dean of Students	Mr. Bruce A. MORGAN
37	Director of Financial Aid	Mr. David L. HAGGARD
14	Director of Information Systems	Mr. James SULLIVAN
06	Registrar	Ms. Janet M. PIATT
08	Director of Library Sciences	Dr. Gary N. FITSIMMONS
15	Director Personnel Services	Mrs. Angie C. PRICE
41	Athletic Director	Mr. Taylor HASTY
18	Director of Physical Plant	Mr. David A. MORGAN
29	Director of Alumni Affairs	Mrs. Paulakay HALL
07	Director of Admissions	Mr. Joshua D. HOOD
88	Accreditation Liaison	Mr. Samuel J. YOUNGS

Carson-Newman University (H)

1646 Russell Avenue, PO Box 557,
Jefferson City TN 37760-2204
County: Jefferson FICE Identification: 003481
Unit ID: 219806
Telephone: (865) 471-2000 Carnegie Class: Masters/M
FAX Number: (865) 471-3502 Calendar System: Semester
URL: www.cn.edu
Established: 1851 Annual Undergrad Tuition & Fees: $26,360
Enrollment: 2,528 Coed
Affiliation or Control: Southern Baptist IRS Status: 501(c)3
Highest Offering: Doctorate
Accreditation: SC, AAFCS, ART, CACREP, CAEPN, DIETD, MUS, NURSE

Code	Title	Name
01	President	Dr. J. Randall O'BRIEN
05	Vice Pres Academic Affairs/Provost	Dr. Paul PERCY
30	Vice President for Advancement	Vacant
32	Vice President Student Affairs	Dr. Ross BRUMMETT
35	Dean of Student Affairs	Mrs. Shelley BALL
08	Dean of Library Services	Mr. Bruce KOCOUR
26	Exec Dir University Relations	Mr. Charles KEY
37	Director Financial Aid	Mrs. Danette SEALE
38	Director Counseling Services	Mrs. Jennifer CATLETT
13	Director of IT	Mr. David TUELL
18	Chief Facilities/Physical Plant	Mr. Ondes WEBSTER
84	Dean of Enrollment Management	Mr. Aaron PORTER
92	Director of Honors Program	Dr. Andrew SMITH
15	Director of Human Resources	Mrs. Elaine SMITH
41	Athletic Director	Mr. Allen MORGAN
10	Chief Financial/Business Officer	Mrs. Martha CHAMBERS
85	Dean of Global Education	Dr. Regina SULLIVAN
06	Registrar	Mrs. Sheryl GRAY

Chattanooga College (I)

248 Northgate Mall Drive, Suite 130,
Chattanooga TN 37415
County: Hamilton FICE Identification: 022042
Unit ID: 220118
Telephone: (423) 624-0077 Carnegie Class: Assoc/HVT-High Non
FAX Number: (423) 624-1575 Calendar System: Quarter
URL: www.chattanoogacollege.edu
Established: 1968 Annual Undergrad Tuition & Fees: $10,690
Enrollment: 298 Coed
Affiliation or Control: Proprietary IRS Status: Proprietary
Highest Offering: Associate Degree
Accreditation: ACCSC

Code	Title	Name
01	President	Mr. William G. FAOUR
03	Vice President	Mr. Toney C. MCFADDEN
37	Director Financial Aid	Mrs. Evelyn DAVIS

Christian Brothers University (A)

650 East Parkway S, Memphis TN 38104-5581
County: Shelby FICE Identification: 003482
Unit ID: 219833
Telephone: (901) 321-3000 Carnegie Class: Masters/M
FAX Number: (901) 321-3494 Calendar System: Semester
URL: www.cbu.edu
Established: 1871 Annual Undergrad Tuition & Fees: $30,860
Enrollment: 1,842 Coed
Affiliation or Control: Roman Catholic IRS Status: 501(c)3
Highest Offering: Master's
Accreditation: **SC**, CAEPN, ENG, NURSE

01 President .... Dr. John SMARRELLI, JR.
05 VP Academics & Student Life .... Dr. Paul HAUGHT
10 CFO & VP Administration .... Ms. Carolyn HEAD
111 Vice Pres Institutional Advancement .... Vacant
84 VP for Enrollment Management .... Dr. Anne KENWORTHY
26 VP for Communications & Marketing .. Ms. Deborah BLANCHARD
20 Assoc VP of Acad & Strategic Init .... Dr. Jack HARGETT
32 Dean of Students .... Ms. Karen CONWAY
13 Associate VP for ITS .... Mr. Brett DOTY
06 Registrar .... Mr. Scott SUMMERS
36 Director Career Center .... Mrs. Amy WARE
08 Director of Plough Library .... Ms. Kay CUNNINGHAM
07 Director of Admissions .... Ms. Kristi FORMAN
38 Director of Counseling .... Mrs. Sadie LISENBY
37 Director Financial Resources .... Dr. John LEWIS
09 Dir Inst Research/Effectiveness .... Ms. Melissa S. ANDREWS
39 Director Residence Life .... Mr. Alton WADE
35 Associate VP for Student Life .... Dr. Timothy DOYLE
42 Director of Ministry and Mission .... Br. Dominic EHRMANTRAUT
92 Director Honors Program .... Dr. Tracie L. BURKE
41 Athletic Director .... Mr. Brian SUMMERS
30 Sr Director Development .... Ms. Jordan SCARLESKI
29 Director Alumni .... Mr. Terez WILSON
21 Controller .... Mr. Thomas COCHRAN
15 Director of Personnel .... Mr. Greg ELLER
18 Chief Facility/Physical Plant .... Mr. Philip R. YELVINGTON
19 Director of Security .... Mr. John D. LOTRIONTE
40 Director Bookstore .... Ms. Shannon DAVIS
50 Dean School of Business .... Dr. Bjoern A. CLAASSEN
54 Dean School of Engineering .... Dr. Pong MALASRI
49 Interim Dean School of Arts .... Dr. Scott GEIS
81 Dean School of Science .... Dr. James MCGUFFEE
107 Dir Graduate/Professional Stds Pgms .... Ms. Toni BENNETT
58 Director Graduate Education Program .... Dr. Samantha ALPERIN
58 Director MBA Program .... Dr. Scott LAWYER
66 Director Nursing Program .... Dr. Jennifer HITT
88 Director Physician Assistant Stds .... Ms. Teresa PRESTON
04 Senior Executive Asst to President .... Mrs. Donna M. FREEMAN
104 Director Study Abroad .... Dr. Emily FORSDICK
25 Chief Contracts/Grants Admin .... Mr. Robert ARNOLD
101 Secretary of the Institution/Board .... Ms. Melanie BREMER

Concorde Career College (B)

5100 Poplar Avenue, Suite 132, Memphis TN 38137-0132
County: Shelby FICE Identification: 021571
Unit ID: 219903
Telephone: (901) 761-9494 Carnegie Class: Spec 2-yr-Health
FAX Number: (901) 761-3293 Calendar System: Semester
URL: www.concorde.edu
Established: 1967 Annual Undergrad Tuition & Fees: N/A
Enrollment: 1,258 Coed
Affiliation or Control: Proprietary IRS Status: Proprietary
Highest Offering: Associate Degree
Accreditation: **COE**, COARC, DA, DH, MLTAD, OTA, POLYT, PTAA, RAD, SURGT

01 Campus President .... Mrs. Lori SPENCER
11 Regional Vice President Operations .... Mr. Tommy STEWART

The Crown College of the Bible (C)

2307 W. Beaver Creek Drive, Powell TN 37849
County: Knox Identification: 667141
Telephone: (865) 938-8186 Carnegie Class: Not Classified
FAX Number: (865) 938-8188 Calendar System: Semester
URL: thecrowncollege.com
Established: 1991 Annual Undergrad Tuition & Fees: N/A
Enrollment: N/A Coed
Affiliation or Control: Baptist IRS Status: 501(c)3
Highest Offering: Master's
Accreditation: **TRACS**

01 Founder & President .... Clarence SEXTON
05 Vice President of Academics .... Tim TOMLINSON
11 Vice President of Operations .... M. Shannon SEXTON

Cumberland University (D)

1 Cumberland Square, Lebanon TN 37087-3554
County: Wilson FICE Identification: 003485
Unit ID: 219949
Telephone: (615) 444-2562 Carnegie Class: Masters/M
FAX Number: (615) 444-2569 Calendar System: Semester
URL: www.cumberland.edu
Established: 1842 Annual Undergrad Tuition & Fees: $21,210
Enrollment: 1,550 Coed
Affiliation or Control: Independent Non-Profit IRS Status: 501(c)3
Highest Offering: Master's
Accreditation: **SC**, ACBSP, #CAATE, CAEPN, NURSE

01 President .... Dr. Paul STUMB
05 Provost/Vice Pres Academic Affairs .... Dr. William MCKEE
10 Vice President of Finance .... Ms. Judy G. JORDAN
111 Vice President of Advancement .... Mr. Rusty RICHARDSON
13 Vice Pres IT/Campus Services .... Mr. Joe GRAY
32 AVP/Dean of Students .... Ms. Stephanie WALKER
66 Dean Nursing and Health Sciences .... Dr. Joy KIMBRELL
100 Executive Coordinator to President .... Ms. Leslie STEELE
30 Exec Dir Development/Alumni Rels .... Vacant
08 Director Library Services .... Ms. Bettina WARKENTIN
84 Exec Director Enrollment Services .... Mr. Eddie LOVIN
41 Director of Athletics .... Mr. Ron PAVAN
06 Registrar .... Ms. Tammi PAVAN
15 Human Resources Generalist .... Ms. Renee JONES
14 Director of Information Technology .... Mr. Jerry ENGLAND
09 Director of Institutional Research .... Mr. Larry F. VAUGHAN
26 Exec Dir Communications/Marketing .... Mr. Phillip CARTER
36 Dir of Career Services/Internships .... Ms. Courtney VICK
37 Director Student Financial Aid .... Ms. Beatrice LACHANCE
39 Director Student Housing .... Ms. Catie STRAUBE
50 Dean Labry School of Business .... Dr. Chris FULLER
53 Dean of Humanities/Education & Art .... Dr. Eric CUMMINGS

Daymar College (E)

2691 Trenton Road, Clarksville TN 37040-6718
Telephone: (931) 552-7600 Identification: 666492
Accreditation: **ACICS**, PTAA

† Branch campus of Daymar College, Nashville, TN.

Daymar College (F)

415 Golden Bear Court, Murfreesboro TN 37128-5508
Telephone: (615) 217-9347 Identification: 666392
Accreditation: **ACICS**

† Branch campus of Daymar College, Nashville, TN.

Daymar College (G)

560 Royal Parkway, Nashville TN 37214
County: Davidson FICE Identification: 004934
Unit ID: 220002
Telephone: (615) 361-7555 Carnegie Class: Bac/Assoc-Mixed
FAX Number: (615) 367-2736 Calendar System: Quarter
URL: www.daymarcollege.edu
Established: 1884 Annual Undergrad Tuition & Fees: $15,000
Enrollment: 153 Coed
Affiliation or Control: Proprietary IRS Status: Proprietary
Highest Offering: Baccalaureate
Accreditation: **ACICS**

01 President .... Mr. Joel MUSGROVE
05 Campus Dean .... Ms. Laurna TAYLOR
10 Director of Financial Services .... Ms. Denise JERNIEAN
36 Director of Career Services .... Ms. Angela PEARROW
06 Registrar .... Mr. Ryan PALOMBO

East Tennessee State University (H)

1276 Gilbreath Drive, Johnson City TN 37614-1700
County: Washington FICE Identification: 003487
Unit ID: 220075
Telephone: (423) 439-1000 Carnegie Class: DU-Mod
FAX Number: (423) 439-5770 Calendar System: Semester
URL: www.etsu.edu
Established: 1911 Annual Undergrad Tuition & Fees (In-State): $8,341
Enrollment: 14,334 Coed
Affiliation or Control: State IRS Status: 501(c)3
Highest Offering: Doctorate
Accreditation: **SC**, ART, AUD, CACREP, CAEPN, CIDA, CLPSY, COARC, CS, CSHSE, DH, DIETD, DIETI, ENGR, ENGT, MED, MUS, NURSE, PH, PHAR, PTA, RAD, SP, SW, THEA

02 President .... Dr. Brian E. NOLAND
100 Chief of Staff/Assoc VP Health Affs .... Dr. Jane M. JONES
11 Acting Chief Operating Officer .... Mr. Jeremy B. ROSS
05 Provost/Vice Pres Academic Affairs .... Dr. Bert C. BACH
10 Acting Chief Financial Officer .... Dr. B. J. KING
17 Vice President Health Affairs .... Dr. Wilsie S. BISHOP
111 VP University Advancement .... Ms. Pamela S. RITTER
101 Secretary of the Board .... Dr. M. David LINVILLE, JR.
41 Athletic Director .... Dr. Richard L. SANDER
28 Spec Asst to Pres Equity/Diversity .... Ms. Mary V. JORDAN
116 Director of Internal Audit .... Ms. Rebecca B. LEWIS
43 University Counsel .... Mr. Edward J. KELLY
26 Exec Director of Univ Relations/CCO .... Mr. Joseph E. SMITH
84 Vice Provost Enrollment Services .... Dr. Ramona A. WILLIAMS
51 Dean Cont Studies & Acad Outreach .... Dr. Richard E. OSBORN
46 Vice Prov Research/Sponsored Pgms .... Dr. William R. DUNCAN
32 Vice Pres Student Affairs .... Dr. Joe H. SHERLIN
20 Vice Provost Academic Affairs .... Dr. M. Marshall GRUBE
20 Vice Provost Undergraduate Ed .... Dr. William G. KIRKWOOD
18 Assoc VP for Facilities Management .... Mr. William B. RASNICK, JR.
35 Assoc VP Student Engagement .... Dr. Jeffery S. HOWARD
13 CIO/Sr Vice Provost for ITS .... Dr. Karen D. KING
11 Assoc VP Administrative Services .... Dr. Katherine M. KELLEY
21 Sr Assoc VP Finance & Admin .... Dr. B. J. KING
112 Exec Director for Planned Giving .... Ms. Sunny SANDOS
29 Assoc VP Univ Adv/Exec Dir Alumni .... Dr. Robert M. PLUMMER
86 Assoc VP for Comm & Gov Relations .... Ms. Bridget R. BAIRD
49 Dean College Arts & Science .... Dr. Gordon K. ANDERSON
50 Dean College of Business/Technology .... Dr. Dennis R. DEPEW
76 Dean College of Clin/Rehab Sci .... Dr. Donald A. SAMPLES
53 Dean College of Education .... Dr. Gregory F. ALOIA
92 Interim Dean Honors College .... Dr. Judith B. SLAGLE
63 Dean College of Medicine .... Dr. Robert T. MEANS, JR.
67 Dean College of Pharmacy .... Dr. Debbie C. BYRD
66 Dean College of Nursing .... Dr. Wendy M. NEHRING
69 Dean College of Public Health .... Dr. Randolph F. WYKOFF
58 Dean School of Graduate Studies .... Dr. Cecilia A. MCINTOSH
08 Dean of Libraries .... Ms. Patricia R. VAN ZANDT
06 University Registrar .... Ms. Sheryl L. BURNETTE
07 Director of Admissions .... Mr. Brian L. HENLEY
36 Director University Career Services .... Dr. David E. MAGEE, JR.
38 Director Counseling Center .... Dr. Dan L. JONES
37 Director of Financial Aid .... Ms. Catherine A. MORGAN
92 Director University Honors Program ... Dr. Karen R. KORNWEIBEL
39 Director Student Housing .... Dr. Bonnie L. BURCHETT
85 Dir International Programs/Services .... Dr. Maria D. COSTA
93 Multicultural Director .... Ms. Laura C. TERRY
19 Director Public Safety .... Chief Jack R. COTREL
25 Director of Sponsored Programs .... Ms. Wendy ECKERT
87 Director Summer & Winter Sessions .... Dr. Sarah E. HARKNESS
94 Director of Women's Studies .... Dr. Phyllis A. THOMPSON
105 Web Manager .... Ms. Michaele D. LAWS
15 Dir Empl Relations/Compensation/Dev .... Ms. Diana D. MCCLAY
118 Director Benefits/Retirement/HRIS .... Ms. Tammy S. HAMM
108 Dir Institutional Effectiveness .... Dr. Cheri CLAVIER
45 Assoc VP/Chief Planning Officer .... Dr. Michael B. HOFF

Fisk University (I)

1000 17th Avenue N, Nashville TN 37208-3051
County: Davidson FICE Identification: 003490
Unit ID: 220181
Telephone: (615) 329-8500 Carnegie Class: Bac-A&S
FAX Number: N/A Calendar System: Semester
URL: www.fisk.edu
Established: 1866 Annual Undergrad Tuition & Fees: $21,480
Enrollment: 855 Coed
Affiliation or Control: Independent Non-Profit IRS Status: 501(c)3
Highest Offering: Master's
Accreditation: **SC**, MUS

01 President .... Dr. Kevin D. ROME
05 VP of Academic Affairs & Provost .... Dr. Rodney S. HANLEY
10 Vice President for Finance and CFO .... Ms. Willie R. HUGHEY
04 Exec Assistant to the President .... Mrs. Sherri B. RUCKER
111 Vice President of Inst Advancement .... Dr. Jens FREDERIKSEN
09 AVP for Inst Effectiveness Accredit .... Dr. Jason R. CURRY
32 VP of Student Engagement & Enroll .... Vacant
20 Vice Provost Academic Initiatives .... Dr. Arnold BURGER
13 Infrastructure Manager .... Mr. Chris ESTES
29 Exec Director of Alumni Affairs .... Mrs. Adrienne LATHAM
07 Dean of Recruitment & Admission .... Ms. Juliet JOHNSON
37 Director of Financial Aid .... Ms. Bianca MATLOCK
06 Registrar .... Ms. Fantina CARTER
08 University Librarian .... Dr. Jessie C. SMITH
81 Dean Sch Natural Science/Math/Bus .... Dr. Cathy MARTIN
79 Dean School Humanities/Social Sci .... Dr. Reavis MITCHELL
41 Dir of Athletics & Intramural Pgms .... Dr. Larry GLOVER
42 Dean of the Chapel .... Dr. Jason CURRY
25 Dir Sponsored Research & Programs .... Dr. Amelia HUNTER
112 Director of Planned Giving .... Ms. Sheila SMITH
18 Director of Facilities .... Mr. Norman RAPP
19 Chief/Director of Campus Safety .... Mr. Mickey WEST
96 Director of Purchasing .... Vacant
36 Director Career Development .... Ms. Latreace WELLS
38 Coordinator of Student Counseling .... Dr. Sheila PETERS
15 Director of Human Resources .... Dr. JaCenda DAVIDSON
21 Comptroller .... Mr. Warren IRONS
102 Dir Foundation/Corporate Relations .... Mr. Van PINNOCK
105 Webmaster .... Mr. George DOTSON
39 Director Student Housing .... Dr. Christopher DUKE
43 Dir Legal Services/General Counsel .... Ms. Stacey GARRETT
106 Dir Online Education/E-learning .... Dr. Shirley BROWN
86 Director Government Relations .... Dr. Edwina HAMBY
101 Secretary of the Board .... Ms. Sherri RUCKER
26 Chief Public Relations .... Mr. Raymond WADE
35 Asst VP/Dean of Student Engagement .... Ms. Natara GARVIN

Fortis Institute (J)

1025 Highway 111, Cookeville TN 38501-4305
County: Putnam FICE Identification: 023263
Unit ID: 418870
Telephone: (931) 526-3660 Carnegie Class: Spec 2-yr-Health
FAX Number: (931) 372-2603 Calendar System: Quarter
URL: www.fortis.edu/cookeville-tennessee.php
Established: 1970 Annual Undergrad Tuition & Fees: $14,517
Enrollment: 212 Coed
Affiliation or Control: Proprietary IRS Status: Proprietary
Highest Offering: Associate Degree
Accreditation: **COE**, MLTAD, RAD, SURGT

01 Campus President .... Mr. James WILLIAMSON
06 Registrar .... Ms. Wendy BANDY
07 Director of Admissions .... Mr. Solomon WILLIAMS
10 Chief Business Officer .... Ms. Melissa LEWIS
36 Director Student Placement .... Ms. Cindy GARRISON
37 Director Student Financial Aid .... Ms. Lisa WALLING

Fortis Institute-Nashville (A)

3354 Perimeter Hill Drive Ste 105, Nashville TN 37211
Telephone: (615) 320-5917 Identification: 770509
Accreditation: ABHES, CVT, MLTAD, RAD, SURGT, SURTEC

† Branch campus of Fortis Institute, Baton Rouge, LA.

Fountainhead College of Technology (B)

3203 Tazewell Pike, Knoxville TN 37918
County: Knox FICE Identification: 007439
Unit ID: 221795
Telephone: (865) 688-9422 Carnegie Class: Spec-4-yr-Other Tech
FAX Number: (865) 688-2419 Calendar System: Semester
URL: www.fountainheadcollege.edu
Established: 1947 Annual Undergrad Tuition & Fees: $14,750
Enrollment: 94 Coed
Affiliation or Control: Proprietary IRS Status: Proprietary
Highest Offering: Baccalaureate
Accreditation: ACCSC

00 CEO .... Mr. Richard W. RACKLEY
01 Campus President .... Ms. Casey C. RACKLEY
32 Director Student Services .... Ms. Fran CLEMMONS

Freed-Hardeman University (C)

158 E Main, Henderson TN 38340-2398
County: Chester FICE Identification: 003492
Unit ID: 220215
Telephone: (731) 989-6000 Carnegie Class: Masters/S
FAX Number: N/A Calendar System: Semester
URL: www.fhu.edu
Established: 1869 Annual Undergrad Tuition & Fees: $21,500
Enrollment: 1,828 Coed
Affiliation or Control: Churches Of Christ IRS Status: 501(c)3
Highest Offering: Doctorate
Accreditation: SC, ACBSP, CAEPN, NURSE, SW, THEOL

01 President .... Mr. David R. SHANNON
04 Executive Assistant to President .... Mrs. Donna STEELE
05 Provost and VP Academics .... Dr. Charles VIRES
10 Exec VP and CFO .... Dr. Dwayne WILSON
111 VP for Community Engagement .... Mr. Dave CLOUSE
32 VP Student Services .... Dr. Wayne SCOTT
20 Associate VP for Academics .... Dr. Vicki JOHNSON
110 Associate VP for Advancement .... Mr. Kyle LAMB
84 Associate VP Enrollment Management .... Mr. Joseph ASKEW
115 Associate VP of Finance .... Mr. Jay SATTERFIELD
41 Director of Athletics .... Mr. Michael MCCUTCHEN
44 Director Annual Giving .... Mr. Ryan MALECHA
07 Director of Admissions .... Mrs. Kaylan STEWART
29 Director of Alumni Relations .... Mrs. Donna STEELE
35 Dean of Students .... Mr. Stuart VARNER
35 Dean of Student Life .... Mr. Tony ALLEN
06 Registrar .... Mr. Jared GOTT
37 Director Student Financial Services .... Mrs. Summer JUDD
08 Library Director .... Mr. Wade OSBURN
70 Director of Social Work Program .... Mrs. Nadine MCNEAL
24 A-V Supervisor .... Mrs. Gail NASH
21 Controller .... Mrs. Courtney INSELL
108 Dir Institutional Effectiveness .... Mr. A.B WHITE
09 Director of Institutional Research .... Mr. Micah SMITH
18 Director of Facilities and Grounds .... Mr. Shannon SEWELL
73 Dean College of Biblical Studies .... Dr. Billy R. SMITH
50 Dean College of Business .... Dr. Jason BRASHIER
53 Dean College of Educ & Behav Sci .... Dr. Sharen CYPRESS
49 Dean College of Arts & Sciences .... Dr. LeAnn SELF-DAVIS
92 Dean of Honors College .... Dr. Jenny JOHNSON
104 Dir of International Studies .... Dr. Jenny JOHNSON
38 Director of Counseling .... Mrs. Nicole YOUNG
36 Director of Univ Career Center .... Dr. Wayne SCOTT
96 Purchasing Coordinator .... Mr. Chris CURRY
40 University Book Store Manager .... Ms. Katie NIXON
19 Director Security/Safety .... Mr. Rodney WEAVER

Harding School of Theology (D)

1000 Cherry Road, Memphis TN 38117-5499
Telephone: (901) 761-1350 FICE Identification: 004081
Accreditation: &NH, THEOL

† Regional accreditation is carried under Harding University, Searcy, AR.

Hiwassee College (E)

225 Hiwassee College Drive, Madisonville TN 37354
County: Monroe FICE Identification: 003494
Unit ID: 220312
Telephone: (423) 442-2001 Carnegie Class: Bac/Assoc-Mixed
FAX Number: (423) 420-1929 Calendar System: Semester
URL: www.hiwassee.edu
Established: 1850 Annual Undergrad Tuition & Fees: $15,543
Enrollment: 280 Coed
Affiliation or Control: United Methodist IRS Status: 501(c)3
Highest Offering: Baccalaureate
Accreditation: TRACS, DH

01 President .... Dr. Robin J. TRICOLI
05 Vice Pres for Academic Affairs .... Dr. Jason LEONARD
10 VP Business Affairs & Treasurer .... Mr. David WATTS
84 Vice Pres Enrollment Management .... Mr. Richard BEAUBIEN
06 Registrar .... Jane DYE

Huntington College of Health Sciences (F)

117 Legacy View Way, Knoxville TN 37918
County: Knox Identification: 666971
Unit ID: 488068
Telephone: (865) 524-8079 Carnegie Class: Not Classified
FAX Number: (865) 524-8339 Calendar System: Semester
URL: www.hchs.edu
Established: 1985 Annual Undergrad Tuition & Fees: $6,155
Enrollment: N/A Coed
Affiliation or Control: Proprietary IRS Status: Proprietary
Highest Offering: Doctorate
Accreditation: DEAC

01 Chief Executive Officer/President .... Dr. Art PRESSER
05 Provost .... Mr. Gene BRUNO
10 Chief Financial Officer .... Mr. Robert SCHMAEF
11 Sr VP Admin & Academic Affairs .... Ms. Jennifer GREEN
07 Director of Admissions .... Ms. Kim MARQUIS
21 Director of Finance .... Ms. Jeannette MINIX
37 Director of Financial Aid .... Ms. Heather MORRISON-MONGER
06 Registrar .... Ms. Brittany LONGNECKER
08 Head Librarian .... Ms. Pam WREN
09 Director of Institutional Research .... Dr. Denise WOOD

John A. Gupton College (G)

1616 Church Street, Nashville TN 37203-2920
County: Davidson FICE Identification: 008859
Unit ID: 220464
Telephone: (615) 327-3927 Carnegie Class: Spec 2-yr-A&S
FAX Number: (615) 321-4518 Calendar System: Semester
URL: www.guptoncollege.edu
Established: 1946 Annual Undergrad Tuition & Fees: $11,070
Enrollment: 120 Coed
Affiliation or Control: Independent Non-Profit IRS Status: 501(c)3
Highest Offering: Associate Degree
Accreditation: SC, FUSER

01 President .... Mr. B. Steven SPANN
08 Library Director .... Mr. William P. BRUCE
06 Registrar .... Ms. Lisa MOFFITT

Johnson University (H)

7900 Johnson Drive, Knoxville TN 37998-0001
County: Knox FICE Identification: 003495
Unit ID: 220473
Telephone: (865) 573-4517 Carnegie Class: Spec-4-yr-Faith
FAX Number: (865) 251-2337 Calendar System: Semester
URL: www.johnsonu.edu
Established: 1893 Annual Undergrad Tuition & Fees: $13,950
Enrollment: 1,171 Coed
Affiliation or Control: Christian Churches And Churches of Christ
IRS Status: 501(c)3
Highest Offering: Doctorate
Accreditation: SC, BI, CACREP, CAEPN

01 President .... Dr. Gary E. WEEDMAN
05 VP for Academic Affairs/Provost .... Dr. Thomas SMITH
84 VP for Enrollment Services .... Vacant
26 VP for External Relations .... Richard CLARK
32 VP for Student Services .... David LEGG
11 VP for Administration .... Cliff MCCARTNEY
10 VP for Finance .... Cindy BARNARD
03 Chancellor/Vice Provost Florida .... Dr. Michael CHAMBERS
120 Assoc Provost for Online Education .... Dr. John KETCHEN
42 Dean of the Chapel .... Bill WOLF
20 Vice Provost for Academic Services .... Dr. Greg LINTON
13 Director of IT .... Glenn FEASTER
41 Athletic Director .... Ken UNDERWOOD
123 Director of Graduate Admissions .... Lisa TARWATER
20 Director of Program Administration .... Joy WINGFIELD
08 Library Director .... Carrie Beth LOWE
108 IE/Director of Assessment .... Emili WILLIAMS
07 Director of Undergrad Admissions .... Julee SCHULTZ
15 Director Human Resources .... Ruthanne BEAM
18 Director of Plant Services .... Ben LUTZ, JR.
37 Director of Financial Aid .... Kayla WILLIAMS
06 Registrar .... Andrew FRAIZER
121 Director of Academic Support .... Kelly ESTES
35 Assoc Dean of Students .... Deborah LANE
49 Dean Arts & Sciences .... Dr. Gary STRATTON
73 Dean Bible & Theology .... Dr. Jon WEATHERLY
50 Dean Business & Public Leadership .... Dr. Catherlyn BRIM
60 Dean Communication & Creative Arts .... Dr. Matthew BROADDUS
73 Dean Congregational Ministry .... Dr. Daniel OVERDORF
82 Dean Intercultural Studies .... Dr. Linda WHITMER
83 Dean Social & Behavioral Sciences .... Dr. Sean RIDGE
53 Dean Templar School of Education .... Dr. Roy MILLER

King University (I)

1350 King College Road, Bristol TN 37620-2699
County: Sullivan FICE Identification: 003496
Unit ID: 220516
Telephone: (423) 968-4861 Carnegie Class: Masters/L
FAX Number: (423) 968-4456 Calendar System: Other
URL: www.king.edu
Established: 1867 Annual Undergrad Tuition & Fees: $27,276
Enrollment: 2,920 Coed
Affiliation or Control: Presbyterian Church (U.S.A.) IRS Status: 501(c)3
Highest Offering: Doctorate
Accreditation: SC, #CAATE, NURSE, SW

01 President .... Mr. Alexander W. WHITAKER, IV
05 Vice Pres Acad Affairs/Acad Dean .... Dr. Matthew ROBERTS
10 Vice President for Admin & Finance .... Mr. James P. DONAHUE
32 Vice President for Student Affairs .... Dr. Robert A. LITTLETON
84 Assoc VP of Enrollment Mgmt .... Mr. Micah R. CREWS
26 Vice Pres Marketing .... Mrs. A. LeAnn HUGHES
08 Dean of Library Services .... Ms. Erika BRAMMER
35 Assoc VP/Dean of Student Success .... Mr. Matthew S. PELTIER
04 Executive Assistant to President .... Ms. Holly L. STEVENS
06 Registrar/Dir Regist & Records .... Mrs. Jessica SWINEY
30 Director of Development .... Mrs. Denise ASBURY
42 Chaplain .... Dr. Brian ALDERMAN
21 Director of Business Operations .... Mr. Thomas R. LARSON
36 Director of Career Development .... Ms. Donna H. FELTY
41 Athletic Director .... Mr. J. David HICKS
38 Director of Counseling .... Mr. Charles S. THOMPSON
88 Sports Information Director .... Mr. Travis L. CHELL
40 Bookstore Manager .... Ms. Susan D. MARSHALL
37 Director Student Financial Aid .... Mr. Richard BRAND
18 Chief Facilities/Physical Plant .... Mr. Todd THOMAS
92 Director of Honors Program .... Dr. Craig STREETMAN
27 Director Marketing & Communications .... Ms. Sarah CLEVINGER
27 Assoc Director of Communication .... Mrs. Laura K. BOGGAN
100 Chief of Staff .... Mrs. Rebecca J. THOMAS

Lane College (J)

545 Lane Avenue, Jackson TN 38301-4598
County: Madison FICE Identification: 003499
Unit ID: 220598
Telephone: (731) 426-7500 Carnegie Class: Bac-Diverse
FAX Number: (731) 427-3987 Calendar System: Semester
URL: www.lanecollege.edu
Established: 1882 Annual Undergrad Tuition & Fees: $10,280
Enrollment: 1,376 Coed
Affiliation or Control: Christian Methodist Episcopal IRS Status: 501(c)3
Highest Offering: Baccalaureate
Accreditation: SC

01 President .... Dr. Logan C. HAMPTON
03 Executive Vice President/Chaplain .... Dr. Moses GOLDMON
05 Vice President Academic Affairs .... Dr. Michelle STEWART
11 Exec Vice Pres Administration .... Ms. Sherrill B. SCOTT
32 Vice President Student Affairs .... Mr. Darryl MCGEE
111 Vice Pres Inst Advance/Dir Alum Aff .... Ms. Tori HALIBURTON
13 Assoc VP Information Technology .... Mr. Earnest L. MITCHELL, III
100 Chief of Staff .... Ms. Darlette C. SAMUELS
18 Chief Facilities/Physical Plant .... Mr. Mack CHAVIS, JR.
09 Director Institutional Research .... Ms. Charlise ANDERSON
08 Librarian .... Ms. Lan WANG
07 Director of Admissions .... Mr. Derrick MAYS
06 Registrar .... Mr. Terry W. BLACKMON
37 Director of Financial Aid .... Ms. Lori MITCHUM
20 Director Academic Assessment .... Vacant
96 Director of Purchasing .... Ms. Tammy MCDOUGAL
36 Assistant Director of Career Svcs .... Ms. Katrina TATE
40 Director Bookstore .... Mr. Shaquilla SMITH
19 Director of Safety/Security .... Mr. Steaven JOY
41 Director of Athletics .... Mr. Derrick BURROUGHS
29 Director Alumni Relations .... Ms. Tori HALIBURTON
27 Chief Information Officer .... Vacant
103 Dir Workforce/Career Development .... Mrs. Sherry RUTHERFORD
105 Director Web Services .... Mr. Andy JONES
39 Director Student Housing .... Mr. Macklin GIPSON
43 Dir Legal Services/General Counsel .... Mr. Nathan PRIDE
44 Director Annual Giving .... Ms. Lisa PEOPLES
86 Director Government Relations .... Mr. Richard DONNELL

L'Ecole Culinaire Memphis (K)

1245 North Germantown Parkway, Cordova TN 38016
Telephone: (901) 754-7115 Identification: 770841
Accreditation: ACCSC

† Branch campus of Vatterott College-Des Moines, Des Moines, IA

Lee University (L)

1120 N Ocoee Street, Cleveland TN 37320-3450
County: Bradley FICE Identification: 003500
Unit ID: 220613
Telephone: (423) 614-8000 Carnegie Class: Masters/M
FAX Number: (423) 614-8083 Calendar System: Semester
URL: www.leeuniversity.edu
Established: 1918 Annual Undergrad Tuition & Fees: $15,770
Enrollment: 5,041 Coed
Affiliation or Control: Church Of God IRS Status: 501(c)3
Highest Offering: Beyond Master's But Less Than Doctorate
Accreditation: SC, ACBSP, CAATE, CAEPN, MFCD, MUS, NURSE

01 President .... Dr. C. Paul CONN
04 Executive Assistant to President .... Mrs. Stephanie TAYLOR
10 Vice President Business & Finance .... Mr. Chris CONINE
05 Vice President for Academic Affairs .... Dr. Deborah MURRAY

84 Vice President for Enrollment ... Mr. Phil COOK
26 VP for University Relations ... Dr. Jerome HAMMOND
32 VP for Student Development ... Dr. Mike HAYES
13 VP for Information Services ... Dr. Jayson VANHOOK
20 Assistant VP for Academic Affairs ... Dr. Eric MOYEN
11 Assistant VP for Operations ... Mr. Cole STRONG
21 Comptroller ... Mr. Duane PACE
37 Director of Financial Aid ... Mrs. Marian DILL
35 Dean of Students ... Mr. Alan MCCLUNG
15 Director of Human Resources ... Mrs. Ann MCELRATH
14 Director of IT Operations ... Mr. Chris GOLDEN
14 Director of IT Systems ... Mr. Nate TUCKER
29 Director of Alumni Relations ... Mrs. Patti CAWOOD
39 Director of Residential Life ... Mr. George BOSTANIC
06 Registrar ... Ms. Cathy THOMPSOM
113 Bursar ... Ms. Kristy HARNER
08 Librarian ... Dr. Louis MORGAN
42 Director of Campus Ministries ... Rev. Jimmy HARPER
25 Director of Grants ... Mrs. Vanessa HAMMOND
19 Director of Campus Safety ... Mr. Matt BRINKMAN
23 Director of Health Services ... Mr. Mickey MOORE
27 Director of Public Information ... Mr. Brian CONN
73 Dean School of Religion ... Dr. Terry CROSS
49 Dean College of Arts & Sciences ... Dr. Matthew MELTON
53 Dean College of Education ... Dr. William ESTES
64 Dean School of Music ... Dr. William GREEN
66 Dean School of Nursing ... Dr. Sara CAMPBELL
51 Exec Dir of Div of Adult Learning ... Dr. Joshua BLACK
123 Director of Graduate Enrollment ... Dr. Jeffery MCGIRT
38 Director of Counseling Center ... Dr. David QUAGLIANA
18 Director of Physical Plant ... Mr. Larry BERRY
41 Athletic Director ... Mr. Larry CARPENTER
104 Director of Global Perspectives ... Mrs. Angeline MCMULLIN
36 Director of Calling and Career ... Dr. Sheila CORNEA
07 Director of Admissions ... Mr. Darren ECHOLS
09 Director of Institutional Research ... Vacant

LeMoyne-Owen College (A)

807 Walker Avenue, Memphis TN 38126-6595
County: Shelby FICE Identification: 003501
Unit ID: 220604
Telephone: (901) 435-1000 Carnegie Class: Bac-Diverse
FAX Number: (901) 435-1699 Calendar System: Semester
URL: www.loc.edu
Established: 1862 Annual Undergrad Tuition & Fees: $10,880
Enrollment: 945 Coed
Affiliation or Control: Multiple Protestant Denominations
IRS Status: 501(c)3
Highest Offering: Baccalaureate
Accreditation: SC, CAEPN

01 President ... Dr. Andrea LEWIS MILLER
05 VP Academic and Student Affairs ... Vacant
10 VP Finance and Administration ... Ms. Loretta STUBBS
88 Director Title III Administration ... Ms. Shirley HILL
32 Dean of Students ... Mr. Kenneth QUINN
111 VP Institutional Advancement ... Ms. Brenda GAINES-OLLIE
13 VP Information Technology ... Mr. Dwayne CABLE
84 Exec Dir Strategic Enrollment Mgmt ... Dr. Delphia HARRIS
15 Director of Human Resources ... Ms. Neva BURKE
08 Librarian ... Ms. Annette BERHE
37 Director Student Financial Services ... Ms. Phyllis TORRY
06 Registrar ... Mr. Addie HARVEY
100 Chief of Staff ... Vacant
29 Director of Alumni Relations ... Ms. Frankie JEFFRIES
21 Executive Finance Director ... Ms. Yolanda EMODOGO
09 Director Institutional Research ... Mr. Reoungeneria MCFARLAND
92 Director Du Bois Honors Program ... Mr. Dorsey PATTERSON
50 Chair Div Business & Econ Devel ... Dr. Katherine CAUSEY
53 Chair Education Division ... Dr. Ralph CALHOUN
57 Chair Div Fine Arts & Humanities ... Mr. Claybourne FOSTER
65 Chair Div Natural & Math Science ... Dr. Sherry PAINTER
83 Chair Div Social & Behavioral Sci ... Mr. Michael ROBINSON
38 Director Student Counseling ... Mr. Tony WHITSON
26 Dir Public Relations & Marketing ... Vacant
41 Director of Athletics ... Mr. Clint JACKSON
11 Director Administrative Services ... Mr. Jesse CHATMAN
88 Exec Director Engaged Student Learn ... Dr. Linda WHITE
07 Director of Admissions ... Mr. Samuel KING
04 Administrative Asst to President ... Ms. Velma GRAY
18 Chief Facilities/Physical Plant ... Mr. Anthony COWAN
39 Director of Campus Living and Learn ... Mr. Shawn RUCKER
25 Grant Writer ... Ms. Michelle COWAN
35 Director of Student Development ... Ms. Jean SAULSBERRY
88 Director Freshmen Seminar ... Ms. Meridith RUCKER

Lincoln College of Technology Nashville (B)

1524 Gallatin Avenue, Nashville TN 37206-3298
County: Davidson FICE Identification: 007440
Unit ID: 221148
Telephone: (615) 226-3990 Carnegie Class: Spec 2-yr-Tech
FAX Number: (615) 262-8466 Calendar System: Other
URL: www.lincolncollegeoftechnology.com
Established: 1919 Annual Undergrad Tuition & Fees: N/A
Enrollment: 1,609 Coed
Affiliation or Control: Proprietary IRS Status: Proprietary
Highest Offering: Associate Degree
Accreditation: ACCSC

01 President ... Mr. Jim COAKLEY
05 Academic Dean ... Ms. Jackie RODDY
07 Vice President of Admissions ... Mr. Shayne PULVER
37 Director of Financial Aid ... Mr. Chris BIDDLE
06 Registrar ... Mr. Gary WHITE

Lincoln Memorial University (C)

6965 Cumberland Gap Parkway, Harrogate TN 37752-1901
County: Claiborne FICE Identification: 003502
Unit ID: 220631
Telephone: (423) 869-3611 Carnegie Class: Masters/L
FAX Number: (423) 869-6250 Calendar System: Semester
URL: www.lmunet.edu
Established: 1897 Annual Undergrad Tuition & Fees: $21,050
Enrollment: 3,983 Coed
Affiliation or Control: Independent Non-Profit IRS Status: 501(c)3
Highest Offering: Doctorate
Accreditation: SC, ACBSP, ADNUR, ANEST, ARCPA, CAATE, CACREP, CAEPN, #LAW, MT, NUR, OSTEO, SW, @VET

01 President ... Dr. E. Clayton HESS
11 VP for Administration ... Ms. Lisa B. COX
30 VP University Advancement ... Ms. Cynthia L. WHITT
05 VP Academic Affairs ... Dr. Amiel JARSTFER
46 VP Research ... Dr. Dennis KIICK
10 Vice President of Finance ... Ms. Christy GRAHAM
32 VP of Student/Enrollment Services ... Dr. Jonathan LEO
61 VP/Dean School of Law ... Judge Gary WADE
84 VP Enrollment/Athletic/Public Rels ... Dr. James HURLEY
74 VP & Dean College of Veterinary Med ... Dr. Jason JOHNSON
88 VP/Dean College of Osteopathic Med ... Dr. Brian KESSLER
35 Dean of Students ... Ms. Mary Ann SEARLE
53 Dean of School of Education ... Dr. Sylvia LYNCH
81 Dean of Mathematics & Sciences ... Dr. Amiel JARSTFER
66 Dean Sch of Nursing/VP Ext Sites ... Dr. Mary Anne MODRCIN
50 Dean School of Business ... Dr. James HURLEY
04 Exec Assistant to the President ... Mrs. Janet SMITH
37 Executive Director of Financial Aid ... Ms. Tammy TOMFOHRDE
09 Director of Institutional Research ... Vacant
41 Athletic Director ... Mr. Matthew GREEN
18 Director Properties/Physical Plant ... Mr. Rodney COCHRAN
15 Director of Human Resources ... Ms. Libby KING
96 Director Purchasing ... Ms. Pat TENNYSON
06 Registrar ... Ms. Helen BAILEY
42 University Chaplain ... Vacant
43 Legal Counsel/VP Public Affairs ... Mr. Mark CUSHING
13 Chief Information Officer ... Mr. Jason MCCONNELL
26 Senior Director of Marketing ... Mrs. Kate M. REAGAN
29 Director Alumni Services ... Ms. Sheliah COSBY
40 Bookstore Manager ... Mr. Nathan ADKINS
49 Dean of Arts/Humanities/Social Sci ... Dr. Martin SELLERS
121 VP Academic/Student Support Svcs ... Dr. Travis WRIGHT

Lipscomb University (D)

One University Park Dr., Nashville TN 37204-3951
County: Davidson FICE Identification: 003486
Unit ID: 219976
Telephone: (615) 966-1000 Carnegie Class: DU-Mod
FAX Number: (615) 966-1798 Calendar System: Semester
URL: www.lipscomb.edu
Established: 1891 Annual Undergrad Tuition & Fees: $29,756
Enrollment: 4,680 Coed
Affiliation or Control: Churches Of Christ IRS Status: 501(c)3
Highest Offering: Doctorate
Accreditation: SC, ACBSP, CACREP, CAEPN, DIETD, DIETI, ENG, MUS, NUR, PHAR, SW, THEOL

01 President ... Dr. L. Randolph LOWRY, III
05 Provost ... Dr. W. Craig BLEDSOE
32 Senior VP Student Life ... Dr. Scott MCDOWELL
10 Senior VP Finance & Administration ... Mr. Danny H. TAYLOR
53 Int VP & Dean Col of Education ... Dr. Deborah BOYD
26 VP University Relations ... Mr. Walt LEAVER
29 Vice Pres Alumni Relations ... Mr. Phil ELLENBURG
84 VP Enrollment Management ... Mr. Rick HOLAWAY
86 VP External Affairs ... Dr. John LOWRY
42 Vice President for Church Services ... Dr. Scott SAGER
13 Vice President Info Technology/CIO ... Mr. Mike GREEN
20 Vice Prov Acad Admin & Fin Affairs ... Dr. Susan C. GALBREATH
100 Senior Advisor to the President ... Dr. Jim THOMAS
43 General Counsel ... Dr. David WILSON
30 Senior Development Counsel ... Mr. Dale ARMSTRONG
41 Director of Athletics ... Mr. Philip HUTCHESON
20 Associate Provost Academic Support ... Mr. Steve PREWITT
58 Vice Provost for Grad Studies ... Dr. Randy BOULDIN
88 Assoc Prov for Inst Effectiveness ... Dr. Elaine GRIFFIN
79 Dean College of Arts & Sciences ... Dr. Norma BURGESS
73 Dean College of Bible & Ministry ... Dr. C. Leonard ALLEN
50 Int Dean College of Business ... Dr. Ray ELDRIDGE
81 Dean College of Engineering ... Dr. Justin MYRICK
67 Dean College of Pharmacy ... Dr. Roger DAVIS
107 Int Dean College of Prof Studies ... Dr. Nina MOREL
55 Dean School of Computing/Technology ... Dr. Fortune MHLANGA
35 Dean of Student Life ... Dr. Sam SMITH
21 Associate VP Finance ... Mr. Darrell DUNCAN
102 Assoc VP Donor Rel & Stewardship ... Mr. David ENGLAND
44 Asst VP Annual Giving & Advanc Svcs ... Mrs. Carrie THOMPSON
06 Registrar ... Ms. Teresa WILLIAMS
37 Director of Financial Aid ... Ms. Tiffany SUMMERS
08 Director of Library Services ... Ms. Sandra PARHAM
19 Dir of Campus Security & Safety ... Mr. Darrin BELLOWS
36 Director of Career Development Ctr ... Mrs. Monica WENTWORTH
88 Senior Director of Student Success ... Dr. Brian MAST
55 Int Dean Adult Degree Program ... Dr. Nina MOREL
73 Assoc Dir Hazelip Sch of Theology ... Dr. Mark BLACK
83 Chair Grad Studies in Psychology ... Dr. Shanna RAY
88 Managing Dir Inst for Conflict Mgmt ... Dr. Steve JOINER
88 Dir Inst for Christian Spirituality ... Dr. Kris MILLER
88 Dir Inst for Law Justice & Society ... Dr. Randy SPIVEY
88 Found Dir Inst for Civic Leadership ... Ms. Linda SCHACHT
88 Found Dir Inst for Sustain Practice ... Mr. Dodd GALBREATH
88 Director of Global Learning ... Mr. Michael WINEGEART
38 Director Counseling Center ... Dr. Frank SCOTT
88 Senior Campus Minister ... Mr. Steve DAVIDSON
28 Asst Dean Intercultural Development ... Ms. Lisa STEELE
09 Director of Institutional Research ... Mr. Matt REHBEIN
15 Assoc Vice Pres Human Resources ... Ms. Cindy HOOPER
18 Director of Campus Plant ... Mr. Jeff WILSON
105 Director of Information Security ... Mr. Dave WAGNER

Martin Methodist College (E)

433 W Madison Street, Pulaski TN 38478-2799
County: Giles FICE Identification: 003504
Unit ID: 220701
Telephone: (931) 363-9800 Carnegie Class: Bac-Diverse
FAX Number: (931) 363-9818 Calendar System: Semester
URL: www.martinmethodist.edu
Established: 1870 Annual Undergrad Tuition & Fees: $23,708
Enrollment: 1,105 Coed
Affiliation or Control: United Methodist IRS Status: 501(c)3
Highest Offering: Master's
Accreditation: SC, NURSE

01 President ... Dr. Mark D. LA BRANCHE
05 Vice President of Academic Affairs ... Dr. Judy B. CHEATHAM
10 VP for Finance & Administration ... Ms. Rhonda CLINARD
111 Vice Pres for College Advancement ... Mr. David JONES
06 Registrar ... Mrs. Mary Jane PINSON
41 Athletic Director ... Mr. Jeff N. BAIN
42 Chaplain ... Rev. Laura KIRKPATRICK
08 Librarian ... Mr. Richard MADDEN
40 Director of Bookstore ... Mrs. Margaret W. JACKSON
29 Alumni Affairs Director ... Mrs. Edna LUNA
04 Assistant to the President ... Mrs. Kim W. HARRISON
07 Director of Admissions ... Mr. Tyler COX
15 Director Personnel Services ... Mr. James R. HLUBB
37 Director Student Financial Aid ... Mrs. Emma HLUBB
18 Chief Facilities/Physical Plant ... Mr. Melvin EARLS
26 Director of Public Relations ... Ms. Sissy GARNER
38 Dir Student Counseling/Career/Svcs ... Ms. Doris F. WOSSUM
85 Director Foreign Students ... Mrs. Robin HOOD
13 Director of Technology ... Mr. Cedric NKULU
09 Director of Institutional Research ... Vacant
19 Director Security/Safety ... Mr. Joe MCNAIRY

Maryville College (F)

502 E Lamar Alexander Parkway, Maryville TN 37804-5907
County: Blount FICE Identification: 003505
Unit ID: 220710
Telephone: (865) 981-8000 Carnegie Class: Bac-A&S
FAX Number: (865) 981-8010 Calendar System: Semester
URL: www.maryvillecollege.edu
Established: 1819 Annual Undergrad Tuition & Fees: $33,524
Enrollment: 1,213 Coed
Affiliation or Control: Presbyterian Church (U.S.A.) IRS Status: 501(c)3
Highest Offering: Baccalaureate
Accreditation: SC, MUS

01 President ... Dr. William T. BOGART
04 Assistant to President ... Ms. Laura M. CASE
00 Chairman of the Board ... Dr. Mary Kay SULLIVAN
05 Vice President & Dean of College ... Dr. Barbara WELLS
10 VP of Finance & Administration ... Mr. Jeffery S. INGLE
32 Vice President & Dean of Students ... Dr. Melanie V. TUCKER
111 VP for Institutional Advancement ... Ms. Suzy BOOKER
07 Exec Dir Admissions/Fin Aid ... Ms. Cyndi SWEET
26 Exec Dir for Mktg & Communications ... Ms. Karen ELDRIDGE
20 Associate Dean & Dir of IR ... Dr. Mardi P. CRAIG
06 Registrar ... Ms. Kathi WILSON
21 Controller ... Ms. Julie RAMSEY
35 Assistant Dean of Students ... Ms. Kristin GOURLEY
85 Director of International Education ... Ms. Kirsten SHEPPARD
13 Director of Information Technology ... Mr. John BERRY
121 Director Academic Support Center ... Ms. Kim D. OCHSENBEIN
36 Director of the Career Center ... Ms. Christy MCDONALD
37 Director of Financial Aid ... Ms. Alayne BOWMAN
41 Athletic Director ... Ms. Kandis SCHRAM
08 Director of the Library ... Ms. Angela QUICK
18 Director of Physical Plant ... Mr. Andy K. MCCALL
42 Campus Minister ... Rev. Anne MCKEE
15 Director of Human Resources ... Ms. Keni LANAGAN
38 Director of Counseling ... Mr. Bruce HOLT
30 Director of Development ... Mr. Eric BELLAH
88 Asst Director of Maryville Fund ... Ms. Meghan FAGG
29 Dir of Alumni Affairs & Stewardship ... Ms. Angela MILLER
44 Director of Major Gifts ... Ms. Diana CANACARIS
22 Director of Multicultural Affairs ... Mr. Larry ERVIN
40 Bookstore Manager ... Ms. Morgan STRAIN

88 Gen Mgr Clayton Center for the Arts .... Mr. Blake SMITH
19 Director of Safety & Security .... Mr. Jack PIEPENBRING
39 Housing Coordinator .... Mrs. Raeann REIHL

Meharry Medical College (A)

1005 Dr. D. B. Todd Jr. Boulevard,
Nashville TN 37208-3501

County: Davidson FICE Identification: 003506
Unit ID: 220792
Telephone: (615) 327-6111 Carnegie Class: Spec-4-yr-Med
FAX Number: (615) 327-6540 Calendar System: Semester
URL: www.mmc.edu
Established: 1876 Annual Graduate Tuition & Fees: N/A
Enrollment: 829 Coed
Affiliation or Control: Independent Non-Profit IRS Status: 501(c)3
Highest Offering: Doctorate; No Undergraduates
Accreditation: SC, DENT, MED, PH

01 President/Chief Executive Ofcr .... Dr. James E.K HILDRETH
03 Executive Vice President .... Dr. Peter E. MILLET
63 Sr VP Health/Dean Sch of Medicine ..... Dr. Veronica T. MALLETT
11 Sr Vice Pres Administration .... Dr. Saletta HOLLOWAY
26 VP Marketing/Communications .... Ms. Janet CALDWELL
10 Sr Vice President Finance/CFO .... Mrs. LaMel BANDY-NEAL
32 Sr Vice Pres Student Affairs .... Dr. A. Dexter SAMUELS
46 Vice President for Research .... Vacant
88 VP Development/Faculty
Affairs .... Dr. Patricia MATTHEWS-JUAREZ
26 VP External Affairs .... Mr. Lawrence HALL, JR.
13 Assoc VP Information Technology .... Mr. Anthony WILLIAMS
15 Assoc Vice Pres Human Resources .... Mr. Mark SMITH
21 Assoc Vice Pres Financial Systems .... Mr. Larry HOLDEN
111 SVP Institutional Advancement .... Mr. Patrick H. JOHNSON
25 Asst Controller Grants/Contracts .... Ms. Zulfat A. SUARA
43 SVP/General Counsel/Corp Sec ... Mrs. Ivanetta DAVIS-SAMUELS
58 Dean Graduate Studies and
Research .... Dr. Maria DE FATIMA LIMA
32 Int Assoc Dean Student/Academic Aff ..... Dr. Mildred D. COLLINS
51 Director Lifelong Learning .... Dr. Allyson FLEMING
76 Dean Allied Health Professions .... Vacant
52 Dean School of Dentistry .... Dr. Cherae FARMER-DIXON
29 Executive Director Alumni Affairs .... Dr. Henry MOSES
07 Dir Admissions & Recruitment .... Ms. April E. CURRY-ROBERTS
08 AVP Director of Library .... Ms. Brenda F. GREEN
19 Director Campus Safety & Security .... Ms. Theresa MCKINNON
37 Director Student Financial Aid .... Ms. Barbara THARPE
09 Director Institutional Research .... Dr. Chau-Kuang CHEN
100 Chief of Staff/Dir Title III
Adm .... Mrs. Sandra ANDERSON-WILLIAMS
18 Director Facilities .... Mr. George N. KELLY
38 Director Counseling Center .... Ms. Sharda D. MISHRA
06 Registrar .... Ms. Sonja COGGINS VIENTOS
45 Dir Inst Effectiveness & Planning .... Dr. Juanita BUFORD
04 Executive Assistant to the Pres .... Ms. Kimberly STEVENSON

Memphis College of Art (B)

1930 Poplar Avenue, Memphis TN 38104

County: Shelby FICE Identification: 003507
Unit ID: 220808
Telephone: (901) 272-5100 Carnegie Class: Spec-4-yr-Arts
FAX Number: (901) 272-5104 Calendar System: Semester
URL: www.mca.edu
Established: 1936 Annual Undergrad Tuition & Fees: $31,700
Enrollment: 410 Coed
Affiliation or Control: Independent Non-Profit IRS Status: 501(c)3
Highest Offering: Master's
Accreditation: SC, ART

01 President .... Dr. Ronald L. JONES
05 Dean & VP Academic Affairs .... Mr. Remy MILLER
10 VP Operation/Chf Financial Ofcr .... Mr. George NINAN
30 Vice President Advancement .... Ms. Laura HINE
32 Vice President Student Affairs .... Ms. Susan S. MILLER
26 Vice Pres Communications/Mrktng .... Ms. Carrie CORBETT
21 Assoc Vice Pres for Operations .... Mr. Jonathan WELDEN
08 Librarian .... Mr. Derrick CASEY
04 Assistant to President .... Ms. Anne BALLAM
07 Dean of Admissions .... Ms. Annette JAMES-MOORE
35 Director Student Life .... Ms. Nicholous DARMSTAEDTER
37 Director Financial Aid .... Mr. Aaron WHITE
06 Registrar .... Ms. Erica SIMPSON
36 Director Career Development .... Ms. Carrie Allison BROOKS
19 Director Campus Security .... Vacant
109 Business Office Manager .... Ms. Heather RAGLAND
31 Director Community Education .... Ms. Cecelia PALAZOLA

Memphis Theological Seminary (C)

168 East Parkway S at Union, Memphis TN 38104-4395

County: Shelby FICE Identification: 010529
Unit ID: 220871
Telephone: (901) 458-8232 Carnegie Class: Spec-4-yr-Faith
FAX Number: (901) 452-4051 Calendar System: Semester
URL: www.memphisseminary.edu
Established: 1852 Annual Graduate Tuition & Fees: N/A
Enrollment: 267 Coed
Affiliation or Control: Cumberland Presbyterian IRS Status: 501(c)3
Highest Offering: Doctorate; No Undergraduates
Accreditation: SC, THEOL

01 President .... Dr. Daniel J. EARHEART-BROWN
05 Vice President Academic Affs & Dean .... Dr. Peter GATHJE
30 Vice President of Advancement .... Dr. Keith GASKIN
08 Librarian .... Dr. Deborah TAYLOR
10 Vice President of Operations/
CFO .... Mrs. Cassandra F. PRICE-PERRY
32 Director of Student Services .... Dr. Barry L. ANDERSON
108 Assoc Dean Inst Effectiveness .... Dr. Gail ROBINSON
06 Dir Acad Rec/Regist & Accreditation .... Dr. Gail D. ROBINSON
26 Communications Coordinator .... Ms. Felecia DONELSON

Meridian Institute of Surgical Assisting (D)

1507 County Hospital Road, Nashville TN 37218

County: Davidson FICE Identification: 041650
Unit ID: 461324
Telephone: (877) 954-1500 Carnegie Class: Not Classified
FAX Number: (615) 746-6765 Calendar System: Semester
URL: www.meridian-institute.edu
Established: 1999 Annual Undergrad Tuition & Fees: N/A
Enrollment: 402 Coed
Affiliation or Control: Proprietary IRS Status: Proprietary
Highest Offering: Associate Degree
Accreditation: ABHES, SURGA, SURTEC

01 President .... Mr. Dennis STOVER

Mid-America Baptist Theological Seminary (E)

2095 Appling Road, Cordova TN 38016-4911

County: Shelby FICE Identification: 029172
Unit ID: 220914
Telephone: (901) 751-8453 Carnegie Class: Not Classified
FAX Number: (901) 751-8454 Calendar System: Semester
URL: www.mabts.edu
Established: 1972 Annual Undergrad Tuition & Fees: N/A
Enrollment: N/A Coed
Affiliation or Control: Independent Non-Profit IRS Status: 501(c)3
Highest Offering: Doctorate
Accreditation: SC

01 President .... Dr. Michael R. SPRADLIN
03 Executive Vice President .... Dr. Bradley THOMPSON
05 Academic Vice President .... Dr. Timothy SEAL
10 Vice Pres for Finance & Operations .... Mr. Randy REDD
30 VP of Institutional Advancement .... Mr. Nathan COLE
12 Director NE Branch .... Dr. Michael HAGGARD
06 Registrar .... Mrs. Rose MINK
08 Director of Library Services .... Mr. Terrence BROWN
07 Director of Admissions .... Dr. Tanner HICKMAN
04 Admin Assistant to the President .... Mrs. Maria WOOTEN
18 Supt of Buildings & Grounds .... Mr. Gene APPLEBURY
40 Manager Bookstore .... Mr. David FOUST

Mid-South Christian College (F)

PO Box 181056, Memphis TN 38181

County: Shelby Identification: 667046
Unit ID: 481225
Telephone: (901) 375-4400 Carnegie Class: Spec-4-yr-Faith
FAX Number: (901) 375-4085 Calendar System: Semester
URL: www.midsouthchristian.edu
Established: 1959 Annual Undergrad Tuition & Fees: $5,018
Enrollment: 22 Coed
Affiliation or Control: Independent Non-Profit IRS Status: 501(c)3
Highest Offering: Baccalaureate
Accreditation: BI

01 President .... Mr. Larry GRIFFIN
05 Academic Dean .... Dr. Robert GRIFFIN
32 Director of Student Services .... Mr. Brent LINN
04 Executive Assistant .... Mrs. Jane GIBSON
06 Registrar .... Mr. Keith GRAHAM
08 Head Librarian .... Mrs. Judi HOMAN
10 Business Manager .... Mrs. Renae MASK
37 Director Student Financial Aid .... Mrs. Mary JACKSON

Middle Tennessee School of Anesthesia (G)

PO Box 417, 315 Hospital Drive, Madison TN 37116-6414

County: Davidson FICE Identification: 007783
Unit ID: 220996
Telephone: (615) 868-6503 Carnegie Class: Spec-4-yr-Other Health
FAX Number: (615) 868-9885 Calendar System: Quarter
URL: www.mtsa.edu
Established: 1950 Annual Graduate Tuition & Fees: N/A
Enrollment: 224 Coed
Affiliation or Control: Independent Non-Profit IRS Status: 501(c)3
Highest Offering: Doctorate; No Undergraduates
Accreditation: SC, ANEST

01 President .... Dr. Christopher P. HULIN
05 Dean .... Dr. Mana OVERSTREET
10 VP for Finance & Administration .... Sam L. MINTEN
30 VP for Advancement & Alumni .... James B. CLOSSER
20 Program Administrator .... Dr. Rusty GENTRY
88 Dir of Inst Effectiveness & LR .... Dr. Amy C. GIDEON
07 Coord Admissions/Recruitment .... Pam NIMMO

Middle Tennessee State University (H)

1301 E Main Street, Murfreesboro TN 37132-0001

County: Rutherford FICE Identification: 003510
Unit ID: 220978
Telephone: (615) 898-2300 Carnegie Class: DU-Mod
FAX Number: (615) 898-5538 Calendar System: Semester
URL: www.mtsu.edu
Established: 1911 Annual Undergrad Tuition & Fees (In-State): $8,280
Enrollment: 22,511 Coed
Affiliation or Control: State IRS Status: 501(c)3
Highest Offering: Doctorate
Accreditation: SC, AAB, AAFCS, ART, CAATE, CACREP, CAEPN, #CIDA, CS, DIETD, ENGT, JOUR, MUS, NAIT, NRPA, NURSE, SW, THEA

02 President .... Dr. Sidney A. MCPHEE
05 Interim University Provost .... Dr. Mark E. BYRNES
10 VP Business & Finance .... Mr. Alan R. THOMAS
111 Vice President Univ Advancement .... Mr. William J. BALES
32 VP Student Affairs .... Dr. Debra K. SELLS
13 VP Info Tech/Chief Info Officer .... Mr. Bruce PETRYSHAK
58 Vice Provost Rsrch/Dean Grad Stds .... Dr. David BUTLER
121 Vice Provost for Student Success .... Dr. Richard SLUDER
43 Univ Counsel & Asst to the Pres .... Ms. Heidi ZIMMERMAN
04 Exec Assistant to the President .... Ms. Kimberly S. EDGAR
22 Exec Dir Institutional Equity/Com .... Ms. Barbara L. PATTON
07 Assoc Vice Prov UG Recruitment .... Dr. Laurie B. WITHEROW
14 Assoc Vice Pres Info Technology .... Mr. Tom WALLACE
21 Assoc Vice Pres Business Office .... Ms. Kathy THURMAN
35 Assoc Vice Pres/Dean Student Life .... Ms. Sarah SUDAK
15 Asst Vice Pres Human Resource
Svcs .... Ms. Kathy I. MUSSELMAN
18 Asst Vice Pres Facilities Services .... Mr. Joe WHITEFIELD
11 Asst Vice Pres Admin/Business Svcs .... Ms. Kathryn CRISP
91 Assoc Vice Pres Enterprise Res Plng .... Mrs. Lisa C. ROGERS
90 Asst Vice Pres Acad & Instruct Tech .... Ms. Barbara J. DRAUDE
81 Dean Col Basic/Applied Science .... Dr. Robert U. FISCHER, JR.
83 Dean College Behavioral & Hlth Sci .... Dr. Harold D. WHITESIDE
60 Dean College Media & Entertain .... Dr. Ken A. PAULSON
50 Dean College of Business .... Dr. David J. URBAN
53 Dean College of Education .... Dr. Lana C. SEIVERS
49 Interim Dean Col of Liberal Arts .... Dr. Karen K. PETERSEN
51 Assoc Dean University College .... Dr. David GOTCHER
92 Dean University Honors College .... Dr. John R. VILE
08 Dean University Library .... Ms. Bonnie J. ALLEN
09 Asst Vice Provost for IEPR .... Mr. Chris BREWER
36 Dir Career & Employment Center .... Mr. Bill FLETCHER
88 Asst Vice Prov Student Success .... Mr. Vincent WINDROW
37 Dir of Financial Aid & Scholarship .... Mr. Stephen F. WHITE
25 Dir Research Services .... Mr. Jeffry PORTER
29 Director Alumni Relations .... Ms. Ginger C. FREEMAN
40 Director Bookstore .... Mr. Jeff WHITWELL
24 Manager Center for Educational Med .... Mr. Anthony TATE
38 Interim Dir Counseling Services .... Dr. MaryKaye ANDERSON
30 Director Development Office .... Ms. Patricia BRANAM
84 Director Enrollment Technical Sys .... Ms. Teresa W. THOMAS
27 Director News & Media Relations .... Mr. Jimmy W. HART
41 Director of Athletics .... Mr. Chris J. MASSARO
23 Director of Health Services .... Mr. Richard L. CHAPMAN
06 Registrar .... Ms. Susan FIELDHOUSE
19 Chief of Police/Dir Public Safety .... Mr. Carl S. PEASTER

Miller-Motte Technical College (I)

6397 Lee Highway, Suite 100, Chattanooga TN 37421
Telephone: (423) 510-9675 Identification: 770781
Accreditation: ACICS, MAC, SURGT

Miller-Motte Technical College (J)

1820 Business Park Drive, Clarksville TN 37040-6023

County: Montgomery FICE Identification: 026142
Unit ID: 382771
Telephone: (931) 553-0071 Carnegie Class: Spec 2-yr-Health
FAX Number: (931) 552-2916 Calendar System: Quarter
URL: www.miller-motte.edu
Established: 1916 Annual Undergrad Tuition & Fees: $9,800
Enrollment: 334 Coed
Affiliation or Control: Proprietary IRS Status: Proprietary
Highest Offering: Associate Degree
Accreditation: ACICS, MAC, SURGT

01 Campus Director .... Ms. Kala FIELDER
05 Director of Education .... Ms. Shannon MANZELLA
37 Financial Aid Director .... Ms. Debbie STRATMAN
36 Director of Career Development .... Mr. John MCCASLIN
07 Director of Admissions .... Ms. Gail MASSEY

† No longer accepting campus-based students.

Miller-Motte Technical College (K)

1515 North Gallatin Pike, Madison TN 37115
Telephone: (615) 859-8090 Identification: 770782
Accreditation: ACICS

† Branch campus of Miller-Motte Technical College, Clarksville, TN. No longer accepting campus-based students

Milligan College (A)

2010 Milligan College PO Box 500,
Milligan College TN 37682-4000
County: Carter FICE Identification: 003511
Unit ID: 486901
Telephone: (423) 461-8700 Carnegie Class: Masters/S
FAX Number: (423) 461-8755 Calendar System: Semester
URL: www.milligan.edu
Established: 1866 Annual Undergrad Tuition & Fees: $31,450
Enrollment: 1,193 Coed
Affiliation or Control: Independent Non-Profit IRS Status: 501(c)3
Highest Offering: Doctorate
Accreditation: SC, CAEPN, NURSE, OT, THEOL

01 President ... Dr. William B. GREER
05 Vice Pres Academic Affairs/Dean ... Dr. Garland YOUNG
32 Vice Pres Student Devel & Athletics ... Mr. Mark FOX
111 Vice Pres Institutional Advancement ... Mr. Jack SIMPSON
84 Vice Pres Enrollment Management ... Dr. Lee HARRISON
10 Vice Pres Business & Finance ... Mrs. Jacqui STEADMAN
06 Registrar/Assoc Dean ... Mrs. Sue SKIDMORE
07 Director of Admissions ... Ms. Kristin WRIGHT
08 Director of Library Services ... Mr. Gary DAUGHT
35 Director of Student Activities ... Mr. Jason ONKS
29 Director of Alumni Relations ... Ms. Theresa GARBE
15 Director Personnel Services ... Ms. Robbyn MAYLOTT
09 Director of Institutional Research ... Ms. Cindy WYMER
37 Coordinator of Financial Aid ... Ms. Diane KEASLING
26 Director of Church Relations ... Mr. Kit DOTSON
36 Director Student Placement ... Ms. Beth ANDERSON
18 Service Manager Facilities ... Mr. Ken BROYLES
28 Director Multicultural Engagement ... Ms. Rachel OWENS
27 Dir of Public Relations/Marketing ... Ms. Chandrea SHELL
19 Director Property & Risk Management ... Mr. Brent NIPPER
44 Director Annual Giving ... Mrs. Rhajon SMITH
90 Director of Information Technology ... Mrs. Amanda BRISTOL

National College (B)

5760 Stage Road, Bartlett TN 38134
Telephone: (901) 213-1681 Identification: 770783
Accreditation: ACICS, MAC

National College (C)

2526 Thousand Oaks Cove, Memphis TN 38118
Telephone: (901) 363-9046 Identification: 770785
Accreditation: ACICS, CAHIIM, MAC

National College (D)

1638 Bell Road, Nashville TN 37211
County: Davidson FICE Identification: 004617
Unit ID: 388043
Telephone: (615) 333-3344 Carnegie Class: Assoc/HVT-High Non
FAX Number: (615) 333-3429 Calendar System: Quarter
URL: www.national-college.edu
Established: 1991 Annual Undergrad Tuition & Fees: $11,466
Enrollment: 507 Coed
Affiliation or Control: Proprietary IRS Status: Proprietary
Highest Offering: Baccalaureate
Accreditation: ACICS, MAC

01 Director ... Ms. Patricia WHITT

North Central Institute (E)

168 Jack Miller Boulevard, Clarksville TN 37042-4810
County: Montgomery FICE Identification: 030791
Unit ID: 418889
Telephone: (931) 431-9700 Carnegie Class: Spec 2-yr-Tech
FAX Number: (931) 431-9771 Calendar System: Semester
URL: www.nci.edu
Established: 1988 Annual Undergrad Tuition & Fees: N/A
Enrollment: 99 Coed
Affiliation or Control: Proprietary IRS Status: Proprietary
Highest Offering: Associate Degree
Accreditation: COE

01 President ... Tamela K. TALIENTO
06 Registrar ... Michelle HARTSON
07 Director of Admissions ... Dale WOOD
37 Director of Financial Aid ... Cathy ROYALS
13 Director of Information Technology ... Leo JORDAN

Nossi College of Art (F)

590 Cheron Road, Nashville TN 37115
County: Davidson FICE Identification: 025782
Unit ID: 368452
Telephone: (615) 514-2787 Carnegie Class: Spec-4-yr-Arts
FAX Number: (615) 514-2788 Calendar System: Trimester
URL: www.nossi.edu
Established: 1973 Annual Undergrad Tuition & Fees: $17,800
Enrollment: 259 Coed
Affiliation or Control: Proprietary IRS Status: Proprietary
Highest Offering: Baccalaureate
Accreditation: ACCSC

01 President ... Ms. Nossi VATANDOOST
03 Executive Vice President ... Mr. Cyrus VATANDOOST
05 Vice President for Academic Affairs ... Dr. Byron EDWARDS
07 Admissions Director ... Ms. Mary ALEXANDER
37 Financial Aid Director ... Ms. Mary KIDD
06 Registrar ... Mrs. Mindy GILBERT
08 Head Librarian ... Mrs. Kolleen LONGMIRE
26 Chief Public Relations/Marketing ... Mrs. Libby LUFF
10 Business Office Manager ... Mrs. Kristi BINKLEY
32 Chief Student Affairs/Student Life ... Ms. Libby FUNKE-LUFF
36 Director Student Placement ... Mr. Dax GOMEZ

O'More College of Design (G)

423 S Margin Street, Franklin TN 37064
County: Williamson FICE Identification: 021064
Unit ID: 221254
Telephone: (615) 794-4254 Carnegie Class: Spec-4-yr-Arts
FAX Number: (615) 790-1662 Calendar System: Semester
URL: www.omorecollege.edu
Established: 1970 Annual Undergrad Tuition & Fees: $28,176
Enrollment: 167 Coed
Affiliation or Control: Independent Non-Profit IRS Status: 501(c)3
Highest Offering: Baccalaureate
Accreditation: ACCSC, CIDA

01 President ... Mrs. Shari FOX
26 Director of Marketing & Development ... Ms. Amy SHELTON
11 Director of Operations ... Mr. Steve BANKS
19 Director of Security ... Mr. DeWayne PULLIAM
07 Manager of Admissions ... Mrs. Tori BAGSBY
08 Director of Information Resources ... Ms. Nicole FOX
88 Chair School of Fashion ... Mrs. Jamie ATLAS
88 Chair School of Interior Design ... Ms. Rebecca BREWER
88 Chair School of Visual Design ... Mrs. Jess SMITH
05 Director of Academic Affairs ... Mrs. Jamie SHAFFER
18 Director of Facilities ... Mr. Jimmy FOX
06 Registrar ... Ms. Lauren RICHERT
32 Director of Student Affairs ... Mrs. Emily KYNERD
37 Director of Financial Aid ... Ms. Lea VOIGT
07 Director of Enrollment/Admissions ... Mrs. Sara MARTIN
30 Development Coordinator ... Mrs. Amy HIRT

Oxford Graduate School (H)

500 Oxford Drive, Dayton TN 37321-6736
County: Rhea FICE Identification: 038403
Unit ID: 461120
Telephone: (423) 775-6596 Carnegie Class: Spec-4-yr-Faith
FAX Number: (423) 775-6599 Calendar System: Semester
URL: www.ogs.edu
Established: 1981 Annual Graduate Tuition & Fees: N/A
Enrollment: 93 Coed
Affiliation or Control: Independent Non-Profit IRS Status: 501(c)3
Highest Offering: Doctorate; No Undergraduates
Accreditation: TRACS

01 President ... Dr. Kimberly GEIGER
00 Chancellor ... Dr. David ANDERSON
05 Dean of Faculty ... Dr. Robert ANDREWS
11 Vice President of Administration ... Dr. Paul LAWHORN
07 Director of Admissions & Phys Opers ... Dr. Gwen BOLLANT
108 Institutional Assessment Officer ... Dr. Joshua REICHARD
10 Business Officer ... Ms. Sharlene DANIEL
29 Director Alumni Relations ... Dr. Bonnie LIBHART
08 Director of Library Operations ... Dr. David WARD
06 Registrar ... Dr. Paul LAWHORN

Pentecostal Theological Seminary (I)

900 Walker Street, NE, Cleveland TN 37311
County: Bradley FICE Identification: 021883
Unit ID: 219842
Telephone: (423) 478-1131 Carnegie Class: Spec-4-yr-Faith
FAX Number: (423) 478-7711 Calendar System: 4/1/4
URL: www.ptseminary.edu
Established: 1975 Annual Graduate Tuition & Fees: N/A
Enrollment: 379 Coed
Affiliation or Control: Church Of God IRS Status: 501(c)3
Highest Offering: Doctorate; No Undergraduates
Accreditation: SC, THEOL

01 President ... Dr. Michael L. BAKER
05 Dean of Faculty/VP for Academics ... Dr. David S. HAN
108 VP for Inst Effect/Accreditation ... Dr. Oliver L. MCMAHAN
10 Director of Finance ... Mr. Caleb PEACOCK
04 Exec Assistant to the President ... Mrs. Teresa GILBERT
06 Director of Acad Records/Registrar ... Ms. Anita F. BLEVINS
15 Director of Administrative Services ... Rev. Joylita W. TERPSTRA
18 Dir of Facilities/Support Services ... Mr. Phillip WOOD
32 Director of Student Services ... Dr. Welton WRISTON
37 Director of Financial Aid ... Mrs. Robin SLUDER
07 Director of Admissions ... Ms. Regina WILHELM
106 Director Online Learning ... Dr. Robert BLACKABY
29 Director Alumni Relations & PR ... Mrs. Sharon BAKER

Remington College (J)

2710 Nonconnah Boulevard, Memphis TN 38132-2110
Telephone: (901) 345-1000 Identification: 666062
Accreditation: ACCSC

† Branch campus of Remington College, Mobile, AL.

Remington College (K)

441 Donelson Pike, Suite 150, Nashville TN 37214-3558
Telephone: (615) 889-5520 Identification: 666307
Accreditation: ACCSC, DH

† Branch campus of Remington College, Mobile, AL.

Rhodes College (L)

2000 North Parkway, Memphis TN 38112-1690
County: Shelby FICE Identification: 003519
Unit ID: 221351
Telephone: (901) 843-3000 Carnegie Class: Bac-A&S
FAX Number: N/A Calendar System: Semester
URL: www.rhodes.edu
Established: 1848 Annual Undergrad Tuition & Fees: $44,942
Enrollment: 2,063 Coed
Affiliation or Control: Presbyterian Church (U.S.A.) IRS Status: 501(c)3
Highest Offering: Master's
Accreditation: SC, MUS

01 President ... Dr. Marjorie HASS
05 Dean of Academic Affairs ... Dr. Milton MORELAND
10 VP for Finance & Business Affairs ... Mr. Kyle WEBB
13 Vice Pres for Information Services . Dr. Robert M. JOHNSON, JR.
30 Vice President for Development ... Ms. Jennifer G. WADE
84 Vice Pres Enrollment/Communications ... Mr. Carey THOMPSON
32 Dean of Students ... Ms. Carol E. CASEY
35 Associate Dean of Students ... Vacant
20 Assoc Dean of Academic Affairs ... Dr. Brian W. SHAFFER
28 Assoc Dean of Diversity & Inclusion ... Dr. Nicole CHADDOCK
20 Assoc Dean of Academic Affairs ... Dr. Michelle MATTSON
06 Registrar ... Ms. DeAnna ADAMS
37 Director of Financial Aid ... Mr. Michael MORGAN
08 Director of Library ... Ms. Darlene D. BROOKS
29 Director of Alumni Relations ... Ms. Tracy PATTERSON
15 Director of Human Resources ... Ms. Claire R. SHAPIRO
14 Director of Info Tech Services ... Mr. Richard TRENTHEM
19 Director of Campus Safety ... Mr. Ike SLOAS
41 Director of Athletics ... Mr. Jeff CLEANTHES
36 Director of Career Services ... Ms. Sandra G. TRACY
38 Director of Counseling Services ... Mr. Robert B. DOVE
18 Director of Physical Plant ... Mr. Brian E. FOSHEE
44 Director of Planned Giving ... Mr. Jim DUNCAN
26 Director of Communications ... Ms. Lynn CONLEE
09 Director of Institutional Research . Ms. Dawn CLEMENT CORNIES
04 Exec Assistant to the President ... Ms. Melody H. RICHEY
07 Director of Admissions ... Mr. Jeffery NORRIS

Richmont Graduate University (M)

1815 McCallie Avenue, Chattanooga TN 37404
County: Hamilton FICE Identification: 033554
Unit ID: 441104
Telephone: (423) 266-4574 Carnegie Class: Spec-4-yr-Other Health
FAX Number: (423) 265-7375 Calendar System: Semester
URL: www.richmont.edu
Established: 1933 Annual Graduate Tuition & Fees: N/A
Enrollment: 258 Coed
Affiliation or Control: Independent Non-Profit IRS Status: 501(c)3
Highest Offering: Master's; No Undergraduates
Accreditation: SC, CACREP

01 President ... Dr. Timothy QUINNAN
05 Academic Dean/Dean Sch Counseling ... Dr. Stephen BRADSHAW
10 VP of Finance ... Mr. Tim MCPHERSON
13 VP of Information Technology ... Mr. Darwin BLANDON
84 VP of Enrollment Management ... Ms. Roxanne SHELLABARGER
88 VP of Integration ... Dr. Dan SARTOR
32 Dean of Students ... Dr. Amanda BLACKBURN
73 Dean School of Ministry ... Dr. Josh RICE
88 Dean of Clinical Affairs ... Dr. Vanessa SNYDER
04 Assistant to the President ... Mr. Philip BURNS
06 Registrar ... Ms. Amy COXWELL
08 Director of Libraries ... Mr. John HUGHES
09 Director of Institutional Research ... Dr. Mary PLISCO
108 Dir Institutional Effectiveness ... Dr. Sonja SUTHERLAND
18 Facilities Manager ... Mr. Neil ANDERSON
26 Director of Communications ... Mr. Scottie BLACKBURN
29 Director Alumni Relations ... Ms. Martha BUSBY
30 Director of Development ... Ms. Kelly KING-LINSTEDT
37 Director of Financial Aid ... Mr. Morris LUTES

SAE Institute Nashville (N)

7 Music Circle North, Nashville TN 37203
County: Davidson FICE Identification: 038303
Unit ID: 446525
Telephone: (615) 244-5848 Carnegie Class: Assoc/HVT-High Trad
FAX Number: (615) 244-3192 Calendar System: Semester
URL: nashville.sae.edu
Established: 1976 Annual Undergrad Tuition & Fees: $25,061
Enrollment: 141 Coed
Affiliation or Control: Proprietary IRS Status: Proprietary
Highest Offering: Associate Degree
Accreditation: ACCSC

01 Director ... Ms. Lynn DORTON

Sewanee: The University of the South (A)

735 University Avenue, Sewanee TN 37383-1000
County: Franklin FICE Identification: 003534
Unit ID: 221519
Telephone: (931) 598-1000 Carnegie Class: Bac-A&S
FAX Number: (931) 598-1145 Calendar System: Semester
URL: www.sewanee.edu
Established: 1857 Annual Undergrad Tuition & Fees: $42,400
Enrollment: 1,797 Coed
Affiliation or Control: Protestant Episcopal IRS Status: 501(c)3
Highest Offering: Doctorate
Accreditation: SC, THEOL

01 Vice Chancellor & President .... Dr. John M. MCCARDELL, JR.
05 Provost .... Dr. Nancy BERNER
111 Vice President for Advancement .... Mr. Jay FISHER
88 Special Assistant to the VC .... Mr. Frank GLADU
45 Vice Provost for Planning and Admin .... Vacant
117 Vice President Risk Management .... Mr. Eric HARTMAN
13 Assoc Provost Info Tech/Librarian .... Dr. Vicki G. SELLS
49 Dean College of Arts & Sciences .... Dr. Terry L. PAPILLON
73 Dean School of Theology .... Rt Rev. J. Neil ALEXANDER
32 Dean of Students .... Dr. Marichal GENTRY
09 Asst Dir of Inst Research .... Vacant
06 Assistant Provost for Academic Svcs .... Dr. Paul G. WILEY
07 Dean of Admission & Financial Aid . Ms. Lee Ann M. BACKLUND
37 Assoc Dean Student Financial Aid .... Ms. Beth CRAGAR
20 Associate Dean for Academic Affairs .... Dr. Alex M. BRUCE
26 Exec Dir Marketing/Communications .... Mr. Parker OLIVER
15 Director of Human Resources .... Ms. Mary WILSON
41 Director of Athletics .... Mr. Mark F. WEBB
29 Director of Alumni Relations .... Ms. Susan S. ASKEW
36 Director of Career Services .... Ms. Kim D. HEITZENRATER
38 Director of Wellness Center .... Dr. Nicole NOFFSINGER-FRAZIER
93 Director of Minority Affairs .... Mr. Eric V. BENJAMIN
18 Director of Physical Plant Services .... Mr. Michael D. GARDNER
43 University Legal Counsel .... Ms. Donna L. PIERCE
19 Chief of Police .... Ms. Marie ELDRIDGE
10 VP for Finance and Treasurer .... Dr. Douglass WILLIAMS
23 Director of Univ Health Services .... Ms. Karen THARP
24 Director of Media Services .... Mr. Larry E. WOOD
42 University Chaplain & Dean .... VRev. Thomas E. MACFIE
28 Assoc Dean Fac Dev & Inclu .... Dr. Elizabeth SKOMP
104 Assoc Dean of Global Education .... Dr. Scott WILSON

South College (B)

3904 Lonas Drive, Knoxville TN 37909-3323
County: Knox FICE Identification: 004938
Unit ID: 220552
Telephone: (865) 251-1800 Carnegie Class: Masters/S
FAX Number: (865) 584-7335 Calendar System: Quarter
URL: www.southcollegetn.edu
Established: 1882 Annual Undergrad Tuition & Fees: $18,375
Enrollment: 1,335 Coed
Affiliation or Control: Proprietary IRS Status: Proprietary
Highest Offering: Doctorate
Accreditation: SC, ARCPA, DMS, MAC, NMT, NUR, OTA, PHAR, PTA, PTAA, RAD

01 President .... Mr. Stephen A. SOUTH
05 Executive VP and Provost .... Dr. Kim B. HALL
20 Vice President of Academic Affairs .... Dr. Lisa SATTERFIELD
32 VP Acad Supp & Student Services .... Dr. Stacy WADDELL
84 VP Enrollment Management .... Mr. Walter HOSEA
13 VP Information Tech/Facilities .... Mr. Ron HALL
86 VP Admin & Regulatory Compliance .... Mr. Steve WOODFORD
08 Head Librarian .... Ms. Anya MCKINNEY
10 Chief Financial Officer .... Mr. Brad ADAMS
06 Registrar .... Ms. Kim WOOD
36 Career Services Coordinator .... Mr. Gary TAYLOR
37 Sr Director of Financial Aid .... Mr. Larry BROADWATER
72 Director Instructional Technology .... Mr. Stephen JAMES
07 Director for Admissions .... Ms. Carrie MAJOR

Southern Adventist University (C)

Box 370, 5010 University Drive,
Collegedale TN 37315-0370
County: Hamilton FICE Identification: 003518
Unit ID: 221661
Telephone: (423) 236-2000 Carnegie Class: Masters/M
FAX Number: (423) 236-1000 Calendar System: Semester
URL: www.southern.edu
Established: 1892 Annual Undergrad Tuition & Fees: $21,150
Enrollment: 3,125 Coed
Affiliation or Control: Seventh-day Adventist IRS Status: 501(c)3
Highest Offering: Doctorate
Accreditation: SC, ADNUR, CACREP, CAEPN, CS, IACBE, MUS, NUR, SW

01 President .... Dr. David C. SMITH
05 Vice Pres Academic Administration .... Dr. Robert YOUNG
10 Vice President Financial Admin .... Mr. Tom VERRILL
32 Vice President Student Services .... Mr. Dennis NEGRON
45 Director Strategic Initiatives .... Mrs. Barb EDENS
30 Vice President Advancement .... Mrs. Carolyn HAMILTON
84 Vice Pres Enrollment Management .... Mr. Marc A. GRUNDY
20 Int Associate VP Academic Admin .... Dr. Tyson HALL
21 Associate VP Financial Admin .... Mr. Marty HAMILTON
13 Assoc VP Information Systems .... Mr. Gary SEWELL
09 Director Inst Research/Planning .... Dr. Hollis JAMES
07 Director of Admissions .... Mr. Rick ANDERSON
08 Director of Libraries .... Mr. Deyse BRAVO
06 Director Records & Advisement .... Mrs. Joni I. ZIER
15 Director Human Resources .... Mrs. Brenda FLORES-LOPEZ
26 Vice Pres Marketing/University Rels .... Ms. Ingrid SKANTZ
29 Director Alumni Relations .... Ms. Evonne CROOK
38 Director Student Success Center .... Dr. Jim WAMPLER
33 Dean of Men .... Mr. Dwight E. MAGERS
34 Dean of Women .... Ms. Lisa HALL
50 Dean School of Business/Mgmt .... Dr. Mark HYDER
53 Dean School of Education/Psych .... Dr. John MCCOY
57 Dean School of Visual Art/Design .... Mr. Randy CRAVEN
60 Dean School of Journalism/Comm .... Dr. Rachel WILLIAMS-SMITH
64 Dean School of Music .... Dr. Peter COOPER
66 Dean School of Nursing .... Dr. Barbara JAMES
68 Dean Sch of Phys Ed/Health/Wellness .... Dr. Robert BENGE
73 Dean School of Religion .... Dr. Greg KING
77 Dean School of Computing .... Dr. Rick HALTERMAN
70 Dean Social Work/Family Studies .... Dr. Kristie WILDER
72 Chair Technology .... Dr. Mark HYDER
81 Chair Mathematics .... Dr. Kevin BROWN
76 Chair Biology/Allied Health .... Dr. Keith SNYDER
88 Chair Chemistry .... Dr. Brent HAMSTRA
88 Chair English .... Dr. Keely TARY
88 Chair History & Political Studies .... Dr. Marc PEACH
88 Chair Physics .... Dr. Chris HANSEN
18 Director Plant Services .... Mr. Eric SCHOONARD
35 Director Student Affairs & Life Act .... Ms. Kari SHULTZ
37 Director Student Finance .... Mrs. Paula WALTERS
96 Assoc VP of Retail/Auxilliary Ops .... Mr. Russell ORRISON
04 Administrative Asst to President .... Mrs. Joylynn SCOTT

Southern College of Optometry (D)

1245 Madison Avenue, Memphis TN 38104-2222
County: Shelby FICE Identification: 003517
Unit ID: 221670
Telephone: (901) 722-3200 Carnegie Class: Spec-4-yr-Other Health
FAX Number: (901) 722-3279 Calendar System: Trimester
URL: www.sco.edu
Established: 1932 Annual Graduate Tuition & Fees: N/A
Enrollment: 528 Coed
Affiliation or Control: Independent Non-Profit IRS Status: 501(c)3
Highest Offering: Doctorate; No Undergraduates
Accreditation: SC, OPT, OPTR

01 President .... Dr. Lewis REICH
04 Executive Admin Assistant to Pres .... Ms. Sandra S. STEPHENS
05 VP for Academic Affairs .... Dr. John B. CAMPBELL
111 Vice President for Inst Advancement ..... Dr. Kristin K. ANDERSON
102 Dir of Corp & Foundation Relations .... Ms. Christine M. WEINREICH
10 Vice President for Finance & Admin .... Mr. David L. WEST
13 Exec Dir of Information Services .... Mr. Dean SWICK
18 Director of Physical Plant .... Mr. Danny ANDERSON
17 Vice Pres for Clinical Programs .... Dr. James E. VENABLE
23 Director of Clinic Operations .... Mr. Gary SNUFFIN
32 Vice President for Student Services .... Mr. Joseph H. HAUSER
07 Dir of Admissions/Enrollment Svcs . Mr. Michael N. ROBERTSON
07 Director of Student Recruitment .... Ms. Sunnie EWING
08 Director of Library .... Ms. Leslie HOLLAND
26 Dir of Communications/Media Svcs .... Mr. Jim HOLLIFIELD
15 Vice President for Human Resources .... Ms. Ann Z. FIELDS
37 Director of Financial Aid .... Ms. Cindy GARNER
09 Director of Institutional Research .... Dr. Michael CHRISTENSEN
108 Director Institutional Assessment .... Ms. Pamela MOSS
19 Manager of Security/Safety .... Mr. Don HENSON
101 Secretary of the Institution/Board .... Ms. Sandra STEPHENS
29 Director of Alumni & Spec Events .... Ms. Beth FISHER
44 Annual Giving Coordinator .... Ms. Cecily FREEMAN

*Tennessee Board of Regents Office (E)

1 Bridgestone Park, Nashville TN 37214
County: Davidson FICE Identification: 029031
Unit ID: 409379
Telephone: (615) 366-4400 Carnegie Class: N/A
FAX Number: (615) 366-3922
URL: www.tbr.edu

01 Chancellor .... Dr. Flora TYDINGS
05 Vice Chanc Academic Affairs .... Vacant
10 Vice Chanc Business & Finance .... Mr. Danny GIBBS
11 Vice Chanc Admin & Fac Mgmt .... Mr. David B. GREGORY
12 EVC TN Colleges of Applied Tech .... Mr. James KING
13 Chief Information Officer .... Mr. Stephen VIEIRA
88 Vice Chanc for Community Colleges .... Vacant
43 General Counsel .... Ms. Mary MOODY
09 Asst Vice Chanc Research/Assessment .... Mr. Chris TINGLE
32 Assoc Vice Chanc Student Success .... Ms. Heidi LEMING
20 Int Vice Chance Academic Affairs .... Mr. Randy SCHULTE
15 Asst Vice Chanc for Human Resources .... Ms. April PRESTON
21 Asst Vice Chanc Business/Finance .... Ms. Renee STEWART
26 Communications Director .... Mr. Rick LOCKER

*Chattanooga State Community College (F)

4501 Amnicola Highway, Chattanooga TN 37406-1097
County: Hamilton FICE Identification: 003998
Unit ID: 219824
Telephone: (423) 697-4400 Carnegie Class: Assoc/MT-VT-High Trad
FAX Number: N/A Calendar System: Semester
URL: www.chattanoogastate.edu
Established: 1965 Annual Undergrad Tuition & Fees (In-State): $4,063
Enrollment: 9,374 Coed
Affiliation or Control: State IRS Status: 501(c)3
Highest Offering: Associate Degree
Accreditation: SC, ACBSP, ADNUR, CAHIIM, COARC, DA, DH, DMS, EMT, ENGR, ENGT, MAC, NMT, PTAA, RAD, RTT, SURGT

02 President .... Dr. Rebecca ASHFORD
45 Interim VP Inst Effect Rsrch Plan .... Dr. Traci WILLIAMS
05 Vice Pres Academic Affairs .... Dr. Dana NICHOLS
10 Exec Vice Pres Business & Finance .... Ms. Tammy SWENSON
32 Vice President Student Services .... Ms. Debbie ADAMS
72 Exec VP Technical College .... Dr. James BARROTT
13 Vice Pres Information Technology .... Dr. Gardner LONG
111 Vice Pres Col Advance & Public Rels ..... Ms. Nancy PATTERSON
21 Asst Vice Pres Business & Finance .... Ms. Susan JOSEPH
35 Asst Vice Pres Student Affairs .... Mr. Brad MCCORMICK
18 Executive Director Plant Operations .... Mr. Guy DAVIS
56 Asst VP Distributed Education .... Ms. Judy LOWE
09 Director Institutional Research .... Ms. Bonnie RIGGS
26 Director Marketing .... Ms. Patty BROWN
37 Director Student Financial Aid .... Mr. Reed ALLISON
07 Director of Admissions .... Ms. Gail CAMPBELL
28 Director Multicultural Services .... Ms. Mary KNAFF
41 Athletic Director .... Vacant
88 Dean Acad Assessment/Accred/Compl .... Mr. John HAWORTH
08 Dean Library Services .... Ms. Susan JENNINGS
76 Dean Allied Health & Nursing .... Dr. Mark KNUTSEN
79 Dean Humanities & Fine Arts .... Mr. Darrin HASSEVOORT
83 Assc VP AC Aff Dean Soci/Behav Sci .... Dr. Mosunmola GEORGE-TAYLOR
81 Dean Math & Sciences .... Mr. Roy SOFIELD
50 Dean Business/Info Tech .... Mr. Barry JENNISON
32 Dean Student Life/Judicial Affairs .... Ms. Sandy RUTTER
75 Dean Tennessee Technology Center .... Dr. Mike RICKETTS
54 Interim Dean Engineering Technology .... Ms. Lyn POTTER
84 Dir Welcome Center/Recruiting .... Ms. Kisha CALDWELL
108 Director Assessment & Planning .... Dr. Traci WILLIAMS
06 Director of Records .... Ms. Laqueta SOULE
105 Coordinator Web Services .... Ms. Vickie BOLES
15 Exec Dir HR/Affirm Action/Title I .... Mr. Brian EVANS

*Cleveland State Community College (G)

PO Box 3570, Cleveland TN 37320-3570
County: Bradley FICE Identification: 003999
Unit ID: 219879
Telephone: (423) 472-7141 Carnegie Class: Assoc/HT-High Trad
FAX Number: (423) 478-6255 Calendar System: Semester
URL: www.clevelandstatecc.edu
Established: 1967 Annual Undergrad Tuition & Fees (In-State): $4,043
Enrollment: 3,509 Coed
Affiliation or Control: State IRS Status: 501(c)3
Highest Offering: Associate Degree
Accreditation: SC, ACBSP, ADNUR, MAC, NAIT

02 President .... Dr. William SEYMOUR
05 Vice President for Academic Affairs .... Dr. Denise KING
32 Vice President for Student Services .... Dr. Michael STOKES
30 VP Finance & Advancement .... Dr. Thomas WRIGHT
09 Director of Institutional Research .... Mr. David KNOPP
37 Director of Financial Aid .... Mrs. Jamie HAMBY
26 Director Marketing & Promotions .... Mr. Tony BARTOLO
06 Asst Dir Enrollment Svcs/Registrar .... Mrs. Gail GREENWOOD
15 Director of Human Resources .... Mrs. Joan BATES
08 Director of the Library .... Vacant
13 Director of Information Technology .... Mr. Chris MOWERY
19 Coordinator Campus Security .... Mr. Mike HODGES
50 Dean of Business & Technology .... Ms. Susan WEBB-CURTIS
66 Director of Nursing .... Mrs. Nancy LABINE
79 Dean Humanities/Social Sciences .... Dr. Robert BRANDON
81 Dean Math/Science/Health/Wellness .... Dr. Mitchell RHEA
38 Dir Student Development/ACCESS Ctr .... Mr. Mark WILSON
103 Dir Workforce Development .... Mr. Rick CREASY
18 Director of Plant Operations .... Vacant
21 Asst VP Finance & Operations .... Ms. Alisha FOX
84 Director of Enrollment Services .... Mr. Jason SEWELL
07 Asst Director of Admissions .... Ms. Suzanne BAYNE
41 Athletic Director .... Mr. Mike POLICASTRO

*Columbia State Community College (H)

1665 Hampshire Pike, Columbia TN 38401-5653
County: Maury FICE Identification: 003483
Unit ID: 219888
Telephone: (931) 540-2722 Carnegie Class: Assoc/HT-High Trad
FAX Number: (931) 540-2535 Calendar System: Semester
URL: www.columbiastate.edu
Established: 1966 Annual Undergrad Tuition & Fees (In-State): $4,015
Enrollment: 5,297 Coed
Affiliation or Control: State IRS Status: 501(c)3

Highest Offering: Associate Degree
Accreditation: SC, ACBSP, ADNUR, COARC, EMT, NAIT, RAD

02 President ... Dr. Janet F. SMITH
05 Interim VP for Academic Affairs ... Ms. Joni LENIG
10 VP for Financial & Admin Affairs ... Ms. Elaine CURTIS
111 VP for Advancement ... Ms. Bethany LAY
20 Assoc VP Faculty/Curric & Programs ... Ms. Joni L. LENIG
32 Interim VP for Student Affairs ... Ms. Ruth Ann HOLT
13 Assoc VP for Info Technology ... Dr. Emily SICIENSKY
21 Assoc VP for Business Services ... Mr. Keith ISBELL
26 Director of Communications ... Ms. Amy SPEARS-BOYD
28 Asst to Pres for Access & Diversity ... Dr. Christa S. MARTIN
06 Director Records ... Ms. Sharon G. BOWEN
15 Director Human Resources ... Ms. Christie MILLER
08 Director Library ... Mr. Aaron WIMER
45 Assoc VP for Plng/Effect & Reten ... Ms. Tammy BORREN
37 Director Financial Aid ... Mr. John CAGE
41 Director Athletics ... Mr. Johnny LITTRELL
18 Director Facility Services & Safety ... Mr. Tim HALLMARK
56 Assoc VP Wiliamson Campus ... Dr. Shanna JACKSON
96 Coordinator Purchasing ... Mr. Jon ARNOLD
84 Chief Enrollment Svcs Officer ... Ms. Jill RILEY
103 Dir Workforce/Career Development ... Ms. LK BROWNING
104 Director Study Abroad ... Mr. Wes DULANEY
106 Dir Online Education/E-learning ... Dr. Marilia GERGES
108 Director Institutional Assessment ... Mr. Harjanto DJUNAIDI
19 Director Security/Safety ... Mr. Randy CARROLL

*Dyersburg State Community College (A)

1510 Lake Road, Dyersburg TN 38024-2450
County: Dyer FICE Identification: 006835
Unit ID: 220057
Telephone: (731) 286-3200 Carnegie Class: Assoc/HT-Mix Trad/Non
FAX Number: (731) 286-3333 Calendar System: Semester
URL: www.dscc.edu
Established: 1967 Annual Undergrad Tuition & Fees (In-State): $4,229
Enrollment: 2,857 Coed
Affiliation or Control: State IRS Status: 501(c)3
Highest Offering: Associate Degree
Accreditation: SC, ACBSP, ADNUR, CAHIIM, EMT

02 President ... Dr. Karen A. BOWYER
05 Vice President for the College ... Dr. Tamara DANIEL
10 Vice President Finance/Admin Svcs ... Dr. Charlene WHITE
111 VP Inst Advancement/Cont Education ... Dr. Kimberly MARTIN
13 Vice President Technology ... Mr. Josh DUGGIN
32 Dean of Student Services ... Ms. Larenda FULTZ
08 Dean Learning Resources Center ... Ms. Susan CHARLEY
37 Director of Financial Aid ... Mrs. Kacee HARDY
09 Institutional Research Specialist ... Ms. Mary RICKS
15 Director Human Resources ... Ms. Sheila GILLAHAN
103 Director of Workforce Development ... Ms. Margaret PRATER
29 Director of Alumni Relations ... Ms. Amy FINCH
121 Academic/Career Counselor ... Ms. Sherry BAKER
41 Director of Athletics ... Mr. Alan BARNETT
18 Director of Physical Plant ... Mr. Kent JETTON
07 Director of Admissions & Records ... Ms. Heather PAGE
26 Director of Public Information ... Ms. Amy FINCH
96 Director of Purchasing ... Ms. Beth MULLINS
21 Business & Student Fin Svcs Manager ... Ms. Donna MEALER
49 Dean Arts & Sciences ... Mr. James BARHAM
72 Dean Business/Tech/Allied Health ... Ms. Julie FRAZIER
66 Dean Nursing/Allied Health Div ... Ms. Amy JOHNSON
04 Administrative Asst to President ... Ms. Edith CARLTON

*Jackson State Community College (B)

2046 North Parkway, Jackson TN 38301-3797
County: Madison FICE Identification: 004937
Unit ID: 220400
Telephone: (731) 424-3520 Carnegie Class: Assoc/HT-Mix Trad/Non
FAX Number: (731) 425-2647 Calendar System: Semester
URL: www.jscc.edu
Established: 1965 Annual Undergrad Tuition & Fees (In-State): $4,029
Enrollment: 4,746 Coed
Affiliation or Control: State IRS Status: 501(c)3
Highest Offering: Associate Degree
Accreditation: SC, ACBSP, ADNUR, EMT, MLTAD, NAIT, OTA, PTAA, RAD

02 President ... Dr. Allana HAMILTON
05 VP of Academic Affairs ... Dr. Larry BAILEY
10 Vice Pres of Finance & Admin Affs ... Mr. Horace W. CHASE
30 Dir of Development/Cmty Relations ... Ms. Dee HENDERSON
32 VP of Student Services ... Mr. Brian GANN
111 VP of Institutional Advancement ... Mr. Bobby SMITH
116 Internal Auditor ... Mrs. Angela P. BROWN
15 Dir Human Resources/Affirm Action ... Ms. Amy WEST
09 Dir Inst Research & Accountability ... Mrs. Sara VONDERHEIDE
13 Director of Information Technology ... Ms. Dana NAILS
21 Director of Business Services ... Mr. Tim DELLINGER
18 Director of Physical Plant ... Mr. Preston TURNER
96 Director of Purchasing ... Mr. Robert D. HEMRICK
12 Director Lexington Campus ... Ms. Sandy STANFILL
12 Director Savannah Campus ... Mrs. Meda FALLS
12 Director Humboldt Campus ... Ms. Lisa BARKER
26 Director of PR and Marketing ... Mr. John MCCOMMON
37 Director Student Financial Aid ... Ms. Dewana LATIMER
07 Director of Admissions and Records ... Ms. Robin MAREK
08 Head Librarian ... Mr. Scott COHEN
19 Director Security/Safety ... Mr. Darron BILLINGS
41 Athletic Director ... Vacant

*Motlow State Community College (C)

PO Box 8500, Lynchburg TN 37352-8500
County: Moore FICE Identification: 006836
Unit ID: 221096
Telephone: (931) 393-1500 Carnegie Class: Assoc/HT-High Trad
FAX Number: (931) 393-1681 Calendar System: Semester
URL: www.mscc.edu
Established: 1969 Annual Undergrad Tuition & Fees (In-State): $4,051
Enrollment: 5,256 Coed
Affiliation or Control: State IRS Status: 501(c)3
Highest Offering: Associate Degree
Accreditation: SC, ACBSP, ADNUR, NAIT

02 Interim President ... Ms. Hilda TUNSTILL
05 Interim VP for Academic Affairs ... Ms. Melody EDMONDS
10 Vice Pres for Finance & Admin ... Ms. Hilda TUNSTILL
26 VP Marketing & Campus Activities ... Ms. Terri BRYSON
88 VP Quality Assur & Performance Fund ... Dr. Scott COOK
13 Chief Information Officer ... Ms. Cynthia LOGAN
32 Vice Pres for Student Affairs ... Ms. Cheryl HYLAND
72 Dean Career & Tech Programs ... Mr. Fred RASCOE
88 Asst Dean CTP & DE ... Ms. Debra SMITH
12 Interim Dean McMinnville Campus ... Mr. Shane BUCHANAN
76 Dean Allied Health/Dir of Nursing ... Ms. Pat HENDRIX
12 Dean of Moore County Campus ... Ms. Cheryl NORRIS
12 Assn Dean Fayetteville Campus ... Ms. Lisa SMITH
12 Dean of Smyrna Campus ... Ms. Elizabeth FITCH
35 Dean of Students ... Ms. Kirsten MOSS
18 Director of Facilities ... Mr. Brian GAFFORD
14 Director of Technical Operations ... Mr. Michael BOATMAN
88 Director of Special Events ... Ms. Brenda CANNON
36 Director of Career Readiness ... Mr. Shane BUCHANAN
08 Director of Libraries ... Mr. Chris BRYANT
102 Director of the Foundation ... Ms. Lane YODER
37 Executive Director of Financial Aid ... Mr. Joe MYERS
38 Director of Disability & Testing ... Ms. Belinda CHAMPION
07 Director of Admissions & Records ... Ms. Mae SANDERS
19 Director of Public Safety ... Mr. Ray HIGGINBOTHAM
41 Director of Athletics ... Mr. C. Scott SHASTEEN
91 Director Admin Computing ... Vacant
121 Director Student Success ... Ms. Rhonda COTHAM
84 Director of Recruitment ... Mr. Jeremy MILLS
103 Dir of Workforce Dev & Extended ... Mr. Tom DILLINGHAM
15 Director of Human Resources ... Ms. Laura JENT
21 Director of Fiscal Services ... Ms. Sandy SCHAFFER
04 Admin Assistant to the President ... Ms. Christy GLENN

*Nashville State Community College (D)

120 White Bridge Road, Nashville TN 37209-4515
County: Davidson FICE Identification: 008145
Unit ID: 221184
Telephone: (615) 353-3333 Carnegie Class: Assoc/HT-Mix Trad/Non
FAX Number: (615) 353-3713 Calendar System: Semester
URL: www.nscc.edu
Established: 1969 Annual Undergrad Tuition & Fees (In-State): $3,969
Enrollment: 10,192 Coed
Affiliation or Control: State IRS Status: 501(c)3
Highest Offering: Associate Degree
Accreditation: SC, ACBSP, ACFEI, ADNUR, NAIT, OTA, SURGT

02 President ... Dr. George H. VAN ALLEN
05 Vice Pres of Academic Affairs ... Dr. William T. BROWN
10 Vice Pres Finance & Administration ... Mrs. Mary M. CROSS
09 VP of Institutional Effectiveness ... Dr. Flora R. SETAYESH
45 Assoc VP Planning/Assessment ... Mr. Ted M. WASHINGTON
30 Exec Dir of Devel/Dir Public Affs ... Mrs. Lauren P. BELL
32 Dean of Students ... Dr. Carol J. MARTIN-OSORIO
116 Internal Auditor ... Mr. Andrew MCARTHUR
06 Registrar ... Mr. Lance L. WOODARD
07 Director of Admissions ... Mrs. Laura P. MORAN
13 Director of Computer Services ... Mr. Paul A. KAMINSKY
19 Director of Safety and Security ... Mr. Derrek G. SHEUCRAFT
37 Director of Financial Aid ... Ms. Jennifer D. BYRD
15 Dir Human Res/Affirm Act/Diversity ... Mrs. Sheryl R. GOSSARD
18 Director of Operations/Maintenance ... Mr. Jim T. DAWSON
103 Dir Workforce and Community Dev ... Vacant
26 Manager of Publications ... Ms. Ellen L. ZINK
106 Director of Online Learning ... Ms. Shelley J. GROSS-GRAY
83 Dean of Social and Life Sciences ... Dr. Julie E. WILLIAMS
72 Dean of Comp/Eng Technologies ... Dr. Reginald J. GARDNER
81 Dean Math & Natural Sciences ... Dr. Sarah E. ROBERTS
79 Dean English/Humanities & Arts ... Dr. Patricia J. ARMSTRONG
62 Dean Lrng Resources & Distance Educ ... Dr. Faye M. JONES
50 Dean Business & Applied Arts ... Ms. Karen L. STEVENSON
96 Director of Purchasing ... Ms. Jo SMITH
66 Director of Nursing ... Dr. Cynthia G. WALLER
04 Administrative Asst to President ... Mrs. Judy I. COOK
36 Director Student Placement ... Mr. Stephen L. HOOKS

*Northeast State Community College (E)

PO Box 246, 2425 Highway 75, Blountville TN 37617-0246
County: Sullivan FICE Identification: 005378
Unit ID: 221908
Telephone: (423) 323-3191 Carnegie Class: Assoc/HT-High Trad
FAX Number: (423) 279-7636 Calendar System: Semester
URL: www.northeaststate.edu
Established: 1965 Annual Undergrad Tuition & Fees (In-State): $4,056
Enrollment: 6,084 Coed
Affiliation or Control: State IRS Status: 501(c)3
Highest Offering: Associate Degree
Accreditation: SC, ACBSP, ADNUR, CVT, DA, EMT, MLTAD, NAIT, SURGT

02 Interim President ... Mr. James KING
04 Exec Assistant to the President ... Ms. Cindy S. CHRISTIAN
05 Int Vice Pres Academic Affairs ... Dr. Sam ROWELL
10 Chief Financial Officer ... Col. James CLINE, RET.
11 Vice Pres Administrative Svcs ... Mr. Fred LEWIS
32 Vice President Student Affairs ... Mr. Matt DELOZIER
103 VP Economic & Workforce Development ... Mr. Jeff D. MCCORD
56 Asst VP Evening/Distance Educ ... Dr. Pashia HOGAN
20 Asst Vice Pres Academic Affairs ... Mr. Don COLEMAN
30 Chief Advancement Officer ... Dr. Leigh HORNSBY
06 Registrar/Admissions & Records ... Ms. Deidra CLOSE
15 Exec Director Human Resources ... Ms. Tyra COPAS
31 Director Community Relations ... Mr. Robert CARPENTER
26 Director of Marketing ... Ms. Amanda ADAMS
45 Director Planning & Assessment ... Mr. John GRUBB
08 Dean Library ... Mr. Christopher DEMAS
79 Dean Humanities ... Mr. William WILSON
81 Dean Mathematics ... Ms. Malissa TRENT
76 Dean Health Related Profession ... Ms. Connie MARSHALL
72 Dean Advance Technologies ... Mr. Sam S. ROWELL
83 Dean Behavior/Social Sciences ... Dr. Xiaoping WANG
81 Dean Science ... Dr. Carolyn MCCRACKEN
50 Dean Business Technologies ... Mr. Danny L. LAWSON
66 Interim Dean Nursing ... Dr. Johanna NEUBRANDER
84 Dean of Enrollment Management ... Ms. Jennifer STARLING
07 VA Admissions/Records Tech Clerk ... Mr. John ADCOX

*Pellissippi State Community College (F)

PO Box 22990, Knoxville TN 37933-0990
County: Knox FICE Identification: 012693
Unit ID: 221643
Telephone: (865) 694-6400 Carnegie Class: Assoc/HT-Mix Trad/Non
FAX Number: (865) 539-7240 Calendar System: Semester
URL: www.pstcc.edu
Established: 1974 Annual Undergrad Tuition & Fees (In-State): $4,084
Enrollment: 10,325 Coed
Affiliation or Control: State IRS Status: 501(c)3
Highest Offering: Associate Degree
Accreditation: SC, ACBSP, ACFEI, ADNUR, NAIT

02 President ... Dr. L. Anthony WISE
125 President Emeritus ... Dr. Allen G. EDWARDS
05 Vice President of Academic Affairs ... Dr. Ted A. LEWIS
13 Vice President Information Services ... Ms. Audrey J. WILLIAMS
10 Vice President Business & Finance ... Mr. Ronald L. KESTERSON
102 Exec Director of Foundation ... Ms. Aneisa L. MCDONALD
32 Vice President of Student Affairs ... Vacant
103 Exec Dir Business/Workforce Dev ... Mr. Teri T. BRAHAMS
12 Campus Dean Blount County Programs ... Ms. Holly L. BURKETT
12 Campus Dean Strawberry Pl Program ... Dr. Mike NORTH
12 Campus Dean Magnolia Ave Programs .. Ms. Rosalyn P. TILLMAN
12 Campus Dean Division Street Program ... Ms. Esther L. DYER
35 Dean of Students ... Mr. Travis C. LOVEDAY
21 Asst VP Business Services ... Ms. Renee MOORE
88 Manager Accounts Payable ... Ms. Debra CLARK
20 Asst VP of Academic Affairs ... Dr. Beth NORTON
84 Asst VP Enrollment Services ... Ms. Leigh A. TOUZEAU
22 Exec Director Equity & Compliance ... Dr. Patrick SHIPWASH
35 Dir of Student Life & Recreation ... Ms. Kim THOMAS-LARUE
36 Director of Placement ... Ms. Cynthia ATCHLEY
22 Director of Disability Services ... Ms. Ann E. SATKOWIAK
38 Director Counseling Department ... Dr. Elizabeth E. FIRESTONE
26 Director Marketing & Communications ... Ms. Julia H. WOOD
07 Dir of Admiss & Records/Registrar ... Ms. Melanie M. PARADISE
08 Director of Library Services ... Mr. J. Peter NERZAK
24 Dir Educ Technology Svcs ... Ms. Kristy M. CONGER
37 Director of Financial Aid ... Mr. Dick W. SMELSER
108 Dir Inst Effective/Assess/Planning ... Ms. Nancy A. RAMSEY
18 Director of Facilities ... Ms. Regina MCNEW
19 Chief of Police Safety/Security ... Mr. Fred J. BREINER
114 Director Budget & Payroll ... Ms. Nancy DONAHUE
96 Director of Purchasing ... Mr. John S. CLARK
15 Director Human Resources ... Ms. Carole GARY
25 Interim Director Grant Development ... Mr. David CAZALET
104 Exec Dir TnCIS/International Educ ... Ms. Tracey BRADLEY
112 Director Major Gift Development ... Ms. Marilyn RODDY
44 Dir Annual Giving & Scholarhships ... Vacant
88 Dir Cmty Outreach/Donor Engagement ... Ms. Patricia T. MYERS
91 Dir Applications Programming Sup ... Mr. James (Dean) COPPLE
88 Dir of Network & Technical Services ... Mr. Larry BATES
28 Director of Access & Diversity ... Ms. Gayle E. WOOD
88 Director of Academic Testing ... Ms. Joan NEWMAN
88 Dir Curriculum & New Programs ... Ms. Judy GOSCH
121 Director of Advising ... Ms. Rachael C. CRAGLE
88 Dir Academic Support Programs ... Ms. Jan T. SHARP
113 Bursar ... Ms. Mandy BENTZ
116 Director of Internal Audit ... Ms. Suzanne WALKER
89 Director of QEP ... Ms. Kellie TOON
88 Director of New Student Orientation ... Ms. Rebecca MILAM
88 Director TRIO Student Support Svcs ... Dr. Mark S. COTTER
88 Director Veteran Services ... Mr. Eric D. BOLLMANN

*Roane State Community College (A)

276 Patton Lane, Harriman TN 37748-5011
County: Roane FICE Identification: 009914
Unit ID: 221397
Telephone: (865) 354-3000 Carnegie Class: Assoc/HT-High Trad
FAX Number: (865) 882-4585 Calendar System: Semester
URL: www.roanestate.edu
Established: 1971 Annual Undergrad Tuition & Fees (In-State): $4,047
Enrollment: 5,861 Coed
Affiliation or Control: State IRS Status: 501(c)3
Highest Offering: Associate Degree
Accreditation: SC, ACBSP, ADNUR, CAHIIM, COARC, COMTA, DH, EMT, OPD, OTA, POLYT, PTAA, RAD

02 President ... Dr. Chris WHALEY
05 Vice Pres for Student Learning/CAO ... Dr. Diane WARD
10 Exec Vice Pres Business & Finance ... Vacant
103 VP Workforce Develop/Student Affs ... Ms. Teresa S. DUNCAN
12 Exec Dir of Oak Ridge & Cmty Rel ... Dr. Owen DRISKILL
32 Dean of Students ... Mrs. Brenda RECTOR
21 Director of Accounting Services ... Ms. Marsha MATHEWS
13 Interim Computer Info Officer ... Ms. Keri PHILLIPS
09 VP Institutional Research ... Ms. Karen L. BRUNNER
22 Coordinator Affirmative Action ... Mr. Odell FEARN
08 Director of Library Services ... Mr. Robert M. BENSON
06 Director of Records & Registration ... Ms. Donna MACK
18 Director Physical Plant & Expo Ctr ... Mr. Stan R. STARKEY
29 Director Alumni Relations ... Ms. Tamsin MILLER
96 Director of Purchasing ... Mrs. Dana WEST
36 Workforce Placement & Job Placement ... Ms. Kim HARRIS
04 Executive Assistant to President ... Vacant
19 Director Security/Safety ... Mr. Thomas STUFANO
41 Athletic Director ... Mr. Randy NESBIT
104 Director Study Abroad ... Dr. Adolf KING
121 Dean of Student Academic Services ... Ms. Kathryn RHODES

*Southwest Tennessee Community College (B)

PO Box 780, Memphis TN 38101-0780
County: Shelby FICE Identification: 010439
Unit ID: 221485
Telephone: (901) 333-5000 Carnegie Class: Assoc/MT-VT-Mix Trad/Non
FAX Number: (901) 333-4645 Calendar System: Semester
URL: www.southwest.tn.edu
Established: 2000 Annual Undergrad Tuition & Fees (In-State): $4,059
Enrollment: 9,135 Coed
Affiliation or Control: State IRS Status: 501(c)3
Highest Offering: Associate Degree
Accreditation: SC, ACBSP, ACFEI, ADNUR, #DIETT, EMT, ENGT, MLTAD, PHLEB, PTAA, RAD

02 President ... Dr. Tracy D. HALL
04 Assistant to the President ... Ms. LaTorya CERUTI
05 Vice President of Academic Affairs ... Dr. Christopher C. EZELL
86 Exec Asst to Pres/Govt Relations ... Mr. Sherman D. GREER
111 Vice Pres Institutional Advancement ... Mrs. Karen F. NIPPERT
10 Vice Pres Finance & Admin Services ... Mrs. Anita LOCKRIDGE
32 Vice Pres Student Affairs ... Mrs. Jacqueline A. FAULKNER
84 Exec Dir of Enrollment Services ... Dr. Steven SMITH
26 Exec Director of Comm & Marketing ... Ms. Daphne THOMAS
15 Exec Director Human Resources ... Ms. Terrie STARLING
06 Registrar ... Ms. Barbara WELLS
18 Director Physical Plant ... Mr. Gerald BATCHELOR
96 Director of Purchasing ... Vacant
37 Director of Financial Aid ... Mrs. Lechelle D. DAVENPORT
09 Institutional Research Analyst ... Mr. Donald C. MYERS
13 Exec Dir Info Systems (CIO) ... Mr. Michael D. BOYD
19 Director Public Safety ... Mrs. Lezley A. WEBB
22 Exec Dir Equity and Compliance ... Mrs. Monika L. JOHNSON
103 Assoc Vice Pres of Workforce Dev ... Vacant

*Volunteer State Community College (C)

1480 Nashville Pike, Gallatin TN 37066-3188
County: Sumner FICE Identification: 009912
Unit ID: 222053
Telephone: (615) 452-8600 Carnegie Class: Assoc/MT-VT-Mix Trad/Non
FAX Number: (615) 230-3577 Calendar System: Semester
URL: www.volstate.edu
Established: 1970 Annual Undergrad Tuition & Fees (In-State): $4,037
Enrollment: 8,098 Coed
Affiliation or Control: State IRS Status: 501(c)3
Highest Offering: Associate Degree
Accreditation: SC, ACBSP, CAHIIM, COARC, DA, DMS, EMT, MLTAD, POLYT, PTAA, RAD

02 President ... Dr. Jerry FAULKNER
05 Vice President Academic Affairs ... Dr. George PIMENTEL
10 Vice President Business & Finance ... Ms. Beth COOKSEY
32 Vice President Student Services ... Dr. Emily SHORT
30 Vice Pres for Resource Development ... Ms. Karen MITCHELL
45 Vice Pres Inst Planning/Research ... Ms. Jane MCGUIRE
20 Asst VP of Academic Affairs ... Dr. Michael TORRENCE
21 Asst Vice Pres Business & Finance ... Ms. Renee AUSTIN
35 Asst VP Student Svcs/Enrollment Mgt . Dr. Talia KORONKIEWICZ
51 Asst VP/Dean Continuing Education ... Mrs. Hilary B. MARABETI
76 Dean of Health ... Mr. Elvis BRANDON
79 Dean Humanities ... Dr. Jennifer BREZINA
53 Dean Social Science/Education ... Ms. Phyllis FOLEY
81 Dean Math & Science ... Dr. Philip CLIFFORD
50 Dean of Business ... Ms. Patricia ANDERSON
88 Director of Development Studies Pgm ... Ms. Kay DAYTON
15 Dir Personnel/Affirm Act/Human Res ... Ms. Lori CUTRELL
08 Director Library Services ... Ms. Sarah SMITH
07 Dir Admissions & College Registrar ... Mr. Tim AMYX
13 Director Information Technology ... Mr. Kevin BLANKENSHIP
37 Director Student Financial Aid ... Mrs. Sue H. PEDIGO
26 Director Public Relations ... Mrs. Tami WALLACE
18 Senior Director Physical Plant ... Mr. William NEWMAN
19 Chief Security & Safety ... Mr. William D. ROGAN
41 Director of Athletics ... Mr. Bobby HUDSON
106 Director Distance Learning ... Mrs. Rhonda GREGORY
88 Special Adult Programs/ADA Director ... Ms. Kathy SOWELL
09 Director of Institutional Research ... Mrs. Ann Marie CALDERON
96 Director Purchasing ... Mr. Chris HARRISON
24 Director Media Services ... Mr. Terry HEINEN
124 Director Retention Support Services ... Ms. Heather HARPER
36 Director of Career Placement ... Dr. Rick PARRENT
38 Director Counseling & Testing ... Mr. Terry BUBB
28 Director Student Life & Diversity ... Dr. Kenny YARBROUGH
88 Dir Health Sciences Ctr of Emphasis ... Ms. Terri CRUTCHER
110 Director of Development ... Ms. Alison MUNCY
06 Registrar ... Mr. Tim AMYX
04 Administrative Asst to President ... Ms. Karen WALLER

*Walters State Community College (D)

500 S Davy Crockett Parkway, Morristown TN 37813-6899
County: Hamblen FICE Identification: 008863
Unit ID: 222062
Telephone: (423) 585-2600 Carnegie Class: Assoc/HT-High Trad
FAX Number: (423) 585-6853 Calendar System: Semester
URL: www.ws.edu
Established: 1969 Annual Undergrad Tuition & Fees (In-State): $4,032
Enrollment: 5,947 Coed
Affiliation or Control: State IRS Status: 501(c)3
Highest Offering: Associate Degree
Accreditation: SC, ACBSP, ACFEI, ADNUR, CAHIIM, COARC, EMT, NAIT, PTAA, SURGT

02 President ... Dr. Anthony R. MIKSA
04 Int Exec Director to the President ... Ms. Leann LONG
05 Vice President Academic Affairs ... Dr. Lori CAMPBELL
10 Int Vice President Business Affairs ... Dr. Mark HURST
32 Vice President Student Affairs ... Ms. Angi SMITH
111 Vice Pres for College Advancement ... Mr. Chris CATES
45 VP for Planning/Research/Assessment . Dr. Debbie L. MCCARTER
20 Asst Vice Pres for Academic Affairs ... Dr. John LAPRISE
35 Asst Vice Pres Student Affairs ... Mr. Michael A. CAMPBELL
18 Asst Vice Pres Facilities Mgmt ... Mr. Max E. WILLIAMS
21 Asst Vice Pres Business Affairs ... Ms. Heather CARRIER
28 Spec Asst to Pres for Diversity ... Ms. W. Ann BOWEN
08 Dean of Library ... Dr. Jamie POSEY
31 Dean of Workforce Training ... Dr. Joseph L. COMBS
19 Dean of Public Safety Division ... Mr. Thomas STRANGE
17 Dean Health Programs ... Ms. Marty K. RUCKER
12 Dean Greenville/Greene Co Center ... Ms. Drucilla W. MILLER
12 Dean Sevier County Campus ... Dr. Jama SUTTON
83 Dean of Behavioral/Social Sciences ... Mr. Darrel MCGHEE
50 Dean of Business ... Dr. Amy ROSS
79 Dean of Humanities ... Mr. Chippy MCLAIN
81 Dean of Mathematics ... Mr. John C. KNIGHT
49 Dean of Natural Science ... Dr. Jeffrey T. HORNER
75 Dean of Technical Education ... Mr. Thomas R. SEWELL
06 Dean Student Info System/Records ... Ms. Linda MASON
103 Dean Ctr for Workforce Development ... Ms. Donna STANSBERRY
37 Dean of Financial Aid ... Ms. Ashley EDENS
38 Exec Director Counseling/Testing ... Dr. Andy HALL
15 Exec Dir of Human Resources ... Ms. Tammy GOODE
26 Vice President Public Information ... Mr. James B. PECTOL
13 Exec Director for Information ... Mr. Joe E. SARGENT
41 Director of Athletics ... Mr. Mike CAMPBELL
07 Director of Admissions ... Ms. Avery SWINSON
19 Chief of Campus Police ... Ms. Sarah ROSE
89 Director Freshmen Studies ... Vacant
36 Director Student Placement ... Dr. Andy HALL
92 Director Honors Program ... Ms. Janice M. DONAHUE
96 Director of Purchasing ... Ms. Renee JARNIGAN
105 Director of Network Services ... Mr. Bill R. MOREFIELD
29 Coordinator of Alumni Relations ... Ms. Wanda HARRELL
84 Director Enrollment Development ... Ms. Avery SWINSON
93 Coord Minority Student Recruit ... Ms. Roxanne BOWEN
108 Exec Dir of Planning & Assessment ... Dr. Deanna GARMAN

Tennessee State University (E)

3500 John A Merritt Boulevard, Nashville TN 37209-1561
County: Davidson FICE Identification: 003522
Unit ID: 221838
Telephone: (615) 963-5000 Carnegie Class: DU-Mod
FAX Number: (615) 963-7412 Calendar System: Semester
URL: www.tnstate.edu
Established: 1912 Annual Undergrad Tuition & Fees (In-State): $7,256
Enrollment: 9,167 Coed
Affiliation or Control: State IRS Status: 501(c)3
Highest Offering: Doctorate
Accreditation: SC, AAFCS, ADNUR, ART, CAEPN, CAHIIM, COARC, COPSY, CS, DH, DIETD, ENG, MUS, NAIT, NUR, OT, PH, PTA, SP, SPAA, SW

02 President ... Dr. Glenda GLOVER
05 Vice President Academic Affairs ... Dr. Mark G. HARDY
04 Senior Office Assistant ... Ms. Zanetta GOOCH
10 VP Business & Finance ... Mrs. Cynthia BROOKS
11 VP Administrative Affairs ... Ms. Jane JACKSON
32 Vice Pres Student Affairs ... Ms. Tracey FORD
30 VP Institutional Advancement ... Vacant
41 Athletic Director ... Mrs. Teresa LAWRENCE-PHILLIPS
43 University Legal Counsel ... Mr. Laurence PENDLETON
84 Assoc Provost Enrollment Mgmt ... Dr. John CADE
20 Assoc VP Academic Affairs ... Dr. Patricia CROOK
20 AVP Academic Affairs/Extended Educ ... Dr. Evelyn NETTLES
15 Assoc VP/Dir Human Resources ... Ms. Linda C. SPEARS
21 Assoc VP Financial Services ... Mr. Bradley WHITE
88 Asst VP Budget/Travel ... Mr. Bradley WHITE
37 Asst VP Financial Aid ... Ms. Amy B. WOOD
26 Asst VP Public Rels/Communication ... Ms. Kelli SHARPE
09 Asst VP Inst Effectiveness/Research . Dr. G. Pamela BURCH-SIMS
18 Director Facilities/Physical Plant ... Mr. Daniel WOOTEN
28 Dir Equity Diversity & Compliance ... Ms. Tiffa COX
06 Registrar ... Mrs. Thelria HARDAWAY
19 Chief TSU Police Department ... Mr. Richard BRIGGANCE
08 Dean Libraries & Media Centers ... Dr. Murle KENERSON
49 Dean College of Liberal Arts ... Dr. Gloria C. JOHNSON
50 Dean College of Business ... Dr. Millicent LOWNES-JACKSON
53 Int Dean College of Education ... Dr. Celeste WILLIAMS
54 Dean College of Engr/Tech/Comp Sci ... Dr. S. Keith HARGROVE
47 Dn Agriculture/Human & Natural Sci ... Dr. Chandra REDDY
76 Int Dean Col Health Sciences ... Dr. Ronald BARREDO

Tennessee Technological University (F)

1000 N Dixie Avenue, Cookeville TN 38505-0001
County: Putnam FICE Identification: 003523
Unit ID: 221847
Telephone: (931) 372-3101 Carnegie Class: DU-Mod
FAX Number: (931) 372-3898 Calendar System: Semester
URL: www.tntech.edu
Established: 1915 Annual Undergrad Tuition & Fees (In-State): $8,203
Enrollment: 10,900 Coed
Affiliation or Control: State IRS Status: 501(c)3
Highest Offering: Doctorate
Accreditation: SC, AAFCS, ART, CACREP, CAEPN, CS, DIETD, ENG, ENGT, MUS, NURSE

02 President ... Dr. Philip B. OLDHAM
05 Interim Provost/Vice President ... Dr. Mark STEPHENS
10 Vice Pres Planning & Finance ... Dr. Claire STINSON
32 Vice President Student Affairs ... Mr. Marc BURNETT
35 Asst VP Student Affairs ... Mr. Ed BOUCHER
46 VP Research & Economic Development ... Dr. Bharat SONI
86 Director Government Relations ... Dr. Terry SALTSMAN
88 Assoc VP for Research ... Dr. Francis O. OTUONYE
111 Vice President Univ Advancement ... Dr. Kevin BRASWELL
20 Sr Assoc VP Academic Affairs ... Dr. Mark STEPHENS
20 Assoc Provost/Vice Pres Acad Affs ... Dr. Xiaoming (Sharon) HUO
13 Interim CIO Info Tech Svcs ... Dr. Terry SALTSMAN
37 Director Financial Aid ... Mr. Lester MCKENZIE
08 Director Library & Learning Asst ... Dr. Doug BATES
09 Director Institutional Research ... Dr. Glenn W. JAMES
45 Director of Institutional Planning ... Dr. Claire STINSON
15 Assoc VP Human Resources ... Dr. Leslie CRICKENBERGER
19 Director of University Police ... Mr. Tony NELSON
39 Director of Housing ... Mr. Charles MACKE
41 Director of Athletics ... Mr. Mark WILSON
18 Assoc VP Physical Plant ... Mr. Jack BUTLER
38 Director Counseling Center ... Ms. Patricia SMITH
23 Director of Health Svcs ... Ms. Leigh A. RAY
36 Director Career Services ... Ms. Lynn HALEY
26 Assoc VP Communications & Mkting ... Ms. Karen LYKINS
85 Director International Education ... Mr. Charles WILKERSON
06 Registrar ... Ms. Brandi HILL
92 Director Honors Program ... Dr. Rita BARNES
93 Asst VP Multicultural Affairs ... Dr. Robert OWENS
96 Director of Purchasing ... Ms. Judy M. HULL
21 Associate VP Business ... Mr. Jeff YOUNG
43 Director University Counsel ... Ms. Kae CARPENTER
29 Dir Alumni Engagement & Annual Giv ... Mr. Brandon BOYD
116 Director of Internal Audit ... Ms. Deanna METTS
22 Dir of AA & Employee Relations ... Ms. Elizabeth GAYS
07 Director of Admissions ... Ms. Judy RIGGSBEE
19 Dir Capital Proj Envir Health & Saf ... Mr. James COBB
84 Interim AVP Enr Mgt & Student Succ ... Dr. Leslie CRICKENBERGER
49 Dean of Arts & Sciences ... Dr. Paul SEMMES
54 Dean of Engineering ... Vacant
47 Dean Agric & Human Ecology ... Dr. Liz MULLENS
50 Dean of Business Admin ... Dr. Thomas PAYNE
53 Dean College of Education ... Dr. Jennifer SHANK
66 Dean School of Nursing ... Dr. Huey-Ming TZENG
88 Dean Interdisciplinary Studies ... Dr. Mike GOTCHER
58 Assoc Dean of Graduate Studies ... Dr. Alice CAMUTI
04 Administrative Asst to President ... Ms. Terri TAYLOR
105 Director Web Services ... Mr. David WILLIS
108 Director Institutional Assessment ... Dr. Theresa ENNIS
90 Director Academic Computing ... Ms. Yvette CLARK
91 Director Administrative Computing ... Mr. Rick CUMBY
106 Assoc VP Digital & Distance Educ ... Dr. Patrick WILSON
102 Dir Foundation/Corporate Relations ... Ms. Tracey DUNCAN
104 Director Study Abroad ... Ms. Amy MILLER

Tennessee Wesleyan University (A)

204 East College St., Athens TN 37303
County: McMinn FICE Identification: 003525
Unit ID: 221731
Telephone: (423) 745-7504 Carnegie Class: Bac-Diverse
FAX Number: (423) 744-9968 Calendar System: Semester
URL: www.tnwesleyan.edu
Established: 1857 Annual Undergrad Tuition & Fees: $23,000
Enrollment: 1,027 Coed
Affiliation or Control: United Methodist IRS Status: 501(c)3
Highest Offering: Master's
Accreditation: SC, NURSE, @SW

01 President .... Dr. Harley KNOWLES
05 Vice President for Academic Affairs .... Dr. Grant WILLHITE
10 Vice Pres Financial/Business Affs .... Mrs. Gail HARRIS
32 Vice President for Student Life .... Dr. Scott MASHBURN
111 Vice President of Advancement .... Mr. Randy NELSON
07 Vice President for Admissions .... Ms. Joanne LANDERS
04 Executive Assistant to President .... Mrs. Gail ROGERS
08 Dir of Library & Info Svcs .... Ms. Julie ADAMS
06 Registrar .... Mrs. Julie MCCASLIN
37 Director of Financial Aid .... Mrs. Lacey WEESE
41 Athletic Director .... Mr. Donny MAYFIELD
15 Human Resources Director .... Mr. Kyle FULBRIGHT
18 Chief of Facilities/Physical Plant .... Mr. Mike INGRAM
26 Director of Communications .... Ms. Bridgette RAPER
35 Assoc Dean of Students .... Ms. Kerrie LYNN
13 Exec Director of Information Tech .... Mr. Brandon LAMBDIN

Trevecca Nazarene University (B)

333 Murfreesboro Road, Nashville TN 37210-2877
County: Davidson FICE Identification: 003526
Unit ID: 221892
Telephone: (615) 248-1200 Carnegie Class: DU-Mod
FAX Number: (615) 248-7728 Calendar System: Semester
URL: www.trevecca.edu
Established: 1901 Annual Undergrad Tuition & Fees: $24,624
Enrollment: 2,640 Coed
Affiliation or Control: Church Of The Nazarene IRS Status: 501(c)3
Highest Offering: Doctorate
Accreditation: SC, ARCPA, CACREP, CAEPN, MUS, NURSE, SW

01 President .... Dr. Dan BOONE
04 Assistant to the President .... Ms. Anne TWINING
05 University Provost .... Dr. Stephen M. PUSEY
10 Exec Vice Pres Finance & Admin .... Mr. David CALDWELL
26 Vice President External Relations .... Mrs. Peggy J. COONING
58 Assoc Provost/VP Grad & Cont Stds .... Dr. Tim EADES
20 Assoc Provost/Dean Academic Affairs .... Dr. Tom MIDDENDORF
20 Assoc Vice Pres Academic Programs .... Dr. Jim HIATT
88 Assoc VP Accred/State Authorization .... Dr. Jonathan BARTLING
51 Assoc Vice Pres Graduate/Cont Stds .... Dr. Ricky CHRISTMAN
27 Assoc Vice Pres Marketing & Comm .... Mr. Matthew TOY
32 Assoc Provost/Dean of Student Dev .... Mr. Stephen A. HARRIS
84 Assoc Provost/Dean of Enroll Mgmt .... Ms. Holly WHITBY
42 University Chaplain .... Ms. Shawna GAINES
73 Dean School of Theol/Christian Min .... Dr. Timothy M. GREEN
88 Assoc Dean Doctoral Programs .... Dr. Heidi FREDERICK
35 Assoc Dean Student Community Life .... Mr. Matt SPRAKER
39 Asc Dean Students Residential Life .... Mrs. Ronda LILIENTHAL
53 Dean of the School of Education .... Dr. Suzann HARRIS
49 Dean of School of Arts & Science .... Dr. Lena WELCH
64 Dean School of Music & Worship Arts .... Dr. David DIEHL
13 Chief Information Officer/ITS .... Mr. John EBERLE
08 Director Library Services .... Dr. Ruth KINNERSLEY
108 Dir Institutional Effectiveness .... Ms. Donna K. TUDOR
09 Director of Academic Data Mgmt .... Dr. Eugenia HARRIS
06 Registrar .... Ms. Katrina CHAPMAN
19 Director of Security .... Mr. Greg DAWSON
07 Director of Admissions .... Ms. Melinda MILLER
41 Athletic Director .... Mr. Mark ELLIOTT
88 Director Ctr/Ldrshp Calling Service .... Ms. Michelle GAERTNER
38 Director Counseling Services .... Dr. Sara HOPKINS
28 Coord Student Engagement/Diversity .... Mr. Brodrick THOMAS
88 Coord Counseling/Vocation Engagemnt .... Ms. Jennifer NEELY
36 Coordinator of Career Services .... Ms. Nicole HUBBS
106 Director Online Learning .... Ms. LaMetrius DANIELS
21 Director of Financial Services .... Mr. Chuck SEAMAN
15 Director Human Resources .... Mr. Steve SEXTON
37 Director of Financial Aid .... Mr. Eddie WHITE
76 Director Physician Asst Pgm .... Mr. Bret REEVES
18 Director Plant Operations .... Mr. Glen LINTHICUM
29 Director Alumni/Church Engagement .... Mr. Michael JOHNSON
30 Director of Development Operations .... Ms. Christy GRANT
27 Mgr of Content & Media Relations .... Ms. Mandy CROW
89 Coordinator Freshman Year Exper .... Ms. Megan MCGHEE
124 Coordinator of Assessment/Retention .... Mr. Jeffrey SWINK

Tusculum College (C)

60 Shiloh Road, Greeneville TN 37743-9997
County: Greene FICE Identification: 003527
Unit ID: 221953
Telephone: (423) 636-7300 Carnegie Class: Masters/M
FAX Number: (423) 638-7166 Calendar System: Semester
URL: www.tusculum.edu
Established: 1794 Annual Undergrad Tuition & Fees: $23,125
Enrollment: 1,809 Coed
Affiliation or Control: Presbyterian Church (U.S.A.) IRS Status: 501(c)3
Highest Offering: Master's
Accreditation: SC, #CAATE, NURSE

01 President .... Dr. Nancy B. MOODY
05 VP Academic Affairs .... Dr. Jason PIERCE
30 VP Institutional Advancement .... Ms. Heather PATCHETT
10 Vice Pres/Chief Financial Officer .... Mr. Steve GEHRET
84 VP for Enrollment Management .... Dr. Paul PINCKLEY
20 Asst VP for Academic Affairs .... Dr. Lisa JOHNSON
32 Dean of Students .... Dr. David MCMAHAN
35 Associate Dean of Students .... Ms. Jonita ASHLEY-PAULEY
06 Registrar .... Ms. Bobbie CLARKSTON
21 Controller .... Ms. Tracey JULIAN
07 Director of Operations/Admissions .... Ms. Melissa RIPLEY
20 Asst VP for Academic Affairs .... Dr. Carl LARSEN
15 Director Human Resources .... Ms. Mary SONNER
36 Director Career Counseling .... Ms. Robin LAY
08 Librarian .... Ms. Kathy HICKS
37 Director of Financial Aid .... Ms. Karen SARTAIN
41 Athletic Director .... Mr. Doug JONES
26 Director of Communications .... Ms. Suzanne RICHEY
13 Director of Information Systems .... Dr. Blair HENLEY
18 Director Facilities Management .... Mr. David MARTIN
92 Director of Honors Program .... Ms. Megan STARK
40 Bookstore Manager .... Mr. Cliff HOY
19 Director of Campus Safety .... Mr. Jonathan GRESHAM
49 Dean School of Arts and Sciences .... Mr. Wayne THOMAS
50 Dean School of Business .... Dr. Michael DILLON
53 Dean School of Education .... Dr. Tricia HUNSADER
66 Dean School of Nursing .... Dr. Lois EWEN

Union University (D)

1050 Union University Drive, Jackson TN 38305-3697
County: Madison FICE Identification: 003528
Unit ID: 221971
Telephone: (731) 668-1818 Carnegie Class: DU-Mod
FAX Number: (731) 661-5175 Calendar System: 4/1/4
URL: www.uu.edu
Established: 1823 Annual Undergrad Tuition & Fees: $30,330
Enrollment: 3,583 Coed
Affiliation or Control: Southern Baptist IRS Status: 501(c)3
Highest Offering: Doctorate
Accreditation: SC, ANEST, ART, CAATE, CAEPN, ENG, MUS, NURSE, PHAR, SW

01 President .... Dr. Samuel (Dub) W. OLIVER
05 Provost/VP Academic Affairs .... Dr. C. Ben MITCHELL
10 Sr Vice Pres Business Services .... Mr. Gary L. CARTER
111 Vice Pres Institutional Advancement .... Mrs. Catherine KWASIGROH
84 Vice Pres Enrollment Services .... Mr. Dan GRIFFIN
32 Dean of Students .... Dr. Bryan CARRIER
42 Vice Pres for University Ministries .... Dr. Todd BRADY
108 Asst Provost Accred & Research .... Dr. Michele ATKINS
04 Exec Assistant to the President .... Mrs. Gaye CHRISTY
21 Assoc Vice Pres Business Svcs .... Mr. Robert SIMPSON
08 Director of the Library .... Mrs. Melissa MOORE
26 Assoc VP University Communications .... Mr. Tim ELLSWORTH
13 Assoc VP Information Technology .... Mr. James AVERY
15 Assoc VP Business Svcs/Human Res .... Dr. John CARBONELL
07 Asst VP for Undergraduate Admiss .... Mr. Robbie GRAVES
37 Director Student Financial Planning .... Mr. John WINDHAM
49 Dean College Arts & Sciences .... Dr. John NETLAND
50 Dean School of Business .... Dr. Jason GARRETT
66 Dean School of Nursing .... Dr. Kelly HARDEN
53 Exec Dean College of Education .... Dr. Tom ROSEBROUGH
88 Dean Sch of Theology Missions .... Dr. Nathan FINN
67 Dean School of Pharmacy .... Dr. Sheila MITCHELL
91 Assoc Dir Information Technology .... Miss Karen MCWHERTER
36 Dir Vocation Ctr/Life Call/Career .... Mr. Alex HUGUENARD
14 Director of Data Management .... Mr. David PORTER
06 Registrar .... Mrs. Susan HOPPER
19 Director of Security/Safety .... Mr. Yancey PETTIGREW
41 Director of Athletics .... Mr. Tommy SADLER
18 Chief Facilities/Physical Plant .... Mr. David MCBRIDE
70 Dean School of Social Work .... Mrs. Mary Anne POE
51 Dean School Adult & Prof Studies .... Dr. Beverly ABSHER

The University of Memphis (E)

Southern Avenue, Memphis TN 38152
County: Shelby FICE Identification: 003509
Unit ID: 220862
Telephone: (901) 678-2000 Carnegie Class: DU-Higher
FAX Number: N/A Calendar System: Semester
URL: www.memphis.edu
Established: 1912 Annual Undergrad Tuition & Fees (In-State): $9,125
Enrollment: 20,585 Coed
Affiliation or Control: State IRS Status: 501(c)3
Highest Offering: Doctorate
Accreditation: SC, ART, AUD, CACREP, CAEPN, CIDA, CLPSY, COPSY, CS, DIETD, DIETI, ENG, ENGT, HSA, IPSY, JOUR, LAW, MUS, NURSE, PH, PLNG, SCPSY, SP, SPAA, SW, THEA

02 President .... Dr. M. David RUDD
05 Provost .... Dr. Karen WEDDLE-WEST
20 Vice Provost Academic Innovation .... Dr. Richard IRWIN
10 Interim VP Business & Finance .... Ms. Jeannie SMITH
88 Asst VP Campus Planning Design .... Mr. Tony POTEET
18 Asst VP Physical Plant .... Mr. Ron BROOKS
21 Asst VP Business Services .... Dr. Edwina WASHINGTON
19 Int Chief of Police .... Mr. Derek MYERS
116 Int Chief Audit Executive .... Ms. Vicki DEATON
30 Chief Development Officer .... Mr. Bobby A. PRINCE
32 Vice President Student Affairs .... Dr. Darrell RAY
35 Asst VP Student Aff/Dev .... Vacant
26 VP External Relations .... Ms. Tammy HEDGES
46 Vice President for Research .... Dr. Andrew W. MEYERS
41 Director of Athletics .... Mr. Tom BOWEN
43 University Counsel .... Ms. Melanie MURRY
22 Dir of Institutional Equity .... Mr. Michael S. WASHINGTON
13 CIO/Vice Provost for Info Tech .... Dr. Robert JACKSON
84 Int Vice Provost Enrollment Svcs .... Dr. William AKEY
58 Vice Prov/Dean Graduate School .... Dr. Jasbir DHALIWAL
21 Int Assistant VP Finance .... Ms. Deborah BECKER
15 Asst Vice Pres Human Resources .... Ms. Maria ALAM
08 Dean U of M Libraries .... Dr. Sylverna V. FORD
09 Int Director Institutional Research .... Ms. Bridgette DECENT
36 Director Career & Employment Svcs .... Ms. Alisha D. ROSE
06 Registrar .... Ms. Darla KEEL
37 Director of Student Aid .... Ms. Karen SMITH
96 Director of Purchasing .... Ms. Canty ROBBINS
29 Director of Alumni Relations .... Ms. Kristie GOLDSMITH
92 Director University Honors Program .... Dr. Melinda L. JONES
07 Director of Admissions .... Dr. William AKEY
28 Director of Diversity Initiatives .... Dr. Karen WEDDLE-WEST
88 Int Dn Com Sciences Disorders .... Dr. Linda D. JARMULOWICZ
49 Dean of Arts & Sciences .... Dr. Thomas J. NENON
50 Dean Business & Economics .... Dr. Rajiv GROVER
53 Dean of Educ Health/Human Sci .... Dr. Kandi HILL-CLARKE
54 Dean of Engineering .... Dr. Richard J. SWEIGARD
88 Dean University College .... Dr. Dan L. LATTIMORE
57 Dean Communication & Fine Arts .... Dr. Anne HOGAN
61 Dean School of Law .... Mr. Peter V. LETSOU
66 Dean School of Nursing .... Dr. Lin ZHAN
69 Int Dean School of Public Health .... Dr. James G. GURNEY
76 Dir School of Health Studies .... Dr. Richard J. BLOOMER
104 Director Study Abroad .... Ms. Rebecca DYCK-LAUMANN
108 Director Institutional Assessment .... Dr. Colton COCKRUM
38 Director Student Counseling .... Dr. Jane CLEMENT
112 Director of Planned Giving .... Mr. Dan MURRELL

University of Phoenix Memphis Campus (F)

65 Germantown Court, Cordova TN 38018-7290
Telephone: (901) 751-1086 Identification: 770224
Accreditation: &NH, ACBSP

† No longer accepting campus-based students.

University of Phoenix Nashville Campus (G)

616 Marriott Drive, Nashville TN 37214-5048
Telephone: (615) 872-0188 Identification: 770225
Accreditation: &NH, ACBSP

† No longer accepting campus-based students.

*University of Tennessee System Office (H)

800 Andy Holt Tower, Knoxville TN 37996-0180
County: Knox FICE Identification: 008051
Unit ID: 221722
Telephone: (865) 974-1000 Carnegie Class: N/A
FAX Number: (865) 974-3753
URL: www.tennessee.edu

01 President .... Dr. Joe DIPIETRO
11 Exec VP/Chief Operating Officer .... Dr. Tonjanita JOHNSON
05 VP Academic Affairs/Student Success .... Dr. Katherine N. HIGH
30 CEO Foundation/VP Devel/Alumni .... Mr. Ricky N. MCCURRY
86 VP for Government Rels/Advocacy .... Mr. Anthony HAYNES
45 Int VP Research/Outreach/Econ Dev .... Dr. Stacey PATTERSON
10 CFO .... Mr. David L. MILLER
43 General Counsel/Secretary .... Mr. Matthew SCOGGINS
15 Vice President for Human Resources .... Ms. Linda HENDRICKS HARIG
86 Vice Pres Institute for Public Svc .... Dr. Herb BYRD
26 Assoc VP Communications/Marketing .... Ms. Tiffany CARPENTER
13 Chief Information Officer .... Mr. Les MATHEWS
04 Exec Assistant to the President .... Dr. David GOLDEN
21 Exec Dir Auditing/Consulting Svcs .... Ms. Sandy JANSEN
29 Asst VP UTN Alumni Affairs .... Ms. Kerry WITCHER

*University of Tennessee, Knoxville (I)

1331 Circle Park, Andy Holt Tower,
Knoxville TN 37996-0184
County: Knox FICE Identification: 003530
Unit ID: 221759
Telephone: (865) 974-1000 Carnegie Class: DU-Highest
FAX Number: (865) 974-1182 Calendar System: Semester
URL: www.utk.edu
Established: 1794 Annual Undergrad Tuition & Fees (In-State): $12,724
Enrollment: 27,845 Coed
Affiliation or Control: State IRS Status: 501(c)3
Highest Offering: Doctorate
Accreditation: SC, ANEST, ART, CACREP, CAEPN, CIDA, CLPSY, COPSY, CS, DENT, DIETD, DIETI, ENG, IPSY, JOUR, LAW, LIB, LSAR, MT, MUS, NRPA, NURSE, PAST, PH, RAD, SCPSY, SW, THEA, VET

02 Chancellor .... Dr. Beverly J. DAVENPORT
100 Chancellor's Executive Assistant .... Ms. Debra K. THOMAS
05 Interim Provost/Vice Chancellor .... Dr. John ZOMCHICK
32 Vice Chancellor for Student Life .... Dr. Vincent CARILLI

46 Vice Chancellor Research/Engagement ... Vacant
10 Vice Chanc Finance & Administration ... Mr. Chris CIMINO
26 Vice Chanc for Communications ... Mr. Ryan ROBINSON
30 Vice Chancellor for Development ... Mr. Chip BRYANT
20 Vice Provost for Academic Affairs ... Dr. RJ HINDE
58 Vice Provost/Dean Graduate School ... Dr. Dixie THOMPSON
35 AVC Student Life/Dean of Students ... Vacant
39 Asst VC/Exec Dir Univ Housing ... Dr. Frank CUEVAS
51 Asst Provost Univ Outrch/Cont Educ ... Dr. Norvel BURKETT
84 Asst Provost Enrollment Svcs ... Ms. Kari ALLDREDGE
18 Assoc Vice Chanc Facilities Svcs ... Mr. Dave IRVIN
41 Vice Chancellor/Dir Athletics ... Mr. John CURRIE
28 Assoc Vice Chanc Equity & Diversity ... Ms. Jennifer RICHTER
37 Director of Financial Aid ... Mr. Jeffrey G. GERKIN
09 Dir Inst Research/Assessment ... Ms. Denise GARDNER
38 Director of Student Counseling ... Dr. Victor BARR
06 Registrar ... Ms. Monique W. ANDERSON
27 Director of Marketing ... Ms. Caitlin MCCLEARY
47 Dean Ag Sciences/Natural Resources ... Dr. Caula BEYL
48 Dean of Architecture and Design ... Dr. Scott POOLE
50 Dean Business Administration ... Dr. Steve MANGUM
60 Dean Communication/Information ... Dr. Michael WIRTH
53 Dean Educ/Health/Human Sciences ... Dr. Robert RIDER
54 Dean of Engineering ... Dr. Wayne DAVIS
61 Dean of Law ... Prof. Melanie WILSON
49 Dean of Arts & Sciences ... Dr. Theresa LEE
66 Dean of Nursing ... Dr. Victoria NIEDERHAUSER
70 Dean of Social Work ... Dr. Karen SOWERS
74 Dean of Veterinary Medicine ... Dr. James P. THOMPSON
47 Dean of Agricultural Extension Svc ... Dr. Tim L. CROSS
08 Dean of Libraries ... Dr. Steve SMITH

*University of Tennessee at Chattanooga (A)

615 McCallie Avenue, Chattanooga TN 37403-2504
County: Hamilton FICE Identification: 003529
Unit ID: 221740
Telephone: (423) 425-4111 Carnegie Class: Masters/L
FAX Number: (423) 425-2200 Calendar System: Semester
URL: www.utc.edu
Established: 1886 Annual Undergrad Tuition & Fees (In-State): $8,544
Enrollment: 11,387 Coed
Affiliation or Control: State IRS Status: 501(c)3
Highest Offering: Doctorate
Accreditation: **SC**, ANEST, ART, CAATE, CACREP, CAEPN, CIDA, CS, DIETD, ENG, ENGT, JOUR, MUS, NURSE, OT, PTA, SPAA, SW, THEA

02 Chancellor ... Dr. Steven R. ANGLE
05 Provost & Sr Vice Chancellor ... Dr. Jerald AINSWORTH
108 Vice Provost for Academic Affairs ... Dr. David RAUSCH
111 Vice Chanc University Advancement ... Dr. Bryan ROWLAND
10 Exec Vice Chanc Fin/Operations & IT ... Dr. Richard BROWN
46 Vice Chancellor for Research ... Dr. Joanne ROMAGNI
32 Interim Vice Chanc Student Dev ... Dr. Dee Dee ANDERSON
20 Assoc Provost for Academic Affairs ... Vacant
21 Assoc Vice Chanc Business/Fin Affs .. Ms. Vanasia Conley PARKS
26 Sr Assoc Vice Chanc Comm & Mktg .. Mr. George HEDDLESTON
41 Interim Vice Chanc & AD ... Mr. Scott ALTIZER
26 Assoc VC University Relations ... Mr. Chuck CANTRELL
18 Asst VC Operations/Fac Plng & Mgt ... Mr. Tom M. ELLIS
91 Assoc VC & CIO ... Mr. Tom HOOVER
100 Chief of Staff ... Ms. Terry DENNISTON
08 Dean of UTC Library ... Ms. Theresa LIEDTKA
88 Assoc Dean of Student Life ... Mr. Jim HICKS
84 Asst Provost Enrollment Services ... Mr. Yancy FREEMAN
06 Int Director Records & Registrar ... Ms. Sandy ZITKUS
13 Manager Client Solutions/IT ... Mr. Ron BAKER
09 Dir of Planning/Eval/Inst Research ... Ms. Eva LEWIS
36 Int Dir Placemt/Student Employment ... Mrs. Donna COOPER
15 Exec Director of Human Resources ... Ms. Laure POU
38 Interim Director of Counseling ... Dr. Elizabeth O'BRIEN
37 Director of Financial Aid ... Ms. Jennifer BUCKLES
58 Dean of the Graduate School ... Dr. Joanne ROMAGNI
49 Dean of Arts & Sciences ... Dr. Jeff ELWELL
50 Dean of Business Administration ... Dr. Robert DOOLEY
53 Dean of Health/Educ/Prof Studies ... Dr. Valerie RUTLEDGE
54 Dean Engineering/Comp Science ... Dr. Daniel PACK
66 Director of Nursing ... Dr. Chris SMITH
22 Director of Equity & Diversity ... Dr. Bryan SAMUEL
25 Director of Sponsored Programs ... Ms. Meredith PERRY
29 Director of Alumni Affairs ... Ms. Jayne HOLDER
96 Mgr of Business Svcs (Purchasing) ... Mr. Charles SCOTT
19 Chief of Police ... Mr. Robert RATCHFORD
39 Director Student Housing ... Ms. Valara SAMPLE
92 Dean Honors College ... Dr. Linda FROST
88 Director of Community Partnerships ... Ms. Ann YOACHIM
104 Exec Director International Program ... Mr. Takeo SUZUKI
43 Dir Legal Services/General Counsel ... Mr. Yousef A. HAMADEH

*University of Tennessee at Martin (B)

554 University Street, Martin TN 38238-0001
County: Weakley FICE Identification: 003531
Unit ID: 221768
Telephone: (731) 881-7000 Carnegie Class: Masters/M
FAX Number: (731) 881-7019 Calendar System: Semester
URL: www.utm.edu
Established: 1900 Annual Undergrad Tuition & Fees (In-State): $9,088
Enrollment: 6,827 Coed
Affiliation or Control: State IRS Status: 501(c)3
Highest Offering: Master's
Accreditation: **SC**, AAFCS, CAEPN, CEA, DIETD, DIETI, ENG, JOUR, MUS, NUR, SW

02 Chancellor ... Dr. Keith S. CARVER, JR.
05 Interim Provost & VC for Acad Affs ... Dr. Richard HELGESON
10 Int Vice Chanc for Finance & Admin ... Ms. Petra R. MCPHEARSON
32 Vice Chancellor for Student Affairs ... Dr. Margaret Y. TOSTON
111 Vice Chancellor for Univ Advancemnt ... Mr. Andrew A. WILSON
20 Assoc Vice Chanc for Academic Affr ... Dr. Victoria S. SENG
13 Interim Chief Information Officer ... Ms. Amy BELEW
114 Int Dir Budget & Mgmt Report ... Ms. Carol WILLIAMS
35 Asst Vice Chanc for Student Affairs ... Mr. John ABEL
30 Asst VChanc Devel & Planned Giving .Ms. Jeanna C. SWAFFORD
04 Exec Assistant to the Chancellor ... Ms. Edie B. GIBSON
29 Assoc Vice Chanc for Alumni Rels ... Dr. Charley T. DEAL
06 Int Dir of Acad Records & Registrar ... Ms. Martha BARNETT
28 Int Equity & Diversity Ofcr-AA/EEO ... Mr. Joe T. HENDERSON
15 Director of Human Resources ... Mr. James (Phillip) BRIGHT
09 Director Institutional Research ... Dr. Desiree A. MCCULLOUGH
41 Dir Intercollegiate Athletics ... Mr. Kurt MCGUFFIN
08 Director of Library ... Dr. John BURCH
18 Director of Physical Plant Opers ... Dr. Tim J. NIPP
19 Director of Public Safety ... Mr. Scott D. ROBBINS
96 Purchasing Agent ... Ms. Lori A. DONAVANT
23 Dir Student Health & Counseling Svc ... Ms. Shannon DEAL
39 Asst VC Student/Residential Life ... Ms. Gina MCCLURE
26 Chief Communications Officer ... Mr. Robert (Bud) D. GRIMES
85 Dir Tenn Intensive English Pgm ... Ms. Amy E. FENNING
47 Dean Col Agri & App Sciences ... Dr. Todd A. WINTERS
50 Dean Col Business & Global Affairs ... Dr. Ross N. DICKENS
53 Dean Col Educ/Health/Behav Sci ... Ms. Cynthia L. WEST
79 Dean Col Humanities/Fine Arts ... Dr. Lynn M. ALEXANDER
54 Int Dean Col Engr & Natural Sci ... Dr. Jennifer GREENWOOD
105 Director Web Services ... Mr. Brian C. INGRAM
106 Int Dir Exec Online Educ/E-learning ... Dr. Brian DONAVANT
25 Chief Contracts/Grants Admin ... Dr. Joan K. WEST
84 Exec Dir Enroll Svcs/Stdnt Engagmnt ... Dr. James D. MANTOOTH
07 Director of Admissions ... Ms. Destin TUCKER
104 Dir International Education ... Dr. Malcolm KOCH
37 Asst Dir Financial Aid/Scholarship ... Ms. Amy MISTRIC

*University of Tennessee Health Science Center (C)

910 Madison Avenue, Memphis TN 38163
County: Shelby FICE Identification: 006725
Unit ID: 487010
Telephone: (901) 448-5500 Carnegie Class: Not Classified
FAX Number: N/A Calendar System: Semester
URL: www.uthsc.edu
Established: 1911 Annual Undergrad Tuition & Fees (In-State): N/A
Enrollment: 3,075 Coed
Affiliation or Control: State IRS Status: 501(c)3
Highest Offering: Doctorate
Accreditation: **SC**, ANEST, #ARCPA, AUD, CAHIIM, CYTO, DENT, DH, HT, IPSY, MED, MT, NURSE, OT, PHAR, PTA, SP

02 Chancellor ... Dr. Steve J. SCHWAB
03 Executive Vice Chancellor/COO ... Dr. Kennard D. BROWN
05 VC Academic/Faculty/Student Affs ... Dr. Lori GONZALEZ
10 Vice Chancellor Finance/Operations ... Anthony A. FERRARA
13 VC Information Technology Services ... Dr. Jan VAN DER AA
46 Vice Chancellor Research ... Dr. Steven R. GOODMAN
30 VC Development and Alumni Affairs ... Love COLLINS, III
32 Assoc VC Student Affairs ... Dr. Susan DAVIES
52 Dean Dentistry ... Dr. Timothy L. HOTTEL
58 Dean Graduate Health Sciences ... Dr. Donald B. THOMASON
76 Dean Health Professions ... Vacant
63 Executive Dean Medicine ... Dr. David M. STERN
63 Dean Medicine Chattanooga ... Dr. Robert B. SHACK
63 Dean Medicine Knoxville ... Dr. James J. NEUTENS
66 Dean Nursing ... Dr. Wendy M. LIKES
67 Dean Pharmacy ... Dr. Marie A. CHISHOLM-BURNS
06 Registrar ... Dr. Matthew MOORE
07 Director of Admissions ... Ann SALINA
37 Director of Financial Aid ... Samuel MATHENY
08 Director Library ... Dr. Rick FOUGHT
15 Assc VC Human Resources ... Dr. Chandra ALSTON
18 Assoc VC Facilities Administration ... Emile DAVID
19 Chief of Police ... Anthony BERRYHILL
22 Asst VC Equity and Diversity ... Dr. Michael ALSTON
26 Asst VC Communications & Marketing ... Sally BADOUD

Vanderbilt University (D)

2305 West End Avenue, Nashville TN 37203
County: Davidson FICE Identification: 003535
Unit ID: 221999
Telephone: (615) 322-7311 Carnegie Class: DU-Highest
FAX Number: (615) 343-7765 Calendar System: Semester
URL: www.vanderbilt.edu
Established: 1873 Annual Undergrad Tuition & Fees: $45,610
Enrollment: 12,567 Coed
Affiliation or Control: Independent Non-Profit IRS Status: 501(c)3
Highest Offering: Doctorate
Accreditation: **SC**, AUD, CACREP, CLPSY, CS, DENT, DIETI, DMS, ENG, IPSY, LAW, MED, MIDWF, MT, MUS, NDT, NMT, NURSE, PERF, PH, SP, THEOL

01 Chancellor ... Dr. Nicholas ZEPPOS
05 Provost/Vice Chancellor ... Dr. Susan R. WENTE
17 Dean School of Medicine ... Dr. Jeffrey R. BALSER
10 Vice Chancellor Finance/CFO ... Mr. Brett SWEET
11 Vice Chanc Administration ... Mr. Eric KOPSTAIN
30 Vice Chanc Dev & Alumni Relations ... Ms. Susie STALCUP
12 Vice Provost for Research ... Dr. Padma RAGHAVAN
115 Vice Chanc for Investments ... Mr. Anders W. HALL
28 VC Equity/Diversity/Inclusion ... Dr. George C. HILL
15 Chief Human Resources Ofcr ... Ms. Barbara CARROLL
41 Vice Chanc Athletics & Univ Affairs ... Dr. David WILLIAMS
20 Assoc Vice Chanc Academic Affairs ... Ms. Susan HART
26 Vice Chancellor for Communications ... Mr. Steve ERTEL
13 Vice Chancellor Information Tech ... Mr. John M. LUTZ
09 Interim Dir Institutional Research ... Dr. Richard IANNELLI
20 Vice Provost Learning & Res Affairs ... Ms. Cynthia J. CYRUS
88 Vice Prov Acad & Strat Affairs ... Dr. John G. GEER
58 Dean of the Graduate School ... Dr. Mark T. WALLACE
08 University Librarian ... Dr. Valerie HOTCHKISS
27 Dean of Student Publicats/Comm ... Mr. F. Clark WILLIAMS
21 Asst V Chanc for Finance/Controller ... Ms. Dalana ROBERTSON
06 Registrar ... Mr. Bart P. QUINET
84 Vice Provost Univ Enrollment Affs ... Dr. Douglas CHRISTIANSEN
07 Dir Undergraduate Admissions ... Mr. John GAINES
37 Director Student Financial Aid ... Mr. Brent B. TENER
38 Director Psych Counseling Center ... Dr. Catherine FUCHS
36 Exec Dir Career Center ... Dr. Katharine S. BROOKS
25 Assoc Director Sponsored Programs ... Mr. Jeff NEWMAN
32 Dean of Students/Assoc Provost ... Mr. Mark BANDAS
106 Assoc Provost for Digital Learning ... Dr. John M. SLOOP
49 Dean College of Arts and Science ... Dr. Lauren BENTON
54 Dean School of Engineering ... Dr. Philippe M. FAUCHET
66 Dean School of Nursing ... Dr. Linda NORMAN
53 Dean Education & Human Development ... Dr. Camilla P. BENBOW
64 Dean Blair School of Music ... Dr. Mark WAIT
73 Dean of the Divinity School ... Dr. Emilie M. TOWNES
61 Dean of the School of Law ... Dr. Chris GUTHRIE
50 Dean Owen Grad School of Mgmt ... Dr. M. Eric JOHNSON
88 Dean of the Ingram Commons ... Dr. Vanessa BEASLEY
42 Associate Chaplain ... Rev. Gretchen PERSON
19 Chief of Police/Asst Vice Chanc ... Mr. August J. WASHINGTON
22 Dir EO/AA & Disability Svcs ... Ms. Anita JENIOUS
41 Dir Sport Operations/Asst Vice Chan ... Mr. Brockton WILLIAMS
39 Sr Director Housing Operations ... Mr. James S. KRAMKA
43 Vice Chancellor/General Counsel ... Ms. Audrey J. ANDERSON
44 Asst Vice Chancellor Annual Giving ... Mr. Kyle D. MCGOWAN
86 Asst Vice Chanc Federal Relations ... Ms. Christina D. WEST

Vatterott Career College (E)

6991 Appling Farms Parkway, Memphis TN 38133
Telephone: (901) 372-2399 Identification: 770592
Accreditation: **ACCSC**

† Branch campus of Vatterott College-Des Moines, Des Moines, IA

Vatterott College-Memphis (F)

2655 Dividend Drive, Memphis TN 38132-1713
Telephone: (901) 761-5730 Identification: 666308
Accreditation: **ACCSC**

† Branch campus of Vatterott College-NorthPark, Berkeley, MO.

Virginia College School of Business and Health (G)

721 Eastgate Loop, Chattanooga TN 37411-5600
Telephone: (423) 893-2000 Identification: 666136
Accreditation: **ACICS**, ACFEI

† Branch campus of Virginia College, Birmingham, AL

Virginia College School of Business and Health (H)

5003 North Broadway Street, Knoxville TN 37918
Telephone: (865) 745-4500 Identification: 770828
Accreditation: **ACICS**, SURGT

† Branch campus of Virginia College, Birmingham, AL

Visible Music College (I)

200 Madison Avenue, Memphis TN 38103
County: Shelby FICE Identification: 039823
Unit ID: 449764
Telephone: (901) 381-3939 Carnegie Class: Spec-4-yr-Arts
FAX Number: (901) 377-0544 Calendar System: Semester
URL: www.visible.edu
Established: 2000 Annual Undergrad Tuition & Fees: $19,500
Enrollment: 109 Coed
Affiliation or Control: Independent Non-Profit IRS Status: 501(c)3
Highest Offering: Baccalaureate
Accreditation: **TRACS**

01 President ... Dr. Ken STEORTS
05 Vice President of Academics ... Dr. Cameron HARVEY
30 Vice President of Advancement ... Geordy WELLS
10 Vice President of Business ... Ben RAWLEY
32 Director of Students ... JD WILSON
07 Director of Admissions ... Brian DUFFY
37 Director of Financial Aid ... Cynthia BROWN
06 Registrar ... Scott LENCKE
21 Business Office Manager/HR Coord ... Toni MELTON
18 Operations/IT Manager ... Matt BROWN
84 Manager Enrollment Management ... Amy SPICER

Watkins College of Art, Design & Film (A)

2298 Rosa L. Parks Boulevard, Nashville TN 37228-1306
County: Davidson FICE Identification: 030888
Unit ID: 392840
Telephone: (615) 383-4848 Carnegie Class: Spec-4-yr-Arts
FAX Number: (615) 383-4849 Calendar System: Semester
URL: www.watkins.edu
Established: 1885 Annual Undergrad Tuition & Fees: $23,700
Enrollment: 292 Coed
Affiliation or Control: Independent Non-Profit IRS Status: 501(c)3
Highest Offering: Master's
Accreditation: SC, ART

01 President ... Dr. J. KLINE
111 Vice Pres Institutional Advancement ... Ms. Autumn PARROT
05 Vice President for Academic Affairs ... Ms. Joy MCKENZIE
10 Vice Pres Finance and Operations ... Ms. Mary Ellen LOTHAMER
84 Vice Pres Strategic Enrollment Mgmt ... Ms. Alison MIYAUCHI
26 Director of Communications ... Mr. Brendan TAPLEY
06 Registrar ... Ms. Tracie JOHNSON
37 Director Financial Aid ... Ms. Regina GILBERT
08 Library Director ... Ms. Amy KAMMERMAN
13 Director Information Technology ... Mr. Shawn MAGGARD
18 Director of Facilities ... Mr. Martin DILLINGHAM
88 Chair Film School ... Mr. Richard GERSHMAN
57 Chair Fine Art Department ... Ms. Kristi HARGROVE
88 Chair Graphic Design Department ... Mr. Dan BRAWNER
88 Chair Interior Design Department ... Vacant
88 Chair Photography Department ... Ms. Kristy HARGROVE
97 Director General Education ... Ms. Cary Beth MILLER
51 Director Community Education ... Ms. Anna MCKEOWN
32 Director Student Life ... Ms. Kristina KRAU WAYMIRE

Welch College (B)

1045 Bison Trail, Gallatin TN 37066
County: Sumner FICE Identification: 030018
Unit ID: 220206
Telephone: (615) 675-5255 Carnegie Class: Bac-Diverse
FAX Number: (615) 296-0400 Calendar System: Semester
URL: www.welch.edu
Established: 1942 Annual Undergrad Tuition & Fees: $17,920
Enrollment: 346 Coed
Affiliation or Control: Free Will Baptist IRS Status: 501(c)3
Highest Offering: Master's
Accreditation: SC, BI

01 President ... Dr. J. Matthew PINSON
05 Provost ... Dr. Matthew J. MCAFFEE
45 Vice Pres for Stategic Initiatives ... Dr. P. Greg KETTEMAN
10 Vice President Financial Affairs ... Mr. Craig MAHLER
32 VP Student Svcs/Dean of Students ... Dr. Jon FORLINES
30 Vice Pres Institutional Advancement ... Mr. David WILLIFORD
108 Vice Pres for Inst Effectiveness ... Dr. Kevin HESTER
20 Vice Provost for Academic Administr ... Mr. Matthew BRACEY
34 Dean of Women ... Mrs. Susan FORLINES
55 Dean of Enriched Adult Studies ... Mr. William SLATER
08 Librarian ... Mrs. Carol REID
09 Director of Institutional Research ... Mr. Wayne SPRUILL
84 Dir of Enrollment Services ... Mr. Daniel WEBSTER
26 Chief Public Relations/Marketing ... Mr. Josh OWENS
106 Dir of Online and Adult Studies ... Mr. Allan CROWSON
44 Director of the Annual Fund ... Mr. Mike EDWARDS
18 Director of Plant Operations ... Mr. Sandy GOODFELLOW
41 Athletic Director ... Mr. Greg FAWBUSH
37 Student Financial Aid Coordinator ... Mrs. Angie EDGMON
06 Registrar ... Dr. Sharon RODGERS
04 Exec Assistant to the President ... Mrs. Martha FLETCHER
21 Staff Accountant ... Mrs. Leigh Ann SMITH

Williamson College (C)

274 Mallory Station Road, Franklin TN 37067
County: Williamson FICE Identification: 035135
Unit ID: 443340
Telephone: (615) 771-7821 Carnegie Class: Spec-4-yr-Faith
FAX Number: (615) 771-7810 Calendar System: Other
URL: www.williamsoncc.edu
Established: 1996 Annual Undergrad Tuition & Fees: $12,075
Enrollment: 70 Coed
Affiliation or Control: Non-denominational IRS Status: 501(c)3
Highest Offering: Baccalaureate
Accreditation: BI

01 President ... Dr. Ed SMITH
88 Dean Emeritus ... Dr. Sharon LANDER
11 Vice President for Operations ... Ms. Susan MAYS
06 Registrar/Dir Instl Effectiveness ... Ms. Karen HUDSON
37 Dir Financial Aid/Veteran Affairs ... Ms. Cristina MAJORS
04 Executive Team Coordinator ... Ms. Laura FLOWERS

TEXAS

Abilene Christian University (D)

ACU Box 29100, Abilene TX 79699-9100
County: Taylor FICE Identification: 003537
Unit ID: 222178
Telephone: (325) 674-2000 Carnegie Class: Masters/L
FAX Number: (325) 674-2202 Calendar System: Semester
URL: www.acu.edu
Established: 1906 Annual Undergrad Tuition & Fees: $32,070
Enrollment: 4,544 Coed
Affiliation or Control: Churches Of Christ IRS Status: 501(c)3
Highest Offering: Doctorate
Accreditation: SC, CIDA, CS, DIETD, @DIETI, JOUR, MFCD, MUS, NURSE, OT, SP, SW, THEOL

01 President ... Dr. Phil SCHUBERT
100 Senior Advisor to the President ... Ms. Suzanne ALLMON
03 Vice President of the University ... Dr. Gary D. MCCALEB
05 Provost ... Dr. Robert RHODES
111 VP for Advancement ... Mr. Jim ORR
32 VP for Student Life ... Mr. Chris RILEY
10 VP & Chief Business Officer ... Mr. Steven HOLLEY
20 VP Academic Affairs-Dallas ... Dr. Stephen JOHNSON
115 Chief Investment Ofcr/Pres ACIMCO ... Mr. Jack W. RICH
43 Vice President & General Counsel ... Mr. Slade SULLIVAN
00 Chancellor ... Dr. Royce MONEY
88 Exec Assistant to the Chancellor ... Mr. Jim HOLMANS
102 Vice Chancellor/Pres ACU Foundation ... Mr. Dan T. GARRETT
20 Vice Provost ... Dr. Susan LEWIS
84 Asst VP Enrollment-Dallas ... Ms. Jessica MANNING
49 Dean College of Arts & Sciences ... Dr. Greg STRAUGHN
73 Dean College of Biblical Studies ... Dr. Ken R. CUKROWSKI
50 Dean College of Business Admin ... Dr. Brad CRISP
53 Dean College of Educ & Human Svcs ... Dr. Donnie SNIDER
92 Dean Honors College ... Dr. Jason MORRIS
58 Dean Graduate School ... Dr. Donnie SNIDER
66 Dean School of Nursing ... Dr. Becky HAMMACK
08 Dean Library/Educational Technology ... Dr. John WEAVER
104 Director of the Ctr Intl Educ ... Dr. Stephen SHEWMAKER
106 Managing Director Online Programs ... Mr. Corey PATTERSON
35 Dean of Students ... Mr. Mark LEWIS
36 Director Career Center ... Mrs. Jill FORTSON
06 Registrar/Dir of Academic Records ... Dr. Eric GUMM
84 Chief Enroll Ofcr/Dir Stdnt Fin Svc ... Mr. Kevin CAMPBELL
26 Chief Marketing Officer ... Mr. Jason GROVES
39 Director Residence Life ... Ms. Jennifer BUTLER
38 Director Univ Counseling Center ... Mr. Steve ROWLANDS
18 Exec Dir Facilities/Campus Develop ... Mr. Corey RUFF
13 Exec Dir of Information Technology ... Mrs. Kay REEVES
24 Exec Dir Adams Ctr Teaching/Lrng ... Dr. Jennifer SHEWMAKER
29 Dir of Alumni Rels & Annual Project ... Mr. Craig FISHER
19 Chief of Police ... Mr. Jimmy ELLISON
112 Director of Major Gifts ... Mr. Don GARRETT
41 Director of Athletics ... Mr. Lee DE LEON
15 Director of HR ... Mrs. Wendy JONES
88 Director of Faculty Enrichment ... Dr. Laura CARROLL
09 Asst Provost for Inst Effectiveness ... Dr. Tom A. MILHOLLAND
96 Director of Procurement ... Ms. Sandy HALL
101 Secretary to the Board of Trustees ... Mr. Slade SULLIVAN
04 Exec Assistant Office of President ... Mrs. Stephanie A. WOODLEE
46 Director Research/Sponsored Progams ... Dr. Megan ROTH
58 Dean College Grad/Professional Stds ... Dr. Jamie GOFF
07 Director of Admissions ... Ms. Tamara LONG
88 Title IX Coordinator ... Mrs. Sherita NICKERSON

*Alamo Community College District Central Office (E)

201 W. Sheridan, San Antonio TX 78204-1429
County: Bexar FICE Identification: 003607
Unit ID: 222497
Telephone: (210) 485-0020 Carnegie Class: N/A
FAX Number: (210) 486-9166
URL: www.alamo.edu

01 Chancellor ... Dr. Bruce LESLIE
05 Vice Chanc for Academic Success ... Dr. Jo-Carol FABIANKE
11 Vice Chanc for Finance & Admin ... Ms. Diane E. SNYDER
32 Vice Chancellor for Student Success ... Dr. Adelina SILVA
103 Vice Chanc Economic/Workforce Devel ... Dr. Federico ZARAGOZA
13 VC Plng/Performance/Info Systems ... Dr. Thomas CLEARY
15 Assoc Vice Chanc Human Resources ... Ms. Linda BOYER-OWENS
26 Assoc Vice Chanc Communications ... Mr. Leo ZUNIGA
18 Assoc Vice Chanc Facilities ... Mr. John STRYBOS
10 Assoc VC Finance & Fiscal Services ... Ms. Pamela ANSBOURY
04 Deputy to the Chancellor ... Ms. Michelle PERALES
111 Exec Director Inst Advancement ... Mr. Jim ESKIN
116 Director of Internal Audit ... Mr. Bill WULLENJOHN
96 Director Acquisitions & Admin Svcs ... Mr. Gary O'BAR
19 Chief Department of Public Safety ... Mr. Don ADAMS
21 Comptroller ... Ms. Gettie MORENO
12 President Northwest Vista College ... Dr. Ric BASER
12 President San Antonio College ... Dr. Robert VELA
12 President St Philip's College ... Dr. Adena WILLIAMS LOSTON
12 President Palo Alto College ... Dr. Michael FLORES
12 Pres Northeast Lakeview College ... Dr. Veronica GARCIA
37 Director Student Financial Aid ... Mr. Harold WHITIS
43 Dir Legal Services/General Counsel ... Mr. Ross LAUGHEAD
09 Dist Dir Inst Rsch/Effect/Planning ... Mr. Velda VILLARREAL

*Northeast Lakeview College (F)

1201 Kitty Hawk Road, Universal City TX 78148
County: Bexar Identification: 667278
Telephone: (210) 486-5000 Carnegie Class: Not Classified
FAX Number: N/A Calendar System: Semester
URL: www.alamo.edu/nlc
Established: 2007 Annual Undergrad Tuition & Fees (In-District): N/A
Enrollment: N/A Coed
Affiliation or Control: Local IRS Status: 501(c)3
Highest Offering: Associate Degree
Accreditation: @SC

02 President ... Dr. Veronica GARCIA
05 Int VP Academic Success ... Dr. Alan COTTRELL
11 Vice Pres of College Services ... Dr. Tangila DOVE
32 Vice Pres Student Success ... Dr. Debbie C. HAMILTON

*Northwest Vista College (G)

3535 N Ellison Drive, San Antonio TX 78251-4217
County: Bexar FICE Identification: 033723
Unit ID: 420398
Telephone: (210) 486-4000 Carnegie Class: Assoc/HT-High Trad
FAX Number: (210) 486-9105 Calendar System: Semester
URL: www.alamo.edu/nvc
Established: 1995 Annual Undergrad Tuition & Fees (In-District): $2,188
Enrollment: 16,656 Coed
Affiliation or Control: Local IRS Status: 501(c)3
Highest Offering: Associate Degree
Accreditation: SC

02 President ... Dr. Ric N. BASER
03 Vice President for College Services ... Mrs. Erin L. SHERMAN
05 Vice President for Academic Success ... Dr. Amy F. WHITWORTH
32 Vice President for Student Success ... Mrs. Deborah GAITAN
111 Director Institutional Advancement ... Mrs. Lynne DEAN
08 Learning Resources Chair ... Vacant
121 Dean of Student Success ... Mrs. Jennifer COMEDY-HOLMES
26 Dir of Public Relations & Marketing ... Mrs. Renata SERAFIN
13 Director Info/Communications Tech ... Mr. Felix SALINAS
37 Associate Director of Financial Aid ... Mrs. Rosalinda ENCINA
113 Assistant Bursar ... Mrs. Patricia SANCHEZ
15 Sr Human Resources Generalist ... Mrs. Jessica SACAL-TRENT
45 Director of Resources & College Dev ... Ms. Judy V. CAMARGO
18 Superintendent NVC ... Mr. Bernie ZERTUCHE
103 Dean of Workforce Development ... Mr. Patrick FONTENOT
49 Dean of Arts and Sciences ... Dr. Russell FROHARDT
09 Director of Institutional Research ... Dr. Eliza HERNANDEZ
84 Director of Enrollment Management ... Mrs. Robin SANDBERG
07 Associate Director of Admissions ... Mrs. Yvonne GUERRA
04 Executive Assistant to President ... Mrs. Lisa MCGOLDRICK

*Palo Alto College (H)

1400 W Villaret Boulevard, San Antonio TX 78224-2499
County: Bexar FICE Identification: 023413
Unit ID: 246354
Telephone: (210) 486-3000 Carnegie Class: Assoc/HT-High Non
FAX Number: (210) 921-5005 Calendar System: Semester
URL: www.alamo.edu
Established: 1985 Annual Undergrad Tuition & Fees (In-District): $2,188
Enrollment: 8,671 Coed
Affiliation or Control: Local IRS Status: 501(c)3
Highest Offering: Associate Degree
Accreditation: SC

02 President ... Dr. Mike FLORES
05 Vice President for Academic Success ... Ms. Elizabeth TANNER
10 Vice President of College Services ... Dr. Beatriz JOSEPH
32 Vice President for Student Success ... Mr. Gilberto BECERRA
49 Dean Arts & Sciences ... Vacant
72 Dean Career/Technical Education ... Vacant
08 Dean of Learning Resources ... Ms. Tina MESA
35 Dean of Student Success ... Ms. Katherine BEAUMONT DOSS
26 Director of Public Relations ... Mr. Jerry ARELLANO
113 Assistant Bursar ... Ms. Teresa FREEMAN
84 Director of Enrollment Management ... Ms. Elizabeth AGUILAR-VILLARUAL
37 Assc Dir Student Financial Services ... Ms. Shirley LEIJA
41 Athletic Director ... Miss Shanea ALLEN
18 Facilities Superintendnt/Phys Plant ... Mr. Sergio RIVERA
29 Coordinator Alumni Relations ... Ms. Leticia INOCENCIO
09 Dir Inst Rsrch/Plng/Effectiveness ... Mr. George GUAJARDO
25 Director of Advancement & Grants ... Ms. Stephanie VASQUEZ
06 Chief Records Officer ... Ms. Diane BURRESS
04 Administrative Asst to President ... Mrs. Connie ACOVIO
13 Chief Info Technology Director ... Mr. Christopher DELGADO
102 Exec Dir Alamo Colleges Found ... Mr. Jim ESKIN

*St. Philip's College (I)

1801 Martin Luther King, San Antonio TX 78203-2098
County: Bexar FICE Identification: 003608
Unit ID: 227854
Telephone: (210) 486-2000 Carnegie Class: Assoc/HVT-High Non
FAX Number: N/A Calendar System: Semester
URL: www.alamo.edu/spc/
Established: 1898 Annual Undergrad Tuition & Fees (In-District): $2,188
Enrollment: 11,198 Coed
Affiliation or Control: Local IRS Status: 501(c)3
Highest Offering: Associate Degree
Accreditation: SC, ACFEI, CAHIIM, COARC, CVT, HT, MLTAD, OTA, PTAA, RAD, SURGT

02 President ... Dr. Adena WILLIAMS LOSTON
05 Vice Pres of Academic Success ... Ms. Maureen CARTLEDGE
32 Vice Pres of Student Success ... Dr. Mordecai BROWNLEE
11 Vice President for College Svcs ... Ms. Lacy HAMPTON
35 Dean Student Success ... Dr. Paul MACHEN
08 Dean Interdisciplinary Programs ... Dr. Natasha SCHMITTOU
75 Dean Applied Science & Tech ... Mr. Christopher BEARDSALL
49 Interim Dean Arts & Science ... Mr. George JOHNSON

76 Dean of Health Sciences .... Ms. Rose STERLING
37 Asst Director of Financial Aid .... Ms. Grace ZAPATA
45 Director Planning & Research .... Dr. Maria HINOJOSA
113 Assistant Bursar .... Ms. Sophia GONZALEZ
26 Dir Community & Public Relations .... Ms. Tracy ROSS-GARCIA
111 Director Institutional Advancement .... Dr. Sharon CROCKETT-RAY
72 Director Instructional Technology .... Mr. John ORONA
18 Chief Facilities/Physical Plant .... Ms. Bertha NORWOOD
29 Director Alumni Relations .... Dr. Sharon CROCKETT-RAY
84 Director Enrollment Management .... Ms. Beatrice BUTLER
114 Chief Budget Manager .... Mr. Paul BORREGO

*San Antonio College (A)

1300 San Pedro Avenue, San Antonio TX 78212-4299
County: Bexar FICE Identification: 009163
Unit ID: 227924
Telephone: (210) 486-0000 Carnegie Class: Assoc/HT-Mix Trad/Non
FAX Number: N/A Calendar System: Semester
URL: www.alamo.edu/sac
Established: 1925 Annual Undergrad Tuition & Fees (In-District): $2,188
Enrollment: 20,640 Coed
Affiliation or Control: Local IRS Status: 501(c)3
Highest Offering: Associate Degree
Accreditation: SC, ADNUR, CEA, DA, EMT, FUSER, MAC

02 President .... Dr. Robert H. VELA
32 Vice Pres Student Success .... Dr. Lisa ALCORTA
11 Vice President of College Services .... Dr. Stella LOVATO
05 Vice Pres for Academic Success .... Dr. Jothany BLACKWOOD
32 Dean of Student Success .... Mr. Richard FARIAS
72 Dean Professional & Tech Educ .... Ms. Vernell E. WALKER
49 Dean of Arts & Sciences .... Dr. Conrad KRUEGER
51 Dean Cont Educ/Training Network .... Mr. Tim ROCKEY
08 Library Director .... Mr. Johnathan WILSON
88 Dean of Performance Excellence .... Dr. Francisco SOLIS
84 Director of Enrollment Services .... Mr. J. Martin ORTEGA
85 Coordinator International Students .... Ms. Patrice BALLARD
26 Director Public Relations .... Ms. Vanessa TORRES
45 Director of Grants Development .... Ms. Susan B. ESPINOZA
18 Chief Facilities/Physical Plant .... Mr. David ORTEGA
23 Director Health Services .... Ms. Paula DAGGETT
37 Coordinator of Financial Aid .... Mr. Daniel BARRETO

Altierus Career College (B)

300 Six Flags Drive, Suite 100, Arlington TX 76011
Telephone: (817) 652-7790 Identification: 770788
Accreditation: ACICS

† Branch campus of Altierus Career College, Henderson, NV

Alvin Community College (C)

3110 Mustang Road, Alvin TX 77511-4898
County: Brazoria FICE Identification: 003539
Unit ID: 222567
Telephone: (281) 756-3500 Carnegie Class: Assoc/MT-VT-Mix Trad/Non
FAX Number: (281) 756-3854 Calendar System: Semester
URL: www.alvincollege.edu
Established: 1948 Annual Undergrad Tuition & Fees (In-District): $1,562
Enrollment: 5,114 Coed
Affiliation or Control: Local IRS Status: 501(c)3
Highest Offering: Associate Degree
Accreditation: SC, ADNUR, COARC, DMS, EMT, NDT, POLYT

01 President .... Dr. Christal M. ALBRECHT
05 Vice President Instruction .... Dr. Cynthia GRIFFITH
10 VP Administrative Services .... Mr. Karl STAGER
32 VP Student Services .... Ms. Marilyn DEMENT
49 Dean of Arts & Sciences .... Vacant
76 Dean Legal and Health Sciences .... Dr. John BETHSCHEIDER
51 Dean/Exec Dir Cont Ed/Wkforce Devel .... Mr. Jim SIMPSON
97 Dean General Educ/Academic Support .... Dr. Nadezhda (Nadia) NAZARENKO
88 Dean Prof/Tech/Human Performance .... Dr. Linda AUSTIN
06 Registrar .... Ms. Irene M. ROBINSON
08 Director Library Services .... Ms. Rebecca MCCLAIN
21 Director Fiscal Affairs/Controller .... Ms. Deborah KRAFT
13 Director Information Technology .... Mr. Kelly KLIMPT
37 Dir Student Financial Aid Placement .... Ms. Dora SIMS
15 Exec Director Human Resources .... Ms. Karen EDWARDS
18 Director Physical Plant .... Mr. Patrick GEBHART
29 Director Alumni Relations .... Ms. Wendy DEL BELLO
07 Director Advising Services .... Ms. Stephanie STOCKSTILL
09 Director of Inst Effective/Research .... Mr. Patrick SANGER
30 Chief Development .... Ms. Wendy DEL BELLO
26 Chief Public Relations Officer .... Ms. Wendy DEL BELLO
88 Assistant Director Fiscal Affairs .... Ms. Laurel JOSEPH
35 Coordinator Student Activities .... Ms. Amanda SMITHSON
04 Administrative Asst to President .... Ms. Tammy GIFFROW
19 Director Security/Safety .... Mr. Howard I. HAMRICK

Amarillo College (D)

PO Box 447, Amarillo TX 79178-0001
County: Potter FICE Identification: 003540
Unit ID: 222576
Telephone: (806) 371-5000 Carnegie Class: Assoc/MT-VT-High Trad
FAX Number: (806) 371-5370 Calendar System: Semester
URL: www.actx.edu
Established: 1929 Annual Undergrad Tuition & Fees (In-District): $2,010
Enrollment: 9,936 Coed
Affiliation or Control: State/Local IRS Status: 501(c)3
Highest Offering: Associate Degree
Accreditation: SC, ADNUR, COARC, DA, DH, EMT, FUSER, MLTAD, MUS, NMT, OTA, PTAA, RAD, RTT, SURGT

01 President .... Dr. Russell D. LOWERY-HART
03 Executive Vice President .... Mr. Mark D. WHITE
05 VP of Academic Affairs .... Dr. Tamara T. CLUNIS
10 VP of Business Affairs .... Mr. Steve G. SMITH
26 VP Communications & Marketing .... Mr. Kevin J. BALL
51 Dean of Continuing Education .... Ms. Toni B. GRAY
32 VP of Student Affairs .... Mr. Robert C. AUSTIN
20 Assoc VP Academic Affairs .... Mr. Frank E. SOBEY
102 Dir AC Foundation/Development .... Mrs. Kathleen B. DOWDY
76 Associate Dean of Health Sciences .... Mrs. Kimberly A. CROWLEY
18 Manager Physical Plant .... Mr. Jim BACA
37 Director Financial Aid .... Ms. Kelly PRATER
08 Director AC Library Network .... Ms. Emily R. GILBERT
06 Registrar .... Mrs. Diane BRICE
15 VP for Employee and Org Dev .... Ms. Lyndy D. FORRESTER
19 Chief of Police .... Mr. Steve L. CHANCE
26 Dir Foundation Mktg/Special Events .. Mrs. Tracy D. DOUGHERTY
09 Exec Dir Decision Analytics & IR .. Mr. Collin C. WITHERSPOON
121 Director of Advising .... Mr. Ernesto F. OLMOS
88 Director Amarillo Museum of Art .... Mrs. Kim B. MAHAN
88 Director Criminal Justice Program .... Mr. Eric C. WALLACE
96 Director of Purchasing/Records Ret .... Ms. Kimberly L. CARLILE
81 Dean of STEM .... Dr. Carol BUSE
76 Dean of Health Sciences .... Mr. Mark E. ROWH
72 Dean of Technical Education .... Ms. Megan E. EIKNER
49 Dean of Liberal Arts .... Ms. Victoria TAYLOR-GORE
88 Dean Academic Success .... Ms. Edythe L. CARTER
100 Chief of Staff .... Ms. Cara J. CROWLEY
84 Recruitment Spec/Enrollment Mgmt .... Mr. Richie GARZA
13 Chief Information Officer .... Mr. Terry L. KLEFFMAN
04 Administrative Asst to President .... Ms. Joy D. BRENNEMAN
106 Dir Online Education/E-learning .... Ms. Heather L. VORAN
108 Director Inst Effectivenes .... Ms. Tina M. BABB
25 Chief Contracts/Grants Admin .... Ms. Teresa G. CLEMONS

Amberton University (E)

1700 Eastgate Drive, Garland TX 75041
County: Dallas FICE Identification: 022594
Unit ID: 222628
Telephone: (972) 279-6511 Carnegie Class: Masters/L
FAX Number: (972) 279-9773 Calendar System: Semester
URL: www.amberton.edu
Established: 1971 Annual Undergrad Tuition & Fees: N/A
Enrollment: 1,379 Coed
Affiliation or Control: Independent Non-Profit IRS Status: 501(c)3
Highest Offering: Master's
Accreditation: SC

01 President .... Dr. Melinda REAGAN
05 Academic Dean .... Dr. Deborah HILL
111 Dean Univ Advance/VP Strategic Svcs .... Dr. Jo Lynn LOYD
10 Chief Business Officer .... Mr. Brent BRADSHAW
06 Registrar .... Ms. Marge MASSEY
32 Director Student Services .... Ms. Heather MILLER
84 Director for Recruiting .... Mr. Glenn SORRELLS
08 Head Librarian .... Ms. Bridget BARRY THIAS
29 Dir Alumni Relations & Inst Rsrch .... Dr. Jo Lynn LOYD
07 Director of Admissions .... Dr. Jonathan SCHULTZ

American College of Acupuncture and Oriental Medicine (F)

9100 Park West Drive, Houston TX 77063-4104
County: Harris FICE Identification: 031533
Unit ID: 429085
Telephone: (713) 780-9777 Carnegie Class: Spec-4-yr-Other Health
FAX Number: (713) 781-5781 Calendar System: Trimester
URL: www.acaom.edu
Established: 1991 Annual Graduate Tuition & Fees: N/A
Enrollment: 138 Coed
Affiliation or Control: Proprietary IRS Status: Proprietary
Highest Offering: Doctorate; No Undergraduates
Accreditation: SC, ACUP

01 President .... Dr. John Paul LIANG
11 Vice President of Operations .... Ms. Angel GUINARA
05 Dean of Academic Affairs .... Dr. Wen HUANG
20 Dean of Clinical Training .... Dr. Baisong ZHONG
06 Registrar .... Ms. Vicki ROSSMAN
09 Dir Inst Research/Effectiveness .... Mr. Michael Dale STAFFORD
37 Financial Aid Ofcr/Inst Compliance .... Ms. Theresa LIGON

American InterContinental University-Houston Campus (G)

9999 Richmond Avenue, Houston TX 77042-4516
Telephone: (832) 201-3600 Identification: 666335
Accreditation: &NH, ACBSP

† Regional accreditation is carried under the parent institution in Hoffman Estates, IL.

Ana G. Mendez University System-Dallas (H)

3010 N. Stemmons Fwy, Dallas TX 75247
Telephone: (469) 341-7300 Identification: 770947
Accreditation: &M

† Branch campus of Sistema Universitario Ana G. Mendez, Rio Piedras, PR

Angelina College (I)

PO Box 1768, Lufkin TX 75902-1768
County: Angelina FICE Identification: 006661
Unit ID: 222822
Telephone: (936) 639-1301 Carnegie Class: Assoc/MT-VT-Mix Trad/Non
FAX Number: (936) 639-4299 Calendar System: Semester
URL: www.angelina.edu
Established: 1966 Annual Undergrad Tuition & Fees (In-District): $2,370
Enrollment: 5,141 Coed
Affiliation or Control: State/Local IRS Status: 501(c)3
Highest Offering: Associate Degree
Accreditation: SC, COARC, DMS, EMT, RAD, SURGT

01 President .... Dr. Michael SIMON
05 Vice Pres Academic Affairs .... Dr. Cynthia CASPARIS
10 Vice President Business Services .... Mr. Chris SULLIVAN
31 Dean of Community Services .... Mr. Tim DITORO
32 Dean of Student Services .... Mr. Steve HUDMAN
13 Dir Management Information Systems .... Mr. Kenneth STREET
37 Director Student Financial Aid .... Mrs. Sue JONES
18 Chief Facilities/Physical Plant .... Mr. Steve CAPPS
88 Coord of QE & Innovative Projects .... Dr. Monica PETERS
26 Coord of Communications .... Mrs. Nancy REYNOLDS
15 Director Human Resources .... Mrs. Tifini WHIDDON
06 Registrar .... Mrs. Sandra COX
121 Assoc Dean Academic Support Svcs .... Ms. Sellestine HUNT
106 Director Distance Education .... Mrs. Judy WRIGHT
21 Controller .... Mrs. Michaelyn GREENE
04 Administrative Asst to President .... Ms. Tracy NEAL

AOMA Graduate School of Integrative Medicine (J)

4701 West Gate Boulevard, Austin TX 78745
County: Travis FICE Identification: 031564
Unit ID: 429094
Telephone: (512) 454-1188 Carnegie Class: Spec-4-yr-Other Health
FAX Number: (512) 454-7001 Calendar System: Quarter
URL: www.aoma.edu
Established: 1993 Annual Graduate Tuition & Fees: N/A
Enrollment: 176 Coed
Affiliation or Control: Proprietary IRS Status: Proprietary
Highest Offering: Doctorate; No Undergraduates
Accreditation: SC, ACUP

01 President .... Dr. Betty EDMOND
05 Vice President of Faculty .... Dr. Qianzhi (Jamie) WU
88 VP of Academics & Accreditation .... Dr. Lesley HAMILTON
125 President Emeritus .... Dr. William MORRIS
32 Dean of Students .... Mr. Robert LAGUNA
45 Program and Research Director .... Dr. John FINNELL
10 Sr Director of Finance .... Ms. Kelly DOGGETT
88 Director of Clinical Education .... Dr. Jing FAN
11 Director of Operations .... Ms. Inge BOTHMA
08 Head Librarian .... Mr. David YORK
07 Director of Admissions .... Ms. Jessica DU
06 Registrar .... Ms. Taryn ALTENDORFER
58 Dean of Academics .... Dr. Yuxin HE
88 Director of Herbal Studies .... Dr. Violet SONG
88 Director Acupuncture .... Dr. Yuxing LIU
23 Clinic Business Director .... Ms. Stephanee OWENBY
121 Academic Advisor .... Mr. Robert LAGUNA
26 Dir of Marketing and Outreach .... Mr. Rob DAVIDSON
37 Director Student Financial Aid .... Ms. Estella SEARS
81 Director of Biomedical Sciences .... Dr. Raja MANDYAM
09 Dir Inst Effectiveness/Cont Educ .... Ms. Cara EDMOND

Argosy University, Dallas (K)

5001 Lyndon B. Johnson Freeway, Farmers Branch TX 75244
Telephone: (214) 890-9900 Identification: 666181
Accreditation: &WC, ACBSP, CACREP, HT, MLTAD, NURSE

† Regional accreditation is carried under the parent institution in Orange, CA.

Arlington Baptist University (L)

3001 W Division, Arlington TX 76012-3497
County: Tarrant FICE Identification: 020814
Unit ID: 222877
Telephone: (817) 461-8741 Carnegie Class: Spec-4-yr-Faith
FAX Number: (817) 274-1138 Calendar System: Semester
URL: www.ABU.edu
Established: 1939 Annual Undergrad Tuition & Fees: $11,500
Enrollment: 204 Coed
Affiliation or Control: Baptist IRS Status: 501(c)3
Highest Offering: Master's
Accreditation: BI

01 President .... Dr. D. L MOODY
05 Academic Dean .... Ms. Janie TAYLOR
32 Dean of Students .... Vacant
10 Business Manager/Dir Financial Aid .... Mr. David INGRAM
06 Registrar .... Ms. Janie TAYLOR
08 Acting Head Librarian .... Ms. Amy SCHAEFFER
18 Director Physical Plant .... Mr. T. J HUDSON
40 Director Bookstore .... Mrs. Vickie BRYANT
111 Director Institutional Advancement .... Mrs. Kim MARVIN

41 Athletic Director Mr. Cliff MCDANIEL
106 Dir Online Education/E-learning Dr. Carl JOHNSON
37 Director Student Financial Aid Mrs. Cindy TREAT
13 Chief Info Technology Officer (CIO) Dr. Chris ROLLWITZ

The Art Institute of Austin (A)

101 W. Louis Henna Blvd, Ste 100, Austin TX 78728
Telephone: (512) 691-1707 Identification: 770973
Accreditation: &SC, CIDA

Art Institute of Dallas (B)

8080 Park Lane, Suite 100, Dallas TX 75231-5993
Telephone: (214) 692-8080 FICE Identification: 025396
Accreditation: &SC, ACFEI, CIDA

† Regional accreditation is carried under the parent institution, Miami International University, Miami, FL.

The Art Institute of Houston (C)

4140 Southwest Freeway, Houston TX 77027
County: Harris FICE Identification: 021171
Unit ID: 222938
Telephone: (713) 623-2040 Carnegie Class: Spec-4-yr-Arts
FAX Number: (713) 966-2700 Calendar System: Quarter
URL: www.aih.aii.edu
Established: 1978 Annual Undergrad Tuition & Fees: $17,664
Enrollment: 1,642 Coed
Affiliation or Control: Proprietary IRS Status: Proprietary
Highest Offering: Baccalaureate
Accreditation: #SC, ACFEI, CIDA

01 President Susanne BEHRENS
05 Provost Dr. Gary EATON
32 Dean of Student Affairs LaToya NORTHINGTON
07 Senior Director of Admissions Jane CHASTANT
15 Human Resources Generalist Elizabeth WHITTINGTON
37 Dir of Student Financial Services Kelly GARRETT
06 Registrar Grace JACKSON
04 Administrative Asst to President Teresa SMITH

The Art Institute of San Antonio (D)

10000 IH-10 W, Ste 200, San Antonio TX 78230
Telephone: (210) 338-7320 Identification: 770974
Accreditation: &SC, CIDA

Auguste Escoffier School of Culinary Arts (E)

6020-B Dilliard Circle, Austin TX 78752-4438
County: Travis FICE Identification: 037276
Unit ID: 444556
Telephone: (512) 451-5743 Carnegie Class: Not Classified
FAX Number: (512) 467-9120 Calendar System: Quarter
URL: www.escoffier.edu
Established: 1997 Annual Undergrad Tuition & Fees: N/A
Enrollment: 304 Coed
Affiliation or Control: Proprietary IRS Status: Proprietary
Highest Offering: Associate Degree
Accreditation: COE

Austin College (F)

900 N Grand Avenue, Sherman TX 75090-4400
County: Grayson FICE Identification: 003543
Unit ID: 222983
Telephone: (903) 813-2000 Carnegie Class: Bac-A&S
FAX Number: (903) 813-3199 Calendar System: 4/1/4
URL: www.austincollege.edu
Established: 1849 Annual Undergrad Tuition & Fees: $37,315
Enrollment: 1,255 Coed
Affiliation or Control: Presbyterian Church (U.S.A.) IRS Status: 501(c)3
Highest Offering: Master's
Accreditation: SC

01 President Mr. Steven P. O'DAY
05 Exec VP Acad Aff & Spec Initiative Dr. Sheila A. PINERES
32 Vice Pres Student Affairs/Athletics Mr. Timothy P. MILLERICK
111 Vice Pres Institutional Advancement Ms. Allison M. DAWSON
10 Vice President for Business Affairs Ms. Heidi B. ELLIS
84 Vice President for Inst Enrollment Ms. Nan M. DAVIS
21 Assoc VP Business Affairs Ms. Rana ASKINS
110 Assoc VP for Inst Advancement Ms. Cary E. WACKER
29 Dir Alumni Programming Ms. Sarah MOORE
37 AVP/Exec Director Financial Aid Ms. Laurie COULTER
07 Exec Dir Admission Ms. Baylee L. KOWERT
42 Chaplain/Dir of Church Relations Dr. John D. WILLIAMS
35 Dean of Students Mr. Michael DEEN
06 Registrar Dr. Dawn REMMERS
08 College Librarian/Library Director Ms. Barbara CORNELIUS
79 Dean of Humanities Dr. Max GROBER
81 Dean of Sciences Dr. Steve GOLDSMITH
83 Dean of Social Sciences Dr. David GRIFFITH
15 Director of Human Resources Mr. Keith L. LAREY
36 Director Career Services Ms. Margie A. NORMAN
13 Exec Director IT Mr. Charles CURTIS
53 Chair of Education Dept Dr. Julia SHAHID
104 International Education Coordinator Ms. Cheryl MARCELO
26 Director of Public Affairs Dr. Lynn Z. WOMBLE
19 Chief of Police Mr. James PERRY
40 Interim Manager of Campus Store Ms. Linda FRANZEO
27 Exec Dir Editorial Communications Ms. Vickie S. KIRBY
18 Exec Director of Facilities Mr. David TURK
96 Purchasing Representative Ms. Debra REED
102 Dir Corp & Foundation & Gov Reltns Ms. Britanny DEREBERY
41 Director of Athletics Mr. David NORMAN
09 Dir Institutional Research & Assess Mr. David SNYDER
101 Asst to Pres/Asst Sec of Board Ms. Genna BETHEL
38 Coordinator Student Counseling Vacant
39 Director of Residence Life Ms. Christina HERRERA

Austin Community College District (G)

5930 Middle Fiskville Road, Austin TX 78752-4390
County: Travis FICE Identification: 012015
Unit ID: 222992
Telephone: (512) 223-7000 Carnegie Class: Assoc/MT-VT-High Non
FAX Number: (512) 223-7185 Calendar System: Semester
URL: www.austincc.edu
Established: 1972 Annual Undergrad Tuition & Fees (In-District): $2,550
Enrollment: 41,574 Coed
Affiliation or Control: State/Local IRS Status: 501(c)3
Highest Offering: Associate Degree
Accreditation: SC, ACBSP, ACFEI, ADNUR, CAHIIM, DH, DMS, EMT, MLTAD, OTA, PHLEB, PNUR, PTAA, RAD, SURGT

01 President/CEO Dr. Richard M. RHODES
03 Provost/Exec Vice Pres Dr. Charles COOK
10 EVP Finance & Administration Mr. Neil W. VICKERS
05 VP Instruction Mr. Michael T. MIDGLEY
32 VP Student Services Dr. Virginia FRAIRE
15 VP Human Resources Ms. Geraldine TUCKER
09 VP Effectiveness & Accountability Mrs. Soon O. MERZ
20 AVP College Access Programs Dr. Stephanie HAWLEY
13 VP Information Technology Mr. Stanley T. GUNN
121 AVP Student Success Dr. Richard R. ARMENTA
26 VP Cmty Engagement & Public Affairs Dr. Molly Beth MALCOLM
45 VP Inst Planning/Develop & Eval Dr. Mary E. HARRIS
18 VP Facilities & Construction Mr. William S. MULLANE
26 Exec Dir Public Info & College Mktg Ms. Brette E. LEA
102 Executive Director ACC Foundation Ms. Stephanie C. DEMPSEY
06 Registrar Ms. Glynis MILLER
07 Executive Director of Admissions Ms. Linda KLUCK
08 Dean Library Services Dr. Julie TODARO
19 Chief of Police Mr. Lynn DIXON
37 Executive Director Financial Aid Ms. Teresita BAZAN
96 Director of Purchasing Mr. Anthony OWENS
29 Director Alumni Relations Ms. Mary Ann CICALA

Austin Graduate School of Theology (H)

7640 Guadalupe Street, Austin TX 78752
County: Travis FICE Identification: 023628
Unit ID: 247825
Telephone: (512) 476-2772 Carnegie Class: Spec-4-yr-Faith
FAX Number: (512) 476-3919 Calendar System: Semester
URL: www.austingrad.edu
Established: 1976 Annual Undergrad Tuition & Fees: N/A
Enrollment: 44 Coed
Affiliation or Control: Independent Non-Profit IRS Status: 501(c)3
Highest Offering: Master's
Accreditation: SC

01 President Dr. Stanley G. REID
37 Vice President/Dir Financial Aid Mr. Dave ARTHUR
07 Director Recruiting & Admissions Mrs. Dawn BOND
06 Registrar Ms. Dawn BOND

Austin Presbyterian Theological Seminary (I)

100 E 27th Street, Austin TX 78705-5797
County: Travis FICE Identification: 003544
Unit ID: 223001
Telephone: (512) 472-6736 Carnegie Class: Spec-4-yr-Faith
FAX Number: (512) 479-0738 Calendar System: Semester
URL: www.austinseminary.edu
Established: 1902 Annual Graduate Tuition & Fees: N/A
Enrollment: 159 Coed
Affiliation or Control: Presbyterian Church (U.S.A.) IRS Status: 501(c)3
Highest Offering: Doctorate; No Undergraduates
Accreditation: SC, THEOL

01 President Rev. Theodore J. WARDLAW
05 Academic Dean Dr. David H. JENSEN
10 Vice Pres Finance/Administration Ms. Heather ZDANCEWICZ
111 Vice Pres Institutional Advancement Ms. Donna SCOTT
32 Vice Pres Student Affairs/Vocation Rev. Sarah GAVENTA
07 Vice President for Admissions Rev. John H. BARDEN
51 VP Education Beyond the Walls Ms. Melissa WIGINTON
29 Director Alumni & Church Relations Mr. Gary MATHEWS
08 Director of the Stitt Library Dr. Timothy LINCOLN
06 Asst Dean Academic Affs/Registrar Ms. Jacqueline D. HEFLEY
37 Director of Financial Aid Ms. Glenna BALCH
100 Exec Assistant to the President Ms. Mona SANTANDREA
13 Director of Information Technology Ms. Julie NEWTON
15 Director Personnel Services Ms. Pamela OWENS
18 Chief Facilities/Physical Plant Mr. John EVERETT
44 Director Annual Giving Ms. Claire MATHIAS

Bakke Graduate University (J)

8515 Greenville Ave, S206, Dallas TX 75243-7039
County: Dallas FICE Identification: 031108
Unit ID: 420705
Telephone: (214) 329-4447 Carnegie Class: Spec-4-yr-Faith
FAX Number: (214) 347-9367 Calendar System: Semester
URL: www.bgu.edu
Established: 1990 Annual Graduate Tuition & Fees: N/A
Enrollment: 174 Coed
Affiliation or Control: Independent Non-Profit IRS Status: 501(c)3
Highest Offering: Doctorate; No Undergraduates
Accreditation: TRACS

01 President Dr. Brad SMITH
05 Academic Dean Dr. Judi MELTON
10 Chief Operations/Financial Ofcr Ms. Carolyn COCHRAN
06 Registrar Dr. Judi MELTON
07 Admissions Coordinator Ms. Traci TUCKER
08 Head Librarian Ms. Jennifer ROMAN
106 Dir Online Education/E-learning Dr. Judi MELTON
37 Director Student Financial Aid Ms. Carolyn COCHRAN

Baptist Health System School of Health Professions (K)

8400 Datapoint Drive, San Antonio TX 78229
County: Bexar FICE Identification: 006606
Unit ID: 223083
Telephone: (210) 297-9636 Carnegie Class: Spec-4-yr-Other Health
FAX Number: (210) 297-0075 Calendar System: Semester
URL: www.bshp.edu
Established: 1903 Annual Undergrad Tuition & Fees: N/A
Enrollment: 686 Coed
Affiliation or Control: Proprietary IRS Status: Proprietary
Highest Offering: Baccalaureate
Accreditation: ABHES, ADNUR, NUR, RAD, SURGT, SURTEC

01 Interim President Dr. Patricia E. ALVOET
04 Administrative Asst to President Diane TYLER
07 Director of Admissions Jillian DENMAN
08 Director of Library Anita SHAW
05 Director of Gen Educ and Online Lucinda FLORES
10 Director of Finance Priti LAXMI
37 Director of Student Financial Aid Patrick REYNA
13 Director of Information Systems Nancy ORTIZ
06 Registrar Rebecca WATTS
06 Registrar Tavianna SIEGEL

† Tuition varies by degree program.

Baptist Hospitals of Southeast Texas School of Radiologic Technology (L)

3030 Fannin Ste A, Beaumont TX 77704
County: Jefferson Identification: 667153
Telephone: (409) 212-5724 Carnegie Class: Not Classified
FAX Number: N/A Calendar System: Semester
URL: www.bhset.net
Established: 1952 Annual Undergrad Tuition & Fees: N/A
Enrollment: N/A Coed
Affiliation or Control: Independent Non-Profit IRS Status: 501(c)3
Highest Offering: Associate Degree
Accreditation: RAD

01 Program Director Deborah SMITH
11 Chief of Administration David PARMER

Baptist Missionary Association Theological Seminary (M)

P.O. Box 670, 1530 East Pine Street, Jacksonville TX 75766-5407
County: Cherokee FICE Identification: 023312
Unit ID: 223117
Telephone: (903) 586-2501 Carnegie Class: Spec-4-yr-Faith
FAX Number: (903) 586-0378 Calendar System: Semester
URL: www.bmats.edu
Established: 1957 Annual Undergrad Tuition & Fees: $5,800
Enrollment: 133 Coed
Affiliation or Control: Baptist IRS Status: 501(c)3
Highest Offering: Master's
Accreditation: SC, THEOL

01 President Dr. Charley HOLMES
05 Dean/Registrar Dr. Philip ATTEBERY
04 Assistant to the President Keri SOUTHERN
32 Director of Student Services Ronnie J. JOHNSON
08 Library Director Dr. James BLAYLOCK
10 Chief Business Officer Chris PROCTOR

Baptist University of the Americas (N)

7838 Barlite Blvd., San Antonio TX 78224-1336
County: Bexar FICE Identification: 037333
Unit ID: 444398

Telephone: (210) 924-4338 Carnegie Class: Spec-4-yr-Faith
FAX Number: (210) 924-0888 Calendar System: Semester
URL: www.bua.edu
Established: 1947 Annual Undergrad Tuition & Fees: $6,240
Enrollment: 195 Coed
Affiliation or Control: Baptist IRS Status: 501(c)3
Highest Offering: Baccalaureate
Accreditation: **BI**

01 Acting President Dr. Moises RODRIGUEZ
03 Executive Vice President Dr. Moises RODRIGUEZ
10 Vice Pres for Admin and Finance Mr. Barry TYLER
30 Vice Pres for Development Mr. Teo CISNEROS
05 Vice Pres for Academic Affairs Dr. Marconi MONTEIRO
32 Vice Pres for Student Svcs/Enroll Ms. Mary RANJEL
37 Financial Aid Administrator Mrs. Araceli ACOSTA

Baylor College of Medicine (A)

One Baylor Plaza, Houston TX 77030-3411
County: Harris FICE Identification: 004949
Unit ID: 223223
Telephone: (713) 798-4951 Carnegie Class: Spec-4-yr-Med
FAX Number: (713) 798-3692 Calendar System: Quarter
URL: www.bcm.edu
Established: 1900 Annual Graduate Tuition & Fees: N/A
Enrollment: 1,572 Coed
Affiliation or Control: Independent Non-Profit IRS Status: 501(c)3
Highest Offering: Doctorate; No Undergraduates
Accreditation: **SC**, ANEST, ARCPA, IPSY, MED, OPE

00 Chancellor Vacant
01 President and CEO Dr. Paul KLOTMAN
05 Provost/SVP Acad & Faculty Affairs Dr. Alicia MONROE
17 Vice Pres/Chief Medical Officer Dr. Steve SIGWORTH
10 Sr VP/Chief Business Officer Mrs. Kimberly C. DAVID
30 Vice Pres Philanthropy Vacant
43 Sr Vice Pres/General Counsel Mr. Robert F. CORRIGAN, JR.
26 VP Communications/Public Affairs Ms. Claire M. BASSETT
15 Vice President Human Resources Mr. Dane FRIEND
46 Sr Vice President/Dean Research Dr. Adam KUSPA
13 VP Information Technology Vacant
86 Vice Pres Government Relations Mr. Tom KLEINWORTH
88 Dean Natl Sch Tropical Medicine Dr. Peter J. HOTEZ
21 VP Finance/CFO Ms. Julie NICKELL
63 Dean of Medical Education Dr. Jennifer CHRISTNER
58 Int Dean Grad Sch Biomed Sciences Dr. Adam KUSPA
76 Dean School Allied Health Sciences Dr. Robert MCLAUGHLIN
28 Sr Assoc Dean Diversity Dr. James L. PHILLIPS
63 Sr VP/Dean of Medical Education Dr. C. Michael FORDIS, JR.
20 Sr Assoc Dean Med Education Dr. Mary L. BRANDT
88 Associate Dean Res Assurances Dr. Stacey L. BERG
88 Asst Dean Graduate Medical Educ Dr. Jacqueline LEVESQUE
07 Assistant Dean for Admissions Dr. Jesus G. VALLEJO
35 Assistant Dean Student Affairs Dr. Andrea Gail STOLAR
88 Assoc Dean Medical Education Dr. Jerry C. GOODMAN
21 Controller Mr. Douglas R. SPADE
09 Exec Dir Inst Effectivenesness Ms. Lilly SHIH
37 Director Student Financial Planning Ms. Hilda DELEON
32 Assoc Dean of Student Affairs Mr. Joseph KASS
88 Exec Director Environmental Safety Mr. Paul MURACA
75 Director Occupational Medicine Dr. James E. KELAHER
29 Director Alumni Affairs Mr. Alexander M. HOPKINS
19 Exec Director of Security Mr. John A. ROBERSON
96 Director Supply Chain Management Mr. Miguel MACHADO
06 Registrar Ms. Latoya R. WHITAKER

Baylor University (B)

One Bear Place #97096, Waco TX 76798-7096
County: McLennan FICE Identification: 003545
Unit ID: 223232
Telephone: (254) 710-3555 Carnegie Class: DU-Higher
FAX Number: (254) 710-3557 Calendar System: Semester
URL: www.baylor.edu
Established: 1845 Annual Undergrad Tuition & Fees: $42,006
Enrollment: 16,787 Coed
Affiliation or Control: Baptist IRS Status: 501(c)3
Highest Offering: Doctorate
Accreditation: **SC**, CAATE, CIDA, CLPSY, CS, DIETD, DIETI, ENG, HSA, JOUR, LAW, MIDWF, MUS, NURSE, PH, PTA, SP, SW, THEA, THEOL

01 President Dr. Linda A. LIVINGSTONE
05 Interim Provost Dr. Michael MCLENDON
100 Chief of Staff to the President Dr. Robyn L. DRISKELL
10 Senior VP & COO Dr. Reagan M. RAMSOWER
22 Chief Compliance Officer Mr. G. Doug WELCH
30 Sr VP for Univ Development Mr. David ROSSELLI
32 Vice President Student Life Dr. Kevin P. JACKSON
26 VP Marketing & Comm/CMO Mr. Jason D. COOK
29 Vice Pres Constituent Engagement Ms. Tommye Lou DAVIS
43 Gen Counsel/CLO & Corp Sec Mr. Christopher W. HOLMES
41 VP & Director of Athletics Mr. Mack RHOADES, IV
117 VP for Governance & Risk Dr. Juan ALEJANDRO, JR.
09 Director Inst Research/Testing Dr. Kathleen MORLEY
21 VP of Financial Operations Mrs. Susan D. ANZ
45 AVP of Budget & Planning Mr. Brian S. DENMAN
18 VP for Facilities & Oper Mgmt Mr. Brian W. NICHOLSON
15 VP & Chief Human Resource Officer Mrs. Cheryl GOCHIS
13 Interim VP InfoTech/Dpty CIO Mrs. Becky L. KING
08 Interim Dean of Libraries Mr. John WILSON
35 Associate Vice Pres Student Life Dr. Martha Lou SCOTT
06 Registrar Mr. Jonathan C. HELM
102 Assoc VP Corp/Foundation Relations Mr. Chris KRAUSE
90 Assoc Vice Pres Electronic Library Mr. Timothy M. LOGAN
108 Dir of Inst Planning & Assessment Dr. J. Ben COX
97 Vice Provost Undergrad Education Dr. Wesley NULL
20 Vice Prov/Academic Affs & Policy Dr. James BENNIGHOFF
46 Vice Prov Research/Dir CASPER Dr. Truell HYDE
07 Assoc VP of Enrollment Mgt Ms. Jennifer CARRON
115 VP & Chief Investment Officer Mr. R. Brian WEBB
19 Chief of Police Mr. Brad WIGTIL
93 Director Multiculture Affairs Mrs. Pearlie BEVERLY
121 Director Academic Support Programs Ms. Sally FIRMIN
23 Medical Director Health Center Dr. Sharon STERN
36 Exec Dr Career & Professional Dev Dr. Marjorie N. ELLIS
25 Asst Vice Prov Res & Dir Spons Prog Ms. Lisa H. MCKETHAN
38 Exec Director Counseling Svcs Dr. James G. MARSH
40 Director Baylor Bookstore Mr. Allen A. PINE
86 Director Governmental Relations Ms. Rochonda FARMER-NEAL
96 Asst VP for Procurement Services Mr. Tom HOFFMEYER
31 Dir Cmty Relations & Continued Ed Ms. Gabriela COLMAN
49 Dean College of Arts/Sciences Dr. Lee C. NORDT
50 Dean School of Business Dr. Terry S. MANESS
53 Dean School of Education Dr. Michael K. MCLENDON
61 Dean School of Law Mr. Bradley TOBEN
64 Dean School of Music Dr. Gary MORTENSON
66 Dean School of Nursing Dr. Shelley F. CONROY
58 Vice Provost & Dean Graduate School Dr. Larry LYON
73 Dean Truett Theological Sem Dr. Todd D. STILL
54 Dean Engineering & Computer Science Dr. Dennis L. O'NEAL
92 Dean Honors College/Dir BU in DC Dr. Thomas S. HIBBS
85 Vice Provost for Global Engagement Dr. Jeffrey S. HAMILTON
35 Dean Student Development Dr. Elizabeth PALACIOS
35 Dean Student Learning & Engagement Dr. Jeff DOYLE
42 University Chaplain Dr. Burt BURLESON
88 Assoc Dean Student Conduct Admin Ms. Bethany J. MCCRAW
37 Student Financial Aid Ms. Jennifer CARRON
88 Assoc VP Public Safety & Security Mr. Mark CHILDERS

B.H. Carroll Theological Institute (C)

6500 N Belt Line Road, Suite 100, Irving TX 75063-6056
County: Tarrant Identification: 667089
Telephone: (972) 580-7600 Carnegie Class: Not Classified
FAX Number: (972) 756-0600 Calendar System: Semester
URL: www.bhcarroll.edu
Established: 2004 Annual Graduate Tuition & Fees: N/A
Enrollment: N/A Coed
Affiliation or Control: Southern Baptist IRS Status: 501(c)3
Highest Offering: Doctorate; No Undergraduates
Accreditation: **BI**, THEOL

01 President Dr. C. Gene WILKES
10 CFO/Director Business Affairs Dr. Shane BENDER
06 Registrar Dr. Stan MOORE
07 Director of Admissions Ms. Meredith CHACIN
08 Dir Library & Information Services Mr. Don DAY
09 Dir of Institutional Effectiveness Ms. Amanda CRANE

Blinn College (D)

902 College Avenue, Brenham TX 77833-4098
County: Washington FICE Identification: 003549
Unit ID: 223427
Telephone: (979) 830-4000 Carnegie Class: Assoc/HT-High Trad
FAX Number: (979) 830-4030 Calendar System: Semester
URL: www.blinn.edu
Established: 1883 Annual Undergrad Tuition & Fees (In-District): $2,424
Enrollment: 19,780 Coed
Affiliation or Control: State/Local IRS Status: 501(c)3
Highest Offering: Associate Degree
Accreditation: **SC**, ADNUR, CAHIIM, DH, EMT, IFSAC, PTAA, RAD

01 Chancellor Dr. Mary HENSLEY
43 Exec Vice Chanc/General Counsel Mr. Mel WAXLER
101 Special Asst to Chancellor/BOT Ms. Laurie CLARK
32 Vice Chancellor Student Services Dr. Dennis CROWSON
10 Vice Chanc Business/Finance/CFO Mr. Richard CERVANTES
05 Vice Chancellor Admin/Operations Ms. Karen BUCK
12 Executive Dean Bryan Campus Dr. Jimmy BYRD
20 Dean Academic Affairs Dr. John BEAVER
09 Dean Inst Research/Effectiveness Dr. Amanda CLARK
06 Dean Admissions/Records/Registrar Ms. Andrea LINER
88 Judicial Officer Ms. Betty HEGEMEYER
35 Dean of Student Success Mr. Jeremy THOMAS
43 Legal Counsel Mr. Ted HAJOVSKY
102 Executive Director Foundation Ms. Susan MYERS
18 AVC Facilities/Planning/Constr Mr. Richard O'MALLEY
12 Dean Schulenburg Campus Ms. Rebecca GARLICK
12 Dean Sealy Campus Ms. Lisa CATON
72 Dean Technical/Prof Programs Mr. Jon (Jay) ANDERSON
22 Director Disability Services (Bre) Ms. Patricia MORAN
22 Dir Disability Services (Bryan) Ms. Brenda JONES-WILKINS
04 Admin Asst to the Chancellor Ms. Becky KREBS
21 Director Accounting Mr. Thomas BRAZZEL
08 Interim Dean Library Services Dr. John BEAVER
38 Director of Counseling Mr. Robert LOVELIDGE
13 Dir Administrative Computing Svcs Ms. Christine WIED
37 Dean Financial Aid/Scholarships Mr. Brent WILLIFORD
15 Asst Vice Chanc Human Resources Ms. Marie KIRBY
41 Athletic Dir/Mens Head Bsktbl Coach Mr. Scott SCHUMACHER
19 Chief College Police Department Mr. John CHANCELLOR
96 Director Purchasing/Transportation Mr. Ross SCHROEDER
07 Director Admissions & Records Ms. Kristi URBAN
26 Dir Marketing/Media Relations Mr. Jeff TILLEY
35 Dir Student Leadership/Activities Mr. David G. MICHENER
39 Housing Director Vacant
27 Dir Communications/Media Relations Mr. Richard BRAY

Brazosport College (E)

500 College Drive, Lake Jackson TX 77566-3199
County: Brazoria FICE Identification: 007287
Unit ID: 223506
Telephone: (979) 230-3000 Carnegie Class: Bac/Assoc-Assoc Dom
FAX Number: (979) 230-3443 Calendar System: Semester
URL: www.brazosport.edu
Established: 1968 Annual Undergrad Tuition & Fees (In-District): $2,385
Enrollment: 4,221 Coed
Affiliation or Control: Local IRS Status: 501(c)3
Highest Offering: Baccalaureate
Accreditation: **SC**, EMT

01 President Dr. Millicent M. VALEK
05 VP Academic & Student Affairs Dr. Lynda VILLANUEVA
103 VP Industry & Community Resources Ms. Anne BARTLETT
111 VP College Advancement Ms. Serena ANDREWS
15 VP Human Resources Mr. Marshall CAMPBELL
10 VP Financial Services & CFO Mr. David MARSHALL
32 Dean of Student Services Ms. Jo GREATHOUSE
20 Dean of Instruction Mr. Jeffrey DETRICK
09 Dean Planning/Int Effectiv/Research Vacant
07 Director Admissions/Registrar Ms. Priscilla SANCHEZ
38 Director Counseling and Testing Mr. Arnold RAMIREZ
26 Director Marketing & Communications Mr. Kyle SMITH
13 Director Information Technology Mr. Ron PARKER
37 Director of Financial Aid Ms. Kay WRIGHT
08 Director Library & Learning Service Ms. Cassie BRUNER
18 Director Facility Services Mr. John DITTO
88 Director Small Business Dev Center Dr. Janice GOINES
31 Director Community Education Ms. Catherine HANSON
88 Director Children's Center Ms. Julie LITTLEFIELD
25 Director Grant Administration Vacant
109 Director Business Services Ms. Ginger WOOSTER
21 Internal Auditor Ms. Cynthia STRADER

Brightwood College (F)

2241 South Watson Road, Arlington TX 76010
Telephone: (972) 623-4700 Identification: 770544
Accreditation: **ACICS**

Brightwood College (G)

6115 Eastex Freeway, Suite A-142, Beaumont TX 77706
Telephone: (409) 833-2722 Identification: 770545
Accreditation: **ACICS**

Brightwood College (H)

1900 North Expressway, Brownsville TX 78521
Telephone: (956) 547-8200 Identification: 770595
Accreditation: **ACICS**

Brightwood College (I)

1620 S Padre Island Drive, Ste 600,
Corpus Christi TX 78416
Telephone: (361) 852-2900 Identification: 770597
Accreditation: **ACICS**

Brightwood College (J)

12005 Ford Road, Suite 100, Dallas TX 75234
County: Dallas FICE Identification: 032723
Unit ID: 382896
Telephone: (972) 385-1446 Carnegie Class: Assoc/HVT-Mix Trad/Non
FAX Number: (972) 385-0641 Calendar System: Other
URL: www.brightwood.edu
Established: 1983 Annual Undergrad Tuition & Fees: N/A
Enrollment: 433 Coed
Affiliation or Control: Proprietary IRS Status: Proprietary
Highest Offering: Associate Degree
Accreditation: **ACICS**, PTAA

01 Campus President Ms. Michelle OWENS

Brightwood College (K)

8360 Burnham Road, Ste 100, El Paso TX 79907
County: El Paso FICE Identification: 025919
Unit ID: 246266
Telephone: (915) 595-1935 Carnegie Class: Assoc/HVT-High Non
FAX Number: (915) 595-6619 Calendar System: Other
URL: www.brightwood.edu
Established: 1983 Annual Undergrad Tuition & Fees: N/A
Enrollment: 587 Coed
Affiliation or Control: Proprietary IRS Status: Proprietary
Highest Offering: Associate Degree
Accreditation: **ACICS**

01 President Ms. Dawn MICHELLE
05 Director of Education Ms. Ramona GARCIA

Brightwood College **(A)**
2001 Beach Street, Suite 201, Fort Worth TX 76103
Telephone: (817) 413-2000 Identification: 770598
Accreditation: ACICS

Brightwood College (B)
711 East Airtex Drive, Houston TX 77073
County: Harris FICE Identification: 023122
Unit ID: 229036
Telephone: (281) 443-8900 Carnegie Class: Not Classified
FAX Number: (281) 443-0777 Calendar System: Other
URL: www.brightwood.edu
Established: 1983 Annual Undergrad Tuition & Fees: N/A
Enrollment: 336 Coed
Affiliation or Control: Proprietary IRS Status: Proprietary
Highest Offering: Associate Degree
Accreditation: ACICS

01 Campus President .... Mr. Richard SAMBRANO

Brightwood College **(C)**
6410 McPherson, Laredo TX 78041
Telephone: (956) 717-5909 Identification: 770546
Accreditation: ACICS

Brightwood College **(D)**
1500 S Jackson Road, McAllen TX 78503
Telephone: (956) 630-1499 Identification: 770596
Accreditation: ACICS

Brightwood College (E)
7142 San Pedro Avenue, Suite 100,
San Antonio TX 78216
County: Bexar FICE Identification: 009466
Unit ID: 364955
Telephone: (210) 733-0777 Carnegie Class: Assoc/HVT-Mix Trad/Non
FAX Number: (210) 340-6603 Calendar System: Other
URL: brightwood.edu
Established: 1983 Annual Undergrad Tuition & Fees: N/A
Enrollment: 542 Coed
Affiliation or Control: Proprietary IRS Status: Proprietary
Highest Offering: Associate Degree
Accreditation: ACICS

01 President .... Sandra MUSKOPS

Brightwood College (F)
6441 NW Loop 410, San Antonio TX 78238
County: Bexar FICE Identification: 031158
Unit ID: 431886
Telephone: (210) 308-8584 Carnegie Class: Spec 2-yr-Health
FAX Number: (210) 308-8985 Calendar System: Other
URL: www.brightwood.edu
Established: 1983 Annual Undergrad Tuition & Fees: N/A
Enrollment: 506 Coed
Affiliation or Control: Proprietary IRS Status: Proprietary
Highest Offering: Associate Degree
Accreditation: ACICS, CAHIIM

01 President .... Mr. Eric RUDIE

Brightwood College-Friendswood **(G)**
3208 FM 528, Friendswood TX 77546
Telephone: (281) 648-0880 Identification: 667051
Accreditation: ACICS, MAC

† Branch campus of Brightwood College, Houston, TX.

Brite Divinity School (H)
2925 Princeton Street, Fort Worth TX 76129-0001
County: Tarrant Identification: 666228
Unit ID: 450304
Telephone: (817) 257-7575 Carnegie Class: Spec-4-yr-Faith
FAX Number: (817) 257-6932 Calendar System: Semester
URL: www.brite.tcu.edu
Established: 1873 Annual Graduate Tuition & Fees: N/A
Enrollment: 217 Coed
Affiliation or Control: Independent Non-Profit IRS Status: 501(c)3
Highest Offering: Doctorate; No Undergraduates
Accreditation: SC, THEOL

01 President & Chief Executive Officer .... Dr. D. Newell WILLIAMS
05 Exec Vice President/Dean .... Dr. Joretta MARSHALL
10 Vice President Business/Finance .... Ms. Michele G. SMITH
32 Asst Dean for Common Life .... Dr. Valerie FORSTMAN

Brown Mackie College - San Antonio **(I)**
4715 Fredericksburg Road, Suite 100,
San Antonio TX 78229
Telephone: (877) 460-1714 Identification: 770799
Accreditation: ACICS

† In teach-out mode. Branch campus of The Art Institute of Phoenix, Phoenix, AZ

Carrington College - Mesquite **(J)**
3733 West Emporium Circle, Mesquite TX 75150
Telephone: (972) 682-2800 Identification: 770967
Accreditation: &WJ

† Branch campus of Carrington College - Sacramento, Sacramento, CA

Center for Advanced Legal Studies (K)
800 W Sam Houston Pkwy, S Suite 100,
Houston TX 77042
County: Harris FICE Identification: 026047
Unit ID: 379782
Telephone: (713) 529-2778 Carnegie Class: Spec-4-yr-Other
FAX Number: (855) 422-4466 Calendar System: Other
URL: www.paralegal.edu
Established: 1987 Annual Undergrad Tuition & Fees: N/A
Enrollment: 212 Coed
Affiliation or Control: Proprietary IRS Status: Proprietary
Highest Offering: Associate Degree
Accreditation: ACICS, COE

01 School Director/Co-Founder .... Mr. Doyle HAPPE
05 Dean .... Mr. Thomas SWANSON
07 Director of Admissions .... Mr. James SCHEFFER

Central Texas College (L)
PO Box 1800, Killeen TX 76540-9990
County: Bell FICE Identification: 004003
Unit ID: 223816
Telephone: (254) 526-7161 Carnegie Class: Assoc/HT-High Non
FAX Number: (254) 526-0817 Calendar System: Semester
URL: www.ctcd.edu
Established: 1965 Annual Undergrad Tuition & Fees (In-District): $2,280
Enrollment: 19,562 Coed
Affiliation or Control: Local IRS Status: 501(c)3
Highest Offering: Associate Degree
Accreditation: SC, ADNUR, EMT, MLTAD

01 Chancellor .... Mr. Jim YEONOPOLUS
03 Deputy Chanc US Campus Operations .... Dr. Tina ADY
11 Deputy Chanc Finance & Admin .... Ms. Michele CARTER
05 Deputy Chanc Acad & Student Svcs .... Dr. Robin GARRETT
12 Dean Continental & Ft Hood Campuses .... Mr. Raul GARCIA
12 Dean Central Campus .... Ms. Janice ANDERSON
32 Dean Student Services .... Dr. Johnelle WELSH
08 Dean Library Services .... Ms. Lori PURSER
38 Director Guidance/Counseling .... Vacant
06 Associate Dean Admin/Reg/Records ...... Mr. Stephen O'DONOVAN
10 Comptroller .... Mr. Bob LIBERTY
15 Director Human Resource Mgmt .... Ms. Holly JORDAN
106 Director Distance Education/Ed Tech .... Ms. Sharon DAVIS
18 Director Facilities Management .... Mr. Mark HARMSEN
21 Director Business Services .... Mr. Ted GONZALEZ
30 Director College Development .... Ms. Amy BAWCOM
09 Director Institutional Effectivenes .... Dr. Lelia HACKETT
13 Director Information Technology .... Mr. Cliff GAINES
07 Director Admissions/Recruitment .... Ms. Shannon BRALLEY
88 Director Testing .... Mr. Victor GATES
85 Director International Student Svcs .... Ms. Rebecca LOPEZ
22 Director Disability Support Svcs .... Dr. Christy SHANK
88 Director Substance Abuse Resource . Dr. Gerald MAHONE-LEIWS
36 Director Career Planning/Placement .... Ms. Keisha HOLMAN
26 Dir Community Relations/Marketing .... Ms. Barbara MERLO
88 Liaison Military Programs .... Ms. Diana CASTILLO
19 Chief Police/Security Services .... Ms. Mary WHEELER
40 Manager Bookstore .... Ms. Regina MARTINEZ-WOODRUFF
37 Director Student Financial Aid .... Ms. Annabelle SMITH
96 Director of Purchasing .... Mr. Ted GONZALEZ
04 Administrative Asst to President .... Ms. Debra HAVENS
43 Dir Legal Services/General Counsel .... Ms. Deborah SHIBLEY
86 Director Government Relations .... Mr. Brian SUNSHINE

Chamberlain University-Houston **(M)**
11025 Equity Drive, Houston TX 77041
Telephone: (713) 277-9800 Identification: 770500
Accreditation: &NH, NURSE

† Branch campus of Chamberlain University-Addison, Addison, IL

Chamberlain University-Irving **(N)**
4800 Regent Blvd., Irving TX 75063
Telephone: (469) 706-6705 Identification: 770853
Accreditation: &NH, NURSE

† Branch campus of Chamberlain University-Addison, Addison, IL

Chamberlain University-Pearland **(O)**
12000 Shadow Creek Pkwy, Pearland TX 77584
Telephone: (832) 664-7000 Identification: 770934
Accreditation: &NH, NURSE

† Branch campus of Chamberlain College of Nursing-Addison, Addison, IL.

Christ Mission College (P)
10822 FM 1560, San Antonio TX 78254
County: Bexar Identification: 667320
Telephone: (210) 688-3101 Carnegie Class: Not Classified
FAX Number: N/A Calendar System: Semester
Established: 1926 Annual Undergrad Tuition & Fees: N/A
Enrollment: N/A Coed
Affiliation or Control: Independent Non-Profit IRS Status: 501(c)3
Highest Offering: Baccalaureate
Accreditation: @BI

01 President .... Dr. Monte MADSEN

Cisco College (Q)
101 College Heights, Cisco TX 76437-1900
County: Eastland FICE Identification: 003553
Unit ID: 223898
Telephone: (254) 442-5000 Carnegie Class: Assoc/MT-VT-High Trad
FAX Number: (254) 442-5100 Calendar System: Semester
URL: www.cisco.edu
Established: 1940 Annual Undergrad Tuition & Fees (In-State): $3,810
Enrollment: 3,608 Coed
Affiliation or Control: State IRS Status: 501(c)3
Highest Offering: Associate Degree
Accreditation: SC, COARC, MAC, SURGT

01 President .... Dr. Thad ANGLIN
05 Chief Instruction Officer .... Dr. Carol DUPREE
32 Vice President for Student Services .... Dr. Jerry DODSON
13 Exec Dir of Information Technology .... Mr. Steve POWELL
30 Director of Development .... Ms. Martha MONTGOMERY
37 Director of Financial Aid .... Ms. Linda SELLERS
15 Director of Human Resources .... Ms. Pamela G. PAGE
08 Director of Library Services .... Ms. Donna CLARK
19 Director Campus Safety .... Mr. Roger TIGHE
07 Director of Enrollment Services .... Ms. Shirley DOVE
04 Executive Asst to President .... Ms. Sydni RABB
103 Dir Workforce/Career Development .... Ms. Charlotte SPEEGLE
106 Dir Online Education/E-learning .... Ms. Sheron CATON
39 Director Student Housing .... Mr. Ryan JOHNSON
10 Dean of Business Svcs/CFO .... Ms. Audra TAYLOR
96 Director of Purchasing .... Ms. Beverly MASSEY

Clarendon College (R)
PO Box 968, Clarendon TX 79226-0968
County: Donley FICE Identification: 003554
Unit ID: 223922
Telephone: (806) 874-3571 Carnegie Class: Assoc/HVT-Mix Trad/Non
FAX Number: (806) 874-3201 Calendar System: Semester
URL: www.clarendoncollege.edu
Established: 1898 Annual Undergrad Tuition & Fees (In-District): $2,424
Enrollment: 1,346 Coed
Affiliation or Control: State/Local IRS Status: 501(c)3
Highest Offering: Associate Degree
Accreditation: SC

01 President .... Dr. Robert RIZA
05 Exec VP Academic/Student Affairs .... Mr. Tex BUCKHAULTS
20 Vice President of Academic Affairs .... Mr. Brian FULLER
100 Chief of Staff .... Mrs. Ashlee ESTLACK
41 Athletic Director .... Mr. Brad VANDEN BOOGAARD
10 Vice Pres Administrative Services .... Mrs. Lana RITCHIE
37 Associate Dean of Financial Aid .... Mrs. Susan RUSSELL
84 Assoc Dean of Enrollment Services .... Mrs. Becky GREEN
13 Director of Information Technology .... Mr. Will THOMPSON
09 Director of Institutional Research .... Dr. Robert TAYLOR
08 Librarian .... Ms. Pamela REED
81 Division Chair Science/Health .... Mrs. Scarlet ESTLACK
49 Division Chair Liberal Arts .... Mrs. Kim JEFFREY

Coastal Bend College (S)
3800 Charco Road, Beeville TX 78102-2197
County: Bee FICE Identification: 003546
Unit ID: 223320
Telephone: (361) 358-2838 Carnegie Class: Assoc/HVT-High Trad
FAX Number: (361) 354-2333 Calendar System: Semester
URL: www.coastalbend.edu
Established: 1965 Annual Undergrad Tuition & Fees (In-District): $2,646
Enrollment: 4,450 Coed
Affiliation or Control: State/Local IRS Status: 501(c)3
Highest Offering: Associate Degree
Accreditation: SC, DH, RAD

01 President .... Dr. Beatriz T. ESPINOZA
05 VP of Instruction/Econ Development .... Dr. Matilda SAENZ
20 Dean of Academics .... Mr. Mark SECORD
20 Assistant Dean of Academics .... Ms. Kayla JONES
32 Exec Dean of Student Services .... Ms. Lupe GANCERES
07 Director of Admissions/Registrar .... Ms. Candy FULLER
26 Director of Marketing & Public Rels .... Mr. Bernard SAENZ
37 Director of Financial Aid .... Ms. Nora MORALES
12 Director of Alice Campus .... Mr. David SULLIVAN
12 Director of Kingsville Campus .... Dr. Cynthia ALVARADO-STINSON
45 VP of Strategic Planning and Admin ... Ms. Shannon MCCARRON
10 Exec Director of Business Services .... Vacant
08 Director Library Services .... Dr. Hong "Anna" XU

15 Human Resources Director .... Ms. Esther MARTINEZ
13 Director of IT Services/Webmaster .... Mr. Amador RAMIREZ
18 Chief Facilities/Physical Plant .... Mr. Jacinto (JC) COLMENERO
04 Executive Asst to President .... Ms. Stacie YANTA
103 Dean of Workforce Training .... Ms. Julia GARCIA
39 Director Student Housing .... Mr. Domingo MARTINEZ
09 Director of Institutional Research .... Mr. Miguel AGUILAR
102 Exec Dir CBC Foundation .... Ms. Madeline MADDEN
19 Director Security/Safety .... Dr. Kevin BEHR
41 Athletic Director .... Mr. Paul CANTRELL
76 Assistant Dean of Allied Health .... Ms. Loana HERNANDEZ
88 Director of Dual Enrollment .... Ms. Susie GAITAN

College of Biblical Studies-Houston (A)

7000 Regency Square Boulevard, Houston TX 77036-3298
County: Harris FICE Identification: 034224
Unit ID: 388520
Telephone: (713) 785-5995 Carnegie Class: Spec-4-yr-Faith
FAX Number: (713) 785-5998 Calendar System: Semester
URL: www.cbshouston.edu
Established: 1976 Annual Undergrad Tuition & Fees: $6,946
Enrollment: 423 Coed
Affiliation or Control: Independent Non-Profit IRS Status: 501(c)3
Highest Offering: Baccalaureate
Accreditation: **SC**, BI

01 President .... Dr. Bill BLOCKER
04 Executive Assistant .... Mrs. Vicki PATTERSON
05 VP Academic Affairs/Acad Dean .... Dr. Joseph D. PARLE
03 VP Admin and Student Affairs .... Mr. Paul KEITH
10 Chief Financial Officer .... Mr. Andy LIVELY
84 Exec Director Enrollment Services .... Dr. Lisa STEWART
26 Exec Director of Marketing and PR .... Vacant
11 Dean of Operations .... Mr. Shane BOOTH
18 Dir Real Estate Operations .... Mr. Terry BRYAN
15 Director of Human Resources .... Mr. Paul KEITH
06 Registrar .... Mr. Chad KNIFFEN
08 Director of Library Services .... Mr. Artis LOVELADY, III
09 Dir Inst Effect and Accreditation .... Dr. Bryce F. HANTLA
07 Director of Admissions .... Dr. Lisa STEWART
106 Assoc Dean Dist Educ Operations .... Mr. Shane BOOTHE
20 Assoc Dean Faculty and Curr Dev .... Dr. Brittany BURNETTE
37 Senior Financial Aid Officer .... Vacant

The College of Health Care Professions (B)

6330 East Highway 290, Suite 180, Austin TX 78723
County: Travis FICE Identification: 034263
Unit ID: 437635
Telephone: (512) 617-5700 Carnegie Class: Spec 2-yr-Health
FAX Number: (512) 892-6643 Calendar System: Other
URL: www.chcp.edu
Established: 1988 Annual Undergrad Tuition & Fees: N/A
Enrollment: 301 Coed
Affiliation or Control: Proprietary IRS Status: Proprietary
Highest Offering: Associate Degree
Accreditation: **ABHES**

01 President .... Ms. Sara RAMBIKUR

The College of Health Care Professions (C)

240 Northwest Mall Boulevard, Houston TX 77092
County: Harris FICE Identification: 031281
Unit ID: 392257
Telephone: (713) 425-3100 Carnegie Class: Spec 2-yr-Health
FAX Number: (713) 425-3192 Calendar System: Other
URL: www.chcp.edu
Established: 1988 Annual Undergrad Tuition & Fees: N/A
Enrollment: 1,246 Coed
Affiliation or Control: Proprietary IRS Status: Proprietary
Highest Offering: Associate Degree
Accreditation: **ABHES**, SURGT, SURTEC

01 Campus President .... Dr. Himesh LAKHLANI

The College of Health Care Professions-Dallas (D)

8390 Lyndon B. Johnson Fwy, Ste 300, Dallas TX 75243
Telephone: (214) 420-3400 Identification: 770531
Accreditation: **ABHES**

The College of Health Care Professions-Fort Worth (E)

4248 North Freeway, Fort Worth TX 76137
Telephone: (817) 632-5900 Identification: 770532
Accreditation: **ABHES**

The College of Health Care Professions-McAllen (F)

1917 Nolana Avenue, Ste 100, McAllen TX 78504
Telephone: (713) 425-3125 Identification: 770963
Accreditation: **ABHES**

The College of Health Care Professions-San Antonio (G)

4738 Northwest Loop 410, San Antonio TX 78229
Telephone: (210) 298-3600 Identification: 770964
Accreditation: **ABHES**, SURTEC

College of the Mainland (H)

1200 Amburn Road, Texas City TX 77591-2499
County: Galveston FICE Identification: 007096
Unit ID: 226408
Telephone: (409) 933-8271 Carnegie Class: Assoc/MT-VT-High Trad
FAX Number: (409) 933-8010 Calendar System: Semester
URL: www.com.edu
Established: 1966 Annual Undergrad Tuition & Fees (In-District): $1,773
Enrollment: 4,013 Coed
Affiliation or Control: Local IRS Status: 501(c)3
Highest Offering: Associate Degree
Accreditation: **SC**, ADNUR, CAHIIM, EMT, MAC

01 President .... Dr. Warren NICHOLS
05 Int Vice President for Instruction .... Dr. James TEMPLER
10 Vice President for Fiscal Affairs .... Dr. Clen BURTON
32 Vice President for Student Services .... Dr. Vicki STANFIELD
111 Vice Pres Inst Advancement .... Ms. Mary Ann AMELANG
35 Assoc VP Student Success & Conduct .... Ms. Kris KIMBARK
06 Assoc VP for Enrollment/Registrar .... Mrs. Kelly MUSICK
18 Assoc VP Facility Services .... Mr. Charles KING
08 Director Library Services .... Ms. Kathryn PARK
37 Director of Student Financial Svcs .... Mr. Carl GORDON
28 Director of Diversity & Equity .... Ms. Lonica BUSH
96 Director of Purchasing .... Ms. Sonja BLINKA
09 Research Specialist .... Ms. Cheryl YOUNG

Collin County Community College District (I)

3452 Spur 399, McKinney TX 75069
County: Collin FICE Identification: 023614
Unit ID: 247834
Telephone: (972) 758-3805 Carnegie Class: Assoc/HT-Mix Trad/Non
FAX Number: (972) 758-3807 Calendar System: Semester
URL: www.collin.edu
Established: 1985 Annual Undergrad Tuition & Fees (In-District): $1,264
Enrollment: 28,187 Coed
Affiliation or Control: State/Local IRS Status: 501(c)3
Highest Offering: Associate Degree
Accreditation: **SC**, ACFEI, ADNUR, CAHIIM, COARC, DH, EMT, POLYT, SURGT

01 District President .... Dr. H. Neil MATKIN
04 Exec Asst to President/Board Sec .... Ms. Shirley K. HARMON
05 Exec VP/Chief Academic Officer .... Dr. Brenda K. KIHL
20 Sr VP Acad/Workforce/Enroll Svcs .... Dr. Sherry L. SCHUMANN
108 Sr VP Org Effectiveness .... Ms. Kimberly K. DAVISON
10 Dist VP Admin Services & CFO .... Vacant
26 Chief Public Relations Officer .... Mr. Thomas R. DELAMATER
15 VP Human Resources .... Mr. Floyd W. NICKERSON
111 VP Advancement .... Ms. Lisa R. VASQUEZ
103 VP Workforce & Economic Dev .... Dr. Jennifer BLALOCK
20 VP Academic Services .... Dr. Dani R. DAY
32 VP Student & Enrollment Services .... Dr. Albert TEZENO
12 VP/Provost Spring Creek Campus .... Dr. Mary S. MCRAE
12 VP/Provost Preston Ridge Campus .... Dr. Abe JOHNSON
12 VP/Provost Central Park Campus .... Dr. Jon H. HARDESTY
09 Assoc VP Institutional Research .... Dr. Thomas K. MARTIN
21 Assoc VP Financial Svcs & Reporting .... Ms. Barbara A. JOHNSTON
21 Assoc VP Controller/Stdnt Fin Svcs .... Ms. Julie M. BRADLEY
88 Assoc VP P-12 Partnerships .... Mr. Raul J. MARTINEZ
103 Dean Workforce Educ Preston Ridge .... Mr. James N. BARKO
103 Dean Workforce Educ Spring Creek .... Ms. Gaye M. COOKSEY
76 Dean Health Sci/Emergency Svcs .... Mr. Gary B. HODGE
66 Dean Nursing .... Ms. Donna M. HATCH
20 Dean Academic Affairs Central Park .... Ms. Brenda C. CARTER
20 Dean Academic Affairs Preston Ridge .... Ms. Wendy A. GUNDERSON
79 Dean Humanities/Bus Spring Creek .... Dr. Donald L. WEASENFORTH
81 Dean Math & Sciences Spring Creek ... Dr. L. Cameron NEAL, JR.
45 Dean Strategic Initiatives .... Mr. Mark S. GARCIA
84 Dean Student Enrol Svcs Central Pk .... Dr. Alicia L. HUPPE
84 Dean Stdnt Enrol Svcs Spring Creek .... Mr. Douglas G. WILLIS
84 Dean Stdnt Enrol Svcs Preston Ridge .... Ms. Stephanie MEINHARDT
35 Dean of Students .... Mr. Terrence P. BRENNAN
38 Assoc Dean Counseling/Career Svcs .... Dr. Linda R. QUALIA
06 Director of Admissions/Registrar .... Mr. Todd E. FIELDS
13 Assoc VP/Chief Info Sys Officer .... Mr. David R. HOYT
18 Executive Director Facilities .... Mr. William L. KING
19 Chief of Police .... Mr. William F. TAYLOR
08 Exec Dir Central Park Library .... Vacant
08 Exec Dir Preston Ridge Library .... Mr. John C. MULLIN
08 Exec Dir Spring Creek Library .... Ms. Linda A. KYPRIOS
41 Director Athletics .... Dr. Albert TEZENO
96 Director Purchasing .... Ms. Cynthia L. WHITE
37 Director Financial Aid/Vets Affairs .... Mr. Alan D. PIXLEY
88 Director Weekend College .... Mr. Brian L. LENHART
85 Coordinator International Studies .... Vacant

Commonwealth Institute of Funeral Service (J)

415 Barren Springs, Houston TX 77090-5913
County: Harris FICE Identification: 003556
Unit ID: 366261
Telephone: (281) 873-0262 Carnegie Class: Spec 2-yr-A&S
FAX Number: (281) 873-5232 Calendar System: Quarter
URL: www.commonwealth.edu
Established: 1936 Annual Undergrad Tuition & Fees: $12,495
Enrollment: 228 Coed
Affiliation or Control: Independent Non-Profit IRS Status: 501(c)3
Highest Offering: Associate Degree
Accreditation: **FUSER**

01 President/CEO .... Dr. Jason C. ALTIERI
10 Vice President/Treasurer .... Mr. W. Blair WALTRIP
05 Dean of Academic Affairs .... Mr. Stuart MOEN
32 Dean of Students .... Mr. Christopher LAYTON
37 Director Student Financial Aid .... Ms. Marlene PERRY
06 Registrar .... Ms. Patricia MORENO
08 Head Librarian .... Ms. Melissa DAVIS

Concorde Career College (K)

12606 Greenville Avenue, Suite 130, Dallas TX 75243
Telephone: (469) 221-3411 Identification: 770593
Accreditation: **ACCSC**, #COARC, DH, PTAA, SURGT

† Branch campus of Concorde Career College, Aurora, CO

Concorde Career College (L)

4803 NW Loop 410, Suite 200, San Antonio TX 78229
Telephone: (210) 428-2000 Identification: 770594
Accreditation: **ACCSC**, COARC, DH, PTAA

† Branch campus of Concorde Career College, Kansas City, MO

Concorde Career Institute (M)

3015 West I-20, Grand Prairie TX 75052
County: Tarrant FICE Identification: 035423
Unit ID: 441742
Telephone: (469) 348-2500 Carnegie Class: Spec 2-yr-Health
FAX Number: (469) 348-2580 Calendar System: Semester
URL: www.concorde.edu
Established: 1991 Annual Undergrad Tuition & Fees: N/A
Enrollment: 808 Coed
Affiliation or Control: Proprietary IRS Status: Proprietary
Highest Offering: Associate Degree
Accreditation: **ACCSC**, NDT, POLYT, SURGT

01 Campus President .... Mr. Mike LOVEJOY

Concordia University Texas (N)

11400 Concordia University Drive, Austin TX 78726
County: Travis FICE Identification: 003557
Unit ID: 224004
Telephone: (512) 313-3000 Carnegie Class: Masters/L
FAX Number: (512) 313-3999 Calendar System: Semester
URL: www.concordia.edu
Established: 1926 Annual Undergrad Tuition & Fees: $29,260
Enrollment: 2,559 Coed
Affiliation or Control: Lutheran Church - Missouri Synod
IRS Status: 501(c)3
Highest Offering: Doctorate
Accreditation: **SC**, IACBE, NURSE

01 President/CEO .... Dr. Donald CHRISTIAN
04 Executive Asst to Pres/CEO .... Ms. Kathy ARNOLD
05 Provost & Executive VP .... Dr. Kristi KIRK
11 VP Administration & COO .... Ms. Beth ATHERTON
10 Chief Financial Officer .... Ms. Sarah LOGHIN
45 Chief Strategy Officer .... Dr. Shane SOKOLL
42 Campus Pastor .... Rev. Steve FICK
20 AVP Academics .... Dr. Lynette GILLIS
88 Assistant to the Provost .... Dr. Allen BROWN
07 AVP of Admissions .... Ms. Jennielle STROTHER
30 AVP External Relations .... Mr. James CANDIDO
26 AVP Marketing/Communications .... Ms. Lisa KESSLER
18 AVP Facilities Services .... Mr. Dan GREGORY
21 Controller .... Ms. Maria ANAYA
107 Dean Professional Studies .... Vacant
49 Dean Arts & Sciences .... Dr. Carl TROVALL
106 Center Dean Online .... Dr. Alex HERRON
66 Dir School of Nursing Program .... Dr. Kathy LAUCHNER
53 Dir School of Education .... Dr. James MCCONNELL
50 Dir School of Business/Comm .... Dr. Randolph WILT
57 Dir School of Fine Arts .... Dr. Kelly GORDON
81 Dir School of Nat/Applied Sciences .... Dr. Philip SCHIELKE
79 Dir School of Humanities .... Vacant
06 Registrar .... Ms. Connie BERAN
37 Director Student Financial Services .... Mr. Russell JEFFREY
41 Athletic Director .... Ms. Ronda SEAGRAVES
121 Director Student Success Center .... Ms. Ruth COOPER
36 Director Career Center .... Ms. Randa SCOTT
32 AVP Student Life/Dean of Students .... Dr. Elizabeth MEDINA
39 Director of Residential Life .... Mr. Jakob ADAM
08 Director of Library Services .... Ms. Mikail MCINTOSH-DOTY

58 Director MBA Graduate Program .... Dr. Elise BRAZIER
13 Chief Technology Officer .... Mr. Ian VARGA
19 Chief of Police .... Vacant
43 Inside Counsel/Sr Dir Risk & Comp .... Ms. Rachael MARESH
15 AVP Human Resources .... Ms. Angela CLEMENTS
29 Dir Donor & Alumni Relations .... Mr. Jeff FROSCH
102 Dir Foundation Relations .... Ms. Meghann BOLTON
44 Dir Donor Relations .... Ms. Tina HAMILTON
90 Mgr Instructional Technology .... Mr. Joel RAHN
40 Bookstore Manager .... Ms. Jessica BRIGHT
09 Dir Inst Research & Effectiveness .... Dr. Trey BUCHANAN
96 Director Support Services .... Mr. Eric SILBER
105 Web Administrator .... Mr. Bryan GILBERT

Criswell College (A)

4010 Gaston Avenue, Dallas TX 75246-1537
County: Dallas FICE Identification: 041218
Unit ID: 475608
Telephone: (214) 821-5433 Carnegie Class: Not Classified
FAX Number: (214) 370-0497 Calendar System: Semester
URL: www.criswell.edu
Established: 1970 Annual Undergrad Tuition & Fees: $8,950
Enrollment: 305 Coed
Affiliation or Control: Independent Non-Profit IRS Status: 501(c)3
Highest Offering: Master's
Accreditation: SC

01 President .... Barry CREAMER
05 Vice President Academic Affairs .... Joseph WOODDELL
10 Chief Business Officer/VP Finance .... Kevin STILLEY
84 Vice Pres Enrollment Services .... Russell MARRIOTT
111 Vice Pres Advancement .... Michael CLAYTON
100 Chief of Staff .... Daisy REYNOLDS

Culinary Institute LeNotre (B)

7070 Allensby Street, Houston TX 77022-4322
County: Harris FICE Identification: 037233
Unit ID: 444565
Telephone: (713) 692-0077 Carnegie Class: Spec 2-yr-A&S
FAX Number: (713) 692-7399 Calendar System: Other
URL: www.culinaryinstitute.edu
Established: 1998 Annual Undergrad Tuition & Fees: $15,938
Enrollment: 421 Coed
Affiliation or Control: Proprietary IRS Status: Proprietary
Highest Offering: Associate Degree
Accreditation: ACCSC, ACFEI

01 School Director .... Isabel OLIVAS

Culinary Institute of America San Antonio (C)

312 Pearl Parkway, Bldg 3, San Antonio TX 78215
Telephone: (210) 554-6400 Identification: 770131
Accreditation: &M

† Branch campus of The Culinary Institute of America, Hyde Park, NY

Dallas Baptist University (D)

3000 Mountain Creek Parkway, Dallas TX 75211-9299
County: Dallas FICE Identification: 003560
Unit ID: 224226
Telephone: (214) 333-7100 Carnegie Class: DU-Mod
FAX Number: (214) 333-5447 Calendar System: 4/1/4
URL: www.dbu.edu
Established: 1898 Annual Undergrad Tuition & Fees: $26,180
Enrollment: 5,319 Coed
Affiliation or Control: Baptist IRS Status: 501(c)3
Highest Offering: Doctorate
Accreditation: SC, ACBSP, CEA, MUS

00 Chancellor .... Dr. Gary COOK
01 President .... Dr. Adam WRIGHT
04 Assistant to the President .... Mrs. Alyssa FURR
46 Vice Pres for Executive Affairs .... Dr. Norma HEDIN
10 Vice President Financial Affairs .... Dr. Matt MURRAH
05 Provost .... Dr. Denny DOWD
11 Vice President for Admin Affairs .... Mr. Jonathan TEAT
84 Vice President for Enrollment .... Dr. Cory HINES
32 Vice President for Student Affairs .... Dr. Jay HARLEY
26 Vice President for Communications .. Dr. Blake KILLINGSWORTH
111 Vice President for Advancement .... Mr. Jeff JOHNSON
85 Vice Pres for International Affairs .... Mr. Randy BYERS
20 Associate Provost .... Mrs. Deemie NAUGLE
20 Asst Provost/Director Hybrid Educ .... Dr. Mark HALE
20 Academic Dean .... Dr. Gail LINAM
06 Registrar .... Ms. Linda RONEY
35 Dean of Students .... Mr. Dan GIBSON
42 Dean of Spiritual Life .... Mr. John BORUM
58 Dean of Cook School of Leadership .... Dr. Jack GOODYEAR
50 Dean College of Business .... Dr. Dale SIMS
81 Dean College Natural Science & Math .... Dr. Dionisio FLEITAS
53 Dean College of Education .... Dr. Neil DUGGER
57 Dean College of Fine Arts .... Mr. Ron BOWLES
73 Dean College of Christian Faith .... Dr. Steve MULLEN
79 Dean Col Humanities/Social Sciences .... Dr. Rob SULLIVAN
88 Dean College Professional Studies .... Mr. Jeremy VICKERS
120 Director of Online Education .... Mr. Matt WINN
114 Asst VP for Financial Affairs .... Mr. Danny HASSETT
21 Director of Financial Affairs .... Mr. Matthew STREETT
21 Controller .... Mrs. Mendi MCMAHAN
37 Acting Director of Financial Aid .... Mr. Justin SILCOX
113 Dir of Student Account Services .... Mr. Max BUSSE
07 Assoc Vice Pres for Enrollment .... Mr. Jason WILLIAMS
14 Director of Information Technology .... Mr. Weston SCHUBERT
90 Dir of Customer Service/Info Tech .... Mr. Michael STEWART
105 Web Developer .... Mrs. Anu CHIVUKULA
29 Director of Alumni Relations .... Mrs. Janae GIBSON
08 Interim Director of Library .... Mr. Scott JEFFRIES
15 Director of Human Resources .... Mrs. Tamy ROGERS
43 General Counsel .... Vacant
85 Dir Intl Admissions & Immigration .... Mr. Timothy WATTS
85 Director of Intl Student Services .... Mrs. Susie CASSEL
41 Director of Athletics .... Mr. Connor SMITH
122 Director of Student Life .... Mr. Jacob WINSLAGER
121 Director of Student Success .... Mrs. Molly TAYLOR
36 Director of Career Services .... Mrs. Marion HILL-HUBBARD
38 Dir Counseling & Spiritual Care .... Dr. Jordan DAVIS
27 Director of Marketing .... Mrs. Layna EVANS
39 Director of University Housing .... Mr. Zach BEAN
24 Director of Media Services .... Mr. Rob LEWIS
19 Chief of University Police .... Mr. John SHAW
19 Director of Campus Security .... Mr. Donald KABETZKE
108 Coord Institutional Effectiveness .... Mrs. Carol REID
09 Coord of Institutional Research .... Mrs. Pam NEUMANN
88 Academic Projects Administrator .... Ms. Lou ESPARZA
40 Manager Bookstore .... Mr. Cole MARTIN

Dallas Christian College (E)

2700 Christian Parkway, Dallas TX 75234-7299
County: Dallas FICE Identification: 006941
Unit ID: 224244
Telephone: (972) 241-3371 Carnegie Class: Spec-4-yr-Faith
FAX Number: (972) 241-8021 Calendar System: 4/1/4
URL: www.dallas.edu
Established: 1950 Annual Undergrad Tuition & Fees: $17,454
Enrollment: 316 Coed
Affiliation or Control: Christian Churches And Churches of Christ
IRS Status: 501(c)3
Highest Offering: Baccalaureate
Accreditation: BI

01 President .... Dr. Brian D. SMITH
05 Interim VP for Academic Affairs .... Mr. Bruce LONG
84 VP for Enrollment Management .... Mr. Mac INGMIRE
111 VP for Institutional Advancement .... Mr. Mark WORLEY
10 VP of Finance & Operations .... Ms. Andrea SHORT
108 Dir Institutional Effectiveness .... Mr. Bruce LONG
06 Registrar .... Mrs. Crystal LAIDACKER
37 Dir of Student Financial Svcs .... Ms. Breanda GILLASPIE
18 Director of Facilities .... Mr. Gary ADAMS
04 Executive Assistant to the Pres .... Ms. Dottie FARLEY
08 Director of Library Services .... Ms. Jane REYNOLDS

*Dallas County Community College District Office (F)

1601 South Lamar Street, Dallas TX 75215
County: Dallas FICE Identification: 009331
Unit ID: 224253
Telephone: (214) 378-1601 Carnegie Class: N/A
FAX Number: (214) 378-1810
URL: www.dcccd.edu

01 Chancellor .... Dr. Joe D. MAY
05 Interim Vice Chanc Educ Policy .... Ms. Anna MAYS
100 Exec Vice Chanc/Chief of Staff .... Dr. Justin LONON
103 Vice Chanc Workforce/EconDev .... Mr. Mark HAYS
88 Exec Dist Dir WF Educ & Compliance .... Mr. Don PERRY
18 Asc Vice Chanc Facil Mgmt/Architect .... Mr. Clyde PORTER
43 District General Counsel .... Mr. Robert WENDLAND
86 Assoc VChanc of Public/Govt Affairs .... Mr. Isaac FAZ
15 Chief Talent Officer .... Mrs. Susan HALL
45 Chief Strategy Officer .... Ms. Mary BRUMBACH
96 Director of Purchasing .... Mr. Steve PARK
10 Chief Financial Officer .... Mr. John ROBERTSON
13 Chief Innovation Officer (CIO) .... Dr. Tim MARSHALL
09 Director of Institutional Research .... Dr. Richard PLOTT
101 Board Relations Executive .... Ms. Perla MOLINA
102 Exec Director DCCCD Foundation .... Mrs. Pyeper WILKINS
88 Dist Director Internet Publishing .... Mrs. Georgeann MOSS
19 Chief Public Safety & Security .... Ms. Lauretta HILL
26 Dist Director Marketing & Comm .... Mrs. Kathy COOK
37 Exec Dist Director Financial Aid .... Ms. Cynthia BUTLER

*Brookhaven College (G)

3939 Valley View, Dallas TX 75244-4997
County: Dallas FICE Identification: 021002
Unit ID: 223524
Telephone: (972) 860-4700 Carnegie Class: Assoc/HT-High Non
FAX Number: (972) 860-4897 Calendar System: Semester
URL: www.brookhavencollege.edu
Established: 1978 Annual Undergrad Tuition & Fees (In-District): $1,770
Enrollment: 10,553 Coed
Affiliation or Control: State/Local IRS Status: 501(c)3
Highest Offering: Associate Degree
Accreditation: SC, ADNUR, ART, EMT, RAD

02 President .... Dr. Thom D. CHESNEY
05 Vice President of Academic Affairs .... Mr. Donald SMITH
10 Vice President of Business Services .... Mr. George HERRING
32 Vice Pres Student Dev/Enroll Mgmt .... Mr. Oscar LOPEZ
04 Exec Assistant to President .... Ms. Edna LOVE
50 Exec Dean Business Studies .... Mr. Sandy WYCHE
103 Assoc VP Workforce/Continuing Educ .... Mr. Vernon L. HAWKINS
30 Assoc Vice Pres Development .... Ms. Marilyn K. LYNCH
45 Exec Dean Educational Resources .... Ms. Sarah FERGUSON
57 Exec Dean Fine Arts/Physical Educ .... Mr. Rick MAXWELL
81 Exec Dean Science/Math .... Dr. Kathryn WETZEL
23 Exec Dean of Health/Human Svcs .... Dr. Juanita FLINT
09 Exec Dir Plng/Rsrch/Inst Effective .... Dr. Michael DENNEHY
13 Director Information Technology .... Mr. Michael DEASON
83 Exec Dean Social Sci/Distance Lrng .... Mr. Sam GOVEA
26 Executive Dean Communications .... Mrs. Kendra VAGLIENTI
84 Exec Dean Stdnt Success/Enroll Svcs .... Ms. Brenda DALTON
27 Asst Dir Marketing & Public Info .... Vacant
07 Director of Admissions/Registrar .... Ms. Thoa Hoang VO
41 Director of Athletics .... Vacant
21 Director of Business Operations .... Ms. Willadean MARTIN
36 Director Career Services .... Ms. Dominica MCCARTHY
88 Dir Brookhaven Geotech Institute .... Ms. Melanie GAMBLE
18 Director of Facilities .... Vacant
15 Exec Dir of Human Resources .... Ms. Terri EDRICH
35 Admin Office of Student Life .... Mr. Brian BORSKI
19 Captain of College Police .... Vacant
04 Assistant to President .... Ms. Carrie SCHWEITZER

*Cedar Valley College (H)

3030 N Dallas Avenue, Lancaster TX 75134-3799
County: Dallas FICE Identification: 003561
Unit ID: 223773
Telephone: (972) 860-8201 Carnegie Class: Assoc/MT-VT-High Non
FAX Number: (972) 682-7075 Calendar System: Semester
URL: www.cedarvalleycollege.edu
Established: 1974 Annual Undergrad Tuition & Fees (In-District): $1,770
Enrollment: 5,635 Coed
Affiliation or Control: State/Local IRS Status: 501(c)3
Highest Offering: Associate Degree
Accreditation: SC

02 President .... Dr. Joseph SEABROOKS
05 Vice President for Instruction .... Ms. Audra BARRETT
32 VP Student Services/Enrollment Mgmt .... Dr. Karen LALJIANI
10 Vice President Business Services .... Mr. Huan LUONG
81 Executive Dean Math/Science/Health .... Mr. Eddy RAWLINSON
49 Executive Dean Liberal Arts .... Dr. Solomon CROSS
50 Exec Dean Bus/Science/Technology .... Dr. Ruben JOHNSON
20 Int Dean Instr Supp Distance Educ ...... Dr. Maria BOCCALANDRO
51 Executive Dean Cmty & Resource Dev .... Mrs. Patricia DAVIS
35 Dean Student Support Services .... Ms. Grenna ROLLINGS
84 Exec Dean Student/Enrollment Svcs .... Ms. Jarlene DECAY
08 Director Library Services .... Ms. Vidya KRISHNASWAMY
09 Dir Inst Research/Effectiveness .... Ms. Nicole NAAN
07 Asst Director of Admissions .... Ms. Lucia JOHNSON
18 Director Facilities Management .... Mrs. Cindy A. ROGERS
26 Assoc Dir Marketing/Public Rela .... Mr. Henry MARTINEZ
15 Executive Director Human Resources .... Ms. Mary MALLARD
37 Director of Financial Aid .... Vacant
36 Career Services Coordinator .... Ms. Lathera ADDISON
06 Associate Registrar .... Ms. Megan DEAL
29 Director Alumni Relations .... Ms. Patricia DAVIS
21 Assoc Director of Business Services .... Ms. Susan PIERCE

*Eastfield College (I)

3737 Motley Drive, Mesquite TX 75150-2099
County: Dallas FICE Identification: 008510
Unit ID: 224572
Telephone: (972) 860-7100 Carnegie Class: Assoc/MT-VT-High Non
FAX Number: (972) 860-8373 Calendar System: Semester
URL: www.eastfieldcollege.edu
Established: 1970 Annual Undergrad Tuition & Fees (In-District): $1,770
Enrollment: 12,498 Coed
Affiliation or Control: State/Local IRS Status: 170(c)1
Highest Offering: Associate Degree
Accreditation: SC

02 President .... Dr. Jean L. CONWAY
05 Exec VP Academic Affairs .... Mr. Michael J. GUTIERREZ
10 VP Business Services .... Dr. Adrian H. DOUGLAS
15 Exec Director Human Resources .... Mr. Larry L. WILSON
32 Exec Dean Student Development .... Mr. Paul M. GOERTEMILLER
35 Executive Dean Student Services .... Ms. Mayra OLIVARES-URUETA
12 Exec Dir Pleasant Grove Campus .... Mr. Javier E. OLGUIN
09 Director Institutional Research .... Mr. Ricardo RODRIGUEZ
20 Assoc VP Academic Affairs .... Ms. Rachel B. WOLF
103 Associate Dean of Workforce Dev .... Mr. Johnnie O. BELLAMY
81 Executive Dean STEM .... Vacant
83 Executive Dean Social Sciences .... Dr. Michael D. WALKER
103 Director Workforce Devel .... Mrs. Christa K. JONES
08 Executive Dean Library .... Ms. Karla J. GREER
20 Assoc VP Academic Affairs .... Dr. Kimberly M. LOWRY
57 Exec Dean Arts and Communications .... Ms. Courtney CARTER-HARBOUR
21 Exec Dean of Financial Affairs .... Ms. Heidi M. BASSETT
18 Director Facilities Management .... Mr. Michael BRANTLEY
45 Dean Planning/Research/Inst Effect ... Dr. Kimberly K. CHANDLER
46 Dean Resource Development ..... Dr. Tricia THOMAS-ANDERSON
51 Exec Dean Continuing Education .... Ms. Judith C. DUMONT
26 Director of Marketing .... Ms. Donielle R. JOHNSON
106 Dean Inst Support & Distance Educ .... Mr. Abuzafar M. BASHET

27 Associate Director College Comm ... Ms. Sharon L. COOK
07 Exec Dean Student & Enrollment ... Mr. Robert C. HARPER
88 Assoc Dean Educational Resources ... Ms. Lucinda A. GONZALES
88 Associate Dean Police Academy ... Mr. James R. STEWART
81 Associate Dean STEM ... Ms. Amy M. VANCE

*El Centro College (A)

801 Main Street, Dallas TX 75202-3604
County: Dallas FICE Identification: 004453
Unit ID: 224615
Telephone: (214) 860-2000 Carnegie Class: Assoc/MT-VT-High Non
FAX Number: (214) 860-2335 Calendar System: Semester
URL: www.elcentrocollege.edu
Established: 1966 Annual Undergrad Tuition & Fees (In-District): $1,770
Enrollment: 9,002 Coed
Affiliation or Control: State/Local IRS Status: 501(c)3
Highest Offering: Associate Degree
Accreditation: SC, ACFEI, ADNUR, COARC, CVT, DH, DMS, EMT, MAC, MLTAD, PNUR, RAD, SURGT

02 President ... Dr. Jose ADAMES
05 VP Academic Affairs ... Dr. Charles MORRIS
32 VP of Student Svcs & Enrollment ... Dr. Chemene L. CRAWFORD
10 Interim VP Business Services ... Ms. Lenora REECE
30 Manager of Development ... Ms. Paige BLUEJACKET
17 Int Exec Dean/Health & Legal Stds ... Mr. Ceaser ESPINOZA
88 Exec Dean Academic Transfer ... Dr. Anthony MANSUETO
81 Exec Dean STEM ... Ms. Beth STALL
50 Exec Dean Bus/Des/Pub Svc ... Ms. Sherry JONES
103 Exec Dean Workforce/Cont Educ ... Vacant
106 Dean Instruct Innovation/Acad Sup ... Ms. Karla DAMRON
108 Dean Curriculum Assessment ... Ms. Karen MONGO
09 Dean Institutional Effectiveness ... Ms. Teresa S. ISBELL
35 Dean Student Support Services ... Ms. Karen ROYSTER
121 Dean Student Success ... Mr. Cornelius JOHNSON
08 Asst Dean Educational Resources ... Dr. Norman HOWDEN
07 Assoc Dean Enroll Services ... Ms. Rebecca J. GARZA
12 Exec Director West Campus ... Ms. Kathy ACOSTA
15 Exec Director Human Resources ... Ms. Dawn M. SEGROVES
19 College Director College Police ... Mr. Joseph HANNIGAN
26 Dir Marketing/Communications ... Ms. Priscilla A. STALEY
18 Col Director Facilities Services ... Mr. Jeremy MCCLELLAND
21 Dir Business Operations ... Ms. Keisha FARRINGTON
37 Dir Student Financial Aid ... Ms. Pam A. LUCAS
13 Director Information Technology ... Mr. Michael C. JOHNSON
85 Director College Programs ... Mr. Robert G. REYES
36 Pgm Svcs Coord Career Services ... Ms. Christol JOHNSON
38 Licensed Psychologist ... Dr. Katherine WOODS
04 Administrative Asst to President ... Ms. Ida KELLER
40 Manager Bookstore ... Mr. Richard SCHLEIFFER

*Mountain View College (B)

4849 W Illinois Avenue, Dallas TX 75211-6599
County: Dallas FICE Identification: 008503
Unit ID: 226930
Telephone: (214) 860-8680 Carnegie Class: Assoc/HT-High Non
FAX Number: (214) 860-8521 Calendar System: Semester
URL: www.mountainviewcollege.edu
Established: 1970 Annual Undergrad Tuition & Fees (In-District): $1,770
Enrollment: 8,539 Coed
Affiliation or Control: State/Local IRS Status: 501(c)3
Highest Offering: Associate Degree
Accreditation: SC

02 President ... Dr. Robert GARZA
05 Vice President of Instruction ... Dr. Lori DODDY
32 VP Student Svcs/Enrollment Mgmt ... Dr. Leonard GARRETT
10 Vice President of Business Services ... Dr. Sharon DAVIS
84 Exec Dean Student Support Svcs ... Mr. Matthew SANCHEZ
90 Exec Dean Curriculum & Instruction ... Dr. Karen VALENCIA
45 Dean Education Center/Dir Title V ... Vacant
06 Assoc Dean Admission/Enrollment ... Ms. Glenda GARRETT
18 Director Facilities Services ... Mr. Allan KNOTT
09 Dir of Planning/Research & IE ... Ms. Iva BERGERON
35 Director of Student Life ... Ms. Cathy EDWARDS
103 Exec Dean of Workforce/Cont Educ ... Ms. Pat WEBB
26 Director Public Info/Marketing ... Ms. Jill LAIN
21 Director of Business Operations ... Mr. Jose RODRIGUEZ
15 Exec Director Human Resources ... Mr. Jarred DAVIS
36 Director Career Development ... Ms. Regina GARNER
45 Dean Resource Development ... Ms. Heather A. MARSH
04 Administrative Asst to President ... Ms. Brenda EPPERSON
08 Head Librarian ... Ms. Jean BAKER
41 Athletic Director ... Mr. Keith MCKINNON

*North Lake College (C)

5001 N MacArthur Boulevard, Irving TX 75038-3899
County: Dallas FICE Identification: 020774
Unit ID: 227191
Telephone: (972) 273-3000 Carnegie Class: Assoc/HT-High Non
FAX Number: (972) 273-3014 Calendar System: Semester
URL: www.dcccd.edu
Established: 1977 Annual Undergrad Tuition & Fees (In-District): $1,770
Enrollment: 9,871 Coed
Affiliation or Control: State/Local IRS Status: 501(c)3
Highest Offering: Associate Degree
Accreditation: SC, CONST

02 President ... Dr. Christa SLEJKO
05 Vice President Academic Affairs ... Dr. Shawnda FLOYD
103 VP Workforce Education ... Dr. Paul KELEMEN
10 Interim Vice Pres Business Services ... Dr. Eddie TEALER
45 Vice Pres Planning & Development ... Ms. Candace CASTILLO
84 VP Stdnt Svcs/Enrollment Mgmt ... Ms. Mary CIMINELLI
88 Director of Learning Resources ... Mr. Kent SEAVER
07 Director Admissions & Registration ... Ms. Francyenne MAYNARD
26 Director Marketing & Public Info ... Ms. Gina FEDERER
12 Ex Director North and South Campus ... Mr. Arthur JAMES
08 Head Librarian ... Dr. Enrique CHAMBERLAIN
18 Director Facilities Services ... Mr. John WATSON
19 Director Campus Police ... Mr. Randy REED
88 Int Director of Decision Support ... Ms. Peggy SINDELAR
15 Director Human Resources ... Mr. Willie NEAL
21 Director Business Operations ... Ms. Elsy CARRANZA
32 Dir Student Programs/Resources ... Ms. Beth NIKOPOULOS
103 Director Workforce Dev/CE ... Mr. Tim SAMUELS
83 Executive Dean Liberal Arts ... Dr. Kristopher COPELAND
81 Exec Dean Math/Science ... Dr. Matthew DEMPSEY
50 Exe Dean Arts/Bus/Sports Sci Tech ... Dr. David EVANS
12 Exec Dean West Campus ... Mr. Mike COOLEY
04 Administrative Asst to President ... Ms. Kari ANDREWS
41 Athletic Director ... Mr. Greg SOMMERS

*Richland College (D)

12800 Abrams Road, Dallas TX 75243-2199
County: Dallas FICE Identification: 008504
Unit ID: 227766
Telephone: (972) 238-6194 Carnegie Class: Assoc/HT-High Non
FAX Number: (972) 238-6978 Calendar System: Semester
URL: www.rlc.dcccd.edu
Established: 1972 Annual Undergrad Tuition & Fees (In-District): $1,770
Enrollment: 16,687 Coed
Affiliation or Control: State/Local IRS Status: 501(c)3
Highest Offering: Associate Degree
Accreditation: SC, MAC

02 President ... Dr. Kathryn K. EGGLESTON
04 Dean/Exec Assistant to President ... Ms. Janet C. JAMES
05 Exec VP Acad Affs & Stdnt Success ... Vacant
10 VP for Business Services ... Mr. Ron M. CLARK
84 Assoc VP Enrollment/Supt RCHS ... Ms. Donna WALKER
50 Exec Dean Sch of Engr/Business/Tech ... Ms. Martha A. HOGAN
79 Exec Dean Human/Fine & Perf Arts ... Ms. Diane HILBERT
81 Exec Dean of Math/Science/Hlth Prof ... Dr. Raymond P. CANHAM
09 Assoc VP Plng/Rsrch/Inst Effect ... Ms. Fonda L. VERA
60 Exec Dean World Lang/Cultures/Comm ... Ms. Susan E. BARKLEY
88 Inst Dean Lrng Enrich & Acad Dev ... Mr. Thales GEORGIOU
83 Inst Dean School of Social Science ... Dr. LaQueta WRIGHT
06 Registrar ... Vacant
41 Director Athletic Programs ... Mr. Guy SIMMONS
32 Director of Student Life ... Ms. Erin LEWIS
08 Dean Educational Services ... Ms. Laura MCKINNON
26 Dir College Comm and Marketing ... Ms. Whitney ROSENBALM
18 Director of Facilities Services ... Mr. Kenneth DUNSON
15 Executive Director Human Resources ... Dr. Bill DIAL
19 Chief of College Police ... Mr. Robert D. BAKER
88 Principal Richland Collegiate HS ... Mr. Craig HINKLE

Dallas Institute of Funeral Service (E)

3909 S Buckner Boulevard, Dallas TX 75227-4314
County: Dallas FICE Identification: 010761
Unit ID: 224271
Telephone: (214) 388-5466 Carnegie Class: Spec 2-yr-A&S
FAX Number: (214) 388-0316 Calendar System: Quarter
URL: www.dallasinstitute.edu
Established: 1945 Annual Undergrad Tuition & Fees: $11,170
Enrollment: 145 Coed
Affiliation or Control: Independent Non-Profit IRS Status: 501(c)3
Highest Offering: Associate Degree
Accreditation: FUSER

01 President ... Mr. James M. SHOEMAKE

Dallas Nursing Institute (F)

12170 North Abrams Road, Suite 125, Dallas TX 75243
County: Dallas FICE Identification: 034165
Unit ID: 437732
Telephone: (469) 941-8300 Carnegie Class: Spec 2-yr-Health
FAX Number: (214) 575-9090 Calendar System: Semester
URL: www.dni.edu
Established: 1991 Annual Undergrad Tuition & Fees: N/A
Enrollment: 211 Coed
Affiliation or Control: Proprietary IRS Status: Proprietary
Highest Offering: Baccalaureate
Accreditation: ABHES

01 Executive Director ... Dr. Charlita SHELTON
32 Director of Student Affairs ... Ms. Brigit MATTIX

Dallas Theological Seminary (G)

3909 Swiss Avenue, Dallas TX 75204-6493
County: Dallas FICE Identification: 003562
Unit ID: 224305
Telephone: (214) 887-5000 Carnegie Class: Spec-4-yr-Faith
FAX Number: (214) 887-5532 Calendar System: Semester
URL: www.dts.edu
Established: 1924 Annual Graduate Tuition & Fees: N/A
Enrollment: 2,132 Coed
Affiliation or Control: Independent Non-Profit IRS Status: 501(c)3
Highest Offering: Doctorate; No Undergraduates
Accreditation: SC, THEOL

01 President ... Dr. Mark L. BAILEY
05 Vice Pres Academic Affs/Acad Dean ... Dr. Mark M. YARBROUGH
32 VP for Student Life & Dean of Stdnt ... Dr. George HILLMAN
10 Vice President Business & Finance ... Mr. Dale C. LARSON
111 Vice President for Advancement ... Ms. Kimberly B. TILL
11 Vice President Campus Operations ... Mr. Robert F. RIGGS
26 Exec Dir Communications/Ed Tech ... Mr. John C. DYER
102 President Dallas Sem Foundation ... Mr. Stephen M. GOLDING
108 Dean of Assessment ... Vacant
20 Dean of Academic Administration ... Dr. James H. THAMES
12 Dean of DTS Houston ... Dr. Bruce W. FONG
58 Director of PhD Studies ... Dr. Richard A. TAYLOR
58 Director of DMin Studies ... Dr. D. Scott BARFOOT
09 Dir of Institutional Effectiveness ... Mr. David HIONIDES
06 Registrar ... Mr. Billy R. TODD, JR.
88 Exec Dir of Leadership Center ... Dr. Bill HENDRICKS
88 Exec Dir of Cultural Engagement ... Dr. Darrell L. BOCK
07 Director of Admissions ... Mr. Nate MCKANNA
08 Library Director ... Mr. Marvin T. HUNN, II
29 Dean of Enrollment/Alumni Services ... Mr. Gregory A. HATTEBERG
36 Director of Placement ... Dr. Paul E. PETTIT
24 Director of Audio/Visual Support ... Mr. James W. HOOVER
42 Campus Pastor ... Dr. Joe ALLEN
34 Adviser to Women Students ... Ms. Lynn Etta G. MANNING
93 Adviser to African-American Studnts ... Dr. Terrance S. WOODSON
13 Director of Information Technology ... Mr. Kevin COX
19 Chief of Campus Police ... Mr. John S. BLOOM
39 Director of Housing & Food Services ... Mr. Drew H. WILLIAMS
106 Dir Online and External Studies ... Mr. Robert M. ABEGG
88 Director of Online Chinese Studies ... Dr. Samuel CHIA
38 Director of Counseling Services ... Dr. Kelly CHEATHAM
21 Controller ... Ms. Patricia MAYABB
40 Bookstore Manager ... Mr. Kevin D. STERN
85 International Student Adviser ... Ms. Rachel O'BRIEN
04 Administrative Asst to President ... Ms. Michelle B. SCHIWIETZ
15 Director Human Resources ... Ms. Karen G. HOLDER
91 Director AdministrativeTechnology ... Mr. Gary HOYER
105 Director Web Development ... Mr. John C. DYER
101 Admin Coordinator for Board Mtgs ... Ms. Margaret TOLLIVER

Del Mar College (H)

101 Baldwin Blvd., Corpus Christi TX 78404-3897
County: Nueces FICE Identification: 003563
Unit ID: 224350
Telephone: (361) 698-1200 Carnegie Class: Assoc/MT-VT-High Trad
FAX Number: (361) 698-1559 Calendar System: Semester
URL: www.delmar.edu
Established: 1935 Annual Undergrad Tuition & Fees (In-District): $2,546
Enrollment: 10,852 Coed
Affiliation or Control: Local IRS Status: 501(c)3
Highest Offering: Associate Degree
Accreditation: SC, ACFEI, ADNUR, ART, CAHIIM, COARC, DA, DH, DMS, EMT, MLTAD, MUS, #OTA, PTAA, RAD, SURGT, THEA

01 President ... Dr. Mark ESCAMILLA
43 General Counsel ... Mr. Augustin RIVERA, JR.
05 Provost/VP for Academic Affairs ... Dr. Beth LEWIS
32 Vice President for Student Affairs ... Dr. Rito SILVA
10 Int Chief Financial Officer ... Dr. Cathy WEST
103 VP Workforce Dev/Strategic Init ... Ms. Lenora KEAS
26 Exec Dir Strategic Communications ... Ms. Claudia JACKSON
30 Exec Director of Development ... Ms. Mary MCQUEEN
07 Dean Student Outreach/Enroll Svcs ... Ms. Patricia BENAVIDES-DOMINGUEZ
124 Dean Student Engagement & Retention ... Ms. Cheryl SANDERS
49 Dean Division Arts & Sciences ... Dr. Jonda HALCOMB
17 Dean Health Sciences & Prof ... Dr. Shannon YDOYAGA
75 Dean Bus/Ind/Public Safety ... Mr. Charles MCKINNY
51 Dean CE & Off Campus Programs ... Dr. Leonard RIVERA
88 Dean Workforce Pgms/Corporate Svcs ... Mr. Daniel KORUS
15 Exec Director HR & Administration ... Ms. Tammy MCDONALD
21 Comptroller ... Mr. John J. JOHNSON
96 Director of Purchasing/Business Svc ... Mr. David DAVILA
13 Chief Information Officer ... Mr. August ALFONSO
19 Chief of Security ... Ms. Lauren WHITE
88 Dir Environmental/Health/Safety ... Mr. Kelly L. WHITE
37 Director of Financial Aid ... Ms. Nancy M. BRISENO
06 Registrar ... Ms. Elizabeth ADAMSON
32 Dir Student Leadership/Campus Life ... Ms. Beverly CAGE
113 Dir of Financial Services/Bursar ... Ms. D'Ann POLAND
08 Int Director of Libraries ... Ms. Sally BICKLEY
09 Director of Institutional Research ... Mr. Sushil PALLEMONI
16 Director of Human Resources ... Mr. Jerry W. HENRY
88 Director of Payroll ... Ms. Katrina GARCIA

DeVry University - Irving Campus (I)

4800 Regent Boulevard, Ste 200, Irving TX 75063-2439
Telephone: (972) 929-6777 FICE Identification: 010139
Accreditation: &NH, ENGT

† Regional accreditation is carried under the parent institution in Downers Grove, IL.

East Texas Baptist University (J)

One Tiger Drive, Marshall TX 75670-1498
County: Harrison FICE Identification: 003564
Unit ID: 224527

Telephone: (903) 935-7963 Carnegie Class: Bac-Diverse
FAX Number: (903) 938-7798 Calendar System: Semester
URL: www.etbu.edu
Established: 1912 Annual Undergrad Tuition & Fees: $24,700
Enrollment: 1,308 Coed
Affiliation or Control: Baptist IRS Status: 501(c)3
Highest Offering: Master's
Accreditation: SC, #CAATE, MUS, NURSE

01 President .... Dr. J. Blair BLACKBURN
05 Provost/Vice Pres Academic Affairs .... Dr. Thomas SANDERS
10 Sr Vice Pres Financial Affairs .... Mr. Ned CALVERT
84 Vice Pres Enrollment/Admin Affairs .... Mr. Kevin CAFFEY
111 Vice Pres University Advancement .... Dr. Scott BRYANT
32 Vice President for Student Affairs .... Dr. Heather HADLOCK
41 Vice President for Athletics .... Mr. Ryan ERWIN
20 Assistant Provost for Acad Affairs .... Dr. Emily PREVOST
110 Assoc Vice Pres Univ Advancement .... Mrs. Allison PETEET
21 Assoc Vice Pres for Financial Serv .... Mr. Lee FERGUSON
09 Dean Acad Services & Inst Research .... Dr. Marty WARREN
107 Dean School of Professional Studies .... Dr. Joseph BROWN
53 Dean School of Education .... Dr. John SARGENT
88 Dean School of Christian Studies .... Dr. John HARRIS
83 Dean School of Nat/Soc Sciences .... Dr. Lynn NEW
50 Dean School of Business .... Dr. Barry EVANS
79 Dean School of Humanities .... Dr. Jerry SUMMERS
57 Dean School of Comm & Perf Arts .... Dr. Tom WEBSTER
106 Dean of Online Learning .... Dr. Colleen HALUPA
66 Dean School of Nursing .... Dr. Rebekah GRIGSBY
55 Director for Adult Education .... Mr. Vince BLANKENSHIP
35 Dean of Students .... Mr. Blair PREVOST
07 Director of Admissions .... Mrs. Meredith PALMER
13 Director of Inst Technology .... Mr. Barry HALE
08 Director of Library .... Ms. Cynthia PETERSON
26 Director of Public Relations/Mktg .... Ms. Becky DAVIS
37 Director of Financial Aid .... Mr. Nathan FLORY
88 Director Baptist Student Ministry .... Mr. Mark YATES
40 Director of Bookstore .... Ms. Karan SUSTAIRE
18 Director of Physical Operations .... Mr. Stephen RATCLIFF
85 Dir Global Educ/Grt Commission Ctr .... Dr. Lisa SEELEY
121 Director of Student Success .... Mrs. Kelley PAUL
11 Director of University Operations .... Mr. Chris CRAWFORD
19 Director of Security/Safety .... Mr. Larry NORTHCUTT
123 Director of Graduate Admissions .... Mr. Den MURLEY
39 Director of Res Life/Student Hsg .... Ms. Lauren MOORE
88 Director of Student Activities .... Ms. Madison KAUFFMAN
06 University Registrar .... Mr. Troy WHITE
42 Chaplain/Dir of Campus Ministry .... Dr. Scott STEVENS

El Paso Community College (A)

P.O. Box 20500, El Paso TX 79998
County: El Paso FICE Identification: 010387
Unit ID: 224642
Telephone: (915) 831-2000 Carnegie Class: Assoc/HT-High Trad
FAX Number: N/A Calendar System: Semester
URL: www.epcc.edu
Established: 1969 Annual Undergrad Tuition & Fees (In-District): $2,746
Enrollment: 28,764 Coed
Affiliation or Control: Local IRS Status: 501(c)3
Highest Offering: Associate Degree
Accreditation: SC, ADNUR, CAHIIM, COARC, DA, DH, DMS, EMT, MAC, MLTAD, PTAA, RAD, SURGT

01 President .... Dr. William SERRATA
05 Vice President Instruction .... Mr. Steve SMITH
11 Vice Pres Financial and Admin Ops . Ms. Josette SHAUGHNESSY
13 Vice Pres Information Tech/CIO .... Dr. Jenny GIRON
32 Int Vice President Student Services .... Mr. Raul H. LERMA
10 AVP Budget and Financial Svcs .... Mr. Fernando FLORES
20 AVP Instruction and Student Success .... Dr. Julie PENLEY
103 AVP Workforce and CE .... Dr. Jaime FARIAS
15 Assoc VP Employee Relations .... Ms. Victoria D. LIPSCOMB
26 Dir Marketing & Community Rels .... Ms. Joyce Y. CORDELL
12 Dean Instruct Programs-MDP Campus .... Mr. Joshua I. VILLALOBOS
76 Dean Health Career/TechEd/Math/Sci .... Dr. Paula MITCHELL
60 Dean Arts/Comm/Career/TechEd/SoSc .... Dr. Eileen G. CONKLIN
83 Dean Arts/Comm & Soc Sci .... Ms. Janet L. EVELER
79 Dean ESL Reading Social Science .... Ms. Susana RODARTE
57 Dean Comm/Performing Arts .... Mr. Blayne J. PRIMOZICH
53 Dean Education/Career/Tech Pgms .... Dr. Myshie M. PAGEL
66 Dean Nursing .... Ms. Paula G. MEAGHER
12 Dean Instructional Pgms-NW Campus .... Dr. Lydia TENA
81 Dean Math/Sci/Career Tech Educ .... Mr. Ernest R. WEBB, II
88 Dean Dual Credit & Early Col .... Ms. Maria Antonieta BADILLO
37 Assoc Dir Student Financial Aid .... Ms. Ines LOPEZ
45 Dir Institutional Effectiveness .... Dr. Ron STROUD
08 Director Library Technical Services .... Mr. Luis CHAPARRO
21 Comptroller .... Mr. Fernando FLORES
36 Director Career Services .... Ms. Carla CARDOZA
18 Executive Director Physical Plant .... Mr. Richard L. LOBATO
19 Chief of Police .... Mr. Jose L. RAMIREZ
16 Exec Dir Human Resources ORMS .... Vacant
07 Exec Director Admissions/ Registrar .... Dr. Cassandra M. LACHICA-CHAVEZ
96 Dir Purchasing & Contract Mgmt .... Mr. Ruben C. GALLARDO
09 Director Institutional Research .... Dr. Carol KAY
88 Director Human Resources Devel .... Mr. Alex HERNANDEZ
21 Director Budget .... Ms. Laura TELLEZ
88 Dir College Access/Development Ctr .... Vacant
102 Exec Dir Resource Dev/Foundation .... Ms. Dolores GROSS
22 Dir Ctr for Students w/Disabilities .... Ms. Janet M. LOCKHART
88 Director Recruitment/School Rels .... Ms. Nita CORRAL-NAVA
88 Exec Dir Outreach Transition Svcs .... Dr. Marisa E. PIERCE
25 Director Grants Management .... Mr. Alfred C. LAWRENCE
103 Director Workforce Development .... Ms. Luz E. TABOADA
106 Director Distance Education .... Mr. Robert P. JONES
88 Director Student Success .... Ms. Lucia M. RODRIGUEZ
88 Dir Law Enforcement Trng Academy .... Mr. Barry J. BOGLE
28 Director of Diversity Programs .... Mrs. Olga CHAVEZ
41 Athletic Director .... Mr. Felix HINOJOSA

Fortis College (B)

401 East Palace Pkwy Ste 100, Grand Prairie TX 75050
Telephone: (972) 375-0006 Identification: 770937
Accreditation: ABHES, RAD, SURGT, SURTEC

† Branch campus of Fortis Institute, Baton Rouge, LA.

Fortis College (C)

1201 West Oaks Mall, Houston TX 77082
County: Harris FICE Identification: 034244
Unit ID: 392415
Telephone: (713) 266-6594 Carnegie Class: Not Classified
FAX Number: (713) 782-5873 Calendar System: Quarter
URL: fortiscollege.edu
Established: Annual Undergrad Tuition & Fees: N/A
Enrollment: 210 Coed
Affiliation or Control: Proprietary IRS Status: Proprietary
Highest Offering: Associate Degree
Accreditation: COE, SURGT

01 Campus President .... Art CERVANTES

Frank Phillips College (D)

PO Box 5118, Borger TX 79008-5118
County: Hutchinson FICE Identification: 003568
Unit ID: 224891
Telephone: (806) 457-4200 Carnegie Class: Assoc/HVT-High Non
FAX Number: (806) 457-4224 Calendar System: Semester
URL: www.fpctx.edu
Established: 1948 Annual Undergrad Tuition & Fees (In-District): $3,052
Enrollment: 1,459 Coed
Affiliation or Control: Local IRS Status: 501(c)3
Highest Offering: Associate Degree
Accreditation: SC

01 President .... Dr. Jud HICKS
11 Vice Pres Administrative Services .... Dr. Jud HICKS
05 Vice President of Academic Affairs .... Dr. Shannon CARROLL
103 Dean of Career & Technical Educ .... Ms. Tiffany THOMAS
08 Director of the Library .... Mr. Jason PRICE
18 Director Physical Plant .... Ms. Regina HANEY
30 Director Advancement .... Ms. Nicole SIDDENS
37 Dir Student Financial Services .... Ms. Beverly FIELDS
38 Director Student Counseling/Testing .... Ms. Deborah JOHNSON
07 Director Admissions & Records .... Ms. Michele STEVENS
56 Director of Extended Education .... Ms. Tiffany THOMAS
10 Director of Accounting .... Ms. Renee PRATHER

Galen College of Nursing (E)

7411 John Smith Drive, Suite 300, San Antonio TX 78229
Telephone: (210) 733-3056 Identification: 770538
Accreditation: &SC

† Branch campus of Galen College of Nursing, Louisville, KY

Galveston College (F)

4015 Avenue Q, Galveston TX 77550-7496
County: Galveston FICE Identification: 004972
Unit ID: 224961
Telephone: (409) 944-4242 Carnegie Class: Assoc/MT-VT-High Non
FAX Number: (409) 944-1500 Calendar System: Semester
URL: www.gc.edu
Established: 1966 Annual Undergrad Tuition & Fees (In-District): $2,050
Enrollment: 2,071 Coed
Affiliation or Control: State/Local IRS Status: 501(c)3
Highest Offering: Associate Degree
Accreditation: SC, ADNUR, EMT, NMT, RAD, RTT

01 President .... Dr. Myles SHELTON
05 Vice President of Instruction .... Dr. Cissy MATTHEWS
11 Vice President for Administration .... Dr. Gaynelle HAYES
32 Actg VP of Student Services .... Mr. Ron C. CRUMEDY
75 Dean of Tech & Prof Education .... Ms. Vera LEWIS-JASPER
30 Dir of Development/GC Foundation .... Ms. Maria TRIPOVICH
10 Comptroller/CFO .... Mr. M. Jeff ENGBROCK
13 Director of Info Technology .... Mr. George CROSSLAND
26 Director of Public Affairs .... Mr. Joseph E. HUFF, III
15 Dir Human Resources/Risk Management .... Dr. Mary Jan LANTZ
41 Athletic Director/Head Coach .... Mr. Ken DELCAMBRE
07 Director Admissions/Registrar .... Mr. Scott BRANUM
66 Director of Nursing .... Dr. Sandra BRANNAN
09 Director Inst Effectiveness/Rsrch .... Dr. Larry ROOT
18 Director of Facilities/Security .... Mr. Tim W. SETZER
62 Dir of Library/Learning Resources .... Dr. Alan M. UYEHARA
37 Director of Financial Aid .... Ms. Meghann NASH
04 Executive Assistant .... Ms. Carla D. BIGGERS

Golf Academy of America (G)

1861 Valley View Lane, Suite 100, Farmers Branch TX 75234
Telephone: (972) 763-8100 Identification: 770621
Accreditation: ACICS

† Branch campus of Virginia College, Birmingham, AL

Grace School of Theology (H)

3705 College Park Drive, The Woodlands TX 77384
County: Montgomery Identification: 667100
Unit ID: 481401
Telephone: (877) 476-8674 Carnegie Class: Not Classified
FAX Number: (877) 735-2867 Calendar System: Semester
URL: www.gsot.edu
Established: 2002 Annual Undergrad Tuition & Fees: $5,280
Enrollment: 313 Coed
Affiliation or Control: Independent Non-Profit IRS Status: 501(c)3
Highest Offering: Doctorate
Accreditation: THEOL, TRACS

01 President .... Dr. Dave ANDERSON
43 Exec Vice President/General Counsel .... Mr. Tom KRUPPSTADT
05 Vice Pres Academic Affairs .... Dr. Al LETTING, III
30 Vice Pres Advancement .... Mr. Daniel LABRY

Graduate Institute of Applied Linguistics (I)

7500 W Camp Wisdom Road, Dallas TX 75236-5629
County: Dallas FICE Identification: 038513
Telephone: (972) 708-7340 Carnegie Class: Not Classified
FAX Number: (972) 708-7292 Calendar System: Other
URL: www.gial.edu
Established: 1999 Annual Undergrad Tuition & Fees: N/A
Enrollment: N/A Coed
Affiliation or Control: Independent Non-Profit IRS Status: 501(c)3
Highest Offering: Master's
Accreditation: SC

01 President .... Dr. Doug TIFFIN
05 Dean of Academic Affairs .... Vacant
10 Vice President of Finance .... Mr. Rod JENKINS
11 Vice President of Operations .... Mr. Jeff MINARD
32 Dean of Students .... Ms. Meg TRIHUS
06 Registrar .... Mrs. Lynne M. LAMIMAN
07 Director of Admissions .... Mrs. Maggie A. JOHNSON
08 Library Director .... Ms. Ferne L. WEIMER
30 Director of Development .... Ms. Judy POLLOCK
09 Director of Inst Research/Svcs .... Mr. Richard E. LYNCH
13 Director of Computing Services .... Mr. Chuck WALEK
21 Business Manager .... Mr. Paul W. SETTER
37 Financial Aid Administrator .... Ms. Margaret JOHNSON
88 Veterans' Officer .... Ms. Margaret JOHNSON
42 Chaplain .... Mr. Victor JACKSON
29 Alumni Relations .... Mrs. Allison PYLE
04 Administrative Asst to President .... Ms. Gail DYKSTRA

Grayson College (J)

6101 Grayson Drive, Denison TX 75020-8299
County: Grayson FICE Identification: 003570
Unit ID: 225070
Telephone: (903) 465-6030 Carnegie Class: Assoc/MT-VT-Mix Trad/Non
FAX Number: (903) 463-5284 Calendar System: Semester
URL: www.grayson.edu
Established: 1963 Annual Undergrad Tuition & Fees (In-District): $1,956
Enrollment: 4,591 Coed
Affiliation or Control: State/Local IRS Status: 501(c)3
Highest Offering: Associate Degree
Accreditation: SC, ACFEI, ADNUR, DA, EMT, MLTAD

01 President .... Dr. Jeremy P. MCMILLEN
05 Vice President of Instruction .... Dr. Dava WASHBURN
32 Vice President of Student Affairs .... Dr. Regina ORGAN
10 Vice President of Business Services .... Mr. Giles BROWN
13 VP Info Technology/Dir of Library .... Mr. Gary PAIKOWSKI
04 Assistant to the President .... Dr. Molly HARRIS
102 Exec Dir Grayson College Foundation .... Mr. Randy TRUXAL
07 Director of Admissions/Registrar .... Mrs. Christy KLEMIUK
37 Director of Financial Aid .... Ms. Donna KING
14 Director of Network Services .... Mr. Mike BROWN
19 Chief of Campus Police .... Mr. Andrew MACPHERSON
26 Dir Marketing/Public Information .... Mrs. Amy EVANS
21 Director of Fiscal Services .... Mr. Danny HYATT
41 Athletic Director .... Mr. Mike MCBRAYER
40 Bookstore Manager .... Ms. Venus MCGUIRE

Hallmark University (K)

10401 IH-10 W, San Antonio TX 78230-1737
County: Bexar FICE Identification: 010509
Unit ID: 225201
Telephone: (210) 690-9000 Carnegie Class: Bac/Assoc-Assoc Dom
FAX Number: (210) 697-8225 Calendar System: Semester
URL: www.hallmarkuniversity.edu
Established: 1969 Annual Undergrad Tuition & Fees: N/A
Enrollment: 859 Coed
Affiliation or Control: Independent Non-Profit IRS Status: 501(c)3
Highest Offering: Master's

Accreditation: ACCSC

00 Chancellor Mr. Joseph B. FISHER
01 University President Mr. Brent FESSLER
05 Provost Mr. Donald (Jay) GREGSON
10 VP Finance/Chief Business Officer Ms. Roxanne DARTY
111 Vice President of Advancement Mr. Clarence (Reggie) WILLIAMS
20 Dean of Academics Ms. Rebecca WADLER
26 Director of Marketing Mr. Micah BELL
06 Registrar Ms. Racquel SULLEMUN
32 Director of Student Affairs Ms. Evonn SHORT
37 Director Student Financial Aid Ms. Grace CALIXTO
07 Director of Admissions Ms. Jennifer SANCHEZ
08 Library Director Ms. Sarah WALCH
13 Chief Info Technology Officer (CIO) Mr. Taylor MERCIER
100 Executive Chief of Staff Mr. Christopher SHORT
88 Director of Regulatory Compliance Ms. Joyce M. GREAVES
42 Chaplain Mr. Douglas HEINTZ
16 Human Resources Generalist Ms. Monica BRUNKEN

Hardin-Simmons University (A)

2200 Hickory, Abilene TX 79698-0001
County: Taylor FICE Identification: 003571
Unit ID: 225247
Telephone: (325) 670-1000 Carnegie Class: Masters/M
FAX Number: (325) 670-1267 Calendar System: Semester
URL: www.hsutx.edu
Established: 1891 Annual Undergrad Tuition & Fees: $25,830
Enrollment: 2,112 Coed
Affiliation or Control: Baptist IRS Status: 501(c)3
Highest Offering: Doctorate
Accreditation: SC, ACBSP, #ARCPA, CAATE, CACREP, MUS, NURSE, PTA, SW, THEOL

01 President Dr. Eric I. BRUNTMYER
05 Provost & Chief Academic Officer Dr. Thomas V. BRISCO
10 Vice President for Finance Dr. Jodie MCGAUGHEY
30 VP for Institutional Advancement Mr. Mike HAMMACK
32 Vice Pres for Student Life Dr. Dave ROZEBOOM
84 VP for Enrollment Management Mrs. Vicki HOUSE
07 Assoc VP for Enrollment Svcs Mr. Jim JONES
53 Dean Col Human Sci/Education Stds Dr. Perry HALEY BROWN
49 Dean College of Liberal Arts Dr. Stephen COOK
50 Dean Kelley College of Business Mr. Michael MONHOLLON
64 Dean College of Fine Arts Dr. Robert TUCKER
73 Assoc Dean Logsdon Sch of Theology Dr. Larry MCGRAW
58 Dean of Graduate Studies Dr. Nancy KUCINSKI
66 Dean School of Nursing Dr. Nina OUIMETTE
81 Dean School Sciences/Mathematics Dr. Christopher L. MCNAIR
13 Assoc Vice Pres Technical Services Mr. Travis P. SEEKINS
21 Asst VP For Finance/Controller Mrs. Jessica GARCIA
38 Assoc VP Academic Advising/Retent Mrs. Gracie CARROLL
08 Dean/Dir of University Libraries Mrs. Elizabeth J. WORLEY
09 Director of Institutional Research Mrs. Lori BLAKE
06 Registrar Mrs. Kacey HIGGINS
35 Dean of Students Mr. Brian DAWSON
29 Director of Alumni Relations Mrs. Britt E. JONES
19 Chief of Police Mr. Frank LOZA
23 University Nurse Mrs. Sue A. BIGGS
42 Chaplain Dr. Kelly PIGOTT
39 Director of Residence Life Ms. Hollly EDWARDS
15 Director of Human Resources Mr. John SNAPP
27 Dir of Univ Communications Mr. James STONE
37 Dir Student Fin Aid & Scholarships Mrs. Bridget MOORE
18 Facilities Services Director Mr. Tim MCCARRY
41 Athletic Director Mr. John M. NEESE
85 Director of International Studies Dr. Allan J. LANDWER
26 Public Relations Director Mrs. Cheryl SAWYERS
93 Coordinator of Minority Studies Dr. Joe H. ALCORTA
28 Coord of Student Diversity Programs Dr. Kelvin J. KELLEY

Hill College (B)

112 Lamar Drive, Hillsboro TX 76645-2711
County: Hill FICE Identification: 003573
Unit ID: 225371
Telephone: (254) 659-7500 Carnegie Class: Assoc/HVT-Mix Trad/Non
FAX Number: (254) 582-7591 Calendar System: Semester
URL: www.hillcollege.edu
Established: 1923 Annual Undergrad Tuition & Fees (In-District): $1,995
Enrollment: 4,014 Coed
Affiliation or Control: Local IRS Status: 501(c)3
Highest Offering: Associate Degree
Accreditation: SC, CVT, EMT

01 President Dr. Pamela BOEHM
04 Executive Asst to the President Ms. Vonnie MORPHEW
05 Vice President Instruction Mr. Rex PARCELLS
25 Vice President External Affairs Ms. Jessyca BROWN
10 Vice Pres Administrative Services Mr. Billy D. CURBO
32 Vice President Student Services Ms. Lizza TRENKLE
13 Vice Pres Information Technology Mrs. Jessie WHITE
21 Dean Financial Services Mrs. Debbie GERIK
08 Librarian - Hill Campus Mr. Joseph SHAUGHNESSY
08 Librarian - Cleburne Campus Mr. John LAMBERTH
15 Director Human Resources Mrs. Jamie JASKA
12 Exec Dir JCC/Dean of Students Mr. Bill GILKER
41 Athletic Director Mr. Paul BROWN
26 Director of Marketing & Public Rels Mrs. Robin DEMOTT
09 Dir of Institutional Effectiveness Ms. Sherry DAVIS
37 Director of Financial Aid Ms. Kathleen PUSTEJOVSKY
18 Director Physical Plant Mr. Frank WILLIAMS
29 Director Alumni Relations Mr. Preston MCREYNOLDS

Houston Baptist University (C)

7502 Fondren Road, Houston TX 77074-3298
County: Harris FICE Identification: 003576
Unit ID: 225399
Telephone: (281) 649-3000 Carnegie Class: Masters/M
FAX Number: (281) 649-3012 Calendar System: Semester
URL: www.hbu.edu
Established: 1960 Annual Undergrad Tuition & Fees: $30,800
Enrollment: 3,160 Coed
Affiliation or Control: Southern Baptist IRS Status: 501(c)3
Highest Offering: Doctorate
Accreditation: SC, NUR

01 President Dr. Robert B. SLOAN, JR.
05 Provost Dr. Cynthia SIMPSON
10 Vice President Financial Operations Mrs. Sandra N. MOONEY
30 Vice President for Advancement Mrs. Sharon E. SAUNDERS
26 Vice Pres University Relations Mrs. Sharon E. SAUNDERS
84 Vice Pres Enrollment Management Mr. James STEEN
20 Associate Provost Ms. Ritamarie TAUER
20 Associate Provost Dr. Michael ROSATO
21 Planning & Budget Director Mr. Michael DEI
79 Dean School of Humanities Dr. Jodey HINZE
50 Dean School of Business Dr. Michael WEEKS
81 Dean College of Science & Math Dr. Doris C. WARREN
92 Director Honors College Dr. Gary HARTENBURG
53 Interim Dean School of Education Dr. Teresa MCINTYRE
57 Dean School of Fine Arts Dr. Jason LESTER
66 Dean Sch Nursing & Allied Hlth Dr. Renae SCHUMANN
41 Athletic Director Mr. Steve C. MONIACI
06 University Registrar Ms. Erinn HUGHES
08 Interim Director of Libraries Mr. Dean RILEY
42 University Minister Vacant
21 Assoc VP Financial Operations Ms. Loree WATSON
39 Director Housing Operations Vacant
13 Chief Information Officer (IT) Mr. Glen JOHNSON
09 Dir Inst Research & Effectiveness Mr. Todd COCKRELL
32 Vice President Student Life Mr. Whittington GOODWIN
88 SACS Liaison Ms. Ritamarie TAUER
04 Admin Asst to the President Mrs. Karen FRANCIES
15 Director of Human Resources Ms. Jennifer DELANTER
18 Dir of Maintenance & Operations Mr. Gary DYKE
36 Dir of Career & Calling Ms. Colette CROSS
37 Sr Dir Financial Aid & Scholarships Ms. Veronica GABBARD
96 Cost Control Analyst Ms. Jody WILDING
105 Director Web Services Mr. Alan PRESLEY

Houston Community College (D)

3100 Main Street, Houston TX 77002
County: Harris FICE Identification: 010633
Unit ID: 225423
Telephone: (713) 718-2000 Carnegie Class: Assoc/HT-High Trad
FAX Number: N/A Calendar System: Semester
URL: www.hccs.edu
Established: 1971 Annual Undergrad Tuition & Fees (In-State): $1,632
Enrollment: 56,522 Coed
Affiliation or Control: State IRS Status: 501(c)3
Highest Offering: Associate Degree
Accreditation: SC, ACBSP, ACFEI, ART, CAHIIM, COARC, DA, DH, DMS, EMT, ENGT, HT, MAC, MLTAD, NMT, OTA, PTAA, RAD, SURGT

01 Chancellor Dr. Cesar MALDONADO
100 Chief of Staff Dr. Melissa GONZALEZ
04 Exec Assistant to the Chancellor Ms. Keiana BLAKE
10 Senior VC Finance & Administration Ms. Teri ZAMORA
43 General Counsel Mr. E. Ashley SMITH
05 VC Instructional Services/CAO Dr. Kimberly BEATTY
32 Vice Chancellor Student Services Dr. Athos BREWER
13 Vice Chancellor Information Tech Dr. William E. CARTER
45 VC Planning and Inst Effectiveness Dr. Kurt EWEN
20 Assoc VC of Instructional Services Dr. Steve LEVEY
21 Assoc VC Finance & Accounting Ms. Carin HUTCHINS
88 Assoc VC of College Readiness Dr. Catherine O'BREIN
84 Assoc VC of Enrollment Services Ms. Shantay GRAYS
35 Assoc VC of Student Success Dr. Cheryl STERLING
85 Assoc VC of Intl Students Vacant
18 Chief Facilities Officer Vacant
15 Chief Human Resource Officer Ms. Janet MAY
22 Director EEO/Compliance Mr. David CROSS
21 Controller Dr. Karla BENDER
21 Treasurer Mr. Ron E. DEFALCO
26 Assoc VC Communications & Marketing Ms. Linda TOYOTA
66 Department Chair Vocational Nursing Ms. Deborah SIMMONS-JOHNSON
07 Director of Admissions & Registrar Ms. Mary LEMBURG
09 Exec Dir of Inst Research & Innov Dr. Martha OBURN
46 Director of Resource Development Vacant
102 Executive Director Foundation Ms. Carmetha WILLIAMS
12 President-Northeast College Dr. Margaret FORD FISHER
12 President-Southwest College Dr. Madeline BURILLO
12 President-Central College Dr. Muddassir SIDDIQI
12 President-Southeast College Dr. Irene PORCARELLO
12 President-Northwest College Dr. Zachary HODGES
12 President-Coleman College Dr. Phillip NICOTERA
29 Alumni Relations Specialist Ms. Zandra HENDERSON
96 Ex Dir Purchasing/Procurement Oper Mr. Rogelio ANASAGASTI
88 Director Student/Financial Services Mr. Hernando BALDONADO
37 Exec Director Student Financial Aid Ms. JoEllen SOUCIER
116 Director Internal Auditing Mr. Terrance CORRINGAN
50 COE Dean Business Mr. Jesus RODRIGUEZ
88 COE Dean English Ms. Amy TAN
46 COE Director Construction Mr. Kris ASPER
88 COE Director Consumer Arts & Sci Mr. Anthony HANCOCK
88 COE Director Digital & Info Tech Mr. Doug ROWLETT
88 COE Dean Earth Life Natural Sci Mr. Jerome DRAIN
54 COE Director Engineering Mr. John VASSELLI
88 COE Director Global Energy Mr. Morteza SAMEEI
76 COE Director Health Science Vacant
49 COE Dean Liberal Arts & Humanities Mr. Theodore HANLEY
88 COE Director Logistics Ms. Cynthia GARZA
88 COE Director Manufacturing Mr. Frederick HEARD
88 COE Director Material Science Dr. Tam LE
81 COE Dean Mathematics Mr. Timor SERVER
72 COE Director Media Arts & Tech Mr. Jimmy ADAMS
88 COE Director Public Safety Mr. Johnny SESSUMS
83 COE Dean Social & Behavioral Sci Mr. Aaron KNIGHT
86 AVC Government & External Relations Mr. Remmele YOUNG

Houston Graduate School of Theology (E)

4300-C West Bellfort, Houston TX 77035
County: Harris FICE Identification: 023202
Unit ID: 246345
Telephone: (713) 942-9505 Carnegie Class: Spec-4-yr-Faith
FAX Number: (713) 942-9506 Calendar System: Semester
URL: www.hgst.edu
Established: 1983 Annual Graduate Tuition & Fees: N/A
Enrollment: 154 Coed
Affiliation or Control: Independent Non-Profit IRS Status: 501(c)3
Highest Offering: Doctorate; No Undergraduates
Accreditation: THEOL

01 President Dr. James H. FURR
05 Interim Academic Dean Dr. Becky L. TOWNE
10 Chief Financial Officer Ms. Tracee FLETCHER
07 Dir of Admissions/Recruiting Ms. Gloria FIKES
06 Registrar Ms. Laura HAMILTON
08 Director of Library Services Ms. Janet KENNARD

Houston International College-Cardiotech Ultrasound School (F)

12135 Bissonnet, Ste E, Houston TX 77099
County: Harris FICE Identification: 041385
Unit ID: 458034
Telephone: (281) 495-0078 Carnegie Class: Not Classified
FAX Number: (281) 495-5618 Calendar System: Semester
URL: www.cardiotech.org
Established: 2003 Annual Undergrad Tuition & Fees: $10,233
Enrollment: 50 Coed
Affiliation or Control: Proprietary IRS Status: Proprietary
Highest Offering: Associate Degree
Accreditation: ABHES

01 Director Ms. Joan DOUGLAS

Howard College (G)

1001 Birdwell Lane, Big Spring TX 79720-3799
County: Howard FICE Identification: 003574
Unit ID: 225520
Telephone: (432) 264-5000 Carnegie Class: Assoc/HT-High Trad
FAX Number: (432) 264-5082 Calendar System: Semester
URL: www.howardcollege.edu
Established: 1945 Annual Undergrad Tuition & Fees (In-District): $2,560
Enrollment: 4,044 Coed
Affiliation or Control: State/Local IRS Status: 501(c)3
Highest Offering: Associate Degree
Accreditation: SC, ADNUR, COARC, DH, EMT, RAD, SURGT

01 President Dr. Cheryl T. SPARKS
05 Vice President Academic Affairs Dr. Amy BURCHETT
20 Dean Academic Affairs SWCID Mr. Danny CAMPBELL
32 Dean Student Affairs SWCID Ms. Nancy BONURA
103 Workforce & Cmty Dev Officer-SA Ms. Jamie RAINEY
12 Admin Dean Big Spring Area Mrs. Erin MACKENZIE
10 Chief Business Officer Mr. Steve SMITH
18 Chief Operations Officer Mr. Terry HANSEN
10 Chief Financial Officer Ms. Brenda CLAXTON
08 Dean of Libraries Mr. Luis KINCADE
13 Dean Information Technology Mr. Eric HANSEN
106 Director eLearning Services Ms. Kym CLARK
37 Dean Financial Aid Mrs. Candice MALDONADO
26 Director Effectiveness/Information Ms. Cindy SMITH
41 Athletic Director Mr. Terry HANSEN
103 Workforce & Cmty Dev Officer-BS Mr. Fabian SERRANO
15 Director Human Resources/Payroll Ms. Rhonda KERNICK
12 Admin Dean-San Angelo Ms. Pam CALLAN
06 District Registrar Mrs. TaNeal RICHARDSON
21 Director Student Accounting Ms. Laura FITZPATRICK
30 Director Institutional Advancement Mrs. Jan FORESYTH
76 Dean Health Professions Ms. Luci GABEHART
09 Research and Reporting Officer Ms. Rebecca VILLANUEVA
21 Director Financial Accounting Ms. Jeannie CARROLL
04 Executive Asst to the President Ms. Julie BAILEY

Howard Payne University (H)

1000 Fisk Street, Brownwood TX 76801-2794
County: Brown FICE Identification: 003575
Unit ID: 225548
Telephone: (325) 646-2502 Carnegie Class: Bac-Diverse

FAX Number: (325) 649-8975 Calendar System: Semester
URL: www.hputx.edu
Established: 1889 Annual Undergrad Tuition & Fees: $26,630
Enrollment: 1,163 Coed
Affiliation or Control: Baptist IRS Status: 501(c)3
Highest Offering: Master's
Accreditation: SC, CAATE, MUS, SW

01 President .... Dr. William N. ELLIS
05 Provost/Chief Academic Officer .... Dr. Mark TEW
10 Int Chief Financial Officer .... Mr. Mike RODGERS
32 Vice Pres Stdnt Life/Dean Stdnts .... Dr. Magen BUNYARD
44 Vice President Development .... Mr. Randy YEAKLEY
84 Assoc VP for Enrollment Management .... Mr. Kevin KIRK
15 Asst VP for Bus & Hum Resources .... Mr. Bill FISHBACK
18 AVP Facilities/Planning .... Mr. Terry PRITCHETT
13 Asst VP Information Technology .... Ms. Jodi GOODE
06 Registrar .... Mrs. Lana WAGNER
37 Director Financial Aid .... Mrs. Glenda HUFF
07 Director of Admission .... Mrs. P.J GRAMLING
36 Dir Academic Testing/Career Svcs .... Ms. Wendy MCNEELEY
26 Director of Publications .... Mr. Kyle C. MIZE
09 Director Institutional Research .... Vacant
41 Athletic Director .... Mr. Hunter SIMS
91 Database Administrator .... Mr. Tyler CHRISTIANSEN
90 Computer Network Administrator .... Mr. Russell EZZELL
29 Coordinator of Alumni Relations .... Mr. Stephen SULLIVAN
88 Special Events Coordinator .... Ms. Kathy JAMES
04 Executive Assistant to President .... Ms. Tammy LOWREY
38 University Counselor .... Mrs. Toni DAMRON
56 Dean Extended Education .... Dr. Robert BICKNELL
08 Dean of Libraries .... Mrs. Alexia RIGGS
81 Dean School of Science & Math .... Dr. Pam BRYANT
50 Dean School of Business .... Dr. Brad LEMLER
53 Dean School of Education .... Dr. Kylah CLARK-GOFF
64 Dean School of Music & Fine Arts .... Dr. Richard FIESE
73 Dean School of Christian Studies .... Dr. Donnie AUVENSHINE
79 Dean School of Humanities .... Dr. Millard KIMERY

Huston-Tillotson University (A)

900 Chicon Street, Austin TX 78702-2795
County: Travis FICE Identification: 003577
Unit ID: 225575
Telephone: (512) 505-3000 Carnegie Class: Bac-Diverse
FAX Number: (512) 505-3190 Calendar System: Semester
URL: www.htu.edu
Established: 1875 Annual Undergrad Tuition & Fees: $14,346
Enrollment: 1,023 Coed
Affiliation or Control: Multiple Protestant Denominations
IRS Status: 501(c)3
Highest Offering: Master's
Accreditation: SC, ACBSP

01 President & CEO .... Dr. Colette PIERCE BURNETTE
04 Executive Assistant to President .... Vacant
100 Chief of Staff/Clerk to Board .... Mr. Wayne KNOX
10 VP for Administration & Finance .... Mr. Damon JOHNSON
111 Vice Pres Institutional Advancement . Ms. Angela HALL WATKINS
05 Provost/VP Academic & Student Affs .... Dr. Archibald W. VANDERPUYE
32 Dean of Student Affairs .... Ms. Ericka JONES
84 Dean of Enrollment Management .... Dr. Rhonda M. MOSES
08 Media Librarian/Archivist .... Ms. Josie RAGOLIA
36 Director Career & Grad Development .... Mr. Steven HATCHETT
41 Director of Athletics .... Mr. Charles H. DUBRA
06 University Registrar .... Mrs. Earnestine J. STRICKLAND
25 Dir Sponsored PRGs/Title III Coord .... Dr. Beverly L. DOWNING
09 Director IR/Planning/Assessment .... Vacant
13 Int Director Information Technology .... Mr. Jon ALBRECHT
26 Director of Public Relations .... Ms. Julianne HANCKEL
18 Director of Facilities .... Ms. Kim HAMMOND
30 Senior Development Officer .... Ms. Linda Y. JACKSON
29 Director of Alumni Affairs .... Ms. LaJuana SANFORD
35 Coordinator of Campus Life .... Mr. Delton PIERCE
88 Dir of Ctr for Academic Excellence .... Ms. Autumn CAVINESS
15 Director of Human Resources .... Ms. Tracy NICHOLS
38 Dir Counseling & Consultation Ctr .... Ms. Dawn LEISCH
42 University Chaplain .... Rev. Donald E. BREWINGTON
07 Director of Admission .... Mr. Jeffrey PIERCE, II
49 Dean College of Arts & Sciences .... Dr. Michael HIRSCH
50 Dean School of Business/Technology .... Dr. Steven EDMOND
37 Int Asst Director of Financial Aid .... Ms. Karen PRICE-SCOTT
22 Coord Counseling/Disability Svcs .... Ms. Bianca SANDOVAL

Interactive College of Technology (B)

213 West Southmore, Ste 101, Pasadena TX 77502
County: Harris FICE Identification: 023313
Unit ID: 440776
Telephone: (713) 920-1120 Carnegie Class: Not Classified
FAX Number: (713) 477-0348 Calendar System: Semester
URL: www.ict.edu
Established: Annual Undergrad Tuition & Fees: N/A
Enrollment: 28 Coed
Affiliation or Control: Proprietary IRS Status: Proprietary
Highest Offering: Associate Degree
Accreditation: COE

01 Campus Director .... Bill MCGUIRE

Jacksonville College (C)

105 B. J. Albritton Drive, Jacksonville TX 75766-4759
County: Cherokee FICE Identification: 003579
Unit ID: 225876
Telephone: (903) 586-2518 Carnegie Class: Assoc/HT-High Non
FAX Number: (903) 586-0743 Calendar System: Semester
URL: www.jacksonville-college.edu
Established: 1899 Annual Undergrad Tuition & Fees: $7,900
Enrollment: 582 Coed
Affiliation or Control: Baptist IRS Status: 501(c)3
Highest Offering: Associate Degree
Accreditation: SC

01 President .... Dr. Mike SMITH
03 Vice President Executive Affairs .... Dr. Blanton FEASTER
05 Academic Dean/Registrar .... Mrs. Marolyn WELCH
32 Dean of Students .... Mr. Donny SADLER
10 Business Officer .... Ms. Jennifer HUGHES
41 Athletic Director .... Ms. Leasa AILSHIE
06 Registrar .... Ms. Jodye JAY
07 Director of Admissions .... Mrs. Sandra CLAY
18 Chief Facilities/Physical Plant .... Mr. Dan SHOFFNER
26 Chief Public Relations Officer .... Dr. David HEFLIN
29 Director of Alumni Relations .... Mr. Randy DECKER
37 Director Student Financial Aid .... Mr. Paul GALYEAN
39 Director Student Housing .... Mr. David WHITE
19 Chief of Security .... Mr. Micael MORSE

Jarvis Christian College (D)

Highway 80 E., PR 7631, Hawkins TX 75765-1470
County: Wood FICE Identification: 003637
Unit ID: 225885
Telephone: (903) 730-4890 Carnegie Class: Bac-Diverse
FAX Number: (903) 769-4842 Calendar System: Semester
URL: www.jarvis.edu
Established: 1912 Annual Undergrad Tuition & Fees: $11,720
Enrollment: 863 Coed
Affiliation or Control: Christian Church (Disciples Of Christ)
IRS Status: 501(c)3
Highest Offering: Baccalaureate
Accreditation: SC, ACBSP, @SW

01 President .... Dr. Lester C. NEWMAN
05 Provost/Vice Pres Academic Affairs .... Dr. Glenell PRUITT
10 Vice Pres Administration & Finance .... Mr. Melvin HAMLET
30 VP Institutional Advancement/Devel .... Mr. Lee MONROE
45 Vice Pres for Inst Effectiveness .... Vacant
32 AVP Student/Enrollment Services .... Vacant
108 AVP Inst Effect/Rsch/Assessment .... Dr. Belinda PRIHODA
13 Int Director Information Technology .... Mr. Stan FRIDIE
06 Registrar .... Mrs. Adrienne A. WYATT
39 Director Student Facilities/Housing .... Mr. Cory GIPSON
84 Exec Director Enrollment Management .... Ms. Micheline LAMBERT-GIBSON
26 Director Public Relations/Publicity .... Ms. Sherry SHEPHARD
100 Chief of Staff/Director Title III . Mrs. Cynthia HOLLMAN-STANCIL
08 Head Librarian .... Mr. Rodney ATKINS
38 Director Career Services .... Mr. Chestley TALLEY
37 Director of Financial Aid .... Ms. Cecelia JONES
41 Athletic Director .... Mr. Bobby LADNER
42 Chaplain/Director of Religious Life . Pastor Cherisna JEAN-MARIE
15 Director Human Resources .... Dr. Daphne SINGLETON
09 Director Institutional Research .... Vacant
18 Chief Facilities/Physical Plant .... Mr. Willie SANDIFER

KD Conservatory College of Film and Dramatic Arts (E)

2600 N Stemmons Fwy, Suite 117, Dallas TX 75207-2111
County: Dallas FICE Identification: 023182
Unit ID: 225991
Telephone: (214) 638-0484 Carnegie Class: Spec 2-yr-A&S
FAX Number: (214) 630-5140 Calendar System: Semester
URL: www.kdstudio.com
Established: 1979 Annual Undergrad Tuition & Fees: $16,625
Enrollment: 126 Coed
Affiliation or Control: Proprietary IRS Status: Proprietary
Highest Offering: Associate Degree
Accreditation: THEA

01 President/CEO .... Ms. Kathy TYNER
05 Director/CAO .... Mr. T. A TAYLOR
88 Program Chair - MT .... Mr. Michael SERRECCHIA
88 Program Chair - Film Program .... Mr. Dennis BISHOP
11 Head of Operations .... Vacant
32 Head of Student Services .... Ms. Ashlyn NICHOLS
37 Student Financial Aid .... Ms. Linda CRAFT
08 Chief Library Officer .... Ms. Judith HEAD

Kilgore College (F)

1100 Broadway, Kilgore TX 75662-3299
County: Gregg FICE Identification: 003580
Unit ID: 226019
Telephone: (903) 984-8531 Carnegie Class: Assoc/MT-VT-High Trad
FAX Number: (903) 983-8600 Calendar System: Semester
URL: www.kilgore.edu
Established: 1935 Annual Undergrad Tuition & Fees (In-District): $1,632
Enrollment: 5,666 Coed
Affiliation or Control: Local IRS Status: 501(c)3
Highest Offering: Associate Degree
Accreditation: SC, ADNUR, EMT, PTAA

01 President .... Dr. Brenda S. KAYS
05 Vice President of Instruction .... Dr. Michael H. TURPIN
11 Vice Pres Administrative Services .... Mr. Duane MCNANEY
32 Vice President Student Development .... Dr. Mike JENKINS
09 Vice Pres Institutional Planning .... Mrs. Staci MARTIN
57 Div Dean Liberal & Fine Arts .... Mrs. Becky JOHNSON
81 Div Dean Science/Math/Health Sci .... Mrs. Louise WILEY
50 Div Dean Business/Tech/Lang Devel/ .... Mr. Randy LEWELLEN
75 Dir of Adult Voc Educ .... Ms. Martha WOODRUFF
12 Div Dean of Longview Center .... Dr. Julie H. FOWLER
06 Registrar .... Mr. Chris GORE
15 Director of Human Resources .... Mr. Tony JOHNSON
13 Director of Information Technology .... Mr. John COLVILLE
08 Director Library .... Ms. Kathy FAIR
40 Manager of Bookstore .... Mr. Corrie THIBODEAUX
19 Chief of Police .... Chief Heath CARIKER
84 Dir of Marketing & Enrollment Mgmt .... Mr. Trey HATTAWAY
04 Assistant to the President .... Mrs. Nancy LAW
30 Director of Development .... Mrs. Leah GORMAN
37 Financial Aid Officer .... Mr. Reggie BRAZZLE
85 International Student Advisor .... Ms. Estonia GRAVES
26 Coordinator of Public & Sports Info .... Mr. Chris CRADDOCK
09 Coord of Institutional Research .... Ms. Jane LEWIS
38 Coordinator of Counseling .... Mrs. Pam GATTON
96 Purchasing Agent .... Ms. Tammie PASCOE
39 Director of Residential Life .... Vacant
07 Director of Admissions .... Mr. Chris GORE
106 Dir Online Education/E-learning .... Ms. Charleen WORSHAM
18 Chief Facilities/Physical Plant .... Mr. Jeff WILLIAMS
41 Athletic Director .... Mr. Jimmy RIEVES

The King's University (G)

2121 E. Southlake Boulevard, South Lake TX 76092-6507
County: Tarrant FICE Identification: 035163
Unit ID: 439701
Telephone: (817) 722-1700 Carnegie Class: Spec-4-yr-Faith
FAX Number: N/A Calendar System: Quarter
URL: tku.edu/
Established: 1997 Annual Undergrad Tuition & Fees: $13,650
Enrollment: 764 Coed
Affiliation or Control: Independent Non-Profit IRS Status: 501(c)3
Highest Offering: Doctorate
Accreditation: BI, TRACS

01 President .... Dr. David COLE
09 Vice Pres Institutional Effective .... Dr. Linda RINN
11 Vice Pres Business Admin/CFO .... Ms. Ashley GREEN
84 Vice Pres Enrollment Management .... Dr. Rhonda DAVIS
05 Academic Dean .... Dr. Daniel DAVIS
10 Director of Finance .... Ms. Ashley GREEN
106 Dean Distance Education .... Dr. Frank MARKOW
09 Dir Institutional Effectiveness .... Dr. Bobbi STRINGER
32 Dean of Student Life .... Mr. Shawn BRANN
07 Assoc Director of Admissions .... Ms. Courtney WIDELITZ
06 Assoc Dir Student Recruitment .... Ms. Angela TRANEL
37 Int Director Financial Aid .... Mr. Travis TERMIN
08 Director of Library Services .... Mr. Tracey R. LANE
30 Chief Development .... Mr. Lee S. MIMMS
13 Director Information Management .... Ms. Esther KUHN
21 Student Accounts Officer .... Ms. June M. HADLEY
90 Dir Acad Computing/Dir Student Affs .... Prof. Donald C. BRUBAKER
29 Director Alumni Relations .... Ms. Maureen A. BRODERSON
96 Director of Purchasing .... Mr. Bob CARON
28 Director of Diversity .... Dr. Michael J. GREGG
102 Dir Foundation/Corporate Relations .... Mr. Lee S. MIMMS
26 Dir of Marketing/Communications .... Mr. Michael KEITH

Laredo Community College (H)

West End Washington Street, Laredo TX 78040-4395
County: Webb FICE Identification: 003582
Unit ID: 226134
Telephone: (956) 722-0521 Carnegie Class: Assoc/MT-VT-High Trad
FAX Number: (956) 721-5381 Calendar System: Semester
URL: www.laredo.edu
Established: 1946 Annual Undergrad Tuition & Fees (In-District): $3,780
Enrollment: 8,749 Coed
Affiliation or Control: Local IRS Status: 501(c)3
Highest Offering: Associate Degree
Accreditation: SC, ADNUR, OTA, PTAA, RAD

01 President .... Dr. Ricardo SOLIS
05 Sr VP of Student and Academic Aff .... Dr. Vincent R. SOLIS
25 VP for Resource Development .... Dr. Nora R. GARZA
11 VP for Institutional Operations .... Dr. Federico SOLIS
10 Chief Financial Officer .... Dr. Nora STEWART
111 Exec Dir Strategic & External Init .... Mr. Rodney RODRIGUEZ
35 Associate VP of Student Services .... Mr. Robert OCHOA
49 Dean of Arts & Sciences .... Dr. Marisela RODRIGUEZ
103 Dean of Workforce Education ... Mr. J. Alfredo INIGUEZ-JIMENEZ

Lee College (I)

511 S Whiting, PO Box 818, Baytown TX 77522-0818
County: Harris FICE Identification: 003583
Unit ID: 226204
Telephone: (281) 427-5611 Carnegie Class: Assoc/HVT-High Trad
FAX Number: (281) 425-6555 Calendar System: Semester
URL: www.lee.edu

Established: 1934 Annual Undergrad Tuition & Fees (In-District): $1,672
Enrollment: 6,202 Coed
Affiliation or Control: State/Local IRS Status: 501(c)3
Highest Offering: Associate Degree
Accreditation: SC, ADNUR, CAHIIM

01 President .... Dr. Dennis BROWN
100 Senior Assistant to the President .... Ms. Leslie D. GALLAGHER
03 Executive Vice President .... Dr. Christina PONCE
10 VP Finance & Administration .... Mr. Steve EVANS
05 VP Instruction .... Dr. Veronique TRAN
32 VP Student Affairs .... Dr. Donnetta SUCHON
12 Dean of Huntsville Center at TDCJ .... Ms. Donna P. ZUNIGA
09 Exec Dir Institutional Research .... Dr. Michael K. FLEMING
13 Chief Information Officer .... Dr. Carolyn A. LIGHTFOOT
103 VP Workforce & Corporate Partnershp .... Dr. Angela ORIANO
06 Registrar .... Mr. Scott BENNETT
15 Director Human Resources .... Ms. Amanda SUMMERS
26 Director Marketing & Public Affairs .... Ms. Susan SMEDLEY
37 Interim Director Financial Aid .... Ms. Rachel OLIVER
102 Exec Dir Foundation & Resource Dev .... Ms. Pam WARFORD
96 Director Purchasing .... Mr. Mike SPARKES

LeTourneau University (A)

PO Box 7001, 2100 S Mobberly Ave,
Longview TX 75607-7001
County: Gregg FICE Identification: 003584
Unit ID: 226231
Telephone: (903) 233-3000 Carnegie Class: Masters/M
FAX Number: (903) 233-3101 Calendar System: Semester
URL: www.letu.edu
Established: 1946 Annual Undergrad Tuition & Fees: $28,480
Enrollment: 2,795 Coed
Affiliation or Control: Independent Non-Profit IRS Status: 501(c)3
Highest Offering: Master's
Accreditation: SC, ENG, ENGT, NURSE

01 President .... Dr. Dale A. LUNSFORD
05 Provost & VP for Academic Affairs .... Dr. Steven D. MASON
30 Vice President for Development .... Dr. Terry ZEITLOW
10 VP Finance/Administration .... Mr. Mike HOOD
32 Dean of Students .... Ms. Kristy MORGAN
84 VP Residential Enrollment Services .... Mr. Carl ARNOLD
26 VP Marketing & Communications .... Mr. Don EGLE
88 Assoc Prov for Residential Admin .... Dr. Benjamin CALDWELL
88 VP for Global Operations .... Dr. Melanie ROUDKOVSKI
07 Associate VP Global Enrollment Svcs .... Mr. Christopher W. FONTAINE
18 Asst VP of Facilities Services .... Mr. Ben HAYWOOD
53 Dean School of Education .... Dr. Larry FRAZIER
50 Dean School of Business .... Dr. Van GRAHAM
54 Dean Sch Engineering & Engr Tech .... Dr. Steve STARRETT
49 Dean School of Arts & Sciences .... Dr. Larry FRAZIER
88 Dean School of Aeronautical Science .... Mr. Fred L. RITCHEY
35 Assoc Dean Student Engagement .... Mr. Steve CONN
08 Director Learning Resource Center .... Shelby WAVE
41 Director of Athletics .... Ms. Terri DEIKE
25 Director Office of Sponsored Pgms .... Mr. Paul R. BOGGS
13 Chief Information Officer .... Mr. Matthew HENRY
15 Director of Human Resources .... Mrs. Phyllis TURNER
23 Director Health Services .... Mrs. Jerrie REYNOLDS
19 Chief of Police .... Mr. Michael SCHULTZ
36 Director of Career Services .... Mrs. Deena SHELTON
06 University Registrar .... Mr. Texas RUEGG
07 Director of Admissions .... Mr. Michael VANBROCKLIN
29 Director of Alumni & Parent Rels .... Ms. Jamie DEYOUNG
27 Director of University Relations .... Ms. Janet RAGLAND
27 Director Marketing & Communication .... Ms. Kate GRONEWALD
21 Controller .... Ms. Vikki KEILERS
09 Asst VP for Accreditation & QA .... Dr. Karl PAYTON
88 Executive Dir Ctr for Faith & Work .... Mr. Bill PEEL
04 Administrative Asst to President .... Mrs. Denise BAILEY
106 Assoc VP for Global Student Success .... Mr. Carlton MITCHELL
37 Director Student Financial Aid .... Ms. Tracy WATKINS
38 Director Center for Counseling .... Mrs. Treva BARHAM
104 Chief Global Initiatives Officer .... Mr. Alan CLIPPERTON
83 Dean Col Hlth Sciences/Prof Studies .... Dr. Melanie ROUDKOVSKI
73 Dean School of Theology & Vocation .... Dr. Kelly LIEBENGOOD
66 Dean School of Nursing .... Dr. Kimberly QUIETT
101 Secretary of the Institution/Board .... Mr. Merle STOLTZFUS
105 Director Web Services .... Mr. Mark ROEDEL
39 Director Student Housing .... Mr. Tony ZAPPASODI

Lincoln College of Technology (B)

2915 Alouette Drive, Grand Prairie TX 75052
County: Tarrant FICE Identification: 008353
Unit ID: 226277
Telephone: (972) 660-5701 Carnegie Class: Not Classified
FAX Number: (972) 660-6148 Calendar System: Other
URL: www.lincolntech.com
Established: Annual Undergrad Tuition & Fees: N/A
Enrollment: 872 Coed
Affiliation or Control: Proprietary IRS Status: Proprietary
Highest Offering: Associate Degree
Accreditation: ACCSC

01 Campus President .... Mr. Mike COULING

Lone Star College System (C)

5000 Research Forest Drive,
The Woodlands TX 77381-4356
County: Harris FICE Identification: 011145
Unit ID: 227182
Telephone: (832) 813-6500 Carnegie Class: Assoc/HT-Mix Trad/Non
FAX Number: N/A Calendar System: Semester
URL: www.lonestar.edu
Established: 1972 Annual Undergrad Tuition & Fees (In-District): $1,552
Enrollment: 70,724 Coed
Affiliation or Control: State/Local IRS Status: 501(c)3
Highest Offering: Associate Degree
Accreditation: SC, ADNUR, CAHIIM, CEA, COARC, DH, DMS, EMT, MAC, MUS, OTA, PTAA, RAD, SURGT

01 Chancellor .... Dr. Stephen HEAD
03 Executive Vice Chancellor .... Dr. Alicia HARVEY-SMITH
10 Vice Chanc for Admin & Finance .... Ms. Jennifer OLENICK
13 Vice Chanc/Chief Info Officer .... Mr. Link ALANDER
26 Vice Chanc Govt & Public Relations .... Mr. Amos MCDONALD
05 AVC Academic Affairs .... Mr. Michael KRALL
32 AVC Student Success .... Dr. Chantell HINES
43 General Counsel .... Mr. Mario CASTILLO
100 Vice Chanc/Chief of Staff .... Ms. Helen CLOUGHERTY
12 President of LSC-Kingwood .... Dr. Katherine PERSSON
12 President of LSC-Tomball .... Dr. Lee Ann NUTT
12 President of LSC-North Harris .... Dr. Gerald NAPOLES
12 President of LSC-Montgomery .... Dr. Rebecca RILEY
12 President of LSC-CyFair .... Dr. Seelpa KESHVALA
12 President of LSC-University Park .... Mr. Shah ARDALAN
18 Vice Chanc Facilities/Construction .... Vacant
15 AVC Human Resources .... Mr. Mark YURAN
105 Director Portal Services .... Mr. Harry KHEHRA
21 AVC Admin & Finance .... Ms. Tammy CORTES
106 AVC LSC-Online .... Vacant
45 Exec Dir Strategic Plng & Assess .... Dr. Christopher TKACH
14 AVC Office Tech Services .... Vacant
08 Director Library/LSC-Kingwood .... Mr. Anthony MCMILLIAN
08 Director Library/LSC-Tomball .... Ms. Pamela SHAFER
08 Director Library/LSC-North Harris .... Ms. Pradeep LELE
08 Director Library/LSC-Cy Fair .... Mr. Michael STAFFORD
08 Director Library/LSC-Montgomery .... Dr. Janice PEYTON
08 Director Library/LSC-Univ Park .... Ms. Shannon HAUSINGER
37 Exec Dir Financial Aid .... Ms. Tracie HUNTER
116 Exec Director Internal Audit .... Ms. Leticia CHARBONNEAU
19 Chief of Police/Dir Pub Safety .... Mr. Paul WILLINGHAM
96 Director of Purchasing .... Mr. William DODD
04 Executive Asst to Chancellor .... Ms. Elva BORSCH
111 Chief Advancement Officer .... Vacant
29 Director of Constituent Engagement .... Ms. Susan SUMMERS

Lubbock Christian University (D)

5601 19th Street, Lubbock TX 79407-2099
County: Lubbock FICE Identification: 003586
Unit ID: 226383
Telephone: (806) 796-8800 Carnegie Class: Masters/M
FAX Number: (806) 720-7255 Calendar System: Semester
URL: www.lcu.edu
Established: 1957 Annual Undergrad Tuition & Fees: $21,166
Enrollment: 1,958 Coed
Affiliation or Control: Churches Of Christ IRS Status: 501(c)3
Highest Offering: Master's
Accreditation: SC, NUR, SW, @THEOL

01 President .... Mr. L. Timothy PERRIN
03 Executive Vice President .... Dr. Brian STARR
05 Provost & Chief Academic Officer .... Dr. Rodney B. BLACKWOOD
43 General Counsel .... Dr. Bart PRUITT
30 Vice Pres University Advancement .... Mr. Raymond RICHARDSON
10 Chief Financial Officer .... Mr. Brandon GOEN
13 Vice President for Technology .... Dr. Karl MAHAN
26 Vice Pres for University Relations .... Mr. Warren MCNEILL
107 Dean Col of Professional Studies .... Dr. Toby ROGERS
49 Dean College Liberal Arts/Education .... Dr. Susan BLASSINGAME
73 Dean Col Biblical Stds/Behavior Sci .... Dr. Jesse LONG
09 Asst VP for Instl Effectiveness .... Mr. Randy SELLERS
41 Athletic Director .... Mr. Paul HISE
06 Registrar .... Mrs. Janice STONE
37 Director of Financial Assistance .... Mrs. Amy HARDESTY
32 Dean of Students .... Mr. Josh STEPHENS
08 Director of Library Services .... Ms. Paula GANNAWAY
18 Director of Campus Facilities .... Mr. Mike SELLECK
38 Director Student Counseling .... Mr. John MAPLES
92 Director of Honors Program .... Dr. Stacy PATTY
23 Director of Medical Clinic .... Dr. Jeff SMITH
14 Director of Technology Services .... Mr. Robert SMITH
88 Director of Disability Services .... Vacant
39 Director of Residential Life .... Mrs. Sunny PARK
07 Director of Admissions .... Mr. Chris HAYES
15 Human Resources Director .... Mrs. Brenda LOWE
29 Director Alumni Relations .... Mrs. Sheila DYE
19 Director of Security .... Mr. Michael SMITH
40 Bookstore Manager .... Mrs. Denise MCNEILL
04 Administrative Asst to President .... Ms. Rhonda SHOOTER
84 Director Enrollment Management .... Mr. Mondy BREWER
50 Dean School of Business .... Mr. Tracy MACK

McLennan Community College (E)

1400 College Drive, Waco TX 76708-1498
County: McLennan FICE Identification: 003590
Unit ID: 226578
Telephone: (254) 299-8000 Carnegie Class: Assoc/MT-VT-Mix Trad/Non
FAX Number: (254) 299-8654 Calendar System: Semester
URL: www.mclennan.edu
Established: 1965 Annual Undergrad Tuition & Fees (In-District): $2,760
Enrollment: 8,305 Coed
Affiliation or Control: State/Local IRS Status: 501(c)3
Highest Offering: Associate Degree
Accreditation: SC, ADNUR, CAHIIM, COARC, EMT, MAC, MLTAD, OTA, PTAA, RAD, SURGT

01 President .... Dr. Johnette MCKOWN
10 Vice Pres Finance & Administration .... Dr. Stephen BENSON
05 Vice President Instruction .... Dr. Fred HILLS
22 Equal Employment Opportunity Ofcr .... Mr. Al POLLARD
32 Vice President Student Success .... Dr. Drew CANHAM
09 Vice Pres Research/Effectiveness .... Dr. Phil RHODES
102 Exec Director MCC Foundation .... Ms. Kim PATTERSON
11 Director Administrative Services .... Ms. Lori SOUTHERN
37 Director Financial Aid .... Mr. James KUBACAK
26 Director Marketing & Communication .... Ms. Lisa WILHELMI
41 Director Athletics .... Mrs. Shawn TROCHIM
06 Director Records & Registration .... Mr. Herman V. TUCKER
07 Director Admissions & Recruitment .... Mrs. Karen CLARK
08 Director Library Services .... Mr. Daniel MARTINSEN
15 Director Human Resources .... Ms. Missy KITTNER
18 Director Physical Plant .... Mrs. Dianne E. FEYERHERM
21 Director Financial Services .... Mrs. Terry LECHLER
76 Dean Health Professions .... Ms. Glynnis GAINES
49 Dean Arts & Sciences .... Dr. Fred HILLS
51 Dean Continuing Education .... Mr. Frank GRAVES

McMurry University (F)

1400 Sayles Boulevard, Abilene TX 79697
County: Taylor FICE Identification: 003591
Unit ID: 226587
Telephone: (325) 793-3800 Carnegie Class: Bac-Diverse
FAX Number: (325) 793-6800 Calendar System: Semester
URL: www.mcm.edu
Established: 1923 Annual Undergrad Tuition & Fees: $26,275
Enrollment: 1,071 Coed
Affiliation or Control: United Methodist IRS Status: 501(c)3
Highest Offering: Master's
Accreditation: SC, NURSE

01 President .... Dr. Sandra HARPER
05 Vice Pres Academic Affairs .... Dr. James HUNT
10 Vice Pres Finance & Administration .... Mrs. Lisa L. WILLIAMS
111 Vice Pres Institutional Advancement .... Ms. Debra HULSE
18 AVP Facilities & Campus Planning .... Mr. Brad POORMAN
84 Vice Pres for Enrollment Management .... Mr. David HERINGER
105 Webmaster .... Mr. Jim QUINNETT
14 Director of Customer Services .... Mr. Freddie FAMBLE, JR.
13 Director of Administrative Systems .... Ms. Kathy DENSLOW
06 Registrar .... Mrs. Carolyn A. CALVERT
08 Director Jay-Rollins Library .... Ms. Terry YOUNG
32 Dean of Students & Campus Life .... Mr. Allen WITHERS
66 Interim Dean School of Nursing .... Dr. Sheila GARLAND
35 Director of Student Activities .... Vacant
37 Director of Financial Aid .... Mr. Tim SEHRIST
21 Controller .... Ms. Tina SCHUELLER
15 Director of Human Resources .... Ms. Lecia HUGHES
108 Dir of Institutional Effectiveness .... Dr. Thomas BENOIT
09 Director of Institutional Research .... Ms. Terry NIXON
26 AVP of Marketing & Communications .... Mr. Daniel MANSON
29 Director Alumni Relations .... Ms. Suzann COUTS
38 Director Counseling & Career Svcs .... Mr. James GREER
41 Director of Athletics .... Mr. Sam FERGUSON
42 Dir of Religious Life/Univ Chaplain .... Rev. Marty CASHBURLESS
19 Director of Campus Security .... Mr. Mark R. ODOM
23 Director of Health Services .... Ms. Ronda HOELSCHER
39 Director of Residence Life .... Vacant
102 Executive Director Donor Relations .... Ms. Nancy SMITH
92 Director Honors Program .... Dr. Philip LE MASTERS
106 Director of Online Education .... Vacant
04 Executive Asst to President .... Ms. Jerri GAZAILLE
50 Dean School of Business .... Dr. Paul MASON

Messenger College (G)

400 S Industrial Boulevard, Euless TX 76040
County: Tarrant FICE Identification: 030926
Unit ID: 417752
Telephone: (817) 554-5950 Carnegie Class: Spec-4-yr-Faith
FAX Number: (817) 391-4003 Calendar System: Semester
URL: www.messengercollege.edu
Established: 1987 Annual Undergrad Tuition & Fees: $9,120
Enrollment: 111 Coed
Affiliation or Control: Pentecostal Church of God IRS Status: 501(c)3
Highest Offering: Baccalaureate
Accreditation: TRACS

01 President .... Rev. Randall K. LAWRENCE
04 Administrative Asst to President .... Sharon TOW
05 VP of Academic Affairs .... Dr. Candace RAYBURN
07 Director of Enrollment Services .... Carrie UNDERWOOD
08 Head Librarian .... Mary THOMASON
10 VP of Business Affairs .... Angela HEPPNER
32 VP of Student Development .... Fiona PARKER
37 Director Student Financial Aid .... Diana SPEEGLE

MIAT College of Technology (A)

533 Northpark Central Dr, Houston TX 77073
Telephone: (713) 401-3399 Identification: 770972
Accreditation: ACCSC

† Branch campus of MIAT College of Technology, Canton, MI

Midland College (B)

3600 N Garfield, Midland TX 79705-6397
County: Midland FICE Identification: 009797
Unit ID: 226806
Telephone: (432) 685-4500 Carnegie Class: Bac/Assoc-Assoc Dom
FAX Number: (432) 685-4714 Calendar System: Semester
URL: www.midland.edu
Established: 1969 Annual Undergrad Tuition & Fees (In-District): $2,580
Enrollment: 5,430 Coed
Affiliation or Control: Local IRS Status: 501(c)3
Highest Offering: Baccalaureate
Accreditation: SC, CAHIIM, COARC, DMS, EMT

01 President .... Dr. Steve THOMAS
03 Executive Vice President .... Dr. Richard C. JOLLY
88 Special Advisor to President .... Dr. Deana SAVAGE
10 Vice Pres Administrative Services .... Mr. Rick BENDER
32 Vice President Student Services .... Ms. Rita Nell DIFFIE
13 Vice Pres Info Tech/Facilities .... Mr. Dennis SEVER
101 Asst to President/Sec to Board .... Mrs. Bahola EDWARDS
106 Dean of Distance Learning/Cont Educ .... Mr. Dale BEIKIRCH
57 Dean of Fine Arts/Communication .... Mr. William FEELER
72 Dean of Applied Technology .... Mr. Curt PERVIER
76 Dean of Health Sciences .... Ms. Carmen EDWARDS
81 Dean of Math/Natural Sciences .... Dr. Margaret WADE
83 Dean Adult/Developmental Education .... Mrs. Lynda WEBB
26 Dean of Public Information .... Ms. Rebecca BELL
30 Exec Dir Inst Advancement/Col Found .... Vacant
06 Registrar .... Mrs. Angela BALCH
08 Head Librarian .... Mr. John DEATS
15 Director of Human Resources/Payroll .... Mrs. Natasha MORGAN
18 Director Physical Plant .... Mr. Ken RILEY
19 Chief of Police .... Mr. Richard MCKEE
35 Student Life Director .... Mr. Ty SOLIZ
41 Athletic Director .... Mr. Forrest ALLEN
09 Dir Institutional Effect/Planning .... Ms. Karen WAGGONER
37 Director Student Financial Aid .... Ms. Yolanda RAMOS
96 Director Purchasing .... Ms. Barbara FENNELL
84 Dean of Enrollment Management .... Ms. Liz ZENTENO
07 Director of Admissions/Recruitment .... Mr. Jeremy MARTINEZ

Midwestern State University (C)

3410 Taft Boulevard, Wichita Falls TX 76308-2095
County: Wichita FICE Identification: 003592
Unit ID: 226833
Telephone: (940) 397-4000 Carnegie Class: Masters/M
FAX Number: (940) 397-4042 Calendar System: Semester
URL: www.mwsu.edu
Established: 1922 Annual Undergrad Tuition & Fees (In-State): $8,620
Enrollment: 6,043 Coed
Affiliation or Control: State IRS Status: 501(c)3
Highest Offering: Master's
Accreditation: SC, ART, CAATE, CAEPN, COARC, DH, ENG, MUS, NURSE, RAD, SW, THEA

01 President .... Dr. Suzanne SHIPLEY
05 Provost .... Dr. James JOHNSTON
10 VP Business Affairs & Finance .... Dr. Marilyn FOWLE
111 VP Univ Advancement & Student Affs .... Mr. Anthony VIDMAR
32 VP Student Affairs/Enrollment Mgmt .... Dr. Keith LAMB
18 Assoc VP Facilities Services .... Mr. Kyle OWEN
35 Assoc VP Student Affairs/Enrol Mgmt .... Mr. Matthew PARK
13 Chief Information Systems .... Dr. David SANCHEZ
06 Registrar .... Ms. Darla INGLISH
08 University Librarian .... Dr. Clara LATHAM
37 Director of Student Financial Aid .... Ms. Kathy PENNARTZ-BROWNING
38 Director of Counseling Center .... Dr. Pam MIDGETT
51 Director of Extended Education .... Dr. Pamela MORGAN
07 Director of Admissions .... Ms. Gayonne BEAVERS
19 Chief of Police .... Mr. Patrick COGGINS
26 Director Public Info/Marketing .... Ms. Julie GAYNOR
88 Dir Donor Services and Scholarships .... Ms. Laura PETERSON
36 Director Career Management Center .... Mr. Dirk WELCH
41 Interim Director of Athletics .... Mr. Kyle WILLIAMS
15 Director of Human Resources .... Ms. Dawn FISHER
09 Director Inst Research & Planning .... Mr. Mark MCCLENDON
21 Controller .... Mr. Chris STOVALL
23 Director Vinson Health Center .... Dr. Keith WILLIAMSON
20 Associate VP Academic Affairs .... Vacant
50 Dean College Business Admin .... Dr. Terry PATTON
53 Dean College of Education .... Dr. Matthew CAPPS
57 Dean College of Fine Arts .... Dr. Martin CAMACHO
76 Int Dean Col Health Sci/Human Svcs .... Dr. Jeffrey KILLION
79 Dean College Humanities/Social Sci .. Dr. Samuel E. WATSON, III
81 Dean College of Science & Math .... Dr. Margaret BROWN MARSDEN
86 Director Board & Govt Relations .... Ms. Deborah L. BARROW
29 Director of Alumni Relations .... Ms. Leslee PONDER
121 Director of Academic Success Center .... Vacant
105 Webmaster .... Mr. Jonathan SHIREY
96 Director of Purchasing .... Mr. Stephen SHELLEY
22 Dir Disability Support Services .... Ms. Debra HIGGINBOTHAM
39 Director Housing & Residence Life .... Ms. Kristi SCHULTE
30 Director University Development .... Mr. Steve SHIPP
104 Director of International Education .... Dr. Michael MILLS
88 Director Testing Center .... Ms. Lynn DUCIOAME
85 Director International Services .... Dr. Randy GLEAN
114 Director Budget & Management .... Ms. Valarie MAXWELL
88 Director Museum .... Dr. Francine CARRARO
88 Director Student Support Services .... Ms. Lisa ESTRADA-HAMBY
88 Campus Postal Supervisor .... Mr. Jon LANE
92 Coordinator Honors Program .... Mrs. Juliana LEHMAN-FELTS
43 Dir Legal Services/General Counsel .... Mr. Barry MACHA

National American University-Austin (D)

13801 Burnet Road, Suite 300, Austin TX 78727
Telephone: (512) 651-4700 Identification: 770411
Accreditation: &NH, CVT

† Branch campus of National American University, Rapid City, SD

National American University-Georgetown (E)

1015 W University Avenue, Suite 700, Georgetown TX 78628
Telephone: (512) 942-6750 Identification: 770413
Accreditation: &NH, MAC

† Branch campus of National American University, Rapid City, SD

National American University-Houston (F)

11511 Katy Freeway Ste 200, Houston TX 77079
Telephone: (832) 619-7300 Identification: 770930
Accreditation: &NH

† Branch campus of National American University, Rapid City, SD.

National American University-Lewisville (G)

475 State Hwy 121 Bypass #150, Lewisville TX 75067
Telephone: (972) 829-2150 Identification: 770415
Accreditation: &NH

† Branch campus of National American University, Rapid City, SD

National American University-Mesquite (H)

18600 LBJ Freeway, Mesquite TX 75150
Telephone: (972) 773-8800 Identification: 770416
Accreditation: &NH, MAC

† Branch campus of National American University, Rapid City, SD

National American University-Richardson (I)

300 N Coit Road, Suite 225, Richardson TX 75080
Telephone: (972) 773-8650 Identification: 770414
Accreditation: &NH

† Branch campus of National American University, Rapid City, SD

Navarro College (J)

3200 W Seventh Avenue, Corsicana TX 75110-4899
County: Navarro FICE Identification: 003593
Unit ID: 227146
Telephone: (903) 874-6501 Carnegie Class: Assoc/MT-VT-High Trad
FAX Number: (903) 874-4636 Calendar System: Semester
URL: www.navarrocollege.edu
Established: 1946 Annual Undergrad Tuition & Fees (In-District): $2,400
Enrollment: 9,592 Coed
Affiliation or Control: Local IRS Status: 501(c)3
Highest Offering: Associate Degree
Accreditation: SC, ADNUR, EMT, MLTAD, OTA, PTAA

01 District President .... Dr. Richard M. SANCHEZ
12 President Ellis Co Campuses .... Dr. Kenneth MARTIN
05 Vice Pres Academic Affairs .... Ms. Carol HANES
10 Vice President Finance & Admin .... Ms. Thomas TERESA
111 VP Oper/Institutional Advancement .... Dr. Harold HOUSLEY
32 Vice President Student Services .... Ms. Maryann HAILEY
84 VP Enroll Mgmt/Inst Effect .... Ms. Sina RUIZ
15 VP Human Resources .... Ms. Marcy BALLEW
88 Dean of Midlothian Campus .... Dr. Alex KAJSTURA
26 Director of Mktg/Public Relations .... Ms. Stacie SIPES
41 Athletic Director .... Mr. Roark MONTGOMERY
20 Interim Exec Dean of Acad Studies .... Mr. Terry PETERMAN
75 Exec Dean Career and Tech Ed .... Dr. Eileen HAMBY
106 Dean of Online Instruction .... Mr. Matthew MILLER
76 Dean of Health Professions .... Mr. Guy FEATHERSTON
12 Dean of Navarro College South .... Dr. Joel MICHAELIS
21 Comptroller .... Ms. Aaron LANGSTON
103 Dean of Workforce & Cont Ed .... Ms. Darla LITTREL
08 Dean of Libraries .... Mr. Tim KEVIL
07 Dir of Admissions/Registrar .... Ms. Tammy ADAMS
18 Exec Director of Facilities .... Mr. Karl HUMPHRIES
13 Interim CIO .... Ms. Karen HEINEMANN
37 Director Student Financial Aid .... Ms. Kristal NICHOLSON
39 Director of Residence Life .... Mr. Charles BETTS
104 Director of International Programs .... Ms. Elizabeth PILLANS
88 Academic Dean of Ellis County .... Ms. Terry GIBSON
88 Interim Dean of Sci/Kines/Dev Stds .... Ms. Christina MIMS
71 Dir Navarro College TJJD Program .... Ms. Sheri SHORT
35 Dean of Student Guidance .... Mr. Michael DAVILA
35 Dean of Student Services Ellis Cty .... Ms. Kristin WALKER
09 Director of Institutional Research .... Ms. Elizabeth CHIVERS
04 Exec Asst to District President .... Ms. Leslie SMITH

North American University (K)

11929 W. Airport Boulevard, Stafford TX 77477
County: Fort Bend FICE Identification: 041795
Unit ID: 461795
Telephone: (832) 230-5555 Carnegie Class: Bac-Diverse
FAX Number: N/A Calendar System: Semester
URL: www.na.edu
Established: 2010 Annual Undergrad Tuition & Fees: $11,900
Enrollment: 660 Coed
Affiliation or Control: Non-denominational IRS Status: 501(c)3
Highest Offering: Master's
Accreditation: ACICS

01 President .... Dr. Serif A. TEKALAN
05 Vice Pres Academic Affairs-Provost .... Dr. John C. TOPUZ
11 VP Admin Affairs/Assoc Prof .... Dr. Kadir ALMUS
04 Administrative Asst to President .... Jill SELTZER
06 Registrar .... Edra EDWARDS
07 Associate Director of Admissions .... Shawn WASHINGTON
08 Head Librarian .... Gary CHAUFFEE
106 Dir Online Education/E-learning .... Mustafa MALDAR
13 Chief Info Technology Officer (CIO) .... Khudoyor S. ORTIKOV
32 Chief Student Affairs/Student Life .... Osman KANLIOGLU
37 Assoc Dir Student Financial Aid .... Tia SIMON
10 Chief Business Officer .... Dovran OVEZOV

North Central Texas College (L)

1525 W. California Street, Gainesville TX 76240-4699
County: Cooke FICE Identification: 003558
Unit ID: 224110
Telephone: (940) 668-7731 Carnegie Class: Assoc/HT-High Trad
FAX Number: (940) 668-6049 Calendar System: Semester
URL: www.nctc.edu
Established: 1924 Annual Undergrad Tuition & Fees (In-District): $1,824
Enrollment: 9,618 Coed
Affiliation or Control: State/Local IRS Status: 501(c)3
Highest Offering: Associate Degree
Accreditation: SC, ADNUR, EMT, SURGT

01 President .... Dr. G. Brent WALLACE
05 Vice Pres Instruction/Student Svcs .... Dr. Andrew FISHER
32 Vice President of Student Services .... Vacant
10 Vice President Fiscal Affairs .... Dr. Janie NEIGHBORS
11 Vice Pres Administrative Affairs .... Mr. Robbie BAUGH
30 Vice Pres External Affairs .... Ms. Debbie SHARP
103 Associate VP Academic Partnerships .... Dr. Emily KLEMENT
108 Assoc VP Strategic Partnership .... Dr. Emily KLEMENT
13 Chief Information Officer .... Ms. Denise CASON
08 Dean of Libraries .... Ms. Diane ROETHER
15 Sr Director Human Resources .... Ms. Lynn PETERS
37 Director Financial Aid .... Ms. Ashley TATUM
06 Registrar/Director of Admissions .... Ms. Melinda CARROLL
38 Director Advisement .... Ms. Tracey FLENIKEN
26 Dir Marketing and Public Relations .... Mrs. Dianne WALTERSCHEID
41 Athletic Director .... Mr. Van HEDRICK
35 Director of Student Life .... Ms. Daisy GARCIA
76 Dean of Health Science .... Mrs. Gie ARCHER
72 Dean of Instruction Gainesville .... Ms. Sara FLUSCHE
49 Dean of Instruction Corinth .... Dr. Larry GILBERT
49 Dean of Instruction Flower Mound .... Mrs. Sara ALFORD
19 Police Chief .... Mr. James FITCH
35 Dean of Students .... Dr. Rodney LIPSCOMB
12 Dean of Denton County Campuses .... Mr. Roy CULBERSON
12 Director of Flower Mound Campus .... Ms. Jessica DEROCHE
12 Director of Bowie Campus .... Dr. Jose DASILVA
12 Director of Graham Campus .... Ms. Kim BIRDWELL

Northeast Texas Community College (M)

PO Box 1307, Mount Pleasant TX 75456-1307
County: Titus FICE Identification: 023154
Unit ID: 227225
Telephone: (903) 434-8100 Carnegie Class: Assoc/MT-VT-Mix Trad/Non
FAX Number: (903) 572-6712 Calendar System: Semester
URL: www.ntcc.edu
Established: 1984 Annual Undergrad Tuition & Fees (In-District): $2,682
Enrollment: 2,989 Coed
Affiliation or Control: Local IRS Status: 501(c)3
Highest Offering: Associate Degree
Accreditation: SC, EMT, MAC, MLTAD, PTAA

01 President .... Dr. Brad W. JOHNSON
04 Executive Asst to the President .... Ms. Pat L. TALLANT
05 Executive Vice Pres for Instruction .... Dr. Ron CLINTON
11 Vice Pres Administrative Services .... Mr. Jeffrey CHAMBERS
111 Vice Pres Institutional Advancement .... Dr. Jonathan W. MCCULLOUGH
32 VP for Student & Outreach Services .... Dr. Josh STEWART
103 Assoc VP for Workforce Development .... Dr. Kevin ROSE
37 Dean Enroll/Dir Student Fin Assist .... Ms. Kim IRVIN
76 Dean of Allied Health Professions .... Dr. Shannon COX-KELLEY
84 Associate Dean of Outreach Services .... Ms. Melody HENRY

18 Director of Plant Services .... Mr. Tom RAMLER
08 Director Learning Resource Center .... Mr. Ron BOWDEN
13 Director of Computer Services .... Mr. Kenneth GOODSON
26 Director Marketing/Public Relations .... Ms. Jodi WEBER
06 Registrar .... Ms. Betsy GOODING
15 Director Human Resources .... Ms. Amy ADKINS
10 Controller .... Ms. Brandi M. DERRICK
09 Dir Institutional Effectiveness .... Ms. Toni LABEFF
07 Director of Admissions .... Ms. Melissa HARRISON
36 Career Development/Advisor .... Ms. Lynda WATSON

Northwood University (A)

1114 West FM 1382, Cedar Hill TX 75104
Telephone: (972) 293-5400 Identification: 770280
Accreditation: &NH, ACBSP

† Branch campus of Northwood University, Midland, MI

Oblate School of Theology (B)

285 Oblate Drive, San Antonio TX 78216-6693
County: Bexar FICE Identification: 003595
Unit ID: 227289
Telephone: (210) 341-1366 Carnegie Class: Spec-4-yr-Faith
FAX Number: (210) 341-4519 Calendar System: Semester
URL: www.ost.edu
Established: 1903 Annual Graduate Tuition & Fees: N/A
Enrollment: 134 Coed
Affiliation or Control: Roman Catholic IRS Status: 501(c)3
Highest Offering: Doctorate; No Undergraduates
Accreditation: SC, PAST, THEOL

01 President .... Rev. Ronald ROLHEISER
05 Vice Pres Academic Affairs/Dean .... Dr. Scott WOODWARD
10 Vice Pres Finance/Human Resources .... Mr. Rene ESPINOSA
11 Vice Pres Administrative Affairs .... Rev. David KALERT
30 Vice Pres Institutional Advancement .... Mrs. Lea KOCHANEK
20 Associate Dean .... Sr. Linda GIBLER
51 Assoc Dean of Continuing Education .... Mrs. Rose MARDEN
88 Director Oblate Renewal Center .... Mrs. K.T COCKERELL
18 Director of Physical Plant .... Mr. Pedro CANTU
08 Director of the Library .... Ms. Maria GARCIA
06 Registrar & Director of Admissions .... Mr. Mario PORTER
88 Director Lay Ministry Institute .... Mrs. Bonnie ABADIE
88 Director Ministry to Ministers Pgm .... Rev. James MYERS
09 Dir Instl Research/Plng/Assessment .... Rev. David KALERT
88 Director DMin Program .... Rev. Wayne CAVALIER
88 Director PhD Program .... Rev. John MARKEY
26 Director of Communications .... Mr. Michael PARKER

Odessa College (C)

201 W University Boulevard, Odessa TX 79764-7127
County: Ector FICE Identification: 003596
Unit ID: 227304
Telephone: (432) 335-6400 Carnegie Class: Assoc/MT-VT-Mix Trad/Non
FAX Number: (432) 335-6860 Calendar System: Semester
URL: www.odessa.edu
Established: 1946 Annual Undergrad Tuition & Fees (In-District): $2,808
Enrollment: 5,473 Coed
Affiliation or Control: Local IRS Status: 501(c)3
Highest Offering: Associate Degree
Accreditation: SC, ADNUR, EMT, MUS, PTAA, RAD, SURGT

01 President .... Dr. Gregory D. WILLIAMS
05 Vice President for Instruction .... Ms. Valerie JONES
10 Vice President Business Affairs .... Ms. Virginia E. CHISUM
32 VP Student Svcs/Enrollment Mgmt .... Ms. Kimberly MCKAY
13 Vice President for Information Tech .... Mr. Shawn SHREVES
09 VP for Institutional Effectiveness .... Dr. Donald WOOD
30 Exec Director for Advancement .... Mr. Jeffrey MEYERS
11 Exec Dir of Administration & HR .... Mr. Ken ZARTNER
49 Dean of Arts & Sciences .... Dr. Eric YEAGER
84 Exec Director Enrollment Services .... Mr. Louis GONZALES
06 Registrar .... Ms. Karen DOUGHTY
41 Director Intercollegiate Athletics .... Mr. Wayne BAKER
37 Director Student Financial Svcs .... Ms. Ashley WARREN
18 Director Facilities & Construction .... Mr. Bryan HEIFNER
26 Exec Director of Marketing .... Mr. Frank RICH
38 Exec Director Student Completion .... Ms. Kristi CLEMMER
96 Dir of Purchasing/Business Services .... Ms. Cindy CURNUTT

Our Lady of the Lake University (D)

411 SW 24th Street, San Antonio TX 78207-4689
County: Bexar FICE Identification: 003598
Unit ID: 227331
Telephone: (210) 434-6711 Carnegie Class: Masters/L
FAX Number: (210) 431-3928 Calendar System: Semester
URL: www.ollusa.edu
Established: 1895 Annual Undergrad Tuition & Fees: $27,160
Enrollment: 3,334 Coed
Affiliation or Control: Roman Catholic IRS Status: 501(c)3
Highest Offering: Doctorate
Accreditation: SC, ACBSP, COPSY, MFCD, SP, SW

01 President .... Dr. Diane MELBY
11 Vice President Administration .... Ms. Rosalinda GARCIA
05 Vice President for Academic Affairs .... Dr. Marcheta EVANS
32 Vice President of Student Life .... Mr. Jack L. HANK
10 Vice President Finance & Facilities .... Mr. Anthony TURRIETTA
30 Vice Pres Institutional Advancement .... Mr. Daniel YOXALL
84 Vice Pres of Enrollment Management .... Ms. Mary SCOTKA
26 Vice Pres Communications/Marketing .... Mr. Daniel YOXALL
42 University Chaplain .... Fr. Kevin FAUSZ
13 Chief Technology Officer .... Mr. Curtis L. SPEARS
108 Asst VP for I/E & Accreditation .... Dr. Kara LARKAN-SKINNER
18 Director Physical Plant .... Mr. Darrell R. GLASSCOCK
15 Director Human Resources .... Mr. Phillip VARGAS
06 Registrar .... Ms. Betty GALVAN
14 Director Network & Telecomm .... Mr. David LYTLE
19 Chief of Police/Dir Campus Safety .... Mr. Ramon ZERTUCHE
39 Director Residence Life .... Mr. Mark R. CENTER
36 Director Career Counsel/Placement .... Mr. Andres JAIME
38 Director of Counseling Services .... Dr. Rosa ESPINOSA
23 Director of Health Services .... Ms. Julie STUCKEY
40 Director Bookstore .... Ms. Jennifer WOLFF
102 Corporate Relations Officer .... Ms. Roxanne SANCHEZ
44 Dir Advancement Svcs/Annual Giving .... Mr. John SANCHEZ
29 Dir Alumni/Stewardship Relations .... Mrs. Debora GUZMAN
37 Director of Financial Aid .... Ms. Esmarelda FLORES
09 Dir Institutional Research .... Ms. Frances FREY
07 Asst Dir of Undergrad Admissions .... Ms. Shannon TIJERINA

Panola College (E)

1109 West Panola Street, Carthage TX 75633-2397
County: Panola FICE Identification: 003600
Unit ID: 227386
Telephone: (903) 693-2000 Carnegie Class: Assoc/HT-High Trad
FAX Number: (903) 693-1167 Calendar System: Semester
URL: www.panola.edu
Established: 1947 Annual Undergrad Tuition & Fees (In-District): $1,824
Enrollment: 2,675 Coed
Affiliation or Control: Local IRS Status: 501(c)3
Highest Offering: Associate Degree
Accreditation: SC, ADNUR, CAHIIM, EMT, MLTAD, OTA

01 President .... Dr. Gregory S. POWELL
05 Vice President of Instruction .... Dr. Billy W. ADAMS
32 Vice President of Student Services .... Mr. Don CLINTON
10 Vice President of Fiscal Services .... Mr. Troy CASERTA
49 Dean of Arts/Sciences/Technology .... Mrs. Natalie OSWALT
106 Dean of Distance/Digital Learning .... Mrs. Teresa BROOKS
76 Dean of Health Sciences .... Mrs. Kelly REED-HIRSCH
11 Director of Administrative Services .... Mr. Mike EDENS
07 Director of Admissions/Registrar .... Mr. Jeremy DORMAN
30 Dir Institutional Advancement .... Mrs. Jessica PACE
08 Director of Library .... Mrs. Cristie FERGUSON
103 Dir of Workforce & Economic Devel .... Mrs. Whitney MCBEE
09 Director of Institutional Research .... Mrs. Trythena WALKER
12 Director of Shelby County Operation .... Mrs. Cancee LESTER
12 Director of Marshall Operations .... Mrs. Laura WOOD
13 Director of IT Service .... Mr. Allen WEST
19 Campus Police Chief .... Mr. Bryan RICKERT
37 Director Student Financial Aid .... Mrs. Denise WELCH
26 Marketing Coordinator .... Ms. Teresa BEASLEY
18 Dir of Facilities/Physical Plant .... Mr. Alan MOON

Paris Junior College (F)

2400 Clarksville Street, Paris TX 75460-6298
County: Lamar FICE Identification: 003601
Unit ID: 227401
Telephone: (903) 785-7661 Carnegie Class: Assoc/HVT-Mix Trad/Non
FAX Number: (903) 782-0370 Calendar System: Semester
URL: www.parisjc.edu
Established: 1924 Annual Undergrad Tuition & Fees (In-District): $2,250
Enrollment: 4,999 Coed
Affiliation or Control: State/Local IRS Status: 501(c)3
Highest Offering: Associate Degree
Accreditation: SC, ADNUR, EMT, RAD, SURGT

01 President .... Dr. Pamela D. ANGLIN
05 Vice President of Academic Studies .... Dr. Pamela MILLSAY
103 Vice President Workforce Education .... Mr. John SPRADLING
32 VP Student Access/Success .... Mrs. Sheila REECE
60 Dean Communications/Arts .... Dr. Ken HALEY
07 Director of Admissions .... Mrs. Amie CATO
06 Registrar .... Mrs. Amie CATO
10 Controller .... Mrs. Keitha CARLTON
37 Director Student Financial Aid .... Mrs. Linda SLAWSON
09 Director Institutional Research .... Mrs. Beverly MATTHEWS
111 Director Institutional Advancement .... Mr. Derald BULLS
35 Director Student Life .... Mr. Kenneth WEBB
13 Director Information Technology .... Mr. Eddie MAHAR
26 Chief Public Relations Officer .... Ms. Margaret RUFF
18 Manager Plant Operations .... Mr. Randall COX
15 Director Personnel Services .... Mrs. Paula WHITE

Parker University (G)

2540 Walnut Hill Lane, Dallas TX 75229-5609
County: Dallas FICE Identification: 023053
Unit ID: 243823
Telephone: (972) 438-6932 Carnegie Class: Spec-4-yr-Other Health
FAX Number: (214) 902-2496 Calendar System: Trimester
URL: www.parker.edu
Established: 1982 Annual Undergrad Tuition & Fees: $15,276
Enrollment: 1,015 Coed
Affiliation or Control: Independent Non-Profit IRS Status: 501(c)3
Highest Offering: Doctorate
Accreditation: SC, CAHIIM, CHIRO, COMTA, OTA

01 President .... Dr. William E. MORGAN
05 Vice Pres Academic Operations .... Dr. Janell E. GIBSON
63 Vice Pres College of Chiropractic .... Dr. Ashley E. CLEVELAND
30 Vice Pres Inst Advancement .... Dr. R. Fred ZUKER

Paul Quinn College (H)

3837 Simpson Stuart Road, Dallas TX 75241-4398
County: Dallas FICE Identification: 003602
Unit ID: 227429
Telephone: (214) 376-1000 Carnegie Class: Bac-Diverse
FAX Number: (214) 379-5559 Calendar System: Semester
URL: www.pqc.edu
Established: 1872 Annual Undergrad Tuition & Fees: $8,318
Enrollment: 424 Coed
Affiliation or Control: African Methodist Episcopal IRS Status: 501(c)3
Highest Offering: Baccalaureate
Accreditation: TRACS

01 President .... Dr. Michael J. SORRELL
05 Vice Pres Academic Affairs .... Dr. Kizuwanda GRANT
10 Chief Financial Officer .... Mr. Bruce BRINSON
06 Registrar .... Ms. Twyla GILLS
08 Librarian/Director LRC .... Ms. Clarice MEDLEY-WEEKS
13 Director of Technology .... Vacant
41 Dir Athletics/Intramural Sports .... Ms. Kelsel THOMPSON
37 Director of Financial Aid .... Ms. Dana MINGO
35 Dean Student Support Services .... Dr. Felicia SHEPHARD
18 Director of Facilities .... Vacant
09 Instl Research Representative .... Dr. Chris DOWDY
30 Director of Development .... Mr. Dennis COLEMAN
23 Nurse .... Ms. Glenda DAVIS
07 Director of Recruiting .... Mrs. Jessika LARA

Pima Medical Institute-El Paso (I)

6926 Gateway Blvd., E., El Paso TX 79915
Telephone: (915) 633-1133 Identification: 770962
Accreditation: ABHES

† Branch campus of Pima Medical Institute-Tucson, Tucson, AZ

Pima Medical Institute-Houston (J)

10201-C Katy Freeway, Houston TX 77024
Telephone: (713) 778-0778 Identification: 770510
Accreditation: ABHES, #COARC, DH, OTA, PTAA, RAD

† Branch campus of Pima Medical Institute-Tucson, Tucson, AZ

Quest College (K)

5430 Fredericksburg Road, Ste 310,
San Antonio TX 78229
County: Bexar FICE Identification: 034003
Unit ID: 439507
Telephone: (210) 366-2701 Carnegie Class: Not Classified
FAX Number: (210) 366-0738 Calendar System: Semester
URL: www.questcollege.edu
Established: 1995 Annual Undergrad Tuition & Fees: N/A
Enrollment: 221 Coed
Affiliation or Control: Proprietary IRS Status: Proprietary
Highest Offering: Associate Degree
Accreditation: COE

00 Owner/Administrator .... Ms. Jeanne MARTIN
01 School Director .... Ms. Sandy CLAUSS

Ranger College (L)

1100 College Circle, Ranger TX 76470-3298
County: Eastland FICE Identification: 003603
Unit ID: 227687
Telephone: (254) 647-3234 Carnegie Class: Assoc/HVT-High Trad
FAX Number: (254) 647-1656 Calendar System: Semester
URL: www.rangercollege.edu
Established: 1926 Annual Undergrad Tuition & Fees (In-District): $2,590
Enrollment: 2,063 Coed
Affiliation or Control: Local IRS Status: 501(c)3
Highest Offering: Associate Degree
Accreditation: SC

01 President .... Dr. William J. CAMPION
12 Vice President Brown County .... Dr. Orlando MORENO
12 Vice President Erath County .... Dr. Kerry SCHINDLER
05 Vice President of Instruction .... Dr. Billy ADAMS
10 Vice President Business Service/CFO .... Mr. Paul WOODFIN
103 Vice President Workforce Devlopmnt .... Mr. Dixon BAILEY
32 Vice President of Student Services .... Mr. Manuel MCGRIFF
11 Assoc VP of Administration .... Mrs. Cherie BELTRAN
09 Director of Institutional Research .... Mr. John SLAUGHTER
84 Dean of Enrollment Management .... Mr. Robert CULVERHOUSE
18 Director of Physical Plant .... Mr. Charles LEMASTER
37 Director of Financial Aid .... Mr. Don HILTON
38 Director of Counseling .... Mr. Gabe LEWIS
08 Director of Learning Resources .... Mrs. Crystal STANLEY
121 Director of Advising .... Mrs. Crystal ROSE
15 Human Resources .... Ms. Delinda SPENCER
113 Bursar .... Ms. Evonne CHERRY
41 Athletic Director .... Mr. Billy GILLISPIE
40 Director Bookstore .... Miss Cindy STRINGER

Reformed Theological Seminary (A)

6060 N Central Expressway, Ste. 700, Dallas TX 75206
Telephone: (601) 923-1600 Identification: 667055
Accreditation: THEOL

† Branch campus of Reformed Theological Seminary, Jackson, MS

Remington College-Dallas Campus (B)

1800 Eastgate Drive, Garland TX 75041-5513
County: Dallas FICE Identification: 030265
Unit ID: 223463
Telephone: (972) 686-7878 Carnegie Class: Bac/Assoc-Assoc Dom
FAX Number: (972) 686-5116 Calendar System: Quarter
URL: www.remingtoncollege.edu
Established: 1987 Annual Undergrad Tuition & Fees: $14,953
Enrollment: 890 Coed
Affiliation or Control: Independent Non-Profit IRS Status: 501(c)3
Highest Offering: Baccalaureate
Accreditation: ACCSC

01 Campus President .... Mr. Skip WALLS
05 Academic Dean .... Mr. Charles STRATTON
07 Director of Admissions .... Ms. Macy MONDICS

Remington College-Fort Worth Campus (C)

300 E Loop 820, Fort Worth TX 76112-1225
Telephone: (817) 451-0017 Identification: 666063
Accreditation: ACCSC

Remington College-Houston Southeast Campus (D)

20985 Interstate 45 South, Webster TX 77598
Telephone: (281) 554-1700 Identification: 770601
Accreditation: ACCSC

Remington College-North Houston Campus (E)

11310 Greens Crossing, Suite 300, Houston TX 77067
Telephone: (281) 885-4450 Identification: 770600
Accreditation: ACCSC

Rice University (F)

PO Box 1892, Houston TX 77251-1892
County: Harris FICE Identification: 003604
Unit ID: 227757
Telephone: (713) 348-0000 Carnegie Class: DU-Highest
FAX Number: N/A Calendar System: Semester
URL: www.rice.edu
Established: 1891 Annual Undergrad Tuition & Fees: $43,918
Enrollment: 6,719 Coed
Affiliation or Control: Independent Non-Profit IRS Status: 501(c)3
Highest Offering: Doctorate
Accreditation: SC, ENG

01 President .... Mr. David W. LEEBRON
101 Deputy Sec to Board of Trustees .... Ms. Cynthia L. WILSON
05 Provost .... Dr. Marie L. MIRANDA
11 Vice President Administration .... Dr. Kevin KIRBY
10 Vice President Finance .... Ms. Kathy COLLINS
30 Vice Pres Development/Alumni Rels .... Mr. Darrow ZEIDENSTEIN
115 Vice Pres Investments/Treasurer .... Ms. Allison THACKER
84 Vice President for Enrollment .... Ms. Yvonne DASILVA
26 Vice President for Public Affairs .... Ms. Linda THRANE
13 Vice President IT & CIO .... Ms. Klara JELINKOVA
46 Vice Provost Research .... Dr. Yousif SHAMOO
20 Vice Provost for Academic Affairs .... Dr. Fred HIGGS
08 Vice Provost/University Librarian .... Ms. Sara LOWMAN
45 Vice President Strategic Inits .... Dr. Caroline LEVANDER
15 Associate Vice Pres Human Resources .... Ms. Mary A. CRONIN
91 Assoc Vice Pres for Admin Systems .... Mr. Randy CASTIGLIONI
43 VP & General Counsel .... Mr. Richard A. ZANSITIS
06 Registrar .... Mr. David TENNEY
29 Asst VP for Alumni Relations .... Ms. Marthe GOLDEN
37 Director Student Financial Services .... Ms. Anne E. WALKER
25 AVP Sponsored Proj/Res Compliance .... Ms. Krystal TOUPS
41 Director of Athletics .... Dr. Joseph KARLGAARD
85 Assoc Vice Provost Intl Education .... Dr. Adria BAKER
39 Assoc Vice Pres Housing & Dining .... Mr. Mark DITMAN
23 Director Student Health Services .... Dr. Stacy WARE
09 Assoc VP Institutional Research .... Mr. Sivakumar JAGANATHAN
21 University Controller .... Mr. Bradley FRALIC
21 Director of Internal Audit .... Ms. Janet COVINGTON
19 Chief of Campus Police .... Mr. James TATE
22 Director of Affirmative Action .... Mr. Russell BARNES
27 Sr Dir of News & Media Relations .... Mr. B.J ALMOND
21 Director Administrative Services .... Mr. Eugen RADULESCU
07 Director of Admissions .... Mr. Dan WARNER
28 Director of Diversity .... Dr. Roland B. SMITH
38 Director of Student Counseling .... Dr. Timothy K. BAUMGARTNER
36 Dir Center for Career Development .... Ms. Nicole VAN DEN HEUVEL
96 Director of Procurement .... Mr. Brian SOIKA
79 Dean of School of Humanities .... Dr. Kathleen CANNING
58 Dean Graduate/Postdoctoral Stds .... Dr. Seiichi MATSUDA
97 Dean of Undergraduate Education .... Dr. John S. HUTCHINSON
48 Dean of Architecture .... Dr. Sarah M. WHITING
64 Dean of Shepherd School of Music .... Dr. Robert YEKOVICH
54 Dean GR Brown School Engineering .... Dr. Reginal DESROCHES
50 Dean JH Jones Graduate Sch Business .... Dr. Peter RODRIGUEZ
83 Dean of Social Sciences .... Dr. Antonio MERLO
81 Dean of Wiess Sch Natural Science .... Dr. Peter ROSSKY
51 Dean Glasscock Sch Continuing Stds .... Dr. Mary MCINTIRE
88 Asst Dean Stdnt Counsel/Jud Pgms .... Dr. Donald OSTDIEK
22 Director of Compliance .... Mr. Ken LIDDLE
18 Chief Facilities/Physical Plant .... Ms. Kathy JONES

Rio Grande Bible Institute (G)

4300 South US Highway 281, Edinburg TX 78539-9650
County: Hidalgo Identification: 666395
Unit ID: 475185
Telephone: (956) 380-8100 Carnegie Class: Spec-4-yr-Faith
FAX Number: (956) 380-8256 Calendar System: Semester
URL: www.riogrande.edu
Established: 1946 Annual Undergrad Tuition & Fees: $2,900
Enrollment: 136 Coed
Affiliation or Control: Independent Non-Profit IRS Status: 501(c)3
Highest Offering: Baccalaureate
Accreditation: BI

01 President .... Dr. Lawrence B. WINDLE
04 Administrative Assistant to Pres .... Mrs. Ruth WINDLE
05 Vice President of Education .... Mr. David LOYOLA
32 Dean of Students .... Mr. Nelson MATUS
21 Comptroller .... Mr. Jonathan WHITE
08 Librarian .... Mrs. Donna ANTONIUK
06 Registrar .... Mr. Keith SWARTZBAUGH
15 Personnel Director .... Mr. Daniel DELEON
26 Vice Pres Ministerial Advancement .... Mr. Bob ALLEN

Roueche Graduate Center of National American University (H)

6836 Austin Center Blvd, Ste 270, Austin TX 78731
Telephone: (512) 813-2300 Identification: 770931
Accreditation: &NH

† Graduate Center of National American University, Austin, TX.

St. Edward's University (I)

3001 S Congress Avenue, Austin TX 78704-6489
County: Travis FICE Identification: 003621
Unit ID: 227845
Telephone: (512) 448-8400 Carnegie Class: Masters/L
FAX Number: (512) 448-8492 Calendar System: Semester
URL: www.stedwards.edu
Established: 1885 Annual Undergrad Tuition & Fees: $41,178
Enrollment: 4,620 Coed
Affiliation or Control: Independent Non-Profit IRS Status: 501(c)3
Highest Offering: Master's
Accreditation: SC, SW

01 President .... Dr. George E. MARTIN
05 Exec VP/Interim VP for Acad Affairs .... Sr. Donna M. JURICK
10 Vice President Financial Affairs .... Ms. Kimberly KVAAL
111 Vice President for Advancement .... Mr. Joe DEMEDEIROS
26 Vice Pres Marketing/Enrollment Mgmt .... Ms. Paige BOOTH
32 Vice President for Student Affairs .... Dr. Lisa L. KIRKPATRICK
13 Vice President Information Tech .... Mr. David E. WALDRON
42 Director of Campus Ministry .... Fr. Peter J. WALSH
09 Assoc VP Inst Effectiveness/Rsrch .... Mr. Bhuban R. PANDEY
88 Assoc VP for Global Initiatives .... Mr. William J. CLABBY
21 Assoc VP for Finance .... Mr. Erin DELFFS
20 Assoc VP for Academic Affairs .... Dr. Molly E. MINUS
88 Assoc VP Faculty Development .... Ms. Lori W. PETERSON
07 Assoc VP/Dean of Admission .... Ms. Tracy L. MANIER
37 Assoc VP Student Financial Services .... Ms. Doris F. CONSTANTINE
35 Dean of Students .... Mr. Steven J. PINKENBURG
121 Assoc VP Stdnt Acad Support Svcs .... Ms. Nicole G. TREVINO
27 Assoc VP for Marketing .... Ms. Christie CAMPBELL
110 Executive Director of Development .... Mr. Michael V. MORELIUS
18 Assoc VP Facilities .... Mr. Michael W. PETERSON
91 Assoc VP Digital Effectiveness .... Ms. Angela M. SVOBODA
109 Associate VP for Business Services .... Ms. Cyndy JOHNSON
88 Assoc VP Master Planning .... Mr. Kit JOHNSON
15 Assistant VP of Human Resources .... Ms. Kimberly M. VAN SAVAGE
19 Assistant VP for Campus Safety .... Mr. Scott G. BURNOTES
100 Chief of Staff/Sustainability Coord .... Ms. Cristina L. BORDIN
88 Chief Data Officer/Data Strategy .... Mr. Justin M. SLOAN
83 Dean Behavioral & Social Sciences .... Dr. Brenda J. VALLANCE
50 Dean The Munday School of Business .... Dr. Nancy SCHREIBER
53 Dean School of Education .... Dr. Glenda BALLARD
79 Dean School of Humanities .... Dr. Sharon D. NELL
81 Dean School of Natural Sciences .... Dr. Gary MORRIS
55 Interim Dean of New College .... Dr. Ramsey FOWLER
97 Director of General Education .... Dr. Cory LOCK
89 Director Freshman Studies .... Ms. Alexandra L. BARRON
88 Director Capstone Program .... Dr. Todd D. ONDERDONK
92 Director Honors Program .... Dr. Steven M. RODENBORN
08 Director of Munday Library .... Mr. Pongracz SENNYEY
06 Registrar .... Dr. Lance R. HAYES
36 Dir Career & Prof Development .... Mr. Raymond C. ROGERS
29 Director of Alumni & Parent Pgms .... Ms. Karin DICKS
108 Dir of Institutional Assessment .... Mr. David A. BLAIR
104 Director Ofc of Global Engagement .... Ms. Lesley J. ROBINSON
24 Interim Dir Info Tech Resources .... Mr. Antonio T. CHAVEZ
90 Dir Instructional & Emerging Tech .... Ms. Rebecca F. DAVIS
105 Midware/User Experience Architect .... Mr. Tim TASHJIAN
27 Director of Communications .... Ms. Mischelle R. DIAZ
38 Director of Health & Counseling Ctr .... Dr. Calvin A. KELLY
102 Director Foundation Relations .... Ms. Allison M. RASP
37 Director Student Financial Services .... Ms. Jennifer M. BECK
41 Associate VP Athletics .... Ms. Debora W. TAYLOR
35 Director of Student Life .... Mr. Thomas B. SULLIVAN
39 Director Residence Life .... Ms. Alicia L. VELA
04 Admin Assistant to President .... Ms. Lorraine M. PAGAN
40 Campus Stores Director .... Mr. Tim JACKSON

St. Mary's University (J)

One Camino Santa Maria, San Antonio TX 78228-8572
County: Bexar FICE Identification: 003623
Unit ID: 228149
Telephone: (210) 436-3011 Carnegie Class: Masters/L
FAX Number: (210) 436-3500 Calendar System: Semester
URL: www.stmarytx.edu
Established: 1852 Annual Undergrad Tuition & Fees: $28,200
Enrollment: 3,625 Coed
Affiliation or Control: Roman Catholic IRS Status: 501(c)3
Highest Offering: Doctorate
Accreditation: SC, CACREP, ENG, LAW, MFCD, MUS

01 President .... Mr. Thomas M. MENGLER
05 Provost/VP Academic Affairs .... Dr. Aaron TYLER
10 Vice Pres Administration & Finance .... Ms. Peggy DEBARTOLO
84 Vice Prov Enrollment Management .... Dr. Rosalind ALDERMAN
32 Assoc Provost Student Dev .... Mr. Timothy BESSLER
30 Vice Pres University Advancement .... Mr. Richard (Rick) KIMBROUGH, II
88 Vice President Mission & Rector .... Rev. Tim EDEN, SM
50 Dean/Bill Greehey Sch Business .... Dr. Tanuja SINGH
79 Dean Humanities & Social Science .... Dr. Christopher FROST
54 Dean Science/Engrng/Technology .... Dr. Winston EREVELLES
61 Dean of Law .... Mr. Steve SHEPPARD
39 Director Residence Life .... Mr. James VILLARREAL
100 Chief of Staff/Office of President .... Ms. Dianne L. PIPES
06 Registrar .... Ms. Christina VILLANUEVA
07 Dean of Admission .... Vacant
08 Exec Director Louis J Blume Library .... Ms. Caroline BYRD
37 Director Financial Assistance .... Mr. David R. KRAUSE
38 Int Director Student Counseling .... Ms. Deidra COLEMAN
90 Exec Dir/Instructor Acad Tech .... Mr. Jeff SCHOMBURG
15 Director Human Resources .... Ms. Elsa YBANEZ
72 Vice Pres Information Services .... Mr. Curtis WHITE
13 Dir Network Security Administration .... Mr. Robert STOOKSBERRY
14 Director Systems Support Services .... Mr. Frank NIEWIERSKI
42 Director University Ministry .... Mr. Wayne ROMO
29 Executive Director Alumni Relations .... Mr. Peter HANSEN
21 Director of Finance .... Ms. Mei-Lin LEE
21 Director of Accounting Operations .... Ms. Sheila NIX
26 Dir Media Relations/Communications .... Mrs. Gina FARRELL
18 Exec Dir Facilities Administration .... Mr. Aaron HANNA

*San Jacinto College District (K)

4624 Fairmont Parkway, Pasadena TX 77504-3323
County: Harris FICE Identification: 029137
Unit ID: 227988
Telephone: (281) 998-6150 Carnegie Class: N/A
FAX Number: N/A
URL: www.sanjac.edu

01 Chancellor .... Dr. Brenda HELLYER
03 Deputy Chancellor and President .... Dr. Laurel WILLIAMSON
10 Vice Chancellor Fiscal Affairs .... Mr. Chet LEWIS
15 Vice Chanc Human Resources .... Mr. Stephen TRNCAK
13 CIO .... Mr. Rob STANICIC
26 Vice Chanc Marketing/Govt Rels .... Mrs. Teri CRAWFORD
45 Vice Chanc Strategic Initiatives .... Dr. Allatia HARRIS
84 Dean Enroll Mgmt/College Registrar .... Ms. Wanda MUNSON
09 Director of Research .... Mr. George GONZALEZ
37 Dean Financial Aid Services .... Mr. Robert MERINO
96 Director Contracts & Purchasing .... Ms. Ann KOKX-TEMPLET
04 Administrative Asst to President .... Ms. Mandi REILAND
19 Director Security/Safety .... Ms. Ginger LAMBERT
25 Chief Contracts/Grants Admin .... Mr. Michael MOORE
29 Director Alumni Relations .... Ms. Ruth KEENAN
32 Chief Student Affairs/Student Life .... Ms. Joanna ZIMMERMANN
43 Dir Legal Services/General Counsel .... Ms. Clare IANNELLI

*San Jacinto College Central (L)

8060 Spencer Highway, Pasadena TX 77505-5903
County: Harris FICE Identification: 003609
Unit ID: 227979
Telephone: (281) 998-6150 Carnegie Class: Assoc/MT-VT-Mix Trad/Non
FAX Number: (281) 476-1892 Calendar System: Semester
URL: www.sanjac.edu
Established: 1960 Annual Undergrad Tuition & Fees (In-District): $1,500
Enrollment: 28,326 Coed
Affiliation or Control: Local IRS Status: 501(c)3
Highest Offering: Associate Degree
Accreditation: &SC, ACFEI, ADNUR, COARC, DMS, MLTAD, RAD, SURGT

02 Deputy Chancellor and President .... Dr. Laurel WILLIAMSON
05 Provost .... Mr. Van A. WIGGINTON
32 Associate VC Student Services .... Ms. Joanna ZIMMERMANN
06 College Registrar .... Dr. Wanda MUNSON

49 Dean Liberal Arts & Science .... Dr. Kelly SIMONS
75 Dean Business & Technology .... Mr. Jeffrey PARKS
76 Dean Health Sciences .... Dr. Michael KANE
11 Dean Administration .... Dr. James BRASWELL
07 Dean Enrollment Services .... Mr. Kevin MCKISSON
35 Dean Student Development .... Ms. Shelley RINEHART
37 Dean Financial Aid Services .... Mr. Robert MERINO
88 Dean Compliance & Judicial Affairs .... Ms. Clare IANNELLI
92 Director Honors Program .... Dr. Eddie WELLER
88 Director Dual Credit .... Ms. Nicole BARNES
08 Director Library .... Ms. Karen BLANKENSHIP
88 Director Campus Services .... Mr. Christopher CRUMLEY
41 Athletic Director .... Ms. Sharon NELSON
121 Director Student Success .... Ms. Dawn SHEDD
88 Dir Educ Planning/Couns/Completion .... Ms. Christine TORRES
84 Director Enrollment Management .... Vacant

† Regional accreditation is carried under the parent institution (district office) in Pasadena, TX.

*San Jacinto College North (A)

5800 Uvalde Road, Houston TX 77049-4599

County: Harris | Identification: 666747
Unit ID: 227997
Telephone: (281) 458-4050 | Carnegie Class: Not Classified
FAX Number: (281) 459-7125 | Calendar System: Semester
URL: www.sanjac.edu
Established: 1974 | Annual Undergrad Tuition & Fees (In-District): N/A
Enrollment: N/A | Coed
Affiliation or Control: Local | IRS Status: 501(c)3
Highest Offering: Associate Degree
Accreditation: &SC, ACFEI, CAHIIM, EMT, MAC

02 Deputy Chancellor and President .... Dr. Laurel WILLIAMSON
05 Provost .... Dr. William RAFFETTO
32 Associate VC Student Services .... Ms. Joanna ZIMMERMAN
07 Dean Enrollment Services .... Mr. Kevin MCKISSON
11 Dean Administration .... Dr. Jerrel WADE
76 Dean Natural and Health Sciences .... Ms. Rhonda BELL
50 Dean Business and Technology .... Mr. Mark JOHNSON
88 Dean Comp & Judicial Affairs .... Ms. Clare IANNELLI
62 Director Library .... Ms. Lyn GARNER
49 Dean Liberal Arts .... Mr. Shawn SILMAN
06 College Registrar .... Dr. Wanda MUNSON
41 Athletic Director .... Mr. Tom ARRINGTON
92 Director Honors Program .... Dr. Eddie WELLER
88 Dual Credit Director .... Dr. Anne DICKENS
55 Director Evening/Weekend Services .... Mr. Don SPIES
121 Director Student Success Center .... Ms. Erika HERNANDEZ
37 Dean Financial Aid Services .... Mr. Robert MERINO
32 Dean Student Development .... Ms. Tami KELLY
88 Dir Educational Planning & Counsel .... Ms. Sonia TOWNSEND

† Regional accreditation is carried under the parent institution (district office) in Pasadena, TX.

*San Jacinto College South (B)

13735 Beamer Road, Houston TX 77089-6099

County: Harris | Identification: 666748
Unit ID: 22797902
Telephone: (281) 484-1900 | Carnegie Class: Not Classified
FAX Number: (281) 922-3401 | Calendar System: Semester
URL: www.sanjac.edu
Established: 1979 | Annual Undergrad Tuition & Fees (In-District): N/A
Enrollment: N/A | Coed
Affiliation or Control: Local | IRS Status: 501(c)3
Highest Offering: Associate Degree
Accreditation: &SC, ADNUR, PTAA

02 Deputy Chancellor and President .... Dr. Laurel WILLIAMSON
05 Provost .... Dr. Brenda JONES
32 Associate VC Student Services .... Ms. Joanna ZIMMERMANN
49 Dean of Liberal Arts & College Prep .... Ms. Ann TATE
50 Dean Business & Technology .... Mr. Kevin MORRIS
76 Dean Health and Natural Sciences .... Dr. Alexander OKWONNA
11 Dean Administration .... Mr. Joseph HEBERT
84 Dean Enrollment Services .... Mr. Kevin MCKISSON
88 Dean Comp & Judicial Affairs .... Ms. Clare IANNELLI
92 Director Honors Program .... Dr. Eddie WELLER
55 Director Evening Division .... Mr. Ross KELSEY
62 Director Library .... Mr. Richard MCKAY
41 Director Athletics .... Ms. Kelly SAENZ
88 Dual Credit Director .... Ms. Kristen ROSS
06 College Registrar .... Dr. Wanda MUNSON
32 Dean Student Development .... Ms. Debbie SMITH
88 Director Education Planning .... Ms. Tanesha ANTOINE
88 Director Student Success Center .... Ms. Diana SHOKRALLA
37 Dean Financial Aid Services .... Mr. Robert MERINO

† Regional accreditation is carried under the parent institution (district office) in Pasadena, TX.

School of Automotive Machinists & Technology (C)

1911 Antoine Drive, Houston TX 77055

County: Harris | FICE Identification: 030323
Unit ID: 377218
Telephone: (713) 683-3817 | Carnegie Class: Not Classified
FAX Number: (713) 683-7077 | Calendar System: Semester
URL: www.samtech.edu
Established: 1985 | Annual Undergrad Tuition & Fees: N/A
Enrollment: 212 | Coed
Affiliation or Control: Proprietary | IRS Status: Proprietary
Highest Offering: Associate Degree
Accreditation: ACCSC

01 President/Dir of Education .... Judson MASSINGILL
11 CEO/Sch Exec Director/Administrator .... Linda MASSINGILL
07 Director of Admissions .... Scott MORRIS
37 Financial Aid Director .... Susie FAERMAN

Schreiner University (D)

2100 Memorial Boulevard, Kerrville TX 78028-5611

County: Kerr | FICE Identification: 003610
Unit ID: 228042
Telephone: (830) 896-5411 | Carnegie Class: Bac-A&S
FAX Number: (830) 896-3232 | Calendar System: Semester
URL: www.schreiner.edu
Established: 1923 | Annual Undergrad Tuition & Fees: $25,750
Enrollment: 1,230 | Coed
Affiliation or Control: Presbyterian Church (U.S.A.) | IRS Status: 501(c)3
Highest Offering: Master's
Accreditation: SC, NURSE

00 Chancellor .... Dr. Timothy SUMMERLIN
01 President .... Dr. Charlie MCCORMICK
05 Provost/Vice Pres Academic Affairs .... Dr. Diana COMUZZIE
10 Vice Pres Administration & Finance .... Mr. Bill MUSE
30 Vice Pres Advancement .... Mr. Mark TUSCHAK
84 Vice Pres Enrollment Services .... Dr. Larry CANTU
26 Vice President for Marketing .... Ms. Lane H. TAIT
06 Assistant Provost & Registrar .... Ms. Darlene BANNISTER
20 Dean of Student Success .... Dr. Candice SCOTT
84 Dean of Enrollment Services .... Ms. Toni BRYANT
21 Controller .... Ms. Helen WILHELM
42 Campus Minister .... Rev. Virginia NORRIS-LANE
32 Dean of Students .... Dr. Charlie HUEBER
27 Director of Communications .... Ms. Amy ARMSTRONG
41 Athletic Director .... Mr. Bill RALEIGH
15 Director of Human Resource Services .... Ms. Wendy BLAETTNER
18 Director Campus Operations .... Mr. Ed WINGARD
29 Director Alumni Relations .... Ms. Tammi CLANTON
38 Director Student Counseling .... Ms. Kimberly J. WOODS
36 Director Advising & Career Devel .... Ms. Cristina MARTINEZ
09 Director of Institutional Research .... Dr. Lucien COSTLEY

Seminary of the Southwest (E)

Box 2247, Austin TX 78768-2247

County: Travis | FICE Identification: 003566
Unit ID: 224712
Telephone: (512) 472-4133 | Carnegie Class: Spec-4-yr-Faith
FAX Number: (512) 472-3098 | Calendar System: 4/1/4
URL: www.ssw.edu
Established: 1952 | Annual Graduate Tuition & Fees: N/A
Enrollment: 96 | Coed
Affiliation or Control: Protestant Episcopal | IRS Status: 501(c)3
Highest Offering: Master's; No Undergraduates
Accreditation: SC, CACREP, THEOL

01 Dean & President .... V.Rev. Cynthia Briggs KITTREDGE
05 Academic Dean .... Dr. Scott BADER-SAYE
03 Executive Vice President .... Mr. Fred CLEMENT
07 Director of Admissions .... Rev. Hope BENKO
26 Director of Communications .... Mr. Eric SCOTT
10 Accounting Director .... Ms. Kathy LEBRUN
06 Registrar/Director of Assessment .... Ms. Madelyn SNODGRASS
08 Director of the Booher Library .... Ms. Alison POAGE
18 Director of Facilities Management .... Mr. Tigh WALTERS
13 Director Information Technology .... Mr. Erik MORROW
04 Administrative Asst to President .... Ms. Lesley WILDER
29 Director Alumni Relations .... Ms. Kelly ROWLEY

South Plains College (F)

1401 College Avenue, Levelland TX 79336-6595

County: Hockley | FICE Identification: 003611
Unit ID: 228158
Telephone: (806) 894-9611 | Carnegie Class: Assoc/MT-VT-Mix Trad/Non
FAX Number: (806) 894-5274 | Calendar System: Semester
URL: www.southplainscollege.edu
Established: 1957 | Annual Undergrad Tuition & Fees (In-State): $2,240
Enrollment: 9,126 | Coed
Affiliation or Control: State | IRS Status: 501(c)3
Highest Offering: Associate Degree
Accreditation: SC, ADNUR, COARC, EMT, PTAA, SURGT

01 President .... Dr. Robin SATTERWHITE
05 Vice President Academic Affairs .... Dr. Ryan GIBBS
10 Vice Pres Business Affairs .... Ms. Teresa GREEN
32 Vice President of Student Affairs .... Vacant
111 Vice Pres Institutional Advancement .... Mr. Stephen S. JOHN
49 Dean of Arts & Sciences .... Mr. Yancy NUNEZ
76 Dean of Health Occupations .... Ms. Sue Ann LOPEZ
75 Dean of Technical Education .... Mr. Robbie M. BLAIR
51 Dean Continuing & Distance Educ .... Mr. Ronald SPEARS
11 Dean Administrative Services .... Mr. Ronnie WATKINS
07 Dean of Admissions & Records .... Mrs. Andrea RANGEL
12 Dean of Reese Center .... Ms. Kara MARTINEZ
09 Assoc Dean of Research & Reports .... Mr. Ryan FITZGERALD
26 Assoc Dean of College Relations .... Mr. Dane DEWBRE
13 Assoc Dean Information Technology .... Mr. James HOWELL
88 Assoc Dean Dual Credit .... Mr. Ron SPEARS
103 Assoc Dean Workforce Development .... Vacant
35 Assoc Dean of Students .... Ms. Kathryn PEREZ
121 Director of Advising and Testing .... Mrs. Lola HERNANDEZ
37 Director of Financial Aid .... Ms. Susan NAZWORTH
08 Director of Libraries .... Mr. James BELCHER
30 Director of Development .... Ms. Julie GERSTENBERGER
15 Director of Human Resources .... Mrs. Jeri Ann DEWBRE
41 Director of Athletics .... Mr. Roger REDING
06 Registrar .... Mr. Andrew RUIZ
18 Director of Physical Plant .... Mr. Cary MARROW
40 Bookstore Manager .... Mr. Roger SHULL
28 Diversity Coord/Career Counselor .... Ms. Maria LOPEZ-STRONG

South Texas College (G)

3201 W Pecan, McAllen TX 78501

County: Hidalgo | FICE Identification: 031034
Unit ID: 409315
Telephone: (956) 872-5051 | Carnegie Class: Bac/Assoc-Assoc Dom
FAX Number: (956) 971-3739 | Calendar System: Semester
URL: www.southtexascollege.edu
Established: 1993 | Annual Undergrad Tuition & Fees (In-District): $3,606
Enrollment: 34,371 | Coed
Affiliation or Control: State/Local | IRS Status: 501(c)3
Highest Offering: Baccalaureate
Accreditation: SC, ACBSP, CAHIIM, COARC, EMT, OTA, PTAA

01 President .... Dr. Shirley A. REED
05 Int Vice Pres Academic Affs/CAO .... Dr. Anahid PETROSIAN
10 VP Finance/Administrative Svcs .... Ms. Maria G. ELIZONDO
32 VP Student Affairs/Enroll Mgmt .... Mr. Matthew HEBBARD
13 VP Info Services/Planning .... Dr. David PLUMMER
111 Vice Pres Institutional Advancement .... Vacant
88 Associate Dean for Industry & Econ .... Mr. Carlos MARGO
83 Dean Liberal Arts/Soc Sci .... Dr. Margaretha BISCHOFF
50 Dean Business/Technology .... Mr. Mario REYNA
76 Int Dean Nursing/Allied Health .... Ms. Melba TREVINO
81 Dean Math/Science/BA Programs .... Dr. Ali ESMAEILI
24 Dir Instructional Technologies .... Mr. Cody GREGG
37 Assoc Dean Student Financial Svcs .... Mr. Mike CARRANZA
21 Comptroller .... Ms. Myriam LOPEZ
15 Director Human Resources .... Ms. Brenda Jo BALDERAZ
51 Dir Cont/Prof & Workforce Education .... Mr. Juan Carlos AGUIRRE
96 Director Purchasing .... Ms. Rebecca CAVAZOS
09 Dir Research/Analytical Svcs .... Mr. Serkan CELTEK
121 Dean Student Support Svcs .... Mr. Paul HERNANDEZ, JR.
18 Director Operations/Maintenance .... Mr. George MCCALEB
18 Director Facilities Plan/Construct .... Mr. Ricardo DE LA GARZA
25 Grants/Contracts Compliance Officer .... Ms. Samantha URIEGAS
12 Campus Administrator Starr Cty .... Dr. Arthuro MONTIEL
12 Campus Administrator Mid-Valley .... Mr. Daniel MONTEZ
88 Employee Relations Officer .... Ms. Laura REQUENA
106 Dean Distance Learning .... Vacant
26 Director Public Rels/Marketing .... Mr. Daniel RAMIREZ
88 Dir of Student Activ & Wellness .... Mr. Elibariki NGUMA
84 Dean Enrollment Services/Registrar .... Mr. Matthew HEBBARD
20 Asst to VP Instructional Svcs .... Dr. Anahid PETROSIAN
19 Director Security .... Mr. Paul VARVILLE
62 Dean Library Services/Instr Tech .... Mr. Cody GREGG
13 Chief Information Officer .... Ms. Alicia GOMEZ
14 Director for IT Services .... Mr. Daniel DE LEON
08 Director Library Technical Services .... Mr. Jesus CAMPOS
08 Director Library Public Services .... Ms. Noemi GARZA
88 Dir Centers for Lrg Excellence .... Ms. Teresa GARCIA
88 Administrator High School Programs .... Mr. Nicolas GONZALEZ
90 Dir Info Commons Open Labs .... Dr. Lelia SALINAS
35 Dean Student Affairs .... Mr. Pablo HERNANDEZ, JR.
119 Chief Information Security Officer .... Mr. Victor GONZALEZ
88 Assoc Dean Curriculum/Student Lrng .... Ms. Kristina WILSON

South Texas College of Law Houston (H)

1303 San Jacinto Street, Houston TX 77002-7000

County: Harris | FICE Identification: 004977
Unit ID: 228194
Telephone: (713) 659-8040 | Carnegie Class: Spec-4-yr-Law
FAX Number: (713) 646-2909 | Calendar System: Semester
URL: www.stcl.edu
Established: 1923 | Annual Graduate Tuition & Fees: N/A
Enrollment: 1,042 | Coed
Affiliation or Control: Independent Non-Profit | IRS Status: 501(c)3
Highest Offering: First Professional Degree; No Undergraduates
Accreditation: LAW

01 President & Dean .... Mr. Donald J. GUTER
03 Executive Vice President .... Vacant
30 Sr VP of Institutional Advancement .... Ms. Mindy GUTHRIE
05 Vice President & Associate Dean .... Ms. Maxine GOODMAN
04 Sr Exec Assistant to President/Dean .... Ms. Jennifer M. HUDSON
10 Vice President and CFO .... Mr. Gregory A. BROTHERS
09 Vice Pres Strategic Plng/Inst Rsrch .... Mr. Jeffrey L. RENSBERGER
08 Director Library Svcs .... Ms. Colleen MANNING
20 Vice President & Associate Dean .... Mr. T. Gerald TREECE
20 Vice President & Associate Dean .... Ms. Catherine G. BURNETT
20 Vice President & Associate Dean .... Mr. John WORLEY
13 Vice President Technology .... Mr. Randy MARAK
15 VP for HR and General Counsel .... Mr. Steve ALDERMAN
38 Asst Dean for Academic Assistance .... Ms. Gena L. SINGLETON
06 Registrar .... Ms. Mandi GIBSON
36 Director of Career Resources .... Ms. Nazleen JIWANI

07 Assistant Dean for Admissions .... Ms. Alicia CRAMER
21 Controller .... Ms. Nancy N. JOHNSON
37 Director of Financial Aid .... Ms. Emily SILLCOCKS
26 Dir Marketing/Communications .... Ms. Diane SUMMERS
32 Assistant Dean .... Ms. Wanda MORROW
19 Director Security .... Mr. Kent BRAZELTON
09 Exec Dir of Institutional Research .... Dr. Francesca BONADUCE DE NIGRIS
24 Dir Instructional Technology Svcs .... Mr. Terry SMITH
14 Director Information Services .... Mr. George MILZ
43 General Counsel .... Mr. Steve ALDERMAN
30 Director of Development/Major Gifts .... Ms. Mindy GUTHRIE
44 Director of Annual Giving .... Vacant
29 Director of Alumni Relations .... Ms. Megan GRAF
102 Dir of Foundation & Govt Relations .... Ms. Ashley ESTES
18 Chief Facilities/Physical Plant .... Mr. William HILL
96 Manager of Purchasing .... Ms. Sandra KASPER
26 Manager of Public Relations .... Ms. Claire CATON

South University (A)

1220 W. Louis Henna Boulevard, Round Rock TX 78681
Telephone: (512) 516-8800 Identification: 770917
Accreditation: &SC, ACBSP, NURSE, PTAA

† Branch campus of South University, Savannah, GA

Southern Methodist University (B)

6425 Boaz Lane, Dallas TX 75205-0100
County: Dallas FICE Identification: 003613
Unit ID: 228246
Telephone: (214) 768-2000 Carnegie Class: DU-Higher
FAX Number: (214) 768-1001 Calendar System: Semester
URL: www.smu.edu
Established: 1911 Annual Undergrad Tuition & Fees: $50,358
Enrollment: 11,643 Coed
Affiliation or Control: United Methodist IRS Status: 501(c)3
Highest Offering: Doctorate
Accreditation: SC, ART, CLPSY, CS, DANCE, ENG, LAW, MUS, THEA, THEOL

01 President .... Dr. R. Gerald TURNER
05 Provost/VP Academic Affairs .... Dr. Steven C. CURRALL
10 Vice President Business & Finance .... Ms. Chris C. REGIS
32 VP for Student Affairs .... Dr. Kenechukwu (K.C.) MMEJE
30 Vice Pres Devel & External Affairs .... Mr. Brad E. CHEVES
43 Gen Counsel/VP Leg Affs/Govt Rels .... Mr. Paul J. WARD
11 Vice President Executive Affairs .... Dr. Harold W. STANLEY
49 Dean Dedman College .... Dr. Thomas DIPIERO
35 Assoc VP/Dean of Student Life .... Dr. Joanne E. VOGEL
117 Assoc VP/Chief Risk Officer .... Ms. Ellen S. HOLLAND
114 Associate Vice President/Budgets .... Mr. Ernie BARRY
110 Asst Vice Pres Univ Development .... Ms. Pam CONLIN
15 Assoc VP/Chief Human Res Officer .... Ms. Sheri STARKEY
84 Assoc VP Enroll Management .... Mr. Wes K. WAGGONER
109 Assoc VP of Campus Services .... Ms. Alison TWEEDY
20 Assoc Provost .... Dr. Peter K. MOORE
100 Asst Provost/Chief of Staff .... Mr. Daniel P. EADY
88 Exec Dir of Program Services .... Ms. Dana AYRES
57 Dean Meadows Sch of the Arts .... Dr. Sam HOLLAND
61 Dean Dedman School of Law .... Ms. Jennifer M. COLLINS
54 Dean Lyle School of Engr .... Dr. Marc CHRISTENSEN
73 Dean Perkins School of Theology .... Dr. Craig C. HILL
50 Dean Cox School of Business .... Dr. Matthew B. MYERS
58 Director of Graduate Studies .... Ms. Reva POLLACK
46 Assoc VP Research/Dean Grad Studies .... Dr. James E. QUICK
53 Dean Sch of Educ/Human Dev .... Dr. Stephanie L. KNIGHT
08 Int Dean/Dir Central Univ Libraries .... Ms. Elizabeth KILLINGSWORTH
20 Assoc Provost .... Ms. Julie FORRESTER
20 Assoc Provost .... Dr. Douglas A. REINELT
25 Director of Sponsored Projects .... Vacant
41 Director of Athletics .... Mr. Richard L. HART
06 Registrar .... Mr. John A. HALL
37 Exec Director Financial Aid .... Mr. Marc PETERSON
13 Chief Information Officer .... Dr. Michael H. HITES
38 Director of Counseling Services .... Dr. Cathey SOUTTER
23 Assoc Dean of Health Services .... Dr. Randy P. JONES
04 Ex Ast to Pres/Ex Dir Inst Acc/Eqt .... Ms. Samantha THOMAS
09 Director of Institutional Research .... Dr. Michael D. TUMEO
21 Treasurer/Chief Investment Officer .... Mr. Rakesh DAHIYA
96 Director of Procurement .... Ms. Shannon BROWN
42 University Chaplain .... Dr. Stephen RANKIN
24 Asst Dean Central Univ Libraries .... Dr. Bill DWORACZYK
29 Exec Dir Alumni Relations .... Ms. Marianne B. PIEPENBURG
12 Executive Director SMU-in-Taos .... Mr. Michael ADLER
12 Interim Campus Dir SMU-in-Plano .... Mr. Jim KRAMB
104 Director Study Abroad .... Dr. Catherine WINNIE
108 Director Assessment/Accreditation .... Dr. Patricia ALVEY
18 Assoc VP Facilities Plng/Management .... Mr. Philip JABOUR
27 Exec Dir of Integrated Marketing .... Mr. Neil ROBINSON
19 Chief of Police .... Mr. Richard SHAFER
07 Dean of Undergraduate Admissions .... Ms. Elena D. HICKS

Southwest Texas Junior College (C)

2401 Garner Field Road, Uvalde TX 78801-6221
County: Uvalde FICE Identification: 003614
Unit ID: 228316
Telephone: (830) 278-4401 Carnegie Class: Assoc/HT-High Trad
FAX Number: (830) 591-7354 Calendar System: Semester
URL: www.swtjc.edu
Established: 1946 Annual Undergrad Tuition & Fees (In-District): $2,116
Enrollment: 5,661 Coed
Affiliation or Control: Local IRS Status: 501(c)3
Highest Offering: Associate Degree
Accreditation: SC

01 President .... Dr. Hector GONZALES
11 Vice President Administrative Svcs .... Mr. Derek SANDOVAL
32 Vice President Student Services .... Mrs. Margot MATA
10 Vice President Finance .... Dr. Anne TARSKI
05 Vice President Academic Services .... Dr. Mark UNDERWOOD
30 AVP Institutional Advancement .... Vacant
12 Vice President Del Rio .... Mr. Derek M. SANDOVAL
12 Vice President Eagle Pass .... Mr. Gilbert S. BERMEA
88 Dean of College of Applied Science .... Mr. Juan Johnny C. GUZMAN
103 Dean of Workforce Education .... Ms. Romelia ARANDA
49 Dean of College of Liberal Arts .... Dr. Cheryl L. SANCHEZ
121 Director of Academic Advising .... Ms. Stephanie P. CERNA
37 Director of Financial Aid .... Ms. Yvette HERNANDEZ
13 Director of Information Technology .... Mr. Scott BAKER
18 Physical Plant Director .... Mr. Kirk M. PALERMO
35 Director Student Success .... Ms. Randa SCHELL
15 Human Resources Coordinator .... Mr. Oscar S. GARCIA
09 Director of Institutional Research .... Ms. Renee ZIMMERMAN
06 Registrar .... Mr. Luis FERNANDEZ
08 Head Librarian .... Dr. Juanita FLORES
19 Director Security/Safety .... Mr. Robert DOUCET
96 Purchasing Manager .... Mr. Santos DIAZ

Southwest University at El Paso (D)

1414 Geronimo Drive, El Paso TX 79925
County: El Paso FICE Identification: 041317
Unit ID: 451556
Telephone: (915) 778-4001 Carnegie Class: Bac/Assoc-Assoc Dom
FAX Number: (915) 778-1575 Calendar System: Other
URL: www.southwestuniversity.edu
Established: 2001 Annual Undergrad Tuition & Fees: $15,000
Enrollment: 1,469 Coed
Affiliation or Control: Proprietary IRS Status: Proprietary
Highest Offering: Baccalaureate
Accreditation: ABHES, DMS, RAD

01 President .... Ms. Yolanda ARRIOLA
05 School Director .... Ms. Marisol GUTIERREZ

Southwestern Adventist University (E)

100 W Hillcrest Street, Keene TX 76059-0567
County: Johnson FICE Identification: 003619
Unit ID: 228468
Telephone: (817) 645-3921 Carnegie Class: Bac-Diverse
FAX Number: (817) 202-6744 Calendar System: Semester
URL: www.swau.edu
Established: 1893 Annual Undergrad Tuition & Fees: $20,276
Enrollment: 789 Coed
Affiliation or Control: Seventh-day Adventist IRS Status: 501(c)3
Highest Offering: Master's
Accreditation: SC, IACBE, NURSE

01 President .... Dr. Ken SHAW
05 VP for Academic Administration .... Dr. Amy ROSENTHAL
10 VP for Financial Administration .... Mr. Joel WALLACE
84 VP for Enrollment .... Ms. Enga ALMEIDA
32 VP for Student Services .... Mr. James THE
42 VP for Spiritual Development .... Mr. Russ LAUGHLIN
30 VP for Univ Advancement .... Mrs. Tami CONDON
09 Director of Institutional Research .... Dr. Thomas G. BUNCH
37 Asst VP for Student Finance .... Mr. Duane VALENCIA
21 Asst VP Financial Administration .... Mr. Greg A. WICKLUND
06 Registrar .... Mr. Jason KOWARSCH
08 Librarian .... Ms. Cristina M. THOMSEN
34 Dean of Women .... Mrs. Janelle D. WILLIAMS
33 Dean of Men .... Mr. William IVERSON
13 Dir Information Technology Svcs .... Mr. E. Charles LEWIS
18 Plant Engineer .... Mr. Dale E. HAINEY
26 Director of Marketing .... Ms. Darcy FORCE
29 Director of Alumni Relations .... Mrs. Vonda SEALS
38 Director of Counseling & Testing .... Dr. R. Mark ALDRIDGE
22 Director of Disability Services .... Ms. Lillian LOPEZ
121 Dir Ctr for Acad Success/Advising .... Mrs. Renata OCAMPO
07 Director of Admissions .... Ms. Rahneeka HAZELTON
15 Director of Human Resources .... Mrs. Denise RIVERA
19 Director Security/Safety .... Mr. Keith BEUCLER

Southwestern Assemblies of God University (F)

1200 Sycamore, Waxahachie TX 75165-2397
County: Ellis FICE Identification: 003616
Unit ID: 228325
Telephone: (972) 937-4010 Carnegie Class: Masters/S
FAX Number: (972) 923-0488 Calendar System: Semester
URL: www.sagu.edu
Established: 1927 Annual Undergrad Tuition & Fees: $19,560
Enrollment: 1,974 Coed
Affiliation or Control: Assemblies Of God Church IRS Status: 501(c)3
Highest Offering: Doctorate
Accreditation: SC, IACBE

01 President .... Dr. Kermit S. BRIDGES
05 Vice President for Academics .... Dr. Paul BROOKS
32 Vice President for Student Develop .... Rev. Terry PHIPPS
10 Vice Pres for Business & Finance .... Rev. David W. WILLEMSEN
111 Vice President for Univ Advancement .... Rev. Irby MCKNIGHT
84 Vice Pres Enrollment & Retention .... Rev. Eddie DAVIS
20 Dean of Academic Services .... Rev. Donny LUTRICK
58 Dean of Graduate Studies .... Dr. Robert HARDEN
73 Dean Col Bible & Church Ministries .... Dr. Michael CLARENSAU
50 Dean Col of Business & Education .... Vacant
64 Dean Col of Music & Comm Arts .... Mr. Del GUYNES
09 Vice Pres for Inst Effectiveness .... Dr. Kim BERNECKER
106 Asst Dean for Distance Education .... Rev. Joseph HARTMAN
06 Registrar .... Ms. Heather FRANCIS
35 Dean of Students .... Rev. Lance MECHE
88 Director of Learning Centers .... Mr. Nolan JONES
13 Sr Dir Information Technology .... Mr. Kirk PASCHALL
29 Director of Alumni Relations .... Mr. Devin FERGUSON
08 Director of Learning Resources .... Ms. Radonna HOLMES
14 Director of Campus Software .... Mr. Mark WALKER
21 Dir of Business Services .... Ms. Katie WHITE
88 Senior Director of Accounting .... Ms. Candee LUTRICK
37 Sr Director of Financial Aid .... Mr. Jeff FRANCIS
19 Director of Security .... Mr. Ron CRANE
07 Assistant Dean of Admissions .... Mr. Joshua MARTIN
24 Director of Media Services .... Mr. John COOKMAN
88 Director of Accounts Receivable .... Mr. Chris BACA
36 Director of Career Services .... Ms. Beverly ROBINSON
41 Athletic Director .... Mr. Jesse GODDING
26 Director of University Marketing .... Mr. Ryan MCELHANY
15 Director of Human Resources .... Mrs. Ruth ROBERTS
38 Counselor .... Dr. Tim MYERS
88 Director of On Campus Admissions .... Mr. Joshua DUNN
88 Director of Admissions Info Systems .... Mr. Jarrod PACE
04 Executive Asst to President .... Ms. Patricia BROOKS

Southwestern Baptist Theological Seminary (G)

PO Box 22607, Fort Worth TX 76122-0150
County: Tarrant FICE Identification: 003617
Unit ID: 228477
Telephone: (817) 923-1921 Carnegie Class: Not Classified
FAX Number: (817) 921-8766 Calendar System: Semester
URL: www.swbts.edu
Established: 1908 Annual Undergrad Tuition & Fees: N/A
Enrollment: N/A Coed
Affiliation or Control: Southern Baptist IRS Status: 501(c)3
Highest Offering: Doctorate
Accreditation: SC, MUS, THEOL

01 President .... Dr. Paige PATTERSON
05 Executive Vice President/Provost .... Dr. Craig A. BLAISING
10 Vice Pres Business Administration .... Mr. Kevin ENSLEY
111 Vice Pres Institutional Advancement .... Mr. Mike C. HUGHES
32 Vice Pres for Student Services .... Dr. Kyle WALKER
45 Vice Pres of Strategic Initiatives .... Dr. Charles PATRICK
108 Assoc VP Inst Assessment .... Dr. Mark LEEDS
73 Dean of the School of Theology .... Dr. Jeffrey BINGHAM
53 Dean Sch of Church & Fam Ministries .... Dr. Waylan OWENS
64 Dean School of Church Music .... Dr. Leo DAY
12 Dean Havard Sch for Theol Studies .... Dr. Denny AUTREY
73 Dean Sch of Evangelism & Missions .... Dr. Keith EITEL
49 Dean College at Southwestern .... Dr. Mike WILKINSON
94 Dean of Women's Programs .... Dr. Terri STOVALL
56 Dean Center for Extension Education .... Dr. Deron BILES
88 Dean of the School of Preaching .... Mr. David ALLEN
100 Chief of Staff/President's Office .... Mr. Scott COLTER

Southwestern Christian College (H)

Box 10, Terrell TX 75160-9002
County: Kaufman FICE Identification: 003618
Unit ID: 228486
Telephone: (972) 524-3341 Carnegie Class: Bac/Assoc-Assoc Dom
FAX Number: (972) 563-7133 Calendar System: Semester
URL: www.swcc.edu
Established: 1949 Annual Undergrad Tuition & Fees: $8,136
Enrollment: 150 Coed
Affiliation or Control: Churches Of Christ IRS Status: 501(c)3
Highest Offering: Baccalaureate
Accreditation: SC

01 President .... Dr. Jack EVANS, SR.
30 Vice President for Instl Expansion .... Dr. James MAXWELL
05 Vice President Academic Affairs .... Mrs. Zoa Ann TURNER
10 Vice President Fiscal Affairs .... Mr. Douglas HOWIE
32 Vice President Student Affairs .... Mr. Ben FOSTER
26 Vice President Public Relations .... Mr. Jack EVANS, JR.
08 Librarian .... Mrs. Doris JOHNSON
07 Director Admissions/Retention Coord .... Mr. Warren ROBERTS
37 Director of Financial Aid .... Ms. Tonya DEAN
44 Director of Development .... Mr. Jack EVANS, JR.

Southwestern University (I)

1001 E University Avenue, Georgetown TX 78626-6144
County: Williamson FICE Identification: 003620
Unit ID: 228343
Telephone: (512) 863-6511 Carnegie Class: Bac-A&S
FAX Number: (512) 863-5788 Calendar System: Semester
URL: www.southwestern.edu
Established: 1840 Annual Undergrad Tuition & Fees: $39,060
Enrollment: 1,515 Coed
Affiliation or Control: United Methodist IRS Status: 501(c)3
Highest Offering: Baccalaureate

Accreditation: SC, MUS

01 President Dr. Edward B. BURGER
42 University Chaplain Rev. Megan DANNER
04 Exec Asst for Pres/Board Liaison Ms. Patricia WITT
05 Dean of Faculty Dr. Alisa GAUNDER
32 Vice President for Student Life Ms. Jaime WOODY
13 VP for Information Services and CIO Vacant
10 VP for Finance and Administration Mr. Craig ERWIN
30 Vice Pres for University Relations Mr. Paul SECORD
20 Assoc VP Academic Administration Ms. Julie A. COWLEY
26 VP Integrated Communications/CMO Mr. Tim COBB
15 Assoc VP for Human Resources Ms. Elma F. BENAVIDES
35 Dean of Students Ms. Shelley STORY
29 Assoc VP for Alumni & Parents Ms. Megan FRISQUE
41 Assoc VP/Dir Intercollegiate Athl Dr. Glada C. MUNT
21 Dir Finance Acct/Controller Ms. Brenda THOMPSON
19 Chief of Police Mr. Brad DUNN
37 Director of Financial Aid Mr. James GAETA
36 Director Career Services Mr. Daniel OROZCO
121 Dir Academic Success Mr. David SEILER
88 Dir Paideia Program/Assoc Professor Dr. Sherry E. ADRIAN
85 Director Intercultural Learning Ms. Tisha TEMPLE
09 Dir Inst Research/Effectiveness Ms. Natasha WILLIAMS
28 Asst Dean Multicultural Affairs Ms. Terri JOHNSON
31 Director Community Engaged Learning Dr. Sarah BRACKMANN
07 Director of Admission Mr. Robert BALDWIN
08 Dir of Library Resources Ms. Amy ANDERSON
84 Dean of Enrollment Services Ms. Christine D. BOWMAN
91 Director Administrative Computing Ms. Jennifer O'DANIEL
102 Senior Dir Foundation Relations Ms. Larkin TOM
105 Webmaster Mr. Ed HILLIS
18 Assoc VP Facilities Mgmt Mr. Michael MILLER
44 Director Annual Giving Ms. Melissa MILLER

Stephen F. Austin State University (A)

2008 Alumni Drive, Rusk 206,
Nacogdoches TX 75961-3940

County: Nacogdoches FICE Identification: 003624
Unit ID: 228431
Telephone: (936) 468-2011 Carnegie Class: Masters/L
FAX Number: (936) 468-2202 Calendar System: Semester
URL: www.sfasu.edu
Established: 1921 Annual Undergrad Tuition & Fees (In-State): $7,716
Enrollment: 12,606 Coed
Affiliation or Control: State IRS Status: 501(c)3
Highest Offering: Doctorate
Accreditation: SC, AAFCS, ART, CAATE, CACREP, CAEPN, CEA, CIDA, CS, DIETD, DIETI, MUS, NUR, SP, SW, THEA

01 President Dr. Baker PATTILLO
05 Provost/VP Academic Affairs Dr. Stephen A. BULLARD
10 Vice Pres Finance/Administration Dr. Danny R. GALLANT
32 Vice Pres for University Affairs Dr. Steve WESTBROOK
111 Vice Pres University Advancement Ms. Jill STILL
29 Exec Director Alumni Mr. Craig A. TURNAGE
20 Assoc Provost/VP Academic Affairs Dr. Mary Nelle BRUNSON
84 Exec Dir of Enrollment Management Ms. Monique COSSICH
26 Exec Dir Univ Mktg Comm Dr. Shirley A. LUNA
43 General Counsel Mr. Damon DERRICK
06 Registrar Ms. Lynda LANGHAM
09 Director Institutional Research Ms. Karyn HALL
08 Library Director Ms. Shirley DICKERSON
39 Director of Residence Life Mr. Winston BAKER
18 Director of Physical Plant Mr. Lee BRITTAIN
37 Director of Financial Aid Ms. Rachele GARRETT
22 Director Affirmative Action Vacant
13 Interim Chief Information Officer Mr. Michael P. COFFEE
15 Director of Human Resources Ms. Loretta C. DOTY
19 Chief of University Police Mr. Marc COSSICH
23 Director Health Services Vacant
41 Director of Intercol Athletics Mr. Robert W. HILL
35 Dean Student Affairs Dr. Adam PECK
38 Director of Counseling Ms. Jill MILEM
96 Director of Procurement Ms. Kay JOHNSON
46 Dir Research/Sponsored Programs Vacant
58 Dean Graduate School Dr. Richard BERRY
49 Dean College Liberal/Applied Arts Dr. Brian MURPHY
47 Dean College Forestry/Agriculture Vacant
53 Dean of College of Education Dr. Judy A. ABBOTT
57 Dean College Fine Arts Dr. A.C. (Buddy) HIMES
50 Dean College of Business Dr. Timothy BISPING
81 Dean College Sciences & Math Dr. Kimberly M. CHILDS
04 Special Asst to President Ms. Susan H. WILLLIAMS
101 Coordinator of Board Affairs Ms. Judith P. BUCKINGHAM
30 Exec Director of Development Dr. Joel L. TURNER, III
104 Director International Programs Ms. Heather CATTON
105 University Webmaster Mr. Jason L. JOHNSTONE
106 Int Dir Instructional Technology Ms. Mary D. SMITH
108 Director Institutional Assessment Vacant
121 Asst Dean Stdnt Affairs Support Dr. Michael E. WALKER
07 Associate Director of Admissions Mr. Kevin L. DAVIS

Tarrant County College District (B)

1500 Houston Street, Fort Worth TX 76102-6599

County: Tarrant FICE Identification: 003626
Unit ID: 228547
Telephone: (817) 515-5100 Carnegie Class: Assoc/HT-Mix Trad/Non
FAX Number: (817) 515-5350 Calendar System: Semester
URL: www.tccd.edu
Established: 1965 Annual Undergrad Tuition & Fees (In-District): $1,416
Enrollment: 51,688 Coed
Affiliation or Control: State/Local IRS Status: 501(c)3
Highest Offering: Associate Degree
Accreditation: SC, ACFEI, ADNUR, CAHIIM, COARC, CONST, DH, DIETT, EMT, PTAA, RAD, SURGT

01 Chancellor Dr. Eugene V. GIOVANNINI
43 Vice Chanc Admin and Gen Counsel Mrs. Angela ROBINSON
10 Vice Chancellor for Finance Dr. Mark MCCLENDON
13 Vice Chanc for Info & Technology Mr. Guhan RAGHU
05 Exec Vice Chancellor & Provost Dr. Elva C. LEBLANC
18 Vice Chanc Real Estate/Facilities Ms. Nina PETTY
26 VC Communications/External Affairs Mr. Reginald GATES
20 VP Academic Affairs SO Dr. Dana GROVE
20 VP Academic Affairs NE Dr. Linda S. BRADDY
20 VP Academic Affairs NW Dr. Judith GALLAGHER
20 VP Academic Affairs SE Dr. Zena JACKSON
20 VP Academic Affairs TR Dr. Bryan STEWART
20 VP Academic Affairs TCC Connect Dr. Kelvin BENTLEY
32 VP Student Dev Services NE Dr. Magdalena DELA TEJA
32 VP Student Dev Services SE Dr. Lyvier LEFFLER
32 VP Student Dev Services SO Dr. Larry RIDEAUX
32 VP Student Dev Services TR Mr. Adrian RODRIGUEZ
32 VP Student Dev Services NW Dr. Joe RODE
32 VP Acad Outreach & SS TCC Connect Dr. Aubra J. GANNT
12 President South Campus Dr. Peter JORDAN
12 President Northwest Campus Dr. Zarina BLANKENBAKER
12 President Northeast Campus Dr. Allen GOBEN
12 President Southeast Campus Dr. William COPPOLA
12 President Trinity River Campus Dr. Stephen S. MADISON
12 President TCC Connect Dr. Carlos MORALES
84 Assoc Vice Chanc Enrollment Svcs Mr. David XIMENEZ
88 Assoc Vice Chanc Student Success Dr. Jade BORNE
15 Assoc Vice Chanc Human Resources Dr. Ricardo CORONADO
25 Assoc Vice Chanc Grants Dev/Compl Ms. Jackie MAKI
21 Assoc Vice Chancellor Finance Mrs. Nancy H. CHANG
20 Assoc Vice Chanc Academic Affairs Dr. Nancy CURE
103 Assoc Vice Chanc Econ/Workforce Dev Mr. Benjamin RAND
102 Executive Director TCC Foundation Dr. Joe MCINTOSH
09 Exec Dir Inst Intell & Research Dr. Rosemary REYNOLDS
27 Exec Dir Comm/PR/Marketing Ms. Suzanne GROVES
18 Assoc Vice Chan Real Estate/Facs Mr. Gary PREATHER
19 Chief of Police Mr. Shaun WILLIAMS
20 Dist Reg & Dir Academic Supp Svcs Mr. John D. SPENCER
88 Exec Dir International Initiatives Dr. Sheryl OLIVEREZ HARRIS
08 Director Library Services NE Mr. Mark DOLIVE
08 Director Library Services SO Ms. Linda JENSON
08 Director Library Services NW Ms. Kristyn S. HELGE
08 Director Library Services SE Ms. Jotisa KLEMM
08 Director Library Services TR Ms. Suzanne BECKETT
06 Registrar South Campus Ms. Vanessa WALKER
06 Registrar Northeast Campus Mr. Brian D. BARRETT
06 Registrar Northwest Campus Ms. Rebecca (Becki) GRIFFITH
06 Registrar Southeast Campus Mr. Kenne EVANS
06 Registrar Trinity Campus Mr. Vikas RAJPUROHIT
38 Director of Counseling SO Ms. Ticily MEDLEY
38 Director of Counseling NE Dr. Condoa PARRENT
38 Director of Counseling NW Dr. Charles (Ricks) EDMONDSON
38 Director of Counseling SE Dr. Michael DUPONT
38 Director of Counseling TR Dr. Louann T. SCHULZE
37 District Director Financial Aid Ms. Samantha STALNAKER
37 Director of Financial Aid SO Ms. JoLynn H. SPROLE
37 Director of Financial Aid NE Ms. Mary BLEDSOE
37 Director of Financial Aid NW Ms. Trina SMITH-PATTERSON
37 Director of Financial Aid SE Ms. Elizabeth LANDWERMEYER
37 Director of Financial Aid TR Mr. William MCMULLEN
35 Dir Student Develop Svcs NE Mr. Victor BALLESTEROS
35 Dir Student Develop Svcs SO Dr. Jared M. COBB
35 Dir Student Develop Svcs NW Dr. Vesta M. MARTINEZ
35 Dir Student Develop Svcs SE Mr. Douglas C. PEAK
35 Dir Student Develop Svcs TR Mr. Carter BEDFORD
88 Director of Business Services Mrs. Kathy M. CRUSTO-WAY
96 Exec Dir of Procurement Mr. Michael (Mike) HERNDON
18 Exec Dir Inst Strategic Development Ms. Margaret K. LUTTON
07 Dist Dir of Admissions & Records Ms. Nichole MANCONE
28 Dir of Inst Div & Inclusion Mr. Andrew DUFFIELD
29 Alumni and Comm Specialist Ms. Gloria FISHER

Temple College (C)

2600 S First Street, Temple TX 76504-7435

County: Bell FICE Identification: 003627
Unit ID: 228608
Telephone: (254) 298-8282 Carnegie Class: Assoc/HT-High Trad
FAX Number: (254) 298-8266 Calendar System: Semester
URL: www.templejc.edu
Established: 1926 Annual Undergrad Tuition & Fees (In-District): $2,136
Enrollment: 5,716 Coed
Affiliation or Control: Local IRS Status: 501(c)3
Highest Offering: Associate Degree
Accreditation: SC, ADNUR, COARC, DH, DMS, EMT, SURGT

01 President Dr. Glenda O. BARRON
05 Vice Pres of Educational Services Dr. Mark A. SMITH
10 Vice Pres Administrative Svcs/CIO Dr. Van MILLER
13 AVP Finance/Information Tech Svcs Mr. Gary JACKSON
31 AVP Acad Outreach & Ext Programs Dr. Dan SPENCER
15 Assoc VP Resource Management Dr. Randy BACA
31 AVP Cmty Initiatives/Special Pgms Dr. Jimmy ROBERTS
106 Dir Web Applications & System Mr. Joe TEAKELL
84 Div Dir Student & Enrollment Svcs Mrs. Carey ROSE
08 Div Director of Learning Resources Mr. Kevin HENARD
30 Exec Dir Institutional Advancement Mrs. Jennifer GRAHAM
38 Director Student Advising Ms. Danya BAILEY
04 Assistant to the President & Board Mrs. Judith DOHNALIK
37 Director of Financial Aid Ms. Peggy WATTS
26 Director Marketing/Public Relations Ms. Ellen DAVIS
18 Dir Facilities/Physical Plant Mr. Al KENT
96 Director of Purchasing Mr. Brian SUPAK
32 Director Student Life Mrs. Ruth BRIDGES
06 Registrar Mrs. Toni CUELLAR
41 Athletic Director Mr. Craig MCMURTRY
19 Chief of Police Mr. Michael MARKUM

Texarkana College (D)

2500 N Robison Road, Texarkana TX 75599

County: Bowie FICE Identification: 003628
Unit ID: 228699
Telephone: (903) 823-3456 Carnegie Class: Assoc/HVT-Mix Trad/Non
FAX Number: (903) 823-3451 Calendar System: Semester
URL: www.texarkanacollege.edu
Established: 1927 Annual Undergrad Tuition & Fees (In-District): $2,116
Enrollment: 4,165 Coed
Affiliation or Control: Local IRS Status: 501(c)3
Highest Offering: Associate Degree
Accreditation: SC, ADNUR, EMT

01 President Mr. James H. RUSSELL
05 Vice President of Instruction Dr. Donna MCDANIEL
10 Chief Finance Officer Mrs. Kim JONES
32 Dean of Students Mr. Robert JONES
13 Chief Info Technology Officer Mr. Mike DUMDEI
30 Director Foundation/Development Mrs. Katie ANDRUS
09 Director Inst Rsrch & Effectiveness Mrs. Phyllis DEESE
18 Director Facilities Services Mr. Rick BOYETTE
26 Director Inst Adv/Public Relations Mrs. Suzy IRWIN
88 Director KTXK Radio Mr. Steve MITCHELL
15 Director Human Resources Mrs. Phyllis DEESE
103 Dean Workforce & Cont Education Mr. Brandon WASHINGTON
81 Dean STEM Dr. Catherine HOWARD
76 Dean Health Sciences Mrs. Courtney SHOALMIRE
49 Dean Liberal & Performing Arts Mrs. Mary E. YOUNG
07 Director of Admissions Mr. Lee WILLIAMS
88 Director Advising & Registration Dr. Lori ROCHELLE
08 Director Library/Student Support Dr. Tonja MACKEY
06 Registrar Mr. Brandon HIGGINS
37 Director Student Financial Aid Mrs. Susan JOHNSTON
04 Presidential Events Coordinator Mrs. Mindy PRESTON

*The Texas A & M University System Office (E)

301 Tarrow Street, 7th Floor, College Station TX 77840

County: Brazos FICE Identification: 003629
Unit ID: 228732
Telephone: (979) 458-6000 Carnegie Class: N/A
FAX Number: (979) 458-6044
URL: www.tamus.edu

01 Chancellor Mr. John SHARP
05 Vice Chanc for Academic Affairs Dr. James HALLMARK
86 Vice Chanc for Federal & State Rels Mr. Tommy WILLIAMS
10 Exec VC & Chief Financial Officer Mr. Billy HAMILTON
26 Vice Chanc for Marketing & Comm Mr. Laylan COPELIN
116 Chief Auditor Ms. Charlie HRNCIR
43 General Counsel Mr. Ray BONILLA
46 Vice Chancellor for Research Dr. Jon MOGFORD
21 Vice Chanc for Business Affairs Mr. Phillip RAY
13 Chief Information Officer Mr. Mark STONE
21 Treasurer Ms. Maria ROBINSON
100 Exec Assistant to the Chancellor Ms. Stephanie BJUNE

*Prairie View A & M University (F)

P.O. Box 519, Prairie View TX 77446-0519

County: Waller FICE Identification: 003630
Unit ID: 227526
Telephone: (936) 261-3311 Carnegie Class: DU-Mod
FAX Number: (936) 261-2115 Calendar System: Semester
URL: www.pvamu.edu
Established: 1876 Annual Undergrad Tuition & Fees (In-State): $10,059
Enrollment: 8,315 Coed
Affiliation or Control: State IRS Status: 501(c)3
Highest Offering: Doctorate
Accreditation: SC, CS, DIETD, DIETI, ENG, ENGT, MUS, NUR, NURSE, SW

02 Interim President Dr. Ruth J. SIMMONS
05 Provost/Sr VP Academic Affairs Dr. Felicia M. NAVE
20 Assoc Prov & Assoc VP Acad Afairs Dr. James J. WILSON, JR.
10 Sr Vice President Business Affairs Dr. Corey S. BRADFORD, SR.
32 VP for Student Affs/Inst Relations Dr. Lauretta F. BYARS
46 VP for Research/Innov/Spons Pgm Dr. Cajetan M. AKUJUOBI
109 Vice Pres Auxiliary Services Mr. Fred E. WASHINGTON
11 Vice President Administration Dr. Michael L. MCFRAZIER
100 Chief of Staff Dr. Michael L. MCFRAZIER
84 Assoc Provost Enrollment Mgmt Vacant
88 Asst VP for Financial Accounting Mr. Rod MIRELES
21 Asst VP for Financial Services Ms. Patricia BAUGHMAN
92 Director of Honors Program Dr. James J. WILSON, JR.
88 Asst VP Auxiliary Enterprises Ms. Tressey D. WILSON
30 Executive Director of Development Ms. Deidra FONTAINE
09 Director Institutional Research Mr. Dean WILLIAMSON
07 Int Dir of Undergraduate Admissions Ms. Lenice BROWN
18 Int Assistant VP of Physical Plant Mr. Charles MUSE
08 Director of Library Dr. Rosie L. ALBRITTON
15 Director of Human Resources Ms. Radhika AYYAR

37 Director of Financial Aid ... Mr. Ralph PERRI
36 Program Coord Residence Life ... Mr. Charles E. CROCKETT
63 Director Undergrad Med Acad ... Dr. Dennis E. DANIELS
41 Vice President/Athletics Director ... Mr. Ashley N. ROBINSON
13 Interim Chief Information Officer ... Mr. Midhat ASGHAR
58 Acting Dean Graduate Studies ... Dr. Carmen CARTER
50 Dean College of Business ... Dr. Munir QUDDUS
53 Dean College of Education ... Dr. Phyllis TURNER-METCALF
54 Dean College of Engineering ... Dr. Kendall T. HARRIS
47 Int Dean Col Agriculture/Human Sci ... Dr. James PALMER
66 Dean College of Nursing ... Dr. Betty ADAMS
49 Dean College of Arts & Sciences ... Dr. Danny R. KELLEY
48 Dean School of Architecture ... Dr. Ikhlas SABOUNI
88 Dean Col of Juv Just/Psychology ... Dr. Tamara L. BROWN
21 Director of Treasury Services ... Ms. Equilla JACKSON
23 Director Health Center ... Ms. Thelma J. PIERRE
56 Administrator Coop Extension ... Dr. Carolyn J. WILLIAMS
19 Chief of Police ... Vacant
29 Director Alumni Affairs ... Ms. Carol CAMPBELL
06 Registrar/Records ... Ms. Deborah J. DUNGEY
12 Exec Dir University College ... Ms. Lettie M. RAAB
28 Director of Diversity ... Ms. Elma D. GONZALEZ
85 Immigration Services Coord ... Mrs. Evelyn J. MCGINTY
96 Procurement Sup/HUB Coordinator ... Mr. Jim A. NELMS
114 Director Budget & Reconciliation ... Mrs. Diane T. EVANS

*Tarleton State University (A)

1333 W Washington, Box T-0001,
Stephenville TX 76402-0001

County: Erath FICE Identification: 003631
Unit ID: 228529
Telephone: (254) 968-9000 Carnegie Class: Masters/L
FAX Number: (254) 968-9920 Calendar System: Semester
URL: www.tarleton.edu
Established: 1899 Annual Undergrad Tuition & Fees (In-State): $7,140
Enrollment: 12,330 Coed
Affiliation or Control: State IRS Status: 501(c)3
Highest Offering: Doctorate
Accreditation: SC, ACBSP, CACREP, DMOLS, ENG, HT, MLTAD, MT, MUS, NURSE, SW

02 President ... Dr. F. Dominic DOTTAVIO
100 Chief of Staff ... Vacant
05 Provost/Exec VPAA ... Dr. Karen MURRAY
30 Vice Pres Inst Advancement ... Dr. Kyle W. MCGREGOR
10 Vice Pres Finance/Administration ... Mr. Tye MINCKLER
32 VP Student Affairs ... Ms. Laura BOREN
84 Asst VP Enrollment Mgmt ... Dr. Javier GARZA
20 AVP Outreach & Off Campus Programs ... Dr. Rusty FREEED
20 Assoc VP for Academic Affairs ... Dr. Dwayne SNIDER
20 Assoc VP Curriculum/Assess/Faculty ... Dr. Diane TAYLOR
36 Director of Career Services ... Ms. Alana HEFNER
18 Director of Facilities ... Mr. Aaron WAND
21 Asst VP Finance/Controller ... Ms. Lori BEATY
35 AVP Student Success/Multicul Init ... Dr. Jennifer T. EDWARDS
30 Asst VP Development ... Ms. Janice HORAK
76 Dean Col Health Sci & Human Svcs ... Dr. David WEISSENBURGER
81 Dean College Science & Technology ... Dr. James PIERCE
50 Dean Col of Business Administration ... Dr. Steve STEED
47 Dean Col Agricul & Environ Sciences ... Dr. Steve DAMRON
53 Dean College of Education ... Dr. Jordan BARKLEY
49 Dean College Liberal/Fine Arts ... Ms. Kelli STYRON
58 Dean College of Graduate Studies ... Dr. Barry LAMBERT
07 Director Undergraduate Admissions ... Ms. Cynthia HESS
22 Dir Student Disability Services ... Ms. Trina GEYE
08 University Librarian ... Mrs. Donna SAVAGE
92 Exec Dir of Honors College ... Dr. Craig CLIFFORD
37 Director Student Financial Aid ... Ms. Kathy PURVIS
09 Director Institutional Research ... Dr. Mike HAYNES
13 CIO/Exec Dir Information Tech Svcs ... Ms. Rebecca GRAY
15 Asst VP Employee Services ... Ms. Angela C. BROWN
35 Asst VP for Student Affairs ... Dr. ShaRhonda MACKLIN
35 AVP Student Affairs/Dean of Student ... Dr. Mike LEESE
41 Athletic Director ... Mr. Lonn REISMAN
23 Director Student Health Center ... Ms. Bridgette BEDNARZ
38 Director Student Counseling ... Dr. Brenda FAULKNER
19 University Police Chief ... Mr. Matt WELCH
88 Exec Dir of Student Engagement ... Mr. Darrell BROWN
24 Dir Center for Instr Innovation ... Dr. Kelli SHAFFER
44 Asst VP Advancement & Ext Relations ... Ms. Sabra GUERRA
104 Dir International Academic Programs ... Dr. Marilyn ROBITAILLE
06 Registrar ... Mr. David SUTTON
96 Director of Purchasing/HUB ... Ms. Elaine CHEW
25 Contract Specialist ... Ms. Kim MEDFORD
40 Manager Campus Store ... Ms. Carrie MCCANN
105 Web Administrator ... Ms. Daphne HUNT
04 Administrative Asst to President ... Ms. Tauna BERTSCH
29 Director Alumni Relations ... Ms. Jessica EVANS
117 Dir & Univ Compliance Officer ... Mr. Kent STYRON
26 Asst VP Marketing & Communications ... Mr. Harry BATTSON

*Texas A & M International University (B)

5201 University Boulevard, Laredo TX 78041-1900

County: Webb FICE Identification: 009651
Unit ID: 226152
Telephone: (956) 326-2001 Carnegie Class: Masters/L
FAX Number: (956) 326-2348 Calendar System: Semester
URL: www.tamiu.edu
Established: 1969 Annual Undergrad Tuition & Fees (In-State): $7,016
Enrollment: 7,192 Coed
Affiliation or Control: State IRS Status: 501(c)3
Highest Offering: Doctorate
Accreditation: SC, NUR, SPAA

02 President ... Dr. Pablo ARENAZ
05 Provost ... Dr. Thomas R. MITCHELL
10 Vice Pres Finance & Administration ... Mr. Juan J. CASTILLO, JR.
111 Vice Pres Institutional Advancement ... Ms. Rosanne PALACIOS
32 Vice Pres for Student Success ... Dr. Minita RAMIREZ
11 Assoc Vice Pres for Administration ... Mr. Trevor C. LIDDLE
88 Interim Dir of Compliance ... Ms. Lauren A. PAUL
13 Assoc VP Information Technology/CIO ... Dr. Leebrian E. GASKINS
20 Associate Provost ... Dr. Kevin D. LINDBERG
49 Dean College Arts & Sciences ... Dr. Claudia E. SAN MIGUEL
50 Dean AR Sanchez Jr Sch of Business ... Dr. Steve R. SEARS
66 Dean Canseco School of Nursing ... Dr. Glenda C. WALKER
08 Dir Sue & Radcliffe Killam Library ... Mr. Douglas M. FERRIER
07 Director Admissions ... Mrs. Rosie A. DICKINSON
06 Associate VP/Univ Registrar ... Mr. Juan G. GARCIA, JR.
15 Director of Human Resources ... Ms. Martha O. GONZALEZ
26 Director Public Rels Mktg/Info Svcs ... Mr. Steve K. HARMON
37 Director Financial Aid ... Mrs. Laura M. ELIZONDO
41 Director of Athletics ... Mr. Gilbert G. ZIMMERMANN
18 Director Physical Plant ... Mr. Roberto A. GARZA
29 Director Alumni Relations ... Mrs. Yelitza M. HOWARD
36 Executive Director Career Services ... Mrs. Cassandra L. WHEELER
39 Director of Residence Life/Housing ... Ms. Mirasol TABAREZ
38 Dir Student Couns/Disb Svcs ... Ms. Aracely C. HERNANDEZ
96 Dir Purchasing & Support Services ... Ms. Ann E. GUTIERREZ
92 Assoc Prof Director Honors Pgm ... Dr. Deborah L. BLACKWELL
21 Comptroller ... Ms. Elena M. MARTINEZ
35 Associate VP Student Success ... Ms. Gina D. GONZALEZ
88 Dir Recruitment/School Relations ... Ms. Scheiby C. FISHER
88 Assoc Dir Student Orien Lead Engage ... Mr. Miguel A. TREVINO
108 Assoc VP Institutional Assessment ... Vacant
54 Dean of University College ... Dr. Catheryn J. WEITMAN

*Texas A & M University (C)

1246 TAMU, College Station TX 77843-1246

County: Brazos FICE Identification: 003632
Unit ID: 228723
Telephone: (979) 845-2217 Carnegie Class: DU-Highest
FAX Number: (979) 845-5027 Calendar System: Semester
URL: www.tamu.edu
Established: 1876 Annual Undergrad Tuition & Fees (In-State): $11,036
Enrollment: 63,813 Coed
Affiliation or Control: State IRS Status: 501(c)3
Highest Offering: Doctorate
Accreditation: SC, CAATE, CLPSY, CONST, COPSY, CS, DENT, DH, DIETD, DIETI, ENG, ENGT, FEPAC, HSA, IPSY, LAW, LSAR, MED, NRPA, NURSE, PH, PLNG, SCPSY, SPAA, VET

02 President ... Mr. Michael K. YOUNG
05 Provost/Exec Vice President ... Dr. Carol A. FIERKE
03 Senior Vice President HSC ... Dr. Carrie L. BYINGTON
10 Exec VP Fin & Admin (CFO) ... Dr. Jerry STRAWSER
26 Sr VP Marketing/Communications ... Ms. Amy B. SMITH
13 Vice President IT & CIO ... Ms. M. Dee CHILDS
15 VP HR & Org Effectiveness ... Dr. Barbara A. ABERCROMBIE
32 Vice President Student Affairs ... Dr. Daniel J. PUGH, SR.
46 Interim VP Research ... Dr. Karen L. BUTLER-PURRY
86 Vice Pres Governmental Relations ... Mr. Michael O'QUINN
26 Vice President Brand & Business Dev ... Mr. Shane HINCKLEY
12 VP TAMU/COO TAMU-Galveston Campus ... Col. Michael E. FOSSUM
28 Vice Pres/Assoc Prov Diversity ... Dr. Christine A. STANLEY
20 Vice Provost for Academic Affairs ... Dr. Michael BENEDIK
84 VP Enrollment & Acad Svcs ... Mr. Joseph P. PETTIBON, II
20 Assoc VP Academic Affairs ... Dr. Michael STEPHENSON
43 Deputy General Counsel ... Mr. Scott A. KELLY
47 Dean Agriculture & Life Science ... Dr. Mark A. HUSSEY
48 Dean Architecture ... Dr. Jorge VANEGAS
50 Dean Business ... Dr. Eli JONES
52 Dean Dentistry ... Dr. Lawrence E. WOLINSKY
53 Dean Education & Human Development ... Dr. Joyce M. ALEXANDER
54 Dean Engineering ... Dr. M. Katherine BANKS
65 Interim Dean Geosciences ... Dr. Debbie THOMAS
80 Dean Govt & Public Policy ... Gen. Mark A. WELSH, III
61 Dean Law ... Dr. Andrew P. MORRISS
49 Dean Liberal Arts ... Dr. Pamela R. MATTHEWS
63 Dean Medicine ... Dr. Carrie L. BYINGTON
66 Dean Nursing ... Dr. Sharon A. WILKERSON
67 Dean Pharmacy ... Dr. Indra K. REDDY
69 Dean Public Health ... Dr. Jay MADDOCK
81 Dean Science ... Dr. Meigan C. ARONSON
74 Dean Vet Med & Biomed Sciences ... Dr. Eleanor M. GREEN
08 Dean/Director Libraries ... Mr. David H. CARLSON
88 Dir Inst Biosciences & Tech ... Dr. Cheryl L. WALKER
12 Dean & COO TAMU Qatar Campus ... Dr. Cesar MALAVE
20 Dean of Faculties/Assoc Prov ... Dr. John R. AUGUST
20 Assoc Prov Undergrad Studies ... Dr. Ann KENIMER
107 Actg Assoc Prov Grad/Prof Studies ... Dr. Mark ZORAN
07 Interim Dir Admissions ... Mr. Lynn BARNES
37 Exec Dir Student Financial Aid ... Ms. Delisa F. FALKS
06 Registrar ... Ms. Venesa A. HEIDICK
36 Exec Dir Career Center ... Dr. J. Leigh TURNER
14 Exec Dir Computing & Info Svcs ... Mr. Pete MARCHBANKS
23 Director Student Health Center ... Dr. Martha C. DANNENBAUM
38 Exec Dir Student Counseling Svcs ... Dr. Maggie GARTNER
39 Director Residence Life/Housing ... Ms. Chareny L. RYDL
92 Exec Director Honors Programs ... Dr. Sumana DATTA
104 Director Study Abroad ... Dr. Jane FLAHERTY
09 Exec Dir Data & Research Svcs ... Dr. David J. MARTIN
102 President Texas A&M Foundation ... Mr. Tyson VOELKEL
29 Pres Assoc of Former Students ... Mr. Porter GARNER
100 Chief of Staff ... Vacant
19 Chief University Police ... Mr. J. Michael E. REAGAN
41 Athletic Director ... Mr. Scott WOODWARD

*Texas A & M University - Central Texas (D)

1001 Leadership Place, Killeen TX 76549

County: Bell Identification: 667086
Unit ID: 483036
Telephone: (245) 519-5400 Carnegie Class: Masters/L
FAX Number: (245) 519-5482 Calendar System: Semester
URL: www.tamuct.edu
Established: 1999 Annual Undergrad Tuition & Fees (In-State): N/A
Enrollment: 2,466 Coed
Affiliation or Control: State IRS Status: 501(c)3
Highest Offering: Master's
Accreditation: SC, ACBSP, NURSE, SW

02 President ... Dr. Marc A. NIGLIAZZO
46 Vice President of Research ... Dr. Russell PORTER
04 Administrative Asst to President ... Ms. Vicky FERGUSON
05 Chief Academic Officer ... Dr. Peg GRAY-VICKREY
07 Director of Admissions ... Mr. Joshua SMITH
08 Head Librarian ... Ms. Bridgit MCCAFFERTY
09 Director of Institutional Research ... Mr. Paul TURCOTTE
10 Chief Business Officer ... Ms. Gaylene NUNN
13 Chief Info Technology Officer (CIO) ... Mr. Todd LUTZ
15 Director Personnel Services ... Mr. Tina FLOREZ-NEVAREZ
18 Chief Facilities/Physical Plant ... Ms. Gaylenne NUNN
22 Dir Affirmative Action/EEO ... Ms. Deserie RIVERA
26 Chief Public Relations/Marketing ... Vacant
30 Exec Dir Advancement & Alumni Svcs ... Dr. Karen CLOS
32 Chief Student Affairs/Student Life ... Mr. Brandon GRIGGS
36 Director Student Placement ... Ms. Heather WHEELER
37 Director Student Financial Aid ... Ms. Irene MONTALVO
50 Dean of Business ... Dr. Larry GARNER
53 Dean of Education ... Dr. Edward HILL
86 Director Government Relations ... Vacant
49 Dean of Arts & Science ... Dr. Jerry JONES
06 Registrar ... Mr. Lester LUGO
106 Dir Online Education/E-learning ... Dr. Richard SCHILKE
108 Director Institutional Assessment ... Mr. Paul TURCOTTE
19 Chief of Police ... Mr. Charles RODRIGUEZ
28 Director of Diversity ... Mr. Shailen SINGH
29 Director Alumni Relations ... Dr. Karen CLOS
84 Director Enrollment Management ... Mr. Clifton JONES
96 Director of Purchasing ... Mr. Johnathan FUSELIER

*Texas A & M University - Commerce (E)

PO Box 3011, Commerce TX 75429-3011

County: Hunt FICE Identification: 003565
Unit ID: 224554
Telephone: (903) 886-5102 Carnegie Class: DU-Higher
FAX Number: (903) 886-5888 Calendar System: Semester
URL: www.tamuc.edu
Established: 1889 Annual Undergrad Tuition & Fees (In-State): $7,750
Enrollment: 12,928 Coed
Affiliation or Control: State IRS Status: 501(c)3
Highest Offering: Doctorate
Accreditation: SC, ART, CACREP, ENG, MUS, NURSE, SW

02 President & CEO ... Dr. Ray M. KECK, III
05 Provost & VP Academic Affairs ... Dr. John HUMPHREYS
10 VP Business & Administration ... Ms. Alicia CURRIN
111 Int VP Institutional Advancement ... Mr. Wyman WILLIAMS
26 VP Media Relations & Comm Engagment ... Mr. Noah NELSON
100 Chief of Staff ... Ms. Linda KING
88 Chief Compliance Officer ... Ms. Heidi R. WRIGHT
41 Athletic Director ... Mr. Tim MCMURRAY
27 Chief Marketing Officer ... Mr. Scott CASON
108 Assoc Provost Institional Effectvns ... Dr. Shonda GIBSON
20 Assoc Provost Academic Foundations ... Dr. Ricky DOBBS
20 Assoc Provost Faculty & Admin Affrs ... Dr. Madeline JUSTICE
84 Assoc VP Enrollment Management ... Dr. Lee YOUNG
21 Assoc VP Business Admin/Comptroller ... Ms. Paula HANSON
114 Asst VP and Chief Budget Officer ... Ms. Tina LIVINGSTON
06 Registrar ... Ms. Paige BUSSELL
88 Dir of Acct & Financial Reporting ... Ms. Sarah BAKER
08 Library Director ... Mr. Gregory MITCHELL
12 Exec Dir Extended University ... Dr. Berri O'NEAL
13 Chief Information Officer ... Mr. Tim MURPHY
37 Director of Fin Aid & Scholarships ... Ms. Maria RAMOS
58 Vice Provost & Dean Grad Studies ... Dr. Jacob WARREN
53 Dean Education & Human Services ... Dr. Tim LETZRING
79 Dean of Humanities/Soc Sci & Art ... Dr. Salvatore ATTARDO
92 Dean of the Honors College ... Dr. Ray GREEN
81 Dean of Science & Engineering ... Dr. Brent DONHAM
50 Dean of Business ... Dr. Shanan GIBSON
47 Director of School of Agriculture ... Dr. Randy HARP
88 Dean of University College ... Dr. Tabetha ADKINS-SHATO
07 Director of Undergrad Admissions ... Mr. Jody TODHUNTER
88 Director of Academic Testing ... Dr. Hattie POWELL
32 Asst VP & Dean of Students ... Dr. Tomas A. AGUIRRE
29 Director of Alumni Relations ... Mr. Derryle PEACE
19 Chief of Police ... Mrs. Donna SPINATO

12 Director Metroplex Center ... Mr. Russell BLANCHETT
12 Director Navarro Partnership ... Dr. Jeanetta GROCE
38 Director Counseling Center ... Dr. Linda T. CLINTON
39 Dir Residential Living & Learning ... Mr. Michael STARK
88 Dir of Campus Operations & Safety ... Mr. Derek PREAS
23 Director Student Health Center ... Ms. Maxine MENDOZA-WELCH
104 Exec Dir Global Prog/Study Abroad ... Mr. Jacques FUQUA
96 Chief Procurement Ofcr & HUB Coord ... Mr. Travis BALL
04 Assistant to the President ... Ms. Rhonda FERGUSON
85 Dir International Student Services ... Vacant
105 Web Application Developer ... Mr. Rick BARR
15 Chief HR & Diversity Officer ... Dr. Edward W. ROMERO
18 Exec Dir Facilities Support Svcs ... Mr. David MCKENNA
22 Interim Title IX Coordinator ... Mr. James VANBEBBER
110 Director of Advancement Services ... Mrs. Brenda MORRIS

*Texas A & M University - Corpus Christi (A)

6300 Ocean Drive, Corpus Christi TX 78412

County: Nueces FICE Identification: 011161
Unit ID: 224147
Telephone: (361) 825-5700 Carnegie Class: DU-Mod
FAX Number: (361) 825-5887 Calendar System: Semester
URL: www.tamucc.edu
Established: 1947 Annual Undergrad Tuition & Fees (In-State): $8,424
Enrollment: 11,661 Coed
Affiliation or Control: State IRS Status: 501(c)3
Highest Offering: Doctorate
Accreditation: SC, CAATE, CACREP, CS, ENGR, ENGT, MT, MUS, NURSE

02 President/CEO ... Dr. Kelly M. QUINTANILLA
05 Interim Prov/VP for Acad Affairs ... Dr. Ted GUFFY
10 Exec VP for Finance/Admin ... Mr. Terry TATUM
111 Vice Pres Institutional Advancement ... Dr. Mary Jane GARZA
32 VP Student Engagement & Success ... Dr. Don ALBRECHT
46 VP Rsrch/Commercialization/Outreach ... Dr. Luis CIFUENTES
20 Assoc Vice Pres Academic Affairs ... Dr. Amy ALDRIDGE SANFORD
100 Chief of Staff ... Dr. Mary SHERWOOD
13 Assoc VP for Info Technology/CIO ... Mr. Edward EVANS
20 Assoc VP for Academic Affairs ... Dr. David BILLEAUX
84 Assoc VP Enrollment Management ... Ms. Margaret DECHANT
35 Assoc Vice Pres/Dean of Students ... Ms. Ann DEGAISH
20 Assoc VP Academic Affairs ... Ms. Christine SHUPALA
08 Director Bell Library ... Dr. Catherine RUDOWSKY
09 Assoc VP Planning & Inst Research ... Dr. Leona URBISH
26 Director of Marketing ... Ms. Ashley LARRABEE
30 Exec Director Development ... Ms. Jaime NODARSE
06 Univ Registrar/Dir Veterans Affrs ... Mr. Michael RENDON
07 Exec Director of Admissions ... Mr. Oscar REYNA
37 Director of Financial Assistance ... Ms. Jeannie GAGE
31 Director Community Outreach ... Mr. Joseph MILLER
15 Director of Human Resources ... Ms. Debra CORTINAS
36 Director Career Services ... Ms. Terri HOWE
38 Dir Student Counseling/Development ... Vacant
28 Dir Employee Develop/Compliance Svc ... Mr. Sam RAMIREZ
11 Exec Dir Administrative Services ... Ms. Judy HARRAL
96 Dir Procurement & Disbursements ... Mr. Will HOBART
113 Bursar ... Ms. Christina HOLZHEUSER
58 Dean College of Graduate Studies ... Dr. Jo Ann CANALES
49 Dean College of Liberal Arts ... Dr. Mark HARTLAUB
50 Dean College of Business ... Dr. John E. GAMBLE
53 Dean College of Education ... Dr. Dean SCOTT
54 Dean College of Science & Engr ... Dr. Frank PEZOLD
66 Dean College of Nursing/Health Sci ... Dr. Julie HOFF

*Texas A & M University - Kingsville (B)

700 University Boulevard, Kingsville TX 78363-8202

County: Kleberg FICE Identification: 003639
Unit ID: 228705
Telephone: (361) 593-2111 Carnegie Class: DU-Mod
FAX Number: (361) 593-3107 Calendar System: Semester
URL: www.tamuk.edu
Established: 1925 Annual Undergrad Tuition & Fees (In-State): $8,049
Enrollment: 9,207 Coed
Affiliation or Control: State IRS Status: 501(c)3
Highest Offering: Doctorate
Accreditation: SC, CS, DIETD, DIETI, ENG, MUS, NAIT, PHAR, SP, SW

02 President ... Dr. Steven H. TALLANT
100 Chief of Staff ... Mr. Randy HUGHES
43 Director of Compliance ... Ms. Karen B. ROYAL
05 Provost & Vice Pres Acad Affs ... Dr. Heidi ANDERSON
32 Sr VP Student Affairs & Admin ... Dr. Terisa RILEY
10 VP Finance/Chief Financial Officer ... Mr. Raaj KURAPATI
21 Exec Director Financial Reporting ... Ms. Joanne MACIAS
117 Risk Management ... Dr. Shane CREEL
36 Exec Director of Career Services ... Mr. Christian FERRIS
109 Director of Auxiliary Services ... Mr. Crispin TREVINO
88 Dir of Campus Rec & Fitness ... Mr. Anthony KREITZER
84 VP Enrollment Management ... Vacant
13 Chief Information Officer ... Mr. Robert PAULSON
14 Assoc CIO ... Mr. Lonnie NAGEL
88 Dir Enterprise Applications ... Mr. Lee MOORE
35 Dean of Students ... Ms. Kristin COMPARY
20 Associate VP Academic Affairs ... Dr. Duane GARDINER
85 Dir International Studies ... Mr. Peter LI
88 Dir Center Teaching Effectiveness ... Dr. Jaya GOSWAMI
58 Assoc VP Research & Grad Studies ... Dr. Allen RASMUSSEN
88 Asst VP Student Access ... Dr. Mary GONZALEZ
47 Dean College Agriculture ... Dr. Shad NELSON
49 Dean Arts & Sciences ... Dr. Dolores GUERRERO
50 Dean Business Administration ... Dr. Natalya DELCOURE
53 Dean Education & Human Performance ... Dr. Alberto RUIZ
54 Dean Engineering ... Dr. Mohammad ALAM
121 Assoc VP for Student Success ... Dr. Jaya GOSWAMI
26 Exec Dir Markting/Communications ... Ms. Cheryl CAIN
08 Librarian ... Mr. Bruce R. SCHUENAMAN
108 Dir Planning & Assessment ... Ms. Miao ZHUANG
88 Director Citrus Center ... Dr. John DA GRACA
88 Director King Ranch Institute ... Dr. Clay P. MATHIS
88 Exec Director CKWRI ... Dr. David HEWITT
88 Exec Co-Director Nat Toxins Res Ctr ... Dr. Elda E. SANCHEZ
88 Director Inst Sust Energy & Env ... Dr. Kim JONES
06 Interim Registrar ... Ms. Mildred SLAUGHTER
07 Director of Admissions ... Ms. Shelly KEY
111 VP Insitutional Advancement ... Mr. Bradley WALKER
29 Director Development and Alumni Rel ... Vacant
41 VP Intercollegiate Athletics & Camp ... Dr. Scott GINES
40 Director Bookstore ... Ms. Mary GUTIERREZ
106 Director Distance Learning ... Ms. Michelle DURAN
30 Exec Dir Development & Alumni ... Ms. Lori RUSSEK
23 Director Student Health & Wellness ... Ms. Jo Elda CASTILLO-ALANIZ
09 Director Institutional Research ... Ms. Miao ZHUANG
88 Director John E Conner Museum ... Mr. Jonathan PLANT
15 Exec Dir Human Resources ... Mr. Leon BAZAR
18 Exec Director Physical Plant ... Mr. John CAMISCIONI
96 Assoc VP Support Services ... Mr. Ralph STEPHENS
25 Contract Administrator ... Ms. Rachel L. BUENTELLO
39 Director Residence Life ... Mr. Tom MARTIN
46 Exec Dir Strategic Sourcing ... Ms. Maricelda ZARATE
35 Director Student Activities ... Ms. Erin MCCLURE
19 Director of University Police ... Mr. Felipe GARZA
37 Director Student Financial Aid ... Mr. Arnold TREJO
38 Asst Director Counseling Services ... Ms. Renee WIESS
113 Dir Student Accts & Bursar ... Mr. Carlos MARTINEZ
88 Advisor Pre-profession Programs ... Ms. Amanda MUNIZ
88 Bible Chair Baptist ... Mr. Mike CERVANTES
88 Bible Chair Catholic ... Ms. Nina JOINER
04 Sr Exec Asst to President ... Ms. Margarita M. GALVAN
104 Director Study Abroad ... Mr. Peter LI
25 Exec Dir Research & Spons Programs ... Ms. Maria MARTINEZ
86 Director Government Relations ... Mr. Luis GONZALEZ

*Texas A & M University-San Antonio (C)

One University Way, San Antonio TX 78224

County: Bexar Identification: 666689
Unit ID: 459949
Telephone: (210) 784-1000 Carnegie Class: Not Classified
FAX Number: (210) 784-6219 Calendar System: Semester
URL: www.tamusa.edu
Established: 2009 Annual Undergrad Tuition & Fees (In-District): $6,562
Enrollment: 4,564 Coed
Affiliation or Control: State/Local IRS Status: 501(c)3
Highest Offering: Master's
Accreditation: SC

02 President ... Dr. Cynthia TENIENTE-MATSON
05 Provost/VP Academic Affairs ... Dr. Michael O'BRIEN
10 Vice Pres Finance/Administration ... Dr. William SPINDLE
32 Vice President for Student Affairs ... Dr. Melissa MAHAN
30 VP for University Advancement ... Dr. Richard ORTEGA
09 Director of Institutional Research ... Ms. Jane MIMS
50 Dean College of Business ... Dr. Tracy HURLEY
49 Dean College of Arts & Sciences ... Dr. Mirley BALASUBRAMANYA
53 Dean College of Education & Devel ... Dr. Wowek (Sean) KEARNY
100 Chief of Staff ... Ms. Jennifer HAFT
29 Director Alumni Affairs ... Dr. Mary Kay COOPER
26 Dir of Marketing/Communications ... Mr. David PERRYMAN
07 Director of Admissions ... Ms. Chryssa DELGADO
37 Director of Student Financial Aid ... Ms. Angelika WILLIAMS

*Texas A & M University - Texarkana (D)

7101 University Avenue, Texarkana TX 75503

County: Bowie FICE Identification: 031703
Unit ID: 224545
Telephone: (903) 223-3000 Carnegie Class: Masters/M
FAX Number: (903) 832-8890 Calendar System: Semester
URL: www.tamut.edu
Established: 1971 Annual Undergrad Tuition & Fees (In-State): $6,840
Enrollment: 1,848 Coed
Affiliation or Control: State IRS Status: 501(c)3
Highest Offering: Doctorate
Accreditation: SC, CACREP, NURSE

02 President ... Dr. Emily FOURMY CUTRER
05 Provost/Vice Pres Academic Affairs ... Dr. David YELLS
10 VP Finance & Administration ... Mr. James SCOGIN
32 Asst Vice Pres for Student Success ... Mrs. Elizabeth PATTERSON
30 Assoc VP University Advancement ... Mrs. LeAnne WRIGHT
03 VP Student Engagement/Enrol/Success ... Mrs. Kathy WILLIAMS
100 Chief of Staff President's Office ... Mrs. Vicki HUCKABEE
13 Chief Information Technology ... Mr. Jeff HINTON
20 Assoc Provost/SACSCOC Liaison ... Dr. Nancy JORDAN
49 Dean Col Arts & Sciences/Education ... Dr. Delbert DOUGHTY
50 Dean Col of Bus/Engineering/Tech ... Dr. Gary STADING
21 Controller ... Mrs. Jackie ELDER
37 Dir Financial Aid & Veteran Svcs ... Mr. Michael FULLER
15 Director Human Resources & EEO ... Mr. Ricky NORTON
08 Director Library ... Mrs. Teri STOVER
18 Director Physical Plant ... Mr. Richard LYNES
18 Police Chief/Director Security ... Mr. Alex SERRANO
96 Director Purchasing ... Mrs. Cynthia HENDERSON
88 Director Payroll ... Mrs. Ramona GREEN
35 Director Student & Career Services ... Mr. Carl GREIG
84 Director Enrollment Management ... Mr. Toney FAVORS
26 Director Communications ... Ms. Carol LANGSTON
104 Director of International Studies ... Ms. Jennifer FELPS
41 Director of Athletics ... Mr. Michael GALVAN
04 Exec Admin Assistant to President ... Ms. Loren LOFTIN
06 Registrar ... Mrs. Jana BOATRIGHT
38 Director Student Counseling ... Mrs. Barbara WILSON
29 Alumni Relations Coordinator ... Mr. Mark MISSILDINE

*West Texas A & M University (E)

2403 Russell C. Long Blvd., Canyon TX 79015

County: Randall FICE Identification: 003665
Unit ID: 229814
Telephone: (806) 651-0000 Carnegie Class: Masters/L
FAX Number: (806) 651-2126 Calendar System: Semester
URL: www.wtamu.edu
Established: 1910 Annual Undergrad Tuition & Fees (In-State): $7,699
Enrollment: 9,489 Coed
Affiliation or Control: State IRS Status: 501(c)3
Highest Offering: Doctorate
Accreditation: SC, #CAATE, CS, ENG, MUS, NURSE, SP, SW, THEA

02 President ... Dr. Walter V. WENDLER
05 Provost/Vice Pres Acad Affairs ... Dr. Wade SHAFFER
10 Vice Pres for Business and Finance ... Mr. Randy RIKEL
32 Vice President for Student Affairs ... Mr. Michael J. KNOX
30 Vice Pres Institutional Advancement ... Mr. Tim BYNUM
84 Vice Pres of Enrollment Management ... Mr. Dan D. GARCIA
28 Chief Diversity/Inclusion Officer ... Ms. Angela ALLEN
100 Chief of Staff/Asst VP Strat Plng ... Ms. Tracee POST
06 Registrar ... Ms. Tana J. MILLER
07 Director of Admissions ... Mr. Kyle MOORE
08 Dir Information/Library Resources ... Ms. Shawna J. KENNEDY-WITTHAR
36 Dir Career Planning/Placement ... Ms. Denese SKINNER
37 Director Student Financial Aid ... Ms. Marian K. GIESECKE
51 Dir Education on Demand ... Ms. Andrea PORTER
23 Director Medical Service ... Dr. Jim GIBBS
19 Police Chief ... Chief Shawn G. BURNS
26 Director Communication Services ... Ms. Ann UNDERWOOD
29 Director of Alumni Relations ... Ms. Becky STOGNER
38 Director Counseling Services ... Ms. Dayna SCHERTLER
41 Director of Athletics ... Mr. Michael MCBROOM
09 Director Institutional Research ... Mr. Jarvis D. HAMPTON
13 Chief Information Officer ... Mr. James D. WEBB
96 Director of Purchasing ... Mr. Brian GLENN
40 Manager Bookstore ... Mr. Terry S. NEPPER
15 Director Personnel Services ... Mr. David KOHLER
47 Dean Col Agr/Nat Sciences ... Dr. Dean HAWKINS
50 Dean College of Business ... Dr. Neil W. TERRY
53 Dean Col Education & Social Science ... Dr. Eddie W. HENDERSON
57 Dean College Fine Arts/Humanities ... Dr. Jessica MALLARD
54 Dean Col Eng/Comp Sci/Mathematics ... Dr. Emily HUNT
46 VP for Research & Compliance ... Dr. Angela SPAULDING
66 Dean College of Nursing/Health Sci ... Dr. Dirk NELSON
104 Director Study Abroad ... Ms. Carolina GALLOWAY

*Texas A & M University at Galveston (F)

PO Box 1675, Galveston TX 77553-1675

Telephone: (409) 740-4414 FICE Identification: 010298
Accreditation: &SC, ENG, ENGT

† Regional accreditation is carried under the parent institution Texas A & M University, College Station, TX.

Texas Chiropractic College (G)

5912 Spencer Highway, Pasadena TX 77505-1699

County: Harris FICE Identification: 003635
Unit ID: 228866
Telephone: (281) 487-1170 Carnegie Class: Spec-4-yr-Other Health
FAX Number: (281) 487-2009 Calendar System: Trimester
URL: www.txchiro.edu
Established: 1908 Annual Undergrad Tuition & Fees: N/A
Enrollment: 282 Coed
Affiliation or Control: Independent Non-Profit IRS Status: 501(c)3
Highest Offering: Doctorate
Accreditation: SC, CHIRO

01 President ... Dr. Steve FOSTER
10 Chief Financial Officer ... Ms. Ann DOMINICK
05 VP for Academic Affairs ... Dr. John MROZEK
11 VP of Administrative Services ... Dr. Sandra HUGHES
111 Exec Dir of Institution Advancement ... Ms. Monique LEWIS
32 Exec Director of Student Services ... Ms. Kristina HANSON
63 Interim Assoc VP of Clinics ... Dr. Lawrence WYATT
06 Registrar ... Ms. Sarah TROTMAN
15 Director of Human Resources ... Mrs. Sue ARNOLD
26 Director of Communications ... Ms. Elise FEATHERLY
08 Director of Library Services ... Ms. Carol WEBB

37 Director of Financial Aid ... Mr. Arthur GOUDEAU
29 Development & Alumni Relations Coor ... Ms. Taylor BALLARD
07 Assistant Director of Admissions ... Ms. Emery CARTER
101 Secretary of the Institution/Board ... Mrs. Sue ARNOLD

Texas Christian University (A)

2800 S University Drive, Fort Worth TX 76129-2800
County: Tarrant FICE Identification: 003636
Unit ID: 228875
Telephone: (817) 257-7000 Carnegie Class: DU-Higher
FAX Number: (817) 257-7333 Calendar System: Semester
URL: www.tcu.edu
Established: 1873 Annual Undergrad Tuition & Fees: $42,670
Enrollment: 10,323 Coed
Affiliation or Control: Christian Church (Disciples Of Christ)
IRS Status: 501(c)3
Highest Offering: Doctorate
Accreditation: SC, ANEST, ART, CAATE, CIDA, CS, DANCE, DIETC, DIETD, ENG, #JOUR, MUS, NURSE, SP, SW

01 Chancellor ... Dr. Victor J. BOSCHINI, JR.
05 Provost/Vice Chanc Academic Affairs ... Dr. R. Nowell DONOVAN
10 Vice Chanc Finance & Administration ... Mr. Brian G. GUTIERREZ
30 Vice Chanc University Advancement . Mr. Donald J. WHELAN, JR.
32 Vice Chancellor Student Affairs ... Dr. Kathryn CAVINS-TULL
26 Vice Chanc Mktg & Communication ... Ms. Tracy SYLER-JONES
15 Vice Chancellor Human Resources ... Ms. Yohna CHAMBERS
41 Director Athletics ... Mr. Christopher DEL CONTE
88 Chief Investment Officer ... Mr. Jim HILLE
13 Chief Technology Officer ... Mr. Bryan LUCAS
88 Chief University Compliance Officer ... Ms. Andrea NORDMANN
100 Chief of Staff ... Ms. Jean MRASEK
88 Chancellor's Intern ... Ms. Lauren NIXON
29 Assoc Vice Chanc Alumni Relations ... Ms. Kristi M. HOBAN
88 Assoc Vice Chanc Advancement Ops ... Dr. Roby V. KEY
35 Assoc VC/Dean Student Development ... Dr. Barbara B. HERMAN
35 Assoc Vice Chanc/Dean Campus Life ... Dr. David COZZENS
21 Assoc Vice Chanc & Controller ... Ms. Cheryl L. WILSON
18 Assoc Vice Chanc for Facilities ... Mr. Todd S. WALDVOGEL
88 Associate VC Donor Relations ... Julie WHITT
28 Chief Incl Ofcr & Title IX Coord ... Mr. Darron TURNER
44 Assoc VC University Development ... Mr. David NOLAN
88 Asst VC School & College Dev ... Mr. Adam BAGGS
09 Assoc Provost Research ... Dr. Bonnie MELHART
20 Assoc Provost Academic Support ... Dr. Leo W. MUNSON
20 Asst Provost Academic Plng/Budget ... Ms. Megan M. SOYER
108 Assoc Provost Inst Effectiveness ... Dr. Catherine WEHLBURG
88 Assoc Provost Devel Academic Future ... Dr. David WHILLOCK
49 Dean Addran College of Liberal Arts ... Dr. Andrew SCHOOLMASTER
50 Dean Neeley School of Business ... Dr. Homer EREKSON
60 Dn Bob Schieffer Col Communication ... Dr. Kristie BUNTON
53 Dean College of Education ... Dr. Mary PATTON
57 Dean College of Fine Arts ... Dr. Anne HELMREICH
66 Dean Harris Col Nursing/Hlth Sci ... Dr. Susan WEEKS
54 Dean Col of Science & Engineering ... Dr. Phil HARTMAN
92 Dn John V Roach Honors College ... Dr. Diane SNOW
08 Dean of the Library ... Dr. June KOELKER
07 Int Dean of Admission ... Mr. Heath A. EINSTEIN
22 Affirmative Action Officer ... Ms. Kristen TAYLOR
06 Registrar/Dir Enrollment Management ... Ms. Mary KINCANNON
19 Chief TCU Police ... Mr. Steve G. MCGEE
42 Minister to the University ... Rev. Angela KAUFMAN
106 Asst Provost of Educ Tech/Fac Dev ... Ms. Romana HUGHES
85 Assoc Dir International Education ... Dr. Tracy RUNDSTROM WILLIAMS
25 Director Contract Administration ... Mr. Matthew WALLIS
16 Director Employee Relations ... Ms. Kristen TAYLOR
51 Director Extended Education ... Mr. David A. GREBEL
88 Assoc Dean Dir Freshman Admission ... Mr. Mike MOONEYHAM
88 Director Transfer Admission ... Ms. Amanda NICKERSON
23 Director Health Services ... Dr. Jane TORGERSON
09 Director Institutional Research ... Dr. Cathan COGHLAN
24 Int Dir Instructional Services ... Ms. Deana RAY
85 Director International Student Svcs ... Mr. John L. SINGLETON
38 Director Mental Health Services ... Dr. Linda WOLSZON
96 Warehouse/Purchasing Agent ... Mr. Roger D. FULLER
39 Director Housing & Residential Life ... Mr. Craig ALLEN
37 Dir Scholarships & Financial Aid ... Mr. Michael H. SCOTT
105 Int Director Website Management ... Ms. Elaine TUBRE
25 Director Sponsored Programs ... Ms. Linda FREED
36 Exec Director Career Services ... Dr. John THOMPSON

Texas College (B)

2404 N Grand Avenue, Tyler TX 75702-1962
County: Smith FICE Identification: 003638
Unit ID: 228884
Telephone: (903) 593-8311 Carnegie Class: Bac-Diverse
FAX Number: (903) 593-0588 Calendar System: Semester
URL: www.texascollege.edu
Established: 1894 Annual Undergrad Tuition & Fees: $10,008
Enrollment: 853 Coed
Affiliation or Control: Christian Methodist Episcopal IRS Status: 501(c)3
Highest Offering: Baccalaureate
Accreditation: SC

01 President ... Dr. Dwight FENNELL
05 Vice President Academic Affairs ... Dr. Stephen JONES
10 Vice Pres Business & Finance ... Mr. James HARRIS
32 Dean of Students ... Mr. Isaac WILLIAMS
30 Development Officer ... Mrs. Angelia FENNELL
07 Coordinator of Admission ... Mr. Ronald MCDOWELL
06 Registrar ... Mr. John ROBERTS
09 Dir Inst Research/ Effectiveness ... Dr. Cynthia MARSHALL-BIGGINS
08 Director of Library Services ... Mrs. Linda SIMMONS-HENRY
13 Asst Dir Information Technology ... Mr. Ocie FISHER
15 Director Human Resources ... Ms. Lois BOWIE
21 Comptroller ... Mr. Walter MOSLEY
41 Athletic Director ... Ms. Elissia BURWELL
37 Director Financial Aid ... Ms. Gail JOHNSON
18 Director Physical Plant ... Mr. Anthony PARKER
26 Coordinator Public Relations ... Mr. Jake MARTIN
29 Coordinator Alumni Affairs ... Ms. Orenthia MASON
19 Director Security/Safety ... Dr. Willie CHAMPION

Texas Health and Science University (C)

4005 Manchaca Road, Austin TX 78704-6737
County: Travis FICE Identification: 031795
Unit ID: 430704
Telephone: (512) 444-8082 Carnegie Class: Spec-4-yr-Other Health
FAX Number: (512) 444-6345 Calendar System: Trimester
URL: www.thsu.edu
Established: 1990 Annual Undergrad Tuition & Fees: N/A
Enrollment: 128 Coed
Affiliation or Control: Proprietary IRS Status: Proprietary
Highest Offering: Master's; No Lower Division
Accreditation: ACICS, ACUP

01 President ... Ms. Lisa (Ping-Hui) LIN
11 VP of Operations/Assessment ... Dr. David VEQUIST
05 Senior Administrator ... Ms. Wai Lan KUO
30 Director of Development/Operations ... Mr. Paul LIN
81 Academic Dean/Biomed Dir ... Dr. Maoyi CAI
88 Director of Acupuncture/Clinic Dir ... Dr. Hai Tao CAO
88 Director of Herbal Department ... Ms. Allison YU
03 DAOM Director ... Dr. Wenjie SUN
32 Dean of Students/Assoc Dir DAOM ... Ms. Marty CALLIHAM
06 Registrar/Administrator ... Ms. Erin WALLACE
37 Financial Aid/Intl Student Advisor ... Mr. Antonio HOLLOWAY
08 Librarian/IT Manager ... Mr. Ryan HAECKER
07 Marketing & Admissions Officer ... Mr. Kanok LI
12 Academic Dean/Dean of Students SA ... Dr. Roberto GUERRERO

† Granted candidacy at the Doctorate level by ACAOM.

Texas Lutheran University (D)

1000 W Court Street, Seguin TX 78155-5999
County: Guadalupe FICE Identification: 003641
Unit ID: 228981
Telephone: (830) 372-8000 Carnegie Class: Bac-Diverse
FAX Number: (830) 372-8096 Calendar System: Semester
URL: www.tlu.edu
Established: 1891 Annual Undergrad Tuition & Fees: $28,910
Enrollment: 1,373 Coed
Affiliation or Control: Evangelical Lutheran Church In America
IRS Status: 501(c)3
Highest Offering: Master's
Accreditation: SC, ACBSP, CAATE, MUS, NURSE

01 President ... Dr. Stuart B. DORSEY
05 Vice Pres for Academic Affairs ... Dr. Debbie COTTRELL
10 Vice President Finance ... Mr. Andrew NELSON
84 Vice President Enrollment Services ... Ms. Sarah STORY
30 VP for Development/Alumni Relations ... Mr. Rick ROBERTS
32 VP/Dean of Student Life & Learning ... Ms. Kristi QUIROS
26 Vice President for Marketing Comm ... Ms. Sarah STORY
06 Director of Records & Registration ... Mr. Glenn YOCKEY
08 Library Director ... Ms. Martha RINN
37 Director of Financial Aid ... Ms. Bonnie TREVINO
42 Campus Pastor ... Rev. Kara STEWART
36 Director Career Development ... Ms. LaTonya HENRY
38 Director Counseling Services ... Vacant
07 Director of Admissions ... Ms. ALecia MCCAIN
15 Director of Human Resources ... Ms. Toi TURNER
41 Director of Athletics ... Mr. Bill MILLER
09 Director of Institutional Research ... Ms. Jean CONSTABLE
04 Exec Assistant to the President ... Ms. Susan RINN
101 Secretary of the Institution/Board ... Ms. Susan RINN
102 Dir Foundation/Corporate Relations ... Mr. Sam EHRLICH
104 Director Study Abroad ... Ms. Charla BAILEY
27 Director of Marketing/Communication ... Ms. Ashlie FORD
108 Director of Academic Assessment ... Dr. Michael CZUCHRY
13 Chief Info Technology Officer (CIO) ... Mr. William SENTER
18 Chief Facilities/Physical Plant ... Mr. Kirk HERBOLD
19 University Police Chief ... Chief Irene GARCIA
29 Director Alumni Relations ... Ms. Taylor CARLETON
39 Director of Residence Life ... Ms. Pesha MABRIE
44 Director Annual Giving ... Ms. Taylor CARLETON
86 Director Government Relations ... Vacant
22 Dir Affirm Action/EEO/Diversity ... Ms. Toi TURNER
43 Dir Legal Services/General Counsel ... Mr. James FROST

Texas Southern University (E)

3100 Cleburne Street, Houston TX 77004-4584
County: Harris FICE Identification: 003642
Unit ID: 229063
Telephone: (713) 313-7011 Carnegie Class: DU-Mod
FAX Number: (713) 313-1092 Calendar System: Semester
URL: www.tsu.edu
Established: 1927 Annual Undergrad Tuition & Fees (In-State): $9,000
Enrollment: 8,965 Coed
Affiliation or Control: State IRS Status: 170(c)1
Highest Offering: Doctorate
Accreditation: SC, CAEPN, CAHIIM, COARC, DIETD, ENGT, LAW, MT, NAIT, PHAR, PLNG, SPAA, SW

01 President ... Dr. Austin A. LANE
05 Int Provost/VP Academic Affairs ... Dr. Bobby WILSON
10 Vice President for Admin & Finance ... Mr. Kenneth HUEWITT
111 Vice Pres University Advancement ... Vacant
100 Chief of Staff ... Ms. Heidi SMITH
43 General Counsel ... Mr. Andrew C. HUGHEY
41 VP Intercollegiate Athletics ... Dr. Charles F. MCCLELLAND
32 VP Student Svcs/Dean of Students ... Dr. Raphael X. MOFFETT
09 Int Assoc Provost/Assoc VP Research ... Dr. Adebayo O. OYEKAN
88 Dir Title III & Ofc of Sponsored Pr ... Ms. Demetria JOHNSON-WEEKS
15 Assoc VP of Human Resources ... Ms. Keisha DAVID
26 Assoc VP of Communications ... Vacant
84 Assoc VP Enrollment Management ... Mr. Wendell WILLIAMS
06 University Registrar ... Ms. Marilyn C. SQUARE
08 Exec Director Libraries/Museums ... Dr. Janice L. PAYTON
50 Int Dean School of Business ... Dr. John H. WILLIAMS
51 Int Dir Office of Cont Education ... Dr. Melanie LAWSON
53 Dean College of Education ... Dr. Lillian B. POATS
80 Int Dean School of Public Affairs ... Dr. Michael ADAMS
61 Int Dean School of Law ... Dr. James DOUGLAS
67 Int Dean Col Pharmacy & Health Sci ... Dr. Shirlette MILTON
72 Int Dean College of Science/Tech ... Dr. John B. SAPP
60 Dean School of Communications ... Dr. Reza J. POUDEH
19 Chief of Police ... Chief Mary YOUNG
39 Director of Student Housing ... Ms. Yvette BARKER
92 Int Dean Freeman Honors College ... Dr. Elizabeth A. BROWN-GUILLORY
96 Exec Dir Procurement Services ... Mr. Gregory G. WILLIAMS
18 Exec Director Facilities & Maint ... Vacant
13 Chief Information Officer ... Mr. Luis VILLARREAL
58 Dean Graduate School ... Dr. Gregory H. MADDOX
21 Exec Dir Provost of Business Svcs ... Mr. Charles E. HENRY
21 Controller ... Ms. Christina ORDONEZ-CAMPOS
124 Dir Acad Ret Svcs Spec Asst/Provost ... Ms. Lori A. LABRIE
88 Exec Director Budget ... Mr. Elias HAILU
114 Assoc VP Treasurer & Budget ... Mr. Louis W. EDWARDS
108 Exec Dir Inst Assess/Plng/Effect ... Dr. Rajanel CROCKEM
29 Exec Dir Alumni Rels/Spec Events ... Ms. Connie L. COCHRAN
88 Director of Student Activities ... Mr. Kavaris SIMS
88 Director of Scholarships ... Ms. Cynthia LEE
88 Associate Dean for Academic Affairs ... Dr. Bernnell PELZIER-GLAZE
88 Senior Academic Technology Officer ... Mr. Darnell JOSEPH
88 Associate Director of QEP Office ... Dr. Arbolina L. JENNINGS
106 Dir Online Education/E-learning ... Mr. Remi ADEMOLA
37 Director Student Financial Aid ... Ms. Linda BALLARD
31 Director Community Relations ... Dr. Leonard H. SPEARMAN
86 Director of Governmental Relations ... Mr. Dominique CALHOUN
04 Administrative Asst to President ... Ms. Regina WILLIAMS

Texas Southmost College (F)

80 Fort Brown, Brownsville TX 78520-4993
County: Cameron FICE Identification: 003643
Unit ID: 227377
Telephone: (956) 295-3600 Carnegie Class: Assoc/HT-Mix Trad/Non
FAX Number: (956) 295-3384 Calendar System: Semester
URL: www.tsc.edu
Established: 1926 Annual Undergrad Tuition & Fees (In-District): $3,198
Enrollment: 4,029 Coed
Affiliation or Control: State/Local IRS Status: 501(c)3
Highest Offering: Associate Degree
Accreditation: SC

01 Interim President ... Mr. Mike SHANNON
05 Vice President of Instruction ... Vacant
10 Vice President of Finance and Admin ... Mr. Santos ALARCON
111 Vice President of Institutional Adv ... Ms. Melinda RODRIGUEZ
20 Associate VP of Instruction ... Mr. Donald CROUSE
88 Dean of College Preparatory Studies ... Dr. Angelica M. FUENTES
81 Interim Dean of STEM and CTE ... Dr. Murad ABUSALIM
79 Interim Dean of Humanities ... Dr. Deborah HUERTA
76 Interim Dean of Allied Health ... Mr. Scott NELSON
07 Director of Admissions and Records ... Mr. Alex SALINAS
09 Director of Inst Planning/Research ... Mr. Oscar O. HERNANDEZ
103 Executive Director of WTCE ... Ms. Diana LLAMAS
106 Dir Educ Technology & Curricular I ... Ms. Antonia SALDIVAR
13 Chief Info Technology Officer (CIO) ... Mr. Daniel DELEON
15 Executive Director of Human Resourc ... Ms. Lissa FRAUSTO
18 Director Facilities/Physical Plant ... Mr. Antonio GUEVARA
25 Coordinator Grants Dev and Admin ... Dr. Prisci TIPTON
32 Director of Student Life ... Mr. Armando PONCE
36 Coordinator of Transfer/Career and ... Ms. Thelma SULLIVAN
37 Director Student Financial Aid ... Ms. Ana DE LA GARZA
96 Coordinator of Purchasing ... Ms. Patricia SALDIVAR

Texas State Technical College Waco (G)

3801 Campus Drive, Waco TX 76705-1695
County: McLennan FICE Identification: 003634
Unit ID: 487320
Telephone: (254) 867-4893 Carnegie Class: Assoc/HVT-High Trad
FAX Number: (254) 867-3973 Calendar System: Semester
URL: www.tstc.edu
Established: 1965 Annual Undergrad Tuition & Fees (In-State): $4,665

Enrollment: 11,316 Coed
Affiliation or Control: State IRS Status: 501(c)3
Highest Offering: Associate Degree
Accreditation: SC, CAHIIM, DH, EMT, MAC, SURGT

01 Chancellor .... Mr. Mike REESER
05 Provost Waco .... Mr. Adam C. HUTCHISON
11 VC & Chief Operations Officer .... Dr. Elton E. STUCKLY, JR.
86 VC & Chief Govt Affairs Officer .... Mr. Roger MILLER
10 VC & Chief Financial Officer .... Mr. Jonathan HOEKSTRA
100 Chief Culture Officer .... Mrs. Gail LAWERENCE
13 VC & Chief Technology Officer .... Mr. Rick HERRERA
26 VC & Chief Marketing Officer .... Mr. Jeff KILGORE
43 VC & Chief Legal Officer .... Mr. Ray RUSHING
88 VC & Chief Policy Officer .... Mr. Michael A. BETTERSWORTH
12 Provost Fort Bend County .... Mr. Randall WOOTEN
12 Provost Harlingen .... Mr. Rick HERRERA
12 Provost Marshall .... Mr. Barton DAY
12 Provost West Texas .... Ms. Marina WILCOX
12 Provost West Texas .... Mr. Rick DENBOW
12 Provost North Texas .... Mr. Marcus BALCH
12 Provost Williamson County .... Mr. Edgar PADILLA
111 Sr Exec Dir Inst Advancement .... Dr. Terry CONROY

*The Texas State University System (A)

208 E 10th Street, Suite 600, Austin TX 78701-2407
County: Travis FICE Identification: 033442
Telephone: (512) 463-1808 Carnegie Class: N/A
FAX Number: (512) 463-1816
URL: www.tsus.edu

01 Chancellor .... Brian MCCALL
05 Vice Chanc for Academic Affairs .... John HAYEK
43 Vice Chanc & General Counsel .... Fernando C. GOMEZ
10 Vice Chancellor for Finance .... Roland K. SMITH
86 Vice Chanc Government Relations .... Sean CUNNINGHAM
25 Vice Chanc Contract Administration .... Peter E. GRAVES
88 Associate General Counsel .... Nelly R. HERRERA
18 Assoc Vice Chanc Facilities .... Rob Roy PARNELL
26 Deputy Dir Mktg & Communications .... Mike WINTEMUTE
116 Director of Audits & Analysis .... Carole M. FOX
11 Director of Administration .... Carol TREADWAY

*Lamar Institute of Technology (B)

PO Box 10043, Beaumont TX 77710-0043
County: Jefferson FICE Identification: 036273
Unit ID: 441760
Telephone: (409) 880-8321 Carnegie Class: Assoc/HVT-High Trad
FAX Number: (409) 880-1711 Calendar System: Semester
URL: www.lit.edu
Established: 1995 Annual Undergrad Tuition & Fees (In-State): $4,534
Enrollment: 2,845 Coed
Affiliation or Control: State IRS Status: 501(c)3
Highest Offering: Associate Degree
Accreditation: SC, CAHIIM, COARC, DH, DMS, EMT, RAD

02 President .... Dr. Lonnie HOWARD
05 Vice Pres Student & Acad Success .... Ms. Melissa ARMENTOR
10 Chief Business and Financial Office .... Ms. Bonnie ALBRIGHT
15 Vice President for Human Resources .... Mrs. Catherine BLANCHARD
103 Exec Director of Workforce Educ .... Mr. Patrick CALHOUN
37 Director of Student Financial Aid .... Vacant
13 Director of Information Technology .... Mrs. Susan COOK
30 Exec Dir Devel/Dir LIT Foundation .... Ms. Joanne BROWN
26 Exec Dir Marketing & Strategic Comm .... Ms. Lana PIGAO
18 Director of Facilities .... Mr. Stephen ARNOLD
45 Vice President for Strategic Init .... Mr. David MOSLEY
04 Exec Assistant to the President .... Ms. Veronica COLLIER
06 Registrar .... Mr. David SHORT

*Lamar University (C)

PO Box 10001, Beaumont TX 77710-0009
County: Jefferson FICE Identification: 003581
Unit ID: 226091
Telephone: (409) 880-7011 Carnegie Class: DU-Mod
FAX Number: (409) 880-8404 Calendar System: Semester
URL: www.lamar.edu
Established: 1923 Annual Undergrad Tuition & Fees (In-State): $8,146
Enrollment: 14,965 Coed
Affiliation or Control: State IRS Status: 501(c)3
Highest Offering: Doctorate
Accreditation: SC, ACFEI, ART, AUD, CACREP, CAEPN, CONST, CS, DIETD, DIETI, ENG, MUS, NUR, SP, SW

02 President .... Dr. Kenneth R. EVANS
05 Provost/Vice Pres Academic Affairs .... Dr. James W. MARQUART
10 Vice Pres Finance/Operations .... Mr. Edward Craig NESS
111 Vice Pres University Advancement .... Mr. Juan ZABALA
13 Vice Pres Information Technology .... Ms. Priscilla PARSONS
20 Sr Assoc Provost for Academic Affs .... Dr. Kevin B. SMITH
106 Vice Provost for Digital Learning .... Dr. Brenda NICHOLS
15 Assoc Vice Pres Human Resources .... Ms. Catherine BLANCHARD
18 Assoc Vice Pres Facilities Mgmt .... Mr. Michael RULAND
21 Assoc Vice Pres Finance/Controller .... Vacant
124 Int Exec Dir Stdnt Achieve & Retent .... Dr. Daniel BARTLETT
58 Dean of Graduate Studies .... Dr. William HARN
49 Int Dean College Arts & Sciences .... Dr. Joeseph NORDGREN
50 Dean College of Business .... Dr. Henry VENTA
53 Dean College of Edu & Human Develop .... Dr. Robert SPINA
54 Dean College of Engineering .... Dr. Srinivas PALANKI
57 Dean College of Fine Arts & Comm .... Dr. Derina HOLTZHAUSEN
08 Director Library Services .... Mr. David J. CARROLL
06 Registrar .... Mr. David SHORT, JR.
88 Assoc Provost of Distance Learning .... Dr. Paula NICHOLS
20 Director Strategic Implementation .... Ms. Deidra MAYER
30 Director of Development .... Vacant
09 Director Institutional Research .... Dr. Gregory MARSH
36 Assoc Dir Career Services .... Ms. Angela THOMAS
23 Director Health Services .... Ms. Shawn GRAY
19 Chief University Police .... Mr. Hector FLORES
26 Public Relations Director .... Mr. Brian SATTLER
29 Director Alumni Relations .... Ms. Shannon COPELAND
37 Director Student Financial Aid .... Ms. Jill ROWLEY
96 Director of Purchasing .... Ms. Stacy CARTER-ELIZONDO
07 Director of Admissions .... Vacant

*Lamar State College-Orange (D)

410 Front Street, Orange TX 77630-5802
County: Orange FICE Identification: 023582
Unit ID: 226107
Telephone: (409) 883-7750 Carnegie Class: Assoc/HVT-High Trad
FAX Number: (409) 882-3374 Calendar System: Semester
URL: www.lsco.edu
Established: 1969 Annual Undergrad Tuition & Fees (In-State): $4,120
Enrollment: 2,318 Coed
Affiliation or Control: State IRS Status: 501(c)3
Highest Offering: Associate Degree
Accreditation: SC

02 President .... Dr. J. Michael SHAHAN
05 Vice President Academic Affairs .... Dr. Gwen WHITEHEAD
10 Vice President Finance & Operations .... Mrs. Dana ROGERS
32 VP Student Svcs & Auxiliary Ent .... Mr. Michael YEATER
08 Director of Library Services .... Ms. Mary MCCOY
06 Registrar .... Mrs. Becky J. MCANELLEY
37 Director Student Financial Aid .... Mr. Kerry J. OLSON
15 Human Resources Director .... Ms. Patty COLLINS
18 Director of Physical Plant .... Mr. David GOINS
13 Coord Information Resources .... Ms. Linda G. BURNETT
09 Coordinator Institutional Research .... Dr. Hunter KEENEY
25 Contracts/Grants Administrator .... Mrs. Dana N. ROGERS
76 Dean Health Sciences/Workforce Educ .... Ms. Gina A. SIMAR
81 Director Education & Mathematics .... Ms. Suzonne CROCKETT
49 Dir Arts/Humanities/Social Sciences .... Mr. Andy PRESLAR
96 Director of Purchasing .... Ms. Maria GARCIA

*Lamar State College-Port Arthur (E)

1500 Procter Street, Port Arthur TX 77640-6604
County: Jefferson FICE Identification: 023485
Unit ID: 226116
Telephone: (409) 983-4921 Carnegie Class: Spec 2-yr-Health
FAX Number: (409) 984-6032 Calendar System: Semester
URL: www.lamarpa.edu
Established: 1909 Annual Undergrad Tuition & Fees (In-State): $5,698
Enrollment: 1,802 Coed
Affiliation or Control: State IRS Status: 501(c)3
Highest Offering: Associate Degree
Accreditation: SC, SURGT

02 President .... Dr. Betty REYNARD
05 Vice President Academic Affairs .... Dr. Gary D. STRETCHER
10 Vice President Finance & Operations .... Ms. Mary WICKLAND
32 Dean of Student Services .... Dr. Deborrah HEBERT
04 Admin Assistant to the President .... Mrs. Donna SCHION
08 Dean Library Services .... Ms. Helena ARTHUR-OKOR
06 Registrar .... Ms. Jennifer WAGNER
37 Director Financial Aid .... Ms. Connie RILEY
45 Director Inst Effectiveness .... Mr. James M. KNOWLES
18 Director of Physical Plant .... Mr. Warren S. ODOM
26 Public Information Officer .... Mr. Gerry DICKERT
56 Dir Inmate Instructional Program .... Dr. Barbara HUVAL
13 Dir Information Technology Services .... Mr. Samir GHORAYEB
15 Director Human Resources .... Ms. Tammy RILEY
09 Director of Institutional Research .... Mrs. Petra UZORUO
51 Dean Workforce/Continuing Educ Pgms .... Dr. Ben STAFFORD
72 Dean Technical Programs .... Ms. Shelia TRAHAN
81 Department Head Science & Math .... Dr. Percy JORDAN
50 Dept Head Business/CIS Technology .... Mrs. Sheila GUILLOT
39 Director Student Housing .... Dr. Deborrah HEBERT
41 Athletic Director .... Mr. Scott STREET
96 Director of Purchasing .... Mrs. Allison WRIGHT

*Sam Houston State University (F)

1806 Avenue J, Suite 303, Huntsville TX 77341-0001
County: Walker FICE Identification: 003606
Unit ID: 227881
Telephone: (936) 294-1111 Carnegie Class: DU-Mod
FAX Number: (936) 294-1465 Calendar System: Semester
URL: www.shsu.edu
Established: 1879 Annual Undergrad Tuition & Fees (In-State): $7,762
Enrollment: 20,031 Coed
Affiliation or Control: State IRS Status: 501(c)3
Highest Offering: Doctorate
Accreditation: SC, ART, CAATE, CACREP, CAEPN, CIDA, CLPSY, CS, DIETD, DIETI, FEPAC, MUS, NURSE

02 President .... Dr. Dana G. HOYT
05 Provost/VPAA .... Dr. Richard EGLSAER
10 VP for Finance & Operations .... Dr. Carlos HERNANDEZ
111 VP for University Advancement .... Mr. Frank HOLMES
84 VP for Enrollment Management .... Dr. Heather THIELEMANN
32 VP for Student Affairs .... Mr. Frank PARKER
13 VP for Information Technology .... Mr. Mark ADAMS
41 Athletic Director .... Mr. Bobby WILLIAMS
100 Chief of Staff .... Ms. Kathy GILCREASE
20 Vice Provost .... Dr. Mary ROBBINS
58 Dean Graduate Studies .... Dr. Ken HENDRICKSON
25 Assoc VP Research/Sponsored Program .... Dr. Jerry COOK
106 Assoc VP Distance Learning .... Dr. William ANGROVE
21 Asst VP Finance & Operations .... Ms. Sylvia RAPPE
18 Assoc VP Facilities Management .... Mr. Juan NUNEZ
15 Assoc VP for HR & Risk Management .... Mr. David HAMMONDS
26 Assoc VP Marketing & Comm .... Ms. Kris KASKEL-RUIZ
30 Assoc VP for Development .... Ms. Thelma MOONEY
88 Assoc VP Enrollment Management .... Mr. Scot MERTZ
35 Assoc VP Student Affairs/Rec Sports .... Dr. Keith JENKINS
14 Assoc VP Infrustructure/Support Svc .... Mr. Terrance HARRIS
105 Assoc VP Enterprise Services .... Vacant
09 Asst VP Institutional Effectiveness .... Ms. Donna ARTHO
50 Dean of Business Administration .... Dr. Mitchell MUEHSAM
61 Dean of Criminal Justice .... Dr. Phillip LYONS
53 Dean of Education .... Dr. Stacey EDMONSON
57 Dean of Fine Arts/Mass Comm .... Dr. Ronald SHIELDS
76 Interim Dean of Health Sciences .... Dr. Rhonda CALLAWAY
83 Dean of Humanities/Social Sciences .... Dr. Abbey ZINK
81 Dean of Sciences .... Dr. John PASCARELLA
08 Director Library Services .... Ms. Ann HOLDER
63 Dean of Osteopathic Medicine .... Dr. Charles HENLEY
19 Director Public Safety Services .... Mr. Kevin MORRIS
06 Registrar .... Ms. Teresa RINGO
07 Director Undergraduate Admissions .... Ms. Angie TAYLOR
37 Director Financial Aid .... Ms. Lydia HALL
39 Director Residence Life .... Ms. Joellen TIPTON
23 AVP SA/Student Hlth & Couns Center .... Dr. Drew MILLER
29 Director Alumni Relations .... Mr. Charlie VIENNE
35 Dean of Students .... Mr. John YARABECK
108 Asst VP Planning & Assessment .... Dr. Somer FRANKLIN
43 Dir Legal Services/General Counsel .... Ms. Rhonda BEASSIE
21 Interim Controller .... Ms. Amanda WITHERS
88 Treasurer .... Mr. David VERGHESE
114 Director of University Budget .... Mr. Edgar SMITH
110 Director Advancement Services .... Ms. Patricia LEWIS
88 Museum Director .... Mr. Mac WOODWARD
88 Asst VP Enrollment Management .... Ms. Leah MULLIGAN
88 Asst VP Student Affairs .... Dr. Kristy VIENNE
35 Director of Student Activities .... Mr. Brandon COOPER
88 Dir Stdnt Affairs Finance & Budget .... Ms. Lynn CLOPTON
28 Dir Equity & Inclusion & Title IX .... Ms. Jeanine BIAS
88 Dir of Leadership Initiatives .... Ms. Meredith CONREY
88 Assoc VP Client Services .... Mr. Terry BLAYLOCK
88 Director IT Project Management .... Ms. Linda MCINTOSH
119 Director Information Security .... Mr. Steven FREY
88 Director IT Finance & Budget .... Ms. Deborah MCKERALL

*Sul Ross State University (G)

PO Box C-100, Alpine TX 79832-0001
County: Brewster FICE Identification: 003625
Unit ID: 228501
Telephone: (432) 837-8011 Carnegie Class: Masters/L
FAX Number: (432) 837-8334 Calendar System: Semester
URL: www.sulross.edu
Established: 1917 Annual Undergrad Tuition & Fees (In-State): $6,419
Enrollment: 2,967 Coed
Affiliation or Control: State IRS Status: 501(c)3
Highest Offering: Master's
Accreditation: SC, NURSE

02 President .... Dr. Bill KIBLER
05 Exec VP Academic/Stdnt Affs/Provost .... Dr. Jim CASE
10 Vice Pres for Finance & Operations .... Mr. Cesario E. VALENZUELA
84 Vice Pres Enrollment Management .... Ms. Mary Beth MARKS
30 Assoc Vice Pres University Services .... Mr. Leo G. DOMINGUEZ
12 RGC Dean .... Dr. Veronica MENDEZ MAQUEO
11 Director of Administration .... Ms. Yvonne REALIVASQUEZ
06 Director Records & Registration .... Ms. Pamela S. PIPES
08 Dean Library & Info Technology .... Ms. April AULTMAN BECKER
32 Dean of Students .... Mr. Leo DOMINGUEZ
92 Dir Honors Prog/Acad Ctr Excellence .... Dr. Kathy STEIN
26 Director News & Publications .... Mr. Stephen W. LANG
37 Dir Financial Assistance .... Mr. Mickey CORBETT
49 Dean Arts & Science .... Dr. Jay DOWNING
107 Dean Education & Professional Stds .... Dr. Hamin SHABAZZ
47 Dean Agricult/Natural Resource Sci .... Dr. Robert J. KINUCAN
15 Director of Human Resources .... Mrs. Gail COLLIER
18 Asst Director of Physical Plant .... Mr. Edmundo NATERA
19 Director Dept of Public Safety .... Mr. Johnnie L. HOLBROOKS
21 Director of Accounting Services .... Mr. Santiago CASTILLO
39 Director Residential Living .... Mr. Bradley GWATNEY
41 Director of Athletics .... Mr. Bobby S. MESKER
38 Director of Counseling Ctr .... Ms. Mary SCHWARTZE
13 Chief Information Officer .... Mr. David W. GIBSON
96 Director of Purchasing .... Mr. Noe HERNANDEZ
88 Dir Center for Big Bend Studies .... Mr. Andy CLOUD
29 Director Alumni Relations .... Ms. Aida LUEVANOS
88 Director of Upward Bound .... Ms. Barbara VEGA
88 Director of University Archives .... Ms. Melleta BELL
88 Director Small Business Devel Ctr .... Ms. Patricia K. LONG
88 Law Enforcement Academy Coord .... Ms. Clariza PINA

07 Director Admissions & Records .... Ms. Claudia WRIGHT
88 Mail Service Supervisor .... Ms. Leticia GONZALES
116 Internal Auditor .... Mr. Scott A. CUPP
36 Coord Career Services & Testing .... Ms. Jan L. RUEB
09 Dir of Institutional Effectiveness .... Dr. Jeanne QVARMSTROM
50 Dean Graduate Studies .... Dr. Sharon HILEMAN

*Texas State University (A)

601 University Drive, San Marcos TX 78666-4615
County: Hays FICE Identification: 003615
Unit ID: 228459
Telephone: (512) 245-2111 Carnegie Class: DU-Higher
FAX Number: (512) 245-3040 Calendar System: Semester
URL: www.txstate.edu
Established: 1899 Annual Undergrad Tuition & Fees (In-State): $9,605
Enrollment: 37,979 Coed
Affiliation or Control: State IRS Status: 170(c)1
Highest Offering: Doctorate
Accreditation: SC, CAATE, CACREP, CAEPT, CAHIIM, CEA, CIDA, COARC, COARCP, CONST, CS, DIETD, DIETI, ENG, HSA, IPSY, JOUR, MT, MUS, NRPA, NURSE, PTA, RTT, SP, SPAA, SW

02 President .... Dr. Denise M. TRAUTH
05 Provost/Vice Pres Academic Affairs .... Dr. Gene BOURGEOIS
100 Special Assistant to the President .... Dr. Vicki S. BRITTAIN
32 Vice President Student Affairs .... Dr. Joanne H. SMITH
10 Vice Pres Finance/Support Services .... Mr. Eric ALGOE
111 Vice Pres University Advancement .... Dr. Barbara BREIER
13 Vice Pres Information Technology .... Mr. Kenneth PIERCE
83 Dean College of Applied Arts .... Dr. T. Jaime CHAHIN
50 Dean McCoy Col of Business Admin .... Dr. Denise T. SMART
57 Dean College Fine Arts & Comm .... Dr. John FLEMING
53 Dean College of Education .... Dr. Stan CARPENTER
76 Dean College Health Professions .... Dr. Ruth B. WELBORN
83 Dean College Liberal Arts .... Dr. Michael HENNESSY
81 Dean College of Science & Engr .... Dr. Christine HAILEY
58 Dean The Graduate College .... Dr. Andrea GOLATO
97 Dean Univ Col & Dir PACE Center .... Dr. Daniel BROWN
92 Dean Honors College .... Dr. Heather GALLOWAY
20 Assoc Vice Pres Academic Affairs .... Dr. Vedaraman SRIRAMAN
15 Asst VP of Human Resources .... Mr. John E. MCBRIDE
20 Associate Provost .... Dr. Debbie M. THORNE
18 Associate VP of Facilities .... Mr. Thomas F. SHEWAN
86 Assoc VP Research & Dir of Fed Rels .... Dr. Walter E. HORTON
35 Assoc VP Stdnt Affs/Dean of Stdnt .. Dr. Margarita M. ARELLANO
20 Assoc Vice Pres for Inst Effective .... Dr. Beth E. WUEST
21 Assoc VP Financial Services .... Mr. Darryl BORGONAH
84 Assoc VP Enroll Mgmt/Marketing .... Mr. Gary T. RAY
08 Associate VP University Library .... Ms. Joan L. HEATH
20 Assistant VP for Academic Services .... Dr. Ronald C. BROWN
38 Director Counseling Center .... Dr. Kathlyn C. DAILEY
07 Asst VP Enroll Mgmt/Dir Ungrad Adm .... Ms. Stephanie ANDERSON
28 AVP/Dir Student Diversity/Inclusion .... Dr. Sherri BENN
30 Asst VP University Advancement .... Mr. Dan PERRY
112 Asst VP Development/Major Gifts .... Mr. Tim PLOCICA
88 Asst VP Univ Advance/Communication .... Mr. Matt FLORES
88 Assoc VP Finance/Support Svcs Plng .... Ms. Nancy NUSBAUM
14 Assoc VP for Technology Resources .... Mr. Mark HUGHES
90 Assoc VP Instructional Tech Supp .... Dr. Carlos SOLIS
106 Dir Distance & Extended Learning .... Mr. Dana WILLETT
06 University Registrar .... Mr. Louis E. JIMENEZ
91 Director Enterprise Systems .... Mr. Martin MILLS
37 Director of Fin Aid & Scholarships .... Dr. Christopher MURR
36 Director Career Services .... Ms. Norma GUERRA GAIER
41 Director of Athletics .... Dr. Lawrence B. TEIS
29 Director of Alumni Affairs .... Ms. Kim GANNON
27 Director Univ News Services .... Mr. Jayme L. BLASCHKE
12 Asst VP Round Rock Campus .... Dr. Edna REHBEIN
25 Director of Sponsored Programs .... Vacant
19 Director University Police .... Mr. Jose BANALES
23 Director Student Health Center .... Dr. Emilio CARRANCO
39 Director Housing & Residential Life .... Dr. Rosanne PROITE
40 Manager University Bookstore .... Mr. John ROOT
24 Director Instructional Media .... Ms. Laura TRIAL
09 Asst VP of Institutional Research .... Mr. Joseph M. MEYER
22 Chief Diversity/Dir Equity & Access .... Dr. Gilda GARCIA
93 Dir Center for Multicul/Gender Stds .... Dr. Audwin ANDERSON
96 Director Purchasing .... Mr. Dan ALDEN
26 Director of University Marketing .... Mr. Daniel W. EGGERS
116 Director of Audit & Compliance .... Mr. Steve R. MCGEE
88 Interim Director Campus Recreation .... Dr. Margarita ARELLANO
88 Director LBJ Student Center .... Mr. Jack RAHMANN
124 Director Retention Mgmt & Planning .... Dr. Jen BECK
22 Int Director Disability Services .... Dr. Sherri BENN
108 Dir Univ Planning & Assessment .... Dr. Ana Lisa GARZA
104 Asst VP for International Affairs .... Dr. Ryan BUCK
88 Director Learning Spaces .... Mr. Brian SHANKS

*Texas Tech University System (B)

1508 Knoxville Ave, Lubbock TX 79409-2013
County: Lubbock Identification: 667242
Telephone: (806) 742-0012 Carnegie Class: N/A
FAX Number: N/A
URL: www.texastech.edu

01 Chancellor .... Mr. Robert L. DUNCAN
05 Vice Chancellor Academic Affairs .... Dr. John OPPERMAN
10 Vice Chancellor & CFO .... Mr. Jim BRUNJES
30 Vice Chancellor Inst Advancement .... Ms. Lisa D. CALVERT
86 Vice Chanc Government Relations .... Ms. Martha BROWN
18 Vice Chanc Facil Plng/Construction .... Mr. Michael MOLINA
43 Vice Chancellor General Counsel .... Mr. John HUFFAKER
116 Vice Chancellor Audit .... Mrs. Kim TURNER
26 Vice Chancellor Communications .... Mr. Brett ASHWORTH

*Angelo State University (C)

2601 West Avenue N, San Angelo TX 76909-0001
County: Tom Green FICE Identification: 003541
Unit ID: 222831
Telephone: (325) 942-2555 Carnegie Class: Masters/L
FAX Number: N/A Calendar System: Semester
URL: www.angelo.edu
Established: 1928 Annual Undergrad Tuition & Fees (In-State): $7,047
Enrollment: 8,483 Coed
Affiliation or Control: State IRS Status: 501(c)3
Highest Offering: Doctorate
Accreditation: SC, ACBSP, CAEPN, MUS, NURSE, PTA, SW

02 President .... Dr. Brian J. MAY
05 Provost/Vice Pres Academic Affairs .... Dr. Donald R. TOPLIFF
30 VP for Development & Alumni Rels .... Ms. Jamie AKIN
10 VP for Finance and Administration .... Ms. Angelina WRIGHT
32 VP for Student Affs & Enroll Mgmt .... Dr. Javier FLORES
58 Dean Col of Grad Studies & Research .... Dr. Susan KEITH
54 Dean of College of Sci & Engr .... Dr. Paul SWETS
50 Dean College Business .... Dr. Clifton JONES
53 Dean College of Education .... Dr. John MIAZGA
66 Dean College Health & Human Service .... Dr. Leslie MAYRAND
79 Dean College of Arts & Humanities ...... Ms. Carolyn GASCOIGNE
06 Director of Registrar Services .... Ms. Cindy WEEAKS
89 Dean Freshman College .... Dr. John WEGNER
09 Director of Accountability .... Ms. Brandy HAWKINS
08 Exec Director of Library .... Dr. Maurice G. FORTIN
36 Director Career Development .... Ms. Julie J. RUTHENBECK
15 Director of Human Resources .... Mr. Kurtis R. NEAL
37 Director of Student Financial Aid .... Mr. William BLOOM
26 Director of Communications & Mktg .... Ms. Rebekah BRACKIN
29 Director Development & Alumni Svcs .... Ms. Kimberly ADAMS
35 Exec Director of Student Affairs .... Dr. Bradley PETTY
18 Director of Facilities Management .... Mr. Jay HALBERT
39 Dir of Housing & Residential Pgm .... Ms. Tracy W. BAKER
40 Manager Bookstore .... Ms. Michaela REYNOLDS
41 Athletic Director .... Mr. James REID
19 Chief of University Police .... Mr. James E. ADAMS
13 Assoc VP Information Technology/CIO .... Mr. Douglas FOX
21 Director of Business Services .... Ms. Jessica MANNING
96 Director Purchasing and Travel .... Ms. Michelle MICHAELIS
92 Director of Honors Program .... Dr. Shirley EOFF
04 Executive Asst to the President .... Ms. Adelina C. MORALES
104 Director of International Studies .... Ms. Meghan PACE
07 Director of Admissions .... Ms. Sharla ADAM
38 Director of Counseling Services .... Mr. Cleave POOL
84 Director Enrollment Management .... Mr. Jeffrey SEFCIK
43 Sr Exec Asst to Pres/Gen Counsel .... Mr. Joe MUNOZ

† Affiliated with Texas Tech University in Lubbock, TX

*Texas Tech University (D)

2500 Broadway, Lubbock TX 79401
County: Lubbock FICE Identification: 003644
Unit ID: 229115
Telephone: (806) 742-2121 Carnegie Class: DU-Highest
FAX Number: (806) 742-2138 Calendar System: Semester
URL: www.ttu.edu
Established: 1923 Annual Undergrad Tuition & Fees (In-State): $8,428
Enrollment: 35,859 Coed
Affiliation or Control: State IRS Status: 170(c)1
Highest Offering: Doctorate
Accreditation: SC, ARCPA, ART, CACREP, CAEPN, #CIDA, CLPSY, COPSY, CS, DANCE, DIETD, DIETI, ENG, IPSY, LAW, LSAR, MFCD, MIDWF, MUS, SPAA, SW, THEA

00 Chancellor .... Mr. Robert L. DUNCAN
02 President .... Dr. Lawrence SCHOVANEC
101 Sec Board Regents/Ex Asst to Chanc ..... Ms. Christina MARTINEZ
05 Provost and Senior Vice President .... Dr. Michael GALYEAN
10 Chief Operating Ofcr/SVP Admin/Fin .... Ms. Noel SLOAN
111 Vice Chanc Inst Advancement .... Ms. Lisa CALVERT
86 Vice Chancellor Govt Relations .... Ms. Martha BROWN
43 Vice Chanc & General Counsel .... Mr. John HUFFAKER
18 VC Facilities Planning Construction .... Mr. Michael MOLINA
20 Sr Vice Provost Academic Affairs .... Dr. Rob STEWART
100 President's Chief of Staff .... Ms. Grace HERNANDEZ
29 EVP & CEO Texas Tech Alumni Assoc .... Dr. Bill DEAN
46 Vice President for Research .... Dr. Joseph HEPPERT
28 Vice Pres Institutional Diversity .... Vacant
84 Assoc VP Enrollment Management .... Dr. Ethan LOGAN
20 Vice Provost Academic Affairs .... Ms. Genevieve DURHAM DECESARO
21 Asst Vice Pres & Controller .... Ms. Sharon WILLIAMSON
82 Vice Prov International Affairs .... Amb. Tibor P. NAGY
13 Assoc VP Info Tech and CIO .... Mr. Sam SEGRAN
08 Dean of Libraries .... Dr. Bella GERLICH
60 Dean Media & Communications .... Dr. David PERLMUTTER
32 Asst Dean of Students .... Ms. Denise TIJERINA
37 Executive Director Fin Aid .... Vacant
14 Chief Information Officer .... Ms. Kay RHODES
06 Registrar .... Ms. Bobbie BROWN
07 Executive Director of Admissions .... Ms. Jamie HANSARD
27 Managing Dir Commun & Marketing .... Mr. Chris COOK
04 Executive Asst to President .... Ms. Mikki ROSS
31 Director Community Engagment .... Vacant
44 Managing Director Annual Giving .... Mr. Daniel BURGNER
23 Managing Dir Student Health Serv .... Ms. Evelyn MCPHERSON
39 Managing Dir Student Housing .... Mr. Sean DUGGAN
36 Managing Director Career Center .... Mr. Jay KILLOUGH
15 Managing Director of HR Management .. Ms. Jodie BILLINGSLEY
22 Asst Vice Chanc Admin/Mng Dir EEO ..... Ms. Charlotte BINGHAM
38 Director Student Counseling .... Dr. Richard LENOX
41 Director of Athletics .... Mr. Kirby HOCUTT
47 Interim Dean Ag Sci/Natural Res .... Dr. Steve FRAZE
49 Dean of Arts & Sciences .... Dr. Brent LINDQUIST
48 Dean of Architecture .... Dr. James P. WILLIAMSON
50 Dean Business Administration .... Dr. Margaret L. WILLIAMSON
53 Dean of Education .... Dr. Scott RIDLEY
54 Dean of Engineering .... Dr. Albert SACCO, JR.
88 Dean of Human Sciences .... Dr. Linda HOOVER
61 Dean School of Law .... Dr. Jack NOWLIN
58 Dean of Graduate School .... Dr. Mark SHERIDAN
92 Dean Honors College .... Dr. Michael SAN FRANCISCO
57 Dean Visual & Performing Arts .... Dr. Noel ZAHLER
19 Chief of Police .... Mr. Kyle K. BONATH
09 Managing Dir Institutional Research .... Ms. Vicki WEST
96 Managing Dir Procurement Services .... Ms. Jennifer ADLING

*Texas Tech University Health Sciences Center (E)

3601 4th Street, Lubbock TX 79430-0001
County: Lubbock FICE Identification: 010674
Unit ID: 229337
Telephone: (806) 743-1000 Carnegie Class: Spec-4-yr-Med
FAX Number: N/A Calendar System: Semester
URL: www.ttuhsc.edu
Established: 1969 Annual Undergrad Tuition & Fees (In-State): N/A
Enrollment: 4,998 Coed
Affiliation or Control: State IRS Status: 501(c)3
Highest Offering: Doctorate
Accreditation: SC, AUD, CAATE, CACREP, DMOLS, MED, MT, NURSE, OT, PHAR, PTA, SP

02 President .... Dr. Tedd L. MITCHELL
10 Exec Vice Pres for Finance Admin .... Mr. Elmo M. CAVIN, JR.
05 Exec Vice Pres Academic Affairs .... Dr. Rial D. ROLFE
26 Exec Dir Communications & Mktg .... Ms. Mary CROYLE
17 Exec Vice Pres Rural/Community Hlth .. Dr. Billy U. PHILIPS, JR.
46 Senior Vice President for Research .... Dr. Quentin SMITH
13 Vice Pres Info Tech/Chief Info Ofcr .... Dr. Chip SHAW
86 VP Federal and State Relations .... Mr. Ryan HENRY
88 Vice President of Health Policy .... Dr. Cynthia JUMPER
28 VP of Diversity & Inclusion .... Dr. Kim PECK
100 Chief of Staff .... Ms. Didit MARTINEZ
43 Senior Assoc General Counsel .... Mr. Jon MCGOUGH
21 Assoc Vice Pres Business Affairs .... Mr. Mike CROWDER
15 Int AVP of Human Resources .... Dr. Janet COQUELLIN
108 Asst VP Academic Affairs .... Dr. Kari DICKSON
30 Asst VC Institutional Advancement .... Ms. Kendra BURRIS
21 Asst Vice Pres of Budget .... Vacant
32 AVP Student Services .... Ms. Margret DURAN
22 Asst Vice Pres Compliance .... Ms. Sonya CASTRO-QUIRINO
18 Int AVP of Physical Plant .... Mr. Greg LOVETT
63 Dean of Medical School .... Dr. Steven L. BERK
58 Dean Grad Sch Biomed Sciences .... Dr. Brandt L. SCHNEIDER
66 Dean of Nursing School .... Dr. Michael L. EVANS
76 Dean of Allied Health Sciences Sch .... Dr. Lori RICE-SPEARMAN
67 Dean of Pharmacy School .... Dr. Quentin R. SMITH
63 Reg Dean Medicine Amarillo Campus .... Dr. Richard JORDAN
63 Reg Dean Medicine Odessa Campus .... Dr. Gary VENTOLINI
66 Reg Dean Nursing Abilene .... Ms. Pearl E. MERRITT
66 Reg Dean Nursing Odessa Campus .... Dr. Sharon CANNON
76 Reg Dean Allied Health Amarillo .... Dr. Michael HOOTEN
76 Reg Dean Allied Health Odessa .... Dr. Neeraj KUMAR
67 Reg Dean Pharmacy Abilene .... Dr. Cindy RAEHL
67 Reg Dean Pharmacy Amarillo .... Dr. Thomas THEKKUMKARA
67 Reg Dean Pharmacy Dallas .... Dr. Roland PATRY
67 Reg Dean Pharmacy Lubbock .... Dr. Charles E. SEIFERT
06 Registrar .... Ms. Tamara N. KRAUSER
08 Exec Director of HSC Libraries .... Dr. Richard NOLLAN
21 Managing Dir Accounting Services .... Ms. Melody OLIPHINT
22 Director of Equal Employment .... Ms. Charlotte BINGHAM
25 Director of Sponsored Programs .... Ms. Erin WOODS
37 Director of Financial Aid .... Mr. Marcus WILSON
25 Sr Director of Contracting .... Mr. Jim LEWIS
19 Information Security Officer .... Mr. Andrew HOWARD
96 Managing Director of Purchasing .... Mr. John G. HAYNES
09 Chief Analyst Inst Research .... Mr. Kevin MCINTYRE
29 Director of Alumni Relations .... Ms. Julie DOSS
88 Sr Director Office of Global Health ...... Ms. Michelle ENSMINGER

*Texas Tech University Health Sciences Center at El Paso (F)

5001 El Paso Drive, El Paso TX 79905
Telephone: (915) 215-4300 Identification: 667243
Accreditation: &SC, MED, NURSE

Texas Wesleyan University (G)

1201 Wesleyan, Fort Worth TX 76105-1536
County: Tarrant FICE Identification: 003645
Unit ID: 229160
Telephone: (817) 531-4444 Carnegie Class: DU-Mod
FAX Number: (817) 531-4425 Calendar System: Semester
URL: www.txwes.edu

Established: 1890 Annual Undergrad Tuition & Fees: $26,050
Enrollment: 2,474 Coed
Affiliation or Control: United Methodist IRS Status: 501(c)3
Highest Offering: Doctorate
Accreditation: SC, ACBSP, ANEST, CAATE, MFCD, MUS

01 President Mr. Frederick G. SLABACH
05 Provost/Sr Vice President Dr. Allen HENDERSON
10 VP Finance & Administration Mrs. Donna NANCE
30 VP University Advancement Mr. Jim LEWIS
84 VP for Enrollment & Student Svcs Ms. Pati ALEXANDER
26 Vice Pres Marketing/Communications Mr. John VEILLEUX
32 VP Student Affairs/Dean of Students Mr. Dennis HALL
20 Assoc Provost Academic Affairs Dr. Steven DANIELL
20 Associate Provost Dr. Helena BUSSELL
41 Athletic Director Mr. Steven TRACHIER
53 Dean School of Education Dr. Carlos MARTINEZ
50 Dean of School of Business Dr. Hector QUINTANILLA
49 Dean School Arts & Letters Dr. Mark HANSHAW
83 Dean School of Natural & Social Sci Dr. Ricardo RODRIGUEZ
39 Asst Dn Stdnts/Dir Residence Life Mr. Jon BARTLETT
06 Registrar Mr. Sloan WHITE
08 Library Science Assoc Professor Ms. Elizabeth HOWARD
21 Controller Ms. Jacqueline RUTLEDGE
07 Enrollment Services Assistant VP Mr. Chadd BRIDWELL
37 Director Financial Aid Ms. Laurie ROSENKRANTZ
42 Interim Chaplain Ms. Gladys CHILDS
38 Director of Counseling Dr. Linda METCALF
29 Director Alumni Relations Mrs. DeAwna WOOD
15 AVP of Human Resources Ms. Angela DAMPEER
96 Director of Purchasing Ms. Deborah CAVITT
36 Director of Career Services Ms. Robyn BONE
18 Exec Dir of Facil/Opers/Emr Svcs Mr. Brian FRANKS
25 Sr Dir of Sponsored Programs Mr. Shawn FARRELL
13 Associate Vice President & CIO Mr. Marcus KERR
04 Executive Assistant to the Pres Ms. Judi D. PARDUE
04 Executive Assistant to the Pres Mrs. Sherry SANDLES
09 Director Institutional Research Ms. Sherri CARABALLO
100 Chief of Staff and General Counsel Ms. Patti GEARHART TURNER
103 Director Career Services/Counselor Ms. Robyn BONE

Texas Woman's University (A)

Box 425587, Denton TX 76204-5587
County: Denton FICE Identification: 003646
Unit ID: 229179
Telephone: (940) 898-2000 Carnegie Class: DU-Mod
FAX Number: (940) 898-3198 Calendar System: Semester
URL: www.twu.edu
Established: 1901 Annual Undergrad Tuition & Fees (In-State): $7,238
Enrollment: 15,286 Coed
Affiliation or Control: State IRS Status: 501(c)3
Highest Offering: Doctorate
Accreditation: SC, ACBSP, CACREP, COPSY, DANCE, DH, DIETD, DIETI, HSA, IPSY, LIB, MUS, NURSE, OT, PTA, SCPSY, SP, SW

01 Chancellor & President Dr. Carine FEYTEN
05 Provost & VP Academic Affairs Dr. Robert NEELY
10 Interim VP Finance/Administration Ms. Betty CRAIN
32 Vice President Student Life Dr. Monica MENDEZ-GRANT
13 Assoc Provost for Technology & CIO Dr. Rob PLACIDO
20 Senior Associate Provost Dr. Jennifer MARTIN
09 Assoc Prov Inst Improve & Data Mgmt Dr. Mark S. HAMNER
26 Assoc Vice Pres Mktg/Communication Ms. Cindy POLLARD
84 Int Vice Pres Enrollment Services Ms. Babrara LERNER
21 Associate Vice President Finance Ms. Pam WILSON
18 Assoc Vice Pres Facilities Mr. Joe STANDRIDGE, JR.
15 Assoc Vice Pres Human Resources Mr. Lewis BENAVIDES
49 Dean College Arts & Sciences Dr. Abigail TILTON
69 Dean College Health Sciences Dr. Christopher T. RAY
107 Int Dean College Prof Education Dr. Jerry WHITWORTH
58 Dean Graduate School Dr. Larry LEFLORE
07 Director of Admissions Ms. Erma M. NIETO-BRECHT
43 General Counsel Ms. Destinee WAITERS
08 Director of Libraries Ms. Suzanne SEARS
37 Director Student Financial Aid Mr. Governor E. JACKSON
36 Director Career & Employment Svcs Ms. Lisa GARZA
38 Director Counseling Center Dr. Denise LUCERO-MILLER
19 Director of Public Safety Ms. Liz PAULEY
06 Registrar Mr. Bobby LOTHRINGER
41 Athletic Director Ms. Chalese CONNORS
23 Director Student Health Services Dr. Connie MENARD
39 Director University Housing Ms. Jill ECKARDT
29 Director Alumni Relations Ms. Anne SCOTT
96 Procurement Services Ms. Vanna PARR
04 Executive Asst to Chancellor/Pres Ms. Lorie HUSLIG
04 Coord Events Outreach & Communic Ms. Rachel PRIDE
100 Chief of Staff Mr. Christopher JOHNSON
104 Director Study Abroad Ms. Annie PHILLIPS
106 Dir Teach & Learn w/Technology Dr. Lynda MURPHY
108 Director Academic Assessment Dr. Terry SENNE
30 Vice President Advancement Ms. Heidi TRACY
50 Director School of Management Dr. Margaret A. YOUNG
86 Dir Governmental & Legis Affairs Mr. Kevin CRUSER

Trinity University (B)

One Trinity Place, San Antonio TX 78212-7200
County: Bexar FICE Identification: 003647
Unit ID: 229267
Telephone: (210) 999-7011 Carnegie Class: Masters/S
FAX Number: (210) 999-7696 Calendar System: Semester
URL: www.trinity.edu
Established: 1869 Annual Undergrad Tuition & Fees: $39,560
Enrollment: 2,438 Coed
Affiliation or Control: Independent Non-Profit IRS Status: 501(c)3
Highest Offering: Master's
Accreditation: SC, CAEPN, ENG, HSA

01 President Dr. Danny ANDERSON
05 Vice Pres Academic Affairs Dr. Deneese JONES
10 VP Finance and Administration Mr. Gary LOGAN
111 VP Alumni Relations & Development Mr. Michael BACON
26 VP Info Resources/Marketing & Comm Dr. Charles B. WHITE
84 VP Enrollment/Student Retention Mr. Eric MALOOF
32 Vice Pres Student Life Dr. Sheryl R. TYNES
20 Assoc VP Faculty Recruitment & Dev Dr. Duane COLTHARP
20 Assoc VP Budget & Research Dr. Mark BRODL
21 Assoc VP for Finance Ms. Diana HEEREN
32 Assoc VP Stdnt Affs/Dean of Stdnt Mr. David M. TUTTLE
09 Assoc VP/Dir Institutional Research Dr. Diane G. SAPHIRE
51 AVP Conferences/Special Pgms Ms. Ann G. KNOEBEL
37 Asst VP Student Financial Svcs Ms. Glendi GADDIS
27 Asst VP External Relations Ms. Sharon JONES SCHWEITZER
08 Asst VP/University Librarian Ms. Diane J. GRAVES
19 Asst VP Public Safety/Ent Risk Mgmt Mr. Paul CHAPA
15 Assistant VP Human Resources Ms. Pamela JOHNSTON
06 Registrar Mr. Alfred RODRIGUEZ
07 Director Admissions/Operations Ms. Valerie SCHWEERS
38 Director Counseling/Health Svcs Dr. Gary W. NEAL
31 Director Student Involvement Ms. Jamie THOMPSON
36 Director of Career Services Ms. Twyla HOUGH
13 Dir/Chief Info Technology Officer Mr. Fred ZAPATA
44 Sr Director of Annual Giving Pgms Ms. Kathy MCNEILL
29 Senior Director of Alumni Relations Mr. Hugh DASCHBACH
04 Assistant to the President Ms. Claire SMITH
18 Director Facility Services Mr. James BAKER
42 Chaplain Rev. Stephen R. NICKLE
96 Director of Purchasing Vacant
28 Director Diversity Ms. Jamie THOMPSON
41 Athletic Director Mr. Bob KING
40 Manager of Bookstore Ms. Susie JUVERA

Trinity Valley Community College (C)

100 Cardinal Drive, Athens TX 75751-2734
County: Henderson FICE Identification: 003572
Unit ID: 225308
Telephone: (903) 677-8822 Carnegie Class: Assoc/MT-VT-High Non
FAX Number: (903) 675-6316 Calendar System: Semester
URL: www.tvcc.edu
Established: 1946 Annual Undergrad Tuition & Fees (In-District): $2,460
Enrollment: 4,668 Coed
Affiliation or Control: State/Local IRS Status: 501(c)3
Highest Offering: Associate Degree
Accreditation: SC, ADNUR, EMT, SURGT

01 President Dr. Jerry KING
05 Vice President for Instruction Dr. Wendy ELMORE
30 VP of Institutional Advancement Ms. Kristen BENNETT
32 Vice President Student Services Dr. Jay KINZER
13 VP of Information Technology Mr. Brett DANIEL
10 Vice Pres Administrative Services Mrs. Jean MCSPADDEN
20 Assoc VP Instruction Academic Educ Mrs. Kristin SPIZZIRRI
103 Associate VP of Workforce Education Mr. David MCANALLY
91 Assoc VP of Information Technology Vacant
21 Associate Business Officer Ms. Courtney WALKER
12 Assoc VP of TDCJ Programs Dr. Sam HURLEY
18 Asst VP of Facilities Management Mr. David GRAEM
76 Provost Health Occupations Dr. Helen REID
12 Provost Kaufman County Campus Dr. Algia ALLEN
12 Provost Anderson County Campus Dr. Jeff WATSON
06 AVP of Enrollment Mgmt/Registrar Dr. Colette HILLIARD
09 Dir Strategic Planning/SACS Ms. Tina RUMMEL
08 Director Learning Resource Center Ms. Karla BRYAN
36 Dir of Student Pathways/Success Ms. Tammy DENNEY
26 Public Information Officer Mr. Mark MEREDITH
07 Director School Relations Ms. Audrey HAWKINS
37 Dir Student Finan Aid/Veteran's Svc Ms. Jennifer EVILSIZER
41 Athletic Director Mr. Brad SMILEY
19 Director of Campus Police Mr. Stewart NEWBY
36 Placement Officer Vacant
40 Bookstore Manager Mrs. Beth Ann KIDD
35 Director Student Activities Mr. Harold JONES
31 Director Community Services Ms. Gayla ROBERTS
15 Director of Human Resources Ms. Janene DOTTS
96 Director of Purchasing Ms. Judith MCGILVRAY

Tyler Junior College (D)

PO Box 9020, Tyler TX 75711-9020
County: Smith FICE Identification: 003648
Unit ID: 229355
Telephone: (903) 510-2200 Carnegie Class: Assoc/MT-VT-High Trad
FAX Number: (903) 510-2632 Calendar System: Semester
URL: www.tjc.edu
Established: 1926 Annual Undergrad Tuition & Fees (In-District): $2,634
Enrollment: 10,934 Coed
Affiliation or Control: State/Local IRS Status: 170(c)1
Highest Offering: Baccalaureate
Accreditation: SC, CAHIIM, COARC, #COARCP, DA, DH, DMS, EMT, MLTAD, OTA, PTAA, RAD, SURGT

01 President Dr. L. Michael METKE
04 Exec Asst to President Ms. Ellen MATTHEWS
10 Vice President Financial AffairsCFO Ms. Sarah E. VAN CLEEF
05 Provost/Vice Pres Acad & Stdnt Affs Dr. Juan E. MEJIA
111 Exec Dir Inst Advance/Foundation Mr. Dennis M. ANDREWS
09 Exec Dir Inst Effect Plng & Rsrch Dr. Cheryl L. ROGERS
51 Dean Continuing Studies Dr. Aubrey D. SHARPE
15 Exec Dir Human Resources Mr. S. Kevin FOWLER
18 Exec Dir Facilities & Construction Vacant
26 Exec Dir Marketing Media Comm Mrs. Kimberly LESSNER
13 Chief Information Officer Mr. Larry MENDEZ
20 Asst Vice Pres Academic Affairs Ms. Tampa J. NANNEN
32 Asst Vice Pres Student Affairs Dr. Thomas A. JOHNSON
32 Asst Vice Pres Student Engagement Dr. Timothy S. DRAIN
81 Dean Engineering Math and Sciences Dr. Kenneth R. MURPHY
76 Dean Nursing Health Sciences Mr. Paul R. MONAGAN
79 Dean Humanities Comm Fine Arts Ms. Linda GARY
107 Dean Professional Tech Programs Mr. Bryan RENFRO
84 Dean Enrollment Management Mrs. Janna L. CHANCEY
20 Dean Academic Success Mr. Dometrius HILL
88 Dean Curriculum Compliance Ms. Lisa M. HARPER
41 Athletic Director Dr. Timothy S. DRAIN
21 Controller Mr. Hunter THROCKMORTON
14 Exec Dir Informational Technology Mr. Rick BESCH
06 Dir Academic Services Registrar Mr. Thomas ELDER
07 Director Admissions Ms. Nidia HASSAN
27 Dir Public Affairs Media Relations Mrs. Rebecca SANDERS
09 Dir Institutional Research Ms. Jacquelyn MESSINGER
37 Director Financial Aid Ms. Devon WIGGINS
08 Director Learning Resource Center Ms. Marian D. JACKSON
96 Director Campus Services Vacant
35 Director Student Life Mrs. Lauren TYLER
109 Director Auxiliary Services Ms. Diana KAROL
39 Director Student Housing Ms. Diana KAROL
88 Director Testing Mr. Roger GRIMM
121 Director Academic Advising Mrs. Jan ADAMS
29 Director Alumni Relations Vacant
88 Director SBDC Mr. Donald W. PROUDFOOT
44 Director Annual Giving Mr. Robert SPRINGER
106 Director Distance Education Mr. Ken CRAVER
19 Director Campus Police Mr. Randy MELTON
92 Director Honors Program Mr. David FUNK
112 Director Major Gifts Ms. Barabara KING
102 Director Foundation Ms. Shelby GOULD
119 Director Information Security Mr. Carl SHOTTS
16 Assistant Director Human Resources Mrs. Connie J. RUSSELL
16 Assistant Dir Human Res Title IX Mr. Andrew CANTEY
118 Manager Benefits Compensation Ms. DeVonne CAGLE
38 Counselor Learning Specialist Mrs. Tracey WILLIAMS
36 Coordinator Career Services Mrs. Jennifer RENFRO

University of Dallas (E)

1845 E Northgate Drive, Irving TX 75062-4736
County: Dallas FICE Identification: 003651
Unit ID: 224323
Telephone: (972) 721-5000 Carnegie Class: Masters/L
FAX Number: (972) 721-5017 Calendar System: Semester
URL: www.udallas.edu
Established: 1956 Annual Undergrad Tuition & Fees: $37,230
Enrollment: 2,387 Coed
Affiliation or Control: Roman Catholic IRS Status: 501(c)3
Highest Offering: Doctorate
Accreditation: SC

01 President Mr. Thomas W. KEEFE
04 Exec Admin Asst to the President Ms. Cathy MCCALEB
84 Sr VP Enroll Mgmt & Student Service Dr. John PLOTTS
10 VP and Chief Financial Officer Dr. Brian MURRAY
05 Provost and Chief Academic Officer Vacant
111 VP for Advancement Ms. Joan CANTY
26 Executive VP for External Affairs Mr. Robert M. GALECKE
43 General Counsel Ms. Karin RILLEY
11 Assoc VP for Administration Vacant
50 Dean College of Business Dr. Brett LANDRY
49 Dean of Constantin College Dr. Jonathan J. SANFORD
58 Dean Grad School of Liberal Arts Dr. Joshua S. PARENS
73 Dean School of Ministry Dr. Ted WHAPHAM
08 Dean of Libraries and Research Ms. Cherie L. HOHERTZ
88 Assoc Dean for Constantin College Dr. Scott CRIDER
06 Registrar Mrs. Kathy MCGRAW
19 Campus Safety Supervisor Mr. Charles STEADMAN
13 Director Information Technology Mr. Richard HAYTER
14 Director of IT User Support Service Mr. Sabyasachi SANYAL
41 Director of Athletics Mr. Richard STROCKBINE
42 Director of Campus Ministry Mrs. Denise PHILLIPS
18 Director of Facilities Mr. Jerry HABA
21 Director of Finance Mr. Leonard A. ROBERTSON
15 Asst Vice President for HR Dr. Richard HUNTLEY
09 Director of Institutional Research Ms. Vicky MORRIS-DUEER
27 Director of Marketing & Comm Vacant
96 Director of Purchasing Mr. Alan STERLING
104 Director for Rome/Summer Programs Mrs. Becky DAVIES
23 Director of Student Health Dr. Lora RODRIGUEZ
36 Director of Career Services Ms. Julie JERNIGAN

*University of Houston System (F)

4302 University Dr., 212 E. Cullen, Houston TX 77204-2018
County: Harris FICE Identification: 011721
Unit ID: 229407
Telephone: (713) 743-1000 Carnegie Class: N/A
FAX Number: N/A
URL: www.uhsa.uh.edu

01 Chancellor Dr. Renu KHATOR

05 Sr VC for Academic Affairs/Provost ....Dr. Paula M. SHORT
43 Vice Chancellor/General Counsel ....Ms. Dona H. CORNELL
10 VC Administration/Finance ....Mr. Jim MCSHAN
32 Vice Chancellor Student Affairs ....Dr. Richard WALKER
111 VC University Advancement ....Ms. Eloise D. BRICE
26 Assoc VP Mktg/Comm/Media ....Ms. Lisa K. HOLDEMAN
13 Assoc VC CIO/Information Technology ....Dr. Dennis FOUTY
21 Associate Vice Chancellor Finance ....Mr. Raymond BARTLETT
11 Assoc VC Administration ....Dr. Emily MESSA
86 Vice Chanc Govt Relations ....Mr. Jason S. SMITH
45 Asst VC for Planning & Policy ....Mr. Chris STANICH
15 Exec Director Human Resources ....Ms. Joan M. NELSON
116 Director Internal Auditing ....Mr. Don GUYTON
88 Treasurer ....Ms. Roberta (Robbi) PURYEAR
100 Chief of Staff ....Mr. Michael JOHNSON

*University of Houston (A)

4302 University Dr., 212 E. Cullen,
Houston TX 77204-2018

County: Harris FICE Identification: 003652
Unit ID: 225511
Telephone: (713) 743-1000 Carnegie Class: DU-Highest
FAX Number: N/A Calendar System: Semester
URL: www.uh.edu
Established: 1927 Annual Undergrad Tuition & Fees (In-State): $9,519
Enrollment: 42,704 Coed
Affiliation or Control: State IRS Status: Exempt
Highest Offering: Doctorate
Accreditation: SC, AAFCS, CAATE, CAEP, CEA, CLPSY, CONST, COPSY, CS, DIETD, DIETI, ENG, ENGT, IPSY, LAW, MUS, NAIT, OPT, OPTR, PHAR, SCPSY, SP, SW

02 President ....Dr. Renu KHATOR
05 Sr VC/VP Academic Affs/Provost ....Dr. Paula M. SHORT
10 VC/VP Administration/Finance ....Mr. Jim MCSHAN
111 VC/VP University Advancement ....Ms. Eloise D. BRICE
32 VC/VP Student Affairs ....Dr. Richard WALKER
26 Int AVP for Mtkg/Commun/Media Rels ...Ms. Lisa K. HOLDEMAN
20 Vice Provost Academic Programs ....Dr. Bruce A. JONES
86 VC/VP Govt & Community Relations ....Mr. Jason S. SMITH
43 VC/VP Legal Affairs & Gen Counsel ....Ms. Dona H. CORNELL
46 Int VC/VP Research/Tech Transfer ....Dr. Ramanan KRISHNAMOORTI
100 Chief of Staff ....Mr. Mike JOHNSON
31 VP for Community Rels & Inst Access ....Dr. Elwyn C. LEE
88 Vice Provost Global Strategies ....Dr. Jaime ORTIZ
29 Assoc VP Alumni Association ....Mr. Mike PEDE
13 Assoc VP Information Tech/CIO ....Dr. Dennis FOUTY
27 Executive Director Media Relations ....Mr. Mike S. ROSEN
20 Vice Provost & Dean UG Stdnts ....Dr. Teri E. LONGACRE
58 Vice Provost & Dean Grad School ....Mr. Dimitri LITVINOV
88 Int Assoc Provost Fac Dev/Affairs ....Dr. Mark CLARKE
21 Assoc Provost Finance & Admin ....Dr. Sabrina HASSUMANI
30 Assoc VP for Univ Development ....Mr. Cliff REDD
35 Assoc VC/VP Student Affairs ....Mr. Daniel MAXWELL
88 Assoc VP Stdnt Affs/Dean of Stdnts ....Dr. William MUNSON
91 Assoc VP Enterprise Sys Adm ....Dr. Arun JAIN
21 Associate VC/VP Finance ....Mr. Raymond BARTLETT
88 Assoc Prov Educ Innov & Tech ....Dr. Jeff MORGAN
22 Asst VC/VP Equal Opportunity ....Dr. Richard A. BAKER
45 AVC/Assoc Prov Inst Plng/Analy ....Mr. Chris M. STANICH
88 Assoc Prov Strategic Enroll Plng ....Dr. Maureen G. CROFT
41 VP Intercollegiate Athletics ....Mr. Hunter YURACHEK
37 Exec Dir Scholarships & Fin Aid ....Mr. Sal LORIA
15 Exec Director Human Resources ....Ms. Joan NELSON
51 Director Continuing Education ...Ms. Mercedes SURATY-CLARKE
06 University Registrar ....Ms. Debbie HENRY
07 Executive Director of Admissions ....Mr. Mardell MAXWELL
19 Asst VC/VP Public Safety/Security ....Mr. Malcolm DAVIS
96 Director of Purchasing ....Mr. Jack TENNER
49 Dean Col Liberal Arts/Soc Sci ....Dr. Antonio TILLIS
81 Dean Col Natural Sci & Math ....Dr. Dan WELLS
88 Dean College of Optometry ....Dr. Earl L. SMITH
72 Dean College of Technology ....Dr. Tony AMBLER
66 Dean School of Nursing ....Dr. Kathryn M. TART
54 Dean Cullen College of Engineering ....Dr. Joseph W. TEDESCO
48 Dean College of Architecture ....Ms. Patricia Belton OLIVER
70 Dean Graduate Col of Social Work ....Dr. Alan DETLAFF
67 Dean College of Pharmacy ....Dr. Lamar PRITCHARD
53 Dean College of Education ....Dr. Robert MCPHERSON
50 Dean Bauer Col Business Admin ....Dr. Latha RAMCHAND
88 Dean Hilton Col Htl/Restaurant Mgt ....Dr. Dennis REYNOLDS
08 Dean University Libraries ....Ms. Lisa A. GERMAN
92 Dean Honors College ....Dr. William MONROE
61 Dean UH Law Center ....Mr. Leonard M. BAYNES
11 Assoc VC/VP Administration ....Dr. Emily MESSA
88 Chief Energy Officer ....Dr. Ramanan KRISHNAMOORTI
57 Dean McGovern College of the Arts ....Dr. Andrew DAVIS

*University of Houston - Clear Lake (B)

2700 Bay Area Boulevard, Houston TX 77058

County: Harris FICE Identification: 011711
Unit ID: 225414
Telephone: (281) 283-7600 Carnegie Class: Masters/L
FAX Number: (281) 283-2219 Calendar System: Semester
URL: www.uhcl.edu
Established: 1971 Annual Undergrad Tuition & Fees (In-State): $6,502
Enrollment: 8,906 Coed
Affiliation or Control: State IRS Status: 501(c)3
Highest Offering: Doctorate
Accreditation: SC, CAEPN, CS, ENG, ENGR, IPSY, MFCD, NUR, SW

02 President ....Dr. Ira K. BLAKE
05 Int Sr Vice Pres for Acad Affairs ....Dr. Glen HOUSTON
10 Int VP Administration & Finance ....Ms. Jean CARR
04 Executive Assoc to the President ....Vacant
13 Assoc VP Information Resources ....Dr. A. Glen HOUSTON
20 Int Assoc VP Academic Affairs ....Dr. Kathryn MATTHEW
111 Assoc VP University Advancement ....Ms. Rhonda THOMPSON
32 Assoc Vice Pres Student Services ....Dr. Darlene BIGGERS
21 Associate Vice President Finance ....Ms. Usha MATHEW
84 Assoc Vice Pres Enrollment Mgmt ....Dr. Yvette BENDECK
18 Assoc VP Facilities Mgmt/Construct ....Mr. Ward MARTAINDALE
50 Dean College Business ....Dr. Edward WALLER
81 Int Dean College Science/Engr ....Dr. Ju H. KIM
79 Dean College Human Sci/Humanities ....Dr. Rick SHORT
53 Dean College Education ....Dr. Mark D. SHERMIS
35 Dean of Students ....Mr. David A. RACHITA
28 Asst Dean Student Diversity ....Ms. Darlene BIGGERS
08 Exec Director Neumann Library ....Ms. Karen WIELHORSKI
85 Exec Dir Intl Admissions/Programs ....Vacant
45 Exec Dir Planning and Assessment ....Ms. Pat CUCHENS
15 Executive Director Human Resources ....Ms. Nichole ESLINGER
14 Exec Director University Computing ....Mr. Rodger CARR
21 Exec Dir of Procurement & Payables ....Ms. Debra CARPENTER
25 Exec Dir Sponsored Programs ....Dr. Kathryn MATTHEW
37 Executive Director Financial Aid ....Dr. Billy SATTERFIELD
88 Exec Dir Environment Inst Houston ....Dr. George GUILLEN
06 Registrar/Director Academic Records ....Dr. Billy SATTERFIELD
106 Director Distance/Off-Campus Educ ....Ms. Lisa GABRIEL
26 Exec Dir University Communications ...Ms. Theresa PRESSWOOD
29 Dir Development & Alumni Relations ....Mr. Dwayne BUSBY
19 Chief of Police ....Mr. Allen HILL, JR.
36 Ex Dir Counseling/Hlth/Career Svcs ....Dr. Cindy COOK
12 Dir Camp Operat/UHCL Pearland Camp ....Dr. Kathy DUPREE
23 Dir Health & Disability Services ....Ms. Regina PICKETT
07 Exec Director of Admissions ....Ms. Rauchelle JONES
40 Manager Bookstore ....Mr. Devin WHIPP

*University of Houston - Downtown (C)

One Main Street, Houston TX 77002-1014

County: Harris FICE Identification: 003612
Unit ID: 225432
Telephone: (713) 221-8001 Carnegie Class: Masters/S
FAX Number: (713) 221-8075 Calendar System: Semester
URL: www.uhd.edu
Established: 1974 Annual Undergrad Tuition & Fees (In-State): $5,978
Enrollment: 14,262 Coed
Affiliation or Control: State IRS Status: Exempt
Highest Offering: Master's
Accreditation: SC, ENGT, SW

02 President ....Dr. Juan S. MUNOZ
04 Executive Assoc to President ....Ms. Vanessa PIGEON
05 Int Provost/Sr VP Acad & Stdnt Affs ....Mr. Edward T. HUGETZ
20 Assoc VP for Academic Affairs ....Dr. Faiza KHOJA
84 VP Student Affairs/Enroll Mgmt ....Dr. Tomikia P. LEGRANDE
50 Dean Davies College of Business ....Dr. Michael FIELDS
79 Dean Col Humanities/Social Sci ....Dr. DoVeanna FULTON
88 Int Dean College of Public Service ....Dr. Leigh VAN HORN
81 Dean Col Sciences & Tech ....Dr. Akif UZMAN
88 Dean University College ....Dr. Chris BIRCHAK
88 Dir QEP & CCESL ....Dr. Poonam SALHOTRA
08 Executive Director WI Dykes Library ....Ms. Pat ENSOR
106 Exec Dir Off Campus/OL Coordinator ....Mr. Louis D. EVANS, III
88 Asst VP Research/Sponsored Pgms ....Dr. Jerry JOHNSON
09 Director of Institutional Research ....Ms. Carol M. TUCKER
108 Dir Institutional Assessment ....Dr. Lea CAMPBELL
88 Director Creative Services ....Vacant
88 Director O'Kane Gallery ....Mr. Mark CERVENKA
88 Exec Director of Scholars Academy ....Dr. Mary Jo PARKER
88 Dir Teaching & Learning Excel ....Dr. Gregory DEMENT
88 Director FTIC Retention Services ....Ms. Jemma SYLVESTER-CAESAR
88 Director of Advising Services ....Ms. Reyna ROMERO
88 Director of Academic Support Center ....Dr. Isidro GRAU
88 Exec Dir Academic Admin & Ops ....Ms. Elaine PEARSON
88 Dir Strategic Initiatives & Project ....Ms. Lucy BOWEN
92 Director Honors Program ....Dr. Mari NICHOLSON-PREUSS
88 Dir Applied Business/Technology Ctr ....Mr. G. V. KRISHNAN
88 Director English Language Institute ....Dr. Gail KELLERSBERGER
88 Dir Criminal Justice Center ....Mr. Steven BRACKEN
88 Dir Ctr Public Svc & Fam Strengths ....Mr. Steven VILLANO
51 Int Dir Continuing Education ....Mr. William DUDLEY
88 Dir Center for Entrepreneurship ....Mr. William DUDLEY
88 Dir Insurance & Risk Management Ctr ....Ms. Priscilla OEHLERT
36 Dir Davies COB Career Dev Center ....Mr. Brett HOBBY
88 Exec Dir Inst & Faculty DCOB ....Dr. Sedef SMITH
88 Dir Business Analytics & Dec ....Ms. Emily LEFFLER
88 Dir of Retail Mgmt Center ....Mr. Tracy DAVIS
88 Exec Dir Process Improvement ....Mr. Charles ROCKWELL
10 VP Administration & Finance ....Mr. David M. BRADLEY
13 Assoc VP Information Technology ....Mr. Hossein SHAHROKHI
91 Director Enterprise Systems ....Mr. Kong YIN
88 Dir Technology Learning Services ....Mr. John LANE
88 Director Technical Services ....Ms. Grace DAVILA
88 Dir Comp/Telecom & Video Networks ....Mr. Miguel RUIZ
90 Director User Support Services ....Mr. Said FATTOUH
88 Dir IT Business Services ....Ms. Jacqueline SMITH
119 Dir Info Security & IT Compliance ....Mr. Jon GARZA
88 Dir IT Project Management Office ....Ms. Kimberly SOLOMON
88 Dir University Business Services ....Ms. Mary TORRES
88 Director Emergency Management ....Ms. Carol MANOUSOS
114 Exec Dir Budget/Proc & Contr Proc ....Ms. Theresa MENELEY

21 Asst VP Business Affairs ....Mr. George W. ANDERSON
88 Dir Financial Reporting ....Ms. Delethia MURRAY
117 Director Risk Mgmt & Compliance ....Ms. Mary COOK
18 Asst VP Facilities Management ....Mr. Chris MCCALL
88 Dir Building Maintenance ....Mr. Abraham FLORES
88 Dir MEP ....Mr. Kris ZIMMERMAN
19 Chief of Police ....Mr. Michael BENFORD
88 Dir Student Accounts & Collection ....Ms. Lauren BELLENGER
88 Dir Accounts Payable ....Ms. Cynthia CONNER
15 VP Employment Svcs & Operations ... Ms. Ivonne MONTALBANO
118 Dir Benefits & Compensation ....Ms. Erica MORALES
88 Director Payroll & Records ....Ms. April FRANK
88 Asst Dean Enrollment Management .. Mr. Christopher CHEATHAM
35 Asst VP Stdnt Success/Dean of Stdnt ....Mr. Samuel SANTOS
88 Asst Dn Student Affs/Title IV Coord ....Mr. Tommy THOMASON
88 Director Student Activities ....Mr. Tremaine KWASIKPUI
28 Dir Ctr Stdnt Diversity Equ & Incl ....Dr. John HUDSON
07 Director Undergraduate Admissions ....Ms. Ceshia LOVE
37 Director Financial Aid ....Ms. LaTasha GOUDEAU
41 Director Sports & Fitness ....Mr. Richard SEBASTIANI
36 Int Dir Career Development Center ....Ms. Katherine KNAPP
88 Director Disability Services ....Dr. Meritza TAMEZ
88 Director Veterans Services ....Mr. Richard SELVERA
88 Dir Minority Male Recruitment ....Dr. Jerry WALLACE, JR.
88 Director Testing Services ....Mr. Robert ALONZO
88 Dir Events & Conference Services ....Ms. Mary A. WHITE
88 Director Talent Search ....Ms. Carrie HAYS
88 Director Upward Bound ....Ms. Dawanna LEWIS
88 Int Pgm Dir Title V Stdnt Success ....Mr. Branden KUZMICK
111 VP Advancement & External Rels ....Ms. Johanna WOLFE
26 Exec Dir of University Relations ....Ms. Elisa CROSSLAND
102 Director Corporate Relations ....Mr. Jacob LIPP
44 Dir Annual Fund & Individual Giving ....Mr. Jonathan BROOKS
88 Dir Advancement Services & Bus Ops ....Mr. Brian DRAKE
29 Director Alumni Relations ....Dr. Liza ALONZO
88 Director Communications ....Mr. P. Michael EMERY
88 Director Marketing ....Ms. Toye SIMMONS

*University of Houston - Victoria (D)

3007 N Ben Wilson, Victoria TX 77901-4450

County: Victoria FICE Identification: 013231
Unit ID: 225502
Telephone: (361) 570-4848 Carnegie Class: Masters/L
FAX Number: (361) 580-5534 Calendar System: Semester
URL: www.uhv.edu
Established: 1973 Annual Undergrad Tuition & Fees (In-State): $7,369
Enrollment: 4,152 Coed
Affiliation or Control: State IRS Status: 501(c)3
Highest Offering: Master's
Accreditation: SC, CACREP, NURSE

02 President ....Dr. Raymond V. MORGAN, JR.
11 Vice Pres Administration & Finance ....Mr. Wayne B. BERAN
05 Interim Provost/VP Acad Affairs ....Dr. Dave COCKRUM
32 Vice President Student Affairs ....Dr. Jay LAMBERT
49 Dean Arts & Sciences ....Dr. Jeffrey DI LEO
50 Dean Business Administration ....Dr. Farhang NIROOMAND
53 Dean Education & Human Development ....Dr. Freddie LITTON
111 VP Advancement & External Relations ....Mr. Jesse D. PISORS
08 Senior Director of Library ....Dr. Joe F. DAHLSTROM
13 Sr Director Technology Services ....Mr. Randy FAULK
15 Dir Human Res/Deputy EO/Title IX ....Ms. Laura L. SMITH
84 Asst VP for Enrollment Mgmt ....Dr. Denee THOMAS
88 Dir Small Business Development Ctr ....Mr. Joe HUMPHREYS
06 Registrar ....Ms. Trudy WORTHAM
37 Director Financial Aid ....Ms. Lashon WILLIAMS
18 Director Facilities ....Mr. John BURKE
10 Director Business Services ....Mr. Tim MICHALSKI
21 Comptroller ....Ms. Valerie WALDEN
41 Director Athletics ....Mr. Ashley WALYUCHOW
26 Director Marketing & Communications ....Ms. Paula COBLER
38 Director of Counseling Center ....Vacant
35 Director of Student Life & Services ....Mr. Michael WILKINSON
114 Director of Budget ....Ms. Karen SANDERS
39 Director Residence Life & Univ Comm ....Mr. Brandon W. LEE
88 Director Capital Projects ....Ms. Brenda SVETLIK
04 Executive Adm Asst to President ....Ms. Kathy WALTON
25 Dir Research Adm & Sponsored Pgms ...Ms. Angela HARTMANN
108 Dir Inst Research/Effectiveness ....Dr. Sharon M. BAILEY
102 Sr Dir Corp/Foundation Relations ....Ms. Courtney M. SIDES
29 Dir Alumni/Annual Giving ....Ms. Kira MUDD
20 Assoc Prov Univ Col Implementation ....Dr. Beverly TOMEK
85 Director International Programs ....Ms. Ludmi HERATH
88 Sr Dir Enroll Mgmt/External Rels ....Ms. Karla DECUIR
88 Coordinator Title IX ....Ms. Rebecca LAKE
07 Director Admissions/Recruitment ....Mr. Billy LAGAL

University of the Incarnate Word (E)

4301 Broadway, San Antonio TX 78209-6397

County: Bexar FICE Identification: 003578
Unit ID: 225627
Telephone: (210) 829-6000 Carnegie Class: Masters/L
FAX Number: (210) 829-1220 Calendar System: Semester
URL: www.uiw.edu
Established: 1881 Annual Undergrad Tuition & Fees: $28,898
Enrollment: 8,666 Coed
Affiliation or Control: Roman Catholic IRS Status: 501(c)3
Highest Offering: Doctorate
Accreditation: SC, ACBSP, #CAATE, CIDA, DIETD, DIETI, HSA, MUS, NMT, NURSE, OPT, OPTR, @OSTEO, #OTA, PHAR, PTA, THEA

01 President ... Dr. Thomas EVANS
00 Chancellor ... Dr. Denise DOYLE
88 Vice President Mission and Ministry ... Sr. Walter MAHER
04 Executive Assistant to President ... Ms. Vanessa LOPEZ
26 Asst to the President/Communication ... Mr. Lou FOX
43 Vice President/General Counsel ... Ms. Cindy ESCAMILLA
05 Provost ... Dr. Kathleen LIGHT
84 Vice Pres Enrollment Mgt/Stdnt Svcs . Dr. David M. JURENOVICH
111 Vice Pres Institutional Advancement ... Sr. Kathleen COUGHLIN
10 Vice Pres for Business & Finance ... Mr. Douglas ENDSLEY
104 Vice Pres International Programs ... Mr. Marcos FRAGOSO
56 Vice Pres of Ext Academic Programs ... Dr. Cyndi WILSON-PORTER
13 Vice Pres Information Resources/CIO ... Ms. Lisa BAZLEY
21 Comptroller ... Ms. Edith COGDELL
50 Dean H-E-B Sch Business & Admin ... Dr. Forrest F. AVEN
57 Dean Humanities Arts & Social Sci ... Dr. Kevin VICHCALES
66 Dean Nursing & Health Professions ... Dr. Mary HOKE
53 Dean Dreeben School of Education ... Dr. Denise STAUDT
54 Dean Math Science Engineering ... Dr. Carlos GARCIA
88 Dean Interactive Media & Design ... Dr. Sharon WELKEY
67 Dean Feik School of Pharmacy ... Dr. David MAIZE
88 Dean School of Optometry ... Dr. Timothy WINGERT
58 Dean of Grad Studies/Research ... Dr. Osman OZTURGUT
62 Dean of Library Services ... Dr. Cheryl ANDERSON
108 Assoc Provost/Dir of Assessment ... Dr. Glenn JAMES
55 Dean Sch of Extended Studies ... Mr. Vincent PORTER
89 Dean Univ Preparatory Programs ... Mr. Daniel OCHOA
88 Dean School Physical Therapy ... Dr. Caroline GOULET
29 Director of Alumni/Parent Relations ... Dr. Lisa MCNARY
27 Director of Comm/Marketing ... Ms. Debra DEL TORO
84 Dean of Enrollment ... Ms. Heather RODRIGUEZ
32 Dean of Student Success ... Ms. Sandy MCMAKIN
38 Director of Counseling ... Dr. Christie MELONSON
20 Director of Academic Advising ... Dr. Sonia JASSO
88 Director Learning Assistance Center ... Ms. Cristina ARIZA
06 Registrar ... Dr. Bobbye G. FRY
37 Director of Financial Aid ... Ms. Amy CARCANAGUES
32 Dean of Campus Life ... Dr. Renee MOORE
39 Director of Residence Life ... Ms. Diane SANCHEZ
35 Director of Campus Engagement ... Mr. Paul AYALA
23 Associate Dean Health Services ... Dr. Corinne JEDYNAK-BELL
42 Chaplain ... Fr. Tom DYMOWSKI
42 Director of Campus Ministry ... Ms. Elisabeth VILLARREAL
15 Director of Human Resources ... Ms. Annette THOMPSON
96 Director of Purchasing ... Mr. Sam WAGES
18 Director Facilities Mgmt & Services ... Mr. Steve HEYING
41 Interim Director of Athletics ... Mr. Mark PAPICH
88 Sr Director Infrastructure Svcs ... Mr. Neil SCHROEDER
88 Director of Enterprise Applications ... Ms. Iris SOLCHER
88 Director Instructional Technology ... Ms. Ana GONZALES
72 Director of Technology Support ... Mr. Anthony RAMOS
09 Director of Institutional Research ... Ms. Robin LOGAN
07 Director of Admissions ... Mr. Javier LARA
36 Coordinator of Career Services ... Ms. Abreeta GOODE
100 Chief of Staff ... Mr. Vincent RODRIGUEZ
102 Dir Foundation/Corporate Relations ... Mr. Jon GILLESPIE
105 Director Web Development ... Mr. Troy KNICKERBOCKER
19 Chief of Police ... Mr. Robert CHAVEZ
44 Dir of Major Gifts/Planned Giving ... Mr. Alex CASTANEDA
63 Dean School of Osteopathic Medicine ... Dr. Robyn PHILLIPS-MADSON
30 Director of Development ... Ms. Rosie GARCIA
88 Director Print Svcs/Graphic Design ... Mr. Michael HOOD

University of Mary Hardin-Baylor (A)

900 College Street, Belton TX 76513-2578
County: Bell — FICE Identification: 003588
Unit ID: 226471
Telephone: (254) 295-8642 — Carnegie Class: Masters/M
FAX Number: (254) 295-4535 — Calendar System: Semester
URL: www.umhb.edu
Established: 1845 — Annual Undergrad Tuition & Fees: $26,550
Enrollment: 3,898 — Coed
Affiliation or Control: Southern Baptist — IRS Status: 501(c)3
Highest Offering: Doctorate
Accreditation: SC, ART, CACREP, MUS, NURSE, @PTA, SW

01 President/CEO ... Dr. Randy G. O'REAR
03 Sr Vice Pres Admin/COO ... Dr. Steve THEODORE
05 Provost/Sr VP Academic Affs ... Dr. John VASSAR
45 Int VP Campus Planning & Support ... Mr. Edd MARTIN
30 Vice Pres for Development ... Dr. Rebecca O'BANION
26 Vice Pres Communication/Spec Proj ... Dr. Paula TANNER
32 Vice Pres for Student Life ... Dr. Brandon SKAGGS
41 Vice Pres Athletics ... Mr. Randy MANN
10 Vice Pres Business/Finance/CFO ... Mrs. Jennifer RAMM
15 Vice Pres Human Resources ... Mrs. Susan OWENS
13 Vice Pres Information Tech ... Mr. Brent HARRIS
84 Vice Pres Enrollment Mgmt ... Dr. Gary LAMM
18 Assoc Vice Pres for Campus Planning ... Mr. Bob PATTEE
21 Controller ... Mrs. Charla KAHLIG
50 Dean McLane College of Business ... Dr. Ken SMITH
79 Dean of Humanities & Sciences ... Dr. Danny MYNATT
66 Dean of Nursing ... Dr. Sharon SOUTER
53 Dean of Education ... Dr. Marlene ZIPPERLEN
58 Dean Graduate School ... Dr. Colin WILBORN
88 Dean of Christian Studies ... Dr. Tim CRAWFORD
57 Dean Visual/Performing Arts ... Mr. Ted BARNES
35 Dean of Students ... Mr. Ray MARTIN
39 Assoc Dean Students/Dir Residence ... Ms. Donna PLANK
04 Executive Assistant ... Mrs. Phyllis ROGERS
06 Registrar ... Mrs. Amy MCGILVRAY
88 Dir Grad Student Services/Engagemt ... Ms. Melissa WILLIAMS
07 Director of Admissions & Recruiting ... Dr. Brent BURKS
08 Director Learning Resources ... Ms. Denise KARIMKHANI
27 Director Marketing/Public Relations ... Mr. James STAFFORD
09 Director Institutional Research ... Ms. Jen JONES
37 Director Financial Aid ... Mr. Ron BROWN
92 Director Honors Program ... Dr. David HOLCOMB
19 Director Campus Police ... Mr. Gary SARGENT
96 Purchasing Manager ... Mrs. Jennifer WEBB
29 Director Alumni Relations ... Mr. Jeff SUTTON
42 University Chaplain ... Dr. George LOUTHERBACK
36 Director Career Services ... Mr. Don OWENS
38 Director Couns Testing & Health ... Mr. Nate WILLIAMS
85 Dir International Student Services ... Mrs. Elizabeth TANAKA
112 Director Planned Giving ... Mrs. Melissa BRAGG
40 Bookstore Manager ... Ms. Debbie COTTRELL

University of North Texas (B)

1155 Union Circle #311277, Denton TX 76203-5013
County: Denton — FICE Identification: 003594
Unit ID: 227216
Telephone: (940) 565-2000 — Carnegie Class: DU-Highest
FAX Number: (940) 565-7600 — Calendar System: Semester
URL: www.unt.edu
Established: 1890 — Annual Undergrad Tuition & Fees (In-State): $10,153
Enrollment: 37,299 — Coed
Affiliation or Control: State — IRS Status: 501(c)3
Highest Offering: Doctorate
Accreditation: SC, ART, AUD, CACREP, CAEPN, CEA, CIDA, CLPSY, COPSY, CS, ENG, ENGT, FEPAC, JOUR, LIB, MUS, SP, SPAA, SW

01 President ... Dr. Neal SMATRESK
00 Chancellor ... Mr. Lee F. JACKSON
05 Provost/Vice Pres Academic Affairs ... Dr. Jennifer EVANS-COWLEY
10 Vice Pres Finance/Administration ... Mr. Bob BROWN
46 VP Research/Innovation ... Dr. Thomas J. MCCOY
32 Vice President Student Affairs ... Dr. Elizabeth WITH
43 Vice Chancellor/General Counsel ... Ms. Nancy S. FOOTER
26 Vice President University Relations ... Ms. Deborah S. LELIAERT
30 Associate Dean for Development ... Ms. Eileen P. MORAN
84 VP for Enrollment ... Mr. Shannon M. GOODMAN
13 Vice President for Univ Info Svcs ... Dr. Vernon A. CLARK
20 Vice Provost for Academic Affairs ... Dr. Christy CRUTSINGER
20 Vice Provost for Academic Resources ... Mr. Robert A. WATLING
20 Vice Provost for Faculty Success ... Dr. Michael MCPHERSON
88 Vice Provost for Academic Admin ... Dr. Terri DAY
88 Vice Provost for Academic Outreach ... Dr. Brenda MCCOY
41 Deputy Athletic Director ... Mr. Henry H. DICKENSON
35 Dean Students ... Dr. Maureen MCGUINNESS
13 Vice President for Information Tech ... Vacant
114 Assoc VP Budget & Analytics ... Ms. Beverly COTTON
88 Assoc Vice Prov Lrng Enhancement ... Dr. Patrick PLUSCHT
28 VP Institutional Equity & Diversity ... Dr. Joanne WOODARD
88 Vice Prov for Transfer Articulation ... Dr. Jean KELLER
18 Assoc Vice President for Facilities ... Mr. David REYNOLDS
08 Dean of Libraries ... Ms. Cathy HARTMAN
37 Director Financial Aid ... Ms. Zelma DELEON
49 Dean College of Liberal Arts & SSci ... Dr. David HOLDEMAN
81 Dean College of Science ... Dr. Su GAO
50 Dean College Business ... Dr. Marilyn WILEY
53 Dean College of Education ... Dr. Bertina COMBES
11 Associate Dean of Admin Affairs ... Dr. Eric LIGON
88 Dean Col Public Affs/Community Svc ... Dr. Linda HOLLOWAY
64 Dean College of Music ... Dr. John W. RICHMOND
59 Dean Col of Merch/Hosp & Tourism ... Dr. Judith FORNEY
62 Dean College of Information ... Dr. KINSHUK
58 Vice Provost Toulouse Grad School ... Dr. Victor PRYBUTOK
88 Dean of TAMS ... Dr. Glenisson DE OLIVEIRA
60 Dean Mayborn Sch of Journalism ... Dr. Dorothy BLAND
54 Dean College of Engineering ... Dr. Costas TSATSOULIS
90 Director Acad Computing/User Svcs ... Dr. Philip C. BACZEWSKI
09 Director Institutional Research ... Dr. Mary BARTON
108 Assistant Vice President DAIR ... Dr. Jason F. SIMON
88 Director of Accreditation ... Ms. Elizabeth VOGT
07 Director of Admissions ... Dr. Rebecca LOTHRINGER
51 Dir Ctr for Achvmnt & Lifelng Lrng ... Ms. Marilyn D. WAGNER
06 Registrar ... Ms. Lynn MCCREARY
15 Assoc Vice Chancellor HR ... Mr. Luis LEWIN
36 Dir Career & Counseling Svcs ... Mr. Dan NAEGELI
19 Director/Chief of Police ... Mr. Ed REYNOLDS
39 Director Housing ... Mr. Gina VANACORE
85 Vice Provost International Affairs ... Ms. Amy SHENBERGER
23 Dir Stdnt Health Ctr/Wellness Svcs ... Dr. Herschel VOORHEES
29 Exec Dir Advancement Services ... Mr. Robert MCINTURF
04 Administrative Asst to President ... Ms. Ruby RAINES
101 Secretary of the Institution/Board ... Dr. Rosemary R. HAGGETT
25 Asst VP Research/Sponsored Pgm ... Dr. David SCHULTZ
104 Director Study Abroad ... Ms. Amy SHENBERGER

University of North Texas at Dallas (C)

7300 University Hills Blvd, Dallas TX 75241
County: Dallas — Identification: 667124
Unit ID: 484905
Telephone: (972) 780-3600 — Carnegie Class: Not Classified
FAX Number: (972) 780-3606 — Calendar System: Semester
URL: www.untdallas.edu
Established: 2000 — Annual Undergrad Tuition & Fees (In-State): $7,848
Enrollment: 2,488 — Coed
Affiliation or Control: State — IRS Status: 501(c)3
Highest Offering: Doctorate
Accreditation: SC

01 President ... Mr. Robert MONG
10 Chief Financial Officer ... Dr. Daniel EDELMAN
05 Provost ... Dr. Betty STEWART

University of North Texas Health Science Center at Fort Worth (D)

3500 Camp Bowie Boulevard, Fort Worth TX 76107-2699
County: Tarrant — FICE Identification: 009768
Unit ID: 228909
Telephone: (817) 735-2000 — Carnegie Class: Spec-4-yr-Med
FAX Number: (817) 735-2486 — Calendar System: Semester
URL: www.unthsc.edu
Established: 1966 — Annual Graduate Tuition & Fees: N/A
Enrollment: 2,382 — Coed
Affiliation or Control: State — IRS Status: 501(c)3
Highest Offering: Doctorate; No Undergraduates
Accreditation: SC, ARCPA, HSA, OSTEO, PH, PHAR, PTA

01 President ... Dr. Michael WILLIAMS
10 Senior VP for Finance and CFO ... Mr. Gregory R. ANDERSON
17 Executive VP Clinical Affairs ... Mr. Michael R. HICKS
05 Interim Provost and Exec VP ... Dr. Claire PEEL
86 Vice President Governmental Affairs ... Mr. Dan JENSEN
63 Dean Texas Col of Osteopathic Med ... Dr. Don PESKA
32 Vice Pres Student Affairs ... Dr. Thomas MOORMAN
15 Vice Pres Human Resource Svcs ... Vacant
45 Interim VP Research ... Dr. Anuja GHORPADE
51 Assoc VP for Professional/Cont Edu ... Ms. Pam MCFADDEN
58 Dean Grad Sch Biomedical Sciences ... Dr. Meharvan SINGH
76 Interim Dean School of Health Prof ... Dr. Nicoleta BUGNARIU
69 Dean of School of Public Health ... Dr. Dennis THOMBS
37 Director Student Financial Aid ... Mr. Joseph SANCHEZ
84 Executive Director Enrollment Svcs ... Mr. A.J RANDOLPH
19 Chief of Police ... Ms. Laurie CLOUSE
111 VP Institutional Advancement ... Mr. Doug WHITE
09 VP Strategy & Measurement ... Dr. Thomas FAIRCHILD
21 Vice President Finance & Planning ... Mr. Geoff SCARPELLI
07 Asst Dean of Admissions & Outreach ... Vacant
06 Registrar ... Mr. A.J RANDOLPH
03 Executive VP/Chief People Officer ... Mr. Steven R. SOSLAND
08 Director of Lewis Library ... Mr. Daniel BURGARD
13 Chief Info Technology Officer (CIO) ... Ms. Lynley DUNGAN

University of Phoenix Dallas Campus (E)

12400 Coit Road, Dallas TX 75251-2004
Telephone: (972) 385-1055 — Identification: 770227
Accreditation: &NH, ACBSP

† Branch campus of University of Phoenix, Tempe, AZ

University of Phoenix El Paso Campus (F)

1340 Adabel Drive, El Paso TX 79936-5900
Telephone: (915) 599-5900 — Identification: 770228
Accreditation: &NH, ACBSP

† No longer accepting campus-based students.

University of Phoenix Houston Campus (G)

11451 Katy Freeway, Houston TX 77079-2004
Telephone: (713) 465-9966 — Identification: 770229
Accreditation: &NH, ACBSP

† No longer accepting campus-based students.

University of Phoenix San Antonio Campus (H)

8200 IH-10 West, Suite 1000, San Antonio TX 78230-3876
Telephone: (210) 524-2100 — Identification: 770231
Accreditation: &NH, ACBSP

† Branch campus of University of Phoenix, Tempe, AZ

University of St. Augustine for Health Sciences (I)

5401 La Crosse Ave, Austin TX 78739
Telephone: (512) 394-9766 — Identification: 770940
Accreditation: &WC, OT, PTA

† Branch campus of University of St. Augustine for Health Sciences, San Marcos, CA.

University of St. Thomas (J)

3800 Montrose Boulevard, Houston TX 77006-4696
County: Harris — FICE Identification: 003654
Unit ID: 227863
Telephone: (713) 522-7911 — Carnegie Class: Masters/L
FAX Number: (713) 525-2125 — Calendar System: Semester
URL: www.stthom.edu
Established: 1947 — Annual Undergrad Tuition & Fees: $31,520
Enrollment: 3,359 — Coed
Affiliation or Control: Roman Catholic — IRS Status: 501(c)3
Highest Offering: Doctorate
Accreditation: SC, CAEPT, NURSE, THEOL

01 President Dr. Richard LUDWICK
04 Special Assistant to the President Ms. Cindy VIAUD
04 Exec Assistant to the President Ms. Anne LAMBERT
10 Vice President for Finance Ms. Elizabeth CONDIC
05 Provost and VP Academic Affairs Dr. Dominic AQUILA
11 Assoc VP of Human Resources Mr. Randy GRAHAM
20 AVP Acad Affs/Dean Extended Pgms Dr. Ravi SRINIVAS
66 Dean School of Nursing Dr. Poldi TSCHIRCH
49 Dean Arts & Sciences Dr. Chris EVANS
73 Dean School of Theology Dr. Sandra C. MAGIE, CM
50 Dean Cameron School of Business Dr. Beena GEORGE
53 Dean School of Educ & Human Svcs Dr. Paul PAESE
08 Dean of Libraries Mr. James PICCININNI
58 Dir Center for Thomistic Studies Dr. Steven JENSEN
82 Director Center for Intl Studies Dr. Hans STOCKTON
88 Director Center for Irish Studies Ms. Lori GALLAGHER
88 Dir Center for Ethical Leadership Dr. Joseph CERAMI
13 Vice Pres Information Technology Mr. Gary MCCORMACK
30 Int Vice Pres for Inst Advancement Ms. Cynthia COLBERT RILEY
84 Int Vice Pres Marketing/Enroll Mgmt Mr. Arthur ORTIZ
88 Director Center for Faith & Culture Fr. Christopher VALKA
06 Interim Registrar Ms. Michele WILLIAMS
90 Dir of Network & Campus Computing Mr. Tony REYNA
90 Director Technology Support Svcs Mr. Mark HENDERSON
91 Dir Administrative Computing Svcs Ms. Joanna E. PALASOTA
32 Vice Pres Student Affairs Ms. Patricia MCKINLEY
35 Asst VP Student Affs/Dean Students Ms. Lindsey MCPHERSON
38 Exec Dir Counseling & Disability Dr. Rose SIGNORELLO
42 Dir of Campus Ministry/Chaplain Fr. David BITTNER
39 Director Residence Life Ms. Ana Alicia LOPEZ
88 Asst Dir of Recreational Sports Ms. Mary Ann SHAW
18 Asst VP Facilities Operations Mr. Howard A. ROSE
21 Controller Ms. Brandy SHAW
88 Treasurer Ms. Susan ROSE
84 Asst VP of Enrollment Management Vacant
07 Dir of Transfer Adm & Veteran Svcs Mr. Phil BUTCHER
37 Dean of Scholarships/Financial Aid Ms. Lynda MCKENDREE
26 Director of Communications Ms. Sandra SOLIZ
88 Director of Creative Services Ms. Marionette MITCHELL
108 Assoc VP Institutional Assessment Dr. Siobhan FLEMING
19 Chief of Police Mr. H. E JENKINS
41 Athletic Director Mr. Todd SMITH
104 Director Study Abroad Dr. Ravi SRINIVAS
29 Director Alumni Relations Mr. Hank EMERY

*University of Texas System Administration (A)

210 West 7th Street, Austin TX 78701-2982
County: Travis FICE Identification: 003655
Unit ID: 229090
Telephone: (512) 499-4201 Carnegie Class: N/A
FAX Number: N/A
URL: www.utsystem.edu

01 Chancellor Mr. William H. MCRAVEN
03 Deputy Chancellor Mr. David E. DANIEL
05 Exec VC Academic Affairs Dr. Steve LESLIE
17 Exec Vice Chanc Health Affairs Dr. Raymond S. GREENBERG
10 Exec Vice Chanc Business Affairs Dr. Scott C. KELLEY
43 Vice Chanc & General Counsel Mr. Dan SHARPHORN
86 Vice Chanc for Govt Relations Mr. Barry MCBEE
26 Vice Chanc for External Relations Dr. Randa S. SAFADY
86 Vice Chanc Federal Relations Mr. William SHUTE
45 Vice Chanc Strategic Initiatives Dr. Stephanie A. BOND-HUIE
18 Assoc VC Facil Plng/Construction Mr. Michael O'DONNELL
13 Assoc VC & Chief Info Officer Mr. Mark MILSTEIN
21 Assc VC/Controller/Chief Budget Ofc Mr. Randy WALLACE
15 Assoc Vice Chanc Employee Services Mr. Dan STEWART
27 Executive Director Public Affairs Ms. Jenny LACOSTE-CAPUTO
88 Executive Director Real Estate Mr. Kirk TAMES
30 Dir Development/Gift Planning Svcs Ms. Julie LYNCH
19 Director of Police Mr. Michael J. HEIDINGSFIELD
04 Administrative Asst to President Ms. Katherine IANNESSA

*The University of Texas at Arlington (B)

701 S Nedderman Drive, Arlington TX 76013
County: Tarrant FICE Identification: 003656
Unit ID: 228769
Telephone: (817) 272-2101 Carnegie Class: DU-Highest
FAX Number: (817) 272-5656 Calendar System: Semester
URL: www.uta.edu
Established: 1895 Annual Undergrad Tuition & Fees (In-State): $9,616
Enrollment: 41,988 Coed
Affiliation or Control: State IRS Status: 170(c)1
Highest Offering: Doctorate
Accreditation: SC, ART, CAATE, CAEPN, CEA, CIDA, CS, ENG, LSAR, MUS, NURSE, PLNG, SPAA, SW

02 President Dr. Vistasp M. KARBHARI
05 Provost & VP Acad Affairs Dr. Teik LIM
10 Chief Financial Officer and VP Ms. Kelly DAVIS
32 VP Student Affairs Ms. Lisa NAGY
30 VP Development and Alumni Relations Mr. Michael KINGAN
46 Vice President Research Dr. Duane DIMOS
13 Chief Information Officer Vacant
11 Vice Pres Admin & Campus Operations Mr. John D. HALL
26 Vice President of Communications Ms. Lynne WATERS
15 Vice President for Human Resources Ms. Jean HOOD
84 VP for Enrollment Management Dr. Troy JOHNSON
45 Assoc Vice Provost Inst Eff/Report Dr. Loraine PHILLIPS
16 Asst Vice Pres Human Resources Ms. Eunice M. CURRIE
18 Asst VP Campus Operation/Facilities Mr. Bill POOLE
88 Interim Director for Univ College Ms. Liz HANNABAS
100 Chief of Staff and Assoc VP Ms. Salma ADEM
58 Assoc Dean of Graduate Studies Mr. Raymond L. JACKSON
48 Int Dean Arch/Urban & Pub Affairs Dr. Ron ELSENBAUMER
50 Interim Dean College of Business Dr. Chandra SUBRAMANIAM
54 Dean of Engineering Dr. Peter CROUCH
49 Dean of Liberal Arts Dr. Elisabeth CAWTHON
66 Dean of Nursing Dr. Anne BAVIER
81 Dean of Science Dr. Morteza KHALEDI
70 Dean School of Social Work Dr. Scott RYAN
53 Dean College of Education Dr. Teresa TABER DOUGHTY
92 Interim Dean Honors College Dr. Kevin GUSTAFSON
08 Dean of Libraries Dr. Rebecca BICHEL
12 Exec Dir of UTA Ft Worth Center Mr. Mike WEST
37 Director of Financial Aid Dr. Karen KRAUSE
23 Director Student Health Center Mr. Robert BLUM
22 Director Equal Opportunity Services Mr. Eddie FREEMAN
24 Director of Art Services Mr. Joel QUINTANS
41 Athletic Director Mr. Jim BAKER
19 Dir Environmental Health Safety Ms. Leah HOY
85 Executive Director Intl Education Mr. Jay HORN
88 Director Multicultural Outreach Mr. Casey GONZALES
88 Director Multicultural Affairs Ms. Leticia MARTINEZ
86 Assoc VP Government Relations Mr. Jeff JETER
09 Director of Institutional Research Ms. Loraine PHILLIPS
43 Dir Legal Services/General Counsel Mr. Shelby BOSEMAN
96 Director of Purchasing Ms. Julia CORNWELL
29 Exec Dir for Alumni & Donor Rels Ms. Julie BARFIELD
04 Administrative Assoc to President Ms. Elsa CORRAL

*University of Texas at Austin (C)

110 Inner Campus Drive, Austin TX 78712-1111
County: Travis FICE Identification: 003658
Unit ID: 228778
Telephone: (512) 471-3434 Carnegie Class: DU-Highest
FAX Number: (512) 471-2942 Calendar System: Semester
URL: www.utexas.edu
Established: 1883 Annual Undergrad Tuition & Fees (In-State): $10,092
Enrollment: 50,950 Coed
Affiliation or Control: State IRS Status: 170(c)1
Highest Offering: Doctorate
Accreditation: SC, ART, AUD, CAATE, CACREP, CEA, CIDA, CLPSY, COPSY, DANCE, DIETC, DIETD, ENG, IPSY, JOUR, LAW, LIB, LSAR, #MED, MUS, NURSE, PHAR, PLNG, SCPSY, SP, SPAA, SW

02 President Dr. Gregory L. FENVES
05 Executive VP & Provost Dr. Maurie MCINNIS
10 VP & Chief Financial Officer Mr. Darrell BAZZELL
28 Int VP Diversity/Cmty Engagement Mr. Leonard MOORE
11 Vice Pres for University Operations Dr. Patricia L. CLUBB
46 Vice President Research Dr. Daniel JAFFE
32 Vice President Student Affairs Dr. Gage E. PAINE
63 Vice President for Medical Affairs Dr. S. Claiborne JOHNSTON
30 Vice Pres for Development Mr. Scott RABENOLD
35 Vice President Student Affairs Dr. Soncia R. REAGINS-LILLY
13 Chief Information Officer Mr. Michael CUNNINGHAM
27 Chief Communications Officer Mr. Gary SUSSWEIN
43 Vice President Legal Affairs Ms. Patricia A. OHLENDORF
88 Deputy to the Pres Strategy/Policy Dr. Harrison A. KELLER
100 Deputy to the President Ms. Nancy A. BRAZZIL
04 Executive Assistant to President Ms. Rebecca L. BAUGHMAN
88 Sr Vice Prov Resource Management Dr. Daniel T. SLESNICK
84 Sr Vice Provost Enroll/Grad Mgmt Ms. Rachelle HERNANDEZ
88 Sr Vice Pres Strategic Initiatives Dr. David A. LAUDE
20 Sr Vice Provost for Faculty Affairs Dr. Janet M. DUKERICH
88 Vice Provost for Biomed Sciences Dr. Robert O. MESSING
46 Assoc VP Rsrch/Dir Spnsrd Projects Dr. Jason D. RICHTER
08 Vice Provost/Director UT Libraries Dr. Lorraine J. HARICOMBE
06 Vice Provost & Registrar Mr. Vincent (Shelby) STANFIELD
104 Vice Provost International Programs Dr. Janet L. ELLZEY
58 Interim Dean Graduate Studies Dr. Marvin L. HACKERT
88 Vice Provost Inst Accred Dr. Linda N. DICKENS
86 Assoc VP for Governmental Relations Mr. Carlos E. MARTINEZ
86 Assoc VP for Governmental Relations Ms. Gwen W. GRIGSBY
21 Associate VP for Finance Ms. Mary E. KNIGHT
21 Budget Director Ms. Elvia H. ROSALES
09 Director Institutional Research Ms. Tracy H. BROWN
88 Assoc Vice Prov Acad Business Affs Ms. Kathryn V. FOSTER
121 Assoc Vice Prov Student Success Ms. Carolyn K. CONNERAT
88 Associate Vice Provost Mr. Phil D. LONG
88 Associate Vice President Ms. Renee L. WALLACE
19 Assoc VP Campus Safety/Security Dr. Gerald (Bob) R. HARKINS
18 Assoc VP Facilities Management Mr. Juan ONTIVEROS
15 Associate Vice Pres Human Resources Dr. Debra G. KRESS
22 Asst VP Institutional Equity Dr. Sherri L. SANDERS
23 Director University Health Services Ms. Jamie L. SHUTTER
37 Director Student Financial Svcs Ms. Diane C. TODD SPRAGUE
39 Director Housing & Food Service Mr. Rene RODRIGUEZ
41 Interim Athletics Director Mr. Michael PERRIN
41 Women's Athletics Director Ms. Christine A. PLONSKY
29 CEO/Exec Director Texas Exes Ms. Leslie CEDAR
19 Chief University Police Mr. David CARTER
48 Dean of Architecture Dr. Michelle ADDINGTON
50 Dean McCombs School of Business Dr. Jay C. HARTZELL
60 Dean of Communication Dr. Jay M. BERNHARDT
53 Dean of Education Dr. Manuel J. JUSTIZ
54 Dean of Engineering Dr. Sharon L. WOOD
57 Dean of Fine Arts Dr. Douglas J. DEMPSTER
62 Int Dean School of Information Dr. Randolph BIAS
65 Dean Jackson School of Geosciences Dr. Sharon MOSHER
61 Dean School of Law Mr. Ward FARNSWORTH
49 Dean of Liberal Arts Dr. Randy L. DIEHL
81 Dean of Natural Sciences Dr. Linda A. HICKE
66 Dean of Nursing Dr. Alexa M. STUIFBERGEN
67 Dean of Pharmacy Dr. M. Lynn CRISMON
80 Dean LBJ School Public Affs Dr. Angela EVANS
70 Dean Social Work Dr. Luis H. ZAYAS
97 Dean of Undergrad Studies Dr. Brent L. IVERSON
26 Director Communications Mr. Joey WILLIAMS
51 Associate Director Internal Audits Mr. Jeff D. TREICHEL
88 Director Internal Audits Mr. Michael W. VANDERVORT
18 Associate VP Utilities/Energy Mgmt Mr. Juan M. ONTIVEROS
88 Executive Director Univ Union Mr. Mulugeta FEREDE
27 Director Univ of Texas Press Mr. David S. HAMRICK
88 Assoc Athl Dir/Dir Spec Events Ctr Mr. John M. GRAHAM
07 Director of Admissions Ms. Susan L. KEARNS

*The University of Texas at Dallas (D)

800 West Campbell Road, Richardson TX 75080
County: Collin FICE Identification: 009741
Unit ID: 228787
Telephone: (972) 883-2111 Carnegie Class: DU-Highest
FAX Number: (972) 883-2237 Calendar System: Semester
URL: www.utdallas.edu
Established: 1969 Annual Undergrad Tuition & Fees (In-State): $11,192
Enrollment: 24,554 Coed
Affiliation or Control: State IRS Status: 501(c)3
Highest Offering: Doctorate
Accreditation: SC, ACAE, AUD, CS, ENG, IPSY, SP, SPAA

02 President Dr. Richard BENSON
03 Executive Vice President Dr. B. Hobson WILDENTHAL
05 Interim Provost Dr. Inga MUSSELMAN
10 Vice President for Business Affairs Dr. Calvin D. JAMISON
32 Vice President Student Affairs Dr. Gene FITCH
46 Interim VP for Research Mr. Rafael MARTIN
20 Vice Provost Dr. John WIORKOWSKI
30 Vice President for Development Dr. Kyle EDGINGTON
13 VP Info Technology and CIO Mr. Frank FEAGANS
28 Vice President of Diversity Dr. George W. FAIR
114 Interim Asst VP Budget Mr. Orkun TOROS
21 VP Finance & Controller Mr. Terry PANKRATZ
26 VP Public Affairs Ms. Amanda O. ROCKOW
45 Exec Director Strategic Planning Dr. Lawrence J. REDLINGER
35 Dean of Students Dr. Amanda SMITH
58 Dean Graduate Studies Dr. Marion UNDERWOOD
53 Dean Undergraduate Education Dr. Andrew BLANCHARD
79 Dean School Arts & Humanities Dr. Dennis KRATZ
50 Dean School of Management Dr. Hasan PIRKUL
81 Dean Sch of Natural Science/Math Dr. Bruce NOVAK
83 Dean School of Econ/Pol/Policy Sci Dr. Denis J. DEAN
76 Dean Sch Behavioral/Brain Science Dr. James BARTLETT
97 Dean School General Studies Dr. George W. FAIR
54 Dean EJ Sch of Engr/Computer Sci Dr. Mark W. SPONG
88 Dean Sch Arts/Tech & Emerg Media Dr. Anne BALSAMO
92 Dean Honors College Dr. Edward HARPHAM
08 Dean of Libraries Dr. Ellen SAFLEY
06 Registrar Ms. Jennifer MCDOWELL
12 Exec Director of Callier Center Dr. Thomas F. CAMPBELL
18 Assoc VP Facilities Management Mr. Richard DEMPSEY
15 Assoc VP Human Resources Ms. Colleen DUTTON
96 Exec Dir Procurement Management Ms. Deborah REYNOLDS
19 Chief of Police Mr. Larry ZACHARIAS
36 Director Career Services Vacant
38 Director Student Counseling Mr. James P. CANNICI
116 Institutional Chief Audit Executive Ms. Toni STEPHENS
41 Director Intercollegiate Athletics Mr. Bill PETITT
78 Assoc Dir Co-operative Education Mr. Michael J. CHOATE
90 Director Tech Customer Services Mr. Donald L. DAVIS
29 Senior Director of Alumni Relations Ms. Melinda MENDOZA
04 Executive Associate to President Ms. Kimberly GOODFRIEND
105 Assistant VP Web Services Mr. Cary DELMARK
106 Asst Provost Learning Tech Mr. Darren CRONE
39 Asst VP Residential Life Mr. Ryan WHITE
104 Director Study Abroad Ms. Lisabeth LASSITER
37 Director Student Financial Aid Ms. Beth TOLAN
43 University Attorney Mr. Timothy SHAW
84 Asst Provost Enrollment Management Mr. Wray WELDON

*University of Texas at El Paso (E)

500 W University Avenue, El Paso TX 79968-8900
County: El Paso FICE Identification: 003661
Unit ID: 228796
Telephone: (915) 747-5000 Carnegie Class: DU-Higher
FAX Number: (915) 747-5111 Calendar System: Semester
URL: www.utep.edu
Established: 1914 Annual Undergrad Tuition & Fees (In-State): $7,548
Enrollment: 23,397 Coed
Affiliation or Control: State IRS Status: 501(c)3
Highest Offering: Doctorate
Accreditation: SC, CACREP, CS, ENG, MT, MUS, NURSE, OT, PH, @PHAR, PTA, SP, SPAA, SW

02 President Dr. Diana S. NATALICIO
05 Provost Dr. Carol A. PARKER
03 Executive Vice President Mr. Ricardo ADAUTO, III
04 Assistant to the President Ms. Estrella ESCOBAR
10 Interim VP Business Affairs Mr. Ricardo ADAUTO

46 Vice President for Research .... Dr. Roberto OSEGUEDA
13 Vice Pres Info Resources & Planning .... Dr. Steve RITER
58 Dean of Graduate School .... Dr. Charles AMBLER
32 Vice President Student Affairs .... Dr. Gary EDENS
50 Dean of Business Administration .... Dr. Robert NACHTMANN
53 Dean of Education .... Vacant
54 Dean of Engineering .... Dr. Theresa MALDONADO
49 Interim Dean of Liberal Arts .... Dr. Stephen CRITES
76 Dean of Health Sciences .... Dr. Shafik DHARAMSI
81 Dean of Science .... Dr. Robert KIRKEN
66 Dean of School of Nursing .... Dr. Elias PROVENCIO-VASQUEZ
18 Assoc VP Business Affs/Facilities .... Mr. Greg L. MCNICOL
08 Assoc Vice President Library .... Mr. Robert L. STAKES
111 Asst Vice Pres Inst Advancement .... Mr. Beto LOPEZ
26 Assoc VP University Communications .... Ms. Robin STANTON GERROW
22 Asst Vice Pres EO/AA Dept .... Ms. Sandy VASQUEZ
29 Asst VP Alumni Affairs .... Ms. Maribel VILLALVA
46 Assoc Provost for Resource Mgmt .... Ms. Elizabeth FLORES
84 Asst VP Enrollment Services .... Ms. Amanda VASQUEZ
15 Assoc VP Human Resources Svcs .... Dr. Victor PACHECO
19 Chief Campus Police .... Mr. Clifton WALSH
37 Assoc VP for Financial Services .... Ms. Heidi GRANGER
23 Director of Student Health Center .... Ms. Louise P. CASTRO
36 Director of Career Services .... Ms. Betsy CASTRO-DUARTE
35 Associate VP/Dean of Students .... Ms. Catherine M. MCCORRY-ANDALIS
108 Assoc VP Inst Eval/Rsrch & Planning .... Dr. Roy MATHEW
39 Director of Housing Services .... Mr. Charlie E. GIBBENS
40 Director of University Bookstore .... Mr. Fernando PADULA
41 Athletics Director .... Mr. Robert W. STULL
38 Director Counseling Services .... Ms. Sherri I. TERRELL
96 Dir Purchasing/General Services .... Ms. Diane N. DEHOYOS
21 Interim Vice Pres Business Affairs .... Mr. Richard ADAUTO, III
30 VP Asset Mgmt/Development .... Mr. Benjamin GONZALEZ

*The University of Texas Rio Grande Valley (A)

1201 W University Drive, Edinburg TX 78539-2970
County: Hidalgo FICE Identification: 003599
Unit ID: 227368
Telephone: (888) 882-4026 Carnegie Class: DU-Mod
FAX Number: (956) 665-2150 Calendar System: Semester
URL: www.utrgv.edu
Established: 2015 Annual Undergrad Tuition & Fees (In-State): $7,438
Enrollment: 28,584 Coed
Affiliation or Control: State IRS Status: 501(c)3
Highest Offering: Doctorate
Accreditation: #SC, ARCPA, CACREP, CAEPN, ENG, #MED, MT, MUS, NURSE, OT, SP, SW, THEA

02 President .... Dr. Guy BAILEY
03 Deputy President .... Dr. Janna ARNEY
05 Provost/EVP Academic Affairs .... Dr. Havidan RODRIGUEZ
10 EVP for Finance and Administration .... Mr. Rick ANDERSON
46 Interim Sr VP Research/Innov & Econ .... Dr. Juan SANCHEZ
111 VP for Advancement .... Dr. Kelly SCRIVNER
86 VP for Governmental & Community Rel . Ms. Veronica GONZALES
20 Deputy Provost .... Dr. Cynthia BROWN
88 Vice Provost for Faculty Affairs .... Dr. Ala QUBBAJ
100 Assistant Provost & Chief of Staff .... Ms. Nina YOUNG
32 VP for Student Success .... Dr. Kristin CROYLE
84 VP for Strategic Enrollment .... Dr. Maggie HINOJOSA
21 Interim Assoc VP Fiscal Svcs/Comptr .... Ms. Karla LOYA
11 Sr Assoc VP for Operations .... Mr. Doug ARNEY
45 Assoc VP for Planning & Analysis .... Mr. Juan C. GONZALEZ
18 Assoc VP for Facilities .... Ms. Marta SALINAS-HOVAR
19 Assoc VP Campus Safety & Security .... Mr. Ben REYNA
30 Assoc VP for Development .... Mr. Alicia M. KING
110 Assoc VP for Advancement Services .... Ms. Lydia ALEMAN
88 Assoc VP for Governmental Relations .... Mr. Richard P. SANCHEZ
26 Assoc VP for University Marketing .... Mr. Patrick GONZALES
88 Acting Assoc VP Econ Development .. Dr. Andreas HOLZENBURG
21 Asst VP for Finance & Admin .... Ms. Karla LOYA
109 Asst VP for Campus Auxiliary Svcs .... Ms. Leticia BENAVIDES
31 Asst VP for Community Engagement .... Ms. Cris TREJO
09 AVP Strategic Analysis and Inst Res .... Ms. Susan BROWN
53 Dean College of Education & P-16 ..... Dr. Patricia A. MCHATTON
50 Dean Col Business Entrepreneurship .... Dr. Mark KROLL
81 Dean College of Sciences .... Dr. Parwinder GREWAL
54 Dean College Engr/Computer Science .... Dr. Alex DOMIJAN
76 Dean College of Health Affairs .... Dr. Michael LEHKER
49 Dean College of Fine Arts .... Dr. Steven BLOCK
83 Dean College of Liberal Arts .... Dr. Walter DIAZ
63 VP Med Affairs & Dean School of Med .... Dr. John KROUSE
17 Interim Assoc Dean Clinical Affairs .... Dr. Nancy BARONE
43 Chief Legal Officer .... Ms. Karen ADAMS
15 Chief Human Resources Officer .... Mr. Mike JAMES
22 Chief Compliance Officer .... Ms. Diane SHEPPARD
13 Chief Information Officer .... Dr. Jeffrey GRAHAM
29 Exec Dir of Alumni Relations .... Ms. Isis LOPEZ
41 Athletics Director .... Mr. Christopher KING
46 Director for Strategic Research Dev .... Dr. Pam MEREDITH

*University of Texas at San Antonio (B)

One UTSA Circle, San Antonio TX 78249-0169
County: Bexar FICE Identification: 010115
Unit ID: 229027
Telephone: (210) 458-4011 Carnegie Class: DU-Higher
FAX Number: (210) 458-4187 Calendar System: Semester
URL: www.utsa.edu
Established: 1969 Annual Undergrad Tuition & Fees (In-State): $7,700
Enrollment: 28,787 Coed
Affiliation or Control: State IRS Status: 501(c)3
Highest Offering: Doctorate
Accreditation: SC, ART, CACREP, CEA, #CIDA, CONST, ENG, MUS, SPAA, SW

02 President .... Dr. T. Tyler EIGHMY
05 Int Provost/Vice Pres Academic Affs .... Dr. Mauli AGRAWAL
10 Vice Pres for Business Affairs .... Ms. Kathryn FUNK-BAXTER
46 Int Vice President for Research .... Dr. Bernard ARULANANDAM
32 Vice President for Student Affairs .... Mr. Samuel GONZALES
31 Vice President Community Services .... Dr. Jude VALDEZ
30 VP External Rels/Chief Dev Ofcr .... Ms. Marjorie M. FRENCH
20 Exec Vice Provost/Sr Intl Ofcr .... Ms. Rene ZENTENO
09 Assoc V Prov Acad Compl/Inst Effect .. Mr. Steve L. WILKERSON
12 Vice Provost for Downtown Campus .... Dr. Jesse T. ZAPATA
13 Vice Provost Information Tech/CIO .... Mr. Bryan WILSON
20 Int V Prov/Dean University College .... Dr. Heather J. SHIPLEY
21 Associate VP Financial Affairs .... Ms. Lenora CHAPMAN
15 Associate VP Human Resources .. Ms. Barbara BARAN-CENTENO
08 Dean of Libraries .... Dr. Dean D. HENDRIX
92 Dean of Honors College .... Dr. Richard A. DIEM
58 Vice Provost/Dean Graduate School .... Dr. DeBrenna LaFa AGBENYIGA
50 Dean of College of Business .... Dr. Wm Gerard (Gerry) Y. SANDERS
57 Dean College of Liberal & Fine Arts .... Dr. Daniel J. GELO
54 Dean of College of Engineering .... Dr. Joann BROWNING
83 Dean of College of Sciences .... Dr. George PERRY
48 Dean School of Architecture .... Prof. John MURPHY
53 Dean College Educ/Human Development .... Dr. Margo DELLI CARPINI
80 Dean of College of Public Policy .... Dr. Rogelio SAENZ
19 AVP Public Safety/Chief of Police .... Mr. Gerald LEWIS
41 Assoc VP Director Intcollegiate Ath .... Ms. Lynn HICKEY
29 Director Alumni Programs .... Ms. Anne ENGLERT
43 Interim Chief Legal Officer .... Mr. John P. DANNER
26 Associate VP for Comm/Marketing .... Mr. Joe IZBRAND
86 AVP Government Relations & Policy .. Mr. Albert A. CARRISALEZ
04 Executive Assistant Office of Pres .... Ms. Patricia CARDENAS
06 Assoc Vice Pres & Univ Registrar .... Dr. Joseph R. DECRISTOFORO
07 Director of Admissions .... Ms. Beverly WOODSON DAY
100 Executive Director of Operations .... Ms. Elvira E. JACQUEZ
36 Director of Career Services .... Ms. Audrey J. MAGNUSON
104 Interim Dir of Educ Abroad Services .... Ms. Cristina SANCHEZ
105 Associate Director of Web/Portal .... Mr. Shashi B. PINHEIRO
106 Director of Online Learning .... Ms. Marcela V. RAMIREZ
108 Assistant Vice Provost Assessment .... Dr. Kasey NEECE-FIELDER
18 Associate VP for Facilities .... Mr. David J. RIKER
22 Director Equal Opportunity Services .... Mr. Leonard FLAUM
25 Director of Grants/Contracts .... Ms. Shannyn ADKINS
28 Associate Provost .... Col. Lisa C. FIRMIN
37 Director of Student Financial Aid .... Ms. Diana S. MARTINEZ
38 Director of Counseling Services .... Mr. Thomas BAEZ
39 Director Student Housing/Residence .... Mr. Daniel L. GOCKLEY
30 Asst VP Ops/Advancement Services ...... Ms. Rebecca ANDERSON
84 Director Student Enrollment Svcs .... Ms. Erika M. COX
90 Director of Academic Computing .... Mr. John P. SOUDAH
91 Exec Director of Enterprise System .... Mr. Bryan P. WILSON
96 Director Business Contracts .... Mr. Robert L. DICKENS

*University of Texas at Tyler (C)

3900 University Boulevard, Tyler TX 75799-6699
County: Smith FICE Identification: 011163
Unit ID: 228802
Telephone: (903) 566-7000 Carnegie Class: Masters/L
FAX Number: (903) 566-7068 Calendar System: Semester
URL: www.uttyler.edu
Established: 1971 Annual Undergrad Tuition & Fees (In-State): $7,602
Enrollment: 8,785 Coed
Affiliation or Control: State IRS Status: 501(c)3
Highest Offering: Doctorate
Accreditation: SC, CACREP, ENG, MUS, NAIT, NURSE, @PHAR

02 President .... Dr. Michael TIDWELL
05 Provost/VP Academic Affairs .... Dr. Amir MIRMIRAN
30 Vice President Univ Advancement .... Mr. Jerre IVERSEN
32 Vice Pres for Student Affairs .... Dr. Howard PATTERSON
13 Vice President & CIO IT .... Dr. Sherri WHATLEY
20 Vice Provost AA/Grad Studies .... Dr. William GEIGER
46 VP for Research & Technology Transf .... Dr. Michael ODELL
10 VP for Business Affairs .... Mr. William O'DONNELL
15 Director of Human Resources .... Ms. Amy CLEM
21 Assoc VP for Business Affairs .... Ms. Carrie CLAYTON
86 AVP for Legislative Relations .... Ms. Laura JACKSON
84 AVP for Enrollment Management .... Ms. Sarah BOWDIN
108 Asst Vice Pres for Assessment/IE .... Dr. Lou Ann BERMAN
35 Asst VP Student Affs/Dean Students .... Ms. Ona TOLLIVER
49 Dean College of Arts & Sciences .... Dr. Martin SLANN
50 Dean College Business & Technology .... Dr. James LUMPKIN
53 Dean College Educ & Psych .... Dr. Ross SHERMAN
54 Interim Dean College Engineering .... Dr. Michael MCGINNIS
66 Dean College Nursing & Health Sci .... Dr. Yong TAI WANG
67 Dean College of Pharmacy .... Dr. Lane BRUNNER
08 Exec Director of the Library .... Ms. Jeanne STANDLEY
21 Director of Financial Services .... Ms. Cindy TROYER
18 AVP for Facilities Management .... Mr. Jerry STUFF
29 Director of Alumni Relations .... Ms. Brittany CHILDS
26 Exec Dir Marketing & Communication .... Ms. Beverley GOLDEN
38 Dir Stdnt Svc/Stdnt Couns/Test Ctr .... Ms. Kim HARVEY-LIVINGSTON
39 Director of Residence Life .... Dr. Jennifer WATERS
06 Registrar .... Ms. Sonja MORALE
09 Interim Dir Institutional Analysis .... Ms. Cindy STRAWN
19 Chief University Police .... Mr. Mike W. MEDDERS
04 Executive Asst to President .... Ms. Janet ROBERTSON
07 Interim Director of Admissions .... Ms. Angela COPELAND
37 Director of Student Financial Aid .... Mr. Scott LAPINSKI
43 Chief Legal Officer .... Mr. Michael DONLEY

*The University of Texas Health Science Center at Houston (UTHealth) (D)

PO Box 20036, Houston TX 77225-0036
County: Harris FICE Identification: 004951
Unit ID: 229300
Telephone: (713) 500-4472 Carnegie Class: Spec-4-yr-Med
FAX Number: (713) 500-3026 Calendar System: Semester
URL: www.uth.edu
Established: 1972 Annual Undergrad Tuition & Fees (In-State): N/A
Enrollment: 4,795 Coed
Affiliation or Control: State IRS Status: 501(c)3
Highest Offering: Doctorate
Accreditation: SC, ANEST, DENT, DH, DIETI, ENGR, IPSY, MED, NURSE, PERF, PH

02 President .... Dr. Giuseppe N. COLASURDO
11 CFO/COO & Exec VP for Admin .... Mr. T. Kevin DILLON
63 Dean Medical School .... Dr. Barbara J. STOLL
69 Dean School of Public Health .... Dr. Eric BOERWINKLE
52 Dean School of Dentistry .... Dr. John A. VALENZA
58 Dean Grad Sch Biomedical Sciences ..... Dr. Michael BLACKBURN
66 Dean School of Nursing .... Dr. Lorraine FRAZIER
88 Dean Sch of Biomed Informatics .... Dr. Jiajie W. ZHANG
05 Exec VP & Chief Academic Officer ... Dr. Michael R. BLACKBURN
45 Senior VP for Strategic Planning .... Dr. Osama I. MIKHAIL
10 Sr VP Finance & Business Svcs .... Mr. Michael TRAMONTE
46 Vice Dn Rsrch/Dir Molecular Med .... Dr. John HANCOCK
30 Vice Pres Development .... Mr. Kevin J. FOYLE
15 VP/Chief Human Resources Officer .... Mr. Eric FERNETTE
43 VP/Chief Legal Officer .... Mr. Daniel J. REAT
86 VP Govt Relations .... Mr. Scott FORBES
88 VP Research & Technology .... Dr. Bruce D. BUTLER
109 VP Auxiliary Enterprises .... Mr. Charles A. FIGARI
13 VP/Chief Information Officer .... Mr. Richard L. MILLER
18 VP Facilities Planning & Engr .... Mr. Richard L. MCDERMOTT
90 Asst VP Academic Technology .... Dr. William A. WEEMS
116 Asst VP & Chief Audit Officer .... Mr. Daniel SHERMAN
06 Registrar .... Mr. Robert JENKINS
19 Chief of Police .... Mr. William ADCOX
41 Director Recreation/Intramural Pgms .... Ms. Pauline M. HABETZ
85 Director International Affairs .... Ms. Rose Mary VALENCIA
39 Director University Housing .... Mr. Billy C. HINTON
26 Executive Director Communications .... Ms. Meredith RAINE
37 Director Student Financial Svcs .... Ms. Araceli ALVAREZ
25 Assoc VP Sponsored Projects Admin ...... Ms. Kathleen KREIDLER
14 Director Data Center Operations .... Mr. Kevin B. GRANHOLD
88 Director Educational Tech Nursing .... Ms. Linda L. CRAYS
88 Director Biomedical Info Tech Med .... Dr. Stephen J. FATH
07 Vice Dean Admissions/Stdt Aff-Med .... Dr. Margaret MCNEESE
32 Assoc Dean Student & Acad Affs UTSD ..... Dr. Robert D. SPEARS
32 Assoc Dean of Student Affairs-SPH .... Dr. Mary A. SMITH
35 Dir of Student Affairs-SBMI .... Ms. Jaime HARGRAVE
35 Director Student Affairs-SON .... Ms. Diana PRESSLEY
09 Director of Institutional Research .... Ms. Deanne HERNANDEZ

*University of Texas Health Science Center at San Antonio (E)

7703 Floyd Curl Drive, San Antonio TX 78229-3900
County: Bexar FICE Identification: 003659
Unit ID: 228644
Telephone: (210) 567-7000 Carnegie Class: Spec-4-yr-Med
FAX Number: (210) 567-2025 Calendar System: Other
URL: www.uthscsa.edu
Established: 1959 Annual Undergrad Tuition & Fees (In-State): N/A
Enrollment: 3,130 Coed
Affiliation or Control: State IRS Status: 501(c)3
Highest Offering: Doctorate
Accreditation: SC, ARCPA, COARC, DENT, DH, DIETC, EMT, HT, IPSY, MED, MT, NURSE, OT, PTA, RADDOS

02 President .... Dr. William L. HENRICH
03 Sr Exec Vice President & COO .... Mr. Michael E. BLACK
11 Exec VP for Facility Planning/Admin .... Mr. James D. KAZEN
10 Vice President & CFO .... Ms. Andrea M. MARKS
05 VP Acad/Fac & Student Affairs .... Dr. Jacqueline L. MOK
13 Vice Pres & Chief Information Ofcr .... Mr. Yeman COLLIER
46 Vice President for Research .... Dr. Andrea GIUFFRIDA
86 VP for Governmental Relations .... Mr. Armando DIAZ
30 VP Inst Advancement/Chief Dev Ofcr ... Ms. Deborah H. MORRILL
26 VP & Chief Marketing/Comm Officer .... Ms. Heather ADKINS
15 Vice Pres of Human Resources .... Mr. J. Michael TESH
100 VP & Chief of Staff .... Ms. Mary G. DELAY
21 Asst Vice Pres for Business Affairs .... Mr. Gerard E. LONG
09 Asst VP Research .... Dr. Mark J. NIJLAND
43 Asst VP/Chief Legal Officer .... Mr. Jack C. PARK
63 Interim Dean School of Medicine .... Dr. Ron RODRIGUEZ
52 Dean School of Dentistry .... Dr. William W. DODGE
58 Dean Graduate Biomed Science .... Dr. David WEISS
76 Dean School Health Professions .... Dr. David C. SHELLEDY
66 Dean School of Nursing .... Dr. Eileen T. BRESLIN

32 Director for Student Life ....Ms. Le Keisha JOHNSON
06 Registrar ....Ms. Blanca GUERRA
08 Senior Director of Libraries ....Mr. Owen H. ELLARD
19 Chief of Police ....Mr. Michael PARKS
88 Exec Dir Acad/Fac/Studnt Ombudspers ....Dr. Bonnie L. BLANKMEYER
37 Director of Financial Aid ....Ms. Ellen NYSTROM
38 Director of Student Counseling ....Dr. Mia VEVE
96 Sr Dir Supply Chain Mngmt/HUB Coord ....Mr. Eric R. WALLS
07 Director of Admissions ....Vacant
102 Development Officer ....Ms. Leslie M. PAYNE
44 Interim Director Planned Giving ....Ms. Jennifer M. CLARK

*The University of Texas Health Science Center at Tyler (A)

11937 US Hwy 271, Tyler TX 75708-3154

County: Smith Identification: 667206
Unit ID: 485537
Telephone: (903) 877-7777 Carnegie Class: Not Classified
FAX Number: N/A Calendar System: Semester
URL: www.uthct.edu
Established: 1977 Annual Graduate Tuition & Fees: N/A
Enrollment: 17 Coed
Affiliation or Control: State IRS Status: 501(c)3
Highest Offering: Master's; No Undergraduates
Accreditation: **SC**, IPSY

02 President and CEO ....Dr. Kirk A. CALHOUN
11 Exec VP/Chief Operating Officer ....Joseph F. WOELKERS
05 Sr VP Academic Affairs/Provost ....Dr. Jeffrey L. LEVIN
46 Sr VP Research & Graduate Studies ....Dr. Steven IDELL
23 Sr VP/CMO & Physician in Chief ....Dr. Steven W. COX
88 Sr VP Population Health ....Dr. David L. LAKEY
17 Sr VP/CAO Hospital & Clinics ....Timothy G. OCHRAN
10 VP/Chief Financial Officer ....Kris KAVASCH
15 VP Human Resources/CHRO ....Cynthia SCOTT-LUNAU
43 VP/Chief Legal Officer ....Terry WITTER
45 VP Planning & Public Policy ....Daniel DESLATTE
13 VP Information Technology (CIO) ....John YODER
30 VP Institutional Advancement ....Derrith BONDURANT
18 Assoc VP Physical Plant ....Thomas BRUNETTE
20 Assoc VP Academic Affairs ....Dr. Pierre F. NEUENSCHWANDER
32 Director of Student Affairs ....Dr. Mickey SLIMP
08 Director of Library Services ....Thomas CRAIG
09 Director of Institutional Research ....Sara SHEPHERD
86 Dir University & Community Affairs ....Kimberly ASHLEY
96 Director of Purchasing ....Crystal SMITH
37 Director Student Financial Aid ....Araceli ALVAREZ
06 Registrar ....Robert JENKINS
04 Administrative Asst to President ....Carol DAVIS
19 Chief of Police ....Chief Robert CROMLEY
26 Chief Public Affair/Market Exec ....Rhonda SCOBY

*The University of Texas MD Anderson Cancer Center (B)

1515 Holcombe Boulevard, Houston TX 77030-4000

County: Harris FICE Identification: 025554
Unit ID: 416801
Telephone: (713) 792-6161 Carnegie Class: Spec-4-yr-Other Health
FAX Number: N/A Calendar System: Semester
URL: www.mdanderson.org
Established: 1941 Annual Undergrad Tuition & Fees (In-District): N/A
Enrollment: 320 Coed
Affiliation or Control: State/Local IRS Status: 501(c)3
Highest Offering: Doctorate
Accreditation: **SC**, CGTECH, CYTO, DENT, DMOLS, HT, MT, PAST, RAD, RADDOS, RADMAG, RTT

02 President ....Dr. Ronald DEPINHO
10 Sr Exec Vice Pres Business Affairs ....Mr. Dan FONTAINE
88 Exec Vice Pres/Physician-in-Chief ....Dr. Thomas BUCHHOLZ
05 Provost/Executive Vice President ....Dr. Ethan DMITROVSKY
100 Chief of Staff ....Vacant

*The University of Texas Medical Branch (C)

301 University Boulevard, Galveston TX 77555-0100

County: Galveston FICE Identification: 004952
Unit ID: 228653
Telephone: (409) 772-1011 Carnegie Class: Spec-4-yr-Med
FAX Number: N/A Calendar System: Semester
URL: www.utmb.edu
Established: 1891 Annual Undergrad Tuition & Fees (In-State): N/A
Enrollment: 3,169 Coed
Affiliation or Control: State IRS Status: 170(c)1
Highest Offering: Doctorate
Accreditation: **SC**, ARCPA, BBT, COARC, DENT, DIETI, MED, MT, NURSE, OT, PH, PTA

02 President ....Dr. David L. CALLENDER
04 Exec Asst to the President ....Ms. Mary Ann PEDRAZA
05 Exec VP/Provost/Dean Sch of Med ....Dr. Danny O. JACOBS
23 Exec VP & CEO Health System ....Ms. Donna K. SOLLENBERGER
10 Exec VP & Chief Business/Fin Ofcr ....Ms. Cheryl SADRO
86 Sr VP Health Policy & Legis Affairs ....Dr. Ben G. RAIMER
88 VP & Chief Physician Executive ....Dr. Rex M. MCCALLUM
17 Chief Medical Officer ....Dr. Gulshan SHARMA
20 VP Education & Dean Sch of Nursing ....Dr. Pamela G. WATSON
76 VP & Dean Sch of Health Professions ....Dr. Elizabeth J. PROTAS
58 VP & Dean Grad Sch of Biomed Sci ....Dr. David W. NIESEL
15 VP HR & Employee Services ....Dr. Ronald B. MCKINLEY
13 VP Information Services & CIO ....Mr. Todd A. LEACH
21 VP Finance Academic Enterprise ....Ms. Frances HUTCHISON
18 VP Business Oper & Facilities ....Mr. Michael B. SHRINER
11 VP/Chief Admin Officer AE ....Mr. Loren SKINNER
21 VP Finance Clinical Enterprise ....Mr. David M. CONNAUGHTON
45 VP for Strategic Mgmt ....Dr. Rebecca SAAVEDRA
43 Sr VP General Counsel ....Ms. Carolee KING
26 VP Marketing & Communications ....Mr. Stephen CAMPBELL
81 Assoc Dean Grad Sch Biomed Sci ....Dr. Jose M. BARRAL
07 Assoc Dean Admissions Sch of Med ....Dr. Jeffrey RABEK
32 Assoc Dean Student Affairs/Adm SON ....Ms. Dorothy PEARROW
46 Assoc VP Research Admin ....Ms. Toni J. D'AGOSTINO
08 Assoc VP Academic Res/Library ....Ms. Patricia A. CIEJKA
09 Assoc VP Inst Effectiveness ....Dr. John C. MCKEE
27 Assoc VP Public Affairs ....Ms. Mary G. HAVARD
21 Assoc VP Fin Plng & Perf Mgmt ....Mr. Matthew FURLONG
114 Assoc VP Budget & Analysis ....Ms. Celia BAILEY-OCHOA
116 Assoc VP Audit Services ....Ms. Kimberly K. HAGARA
30 Assoc VP Chief Develop Officer ....Ms. Betsy B. CLARDY
29 Asst VP Alumni Relations ....Vacant
88 VP & Chief Compliance Officer ....Mr. Tobin R. BOENIG
06 AVP Univ Student Svcs & Registrar ....Mr. William S. BOEH
19 Chief of University Police ....Mr. Thomas ENGELLS
28 Dir of Diversity and Inclusion ....Vacant
96 AVP Supply Chain Management ....Mr. Frank REIGHARD
38 Director Student Counseling ....Ms. Cynthia DESANTOS
100 Chief of Staff ....Ms. Sheila LIDSTONE
16 Assoc VP HR Talent Manager ....Mr. Ian BARRETT
105 Director Digital Communications ....Mr. Eduardo VALDES
106 Dir Online Education/E-learning ....Dr. Trish RICHARD
108 Asst Dir Institutional Effectivenes ....Mr. Jay HOWELL
37 Director Student Financial Aid ....Ms. Carol CROMIE
39 AVP BOF Student Housing ....Mr. Carlos ESCOBAR
41 Athletic Director ....Mr. Gerald CLEVELAND
44 Director Annual or Planned Giving ....Ms. Marie MACZAK
90 Asst Director Academic Computing ....Mr. David DEL PINO KLOQUES

*University of Texas of the Permian Basin (D)

4901 E University Boulevard, Odessa TX 79762-0001

County: Ector FICE Identification: 009930
Unit ID: 229018
Telephone: (432) 552-2020 Carnegie Class: Masters/M
FAX Number: (432) 552-2374 Calendar System: Semester
URL: www.utpb.edu
Established: 1969 Annual Undergrad Tuition & Fees (In-State): $5,774
Enrollment: 6,077 Coed
Affiliation or Control: State IRS Status: 501(c)3
Highest Offering: Master's
Accreditation: **SC**, ART, CAATE, CAEPN, ENG, MUS, NURSE, SW

02 President ....Dr. Sandra WOODLEY
04 Assistant to the President ....Ms. Danielle JESENSKY
05 Provost/Vice Pres Academic Affairs ....Dr. Dan HEIMMERMANN
10 Vice President Business Affairs ....Mr. Mark MCGURK
32 Sr AVP Academic & Student Services ....Ms. Teresa SEWELL
58 AVP Research/Dean Graduate Studies ....Dr. Juli RATHEAL
13 Chief Information Officer ....Mr. Lowell BALLARD
49 Dean College of Arts & Science ....Dr. Michael ZAVADA
50 Dean School of Business ....Dr. William PRICE
53 Int Dean School of Education ....Dr. Roy HURST
111 Director Institutional Advancement ....Ms. Lee Anna GOOD
07 Director Admissions ....Mr. Scott SMILEY
06 Registrar ....Mr. Joe SANDERS
37 Director Financial Aid ....Mr. C. Edward KERESTLY
08 Director of Library Services ....Mr. Howard MARKS
15 Director Human Resources ....Ms. Sharon BURKE
51 Director Continuing Education ....Mr. Rey LASCANO
26 Interim Public Information Officer ....Ms. Travis WOODWARD
41 Director Athletics ....Mr. Andy NEWMAN
19 Chief of Police ....Chief Tom HAIN
18 Chief Facilities/Physical Plant ....Mr. Jay HANEY
36 Dir Student Placement/Counseling ....Mr. Tony LOVE
96 Interim Director of Purchasing ....Ms. Ynez ALDERSON
09 Director of Institutional Research ....Dr. Denise WATTS
29 Alumni Relations ....Mrs. Maribea MERRITT
39 Director Student Housing ....Ms. Chermae PEEL

*University of Texas Southwestern Medical Center (E)

5323 Harry Hines Boulevard, Dallas TX 75390-9002

County: Dallas FICE Identification: 010019
Unit ID: 228635
Telephone: (214) 648-3111 Carnegie Class: Spec-4-yr-Med
FAX Number: N/A Calendar System: Semester
URL: www.utsouthwestern.edu
Established: 1943 Annual Undergrad Tuition & Fees (In-State): N/A
Enrollment: 2,295 Coed
Affiliation or Control: State IRS Status: 501(c)3
Highest Offering: Doctorate
Accreditation: **SC**, ARCPA, CACREP, CLPSY, DIETC, IPSY, MED, OPE, PAST, PTA, RTT

02 President ....Dr. Daniel K. PODOLSKY
100 Vice President & Chief of Staff ....Dr. Robin M. JACOBY
05 Exec VP Acad Affs/Provost/Dean SMS ....Dr. Gregory FITZ
03 Exec VP Health System Affairs ....Vacant
10 Exec Vice Pres Business Affairs ....Mr. Arnim DONTES
46 Vice Provost/Dean of Basic Research ....Dr. David W. RUSSELL
23 Vice President Clinical Operations ....Dr. John D. RUTHERFORD
88 Vice President/CEO University Hosp ....Dr. John WARNER
88 Chief Quality Officer ....Dr. Gary REED
21 Vice President Financial Affairs ....Mr. Michael SERBER
86 Vice Pres Govt Affairs & Policy ....Ms. Angelica MARIN-HILL
26 Vice Pres Comm Mktg & Public Affs ....Vacant
15 Vice President Chief HR Officer ....Mr. Ivan THOMPSON
43 Vice President Legal Affairs ....Ms. Leah A. HURLEY
88 Vice Pres Technology Development ....Mr. Frank P. GRASSLER
30 Vice President Development ....Ms. Amanda BILLINGS
102 Vice Pres Community and Corp Rels ....Mr. Ruben E. ESQUIVEL
13 Vice Pres Information Resources ....Mr. Marc MILSTEIN
18 Vice President Facilities Mgmt ....Mr. Juan M. GUERRA, JR.
09 Asst Vice Pres COI Research Reg Aff ....Ms. Angela WISHON
20 Vice Pres Chief COO Academic Affairs ....Mr. Cameron SLOCUM
88 Assoc Vice Pres Ambulatory Care ....Dr. Stan TAYLOR
17 Chief Med Officer University Hosp ....Dr. Steven LEACH
88 Assoc Vice Pres Chief Nursing Ofcr ....Ms. Susan HERNANDEZ
96 Asst Vice Pres Materials Mgmt ....Mr. Charles COBB
88 Assoc Vice Pres & Clinical Exec Neu ....Dr. Christopher MADDEN
88 Assoc Vice Pres Parkland HHS Aff ....Dr. Carlos GIROD
27 Asst Vice Pres Marketing ....Ms. Dorothea BONDS
27 Asst Vice President Communication ....Mr. Mark LANE
21 Asst Vice Pres Acctg Fiscal Svcs ....Ms. Sharon LEARY
08 Asst Vice Pres Library Services ....Ms. Kelly GONZALEZ
20 Vice Provost Sr Assoc Dean Ed ....Dr. Charles M. GINSBURG
20 Vice Provost Sr Assoc Dean Faculty ....Dr. Dwain L. THIELE
28 Assoc Dean Faculty Diversity & Dev ....Dr. Byron L. CRYER
88 Assoc Dean Global Health ....Dr. Fiemu E. NWARIAKU
63 Assoc Dean Grad Medical Education ....Dr. Bradley MARPLE
63 Assoc Dean Undergrad Medical Educ ....Dr. Robert REGE
32 Assoc Dean Student Affairs ....Dr. Angela MIHALIC
88 Assoc Dean Credentialing Ed Outcome ....Dr. James M. WAGNER
32 Assoc Dean Student Affairs ....Dr. Blake BARKER
93 Assoc Dean Student Diversity & Incl ....Dr. Shawna NESBITT
58 Dean Grad School Biomedical Science ....Dr. Andrew ZINN
76 Dean School of Health Professions ....Dr. Jon WILLIAMSON
06 Assistant Registrar ....Ms. Deborah CHEN
07 Assoc Director of Admissions ....Ms. Anne P. MCLANE
11 Assoc VP/Chief Operating Officer ....Ms. Becky MCCULLEY
88 Assoc Vice Pres Health System Mgmt ....Mr. Suresh GUNASEKARAN
108 Asst Vice Pres Academic Plng Assmnt ....Mr. James DRAKE
111 Exec VP Institutional Advancement ....Dr. Marc A. NIVET
37 Director Student Financial Aid ....Ms. Melet LEAFGREEN
84 Director Enrollment Services ....Ms. Shannon WILLIAMS

Vernon College (F)

4400 College Drive, Vernon TX 76384-4092

County: Wilbarger FICE Identification: 010060
Unit ID: 229504
Telephone: (940) 552-6291 Carnegie Class: Assoc/MT-VT-High Non
FAX Number: (940) 553-3902 Calendar System: Semester
URL: www.vernoncollege.edu
Established: 1970 Annual Undergrad Tuition & Fees (In-District): $3,150
Enrollment: 2,891 Coed
Affiliation or Control: State/Local IRS Status: 501(c)3
Highest Offering: Associate Degree
Accreditation: **SC**, CAHIIM, SURGT

01 President ....Dr. Dusty R. JOHNSTON
04 Admin Secretary to the President ....Ms. Mary KING
05 Dean of Instructional Services ....Vacant
10 Dean of Administrative Services ....Mr. Garry DAVID
32 Dean of Student Services ....Mr. James NORDONE, JR.
07 Dean Admiss/Registr/Financial Aid ....Mr. Joe HITE
103 Assoc Dean of Instructional Service ....Ms. Shana DRURY
30 Dir Inst Advance/VC Foundation ....Ms. Michelle ALEXANDER
88 Director of Quality Enhancement ....Ms. Criquett LEHMAN
09 Dir of Institutional Effectiveness ....Mrs. Betsy HARKEY
37 Director Financial Aid ....Mrs. Melissa J. ELLIOTT
08 Director of Library Services ....Ms. Marion GRONA
18 Director Physical Plant ....Mr. Lyle BONNER
15 Director of Human Resources ....Mrs. Haven DAVID
39 Director of Housing ....Ms. Kelly EASON
35 Assoc Dean of Student Services ....Mrs. Kristin HARRIS
06 Director of Admissions & Records ....Mrs. Amanda RAINES
66 Dir Associate Degree in Nursing ....Mrs. Mary RIVARD
66 Dir Licensed Vocational Nursing ....Ms. Sherri DENHEM
35 Director of Student Activities ....Ms. Shealeigh JONES
19 Director of Campus Police ....Mr. Kevin HOLLAND
41 Athletic Director ....Mr. James NORDONE, JR.

Vet Tech Institute of Houston (G)

4669 Southwest Freeway, Suite 100, Houston TX 77027

County: Harris FICE Identification: 021448
Unit ID: 223472
Telephone: (713) 629-8940 Carnegie Class: Spec 2-yr-Health
FAX Number: (713) 629-0059 Calendar System: Semester
URL: www.vettechinstitute.edu/houston
Established: 2007 Annual Undergrad Tuition & Fees: $14,320
Enrollment: 254 Coed
Affiliation or Control: Proprietary IRS Status: Proprietary
Highest Offering: Associate Degree
Accreditation: **ACICS**

01 Director/Chief Academic Officer ....Mr. Elbert HAMILTON, JR.

Victoria College (A)

2200 E Red River, Victoria TX 77901-4494
County: Victoria FICE Identification: 003662
Unit ID: 229540
Telephone: (361) 573-3291 Carnegie Class: Assoc/MT-VT-High Trad
FAX Number: (361) 572-3850 Calendar System: Semester
URL: www.victoriacollege.edu
Established: 1925 Annual Undergrad Tuition & Fees (In-District): $2,640
Enrollment: 4,051 Coed
Affiliation or Control: Local IRS Status: 501(c)3
Highest Offering: Associate Degree
Accreditation: SC, ADNUR, #COARC, EMT, PTAA

01 President .... Dr. David HINDS
05 Int Vice President of Instruction .... Ms. Cindy BUCHHOLZ
10 Vice Pres Administrative Svcs .... Mr. Keith BLUNDELL
32 Interim Dean of Student Services .... Ms. Jackie MIKESH
111 VP College Advance/External Affairs .... Ms. Jennifer L. YANCEY
09 Dir Inst Effect/Research/Assess .... Ms. Patricia REHAK
08 Director of Libraries .... Dr. Joe F. DAHLSTROM
07 Director of Enrollment Services .... Dr. Edrel STONEHAM
18 Director Physical Plant .... Dr. Larry GARRETT
37 Director Financial Aid .... Ms. Kim OBSTA
15 Director Human Resources .... Ms. Terri KURTZ
26 Dir Marketing & Communications .... Mr. Darin KAZMIR
38 Director Advising/Counseling .... Mr. Robert CUBRIEL, III
96 Director of Purchasing .... Ms. Lydia HUBER
21 Director of Finance .... Ms. Tracey BERGSTROM
35 Student Center/Activities Director .... Ms. Elaine EVERETT-HENSLEY
13 Director Technology Services .... Mr. Andy FARRIOR
04 Exec Admin Asst to President .... Ms. Mary Ann RODRIGUEZ
102 Exec Dir of College Advance & Found .... Ms. Amy MUNDY

Virginia College (B)

5005 50th Street, Lubbock TX 79414
Telephone: (806) 784-1900 Identification: 770547
Accreditation: ACICS

† Branch campus of Virginia College, Birmingham, AL

Virginia College Austin (C)

14200 North Interstate 35, Austin TX 78728
Telephone: (512) 371-3500 Identification: 666074
Accreditation: ACICS, #COARC, DMS, SURGT

† Branch campus of Virginia College, Birmingham, AL.

Vista College (D)

3440 Bell Street, Suite 100, Amarillo TX 79109
Telephone: (806) 372-3700 Identification: 770548
Accreditation: COE

Vista College (E)

6101 Montana Avenue, El Paso TX 79925-2021
County: El Paso FICE Identification: 025720
Unit ID: 365204
Telephone: (915) 779-8031 Carnegie Class: Assoc/HVT-High Non
FAX Number: (915) 779-8097 Calendar System: Semester
URL: www.vistacollege.edu
Established: 1987 Annual Undergrad Tuition & Fees: $15,550
Enrollment: 4,349 Coed
Affiliation or Control: Proprietary IRS Status: Proprietary
Highest Offering: Associate Degree
Accreditation: COE

01 Campus Director .... Mr. Antonio RICO
06 Registrar .... Ms. Valerie PARKS
07 Assoc Director of Admissions .... Mr. Andre RAYOS
37 Director Student Financial Aid .... Ms. Adrianna DURAN
63 Program Director Allied Health .... Ms. Juana CERVANTES
36 Sr Career Services Coordinator .... Ms. Amanda CUSEO

Vista College (F)

4620 50th Street, Lubbock TX 79414
Telephone: (806) 785-2100 Identification: 770549
Accreditation: COE

Vista College-Online (G)

300 N. Coit Road, Suite 300, Richardson TX 75080
County: Davis FICE Identification: 025728
Unit ID: 377342
Telephone: (972) 707-8600 Carnegie Class: Bac/Assoc-Assoc Dom
FAX Number: (972) 707-8575 Calendar System: Other
URL: www.vistacollege.edu/online/
Established: Annual Undergrad Tuition & Fees: N/A
Enrollment: 345 Coed
Affiliation or Control: Proprietary IRS Status: Proprietary
Highest Offering: Baccalaureate
Accreditation: ACCSC

01 Director .... Mr. Art WALLER

Wade College (H)

1950 Stemmons Fwy, Ste 4080, LB 562, Dallas TX 75207
County: Dallas FICE Identification: 010130
Unit ID: 226879
Telephone: (214) 637-3530 Carnegie Class: Bac/Assoc-Mixed
FAX Number: (214) 637-0827 Calendar System: Trimester
URL: www.wadecollege.edu
Established: 1962 Annual Undergrad Tuition & Fees: $13,675
Enrollment: 202 Coed
Affiliation or Control: Proprietary IRS Status: Proprietary
Highest Offering: Baccalaureate
Accreditation: SC

01 President .... Dr. Harry DAVROS
03 Vice President .... Mr. John CONTE
05 Director of Academic Affairs .... Ms. Elizabeth JOHNSTON
11 Director of Institutional Support .... Ms. Kim PARKER
08 Head Librarian .... Mrs. Bobbie BAUMGARTEN
36 Director of Career Services .... Mrs. Jennifer MAGEE
07 Director of Admissions .... Mr. John FLORES
37 Director Student Financial Aid .... Ms. Lisa HOOVER

Wayland Baptist University (I)

1900 West Seventh Street, Plainview TX 79072-6998
County: Hale FICE Identification: 003663
Unit ID: 229780
Telephone: (806) 291-1000 Carnegie Class: Masters/L
FAX Number: (806) 291-1960 Calendar System: Semester
URL: www.wbu.edu
Established: 1908 Annual Undergrad Tuition & Fees: $15,060
Enrollment: 5,231 Coed
Affiliation or Control: Southern Baptist IRS Status: 501(c)3
Highest Offering: Doctorate
Accreditation: SC, MUS, NUR

01 President .... Dr. Bobby L. HALL
05 Vice Pres of Academic Affairs .... Dr. Cindy M. MCCLENAGAN
84 Vice Pres Enrollment Management .... Dr. D. Claude LUSK
20 Vice Pres of External Campuses .... Dr. Elane SEEBO
10 Chief Financial Officer .... Mrs. Lezlie HUKILL
12 Exec Dir/Campus Dean Albuquerque .... Dr. Tom FISHER
12 Exec Dir/Campus Dean Altus .... Dr. Jerry FAUGHT
12 Exec Dir/Campus Dean Amarillo .... Dr. J. B BOREN
12 Exec Dir/Campus Dean Anchorage .... Dr. Eric ASH
12 Exec Dir/Campus Dean Clovis .... Dr. Gary MITCHELL
12 Exec Dir/Campus Dean Fairbanks .... Dr. Ernie RAHN
12 Exec Dir/Campus Dean Hawaii .... Dr. Dan JACOBSON
12 Exec Dir/Campus Dean Lubbock .... Dr. David BISHOP
12 Exec Dir/Campus Dean Phoenix .... Dr. D. Glenn SIMMONS
12 Exec Dir/Campus Dean San Antonio .... Dr. James ANTENEN
12 Exec Dir/Campus Dean Sierra Vista .... Vacant
12 Exec Dir/Campus Dean Wichita Falls .... Dr. Dean DANIEL
83 Acad Dean School Behav & Soc Sci .... Dr. Peter BOWEN
50 Academic Dean School of Business .... Dr. Barry W. EVANS
53 Academic Dean School of Education .... Dr. Gene WHITFILL
57 Academic Dean School of Fine Arts .... Dr. Marti R. RUNNELS
79 Academic Dean School of Lang & Lit .... Dr. Laura C. BRANDENBURG
81 Academic Dean School Math/Sciences .... Dr. Scott FRANKILIN
64 Academic Dean School of Music .... Dr. Ann B. STUTES
66 Academic Dean School of Nursing .... Dr. Diane FRAZOR
73 Academic Dean School Rel & Phil .... Dr. Clinton LOWIN
06 University Registrar .... Mrs. Julie BOWEN
32 Exec Dir Student Services .... Mr. Brad MILES
30 Executive Dir Univ Advancement .... Mr. Mike MELCHER
41 Dir of Intercollegiate Athletics .... Mr. Rick COOPER
07 Exec Dir Admissions & Recruiting .... Mr. Chad CAIN
07 Director of Admissions .... Mrs. Debbie STENNETT
29 Director Alumni Relations .... Mrs. Teresa YOUNG
88 Dir Church & Denominational Rel .... Dr. Paul SADLER
44 Director of Annual Fund .... Vacant
30 Director of Development .... Mrs. Amber MCCLOUD
37 Director of Financial Aid .... Mrs. Karen LAQUEY
58 Director of Graduate Studies .... Ms. Amanda STANTON
15 Director of HR & Wellness Mgr .... Mr. Ron APPLING
13 Director Information Technology .... Mrs. Katrina SMITH
09 Dir Inst Research/Effectiveness .... Dr. Andy PAGEL
12 Director of the Kenya Program .... Dr. Richard SHAW
08 Director of Libraries .... Dr. Polly R. LACKEY
88 Director Property Management .... Mr. Danny W. MURPHREE
26 Director of Communications .... Mr. Jonathan PETTY
23 Director of Health Services .... Vacant
39 Coordinator of Student Housing .... Mrs. Nancy KEITH
38 Dir Counseling/Career/Disability .... Ms. Teresa MOORE
40 Director of University Store .... Mr. Brad HENDERSON
106 Director of Virtual Campus .... Dr. Trish RITSCHEL-TRIFILO
105 Director of Web Services .... Mrs. Charlotte SCHUMACHER
88 Dir BAS/BCM & Assoc Registrar .... Dr. Daniel BROWN
19 WBU Chief of Police .... Mr. Lonnie BURTON
18 Chief Facilities/Physical Plant .... Mr. David MURPHREE
04 Exec Asst to President .... Mrs. Cynthia TREVINO

Weatherford College (J)

225 College Park Drive, Weatherford TX 76086-5699
County: Parker FICE Identification: 003664
Unit ID: 229799
Telephone: (817) 594-5471 Carnegie Class: Assoc/HT-High Trad
FAX Number: (817) 598-6210 Calendar System: Semester
URL: www.wc.edu
Established: 1869 Annual Undergrad Tuition & Fees (In-District): $2,440
Enrollment: 5,483 Coed
Affiliation or Control: Local IRS Status: 501(c)3
Highest Offering: Associate Degree
Accreditation: SC, ADNUR, COARC, DMS, EMT, OTA, PHLEB, PTAA, RAD

01 Interim President .... Mr. Brent BAKER
04 Exec Asst to the President .... Mrs. Theresa R. HUTCHISON
32 VP of Inst & Student Services .... Mr. Michael ENDY
10 Exec VP Financial/Admin Affairs .... Mrs. Andra R. CANTRELL
30 Vice Pres Institutional Advancement .... Mr. Brent BAKER
76 Dean of Health & Human Sciences .... Ms. Katherine BOSWELL
05 Executive Dean of Academics .... Vacant
53 Dean Educational/Instructional Sppt .... Ms. Rhonda TORRES
35 Executive Dean of Student Services .... Mr. Adam FINLEY
103 Assoc Dean Workforce/Economic Devel .... Mrs. Janetta KRUSE
26 Dir Communications/Public Relations .... Mrs. Crystal WOERLY
31 Dean of Community Programs .... Mr. Duane DURRETT
88 Director Industrial/Transportation .... Mr. Terry PILGRIM
09 Dir Inst Research and Assessment .... Mr. Lee BUTLER
35 Exec Director Student Development .... Mr. Doug JEFFERSON
36 Dir of Career and Transfer Center .... Mr. John TURNTINE
109 Director Food Services .... Ms. Erin DAVIDSON
37 Director Student Financial Aid .... Mr. Donnie PURVIS
21 Controller .... Mrs. Rebecca DEPUY
15 Director Human Resources .... Mrs. Ralinda STONE
07 Director of Admissions/Veterans .... Mr. Ralph WILLINGHAM
13 Director Technology Services .... Mr. Greg SHRADER
08 Director of Library Services .... Mrs. Valorie STARR
18 Director of Facilities .... Ms. Rhonda SWAN
96 Director of Purchasing .... Mrs. Jeanie HOBBS
45 Director of Resource Development .... Vacant
19 Chief of Campus Police .... Mr. Paul STONE
38 Student Counseling .... Ms. Phyllis TIFFIN
88 Director Upward Bound .... Mr. Jeff KHALDEN
29 Director Alumni Relations .... Mr. Brent BAKER
103 Director of Workforce Education .... Ms. Janetta KRUSE
53 Director of Teacher Education .... Dr. Joyce MELTON PAGES
06 Registrar .... Mrs. Vicki TRAWEEK
88 Director of Testing .... Ms. Lela MORRIS
88 Dir of Outreach/Student Success .... Ms. Kay LANDRUM
88 Director Special Populations .... Mrs. Dawn KAHLDEN
39 Director Student Housing .... Miss Faith STIFFLER
41 Athletic Director .... Mr. Bob MCKINLEY

West Coast University (K)

8435 N Stemmons Freeway, Dallas TX 75247-3900
Telephone: (214) 453-4533 Identification: 770485
Accreditation: &WC

† Branch campus of West Coast University, North Hollywood, CA

Western Technical College (L)

9624 Plaza Circle, El Paso TX 79927-2105
County: El Paso FICE Identification: 020983
Unit ID: 224679
Telephone: (915) 532-3737 Carnegie Class: Assoc/HVT-High Trad
FAX Number: (915) 532-6946 Calendar System: Other
URL: www.westerntech.edu
Established: 1969 Annual Undergrad Tuition & Fees: N/A
Enrollment: 1,020 Coed
Affiliation or Control: Proprietary IRS Status: Proprietary
Highest Offering: Associate Degree
Accreditation: ACCSC, PTAA

01 President/Director .... Mr. Allan SHARPE
88 Assistant Director .... Mr. Randy KUYKENDALL
11 Chief Administrative Officer .... Mr. Bill TERRELL
12 Executive VP/Campus School Director .... Ms. Mary CANO
07 VP Admissions/Marketing .... Ms. Lynda CERVANTES
05 Academic Dean (Diana) .... Ms. Marsha LAWLER
10 Accounting Controller .... Ms. Laura PLUMMER
37 Student Financial Services Director .... Ms. Danielle PICCHI
36 Director Career Services .... Ms. Helen GARCIA
13 Director Information Technology .... Mr. Jose PEREZ

Western Technical College (M)

9451 Diana Drive, El Paso TX 79924-6936
Telephone: (915) 566-9621 Identification: 666103
Accreditation: ACCSC

Western Texas College (N)

6200 College Avenue, Snyder TX 79549-6189
County: Scurry FICE Identification: 009549
Unit ID: 229832
Telephone: (325) 573-8511 Carnegie Class: Assoc/MT-VT-High Non
FAX Number: (325) 573-9321 Calendar System: Semester
URL: www.wtc.edu
Established: 1969 Annual Undergrad Tuition & Fees (In-District): $2,018
Enrollment: 2,124 Coed
Affiliation or Control: State/Local IRS Status: 501(c)3
Highest Offering: Associate Degree
Accreditation: SC

01 President .... Dr. Barbara R. BEEBE
04 Assistant to the President .... Ms. Melanie SCHWERTNER
10 Chief Financial Officer .... Ms. Patricia CLAXTON
11 Chief Operation Officer .... Mr. Mike THORTON
09 Dean Inst Research & Effectiveness .... Mr. Britt CANADA
05 Dean of Instructional Affairs .... Ms. Stephanie DUCHENEAUX

32 Dean of Student Services .... Mr. Ralph RAMON
72 Dean of Technology .... Mr. Roy BARTELS
103 Dean Workforce Development .... Vacant
41 Athletic Director .... Ms. Tammy DAVIS
06 Registrar .... Ms. Ann GALYEAN
37 Director Financial Aid .... Mr. Greg TORRES
21 Controller .... Ms. Marjann MORROW
15 Director of Human Resources .... Ms. Sheila WILLIAMSON
85 Dir International Student Services .... Ms. Melissa DOUCETTE
96 Director of Purchasing & Compliance .... Mr. Mitch CALHOUN

Wharton County Junior College (A)

911 Boling Highway, Wharton TX 77488-3298
County: Wharton FICE Identification: 003668
Unit ID: 229841
Telephone: (979) 532-4560 Carnegie Class: Assoc/MT-VT-Mix Trad/Non
FAX Number: (979) 532-6526 Calendar System: Semester
URL: www.wcjc.edu
Established: 1946 Annual Undergrad Tuition & Fees (In-District): $2,222
Enrollment: 7,416 Coed
Affiliation or Control: Local IRS Status: 501(c)3
Highest Offering: Associate Degree
Accreditation: **SC**, CAHIIM, CSHSE, DH, EMT, PTAA, RAD, SURGT

01 President .... Ms. Betty A. MCCROHAN
05 Vice President of Instruction .... Ms. Leigh Ann COLLINS
11 Vice President Administrative Svcs .... Mr. Bryce KOCIAN
13 Vice President of Technology & IR .... Ms. Pamela YOUNGBLOOD
32 Vice President of Student Services .... Mr. David LEENHOUTS
21 Dean of Financial & Business Svcs .... Mr. Gus WESSELS
26 Director of Marketing & Comm .... Ms. Zina CARTER
06 Registrar .... Ms. Karen PREISLER
37 Director of Financial Aid .... Mr. Richard D. HYDE
08 Director Library Info/Tech Services .... Ms. Kwei HSU
18 Director of Facilities Management .... Mr. Mike FEYEN
15 Director of Human Resources .... Ms. Judy JONES
09 Director of Inst Effectiveness .... Vacant
96 Director of Purchasing .... Mr. Philip WUTHRICH
101 Secretary of the Institution/Board .... Mrs. Deanna FEYEN
19 Director Security/Safety .... Mr. Danny TERRONEZ
41 Athletic Director .... Mr. Gene BAHNSEN

Wiley College (B)

711 Wiley Avenue, Marshall TX 75670-5199
County: Harrison FICE Identification: 003669
Unit ID: 229887
Telephone: (903) 927-3300 Carnegie Class: Bac-Diverse
FAX Number: (903) 938-8100 Calendar System: Semester
URL: www.wileyc.edu
Established: 1873 Annual Undergrad Tuition & Fees: $12,064
Enrollment: 1,172 Coed
Affiliation or Control: United Methodist IRS Status: 501(c)3
Highest Offering: Baccalaureate
Accreditation: **SC**, ACBSP

01 President and CEO .... Dr. Haywood L. STRICKLAND
03 Executive Vice President .... Dr. Glenda F. CARTER
10 Vice Pres for Business & Finance .... Dr. James BATTEN
05 Provost/VP Academic Affairs .... Dr. Gloria P. JAMES
32 Vice President Student Affairs .... Dr. Joseph L. MORALE
111 Vice Pres Institutional Advancement .... Vacant
84 Vice Pres for Enrollment Services .... Mr. Antonio M. BOYLE
13 Director Info Technology .... Mr. Chris WATSON
21 Director of Finance .... Mrs. Dawn JONES
53 Dean of Education .... Dr. Calandra LOCKHART
42 College Chaplain .... Rev. Tabitha RANKIN
04 Special Assistant to the President .... Mrs. Karen HELTON
50 Dean of Business & Technology .... Dr. Abdalla F. HAGAN
49 Dean of Sciences .... Dr. John G. STUART
79 Dean Social Sciences & Humanities .... Dr. Bernadette L. BRUSTER
26 Director of Public Relations .... Ms. Tammy TAYLOR
08 Director of Library Services .... Mr. Christopher ALTNAU
06 Registrar .... Ms. Laura LANDER
07 Director of Admissions .... Ms. Jamecia MURRAY
15 Director of Human Resources .... Mrs. Krystal MOODY
18 Superintendent of Facilities .... Vacant
37 Director of Financial Aid .... Mr. Kareem MCELMORE
29 Director of Alumni Relations .... Ms. Alvena JONES
09 Director of Institutional Research .... Mr. Daniel NYACHUBA
11 Director Administrative Svcs .... Mr. O. Ivan WHITE
23 College Nurse .... Ms. Shonte EPPERSON
41 Acting Director of Athletics .... Dr. Joseph L. MORALE
96 Director of Purchasing .... Mr. Darius Z. KIMBLE
35 Director of Student Development .... Vacant
101 Secretary of the Institution/Board .... Mrs. Cassandra M. JOHNSON
106 Dir Online Education/E-learning .... Vacant
19 Director Security/Safety .... Mr. Winston ROBINSON
39 Director of Residence Life .... Mr. Howard FISHER
43 Dir Legal Services/General Counsel .... Dr. Kim BEATON
112 Director Major Gifts/Planned Giving .... Mr. Charles CORNISH
90 Director Academic Computing .... Vacant
100 Chief of Staff .... Dr. Charles N. SMITH

UTAH

Argosy University, Salt Lake City (C)

121 Election Road Suite 300, Draper UT 84020-7724
Telephone: (801) 601-5000 Identification: 666655
Accreditation: **&WC**, ACBSP, MFCD

† Regional accreditation is carried under the parent institution in Orange, CA.

The Art Institute of Salt Lake City (D)

121 West Election Road, Draper UT 84020
Telephone: (801) 601-4700 Identification: 666694
Accreditation: **#ACICS**

† Branch campus of The Art Institute of Phoenix, AZ. School is in teach-out plan.

Brigham Young University (E)

Provo UT 84602-0002
County: Utah FICE Identification: 003670
Unit ID: 230038
Telephone: (801) 422-4000 Carnegie Class: DU-Higher
FAX Number: (801) 422-0684 Calendar System: Semester
URL: www.byu.edu
Established: 1875 Annual Undergrad Tuition & Fees: $5,300
Enrollment: 33,469 Coed
Affiliation or Control: Latter-day Saints IRS Status: 501(c)3
Highest Offering: Doctorate
Accreditation: **NW**, ART, CAATE, CAEPT, CLPSY, COPSY, CS, DANCE, DIETD, DIETI, ENG, ENGR, ENGT, IPSY, JOUR, LAW, MFCD, MT, MUS, NRPA, NURSE, PH, SP, SPAA, SW, THEA

01 President .... Dr. Kevin J. WORTHEN
05 Academic Vice President .... Mr. James R. RASBAND
11 Administrative Vice President .... Mr. Brian K. EVANS
111 Advancement Vice President .... Dr. Matthew O. RICHARDSON
13 Vice Pres Info Tech/Chief Info Ofcr .... Dr. J. Kelly FLANAGAN
88 International Vice President .... Dr. Sandra ROGERS
32 Student Life Vice President .... Dr. Janet S. SCHARMAN
43 Asst to President/General Counsel .... Mr. Michael R. ORME
45 Asst to Pres Planning/Assessment .... Mr. James D. GORDON, III
26 Asst to Pres Univ Communications .... Mrs. Carri P. JENKINS
20 Assoc Acad Vice President Faculty .... Dr. Craig H. HART
20 Assoc Acad VP Undergraduate Stds .... Dr. Brad L. NEIGER
46 Assoc Acad VP Research/Grad Stds .... Dr. Alan R. HARKER
35 Assoc Student Life Vice Pres .... Dr. Ronald K. CHAPMAN
10 Chief Financial Officer .... Mr. Brian K. EVANS
18 Asst Admin VP Physical Facilities .... Mr. Ole M. SMITH
15 Asst Admin VP Human Resource Svcs .... Mr. Brad TAYLOR
35 Asst Admin VP/Stdnt Auxiliary Svc .... Mr. Carr KRUEGER
29 Managing Dir Alumni/Ext Rels .... Mr. McKay CHRISTENSEN
30 Managing Dir LDS Philanthropies .... Dr. Tanise CHUNG-HOON
121 Exec Dir Stdnt Acad/Advisement Svcs .... Mr. Christian FAULCONER
35 Dean Student Life .... Mr. Vernon L. HEPERI
37 Director Financial Aid/Scholarships .... Mr. Steven E. HILL
88 Dean Undergraduate Education .... Dr. Susan RUGH
08 University Librarian .... Ms. Jennifer PAUSTENBAUGH
58 Dean Graduate Studies .... Dr. Wynn C. STIRLING
51 Dean Continuing Education .... Dr. Lee GLINES
47 Dean Life Sciences .... Dr. James P. PORTER
54 Dean Engineering & Technology .... Dr. Michael E. JENSEN
83 Dean Family Home & Social Science .... Dr. Benjamin M. OGLES
57 Dean Fine Arts & Communications .... Dr. Edward E. ADAMS
79 Dean Humanities .... Dr. J. Scott MILLER
61 Dean Law School .... Dr. D. Gordon SMITH
50 Dean Marriott School Management .... Dr. Lee T. PERRY
53 Dean McKay School of Education .... Dr. Mary Ann PRATER
81 Dean Physical & Math Science .... Dr. Scott D. SOMMERFELDT
66 Dean Nursing .... Dr. Patricia RAVERT
73 Dean Religious Education .... Dr. Brent TOP
38 Director Counseling & Career Ctr .... Dr. Steve A. SMITH
09 Dir Institutional Assess/Analysis .... Dr. Danny R. OLSEN
06 Registrar .... Mr. Barry ALLRED
07 Director of Admissions .... Ms. Lori GARDINER
96 Director of Purchasing .... Mr. W. Timothy HILL
88 Dir University Accessibility Center .... Dr. Gerilynn VORKINK
19 Director Security/Safety .... Mr. Larry STOTT
39 Director Student Housing .... Ms. Julie FRANKLIN
41 Athletic Director .... Mr. Tom HOLMOE

Broadview Entertainment Arts University (F)

240 East Morris Avenue, Salt Lake City UT 84115
Telephone: (801) 300-4300 Identification: 770809
Accreditation: **ACICS**

Broadview University (G)

1902 W 7800 S, West Jordan UT 84088-4021
County: Salt Lake FICE Identification: 011166
Unit ID: 230056
Telephone: (801) 542-7600 Carnegie Class: Spec-4-yr-Other Health
FAX Number: (801) 542-7601 Calendar System: Quarter
URL: www.broadviewuniversity.edu
Established: 1971 Annual Undergrad Tuition & Fees: $14,400
Enrollment: 160 Coed
Affiliation or Control: Proprietary IRS Status: Proprietary
Highest Offering: Master's
Accreditation: **ACICS**, MAAB

01 President .... Mr. Terry MYHRE
05 Director .... Ms. Crystal DEWEERD

Eagle Gate College (H)

915 North 400 West, Layton UT 84041
Telephone: (801) 546-7500 Identification: 770812
Accreditation: **ACICS**

Eagle Gate College (I)

5588 S Green Street, Suite 150, Murray UT 84123-6965
County: Salt Lake FICE Identification: 021785
Unit ID: 230366
Telephone: (801) 333-8100 Carnegie Class: Bac/Assoc-Mixed
FAX Number: (801) 263-6520 Calendar System: Other
URL: www.eaglegatecollege.edu
Established: 1979 Annual Undergrad Tuition & Fees: $14,297
Enrollment: 353 Coed
Affiliation or Control: Proprietary IRS Status: Proprietary
Highest Offering: Baccalaureate
Accreditation: **ACICS**, NURSE

01 Campus President .... Mr. Todd SMITH

Fortis College (J)

3949 South 700 East, Suite 150, Salt Lake City UT 84107
Telephone: (801) 713-0915 Identification: 666762
Accreditation: **ACCSC**, ADNUR, DH

† Tuition varies by degree program.

Independence University (K)

4021 South 700 East, Suite 400,
Salt Lake City UT 84107-2453
County: Salt Lake FICE Identification: 022061
Unit ID: 465812
Telephone: (801) 290-3240 Carnegie Class: Spec-4-yr-Other Health
FAX Number: (801) 263-0345 Calendar System: Other
URL: www.independence.edu
Established: 1978 Annual Undergrad Tuition & Fees: $16,968
Enrollment: 6,025 Coed
Affiliation or Control: Independent Non-Profit IRS Status: 501(c)3
Highest Offering: Master's
Accreditation: **ACCSC**, #COARC, NURSE

01 President .... Mr. Eric JUHLIN

LDS Business College (L)

95 North 300 West, Salt Lake City UT 84101-3500
County: Salt Lake FICE Identification: 003672
Unit ID: 230418
Telephone: (801) 524-8100 Carnegie Class: Assoc/MT-VT-High Trad
FAX Number: (801) 524-1900 Calendar System: Semester
URL: www.ldsbc.edu
Established: 1886 Annual Undergrad Tuition & Fees: $3,240
Enrollment: 2,153 Coed
Affiliation or Control: Latter-day Saints IRS Status: 501(c)3
Highest Offering: Associate Degree
Accreditation: **NW**, #MAC

01 President .... Dr. Bruce C. KUSCH
04 Executive Admin Asst .... Ms. Jolynn T. WOLFGRAMM
05 Chief Academic Officer .... Craig D. BELL
13 Chief Information Officer .... Mr. Mark R. AUGHENBAUGH
50 Director of Strategic Initiatives .... Mr. Robert O. SALMON
88 Director of Academic Programs .... Ms. Cathy T. CAREY
20 Dean of Instructional Support .... Mr. Tyler S. MORGAN
15 Director of Human Resources .... Mr. Brady J. KIMBER
26 Director of Public Affairs .... Mr. Howard M. COLLETT
36 Director of Career Services .... Mr. Justin K. JONES
06 Registrar .... Ms. Tamra TAYLOR
08 Dir of Library/Inform Resources .... Ms. Sarah SORENSEN
21 Controller .... Mr. Chris REITZ
37 Student Financial Services Manager .... Ms. Melanie CONOVER
40 Bookstore Manager .... Ms. Rachel BINGHAM

Midwives College of Utah (M)

1174 E Graystone Way Suite 2,
Salt Lake City UT 84106-2671
County: Utah Identification: 666281
Unit ID: 480985
Telephone: (866) 680-2756 Carnegie Class: Spec-4-yr-Other Health
FAX Number: (866) 207-2024 Calendar System: Semester
URL: www.midwifery.edu
Established: 1980 Annual Undergrad Tuition & Fees: $6,349
Enrollment: 236 Coed
Affiliation or Control: Independent Non-Profit IRS Status: 501(c)3
Highest Offering: Master's
Accreditation: **MEAC**

01 President .... Ms. Kristi RIDD-YOUNG
05 Academic Dean .... Ms. Tamara TAITT
17 Clinical Director .... Ms. Maria CRANFORD
06 Registrar .... Ms. Laura PARK
08 Head Librarian .... Ms. Kaylee RIDD
07 Admissions .... Ms. Mel SMITH-TOURVILLE
13 Chief Info Technology Officer (CIO) .... Mr. Alan BELLOWS
37 Financial Aid Director .... Ms. Whitney MESYEF
58 Graduate Dean .... Ms. Courtney EVERSON
10 Chief Business Officer .... Ms. Julie DELONG
101 Secretary of the Institution/Board .... Ms. Jodie PALMER
26 Chief Public Relations/Marketing .... Ms. Masha MESYEF
28 Director of Diversity .... Dr. Courtney EVERSON
32 Chief Student Affairs/Student Life .... Ms. Cheryl FURER
53 Dean of Education .... Ms. Jana STUDELSKA

Neumont University (A)

143 South Main, Salt Lake City UT 84111
County: Salt Lake FICE Identification: 010098
Unit ID: 445692
Telephone: (801) 302-2800 Carnegie Class: Spec-4-yr-Other Tech
FAX Number: (801) 302-2811 Calendar System: Quarter
URL: www.neumont.edu
Established: 2003 Annual Undergrad Tuition & Fees: $24,750
Enrollment: 472 Coed
Affiliation or Control: Proprietary IRS Status: Proprietary
Highest Offering: Master's
Accreditation: ACICS

01 President/Campus Dir Utah .... Shaun MCALMONT
05 Provost .... Aaron REED
32 Dean of Student Affairs .... Corrine PADILLA
06 Registrar .... Alice NGUYEN
07 Director of Admissions .... Karick HEATON

New Charter University (B)

50 W. Broadway, Suite 300, Salt Lake City UT 84101
County: Salt Lake FICE Identification: 041292
Unit ID: 420361
Telephone: (801) 883-8336 Carnegie Class: Not Classified
FAX Number: (801) 855-5922 Calendar System: Trimester
URL: www.new.edu
Established: 1994 Annual Undergrad Tuition & Fees: N/A
Enrollment: N/A Coed
Affiliation or Control: Proprietary IRS Status: Proprietary
Highest Offering: Master's
Accreditation: DEAC

01 President .... Ms. Diane JOHNSON
05 Academic Dean .... Ms. Mary Beth FINN
10 Exec Director Business Operations .... Ms. Debbie AUSTIN
32 Manager Operations/Student Affairs .... Vacant

Nightingale College (C)

4155 Harrison Blvd, Ste 100, Ogden UT 84403
County: Weber FICE Identification: 038383
Unit ID: 444787
Telephone: (801) 689-2160 Carnegie Class: Not Classified
FAX Number: (801) 689-3114 Calendar System: Semester
URL: www.nightingale.edu
Established: 2010 Annual Undergrad Tuition & Fees: N/A
Enrollment: 237 Coed
Affiliation or Control: Proprietary IRS Status: Proprietary
Highest Offering: Baccalaureate
Accreditation: ABHES, ADNUR, NURSE

01 President/CEO .... Mr. Mikhail SHNEYDER
10 Vice Pres Operations/Controller .... Ms. Kara HARMON
26 Vice Pres Marketing & Admission .... Mr. Jonathan TANNER

Ogden-Weber Applied Technology College (D)

200 North Washington Boulevard, Ogden UT 84404-4089
County: Weber FICE Identification: 023465
Unit ID: 230490
Telephone: (801) 627-8300 Carnegie Class: Not Classified
FAX Number: (801) 395-3727 Calendar System: Other
URL: www.owatc.edu
Established: 1971 Annual Undergrad Tuition & Fees (In-District): N/A
Enrollment: 2,433 Coed
Affiliation or Control: State/Local IRS Status: 501(c)3
Highest Offering: Associate Degree
Accreditation: COE, MAC, PNUR

01 President & Chief Executive Officer .... Collette MERCIER
05 VP for Instructional Services .... James R. TAGGART
32 VP for Student Services .... Chad BURCHELL
10 VP for College Services/CFO .... Tyler CALL
04 Administrative Asst to President .... Tina SMITH
06 Registrar .... Kari MARLER
102 Dir Foundation/Corporate Relations .... Monica SCHWENK
15 Director Personnel Services .... Theresa WALKER
19 Director Security/Safety .... Fred FRAZIER
26 Dir Marketing & Diversity .... Juliane KETTERING
37 Director Student Financial Aid .... Jan BURTON

† Campus of Utah College of Applied Technology, Salt Lake City, UT.

Provo College (E)

1450 W 820 N, Provo UT 84601-1305
County: Utah FICE Identification: 023608
Unit ID: 380438
Telephone: (801) 818-8900 Carnegie Class: Assoc/HVT-High Non
FAX Number: (801) 375-9728 Calendar System: Other
URL: www.provocollege.edu
Established: 1984 Annual Undergrad Tuition & Fees: $13,516
Enrollment: 364 Coed
Affiliation or Control: Proprietary IRS Status: Proprietary
Highest Offering: Associate Degree
Accreditation: ACICS, NURSE, PTAA

01 Campus President .... Mr. Todd SMITH
05 Academic Dean .... Mrs. Jana COLYAR
10 Business Manager .... Ms. Julie BRADFORD
07 Director of Admissions .... Vacant
37 Financial Services Assoc Director .... Ms. Julie TRUJILLO
06 Registrar .... Mrs. April ACUNA
32 Dir of Placement/Student Services .... Ms. Christine ANDERSON

Rocky Mountain University of Health Professions (F)

122 East 1700 South, Building C, Provo UT 84606-7379
County: Utah FICE Identification: 041932
Unit ID: 475495
Telephone: (801) 375-5125 Carnegie Class: Spec-4-yr-Other Health
FAX Number: (801) 375-2125 Calendar System: Trimester
URL: www.rmuohp.edu
Established: 1998 Annual Graduate Tuition & Fees: N/A
Enrollment: 567 Coed
Affiliation or Control: Proprietary IRS Status: Proprietary
Highest Offering: Doctorate; No Undergraduates
Accreditation: NW, #ARCPA, NURSE, PTA, @SP

01 President .... Dr. Richard P. NIELSEN
05 Exec VP Academic Affairs/Provost .... Dr. Mark HORACEK
11 Chief Operation Officer .... Mr. Jeff B. BATE
10 Vice President Finance .... Mr. Jeff B. BATE
31 VP Inst Effect/Cmty Engagement .... Dr. Jessica D. EGBERT
84 AVP Enrollment Management .... Mr. Bryce GREENBERG
09 Exec VP Inst Effect/Strategic Int .... Dr. Sandra PENNINGTON
46 Director of Research .... Vacant
51 Director Continuing Education .... Dr. Michael SKURJA
32 Director Student Services .... Ms. Lori GORDON

Stevens-Henager College (G)

755 South Main Street, Logan UT 84321
Telephone: (435) 792-6970 Identification: 770603
Accreditation: ACCSC, MAC

Stevens-Henager College (H)

1890 South 1350 West, Ogden UT 84401
County: Weber FICE Identification: 003674
Unit ID: 230621
Telephone: (801) 622-1567 Carnegie Class: Spec-4-yr-Other Health
FAX Number: (801) 621-0853 Calendar System: Quarter
URL: www.stevenshenager.edu
Established: 1891 Annual Undergrad Tuition & Fees: $16,968
Enrollment: 226 Coed
Affiliation or Control: Independent Non-Profit IRS Status: 501(c)3
Highest Offering: Baccalaureate
Accreditation: ACCSC, MAC, SURGT

01 Pres of Ogden Campus/Regional Dir .... Ms. Vicky DEWSNUP
07 Director of Admissions .... Mr. Eric SIMPSON
32 Director of Student Services .... Mr. Doug BURCH
05 Chief Academic Officer .... Dr. Wayne HUNSAKER
10 Chief Business Officer .... Mr. Leland NEIL
36 Director Career Services .... Mr. Doug BURCH

Stevens-Henager College (I)

1476 S Sandhill Road, Orem UT 84058-7310
Telephone: (801) 418-1450 FICE Identification: 030030
Accreditation: ACCSC, MAC

Stevens-Henager College (J)

720 South River Road, Suite C-130, St. George UT 84790
Telephone: (435) 628-9902 Identification: 770604
Accreditation: ACCSC

Stevens-Henager College (K)

383 W Vine Street, Salt Lake City UT 84123
Telephone: (801) 281-7620 Identification: 666038
Accreditation: ACCSC, COARC

† Branch campus of Stevens-Henager College, Ogden, UT.

Uintah Basin Technical College (L)

1100 East Lagoon Street, Roosevelt UT 84066
County: Duchesne FICE Identification: 011165
Unit ID: 230676
Telephone: (435) 722-6900 Carnegie Class: Not Classified
FAX Number: (435) 722-6999 Calendar System: Semester
URL: www.ubtech.edu
Established: 1968 Annual Undergrad Tuition & Fees (In-State): N/A
Enrollment: 1,283 Coed
Affiliation or Control: State IRS Status: 501(c)3
Highest Offering: Associate Degree
Accreditation: COE, PNUR

01 Campus President .... Aaron K. WEIGHT
32 Vice Pres of Student Services .... Robert PETERSON
10 Vice President Fiscal Services .... Keith SPROUSE
05 Vice President Instruction .... Tammy WILKERSON
04 Exec Assistant to the President .... Trenna BALLOU
06 Registrar .... Julene OLSEN
37 Financial Aid Coordinator .... Karen SECREST
07 Admissions .... Jim LAMUTH
15 Human Resources Dir/Controller .... Shawn METCALF

† Campus of Utah College of Applied Technology, Salt Lake City, UT.

University of Phoenix Utah Campus (M)

5373 South Green Street, Salt Lake City UT 84123-4642
Telephone: (801) 263-1444 Identification: 770232
Accreditation: &NH, ACBSP, CACREP, CAEPN

† No longer accepting campus-based students.

The Utah College of Dental Hygiene at Careers Unlimited (N)

1176 S 1480 W, Orem UT 84058-4905
County: Utah FICE Identification: 034633
Unit ID: 448239
Telephone: (801) 426-8234 Carnegie Class: Spec-4-yr-Other Health
FAX Number: (801) 224-5437 Calendar System: Other
URL: www.ucdh.edu
Established: 2006 Annual Undergrad Tuition & Fees: N/A
Enrollment: 120 Coed
Affiliation or Control: Proprietary IRS Status: Proprietary
Highest Offering: Baccalaureate
Accreditation: ACCSC, DH

01 College President .... Mr. Brent MOLEN
05 College Academic Vice President .... Ms. Krista MCCLURE
00 Director Emeritus/CEO .... Mr. Kenneth MOLEN

*Utah System of Higher Education (O)

The Gateway, 60 S 400 W, Salt Lake City UT 84101-1284
County: Salt Lake FICE Identification: 009339
Telephone: (801) 321-7101 Carnegie Class: N/A
FAX Number: (801) 321-7199
URL: www.higheredutah.org

01 Exec Ofcr/Comm of Higher Education .... Dr. David L. BUHLER
05 Assoc Commissioner Academic Affairs .... Dr. Elizabeth J. HITCH
10 Assoc Commissioner Fin/Facilities .... Dr. Kimberly HENRIE
37 Exec Director Student Financial Aid .... Mr. David A. FEITZ
88 UESP Executive Director .... Ms. Lynne WARD

*The University of Utah (P)

201 South 1460 East, Salt Lake City UT 84112-1107
County: Salt Lake FICE Identification: 003675
Unit ID: 230764
Telephone: (801) 581-7200 Carnegie Class: DU-Highest
FAX Number: (801) 581-3007 Calendar System: Semester
URL: www.utah.edu
Established: 1850 Annual Undergrad Tuition & Fees (In-State): $8,518
Enrollment: 31,592 Coed
Affiliation or Control: State IRS Status: 501(c)3
Highest Offering: Doctorate
Accreditation: NW, ARCPA, AUD, CAATE, CAEP, CEA, CLPSY, COPSY, CYTO, DANCE, DENT, DIETC, ENG, ENGR, HSA, IPSY, LAW, MED, MIDWF, MT, MUS, NMT, NRPA, NURSE, OT, PH, PHAR, PLNG, PTA, SCPSY, SP, SPAA, SW

02 President .... Dr. David W. PERSHING
05 Sr Vice Pres Academic Affairs .... Dr. Ruth WATKINS
17 Sr VP Hlth Sci/CEO Univ Ut Hlth Ctr .... Dr. A. Lorris BETZ
43 Chief General Counsel .... Ms. Elizabeth DOLAN WINTER
11 Vice Pres Administrative Services .... Mr. John R. NIXON
32 Vice President Student Affairs .... Dr. Barbara H. SNYDER
111 Vice Pres Institutional Advancement .... Mr. Fred C. ESPLIN
86 Vice President Government Relations .... Mr. Jason P. PERRY
15 Assoc Vice Pres for Human Resources .... Ms. Joan GINES
46 Vice President Research .... Dr. Andrew S. WEYRICH
04 Exec Asst to the President .... Ms. Julia A. JONES
13 Chief Information Officer .... Mr. Stephen HESS
21 Chief Strategy Officer .... Ms. Patricia A. ROSS
88 Chief Global Officer .... Dr. Michael L. HARDMAN
16 Chief Human Resources Officer .... Mr. Jeff HERRING
26 Chief Mktg & Communications Officer .... Mr. William J. WARREN
20 Sr AVP AA & Dean Undergrad Studies .... Dr. Martha S. BRADLEY
84 Sr Assoc VP for Enrollment Mgmt .... Ms. Mary G. PARKER
10 Chief Financial Officer Main Campus .... Ms. Cathy ANDERSON
18 Chief Design & Construction Officer .... Ms. Robin BURR
21 Assoc VP Admin/Finance & Bus Svcs .... Mr. Jeffrey J. WEST
22 Assoc VP Equity/Diversity .... Dr. Kathryn B. STOCKTON
88 Associate Vice President Research .... Dr. Cynthia M. FURSE
88 Assoc VP Acad Affairs/Faculty .... Dr. Amy WILDERMUTH
35 AVP Student Affs/Bus/Auxil Svcs .... Dr. Jerry L. BASFORD
109 Assoc VP Admin Svc/Auxiliary Svc .... Mr. Gordon N. WILSON
58 Dean Graduate School .... Dr. David B. KIEDA
48 Dean Architecture & Planning .... Dr. Keith D. MOORE
50 Dean David Eccles Sch of Business .... Dr. Taylor RANDALL
52 Dean School of Dentistry .... Dr. Wyatt HUME
53 Dean College of Education .... Dr. Elaine CLARK
54 Dean College of Engineering .... Dr. Richard B. BROWN
57 Dean Col of Fine Arts/AVP the Arts .... Dr. John W. SCHEIB
68 Dean College of Health .... Dr. David H. PERRIN
92 Dean Honors College .... Dr. Sylvia TORTI
79 Dean College of Humanities .... Dr. Dianne HARRIS
61 Dean S J Quinney College of Law .... Dr. Robert ADLER
65 Dean Coll of Mines & Earth Science .... Dr. Darryl P. BUTT

63 Interim Dean School of Medicine ...... Dr. Wayne M. SAMUELSON
66 Dean College of Nursing .... Dr. Patricia MORTON
67 Dean College of Pharmacy .... Dr. Randall T. PETERSON
81 Dean College of Science .... Dr. Henry WHITE
83 Dean Col Social/Behav Science .... Dr. Cynthia BERG
70 Dean College of Social Work .... Dr. Martell L. TEASLEY
35 Dean of Students .... Dr. Lori MCDONALD
06 University Registrar .... Mr. Timothy J. EBNER
88 Int CEO Univ Hospitals & Clinics .... Mr. Gordon L. CRABTREE
88 Director Institutional Review Board .... Mr. John P. STILLMAN
96 Director Procurement .... Mr. Glendon G. MITCHELL
94 Chair Gender Studies .... Dr. Susie PORTER
77 Directory School of Computing .... Mr. Ross T. WHITAKER
88 Director Dental Clinic/Gen Residenc .... Dr. Craig PROCTOR
88 Asst Dean Clinical Affairs/Care .... Dr. A. J. SMITH
07 Interim Director Admissions .... Ms. Mary G. PARKER
29 Exec Director Alumni Association .... Mr. M. John ASHTON
112 Director Planned Giving .... Ms. Karin S. HARDY
37 Dir Financial Aid & Scholarships .... Ms. Brenda BURKE
08 Dean MLIB/University Librarian .... Ms. Alberta COMER
08 Interim Dir Eccles Health Sci Lib .... Ms. Melissa L. RETHLEFSEN
08 Dir S J Quinney Col of Law/Lib .... Ms. Melissa BERNSTEIN
36 Director of Career Services .... Mr. Stan D. INMAN
38 Director Counseling Center .... Dr. Lauren WEITZMAN
39 Director Housing & Res Education .... Ms. Barbara REMSBURG
39 Director Univ Student Apartments .... Ms. Jennifer G. REED
88 Dir Natural History Museum of Utah .... Dr. Sarah B. GEORGE
19 Chief of Police .... Mr. Dale G. BROPHY
40 Director Campus Bookstore .... Mr. Daniel L. ARCHER
85 Director International Center .... Ms. Chalimar L. SWAIN
41 Director Athletics .... Dr. Chris HILL
25 Dir Office of Sponsored Projects .... Mr. Brent K. BROWN
31 Dir Univ Neighborhood Partners .... Dr. Sarah MUNRO
09 Director Institutional Analysis .... Dr. Michael D. MARTINEAU

*Southern Utah University (A)

351 W University Blvd, Cedar City UT 84720-2470
County: Iron FICE Identification: 003678
Unit ID: 230603
Telephone: (435) 586-7700 Carnegie Class: Masters/L
FAX Number: (435) 586-5475 Calendar System: Semester
URL: www.suu.edu
Established: 1897 Annual Undergrad Tuition & Fees (In-State): $6,530
Enrollment: 8,881 Coed
Affiliation or Control: State IRS Status: 501(c)3
Highest Offering: Master's
Accreditation: NW, ART, CAATE, CAEP, CS, DANCE, ENG, ENGT, MUS, NURSE, SPAA

02 President .... Mr. Scott L. WYATT
05 Provost .... Dr. Bradley COOK
10 Vice Pres of Finance & Admin .... Mr. Marvin DODGE
32 Asst VP/Dean Student Services .... Mr. Jason RAMIREZ
30 Vice Pres Advance/Enrollment Mgmt .... Mr. Stuart JONES
58 Assoc Provost .... Dr. James SAGE
07 Exec Director of Admissions .... Mr. Brandon WRIGHT
18 Executive Director of FM .... Mr. Tiger FUNK
26 Exec Director Brand Strategy .... Ms. Ellen TREANOR
08 Dean/Director Library/Univ Studies .... Dr. Richard SAUNDERS
51 Dean of Continuing/Profess Studies .... Dr. Mark ATKINSON
21 Asst VP of Budget and Planning .... Mr. Mitchell BEALER
75 Director CTE .... Vacant
06 Registrar .... Mr. John ALLRED
15 Director Human Resources .... Mr. David T. MCGUIRE
88 Dean Integrative/Engaged Learning .... Dr. Patrick CLARKE
37 Director of Financial Aid .... Mr. David HUGHES
29 Vice Pres Alumni/Community Rels .... Ms. Mindy BENSON
41 Athletic Director .... Mr. Jason BUTIKOFER
43 Legal Counsel .... Ms. Ann Marie ALLEN
79 Dean Col Humanities/Soc Sci .... Vacant
50 Dean School of Business .... Vacant
53 Dean College of Education .... Dr. Shawn L. CHRISTIANSEN
81 Dean College of Sci and Engineering .... Dr. Robert EVES
57 Dean College Performing/Visual Arts .... Mrs. Shauna MENDINI
96 Director of Purchasing .... Mr. Bradley BROWN
09 Exec Dir Inst Research/Assessment .... Mr. Christian REINER
38 Director Student Counseling .... Dr. Curtis HILL

*Dixie State University (B)

225 S University Avenue, Saint George UT 84770-3876
County: Washington FICE Identification: 003671
Unit ID: 230171
Telephone: (435) 652-7500 Carnegie Class: Bac/Assoc-Mixed
FAX Number: (435) 656-4001 Calendar System: Semester
URL: www.dixie.edu
Established: 1911 Annual Undergrad Tuition & Fees (In-State): $4,840
Enrollment: 8,503 Coed
Affiliation or Control: State IRS Status: 501(c)3
Highest Offering: Baccalaureate
Accreditation: NW, ACBSP, ADNUR, CAEPT, COARC, DH, EMT, MLTAD, MT, MUS, NUR, PTAA, RAD, SURGT

02 President .... Dr. Richard B. WILLIAMS
11 Vice Pres Administrative Services .... Mr. Paul MORRIS
05 Provost/VP Academic Affairs .... Dr. Michael LACOURSE
32 Vice Pres Student Affairs .... Dr. Peter GITAU
111 Vice Pres Advancement .... Mr. Brad LAST
86 Vice President Government Relations .... Mr. Frank LOJKO
79 Dean College Humanities/Social Sci .... Dr. Richard FEATHERSTONE
66 Dean College Health Sciences .... Dr. Eliezer BERMUDEZ
50 Dean Col Business & Communication .... Dr. Kyle WELLS
81 Dean College Science & Technology .... Dr. Eric PEDERSEN
53 Dean College Education .... Dr. Brenda SABEY
51 Assoc Prov Cmty Global Outreach .... Dr. Nancy HAUCK
35 Dean of Students .... Mr. Del BEATTY
13 Chief Information Officer .... Mr. Gary J. KOEVEN
10 Asst VP of Business Services .... Mr. A. Scott TALBOT
15 Exec Director of Human Resources .... Mr. Travis ROSENBERG
18 Exec Dir Facilities Management .... Ms. Sherry RUESCH
08 Dean of the Library .... Ms. Kelly PETERSEN-FAIRCHILD
109 Executive Director Auxiliaries .... Mr. Don STECK
37 Exec Director Financial Aid .... Mr. J. D ROBERTSON
84 Asst VP Enrollment Services .... Ms. Darlene DILLEY
06 Registrar .... Ms. Julie STENDER
89 Director of New Student Programs .... Mr. Brett SCHWARTZ
121 Director of Advisement .... Mr. Mike OLSEN
26 Chief Mktg & Communication Officer .... Dr. Jordan SHARP
18 Director Facilities Operation .... Mr. Doug WHITEHEAD
19 Security Officer .... Capt. Ron ISSACSON
41 Exec Director of Athletics .... Dr. Jason BOOTHE
39 Director Housing & Residential Life .... Mr. Seth GUBLER
09 Director of Institutional Research .... Ms. Andrea BROWN
04 Assistant to the President .... Ms. Theresa BONDAD
35 Dir Student Involvement & Ldrshp .... Mr. Luke KEROUAC
96 Director of Purchasing .... Ms. Jackie FREEMAN
29 Director of Alumni Relations .... Mr. John BOWLER
36 Director of Career Services .... Ms. Ali THREET
105 Director of Network Services .... Mr. Allen FOX
25 Director of Payroll & Grants .... Ms. Krystal THOMPSON
28 Dir Multicultural Inclusion Ctr .... Ms. Daneka SOUBERBIELLE
43 General Counsel .... Mr. Doajo HICKS
91 Director Administrative Computing .... Mr. James MILLER
100 Chief of Staff .... Mr. Courtney WHITE
104 Director of Global Education .... Dr. Luis AREVALO
88 Exec Dir Acad Innovation & Ldrshp .... Mr. Bruce HARRIS
108 Director of Assessment .... Dr. Laura SNELSON

*Utah State University (C)

Logan UT 84322-0001
County: Cache FICE Identification: 003677
Unit ID: 230728
Telephone: (435) 797-1000 Carnegie Class: DU-Higher
FAX Number: (435) 797-3880 Calendar System: Semester
URL: www.usu.edu
Established: 1888 Annual Undergrad Tuition & Fees (In-State): $7,426
Enrollment: 28,622 Coed
Affiliation or Control: State IRS Status: 501(c)3
Highest Offering: Doctorate
Accreditation: NW, ART, AUD, CACREP, CAEPT, CEA, CIDA, CS, DIETC, DIETD, DIETI, ENG, ENGR, IPSY, LSAR, MFCD, MUS, PSPSY, SP, SW

02 President .... Dr. Noelle E. COCKETT
05 Interim Provost .... Dr. Laurens H. SMITH
43 General Counsel .... Ms. Mica MCKINNEY
10 Vice President Business & Finance .... Mr. Dave COWLEY
32 Vice President Student Services .... Mr. James MORALES
56 Vice Pres Extension & Agriculture .... Dr. Kenneth L. WHITE
46 VP Research/Dn Sch Graduate Stds .... Dr. Mark R. MCLELLAN
30 VP Univ Advance/Commercialization .... Mr. Robert BEHUNIN
13 CIO/Assoc VP Information Technology .... Dr. Eric HAWLEY
18 Associate VP for Facilities .... Mr. Charles DARNELL
07 Asst VP Recruitment/Enrollment Svcs .... Mr. John MORTENSEN
20 VP for Academic/Instructional Svcs .... Dr. Robert WAGNER
08 Dean Libraries .... Mr. Brad COLE
26 Exec Dir Public Relations/Marketing .... Mr. Tim VITALE
09 Dir Analysis Assess/Accreditation .... Mr. Michael TORRENS
22 Director Affirmative Action/EEO .... Ms. Stacy STURGEON
41 Athletic Director .... Mr. John HARTWELL
25 Exec Director Sponsored Programs .... Mr. Kevin PETERSON
86 Director Government Relations .... Mr. Neil N. ABERCROMBIE
15 Interim Exec Dir of Human Resources .... Mr. Chris NELSON
19 Director University Police Dept .... Mr. Steven J. MECHAM
06 Registrar .... Mr. Fran HOPKIN
36 Exec Dir Career Services/Coop Educ .... Ms. Donna E. CROW
37 Director of Financial Aid .... Ms. Patti KOHLER
38 Director Counseling Center .... Dr. David BUSH
40 Director of Campus Store .... Mr. David HANSEN
92 Director of Honors .... Ms. Kristine MILLER
96 Director of Purchasing .... Mr. Jeff CROSBIE
47 Dean of Agriculture .... Dr. Kenneth L. WHITE
57 Dean of Arts .... Dr. Craig JESSOP
50 Dean of Business .... Mr. Douglas D. ANDERSON
53 Dean of Education .... Dr. Beth FOLEY
54 Interim Dean of Engineering .... Dr. Jagath KALUARACHCHI
79 Dean Humanities/Social Science .... Dr. John C. ALLEN
65 Dean of Natural Resources .... Dr. Chris LUECKE
81 Interim Dean of Science .... Ms. Lisa BERREAU

*Utah Valley University (D)

800 W University Parkway, Orem UT 84058-5999
County: Utah FICE Identification: 004027
Unit ID: 230737
Telephone: (801) 863-8000 Carnegie Class: Masters/S
FAX Number: (801) 226-5207 Calendar System: Semester
URL: www.uvu.edu
Established: 1941 Annual Undergrad Tuition & Fees (In-State): $5,530
Enrollment: 33,211 Coed
Affiliation or Control: State IRS Status: 501(c)3
Highest Offering: Master's
Accreditation: NW, ADNUR, CAEP, CAEPT, CEA, CS, DH, EMT, ENG, IFSAC, MUS, NUR, SW

02 President .... Dr. Matthew S. HOLLAND
05 Senior Vice Pres Academic Affairs .... Dr. Jeffery E. OLSON
11 Vice Pres Finance & Administration .... Dr. Val L. PETERSON
32 Vice President Student Affairs .... Dr. Michelle O. TAYLOR
30 Vice Pres Development/Alumni .... Mr. Scott COOKSEY
26 Vice Pres University Relations .... Dr. Cameron K. MARTIN
45 VP Planning/Budgets & HR .... Ms. Linda MAKIN
10 Assoc Vice Pres Finance .... Vacant
20 Assoc Vice Pres Engaged Learning .... Dr. Frederick H. WHITE
18 Assoc Vice Pres Facilities Planning .... Mr. Frank YOUNG
20 Assoc VP Programs .... Vacant
27 Assoc VP College Mktg/Communication .... Mr. Stephen L. WHITE
20 Assoc VP Academic Affairs/Admin .... Dr. Kathren BROWN
124 Assoc VP Student Success/Retention .... Ms. Michelle KEARNS
88 Sr Dir Community College Programs .... Dr. Darrel L. HAMMON
21 Asst VP/Controller Business Svcs .... Mr. Kedric BLACK
07 Sr Director Admissions/One Stop .... Vacant
72 Dean Computing/Technology .... Dr. Saeed MOAVENI
57 Dean School of the Arts .... Dr. Newell DAYLEY
81 Dean Science & Health .... Dr. Daniel FAIRBANKS
50 Dean School of Business .... Dr. Norman WRIGHT
97 Dean University College .... Dr. Forrest G. WILLIAMS
75 Dean Aviation and Public Services .... Dr. David MCENTIRE
53 Dean School of Education .... Dr. Parker C. FAWSON
15 Assoc VP Human Res/Equity Officer .... Mr. Mark WIESENBERG
37 Director Financial Aid/Scholarship .... Ms. Trish HOWARD
19 Dir Public Safety/Chief of Police .... Mr. John BREWER
112 Director of Planned Giving .... Ms. Cristina PIANEZZOLA
09 Director Institutional Research .... Mr. Robert LOVERIDGE
41 Assoc VP Athletics .... Mr. Vince OTOUPAL
24 Director Studios & Engineering .... Mr. Will MCKINNON
40 Director Bookstore .... Ms. Louise BRIDGE
06 Registrar .... Ms. LuAnn SMITH
28 Dir Multicultural Student Services .... Mr. Barney NYE
29 Director Alumni Relations .... Ms. Jeri L. ALLPHIN
38 Dir Career & Academic Counseling .... Mr. Adam BLACK
96 Director of Purchasing .... Mr. Ryan LINDSTROM
04 Executive Asst to President .... Ms. Candice L. GARDNER
08 Director Library .... Ms. Lesli BAKER
102 Dir Foundation/Corporate Relations .... Vacant
103 Dir Workforce/Career Development .... Ms. Sherry HARWARD
104 Director Study Abroad .... Mr. Baldomero LAGO
105 Director Web Services .... Mr. Nathan GERBER
108 Institutional Review Board Chair .... Mr. Andrew CREER
13 Assoc Vice Pres CIO/IT .... Mr. Ray WALKER
90 Director Academic IT & Analytics .... Ms. Laura BUSBY

*Weber State University (E)

3850 Dixon Parkway, Ogden UT 84408
County: Weber FICE Identification: 003680
Unit ID: 230782
Telephone: (801) 626-6000 Carnegie Class: Masters/L
FAX Number: (801) 626-7922 Calendar System: Semester
URL: www.weber.edu
Established: 1889 Annual Undergrad Tuition & Fees (In-State): $5,523
Enrollment: 25,955 Coed
Affiliation or Control: State IRS Status: 501(c)3
Highest Offering: Master's
Accreditation: NW, ADNUR, ART, CAATE, CAEPT, CAHIIM, CEA, CIDA, COARC, CS, DH, EMT, ENG, ENGT, HSA, MLTAD, MT, MUS, NUR, SW

02 President .... Dr. Charles A. WIGHT
05 Provost .... Dr. Madonne MINER
10 Vice Pres Administrative Services .... Dr. Norm TARBOX
111 Vice Pres for Univ Advancement .... Dr. Brad MORTENSEN
32 Interim VP Student Affairs .... Dr. Brett PEROZZI
13 VP for Information Technology .... Dr. Bret ELLIS
20 Vice Provost .... Dr. Bruce DAVIS
35 Assoc VP for Student Affairs .... Dr. Brett PEROZZI
21 Asst VP for Financial Services .... Mr. Steven E. NABOR
15 Asst Vice Pres for Human Resources .... Ms. Cherrie NELSON
18 Assoc VP for Facilities Management .... Mr. Mark HALVERSON
84 Asst Prov for Enrollment Services .... Dr. Bruce BOWEN
20 Asst Prov & Dean of Undergraduates .... Dr. Brenda MARSTELLER-KOWALEWSKI
76 Dean Health Professions .... Dr. Yasmen SIMONIAN
50 Dean Business/Economics .... Dr. Jeffrey STEAGALL
53 Dean of Education .... Dr. Jack L. RASMUSSEN
83 Dean Social Behavioral Science .... Dr. Frank HARROLD
79 Dean of Arts & Humanities .... Dr. Scott SPRENGER
81 Dean of Science .... Dr. David MATTY
72 Dean of Applied Science & Tech .... Dr. David FERRO
35 Dean of Students .... Dr. Jeffrey J. HURST
06 Registrar .... Mr. Casey D. BULLOCK
19 Director Public Safety .... Vacant
29 Exec Director Alumni Association .... Ms. Nancy COLLINWOOD
38 Dir Counseling & Psycholog Services .... Dr. Dianna K. ABEL
36 Director of Career Services .... Dr. Winn STANGER
37 Director of Financial Aid .... Mr. Jed SPENCER
27 Director of Media Relations .... Mr. John L. KOWALEWSKI
07 Director of Admissions .... Mr. Scott TEICHERT
08 University Librarian .... Ms. Joan HUBBARD
22 Dir Equal Opportunity/Affirm Action .... Dr. Barry G. GOMBERG
41 Dir of Intercollegiate Athletics .... Mr. Jerry BOVEE
40 Bookstore Director .... Mr. Tim ECK
25 Director Sponsored Projects .... Mr. James TAYLOR
85 Director Services Intl Students .... Dr. Mary A. MACHIRA
23 Director Student Health Center .... Dr. Shawn D. MCQUILKIN
26 Director Public Relations .... Ms. Allison B. HESS

91 Director Administrative Computing .... Vacant
43 University Counsel .... Dr. G. Richard HILL
39 Director Housing & Residence Life .... Mr. Daniel KILCREASE
96 Director of Purchasing .... Ms. Nancy E. EMENGER
28 Chief Diversity Officer .... Dr. Adrienne G. GILLESPIE
92 Director of Honors Program .... Dr. Judy ELSLEY
114 Director Budget & Investments .... Mr. Brian L. SHUPPY
94 Director Women's Center .... Ms. Stephanie MCCLURE

*Snow College (A)

150 College Avenue, Ephraim UT 84627-1299
County: Sanpete FICE Identification: 003679
Unit ID: 230597
Telephone: (435) 283-7000 Carnegie Class: Bac/Assoc-Assoc Dom
FAX Number: (435) 283-6879 Calendar System: Semester
URL: www.snow.edu
Established: 1888 Annual Undergrad Tuition & Fees (In-State): $3,592
Enrollment: 5,111 Coed
Affiliation or Control: State IRS Status: 501(c)3
Highest Offering: Baccalaureate
Accreditation: NW, ACBSP, ADNUR, MUS, PNUR, THEA

02 President .... Dr. Gary L. CARLSTON
05 Vice President for Academic Affairs .... Dr. Steven HOOD
10 VP Finance/Administrative Services .... Mr. Jacob DETTINGER
32 Vice President Student Success .... Mr. Craig MATHIE
35 Director of Student Life .... Ms. Michelle BROWN
75 Dean Business & Applied Tech .... Mr. Mike MEDLEY
36 Director of Student Success .... Vacant
08 Director Library/Information Svcs .... Mr. Jon OSTLER
09 Director Institutional Research .... Ms. Beckie HERMANSEN
15 Director Human Resource Development .... Mr. Wayne SQUIRE
18 Director Campus Services Ephraim .... Ms. Leslee COOK
24 Director TTC .... Mr. Chase MITCHELL
39 Director Student Housing .... Ms. Jessica SIEGFRIED
41 Athletic Director .... Mr. Robert NIELSON
06 Registrar .... Mr. Micah STRAIT
07 Director Admissions .... Mr. Jeffrey SAVAGE
21 Budget Director .... Ms. Sherri HANSEN
26 Director Public Relations .... Mr. John STEVENS
35 Director Student Affairs .... Mr. Mike ANDERSON
37 Director Student Financial Aid .... Mr. Jack DALENE
38 Director Student Counseling .... Mr. Allen RIGGS
96 Director of Purchasing .... Mr. Michael JORGENSEN
30 Chief Development Officer .... Ms. Rosie CONNOR
27 Director of Campus Relations .... Ms. Heidi STRINGHAM
04 Administrative Asst to President .... Ms. Marci LARSEN
13 Chief Info Technology Officer (CIO) .... Mr. Phil ALLRED

*Salt Lake Community College (B)

4600 S Redwood Road, Salt Lake City UT 84123-3197
County: Salt Lake FICE Identification: 005220
Unit ID: 230746
Telephone: (801) 957-4111 Carnegie Class: Assoc/HT-Mix Trad/Non
FAX Number: (801) 957-4444 Calendar System: Semester
URL: www.slcc.edu
Established: 1948 Annual Undergrad Tuition & Fees (In-State): $3,690
Enrollment: 29,350 Coed
Affiliation or Control: State IRS Status: 501(c)3
Highest Offering: Associate Degree
Accreditation: NW, ACFEI, ADNUR, DH, FUSER, MAC, OTA, PTAA, RAD, SURGT

02 President .... Dr. Deneece HUFTALIN
05 Provost for Academic Affairs .... Dr. Clifton SANDERS
10 Vice Pres Business Services .... Mr. Dennis KLAUS
32 Vice President Student Affairs .... Dr. Charles LEPPER
30 Vice Pres Institutional Advancement .... Ms. Alison MCFARLANE
86 VP Govt & Community Relations .... Mr. Tim SHEEHAN
108 Vice Pres Inst Effectiveness .... Ms. Barbara GROVER
28 Spec Asst to President .... Dr. Roderic LAND
103 Assoc Provost/Workforce & Econ Dev .... Mr. Rick BOUILLON
20 Assoc Provost Academic Support .... Dr. Nate SOUTHERLAND
121 Int AVP Student Success/Completion .... Ms. Candida DARLING
88 Asst Provost Learning Advancement .... Dr. David HUBERT
21 Asst Vice Pres of Budget Services .... Mr. Darren MARSHALL
35 Dean of Students/Asst Vice Pres .... Dr. Kenneth STONEBROOK
15 Asst Vice Pres of Human Resources .... Mr. Craig GARDNER
18 Asst Vice Pres of Facilities .... Mr. Robert ASKERLUND
39 Asst Vice Pres Student Life .... Mr. Curt LARSEN
84 Asst VP Student Enrollment Services .... Mr. Eric WEBER
26 Asst VP Inst Mktg/Communications .... Mr. Michael NAVARRE
09 Asst VP Strategy & Analysis .... Mr. Jeff AIRD
60 Dean Arts/Communication/Media .... Mr. Richard SCOTT
50 Dean School of Business .... Dr. Dennis BROMLEY
79 Int Dean Humanities/Social Sciences .... Dr. Paul ALLEN
76 Dean School of Health Sciences .... Dr. JoAnne WRIGHT
81 Dean Science/Math & Engineering .... Dr. Craig CALDWELL
75 Dean Technical Specialties .... Mr. Rick BOUILLON
88 Dean SAT/Prof Development .... Mr. Kevin BROCKBANK
41 Director Athletics & Recreation .... Mr. Kevin M. DUSTIN
109 Sr Dir Student Ctr/Auxiliary Svc .... Mr. Jason BEAL
24 Director Technical Productions .... Mr. Seth MILLER
121 Director Academic Advising .... Ms. Sonia PARKER
36 Director Career/Student Employment .... Mr. Jack HESLEPH
88 Director Testing & Placement .... Ms. Diana HARVEY
06 Registrar .... Ms. MaryEtta CHASE
37 Director Financial Aid .... Ms. Cristi MILLARD
19 Director Public Safety .... Mr. Shane CRABTREE
13 Chief Information/Security Officer .... Mr. Bill ZOUMADAKIS

21 Controller/Business Manager .... Mr. Douglas HANSEN
22 EEO Director .... Ms. Mozelle ORTON
96 Purchasing Director .... Mr. Brandon THOMAS
25 Director Sponsored Projects .... Ms. Nicole OMER
30 Exec Director of Development .... Ms. Nancy MICHALKO
117 Risk Manager .... Ms. Mikel BIRCH
04 Admin Asst to President & Board Sec .... Ms. Janice SCHMIDT

*Utah State University Eastern (C)

451 E 400 N, Price UT 84501-2699
Telephone: (435) 613-5000 FICE Identification: 003676
Accreditation: &NW, ADNUR, PNUR

† Regional accreditation is carried under the parent institution in Logan, UT.

Western Governors University (D)

4001 S 700 E, Suite 700, Salt Lake City UT 84107-2533
County: Salt Lake FICE Identification: 033394
Unit ID: 433387
Telephone: (801) 274-3280 Carnegie Class: Masters/L
FAX Number: (801) 274-3305 Calendar System: Other
URL: www.wgu.edu
Established: 1996 Annual Undergrad Tuition & Fees: $6,070
Enrollment: 70,504 Coed
Affiliation or Control: Independent Non-Profit IRS Status: 501(c)3
Highest Offering: Master's
Accreditation: NW, CAEPN, CAHIIM, NURSE

01 President .... Dr. Scott D. PULSIPHER
05 Provost/Chief Academic Officer .... Dr. Marni B. STEIN
10 Vice Pres Finance/Administration .... David GROW
09 Vice Pres Quality/Inst Research .... Jason LEVIN
26 Vice President of Marketing .... Carey HILDERBRAND
15 Vice President of Human Resources .... Bonnie PATTEE
37 Vice Pres of Financial Aid .... Bob COLLINS
27 Vice President of Public Relations .... Joan MITCHELL
88 Associate Provost Student Mentoring .... Mitsu FRAZIER
20 Associate Provost Academic Services .... Dr. Stacey LUDWIG-JOHNSON
76 Dean College of Health Professions .... Jan JONES-SCHENK
27 Chief Marketing Officer .... Patrick PARTRIDGE
86 Director Government Relations .... Chris BONNELL
100 Chief of Staff .... Gilbert ROJAS
13 Chief Information Office .... Boyd BISCHOFF

Westminster College (E)

1840 S 1300 E, Salt Lake City UT 84105-3697
County: Salt Lake FICE Identification: 003681
Unit ID: 230807
Telephone: (801) 484-7651 Carnegie Class: Masters/L
FAX Number: (801) 466-6916 Calendar System: Semester
URL: www.westminstercollege.edu
Established: 1875 Annual Undergrad Tuition & Fees: $32,404
Enrollment: 2,821 Coed
Affiliation or Control: Independent Non-Profit IRS Status: 501(c)3
Highest Offering: Master's
Accreditation: NW, AAB, ACBSP, ANEST, CAEPT, MACTE, NURSE, PH

01 President .... Mr. Stephen R. MORGAN
05 Provost .... Dr. Lisa GENTILE
111 Vice Pres Institutional Advancement .... Mrs. Staci CARSON
10 Vice Pres Finance & Administration .... Mr. Curtis W. RYAN
84 Vice President Enrollment Mgmt .... Mr. Ron HEADINGS
26 Chief Marketing Officer .... Ms. Sheila YORKIN
49 Dean School of Arts & Sciences .... Dr. Lance NEWMAN
66 Dean School of Nursing/Hlth Science .... Dr. Sheryl STEADMAN
50 Dean School of Business .... Mrs. Melissa KOERNER
53 Dean School of Education .... Dr. Melanie AGNEW
32 Dean of Students .... Mr. Mark FERNE
29 Director Alumni Relations .... Ms. Kayla SMITH
09 Director of Inst Research/Assess .... Ms. Nichole GREENWOOD
45 Chief Strategy Officer .... Ms. Annalisa HOLCOMBE
13 Chief Information Officer .... Mr. Robert ALLRED
43 General Counsel/Risk Management .... Ms. Kathryn HOLMES
21 Director of Accounting Services .... Ms. Jennifer MEDRANO
15 Director of Human Resources .... Ms. Julie FREESTONE
06 Registrar .... Mr. Michael SANTAROSA
37 Director of Financial Aid .... Ms. Jenny RYAN
07 Director of Admissions .... Vacant
18 Director Plant/Facilities .... Mr. Richard A. BROCKMYER
36 Director of Career Resource Center .... Ms. Brianna KOUCOS
08 Director Giovale Library .... Mr. Robert ALLRED
35 Assistant Dean of Students .... Mr. Karnell BLACK
39 Director of Student Involvement .... Mr. Ryan COOK
88 Director of Conferences .... Mr. Jeff BROWN
19 Director of Campus Security .... Mr. Tony RUSSELL
41 Director of Athletics .... Mr. Shay WYATT
42 Director of Spiritual Life .... Ms. Jan SAAED
38 Director of Campus Counseling .... Ms. Lisa JONES
92 Dean of Honors College .... Dr. Richard BADENHAUSEN
91 Database Administrator .... Mr. Kyle RIMA
04 Executive Asst to President .... Ms. Emmalee SZWEDKO
22 Title IX Coordinator/EEO Complaince .... Mr. Jason SCHWARTZ
101 Secretary of the Institution/Board .... Ms. Annalisa HOLCOMBE
28 VP of Diversity/Equity & Inclusion .... Dr. Marco BARKEER

† Granted candidacy at the Doctorate level.

VERMONT

Bennington College (F)

One College Drive, Bennington VT 05201-6003
County: Bennington FICE Identification: 003682
Unit ID: 230816
Telephone: (802) 442-5401 Carnegie Class: Bac-A&S
FAX Number: (802) 447-4269 Calendar System: Semester
URL: www.bennington.edu
Established: 1932 Annual Undergrad Tuition & Fees: $50,100
Enrollment: 801 Coed
Affiliation or Control: Independent Non-Profit IRS Status: 501(c)3
Highest Offering: Master's
Accreditation: EH

01 President .... Dr. Mariko SILVER
05 Provost/Dean of the College .... Ms. Isabel ROCHE
10 VP for Finance & Administration .... Mr. Brian MURPHY
45 Sr VP for Institutional Initiatives .... Mr. David G. REES
88 Sr VP for Strategic Partnerships .... Ms. Paige BARTELS
111 VP for Institutional Advancement .... Mr. Matt RIZZO
07 VP/Dean of Admissions & Fin Aid .... Mr. Hung BUI
18 AVP for Facilities Mgmt & Planning .... Mr. Andy SCHLATTER
88 Advisor to the President .... Mr. Duncan DOBBELMANN
32 Dean of Students .... Ms. Xenia MARKOWITT
09 Dean of Research/Plng/Assessment .... Mr. Zeke BERNSTEIN
08 Dean of the Library .... Ms. Oceana WILSON
15 Director of Human Resources .... Ms. Heather FALEY
37 Director of Financial Aid .... Ms. Heather CLIFFORD

Champlain College (G)

163 S Willard Street, Burlington VT 05402-0670
County: Chittenden FICE Identification: 003684
Unit ID: 230852
Telephone: (802) 860-2700 Carnegie Class: Masters/M
FAX Number: (802) 860-2750 Calendar System: Semester
URL: www.champlain.edu
Established: 1956 Annual Undergrad Tuition & Fees: $38,660
Enrollment: 4,006 Coed
Affiliation or Control: Independent Non-Profit IRS Status: 501(c)3
Highest Offering: Master's
Accreditation: EH, ART, RAD, SW

01 President .... Donald J. LAACKMAN
05 Provost .... Dr. Laurie QUINN
10 Vice President Finance and Planning .... Shelley NAVARI
84 Vice President Enrollment .... Dr. Lisa BLUNDERS
111 Vice President Advancement .... Robert M. CALDWELL
32 Vice President Student Life .... Dr. Leslie AVERILL
15 Vice President People & Technology .... Mary Margaret LEE
101 VP Strategic Communications & Exten .... Katie HAWLEY
21 Director of Finance & Asst Treasure .... April O'DELL
13 Asst Vice Pres Information Systems .... Theodore LASKARIS
36 Director Career Collaborative .... Dr. Tanja HINTERSTOISSER
20 Senior Associate Provost .... Dr. Michelle MILLER
53 Dean Education/Human Stds Div .... Dr. Laurel BONGIORNO
88 Dean Comm/Creative Media Div .... Dr. Paula WILLOQUET-MARICONDI
50 Dean Business Division .... Dr. Scott BAKER
77 Dean Information Tech/Science .... Dr. Scott STEVENS
107 Dean Continuing Professional Stds .... Dr. Mika NASH
07 Director of Undergrad Admissions .... Chris PERLONGO
06 Registrar .... Rebecca PETERSON
37 Director of Financial Aid .... Kristi JOVELL
38 Dir of Counseling & Accommodations .... Skip HARRIS
18 Director of Physical Plant .... Thomas BONNETTE
19 Director of Security & Safety .... Bruce BOVAT
23 Director Health Services .... Skip HARRIS
22 Director of Affirmative Action .... Dana HUTCHINSON
39 Director of Residential Life .... Danelle BERUBE
85 Asst Dir International Education .... Jessa KARKI
26 Public Information & News Director .... Stephen MEASE
29 Director of Alumni Relations .... Hannah CAMPBELL
08 Director Library .... Janet COTTRELL
28 Spec Adv to the President D&I .... Angela BATISTA
103 Director Workforce Development .... Melissa HERSH
30 Director Institutional Advancement .... Sarah ANDRIANO
04 Executive Assistant .... Linda MURPHY
40 Bookstore Manager .... Kevin MCCANN
106 Director E-learning .... Ursula JONES
108 Director Learning Assessment .... Ellen ZEMAN
105 Director Web Services .... Brian ANDREWS
25 Chief Contracts/Grants Admin .... Ted WINOKUR

College of St. Joseph (H)

71 Clement Road, Rutland VT 05701-3899
County: Rutland FICE Identification: 003685
Unit ID: 231077
Telephone: (802) 773-5900 Carnegie Class: Bac-Diverse
FAX Number: (802) 776-5258 Calendar System: Semester
URL: www.csj.edu
Established: 1956 Annual Undergrad Tuition & Fees: $22,650
Enrollment: 327 Coed
Affiliation or Control: Roman Catholic IRS Status: 501(c)3
Highest Offering: Master's
Accreditation: EH

01 President .... Mr. Larry JENSEN

03 Sr VP of College Affairs .... Mr. Jeffrey BROWN
05 VP Academic Affs .... Dr. Robert GODDARD
10 Business Manager .... Ms. Karen REYNOLDS
32 VP Student Affs .... Ms. Melissa PARADEE
15 Vice Pres Human Resources .... Mrs. Jody BREAULT
26 VP of External Affairs .... Mr. James LAMBERT
37 Director of Financial Aid .... Mrs. Julie ROSMUS
07 Director of Admissions .... Mr. Ken LABATE
30 Dir Development/Alumni Relations .... Ms. Nanci GORDON
06 Registrar .... Mr. Greg CHAMBERLAND
13 CIS Administrator .... Mr. Raymond GIBBS
121 Director of Learning Center .... Ms. Susan BOYCE
21 Controller .... Mrs. Karen REYNOLDS
18 Director of Maintenance .... Mr. Thomas BELAND
08 Librarian .... Ms. Doreen MCCULLOUGH
49 Chair Arts & Sciences Division .... Dr. David BALFOUR
50 Chair Business Division .... Dr. Erika BERNER
53 Chair Education Division .... Dr. David ST. GERMAIN
83 Chair Psychology/Human Services Div .... Dr. Michael W. KESLER

Goddard College (A)

123 Pitkin Road, Plainfield VT 05667-9432

County: Washington FICE Identification: 003686
Unit ID: 230889
Telephone: (800) 468-4888 Carnegie Class: Masters/M
FAX Number: (802) 454-1029 Calendar System: Semester
URL: www.goddard.edu
Established: 1863 Annual Undergrad Tuition & Fees: $15,786
Enrollment: 512 Coed
Affiliation or Control: Independent Non-Profit IRS Status: 501(c)3
Highest Offering: Master's
Accreditation: EH

01 President .... Mr. Robert KENNY
05 Academic Dean .... Dr. Lewis JONES
10 Interim CFO .... Ms. Sherri MOLLEUR
111 Chief Advancement Officer .... Vacant
32 Dean of Community Life .... Ms. Susan A. WILSON
06 Registrar .... Mr. Josh CASTLE
15 Director of Human Resources .... Vacant
37 Director of Financial Aid .... Ms. Beverly JENE
88 Director of Campus Services .... Mr. Paul SHPER
08 Director of Information Access .... Ms. Clara BRUNS
18 Director of Facilities Operations .... Mr. Scott BLANCHARD
07 Director of Admissions .... Mr. Gariot LOUIMA
88 Director of WGDR/WGDH Radio .... Mr. Kris GRUEN

Green Mountain College (B)

1 Brennan Circle, Poultney VT 05764-1199

County: Rutland FICE Identification: 003687
Unit ID: 230898
Telephone: (802) 287-8000 Carnegie Class: Masters/S
FAX Number: (802) 287-8099 Calendar System: Semester
URL: www.greenmtn.edu
Established: 1834 Annual Undergrad Tuition & Fees: $37,002
Enrollment: 864 Coed
Affiliation or Control: Independent Non-Profit IRS Status: 501(c)3
Highest Offering: Master's
Accreditation: EH

01 President .... Mr. Robert W. ALLEN
03 Executive Vice President .... Mr. Chris HALNON
05 Vice President Academic Affairs .... Dr. Thomas MAUHS-PUGH
32 Vice President Student Affairs .... Vacant
84 Director of Enrollment Management .... Mr. Ryan LONGE
04 Executive Assistant to President .... Vacant
20 Dean of Faculty .... Dr. James HARDING
07 Director of Admissions .... Mr. Ryan LONGE
30 Director of Development .... Ms. Michele ALMEIDA
06 Registrar .... Ms. Sharon L. HOFFMAN
18 Director of Facilities .... Mr. William BALLARD
19 Director of Public Safety .... Mr. Timothy OLIVER
26 Dir of Public Relations/Marketing .... Dr. Karen FLEMING
41 Athletic Director .... Mr. Kip SHIPLEY
08 Director Library & Information Svcs .... Mr. Paul MILLETTE
85 Director of International Pgms .... Vacant
13 Director Computing & Info Mgmt .... Mr. Jeffrey WRIGHT
42 Chaplain .... Ms. Shirley OSKAMP
29 Dir Alumni Relations/Annual Giving .... Ms. Michele ALMEIDA
36 Director of Career Counseling .... Ms. Serena GUILES
92 Director of College Honors Program .... Dr. Jennifer SELLERS
37 Director Student Financial Aid .... Ms. Wendy ELLIS
15 Director Human Resources .... Ms. Janie EVANS
38 Director Student Counseling .... Vacant
09 Director of Institutional Research .... Ms. Sharon L. HOFFMAN
123 Director of Graduate Admissions .... Dr. Mark FAZIOLI
23 Director of Wellness Center .... Ms. Peggy GREGORY

Landmark College (C)

19 River Road South, Putney VT 05346

County: Windham FICE Identification: 025326
Unit ID: 247649
Telephone: (802) 387-4767 Carnegie Class: Bac/Assoc-Assoc Dom
FAX Number: (802) 387-6868 Calendar System: Semester
URL: www.landmark.edu
Established: 1985 Annual Undergrad Tuition & Fees: $52,650
Enrollment: 466 Coed
Affiliation or Control: Independent Non-Profit IRS Status: 501(c)3
Highest Offering: Baccalaureate
Accreditation: EH

01 President .... Dr. Peter A. EDEN
03 Executive Vice President .... Mr. Jon A. MACCLAREN
05 VP Academic Affairs .... Dr. Gail GIBSON SHEFFIELD
111 VP Institutional Advancement .... Ms. Ellen SMITH
32 VP Student Affairs .... Mr. Michael LUCIANI
84 VP Enrollment Management .... Mr. Kevin MAYNE
88 VP Educational Research/Innovation .... Ms. Manju BANERJEE
04 Assistant to the President .... Ms. Tiffany KERYLOW
88 Dir Transfer/Career/Internship Svc .... Ms. Jan COPLAN
26 Director Marketing & Communications .... Mr. Mark DIPIETRO
18 Director Facilities .... Mr. Kyle SKROCKI
08 Head Librarian .... Ms. Jennifer LANN
13 Chief Technology Officer .... Ms. Corinne BELL
06 Registrar .... Ms. Lindsay COX
41 Director Athletics .... Mr. Steve STANLEY
37 Director Student Financial Aid .... Mr. Michael MERTES
38 Director of Counseling/Wellness .... Ms. Jacala MILLS
23 Director of Health Services .... Vacant
40 Bookstore Manager .... Ms. Kimberly JUDD
15 Dir of Human Resources .... Ms. Carolyn LEBAIL
21 Controller .... Mr. Mark HIGGINS
35 Dean of Students .... Mr. Patrick CONNELLY
07 Sr Dir Recruitmt/Outreach/Engagemt .... Ms. Carroll PARE
19 Director Campus Safety .... Vacant
29 Associate Director Alumni Affairs .... Ms. Tricia STANLEY
101 Secretary of the Institution/Board .... Ms. Carol NARDINO
104 Director International Education .... Ms. Peg ALDEN
106 Dir Online Learning .... Ms. Marie-Pierre HUGUET

Marlboro College (D)

PO Box A, Marlboro VT 05344-9999

County: Windham FICE Identification: 003690
Unit ID: 230940
Telephone: (802) 257-4333 Carnegie Class: Bac-A&S
FAX Number: (802) 257-4154 Calendar System: Semester
URL: www.marlboro.edu
Established: 1946 Annual Undergrad Tuition & Fees: $40,030
Enrollment: 189 Coed
Affiliation or Control: Independent Non-Profit IRS Status: 501(c)3
Highest Offering: Master's
Accreditation: EH

01 President .... Mr. Kevin F. QUIGLEY
114 Chief Planning & Budget Officer .... Mr. Robert WEBBER
05 Dean of Faculty/Chief Academic Ofcr .... Mr. Richard GLEJZER
07 Dean of Admissions .... Ms. Brigid LAWLER
32 Dean of Students .... Mr. Luis ROSA
58 Assoc Dean Graduate/Professional St .... Ms. Kate JELLEMA
08 Library Director .... Ms. Beth RUANE
06 Asst Registrar .... Ms. Rebecca CATARELLI
102 Dir Corp & Foundation Relations .... Ms. Hillary TWINING
26 Dir of Marketing/Communications .... Vacant
18 Director of Plant Operations .... Mr. Dan J. COTTER
82 World Studies Director .... Mr. Seth HARTER
04 Asst to President .... Ms. Vanessa REDFIELD
29 Director Alumni Relations .... Ms. Kathy WATERS
104 Director Study Abroad .... Ms. Maggie STRASSMAN
13 Chief Info Technology Officer (CIO) .... Mr. John BAKER
30 Chief External Relations Officer .... Mr. Matthew BARONE
41 Athletic Director .... Mr. Randy KNAGGS

Marlboro College Graduate School (E)

PO Box A, Marlboro VT 05344

Telephone: (802) 258-9200 Identification: 770120
Accreditation: &EH

Middlebury Bread Loaf School of English (F)

75 Franklin Street, Middlebury VT 05753

Telephone: (802) 443-5418 Identification: 770119
Accreditation: &EH

† Bread Loaf School of English is a summer graduate program and the enrollment figure is for the summer term.

Middlebury College (G)

Old Chapel, Middlebury VT 05753-6200

County: Addison FICE Identification: 003691
Unit ID: 230959
Telephone: (802) 443-5000 Carnegie Class: Bac-A&S
FAX Number: (802) 443-2071 Calendar System: 4/1/4
URL: www.middlebury.edu
Established: 1800 Annual Undergrad Tuition & Fees: $50,063
Enrollment: 2,558 Coed
Affiliation or Control: Independent Non-Profit IRS Status: 501(c)3
Highest Offering: Doctorate
Accreditation: EH

01 President .... Dr. Laurie L. PATTON
05 Provost .... Dr. Susan BALDRIDGE
88 VP for Academic Development .... Dr. Tim SPEARS
10 Exec VP Finance & Administration .... Mr. David J. PROVOST
03 Sr Vice Pres/Philanthropic Advisor .... Mr. Michael SCHOENFELD
15 VP for HR/Chief Risk Officer .... Karen MILLER
111 VP for Advancement .... Colleen FITZPATRICK
20 VP Academic Affairs/Dean of Faculty .... Dr. Andrea LLOYD
26 VP for Communications & Marketing .... Mr. Bill BURGER
32 VP Student Affairs/Dean of College .... Dr. Katy SMITH ABBOTT
58 VP Acad Affs/Dean of the Institute .... Dr. Jeffrey DAYTON-JOHNSON
07 Dean of Admissions .... Mr. Gregory B. BUCKLES
104 Dean of International Programs .... Dr. Jeffrey CASON
101 Special Asst to Pres/Sec of Corp .... Mr. David A. DONAHUE
45 Assoc Provost for Planning .... Mr. LeRoy GRAHAM
08 Dean of the Library .... Mr. Michael D. ROY
37 Assoc VP Student Financial Services ... Ms. Kim DOWNS-BURNS
13 AVP Information Technology .... Mr. Jim STUART
79 Dean of the Language Schools .... Dr. Stephen SNYDER
20 Dean of Curriculum .... Dr. Suzanne GURLAND
09 Dean for Faculty Dev & Research .... Dr. James RALPH
21 Asst Treasurer/Dir of Business Svcs .... Mr. Thomas CORBIN
29 Assoc VP Alumni Rels/Annual Giving .... Ms. Margaret STOREY GROVES
23 Exec Dir Health & Counseling Svcs .... Dr. Augustus JORDAN
42 Chaplain .... Ms. Laurie JORDAN
41 Director of Athletics .... Mr. Erin QUINN
35 Assoc Dn of the Col/Dir Pub Safety .Ms. Elizabeth B. BURCHARD
06 Registrar .... Ms. Jennifer THOMPSON
15 Director of Human Resources .... Ms. Cheryl MULLINS
40 Bookstore Manager .... Ms. Erin JONES-POPPE

† Tuition figure is a comprehensive fees figure.

New England Culinary Institute (H)

7 School Street, Montpelier VT 05602-9720

County: Washington FICE Identification: 022540
Unit ID: 230977
Telephone: (802) 225-3200 Carnegie Class: Spec-4-yr-Other
FAX Number: (802) 225-3280 Calendar System: Quarter
URL: www.neci.edu
Established: 1980 Annual Undergrad Tuition & Fees: N/A
Enrollment: 379 Coed
Affiliation or Control: Proprietary IRS Status: Proprietary
Highest Offering: Baccalaureate
Accreditation: ACCSC

01 CEO/President .... Mr. Francis VOIGT
10 Chief Financial Officer .... Mr. Phillip HARKER
05 Dean of Education/Dept Chr Cul Arts .... Mr. Lyndon VIRKLER
88 Exec Chef & VP Culinary Operations .... Chef Jean-Louis GERIN
88 Chair Baking & Pastry Programs .... Chef Kathleen KESSLER
88 Chair Food/Beverage Business Mgmt .... Ms. Michelle FORD
20 Director of Compliance/Academics .... Ms. Laureen GAUTHIER
106 Chair Online Programs .... Chef Peg CHECCI
06 Registrar .... Ms. Gail MACDONALD
07 Director of Admissions .... Mr. Dwight CROSS
08 Head Librarian .... Ms. Rachel BORNSTEIN
15 Director Human Resources .... Ms. Karen MADIGAN
18 Director of Facilities .... Mr. William COLGAN
36 Career Services Manager .... Ms. Eunice JORDAN
20 Sr Dir Operations & Education .... Chef David MILES
37 Director Financial Aid .... Ms. Jessica CHAPPEL

Norwich University (I)

158 Harmon Drive, Northfield VT 05663-1000

County: Washington FICE Identification: 003692
Unit ID: 230995
Telephone: (802) 485-2000 Carnegie Class: Masters/L
FAX Number: (802) 485-2032 Calendar System: Semester
URL: www.norwich.edu
Established: 1819 Annual Undergrad Tuition & Fees: $37,354
Enrollment: 3,870 Coed
Affiliation or Control: Independent Non-Profit IRS Status: 501(c)3
Highest Offering: Master's
Accreditation: EH, ACBSP, CAATE, ENG, NURSE

01 President .... Dr. Richard W. SCHNEIDER
05 Provost & Dean of Faculty .... Dr. Sandra AFFENITO
58 VP & Dean Col of Grad/Cont Studies .... Dr. William CLEMENTS
32 VP Student Affairs & Technology .... Dr. Frank VANECEK
30 VP Alumni & Development Relations .... Mr. David J. WHALEY
88 VP Strategic Partnership .... Mr. Phillip SUSMANN
84 VP of Enrollment Management .... Mr. Greg MATTHEWS
10 Chief Financial Officer .... Ms. Lauren WOBBY
11 Chief Administrative Officer .... Mr. David MAGIDA
107 Dean Col of Professional Schools .... Mr. Aron TEMKIN
83 Dean College of Liberal Arts .... Dr. Edward KOHN
81 Dean College of Science/Mathematics .... Dr. Michael MCGINNIS
88 Dean College of National Services .... Col. Andrew HIRD
29 Assoc VP Alumni Relations .... Ms. Diane SCOLARO
20 Assoc VP Academic Affairs .... Dr. Natalia BLANK
26 Asst VP Office of Communications .... Ms. Kathy MURPHY-MORIARITY
04 Exec Assistant to President .... Ms. Laura AMELL
35 Dean of Students .... Ms. Martha MATHIS
08 Interim Head Librarian .... Mr. Greg SAUER
41 Athletic Director .... Mr. Anthony A. MARIANO
18 Director Facilities/Operations .... Mr. Bizhan YAHYAZADEH
37 Director of Student Financial Aid .... Vacant
38 Director Student Counseling .... Vacant
07 Director of Admissions .... Mr. Tim REARDON
06 Registrar & Inst Research Dir .... Dr. Diane DOUGLAS
102 Dir Foundation/Corporate Relations .... Ms. Jess JAGGARS
103 Dir Career Development .... Ms. Kathryn PROVOST
19 Director Security/Safety .... Mr. Larry ROONEY
15 Director of Human Resources .... Vacant

Saint Michael's College (A)

One Winooski Park, Colchester VT 05439-0001

County: Chittenden | FICE Identification: 003694 | Unit ID: 231059
Telephone: (802) 654-2000 | Carnegie Class: Bac-A&S
FAX Number: (802) 654-2297 | Calendar System: Semester
URL: www.smcvt.edu
Established: 1904 | Annual Undergrad Tuition & Fees: $41,975
Enrollment: 2,367 | Coed
Affiliation or Control: Roman Catholic | IRS Status: 501(c)3
Highest Offering: Master's
Accreditation: EH, CEA

Code	Title	Name
01	President	Dr. John J. NEUHAUSER
04	Assistant to the President	Ms. Tara L. ARCURY
05	Vice Pres Academic Affairs	Dr. Karen A. TALENTINO
10	Vice President for Finance	Vacant
32	Vice President for Student Affairs	Dr. Dawn M. ELLINWOOD
84	Vice Pres Enrollment/Marketing	Dr. Sarah M. KELLY
15	Vice President for HR & Admin Svcs	Vacant
111	VP for Institutional Advancement	Mr. Patrick J. GALLIVAN
20	Dean of the College	Dr. Jeffrey TRUMBOWER
42	Director Edmundite Campus Ministry	Rev. Brian J. CUMMINGS, SSE
07	Director of Admission	Mr. Michael STEFANOWICZ
37	Director Student Financial Services	Mr. Daniel R. COUTURE
06	Registrar	Mr. David BARROWCLOUGH
29	Director of Alumni/Parent Relations	Ms. Angela ARMOUR
35	Director Student Activities	Vacant
93	Dir Multicultural Student Affairs	Mr. Moise ST. LOUIS
39	Director of Residence Life	Mr. Louis DIMASI
88	Associate Dean of the College	Dr. Jonathan L. D'AMORE
104	Director of Study Abroad	Ms. Peggy H. IMAI
92	Honors Program Faculty Coordinator	Dr. Jim BYRNE
94	Coord of Gender/Women's Studies	Vacant
08	Dir Library & Information Services	Mr. John K. PAYNE
13	Chief Information Officer	Mr. William O. ANDERSON
19	Director of Public Safety	Vacant
18	Dir of Facilities/College Architect	Mr. James P. FARRINGTON
38	Director of Personal Counseling	Ms. Kathleen BUTTS
36	Director of Career Development	Vacant
23	Director of Health Services	Ms. Mary MASSON
41	Director of Athletics	Dr. Christopher KENNEY
110	Director of Advancement Services	Ms. Linda V. DONAHUE
102	Director of Foundation Relations	Ms. Angela IRVINE
96	Director of Business Services	Mr. Robert ROBINSON
105	Dir of Web Site Development	Vacant
44	Director of Individual Giving	Ms. Terri P. SELBY
88	Financial Accounting Manager	Ms. Shirley J. GOODELL-LACKEY
40	Bookstore Manager	Mr. Stephen MCMAHON
26	Marketing/Communications Manager	Ms. Lindsay DAMICI

School for International Training (SIT) (B)

1 Kipling Road, Brattleboro VT 05302-0676

County: Windham | FICE Identification: 008860 | Unit ID: 231068
Telephone: (802) 257-7751 | Carnegie Class: Spec-4-yr-Other
FAX Number: (802) 258-3248 | Calendar System: Other
URL: www.sit.edu
Established: 1964 | Annual Undergrad Tuition & Fees: N/A
Enrollment: 358 | Coed
Affiliation or Control: Independent Non-Profit | IRS Status: 501(c)3
Highest Offering: Master's
Accreditation: EH

Code	Title	Name
01	President	Dr. Sophia HOWLETT
10	CFO	Mr. Kote LOMIDZE
100	Chief Of Staff	Ms. Bethaney LACLAIR
43	General Counsel	Ms. Lisa RAE
58	Dean SIT Graduate Institute	Dr. Kenneth WILLIAMS
88	Program Coord Language & Culture	Ms. Sharon BROOKS
15	Executive Director Human Resources	Ms. Anne BRNGER
07	Director of Admissions	Ms. Laura ANDREWS
06	Registrar	Ms. Ginny NELLIS
37	Director Financial Aid	Ms. Cathy MULLINS
32	Dean of Students	Mr. Michael SMALLIS
35	Director of Campus Life	Mr. Stephen SWEET
26	Director of Marketing	Ms. Mary Kate O'BRIEN
04	Executive Asst to CEO & President	Ms. Adelee AUSTIN
104	Vice Provost for Study Abroad	Ms. Priscilla STONE
108	Assoc Dean for Assessment	Dr. Kathryn INSKEEP
13	Vice President IT	Mr. Esteban DELEON
28	Chief Diversity Officer	Dr. Michelle CROMWELL
29	Director of Alumni Engagement	Ms. Carla LINEBACK
38	Director Student Counseling	Ms. Jane BUCKINGHAM
39	Director Student Housing	Mr. David FINCK
36	Director Career & Practicum Service	Ms. Squeak STONE
08	Head Librarian	Mr. Patrick SPURLOCK
41	Athletic Director	Vacant

Southern Vermont College (C)

982 Mansion Drive, Bennington VT 05201-6002

County: Bennington | FICE Identification: 003693 | Unit ID: 231086
Telephone: (802) 442-5427 | Carnegie Class: Bac-Diverse
FAX Number: (802) 447-4695 | Calendar System: Semester
URL: www.svc.edu
Established: 1926 | Annual Undergrad Tuition & Fees: $23,975
Enrollment: 475 | Coed
Affiliation or Control: Independent Non-Profit | IRS Status: 501(c)3
Highest Offering: Baccalaureate
Accreditation: EH, NURSE, RAD

Code	Title	Name
01	President	Dr. David R. EVANS
10	Exec VP Admin and Finance	Ms. Jennifer MACKSEY
07	VP for Enrollment Management	Mr. Daniel SUMMERS, II
111	VP Advancement	Ms. Nina MOSER
32	Dean of Students	Ms. Heather QUIRE
05	Dean of the Faculty	Dr. Jennifer R. BURG
41	Director of Athletics	Mr. Sharief HASHIM
20	Dean of Teaching & Learning	Dr. Melinda MARIS
20	Dean of Academic Operations	Ms. Kimberley GOULD
66	Chair Nursing & Health Services	Dr. Mary BOTTER
79	Chair of Humanities	Dr. Daisy LEVY
81	Chair of Science and Mathematics	Dr. Jennifer NELSON
83	Chair of Social Sciences	Mr. Scott STEIN
09	Director of Institutional Research	Ms. Emma PIAZZA
04	Executive Assistant	Ms. Erica HARMON
08	Director Library	Ms. Sarah SANFILIPPO
06	Registrar	Mr. Alan HATTON
36	Director Career Dev/Internships	Ms. Elizabeth DUNHAM
18	Director of Facilities	Mr. Mark J. KLAUDER
38	Director of Counseling	Ms. Louise BINETTE
39	Director of Residence Life	Vacant
19	Director of Campus Safety	Mr. James G. WALDON
37	Director of Student Fin Svcs	Ms. Susan ROCHETTE
15	Director of Human Resources	Ms. Carole SHERINGHAM
88	Coord Learning Disabilities	Mr. David A. LINDENBERG
13	Director Information Technology	Mr. Michael KEEN
27	Asst Director of Communication	Ms. Marion WHITEFORD
28	Director of Diversity Initiatives	Dr. Ivan FIGUEROA
44	Annual Giving Officer	Ms. Christina COLE

Sterling College (D)

PO Box 72, Craftsbury Common VT 05827-0072

County: Orleans | FICE Identification: 021435 | Unit ID: 231095
Telephone: (802) 586-7711 | Carnegie Class: Bac-A&S
FAX Number: (802) 586-2596 | Calendar System: Semester
URL: www.sterlingcollege.edu
Established: 1958 | Annual Undergrad Tuition & Fees: $36,495
Enrollment: 117 | Coed
Affiliation or Control: Independent Non-Profit | IRS Status: 501(c)3
Highest Offering: Baccalaureate
Accreditation: EH

Code	Title	Name
01	President	Mr. Matthew DERR
05	Dean of Academics	Dr. Carol DICKSON
07	Director of Admission	Mr. Tim PATTERSON
111	Director of Advancement Services	Ms. Michelle MARTIN
10	Director of Finance/Operations	Mr. Bill WHITE
08	Librarian	Ms. Petra VOGEL
18	Director of Facilities	Mr. Kelly JONES
32	Dean of Community	Ms. Favor ELLIS
06	Registrar	Ms. Laura Lea BERRY
26	Director of Communications	Ms. Christian FEUERSTEIN
29	Director of Alumni Relations	Mr. Topher BORDEAU
37	Director of Financial Aid	Ms. Barbara STUART
84	Chief Enrollment Officer	Ms. Beana BERN

University of Vermont (E)

South Prospect Street, Burlington VT 05405-0160

County: Chittenden | FICE Identification: 003696 | Unit ID: 231174
Telephone: (802) 656-3131 | Carnegie Class: DU-Higher
FAX Number: N/A | Calendar System: Semester
URL: www.uvm.edu
Established: 1791 | Annual Undergrad Tuition & Fees (In-State): $17,300
Enrollment: 12,815 | Coed
Affiliation or Control: State | IRS Status: 501(c)3
Highest Offering: Doctorate
Accreditation: EH, CAATE, CACREP, CAEPN, CLPSY, DENT, DIETC, DIETD, ENG, IPSY, MED, MT, NMT, NURSE, PTA, RTT, SP, SPAA, SW

Code	Title	Name
01	President	Dr. E. Thomas SULLIVAN
05	Senior Vice President & Provost	Dr. David V. ROSOWSKY
10	VP for Finance & Treasurer	Mr. Richard H. CATE
86	VP University Relations & Admin	Dr. Thomas J. GUSTAFSON
46	VP Research	Dr. Richard A. GALBRAITH
30	CEO & President The UVM Foundation	Mr. Shane JACOBSON
43	VP Legal Affairs & General Counsel	Ms. Francine T. BAZLUKE
84	VP Enrollment Management	Ms. Stacey R. KOSTELL
15	VP Human Resources	Dr. Wanda HEADING-GRANT
20	Assoc Prov Faculty Affairs	Dr. Jim VIGOREAUX
20	Assoc Provost Teaching & Learning	Dr. Brian V. REED
32	Vice Provost for Student Affairs	Dr. Annie STEVENS
28	VP for Human Resources & Diversity	Dr. Wanda R. HEADING-GRANT
100	VP for Executive Operations	Dr. Gary L. DERR
18	Assoc VP Admin & Facility Services	Mr. William P. BALLARD
118	Director Benefits & Employee Svcs	Mr. Harold J. PIERCE
35	Dean of Students	Dr. David A. NESTOR
29	VP for Alumni Relations	Mr. Alan E. RYEA
63	Dean College of Medicine	Dr. Frederick C. MORIN, III
66	Dean Nursing & Health Sciences	Dr. Patricia A. PRELOCK
49	Dean Arts & Sciences	Dr. William A. FALLS
47	Dean Agriculture & Life Sciences	Dr. Thomas C. VOGELMANN
54	Dean Engineering & Math Sciences	Dr. Luis A. GARCIA
53	Dean Education & Social Svcs	Dr. Scott THOMAS
50	Dean Business Administration	Dr. Sanjay SHARMA
92	Acting Dean Honors College	Dr. David JENEMANN
65	Dean Environment & Natural Resource	Dr. Nancy E. MATHEWS
56	Director Extension	Mr. Chuck ROSS
58	Dean Graduate College	Dr. Cynthia J. FOREHAND
51	Dean Continuing & Distance Educ	Ms. Cynthia L. BELLIVEAU
08	Dean Libraries & Learning Res & CIO	Ms. Mara R. SAULE
06	Registrar	Ms. Veronika CARTER
09	Director Institutional Research	Dr. Alexander C. YIN
26	Director University Communications	Mr. Enrique CORREDERA
13	Assoc Chief Information Officer	Ms. Julia H. RUSSELL
25	Assoc VP Research Admin	Dr. Carol ZUICHES
114	University Budget Director	Mr. Alberto CITARELLA
19	Chief of Police Services	Ms. Lianne M. TUOMEY
41	Director of Athletics	Mr. Jeffrey L. SCHULMAN
36	Director Career Services	Ms. Pamela K. GARDNER
23	Director Ctr for Health & Wellbeing	Dr. Jon K. PORTER
38	Counsel/Psych Services Program Dir	Dr. Todd N. WEINMAN
39	Director Residential Life	Mr. Rafael RODRIGUEZ
40	Director University Bookstore	Mr. Jay E. MENNINGER
85	Director Intl Education Services	Ms. Kimberly A. HOWARD
102	VP The UVM Foundation	Mr. Mark W. DORGAN
44	Asst VP Development & Gift Planning	Ms. Amy PALMER-ELLIS
22	Director AA & EO	Mr. Jes S. KRAUS
123	Director Graduate Admissions	Ms. Kimberly L. HESS
07	Int Dir Undergraduate Admissions	Ms. Stacey KOSTELL
37	Director Student Financial Services	Ms. Marie D. JOHNSON
96	Director Purchasing Services	Ms. Natalie L. GUILLETTE
94	Director Women's Center	Ms. Melissa MURRAY
24	Access/Media Services Librarian	Mr. Aaron F. NICHOLS
101	Board of Trustees Coordinator	Ms. Corinne B. THOMPSON

Vermont College of Fine Arts (F)

36 College Street, Montpelier VT 05602-3145

County: Washington | FICE Identification: 003697 | Unit ID: 455992
Telephone: (802) 828-8600 | Carnegie Class: Masters/M
FAX Number: (802) 828-8649 | Calendar System: Semester
URL: www.vcfa.edu
Established: 2008 | Annual Graduate Tuition & Fees: N/A
Enrollment: 366 | Coed
Affiliation or Control: Independent Non-Profit | IRS Status: 501(c)3
Highest Offering: Master's; No Undergraduates
Accreditation: EH, ART

Code	Title	Name
01	President	Mr. Thomas Christopher GREENE
05	Academic Dean	Mr. Matthew MONK
10	Chief Financial Ofcr/VP for Admin	Ms. Erica HARE
04	Administrative Asst to President	Ms. Angela PALADINO
26	Exec Dir Marketing/Communications	Mr. Alastair HAYES
06	Registrar	Ms. Jody MAUNSELL
08	Head Librarian	Mr. Jim NOLTE
13	Chief Info Technology Officer (CIO)	Mr. Peter TIMPONE
18	Exec Dir Facilities/Operations	Mr. Matthew COYNE
84	Vice Pres Enrollment Management	Mr. David MARKOW

† Carnegie Graduate Instructional Program classification is Postbac-A&S

Vermont Law School (G)

164 Chelsea Street, PO Box 96,
South Royalton VT 05068-0096

County: Windsor | FICE Identification: 011934 | Unit ID: 231147
Telephone: (802) 831-1000 | Carnegie Class: Spec-4-yr-Law
FAX Number: (802) 831-1163 | Calendar System: Semester
URL: www.vermontlaw.edu
Established: 1972 | Annual Graduate Tuition & Fees: N/A
Enrollment: 583 | Coed
Affiliation or Control: Independent Non-Profit | IRS Status: 501(c)3
Highest Offering: First Professional Degree; No Undergraduates
Accreditation: EH, LAW

Code	Title	Name
01	President and Dean	Mr. Thomas MCHENRY
05	Vice Dean for Faculty	Mrs. Stephanie WILLBANKS
32	Vice Dean for Students	Ms. Beth MCCORMACK
10	Vice President for Finance	Ms. Lorraine ATWOOD
07	Vice President for Enrollment	Mr. John MILLER
111	Vice President of Advancement	Ms. Mary WELZ
100	Chief of Staff	Ms. Kimberly EVANS
88	Director Environmental Law Ctr	Mr. David MEARS
35	Assoc Dean Student Affs & Diversity	Ms. Shirley JEFFERSON
20	Associate Dean of Faculty	Mr. Sean NOLON
106	Director of Distance Learning	Ms. Linda HIEMER
15	Human Resources Manager	Ms. Chantelle BRACKETT
08	Library Director	Mr. Cynthia LEWIS
21	Comptroller	Mr. Robert WEBBER
06	Registrar	Ms. Maureen MORIARTY
37	Director of Financial Aid	Ms. Melody DEFLORIO
18	Facilities Manager	Mr. Andrew BRACKETT
26	Director of Communications	Ms. Maryellen APELQUIST
13	Technology Operations Manager	Mr. Sean LEE
04	Exec Asst to the President/Dean	Ms. Stephanie CHIARELLA
40	Bookstore Manager	Ms. Amy MCDOWELL
29	Asst Director of Alumni Affairs	Ms. Melissa HARWOOD

*Vermont State Colleges Office of the Chancellor (H)

PO Box 7, Montpelier VT 05601

County: Washington | FICE Identification: 029162 | Unit ID: 231156
Telephone: (802) 224-3000 | Carnegie Class: N/A

FAX Number: (802) 224-3035
URL: www.vsc.edu

01 Chancellor .... Mr. Jeb SPAULDING
04 Exec Assistant to the Chancellor .... Ms. Harriet JOHNSON
43 Vice President/General Counsel .... Ms. Sophie ZDATNY
10 Vice Pres/Chief Financial Officer .... Mr. Stephen WISLOSKI
05 Chief Academic/Tech Officer .... Dr. Yasmine ZIESLER
86 Dir External/Governmental Affairs .... Ms. Tricia COATES
26 Chief Information Officer .... Mr. Kevin CONROY
18 Director of Facilities .... Mr. Richard ETHIER
13 Director of System Info Tech .... Vacant
15 Director of Human Resources .... Ms. Nancy SHAW
09 Director of Institutional Research .... Mr. Zuan ZHANG
88 Director of Payroll/Benefits .... Ms. Tracy SWEET
25 Grants Coordinator .... Mr. David RUBIN

*Castleton University (A)

62 Alumni Drive, Castleton VT 05735-4454
County: Rutland | FICE Identification: 003683
Unit ID: 230834
Telephone: (802) 468-5611 | Carnegie Class: Bac-Diverse
FAX Number: (802) 468-6470 | Calendar System: Semester
URL: www.castleton.edu
Established: 1787 | Annual Undergrad Tuition & Fees (In-State): $11,314
Enrollment: 2,246 | Coed
Affiliation or Control: State | IRS Status: 501(c)3
Highest Offering: Master's
Accreditation: EH, CAATE, NURSE, SW

02 President .... Mr. David S. WOLK
04 Exec Assistant to the President .... Ms. Rita B. GENO
05 Academic Dean .... Dr. Jonathan SPIRO
11 Dean of Administration .... Mr. Scott DIKEMAN
10 Director of Finance .... Ms. Laura JAKUBOWSKI
32 Dean of Students .... Mr. Dennis PROULX
84 Dean of Enrollment .... Mr. Maurice OUIMET
15 Director of Human Resources .... Ms. Janet HAZELTON
35 Associate Dean of Students .... Ms. Victoria ANGIS
06 Registrar .... Ms. Lori ARNER
08 Director Calvin Coolidge Library .... Ms. Jami YAZDANI
37 Director Student Financial Aid .... Ms. Kathy O'MEARA
53 Director of Education .... Dr. Richard REARDON
18 Director of Physical Plant .... Mr. Chuck LAVOIE
30 Dean of Advancement .... Mr. Jeff WELD
36 Dir of Career Development .... Ms. Renee BEAUPREWHITE
23 Wellness Center Director .... Ms. Martha COULTER
38 Director Student Counseling .... Vacant
13 Chief Technology Officer .... Ms. Gayle MALINOWSKI
86 Dean of Entrepreneurial Programs .... Mr. Lyle JEPSON

*Community College of Vermont (B)

PO Box 489, Montpelier VT 05601
County: Washington | FICE Identification: 011167
Unit ID: 230861
Telephone: (802) 828-2800 | Carnegie Class: Assoc/HT-High Non
FAX Number: (802) 828-2805 | Calendar System: Semester
URL: www.ccv.edu
Established: 1970 | Annual Undergrad Tuition & Fees (In-State): $6,222
Enrollment: 5,983 | Coed
Affiliation or Control: State | IRS Status: 501(c)3
Highest Offering: Associate Degree
Accreditation: EH

02 President .... Ms. Joyce M. JUDY
11 Dean of Administration .... Dr. Barbara MARTIN
05 Dean of Academic Services .... Ms. Deborah STEWART
32 Dean of Student Services .... Ms. Heather WEINSTEIN
84 Dean Enrollment Services .... Ms. Pam CHISHOLM
20 Associate Academic Dean .... Ms. Diane HERMANN-ARTIM
12 Exec Director of Academic Center .... Mr. Eric SAKAI
12 Exec Director of Academic Center .... Ms. Katie MOBLEY
12 Exec Director of Academic Center .... Ms. Tapp BARNHILL
15 Director Human Resources .... Mr. Robert FINNEGAN
06 Registrar .... Mr. John Paul REES
07 Director of Admissions .... Mr. Adam WARRINGTON
09 Dir Institutional Research/Planning .... Ms. Laura MASSELL
26 Chief Public Relations Officer .... Mr. Josh LARKIN
88 Director of Secondary Initiatives .... Ms. Natalie SEARLE
36 Director of Career Training Program .... Vacant
27 Dir of Marketing/Communications .... Ms. Janette SHAFFER
10 Chief Financial/Business Officer .... Mr. Nathan HOCK

*Johnson State College (C)

337 College Hill, Johnson VT 05656
County: Lamoille | FICE Identification: 003688
Unit ID: 230913
Telephone: (802) 635-1240 | Carnegie Class: Masters/S
FAX Number: (802) 635-1230 | Calendar System: Semester
URL: www.jsc.edu
Established: 1828 | Annual Undergrad Tuition & Fees (In-State): $11,290
Enrollment: 1,514 | Coed
Affiliation or Control: State | IRS Status: 501(c)3
Highest Offering: Master's
Accreditation: EH

02 President .... Dr. Elaine C. COLLINS
05 Provost .... Dr. Nolan T. ATKINS
11 Dean of Administration .... Ms. Sharron R. SCOTT
32 Dean of Students .... Mr. Jonathan M. DAVIS
84 Associate Dean of Enrollment .... Ms. Penny HOWRIGAN
35 Associate Dean of Students .... Ms. Michele WHITMORE
06 Registrar .... Mr. Douglas EASTMAN
106 Assoc Dean of Distance Education .... Ms. Bobbi Jo CARTER
18 Director of Physical Plant .... Mr. Tom ARCHER
41 Director of Athletics & Recreation .... Mr. Jamey VENTURA
38 Director of Counseling Services .... Ms. Kate MCCARTHY
30 Director of Development/Alumni Rels .... Ms. Lauren PHILIE
36 Director of Advising .... Ms. Sara KINERSON
89 Director of First-Year Experience .... Ms. Margo WARDEN
19 Director of Public Safety .... Mr. Michael PALAGONIA
26 Interim Communications Manager .... Ms. Melissa WEINSTEIN
37 Director of Financial Aid .... Ms. Lisa CUMMINGS
15 Director of Human Resources .... Ms. Sandra FRANZ
07 Director of Admissions .... Mr. Patrick ROGERS
08 Faculty Librarian .... Mr. Joseph FARARA
79 Chair Humanities .... Dr. Lisa CLINE
53 Chair Education .... Dr. Rob SCHULZE
65 Chair Environ/Health Sciences .... Dr. Elizabeth DOLCI
88 Chair Performing Arts .... Ms. Bethany PLISSEY
57 Chair Fine Arts .... Mr. Ken LESLIE
50 Chair Business/Economics .... Mr. James BLACK
60 Chair Writing/Literature .... Dr. Sharon TWIGG
81 Chair Mathematics .... Dr. Julie THEORET
83 Chair Behavioral Sciences .... Dr. Susan GREEN
04 Executive Asst to President .... Ms. Cecilia NORTH
13 Chief Info Technology Officer (CIO) .... Mr. Michael DENTE

*Lyndon State College (D)

1001 College Road, PO Box 919,
Lyndonville VT 05851-0919
County: Caledonia | FICE Identification: 003689
Unit ID: 230931
Telephone: (802) 626-6200 | Carnegie Class: Bac-Diverse
FAX Number: (802) 626-9770 | Calendar System: Semester
URL: www.lyndonstate.edu
Established: 1911 | Annual Undergrad Tuition & Fees (In-State): $11,290
Enrollment: 1,266 | Coed
Affiliation or Control: State | IRS Status: 501(c)3
Highest Offering: Master's
Accreditation: EH, EXSC

02 President .... Dr. Elaine C. COLLINS
05 Provost .... Dr. Nolan T. ATKINS
11 Dean of Administration .... Ms. Sharron R. SCOTT
20 Associate Dean of Faculty .... Mr. Thomas K. ANDERSON
32 Dean of Student Affairs .... Mr. Jonathan M. DAVIS
07 Director of Admissions .... Mr. Vincent U. MALONEY
18 Director of Physical Plant .... Mr. Thomas R. ARCHER
13 Chief Technology Officer .... Mr. Michael A. DENTE
30 Director of Development .... Ms. Jennifer K. HARRIS
08 Library Director .... Mr. Samuel C. BOSS
06 Registrar .... Ms. Miranda D. FOX
35 Director of Student Life .... Ms. Erin S. ROSSETTI
41 Director of Athletics .... Mr. Christopher T. UMMER
37 Director of Financial Aid .... Ms. Tanya W. BRADLEY
36 Director of Career Services .... Ms. Amy L. WRIGHT
88 Dir of Student Academic Development .... Ms. Debra M. BAILIN
26 Executive Director of Communication .... Ms. Sylvia PLUMB
121 Director of Advising Resources .... Ms. Kathleen E. GOLD
15 Director of Human Resources .... Ms. Sandra L. FRANZ

*Vermont Technical College (E)

PO Box 500, Randolph Center VT 05061-0500
County: Orange | FICE Identification: 003698
Unit ID: 231165
Telephone: (802) 728-1000 | Carnegie Class: Bac/Assoc-Mixed
FAX Number: (802) 728-1508 | Calendar System: Semester
URL: www.vtc.edu
Established: 1866 | Annual Undergrad Tuition & Fees (In-State): $14,026
Enrollment: 1,559 | Coed
Affiliation or Control: State | IRS Status: 501(c)3
Highest Offering: Master's
Accreditation: EH, ADNUR, COARC, DH, ENGT, NUR, PNUR

02 President .... Ms. Patricia L. MOULTON
05 Interim Dean Academic Affairs .... Mr. Allan ROGERS
32 Dean of Student Affairs .... Mr. John PATERSON
20 Dean Academic Pgm Development .... Mr. Brent SARGENT
11 Dean of Administration .... Mr. Littleton TYLER
13 Chief Technology Officer .... Mr. James SMITH
30 Assoc Dean Inst Advancement .... Vacant
66 Assoc Dean of Nursing .... Ms. Sarah BILLINGS-BERG
06 Registrar .... Ms. Shelly RUSS
10 Controller .... Ms. Eileen DONOVAN
37 Director Financial Aid .... Ms. Catherine MCCULLOUGH
29 Assoc Dean Enrollment/Alumni Affs .... Mr. Dwight CROSS
19 Director Public Safety .... Mr. Emile FREDETTE
18 Director Facilities .... Mr. Theodore MANAZIR
36 Director Career Development .... Ms. Karry BOOSKA
15 Director of Human Resources .... Ms. Pamela ANKUDA
26 Dir Marketing/Communications .... Ms. Amanda CHAULK
40 Manager Bookstore .... Mr. Joe HIRAK
07 Asst Director of Admissions .... Ms. Jessica VAN DEREN
08 Library Director .... Ms. Jane KEARNS

VIRGINIA

Advanced Technology Institute (F)

5700 Southern Boulevard, Virginia Beach VA 23462-2409
County: City of Virginia Beach | FICE Identification: 031275
Unit ID: 231411
Telephone: (757) 490-1241 | Carnegie Class: Spec 2-yr-Tech
FAX Number: (757) 499-5929 | Calendar System: Semester
URL: www.auto.edu
Established: 1993 | Annual Undergrad Tuition & Fees: $13,250
Enrollment: 633 | Coed
Affiliation or Control: Proprietary | IRS Status: Proprietary
Highest Offering: Associate Degree
Accreditation: ACCSC

01 Campus President .... Mr. Dick DAIGLE
05 Chief Academic Officer .... Mr. Chenek PICKA
07 Director of Admissions .... Mr. Mike CORCORAN
32 Director of Student Services .... Mr. Kirk CLAYTON
37 Director Student Financial Aid .... Mr. Chad MARTS
06 Registrar .... Mrs. Shannon VOIGT
15 Director Personnel Services .... Mr. Rey LIZAN
36 Director Student Placement .... Mr. Kirk CLAYTON
39 Director Student Housing .... Mr. Kirk MANGHAM

American National University (G)

1813 E Main Street, Salem VA 24153-4598
County: Independent City | FICE Identification: 003726
Unit ID: 232797
Telephone: (540) 986-1800 | Carnegie Class: Bac/Assoc-Mixed
FAX Number: (540) 986-1344 | Calendar System: Quarter
URL: www.an.edu
Established: 1886 | Annual Undergrad Tuition & Fees: $14,886
Enrollment: 1,207 | Coed
Affiliation or Control: Proprietary | IRS Status: Proprietary
Highest Offering: Master's
Accreditation: ACICS, CEA, MAC, NURSE

01 President .... Mr. Frank E. LONGAKER
10 Exec VP of Campus Operations .... Mr. Jason TOWERS
21 Exec VP of Campus Support Operation .... Ms. Cathy PLUNKETT

American National University (H)

3926 Seminole Trail, Charlottesville VA 22911-8397
Telephone: (434) 295-0136 | Identification: 666501
Accreditation: ACICS, MAC

American National University (I)

336 Old Riverside Drive, Danville VA 24541-1819
Telephone: (434) 793-6822 | Identification: 666502
Accreditation: ACICS, MAC

American National University (J)

1515 Country Club Road, Harrisonburg VA 22801-9709
Telephone: (540) 432-0943 | Identification: 666503
Accreditation: ACICS, MAC, SURGT

American National University (K)

104 Candlewood Court, Lynchburg VA 24502-2653
Telephone: (434) 239-3500 | Identification: 666504
Accreditation: ACICS, MAC

Appalachian College of Pharmacy (L)

1060 Dragon Road, Oakwood VA 24631
County: Buchanan | FICE Identification: 041806
Unit ID: 449922
Telephone: (276) 498-4190 | Carnegie Class: Spec-4-yr-Other Health
FAX Number: (276) 498-4193 | Calendar System: Semester
URL: www.acpharm.org
Established: 2003 | Annual Graduate Tuition & Fees: N/A
Enrollment: 202 | Coed
Affiliation or Control: Independent Non-Profit | IRS Status: 501(c)3
Highest Offering: Doctorate; No Undergraduates
Accreditation: SC, PHAR

01 President .... Mr. Michael G. MCGLOTHLIN
05 Dean .... Dr. Susan L. MAYHEW
10 Chief Financial Officer .... Ms. Holli HARMAN
07 Dir of Admissions/Fin Aid/Registrar .... Ms. Vickie KEENE
103 Dir of Institutional Development .... Mr. Terry KILGORE
32 Dir Student Services/Alumni Affairs .... Mr. Jason MCGLOTHLIN
13 Dir Safety/Information Technology .... Mr. Michael DEEL

Appalachian School of Law (M)

1169 Riverside Drive, Grundy VA 24614-2825
County: Buchanan | FICE Identification: 035593
Unit ID: 432348
Telephone: (800) 895-7411 | Carnegie Class: Spec-4-yr-Law
FAX Number: (276) 935-8261 | Calendar System: Semester
URL: www.asl.edu
Established: 1995 | Annual Undergrad Tuition & Fees: N/A
Enrollment: 109 | Coed
Affiliation or Control: Independent Non-Profit | IRS Status: 501(c)3

Highest Offering: First Professional Degree
Accreditation: LAW

01 Interim Dean and COO Ms. Sandra K. MCGLOTHLIN
05 Assoc Dean of Academic Affairs Mr. Mason HEIDT
08 Acting Director of Library Ms. Glenna OWENS
36 Director of Career Services Mr. Jeremy WILLIAMS
13 Director of Information Services Mr. Brian PRESLEY
15 Director Cmty Service & Personnel Ms. Jina M. SAULS
07 Director of Admissions Ms. Kelsea WAGNER
06 Registrar Ms. Beth STANLEY
37 Financial Aid Officer Mr. David BROOKSHIRE

Argosy University, Washington DC (A)

1550 Wilson Boulevard, Suite 600,
Arlington VA 22209-2435
Telephone: (703) 526-5800 Identification: 666788
Accreditation: &WC, ACBSP, CACREP, CLPSY

† Regional accreditation is carried under the parent institution in Orange, CA.

The Art Institute of Virginia Beach (B)

4500 Main Street, Ste 100, Virginia Beach VA 23462
Telephone: (757) 493-6700 Identification: 770977
Accreditation: &SC, ACFEI

† Branch campus of The Art Institute of Atlanta, Atlanta, GA

The Art Institute of Washington (C)

1820 North Fort Myer Drive, Arlington VA 22209-1802
Telephone: (703) 358-9550 Identification: 770945
Accreditation: &SC, CIDA

† Branch campus of The Art Institute of Atlanta, Atlanta, GA.

Atlantic University (D)

215 67th Street, Virginia Beach VA 23451-8101
County: Virginia Beach Identification: 666653
Unit ID: 231402
Telephone: (757) 631-8101 Carnegie Class: Not Classified
FAX Number: (757) 631-8096 Calendar System: Trimester
URL: www.atlanticuniv.edu
Established: 1930 Annual Graduate Tuition & Fees: N/A
Enrollment: N/A Coed
Affiliation or Control: Independent Non-Profit IRS Status: 501(c)3
Highest Offering: Master's; No Undergraduates
Accreditation: DEAC

01 CEO Kevin TODESCHI
05 Dir Academic & Administrative Affs James VAN AUKEN
84 Assoc VP Enrollment Management Rachel VINCITORE

Averett University (E)

420 W Main Street, Danville VA 24541-3692
County: Independent City FICE Identification: 003702
Unit ID: 231420
Telephone: (434) 791-5600 Carnegie Class: Bac-Diverse
FAX Number: (434) 791-7181 Calendar System: Semester
URL: www.averett.edu
Established: 1859 Annual Undergrad Tuition & Fees: $31,980
Enrollment: 878 Coed
Affiliation or Control: Independent Non-Profit IRS Status: 501(c)3
Highest Offering: Master's
Accreditation: SC, #CAATE, NURSE

01 President Dr. Tiffany M. FRANKS
32 Executive Vice President Mr. Charles S. HARRIS
05 Vice Pres for Academic Affairs Dr. Timothy FULOP
10 Vice President Business & Finance Mr. Aaron HOWELL
30 Vice Pres Institutional Advancement Mr. Albert RAWLEY
15 Director of Human Resources Mrs. Kathie TUNE
84 Vice Pres Enrollment Management Ms. Stacy GATO
37 Director Student Financial Services Mr. Carl BRADSHER
21 Controller Ms. Lisa STEWART
08 Director of Library Ms. Elaine DAY
36 Director of Career Development Ms. Angie MCADAMS
06 Registrar Mrs. Janet ROBERSON
26 Dir of Marketing/Communications Ms. Cassie JONES
29 Director Alumni Relations Mr. Dan HAYES
09 Dir Institutional Research/Effect Dr. Pam MCKIRDY
07 Director of Admissions Mr. Joel NESTER
18 Chief Facilities/Physical Plant Vacant
35 Director of Student Affairs Ms. Lesley VILLAROSE
38 Director of Student Counseling Mrs. Joan KAHWAJY-ANDERSON

Baptist Theological Seminary at Richmond (F)

8040 Villa Park Drive, Richmond VA 23228
County: Independent City FICE Identification: 031169
Unit ID: 366793
Telephone: (804) 355-8135 Carnegie Class: Spec-4-yr-Faith
FAX Number: (804) 355-8182 Calendar System: Semester
URL: www.btsr.edu
Established: 1991 Annual Graduate Tuition & Fees: N/A
Enrollment: 70 Coed
Affiliation or Control: Independent Non-Profit IRS Status: 501(c)3
Highest Offering: Doctorate; No Undergraduates
Accreditation: THEOL

01 President Dr. Linda M. BRIDGES
05 Acting VP of Acad Affairs & Dean Dr. Tracy HARTMAN
111 VP Institutional Advancement Mr. Rob FOX
10 Dir Business Affairs & Facilities Dr. James F. PEAK, JR.
07 Director Admissions & Recruitment Dr. Melissa FALLEN
06 Registrar Rev. Susan BLANCHARD
13 Chief Info Technology Officer (CIO) Ms. Eryn VAN LEAR
26 Communications Manager Ms. Lacy KENDRICK

Bethel College (G)

1705 Todds Lane, Hampton VA 23666
County: Hampton City FICE Identification: 041538
Unit ID: 458113
Telephone: (757) 826-1883 Carnegie Class: Spec-4-yr-Faith
FAX Number: (757) 826-5436 Calendar System: Semester
URL: www.bethel-college.com
Established: 2004 Annual Undergrad Tuition & Fees: $8,100
Enrollment: 58 Coed
Affiliation or Control: Assemblies Of God Church IRS Status: 501(c)3
Highest Offering: Baccalaureate
Accreditation: BI

01 President Dr. Mark WOOTTON
05 Academic Dean/Exec Vice President Dr. Ron DEBERRY
32 Student Affairs Ms. Nanette BARTHOLOMEW
06 Registrar Mrs. Shawn LABADIE
08 Librarian Ms. Janell SANFORD
30 Director Institutional Advancement Ms. Audrey SOMERO

Bluefield College (H)

3000 College Avenue, Bluefield VA 24605-1799
County: Tazewell FICE Identification: 003703
Unit ID: 231554
Telephone: (276) 326-3682 Carnegie Class: Bac-Diverse
FAX Number: (276) 326-4288 Calendar System: Semester
URL: www.bluefield.edu
Established: 1922 Annual Undergrad Tuition & Fees: $24,380
Enrollment: 976 Coed
Affiliation or Control: Baptist IRS Status: 501(c)3
Highest Offering: Master's
Accreditation: SC, CAEPT, NURSE

01 President Dr. David W. OLIVE
04 Assistant to the President Mrs. Diane T. SHOTT
05 VP for Academic Affairs Dr. Marshall FLOWERS
111 VP for Advancement Mrs. Ruth BLANKENSHIP
10 VP for Finance & Admin Mrs. Ruth BLANKENSHIP
84 VP for Enrollment Mgmt/Student Dev Mr. Michael J. WHITE
06 Registrar Ms. Jennifer LAMB
08 Director of Library Services Ms. Barbara GILLESPIE
26 Director of Public Relations Mr. Chris SHOEMAKER
29 Director of Alumni Relations Mr. Josh GRUBB
09 Director of Institutional Research Mr. Bryan FRAZIER
37 Interim Director of Financial Aid Ms. Cary WRIGHT
42 Campus Minister Dr. Henry CLARY
41 Athletic Director Mr. Mike WHITE
40 Campus Store Manager Ms. Beth KINSER
18 Director of Maintenance Ms. Elizabeth STANTON
19 Coordinator of Campus Safety Mr. Gary RUTH
15 Human Resources Director Ms. Judy PEDNEAU
13 Chief Info Technology Officer Mr. Steve KESSINGER
53 Dean School of Education Dr. Tom BREWSTER

Bon Secours Memorial College of Nursing (I)

8550 Magellan Parkway, Ste 1100, Richmond VA 23227
County: Henrico FICE Identification: 010043
Unit ID: 233356
Telephone: (804) 627-5300 Carnegie Class: Spec-4-yr-Other Health
FAX Number: (804) 627-5330 Calendar System: Semester
URL: www.bsmcon.edu
Established: 1961 Annual Undergrad Tuition & Fees: N/A
Enrollment: 500 Coed
Affiliation or Control: Independent Non-Profit IRS Status: 501(c)3
Highest Offering: Baccalaureate
Accreditation: ACICS, NURSE

05 Vice Pres Academic Affairs/Provost Dr. Melanie H. GREEN
66 Dean of Nursing Dr. Barbara C. SORBELLO
10 Dean of Finance and Administration Vacant
32 Dean of Student Services Ms. Leslie WINSTON
88 Dean of Clinical Simulation Center Ms. Holly PUGH
09 Director of Inst Effectiveness Dr. Benji N. DJEUKENG
88 Associate Dean of Nursing Dr. Chris-Tenna M. PERKINS
06 Registrar Ms. Lydia LISNER
07 Director of Admissions Ms. Carrie NEWCOMB
08 Head Librarian Ms. Kathleen HIERHOLZER
29 Director Alumni Relations Ms. Jennifer GOINS
36 Director Student Placement Ms. Allison PETERSON
37 Director Student Financial Aid Ms. Kelley FLORIAN

Bridgewater College (J)

402 E College Street, Bridgewater VA 22812-1599
County: Rockingham FICE Identification: 003704
Unit ID: 231581
Telephone: (540) 828-8000 Carnegie Class: Bac-A&S
FAX Number: (540) 828-5479 Calendar System: Semester
URL: www.bridgewater.edu
Established: 1880 Annual Undergrad Tuition & Fees: $32,590
Enrollment: 1,834 Coed
Affiliation or Control: Church Of The Brethren IRS Status: 501(c)3
Highest Offering: Master's
Accreditation: SC, CAATE

01 President Dr. David W. BUSHMAN
03 Executive Vice President Mr. Roy W. FERGUSON, JR.
05 Provost/VP for Academic Affairs Dr. Leona SEVICK
10 Vice Pres for Finance & Treasurer Ms. Anne B. KEELER
111 Vice Pres for Institutional Advance Dr. Maureen SILVA
26 Assoc VP Marketing & Communications Ms. Abbie PARKHURST
84 Vice President for Enrollment Mgmt Mr. Reggie WEBB
18 Director of Sustainability Mr. Teshome H. MOLALENGE
40 Bookstore Manager Ms. Sarah LANDIS
20 Associate Dean of Academic Affairs Dr. Robert B. ANDERSEN
32 VP for Student Life/Dean of Student Dr. Leslie FRERE
36 Director of Career Services Ms. Sherry TALBOTT
121 Director of Academic Support Svcs Dr. Raymond W. STUDWELL, II
42 Chaplain Rev. Robert R. MILLER
07 Director of Admissions Mr. Jarret L. SMITH
37 Director of Financial Aid Mr. Scott D. MORRISON
21 Director of Finance & Budget Ms. Penny E. REARDON
13 Director of Info Tech Center Ms. Kristy K. RHEA
41 Director of Athletics Mr. Curtis L. KENDALL
38 Director of Counseling Services Mr. Randall HOOK
29 Director of Alumni Relations Ms. Ellen B. MILLER
09 Director of Institutional Research Ms. Dawn S. DALBOW
15 Director of Human Resources Mrs. Kimberly P. HARPER
08 Library Director Mr. Andrew L. PEARSON
06 Registrar Ms. Cynthia K. HOWDYSHELL
21 Controller Ms. Mary S. SCHWAB
27 Editor/Dir of Media Relations Mr. Charles R. CULBERTSON
18 Director of Facilities Mr. David R. VANDEVANDER
19 Campus Police Chief Mr. Milton S. FRANKLIN
28 Minority Mentor Mr. James E. RAEFORD
23 Director of Student Health Services Ms. Paige FRENCH
28 Director of Multicultural Services Ms. Joanne HARRIS-DUFF
109 Director of Dining Services Ms. Mary SPEIR
04 Administrative Asst to President Mrs. Elaine C. DELLINGER
39 Director Student Housing Ms. Dawn OHANESSIAN
104 Director International Education Mrs. Anne MARSH

Bryant & Stratton College (K)

8141 Hull Street Road, North Chesterfield VA 23235-6411
Telephone: (804) 745-2444 Identification: 666496
Accreditation: &M, ADNUR, MAC, NURSE

† Regional accreditation is carried under the parent institution (corporate office) in Buffalo, NY.

Bryant & Stratton College (L)

301 Centre Pointe Drive, Virginia Beach VA 23462-4417
Telephone: (757) 499-7900 FICE Identification: 010061
Accreditation: &M, MAC

† Regional accreditation is carried under the parent institution (corporate office) in Buffalo, NY.

California University of Management and Sciences Virginia (M)

4300 Wilson Blvd, Suite 140, Arlington VA 22203
Telephone: (703) 663-8088 Identification: 666734
Accreditation: ACICS

† Branch campus of California University of Management and Sciences, Anaheim, CA.

Centra College of Nursing (N)

905 Lakeside Drive, Suite A, Lynchburg VA 24501
County: Independent City FICE Identification: 021758
Unit ID: 232618
Telephone: (434) 200-3070 Carnegie Class: Spec 2-yr-Health
FAX Number: (434) 200-5505 Calendar System: Semester
URL: www.centracon.edu
Established: 2011 Annual Undergrad Tuition & Fees: $11,490
Enrollment: 142 Coed
Affiliation or Control: Independent Non-Profit IRS Status: 501(c)3
Highest Offering: Associate Degree
Accreditation: ABHES, ADNUR, PNUR

01 Dean Dr. Melody SHARP
66 Assoc Director ADN Program Dr. Jim EMERSON
66 Assoc Director PN Program Ms. Dana GRANT
05 Director of Academic Progression Dr. Diane ELMORE
37 Financial Aid/Enrollment Manager Mr. Aaron ELLENBURG

Centura College (O)

932 Ventura Way, Chesapeake VA 23320
Telephone: (757) 549-2121 Identification: 770608
Accreditation: ACCSC

Centura College (A)

616 Denbigh Boulevard, Newport News VA 23608
Telephone: (757) 874-2121 Identification: 770606
Accreditation: ACCSC

Centura College (B)

7020 N Military Highway, Norfolk VA 23518-4202
Telephone: (757) 853-2121 Identification: 770605
Accreditation: ACCSC

Centura College (C)

7914 Midlothian Turnpike, North Chesterfield VA 23235
County: Chesterfield FICE Identification: 031264
Unit ID: 427982
Telephone: (804) 330-0111 Carnegie Class: Spec 2-yr-Health
FAX Number: (804) 330-3809 Calendar System: Semester
URL: www.centuracollege.edu
Established: 1992 Annual Undergrad Tuition & Fees: $16,337
Enrollment: 148 Coed
Affiliation or Control: Proprietary IRS Status: Proprietary
Highest Offering: Associate Degree
Accreditation: ACCSC

01 Campus Executive Director .... Susam MERRITT

Centura College (D)

2697 Dean Drive, Suite 100,
Virginia Beach VA 23452-7431
County: City of Virginia Beach FICE Identification: 023344
Unit ID: 232016
Telephone: (757) 340-2121 Carnegie Class: Bac/Assoc-Mixed
FAX Number: (757) 340-9704 Calendar System: Semester
URL: www.centuracollege.edu
Established: 1969 Annual Undergrad Tuition & Fees: $15,887
Enrollment: 164 Coed
Affiliation or Control: Proprietary IRS Status: Proprietary
Highest Offering: Baccalaureate
Accreditation: ACCSC

01 Campus Executive Director .... Wendy DAVIDSON
11 Assistant Campus Executive Director .... Dennis RYAN
05 Director of Education .... Emily SIMMONS
07 Director of Admissions .... Vacant
06 Registrar .... Dennis RYAN
37 Financial Aid Officer ....Jennifer BROADWELL
10 Bursar .... Sarah TROUT
32 Student Services Coordinator ....Megan DE HART
36 Career Services Coordinator ....Alexis PALMER
08 Librarian .... Jeffery BARBOUR

Chamberlain University-Arlington Campus (E)

2450 Crystal Drive, Arlington VA 22202
Telephone: (703) 416-7300 Identification: 770497
Accreditation: &NH, NURSE

† Branch campus of Chamberlain University-Addison, Addison, IL

Chester Career College (F)

751 West Hundred Road, Chester VA 23836-2516
County: Chesterfield FICE Identification: 034095
Unit ID: 437769
Telephone: (804) 751-9191 Carnegie Class: Not Classified
FAX Number: (804) 751-2599 Calendar System: Semester
URL: www.chestercareercollege.edu
Established: 1997 Annual Undergrad Tuition & Fees: N/A
Enrollment: 154 Coed
Affiliation or Control: Proprietary IRS Status: Proprietary
Highest Offering: Associate Degree
Accreditation: COE

01 Campus Director ....Ms. Debbie HARRIS
05 Academic Dean/Dir Allied Health ....Ms. Sandra KERRICK
06 Registrar ....Ms. Annette WHITE
08 Head Librarian .... Ms. Kathy PHILO
36 Director Job Placement ....Mrs. Tamara KNIGHT
37 Director Student Financial Aid ....Ms. Jennifer GLOVER

Christendom College (G)

134 Christendom Drive, Front Royal VA 22630-6534
County: Warren FICE Identification: 036653
Unit ID: 231703
Telephone: (540) 636-2900 Carnegie Class: Not Classified
FAX Number: (540) 636-1655 Calendar System: Semester
URL: www.christendom.edu
Established: 1977 Annual Undergrad Tuition & Fees: N/A
Enrollment: N/A Coed
Affiliation or Control: Roman Catholic IRS Status: 501(c)3
Highest Offering: Master's
Accreditation: SC

01 President ....Dr. Timothy T. O'DONNELL
10 Executive Vice President/CFO/COO ....Mr. Kenneth H. FERGUSON
05 Vice President Academic Affairs .... Dr. Gregory TOWNSEND
30 Vice President for Advancement ....Mr. Paul JALSEVAC
18 Vice Pres Operations/Facility Plng ....Mr. Michael S. FOECKLER
84 Vice Pres Enrollment & Marketing .... Mr. Thomas MCFADDEN
21 Controller ....Mr. Luke FIER
32 Dean of Student Life .... Mr. Chris VANDER WOUDE
20 Academic Dean ....Mr. Mark WUNSCH
06 Registrar .... Mr. Walter A. JANARO
07 Director of Admissions ....Mr. Sam PHILLIPS
08 Director of Christendom Library ...... Mr. Andrew V. ARMSTRONG
37 Financial Aid Officer ....Mrs. Alisa L. POLK
29 Asst Dir Alumni/Donor Relations ....Mr. Vince CRISTE
13 Director of Computer Services ....Mr. Douglas S. BRIGGS
88 Registrar/Business Officer NDGS .... Miss Maura MCMAHON
41 Athletic Director ....Mr. Patrick QUEST
04 Exec Assistant to the President ....Ms. Brenda SEELBACH
58 Dean of the Graduate School ....Dr. Robert J. MATAVA

Christopher Newport University (H)

1 Avenue of the Arts, Newport News VA 23606-3072
County: Independent City FICE Identification: 003706
Unit ID: 231712
Telephone: (757) 594-7000 Carnegie Class: Masters/S
FAX Number: N/A Calendar System: Semester
URL: www.cnu.edu
Established: 1960 Annual Undergrad Tuition & Fees (In-State): $13,054
Enrollment: 5,172 Coed
Affiliation or Control: State IRS Status: 501(c)3
Highest Offering: Master's
Accreditation: SC, ENG, MUS, SW, THEA

01 President ....Hon. Paul S. TRIBLE, JR.
100 Chief of Staff ....Mrs. Cynthia R. PERRY
05 Provost ....Dr. David C. DOUGHTY
10 Executive Vice President/CFO ....Mr. William L. BRAUER
43 University Counsel ....Ms. Maureen MATSEN
111 Vice Pres for Univ Advancement ....Mrs. Adelia P. THOMPSON
15 Director of Human Resources ....Mrs. Lorraine M. WESTPHAL
04 Exec Assistant to President/Board ......Mrs. Beverley D. MUELLER
07 Dean of Admission...Mr. Robert J. LANGE
84 VP for Enrollment/Student Success .....Dr. Lisa DUNCAN RAINES
32 Vice President of Student Affairs ....Dr. Kevin M. HUGHES
49 Dean College Arts & Humanities ....Dr. Lori J. UNDERWOOD
83 Dean College of Social Sciences .... Dr. Quentin KIDD
83 Dean College Nat/Behav Science .... Dr. Nicole R. GUAJARDO
50 Dean Luter School of Business ....Dr. George H. EBBS
41 Director of Athletics ....Mr. Kyle S. MCMULLIN
21 University Comptroller ....Mrs. Diane REED
06 University Registrar ....Mrs. Julianna M. WAIT
37 Director of Financial Aid ....Ms. Christina L. RUSSELL
39 Director of Housing ....Mr. Andrew H. KOERNERT
09 Director of Institutional Research ....Ms. Donna A. VARNER
13 Chief Information Officer ....Mr. Andrew B. CRAWFORD
45 Director of Planning & Budget ....Ms. Patricia L. MCDERMOTT
116 Director of University Audit ....Ms. Faith D. BELOTE
108 Director of Assessment & Evaluation ....Mr. Jason C. LYONS
96 Director of Material Management .... Mr. Ryan A. FEREBEE
08 University Librarian ....Ms. Mary K. SELLEN
19 Sr Commander Police Operations ....Mr. Scott AUSTIN
18 Director of Facilities Mgmt ....Mr. Scott GESELE
112 Sr Dir Advancement/Gift Planning .... Ms. Lucy L. LATCHUM
102 Dir Foundation & Corporate Giving ....Mr. Keith D. ROOTS
26 Exec Dir of University Relations ....Mrs. Amie G. DALE
27 Director of External Relations ....Mr. Thomas E. KRAMER
29 Director of Alumni Relations ....Mr. Baxter VENDRICK
22 Director of Title IX and EO .... Ms. Michelle L. MOODY
38 Exec Dir Counseling/Health Services ....Dr. William V. RITCHEY
36 Director Center of Career Planning ...... Ms. Elizabeth K. WESTLEY
104 Director of Study Abroad ....Ms. Amanda K. PIERCE

College of William & Mary (I)

PO Box 8795, Williamsburg VA 23187-8795
County: Independent City FICE Identification: 003705
Unit ID: 231624
Telephone: (757) 221-4000 Carnegie Class: DU-Higher
FAX Number: (757) 221-1259 Calendar System: Semester
URL: www.wm.edu
Established: 1693 Annual Undergrad Tuition & Fees (In-State): $21,234
Enrollment: 8,484 Coed
Affiliation or Control: State IRS Status: 501(c)3
Highest Offering: Doctorate
Accreditation: SC, CACREP, CAEPN, IPSY, LAW

01 President .... Mr. W. Taylor REVELEY, III
05 Provost .... Dr. Michael HALLERAN
10 Sr VP for Finance & Administration ....Mr. Samuel E. JONES
111 VP for University Advancement ....Dr. Matthew T. LAMBERT
45 Vice Pres for Strategic Initiatives ....Mr. Henry R. BROADDUS
32 Vice President for Student Affairs ....Dr. Virginia M. AMBLER
41 Director of Athletics ....Ms. Samantha HUGE
29 Assoc VP/Ex Dir Alumni Engagement .Ms. Marilyn W. MIDYETTE
49 Dean Faculty of Arts & Sciences .... Dr. Katharine CONLEY
50 Dean Mason School of Business .... Mr. Lawrence B. PULLEY
53 Dean School of Education ....Dr. Spencer NILES
61 Dean William & Mary Law School ...... Mr. Davison M. DOUGLAS
88 Dean and Director of VIMS ....Dr. John T. WELLS
08 Dean University Libraries .... Ms. Carrie COOPER
43 University Counsel ....Ms. Deborah A. LOVE
20 Vice Prov Academic & Faculty Affs .... Ms. Ann Marie STOCK
82 Vice Prov Intl Affairs/Reves Ctr ....Dr. Stephen E. HANSON
46 Vice Provost Rsch & Grad Prof Stds ....Dr. Dennis M. MANOS
13 Chief Information Officer .... Mr. Courtney CARPENTER
14 Deputy CIO ....Ms. Bernadette KENNEY
108 Assoc Provost Inst Accred ....Dr. Susan L. BOSWORTH
07 Dean of Admission/Assoc Prov Enroll .... Mr. Tim A. WOLFE
06 Assoc Provost & Univ Registrar ....Ms. Sara L. MARCHELLO
09 Director of Institutional Research ....Mr. Evan DAVIES
106 Assoc Provost ELearning Initiatives ....Dr. Michele H. JACKSON
88 Dean for Educational Policy ....Dr. Lu Ann HOMZA
58 Dean Graduate Studies & Research .... Dr. Virginia TORCZON
92 Dean Honors/Interdisciplinary Stds ....Dr. Joel D. SCHWARTZ
88 Dean of Undergraduate Studies ....Dr. Janice L. ZEMAN
104 Director of Global Education ....Ms. Sylvia MITTERNDORFER
86 Assoc VP Government Relations ....Ms. Frances C. BRADFORD
26 Chief Com Officer Univ Web/Design ....Mr. Brian WHITSON
88 Assoc VP Development/Campaign Dir .... Mr. Mark L. BEGLY
30 Assoc VP University Development ....Mr. Earl T. GRANGER
18 Assoc Vice Pres Facilities Mgmt ....Mr. Van DOBSON
35 Dean of Students ....Ms. Marjorie THOMAS
25 Director of Sponsored Programs .... Ms. Jane LOPEZ
22 Asst Director of Equal Opportunity .... Ms. Sharron GATLING
37 Director Student Financial Aid .... Mr. Joseph DOBROTA
15 Chief Human Resources Officer ....Mr. John POMA
38 Director Counseling Center ....Dr. Warrenetta C. MANN
36 Director Career Development ....Ms. Kathleen L. POWELL
19 Chief W&M Police Department ....Ms. Deborah CHEESEBRO
114 Chief Budget Officer ....Ms. Amy SEBRING
23 Director Student Health Services ....Dr. Virginia D. WELLS
39 Assoc VP Stdnt Affs/Dir of Res Life ....Maggie EVANS
96 Director of Procurement ....Ms. Erma BAKER
40 Manager W&M Bookstore ....Ms. Cathy PACHECO
100 Asst to President/Chief of Staff ....Mr. Michael J. FOX
101 Secretary to the Board of Visitors ....Mr. Michael J. FOX
04 Executive Asst to President .... Ms. Cynthia A. BRAUER
105 Director of University Web & Design ....Ms. Tina L. COLEMAN
88 Assoc VP for Health & Wellness .... Dr. Robert K. CRACE
28 Chief Diversity Officer ....Dr. Fanchon GLOVER
84 Vice Prov Enroll & Dean Admissions ....Mr. Timothy A. WOLFE

Columbia College (J)

8620 Westwood Center Drive, Vienna VA 22182
County: Fairfax FICE Identification: 041273
Unit ID: 455983
Telephone: (703) 206-0508 Carnegie Class: Assoc/HT-High Trad
FAX Number: (703) 206-0488 Calendar System: Other
URL: www.ccdc.edu
Established: 1999 Annual Undergrad Tuition & Fees: N/A
Enrollment: 424 Coed
Affiliation or Control: Proprietary IRS Status: Proprietary
Highest Offering: Associate Degree
Accreditation: ACICS, COE

01 President/Founder ....Dr. Richard K. KIM

Culinary Institute of Virginia (K)

2428 Almeda Avenue, Ste 106, Norfolk VA 23513
Telephone: (757) 858-2433 Identification: 770960
Accreditation: &SC

Danville Regional Medical Center School of Health Professions (L)

142 South Main Street, Danville VA 24541
County: Independent City FICE Identification: 021116
Unit ID: 232724
Telephone: (434) 799-4510 Carnegie Class: Not Classified
FAX Number: (434) 799-3718 Calendar System: Semester
URL: www.danvilleregional.com
Established: 1898 Annual Undergrad Tuition & Fees: N/A
Enrollment: 19 Coed
Affiliation or Control: Proprietary IRS Status: Proprietary
Highest Offering: Associate Degree
Accreditation: ABHES, RAD

01 Director Radiology Pgms/Tech .... Mr. Kevin MURRAY

DeVry University - Arlington Campus (M)

2450 Crystal Drive, Arlington VA 22202-3887
Telephone: (703) 414-4000 Identification: 666220
Accreditation: &NH, ENGT

† Regional accreditation is carried under the parent institution in Downers Grove, IL.

Divine Mercy University (N)

2001 Jefferson Davis Hwy, Ste 511,
Arlington VA 22202-3609
County: Arlington FICE Identification: 038724
Unit ID: 445869
Telephone: (703) 416-1441 Carnegie Class: Spec-4-yr-Other Health
FAX Number: (703) 416-8588 Calendar System: Semester
URL: www.divinemercy.edu
Established: 1998 Annual Graduate Tuition & Fees: N/A
Enrollment: 150 Coed
Affiliation or Control: Independent Non-Profit IRS Status: 501(c)3
Highest Offering: Doctorate; No Undergraduates
Accreditation: SC, CLPSY

01 President ....Fr. Charles SIKORSKY

Eastern Mennonite University (A)

1200 Park Road, Harrisonburg VA 22802-2462
County: Independent City FICE Identification: 003708
Unit ID: 232043
Telephone: (540) 432-4000 Carnegie Class: Masters/S
FAX Number: (540) 432-4444 Calendar System: Semester
URL: www.emu.edu
Established: 1917 Annual Undergrad Tuition & Fees: $34,200
Enrollment: 1,773 Coed
Affiliation or Control: Mennonite Church IRS Status: 501(c)3
Highest Offering: Master's
Accreditation: SC, CACREP, CAEPN, NURSE, PAST, SW, THEOL

01 President .... Dr. Susan SCHULTZ-HUXMAN
05 Provost .... Dr. Fred L. KNISS
111 Vice President for Advancement .... Mr. Kirk L. SHISLER
10 Vice President for Finance .... Mr. Daryl W. BERT
84 Vice Pres Enrollment & Student Life .... Dr. Jim SMUCKER
20 Vice Pres & Undergrad Academic Dean .... Dr. Deirdre SMELTZER
73 Interim Seminary Dean .... Dr. Fred L. KNISS
06 University Registrar .... Mr. David A. DETROW
26 Director of Marketing Services .... Ms. Andrea S. WENGER
07 Director Undergraduate Admissions .... Mr. Matthew RUTH
08 Director of Libraries .... Dr. G. Marcille H. FREDERICK
37 Director of Financial Assistance .... Ms. Michele R. HENSLEY
36 Director Career Services/Testing .... Ms. Kimberly PHILLIPS
29 Director of Alumni/Parent Relations .... Mr. Jeffrey A. SHANK
09 Director Institutional Research .... Dr. Scott BARGE
04 Assistant to the President .... Ms. Twila K. YODER
41 Athletic Director .... Mr. David A. KING
42 Campus Pastor .... Mr. Brian M. BURKHOLDER
13 Director of Information Systems .... Mr. Benjamin S. BEACHY
18 Director of Physical Plant .... Mr. Ed LEHMAN
15 Director Human Resources .... Ms. Marcia J. ENGLE
21 Controller .... Mr. Timothy STUTZMAN
27 Chief Public Information Officer .... Ms. Mia KIVLIGHAN
35 Director Student Affairs .... Ms. Rachel R. SAWATZKY
38 Director Student Counseling .... Vacant

Eastern Virginia Career College (B)

10304 Spotsylvania Avenue, Ste. 400,
Fredericksburg VA 22408-8605
County: Spotsylvania FICE Identification: 036543
Unit ID: 441858
Telephone: (540) 373-2200 Carnegie Class: Spec 2-yr-Health
FAX Number: (540) 373-4465 Calendar System: Other
URL: www.evcc.edu
Established: 2000 Annual Undergrad Tuition & Fees: N/A
Enrollment: 217 Coed
Affiliation or Control: Proprietary IRS Status: Proprietary
Highest Offering: Associate Degree
Accreditation: COE, OTA

01 Chief Executive Officer/President .... Ms. A. Christine CARROLL

Eastern Virginia Medical School (C)

Box 1980, Norfolk VA 23501-1980
County: Independent City FICE Identification: 010338
Unit ID: 231970
Telephone: (757) 446-5600 Carnegie Class: Spec-4-yr-Med
FAX Number: (757) 446-5135 Calendar System: Other
URL: www.evms.edu
Established: 1973 Annual Graduate Tuition & Fees: N/A
Enrollment: 1,096 Coed
Affiliation or Control: Independent Non-Profit IRS Status: 501(c)3
Highest Offering: Doctorate; No Undergraduates
Accreditation: SC, ARCPA, CLPSY, IPSY, MED, PH, SURGA

01 President/Provost/Dean .... Dr. Richard V. HOMAN
04 Sr Exec Assistant to the President .... Ms. Tracy L. MORTON
116 Director Internal Audit .... Mr. Robert B. WOOD
100 VP of Operations/Chief of Staff .... Mr. Brant M. COX
17 Vice Pres/Dean Sch of Health Prof .... Dr. Charles D. COMBS
88 Assoc Dean for Health Professions .... Dr. Jeffrey A. JOHNSON
10 Vice Pres Administration/Finance ..... Mr. Mark R. BABASHANIAN
19 Chief of Police .... Mr. Andrew J. MITCHELL
18 Director Facilities/Physical Plant .... Mr. Doug MARTIN
28 Vice President for Diversity .... Mr. Mekbib L. GEMEDA
88 Vice Dean for Faculty Affairs .... Dr. Elza MYLONA
88 Vice Dean Clinical Affairs .... Dr. Alfred Z. ABUHAMAD
23 CEO EVMS Medical Group .... Mr. James F. LIND
05 Vice Dean Academic Affairs .... Dr. Ronald W. FLENNER
43 Vice President and General Counsel .... Ms. Stacy R. PURCELL
58 Vice Dean Grad Medical Education .... Dr. Linda R. ARCHER
46 Vice Dean for Research .... Dr. Jerry L. NADLER
09 Sr Assoc Dean for Research .... Dr. William J. WASILENKO
88 Assoc Dean Hum Sub Protection/IRB .... Dr. Harry J. TILLMAN
50 Assoc Dean Business/Admin Affairs .... Mr. David E. HUBAND
84 Assoc Dean Admissions and Enroll .... Dr. Thomas D. KIMBLE
32 Assoc Dean for Student Affairs .... Dr. Ann E. CAMPBELL
20 Asst Dean for Academic Affairs ..... Dr. Senthil K. RAJASEKARAN
08 Director of Library Services .... Ms. Kerrie S. SHAW
35 Asst Dean Student Affairs .... Dr. Allison P. KNIGHT
93 Asst Dean for Diversity .... Ms. Gail C. WILLIAMS
06 Registrar .... Mr. Michael J. DONLAN
15 Director Human Resources .... Mr. Matthew R. SCHENK
21 Asst VP for Financial Services .... Ms. Helen S. HESELIUS
88 Director for Technology Transfer .... Mr. Paul B. DIMARCO
37 Director Student Financial Aid .... Ms. Deborah R. BROWN
21 Director for Business Management ...... Ms. Tammy A. CHRISMAN
96 Director of Materials Management .... Mr. Steven LEE
13 Chief Information Officer .... Ms. Deborah A. TAYLOR
26 Chief Comm and Marketing Officer .... Dr. Vincent A. RHODES
29 Exec Director for Alumni Affairs .... Ms. Melissa W. LANG
30 Asst VP Development .... Ms. Connie L. MCKENZIE
88 Director of the Brock Institute .... Dr. Cynthia ROMERO
51 Director for Continuing Med Educ .... Ms. Drucie A. PAPAFIL
88 Director Occupational Health .... Ms. Heather SINGLETON
25 Director Sponsored Programs .... Ms. Yolanda F. DEMORY
88 Director Rad Safety Env Health .... Mr. Courtney A. KERR
117 Director Risk Management .... Ms. Donita M. LAMARAND

† Member of Virginia Consortium for Professional Psychology.

ECPI University (D)

5555 Greenwich Road, Virginia Beach VA 23462-6554
County: Independent City FICE Identification: 010198
Unit ID: 248934
Telephone: (757) 671-7171 Carnegie Class: Bac/Assoc-Mixed
FAX Number: (757) 671-8661 Calendar System: Semester
URL: www.ecpi.edu
Established: 1966 Annual Undergrad Tuition & Fees: $14,775
Enrollment: 11,735 Coed
Affiliation or Control: Proprietary IRS Status: Proprietary
Highest Offering: Master's
Accreditation: SC, ACFEI, MAAB, NUR, NURSE

01 President .... Mr. Mark B. DREYFUS
12 Campus President .... Mr. Kevin PAVEGLIO
13 VP Info Systems/Financial Aid .... Mr. Jeff ARTHUR

ECPI University-Northern Virginia (E)

10021 Balls Ford Road, Ste 100, Manassas VA 20109
Telephone: (703) 348-4062 Identification: 770957
Accreditation: &SC, MAAB, RAD, SURTEC

ECPI University-Richmond/Innsbrook (F)

4305 Cox Road, Glen Allen VA 23060
Telephone: (804) 934-0100 Identification: 770961
Accreditation: &SC

ECPI University-Richmond/Moorefield (G)

800 Moorefield Park Drive, Richmond VA 23236
Telephone: (804) 330-5533 Identification: 770958
Accreditation: &SC, CAHIIM, MAAB, SURTEC

ECPI University-Roanoke (H)

5234 Airport Road, Ste 200, Roanoke VA 24012
Telephone: (540) 563-8000 Identification: 770959
Accreditation: &SC, MAAB

Edward Via College of Osteopathic Medicine (I)

2265 Kraft Drive, Blacksburg VA 24060
County: Montgomery FICE Identification: 037093
Unit ID: 442806
Telephone: (540) 231-4000 Carnegie Class: Spec-4-yr-Med
FAX Number: (540) 231-5252 Calendar System: Semester
URL: www.vcom.vt.edu
Established: 2002 Annual Graduate Tuition & Fees: N/A
Enrollment: 1,637 Coed
Affiliation or Control: Independent Non-Profit IRS Status: 501(c)3
Highest Offering: Doctorate; No Undergraduates
Accreditation: OSTEO

01 President .... Dr. Dixie TOOKE-RAWLINS
05 Provost/EVP & Founding Dean .... Dr. Dixie TOOKE-RAWLINS
10 Vice President Finance/CFO .... Mr. Chuck SWAHA
32 Vice Pres Student Services .... Mr. William KING
46 Vice Provost for Research .... Dr. Gunnar BROLINSON
11 Vice President Operations .... Mr. Bill PRICE
12 Dean Carolinas Campus .... Dr. Timothy J. KOWALSKI
12 Dean Virginia Campus .... Dr. Jan M. WILLCOX
63 Dean Grad Cert/Pre-Med Program .... Dr. Brian W. HILL
21 Sr Exec Dir Administrative Svcs .... Ms. Patty SMITH

Emory & Henry College (J)

PO Box 947, 30461 Garnand Drive,
Emory VA 24327-0947
County: Washington FICE Identification: 003709
Unit ID: 232025
Telephone: (276) 944-4121 Carnegie Class: Bac-A&S
FAX Number: (276) 944-6934 Calendar System: Semester
URL: www.ehc.edu
Established: 1836 Annual Undergrad Tuition & Fees: $33,700
Enrollment: 1,117 Coed
Affiliation or Control: United Methodist IRS Status: 501(c)3
Highest Offering: Doctorate
Accreditation: SC, #ARCPA, CAATE, CAEPT, @PTA

01 President .... Mr. Jake B. SCHRUM
43 Exec Asst to Pres/General Counsel .... Mr. Mark R. GRAHAM
05 Int VP Academic Affairs/Dean .... Dr. Melissa TAVERNER
10 VP for Business and Finance .... Mr. Richard K. GAUMER
32 VP Student Life/Student Success .... Ms. Pamela L. GOURLEY
111 VP for Institutional Advancement .... Mr. Joseph P. TAYLOR
84 Vice Pres for Enrollment Management .... Mr. Dave VOSKUIL
09 Dir Institutional Research/Effect .... Mr. Gregory G. STEINER
29 Director of Alumni Affairs .... Ms. Monica S. HOEL
37 Director of Financial Aid .... Ms. Scarlett BLEVINS
06 Registrar .... Ms. Tammy SHEETS
36 Director of Career Services .... Ms. Amanda GARDNER
38 Director Student Counseling .... Mr. Todd STANLEY
26 Director Internal/Integrated Comm .... Mr. Dirk S. MOORE
13 Chief Information Officer/Librarian ...... Ms. Lorraine N. ABRAHAM
18 Dir of Facilities Plng/Management .... Mr. Scott E. WILLIAMS
40 Bookstore Manager .... Mr. Terry RICHARDSON
42 Chaplain .... Rev. Mary K. BRIGGS
15 Director Human Resources .... Ms. Kim STEINER
20 Associate VP Academic Affairs .... Dr. Michael J. PUGLISI
35 Dean of Students .... Mr. Kyle CUTSHAW
21 Associate VP Business/Finance .... Ms. Benita BARE
07 Director of Admissions .... Mr. Matthew CRISMAN
39 Director of Housing .... Ms. Lacey SOUTHWICK
41 Director of Athletics .... Ms. Myra SIMS
19 Chief of Campus Police .... Mr. Scott POORE
102 Director Foundation Relations .... Ms. Cassidy MOORE
104 Director Study Abroad .... Dr. Celeste GAIA
105 Director Web Services .... Mr. Kevin CALL
44 Director Annual or Planned Giving .... Ms. Ronan KING
53 Director of Education Center .... Dr. Janet CRICKMER

Faith Bible College (K)

6330 Newtown Road, Suite 211, Norfolk VA 23502
County: Independent City Identification: 667285
Telephone: (757) 423-2095 Carnegie Class: Not Classified
FAX Number: (757) 222-1341 Calendar System: Semester
URL: www.faithbiblecollege.com
Established: 1995 Annual Undergrad Tuition & Fees: N/A
Enrollment: N/A Coed
Affiliation or Control: Independent Non-Profit IRS Status: 501(c)3
Highest Offering: Associate Degree
Accreditation: @BI

01 President .... Dr. Hap STRUTHERS
05 Vice Pres Academic Affairs .... Dr. Cherral MASON
42 Vice Pres Church Relations .... Capt. Dale PARKER

Ferrum College (L)

PO Box 1000, 215 Ferrum Mtn Road,
Ferrum VA 24088-9001
County: Franklin FICE Identification: 003711
Unit ID: 232089
Telephone: (540) 365-2121 Carnegie Class: Bac-Diverse
FAX Number: (540) 365-4269 Calendar System: Semester
URL: www.ferrum.edu
Established: 1913 Annual Undergrad Tuition & Fees: $31,915
Enrollment: 1,334 Coed
Affiliation or Control: United Methodist IRS Status: 501(c)3
Highest Offering: Baccalaureate
Accreditation: SC, SW

01 Interim President .... Dr. Jennifer L. BRAATEN
05 Provost .... Dr. Aime SPOSATO
10 VP for Business and Finance .... Mr. Chris BURNLEY
111 Vice Pres Institutional Advancement .... Mr. George SEALS
84 VP for Enrollment Management .... Mr. James A. PENNIX
32 Dean of Student Life .... Ms. Nicole LENEZ
42 Dean of Chapel .... Dr. Jan C. NICHOLSON ANGLE
04 Special Asst to the President .... Ms. Courtney L. BROWN
06 Registrar .... Mrs. Yvonne S. WALKER
07 Dean of Admissions .... Mr. Jason D. BYRD
09 Director of Inst Research .... Mrs. Ursa JOHNSON
08 Director Stanley Library .... Ms. Brandi PORTER
37 Director of Financial Aid .... Ms. Heather HOLLANDSWORTH
29 Director Alumni & Family Programs .... Mrs. Tracy S. HOLLEY
26 Director of Public Relations .... Vacant
41 Director of Athletics .... Mr. J. Abraham NAFF
44 Regional Gift Officer .... Mr. Gene BOURNE
18 Director of Physical Plant .... Mr. Brad BISHOP
35 Dir Student Leadership & Engagement .... Mr. Justin MUSE
13 Dir of Network Services .... Mr. Eugene HACKER
15 Dir of Human Resources .... Mr. Chris CHANDLER
40 Bookstore Manager .... Mr. Christopher HUNNICUTT
19 Chief of Ferrum College Police Dept .... Chief J. F. OWENS
36 Dir Career Svcs/Student Employment .... Vacant
88 Director of Academic Accessibility .... Ms. Nancy S. BEACH
91 Dir Administrative Computing .... Mr. Shawn SHIRLEY
79 Dean School Arts & Humanities .... Dr. David B. HOWELL
81 Dean School Natural Science & Math .... Dr. Jinnie GARRETT
83 Dean School Social Sciences .... Dr. Kevin REILLY

Fortis College (M)

6300 Center Drive, Building 22, Norfolk VA 23502
County: Independent City FICE Identification: 023427
Unit ID: 233329
Telephone: (757) 499-5447 Carnegie Class: Spec 2-yr-Health
FAX Number: N/A Calendar System: Quarter
URL: www.fortis.edu/campuses
Established: Annual Undergrad Tuition & Fees: $14,087
Enrollment: 292 Coed
Affiliation or Control: Proprietary IRS Status: Proprietary
Highest Offering: Associate Degree

Accreditation: **ACICS**

01 President .... Mr. Matthew BANO

Fortis College (A)

2000 Westmoreland Street, Suite A, Richmond VA 23230
Telephone: (804) 323-1020 Identification: 770815
Accreditation: **ACICS**, DA, SURGT

George Mason University (B)

4400 University Drive - MSN 3A1, Fairfax VA 22030-4444
County: Fairfax FICE Identification: 003749
Unit ID: 232186
Telephone: (703) 993-1000 Carnegie Class: DU-Highest
FAX Number: N/A Calendar System: Semester
URL: www.gmu.edu
Established: 1957 Annual Undergrad Tuition & Fees (In-State): $11,300
Enrollment: 33,929 Coed
Affiliation or Control: State IRS Status: 501(c)3
Highest Offering: Doctorate
Accreditation: **SC**, ART, CAATE, CAEPN, CEA, CLPSY, CS, ENG, EXSC, HSA, IPSY, LAW, MUS, NRPA, NURSE, PH, SPAA, SW

01 President .... Dr. Ángel CABRERA
05 Provost & Executive Vice President .... Dr. S. David WU
10 Senior VP of Administration/Finance .... Ms. Jennifer (J.J.) DAVIS
100 Chief of Staff/VP Comm & Marketing .... Mr. Frank NEVILLE
84 Vice Pres Enrollment Management .... Mr. David BURGE
18 Interim Vice Pres for Facilities .... Mr. Frank STRIKE
86 VP Government & Community Relations .... Mr. Paul LIBERTY
111 VP Univ Advancement & Alumni Rels .... Dr. Janet BINGHAM
13 VP Information Technology/CIO .... Ms. Marilyn SMITH
32 Vice President for University Life .... Ms. Rose PASCARELL
46 Vice President for Research .... Dr. Deborah CRAWFORD
28 VP Compliance/Diversity & Ethics .... Mr. Julian WILLIAMS
15 VP for HR/Payroll & Fac/Staff Life .... Ms. Linda HARBER
43 University Counsel .... Mr. Thomas M. MONCURE
45 Asst VP & Chief Budget Officer .... Mr. David B. MOORE
21 Assoc VP/Controller Fiscal Services .... Ms. Lisa KEMP
20 VP Acad Innovation & New Ventures .... Dr. Michelle MARKS
20 Assoc Prov Acad Initiatives & Svcs .... Dr. Janette MUIR
88 Assoc Prov for Academic Admin .... Ms. Renate H. GUILFORD
58 Assoc Prov for Graduate Education .... Dr. Cody EDWARDS
35 Exec Dir Office Student Involvement .... Ms. Lauren LONG
35 Assistant Vice Pres University Life .... Dr. Kahan SABLO
06 Assoc Provost/University Registrar .... Ms. Eve DAUER
37 Director Student Financial Aid .... Dr. Sandra TARBOX
36 Assoc Dir Univ Career Services .... Ms. Saskia CLAY-ROOKS
08 Dean of Libraries/Univ Librarian .... Mr. John G. ZENELIS
23 Administrator Student Health Svcs .... Dr. Wagida A. ABDALLA
29 Assoc VP Alumni Relations .... Ms. Christine CLARK-TALLEY
41 Asst VP/Dir Intercolleg Athletics .... Mr. Brad EDWARDS
19 Chief of Police .... Mr. Carl ROWAN
49 Dean Col of Humanities/Social Sci .... Dr. Deborah BOEHM-DAVIS
61 Dean School of Law .... Dr. Henry BUTLER
80 Dean Schar School of Policy & Govt .... Dr. Mark ROZELL
50 Dean School of Business .... Dr. Maury PEIPERL
53 Dean College of Educ & Human Devel .... Dr. Mark R. GINSBERG
54 Dean Volgenau School of Engineering .... Dr. Kenneth BALL
66 Dean College of Health & Human Svcs .... Dr. Thomas R. PROHASKA
81 Dean College of Science .... Dr. Peggy AGOURIS
88 Dean Sch Conflict Analysis & Resol .... Dr. Kevin AVRUCH
88 Dean CVPA/Exec Dir HPAC .... Dr. Rick DAVIS
38 Exec Dir Counseling & Psych Svcs .... Dr. Rachel WERNICKE
09 Assoc Prov Institutional Research .... Dr. Thulasi KUMAR
96 Director of Purchasing & Acct Pay .... Mr. Cliff SHORE
04 Director of Presidential Admin .... Ms. Sharon CULLEN
101 Sec Pro Tem to Board of Visitors .... Ms. Kathy CAGLE
39 Dir of Housing Services & Finance .... Ms. Maria FIORE
108 Asst Dir Inst Rsrch & Assessment .... Dr. Stephanie FOSTER
25 Asc VP Rsrch Ops Ofc Sponsored Pgms .... Mr. Mike LASKOFSKI
44 Director Annual Giving/Ofc Advance .... Mr. Nick HERMAN
102 Dir Corporate/Foundation Relations .... Mr. Ted WYNN
103 Asoc Dir Career Development .... Ms. Ann M. GARNER
105 Mgr Web Applications & Services ITS .... Mr. Mohammad FALLAH ASL
106 Dir Online Education .... Mr. Stanley ZOLTEK
88 Assoc Dir Enrollment Management .... Ms. Kathy ZUPAN
90 Dir/System Admin Computing Svcs .... Mr. Mitchell FLETCHER

Global Health College (C)

6101 Stevenson Avenue, Alexandria VA 22304
County: Independent City FICE Identification: 041400
Unit ID: 455390
Telephone: (703) 212-7410 Carnegie Class: Spec 2-yr-Health
FAX Number: (703) 212-7414 Calendar System: Other
URL: www.global.edu
Established: 2004 Annual Undergrad Tuition & Fees: $19,699
Enrollment: 339 Coed
Affiliation or Control: Proprietary IRS Status: Proprietary
Highest Offering: Baccalaureate
Accreditation: **ACICS**, PNUR

01 President .... Mariatu KARGBO
10 Vice Pres Administration/Fiscal Svc .... Bernard FRISBY

Hampden-Sydney College (D)

College Road, PO Box 128,
Hampden-Sydney VA 23943-0667
County: Prince Edward FICE Identification: 003713
Unit ID: 232256
Telephone: (434) 223-6000 Carnegie Class: Bac-A&S
FAX Number: (434) 223-6350 Calendar System: Semester
URL: www.hsc.edu
Established: 1775 Annual Undergrad Tuition & Fees: $42,962
Enrollment: 1,087 Male
Affiliation or Control: Presbyterian Church (U.S.A.) IRS Status: 501(c)3
Highest Offering: Baccalaureate
Accreditation: **SC**

01 President .... Dr. John L. STIMPERT
05 Provost .... Dr. Dennis G. STEVENS
20 Interim Dean of the Faculty .... Dr. Walter M. MCDERMOTT
10 VP Business Affairs & Finance .... Mr. W. Glenn CULLEY, JR.
111 VP Institutional Advancement .... Dr. H. Lee KING, JR.
07 Dean of Admissions .... Ms. Anita H. GARLAND
32 Dean of Students .... Dr. Robert P. SABBATINI
121 Associate Dean Academic Success .... Ms. Lisa A. BURNS
41 Director of Athletics .... Vacant
08 Director of the Library & Computing .... Ms. Shaunna E. HUNTER-MCKINNEY
06 Registrar .... Ms. Dawn L. CONGLETON
37 Director of Financial Aid .... Ms. Zita M. BARREE
29 Director of Alumni Relations .... Mr. Aaron VAN ALLEN
18 Director of Physical Plant .... Mr. John C. PRENGAMAN
36 Dir Career Ed/Vocational Reflection .... Vacant
23 Director of Student Health Center .... Ms. Andrea R. JONES
15 Director of Human Resources .... Ms. Sue V. CARTER
19 Dir Public Safety/Chief of Police .... Mr. T. Mark FOWLER
40 Bookstore Manager .... Ms. Kimberly S. MICHAUX
09 Assoc Dean Inst Effectiveness .... Dr. Christine C. ROSS
26 Director Communications & Marketing .... Mr. Gordon W. NEAL
21 Controller .... Mr. Michael A. SMITH
35 Dir of Student Affairs Operations .... Ms. Sandy P. COOKE
39 Director of Residence Life .... Mr. John R C. RAMSAY
25 Director of College Grants .... Ms. P. J. TOWNSEND
104 Dir Global Education & Study Abroad .... Dr. Daniella WIDDOWS

Hampton University (E)

100 E. Queen Street, Hampton VA 23668
County: Independent City FICE Identification: 003714
Unit ID: 232265
Telephone: (757) 727-5000 Carnegie Class: Masters/M
FAX Number: (757) 727-5085 Calendar System: Semester
URL: www.hamptonu.edu
Established: 1868 Annual Undergrad Tuition & Fees: $24,242
Enrollment: 4,269 Coed
Affiliation or Control: Independent Non-Profit IRS Status: 501(c)3
Highest Offering: Doctorate
Accreditation: **SC**, AAB, CACREP, CAEPN, CS, ENG, IACBE, JOUR, MUS, NURSE, #PHAR, PTA, SP

01 President .... Dr. William R. HARVEY
03 Senior Vice President .... Mr. Paul C. HARRIS
05 Chancellor & Provost .... Dr. JoAnn W. HAYSBERT
10 Vice Pres Business Affs/Treasurer .... Mrs. Doretha J. SPELLS
11 Vice Pres for Administrative Svcs .... Dr. Barbara L. INMAN
43 Vice President/General Counsel .... Atty. Faye HARDY-LUCAS
30 Interim VP for Development .... Mr. Laron CLARK
100 Chief of Staff .... Dr. Charrita D. DANLEY
21 Asst VP Business Affs/Comptroller .... Mrs. Denise NICHOLS
25 Asst Vice Pres Grants Management .... Mrs. Lillie F. GREEN
20 Asst Provost Academic Affairs .... Dr. Pollie MURPHY
26 Asst VP for Marketing .... Ms. B. DaVida PLUMMER
45 Asst Prov Research & Grantsmanship .... Dr. Michelle PENN-MARSHALL
88 Dean of Judicial Affairs .... Mr. Woodson H. HOPEWELL, JR.
39 Dean of Residential Life .... Miss Jewel B. LONG
07 Dean of Admissions .... Mrs. Angela BOYD
06 Registrar .... Mrs. Jorsene COOPER
36 Dir Career Counsel/Planning Ctr .... Mrs. Bessie WILLIS
38 Director Counseling Center .... Ms. Valerie PROCTOR
08 Administrator University Libraries .... Mrs. Tina ROLLINS
29 Director of Alumni Affairs .... Ms. Brint MARTIN
15 Director of Human Resources .... Ms. Rikki THOMAS
14 Director Computer Center .... Mr. Darien HAWKINS
37 Financial Aid Officer .... Mr. Martin MILES
27 Director of University Relations .... Vacant
09 Director Institutional Research .... Mrs. Michelle CLAWSON
23 Director Student Health Services .... Dr. Karen WILLIAMS
42 University Chaplain .... Rev. Debra L. HAGGINS
18 Director Buildings & Grounds .... Mr. Randall HARDY
87 Director of Summer Sessions .... Dr. Pollie MURPHY
19 Chief of Campus Police .... Mr. David GLOVER
86 Director Government Relations .... Mr. Wilbert L. THOMAS
96 Director of Purchasing .... Vacant
40 University Bookstore Manager .... Ms. Michelle R. MILLER
53 Dean School of Liberal Arts & Educ .... Dr. Linda MALONE-COLON
66 Dean School of Nursing .... Dr. Shevallanie LOTT
81 Assistant Dean School of Science .... Dr. Michelle CLAVILLE
50 Dean School of Business .... Dr. Sid H. CREDLE
54 Dean Sch of Engineering/Technology .... Dr. Joyce SHIRAZI
67 Dean School of Pharmacy .... Dr. Wayne HARRIS
58 Dean the Graduate College .... Dr. Michelle PENN-MARSHALL
60 Dean Scripps Howard Sch Journ/Comm .... Ms. DaVida PLUMMER
88 Dean University College .... Dr. Kim LUCKES

Hollins University (F)

PO Box 9688, Roanoke VA 24020-1688
County: Roanoke FICE Identification: 003715
Unit ID: 232308
Telephone: (540) 362-6000 Carnegie Class: Bac-A&S
FAX Number: (540) 362-6642 Calendar System: 4/1/4
URL: www.hollins.edu
Established: 1842 Annual Undergrad Tuition & Fees: $36,835
Enrollment: 802 Female
Affiliation or Control: Independent Non-Profit IRS Status: 501(c)3
Highest Offering: Master's
Accreditation: **SC**, CAEPT

01 President .... Dr. Pareena G. LAWRENCE
10 Vice Pres Finance/Administration .... Ms. Kerry EDMONDS
30 Vice Pres for External Relations .... Ms. Audrey STONE
84 Vice President of Enrollment .... Mr. Jason HAMILTON
05 Chair of the Faculty .... Ms. Rachel NUNEZ
32 Dean of Students .... Ms. Patty O'TOOLE
20 Dean Academic Services .... Mr. Michael GETTINGS
28 Associate Dean Intercultural Pgms .... Ms. Jeri L. SUAREZ
04 Executive Assistant to President .... Ms. Brook E. DICKSON
88 Director Alumnae & Donor Relations .... Vacant
06 Registrar .... Ms. Patricia BROKKEN
08 Director of the Library .... Mr. Luke VILELLE
15 Director of Human Resources .... Ms. Alicia GODZWA
26 Director of Public Relations .... Mr. Jeff HODGES
29 Director of Alumnae Relations .... Vacant
36 Director Career Development Center .... Ms. Ashley GLENN
37 Director Financial Aid .... Ms. Mary Jean CORRISS
41 Director of Athletics .... Mr. William MANNINO
09 Asst Dir Institutional Research .... Ms. Katie READ
18 Director Plant Operations/Services .... Ms. Mae RAMSEY
104 Director International Programs .... Ms. Jeanette BARBIERI
13 Chief Info Technology Officer .... Ms. Carol REED
19 Director Security/Safety .... Mr. David CARLSON
39 Dir Housing & Residential Life .... Ms. Melissa HINE
07 Director of Admissions .... Ms. Ashley BROWNING

iGlobal University (G)

7700 Little River Turnpike, Ste 600, Annandale VA 22003
County: Fairfax Identification: 667105
Unit ID: 483780
Telephone: (703) 941-2020 Carnegie Class: Not Classified
FAX Number: (703) 941-2025 Calendar System: Quarter
URL: www.iglobaluniversity.org
Established: 2008 Annual Undergrad Tuition & Fees: $13,820
Enrollment: 286 Coed
Affiliation or Control: Proprietary IRS Status: Proprietary
Highest Offering: Master's
Accreditation: **ACICS**

01 President & CEO .... Dr. David Y. SOHN
05 Director .... Mr. Dustin CASSELL

Ivy Christian College (H)

9401 Mathy Drive, Ste 200, Fairfax VA 22031
County: Fairfax Identification: 667213
Telephone: (703) 425-4143 Carnegie Class: Not Classified
FAX Number: (703) 425-4148 Calendar System: Quarter
URL: www.ivy.edu
Established: 2006 Annual Undergrad Tuition & Fees: N/A
Enrollment: N/A Coed
Affiliation or Control: Independent Non-Profit IRS Status: 501(c)3
Highest Offering: Baccalaureate
Accreditation: **TRACS**

01 President .... Dr. David Y. PAK
05 Academic Dean .... Pastor Youn LEE

James Madison University (I)

800 S Main Street, Harrisonburg VA 22807-0001
County: Independent City FICE Identification: 003721
Unit ID: 232423
Telephone: (540) 568-6211 Carnegie Class: Masters/L
FAX Number: N/A Calendar System: Semester
URL: www.jmu.edu
Established: 1908 Annual Undergrad Tuition & Fees (In-State): $10,390
Enrollment: 21,227 Coed
Affiliation or Control: State IRS Status: 501(c)3
Highest Offering: Doctorate
Accreditation: **SC**, ARCPA, ART, AUD, CAATE, CACREP, CAEPN, CS, DANCE, DIETD, ENG, ENGR, IPSY, MUS, NURSE, OT, PSPSY, SP, SPAA, SW, THEA

01 President .... Mr. Jonathan R. ALGER
05 Provost/Senior VP Academic Affairs .... Dr. Heather COLTMAN
10 Sr Vice Pres Administration/Finance .... Mr. Charles W. KING
32 Sr VP Student Affairs .... Dr. Mark J. WARNER
111 Vice Pres University Advancement .... Dr. Nick LANGRIDGE
84 VP Access and Enrollment Mgmt .... Ms. Donna L. HARPER
13 AVP Information Technology .... Mr. Dale B. HULVEY
81 Dean College Science/Math .... Dr. Cynthia BAUERLE
49 Interim Dean College Arts/Letters .... Dr. Chris ARNDT
76 Dean Col of Health & Behav Studies .... Dr. Sharon LOVELL
50 Dean College of Business .... Dr. Mary GOWAN
57 Dean College Visual Performing Arts .... Dr. George E. SPARKS
53 Dean College of Education .... Dr. Phillip M. WISHON

72 Dean College of Int Science & Engr ... Dr. Robert KOLVOORD
58 Dean Graduate School ... Dr. Jie CHEN
97 Dean University Studies ... Dr. Linda C. HALPERN
08 Dean of Libraries/Educ Technologies ... Dr. Adam A. MURRAY
43 University Counsel ... Ms. Susan L. WHEELER
114 Asst Vice Pres Budget Management ... Ms. Diane L. STAMP
07 Dean of Admissions ... Mr. Michael D. WALSH
37 Dir Financial Aid & Scholarships ... Mr. Brad BARNETT
15 Director Human Resources ... Ms. Diane YERIAN
09 Director Institutional Research ... Dr. Frank J. DOHERTY
41 Director of Athletics ... Mr. Jeffrey T. BOURNE
26 Dir Comm & Univ Spokesperson ... Mr. Bill J. WYATT
06 University Registrar ... Ms. Michele M. WHITE
19 Chief of Police ... Mr. Lee A. SHIFFLETT
22 Dir of EEO ... Mr. James R. ROBINSON
29 Director Alumni Relations ... Ms. Ashley E. PRIVOTT
27 Senior Advancement Marketing Dir ... Mr. David R. TAYLOR

Jefferson College of Health Sciences (A)

101 Elm Avenue S.E., Roanoke VA 24013
County: Independent City — FICE Identification: 006622
Unit ID: 231837
Telephone: (540) 985-8483 — Carnegie Class: Spec-4-yr-Other Health
FAX Number: (540) 224-6703 — Calendar System: Semester
URL: www.jchs.edu
Established: 1982 — Annual Undergrad Tuition & Fees: $25,150
Enrollment: 1,062 — Coed
Affiliation or Control: Independent Non-Profit — IRS Status: 501(c)3
Highest Offering: Doctorate
Accreditation: SC, ARCPA, COARC, EMT, MT, NURSE, OT, OTA, PTAA, SURGT

01 President ... Dr. Nathaniel L. BISHOP
05 Dean of the Coillege ... Dr. Julie A. DELOIA
11 Dean Administrative Services ... Ms. Anna S. MILLIRONS
84 Dean Enrollment Management ... Dr. Steven W. NAPE
32 Dean Student Affairs ... Mr. B. Scott HILL
18 Safety & Clery Act Liaison ... Ms. Susan L. BOOTH
108 Dean Institutional Effectiveness ... Dr. Glen R. MAYHEW
30 Director of Development ... Mr. Erik W. WILLIAMS
88 Pgm Director Physician Assistant ... Dr. Sarah L. NICELY
88 Pgm Director Health & Exercise Sci . Dr. Allison H. BOWERSOCK
88 Pgm Director Emergency Services ... Mr. John C. COOK
88 Pgm Director Biomedical Sciences ... Dr. Robin L. DAVIES
88 Pgm Director Physical Therapy Asst ... Ms. Rebecca DUFF
88 Pgm Director Doctor Occ Therapy ... Dr. David A. HAYNES
79 Director Humanities & Soc Sciences ... Dr. Courtney D. WATSON
88 Pgm Director Medical Lab Science ... Ms. Laura R. LINK
88 Pgm Director Occ Therapy Assistant ... Ms. Ave M. MITTA
66 Program Director RN - BSN ... Dr. Patty M. VARI
88 Pgm Director Healthcare Mgmt BS ... Ms. Carey H. PEERMAN
88 Pgm Dir Master Healthcare Admin ... Dr. Rebecca F. MCINTYRE
88 Pgm Director Respiratory Therapy ... Dr. Chase POULSEN
88 Pgm Director Surgical Technology ... Mr. John D. RATLIFF
88 Pgm Director Health Psychology ... Dr. Robert C. REESE
88 Program Dir Doctor Health Sciences ... Dr. Diana L. WILLEMAN-BUCKELEW
88 Pgm Dir Family Nurse Practitioner ... Dr. Milena STAYKOVA
88 Director InterProf Educ/Faculty Dev ... Ms. Kimberly WHITER
76 Int Pgm Director Health Sciences ... Dr. F. Jeannine EVERHART
66 Program Director Traditional BSN ... Dr. Cathy A. HILER
66 Pgm Director Accelerated BSN ... Dr. Kimberly M. WILSON
113 Bursar ... Ms. Tonia Y. ANDREWS
40 Manager Bookstore ... Ms. Suzanne M. ANDERSON
35 Director Student Life ... Ms. Elizabeth A. COSTA
25 Grants Management Administrator ... Ms. Amanda M. ELLINGER
04 Admin Assistant to President ... Ms. Janel BEEHNER
26 Senior Consultant Communications ... Mr. Mark A. LAMBERT
09 Dir Institutional Research & Plng ... Dr. Timothy R. MILLARD
121 Director of Academic Support Svcs ... Mr. Al W. OVERSTREET
39 Residence Life Coordinator ... Ms. Stephanie SIMPSON
38 Director Counseling and Wellness ... Dr. Jennifer J. SLUSHER
08 Director Library ... Ms. Ramona H. THISS
106 Dir Online & Continuing Education ... Ms. Margie B. VEST
06 Registrar ... Ms. Megan L. COULTER
88 Title IX & Disability Svcs Coord ... Ms. Shannon K. KINZIE
07 Director of Admissions ... Ms. Sarah R. BOSWELL
37 Director Student Financial Aid ... Ms. Debra J. JOHNSON

The John Leland Center for Theological Studies (B)

1306 N Highland Street, Arlington VA 22201
County: Arlington — Identification: 666340
Telephone: (703) 812-4757 — Carnegie Class: Not Classified
FAX Number: (703) 812-4764 — Calendar System: Other
URL: www.leland.edu
Established: 1998 — Annual Graduate Tuition & Fees: N/A
Enrollment: N/A — Coed
Affiliation or Control: Baptist — IRS Status: 501(c)3
Highest Offering: Master's; No Undergraduates
Accreditation: THEOL

01 President ... Dr. Mark J. OLSON
05 Academic Dean ... Dr. John LEE
04 Assistant to the President ... Ms. Shana WRIGHT
08 Librarian ... Ms. Monica LEAK
06 Registrar ... Ms. Andrea BAKKE
07 Director Recruiting/Admissions ... Mr. Daniel BRIDGEFORTH
10 Director of Finance ... Mr. Mel HARRIS
26 Chief Public Relations Officer ... Ms. Vicki BOHANNON

Kings Park University (C)

4613-D Pinecrest Office Park Drive, Alexandria VA 22312
County: Fairfax — Identification: 667158
Telephone: (703) 354-3533 — Carnegie Class: Not Classified
FAX Number: (703) 354-3577 — Calendar System: Trimester
URL: www.kpu.us
Established: 2000 — Annual Graduate Tuition & Fees: N/A
Enrollment: N/A — Coed
Affiliation or Control: Independent Non-Profit — IRS Status: 501(c)3
Highest Offering: Master's; No Undergraduates
Accreditation: ACUP

01 President ... Rev. Tae JONG PARK

Liberty University (D)

1971 University Boulevard, Lynchburg VA 24515
County: Independent City — FICE Identification: 020530
Unit ID: 232557
Telephone: (434) 582-2000 — Carnegie Class: DU-Mod
FAX Number: N/A — Calendar System: Semester
URL: www.liberty.edu
Established: 1971 — Annual Undergrad Tuition & Fees: $21,292
Enrollment: 80,494 — Coed
Affiliation or Control: Other — IRS Status: 501(c)3
Highest Offering: Doctorate
Accreditation: SC, ACBSP, CAATE, CACREP, CAEPN, CS, ENG, EXSC, LAW, MUS, NURSE, @OSTEO, @SW

01 President ... Mr. Jerry FALWELL, JR.
03 Executive Vice President & COO ... Mr. Randy SMITH
05 Chief Academic Officer & Provost ... Dr. Ronald E. HAWKINS
05 Co-Provost & VP for Acad Affairs ... Dr. Ben GUTIERREZ
10 Chief Financial Officer ... Mr. Don MOON
32 Sr Vice President Student Affairs ... Dr. Mark L. HINE
84 Executive VP of Res Enrollment ... Mr. Chris JOHNSON
26 VP of Marketing & Communication ... Ms. Kristin CONRAD
109 Senior VP for Auxiliary Services ... Mr. Lee BEAUMONT
84 Executive VP of Online Enrollment ... Mr. Ron KENNEDY
15 Vice President Human Resources ... Mrs. Laura J. WALLACE
88 Vice Pres for Spiritual Development ... Mr. David NASSER
45 AVP for Institutional Effectiveness ... Mr. H. Skip KASTROLL
13 Chief Information Officer ... Mr. John GAUGER
06 University Registrar ... Mrs. Helene VANCE
43 General Counsel ... Mr. David M. CORRY
29 Director of Alumni Affairs ... Mr. Tyler FALWELL
08 Dean Jerry Falwell Library ... Mrs. Angela RICE
80 Dean Helms School of Government ... Mr. Shawn D. AKERS
37 Sr VP Student Financial Services ... Dr. Robert L. RITZ
18 Sr VP Campus Facilities & Transport ... Mr. Charles SPENCE
88 VP of Major Construction ... Mr. Daniel DETER
30 VP of Development ... Mr. Tom ARNOLD
88 VP Outreach & Strategic Partnership ... Dr. Barry MOORE
11 VP of Business Administration ... Mr. Chris CARROLL
41 Director of Athletics ... Mr. Ian MCCAW
49 Dean College of Arts & Sciences ... Dr. Roger D. SCHULTZ
83 Dean School of Behavioral Sciences ... Dr. Steve WARREN
50 Interim Dean School of Business ... Dr. David CALLAND
60 Dean School of Comm & Digital Cont ... Dr. Bruce KIRK
57 Dean School of Visual & Perf Arts ... Mr. Scott HAYES
97 Dean CASAS ... Dr. Brian YATES
73 Dean School of Divinity ... Dr. Ed HINDSON
53 Dean School of Education ... Dr. Heather SCHOFFSTALL
35 VP of Campus Recreation ... Mr. Chris MISIANO
88 VP of Off-Campus Facilities ... Mr. Scott STARNES
19 Chief of Police LUPD ... Col. Richard HINKLEY
54 Dean School of Engineering and CSCI ... Mr. David DONAHOO
28 Dir Ctr for Multicltrl Enrichment ... Ms. Melany PEARL
61 Dean School of Law ... Mr. Keith FAULKNER
88 Dean School of Aeronautics ... Mr. Jim MOLLOY
88 Dir Center for Teaching Excellence ... Mr. Shawn BIELICKI
97 Vice Provost for UG Education ... Dr. Gabriel ETZEL
58 Vice Provost for Grad Education ... Dr. Scott HICKS
76 Dean School of Health Sciences ... Dr. Ralph LINSTRA
63 Dean College of Osteopathic Med ... Dr. Peter BELL
64 Dean School of Music ... Dr. Vernon WHALEY
35 Dean of Students ... Mr. Robert MULLEN
66 Dean School of Nursing ... Dr. Deanna BRITT
88 Dean of Resident Admissions ... Dr. Terry ELAM

Longwood University (E)

201 High Street, Farmville VA 23909-1801
County: Prince Edward — FICE Identification: 003719
Unit ID: 232566
Telephone: (434) 395-2000 — Carnegie Class: Masters/M
FAX Number: (434) 395-2635 — Calendar System: Semester
URL: www.longwood.edu
Established: 1839 — Annual Undergrad Tuition & Fees (In-State): $12,240
Enrollment: 5,087 — Coed
Affiliation or Control: State — IRS Status: 501(c)3
Highest Offering: Master's
Accreditation: SC, CAATE, CAEPN, EXSC, MUS, NRPA, NURSE, SP, SW, THEA

01 President ... Mr. W. Taylor REVELEY, IV
05 Provost/Vice Pres Academic Affairs ... Dr. Joan NEFF
10 Vice Pres Administration & Finance ... Mr. Kenneth COPELAND
32 Vice President for Student Affairs ... Dr. Tim J. PIERSON
111 VP for Institutional Advancement ... Ms. Courtney HODGES
45 VP for Strategic Operations ... Ms. Victoria KINDON
13 Chief Information Officer ... Ms. Victoria KINDON
84 Assoc VP Enrollment Management ... Dr. Jennifer K. GREEN
26 Assoc VP Publ/Mktg/Communications ... Ms. Sabrina BROWN
96 Assoc VP for Admin & Finance ... Ms. Cathryn B. MOBLEY
29 AVP for Alumni & Career Services ... Mr. Ryan CATHERWOOD
09 Int Dir Assessment/Inst Research ... Dr. David LEHR
06 Registrar ... Mrs. Susan HINES
07 Dean of Admissions ... Mr. Jason C. FAULK
08 Dean of Library ... Mr. Brent ROBERTS
28 Dir Citizen Ldrshp/Soc Justice Educ ... Mr. Jonathan E. PAGE
38 Director Student Counseling ... Dr. Maureen J. WALLS-MCKAY
36 Associate Director Career Services ... Ms. Ashley CRUTE
37 Int Director Student Financial Aid ... Ms. Gayle J. COVINGTON
15 Chief Human Resources Officer ... Ms. Lisa MOONEY
18 Dir Facilities Operations Services ... Mr. Alvin B. MYERS
100 Chief of Staff ... Mr. Justin POPE
41 Athletic Director ... Mr. Troy AUSTIN

Lynchburg College (F)

1501 Lakeside Drive, Lynchburg VA 24501-3199
County: Independent City — FICE Identification: 003720
Unit ID: 232609
Telephone: (434) 544-8100 — Carnegie Class: Masters/M
FAX Number: (434) 544-8499 — Calendar System: Semester
URL: www.lynchburg.edu
Established: 1903 — Annual Undergrad Tuition & Fees: $36,620
Enrollment: 2,794 — Coed
Affiliation or Control: Christian Church (Disciples Of Christ) — IRS Status: 501(c)3
Highest Offering: Doctorate
Accreditation: SC, ACBSP, #ARCPA, CAATE, CACREP, EXSC, MUS, NURSE, PTA

01 President ... Dr. Kenneth R. GARREN
05 Vice Pres & Dean for Academic Affs ... Dr. Sally SELDEN
10 Vice President Business & Finance ... Mr. Steve BRIGHT
111 Sr Vice President Advancement ... Dr. J. Michael BONNETTE
84 Vice Pres Enrollment Management ... Mrs. Rita DETWILER
32 Vice Pres & Dean of Student Devel ... Mr. Hayward GUENARD
45 VP Inst Planning/Effectiveness ... Dr. Debbie DRISCOLL
26 AVP Communications & Marketing ... Mr. Mike JONES
50 Dean School Business & Economics ... Dr. Daniel MESSERSCHMIDT
53 Dean Sch Education/Leadership Stds ... Dr. Roger JONES
60 Dean Sch Communications & The Arts ... Dr. Oeida HATCHER
79 Dean Sch Humanities/Social Science ... Dr. Charles WALTON
81 Dean School of Sciences ... Dr. William LOKAR
76 Dean Sch Health Science/Human Perf ... Dr. Jean ST. CLAIR
06 Interim Registrar/Acad/Stdnt Info ... Mrs. Susan KENNON
08 Director of the Library ... Mrs. Jennifer HORTON
37 Director of Financial Aid ... Mr. Timothy SAULNIER
07 Director of Admissions ... Ms. Sharon WALTERS-BOWER
102 Director of Grants Management ... Ms. Carol HARDIN
13 Director Information and Technology ... Mrs. Jackie ALMOND
15 Human Resource Director ... Ms. Linda HALL
19 Director Security/Safety ... Mr. Bob DRISKILL
28 Diversity and Inclusion Officer ... Mr. Aaron SMITH
29 Director Alumni Relations ... Ms. Heather GARNETT
39 Director Residence Life ... Ms. Kristen COOPER
41 Athletic Director ... Mr. Jon WATERS
96 Purchasing and Logistics Coord ... Mrs. Cynthia PONTON

Mary Baldwin University (G)

318 Prospect Street, Staunton VA 24401
County: Augusta — FICE Identification: 003723
Unit ID: 232672
Telephone: (540) 887-7000 — Carnegie Class: Bac-A&S
FAX Number: (540) 886-5561 — Calendar System: Other
URL: www.marybaldwin.edu
Established: 1842 — Annual Undergrad Tuition & Fees: $30,635
Enrollment: 1,666 — Female
Affiliation or Control: Presbyterian Church (U.S.A.) — IRS Status: 501(c)3
Highest Offering: Doctorate
Accreditation: SC, #ARCPA, CAEPT, NURSE, OT, PTA, SW

01 President ... Dr. Pamela FOX
05 Provost/VP for Academic Affairs ... Dr. Ty BUCKMAN
10 Exec Vice President Finance/Admin ... Mr. David MOWEN
84 VP Enrollment Mgmt ... Vacant
111 VP University Advancement ... Ms. Brooke HERNDON
26 VP University Relations ... Vacant
76 VP MDCHS ... Dr. Linda SEESTEDT-STANFORD
88 Assoc VP for Inclusive Excellence ... Rev. Andrea CORNELL-SCOTT
88 Commandant VWIL/Spec Asst to Pres ... BGen. Teresa A. DJURIC
11 Dir of Admin & Student Success ... Ms. Lallon POND
09 Institutional Repts/Research Coord ... Ms. Carrie BOYD
13 Chief Information Officer ... Mr. Angus MCQUEEN
06 Registrar ... Ms. Kimberlely D. ROBINSON
08 Director of Library ... Ms. Carol CREAGER
49 Dean of College of Arts & Sciences ... Dr. Martha J. WALKER
50 Dean of Col Business & Prof Stds ... Dr. Joseph R. SPRANGEL, JR.
53 Dean of College of Education ... Dr. Rachel POTTER
57 Director MLitt/MFA ... Dr. Paul MENZER
15 Director of Human Resources ... Ms. Shelly IRVINE
32 Assoc VP of Student Life ... Ms. Lisa WELLS
18 Director Facilities Management ... Mr. Brent DOUGLASS
21 Dir of Budgets/Business Operation ... Mr. Rick CZERWINSKI
29 Director of Alumni Engagement ... Ms. Clare EAKIN
36 Director Career to Career Center ... Ms. Nell DESMOND

37 Director of Financial Aid ....Ms. Robin DIETRICH
04 Executive Presidential Assistant .... Ms. Sharon S. BOSSERMAN
41 Athletic Director ....Ms. Lynda J. ALANKO
07 Dir of Admiss for Adult & Grad Stds ....Mr. Daryl L. KINGREY
19 Director Security/Safety .... Mr. Thomas L. BYERLY

Marymount University (A)

2807 N Glebe Road, Arlington VA 22207-4299
County: Arlington FICE Identification: 003724
Unit ID: 232706
Telephone: (703) 522-5600 Carnegie Class: Masters/L
FAX Number: (703) 284-1637 Calendar System: Semester
URL: www.marymount.edu
Established: 1950 Annual Undergrad Tuition & Fees: $29,780
Enrollment: 3,363 Coed
Affiliation or Control: Roman Catholic IRS Status: 501(c)3
Highest Offering: Doctorate
Accreditation: SC, ACBSP, CACREP, CAEP, CAEPN, CIDA, HSA, NURSE, PTA

01 President ....Dr. Matthew D. SHANK
05 Provost & VP Acad Affairs .... Dr. William EHMANN
10 Vice Pres for Financial Affairs ....Mr. Alphonso V. DIAZ
111 Vice Pres University Advancement .... Mr. Joseph FOSTER
32 Vice Pres for Student Affairs .... Dr. Linda MCMURDOCK
09 Assoc VP Planning & Inst Effect .... Mr. Michael SCHUCHERT
20 Assoc VP Academic Affairs .... Mrs. Bridget MURPHY
84 Assoc VP Enrollment Mgmt & Dir Grad ...... Mrs. Francesca REED
21 Asst Vice Pres and Controller ....Mr. Ronald SOMERVELL
109 Asst Vice Pres Campus Plng & Mgmt ....Mr. Upendra MALANI
08 Dean Library & Learning Services ....Dr. Zary MOSTASHARI
35 Dean Student Life ....Mrs. Christina RAJMAIRA
121 Dean Student Success .... Dr. Demetrius JOHNSON
49 Dean Arts & Sciences ....Dr. Christina CLARK
50 Dean Business Administration .. Dr. Marianne WARD-PERADOZA
53 Dean Education & Human Services ....Dr. Lois STOVER
66 Dean Health Professions ....Dr. Jeanne MATTHEWS
58 Assoc Provost Research & Grad Ed ....Dr. Rita WONG
89 Assoc Dean First Year Experience .... Dr. Yolanda GIBSON
124 Asst Dean Student Engagement .... Dr. Vernon WILLIAMS
06 University Registrar ....Mrs. Simone WOUNG
12 Executive Director Reston Center ....Mr. Lawrence HOFFMAN
13 Exec Director IT Services .... Mr. Steve MUNSON
15 Exec Dir Human Resource Svcs ....Vacant
104 Exec Dir Center for Global Studies ....Mr. Victor BETANCOURT SANTIAGO
88 Exec Dir Ctr Teaching/Learning ....Ms. Michelle STEINER
07 Director of Undergrad Admissions ....Ms. Dana MATASSINO
18 Director of Physical Plant ....Vacant
19 Dir of Campus Safety/Transportation ....Mr. Eric HOLS
23 Director Student Health Center .... Mrs. Catherine BROCKER
25 Dir Office of Sponsored Research .... Mrs. Cheryl GREEN
29 Director Alumni Relations ....Ms. Anna SODY
37 Director Financial Aid ....Ms. Deborah RAINES
38 Interim Director Student Counseling ....Ms. Jennifer TELFAIR
39 Dir Campus & Residential Svcs .... Ms. Tina SHEPPARD
41 Director Athletics ....Ms. Jamie REYNOLDS
42 Director Campus Ministry ....Fr. Thomas YEHL
44 Director Annual Fund ....Vacant
85 Director International Student Svcs ....Mrs. Aline ORFALI
91 Dir of Admin Information Services ....Vacant
92 Director Honors Program .... Dr. Stacy LOPRESTI-GOODMAN
108 Dir Assessment & Inst Effectiveness ....Ms. Ann BOUDINOT
114 Director Budget & Risk Mgmt .... Mrs. Margaret AXELROD
119 Director Infrastructure & Security .... Mr. David LUTES
120 Int Dir Distance Ed & Instr Design ....Dr. Joseph PROVENZANO
88 Director Acad Affairs Info Systems ....Mr. Louis FRISENDA
88 Dir Campus Pgms & Leadership Dev .... Mr. Vincent STOVALL
88 Director Enrollment Mgmt Systems .... Mrs. Sara MEEHAN
88 Director Experiential Learning ....Mr. David POMEROY
88 Director IT Support Services ...... Mr. Oscar VENTURA-MENDOZA
88 Director Planning & Service Quality .... Mrs. Anne STANCIL
88 Conference Services Manager .... Ms. Joy COLEMAN
88 Interim Dir Student Access Services .... Dr. Jennifer SPAFFORD
88 Dir Stdnt Conduct & Acad Integrity ..... Mr. Christopher FIORELLO
88 Director Training/Org Development ....Vacant
16 Asst Director Employment .... Ms. Lisa IGIEHON
105 Web Application Manager ....Mr. Yong SHIN
113 Bursar ....Mr. Anantha GORTI
118 Human Resource Manager Benefits ....Mrs. Paula POLSON
88 Title IX Coordinator .... Ms. Angela NASTASE
40 Manager B&N Bookstore ....Ms. Kandice LARGE
96 Coordinator of Purchasing ....Mrs. Amy PAPPAS
04 Administrative Asst to President ....Mrs. Hilary PHILLIPS

Medical Careers Institute (B)

1001 Omni Boulevard Suite 200,
Newport News VA 23606-4388
Telephone: (757) 873-2423 FICE Identification: 022472
Accreditation: &SC, CAHIIM, MAAB, PTAA, RAD

† Regional accreditation is carried under the parent institution, ECPI College of Technology, in Virginia Beach, VA.

Medical Careers Institute (C)

2809 Emerywood Parkway, Suite 400,
Richmond VA 23294
Telephone: (804) 521-5999 Identification: 667038
Accreditation: &SC, MAAB

† Regional accreditation is carried under the parent institution ECPI College of Technology, Virginia Beach, VA.

Miller-Motte Technical College (D)

1011 Creekside Lane, Lynchburg VA 24502-4353
County: Lynchburg FICE Identification: 004992
Unit ID: 233091
Telephone: (434) 239-5222 Carnegie Class: Assoc/HVT-High Non
FAX Number: (434) 239-1069 Calendar System: Quarter
URL: www.miller-motte.edu
Established: 1997 Annual Undergrad Tuition & Fees: $10,288
Enrollment: 323 Coed
Affiliation or Control: Proprietary IRS Status: Proprietary
Highest Offering: Associate Degree
Accreditation: ACICS, MAC, SURGT

01 Director .... Ms. Susie ROWLAND

† No longer accepting campus-based students.

Miller-Motte Technical College (E)

4444-A Electric Road, Roanoke VA 24018
Telephone: (540) 597-1010 Identification: 770816
Accreditation: ACICS

† Branch campus of Miller-Motte Technical College, Lynchburg, VA. No longer accepting campus-based students

Norfolk State University (F)

700 Park Avenue, Norfolk VA 23504-8000
County: Independent City FICE Identification: 003765
Unit ID: 232937
Telephone: (757) 823-8600 Carnegie Class: Masters/M
FAX Number: (757) 823-2067 Calendar System: Semester
URL: www.nsu.edu
Established: 1935 Annual Undergrad Tuition & Fees (In-State): $8,738
Enrollment: 5,107 Coed
Affiliation or Control: State IRS Status: 501(c)3
Highest Offering: Doctorate
Accreditation: SC, CAEPN, CLPSY, CS, DIETD, ENG, JOUR, #KIN, MT, MUS, NAIT, NUR, SW

01 President ....Mr. Eddie N. MOORE, JR.
05 Provost/Vice Pres Academic Affs ....Dr. Stacey F. JONES
10 Vice Pres Finance and Admin ....Mr. Gerald E. HUNTER
111 Vice Pres Univ Advancement .... Dr. Deborah C. FONTAINE
32 Vice Pres Student Affs/Enroll Mgmt ....Dr. Michael M. SHACKLEFORD
20 Interim Vice Provost ....Dr. Leroy HAMILTON, JR.
43 University Counsel ....Ms. Pamela F. BOSTON
07 Exec Director of Admissions ....Dr. Juan M. ALEXANDER
19 Chief of Campus Police ....Mr. Troy COVINGTON
38 Director of Counseling ....Ms. Vanessa C. JENKINS
06 Registrar ....Mr. Michael CARPENTER
08 Dean of Library Services ....Mr. Marc L. FINNEY
37 Director of Financial Aid ....Dr. Melissa BARNES
36 Director of Career Services ....Ms. Alisha BAZEMORE
15 Assoc VP Human Resources .... Ms. Mona ADKINS-EASLEY
29 Dir Alumni Relations/Annual Giving ....Ms. Michelle D. HILL
49 Interim Dean of Liberal Arts .... Dr. Cassandra NEWBY-ALEXANDER
50 Interim Dean of Business ....Mr. Glen R. CARRINGTON
53 Dean of Education ....Dr. Denise LITTLETON
76 Act Dean of Science/Eng/Technology ....Dr. Joseph C. HALL
70 Dean of Social Work ....Dr. Rowena G. WILSON
92 Dean of Honors College ....Dr. Page LAWS
58 Dean of Graduate Studies & Research . Dr. George E. MILLER, III
86 Legislative Liaison ....Mr. Robert L. TURNER
26 Exec Dir Communications & Marketing .Ms. Stevalynn R. ADAMS
09 Dir Institutional Research ....Mr. Ephraim BENNETT
39 Exec Dir Housing & Residence Life ...Mrs. Faith M. FITZGERALD
40 Bookstore Manager ....Ms. Angela HARRISON
41 Athletics Director ....Mr. Marty L. MILLER
18 Assoc Vice Pres Facilities Mgmt ....Mr. Anton KASHIRI
85 Dir International Student Services ....Mrs. Beverly HARRIS
96 Director of Procurement .... Mr. Eugene ANDERSON
21 University Controller ....Mrs. Karla J. AMAYA GORDON
35 Dean of Students ....Ms. Tracci JOHNSON
35 Assoc Vice Pres for Student Affairs .... Mrs. Julia WINGARD

† Member of Virginia Consortium for Professional Psychology.

Old Dominion University (G)

5115 Hampton Boulevard, Norfolk VA 23529-0001
County: Independent City FICE Identification: 003728
Unit ID: 232982
Telephone: (757) 683-3000 Carnegie Class: DU-Higher
FAX Number: (757) 683-4505 Calendar System: Semester
URL: www.odu.edu
Established: 1930 Annual Undergrad Tuition & Fees (In-State): $9,750
Enrollment: 24,672 Coed
Affiliation or Control: State IRS Status: 501(c)3
Highest Offering: Doctorate
Accreditation: SC, ANEST, ART, CAATE, CACREP, CAEPN, CLPSY, CYTO, DH, ENG, ENGT, EXSC, MT, MUS, NMT, NRPA, NURSE, PH, PTA, SP, SPAA, THEA

01 President ....Mr. John R. BRODERICK
05 Provost/VP Academic Affairs ....Dr. Austin AGHO
10 Vice President Admin & Finance ....Mr. Gregory DUBOIS
46 Vice President for Research ....Dr. Morris W. FOSTER
15 Vice Pres for Human Resources ...Ms. September C. SANDERLIN
30 Vice Pres University Advancement ....Mr. Alonzo C. BRANDON
32 VP Student Engagement & Enroll Svcs ......Dr. Ellen J. NEUFELDT
88 Vice Provost for Faculty/Pgm Devel ....Vacant
88 Vice Prov Academic Programs .... Dr. Brian K. PAYNE
20 Assoc Vice Pres Academic Affairs .... Mr. James P. DUFFY
21 Assoc VP for Financial Services ...... Ms. Deborah L. SWIECINSKI
88 Asst VP Regional/Higher Educ Ctrs ....Ms. Renee E. OLANDER
56 Assoc VP Distance Learning .... Mr. Andrew R. CASIELLO
84 Assoc Vice Pres Enrollment Mgmt ....Ms. Jane H. DANE
44 Assoc Vice Pres for Advancement ....Mr. Daniel J. GENARD
88 Assoc VP Student Engagement ....Dr. Johnny W. YOUNG
109 Asst Vice Pres Auxiliary Services ....Mr. Todd K. JOHNSON
21 Asst VP Finance/Univ Controller ....Ms. Mary C. DENEEN
13 CIO/Assoc VP for University Svcs ..... Mr. James R. WATERFIELD
31 Asst Vice Pres Community Engagement ....Ms. Karen F. MEIER
35 Dean Students/AVP Stdnt Engagement .... Dr. Donald M. STANSBERRY
20 Asst VP Undergraduate Studies .... Ms. Judith M. BOWMAN
29 Asst Vice Pres of Alumni Relations .... Ms. Joy L. JEFFERSON
26 AVP Marketing & Communications ..... Ms. Giovanna M. GENARD
22 Asst VP Inst Equity & Diversity ....Ms. ReNee S. DUNMAN
58 Associate VP for Graduate Studies .... Dr. Robert WOJTOWICZ
49 Dean College Arts & Letters .... Dr. Kent SANDSTROM
81 Dean College of Sciences ....Dr. Gail DODGE
76 Int Dean College Health Sciences ....Dr. Richardean BENJAMIN
50 Dean Strome College of Business ....Dr. Jeff F. TANNER
53 Dean Darden College of Education ....Dr. Jane S. BRAY
54 Dean Batten Col Engineering & Tech ......Dr. Stephanie G. ADAMS
92 Dean Honors College ....Dr. David D. METZGER
20 Exec Dir Ctr High Impact Practices ....Ms. Lisa MAYES
36 Int Exec Dir Career Management Ctr .... Ms. Beverly FORBES
93 Exec Dir of Intercultural Relations ....Ms. Lesa C. CLARK
43 Asst Atty Gen/Assoc Univ Counsel ....Mr. Richard E. NANCE
85 Int Exec Dir International Programs ....Dr. Steven BELL
08 University Librarian ....Mr. George J. FOWLER
06 Interim University Registrar ....Mr. Humberto PORTELLEZ
07 Exec Director of Admissions .... Dr. J. Christopher FLEMING
41 Director of Athletics ....Dr. C. Wood SELIG
37 Director Student Financial Aid .... Ms. Vera E. RIDDICK
31 Director of Community Relations ....Ms. Cecelia T. TUCKER
88 Director Military Affairs ....Mr. Robert E. CLARK
38 Sr Exec Director Counseling Svcs .... Dr. Nancy BADGER
23 Director Student Health Center ....Ms. Jennifer J. FOSS
85 Director Intl Students/Scholar Svcs .... Ms. Robbin S. FULMORE
39 Exec Director of Student Housing ....Vacant
18 Director Facilities Management .... Mr. R. Dillard GEORGE
19 VP for Public Safety & Chief Police ....Ms. Rhonda L. HARRIS
28 Dir Inst Equity/Diversity/EO/AA ....Ms. Lanay NEWSOM
109 Actg Dir of Procurement Services ....Ms. Etta A. HENRY
94 Director Women's Studies ....Dr. Jennifer N. FISH
16 Dir of HR Employee Rels/Strat Init .... Ms. JaRenae WHITEHEAD
35 Dir Leadership/Student Involvement .... Ms. Nicole C. KIGER
40 University Bookstore Manager .... Mr. Darryl ATKINSON
04 Asst to the President ....Ms. Velvet L. GRANT
86 Asst to Pres for Govt Relations ....Ms. Elizabeth A. KERSEY

† Member of Virginia Consortium for Professional Psychology.

Patrick Henry College (H)

Ten Patrick Henry Circle, Purcellville VA 20132
County: Loudoun FICE Identification: 039513
Telephone: (540) 338-1776 Carnegie Class: Not Classified
FAX Number: (540) 441-8709 Calendar System: Semester
URL: www.phc.edu
Established: 2000 Annual Undergrad Tuition & Fees: N/A
Enrollment: N/A Coed
Affiliation or Control: Independent Non-Profit IRS Status: 501(c)3
Highest Offering: Baccalaureate
Accreditation: TRACS

125 Chancellor Emeritus ....Dr. Michael P. FARRIS
01 President ....Mr. Jack HAYE
03 Executive Vice President .... Mr. Howard SCHMIDT
10 VP for Administration & Finance ....Mr. Daryl WOLKING
09 VP for Institutional Effectiveness .... Mr. Rodney J. SHOWALTER
30 Vice President for Advancement ....Mr. Tom ZIEMNICK
05 Dean of Academic Affairs ....Dr. Frank GULIUZZA
32 Dean of Student Affairs ....Ms. Sandra K. CORBITT
08 Director of the Library .... Ms. Sara E. PENSGARD
07 Director of Admissions .... Mr. Stephen C. ALLEN

Protestant Episcopal Theological Seminary in Virginia (I)

3737 Seminary Road, Alexandria VA 22304-5201
County: Independent City FICE Identification: 003731
Unit ID: 233259
Telephone: (703) 370-6600 Carnegie Class: Not Classified
FAX Number: N/A Calendar System: Semester
URL: www.vts.edu
Established: 1823 Annual Graduate Tuition & Fees: N/A
Enrollment: N/A Coed
Affiliation or Control: Protestant Episcopal IRS Status: 501(c)3
Highest Offering: Doctorate; No Undergraduates
Accreditation: THEOL

01 Dean and President .... Rev. Ian S. MARKHAM
05 VP of Academic Affairs .... Rev. Melody D. KNOWLES
111 VP of Institutional Advancement ....Rev. J. Barney HAWKINS
15 VP for HR and Inst Effectiveness ....Ms. Katie GLOVER
32 Interim Assoc Dean of Students ....Rev. Francis H. WADE
10 Comptroller .... Ms. Olivine PILLING

06 Registrar .... Mrs. Tamara A. SHEPHERD
08 Head Librarian .... Dr. Mitzi J. BUDDE
26 Director of Communications .... Mr. Curtis PRATHER
07 Director of Admissions .... Vacant

Radford University (A)

801 East Main Street, Radford VA 24142
County: Radford City FICE Identification: 003732
Unit ID: 233277
Telephone: (540) 831-5000 Carnegie Class: Masters/L
FAX Number: N/A Calendar System: Semester
URL: www.radford.edu
Established: 1910 Annual Undergrad Tuition & Fees (In-State): $10,081
Enrollment: 9,743 Coed
Affiliation or Control: State IRS Status: 170(c)1
Highest Offering: Doctorate
Accreditation: SC, ART, CAATE, CACREP, CAEPN, CIDA, COPSY, CS, DANCE, DIETD, MUS, NRPA, NURSE, OT, PTA, SP, SW, THEA

01 President .... Dr. Brian O. HEMPHILL
05 Provost/VP Academic Affairs .... Dr. Graham GLYNN
10 VP Finance and Administration/CFO .... Mr. Richard ALVAREZ
13 VP Information Technology/CIO .... Mr. Danny KEMP
32 Interim VP Student Affairs .... Ms. Susan TRAGESER
26 VP University Relations/CCO .... Mr. Larry CARPENTER
111 VP University Advancement .... Ms. Wendy LOWERY
50 Dean Business and Economics .... Dr. George LOW
53 Dean Education and Human Devel .... Dr. Kenna COLLEY
76 Dean Health and Human Services .... Dr. Kenneth COX
83 Dean Humanities and Behavioral Sci .... Dr. Katherine HAWKINS
81 Dean Science and Technology .... Dr. J. Orion ROGERS
57 Dean Visual and Performing Arts .... Ms. Margaret DEVANEY
58 Acting Dean Graduate Studies/Resear .... Dr. Laura JACOBSEN
84 VP Enrollment Mgmt .... Ms. Katherine MCCARTHY
08 Dean of the Library .... Mr. Steven HELM
06 Registrar .... Mr. Matthew BRUNNER
37 Director of Financial Aid .... Ms. Barbara PORTER
29 Executive Dir of Alumni Relations .... Ms. Laura TURK
41 Director Intercollegiate Athletics .... Mr. Robert LINEBURG
15 Asst VP for Human Resources .... Mr. John BROOKS
19 Interim Deputy Chief .... Mr. David UNDERWOOD
09 Director of Institutional Research .... Dr. Eric LOVIK
101 Secretary of the Board of Visitors .... Ms. Mary WEEKS

Randolph College (B)

2500 Rivermont Avenue, Lynchburg VA 24503-1555
County: Independent City FICE Identification: 003734
Unit ID: 233301
Telephone: (434) 947-8000 Carnegie Class: Bac-A&S
FAX Number: (434) 947-8139 Calendar System: Semester
URL: www.randolphcollege.edu
Established: 1891 Annual Undergrad Tuition & Fees: $36,770
Enrollment: 688 Coed
Affiliation or Control: United Methodist IRS Status: 501(c)3
Highest Offering: Master's
Accreditation: SC, CAEP

01 President .... Dr. Bradley W. BATEMAN
05 VP Academic Affs & Dean of College .... Dr. Carl A. GIRELLI
111 Vice Pres Institutional Advancement .... Ms. Farah MARKS
10 Vice Pres Finance & Administration .... Mr. James MANARO
32 VP Student Affs & Dean of Students .... Dr. Matha THORNTON
84 VP Enrollment Management .... Mr. Michael J. QUINN
100 VP & Chief of Staff .... Mr. Wesley FUGATE
20 Associate Dean of the College .... Ms. Paula J. WALLACE
29 Director Alumnae & Alumni Pgm .... Ms. Phebe WESCOTT
09 Dir IR/Planning & Assessment .... Dr. John F. KEENER
15 Director Human Resources .... Ms. Sharon SAUNDERS
18 Chief Facilities/Physical Plant .... Mr. John LEARY
21 Director of Finance .... Mr. Jonathan TYREE
38 Director Student Counseling .... Dr. Anne HERSHBELL
08 Librarian .... Ms. Lisa BROUGHMAN
06 Registrar .... Ms. Barbara S. THRASHER
37 Dir Student Financial Services .... Ms. Debi WOODALL-STEVENS
36 Director of Career Development .... Ms. Christine HARRIGER
13 Director of Information Technology .... Mr. Victor GOSNELL
04 Administrative Asst to President .... Ms. Cindy LYONS
07 Director of Admissions .... Ms. Nelson DAVIS
19 Director Security/Safety .... Mr. Kris IRWIN
41 Athletic Director .... Ms. Tina HILL
104 Director Study Abroad .... Ms. Maureen KIERNAN
26 Chief Public Relations/Marketing .... Ms. Brenda EDSON

Randolph-Macon College (C)

204 Henry Street, PO Box 5005, Ashland VA 23005-5505
County: Hanover FICE Identification: 003733
Unit ID: 233295
Telephone: (804) 752-7200 Carnegie Class: Bac-A&S
FAX Number: (804) 752-7231 Calendar System: Other
URL: www.rmc.edu
Established: 1830 Annual Undergrad Tuition & Fees: $38,730
Enrollment: 1,418 Coed
Affiliation or Control: United Methodist IRS Status: 501(c)3
Highest Offering: Baccalaureate
Accreditation: SC, #CAEP

01 President .... Mr. Robert R. LINDGREN
05 Provost/VP for Academic Affairs .... Dr. William T. FRANZ
10 Vice Pres of Admin & Finance .... Mr. Paul DAVIES
111 Vice Pres for College Advancement .... Ms. Diane M. LOWDER
84 Vice Pres for Enroll/Admiss/Fin Aid .... Dr. David L. LESESNE
32 Vice President for Student Affairs .... Dr. Grant L. AZDELL
04 Executive Assistant to the Pres .... Ms. Jennifer L. THOMPSON
07 Director of Admissions .... Vacant
29 Exec Director Alumni Relations .... Ms. Alice D. LYNCH
26 Dir of Marketing & Communications .... Mrs. Anne Marie LAURANZON
37 Director of Financial Aid .... Mrs. Mary Y. NEAL
13 CIO and ITS Director .... Mr. Kirk BAUMBACH
06 Registrar .... Mrs. Alana DAVIS
38 Director of Counseling Services .... Dr. D. Craig ANDERSON
09 Director of Institutional Research .... Dr. Katherine D. WALKER
18 Dir of Operations & Physical Plant .... Mr. Thomas P. DWYER
42 Chaplain .... Rev. Kendra S. GRIMES
19 Director of Campus Safety .... Mr. Maurice J. KIELY
41 Athletic Director .... Mr. Jeffrey S. BURNS
15 Director Human Resources .... Mrs. Sharon S. JACKSON
21 Controller .... Ms. Barbara A. DAUBERMAN
20 Associate Dean of the College .... Dr. Lauren C. BELL
36 Director of Professional Develop .... Ms. Catherine A. ROLLMAN
35 Asst Dean of Students .... Mr. James D. MCGHEE, JR.
40 Bookstore Manager .... Mrs. Barclay F. DUPRIEST
114 Director of Budget/Financial Analys .... Mrs. Caroline C. BUSCH
08 Head Librarian .... Ms. Nancy K. FALCIANI-WHITE
102 Dir Foundation/Corporate Relations .... Mr. Robert H. PATTERSON
104 Director Study Abroad .... Ms. Tammi L. REICHEL
28 Director of Diversity .... Ms. Alicia C. ELMS
39 Director Student Housing .... Ms. Melissa LEECY
44 Director Annual or Planned Giving .... Mr. Richard M. GOLEMBESKI

Reformed Theological Seminary (D)

1651 Old Meadow Road, Suite 300, McLean VA 22102
Telephone: (703) 448-3393 Identification: 666079
Accreditation: &SC, THEOL

† Regional accreditation is carried under the parent institution in Jackson, MS.

Regent University (E)

1000 Regent University Drive, Virginia Beach VA 23464-9800
County: Independent City FICE Identification: 030913
Unit ID: 231651
Telephone: (757) 352-4127 Carnegie Class: DU-Mod
FAX Number: (757) 352-4381 Calendar System: Semester
URL: www.regent.edu
Established: 1977 Annual Undergrad Tuition & Fees: $16,438
Enrollment: 6,950 Coed
Affiliation or Control: Independent Non-Profit IRS Status: 501(c)3
Highest Offering: Doctorate
Accreditation: SC, ACBSP, CACREP, CAEPT, CLPSY, LAW, THEOL

01 Chancellor & CEO .... Dr. M.G. (Pat) ROBERTSON
05 Executive VP for Academic Affairs .... Dr. Gerson MORENO-RIANO
10 Chief Financial Officer .... Mr. Robert OWEN
32 Executive VP for Student Life .... Dr. Joseph UMIDI
43 Senior VP & General Counsel .... Mr. Louis A. ISAKOFF
29 Vice President for Alumni Relations .... Mrs. Ann LEBLANC
26 VP for Marketing & Public Relations .... Mrs. Sherri MILLER
10 Vice President for Finance .... Mr. Dean A. WOOTEN
15 VP for Human Resources & Admin .... Mrs. Martha J. SMITH
20 Associate VP for Academic Affairs .... Mr. Douglas COOK
88 Associate VP for Teaching/Learning .... Dr. Jason BAKER
61 Dean School of Law .... Mr. Michael HERNANDEZ
49 Dean College of Arts & Sciences .... Dr. Robert HERRON
08 Dean of University Library .... Dr. Esther GILLIE
50 Dean School of Business/Leadership .... Dr. Doris GOMEZ
80 Dean School of Government .... Dr. Eric PATTERSON
53 Dean School of Education .... Dr. Donald FINN
83 Dean Psychology & Counseling .... Dr. William HATHAWAY
73 Dean School of Divinity .... Dr. Corne BEKKER
06 Registrar .... Ms. Erica LEMELLE
84 Assistant VP of Enrollment Mgmt .... Mrs. Heidi CECE
35 Director of Student Activities .... Mr. Roger CHEEKS
106 Director of CTL .... Dr. Tonya AMANKWATIA
37 Sr Assoc Dir Financial Aid .... Mr. Tim PARRY
09 Director of Institutional Research .... Dr. Amanda WYNN
18 Dir of Facilities & Engineering .... Mr. Richard JEMIOLA
88 Director of Alumni Relations .... Ms. Melissa FUQUAY
42 Director of Campus Ministries .... Vacant
108 Director of Assessment .... Dr. Ryan MURNANE
123 Dir of Graduate & Military Admiss .... Mr. Bob HABIB
39 Assistant VP for Student Life .... Mr. Adam WILLIAMS
96 Manager of Purchasing .... Mrs. Pauline CARRAWAY
04 Assistant to the Chancellor .... Mrs. Carol DIXON
13 Executive Director of IT .... Mr. Jonathan HARRELL
41 Athletic Director .... Mr. Roger CHEEKS

Richard Bland College (F)

11301 Johnson Road, South Prince George VA 23805-7100
County: South Prince George FICE Identification: 003707
Unit ID: 233338
Telephone: (804) 862-6100 Carnegie Class: Spec 2-yr-Other
FAX Number: (804) 862-6207 Calendar System: Semester
URL: www.rbc.edu
Established: 1960 Annual Undergrad Tuition & Fees (In-State): $7,140
Enrollment: 2,255 Coed
Affiliation or Control: State IRS Status: 501(c)3
Highest Offering: Associate Degree
Accreditation: SC

01 President .... Dr. Debbie L. SYDOW
05 Provost .... Dr. Kenneth LATESSA
10 Chief Financial Officer .... Ms. Penny HOWARD
18 Director Capital Assets/Operations .... Mr. Eric KONDZIELAWA
04 Executive Assistant to President .... Ms. Laschrecse AIRD
26 Director of Communications .... Ms. Joanne WILLIAMS
15 Director of Human Resources .... Ms. Takeya M. MCLAURIN
30 Chief Development Officer .... Dr. James T. HART
19 Chief Campus Safety/Police .... Mr. Jeffrey BROWN
43 College Counsel .... Ms. Cynthia NORWOOD
20 Dean of Faculty/CAO .... Dr. Vern L. LINDQUIST
84 Asst Provost Enrollment Management .... Dr. Danielle E. WILLIAMS
39 Asst Provost Resid & Student Life .... Dr. Corey SCOTT
121 Asst Provost Student Success .... Ms. Kim DUPRE
41 Director Athletics & Recreation .... Mr. Chuck MOORE
09 Director of Institutional Research .... Ms. Carol KELEJIAN
13 Director of Information Technology .... Vacant
08 Associate Dean Instruct Resources .... Ms. Aimee JOYAUX
37 Director of Financial Aid .... Ms. Lisa JOHNSON
06 Director of Records & Registration .... Vacant
07 Director of Admissions .... Ms. Judy WACHSMANN
38 Dir of Counseling/Student Support .... Dr. Evanda WATTS-MARTINEZ
88 Director Athletic Communications .... Mr. Greg PROUTY
35 Director of Student Activities .... Mr. Michael ROGERS
109 Assoc Director Aux Enterprises .... Ms. Jamie CAMP
21 Controller .... Ms. Denise L. DAVIS
113 Bursar .... Ms. Melissa MAHONEY
96 Procurement Manager .... Ms. Trinika LEWIS-WILSON
119 Information Security Officer .... Ms. Deborah JAMES
14 Manager Projects & Telecom .... Mr. George JELLERSON
14 Technology Support Manager .... Mr. Clifton YOUNG
16 HR Specialist .... Ms. Alice JABBOUR

Riverside College of Health Careers (G)

316 Main Street, Newport News VA 23601
County: Independent City FICE Identification: 021400
Unit ID: 233408
Telephone: (757) 240-2200 Carnegie Class: Spec 2-yr-Health
FAX Number: (757) 240-2225 Calendar System: Semester
URL: www.riverside.edu
Established: 1916 Annual Undergrad Tuition & Fees: $15,849
Enrollment: 208 Coed
Affiliation or Control: Independent Non-Profit IRS Status: 501(c)3
Highest Offering: Associate Degree
Accreditation: ABHES, PNUR, PTAA, RAD, SURGT, SURTEC

01 System Director of Education .... Robin M. NELHUEBEL
06 Registrar .... Lori ARNDER
08 Head Librarian .... Cassandra MOORE
10 Director of Campus Resources .... Michael HAMILTON
07 Recruitment Coordinator .... Cynthia REDDINGTON

Roanoke College (H)

221 College Lane, Salem VA 24153-3747
County: Independent City FICE Identification: 003736
Unit ID: 233426
Telephone: (540) 375-2500 Carnegie Class: Bac-A&S
FAX Number: (540) 375-2205 Calendar System: Semester
URL: www.roanoke.edu
Established: 1842 Annual Undergrad Tuition & Fees: $41,429
Enrollment: 2,001 Coed
Affiliation or Control: Evangelical Lutheran Church In America
IRS Status: 501(c)3
Highest Offering: Baccalaureate
Accreditation: SC, ACBSP, CAATE, CAEPT

01 President .... Mr. Michael C. MAXEY
05 Vice President/Dean of the College .... Dr. Richard A. SMITH
84 VP of Enroll Svcs/Dean Adm/Fin Aid .... Dr. Brenda P. POGGENDORF
32 Vice President Student Affairs .... Mr. Aaron L. FETROW
10 Vice President Business Affairs .... Mr. Mark P. NOFTSINGER
30 Vice President Resource Development .... Mr. Aaron L. FETROW
37 VP Enrollment/Dir Admiss/Fin Aid .... Dr. Brenda P. POGGENDORF
43 General Counsel .... Mr. G. Michael PACE, JR.
13 Chief Information Officer .... Mr. Mark D. POORE
09 Dir Institutional Research .... Dr. Jack K. STEEHLER
20 Assoc Dean Academic Affairs/Admin .... Dr. Jennifer K. BERENSON
06 Assoc Dean Acad Affairs/Registrar .... Ms. Leah L. RUSSELL
07 Director of Recruitment .... Mr. Courtney PENN
35 AVP/Dean of Students/Student Affs .... Dr. Brian T. CHISOM
39 Director of Residence Life/Housing .... Mr. Jimmy R. WHITED
92 Director of Honors Programs .... Dr. Chad T. MORRIS
08 Director of the Library .... Ms. Elizabeth MCCLENNEY
36 Director of Career Services .... Ms. Toni D. MCLAWHORN
24 Media Technology Director .... Mr. David H. MULFORD
31 Dir of Community Programs .... Ms. Tanya RIDPATH
26 Director of Public Relations .... Ms. Teresa T. GEREAUX
44 Director of Gift Planning .... Mr. Richard J. POGGENDORF
29 Dir of Alumni/Family Relations .... Mr. Jonathan E. LEE
114 Director of Finance & Budget .... Ms. Kathryn A. VANNESS
91 Database Director .... Ms. Mitzi B. STEELE
15 Director Human Resources .... Ms. Kathy MARTIN
40 Bookstore Coordinator/Buyer .... Ms. Melissa B. RUTLEDGE
19 Director Campus Safety .... Mr. Thomas A. RAMBO
23 Dir Student Health/Counseling Svcs .... Ms. Sandra W. MCGHEE

41 Athletic Director ... Mr. M. Scott ALLISON
42 Chaplain/Dean of the Chapel ... Rev. Christopher M. BOWEN
104 Director International Education ... Dr. Pamela A. SEROTA COTE
28 Director of Multicultural Affairs ... Ms. Juliet J. LOWERY
04 Executive Assistant to President ... Mrs. Whitney C. ALDRIDGE

Saint Michael College of Allied Health (A)

8305 Richmond Hwy, Ste 10A, Alexandria VA 22309
County: Independent City | Identification: 667226
Unit ID: 486424
Telephone: (703) 746-8708 | Carnegie Class: Not Classified
FAX Number: (703) 746-8709 | Calendar System: Other
URL: www.stmichaelcollegeva.us
Established: 2007 | Annual Undergrad Tuition & Fees: $16,300
Enrollment: 90 | Coed
Affiliation or Control: Proprietary | IRS Status: Proprietary
Highest Offering: Associate Degree
Accreditation: **COE**

01 Director ... Dr. Michael ADEDOKUN

Sentara College of Health Sciences (B)

1441 Crossways Boulevard, Ste 105,
Chesapeake VA 23320
County: Chesapeake City | FICE Identification: 031065
Unit ID: 232885
Telephone: (757) 388-2900 | Carnegie Class: Spec-4-yr-Other Health
FAX Number: (757) 222-7694 | Calendar System: Semester
URL: www.sentara.edu
Established: 1892 | Annual Undergrad Tuition & Fees: N/A
Enrollment: 445 | Coed
Affiliation or Control: Independent Non-Profit | IRS Status: 501(c)3
Highest Offering: Baccalaureate
Accreditation: **ABHES**, CVT, NURSE, SURGT, SURTEC

01 Executive Director & Dean ... Mrs. Angela TAYLOR
45 Asst Dean Institutional Effective ... Ms. Metta ALSOBROOK
10 Asst Dean Administration & Finance ... Mr. Christopher NELSON
84 Director of Enrollment Management ... Mr. Joseph HOWE
08 Librarian ... Ms. Suzanne DUNCAN
37 Financial Aid Advisor ... Ms. Mary Ann RIVERA
07 Admissions Recruiter ... Mr. Jeremy BROFFT
07 Admissions Recruiter ... Mr. Kevin LAWRENCE

Shenandoah University (C)

1460 University Drive, Winchester VA 22601-5195
County: Independent City | FICE Identification: 003737
Unit ID: 233541
Telephone: (540) 665-4500 | Carnegie Class: DU-Mod
FAX Number: N/A | Calendar System: Semester
URL: www.su.edu
Established: 1875 | Annual Undergrad Tuition & Fees: $31,322
Enrollment: 3,820 | Coed
Affiliation or Control: United Methodist | IRS Status: 501(c)3
Highest Offering: Doctorate
Accreditation: **SC**, ARCPA, CAATE, CAEPT, COARC, MIDWF, MUS, NURSE, OT, PHAR, PTA

01 President ... Dr. Tracy FITZSIMMONS
05 VP for Academic Affairs ... Dr. Adrienne G. BLOSS
10 Vice Pres Administration/Finance ... Mr. Robert L. KEASLER
32 Vice President for Student Life ... Rev Dr. Rhonda VANDYKE
111 Senior VP & VP for Advance & Plng ... Mr. Mitchell L. MOORE
84 VP for Enrol Mgmt & Student Success ... Dr. Clarresa MORTON
35 Dean of Students ... Ms. Sue O'DRISCOLL
30 Assoc Vice Pres for Leadership Gift ... Ms. Jane D. PITTMAN
26 Director of Media Relations ... Ms. Emily BURNER
49 Dean of College of Arts & Sciences ... Dr. Jeff COKER
50 Dean of Byrd School of Business ... Dr. Miles DAVIS
64 Dean of Shenandoah Conservatory ... Dr. Michael J. STEPNIAK
67 Dean of Dunn School of Pharmacy ... Dr. Robert DICENZO
07 Exec of Recruitment & Admissions ... Mr. Andy WOODALL
124 Dir of Student Engagement ... Mr. Doug STUMP
08 Director of Library Services ... Mr. Christopher A. BEAN
06 Registrar ... Ms. Emily HOLLINS
21 Asst VP for Admin & Finance ... Ms. Courtney JARRETT
37 Director of Financial Aid ... Ms. Karen H. BUCHER
36 Director of Career Services ... Ms. Jennifer A. SPATARO-WILSON
18 Director of Physical Plant ... Mr. Barry SCHNOOR
23 Director of Wellness Center ... Mr. Ronald G. STICKLEY
15 Director of Human Resources ... Ms. Marie C. LANDES
41 Athletic Director ... Mr. Doug ZIPP
91 Database & System Administrator ... Mr. Seth BURKE
13 Director of Institutional Computing ... Mr. Quaiser ABSAR
66 Dean Custer School of Nursing ... Dr. Kathleen LASALA
88 Director Div of Athletic Training ... Dr. Rose A. SCHMIEG
88 Dir Div of Occupational Therapy ... Dr. Cathy SHANHOLTZ
88 Interim Dir Div of Physical Therapy ... Dr. Sheri HALE
112 Director of Planned & Major Gifts ... Vacant
19 Chief of Public Safety ... Mr. Paul WIEBER
102 Dir of Grant Supp & Foundation Rels ... Ms. Marguerite LANDENBURGER
109 Director Auxiliary Services ... Ms. Pamela B. BURKE
88 Dir Div of Physician Asst Studies ... Dr. Tony MILLER
20 Director Learning Services ... Ms. Holli PHILLIPS
42 Dean of Spiritual Life ... Rev Dr. Justin ALLEN
88 Dir Division of Respiratory Care ... Ms. Stephanie CROSS
09 Director Institutional Research ... Dr. Howard BALLENTINE
40 Bookstore Manager ... Ms. Kimberly OTYENOH
96 Purchasing/Accounts Payable Manager ... Ms. Mary LEMASTER
24 Coordinator Media Services ... Ms. Val GANGWER
38 Counseling Center Director ... Ms. Emily PETKUS
04 Executive Asst to President ... Ms. Kim KECKLEY
101 Secretary of the Board of Trustees ... Ms. Kelly NEMZEK
53 Director School of Education ... Dr. Dennis KELLISON
104 Director International Programs ... Ms. Bethany GALIPEAU-KONATE
44 Director Annual Giving ... Ms. Kara JENKINS
90 Director Insitutional Computing ... Mr. Quaiser ABSAR
43 General Counsel ... Mr. Philip EVANS

South Baylo University (D)

7535 Little River Tnpk Unit 325-A, Annandale VA 22003
Telephone: (703) 642-7518 | Identification: 770912
Accreditation: **@ACUP**

† Branch campus of South Baylo University, Anaheim, CA

South University (E)

2151 Old Brick Road, Richmond VA 23060
Telephone: (804) 727-6800 | Identification: 770919
Accreditation: **&SC**, ACBSP, #ARCPA, CACREP, NURSE, OTA, PTAA

† Branch campus of South University, Savannah, GA

South University (F)

301 Bendix Road, Suite 100, Virginia Beach VA 23452
Telephone: (757) 493-6900 | Identification: 770920
Accreditation: **&SC**, ACBSP, CACREP, NURSE, OTA, PTAA

† Branch campus of South University, Savannah, GA

Southern Virginia University (G)

1 University Hill Drive, Buena Vista VA 24416-3097
County: Rockbridge | FICE Identification: 003738
Unit ID: 233611
Telephone: (540) 261-8400 | Carnegie Class: Bac-A&S
FAX Number: (540) 266-3859 | Calendar System: Semester
URL: www.svu.edu
Established: 1867 | Annual Undergrad Tuition & Fees: $14,900
Enrollment: 732 | Coed
Affiliation or Control: Independent Non-Profit | IRS Status: 501(c)3
Highest Offering: Baccalaureate
Accreditation: **SC**

01 President ... Dr. Reed N. WILCOX
05 Provost ... Dr. Scott DRANSFIELD
10 VP Finance ... Mr. Robert E. HUCH
30 VP Institutional Advancement ... Mr. Todd BROTHERSON
84 VP Enrollment Marketing/Strategy ... Mr. Brett GARCIA
32 VP Student Life ... Mr. Michael GIBBONS
46 VP Educational Research & Dev ... Dr. Karen M. WALKER
11 Exec Dir of Campus Operations ... Mr. Arthur FURLER
04 Administrative Asst to President ... Mrs. Kristie GIBBONS
06 Registrar ... Ms. Whitney M. LARSEN
08 Director of Library Services ... Mrs. Stephanie K. HARDY
104 Director of Travel Study ... Mrs. Carrie P. BROTHERSON
20 Associate Provost ... Dr. Jeremy JOHN
57 Division Chair Fine & Perf Arts ... Dr. Brent HANSON
79 Division Chair Humanities ... Dr. John ARMSTRON
81 Div Chair Science & Mathematics ... Dr. Richard GARDNER
83 Div Chair Social & Behavioral Sci ... Dr. Lora KNIGHT
53 Director of Teacher Education ... Mrs. Kimberly KEARNEY
09 Dir of Institutional Effectiveness ... Dr. Jon WALLIN
21 Controller & Dir of Business Ops ... Mr. Jesse SEEGMILLER
37 Director of Financial Aid ... Mr. John BRANDT
15 Human Resources Manager ... Mr. Robbie BAILEY
88 Title IX Coordinator ... Ms. Deidra DRYDEN
96 Senior Accountant ... Mr. Trenton DESPAIN
07 Director of Admissions ... Mr. Chris PENDELTON
41 Athletic Director ... Mr. Jason LAMB
26 Director of Communications ... Mr. Chris PENDLETON
88 Senior Women's Athletic Admin ... Ms. Deidra DRYDEN
29 Alumni Relations Coordinator ... Mr. Cameron CROWTHER
35 Dean of Students ... Mr. Michael GIBBONS
38 Director of Student Support ... Dr. Chad KELLAND
36 Director Career Development Center ... Mr. Cameron T. CROWTHER
23 Director of Student Health Services ... Mrs. Ginger LANIER
85 Foreign Students PDSO ... Ms. Whitney M. LARSEN
19 Director Security/Safety ... Mr. Jacob SMITH
11 Director of Campus Operations ... Mr. Joseph WHETSTONE
109 Director of Food Services ... Mrs. Effie WALLACE
18 Asst Dir Facilities/Physical Plant ... Mr. Byron PORTER
13 IT Support Manager ... Ms. Stephanie GILMER

Southside Regional Medical Center Professional Schools (H)

430 Clairmont Court, Suite 200,
Colonial Heights VA 23834
County: Independent City | FICE Identification: 012744
Unit ID: 233082
Telephone: (804) 765-5800 | Carnegie Class: Spec 2-yr-Health
FAX Number: (804) 765-5944 | Calendar System: Semester
URL: www.srmconline.com
Established: 1895 | Annual Undergrad Tuition & Fees: $13,545
Enrollment: 113 | Coed
Affiliation or Control: Proprietary | IRS Status: Proprietary
Highest Offering: Associate Degree
Accreditation: **ABHES**, ADNUR, DMS, RAD

01 Vice Pres for Professional Schools ... Ms. Cynthia PARSONS

Standard Healthcare Services College of Nursing (I)

7704 Leesburg Pike, Suite 1000, Falls Church VA 22043
County: Fairfax | Identification: 667129
Unit ID: 483814
Telephone: (703) 891-1787 | Carnegie Class: Not Classified
FAX Number: (703) 891-1789 | Calendar System: Other
URL: www.standardcollege.edu
Established: 2004 | Annual Undergrad Tuition & Fees: N/A
Enrollment: 201 | Coed
Affiliation or Control: Proprietary | IRS Status: Proprietary
Highest Offering: Associate Degree
Accreditation: **ABHES**

01 Executive Director ... Ms. Isibor J. NOSEGBE
06 Registrar ... Ms. Lisley M. ANCO
05 Director of Education ... Mr. Sakpa S. AMARA
32 Dean of Student Services ... Mrs. Sondra BROWN
37 Financial Aid ... Mrs. Brenda GARCES
07 Admissions ... Mrs. Candice SAVICE
10 Business Office ... Mrs. Nganya M. NANYARO

Stratford University (J)

7777 Leesburg Pike, Suite 1LN, Falls Church VA 22043
County: Fairfax | FICE Identification: 025412
Unit ID: 438498
Telephone: (703) 821-8570 | Carnegie Class: Masters/L
FAX Number: N/A | Calendar System: Quarter
URL: www.stratford.edu
Established: 1976 | Annual Undergrad Tuition & Fees: $15,135
Enrollment: 3,303 | Coed
Affiliation or Control: Proprietary | IRS Status: Proprietary
Highest Offering: Master's
Accreditation: **ACICS**, CEA, MAAB, NURSE

01 President ... Dr. Richard SHURTZ
05 VP Faculty and Academic Affairs ... Dr. Lee SMITH
88 VP Accreditation/State Licensu ... Dr. James FLAGGERT
88 VP International ... Mr. Feroze KHAN
12 Main Campus President ... Dr. Valerie TRIMARCHI
13 Chief Information Officer (CIO) ... Mr. Kevin COUGHENOUR
26 EVP Marketing ... Ms. Mary Ann SHURTZ

† University administration building is located at 3201 Jermantown Rd, Ste 500 Fairfax, VA 22030.

Stratford University Alexandria Campus (K)

2900 Eisenhower Avenue, Alexandria VA 22314
Telephone: (571) 777-0130 | Identification: 770856
Accreditation: **ACICS**, ACFEI, MAAB

Stratford University Glen Allen Campus (L)

11104 West Broad Street, Glen Allen VA 23060
Telephone: (804) 290-4231 | Identification: 770819
Accreditation: **ACICS**, ACFEI, MAAB

Stratford University Newport News Campus (M)

836 J. Clyde Morris Boulevard,
Newport News VA 23601-1303
Telephone: (757) 873-4235 | Identification: 770818
Accreditation: **ACICS**, ACFEI, MAAB

Stratford University Virginia Beach Campus (N)

555 S. Independent Blvd., Virginia Beach VA 23452
Telephone: (757) 448-3151 | Identification: 770857
Accreditation: **ACICS**, MAAB

Stratford University Woodbridge Campus (O)

14349 Gideon Drive, Woodbridge VA 22192
Telephone: (703) 897-1982 | Identification: 770817
Accreditation: **ACICS**, ACFEI, MAAB

Sweet Briar College (P)

134 Chapel Road, Sweet Briar VA 24595-9998
County: Amherst | FICE Identification: 003742
Unit ID: 233718
Telephone: (434) 381-6100 | Carnegie Class: Bac-A&S
FAX Number: (434) 381-6173 | Calendar System: Semester
URL: www.sbc.edu
Established: 1901 | Annual Undergrad Tuition & Fees: $36,425
Enrollment: 320 | Female
Affiliation or Control: Independent Non-Profit | IRS Status: 501(c)3
Highest Offering: Master's
Accreditation: **SC**, ENG

01 President ... Dr. Meredith WOO
10 Vice Pres Finance and Treasurer ... Mr. Timothy KLOCKO
04 Exec Asst Office of the President ... Mrs. Dawn GATEWOOD
09 Dir of Institutional Effectiveness ... Ms. Christy C. COLE
05 Dean of Academic Affairs ... Ms. Pamela DEWEESE
84 Dean of Enrollment Management ... Mr. Bill ALLEN
08 Dir Integrated Information Systems ... Mr. Joe MALLOY
41 Director of Athletics ... Vacant
104 Director Junior Year in Spain ... Ms. Giulia V. WITCOMBE
32 Dean of Student Life/Academic Supp ... Mrs. Kelly KRAFT-MEYER
21 Assoc VP Finance/Administration ... Ms. Debbie FARIS
15 Director of Human Resources ... Ms. Nicole WHITEHEAD
18 Director Physical Plant ... Mr. Steve BAILEY
19 Director of Campus Safety ... Mr. Brian MARKER
37 Director Financial Aid ... Ms. Wanda SPRADLEY
40 Book Shop Manager ... Ms. Lynn LEWIS
96 Director Purchasing ... Ms. Cynthia L. PONTON
88 Director of Hospitality ... Ms. Cathy MAYS
30 Vice Pres Alumnae Relations/ Develop ... Ms. Mary Pope M. HUTSON
38 Mental Health Counselor/Health Svcs ... Ms. Pamela CALDWELL
36 Director Career Services ... Ms. Barbara WATTS
39 Director Residence Life & Housing ... Ms. Kerri BOND
26 Director of Media/Marketing & Comm ... Vacant
06 Registrar ... Ms. Deborah POWELL
07 Director of Admissions Operations ... Ms. Melanie CAMPBELL
13 Chief Info Technology Officer (CIO) ... Mr. Aaron MAHLER
25 Chief Contracts/Grants Admin ... Ms. Kathleen PLACIDI
29 Director Alumni Relations ... Ms. Priscilla CARROLL
43 Dir Legal Services/General Counsel ... Ms. Nancyellen KEANE
54 Chair Engineering/Computer Sci/Phys ... Mr. Henry YOCHUM

Union Presbyterian Seminary (A)

3401 Brook Road, Richmond VA 23227-4597
County: Independent City FICE Identification: 003743
Unit ID: 233842
Telephone: (804) 355-0671 Carnegie Class: Spec-4-yr-Faith
FAX Number: (804) 355-3919 Calendar System: Semester
URL: www.upsem.edu
Established: 1812 Annual Graduate Tuition & Fees: N/A
Enrollment: 184 Coed
Affiliation or Control: Presbyterian Church (U.S.A.) IRS Status: 501(c)3
Highest Offering: Doctorate; No Undergraduates
Accreditation: SC, THEOL

01 President ... Dr. Brian K. BLOUNT
10 Vice Pres Finance & Administration ... Mr. Michael B. CASHWELL
30 Vice President Advancement ... Mr. Richard WONG
84 VP Student Life/Enrollment Mgmt ... Ms. Michelle WALKER
05 Dean Union Presby Sem (Richmond) .. Dr. Kenneth J. MCFAYDEN
12 Dean Union Presby Sem (Charlotte) ... Dr. Richard N. BOYCE
20 Associate Dean Academic Programs ... Dr. E. Carson BRISSON
07 Director of Admissions ... Ms. Mairi RENWICK
06 Registrar ... Mr. J. Stanley HARGRAVES
08 Seminary Librarian ... Dr. Christopher RICHARDSON
13 Director Technology Services ... Mr. John R. WILSON
36 Director Student Placement ... Dr. Susan E. FOX
37 Director of Financial Aid ... Ms. Michelle WALKER

University of Fairfax (B)

3361 Melrose Ave, NW, Roanoke VA 24017
County: Independent City Identification: 667094
Telephone: (888) 980-9151 Carnegie Class: Not Classified
FAX Number: N/A Calendar System: Other
URL: www.ufairfax.edu
Established: 2002 Annual Undergrad Tuition & Fees: N/A
Enrollment: N/A Coed
Affiliation or Control: Other IRS Status: Proprietary
Highest Offering: Doctorate
Accreditation: DEAC

05 Dean/Chief Academic Officer ... Dr. Scott MENSCH
11 Administrative Dean ... Keith NORDMANN
26 VP Marketing & Communications ... Chuck STEENBURGH

† Tuition is $895 per semester credit.

University of Management & Technology (C)

1901 Fort Myer Drive, Suite 700, Arlington VA 22209-1609
County: Arlington FICE Identification: 041103
Unit ID: 437097
Telephone: (703) 516-0035 Carnegie Class: DU-Mod
FAX Number: (703) 516-0985 Calendar System: Semester
URL: www.umtweb.edu
Established: 1998 Annual Undergrad Tuition & Fees: $9,450
Enrollment: 1,260 Coed
Affiliation or Control: Proprietary IRS Status: Proprietary
Highest Offering: Doctorate
Accreditation: DEAC

01 President ... Dr. Yanping CHEN
05 Academic Dean ... Dr. J. Davidson FRAME

University of Mary Washington (D)

1301 College Avenue, Fredericksburg VA 22401-5300
County: Independent City FICE Identification: 003746
Unit ID: 232681
Telephone: (540) 654-1000 Carnegie Class: Masters/L
FAX Number: (540) 654-1073 Calendar System: Semester
URL: www.umw.edu
Established: 1908 Annual Undergrad Tuition & Fees (In-State): $11,630
Enrollment: 4,647 Coed
Affiliation or Control: State IRS Status: 501(c)3
Highest Offering: Master's
Accreditation: SC, NURSE

01 President ... Dr. Troy PAINO
05 Provost ... Dr. Jonathan LEVIN
100 Chief of Staff ... Dr. Martin A. WILDER
10 VP for Admin & Finance ... Mr. Richard R. PEARCE
32 Vice President Student Affairs ... Dr. Juliette LANDPHAIR
111 Vice Pres for Advance & Univ Rels ... Vacant
102 CEO of UMW Foundation ... Mr. Jeffrey W. ROUNTREE
13 Actg CIO ... Mr. Hall CHESHIRE
88 Exec Dir Economic Development ... Mr. Brian J. BAKER
15 Asst Vice Pres/Human Res/AAEEO ... Ms. Sabrina C. JOHNSON
105 Director of Digital Communication ... Ms. Shelley KEITH
21 Asst Vice Pres Business Svcs/CPO ... Ms. Erma A. BAKER
20 Associate Provost ... Dr. John T. MORELLO
18 Assoc Vice Pres Facilities Services ... Mr. John P. WILTENMUTH, III
09 Asst Prov Inst Analy & Effect ... Mr. Taiwo A. ANDE
84 Assoc Prov for Enrollment Mgmt ... Ms. Kimberley BUSTER-WILLIAMS
53 Int Dean of College of Education ... Dr. Nina MIKHALEVSKY
50 Dean College of Business ... Dr. Lynne D. RICHARDSON
49 Dean College of Arts & Sciences ... Dr. Richard FINKELSTEIN
35 Dean of Student Life ... Mr. Cedric B. RUCKER
37 Director of Financial Aid ... Ms. Heidi HUNTER-GOLDSWORTHY
09 Director of Institutional Research ... Mr. Mathew C. WILKERSON
116 Internal Audit Director ... Ms. Tera D. KOVANES
39 Director of Residence Life ... Ms. Christine M. PORTER
06 Registrar ... Ms. Rita DUNSTON
41 Director of Athletics ... Mr. Ken D. TYLER
08 University Librarian ... Ms. Rosemary ARNESON
88 Director of Publications ... Ms. Neva S. TRENIS
88 Director of Dodd Auditorium ... Mr. Doug NOBLE
121 Assoc Dean of Advising Services ... Ms. Sallie W. BRAXTON
19 Chief of University Police ... Mr. Michael W. HALL
29 Exec Director Alumni Relations ... Mr. Mark THADEN
38 Director of Counseling/Psych Svcs ... Mr. Tevya ZUKOR
88 Director of Disability Resources ... Ms. Sandra FRITTON
23 University Physician ... Dr. P. Thomas RILEY
88 Director of University Galleries .. Ms. Rosemary K. JESIONOWSKI
28 Spec Asst Diversity & Inclusion ... Dr. Leah COX
26 Associate VP University Rels ... Ms. Anna B. BILLINGSLEY
27 Director Media & Public Relations ... Ms. Marty G. MORRISON
27 Director of Marketing ... Mr. Malcolm HOLMES
88 Director of Design Services ... Ms. AJ NEWELL
30 Assoc VP Univ Advancemnt/Alumni Rel ... Mr. Kenneth L. STEEN

University of North America (E)

8618 Westwood Center Dr., Ste 100, Vienna VA 22182
County: Fairfax Identification: 667241
Telephone: (571) 633-9651 Carnegie Class: Not Classified
FAX Number: (703) 890-3372 Calendar System: Semester
URL: www.uona.edu
Established: Annual Undergrad Tuition & Fees: N/A
Enrollment: N/A Coed
Affiliation or Control: Independent Non-Profit IRS Status: 501(c)3
Highest Offering: Master's
Accreditation: ACICS

00 Chancellor ... Marty MARTIN
01 President ... Jill MARTIN
05 VP of Academics/Outreach ... John HOUGH
20 VP of Educational Operations ... Jason KOO
37 Director Student Financial Affairs ... Padmanjali POKHAREL

University of the Potomac (F)

2070 Chain Bridge Road Suite G100, Vienna VA 22182
Telephone: (888) 380-1192 Identification: 666178
Accreditation: &M

† Regional accreditation is carried under the parent institution in Washington, DC.

University of Richmond (G)

28 Westhampton Way, Richmond VA 23173-1903
County: Independent City FICE Identification: 003744
Unit ID: 233374
Telephone: (804) 289-8000 Carnegie Class: Bac-A&S
FAX Number: (804) 287-6540 Calendar System: Semester
URL: www.richmond.edu
Established: 1830 Annual Undergrad Tuition & Fees: $49,420
Enrollment: 4,181 Coordinate
Affiliation or Control: Independent Non-Profit IRS Status: 501(c)3
Highest Offering: Doctorate
Accreditation: SC, CAEPT, LAW

01 President ... Dr. Ronald A. CRUTCHER
05 Executive VP & Provost ... Dr. Jeffrey LEGRO
10 EVP & COO Business & Finance ... Mr. David B. HALE
32 Vice President Student Affairs ... Dr. Stephen D. BISESE
111 Vice President Advancement ... Mr. Thomas C. GUTENBERGER
13 Vice Pres for Information Services ... Mr. Keith J. MCINTOSH
84 Vice Pres Enrollment Management ... Dr. Stephanie DUPAUL
45 Vice President Planning & Policy ... Dr. Lori G. SCHUYLER
101 VP & Secretary Board of Trustees ... Dr. Ann Lloyd BREEDEN
04 Executive Assistant to President ... Vacant
88 President Spider Mgmt Company ... Mr. Rob BLANDFORD
15 Senior Assoc VP Human Resources ... Mr. Carl K. SORENSEN
18 Assoc Vice Pres Facilities ... Mr. Andrew S. MCBRIDE
29 Asst VP Alumni & Career Services ... Ms. Denise D. SMITH
102 Asst VP Foundation/Corp/Govt Rels ... Ms. Michelle E. WAMSLEY
42 University Chaplain ... Rev. Craig T. KOCHER
07 Assoc VP and Dean of Admissions ... Mr. Gil VILLANUEVA
08 University Librarian ... Mr. Kevin BUTTERFIELD
09 Dir Institutional Effectiveness ... Ms. Melanie JENKINS
06 University Registrar ... Ms. Susan D. BREEDEN
37 Director of Financial Aid ... Ms. Cynthia B. DEFFENBAUGH
36 Director Career Services ... Ms. Leslie W. STEVENSON
38 Director of CAPS ... Dr. Peter O. LEVINESS
96 Director Strategic Sourcing ... Ms. Jean C. HINES
35 Assoc VP Student Development ... Dr. Tinina Q. CADE
41 Director of Athletics ... Vacant
104 Director Study Abroad ... Ms. Michele D. COX
105 Director Web Services ... Mr. Eric F. PALMER
33 Dean of Richmond College ... Dr. Joseph R. BOEHMAN
34 Dean Westhampton College ... Dr. Mia R. GENONI
49 Dean School of Arts & Sciences ... Dr. Patrice D. RANKINE
50 Dean School of Business ... Dr. Nancy A. BAGRANOFF
61 Dean School of Law ... Dr. Wendy C. PERDUE
51 Dean School Continuing Studies ... Dr. Jamelle WILSON
88 Dean Jepson School Leader Stds ... Dr. Sandra J. PEART
19 Assc VP Public Sfty/Chief of Police ... Mr. David M. MCCOY
23 Director Health Center ... Dr. Lynne P. DEANE
26 Asst VP for Communications ... Mr. John M. BARRY
40 Manager University Bookstore ... Mr. Roger L. BROOKS
28 Director Common Ground ... Dr. Glyn HUGHES
39 Director Student Housing ... Mr. Patrick B. BENNER
43 VP & General Counsel ... Ms. Shannon E. SINCLAIR
91 Manager Admin Systems ... Mr. Lee PARKER, III

University of Virginia (H)

1827 University Avenue, Charlottesville VA 22904
County: Independent City FICE Identification: 003745
Unit ID: 234076
Telephone: (434) 924-0311 Carnegie Class: DU-Highest
FAX Number: (434) 924-0938 Calendar System: Semester
URL: www.virginia.edu
Established: 1819 Annual Undergrad Tuition & Fees (In-State): $16,412
Enrollment: 23,883 Coed
Affiliation or Control: State IRS Status: 501(c)3
Highest Offering: Doctorate
Accreditation: SC, CACREP, CAEPT, CLPSY, CS, DENT, DIETI, ENG, IPSY, LAW, LSAR, MED, NURSE, PAST, PCSAS, PH, PLNG, PSPSY, SP

01 President ... Dr. Teresa A. SULLIVAN
101 Secretary Board of Visitors ... Ms. Susan G. HARRIS
05 Exec Vice President & Provost ... Dr. Thomas C. KATSOULEAS
17 Exec Vice Pres for Health Affairs ... Dr. Richard P. SHANNON
111 Vice Pres for Advancement ... Mr. Mark M. LUELLEN
03 Exec Vice Pres/Chief Operating Ofcr ... Mr. Patrick D. HOGAN
32 Vice Pres/Chief Student Affs Ofcr ... Ms. Patricia M. LAMPKIN
46 Vice Pres for Research ... Mr. Melur RAMASUBRAMANIAN
28 VP/Chief Officer Diversity/Equity ... Mr. Marcus L. MARTIN
41 Dir Intercollegiate Athletic Pgms ... Mr. Craig K. LITTLEPAGE
23 CEO Medical Center ... Ms. Pamela M. SUTTON-WALLACE
15 VP/Chief HR Officer ... Ms. Kelley STUCK
11 Sr Vice President for Operations ... Ms. Colette SHEEHY
10 Vice President for Finance ... Ms. Melody BIANCHETTO
13 VP for Information Technology ... Mr. Ronald R. HUTCHINS
88 Health Sys CFO/Bus Dev Officer ... Mr. Larry L. FITZGERALD
100 Chief of Staff/Assoc VP for Admin ... Ms. Nancy A. RIVERS
20 Vice Prov for Academic Affairs ... Mr. Archie L. HOLMES, JR.
88 Vice Prov Faculty Affairs ... Ms. Kerry ABRAMS
88 Vice Prov for Global Affairs ... Mr. Jeffrey W. LEGRO
11 Vice Prov for Admin/Chief of Staff ... Ms. Anda L. WEBB
88 Vice Prov for the Arts ... Mr. Jody K. KIELBASA
21 Assoc VP Business Operations ... Mr. Richard A. KOVATCH
37 Asst Vice Pres Student Finan Svcs ... Mr. Stephen A. KIMATA
25 Asst VP Research Admin ... Ms. Elizabeth H. ADAMS
26 VP Communication/Chief Mktg Officer ... Mr. David W. MARTEL
18 Assoc VP & Chief Facilities Officer ... Mr. Donald E. SUNDGREN
115 Chief Investment Officer ... Mr. Lawrence E. KOCHARD
06 Registrar ... Ms. Carol A J. STANLEY
07 Dean of Admission ... Mr. Gregory W. ROBERTS
61 Dean School of Law ... Ms. Risa L. GOLUBOFF
49 Dean School of Arts & Sciences ... Mr. Ian BAUCOM
63 Dean School of Medicine ... Dr. David S. WILKES
66 Dean School of Nursing ... Ms. Dorrie K. FONTAINE
54 Dean Schl Engr/Applied Science ... Mr. Craig BENSON
48 Dean School of Architecture ... Ms. Ila BERMAN
50 Dean School of Commerce ... Mr. Carl P. ZEITHAML
80 Dean Sch Leadership/Public Policy ... Mr. Allan C. STAM
53 Dean School of Education ... Mr. Robert C. PIANTA
50 Dean Grad School Business Admin ... Mr. Scott C. BEARDSLEY
51 Interim Dean Cont & Prof Studies ... Mr. Steven E. LAYMON
35 Associate VP/Dean of Students ... Mr. Allen W. GROVES
23 Exec Director Student Health ... Dr. Christopher HOLSTEGE
43 Gen Counsel & Corporate Secretary ... Mr. Roscoe C. ROBERTS
22 Assoc VP Equal Opp Pgms/Civ Rights ... Ms. Catherine SPEAR
08 Univ Librarian/Dean of Libraries ... Mr. John M. UNSWORTH
108 Assoc Prov Inst Assess & Studies ... Ms. Christina MORELL
88 Exec Director The Jefferson Trust ... Mr. Wayne COZART
36 Assoc VP Career & Prof Development ... Mr. Everette FORTNER
88 Dir Summer & Special Academic Pgms ... Mr. Dudley J. DOANE
104 Dir International Studies Office ... Mr. Dudley J. DOANE

19 Chief of Police .... Mr. Michael A. GIBSON
39 Exec Dir Housing & Residence Life .... Ms. Gay PEREZ
40 Executive Director of UVa Bookstore .... Mr. Jonathan A. KATES
93 Dean African-American Affairs .... Dr. Maurice APPREY
94 Dir Study in Women Gender Sexuality .... Ms. Charlotte PATTERSON
96 Director of Procurement Services .... Mr. Eric N. DENBY

The University of Virginia's College at Wise (A)

One College Avenue, Wise VA 24293-4412
County: Wise FICE Identification: 003747
Unit ID: 233897
Telephone: (276) 328-0100 Carnegie Class: Bac-A&S
FAX Number: (276) 376-1012 Calendar System: Semester
URL: www.uvawise.edu
Established: 1954 Annual Undergrad Tuition & Fees (In-State): $9,539
Enrollment: 2,027 Coed
Affiliation or Control: State IRS Status: 501(c)3
Highest Offering: Baccalaureate
Accreditation: SC, CAEP, CS, ENG, NURSE

01 Chancellor .... Dr. Donna P. HENRY
05 Provost/Vice Chan for Acad Affairs .... Dr. Sanders HUGUENIN
30 Vice Chanc Devel/College Relations .... Mr. Robert S. BRAGG
10 Vice Chanc Finance/Administration .... Mr. Sim E. EWING
84 Vice Chancellor Enrollment Mgmt .... Mr. Russell D. NECESSARY
20 Academic Dean .... Dr. Amelia J. HARRIS
32 Dean of Students .... Vacant
21 Comptroller .... Mrs. Kristy KISER
06 Registrar .... Ms. Narda PORTER
08 Director of the Library .... Mr. Robin P. BENKE
15 Director of Human Resources .... Ms. Stephanie D. PERRY
88 Director of College Services .... Mr. Joseph B. KISER
26 Director of News & Media Relations .... Ms. Kathy STILL
110 Director of Development .... Ms. Valerie LAWSON
29 Director of Alumni Relations .... Ms. Elizabeth BOYD
37 Director of Financial Aid .... Ms. Rebecca HUFFMAN
35 Asst Dir of Student Activities .... Ms. Sarah SMITH
36 Director of Career Development .... Ms. Neva BRYAN
38 Personal Counselor/Health Services .... Ms. Rachel ROSE
19 Campus Police Chief .... Mr. Ronnie SHORTT
12 Site Director UVA-Wise Programs .... Ms. Courtney L. CONNER
18 Interim Dir Facility Planning/Mgmt .... Mr. David SHORT
27 Associate Vice Chancellor of Info .... Dr. P. Scott BEVINS
24 Director of Media Services .... Ms. Rosa BOTT
40 Bookstore Manager .... Mr. Scott LAWSON
39 Director of Residence Life .... Mr. Josh JUSTICE
108 Director Institutional Assessment .... Mr. David KLOCEK
100 Chief of Staff .... Ms. Huda ADEN

Virginia Baptist College (B)

4105 Plank Road, Fredericksburg VA 22407-4803
County: Spotsylvania FICE Identification: 038626
Unit ID: 482228
Telephone: (540) 785-5440 Carnegie Class: Spec-4-yr-Faith
FAX Number: (540) 785-5441 Calendar System: Semester
URL: www.vbc.edu
Established: 1984 Annual Undergrad Tuition & Fees: $5,560
Enrollment: 108 Coed
Affiliation or Control: Baptist IRS Status: 501(c)3
Highest Offering: Master's
Accreditation: TRACS

00 Chancellor .... Dr. Don FORRESTER
01 President .... Daniel STEVENS
05 Chief Academic Officer .... John EDMONDS
32 Chief Student Affairs/Student Life .... Adam DAVIS
10 Chief Financial Officer .... Sherry DAVIS
37 Director Student Financial Aid .... Meg POLIVKA
39 Director Student Housing .... Adam DAVIS
108 Director Institutional Assessment .... Ann RILL

Virginia Beach Theological Seminary (C)

2221 Centerville Turnpike, Virginia Beach VA 23464-6847
County: Virginia Beach FICE Identification: 039663
Unit ID: 449834
Telephone: (757) 479-3706 Carnegie Class: Not Classified
FAX Number: N/A Calendar System: Semester
URL: www.vbts.edu
Established: 1995 Annual Graduate Tuition & Fees: $7,970
Enrollment: 40 Coed
Affiliation or Control: Baptist IRS Status: 501(c)3
Highest Offering: Master's; No Undergraduates
Accreditation: TRACS

01 President .... Dr. Daniel K. DAVEY
05 Chief Academic Officer .... Dr. Eric J. LEHNER
07 Director of Admissions/Registrar .... Mr. Edward R. ESTES, IV
10 Financial Officer .... Capt. Tony A. BRAZAS
08 Head Librarian .... Dr. Michael H. WINDSOR

Virginia College (D)

7200 Midlothian Turnpike, Richmond VA 23225
Telephone: (804) 977-5100 Identification: 770837
Accreditation: ACICS, ACFEI, OTA

† Branch campus of Virginia College, Birmingham, AL

Virginia Commonwealth University (E)

901 W Franklin Street, Box 842527, Richmond VA 23284-2527
County: Independent City FICE Identification: 003735
Unit ID: 234030
Telephone: (804) 828-0100 Carnegie Class: DU-Highest
FAX Number: N/A Calendar System: Semester
URL: www.vcu.edu
Established: 1838 Annual Undergrad Tuition & Fees (In-State): $13,130
Enrollment: 30,918 Coed
Affiliation or Control: State IRS Status: 501(c)3
Highest Offering: Doctorate
Accreditation: SC, ANEST, ART, CACREP, CAEPN, CEA, CIDA, CLPSY, COPSY, CS, DANCE, DENT, DH, DIETI, EMT, ENG, FEPAC, HSA, IPSY, JOUR, MED, MT, MUS, NMT, NUR, NURSE, OT, PAST, PDPSY, PH, PHAR, PLNG, PTA, RAD, RTT, SPAA, SW, THEA

01 Pres VCU/Pres & Chair VCU Hlth Sys .... Dr. Michael RAO
05 Provost & VP for Academic Affair .... Dr. Gail HACKETT
17 VP Health Sci/CEO VCU Health Sys .... Dr. Marsha RAPPLEY
17 VP Clinical Svcs/CEO VCU Hospital .... Ms. Deborah DAVIS
10 VP for Finance and Budget .... Ms. Karol GRAY
46 Vice President for Research .... Dr. Francis L. MACRINA
30 Int VP Development/Alumni Relations .... Mr. Ed GRIER
86 Exec Dir Government Relations .... Ms. Karah L. GUNTHER
32 Sr Vice Prov Student Affairs .... Dr. Charles J. KLINK
88 Vice Prov for Life Sciences .... Dr. Robert M. TOMBES
09 Vice Prov Planning & Decision Supp .... Ms. Kathleen SHAW
84 Interim Vice Prov Strategic Enrol .... Ms. Sybil HALLORAN
13 Chief Information Officer Tech Svcs .... Mr. Alexander L. HENSON
18 Assoc Vice Pres Facilities Mgmt .... Mr. Richard F. SILWOSKI
84 AVP Strategic Enrollment Svcs .... Ms. Anjour HARRIS
15 Asst Vice Pres for Human Resource .... Ms. Cathleen C. BURKE
08 University Librarian .... Mr. John E. ULMSCHNEIDER
43 University Counsel .... Ms. Stephanie L. HAMLETT
41 Assoc VP and Director of Athletics .... Mr. Edward K. MCLAUGHLIN
21 Asst Vice Pres of Business Services .... Ms. Diane L. REYNOLDS
39 Asst VProvost/Exec Dir Res Life Hou .... Mr. Curtis ERWIN
06 Univ Registrar & Dir Records/Regis .... Mr. Bernard C. HAMM
37 Executive Director of Financial Aid .... Mr. Marc VERNON
38 Dir of Counseling Services .... Dr. Jihad N. AZIZ
36 Dir of University Career Center .... Ms. Heidi A. MCCORMICK
35 Assoc Vice Prov/Dean Student Affs .... Dr. Reuban B. RODRIGUEZ
29 Assoc VP University Alum Relations .. Ms. Diane STOUT BROWN
88 Exec Dir Global Education Office .... Dr. R. McKenna BROWN
88 Dir Ctr for Environmental Studies .... Dr. Gregory C. GARMAN
25 Sr Assoc VP Rsrch Admin/Compliance .... Ms. Susan E. ROBB
19 Asst Vice Pres Campus Police .... Mr. John A. VENUTI
31 VProv/Div Community Engagement .... Dr. Catherine W. HOWARD
92 Dean Honors College .... Dr. Barry L. FALK
67 Dean of Pharmacy .... Dr. Joseph T. DIPIRO
66 Dean of School of Nursing .... Dr. Jean GIDDENS
63 Dean of School of Medicine .... Dr. Peter F. BUCKLEY
53 Dean School of Education .... Dr. Andrew P. DAIRE
52 Dean of Dentistry .... Dr. David C. SARRETT
50 Interim Dean School of Business .... Mr. Kenneth B. KAHN
49 Dean Humanities & Sciences .... Dr. Monsterrat FUENTES
57 Dean School of Arts .... Mr. Shawn BRIXEY
70 Interim Dean School of Social Work .... Dr. Timothy L. DAVEY
76 Dean Allied Health Professions .... Dr. Cecil B. DRAIN
58 Dean Graduate School .... Dr. F. Douglas BOUDINOT
54 Dean of School of Engineering .... Dr. Barbara D. BOYAN
96 Director Procurement Svcs .... Ms. Brenda MOWEN
26 Vice President University Relations .... Ms. Pamela D. LEPLEY
104 Director Study Abroad .... Ms. Stephanie DAVENPORT TIGNOR
28 Sr Asst to Pres & Int VP Inclusiv .... Dr. Kevin ALLISON
100 Sr Exec Dir Ofc of the President .... Mr. Brian D. SHAW
106 Exec Director Online @VCU .... Ms. Monica J. OROZCO
90 Dir Academic Technologies .... Ms. Colleen BISHOP
108 Dir Academic Integrity & Assessment .... Dr. Scott F. OATES
22 Int VP Inclusive Excellence .... Dr. Kevin ALLISON

*Virginia Community College System Office (F)

300 Arboretum Place, Suite 200, Richmond VA 23236
County: Independent City FICE Identification: 008904
Unit ID: 234146
Telephone: (804) 819-4901 Carnegie Class: N/A
FAX Number: (804) 819-4760
URL: www.vccs.edu

01 Chancellor .... Dr. Glenn DUBOIS
10 Vice Chanc Administrative Services .... Ms. Donna VANCLEAVE
05 Vice Chancellor Academic Services .... Dr. Sharon MORRISSEY
103 Vice Chanc Workforce Development .... Dr. Craig HERNDON
13 Vice Chanc Information Tech Svcs .... Dr. James DAVIS
111 Vice Chanc Institutional Advance .... Dr. Jennifer SAGER GENTRY
15 Assoc Vice Chanc Human Resource Svc .... Dr. Christopher LEE
18 Assoc Vice Chanc/Facility Mgmt .... Mr. Bert JONES
43 General Counsel .... Ms. Greer SAUNDERS
116 Director of Internal Audit .... Mr. Whit MADERE
21 Controller .... Mr. Dave MAIR
04 Exec Assistant to the Chancellor .... Ms. Rose Marie OWEN

*Blue Ridge Community College (G)

PO Box 80, Weyers Cave VA 24486-0080
County: Augusta FICE Identification: 006819
Unit ID: 231536
Telephone: (540) 234-9261 Carnegie Class: Assoc/HT-Mix Trad/Non
FAX Number: (540) 234-8189 Calendar System: Semester
URL: www.brcc.edu
Established: 1967 Annual Undergrad Tuition & Fees (In-State): $5,132
Enrollment: 4,192 Coed
Affiliation or Control: State IRS Status: 501(c)3
Highest Offering: Associate Degree
Accreditation: SC, ADNUR

02 President .... Dr. John A. DOWNEY
32 Vice Pres Instruction/Student Svcs .... Dr. Robert YOUNG
10 VP Finance/Administrative Svcs .... Ms. Cynthia PAGE
15 Director of Human Resources .... Mr. Tim NICELY
30 Executive Director Development .... Ms. Amy LASER KIGER
05 Dean of Academic Affairs .... Ms. Marlena JARBOE
05 Dean of Academic Affairs .... Dr. David URSO
103 Dean of Workforce & Continuing Ed .... Dr. Kevin B. RATLIFF
88 Dean Student Support Services .... Ms. Annette WILLIAMS
08 Head Librarian .... Mr. Kyle MCCARRELL
26 Chief Public Relations Officer .... Ms. Bridget BAYLOR
06 Registrar/Admissions .... Ms. Lisa ADKINS
21 Financial Services Manager .... Ms. Franki HAMPTON
09 Coordinator Institutional Research .... Dr. Susan E. CROSBY
37 Financial Aid Coordinator .... Ms. Megan HARTLESS
36 Coord Career Services/ Recruitment .... Ms. Carmel MURPHY-NORRIS
84 Enrollment Services Specialist .... Vacant

*Central Virginia Community College (H)

3506 Wards Road, Lynchburg VA 24502-2498
County: Independent City FICE Identification: 004988
Unit ID: 231697
Telephone: (434) 832-7600 Carnegie Class: Assoc/HT-High Non
FAX Number: (434) 386-4700 Calendar System: Semester
URL: www.cvcc.vccs.edu
Established: 1966 Annual Undergrad Tuition & Fees (In-State): $4,598
Enrollment: 4,433 Coed
Affiliation or Control: State IRS Status: 501(c)3
Highest Offering: Associate Degree
Accreditation: SC, COARC, EMT, RAD

02 President .... Dr. John CAPPS
05 VP Student & Academic Services .... Dr. Muriel MICKLES
10 Vice President Finance & Admin Svcs .... Mr. Lewis BRYANT, III
30 Vice Pres Institutional Advancement .... Mr. Michael BRADFORD
13 Vice Pres of Information Technology .... Mr. David LIGHTFOOT
45 Dean Inst Effectiveness/Planning .... Ms. Kristen OGDEN
32 Dean of Student Services .... Ms. Patricia SAFFIOTI
88 Director of Strategic Initiatives .... Mr. William SANDIDGE
29 Director Alumni/Public Relations .... Mr. Kenneth BUNCH
84 Dean of Enrollment Management .... Mr. Michael FARRIS
15 Human Resource Manager .... Mr. Randall FRANKLIN
56 Distance Education Supervisor .... Mr. Ed MCGEE
08 Coordinator of Library Services .... Mr. Michael T. FEIN
78 Coord Apprenticeship/Coop Education .... Vacant
79 Dean Humanities/Social Science .... Dr. Peter DORMAN
50 Dean of Business & Allied Health .... Dr. James LEMONS
81 Dean of Science/Math/Engineering .... Dr. Jeffrey W. LAUB
04 General Administration Coordinator .... Ms. Dianne SYKES
38 Director Student Counseling .... Ms. Lisa CHILTON

*Dabney S. Lancaster Community College (I)

1000 Dabney Drive, Clifton Forge VA 24422-1000
County: Alleghany FICE Identification: 004996
Unit ID: 231873
Telephone: (540) 863-2820 Carnegie Class: Assoc/HT-High Non
FAX Number: (540) 863-2915 Calendar System: Semester
URL: www.dslcc.edu
Established: 1962 Annual Undergrad Tuition & Fees (In-State): $4,478
Enrollment: 1,236 Coed
Affiliation or Control: State IRS Status: 501(c)3
Highest Offering: Associate Degree
Accreditation: SC, ACFEI, ADNUR

02 President .... Dr. John J. RAINONE
05 Vice President of Academic Affairs .... Dr. Benjamin WORTH
10 Vice President Finance/Admin Svcs .... Mrs. Angela GRAHAM
51 VP Continuing Educ/Workforce Svcs .... Mr. Gary S. KEENER
09 AVP of Institutional Effectiveness .... Mr. Matthew MCGRAW
32 Int Director of Student Services .... Mr. Joseph HAGY
111 Director of Inst Advancement .... Ms. Rachael G. THOMPSON
08 Director of Learning Resources .... Ms. Nova WRIGHT
13 Director of Technology Services .... Ms. Tamra LIPSCOMB
15 Director of Human Resources .... Ms. April TOLLEY
18 Buildings & Grounds Supervisor .... Mr. Steven N. RICHARDS
21 Business Manager .... Ms. Deidre WOLFE
88 Special Assistant to President .... Ms. Gail JOHNSON
37 Coord of Student Financial Aid .... Mrs. Joy BROYLES
06 Registrar .... Vacant
04 Executive Asst to President .... Ms. Phyllis BARTLEY
07 Admissions Officer .... Ms. Suzanne OSTLING
29 Alumni Relations Coordinator .... Ms. Jodi BURGESS

*Danville Community College (J)

1008 S Main Street, Danville VA 24541-4088
County: Independent City FICE Identification: 003758
Unit ID: 231882
Telephone: (434) 797-2222 Carnegie Class: Assoc/MT-VT-High Non
FAX Number: (434) 797-8514 Calendar System: Semester
URL: www.danville.edu

Established: 1967 Annual Undergrad Tuition & Fees (In-State): $4,455
Enrollment: 3,561 Coed
Affiliation or Control: State IRS Status: 501(c)3
Highest Offering: Associate Degree
Accreditation: SC

02 President ....Dr. Bruce R. SCISM
05 Vice Pres Academic/Student Services ....Dr. Debra HOLLEY
10 Vice Pres Financial/Admin Services ....Mr. Charles TOOTHMAN
30 Vice President of Development ....Mr. Shannon HAIR
09 Dir of Plng/Effectiveness/Research ....Mr. George STILL
26 Public Relations/Marketing Manager ....Ms. Kimberly BUCK

*Eastern Shore Community College (A)

29300 Lankford Highway, Melfa VA 23410-9755
County: Accomack FICE Identification: 003748
Unit ID: 232052
Telephone: (757) 789-1789 Carnegie Class: Assoc/MT-VT-Mix Trad/Non
FAX Number: (757) 789-1737 Calendar System: Semester
URL: www.es.vccs.edu
Established: 1971 Annual Undergrad Tuition & Fees (In-State): $4,538
Enrollment: 745 Coed
Affiliation or Control: State IRS Status: 501(c)3
Highest Offering: Associate Degree
Accreditation: SC

02 President ....Dr. Linda THOMAS-GLOVER
05 VP of Academic & Student Svcs ....Dr. Kimberly BRITT
10 Vice Pres Finance & Administration ....Mrs. Annette EDWARDS
32 Coordinator of Student Services ....Mrs. Cheryll MILLS
08 Director Learning Resources ....Mrs. Janet JUSTIS
06 Registrar ....Mrs. Artima TAYLOR-THORNTON
09 Director of Institutional Research ....Ms. Judith GRIER
26 Marketing and Development Officer ....Mr. William LECATO
37 Financial Aid Coordinator ....Ms. Carole READ
15 Human Resource Officer ....Mr. Michael DRISCOLL
18 Chief Facilities/Physical Plant ....Mr. Bobby MEARS
29 Director Alumni Relations/Devel ....Ms. Eve BELOTE
88 Assistant to the VP of Academics ....Mrs. Robin RICH-COATES

*Germanna Community College (B)

2130 Germanna Highway, Locust Grove VA 22508-2102
County: Orange FICE Identification: 008660
Unit ID: 232195
Telephone: (540) 423-9030 Carnegie Class: Assoc/HT-Mix Trad/Non
FAX Number: (540) 727-3207 Calendar System: Semester
URL: www.germanna.edu
Established: 1970 Annual Undergrad Tuition & Fees (In-State): $4,681
Enrollment: 6,993 Coed
Affiliation or Control: State IRS Status: 501(c)3
Highest Offering: Associate Degree
Accreditation: SC, ADNUR, DA, PTAA

02 President ....Dr. Janet GULLICKSON
04 Exec Assistant to the President ....Ms. Pamela S. DUFF
05 VP Academic & Student Services ....Mr. Thomas PERIN
10 VP Finance & Administrative Svcs ....Vacant
103 VP Workforce & Community Educ ....Dr. Jeanne WESLEY
111 VP Institutional Advancement ....Vacant
32 Dean of Student Services ....Ms. Pam FREDERICK
45 Exec Dir of Planning & Assessment ....Dr. John M. DAVIS
08 Head Librarian ....Ms. Tamara REMHOF
06 Registrar ....Ms. Cheri MAEA
72 Dean Professional & Technical Study ....Ms. Denise GUEST
106 Dean Distance Educ & Lrng Resources ....Dr. Yanyan YONG
66 Dean of Nursing & Health Technology ....Dr. Patti LISK
15 Associate VP of Human Resources ....Mrs. Laurie BOURNE
18 Building & Ground Supervisor ....Mr. Garland FENWICK
13 Manager Technology Services ....Vacant
26 Director of Marketing ....Vacant
49 Dean of Arts & Sciences ....Dr. Shashuna GRAY
88 Dean of Workforce Prof Development ....Ms. Martha O'KEEFE
19 Chief of Police ....Mr. Craig BRANCH
37 Director Student Financial Aid ....Mr. Aaron WHITACRE

*J. Sargeant Reynolds Community College (C)

PO Box 85622, Richmond VA 23285-5622
County: Henrico FICE Identification: 003759
Unit ID: 232414
Telephone: (804) 371-3000 Carnegie Class: Assoc/MT-VT-Mix Trad/Non
FAX Number: (804) 371-3650 Calendar System: Semester
URL: www.reynolds.edu
Established: 1972 Annual Undergrad Tuition & Fees (In-State): $4,766
Enrollment: 10,889 Coed
Affiliation or Control: State IRS Status: 501(c)3
Highest Offering: Associate Degree
Accreditation: SC, ACFEI, ADNUR, COARC, DA, DT, EMT, MLTAD, OPD

02 President ....Dr. Gary L. RHODES
03 Executive Vice President ....Dr. Genene D. LEROSEN
05 Vice President Academic Affairs ....Vacant
111 Vice President Advancement ....Mrs. Elizabeth S. LITTLEFIELD
103 VP Comm Col Workforce Alliance ....Vacant
10 VP Finance and Administration ....Ms. Amelia M. BRADSHAW
32 VP Student Affairs/Title IX Coord ....Dr. Thomas N. HOLLINS, JR.
45 Assoc VP Policy/Inst Effectiveness ....Dr. Timothy MERRILL
13 Vice President Technology ....Dr. Mark D. WEBSTER
79 Dean School of Humanities/Soc Sci ....Dr. Barbara M. GLENN
50 Dean School of Business ....Mr. David J. BARRISH
76 Dean School of Nursing/Allied Hlth ....Dr. Susan S. HUNTER
81 Dean School of Math Sci Engineering ....Mr. Raymond A. BURTON
20 Asst VP Academic Affairs ....Mr. Ty CORBIN
09 Director Office Inst Effectiveness ....Dr. Jackie R. BOURQUE
15 Assoc VP HR/Equal Emp Oppty Ofcr ....Ms. Corliss B. WOODSON
37 Director of Financial Aid ....Mrs. Kiesha L. POPE
07 Director of Admissions & Records ....Mrs. Karen M. PETTIS-WALDEN
88 Director Outreach and Recruitment ....Ms. Tracy S. GREEN
27 Director Communications ....Mr. Joseph SHILLING
26 Director of Marketing ....Ms. Kelly A. SMITH
08 Director of Info/Library Services ....Ms. Hong WU
88 Director of Learning Communities ....Mr. Charles PETERSON, JR.
18 Director Facilities Mgmt/Planning ....Mr. Michael VERDU
21 Director of Financial Operations ....Ms. Shirley L. HOPKINS
30 Director of Development ....Ms. Marianne S. MCGHEE
88 Director of Middle College ....Ms. Mary Jo WASHKO
84 Director of Enrollment Services ....Mr. Brian A. RICHARDSON
06 Registrar ....Ms. Denise S. TUNSTALL
96 Purchasing Manager ....Mr. Christopher L. COLE
19 Chief of Police ....Mr. Paul L. RONCA

*John Tyler Community College (D)

13101 Jefferson Davis Highway, Chester VA 23831-5316
County: Chesterfield FICE Identification: 004004
Unit ID: 232450
Telephone: (804) 796-4000 Carnegie Class: Assoc/HT-Mix Trad/Non
FAX Number: (804) 796-4163 Calendar System: Semester
URL: www.jtcc.edu
Established: 1965 Annual Undergrad Tuition & Fees (In-State): $4,473
Enrollment: 10,035 Coed
Affiliation or Control: State IRS Status: 501(c)3
Highest Offering: Associate Degree
Accreditation: SC, ADNUR, FUSER

02 President ....Dr. Edward (Ted) E. RASPILLER
04 Executive Assistant to President ....Ms. Mara M. HILLIAR
05 VP Learning & Student Success ....Dr. William FIEGE
10 Interim VP Administration ....Ms. Susan GRINNAN
111 VP Institutional Advancement ....Ms. Rachel BIUNDO
103 Vice Pres for CC Workforce Alliance ....Mr. Mac L. MCGINTY
32 VP of Student Success ....Dr. Julie RANSON
35 Dean of Students ....Ms. Sandra KIRKLAND
49 Dean Arts/Humanities/Soc Sciences ....Dr. Mikell BROWN
81 Dean Math/Natural & Health Sci ....Dr. Johanna WEISS
09 Dir Institutional Effectiveness ....Dr. Donna JOVANOVICH
08 Librarian Chester Campus ....Ms. Linda LUEBKE
15 AVP of Human Resources ....Ms. Susan GRINNAN
37 Director Financial Aid ....Mr. Tony JONES
19 Security Manager ....Mr. Frank MEDAGLIA
26 Public Relations Manager ....Ms. Holly WALKER
36 Int Dir Advising Chester Campus ....Ms. Altrice SMITH
36 Dir Counseling Midlothian Campus ....Dr. Ruth VARNEY
18 Dir Facilities Operations/Safety ....Mr. Greg A. DUNAWAY
08 Librarian Midlothian Campus ....Ms. Helen MCKANN
06 Registrar ....Ms. Joy L. JAMES
96 Director of Purchasing ....Ms. Nancy M. JIMISON

*Lord Fairfax Community College (E)

173 Skirmisher Lane, Middletown VA 22645-1745
County: Frederick FICE Identification: 008659
Unit ID: 232575
Telephone: (540) 868-7000 Carnegie Class: Assoc/HT-Mix Trad/Non
FAX Number: (540) 868-7100 Calendar System: Semester
URL: www.lfcc.edu
Established: 1970 Annual Undergrad Tuition & Fees (In-State): $4,507
Enrollment: 7,002 Coed
Affiliation or Control: State IRS Status: 501(c)3
Highest Offering: Associate Degree
Accreditation: SC, ADNUR, CAHIIM, EMT, SURGT

02 President ....Dr. Cheryl THOMPSON-STACY
12 Provost Fauquier Campus ....Dr. Christopher COUTTS
05 VP of Academic & Student Affairs ....Dr. Kim BLOSSER
10 VP of Finance & Admin Services ....Mr. Chris BOIES
103 VP of Workforce & Prof Development ....Ms. Jeanian CLARK
30 Assoc VP of Inst Advance/Educ Fdn ....Ms. Liv HEGGOY
25 Director TAACCCT Project/K2W ....Dr. John MILAM
76 Dean Health Professions ....Ms. Patricia P. LAWSON
50 Dean Business/Educ/HLM & Technology ....Dr. Karen KELLISON
81 Dean Science/Eng/Math & Health ....Dr. J. Brandon SHAW
83 Dean Hum/Social Sciences/Stdnt Dev ....Dr. James GILLISPIE
32 Dean Academic/Stdnt Aff & Outreach ....Ms. Brenda K. BYARD
08 Director Learning Resources Center ....Mr. David R. GRAY
38 Director Advising & Stdnt Support ....Ms. Amber FOLTZ
37 Director of Financial Aid ....Mr. Steven WILSON
88 Librarian/Tutor Coordinator ....Mr. Gregory ARMSTRONG
88 Librarian ....Ms. Kerry KILPATRICK
88 Dir Transition Programs/Title IX ....Ms. Lyda KISER
26 Dir Marketing & Outreach ....Ms. Brandy BOIES
71 Assoc Dean Acad Support/Student Eng ....Dr. Mia S. DEZURA
88 Director TRIO Student Support Svcs ....Ms. Sarah WILLIAMS
88 Coord Business/Industry Trng ....Mr. Bill PENCE
88 Coord Business/Industry Trng ....Mr. Larry BAKER
88 Dir Marketing/Business/Ind Trng ....Mr. Guy E. CURTIS, III
84 Associate Dean of Instruction ....Ms. Heather BURTON
88 Counselor - Fauquier Campus ....Ms. Andrea M. LO
88 Counselor ....Ms. Kelly REDMON
88 Director Small Business Dev Center ....Ms. Christine KRIZ

*Mountain Empire Community College (F)

3441 Mountain Empire Road, Big Stone Gap VA 24219-4634
County: Wise FICE Identification: 009629
Unit ID: 232788
Telephone: (276) 523-2400 Carnegie Class: Assoc/MT-VT-Mix Trad/Non
FAX Number: (276) 523-8297 Calendar System: Semester
URL: www.mecc.edu
Established: 1972 Annual Undergrad Tuition & Fees (In-State): $4,478
Enrollment: 2,718 Coed
Affiliation or Control: State IRS Status: 501(c)3
Highest Offering: Associate Degree
Accreditation: SC, ADNUR, COARC, NAIT

02 President ....Dr. Kristen WESTOVER
05 VP Academic & Student Services ....Ms. Vickie RATLIFF
10 Vice Pres Finance & Admin Services ....Mr. Ron VICARS
111 Vice Pres Institutional Advancement ....Ms. Donna G. STANLEY
32 Dean of Student Services ....Ms. Lelia BRADSHAW
07 Dean Admission/Financial Aid ....Ms. Kristy HALL
08 Director of Library Services ....Mr. Michael GILLEY
76 Dean of Health Sciences ....Ms. Kim DORTON
13 Dir Ctr Computing & Info Technology ....Mr. Tony ROBINSON
15 Director Personnel Services ....Ms. Pam GILES
18 Chief Facilities/Physical Plant ....Mr. Preston LAYNE
49 Dean Arts & Sciences ....Ms. Harriett ARRINGTON
72 Dean of Industrial Tech/Health Sci ....Mr. Tommy CLEMENTS
26 Chief Public Relations Officer ....Ms. Amy GREEAR
19 Chief of Police ....Mr. Russell CYPHERS

*New River Community College (G)

5251 College Drive, Dublin VA 24084-1127
County: Pulaski FICE Identification: 005223
Unit ID: 232867
Telephone: (540) 674-3600 Carnegie Class: Assoc/HT-High Non
FAX Number: (540) 674-3642 Calendar System: Semester
URL: www.nr.edu
Established: 1969 Annual Undergrad Tuition & Fees (In-State): $4,464
Enrollment: 4,477 Coed
Affiliation or Control: State IRS Status: 501(c)3
Highest Offering: Associate Degree
Accreditation: SC

02 President ....Dr. Patricia B. HUBER
05 Int VP for Instruction/Student Svcs ....Mr. Peter T. ANDERSON
10 Vice Pres for Finance & Technology ....Mr. John L. VAN HEMERT
30 VP for WD and External Relations ....Dr. Mark C. ROWH
09 Dir Inst Effectiveness/Research ....Dr. Frederick M. STREFF
102 Executive Director of Foundation ....Ms. Angie E. COVEY
49 Dean of Arts & Sciences ....Dr. Janice SHELTON
50 Interim Dean of Bus & Technologies ....Ms. Debra BOND
32 Dean of Student Services ....Dr. Deborah KENNEDY
15 Dir of Human Resources & Bus Oper ....Ms. Melissa P. ANDERSON
06 Registrar ....Mrs. Tammy SMITH
37 Director of Student Financial Aid ....Ms. Lori A. NUNN
88 Director of ASLP ....Mrs. Jill WILLIAMS
88 Emer Prep Coord/Assoc Dir ASLP ....Dr. Amy J. HALL
96 Inventory and Purchasing Technician ....Ms. Monica W. CARDEN
106 Director Distance Education ....Mrs. Linda C. CLAUSSEN
08 Coordinator of Library Services ....Mrs. Sandra B. SMITH
07 Coord Admissions/Records/Stdnt Svcs ....Mrs. Tammy SMITH
18 Chief Facilities/Physical Plant ....Mr. Anthony J. NICOLO
88 Coordinator of WorkKeys Center ....Mrs. Patricia RYAN
88 Enrollment Coordinator ....Mrs. Lori MITCHELL
26 Public Relations Specialist ....Ms. Joyce K. TAYLOR
22 Coord Ctr for Disability Services ....Ms. Lucy J. HOWLETT
04 Administrative Asst to President ....Mrs. Kathy T. RIDPATH

*Northern Virginia Community College (H)

4001 Wakefield Chapel Road, Annandale VA 22003-3796
County: Fairfax FICE Identification: 003727
Unit ID: 232946
Telephone: (703) 323-3000 Carnegie Class: Assoc/HT-Mix Trad/Non
FAX Number: (703) 323-3767 Calendar System: Semester
URL: www.nvcc.edu
Established: 1965 Annual Undergrad Tuition & Fees (In-State): $5,313
Enrollment: 52,078 Coed
Affiliation or Control: State IRS Status: 501(c)3
Highest Offering: Associate Degree
Accreditation: SC, ADNUR, CAHIIM, COARC, DA, DH, DMS, EMT, MLTAD, OTA, PTAA

02 President ....Dr. Scott RALLS
05 Exec VP/Chief Academic Officer ....Dr. Mel D. SCHIAVELLI
10 VP Finance/Chief Admin Officer ....Ms. Dimitrina DIMKOVA
13 Vice Pres of Information Technology ....Dr. Steven G. SACHS
103 VP of Workforce Development ....Mr. Steve PARTRIDGE
09 VP Inst Effectiveness & Student Suc ....Dr. George E. GABRIEL
20 Assoc VP Academic Services ....Dr. Sharon N. ROBERTSON
111 VP of Institutional Advancement ....Ms. Elizabeth WEATHERLY
84 Assoc VP Stdnt Svcs & Enroll Mgmt ....Dr. Elizabeth HARPER
12 Provost Alexandria Campus ....Dr. Annette HAGGRAY
12 Provost Annandale Campus ....Dr. Pamela HILBERT
12 Provost Loudoun Campus ....Dr. Julie LEIDIG
12 Provost Manassas Campus ....Dr. Molly LYNCH

12 Acting Provost Medical Educ Campus ....Mr. Andrew CORNELL
12 Provost Woodbridge Campus ....Dr. Sam HILL
102 Exec Dir NVCC Education Foundation ....Mr. John J. RUFFINO
06 College Registrar ....Ms. Alethea HAMILTON
22 Director of Diversity ....Mr. Everett V. EBERHARDT
102 Assistant Dir NVCC Educ Foundation ....Ms. Mary BRAMLEY
25 Director of Grants ....Dr. Syedur RAHMAN
15 Director of Human Resources ....Ms. Charlotte M. CALOBRISI
96 Director of Purchasing ....Mr. Edward J. MELLON
37 Dir Stdnt Financial Aid/Support Svc ....Ms. Joan A. ZANDERS
21 Acting Associate VP ....Mr. Cory THOMPSON
18 Director of Facilities ....Mr. Steven PATTERSON
26 Director of Media Relations ....Ms. Kathy THOMPSON
19 Director Security/Safety ....Chief Daniel DUSSEAU
86 Director Government Affs/Cmty Rels ....Mr. Dana KAUFFMAN

*Patrick Henry Community College (A)

645 Patriot Avenue, Martinsville VA 24112
County: Henry FICE Identification: 003751
Unit ID: 233019
Telephone: (276) 638-8777 Carnegie Class: Assoc/HT-High Non
FAX Number: (276) 656-0320 Calendar System: Semester
URL: www.ph.vccs.edu
Established: 1962 Annual Undergrad Tuition & Fees (In-State): $4,473
Enrollment: 2,594 Coed
Affiliation or Control: State IRS Status: 501(c)3
Highest Offering: Associate Degree
Accreditation: SC, ADNUR, EMT

02 President ....Dr. Angeline D. GODWIN
05 VP Academic/Student Develop Svcs ....Dr. Greg HODGES
10 VP Finance & Admin Services ....Mr. John HANBURY
103 VP Workforce/Economic/Community Dev ....Mrs. Rhonda HODGES
111 VP Institutional Advancement ....Vacant
20 Dean Academic Success/Col Transfer ....Mr. Terry YOUNG
81 Dean Science/Tech/Engineering/Math ....Dr. Colin FERGUSON
76 Dean Prof Tech/Health Sciences ....Ms. Amy WEBSTER
72 Dean of Technology ....Mr. David DEAL
15 Director of Human Resources ....Ms. Belinda STOCKTON
84 Dir of Enrollment Mgmt ....Vacant
07 Coord Admiss & Accel Lrng ....Ms. Meghan EGGLESTON
26 Public Relations & Mktg Mgr ....Mr. Randy FERGUSON
06 Registrar ....Ms. Jessica CARTER
37 Financial Aid/Veterans Admin ....Mrs. Cindy KELLER
08 Head Librarian ....Mr. Barry REYNOLDS
25 Chief Contracts/Grants Admin ....Ms. Sarah B. MORRISON
41 Athletic Director ....Mr. Brian HENDERSON
09 Research Analyst ....Ms. Lisa FINLEY
18 Chief Facilities/Physical Plant ....Ms. Roberta WRIGHT
19 Director Security/Safety ....Mr. Gary DOVE
96 Director of Purchasing ....Ms. Lori CONNER
04 Administrative Asst to President ....Ms. Jencie GIBSON

*Paul D. Camp Community College (B)

100 N College Drive, Franklin VA 23851-0737
County: Independent City FICE Identification: 009159
Unit ID: 233037
Telephone: (757) 569-6700 Carnegie Class: Assoc/HT-High Non
FAX Number: (757) 569-6795 Calendar System: Semester
URL: www.pdc.edu
Established: 1970 Annual Undergrad Tuition & Fees (In-State): $4,453
Enrollment: 1,473 Coed
Affiliation or Control: State IRS Status: 501(c)3
Highest Offering: Associate Degree
Accreditation: SC, ADNUR

02 President ....Dr. Daniel W. LUFKIN
05 VP Academic/Student Development ....Dr. Tara ATKINS-BRADY
11 Operations Manager ....Mr. Phillip BRADSHAW
111 VP Institutional Advancement & WFD ....Dr. Renee FELTS
32 Dean Student Services ....Ms. Trina JONES
20 Dean of Suffolk Academic Programs ....Dr. Justin OLIVER
08 Librarian ....Vacant
12 Academic Director-Smithfield ....Mrs. Antoinette JOHNSON
103 Dir of Workforce Development ....Mrs. Angela LAWHORNE
09 Coord Inst Research/Assessment ....Ms. Damay J. BULLOCK
18 Chief Facilities/Physical Plant ....Vacant
15 Human Resources Analyst ....Mr. Shawn BURKS
26 Public Relations Specialist ....Mrs. Wendy HARRISON
37 Financial Aid Coordinator ....Ms. Teresa HARRISON
04 Assistant to the President ....Ms. Cathy CUTCHINS

*Piedmont Virginia Community College (C)

501 College Drive, Charlottesville VA 22902-7589
County: Independent City FICE Identification: 009928
Unit ID: 233116
Telephone: (434) 977-3900 Carnegie Class: Assoc/HT-High Non
FAX Number: (434) 971-8232 Calendar System: Semester
URL: www.pvcc.edu
Established: 1972 Annual Undergrad Tuition & Fees (In-State): $4,558
Enrollment: 5,438 Coed
Affiliation or Control: State IRS Status: 501(c)3
Highest Offering: Associate Degree
Accreditation: SC, ADNUR, DMS, EMT, RAD, SURGT

02 President ....Dr. Frank FRIEDMAN
05 VP Instruction/Student Svcs ....Dr. John DONNELLY
10 Vice President Finance/Admin Svcs ....Mr. Kim MCMANUS
30 Vice Pres Advancement/Development ....Mr. Harry STILLERMAN
79 Dean Humanities/Fine Arts/Soc Sci ....Dr. Leonda KENISTON
50 Dean Business/Math/Technologies ....Dr. Adam HASTINGS
17 Dean Health & Life Sciences ....Dr. Jean CHAPPELL
103 Dean Workforce Services ....Ms. Valerie PALAMOUNTAIN
32 Dean of Student Services ....Ms. Mary Lee WALSH
13 Chief Information Officer ....Ms. Sue HAAS
09 Dir Instl Research/Planning/Effect ....Dr. Jolene HAMM
06 Registrar ....Ms. Allyson REA
96 Business Manager ....Ms. Tracy CERSLEY
18 Facilities Manager ....Vacant
15 Human Resources Director ....Mrs. Teresa WILLIS
26 Marketing/Media Relations Director ....Ms. Leigh-Anne LAWRENCE
108 Outreach Manager ....Ms. Denise MCCLANAHAN
08 Director Library Services ....Ms. Crystal NEWELL
37 Director Financial Aid ....Ms. Crystal FILER-OGDEN
36 Director Advising & Transfer ....Mr. Kemper STEELE

*Rappahannock Community College (D)

12745 College Drive, Glenns VA 23149-0287
County: Gloucester FICE Identification: 009160
Unit ID: 233310
Telephone: (804) 758-6700 Carnegie Class: Assoc/HT-High Non
FAX Number: (804) 758-3852 Calendar System: Semester
URL: www.rappahannock.edu
Established: 1970 Annual Undergrad Tuition & Fees (In-State): $4,588
Enrollment: 3,566 Coed
Affiliation or Control: State IRS Status: 501(c)3
Highest Offering: Associate Degree
Accreditation: SC, ADNUR

02 President ....Dr. Elizabeth H. CROWTHER
32 VP Instruction/Student Development ....Dr. A. Donna ALEXANDER
10 Vice Pres Finance/Admin Services ....Mr. William DOYLE
103 Vice Pres Workforce/Cmty Devel ....Mr. Jason PERRY
05 Interim Academic Dean ....Mr. Matthew BRENT
35 Dean Student Development ....Dr. Dave KEEL
106 Dean of Distance Learning/Tech ....Ms. Virginia JONES
30 Dean of College Advancement ....Ms. Sarah POPE
108 Dean Research/Effectiveness/Plng ....Dr. Glenda D. HAYNIE
37 Financial Aid/Veteran Affairs Ofcr ....Ms. Sherika CHARITY
15 Director Human Resources ....Mrs. Caroline W. STELTER
18 Facilities/Physical Plant Supv ....Mr. John LEONARD
10 Business Manager ....Ms. Susan S. BROADDUS
06 Student Records/Information Coord ....Ms. Felicia B. PACKETT
08 Library Coordinator ....Mr. Dan REAM

*Southside Virginia Community College (E)

109 Campus Drive, Alberta VA 23821-2930
County: Brunswick FICE Identification: 008661
Unit ID: 233639
Telephone: (434) 949-1000 Carnegie Class: Assoc/MT-VT-High Non
FAX Number: (434) 949-7863 Calendar System: Semester
URL: www.southside.edu
Established: 1970 Annual Undergrad Tuition & Fees (In-State): $4,463
Enrollment: 4,439 Coed
Affiliation or Control: State IRS Status: 501(c)3
Highest Offering: Associate Degree
Accreditation: SC, ADNUR, EMT

02 President ....Dr. Al ROBERTS
05 Vice Pres Academics/Student Affs ....Dr. Tara BLACKWELL
10 Vice Pres Finance & Administration ....Mrs. Shannon V. FEINMAN
30 Chief Development Officer ....Mrs. Mary Jane ELKINS
44 Dean of Institutional Advancement ....Mrs. Mary Jane ELKINS
13 Chief Information Officer ....Mr. Chad WOLLENBERG
84 Dean Enrollment Management ....Ms. Dorothea SIZEMORE
20 Dean of Instruction ....Dr. Dixie DALTON
20 Dean of Instruction ....Dr. Chad PATTON
20 Dean of Instruction ....Dr. Michelle EDMONDS
09 Dean Institutional Effectiveness ....Dr. Anne HAYES
66 Dean of Nursing/Health Technology ....Dr. Michelle K. EDMONDS
102 Exec Director SVCC Foundation ....Mrs. Mary Jane ELKINS
08 College Librarian ....Ms. Marika PETERSON
26 Public Relations & Mktg Specialist ....Mrs. Christie C. HALES
37 Director of Financial Aid ....Mrs. Sally THARRINGTON
28 Director of Diversity ....Dr. Anne HAYES
15 Human Resources Manager ....Ms. Bethany W. HARRIS
18 Buildings/Grounds Supt Christanna ....Mr. Roger WRAY
18 Buildings/Grounds Superintendent ....Mr. Eddie BENNETT
38 Director Student Counseling Daniel ....Mrs. Bernadette BATTLE
21 Business Manager ....Mrs. Toni LAMBERT
29 Alumni Relations SVCC ....Mrs. Mary Jane ELKINS

*Southwest Virginia Community College (F)

Box SVCC, Richlands VA 24641-1101
County: Tazewell FICE Identification: 007260
Unit ID: 233648
Telephone: (276) 964-2555 Carnegie Class: Assoc/HT-Mix Trad/Non
FAX Number: (276) 964-9307 Calendar System: Semester
URL: www.sw.edu
Established: 1967 Annual Undergrad Tuition & Fees (In-State): $4,463
Enrollment: 2,563 Coed
Affiliation or Control: State IRS Status: 501(c)3
Highest Offering: Associate Degree
Accreditation: SC, ADNUR, EMT, OTA, RAD

02 President ....Dr. J. Mark ESTEPP
05 Interim VP Acad & Student Services ....Dr. Ronald PROFFITT
10 Vice Pres Finance & Admin Svcs ....Mr. Windell TURNER
04 General Admin Coordinator ....Mrs. Rhonda L. VANDYKE
79 Dean Humanit/Sci/Math/Health Tech ....Mrs. Cathy SMITH-COX
50 Dean Business/Engr & Indust Tech ....Mr. James DYE
103 Pgm Developer Workforce Solutions ....Mr. Thomas LESTER
32 Dean Student Success ....Mrs. Dyan E. LESTER
09 Institutional Research Officer ....Dr. Edmond C. SMITH
102 Exec Dir SWCC Educ Foundation & Dev ....Mrs. Susan L. LOWE
15 Human Resources Director ....Ms. Martha L. RASNAKE
19 Campus Police Chief ....Mr. Ronnie KISER
21 Business Manager ....Mr. Michael BALES
18 Physical Plant Superintendent ....Mr. Tony MCGHEE
26 Public Relations Coordinator ....Ms. Patsy G. BUSSARD
08 Coordinator of Library Services ....Ms. Teresa A. YEAROUT
106 Distance Learning ....Mrs. Dyan E. LESTER
25 Grants Coordinator ....Ms. Phyllis ROBERTS
105 Director Web Services ....Ms. Teresa PRUETT
13 Chief Info Technology Officer (CIO) ....Mr. Charles MUSICK

*Thomas Nelson Community College (G)

99 Thomas Nelson Drive, Hampton VA 23666
County: Independent City FICE Identification: 006871
Unit ID: 233754
Telephone: (757) 825-2700 Carnegie Class: Assoc/HT-Mix Trad/Non
FAX Number: (757) 825-2763 Calendar System: Semester
URL: www.tncc.edu
Established: 1967 Annual Undergrad Tuition & Fees (In-State): $4,544
Enrollment: 9,316 Coed
Affiliation or Control: State IRS Status: 501(c)3
Highest Offering: Associate Degree
Accreditation: SC, ADNUR, DH

02 President ....Dr. John T. DEVER
05 Vice Pres for Academic Affairs ....Dr. Susan ENGLISH
32 Int Vice Pres for Student Affairs ....Ms. Kris RARIG
11 Vice President for Admin/Finance ....Mr. Charles A. NURNBERGER
103 Vice Pres for Workforce Development ....Dr. Deborah G. WRIGHT
111 Vice Pres Institutional Advancement ....Ms. Cynthia CALLAWAY
88 Provost Historic Triangle Campus ....Dr. Gregory MCLEOD
35 Assoc VP for Student Affairs ....Dr. Vicki RICHMOND
13 Int Director of Information Tech ....Ms. Debra HUDGINS
120 Dir Distance/Distributive Learning ....Ms. Ruth SMITH
84 Int Dean of Enrollment Management ....Dr. Tiffany RAY
121 Dir Student Success/Advising ....Ms. Crystal ANDERSON
10 Assoc VP for Financial Services ....Ms. Teresa BAILEY
88 Assoc VP for Workforce Training/CE ....Dr. Carmen BURROWS
60 Dean Communications/Social Sciences ....Dr. Patrick TOMPKINS
81 Dean Science/Engr/Technology ....Mr. Seyed AKHAVI
50 Dean Bus/Public Svcs/IT/Math ....Dr. Charles SWAIM
76 Dean Health Professions ....Dr. Christy HAWKINS
37 Dir Financial Aid/Veteran Affairs ....Ms. Kathryn ANDERSON
18 Mgr Facilities/Plan/Capital Outlay ....Mr. Mark KRAMER
26 Director Public Relations/Marketing ....Ms. Cecilia RAMIREZ
30 Director of Development ....Ms. Tracy ASHLEY
08 Director of Learning Resources ....Dr. Richard HODGES
09 Dir Inst Research and Effectiveness ....Mr. Steven FELKER
21 Business Office Manager ....Vacant
15 Director of Human Resources ....Ms. Joy COOKE

*Tidewater Community College (H)

121 College Place, Norfolk VA 23510
County: Independent City FICE Identification: 003712
Unit ID: 233772
Telephone: (757) 822-1122 Carnegie Class: Assoc/HT-Mix Trad/Non
FAX Number: (757) 822-1060 Calendar System: Semester
URL: www.tcc.edu
Established: 1968 Annual Undergrad Tuition & Fees (In-State): $5,299
Enrollment: 25,927 Coed
Affiliation or Control: State IRS Status: 501(c)3
Highest Offering: Associate Degree
Accreditation: SC, ACFEI, ADNUR, CAHIIM, COARC, DMS, EMT, FUSER, MLTAD, OTA, PTAA, RAD

02 President ....Dr. Edna V. BAEHRE-KOLOVANI
05 VP Academic Affairs/Chief Acad Ofcr ....Dr. Daniel T. DEMARTE
32 Int VP for Student Affairs ....Dr. Michael D. SUMMERS
10 Vice President Finance ....Ms. Phyllis F. MILLOY
26 VP Public Affairs & Communications ....Dr. James P. TOSCANO
111 Acting VP Inst Advancement ....Dr. James P. TOSCANO
18 Exec Dir Real Estate Dev/COO Facil ....Mr. Matthew J. BAUMGARTEN
13 Acting VP Information Systems ....Mr. Curtis K. AASEN
103 VP for Workforce Solutions ....Dr. Corey L. MCCRAY
12 Provost Chesapeake Campus ....Dr. Lisa B. RHINE
12 Provost Portsmouth Campus ....Dr. Michelle W. WOODHOUSE
12 Provost Norfolk Campus ....Dr. Jeffrey S. BOYD
12 Provost Virginia Beach Campus ....Dr. Michael D. SUMMERS
09 Dir Institutional Effectiveness ....Mr. Curtis K. AASEN
15 Associate VP for Human Resources ....Ms. Beth LUNDE
100 Chief of Staff ....Ms. Susan M. JAMES
20 AVP Academics ....Dr. Kellie C. SOREY
20 AVP Faculty Professional Dev ....Mr. Frederick E. STEMPLE, JR.
20 AVP Learning Tech Applications ....Mr. John MOREA
08 AVP for Libraries ....Mr. Steve E. LITHERLAND
84 AVP Recruitment/Admission/Enroll ....Dr. Karen D. CAMPBELL

106 Dean for the Center of eLearning ... Ms. Virginia K. ZILLGES
27 AVP Interactive Com/Pub Info Office ... Ms. Marian L. ANDERFUREN
121 AVP for Student Success ... Ms. Christine DAMROSE-MAHLMANN
21 Associate VP for Finance ... Ms. Heather H. TAYLOR
21 AVP Finance Designated Finance ... Ms. Reyne D. BUCHHOLZ
50 Int Dn Bus/Pub Svc/Tech Chesapeake ... Dr. Kelly GILLERLAIN
79 Dean of Hum & Soc Sci Chesapeake ... Ms. Diane N. RYAN
81 Dean Sci/Tech/Eng/Math Chesapeake ... Mr. Thomas B. STOUT
35 Dean of Student Svcs Chesapeake ... Dr. James E. EDWARDS
50 Dean Bus/SC/P Svcs/Tech Norfolk ... Ms. Johnna C. HARRELL
81 Dean Lang/Math/Science Norfolk ... Dr. Kerry S. RAGNO
35 Dean of Student Svcs Norfolk ... Mr. Emmanuel CHESTNUT
50 Interim Dean Bus/Pub Svcs/Tech PT ... Mr. Peter T. AGBAKPE
81 Dean Lang/Math/Science Portsmouth ... Ms. Jenefer D. SNYDER
35 Dean of Student Svcs Portsmouth ... Ms. Dana M. SINGLETON
66 Dean Beazley School Nurs Portsmouth ... Dr. Phyllis M. EATON
54 Dean Math Eng & Ind Tech Va Beach ... Mr. David A. EKKER
76 Dean Health Professions ... Mr. Thomas G. CALOGRIDES, JR.
50 Dean IT & Business Va Beach ... Mr. William CLEMENT
81 Dean Natural Sciences Va Beach ... Mr. Gregory P. FRANK
83 Dean Social Sci/Pub Svcs Va Beach ... Mr. Joseph J. FAIRCHILD
79 Dean Humanities Va Beach ... Ms. Marcanne ANDERSEN
35 Dean of Student Svcs Va Beach ... Dr. Marilyn R. HODGE
88 Dir Reg Automotive Ctr Chesapeake ... Mr. Beno RUBIN
14 Dir Programming Systems & Develop ... Mr. Ken BALLARD
06 College Registrar ... Mrs. Laura BURNHAM
57 Interim Director Visual Arts Center ... Ms. Corrine LILYARD-MITCHELL
18 Interim Director Facilities ... Mr. Albert THOMPSON
19 Director Safety & Security ... Mr. George J. OKATY
88 Exec Dir Ctr Military Veterans Educ ... Mr. William E. BROWN, III
88 Director of Apprenticeship Inst ... Mr. Michael T. ESTES
88 Exec Dir Roper Performing Arts Ctr ... Mr. Paul H. LASAKOW
96 Dir Material Mgmt & Procurement Se ... Ms. Robin S. MOORE
37 Director Central Financial Aid ... Ms. Jennifer E. HARPHAM
109 Director Auxiliary Services ... Ms. Bridgett M. PASSAUER
88 Dir Gen Educ Assess Trans Partnrshp ... Ms. Jennifer FERGUSON
88 Dir Std Mental Health & Behavior ... Dr. Jessica SMITH
45 Dir of Planning & Accountability ... Dr. Kimberly M. BOVEE
45 Director Grants/Sponsored Programs ... Ms. Laverne ELLERBE
30 Interim Chief Development Officer ... Ms. Donna HENDERSON
88 Director of Intercultural Learning ... Dr. Jeanne B. NATALI
88 Director Marketing ... Mr. Curt J. WYNN
105 Chief Web Communications Officer ... Ms. Allison H. TRELOAR
04 Administrative Asst to President ... Ms. Latesha JOHNSON
22 Affirmative Action/EEO ... Ms. Jill J. ADAMS
28 Diversity Officer ... Ms. Susan M. JAMES

*Virginia Highlands Community College (A)

PO Box 828, Abingdon VA 24212-0828

County: Washington FICE Identification: 007099
Unit ID: 233903
Telephone: (276) 739-2400 Carnegie Class: Assoc/HT-Mix Trad/Non
FAX Number: (276) 739-2590 Calendar System: Semester
URL: www.vhcc.edu
Established: 1967 Annual Undergrad Tuition & Fees (In-State): $4,478
Enrollment: 2,365 Coed
Affiliation or Control: State IRS Status: 501(c)3
Highest Offering: Associate Degree
Accreditation: SC, ADNUR

02 President ... Dr. Gene C. COUCH, JR.
05 VP Instruction & Student Services ... Dr. Stacy THOMAS
10 VP Financial/Administrative Svcs ... Ms. Christine FIELDS
111 Vice Pres Institutional Advancement ... Dr. Joey GILBERT
49 Business Humanities & Science Div ... Ms. Barbara MANUEL
09 Dir of Institutional Rsrch/Effectiv ... Mr. Robert E. MAY
66 Dean of Nursing and Allied Health ... Ms. Kathy J. MITCHELL
103 VP Workforce Training & Cont Educ ... Ms. Melinda T. LELAND
08 Coordinator of Library Services ... Mr. Joel RUDY
37 Director of Financial Aid ... Ms. Nancy HOPE
07 Director Admission/Records ... Vacant
06 Registrar ... Ms. Charlene EASTRIDGE
15 Human Resource Manager ... Ms. Laura MCCLELLAN
26 Coord Public Rels & Marketing ... Ms. Anne DUNHAM
88 Director Project EXCEL ... Ms. Karen CHEERS
21 Business Manager ... Ms. Mary SNEAD
96 Director of Purchasing ... Ms. Chelsa TAYLOR
90 Coord Academic Computing/Technology ... Mr. Glen JOHNSON
09 Institutional Research Officer ... Mr. Jeff D. RUSSELL
18 Chief Facilities/Physical Plant ... Mr. Ernest L. NUNLEY
19 Campus Police Chief ... Mr. Blake ANDIS
36 Career Plng/Placement Specialist ... Mr. Michael MCBRIDE

*Virginia Western Community College (B)

3093 Colonial Avenue SW, Roanoke VA 24015-4705

County: Independent City FICE Identification: 003760
Unit ID: 233949
Telephone: (540) 857-8922 Carnegie Class: Assoc/HT-High Non
FAX Number: (540) 857-6526 Calendar System: Semester
URL: www.virginiawestern.edu
Established: 1966 Annual Undergrad Tuition & Fees (In-State): $5,093
Enrollment: 7,932 Coed
Affiliation or Control: State IRS Status: 501(c)3
Highest Offering: Associate Degree
Accreditation: SC, ACBSP, ACFEI, DH, RAD, RTT

02 President ... Dr. Robert H. SANDEL
10 Vice Pres of Finance/Admin Services ... Ms. Lisa RIDPATH
05 Vice Pres Academic/Student Affs ... Dr. Elizabeth WILMER
111 Vice Pres Institutional Advancement ... Vacant
103 Vice Pres Workforce Development Svc ... Dr. Milian HAYWARD
45 Dean Institutional Effectiveness ... Ms. Rachelle KOUDELIK-JONES
49 Dean Liberal Arts/Social Sciences ... Ms. Amy ANGUIANO
76 Dean Health Professions ... Ms. Carole GRAHAM
81 Dean Science/Tech/Engineering/Math ... Dr. John ANDERSON
50 Dean Business/Trades/Technology ... Ms. Deborah YANCEY
24 Dean Learning Resources ... Mr. Christopher PORTER
32 Dean of Student Services ... Ms. Lori BAKER
09 Director Institutional Research ... Ms. Carol ROWLETT
18 Director of Facilities Planning ... Mr. Kevin G. WITTER
26 Director Marketing/Strategic Comm ... Mr. Josh MEYER
06 Registrar ... Ms. Karin COLE
19 Campus Police Chief ... Mr. Craig HARRIS
37 Coord Financial Aid/Veterans Affs ... Mr. Chad SARTINI
103 Workforce Operations Supervisor ... Ms. Cassandra DOVE
13 Dir Information Educ Technology ... Mr. Shivaji SAMANTA
15 Assoc VP of Human Resources ... Ms. Jennifer PITTMAN
21 Business Manager ... Mrs. Fredona AARON
84 Coordinator for Enrollment Services ... Ms. Brooke FERGUSON
08 Coordinator of the Library ... Vacant
36 Coordinator Career Services ... Ms. Rhonda PERDUE
25 Coord Grants Dev & Special Projects ... Ms. Marilyn J. HERBERT-ASHTON
30 Coordinator of Development ... Ms. Carole TARRANT

*Wytheville Community College (C)

1000 E Main Street, Wytheville VA 24382-3308

County: Wythe FICE Identification: 003761
Unit ID: 234377
Telephone: (276) 223-4700 Carnegie Class: Assoc/HT-Mix Trad/Non
FAX Number: (276) 223-4778 Calendar System: Semester
URL: www.wcc.vccs.edu
Established: 1963 Annual Undergrad Tuition & Fees (In-State): $4,493
Enrollment: 2,915 Coed
Affiliation or Control: State IRS Status: 501(c)3
Highest Offering: Associate Degree
Accreditation: SC, ADNUR, DH, MLTAD, PTAA

02 President ... Dr. Dean SPRINKLE
05 Vice Pres Instruction/Student Devel ... Dr. Lorri HUFFARD
10 Vice Pres Finance & Admin Services ... Ms. Crystal Y. CREGGER
09 Director of Institutional Research ... Dr. Kent E. GLINDEMANN
30 Vice Pres of College Development ... Dr. Rhonda K. CATRON-WOOD
103 Director of Workforce Development ... Mr. Perry HUGHES
83 Dean of Transfer & Social Sciences ... Mr. Jacob SURRATT
76 Dean of Health & Occupational Pgms ... Mr. Jamie EDWARDS
32 Dean of Student Services ... Ms. Renee THOMAS
13 Director Acad/Admin Computing ... Mr. Shawn MCREYNOLDS
06 Registrar ... Ms. Karen ALEXANDER
15 Human Resources Manager ... Ms. Malinda EVERSOLE
26 Public Relations Coordinator ... Vacant
08 Coordinator of Library Services ... Mr. George E. MATTIS, JR.
96 Procurement Officer ... Ms. Vivian FANNING
106 Dir of Distance & Distrib Learning ... Mr. Kenneth E. FAIRBANKS
37 Coordinator Financial Aid ... Ms. Mary Beth GALLAGHER
04 Administrative Asst to President ... Ms. Denita BURNETT
29 Development Svcs/Alumni Coordinator ... Ms. Jill W. ROSS

Virginia International University (D)

11200 Waples Mill Road, Suite 360, Fairfax VA 22030

County: Fairfax FICE Identification: 041440
Unit ID: 460376
Telephone: (703) 591-7042 Carnegie Class: Not Classified
FAX Number: (703) 591-7046 Calendar System: Semester
URL: www.viu.edu
Established: 1998 Annual Undergrad Tuition & Fees: $9,608
Enrollment: N/A Coed
Affiliation or Control: Independent Non-Profit IRS Status: 501(c)3
Highest Offering: Master's
Accreditation: ACICS, CEA

01 President ... Dr. Isa SARAC
10 Exec Vice Pres Finance & IT ... Mr. Prashish SHRESTHA
09 Assoc Vice Pres Inst Effectiveness ... Ms. Christine KOONTS

Virginia Military Institute (E)

319 Letcher Avenue, Lexington VA 24450-0304

County: Independent City FICE Identification: 003753
Unit ID: 234085
Telephone: (540) 464-7230 Carnegie Class: Bac-A&S
FAX Number: (540) 464-7583 Calendar System: Semester
URL: www.vmi.edu
Established: 1839 Annual Undergrad Tuition & Fees (In-State): $17,492
Enrollment: 1,717 Coed
Affiliation or Control: State IRS Status: 501(c)3
Highest Offering: Baccalaureate
Accreditation: SC, ENG

01 Superintendent ... Gen. J. H. Binford PEAY
05 Dean of the Faculty ... BGen. Jeffrey G. SMITH
10 Director Finance/Admin ... Col. Dallas B. CLARK
32 Commandant of Cadets ... Col. William J. WANOVICH
100 Chief of Staff ... Col. James P. INMAN
04 Exec Asst to the Superintendent ... LtCol. Sean P. HARRINGTON
21 Assoc Business Exec/Treasurer ... Col. Jeffrey L. LAWHORNE
07 Director of Admissions ... Col. Vernon L. BEITZEL
88 Exec Director Museum Programs ... Col. Keith E. GIBSON
37 Director of Financial Aid ... Capt. Brian L. QUISENBERRY
35 Deputy Commandant ... Col. L. E. HURLBUT
36 Director of Career Services ... Col. R. Samuel RATCLIFFE
41 Director Intercollegiate Athletics ... Mr. David L. DILES
26 Director Communications & Marketing ... Col. Stewart D. MACINNIS
29 Executive VP Alumni Association ... Col. Adam C. VOLANT
102 Exec VP VMI Foundation/Fund Raising ... Mr. Warren J. BRYAN
88 Exec VP Keydet Club/Athletic Fund ... Mr. Gregory M. CAVALLARO
06 Registrar ... Col. Janet M. BATTAGLIA
15 Director Human Resources ... LtCol. Richard A. PARELLA, JR.
18 Director Physical Plant ... LtCol. Richard A. FLETCHER
09 Director Institutional Research ... LtCol. Lee L. RAKES
109 Director Auxiliary Services ... Col. David P. WILLIAMS
40 Manager Bookstore ... Mr. Bradley N. MCDOUGAL
42 Institute Chaplain ... Col. Robert E. PHILLIPS, SR.
17 Institute Physician ... Dr. David L. COPELAND
88 Director of Athletic Communications ... Mr. Wade H. BRANNER
08 Head Librarian ... Col. Dorothy C. LOCKABY
38 Director of Cadet Counseling ... LtCol. Sarah L. JONES
13 Director Information Technology ... Col. Thomas F. HOPKINS
96 Director of Purchasing ... Maj. Kathy H. TOMLIN

† Tuition includes required room and board and quartermaster charges.

Virginia Polytechnic Institute and State University (F)

Blacksburg VA 24061-0202

County: Montgomery FICE Identification: 003754
Unit ID: 233921
Telephone: (540) 231-6000 Carnegie Class: DU-Highest
FAX Number: (540) 231-9263 Calendar System: Semester
URL: www.vt.edu
Established: 1872 Annual Undergrad Tuition & Fees (In-State): $12,852
Enrollment: 32,663 Coed
Affiliation or Control: State IRS Status: 501(c)3
Highest Offering: Doctorate
Accreditation: SC, ART, CACREP, CAEPN, CEA, CIDA, CLPSY, CONST, CS, DIETD, DIETI, ENG, IPSY, LSAR, MFCD, MUS, PCSAS, PH, PLNG, SPAA, THEA, VET

01 President ... Timothy D. SANDS
05 Executive Vice President & Provost ... Thanassis RIKAKIS
11 Vice President for Administration ... Sherwood G. WILSON
13 Vice Pres for Information Tech ... Scott F. MIDKIFF
32 Vice President Student Affairs ... Patricia A. PERILLO
111 Vice Pres for Advancement ... Charles D. PHLEGAR
29 Sr Assoc Vice Pres Alumni Relations ... Matthew M. WINSTON, JR.
28 Vice Provost Inclusion & Diversity ... Menah PRATT-CLARKE, JR.
46 Vice Provost Research & Innovation ... Theresa MEYER
20 Vice Prov for Undergrad Acad Affs ... Rachel L. HOLLOWAY
58 Vice President and Dean Grad Educ ... Karen P. DEPAUW
56 VP Outreach/International Affs ... Guru GHOSH
10 Vice President for Finance and CFO ... M. Dwight SHELTON, JR.
07 Assoc VP/Dir Undergrad Admissions ... Mildred JOHNSON
35 Dean of Students ... Thomas BROWN
15 Assoc Vice Pres for Administration ... Lisa WILKES
09 Assoc Prov Acad Decision Support ... Vacant
43 University Counsel ... Kay K. HEIDBREDER
84 Vice Prov for Enroll & Degree Mgmt ... Luisa HAVENS
37 Dir of Scholarships/Financial Aid ... Elizabeth ARMSTRONG
20 Vice Provost Faculty Affairs ... Jack FINNEY
45 Vice Provost Resource Management ... Kenneth SMITH
23 Director Schiffert Health Center ... Kanitta CHAROENSIRI
18 Assoc Vice Pres/Chief Facilities ... Christopher KIWUS
109 Director of Dining Services ... Ted FAULKNER
39 Dir Housing and Residential Life ... Eleanor FINGER
41 Athletic Director ... Whit BABCOCK
26 Assoc Vice Pres Univ Relations ... Tracy VOSBURGH
38 Director Student Counseling ... Chris FLYNN
40 Executive Director Bookstore ... Donald J. WILLIAMS
62 Dean of Libraries ... Tyler WALTERS
47 Dean of Agriculture/Life Sciences ... Alan GRANT
48 Dean of Architecture/Urban Studies ... Jack DAVIS
49 Dean College of Science ... Sally C. MORTEN
50 Dean of Business ... Robert T. SUMICHRAST
54 Int Dean of Engineering ... G. Don TAYLOR
79 Dean Liberal Arts & Human Sciences ... Elizabeth SPILLER
74 Dean of Veterinary Medicine ... Cyril R. CLARKE
65 Dean of Natural Resources & Environ ... Paul M. WINISTORFER
96 Director of Procurement ... Mary HELMICK
91 Assoc Vice Pres for Enterprise Sys ... Deborah M. FULTON
12 VP for the National Capital Region ... Steven H. MCKNIGHT
102 CEO Virginia Tech Foundation ... John E. DOOLEY
04 Sr Executive Asst to President ... Sandy SMITH
06 University Registrar ... Rick SPARKS
100 Chief of Staff ... Kim O'ROURKE
104 Director Global Education Office ... Theresa C. JOHANSSON
105 Director Web Communications ... John JACKSON
106 Exec Dir Tech-enhanced Learning ... Dale PIKE
88 Asst Provost Regional Accreditation ... Kristen BUSH
19 Chief of Police/Dir of Security ... Kevin FOUST
22 Dir Affirmative Action/EEO ... Karisa MOORE
25 Chief Contracts/Grants Admin ... Frank FITZGERALD
44 Director Annual or Planned Giving ... Randy HOLDEN
86 Exec Director Government Relations ... Chris YIANILOS

Virginia State University (A)

One Hayden Drive,
Virginia State University VA 23806-0001
County: Chesterfield   FICE Identification: 003764
Unit ID: 234155
Telephone: (804) 524-5000   Carnegie Class: Masters/M
FAX Number: (804) 524-6506   Calendar System: Semester
URL: www.vsu.edu
Established: 1882   Annual Undergrad Tuition & Fees (In-State): $8,472
Enrollment: 4,696   Coed
Affiliation or Control: State   IRS Status: 501(c)3
Highest Offering: Doctorate
Accreditation: SC, ART, CAEPN, CS, DIETD, DIETI, ENG, ENGR, ENGT, MUS, NAIT, SW

01 President .... Dr. Makola M. ABDULLAH
10 Vice President for Finance .... Mr. Kevin DAVENPORT
05 Provost/VP for Academic Affairs .... Dr. Donald PALM
32 VP for Student Success & Engagement .... Dr. Letizia GAMBRELL-BOONE
111 VP for Institutional Advancement .... Ms. Reshunda MAHONE
11 Vice President for Administration .... Mr. Hubert D. HARRIS
20 Vice Provost .... Vacant
84 Asst VP/Student Enrollment Services .... Dr. Jame'l HODGES
21 Assoc Vice President for Finance .... Ms. Sheila MCNAIR
50 Dean Reginald F Lewis Col Business . Dr. Emmanuel OMOJOKUN
54 Dean College of Engineering & Tech . Dr. Keith M. WILLIAMSON
79 Dean Col of Humanities & Soc Sci .... Dr. Andrew KANU
47 Dean College of Agriculture .... Dr. Marion R. MCKINNEY
58 Dean Graduate Studies .... Vacant
62 Dean Library & Library Services .. Dr. Elsie S. WEATHERINGTON
76 Dean College of Natural Health Sci .... Dr. Larry BROWN
53 Dean College of Education .... Dr. Willis W. WALTER
06 Registrar .... Mrs. Debera BONNER
09 Director Inst Planning/Assessment .... Dr. Emmett L. RIDLEY
37 Director of Financial Aid .... Mrs. Myra PHILLIPS
19 Chief of Police and Public Safety .... Mr. David BRAGG
27 Media Specialist .... Mr. Jesse VAUGHAN
18 Director of Facilities .... Mr. Gilbert HANZLIK
07 Director for Enrollment Services .... Mr. Rodney HALL
26 Interim Director for Communication .... Mrs. Gwen WILLIAMS DANDRIDGE
15 Interim HR Director .... Ms. Karen GULLIFORD
39 Director Residence Facilities .... Dr. Kelvin RACHELL
36 Director Career Services .... Mr. Joseph LYONS
40 Bookstore Manager .... Mr. Kevin POWELL
92 Director Honors Program .... Mr. Daniel M. ROBERTS
41 Athletic Director .... Mrs. Peggy DAVIS
42 Minister .... Rev. Delano DOUGLAS
29 Director of Alumni Relations .... Ms. Charmica D. EPPS
13 Deputy Chief Information Officer .... Vacant
23 Director of Student Health Services .... Dr. Darylnet LYTTLE
25 Contract Manager .... Ms. Linda SCOTT
87 Director Summer School Session .... Dr. Vykuntapathi THOTA
96 Director of Purchasing .... Mr. Ryan FEREBEE
38 Director University Counseling .... Vacant
88 Special Assistant to the President .... Mr. Osubi CRAIG
04 Executive Assistant to President .... Mrs. Danette JOHNSON
101 Special Asst to President & Board .... Dr. Annie REDD
43 General Counsel .... Ms. Ramona L. TAYLOR

Virginia Tech Carilion School of Medicine (B)

2 Riverside Circle, Suite M140, Roanoke VA 24016
County: Independent City   Identification: 667148
Unit ID: 459082
Telephone: (540) 526-2559   Carnegie Class: Not Classified
FAX Number: (540) 581-0741   Calendar System: Other
URL: www.vtc.vt.edu
Established: 2007   Annual Graduate Tuition & Fees: N/A
Enrollment: 165   Coed
Affiliation or Control: Independent Non-Profit   IRS Status: 501(c)3
Highest Offering: Doctorate; No Undergraduates
Accreditation: SC, MED

01 President & Dean .... Dr. Cynda Ann JOHNSON
05 Vice Dean .... Dr. Daniel P. HARRINGTON

Virginia Union University (C)

1500 N Lombardy Street, Richmond VA 23220-1784
County: Independent City   FICE Identification: 003766
Unit ID: 234164
Telephone: (804) 257-5600   Carnegie Class: Bac-A&S
FAX Number: (804) 257-5818   Calendar System: Semester
URL: www.vuu.edu
Established: 1865   Annual Undergrad Tuition & Fees: $17,034
Enrollment: 1,922   Coed
Affiliation or Control: Baptist   IRS Status: 501(c)3
Highest Offering: Doctorate
Accreditation: SC, ACBSP, CAEPN, SW, THEOL

01 Acting President .... Dr. Joseph F. JOHNSON
05 VP Academic Affairs .... Dr. Joy P. GOODRICH
32 VP Enroll Mgmt & Student Affs .... Vacant
10 VP Financial Affairs .... Mr. Gregory LEWIS
111 Vice Pres Institutional Advancement .... Mr. Dennis C. WASHINGTON
09 VP Research/Planning & Spec Pgms .... Dr. Joy P. GOODRICH
26 Dir Public Relations .... Vacant
53 Dean Evelyn R Syphax Sch Ed/Psy .... Dr. David A. ADEWUYI
81 Dean Math/Science & Technology .... Dr. Latrelle A. GREEN
50 Dean Sydney Lewis Sch of Business .... Dr. Brenda J. PONSFORD
79 Dean Sch of Humanities/Soc Sci .... Dr. Michael OROK
73 Sr VP/Dean School of Theology .... Dr. John W. KINNEY
25 Asst to President Title III Pgms .... Mr. Samuel T. RHOADES
15 Director Human Resources .... Ms. Debra A. JONES
06 Registrar .... Ms. Marilyn A. BROOKS
38 Director Counseling .... Dr. Remy J. THOMPSON
29 Director of Alumni Relations .... Vacant
08 Library Director .... Ms. Pamela B. FOREMAN
37 Director Financial Aid .... Ms. Karen L. GEE
13 Director Information Technology .... Mr. Robert R. GRAY
36 Director Career Services .... Ms. Takeish N. BROWN
42 University Pastor .... Rev. Angelo V. CHATMON
41 Athletic Director .... Mr. Joseph TAYLOR
19 Chief University Police .... Col. Carlton G. EDWARDS
24 Audio Visual Coordinator .... Mr. JaPrince L. CARTER
21 Asst VP Finan Affairs/Comptroller .... Ms. Stephanie M. WHITE
40 Bookstore Manager .... Ms. Terri WYATT
39 Director of Residence Life .... Mr. Mandrake T. MILLER
31 Coordinator Student & Community Eng .... Ms. Claudia E. WALL
18 Director Facilities .... Mr. David E. GORDON
96 Director of Purchasing .... Vacant
04 Administrative Asst to President .... Ms. Renee W. JOLLEY
104 Dir Ctr for International Studies .... Dr. David A. ADEWUYI
106 Dir Online Education/E-learning .... Dr. Laurene E. COLLINS
108 Director Institutional Assessment .... Dr. Samantha M. NASH
22 Dir Affirmative Action/EEO .... Ms. Debra A. JONES
44 Director Annual or Planned Giving .... Ms. Lisa D. WINN
07 Director of Admissions .... Ms. Kristie L. WHITE
101 Secretary of the Institution/Board .... Ms. Renee W. JOLLEY

Virginia University of Lynchburg (D)

2058 Garfield Avenue, Lynchburg VA 24501-6417
County: Independent City   FICE Identification: 003762
Unit ID: 234137
Telephone: (434) 528-5276   Carnegie Class: Spec-4-yr-Faith
FAX Number: (434) 528-4257   Calendar System: Semester
URL: www.vul.edu
Established: 1886   Annual Undergrad Tuition & Fees: $7,880
Enrollment: 402   Coed
Affiliation or Control: Independent Non-Profit   IRS Status: 501(c)3
Highest Offering: Doctorate
Accreditation: TRACS

01 President .... Dr. Kathy C. FRANKLIN
05 Provost/Executive Vice President .... Dr. John BOREK
10 Vice President of Finance .... Dr. Donald LESLIE
32 Vice Pres Div Student Affairs .... Dr. Kyle REICHLE
06 Registrar .... Mr. Chris SHANKS
84 Dir Enrollment Management/Fin Aid .... Ms. Rita B. WALKER
18 Dir of Facilities/Maintenance .... Mr. Houston D. WALTHALL
106 Dir Online Education/E-learning .... Ms. Katrina V. FRANKLIN
19 Director Security/Safety .... Mr. Robert CABLER, JR.
11 Chief Operating Officer .... Mr. Jason J. RANDOO
37 Acting Director of Financial Aid .... Ms. Romena MORGAN
04 Administrative Asst to President .... Ms. Megan DEN BLEYKER
08 Head Librarian .... Ms. Lisa KRAJECKI
13 IT Director .... Mr. Scott BROWN

Virginia University of Oriental Medicine (E)

9401 Mathy Drive, Fairfax VA 22031
County: Fairfax   Identification: 667208
Telephone: (703) 323-5690   Carnegie Class: Not Classified
FAX Number: (703) 323-5692   Calendar System: Quarter
URL: www.vuom.org
Established: Annual Undergrad Tuition & Fees: N/A
Enrollment: N/A   Coed
Affiliation or Control: Independent Non-Profit   IRS Status: 501(c)3
Highest Offering: Master's
Accreditation: ACUP

01 President .... John SHIN
05 Vice Pres Academic Affairs/CEO .... Tae CHEONG-CHOO
11 COO/Director of Admissions .... John YOO

Virginia Wesleyan University (F)

5817 Wesleyan Drive, Virginia Beach VA 23455
County: Independent City   FICE Identification: 003767
Unit ID: 234173
Telephone: (757) 455-3200   Carnegie Class: Bac-A&S
FAX Number: (757) 461-4944   Calendar System: 4/1/4
URL: www.vwu.edu
Established: 1961   Annual Undergrad Tuition & Fees: $35,610
Enrollment: 1,441   Coed
Affiliation or Control: United Methodist   IRS Status: 501(c)3
Highest Offering: Master's
Accreditation: SC, NRPA, SW

01 President .... Dr. Scott D. MILLER
05 Provost and Vice President .... Dr. Timothy G. O'ROURKE
03 Senior Vice President .... Dr. Mort GAMBLE
10 Vice President for Finance & Admin .... Mr. James E. COOPER
32 VP for Student Affairs .... Dr. Keith MOORE
07 Vice President for Enrollment .... Mr. David WAGGONER
13 Chief Information Officer .... Mr. Robert LEITGEB
41 Executive Director of Athletics .... Ms. Joanne M. RENN
04 Exec Assistant to the President .... Ms. Stephanie SMAGLO
88 Exec Dir Quality Enhancement Plan .... Dr. Sara SEWELL
26 Director of Communications .... Ms. Leona BAKER
111 Assoc VP for Advancement/Board Rel .... Ms. Suzanne SAVAGE
20 Assistant Provost .... Ms. Debbie L. HICKS
39 Director of Residence Life .... Mr. Chittams RALPH
45 Exec Dir of College Rel/Strat Plng .... Ms. Laynee H. TIMLIN
55 Coord of the Adult Studies Program .... Ms. Pamela PARAMORE
08 Library Director .... Mrs. Susan ERICKSON
15 Director of Human Resources .... Ms. Karla R. RASMUSSEN
06 Registrar .... Ms. Regina BYNUM
37 Director of Financial Aid .... Ms. Teresa L. RHYNE
96 Director of Purchasing .... Ms. Midge ZIMMERMAN
31 Director of Community Service .... Ms. Diane E. HOTALING
36 Dir of Career Dev & Internships .... Ms. Rosalie ROBERTSON
19 Director of Campus Security .... Mr. Jerry MANCE, JR.
18 Director of Physical Plant .... Mr. Robert LEVINSKY
42 Chaplain .... Rev. Greg WEST
38 Director of Counseling Services .... Mr. Bill BROWN
44 Exec Dir of Annual Giv/Alumni Rel .... Ms. Lori HARRIS
92 Director Honors and Scholars .... Dr. Joyce B. EASTER
88 Director of Student Activities .... Ms. Kate GRIFFIN
40 Bookstore Manager .... Ms. Kim S. BROWN
79 Dean .... Dr. Travis MALONE
81 Dean .... Dr. Christopher HALEY
83 Dean .... Dr. Robert ALBERTSON
09 Senior Researcher/Policy Analyst .... Mr. Donald STAUFFER
102 Dir of Corp Rel/Coord of Boyd Inst .... Ms. Kelly CORDOVA
104 Director of Study Away Programs .... Ms. Amanda REINIG

Washington and Lee University (G)

204 W Washington Street, Lexington VA 24450-2116
County: Independent City   FICE Identification: 003768
Unit ID: 234207
Telephone: (540) 458-8400   Carnegie Class: Bac-A&S
FAX Number: (540) 458-8945   Calendar System: Other
URL: www.wlu.edu
Established: 1749   Annual Undergrad Tuition & Fees: $48,267
Enrollment: 2,172   Coed
Affiliation or Control: Independent Non-Profit   IRS Status: 501(c)3
Highest Offering: Doctorate
Accreditation: SC, CAEPT, JOUR, LAW

01 President .... Dr. William C. DUDLEY
05 Provost .... Dr. Marc CONNER
20 Associate Provost .... Dr. Marcia FRANCE
10 Vice Pres for Finance and Admin .... Mr. Steven G. MCALLISTER
111 Vice Pres University Advancement .... Mr. Dennis W. CROSS
32 VP Student Affs & Dean of Students .... Ms. Sidney S. EVANS
101 Sr Asst to Pres/Sec of University .... Mr. James D. FARRAR
43 General Counsel .... Ms. Leanne M. SHANK
22 Assoc Gen Counsel Compliance Spprt .... Ms. Jennifer E. KIRKLAND
49 Dean of the College .... Dr. Suzanne P. KEEN
50 Dean of Commerce/Economics/Politics .... Mr. Robert D. STRAUGHAN
61 Dean of Law School .... Mr. Brant J. HELLWIG
26 Exec Dir of Comm/Public Affairs .... Ms. Jessica WILLETT
35 Dean of Student Life .... Mr. David M. LEONARD
35 Assoc Dean of Students .... Ms. Tamara Y. FUTRELL
35 Assoc Dean of Students .... Ms. Tammi R. SIMPSON
30 Exec Dir of University Development .... Mr. Tres MULLIS
41 Director of Athletics .... Ms. Janine M. HATHORN
89 Asst Dean for 1st Yr Experience .... Mr. Jason L. RODOCKER
07 Dean of Admissions/Financial Aid .... M. Sally S. RICHMOND
09 Asst Provost for Inst Effectiveness .... Mr. Bryan PRICE
06 University Registrar .... Mr. Scott DITTMAN
08 University Librarian .... Mr. John TOMBARGE
85 Director International Education .... Dr. Mark E. RUSH
29 Exec Director of Alumni Affairs .... Mr. Waller T. DUDLEY
15 Exec Director of Human Resources .... Ms. Mary E. MAIN
37 Director of Financial Aid .... Mr. James D. KASTER
18 Exec Dir Facilities/Capital Plng .... Mr. Randolph HARE
21 Associate Treasurer & Controller .... Mrs. Deborah Z. CAYLOR
13 Chief Technology Officer .... Mr. David SAACKE
24 Senior Academic Technologist .... Mr. Brandon R. BUCY
36 Director Career Development .... Mr. John A. JENSEN
23 Director Student Health/Counseling .... Dr. Jane T. HORTON
109 Interim Director of Dining Services .... Mr. Dwight D. BITZ
40 Director of Administrative Services .... Mr. K. C SCHAEFER

Washington University of Virginia (H)

4300 Evergreen Lane, Annandale VA 22003
County: Fairfax   Identification: 666234
Telephone: (703) 333-5904   Carnegie Class: Not Classified
FAX Number: (703) 333-5906   Calendar System: Semester
URL: www.wuv.edu
Established: 1982   Annual Undergrad Tuition & Fees: N/A
Enrollment: N/A   Coed
Affiliation or Control: Baptist   IRS Status: 501(c)3
Highest Offering: Doctorate
Accreditation: BI, THEOL

01 President .... Dr. Peter M. CHANG
03 Executive Vice President .... Mrs. Joyce G. PARK
07 Dean of Enrollment .... Mr. David Y. LEE
08 Head Librarian .... Mr. Robert ROSE, JR.
50 Dean School of Business .... Mr. Won Eog KIM

Wave Leadership College (A)

1000 North Great Neck Road, Virginia Beach VA 23454
County: Independent City Identification: 667210
Unit ID: 486594
Telephone: (757) 481-5005 Carnegie Class: Not Classified
FAX Number: (757) 496-6697 Calendar System: Semester
URL: www.wavecollege.com
Established: 2000 Annual Undergrad Tuition & Fees: $6,680
Enrollment: 66 Coed
Affiliation or Control: Independent Non-Profit IRS Status: 501(c)3
Highest Offering: Associate Degree
Accreditation: @BI

01 President .... Steve KELLY
03 Executive Vice President .... Derek P. HOLSER
05 Academic Dean .... Sarah HUMMEL
32 Dean of Students .... James KNARR
06 Registrar .... Jacquie EVANS
08 Librarian .... Sasha MATTHEWS
37 Financial Aid Director .... James KNARR
85 International Student Liaison .... Jimada ROBINSON

WASHINGTON

Antioch University Seattle (B)

2400 3rd Avenue, Seattle WA 98121-1814
Telephone: (206) 441-5352 Identification: 666812
Accreditation: &NH, CACREP, MFCD

† Regional accreditation is carried under the parent institution in Yellow Springs, Ohio.

Argosy University, Seattle (C)

2601 A Elliott Avenue, Seattle WA 98121-1318
Telephone: (206) 283-4500 Identification: 666080
Accreditation: &WC, ACBSP

† Regional accreditation is carried under the parent institution in Orange, CA.

The Art Institute of Seattle (D)

2323 Elliott Avenue, Seattle WA 98121-1622
County: King FICE Identification: 022913
Unit ID: 234492
Telephone: (206) 448-0900 Carnegie Class: Spec-4-yr-Arts
FAX Number: (206) 448-2501 Calendar System: Quarter
URL: www.ais.edu
Established: 1946 Annual Undergrad Tuition & Fees: $17,556
Enrollment: 1,190 Coed
Affiliation or Control: Proprietary IRS Status: Proprietary
Highest Offering: Baccalaureate
Accreditation: NW, ACFEI, CIDA

01 President .... Carol MENCK
05 Dean of Academic Affairs .... Dr. Scott CARNZ
26 Director of Campus Relations .... Samuel KING
32 Dean of Student Affairs .... Angela HEDWALL
07 Senior Director of Admissions .... Anthony NAVETTA
10 Regional Finance Director .... Greg WOODARD
36 Director of Career Services .... Angela HEDWALL

Bastyr University (E)

14500 Juanita Drive NE, Kenmore WA 98028-4966
County: King FICE Identification: 022425
Unit ID: 235547
Telephone: (425) 602-3000 Carnegie Class: Spec-4-yr-Other Health
FAX Number: (425) 823-6222 Calendar System: Quarter
URL: www.bastyr.edu
Established: 1978 Annual Undergrad Tuition & Fees: N/A
Enrollment: 1,264 Coed
Affiliation or Control: Independent Non-Profit IRS Status: 501(c)3
Highest Offering: Doctorate
Accreditation: NW, ACUP, DIETD, DIETI, MEAC, NATUR

01 Interim President .... Mr. Harlan PATTERSON
05 Senior Vice President/Provost .... Dr. Dave RULE
10 Vice President for Finance & Admin .... Mr. Glenn R. FORD
100 Chief of Staff .... Ms. Coquina L. DEGER
32 Vice President of Student Affairs .... Ms. Susan WEIDER
15 Vice President of Human Resources .... Mr. Keith W. WOODY

Bates Technical College (F)

1101 S Yakima Avenue, Tacoma WA 98405-4895
County: Pierce FICE Identification: 005306
Unit ID: 235671
Telephone: (253) 680-7000 Carnegie Class: Assoc/HVT-High Non
FAX Number: (253) 680-7101 Calendar System: Quarter
URL: www.bates.ctc.edu
Established: 1940 Annual Undergrad Tuition & Fees (In-State): $4,601
Enrollment: 3,272 Coed
Affiliation or Control: State IRS Status: 501(c)3
Highest Offering: Associate Degree
Accreditation: NW, ACBSP, ACFEI, DA, DT, OTA

01 President .... Dr. Ron LANGRELL
05 Exec VP of Instruction/Student Svcs .... Mr. Al GRISWOLD
04 Exec Asst to the President .... Ms. Becky WELCH
32 Vice President of Student Services .... Ms. Lin ZHOU
15 Director of Human Resources .... Mr. Gary NILSSON
11 Vice Pres Administrative Services .... Ms. Holly WOODMANSEE
07 Dir of Admissions/Recruitment/Mktg .... Ms. Kimberly PLEGER
18 Exec Dir Facilities/Operations .... Mr. Marty MATTES
96 General Services Manager .... Mr. Alexander KENESSON
37 Financial Aid Director .... Ms. Susan NEESE
13 Exec Director of IT .... Mr. Pat TAYLOR
84 Dir of Enrollment Mgt/Admission .... Ms. Jaime LUJAN
09 Director of Institutional Research .... Mr. Jon BOLAS
19 Director Security/Safety .... Mr. Derick NELONS
08 Head Librarian .... Mr. Mike WOOD
30 Exec Dir of Resource Development .... Ms. Erin ZEIGER

Bellevue College (G)

3000 Landerholm Circle, SE, Bellevue WA 98007-6484
County: King FICE Identification: 003769
Unit ID: 234669
Telephone: (425) 564-1000 Carnegie Class: Bac/Assoc-Assoc Dom
FAX Number: (425) 564-4065 Calendar System: Quarter
URL: www.bellevuecollege.edu
Established: 1965 Annual Undergrad Tuition & Fees (In-State): $3,624
Enrollment: 13,398 Coed
Affiliation or Control: State IRS Status: 501(c)3
Highest Offering: Baccalaureate
Accreditation: NW, ADNUR, CIDA, DMS, NDT, NMT, NURSE, RADDOS, RTT

01 President .... Dr. Jerry WEBER
04 Exec Asst to the President .... Vacant
11 Vice Pres Administrative Services .... Mr. Ray WHITE
05 Int Vice Pres of Instruction .... Dr. Gita BANGERA
15 Vice President of Human Resources .... Mr. Aaron HILLIARD
111 Vice Pres Institutional Advancement .... Ms. Gayle BARGE
32 Vice President of Student Affairs .... Dr. Ata KARIM
103 Vice Pres of Econ & Wkfrc Dev .... Mr. Albert LEWIS
28 Int Vice President of Diversity .... Dr. Sayumi IREY
13 Vice Pres of Information Resources .... Mr. Russell BEARD
09 Int Assoc VP Effect & Strat Plng .... Mr. Alec CAMPBELL
51 Dean Continuing Education .... Vacant
79 Dean of Arts and Humanities .... Ms. Margaret HARADA
76 Dean of HSEWI .... Ms. Leslie HEIZER NEWQUIST
83 Dean of Social Science .... Ms. Virginia BRIDWELL
88 Associate Dean of Student Programs .... Mr. Faisal JASWAL
35 Dean of Student Affairs .... Ms. Kathleen HATHAWAY
85 Dean of Intl Educ & Global Init .... Mr. Jean D'ARC CAMPBELL
10 Exec Dir of Finance & Auxiliary Svc .... Ms. Jennifer STROTHER
08 Dean of Library Media Center .... Ms. Vivienne MCCLENDON
26 Director of Marketing .... Vacant
37 Director Financial Aid .... Ms. Melanie RUIZ
19 Director of Public Safety .... Mr. My TRAN
13 Director Computing Services .... Mr. Jason AQUI
91 Manager Networking Svcs & Security .... Mr. Gary FARRIS
41 Director of Athletics .... Mr. Bill O'CONNOR
38 Student Counseling .... Mr. Harlan LEE
40 Director Bellevue College Bookstore .... Ms. Kristen CONNELY
96 Exec Director Physical Plant Ops .... Mr. Dexter JOHNSON

Bellingham Technical College (H)

3028 Lindebergh Avenue, Bellingham WA 98225-1599
County: Whatcom FICE Identification: 004999
Unit ID: 234696
Telephone: (360) 752-7000 Carnegie Class: Assoc/HVT-High Non
FAX Number: (360) 676-2798 Calendar System: Quarter
URL: www.btc.edu
Established: 1957 Annual Undergrad Tuition & Fees (In-District): $3,394
Enrollment: 2,403 Coed
Affiliation or Control: State/Local IRS Status: 501(c)3
Highest Offering: Associate Degree
Accreditation: NW, ACFEI, ADNUR, DA, DH, SURGT

01 President .... Dr. Kimberly PERRY
04 Exec Assistant to the President .... Ms. Ronda LAUGHLIN
05 Vice President of Instruction .... Dr. Frank POWERS
32 Vice President of Student Services .... Dr. Linda FOSSEN
11 VP of Administrative Services .... Ms. Chad STITELER
72 Dean of Professional Technical Educ .... Ms. Tonya MCCABE
72 Dean of Professional Technical Educ .... Mr. Walter HUDSICK
111 Exec Director College Advancement .... Mr. Dean FULTON
15 Director Human Resources .... Ms. Camille GATZA
37 Director Financial Aid .... Ms. Crystal BAGBY
06 Director Registration/Enrollment .... Ms. Joan KAMMERZELL
13 Dir Computer/Inform Support Svcs .... Mr. Curtis PERERA
08 Director Library .... Ms. Jane BLUME
18 Chief Facilities/Physical Plant .... Mr. David JUNGKUNTZ
26 Director of Communications .... Ms. Marni SALING MAYER
07 Director of Admissions .... Ms. Karen BADE
36 Director Advising & Career Svcs .... Ms. Caryn REGIMBAL
09 Dir of Inst Research & Planning .Ms. RaeLyn AXLUND MCBRIDE
19 Director Security/Safety .... Mr. Al JENSEN
38 Student Counseling .... Ms. Nara SAMUELS

† Granted candidacy at the Baccalaureate level.

Big Bend Community College (I)

7662 Chanute Street NE, Moses Lake WA 98837-3299
County: Grant FICE Identification: 003770
Unit ID: 234711
Telephone: (509) 793-2222 Carnegie Class: Assoc/MT-VT-Mix Trad/Non
FAX Number: (509) 762-6329 Calendar System: Quarter
URL: www.bigbend.edu
Established: 1962 Annual Undergrad Tuition & Fees (In-State): $3,851
Enrollment: 2,070 Coed
Affiliation or Control: State IRS Status: 501(c)3
Highest Offering: Associate Degree
Accreditation: NW, ADNUR

01 President .... Dr. Terry LEAS
10 Vice Pres Administrative Services .... Ms. Linda SCHOONMAKER
05 VPLearning & Student Success .... Dr. Bryce HUMPHERYS
15 VP of Human Resources & Labor .... Mrs. Kim GARZA
103 Dean Workforce Education .... Ms. Daneen BERRY-GUERIN
88 Dean of Transitional Studies .... Ms. Faviola BARBOSA
32 Dean of Student Services .... Dr. Dawna HAYNES
49 Dean of Arts & Sciences .... Ms. Kathleen DUVLL
53 Dean Educ/Health/Language Skills .... Vacant
35 Director of Student Programs .... Ms. Kim JACKSON
37 Director of Financial Aid .... Mr. Jeremy IVERSON
06 Registrar .... Ms. Ruth COFFIN
08 Director of Library Resources .... Mr. Tim FUHRMAN
41 Director of Athletics .... Mr. Mark POTH
102 Dir Inst Advancement/Exec Dir Found .... Mrs. LeAnne PARTON
26 Director of Communications .... Mr. Matt KILLEBREW
21 Exec Director of Business Services .... Ms. Charlene RIOS
40 Director of Bookstore .... Mrs. Caren COURTRIGHT
96 Director of Purchasing .... Mr. Joe AUVIL
39 Residence Hall Coordinator .... Mr. Hugh SCHOLTE
09 Dean of Institutional Research .... Ms. Valerie PARTON
13 Chief Info Technology Officer (CIO) .... Mr. Rick SPARKS
19 Director Security/Safety .... Mr. Kyle FOREMAN
04 Administrative Asst to President .... Ms. Melinda DOURTE
18 Chief Facilities/Physical Plant .... Mr. James SAUCEDA

Carrington College - Spokane (J)

10102 E Knox Ave., Suite 200, Spokane WA 99206-4187
Telephone: (509) 462-3722 Identification: 666385
Accreditation: &WJ, MAAB, RAD

† Regional accreditation is carried under the parent institution in Sacramento, CA.

Cascadia College (K)

18345 Campus Way, NE, Bothell WA 98011-8205
County: King FICE Identification: 034835
Unit ID: 439190
Telephone: (425) 352-8000 Carnegie Class: Assoc/HT-Mix Trad/Non
FAX Number: (425) 352-8313 Calendar System: Quarter
URL: www.cascadia.edu
Established: 2000 Annual Undergrad Tuition & Fees (In-District): $3,753
Enrollment: 3,497 Coed
Affiliation or Control: State/Local IRS Status: Exempt
Highest Offering: Baccalaureate
Accreditation: NW

01 President .... Dr. Eric MURRAY
101 Exec Assist to the President .... Vicki NEWTON
11 VP Administrative Services .... Terence HSIAO
10 Dir of Finance .... Sharon WAYMIRE
13 Dir of Information Services .... Brian CULVER
88 Org Ch Mgmnt/Project Manager .... Scott MCKEAN
18 Asst Director of Facilities .... Kimberlee CLARK
05 VP Student Learning & Success .... Dr. Rosemary SUTTON
20 Dean of Student Learning .... Dr. Erik TINGELSTAD
20 Dean of Student Learning .... Dr. Todd LUNDBERG
32 Dean of Student Success Services .... Erin BLAKENEY
20 Asst Dean of Student Learning .... Lyn EISENHOUR
45 Dir Institutional Effectiveness .... Glenn COLBY
84 Dir Enrollment Services .... Shawn MILLER
37 Dir Student Financial Services .... Deann HOLLIDAY
121 Dir Student Adv & Support Services .... Gordon DUTRISAC
35 Dir of Student Life .... Becky RIOPEL
111 VP College Relations & Advancement .... Meagan WALKER
85 Dir of International Programs .... Yukari ZEDNICK
30 Asst Dir of Development .... Mark COLLINS
27 Manager Recruitment & Outreach .... Sara GOMEZ-TAYLOR
15 Executive Director of HR .... Martin LOGAN
118 Manager Payroll .... Rod COWLEY
88 Manager of Professional Development .... Samantha BROWN
16 Human Resources Generalist .... Haley GREEN
16 Human Resources Generalist .... Katherine KAMERON

Central Washington University (L)

400 E University Way, Ellensburg WA 98926-7501
County: Kittitas FICE Identification: 003771
Unit ID: 234827
Telephone: (509) 963-2111 Carnegie Class: Masters/L
FAX Number: (509) 963-3206 Calendar System: Quarter
URL: www.cwu.edu
Established: 1890 Annual Undergrad Tuition & Fees (In-State): $7,719
Enrollment: 11,993 Coed
Affiliation or Control: State IRS Status: 501(c)3
Highest Offering: Master's
Accreditation: NW, CACREP, CONST, DIETD, DIETI, EMT, ENGT, IPSY, MUS

01 President .... Dr. James L. GAUDINO
05 Provost/VP Academic & Student Life .... Dr. Katherine FRANK
10 VP Business & Financial Affairs .... Mr. Joel KLUCKING
100 Chief of Staff .... Ms. Linda SCHACTLER
20 Assoc Provost UG/Faculty Affairs .... Dr. Gail MACKIN

56 Assoc Provost Ext Learn & Outreach ... Dr. Gayla STONER
88 Assoc Provost Accreditation ... Dr. Bernadette JUNGBLUT
84 Vice Pres Enrollment Management ... Ms. Sharon O'HARE
32 Dean of Student Success ... Mr. Richard DESHIELDS
11 VP of Operations ... Mr. Joseph HAN
58 Dean Graduate Studies/Research ... Dr. Kevin ARCHER
49 Dean College of Arts/Humanities ... Dr. Todd SHIVER
50 Dean College of Business ... Dr. Kathryn MARTELL
53 Dean College of Educ/Prof Studies ... Dr. Paul BALLARD
83 Dean College of the Sciences ... Dr. Tim ENGLUND
08 Interim Dean of Library Services ... Dr. Gregory PAVEZA
30 Vice Pres University Advancement ... Mr. Scott WADE
07 Assoc VP of Admissions & Enrollment ... Mr. Josh HIBBARD
26 Vice Pres of Public Affairs ... Ms. Kremiere JACKSON
28 Vice Pres of Diversity ... Dr. Delores CLEARY
13 Assoc VP Info Svcs & Security ... Mr. Andreas BOHMAN

Centralia College (A)

600 Centralia College Boulevard,
Centralia WA 98531-4035

County: Lewis — FICE Identification: 003772
Unit ID: 234845
Telephone: (360) 736-9391 — Carnegie Class: Bac/Assoc-Assoc Dom
FAX Number: (360) 330-7108 — Calendar System: Quarter
URL: www.centralia.edu
Established: 1925 — Annual Undergrad Tuition & Fees (In-State): $4,188
Enrollment: 3,260 — Coed
Affiliation or Control: State — IRS Status: 501(c)3
Highest Offering: Baccalaureate
Accreditation: **NW**

01 President ... Dr. Robert MOHRBACHER
05 Vice President Instruction ... Mr. John MARTENS
32 Vice President of Students ... Mr. Robert COX
10 Vice Pres Finance/Administration ... Mr. Steve WARD
15 VP Human Resources/Legal Affairs ... Ms. Julie HUSS
103 Dean Workforce Education ... Ms. Durelle SULLIVAN
08 Dean of Library Services/E-Learning ... Ms. Sue KENNEDY
88 Dean of Academic Transfer Programs ... Mr. Christian BRUHN
09 Director of Institutional Research ... Vacant
103 Dir WorkFirst & Worker Retraining ... Ms. Margret FRIEDLEY
84 Director of Enrollment Services ... Ms. Kimberly INGRAM
37 Director of Financial Aid ... Ms. Tracy DAHL
13 Director Information Technology ... Mr. Patrick ALLISON
41 Director of Sports Programs ... Mr. Bob PETERS
29 Director Alumni Relations ... Ms. Julia JOHNSON
96 Director of Purchasing ... Ms. Bonnie MYER
26 Dir College Relations & Events ... Ms. Amanda HAINES
06 Registration Specialist ... Ms. Rosanna SCHLAGEL
40 Bookstore Manager ... Ms. Tammy STRODEMIER
97 Program Coordinator ... Ms. Joanie ROGERSON

Charter College (B)

17200 SE Mill Plain Blvd, Suite 100, Vancouver WA 98683
Telephone: (360) 448-2000 — Identification: 770822
Accreditation: **ACICS**

† Branch campus of Charter College, Anchorage, AK

Charter College-Fife (C)

3700 Pacific Highway E, Suite 407, Fife WA 98424
Telephone: (775) 525-2117 — Identification: 770623
Accreditation: **ACICS**

† Branch campus of Charter College, Anchorage, AK

City University of Seattle (D)

521 Wall Street, Suite 100, Seattle WA 98121
County: King — FICE Identification: 013022
Unit ID: 234915
Telephone: (206) 239-4500 — Carnegie Class: Masters/L
FAX Number: (206) 239-4802 — Calendar System: Quarter
URL: www.cityu.edu
Established: 1973 — Annual Undergrad Tuition & Fees: $16,748
Enrollment: 2,347 — Coed
Affiliation or Control: Independent Non-Profit — IRS Status: 501(c)3
Highest Offering: Doctorate
Accreditation: **NW**, ACBSP, CACREP, CS

01 President ... Mr. Randy C. FRISCH
101 Exec Asst Office of the President ... Ms. Miranda HOLTMANN
32 Vice President Student Services ... Dr. Melissa E. MECHAM
05 Provost/Vice Pres Academic Affairs ... Dr. Kurt KIRSTEIN
10 Int Chief Financial Officer ... Vacant
88 Vice President European Operations ... Dr. Jan REBRO
84 Vice Pres Enrollment Management ... Mr. Matt HANUSA
50 Dean School of Management ... Mr. Tom CAREY
53 Dean School of Education ... Dr. Kelly FLORES
108 Director of Inst Effectiveness ... Mr. Christopher JOHNSON
21 Director of Finance ... Mr. Christopher BRYAN
15 Director of Human Resources ... Ms. Janet O'LEARY
08 Director Library Services ... Ms. Mary MARA
37 Assoc Dir Student Financial Svcs ... Ms. Linda COOKE
29 Alumni Relations Manager ... Mr. Alex WEBSTER
90 Director of Information Technology ... Mr. Kevin H. BROWN
07 Director Admissions ... Ms. Amy PORTWOOD
85 Director Intl Student Office ... Ms. Sabine SAWAY
18 Facilities Manager ... Mr. Troy CRABREE

Clark College (E)

1933 Fort Vancouver Way, Vancouver WA 98663-3598
County: Clark — FICE Identification: 003773
Unit ID: 234933
Telephone: (360) 992-2000 — Carnegie Class: Assoc/MT-VT-Mix Trad/Non
FAX Number: (360) 992-2871 — Calendar System: Quarter
URL: www.clark.edu
Established: 1933 — Annual Undergrad Tuition & Fees (In-State): $3,498
Enrollment: 10,477 — Coed
Affiliation or Control: State — IRS Status: 501(c)3
Highest Offering: Associate Degree
Accreditation: **NW**, ADNUR, DH, MAC

01 President ... Mr. Robert KNIGHT
05 Vice President of Instruction ... Dr. Tim COOK
32 Vice President of Student Affairs ... Mr. William BELDEN
11 Vice President of Admin Services ... Mr. Bob WILLIAMSON
15 Assoc Vice Pres of Human Resources ... Darcy ROURK
45 Assoc VP Planning/Inst Effective ... Ms. Shanda DIEHL
51 Assoc VP Corp & Continuing Educ ... Mr. Kevin WITTE
84 Dir of Enrollment/Registrar ... Ms. Mirranda SAARI
50 Dean Business/Technology ... Ms. Genevieve HOWARD
79 Int Dean Engl/Comm/Hum/Basic Educ ... Ms. Deena GODWIN
76 Int Assoc Dean of Health Science ... Ms. Linda VALENZUELA
83 Dean Social Sciences/Fine Arts ... Mr. Miles JACKSON
52 Director of Dental Hygiene ... Ms. Brenda WALSTEAD
04 Exec Assistant to the President ... Ms. Leigh KENT
41 Director of Athletics ... Mr. Chris JACOBS
16 Associate Director Human Resources ... Ms. Sue WILLIAMS
08 Dir of Library Services ... Vacant
18 Director of Plant Services ... Mr. Tim PETTA
26 Chief Comm & Information Officer ... Mr. Chato HAZELBAKER
36 Director Career/Employment Services ... Ms. Edie BLAKELY
37 Director of Financial Aid ... Ms. Chippi BELLO
10 Director of Business Services ... Ms. Sabra SAND
35 Dir Stdnt Life/Multicult Stdnt Affs ... Ms. Sarah GRUHLER
121 Director of Advising Center ... Mr. John MADUTA
25 Director of Grant Development ... Ms. Julie MADSEN
28 Director of Equity & Diversity ... Ms. Loretta CAPEHEART
19 Director of Security & Safety ... Vacant
85 International Recruitment Manager ... Ms. Jane WALSTER
40 Bookstore Manager ... Ms. Monica KNOWLES
88 Mature Learning & Travel Stds Mgr ... Ms. Tracy REILLY-KELLY
96 Purchasing Manager ... Ms. Lisa NELSON
102 Foundation CEO ... Ms. Lisa GIBERT
105 Information Technology Specialist ... Mr. Chris CONCANNON
29 Director Alumni Relations ... Ms. Vivian MANNING

† Granted candidacy at the Baccalaureate level.

Clover Park Technical College (F)

4500 Steilacoom Boulevard, SW,
Lakewood WA 98499-4004
County: Pierce — FICE Identification: 005752
Unit ID: 234951
Telephone: (253) 589-5800 — Carnegie Class: Bac/Assoc-Assoc Dom
FAX Number: (253) 589-5851 — Calendar System: Quarter
URL: www.cptc.edu
Established: 1942 — Annual Undergrad Tuition & Fees (In-State): $5,865
Enrollment: 3,650 — Coed
Affiliation or Control: State — IRS Status: 501(c)3
Highest Offering: Associate Degree
Accreditation: **NW**, DA, HT, MAC, MLTAD, SURGT

01 President ... Dr. Joyce LOVEDAY
04 Executive Assistant ... Cherie STEELE
05 Int Vice President Instruction ... Mabel EDMONDS
10 Vice President Finance & Admin Svcs ... Larry CLARK
32 VP Student Success ... Scott LATIOLAIS
26 VP Strategic Development ... Tawny DOTSON
15 Human Resources Director ... Vacant
103 Dir of Workforce Development ... Cristeen CROUCHET
13 Dir Information Technology ... Pamela JETER
37 Director Financial Aid ... Wendy JOSEPH
18 Director Facilities Services ... John KANISS
12 Dir Northwest Career/Technical HS ... Loren DAVIS
84 Director of Enrollment Services ... Cynthia MOWRY
96 Purchasing & Supply Specialist ... Kimberly BILLS
27 Marketing/Outreach Coordinator ... Janet HOLM
09 Institutional Researcher ... Dr. Margie TOMSIC
40 Bookstore Coordinator ... Donna KOEHLER
06 Registrar ... Cynthia MOWRY
88 Dean Division B ... Claire KORSCHINOWSKI
88 Dean Division C ... Michelle HILLESLAND
88 Dean Division A ... Tanya SORENSON

† Granted candidacy at the Baccalaureate level.

Columbia Basin College (G)

2600 N 20th Avenue, Pasco WA 99301-3397
County: Franklin — FICE Identification: 003774
Unit ID: 234979
Telephone: (509) 547-0511 — Carnegie Class: Bac/Assoc-Assoc Dom
FAX Number: (509) 546-0404 — Calendar System: Quarter
URL: www.columbiabasin.edu
Established: 1955 — Annual Undergrad Tuition & Fees (In-State): $4,163
Enrollment: 6,422 — Coed
Affiliation or Control: State — IRS Status: 170(c)1
Highest Offering: Baccalaureate
Accreditation: **NW**, ADNUR, DH, EMT, MAC, SURGT

01 President ... Dr. Richard CUMMINS
05 Vice President Instruction ... Dr. Virginia TOMLINSON
10 Vice Pres Administrative Services ... Mr. Tyrone BROOKS
32 Vice President of Student Services ... Ms. Cheryl HOLDEN
15 VP Human Resources/Legal Affairs ... Ms. Camilla GLATT
13 Asst VP Infrastructure Services ... Mr. Brian DEXTER
09 Dean for Organizational Learning ... Dr. Jason ENGLE
49 Dean Arts & Humanities ... Mr. Bill MCKAY
62 Assoc Dean Library Services ... Ms. Melissa MCBURNEY
102 Executive Director Foundation ... Ms. Alissa WATKINS
40 Bookstore Director ... Ms. Debra BRUCE
18 Director of Plant Operations ... Mr. Chuck SCHMIDT
41 Athletic Director ... Mr. Scott ROGERS
26 Communications Director ... Mr. Frank MURRAY
35 Director of Student Activities ... Ms. Alice SCHLEGEL
37 Director Student Financial Aid ... Mr. Ben BEUS
96 Director of Purchasing ... Ms. Sarah BROOKS
06 Associate Registrar ... Ms. Donna KORSTAD

*Community Colleges of Spokane District 17 (H)

501 N Riverpoint Boulevard, Ste 126,
Spokane WA 99217-6000
County: Spokane — FICE Identification: 010784
Telephone: (509) 434-5107 — Carnegie Class: N/A
FAX Number: (509) 434-5120
URL: www.ccs.spokane.edu

01 Chancellor ... Dr. Christine JOHNSON
02 Pres Spokane Community College ... Dr. Ryan CARSTENS
02 Pres Spokane Falls Comm College ... Dr. Darren PITCHER
05 Provost/Chief Learning Officer ... Dr. Nancy FAIR-SZOFRAN
20 Vice President of Learning SCC ... Ms. Jenni MARTIN
20 Vice President of Learning SFCC ... Dr. Andrew FELDMAN
32 VP of Student Services SCC ... Dr. Glen COSBY
32 VP of Student Services SFCC ... Dr. Chrissy DAVIS JONES
10 Chief Financial Officer ... Ms. Lisa HJALTALIN
11 Chief Administration Officer ... Mr. Greg L. STEVENS
13 Chief Information Officer ... Dr. Steve CHEN
26 Public Information Officer ... Ms. Carolyn CASEY
41 Dist Director of Athletics PE/Rec ... Mr. Ken BURRUS
102 Executive Director CCS Foundation ... Ms. Heather BEEBE STEVENS
40 Director College Bookstores ... Ms. Shami R. RUGGLES
18 District Director of Facilities ... Mr. John GILLETTE
103 Dist Dir Wkforce/Cont Ed/Corp Trng ... Ms. Sara SEXTON-JOHNSON
07 District Outreach Coordinator ... Mr. Tim CHURCHILL
96 Purchasing Manager ... Mr. Steve HOPF
106 Dir Online Education/E-learning ... Mr. Patrick MCEACHERN

*Spokane Community College (I)

North 1810 Greene Street, Spokane WA 99217-5499
County: Spokane — FICE Identification: 003793
Unit ID: 236692
Telephone: (509) 533-7000 — Carnegie Class: Assoc/HVT-Mix Trad/Non
FAX Number: (509) 533-8839 — Calendar System: Quarter
URL: www.scc.spokane.edu
Established: 1963 — Annual Undergrad Tuition & Fees (In-State): $3,393
Enrollment: 10,218 — Coed
Affiliation or Control: State — IRS Status: 501(c)3
Highest Offering: Associate Degree
Accreditation: **NW**, ACFEI, ADNUR, CAHIIM, COARC, CVT, DA, DMS, MAC, RAD, SURGT

00 District Chancellor ... Dr. Christine JOHNSON
02 Acting President ... Dr. Kevin BROCKBANK
05 VP of Instruction ... Ms. Jenni MARTIN
32 Vice President of Student Services ... Dr. Glen COSBY
121 Director Student Success & Outreach ... Ms. Lori HUNT
07 Director Admissions & Registration ... Ms. Chantel BLACK
35 Associate Dean Student Development ... Mr. Connan CAMPBELL
51 Acting Dean Adult Basic Education ... Ms. Linda AMES
49 Interim Dean Arts & Sciences ... Ms. Gwendolyn JAMES
50 Dean Business/Hospitality/Info Tech ... Mr. Jeff BROWN
88 Assoc Dean Corrections Education ... Mr. Kevin HOUSE
56 Acting Dean Extended Learning ... Ms. Jaclyn JACOT
76 Dean Health & Environmental Science ... Dr. J.L HENRIKSEN
66 Associate Dean of Nursing ... Dr. Cheri OSLER
75 Dean for Technical Education ... Mr. Dave COX
41 Director Athletics/PE/Recreation ... Mr. Ken BURRUS
09 Sr Dir Inst Effectiveness/Planning ... Dr. Colin ORMSBY
88 Assistant Dean PACE Services ... Ms. Linda AMES
06 Registrar ... Ms. Chantel BLACK
37 Director Financial Aid ... Ms. Tammy ZIBELL
10 Chief Financial Officer ... Ms. Lisa HJALTALIN
40 Director of College Bookstores ... Ms. Shami RUGGLES
11 Chief Administration Officer ... Mr. Greg STEVENS
26 Chief Public Information Officer ... Ms. Carolyn CASEY
30 District Development Officer ... Ms. Heather BEEBE-STEVENS
20 District Provost ... Dr. Nancy FAIR-SZOFRAN
38 Student Counseling Department Chair ... Mr. Bill RAMBO
96 Director of Purchasing ... Mr. Steve HOPF
04 Executive Asst to President ... Ms. Joanne ARSENAULT
13 Chief Info Technology Officer (CIO) ... Dr. Steve CHEN

† Granted candidacy at the Baccalaureate level.

*Spokane Falls Community College (A)

3410 W Fort George Wright Drive,
Spokane WA 99224-5288
County: Spokane — FICE Identification: 009544
Unit ID: 236708
Telephone: (509) 533-3500 — Carnegie Class: Assoc/HT-High Non
FAX Number: (509) 533-3237 — Calendar System: Quarter
URL: www.spokanefalls.edu
Established: 1967 — Annual Undergrad Tuition & Fees (In-State): $3,393
Enrollment: 5,909 — Coed
Affiliation or Control: State — IRS Status: Exempt
Highest Offering: Baccalaureate
Accreditation: NW, OTA, PTAA

02 Acting President .... Dr. Darren PITCHER
04 Exec Asst to the President .... Ms. Jan CARPENTER
05 Vice President of Learning .... Dr. Andrew FELDMAN
32 Acting Vice President of Stdnt Svcs .... Dr. Chrissy DAVIS JONES
81 Dean Computing/Math & Science .... Mr. James BRADY
83 Dean Soc Sci/Acct/Econ/Hum Svcs .... Vacant
79 Dean Humanities .... Dr. Linda BEANE-BOOSE
57 Dean Visual & Performing Arts .... Dr. Bonnie BRUNT
50 Dean Bus/Prof Stds/Workforce .... Ms. Lora SENF
121 Dean Student Support Services .... Vacant
07 Dir Recruit/New Stdnt Entry Center .... Vacant
38 Counseling Deptartment Chair .... Ms. Cynthia VIGIL
37 Director of Financial Aid .... Ms. Marjorie DAVIS
06 Acting Registrar .... Ms. Kari COLLEN
41 Athletic Director .... Mr. Ken BURRUS
19 Security & Safety Supervisor .... Mr. Kenneth DEMELLO
09 Dir Inst Effectiveness/Research .... Ms. Sally JACKSON
15 Chief Human Resources Officer .... Mr. Greg STEVENS
10 Chief Business Officer .... Ms. Lisa HJALTALIN
13 Chief Info Technology Officer (CIO) .... Dr. Steve CHEN
102 Exec Director CCS Foundation .... Mr. Tony HIGLEY
85 Vice Prov Strategic Partnerships .... Dr. Kevin BROCKBANK
08 District Director of Libraries .... Dr. Mary Ann GOODWIN
106 District Director of e-Learning .... Mr. Patrick MCEACHERN
103 Chief Workforce Development Officer .... Mr. Mark MATTKE
26 Public Information Officer .... Ms. Carolyn CASEY
18 Director of Facilities .... Mr. John GILLETTE
96 Director of Purchasing .... Mr. Steve HOPF

Cornish College of the Arts (B)

1000 Lenora Street, Seattle WA 98121-2707
County: King — FICE Identification: 012315
Unit ID: 235024
Telephone: (206) 726-5151 — Carnegie Class: Spec-4-yr-Arts
FAX Number: (206) 720-1011 — Calendar System: Semester
URL: www.cornish.edu
Established: 1914 — Annual Undergrad Tuition & Fees: $38,820
Enrollment: 724 — Coed
Affiliation or Control: Independent Non-Profit — IRS Status: 501(c)3
Highest Offering: Baccalaureate
Accreditation: NW, ART

01 Interim President .... Mr. Chris KEVORKIAN
05 Interim Provost .... Ms. Star RUSH
111 VP Institutional Advancement .... Ms. Anne DERIEUX
10 Chief Financial Officer .... Ms. Diane HAGER
84 VP of Enrollment Management .... Mr. Ryan O'MEALEY
15 VP of Human Resources .... Mr. Joe CANFIELD
32 Dean of Student Life .... Vacant
06 Dean of Academic Services/Registrar .... Ms. Adrienne M. BOLYARD
13 Director of Information Technology .... Mr. Mark LEDESMA
21 Controller .... Ms. Tina CHAMBERLAIN
08 Director of Library Services .... Ms. Hollis NEAR
07 Director of Admissions .... Ms. Sharron STARLING
26 Director of Communications .... Ms. Rosemary JONES
19 Dir of Operations & Security .... Mr. Brandon BIRD
38 Director Student Counseling .... Ms. Lori KORSHORK
37 Asst Director of Financial Aid .... Ms. Margaret MURRAY

DigiPen Institute of Technology (C)

9931 Willows Road, NE, Redmond WA 98052
County: King — FICE Identification: 037243
Unit ID: 443410
Telephone: (425) 558-0299 — Carnegie Class: Bac-Diverse
FAX Number: (425) 558-0378 — Calendar System: Semester
URL: www.digipen.edu
Established: 1988 — Annual Undergrad Tuition & Fees: $29,000
Enrollment: 1,076 — Coed
Affiliation or Control: Proprietary — IRS Status: Proprietary
Highest Offering: Master's
Accreditation: ACCSC, ENG

01 President .... Mr. Claude COMAIR
32 Sr VP Student & External Affairs .... Ms. Angela KUGLER
35 Dean of Students .... Mr. Marshall TRAVERSE
07 Director of Admissions .... Ms. Danial POWERS
37 Director Student Financial Aid .... Ms. Trinity HUTTNER

Eastern Washington University (D)

526 5th Street, Cheney WA 99004-1619
County: Spokane — FICE Identification: 003775
Unit ID: 235097
Telephone: (509) 359-6200 — Carnegie Class: Masters/L
FAX Number: (509) 359-6927 — Calendar System: Quarter
URL: www.ewu.edu
Established: 1882 — Annual Undergrad Tuition & Fees (In-State): $6,951
Enrollment: 12,361 — Coed
Affiliation or Control: State — IRS Status: 501(c)3
Highest Offering: Doctorate
Accreditation: NW, CAATE, CACREP, CS, DH, ENG, ENGT, MUS, NRPA, OT, PLNG, PTA, SP, SPAA, SW

01 President .... Dr. Mary CULLINAN
05 Provost/VP of Academic Affairs .... Dr. Scott GORDON
10 Vice President for Business/Finance .... Ms. Mary VOVES
32 Vice President for Student Affairs .... Ms. Stacey MORGAN FOSTER
30 Vice President of Advancement .... Mr. Michael WESTFALL
13 VP Info Technology/CIO .... Dr. Gary PRATT
20 Vice Prov Academic Admin .... Dr. Linda KIEFFER
88 Vice Prov Acad Plng/Grants & Res .... Dr. Colin ORMSBY
88 Vice Prov Undergrad & Stdnt Success .... Dr. Chuck LOPEZ
08 Dean of Libraries .... Dr. Suzanne MILTON
06 Registrar .... Ms. Angela ANDERSON
41 Director Intercollegiate Athletics .... Mr. William CHAVES
21 Assoc VP Finance/Chief Fin Officer .... Ms. Toni HABEGGER
18 Assoc Vice Pres for Facilities .... Mr. Shawn KING
84 Assoc Vice Pres Enrollment Mgmt .... Dr. Neil WOOLF
86 Asst Dir of Government Affairs .... Ms. Alicia KINNE-CLAWSON
36 Asst VP Student Svcs/Dir Career Dev .... Ms. Virginia (Gini) HINCH
15 AVP of Human Resources .... Ms. Deborah DANNER
101 Exec Assistant to the President/BOT .... Ms. Marilyn DREIS
100 Chief of Staff .... Ms. Angela JONES
92 Director of University Honors .... Dr. Dana ELDER
07 Director of Admissions .... Ms. Cathy SLEETH
37 Director of Fin Aid & Scholarships .... Mr. Bruce DEFRATES
40 Bookstore Director .... Ms. Devon TINKER
51 Dir of Continuing Education & RS .... Vacant
06 Director of Registration & Records .... Ms. Debra FOCKLER
58 Vice Provost/Graduate Research .... Dr. Colin ORMSBY
29 Director of Alumni Advancement .... Ms. Lisa POPLAWSKI
109 Assoc VP/Business Auxiliary Svcs .... Ms. LeeAnn CASE
39 Sr Director Housing/Residence Life .... Mr. Josh ASHCROFT
38 Director Counseling & Psych Svcs .... Dr. Robert QUACKENBUSH
19 Director Public Safety/Chief Police .... Chief Timothy L. WALTERS
27 Director of Media Relations .... Mr. David MEANY
22 Dir Equal Opp/Affirm Action Coord .... Ms. Gayla THOMAS
50 Int Dean Business & Public Admin .... Dr. Danny ARNOLD
49 Dean College Arts/Letters/Education .... Dr. Roy SONNEMA
83 Int Dean Col Soc/Behav Sci/Soc Work .... Dr. Jonathan ANDERSON
81 Dean Col Science/Technology/Math .... Dr. David BOWMAN
66 Dean Health Science & Public Health .... Dr. Laureen O'HANLON
35 Assoc VP/Dean of Student Life .... Dr. Amy JOHNSON
09 Assoc Director/Institutional Rsrch .... Ms. Bamby FIELDS
44 Assoc Director of Annual Giving .... Ms. Pat SPANJER
26 Dir Marketing/Communications .... Ms. Teresa CONWAY
104 Dir Office of Global Initiatives .... Ms. Catherine DIXON
106 Exec Director E-Learning .... Mr. Ben MEREDITH
25 Exec Dir Grants & Research Dev .... Ms. Ruth GALM

Edmonds Community College (E)

20000 68th Avenue W, Lynnwood WA 98036-5999
County: Snohomish — FICE Identification: 005001
Unit ID: 235103
Telephone: (425) 640-1459 — Carnegie Class: Assoc/MT-VT-High Non
FAX Number: (425) 771-3366 — Calendar System: Quarter
URL: www.edcc.edu
Established: 1967 — Annual Undergrad Tuition & Fees (In-State): $3,756
Enrollment: 8,571 — Coed
Affiliation or Control: State — IRS Status: 501(c)3
Highest Offering: Associate Degree
Accreditation: NW, CA, CONST

01 President .... Dr. Jean HERNANDEZ
05 Exec Vice President Instruction .... Dr. Charlie CRAWFORD
10 Vice Pres Finance & Operations .... Mr. Kevin MCKAY
30 Vice Pres Col Relations/Advancement .... Dr. Tonya DRAKE
15 AVP HR & Title IX Compliance .... Mr. Dennis CURRAN
32 Vice President Student Services .... Ms. Christina CASTORENA
103 VP Workforce Development/Training .... Dr. Terry COX
85 Vice Pres International Education .... Mr. David CORDELL
84 Dean Student Enroll/Financial Svcs .... Mr. Saovra EAR
35 Dean Student Life/Development .... Mr. Jorge DE LA TORRE
04 Executive Asst to the President .... Ms. Patty MICHAJLA
36 Dean Student Success/Retention .... Dr. Steve WOODARD
102 Director College Foundation .... Mr. Brad THOMAS
88 Director Advising .... Ms. Olla IBRAHIM
25 Exec Director Grants & Research .... Ms. Cat CAROTHERS
26 Dir Marketing/Public Information .... Ms. Marisa PIERCE
13 Director Information Technology .... Ms. Eva SMITH
18 Dir Facilities/Planning/Operations .... Ms. Stephanie TEACHMAN
41 Athletic Director .... Mr. Spencer STARK
85 Dir International Student Services .... Ms. Lisa THOMPSON
09 Institutional Researcher .... Ms. Pat HUFFMAN
28 Assoc VP Equity & Inclusion .... Dr. Yvonne TERRELL-POWELL
108 Exec Dir Inst Effect/Strategic Plng .... Mr. James MULIK
96 Director of Finance .... Ms. Janie BARNETT-PARKER
27 Marketing Manager .... Vacant
19 Interim Director Safety & Security .... Mr. Vincent LIVINGSTON
06 Dir Enrollment Svcs/Registrar .... Ms. Christina RUSS
21 Director of Accounting .... Ms. Geni TEAGUE
102 Executive Director EDCC Foundation .... Mr. Brad THOMAS
37 Director Financial Aid .... Ms. MiChelle THORSEN
38 Dir Counseling & Resource Center .... Ms. Jessica BURWELL

† Granted candidacy at the Baccalaureate level.

Everett Community College (F)

2000 Tower Street, Everett WA 98201-1390
County: Snohomish — FICE Identification: 003776
Unit ID: 235149
Telephone: (425) 388-9100 — Carnegie Class: Assoc/MT-VT-High Non
FAX Number: (425) 388-9129 — Calendar System: Quarter
URL: www.everettcc.edu
Established: 1941 — Annual Undergrad Tuition & Fees (In-State): $3,648
Enrollment: 7,505 — Coed
Affiliation or Control: State — IRS Status: 501(c)3
Highest Offering: Associate Degree
Accreditation: NW, ADNUR, MAC

01 President .... Dr. David BEYER
04 Sr Exec Asst to President .... Ms. Melissa GERAGHTY
05 Int EVP Instruction/Student Svcs .... Dr. Tammy FRANKLAND
111 Vice Pres of College Advancement .... Dr. John OLSON
10 Vice Pres of Administrative Svcs .... Ms. Jennifer L. HOWARD
26 Vice Pres of College Services .... Mr. Patrick SISNEROS
60 Dean Communication/Social Sciences .... Mr. Eugene MCAVOY
32 Dean of Student Development .... Mr. Anthony WILLIAMS
81 Dean of Math & Science .... Mr. Al FRIEDMAN
62 Dean of Arts & Learning Resources .... Ms. Jeanne LEADER
76 Dean Health Sciences/Public Safety .... Mr. Jason SMITH
53 Dean of Basic & Adult Education .... Ms. Katie JENSEN
28 Chief Diversity & Equity Officer .... Ms. Maria PENA
51 Director Continuing Education .... Ms. Karen LANDRY
84 Dean Enrollment/Student Finan Svcs .... Ms. Laurie FRANKLIN
50 Dean of Business & Applied Tech .... Mr. Ryan DAVIS
19 Dir of Campus Safety & Security .... Mr. Charles MACKLIN
88 Vice Pres of Corporate Training .... Mr. John B. BONNER
09 Director Institutional Research .... Mr. Sean GEHRKE
41 Director of Athletics .... Mr. Garet STUDER
40 Director of Bookstore .... Ms. Rachael WATSON
22 Dir Center for Disability Services .... Vacant

The Evergreen State College (G)

2700 Evergreen Parkway, NW, Olympia WA 98505-0005
County: Thurston — FICE Identification: 008155
Unit ID: 235167
Telephone: (360) 867-6000 — Carnegie Class: Masters/M
FAX Number: N/A — Calendar System: Quarter
URL: www.evergreen.edu
Established: 1967 — Annual Undergrad Tuition & Fees (In-State): $7,414
Enrollment: 4,190 — Coed
Affiliation or Control: State — IRS Status: 501(c)3
Highest Offering: Master's
Accreditation: NW

01 President .... Dr. George S. BRIDGES
05 VP Academic Affairs & Provost .... Dr. Jennifer DRAKE
32 Vice President Student Affairs .... Dr. Wendy ENDRESS
10 Vice President Finance/Admin .... Dr. John HURLEY
111 Vice President College Advancement .... Ms. Amanda WALKER
26 Vice President College Relations .... Ms. Sandy KAISER
84 Assoc Vice Pres for Enrollment Mgmt .... Mr. Steve HUNTER
15 Assoc Vice Pres for Human Resources .... Ms. Laurel UZNANSKI
08 Dean of Library Services .... Mr. Greg MULLINS
121 Dir of Academic and Career Advising .... Ms. Kitty JONES
100 Chief of Staff/Secretary to BOT .... Mr. John CARMICHAEL
22 Affirm Act/Equal Opp Officer .... Ms. Lorie MASTIN
13 Director Computing/Communications .... Mr. Antonio ALFONSO
37 Director of Financial Aid .... Ms. Tracy HALL
06 Registrar .... Ms. Elaine HAYASHI-PETERSEN
09 Director of Institutional Research .... Ms. Laura COGHLAN
18 Director of Facilities .... Ms. Jeanne RYNNE
21 Director of Business Services .... Mr. Dave KOHLER
38 Dir Counseling & Health Services .... Ms. Elizabeth MCHUGH
96 Purchasing and Contracts Manager .... Mr. Brant EDDY
07 Director of Admissions .... Mr. Eric PEDERSEN
88 Director of Sustainability .... Mr. Scott MORGAN

Faith International University (H)

3504 N Pearl Street, Tacoma WA 98407-2607
County: Pierce — FICE Identification: 036894
Unit ID: 443049
Telephone: (253) 752-2020 — Carnegie Class: Spec-4-yr-Faith
FAX Number: (253) 759-1790 — Calendar System: Quarter
URL: www.faithseminary.edu
Established: 1969 — Annual Undergrad Tuition & Fees: $7,840
Enrollment: 370 — Coed
Affiliation or Control: Interdenominational — IRS Status: 501(c)3
Highest Offering: Doctorate
Accreditation: TRACS

01 President .... Dr. Michael J. ADAMS
05 Vice Pres Academic Affs/Provost .... Dr. H. Wayne HOUSE
104 VP Intl Affs/Dean Korean Division .... Dr. Kyu H. LEE
11 VP Administrative Affs/Registrar .... Mr. John WHEELER
88 Admin Dean Korean Division .... Dr. Miae LEE
10 Chief Financial Officer .... Dr. Douglas COLLIER
07 Director of Admissions .... Ms. Karen BURNWORTH
08 Director Library Services .... Dr. Timothy HYUN
32 Director Student Services .... Ms. Nor BOICE
04 Exec Administrative Assistant .... Ms. Kimberly ADAMS
06 Registrar .... Ms. Mary VELONI

Gonzaga University (A)

502 East Boone Avenue, Spokane WA 99258-0102
County: Spokane FICE Identification: 003778
Unit ID: 235316
Telephone: (800) 986-9585 Carnegie Class: Masters/L
FAX Number: (509) 313-5718 Calendar System: Semester
URL: www.gonzaga.edu
Established: 1887 Annual Undergrad Tuition & Fees: $39,730
Enrollment: 7,491 Coed
Affiliation or Control: Roman Catholic IRS Status: 501(c)3
Highest Offering: Doctorate
Accreditation: NW, ANEST, CACREP, CAEPN, CEA, CS, ENG, LAW, MUS, NURSE

01 President ... Dr. Thayne M. MCCULLOH
100 Chief of Staff ... Mr. John SKLUT
05 Academic Vice President ... Dr. Patricia OCONNELL KILLEN
10 Vice President for Finance ... Mr. Charles J. MURPHY
88 VP for Mission & Ministry ... Fr. Patrick LEE, SJ
32 VP for Student Development ... Dr. Judith BIGGS GARBUIO
111 VP for University Advancement ... Mr. Joe POSS
45 VP for Policy/Planning & Admin ... Vacant
20 Assoc Academic Vice President ... Dr. Ron LARGE
28 Assoc AVP/Chief Diversity Officer ... Dr. Raymond REYES
06 Assoc Academic Vice Pres/Registrar ... Ms. Jolanta A. WEBER
15 Asst Vice President Human Resources ... Mr. Kirk WOOD-GAINES
26 Associate VP for Marketing/Comm ... Mr. Dave SONNTAG
88 Assistant VP for Mission ... Fr. Jim VOISS, SJ
36 Asst VP for Student Devel/Career ... Mr. O. Ray ANGLE
88 Vice President for University ... Fr. Frank E. CASE, SJ
07 Dean of Admission ... Ms. Julie A. MCCULLOH
88 Asst VP Student Well Being/Healthy ... Mr. Eric BALDWIN
08 Dean of Library Services ... Mr. Paul J. BRACKE
37 Dean of Student Finance Services ... Mr. James WHITE
13 Chief Information Officer ... Mr. Borre ULRICHSEN
26 Director Cmty/Public Relations ... Ms. Mary Joan HAHN
29 Director of Engagement ... Ms. Kara HERTZ
36 Director Career Center ... Dr. Mary HEITKEMPER
38 Director of Counseling Services ... Dr. Fernando ORITZ
49 Dean Arts & Sciences ... Dr. Elisabeth MERMANN-JOZWIAK
50 Dean School of Business ... Dr. Kenneth ANDERSON
53 Dean of Education ... Dr. Vincent C. ALFONSO
54 Dean of Engineering & Applied Scien ... Dr. Steve SILLIMAN
61 Dean of Law ... Ms. Jane KORN
09 Director of Institutional Research ... Mr. Maxwell KWENDA
41 Director of Athletics ... Mr. Michael L. ROTH
43 General Counsel ... Ms. Maureen MCGUIRE
18 Director Plant Services ... Mr. Kenneth R. SAMMONS
92 Director Honors Program ... Rev. Tim R. CLANCY, SJ
96 Director Purchasing ... Mr. Steve M. LUNDEN
104 Director Study Abroad ... Mr. Richard O. MENARD
25 Director Sponsored Research & Pgm ... Dr. Joann WAITE
108 Faculty Director of Assessment ... Dr. Patrick T. MCCORMICK
66 Interim Dean of Nurs & Human Phys ... Dr. Lin MURPHY
20 Asst AVP for Global Engagement ... Dr. Joseph J. KINSELLA
35 Dean of Student Engagement ... Mr. Matt LAMSMA
106 Dean of Virtual Campus ... Dr. Michael CAREY
71 Director of Gonzaga-In-Florence ... Dr. Jason HOUSTON
100 Faculty Advisor to the President ... Dr. Ellen M. MACCARONE
21 Assoc Vice President of Finance ... Mr. Joe SMITH
88 Controller ... Ms. Deena PRESNELL
88 Sr Publications Ed & Content Strat ... Ms. Kathryn VANSKIKE
19 Director Security/Safety ... Mr. Scott SNIDER
22 Dir Affirmative Action/EEO ... Ms. Chris PURVIANCE
39 Director Student Housing ... Mr. Dennis COLESTOCK
04 Executive Asst to President ... Ms. Julia BJORDAHL
101 Secretary of the Institution/Board ... Ms. Maureen MCGUIRE
44 Director of Annual Giving ... Ms. Stephanie ROCKWELL

Grays Harbor College (B)

1620 Edward P. Smith Drive, Aberdeen WA 98520-7500
County: Grays Harbor FICE Identification: 003779
Unit ID: 235334
Telephone: (360) 532-9020 Carnegie Class: Assoc/HVT-High Non
FAX Number: (360) 538-4299 Calendar System: Quarter
URL: www.ghc.edu
Established: 1930 Annual Undergrad Tuition & Fees (In-District): $3,746
Enrollment: 1,804 Coed
Affiliation or Control: State/Local IRS Status: 501(c)3
Highest Offering: Associate Degree
Accreditation: NW, ADNUR

01 President ... Dr. James MINKLER
04 Senior Admin Assistant to President ... Ms. Sandra ZELASKO
05 Vice President for Instruction ... Dr. Emily LARDNER
10 Chief Financial Officer ... Mr. Nicholas LUTES
32 Vice President for Student Services ... Mr. Jason HOSENEY
13 Chief Exec Information Technology ... Mr. Andrew GLASS
75 Dean Vocational Instruction ... Vacant
35 Assoc Dean for Student Services ... Mr. Jerad SORBER
08 Assoc Dean Library/Media Services ... Mr. Ahniwa FERRARI
07 Assoc Dean of Admissions ... Vacant
15 Chief Human Resources Officer ... Mr. Darrin JONES
37 Director Student Financial Aid ... Ms. Stacey SAVINO
18 Dir Campus Operations/Sfty/Security ... Mr. Lance JAMES
38 Director of Counseling ... Vacant
30 Chief Development Officer ... Ms. Lisa SMITH
26 Director Public Relations ... Ms. Jane F. GOLDBERG
09 Chief Instl Effect/Research/Plng ... Ms. Kristy ANDERSON
06 Registrar ... Mr. Gerad SORBER
41 Athletic Director ... Mr. Tom SUTERA
106 Dir Online Education/E-Learning ... Mr. James UMPHRES

† Granted candidacy at the Baccalaureate level.

Green River College (C)

12401 SE 320th Street, Auburn WA 98092-3699
County: King FICE Identification: 003780
Unit ID: 235343
Telephone: (253) 288-3340 Carnegie Class: Bac/Assoc-Assoc Dom
FAX Number: (253) 288-3470 Calendar System: Quarter
URL: www.greenriver.edu
Established: 1965 Annual Undergrad Tuition & Fees (In-State): $4,597
Enrollment: 8,153 Coed
Affiliation or Control: State IRS Status: 501(c)3
Highest Offering: Baccalaureate
Accreditation: NW, OTA, PTAA

01 President ... Dr. Suzanne JOHNSON
05 Int Vice Pres of Instruction ... Dr. Rebecca WILLIAMSON
13 Exec Dir of Information Technology ... Camella MORGAN
10 Vice President Business Affairs ... Shirley BEAN
15 Vice President for Human Resources ... Marshall SAMPSON
32 Vice President of Student Services . Dr. Deborah CASEY POWELL
56 VP Intl Programs/Extended Learning ... Wendy STEWART
75 Int Dn Prof/Tech Ed/Trades & Tech ... Barry ROBINSON
72 Int Dn Prof/Tech Ed/Trades & Tech ... Timm LOVITT
49 Dean Fine Arts/Math/Soc Sci/Library ... Christie GILLILAND
84 Dean of Enrollment & Completion ... David LARSEN
06 Director of Enrollment Services ... Denise BENNATTS
37 Director of Financial Aid ... Teresa BUCHMANN
30 Exec Director of Development/Found ... George FRASIER
114 Director of Budget ... Janee SOMMERFELD
21 Senior Director of Financial Svcs ... Micki CHIKWINYA
18 Director of Facilities ... Robert OLSON
26 Exec Director of College Relations ... Allison FRIEDLY
51 Dean for Branch Campuses & CE ... Leslie MOORE
09 Int Director of Planning & Research ... Fia ELIASSON-CREEK
28 Dir Diversity/Equity & Inclusion ... Marwa ALMUSAWI
96 Director of Procurement ... Laura LOWE
19 Director of Campus Safety ... Derek RONNFELDT
41 Director Athletics ... Bob KICKNER
04 Executive Assistant to President ... Suzanne MCCUDDEN

Heritage University (D)

3240 Fort Road, Toppenish WA 98948-9599
County: Yakima FICE Identification: 003777
Unit ID: 235422
Telephone: (509) 865-8500 Carnegie Class: Masters/S
FAX Number: (509) 865-7976 Calendar System: Semester
URL: www.heritage.edu
Established: 1982 Annual Undergrad Tuition & Fees: $19,122
Enrollment: 1,219 Coed
Affiliation or Control: Independent Non-Profit IRS Status: 501(c)3
Highest Offering: Master's
Accreditation: NW, #ARCPA, MT, SW

01 President ... Dr. Andrew C. SUND
05 Provost/VP Academic Affairs ... Dr. Laurie FATHE
32 VP Student Affairs & Enrollment ... Dr. Celestino LIMAS
100 Chief of Staff ... Ms. Veronica NARANJO
30 VP Advancement & Marketing ... Mr. David WISE
84 Assoc VP Enrollment Management ... Vacant
06 Registrar ... Mr. Luis GUTIERREZ
53 Dean of Education & Psychology ... Ms. Merrilou HARRISON
18 Director Physical Plant/Maintenance ... Mr. Jeff BEEHLER
37 Director of Financial Aid ... Ilda MEZA
08 Library Director ... Mr. Daniel LIESTMAN
13 VP Information Technology/CIO ... Mr. Jim BUSH
07 Director of Recruitment ... Ms. Erica TAIT
26 Communications Officer ... Ms. Bonnie HUGHES
04 Manager President's Office ... Ms. Betty J. SAMPSON
09 Director of Institutional Research ... Vacant
15 Director Human Resources ... Ms. Veronica NARANJO
49 Dean Arts & Sciences ... Dr. Kazuhiro SONODA
35 Asst VP Student Affairs ... Ms. Melissa HILL
21 Controller ... Mr. Mark MCNABB
29 Director of Alumni Relations ... Vacant

Highline College (E)

PO Box 98000, 2400 S 240th Street,
Des Moines WA 98198-9800
County: King FICE Identification: 003781
Unit ID: 235431
Telephone: (206) 878-3710 Carnegie Class: Bac/Assoc-Assoc Dom
FAX Number: (206) 870-3779 Calendar System: Quarter
URL: www.highline.edu
Established: 1961 Annual Undergrad Tuition & Fees (In-State): $3,851
Enrollment: 6,560 Coed
Affiliation or Control: State IRS Status: 501(c)3
Highest Offering: Baccalaureate
Accreditation: NW, ADNUR, COARC, MAC

01 President ... Dr. Jack BERMINGHAM
11 Vice Pres Administrative Services ... Mr. Michael PHAM
05 Vice Pres for Academic Affairs ... Mr. Jeff WAGNITZ
30 VP Inst Advancement/Cmty Rels ... Dr. Lisa SKARI
32 Vice Pres for Student Services ... Ms. Toni CASTRO
20 Dean of Instruction-Vocational ... Ms. Alice MADSEN
20 Dean of Instruction-Academics ... Dr. Rolita EZEONU
24 Dean Instructional Resources ... Ms. Monica LUCE
35 Assoc Dean CLS/Engage/Assessment ... Mr. Jonathan BROWN
31 Exec Dir Community Education ... Ms. Judy PERRY
84 Assoc Dean Enrollment Services ... Ms. Lorraine ODOM
26 Director Communications & Marketing ... Mr. Tony JOHNSON
15 Exec Director of Human Resources ... Ms. Sue WILLIAMSON
10 Director Financial Services ... Ms. Cathy CARTWRIGHT
13 Executive Director and CIO ... Mr. Tim WRYE
18 Director Facilities & Operations ... Mr. Barry HOLLDORF
19 Dir Safety/Sec & Emergency Manager ... Mr. David MENKE
41 Director Athletics ... Mr. John DUNN
30 Director Development/Foundation ... Ms. Sharon CUPP
09 Director Institutional Research ... Ms. Emily COATES
40 Bookstore Manager ... Ms. Kristi DOPP
96 Manager of Purchasing ... Ms. Dianna THIELE
06 Registrar ... Ms. Lorraine ODOM
07 Director of Admissions ... Ms. L. Michelle KUWASAKI
85 Dir International Student Program ... Ms. Mariko FUJIWARA

Lake Washington Institute of Technology (F)

11605 132nd Avenue NE, Kirkland WA 98034-8506
County: King FICE Identification: 005373
Unit ID: 235699
Telephone: (425) 739-8100 Carnegie Class: Bac/Assoc-Assoc Dom
FAX Number: (425) 739-8299 Calendar System: Quarter
URL: www.lwtech.edu
Established: 1949 Annual Undergrad Tuition & Fees (In-State): $4,059
Enrollment: 3,531 Coed
Affiliation or Control: State IRS Status: 170(c)1
Highest Offering: Baccalaureate
Accreditation: NW, ACFEI, ADNUR, DA, DH, FUSER, MAC, OTA, PTAA

01 President ... Dr. Amy M. MORRISON GOINGS
04 Exec Assistant to the President ... Ms. Heather DEGRAW
32 VP Student Services ... Dr. Ruby HAYDEN
05 VP of Instruction ... Dr. Elliot STERN
10 VP Administrative Services ... Mr. Bill THOMAS
20 Dean of Instruction ... Mr. Douglas J. EMORY
86 Exec Dir Legislative & Ext Rels ... Ms. Terry BYINGTON
13 Chief Information Officer ... Mr. Christopher WEEKS
30 Exec Director Development ... Ms. Elisabeth SORENSEN
15 Exec Director Human Resources ... Ms. Melissa LAMY
88 Spec Asst to Pres College Advance ... Ms. Andrea I. OLSON
76 Dean Instruction Allied Health ... Ms. Jamilyn PENN
72 Dean Design/IT/BAS Development ... Dr. Suzanne AMES
89 Principal/Dean High School Programs ... Dr. Kim INFINGER
08 Library Program Coordinator ... Ms. Cheyenne M. RODUIN
26 Director Communications/Marketing ... Ms. Leslie SHATTUCK
76 Dir Phys Therapist Assistant Pgm ... Ms. Molly VERSCHUYL
88 Director Funeral Services ... Ms. Jamye CAMERON
66 Director of Nursing Program ... Ms. Chitra SHARIFIAN
104 Director International Programs ... Ms. Sarah ROSS
106 Director of eLearning ... Ms. Rhonda DEWITT
18 Director Facilities & Operations ... Mr. Tim WHEELER
37 Director Financial Aid ... Mr. Bill CHANEY
103 Director Workforce Development ... Ms. Demetra BIROS
25 Dir of Research & Grant Development ... Ms. Cathy COPELAND
07 Director Admissions & Outreach ... Ms. Christina HARTER
88 Assoc Dean TRiO Student Spprt Svcs ... Dr. Patricia HUNTER
21 Director of Financial Services ... Mr. Xieng LIM
88 Director Student Programs ... Ms. Sheila WALTON
109 Manager Food Service Operations ... Mr. Joe TREVINO
96 Manager Purchasing Service ... Mr. Gordy FUNAI
105 Website/Digital Content Specialist ... Ms. Alisa SHTROMBERG
40 Manager Bookstore ... Mr. Russ MERKOW
19 Director Security/Safety ... Mr. Anthony BOWERS
84 Director Enrollment Services ... Ms. Larisa AKSELRUD
35 Director Student Development ... Ms. Katie VIOLA
09 Director Research & Grants ... Ms. Cathy COPELAND
124 Student Devel/Retention Counselor ... Ms. Neera MEHTA

Lower Columbia College (G)

PO Box 3010, Longview WA 98632-0310
County: Cowlitz FICE Identification: 003782
Unit ID: 235750
Telephone: (360) 442-2311 Carnegie Class: Assoc/HVT-High Non
FAX Number: (360) 442-2109 Calendar System: Quarter
URL: www.lowercolumbia.edu
Established: 1934 Annual Undergrad Tuition & Fees (In-State): $4,131
Enrollment: 2,969 Coed
Affiliation or Control: State IRS Status: 170(c)1
Highest Offering: Associate Degree
Accreditation: NW, ADNUR, MAC

01 President ... Mr. Christopher C. BAILEY
05 Vice President of Instruction ... Mr. Brendan GLASER
11 Vice President Administrative Svcs ... Mr. Nolan WHEELER
32 Vice President of Student Services ... Ms. Sue ORCHARD
103 Int Dean Workforce/Continuing Educ ... Ms. Tamra BELL
20 Dean Instructional Programs ... Mr. Kyle HAMMON
76 Executive Dean Allied Health/Nurse ... Ms. Karen JOINER
09 Director Effectiveness & Marketing ... Ms. Wendy HALL
18 Director of Campus Services ... Mr. Richard HAMILTON
102 Director of Foundation ... Ms. Kendra SPRAGUE
41 Athletic Director ... Mr. Kirc J. ROLAND
21 Controller ... Ms. Kelley WEST
15 Director of Personnel Services ... Ms. Kendra SPRAGUE
37 Financial Aid Officer ... Ms. Marisa GEIER
08 Associate Dean Resource Svcs ... Ms. Melinda HARBAUGH

13 Director of Information Technology ... Mr. Brandon RAY
40 Director of Bookstore ... Mr. Cliff HICKS
07 Director Admissions/Registrar ... Ms. Nichole SEROSHEK
10 Chief Business Officer ... Mr. Nolan WHEELER
96 Director of Purchasing ... Mr. Rod RAMER
04 Executive Assistant ... Ms. Linda J. CLARK
06 Registrar ... Ms. Nichole SEROSHEK
106 Dir Online Education/E-learning ... Ms. Sarah GRIFFITH
19 Director Security/Safety ... Mr. Jason ARROWSMITH
29 Director Alumni Relations ... Ms. Sheila BURGIN
108 Director Institutional Assessment ... Ms. Wendy HALL

Moody Bible Institute-Spokane (A)

611 E Indiana Avenue, Spokane WA 99207
Telephone: (509) 570-5900 Identification: 770082
Accreditation: &NH

† Branch campus of Moody Bible Institute, Chicago, IL

Northwest College of Art & Design (NCAD) (B)

16301 Creative Drive NE, Poulsbo WA 98370-8651
County: Kitsap FICE Identification: 026021
Unit ID: 377546
Telephone: (360) 779-9993 Carnegie Class: Spec-4-yr-Arts
FAX Number: (360) 779-9933 Calendar System: Semester
URL: www.ncad.edu
Established: 1982 Annual Undergrad Tuition & Fees: $19,075
Enrollment: 100 Coed
Affiliation or Control: Proprietary IRS Status: Proprietary
Highest Offering: Baccalaureate
Accreditation: ACCSC

01 President ... Craig FREEMAN
05 Director of Education ... Julius FINLEY
11 Director of Operations ... Kim PERIGARD
06 Registrar ... Reginald WEST
13 IT Admin ... Skye CARLSON
07 Admissions Representative ... Cardell SIMMONS
37 Financial Aid ... Julie PERIGARD
08 Head Librarian ... Tiffany SUDELA

Northwest Indian College (C)

2522 Kwina Road, Bellingham WA 98226-9278
County: Whatcom FICE Identification: 021800
Unit ID: 380377
Telephone: (360) 676-2772 Carnegie Class: Tribal
FAX Number: (360) 738-0136 Calendar System: Quarter
URL: www.nwic.edu
Established: 1978 Annual Undergrad Tuition & Fees: $4,407
Enrollment: 641 Coed
Affiliation or Control: Tribal Control IRS Status: 501(c)3
Highest Offering: Baccalaureate
Accreditation: NW

01 President ... Dr. Justin GUILLORY
10 Chief Financial Officer ... Mr. Steve ZAWOYSKY
05 Vice Pres Instruction/Student Svcs ... Ms. Carole RAVE
11 Vice Pres Campus Development ... Mr. David OREIRO
46 VP for Research/Sponsored Programs ... Ms. Barbara ROBERTS
04 Exec Assistant to the President ... Ms. Frances SELLARS
106 Dean of Academic/Distant Learning ... Ms. Bernice PORTERVINT
32 Dean of Student Life ... Ms. Victoria RETASKET
37 Asc Dn Students/Fin Aid Dir/Admiss ... Ms. Shayna NISHIYAMA
13 IS Director ... Mr. Michael JAMES
08 Library Director ... Ms. Valerie MCBETH
06 Registrar ... Ms. Patricia CUEVA
09 Director of Institutional Research ... Ms. Carmen BLAND
15 Director Human Resources ... Ms. Linda SCHNELL
18 Director of Facilities Maintenance ... Mr. Jon DAVIS
19 Security Manager ... Ms. Lavonne BALLEW
30 Director of NWIC Foundation ... Mr. Greg MASTEN
41 Athletic Director ... Ms. Krista MAHLE
96 Purchasing Manager ... Mr. Charlie ROBERTS
26 Chief Public Relations/Marketing ... Ms. Barbara LEWIS

Northwest School of Wooden Boatbuilding (D)

42 N Water Street, Port Hadlock WA 98339-8706
County: Jefferson FICE Identification: 041550
Unit ID: 458140
Telephone: (360) 385-4948 Carnegie Class: Spec 2-yr-Tech
FAX Number: (360) 385-5089 Calendar System: Other
URL: www.nwswb.edu
Established: 1981 Annual Undergrad Tuition & Fees: $14,550
Enrollment: 62 Coed
Affiliation or Control: Independent Non-Profit IRS Status: 501(c)3
Highest Offering: Associate Degree
Accreditation: ACCSC

01 Executive Director ... Ms. Betsy DAVIS

Northwest University (E)

PO Box 579, Kirkland WA 98083-0579
County: King FICE Identification: 003783
Unit ID: 236133
Telephone: (425) 822-8266 Carnegie Class: Masters/M
FAX Number: (425) 889-5224 Calendar System: Semester
URL: www.northwestu.edu
Established: 1934 Annual Undergrad Tuition & Fees: $29,200
Enrollment: 1,236 Coed
Affiliation or Control: Assemblies Of God Church IRS Status: 501(c)3
Highest Offering: Doctorate
Accreditation: NW, ACBSP, NURSE

01 President ... Dr. Joseph CASTLEBERRY
05 Provost ... Dr. Jim HEUGEL
10 Chief Financial Officer ... Mr. John JORDAN
111 Senior VP of Advancement ... Mr. Ken CORNELL
42 Campus Pastor ... Rev. Phil RASMUSSEN
06 Registrar ... Mrs. Sandy HENDRICKSON
07 Director of Admissions ... Mr. Andy HALL
37 Director of Financial Aid ... Mr. Roger WILSON
41 Athletic Director ... Mr. Gary MCINTOSH
08 College Librarian ... Mr. Adam EPP
38 Director of Counseling Services ... Vacant
29 Dir of Alumni Svcs/Parent Rels ... Ms. Leanne KONZELMAN
15 Director Human Resources ... Ms. Victoria CLARK
121 Director Student Success ... Mrs. Amy JONES
32 Dean of Students ... Mr. Rick ENGSTROM
26 Director of Marketing ... Mr. Steve BOSTROM
04 Administrative Asst to President ... Mrs. Patti THOMAS
50 Dean College of Business ... Dr. Teresa GILLESPIE
53 Dean College of Education ... Dr. Molly QUICK
28 Director of Multicultural Life ... Dr. Nina HANSON
39 Director of Res Life and Housing ... Ms. Sarah JOBSON

Olympic College (F)

1600 Chester Avenue, Bremerton WA 98337-1699
County: Kitsap FICE Identification: 003784
Unit ID: 236188
Telephone: (360) 792-6050 Carnegie Class: Bac/Assoc-Assoc Dom
FAX Number: (360) 475-7151 Calendar System: Quarter
URL: www.olympic.edu
Established: 1946 Annual Undergrad Tuition & Fees (In-State): $3,618
Enrollment: 7,177 Coed
Affiliation or Control: State IRS Status: 501(c)3
Highest Offering: Baccalaureate
Accreditation: NW, ACFEI, ADNUR, MAC, NURSE, PTAA

01 President ... Dr. David C. MITCHELL
05 Vice President for Instruction ... Dr. Mary GARGUILE
10 Vice President for Administration ... Dr. Kay ASH
32 Vice President for Student Services ... Dr. Damon BELL
26 Vice President Equity & Inclusion ... Ms. Cheryl NUÑEZ
15 Exec Director Human Resource Svcs ... Dr. Joan HANTEN
51 Director of Continuing Education ... Vacant
04 Exec Assistant to the President ... Ms. Shawna BLISS
37 Director Student Financial Services ... Ms. Heidi TOWNSEND
27 Director of Communications ... Mr. Shawn DEVINE
84 Dean of Enrollment Services ... Ms. Jennifer GLASIER
18 Dir Facilities Svcs/Capital Project ... Mr. Dan WHITTIER
21 Director of Business Services ... Ms. Janell WHITELEY
96 Procurement Officer ... Ms. Diana LAKE
36 Director Career Center ... Ms. Teresa MCDERMOTT
09 Exec Dir InstitutionalEffectiveness ... Vacant
28 Supervisor Multicltrl/Student Pgms ... Ms. Jodie COLLINS
103 Dean Workforce Development ... Ms. Amy HATFIELD
08 Dean Library/Lrng Resources/eLrng ... Ms. Erica COE
50 Dean Business & Technology ... Dr. Norma WHITACRE
81 Dean Math/Engineer/Sci/Health ... Dr. Mark HARRISON
79 Dean Humanities/Social Science ... Dr. Rebecca SEAMAN
13 Exec Dir of Technical Services ... Ms. Evelyn HERNANDEZ
19 Director of Campus Safety ... Mr. Daniel WALKUP
25 Director of Grants ... Ms. Sharon KLINE
29 Exec Dir of Foundation/Alumni Assn ... Mr. David EMMONS
41 Director of Athletics ... Mr. Barry JANUSCH

Pacific Lutheran University (G)

12180 Park Avenue S., Tacoma WA 98447-0003
County: Pierce FICE Identification: 003785
Unit ID: 236230
Telephone: (253) 531-6900 Carnegie Class: Masters/M
FAX Number: (253) 535-8320 Calendar System: 4/1/4
URL: www.plu.edu
Established: 1890 Annual Undergrad Tuition & Fees: $39,450
Enrollment: 3,170 Coed
Affiliation or Control: Evangelical Lutheran Church In America
IRS Status: 501(c)3
Highest Offering: Master's
Accreditation: NW, CAEPN, CS, ENG, MFCD, MUS, NURSE, SW

01 Acting President ... Mr. Allan BELTON
100 Senior Advisor to the President ... Ms. Kris H. PLAEHN
04 Senior Admin Asst to the President ... Ms. Julie L. MIX
101 Director of Admin & Sec to Board ... Ms. Vicky L. WINTERS
05 Acting Provost ... Dr. Joanna GREGSON
10 Senior VP & Chief Admin Officer ... Mr. Allan BELTON
111 Vice Pres for Advancement ... Mr. Daniel J. LEE
32 Vice Pres for Student Life ... Dr. Joanna C. ROYCE-DAVIS
84 Dean for Enrollment Management ... Mr. Michael T. FRECHETTE
26 Vice Pres Marketing & Communication ... Ms. Donna L. GIBBS
20 Assoc Provost Undergrad Programs ... Dr. Jan P. LEWIS
21 Controller ... Mr. Steve M. WHITEHOUSE
42 University Pastor ... Rev. Jen RUDE
57 Dean School of Arts & Communication ... Dr. Cameron D. BENNETT
50 Dean of School of Business ... Dr. Chung-Shing LEE
53 Dean School of Educ & Kinesiology ... Dr. Terry M. BERGESON
66 Dean School of Nursing ... Dr. Sheila K. SMITH
79 Dean of Humanities ... Dr. Kevin J. O'BRIEN
81 Dean of Natural Sciences ... Dr. Ann J. AUMAN
83 Dean of Social Sciences ... Dr. David R. HUELSBECK
35 Dean of Students ... Dr. Eva R. FREY
51 Assoc Provost for Grad & Cont Educ ... Dr. Geoffrey E. FOY
88 Exec Dir Wang Ctr for Global Educ ... Dr. Tamara R. WILLIAMS
121 Director Academic Advising ... Dr. Hal R. DELAROSBY
41 Director Athletics & Recreation ... Ms. Laurie L. TURNER
06 Registrar ... Mr. Kevin A. BERG
39 Assoc VP for Campus Life ... Mr. Tom A. HUELSBECK
18 Assoc VP for Facilities Management ... Mr. Ray ORR
19 Director of Campus Safety & Info ... Mr. Greg V. PREMO
36 Director of Career Connections ... Ms. Donna L. MILLER
23 Director Health Services ... Ms. Elizabeth A. HOOPER
15 Assoc Vice Pres Human Resources ... Ms. Teri P. PHILLIPS
90 Dir of Enterprise Systems & Comm ... Mr. David P. ALLEN
13 Director Information Services ... Ms. Ardys E. CURTIS
37 Interim Director of Financial Aid ... Mr. Ronald M. NOBORIKAWA
40 Manager of Bookstore ... Ms. Amanda B. HAWKINS
09 Dir Assessment/Accreditation/Rsrch ... Ms. Summer S. KENESSON
102 Corporate & Foundation Mgr ... Ms. Danielle N. CRYER
44 Director Annual Giving ... Ms. Alicia A. HINCKLEY
22 Dir Affirmative Action/EEO ... Ms. Teri P. PHILLIPS
28 Asst VP Diversity/Justice/Sustain ... Ms. Angie Z. HAMBRICK
29 Director Alumni Relations ... Ms. Jessica L. PAGEL
38 Interim Director Counseling Ctr ... Dr. Joanna ROYCE-DAVIS

† Granted candidacy at the Doctorate level.

Pacific Northwest University of Health Sciences (H)

111 University Parkway, Suite 202, Yakima WA 98901
County: Yakima FICE Identification: 041305
Unit ID: 455406
Telephone: (509) 452-5100 Carnegie Class: Spec-4-yr-Med
FAX Number: (509) 452-5101 Calendar System: Semester
URL: www.pnwu.edu
Established: 2005 Annual Graduate Tuition & Fees: N/A
Enrollment: 495 Coed
Affiliation or Control: Independent Non-Profit IRS Status: 501(c)3
Highest Offering: Doctorate; No Undergraduates
Accreditation: @NW, OSTEO

01 President ... Dr. Keith WATSON
100 Senior Advisor to the President ... Dr. Robert E. SUTTON
05 Provost ... Dr. Edward BILSKY
10 Chief Financial Officer ... Ms. Ann HITTLE
11 Chief Operations Officer ... Mr. Frank D. ALVAREZ
30 Chief Development Officer ... Ms. Michele ERICKSON
63 Dean Col of Osteopathic Medicine ... Dr. Thomas SCANDALIS
09 Chief Research Officer ... Ms. Michele MCCARROLL
08 Head Librarian ... Ms. Anita CLEARY
13 Chief Info Technology Officer (CIO) ... Mr. John DEVORE
15 Director Personnel Services ... Ms. Stefanie DURAND
18 Chief Facilities/Physical Plant ... Mr. Dave WARNER
19 Director Security/Safety ... Mr. Ben HITTLE
26 Chief Public Relations/Marketing ... Mr. Dean O'DRISCOLL
29 Director Alumni Relations ... Ms. Jan JORGENSON
37 Director Student Financial Aid ... Ms. Laura PENDLETON
45 Chief Institutional Planning ... Ms. Angie GIRARD
04 Administrative Asst to President ... Ms. Vikki GORE
07 Director of Enrollment Services ... Ms. LeAnn HUNTER
108 Dir Institutional Effectiveness ... Ms. Lori FULTON
32 Assoc Dean Student Affairs ... Dr. Stephen LAIRD
96 Asst Dir Procurement/Asset Mgmt ... Ms. Barbara ANDERSON

Peninsula College (I)

1502 East Lauridsen Boulevard,
Port Angeles WA 98362-6698
County: Clallam FICE Identification: 003786
Unit ID: 236258
Telephone: (360) 452-9277 Carnegie Class: Bac/Assoc-Assoc Dom
FAX Number: (360) 457-8100 Calendar System: Quarter
URL: www.pencol.edu
Established: 1961 Annual Undergrad Tuition & Fees (In-District): $4,344
Enrollment: 2,271 Coed
Affiliation or Control: State/Local IRS Status: 501(c)3
Highest Offering: Baccalaureate
Accreditation: NW, ADNUR, MAC

01 President ... Dr. Luke ROBINS
05 Vice President Instruction ... Dr. Sharon BUCK
11 Vice President Administrative Svcs ... Ms. Deborah FRAZIER
32 Vice President Student Services ... Mr. Jack HULS
45 VP Institutional Effectiveness ... Dr. Paula DOHERTY
50 Dir Cmty/Business Education ... Ms. Linty HOPIE
55 Dean Adult Basic Education ... Dr. Evelyn SHORT
35 Dean of Student Services ... Ms. Maria PENA
37 Assoc Dean Fin Aid/Enrollment Svcs ... Ms. Krista FRANCIS
41 Assoc Dean Athletics/Student Prgms ... Mr. Rick ROSS
13 Director Information Technology ... Mr. Steven BAXTER
04 Executive Asst to the President ... Ms. Kelly GRIFFITHS
26 Director Public Information ... Ms. Phyllis L. VAN HOLLAND
15 Director Human Resources ... Mr. Kraig MICHELS
85 Dir Intl Stdnt Pgm/Stdnt Recruit ... Ms. Sophia ILIAKIS-DOHERTY
102 Director College Foundation ... Ms. Getta ROGERS
09 Int Dir of Institutional Research ... Ms. Katie BRENKMAN

18 Director Physical Plant .... Mr. Rick CROOT
40 Bookstore Manager .... Mrs. Camilla RICO
88 Manager High School Program .... Ms. Cindy LAUDERBACK

Perry Technical Institute (A)

2011 W. Washington Avenue, Yakima WA 98903
County: Yakima FICE Identification: 009387
Unit ID: 236212
Telephone: (509) 453-0374 Carnegie Class: Not Classified
FAX Number: (509) 453-0375 Calendar System: Quarter
URL: www.perrytech.edu
Established: 1939 Annual Undergrad Tuition & Fees: N/A
Enrollment: 825 Coed
Affiliation or Control: Independent Non-Profit IRS Status: 501(c)3
Highest Offering: Associate Degree
Accreditation: **ACCSC**

01 President .... Christine COTE
04 Administrative Asst to President .... Renee KABRICH
06 Registrar .... Jill COPE
07 Director of Student Enrollment .... Nicole TRAMMELL
10 Chief Business Officer .... Cathy STERBENZ
102 Foundation/PR Director .... Erin FISHBURN
13 Chief Info Technology Officer (CIO) .... Josh PHILLIPS
15 Human Resource Manager .... Carol HELMS
19 Director of Facilities/Safety .... Kaila LOCKBEAM
22 Dir of Institutional Effectiveness .... Emily JAMESON DUBOW
36 Director Student Placement .... Chelsea SNODGRASS
37 Director Student Financial Aid .... Mayra FERNANDEZ
50 Dean of Education .... Nathan HULL
53 Associate Dean .... Jason LAMIQUIZ
96 Purchasing Manager .... Maria PULIDO

Pierce College District (B)

1601 39th Avenue SE, Puyallup WA 98374
County: Pierce FICE Identification: 005000
Unit ID: 439145
Telephone: (253) 964-6500 Carnegie Class: Assoc/HT-High Non
FAX Number: N/A Calendar System: Quarter
URL: www.pierce.ctc.edu
Established: 1967 Annual Undergrad Tuition & Fees (In-State): $3,696
Enrollment: 4,154 Coed
Affiliation or Control: State IRS Status: 501(c)3
Highest Offering: Baccalaureate
Accreditation: **NW**, ADNUR, DH

01 District Chancellor .... Dr. Michele JOHNSON
12 President Pierce College Puyallup .... Dr. Marty CAVALLUZZI
12 President Fort Steilacoom .... Ms. Denise YOCHUM
05 VP Learning/Student Success-PY .... Dr. Matthew CAMPBELL
05 Vice Pres Learning/Stdnt Success-FS .... Dr. Debra GILCHRIST
10 Vice Pres Administrative Services .... Mr. Choi HALLADAY
30 VP Advancement/Dir Foundation .... Ms. Deidre SOILEAU
15 Vice President for Human Resources .... Ms. Holly GORSKI
13 Dean of Institutional Technology .... Mr. Mike STOCKE
84 Dean Enroll Svcs/Fin Aid/Registrar .... Ms. Anne WHITE
08 Dean Libraries & Learning Resources .... Ms. Christie FLYNN
26 Dir Marketing and Communications .... Mr. Brian BENEDETTI
32 Dean of Student Success .... Ms. Agnes STEWARD
35 Dir Student Programs-Ft Steilacoom .... Mr. Cameron COX
41 Director District Athletics .... Mr. Duncan STEVENSON
18 Director of Facilities & Const Mgt .... Mr. Jim TAYLOR
35 Dir of Student Life-Puyallup .... Mr. Sean COOKE
85 Exec Dir of International Education .... Ms. Myung PARK
19 District Manager Campus Safety .... Mr. Chris MACKERSIE
21 Director Fiscal Services .... Ms. Sylvia JAMES
37 Director Financial Aid .... Ms. Isabelle MORA
84 Director Enrollment Services-Puy .... Ms. Els DEMING
96 Procurement Officer .... Mr. Curtis LEE
29 Alumni Relations Manager .... Ms. Marion SHARP
09 Director Institutional Research .... Mr. Erik GIMNESS
49 Dean Arts & Humanities .... Dr. Holly SMITH
88 Dean Transitional Education .... Ms. Lori GRIFFIN
76 Dean Tech/Allied Health .... Mr. Ronald MAY
81 Dean Natural Sciences .... Mr. Thomas BROXSON
83 Dean Business/Social Sciences .... Dr. Sachi HORBACK

Pima Medical Institute-Renton (C)

555 South Renton Village Place, Renton WA 98057
Telephone: (425) 228-9600 Identification: 770517
Accreditation: **ABHES**, COARC, OTA

† Branch campus of Pima Medical Institute-Tucson, Tucson, AZ

Pima Medical Institute-Seattle (D)

9709 3rd Avenue NE, Suite 400, Seattle WA 98115-2052
Telephone: (206) 322-6100 Identification: 666172
Accreditation: **ABHES**, DH, OTA, PTAA, RAD

† Branch campus of Pima Medical Institute-Tucson, Tucson, AZ

Renton Technical College (E)

3000 NE Fourth Street, Renton WA 98056-4123
County: King FICE Identification: 010434
Unit ID: 236382
Telephone: (425) 235-2352 Carnegie Class: Assoc/HVT-High Non
FAX Number: (425) 235-7832 Calendar System: Quarter
URL: www.rtc.edu
Established: 1942 Annual Undergrad Tuition & Fees (In-State): $4,836
Enrollment: 3,961 Coed
Affiliation or Control: State IRS Status: 501(c)3
Highest Offering: Associate Degree
Accreditation: **NW**, ACFEI, DA, MAC, SURGT

01 President .... Dr. Kevin D. McCARTHY
10 VP Finance/Administration .... Ms. Melinda M. MERRELL
05 Vice President Instruction .... Mr. Angel REYNA
32 VP Student Services .... Ms. Jessica GILMORE ENGLISH
97 Dean Basic Studies .... Ms. Jodi NOVOTNY
76 Dean Allied Health .... Mr. Christopher CARTER
103 Executive Dean Workforce/Econ Dev .... Mr. Jacob JACKSON
50 Dean Bus/Educ/Hum Svcs/Gen Educ .... Ms. Sarah WAKEFIELD
72 Dean Automotive/Tech/Distance Educ .... Vacant
102 Foundation Executive Director .... Ms. Carrie SHAW
13 Chief Information Officer .... Mr. Paul CORRIGLIANO
07 Director Enrollment Services .... Mr. Patrick BROWN
111 Exec Dir Institutional Advancement .... Ms. Michelle CAMPBELL
08 Director Library .... Ms. Cheyenne RODUIN
21 Director Financial Services .... Mr. Mark JOHNSON
15 Executive Director Human Resources .... Ms. Lesley HOGAN
37 Director Financial Aid .... Ms. Donna HARTMANN-TURNER
18 Director Plant Operations .... Mr. Barry A. BAKER
40 Bookstore Manager .... Mr. Jose A. PERDOMO
19 Safety & Security Manager .... Mr. Matthew VIELBIG
88 Dean Culinary Arts .... Mr. Doug MEDBURY
26 Dir College Relations/ Marketing .... Ms. Katherine HEDLAND HANSEN
38 Dean Counseling & Advising .... Mr. Scott LATIOLAIS
35 Director Student Programs .... Ms. Jessica SUPINSKI
06 Registration Coordinator .... Ms. Ly CHANG
88 Custodial Manager .... Mr. Mark DANIELS
88 Director Outreach/Entry Services .... Ms. Andrea LANCASTER
04 Executive Asst to President .... Ms. Di BEERS

† Granted candidacy at the Baccalaureate level.

Saint Martin's University (F)

5000 Abbey Way, SE, Lacey WA 98503-7500
County: Thurston FICE Identification: 003794
Unit ID: 236452
Telephone: (360) 491-4700 Carnegie Class: Masters/M
FAX Number: (360) 459-4124 Calendar System: Semester
URL: www.stmartin.edu
Established: 1895 Annual Undergrad Tuition & Fees: $34,356
Enrollment: 1,719 Coed
Affiliation or Control: Roman Catholic IRS Status: 501(c)3
Highest Offering: Master's
Accreditation: **NW**, ACBSP, CAEPT, ENG, NURSE, SW

00 Chancellor .... Abbot Neal G. ROTH, OSB
01 President .... Dr. Roy F. HEYNDERICKX
05 Provost & Vice President .... Dr. Molly E. SMITH
10 Vice President of Finance .... Mr. Ed BARTON
30 Vice Pres Inst Advancement .... Ms. Cecelia LOVELESS
85 Vice Pres Intl Programs/Development .... Ms. Josephine YUNG
26 VP of Marketing/ Communications .... Ms. Genevieve CANCEKO CHAN
13 Associate Vice President/CIO .... Mr. Greg DAVIS
15 Associate VP of Human Resources .... Ms. Cynthia JOHNSON
49 Dean Col of Arts & Sciences .... Dr. Jeff CRANE
53 Dean of Education .... Dr. Kate BOYLE
50 Dean of Business .... Dr. Richard BEER
54 Dean of Engineering .... Dr. David OLWELL
32 Dean Student Services .... Ms. Melanie RICHARDSON
84 Dean Enrollment Management .... Ms. Pamela HOLSINGER-FUCHS
07 Dean Admission/Stdnt Financial Svcs .... Vacant
21 Controller .... Ms. Linda NEWMAN
37 Director Financial Aid .... Mr. Michael GROSSO
29 Director Alumni Relations .... Vacant
06 Assistant Registrar .... Ms. Ronda VANDERGIFF
18 Director Facilities Management .... Mr. Philip CHEEK
44 Dir of Development/Planned Giving .... Ms. Katie WOJKE
36 Director of Career Placement .... Ms. Ann ADAMS
41 Athletic Director .... Mr. Bob GRISHAM
56 Director Extension Programs .... Mr. Cruz ARROYO
08 Library Director .... Mr. Scot HARRISON
42 Director Campus Ministry .... Ms. Angela CARLIN
39 Director of Housing/Residence Life .... Mr. Tim MCCLAIN
38 Director Counseling Center .... Ms. Jan BERNEY
09 Director Institutional Grants/Rsrch .... Ms. Erin HOILAND

*Seattle Colleges (G)

1500 Harvard Avenue, Seattle WA 98122-3803
County: King FICE Identification: 010106
Unit ID: 236498
Telephone: (206) 934-4100 Carnegie Class: N/A
FAX Number: (206) 934-3883
URL: www.seattlecolleges.edu

01 Chancellor .... Dr. Shouan PAN
03 Interim Vice Chancellor .... Dr. Mary Ellen O'KEEFFE
10 Vice Chanc for Finance & Technology .... Dr. Kurt BUTTLEMAN
15 Chief Human Resources Officer .... Dr. David BLAKE
26 Exec Director of Communications .... Dr. Earnest PHILLIPS
30 Assoc Vice Chanc for Advancement .... Ms. Wendy SCHNEIDER
12 President South Seattle College .... Mr. Gary OERTLI
12 President North Seattle College .... Dr. Warren BROWN
12 President Seattle Central College .... Dr. Sheila EDWARDS LANGE

*North Seattle College (H)

9600 College Way N, Seattle WA 98103-3599
County: King FICE Identification: 009704
Unit ID: 236072
Telephone: (206) 934-3600 Carnegie Class: Bac/Assoc-Assoc Dom
FAX Number: (206) 934-3606 Calendar System: Quarter
URL: www.northseattle.edu
Established: 1970 Annual Undergrad Tuition & Fees (In-State): $3,819
Enrollment: 6,310 Coed
Affiliation or Control: State IRS Status: 170(c)1
Highest Offering: Baccalaureate
Accreditation: **NW**, ADNUR, MAC

02 President .... Dr. Warren J. BROWN
05 Vice President for Instruction .... Dr. Kristen JONES
32 Vice Pres Student Development .... Mr. Joseph BARRIENTOS
11 Vice President of Administration .... Ms. Andrea JOHNSON
36 Exec Dean Career/Workforce Educ .... Dr. John LEDERER
79 Dean Art/Humanities/Social Sciences .... Mr. Brian PALMER
81 Dean Math & Science .... Ms. Alissa AGNELLO
103 Dean Workforce Instruction .... Dr. Laura HOPKINS
08 Dean Library & Media Services .... Dr. Aryana BATES
35 Assoc Dean Student Devel Svcs .... Ms. Alice MELLING
88 Dean Basic/Transitional Stds .... Mr. Curtis BONNEY
30 Executive Director of Advancement .... Ms. Traci RUSSELL
26 Dir Marketing & Public Relations .... Ms. Melissa MIXON
84 Dean Enrollment Svcs/Registrar .... Ms. Kathy RHODES
51 Director Continuing Education .... Ms. Christy ISAACSON
37 Director Financial Aid Services .... Ms. Brianne SANCHEZ
35 Dir Student Ldrshp/Multi Cult Pgms .... Mr. Jeffrey VASQUEZ
103 Director Workforce Education .... Ms. Lindsay CAEL
09 Dir Institutional Effectiveness .... Dr. Stephanie DYKES
104 Director International Programs .... Dr. Cathy Lee ARCUINO
15 Director of Human Resources .... Vacant
18 Dir Facilities & Plant Operations .... Mr. Jeffrey CAULK
38 Lead Counselor .... Dr. Lydia MINATOYA
13 Chief Info Technology Officer .... Dr. Cindy RICHE
19 Director Security/Safety .... Mr. Darryl JOHNSON
28 Director of Diversity & Inclusion .... Ms. Pam RACANSKY
07 Coordinator Admissions/Residency .... Mr. Fleetwood L. WILSON
04 Executive Asst to President .... Ms. Toni STANKOVIC
10 Director Business Operations .... Mr. Dennis YASUKOCHI
25 Director of Grants .... Ms. Ann RICHARDSON
41 Athletic Director .... Ms. Carianya NAPOLI

*Seattle Central College (I)

1701 Broadway, Seattle WA 98122-2400
County: King FICE Identification: 003787
Unit ID: 236513
Telephone: (206) 587-3800 Carnegie Class: Bac/Assoc-Assoc Dom
FAX Number: (206) 344-4390 Calendar System: Quarter
URL: seattlecentral.edu
Established: 1966 Annual Undergrad Tuition & Fees (In-State): $3,925
Enrollment: 6,574 Coed
Affiliation or Control: State IRS Status: 170(c)1
Highest Offering: Baccalaureate
Accreditation: **NW**, ACFEI, ADNUR, COARC, DH, SURGT

02 President .... Dr. Sheila EDWARDS LANGE
05 Vice Pres of Instruction .... Mr. Bradley LANE
11 Vice Pres Administrative Services .... Mr. Bruce RIVELAND
32 Vice Pres Student Services .... Ms. Yoshiko HARDEN
103 Executive Dean Workforce Educ .... Mr. Chris SULLIVAN
09 Exec Dir Inst Effectiveness .... Ms. Naina ESHWAR
37 Director of Financial Aid .... Vacant
102 Executive Director Foundation .... Ms. Lauren GUZAUSKAS
26 Director of Communications .... Mr. David SANDLER
08 Dean of Library Svcs/E-learn .... Ms. Lynn KANNE
49 Dean Basic Studies .... Ms. Laura DIZAZZO
50 Dean Business IT & Creative Arts .... Vacant
76 Dean of Allied Health .... Mr. David GOURD
81 Dean of STEM .... Dr. Wendy ROCKHILL
83 Dean Arts Humanities/Social Science .... Ms. Kayleen OKA
88 Assoc VP International Education .... Dr. Andrea INSLEY
35 Dean Student Development .... Mr. Ricardo LEYVA-PUEBLA
13 Director Information Technology .... Mr. Tim RAGER
12 Director Seattle Maritime Academy .... Ms. Sarah SCHERER
12 Assoc Dean Seattle Culinary Academy .... Ms. Katherine KEHRLI
51 Director Cmty Educ/Evening Pgm .... Ms. Gabrielle BACHMEIER
84 Dean Enrollment Services/Registrar .... Ms. Diane COLEMAN
19 Director Public Safety .... Mr. Elman MCCLAIN
18 Dir Facilities/Plant Operations .... Mr. Chuck DAVIS
20 Dean Business/Behavioral Science .... Dr. Debra SULLIVAN
04 Executive Admin Asst to President .... Ms. Angelique ODOM
10 Chief Business Officer .... Ms. Phyllis GRETCHENUK
15 Director Human Resources .... Ms. Christina NELSON
28 Director Diversity/Equity & Inclu .... Ms. Tina YOUNG

*South Seattle College (J)

6000 16th Avenue, SW, Seattle WA 98106-1499
County: King FICE Identification: 009706
Unit ID: 236504
Telephone: (206) 934-5300 Carnegie Class: Bac/Assoc-Assoc Dom
FAX Number: (206) 934-5393 Calendar System: Quarter
URL: www.southseattle.edu
Established: 1969 Annual Undergrad Tuition & Fees (In-State): $3,854
Enrollment: 6,076 Coed
Affiliation or Control: State IRS Status: 501(c)3
Highest Offering: Baccalaureate
Accreditation: **NW**

02 President ....Mr. Gary L. OERTLI
05 Vice Pres Instruction ....Mr. Pete LORTZ
11 Vice Pres Administrative Svcs ....Dr. Elizabeth PLUNTA
32 Vice President Student Services ....Dr. Rosie RIMANDO
30 Director Advancement ....Ms. Heather FOSS
45 Dean Instructional Resources ....Ms. Mary Jo WHITE
12 Exec Dean of Georgetown Campus ....Ms. Holly MOORE
97 Dean Basic & Transitional Studies ....Mr. John BOWERS
20 Dean of Academic Programs ....Ms. Stephanie DELANEY
35 Dean Student Life ....Mr. Daniel JOHNSON
103 Dn Professional/Tech/Workforce Educ ....Ms. Veronica WADE
17 Dean Hosp & Service Occupations ....Mr. Robert GLATT
72 Dean Multi-Trades/Info Tech/Bus ....Mr. Duncan BURGESS
84 Dean Enrollment Services ....Ms. Joyce ALLEN
88 Dean of Aviation ....Ms. Kim ALEXANDER
20 Assoc Dean Academic Programs ....Ms. Laura KINGSTON
20 Assoc Dean Academic Programs ....Mr. Johnny HU
06 Assistant Registrar ....Ms. Marilyn ANDERSON-BURT
104 Exec Dir Ctr for Intl Education ....Ms. Kathie KWILINSKI
51 Director Continuing Education ....Ms. Luisa MOTTEN
103 Int Dir Workforce Dev/Employ Svcs ....Ms. Stephanie GUY
37 Dir Student Financial Assistance ....Ms. Corinne SOLTIS
26 Director Communications ....Mr. Ty SWENSON
15 Director Human Resources ....Ms. Linda MANNING
108 Chief Data and Strategy Officer ....Mr. Greg DEMPSEY
13 Director Business Operation ....Ms. Rob'n LEWIS
18 Dir Facilities & Plant Operations ....Mr. Eric STEEN
28 Dir of Equity/Diversity/Inclusion ....Vacant
19 Manager Safety/Security ....Mr. James E. LEWIS
40 Manager Bookstore ....Ms. Danica GOODMAN

Seattle Institute of Oriental Medicine (A)

444 Ravenna Boulevard, Suite 208, Seattle WA 98115
County: King FICE Identification: 032803
Unit ID: 439914
Telephone: (206) 517-4541 Carnegie Class: Spec-4-yr-Other Health
FAX Number: (206) 299-3538 Calendar System: Trimester
URL: www.siom.edu
Established: 1994 Annual Undergrad Tuition & Fees: N/A
Enrollment: 37 Coed
Affiliation or Control: Proprietary IRS Status: Proprietary
Highest Offering: Master's; No Lower Division
Accreditation: ACUP

01 President ....Craig MITCHELL
05 Academic Dean ....Vacant
06 Academic Coordinator ....Corey OJIMA

Seattle Pacific University (B)

3307 Third Avenue W, Seattle WA 98119-1997
County: King FICE Identification: 003788
Unit ID: 236577
Telephone: (206) 281-2111 Carnegie Class: DU-Mod
FAX Number: (206) 281-2115 Calendar System: Quarter
URL: www.spu.edu
Established: 1891 Annual Undergrad Tuition & Fees: $38,940
Enrollment: 4,204 Coed
Affiliation or Control: Free Methodist IRS Status: 501(c)3
Highest Offering: Doctorate
Accreditation: NW, CACREP, CLPSY, DIETD, ENG, MFCD, MUS, NURSE, THEOL

01 President ....Dr. Daniel J. MARTIN
05 Provost ....Dr. Jeffrey B. VAN DUZER
11 Sr VP for Planning & Administration ....Mr. Donald W. MORTENSON
32 VP for Student Life ....Dr. Jeffrey C. JORDAN
111 VP for Advancement ....Mrs. Louise S. FURROW
10 VP for Business & Finance ....Mr. Craig G. KISPERT
84 VP for Enrollment Mgmt & Mktg ....Mr. Nate MOUTTET
28 VP for Diversity/Equity/Inclusion ....Ms. Sandra MAYO
20 Vice Provost Academic Affairs ....Dr. Cynthia J. PRICE
18 Asst VP Facility Management ....Mr. David B. CHURCH
43 Asst VP Risk Mgmt & Univ Counsel ....Mr. Nick GLANCY
13 Asst VP Technology Services ....Mr. David W. TINDALL
37 Asst VP UG Enrollment Oper & SFS ....Mr. Jordan L. GRANT
50 Dean School of Business/Govt/Econ ....Dr. Ross STEWART
53 Dean School of Education ....Dr. Rick EIGENBROOD
66 Dean School of Health Sciences ....Dr. Lorie WILD
81 Dean CAS - Sciences Division ....Dr. Bruce D. CONGDON
49 Dean CAS - Arts & Humanities Div ....Dr. Debra-L SEQUEIRA
88 Dean School of Psych/Fam & Cmty ....Dr. Katy TANGENBERG
73 Dean School of Theology ....Dr. Douglas M. STRONG
35 Dean of Students for Cmty Life ....Mr. Chuck STRAWN
36 Dean Stdnt Lrng/Dir Ctr Career Coun ....Dr. Jacqui S. SMITH-BATES
08 University Librarian ....Mr. Michael PAULUS
38 Director Student Counseling Center ....Dr. Steven A. MAYBELL
07 Sr Dir Recruitment and Admissions ....Mr. Jobe S. KORB-NICE
07 Director Undergraduate Admissions ....Ms. Ineliz SOTO FULLER
09 Interim Dir IR & Assessment Coord ....Mr. Stan LAN
06 University Registrar ....Mrs. Kenda GATLIN
26 Sr Dir Univ Comm & Marketing ....Mrs. Alison ESTEP
27 News & Media Relations Manager ....Mrs. Tracy C. NORLEN
109 Director of University Services ....Ms. Alexis CRUIKSHANK
19 Director of Safety & Security ....Mr. Mark REID
110 Director of Advancement ....Ms. Maribeth MARTIN LOPIT
29 Director of Alumni/Parent Relations ....Mr. Bryan H. JONES
41 Athletic Director ....Mr. Jackson STAVA
15 Director of Human Resources ....Mr. Gary E. WOMELSDUFF
39 Director of Residence Life ....Mr. Gabe JACOBSEN
35 Director Student Programs ....Ms. Whitney BROETJE
88 Dean of Multi-Ethnic/Wellness Pgms ....Mrs. Susan OKAMOTO LANE
104 Director of Study Abroad ....Ms. Gail DEBELL
04 Executive Asst to President ....Mrs. Ruth JACOBSEN

The Seattle School of Theology and Psychology (C)

2501 Elliot Avenue, Seattle WA 98121-1177
County: King FICE Identification: 034664
Unit ID: 441131
Telephone: (206) 876-6100 Carnegie Class: Spec-4-yr-Other Health
FAX Number: (206) 876-6195 Calendar System: Trimester
URL: www.theseattleschool.edu
Established: 2001 Annual Graduate Tuition & Fees: N/A
Enrollment: 302 Coed
Affiliation or Control: Independent Non-Profit IRS Status: 501(c)3
Highest Offering: Master's; No Undergraduates
Accreditation: THEOL

01 President ....Dr. Keith R. ANDERSON
05 Sr Vice Pres Academic Affs/CAO ....Dr. J. Derek MCNEIL
10 Chief Financial Officer ....Mr. Phil BISHOP
30 Vice Pres Advancement ....Ms. Cathy LOERZEL
32 VP Students & Alumni/Dn of Students ....Mr. Paul STEINKE
08 Dir Library Svcs/Inst Assessment ....Ms. Cheryl GOODWIN
06 Dir Academic Services/Registrar ....Ms. Kristen HOUSTON
84 Director of Enrollment Management ....Ms. Nicole GREENWALD
13 Director Computer & Info Services ....Ms. Grace LA TORRA
15 Human Resources ....Ms. Kartha HEINZ

Seattle University (D)

901 12th Avenue, Seattle WA 98122-1090
County: King FICE Identification: 003790
Unit ID: 236595
Telephone: (206) 296-6000 Carnegie Class: Masters/L
FAX Number: N/A Calendar System: Quarter
URL: www.seattleu.edu
Established: 1891 Annual Undergrad Tuition & Fees: $41,265
Enrollment: 7,405 Coed
Affiliation or Control: Roman Catholic IRS Status: 501(c)3
Highest Offering: Doctorate
Accreditation: NW, CACREP, DMS, ENG, LAW, MFCD, MIDWF, NURSE, SPAA, SW, THEOL

01 President ....Rev. Stephen V. SUNDBORG, SJ
05 Interim Provost ....Dr. Robert DULLEA
11 Executive Vice President Admin ....Dr. Timothy LEARY
10 Chief Financial Officer ....Ms. Connie KANTER
43 Vice Pres and University Counsel ....Ms. Mary S. PETERSEN
111 VP University Advancement ....Mr. Michael PODLIN
32 VP Student Development ....Dr. Michele MURRAY
88 Vice President Mission & Ministry ....Rev. Peter ELY, SJ
108 Assoc VP for Inst Effectiveness ....Dr. Robert DUNIWAY
84 Vice President for Enrollment Svcs ....Ms. Marilyn CRONE
26 Vice President for Communications ....Mr. Scott MCCLELLAN
15 Vice President Human Resources ....Mr. Gerald HUFFMAN
28 Chief Diversity Officer ....Ms. Natasha MARTIN
15 VP Human Resources ....Ms. Michelle CLEMENTS
31 Executive Director Cmty Engagement ....Mr. Kent KOTH
49 Dean of Arts & Sciences ....Dr. David POWERS
50 Dean of Business & Economics ....Dr. Joseph M. PHILLIPS
53 Dean of Education ....Dr. Deanna SANDS
66 Dean of Nursing ....Dr. Kristen SWANSON
54 Dean of Science & Engineering ....Dr. Michael QUINN
79 Interim Dean of Humanities ....Dr. Paulette KIDDER
61 Dean of Law ....Ms. Annette C. CLARK
73 Dean of Theology & Ministry ....Dr. Mark MARKULY
51 Dean Schl New & Continuing Studies ....Dr. Rick FEHRENBACHER
08 University Librarian ....Vacant
20 Assoc Provost Academic Achievement ....Dr. Charles LAWRENCE
87 Director Summer Programs ....Dr. Kevin KRYCKA
20 Assoc Provost Global Engagement ....Dr. Russell POWELL
123 Graduate Admissions ....Ms. Janet SHANDLEY
06 University Registrar ....Ms. Erin MORGAN
13 Chief Information Officer ....Chris VAN LIEW
21 Assoc VP of Finance ....Mr. Andrew O'BOYLE
18 Assoc VP Facilities Administration ....Mr. Robert SCHWARTZ
29 Asst VP Alumni Relations ....Ms. Susan VOSPER
14 Executive Director ....Mr. Dennis GENDRON
112 Sr Director of Planned Giving ....Ms. Sarah FINNEY
44 Director of Annual Giving ....Ms. Cathy REILLY
102 Dir of Foundation & Corporate Rels ....Ms. Jane SPALDING
35 Assoc Vice Pres Student Development ....Dr. Alvin STURDIVANT
06 Associate Registrar ....Mr. Andrew ANDERSON
07 Dean of Admissions ....Ms. Melore NIELSEN
09 Director of Institutional Research ....Dr. Irina VOLOSHIN
42 Director Campus Ministry ....Ms. Tammy LIDDELL
37 Director Student Financial Services ....Mr. Jeff SCOFIELD
41 Director of Athletics ....Mr. Bill HOGAN
19 Executive Director of Public Safety ....Mr. Timothy MARRON
35 Dean of Students ....Mr. Darrell GOODWIN
85 Director International Student Ctr ....Mr. Ryan GREENE
104 Director Education Abroad ....Ms. Gina LOPARDO
36 Executive Director Career Services ....Vacant
38 Director Counseling Center ....Dr. Kimberly CALUZA
28 Director of Multicultural Affairs ....Ms. Tiffany GRAY
39 Dir Housing & Resid Life ....Ms. Kathleen BAKER
25 Director Research & Sponsored Proj ....Dr. Nalini IYER
96 Director of Purchasing ....Ms. Marie PETERSON
23 Director Student Health Center ....Ms. Maura O'CONNOR
04 Executive Secretary to President ....Ms. Liz PILATI
100 Assistant to the President ....Ms. Kathy YBARRA
105 Web Communications Manager ....Mr. Jason BEARD
51 Dean New and Continuing Studies ....Dr. Richard FEHRENBACHER
22 Dir Professional Dev/EEO ....Ms. Helaina SOREY
86 Director of External Affairs ....Mr. Solynn MCCURDY
27 Associate Chief Information Officer ....Mr. Travis NATION

Shoreline Community College (E)

16101 Greenwood Avenue N, Shoreline WA 98133-5696
County: King FICE Identification: 003791
Unit ID: 236610
Telephone: (206) 546-4101 Carnegie Class: Assoc/MT-VT-High Non
FAX Number: (206) 546-4630 Calendar System: Quarter
URL: www.shoreline.edu
Established: 1964 Annual Undergrad Tuition & Fees (In-State): $3,735
Enrollment: 5,751 Coed
Affiliation or Control: State IRS Status: 170(c)1
Highest Offering: Associate Degree
Accreditation: NW, ADNUR, CAHIIM, DH, MLTAD

01 President ....Dr. Cheryl ROBERTS
05 VP Academic & Student Affairs ....Ms. Alison STEVENS
15 VP Human Resources ....Vacant
111 VP Advancement ....Ms. Mary BRUEGGEMAN
26 Exec Dir Communication/Marketing ....Ms. Martha G. LYNN
114 Director Budget ....Vacant
04 Exec Asst to the President ....Ms. Lori YONEMITSU
85 Exec Dir International Programs ....Ms. Diana SAMPSON
72 Director Technology Support Service ....Mr. Gary KALBFLEISCH
06 Registrar ....Ms. Chris MELTON
18 Director Facilities ....Mr. Jason FRANCOIS
19 Director Safety & Security ....Mr. Edwin LUCERO
66 Program Director Nursing ....Ms. Lynn VON SCHLIEDER
37 Director Financial Aid ....Ms. Chris MELTON
38 Assoc Dean Counseling ....Vacant
109 Director Auxiliary Services ....Ms. Leah PEARCE
09 Dir Institutional Effectiveness ....Ms. Bayta MARING
08 Dean Library Services ....Vacant
32 Dean of Students ....Vacant
103 Exec Dean Workforce/Auto ....Mr. Guy HAMILTON
79 Dean Humanities Division ....Ms. Kathy HUNT
70 Dean Social Science ....Ms. Amy KINSEL
81 Exec Dean Math/Science ....Mr. Guy HAMILTON
27 Exec Dir Communication/Marketing ....Ms. Martha LYNN
41 Athletic Director ....Mr. Steve ESKRIDGE

Skagit Valley College (F)

2405 College Way, Mount Vernon WA 98273-5899
County: Skagit FICE Identification: 003792
Unit ID: 236638
Telephone: (360) 416-7600 Carnegie Class: Bac/Assoc-Assoc Dom
FAX Number: (360) 416-7890 Calendar System: Quarter
URL: www.skagit.edu
Established: 1926 Annual Undergrad Tuition & Fees (In-State): $4,200
Enrollment: 5,290 Coed
Affiliation or Control: State IRS Status: 501(c)3
Highest Offering: Baccalaureate
Accreditation: NW, ACFEI, ADNUR, MAC

01 President ....Dr. Thomas KEEGAN
05 Vice President for Instruction ....Dr. Kenneth LAWSON
10 Vice Pres Administrative Services ....Mr. Ed JARAMILLO
12 Vice President of Whidbey Campus ....Dr. Laura CAILLOUX
104 Assoc VP International Education ....Ms. Mari ACOB-NASH
13 Dean of Information Technology ....Mr. Andy HEISER
103 Dean Workforce Education ....Mr. Darren GREENO
20 Dean Academic Education ....Dr. Gabriel MAST
84 Assoc Dean Enrollment Services ....Ms. Sinead PLAGGE
32 Director of Student Life ....Mr. Brian MURPHY
37 Director of Financial Aid ....Ms. Crystal ALLISON
15 Exec Director of Human Resources ....Ms. Carolyn TUCKER
18 Director of Facilities & Operations ....Mr. Dave SCOTT
26 Chief Public Information Officer ....Ms. Arden AINLEY
104 Director of International Programs ....Ms. Christa SCHULZ
40 Bookstore Manager ....Ms. Kim HALL
41 Athletic Director ....Mr. Steve EPPERSON
09 Director of Institutional Research ....Dr. Maureen PETTITT

South Puget Sound Community College (G)

2011 Mottman Road, SW, Olympia WA 98512-6292
County: Thurston FICE Identification: 005372
Unit ID: 236656
Telephone: (360) 754-7711 Carnegie Class: Assoc/MT-VT-High Non
FAX Number: (360) 664-0780 Calendar System: Quarter
URL: www.spscc.edu
Established: 1962 Annual Undergrad Tuition & Fees (In-State): $4,104
Enrollment: 4,839 Coed
Affiliation or Control: State IRS Status: 501(c)3
Highest Offering: Associate Degree
Accreditation: NW, ACFEI, DA, IFSAC, MAC

01 President ....Dr. Timothy STOKES
04 Special Assistant to the President ....Ms. Diana TOLEDO

05 Vice President for Instruction .... Dr. Michelle ANDREAS
32 Vice President for Student Services .... Dr. David PELKEY
11 Vice Pres Administrative Services .... Mr. Albert BROWN
07 Dean of Enrollment Services .... Mr. Steven ASHPOLE
18 Director of Facilities ....Ms. Laura PRICE
26 Dir of Public Relations & Events .... Ms. Kelly GREEN
35 Dean Student Engagement/Retention .... Ms. Jennifer MANLEY
37 Dean of Student Financial Services .... Ms. Johanna DWYER
15 Chief Human Resources Officer .... Mr. Kennith HARDEN
102 Exec Director of College Foundation ....Ms. Tanya MOTE
28 Director of Diversity & Equity ....Vacant
09 Director of Institutional Research .... Ms. Jennifer TUIA
06 Director of Enrollment/Registrar .... Ms. Heidi DEARBORN
08 Dean of Academic Support Services ....Ms. Amy KELLY
19 Director of Safety & Security .... Mr. Robert SHAILOR
13 Chief Information Officer .... Ms. Lori CASILE
72 Dean of Applied Technology .... Ms. Kathy HOOVER
76 Dean of Natural & Applied Sciences .... Dr. Kevin ASMAN
79 Dean of Humanities/Communications .... Ms. Mary SOLTMAN
83 Dean of Social Sciences & Business .... Ms. Valerie SUNDBY-THORP
96 Procurement & Supply Specialist 4 ....Ms. Vida SHERRARD-HANNON

Tacoma Community College (A)

6501 S 19th Street, Tacoma WA 98466-6100

County: Pierce | FICE Identification: 003796 | Unit ID: 236753
Telephone: (253) 566-5000 | Carnegie Class: Assoc/MT-VT-High Non
FAX Number: N/A | Calendar System: Quarter
URL: www.tacomacc.edu
Established: 1965 | Annual Undergrad Tuition & Fees (In-State): $3,686
Enrollment: 7,202 | Coed
Affiliation or Control: State | IRS Status: 501(c)3
Highest Offering: Baccalaureate
Accreditation: NW, ADNUR, CAHIIM, COARC, DMS, EMT, RAD

01 Co-President .... Mr. Bill RYBERG
01 Co-President ....Ms. Mary CHIKWINYA
05 Exec VP Academic/Student Affairs ....Dr. Tod TREAT
11 Vice Pres Administrative Services ....Vacant
32 Vice Pres Student Services ....Ms. Mary CHIKWINYA
88 Dir Conduct/Compliance & Partners .... Ms. Dolores HAUGEN
07 Dean for Entry & Enrollment Svcs .... Ms. Betsy ABTS
38 Dean for Advising and Counseling .... Ms. Shema HANEBUTTE
108 Dean Org Learning & Effectiveness ....Vacant
18 Director Facilities/CapitalProjects ....Mr. Greg RANDALL
35 Director of Student Engagement ....Ms. Sonja MORGAN
37 Director Student Financial Aid ....Ms. Kim MATISON
04 Executive Asst to President ....Ms. Kelly MAXFIELD
09 Director of Institutional Research ....Ms. Kelley SADLER
15 Director of Human Resources ....Ms. Beth BROOKS
111 Vice Pres for College Advancement .... Mr. Bill RYBERG
41 Athletic Director .... Mr. Jason PRENEVOST
10 Director Financial Services ....Vacant
13 Director of IT .... Mr. Clay KRAUSS
106 Dir Online Education/E-learning .... Mr. Chris SORAN
19 Director Security/Safety ....Mr. Will HOWARD
26 Chief Public Relations/Marketing .... Ms. Tamyra HOWSER

University of Phoenix Western Washington Campus (B)

7100 Fort Dent Way, Suite 100, Tukwila WA 98188-8553

Telephone: (425) 572-1600 | Identification: 770234
Accreditation: &NH, ACBSP

† No longer accepting campus-based students.

University of Puget Sound (C)

1500 N Warner St., Tacoma WA 98416-0002

County: Pierce | FICE Identification: 003797 | Unit ID: 236328
Telephone: (253) 879-3100 | Carnegie Class: Bac-A&S
FAX Number: (253) 879-3500 | Calendar System: Semester
URL: www.pugetsound.edu
Established: 1888 | Annual Undergrad Tuition & Fees: $46,552
Enrollment: 2,774 | Coed
Affiliation or Control: Independent Non-Profit | IRS Status: 501(c)3
Highest Offering: Doctorate
Accreditation: NW, IPSY, MUS, OT, PTA

01 President ....Dr. Isiaah CRAWFORD
101 Board Secy/Dir Ofc of President ....Ms. Mary Elizabeth COLLINS
05 Academic VP/Dean of University ....Dr. Kristine M. BARTANEN
10 Vice Pres Finance & Admin .... Ms. Sherry B. MONDOU
26 Vice President University Relations ....Mr. David BEERS
84 Vice President Enrollment .... Ms. Laura E. MARTIN-FEDICH
32 VP Student Affairs/Dean of Students ....Vacant
114 Assoc VP Accounting/Budget Svcs ....Ms. Janet S. HALLMAN
15 Assoc Vice Pres Human Resources .... Ms. Cindy MATERN
21 Assoc Vice Pres Business Services ....Mr. John M. HICKEY
18 Assoc Vice Pres Facilities Services ....Mr. Bob KIEF
37 Assoc VP for Student Financial Svcs .....Ms. Maggie A. MITTUCH
27 Executive Dir of Communications .... Ms. Gayle MCINTOSH
13 Chief Information Officer .... Mr. Jeremy L. CUCCO
28 Dean Diversity and Inclusion ....Dr. Michael BENITEZ
20 Associate Academic Dean .... Dr. Martin JACKSON
20 Associate Academic Dean .... Dr. Sunil KUKREJA
20 Associate Academic Dean ....Dr. Renee HOUSTON

09 Dir Inst Research & Retention .... Ms. C. Ellen PETERS
06 Registrar ....Mr. Michael PASTORE
08 Library Director .... Ms. Jane CARLIN
41 Director of Athletics ....Ms. Amy E. HACKETT
29 Director Alumni & Parent Relations .... Ms. Allison CANNADY-SMITH
85 Director International Programs .... Mr. Roy ROBINSON
53 Dean School of Education ....Dr. Amy RYKEN
50 Dir School of Business/Leadership .... Dr. Alva BUTCHER
64 Director of School of Music .... Dr. Keith C. WARD
88 Director of Occupational Therapy ....Dr. Yvonne SWINTH
88 Director of Physical Therapy ....Dr. Robert BOYLES

University of Washington (D)

1400 NE Campus Parkway, Seattle WA 98195-0001

County: King | FICE Identification: 003798 | Unit ID: 236948
Telephone: (206) 543-2100 | Carnegie Class: DU-Highest
FAX Number: (206) 543-9285 | Calendar System: Quarter
URL: www.washington.edu
Established: 1861 | Annual Undergrad Tuition & Fees (In-State): $10,753
Enrollment: 45,408 | Coed
Affiliation or Control: State | IRS Status: 501(c)3
Highest Offering: Doctorate
Accreditation: NW, ARCPA, AUD, CAHIIM, CEA, CLPSY, CONST, DENT, DIETC, EMT, ENG, HSA, IPSY, JOUR, LAW, LIB, LSAR, MED, MIDWF, MT, NURSE, OPE, OT, PAST, PDPSY, PH, PHAR, PLNG, PTA, SCPSY, SP, SPAA, SW

01 President ....Dr. Ana Mari CAUCE
05 Provost/Exec Vice Pres .... Dr. Gerald J. BALDASTY
12 Chancellor Bothell Campus .... Dr. Bjong W. YEIGH
12 Chancellor Tacoma Campus ....Dr. Mark PAGANO
10 Executive VP Finance and Admin ....Dr. Jeffrey SCOTT
28 VP Minority Affs/Vice Prov Div ....Dr. Rickey HALL
17 Exec VP Med Affs/CEO UW Med/Dean ....Dr. Paul G. RAMSEY
111 Vice Pres for Univ Advancement .... Dr. Connie KRAVAS
15 Vice President Human Resources .... Ms. Mindy KORNBERG
13 Int VP for UW IT .... Mr. Aaron POWELL
26 Chief Marketing & Communications ....Ms. Mary GRESCH
46 Vice Provost Research .... Dr. Mary E. LIDSTROM
51 V Provost UW Continuum College ....Dr. Rovy BRANON
45 Assoc Vice Prov Plng & Budgeting ....Ms. Sarah NORRIS HALL
20 Vice Prov/Dean Undergrad Acad Affs ....Dr. Ed TAYLOR
32 Vice Pres Student Life .... Mr. Denzil SUITE
88 V Provost for Academic Personnel ....Dr. Cheryl A. CAMERON
88 V Prov for Innovation/CoMotion .... Dr. Vikram JANDHYALA
86 Director Federal Relations .... Ms. Sarah CASTRO
43 Division Chief Attorney General ....Ms. Karin NYROP
06 University Registrar .... Ms. Helen GARRETT
29 Assoc VP Alum Relations ....Mr. Paul RUCKER
17 Exec Dir UW Medical Ctr Admin .... Mr. Geoff P. AUSTIN
37 Asst VP Enroll/Exec Dir Fin Aid ....Ms. Kay LEWIS
86 Chief Strategy Officer .... Ms. Margaret A. SHEPHERD
84 Assoc VP Enrollment/Admissions .... Dr. Philip BALLINGER
09 Director Institutional Analysis .... Ms. Carol DIEM
36 Director Career Center .... Ms. Susan TERRY
14 CFO/UW Information Technology .... Mr. Bill FERRIS
18 Assoc VP Capital Planning Devel ....Mr. Michael MCCORMICK
92 Director Honors Program .... Dr. Victoria LAWSON
41 Director Athletics .... Ms. Jennifer COHEN
08 VP for Digital Init/Dean Libraries ....Ms. Lizabeth A. WILSON
96 Director Procurement Services .... Mr. Mark CONLEY
58 Vice Prov/Dean Graduate School .... Dr. David L. EATON
49 Dean Arts & Sciences ....Dr. Robert STACEY
47 Dean Col of Built Environments ..... Dr. John SCHAUFELBERGER
22 Dir EOAA .... Mr. Torrey TIBURZI
50 Dean Business School .... Dr. Jim JIAMBALVO
54 Dean Engineering .... Dr. Michael B. BRAGG
61 Int Dean Law School .... Dr. Anita KRUG
70 Dean Social Work .... Dr. Edwina UEHARA
52 Dean Dentistry ....Dr. Joel H. BERG
63 Dean Medicine ....Dr. Paul G. RAMSEY
66 Dean Nursing .... Dr. Azita EMAMI
67 Dean Pharmacy .... Dr. Sean SULLIVAN
69 Int Dean School of Public Health ....Dr. Joel KAUFMAN
53 Dean College of Education ....Dr. Mia TUAN
80 Dean of Public Affairs .... Dr. Sandra O. ARCHIBALD
88 Assoc Dean Information School ....Dr. Carole PALMER
88 Dean Col of the Environment .... Dr. Lisa GRAUMLICH
04 Executive Asst to President .... Ms. Lenina ARENAS-FUENTES
07 Director of Admissions .... Mr. Paul SEEGERT
104 Director Study Abroad .... Mr. Peter MORAN
108 Int Assc Dir Educational Assessment .... Ms. Debbie MCGHEE
19 Director Security/Safety .... Mr. John N. VINSON
38 Director Student Counseling ....Dr. Natacha F. KUNE
39 Director Student Housing .... Ms. Pam SCHREIBER
101 Secretary to the Board of Regents ....Mr. Tyler LANGE
102 Asst Vice Pres Constituency Pgms ....Ms. Joanna GLICKLER
44 Sr Director Annual Philanthropy ...... Ms. Jennifer MACCORMACK

Walla Walla Community College (E)

500 Tausick Way, Walla Walla WA 99362-9267

County: Walla Walla | FICE Identification: 005006 | Unit ID: 236887
Telephone: (509) 522-2500 | Carnegie Class: Assoc/HVT-High Non
FAX Number: (509) 527-4480 | Calendar System: Quarter
URL: www.wwcc.edu
Established: 1967 | Annual Undergrad Tuition & Fees (In-State): $4,203
Enrollment: 4,617 | Coed
Affiliation or Control: State | IRS Status: 170(c)1
Highest Offering: Associate Degree
Accreditation: NW, ADNUR, MAC

01 President ....Dr. Derek R. BRANDES
05 Vice President of Instruction ....Dr. Marleen RAMSEY
32 Vice Pres of Student Affairs ....Dr. Jose DA SILVA
10 VP Financial & Admin Services ....Mrs. Davina K. FOGG
76 Dean of Health Sciences Education .... Ms. Kathleen ADAMSKI
111 Vice President of Advancement ....Mr. Doug BAYNE
07 Director of Admissions/Registrar ....Mr. Carlos E. DELGADILLO
121 Exec Director Strategic Initiatives .... Ms. Kristi WELLINGTON-BAKER
37 Financial Aid Director ....Ms. Danielle HODGEN
08 Director of Library Services ....Mrs. Stacy PREST
12 Dean Clarkston Campus ....Dr. Chad MILTENBERGER
41 Athletic Director ....Mr. Jeffrey E. REINLAND
15 Vice President of Human Resources ..Mrs. Sharon M. HARTFORD
18 Dir Facility Svcs/Capital Projects ....Mr. Shane LOPER
106 Director of eLearning ....Ms. Lisa CHAMBERLIN
88 Dean of Transitional Studies ....Ms. Darlene SNIDER
40 Bookstore Manager .... Ms. Alecia ANGELL
56 Director of Extended Learning ....Ms. Jodi WORDEN
26 Exec Dir Communications/Marketing ....Ms. Melissa THIESSEN
06 Registrar ....Mr. Carlos DELGADILLO
09 Exc Dir Institutional Effectiveness .... Dr. Nicholas VELLUZZI
103 Dean Workforce Education ....Mr. Jerry ANHORN, JR.
13 Director Technology Svcs .... Mr. Kevin COMBS

Walla Walla University (F)

204 S College Avenue, College Place WA 99324-1198

County: Walla Walla | FICE Identification: 003799 | Unit ID: 236896
Telephone: (509) 527-2615 | Carnegie Class: Masters/M
FAX Number: (509) 527-2397 | Calendar System: Quarter
URL: www.wallawalla.edu
Established: 1892 | Annual Undergrad Tuition & Fees: $26,982
Enrollment: 1,840 | Coed
Affiliation or Control: Seventh-day Adventist | IRS Status: 501(c)3
Highest Offering: Master's
Accreditation: NW, ACBSP, ACFEI, ENG, MUS, NUR, NURSE, SW

01 President .... Dr. John MCVAY
05 Vice Pres Academic Administration ....Vacant
10 Vice Pres Financial Administration .... Mr. Steve ROSE
32 Vice Pres Student Life and Mission .... Dr. Doug TILSTRA
84 VP University Relations and Advance ....Ms. Jodi WAGNER
28 Asst to President for Diversity ....Dr. Pedrito MAYNARD-REID
04 Executive Asst Office of President ....Ms. Deirdre BENWELL
20 Associate Vice Pres Academic Admin ....Dr. Scott LIGMAN
21 Associate Vice Pres Financial Admin .... Mr. Ken VYHMEISTER
35 Asst VP/Dean of Students ....Ms. Hilary CATLETT
08 Director of Libraries ....Ms. Carolyn GASKELL
06 Registrar ....Ms. Carolyn DENNEY
42 Chaplain .... Mr. Paddy MCCOY
29 Director of Alumni Relations .... Mrs. Claudia SANTELLANO
13 Director Information Services ....Mr. Scott MCFADDEN
37 Assoc Director Financial Aid .... Ms. Nancy CALDERA
15 Director Human Resources .... Ms. Jennifer CARPENTER
18 Director of Facility Services ....Mr. George BENNETT
26 Dir Marketing/University Relations ..Ms. Emily MUTHERSBAUGH
07 Director of Admissions ....Mr. Dallas WEIS
36 Director Career Development Center .... Mr. David LINDSTROM
38 Director Counseling/Testing ....Ms. Michelle NADEN
09 Director of Institutional Research ....Mr. Brian HARTMAN
41 Athletic Director ....Mr. Jordan STIMMEL
19 Campus Security Director ....Ms. Courtney BRYANT
44 Director Gift Planning ....Ms. Dorita TESSIER
58 Dean of Graduate Programs .... Dr. Pam CRESS
66 Dean of School of Nursing ....Dr. Lucille KRULL
73 Dean of School of Theology ....Dr. David THOMAS
54 Dean of School of Engineering .... Dr. Doug LOGAN
50 Dean of Business ....Mr. Josefer MONTES
53 Dean of Education ....Vacant
70 Dean of Social Work/Sociology ....Dr. Susan SMITH

Washington State University (G)

PO Box 645910, Pullman WA 99164-5910

County: Whitman | FICE Identification: 003800 | Unit ID: 236939
Telephone: (509) 335-3564 | Carnegie Class: DU-Highest
FAX Number: N/A | Calendar System: Semester
URL: www.wsu.edu
Established: 1890 | Annual Undergrad Tuition & Fees (In-District): $11,041
Enrollment: 29,686 | Coed
Affiliation or Control: State/Local | IRS Status: 501(c)3
Highest Offering: Doctorate
Accreditation: NW, CAATE, CEA, CIDA, CLPSY, CONST, COPSY, CS, DIETC, ENG, HSA, IPSY, LSAR, MUS, NURSE, PHAR, SP, SPAA, VET

01 President .... Dr. Kirk SCHULZ
05 Provost/Exec Vice President .... Dr. Daniel BERNADO
10 VP Finance/Administration ....Ms. Stacy PEARSON
111 VP Advancement/CEO WSU Foundation .... Mr. Gil PICCIOTTO
106 VP Academic Outreach/Innovation .... Dr. David CILLAY
32 VP Student Affairs ....Dr. Mary Jo GONZALES
13 VP Information Tech & CIO ....Mr. Sasi PILLAY
46 Vice President Research ....Dr. Christopher KEANE
86 VP External AffairsGovernment Rels ....Ms. Colleen KERR
26 Vice President Marketing & Comm .... Mr. Phil WEILER
20 Vice Provost for Faculty Affairs ....Vacant
12 Chancellor WSU Everett ....Dr. Paul PITRE
12 Chancellor WSU Spokane .... Dr. Daryll DEWALD

12 Chancellor WSU Tri-Cities ....Dr. Keith MOO-YOUNG
12 Chancellor WSU Vancouver ....Dr. Mel NETZHAMMER
43 Div Chief State Attorney Gen Office ....Ms. Danielle HESS
47 Dean Agric/Human Natl Res Sci ....Dr. Ron MITTELHAMMER
50 Dean Carson College of Business ....Dr. Chip HUNTER
53 Dean College of Education ....Dr. Michael TREVISAN
54 Int Dean Engineering & Architecture ....Dr. Don BENDER
66 Dean College of Nursing ....Dr. Joyce GRIFFIN-SOBEL
67 Dean College of Pharmacy ....Dr. Gary POLLACK
60 Int Dean College of Communication ....Dr. Bruce PINKLETON
49 Dean College of Arts & Sciences ....Dr. Daryll DEWALD
74 Dean College of Veterinary Medicine ....Dr. Bryan K. SLINKER
92 Dean Honors College ....Dr. M. Grant NORTON
21 Assoc VP & Chief Budget Officer ....Ms. Joan KING
18 Assoc VP Facilities Services ....Ms. Olivia YANG
71 Dean University College ....Dr. Mary F. WACK
08 Dean Libraries ....Mr. Joseph STARRATT
06 Interim University Registrar ....Mr. Matthew ZIMMERMAN
07 Director Admissions ....Ms. Wendy PETERSON
09 Assoc Dir Institutional Research ....Ms. Fran HERMANSTON
37 Director Financial Aid ....Mr. Brian DIXON
41 Director Intercollegiate Athletics ....Mr. William H. MOOS
116 Director Internal Audit ....Ms. Heather LOPEZ
04 Administrative Asst to President ....Mrs. Ginger DRUFFEL

Washington State University-Spokane (A)

412 East Spokane Falls Blvd, Spokane WA 99207-9600
Telephone: (509) 358-7500 Identification: 770948
Accreditation: &NW, #MED

Washington State University-Tri Cities (B)

2710 Crimson Way, Richland WA 99354-1671
Telephone: (509) 372-7000 Identification: 770949
Accreditation: &NW, CEA

Washington State University-Vancouver (C)

14204 NE Salmon Creek Ave, Vancouver WA 98686-9600
Telephone: (360) 549-9788 Identification: 770950
Accreditation: &NW

Wenatchee Valley College (D)

1300 Fifth Street, Wenatchee WA 98801-1799
County: Chelan FICE Identification: 003801
Unit ID: 236975
Telephone: (509) 682-6800 Carnegie Class: Assoc/MT-VT-Mix Trad/Non
FAX Number: (509) 682-6541 Calendar System: Quarter
URL: www.wvc.edu
Established: 1939 Annual Undergrad Tuition & Fees (In-State): $3,678
Enrollment: 3,218 Coed
Affiliation or Control: State IRS Status: 501(c)3
Highest Offering: Associate Degree
Accreditation: NW, ADNUR, MAC, MLTAD

01 President ....Mr. James RICHARDSON
04 Exec Assistant to President ....Ms. Janet FRANZ
05 Vice President of Instruction ....Dr. Carli SCHIFFNER
11 VP of Administrative Services ....Mr. Brett RILEY
38 Vice President Student Development ....Dr. Chio FLORES
49 Dean Lib Arts/Sciences/Basic Skills ....Ms. Lori KELLER
12 Dean Omak Campus ....Vacant
103 Dean Workforce Education ....Vacant
76 Dean Allied Health/Nursing ....Ms. Jenny CAPELO
15 Director Human Resources ....Ms. Reagan BELLAMY
32 Director Student Programs/Outreach ....Ms. Laura SINGLETARY
37 Director Financial Aid ....Mr. Kevin BERG
18 Facilities & Operations Manager ....Mr. Rich PETERS
06 Registrar ....Mr. Bruce MAXWELL
08 Dn Libraries/Learning Technologies . Mr. Andrew HERSH-TUDOR
10 Director of Fiscal Services ....Ms. Janice FREDSON
26 Communications Manager ....Ms. Libby SIEBENS
20 Coordinator of Adult Basic Skills ....Mr. Aaron PARROTT
27 Marketing/Graphic Design Specialist ....Mr. Nick WINTERS

† Granted candidacy at the Baccalaureate level.

Western Washington University (E)

516 High Street, Bellingham WA 98225-5950
County: Whatcom FICE Identification: 003802
Unit ID: 237011
Telephone: (360) 650-3000 Carnegie Class: Masters/L
FAX Number: (360) 650-3022 Calendar System: Quarter
URL: www.wwu.edu
Established: 1893 Annual Undergrad Tuition & Fees (In-State): $7,903
Enrollment: 15,332 Coed
Affiliation or Control: State IRS Status: 501(c)3
Highest Offering: Beyond Master's But Less Than Doctorate
Accreditation: NW, ART, @AUD, CACREP, CAEPN, CEA, CS, ENGT, MUS, NRPA, NURSE, PLNG, SP

01 President ....Dr. Sabah RANDHAWA
05 Vice Pres Academic Affairs/Provost ....Dr. Brent CARBAJAL
10 Vice Pres Business/Financial Affs ..Mr. Richard D. VAN DEN HUL
84 VP Enrollment/Student Services ....Dr. Melynda HUSKEY
26 Vice Pres for University Relations ....Mr. Steve SWAN
111 Vice Pres University Advancement ....Ms. Stephanie BOWERS
32 Asst VP Enrollment/Student Services ....Dr. Kunle OJIKUTU
13 Vice Prov Info/Chief Info Officer ....Dr. Chuck LANHAM
58 Vice Prov Rsch/Dean Grad Sch ....Dr. Kathleen KITTO
20 Vice Prov Undergraduate Education ....Dr. Steven L. VANDERSTAAY
22 Vice Prov Equal Oppty/Employmt Div ....Dr. Sue GUENTER-SCHLESINGER
51 Vice Provost Extended Education ....Dr. Earl F. GIBBONS
35 Dean of Students ....Mr. Theodore W. PRATT, JR.
15 Asst VP for Human Resources ....Ms. Chyerl WOLFE-LEE
06 Registrar ....Mr. David BRUNNEMER
07 Director of Admissions ....Mr. Cezar MESQUITA
36 Director Career Services Center ....Ms. Tina LOUDON
37 Director Financial Aid ....Ms. Clara CAPRON
29 Executive Director Alumni Relations ....Ms. Deborah DEWEES
27 Director University Communications ....Mr. Paul COCKE
08 Dean of Libraries ....Dr. Mark GREENBERG
39 Director University Residences ....Mr. Leonard JONES
04 Sr Executive Assistant to President ....Dr. Paul DUNN
09 Director of Institutional Research ....Dr. Ming ZHANG
18 Director of Facilities Management ....Mr. John A. FURMAN
19 Director of Public Safety ....Mr. Darin RASMUSSEN
41 Athletic Director ....Mr. Steven CARD
92 Director of Honors Program ....Dr. Scott LINNEMAN
96 Director of Business Services ....Mr. Pete HEILGEIST
79 Dean College of Humanities/Soc Sci .. Dr. Brent MALLINCKRODT
72 Dean College of Science/Technology ....Dr. Brad JOHNSON
50 Dean College Business & Econ ....Dr. Scott YOUNG
65 Dean Huxley Col of the Environment . Dr. Steven HOLLENHORST
57 Dean College of Fine & Perf ....Dr. Christopher SPICER
53 Dean Woodring College of Education ....Dr. Francisco RIOS
12 Dean Fairhaven College ....Dr. Jack HERRING
101 Secretary to the Board of Trustees ..... Ms. Barbara A. SANDOVAL
104 Director Intl Programs & Exchanges ... Ms. Liz PARTOLAN-FRAY
25 Contracts Assistant ....Ms. Andrea RODGER
38 Director Counseling Center ....Dr. Nancy CORBIN
43 AAG/Chief Legal Advisor ....Ms. Kerena HIGGINS
86 Director Government Relations ....Ms. Becca KENNA-SCHENK

† Granted candidacy at the Doctorate level.

Whatcom Community College (F)

237 W Kellogg Road, Bellingham WA 98226-8003
County: Whatcom FICE Identification: 010364
Unit ID: 237039
Telephone: (360) 383-3000 Carnegie Class: Assoc/HT-Mix Trad/Non
FAX Number: (360) 383-4000 Calendar System: Quarter
URL: www.whatcom.ctc.edu
Established: 1970 Annual Undergrad Tuition & Fees (In-State): $4,316
Enrollment: 4,391 Coed
Affiliation or Control: State IRS Status: 501(c)3
Highest Offering: Associate Degree
Accreditation: NW, ADNUR, MAC, PTAA

01 President ....Dr. Kathi HIYANE-BROWN
05 Vice President for Instruction ....Mr. Ed HARRI
11 Int VP for Administrative Services ....Mr. Nate LANGSTRAAT
32 Vice Pres for Student Services ....Dr. Luca LEWIS
20 Dean for Instruction ....Vacant
08 Library Director ....Mr. Howard FULLER
10 Director for Business & Finance ....Mr. Ken BRONSTEIN
06 Registrar ....Mr. Michael SINGLETARY
37 Director of Financial Aid ....Mr. David KLAFFKE
85 Director of International Programs ....Mr. Kelly KESTER
40 Bookstore Manager ....Mr. Jon SPORES
18 Senior Facilities Director ....Mr. Brian KEELEY
04 Special Assistant to the President ....Ms. Rafeeka KLOKE
15 Executive Director Human Resources ....Ms. Becky RAWLINGS
09 Director for Institutional Research ....Dr. Anne Marie KARLBERG

† Granted candidacy at the Baccalaureate level.

Whitman College (G)

345 Boyer Avenue, Walla Walla WA 99362-2083
County: Walla Walla FICE Identification: 003803
Unit ID: 237057
Telephone: (509) 527-5411 Carnegie Class: Bac-A&S
FAX Number: (509) 527-5859 Calendar System: Semester
URL: www.whitman.edu
Established: 1882 Annual Undergrad Tuition & Fees: $47,862
Enrollment: 1,470 Coed
Affiliation or Control: Independent Non-Profit IRS Status: 501(c)3
Highest Offering: Baccalaureate
Accreditation: NW

01 President ....Dr. Kathleen MURRAY
05 Provost/Dean of Faculty ....Dr. Alzada TIPTON
30 Vice President for Development ....Mr. John W. BOGLEY
10 Treasurer/Chief Financial Officer ....Mr. Peter W. HARVEY
32 Dean of Students ....Mr. Daren MOOKO
20 Associate Dean of Faculty ....Dr. Lisa R. PERFETTI
07 Dean of Admission/Financial Aid ....Mr. Tony A. CABASCO
13 Chief Technology Officer ....Mr. Dan M. TERRIO
18 Chief Facilities/Physical Plant ....Mr. Daniel L. PARK
08 Librarian ....Mrs. Dalia L. CORKRUM
91 Director of Enterprise Technology ....Mr. Michael OSTERMAN
09 Director of Institutional Research ....Dr. Neal J. CHRISTOPHERSON
20 Assistant Dean of Faculty ....Dr. Kendra J. GOLDEN
35 Associate Dean of Students ....Mrs. Barbara A. MAXWELL
26 Chief Communications Officer ....Dr. Joshua JENSEN
38 Director Student Counseling ....Mr. F. 'Thatcher' CARTER
39 Director Residence Life & Housing ....Ms. Nancy J. TAVELLI
29 Director Alumni Relations ....Ms. Nancy L. MITCHELL
104 Director of Off-Campus Studies ....Ms. Susan H. HOLME
15 Director Human Resources ....Mr. Dennis T. HOPWOOD
06 Registrar ....Ms. Stacey J. GIUSTI
19 Director of Security ....Mr. Mattew STROE
23 Director Health Services ....Ms. Claudia L. NESS
36 Director of Career Center ....Ms. Gayle TOWNSEND
37 Director of Financial Aid Services ....Ms. Marilyn K. PONTI
41 Athletic Director ....Mr. Dean C. SNIDER
42 Coordinator of Spiritual Life ....Mr. Adam M. KIRTLEY
04 Executive Assistant to President ....Ms. Jennifer A. CASPER
44 Director of Annual Giving ....Mr. Brian DOHE

Whitworth University (H)

300 W Hawthorne Road, Spokane WA 99251-0001
County: Spokane FICE Identification: 003804
Unit ID: 237066
Telephone: (509) 777-1000 Carnegie Class: Masters/S
FAX Number: (509) 777-4763 Calendar System: 4/1/4
URL: www.whitworth.edu
Established: 1890 Annual Undergrad Tuition & Fees: $40,562
Enrollment: 2,650 Coed
Affiliation or Control: Presbyterian IRS Status: 501(c)3
Highest Offering: Master's
Accreditation: NW, CAATE, MUS

01 President ....Dr. Beck A. TAYLOR
05 Provost & Executive Vice President ....Dr. Caroline SIMON
04 Exec Asst to President/Board Secy ....Ms. Ruth PELLS
10 VP Finance & Administration ....Mr. Lawrence PROBUS
32 VP for Student Life/Title IX ....Ms. Rhosetta RHODES
07 VP Admissions & Financial Aid ....Mr. Greg ORWIG
111 VP Institutional Advancement ....Dr. Scott MCQUILKIN
15 Assoc VP Human Resources ....Ms. Dolores HUMISTON
21 Assoc VP Finance & Administration ....Ms. Luz MERKEL
13 Chief Information Officer ....Mr. Kenneth BROWN
42 Dean Spiritual Life ....Dr. Forrest BUCKNER
41 Director of Athletics ....Mr. Timothy DEMANT
28 Chief Diversity Officer ....Dr. Lorna HERNANDEZ JARVIS
20 Associate Provost ....Dr. Brooke KIENER
108 Dir of Assessment/Accreditation ....Dr. Deanna OJENNUS
102 Dir Office of Church Engagement ....Dr. Terry MCGONIGAL
25 Dir Sponsored Program/Grants ....Ms. Lynn NOLAND
53 Interim Dean School of Education ....Dr. Randall MICHAELIS
50 Dean School of Business ....Dr. Timothy WILKINSON
49 Dean College of Arts & Sciences ....Dr. Noelle WIERSMA
06 Registrar ....Mr. Jose ORTIZ
51 AVP Grad Admissions & Cont Studies ....Ms. Cheryl VAWTER
58 Dir Graduate Studies in Education ....Ms. Roberta WILBURN
90 Dir Instructional Resources ....Mr. Kenneth PECKA
88 Assoc Dean Com Standards/Compliance ... Dr. Craig CHATRIAND
29 Dir Alumni/Parent Relations ....Mr. Dale HAMMOND
07 Director of Admissions ....Vacant
18 Director of Facilities Services ....Mr. Christopher EICHORST
23 Interim Director of Health Center ....Ms. Amy CUTLER
37 Director of Financial Aid ....Ms. Traci STENSLAND
35 Assoc Dean of Students/Dir HUB ....Vacant
93 Asst Dean Student Diversity ....Mr. David GARCIA
39 Director of Residence Life ....Mr. Timothy CALDWELL
68 Director of Athletic Training ....Dr. Cynthia WRIGHT
26 Director of Communications ....Ms. Nancy HINES
38 Director of Counseling Services ....Ms. Monica WHITLOCK
46 Director of Institutional Research ....Ms. Wendy OLSON
08 Director Library ....Dr. Amanda CLARK
53 Director MIT ....Dr. David CHERRY
19 Director Security Services ....Ms. Jacquelyn CHRISTENSEN
73 Director MA Theology ....Dr. Jeremy WYNNE
104 Dir of International Education Ctr ....Ms. Sue JACKSON
79 Dir US Cultural Studies ....Dr. Stacy KEOGH GEORGE
50 Int Asst Dir Grad Studies Business ....Ms. Sinead VOORHEES
51 Dir Evening Teacher Certification ....Dr. Stacey HILL
107 Assoc Dean Evening Business Pgm ....Ms. Christie ANDERSON
40 Manager of Bookstore ....Mr. Robin SCHULTZ

Yakima Valley College (I)

PO Box 22520, S 16th Ave & Nob Hill,
Yakima WA 98907-2520
County: Yakima FICE Identification: 003805
Unit ID: 237109
Telephone: (509) 574-4600 Carnegie Class: Bac/Assoc-Assoc Dom
FAX Number: (509) 574-6860 Calendar System: Quarter
URL: www.yvcc.edu
Established: 1928 Annual Undergrad Tuition & Fees (In-State): $4,230
Enrollment: 3,960 Coed
Affiliation or Control: State IRS Status: 170(c)1
Highest Offering: Baccalaureate
Accreditation: NW, ADNUR, DH, MAC, SURGT

01 President ....Dr. Linda KAMINSKI
05 Vice Pres Instruction/Student Svcs ....Mr. Tomas YBARRA
10 Vice Pres Administrative Services ....Dr. Teresa RICH
12 Dean Grandview Campus ....Ms. Marcia SOMER
75 Dean Basic Skills ....Mr. Marc COOMER
13 Director Tech Services ....Mr. Scott TOWSLEY
32 Dean Student Services ....Ms. Leslie BLACKABY
49 Dean Arts & Sciences ....Ms. Kerrie CAVANESS
103 Dean Workforce Education ....Ms. Paulette LOPEZ
08 Library Director ....Ms. Tammy SIEBENBERG
37 Director Student Financial Aid ....Mr. Oscar VERDUZCO

06 Registrar/Director of Admissions .... Ms. Lorena ALVARADO-VALDOVINOS
108 Dir Institutional Effectiveness ....Ms. Sheila DELQUADRI
29 Director Alumni Relations ....Ms. Deborah WILSON
26 Community Relations Coordinator ....Mr. Jay FRANK
15 Director Human Resources ....Mr. Mark ROGSTAD
18 Director Facilities/Physical Plant ....Mr. Jeff WOOD
21 Director Accounting Services ....Ms. Clarissa WOLFE
35 Student Life Coordinator ....Ms. Caitlin GOODWILL
04 Executive Asst to President ....Ms. Megan JENSEN

WEST VIRGINIA

Alderson Broaddus University (A)

101 College Hill Drive, Philippi WV 26416-4600
County: Barbour FICE Identification: 003806
Unit ID: 237118
Telephone: (304) 457-1700 Carnegie Class: Bac-Diverse
FAX Number: (304) 457-6239 Calendar System: Semester
URL: www.ab.edu
Established: 1871 Annual Undergrad Tuition & Fees: $25,350
Enrollment: 1,154 Coed
Affiliation or Control: American Baptist IRS Status: 501(c)3
Highest Offering: Master's
Accreditation: #NH, ARCPA, CAATE, CAEPT, NUR

01 President ....Dr. James (Tim) BARRY
05 Provost/Executive Vice President ....Dr. Joan L. PROPST
11 Vice Pres for Administration ....Mr. Bruce A. BLANKENSHIP
84 Vice Pres Enrollment Management ....Dr. Eric M. SHOR
10 Vice Pres for Finance/CFO ....Mr. Dennis E. STARK
32 Dean of Student Affairs ....Mr. Bruce A. BLANKENSHIP
20 Associate Provost ....Dr. Andrea J. BUCKLEW
63 Dean Col of Physician Asst Studies ....Mr. Thomas F. MOORE
76 Dean College of Health Sciences ....Ms. Kimberly L. WHITE
53 Dean College of Education and Music ....Dr. Jeffrey BUSH
50 Dean Col of Business & Management ....Mr. Richard T. FOLEY
79 Dean Col of Humanities & Soc Sci ....Dr. James M. OWSTON
81 Dean College of Science/Tech/Math ....Dr. Ross A. BRITTAIN
06 Registrar ....Dr. Saundra E. HOXIE
08 Director of Library Services ....Mr. David E. HOXIE
41 Athletic Director ....Mr. Dennis W. CREEHAN
42 Chaplain ....Dr. Carl W. GITTINGS
08 Dir Academic Ctr for Educ Success ....Dr. Amy MASON
21 Controller ....Mr. Jeff ROGERS
29 Director of Alumni Relations ....Mr. Joshua D. ALLEN
44 Director of Annual Giving ....Ms. Christy L. MULLENS-SHAW
40 Director of Campus Services ....Mr. Ed BURDA
36 Director of Career Services ....Ms. Teresa D. VAN ALSBURG
38 Director of Counseling Services ....Mr. Chad HOSTETLER
37 Director of Financial Aid ....Ms. Amy L. KING
18 Director of Facilities ....Mr. Lawrence J. TALLMAN
27 Dir of Information and Research ....Ms. Julia M. MORRIS
13 Director of Information Technology ....Ms. Carol WEAVER
26 Director of Mktg/Communications ....Mr. Craig J. BUTLER
39 Director Student Housing ....Mr. David A. FALLETA
19 Director Security/Safety ....Mr. Matthew SISK
04 Exec Asst to Pres/Sec to the Board ....Mrs. Karla R. HIVELY
105 Web Content Editor ....Vacant
07 Director of Admissions ....Ms. Erika L. THON
09 Director of Institutional Research ....Dr. Bob S. BUCKINGHAM
102 Dir Foundation/Corporate Relations ....Ms. Vicki W. GLASOW

American National University (B)

110 Park Center Drive, Parkersburg WV 26101
Telephone: (304) 699-3005 Identification: 770787
Accreditation: ACICS, MAC

† Branch campus of American National University, Salem, VA

American National University (C)

421 Hilltop Drive, Princeton WV 24740
Telephone: (304) 487-3845 Identification: 666499
Accreditation: ACICS, MAC

† Branch campus of American National University, Salem, VA

American Public University System (D)

111 W Congress Street, Charles Town WV 25414-1621
County: Jefferson FICE Identification: 035393
Unit ID: 449339
Telephone: (304) 724-3700 Carnegie Class: Masters/L
FAX Number: (304) 724-3780 Calendar System: Other
URL: www.apus.edu
Established: 1991 Annual Undergrad Tuition & Fees: $6,880
Enrollment: 52,361 Coed
Affiliation or Control: Proprietary IRS Status: Proprietary
Highest Offering: Doctorate
Accreditation: NH, ACBSP, IFSAC, NURSE, PH

01 President ....Dr. Karan H. POWELL
05 SVP & Provost ....Dr. Vernon SMITH
100 SVP/Chief of Staff ....Dr. Gwen HALL
11 SVP/COO ....Mr. Bob GAY
10 Exec VP & CFO ....Mr. Richard SUNDERLAND, JR.
108 VP Accreditation ....Dr. Jennifer STEPHENS HELM
13 SVP/Chief Information Officer ....Ms. Tracy WOODS
32 VP Student Services ....Ms. Caroline SIMPSON
06 VP/Registrar ....Ms. Michelle NEWMAN
20 Dean of Academic Services ....Dr. Conrad LOTZE
124 Dean Faculty & Student Success ....Dr. Grady BATCHELOR
90 VP Academic & Instructional Tech ....Ms. Karen V. SRBA
43 University Counsel ....Ms. Jennifer J. HERBERT
88 VP Military/Veteran & CC Outreach ....Mr. John ALDRICH
37 VP Financial Aid & Compliance ....Mr. Keith WELLINGS
84 VP Enrollment Mgt & Student Support ....Ms. Terry GRANT
26 VP Marketing ....Ms. Beth LAGUARDIA COOPER
15 VP Human Resources ....Ms. Wendy ANSON
09 VP Institutional Research ....Dr. Dave BECHER
82 Dean Security & Global Studies ....Dr. Mark T. RICCARDI
76 Dean Health Sciences ....Dr. Brian FREELAND
81 Interim Dean STEM ....Dr. Daniel WELSCH
79 Dean Arts & Humanities ....Dr. Grace GLASS
50 Dean Business ....Dr. Chad PATRIZI

Appalachian Bible College (E)

161 College Drive, Mount Hope WV 25880
County: Raleigh FICE Identification: 007544
Unit ID: 237136
Telephone: (304) 877-6428 Carnegie Class: Spec-4-yr-Faith
FAX Number: (304) 877-5082 Calendar System: Semester
URL: abc.edu
Established: 1950 Annual Undergrad Tuition & Fees: $14,000
Enrollment: 281 Coed
Affiliation or Control: Independent Non-Profit IRS Status: 501(c)3
Highest Offering: Master's
Accreditation: NH, BI

01 President ....Dr. Daniel L. ANDERSON
05 Vice President for Academics ....Mr. Daniel S. HANSHEW
10 Vice President for Business ....Mr. Kenneth E. LILLY
30 Vice President for Development ....Rev. Jonathan A. RINKER
32 Vice President for Student Services ....Rev. David E. CHILDS
42 Vice Pres for Extension Ministries ....Mr. David J. HOLLOWAY
33 Dean of Men ....Mr. Kevin GULLION
34 Dean of Women ....Mrs. Linda J. CHILDS
06 Registrar ....Mr. Tim ROWE
07 Director of Admissions ....Mr. Benjamin CALE
08 Librarian ....Mr. David W. DUNKERTON
37 Director of Financial Aid ....Mrs. Laura MARTIN
04 Admin Assistant to the President ....Mrs. Aimee STILES
26 Director of Public Relations ....Miss Karisa A. CLARK

Bethany College (F)

31 E. Campus Drive, Bethany WV 26032-3002
County: Brooke FICE Identification: 003808
Unit ID: 237181
Telephone: (304) 829-7000 Carnegie Class: Bac-A&S
FAX Number: (304) 829-7700 Calendar System: 4/1/4
URL: www.bethanywv.edu
Established: 1840 Annual Undergrad Tuition & Fees: $27,696
Enrollment: 737 Coed
Affiliation or Control: Christian Church (Disciples Of Christ)
IRS Status: 501(c)3
Highest Offering: Master's
Accreditation: NH, CAEPN, SW

01 President ....Dr. Tamara N. RODENBERG
05 Provost/Vice Pres Academic Affairs ....Dr. Joseph LANE
10 Interim Vice President for Finance ....Mrs. Deidra PARR
03 Senior Vice President ....Mr. Sven DE JONG
11 Chief Operations Officer ....Mr. John LIPINSKI
04 Asst to the President ....Ms. Stephanie GORDON
20 Asst Vice President Academic Affs ....Ms. Katherine SHELEK-FURBEE
32 Dean of Students ....Mr. Gerald STEBBINS
37 Director of Financial Aid ....Mr. Jason MCCLAIN
41 Director of Athletics & Recreation ....Mr. Brian ROSE
09 Dir Institutional Research/Records ....Mr. Richard MILLER
88 Director of McCann Learning Center ....Ms. Heather TAYLOR
88 Dir Student Engag/Responsibility ....Ms. Alyssa FEDEROFF
89 Co-Director First Year Experience ....Ms. Angela ICARD
89 Co-Director First Year Experience ....Mr. Travis STRAUB
104 Director of International Programs ....Dr. Harald MENZ
36 Director of Career Services ....Mr. John OSBORNE
23 Director of the Byrd Health Center ....Mrs. Carol TYLER
26 Dir Communications/Integrated Mktg ....Mr. Robert OLTMANNS
29 Director of Alumni/Parent Relations ....Ms. Hannah MCNERNEY
30 Director of Advancement Services ....Ms. Shirley KEMP
88 Director of Sports Information ....Mr. Andrew WOODLEY
88 Director of Church Relations ....Dr. Larry GRIMES
18 Director of Physical Plant ....Mr. Jay EISENHAUER
21 Director of Business Affairs ....Ms. Saralyn DAGUE
19 Director of Safety & Security ....Mr. Charles NEIGHOFF
15 Director of Human Resources ....Ms. Helen BRANCAZIO
39 Assistant Dean of Student Life ....Mr. Andrew LEWIS
35 Director of Student Activities ....Mr. Samuel GOODGE
42 Chaplain ....Rev. Scott THAYER
08 Director of the Libraries ....Mrs. Heather MAY-RICCIUTI
24 Dir Media Services/Classroom Tech ....Mr. Thomas V. FURBEE
88 Public Services Librarian ....Vacant
06 Registrar ....Ms. Lisa CUCARESE
84 Vice Pres of Enrollment Management ....Ms. Mollie CECERE
88 General Manager Conference Center ....Ms. Donna WHITE
109 Director of Dining Services ....Mr. John SHAFFER
40 Manager of the Bookstore ....Ms. Cheryl DEYOUNG
38 College Counselor ....Ms. Renee STOCK

Catholic Distance University (G)

115 West Congress Street, Charles Town WV 25414
County: Jefferson FICE Identification: 041242
Unit ID: 475398
Telephone: (304) 724-5000 Carnegie Class: Not Classified
FAX Number: (304) 724-5017 Calendar System: Other
URL: www.cdu.edu
Established: 1983 Annual Undergrad Tuition & Fees: $10,175
Enrollment: N/A Coed
Affiliation or Control: Independent Non-Profit IRS Status: 501(c)3
Highest Offering: Master's
Accreditation: DEAC

01 President ....Dr. Marianne E. MOUNT
05 Academic Dean ....Dr. Peter BROWN
20 Faculty Chair ....Dr. Matthew BUNSON
88 Dean of Catechetical Programs ....Sr. Mary Margaret SCHLATHER
06 Registrar ....Mrs. Megan DAVIS
51 Continuing Education Support ....Mrs. Kathleen WOODDELL
26 Director of Communications ....Vacant
07 Director of Admissions ....Mrs. Carol CIULLO
37 Financial Aid Officer ....Mrs. Amy SHOUSE
13 Director of Technology ....Mrs. Carol DALEY

Davis & Elkins College (H)

100 Campus Drive, Elkins WV 26241-3996
County: Randolph FICE Identification: 003811
Unit ID: 237358
Telephone: (304) 637-1900 Carnegie Class: Bac-A&S
FAX Number: (304) 637-1413 Calendar System: 4/1/4
URL: www.dewv.edu
Established: 1904 Annual Undergrad Tuition & Fees: $28,842
Enrollment: 796 Coed
Affiliation or Control: Presbyterian Church (U.S.A.) IRS Status: 501(c)3
Highest Offering: Baccalaureate
Accreditation: NH, ADNUR, THEA

01 President ....Mr. Chris A. WOOD
10 VP for Business & Administration ....Mr. Robert O. HARDMAN, II
05 Int Vice Pres for Academic Affairs ....Dr. Robert J. PHILLIPS
32 Vice President for Student Affairs ....Mr. Scott D. GODDARD
30 Vice Pres Institutional Advancement ....Dr. Rosemary M. THOMAS
15 Director Human Resources ....Ms. M. J. COREY
06 Registrar ....Dr. Stephanie C. HAYNES
18 Director of Physical Plant ....Mr. James OWENS
37 Director Financial Planning ....Mr. Matthew A. SUMMERS
08 Assistant Director Booth Library ....Ms. Mary Jo DEJOICE
42 Chaplain ....Vacant
41 Director of Athletics ....Mr. Jamie JOSS
19 Director of Public Safety ....Dr. Michael T. CURTIS
04 Executive Asst to the President ....Ms. Robin PRICE
13 Chief Information Officer ....Mr. Tim GIBSON
29 Director of Alumni Engagement ....Ms. Wendy MORGAN
84 Vice Pres for Enrollment Mgmt ....Dr. Rosemary M. THOMAS
09 Coordinator Institutional Research ....Mr. Guilherme Condolo HUBSCH
26 Dir Communications & Marketing ....Ms. Nanci BROSS-FREGONARA
07 Director of Admission ....Mr. Matthew K. SHIFLETT

Future Generations (I)

390 Road Less Traveled, Franklin WV 26807-9201
County: Pendleton Identification: 666714
Unit ID: 481030
Telephone: (304) 358-2000 Carnegie Class: Spec-4-yr-Other
FAX Number: (304) 358-3008 Calendar System: Other
URL: www.future.edu
Established: 2003 Annual Graduate Tuition & Fees: N/A
Enrollment: 16 Coed
Affiliation or Control: Independent Non-Profit IRS Status: 501(c)3
Highest Offering: Master's; No Undergraduates
Accreditation: NH

01 Executive Director ....Dr. Daniel TAYLOR
11 Chief Operating Officer ....Stephanie HARTMAN
32 Chief Student Affairs/Student Life ....Christie HAND
108 Director Institutional Assessment ....Dr. Jesse PAPPAS
06 Registrar ....Jodie WIMER

Huntington Junior College (J)

900 Fifth Avenue, Huntington WV 25701-2004
County: Cabell FICE Identification: 009047
Unit ID: 237437
Telephone: (304) 697-7550 Carnegie Class: Assoc/HVT-High Non
FAX Number: (304) 697-7554 Calendar System: Quarter
URL: www.huntingtonjuniorcollege.edu
Established: 1936 Annual Undergrad Tuition & Fees: $8,100
Enrollment: 558 Coed
Affiliation or Control: Proprietary IRS Status: Proprietary
Highest Offering: Associate Degree
Accreditation: NH, MAC

01 President ....Carolyn A. SMITH
03 Director ....Dr. Catherine E. SNODDY
05 Academic Affairs Director ....Linda J. WEST
10 Chief Fiscal Officer ....Sharon SNODDY

Martinsburg College (A)

341 Aikens Center, Martinsburg WV 25404
County: Berkeley Identification: 667035
Telephone: (304) 263-6262 Carnegie Class: Not Classified
FAX Number: (866) 703-6611 Calendar System: Other
URL: www.martinsburgcollege.edu
Established: 1980 Annual Undergrad Tuition & Fees: N/A
Enrollment: N/A Coed
Affiliation or Control: Proprietary IRS Status: Proprietary
Highest Offering: Associate Degree
Accreditation: DEAC

01 President .... Paul VIBOCH
05 Chief Academic Officer .... Stella GARLICK
07 Director of Admissions .... Laurie MAURO
06 Registrar .... Debra HAYTAS

Mountain State College (B)

1508 Spring Street, Parkersburg WV 26101
County: Wood FICE Identification: 005008
Unit ID: 237598
Telephone: (304) 485-5487 Carnegie Class: Spec 2-yr-Health
FAX Number: (304) 485-3524 Calendar System: Quarter
URL: www.msc.edu
Established: 1888 Annual Undergrad Tuition & Fees: $8,215
Enrollment: 133 Coed
Affiliation or Control: Proprietary IRS Status: Proprietary
Highest Offering: Associate Degree
Accreditation: ACICS

01 President .... Mrs. Judith SUTTON

Ohio Valley University (C)

1 Campus View Drive, Vienna WV 26105-8000
County: Wood FICE Identification: 003819
Unit ID: 237640
Telephone: (304) 865-6000 Carnegie Class: Bac-Diverse
FAX Number: (304) 865-6001 Calendar System: Semester
URL: www.ovu.edu
Established: 1958 Annual Undergrad Tuition & Fees: $20,460
Enrollment: 451 Coed
Affiliation or Control: Churches Of Christ IRS Status: 501(c)3
Highest Offering: Master's
Accreditation: NH, IACBE

01 President .... Dr. Harold SHANK
00 Chancellor .... Dr. Keith STOTTS
03 EVP/CFO .... Mr. Jeffrey A. DIMICK
100 Chief of Staff .... Mr. Charles MORRIS
05 Provost .... Dr. Joy JONES
111 Director of Advancement .... Mr. Jack THORN
04 President's Office Manager .... Ms. Amanda JIMENEZ
18 Director of Campus Operations .... Mr. David STEWART
36 Director of Career Services .... Mrs. Kathy MULLER
32 Dean of Student Life .... Mrs. Rebecca CLARK
08 Library Director .... Ms. Sonya HESCHT
06 Registrar .... Mrs. Amy GHERKE
07 Director of Admissions Management .... Mrs. Kay GROSE
09 Director of OIE .... Mrs. Kathy DONLEY
13 Chief Info Technology Officer .... Mr. Christopher LANG
26 Director of Marketing .... Vacant
19 Director Security/Safety .... Ms. Hope ASH
37 Director Student Financial Aid .... Mrs. Lindsay COLE
73 Dean College of Bible & Behav Sci .... Dr. Carl M. MOSS
53 Dean College of Education .... Mrs. Glenda J. PENNINGTON
50 Dean College of Business .... Dr. Dan BLAIR
49 Dean College of Arts & Sciences .... Dr. Chris SHROCK
41 Athletic Director .... Mr. Chad PORTER

Salem International University (D)

223 W Main Street, Box 500, Salem WV 26426-0500
County: Harrison FICE Identification: 003820
Unit ID: 237783
Telephone: (304) 326-1109 Carnegie Class: Masters/M
FAX Number: (304) 326-1246 Calendar System: Semester
URL: www.salemu.edu
Established: 1888 Annual Undergrad Tuition & Fees: $14,600
Enrollment: 681 Coed
Affiliation or Control: Proprietary IRS Status: Proprietary
Highest Offering: Master's
Accreditation: NH, CAEPN

01 CEO/Interim President .... Mr. Danny D. FINUF
04 Executive Asst to President .... Mrs. Barbara L. MCCLAIN
03 Executive Vice President .... Dr. Cecil E. KIRKLAND
05 Provost .... Dr. Craig S. MCCLELLAN
37 Dir Financial Aid & Compliance .... Mr. Donald RONAN
13 Director of Information Technology .... Mr. Anthony GRANT
11 VP Operations .... Vacant
07 Director of Admissions .... Ms. Iris ROBERTSON
10 Chief Financial Officer .... Mr. William WINKOWSKI
21 Controller .... Ms. Ginger RICHARDS
85 Intl Student Dir & Business Mgr .... Mrs. Stephanie ROBERTS
06 Registrar .... Mr. Joseph E. FERLIC
50 Dean of Business .... Dr. Marc D. GETTY
53 Dean of Education .... Dr. Craig S. MCCLELLAN
66 Director of Nursing Education .... Mrs. Peggy BEHAN

08 Dean of Library Services .... Dr. Phyllis D. FREEDMAN
32 Dean of Student Affairs .... Dr. Dennis MCNABOE
19 Director of Campus Security .... Mr. Joseph E. SHAVER
41 Director of Athletics .... Mr. Steve POTTS
29 Director Alumni Relations .... Dr. Debra HARRISON
39 Director Student Housing .... Mr. Mark A. NESMITH

University of Charleston (E)

2300 Maccorkle Avenue, SE, Charleston WV 25304-1099
County: Kanawha FICE Identification: 003818
Unit ID: 237312
Telephone: (304) 357-4800 Carnegie Class: Masters/S
FAX Number: (304) 357-4715 Calendar System: Semester
URL: www.ucwv.edu
Established: 1888 Annual Undergrad Tuition & Fees: $29,900
Enrollment: 2,327 Coed
Affiliation or Control: Independent Non-Profit IRS Status: 501(c)3
Highest Offering: Doctorate
Accreditation: NH, ARCPA, CAATE, CIDA, DMS, NUR, OTA, PHAR, RAD

01 President .... Dr. Edwin H. WELCH
05 Exec VP/Provost/Dean of Faculty .... Dr. Kim SPIEZIO
10 Exec VP Administration & Finance .... Mrs. Cleta M. HARLESS
30 Vice Pres for Development .... Ms. Deborah MORRIS
07 Exec VP/Chief Admissions/Mktg Ofcr .... Ms. Joan CLARK
32 Dean of Students .... Ms. Virginia MOORE
26 Director of Marketing .... Mr. David TRAUBE
100 Chief of Staff .... Dr. Jerry FORSTER
06 Registrar .... Ms. Carol SPRADLING
29 Director of Alumni Relations .... Ms. Stephanie MARTIN
21 Controller .... Ms. Terri UNDERHILL
13 Chief Information Officer .... Mr. Scott TERRY
08 Director of Library Services .... Mr. John ADKINS
85 Director International Student Pgms .... Ms. Violetta PETROSYAN
37 Associate Director Financial Aid .... Ms. Michelle MARLOWE
35 Dir of Student Involvement .... Ms. Skyler HUNT
40 Bookstore Manager .... Mr. Glenn JOHNSON
18 Director of Facilities Services .... Mr. Gary BOYD
41 Athletic Director .... Dr. Bren STEVENS
88 VP/Chief Innovation Executive .... Ms. Fonda HOLEHOUSE
09 Director of Institutional Research .... Ms. Lisa DAWKINS
50 Dean Graduate School of Business .... Dr. Scott BELLAMY
67 Dean School of Pharmacy .... Dr. Michelle EASTON
49 Dean School of Arts & Sciences .... Dr. Barbara WRIGHT
76 Dean School of Health Sciences .... Dr. Pamela ALDERMAN
04 Administrative Asst to President .... Ms. Susan LEFEW
15 Director Personnel Services .... Ms. Janice GWINN
19 Director Security/Safety .... Mr. Eric SMITH
38 Director Student Counseling .... Dr. Candace LAYNE
44 Director of Annual Fund .... Ms. Catherine ECKLEY

Valley College - Beckley Campus (F)

120 New River Town Center, Suite C, Beckley WV 25801
County: Raleigh FICE Identification: 030844
Unit ID: 377652
Telephone: (304) 252-9547 Carnegie Class: Spec 2-yr-Other
FAX Number: (304) 252-1694 Calendar System: Other
URL: www.valley.edu
Established: 1983 Annual Undergrad Tuition & Fees: $15,700
Enrollment: 396 Coed
Affiliation or Control: Proprietary IRS Status: Proprietary
Highest Offering: Associate Degree
Accreditation: ACICS

01 President .... Mr. Tony PALMIERI
05 Vice President Campus Operations .... Ms. Beth GARDNER
10 Vice President Administration .... Mr. Matt JENKINS

Valley College - Martinsburg Campus (G)

287 Aikens Center, Martinsburg WV 25404-6203
County: Berkeley FICE Identification: 026094
Unit ID: 377661
Telephone: (304) 263-0979 Carnegie Class: Spec 2-yr-Health
FAX Number: (304) 263-2413 Calendar System: Other
URL: www.valley.edu
Established: 1983 Annual Undergrad Tuition & Fees: N/A
Enrollment: 240 Coed
Affiliation or Control: Proprietary IRS Status: Proprietary
Highest Offering: Associate Degree
Accreditation: ACICS

01 Campus Director .... Mr. Brandon BOWERS

Valley College - Princeton Campus (H)

617 Mercer Street, Princeton WV 24740
County: Mercer FICE Identification: 030842
Unit ID: 377670
Telephone: (304) 425-2323 Carnegie Class: Not Classified
FAX Number: (304) 425-5890 Calendar System: Other
URL: www.valley.edu
Established: 1986 Annual Undergrad Tuition & Fees: N/A
Enrollment: 134 Coed
Affiliation or Control: Proprietary IRS Status: Proprietary
Highest Offering: Associate Degree
Accreditation: ACICS

01 Campus Director .... Ms. Misty TESTERMAN

*West Virginia Council for Community & Technical College Education (I)

1018 Kanawha Boulevard E, Suite 700, Charleston WV 25301-2800
County: Kanawha Identification: 666993
Telephone: (304) 558-0265 Carnegie Class: N/A
FAX Number: (304) 558-1646
URL: www.wvctcs.org

01 Chancellor .... Sarah A. TUCKER

*Blue Ridge Community and Technical College (J)

13650 Apple Harvest Drive, Martinsburg WV 25403
County: Berkeley FICE Identification: 039573
Unit ID: 446774
Telephone: (304) 260-4380 Carnegie Class: Assoc/HT-High Non
FAX Number: (304) 260-1788 Calendar System: Semester
URL: www.blueridgectc.edu
Established: 1974 Annual Undergrad Tuition & Fees (In-State): $3,864
Enrollment: 5,552 Coed
Affiliation or Control: State IRS Status: 501(c)3
Highest Offering: Associate Degree
Accreditation: NH, ADNUR, EMT, PTAA

02 President .... Dr. Peter G. CHECKOVICH
05 Vice President of Instruction .... Dr. George PERRY
103 VP Engineer-Workforce Development .... Dr. Ann M. SHIPWAY
84 VP of Enrollment Management .... Ms. Leslie C. SEE
10 Chief Financial Officer .... Dr. Craig MILLER
06 Registrar .... Dr. Angie M. KINDER
121 Director of Access & Success .... Ms. Brenda NEAL
15 Vice President Human Resources .... Mr. Justin RUBLE
13 Vice President of IT .... Mr. Michael BYERS
37 Director of Financial Aid .... Ms. Anna CRAWFORD

*BridgeValley Community & Technical College (K)

2001 Union Carbide Drive, South Charleston WV 25303
County: Kanawha FICE Identification: 040386
Unit ID: 484932
Telephone: (304) 205-6600 Carnegie Class: Not Classified
FAX Number: N/A Calendar System: Semester
URL: www.bridgevalley.edu
Established: 2014 Annual Undergrad Tuition & Fees (In-District): $4,570
Enrollment: 2,503 Coed
Affiliation or Control: State/Local IRS Status: Exempt
Highest Offering: Associate Degree
Accreditation: NH, ADNUR, COARC, DH, DMS, ENGT, MLTAD, NMT

02 President .... Dr. Eunice BELLINGER
05 VP of Academic Affairs .... Dr. Peter SOSCIA
103 Vice Pres WF/Economic Develop .... Mr. Jeff WYCO
88 VP Community Education .... Ms. Laura MCCULLOUGH
32 Dean of Students .... Mr. James MCDOUGLE
97 Dean of General Education .... Ms. Kim LOVINSKI
76 Dean of Health .... Ms. Suzette BREEDEN
06 Chief Records Officer/Registrar .... Mr. Roy SIMMONS
15 Chief Human Resources Officer .... Ms. Michelle BISSELL
10 Chief Financial Officer .... Ms. Cathy AQUINO
04 Executive Asst to President .... Ms. Alicia SYNER
08 Director of Library Services .... Ms. Heather LAUER
09 Chief Banner Officer .... Mr. James FAUVER
18 Chief IT/Operations Officer .... Mr. Jason STARK
19 Chief of Police .... Mr. Bazra FAKHIR
26 Chief Marketing Officer .... Mr. Brian BOLYARD
50 Dean Business/Legal/Human Svcs .... Ms. Megan LORENZ
72 Dean of Technology .... Mr. Norm MORTENSEN
84 VP Enrollment Mgmt & SS .... Dr. John BERRY
37 Director of Financial Aid .... Ms. Mary BLIZZARD
36 Director of Student Placement .... Ms. Judy WHIPKEY
38 Director of Counseling Svcs .... Ms. Carla BLANKENBUEHLER
96 Chief Procurement Officer .... Mr. John POWELL

*Eastern West Virginia Community and Technical College (L)

316 Eastern Drive, Moorefield WV 26836-1155
County: Hardy FICE Identification: 041190
Unit ID: 438708
Telephone: (304) 434-8000 Carnegie Class: Assoc/MT-VT-High Non
FAX Number: (304) 434-7000 Calendar System: Semester
URL: www.easternwv.edu
Established: 1999 Annual Undergrad Tuition & Fees (In-State): $3,420
Enrollment: 913 Coed
Affiliation or Control: State IRS Status: Exempt
Highest Offering: Associate Degree
Accreditation: NH, ADNUR

02 President .... Dr. Charles TERRELL
11 Exec Dean for Administrative Svcs .... Ms. Penny REARDON
05 Dean for Teaching & Learning .... Ms. Debra BACKUS
32 Dean of Student Access & Success .... Ms. Monica WILSON
31 Dean of Community Engagement .... Ms. Briana LAVORGNA
103 Assoc Dean Workforce Education .... Ms. Sherry WATTS
04 Administrative Asst to President .... Ms. Michael O'LEARY

*Mountwest Community and Technical College (A)

1 Mountwest Way, Huntington WV 25701
County: Cabell FICE Identification: 040414
Unit ID: 444954
Telephone: (304) 710-3141 Carnegie Class: Assoc/HT-High Non
FAX Number: (304) 710-3187 Calendar System: Semester
URL: www.mctc.edu
Established: 1975 Annual Undergrad Tuition & Fees (In-District): $3,888
Enrollment: 1,775 Coed
Affiliation or Control: State/Local IRS Status: 501(c)3
Highest Offering: Associate Degree
Accreditation: NH, ACBSP, CAHIIM, COARC, EMT, MAC, PTAA

02 President .... Dr. Keith J. COTRONEO
05 Exec Vice Pres/Chief Academic Ofcr .... Dr. Harry R. FAULK
10 Vice Pres Finance/Business/CFO .... Mr. Daniel J. FIGLER
32 Vice President of Student Services .... Ms. Billie K. BROOKS
13 VP Operations/Info Technology .... Mrs. Terri L. TOMBLIN-BYRD
06 Registrar .... Ms. Angela ROSS

*New River Community and Technical College (B)

280 University Drive, Beaver WV 25813
County: Raleigh FICE Identification: 039603
Unit ID: 447582
Telephone: (304) 929-5450 Carnegie Class: Assoc/MT-VT-Mix Trad/Non
FAX Number: (304) 929-5478 Calendar System: Semester
URL: www.newriver.edu
Established: 2003 Annual Undergrad Tuition & Fees (In-State): $3,966
Enrollment: 1,624 Coed
Affiliation or Control: State IRS Status: 501(c)3
Highest Offering: Associate Degree
Accreditation: NH, EMT, #PTAA

02 President .... Dr. L. Marshall WASHINGTON
04 Exec Secretary to the President .... Ms. Lori A. MIDKIFF
05 Vice Pres Academic Affairs .... Dr. Richard B. PAGAN
11 Vice Pres Administrative Services .... Ms. Leah A. TAYLOR
13 Vice Pres Technology/Library Svcs .... Dr. David J. AYERSMAN
15 Director Human Resources .... Ms. Amanda L. BAKER
26 Chief Communications Officer .... Ms. Elizabeth M. BELCHER
12 Regional Director of Operations .... Ms. Jill HOLLIDAY
12 Regional Director of Operations .... Mr. Roger D. GRIFFITH
12 Regional Director of Operations .... Ms. Mary IGO
06 Registrar .... Ms. Janelle SCHOFIELD
08 Staff Librarian .... Mr. Robert H. COSTON
37 Director of Financial Aid .... Ms. Patricia HARMON
96 Director of Purchasing .... Ms. Twana JACKSON
10 Chief Financial Officer .... Ms. Heike I. SOEFFKER-CULICERTO
18 Director of Physical Plant .... Mr. Robert RUNION
27 Director of Public Relations .... Ms. Jenni CANTERBURY
84 Director of Enrollment Services .... Ms. Tracy L. EVANS
88 Dean of Transfer and Preprof .... Ms. Wendy PATRIQUIN

*Pierpont Community & Technical College (C)

1201 Locust Avenue, Fairmont WV 26554-2470
County: Marion FICE Identification: 040385
Unit ID: 443492
Telephone: (304) 367-4692 Carnegie Class: Assoc/HVT-Mix Trad/Non
FAX Number: (304) 367-4881 Calendar System: Semester
URL: www.pierpont.edu
Established: 1974 Annual Undergrad Tuition & Fees (In-State): $4,684
Enrollment: 2,182 Coed
Affiliation or Control: State IRS Status: 501(c)3
Highest Offering: Associate Degree
Accreditation: NH, ACFEI, CAHIIM, #COARC, EMT, MLTAD, NAIT, PTAA

02 President .... Dr. Johnny M. MOORE
04 Exec Assistant to the President .... Mrs. Cyndee SENSIBAUGH
05 Provost/VP for Academic Affairs .... Mr. Brian FLOYD
10 VP for Finance and Administration .... Mr. Dale R. BRADLEY
86 VP for Organization and Development .... Mr. Stephen E. LEACH
13 VP Information Technology/CIO .... Mr. Rob LINGER
84 AVP Enrollment Management .... Mrs. Lyla D. GRANDSTAFF
50 Dean Sch of Business/Aviation/Tech .... Dr. Gerald BACZA
76 Dean School of Health Careers .... Mr. Michael WAIDE
79 Int Dean School of Human Services .... Mr. David BEIGHLEY
103 Int Dean Sch of Workforce/Econ Dev .... Mr. Robert Dennis MILLS

*Southern West Virginia Community and Technical College (D)

P. O. Box 2900, Mount Gay WV 25637-2900
County: Logan FICE Identification: 003816
Unit ID: 237817
Telephone: (304) 792-7098 Carnegie Class: Assoc/MT-VT-High Trad
FAX Number: (304) 792-7046 Calendar System: Semester
URL: www.southernwv.edu
Established: 1971 Annual Undergrad Tuition & Fees (In-State): $3,556
Enrollment: 1,644 Coed
Affiliation or Control: State IRS Status: 501(c)3
Highest Offering: Associate Degree
Accreditation: NH, ADNUR, COARC, EMT, MLTAD, RAD, SURGT

02 President .... Dr. Robert E. GUNTER
10 VP for Finance & Administration .... Mr. Samuel M. LITTERAL
05 VP Academic Affairs .... Dr. Jack D. DILBECK, SR.
103 VP Economic & Workforce Development .... Mr. Allyn S. BARKER
13 Chief Information Officer .... Mr. Gary HOLEMAN
30 Vice President for Development .... Mr. Ronald E. LEMON
15 Interim Human Resources Director .... Ms. Debbie C. DINGESS
04 Exec Asst to President & BOG .... Ms. Emma L. BAISDEN
09 Dir Institutional Effectiveness .... Vacant
12 Director Wyoming Campus Operations .... Mr. David LORD
12 Dir Williamson Campus Operations .... Ms. Rita G. ROBERSON
12 Director Logan Campus Operations .... Mr. Randy SKEENS
12 Director Boone Campus Operations .... Mr. William COOK
50 Int Div Head Healthcare & Business .... Ms. Tahnee BRYANT
88 Div Head University Transfer .... Ms. Melinda D. SAUNDERS
06 Interim Registrar .... Ms. Teri WELLS
37 Dir Student Financial Assistance .... Ms. Stella ESTEPP
08 Director of Libraries .... Ms. Kimberly L. MAYNARD
84 Dir Enroll Mgmt/Stdnt Engagement .... Mr. Darrell TAYLOR
22 Dir Affirmative Action/EEO .... Ms. Debbie C. DINGESS
26 Director of Media .... Mr. Joseph NELSON

*West Virginia Northern Community College (E)

1704 Market Street, Wheeling WV 26003-3643
County: Ohio FICE Identification: 009054
Unit ID: 238014
Telephone: (304) 233-5900 Carnegie Class: Assoc/MT-VT-Mix Trad/Non
FAX Number: (304) 232-4651 Calendar System: Semester
URL: www.wvncc.edu
Established: 1972 Annual Undergrad Tuition & Fees (In-State): $3,684
Enrollment: 2,013 Coed
Affiliation or Control: State IRS Status: 501(c)3
Highest Offering: Associate Degree
Accreditation: #NH, ACFEI, ADNUR, CAHIIM, MAC, RAD, SURGT

02 President .... Dr. Vicki RILEY
05 VP of Academic Affairs .... Ms. Jill LOVELESS
10 CFO & VP Administrative Services .... Mr. Jeff SAYRE
32 Vice President Student Services .... Mrs. Janet FIKE
31 Dean Community Relations .... Mr. Robert DEFRANCIS
18 Director of Facilities .... Ms. Trish MARKER
15 Chief Human Resource Officer .... Mrs. Peggy CARMICHAEL
103 VP of Economic & Workforce Dev .... Mr. Larry TACKETT
35 Director Student Union Activities .... Mrs. Shannon PAYTON
04 Administrative Asst to President .... Ms. Stephanie KAPPEL

*New River Community and Technical College Greenbrier Valley Campus (F)

653 Church Street, Lewisburg WV 24901-1303
Telephone: (304) 647-6560 Identification: 770468
Accreditation: &NH

*New River Technical College Mercer County Campus (G)

1397 Stafford Drive, Princeton WV 24740-8230
Telephone: (304) 818-2009 Identification: 770469
Accreditation: &NH

*New River Technical College Nicholas County Campus (H)

6101 Webster Road, Summersville WV 26651
Telephone: (304) 872-1236 Identification: 770470
Accreditation: &NH

*Southern West Virginia Community and Technical College-Boone/Lincoln Campus (I)

3505 Daniel Boone Parkway, Suite A,
Foster WV 25608-8126
Telephone: (304) 369-2952 Identification: 770471
Accreditation: &NH

*Southern West Virginia Community and Technical College-Williamson Campus (J)

1601 Armory Drive, Williamson WV 25661
Telephone: (304) 235-6046 Identification: 770473
Accreditation: &NH

*Southern West Virginia Community and Technical College-Wyoming/McDowell Campus (K)

128 College Drive, Saulsville WV 25876
Telephone: (304) 294-8346 Identification: 770472
Accreditation: &NH

*West Virginia Northern Community College (L)

141 Main Street, New Martinsville WV 26155
Telephone: (304) 455-4684 Identification: 770474
Accreditation: &NH

*West Virginia Northern Community College (M)

150 Park Avenue, Weirton WV 26062
Telephone: (304) 723-2210 Identification: 770475
Accreditation: &NH

*West Virginia Higher Education Policy Commission (N)

1018 Kanawha Boulevard E, Ste 700,
Charleston WV 25301-2887
County: Kanawha FICE Identification: 033440
Unit ID: 237941
Telephone: (304) 558-2101 Carnegie Class: N/A
FAX Number: (304) 558-5719
URL: www.wvhepc.edu

01 Chancellor .... Dr. Paul L. HILL
88 Chancellor Community College .... Dr. Sarah TUCKER
88 Director of Science and Research .... Dr. Jan TAYLOR
05 Vice Chancellor for Academic Affs .... Dr. Corley DENNISON
10 Vice Chancellor for Finance .... Dr. Edward MAGEE
32 Vice Chancellor for Student Affairs .... Dr. Adam GREEN
45 Vice Chancellor Policy and Planning .... Vacant
15 Vice Chancellor for Human Resources .... Ms. Trish CLAY
43 General Counsel .... Mr. Bruce R. WALKER
11 Exec Vice Chancellor Administration .... Mr. Matt TURNER
35 Dir Student/Educational Services .... Mr. Daniel E. CROCKETT
37 Senior Director of Financial Aid .... Mr. Brian WEINGART
88 Director Administrative Services .... Ms. Cindy L. ANDERSON

*Bluefield State College (O)

219 Rock Street, Bluefield WV 24701-2198
County: Mercer FICE Identification: 003809
Unit ID: 237215
Telephone: (304) 327-4000 Carnegie Class: Bac-Diverse
FAX Number: (304) 325-7747 Calendar System: Semester
URL: www.bluefieldstate.edu
Established: 1895 Annual Undergrad Tuition & Fees (In-State): $6,408
Enrollment: 1,486 Coed
Affiliation or Control: State IRS Status: 501(c)3
Highest Offering: Baccalaureate
Accreditation: NH, ACBSP, ADNUR, CAEPN, ENGT, NURSE, RAD

02 President .... Dr. Marsha V. KROTSENG
05 Interim VP Academic Affs/Provost .... Dr. Angela LAMBERT
10 Vice Pres Financial/Admin Affairs .... Ms. Shelia JOHNSON
32 Vice President Student Affairs .... Dr. JoAnn ROBINSON
04 Interim Dir Media Rels/Asst to Pres .... Mr. Mark WARNER
88 Executive Dir Title III .... Dr. Guy SIMS
06 Registrar .... Ms. Terry THOMPSON
08 Director Library Services .... Ms. Joanna THOMPSON
13 Director of Computer Services .... Vacant
36 Director of Placement .... Vacant
07 Director of Admissions .... Mr. James SCHLIMMER
37 Director of Financial Aid .... Mr. Thomas ILSE
15 Director of Human Resources .... Ms. Jonette AUGHENBAUGH
18 Admin Asst Senior of Physical Plant .... Ms. Diana GIBSON
19 Director Public Safety .... Mr. Jason BROOKS
09 Director of Institutional Research .... Dr. Tracey ANDERSON
38 Director of Counseling .... Dr. Cravor JONES
29 Director Alumni Affairs .... Ms. Deirdre GUYTON
40 Manager Bookstore .... Ms. Susan PLUMLEY
41 Athletic Director .... Mr. John LEWIS
50 Dean School of Business .... Mr. John SNEAD
49 Dean School of Arts and Sciences .... Dr. Martha EBORALL
54 Dean School of Eng Tech/Comp Sci .... Dr. Shannon BOWLING
53 Dean School of Education .... Dr. Shelia SARGENT-MARTIN
66 Dean School Nursing/Allied Health .... Ms. Angela LAMBERT
66 ADN Program Director .... Ms. Sandra WYNN
66 BSN Program Director .... Ms. Carol COFER
88 Program Dir of Radiologic Tech .... Ms. Melissa HAYE
61 Program Dir Criminal Justice .... Vacant
28 Asst to Pres Equity/Divers/Inclusn .... Dr. Guy SIMS
96 Director of Purchasing .... Mr. Paul RUTHERFORD
30 Director of Advancement/Planning .... Ms. Betty CARROLL

*Concord University (P)

PO Box 1000, Athens WV 24712-1000
County: Mercer FICE Identification: 003810
Unit ID: 237330
Telephone: (304) 384-3115 Carnegie Class: Masters/S
FAX Number: (304) 384-9044 Calendar System: Semester
URL: www.concord.edu
Established: 1872 Annual Undergrad Tuition & Fees (In-State): $7,238
Enrollment: 2,507 Coed
Affiliation or Control: State IRS Status: 501(c)3
Highest Offering: Master's
Accreditation: NH, #CAATE, CAEPN, SW

02 President .... Dr. Kendra BOGGESS
05 VP & Academic Dean .... Dr. Peter VISCUSI
30 VP for Advancement .... Mrs. Alicia BESENYEI
20 Associate Dean .... Dr. Cheryl BARNES
32 VP Student Affairs .... Dr. Marjie FLANIGAN
10 VP for Business & Finance .... Dr. Charles P. BECKER
11 VP of Administration .... Mr. Rick DILLON
13 VP of Information Technology .... Mr. Charles ELLIOTT

84 VP for Enrollment Management ... Mr. Greg KING
06 Registrar ... Mrs. Carolyn COX
08 Director of Libraries ... Mrs. Connie SHUMATE
37 Director of Student Financial Aid ... Mrs. Debra TURNER
29 Director of Alumni Relations ... Ms. Sarah TURNER
88 Director Bonner Scholars Program ... Mrs. Kathy BALL
15 Human Resources Director ... Mr. Daniel FITZPATRICK
18 Director Physical Plant ... Mr. Gerry VONVILLE
19 Director of Public Safety ... Chief Mark STELLA
36 Director of Career Services ... Vacant
38 Director of Counseling ... Mr. David BAILEY
40 Bookstore Manager ... Mr. Randy JONES
41 Athletic Director ... Mr. Kevin GARRETT
21 Financial Reporting Officer ... Ms. Elizabeth J. CAHILL
24 Ctr for Academic Technologies ... Mr. Steve MEADOWS
26 Public Relations/Mktg Specialist ... Mr. Lance MCDANIEL
25 Director of Grants and Contracts ... Mrs. Melanie FARMER
12 Director of the Beckley Center ... Dr. Susan WILLIAMS
96 Contract Specialist ... Mr. Gary HYLTON
88 Director of Retention ... Ms. Sarah BEASLEY
88 Administrative Secretary to Pres ... Mrs. Trena STOVALL
04 Executive Secretary to President ... Mrs. Lora WOOLWINE
102 Interim Director of the Foundation ... Mrs. Bren YEAGER
39 Director Student Housing ... Mr. Bill FRALEY

*Fairmont State University (A)

1201 Locust Avenue, Fairmont WV 26554-2470
County: Marion FICE Identification: 003812
Unit ID: 237367
Telephone: (304) 367-4000 Carnegie Class: Masters/S
FAX Number: (304) 367-4789 Calendar System: Semester
URL: www.fairmontstate.edu
Established: 1865 Annual Undergrad Tuition & Fees (In-State): $6,950
Enrollment: 4,041 Coed
Affiliation or Control: State IRS Status: 501(c)3
Highest Offering: Master's
Accreditation: NH, ACBSP, ADNUR, CAEPN, ENGR, ENGT, NURSE

02 Interim President FSU ... Dr. Stephen B. JONES
05 Provost/VP Academic Affairs ... Dr. Christina M. LAVORATA
10 Vice Pres Admin & Fiscal Affairs ... Mr. Algis SKUDINSKAS
13 VP/Chief Information Officer ... Mr. John LYMPANY
32 Vice Pres Student Services ... Dr. Timothy OXLEY
108 VP Inst Assessment & Effectiveness ... Dr. Timothy OXLEY
04 Executive Asst to the President ... Ms. Serena SCULLY
20 Assoc Provost for Academic Affs ... Dr. Jack R. KIRBY
26 AVP University Communications ... Ms. Misty POE
18 Asst Vice Pres for Facilities ... Mr. Tom T. TUCKER
15 AVP for Human Resources ... Mrs. Cynthia S. CURRY
06 Registrar ... Dr. Shayne GERVAIS
49 Dean College of Liberal Arts ... Dr. Deanna J. SHIELDS
72 Dean College of Science/Tech ... Dr. Donald E. TRISEL
50 Dean School of Business ... Dr. Richard C. HARVEY
53 Dean School Educ/Hlth/Hum Perf ... Dr. Carolyn CRISLIP-TACY
57 Int Dean School of Fine Arts ... Dr. Robert E. MILD
66 Dean School of Nursing ... Dr. Sharon BONI
07 Director of Admissions/Recruitment ... Ms. Amie M. FAZALARE
29 Interim Director Alumni Relations ... Ms. Amie FAZALARE
91 Dir of Applications Develop Svcs ... Mr. Andy RAISOVICH
41 Director of Athletics ... Mr. Timothy A. MCNEELY
19 Dir of Emerg Mgmt/Chief of Police ... Mr. Jack A. CLAYTON
38 Dir of Counseling and Disab Srvs ... Ms. Andrea M. PAMMER
37 Dir Financial Aid/Scholarships ... Ms. Tresa WEIMER
39 Director of Housing ... Ms. Alicia KALKA
08 Interim Director Library Services ... Ms. Sharon MAZURE
96 Director of Procurement ... Ms. Monica J. COCHRAN
27 Director of Public Relations ... Ms. Misty POE
36 Dir of Career Development Center ... Ms. Amy V. DRVAR
90 Director of Solutions Center ... Ms. Joanie RAISOVICH
23 Director of Student Health Services ... Ms. Trish WATSON

*Glenville State College (B)

200 High Street, Glenville WV 26351-1292
County: Gilmer FICE Identification: 003813
Unit ID: 237385
Telephone: (304) 462-7361 Carnegie Class: Bac-Diverse
FAX Number: (304) 462-7610 Calendar System: Semester
URL: www.glenville.edu
Established: 1872 Annual Undergrad Tuition & Fees (In-State): $7,344
Enrollment: 1,732 Coed
Affiliation or Control: State IRS Status: 501(c)3
Highest Offering: Baccalaureate
Accreditation: NH, CAEPN

02 President ... Dr. Tracy L. PELLETT
05 Vice Pres for Academic Affairs ... Dr. Gary Z. MORRIS
10 Vice Pres for Business & Finance ... Mr. John BECKVOLD
26 VP for Student Life/Athletics ... Mr. Rusty VINEYARD
30 Vice President for Advancement ... Mr. Dennis J. POUNDS
04 Executive Assistant to President ... Ms. Teresa G. STERNS
53 Dean of Teacher Education ... Dr. Kevin G. CAIN
15 Chief Human Resources Officer ... Ms. Krystal D. SMITH
37 Financial Aid Manager ... Ms. Stephany HARPER
18 Exec Director of Physical Plant ... Mr. Thomas R. RATLIFF
39 Director of Residence Life ... Mr. Jerry L. BURKHAMMER
23 Director Campus Health Services ... Ms. Ronda L. WILLIAMS
08 Director of Library ... Ms. Gail L. WESTBROOK
21 Controller ... Ms. Lisa NORTHWOOD
96 Director of Purchasing ... Ms. Joyce E. RIDDLE
29 Director of Alumni Affairs ... Ms. Debra A. NAGY
32 Director of Student Activities ... Ms. Jodi WALTERS
06 Registrar ... Ms. Ann M. REED
13 Manager of Database Admin ... Mr. Neal L. BENSON
36 Academic Support Counselor ... Mr. Bill LILLY
38 Professional Counselor ... Mr. Timothy J. UNDERWOOD
84 Vice Pres for Enrollment Management ... Mr. Charles M. CARVER
19 Associate Director of Public Safety ... Mr. Ronald K. TAYLOR

*Marshall University (C)

1 John Marshall Drive, Huntington WV 25755-0001
County: Cabell FICE Identification: 003815
Unit ID: 237525
Telephone: (304) 696-3170 Carnegie Class: Masters/L
FAX Number: (304) 696-6565 Calendar System: Semester
URL: www.marshall.edu
Established: 1837 Annual Undergrad Tuition & Fees (In-State): $7,154
Enrollment: 13,621 Coed
Affiliation or Control: State IRS Status: 501(c)3
Highest Offering: Doctorate
Accreditation: NH, ADNUR, ANEST, #CAATE, CACREP, CAEPN, CAHIIM, CLPSY, COARC, CYTO, DIETD, DIETI, ENG, ENGR, FEPAC, JOUR, MED, MLTAD, MT, MUS, NUR, PHAR, PTA, SP, SW

02 President ... Dr. Jerome A. GILBERT
05 Provost/Sr VP Academic Affairs ... Dr. Gayle L. ORMISTON
43 Sr VP Exec Affairs & Gen Counsel ... Mr. F. Layton COTTRILL
10 Interim Chief Financial Officer ... Mr. Mark ROBINSON
26 Senior VP Communication/Marketing ... Ms. Virginia R. PAINTER
63 Dean of Medicine ... Dr. Joseph I. SHAPIRO
102 CEO MU Foundation Inc ... Dr. Ron AREA
11 Sr VP for Administration ... Ms. Brandi D. JACOBS
46 VP Research ... Mr. John MAHER
88 Assoc VP for External Engagement ... Ms. Sara P. SCARBRO
53 Dean College of Education ... Dr. Teresa EAGLE
29 Executive Director Alumni Relations ... Mr. Matthew D. HAYES
30 Vice President Development ... Mr. Lance WEST
28 Assoc VP Intercultural Affairs ... Mr. Maurice R. COOLEY
13 Chief Technology Officer ... Mr. Allen TAYLOR
07 Dir Admission Undergrad/Grad Pgms ... Ms. Tammy JOHNSON
32 Dean Student Affairs ... Mr. Cedric GATHINGS
106 Asst VP for OnLine learning Lib/IT ... Ms. Monica BROOKS
58 Interim Dean Graduate College ... Dr. David PITTENGER
49 Dean College Liberal Arts ... Dr. Robert BOOKWALTER
50 Interim Dean College of Business ... Dr. Robert SIMPSON
57 Dean College of Arts & Media ... Mr. Donald L. VAN HORN
67 Dean School of Pharmacy ... Dr. Kevin W. YINGLING
66 Dean College of Health Prof ... Dr. Michael PREWITT
54 Dean Col of Info Tech/Engr ... Dr. Wael ZATAR
81 Dean College of Science ... Dr. Charles SOMERVILLE
92 Dean Honors College ... Dr. Nicola LOCASCIO
41 Director of Athletics ... Mr. Mike HAMRICK
06 Registrar ... Ms. Sonja G. CANTRELL
37 Director Student Financial Aid ... Ms. Kathy BIALK
36 Director Career Services ... Ms. Denise HOGSETT
15 Director Human Resource Services ... Mr. Bruce B. FELDER
19 Director of Public Safety ... Mr. James E. TERRY
96 Director of Purchasing ... Ms. Stephanie SMITH
88 Deputy Facilities Officer ... Mr. Travis BAILEY
18 Director Physical Plant ... Mr. Richard D. OSBURN
39 Director Residence Services ... Ms. Mistie BIBBEE
09 Asst to Pres/Sr VP Inst Rsch/Plng ... Mr. Michael J. MCGUFFEY
22 Director Equity Programs ... Ms. Debra HART
88 Director Recruitment ... Ms. Elizabeth WOLFE
43 Assoc General Counsel ... Ms. Jendonnae HOUDYSCHELL
86 Asst to Pres for External Liaison ... Mr. William BURDETTE
114 Interim Budget Director ... Ms. Katrina ESKINS

*Shepherd University (D)

PO Box 5000, Shepherdstown WV 25443-5000
County: Jefferson FICE Identification: 003822
Unit ID: 237792
Telephone: (304) 876-5000 Carnegie Class: Bac-A&S
FAX Number: (304) 876-3101 Calendar System: Semester
URL: www.shepherd.edu
Established: 1871 Annual Undergrad Tuition & Fees (In-State): $7,170
Enrollment: 3,861 Coed
Affiliation or Control: State IRS Status: 501(c)3
Highest Offering: Doctorate
Accreditation: NH, ART, CAEPN, IACBE, MUS, NRPA, NURSE, SW

02 President ... Dr. Mary HENDRIX
05 Acting Provost ... Dr. Scott BEARD
10 Vice President Finance ... Mr. Tony MAJOR
32 Vice President Student Affairs ... Dr. Thomas SEGAR
84 VPEM/Institution Compact Oversight ... Mr. Bill SOMMERS
43 General Counsel ... Mr. K. Alan PERDUE
11 Vice President Administration ... Mr. James VIGIL
81 Actg Dean College of Nat Sci/Math ... Dr. Robert WARBURTON
79 Dean College of Arts & Humanities ... Mr. Dow BENEDICT
50 Dean Col of Business/Social Science ... Dr. Ann M. LEGREID
53 Dean Col of Educ & Professional Std ... Vacant
88 Prog Rev Oversight/Acting HLC Acrd ... Dr. Virginia HICKS
58 Acting Dean Graduate Studies ... Dr. Richie STEVENS
121 Dean Teaching/Learning/Instruc Res ... Dr. Laura RENNINGER
26 Exec Director Univ Communications ... Ms. Valerie OWENS
09 Director Institutional Research ... Ms. Sara MAENE
39 Director Residence Life ... Ms. Elizabeth SECHLER
21 Director of Finance ... Ms. Pamela STEVENS
35 Asst VPSA/Dir Cmty/Congress Rels ... Ms. Holly FRYE
15 Director Human Resources ... Dr. Marie DEWALT
13 Director Info Technology Services ... Mr. Joey DAGG
06 Registrar ... Ms. Tracy SEFFERS
07 Director of Admissions ... Ms. Kristen LORENZ
37 Director of Financial Aid ... Ms. Joyce CABRAL
19 Univ Police Chief ... Mr. John MCAVOY
53 Director Teacher Education ... Dr. Douglas KENNARD
18 Director of Facilities ... Mr. Eric SHULER
41 Athletics Director ... Mr. Chauncey WINBUSH
96 Director of Procurement Services ... Ms. Debra LANGFORD
38 Director Student Counseling ... Ms. Shanan SPENCER
29 Director Alumni Engagement ... Ms. Kim HUTTO
92 Director Honors Program ... Dr. Mark CANTRELL
30 Executive Director of Development ... Ms. Sherri JANELLE
104 Director Study Abroad ... Ms. Yin STAR
25 Dr of Grant Support/Corp/Found Rela ... Ms. Jessica KUMP
08 Dean Library ... Dr. David GANSZ
04 Executive Asst to the President ... Ms. Sonya SHOLLEY
44 Director of Annual Giving ... Ms. Stacy MCFARLAND

*West Liberty University (E)

208 University Drive, West Liberty WV 26074
County: Ohio FICE Identification: 003823
Unit ID: 237932
Telephone: (304) 336-5000 Carnegie Class: Bac-Diverse
FAX Number: (304) 336-8403 Calendar System: Semester
URL: www.westliberty.edu
Established: 1837 Annual Undergrad Tuition & Fees (In-State): $7,038
Enrollment: 2,341 Coed
Affiliation or Control: State IRS Status: 501(c)3
Highest Offering: Master's
Accreditation: NH, ARCPA, CAATE, CAEPN, DH, IACBE, MT, MUS, NURSE, SW

02 President ... Dr. Stephen G. GREINER
05 Provost ... Dr. Brian L. CRAWFORD
43 Vice President & General Counsel ... Vacant
32 VP of Student Services/Registrar ... Mr. Scott A. COOK
10 Executive Vice President & CFO ... Ms. Roberta LINGER
81 Dean College of Sciences ... Dr. Robert KREISBERG
49 Dean College Liberal Arts ... Dr. Gerard NECASTRO
57 Dean College Arts & Comm ... Dr. Matthew HARDER
53 Interim Dean College of Education ... Dr. Catherine MONTEROSO
66 Dir of Nursing Programs ... Dr. Rose M. KUTLENIOS
50 Dean College of Business ... Dr. Michael TURRENTINE
35 Executive Director Student Services ... Ms. Marcella T. SNYDER
15 Chief Human Resources Officer ... Ms. Diana L. HARTO
13 Chief Technology Officer ... Mr. James T. CLARK
09 Dir of Inst Research & Assessment ... Ms. Paula J. TOMASIK
41 Director of Athletics ... Mr. Lynn ULLOM
07 Dir of Admissions & Recruitment ... Ms. Brenda M. KING
51 Director of Cont Educ/Special Pgm ... Vacant
08 Director of Library ... Ms. Cheryl R. HARSHMAN
29 Exec Dir of Alumni/Cmty Relations ... Mr. Ron A. WITT
37 Director Financial Aid ... Mrs. Katie R. COOPER
111 VP of Institutional Advancement ... Mr. Jason W. KOEGLER
109 Director of Auxiliary Services ... Vacant
38 Director of Counseling ... Ms. Bridgette DAWSON
92 Director of the Honors Program ... Dr. Shannon D. HALICKI
88 Director Dental Hygiene Programs ... Ms. Stephanie MEREDITH
88 Dir Clinical Lab Science Program ... Dr. William C. WAGENER
23 Director of Health Services ... Ms. Cheryl C. BENNINGTON
88 Director Physican Assistant Program ... Dr. William A. CHILDERS, JR.
85 Coord International Student Rec ... Ms. Mihaela A. SZABO
26 Executive Director of Marketing ... Ms. Tammi SECRIST
101 Secretary of the Institution/Board ... Ms. Mary A. EDWARDS
104 Director Study Abroad ... Dr. Sannon HALICKI
105 Director Web Services ... Ms. Whitney M. INKSTER
106 Dir Online Education/E-learning ... Ms. Lucy KEFAUVER
18 Director of Physical Plant ... Mr. Joe MILLS
19 Chief of Police/Dir Public Safety ... Vacant
39 Director Housing & Residence Life ... Ms. Marcella T. SNYDER
96 Director of Purchasing ... Ms. Katrina A. HYDE
06 Registrar ... Mr. Scott A. COOK
102 Executive Director Foundation ... Ms. Angela HILL

*West Virginia School of Osteopathic Medicine (F)

400 Lee Street North, Lewisburg WV 24901-1196
County: Greenbrier FICE Identification: 011245
Unit ID: 237880
Telephone: (304) 645-6270 Carnegie Class: Spec-4-yr-Med
FAX Number: (304) 645-4859 Calendar System: Semester
URL: www.wvsom.edu
Established: 1972 Annual Graduate Tuition & Fees: N/A
Enrollment: 832 Coed
Affiliation or Control: State IRS Status: 501(c)3
Highest Offering: First Professional Degree; No Undergraduates
Accreditation: NH, OSTEO

02 President ... Dr. Michael D. ADELMAN
05 Vice Pres Academic Affairs & Dean ... Dr. Craig BOISVERT
10 Vice Pres Finance & Facilities ... Mr. Larry WARE
11 Vice Pres for Administration ... Dr. James W. NEMITZ
15 Associate VP of Human Resources ... Ms. Leslie BICKSLER
100 Associate VP Administrative Affairs ... Ms. Marilea BUTCHER
43 Vice Pres/General Counsel ... Mr. Jeffrey SHAWVER
20 Assoc Dean Osteopathic Medical Educ ... Dr. Robert W. FOSTER
20 Assoc Dean Graduate Med Education ... Dr. Victoria SHUMAN
20 Assoc Dean Preclinical Education ... Dr. Edward BRIDGES
20 Assoc Dean Predoctoral Clin Educ ... Dr. George BOXWELL

108 Assoc Dean Assessment/Educ Devel ... Dr. Machelle LINSENMEYER
32 Assistant Dean Student Affairs ... Dr. Rebecca MORROW
88 Director of Clinical Evaluation Ctr ... Dr. Gail SWARM
88 Director National Boards Office ... Dr. Robert FISK
13 Chief Technology Officer ... Ms. Kimberly RANSOM
16 Human Resources Manager ... Ms. Tiffany BURNS
06 Registrar ... Ms. Jennifer SEAMS
37 Director Financial Aid ... Ms. Lisa SPENCER
30 Director Institutional Development ... Ms. Heather ANTOLINI
29 Director of Alumni Relations ... Ms. Shannon WARREN
07 Director of Admissions ... Ms. Gwen BYRD
96 Director of Contracts ... Ms. Betty BAKER
08 Director of Library ... Ms. Mary ESSIG
26 Director of Marketing and PR ... Ms. Amy GOETZ
24 Director of Media Services ... Mr. Richard MCMAHAN
18 Director of Physical Plant II ... Mr. William ALDER
35 Director of Student Affairs ... Ms. Belinda EVANS
09 Coordinator Institutional Research ... Mr. Lance RIDPATH
40 Business Manager/Bookstore ... Ms. Cindi KNIGHT
04 Executive Administrative Assistant ... Ms. Cheryl BAKER
114 Manager Payroll Senior ... Ms. Stella DODRILL

*West Virginia State University (A)

PO Box 1000, Institute WV 25112-1000
County: Kanawha FICE Identification: 003826
Unit ID: 237899
Telephone: (304) 766-3000 Carnegie Class: Bac-A&S
FAX Number: (304) 720-2075 Calendar System: Semester
URL: www.wvstateu.edu
Established: 1891 Annual Undergrad Tuition & Fees (In-State): $6,996
Enrollment: 3,166 Coed
Affiliation or Control: State IRS Status: 501(c)3
Highest Offering: Master's
Accreditation: **NH**, ACBSP, CAEPN, SW

02 President ... Dr. Anthony L. JENKINS
10 VP for Business and Finance ... Mr. Melvin JONES
05 Provost and VP for Academic Affairs ... Dr. Kumara JAYASURIYA
09 Coord Institutional Research ... Dr. Danny R. CANTRELL
32 Int VP Enroll Mgmt/Student Affairs ... Mr. Joseph ODEN, JR.
111 VP for University Advancement ... Ms. Patricia J. SCHUMANN
20 Assoc Provost & Assoc VP Acad Affs ... Dr. Scott WOODARD
86 Chief of Staff and VP for Leg Affs ... Mr. Thomas BENNETT, II
46 VP for Research & Public Service ... Dr. Orlando F. MCMEANS
79 Int Dean Col of Arts & Humanities ... Dr. Robert WALLACE
81 Dean Col of Natural Sci/Math ... Dr. Naveed ZAMAN
107 Dean Col of Prof Studies ... Dr. Paige CARNEY
50 Dean Col of Bus Admin/Soc Sci ... Vacant
27 Director of Public Relations ... Mr. Jack BAILEY
13 Director of Information Technology ... Mr. Alan SKIDMORE
09 Dir of Inst Research/Effective ... Vacant
18 Director Physical Facilities ... Mr. Marvin SMITH
06 Director Records & Registration ... Ms. Donna L. HUNTER
19 Director of Public Safety ... Chief Joseph SAUNDERS
21 Asst VP for Business & Finance ... Ms. Kristi WILLIAMS
08 Director of Drain-Jordan Library ... Dr. Willette STINSON
37 Director of Student Financial Asst ... Ms. JoAnn L. ROSS
29 Director of Alumni Relations ... Ms. Belinda FULLER
15 Director of Human Resources ... Vacant
36 Dir of Career Services & Coop Educ ... Ms. Sandhya (Sandy) G. MAHARAJ
07 Director of Admissions ... Ms. Ashley WEIR
89 Director of New Student Programs ... Mrs. Sharon S. BANKS
96 Director of Purchasing ... Mrs. Janis A. BENNETT
106 Dir of Center for Online Learning ... Dr. Thomas KIDDIE
41 Athletic Director ... Mr. Nathan BURTON
39 Dir of Residence Life & Services ... Dr. Nancy NKUMSAH
07 Director of Admissions ... Ms. Ashley WEIR

*West Virginia University (B)

1500 University Avenue, Morgantown WV 26506-0002
County: Monongalia FICE Identification: 003827
Unit ID: 238032
Telephone: (304) 293-0111 Carnegie Class: DU-Highest
FAX Number: (304) 293-5883 Calendar System: Semester
URL: www.wvu.edu
Established: 1867 Annual Undergrad Tuition & Fees (In-State): $7,992
Enrollment: 28,776 Coed
Affiliation or Control: State IRS Status: 501(c)3
Highest Offering: Doctorate
Accreditation: **NH**, ART, AUD, CAATE, CACREP, CAEPN, CEA, CLPSY, COPSY, CS, DENT, DH, DIETD, DIETI, DMS, ENG, ENGR, ENGT, FEPAC, HT, IPSY, JOUR, LAW, LSAR, MED, MT, MUS, NMT, NURSE, OT, PA, PAST, PH, PHAR, PTA, RAD, RADMAG, RTT, SP, SPAA, SW, THEA

02 President/Chief Exec Officer ... Mr. E. Gordon GEE
05 Provost & VP Acad Affairs ... Ms. Joyce MCCONNELL
10 Vice President for Admin & Finance ... Mr. Narvel G. WEESE, JR.
26 Vice Pres for University Relations ... Ms. Sharon L. MARTIN
17 Vice Pres & Ex Dean of Hlth Sci ... Dr. Clay B. MARSH
32 Vice President Student Affairs ... Dr. William SCHAFER
46 Vice President for Research ... Mr. Fred L. KING
102 President & CEO WVU Found ... Ms. Cindi ROTH
15 VP for Human Resources ... Mr. Cris DEBORD
58 Vice Pres Health Sci Res/Grad Educ ... Dr. Glen DILLON
20 Vice Provost Academic Affairs ... Dr. John P. CAMPBELL
20 Assoc Provost Academic Personnel ... Dr. Cecil B. WILSON
88 Director Research & Rural Health ... Ms. Jodie JACKSON
100 VP Fed Relations & Sr Advis to Pres ... Mr. John J. COLE
88 Exec Officer for Policy Development ... Dr. Jennifer L. FISHER
43 VP Legal Affairs/General Counsel ... Mr. Rob ALSOP
21 Assoc VP & Chief Financial Officer ... Ms. Paula R. CANGELIO
21 Assoc Vice Pres for Finance ... Ms. Anjali HALABE
56 Dean & Director of Extension Svcs ... Dr. Steve C. BONANNO
13 Assoc Provost IT/CIO ... Ms. Barbara DAWSON
18 Sr Assoc VP Facilities & Svcs ... Mr. Randy HUDAK
35 Assoc Vice Pres Student Affairs ... Mr. Michael A. ELLINGTON
88 Asst VP Hlth Sci & Tech Academy ... Ms. Ann L. CHESTER
84 Assoc VP Enroll Mgmt Svcs ... Mr. Stephen LEE
45 Assoc Vice Pres Planning & Treasury ... Ms. Elizabeth P. REYNOLDS
86 Assoc VP State/Corporate Relations ... Ms. Sarah A. SMITH
25 Asst VP Office of Research Admin ... Mr. Alan B. MARTIN
09 Director of Institutional Research ... Dr. Nicolas VALCIK
39 Director Res Life/Dean of Students ... Ms. Trish CENDANA
41 Director Intercollegiate Athletics ... Mr. Shane LYONS
23 Director of Health Services ... Dr. Jan E. PALMER
27 Spec Asst VP Univ Relations ... Ms. Rebecca B. LOFSTEAD
29 Exec Director Alumni Association ... Mr. Sean FRISBEE
37 Director Financial Aid ... Ms. Sandra K. OERLY-BENNETT
06 University Registrar ... Ms. Aimee D. PFEIFER
08 Dean of Library Services ... Jon E. CAWTHORNE
38 Asst VP Student Wellness ... Dr. Catherine A. YURA
21 Director Financial Services ... Ms. Lisa A. LIVELY
19 Chief of Police/Univ Police Dept ... Capt. Bob E. ROBERTS
96 Asst VP Procurement/Cont & Pay ... Mr. David BEAVER
88 Assoc VP Intl & Global Outreach ... Dr. David C. STEWART
50 Dean Business and Economics ... Dr. Javier REYES
49 Dean of Arts & Sciences ... Dr. Gregory DUNAWAY
57 Dean College Creative Arts ... Dr. Paul K. KREIDER
53 Dean Educ & Human Resources ... Dr. Gypsy M. DENZINE
61 Dean of Law ... Mr. Gregory W. BOWMAN
63 Executive Dean of Medicine ... Dr. Clay MARSH
52 Dean of Dentistry ... Dr. Tom BORGIA
54 Dean of Engr/Mineral Resources ... Dr. Eugene V. CILENTO
47 Dean of Agriculture & Forestry ... Dr. Daniel J. ROBISON
67 Dean of Pharmacy ... Dr. Patricia A. CHASE
60 Dean of College of Media ... Dr. Maryanne REED
68 Dean Physical Education ... Dr. Dana D. BROOKS
66 Dean of Nursing ... Dr. Tara HULSEY
92 Dean of Honors College ... Mr. Kenneth P. BLEMINGS
88 Assoc Provost UG Acad Affairs ... Dr. Susan D. DAY-PERROOTS
36 Director Career Services ... Mr. David L. DURHAM
88 Assoc Provost Intl Acad Affairs ... Dr. Michael LASTINGER
88 Campus Provost-WVUIT ... Dr. Nigel N. CLARK
88 Assoc Provost Grad Acad Affairs ... Dr. Katherine A. KARRAKER
35 Assoc VP & Dean of Students ... Mr. G. Corey FARRIS
28 VP Diversity Equity & Inclusion ... Mr. David M. FRYSON
105 Director Web Services ... Ms. Cathy ORNDORFF
106 Dean WVU Online & CPE ... Mr. Keith BAILEY
88 Asst VP Strategic & Acad Com ... Dr. Ann CLAYCOMB
88 Asst VP Entrepreneurship & Innovat ... Ms. Melinda WALLS

*West Virginia University at Parkersburg (C)

300 Campus Drive, Parkersburg WV 26104-8647
County: Wood FICE Identification: 003828
Unit ID: 237686
Telephone: (304) 424-8000 Carnegie Class: Bac/Assoc-Mixed
FAX Number: (304) 424-8315 Calendar System: Semester
URL: www.wvup.edu
Established: 1961 Annual Undergrad Tuition & Fees (In-State): $3,384
Enrollment: 2,812 Coed
Affiliation or Control: State IRS Status: 501(c)3
Highest Offering: Baccalaureate
Accreditation: **NH**, ACBSP, ADNUR, CAEPN, NUR, SURGT

02 President ... Dr. Fletcher LAMKIN
04 Executive Asst to the President ... Mr. Brady WHIPKEY
05 Vice Pres of Academic Affairs ... Dr. Chad CRUMBAKER
32 Vice President for Student Services ... Mr. Anthony UNDERWOOD
20 Dean for Academic Affairs ... Dr. Cynthia GISSY
103 Exec Dir Workforce/Economic Develop ... Ms. Michele WILSON
10 Vice Pres Finance/Administration ... Ms. Alice HARRIS
26 Director Marketing/Communications ... Mrs. Katie WOOTTON
13 Chief Information Officer ... Mr. Doug ANTHONY
22 Special Asst to President ... Mrs. Debbie RICHARDS
12 Director Jackson County Center ... Mr. John GORRELL
111 VP Institutional Advancement ... Mr. Jeff OLSON
18 Director Facilities & Services ... Mr. David WHITE
15 Director Human Resources ... Mr. Scott POE
09 Dir Inst Rsrch/Outcomes Assessment ... Mr. Jeremy STARKEY
06 Registrar ... Mrs. Leslie SIMS
07 Dean of Enrollment ... Mrs. Christine POST
37 Director of Financial Aid ... Mrs. Heather SKIDMORE
21 Director of Business Services ... Ms. Jeannine RATLIFFE
08 Director of Library ... Mr. Stephen HUPP
50 Chair Business/Economics/Math Div ... Mr. Jeff HOLLAND
53 Chair Education ... Dr. David LANCASTER
76 Chair Health Sciences Division ... Ms. Cheryl MICHAELS
79 Chair Humanities/Fine Arts Div ... Dr. Dale HARTLEY
81 Chair STEM Division ... Dr. Jared GUMP

West Virginia Junior College (D)

1000 Virginia Street East, Charleston WV 25301-2817
County: Kanawha FICE Identification: 010573
Unit ID: 237987
Telephone: (304) 345-2820 Carnegie Class: Assoc/HVT-High Non
FAX Number: (304) 345-1425 Calendar System: Quarter
URL: www.wvjc.edu
Established: 1892 Annual Undergrad Tuition & Fees: $12,625
Enrollment: 149 Coed
Affiliation or Control: Proprietary IRS Status: Proprietary
Highest Offering: Associate Degree
Accreditation: **ABHES**

01 Campus President ... Ms. Michelle MILES
05 Academic Dean ... Ms. Katie HARVEY
06 Registrar ... Ms. Jennifer BIRD
37 Director Student Financial Aid ... Ms. Katherine BARNES

West Virginia Junior College (E)

148 Willey Street, Morgantown WV 26505-5596
County: Monongalia FICE Identification: 005007
Unit ID: 237996
Telephone: (304) 296-8282 Carnegie Class: Assoc/HVT-Mix Trad/Non
FAX Number: (304) 581-6990 Calendar System: Quarter
URL: www.wvjc.edu
Established: 1922 Annual Undergrad Tuition & Fees: $13,090
Enrollment: 428 Coed
Affiliation or Control: Proprietary IRS Status: Proprietary
Highest Offering: Associate Degree
Accreditation: **ABHES**

01 President & CEO ... Mr. Chad CALLEN
05 Academic Director ... Ms. Brittany NUZZO
36 Career Services ... Ms. Samantha ESPOSITO
37 Financial Aid Director ... Ms. Patricia CALLEN

West Virginia Junior College-Bridgeport (F)

176 Thompson Drive, Bridgeport WV 26330
Telephone: (304) 842-4007 Identification: 770823
Accreditation: **ABHES**

West Virginia Wesleyan College (G)

59 College Avenue, Buckhannon WV 26201-2699
County: Upshur FICE Identification: 003830
Unit ID: 237969
Telephone: (304) 473-8000 Carnegie Class: Masters/S
FAX Number: N/A Calendar System: Semester
URL: www.wvwc.edu
Established: 1890 Annual Undergrad Tuition & Fees: $29,752
Enrollment: 1,518 Coed
Affiliation or Control: United Methodist IRS Status: 501(c)3
Highest Offering: Doctorate
Accreditation: **NH**, CAATE, CAEPN, MUS, NURSE

01 President ... Dr. Joel THIERSTEIN
05 VP Academic Affairs & Dean of Col ... Dr. Boyd CREASMAN
32 VP Student Affairs ... Vacant
84 VP Enrollment Mgmt & Admissions ... Mr. John WALTZ
111 VP Advancement ... Mr. Robert SKINNER
42 Dean of the Chapel ... Rev. Christopher SCOTT
102 Director Foundation/Govt Relations ... Ms. Nicki BENTLEY-COLTHART
11 Director of Administrative Services ... Mr. Robert KIMBLE
37 Director Financial Aid ... Ms. Susan GEORGE
29 Assoc VP Adv & Alumni Relations ... Mr. William ARMISTEAD
08 Director of Library Services ... Ms. Paula MCGREW
06 Dir Acad & Career Svcs/Registrar ... Ms. Alice CREASMAN
39 Director Campus Life & Housing ... Ms. Alisa LIVELY
09 Director of Institutional Research ... Ms. Tammy CRITES
15 Director of Human Resources ... Ms. Vickie CROWDER
18 Director of the Physical Plant ... Mr. Kenneth ANDREW
30 Director Advancement Operations ... Ms. Rose Ellen LOUDIN
88 Director of Learning Center ... Dr. Shawn KUBA
41 Director of Athletics ... Mr. Randall TENNEY
10 Controller ... Mr. Randall CRITES
40 Retail Store Manager ... Ms. Bethaney MCKISIC
92 Director Honors Program ... Mr. Douglas VAN GUNDY
93 Director Multicultural Programs ... Mr. Robert QUARLES
112 Planned Giving Coordinator ... Rev. David PETERS
38 Director of Counseling Services ... Ms. Lori THOMPSON
31 Dir of Community Engagement ... Ms. LeeAnn BROWN
13 Director of Computing Services ... Mr. Neil ROTH
23 Director of Health Services ... Ms. Angela MAHAFFEY
04 Administrative Asst to President ... Ms. Deborah K. MULLENS
19 Director of Security ... Mr. David PARKS
43 Dir Legal Services/General Counsel ... Mr. David W. MCCAULEY
36 Director of Career Services ... Mrs. Barbara MORRISSETTE

Wheeling Jesuit University (H)

316 Washington Avenue, Wheeling WV 26003-6295
County: Ohio FICE Identification: 003831
Unit ID: 238078
Telephone: (304) 243-2000 Carnegie Class: Masters/M
FAX Number: (304) 243-2243 Calendar System: Semester
URL: www.wju.edu
Established: 1954 Annual Undergrad Tuition & Fees: $28,110
Enrollment: 1,385 Coed
Affiliation or Control: Roman Catholic IRS Status: 501(c)3
Highest Offering: Doctorate
Accreditation: **NH**, ACBSP, CAATE, CAEPT, COARC, NURSE, PTA

01 President ... Dr. Debra TOWNSLEY
10 Executive VP Operations & Finance ... Mr. Michael FERGUSON
100 Chief of Staff ... Mr. Mark PHILLIPS
05 Interim VP for Academic Affairs ... Ms. Laurie MCCULLOUGH
20 Assoc VP for Academic Affairs ... Dr. Mark DRNACH

32 Vice President Student Services ..... Dr. Daniel DENTINO
88 Dean of Rehabilitation Sciences ..... Mr. Chris PETROSINO
13 Director Information Technology ..... Mr. Eric MENCER
37 Director Financial Aid ..... Ms. Christie L. TOMCZYK
06 Registrar ..... Mr. Wilson TURNER
08 Librarian ..... Ms. Kelly MUMMERT
42 Director of Campus Ministry ..... Mr. Jamey BROGAN
41 Athletic Director ..... Mr. Kevin FORDE
18 Director of Facilities ..... Mr. Bruce MCCOLLOCH
85 Intl Admissions Representative ..... Ms. Jasmin ILOVAR
04 Administrative Asst to President ..... Ms. Mary Jo HABURSKY
106 Dir Online Education/E-learning ..... Mr. D. Jason FRITZMAN
19 Director Security/Safety ..... Mr. Stephen HABURSKY
29 Director Alumni Relations ..... Ms. Kelly KLUBERT
38 Director Student Counseling ..... Mr. Paul BELLOTTE
111 Director of Advancement ..... Mr. Noah MULL
50 Dean Business & Technology ..... Mr. Robert YAHN
07 Director Admissions ..... Mr. Sean DOYLE

WISCONSIN

Alverno College (A)

3400 S 43rd Street, Box 343922,
Milwaukee WI 53234-3922

County: Milwaukee — FICE Identification: 003832
Unit ID: 238193
Telephone: (414) 382-6000 — Carnegie Class: Masters/M
FAX Number: (414) 382-6066 — Calendar System: Semester
URL: www.alverno.edu
Established: 1887 — Annual Undergrad Tuition & Fees: $26,932
Enrollment: 2,209 — Female
Affiliation or Control: Independent Non-Profit — IRS Status: 501(c)3
Highest Offering: Doctorate
Accreditation: NH, MUS, NURSE

01 President ..... Dr. Andrea J. LEE, IHM
10 Sr Vice Pres Finance & Mgmt Svcs ..... Mr. James OPPERMANN
05 Acting Vice Pres Academic Affairs ..... Dr. Kathy LAKE
30 Vice President College Advancement ..... Vacant
20 Vice Pres for Academic Services ..... Sr. Marlene NEISES
84 VP for Enrollment Services ..... Ms. Kate LUNDEEN
32 Assoc VP/Dean of Students ..... Dr. Wendy POWERS
07 Int Dir Admissions/Ops/Recruitment ..... Ms. Becki CARDENAS
20 Vice President for Student Success ..... Vacant
20 Associate Vice President Academic ..... Vacant
06 Registrar ..... Ms. Patricia HARTMANN
08 Director Library ..... Mr. Larry DUERR
36 Director Career Development ..... Vacant
13 Exec Dir Information Technology ..... Ms. Anita EIKENS
37 Director of Financial Aid ..... Ms. Amy CHRISTEN
29 Director Alumnae Relations ..... Ms. Kim MUENCH
38 Director Advising ..... Ms. Kate TISCH
51 Dir Center for Assessment/ Outreach ..... Ms. Judith REISETTER-HART
15 Director Human Resources ..... Ms. Mary CASEY
41 Director of Athletics ..... Ms. Jessica OTT
42 Campus Minister ..... Vacant
96 Purchasing Agent ..... Ms. Anne MCCARRON
14 Chief Information Officer ..... Mr. Jim HILBY
66 Interim Dean School of Nursing ..... Ms. Margaret RAUSCHENBERGER
107 Dean of Professional Studies ..... Dr. Patricia LUEBKE
49 Dean School of Arts & Sciences ..... Dr. Kevin CASEY
50 Director Master of Business Admin ..... Dr. Patricia JENSEN
04 Director of Presidential Operations ..... Ms. Jill DESMOND
101 Office Manager ..... Ms. Anna ARENS
18 Chief Facilities/Physical Plant ..... Mr. John MARKS
19 Director Security/Safety ..... Lt. Michelle ENGEL

The Art Institute of Wisconsin (B)

320 East Buffalo Street, Suite 100, Milwaukee WI 53202
Telephone: (877) 285-4234 — Identification: 770824
Accreditation: #ACICS

† School is in teach-out plan.

Bellin College, Inc. (C)

3201 Eaton Road, Green Bay WI 54311

County: Brown — FICE Identification: 006639
Unit ID: 238324
Telephone: (920) 433-6699 — Carnegie Class: Spec-4-yr-Other Health
FAX Number: (920) 433-1923 — Calendar System: Semester
URL: www.bellincollege.edu
Established: 1909 — Annual Undergrad Tuition & Fees: $20,500
Enrollment: 371 — Coed
Affiliation or Control: Independent Non-Profit — IRS Status: 501(c)3
Highest Offering: Master's
Accreditation: NH, NURSE, RAD

01 President & CEO of the College ..... Dr. Connie J. BOERST
10 VP of Business & Finance ..... Mrs. Ginger B. KRUMMEN SCHRAVEN
66 Dean of Nursing ..... Dr. Stephanie M. STEWART
76 Dean of Allied Health Sciences ..... Dr. Mark A. BAKE
32 Dean of Student Services ..... Dr. Nancy M. BURRUSS
26 VP of Strategic Engagement & PR ..... Mr. Matt G. RENTMEESTER
13 Director of Technology ..... Mr. Travis A. SMITH
06 Registrar ..... Mr. Russell J. LEARY

37 Director Financial Aid ..... Ms. Lena C. GOODMAN
84 Director of Enrollment Mgmt ..... Mrs. Kathryn WALL
04 Administrative Asst to President ..... Ms. Jamie L. CAMPBELL
08 Head Librarian ..... Ms. Cindy M. REINL
111 Executive Director of Advancement ..... Mr. Thomas J. SHEFCHIK

Beloit College (D)

700 College Street, Beloit WI 53511-5595

County: Rock — FICE Identification: 003835
Unit ID: 238333
Telephone: (608) 363-2000 — Carnegie Class: Bac-A&S
FAX Number: (608) 363-2717 — Calendar System: Semester
URL: www.beloit.edu
Established: 1846 — Annual Undergrad Tuition & Fees: $47,060
Enrollment: 1,358 — Coed
Affiliation or Control: Independent Non-Profit — IRS Status: 501(c)3
Highest Offering: Baccalaureate
Accreditation: NH

01 President ..... Dr. Scott BIERMAN
05 Provost ..... Dr. Ann DAVIES
100 Chief of Staff ..... Mr. Daniel J. SCHOOFF
45 VP Budget & Planning ..... Ms. Stacie SCOTT
30 VP Development & Alumni Relations ..... Ms. Beth MONTEIRO
15 VP Human Resources and Operations ..... Ms. Lori RHEAD
84 VP Enrollment ..... Dr. Robert MIRABILE
32 Dean of Students ..... Dr. Christina KLAWITTER
13 Chief Information Officer ..... Dr. Pam MCQUESTEN
26 Chief Comm & Integ Mktg Officer ..... Mr. Tim JONES
108 Dir Strategic Research & Assessment ..... Ms. Ellie ANDERYRNE
09 Dir Strategic Research & Planning ..... Ms. Ruth VATER
06 Registrar ..... Ms. Mary BOROS-KAZAI
07 Director of Admissions ..... Mr. Patrick WALSH
07 Director of Intl Admissions ..... Ms. Erin GUTH
18 Director of Facilities ..... Mr. Michael PHILLIPS
29 Exec Dir of Dev & Alumni Engage ..... Mr. Mark C. WOLD
39 Director Resident Life/Conferences ..... Mr. John F. WINKELMANN
36 Director of Career Development ..... Ms. Jessica FOX-WILSON
38 College Counselor ..... Vacant
37 Director of Financial Aid ..... Vacant
28 Sr Dir Acad Diversity & Inclusion ..... Ms. Nicole TRUESDELL
41 Athletic Director ..... Mr. Tim SCHMIECHEN
40 Bookstore Director ..... Mr. Peter FRONK

Bryant & Stratton College (E)

310 W Wisconsin Avenue, Suite 500 E,
Milwaukee WI 53203
Telephone: (414) 276-5200 — FICE Identification: 005009
Accreditation: &M, ADNUR, MAC

† Regional accreditation is carried under the parent institution (corporate office) in Buffalo, NY.

Cardinal Stritch University (F)

6801 N Yates Road, Milwaukee WI 53217-3985

County: Milwaukee — FICE Identification: 003837
Unit ID: 238430
Telephone: (414) 410-4000 — Carnegie Class: DU-Mod
FAX Number: (414) 410-4239 — Calendar System: Semester
URL: www.stritch.edu
Established: 1937 — Annual Undergrad Tuition & Fees: $28,212
Enrollment: 3,176 — Coed
Affiliation or Control: Roman Catholic — IRS Status: 501(c)3
Highest Offering: Doctorate
Accreditation: NH, ACBSP, CAEPN, NUR, NURSE

01 Acting President ..... Dr. David L. SHROCK
04 Exec Assistant to the President ..... Ms. Kathryn HOWELL
05 Provost & VP Academic Affairs ..... Dr. Jeffrey D. SENESE
111 Vice President for Univ Advancement ..... Ms. Tonya M. MANTILLA
10 Vice President Business & Finance ..... Mr. Thomas J. CONGDON
84 Vice President Undergraduate Enroll ..... Mr. Nathan D. DEHNE
123 Vice President Graduate Enrollment ..... Mr. Allan M. MITCHLER
13 Chief Information Officer ..... Mr. David W. WEINBERG-KINSEY
66 Dean College Nursing/Health Science ..... Dr. Kelly J. DRIES
50 Dean College of Business & Mgmt ..... Dr. Phillip T. ANDERSON
53 Dean College of Education & Ldrship ..... Dr. Freda R. RUSSELL
49 Dean College of Arts & Sciences ..... Dr. Daniel J. SCHOLZ
41 Director of Athletics ..... Dr. Tim M. VAN ALSTINE
15 Director of Human Resources/Payroll ..... Mr. Michael D. HOFFMAN
06 Registrar ..... Ms. Naomi L. TIEFEL
113 Bursar ..... Ms. Lisa M. LEWIN
37 Dir of Financial Aid ..... Mr. Mark W. QUISTORF
117 Dir Treasury & Risk Management ..... Mr. Scott A. HELLRUNG
20 Director of Academic Affairs ..... Vacant
35 Asst VP of Student Affairs ..... Ms. Tracy A. FISCHER
88 Dir of Mission Engagement ..... Mr. Sean T. LANSING
32 Dean of Students ..... Ms. Donney MORONEY
36 Career Education ..... Mr. Tom E. KIPP
38 Dir for Counseling/Mental Wellness ..... Ms. Mary Beth WISNIEWSKI
104 Coord International Education ..... Ms. Sarah R. SWEENEY
108 Dir of Institutional Effectiveness ..... Mr. William L. MARCOU
91 Director of Enterprise Systems ..... Ms. Susan L. INGLES
08 Director of University Library ..... Ms. Laurie G. SWARTWOUT
102 Exec Dir Corporate & Foundation Rel ..... Vacant
112 Director Major Gifts/Planned Giving ..... Ms. Lisa M. HANDLER
26 Sr Dir Media Relations Adv Comm ..... Ms. Kathleen M. HOHL
29 Dir Alumni Relations/Annual Giving ..... Ms. Corrine M. ANSHUS

18 Director of Facilities ..... Mr. John B. GLYNN
19 Director of Security ..... Mr. Andrew DE RUBERTIS

Carroll University (G)

100 N East Avenue, Waukesha WI 53186-5593

County: Waukesha — FICE Identification: 003838
Unit ID: 238458
Telephone: (262) 547-1211 — Carnegie Class: Masters/S
FAX Number: (262) 524-7646 — Calendar System: Semester
URL: www.carrollu.edu
Established: 1846 — Annual Undergrad Tuition & Fees: $30,388
Enrollment: 3,508 — Coed
Affiliation or Control: Presbyterian Church (U.S.A.) — IRS Status: 501(c)3
Highest Offering: Doctorate
Accreditation: NH, ARCPA, CAATE, NURSE, OT, PTA

01 President ..... Dr. Cindy GNADINGER
05 Provost ..... Dr. Joanne PASSARO
10 Vice President for Finance ..... Mr. Ron LOSTETTER
84 Vice President for Enrollment ..... Mr. James V. WISEMAN
111 Vice President for Advancement ..... Mr. Stephen KUHN
32 Vice President Student Affairs ..... Dr. Theresa BARRY
06 Registrar ..... Ms. Ann HANDFORD
21 Controller ..... Ms. Deidre ERWIN
26 Dir of Communications/Marketing ..... Ms. Jeannine SHERMAN
15 Director of Human Resources ..... Ms. Lorraine FORCINITO
08 Interim Library Director ..... Ms. Brittany LARSON
37 Director of Student Financial Svcs ..... Ms. Dawn M. SCOTT
41 Athletic Director ..... Mr. Joe BAKER
88 Assoc Director of Part-Time Studies ..... Ms. Linda SKLANDER
28 Director of Cultural Diversity ..... Ms. Nicole DAVIS
29 Director Alumni Relations ..... Ms. Dolores M. BROWN
96 Director of Purchasing ..... Ms. Char RICHARDS
07 Director of Admissions ..... Ms. Kelly J. HEIMAN
18 Chief Facilities/Physical Plant ..... Mr. Alan PESCHL
38 Director Student Counseling ..... Ms. Angie R. BRANNAN
04 Exec Assistant to the President ..... Ms. Gina M. EHLER

Carthage College (H)

2001 Alford Park Drive, Kenosha WI 53140-1994

County: Kenosha — FICE Identification: 003839
Unit ID: 238476
Telephone: (262) 551-8500 — Carnegie Class: Bac-A&S
FAX Number: (262) 551-6208 — Calendar System: 4/1/4
URL: www.carthage.edu
Established: 1847 — Annual Undergrad Tuition & Fees: $40,265
Enrollment: 2,978 — Coed
Affiliation or Control: Evangelical Lutheran Church In America — IRS Status: 501(c)3
Highest Offering: Master's
Accreditation: NH, CAATE, MUS, SW

01 President ..... Dr. John R. SWALLOW
04 Special Assistant to the President ..... Mr. Paul R. HEGLAND
05 Provost/VP Academic Affairs ..... Dr. David GARCIA
115 Chief Investment Officer ..... Mr. William R. ABT
10 VP/Chief Financial Officer ..... Mr. Randy BARFIELD
111 VP for Institutional Advancement ..... Vacant
26 VP for Communications ..... Ms. Molly POLK
84 VP for Enrollment ..... Mr. Nick MULVEY
32 Dean of Students/VP Student Life ..... Dr. Kimberlie GOLDSBERRY
101 Secretary of the Board of Trustees ..... Mr. Paul R. HEGLAND
100 Chief of Staff/VP Strategic Initiat ..... Mr. Thomas KLINE
108 VP Institutional Effectiveness ..... Dr. Abigail HEINRICHS
41 Director of Athletics ..... Dr. Robert R. BONN
42 Campus Pastor ..... Ms. Kara BAYLOR
06 Registrar ..... Ms. Brigid PATTERSON

College of Menominee Nation (I)

PO Box 1179, Keshena WI 54135-1179

County: Menominee — FICE Identification: 031251
Unit ID: 413617
Telephone: (800) 567-2344 — Carnegie Class: Tribal
FAX Number: (715) 799-1336 — Calendar System: Semester
URL: www.menominee.edu
Established: 1992 — Annual Undergrad Tuition & Fees: $6,200
Enrollment: 433 — Coed
Affiliation or Control: Tribal Control — IRS Status: 501(c)3
Highest Offering: Baccalaureate
Accreditation: NH, ADNUR

01 Interim President ..... Dr. Diana MORRIS
05 Chief Academic Officer ..... Dr. Diana MORRIS
10 Comptroller ..... Mr. Mwata CHISHA
12 Int Vice Pres CMN Green Bay Campus ..... Ms. Kathy DENOR
26 Dean External Relations ..... Vacant
32 Dean of Student Services ..... Ms. Nicole FISH
49 Dean of Letters & Science ..... Mr. Chad WAUKECHON
75 Dean of Technical Education ..... Vacant
51 Dean of Continuing Education ..... Mr. Brian BOWALKOWSKI
04 Assistant to the President ..... Ms. Melinda COOK
09 Director Institutional Research ..... Vacant
30 Director Advancement ..... Ms. Irene KIEFER
25 Director of Sponsored Programs ..... Vacant
13 IT Director ..... Vacant
18 Director of Operations ..... Vacant
21 Business Manager ..... Vacant
15 Human Resources Director ..... Vacant
06 Registrar/Bursar ..... Ms. Geraldine SANAPAW

07 Int Admissions/Financial Aid Mgr .... Ms. Manih BOYD
29 Dir Alumni Relations/Development .... Ms. Tessa JAMES
88 Vocational Rehab Director .... Ms. Myrna WARRINGTON
08 Library Director .... Ms. Maria ESCALANTE
40 Director of Bookstore .... Vacant

College of Menominee Nation Oneida Campus (A)

2733 S Ridge Road, Green Bay WI 54304
Telephone: (920) 965-0070 Identification: 770424
Accreditation: &NH

Columbia College of Nursing (B)

4425 N Port Washington Road, Milwaukee WI 53212-1099
County: Milwaukee FICE Identification: 006640
Unit ID: 238573
Telephone: (414) 326-2330 Carnegie Class: Spec-4-yr-Other Health
FAX Number: (414) 236-2331 Calendar System: Semester
URL: www.ccon.edu
Established: 1901 Annual Undergrad Tuition & Fees: N/A
Enrollment: 154 Coed
Affiliation or Control: Independent Non-Profit IRS Status: 501(c)3
Highest Offering: Master's
Accreditation: NH, NURSE

01 President & Dean .... Dr. Jill M. BERG
10 Chief Financial/Business Officer .... Ms. Christina ITALIANO
05 Associate Dean of Academic Affairs .... Ms. Heather VARTANIAN
04 Exec Assistant to the President .... Ms. Gail PETERSON
37 Director Student Financial Aid .... Ms. Wendy HILVO
24 Director Educational Media .... Mr. Keith JACKSON
07 Admissions Specialist .... Ms. Susan DONDERO

Concordia University Wisconsin (C)

12800 N Lake Shore Drive, Mequon WI 53097-2402
County: Ozaukee FICE Identification: 003842
Unit ID: 238616
Telephone: (262) 243-5700 Carnegie Class: Masters/L
FAX Number: (262) 243-4351 Calendar System: 4/1/4
URL: www.cuw.edu
Established: 1881 Annual Undergrad Tuition & Fees: $27,900
Enrollment: 8,268 Coed
Affiliation or Control: Lutheran Church - Missouri Synod
IRS Status: 501(c)3
Highest Offering: Doctorate
Accreditation: NH, ARCPA, CAATE, DMS, IACBE, MAC, NURSE, OT, PHAR, PTA, SW

01 President .... Rev Dr. Patrick T. FERRY
11 Executive VP & Chief Oper Ofcr .... Mr. Allen J. PROCHNOW
05 Senior VP of Academics .... Dr. William R. CARIO
26 Senior VP University Affairs .... Ms. Gretchen M. JAMESON
111 VP of Advancement .... Rev Dr. Roy PETERSON
102 VP of Foundation .... Mr. Dean D. RENNICKE
13 VP of Information Technology .... Mr. Thomas G. PHILLIP
32 VP of Student Life .... Mr. Steven P. TAYLOR
100 Assistant to the President .... Mr. Kenneth K. GASCHK
51 Asst VP Academics/Cont & Dist Ed .... Dr. Bernard D. BULL
20 Asst VP Academics Faculty Dev .... Dr. Leah M. DVORAK
121 Asst VP Academics/Student Success .... Ms. Elizabeth A. POLZIN
27 Asst VP Strategic Communications .... Ms. Lisa LILJEGREN
42 Campus Pastor .... Rev. Steven N. SMITH
88 Chair Faculty Senate .... Dr. Robert S. BURLAGE
49 Dean School Arts/Sciences .... Dr. Steven R. MONTREAL
50 Dean School of Business .... Dr. Daniel S. SEM
53 Dean School of Education .... Dr. Michael D. UDEN
76 Dean School of Health Professions .... Dr. Linda M. SAMUEL
66 Dean School of Nursing .... Dr. Sharon L. CHAPPY
67 Dean School of Pharmacy .... Dr. Dean L. ARNESON
35 Dean of Students .... Dr. Steven W. GERNER
06 Registrar .... Mr. Carl R. BUTZ
29 Director of Alumni Relations .... Ms. Michelle L. WAGNER
41 Director of Athletics .... Dr. Rob M. BARNHILL
42 Director Campus Ministry .... Dcn. Kim C. BUELTMANN
19 Director Campus Safety .... Mr. Mario VALDES
38 Director of Counseling .... Mr. David T. ENTERS
36 Director of Career Services .... Mr. Ben B. ROHDE
37 Director of Financial Aid .... Mr. Robert J. NOWAK
15 Director Human Resources .... Ms. Hilary F. VATTER
09 Director of Institutional Research .... Dr. Tamara R. FERRY
24 Director Instructional Technology .... Mr. Sean B. YOUNG
08 Director of Library Services .... Mr. Christian R. HIMSEL
39 Director of Residence Life .... Ms. Beckie KRUSE
88 Exec Director Centers & Acceler .... Ms. Rochelle R. REGENAUER
88 Exec Director Cont & Dist Ed .... Ms. Sarah A. PECOR
85 Exec Director International Educ .... Rev Dr. David C. BIRNER
18 Superintendent Buildings & Grounds .... Mr. Steven V. HIBBARD
40 Bookstore Manager .... Ms. Kia LOR

Edgewood College (D)

1000 Edgewood College Drive, Madison WI 53711-1997
County: Dane FICE Identification: 003848
Unit ID: 238661
Telephone: (608) 663-4861 Carnegie Class: DU-Mod
FAX Number: (608) 663-3291 Calendar System: Semester
URL: www.edgewood.edu
Established: 1927 Annual Undergrad Tuition & Fees: $27,530
Enrollment: 2,678 Coed
Affiliation or Control: Roman Catholic IRS Status: 501(c)3
Highest Offering: Doctorate
Accreditation: NH, ACBSP, MFCD, NURSE

01 President .... Dr. Scott FLANAGAN
05 VP Academic Affs/Academic Dean .... Dr. Dean PRIBBENOW
32 VP Student Devel/Dean of Students .... Dr. Tony CHAMBERS
10 VP Business & Finance .... Mr. Michael GUNS
84 VP Enrollment Mgmt .... Ms. Christine BENEDICT
88 VP Dominican Life & Mission .... Sr. Maggie HOPKINS, OP
111 VP Inst Advancement .... Mr. Gary KLEIN
20 Associate Academic Dean .... Dr. Kelley GRORUD
106 Assoc Acad Dean Online & Adult Lrng .... Dr. Karen FRANKER
49 Dean School of Arts & Sciences .... Dr. John FIELDS
50 Dean School of Business .... Dr. Stevie WATSON
53 Dean School of Education .... Dr. Timothy SLEKAR
71 Dean School of Integrative Studies .... Dr. Kristine MICKELSON
66 Dean School of Nursing .... Dr. Margaret NOREUIL
07 Director Freshman Admissions .... Mr. Derek JOHNSON
13 Interim Dir Information Technology .... Mr. Patrick GUMIENY
108 Director Inst Assessment & Research .... Dr. Edward J. KEELEY
06 Registrar .... Ms. Michelle KELLEY
08 Library Director .... Dr. Sylvia CONTRERAS
36 Director Career Development .... Ms. Sara HANSON
29 Alumni Director .... Ms. Cassie WICKERSHAM
26 Exec Dir of Mktg & Strat Comm .... Ms. Amy PIKALEK
27 Director Marketing & Communication .... Mr. Edward TAYLOR
15 Director Human Resources .... Ms. Pamela LAVALLIERE
18 Director Facilities & Operations .... Ms. Susan VANDERSANDEN
38 Director Personal Counseling Svcs .... Dr. Megan COBB
21 Controller .... Ms. Jane WILHELM
28 Director Diversity & Inclusion .... Mr. Tony GARCIA
37 Director Student Financial Aid .... Ms. Kari GRIBBLE
23 Director Student Health Services .... Ms. Kimberly MORELAND
41 Director Athletics .... Mr. Al BRISACK

George Williams College of Aurora University (E)

350 Constance Boulevard, Williams Bay WI 53191
Telephone: (262) 245-5531 Identification: 770066
Accreditation: &NH

† Branch campus of Aurora University, Aurora, IL

Herzing University (F)

5218 E Terrace Drive, Madison WI 53718-8340
County: Dane FICE Identification: 009621
Unit ID: 240392
Telephone: (608) 249-6611 Carnegie Class: Masters/M
FAX Number: (608) 249-8593 Calendar System: Semester
URL: www.herzing.edu
Established: 1965 Annual Undergrad Tuition & Fees: $13,390
Enrollment: 2,753 Coed
Affiliation or Control: Independent Non-Profit IRS Status: 501(c)3
Highest Offering: Master's
Accreditation: NH, ADNUR, IACBE, NURSE

01 President .... Ms. Renee HERZING
12 Campus President .... Mr. William VINSON
10 CFO & Vice President of Finance .... Mr. Robert HERZOG
05 Academic Dean .... Vacant
37 Educational Funding Manager .... Mr. Clayton GROTH
32 Dir of Student Services/Registrar .... Ms. Amy HERFEL
07 Assoc Director of Admissions .... Ms. Danielle OEST
36 Career Development Specialist .... Ms. Marion DUREN

Herzing University Brookfield Campus (G)

555 South Executive Drive, Brookfield WI 53005
Telephone: (262) 649-1710 Identification: 770429
Accreditation: &NH, NURSE, PTAA

Herzing University Kenosha Campus (H)

4006 Washington Road, Kenosha WI 53144
Telephone: (262) 671-0675 Identification: 770430
Accreditation: &NH, MAAB, NURSE

Herzing University Online (I)

W140N8917 Lilly Road, Menomonee Falls WI 53051
Telephone: (866) 508-0748 Identification: 770431
Accreditation: &NH, CAHIIM, MAAB

Lac Courte Oreilles Ojibwa Community College (J)

13466 W Trepania Road, Hayward WI 54843-2181
County: Sawyer FICE Identification: 025322
Unit ID: 260372
Telephone: (715) 634-4790 Carnegie Class: Tribal
FAX Number: (715) 634-5049 Calendar System: Semester
URL: www.lco.edu
Established: 1982 Annual Undergrad Tuition & Fees: $4,590
Enrollment: 371 Coed
Affiliation or Control: Tribal Control IRS Status: 501(c)3
Highest Offering: Associate Degree
Accreditation: NH

01 President .... Dr. Diane VERTIN
05 VP of Academic & Student Affairs .... Ms. Barb LUNDBERG
11 Vice President of Admin Services .... Ms. Rita MUELLER
10 Chief Financial Officer .... Ms. Jill MATCHETT
51 Dean of Continuing Education .... Ms. Amber MARLOW
09 Director of Institutional Research .... Mr. Tyler TURPIN
32 Dean of Student Svcs & Enrollment .... Ms. Karen BREIT
20 Academic Dean .... Ms. Gerralynne BERG
108 Director of Assessment/Accred .... Mr. Tom ANTELL
25 Office of Sponsored Programs Dir .... Mr. Dan GRETZ
37 Financial Aid Director .... Ms. Kelly QUARDERER

Lakeland University (K)

W3718 South Dr, Plymouth WI 53073
County: Sheboygan FICE Identification: 003854
Unit ID: 238980
Telephone: (920) 565-1000 Carnegie Class: Masters/L
FAX Number: (920) 565-1060 Calendar System: Semester
URL: www.lakeland.edu
Established: 1862 Annual Undergrad Tuition & Fees: $26,560
Enrollment: 3,671 Coed
Affiliation or Control: United Church Of Christ IRS Status: 501(c)3
Highest Offering: Master's
Accreditation: NH, CAEPT

01 President .... Dr. David BLACK
04 Assistant to the President .... Ms. LaJill EDGE
05 Provost/Dean of College .... Dr. Margaret L. ALBRINCK
111 Vice President for Advancement .... Ms. Beth BORGEN
07 Director of Admissions .... Mr. Samuel POULETTE
10 VP/Chief Financial Officer .... Mrs. Carole ROBERTSON
06 Registrar .... Ms. Amanda HRUSKA
103 Director of Career Development .... Mrs. Jessica LAMBRECHT
09 Director of Institutional Research .... Mr. Paul WHITE
32 Assoc Provost Student Development .... Ms. Leslie LASTER
08 Director of Library Services .... Ms. Ann K. PENKE
37 Director of Financial Aid .... Ms. Patty L. TAYLOR
26 Director of Communications .... Mr. David D. GALLIANETTI
21 Controller .... Ms. Amy WIRTZ
29 Dir Alumni & Church Relations .... Ms. Linda BOSMAN
15 Manager of Human Resources .... Ms. Ann FLAD-JESION
41 Director of Athletics .... Ms. April ARVAN
18 Manager of Facilities & Grounds .... Mr. Joe BENIGER
38 Director of Student Counselling .... Dr. Carey A. KNIER
19 Director Security/Safety .... Mr. David SIMON
39 Director of Residence Life .... Mr. Jim BAJCZYK
50 Dean School of Business & Enterpren .... Dr. Scott NIEDERJOHN
81 Dean School of Science/Tech & Educ .... Dr. Brian FRINK

Lawrence University (L)

711 E. Boldt Way, Appleton WI 54911
County: Outagamie FICE Identification: 003856
Unit ID: 239017
Telephone: (920) 832-7000 Carnegie Class: Bac-A&S
FAX Number: (920) 832-6978 Calendar System: Other
URL: www.lawrence.edu
Established: 1847 Annual Undergrad Tuition & Fees: $44,844
Enrollment: 1,557 Coed
Affiliation or Control: Independent Non-Profit IRS Status: 501(c)3
Highest Offering: Baccalaureate
Accreditation: NH, MUS

01 President .... Mr. Mark BURSTEIN
04 Executive Asst to the President .... Ms. Alice BOECKERS
05 Provost and Dean of the Faculty .... Ms. Catherine KODAT
10 VP Finance & Administration .... Mr. Christopher LEE
30 VP Development/Alumni Rels .... Mr. Calvin D. HUSMANN
32 VP for Student Life .... Mr. Christopher D. CARD
29 VP Alumni/Constituency Engagement .... Mr. Mark D. BRESEMAN
28 VP for Diversity & Inclusion .... Dr. Kimberly BARRETT
26 Assoc Vice Pres Communications .... Mr. Craig L. GAGNON
44 Campaign Dir/Principal Gifts Ofcr .... Ms. Kristen M. MEKEMSON
30 Assoc Vice Pres Development .... Ms. Stacy J. MARA
21 Controller .... Ms. Amy PRICE
64 Dean Conservatory of Music .... Mr. Brian G. PERTL
36 Dean of Career Services .... Ms. Mary T. MEANY
121 Dean of Academic Success .... Ms. Monita M. GRAY
20 Associate Dean of the Faculty .... Dr. Robert F. WILLIAMS
28 Asst Dean Students Multicul Affs .... Ms. Pa Lee MOUA
09 Director of Research Administration .... Ms. Kristin L. MCKINLEY
07 Dean of Admissions & Financial Aid .... Mr. Kenneth L. ANSELMENT
37 Director of Financial Aid .... Ms. Sara C. HOLMAN
06 Registrar .... Ms. Anne S. NORMAN
08 Librarian .... Mr. Peter J. GILBERT
41 Athletic Director .... Ms. Christyn ABARAY
13 Director Information Tech Svcs .... Mr. Steven M. ARMSTRONG
15 Director of Human Resources .... Ms. Rochelle L. BLINDAUER
18 Director of Facility Services .... Mr. Daniel R. MEYER
38 Assoc Dean Stdnts Health/Wellness .... Mr. Rich L. JAZDZEWSKI

Madison Media Institute-College of Media Arts (M)

2702 Agriculture Drive, Madison WI 53718-6787
County: Dane FICE Identification: 010913
Unit ID: 364168
Telephone: (800) 236-4997 Carnegie Class: Spec-4-yr-Other Tech
FAX Number: (608) 442-0141 Calendar System: Semester
URL: www.mediainstitute.edu
Established: 1969 Annual Undergrad Tuition & Fees: $10,277
Enrollment: 320 Coed

Affiliation or Control: Proprietary IRS Status: Proprietary
Highest Offering: Baccalaureate
Accreditation: ACICS

01 President .... Mr. Mike BAILEY
37 Director Financial Aid .... Ms. Mari HUFFMAN
07 Admissions Director .... Ms. Kristina GROSS
05 Academic Dean .... Mr. Mike BAILEY
06 Registrar .... Ms. Heather SEIBERLICH

Maranatha Baptist University (A)

745 West Main Street, Watertown WI 53094-7600
County: Jefferson FICE Identification: 023172
Unit ID: 239071
Telephone: (920) 261-9300 Carnegie Class: Bac-Diverse
FAX Number: (920) 261-9109 Calendar System: Semester
URL: www.mbu.edu
Established: 1968 Annual Undergrad Tuition & Fees: $14,260
Enrollment: 1,059 Coed
Affiliation or Control: Independent Non-Profit IRS Status: 501(c)3
Highest Offering: Doctorate
Accreditation: NH, NURSE

01 President .... Dr. Martin MARRIOTT
03 Executive Vice President .... Dr. Matthew DAVIS
05 Vice President for Academic Affairs .... Dr. William LICHT
111 Vice President for Inst Advancement .... Dr. Jim H. HARRISON
10 Vice President for Business Affairs .... Dr. Mark W. STEVENS
32 Dean of Students .... Dr. John DAVIS
06 Registrar .... Mr. Steve CARLSON
07 Director of Admissions .... Mr. Jonathan SHEELEY
30 Director of Development .... Mr. Steve BOARD
09 Director of Institutional Research .... Mr. Jonathan COLEMAN
15 Director Personnel Services .... Mr. Curt OBERHOLTZER
26 Chief Public Relations Officer .... Mr. Peter WRIGHT
41 Athletic Director .... Mr. Robert THOMPSON
08 Librarian .... Mr. Mark HANSON
35 Director Student Affairs .... Mr. David ANDERSON
29 Director Alumni Relations .... Dr. John DAVIS
37 Director Student Financial Aid .... Mr. Randy HIBBS
13 Chief Info Technology Officer (CIO) .... Dr. Werner LUMM
19 Director Security/Safety .... Mr. Timothy JOHNS
106 Dir Online Education/E-learning .... Mr. Phillip OLT
108 Director Institutional Assessment .... Mr. Jonathan COLEMAN
105 Director Web Services .... Mr. Peter WRIGHT
18 Chief Facilities/Physical Plant .... Dr. Werner LUMM
50 Director School of Business .... Mr. Tracy FOSTER
53 Director School of Education .... Mr. David HANDYSIDE

Marian University (B)

45 S National Avenue, Fond Du Lac WI 54935-4699
County: Fond Du Lac FICE Identification: 003861
Unit ID: 239080
Telephone: (920) 923-7600 Carnegie Class: Masters/M
FAX Number: (920) 923-7154 Calendar System: Semester
URL: www.marianuniversity.edu
Established: 1936 Annual Undergrad Tuition & Fees: $28,280
Enrollment: 2,099 Coed
Affiliation or Control: Roman Catholic IRS Status: 501(c)3
Highest Offering: Doctorate
Accreditation: NH, CAEPN, IACBE, NURSE, RAD, SW

01 President .... Dr. Andrew P. MANION
05 VP Academic Affairs .... Dr. Russell K. MAYER
10 Interim VP Business & Finance .... Dr. David W. EISINGER
29 VP Alumni/Partnerships/Career Svcs .... Ms. Stacey L. AKEY
32 VP for Student Engagement .... Ms. Kate CANDEE
84 VP Enrollment Management .... Mr. Jason M. HARMON
26 Senior VP for University Relations .... Dr. George E. KOONCE, JR.
111 Vice Pres Advancement .... Ms. Tracy L. MILKOWSKI
04 Executive Assistant to President .... Ms. Carey C. GARDIN
21 Interim Controller .... Ms. Kara L. SUTKIEWICZ
20 Associate VP for Academic Affairs .... Dr. Kelly A. CHANEY
66 Dean College of the Professions .... Dr. Linda K. MATHESON
49 Dean College of Arts/Sciences .... Dr. Michelle MAJEWSKIE
35 Dean of Student Engagement .... Dr. Paul KRIKAU
08 Director of Libraries .... Ms. Kathryn A. JOHNSTON
18 Operations Manager/Facilities .... Mr. Les M. SHARP
06 Registrar .... Ms. Lynda K. SCHULTZ
09 Director of Institutional Research .... Mr. Thomas P. RICHTER
37 Interim Director of Financial Aid .... Mr. John R. SMITH
42 Director of Campus Ministry .... Sr. Marie SCOTT, CSA
27 Director University Relations .... Ms. Tracy QUALMANN
07 Dean of Admission .... Ms. Shannon S. LALUZERNE
15 Director of Human Resources .... Ms. Amanda L. DUVAL
41 Director of Athletics .... Mr. Jason BARTELT
121 Dean Advising/Academic Services .... Ms. Cathy M. MATHWEG
23 Director of Health Services .... Ms. Jodi S. SCHRAUTH
36 Director of Career Services .... Ms. Mary J. HATLEN
109 Director of Campus Dining Services .... Ms. Nikki A. KRAMER
13 Director of Information Technology .... Dr. Daniel C. PARIZO
40 Director of Bookstore .... Ms. Mary MANGAN-FLOOD
38 Director of Counseling .... Ms. Robyn A. WILLIAMS
92 Director Honors Program .... Dr. Mathew P. SZROMBA
108 Director of Inst Assessment .... Dr. Moreen K. CARVAN
39 Director of Residence Life .... Ms. Severa KRUGER
104 Director of International Programs .... Dr. Cooper S. WAKEFIELD
19 Director Security/Safety .... Mr. Matt D. ROSE

Marquette University (C)

PO Box 1881, Milwaukee WI 53201-1881
County: Milwaukee FICE Identification: 003863
Unit ID: 239105
Telephone: (414) 288-7700 Carnegie Class: DU-Higher
FAX Number: (414) 288-3300 Calendar System: Semester
URL: www.marquette.edu
Established: 1881 Annual Undergrad Tuition & Fees: $38,470
Enrollment: 11,491 Coed
Affiliation or Control: Roman Catholic IRS Status: 501(c)3
Highest Offering: Doctorate
Accreditation: NH, ARCPA, CAATE, CACREP, CLPSY, COPSY, DENT, ENG, LAW, MIDWF, MT, NURSE, PTA, SP, THEA

01 President .... Dr. Michael R. LOVELL
05 Provost .... Dr. Daniel J. MYERS
03 Executive Vice President .... Mr. David LAWLOR
31 Vice President Public Affairs .... Ms. Rana H. ALTENBURG
43 Vice President and General Counsel .... Ms. Cynthia M. BAUER
15 Vice President Human Resources .... Mr. Octavio CASTRO
32 Vice President Student Affairs .... Dr. Xavier A. COLE
09 Vice Pres Research and Innovation .... Dr. Jeanne M. HOSSENLOPP
10 Vice President Finance .... Vacant
42 Vice Pres Mission Ministry .... Rev. Thomas KRETTEK, SJ
20 Senior Vice Prov Faculty Affairs .... Dr. Gary MEYER
26 Vice Pres Marketing & Communication .... Mr. David MURPHY
41 Vice Pres and Director of Athletics .... Mr. Bill SCHOLL
111 Vice Pres University Advancement .... Vacant
84 Vice Provost Enrollment Management .... Dr. John BAWOROWSKY
20 Vice Provost Academic Affairs .... Dr. John J. SU
06 Registrar .... Ms. Georgia D. MCRAE
07 Dean of Admissions .... Vacant
76 Dean of Health Sciences .... Dr. William CULLINAN
60 Dean of Communication .... Dr. Kimo AH YUN
53 Dean of Education .... Dr. William A. HENK
49 Dean of Arts & Sciences .... Dr. Richard C. HOLZ
61 Dean of the Law School .... Mr. Joseph D. KEARNEY
52 Dean of Dentistry .... Dr. William K. LOBB
66 Interim Dean of Nursing .... Dr. Janet WESSEL-KREJCI
54 Dean of Engineering .... Dr. Kristina ROPELLA
50 Dean of Business Administration .... Dr. Brian D. TILL
08 Dean of Libraries .... Ms. Janice WELBURN
58 Dean of Graduate School .... Dr. Douglas WOODS
101 Assistant to Pres/Corp Secretary .... Mr. Steven W. FRIEDER
13 Chief Information Officer .... Ms. Kathy J. LANG
35 Dean of Students .... Dr. Stephanie QUADE
28 Exec Director Diversity & Inclusion .... Dr. William WELBURN
121 Assoc Vice Prov Acad Support Pgm .... Ms. Anne D. DEAHL
90 Assoc Vice Provost Educational Tech .... Mr. G. Jon PRAY
30 Senior Director of Development .... Mr. Timothy RIPPINGER
21 Senior Assoc Vice President Finance .... Vacant
45 Assoc VP Finance/Univ Architect .... Ms. Lora STRIGENS
35 Assistant Vice Pres Student Affairs .... Dr. Jeff JANZ
39 Exec Dir Housing and Residence Life .... Ms. Mary JANZ
25 Exec Dir Research & Sponsored Prog .... Ms. Katherine DURBEN
23 Exec Dir University Medical Clinic .... Dr. Carolyn S. SMITH
36 Director Career Services Center .... Ms. Laura F. KESTNER-RICKETTS
38 Director of Counseling Center .... Dr. Michael J. ZEBROWSKI
18 Dir Facilities & Campus Services .... Mr. Gregory ADAMS
37 Director of Financial Aid .... Ms. Susan M. TEERINK
104 Dir International Education Office .... Mr. Terence MILLER
40 Director Marquette Spirit Shop .... Mr. James K. GRAEBERT
29 Engagement Director .... Mr. Daniel DEWEERDT
19 Chief of Police .... Mr. Paul MASCARI
96 Director of Purchasing .... Ms. Jenny ALEXANDER
04 Administrative Asst to President .... Mrs. Stacy ROMANT

Medical College of Wisconsin (D)

PO Box 26509, Milwaukee WI 53226-0509
County: Milwaukee FICE Identification: 024535
Unit ID: 239169
Telephone: (414) 955-8296 Carnegie Class: Spec-4-yr-Med
FAX Number: (414) 955-6560 Calendar System: Other
URL: www.mcw.edu
Established: 1893 Annual Graduate Tuition & Fees: N/A
Enrollment: 1,217 Coed
Affiliation or Control: Independent Non-Profit IRS Status: 501(c)3
Highest Offering: Doctorate; No Undergraduates
Accreditation: NH, AA, DENT, MED, PDPSY, PH, @PHAR

01 President & CEO .... Dr. John R. RAYMOND, SR.
03 Dean/Executive Vice President .... Dr. Joseph E. KERSCHNER
04 Administrative Asst to President .... Ms. Cheryl A. DYER
05 VP Academic Outreach .... Dr. Cheryl A. MAURANA
10 Sr Vice Pres Finance/Administration .... Mr. Christopher KOPS
88 Dean Grad Sch Biomedical Science .... Dr. Ravi P. MISRA
30 Vice Pres of Development .... Ms. Alice ARCHABAL
15 Vice President Human Resources .... Ms. Sherri DUCHARME-WHITE
86 Vice Pres Government/Community Affs .... Ms. Kathryn A. KUHN
117 VP Corporate Compliance/Risk Mgmt .... Mr. Daniel WICKEHAM
26 VP Comm/Experience & Brand Mgmt .... Ms. Mara LORD
13 VP Information Services .... Mr. David C. HOTCHKISS
27 Sr Assoc Vice Pres Communications .... Mr. Richard N. KATSCHKE
20 Sr Assoc Dean for Academic Affs .... Dr. William J. HUESTON
28 Chief Diversity & Inclusion Officer .... Dr. C. Greer JORDAN
32 Assoc Dean Student Affs & Diversity .... Dr. Dawn S. BRAGG
63 Sr Assoc Dean Graduate Med Educ .... Dr. Kenneth B. SIMONS
46 Director Neuroscience Research Ctr .... Dr. Cecilia J. HILLARD
20 Associate Dean Curriculum .... Dr. Travis P. WEBB
114 Interim Director Budget .... Ms. Lisa SCHEELE
13 Director Application Development .... Ms. Rebecca L. MORRISON
08 Director Medical Libraries .... Ms. Ellen N. SAYED
07 Director Admissions .... Ms. Alexis MEYER
06 Registrar .... Ms. Kerry J. GROSSE
18 VP Facilities & Operations .... Mr. Jeffrey BORNEMANN
37 Director Student Financial Services .... Ms. Linda L. PASCHAL
25 Director Grants & Contracts .... Ms. April HAVERTY
29 Exec Director Alumni Relations .... Mr. Seth M. FLYNN
96 Assoc Dir Purchasing & Payables .... Ms. Paulette M. PECARD
40 Manager of Bookstore .... Ms. Cathy GRANFIELD
19 Director Public Safety .... Mr. David C. FELLER
43 General Counsel .... Mr. John NEWSOME
10 Chief Financial Officer .... Mr. Barclay FERGUSON
67 Dean School of Pharmacy .... Dr. George MACKINNON
25 Contract Administrator .... Mr. Jeffrey WOJNOWSKI
45 Sr Assoc Dean for Research .... Dr. Ann NATTINGER
100 Chief of Staff .... Mr. Ryan J. GOERLITZ

Midwest College of Oriental Medicine (E)

6232 Bankers Road, Racine WI 53403-9747
County: Racine FICE Identification: 030612
Unit ID: 383020
Telephone: (800) 593-2320 Carnegie Class: Spec-4-yr-Other Health
FAX Number: (262) 554-7475 Calendar System: Quarter
URL: www.acupuncture.edu
Established: 1979 Annual Undergrad Tuition & Fees: N/A
Enrollment: 65 Coed
Affiliation or Control: Proprietary IRS Status: Proprietary
Highest Offering: Master's; No Lower Division
Accreditation: ACUP

01 President .... Dr. William J. DUNBAR
05 Director of Academics .... Dr. Robert CHELNICK
12 Evanston Campus Director .... Dr. Kristine L. LA POINT
37 Director of Financial Aid .... Ms. Elizabeth M. HOJAN
07 Admissions Coord/Transfer Credit .... Ms. Liz WARKENTIN
06 Records Officer/Registrar .... Ms. Amy L. BENISH
08 Dean of Students/Librarian .... Mr. John BALLARINI
32 Dean of Students .... Ms. Olga GAJDOSIK
09 Research Director .... Mr. Jin Hua XIE
85 Dean of Foreign Students .... Dr. Duckin SUH
108 Clinic Tracking/Inst Evaluation .... Ms. Deirdre M. DUNBAR
91 Information Systems .... Mr. William H. LEHMAN
26 Marketing/Student Affairs .... Mr. Chris A. KRAJNIAK
88 Office Manager .... Ms. Stephanie M. PITTMAN

Milwaukee Career College (F)

3077 North Maryfair Road, Suite 300, Milwaukee WI 53222
County: Milwaukee FICE Identification: 041174
Unit ID: 449861
Telephone: (800) 754-1009 Carnegie Class: Not Classified
FAX Number: (414) 727-9557 Calendar System: Other
URL: www.mkecc.edu
Established: 2002 Annual Undergrad Tuition & Fees: N/A
Enrollment: 126 Coed
Affiliation or Control: Proprietary IRS Status: Proprietary
Highest Offering: Associate Degree
Accreditation: ABHES, SURTEC

01 President .... Jack TAKAHASHI

Milwaukee Institute of Art & Design (G)

273 E Erie Street, Milwaukee WI 53202-6003
County: Milwaukee FICE Identification: 020771
Unit ID: 239309
Telephone: (414) 847-3200 Carnegie Class: Spec-4-yr-Arts
FAX Number: (414) 291-8077 Calendar System: Semester
URL: www.miad.edu
Established: 1974 Annual Undergrad Tuition & Fees: $35,020
Enrollment: 627 Coed
Affiliation or Control: Independent Non-Profit IRS Status: 501(c)3
Highest Offering: Baccalaureate
Accreditation: NH, ART

01 President .... Mr. Jeff MORIN
05 VP of Academic Affairs .... Mr. David MARTIN
84 VP for Enrollment Management .... Ms. Mary C. SCHOPP
04 Executive Assistant to President .... Ms. Mary EGGERT
108 Assoc VP Academic Plng/Assessment .... Ms. Cynthia LYNCH
10 VP for Financial Affairs .... Ms. Brenda JONES
30 VP of Development & Communications .... Ms. Vivian M. ROTHSCHILD
39 Director of Residential Living .... Ms. Marianne HONRATH
32 Dean of Students .... Mr. Tony J. NOWAK
37 Executive Director of Financial Aid .... Ms. Carol MASSE
07 Director of Admissions .... Mr. David SIGMAN
88 Enroll Communications Specialist .... Ms. Stacey STEINBERG
08 Director of Library Services .... Ms. Cynthia D. LYNCH
36 Director of Career Services .... Mr. Duane P. SEIDENSTICKER
51 Dir Pre-College & Adult Learning .... Mr. Corbett TOOMSEN
19 Director Security/Safety .... Mr. Keith A. KOTOWICZ
06 Director of Registration Services .... Ms. Jean WEIMER
121 Director of College Advising .... Ms. Michelle KAMPA

Code	Title	Name
15	Director of Human Resources	Ms. April FORRAY
20	Director of Academic Operations	Ms. Marie KAMINSKI
18	Building Maintenance Manager	Mr. Michael A. GOETZ
13	Director of Technology	Mr. Matt OGDEN
25	Exe Dir AIM HIGH Wisconsin	Ms. Sharon CROWE

Milwaukee School of Engineering (A)

1025 N Broadway, Milwaukee WI 53202-3109
County: Milwaukee — FICE Identification: 003868
Unit ID: 239318
Telephone: (414) 277-7300 — Carnegie Class: Masters/S
FAX Number: (414) 277-7454 — Calendar System: Quarter
URL: www.msoe.edu
Established: 1903 — Annual Undergrad Tuition & Fees: $37,980
Enrollment: 2,906 — Coed
Affiliation or Control: Independent Non-Profit — IRS Status: 501(c)3
Highest Offering: Master's
Accreditation: NH, CONST, ENG, ENGT, NURSE, PERF

Code	Title	Name
01	President	Dr. John WALZ
05	Vice President Academics	Dr. Eric BAUMGARTNER
10	Vice President of Finance and CFO	Ms. Dawn THIBEDEAU
30	VP of Development/Alumni Rels	Mr. Jeff SNOW
18	VP of Operations	Mr. Kevin MORIN
84	VP of Enroll Mgmt & Dean of Student	Dr. Timothy VALLEY
25	Dean Grants & Projects	Mr. Sheku KAMARA
48	Chair Architectural Engr Dept	Dr. Blake WENTZ
50	Int Chair School of Business	Mr. David SCHMITZ
54	Chair Electrical Engr/CPU Sci Dept	Dr. Stephen WILLIAMS
97	Chair General Studies Department	Dr. Alicia DOMACK
81	Chair Mathematics Department	Dr. Matey KALTCHEV
54	Chair Mechanical Engineering Dept	Dr. Matthew PANHAS
81	Chair Physics/Chemistry Dept	Dr. Matey KALTCHEV
66	Chair Nursing Department	Dr. Carol SABEL
06	Registrar	Ms. Mary F. NIELSEN
13	Director of IT Services	Mr. Rick THOMAS
26	Director Marketing Public Affairs	Mr. Sebastian THACHENKARY
27	Director Public & Media Relations	Ms. JoEllen BURDUE
15	Director of Human Resources	Mr. Kevin A. MORIN
37	Director of Financial Aid	Mr. Steve MIDTHUN
44	Director of Development	Mr. Jonathan V. KOWALSKI, JR.
32	Director Student Activities	Mr. Nick SEIDLER
39	Director Residence Halls	Dr. William E. BREESE
41	Director Athletics	Mr. Brian MILLER
08	Director of Library & Info Services	Mr. Gary S. SHIMEK
105	Director of Services/Webmaster	Mr. Kent A. PETERSON
19	Director of Public Safety	Mr. William P. FADROWSKI
29	Director Alumni Affairs	Ms. Cathy VAREBROOK
07	Director of Admissions	Ms. Seandra MITCHELL
36	Director Student Placement	Ms. Mary SPENCER
40	Bookstore Manager	Mr. David P. ABRAHAMSON

Mount Mary University (B)

2900 N Menomonee River Parkway,
Milwaukee WI 53222-4597
County: Milwaukee — FICE Identification: 003869
Unit ID: 239390
Telephone: (414) 930-3000 — Carnegie Class: Masters/M
FAX Number: (414) 930-3712 — Calendar System: Semester
URL: www.mtmary.edu
Established: 1913 — Annual Undergrad Tuition & Fees: $28,380
Enrollment: 1,313 — Female
Affiliation or Control: Roman Catholic — IRS Status: 501(c)3
Highest Offering: Doctorate
Accreditation: NH, CACREP, #CIDA, DIETC, DIETI, OT, SW

Code	Title	Name
01	President	Dr. Christine PHARR
10	Exec VP Admin Services/Interim CFO	Ms. Beth WNUK
05	VP Academic/Student Affairs	Dr. Karen FRIEDLEN
84	Vice Pres Enrollment Services	Mr. David WEGENER
30	Vice Pres Development	Ms. Pamela OWENS
88	Vice President Mission/ Identity	Sr. Joan PENZENSTADLER, SSND
20	Dean Academic Affairs	Dr. Wendy WEAVER
32	Dean Student Affairs	Ms. Sarah OLEJNICZAK
58	Dean of Graduate Education	Vacant
21	Sr Dir of Business Ofc/Controller	Ms. Sharon ROOB
06	Registrar	Dr. Mary KARR
110	Senior Director of Development	Ms. Lisa BREITSPRECKER
26	Senior Dir of Communication & Mktg	Mr. Scott RUDIE
29	Director of Alumnae Relations	Ms. Andrea MILLER
123	Director of Graduate Admission	Mr. Kirk HELLER DE MESSER
07	Director of Undergraduate Admission	Ms. Rebecca SURGES
09	Exec Director of Inst Effectiveness	Dr. Jill MEYER
08	Director of Library	Mr. Eric ROBINSON
13	Senior Director of IT	Mr. Marc BELANGER
37	Director Financial Aid	Ms. Debra DUFF
35	Director of Student Engagement	Ms. Kayla SELL
39	Director of Residence Life	Mr. Erich ZEIMANTZ
36	Dir of Advising/Career Development	Ms. Michelle PLIML
104	Director of International Studies	Ms. Nan METZGER
15	Senior Director of Human Resources	Ms. Alisa BENDICKSON
41	Athletic Director	Mr. Marc HEIDORF
42	Director of Campus Ministry	Ms. Lea ROSENBERG
18	Director of Buildings & Grounds	Ms. Rebecca JOHNSON
19	Director of Public Safety	Mr. Paul LESHOK
40	Mgr Barnes & Noble Bookstore	Mr. Timothy STERNKE
04	Executive Assistant to President	Vacant
102	Dir Foundation/Corporate Relations	Ms. Anne KAHL

Nashotah House (C)

2777 Mission Road, Nashotah WI 53058-9793
County: Waukesha — FICE Identification: 003874
Unit ID: 239424
Telephone: (262) 646-6500 — Carnegie Class: Spec-4-yr-Faith
FAX Number: (262) 646-6504 — Calendar System: Semester
URL: www.nashotah.edu
Established: 1842 — Annual Graduate Tuition & Fees: N/A
Enrollment: 96 — Coed
Affiliation or Control: Protestant Episcopal — IRS Status: 501(c)3
Highest Offering: Doctorate; No Undergraduates
Accreditation: THEOL

Code	Title	Name
01	Dean-President	Rev. Steven A. PEAY
10	Associate Dean of Administration	Rev. Philip J. CUNNINGHAM
13	IT/Database Administrator	Mr. Matt BILLS
05	Associate Dean for Academic Affairs	Rev. Andrew GROSSO
06	Registrar	Rev. Rick HARTLEY
32	Associate Dean of Students	Rev. Rick HARTLEY
07	Admissions Assoc/Asst Registrar	Ms. Laura GROETSCH
08	Library Director	Dr. David G. SHERWOOD
111	Associate Dean of Inst Advancement	Ms. Diane PLANTENBERG
26	Marketing/Communications	Ms. Lisa SWAN
18	Chief Facilities/Physical Plant	Mr. Ricco MEDINA
101	Secretary of the Board of Trustees	Rev. R. Brien KOEHLER
09	Dir of Institutional Research	Rev. Esther KRAMER
29	Dir of Alumni Relations	Mrs. Jan WATTER

Northland College (D)

1411 Ellis Avenue, Ashland WI 54806-3999
County: Ashland — FICE Identification: 003875
Unit ID: 239512
Telephone: (715) 682-1699 — Carnegie Class: Bac-A&S
FAX Number: (715) 682-1308 — Calendar System: Other
URL: www.northland.edu
Established: 1892 — Annual Undergrad Tuition & Fees: $33,432
Enrollment: 541 — Coed
Affiliation or Control: United Church Of Christ — IRS Status: 501(c)3
Highest Offering: Baccalaureate
Accreditation: NH

Code	Title	Name
01	President	Dr. Michael MILLER
05	Academic Dean	Dr. Leslie ALLDRITT
111	VP of Institutional Advancement	Ms. Margot ZELENZ
10	VP Finance & Administration	Mr. Robert JACKSON
32	Dean of Students	Dr. Hal HAYNES
88	Exec Director Environmental Inst	Dr. Alan BREW
30	Exec Director of Development	Ms. Kristy LIPHART
20	Interim Associate Academic Dean	Dr. Wendy GORMAN
07	Exec Director of Admissions	Mr. Teege METTILLE
06	Registrar	Ms. Michelle BITZER
08	Library Director	Ms. Julia WAGGONER
29	Director of Alumni Relations	Ms. Jackie MOORE
13	Information Service Manager	Mr. Todd PYDO
41	Athletic Director	Ms. Kim FALKENHAGEN
15	Exec Director Human Resources	Mr. Paul SKORACZEWSKI
37	Director of Student Financial Aid	Ms. Kelly DUNN
21	Controller	Mr. Todd VYSKOCIL
09	Institutional Research Specialist	Ms. Petra HOFSTEDT
04	Exec Assistant to the President	Ms. Dawn RIVARD
39	Director of Residential Life	Ms. Melissa HARVEY
25	Director of Sponsored Awards	Ms. Lisa WILLIAMSON
26	Exec Director of Inst Marketing	Ms. Demeri MULLIKIN
18	Director of Operations	Mr. Paul WEBB
19	Campus Safety Director	Mr. Dawayne LAMPSON
38	Campus Counselor	Ms. Kathleen SKORACZEWSKI

Ottawa University Wisconsin (E)

245 South Executive Drive, Brookfield WI 53005-4204
Telephone: (262) 879-0200 — Identification: 666084
Accreditation: &NH

† Regional accreditation is carried under the parent institution in Ottawa, KS.

Rasmussen College - Green Bay (F)

904 South Taylor Street, Building 1, Green Bay WI 54303
Telephone: (920) 593-8400 — Identification: 667063
Accreditation: &NH, ADNUR, CAHIIM, MAAB, MLTAD

† Regional accreditation is carried under the parent institution in Saint Cloud, MN. The tuition figure is an average, actual tuition may vary.

Rasmussen College - Wausau (G)

1101 Westwood Drive, Wausau WI 54401
Telephone: (715) 841-8000 — Identification: 667068
Accreditation: &NH, ADNUR, MAAB

† Regional accreditation carried under the parent institution in Saint Cloud, MN. The tuition figure is an average, actual tuition may vary.

Ripon College (H)

300 West Seward Street, PO Box 248,
Ripon WI 54971-0248
County: Fond du Lac — FICE Identification: 003884
Unit ID: 239628
Telephone: (920) 748-8115 — Carnegie Class: Bac-A&S
FAX Number: (920) 748-7243 — Calendar System: Semester
URL: www.ripon.edu
Established: 1851 — Annual Undergrad Tuition & Fees: $39,142
Enrollment: 794 — Coed
Affiliation or Control: Independent Non-Profit — IRS Status: 501(c)3
Highest Offering: Baccalaureate
Accreditation: NH

Code	Title	Name
01	President	Zachariah P. MESSITTE
04	Exec Sec to President & DOF	Claudia M. LEISTIKOW
101	Special Assistant to the President	Margaret A. CARNE
05	VP & Dean of Faculty	Ed WINGENBACH
111	VP for Advancement	Vacant
10	Vice President for Finance	Karl I. SOLIBAKKE
32	Vice President/Dean of Students	Christophor M. OGLE
84	Vice President for Enrollment	Jennifer L. MACHACEK
06	Assoc Dean of Faculty/Registrar	Michele A. WITTLER
36	Asst Dean of Career & Prof Develop	Lindsay A. BLUMER
07	Dean of Admissions	Leigh D. MLODZIK
21	Controller	Lori A. SCHULZE
08	Access Services Librarian	Kate MOODY
35	Dir Student Activities/Orientation	Sharon JACKSON
121	Director Student Support Svcs	Daniel J. KRHIN
39	Director of Residence Life	Jessica L. JOANIS
26	Exec Dir Marketing & Communications	Melissa K. ANDERSON
27	Dir of Creative & Social Media	Richard T. DAMM
30	Exec Director of Development	Vacant
13	Exec Dir of Information Technology	Tara A. LACHAPELL
109	General Manager Food Service	Doug STENFELDT
18	Director Physical Plant	Brian SKAMRA
41	Director of Athletics	Julie H. JOHNSON
102	Dir Foundation & Govt Relations	Terri L. HOLZMAN
110	Senior Development Director	Nancy L. HINTZ
29	Dir Constituent Engagement	Amy L. GERRETSEN
15	Human Resource Administrator	Jennifer FRANZ
38	Director of Counseling Services	Cynthia S. VIERTEL
40	Bookstore Manager	Vacant
37	Director Financial Aid	David B. WOODWARD
28	Dir of Multicultural Affairs	Kyonna HENRY

Sacred Heart Seminary and School of Theology (I)

7335 S Highway 100, P.O. Box 429,
Hales Corners WI 53130-0429
County: Milwaukee — FICE Identification: 020780
Unit ID: 239637
Telephone: (414) 425-8300 — Carnegie Class: Spec-4-yr-Faith
FAX Number: (414) 529-6999 — Calendar System: Semester
URL: www.shsst.edu
Established: 1933 — Annual Graduate Tuition & Fees: N/A
Enrollment: 92 — Coed
Affiliation or Control: Roman Catholic — IRS Status: 501(c)3
Highest Offering: Master's; No Undergraduates
Accreditation: NH, THEOL

Code	Title	Name
01	President-Rector	Rev. Thomas L. KNOEBEL
10	VP Finance	Ms. Sally A. SMITS
05	VP Intellectual Formation	Dr. Patrick J. RUSSELL
20	VP Pastoral Formation	Dr. John OLESNAVAGE
42	VP Spiritual Formation	Rev. Paul KELLY, SCJ
07	VP External Affairs	Dr. Jeremy BLACKWOOD
88	VP Human Formation	Vacant
06	Registrar	Ms. Julie O'CONNOR
08	Director Library & Acad Supp Svcs	Ms. Jennifer BARTHOLOMEW
18	Director Plant Operations	Mr. Michael J. ERATO
26	Director Communications	Mr. Jonathan DRAYNA
13	Information Systems Coordinator	Ms. Mary GRIEGER
04	Executive Asst to President-Rector	Ms. Theresa M. ILLINGWORTH

Saint Norbert College (J)

100 Grant Street, De Pere WI 54115-2099
County: Brown — FICE Identification: 003892
Unit ID: 239716
Telephone: (920) 403-3181 — Carnegie Class: Bac-A&S
FAX Number: (920) 403-4008 — Calendar System: Semester
URL: www.snc.edu
Established: 1898 — Annual Undergrad Tuition & Fees: $35,381
Enrollment: 2,180 — Coed
Affiliation or Control: Roman Catholic — IRS Status: 501(c)3
Highest Offering: Master's
Accreditation: NH

Code	Title	Name
01	President	Dr. Brian BRUESS
05	Vice Pres Acad Affs/Dean of Col	Dr. Jeffrey FRICK
10	Vice President Business & Finance	Ms. Eileen JAHNKE
30	Vice Pres Institutional Advancement	Mr. Phil OSWALD
32	Vice Pres Mission & Student Affairs	Rev. Jay J. FOSTNER
84	Vice Pres Enrollment Mgmt/Comm	Mr. Edward LAMM
44	Assoc Vice Pres Inst Advancement	Ms. Lynette GREEN
09	AVP Institutional Effectiveness	Dr. Ray ZURAWSKI
20	Associate Academic Dean	Dr. Michael ROSEWALL
36	Director Career Services	Ms. Mary Ellen OLSON
35	Associate Dean Student Life	Vacant
38	Dir Counseling/Career Programs	Mr. Bruce ROBERTSON
07	Actg Exec Director of Admissions	Mr. Mark SELIN
29	Director Alumni & Parent Relations	Mr. Todd DANEN
21	Director of Finance	Mr. Curt KOWALESKI
37	Director of Financial Aid	Ms. Jessica RAFELD

26 Director Communications/ Marketing ... Ms. Jennifer CHRISTIANSEN
08 Director of Library ... Dr. Kristin D. VOGEL
15 Director Human Resources ... Ms. Sue BRINKMAN
41 Director Physical Educ/Athletics ... Mr. Tim BALD
06 Registrar ... Ms. Lauren GAECKE
13 Vice Pres & Chief Info Officer ... Mr. Lee REID
104 Assoc Academic Dir Global Affairs ... Ms. Gratzia VILLARROEL
28 Dir Multicultural Student Services ... Ms. Bridgit MARTIN
18 Director Facilities/Physical Plant ... Mr. Patrick WRENN
40 Manager Bookstore Operations ... Ms. Monica WITTROCK
04 Administrative Asst to President ... Ms. Jamie MCGUIRE
102 Dir Foundation/Corporate Relations ... Ms. Amy KUNDINGER
100 Chief of Staff ... Ms. Amy SORENSON
19 Director Security/Safety ... Mr. Steve JAKUPS
39 Director Student Housing ... Mr. Michael PECKHAM

Silver Lake College of the Holy Family (A)

2406 S Alverno Road, Manitowoc WI 54220-9319
County: Manitowoc FICE Identification: 003850
Unit ID: 239743
Telephone: (920) 684-6691 Carnegie Class: Masters/S
FAX Number: (920) 684-7082 Calendar System: Semester
URL: www.sl.edu
Established: 1935 Annual Undergrad Tuition & Fees: $26,340
Enrollment: 522 Coed
Affiliation or Control: Roman Catholic IRS Status: 501(c)3
Highest Offering: Master's
Accreditation: NH, MUS, NURSE

01 Acting President ... Mr. Dan MCGINTY
04 Executive Asst to President ... Ms. RK GREENING
04 Special Assistant to the President ... Ms. Cynthia ST. JOHN
05 VP for Academic Affairs ... Mr. Matthew SOUCY
10 Chief Financial Officer ... Ms. Janeen MEIFERT
111 VP Advancement/External Relations ... Mr. Marc BARBEAU
42 VP for Mission Integration ... Sr. Lorita GAFFNEY
06 Registrar ... Ms. Amy ECKLEY
08 Head Librarian ... Ms. Natalie LONG
37 Director of Financial Aid ... Ms. Erica PLOECKELMAN
30 Dir of Development/Alumni Engagment ... Ms. Colleen COOPER
13 Director Technology Services ... Mr. Jeff RAHMLOW
15 VP of Human Resources ... Ms. Sandy ISSELMANN
36 Dir Career Res/Experiential Lrng ... Ms. Jan L. ALGOZINE
26 Dir PR/Grant Writing ... Ms. Suzanne WEISS
19 Director of Campus Safety ... Mr. Aaron DUSZYNSKI
44 Assoc Dir Annual Giving/Special Eve ... Ms. Libby SPENCER
84 Dean of Enrollment Management ... Ms. Jamie GRANT
41 Interim Athletics Director ... Mr. Derek DOMINO
32 Asst Dean of Student Development ... Ms. Rachel FISCHER
39 Residence Hall Director ... Ms. Juanita SOTO
124 Dir Retention/Enrollment Services ... Mr. Dan CONNOLLY
09 Director of Institutional Research ... Ms. Kinga JACOBSON

*University of Wisconsin System (B)

1220 Linden Dr, 1720 Van Hise Hall,
Madison WI 53706-1559
County: Dane FICE Identification: 003894
Unit ID: 240435
Telephone: (608) 262-2321 Carnegie Class: N/A
FAX Number: (608) 262-3985
URL: www.wisconsin.edu

01 President ... Ray W. CROSS
05 Vice Pres Academic/Student Affairs ... James P. HENDERSON
11 Sr VP Administration/Fiscal Affairs ... Vacant
10 Senior Assoc Vice President Finance ... Julie GORDON
30 Assoc VP Economic Development ... David BRUKARDT
15 Sr AVP Human Res/Workforce Div ... Shenita BROKENBURR
20 Int AVP Acad Pgms/Educ Innovation ... Dr. Carleen VAN ZANDE
13 Assoc VP Learning/Info Tech ... Vacant
45 Assistant VP Budget & Planning ... Renee STEPHENSON
26 Exec Dir Integr Mktg/Communications ... Vacant
43 General Counsel ... Tomas L. STAFFORD
100 Chief of Staff ... Jessica TORMEY

*University of Wisconsin-Madison (C)

500 Lincoln Drive, Madison WI 53706-1380
County: Dane FICE Identification: 003895
Unit ID: 240444
Telephone: (608) 262-1234 Carnegie Class: DU-Highest
FAX Number: (608) 262-0123 Calendar System: Semester
URL: www.wisc.edu
Established: 1848 Annual Undergrad Tuition & Fees (In-State): $10,488
Enrollment: 42,716 Coed
Affiliation or Control: State IRS Status: 501(c)3
Highest Offering: Doctorate
Accreditation: NH, ARCPA, ART, AUD, CAATE, CACREP, CIDA, CLPSY, COPSY, CYTO, DANCE, DIETD, DMS, ENG, IPSY, LAW, LIB, LSAR, MED, MUS, NURSE, OT, PCSAS, PH, PHAR, PLNG, PTA, RAD, SCPSY, SP, SW, THEA, VET

02 Chancellor ... Dr. Rebecca BLANK
05 Provost Academic Affairs ... Dr. Sarah MANGELSDORF
46 Chief Research Officer ... Dr. Marsha R. MAILICK
11 Vice Chancellor Administration ... Mr. Laurent HELLER
100 Chancellor's Chief of Staff ... Mr. Matt MAYRL
26 Vice Chanc University Relations ... Mr. Charles HOSLET
84 Vice Provost Enrollment Management ... Mr. Steven HAHN
13 Int CIO/Vice Provost Inf Technology ... Mr. Michael LEHMANN
18 Int Assoc Vice Chanc Facl Plng/ Mgmt ... Ms. Margaret TENNESSENN
28 Vice Provost Diversity/Climate ... Dr. Patrick SIMS
20 Assoc Vice Chanc Faculty/Staff Pgms ... Dr. Michael BERNARD-DONALS
20 Assoc Vice Chanc Teaching/Learning ... Dr. Steven M. CRAMER
10 Assoc Vice Chanc Business Services ... Ms. Martha KERNER
32 Dean of Students ... Ms. Lori BERQUAM
58 Dean Graduate School ... Dr. William J. KARPUS
49 Dean College Letters & Science ... Dr. John K. SCHOLZ
63 Dean Medicine and Public Health ... Dr. Robert N. GOLDEN
53 Dean School of Education ... Dr. Diana HESS
50 Dean School of Business ... Dr. Anne P. MASSEY
67 Dean School of Pharmacy ... Dr. Steven M. SWANSON
54 Dean of College of Engineering ... Dr. Ian ROBERTSON
47 Dean of Agricultural/Life Sciences ... Dr. Kathryn VANDENBOSCH
66 Dean of School of Nursing ... Dr. Linda SCOTT
59 Dean of Human Ecology ... Dr. Soyeon SHIM
74 Dean of Veterinary Medicine ... Dr. Mark D. MARKEL
61 Dean of the Law School ... Dr. Margaret RAYMOND
82 Dean International Studies ... Dr. Guido PODESTÁ
43 Director of Admin Legal Services ... Mr. Raymond P. TAFFORA
88 Director Environmental Studies ... Dr. Paul ROBBINS
41 Director Intercollegiate Athletics ... Mr. Barry L. ALVAREZ
88 Director of Physical Plant ... Mr. Jeffrey A. POLLEI
88 Int Director of Arboretum ... Dr. Donna M. PAULNOCK
88 Director State Lab of Hygiene ... Dr. James SCHAUER
88 Director of Wisconsin Union ... Mr. Mark C. GUTHIER
07 Director of Admissions ... Mr. Andre PHILLIPS
08 Director of Libraries ... Mr. Edward VANGEMERT
27 Director University Communications ... Mr. John LUCAS
102 President UW Foundation ... Dr. Michael M. KNETTER
37 Director Student Financial Services ... Mr. Derek KINDLE
38 Director Counseling Services ... Ms. Andrea LAWSON
15 Director Human Resources ... Mr. Wayne GUTHRIE
39 Director of University Housing ... Dr. Jeffrey NOVAK
51 Dean Continuing Studies ... Dr. Jeffrey RUSSELL
19 Chief of University Police ... Ms. Kristen ROMAN
88 Director of Archives ... Mr. David NULL
23 Director University Health Service ... Dr. Sarah A. VAN ORMAN
88 Director of Space Management ... Mr. Brent LLOYD
17 President Hospital & Clinics ... Mr. Ron SLIWINSKI
109 Dir Auxiliary Operations Analysis ... Ms. Donna HALLERAN
06 Registrar ... Mr. Scott OWCZAREK
88 Secretary of the Faculty ... Mr. Steven K. SMITH
88 Secretary of Academic Staff ... Ms. Heather M. DANIELS
88 Director of Recreational Sports ... Mr. John HORN
85 Dir International Student Services ... Dr. Roopa RAWJEE
22 Dir Office of Equity & Diversity ... Mr. Luis A. PINERO
96 Director of Purchasing ... Ms. Lori VOSS
09 Dir Inst Rsrch/Acad Plng/Analysis ... Dr. Jocelyn L. MILNER
88 Special Asst to Provost ... Dr. Eden INOWAY-RONNIE
86 Sr Special Asst to Chanc Fed Rels ... Mr. Michael LENN

*University of Wisconsin-Eau Claire (D)

105 Garfield Avenue, PO Box 4004,
Eau Claire WI 54702-4004
County: Eau Claire FICE Identification: 003917
Unit ID: 240268
Telephone: (715) 836-2637 Carnegie Class: Masters/M
FAX Number: (715) 836-2902 Calendar System: Semester
URL: www.uwec.edu
Established: 1916 Annual Undergrad Tuition & Fees (In-State): $8,812
Enrollment: 10,592 Coed
Affiliation or Control: State IRS Status: 501(c)3
Highest Offering: Doctorate
Accreditation: NH, CAATE, JOUR, MUS, NURSE, SP, SW

02 Chancellor ... Dr. James C. SCHMIDT
05 Prov/Vice Chanc Academic Affairs ... Dr. Patricia A. KLEINE
100 Special Assistant to the Chancellor ... Ms. Mary Jane BRUKARDT
32 Vice Chanc Student Affairs ... Dr. Beth A. HELLWIG
46 Asst VC Research/Sponsored Pgm ... Dr. Karen G. HAVHOLM
18 Asst Chanc Facilities/Univ Rels ... Mr. Michael J. RINDO
28 Asst Chanc EDI ... Dr. Tamara JOHNSON
20 Assoc Vice Chanc Academic Affs ... Dr. Darrell NEWTON
20 Assoc Vice Chanc Academic Affairs ... Dr. Michael J. CARNEY
26 Executive Director Mktg & Planning ... Ms. Mary Jane BRUKARDT
22 Director of Affirmative Action ... Ms. Teresa E. O'HALLORAN
102 Pres UWEC Found/Dir Univ Advance ... Ms. Kimera K. WAY
32 Dean of Students ... Dr. Joseph J. ABHOLD
07 Director of Admissions ... Ms. Heather M. KRETZ
08 Interim Director of Libraries ... Dr. Jill S. MARKGRAF
13 Chief Information Officer ... Mr. Chip P. ECKARDT
14 Dir Learning & Technology Services ... Mr. Craig A. MEY
15 Director of Human Resources ... Mr. David J. MILLER
37 Interim Director of Financial Aid ... Ms. Nicole S. ANDREWS
38 Director of Counseling ... Dr. Riley C. MCGRATH
06 Registrar ... Ms. Tessa A. PERCHINSKY
36 Assoc Director Career Services ... Ms. Staci L. HEIDTKE
19 Director of University Police ... Mr. David W. SPRICK
23 Director of Student Health Services ... Ms. Laura G. CHELLMAN
39 Director of Housing & Res Life ... Mr. J. Quincy CHAPMAN
41 Director of Athletics ... Mr. Daniel J. SCHUMACHER
51 Director Continuing Education ... Mr. Durwin LONG
85 Interim Lead Intl Education ... Ms. Colleen C. MARCHWICK
102 Director Corporate Relations ... Mr. John G. BACHMEIER
92 Interim Director of Honors Program ... Dr. David JONES
26 Chief Public Relations Officer ... Mr. Michael J. RINDO
27 Director of Integrated Marketing ... Ms. Rebecca J. DIENGER
30 Chief Development/Alumni Relations ... Ms. Kimera K. WAY
96 Purchasing Agent ... Ms. Carley a. KUKUK
09 Institutional Planner ... Mr. Andrew J. NELSON
108 Interim Director of Assessment ... Dr. Mary F. HOFFMAN
49 Dean College of Arts & Sciences ... Dr. David E. LEAMAN
66 Dean Col of Nursing/Health Sciences ... Dr. Linda K. YOUNG
53 Dean Col Education/Human Sciences ... Dr. Carmen K. MANNING
50 Interim Dean College of Business ... Dr. Timothy S. VAUGHAN
04 Executive Asst to Chancellor ... Ms. Suzanne C. OLSON

*University of Wisconsin-Green Bay (E)

2420 Nicolet Drive, Green Bay WI 54311-7001
County: Brown FICE Identification: 003899
Unit ID: 240277
Telephone: (920) 465-2000 Carnegie Class: Masters/S
FAX Number: (920) 465-2032 Calendar System: Semester
URL: www.uwgb.edu
Established: 1965 Annual Undergrad Tuition & Fees (In-State): $7,878
Enrollment: 6,784 Coed
Affiliation or Control: State IRS Status: 501(c)3
Highest Offering: Doctorate
Accreditation: NH, ART, CAHIIM, DIETD, DIETI, MUS, NURSE, SW

02 Chancellor ... Dr. Gary L. MILLER
05 Provost/Vice Chancellor ... Dr. Gregory DAVIS
10 Vice Chanc Business & Finance ... Ms. Sheryl VAN GRUENSVEN
111 Vice Chanc University Advancement ... Mr. Tony WERNER
32 Vice Chancellor for Student Affairs ... Dr. Eric ARNESON
20 Assoc Provost for Academic Affairs ... Dr. Clifton GANYARD
53 Dean Health/Education/Social Well ... Dr. Susan GALLAGHER-LEPAK
49 Interim Dean of Arts/Humanities ... Dr. Chuck RYBAK
07 Director of Admissions ... Ms. Jennifer JONES
15 Director of Human Resources ... Ms. Christine OLSON
18 Dir Facilities Management/Planning ... Mr. Paul PINKSTON
19 Director Public Safety ... Mr. Thomas KUJAWA
21 Controller ... Ms. SuAnn DETAMPEL
09 Director Institutional Research ... Vacant
84 Dean Enrollment ... Vacant
46 Director of Institute for Research ... Ms. Lidia NONN
37 Director Financial Aid ... Mr. James P. ROHAN
39 Director of Residence Life ... Ms. Gail SIMS-AUBERT
40 Director Bookstore ... Mr. Gregory KANNENBERG
24 Director Media Svcs/Telecomm ... Mr. William HUBBARD
23 Director Health Services ... Ms. Amy HENNIGES
38 Director Counseling Services ... Mr. Gregory L. SMITH
100 Chief of Staff ... Mr. Ron PFEIFER
26 Director University Communications ... Ms. Janet BONKOWSKI
36 Director Career Services ... Ms. Linda G. PEACOCK-LANDRUM
29 Director Alumni Relations ... Ms. Kari MOODY
35 Director Student Life ... Vacant
06 Registrar ... Mr. Daniel VANDE YACHT
04 Administrative Asst to President ... Ms. Paula MARCEC
08 Asst Chancellor for IT & Library ... Ms. Paula GANYARD
104 Director Study Abroad ... Mr. Brent BLAHNIK
28 Senior Advisory ... Ms. Mai LO LEE
30 Director of Development ... Mr. Jacob DEPAS
13 Asst Vice Chancellor for IT ... Ms. Paula GANYARD

*University of Wisconsin-La Crosse (F)

1725 State Street, La Crosse WI 54601-3788
County: La Crosse FICE Identification: 003919
Unit ID: 240329
Telephone: (608) 785-8000 Carnegie Class: Masters/L
FAX Number: (608) 785-8492 Calendar System: Semester
URL: www.uwlax.edu
Established: 1909 Annual Undergrad Tuition & Fees (In-State): $9,091
Enrollment: 10,490 Coed
Affiliation or Control: State IRS Status: 501(c)3
Highest Offering: Doctorate
Accreditation: NH, ANEST, ARCPA, CAATE, MUS, NMT, NRPA, OT, PH, PTA, RADDOS, RTT

02 Chancellor ... Dr. Joe GOW
05 Provost/Vice Chanc Acad Affairs ... Dr. Betsy MORGAN
111 Vice Chancellor Advancement ... Mr. Greg REICHERT
10 Vice Chancellor Admin & Finance ... Dr. Bob HETZEL
50 Dean of Business Administration ... Dr. Laura MILNER
53 Dean School of Education ... Dr. Marcie WYCOFF-HORN
79 Interim Dean of Liberal Studies ... Dr. Kim VOGT
81 Interim Dean Science/Health ... Dr. Mark SANDHEINRICH
32 Asst Chancellor & Dean of Students ... Vacant
13 Chief Information Officer ... Dr. Mohamed ELHINDI
15 Director of Human Resources ... Ms. Madeline HOLZEM
51 Director Continuing Educ/Exten ... Ms. Penny TIEDT
08 Director of Library ... Ms. Catherine LAVALLÉE-WELCH
85 Dir International Education & Engag ... Ms. Emelee VOLDEN
07 Director ES/Admissions ... Mr. Corey SJOQUIST
06 Registrar ... Ms. Janice VONRUDEN
37 Director ES/Financial Aid ... Ms. Louise L. JANKE
38 Director Counseling/Testing ... Ms. Gretchen REINDERS
36 Director of Career Services ... Ms. Becky VIANDEN
41 Athletic Director ... Ms. Kim BLUM
26 Director News and Marketing ... Mr. Brad R. QUARBERG
29 Director Alumni Relations ... Ms. Janie M. MORGAN
23 Director Student Health Center ... Vacant
09 Director Institutional Research ... Ms. Natalie SOLVERSON
19 Chief of University Police ... Mr. Scott MC COLLOUGH
18 Director Physical Plant ... Mr. Hank M. KLOS

28 Assoc Dean Campus Climate/Diversity .Ms. Barbara E. STEWART
22 Director Affirmative Action .... Mr. Nizam ARAIN
106 Dir Online Education/E-learning .... Dr. Brian UDERMANN
39 Director Student Housing .... Ms. Jacque BOLLINGER

*University of Wisconsin-Milwaukee (A)

PO Box 413, Milwaukee WI 53201-0413

County: Milwaukee FICE Identification: 003896
Unit ID: 240453
Telephone: (414) 229-1122 Carnegie Class: DU-Highest
FAX Number: (414) 229-6329 Calendar System: Semester
URL: www.uwm.edu
Established: 1885 Annual Undergrad Tuition & Fees (In-State): $9,493
Enrollment: 26,726 Coed
Affiliation or Control: State IRS Status: 501(c)3
Highest Offering: Doctorate
Accreditation: NH, CAATE, CLPSY, COPSY, CS, DANCE, DMS, ENG, LIB, MT, MUS, NURSE, OT, PH, PLNG, PTA, RAD, SCPSY, SP, SW

02 Chancellor .... Dr. Mark A. MONE
05 Provost/Vice Chanc Academic Affairs .... Dr. Johannes BRITZ
10 Vice Chanc Finance & Admin Affs .... Ms. Robin L. VAN HARPEN
26 Vice Chanc Univ Rels/Communications .... Mr. Thomas L. LULJAK
46 Interim Vice Provost of Research .... Dr. Mark T. HARRIS
32 Int Vice Chancellor Student Affairs .... Mr. James HILL
30 Vice Chancellor Development .... Dr. Patricia A. BORGER
88 Vice Chanc Global Inclusion & Engag .... Dr. Joan M. PRINCE
20 Assoc Vice Chanc Academic Affairs .... Dr. Devarajan VENUGOPALAN
20 Assoc Vice Chanc Academic Affs .... Dr. Phyllis KING
84 Assoc Vice Chanc Enrollment Mgmt .... Vacant
13 Chief Information Officer .... Dr. Robert J. BECK
18 Assoc VC Facilities Planning/Mgmt .... Mr. Geoffrey HURTADO
04 Senior Advisor to the Chancellor .... Mr. David H. GILBERT
76 Int Dean College Health Sciences .... Dr. Ronald A. CISLER
48 Dean Architecture & Urban Planning .... Dr. Robert C. GREENSTREET
50 Int Dean School of Business .... Dr. Kanti PRASAD
53 Dean of the School of Education .... Dr. Alan R. SHOHO
54 Dean Col Engr & Applied Science .... Dr. Brett PETERS
57 Dean Peck School of the Arts .... Dr. Scott EMMONS
88 Senior Dir/Assoc Dean of Research .... Dr. J. Val KLUMP
69 Int Dean School of Public Health .... Dr. Ronald PEREZ
58 Dean Graduate School .... Dr. Marija GAJDARDZISKA-JOSIFOVSKA
49 Acting Dean Col Letters & Science .... Dr. David CLARK
62 Dean School Information Studies .... Dr. Tomas LIPINSKI
66 Dean of College of Nursing .... Dr. Kim LITWACK
70 Dean Helen Bader Sch Social Welfare .... Dr. Stan STOJKOVIC
51 Director School of Continuing Educ .... Dr. Nancy NELSON
35 Dean of Students .... Dr. Timothy GORDON
22 Dir Equity/Diversity Services .... Ms. Nelida CORTES
08 Int AVP/Director of the Library .... Mr. Michael DOYLEN
43 Director Legal Affairs .... Ms. Joely B. URDAN
06 Registrar .... Mr. Seth J. ZLOTOCHA
15 Assoc VC Human Resources .... Mr. Timothy DANIELSON
19 Chief of University Police .... Mr. Joseph LEMIRE
25 Director Office Sponsored Research .... Mr. Thomas MARCUSSEN
23 Director Health Center .... Dr. Julia BONNER
09 Dir Assessment/Institutional Rsrch .... Dr. Gesele DURHAM
85 Int Dir Center for Intl Education .... Dr. Devarajan VENUGOPALAN
37 Director Financial Aid .... Mr. Timothy OPGENORTH
39 Director of Residence Life .... Ms. Kelly HAAG
41 Athletic Director .... Ms. Amanda BRAUN
40 Director Bookstore .... Mr. Scott HOFFLAND
36 Int Dir Career Plng & Resource Ctr .... Ms. Jean SALZER
27 Director of Media Services .... Ms. Michelle JOHNSON
21 Dir Business & Financial Svcs .... Vacant
29 Director Alumni Relations .... Ms. Amy LENSING TATE
96 Int Director Purchasing .... Mr. Tom SCRIVENER
114 Dir Budget & Planning .... Ms. Cindy KLUGE
07 Director of Admissions & Recruiting .... Vacant
105 Director Web Services .... Mr. Mark JACOBSON
106 Dir Online Education/E-learning .... Ms. Laura PEDRICK
44 Director of Gift Planning .... Ms. Gretchen MILLER

*University of Wisconsin-Oshkosh (B)

800 Algoma Boulevard, Oshkosh WI 54901-3551

County: Winnebago FICE Identification: 003920
Unit ID: 240365
Telephone: (920) 424-1234 Carnegie Class: Masters/L
FAX Number: (920) 424-7317 Calendar System: Semester
URL: www.uwosh.edu
Established: 1871 Annual Undergrad Tuition & Fees (In-State): $7,544
Enrollment: 14,051 Coed
Affiliation or Control: State IRS Status: 501(c)3
Highest Offering: Doctorate
Accreditation: NH, ANEST, CAATE, CACREP, CS, CSHSE, EXSC, IFSAC, JOUR, MUS, NURSE, SW

02 Chancellor .... Dr. Andrew J. LEAVITT
05 Interim Provost & Vice Chancellor .... Dr. John KOKER
20 Interim Associate Vice Chancellor ..... Ms. Carmen FAYMONVILLE
20 Asst Vice Chanc Acad Support .... Dr. Sylvia CAREY-BUTLER
51 Asst VC Div of Online & Cont Educ .... Dr. Charles HILL
32 Vice Chancellor Student Affairs .... Dr. Cheryl GREEN
10 Vice Chancellor Administrative Svcs .... Dr. James FLETCHER
21 Associate Vice Chanc Admin Svcs .... Ms. Lori M. WORM
06 Registrar .... Ms. Lisa M. DANIELSON
22 Affirmative Action Officer .... Ms. Ameerah MCBRIDE
09 Director of Institutional Research .... Mr. Michael W. WATSON
38 Director of Counseling Center .... Dr. Sandy COX
13 CIO Director Info Technology .... Ms. Anne MILKOVICH
50 Dean Business .... Dr. Barbara RAU
66 Interim Dean Nursing .... Dr. Judith WESTPHAL
53 Interim Dean Education & Human Svcs . Dr. Elizabeth ALDERTON
49 Interim Dean Letters & Sciences .... Dr. Colleen MCDERMOTT
102 Pres Univ of Wisc Oshkosh Foundatn .... Vacant
29 Director of Alumni Association .... Ms. Christine M. GANTNER
37 Director of Financial Aid .... Mr. Kim DONAT
26 Exec Director Integrated Marketing .... Ms. Jamie CEMAN
25 Director Grants/Faculty Development ...... Mr. Robert W. ROBERTS
35 Dean of Students .... Dr. Art MUNIN
58 Director Graduate Studies .... Mr. Gregory WYPISZYNSKI
07 Director of Admissions .... Mr. Paul GEDLINSKE
15 Director of Human Resources .... Ms. Laurie TEXTOR
18 Facilities/Physical Plant Director .... Mr. Chuck HERMES
36 Director of Career Services .... Ms. Jaime PAGE-STADLER
32 Director University Honors Program .... Dr. Laurence CARLIN
08 Interim Director Library .... Ms. Sarah NEISES
04 Administrative Asst to President .... Ms. Suzette THIBADEAU
104 Director Study Abroad .... Ms. Jenna GRAFF
41 Athletic Director .... Mr. Darryl SIMS
90 Director Academic Computing .... Ms. Laura KNAAPEN

*University of Wisconsin-Parkside (C)

900 Wood Road, Box 2000, Kenosha WI 53141-2000

County: Kenosha FICE Identification: 005015
Unit ID: 240374
Telephone: (262) 595-2345 Carnegie Class: Bac-A&S
FAX Number: (262) 595-2202 Calendar System: Semester
URL: www.uwp.edu
Established: 1968 Annual Undergrad Tuition & Fees (In-State): $7,367
Enrollment: 4,412 Coed
Affiliation or Control: State IRS Status: 501(c)3
Highest Offering: Master's
Accreditation: NH

02 Chancellor .... Deborah L. FORD
05 Provost/Vice Chancellor .... Robert DUCOFFE
10 Vice Chanc Admin/Fiscal Affairs .... Melvin KLINKNER
111 Asst Chanc Univ Rels/Advancement .... John JARACZEWSKI
20 Vice Provost Academic Affairs .... Gary WOOD
32 Vice Provost Student Affs & Enroll .... Tammy MCGUCKIN
28 University Diversity & Inclusion .... Heather KIND-KEPPEL
35 Dean of Students .... Steve WALLNER
50 Dean Col of Bus Econ & Comput .... Dirk BALDWIN
49 Dean College of Arts & Humanities .... Lesley WALKER
81 Dean College of Nat & Hlth Sciences .... Emmanual OTU
83 Dean Social Sci & Prof Studies .... Peggy JAMES
51 Dir Continuing Educ & Cmty Engage .... Debra KARP
08 Director of the Library .... Anna STADICK
13 Interim Chief Information Officer .... Jordania LEON-JORDAN
93 Director Minority Student Services .... Damian EVANS
21 Dir Business Services/Controller .... Scott MENKE
15 Director Human Resources .... Sheronda GLASS
19 Dir Campus Police/Public Safety .... James HELLER
37 Director Financial Aid .... Kristina KLEMENS
29 Coord Donor Relations & Stewardship .... Molly MOORE
06 Registrar .... Rhonda KIMMEL
36 Dir of Advising/Career Center .... Gwen JONES
18 Director Facilities Management .... John BRUCH
94 Director of Women's Studies .... Linda CRAFTON
35 Assoc Dean of Students .... Damien EVANS
38 Dir Health/Counseling/Disability .... Renee KIRBY
40 Manager Bookstore .... Kim FLANNERY
07 Director Recruit & Admissions .... Troy MOLDENHAUER
04 Administrative Asst to Chancellor .... Jean HRPCEK
104 Admin Program Manager Intl Educ .... Elaine PHILIPPA
39 Director Residence Life .... Joseph BERTHIAUME
41 Athletic Director .... Andrew GAVIN
105 Director Web Services .... Vacant
26 Chief Public Relations/Marketing .... John MIELKE

*University of Wisconsin-Platteville (D)

1 University Plaza, Platteville WI 53818-3099

County: Grant FICE Identification: 003921
Unit ID: 240462
Telephone: (608) 342-1491 Carnegie Class: Masters/L
FAX Number: (608) 342-1232 Calendar System: Semester
URL: www.uwplatt.edu
Established: 1866 Annual Undergrad Tuition & Fees (In-State): $7,484
Enrollment: 8,945 Coed
Affiliation or Control: State IRS Status: 501(c)3
Highest Offering: Master's
Accreditation: NH, ENG, MUS, NAIT

02 Chancellor .... Mr. Dennis J. SHIELDS
05 Act Provost/Vice Chanc Acad Affairs .... Dr. Joanne WILSON
26 Vice Chanc University Relations .... Ms. Rose M. SMYRSKI
10 Int Vice Chanc Admin Services .... Mr. Todd CAROTHERS
30 Exec Dir Development/Alumni Rels ..... Mr. Steven M. RAMIG, JR.
58 Director Graduate School .... Dr. Chanaka MENDIS
06 Registrar .... Mr. David S. KIECKHAFER
84 Vice Chanc Enroll/Student Support ... Ms. Angela M. UDELHOFEN
37 Int Director of Financial Aid .... Mr. Brian BIRD
38 Director Student Counseling .... Ms. Deirdre L. DALSING
26 Dir Univ Info/Comm/Public Rels .... Mr. Paul J. ERICKSON
41 Director Intercollegiate Athletics .... Mr. Shannon EALY
39 Director of Residence Life .... Mrs. Linda MULROY-BOWDEN
15 Director Human Resources/AA/EED .... Ms. Janelle CROWLEY
19 Director Security/Safety .... Chief Joseph HALLMAN
93 Dir Multicultural Educ Resource Ctr .... Ms. Angela M. MILLER
96 Director of Purchasing .... Mr. Lewis BETTINGER
08 Head Librarian .... Mr. James HIBBARD
18 Director of Facilities Management .... Mr. Pete D. DAVIS
36 Director of Career Center .... Dr. Jennifer L. WILLIAMSON-MENDEZ
51 Director Continuing Education .... Ms. Kerie WEDIGE
49 Int Dean Col Liberal Arts/Education ...... Dr. Melissa E. GORMLEY
54 Dean Col of Engr/Math/Science .... Dr. Molly GRIBB
47 Dean Business Life Sci/Agric .... Dr. Wayne C. WEBER
28 Chief Diversity Officer .... Ms. Angela M. MILLER
20 Acting Asst Provost Academic Affs .... Dr. Patrick HAGEN
20 Actg Asst Provost Academic Plng .... Dr. Chanaka MENDIS
13 Asst Vice Chanc/Chief Info Ofcr .... Vacant
106 Exe Dir Alternative Delivery System .... Ms. Dawn M. DRAKE
106 Director Distance Learning Center .... Mr. Daniel R. AVENARIUS
106 Asst Exec Director Alt Delivery Sys .... Mr. Michael GAU
21 Comptroller .... Ms. Cathy J. RIEDL-FARREY
35 Dean of Students .... Ms. Sherry C. NEVINS
07 Director Admissions .... Ms. Heidi TUESCHER-GILLE
23 Admin Director Student Health Svcs .... Ms. Rachel HERMAN
88 Director PACCE .... Dr. Kevin J. BERNHARDT
121 Director Student Support Services .... Ms. Laura A. FRANKLIN
104 Director International Programs .... Ms. Donna L. ANDERSON
124 Director Retention Initiatives .... Ms. Karen MCLEER
09 Int Director of Inst Research .... Mr. John SCHLIESMANN
25 Director of Research .... Ms. Stacy SCHWENKE

*University of Wisconsin-River Falls (E)

410 S Third Street, River Falls WI 54022-5013

County: Pierce FICE Identification: 003923
Unit ID: 240471
Telephone: (715) 425-3911 Carnegie Class: Masters/M
FAX Number: (715) 425-4487 Calendar System: Semester
URL: www.uwrf.edu
Established: 1874 Annual Undergrad Tuition & Fees (In-State): $7,981
Enrollment: 5,949 Coed
Affiliation or Control: State IRS Status: 501(c)3
Highest Offering: Beyond Master's But Less Than Doctorate
Accreditation: NH, CACREP, MACTE, MUS, SP, SW

02 Chancellor .... Dr. Dean A. VAN GALEN
05 Int Vice Chancellor & Provost .... Dr. Faye PERKINS
10 Assistant Chancellor Bus/Finance .... Ms. Elizabeth FRUEH
30 Assistant Chancellor of Advancement .... Mr. Chris MUELLER
85 Int Asst VC for International Pgms .... Ms. Katrina LARSEN
20 Associate VC Academic Affairs .... Dr. Wesley CHAPIN
32 Assoc Vice Chanc Student Affs .... Mr. Gregg HEINSELMAN
21 Controller .... Ms. Jody NICHOLS
47 Dean Agricult/Food/Environ Sci .... Dr. Dale GALLENBERG
53 Int Dean Education/Profess Studies .... Dr. Michael HARRIS
49 Int Dean of Arts & Sciences .... Dr. Tricia DAVIS
50 Dean Business & Economics .... Dr. Michael FRONMUELLER
13 Chief Information Officer .... Mr. Joseph KMIECH
15 Human Resources Director .... Ms. Michelle DROST
18 Exec Dir Facilities/Planning/Mgmt .... Mr. Alan SYMICEK
22 Director Affirmative Action .... Ms. Michelle DROST
88 Director Enrollment/Student Success .... Mr. Mark R. MEYDAM
06 Registrar .... Mrs. Kelly BROWNING
07 Executive Director of Admissions .... Mrs. Sarah EGERSTROM
46 Director Grants & Research .... Ms. Diane BENNETT
08 Co-Interim Director of Library .... Mr. Brad GEE
08 Co-Interim Director of Library .... Ms. Maureen OLLE-LAJOIE
41 Interim Athletic Director .... Mrs. Crystal LANNING
37 Director Financial Assistance .... Mr. Robert BODE
45 Director Campus Planning .... Mr. Dale K. BRAUN
19 Director of Protective Services .... Mr. Karl FLEURY
96 Director Purchasing Services .... Ms. Gail ANDERSON
88 Dir Academic Success Center .... Ms. Kelly GRENZOW
35 Asst Chancellor Student Affairs .... Mr. Gregg M. HEINSELMAN
29 Director Alumni Relations .... Mr. Daniel E. MCGINTY
09 Director of Institutional Research .... Mrs. Stacy KARL
92 Director Honors Program .... Ms. Kathleen HUNZER
38 Director Student Counseling .... Ms. Alice REILLY-MYKLEBUST
56 Outreach Program Manager .... Ms. Pamela BOWEN
88 Interim McNair Scholars Director .... Dr. Diane BENNETT
26 Director Communications & Marketing .... Mr. Jeff PAPAS
39 Director of Student Housing .... Ms. Karla THOENNES
40 Manager Bookstore .... Ms. Sherry REHNELT
04 Administrative Asst to Chancellor .... Ms. Sherri SKOGEN
100 Executive Assistant to Chancellor .... Ms. Beth SCHOMMER

*University of Wisconsin-Stevens Point (F)

2100 Main Street, Stevens Point WI 54481-3871

County: Portage FICE Identification: 003924
Unit ID: 240480
Telephone: (715) 346-0123 Carnegie Class: Masters/S
FAX Number: (715) 346-4841 Calendar System: Semester
URL: www.uwsp.edu
Established: 1894 Annual Undergrad Tuition & Fees (In-State): $8,159
Enrollment: 9,265 Coed
Affiliation or Control: State IRS Status: 501(c)3
Highest Offering: Doctorate
Accreditation: NH, ART, AUD, CAATE, CIDA, DANCE, DIETD, ENG, MT, MUS, NURSE, SP, SW, THEA

02 Chancellor .... Dr. Bernie PATTERSON
05 Provost & Vice Chancellor .... Dr. Greg SUMMERS
10 Vice Chancellor Business Affairs .... Mr. Gregory M. DIEMER
32 Vice Chancellor Student Affairs .... Dr. Al THOMPSON
20 AVC for Tech/Learning/Acad Pgms .... Dr. Todd HUSPENI
100 Chief of Staff .... Dr. Robert MANZKE
15 AVC Person/Bdgt/Grants/Summer Pgms .... Dr. Katie JORE
51 Exec Dir UWSP Continuing Education ..... Mr. Wayne SORENSON
07 Director Admissions .... Mr. Bill JORDAN
37 Director of Financial Aid .... Ms. Mandy SLOWINSKI
19 Dir Safety & Loss Control .... Mr. Walter CLARK
111 Vice Chanc Univ Advancement .... Mr. Chris RICHARDS
29 Director of Alumni Affairs .... Ms. Laura GEHRMAN-ROTTIER
26 Interim Dir Univ Relations/Comm .... Mr. Gary WESCOTT
16 Director of Personnel .... Ms. Pam DOLLARD
38 Director Counseling Center .... Dr. Stacey GERKEN
13 Dir of Information Technology .... Mr. Jim BARRETT
22 Director Equity/Affirmative Action .... Ms. Pam DOLLARD
08 Interim Director University Library .... Ms. Mindy KING
06 Registrar .... Mr. Ed LEE
18 Chief Facilities/Physical Plant .... Mr. Paul HASLER
36 Interim Director Career Services .... Ms. Sue KISSINGER
96 Purchasing Manager .... Ms. Heidi WALLNER
57 Dean Col Fine Arts/Commun .... Dr. Valerie CISLER
49 Interim Dean Col of Letters & Sci .... Dr. Eric YONKE
65 Dean Col of Natural Resources .... Dr. Christine L. THOMAS
107 Dean Col of Professional Studies .... Dr. Marty LOY
35 Director Student Affairs .... Dr. Al THOMPSON
04 Administrative Asst to President .... Ms. Jean SCHERER
104 Director Study Abroad .... Dr. Eric YONKE
41 Athletic Director .... Mr. Brad DUCKWORTH
50 Dean of Business .... Dr. Gary MULLINS
84 Director Enrollment Management .... Mr. Jim BARRETT
86 Director Government Relations .... Dr. Robert MANZKE
39 Director Student Housing .... Mr. Brian FAUST

*University of Wisconsin-Stout (A)

712 South Broadway, Menomonie WI 54751-2458
County: Dunn — FICE Identification: 003915
Unit ID: 240417
Telephone: (715) 232-1122 — Carnegie Class: Masters/L
FAX Number: (715) 232-1416 — Calendar System: 4/1/4
URL: www.uwstout.edu
Established: 1891 — Annual Undergrad Tuition & Fees (In-State): $9,395
Enrollment: 9,554 — Coed
Affiliation or Control: State — IRS Status: 501(c)3
Highest Offering: Beyond Master's But Less Than Doctorate
Accreditation: NH, ACBSP, ART, CACREP, CAEP, CIDA, CONST, CS, DIETD, DIETI, ENG, ENGT, MFCD

02 Chancellor .... Dr. Robert MEYER
05 Provost & Vice Chancellor .... Dr. Patrick GUILFOILE
10 Vice Chanc for Admin/Student Life .... Mr. Phil LYONS
20 Associate Vice Chancellor .... Dr. Glendali RODRIQUEZ
30 Vice Chanc Univ Advance/Mktg .... Mr. Mark PARSON
32 Asst VC Student Life Svcs .... Mr. Scott GRIESBACH
45 Asst Chanc Plng/Assess/Rsrch/Qual .. Dr. Meridith DRZAKOWSKI
49 Dean Col Arts/Humanities/Social Sci .... Dr. Maria ALM
53 Dean Col of Ed/Hosp/Hlth/Hum Sci .... Dr. Robert SALT
81 Dean Col of Science/Tech/Engr/Math .... Dr. Charles BOMAR
35 Interim Dean of Students .... Ms. Sandi SCOTT DUEX
06 Registrar .... Mr. Joshua LIND
84 Exec Dir Enrollment & Ret Svcs .... Mr. Aaron AURE
36 Director Career Services .... Mr. Bryan BARTS
08 Director University Library .... Mr. Scott VRIEZE
04 Special Assistant to the Chancellor .... Ms. Kristi KRIMPELBEIN
37 Director Student Financial Aid .... Ms. Beth BOISEN
26 Director University Communications .... Mr. Doug MELL
21 Director Business/Financial Svcs .. Ms. Kim SCHULTE-SHOBERG
13 Chief Information Officer .... Ms. Suzanne TRAXLER
76 Exec Director Health & Safety .... Mr. James UHLIR
15 Interim Director Human Resources .... Ms. Kristi KRIMPELBEIN
38 Director Counseling Center .... Dr. John ACHTER
23 Director Student Health Services .... Ms. Janice LAWRENCE-RAMAEKER
40 Director Bookstore .... Ms. Cathy CLOSE
44 Director of the Annual Fund .... Ms. Jennifer RUDIGER
85 Int Director International Educ .... Ms. Vickie KUESTER
18 Director Physical Plant .... Ms. Shirley KLEBESADEL
96 Director Procurement/Materials Mgmt .... Mr. Brent TILTON
39 Dir University Housing .... Ms. Sandra SCOTT DUEX
41 Director Athletics .... Mr. Duey NAATZ
29 Assoc Director Alumni Relations .... Ms. Mesa COVILL
19 Dir of Safety & Risk Management .... Mr. Jim UHLIR
19 Coordinator University Police .... Mr. Jason SPETZ
106 Assoc Dir Online Educ/E-learning .... Dr. Amy GULLIXSON
07 Director of Admissions .... Mr. Joel HELMS

*University of Wisconsin-Superior (B)

Belknap and Catlin, PO Box 2000,
Superior WI 54880-4500
County: Douglas — FICE Identification: 003925
Unit ID: 240426
Telephone: (715) 394-8101 — Carnegie Class: Bac-Diverse
FAX Number: (715) 394-8454 — Calendar System: Semester
URL: www.uwsuper.edu
Established: 1893 — Annual Undergrad Tuition & Fees (In-State): $8,088
Enrollment: 2,497 — Coed
Affiliation or Control: State — IRS Status: 501(c)3
Highest Offering: Beyond Master's But Less Than Doctorate
Accreditation: NH, MUS, SW

02 Chancellor .... Dr. Renee WACHTER
05 Int Provost/Vice Chanc Acad Affairs .... Dr. Jackie WEISSENBURGER
111 Vice Chanc University Advancement ... Ms. Jeanne E. THOMPSON
10 Vice Chanc Administration/Finance .... Ms. Gigi KOENIG
26 Dir Communications/Government Rels .... Ms. Jordan MILAN
84 Int Dir Enrollment Management .... Dr. Brenda HARMS
41 Interim Athletic Director .... Mr. Nick BURSIK
32 Dean of Students .... Mr. Harry ANDERSON
15 Int Assoc Director Human Resources .... Mr. Steve MARSHALL
22 Director of Diversity & Inclusion .... Mr. Jerel BENTON
06 Registrar .... Mr. Jeff KIRSHLING
07 Director of Admissions .... Mr. Jeremy NERE
21 Controller .... Mr. Robert B. WAKSDAHL
37 Director Student Financial Aid .... Ms. Donna R. DAHLVANG
51 Dir Center Cont Educ/Online Svcs .... Vacant
56 Int Dir Distance Learning/Cont Educ .... Ms. Karen HEIKEL
40 Director Bookstore .... Mr. Vaughn N. RUSSOM
29 Director Alumni Relations .... Ms. Heather THOMPSON
121 Director Academic Advising .... Ms. Courtney ALEXANDER
08 Interim Librarian .... Ms. Laura JACOBS
18 Director Facilities Management .... Mr. Dustin JOHNSON
04 Administrative Asst to President .... Ms. Patty ULLAN
09 Director of Institutional Research .... Ms. Emily ZOBEL

*University of Wisconsin-Whitewater (C)

800 W Main, Whitewater WI 53190-1790
County: Walworth — FICE Identification: 003926
Unit ID: 240189
Telephone: (262) 472-1918 — Carnegie Class: Masters/L
FAX Number: (262) 472-1518 — Calendar System: Semester
URL: www.uww.edu
Established: 1868 — Annual Undergrad Tuition & Fees (In-State): $7,650
Enrollment: 12,360 — Coed
Affiliation or Control: State — IRS Status: 501(c)3
Highest Offering: Doctorate
Accreditation: NH, ART, CACREP, ENGR, MUS, SP, SW, THEA

02 Chancellor .... Dr. Beverly A. KOPPER
05 Prov/Exec Vice Chanc Academic Affs .... Dr. Susan ELROD
32 Int Vice Chancellor Student Affairs .... Dr. Brent BILODEAU
30 VC Univ Advance/Foundation Pres .... Mr. Jonathan ENSLIN
11 Vice Chanc Administrative Affs .... Ms. Grace CRICKETTE
20 Assoc Vice Chanc Academic Affairs .... Dr. Greg COOK
13 Asst Vice Chanc Tech/Info Resource .... Dr. Elena POKOT
84 Asst Vice Chanc Enroll/Retention .... Mr. Matt ASCHENBRENER
09 Director of Institutional Research .... Ms. Lynsey SCHWABROW
37 Director of Financial Aid .... Ms. Carol A. MILLER
26 Chief Public Relations Officer .... Ms. Sara KUHL
36 Director of Career Services .... Mr. Ron BUCHHOLZ
15 Director Human Resources/Diversity .... Ms. Judith M. TRAMPF
85 Dir Center for Global Education ..... Ms. Candace A. CHENOWETH
44 Exec Dir University Development .... Ms. Kate LOFTUS
18 Director Facility Planning/Mgmt .... Mr. Greg SWANSON
28 Interim Chief Diversity Officer .... Mr. Roger PULLIAM
92 Director of Honors Program .... Dr. Elizabeth KIM
57 Dean Arts/Communication .... Dr. Robert MERTENS
50 Dean of Business & Economics .... Dr. John CHENOWETH
53 Dean Education/Professional Studies ..... Dr. Katharina E. HEYNING
49 Dean Letters & Sciences .... Dr. David TRAVIS
58 Dean Grad Stds/Continuing Educ .... Dr. Seth MEISEL
04 Executive Asst to the Chancellor .... Mrs. Kari HEIDENREICH
41 Athletic Director .... Mr. Todd GARZARELLI

*University of Wisconsin Colleges (D)

432 N. Lake Street, Room 401, Madison WI 53706
County: Dane — FICE Identification: 003897
Unit ID: 240055
Telephone: (608) 262-3786 — Carnegie Class: Assoc/HT-High Trad
FAX Number: (608) 262-7872 — Calendar System: Semester
URL: www.uwc.edu
Established: 1964 — Annual Undergrad Tuition & Fees (In-State): $5,159
Enrollment: 13,454 — Coed
Affiliation or Control: State — IRS Status: 501(c)3
Highest Offering: Baccalaureate
Accreditation: NH

02 Chancellor .... Dr. Cathy SANDEEN
05 Provost/Vice Chancellor .... Dr. Gregory P. LAMPE
10 Vice Chancellor Admin & Fin Svcs .... Mr. Steve C. WILDECK
32 Assoc VC Stdt Svcs & Enroll Mgmt .... Dr. Melissa STUTZ
20 Assoc Vice Chancellor Acad Affairs .... Dr. Joseph FOY
21 Assoc VC Admin & Finance .... Ms. Colleen GODFRIAUX
84 Exec Dir Marketing & Enrollment .... Ms. Vicki KEEGAN
13 Chief Information Officer .... Mr. Werner GADE
15 Asst Vice Chanc Human Resources .... Mr. Jason BEIER
06 Registrar .... Mr. Larry GRAVES
37 Director Student Financial Aid .... Mr. William TRIPPETT
26 Exec Director University Relations .... Vacant
28 Dir Equity/Diversity & Inclusion .... Ms. Kelly THOMAS
104 Director International Programs .... Mr. Tim URBONYA
100 Chief of Staff to the Chancellor .... Ms. Molly VIDAL
12 Northeast Regional Dean .... Dr. Martin RUDD
12 Southwest Regional Dean .... Dr. Charles E. CLARK
12 North Regional Dean .... Dr. Keith MONTGOMERY
12 Southeast Regional Dean .... Dr. Jackie JOSEPH-SILVERSTEIN

*University of Wisconsin Baraboo/Sauk County (E)

1006 Connie Road, Baraboo WI 53913
Telephone: (608) 355-5200 — Identification: 770450
Accreditation: &NH

*University of Wisconsin Barron County (F)

1800 College Drive, Rice Lake WI 54868
Telephone: (715) 234-8176 — Identification: 770457
Accreditation: &NH

*University of Wisconsin Fond du Lac (G)

400 University Drive, Fond du Lac WI 54935
Telephone: (920) 929-1100 — Identification: 770451
Accreditation: &NH

*University of Wisconsin Fox Valley (H)

1478 Midway Road, Menasha WI 54952
Telephone: (920) 832-2600 — Identification: 770456
Accreditation: &NH

*University of Wisconsin Manitowoc (I)

705 Viebahn Street, Manitowoc WI 54220-6699
Telephone: (920) 683-4700 — Identification: 770453
Accreditation: &NH

*University of Wisconsin-Marathon County (J)

518 South 7th Avenue, Wausau WI 54401
Telephone: (715) 261-6100 — Identification: 770461
Accreditation: &NH

*University of Wisconsin Marinette (K)

750 W Bay Shore Street, Marinette WI 54143-4253
Telephone: (715) 735-4300 — Identification: 770454
Accreditation: &NH

*University of Wisconsin Marshfield/Wood County (L)

2200 West 5th Street, Marshfield WI 54449
Telephone: (715) 389-6530 — Identification: 770455
Accreditation: &NH

*University of Wisconsin Richland (M)

1200 Highway 14 West, Richland Center WI 53581-1316
Telephone: (608) 647-6186 — Identification: 770458
Accreditation: &NH

*University of Wisconsin Rock County (N)

2909 Kellogg Avenue, Janesville WI 53546
Telephone: (608) 758-6565 — Identification: 770452
Accreditation: &NH

*University of Wisconsin Sheboygan (O)

One University Drive, Sheboygan WI 53081-4760
Telephone: (920) 459-6600 — Identification: 770459
Accreditation: &NH

*University of Wisconsin Washington County (P)

400 University Drive, West Bend WI 53095
Telephone: (262) 335-5200 — Identification: 770462
Accreditation: &NH

*University of Wisconsin Waukesha (Q)

1500 N University Drive, Waukesha WI 53188-2799
Telephone: (262) 521-5200 — Identification: 770460
Accreditation: &NH

Viterbo University (R)

900 Viterbo Court, La Crosse WI 54601-8802
County: La Crosse — FICE Identification: 003911
Unit ID: 240107
Telephone: (608) 796-3000 — Carnegie Class: Masters/L
FAX Number: (608) 796-3050 — Calendar System: Semester
URL: www.viterbo.edu
Established: 1890 — Annual Undergrad Tuition & Fees: $26,150
Enrollment: 2,756 — Coed
Affiliation or Control: Roman Catholic — IRS Status: 501(c)3
Highest Offering: Doctorate
Accreditation: NH, ACBSP, CACREP, CAEPN, DIETC, DIETI, MUS, NURSE, SW

01 President .... Dr. Glena TEMPLE
05 Vice President for Academic Affairs .... Dr. Tracy STEWART
32 Vice President Student Development .... Dr. Diane L. BRIMMER
10 Vice Pres Administration/Finance .... Mr. Todd M. ERICSON
30 VP Institutional Advance/Univ Rels ...... Mr. Wendell SNODGRASS

21 Assistant Vice President Finance ... Mr. Eugene R. ALBERTS
07 Dean of Admission ... Vacant
42 Chaplain ... Fr. Conrad A. TARGONSKI
66 Dean College of Nursing/Health ... Dr. Martha SCHECKEL
53 Dean Col of Education/Science/Math ... Dr. Sara COOK
49 Dean School Letters & Sciences ... Dr. Timothy SCHORR
57 Dean School of Fine Arts/Humanities ... Dr. Timothy B. SCHORR
50 Dean Dahl School of Business ... Dr. Thomas E. KNOTHE
58 Dean Graduate/Prof/Adult Education ... Vacant
88 Director of Ethics in Leadership ... Dr. Richard L. KYTE
06 Registrar ... Ms. Kori SALASKI
08 Interim Director of Library ... Ms. Kim OLSON-KOPP
13 Director Instruct/Info Technology ... Ms. Sarah BEARBOWER
41 Athletic Director ... Mr. Barry J. FRIED
37 Director of Financial Aid ... Ms. Terry W. NORMAN
26 Director of Marketing ... Ms. Audra NOE
29 Director Alumni Relations ... Ms. Kathleen A. DUERWACHTER
36 Director Career Planning/Placement . Ms. Beth D. DOLDER-ZIEKE
15 Director of Human Resources ... Ms. Heather BUTTERFIELD
09 Director Institutional Research ... Ms. Naomi R. STENNES-SPIDAHL
18 Director Physical Plant ... Mr. Eugene M. MCCURDY
38 Dir Counseling/Student Development ... Ms. LeeAnn VAN VREEDE
39 Director of Residence Life ... Ms. Kirsten GABRIEL
53 Director Grad Studies in Education ... Ms. Jeanette ARMSTRONG
88 Dir Faculty Dev/Internship Coord ... Dr. Theresa MOORE
88 Director of Global Education ... Mr. Shaojie JIANG
19 Director Campus Safety ... Mr. Adam MALIN
07 Asst Director of Admissions ... Ms. Caitlin LOCY
04 Executive Admin Asst to President ... Ms. Sheila SEVERSON

Wisconsin Lutheran College (A)

8800 W Bluemound Road, Milwaukee WI 53226-4699
County: Milwaukee — FICE Identification: 021366
Unit ID: 240338
Telephone: (414) 443-8800 — Carnegie Class: Bac-Diverse
FAX Number: (414) 443-8514 — Calendar System: Semester
URL: www.wlc.edu
Established: 1973 — Annual Undergrad Tuition & Fees: $27,984
Enrollment: 1,188 — Coed
Affiliation or Control: Independent Non-Profit — IRS Status: 501(c)3
Highest Offering: Master's
Accreditation: NH, NURSE

01 President ... Dr. Daniel W. JOHNSON
05 Provost & VP of Academic Affairs ... Dr. John D. KOLANDER
32 Vice President Student Life ... Rev. Nathan STROBEL
10 Vice Pres Finance & Administration ... Mr. Gary SCHMID
26 Exec Dir Marketing & Communication ... Vacant
30 Vice Pres Development ... Mr. Richard MANNISTO
15 Vice Pres of Human Resources ... Mr. Steven SCHROEDER
21 Asst Vice Pres Finance ... Mrs. Diane HOEHNKE
07 Executive Director of Admissions ... Mr. Lucas FAUST
06 Registrar ... Mr. Brett VALERIO
08 Director of Library Services ... Mrs. Starla C. SIEGMANN
37 Director Student Financial Aid ... Mrs. Linda L. LOEFFEL
42 Campus Pastor ... Rev. Wayne SHEVEY
53 Director Teacher Education ... Prof. James HOLMAN
39 Director Residential Life/Housing ... Mr. Adam VOLBRECHT
41 Athletic Director ... Mr. Edward NOON
88 Director of Arts Programming ... Mrs. Loni BOYDL
13 Director of Information Technology ... Mr. John MEYER
29 Director of Alumni Relations ... Mrs. Lisa LEFFEL
88 Information Systems Analyst ... Mrs. Olya FINNEGAN
102 Director Corp/Foundation Relations ... Mrs. Sharon PATTERSON
18 Chief Facilities/Physical Plant ... Mr. Gary SCHMID
24 Media Services Coordinator ... Mr. Tim SNYDER

Wisconsin School of Professional Psychology (B)

9120 W Hampton Avenue, Milwaukee WI 53225-4960
County: Milwaukee — FICE Identification: 022713
Unit ID: 240213
Telephone: (414) 464-9777 — Carnegie Class: Spec-4-yr-Other Health
FAX Number: (414) 358-5590 — Calendar System: Semester
URL: www.wspp.edu
Established: 1979 — Annual Graduate Tuition & Fees: N/A
Enrollment: 95 — Coed
Affiliation or Control: Independent Non-Profit — IRS Status: 501(c)3
Highest Offering: Doctorate; No Undergraduates
Accreditation: NH, CLPSY

01 President ... Dr. Kathleen M. RUSCH
05 Dean ... Dr. Dale A. BESPALEC
04 Office Manager ... Ms. Veronica V. EGERSON
17 Director Clinical Training ... Dr. Susan DVORAK
08 Head Librarian ... Ms. Rebecca DOUGHERTY
37 Director Student Financial Aid ... Mr. Erik MOZOLIK

*Wisconsin Technical College System (C)

PO Box 7874, Madison WI 53707-7874
County: Dane — Identification: 666185
Telephone: (608) 266-1207 — Carnegie Class: N/A
FAX Number: (608) 266-1285
URL: www.wtcsystem.edu

01 President ... Ms. Morna K. FOY
03 Executive Vice President ... Mr. James ZYLSTRA
05 Provost/Vice President ... Ms. Kathleen CULLEN
26 Dir Strategic Advancement ... Mr. Conor SMYTH

*Blackhawk Technical College (D)

PO Box 5009, Janesville WI 53547-5009
County: Rock — FICE Identification: 005390
Unit ID: 238397
Telephone: (608) 758-6900 — Carnegie Class: Assoc/HVT-High Trad
FAX Number: (608) 757-7740 — Calendar System: Semester
URL: www.blackhawk.edu
Established: 1912 — Annual Undergrad Tuition & Fees (In-District): $4,107
Enrollment: 2,249 — Coed
Affiliation or Control: State/Local — IRS Status: 501(c)3
Highest Offering: Associate Degree
Accreditation: NH, ACFEI, ADNUR, DA, DMS, MAC, MLTAD, PTAA, RAD

02 President ... Dr. Tracy P. PIERNER
05 Vice President Academic Affairs ... Vacant
10 Vice President Admin Services ... Ms. Renea L. RANGUETTE
15 Exec Director CHRO ... Mr. Brian B. GOHLKE
09 Dir Institutional Research ... Dr. Jon TYSSE
04 Asst to President/Board Liaison ... Ms. Jacqueline J. PINS
13 Exec Director IT Services ... Mr. Peter MIZERA
26 Marketing & Communications Mgr ... Mr. Gary KOHN
97 Dean Gen Education ... Dr. Gina MCCONOUGHEY
88 Learning Support Manager ... Mr. Darian SNOW
76 Dean Health Sciences/Public Safety ... Ms. Nancy R. LIGHTFIELD
19 Assoc Dean Public Safety ... Mr. Gary TRULSON
19 Manager of Campus Safety & Security ... Mr. Brad K. SMITH
88 EMS Fire Service & Paramedic Coord ... Mr. Robert BALSAMO
66 Assoc Dean Nursing ... Vacant
72 Dean Advanced Mfg & Transportation ... Dr. Garry D. KRAUSE
50 Dean Business ... Dr. Gina MCCONOUGHEY
103 Coord Green Co Workforce & Cmty Ed ... Mr. Matthew URBAN
21 Controller ... Mr. Gerri DOWNING
25 Manager Grants Administration ... Mr. Andrew S. MCGRATH
37 Director of Financial Aid ... Ms. Deena WETTSTEIN
06 Registrar ... Ms. Brooke JOHNSON
18 Facilities Director ... Mr. Steve KORMANAK
96 Purchasing Administrator ... Mr. Thomas PELLIZZI
51 Community Enrichment Manager ... Ms. Kerry OSMOND
08 Dir Teaching & Learning Resources ... Dr. Elizabeth REZEL
30 Director Recource Dev & Cmty Rels ... Ms. Terese CRAIG

*Chippewa Valley Technical College (E)

620 W Clairemont Avenue, Eau Claire WI 54701-6162
County: Eau Claire — FICE Identification: 005304
Unit ID: 240116
Telephone: (715) 833-6200 — Carnegie Class: Assoc/HVT-Mix Trad/Non
FAX Number: (715) 833-6470 — Calendar System: Semester
URL: www.cvtc.edu
Established: 1912 — Annual Undergrad Tuition & Fees (In-District): $4,238
Enrollment: 6,017 — Coed
Affiliation or Control: Local — IRS Status: 501(c)3
Highest Offering: Associate Degree
Accreditation: NH, ACBSP, ADNUR, CAHIIM, COARC, DH, DMS, EMT, MAC, MLTAD, PTAA, RAD, SURGT

02 President ... Bruce A. BARKER
05 Vice President Education ... Julie FURST-BOWE
11 Vice President Operations ... Tom G. HUFFCUTT
32 Vice President Student Services ... Margo A. KEYS
12 Exec Dean Health/Emer Svcs & RF ... Shelly OLSON
12 Chippewa Falls Campus Manager ... Angela ECKMAN
12 Menomonie Campus Manager ... Daniel LYTLE
12 Director of B&I Services ... Roxann VANDERWYST
46 Director Plng/Research & Grants ... Margaret A. DICKENS
75 Dean Skilled Trades & Engineering ... Jeff SULLIVAN
06 Registrar ... Jessica SCHWARTZ
84 Director of Enrollment Services ... Paige WEGNER
37 Financial Aid Officer ... Barbara CLOUTIER
26 Dir of Mktg & Community Relations ... Pam HALLER
10 Director of Budget & Finance ... Kirk L. MOIST
88 Director of Prof Development ... Debra WALSH
13 Director of Info Technology ... Tom J. LANGE
35 Student Central Manager ... Laura ERICSON
35 Student Life Specialist ... Alisa S. SCHLEY
96 Purchasing Representative ... Doug D. DEKAN
21 Budget & Purchasing Manager ... Tracy M. DRIER
19 Public Safety Manager ... William HENNING
28 Diversity Manager ... Dang YANG
88 Director Advisement & Services ... Natalyn M. MARLAIRE
20 Dean Academic and Develop Services ... Jennifer ANDEREGG
102 Exec Dir CVTC Found/Alumni Assoc ... Aliesha R. CROWE
25 Grants & Accreditation Manager ... Shana SCHMIDT
108 Intake Assesment Data Analyst ... Philip V. PALSER
50 Dean Business & Academic Initiative ... Lynette LIVINGSTON
18 Director of Facilities ... Rod BAGLEY
15 Human Resources Director ... Tam BURGAU
21 Business Office Manager ... Sara J. NICK
97 Dean Gen Educ & Liberal Arts ... Cherrie BERGANDI
88 Dean Ag/Energy/Transportation ... Adam WEHLING
88 Criminal Justice Director ... Eric ANDERSON
88 Curr Spec/Instr Designer ... Jodi RUST
76 Assoc Dean of Health ... Amy OLSON
04 Executive Asst to President ... Lauren SULLIVAN

*Fox Valley Technical College (F)

1825 N Bluemound Drive, Appleton WI 54914-1643
County: Outagamie — FICE Identification: 009744
Unit ID: 238722
Telephone: (920) 735-5600 — Carnegie Class: Assoc/HVT-High Non
FAX Number: (920) 735-2582 — Calendar System: Semester
URL: www.fvtc.edu
Established: 1967 — Annual Undergrad Tuition & Fees (In-District): $4,436
Enrollment: 10,901 — Coed
Affiliation or Control: State/Local — IRS Status: 501(c)3
Highest Offering: Associate Degree
Accreditation: NH, ACFEI, ADNUR, CAHIIM, DA, DH, EMT, IFSAC, MAC, OTA, PNUR

02 President ... Dr. Susan A. MAY
05 CAO/VP Instructional Services ... Dr. Christopher MATHENY
11 VP Facilities & Operations ... Ms. Jill MCEWEN
32 VP Student/Community Development ... Dr. Patti JORGENSEN
15 VP Human Resources ... Ms. Deb GORMAN
72 Dean Manufacturing & Agriculture ... Mr. Steve STRAUB
10 VP Financial Services/CFO ... Ms. Amy VAN STRATEN
13 VP Information Tech/CIO ... Mr. Troy KOHL
97 Dean General Studies ... Ms. Carol MAY
102 Exec Dir FVTC Foundation/Cmty Rels ... Ms. Mary DOWNS
12 Oshkosh Campus Director ... Ms. Melissa KOHN
37 Director Student Financial Svcs ... Ms. Stacy DORAN
06 Registrar ... Mr. Brian BUSS
26 Director College Marketing ... Ms. Barb DREGER
118 Director Compensation & Benefits ... Ms. Barb KIEFFER
88 Director Venture Center ... Ms. Amy PIETSCH
108 Director College Effectiveness ... Dr. Patti FROHRIB

*Gateway Technical College (G)

3520 30th Avenue, Kenosha WI 53144-1690
County: Kenosha — FICE Identification: 005389
Unit ID: 238759
Telephone: (262) 564-2200 — Carnegie Class: Assoc/HVT-High Non
FAX Number: (262) 564-2201 — Calendar System: Semester
URL: www.gtc.edu
Established: 1912 — Annual Undergrad Tuition & Fees (In-District): $4,152
Enrollment: 8,740 — Coed
Affiliation or Control: State/Local — IRS Status: 501(c)3
Highest Offering: Associate Degree
Accreditation: NH, ACBSP, ADNUR, DA, PTAA, SURGT

02 President ... Dr. Bryan D. ALBRECHT
05 Exec VP/Prov/Chief Academic Officer ... Ms. Zina HAYWOOD
11 Senior VP of Operations ... Mr. Willaim WHYTE
12 Dean Racine Campus ... Mr. Ray KOUKARI
12 Dean Elkhorn Campus ... Mr. Michael O'DONNELL
12 Dean Kenosha Campus ... Mr. Gary FLYNN
86 VP Government/Community Relations ... Ms. Stephanie SKLBA
103 VP Workforce/Economic Develop Div ... Ms. Debbie DAVIDSON
32 Vice Pres Student Svcs & Enroll Mgt ... Ms. Stacy RILEY
108 Asst Provost/VP Inst Effectiveness ... Dr. John THIBODEAU
121 Dean Learning Success ... Dr. Tammi SUMMERS
06 Registrar ... Ms. Chrystal MOEZ
09 Associate VP Institutional Research ... Ms. Anne WHYNOTT
26 Marketing Director ... Ms. Jayne HERRING
07 Director of College Access ... Ms. Amanda VIRZI
21 Controller ... Ms. Sharon JOHNSON
37 Director Student Financial Aid ... Mr. Justin KEHRING
28 Director of Diversity ... Ms. Debbie MILLER
102 Foundation Executive Director ... Dr. Jennifer CHARPENTIER
13 Chief Info Technology Officer (CIO) ... Mr. Jeff ROBSHAW

*Lakeshore Technical College (H)

1290 North Avenue, Cleveland WI 53015-1414
County: Manitowoc — FICE Identification: 009194
Unit ID: 239008
Telephone: (920) 693-1000 — Carnegie Class: Assoc/HVT-High Non
FAX Number: (920) 693-8078 — Calendar System: Semester
URL: www.gotoltc.edu
Established: 1913 — Annual Undergrad Tuition & Fees (In-District): $4,125
Enrollment: 2,837 — Coed
Affiliation or Control: State/Local — IRS Status: 501(c)3
Highest Offering: Associate Degree
Accreditation: NH, ADNUR, EMT, RAD

02 President ... Dr. Paul CARLSEN
04 Executive Assistant ... Ms. Heidi SOODSMA
05 Vice President of Instruction ... Dr. Barbara DODGE
32 Vice President of Student Services ... Dr. Douglas GOSSEN
103 Vice President Workforce & Econ Dev ... Mr. Peter THILLMAN
15 Chief Human Resources Officer ... Ms. Kathleen KOTAJARVI
10 Chief Financial Officer ... Ms. Cindy DROSS
09 Quality/Continuous Improvement Mgr ... Ms. Cheryl TERP
26 Director of Marketing ... Ms. Julie MIRECKI
28 Multicultural Student Advocate ... Ms. Nicole YANG
54 Dean of Advanced Mfg & Engineering ... Ms. Sheila SCHETTER
50 Dean Business & Technology ... Vacant
97 Dean General & Pre-College Educ ... Ms. Meredith SAUER
07 Enrollment Services Manager ... Mr. George HENZE
37 Financial Aid Manager ... Ms. Jessica HEMENWAY
121 Director of Student Resources ... Ms. Foua HANG
18 Physical Plant Supervisor ... Mr. Bryan KOESER
08 Library Manager ... Ms. Kelly CARPENTER
22 Affirmative Action Officer ... Ms. Kathleen KOTAJARVI
40 Bookstore Manager ... Ms. Kelly WOLFERT

13 Director of Information Technology ... Ms. Wendy NASGOVITZ
111 Director of Advancement ... Ms. Karla ZAHN
30 Development Director ... Ms. Katie WILLINGER
47 Dean of Agri/Energy/Transportation ... Mr. Patrick STASZAK
76 Dean of Health & Human Services ... Mr. James LEMEROND
19 Dean of Public Safety ... Mr. Ryan SKABROUD
88 Assoc Dean of Culinary/Hospitality ... Vacant
66 Assoc Dean of Nursing & Nursing Ast ... Ms. Holly EUCLIDE
88 Director of Facilities/Procurement ... Ms. Brenda RIESTERER
14 IT Services Manager ... Mr. James UMBREIT
36 Career Development Manager ... Ms. Jami KAPRAL
88 Dual Credit Manager ... Ms. Jackie HOLLY
88 Organizational Development Manager ... Ms. Melissa BRAESCH
21 Controller ... Ms. Molly O'CONNELL
88 Director Faculty Dev/Instruct Supp ... Ms. Nadine SCHREITER
88 Accommodations Services Manager ... Mr. Patrick NEUENFELDT
88 Director Apprenticeship/Wkforce Dev ... Ms. Polly ABTS
88 Testing Services Manager ... Ms. Susan KINNESTON
88 Business & Mfg Assess Svcs Mgr ... Mr. William PERSINGER
118 Compensation and Benefits Manager ... Ms. Shikara BEAUDOIN

*Madison Area Technical College (A)

1701 Wright Street, Madison WI 53704-2599
County: Dane FICE Identification: 004007
Unit ID: 238263
Telephone: (608) 246-6100 Carnegie Class: Bac/Assoc-Assoc Dom
FAX Number: (608) 246-6880 Calendar System: Semester
URL: www.madisoncollege.edu
Established: 1912 Annual Undergrad Tuition & Fees (In-District): $4,281
Enrollment: 16,520 Coed
Affiliation or Control: State/Local IRS Status: 501(c)3
Highest Offering: Associate Degree
Accreditation: NH, ACFEI, ADNUR, COARC, CSHSE, DH, EMT, MAC, MLTAD, OPTT, OTA, PTAA, RAD, SURGT

02 President ... Dr. Jack E. DANIELS, III
04 Admin Asst to the President ... Ms. Judith CASTRO-ROMAKER
05 Provost ... Dr. Turina BAKKEN
32 Exec VP/CSSO Student Dev & Success ... Dr. Keith T. CORNILLE
26 Dir Commun/Strategic Marketing ... Mr. Cary R. HEYER
15 VP of Human Resources ... Mr. Jeff REEVES
45 VP Institutional Learning/Effect ... Dr. Timothy L. CASPER
11 CFO/VP of Administrative Services ... Mr. Mark THOMAS
13 Chief Information Officer ... Mr. Mirwais QADER
103 Dean Workforce Education ... Ms. Schauna RASMUSSEN
88 Dean Academic Advancement ... Mr. Christopher P. VANDALL
54 Dean Applied Science Engr & Tech ... Ms. Denise REIMER
49 Dean Arts & Sciences ... Dr. Todd H. STEBBINS
50 Int Dean Business & Applied Arts ... Ms. Erin KOHL
76 Dean Health Education ... Dr. Mark C. LAUSCH
88 Asst VP for Strategic Prtnrshp Innv .. Mr. Bryan M. WOODHOUSE
51 Dean Community & Corporate Learning ... Ms. Kathleen A. RADIONOFF
88 Dir of STEM Center ... Mr. Kevin MIRUS
35 Dean of Students ... Dr. Geraldo G. VILACRUZ
88 Dean Human & Protective Services ... Dr. Shawna M. CARTER
35 Director Student Life ... Ms. Renee M. ALFANO
12 Dean of Northern & Eastern Region ... Mr. James FALCO
88 Dean Ctr Excellence Teaching/Learn ... Ms. Sarah FRITZ
19 Director Public Safety ... Mr. James A. BOTTONI
104 Dir International Education ... Dr. Geoffrey W. BRADSHAW
124 Dean Retention & Student Svcs ... Ms. Carlotta V. CALMESE
36 Dir College & Career Transitions ... Ms. Juanita COMEAU
06 Manager Records/Admissions ... Vacant
08 Director Library Services ... Ms. Julie C. GORES
41 Athletic Director ... Mr. Stephen C. HAUSER
114 Budget Director ... Ms. Sylvia RAMIREZ
108 Director Testing and Assessment ... Vacant
10 Controller ... Ms. Lauralynn M. GRIGG
25 Director Grants & Special Projects ... Ms. Emily J. SANDERS
84 Dean Enrollment Services ... Ms. Lori A. SEBRANEK
18 Director Facilities Services ... Mr. Michael M. STARK
102 Chief Exec Officer Foundation ... Ms. Tammy THAYER
09 Dir Inst Research & Effectiveness ... Mr. Ali R. ZARRINNAM
12 Metro Campus Manager ... Ms. Valentina AHEDO
21 Assistant Controller ... Ms. Dorothy CONDUAH
40 Bookstore Manager ... Mr. Scott R. HEIMAN
37 Dean Financial Aid ... Mr. Keyimani ALFORD
28 VP Equity/Diversity/Cmty Relations ... Ms. Lucia NUNEZ

*Mid-State Technical College (B)

500 32nd Street N, Wisconsin Rapids WI 54494-5599
County: Wood FICE Identification: 005380
Unit ID: 239220
Telephone: (715) 422-5300 Carnegie Class: Assoc/HVT-High Non
FAX Number: (715) 422-5345 Calendar System: Semester
URL: www.mstc.edu
Established: 1967 Annual Undergrad Tuition & Fees (In-District): $4,321
Enrollment: 2,636 Coed
Affiliation or Control: State/Local IRS Status: 501(c)3
Highest Offering: Associate Degree
Accreditation: NH, ADNUR, CAHIIM, COARC, EMT, MAC, PHLEB, SURGT

02 President ... Dr. Shelly MONDEIK
05 Vice President of Academics ... Dr. Sandy KIDDOO
32 Vice President of Student Services ... Dr. Mandy LANG
10 Vice President of Finance ... Mr. Robb FISH
15 Vice President Human Resources ... Mr. Richard O'SULLIVAN
103 Vice President Workforce/Econ Dev ... Dr. Bobbi DAMROW
97 Dean Gen Educ & Learning Resource ... Ms. Beth SMITH
50 Dean Business & Technology ... Dr. Missy SKURZEWSKI-SERVANT
65 Dean Trans/Agric/Nat Res & Constru ... Mr. Ronald ZILLMER
88 Dean Health ... Ms. Colleen KANE
75 Dean Advanced Man & Engineering ... Mr. Alan JAVOROSKI
76 Dean Protective & Human Services ... Ms. Barb JASCOR
12 Dean Stevens Point Campus ... Mr. Volker GAUL
12 Dean Marshfield Campus ... Ms. Brenda DILLENBURG
84 Dean Enrollment Management ... Ms. Kerry FROEHLICH-MUELLER
26 Director Marketing & Communication ... Ms. Kolina STIEBER
102 Director Foundation and Alumni ... Ms. Jill STECKBAUER
18 Director Facilities/Procurement ... Mr. Matt SCHNEIDER
35 Director Student Support ... Ms. Christina LORGE-GROVER
06 Registar ... Ms. Denise BORLAND
37 Manager Financial Aid ... Ms. Mary STRUTHERS

*Milwaukee Area Technical College (C)

700 W State Street, Milwaukee WI 53233-1443
County: Milwaukee FICE Identification: 003866
Unit ID: 239248
Telephone: (414) 297-6600 Carnegie Class: Assoc/HVT-High Trad
FAX Number: (414) 297-7990 Calendar System: Semester
URL: www.matc.edu
Established: 1912 Annual Undergrad Tuition & Fees (In-District): $4,426
Enrollment: 15,186 Coed
Affiliation or Control: Local IRS Status: 501(c)3
Highest Offering: Associate Degree
Accreditation: NH, ACFEI, ADNUR, COARC, CVT, DH, FUSER, MAC, MLTAD, OTA, PHLEB, PNUR, PTAA, #RAD, SURGT

02 President ... Dr. Vicki J. MARTIN
05 Provost ... Dr. Mohammad DAKWAR
32 Vice Pres Student Services ... Dr. Johnny CRAIG
10 Vice President of Finance ... Mr. Jeffrey HOLLOW
43 Vice President & Legal Counsel ... Ms. Janice FALKENBERG
13 Assoc VP Information Technology ... Mr. Michael WALSH
23 Dean Health Occupation ... Dr. Nancy VRABEC
50 Int Dean Business & Graphic Arts ... Dr. Richard BUSALACCHI
24 General Manager Public Television ... Mr. Bohdan ZACHARY
35 Director Student Life ... Mr. Archie GRAHAM
08 Director of Library ... Vacant
37 Director Admissions/Financial Aid ... Ms. Camille NICOLAI
90 Director Technical Services ... Mr. Michael GAVIN
21 Controller ... Ms. Eva KUETHER
19 Director Public Safety ... Ms. Aisha BARKOW
06 Registrar ... Ms. Sarah ADAMS
09 Director Institutional Research ... Dr. Yan WANG
84 Manager Recruitment ... Ms. Sophia WILLIAMS
29 Vice Pres Coll Advancement/Ext Comm ... Ms. Laura BRAY
38 Director Counseling & Advising Svcs ... Mr. Walter LANIER
26 Int Dir Communications/Events ... Ms. Kathryn KAESERMANN
96 Procurement Manager ... Ms. Laura MOORE
41 Coordinator Athletics ... Mr. Randy CASEY

*Moraine Park Technical College (D)

235 N National Avenue, Fond Du Lac WI 54936-1940
County: Fond Du Lac FICE Identification: 009256
Unit ID: 239372
Telephone: (920) 922-8611 Carnegie Class: Assoc/HVT-High Non
FAX Number: (920) 929-2471 Calendar System: Semester
URL: www.morainepark.edu
Established: 1967 Annual Undergrad Tuition & Fees (In-District): $4,340
Enrollment: 6,294 Coed
Affiliation or Control: State/Local IRS Status: 501(c)3
Highest Offering: Associate Degree
Accreditation: NH, ADNUR, CAHIIM, COARC, EMT, MAC, MLTAD, RAD, SURGT

02 President ... Bonnie BAERWALD
05 Vice President Academic Affairs ... James R. EDEN
10 VP Finance and Administration ... Carrie KASUBASKI
32 Vice President Student Services ... James BARRETT
15 Vice President Human Resources ... Kathleen M. BROSKE
13 Chief Information Officer ... Jerry RICHARDS
20 Dean of Applied Technology & Trades ... Fred RICE
88 Dean of Health & Human Services ... Kristin M. FINNEL
97 Dean of General Studies ... Jennifer LANTER
06 Registrar ... Lane HOLTE
12 Dean of the West Bend Campus ... Peter J. RETTLER
35 Dean of Students ... Scott LIEBURN
111 Director of College Advancement ... Dana BOURLAND
26 Dir Marketing/Communications ... Patricia LEHN
08 Library Services Coordinator ... Hans BAIERL
18 Director of Facilities ... Richard BOUDREAU
96 Purchasing Manager ... Timothy KEENAN
09 Director of Inst Effectiveness ... Bojan LJUBENKO

*Nicolet Area Technical College (E)

5364 College Drive, PO Box 518,
Rhinelander WI 54501-0518
County: Oneida FICE Identification: 005384
Unit ID: 239442
Telephone: (715) 365-4493 Carnegie Class: Assoc/HVT-Mix Trad/Non
FAX Number: (715) 365-4445 Calendar System: Semester
URL: www.nicoletcollege.edu
Established: 1967 Annual Undergrad Tuition & Fees (In-State): $4,642
Enrollment: 1,048 Coed
Affiliation or Control: State IRS Status: 501(c)3
Highest Offering: Associate Degree
Accreditation: NH, ADNUR, DH, MAC

02 President ... Dr. Richard R. NELSON
05 VP of Academic Services ... Mr. Ron SKALLERUD
32 VP of Student Services ... Ms. Kathleen FERREL
10 Chief Financial Officer ... Mr. John VAN DE LOO
26 Executive Director ... Ms. Sandy KINNEY
15 Director of Human Resources ... Dr. Dan GROLEAU
13 CIO ... Mr. Greg MILJEVICH
66 Dean of Health Occupations ... Dr. Lenore BLEMKE
103 Dean of Workforce/Economic Dev ... Ms. Sandy BISHOP
49 Dean of Liberal Arts/Business ... Dr. Emily STUCKENBRUCK
88 Dean of Trade/Industry/Apprentice ... Mr. Jeff LABS
19 Assoc Dean/Dir Pub Safety/Security ... Mr. Jason GOELDNER
18 Director of Facilities ... Mr. Pete VANNEY
37 Director of Financial Aid ... Ms. Jill PRICE
102 Foundation Executive Director ... Ms. Heather SCHALLOCK
108 Dir Inst Effectiveness/Staff Dev ... Ms. Kelly HAVERKAMPF
45 Managing Dir Strategic Initiative ... Mr. Chuck KOMP
06 Registrar ... Ms. Kyle GRUENING
04 Exec Asst to President/Board ... Ms. Anne E. BONACK
08 Manager of Library Services ... Ms. Nora CRAVEN
28 Diversity and Tribal Outreach Coord ... Ms. Susan CRAZY THUNDER

*Northcentral Technical College (F)

1000 W Campus Drive, Wausau WI 54401-1880
County: Marathon FICE Identification: 005387
Unit ID: 239460
Telephone: (715) 675-3331 Carnegie Class: Assoc/HVT-High Non
FAX Number: (715) 675-9776 Calendar System: Semester
URL: www.ntc.edu
Established: 1912 Annual Undergrad Tuition & Fees (In-District): $4,313
Enrollment: 4,580 Coed
Affiliation or Control: Local IRS Status: 501(c)3
Highest Offering: Associate Degree
Accreditation: NH, ADNUR, DH, EMT, MAC, MLTAD, PHLEB, RAD, SURGT

02 President ... Dr. Lori A. WEYERS
32 Vice President of Student Services ... Dr. Jeannie M. WORDEN
10 Vice President of Finance & CFO ... Ms. Roxanne LUTGEN
13 Chief Information Officer ... Mr. Chet A. STREBE
18 Director of Facilities ... Mr. Rob ELLIOTT
26 Director of Marketing & PR ... Mrs. Katrina FELCH
19 Dean Public Safety ... Ms. Sara GOSSFELD-BENZING
47 Dean Agricultural Sciences ... Dr. Vicky PIETZ
50 Dean Business/Cmty Svc/Intl Educ ... Mr. Christopher SEVERSON
12 Dean Regional Campuses ... Ms. Bobbi DAMROW
76 Dean of Health Sciences ... Ms. Lorraine ZOROMSKI
22 Employment Coord/Affirm Action Ofcr ... Ms. Cindy THELEN
108 Director Quality/Continuous Improv ... Mrs. Beth ELLIE
35 Director of Student Relations ... Mr. Shawn P. SULLIVAN
19 Director of Security ... Mr. Dan JACOBSON
06 Registrar ... Mr. Nick BLANCHETTE
84 Dean of College Enrollment ... Ms. Sarah DILLON
15 Director of Human Resources ... Ms. Karen BRZEZINSKI
97 Dean Center for Teaching & Learning ... Ms. Debra STENCIL
36 Director of Transfer & Placement ... Ms. Suzi MATHIAS
38 Dean of Student Success ... Mrs. Shannon LIVINGSTON
75 Dean of Technical & Trades ... Mr. Darren ACKLEY
51 Dean Continuing Ed/Virtual College ... Mr. Brad GAST
04 Executive Asst to President ... Mrs. PaHnia THAO
09 Director of Institutional Research ... Mrs. Angela M. SERVI
37 Director Student Financial Aid ... Mr. Jeff CICHON

*Northeast Wisconsin Technical College (G)

PO Box 19042, 2740 W Mason Street,
Green Bay WI 54307-9042
County: Brown FICE Identification: 005301
Unit ID: 239488
Telephone: (920) 498-5444 Carnegie Class: Assoc/HVT-Mix Trad/Non
FAX Number: (920) 498-6260 Calendar System: Semester
URL: www.nwtc.edu
Established: 1913 Annual Undergrad Tuition & Fees (In-District): $4,355
Enrollment: 10,096 Coed
Affiliation or Control: State/Local IRS Status: 501(c)3
Highest Offering: Associate Degree
Accreditation: NH, ACBSP, ADNUR, CAHIIM, COARC, DA, DH, DMS, EMT, ENGT, MAC, MLTAD, PNUR, PTAA, RAD, SURGT

02 President ... Dr. H. Jeffrey RAFN
05 Vice President of Learning ... Ms. Lori SUDDICK
32 Vice President of Student Services ... Vacant
30 Vice Pres of College Advancement ... Ms. Karen SMITS
15 Vice President of Human Resources ... Ms. Sandy RYCZKOWSKI
13 Chief Information Officer ... Mr. Daniel MINCHEFF
10 VP Business & Finance ... Mr. Robert MATHEWS
12 Dean Regional Learning ... Ms. Jan SCOVILLE
50 Dn Business/Information Technology ... Mr. Randy SMITH
76 Dean Health Science ... Ms. Kay TUPALA
72 Dean Trades & Engr Technologies ... Dr. Mark WEBER
97 Dean General Education ... Ms. Michaeline SCHMIT
20 Dean Learning Solutions ... Ms. Anne KAMPS
103 Dean Corp Training & Economic Devel ... Mr. Dean STEWART
38 Dean of Student Success ... Ms. Vickie LOCK
07 Dean Enrollment Services/Registrar ... Mr. Mark FRANKS
37 Financial Aid Director ... Ms. Emily YSEBAERT
102 Foundation Director ... Ms. Crystal HARRISON
40 Director Bookstore ... Mr. Patrick SORELLE

26 Public Relations/Comm Specialist ... Ms. Kathleen FRYDA
18 Director of Facilities ... Mr. Chet LAMERS
08 Manager Library Services ... Ms. Kim LAPLANTE
104 Mgr Student Involvement/Intl Pgm ... Ms. Megan POPKEY
21 Director of Financial Operations ... Vacant
04 Administrative Asst to President ... Ms. Mary Jo TILOT
09 Institutional Researcher ... Mr. Jeff GREBINOSKI
105 Director Web Services ... Ms. Erica PLAZA
28 Director of Diversity ... Mr. Mohammed BEY

*Southwest Wisconsin Technical College (A)

1800 Bronson Boulevard, Fennimore WI 53809-9778
County: Grant   FICE Identification: 007669
Unit ID: 239910
Telephone: (608) 822-3262   Carnegie Class: Assoc/HVT-Mix Trad/Non
FAX Number: (608) 822-6019   Calendar System: Semester
URL: www.swtc.edu
Established: 1967   Annual Undergrad Tuition & Fees (In-District): $4,340
Enrollment: 2,114   Coed
Affiliation or Control: State/Local   IRS Status: Exempt
Highest Offering: Associate Degree
Accreditation: NH, ADNUR, MAC, MEAC, MLTAD, PTAA

02 President ... Dr. Jason S. WOOD
10 VP for Administrative Services ... Mr. Caleb WHITE
05 Chief Academic Officer/Exec Dean ... Dr. Kathleen E. GARRITY
47 Dean of Industry/Trades/Agriculture ... Dr. Derek DACHELET
32 Chief Student Services Officer ... Ms. Holly MILLER
15 Chief Human Resources Officer ... Ms. Krista WEBER
108 Director of College Effectiveness ... Ms. Barbara TUCKER
102 Exec Dir of Foundation/Real Estate ... Ms. Holly CLENDENEN
13 Director of IT Services ... Mr. Heath AHNEN
101 Executive Services Director ... Ms. Karen M. CAMPBELL
18 Director of Facilities ... Mr. Dan IMHOFF
37 Financial Aid Manager ... Ms. Joy A. KITE
19 Public Safety Supervisor ... Ms. Kris WUBBEN
88 Business & Industry Services Mgr ... Ms. Amy CHARLES
20 Innovative/Alternative Learning Mgr ... Ms. Kim MAIER
21 Controller ... Ms. Kelly KELLY
88 Supervisor of Pre-College Programs ... Ms. Julie PLUEMER
06 Registrar ... Ms. Danielle SEIPPEL
36 Career Services Manager ... Ms. Heather FIFRICK
88 Dining Services Manager ... Mr. Rex SMITH
88 Dir Health Occupations/Stdnt Lrng ... Ms. Cynde LARSEN

*Waukesha County Technical College (B)

800 Main Street, Pewaukee WI 53072-4696
County: Waukesha   FICE Identification: 005294
Unit ID: 240125
Telephone: (262) 691-5566   Carnegie Class: Assoc/HVT-High Non
FAX Number: (262) 691-5593   Calendar System: Semester
URL: www.wctc.edu
Established: 1923   Annual Undergrad Tuition & Fees (In-District): $4,340
Enrollment: 7,928   Coed
Affiliation or Control: State/Local   IRS Status: 501(c)3
Highest Offering: Associate Degree
Accreditation: NH, ACFEI, ADNUR, CAHIIM, DH, EMT, ENGT, MAC, SURGT

02 President ... Ms. Kaylen A. BETZIG
05 VP Learning ... Dr. Bradley PIAZZA
32 VP Student Services ... Ms. Nicole GAHAGAN
10 VP Finance ... Ms. Cary A. TESSMANN
15 VP Human Resource Svcs ... Mr. David BROWN
11 VP Strat Mktg Innov & Effectiveness .. Dr. Ann KRAUSE-HANSON
13 Chief Information Officer ... Mr. Rodney NOBLES
102 Dir Foundation/Corporate Relations ... Ms. Ellen PHILLIPS
50 Dean Business Occupations ... Ms. Kim EHLERT
75 Dean Industrial Occupations ... Mr. Michael SHIELS
76 Dean Service Occupations ... Dr. Greg WEST
97 Dean Acad Foundation & General Stds ... Ms. Bethany LEONARD
76 Dean Health Occupations ... Ms. Sandra STEARNS
103 Dean Center/Business Performance ... Dr. Joseph WEITZER
35 Director Student Development ... Dr. Rinardo REDDICK
18 Director Facilities Services ... Mr. Jeffrey LEVERENZ
06 Registrar ... Ms. Rachel BURLING
38 Dir Counslng/Advisng/Stdnt Access ... Dr. Christopher DAOOD
36 Mgr Career Development Services ... Ms. Debra WEBER
26 Marketing & Communications Mgr ... Ms. Susan STERN
07 Mgr Admissions/Testing Svcs ... Ms. Kathleen KAZDA
88 Director Academic Excellence ... Mr. Randall COOROUGH
25 Director of Grants & Contracts ... Ms. Linda J. MILLER
09 Director Inst Rsrch & Effectiveness ... Vacant
37 Manager Financial Aid ... Mr. Timothy K. JACOBSON
35 Student Life Coordinator ... Mr. Jonathan N. PEDRAZA
08 Director of Library Services ... Ms. Terry KEMPER
19 Enviro Health & Safety Supervisor ... Mr. Bruce NEUMANN
27 Specialist Public Relations ... Ms. Shelly KUHN
96 Purchasing Specialist ... Ms. Victoria NASH
28 Diversity Coordinator ... Mr. Rolando DELEON
40 Bookstore Manager ... Mr. James DRAEGER
85 International Educ Coordinator ... Mr. K. Austin BAADE
04 Administrative Asst to President ... Ms. Carolyn TINDALL

*Western Technical College (C)

400 N Seventh Street, La Crosse WI 54601-3368
County: La Crosse   FICE Identification: 003840
Unit ID: 240170
Telephone: (608) 785-9200   Carnegie Class: Assoc/HVT-High Trad
FAX Number: (608) 785-9205   Calendar System: Trimester
URL: www.westerntc.edu
Established: 1912   Annual Undergrad Tuition & Fees (In-District): $3,776
Enrollment: 4,044   Coed
Affiliation or Control: State/Local   IRS Status: 501(c)3
Highest Offering: Associate Degree
Accreditation: NH, ADNUR, CAHIIM, COARC, DA, EMT, MAC, MLTAD, OTA, PTAA, RAD, SURGT

02 President ... Dr. Roger STANFORD
10 Vice President Finance/Operations ... Mr. Wade HACKBARTH
05 Vice President of Academic Affairs ... Dr. Cherrie BERGANDI
32 VP Student Development & Success ... Dr. Denise T. VUJNOVICH
45 VP Strategic Effectiveness & Engag ... Ms. Amy THORNTON
12 Director of Ops-Regional Locations ... Ms. Jennifer BRAVE
102 Executive Director Foundation ... Mr. Michael SWENSON
13 Director Computer/Telecomm Svcs ... Mr. Bruce E. MATHEW
37 Financial Aid Manager ... Ms. Jerolyn R. GRANDALL
21 Controller ... Ms. Amy SCHMIDT
103 Dean Workforce & Economic Devel ... Ms. Patti BALACEK
38 Director Counseling Enroll Svcs ... Ms. Ann BRANDAU-HYNEK
29 Manager Alumni Relations ... Ms. Sally EMERSON
07 Manager Admissions/Registration ... Ms. Sandy PETERSON
35 Dean of Students ... Ms. Shelley MCNEELY
08 Manager Library Services ... Vacant
26 Assoc Director Information Services ... Ms. Joan PIERCE
40 Bookstore Manager ... Mr. David R. WIGNES
72 Dean Integrated Technology ... Mr. Josh GAMER
76 Dean Health & Public Safety ... Ms. Diane NEEFE
97 Dean General Education ... Dr. Douglas STRAUSS
50 Dean Business Education ... Mr. Gary BROWN

*Wisconsin Indianhead Technical College (D)

505 Pine Ridge Drive, Shell Lake WI 54871-9300
County: Washburn   FICE Identification: 011824
Unit ID: 240198
Telephone: (715) 468-2815   Carnegie Class: Assoc/HVT-High Non
FAX Number: (715) 468-2819   Calendar System: Semester
URL: www.witc.edu
Established: 1968   Annual Undergrad Tuition & Fees (In-State): $4,598
Enrollment: 2,894   Coed
Affiliation or Control: State   IRS Status: Exempt
Highest Offering: Associate Degree
Accreditation: NH, ADNUR, CAHIIM, OTA

02 President ... Mr. John WILL
10 Vice Pres Business & Tech Svcs/CFO ... Mr. Steven DECKER
05 Vice President Academic Affairs ... Dr. Bonny COPENHAVER
32 Vice President Student Affairs ... Mr. Steve BITZER
51 Vice President Cont Educ/Foundation ... Mr. Craig FOWLER
09 VP Institutional Effectiveness ... Ms. Susan YOHNK LOCKWOOD
15 VP Human Resources/Risk Mgmt ... Ms. Cher VINK
13 Sr Director Technology Services ... Mr. James DAHLBERG
37 Director Financial Aid ... Mr. Terry KLEIN
06 Registrar ... Mr. Shane EVENSON
84 Director of Enrollment Services ... Ms. Laura SULLIVAN
26 Director or Marketing ... Ms. Jena VOGTMAN

*Chippewa Valley Technical College-Gateway (E)

2320 Alpine Road, Eau Claire WI 54703
Telephone: (715) 874-4600   Identification: 770420
Accreditation: &NH

*Chippewa Valley Technical College Menomonie Campus (F)

403 Technology Drive East, Menomonie WI 54751
Telephone: (715) 232-2685   Identification: 770422
Accreditation: &NH

*Chippewa Valley Technical College River Falls Campus (G)

500 South Wasson Lane, River Falls WI 54022
Telephone: (715) 425-3301   Identification: 770423
Accreditation: &NH

*Chippewa Valley Technical College-West (H)

4000 Campus Road, Eau Claire WI 54703
Telephone: (715) 852-1394   Identification: 770421
Accreditation: &NH

*Gateway Technical College Burlington Center (I)

496 McCanna Parkway, Burlington WI 53105
Telephone: (262) 767-5200   Identification: 770426
Accreditation: &NH, EMT

*Gateway Technical College Elkhorn Campus (J)

400 County Road H, Elkhorn WI 53121
Telephone: (262) 741-8200   Identification: 770427
Accreditation: &NH, MAC

*Gateway Technical College Racine Campus (K)

1001 S Main Street, Racine WI 53403
Telephone: (262) 619-6200   Identification: 770428
Accreditation: &NH, CAHIIM

*Madison Area Technical College Commercial Avenue Education Center (L)

2125 Commercial Avenue, Madison WI 53704
Telephone: (608) 246-6100   Identification: 770436
Accreditation: &NH

*Madison Area Technical College Downtown Education Center (M)

211 North Carroll Street, Madison WI 53703
Telephone: (608) 246-6100   Identification: 770437
Accreditation: &NH

*Madison Area Technical College Fort Atkinson (N)

827 Banker Road, Fort Atkinson WI 53538
Telephone: (920) 568-7200   Identification: 770435
Accreditation: &NH

*Madison Area Technical College Portage (O)

330 West Collins Street, Portage WI 53901
Telephone: (608) 745-3100   Identification: 770438
Accreditation: &NH

*Madison Area Technical College Reedsburg (P)

300 Alexander Avenue, Reedsburg WI 53959
Telephone: (608) 524-7800   Identification: 770439
Accreditation: &NH

*Madison Area Technical College Watertown (Q)

1300 West Main Street, Watertown WI 53098
Telephone: (920) 206-8000   Identification: 770440
Accreditation: &NH

*Mid-State Technical College Marshfield Campus (R)

2600 West 5th Street, Marshfield WI 54449
Telephone: (715) 387-2538   Identification: 770441
Accreditation: &NH

*Mid-State Technical College Stevens Point Campus (S)

1001 Centerpoint Drive, Stevens Point WI 54481
Telephone: (715) 344-3063   Identification: 770442
Accreditation: &NH

*Milwaukee Area Technical College (T)

5555 West Highlands Road, Mequon WI 53092
Telephone: (262) 238-2200   Identification: 770443
Accreditation: &NH

*Milwaukee Area Technical College (U)

6665 South Howell Avenue, Oak Creek WI 53154-1107
Telephone: (414) 571-4500   Identification: 770444
Accreditation: &NH

*Milwaukee Area Technical College (V)

1200 South 71st Street, West Allis WI 53214-3110
Telephone: (414) 456-5500   Identification: 770445
Accreditation: &NH, DIETT

*Moraine Park Technical College (W)

700 Gould Street, Beaver Dam WI 53916
Telephone: (920) 887-1428   Identification: 770446
Accreditation: &NH

*Moraine Park Technical College (X)

2151 North Main Street, West Bend WI 53090
Telephone: (262) 335-5713   Identification: 770447
Accreditation: &NH

*Northeast Wisconsin Technical College-Marinette Campus (Y)

1601 University Drive, Marinette WI 54143
Telephone: (715) 735-9361   Identification: 770448
Accreditation: &NH

Northeast Wisconsin Technical College-Sturgeon Bay Campus **(A)**
229 N 14th Avenue, Sturgeon Bay WI 54235
Telephone: (920) 746-4900 Identification: 770449
Accreditation: &NH

Wisconsin Indianhead Technical College-Ashland Campus **(B)**
2100 Beaser Avenue, Ashland WI 54806
Telephone: (715) 682-8040 Identification: 770463
Accreditation: &NH

Wisconsin Indianhead Technical College-New Richmond Campus **(C)**
1019 S Knowles Avenue, New Richmond WI 54017
Telephone: (715) 246-6561 Identification: 770464
Accreditation: &NH, MAC

Wisconsin Indianhead Technical College-Rice Lake Campus **(D)**
1900 College Drive, Rice Lake WI 54868
Telephone: (715) 234-7082 Identification: 770465
Accreditation: &NH, DA, EMT

Wisconsin Indianhead Technical College-Superior Campus **(E)**
600 North 21st Street, Superior WI 54880
Telephone: (715) 394-6677 Identification: 770466
Accreditation: &NH, MAC

Wright Graduate University for the Realization of Human Potential (F)
N7698 County Highway H, Elkhorn WI 53121
County: Walworth Identification: 667224
Unit ID: 486460
Telephone: (262) 742-4444 Carnegie Class: Not Classified
FAX Number: (262) 721-0752 Calendar System: Quarter
URL: www.wrightgrad.edu
Established: 2006 Annual Graduate Tuition & Fees: N/A
Enrollment: 33 Coed
Affiliation or Control: Independent Non-Profit IRS Status: 501(c)3
Highest Offering: Doctorate; No Undergraduates
Accreditation: DEAC

00 CEO .... Dr. Bob WRIGHT
01 Chancellor .... Dr. Michael ZWELL
12 Campus Director .... Ms. Kate HOLMQUEST
05 Chief Academic Officer .... Dr. Judith WRIGHT

WYOMING

Carbon County Higher Education Center/ Rawlins **(G)**
812 E. Murray Street, Rawlins WY 82301-4466
Telephone: (307) 328-9204 Identification: 770481
Accreditation: &NH

Casper College (H)
125 College Drive, Casper WY 82601-2458
County: Natrona FICE Identification: 003928
Unit ID: 240505
Telephone: (307) 268-2110 Carnegie Class: Assoc/MT-VT-High Non
FAX Number: (307) 268-2682 Calendar System: Semester
URL: www.caspercollege.edu
Established: 1945 Annual Undergrad Tuition & Fees (In-District): $2,832
Enrollment: 3,680 Coed
Affiliation or Control: Local IRS Status: 501(c)3
Highest Offering: Associate Degree
Accreditation: NH, ACBSP, ADNUR, ART, COARC, DANCE, EMT, MLTAD, MUS, OTA, RAD, THEA

01 President .... Dr. Darren D. DIVINE
05 Vice President Academic Affairs .... Dr. Shawn POWELL
32 Vice President Student Services .... Ms. Kim BYRD
10 Vice Pres Administrative Services .... Ms. Lynnde COLLING
51 Exec Dean of Continuing Education .... Dr. Laura DRISCOLL
15 Director Human Resources .... Ms. Rhonda FRANKZEN
07 Director Admissions/Student Records .... Ms. Kyla FOLTZ
26 Director of Public Relations .... Mr. Chris LORENZEN
18 Director Physical Plant .... Mr. Michael SAWYER
38 Director Student Counseling .... Ms. Teresa WALLACE
08 Director of the Library .... Mr. Brad MATTHIES
13 Director Information Technology .... Mr. Kent BROOKS
121 Director of Student Success Service .... Ms. Leanne LOYA
39 Director of Housing .... Ms. Barb MERYHEW
41 Athletic Director .... Ms. Angel SHARMAN
19 Director Campus Security .... Mr. Lance JONES
102 Exec Director Foundation .... Ms. Paulann DOANE
09 Institutional Researcher .... Ms. Lynn FLETCHER
37 Director of Student Financial Aid .... Mrs. Shannon ESKAM
21 Dir Financial Services/Controller .... Ms. Robyn LANDEN
96 Purchasing Coordinator .... Mr. Paul CHRISTMAN
06 Registrar .... Ms. Linda NICHOLS
29 Director Alumni Relations .... Ms. Linda NIX
04 Executive Asst to President .... Ms. Tina SILVA
108 Director Institutional Assessment .... Dr. Melissa STAHLEY-CUMMINGS
25 Grant Coordinator .... Ms. Katie MCMILLAN

Central Wyoming College (I)
2660 Peck Avenue, Riverton WY 82501-1520
County: Fremont FICE Identification: 007289
Unit ID: 240514
Telephone: (307) 855-2000 Carnegie Class: Assoc/HT-High Non
FAX Number: (307) 855-2095 Calendar System: Semester
URL: www.cwc.edu
Established: 1966 Annual Undergrad Tuition & Fees (In-District): $2,856
Enrollment: 2,116 Coed
Affiliation or Control: Local IRS Status: 501(c)3
Highest Offering: Associate Degree
Accreditation: NH, ADNUR

01 President .... Dr. Brad TYNDALL
04 Exec Asst to the President/Board .... Ms. Linda BENDER
05 Vice Pres Academic Affairs .... Dr. Katherine WELLS
10 Vice Pres Admin Svcs/CFO .... Mr. Willie NOSEEP
32 Vice Pres Student Affairs .... Ms. Cory DALY
13 Chief Information Officer .... Mr. John WOOD
18 Chief Facilities/Physical Plant .... Mr. Wayne ROBINSON
08 Director of Library Services .... Ms. Nicole POUGET
26 Director of Marketing .... Ms. Lori RIDGWAY
15 Dir for Human Resources .... Mr. Scott MILLER
21 Finance Officer .... Ms. Lindy PASKETT
19 Director of Campus Safety/Security .... Mr. Chuck CARR
103 Dean Business/Technical & Workforce .... Ms. Lynne MCAULIFFE
41 Director of Athletics .... Mr. Steve BARLOW
06 Registrar .... Ms. Connie NYBERG
49 Dean for Arts & Sciences .... Dr. Mark NORDEEN
102 Exec Director CWC Foundation .... Ms. Becky RUTHENBECK

Eastern Wyoming College (J)
3200 W C Street, Torrington WY 82240-1699
County: Goshen FICE Identification: 003929
Unit ID: 240596
Telephone: (307) 532-8200 Carnegie Class: Assoc/HVT-High Non
FAX Number: (307) 532-8229 Calendar System: Semester
URL: ewc.wy.edu/
Established: 1948 Annual Undergrad Tuition & Fees (In-District): $2,808
Enrollment: 1,769 Coed
Affiliation or Control: State/Local IRS Status: 501(c)3
Highest Offering: Associate Degree
Accreditation: NH

01 President .... Dr. Lesley TRAVERS
04 Exec Asst to President/Board .... Ms. Holly L. BRANHAM
05 Acting VP for Academic Services .... Mr. Roger HUMPHREY
10 VP for Admin Services .... Mr. Ron LAHER
32 VP for Student Services .... Dr. Rex COGDILL
20 Associate VP for Converse County .... Mrs. Margaret FARLEY
30 Dir of Institutional Development .... Mr. John HANSEN
08 Director of Library Services .... Mrs. Casey DEBUS
41 Director of College Athletics .... Mr. Tom ANDERSEN
26 Director of College Relations .... Ms. Tami AFDAHL
18 Director of Physical Plant .... Mr. Keith JARVIS
39 Director of Residence Life .... Mr. Kyle RICE
37 Director of Financial Aid .... Ms. Susan STEPHENSON
15 Director Human Resources .... Mr. Edward MEYER
21 Business Office Director .... Ms. Karen PARRIOTT

Eastern Wyoming College-Douglas Campus **(K)**
800 South Wind River Drive, Douglas WY 82633
Telephone: (307) 624-7000 Identification: 770476
Accreditation: &NH

Gillette College **(L)**
300 West Sinclair, Gillette WY 82718
Telephone: (888) 544-5538 Identification: 770478
Accreditation: &NH

IBMC College/Institute of Business and Medical Careers **(M)**
1854 Dell Range Boulevard, Cheyenne WY 82009
Telephone: (307) 433-8363 Identification: 666738
Accreditation: ACICS

† Branch campus of Institute of Business and Medical Careers, Fort Collins, CO.

Laramie County Community College (N)
1400 E College Drive, Cheyenne WY 82007-3299
County: Laramie FICE Identification: 009259
Unit ID: 240620
Telephone: (307) 778-5222 Carnegie Class: Assoc/HT-High Non
FAX Number: (307) 778-1399 Calendar System: Semester
URL: www.lccc.wy.edu
Established: 1968 Annual Undergrad Tuition & Fees (In-District): $3,306
Enrollment: 4,181 Coed
Affiliation or Control: State/Local IRS Status: 501(c)3
Highest Offering: Associate Degree
Accreditation: NH, ADNUR, DH, DMS, EMT, PTAA, RAD, SURGT

01 President .... Dr. Joe SCHAFFER
05 Vice President of Academic Affairs .... Dr. Clark HARRIS
10 Vice Pres of Administration/Finance .... Mr. Rick JOHNSON
32 Vice President of Student Services .... Ms. Judy HAY
13 Chief Technology Officer .... Mr. Chad MARLEY
15 Executive Director Human Resources .... Ms. Tammy MAAS
111 Interim Assoc VP Inst Advancement .... Ms. Lisa TRIMBLE
12 Interim Executive Director ACC .... Ms. Talisha MOTTINGER
45 Assc VP Institutional Effectiveness .... Dr. Kim BENDER
08 Assoc Dean Library/Learning Commons .... Ms. Maura HADAWAY
37 Director of Financial Aid .... Vacant
18 Director of Physical Plant .... Mr. Bill ZINK
21 Comptroller .... Ms. Nola ROCHA
29 Int Dir Alumni Affairs/Event Plans .... Ms. Lisa MURPHY
44 Dir Scholarships & Annual Giving .... Ms. Melissa DISHMAN
09 Manager of Institutional Research .... Ms. Ann MURRAY
07 Dir of Admissions and Welcome Ctr .... Ms. Sarah HANNES
06 Registrar .... Ms. Stacy MAESTAS
49 Dean School of Arts & Humanities .... Dr. Daniel POWELL
50 Dean Sch of Bus/Ag & Tech Studies .... Vacant
76 Dean Sch of Health Sci & Well .... Ms. Terry HARPER
81 Dean School Math & Science .... Mr. Bryan WILSON
103 Dean Sch of Outreach/Workforce Dev .... Ms. Maryellen TAST
19 Director Campus Safety & Security .... Mr. James CROSBY
41 Director of Athletics .... Mr. Scott NOBLE
04 Executive Asst to President .... Ms. Vicki BOREING

Laramie County Community College Albany County Campus **(O)**
1125 Boulder Drive, Laramie WY 82070
Telephone: (307) 721-5138 Identification: 770477
Accreditation: &NH

Northern Wyoming Community College District (P)
PO Box 1500, 3059 Coffeen Avenue, Sheridan WY 82801-1500
County: Sheridan FICE Identification: 003930
Unit ID: 240666
Telephone: (307) 674-6446 Carnegie Class: Assoc/MT-VT-High Non
FAX Number: (307) 674-3355 Calendar System: Semester
URL: www.sheridan.edu
Established: 1948 Annual Undergrad Tuition & Fees (In-District): $3,156
Enrollment: 4,307 Coed
Affiliation or Control: Local IRS Status: 501(c)3
Highest Offering: Associate Degree
Accreditation: NH, ADNUR, DH

01 President .... Dr. Paul R. YOUNG
05 VP Academic Affairs .... Dr. Richard HALL
10 VP Admin & Finance/CFO .... Ms. Cheryl A. HEATH
12 VP Gillette College/CEO .... Dr. Mark G. ENGLERT
32 VP Student Affairs .... Dr. Leah BARRETT
86 VP External Affairs .... Dr. Susan BIGELOW
75 Dean Career/Technical Education .... Mr. Jed JENSEN
15 Director Human Resources .... Ms. Jennifer MCARTHUR
26 Dir Marketing/College Information .... Ms. Wendy M. SMITH
37 Director Financial Aid Services .... Ms. Heidi BALSTER
13 Dir Information Technology Services .... Mr. Brady R. FACKRELL
09 Director of Institutional Research .... Mr. Jason BROWNING
21 Controller .... Ms. Karen B. BURTIS
07 Executive Director of Admissions .... Mr. Joe B. MUELLER
39 Director Housing/Residential Educ .... Ms. Larissa B. BONNET
88 Director Veteran Services-Sheridan .... Mr. Tyler JENSEN
88 Director Veteran Services-Gillette .... Mr. Loren GROVES
18 Director Facilities/Physical Plant .... Mr. Kent A. ANDERSEN
18 Director Gillette Facilities .... Mr. Mark N. ANDERSEN
08 Librarian .... Ms. Katrina M. BROWN
19 Director Security/Safety .... Mr. Jason VELA
41 Athletic Director .... Ms. Jenni WINTER
04 Administrative Asst to President .... Ms. Mary Jo JOHNSON
20 Assoc Academic Officer-Sheridan .... Ms. Martha DAVEY
20 Assoc Academic Officer-Gillette .... Dr. Matt EWERS
29 Alumni Rels/Communications Coord .... Ms. Bobbi MITZEL
102 Dir Foundation/Corp Rels-Sheridan .... Ms. Jen CROUSE
102 Dir Foundation/Corp Rels-Gillette .... Ms. Heidi GROSS
38 Dir Student Counseling-Gillette .... Ms. Susan SERGE
38 Dir Student Counseling-Sheridan .... Vacant
84 Director Enrollment Management .... Mr. Micah OLSEN

Northwest College (Q)
231 W 6th St, Powell WY 82435
County: Park FICE Identification: 003931
Unit ID: 240657
Telephone: (307) 754-6000 Carnegie Class: Assoc/HT-Mix Trad/Non
FAX Number: (307) 754-6245 Calendar System: Semester
URL: www.nwc.edu
Established: 1946 Annual Undergrad Tuition & Fees (In-District): $3,201
Enrollment: 1,694 Coed
Affiliation or Control: State/Local IRS Status: 501(c)3
Highest Offering: Associate Degree
Accreditation: NH, ADNUR, ART, MUS

01 President ... Dr. Stefani HICSWA
05 Vice Pres Academic Affairs ... Dr. Gerald GIRAUD
32 Vice Pres Student Affairs ... Dr. Lourra BARTHULY
11 Vice Pres Admin Services/Finance ... Ms. Lisa WATSON
26 Vice Pres College Relations ... Mr. Mark KITCHEN
102 Executive Director NWC Foundation ... Ms. Shelby WETZEL
20 Dean Student Lrng/Acad Success ... Dr. Greg THOMAS
103 Dean Extended Campus/Workforce ... Mr. Dean BRUCE
08 Library Director ... Dr. Susan RICHARDS
10 Finance Director ... Mr. Brad BOWEN
15 Human Resources Director ... Ms. Jill ANDERSON
13 Computing Services Director ... Mr. Casey DEARCORN
18 Facilities Director ... Mr. David PLUTE
06 Registrar/Admissions Director ... Mr. Brad HAMMOND
37 Financial Aid/Scholarships Director ... Mr. Shaman QUINN
39 Residence/Campus Life Director ... Mr. Dee HAVIG
04 Exec Secretary to President & Board ... Ms. Cindy CICCI
07 Admissions Manager ... Mr. West HERNANDEZ
09 Institutional Researcher ... Ms. Lisa SMITH
105 Web Developer ... Ms. Carey MILLER
108 Assessment Coordinator ... Ms. Aura NEWLIN
19 Campus Security Coordinator ... Mr. Lee BLACKMORE
30 Development Manager ... Ms. Carol BELL

Oyster Ridge Higher Education/Kemmerer (A)

PO Box 423, Kemmerer WY 83101
Telephone: (307) 877-6958 Identification: 770479
Accreditation: &NH

University of Wyoming (B)

1000 E University Avenue, Dept 3434,
Laramie WY 82071-3434
County: Albany FICE Identification: 003932
Unit ID: 240727
Telephone: (307) 766-1121 Carnegie Class: DU-Higher
FAX Number: (307) 766-2271 Calendar System: Semester
URL: www.uwyo.edu
Established: 1886 Annual Undergrad Tuition & Fees (In-State): $5,055
Enrollment: 12,648 Coed
Affiliation or Control: State IRS Status: 501(c)3
Highest Offering: Doctorate
Accreditation: NH, CACREP, CAEPN, CLPSY, CS, DIETD, ENG, LAW, MUS, NURSE, PHAR, SP, SW

01 President ... Dr. Laurie NICHOLS
05 Provost ... Dr. Kate MILLER
10 Vice President Administration ... Mr. Bill MAI
86 Vice Pres Govt & Community Affairs ... Mr. Chris BOSWELL
46 Vice Pres Research & Economic Dev . Dr. Edmund SYNAKOWSKI
32 Vice President Student Affairs ... Mr. Sean BLACKBURN
13 Vice President Information Tech ... Mr. Robert R. AYLWARD
111 Vice Pres Institutional Advancement ... Mr. W. Ben BLALOCK, III
43 Vice President & General Counsel ... Ms. Tara EVANS
41 Director Intercollegiate Athletics ... Mr. Tom BURMAN
20 Associate VP Academic Affairs ... Dr. Anne ALEXANDER
20 Associate VP Academic Affairs ... Dr. Tami BENHAM-DEAL
84 Associate VP Enrollment Management ... Mr. Kyle MOORE
14 Associate VP Budget and Inst Plan ... Mr. David JEWELL
21 Assoc VP Fiscal Administration ... Ms. Janet S. LOWE
88 Assoc Vice President Research ... Ms. Dorothy C. YATES
35 Interim AVP and Dean of Students ... Dr. Nycole COURTNEY
110 Assoc VP Institutional Advancement ... Mr. John D. STARK
26 Assoc VP Communication/Marketing ... Mr. Chad BALDWIN
47 Dean of Agriculture ... Dr. Frank D. GALEY
49 Dean of Arts & Sciences ... Dr. Paula LUTZ
50 Interim Dean of Business ... Dr. David CHICOINE
53 Dean of Education ... Dr. Ray REUTZEL
54 Dean of Engineering ... Dr. Michael PISHKO
76 Interim Dean of Health Sciences ... Dr. David JONES
61 Dean of Law ... Dr. Klint ALEXANDER
12 Assoc Dean/Director UW at Casper ... Dr. Jeff EDGENS
08 Dean of Libraries ... Dr. Ivan GAETZ
65 Director Haub Sch Env/Nat Resources ... Dr. Melinda BENSON
07 Director of Admissions ... Ms. Shelley DODD
36 Director Advising/Career Services ... Ms. Evelyn J. CHYTKA
29 Exec Director Alumni Affairs ... Mr. Keener FRYE
88 Director American Heritage Center ... Ms. Bridget BURKE
88 Director School of Energy Resources ... Dr. Mark NORTHAM
88 Director Art Museum ... Ms. Susan MOLDENHAUER
88 Director Campus Recreation ... Mr. Patrick MORAN
45 Director Facilities Planning ... Mr. Larry BLAKE
109 Director Auxiliary Services ... Ms. Carolyn SMITH
15 Director Human Resources ... Dr. Jeanne DURR
18 Director UW Operations ... Mr. John DAVIS
92 Interim Director Honors Program ... Dr. Susan ARONSTEIN
86 Spec Advis to the Pres for Ext Rels ... Ms. Meredith ASAY
39 Exec Dir Res Life/Dining/Stdnt Un ... Mr. Eric WEBB
37 Director Student Financial Aid ... Ms. Kathy BOBBITT
06 Registrar ... Mr. Lane BUCHANAN
23 Director Student Health Service ... Dr. Joanne E. STEANE
19 Chief University Police Dept ... Mr. Mike SAMP
38 Dir University Counseling Center ... Dr. Keith EVASHEVSKI

Western Wyoming Community College (C)

2500 College Drive, Rock Springs WY 82902-0428
County: Sweetwater FICE Identification: 003933
Unit ID: 240693
Telephone: (307) 382-1600 Carnegie Class: Assoc/MT-VT-High Non
FAX Number: (307) 382-1636 Calendar System: Semester
URL: www.westernwyoming.edu
Established: 1959 Annual Undergrad Tuition & Fees (In-District): $2,576
Enrollment: 3,298 Coed
Affiliation or Control: State/Local IRS Status: 501(c)3
Highest Offering: Associate Degree
Accreditation: NH, ADNUR

01 President ... Dr. Karla N. LEACH
05 VP for Student Learning ... Dr. Kim FARLEY
32 VP for Student Success Services ... Dr. Philip PARNELL
11 VP for Administrative Services ... Mr. Sheldon FLOM
07 Director of Admissions ... Ms. Erin GREY
06 Registrar ... Vacant
37 Director of Financial Aid ... Ms. Nicole CASTILLON
08 Director of Library Services ... Ms. Janice GROVER-ROOSA
18 Director of Physical Resources ... Mr. Michael BRADY
39 Dir Residence Halls/Student Life ... Mr. Dustin CONOVER
40 Bookstore Manager ... Ms. Natalie LANE
41 Athletic Director ... Dr. Lu SWEET
92 Director of Honors Program ... Mr. Richard KEMPA
09 Director of Planning & Improvement ... Ms. Dianna RENZ
15 Director Human Resources ... Vacant
26 Coord of Marketing/Public Info ... Vacant
30 Director Community College Relation ... Mr. David TATE
36 Dir Student Engagement & Completion ... Mr. Mark REMBACZ
10 Director of Finance and Controller ... Ms. Debbie BAKER
38 Dir Student Counseling/Disability ... Ms. Amy GALLEY
96 Director of Purchasing ... Ms. Tammy REGISTER
04 Executive Asst to President ... Ms. Kandy FRINK
19 Protective Services Supervisor ... Mr. Mark PADILLA
106 Director of Distance Learning ... Ms. Nancy JOHNSON
13 Director of Information Technology ... Mr. Derek ROBINSON
20 Dean of Academics ... Dr. Clifford WITTSTRUCK

Western Wyoming Community College Outreach Afton/Star Valley (D)

247 N Washington, Box 1237, Afton WY 83110
Telephone: (307) 886-3834 Identification: 770483
Accreditation: &NH

Western Wyoming Community College Outreach Evanston (E)

1013 Cheyenne Drive, Evanston WY 82930
Telephone: (307) 789-3988 Identification: 770482
Accreditation: &NH

Wyoming Catholic College (F)

306 Main Street, PO Box 750, Lander WY 82520
County: Fremont Identification: 667227
Telephone: (307) 332-2930 Carnegie Class: Not Classified
FAX Number: (307) 332-2918 Calendar System: Semester
URL: www.wyomingcatholiccollege.com
Established: 2005 Annual Undergrad Tuition & Fees: N/A
Enrollment: N/A Coed
Affiliation or Control: Roman Catholic IRS Status: 501(c)3
Highest Offering: Baccalaureate
Accreditation: @NH

01 President ... Dr. Glen ARBERY
05 Academic Dean ... Dr. Thaddeus KOZINSKI
10 Exec VP for Operations/Finance ... Mr. Richard ROLLINO
30 Vice Pres Advancement/Enrollment ... Mr. Jonathan TONKOWICH
04 Executive Assistant to President ... Ms. Mary MURRAY
32 Director of Student Services ... Ms. Hillary ROWNEY

WyoTech (G)

1889 Venture Drive, Laramie WY 82070
County: Albany FICE Identification: 009157
Unit ID: 240718
Telephone: (307) 742-3776 Carnegie Class: Spec 2-yr-Tech
FAX Number: (307) 755-2484 Calendar System: Other
URL: www.wyotech.edu
Established: 1966 Annual Undergrad Tuition & Fees: N/A
Enrollment: 462 Coed
Affiliation or Control: Independent Non-Profit IRS Status: 501(c)3
Highest Offering: Associate Degree
Accreditation: ACCSC

01 President ... Mr. Caleb PERRITON
84 Director of Student Success ... Mr. Kyle MORRIS
36 Director of Career Services ... Mr. Martin AXLUND
88 Manager of Student Finance ... Ms. Brenda COSSITT
88 Enrollment Manager ... Mr. Glenn HALSEY
06 Registrar ... Ms. Revalee WEERHEIM
39 Housing Manager ... Mr. Gabe LUCERO

US SERVICE SCHOOLS

Air Force Institute of Technology (H)

2950 Hobson Way, Wright Patterson AFB OH 45433-7765
County: Greene FICE Identification: 003009
Unit ID: 200697
Telephone: (937) 255-2321 Carnegie Class: DU-Mod
FAX Number: (937) 656-7600 Calendar System: Quarter
URL: www.afit.edu
Established: 1919 Annual Graduate Tuition & Fees: N/A
Enrollment: 910 Coed
Affiliation or Control: Federal IRS Status: Exempt
Highest Offering: Doctorate; No Undergraduates
Accreditation: NH, ENG, ENGR

01 Chancellor ... Dr. Todd I. STEWART
05 Provost/Vice Chancellor ... Dr. Sivaguru S. SRITHARAN
54 Dean Graduate School of Engr & Mgt ... Dr. Adedeji B. BADIRU
46 Dean for Research ... Dr. Heidi R. RIES
10 Chief Financial Officer ... Ms. Amber L. RICHEY
09 Director Institutional Research ... Dr. Nancy J. ROSZELL
07 Director Admissions/Registrar ... Ms. Kathleen K. HALL
32 Dean of Students ... Col. Adam REIMAN
20 Associate Dean for Academic Affairs ... Dr. Paul J. WOLF
13 Dir Communications & Information ... Major Jeremy MILLAR
08 Director D'Azzo Research Library ... Dr. Ellis BETECK
15 Director Personnel Services ... Ms. Leanne HEAGLE
18 Chief Facilities/Physical Plant ... Mr. Anthony KING
29 Manager Alumni Affairs ... Ms. Kathleen E. SCOTT
35 Director Student Services ... Ms. Kathleen HALL
85 Director of Intl Student Affairs ... Vacant
40 Bookstore Supervisor ... Mr. Joseph SCOTT
106 Dir Online Education/E-learning ... Mr. John A. REISNER

Air University (I)

55 LeMay Plaza South, Maxwell AFB AL 36112-6335
County: Montgomery FICE Identification: 001001
Telephone: (334) 953-5613 Carnegie Class: Not Classified
FAX Number: (334) 953-2749 Calendar System: Other
URL: www.au.af.mil
Established: 1946 Annual Undergrad Tuition & Fees: N/A
Enrollment: N/A Coed
Affiliation or Control: Federal IRS Status: Exempt
Highest Offering: Doctorate
Accreditation: SC

01 Commander and President ... LtGen. Steven L. KWAST
03 Vice Commander ... MajGen. Timothy J. LEAHY
05 Chief Academic Officer ... Col. Jeffrey DONNITHORNE
06 Registrar ... Dr. Michael J. MASTERSON
20 Deputy Director Academic Affairs ... Mr. Jay WARWICK
20 Director Academic Affairs ... Mr. John CARTER

† Parent institution of Community College of the Air Force, School of Advanced Air and Space Studies, and the Air Force Institute of Technology

Community College of the Air Force (J)

100 South Turner Blvd,
Maxwell AFB, Gunter Annex AL 36114-3011
Telephone: (334) 649-5000 FICE Identification: 012308
Accreditation: &SC, #PTAA

† Regional accreditation is carried under the parent institution, Air University, Maxwell AFB, AL.

Defense Language Institute (K)

1759 Lewis Road, Monterey CA 93944
County: Monterey FICE Identification: 001195
Unit ID: 428222
Telephone: (831) 242-5291 Carnegie Class: Not Classified
FAX Number: (831) 242-6495 Calendar System: Other
URL: www.dliflc.edu
Established: 1941 Annual Undergrad Tuition & Fees: N/A
Enrollment: N/A Coed
Affiliation or Control: Federal IRS Status: Exempt
Highest Offering: Associate Degree
Accreditation: WJ

01 Commandant ... Col. Phillip DEPPERT
05 Provost ... Dr. Betty Lou LEAVER
20 Associate Provost ... Dr. Hiam KANBAR
06 Registrar ... Mrs. Roshanak BURNSIDES

† Associate Arts in Foreign Language authorized by US Congress in December 2001 and approved by ACCJC/WASC in June 2002.

59th Dental Training Squadron (L)

Bldg 3352, Lackland AFB TX 78236
Telephone: (210) 292-7251 Identification: 770122
Accreditation: &M

† Branch campus of Uniformed Services University of the Health Sciences, Bethesda, MD

Joint Forces Staff College (M)

7800 Hampton Boulevard, Norfolk VA 23511-1702
Telephone: (757) 443-6124 Identification: 770121
Accreditation: &M

† Branch campus of National Defense University, Washington, DC

The Judge Advocate General's Legal Center & School (N)

600 Massie Road, Charlottesville VA 22903-1781
County: Albermarle Identification: 666974
Telephone: (434) 971-3300 Carnegie Class: Not Classified
FAX Number: (434) 971-3338 Calendar System: Quarter
URL: www.jagcnet.army.mil/tjaglcs
Established: 1951 Annual Graduate Tuition & Fees: N/A
Enrollment: N/A Coed

Affiliation or Control: Federal IRS Status: Exempt
Highest Offering: Master's; No Undergraduates
Accreditation: LAW

01 Commander/Commandant .... BGen. R. Patrick HUSTON
05 Dean .... Col. Randall J. BAGWELL
20 Associate Dean of Academics ...... Mr. Maurice A. LESCAULT, JR.
32 Associate Dean of Students .... LtCol. Sally R. MACDONALD

Marine Corps University (A)

2076 South Street, Quantico VA 22134-5068
County: Prince William Identification: 666745
Unit ID: 438513
Telephone: (703) 784-2105 Carnegie Class: Not Classified
FAX Number: (703) 784-1271 Calendar System: Semester
URL: www.mcu.usmc.mil
Established: 1989 Annual Graduate Tuition & Fees: N/A
Enrollment: N/A Coed
Affiliation or Control: Federal IRS Status: Exempt
Highest Offering: Master's; No Undergraduates
Accreditation: SC

01 President .... BGen. William BOWERS
05 Vice President for Academic Affairs .... Dr. James ANDERSON
11 VP for Operations & Planning .... Mr. Jay HATTON
10 VP Business Affairs .... Mr. Keil GENTRY
20 Director Academic Support Division .... Mr. Richard JAQUES
09 Director Institutional Research .... Vacant

National Defense University (B)

Fort Lesley J. McNair, Washington DC 20319-5066
FICE Identification: 031893
Unit ID: 423494
Telephone: (202) 685-3924 Carnegie Class: Not Classified
FAX Number: (202) 685-3920 Calendar System: Semester
URL: www.ndu.edu
Established: 1976 Annual Graduate Tuition & Fees: N/A
Enrollment: N/A Coed
Affiliation or Control: Federal IRS Status: Exempt
Highest Offering: Master's; No Undergraduates
Accreditation: M

01 President .... MajGen. Frederick M. PADILLA
03 Senior Vice President .... Amb. Donald YAMAMOTO
05 Provost/Vice Pres Academic Affairs .... Dr. John W. YAEGER
11 Chief Operating Officer .... Mr. Robert C. KANE
43 General Counsel .... Ms. Mollie MURPHY
46 Sr Dir Research/Strategic Support .... Dr. Richard D. HOOKER, JR.
88 Chancellor CISA .... Dr. Michael S. BELL
88 Commandant ES .... COL. Paul H. FREDENBURGH, III
88 Commandant NWC .... BGen. Darren E. HARTFORD
88 Chancellor iCollege .... Ms. Janice M. HAMBY
88 Commandant JFSC .... RADM. Brad WILLIAMSON
107 Deputy Director CAPSTONE .... Mr. Gerard M. MAUER, JR.
20 Deputy Vice Pres Academic Affairs .... Dr. Tim RUSSO
32 Associate Provost Student/Acad Svcs .... Vacant
06 University Registrar .... Mr. Larry JOHNSON
42 Chaplain .... COL. Jeffery ZUST
26 Director of Strategic Communication .... Mr. Mark PHILLIPS
13 Chief Information Officer .... Ms. Diane WEBBER
105 Web/Social Media Manager .... Ms. Jennifer RUSSELL
10 Director Resource Management .... Mr. Jay HELMING
25 Director Contracting .... Ms. Jenifer CUOZZO
23 Director Health Fitness .... Mr. Tony SPINOSA
15 Director Human Resources .... Mr. Tim ROBERTSON
08 Director Libraries .... Ms. Helen (Meg) TULLOCH
85 Dir International Student Mgmt Ofc .... Dr. John GODWIN
18 Chief Facilities/Physical Plant .... Mr. Charles FANSHAW
19 Director Security .... Mr. Joe PALLANEZ
102 Int President/CEO NDU Foundation .... Amb. Walter STADTLER

National Intelligence University (C)

7400 Pentagon, Washington DC 20301
Identification: 666393
Unit ID: 131380
Telephone: (301) 243-2118 Carnegie Class: Not Classified
FAX Number: N/A Calendar System: Quarter
URL: www.ni-u.edu
Established: 1962 Annual Undergrad Tuition & Fees: N/A
Enrollment: N/A Coed
Affiliation or Control: Federal IRS Status: Exempt
Highest Offering: Master's
Accreditation: M

01 President .... Dr. J. Scott CAMERON
04 Executive Assistant to President .... Ms. Shauna K. OAKLAND
100 Chief of Staff .... Col. Michael E. SENN
05 Exec VP & Provost .... Dr. Susan M. STUDDS
09 VP Research .... Dr. Terrence C. MARKIN
88 Executive Asst to Provost .... Mr. Jeffrey D. KIRKWOOD
46 Dir Ctr for Strategic Intel Rsrch .... Dr. Robert SMITH
108 Dir Institutional Effectiveness .... Ms. Ellen ROSENTHAL
10 VP Finance & Administration .... Mr. Paul LEGERE
11 Director of Univ Operations .... Mr. Stephen J. KERDA
18 Facilities .... Dr. Richard MESTAS
19 Security Officer .... Ms. Thelma FLAMER
06 Registrar/Dir Enrollment Services .... Mr. Eric H. STUPAR
08 Director Library Services .... Ms. Elizabeth E. VENTURA
58 Dean College Strategic Intel .... Dr. Donald HANLE
12 Director NSA Campus .... Mr. Dax NORMAN
12 Director NGA Campus .... Mr. Timothy J. CHRISTENSON
12 Director Reserve Monthly Pgm .... LCDR. Rachael L. LEWIS
12 Director European Academic Ctr .... Dr. Samiah E. BARONI
12 Director Southern Academic Ctr .... Mr. Kevin TALIAFERRO
12 Director Quantico Academic Ctr .... Mr. Kevin LOGAN
58 Dean School of Science & Tech Intel .... Dr. Brian R. SHAW
26 VP Outreach .... Mr. Frederick HAMMERSEN
29 Dir Outreach & Alumni Affairs .... Mr. Thomas VAN WAGNER

Naval Postgraduate School (D)

1 University Circle, Room M10, Monterey CA 93943-5100
County: Monterey FICE Identification: 001310
Unit ID: 119678
Telephone: (831) 656-2441 Carnegie Class: DU-Higher
FAX Number: (831) 656-2921 Calendar System: Quarter
URL: www.nps.edu
Established: 1909 Annual Undergrad Tuition & Fees: N/A
Enrollment: 2,665 Coed
Affiliation or Control: Federal IRS Status: Exempt
Highest Offering: Doctorate
Accreditation: WC, ENG, SPAA

01 President .... VAdm. Ronald A. ROUTE, RET.
05 Provost/Academic Dean .... Dr. Steven R. LERMAN
100 Chief of Staff .... Col. Todd W. LYONS
20 Vice Provost for Academic Affairs .... Dr. Orrin Douglas MOSES
46 Dean of Research .... Dr. Jeffrey D. PADUAN
54 Dean Grad Sch Engr/Applied Sci .... Dr. Clyde SCANDRETT
58 Dean Sch of Intl Graduate Studies .... Dr. James J. WIRTZ
50 Dean Grad Sch Bus/Public Policy .... Dr. William R. GATES
72 Dean Grad Sch Oper & Info Sciences ... Dr. Gordon MCCORMICK
32 Dean of Students .... CDR. Paul E. RASMUSSEN
10 Director Business Operations .... Mr. Les D. MARTIN
21 Comptroller .... Mr. Kevin K. LITTLE
13 Director Information Technology .... Mr. Joseph LOPICCOLO
08 University Librarian .... Ms. Eleanor S. UHLINGER
06 Registrar .... Mr. Mike ANDERSEN
15 Director Human Resources .... Ms. Ermelinda RODRIGUEZ-HEFFNER
56 Director of CED3 .... Mr. Tom M. MASTRE
07 Director of Admissions .... Ms. Sue DOOLEY
88 Director of Programs .... CDR. Yolanda KERN

Naval War College (E)

686 Cushing Road, Newport RI 02841-1207
County: Newport FICE Identification: 003413
Unit ID: 432320
Telephone: (401) 841-3089 Carnegie Class: Not Classified
FAX Number: (401) 841-1297 Calendar System: Trimester
URL: www.usnwc.edu
Established: 1884 Annual Graduate Tuition & Fees: N/A
Enrollment: N/A Coed
Affiliation or Control: Federal IRS Status: Exempt
Highest Offering: Master's; No Undergraduates
Accreditation: EH

01 President .... RADM. Jeffrey A. HARLEY
04 Exec Assistant to the President .... LCDR. Jay BREWER
05 Provost .... Dr. Lewis M. DUNCAN
88 Chief of Staff to the Provost .... Mr. Richard R. MENARD
20 Associate Provost .... Prof. James E. HICKEY
100 Vice Pres/Chief of Staff .... CAPT. Tamara K. GRAHAM
20 Dean of Academic Affairs .... Dr. John GAROFANO
09 Dean Center for Warfare Studies .... Prof. Thomas CULORA
32 Dean of Students .... CAPT. Pat KEYES
08 Director H. E. Eccles Library .... Dr. Allen C. BENSON
56 Dir College of Distance Education .... Dr. Leonard Walter WILDEMANN
06 Registrar .... Ms. Michele BLACKBURN
46 Chairman Strategy & Policy .... Dr. Paul R. MURPHY
88 Chairman National Security Affairs .... Dr. Paul L. MULLER
88 Chairman Joint Military Operations ...... CAPT. Donald Eric BADER
10 Chief Business Officer .... Mr. Robert SAMPSON
15 Director Military Personnel Svcs .... CDR. Melanie HA'O
15 Civilian Human Resources Officer .... Ms. Charlene HANSON
18 Chief Facilities/Physical Plant .... Ms. Beth LEINBERRY
26 Chief Public Relations Officer .... CDR. Kelly BRANNON
13 Chief Information Officer .... Mr. Joseph PANGBORN
19 Director of Security .... Mr. Paul GATELY
29 Director Alumni Affairs .... Ms. Julia GAGE
104 Director International Programs .... Prof. Thomas MANGOLD
88 Dean Col Operatnl/Strategic Ldrshp .... Prof. James KELLY
88 Director of Events .... Ms. Karen SELLERS

School of Advanced Air and Space Studies (F)

125 Chennault Circle, Maxwell AFB AL 36112-6424
Telephone: (334) 953-5155 Identification: 666746
Accreditation: &SC

† Regional accreditation is carried under the parent institution, Air University, Maxwell AFB, AL.

Uniformed Services University of the Health Sciences (G)

4301 Jones Bridge Road, Bethesda MD 20814-4799
County: Montgomery FICE Identification: 021610
Unit ID: 164137
Telephone: (301) 295-3013 Carnegie Class: Not Classified
FAX Number: (301) 295-3431 Calendar System: Quarter
URL: www.usuhs.edu
Established: 1972 Annual Undergrad Tuition & Fees: N/A
Enrollment: N/A Coed
Affiliation or Control: Federal IRS Status: Exempt
Highest Offering: Doctorate
Accreditation: M, ANEST, CLPSY, DENT, ENGR, MED, NURSE, PH

01 President .... Dr. Richard W. THOMAS
05 Sr Vice Pres University Programs .... Dr. Thomas TRAVIS
10 Vice Pres Finance & Admin .... Mr. Walter TINLING
26 Vice Pres External Affairs .... Dr. Jeffrey LONGACRE
46 Vice President for Research .... Dr. Yvonne MADDOX
04 Exec Assistant to the President .... Ms. Lorraine BREEN
06 AVP & University Registrar ...... Ms. Gail-Selina HEWITT-CLARKE
21 AVP Resource Management .... Ms. Antoinette WHITMEYER
100 Chief of Staff .... Mr. Robert J. THOMPSON
63 Dean School of Medicine .... Dr. Arthur KELLERMANN
66 Dean Graduate School of Nursing .... Dr. Carol ROMANO
76 Dean School Allied Health Sci .... Dr. Mitchell SEAL
52 Dean Naval Postgrad Dental School .... CAPT. Glenn MUNRO
52 Dean Air Force Postgrad Dental Sch .... COL. Drew FALLIS
52 Executive Dean Postgrad Dental .... Dr. Thomas R. SCHNEID
58 Assoc Dean Graduate Education .... Dr. Gregory MUELLER
07 Assoc Dean Admiss & Recruiting SOM .... COL. Aaron SAGUIL
88 Assoc Dean Graduate Medical Educ .... CAPT. Jerri CURTIS
32 Assoc Dean Student Affairs .... COL. Lisa MOORES
20 Assoc Dean for Curriculum .... Dr. Arnyce POCK
88 Sr Assoc Dean for Faculty .... Dr. Brian REAMY
88 Assoc Dean for Medical Education .... Dr. William GILLILAND
88 Assistant Dean Academic Support .... Dr. William WITTMAN
88 Assistant Dean Clinical Sciences .... CAPT. Pamela WILLIAMS
20 Assoc Dean Academic Affairs GSN .... Dr. Diane SEIBERT
13 Chief Information Officer .... Mr. Timothy RAPP
43 General Counsel .... Mr. Jason KAAR
46 Director AFRRI .... COL. Lester HUFF
15 Director Civilian Human Res .... Mr. Darryl BROWN
08 Acting University Librarian .... Ms. Alison ROLLINS
18 Director of Facilities .... Ms. Florence RICHARDSON
96 Director of Contracting .... Mr. Anthony REVENIS
29 Director Alumni Relations .... Ms. Sharon HOLLAND

United States Air Force Academy (H)

2304 Cadet Drive, Suite 3800,
USAF Academy CO 80840-5002
County: El Paso FICE Identification: 001369
Unit ID: 128328
Telephone: (719) 333-9751 Carnegie Class: Bac-Diverse
FAX Number: (719) 333-3647 Calendar System: Semester
URL: www.usafa.af.mil/
Established: 1954 Annual Undergrad Tuition & Fees: N/A
Enrollment: 4,111 Coed
Affiliation or Control: Federal IRS Status: Exempt
Highest Offering: Baccalaureate
Accreditation: NH, CS, DENT, ENG

01 Superintendent .... LtGen. Jay B. SILVERIA
05 Chief Academic Officer .... BGen. Andrew ARMACOST
08 Head Librarian .... Dr. Edward A. SCOTT
09 Director of Institutional Research .... Col. David P. KUENZLI
10 Chief Business Officer .... Mr. Strain A. STEVEN
100 Chief of Staff .... Ms. Gail B. COLVIN
101 Secretary of the Institution/Board .... Col. Gary A. PACKARD
103 Dir Workforce/Career Development .... Dr. Steven K. JONES
104 Director Study Abroad .... Col. Daniel URIBE
11 Chief of Administration .... CMS. Heather L. MUSE
13 Chief Info Technology Officer (CIO) .... Mr. David J. HLUSKA
15 Director Personnel Services .... Mr. Dale A. HOGUE
18 Chief Facilities/Physical Plant .... Mr. Carlos R. CRUZ-GONZALEZ
19 Director Security/Safety .... LTC. Kenneth M. SHIRLEY
22 Dir Affirmative Action/EEO .... Mr. Dwayne L. DAVIS
26 Chief Public Relations/Marketing .... LTC. Lisa S. NEENER
28 Director of Diversity .... Mr. Moses STEWART
29 Director Alumni Relations .... Mr. Brian A. BINN
30 Chief Development/Advancement .... Mr. Tom R. MABRY
32 Chief Student Affairs/Student Life .... Col. Carrie J. BAUSANO
36 Director Student Placement .... Ms. Patricia L. HAMRICK
37 Director Student Financial Aid .... LTC. Steven A. STRAIN
39 Director Student Housing .... Mr. Dean S. MILLS
41 Athletic Director .... Mr. James A. KNOWLTON
43 Dir Legal Services/General Counsel .... Col. Dawn M. ZOLDI
45 Chief Institutional Planning .... Col. David N. KINCAID
50 Head Dept of Management .... Col. Troy R. HARTING
54 Pgm Head Environmental Engineering .... Col. John A. CHRIST
84 Director Enrollment Management ...... Col. Carolyn A. BENYSHEK
90 Director Academic Computing .... Mr. Eugene K. KAUPPILA
91 Director Administrative Computing .... Dr. Andrew J. LAFFELY
96 Director of Purchasing .... Mr. James A. ANDERSON

United States Army Command and General Staff College (I)

100 Stimson Avenue, Fort Leavenworth KS 66027
County: Leavenworth FICE Identification: 001947
Unit ID: 156055
Telephone: (913) 684-3097 Carnegie Class: Not Classified
FAX Number: (913) 684-2906 Calendar System: Trimester
URL: usacac.army.mil/cac2/cgsc/
Established: 1881 Annual Graduate Tuition & Fees: N/A
Enrollment: N/A Coed
Affiliation or Control: Federal IRS Status: Exempt
Highest Offering: Master's; No Undergraduates

Accreditation: NH

01 Deputy Commandant .... BGen. Scott EFFLANDT
04 Assistant Deputy Commandant ....Col. Tom BOLEN
05 Dean of Academics ....Dr. James MARTIN
100 Chief of Staff ....Mr. Jeffrey P. LA MOE
58 Director Graduate Degree Programs .... Dr. Robert BAUMANN
08 Director of Library ....Mrs. Beata MOORE
32 Director CGSS School ....Col. Robert AULT
06 Registrar ....Dr. Thomas E. CREVISTON
26 Chief Public Relations Officer ....Mr. Harry SARLES

United States Army War College (A)

122 Forbes Avenue, Carlisle PA 17013-5050

County: Cumberland Identification: 666235
Telephone: (717) 245-4711 Carnegie Class: Not Classified
FAX Number: (717) 245-4721 Calendar System: Other
URL: www.carlisle.army.mil
Established: 1901 Annual Graduate Tuition & Fees: N/A
Enrollment: N/A Coed
Affiliation or Control: Federal IRS Status: Exempt
Highest Offering: Master's; No Undergraduates
Accreditation: M

01 Commandant .... MajGen. John KEM
05 Provost ....Dr. Jim BRECKENRIDGE

United States Coast Guard Academy (B)

15 Mohegan Avenue, New London CT 06320-8100

County: New London FICE Identification: 001415
Unit ID: 130624
Telephone: (860) 444-8444 Carnegie Class: Bac-Diverse
FAX Number: (860) 444-8288 Calendar System: Semester
URL: www.cga.edu
Established: 1876 Annual Undergrad Tuition & Fees: N/A
Enrollment: 898 Coed
Affiliation or Control: Federal IRS Status: Exempt
Highest Offering: Baccalaureate
Accreditation: EH, ENG

01 Superintendent ....RADM. James E. RENDON
03 Assistant Superintendent ....CAPT. Ronald A. LABREC
45 Planning Officer .... CDR. Gregory K. SABRA
05 Dean of Academics .... Dr. Kurt J. COLELLA
20 Associate Dean .... CAPT. Gregory HALL
45 Director of Academic Resources ....Dr. Eric J. PAGE
07 Director of Admissions ....CAPT. Robert E. MCKENNA
32 Commandant of Cadets ....CAPT. Melissa L. RIVERA
06 Registrar ....Mr. Donald E. DYKES
08 Librarian .... Ms. Lucia MAZIAR
10 Comptroller ....LCDR. Francisco A. ESTEVEZ
26 Communication Director ....Mr. David M. SANTOS
09 Institutional Research ....Dr. Leonard M. GIAMBRA
13 Head of Information Services .... CDR. Christopher M. ARMSTRONG
16 Personnel Management Specialist ....Ms. Julie A. KELLY
15 Chief Personnel/Administration .... CDR. David BURNS
18 Chief Facilities Engineer ....CDR. Joshua W. FANT
22 Civil Rights Officer ....Mr. Roy P. ZIEGENGEIST
23 Chief Health Services .... CAPT. Humberto HERNANDEZ-APONTE
38 Chief Cadet Counselor ....Dr. Robert MURRAY
40 Bookstore Manager ....Ms. Lauri KERP
41 Director of Athletics .... Mr. Timothy M. FITZPATRICK
42 Command Chaplain ....CAPT. Michael J. PARISI
43 Staff Legal Officer ....CDR. Ben G. KARPINSKI
85 International Cadet Advisor ....Dr. Kassim M. TARHINI
28 Instructor Inclusion and Diversity ....Dr. Aram DEKOVEN

† There is a one-time entrance fee of $3,000 to cover uniform, laptop, and supplies.

United States Merchant Marine Academy (C)

300 Steamboat Road, Kings Point NY 11024-1634

County: Nassau FICE Identification: 002892
Unit ID: 197027
Telephone: (516) 773-5000 Carnegie Class: Bac-Diverse
FAX Number: (516) 773-5582 Calendar System: Trimester
URL: www.usmma.edu
Established: 1943 Annual Undergrad Tuition & Fees: $1,167
Enrollment: 930 Coed
Affiliation or Control: Federal IRS Status: Exempt
Highest Offering: Master's
Accreditation: M, ENG

01 Superintendent ....RADM. James A. HELIS
03 Deputy Superintendent ....RDML. Susan L. DUNLAP
05 Interim Academic Dean ....CAPT. Preston DEJEAN
32 Commandant of Midshipmen ....CAPT. Mikel STROUD
20 Assistant Academic Dean ....Ms. Dianne TAHA
18 Asst Supt for Facilities .... CAPT. Theodore DOGONNIUCK
26 Director Office of External Affairs ....Vacant
07 Director of Admissions .... CDR. Michael BEDRYK
06 Registrar ....Ms. Lisa JERRY
13 Director Computer/Information Mgmt .... Mr. Kevin CLARKE
15 Director Human Resources ....Vacant
10 Chief Financial Officer .... Mr. David SOCOLOF
29 Director Alumni Relations ....Mr. Jim TOBIN

35 Director Student Affairs ....Vacant
36 Dir of Prof Develop/Career Services ....CAPT. Gene ALBERT
37 Director Student Financial Aid ....Mr. Joseph BECKER
96 Director of Purchasing .... Mr. Max DIAH
09 Director of Institutional Research ....Vacant
41 Athletic Director ....Ms. Maureen WHITE
108 Director Institutional Assessment ....Ms. Lori TOWNSEND
43 Dir Legal Services/General Counsel ....Ms. Ilene KREITZER
11 Chief of Administration ....Mr. John DEMERS
19 Director Security/Safety .... Mr. Jeffrey THOMAS
22 Dir Affirmative Action/EEO ....Mr. Marvin WILLIAMS

United States Military Academy (D)

West Point NY 10996-5000

County: Orange FICE Identification: 002893
Unit ID: 197036
Telephone: (845) 938-4041 Carnegie Class: Bac-A&S
FAX Number: (845) 938-3021 Calendar System: Semester
URL: www.westpoint.edu
Established: 1802 Annual Undergrad Tuition & Fees: N/A
Enrollment: 4,348 Coed
Affiliation or Control: Federal IRS Status: Exempt
Highest Offering: Baccalaureate
Accreditation: M, CS, ENG

01 Superintendent/President ....LTG. Robert CASLEN, JR.
05 Dean of Academic Board ....BG. Cindy JEBB
20 Vice Dean ....Dr. Jean BLAIR
32 Commandant of Cadets ....BG. Diana M. HOLLAND
100 Chief of Staff ....COL. Wayne A. GREEN
88 Garrison Commander ....COL. Andrew HANSON
07 Director of Admissions .... COL. Deborah MCDONALD
06 Assoc Dean Operations/Registrar .... Dr. James DALTON
45 Associate Dean for Research ....LTC. John GRAHAM
09 Institutional Research ....LTC. Holly WEST
13 Chief Information Officer ....LTC. Edward TEAGUE
10 Director of Resource Management ....Mr. Leslie BREHM
26 Public Affairs Officer .... LTC. Kasker CHRISTOPHER
08 USMA Library ....Mr. Christopher BARTH
29 President Association of Graduates .... Mr. Todd BROWNE
38 Dir Center for Personal Development ....LTC. Darcy SCHNACK
41 Director Intercollegiate Athletics ....Mr. Boo CORRIGAN
18 Chief Facilities/Physical Plant ....Mr. Matthew TALABER
15 Dir Center for Faculty Excellence .... Dr. Mark EVANS
35 Dir Ctr for Enhanced Performance ....LTC. Darcy SCHNACK
88 Director of Cadet Activities .... COL. Tom HANSBARGER
43 Chief Legal Assistance .... Mr. Micheal BARRETT
28 Director of Diversity ....Dr. Donald OUTING
108 Director Institutional Assessment ....Mr. Gerald KOBYLSKI

United States Naval Academy (E)

121 Blake Road, Annapolis MD 21402-5000

County: Anne Arundel FICE Identification: 030430
Unit ID: 164155
Telephone: (410) 293-1000 Carnegie Class: Bac-A&S
FAX Number: (410) 293-3734 Calendar System: Semester
URL: www.usna.edu
Established: 1845 Annual Undergrad Tuition & Fees: N/A
Enrollment: 4,525 Coed
Affiliation or Control: Federal IRS Status: Exempt
Highest Offering: Baccalaureate
Accreditation: M, CS, ENG

01 Superintendent ....VADM. Walter E. CARTER, JR.
32 Commandant of Midshipmen ....Capt. Robert B. CHADWICK, II
05 Academic Dean & Provost .... Dr. Andrew T. PHILLIPS
20 Vice Academic Dean ....Dr. Boyd A. WAITE
07 Dean of Admissions ....Capt. Bruce J. LATTA
10 Associate Dean for Finances ....Capt. Peter A. NARDI
20 Assoc Dean for Academic Affairs .... Dr. Jennifer WATERS
08 Assoc Dean Information Svcs/Library .... Mr. James RETTIG
21 CFO/Deputy for Finance ....Mr. Joseph RUBINO
100 Chief of Staff ....Capt. George E. LANG, JR.
11 CO Naval Support Activity Annapolis .... Capt. Vince W. BAKER
06 Registrar ....Dr. Christopher A. DAVIS
26 Public Affairs Officer .... CDR. David MCKINNEY
29 Exec Director Alumni Association .... Mr. William OCONNER
21 Comptroller ....CDR. Todd W. HAUGE
13 Chief Information Officer ....CDR. Louis J. GIANNOTTI
88 Director Academic Center .... Dr. Bruce J. BUKOWSKI
09 Director Institutional Research .... Capt. Glenn F. GOTTSCHALK
18 Public Works Officer ....Capt. Nicholas MERRY
41 Athletic Director ....Mr. Chet GLADCHUK
42 Command Chaplain .... Capt. Francis P. FOLEY
30 Director Officer Development ....Capt. Mike MICHEL
15 Director Human Resources ....Mr. William COFFIN
28 Director of Diversity .... Capt. Timika LINDSAY

AMERICAN SAMOA

American Samoa Community College (F)

PO Box 2609, Pago Pago AS 96799-2609

County: American Samoa FICE Identification: 010010
Unit ID: 240736
Telephone: (684) 699-9155 Carnegie Class: Bac/Assoc-Assoc Dom
FAX Number: (684) 699-6259 Calendar System: Semester
URL: www.amsamoa.edu
Established: 1970 Annual Undergrad Tuition & Fees (In-State): $3,550
Enrollment: 1,285 Coed
Affiliation or Control: State IRS Status: 501(c)3
Highest Offering: Baccalaureate
Accreditation: WJ

01 President ....Dr. Rosevonne M. PATO
09 Director of Inst Effectiveness .... Mr. Sonny J. LEOMITI
05 VP of Academic and Student Affairs .... Dr. Lina SCANLAN
88 Director of Samoan Studies Inst ....Mrs. Okenaisa FAUOLO-MANILA
88 Director of Land Grant/ACNR ....Mr. Ropeti ARETA
88 Director of UCEDD ....Ms. Tafaimamao TUPUOLA
51 Director of Adult Education-LEL ....Mr. Tauvela FALE
88 Director of Small Business Devel .... Dr. Herbert THWEATT
11 VP of Administration and Finance .... Dr. Mikaele ETUALE
20 Dean of Academic Affairs ....Mrs. Letupu MOANANU
53 Director of Teacher Education .... Ms. Shirley DE LA ROSA
72 Director of Trades & Technology ....Vacant
108 Director of Curriculum & Assessment ...... Mrs. Evelyn V. FRUEAN
32 Dean of Student Services .... Dr. Emilia LE'I
10 Chief Financial Officer ....Mrs. Emey SILAFAU-TOA
13 Chief Information Officer ....Mr. Donald NELSON
18 Physical Facilities Maint Officer ....Mr. Loligi SEUMANUTAFA
15 Human Resources Officer ....Mrs. Sereima ASIFOA
96 Procurement Officer ....Mrs. Jessie SU'ESU'E
38 Program Director of Counseling ....Ms. Annie PANAMA
08 Program Director of Library Svcs ....Mr. Elvis ZODIACAL
06 Records Officer ....Mrs. Sifagatogo TUITASI
07 Admission Officer ....Mrs. Elizabeth LEUMA
37 Financial Aid Officer .... Mr. Peteru K. LAM YUEN
40 Bookstore Mgr/Dir Research Found .... Mrs. Alofia AFALAVA

FEDERATED STATES OF MICRONESIA

College of Micronesia-FSM (G)

PO Box 159 Kolonia, Pohnpei FM 96941-0159

FICE Identification: 010343
Unit ID: 243638
Telephone: (691) 320-2480 Carnegie Class: Assoc/HT-High Non
FAX Number: (691) 320-2479 Calendar System: Semester
URL: www.comfsm.fm
Established: 1963 Annual Undergrad Tuition & Fees (In-State): $4,750
Enrollment: 2,215 Coed
Affiliation or Control: State IRS Status: 501(c)3
Highest Offering: Associate Degree
Accreditation: WJ

01 President/CEO .... Dr. Joseph M. DAISY
09 Vice Pres for IEQA .... Dr. Frankie HARRISS
05 Vice Pres for Instructional Affairs .... Mrs. Karen SIMION
84 Vice Pres Enroll Mgmt/Student Svcs ....Mr. Joey ODUCADO
11 Vice President Admin Services ....Mr. Joseph HABUCHMAI
56 Director of CRE (Land Grant) ....Mr. Engly IOANIS
12 Dean Chuuk Campus ....Mr. Kind KANTO
12 Dean Kosrae Campus ....Mr. Nena MIKE
12 Dean Yap Campus ....Ms. Lourdes ROBOMAN
10 Comptroller ....Mrs. Roselle TOGONON
12 Director FSM-FMI Campus ....Mr. Matthias EWARMAI
15 Director Human Resources ....Ms. Rencelly NELSON
20 Dean of Academic Programs ....Mrs. Maria DISION
08 Director Learning Resource Center ....Mrs. Jennifer HELIEISAR
75 Dir Career & Technical Education ....Mr. Grilly JACK
18 Director Physical Plant/Maintenance .....Mr. Francisco MENDIOLA
06 Registrar ....Mr. Doman DAOAS
21 Business Officer Manager ....Ms. Ritchie VALENCIA
37 Director of Financial Aid .... Mr. Faustino YAROFAISUG
38 Counselor ....Ms. Penselyn SAM
13 Director Information Technology ....Mr. Gordon SEGAL
39 Director Residential/Campus Life ....Ms. Krystilyn M. ATKINSON
100 Chief of Staff ....Vacant
19 Supervisor Security/Safety ....Mr. Warren CHING
96 Director of Procurement .... Mr. Roberto (Bobby) J. SANTOS
108 Dean of Assessment .... Dr. Richard ANDREWS

GUAM

Guam Community College (H)

PO Box 23069, Barrigada GU 96921-3069

County: Guam FICE Identification: 015361
Unit ID: 240745
Telephone: (671) 735-5531 Carnegie Class: Assoc/MT-VT-Mix Trad/Non
FAX Number: (671) 734-5238 Calendar System: Semester
URL: www.guamcc.edu
Established: 1977 Annual Undergrad Tuition & Fees (In-District): $3,414
Enrollment: 2,334 Coed
Affiliation or Control: State/Local IRS Status: 501(c)3
Highest Offering: Associate Degree
Accreditation: WJ, ACFEI

01 President ....Dr. Mary Y. OKADA
05 Vice President Academic Affairs ....Dr. R. Ray D. SOMERA
10 Vice Pres Finance & Administration .... Ms. Carmen K. SANTOS
21 Controller ....Mr. Edwin E. LIMTUATCO
75 Dean Trades & Professional Services ....Dr. Virginia C. TUDELA
32 Dean Technology & Student Services .... Dr. Michael L. CHAN
26 Asst Dir Communications & Promo ....Ms. Jayne T. FLORES
04 Private Secretary ....Ms. Esther A. MUNA

101 Admin Secretary II BOT-Pres Ofc .... Ms. Bertha M. GUERRERO
07 Coordinator Admissions/Registration .... Mr. Patrick L. CLYMER
45 Asst Dir Planning & Development .... Ms. Doris U. PEREZ
103 Asst Dir Cont Educ & Workforce Dev .... Ms. Rowena Ellen PEREZ
88 Assoc Dean Trade & Prof Svcs .... Ms. Pilar WILLIAMS
88 Assoc Dean Trade & Prof Svcs .... Dr. Elizabeth A. DIEGO
35 Assoc Dean Tech & Student Svcs .... Mr. Ronald G. HARTZ
15 Administrator Human Resources .... Ms. Joann W. MUNA
18 Facilities Engineer Administrator .... Vacant
08 Librarian .... Ms. Christine B. MATSON
20 Admin Ofcr VP's Ofc-Academic Affs .... Ms. Ana Mari C. ATOIGUE
09 Asst Director AIER .... Ms. Marlena O. MONTAGUE
88 Pgm Spc Adult Basic Educ .... Ms. Ava M. GARCIA
88 Pgm Spc CACGP .... Ms. Fermina A. SABLAN
35 Pgm Spc Ctr Student Involvement .... Ms. Barbara B. LEON GUERRERO
23 School Health Counselor .... Ms. Eva Marie L. MUI
88 Program Specialist .... Mr. Wesley T. GIMA
37 Coordinator Student Financial Aid .... Ms. Esther A. RIOS
88 Pgm Spc TRIO Programs .... Dr. Julie ULLOA-HEATH
29 Pgm Specialist Alum & Fundraising .... Ms. Bonnie Mae M. DATUIN
29 Pgm Spc Alum & Fundraising .... Mr. Danilo Philbert BILONG
96 Supply Management Administrator . Ms. Joleen M. EVANGELISTA
13 Data Processing Administrator .... Mr. Francisco C. CAMACHO
51 Pgm Spc Continuing Educ .... Ms. Terry L. BARNHART
51 Pgm Spc Continuing Educ .... Mr. Philip C. GUERRERO
40 Bookstore Manager .... Mr. Daniel T. OKADA
55 Pgm Spc Night Administrator .... Mr. Huan HOSEI
19 Safety Admin Envir Safety Ofcr .... Mr. Gregorio T. MANGLONA
88 Pgm Spc Accomodative Svcs .... Mr. John F. PAYNE
88 Sustainability Coordinator .... Mr. Francisco E. PALACIOS
88 Pgm Spc P&D .... Ms. Priscilla C. JOHNS

Pacific Islands University (A)

172 Kinney's Road, Mangilao GU 96913
County: Guam FICE Identification: 034383
Unit ID: 439862
Telephone: (671) 734-1812 Carnegie Class: Spec-4-yr-Faith
FAX Number: (671) 734-1813 Calendar System: Semester
URL: www.piu.edu
Established: 1976 Annual Undergrad Tuition & Fees: $5,428
Enrollment: 70 Coed
Affiliation or Control: Independent Non-Profit IRS Status: 501(c)3
Highest Offering: Master's
Accreditation: TRACS

88 President/CEO (On Medical Leave) .... Dr. David L. OWEN
01 Interim President .... Mr. Howard MERRELL
10 VP Finance/Administration .... Mr. Nino T. PATE
05 Provost/Academic Vice President .... Vacant
20 Seminary Dean .... Mr. Malcolm James SAWYER
88 Liberal Studies Chair .... Vacant
88 Biblical Studies Chair .... Ms. Iotaka CHORAM
32 Dean of Students .... Ms. Celeste HEIMBACH
21 Operations Director/Bookkeeper .... Ms. Celia ATOIGE
04 Admin Assistant to the President .... Mr. Joshua COMBS
08 Library Director .... Mr. Paul DRAKE
15 Human Resource Director .... Mr. Nino T. PATE
84 Enrollment Mgmt Director/Registrar .... Mr. Urte SCHERER
37 Financial Aid Officer .... Ms. Delight SUDA

University of Guam (B)

UOG Station, Mangilao GU 96923-1800
County: Guam FICE Identification: 003935
Unit ID: 240754
Telephone: (671) 735-2990 Carnegie Class: Masters/M
FAX Number: (671) 734-2296 Calendar System: Semester
URL: www.uog.edu
Established: 1952 Annual Undergrad Tuition & Fees (In-State): $5,578
Enrollment: 3,991 Coed
Affiliation or Control: State IRS Status: 501(c)3
Highest Offering: Master's
Accreditation: WC, CAEPN, IACBE, NUR, SW

01 President .... Dr. Robert A. UNDERWOOD
05 Sr VP Academic & Student Affairs .... Dr. Anita B. ENRIQUEZ
10 Vice Pres Administration & Finance .... Mr. Randall V. WIEGAND
58 AVP Graduate Studies/Research & SP ..... Dr. John A. PETERSON
43 University Legal Counsel .... Ms. Victorina M Y. RENACIA
13 Chief Information Officer .... Mr. Rommel HILDAGO
22 Director EEO & Title IX/ADA .... Mr. Joseph B. GUMATAOTAO
04 Executive Assistant to President .... Ms. Louise M. TOVES
26 Director Integrated Mktg & Comm .... Mr. Jonas D. MACAPINLAC
45 Chief Planning Officer .... Mr. David S. OKADA
30 Director Develop & Alumni Affairs .... Mr. Norman ANALISTA
102 Exec Director Endowment Foundation ...... Ms. Janiece A. SABLAN
108 AVP Institutional Effectiveness .... Ms. Deborah D. LEON GUERRERO
20 AVP Academic Excellence .... Mr. Troy MCVEY
49 Dean Col of Lib Arts & Social Sci .... Dr. James D. SELLMANN
47 Dean Col of Natural & Applied Sci .... Dr. Lee S. YUDIN
50 Dean Sch Business & Pub Admin .... Dr. Annette T. SANTOS
53 Dean School of Education .... Dr. John SANCHEZ
66 Dean of Nursing & Hlth Sci ...... Dr. Margaret HATTORI-UCHIMA
54 Interim Dean School of Engineering .... Dr. Shahram KHOSROWPANAH
84 Actg Dean Enroll Mgmt & Stdnt Svcs ... Ms. Remy B. CRISTOBAL
06 Registrar .... Ms. Remy B. CRISTOBAL
37 Financial Aid Director .... Mr. Mark A. DUARTE
32 Student Life Officer .... Ms. Eden SUAREZ-GALVEZ
88 Director Guam CEDDERS .... Dr. Heidi E. SAN NICOLAS
08 Interim Director Learning Resources .... Dr. Monique STORIE
13 Dir Info Tech Resource/Computer Ctr .... Dr. Luan P. NGUYEN
88 Dir Micronesia Area Res Center .... Dr. Monique C. STORIE
88 Director Marine Laboratory .... Dr. Tom SCHILS
88 Dir Watr Env Rsrch Inst Wstrn Pac .... Dr. John JENSON
88 Dir Ctr for Island Sustainability .... Dr. John A. PETERSON
88 Actg Director Prof/Intl Program .... Mr. Carlos TAITANO
88 Director TRIO Programs .... Mr. Yoichi K. RENGIIL
15 Chief Human Resources Officer .... Mr. Larry GAMBOA
18 Chief Plant Fac Ofcr Fac & Util .... Mr. Sonny P. PEREZ
41 Field House/Athletics Director .... Mr. Doug PALMER
19 Safety Administrator .... Mr. Felix MANSAPIT
40 Director Bookstore & Auxiliary Svcs .... Ms. Ann S A. LEON GUERRERO
21 Comptroller .... Ms. Zeny ASUNCION-NACE
39 Director of Residence Halls .... Mr. Jonathan TRIPLET

MARSHALL ISLANDS

College of the Marshall Islands (C)

PO Box 1258, Majuro MH 96960-1258
County: Marshalls FICE Identification: 030224
Unit ID: 376695
Telephone: (692) 625-3394 Carnegie Class: Assoc/HT-High Trad
FAX Number: (692) 625-7203 Calendar System: Semester
URL: www.cmi.edu
Established: 1989 Annual Undergrad Tuition & Fees (In-State): $4,885
Enrollment: 995 Coed
Affiliation or Control: State IRS Status: 501(c)3
Highest Offering: Associate Degree
Accreditation: WJ

01 President .... Dr. Theresa B. KOROIVULAONO
05 Actg VP Academic & Student Affairs .... Dr. Melinda NISH
11 Vice Pres Business & Administrative .... Mr. Stevenson KOTTON
10 Chief Financial Officer .... Mr. Stevenson KOTTON
20 Dean of Academic Affairs .... Ms. Vasemaca SAVU
32 Dean of Student Services .... Ms. Rachel SALOMON
06 Registrar .... Ms. Monica GORDON
07 Director of Admissions & Records .... Ms. Jomi CAPELLE
08 Acting Director of Library .... Ms. Lisa GERANN
15 Human Resources Director .... Ms. Agnes KOTOISUVA
51 Director Continuing/Adult Education .... Vacant
18 Director Physical Plant .... Mr. Emil DEBRUM
13 Director Information & Technology .... Mr. Bonifacio SANCHEZ
88 Director Nuclear Institute .... Ms. Mary L. SILK
37 Financial Aid Director .... Ms. Jacinta SAMUEL
49 Chair Liberal Arts .... Ms. Elizabeth SWITAJ
50 Chair Business & IT .... Ms. Meitaka KENDALL-DOMNICK
66 Chair Nursing .... Ms. Florence L. PETER
19 Director Security/Safety .... Mr. David DEBRUM
38 Dir Counseling/TRACC .... Vacant
09 Dir Inst Research/Assessment .... Ms. Cherly T. VILA
108 Dir Inst Integrity & Effectiveness .... Vacant

NORTHERN MARIANAS

Northern Marianas College (D)

PO Box 501250, Saipan MP 96950-1250
FICE Identification: 030330
Unit ID: 240790
Telephone: (670) 234-5498 Carnegie Class: Bac/Assoc-Mixed
FAX Number: (670) 234-1270 Calendar System: Semester
URL: www.marianas.edu
Established: 1976 Annual Undergrad Tuition & Fees (In-District): $4,038
Enrollment: 1,155 Coed
Affiliation or Control: State/Local IRS Status: 501(c)3
Highest Offering: Baccalaureate
Accreditation: WC

01 President .... Dr. Carmen FERNANDEZ
05 Dean of Academic Programs & Svcs .. Ms. Barbara K. MERFALEN
32 Dean of Student Services .... Mr. Leo PANGELINAN
10 Chief Financial Officer .... Mr. Andrew REESE
31 Dean of CREES .... Dr. Timothy KOCK
04 Executive Secretary to President .... Ms. Becky SABLAN
13 Acting Dir Information Technology .... Ms. Daisie C. RENGUUL
09 Dir Institutional Effectiveness .... Ms. Jacqueline CHE
08 Director Library Services .... Mr. Perry PANGELINAN
53 Director School of Education .... Ms. Charlotte R. CEPEDA
51 Director of Adult Basic Education .... Ms. Lorraine C. MAUI
38 Acting Director of Counseling Svcs .... Ms. Joan TORRES
37 Director of Financial Aid .... Ms. Daisy MANGLONA-PROPST
96 Procurement Manager .... Ms. Anita C. CAMACHO
15 Human Resources .... Mr. Joaquin KIYOSHI
21 Chief Accountant .... Ms. Solita K. BARNES
36 Career Planning/Placement Coord .... Ms. Neda C. DELEON GUERRERA
18 Acting Facilities Manager .... Mr. Vince MERFALEN
106 Director of Distance Learning .... Mr. William HUNTER
06 Registrar .... Mr. Roger CROFT
101 Executive Secretary to the Board .... Ms. Helen B. CAMACHO
111 Dean of Institutional Advancement .... Mr. Frankie M. ELIPTICO
84 Director Enrollment Services .... Mr. Manny CASTRO

PALAU

Palau Community College (E)

PO Box 9, Koror PW 96940-0009
County: Koror FICE Identification: 011009
Unit ID: 243647
Telephone: (680) 488-2470 Carnegie Class: Assoc/HVT-High Trad
FAX Number: (680) 488-2447 Calendar System: Semester
URL: www.pcc.palau.edu
Established: 1969 Annual Undergrad Tuition & Fees: $3,250
Enrollment: 627 Coed
Affiliation or Control: Federal IRS Status: Exempt
Highest Offering: Associate Degree
Accreditation: WJ

01 President .... Dr. Patrick U. TELLEI
05 Vice President Education & Training .... Vacant
11 Vice Pres Administration & Finance .... Mr. Jay OLEGERIIL
46 Vice Pres Cooperative Rsrch/Exten .... Mr. Thomas TARO
04 Exec Assistant to the President .... Mr. Todd NGIRAMENGIOR
32 Dean of Students .... Mr. Sherman DANIEL
20 Dean of Academic Affairs .... Mr. Robert RAMARUI
51 Dean of Continuing Education .... Vacant
30 Director of Development .... Mr. Tzuchie TADAO
07 Director Student Financial Aid .... Mrs. Dahlia M. KATOSANG
06 Director of Admission and Records .... Ms. Lesley B. ADACHI
15 Director of Human Resources .... Vacant
18 Director of Physical Plant .... Mr. Clement KAZUMA
13 Director of Computer Systems .... Mr. Bruce RIMIRCH
35 Director of Student Life .... Ms. Hilda REKLAI
10 Director of Finance .... Ms. Uroi N. SALII
91 System Analyst .... Ms. Grace ALEXANDER
88 Accreditation Liaison Officer .... Ms. Deikola OLIKONG
08 Interim Director Library Services .... Ms. Pioria ASITO
09 Director of Institutional Research .... Ms. Deikola OLIKONG

PUERTO RICO

American University of Puerto Rico (F)

Box 2037, Bayamon PR 00960-2037
County: Bayamon FICE Identification: 011941
Unit ID: 241100
Telephone: (787) 620-2040 Carnegie Class: Masters/S
FAX Number: (787) 785-7377 Calendar System: Other
URL: www.aupr.edu
Established: 1963 Annual Undergrad Tuition & Fees: $5,811
Enrollment: 719 Coed
Affiliation or Control: Independent Non-Profit IRS Status: 501(c)3
Highest Offering: Master's
Accreditation: M

01 President .... Mr. Juan C. NAZARIO TORRES
03 Executive Vice President .... Mr. Jaime GONZALEZ
05 Vice President Acad/Student Affairs .... Dr. Jose RAMIREZ-FIGUEROA
10 Vice Pres Finance & Admin Affairs .... Mrs. Magda A. CANCEL-PEREZ
32 Dean Student Affairs .... Prof. Claribel RODRIGUEZ-VARGAS
06 Registrar .... Prof. Maria RODRIGUEZ-PAZ
07 Admissions Officer .... Ms. Keren LLANOS
08 Learning Resources Center Director .... Vacant
37 Director Financial Aid .... Mrs. Yahaira MELENDEZ
21 Director Accounting .... Mrs. Jeanette AVILES-FERRAN
38 Director Guidance Counseling .... Mrs. Luz S. HERNANDEZ
24 Director Educational Media .... Ms. Carol SANTIAGO
41 Athletic Director .... Mr. Manfredo VEGA
15 Director Personnel Services .... Mrs. Ginette OPPENHEIMER
12 Director Manati Campus .... Prof. Milagros RIVERA-OTERO
09 Dir Research/Institutional Planning .... Vacant
18 Chief Facilities/Physical Plant .... Mr. Efrain LUGO
36 Director of Student Placement .... Vacant
96 Director of Purchasing .... Mrs. Celeste TRAVERSO
92 Director of Honors Program .... Prof. Claribel RODRIGUEZ
30 Chief Development .... Mr. Jaime GONZALEZ
20 Associate Academic Officer .... Prof. Zahira GARCIA
13 Director Computer Center .... Mr. Julio VEGA
53 Dept Chair School of Education .... Dr. Jose RAMIREZ
50 Dept Chair Business Admin/Sec Sci .... Vacant
49 Department Chair Arts & Sciences .... Vacant
100 Chief of Staff .... Ms. Rosabel VAZQUEZ
102 Dir Foundation/Corporate Relations .... Dr. Adela VAZQUEZ
105 Director Web Services .... Vacant
19 Director Security/Safety .... Ms. Rosabel VAZQUEZ
45 Chief Institutional Planning .... Prof. Bolivar RAMIREZ-CARLO, III
04 Administrative Asst to President .... Mrs. Carmen ARROYO

Atenas College (G)

Paseo de las Atenas #101, Manati PR 00674
FICE Identification: 035443
Unit ID: 440651
Telephone: (787) 884-3838 Carnegie Class: Spec-4-yr-Other Health
FAX Number: (787) 854-4530 Calendar System: Semester
URL: www.atenascollege.edu
Established: 1996 Annual Undergrad Tuition & Fees: $6,945
Enrollment: 1,337 Coed
Affiliation or Control: Independent Non-Profit IRS Status: 501(c)3
Highest Offering: Baccalaureate

Accreditation: ⓂM, ACCSC, ⓅPTAA

01 President Dra. María L. HERNÁNDEZ NÚÑEZ
05 Vice President Academic Affairs Prof. Widalys GONZÁLEZ
10 VP Finance & Administrative Affairs Mrs. Astrid Y. MELÉNDEZ HERNÁNDEZ
84 VP of Recruitment & Communications Mrs. Yaniri S. MOLINA
13 VP Tech Infrastructure & Innovation Dr. José E. VALENTÍN
32 Vice President of Student Affairs Mrs. María C. MEDINA
45 VP Planning & Inst Development Mrs. Ingrid Y. COLÓN
20 Associate Dean of Academic Affairs Dra. Cenia K. ROMANO
20 Associate Dean Academic Affairs Prof. Rosa M. MORALES
88 Associate Dean Acad & Adm Affairs Mrs. Luz C. REYES
88 Dir Learning Res Ctr Tech & DE Mrs. Annette DAVILA
36 Director Student Placement Mrs. Sally SANTA
15 Human Resources and Security Dir Mrs. Aurea FIGUEROA
18 Operation Manager Mr. Carlos R. VÁZQUEZ
21 Accounting Director Mrs. Zulay SOTO
37 Financial Aid Administrator Mr. Manuel RAMÍREZ
06 Registrar Mrs. Walitza HERNÁNDEZ
38 Guidance and Counseling Mrs. Keila OJEDA FERNÁNDEZ
08 Librarian Mrs. Sonia N. FERRER MEDINA
88 Coordinator Simulation Center Prof. Diana N. RAMOS MARTÍNEZ
04 Admn Svcs Coordinator Mrs. Diana RODRÍGUEZ ALVARADO
07 Coordinator of Recruitment & Comm Mr. Ovidio SOTO

Atlantic University College (A)

PO Box 3918, Guaynabo PR 00970

County: Guaynabo | FICE Identification: 025054 | Unit ID: 241216
Telephone: (787) 720-1022 | Carnegie Class: Spec-4-yr-Other Tech
FAX Number: (787) 720-1092 | Calendar System: Quarter
URL: www.atlanticu.edu
Established: 1983 | Annual Undergrad Tuition & Fees: $7,425
Enrollment: 1,548 | Coed
Affiliation or Control: Independent Non-Profit | IRS Status: 501(c)3
Highest Offering: Baccalaureate
Accreditation: ACICS

01 President Dr. Teresa DE DIOS UNANUE
13 Exec Vice Pres/Dean Technology/Mktg Prof. Heri MARTINEZ DE DIOS
05 Academic Dean Prof. Ivette CARBONELL
10 Dean of Administration Prof. Heriberto MARTINEZ-ABREU
88 Dean of Digital Arts/Sciences Prof. Frances GRAU
06 Registrar Ms. Edna I. GUTIERREZ
38 Dir Student Counseling/Placement Prof. Maria C. LOPEZ-CEPERO RAMOS
37 Director Financial Aid Mrs. Janice RIVERA
08 Head Librarian Mrs. Tania DÍAZ
07 Director of Admissions Mr. Joel MONTERO
21 Director Business Office Mrs. María del C MONTESINO
15 Officer of Human Resources Ms. Viviana SANTIAGO

Caribbean University (B)

Box 493, Bayamon PR 00960-0493

County: Bayamon | FICE Identification: 012525 | Unit ID: 241377
Telephone: (787) 780-0070 | Carnegie Class: Masters/S
FAX Number: (787) 785-0101 | Calendar System: Semester
URL: www.caribbean.edu
Established: 1969 | Annual Undergrad Tuition & Fees: $5,182
Enrollment: 1,914 | Coed
Affiliation or Control: Independent Non-Profit | IRS Status: 501(c)3
Highest Offering: Doctorate
Accreditation: M, ENG

01 President/CEO Dr. Ana E. CUCURELLA-ADORNO
03 Executive Director Mr. Victor T. ADORNO
05 Vice President of Academic Affairs Dr. Luis J. DELGADO
45 Vice President of Planning and Info Mr. Jorge RIEFKOHL
11 Dean Administration Affairs Mr. Israel RODRIGUEZ
32 Dean of Student Affairs Mr. Luis J. DELGADO
13 IT Interim Director Mr. Luis N. PRATTS
15 Human Resources Director Mrs. Teresita RIVERA
37 Director Student Financial Aid Mr. Javier VAZQUEZ
06 Registrar Ms. Maranjani BORRERO
08 Librarian/Director Audio-Visual Mrs. Carmen L. APONTE
07 Director of Admissions Mrs. Rosalie MORALES
12 Director of Carolina Campus Prof. Jose CUETO
12 Director of Ponce Campus Prof. Sonia PACHECO
12 Director Vega Baja Campus Vacant
20 Provost Ms. Lillian MATOS
71 Director Special Service Program Mrs. Maryliz AUBRET
26 Public Relations Director Dr. Enrique ROSARIO
58 Assoc Dean of Graduate Programs Dr. Luis MEJIAS
49 Director Department Arts/Science Prof. William PEREZ
50 Director Dept Business Admin/Sec Sc Mr. Jose M. CUETO
76 Health Services Ms. Mara MEDINA
54 Director Department of Engineering Dr. Hermes CALDERON
66 Director Department of Nursing Dr. Mildred FLORES
53 Director Department Education Dr. Edgardo REYES
77 Director of Computer Science Dr. Augusto CARVAJAL
18 Chief Facilities/Physical Plant Mr. Henry SEVILLA
43 Legal Advisor Mr. Rafael SANTIAGO
38 Director Counseling Center (CIOSE) Dr. David BAEZ MOJICA
41 Athletic Director Mr. Rafael MARRERO PEREZ
22 Director of Compliance Mrs. Elena GARCIA
84 Director Enrollment Management Vacant
09 Director of Institutional Research Dr. Luz D. SERRANO
96 Director of Purchasing Mrs. Carmen J. ROSA

Carlos Albizu University (C)

Box 9023711, San Juan PR 00902-3711

County: San Juan | FICE Identification: 010724 | Unit ID: 241331
Telephone: (787) 725-6500 | Carnegie Class: Spec-4-yr-Other Health
FAX Number: (787) 721-7187 | Calendar System: Semester
URL: www.albizu.edu
Established: 1966 | Annual Undergrad Tuition & Fees: $7,221
Enrollment: 1,367 | Coed
Affiliation or Control: Independent Non-Profit | IRS Status: 501(c)3
Highest Offering: Doctorate
Accreditation: M, CLPSY, IPSY, SP

00 Chair Board of Trustees Mr. Jaime L. ALBORS BIGAS
01 Interim President Dr. Sylvia LOPEZ-JORGE
12 Chancellor of San Juan Campus Dr. Jose J. CABIYA-MORALES
12 Int Chancellor of Miami Campus Dr. Irene BRAVO
07 Director Admissions/Student Affs Mr. Carlos RODRIGUEZ
11 Spec Asst to Chanc for Admin Affs Mr. Luis ECHEGARAY
05 Interim Provost Dr. Daniel MARTINEZ ORTIZ
88 Special Assistant to Vice President Ms. Sylvia LOPEZ
32 Dean of Student Services Ms. Carmen RIVERA
10 Director of Finance Mr. Hector PENA
46 Director Research Training Dr. Lymaries PADILLA-COTTO
88 Director General Psychology Program Dr. Jaime VERAY
51 Director Continuing Education Ms. Isabel HERNANDEZ
88 Director Internship Dr. Aida GARCIA
37 Director Financial Aid Mrs. Doris QUERO-MENDEZ
08 Director Library Ms. Yolanda ROSARIO-ROSARIO
06 Registrar Mr. Nieves RIVERA
88 Dir Industrial/Org Psych Program Dr. Miguel MARTINEZ-LUGO
13 Dir Information Technology Svcs Mr. Luis CAMACHO
88 Administrator Community Svcs Clinic Mr. Rafael ORTIZ
31 Director Community Services Clinic Dr. Jose RODRIGUEZ-QUINONES
88 Dir PhD Clinical Psychology Program Dr. Jose CABIYA
88 Dir PsyD Clinical Psychology Pgm Dr. Julio SANTANA MARINO
15 Exec Director of Human Resources Ms. Angela RAMOS
30 Director Development Vacant
88 Director Clinical Training Dr. Noel QUINTERO-JIMENEZ
88 Director Bachelor's Program Dr. Jaime VERAY
38 President Student Counseling Mr. Ricardo DEL RIO-MORALES
11 Director Administration Mr. John FERNANDEZ
26 Director Communication Ms. Norma BORGES
29 Director Alumni Relations Ms. Angeles PEREZ
09 Dir Inst Research/Assessment Mr. Rafael MELENDEZ

CEM College (D)

Calle Degetau #25, Bayamon PR 00961

Telephone: (787) 780-8900 | Identification: 770590
Accreditation: ACCSC

CEM College (E)

Calle Dr. Vidal #8 y #53, Humacao PR 00791

Telephone: (787) 852-5505 | Identification: 770589
Accreditation: ACCSC

CEM College (F)

Calle Cristy #56, Mayaguez PR 00680

Telephone: (787) 986-7440 | Identification: 770591
Accreditation: ACCSC

CEM College (G)

Calle 13 #1206, Ext San Agustin, Rio Piedras PR 00926

County: San Juan | FICE Identification: 021891 | Unit ID: 241517
Telephone: (787) 765-4210 | Carnegie Class: Spec-4-yr-Other Health
FAX Number: (787) 765-4277 | Calendar System: Semester
URL: www.cempr.edu
Established: 1980 | Annual Undergrad Tuition & Fees: $7,195
Enrollment: 803 | Coed
Affiliation or Control: Independent Non-Profit | IRS Status: 501(c)3
Highest Offering: Baccalaureate
Accreditation: ACCSC

01 President Mr. Juan C. PAGANI-SOTO
05 Academic Dean Dr. Nereida MORA
10 Dean of Administration/Finance Dr. Carlos RODRIGUEZ
06 Registrar Mrs. Margarita RIVERA
21 Finance Director Mr. Carlos RODRIGUEZ
12 Branch Director Mrs. Brenda COLON
15 Human Resources Director Mrs. Lilliana M. LOPEZ-MEDERO

Center for Advanced Studies On Puerto Rico and the Caribbean (H)

PO Box 902-3970, Old San Juan PR 00902-3970

County: San Juan | FICE Identification: 021660 | Unit ID: 241793
Telephone: (787) 723-4481 | Carnegie Class: Spec-4-yr-Other
FAX Number: (787) 723-1023 | Calendar System: Semester
URL: www.ceaprc.edu
Established: 1976 | Annual Graduate Tuition & Fees: N/A
Enrollment: 484 | Coed
Affiliation or Control: Independent Non-Profit | IRS Status: 501(c)3
Highest Offering: Doctorate; No Undergraduates
Accreditation: M

01 Chancellor Mr. Miguel A. RODRIGUEZ-LOPEZ
05 Academic Dean Dr. Jaime L. RODRIGUEZ-CANCEL
06 Registrar Mrs. Mayra I. RAMIREZ
08 Head Librarian Mr. Francis J. MOJICA
11 Administration Dean Mrs. Lizzette CARRILLO
32 Students Affairs Dean Ms. Clarissa SANTIAGO-TORO
26 Marketing Director Mrs. Monica D. GONZALEZ
37 Financial Aid Officer Mrs. Lillian M. OLIVER
07 Admissions Director Mr. Jose F. PEREZ-RODRIGUEZ

Colegio de Cinematografia, Artes y Television (I)

51 Dr. Veve St, Degetau St Corner, Bayamon PR 00961

County: Bayamon | FICE Identification: 031576 | Unit ID: 430935
Telephone: (787) 779-2500 | Carnegie Class: Assoc/MT-VT-High Trad
FAX Number: (787) 995-2525 | Calendar System: Semester
URL: www.ccatpr.com/nosotros/
Established: 1993 | Annual Undergrad Tuition & Fees: $6,560
Enrollment: 1,049 | Coed
Affiliation or Control: Proprietary | IRS Status: Proprietary
Highest Offering: Associate Degree
Accreditation: ACCSC

01 President Ms. Carola GARCIA

Colegio Universitario de San Juan (J)

180 Jose R. Oliver Street, San Juan PR 00918

County: San Juan | FICE Identification: 010567 | Unit ID: 241720
Telephone: (787) 480-2400 | Carnegie Class: Bac-Diverse
FAX Number: (787) 250-7395 | Calendar System: Semester
URL: www.cunisanjuan.edu
Established: 1972 | Annual Undergrad Tuition & Fees (In-District): $2,370
Enrollment: 1,430 | Coed
Affiliation or Control: Local | IRS Status: 501(c)3
Highest Offering: Baccalaureate
Accreditation: M, ADNUR

01 Interim Chancellor Dr. Phaedra GELPI-RODRIGUEZ
45 Dir Planning/Inst Research/Ext Rels Dr. Haydee M. ZAYAS-HERNANDEZ
05 Interim Dean Academic Affairs Prof. Yanid RIVERA-MERCADO
32 Dean Student Affairs Dr. Melvin VEGA-GONZALEZ
11 Dean Administrative Affairs Prof. Gilberto OLIVO-CRUZ
51 Dir Continuing Educ/Extension Pgm Mrs. Annelis RIVERA-MARQUEZ
37 Manager Student Financial Aid Mrs. Kennia I. SANTOS-PEREZ
08 Head Librarian Mrs. Sheila VERA-MORALES
06 Registrar Mrs. Evelyn GUZMAN-LOPEZ
38 Counselor Mrs. Mara MALAVE-LASSO
36 Placement Officer Prof. Waleska Y. ROSA-NUNEZ
13 Administrator Info Systems/Telecomm Mr. Zacarias POUERIET-DE LA CRUZ
72 Director Science & Technology Dept Prof. Marcus DROZ-RAMOS
76 Dir Health Related Science Dept Prof. Elizabeth ROSARIO-RODRIGUEZ
50 Dir Business Administration Dept Prof. Nilda E. RODRIGUEZ-MOLINA
97 Manager General Education Dept Prof. Carmen J. RODRIGUEZ-VINCENTY
88 Dir Behavioral Related Profess Dept Prof. Maria T. PEREZ-CASANOVA

Columbia Central University (K)

PO Box 8517, Caguas PR 00726-8517

County: Caguas | FICE Identification: 008902 | Unit ID: 241304
Telephone: (787) 743-4041 | Carnegie Class: Spec-4-yr-Other Health
FAX Number: (787) 746-5616 | Calendar System: Semester
URL: www.columbiaco.edu
Established: 1966 | Annual Undergrad Tuition & Fees: $6,520
Enrollment: 1,632 | Coed
Affiliation or Control: Proprietary | IRS Status: Proprietary
Highest Offering: Master's
Accreditation: M

01 President Mrs. Daritza MULERO
05 VP Academic Affairs Mrs. Carmen J. LOPEZ
03 Senior VP of Operations Mrs. Carmen M. RIVERA
10 VP Finance and Administration Mrs. Yesenia CARRION
32 VP Student Affairs Mrs. Brendaliz ZAYAS
26 VP Marketing and Communication Mr. Angel QUIÑONES
12 Chancellor of Caguas Campus Mrs. Gladys SERRANO
12 Chancellor of Yauco Branch Ms. Jannette MENDEZ
20 Dean Academic Affairs Mr. Luis LOPEZ
08 Institutional Librarian Ms. Luz NEGRON
11 Administrative Support Director Ms. Carmen I. ROJAS
37 Financial Aid Director Ms. Gloria MIRABAL
06 Registrar Ms. Wilmarie TORRES
38 Student Counselor Ms. Ingrid CARRION
15 Director Human Resources Ms. Elsie M. TORRES
36 Director Student Placement Ms. Iris TIZOL
18 Facilities & Development Director Mr. Jesus M. RIVERA

Columbia Centro Universitario (A)
Box 3062, Yauco PR 00698-3062
Telephone: (787) 856-0945 Identification: 666036
Accreditation: &M

† Regional accreditation is carried under the parent institution in Caguas, PR.

Conservatory of Music of Puerto Rico (B)
951 Ponce de Leon Ave. Miramar, Santurce PR 00907
County: San Juan FICE Identification: 010819
Unit ID: 241766
Telephone: (787) 751-0160 Carnegie Class: Spec-4-yr-Arts
FAX Number: (787) 766-1216 Calendar System: Semester
URL: www.cmpr.edu
Established: 1959 Annual Undergrad Tuition & Fees (In-State): $3,370
Enrollment: 469 Coed
Affiliation or Control: State IRS Status: 501(c)3
Highest Offering: Master's
Accreditation: M

01 Chancellor .... Mr. Luis HERNANDEZ
05 Dean of Academic Affairs .... Mr. Ariel GUZMAN
10 Int Dean of Finance/Administration .... Ms. Gloryber LABOY
32 Dean Financial Aid .... Mr. Luis R. DIAZ
88 Director of Preparatory School .... Mr. Orlando MALDONADO
07 Admission Coordinator .... Mrs. Ana M. ARRAIZA
08 Librarian .... Mrs. Maria del Carmen MALDONADO
30 Development & Public Relations Dir .... Vacant
15 Human Resources Director .... Ms. Alba DAVILA
38 Counselor .... Ms. Mayra I. SIERRA
06 Registrar .... Mrs. Ilsamar HERNANDEZ
09 Director of Institutional Research .... Mrs. Eutimia SANTIAGO
18 Chief Facilities/Physical Plant .... Mr. Jose MATOS

Dewey University (C)
PO Box 19538, San Juan PR 00910-1538
County: San Juan FICE Identification: 031121
Unit ID: 431309
Telephone: (787) 753-0039 Carnegie Class: Not Classified
FAX Number: (787) 764-6303 Calendar System: Trimester
URL: www.dewey.edu
Established: 1992 Annual Undergrad Tuition & Fees: $7,495
Enrollment: 20 Coed
Affiliation or Control: Independent Non-Profit IRS Status: 501(c)3
Highest Offering: Baccalaureate
Accreditation: ACICS

01 President/CEO .... Mr. Carlos A. QUINONES
03 Executive Vice President .... Ms. Yelitza FELICIANO
10 Director of Finance .... Mr. Jaime MARTIR

Dewey University-Bayamon (D)
Road 2 Corujo Industrial Park, Bayamon PR 00959
Telephone: (787) 778-1200 Identification: 770777
Accreditation: ACICS

Dewey University-Carolina (E)
Road 3 Compound 11, Lot 7, Carolina PR 00986
Telephone: (787) 769-1515 Identification: 770776
Accreditation: ACICS

Dewey University-Fajardo (F)
267 General Valero Street, Fajardo PR 00738
Telephone: (787) 860-1212 Identification: 770775
Accreditation: ACICS

Dewey University-Juana Diaz (G)
Rd 149, KM 55.9 Lomas Industrial PK,
Juana Diaz PR 00795
Telephone: (787) 260-1023 Identification: 770774
Accreditation: ACICS

Dewey University-Manati (H)
Rd 604,KM 49.1,Tierra Nueva Salient, Manati PR 00674
Telephone: (789) 854-3800 Identification: 770807
Accreditation: ACICS

Dominican Study Center of the Caribbean (I)
PO Box 1968, Bayamon PR 00960-1968
County: Bayamon Identification: 666337
Telephone: (787) 786-4508 Carnegie Class: Not Classified
FAX Number: (787) 798-2712 Calendar System: Semester
URL: www.cedoc.edu
Established: 1980 Annual Undergrad Tuition & Fees: N/A
Enrollment: N/A Coed
Affiliation or Control: Independent Non-Profit IRS Status: 501(c)3
Highest Offering: Master's
Accreditation: THEOL

01 Dean .... Rev Dr. Yamil A. SAMALOT-RIVERA, OP

EDIC College (J)
PO Box 9120, Caguas PR 00726-9120
County: Caguas FICE Identification: 030219
Unit ID: 376321
Telephone: (787) 704-1020 Carnegie Class: Assoc/HVT-High Non
FAX Number: (787) 746-0048 Calendar System: Semester
URL: ediccollege.edu
Established: 1987 Annual Undergrad Tuition & Fees: $6,700
Enrollment: 1,245 Coed
Affiliation or Control: Proprietary IRS Status: Proprietary
Highest Offering: Associate Degree
Accreditation: ACICS

01 President/CEO .... Mr. Jose A. CORDOVA
11 Administrator .... Mrs. Milagros CARTAGENA
108 Licensing & Accreditation Director .... Mrs. Loida R. RAMIREZ
12 Director of Branch Campus .... Mr. Reinaldo GONZALEZ
12 Director of Branch Campus .... Mr. Ricardo FLORES
05 Chief Academic Officer .... Mrs. Betsy VIDAL
10 Comptroller .... Mr. Francis HILARIO

EDP University of Puerto Rico (K)
PO Box 192303, San Juan PR 00919-2303
County: San Juan FICE Identification: 021651
Unit ID: 243832
Telephone: (787) 765-3560 Carnegie Class: Bac-Diverse
FAX Number: (787) 777-0025 Calendar System: Semester
URL: www.edpuniversity.edu
Established: 1968 Annual Undergrad Tuition & Fees: $5,940
Enrollment: 1,716 Coed
Affiliation or Control: Independent Non-Profit IRS Status: 501(c)3
Highest Offering: Master's
Accreditation: M, ADNUR

01 President .... Mrs. Gladys T. NIEVES
03 Executive Vice President .... Dr. Marilyn PASTRANA
05 Academic Dean .... Mrs. Yadirah SOTO
10 Vice President Finance .... Mr. Luis RIVERA
26 VP Institutional/International Rels .... Dr. Marilyn PASTRANA
108 AVP Accreditation & Inst Assessment .... Dr. Alberto LOPEZ
13 AVP Administration and Technology .... Eng. Luis FUSTER
85 AVP International Affairs/Dist Educ .... Ms. Sandra ARROYO
21 AVP Financial Affairs .... Mrs. Marie Luz PASTRANA
108 AVP Assessment .... Mrs. Nydia RIVERA
14 Inst Information Systems Dean .... Dr. Ramon MALLOL
06 Registrar .... Mrs. Marian DEJESUS
08 Librarian .... Mrs. Igrí ENRIQUEZ
32 Student Services Dean .... Mr. Oscar MORALES
37 Director of Financial Aid .... Mr. Yaitzaenid GONZALEZ
07 Director of Admissions .... Mrs. Dendy VILA
15 Director Human Resources .... Mr. Hector VAZQUEZ

EDP University of Puerto Rico (L)
PO Box 1674, 49 Betances Street,
San Sebastian PR 00685-1674
Telephone: (787) 896-2137 Identification: 666488
Accreditation: &M, ADNUR

† Regional accreditation is carried under the parent institution in San Juan, PR.

Escuela de Artes Plasticas de Puerto Rico (M)
PO Box 9021112, San Juan PR 00902-1112
County: San Juan FICE Identification: 025694
Unit ID: 241951
Telephone: (787) 725-8120 Carnegie Class: Spec-4-yr-Arts
FAX Number: N/A Calendar System: Semester
URL: www.eap.edu
Established: 1966 Annual Undergrad Tuition & Fees (In-State): $3,462
Enrollment: 573 Coed
Affiliation or Control: State IRS Status: 501(c)3
Highest Offering: Baccalaureate
Accreditation: M, ART

01 Interim Chancellor .... Mr. Carlos E. RIVERA PEREZ
11 Int Dean of Administration .... Ms. Limaris SOTO AQUINO
05 Dean Academic Affairs .... Prof. Teresa LOPEZ
06 Registrar .... Ms. Ileana MALDONADO
07 Officer of Admissions .... Ms. Nitza MELENDEZ
13 Chief Information Technology .... Ms. Limaris SOTO AQUINO
37 Director Student Financial Aid .... Mr. Alfred DIAZ
45 Director of Planning & Budget .... Mr. Carlos E. RIVERA
09 Institutional Research .... Dr. Shirley A. TAVARES
10 Chief Financial Officer .... Ms. Mayra E. DIAZ
18 Coord Facilities/Physical Plant .... Mr. Edwin ALICEA
56 Coordinator Extension Program .... Vacant
38 Counselor Stdnt Life/Counseling .... Ms. Susanne GOTAY
88 Coordinator Cultural Activities ... Mr. Adrian O. RIVERA NEGRON
105 Director Web Services .... Mr. Celso E. PORTELA IRIGOYEN
08 Library Director .... Ms. Estrella VAZQUEZ
20 Int Asst Dean Acad/Student Affairs .... Ms. Ivette MUNOZ
15 Director Human Resources .... Ms. Ivette RODRIGUEZ
57 Director Art Education .... Prof. Maria VAZQUEZ
97 Director General Studies .... Dr. Maria VAZQUEZ
88 Director Fashion Design .... Prof. Ana COLORADO
88 Director Industrial Design .... Prof. Vladimir GARCIA
88 Director Digital Art & Design .... Prof. Guillermo VAZQUEZ
88 Director Painting .... Prof. Cacheila SOTO
88 Director Sculpture .... Prof. Linda SANCHEZ PINTOR
88 Director Printmaking .... Prof. Haydee LANDING

Evangelical Seminary of Puerto Rico (N)
Ponce De Leon Avenue 776, San Juan PR 00925-9907
County: San Juan FICE Identification: 006823
Unit ID: 243498
Telephone: (787) 763-6700 Carnegie Class: Spec-4-yr-Faith
FAX Number: (787) 751-0847 Calendar System: Semester
URL: www.se-pr.edu
Established: 1919 Annual Undergrad Tuition & Fees: N/A
Enrollment: 224 Coed
Affiliation or Control: Interdenominational IRS Status: 501(c)3
Highest Offering: Doctorate
Accreditation: M, THEOL

01 President .... Dra. Doris GARCIA RIVERA
05 Academic Dean/Chaplain .... Dr. Francisco J. GOITIA PADILLA
10 Director Administration & Finances .. Ms. Myrna E. PEREZ-LOPEZ
06 Registrar .... Mrs. Keina TRONCOSO FERNANDEZ
08 Head Librarian .... Mrs. Milka VIGO VERESTÍN
30 Official of Development/Planning .... Ms. Ruth M. DIAZ SEMPRIT
37 Student Financial Aid .... Ms. Lourdes JESUS CESAREO
04 Administrative Asst to President .... Mrs. Ruth M. DIAZ SEMPRIT
13 Chief Info Technology Officer ... Mr. Jesus RODRIGUEZ-CORTES
108 Director Institutional Assessment .... Dr. Juan R. MEJIAS

Huertas College (O)
PO Box 8429, Caguas PR 00726-8429
County: Caguas FICE Identification: 022608
Unit ID: 242112
Telephone: (787) 746-1400 Carnegie Class: Assoc/HVT-High Non
FAX Number: (787) 747-0170 Calendar System: Semester
URL: www.huertas.edu
Established: 1945 Annual Undergrad Tuition & Fees: $6,635
Enrollment: 1,278 Coed
Affiliation or Control: Proprietary IRS Status: Proprietary
Highest Offering: Baccalaureate
Accreditation: M, CAHIIM, PTAA

01 President .... Mr. Ruben LOPEZ-HUERTAS
03 Exec Vice President and Compliance .... Raul HERNANDEZ-RODRIGUEZ
05 Vice Pres Academic/Student Affairs ... Amarillys GARCIA-ACOSTA
30 VP Planning and Development .... Ruth BONILLA
15 VP of Human Resources .... Leslie Ann GUZMAN
32 Associate VP of Student Success .... Maribel CONTRERAS
06 Registrar .... Krishna MARQUEZ
08 Head Librarian .... Maribel CONTRERAS
38 Director Student Counseling .... Evelyn COTTO
10 Director of Revenue .... Eva VEGA
22 Compliance Officer .... Vacant
04 Administrative Asst to President .... Iris COLON
07 Director of Admissions .... Hector MORALES
18 Chief Facilities/Physical Plant .... Ruben LOPEZ
26 Chief Public Relations/Marketing .... Amarilis LOPEZ
36 Director Student Placement .... Veronica RUIZ

Humacao Community College (P)
PO Box 9139, Humacao PR 00792-9139
County: Humacao FICE Identification: 023406
Unit ID: 242121
Telephone: (787) 852-1430 Carnegie Class: Bac/Assoc-Mixed
FAX Number: (787) 850-1577 Calendar System: Trimester
URL: www.hccpr.edu
Established: 1978 Annual Undergrad Tuition & Fees: $5,002
Enrollment: 554 Coed
Affiliation or Control: Independent Non-Profit IRS Status: 501(c)3
Highest Offering: Baccalaureate
Accreditation: ACICS

01 President .... Lic. Jorge E. MOJICA
03 Executive Vice President .... Prof. Aida E. RODRIGUEZ
05 Exec Director/Chief Academic Ofcr .... Dr. Brenda L. MORALES
55 Director of Evening Session .... Prof. Ada BAEZ
88 Title V Project Director .... Mrs. Omayra RODRÍGUEZ
81 STEM Projec Director .... Mr. Jaime RIVERA
37 Director Student Financial Aid .... Mrs. Cheryle PEREZ
36 Student Placement Officer .... Mrs. Juana ROSA
36 Student Placement Officer .... Miss Nilkaliz DEL VALLE
07 Director Admissions .... Mrs. Adela APONTE
06 Registrar .... Mrs. Nildalee MELENDEZ
08 Head Librarian .... Mrs. Lourdes ELIZA
10 Treasury Officer (Finance) .... Vacant
38 Student Counselor .... Mrs. Maria RODRIGUEZ
11 Chief College Administrator .... Mrs. Marianne BERRIOS
04 Admin Asst to Pres/Dir Personnel .... Mrs. Nilda E. RODRIGUEZ

ICPR Junior College (Q)
558 Munoz Rivera Avenue, Hato Rey PR 00919-0304
County: San Juan FICE Identification: 011940
Unit ID: 243841
Telephone: (787) 753-6000 Carnegie Class: Assoc/HVT-Mix Trad/Non
FAX Number: (787) 622-3416 Calendar System: Semester
URL: www.icprjc.edu
Established: 1946 Annual Undergrad Tuition & Fees: $6,540

Enrollment: 633 Coed
Affiliation or Control: Proprietary IRS Status: Proprietary
Highest Offering: Associate Degree
Accreditation: M

01 President/Chief Executive Officer .... Dr. Olga RIVERA
12 Hato Rey Campus Director .... Mrs. Maria de los M. RIVERA
05 Academic Affairs Dean .... Mrs. Elsa RODRIGUEZ
07 Dir Admissions/Marketing Hato Rey .... Mrs. Ana IGUINA
07 Dir Admissions/Marketing Mayaguez .... Vacant
07 Dir Admissions/Marketing Arecibo .... Ms. Brendaliz SANTIAGO
07 Dir Admissions/Marketing Manati .... Mrs. Mariela CRUZ
10 Chief Financial Officer .... Mrs. Arelis DIAZ
37 Financial Aid Director .... Ms. Palmira ARROYO
12 Mayaguez Campus Director .... Dr. Sylvia RAMIREZ
12 Arecibo Campus Director .... Mrs. Ivette CHARRIEZ
12 Manati Campus Director .... Mr. Fernando GONZALEZ
06 Registrar Hato Rey .... Ms. Iris TORRES
06 Registrar Mayaguez .... Mrs. Olga NEGRON
06 Registrar Arecibo .... Mrs. Yaritza SANTIAGO
06 Registrar Manati .... Mrs. Vanessa TRINIDAD
06 Registrar Bayamon Extension .... Vacant
26 Enrollment & Advertising Manager .... Ms. Vimarte ASENCIO
13 Chief Information Officer .... Mr. Nelson MEJIAS
08 Learning Res Librarian Hato Rey .... Mrs. Sulynet TORRES
08 Lrng Resources Librarian Mayaguez .... Mrs. Betania FELICIANO
08 Lrng Resources Librarian Arecibo .... Mrs. Irma JIMENEZ
08 Learning Resources Librarian .... Mr. Martin ROSADO
38 Psychologist Mayaguez .... Mrs. Glendalee ARROYO
38 Professional Counselor Arecibo .... Mrs. Carol LUCIANO
38 Professional Counselor Manati .... Mrs. Carmen DIAZ
38 Professional Counselor Hato Rey .... Mrs. Nichole MALDONADO
15 Human Resources Director .... Mrs. Daisy CASTRO
43 Institutional Compliance Director .... Mrs. Lizzette VARGAS
56 Bayamon Extension Assoc Director .... Ms. Sandra RIJOS
20 Academic Coordinator Mayaguez .... Mrs. Ravel BONILLA
20 Academic Coordinator Arecibo .... Mrs. Erudina ROSAS
20 Academic Coordinator Manati .... Mrs. Maribel TORRES
20 Academic Coordinator Hato Rey .... Mr. Lorna RAMOS

ICPR Junior College-Arecibo Campus (A)

20 Ave San Patricio, Arecibo PR 00614
Telephone: (787) 878-6000 Identification: 770166
Accreditation: &M

ICPR Junior College-Manati Branch Campus (B)

PO Box 49, Manati PR 00674-0049
Telephone: (787) 884-6000 Identification: 770168
Accreditation: &M

ICPR Junior College-Mayaguez Campus (C)

PO Box 1108, Mayaguez PR 00681-9913
Telephone: (787) 832-6000 Identification: 770167
Accreditation: &M

Instituto de Banca y Comercio (D)

709 Ferrocarril Street, Ponce PR 00717
Telephone: (787) 840-6119 Identification: 770773
Accreditation: ACICS

Instituto de Banca y Comercio (E)

61 Ponce de Leon Ave, San Juan PR 00917
Identification: 667107
Telephone: (787) 754-7120 Carnegie Class: Not Classified
FAX Number: (787) 754-7143 Calendar System: Other
URL: www.ibanca.net
Established: 1975 Annual Undergrad Tuition & Fees: N/A
Enrollment: N/A Coed
Affiliation or Control: Proprietary IRS Status: Proprietary
Highest Offering: Associate Degree
Accreditation: ACICS

01 President .... Sr. Guillermo NIGAGLIONI
05 Director .... Mrs. Ana Jacqueline RIVERA

*Inter American University of Puerto Rico Central Office (F)

GPO Box 363255, San Juan PR 00936-3255
County: San Juan FICE Identification: 008242
Unit ID: 242671
Telephone: (787) 766-1912 Carnegie Class: N/A
FAX Number: (787) 751-3375
URL: www.inter.edu

01 President .... Mr. Manuel L. FERNOS
05 Vice Pres Academic & Student Affrs .... Mr. Agustin ECHEVARRIA
10 VP Financial Affairs/Services .... Mr. Luis ESQUILIN
42 Vice President Religious Affairs .... Rev. Norberto DOMINGUEZ
20 Associate VP Academic Affairs .... Dr. Rafael CABRERA
21 Assoc VP Financial Affairs/Services .... Ms. Olga LUNA
32 Associate Vice Pres Student Affairs .... Vacant
100 Exec Dir to Pres/Chief of Staff .... Mr. Dominique GILORMINI-DE GRACIA
26 Exec Dir Public Rels/Communications .... Mrs. Zaima NEGRON
84 Int Dir Inst Prom/Stdnt Recruitment .... Mr. Porfirio RIVERA
09 Exec Director Inst Research .... Dr. Isaac SANTIAGO
13 Exec Dir Information/Telecom .... Mrs. Jossie SALGUERO
43 Exec Director Legal Services .... Mrs. Lorraine JUARBE
43 Exec Director Federal Legal Svcs .... Mr. Vladimir ROMAN
15 Exec Director Human Resources .... Ms. Maggie COLON
30 Exec Director Devel/Alumni Affairs .. Dr. Nelda RIVERA-CLAUDIO

*Inter American University of Puerto Rico Aguadilla Campus (G)

Box 20000, Aguadilla PR 00605-9001
County: Aguadilla FICE Identification: 003939
Unit ID: 242626
Telephone: (787) 891-0925 Carnegie Class: Masters/S
FAX Number: (787) 882-3020 Calendar System: Other
URL: www.aguadilla.inter.edu
Established: 1957 Annual Undergrad Tuition & Fees: $5,654
Enrollment: 4,581 Coed
Affiliation or Control: Independent Non-Profit IRS Status: 501(c)3
Highest Offering: Master's
Accreditation: M, ADNUR, CAEPT, NUR, @SW

02 Chancellor .... Dr. Elie AGESILAS
05 Dean of Studies .... Mrs. Nilsa M. ROMAN
32 Dean of Student Affairs .... Mrs. Ana C. LAUSELL
13 Director Information and Technology .... Mr. Asdrubal JIMENEZ
90 Information Systems Administrator .... Mr. Jossue MORALES
10 Dean of Administrative Affairs .... Mr. Israel AYALA
20 Associate Dean of Studies .... Dr. Luis A. ACEVEDO
30 Development Director .... Dra. Sacha M. RUIZ
08 Library Director .... Mrs. Monserrate YULFO
07 Admissions Director .... Mrs. Doris PEREZ
06 Registrar .... Mrs. Maria PEREZ
37 Financial Aid Director .... Mrs. Gloria CORTES
21 Bursar .... Mr. Hancy MUNIZ
15 Human Resources Director .... Mr. Jose R. AREIZAGA
96 Purchasing Officer .... Ms. Wanda VARGAS
35 Student Support Services Director .... Mrs. Ivonne ACEVEDO
81 Director of Science and Technology .... Prof. Jose SOLORZANO
79 Director of Education & Hum Studies .... Mrs. Ramonita ROSA
50 Director Economic Science & Admin .... Dra. Maria G. ROSA
53 Dir of Social & Behavioral Sciences .... Prof. Gerardo LOPEZ
42 Chaplain .... Dr. Pablo E. ROJAS
88 Director of Upward Bound Program .... Mrs. Mayra ROZADA
88 Dir Campus Learning Center .... Ms. Yamilette PROSPER
18 Dir Building Maintenance/Univ Guard .... Mr. Jose CABAN
38 Director of Counseling Office .... Ms. Dary ACEVEDO
41 Sports Director .... Ms. Yolanda PAGAN
84 Enrollment Manager .... Prof. Myriam MARCIAL

*Inter American University of Puerto Rico Arecibo Campus (H)

PO Box 4050, Arecibo PR 00614-4050
County: Arecibo FICE Identification: 005026
Unit ID: 242635
Telephone: (787) 878-5475 Carnegie Class: Masters/M
FAX Number: (787) 880-1624 Calendar System: Semester
URL: www.arecibo.inter.edu
Established: 1957 Annual Undergrad Tuition & Fees: $5,082
Enrollment: 4,536 Coed
Affiliation or Control: Independent Non-Profit IRS Status: 501(c)3
Highest Offering: Master's
Accreditation: M, ANEST, CAEPT, NUR, SW

02 Chancellor .... Dr. Rafael RAMIREZ-RIVERA
05 Dean of Academic Affairs .... Dr. Annette VEGA
11 Dean of Administrative Affairs .... Lic. Antonio PEREZ-LÓPEZ
32 Dean of Student Affairs .... Mrs. Ilvis AGUIRRE
20 Assoc Dean of Academic Affairs .... Dr. Wanda I. BALSEIRO
08 Educational Resources Center Dir .... Mrs. Sara ABREU
113 Bursar .... Mr. Victor MALDONADO
37 Student Financial Aid Director .... Mr. Ramon DE JESUS
06 Registrar .... Mrs. Carmen RODRIGUEZ
07 Director of Admissions .... Mrs. Provi MONTALVO
04 Executive Assistant to Chancellor .... Mrs. Enid ARBELO
56 Distance Learning Director .... Prof. Ebigaly OLIVER
45 Planning Director .... Mrs. Enid ARBELO
42 Religious Life Director .... Mr. Amilcar SOTO
15 Personnel Director .... Dr. Grisel CASTELLANOS
41 Athletic Department .... Ms. Ileana MORALES
50 Director Econ & Adms Sciences Dept .... Prof. Elba TORO
51 Continuing Education Director .... Mrs. Mariel LLERANDI
53 Director of Education Department .... Dr. Auris MARTINEZ
66 Director of Nursing Department .... Dr. Frances CORTES
79 Dir of Humanities Department .... Dr. Angel TRINIDAD
81 Director of Sciences & Tech Dept .... Dr. Lizbeth ROMERO
83 Director of Social Sciences Dept .... Dr. Lourdes CARRION
30 Development Director .... Vacant
38 Director Student Counseling .... Ms. Abigail TORRES
13 Director of Computing Center .... Mr. Jose SEGARRA
58 Director Graduate Program in Educ .... Dra. Ramonita DIAZ
18 Chief Facilities/Physical Plant .... Vacant
84 Director Enrollment Management .... Mrs. Carmen MONTALVO
88 Dir Graduate Program Anesthesia .... Prof. Josue RAMOS
96 Purchasing Officer .... Mrs. Iris GONZALEZ
92 Coordinator Honor Program .... Ms. Vilmaris VAZQUEZ
108 Director Institutional Assessment .... Dr. Pedro RIVERA
26 Director of Marketing .... Mr. Juan RODRIGUEZ

*Inter American University of Puerto Rico Barranquitas Campus (I)

PO Box 517, Barranquitas PR 00794-0517
County: Barranquitas FICE Identification: 005027
Unit ID: 242644
Telephone: (787) 857-3600 Carnegie Class: Bac-Diverse
FAX Number: (787) 857-2244 Calendar System: Semester
URL: www.br.inter.edu
Established: 1957 Annual Undergrad Tuition & Fees: $5,764
Enrollment: 2,067 Coed
Affiliation or Control: Independent Non-Profit IRS Status: 501(c)3
Highest Offering: Master's
Accreditation: M, CAEPT

02 Chancellor .... Dr. Juan A. NEGRON
05 Dean Academic Affairs .... Dr. Filomena CINTRON
11 Dean Administrative Affairs .... Mrs. Marina RIVERA
32 Dean Student Affairs .... Dr. Maribel LOPEZ
84 Enrollment Manager .... Mrs. Lydia ARCE
15 Director Human Resources .... Mr. Victor SANTIAGO
113 Bursar Director .... Mr. Antonio J. ROSARIO
37 Financial Aid Director .... Mr. Eduardo FONTANEZ
06 Registrar .... Mrs. Sandra M. MORALES
07 Director of Admissions .... Mr. Edgardo CINTRON
53 Dir Education/Social Sci/Humanities .... Mrs. Irma TORRES
81 Dir Natural Sciences/Technology .... Mr. Jose PEREZ
76 Dir Health Department .... Dr. Omar GUERRERO
50 Dir Business Administration .... Mrs. Maria MELENDEZ
84 Director Recruitment/Promotion .... Mrs. Ana Isabel COLON
38 Director Upward Bound Program .... Mrs. Saraliz GONZALEZ
51 Director Continuing Education .... Mrs. Aixa SERRANO
88 Evaluation and Monitoring Officer .... Mrs. Carmen ROSADO
29 Director Alumni Relations .... Mr. Elvin J. ORTIZ
08 Librarian .... Mrs. Maria del C RIVERA
41 Athletic Director .... Mr. Israel RIVERA
42 Chaplain .... Mr. Jose RODRIGUEZ

*Inter American University of Puerto Rico Bayamon Campus (J)

500 Dr. John Will Harris Road, Bayamon PR 00957
County: Bayamon FICE Identification: 005028
Unit ID: 242705
Telephone: (787) 279-1912 Carnegie Class: Bac-Diverse
FAX Number: (787) 279-2205 Calendar System: Semester
URL: bayamon.inter.edu
Established: 1912 Annual Undergrad Tuition & Fees: $5,082
Enrollment: 4,630 Coed
Affiliation or Control: Independent Non-Profit IRS Status: 501(c)3
Highest Offering: Master's
Accreditation: M, AAB, ENG, OPTR

02 Chancellor .... Prof. Juan F. MARTINEZ
04 Assistant to Chancellor .... Mr. Antonio L. PANTOJA
30 Chief Development .... Mr. Jaime COLON
05 Chief Academic Officer .... Dr. Carlos J. OLIVARES
20 Associate Academic Officer .... Dra. Nydia I. FELICIANO
08 Head Librarian .... Mrs. Sandra ROSA
88 Internships and Exchanges Officer .... Mrs. Maritza ZAMBRANA
88 Dean School of Aeronautics .... Prof. Jorge CALAF
54 Dean School of Engineering .... Dr. Javier QUINTANA
88 Director Electrical Engr Dept .... Prof. Miguel MUÑIZ
88 Director Industrial Engr Dept .... Prof. Catherine AGUILAR
88 Director Mechanical Engr Dept .... Dr. Eduardo PEREZ
81 Director Mathematics/Sciences .... Dr. Alberto VIVONI
50 Dir Business Administration Dept .... Dra. Grace D. LEO
60 Director Communications Dept .... Prof. Ruth E. HERNANDEZ
77 Director Computer Sciences Dept .... Prof. Jose RODRIGUEZ
76 Director of Health Science .... Prof. Jose M. CRUZ
79 Director Humanities/Language Dept .... Dra. Isabel GARAYTA
75 Director Tech Institute .... Mrs. Liza FREYTES
32 Chief Students Life Officer .... Mrs. Gema C. TORRES
38 Director Student Counseling .... Mrs. Arlette VALPAIS
41 Athletic Director .... Mr. Reynaldo ROLON
10 Chief Financial/Business Officer .... Mr. Juan C. HERNANDEZ
96 Purchasing Officer .... Mrs. Gladys ARROYO
21 Associate Business Officer .... Mr. Serafin RIVERA
18 Chief Facilities/Physical Plant .... Eng. Jose A. FUENTES
15 Human Resources Director .... Mrs. Migdalia ORTIZ
84 Director Enrollment Services .... Miss Ivette NIEVES
35 Director of Students Services .... Mrs. Aurelis BAEZ
06 Registrar .... Mr. Eddie AYALA
13 Director Information Technology .... Mr. Edwin RIVERA
42 Director of Chaplaincy Office .... Rvda. Carmen I. PEREZ
106 Dir Online Education/E-learning .... Dr. Jose G. SANTIAGO
09 Director of Institutional Research .... Vacant
39 Housing Administrator .... Mr. Gerardo BURGOS
88 International Relations Director .... Mr. Luis ALCARAZ
108 Coordinator of Institutional Assess .... Dr. Jonathan VELAZQUEZ

*Inter American University of Puerto Rico Fajardo Campus (K)

Call Box 70003, Fajardo PR 00738-7003
County: Fajardo FICE Identification: 022828
Unit ID: 242680
Telephone: (787) 863-2390 Carnegie Class: Bac-Diverse
FAX Number: (787) 860-3470 Calendar System: Semester
URL: fajardo.inter.edu
Established: 1960 Annual Undergrad Tuition & Fees: $5,102
Enrollment: 2,239 Coed

Affiliation or Control: Independent Non-Profit IRS Status: 501(c)3
Highest Offering: Master's
Accreditation: M, CAEPT, SW

02 Chancellor .... Dr. Javier MARTINEZ-ORTIZ
05 Dean Academic Affairs .... Vacant
11 Dean Administrative Affairs .... Mr. Rafael E. MARIN
32 Dean for Student Affairs .... Mrs. Lyliana CRESPO
06 Registrar .... Mrs. Arlene PARRILLA
07 Director of Admissions .... Mrs. Ada CARABALLO
37 Director Student Financial Aid .... Mrs. Marilyn MARTINEZ
08 Librarian .... Ms. Angie COLON
15 Director of Personnel Office .... Mrs. Maria A. RAMOS
09 Planning Director .... Ms. Hilda L. ORTIZ
41 Athletic Director .... Mr. Jose RUIZ
18 Physical Plant Supervisor .... Mr. Angel J. RUIZ
42 Chaplain/Director Campus Ministry .... Rev. Rafael HIRALDO
50 Chairperson Business Department .... Prof. Wilfredo DEL VALLE
53 Chairperson Educ & Social Sci Dept .... Prof. Lorell RIVERA
79 Chairperson Humanities Dept .... Dr. Ilsa LOPEZ-VALLES
81 Chairperson Math/Science Dept .... Prof. Milagros DONATO
84 Director Enrollment Management .... Mrs. Glenda DIAZ

*Inter American University of Puerto Rico Guayama Campus (A)

Call Box 10004, Guayama PR 00785
County: Guayama FICE Identification: 022827
Unit ID: 242699
Telephone: (787) 864-2222 Carnegie Class: Bac-Diverse
FAX Number: (787) 866-5006 Calendar System: Semester
URL: www.guayama.inter.edu
Established: 1958 Annual Undergrad Tuition & Fees: $5,764
Enrollment: 2,127 Coed
Affiliation or Control: Independent Non-Profit IRS Status: 501(c)3
Highest Offering: Master's
Accreditation: M, CAEPT

02 President .... Mr. Manuel J. FERNOS
00 Chancellor .... Dr. Angela DE JESUS-ALICEA
06 Registrar .... Mr. Luis A. SOTO
08 Librarian .... Mrs. Edny SANTIAGO
113 Bursar .... Ms. Teresa MANAUTOU
05 Dean of Academic Affairs .... Dr. Merla RIVERA
11 Dean of Administration .... Mr. Nestor A. LEBRON
32 Dean of Students .... Dr. Rosa J. MARTINEZ
07 Director Admissions .... Mrs. Laura FERRER
37 Director Financial Aid .... Mr. Jose A. VECHINI
29 Director Alumni Relations .... Dr. Jose ROMERO
51 Director Continuing Education .... Mrs. Merla RIVERA
15 Human Resources Officer .... Mrs. Maria MARES
18 Chief Facilities/Physical Plant .... Mr. Benjamin AYALA
45 Dir Evaluation & Strategic Planning .... Mrs. Claribel RODRIGUEZ
30 Chief Devel/Dir Annual Plan Giv .... Vacant
42 Chaplain Director .... Rvdo. Arnaldo CINTRON
84 Director Enrollment Management .... Mrs. Eileen RIVERA
96 Director of Purchasing .... Mrs. Maria VAZQUEZ
31 Dir of Community & New Student Rels .... Mrs. Luz ORTIZ
23 Director Health Services .... Mrs. Arcilia RIVERA
66 Director Nursing Program .... Dr. Marisol VELAZQUEZ
88 Dir Adult Higher Education Program .... Mrs. Carmen G. RIVERA
50 Dir Dept Business Admin/Econ Sci .... Dr. Rosalia MORALES
53 Dir Dept Education/Soc Sci/Hum Std .... Dr. Ray ROBLES
81 Dir Dept Natural & Applied Science .... Prof. Carmen TORRES
09 Director of Institutional Research .... Mr. Tomas JIMENEZ

*Inter American University of Puerto Rico / Metropolitan Campus (B)

PO Box 191293, San Juan PR 00919-1293
County: San Juan FICE Identification: 003940
Unit ID: 242653
Telephone: (787) 250-1912 Carnegie Class: DU-Mod
FAX Number: (787) 250-0742 Calendar System: Trimester
URL: www.metro.inter.edu
Established: 1962 Annual Undergrad Tuition & Fees: $7,302
Enrollment: 9,110 Coed
Affiliation or Control: Independent Non-Profit IRS Status: 501(c)3
Highest Offering: Doctorate
Accreditation: M, ADNUR, CAEPT, MT, NUR, SW

02 Chancellor .... Prof. Marilina L. WAYLAND
05 Dean of Studies .... Prof. Migdalia TEXIDOR
32 Dean of Students .... Dr. Carmen OQUENDO
10 Dean of Administration .... Mr. Jimmy CANCEL
11 Dean of Faculty Cs Economics & Adm .... Prof. Fredrick VEGA
53 Dean of Education & Behavioral Sci .... Dr. Carmen COLLAZO
83 Director School of Psychology .... Dr. Jaime SANTIAGO
79 Dean Faculty of Humanities .... Dr. Oscar CRUZ
66 Director of Nursing .... Dr. Maria J. COLÓN
72 Director of Medical Technology .... Dr. Ida A. MEJIAS
81 Dean Faculty of Science & Technolog .... Dr. Yogani GOVENDER
06 Registrar .... Ms. Lisette RIVERA
84 Enrollment Management .... Mr. Luis E. RUIZ
20 Associate Dean of Studies .... Ms. Blanca M. GONZALEZ
08 Dir of Ctr for Access Info .... Ms. Maria de Lourdes RESTO
15 Human Resources Officer .... Mrs. Darlin TORRES
37 Director of Financial Aid .... Ms. Lillian CONCEPCION
18 Dir Conservation & General Services .... Ing. Grisel O. MEDINA
38 Dir Student Placement/Guidanc/Couns .... Ms. Beatriz RIVERA
83 Director School of Social Work .... Dr. Sonia ARCHILLA
58 Director School of Education .... Dr. Maria D. RUBERO
85 Coord International Rels Office .... Prof. Ramon AYALA
73 Dir School of Theology .... Dr. Angel VELEZ
88 Dir School of Criminal Justice .... Prof. Luis SOTO
13 Director Informatic/Telecomm Center .... Mr. Eduardo ORTIZ
36 Director Student Placement .... Mrs. Adabel-Vanessa COLON
07 Director of Admissions .... Ms. Janies OLIVIERI
09 Dean Inst Research/External Rsrch .... Vacant
30 Development & Fund Raising .... Mrs. Evelyn VEGA
96 Purchasing Officer .... Mrs. Patricia GONZALEZ
92 Coordinator of Honors Program .... Prof. Mariusz JACKO
113 Bursar .... Ms. Carmen RIVERA
106 Dir Online Education/E-learning .... Mr. Jairo PULIDO
19 Director Security/Safety .... Mr. George RIVERA
41 Athletic Director .... Mr. Jesus CORA

*Inter American University of Puerto Rico Ponce Campus (C)

104 Turpo Industrial Park Road, #1,
Mercedita PR 00715-1602
County: Ponce FICE Identification: 005029
Unit ID: 242662
Telephone: (787) 284-1912 Carnegie Class: Masters/S
FAX Number: (787) 841-0103 Calendar System: Semester
URL: ponce.inter.edu
Established: 1962 Annual Undergrad Tuition & Fees: $5,084
Enrollment: 5,497 Coed
Affiliation or Control: Independent Non-Profit IRS Status: 501(c)3
Highest Offering: Doctorate
Accreditation: M, CAEPT, #OTA, PTAA, RAD

02 Chancellor .... Dr. Vilma E. COLON
05 Dean of Academic Affairs .... Dr. Jacqueline ALVAREZ
32 Dean of Students .... Mrs. Edda COSTAS
11 Dean of Administrative Affairs .... Eng. Victor A. FELIBERTY
10 Financial Officer .... Mrs. Maria DE P. MENDEZ
08 Director Education Resource Center .... Mrs. Maria SILVESTRINI
35 Director Student Services .... Mrs. Miriam MARTINEZ
10 Bursar .... Mr. Brian HERNANDEZ
06 Registrar .... Mrs. Maria del C PEREZ
30 Director of Development .... Mrs. Hilda V. STELLA
07 Director of Admissions .... Mr. Franco L. DIAZ
15 Human Resource Director .... Mrs. Waleska FLORES
19 Supervisor of University Guard .... Mr. Reinaldo ROSADO
37 Director Student Financial Aid .... Ms. Karen CAQUIAS
41 Athletic Director .... Mr. Raul HERNANDEZ
58 Director of Graduate Programs .... Dr. Delma SANTIAGO
50 Director Business & Administration .... Mrs. Vivien MATTEI
51 Director Continuing Education .... Mrs. Evelyn CASTILLO
79 Act Dir Humanistics/Pedagogical Std .... Mrs. Santy CORREA
81 Director Mathematics/Sciences .... Dr. Hector W. COLON
83 Dir Social/Behavioral Science .... Ms. Lidis L. JUSINO
76 Associate Dean of Health Science .... Dr. Omayra CARABALLO
38 Dir Univ Integration Services Ofc .... Mr. Hector MARTINEZ
13 Director Computer Center .... Mr. Antonio RAMOS
26 Public Relations Officer .... Vacant
04 Chief Executive Assistant .... Mrs. Yinaira SANTIAGO
27 Dir Marketing & Student Promotion .... Mrs. Vanessa PAGAN
106 Director Distance Education Program .... Mr. Rolando MENDEZ
88 Accreditation/Certification Officer .... Vacant
45 Director of Evaluation & Planning .... Vacant
18 Chief Facilities/Physical Plant .... Vacant
36 Director Student Placement .... Mr. Hector MARTINEZ
84 Enrollment Manager .... Mrs. Miriam MARTINEZ
42 Chaplain .... Rev. Lucy ROSARIO
51 Adult Education Director .... Mrs. Marilyn OLIVERAS
20 Assoc Dean Acad Affs/Distance Educ .... Dr. Omayra CARABALLO
21 Assoc Dean Administrative Affairs .... Mr. Julio MUNOZ
96 Purchasing Officer .... Mrs. Vivian ARMSTRONG

*Inter American University of Puerto Rico San German Campus (D)

PO Box 5100, San German PR 00683-9801
County: San German FICE Identification: 003938
Unit ID: 242617
Telephone: (787) 264-1912 Carnegie Class: Masters/M
FAX Number: (787) 892-6350 Calendar System: Semester
URL: www.intersg.edu
Established: 1912 Annual Undergrad Tuition & Fees: $4,962
Enrollment: 4,999 Coed
Affiliation or Control: Independent Non-Profit IRS Status: 501(c)3
Highest Offering: Doctorate
Accreditation: M, CAEPT, IACBE, MT, NURSE, RAD

02 Chancellor .... Prof. Agnes MOJICA
05 Dean of Academic Affairs .... Dr. Nyvia ALVARADO
11 Dean of Administration .... Mrs. Frances CARABALLO
32 Dean of Students .... Mr. Raúl MEDINA
20 Associate Dean of Academic Affairs .... Prof. Vilma MARTÍNEZ
109 Auxiliary Dean of Administration .... Mrs. Marisol GONZÁLEZ
15 Director of Human Resources .... Mrs. Evelyn TORRES
18 Chief Facilities/Physical Plant .... Mr. José A. RIVERA
37 Acting Director Financial Aid .... Mrs. Brunilda FERRER
06 Registrar .... Mrs. Arleen SANTANA
07 Director of Admissions .... Mrs. Mildred CAMACHO
08 Director of Library .... Mrs. Mayra RODRÍGUEZ
38 Director Student Counseling .... Mrs. Daisy PÉREZ
09 Planning Evaluation/Inst Studies .... Dr. Caroline AYALA
19 Director of Security .... Mr. Edwin SOTO
13 Director of Computer Center .... Mr. Rogelio TORO-ZAPATA
41 Athletic Director .... Prof. Francisco ACEVEDO
39 Director of Men Student Housing .... Mrs. Erlinda VEGA
39 Director of Women Student Housing .... Mrs. Hilda CRUZ
42 Dir Chaplaincy/Spiritual Well-being .... Rev. Pablo CARABALLO
04 Special Assistant of the Chancellor .... Mrs. Tary GARCÍA
04 Special Assistant of the Chancellor .... Mrs. Janine HADERTHAUER
35 Manager of Student Services .... Mrs. María Gil MARTÍNEZ
51 Director of Continuing Education .... Vacant
58 Director Graduate Programs .... Dr. Ailín PADILLA
109 Manager of Food Services .... Mrs. Judy ROSADO
17 Health Services Officer .... Mrs. Gladys MEJIAS
88 Acting Auxiliary Dean of Students .... Miss Idalmy RAMOS
30 Chief Development Officer .... Miss Leticia MARTÍNEZ
96 Director of Purchasing .... Mr. Israel CRUZ
113 Director Bursar's Office .... Mr. Carlos SEGARRA
53 Director of Education .... Dr. Miriam PADILLA
83 Dir Social Scieces & Liberal Arts .... Dr. Juan R. GONZALEZ
50 Director of Entrepreneurial & Mgmt .... Dr. Milsa MORALES
88 Director of Biology & Environmental .... Prof. Iris SEDA
72 Director of Technical Studies .... Prof. Mildred ORTIZ
57 Director of Fine Arts .... Prof. Samuel ROSADO
76 Director of Health Sciences .... Prof. Ileana ORTIZ
88 Director of Language & Literature .... Dr. Marta VIADA
81 Director of Math & Applied Sciences .... Prof. Yvonne AVILÉS
92 Director of Honor Program .... Miss Sulmarie MORALES
26 Director of External Resources .... Prof. Mildred DE SANTIAGO
106 Dir Online Education/E-learning .... Prof. Luis ZORNOSA

*Inter American University of Puerto Rico School of Law (E)

PO Box 70351, San Juan PR 00936-8351
County: San Juan Identification: 666813
Unit ID: 242723
Telephone: (787) 751-1912 Carnegie Class: Spec-4-yr-Law
FAX Number: (787) 751-2975 Calendar System: Semester
URL: www.derecho.inter.edu
Established: 1961 Annual Graduate Tuition & Fees: N/A
Enrollment: 833 Coed
Affiliation or Control: Independent Non-Profit IRS Status: 501(c)3
Highest Offering: First Professional Degree; No Undergraduates
Accreditation: M, LAW

02 President .... Mr. Manuel J. FERNÓS
61 Dean .... Dr. Julio E. FONTANET-MALDONADO
05 Dean for Academic Affairs .... Dr. Yanira REYES-GIL
32 Dean of Students .... Dr. Iris M. CAMACHO-MELÉNDEZ
11 Dean of Administration .... Mr. Heriberto SOTO-LÓPEZ
06 Registrar .... Mrs. Sonia I. MONTALVO-COLÓN
08 Head Librarian .... Mr. Hector R. SANCHEZ-FERNANDEZ
61 Director of Legal Aid Clinic .... Mr. Rafael E. RODRÍGUEZ-RIVERA
37 Director of Financial Aid .... Mr. Ricardo CRESPO
07 Director of Admissions .... Mrs. Angela TORRES
18 Chief Facilities/Physical Plant .... Mr. Jose A. RIVERA
113 Director of Bursar Office .... Mrs. Ileana PIÑERO
45 Planning/Eval & Development Ofc .... Mrs. Edith C. PABON-RODRIGUEZ
121 Dir of Academic Support Program .... Mrs. Patricia OTÓN-OLIVIERI
88 Master Program Coordinator .... Dr. Luis E. ROMERO-NIEVES
04 Executive Asst to President .... Mr. Dominique GILORMINI
13 Chief Info Technology Officer .... Ms. Olga I. CRUZ-PABÓN
15 Director Personnel Services .... Mrs. Milagros AMALBERT
19 Director Security/Safety .... Mr. Victor RODRIGUEZ-CRUZ
30 Dir Development/Alumni Rels .... Mrs. Sheila GÓMEZ
36 Director Student Placement/Counsel .... Vacant
51 Assoc Dean Acad Affs/Grad Pgm/ CLE .... Mr. Cesar ALVARADO-TORRES
35 Associate Dean for Student Affairs .... Ms. Lin COLLAZO-CARRO

*Inter American University of Puerto Rico School of Optometry (F)

500 John Will Harris Road, Bayamon PR 00957-6257
County: San Juan Identification: 666601
Unit ID: 404222
Telephone: (787) 765-1915 Carnegie Class: Spec-4-yr-Other Health
FAX Number: (787) 767-3920 Calendar System: Semester
URL: www.optonet.inter.edu
Established: 1981 Annual Graduate Tuition & Fees: N/A
Enrollment: 233 Coed
Affiliation or Control: Independent Non-Profit IRS Status: 501(c)3
Highest Offering: First Professional Degree; No Undergraduates
Accreditation: M, OPT

02 Dean .... Dr. Andres PAGAN
05 Dean for Academic Affairs .... Dr. Angel ROMERO
11 Dean of Administration .... Mr. Francisco RIVERA
32 Dean of Student Affairs .... Dra. Iris CABELLO
42 Director Religious Life .... Dra. Ileana VARGAS
30 Director Development .... Mrs. Maria J. AULET
17 Dean of Clinical Affairs .... Dra. Damaris PAGAN
08 Library Director .... Mrs. Wilma MARRERO
15 Director Human Resources .... Mrs. Jackeline MEJIAS
37 Financial Aid Officer .... Mrs. Sirimarie MARTÍNEZ
04 Executive Assistant of the Dean .... Mrs. Arleen E. CORREA
06 Registrar .... Mrs. Luz OCASIO
26 Director Marketing/Promotion .... Mrs. Jaqueline PABON

Mech-Tech College (A)

PO Box 6118, Caguas PR 00726
County: Caguas FICE Identification: 030255
Unit ID: 414461
Telephone: (787) 744-1060 Carnegie Class: Assoc/HVT-High Trad
FAX Number: (787) 744-1035 Calendar System: Quarter
URL: www.mechtech.edu
Established: 1984 Annual Undergrad Tuition & Fees: $9,042
Enrollment: 2,975 Coed
Affiliation or Control: Proprietary IRS Status: Proprietary
Highest Offering: Associate Degree
Accreditation: CNCE

01 President .... Mr. Edwin J. COLON COSME

Monteclaro: Escuela de Hoteleria y Artes Culinarias (B)

PO Box 447 Palmer, Rio Grande PR 00721-0447
FICE Identification: 034143
Unit ID: 437705
Telephone: (787) 888-1135 Carnegie Class: Not Classified
FAX Number: (787) 888-1252 Calendar System: Semester
URL: www.monteclaro.edu
Established: Annual Undergrad Tuition & Fees: N/A
Enrollment: 13 Coed
Affiliation or Control: Independent Non-Profit IRS Status: 501(c)3
Highest Offering: Associate Degree
Accreditation: ACCSC

01 President .... Ana T. GARCIA
05 Vice Pres Academic Affairs .... Wendy E. MALDONADO

National University College (C)

PMB452, PO Box 144035, Arecibo PR 00614-4035
Telephone: (787) 879-5044 Identification: 666489
Accreditation: &M

National University College (D)

P.O. Box 2036, Bayamon PR 00960
County: Puerto Rico FICE Identification: 022606
Unit ID: 242972
Telephone: (787) 780-5134 Carnegie Class: Spec-4-yr-Other Health
FAX Number: (787) 786-9093 Calendar System: Trimester
URL: www.nuc.edu
Established: 1982 Annual Undergrad Tuition & Fees: $6,495
Enrollment: 5,272 Coed
Affiliation or Control: Proprietary IRS Status: Proprietary
Highest Offering: Master's
Accreditation: M, ADNUR, CAEPT, NUR, @PTAA

01 President .... Dr. Gloria E. BAQUERO
88 VP of Compliance .... Mr. Desi LOPEZ
05 VP Academic Affairs .... Dr. Maria ESTRADA
32 VP of Student Affairs .... Ms. Ana M. LUCUMI
108 Institutional Dir of Assessment .... Ms. Lydia COLLAZO
46 Director Research & Development .... Mr. Angel AVILES
37 Institutional Dir Financial Aid .... Ms. Elizabeth CRUZ
06 Inst Director Admissions/Registrar .... Ms. Lilimar VELEZ

National University College (E)

190 Ave Gautier Benítez esquina Ave, Caguas PR 00725
Telephone: (787) 653-4733 Identification: 770928
Accreditation: &M

† Branch campus of National University College, Bayamon, PR.

National University College Ponce Campus (F)

PO Box 80243, Coto Laurel PR 00780
Telephone: (787) 840-4474 Identification: 770169
Accreditation: &M

National University College Rio Grande Campus (G)

La Dolores, Rio Grande PR 00745
Telephone: (787) 809-5100 Identification: 770170
Accreditation: &M

Ponce Paramedical College (H)

1213 Acacia Street Villa Flores Urb,
Ponce PR 00716-2901
County: Ponce FICE Identification: 025349
Unit ID: 243072
Telephone: (787) 848-1589 Carnegie Class: Spec 2-yr-Health
FAX Number: (787) 259-0169 Calendar System: Other
URL: www.popac.edu
Established: 1983 Annual Undergrad Tuition & Fees: N/A
Enrollment: 2,326 Coed
Affiliation or Control: Proprietary IRS Status: Proprietary
Highest Offering: Associate Degree
Accreditation: ACCSC

01 President .... Mrs. Wilda VELEZ
05 Academic Dean .... Mrs. Rosa E. CRUZ
06 Registrar .... Mrs. Ivette OLIVERAS
37 Director Student Financial Aid .... Mr. Xauel CRUZ

Ponce School of Medicine & Health Sciences (I)

PO Box 7004, Ponce PR 00732-7004
County: Ponce FICE Identification: 024824
Unit ID: 243081
Telephone: (787) 840-2575 Carnegie Class: Masters/S
FAX Number: (787) 840-9756 Calendar System: Semester
URL: www.psm.edu
Established: 1977 Annual Undergrad Tuition & Fees: N/A
Enrollment: 809 Coed
Affiliation or Control: Independent Non-Profit IRS Status: 501(c)3
Highest Offering: Doctorate
Accreditation: M, CLPSY, IPSY, MED, PH

01 President/CEO .... Dr. David LENIHAN
05 Vice Pres Academic Affairs .... Dr. Jose TORRES-RUIZ
32 Vice Pres Student Affairs .... Dr. Emil RUIZ
45 Chief Strategy Officer .... Mr. Israel A. RUIZ
10 Chief Financial Officer .... Mr. Carlos ROJAS

The Pontifical Catholic University of Puerto Rico (J)

2250 Las Americas Avenue, Suite 564,
Ponce PR 00717-9997
County: Ponce FICE Identification: 003936
Unit ID: 241410
Telephone: (787) 841-2000 Carnegie Class: DU-Mod
FAX Number: (787) 651-2034 Calendar System: Semester
URL: www.pucpr.edu
Established: 1948 Annual Undergrad Tuition & Fees: $5,250
Enrollment: 7,767 Coed
Affiliation or Control: Roman Catholic IRS Status: 501(c)3
Highest Offering: Doctorate
Accreditation: M, CACREP, CAEPT, LAW, MT, NUR, SW

00 Chancellor .... M.Rev. Ruben A. GONZALEZ MEDINA, CMF
01 President .... Dr. Jorge I. VELEZ AROCHO
04 Executive Assistant to President .... Lic. Liza RIESTRA
05 Vice President Academic Affairs .... Dr. Leandro COLON
10 Vice President of Finance .... Prof. Irma I. RODRIGUEZ
32 Vice President for Student Affairs .... Prof. Freddie MARTINEZ
20 Assoc Vice Pres Academic Affairs .... Prof. Maria MUNIZ
35 Assoc Vice Pres Student Affairs .... Prof. Myriam D. LOPEZ
09 Vice President Inst Rsrch/Dev Plng .... Dr. Felix CORTES
12 Rector Arecibo Branch .... Dr. Edwin HERNANDEZ
12 Rector Mayaguez Branch .... Dr. Olga HERNANDEZ
06 Registrar .... Prof. Ivan DAVILA
07 Interim Director of Admissions .... Prof. Carmen Z. TORRES
08 Director of the Library .... Prof. Magda VARGAS
37 Director of Student Aid .... Mrs. Maria NOLASCO
36 Director of Placement Services .... Vacant
13 Director Computer Center .... Mr. Moises CABRERA
55 Director of Evening Studies .... Prof. Caridad ALVAREZ
24 Director Educational Technology .... Dr. Edgar RODRIGUEZ
79 Dean of Arts & Humanities .... Rev. Juan Luis NEGRON DELGADO
81 Dean of Sciences .... Dra. Alma L. SANTIAGO
61 Dean of the School of Law .... Lic. Jose A. FRONTERA
50 Dean Business Administration .... Dr. David ZAYAS
53 Dean of Education .... Dr. Myriam ZAYAS
58 Dean Institute of Graduate Studies .... Dr. Hernan VERA
48 Dean School of Architecture .... Mr. Luis V. BADILLO-LOZANO
54 Dean of Engineering .... Ing. Armando RODRIGUEZ
51 Coord Continuing Education Inst .... Mrs. Karen G. MORALES
27 Communications .... Mrs. Jalibeth RODRIGUEZ
29 Alumni Relations Officer .... Mrs. Maria S. MASCARO
15 Director Human Resources .... Mr. Wilfredo CORNIER
40 Director Bookstore .... Mrs. Ashley VELEZ
41 Athletic Director .... Mr. Ramon HERNANDEZ
42 Chaplain .... Rev. Juan C. RIVERA
109 Director Auxiliary Enterprises .... Mr. Julio FELIU
26 Director Public Relations .... Mrs. Irem POVENTUD
38 Director Student Counseling .... Dr. Arvin BAEZ
18 Physical Plant/Safety & Security .... Mr. Julio PALMER
113 Treasurer Bursar's Office .... Mr. Juan E. ROMAN
96 Interim Director of Purchasing .... Mrs. Nelly VELAZQUEZ
88 Director of Biotechnology .... Dra. Cariluz SANTIAGO
88 Accreditation Liaison Officer .... Dr. Carmen J. ACOSTA-FUMERO
30 Infrastructure Director .... Ing. Armando RODRIGUEZ
84 Coord Institutional Recruitment .... Sr. Rene MARRERO
89 Director of Freshmen .... Prof. Carmen Z. TORRES
106 Dir Online Education/E-learning .... Dr. Carmen BETANCOURT
19 Director Security/Safety .... Mr. Julio PALMER
43 Dir Legal Services/General Counsel .... Lic. Carolyn COSTAS
86 Director Government Relations .... Vacant
100 Chief of Staff .... Lic. Liza RIESTRA
108 Director Institutional Assessment .... Dr. Jose N. CARABALLO
39 Director Student Housing .... Mr. Francisco LUGO
39 Director Student Housing .... Ms. Magda PEREZ
102 Dir Foundation/Corporate Relations .... Sra. Gladys M. DIAZ
104 Director Study Abroad .... Dra. Enid MIRANDA
105 Webmaster II .... Mr. Francisco SUAREZ
22 Dir Affirmative Action/EEO .... Mr. Wilfredo CORNIER

Pontifical Catholic University of Puerto Rico-Arecibo Campus (K)

Box 144045, Arecibo PR 00614-4045
Telephone: (787) 881-1212 Identification: 666603
Accreditation: &M

† Regional accreditation is carried under the parent institution in Ponce, PR.

Pontifical Catholic University of Puerto Rico-Mayaguez Campus (L)

Box 1326, Mayaguez PR 00681-1326
Telephone: (787) 834-5151 Identification: 666605
Accreditation: &M

† Branch campus of The Pontifical Catholic University of Puerto Rico, Ponce, PR.

San Juan Bautista School of Medicine (M)

PO Box 4968, Carretera 172, Caguas PR 00726-4968
County: San Juan FICE Identification: 031773
Unit ID: 430670
Telephone: (787) 743-3038 Carnegie Class: Spec-4-yr-Med
FAX Number: (787) 746-3093 Calendar System: Semester
URL: www.sanjuanbautista.edu
Established: 1978 Annual Undergrad Tuition & Fees: $9,166
Enrollment: 320 Coed
Affiliation or Control: Proprietary IRS Status: Proprietary
Highest Offering: First Professional Degree
Accreditation: M, MED

01 President/Dean .... Dr. Yocasta BRUGAL-MENA
11 Dean of Administration .... Mr. Carlos F. ABREU
05 Chief Academic Officer .... Dr. Irving MALDONADO
06 Registrar .... Mr. Israel LÓPEZ
08 Head Librarian .... Mr. Carlos ALTAMIRANO
10 Chief Business Officer .... Mr. Juan C. CASTRO
32 Chief Student Affairs/Student Life .... Dr. Yolanda MIRANDA
37 Director Student Financial Aid .... Miss Beatriz DE LEÓN
07 Director of Admissions .... Ms. Jaymi SANCHEZ
108 Director Institutional Assessment .... Mr. Fernando GONZALEZ
13 Chief Info Technology Officer (CIO) .... Mr. Jorge TORRES
38 Director Student Counseling .... Ms. Ilsa CENTENO

Seminario Teologico de Puerto Rico (N)

Calle Jose Canals #458, Oficina 301, San Juan PR 00918
Telephone: (787) 274-1142 Identification: 770142
Accreditation: &M

† Branch campus of Nyack College, Nyack, NY

*Sistema Universitario Ana G. Mendez (O)

Apartado 21345, Rio Piedras PR 00928-1341
County: San Juan FICE Identification: 029078
Unit ID: 242060
Telephone: (787) 751-0178 Carnegie Class: N/A
FAX Number: (787) 766-1706
URL: www.suagm.edu

01 President .... Mr. Jose F. MENDEZ
05 Vice President for Academic Affairs .... Mr. Jorge L. CRESPO
10 Vice Pres Financial Affairs .... Mr. Alfonso L. DAVILA
32 VP Student/Marketing Affairs .... Dr. Mayra CRUZ
45 Vice President Planning & Research .... Mr. Jorge CRESPO
11 Vice Pres Administrative Affairs .... Mr. Ricardo RODRIGUEZ
15 Vice President Human Resources .... Dr. Victoria DE JESUS
104 Vice President International Affs .... Dr. David MENDEZ
13 Chief Information Officer .... Sr. Kenneth MALDONADO
26 Director Public Relations .... Ms. Maria MARTINEZ
04 Exec Assistant to President .... Ms. Lydia I. MASSARI
06 Registrar .... Ms. Elisa QUILES
07 Director of Admissions .... Ms. Ramonita FUENTES

*Universidad Ana G. Mendez (P)

PO Box 21345, Bayamon PR 00928-1345
County: Bayamon Identification: 667292
Telephone: (787) 288-1118 Carnegie Class: Not Classified
FAX Number: (787) 288-1141 Calendar System: Semester
URL: agmvirtual.suagm.edu
Established: Annual Graduate Tuition & Fees: N/A
Enrollment: N/A Coed
Affiliation or Control: Independent Non-Profit IRS Status: 501(c)3
Highest Offering: Master's; No Undergraduates
Accreditation: M

02 Chancellor .... Dr. Migdalia TORRES
03 Vice Chancellor .... Dr. Wilfredo COLON-GUASP
30 Vice Chanc Ext Resources/Devel .... Ms. Gladys CORA-IZQUIERDO

*Universidad del Este (Q)

PO Box 2010, Carolina PR 00984-2010
County: San Juan FICE Identification: 003941
Unit ID: 243346
Telephone: (787) 257-7373 Carnegie Class: Masters/L

FAX Number: (787) 776-1220 Calendar System: Semester
URL: www.suagm.edu/une
Established: 1949 Annual Undergrad Tuition & Fees: $5,820
Enrollment: 13,058 Coed
Affiliation or Control: Independent Non-Profit IRS Status: 501(c)3
Highest Offering: Master's
Accreditation: M, ACBSP, ACFEI, ADNUR, CAEPT, NUR, SW

02 Chancellor ... Dr. Mildred HUERTAS SOLÁ
05 Vice Chancellor Academic Affairs ... Dr. Angel A. TOLEDO LÓPEZ
11 Vice Chanc Admin Affairs ... Mrs. Maria S. DIAZ
32 Vice Chancellor Student Affairs ... Dr. María G. VÉAZ
24 Vice Chanc Information Resources ... Mrs. Carmen ORTEGA
46 Vice Chanc External Resources ... Mrs. Mayra M. FERRAN
20 Assoc VC Licensing/Accreditation . Dr. Marcos A. VÉLEZ RIVERA
88 Assoc Vice Chanc Admin Affairs ... Mrs. Magalie ALVARADO
35 Assoc Vice Chanc Student Affairs ... Mrs. Gisela NEGRON
84 Assoc VC Enrollment Management ... Mrs. Magda E. OSTOLAZA
23 AVC Stdnt Quality of Life/Wellness . Mrs. Carmen G. VELAZQUEZ
07 Asst Vice Chan Admiss/Financial Aid ... Ms. Liz Y. MENDEZ
09 Asst Vice Chanc Academic Effective ... Vacant
36 Exec Director Employment Placement ... Mrs. Diana M. COLON
111 Asst VC for University Advancement ... Mrs. Maria I. DE GUZMAN
15 Asst Vice Pres Human Resources ... Mrs. Marisol MUÑOZ
114 Assistant Vice President of Budget ... Mr. Jorge A. TORRES
45 Asst Vice President of Planning ... Mr. Alberto J. CAMACHO
88 Dean Intl Sch Hosp/Culinary Arts ... Mrs. Terestella GONZÁLEZ
107 Dean Professional Studies ... Mrs. Mildred Y. RIVERA
18 Physical Plant/Operations VC ... Vacant
06 Registrar ... Mrs. Elisa QUILES
37 Director of Financial Aid ... Mrs. Eigna DE JESUS
08 Director of Library ... Mrs. Elsa MARIANI
26 Director Public Relations ... Mrs. Ivonne D. ARROYO
29 Director Alumni ... Ms. Mariana PAGÁN
13 Information/Telecommunications Dir ... Mr. Rigoberto TERRERO
41 Athletic Director ... Mr. Julio FIGUEROA
19 Director Safety & Security ... Mr. José E. MACHUCA
53 Dean of Education ... Dr. Maria del Carmen ARRIBAS
50 Dean of Business Administration ... Dr. José E. BERRÍOS
72 Dean of Science and Technology ... Dr. Marielis E. RIVERA
76 Dean of Health Science ... Dr. Vanessa ORTIZ
83 Dean of Social Science ... Dr. Eloisa GORDON
51 Exec Director Continuing Education ... Vacant
104 Director of International Affairs ... Mrs. Laurie A. MELIN

*Universidad Del Turabo (A)

Estacion Universidad, Box 3030, Gurabo PR 00778-3030
County: Gurabo FICE Identification: 011719
Unit ID: 243601
Telephone: (787) 743-7979 Carnegie Class: DU-Mod
FAX Number: (787) 744-5394 Calendar System: Semester
URL: www.suagm.edu
Established: 1972 Annual Undergrad Tuition & Fees: $5,820
Enrollment: 17,509 Coed
Affiliation or Control: Independent Non-Profit IRS Status: 501(c)3
Highest Offering: Doctorate
Accreditation: M, CAEPT, COPSY, #DIETC, ENG, @NATUR, NURSE, SP, SW

02 Chancellor ... Dr. Dennis ALICEA
11 Vice Chancellor of Admin Affairs ... Dr. Gladys BETANCOURT
05 Vice Chancellor Academic Affairs ... Dr. Roberto LORAN
32 Vice Chancellor of Student Affairs ... Dra. Brunilda APONTE
08 Vice Chancellor Information Res ... Dr. Sarai LASTRA
92 Vice Chancellor Honors Program ... Ms. Maricarmen SANTOS
88 Asst Vice Chanc Eval & Development ... Ms. Keila J. ROCHE
21 Asst Vice Chanc Admin Affairs ... Mrs. Edna ORTA
53 Dean Education ... Mr. Israel RODRIGUEZ
50 Dean Business and Entrepreneurship ... Dr. Juan Carlos SOSA
54 Acting Dean Engineering ... Dr. Rolando GARCIA
72 Dean Natural Science & Technology ... Dr. Teresa LIPSETT
83 Dean Social Sciences & Commun ... Dra. Maria del C. SANTOS
48 Dean Architecture/Design ... Arq. Aurorisa MATEO
76 Dean Health Sciences ... Dra. Nydia BOU
88 Dean Technical Studies ... Ms. Maria E. FLORES
107 Dean Professional Studies ... Ms. Mildred Y. RIVERA
51 Dean Continuing Education ... Mrs. Lizbeth RIVERA
58 Associate Dean of Graduate Studies ... Dr. Sharon CANTRELL
06 Registrar ... Mrs. Zoraida ORTIZ
97 Dean of General Studies ... Mr. Felix R. HUERTAS
27 Director of Marketing ... Ms. Melba G. SANCHEZ
37 Director Office of Financial Aid ... Mrs. Carmen J. RIVERA
26 Director Public Relations ... Ms. Iris SERRANO
18 Chief Facilities/Physical Plant ... Eng. Mayra RODRIGUEZ
29 Coordinator Alumni Relations ... Ms. Rene S. RONDA
30 Chief Development Officer ... Ms. Alba RIVERA
96 Director of Purchasing ... Ms. Norma C. DONEZ
07 Director of Admissions ... Mrs. Diriee Y. RODRIGUEZ
45 Aux Vice President of Planning ... Ms. Mari G. GONZALEZ
15 Director Personnel Services ... Mrs. Iris BERRIOS
36 Assoc Vice Chanc Student Placement ... Ms. Carmen PULLIZA
84 Director Enrollment Management ... Ms. Maria V. FIGUEROA
114 Aux Vice President of Budget ... Ms. Camille LAMBOY
38 Assoc Vice Chanc Student Counseling ... Ms. Samaris COLLAZO
106 Dir Online Education/E-learning ... Dra. Pilar DAVILA
108 Director Institutional Assessment ... Mr. Ernesto ESPINOZA
41 Assoc Dean/Athletic Director ... Mr. Jorge H. GAROFALO

*Universidad Metropolitana (B)

PO Box 21150, Rio Piedras PR 00928-1150
County: San Juan FICE Identification: 025875
Unit ID: 241739
Telephone: (787) 766-1717 Carnegie Class: Masters/L
FAX Number: (787) 759-7663 Calendar System: Semester
URL: www.suagm.edu/umet
Established: 1980 Annual Undergrad Tuition & Fees: $5,820
Enrollment: 13,919 Coed
Affiliation or Control: Independent Non-Profit IRS Status: 501(c)3
Highest Offering: Doctorate
Accreditation: M, ACBSP, ADNUR, CAEPT, NUR

02 SUAGM President ... Dr. José F. MENDEZ
00 Chancellor ... Dr. Carlos M. PADIN
05 Vice Chancellor Academic Affairs ... Dr. Juan OTERO
108 Asst Vice Chanc Inst Assessment ... Dr. Carmen M. LUNA
30 Asst Vice Chanc Inst Development ... Ms. Belissa AQUINO
32 Vice Chanc for Student Affairs ... Mrs. Carmen ROSADO
82 Executive Director Intl Affairs ... Dr. Zaida VEGA
26 Vice Chanc External Resources ... Dr. Gladys CORA
88 Assoc Vice Chanc Accred/Lic ... Mrs. Lina VEGA
11 Assoc Vice Chanc for Admin Affairs ... Dr. Gregorio VILLEGAS
15 Asst Vice Pres for Human Resources ... Mr. Jorge RODRIGUEZ
13 Vice Pres Information Resources ... Mr. Carlos M. DELGADO
110 Int Assoc Vice Chanc Dev/Retention ... Mrs. Claribell OSORIO
114 Asst Vice Pres Analysis & Budget ... Mrs. Aixa ALDARONDO
45 Asst Vice President of Planning ... Dr. Mariela COLLAZO
124 Assoc Vice Chanc Retention/Develop ... Mrs. Awilda PÉREZ
83 Dean Soc Scienc/Human & Comm ... Dr. Mariveliz CABAN
50 Dean of Business ... Dr. Eliel B. IRIZARRY
53 Dean of Education ... Dr. José R. CINTRON
76 Dean of Health Science ... Dr. Lourdes MALDONADO
81 Dean of Science & Technology ... Dr. Karen GONZALEZ
65 Dean of Environmental Affairs ... Dr. María C. ORTIZ
107 Assoc Dean of Professional Studies ... Ms. Melissa GUILLIANI
60 Assoc Dean of Communications ... Mrs. Sugelenia COTTO
79 Assoc Dean of Humanities ... Dr. Roxanna D. DOMENECH
75 Dean of Technical Studies ... Mrs. Laura E. APONTE
51 Exec Director Continuing Education ... Ms. Lorna MARTINEZ
53 Assoc Dean of Education ... Mrs. Barbara PONCE
08 Head Librarian ... Mr. Gabriel LOPEZ
18 Vice Chanc Operations & Facilities ... Eng. Francisco CABALLERO
76 Director of Respiratory Therapy ... Mrs. Katherine GARCÍA
66 Director of Nursing ... Dr. Yanilda RODRIGUEZ
26 Director Public Relations ... Ms. Yvonne GUADALUPE
06 Registrar ... Mrs. Beatriz NIEVES
12 Additional Location Dir Bayam=n ... Dr. Guillermo VAZQUEZ
12 Additional Location Dir Aguadilla ... Mr. Luis A. RUIZ
12 Additional Location Dir Jayuya ... Dr. Irma del Pilar CRUZ
12 Additional Location Dir Comerfo ... Mr. Jessie HERNANDEZ
07 Admissions Director ... Ms. Yadira RIVERA LUGO
41 Athletic Director ... Mr. Ariel ORTIZ
19 Director Security/Safety ... Mr. Wilfredo RONDON
36 Director Student Placement ... Mrs. Lourdes E. MEDINA
37 Director Student Financial Aid ... Mr. Julio A. RODRÍGUEZ
38 Assoc Vice Chanc Student Wellness ... Mrs. Arelis VILLANUEVA

Trinity College of Puerto Rico (C)

PO Box 7313, Ponce PR 00732
FICE Identification: 031159
Unit ID: 431929
Telephone: (787) 848-5739 Carnegie Class: Not Classified
FAX Number: (787) 284-2537 Calendar System: Semester
URL: www.trinitypr.edu
Established: 1969 Annual Undergrad Tuition & Fees: $6,851
Enrollment: 233 Coed
Affiliation or Control: Independent Non-Profit IRS Status: 501(c)3
Highest Offering: Associate Degree
Accreditation: ACICS

01 Executive Director ... Maria DEL PILAR BONNIN OROZCO
05 Academic Director ... Elizabeth PEREZ TOLEDO
10 Director of Finance Office ... Margarita PEREZ DE JESUS
06 Registrar ... Ana SOTO I COLON

Universal Technology College of Puerto Rico (D)

111 Comercio Street, Aguadilla PR 00603
County: Aguadilla FICE Identification: 030297
Unit ID: 376385
Telephone: (787) 882-2065 Carnegie Class: Spec-4-yr-Other Health
FAX Number: (787) 891-2370 Calendar System: Semester
URL: www.unitecpr.edu
Established: 1987 Annual Undergrad Tuition & Fees: N/A
Enrollment: 374 Coed
Affiliation or Control: Independent Non-Profit IRS Status: 501(c)3
Highest Offering: Baccalaureate
Accreditation: ACICS

01 Chief Executive Officer ... Mrs. Keila LOPEZ
11 Administrative Manager ... Vacant
04 Executive Secretary ... Mrs. Marilyn GONZALEZ
05 Chief Academic Officer ... Vacant
06 Registrar ... Ms. Maria ALVAREZ
08 Director of Library ... Ms. Airlyn VAZQUEZ
10 Accountant ... Ms. Nancy MORALES
12 Director of Branch Campus ... Ms. Nelida CARDONA
13 Director Computer Center ... Mr. Zain CORDERO
15 Director Human Resources ... Ms. Luz ESTRELLA
18 Chief Facilities/Physical Plant ... Mr. Danily NIEVES
32 Director Student Affairs ... Vacant
36 Student Placement Officer ... Ms. Luz ESTRELLA
45 Director Planning & Development ... Mrs. Evelyn TORRES
37 Director Student Financial Aid ... Mr. Samuel HERNANDEZ
38 Director Student Counsel ... Mrs. Dalia SANTIAGO
96 Purchasing Officer ... Mrs. Dolores MITJANS
23 Healthcare Services ... Mr. Silverio JIMENEZ
07 Coordinator of Admissions ... Mrs. Teresita RIVERA
50 Dir General Studies/Business Admin ... Mrs. Sandra GONZALEZ
72 Director of Industrial Technology ... Mr. Eduardo FIGUEROA

Universidad Adventista de las Antillas (E)

Box 118, Mayaguez PR 00681-0118
County: Mayaguez FICE Identification: 005019
Unit ID: 241191
Telephone: (787) 834-9595 Carnegie Class: Bac-Diverse
FAX Number: (787) 834-9597 Calendar System: Semester
URL: www.uaa.edu
Established: 1961 Annual Undergrad Tuition & Fees: $6,850
Enrollment: 1,418 Coed
Affiliation or Control: Seventh-day Adventist IRS Status: 501(c)3
Highest Offering: Master's
Accreditation: M, ANEST, #COARC, NUR, NURSE

01 President ... Dr. Obed JIMENEZ
05 Vice President for Academic Affairs ... Dr. Myrna COLON
10 Vice President Financial Affairs ... Mr. Misael JIMENEZ
32 Vice President for Students Affairs ... Mr. Jaime LOPEZ
30 VP Planning and Development ... Dr. Jose D. GOMEZ
42 Religious Affairs Director ... Mr. Abiezer RODRIGUEZ
20 Associate VP Academic Affairs ... Mrs. Yolanda PEREZ
21 Associate Financial Vice President ... Mrs. Madeline CRUZ
88 Director Student Finance Office ... Mr. José TRIGO
66 Dean of the School of Nursing ... Dr. Maria ROSA
66 Director School of Nursing ... Mr. Héctor GONZÁLEZ
53 Dean of the School of Education ... Dr. Maritza LAMBOY
50 Director of Business Administration ... Dr. David L. RAMOS
81 Director Mathematics/Sciences/Comp .. Mrs. Alicia MORADILLOS
73 Director Theology Department ... Dr. Efren PAGAN
06 Registrar ... Mrs. Ana D. TORRES
07 Director of Admissions ... Mrs. Yolanda FERRER
37 Director of Student Financial Aid ... Mrs. Awilda MATOS
26 Dir Public Relations & Promotion ... Miss Lorell VARELA
108 Dir of Institutional Effectiveness ... Dr. Aurea ARAUJO
13 Director Computing and Information ... Mr. Heber VAZQUEZ
08 Librarian ... Mrs. Aixa VEGA
38 Counselor ... Mrs. Ivelisse PEREZ
88 Environmental Services Director ... Mr. Legna VARELA
18 Chief Facilities/Physical Plant ... Mr. Abel RODRIGUEZ
34 Dean of Women ... Mrs. Felicita CRUZ
33 Dean of Men ... Mr. Hector MONTILLA
09 Institutional Researcher ... Dr. Digna M. WILLIAMS

Universidad Central de Bayamon (F)

PO Box 1725, Bayamon PR 00960-1725
County: Bayamon FICE Identification: 005022
Unit ID: 241225
Telephone: (787) 786-3030 Carnegie Class: Masters/M
FAX Number: (787) 740-2200 Calendar System: Semester
URL: www.ucb.edu.pr
Established: 1961 Annual Undergrad Tuition & Fees: $6,220
Enrollment: 1,727 Coed
Affiliation or Control: Roman Catholic IRS Status: 501(c)3
Highest Offering: Master's
Accreditation: M, CACREP, NURSE, SW

01 President ... Dr. Lillian NEGRON
05 Academic Dean ... Dr. Luz C. VALENTIN
11 Interim Administrative Dean ... Mrs. Enid RIVERA
32 Dean of Students ... Mrs. Niza ZAYAS
49 Dir College Liberal Arts/Humanities ... Fr. Yamil SAMALOT
53 Dir Col of Education and Behavior ... Dr. Caroline GONZALEZ
50 Dir Business Development & Tech ... Dr. Nidia COLON
08 Director Learning Resources ... Mrs. Annette VALENTIN
15 Director of Human Resources ... Mrs. Elaine NUNEZ
30 Int Dir Institutional Development ... Mr. Pedro BERMUDEZ
07 Director of Admissions ... Mrs. Wanda APONTE
37 Director Student Financial Aid ... Mrs. Edna ORTIZ
38 Dir Guidance/Counseling Center ... Mrs. Milagros M. RIVERA
06 Registrar ... Mr. Victor COLON
35 Dir Center Learning Stre (CFAEE) ... Mrs. Myrna PEREZ
13 Director of Information System ... Mr. Jose R. AVILES
18 Director Physical Facilities ... Mr. Eliezer GARCIA
26 Int Marketing Director ... Ms. Magdalis LOPEZ
96 Purchase Officer ... Mrs. Jessica OJEDA
09 Institutional Research Officer ... Mrs. Luz M. PALACIOS
66 Nursing Program Coordinator ... Prof. Zaida RUIZ
20 Associate Academic Dean ... Mr. Pedro BERMUDEZ
29 Alumni Relations ... Mrs. Niza ZAYAS
81 Dir College Sciences/Health Profes ... Dr. Pedro ROBLES
03 Executive Vice President ... Mr. Angel VALENTIN
04 Administrative Asst to President ... Mrs. Luz N. VALLELLANES
101 Secretary of the Institution/Board ... Prof. Marcelina VELEZ
105 Director Web Services ... Mr. Manuel ECHEANDIA
106 Dir Online Education/E-learning ... Mr. Jorge L. DIAZ
108 Director Institutional Assessment ... Dr. Judith TORRES
41 Athletic Director ... Mr. Edwin MORALES

Universidad Central Del Caribe (G)

PO Box 60-327, Bayamon PR 00960-6032
County: Bayamon FICE Identification: 021633
Unit ID: 243568
Telephone: (787) 798-3001 Carnegie Class: Spec-4-yr-Med
FAX Number: (787) 798-6836 Calendar System: Semester
URL: www.uccaribe.edu

Established: 1976 Annual Undergrad Tuition & Fees: $10,470
Enrollment: 493 Coed
Affiliation or Control: Independent Non-Profit IRS Status: 501(c)3
Highest Offering: Doctorate
Accreditation: M, MED

01 President .... Dr. Jose Ginel RODRIGUEZ
05 Dean for Academic Affairs .... Dr. Nereida DIAZ-RODRIGUEZ
20 Asst Dean of Curriculum Development .... Dr. Alvaro PEREZ
11 Dean Administrative Affairs .... Ms. Emilia SOTO
32 Dean Student Affairs .... Dr. Omar PEREZ
63 Dean of Medicine .... Dr. Jose Ginel RODRIGUEZ
88 Associate Dean of Medicine .... Mrs. Zilka RIOS
06 Registrar .... Ms. Nilda MONTANEZ-LOPEZ
07 Director of Admissions .... Ms. Irma L. CORDERO
37 Director Student Financial Aid .... Ms. Mayra SERRANO
10 Director of Finances .... Mrs. Iris J. FONT
08 Librarian .... Ms. Mildred RIVERA
51 Director of Continuing Education .... Dr. Frances GARCIA
38 Counselor .... Ms. Mariana T. HERNANDEZ
46 Dean of Research and Graduate Pgms .... Vacant
20 Dean for Clinical & Faculty Affairs .... Dr. Harry MERCADO
30 Director Inst Development Office .... Ms. Yvonne CORSINO

Universidad Pentecostal Mizpa (A)

RR16 Box 4800, San Juan PR 00926
County: San Juan FICE Identification: 031983
Unit ID: 441690
Telephone: (787) 720-4476 Carnegie Class: Spec-4-yr-Faith
FAX Number: (787) 720-2012 Calendar System: Semester
URL: www.mizpa.edu
Established: 1937 Annual Undergrad Tuition & Fees: $4,120
Enrollment: 370 Coed
Affiliation or Control: Pentecostal Church of God IRS Status: 501(c)3
Highest Offering: Master's
Accreditation: BI

01 President .... Miss Naury Y. SANCHEZ CINTRON
05 Dean of Academic Affairs . Mr. Jose G. TORRACA MONDRIGUEZ
10 Dean Administration/Finance ...... Mr. Ismael SOTO MALDONADO
32 Dean of Student Affairs .... Mr. Jorge A. BURGOS
42 Coordinator Ministerial Formation .... Mr. Harry MUNOZ
06 Registrar .... Mr. Leonardo MELENDEZ LEON
08 Librarian .... Mrs. Melanie RODRIGUEZ
37 Student Financial Aid Officer .... Mrs. Myriam JUARBE
26 Chief Public Relations Officer .... Mr. Rafael LABOY
04 Administrative Asst to President .... Mrs. Maria E. VARGAS

Universidad Politecnica De Puerto Rico (B)

Ponce de Leon 377, Box 192017,
San Juan PR 00919-2017
County: San Juan FICE Identification: 021000
Unit ID: 243577
Telephone: (787) 622-8000 Carnegie Class: Spec-4-yr-Eng
FAX Number: (787) 754-8268 Calendar System: Trimester
URL: www.pupr.edu
Established: 1966 Annual Undergrad Tuition & Fees: $8,328
Enrollment: 4,291 Coed
Affiliation or Control: Independent Non-Profit IRS Status: 501(c)3
Highest Offering: Master's
Accreditation: M, ENG, ENGR, IACBE, LSAR

01 President .... Dr. Ernesto VAZQUEZ-BARQUET
03 Executive Vice President .... Eng. Ernesto VAZQUEZ-MARTINEZ
84 Vice Pres Enrollment Management .... Mr. Carlos PEREZ
05 Chief Academic Officer .... Dr. Miguel A. RIESTRA
06 Registrar .... Mrs. Mayra I. LOPEZ
07 Director Admissions .... Mrs. Teresa CARDONA
08 Head Librarian .... Mrs. Mirta COLON
37 Director Financial Aid .... Mr. Sergio VILLOLDO
09 Director of Institutional Research .... Dr. Miguel A. RIESTRA
15 Director Personnel Services .... Ms. Ana CASTELLANO
18 Chief Facilities/Physical Plant .... Mr. Herminio ROMERO
29 Alumni Relations .... Ms. Lourdes ALCRUDO
32 Director Student Affairs .... Mr. Carlos PEREZ
36 Director Student Placement .... Mrs. Angie ESCALANTE
38 Director Student Counseling .... Ms. Sheila VAZQUEZ
10 Associate Business Officer .... Mrs. Olga CANCEL
96 Director of Purchasing .... Mr. Ramon RIVERA
19 Director Security/Safety .... Mr. Miguel ALBARRAN
41 Athletic Director .... Mr. Roberto MEDINA-ORTIZ
50 Dean of Business .... Dr. Eugenio A. LONGO
49 Dean of Arts and Science/Education .... Dr. Catalina VICENS
54 Dean of Engineering .... Dr. Carlos J. GONZALEZ
106 Dir Online Education/E-learning .... Mrs. Heyda DELGADO

Universidad Teologica Del Caribe (C)

PO Box 901, Saint Just PR 00978-0901
County: Trujillo Alto FICE Identification: 023355
Unit ID: 241614
Telephone: (787) 761-0640 Carnegie Class: Spec-4-yr-Faith
FAX Number: (787) 748-9220 Calendar System: Semester
URL: www.utcpr.edu
Established: 1956 Annual Undergrad Tuition & Fees: $3,968
Enrollment: 294 Coed
Affiliation or Control: Church Of God IRS Status: 501(c)3
Highest Offering: Master's
Accreditation: BI

01 President .... Francisco ORTIZ
05 Academic Dean .... Carmen AYALA
06 Registrar .... Maria Judith CARABALLO
10 Administration Dean .... Frankie NEGRON
32 Students Dean .... Wilfredo ADORNO
37 Financial Aid Director .... Claudia RODRIGUEZ
08 Librarian .... Velma Leticia SOSA
45 Planning & Development Officer .... Ana CEPERO
106 Online Program Coordinator .... Luis COLON
58 Graduate School Coordinator .... Glenda VELAZQUEZ
12 North-Central (Dorado) Campus Coord .... Richard D'COSTA
07 Admissions Officer .... Raul MCCLIN

*University of Puerto Rico-Central Administration (D)

1187 Flamboyan Street, San Juan PR 00926-1117
County: San Juan FICE Identification: 003942
Unit ID: 243160
Telephone: (787) 250-0000 Carnegie Class: N/A
FAX Number: (787) 759-6917
URL: www.upr.edu

01 President .... Dr. Uroyoan R. WALKER-RAMOS
03 Executive Director .... Lic. Manuel E. CAMARA-MONTULL
05 Vice President for Academic Affairs .... Dra. Delia M. CAMACHO
09 Vice Pres Research/ Investigation .... Dr. Jose A. LASALDE-DOMINICCI
32 Vice Pres for Student Affairs .... Dra. Margarita E. VILLAMIL-TORRES
12 Chancellor UPR-Rio Piedras Campus .... Dr. Carlos E. SEVERINO-VALDEZ
12 Chancellor UPR-Mayaguez Campus .... Dr. John FERNANDEZ
12 Chanc UPR-Medical Sciences Campus .... Dr. Noel J. AYMAT-SANTANA
12 Chancellor UPR-Cayey Campus .... Dr. Mario MEDINA-CABAN
12 Chancellor UPR-Humacao Campus ..... Dr. Efrain VAZQUEZ-VERA
12 Chancellor UPR-Bayamon Campus .... Prof. Margarita FERNANDEZ-ZAVALA
12 Chancellor UPR-Ponce Campus .... Dr. Leonardo MORALES-TOMASSINI
12 Chancellor UPR-Carolina Campus .. Dr. Moises ORENGO-AVILES
12 Chancellor UPR-Utuado Campus .... Dra. Raquel G. VARGAS-GOMEZ
12 Chancellor UPR-Aguadilla Campus .... Dr. Nelson A. VERA-HERNANDEZ
12 Chancellor UPR-Arecibo Campus . Dr. Otilio GONZALEZ-CORTES
30 Dir Devel & Alumni Affairs Office .... Sra. Gretchen KRANS
88 Dir Ctrl Designer Construction .... Arq. Alejandro ARGUELLES
10 Director Finance Office .... CPA. Norberto GONZALEZ
15 Director Human Resources Office .... Sra. Erika DIAZ-RIOS
11 Director Administrative Service ...... Mr. Juan M. ORTIZ-VAZQUEZ
13 Director Information Systems Office .... Mr. Victor DIAZ-RODRIGUEZ
37 Director Student Financial Aid .... Vacant
43 Director Legal Affairs Office .... Lic. Cristina ALCARAZ-EMMANUELLI
88 Administrator Botanical Garden .... Sr. Juan M. ORTIZ-VAZQUEZ
26 University Press & Communications . Sra. Olga L. VELEZ-ROLON
101 Exec Secretary University Board .... Sra. Mayra M. FLORES-SANTOS
21 Director Budget Office .... Mr. Basilio RIVERA-ARROYO
18 Dir Physical Dev/Infrastrcture Ofc .... Arq. Fernando PLA-GOMEZ

*University of Puerto Rico-Aguadilla (E)

PO Box 6150, Aguadilla PR 00604-6150
County: Aguadilla FICE Identification: 012123
Unit ID: 243106
Telephone: (787) 890-2681 Carnegie Class: Bac-Diverse
FAX Number: (787) 891-3455 Calendar System: Semester
URL: www.uprag.edu
Established: 1972 Annual Undergrad Tuition & Fees (In-State): $2,022
Enrollment: 3,158 Coed
Affiliation or Control: State IRS Status: 501(c)3
Highest Offering: Baccalaureate
Accreditation: M, ACBSP, CAEPN, ENGT

02 Acting Chancellor .... Dr. Herminia M. ALEMAÑY-VALDEZ
05 Acting Dean Academic Affairs . Dr. Evelyn E. GONZALEZ-GARCIA
11 Dean Administration .... Mr. Luis ALVAREZ-RUIZ
32 Dean Student Affairs .... Dr. Migdalia GONZALEZ-GUERRA
06 Registrar .... Mrs. Zaida SERRANO
07 Admissions Officer .... Mrs. Melba SERRANO
08 Head Librarian .... Prof. Elsa MATOS
13 Director of Computer Center .... Mr. Carlos JIMENEZ
15 Director of Personnel .... Mrs. Nilsa MORALES TORRES
19 Director of Security/Safety .... Mr. Edwin VAZQUEZ MEDINA
37 Director Student Financial Aid .... Mrs. Marta A. SOTO
51 Director Continuing Education .... Prof. Luis R. RIVERA
38 Director Student Counseling .... Dr. Gilberto HERRERA
45 Dir Planning/Inst Research Office .... Mr. Gerardo JAVARIZ
18 Chief Facilities/Physical Plant .... Mr. Luis GARCIA
29 Director Alumni Relations .... Mrs. Jeannette AQUINO
96 Purchasing Supervisor .... Mrs. Widylia MEDINA

*University of Puerto Rico at Arecibo (F)

Call Box 4010, Arecibo PR 00614-4010
County: Arecibo FICE Identification: 007228
Unit ID: 243115
Telephone: (787) 815-0000 Carnegie Class: Bac-Diverse
FAX Number: (787) 880-2245 Calendar System: Semester
URL: www.upra.edu
Established: 1967 Annual Undergrad Tuition & Fees (In-State): $2,083
Enrollment: 3,923 Coed
Affiliation or Control: State IRS Status: 501(c)3
Highest Offering: Baccalaureate
Accreditation: #M, ACBSP, ADNUR, CAEPN, CS, ENGT, JOUR, NUR

02 Chancellor .... Prof. Sylka V. TORRES NAVAS
05 Dean of Academic Affairs .. Dra. Weyna M. QUIÑONES CASTILLA
11 Dean of Administrative Affairs .... Prof. José R. FERNÁNDEZ RODRÍGUEZ
32 Dean of Student Affairs .... Dra. Nayla BAEZ
09 Dir Planning/Institutional Research .... Dra. Geissa TORRES
06 Registrar .... Mrs. Widilia RODRIGUEZ
07 Director of Admissions .... Mrs. Magaly MENDEZ
08 Head Librarian .... Prof. Robert ROSADO
15 Director Human Resources .... Dr. Luis LARACUENTE
38 Director Student Counseling .... Dra. Pilar CORDERO
04 Assistant to the Chancellor .... Prof. Juan PUIG
51 Dir Continuing Education/Prof Stds .... Mrs. Carmen TORRES
37 Director Student Financial Aid .... Ms. Daliana FRESSE
41 Athletic Director .... Ms. Ruth NIEVES
13 Computing & Information Management .... Prof. Luis COLON
20 Assoc Dean of Academic Affairs .... Dra. Wanda DELGADO RODRIGUEZ
29 Director Alumni Relations .... Mrs. Mariely ORTIZ
92 Director Honors Program .... Dra. Jane ALBERDESTON
96 Director of Purchasing .... Mrs. Rosaura QUINTANA
18 Chief Facilities/Physical Plant .... Mr. Edwin RAMOS

*University of Puerto Rico at Bayamon (G)

Carr. 174 #170 Industrial Minillas,
Bayamon PR 00959-1911
County: Bayamon FICE Identification: 010975
Unit ID: 243133
Telephone: (787) 993-0000 Carnegie Class: Bac-Diverse
FAX Number: (787) 993-8900 Calendar System: Semester
URL: www.uprb.edu
Established: 1971 Annual Undergrad Tuition & Fees (In-State): $2,083
Enrollment: 4,965 Coed
Affiliation or Control: State IRS Status: 501(c)3
Highest Offering: Baccalaureate
Accreditation: #M, ACBSP, CAEPN, CS, ENGT

02 Chancellor .... Dr. Miguel VÉLEZ-RUBIO
05 Dean Academic Affairs .... Dr. Juan SÁNCHEZ-MÉNDEZ
32 Dean Student Affairs .... Dr. Lenis TORRES-BERRIOS
06 Registrar .... Ms. Carmen CINTRON-OTERO
07 Director Admissions .... Mrs. Carmen MONTES-BURGOS
08 Director Learning Resources .... Prof. Maria de los Angeles ZAVALA-COLÓN
11 Dean Administrative Affairs .... Prof. Jaime LARACUENTE-QUIÑONES
15 Director Human Resources .... Vacant
35 Director Student Activities .... Mrs. Maribelle PERGOLA-RIVERA
36 Director Student Placement .... Prof. Nelson VÁZQUEZ-ESPEJO
37 Director Student Financial Aid .... Mr. Marcos DE JESÚS
38 Director Student Counseling ... Ms. Guadalupe VEGA-GUTIERREZ
81 Director Biology .... Dr. Nilda APONTE-AVELLANET
50 Director Business Administration .... Prof. Norma PÉREZ
09 Director Planning & Inst Research .... Mr. Javier ZAVALA-QUIÑONES
53 Director Education .... Prof. María A. GONZÁLEZ DE RESENDE
54 Director Engineering .... Prof. Jorge VELAR-PRIETO
68 Director Physical Education .... Prof. Carlos MARICHAL-LUGO
79 Director Humanities .... Dr. Nora RODRÍGUEZ-VALLÉS
83 Director Social Sciences .... Dr. Jorge ROVIRA-ALVAREZ
77 Director Computer Science .... Dr. Nelliud TORRES-BATISTA
75 Director Secretarial Sciences .... Prof. Nancy JIMÉNEZ-PÉREZ
72 Director Electronics .... Prof. Jesús ORTIZ-CINTRÓN
23 Director Health Services .... Vacant
96 Director Purchasing .... Ms. María I. CRESPO-MARTÍNEZ
88 Director Special Services .... Ms. Shelciy COLLAZO-CASTRO
81 Director Physics .... Dr. Solange BENITEZ-RAMÍREZ
88 Director English .... Prof. Catherine TORO-CAMACHO
88 Director Spanish .... Dr. Raúl GUADALUPE
81 Director Mathematics .... Prof. Angel MORERA-GONZÁLEZ
88 Director Chemistry .... Dr. Solange BENÍTEZ-RAMÍREZ
18 Coord Facilities/Physical Plant .... Mr. Samuel SAEZ-
10 Director Finance .... Ms. María PÉREZ-SÁNCHEZ
114 Director Budget .... Vacant
13 Director Information Systems .Ms. Barbara LANDRAU-ESPINOSA
105 Director Web Services .... Mr. Orlando ORENGO-ORTEGA
19 Director Security/Safety .... Ms. Yermarie COSME-FERNANDEZ
41 Athletic Director .... Mr. Gerardo BATISTA-SANTIAGO
43 Dir Legal Services/General Counsel ... Ms. Maribel GORBEA-DÍAZ

*University of Puerto Rico-Carolina (H)

PO Box 4800, Carolina PR 00984-4800
County: San Juan FICE Identification: 030160
Unit ID: 243142
Telephone: (787) 257-0000 Carnegie Class: Bac-Diverse
FAX Number: (787) 750-7940 Calendar System: Quarter
URL: www.uprc.edu
Established: 1974 Annual Undergrad Tuition & Fees (In-State): $3,107
Enrollment: 3,796 Coed
Affiliation or Control: State IRS Status: 501(c)3
Highest Offering: Baccalaureate

Accreditation: #M, ACBSP

02 Chancellor ... Dr. Moises ORENGO
05 Dean of Academic Affairs ... Dr. Awilda NUNEZ
11 Dean Administrative Affairs ... Prof. Víctor PÉREZ
32 Dean Student Affairs ... Prof. Nitza AVILA
06 Registrar ... Mr. Abelardo MARTINEZ
15 Human Resources Director ... Mr. Gregory BERMUDEZ
09 Director of Planning/Inst Research ... Prof. Cristina MARTINEZ
08 Director Learning Resources Center ... Prof. Stanley PORTELA
51 Director Continuing Education ... Mrs. Luaida OYOLA
07 Admissions Officer ... Mrs. Celia MENDEZ
13 Coord/Dir Computer Sys Center ... Mr. Liberty ROLON
37 Financial Aid Director ... Mr. Rafael RUIZ
22 Affirmative Action Officer ... Mrs. Rosa QUINONES
48 Director Graphic Arts/Advertising ... Dr. Jorge VALENTIN
50 Director Banking/Finance/Insurance ... Dr. George OTERO
81 Director Natural Sciences ... Dr. Luis TORRES
88 Director Secretarial Sciences ... Dr. Ramonita ROMAN
83 Director Social Sciences ... Dr. Gerardo PERFECTO
68 Director Physical Education ... Prof. Walbert MARCANO
88 Director Auto Tech/Mech Engineering ... Dr. Jose MEZA
79 Director Humanities ... Dr. Heriberto NIEVES
88 Director Spanish ... Prof. Leyda VAZQUEZ
88 Director English ... Prof. Wanda RODRIGUEZ
88 Dean Hotel Administration School ... Dr. Paul RIVERA
23 Director Health Care ... Dr. Zaida DIAZ
18 Supt Operations & Maintenance ... Mr. Herman MUNIZ
41 Athletic Director ... Mr. Arcadio OCASIO
10 Chief Business Officer ... Mrs. Sarahi GUADALUPE

*University of Puerto Rico at Cayey (A)

PO BOX 372230, Cayey PR 00737-2230
County: Cayey FICE Identification: 007206
Unit ID: 243151
Telephone: (787) 738-2161 Carnegie Class: Bac-A&S
FAX Number: (787) 738-8039 Calendar System: Semester
URL: www.cayey.upr.edu
Established: 1967 Annual Undergrad Tuition & Fees (In-State): $2,083
Enrollment: 3,707 Coed
Affiliation or Control: State IRS Status: 501(c)3
Highest Offering: Baccalaureate
Accreditation: #M, ACBSP, CAEPN

02 Chancellor ... Dr. Mario MEDINA
05 Dean of Academic Affairs ... Dr. Raul CASTRO
11 Dean of Administration Affairs ... Prof. Belma BORRAS
32 Dean of Student Affairs ... Dr. Rochellie MARTINEZ
08 Director Library ... Prof. Angel RIOS
06 Registrar ... Mrs. Daisy RAMOS
15 Director Human Resources ... Mrs. Gema FIGUEROA
56 Head Extension Division ... Mr. Jesus MARTINEZ
37 Director Student Financial Aid ... Mrs. Sonia PLACERES
38 Director Student Counseling ... Dr. Lino HERNANDEZ
36 Interim Director Student Placement ... Mrs. Rosa ORTIZ
13 Director Computer Center ... Mrs. Minerva DIAZ
45 Director Planning & Development ... Dr. Luis MATOS
07 Director Admissions ... Mr. Wilfredo LOPEZ
18 Director Facilities/Physical Plant ... Mr. Ricardo SANTIAGO
23 Director Health Services ... Dr. Idellisse BALBES
19 Director Security/Safety ... Mr. Carlos VAZQUEZ
92 Director Honor Program ... Dr. Nilda SANTOS
20 Associate Academic Officer ... Dr. Aurora RIVERA
41 Director Athletic Program ... Mr. Ismael RAMOS
29 Director Alumni Relations ... Mrs. Leilany C. RIVERA
96 Director Purchasing ... Mrs. Maria CORTES
43 Director Legal Services ... Mr. Francisco MORENO
88 Student Ombudsman ... Prof. Rolando CID
53 Education ... Dr. Ricardo MOLINA
79 Humanities ... Dr. Walter MUCHER
83 Social Sciences ... Dr. Angel RODRIGUEZ
88 Hispanic Studies ... Prof. Miguel FORNERIN
88 English ... Prof. David LIZARDI
81 Chemistry ... Dr. Mayra PAGAN
65 Natural Science ... Dr. Glorivee ROSARIO
88 Biology ... Dr. Rosa del C TORRES
94 Women's Studies ... Dr. Irma LUGO
09 Director Assess & Inst Research ... Dr. Luis MATOS
10 Chief Business Officer ... Ms. Wanda CRUZ
114 Director Budgeting ... Mrs. Maria SANTIAGO
81 Mathematics-Physics ... Dr. Jose ALONSO
50 Business Administration ... Prof. Jaime CRUZ
88 RISE Program ... Dr. Robert ROSS
88 Interdisciplinary Research Inst ... Ms. Vionex MARTI
88 Museum ... Mr. Jonathan BERRIOS
100 Chief of Staff ... Prof. Gladys RAMOS
101 Secretary of the Institution/Board ... Mrs. Sylvia TUBENS
104 Director Study Abroad ... Mrs. Rumaliz SANTINI
105 Director Web Services ... Mr. William SANDOVAL
26 Chief Public Relations/Marketing ... Ms. Yari RIVAS
88 Assoc Dean of Administrative Affs ... Mr. Samuel GONZALEZ
88 Director of Cultural Activities ... Mr. Eleric RIVERA
88 Director of Preschool Develop ... Dr. Carmen BERRIOS

*University of Puerto Rico-Humacao (B)

Call Box 860, Humacao PR 00792
County: Humacao FICE Identification: 003943
Unit ID: 243179
Telephone: (787) 850-0000 Carnegie Class: Bac-Diverse
FAX Number: (787) 852-4638 Calendar System: Semester
URL: www.uprh.edu
Established: 1962 Annual Undergrad Tuition & Fees (In-State): $2,083
Enrollment: 3,845 Coed
Affiliation or Control: State IRS Status: 501(c)3
Highest Offering: Baccalaureate
Accreditation: #M, ACBSP, CAEPN, ENGT, NUR, PTAA, SW

02 Interim Chancellor ... Dr. Hector RÍOS
05 Interim Dean of Academic Affairs ... Dr. Carlos O. CORDERO
11 Interim Dean Administrative Affairs ... Mr. Nelson SANTOS
04 Assistant to the Chancellor ... Mr. Juan C. CASTRO
32 Interim Dean of Student Affairs ... Prof. José A. BALDAGUEZ
20 Assistant Dean of Academic Affairs ... Dr. Edgardo RIVERA
45 Interim Dir Planning Office ... Dr. Ivelisse BLASINI
06 Interim Registrar ... Mr. Jorge ACEVEDO
07 Interim Director of Admissions ... Mrs. Carmen RIVERA
08 Interim Director of the Library ... Mr. Luis RODRIGUEZ
13 Interim Dir System Info Ofc ... Mr. Jorge DAVILA
15 Interim Director Human Resources ... Dr. Carlos O. FIGUEROA
10 Interim Director of Finance ... Mr. Nelson SANTOS
37 Interim Dir Financial Aid Officer ... Mrs. Brunilda LÓPEZ
88 Interim Dir Counseling Office ... Dr. Cástula SANTIAGO
51 Dir Continuing Education/Extension ... Mr. Rody RIVERA
23 Director Health Services ... Vacant
18 Chief Facilities/Physical Plant ... Eng. Daniel ROSARIO
19 Interim Director Security/Transit ... Mr. Juan C. CASTRO
96 Purchase Supervisor ... Mr. Javier A. MUYET
88 Student Ombuds Person ... Prof. Elizabeth R. HODGES
41 Athletic Activities Director ... Mr. Elmer WILLIAMS
114 Interim Director of Budget Office ... Mrs. Daisy RIVERA
108 Office of Institutional Assessment ... Vacant
88 Director Svcs Population Disab ... Prof. Magaly RODRIGUEZ
101 Sec of Academic Senate/Adm Board ... Prof. Amelia MALDONADO
29 Alumni Relations ... Mrs. Jose N. GONZALEZ
88 Envir Health & Occupational Safety ... Mrs. Angelica TORRES
26 Press Relations ... Mrs. Meiling VILLAFAÑE
50 Interim Dir Business Administration ... Prof. Enrique SUAREZ
88 Interim Director of Biology Dept ... Dr. Hector AYALA
88 Interim Director of Chemistry Dept ... Dr. Fabio ALAPE
60 Interim Dir of Communication Dept ... Prof. Hector PIÑERO
53 Interim Director of Education Dept ... Dr. Jesús I. COLÓN
88 Interim Director of English Dept ... Dr. Nilsa LUGO
79 Interim Director of Humanities Dept ... Dr. Zoe JIMENEZ
81 Interim Dir of Mathematics Dept ... Dr. José TORO
66 Interim Director of Nursing Dept ... Dr. Alejandro BORRERO
75 Interim Dir Occup Therapy Dept ... Prof. Mayra LEBRON
88 Interim Dir Office System Adm Dept ... Prof. Ivelisse REYES
76 Interim Dir Physical Therapy Dept ... Dr. Moises CARTAGENA
88 Interim Dir Physics & Elect Dept ... Dr. Rogerio FURLAN
83 Interim Dir Social Science Dept ... Dr. María de Lourdes LARA
70 Interim Dir of Social Work Dept ... Dr. Evelyn CRUZ
88 Interim Director of Spanish Dept ... Dr. Carmen I. ORAMA
92 Interim Dir Academic Honor Program ... Prof. Aida KALIL
88 Dir of Communication Competences ... Vacant
88 Graphics Art Supervisor ... Mr. Carlos LAZU
22 Dir Affirmative Action/EEO ... Mrs. Mariolga ROTGER
46 Dir Subsidized Research & Programs ... Vacant
88 Director Day Care Center ... Mrs. Carmen LUNA
88 Museum Director ... Vacant
88 Student Support Service Director ... Prof. Olga L. BERRÍOS
88 Upward Bound Director ... Mrs. Myriam CINTRÓN
88 Director of ExTgesis Journal ... Prof. Carlos R. GÓMEZ

*University of Puerto Rico-Mayaguez Campus (C)

Call Box 9000, Mayaguez PR 00681-9000
County: Mayaguez FICE Identification: 003944
Unit ID: 243197
Telephone: (787) 832-4040 Carnegie Class: Masters/M
FAX Number: (787) 834-3031 Calendar System: Semester
URL: www.uprm.edu
Established: 1911 Annual Undergrad Tuition & Fees (In-State): $2,083
Enrollment: 12,771 Coed
Affiliation or Control: State IRS Status: 501(c)3
Highest Offering: Doctorate
Accreditation: M, ACBSP, CAEPN, ENG, NUR

02 Chancellor ... Dr. John FERNANDEZ VAN CLEVE
05 Dean of Academic Affairs ... Dr. Betsy MORALES
10 Dean of Administration ... Prof. Lucas N. AVILES
32 Dean of Students ... Dr. Francisco MALDONADO FORTUNET
49 Acting Dean of Arts & Sciences ... Dr. Fernando GILBES
54 Dean of Engineering ... Dr. Agustin RULLAN
47 Dean Agricultural Sciences ... Dr. Raul MACCHIAVELLI
50 Dean Business Administration ... Prof. Ana MARTIN
58 Director of Graduate Studies ... Dr. Carlos QUINONEZ
13 Director of Computer Center ... Mr. Martin MELENDEZ
06 Registrar ... Mrs. Xenia RAMIREZ
08 Acting Director of the Library ... Prof. Anidza VALENTIN RODRIGUEZ
07 Director of Admissions ... Mrs. Maria ALEMANY
37 Dir Student Financial Aid ... Mrs. Myriam BARRETO
36 Director Student Placement ... Mrs. Nancy NIEVES
26 Press Office Director ... Mrs. Mariam L. ROSA VELEZ
45 Director Inst Research/Planning ... Prof. Mercedes FERRER
29 Director Alumni Association ... Mr. Yomarachaliff LUCIANO-FIGUEROA
15 Director Personnel Services ... Mrs. Lissette V. GONZALEZ
18 Acting Director Physical Resources ... Eng. Wilson ORTIZ
38 Acting Director Student Counseling ... Dr. Francisco MALDONADO FORTUNET
21 Director Financial Services ... Mr. Angel F. PEREZ PACHECO
51 Director Continuing Education ... Dr. Jose FERRER
19 Acting Director Security/Safety ... Ms. Maria I. FERNANDEZ
23 Director Health Services ... Mrs. Rosie TORRES
41 Director Athletic Activities ... Mr. Ray QUINONES
43 Director Legal Services ... Lcda. Gretchen HUYKE
108 Director Institutional Assessment ... Prof. Mercedes FERRER
100 Special Assistant to the Chancellor ... Mrs. Damaris TORRES
101 Secretary of Administrative Board ... Mrs. Judith RAMIREZ
105 Director Web Services ... Mr. Martin MELENDEZ
22 Dir Affirmative Action/EEO ... Mrs. Vanessa ALEQUIN BAEZ
96 Acting Director of Purchasing ... Mr. Frankie D. PADILLA

*University of Puerto Rico-Medical Sciences Campus (D)

PO Box 365067, San Juan PR 00936-5067
County: San Juan FICE Identification: 024600
Unit ID: 243203
Telephone: (787) 758-2525 Carnegie Class: Spec-4-yr-Med
FAX Number: (787) 758-2556 Calendar System: Other
URL: www.rcm.upr.edu
Established: 1950 Annual Undergrad Tuition & Fees (In-State): N/A
Enrollment: 2,313 Coed
Affiliation or Control: State IRS Status: 501(c)3
Highest Offering: Doctorate
Accreditation: M, ANEST, AUD, CAHIIM, CYTO, DA, DENT, DIETI, HSA, MED, MT, NMT, NURSE, OT, PH, PHAR, PTA, RAD, SP

02 Chancellor ... Dr. Ramon F. GONZALEZ
05 Dean Academic Affairs ... Dr. Jose A. CAPRILES
32 Dean Students Affairs ... Prof. Rosa M. VELEZ
11 Dean of Administration ... Prof. Carlos ORTIZ
63 Dean School of Medicine ... Dr. Edgar COLON NEGRON
52 Dean School Dental Medicine ... Dr. Ana LOPEZ
69 Dean Grad School Public Health ... Dr. Ralph RIVERA
67 Dean School of Pharmacy ... Dr. Wanda MALDONADO
76 Dean School Health Prof ... Dr. Barbara SEGARRA
66 Dean School of Nursing ... Dr. Suane SANCHEZ
100 Chief of Staff ... Mrs. Lilia FIGUERA
20 Associate Academic Officer ... Dr. Arlene SANCHEZ
13 Ctr Informatics/Technology Director ... Mr. Jose Luis QUINONES
43 Director Legal Services ... Lcda. Irene REYES
26 Chief Information Officer ... Mr. Angel HOYOS
06 Registrar ... Mr. Reinaldo POMALES
08 Library Director ... Dr. Irma QUINONES
09 Director Inst & Academic Research ... Dr. Wanda BARRETO
24 Director Educational Media ... Prof. Luis ESTREMERA
35 Assoc Dean Student Affairs ... Dr. Belinda BEAUCHAMP
07 Director of Admissions ... Mrs. Maribel ORTIZ
38 Director of Student Counseling ... Prof. Blanca AMOROS
37 Director of Student Financial Aid ... Mrs. Yolanda RIVERA
10 Chief Financial Officer ... Mrs. Yolanda QUIÑONES
15 Director Personnel Services ... Mrs. Lizette RAMIU
18 Chief Facilities/Physical Plant ... Mr. Julio A. COLLAZO
96 Director of Purchasing ... Mr. Jose CARDONA
19 Director Security Office ... Mr. William FIGUEROA
108 Director Institutional Assessment ... Prof. Lillian RIOS
25 Chief Contracts/Grants Admin ... Dr. Marcia CRUZ

*University of Puerto Rico at Ponce (E)

PO Box 7186, Ponce PR 00732-7186
County: Ponce FICE Identification: 009652
Unit ID: 243212
Telephone: (787) 844-8181 Carnegie Class: Bac-Diverse
FAX Number: (787) 844-8679 Calendar System: Semester
URL: www.uprp.edu
Established: 1970 Annual Undergrad Tuition & Fees (In-State): $2,083
Enrollment: 3,543 Coed
Affiliation or Control: State IRS Status: 501(c)3
Highest Offering: Baccalaureate
Accreditation: #M, ACBSP, CAEPN, ENGT, PTAA

02 Chancellor ... Dr. Doris S. TORRES
04 Executive Officer III ... Vacant
04 Assistant to the Chancellor ... Prof. Lizzette ROIG
05 Dean Academic Affairs ... Prof. Carmen A. BRACERO
11 Dean Administrative Affairs ... Mr. Isaac COLON
32 Dean Student Affairs ... Mrs. Acmin VELAZQUEZ
20 Associate Academic Dean ... Dr. Joycette SANTOS
45 Dir Inst Research/Planning Officer ... Dr. Jennifer ALICEA
08 Director Library ... Prof. Brett DIAZ
06 Registrar ... Mrs. Marya Z. SANTIAGO
38 Director of Student Counseling ... Dr. Efrain RIOS
07 Director of Admissions ... Mrs. Emily MATOS
37 Director of Financial Aid ... Mr. Arturo ALMODOVAR
15 Director of Personnel Services ... Mr. Juan C. LEON
88 Director of Cultural Activities ... Dr. Jose L. PONS
13 Director of Computer Center ... Mr. Juan VEGA
18 Chief Facilities/Physical Plant ... Mr. Alberto GARCIA
40 Director Bookstore ... Vacant
41 Athletic Director ... Mrs. Lesbia COLON
23 Director Health Services ... Dr. Pedro COLLAZO
29 Director Alumni Relations ... Mrs. Valerie DIAZ
30 Chief Development ... Vacant
19 Director of Security/Traffic ... Mr. German PIMENTEL
88 Coordinator Security/Safety ... Mrs. Celia GONZALEZ
22 Coordinator Affirmative Action ... Mrs. Marlene RODRIGUEZ

*University of Puerto Rico-Rio Piedras Campus (F)

PO Box 23300, Rio Piedras PR 00931-3300
County: San Juan FICE Identification: 007108
Unit ID: 243221

Telephone: (787) 763-3930 Carnegie Class: DU-Higher
FAX Number: (787) 764-8799 Calendar System: Semester
URL: www.uprrp.edu
Established: 1903 Annual Undergrad Tuition & Fees (In-State): $2,078
Enrollment: 16,454 Coed
Affiliation or Control: State IRS Status: 501(c)3
Highest Offering: Doctorate
Accreditation: M, ACBSP, CACREP, CAEPN, CS, DIETD, JOUR, LAW, LIB, PLNG, SPAA, SW

00 Interim Chancellor .... Dr. Luis A. FERRAO DELGADO
02 Interim President .... Dr. Darrel HILLMAN BARRERA
05 Dean Academic Affairs .... Vacant
11 Dean of Administration .... Dr. Grisel E. MELÉNDEZ RAMOS
32 Dean of Students .... Dr. Gloria DÍAZ URBINA
20 Associate Dean Academic Affairs .... Vacant
50 Dean Business Administration .. Dr. Carmen FIGUEORA JIMÉNEZ
48 Dean of Architecture .... Arq. Mayra JIMÉNEZ
81 Dean of Natural Sciences .... Dr. Carlos GONZÁLEZ
83 Dean of Social Sciences .... Dr. Isabel MONTAÑEZ
61 Dean of Law .... Ms. Vivian NEPTUNE
97 Dean of General Studies .... Dr. Vicky MUÑIZ
79 Dean of Humanities .... Dr. Agnes BOSCH
58 Dean Graduate Studies/ Research .... Dr. Pedro J. RODRIGUEZ ESQUERDO
53 Dean of Education .... Dr. Roamé TORRES
35 Asst Dean Student Affairs .... Ms. Estela PEREZ RIESTRA
38 Director of Student Counseling ...... Mrs. Maria JIMENEZ CHAFEY
30 Int Dir Devel & Alumni Relations .... Mrs. Elsa MARIN
06 Registrar .... Mr. Juan M. APONTE
08 Director of Library System .... Dr. Miguel SANTIAGO
15 Director of Human Resources .. Mrs. Sheyla M. MÉNDEZ ROMÁN
07 Director of Admissions .... Mr. Ángel ECHEVARRÍA
13 Director of Computer Center .... Mr. José PABÓN
62 Director Grad Sch Library/Info Sci .... Dr. José SÁNCHEZ
60 Director School of Communication .... Dr. Jorge SANTIAGO
58 Dir Graduate Sch of Planning .... Dr. Carmen CONCEPCIÓN
51 Dir Continuing Educ/Extension .... Dr. Carlos ROSADO
09 Director of Institutional Research .... Vacant
18 Chief Planning/Physical Devel Ofc .... Arq. Miguel PAGÁN
26 Chief Public Relations Officer .... Mrs. Lorna CASTRO
37 Director of Student Financial Aid .... Mr. Anibal ALVALLE
96 Director of Purchasing .... Mr. Ángel DÍAZ
114 Director of Budget .... Ms. Rosa M. ALERS RAMOS
19 Director Security/Safety .... Mr. Victor ROSARIO DELGADO

*University of Puerto Rico at Utuado (A)

PO Box 2500, Utuado PR 00641-2500
County: Utuado FICE Identification: 029384
Unit ID: 243188
Telephone: (787) 894-2828 Carnegie Class: Bac/Assoc-Mixed
FAX Number: (787) 894-1081 Calendar System: Semester
URL: www.uprutuado.edu
Established: 1979 Annual Undergrad Tuition & Fees (In-State): $2,083
Enrollment: 1,461 Coed
Affiliation or Control: State IRS Status: 501(c)3
Highest Offering: Baccalaureate
Accreditation: #M, ACBSP, CAEPN

02 Chancellor .... Dr. Raquel G. VARGAS GOMEZ
05 Academic Dean .... Dr. Eneida RODRIGUEZ
10 Chief Business Officer .... Dr. Edgar DEL TORO
32 Chief Student Life Officer .... Mrs. Maria V. ROBLES
08 Library Director .... Prof. Regina OQUENDO
09 Director Institutional Research .... Vacant
06 Registrar .... Mrs. Ivelisse RIVERA
07 Director of Admission .... Vacant
15 Director Human Resources .... Vacant
38 Director Student Counseling .... Mr. Amilcar GONZALEZ
37 Director Student Financial Aid .... Mrs. Edymariel CORTES
13 Director Information Systems .... Mr. Hector L. LOPEZ
19 Director Security/Safety .... Mr. Miguel TORRES
41 Director of Athletics .... Mr. Miguel RODRIGUEZ
47 Director of Agriculture .... Prof. Eladio GONZALEZ
50 Dir Office Systems/Business Admin .... Dr. Carmen L. LEON
96 Director of Purchasing .... Ms. Luz E. MARTINEZ
51 Director Continuing Education .... Vacant
53 Director Education .... Dra. Yolanda MOLINA
65 Director Natural Sciences .... Vacant
79 Director Humanities/Spanish/English .... Vacant

University of the Sacred Heart (B)

PO Box 12383, San Juan PR 00914-8505
County: San Juan FICE Identification: 003937
Unit ID: 243443
Telephone: (787) 728-1515 Carnegie Class: Masters/M
FAX Number: (787) 728-1692 Calendar System: Semester
URL: www.sagrado.edu
Established: 1935 Annual Undergrad Tuition & Fees: $6,000
Enrollment: 5,060 Coed
Affiliation or Control: Roman Catholic IRS Status: 501(c)3
Highest Offering: Master's
Accreditation: M, CAEPN, NURSE, SW

01 President .... Dr. Gilberto MARXUACH-TORROS
84 Chief of Staff/Dir Enrollment Mgmt .... Mrs. Lourdes BERTRAN-PASARELL
05 Chief Academic Officer .... Dr. Eloísa GORDON
11 Dean of Administration .... Mr. Jose L. RICCI
30 VP University Relations and Develop .. Mr. Eduardo AROSEMENA
10 Int Chief Financial Officer .... Mrs. Rebecca QUINTERO
20 Associate Academic Dean .... Prof. Yezmin HERNANDEZ-SOTO
32 Associate Students Dean .... Prof. Pedro FRAILE
09 Director of Inst Research Office .... Dr. Maria DEL C. RODRIGUEZ
07 Director of Admissions .... Mr. Edwin RIOS
06 Registrar .... Ms. Mildred PINEIRO
26 Communications & Digital Media Dir .... Mrs. Sandra POMALES
21 Director of Budgeting .... Mrs. Maribel VALENTIN
91 Chief Information Technology Office .... Mr. Severo ALICEA
18 Chief Facilities/Physical Plant .... Mr. Jose L. RICCI
15 Director Human Resources .... Mrs. Marilyn FIGUEROA
29 Director Alumni Relations .... Mrs. Arelis MARRERO
08 Head Librarian .... Mrs. Sonia DIAZ
37 Director of Financial Aid .... Ms. June C. ANDRADE
39 Director Student Housing .... Mr. Carlos MOLL
41 Athletic Director .... Mrs. Mari BATISTA
50 Director Business Administration .... Prof. Arturo FIGUEROA
53 Director Education Department .... Dr. Migdalia OQUENDO
81 Director Natural Sciences .... Prof. Agda CARDERO
79 Dir Fac Intdspln Human/Social Stds .... Dr. Sylvia ALVAREZ
21 Internal Auditor .... Mr. Ricardo AGUIRRE
51 Assoc Director Continuing Education .... Mrs. Elvia AGOSTO
19 Director Security/Safety .... Capt. Jose LOZADA

VIRGIN ISLANDS

University of the Virgin Islands (C)

#2 John Brewers Bay, Saint Thomas VI 00802-9990
FICE Identification: 003946
Unit ID: 243665
Telephone: (340) 776-9200 Carnegie Class: Masters/S
FAX Number: (340) 693-1005 Calendar System: Semester
URL: www.uvi.edu
Established: 1962 Annual Undergrad Tuition & Fees (In-State): $5,235
Enrollment: 2,321 Coed
Affiliation or Control: State IRS Status: 501(c)3
Highest Offering: Doctorate
Accreditation: M, CAEPN, NUR

01 President .... Dr. David HALL
88 VP/Business Development/Innovation .... Dr. Haldane DAVIES
04 Director of Presidential Operations .... Ms. Una DYER
101 Board Liaison .... Ms. Gail T. STEELE
05 Provost/VP for Academic Affairs .... Dr. Camille A. MCKAYLE
46 Interim Vice Provost/ECC/RPS .... Dr. Frank MILLS
53 Dean School of Education .... Dr. Linda V. THOMAS
81 Dean College of Sci & Math .... Dr. Sandra ROMANO
50 Dean School of Business .... Dr. Stephen A. REAMES
79 Int Dean Col Liberal Arts/Soc Sci .... Dr. Kimarie ENGERMAN
66 Dean School of Nursing .... Ms. Beverley A. LANSIQUOT
104 Assoc Provost/Grad/Global/Acad Affs .. Dr. James S. MADDIRALA
84 VP Access/Enroll Services .... Dr. Kevin L. WILLIAMS
07 Int Dir Undergrad Recruit/Admiss .... Ms. Charmaine I. SMITH
06 Registrar .... Ms. Monifa J. POTTER
37 Director of Financial Aid .... Ms. Cheryl A. ROBERTS
32 Dean of Students-STT Campus .... Ms. Verna J. RIVERS
36 Dir Counseling & Career Services .... Ms. Patricia TOWAL
38 Director of Counseling Services .... Ms. Dahlia STRIDIRON
35 Director of Student Activities .... Mr. Leon A. LAFOND
30 VP Institutional Advancement .... Mr. Mitchell NEAVES
44 Director of Annual Giving .... Ms. Linda SMITH
30 Capital Campaign Manager .... Mr. Jose Raul CARRILLO
102 Dir Corp/Foundation/Govt Relations .... Mr. Richard G. CLEAVER
10 VP Administration & Finance .... Ms. Shirley L. LAKE-KING
21 Controller .... Ms. Muriel "Peggy" SMITH
15 Director of HR/Org Development .... Mr. Charles Ronald MEEK
19 Acting Chief/Campus Police/ Security .... Mr. Theodore E. GLASFORD
18 Director of Physical Plant .... Mr. Charles MARTIN
13 VP Info Tech Services & Assessment .... Vacant
14 Assistant Chief Information Officer .... Ms. Sharlene J. HARRIS
08 Library Manager .... Mrs. Celia P. PRINCE-RICHARD

University of the Virgin Islands-St. Croix (D)

RR1 10,000, Kingshill VI 00850-9781
Telephone: (340) 778-1620 Identification: 770173
Accreditation: &M

Index of Key Administrators

A

ABSHIRE, Martha Ann ... 225-490-1685 191 G
marthaa.absire@ololcollege.edu
ABSTON, Byron .... 205-391-2388.... 3 E
babston@sheltonstate.edu
ABSTON, Kara .... 501-279-4442.. 19 G
kabston@harding.edu
ABT, William, R .... 262-551-6200 506 H
wabt@carthage.edu
ABTS, Betsy .... 253-566-5326 499 A
babts@tacomacc.edu
ABTS, Polly .... 920-693-1720 513 H
polly.abts@gotoltc.edu
ABU-AGEEL, Nayef .... 301-369-2468 202 J
nmabuageel@captechu.edu
ABU-GHAZALEH, Nabil . 619-644-7100.. 45 A
nabil.abu-ghazaleh@gcccd.edu
ABU-SHAHEEN, Dania ... 914-813-9212 323 K
dshaheen@sarahlawrence.edu
ABUHAMAD, Alfred, Z .. 757-446-7979 480 C
abuhamaz@evms.edu
ABUSALIM, Murad .... 956-295-3568 461 F
murad.abusalim@tsc.edu
ABUSHABAN, Sahar ...... 619-660-4654.. 44 L
sahar.abushaban@gcccd.edu
ABUTIN, Albert .... 714-992-7076.. 54 A
aabutin@fullcoll.edu
ABUZNEID,
Abdelshakour, A .... 203-576-4113.. 88 F
abuzneid@bridgeport.edu
ACARDO, John .... 630-637-5754 147 E
jjacardo@noctrl.edu
ACCAPADI, Mamta, M ... 407-646-2185 106 J
maccapadi@rollins.edu
ACCARDI, Michael .... 978-837-5062 221 G
accardim@merrimack.edu
ACCIARDO, Linda, A ..... 401-874-2116 417 E
lindaa@uri.edu
ACEVEDO, Beatriz .... 212-924-5900 330 G
bursar@swedishinstitute.edu
ACEVEDO, Dary .... 787-891-0925 523 G
dacevedo@aguadilla.inter.edu
ACEVEDO, Francisco ..... 787-892-5700 524 D
facevedo@intersg.edu
ACEVEDO, Ivonne .... 787-891-0925 523 G
iaecheva@ns.inter.edu
ACEVEDO, Jorge .... 787-850-9380 528 B
jorge.acevedo4@upr.edu
ACEVEDO, Luis, A .... 787-891-0925 523 G
luacevedo@aguadilla.inter.edu
ACEVES, Salvador, D ..... 303-458-4144.. 82 D
saceves@regis.edu
ACEY, Denise .... 573-334-9181 262 C
denise@metrobusinesscollege.edu
ACHAN, Jennifer .... 661-395-4482.. 47 A
ACHARYA, Raj .... 812-856-1079 159 H
dean@soic.indiana.edu
ACHARYA, Suresh .... 269-749-7666 236 A
sacharya@olivetcollege.edu
ACHEMIRE, Roy .... 918-293-3800 378 B
roy.achemire@okstate.edu
ACHENBACH, David ...... 508-793-3320 213 D
dachenba@holycross.edu
ACHENBACH, USMS,
Gerard .... 231-995-1203 235 B
gachenbach@nmc.edu
ACHESON, Carol .... 503-253-3443 385 B
cacheson@ocom.edu
ACHS, Carol .... 480-461-7742.. 13 I
carol.achs@mesacc.edu
ACHTER, John .... 715-232-2468 512 A
achterj@uwstout.edu
ACHTERBERG,
Cheryl, L .... 614-292-2461 367 H
achterberg.1@osu.edu
ACHTERMAN, Douglas .. 408-848-4809.. 44 B
dachterman@gavilan.edu
ACIERNO, Lou .... 212-752-1530 312 G
lou.acierno@limcollege.edu
ACKERLEY, Roseanne ... 513-487-3234 309 F
rackerley@huc.edu
ACKERMAN, Aidan .... 617-262-5000 212 C
aidan.ackerman@the-bac.edu
ACKERMAN, Debbie ...... 217-732-3155 143 G
dackerman@lincolncollege.edu
ACKERMAN, Denise ...... 845-758-7625 298 I
ackerman@bard.edu
ACKERMAN,
Denise Ann .... 413-528-7297 211 B
ACKERMAN, Kathy .... 828-395-1522 344 A
kackerman@isothermal.edu
ACKERMAN, Tom .... 618-664-6509 139 A
tom.ackerman@greenville.edu
ACKERMAN, Tom .... 352-271-2905 107 E
thomas.ackerman@sfcollege.edu
ACKLAND, Terri .... 520-494-5227.. 11 P
terri.ackland@centralaz.edu
ACKLEH, Azmy .... 337-482-6986 197 F
asa5773@louisiana.edu

ACKLEY, Brian .... 607-844-8222 331 D
ackleyb@tompkinscortland.edu
ACKLEY, Darren .... 715-675-3331 514 F
ackley@ntc.edu
ACKLEY, Lavon .... 229-430-0415 114 J
lackley@albanytech.edu
ACKMAN, Elizabeth, R ... 315-684-6043 329 F
ackmaner@morrisville.edu
ACOB-NASH, Mari .... 360-416-7786 498 F
mari.acobnash@skaagit.edu
ACOLASTE, Ras .... 703-878-2800.. 93 B
ACOSTA, Araceli .... 210-924-4338 443 N
araceli.acosta@bua.edu
ACOSTA, Esmeralda, M . 623-845-3012.. 13 H
esmeralda.acosta@gccaz.edu
ACOSTA, Kathy .... 214-860-1416 448 A
kacosta@dcccd.edu
ACOSTA, Maria .... 773-838-7984 136 A
macosta68@ccc.edu
ACOSTA, Pilar .... 407-708-2432 107 G
acostap@seminolestate.edu
ACOSTA, Vanessa .... 714-966-8500.. 73 D
vacosta@ves.edu
ACOSTA-FUMERO,
Carmen, J .... 787-841-2000 525 J
cacosta@pucpr.edu
ACOVIO, Connie .... 210-486-3960 441 H
cacovio@alamo.edu
ACQUAAH, George .... 301-860-3610 208 E
gacquaah@bowiestae.edu
ACREE, Cheryl .... 229-333-2126 128 G
cheryl.acree@wiregrass.edu
ACREE, Elizabeth, A ...... 520-621-5200.. 16 J
acree@email.arizona.edu
ACREE, Jenny .... 785-243-1435 176 I
jacree@cloud.edu
ACTON, Anne .... 617-422-7282 222 J
aacton@nesl.edu
ACTON, James .... 312-567-5000 140 I
jacton@iit.edu
ACTOR-ENGEL, Rose ..... 215-635-7300 396 B
raengel@gratz.edu
ACUNA, Angela .... 602-787-7029.. 13 J
angela.l.acuna@paradisevalley.edu
ACUNA, Angela .... 408-498-5133.. 38 I
aacuna@cogswell.edu
ACUNA, April .... 801-818-8900 472 E
april.acuna@provocollege.edu
ADA, Raymond .... 719-632-7626.. 80 J
rada@intellitec.edu
ADACHI, Lesley, B .... 680-488-2471 520 E
lbadachi@gmail.com
ADACHI, Themy-Jo .... 510-430-3285.. 52 E
themy@mills.edu
ADADE, Anthony .... 508-929-8714 219 A
aadade@worcester.edu
ADAIR, Adam .... 870-512-7801.. 18 D
adam_adair@asun.edu
ADAIR, Charles .... 631-420-2198 329 D
charles.adair@famingdale.edu
ADAIR, Kathy .... 906-248-3354 227 P
kadair@bmcc.edu
ADAIR, Matt .... 952-829-2459 240 H
matt.adair@bethfel.org
ADAIR, Shandra .... 303-837-0825.. 76 K
sadair@aii.edu
ADAM, Baba .... 209-384-6000.. 51 G
ADAM, Charles, A .... 563-333-6151 173 A
adamcharlesa@sau.edu
ADAM, Iddi .... 651-779-3447 244 D
iddi.adam@century.edu
ADAM, Jakob .... 512-313-3000 446 N
jakob.adam@concordia.edu
ADAM, Janice, K .... 510-981-2852.. 56 F
jadam@peralta.edu
ADAM, Michelle .... 305-809-3279.. 99 L
michelle.adam@fkcc.edu
ADAM, Nabil .... 973-353-5541 290 D
adam@adam.rutgers.edu
ADAM, Sharla .... 325-942-2041 463 C
sharla.adam@angelo.edu
ADAM, Terri .... 207-974-4691 199 L
tadam@emcc.edu
ADAMCHAK, Andrea .... 765-658-4440 157 H
andreaadamchak@depauw.edu
ADAMCZUK, Agata .... 631-794-6250 329 D
ADAMCZYK, Julie, L ..... 989-837-4436 235 C
ADAMES, Jose .... 214-860-2010 448 A
jose.adames@dcccd.edu
ADAMO, Clare .... 860-632-3009.. 87 D
library@holyapostles.edu
ADAMO, Lauren .... 305-237-2738 103 L
ladamo@mdc.edu
ADAMO, Paul, J .... 607-436-2535 325 E
paul.adamo@oneonta.edu
ADAMS, Adam .... 712-722-6006 168 I
adam.adams@dordt.edu

ADAMS, Alexandra .... 215-637-7700 397 G
aadams@holyfamily.edu
ADAMS, Amanda .... 423-354-5143 437 E
acadams@northeaststate.edu
ADAMS, Amy .... 785-833-4340 179 C
amy.adams@kwu.edu
ADAMS, Amy .... 740-389-4636 365 B
adamsa@mtc.edu
ADAMS, Ann .... 312-491-2869 148 C
a-adams@northwestern.edu
ADAMS, Ann .... 360-438-4382 497 F
aadams@stmartin.edu
ADAMS, Ann Clay .... 404-687-4524 118 B
adamsa@ctsnet.edu
ADAMS, Anthony, T ...... 334-229-5176.... 4 A
anthony-adams@alasu.edu
ADAMS, Barbara, L .... 803-536-8980 423 G
badams@scsu.edu
ADAMS, Betty .... 713-797-7000 458 F
bnadams@pvamu.edu
ADAMS, Billy .... 254-267-7039 454 L
badams@rangercollege.edu
ADAMS, Billy, W .... 903-693-2028 454 E
badams@panola.edu
ADAMS, Blake .... 678-839-5053 127 F
badams@westga.edu
ADAMS, Bobby .... 252-335-0821 342 D
bobby_adams@albemarle.edu
ADAMS, Brad .... 865-251-1800 436 B
badams@southcollegetn.edu
ADAMS, Brenda .... 501-450-1226.. 19 I
adams@hendrix.edu
ADAMS, Brett, C .... 443-352-4250 207 C
bcadams@stevenson.edu
ADAMS, Bruce .... 504-286-5432 195 L
badams@suno.edu
ADAMS, Bryan .... 617-353-3635 212 G
bsadams@bu.edu
ADAMS, Carey .... 314-719-3609 260 C
cadams@fontbonne.edu
ADAMS, Carol .... 678-717-2233 127 B
carol.adams@ung.edu
ADAMS, Caroline .... 805-893-3285.. 70 B
caroline.adams@ucsb.edu
ADAMS, Chadd .... 205-665-6155.... 8 E
cadams3@montevallo.edu
ADAMS, Charles, H .... 813-974-3087 111 A
chadams@honors.usf.edu
ADAMS, Chris .... 573-840-9666 267 J
cadams@trcc.edu
ADAMS, Christopher, J . 631-451-4118 330 B
adamsc@sunysuffolk.edu
ADAMS, Clint .... 303-373-2008.. 82 F
president@rvu.edu
ADAMS, Corey .... 607-729-1581 306 F
cadams@davisny.edu
ADAMS, Dana .... 773-508-8077 144 D
dadams2@luc.edu
ADAMS, Dania .... 305-348-3875 109 D
dania.pearson_adams@fiu.edu
ADAMS, Daniel .... 480-461-7000.. 13 I
ADAMS, David .... 502-852-5555 190 C
david.j.adams@louisville.edu
ADAMS, Dean .... 270-384-8036 187 H
adamsd@lindsey.edu
ADAMS, DeAnna .... 901-843-3885 435 L
registrar@rhodes.edu
ADAMS, Debbie .... 423-697-2493 436 F
debbie.adams@chattanoogastate.edu
ADAMS, Denise .... 530-895-2329.. 28 E
adamsde@butte.edu
ADAMS, Don .... 210-485-0088 441 E
dadams@alamo.edu
ADAMS, Edward .... 646-312-1190 301 B
edward.adams@baruch.cuny.edu
ADAMS, Edward, E .... 801-422-8271 471 E
ed_adams@byu.edu
ADAMS, Elizabeth .... 912-583-3242 116 G
eadams@bpc.edu
ADAMS, Elizabeth, H ..... 434-924-4274 486 H
eha3w@virginia.edu
ADAMS, Elizabeth, T ..... 818-677-2969.. 33 B
elizabeth.t.adams@csun.edu
ADAMS, Ellen .... 718-631-6269 303 F
eadams@qcc.cuny.edu
ADAMS, Eve .... 480-858-9100.. 16 D
e.adams@scnm.edu
ADAMS, Gary .... 972-241-3371 447 E
gadams@dallas.edu
ADAMS, Grantley .... 860-738-6333.. 86 C
gadams@nwcc.edu
ADAMS, Gregory .... 414-288-1492 508 C
gregory.adams@marquette.edu
ADAMS, Jacob .... 909-621-8025.. 37 L
jacob.adams@cgu.edu
ADAMS, James, E .... 325-942-2071 463 C
james.adams@angelo.edu

ADAMS, Jan .... 903-510-3287 464 D
jada@tjc.edu
ADAMS, Jane, A .... 352-392-4574 110 D
jane-adams@ufl.edu
ADAMS, Janieth .... 601-979-0928 253 E
janieth.f.wilson_adams@jsums.edu
ADAMS, Jason .... 303-762-6936.. 79 G
jason.adams@denverseminary.edu
ADAMS, Jeff .... 479-788-7221.. 22 A
jeff.adams@uafs.edu
ADAMS, Jeffrey, M .... 336-841-4581 338 E
jeadams@highpoint.edu
ADAMS, Jeffrey, R .... 717-871-7462 407 A
jeffrey.adams@millersville.edu
ADAMS, Jennifer .... 925-473-7302.. 41 A
jadams@losmedanos.edu
ADAMS, Jennifer .... 334-347-2623.... 1 J
jadams@escc.edu
ADAMS, Jennifer .... 315-792-7810 330 A
jennifer.adams@sunyit.edu
ADAMS, Jennifer .... 614-236-6170 358 A
jadams@capital.edu
ADAMS, Jill, J .... 757-822-1709 489 H
jadams@tcc.edu
ADAMS, Jim, J .... 909-599-5433.. 48 E
jjadams@lifepacific.edu
ADAMS, Jimmy .... 713-718-2093 450 D
jimmy.adams@hccs.edu
ADAMS, John, C .... 607-735-1802 307 G
jadams@elmira.edu
ADAMS, Johnnie .... 310-434-4302.. 62 G
adams_johnnie@smc.edu
ADAMS, Jordan .... 918-540-6211 376 F
jordan.m.adams@neo.edu
ADAMS, OSB, Joseph ... 724-805-2534 410 C
joseph.adams@stvincent.edu
ADAMS, Joshua .... 707-524-1731.. 62 H
jadams2@santarosa.edu
ADAMS, Julie .... 423-746-5251 439 A
jadams@tnwesleyan.edu
ADAMS, Karen .... 785-242-5200 180 H
karen.adams@ottawa.edu
ADAMS, Karen .... 812-856-5596 159 H
kadams@iu.edu
ADAMS, Karen .... 956-296-1416 468 A
karen.adams@utrgv.edu
ADAMS, Karen, H .... 812-856-5596 159 G
kadams@indiana.edu
ADAMS, Kate .... 651-604-4101 243 E
kadams@minneapolisbusinesscollege.edu
ADAMS, Kelly, L .... 315-792-3047 332 H
kadams@utica.edu
ADAMS, Ken .... 814-453-6016 412 A
ADAMS, Kenneth .... 718-289-5313 301 D
kenneth.adams@bcc.cuny.edu
ADAMS, Kent .... 620-450-2140 180 K
kenta@prattcc.edu
ADAMS, Kimberly .... 325-942-2122 463 C
kadams15@angelo.edu
ADAMS, Kimberly .... 253-752-2020 494 H
kimadams@faithseminary.edu
ADAMS, Linda .... 706-379-3111 128 H
leadams@yhc.edu
ADAMS, Lita .... 413-748-3641 224 G
ladams@springfieldcollege.edu
ADAMS, Mack .... 575-527-7552 295 E
madams@nmsu.edu
ADAMS, Mark .... 208-885-4977 132 I
marka@uidaho.edu
ADAMS, Mark .... 936-294-1158 462 F
ucs_mca@shsu.edu
ADAMS, Marsha .... 256-824-6345.... 8 C
marsha.adams@uah.edu
ADAMS, Martin .... 813-988-5131.. 99 D
development@floridacollege.edu
ADAMS, Mary, A .... 303-991-1575.. 76 H
mary.adams@americansentinel.edu
ADAMS, Melvin .... 845-431-8974 307 A
melvin.adams@sunydutchess.edu
ADAMS, Michael .... 910-893-1686 336 C
adams@campbell.edu
ADAMS, Michael .... 310-506-4443.. 56 D
michael.adams@pepperdine.edu
ADAMS, Michael .... 713-313-7760 461 E
adams_mo@tsu.edu
ADAMS, Michael, J .... 888-777-7675 494 H
mjadams@faithseminary.edu
ADAMS, Michelle .... 773-291-6100 135 M
madams@ccc.edu
ADAMS, Molly-Dodd ..... 352-588-8291 106 N
molly-dodd.adams@saintleo.edu
ADAMS, Neale, J .... 515-574-1284 170 C
adams_n@iowacentral.edu
ADAMS, Patrick .... 516-876-3194 327 C
adamsp@oldwestbury.edu
ADAMS, Paul .... 785-628-5866 177 D
padams@fhsu.edu

ADAMS, Paul, S ... 570-408-4114 414 H paul.adams@wilkes.edu
ADAMS, Phillip, D ... 912-358-3059 125 C adamsp@savannahstate.edu
ADAMS, Randall ... 202-885-8664.. 94 C radams@wesleyseminary.edu
ADAMS, Rebecca ... 252-940-6321 340 N rebecca.adams@beaufortccc.edu
ADAMS, Robert ... 575-492-2597 294 L radams@nmjc.edu
ADAMS, Robert, J ... 386-226-6119.. 98 C adamsr@erau.edu
ADAMS, Rodney ... 843-525-8219 424 E radams@tcl.edu
ADAMS, Sally Ann ... 479-575-2000.. 21 I
ADAMS, Sarah ... 414-297-6595 514 C adamss4@matc.edu
ADAMS, Sharman ... 605-642-6551 428 F sharman.adams@bhsu.edu
ADAMS, Shawn ... 404-225-4005 115 J sadams@atlantatech.edu
ADAMS, Sheila, V ... 662-329-7299 254 F svadams@muw.edu
ADAMS, Shirley, M ... 860-515-3836.. 84 H sadams@charteroak.edu
ADAMS, Stephanie, G ... 757-683-4244 483 G sgadams@odu.edu
ADAMS, Stevalynn, R ... 757-823-8373 483 F
ADAMS, Susanne, H ... 910-755-7302 341 C adamss@brunswickcc.edu
ADAMS, Tammy ... 903-875-7348 453 J tammy.adams@navarrocollege.edu
ADAMS, Terri ... 202-806-7040.. 92 C tadams-fuller@howard.edu
ADAMS, Tiffany ... 563-425-5959 173 K adamst26@uiu.edu
ADAMS, Tila ... 401-277-4909 417 B madams@risd.edu
ADAMS, Vic ... 606-589-3001 187 B vic.adams@kctcs.edu
ADAMS, Wesley ... 252-940-6423 340 N wesley.adams@beaufortccc.edu
ADAMS COWES, Sheila . 810-762-9532 232 C sadams@kettering.edu
ADAMS-DUNFORD, Jane ... 828-227-7234 352 C jdunford@wcu.edu
ADAMS-GASTON, Javaune ... 614-292-9334 367 H adams-gaston.1@osu.edu
ADAMS-INGRAM, Hannah ... 317-738-8140 157 L hadams-ingram@franklincollege.edu
ADAMS-KEANE, Helen ... 518-861-2596 314 B hadamskeane@mariacollege.edu
ADAMS O'REGAN, Michelle ... 603-641-7243 282 A mkadams@anselm.edu
ADAMS SOMERLOT, Lisa ... 678-839-6428 127 F ladams@westga.edu
ADAMSKI, Kathleen ... 509-527-4240 499 E kathleen.adamski@wwcc.edu
ADAMSKI, M. Patricia ... 516-463-6800 310 D patricia.adamski@hofstra.edu
ADAMSON, Bonnie, J ... 910-630-7307 340 A adamson@methodist.edu
ADAMSON, Craig ... 215-416-3723 397 K craigadamson@iirp.edu
ADAMSON, Elizabeth ... 361-698-1297 448 H eadamson@delmar.edu
ADAMSON, Kenet ... 828-398-7650 340 M kenetmadamson@abtech.edu
ADAMSON, Richard ... 320-363-3164 250 A radamson@csbsju.edu
ADAMSON, Steve ... 602-386-4188.. 10 G steve.adamson@arizonachristian.edu
ADAMSON, Wendy ... 218-855-8062 244 C wadamson@clcmn.edu
ADAMUS, Anne M, G ... 248-204-2208 233 A aadamus@ltu.edu
ADANK, Nicki ... 507-453-2676 245 G nadank@southeastmn.edu
ADANU, Sesime ... 607-778-5024 326 C adanusk@sunybroome.edu
ADAUTO, Ricardo ... 915-747-5555 467 E radauto@utep.edu
ADAUTO, III, Ricardo ... 915-747-5555 467 E radauto@utep.edu
ADAUTO, III, Richard ... 915-747-5555 467 E radauto@utep.edu
ADCOX, John ... 423-354-5198 437 E jmadcox@northeaststate.edu
ADCOX, Kathy, S ... 252-451-8274 345 B ksadcox665@nashcc.edu
ADCOX, William ... 713-792-2275 468 D william.adcox@uth.tmc.edu
ADDANTE, Shylah ... 518-244-2008 321 G addans@sage.edu
ADDERLY-HENRY, Denelta ... 727-873-4838 111 B denelta@usf.edu
ADDINGTON, Eric, J ... 218-299-3010 241 K eaddingt@cord.edu
ADDINGTON, Gary ... 719-384-6859.. 81 G gary.addington@ojc.edu
ADDINGTON, Michelle .. 512-471-1922 467 C maddington@austin.utexas.edu
ADDIS, Edwin ... 717-947-6213 404 S esaddis@pacollege.edu
ADDISON, Andrea ... 716-829-7737 307 B addison@dyc.edu
ADDISON, Lathera ... 972-860-8146 447 H laddison@dcccd.edu
ADDISON, Lynn ... 912-583-3285 116 G laddison@bpc.edu
ADDISON, Marcia ... 330-494-6170 370 G maddison@starkstate.edu
ADDISON, Steve ... 501-450-3199.. 23 I saddison@uca.edu
ADDISON, Trip ... 912-478-5253 120 E taddison@georgiasouthern.edu
ADDLEMAN, Eleanor, M ... 717-796-1800 401 L eaddlema@messiah.edu
ADDLEMAN, John, A ... 651-638-6287 240 J j-addleman@bethel.edu
ADDY, Amanda ... 937-327-7562 374 A addya@wittenberg.edu
ADDY, Cheryl ... 803-777-2808 424 I caddy@mailbox.sc.edu
ADEBANJO, Dave ... 718-804-8233 303 C dadebanjo@mec.cuny.edu
ADEBIYI, Songie ... 708-596-2000 151 H sadebiyi@ssc.edu
ADEDOKUN, Michael ... 703-746-8708 485 A
ADEGBOYE, David, S ... 504-286-5327 195 L dadegboye@suno.edu
ADEKOLA, Abel ... 570-408-4701 414 H abel.adekola@wilkes.edu
ADELABU, Detris Honora ... 617-879-2184 226 A dadelabu@wheelock.edu
ADELAINE, Michael ... 605-688-4988 429 B michael.adelaine@sdstate.edu
ADELMAN, Michael, D .. 304-647-6200 504 F madelman@osteo.wvsom.edu
ADELSPERGER, Donna .. 219-989-2436 163 E adelsper@pnw.edu
ADEM, Salma ... 817-272-2101 467 B adem@uta.edu
ADEMOLA, Remi ... 713-313-4835 461 E ademolara@tsu.edu
ADEN, Huda ... 276-376-3452 487 A ha3d@uvawise.edu
ADEN-FOX, Nancy ... 402-472-4344 277 G naden1@unl.edu
ADER, Elaine ... 916-558-2062.. 50 I adere@scc.losrios.edu
ADER, Meredith ... 585-582-8218 307 C meredithader@elim.edu
ADER, Meredith ... 336-744-0900 336 D meredith.ader@carolina.edu
ADERHOLD, Mary ... 770-537-5719 128 F mary.aderhold@westgatech.edu
ADERO, Chad ... 301-846-2531 203 H cadero@frederick.edu
ADEWUMI, Michael, A .. 814-863-4030 403 F m2a@psu.edu
ADEWUYI, David, A ... 804-257-5742 491 C daadewuyi@vuu.edu
ADEWUYI, David, A ... 804-342-3937 491 C daadewuyi@vuu.edu
ADEY, Penelope, S ... 518-388-6109 332 B adeyp@union.edu
ADEYANJU, Matthew ... 231-591-2342 230 A matthewadeyanju@ferris.edu
ADIA, Trish ... 954-378-2400.. 93 B
ADIA, Trish ... 561-904-3000.. 93 B
ADISHIAN-ASTONE, Deborah ... 559-278-2083.. 32 A debbiea@csufresno.edu
ADISHIAN-ASTONE, Deborah ... 559-278-3902.. 32 A deborah_adishianastone@csufresno.edu
ADKINS, Adele ... 937-328-3857 359 H adkinsa@clarkstate.edu
ADKINS, Alfred ... 314-539-5178 266 E
ADKINS, Amy ... 903-434-8121 453 M aadkins@ntcc.edu
ADKINS, Cathy, L ... 828-689-1395 339 G cadkins@mhu.edu
ADKINS, Ernest ... 480-517-8202.. 14 B ernest.adkins@riosalado.edu
ADKINS, George ... 630-353-7197 134 K gadkins@devry.edu
ADKINS, Heather ... 210-567-2041 468 E adkinsh3@uthscsa.edu
ADKINS, John ... 304-357-4779 502 E johnadkins@ucwv.edu
ADKINS, Justin ... 814-332-3353 388 F jadkins@allegheny.edu
ADKINS, Kay ... 606-326-2043 185 E kay.adkins@kctcs.edu
ADKINS, Kenneth, R ... 734-487-8460 229 K kadkins5@emich.edu
ADKINS, Lisa ... 540-453-2217 487 G adkinsl@brcc.edu
ADKINS, Marc ... 419-251-1512 365 C marc.adkins@mercycollege.edu
ADKINS, Nathan ... 423-869-6306 433 C nathan.adkins@lmunet.edu
ADKINS, Robert ... 724-503-1001 414 A radkins@washjeff.edu
ADKINS, Shannyn ... 210-458-4229 468 B shannyn.adkins@utsa.edu
ADKINS, Sheldon ... 405-425-5250 377 B sheldon.adkins@oc.edu
ADKINS-EASLEY, Mona . 757-823-8160 483 F madkins-easley@nsu.edu
ADKINS-SHATO, Tabetha ... 903-886-5876 459 E tabetha.adkins@tamuc.edu
ADKISON, Steve ... 870-230-5134.. 19 H sadkison@hsu.edu
ADLEBURG, Frances ... 850-973-1603 104 D adleburgf@nfcc.edu
ADLEMAN, Chris ... 517-321-0242 231 A cadleman@glcc.edu
ADLER, Brian ... 610-758-3375 400 B bla212@lehigh.edu
ADLER, Brian, D ... 580-774-3063 380 B brian.adler@swosu.edu
ADLER, Eve ... 310-434-3464.. 62 G adler_eve@smc.edu
ADLER, Kate ... 212-343-1234 315 D kadler@mcny.edu
ADLER, Laurel ... 626-472-5121.. 42 B ladler@esgvrop.org
ADLER, Michael ... 214-768-1864 457 B madler@smu.edu
ADLER, Niall ... 408-855-5127.. 74 C niall.adler@missioncollege.edu
ADLER, Robert ... 801-581-3791 472 P robert.adler@law.utah.edu
ADLER, Shmuel ... 773-463-7738 152 J sadler@telshe.edu
ADLER, Wendy ... 508-541-1542 214 C wadler@dean.edu
ADLER-KASSNER, Linda 805-893-3006.. 70 B adler-kassner@ltsc.ucsb.edu
ADLING, Jennifer ... 806-742-3844 463 D jennifer.adling@ttu.edu
ADLISH, John ... 702-651-5664 278 N john.adlish@csn.edu
ADMIRAAL, Karin ... 513-244-8637 359 E karin.admiraal@ccuniversity.edu
ADNAN, Asma ... 312-939-0111 137 G asma@eastwest.edu
ADNEY, Chris ... 918-444-2500 376 G adneyc@nsuok.edu
ADOLPH, Laurie ... 563-336-3351 168 K ladolph@eicc.edu
ADORNETTO, Anthony ... 740-588-1205 374 G aadornetto1@zanestate.edu
ADORNO, Victor, T ... 787-780-0070 521 B vadorno@caribbean.edu
ADORNO, Wilfredo ... 787-761-0640 527 C decanoestudiantes@utcpr.edu
ADOYO, Pricilla ... 626-448-0023.. 46 K academicdean@itsla.edu
ADRIAN, Janet ... 913-360-7117 175 D jadrian@benedictine.edu
ADRIAN, Loretta, P ... 714-241-6152.. 38 F ladrian@coastline.edu
ADRIAN, Sherry, E ... 512-863-1905 457 I adrians@southwestern.edu
ADRIANCE, Anne ... 212-229-5600 316 E adrianca@newschool.edu
ADRIANZEN, Manuel ... 718-429-6600 333 B manuel.adrianzen@vaughn.edu
ADSIT, Jason ... 716-829-7731 307 B adsitj@dyc.edu
ADU-MIREKU, Samuel .. 910-672-1042 350 B sadu-mireku@uncfsu.edu
ADUKAITIS, Megan ... 610-796-8225 389 A megan.adukaitis@alvernia.edu
ADY, Tina ... 254-526-1402 445 L tady@ctcd.edu
AEFSKY, Fern ... 352-588-7276 106 N fern.aefsky@saintleo.edu
AEILTS, Larry ... 734-973-3480 238 G laeilts@wccnet.edu
AELION, C. Marjorie ... 413-545-2526 216 H maelion@schoolph.umass.edu
AERTS, Kenneth ... 575-835-5623 294 K kenneth.aerts@nmt.edu
AESCHLIMANN, Rodney, L ... 775-784-1113 279 E rod@admin.edu
AFALAVA, Alofia ... 684-699-9155 519 F a.afalava@amsamoa.edu
AFDAHL, Tami ... 307-532-8206 516 J tami.afdahl@ewc.wy.edu
AFFENITO, Sandra ... 802-485-2025 475 I saffenit@norwich.edu
AFFLECK-GRAVES, John, F ... 574-631-4700 165 A affleck-graves.1@nd.edu
AFFONSO, Adeline ... 212-752-1530 312 G
AFFUSO, Paul ... 626-264-8880.. 71 A
AFOLABI ROYES, Rachael, O ... 412-578-6244 391 G roafolabi@carlow.edu
AFRANK, Kim ... 402-465-2418 276 E kafrank@nebrwesleyan.edu
AFROOKHTEH, Afshin ... 714-816-0366.. 67 J afshin.afrookhteh@trident.edu
AFSAHI, Armin ... 303-871-2647.. 83 E armin.afsahi@du.edu
AFUNUGO, Emmanuel, O ... 724-805-2473 410 C emmanuel.afunugo@stvincent.edu
AGAN, Jeffrey ... 706-295-6974 120 C jagan@gntc.edu
AGARWAL, P.K ... 617-373-2000 223 D
AGARWAL, Vaibhav ... 574-631-0946 165 A vagarwal@nd.edu
AGATHA, Rachelle ... 619-388-2990.. 60 D ragatha@sdccd.edu
AGBAKPE, Peter, T ... 757-822-2301 489 H pagbakpe@tcc.edu
AGBARAJI, Casmir ... 505-786-4113 294 I cagbaraji@navajotech.edu
AGBAYANI, Amefil ... 808-956-4567 129 J agbayani@hawaii.edu
AGBENYIGA, DeBrenna LaFa ... 210-458-6878 468 B debrenna.agbenyiga@utsa.edu
AGBOLI-ESEDEBE, Angela ... 703-329-9100.. 93 B
AGEE, Deborah, G ... 530-752-2396.. 68 H dgagee@ucdavis.edu
AGEE, Doug, A ... 636-584-6714 259 L doug.agee@eastcentral.edu
AGEE, Patty, A ... 660-263-3900 258 A pattyagee@cccb.edu
AGEE, Steve ... 405-208-5276 377 D sagee@okcu.edu
AGESILAS, Elie ... 787-891-0925 523 G eagesila@aguadilla.inter.edu
AGGARWAL, Reena ... 202-687-3784.. 92 B aggarwal@georgetown.edu
AGHO, Austin ... 757-683-3079 483 G aagho@odu.edu
AGIDIUS, Erin ... 208-885-4285 132 I erina@uidaho.edu
AGJMURATI, Nick ... 212-592-2002 324 A nagjmurati@sva.edu
AGLAN, Heshmat ... 334-727-8355.... 7 F aglan@mytu.tuskegee.edu
AGNE, Anissa ... 904-620-2698 110 E anissa.agne@unf.edu
AGNELLO, Alissa ... 206-934-3746 497 H alissa.agnello@seattlecolleges.edu
AGNELLO-VELEY, Josephine ... 860-906-5007.. 85 D
AGNER, Susan ... 704-637-4411 336 G sagner@catawba.edu
AGNESI, Peter ... 954-201-5321.. 96 A pagnesi@broward.edu
AGNETTA, Daniel, E ... 269-471-3302 227 B agnetta@andrews.edu
AGNEW, Brian ... 732-987-2244 286 D bagnew@georgian.edu
AGNEW, Donna ... 847-578-8316 150 E donna.agnew@rosalindfranklin.edu
AGNEW, F. Raymond ... 518-327-6317 320 A ragnew@paulsmiths.edu
AGNEW, Ina ... 918-293-4761 378 B ina.agnew@okstate.edu
AGNEW, Kathy ... 575-646-3553 295 B kagnew@nmsu.edu
AGNEW, Melanie ... 801-832-2474 474 E magnew@westminstercollege.edu
AGNOSTAK, Harry, M ... 848-932-3929 290 A harry.agnostak@rutgers.edu
AGO, Emmanuel ... 718-862-7996 313 L emmanuel.ago@manhattan.edu

AGOONS, Akwai .... 478-827-3229 119 C
akwaia@fvsu.edu
AGOSTA, Frank .... 212-592-2620 324 A
fagosta@sva.edu
AGOSTO, Elilzabeth, L ... 603-646-3124 281 C
elizabeth.lee.agosto@dartmouth.edu
AGOSTO, Elvia .... 787-728-1515 529 B
eagosto@sagrado.edu
AGOURIS, Peggy .... 703-993-1362 481 B
pagouris@gmu.edu
AGRAS, James, R .... 412-359-1000 412 A
AGRAS, James, R .... 412-359-1000 412 C
jagras@triangle-tech.edu
AGRAS, James, R .... 412-359-1000 412 B
jagras@triangle-tech.edu
AGRAS, Rudy, J .... 412-359-1000 412 C
ragras@triangle-tech.edu
AGRAWAL, Gail, B .... 319-335-9034 166 G
gail-agrawal@uiowa.edu
AGRAWAL, Mauli .... 210-458-4110 468 B
mauli.agrawal@utsa.edu
AGRE-KIPPENHAN,
Susan .... 503-883-2409 383 H
sagreki@linfield.edu
AGRELA, Ramona .... 949-824-5962.. 69 A
ragrela@uci.edu
AGUE, Paul, E .... 619-201-8701.. 60 A
paul.ague@sdcc.edu
AGUIAR, Aracely .... 310-287-4374.. 49 H
aguiara@wlac.edu
AGUIAR, Jenny .... 617-730-7102 223 B
jenny.aguiar@newbury.edu
AGUILA, Nayda, G .... 617-964-1100 210 G
naguila@ants.edu
AGUILAR, Carmen .... 508-678-2811 219 C
carmen.aguilar@bristolcc.edu
AGUILAR, Catherine ...... 787-279-1912 523 J
caguilar@bayamon.inter.edu
AGUILAR, Charmaine .... 570-674-6247 401 M
caguilar@misericordia.edu
AGUILAR, Cheryl, M ..... 909-607-1232.. 38 A
cheryl.aguilar@cmc.edu
AGUILAR, Jade .... 503-370-6195 388 D
aguilarj@willamette.edu
AGUILAR, Jose, A .... 951-827-3878.. 69 D
jose.aguilar@ucr.edu
AGUILAR, Kate .... 765-455-9203 160 B
kaguilar@iuk.edu
AGUILAR, Miguel .... 361-354-2718 445 S
maguilar@coastalbend.edu
AGUILAR-VILLARUAL,
Elizabeth .... 210-486-3711 441 H
eaguilar-villar@alamo.edu
AGUILERA, Mary .... 503-375-7113 383 A
maguilera@corban.edu
AGUINALDO, Estrella .... 310-834-3065.. 67 L
AGUINALDO, Teresa ...... 847-543-2288 136 E
com401@clcillinois.edu
AGUIRRE, Arturo .... 213-487-0110.. 41 K
facilities@dula.edu
AGUIRRE, Ilvis .... 787-878-5475 523 H
iaguirre@arecibo.inter.edu
AGUIRRE, Isaiah .... 951-343-5067.. 28 G
iaguirre@calbaptist.edu
AGUIRRE, Juan Carlos .. 956-872-6782 456 G
jcaguirre@southtexascollege.edu
AGUIRRE, Katherine ...... 631-451-4022 330 C
aguirrk@sunysuffolk.edu
AGUIRRE, Maria .... 928-317-6180.. 11 B
maria.aguirre@azwestern.edu
AGUIRRE, Raymund ...... 619-388-6411.. 60 B
raguirre@sdccd.edu
AGUIRRE, Ricardo .... 787-728-1515 529 B
raguirre@sagrado.edu
AGUIRRE, Richard .... 534-535-7571 158 A
rraguirre@goshen.edu
AGUIRRE, Tina .... 760-355-6467.. 46 B
tina.aguirre@imperial.edu
AGUIRRE, Tomas, A ...... 607-746-4440 329 B
AGUIRRE, Tomas, A ...... 903-886-5153 459 E
tomas.aguirre@tamuc.edu
AGWUNOBI, Andrew ...... 860-679-2594.. 88 G
agwunobi@uchc.edu
AH YUN, Kimo .... 414-288-7133 508 C
james.ahyun@marquette.edu
AHA, Christian .... 856-225-6042 290 B
christian.aha@camden.rutgers.edu
AHANONU, Chukwuma . 662-254-3618 255 A
cahan@mvsu.edu
AHEARN, Michael, J ..... 978-867-4004 215 D
michael.ahearn@gordon.edu
AHEDO, Valentina .... 608-246-6461 514 A
vahedo@madisoncollege.edu
AHEE, Renee .... 313-927-1438 233 D
rahee@marygrove.edu
AHERN, Catherine .... 585-785-1273 308 D
catherine.ahern@flcc.edu

AHERN, Joseph, F .... 845-758-7178 298 I
ahern@bard.edu
AHERN, Martin .... 617-984-1635 223 H
mahern@quincycollege.edu
AHERON, Michelle .... 919-497-3306 339 F
maheron@louisburg.edu
AHLBAUM, Mitch .... 212-772-4946 302 E
mahlbaum@hunter.cuny.edu
AHLEMANN, Tina .... 843-574-6142 424 G
tina.ahlemann@tridenttech.edu
AHLQUIST, Michelle ...... 320-762-4918 243 J
michellea@alextech.edu
AHLSTRIN, Joseph .... 845-848-7900 306 G
joseph.ahlstrin@dc.edu
AHLUWALIA, Anoop ...... 732-224-1987 284 B
aahluwalia@brookdalecc.edu
AHMAD, Catherine .... 609-921-8300 288 E
AHMAD, Shahzad .... 320-308-4287 247 E
shah@stcloudstate.edu
AHMED, Andrea .... 520-383-8401.. 16 G
aahmed@tocc.edu
AHMED, Haroon .... 909-962-6762.. 38 B
hahmed@cst.edu
AHMED, Haseeb .... 419-448-2284 362 G
hahmed@heidelberg.edu
AHMED, Juzar .... 812-465-7160 165 C
juzar@usi.edu
AHMED, M. Monir .... 909-537-3132.. 33 D
mahmed@csusb.edu
AHMED, Mirza, F .... 313-496-2674 238 H
fahmed1@wcccd.edu
AHMED, Mustaq .... 419-358-3237 357 E
ahmedm@bluffton.edu
AHMED, Shahzad .... 320-308-5151 247 E
shah@stcloudstate.edu
AHMED, Shariq .... 909-748-8352.. 71 H
shariq_ahmed@redlands.edu
AHMIDOUCH, Abdellah . 336-334-7567 350 C
abdellah@ncat.edu
AHN, David .... 805-267-1690.. 48 B
AHN, David .... 213-386-0080.. 52 C
AHN, Hee Young .... 323-731-2383.. 55 E
president@psuca.edu
AHN, Hongjun .... 714-533-3946.. 35 B
hjahn@calums.edu
AHNEN, Heath .... 608-822-2327 515 A
hahnen@swtc.edu
AHO, Lynn .... 906-524-8313 232 D
laho@kbocc.edu
AHO, Marie .... 906-227-2981 235 A
mariaho@nmu.edu
AHOLA, Scott .... 605-642-6359 428 F
scott.ahola@bhsu.edu
AHORRIO, Beatriz .... 212-694-1000 299 L
bahorrio@boricuacollege.edu
AHOUSE, Juli9e .... 828-726-2715 341 D
jahouse@cccti.edu
AHRENS, Emily .... 218-285-2203 247 A
emily.ahrens@rainyriver.edu
AHRENS, Rebecca .... 417-873-7523 259 G
bahrens@drury.edu
AHUJA, Sunil .... 570-941-7673 413 F
sunil.ahuja@scranton.edu
AIELLO, Karen, M .... 973-655-4213 287 D
aiellok@mail.montclair.edu
AIELLO, Ryan, A .... 971-722-7390 386 C
ryan.aiello@pcc.edu
AIKEN, Adel, G .... 724-847-5002 395 J
aaiken@geneva.edu
AIKEN, Donn .... 518-464-8765 308 A
daiken@excelsior.edu
AIKEN, Irene .... 910-521-6271 351 E
irene.aiken@uncp.edu
AIKEN, Ryan .... 413-775-1309 219 F
aikenr@gcc.mass.edu
AIKEN, William, C .... 704-669-4004 342 B
aikenw271@clevelandcc.edu
AIKENS, Jane .... 641-472-7000 171 J
jaikens@mum.edu
AILSHIE, Leasa .... 903-586-2518 451 C
lailshie@jacksonville-college.edu
AILSTOCK, M. Stephen . 410-777-2230 202 D
smailstock@aacc.edu
AIMAR, Craig .... 989-463-7292 226 H
aimarct@alma.edu
AIMONE, Chris .... 812-877-8498 163 G
aimone@rose-hulman.edu
AINLAY, Stephen, C .... 518-388-6101 332 B
ainlays@union.edu
AINLEY, Arden .... 360-416-7716 498 F
arden.ainley@skagit.edu
AINSLEIGH, Susan .... 413-565-1000 211 C
sainsleigh@baypath.edu
AINSLEY, Sharon .... 610-647-4400 397 I
sainsley@immaculata.edu
AINSLIE, Andrew .... 585-275-3316 332 E
andrew.ainslie@simon.rochester.edu

AINSLIE, Carolyn, N ...... 609-258-1447 288 F
ainslie@princeton.edu
AINSWORTH, Emma, L . 662-685-4771 252 D
eainsworth@bmc.edu
AINSWORTH, Jerald ...... 423-425-4633 440 A
jerald-ainsworth@utc.edu
AINSWORTH, Shereen ... 208-282-2566 132 B
ainssher@isu.edu
AIRD, Jeff .... 801-957-4090 474 B
jeffrey.aird@slcc.edu
AIRD, Laschrecse .... 804-862-6100 484 F
laird@rbc.edu
AIRHIHENBUWA,
Collins .... 314-977-8188 266 J
airhihenbuwaco@slu.edu
AIROZO, Paul .... 508-830-5051 218 D
pairozo@maritime.edu
AISTRUP, Joseph .... 334-844-4026.... 4 D
jaa0025@auburn.edu
AITKEN, Derek .... 510-885-3877.. 31 F
derek.aitken@csueastbay.edu
AITSON-ROESSLER,
Mechelle .... 405-733-7308 379 F
maitson-roessler@rose.edu
AIZAWA, Hatsue .... 620-241-0723 176 G
hatsue.aizawa@centralchristian.edu
AIZENSTAT, Stephen ...... 805-969-3626.. 55 G
saizenstat@pacifica.edu
AJE, John .... 609-984-1130 292 B
jaje@tesu.edu
AJIBADE, Victoria .... 718-368-6896 303 A
victoria.ajibade@kbcc.cuny.edu
AKAKPO, Koffi .... 419-755-4702 366 E
kakakpo@ncstatecollege.edu
AKBAR, Maksood .... 847-290-6425 147 J
provost@nwsc.edu
AKBARI, Hamid .... 507-457-5014 248 C
hakbari@winona.edu
AKCHIN, Lisa, G .... 410-455-2889 208 A
akchin@umbc.edu
AKE, Barbara .... 505-566-3218 296 A
akeb@sanjuancollege.edu
AKENS, Cathy .... 305-919-5943 109 D
akens@fiu.edu
AKERMAN, Patricia .... 320-308-5966 247 F
pakerman@sctcc.edu
AKERS, Lex, A .... 309-677-2721 134 G
lakers@bradley.edu
AKERS, Mary Anne .... 443-885-3225 206 A
maryanne.akers@morgan.edu
AKERS, Matthew, P .... 330-972-7954 371 C
akers1@uakron.edu
AKERS, Shawn, D .... 434-592-4986 482 D
sdakers@liberty.edu
AKEY, Lynn .... 507-389-2419 246 A
lynn.akey@mnsu.edu
AKEY, Stacey, L .... 920-923-7652 508 B
sakey@marianuniversity.edu
AKEY, William .... 901-678-3993 439 E
wakey@memphis.edu
AKHATAR, Sumaira .... 510-356-4760.. 76 B
AKHAVI, Seyed .... 757-825-2898 489 G
akhavis@tncc.edu
AKHTAR, Shama .... 301-860-3402 208 E
sakhtar@bowiestate.edu
AKIE, Ronald, E .... 617-928-4790 222 D
reakie@mountida.edu
AKIN, Christopher, L ..... 813-974-0898 111 A
cakin@usf.edu
AKIN, Daniel, L .... 919-761-2222 349 C
dakin@sebts.edu
AKIN, Jacob, J .... 507-933-7510 242 D
jakin@gustavus.edu
AKIN, Jamie .... 325-942-2116 463 C
jamie.akin@angelo.edu
AKIN, Renea .... 270-534-3461 187 C
renea.akin@kctcs.edu
AKINKUOYE, Nicholas .. 760-355-6215.. 46 B
nicholas.akinkuoye@imperial.edu
AKINLEYE, Johnson, O . 919-530-6104 350 D
johnson.akinleye@nccu.edu
AKINS, Ceciley .... 847-866-3971 138 G
ceciley.akins@garrett.edu
AKINS, Mike .... 904-596-2464 112 F
makins@tbc.edu
AKINS, Renate .... 714-241-6146.. 38 F
rakins1@coastline.edu
AKKAWI, Kayed .... 312-935-6025 149 K
kakkawi@robertmorris.edu
AKL, Fred, A .... 610-499-4036 414 F
faakl@widener.edu
AKL, Hatem .... 732-255-0400 288 B
hakl@ocean.edu
AKMAN, Jeffrey, S .... 202-741-2880.. 92 A
akman@gwu.edu
AKO-ADOUNVO, Gifty ... 614-292-5873 367 H
ako-adounvo.1@osu.edu

AKOB, Joe .... 570-422-3291 406 A
jakob@esu.edu
AKRIDGE, Travis .... 478-299-3530 126 A
takridge@southeasterntech.edu
AKRIGHT, Jan .... 217-228-5520 134 F
akrightj@brcn.edu
AKS, Richard, M .... 848-932-3787 290 A
richard.aks@rutgers.edu
AKSELRUD, Larisa .... 425-739-8515 495 F
larisa.akselrud@lwtech.edu
AKSU, Mert .... 313-994-6620 237 F
aksumn@udmercy.edu
AKUJIEZE, II, Justin ..... 773-995-2965 135 F
jakujiez@csu.edu
AKUJUOBI, Cajetan, M . 936-261-1550 458 F
cmakujuobi@pvamu.edu
AL-AMIN, John .... 323-953-4000.. 49 A
alminja@lacitycollege.edu
AL-ASSAF, Yousef .... 585-475-2411 321 D
ymacad@rit.edu
AL-HASSAN, Marilyn ..... 714-620-3700.. 26 I
AL-HAZZAM DAWASARI,
Elizabeth .... 480-860-2700.. 12 N
edawsari@taliesin.edu
ALADE, Ayodele, J .... 410-651-6327 208 C
ajalade@umes.edu
ALAI, Meghan .... 732-906-2622 287 B
malai@middlesexcc.edu
ALAIMO, Joseph .... 215-951-1974 398 F
alaimo@lasalle.edu
ALAM, Maria .... 901-678-2867 439 E
malam@memphis.edu
ALAM, Mohammad .... 212-220-1299 301 C
malam@bmcc.cuny.edu
ALAM, Mohammad .... 361-593-2000 460 B
mohammad.alam@tamuk.edu
ALAMADARI, Jeanne ..... 408-848-4802.. 44 B
jalamdari@gavilan.edu
ALAMEIDA, Marshall ..... 415-485-9326.. 39 E
malameida@marin.edu
ALANDER, Link .... 832-813-6842 452 C
link.s.alander@lonestar.edu
ALANKO, Lynda, J .... 540-887-7161 482 G
lalanko@marybaldwin.edu
ALAPE, Fabio .... 787-850-9387 528 B
fabio.alape@upr.edu
ALARCON, Antonio .... 831-759-6006.. 45 C
alarcon@hartnell.edu
ALARCON, Santos .... 956-295-3379 461 F
santos.alarcon@tsc.edu
ALASIO, Claire .... 732-571-3463 287 C
calasio@monmouth.edu
ALAVALAPATI,
Janaki, R .... 334-844-1007.... 4 D
jra0024@auburn.edu
ALAVI, Maryam .... 404-894-2600 120 A
maryam.alavi@scheller.gatech.edu
ALBA, Suzanna .... 401-456-8086 417 A
salba@ric.edu
ALBAN, Elisa, C .... 909-621-8147.. 57 I
elisa.alban@pomona.edu
ALBANESE, Karli .... 909-599-5433.. 48 E
kalbanese@lifepacific.edu
ALBANESE, Linda .... 516-323-4025 315 J
lalbanese@molloy.edu
ALBANESE, Marc .... 610-282-1100 393 G
marc.albanese@desales.edu
ALBANESE, Steve .... 914-323-5469 314 A
steve.albanese@mville.edu
ALBANO, John .... 209-386-6777.. 51 G
albano.j@mccd.edu
ALBANO, Ralph .... 202-319-5218.. 91 D
albano@cua.edu
ALBANO, Stephen, D .... 609-984-1100 292 B
salbano@tesu.edu
ALBARRAN, Agustin ...... 619-644-7161.. 45 A
agustin.albarran@gcccd.edu
ALBARRAN, Charo .... 707-256-7105.. 53 D
calbarran@napavalley.edu
ALBARRAN, Miguel .... 787-622-8000 527 B
malbarran@pupr.edu
ALBAWANEH,
Mahmoud .... 562-985-5462.. 32 C
mahmoud.albawaneh@csulb.edu
ALBAWANEH,
Mahmoud .... 949-783-4807.. 73 K
malbawaneh@westcoastuniversity.edu
ALBAYYARI, Jay .... 419-586-0341 374 B
jay.albayyari@wright.edu
ALBERDESTON, Jane ..... 787-815-0000 527 F
jane.alberdeston@upr.edu
ALBERS, Carrie .... 651-523-2684 242 E
calbers01@hamline.edu
ALBERS, Christopher ..... 520-206-2692.. 15 L
calbers@pima.edu
ALBERS, Jhett .... 605-642-6885 428 F
jhett.albers@bhsu.edu

ALBERS, Timothy, L ...... 573-341-6292 269 A
alberstl@mst.edu
ALBERT, Barbara, J .... 570-326-3761 404 T
balbert@pct.edu
ALBERT, David .... 773-702-9800 153 F
dalbert@medicine.bsd.uchicago.edu
ALBERT, Gene .... 516-773-5000 519 C
albertg@usmma.edu
ALBERT, Jennifer .... 631-656-2128 308 F
jennifer.albert@ftc.edu
ALBERT, Juline .... 712-274-6400 174 E
juline.albert@witcc.edu
ALBERT, Marianne .... 724-222-5330 403 E
malbert@penncommercial.edu
ALBERT, Neil .... 315-228-7397 304 G
nalbert@colgate.edu
ALBERT, Patricia .... 336-272-7102 338 B
patricia.albert@greensboro.edu
ALBERT, OP, Peg .... 517-264-7000 236 I
palbert@sienaheights.edu
ALBERT, Rita .... 561-237-7231 103 E
ralbert@lynn.edu
ALBERT, Robert .... 606-783-5158 188 C
r.albert@moreheadstate.edu
ALBERT, Scott .... 724-738-9000 407 C
ALBERT, Shelly .... 618-650-3187 152 C
malbert@siue.edu
ALBERT, Wendy .... 717-867-6302 399 J
walbert@lvc.edu
ALBERT-KNOPP,
Heather .... 207-801-5640 199 A
halbert-knopp@coa.edu
ALBERT LINK, Cindy ..... 617-747-3096 212 B
clink@berklee.edu
ALBERTA, Vince .... 702-895-5165 279 D
vince.alberta@unlv.edu
ALBERTINI, Velmarie ..... 561-868-3891 105 A
albertiv@palmbeachstate.edu
ALBERTO, Paul, A .... 404-413-8100 121 A
palberto@gsu.edu
ALBERTS, Eugene, R ..... 608-796-3849 512 R
eralberts@viterbo.edu
ALBERTS, Kristin .... 904-256-7180 102 B
kalbert@ju.edu
ALBERTS, Trev .... 402-554-2305 277 I
talberts@unomaha.edu
ALBERTSON, Hattie .... 701-228-5454 354 G
hattie.c.albertson@dakotacollege.edu
ALBERTSON, Robert .... 757-455-3226 491 F
ralbertson@vwu.edu
ALBERTSON, Ronald, G 315-229-5962 323 D
ralbertson@stlawu.edu
ALBIERI, Guilherme .... 212-938-5500 328 E
galbieri@sunyopt.edu
ALBIN-HILL, Jill .... 708-524-6980 137 F
jalbin@dom.edu
ALBINA, Adam, R .... 603-641-7266 282 A
aalbina@anselm.edu
ALBINI, Marisa .... 401-333-7150 416 B
malbini@ccri.edu
ALBINSON, Erik .... 319-399-8843 167 F
ealbinso@coe.edu
ALBITZ, Becky .... 845-575-3000 314 C
rebecca.albitz@marist.edu
ALBO-LOPEZ, Nicole ..... 213-763-7025.. 49 F
albolonm@lattc.edu
ALBO-LOPEZ, Nicole ..... 310-233-4021.. 49 B
albolonm@lahc.edu
ALBON, Darrell, J .... 740-368-3070 368 N
djalbon@owu.edu
ALBORS BIGAS,
Jaime, L .... 787-725-6500 521 C
jalbors@pfizer.com
ALBRECHT, Bryan, D .... 262-564-3000 513 G
albrechtb@gtc.edu
ALBRECHT, Christal, M . 281-756-3598 442 C
calbrecht@alvincollege.edu
ALBRECHT, Daniel .... 408-278-4343.. 75 B
dalbrecht@jessup.edu
ALBRECHT, Don .... 361-825-2612 460 A
don.albrecht@tamucc.edu
ALBRECHT, Jana .... 309-438-7018 140 L
jlalbre2@ilstu.edu
ALBRECHT, John .... 775-673-7261 279 A
jalbrecht@tmcc.com
ALBRECHT, Jon .... 512-505-3009 451 A
jalbrecht@htu.edu
ALBRECHT, Kelli .... 501-760-4349.. 20 D
kelli.albrecht@np.edu
ALBRIGHT, Bonnie .... 409-880-7633 462 B
bsalbright@lit.edu
ALBRIGHT, Geri .... 205-929-6315.... 2 G
galbright@lawsonstate.edu
ALBRIGHT, Mike .... 845-341-4728 319 H
mike.albright@sunyorange.edu
ALBRIGHT, Polly .... 765-983-1858 157 I
albripo@earlham.edu
ALBRIGHT, Thomas .... 601-979-2580 253 E
thomas.e.albright@jsums.edu
ALBRINCK, Margaret, L . 920-565-1021 507 K
albrinckm@lakeland.edu
ALBRITTON, Kristen ...... 678-359-5009 121 B
kristena@gordonstate.edu
ALBRITTON, Rosie, L .... 936-261-1510 458 F
rlalbritton@pvamu.edu
ALBURCHER, Ronald ..... 650-723-2300.. 66 C
ALBURN, Amelia .... 508-999-8093 217 A
ascott4@umassd.edu
ALBURY, Gary .... 510-464-3536.. 56 H
galbury@peralta.edu
ALBURY, Laurie .... 386-752-1822.. 99 J
laurie.albury@fgc.edu
ALCAINO, Ricardo .... 805-893-4504.. 70 B
ricardo.alcaino@oeosh.ucsb.edu
ALCALA, Celena .... 310-287-4290.. 49 H
alcalac@wlac.edu
ALCALA, Emma .... 719-549-3327.. 81 M
emma.alcala@pueblocc.edu
ALCANTARA, Ryan .... 310-377-5501.. 51 B
ralcantara@marymountcalifornia.edu
ALCARAZ, Luis .... 787-279-1912 523 J
lalcaraz@bayamon.inter.edu
ALCARAZ-EMMANUELLI,
Cristina .... 787-250-0000 527 D
cristina.alcaraz@upr.edu
ALCOCER, David .... 510-987-9112.. 68 F
david.alcocer@ucop.edu
ALCOCK, Sherry, B .... 563-387-1862 171 I
alcock@luther.edu
ALCON, Arnaa .... 508-531-6131 217 D
aalcon@bridgew.edu
ALCORN, Jill .... 916-660-7160.. 63 K
jalcorn1@sierracollege.edu
ALCORTA, Joe, H .... 325-670-1594 450 A
jalcorta@hsutx.edu
ALCORTA, Lisa .... 210-486-0953 442 A
lalcorta@alamo.edu
ALCRUDO, Lourdes .... 787-622-8000 527 B
lalcrudo@pupr.edu
ALDAMA, Ben .... 479-986-6939.. 20 F
baldama@nwacc.edu
ALDARONDO, Aixa .... 787-766-1717 526 B
aialdarondo@suagm.edu
ALDAVA, Jesse .... 310-342-5200.. 72 D
ALDAY, Katherine, E ..... 470-578-6290 122 C
kalday@kennesaw.edu
ALDEN, Dan .... 512-245-2521 463 A
d_a29@txstate.edu
ALDEN, Peg .... 802-387-6821 475 C
palden@landmark.edu
ALDEN-RIVERS,
Bethany .... 573-651-2682 266 M
baldenrivers@semo.edu
ALDER, William .... 304-647-6203 504 F
walder@osteo.wvsom.edu
ALDERFER, Gregg .... 215-368-5000 389 H
galderfer@biblical.edu
ALDERMAN, Brian .... 423-652-4708 432 I
bjalderman@king.edu
ALDERMAN, Debye, B ... 843-953-7458 420 C
aldermanda@cofc.edu
ALDERMAN,
Norman (Mike), M ...... 863-667-5129 108 G
nmalderman@seu.edu
ALDERMAN, Pamela ...... 304-357-4875 502 E
pamelaalderman@ucwv.edu
ALDERMAN, Rosalind ... 210-436-3995 455 J
ralderman@stmarytx.edu
ALDERMAN, Steve .... 713-646-1812 456 H
salderman@stcl.edu
ALDERSON, Diane .... 810-762-9770 232 C
dalderso@kettering.edu
ALDERSON, Ynez .... 432-552-2795 469 D
alderson_y@utpb.edu
ALDERTON, Elizabeth .... 920-424-2430 511 B
aldertone@uwosh.edu
ALDOUS, Mary .... 518-743-2275 328 G
aldousm@sunyacc.edu
ALDRICH, Adrian, M ..... 630-637-5201 147 E
amaldrich@noctrl.edu
ALDRICH, Allison, S ..... 315-268-6590 304 B
aaldrich@clarkson.edu
ALDRICH, B.J .... 907-474-7043.. 10 B
bjaldrich@alaska.edu
ALDRICH, Christine .... 310-900-1600.. 40 C
caldrich@elcamino.edu
ALDRICH, John .... 304-724-3700 501 D
ALDRICH, Kimberly, J ... 269-337-7302 231 F
kim.aldrich@kzoo.edu
ALDRICH, Michael .... 808-675-3851 128 K
michael.aldrich@byuh.edu
ALDRIDGE, Doug .... 417-626-1234 264 J
aldridge.doug@occ.edu
ALDRIDGE, James .... 800-280-0307 155 H
james.aldridge@ace.edu
ALDRIDGE, R. Mark ...... 817-202-6355 457 E
aldridge@swau.edu
ALDRIDGE, Susan, C .... 215-895-0528 394 C
susan.c.aldridge@drexel.edu
ALDRIDGE, Whitney, C . 540-375-2201 484 H
aldridge@roanoke.edu
ALDRIDGE, William, D .. 202-885-8686.. 94 C
caldridge@wesleyseminary.edu
ALDRIDGE SANFORD,
Amy .... 361-825-3996 460 A
amy.aldridge.sanford@tamucc.edu
ALEJANDRO, JR., Juan . 254-710-3867 444 B
juan_alejandro@baylor.edu
ALEMAN, Karla .... 440-366-7278 364 F
ALEMAN, Lydia .... 956-665-2337 468 A
lydia.aleman@utrgv.edu
ALEMAN, Nicolle .... 541-552-7246 386 H
alemann@sou.edu
ALEMANY, Maria .... 787-832-4040 528 C
admisiones@uprm.edu
ALEMANY-VALDEZ,
Herminia, M .... 787-890-2681 527 E
herminia.alemany@upr.edu
ALEMU, Meseret .... 334-874-5700.... 5 B
malemu@ccal.edu
ALEONG, Natasha .... 786-331-1000 104 C
naleong@maufl.edu
ALEQUIN BAEZ,
Vanessa .... 787-832-4040 528 C
vanessa.alequinbaez@upr.edu
ALERS RAMOS,
Rosa, M .... 787-764-0000 528 F
rosa.alers2@upr.edu
ALEWINE, Jerry .... 864-941-8536 423 C
alewine.j@ptc.edu
ALEWINE, Sharon .... 864-225-7653 421 G
sharonalewine@forrestcollege.edu
ALEX-ASSENSOH,
Yvette, M .... 541-346-9170 387 F
yalex@uoregon.edu
ALEXANDER, A. Donna . 804-758-6704 489 D
dalexander@rappahannock.edu
ALEXANDER, Adrian, W 918-631-2356 381 C
adrian-alexander@utulsa.edu
ALEXANDER, Andrea ..... 408-223-6796.. 61 O
andrea.alexander@evc.edu
ALEXANDER, SJ,
Andrew, F .... 402-280-2071 274 D
andrewalexander@creighton.edu
ALEXANDER, Anne .... 307-766-4286 517 B
aalex@uwyo.edu
ALEXANDER, Anthony ... 660-359-3948 264 H
aalexander@mail.ncmissouri.edu
ALEXANDER, Ashley ...... 202-885-3449.. 91 C
ashleya@american.edu
ALEXANDER, Beth, A .... 317-940-6378 156 I
balexand@butler.edu
ALEXANDER, Bruce .... 315-786-2364 311 H
balexander@sunyjefferson.edu
ALEXANDER, Bruce, D .. 203-432-8611.. 89 G
bruce.alexander@yale.edu
ALEXANDER, Bryant ...... 310-338-7430.. 50 J
bryantkeithalexander@lmu.edu
ALEXANDER, Carol .... 701-349-5776 355 G
carolalexander@trinitybiblecollege.edu
ALEXANDER,
Cassandra .... 229-430-4617 114 I
cassandra.alexander@gmail.com
ALEXANDER, Charlene .. 541-737-5936 385 F
ALEXANDER,
Christine, D .... 717-358-4168 395 G
christine.alexander@fandm.edu
ALEXANDER, Cindy .... 864-294-3324 421 I
cindy.alexander@furman.edu
ALEXANDER, Courtney .. 715-394-8580 512 B
calexan9@uwsuper.edu
ALEXANDER, David .... 316-295-5648 177 F
david_alexander@friends.edu
ALEXANDER, Debra .... 989-328-1276 234 D
debraj@montcalm.edu
ALEXANDER, Elmore ..... 508-531-6151 217 D
elmore.alexander@bridgew.edu
ALEXANDER, F. King .... 225-578-2111 193 L
ALEXANDER, Gary .... 617-850-1322 215 I
galexander@hchc.edu
ALEXANDER, Ginny .... 904-646-2205 100 F
ginny.alexander@fscj.edu
ALEXANDER, Grace .... 680-488-2471 520 E
gracea@palau.edu
ALEXANDER, Iwan .... 205-934-8400.... 8 B
ialex@uab.edu
ALEXANDER, J. Neil ..... 931-598-1288 436 A
jnalexan@sewanee.edu
ALEXANDER, Jay .... 908-835-2329 292 G
jayalex@warren.edu
ALEXANDER, Jeff .... 719-549-3253.. 81 M
jeff.alexander@pueblocc.edu
ALEXANDER, Jenny .... 414-288-7362 508 C
jenny.alexander@marquette.edu
ALEXANDER, John .... 205-391-2343.... 3 E
jalexander@sheltonstate.edu
ALEXANDER, John .... 530-642-5615.. 50 H
alexanj@flc.losrios.edu
ALEXANDER, Joyce, M . 979-845-5311 459 C
joycemalexander@tamu.edu
ALEXANDER, Juan, M ... 757-823-8396 483 F
jmalexander@nsu.edu
ALEXANDER, Karen .... 276-223-4702 490 C
kalexander@wcc.vccs.edu
ALEXANDER, Katie .... 734-432-5837 233 C
ksalexander@madonna.edu
ALEXANDER, Kevin, L ... 714-449-7450.. 51 A
kalexander@ketchum.edu
ALEXANDER, Kim .... 206-934-6660 497 J
kim.alexander@seattlecolleges.edu
ALEXANDER, Kim .... 828-395-1759 344 A
kalexander@isothermal.edu
ALEXANDER, Kimberly .. 845-758-7516 298 I
kalexand@bard.edu
ALEXANDER, King .... 225-578-2111 193 M
alexander@lsu.edu
ALEXANDER, Klint .... 307-766-6416 517 B
klint.alexander@uwyo.edu
ALEXANDER, Laura .... 815-753-6565 147 H
lalexander@niu.edu
ALEXANDER, Laura, A .. 603-526-3760 280 H
lalexander@colby-sawyer.edu
ALEXANDER,
Laurence, B .... 870-575-8471.. 22 E
alexanderl@uapb.edu
ALEXANDER, Lea Ann ... 870-230-5305.. 19 H
alexande@hsu.edu
ALEXANDER, LeAnn ...... 662-241-7494 254 F
mlalexander1@muw.edu
ALEXANDER, Lex .... 336-272-7102 338 B
lex.alexander@greensboro.edu
ALEXANDER,
Livingston .... 814-362-5140 412 I
lalexand@pitt.edu
ALEXANDER, Lynn, M .. 731-881-7490 440 B
lalexand@utm.edu
ALEXANDER,
M. Christopher .... 704-894-2337 337 B
chalexander@davidson.edu
ALEXANDER, Mark .... 662-243-2675 253 A
malexander@eastms.edu
ALEXANDER, Mark .... 610-519-7005 413 K
alexander@law.villanova.edu
ALEXANDER, Mary .... 605-995-2656 427 A
maalexan@dwu.edu
ALEXANDER, Mary .... 615-514-2787 435 F
admissions@nossi.edu
ALEXANDER,
Michael, B .... 617-243-2221 216 C
malexander@lasell.edu
ALEXANDER, Michelle ... 940-552-6291 469 F
malexander@vernoncollege.edu
ALEXANDER, Missy .... 203-837-8400.. 85 B
alexanderm@wcsu.edu
ALEXANDER, Otis .... 786-331-1000 104 C
ALEXANDER, Pam .... 228-497-7642 254 D
pamela.alexander@mgccc.edu
ALEXANDER, Pati .... 817-531-4214 463 G
palexander@txwes.edu
ALEXANDER, Paul .... 508-362-2131 219 E
palexander@capecod.edu
ALEXANDER, Paul .... 701-349-5444 355 G
paulalexander@trinitybiblecollege.edu
ALEXANDER, Paul, H .... 714-879-3901.. 45 I
palexander@hiu.edu
ALEXANDER, Pearl .... 404-894-0300 120 A
pearl.alexander@ohr.gatech.edu
ALEXANDER, Peter .... 336-334-5789 351 D
p_alexan@uncg.edu
ALEXANDER, Rebecca ... 770-962-7580 121 G
ralexander@gwinnetttech.edu
ALEXANDER, Robert ...... 601-974-1062 254 A
robert.alexander@millsaps.edu
ALEXANDER, Ross .... 256-765-5950.... 9 A
ralexander3@una.edu
ALEXANDER, Sanquita .. 334-291-4996.... 1 H
sanquita.alexander@cv.edu
ALEXANDER, Scott .... 207-786-6000 198 E
salexan2@bates.edu
ALEXANDER, Seth .... 617-253-4900 221 C
ALEXANDER, Sherry ...... 918-825-6021 379 C
salexander@rsu.edu
ALEXANDER, State, W .. 704-216-6067 339 E
salexan@livingstone.edu
ALEXANDER, Vanessa ... 601-643-8619 252 G
vanessa.alexander@colin.edu
ALEXANDER, Viola .... 706-507-8800 118 C
alexander_viola@columbusstate.edu
ALEXANDER, William .... 205-226-4736.... 4 F
walexand@bsc.edu

ALEXANDER, William, B .... 215-898-7021 412 G
wba2@upenn.edu
ALEXANDER-LEWIS, Sandi .... 812-866-6101 158 C
alexanderlewis@hanover.edu
ALEXANDER-WALLACE, Linda .... 718-518-4432 302 D
lalexander@hostos.cuny.edu
ALEXANDROU, Cyprian . 315-858-0450 310 E
cyprian@hts.edu
ALEXIS, Kosta .... 617-850-1303 215 I
kalexis@hchc.edu
ALEXIS STEPHENS, Marnelle .... 312-922-1884 144 H
chancellor@maccormac.edu
ALEXO, Kenneth .... 973-408-3067 285 E
kalexojr@drew.edu
ALEXO, Michael .... 302-831-4573.. 90 I
malexo@udel.edu
ALEY, Danielle .... 828-395-1633 344 A
daley@isothermal.edu
ALFANO, Anthony .... 610-519-7730 413 K
anthony.alfano@villanova.edu
ALFANO, Cindy .... 309-268-8019 139 D
cindy.alfano@heartland.edu
ALFANO, Michael, P ..... 860-832-2102.. 84 J
malfano@ccsu.edu
ALFANO, Renee, M .... 608-243-4539 514 A
ralfano@madisoncollege.edu
ALFARO, Richard .... 408-855-5145.. 74 C
richard.alfaro@missioncollege.edu
ALFERNESS, Rod .... 805-893-3141.. 70 B
alferness@engineering.ucsb.edu
ALFIE, Rebeca .... 305-642-4104 105 I
ALFIERI, Regina .... 607-778-5477 326 C
ALFONSO, Antonio .... 360-867-6238 494 G
alfonsoa@evergreen.edu
ALFONSO, August .... 361-698-1300 448 H
aalfonso@delmar.edu
ALFONSO, Jorge .... 305-821-3333 100 A
jalfonso@fnu.edu
ALFONSO, Vincent, C ..... 509-313-3444 495 A
alfonso@gonzaga.edu
ALFORD, Andrew .... 601-276-3704 256 A
aalford@smcc.edu
ALFORD, Cynthia .... 336-838-6111 347 G
clalford287@wilkescc.edu
ALFORD, Keri .... 334-386-7179.... 5 I
kalford@faulkner.edu
ALFORD, Keyimani .... 608-246-6320 514 A
klalford@madisoncollege.edu
ALFORD, Perrin .... 706-756-4621 128 F
perrin.alford@westgatech.edu
ALFORD, Randall, L ...... 321-674-8080.. 99 K
rlalford@fit.edu
ALFORD, Rodney .... 256-890-4733.... 1 F
rodney.alford@calhoun.edu
ALFORD, Sara .... 972-899-8414 453 L
salford@nctc.edu
ALFORD, Tarome .... 404-880-6280 117 H
talford@cau.edu
ALFORQUE, Patrick .... 312-341-2277 150 D
palforque@roosevelt.edu
ALFRED, Tangelia .... 323-241-5333.. 49 E
alfredtm@lasc.edu
ALFRED, Valarie .... 256-761-6208.... 7 D
valfred@talladega.edu
ALFULTIS, Michael, A ... 718-409-7271 329 E
ALGATE, Jill .... 800-280-0307 155 H
jill.algate@ace.edu
ALGER, Christopher ...... 315-268-7258 304 B
calger@clarskon.edu
ALGER, Jonathan, R ...... 540-568-6868 481 I
algerjr@jmu.edu
ALGIER, Anne-Marie ..... 585-275-4085 332 E
anne-marie.algier@rochester.edu
ALGOE, Eric .... 512-245-2244 463 A
e_a231@txstate.edu
ALGOZINE, Jan, L .... 920-686-6192 510 A
jan.algozine@sl.edu
ALI, Adel .... 320-308-3110 247 E
alali@stcloudstate.edu
ALI, Aneesah .... 219-980-6853 160 C
aneeali@iun.edu
ALI, Cheryl .... 609-497-7756 288 E
cheryl.ali@ptsem.edu
ALI, Hesham .... 402-554-2380 277 I
hali@unomaha.edu
ALI, Ibrahim .... 909-274-4225.. 52 I
iali@mtsac.edu
ALI, Mahmood .... 641-472-1126 171 J
housing@mum.edu
ALI, Mohammad .... 937-376-6235 358 I
mali@centralstate.edu
ALI, Nicholas, D .... 412-531-4433 393 D
info@deantech.edu
ALI, Richard, D .... 412-531-4433 393 D
info@deantech.edu
ALI, Rita .... 309-694-5561 139 G
rali@icc.edu
ALIBERTI, Fred .... 518-629-7210 310 G
f.aliberti@hvcc.edu
ALIBRANDI, Cynthia, A . 315-445-4462 312 F
alibraca@lemoyne.edu
ALICANDRO, Jean .... 860-832-1664.. 84 J
alicandro@ccsu.edu
ALICEA, Corinne .... 312-362-8490 137 C
cbenedet@depaul.edu
ALICEA, Dennis .... 787-743-7979 526 A
ut_dalicea@suagm.edu
ALICEA, Edwin .... 787-725-8120 522 M
ealicea@eap.edu
ALICEA, Jennifer .... 787-844-8181 528 E
jennifer.alicea@upr.edu
ALICEA, Priscilla .... 765-983-1600 157 I
ALICEA, Priscilla .... 401-232-6715 416 A
palicea@bryant.edu
ALICEA, Severo .... 787-728-1515 529 B
salicea@sagrado.edu
ALICEA, Victor, G .... 212-694-1000 299 L
valicea@boricuacollege.edu
ALICEA-MALDONADO, Rafael .... 585-345-6820 309 C
ralicea-maldonado@genesee.edu
ALIG, Julie .... 978-934-2506 217 B
julie_alig@uml.edu
ALIMO, Craig .... 707-256-7364.. 53 D
calmio@napavalley.edu
ALINIAZEE, M, T .... 847-290-6425 147 J
president@nwsc.edu
ALIPOE, Dovi .... 601-877-6543 251 G
alipoe@alcorn.edu
ALISHIO, Kip, C .... 513-529-4634 365 I
alishikc@miamioh.edu
ALIVISATOS, Paul .... 510-642-1961.. 68 G
palivisatos@berkeley.edu
ALIX, Jeff .... 419-289-5093 356 L
jalix@ashland.edu
ALKALY, Benjamin .... 310-338-7854.. 50 J
benjamin.alkaly@lmu.edu
ALKANAT, Gokhan .... 334-244-4023.... 4 E
galkanat@aum.edu
ALKIRE, Amy .... 612-330-1188 240 G
alkirea@augsburg.edu
ALKIRE, Laurie .... 308-635-6036 278 B
alkirel@wncc.edu
ALL, Jessica .... 803-812-7398 425 D
allj@mailbox.sc.edu
ALLADA, Venkata .... 573-341-4573 269 A
allada@mst.edu
ALLAN, Kevin .... 845-451-1460 306 D
kevin.allan@culinary.edu
ALLAN, Linda .... 412-809-5100 408 D
allan.linda@pti.edu
ALLAN, Mark .... 215-951-1395 398 F
allanm@lasalle.edu
ALLAN, Nancy .... 570-674-6265 401 M
nallan@misericordia.edu
ALLAN, Sarah .... 740-374-8716 373 G
sallan@wscc.edu
ALLARD, Cathy .... 406-756-3900 271 A
callard@fvcc.edu
ALLARD, Elaine .... 603-535-2458 283 B
eallard@plymouth.edu
ALLARD, Ingrid, M .... 518-262-5919 297 L
allardi@mail.amc.edu
ALLARD, Lee .... 518-782-6987 324 C
lallard@siena.edu
ALLARD, Michael .... 518-828-4181 305 D
allard@sunycgcc.edu
ALLARD, Nicholas, W ... 718-780-7901 300 A
nicholas.allard@brooklaw.edu
ALLATT, Ben .... 717-901-5112 397 E
ballatt@harrisburgu.edu
ALLBAUGH, Jonathan ... 714-556-3610.. 72 F
jonathan.allbaugh@vanguard.edu
ALLBRITTEN, Jeffery ...... 239-489-9211 100 E
president@fsw.edu
ALLCORN, Terry, A .... 417-268-6003 257 H
tallcorn@gobbc.edu
ALLCORN, Terry, L .... 407-582-1492 113 F
tallcorn@valenciacollege.edu
ALLDREDGE, Annita ...... 415-749-4560.. 60 G
aalldredge@sfai.edu
ALLDREDGE, Brian .... 415-514-0421.. 70 A
brian.alldredge@ucsf.edu
ALLDREDGE, Kari .... 865-974-1350 439 I
kalldre1@utk.edu
ALLDRITT, Leslie .... 715-682-1358 509 D
lalldritt@northland.edu
ALLEE, Kelly .... 217-234-5215 143 B
kallee@lakeland.cc.il.us
ALLEE, Rodney .... 317-632-5553 162 P
ALLEGRETTA, Kerri .... 516-403-5392 333 E
kallegretta@webb.edu
ALLEMAN, Vickie .... 415-257-1334.. 41 J
vickie.alleman@dominican.edu
ALLEMAN-BEYERS, Natalie .... 913-468-8500 178 F
nalleman@jccc.edu
ALLEN, Al .... 386-822-8808 111 E
aallen@stetson.edu
ALLEN, Algia .... 972-563-9573 464 C
aallen@tvcc.edu
ALLEN, Amy .... 320-762-4591 243 J
amya@alextech.edu
ALLEN, Andrew .... 651-290-6463 248 U
andrew.allen@mitchellhamline.edu
ALLEN, Andrew .... 619-260-4600.. 71 J
andrewt@sandiego.edu
ALLEN, Angela .... 806-651-8482 460 E
aallen@mail.wtamu.edu
ALLEN, Anita, L .... 215-898-4032 412 G
aallen@law.upenn.edu
ALLEN, Ann Marie .... 435-586-7700 473 A
mciffallen@suu.edu
ALLEN, Anna, M .... 215-951-1374 398 F
aallen@lasalle.edu
ALLEN, Anthony .... 718-933-6700 315 K
aallen@monroecollege.edu
ALLEN, Anthony, W .... 573-629-3252 260 G
anthony.allen@hlg.edu
ALLEN, Augusta .... 610-341-5870 394 E
aallen6@eastern.edu
ALLEN, Benjamin, J ...... 515-294-2042 166 F
bjallen@iastate.edu
ALLEN, Betsy .... 270-824-1727 186 D
betsy.allen@kctcs.edu
ALLEN, Bill .... 434-381-6142 485 P
ballen@sbc.edu
ALLEN, Bob .... 956-380-8125 455 G
ballen@riogrande.edu
ALLEN, Bonnie, J .... 615-898-2772 434 H
bonnie.allen@mtsu.edu
ALLEN, Brenda .... 303-315-2104.. 83 D
brenda.j.allen@ucdenver.edu
ALLEN, Brenda .... 336-750-2200 352 D
allenba@wssu.edu
ALLEN, Brenda, A .... 484-365-7400 400 E
ballen@lincoln.edu
ALLEN, Brian .... 815-939-5258 148 F
ballen@olivet.edu
ALLEN, C. Leonard .... 615-966-6064 433 D
leonard.allen@lipscomb.edu
ALLEN, Calhoun .... 318-869-5120 191 C
callen@centenary.edu
ALLEN, Carol, M .... 443-412-2144 204 C
caallen@harford.edu
ALLEN, Carolyn, H .... 479-575-6702.. 21 I
challen@uark.edu
ALLEN, SJ, Charles, H .. 203-254-4000.. 87 A
executive@fairfield.edu
ALLEN, Charley, B .... 270-809-3919 188 D
callen@murraystate.edu
ALLEN, Chris .... 503-223-8188 386 E
ALLEN, Cindy .... 517-787-0800 231 E
allencynthiaa@jccmi.edu
ALLEN, Clifford .... 503-725-5053 386 D
cliffa@pdx.edu
ALLEN, Craig .... 817-257-7865 461 A
c.allen2@tcu.edu
ALLEN, Dana .... 505-277-5808 296 H
ALLEN, Daniel, T .... 267-502-2636 390 F
daniel.allen@brynathyn.edu
ALLEN, Darren .... 205-929-6361.... 2 G
dallen@lawsonstate.edu
ALLEN, David .... 508-678-2811 219 C
david.allen@bristolcc.edu
ALLEN, David .... 817-923-1921 457 G
dallen@swbts.edu
ALLEN, David, D .... 662-915-7265 256 C
allen@olemiss.edu
ALLEN, David, N .... 520-621-7262.. 16 J
allendn@email.arizona.edu
ALLEN, David, P .... 253-535-7524 496 G
david.allen@plu.edu
ALLEN, David, W .... 916-339-4336.. 53 B
dallen@mticollege.edu
ALLEN, Diane .... 312-935-6023 149 K
dallen@robertmorris.edu
ALLEN, Donna, Y .... 870-235-4012.. 21 F
dyallen@saumag.edu
ALLEN, OP, Elizabeth Anne .... 615-297-7545 429 H
sreanne@aquinascollege.edu
ALLEN, Emily .... 302-343-4500.. 32 D
eallen3@calstatela.edu
ALLEN, Eric .... 724-589-2186 411 D
eallen@thiel.edu
ALLEN, Erika .... 208-792-2458 132 C
elallen@lcsc.edu
ALLEN, Erin .... 319-335-3305 166 G
allene@uifoundation.org
ALLEN, Erin .... 704-991-0261 346 I
eallen4640@stanly.edu
ALLEN, Forrest .... 432-685-4580 453 B
fallen@midland.edu
ALLEN, Gary, K .... 573-882-9200 268 B
allengk@umsystem.edu
ALLEN, Gary, K .... 573-882-9200 268 C
allengk@missouri.edu
ALLEN, George .... 517-607-2556 231 C
gallen@hillsdale.edu
ALLEN, Greg .... 402-557-7581 273 E
greg.allen@bellevue.edu
ALLEN, Helen .... 205-348-7949.... 8 A
helen.allen@ua.edu
ALLEN, Hilary .... 919-760-8548 339 H
allenh@meredith.edu
ALLEN, Ivan .... 478-757-3501 117 D
iallen@centralgatech.edu
ALLEN, Ivan, H .... 478-988-6833 117 E
iallen@centralgatech.edu
ALLEN, James .... 603-542-7744 281 A
jallen@ccsnh.edu
ALLEN, JR., James .... 301-387-3006 203 I
james.allen@garrettcollege.edu
ALLEN, Janel, T .... 402-280-1727 274 D
janelallen@creighton.edu
ALLEN, Janine .... 503-581-8166 383 A
jallen@corban.edu
ALLEN, Jason, K .... 816-414-3700 263 D
president@mbts.edu
ALLEN, Jay, S .... 662-862-8001 253 D
jsallen@iccms.edu
ALLEN, Jeff .... 252-492-2061 347 C
allenjl@vgcc.edu
ALLEN, Jeffrey, S .... 651-696-6174 243 B
allen@macalester.edu
ALLEN, Jen .... 706-419-1119 118 E
jen.allen@covenant.edu
ALLEN, Jennie .... 909-447-2502.. 38 B
jallen@cst.edu
ALLEN, Jerry .... 510-594-3641.. 28 K
jallen@cca.edu
ALLEN, Jo .... 919-760-8511 339 H
jallen@meredith.edu
ALLEN, Jody .... 405-692-3130 376 C
jallen@macu.edu
ALLEN, Joe .... 214-887-5362 448 G
jallen@dts.edu
ALLEN, John, A .... 614-885-5585 369 D
jallen@pcj.edu
ALLEN, John, C .... 435-797-1195 473 C
john.allen@usu.edu
ALLEN, John, W .... 580-327-8594 376 K
jwallen@nwosu.edu
ALLEN, Joseph .... 218-935-0417 251 F
joseph.allen@wetcc.edu
ALLEN, Joshua, D .... 304-457-6392 501 A
allenjd@ab.edu
ALLEN, Joyce .... 206-934-5378 497 J
joyce.allen@seattlecolleges.edu
ALLEN, Judy .... 207-801-5680 199 A
jallen@coa.edu
ALLEN, Julia .... 704-922-6511 343 D
allen.julia@gaston.edu
ALLEN, Justin .... 540-535-3561 485 C
jallen3@su.edu
ALLEN, Kanya .... 270-707-3827 186 B
kanya.allen@kctcs.edu
ALLEN, Karen .... 219-464-5289 165 D
karen.allen1@valpo.edu
ALLEN, Karen .... 812-855-6090 159 H
karealle@indiana.edu
ALLEN, Katherine .... 313-593-5300 238 A
kmaallen@umich.edu
ALLEN, Kathleen .... 440-646-8101 373 B
kallen@ursuline.edu
ALLEN, Kathy .... 501-279-4263.. 19 G
kallen@harding.edu
ALLEN, Kathy .... 828-694-1773 341 B
allenkc@blueridge.edu
ALLEN, Kellie .... 606-326-2044 185 E
kellie.allen@kctcs.edu
ALLEN, Kent .... 405-425-5194 377 B
kent.allen@oc.edu
ALLEN, Kirsten .... 316-322-3192 175 I
kallen2@butlercc.edu
ALLEN, Kitty .... 605-995-2612 427 A
kiallen1@dwu.edu
ALLEN, Larry, K .... 518-564-3282 327 E
lalle001@plattsburgh.edu
ALLEN, Linda .... 417-865-2815 260 B
allenl@evangel.edu
ALLEN, Linda, A .... 319-296-4201 169 H
linda.allen@hawkeyecollege.edu
ALLEN, Linda, D .... 617-373-2307 223 D

ALTEMOSE, Rodney, H .. 215-258-7750 390 I
altemose@bucks.edu

ALTENBURG, Deborah, E .... 202-220-1320 321 A
altend@rpi.edu

ALTENBURG, Rana, H ... 414-288-7430 508 C
rana.altenburg@marquette.edu

ALTENDORFER, Taryn ... 512-492-3011 442 J
registrar@aoma.edu

ALTENKIRCH, Robert, A 256-824-6340.... 8 C
robert.altenkirch@uah.edu

ALTERIO, Christopher ... 315-279-5698 312 D
calterio1@keuka.edu

ALTHAUS, Jon .... 217-234-5225 143 B
jalthaus@lakeland.cc.il.us

ALTHOFF, Debra .... 717-901-5147 397 E
dalthoff@harrisburgu.edu

ALTIER, Jeffrey, P .... 386-822-8100 111 E
jaltier@stetson.edu

ALTIERE, Ralph .... 303-724-2887.. 83 D
ralph.altiere@ucdenver.edu

ALTIERI, Anthony .... 561-237-7275 103 E
aaltieri@lynn.edu

ALTIERI, Guy .... 240-500-2000 204 B
galtieri@hagerstowncc.edu

ALTIERI, Jason, C .... 281-873-0262 446 J
j.altieri@commonwealth.edu

ALTIERI, Paul .... 570-484-2278 406 E
paltieri@lockhaven.edu

ALTIERO, Nicholas, J .... 504-865-5764 196 D
altiero@tulane.edu

ALTIKULAC, John .... 770-426-2644 122 F
jaltikulac@life.edu

ALTIZER, Scott .... 423-425-4444 440 A
scott-altizer@utc.edu

ALTMAN, Barbara .... 570-577-1561 390 H

ALTMAN, Carolyn .... 912-486-1149 120 E
caltman@georgiasouthern.edu

ALTMAN, Don .... 480-219-6008 257 A
daltman@atsu.edu

ALTMAN, J.J .... 912-871-1648 123 J
jaltman@ogeecheetech.edu

ALTMAN, Joanne, D ...... 336-841-9613 338 E
jaltman0@highpoint.edu

ALTMAN, Kayla .... 270-686-2110 183 J
kayla.altman@brescia.edu

ALTMAN, Miranda .... 410-778-7261 210 A
maltman2@washcoll.edu

ALTMAN, Patti .... 419-267-1266 366 G
paltman@northweststate.edu

ALTNAU, Christopher .... 903-927-3274 471 B
caltnau@wileyc.edu

ALTOBELLO, Maria, R ... 603-647-3530 281 D
altobellom@franklinpierce.edu

ALTON, Stevan .... 586-445-7374 233 B
altons@macomb.edu

ALTONGY-MAGEE, Kristy .... 508-373-5726 221 E
kristy.altongy-magee@mcphs.edu

ALTSCHULER, Glenn, C . 607-255-7393 306 B
gca1@cornell.edu

ALTSCHULER, Steve, M . 305-243-6545 112 O
saltschuler@med.miami.edu

ALTSHER, Deborah .... 508-626-4534 218 A
daltsher@framingham.edu

ALTSHULER, Gina .... 215-335-0800 400 D
galtshuler@lincolntech.edu

ALTUCHER, Kristine .... 607-844-8222 331 D
altuchk@tompkinscortland.edu

ALTUSKY, Shlomo Avidgor .... 718-868-2300 299 D

ALTWINE, Chad .... 402-375-7274 276 D
chaltwi1@wsc.edu

ALVA, Sylvia, A .... 909-869-4382.. 31 A
saalva@cpp.edu

ALVALLE, Anibal .... 787-764-0000 528 F
anibal.alvalle@upr.edu

ALVARADO, Cecilia .... 951-222-8000.. 58 H
cecilia.alvarado@rcc.edu

ALVARADO, Christian ... 949-582-4340.. 64 J
calvarado@saddleback.edu

ALVARADO, Christian ... 949-582-4340.. 64 H
calvarado@saddleback.edu

ALVARADO, Magalie ..... 787-257-7373 525 Q
ue_malvarado@suagm.edu

ALVARADO, Miguel .... 617-422-7423 222 J
malvarado@nesl.edu

ALVARADO, Nelly .... 310-900-1600.. 40 C

ALVARADO, Norman ...... 718-779-1430 320 C
nalvarado@plazacollege.edu

ALVARADO, Nyvia .... 787-264-0409 524 D
nialvara@intersg.edu

ALVARADO-STINSON, Cynthia .... 361-592-1615 445 S
calvaradostinson2@coastalbend.edu

ALVARADO-TORRES, Cesar .... 787-751-1912 524 E
calvarado@juris.inter.edu

ALVARADO-VALDOVINOS, Lorena .... 509-574-4702 500 I
lalvarado-valdovinos@yvcc.edu

ALVAREZ, Albert .... 818-364-7600.. 49 C
lamcfoundation@lamission.edu

ALVAREZ, Alvin .... 415-338-3326.. 34 C
aalvarez@sfsu.edu

ALVAREZ, Ana .... 305-284-3584 112 O
aalvarez@miami.edu

ALVAREZ, Araceli .... 713-500-3871 468 D
araceli.alvarez@uth.tmc.edu

ALVAREZ, Araceli .... 713-500-3871 469 A
araceli.alvarez@uth.tmc.edu

ALVAREZ, Barry, L .... 608-262-4312 510 C
bla@athletics.wisc.edu

ALVAREZ, Brian .... 516-364-0808 317 B
itsupport@nycollege.edu

ALVAREZ, Caridad .... 787-841-2000 525 J
caridad_alvarez@pucpr.edu

ALVAREZ, Celso .... 718-429-6600 333 B
celso.alvarez@vaughn.edu

ALVAREZ, Celso .... 305-474-6868 107 B
cjalvarez@stu.edu

ALVAREZ, Celso, J .... 305-474-6868 107 B
cjalvarez@stu.edu

ALVAREZ, Frank, D .... 509-452-5100 496 H
falvarez@pnwu.edu

ALVAREZ, Ivonne .... 619-388-2689.. 60 D
ialvarez@sdccd.edu

ALVAREZ, Jackie .... 541-737-2131 385 F
jackie.alvarez@oregonstate.edu

ALVAREZ, Jacqueline .... 413-542-2354 210 F
jalvarez@amherst.edu

ALVAREZ, Jacqueline .... 787-284-1912 524 C
jalvarez@ponce.inter.edu

ALVAREZ, Lourdes .... 203-932-7257.. 89 D
lavarez@newhaven.edu

ALVAREZ, Maria .... 787-882-2065 526 D
registraduria@unitecpr.net

ALVAREZ, Maria, L .... 305-899-3085.. 95 G
malvarez@barry.edu

ALVAREZ, Patricia .... 559-730-3988.. 39 G
patriciaa@cos.edu

ALVAREZ, Richard .... 718-997-5929 303 E
richard.alvarez@qc.cuny.edu

ALVAREZ, Richard .... 540-831-5411 484 A
ralvarez@radford.edu

ALVAREZ, Silvia .... 212-431-2872 317 H
silvia.alvarez@nyls.edu

ALVAREZ, Sylvia .... 787-728-1515 529 B
salvarez@sagrado.edu

ALVAREZ, Timothy .... 701-231-7701 354 D
timothy.alvarez@ndsu.edu

ALVAREZ-ROBINSON, Sonia .... 404-385-3306 120 A
sonia@consulting.gatech.edu

ALVAREZ-RUIZ, Luis ...... 787-890-2681 527 E
luis.alvarez8@upr.edu

ALVARO, Tammy .... 989-386-6622 234 B
talvaro@midmich.edu

ALVATER, Deborah .... 706-886-6831 126 F
dalvater@tfc.edu

ALVERSON, Amelia, J .... 212-851-7929 305 E
amelia.alverson@columbia.edu

ALVES, Eddie .... 541-881-5590 387 D
ealves@tvcc.cc

ALVES, Stephanie .... 925-969-2082.. 40 L
salves@dvc.edu

ALVEY, Patricia .... 214-768-4519 457 B
palvey@smu.edu

ALVINO, Kathleen, M .... 401-865-2430 416 E
kalvino@providence.edu

ALVIS, Robert .... 812-357-6543 164 A
ralvis@saintmeinrad.edu

ALVITI, Eileen .... 617-747-2375 212 B
hroperations@berklee.edu

ALVOET, Patricia, E .... 210-297-9630 443 K
pealvoet@baptisthealthsystem.com

ALZAHABI, Basem .... 810-762-7893 232 C
balzahab@kettering.edu

AMACK, April .... 970-542-3187.. 81 A
april.amack@morgancc.edu

AMADI, Emmanual .... 662-254-3363 255 A
amadi@mvsu.edu

AMADO, Manuel .... 303-458-4122.. 82 D
mamado@regis.edu

AMADOR, Lui .... 657-278-8660.. 32 B
lamador@fullerton.edu

AMADOR, Tristen .... 303-458-4174.. 82 D
tamador@regis.edu

AMAEFULE, Ann .... 708-237-5050 148 A
aamaefule@nc.edu

AMAKER, Corey, L .... 803-535-5075 419 E
camaker@claflin.edu

AMALBERT, Milagros ..... 787-751-1912 524 E
mamalber@juris.inter.edu

AMAN, Rick, K .... 208-535-5366 131 G
rick.aman@my.eitc.edu

AMANKWATIA, Tonya ... 757-352-4886 484 E
tamankwatia@regent.edu

AMANO, Koyoko .... 570-484-2073 406 E
kxa1026@lockhaven.edu

AMAR, Harish .... 626-350-1500.. 29 E

AMAR, Vikram .... 217-333-0931 154 B
amar@illinois.edu

AMARA, Sakpa, S .... 703-891-1787 485 I
samara@standardcollege.edu

AMARI, Neil, D .... 918-836-6886 380 C
neil.amari@spartan.edu

AMARO, Jovana .... 336-322-2122 345 D
jovana.amaro@piedmontcc.edu

AMASON, Allen .... 912-478-2622 120 E
aamason@georgiasouthern.edu

AMASON, Amy .... 706-776-0104 124 E
aamason@piedmont.edu

AMATO, James .... 312-752-2133 142 E
james.amato@kendall.edu

AMATO, John .... 515-271-2849 168 J
john.amato@drake.edu

AMATO, Paula, A .... 603-428-2461 281 F
pamato@nec.edu

AMATO, Roseann .... 407-708-2713 107 G
amator@seminolestate.edu

AMATOR, Shelley .... 505-566-3466 296 A
amators@sanjuancollege.edu

AMATUCCI, Kelly .... 772-462-7674 101 Q
kamatucc@irsc.edu

AMAVIZCA, Gabriela ..... 520-417-4708.. 11 R
amavizcag@cochise.edu

AMAYA, Mercedes .... 305-237-0388 103 L
mamaya@mdc.edu

AMAYA GORDON, Karla, J .... 757-823-8275 483 F
kjagordon@nsu.edu

AMBACH, Robert .... 513-556-2413 371 E
robert.ambach@uc.edu

AMBAR, Carmen, T .... 440-775-8400 367 B
carmen.ambar@0berlin.edu

AMBELANG, Charlie ...... 408-551-1940.. 62 F
cambelang@scu.edu

AMBERG, David .... 315-464-4515 326 B
ambergd@upstate.edu

AMBLER, Charles .... 915-747-5950 467 E
cambler@utep.edu

AMBLER, Tony .... 713-743-6457 465 A
apambler@central.uh.edu

AMBLER, Virginia, M .... 757-221-1236 479 I
vmambl@wm.edu

AMBRA, Stephen .... 603-271-6484 280 N
sambra@ccsnh.edu

AMBRON, Sueann .... 303-315-8001.. 83 D
sueann.ambron@ucdenver.edu

AMBROSE, AnneMarie .. 315-866-0300 310 A
ambroseac@herkimer.edu

AMBROSE, Charles, M .. 660-543-4112 268 A
ambrose@ucmo.edu

AMBROSE, Danielle .... 503-493-6508 382 I
dambrose@cu-portland.edu

AMBROSE, James .... 315-786-2490 311 H
jambrose@sunyjefferson.edu

AMBROSE, Joshua .... 410-857-2280 205 E
jambrose@mcdaniel.edu

AMBROSE, Molly, B ...... 617-228-2457 219 D
mambrose@bhcc.mass.edu

AMBROSE, Susan .... 617-373-2170 223 D

AMBROSIA, Todd .... 212-614-6110 320 B
todd.ambrosia@mountsinai.org

AMBUR, Roberta, S .... 605-677-5661 428 E
roberta.ambur@usd.edu

AMBURGEY, Jeff, S .... 859-985-3082 183 I
jeff_amburgey@berea.edu

AMBUSKE, Joseph .... 614-236-6116 358 A
jambuske@capital.edu

AMDUR, Nick .... 617-619-1900 216 A
nick.amdur@faculty.hult.edu

AMELANG, Mary Ann .... 409-933-8271 446 H

AMELING, Brian, F .... 864-488-8200 422 B
bameling@limestone.edu

AMELL, Laura .... 802-485-2065 475 I
lamell@norwich.edu

AMELSBERG, James ...... 641-585-8164 174 B
amelsbergj@waldorf.edu

AMEN, Barbara, A .... 503-777-7259 386 F
barbara.amen@reed.edu

AMEND, John .... 402-554-2242 277 I
jamend@unomaha.edu

AMENDOLA, Luigi .... 815-836-5875 143 E
amendolu@lewisu.edu

AMENSON-HILL, Brenda .... 218-477-2171 246 B
brenda.amensonhill@mnstate.edu

AMENTA, Paula .... 847-214-7273 138 B
pamenta@elgin.edu

AMERIN, Kylea, C .... 580-327-8601 376 K
kcamerin@nwosu.edu

AMERIO, Barbara .... 661-763-7881.. 67 A
bamerio@taftcollege.edu

AMERO, Carolina .... 678-466-4217 117 I
carolinaamero@clayton.edu

AMERSHEK, Tom .... 620-235-4775 180 J
tamershek@pittstate.edu

AMES, Amy .... 573-897-5000 267 F

AMES, Christopher .... 518-244-2214 321 G
amesc@sage.edu

AMES, David .... 617-964-1100 210 G
dames@ants.edu

AMES, John .... 610-785-6287 409 F
james@scs.edu

AMES, Linda .... 509-279-6258 493 I
linda.ames@scc.spokane.edu

AMES, Linda .... 509-279-6215 493 I
linda.ames@scc.spokane.edu

AMES, Lynda, J .... 518-564-3310 327 E
ameslj@plattsburgh.edu

AMES, Suzanne .... 425-739-8410 495 F
suzanne.ames@lwtech.edu

AMES, Trevor, R .... 612-624-6244 250 E
amesx001@umn.edu

AMEY, Carol, J .... 859-858-3511 183 D
camey@asbury.edu

AMEY, Tracey .... 570-327-4503 404 T
tamey@pct.edu

AMEZQUITA, Anna Marie .... 951-571-6162.. 58 F
annamarie.amezquita@mvc.edu

AMI, Dawn .... 505-346-2339 296 G
dawn.ami@bie.edu

AMICK, Patricia, A .... 816-604-1130 262 F
patricia.amick@mcckc.edu

AMICO, David .... 315-792-5318 315 I
damico@mvcc.edu

AMIDON, Jacob .... 585-785-1418 308 D
jacob.amidon@flcc.edu

AMIDON, Jacob, E .... 585-785-1418 308 D
jacob.amidon@flcc.edu

AMIDON, James, L .... 765-361-6364 166 B
amidonj@wabash.edu

AMIDON, JR., James, L .... 765-361-6364 166 B
amidonj@wabash.edu

AMIE, Torrion .... 952-358-8505 246 D
torrion.amie@normandale.edu

AMINY, Marina .... 949-582-4365.. 64 J
maminy@saddleback.edu

AMIOTTE, Shannon .... 605-455-6012 427 I
samiotte@olc.edu

AMIRI, Mark, N .... 314-935-5608 269 L
mamiri@wustl.edu

AMIRIDIS, Michael .... 312-413-3350 153 H
chancellor@uic.edu

AMIRIDIS, Michael .... 312-413-3350 153 G
amiridis@uic.edu

AMIRTHARAJ, Merlin .... 704-991-0207 346 I
mamirtharaj5283@stanly.edu

AMIS, Eric, J .... 330-972-7500 371 C
amis@uakron.edu

AMLER, Robert, W .... 914-594-4531 318 A
robert_amler@nymc.edu

AMMAR, Nawal, H .... 856-256-5841 289 H
ammar@rowan.edu

AMMETER, Tony .... 662-915-6748 256 C
tammeter@olemiss.edu

AMMIGAN, Ravi .... 302-831-2115.. 90 I
rammigan@udel.edu

AMMON, Darryl, C .... 660-263-3900 258 A
darrylammon@cccb.edu

AMMON, Janice, S .... 609-497-7890 288 E
chapel@ptsem.edu

AMMONS, Brian .... 828-298-3325 353 B
bammons@warren-wilson.edu

AMMONS, Kevin .... 334-347-2623.... 1 J
kammons@escc.edu

AMMONS, Maxwell, J ... 606-783-2014 188 C
m.ammons@moreheadstate.edu

AMMONS, Sandy .... 910-630-7114 340 A
sammons@methodist.edu

AMOA, Kwesi .... 914-606-6789 333 H
kwesi.amoa@sunywcc.edu

AMODIO, Greg .... 203-582-3621.. 88 A
greg.amodio@quinnipiac.edu

AMOKE, William .... 619-298-1829.. 65 G
wamoke@ssu.edu

AMOO, Judith, L .... 308-635-6702 278 B
amooj@wncc.edu

AMORE, Jason .... 607-871-2144 298 A
amore@alfred.edu

AMORIM, Daniel .... 617-730-7018 223 B
daniel.amorim@newbury.edu

AMOROS, Blanca .... 787-758-2525 528 D
blanca.amoros@upr.edu

AMOS, Anthea .... 850-484-4459 105 E
aamos@pensacolastate.edu

ANDERSON, James, T ... 973-655-7022 287 D andersonja@mail.montclair.edu
ANDERSON, Jan .... 320-762-4518 243 J jana@alextech.edu
ANDERSON, Janice .... 254-526-1116 445 L janice.anderson@ctcd.edu
ANDERSON, Jeanette .... 626-571-8811.. 72 C jeanettea@uwest.edu
ANDERSON, Jeff .... 808-245-8384 130 F jeffa@hawaii.edu
ANDERSON, Jeffrey .... 352-588-8657 106 N jeffrey.anderson@saintleo.edu
ANDERSON, Jeffrey .... 518-255-5413 328 C andersjm@cobleskill.edu
ANDERSON, Jeffrey, J ... 847-574-5210 143 A janderson@lfgsm.edu
ANDERSON, Jennifer ..... 203-254-4000.. 87 A janderson@fairfield.edu
ANDERSON, Jennifer ..... 614-287-5581 360 C jander02@cscc.edu
ANDERSON, Jeremy ...... 606-337-1533 184 D jeremy.anderson@ccbbc.edu
ANDERSON, Jeremy ...... 218-751-8670 249 G jeremyanderson@oakhills.edu
ANDERSON, Jerry .... 515-271-3985 168 J jerry.anderson@drake.edu
ANDERSON, Jessica ...... 815-825-9786 142 F jessica.anderson@kishwaukeecollege.edu
ANDERSON, Jill .... 307-754-6401 516 Q jill.anderson@nwc.edu
ANDERSON, Jillian .... 508-929-8072 219 A jillian.anderson@worcester.edu
ANDERSON, Joan, E ...... 508-793-3644 213 D janderso@holycross.edu
ANDERSON, Joanna ...... 660-596-7223 267 E janderson@sfccmo.edu
ANDERSON, John .... 540-857-7273 490 B janderson@virginiawestern.edu
ANDERSON, John, A ..... 470-578-3132 122 C janders2@kennesaw.edu
ANDERSON, John, M .... 717-871-7001 407 A mupresident@millersville.edu
ANDERSON, Jon (Jay) .. 979-209-7296 444 D jay.anderson@blinn.edu
ANDERSON, Jonathan ... 509-359-6081 494 D janderson@ewu.edu
ANDERSON, Jordan ...... 770-534-6126 116 F janderson6@brenau.edu
ANDERSON, Joyce .... 208-376-7731 131 B janderson@boisebible.edu
ANDERSON, JP .... 585-594-6400 321 C anderson_jp@roberts.edu
ANDERSON, Judith .... 507-538-0162 241 E anderson.judith@mayo.edu
ANDERSON, Julie .... 507-222-6824 241 C janderso@carleton.edu
ANDERSON, Justin .... 603-646-3661 281 C justin.anderson@dartmouth.edu
ANDERSON, Karen .... 515-643-6791 171 K kanderson8@mercydesmoines.org
ANDERSON, Katherine, E .... 856-225-2830 290 B katie.anderson@rutgers.edu
ANDERSON, Kathleen .... 410-837-5249 209 D kanderson@ubalt.edu
ANDERSON, Kathleen, M .... 563-333-6344 173 A officeofthepresident@sau.edu
ANDERSON, Kathryn ...... 757-825-2851 489 G andersonk@tncc.edu
ANDERSON, Kay .... 478-445-6286 119 E kay.anderson@gcsu.edu
ANDERSON, Keith .... 704-216-6248 339 E kanderson@livingstone.edu
ANDERSON, Keith, R ..... 206-876-6101 498 C kanderson@theseattleschool.edu
ANDERSON, Kelly .... 505-566-3775 296 A andersonk@sanjuancollege.edu
ANDERSON, Kelly .... 419-772-2073 367 G k-anderson@onu.edu
ANDERSON, Kelly, M .... 419-434-5184 372 B andersonk3@findlay.edu
ANDERSON, Kenneth .... 509-313-3404 495 A anderson@jepson.gonzaga.edu
ANDERSON, Kevin .... 617-747-2359 212 B physicalplant@berklee.edu
ANDERSON, Kevin .... 301-314-0013 207 G kevina@umd.edu
ANDERSON, Kevin .... 239-432-6706 100 E kevin.anderson@fsw.edu
ANDERSON, Kevin, L ..... 563-589-0211 174 D kanderson@wartburgseminary.edu
ANDERSON, Kim .... 484-365-7565 400 E kanderson@lincoln.edu
ANDERSON, Kirk, D ...... 309-794-7203 133 G kirkanderson@augustana.edu
ANDERSON, Kristen ...... 212-517-0458 314 D kanderson@mmm.edu
ANDERSON, Kristin, K .. 901-722-3216 436 D kanderson@sco.edu
ANDERSON, Kristina, C 240-895-5000 206 G kcanderson@smcm.edu
ANDERSON, Kristine ...... 231-777-0447 234 G kristine.anderson@muskegoncc.edu
ANDERSON, Kristy .... 360-538-4151 495 B kanderso@ghc.edu
ANDERSON, Kyle, D ..... 859-238-5371 184 C kyle.anderson@centre.edu
ANDERSON, Larry .... 318-797-5371 194 E larry.anderson@lsus.edu
ANDERSON, Larry .... 218-879-0842 244 F larrya@fdltcc.edu
ANDERSON, Larry .... 218-879-0822 244 F larrya@fdltcc.edu
ANDERSON, OFM, Lawrence .... 518-783-2332 324 C landerson@siena.edu
ANDERSON, Layne .... 218-477-2447 246 B layne.anderson@mnstate.edu
ANDERSON, Leesa, P ... 706-778-3000 124 E landerson@piedmont.edu
ANDERSON, Leif, B .... 612-330-1497 240 G andersol@augsburg.edu
ANDERSON, Leslie .... 870-733-6732.. 18 B landerson@asumidsouth.edu
ANDERSON, Linda .... 256-726-7095.... 6 E landerson@oakwood.edu
ANDERSON, Linda .... 503-297-5544 385 A landerson@ocac.edu
ANDERSON, Linda, S .... 816-604-2380 262 I linda.anderson@mcckc.edu
ANDERSON, Lisa .... 718-270-5000 303 C lisa@mec.cuny.edu
ANDERSON, Lisa .... 479-619-2227.. 20 F landerson7@nwacc.edu
ANDERSON, Lois .... 301-387-3042 203 I lois.anderson@garrettcollege.edu
ANDERSON, Louise .... 269-488-4777 231 G landerson@kvcc.edu
ANDERSON, Maria .... 973-655-4000 287 D andersonmar@mail.montclair.edu
ANDERSON, Marie .... 909-469-5485.. 74 G manderson@westernu.edu
ANDERSON, Mark .... 860-628-4751.. 87 E manderson@lincolncollegene.edu
ANDERSON, Mark, R .... 470-578-6160 122 C mande126@kennesaw.edu
ANDERSON, Marlene .... 701-224-5578 354 F marlene.anderson@bismarckstate.edu
ANDERSON, Martha ...... 602-285-7553.. 14 A martha.anderson@phoenixcollege.edu
ANDERSON, MaryKaye .. 615-898-2670 434 H marykaye.anderson@mtsu.edu
ANDERSON, Maureen ... 352-854-2322.. 97 C andersom@cf.edu
ANDERSON, Melinda, F 318-619-2916 194 A manderson@lsua.edu
ANDERSON, Melissa, K 920-748-8365 509 H andersonmk@ripon.edu
ANDERSON, Melissa, L 336-841-9220 338 E manderson@highpoint.edu
ANDERSON, Melissa, P 540-674-3635 488 G manderson@nr.edu
ANDERSON, Michelle .... 312-788-1125 154 I manderson@vandercook.edu
ANDERSON, Michelle, J .... 718-951-5671 301 E bcpresident@brooklyn.cuny.edu
ANDERSON, Mike .... 435-283-7393 474 A mike.anderson@snow.edu
ANDERSON, Monique, W .... 865-974-2101 439 I manders3@utk.edu
ANDERSON, Myron .... 303-556-3022.. 80 Q mande118@msudenver.edu
ANDERSON, N. Douglas .... 740-376-4536 365 A doug.anderson@marietta.edu
ANDERSON, Nancy .... 978-867-4828 215 D nancy.anderson@gordon.edu
ANDERSON, Neil .... 423-648-2673 435 M nanderson@richmont.edu
ANDERSON, Nickoel ...... 218-733-5990 245 C n.anderson@lsc.edu
ANDERSON, Nina .... 732-571-7551 287 C nanderso@monmouth.edu
ANDERSON, Patricia ...... 775-753-2115 279 A pat.anderson@gbcnv.edu
ANDERSON, Patricia ..... 615-230-3300 438 C patricia.anderson@volstate.edu
ANDERSON, Pauline ...... 954-201-7877.. 96 A panderso@broward.edu
ANDERSON, Per .... 218-299-3932 241 K anderson@cord.edu
ANDERSON, Peter .... 216-987-3538 360 E peter.anderson@tri-c.edu
ANDERSON, Peter, T ..... 540-674-3631 488 G ptanderson@nr.edu
ANDERSON, Phillip, T .. 414-410-4004 506 F ptanderson@stritch.edu
ANDERSON, Randy .... 323-953-4000.. 49 A andersr@lacitycollege.edu
ANDERSON, Ray .... 480-965-0983.. 10 K ray.anderson@asu.edu
ANDERSON, Rayelle ...... 208-769-5978 132 E rayelle_anderson@nic.edu
ANDERSON, Rebecca .... 704-337-2485 348 D andersonr@queens.edu
ANDERSON, Rebecca .... 210-458-4132 468 B rebecca.anderson@utsa.edu
ANDERSON, Rebekah .... 503-251-5718 387 I reanderson@uws.edu
ANDERSON, Renae .... 785-227-3380 175 E andersonra@bethanylb.edu
ANDERSON, Rhonda ..... 989-837-4459 235 C rca@northwood.edu
ANDERSON, Rhonda, C 989-837-4455 235 C rca@northwood.edu
ANDERSON, Richard ..... 775-831-1314 280 C randerson@sierranevada.edu
ANDERSON, Rick .... 252-940-6417 340 N rick.anderson@beaufortccc.edu
ANDERSON, Rick .... 956-665-2121 468 A rick.anderson@utrgv.edu
ANDERSON, Rick .... 423-236-2000 436 C
ANDERSON, Robert .... 517-629-0446 226 G banderson@albion.edu
ANDERSON, Robin, D ... 503-943-7224 387 H anderson@up.edu
ANDERSON, Roger .... 401-232-6088 416 A randerso@bryant.edu
ANDERSON, Ron .... 651-201-1498 243 I ron.anderson@so.mnscu.edu
ANDERSON, Ronald, M 859-858-3511 183 D ron.anderson@asbury.edu
ANDERSON, Russell ...... 601-266-4153 256 E rusty.anderson@usm.edu
ANDERSON, Ryan .... 718-405-3403 304 H ryan.anderson@mountsaintvincent.edu
ANDERSON, Sandy .... 907-745-3201.... 9 D sanderson@akbible.edu
ANDERSON, Scott .... 209-468-4807.. 67 C scanderson@sjcoe.net
ANDERSON, Scott, D .... 651-631-5152 251 C sdanderson3@unwsp.edu
ANDERSON, Scott, R .... 815-599-3604 139 F scott.anderson@highland.edu
ANDERSON, Sharee ...... 208-535-5333 131 G sharee.anderson@my.eitc.edu
ANDERSON, Sharon, D . 336-734-7735 343 C sanderson@forsythtech.edu
ANDERSON, Shawn .... 218-299-6535 245 H shawn.anderson@minnesota.edu
ANDERSON, Shayna ...... 661-362-2203.. 51 C sanderson@masters.edu
ANDERSON, Stephanie .. 512-245-2803 463 A sa35@txstate.edu
ANDERSON, Susan .... 978-656-3483 220 C andersons@middlesex.mass.edu
ANDERSON, Susan .... 216-373-6396 367 A andersons@ndc.edu
ANDERSON, Susan, M .. 530-898-6472.. 31 D sanderson@csuchico.edu
ANDERSON, Suzanne, M .... 540-853-0691 482 A srmcguire@carilionclinic.org
ANDERSON, Sylvia .... 919-530-5214 350 D sander55@nccu.edu
ANDERSON, Tamara ...... 508-565-1661 224 H tanderson@stonehill.edu
ANDERSON, Therese ..... 215-596-8813 413 E registrar@usciences.edu
ANDERSON, Thomas, K 802-626-6497 477 D thomas.anderson@lyndonstate.edu
ANDERSON, Timothy, J 413-545-6388 216 H tjanderson@ecs.umass.edu
ANDERSON, Tina, K ...... 229-333-2119 128 G tina.anderson@wiregrass.edu
ANDERSON, Todd .... 910-521-6371 351 E todd.anderson@uncp.edu
ANDERSON, Todd, J ..... 213-624-1200.. 42 N tjanderson@fidm.edu
ANDERSON, Tracey .... 304-327-4331 503 O tanderson@bluefieldstate.edu
ANDERSON, Ty .... 580-559-5252 375 I tydand@ecok.edu
ANDERSON, Vanessa .... 303-797-5930.. 76 I vanessa.anderson@arapahoe.edu
ANDERSON, Wanda .... 302-736-2443.. 90 J wanda.anderson@wesley.edu
ANDERSON, Warren, R . 717-736-4102 396 G wranders@hacc.edu
ANDERSON, William ..... 336-316-2907 338 C andersonwj@guilford.edu
ANDERSON, William, O 610-660-1276 409 H banderso@sju.edu
ANDERSON, William, O 802-654-2252 476 A wanderson@smcvt.edu
ANDERSON, Yolanda, B 919-530-6738 350 D yandersn@nccu.edu
ANDERSON-BINA, Cindy .... 218-235-2121 248 B c.bina@vcc.edu
ANDERSON-BURT, Marilyn .... 206-934-5144 497 J marilyn.anderson-burt@seattlecolleges.edu
ANDERSON MARTINEZ, Richard .... 207-602-2826 202 A randerson@une.edu
ANDERSON WIECK, Patricia .... 503-594-3300 382 D patricia.anderson@clackamas.edu
ANDERSON-WILLIAMS, Sandra .... 615-327-6683 434 A williamss@mmc.edu
ANDERYRNE, Ellie .... 608-363-2014 506 D anderbyrneek@beloit.edu
ANDINO, Joseph .... 724-846-5100 395 J
ANDINO, Thomas .... 315-445-4110 312 F andinotm@lemoyne.edu
ANDIS, Blake .... 276-739-2582 490 A bandis@vhcc.edu
ANDORF, Carla .... 319-398-9474 171 F carla.andorf@kirkwood.edu
ANDORS, Allison .... 516-686-7737 317 G aandors@nyit.edu
ANDRACKI, Jason .... 814-332-4351 388 F jandrack@allegheny.edu
ANDRADE, Alicia .... 559-453-2220.. 43 J alicia.andrade@fresno.edu
ANDRADE, June, C .... 787-728-1515 529 B jandrade@sagrado.edu
ANDRADE, Kim .... 405-422-1267 379 B andradek@redlandscc.edu
ANDRAOS, Amale .... 212-854-3473 305 E aa3217@columbia.edu
ANDRE, Nicholas .... 570-662-4834 406 F nandre@mansfield.edu
ANDREA, Francine .... 201-559-6181 286 C andreaf@felician.edu
ANDREA, JR., Robert, K .... 518-956-8206 324 G randrea@albany.edu
ANDREANI, Scott .... 330-494-6170 370 G sandreani@starkstate.edu
ANDREAS, Marc .... 616-222-3000 232 F mandreas@kuyper.edu
ANDREAS, Michelle .... 360-596-5209 498 G mandreas@spscc.edu
ANDREASEN, Michael, C .... 541-346-0869 387 F miandrea@uoregon.edu
ANDRECHAK, Michael ... 404-727-9252 119 B michael.j.andrechak@emory.edu
ANDREINI, Janelle .... 402-465-2414 276 E jsa@nebrwesleyan.edu
ANDREJCZYK, Rose, L .. 413-205-3248 210 E rose.andrejczyk@aic.edu
ANDREO, Eddie .... 620-441-7101 176 M andreoe@cowley.edu
ANDREOLA, Michael .... 412-536-1096 398 E michael.andreola@laroche.edu
ANDRESEN, Elena .... 503-494-4460 385 D provost@ohsu.edu
ANDRESEN, Julie, A ...... 573-629-4001 260 G jandresen@hlg.edu
ANDRESEN, Sharla .... 541-383-7208 382 B sandresen@cocc.edu
ANDRESEN REID, Marcia .... 507-284-3627 241 F andresen.marcia@mayo.edu
ANDRESS-MARTIN, Holly .... 583-288-6421 259 E handress@culver.edu
ANDRETTA, Kim .... 570-372-4042 410 H andretta@susqu.edu
ANDREU, Denise .... 863-297-1000 105 F dandreu@polk.edu
ANDREU, Frank .... 305-821-3333 100 A fandreu@fnu.edu
ANDREW, Barbara .... 973-720-3657 292 I andrewb@wpunj.edu
ANDREW, Damon, P ..... 225-578-1258 193 M damonandrew@lsu.edu
ANDREW, Kenneth .... 304-473-8367 505 G andrew_k@wvwc.edu
ANDREW, Marcy .... 575-758-8914 294 H marcya@midwiferycollege.edu

ANYANWU, Fitzpatrick, U .... 337-421-6905 193 F
fitzpatrick.anyanwu@sowela.edu
ANZ, Susan, D .... 254-710-3731 444 B
susan_anz@baylor.edu
ANZALDUA, Ricardo ..... 212-237-8316 302 F
ranzaldua@jjay.cuny.edu
ANZALONE, Alessandro 813-253-7960 101 M
aanzalone2@hccfl.edu
ANZALONE, Roseann .... 518-743-2242 328 G
anzalonr@sunyacc.edu
ANZINGER, John .... 240-629-7858 203 H
janzinger@frederick.edu
AOUN, Joseph, E .... 617-373-2101 223 D
AOYAMA, Yuko .... 508-793-7779 213 C
yaoyama@clarku.edu
APANEL, Stephen, J ...... 570-577-1195 390 H
stephen.apanel@bucknell.edu
APANOVICH, Val .... 570-674-6749 401 M
vapanovi@misericordia.edu
APAW, David .... 410-225-2464 205 C
dapaw@mica.edu
APEKEY, Stella, G .... 571-553-3537.. 92 A
sapekey@gwu.edu
APEL, Scott .... 562-985-4031.. 32 C
scott.apel@csulb.edu
APELQUIST, Maryellen .. 802-831-1228 476 G
mapelquist@vermontlaw.edu
APER, Jeffery, P .... 217-424-6220 145 J
japer@millikin.edu
APFELTHALER, Gerhard . 805-493-3352.. 30 E
apfeltha@callutheran.edu
APGAR, Travis .... 518-276-6266 321 A
apgart@rpi.edu
APICERNO, Amy .... 727-864-8217.. 97 O
apiceral@eckerd.edu
APLIN, Greg .... 334-222-6591.... 2 H
jgaplin@lbwcc.edu
APODACA, Phillip, C ..... 719-389-6613.. 77 J
papodaca@coloradocollege.edu
APOLLO, Richard, M ...... 516-463-5405 310 D
richard.apollo@hofstra.edu
APONTE, Adela .... 787-285-2525 522 P
adela.aponte@hccpr.edu
APONTE, Arcelio .... 973-353-5541 290 D
arcelio.aponte@rutgers.edu
APONTE, Brunilda .... 787-743-7979 526 A
baponte@suagm.edu
APONTE, Carmen, L .... 787-780-0070 521 B
caponte@caribbean.edu
APONTE, Juan, M .... 787-764-0000 528 F
juan.aponte6@upr.edu
APONTE, Julio .... 787-274-1142 319 C
japonte@stdpr.org
APONTE, Laura, E .... 787-766-1717 526 B
um_laponte@suagm.edu
APONTE, Wanda .... 787-786-3030 526 F
waponte@ucb.edu.pr
APONTE-AVELLANET, Nilda .... 787-993-8861 527 G
nilda.aponte2@upr.edu
APOSTOLO, Brennan ..... 405-422-1266 379 B
brennan.apostolo@redlandscc.edu
APPAVOO, Suresh .... 415-482-3598.. 41 J
sappavoo@dominican.edu
APPEANING, Vladimir ... 225-216-8000 192 B
appeaninga@mybrcc.edu
APPEL, Elizabeth, H ...... 410-777-7383 202 D
ehappel@aacc.edu
APPEL, Heidi .... 419-530-6031 372 F
heidi.appel@utoledo.edu
APPEL, Kellie .... 678-547-6397 122 H
appel_k@mercer.edu
APPEL, Marie-Noel .... 212-229-5662 316 E
appelm@newschool.edu
APPELGET, Kristin .... 609-258-3018 288 F
appelget@princeton.edu
APPELT, Uschi .... 812-866-7221 158 C
appelt@hanover.edu
APPIAH-PADI, Stephen, K .... 570-577-3796 390 H
s.appiahpadi@bucknell.edu
APPIARIUS, Donald, B .. 260-399-7700 165 B
dappiarius@sf.edu
APPLE, Carl .... 616-632-2843 227 C
cpa001@aquinas.edu
APPLE, Mark .... 317-955-6775 162 R
mapple@marian.edu
APPLE, Monique .... 605-455-6055 427 I
mapple@olc.edu
APPLE, Ryan .... 517-321-0242 231 A
rapple@glcc.edu
APPLEBURY, Gene .... 901-751-8453 434 E
gapplebury@mabts.edu
APPLEBY, Charley .... 870-680-8717.. 18 D
charley_appleby@asun.edu
APPLEBY, Karen .... 208-282-4143 132 B
applkare@isu.edu
APPLEGATE, J. Phillip ... 918-631-2070 381 C
phil-applegate@utulsa.edu
APPLEGATE, John .... 812-855-9198 159 G
jsapple@iu.edu
APPLEGATE, John, S ..... 812-855-9198 159 H
jsapple@iu.edu
APPLEMAN, Boomer ..... 508-559-5208 375 I
bappleman@ecok.edu
APPLETON, Amber .... 503-253-3443 385 B
amber.appleton@ocom.edu
APPLETON, Judith, A .... 607-255-9970 306 B
jaa2@cornell.edu
APPLETON, Kevin .... 410-651-6230 208 C
kappleton@umes.edu
APPLETON, Kevin .... 502-597-5075 187 E
kevin.appleton@kysu.edu
APPLETON, Lea .... 909-445-2590.. 38 B
lappleton@cst.edu
APPLIN, Cynthia .... 440-366-7578 364 F
APPLIN, Mary Beth .... 601-857-3253 253 B
mary.applin@hindscc.edu
APPLING, Ron .... 806-291-3451 470 I
applingr@wbu.edu
APPREY, Augustine .... 717-290-8747 399 F
aapprey@lancasterseminary.edu
APPREY, Maurice .... 434-924-7923 486 H
ma9h@virginia.edu
APSEY, Curt .... 208-426-1826 131 C
capsey@boisestate.edu
AQUI, Jason .... 425-564-4128 492 G
jason.aqui@bellevuecollege.edu
AQUILA, Dominic .... 713-525-2164 466 J
aquilad@stthom.edu
AQUILA, Jennifer, K ...... 610-799-1120 400 A
jaquila@lccc.edu
AQUILA, Scott, W .... 610-799-1550 400 A
saquila@lccc.edu
AQUINO, Belissa .... 787-766-1717 526 B
beaquino@suagm.edu
AQUINO, Carlos .... 815-740-3398 154 G
caquino@stfrancis.edu
AQUINO, Cathy .... 304-734-6611 502 K
cathy.aquino@bridgevalley.edu
AQUINO, Eli .... 406-395-4875 273 B
AQUINO, Jeannette .... 787-890-2681 527 E
jeanette.aquino@upr.edu
ARADHYA, Jennifer, M . 781-280-3511 220 C
aradhyaj@middlesex.mass.edu
ARAGON, Amanda .... 970-943-0120.. 84 E
ARAGON, Beverly .... 575-769-4001 293 M
beverly.aragon@clovis.edu
ARAGON, Paul .... 575-439-3705 295 C
aragonp@nmsu.edu
ARAGON, Paul .... 575-769-4165 293 M
paul.aragon@clovis.edu
ARAGON, Tammy .... 480-858-9100.. 16 D
t.aragon@scnm.edu
ARAIMO, Angelo, G ...... 718-390-3412 333 D
aaraimo@wagner.edu
ARAIN, Nizam .... 608-785-8541 510 F
narain@uwlax.edu
ARAIZA, Claudia .... 619-298-1829.. 65 G
caraiza@ssu.edu
ARAIZA, William .... 718-780-7520 300 A
bill.araiza@brooklaw.edu
ARALDI, Mary-Jane, S .. 518-471-3260 314 H
maryjane.araldi@sphp.com
ARAMMASH, Fouzi, H ... 803-705-4311 418 G
arammashf@benedict.edu
ARANA, Sloane .... 918-540-6393 376 F
scbrown@neo.edu
ARANAS, Theodore .... 415-239-3546.. 37 H
taranas@ccsf.edu
ARANDA, Eileen .... 909-667-4411.. 37 J
president@claremontlincoln.edu
ARANDA, Romelia .... 830-758-4125 457 C
rdaranda@swtjc.edu
ARANEO, Mary Lou .... 631-451-4611 330 B
araneom@sunysuffolk.edu
ARANT, Mark .... 270-809-3744 188 D
marant1@murraystate.edu
ARANT, T.J .... 678-407-5200 119 F
tjarant@ggc.edu
ARAQUE, Maria .... 312-915-8777 144 D
maraque@luc.edu
ARAQUE, Teresa .... 239-489-9061 100 E
taraque@fsw.edu
ARASIMOWICZ, George 937-376-6453 358 I
garasimowicz@centralstate.edu
ARATA, Raquel .... 916-484-8363.. 50 F
aratar@arc.losrios.edu
ARAUJO, Aurea .... 787-834-9595 526 E
aaraujo@uaa.edu
ARAUJO, Lisa .... 516-877-3230 297 I
araujo@adelphi.edu
ARBALLO, Madelyn .... 909-594-5611.. 52 I
marballo@mtsac.edu
ARBELO, Enid .... 787-878-5475 523 H
earbelo@arecibo.inter.edu
ARBERY, Glen .... 307-332-2930 517 F
garbery@wyomingcatholiccollege.com
ARBIDE, Donna .... 305-284-4111 112 O
darbide@miami.edu
ARBIDE, Donna, A .... 305-284-2873 112 O
darbide@miami.edu
ARBOGAST, Linda .... 440-775-8540 367 B
linda.arbogast@oberlin.edu
ARBUTHNOT, Beth .... 706-864-1440 127 B
beth.arbuthnot@ung.edu
ARCARESE, Chris .... 303-352-3032.. 79 D
chris.arcarese@ccd.edu
ARCARIO, Paul .... 718-482-5400 303 B
arcariop@lagcc.cuny.edu
ARCE, Elsa, M .... 412-365-1282 392 C
arce@chatham.edu
ARCE, Joshua .... 785-749-8482 178 A
jarce@haskell.edu
ARCE, Katherine .... 310-338-2881.. 50 J
katherine.arce@lmu.edu
ARCE, Lydia .... 787-857-3600 523 I
larce@br.inter.edu
ARCELUS, Victor, J .... 860-439-2834.. 86 H
victor.arcelus@conncoll.edu
ARCENEAUX, Alex .... 985-448-4004 197 C
alex.arceneaux@nicholls.edu
ARCH, Xan .... 503-943-7310 387 H
arch@up.edu
ARCHABAL, Alice .... 414-955-4718 508 D
aarchabal@mcw.edu
ARCHAGA, Teresea .... 925-473-7552.. 41 A
tarchaga@losmedanos.edu
ARCHAMBAULT, Karen, L .... 856-222-9311 289 F
karchambault@rcbc.edu
ARCHAMBAULT, Marc ... 270-745-6208 190 F
marc.archambault@wku.edu
ARCHBOLD, David, J .... 248-370-3358 235 J
archbold@oakland.edu
ARCHER, Chris .... 603-623-0313 281 G
chrisarcher@nhia.edu
ARCHER, Chrysta, M ..... 610-914-1402 413 G
cmarcher@valleyforge.edu
ARCHER, Daniel, L .... 801-581-6326 472 P
darcher@campusstore.utah.edu
ARCHER, Elizabeth .... 619-876-4250.. 68 C
earcher@usuniversity.edu
ARCHER, Frank .... 478-827-7594 119 C
archerf@fvsu.edu
ARCHER, III, Frank .... 229-430-3686 114 I
frank.archer@asurams.edu
ARCHER, Gie .... 940-668-7731 453 L
marcher@nctc.edu
ARCHER, Keith, A .... 309-341-7212 142 G
kaarcher@knox.edu
ARCHER, Kevin .... 509-963-3101 492 L
kevin.archer@cwu.edu
ARCHER, Len .... 407-303-5619.. 94 H
len.archer@adu.edu
ARCHER, Linda, R .... 757-446-6190 480 C
archerlr@evms.edu
ARCHER, Lynn .... 412-536-1182 398 E
lynn.archer@laroche.edu
ARCHER, Nicole .... 415-351-3553.. 60 G
narcher@sfai.edu
ARCHER, Rebecca .... 321-674-7571.. 99 K
rarcher@fit.edu
ARCHER, Ron .... 714-879-3901.. 45 I
rarcher@hiu.edu
ARCHER, Ryan .... 316-295-5410 177 F
archerr@friends.edu
ARCHER, Thomas, R ...... 802-626-6454 477 D
thomas.archer@lyndonstate.edu
ARCHER, Tom .... 802-626-6497 477 C
thomas.archer@lyndonstate.edu
ARCHER-RIERSON, Abby .... 620-242-0439 179 G
archera@mcpherson.edu
ARCHEY, Larry .... 413-559-5767 215 F
ARCHIBALD, Michael ..... 909-621-8152.. 63 F
marchiba@scrippscollege.edu
ARCHIBALD, Sandra, O . 206-616-1648 499 D
sarch@uw.edu
ARCHIE, Cephas .... 585-395-2504 326 D
carchie@brockport.edu
ARCHIE, Tiffenia, D .... 215-204-9213 411 B
tiffenia.archie@temple.edu
ARCHILLA, Sonia .... 787-250-1912 524 B
sarchilla@intermetro.edu
ARCHINAL, Ginette .... 336-278-7230 337 G
garchinal@elon.edu
ARCHULETA, Carol .... 864-231-2000 418 E
carchuleta@andersonuniversity.edu
ARCHULETA, Leticia ...... 505-454-2502 294 D
larchuleta@luna.edu
ARCHULETA, Renee .... 303-914-6345.. 82 B
renee.archuleta@rrcc.edu
ARCHULETTA, Justin ..... 907-745-3201.... 9 D
info@akbible.edu
ARCUINO, Cathy Lee .... 206-934-7804 497 H
ARCURI, Cody .... 718-817-4339 308 G
carcuri@fordham.edu
ARCURY, Tara, L .... 802-654-2212 476 A
tarcury@smcvt.edu
ARD, Aaron .... 803-812-7335 425 D
ajard@mailbox.sc.edu
ARDAIOLO, Frank, P ..... 803-323-2251 426 H
ardaiolof@winthrop.edu
ARDALAN, Shah .... 281-290-2777 452 C
shah.ardalan@lonestar.edu
ARDEN, Warwick, A ...... 919-515-2195 350 E
warwick_arden@ncsu.edu
ARDIS, Ann .... 302-831-8697.. 90 I
aardis@udel.edu
ARDNER, Charles .... 419-448-3443 370 K
cardner@tiffin.edu
ARDREY, Melantha .... 843-953-3257 420 C
ardreym@cofc.edu
AREA, Ron .... 304-696-2826 504 C
area@marshall.edu
AREH, Julia .... 678-872-4201 119 G
jareh@highlands.edu
AREIZAGA, Jose, R .... 787-891-0925 523 G
jareizag@aguadilla.inter.edu
ARELLANO, Jerry .... 210-486-3884 441 H
jarellano59@alamo.edu
ARELLANO, Margarita ... 512-245-2124 463 A
ma33@txstate.edu
ARELLANO, Margarita, M .... 512-245-2124 463 A
ma33@txstate.edu
ARENA, Maryanne .... 585-345-6802 309 C
mcarena@genesee.edu
ARENA, Meaghan .... 585-245-5619 327 B
arena@geneseo.edu
ARENAS, Ruben .... 323-265-8678.. 48 L
arenasr@elac.edu
ARENAS-FUENTES, Lenina .... 206-543-5010 499 D
mlenina@uw.edu
ARENAZ, Pablo .... 956-326-2320 459 B
president@tamiu.edu
AREND, Lori .... 412-536-2506 398 E
lori.arend@laroche.edu
AREND, Matthew .... 517-629-0521 226 G
marend@albion.edu
ARENDT, Ben .... 616-526-6892 228 B
barendt@calvin.edu
ARENDT, Thomas, K ..... 562-902-3355.. 65 D
tomarendt@scuhs.edu
ARENIVAS, Marisol .... 520-417-4115.. 11 R
arenivasm@cochise.edu
ARENS, Anna .... 414-382-6064 506 A
anna.arens@alverno.edu
ARENS, Dave .... 712-279-1715 167 B
dave.arens@briarcliff.edu
ARENS, Nan Crystal ...... 315-781-3304 310 C
arens@hws.edu
ARENS, Timothy, E .... 312-329-4191 146 B
timothy.arens@moody.edu
ARENS, Trente .... 630-829-6077 133 I
tarens@ben.edu
ARENSMEYER, Lauri, D . 208-496-1010 131 D
arensmeyerl@byui.edu
ARENTSEN, Marc .... 508-541-1608 214 C
marentsen@dean.edu
ARETA, Ropeti .... 684-699-1575 519 F
a.areta@amsamoa.edu
ARETS, Wiel .... 312-567-3263 140 I
wiel.arets@iit.edu
ARETZ, Anthony .... 406-791-5300 273 C
anthony.aretz@ugf.edu
AREVALO, Luis .... 435-652-7877 473 B
arevalo@dixie.edu
AREVALO-HILLEN, Jessica .... 510-594-3788.. 28 K
jarevalo@cca.edu
AREY, Emily .... 704-669-4139 342 B
areye@clevelandcc.edu
AREY, George, A .... 617-552-4725 212 E
george.arey@bc.edu
AREY, Jason .... 207-216-4399 200 E
jarey@yccc.edu
AREY, Sherrie .... 406-791-5309 273 C
sherrie.arey@ugf.edu
ARGENTIERI, Colleen .... 607-587-3932 328 F
argentch@alfredstate.edu
ARGIRI, Elizabeth .... 586-445-7306 233 B
argiril@macomb.edu
ARGO, Linda .... 202-885-2753.. 91 C
largo@american.edu
ARGO, Mike, A .... 870-235-4083.. 21 F
maargo@saumag.edu

ARGUELLES, Adrianna ... 718-939-5100 313 B
aarguelles@libi.edu
ARGUELLES, Alejandro .. 787-250-0000 527 D
alejandro.arguelles@upr.edu
ARGYRIS, Steven, G ...... 510-649-2430.. 44 J
sargyris@gtu.edu
ARHIN, Afua .... 910-672-1924 350 B
aarhin@uncfsu.edu
ARHIPOV, Sergei, D ...... 570-581-1818 410 A
sergei.arhipov@stots.edu
ARIANO, Patricia .... 630-829-6003 133 I
pariano@ben.edu
ARIAS, Hamlet .... 305-273-4499.. 96 N
hamelet.arias@cbt.edu
ARIAS, Michael, R .... 949-824-3868.. 69 A
mrarias@uci.edu
ARICK, Bruce, E .... 317-940-9481 156 I
barick@butler.edu
ARICK, Elaine, C .... 330-471-8138 364 H
earick@malone.edu
ARIDA, Lisa, A .... 716-839-8218 306 E
larida@daemen.edu
ARILSON, Barbara .... 440-375-7000 364 C
barilson@lec.edu
ARIOLA-SUKISAKI,
Kainoa .... 808-932-7777 129 I
kariola@hawaii.edu
ARISTIZABAL,
Humberto, X .... 410-543-6426 209 B
hxarisitzabal@salisbury.edu
ARIZA, Cristina .... 210-829-3870 465 E
mariza@uiwtx.edu
ARIZA, Diane, M .... 203-582-8939.. 88 A
diane.ariza@quinnipiac.edu
ARLEDGE, Scott .... 520-417-4047.. 11 R
arledges@cochise.edu
ARLINGTON, David, L ... 716-851-1987 307 I
arlington@ecc.edu
ARLITSCH, Kenning .... 406-994-6978 272 A
kenning.arlitsch@montana.edu
ARMACOST, Andrew ...... 719-333-9751 518 H
ARMAGOST, Mark, S .... 814-863-4308 403 F
msa17@psu.edu
ARMBRUSTER, Shirley .. 559-278-2795.. 32 A
shirleya@csufresno.edu
ARMENDARIZ, John ...... 617-373-2133 223 D
ARMENT, Susan .... 660-263-4100 264 C
susana@macc.edu
ARMENTA, Richard, R ... 512-223-7795 443 G
rarmenta@austincc.edu
ARMENTOR, Melissa ...... 409-880-8853 462 B
mfarmentor@lit.edu
ARMENTROUT, Renae ... 319-208-5015 173 G
rarmentrout@scciowa.edu
ARMES, Traci .... 812-941-2260 161 A
trarmes@ius.edu
ARMEZZANI, Aubree ..... 570-702-8938 398 A
aarmezzani@johnson.edu
ARMIJO, Danny .... 575-624-8250 295 A
darmijo@nmmi.edu
ARMIJO, Lillian .... 575-835-6581 294 K
lillian.armijo@nmt.edu
ARMINGTON, Thomas .. 610-526-1391 389 B
tom.armington@theamericancollege.edu
ARMINI, Michael, A ...... 617-373-5718 223 D
ARMINIAK, Anthony ...... 734-374-3227 238 H
aarmini1@wcccd.edu
ARMISTEAD, Katya .... 805-893-8912.. 70 B
katya.armistead@sa.ucsb.edu
ARMISTEAD, Lisa, P ..... 404-413-2091 121 A
larmistead@gsu.edu
ARMISTEAD, Macon ...... 334-833-4455.... 5 M
marmistead@hawks.huntingdon.edu
ARMISTEAD, William ..... 304-473-8509 505 G
armistead_w@wvwc.edu
ARMITAGE, John .... 585-395-2226 326 D
jarmitage@brockport.edu
ARMOND, Pashuan .... 919-466-4400.. 93 B
ARMONY, Ariel .... 412-648-7374 412 I
armony@pitt.edu
ARMOR, Thomas, W ..... 317-738-8045 157 L
tarmor@franklincollege.edu
ARMOUR, Angela .... 802-654-2527 476 A
aarmour@smcvt.edu
ARMOUR, Janet .... 662-862-8383 253 D
jyarmour@iccms.edu
ARMOUR, Lisa .... 352-381-3642 107 E
lisa.armour@sfcollege.edu
ARMOUR, Robert .... 606-546-1799 189 I
rarmour@unionky.edu
ARMOUR, Robin .... 925-473-7501.. 41 A
rarmour@losmedanos.edu
ARMOZA, Marcela .... 718-260-4999 303 D
marmoza@citytech.cuny.edu
ARMS, Gina .... 516-686-7902 317 G
garms@nyit.edu
ARMSTEAD, Cory .... 334-683-2333.... 3 A
carmstead@marionmilitary.edu
ARMSTRON, John .... 540-261-8563 485 G
john.armstrong@svu.edu
ARMSTRONG, Albert ..... 305-899-3250.. 95 G
aarmstrong@barry.edu
ARMSTRONG, Amy .... 830-792-7405 456 D
anarmstrong@schreiner.edu
ARMSTRONG, Andrew ... 310-655-6970.. 54 I
aarmstrong@otis.edu
ARMSTRONG,
Andrew, V .... 540-636-2900 479 G
armstrong@christendom.edu
ARMSTRONG, Booker .... 816-604-4125 262 K
booker.armstrong@mcckc.edu
ARMSTRONG,
Christopher, M .... 860-701-6194 519 B
christopher.m.armstrong@uscg.mil
ARMSTRONG, Dale .... 615-966-5148 433 D
dale.armstrong@lipscomb.edu
ARMSTRONG, Dana .... 508-213-2177 223 C
dana.armstrong@nichols.edu
ARMSTRONG, David .... 507-389-7206 247 H
david.armstrong@southcentral.edu
ARMSTRONG, David, A . 859-344-3348 189 G
darmstrong@thomasmore.edu
ARMSTRONG, David, C . 574-807-7877 156 E
david.armstrong@bethelcollege.edu
ARMSTRONG, David, M 816-501-2423 257 G
david.armstrong@avila.edu
ARMSTRONG, Dayle .... 909-469-5322.. 74 G
darmstrong@westernu.edu
ARMSTRONG, Elizabeth . 540-231-7197 490 F
beth1@vt.edu
ARMSTRONG, Franca .... 315-334-7701 315 I
farmstrong@mvcc.edu
ARMSTRONG, Gary .... 816-415-7651 270 C
armstrongg@william.jewell.edu
ARMSTRONG, Gregory .. 540-868-7275 488 E
garmstrong@lfcc.edu
ARMSTRONG, JR.,
J. David .... 954-201-7401.. 96 A
darmstro@broward.edu
ARMSTRONG, Jeanette .. 608-796-3395 512 R
jearmstrong@viterbo.edu
ARMSTRONG,
Jeffrey, D .... 805-756-1111.. 30 K
presidentsoffice@calpoly.edu
ARMSTRONG, Jerry .... 303-373-2008.. 82 F
jarmstrong@rvu.edu
ARMSTRONG, Julie .... 810-989-5527 236 G
jarmstrong@sc4.edu
ARMSTRONG, Katelynn . 618-634-3270 151 G
katelynna@shawneecc.edu
ARMSTRONG, Keith .... 719-590-6758.. 79 B
karmstrong@coloradotech.edu
ARMSTRONG, Kelli, J ... 617-552-0585 212 E
kelli.armstrong@bc.edu
ARMSTRONG, Kelli, J ... 617-552-3111 212 E
ARMSTRONG, Kevin .... 402-375-7510 276 D
kearmst1@wsc.edu
ARMSTRONG, Kim .... 501-337-5000.. 19 C
karmstrong@coto.edu
ARMSTRONG, Kimberly . 717-358-3985 395 G
kim.armstrong@fandm.edu
ARMSTRONG, LaTonya . 773-291-6613 135 M
tarmstrong11@ccc.edu
ARMSTRONG, Lee, F ..... 334-844-5176.... 4 D
armstlf@auburn.edu
ARMSTRONG, Lori, B .... 410-704-3570 209 C
larmstrong@towson.edu
ARMSTRONG,
Mary Beth .... 205-665-6720.... 8 E
armstrom@montevallo.edu
ARMSTRONG, Myeshia . 909-274-4234.. 52 I
marmstrong@mtsac.edu
ARMSTRONG, Nancy, A 419-772-2251 367 G
n-armstrong@onu.edu
ARMSTRONG, Neal, R ... 520-621-3513.. 16 J
nra@email.arizona.edu
ARMSTRONG,
Patricia, J .... 615-353-3758 437 D
patricia.armstrong@nscc.edu
ARMSTRONG, Peter .... 402-465-2153 276 E
parmstro@nebrwesleyan.edu
ARMSTRONG, Shirley .... 334-291-4964.... 1 H
shirley.armstrong@cv.edu
ARMSTRONG,
Steven, M .... 920-832-6769 507 L
steven.m.armstrong@lawrence.edu
ARMSTRONG, Susan ...... 318-675-5406 194 D
sarmst@lsuhsc.edu
ARMSTRONG, Tonya ..... 919-572-1625 335 F
tarmstrong@apexsot.edu
ARMSTRONG, Vivian ..... 787-284-1912 524 C
varmstro@ponce.inter.edu
ARMUSEWICZ, Allison .. 716-614-6238 318 E
aarmusewicz@niagaracc.suny.edu
ARN, Diana .... 501-977-2001.. 23 B
arn@uaccm.edu
ARNADE, Peter .... 808-956-6460 129 J
parnade@hawaii.edu
ARNDER, Lori .... 757-240-2200 484 G
lori.arnder@rivhs.com
ARNDT, Chris .... 540-568-7044 481 I
arndtjc@jmu.edu
ARNDT, Wayne .... 732-987-2237 286 D
warndt@georgian.edu
ARNER, Joseph .... 352-588-7548 106 N
joseph.arner@saintleo.edu
ARNER, Lori .... 802-468-1211 477 A
lori.arner@castleton.edu
ARNER, Lynette .... 330-263-2139 360 A
larner@wooster.edu
ARNER, Robert .... 610-292-9852 408 I
robert.arner@reseminary.edu
ARNESON, Dean, L .... 262-243-5700 507 C
dean.arneson@cuw.edu
ARNESON, Eric .... 920-465-2511 510 E
arnesone@uwgb.edu
ARNESON, Rosemary .... 540-654-1000 486 D
rarneso3@umw.edu
ARNETT, Amy .... 207-509-7204 200 I
aarnett@unity.edu
ARNETT, David, J .... 978-478-3400 223 E
darnett@northpoint.edu
ARNETT, Donna .... 859-218-2247 190 B
donna.arnett@uky.edu
ARNETT, Harold .... 620-441-6584 176 M
harold.arnett@cowley.edu
ARNEY, Doug .... 956-296-1535 468 A
doug.arney@utrgv.edu
ARNEY, Janna .... 956-882-8833 468 A
janna.arney@utrgv.edu
ARNN, Larry .... 517-607-2301 231 C
larnn@hillsdale.edu
ARNO, Marlene .... 716-851-1431 307 I
arno@ecc.edu
ARNOLD, Angela .... 952-358-9045 246 D
angela.arnold@normandale.edu
ARNOLD, Brian .... 575-492-2104 297 G
barnold@usw.edu
ARNOLD, Brian .... 704-406-4732 337 H
barnold@gardner-webb.edu
ARNOLD, Carl .... 903-233-4310 452 A
carlarnold@letu.edu
ARNOLD, Carolyn .... 510-723-6965.. 36 C
carnold@chabotcollege.edu
ARNOLD, Clinton, E ...... 562-903-4816.. 27 E
clinton.arnold@biola.edu
ARNOLD, Danny .... 509-828-1223 494 D
darnold@ewu.edu
ARNOLD, David .... 575-492-2124 297 G
darnold@usw.edu
ARNOLD, Eli .... 404-364-8514 124 A
earnold@oglethorpe.edu
ARNOLD, Elizabeth .... 570-484-2293 406 E
earnold@lockhaven.edu
ARNOLD, George .... 773-235-5541 149 I
george.arnold@resu.edu
ARNOLD, Gertrude, L .... 208-426-3236 131 C
gertiarnold@boisestate.edu
ARNOLD, Harvey .... 772-462-6210 101 Q
harnold@irsc.edu
ARNOLD, Jane .... 412-536-1786 398 E
jane.arnold@laroche.edu
ARNOLD, Jeanne .... 717-337-6375 396 A
jarnold@gettysburg.edu
ARNOLD, Jill .... 573-629-3103 260 G
jarnold@hlg.edu
ARNOLD, Jon .... 714-895-8183.. 38 G
jarnold@gwc.cccd.edu
ARNOLD, Jon .... 931-540-2538 436 H
jarnold15@columbiastate.edu
ARNOLD, Joseph, E .... 202-885-8649.. 94 C
jearnold@wesleyseminary.edu
ARNOLD, Joshua .... 909-599-5433.. 48 E
jarnold@lifepacific.edu
ARNOLD, Julie .... 419-448-2953 362 G
jarnold3@heidelberg.edu
ARNOLD, Kathy .... 512-313-3000 446 N
kathy.arnold@concordia.edu
ARNOLD, Kenneth, L .... 707-256-3331.. 53 D
karnold@napavalley.edu
ARNOLD, Lester .... 336-750-2000 352 D
arnoldle@wssu.edu
ARNOLD, Lorene, R ...... 260-399-7700 165 B
larnold@sf.edu
ARNOLD, Lorin Basden 845-257-3280 325 D
provost@newpaltz.edu
ARNOLD, Michael, A .... 302-831-1916.. 90 I
marnold@udel.edu
ARNOLD, Patricia .... 314-246-5964 269 N
patriciaarnold01@webster.edu
ARNOLD, Randall .... 303-245-4797.. 81 B
rarnold@naropa.edu
ARNOLD, Robert .... 901-321-4299 431 A
rarnold@cbu.edu
ARNOLD, Rodney .... 870-743-3000.. 20 E
rarnold@northark.edu
ARNOLD, Sally .... 978-232-2029 214 G
sarnold@endicott.edu
ARNOLD, Shirley, E ...... 828-884-8329 335 L
arnoldse@brevard.edu
ARNOLD, Stephen .... 409-839-2073 462 B
swarnold@lit.edu
ARNOLD, Sue .... 281-998-6003 460 G
sarnold@txchiro.edu
ARNOLD, Susan .... 610-606-4609 392 A
swarnold@cedarcrest.edu
ARNOLD, Tai .... 518-587-2100 329 C
tai.arnold@esc.edu
ARNOLD, Timothy .... 716-338-1125 311 F
timothyarnold@mail.sunyjcc.edu
ARNOLD, Tom .... 434-592-6015 482 D
tarnold@liberty.edu
ARNOLD, III, W. Ellis ... 501-450-1223.. 19 I
arnold@hendrix.edu
ARNONE, Lisa .... 818-401-1043.. 40 A
larnone@columbiacollege.edu
ARNOTT, Tamara .... 218-733-5923 245 C
tamara.arnott@lsc.edu
ARNOULD, Karen, A ..... 810-762-3344 238 B
karnould@umflint.edu
ARNOVE, Theresa .... 410-532-5155 206 D
tarnove@ndm.edu
ARNST, Scott .... 810-762-3123 238 B
sarnst@umflint.edu
ARNZEN, Diane .... 636-481-3282 261 B
darnzen@jeffco.edu
AROBBA, Sarah .... 605-856-5880 428 A
sarah.arobba@sintegleska.edu
AROCHO, Ashley .... 212-650-6460 301 F
aarocho@ccny.cuny.edu
AROMANDO, Drew, C .... 609-896-5178 289 E
aromando@rider.edu
ARON, Deborah .... 215-635-7300 396 B
daron@gratz.edu
ARON, Lashun .... 317-788-3442 164 H
aronl@uindy.edu
ARONSON, Ann .... 612-624-6868 250 E
aronson@umn.edu
ARONSON, Ed .... 541-881-5875 387 D
earonson@tvcc.cc
ARONSON, Linda .... 508-849-3458 210 H
laronson@annamaria.edu
ARONSON, Meigan, C .. 979-845-7361 459 C
maronson@tamu.edu
ARONSON, Ray .... 805-893-4535.. 70 B
ray.aronson@dcs.ucsb.edu
ARONSON, Roberta, C .. 412-396-1818 394 D
aronson@duq.edu
ARONSON, Susan .... 213-624-1200.. 42 N
saronson@fidm.edu
ARONSTAM, Robert, S .. 570-389-5333 405 E
aronstam@bloomu.edu
ARONSTEIN, Susan .... 307-766-4110 517 B
aronstei@uwyo.edu
ARORA, Deepa .... 478-934-6588 123 A
deepa.arora@mga.edu
ARORA SINGH, Alka ..... 623-845-3968.. 13 H
alka.arora.singh@gccaz.edu
AROSEMENA, Eduardo .. 787-728-1545 529 B
earosemena@sagrado.edu
AROZ, Susan, D .... 480-732-7075.. 13 E
sue.aroz@cgc.edu
ARP, Dan .... 541-737-2331 385 F
dan.arp@oregonstate.edu
ARP, Robert .... 707-654-1037.. 32 E
rarp@csum.edu
ARPINO, Donald .... 617-879-7899 218 B
darpino@massart.edu
ARQUETTE, Mary .... 419-824-3969 364 G
marquette@lourdes.edu
ARQUETTE, Toby .... 630-844-5614 133 H
tarquett@aurora.edu
ARRAIZA, Ana, M .... 787-751-0160 522 B
aarraiza@cmpr.pr.gov
ARRAMBIDE, Mike .... 719-884-5000 180 B
jmarrambide@nbc.edu
ARREDONDO, Arnold .... 901-572-2455 430 C
arnold.arredondo@bchs.edu
ARREDONDO, Marisol .. 714-628-7339.. 36 G
arredond@chapman.edu
ARRIAZA, Cecilia .... 714-992-7087.. 54 A
carriaza@fullcoll.edu
ARRIBAS,
Maria del Carmen .... 787-257-7373 525 Q
ue_marribas@suagm.edu
ARRINGTON, Cedric ...... 256-306-2598.... 1 F
cedric.arrington@calhoun.edu
ARRINGTON, Doris, B ... 860-906-5085.. 85 D
darrington@ccc.commnet.edu
ARRINGTON, Harriett ... 276-523-2400 488 F
harrington@mecc.edu

ARRINGTON, Jeffrey ...... 334-386-7105.... 5 I
jarrington@faulkner.edu
ARRINGTON, Michelle .. 601-266-6698 256 E
michelle.arrington@usm.edu
ARRINGTON, Pam .... 330-966-5460 370 G
parrington@starkstate.edu
ARRINGTON,
Stephanie, K .... 765-285-8304 156 C
skarrington@bsu.edu
ARRINGTON, Tom .... 281-459-7613 456 A
tom.arrington@sjcd.edu
ARRINGTON, Trey .... 864-587-4396 424 D
arringtont@smcsc.edu
ARRINGTON-JONES,
Angela .... 773-291-6297 135 M
aarrington@ccc.edu
ARRIOLA, Paul .... 630-617-3109 138 C
paula@elmhurst.edu
ARRIOLA, Yolanda .... 915-778-4001 457 D
ARROWOOD, Roarke ..... 828-835-4305 347 B
rarrowood@tricountycc.edu
ARROWSMITH, Jason ... 360-442-2270 495 G
jarrowsmith@lowercolumbia.edu
ARROYO, Carmen .... 787-620-2040 520 F
carroyo@aupr.edu
ARROYO, Cheryl .... 219-989-2977 163 E
cheryla@pnw.edu
ARROYO, Cruz .... 253-964-4688 497 F
carroyo@stmartin.edu
ARROYO, Gladys .... 787-279-1912 523 J
garroyo@bayamon.inter.edu
ARROYO, Glendalee ...... 787-832-6000 522 Q
ARROYO, Ivonne, D ...... 787-257-7323 525 Q
iarroyo@suagm.edu
ARROYO, Palmira .... 787-753-6335 522 Q
ARROYO, Patti .... 303-404-5111.. 79 K
patti.arroyo@frontrange.edu
ARROYO, Sandra .... 787-765-3560 522 K
sarroyo@edpuniversity.edu
ARRUDA, Yvonne, D ..... 401-865-2480 416 E
yarruda@providence.edu
ARRUTTI, Duane .... 505-277-8125 296 H
darruti@unm.edu
ARSENAULT, Joanne ..... 509-533-7042 493 I
joanne.arsenault@scc.spokane.edu
ARTALE, Maureen, P ..... 607-436-3216 325 E
maureen.artale@oneonta.edu
ARTAZ, Nancy .... 316-295-5514 177 F
artaz@friends.edu
ARTEAGA, Elizabeth .... 714-628-5051.. 58 B
arteaga_elizabeth@sccollege.edu
ARTEAGA-JOHNSON,
Craig .... 909-607-6643.. 57 I
craig.arteagajohnson@pomona.edu
ARTECONA, Sarah, N .... 305-284-5490 112 O
sartecona@miami.edu
ARTER, Neil .... 405-425-5906 377 B
neil.arter@oc.edu
ARTERBURN, Dave .... 256-824-6846.... 8 C
david.r.arterburn@uah.edu
ARTHO, Donna .... 936-294-3101 462 F
artho@shsu.edu
ARTHUR, Christon .... 269-471-3404 227 B
christon@andrews.edu
ARTHUR, Dave .... 512-476-2772 443 H
finaid@austingrad.edu
ARTHUR, Gwendolynne . 508-793-7384 213 C
garthur@clarku.edu
ARTHUR, Jeff .... 757-671-7171 480 D
jarthur@ecpi.edu
ARTHUR, Mark .... 405-789-7661 380 A
mark.arthur@swcu.edu
ARTHUR, Scott .... 303-724-8469.. 83 D
scott.arthur@ucdenver.edu
ARTHUR, Virginia .... 651-793-1900 245 E
ginny.arthur@metrostate.edu
ARTHUR-OKOR, Helena 409-984-6216 462 E
arthurh@lamarpa.edu
ARTIBEE, Jessica .... 952-446-4130 242 A
artibeej@crown.edu
ARTIGUES, Jay .... 985-549-2253 197 E
ARTIM, Chris .... 219-844-0100 156 F
christopher.artim@brightwood.edu
ARTIS, Christine .... 718-933-6700 315 K
cartis@monroecollege.edu
ARTIS, Lori .... 618-468-3000 143 D
lartis@lc.edu
ARTIS, Roslyn, C .... 803-253-5000 418 G
ARTLEY, James .... 904-256-1162.. 99 C
jartley@fcsl.edu
ARTMAN, Vickie .... 618-634-3219 151 G
vickiea@shawneecc.edu
ARUK, Janette .... 585-785-1297 308 D
janette.aruk@flcc.edu
ARULANANDAM,
Bernard .... 210-458-6859 468 B
bernard.arulanandam@utsa.edu

ARUM, Richard .... 949-824-8026.. 69 A
richard.arum@uci.edu
ARUNACHALAM,
Vairam .... 573-882-3225 268 C
arunachalam@missouri.edu
ARUSH, Ilan .... 661-824-2977.. 53 G
iarush@ntps.edu
ARVAN, April .... 920-565-2327 507 K
arvanaa@lakeland.edu
ARVELO, Wildolfo .... 603-427-7602 280 J
warvelo@ccsnh.edu
ARVIDSON, Susie .... 620-223-2700 177 E
susiea@fortscott.edu
ARVIN, Ann .... 650-498-6227.. 66 C
aarvin@stanford.edu
ARVIN, Lorraine .... 503-517-7625 386 F
arvinl@reed.edu
ARVISO, Jason .... 505-786-4193 294 I
jarviso@navajotech.edu
ARVIZU, Primavera .... 661-763-7815.. 67 A
parvizu@taftcollege.edu
ARWOOD, Katie .... 989-328-1291 234 D
katiea@montcalm.edu
ARZOLA, JR., Fernando 760-471-1316.. 59 A
farzola@skcca.edu
ARZROUNI-CHAHINIAN,
Chaghig .... 510-925-4282.. 25 P
carzroun@aua.am
ASAD, Ray .... 408-453-9900.. 45 E
rasad@henley-putnam.edu
ASADOORIAN, III,
Malcolm, O .... 781-768-7077 224 A
malcolm.asadoorian@regiscollege.edu
ASAMOAH, Yaw, A .... 724-357-2280 406 C
yaw.asamoah@iup.edu
ASANTE, Javonda .... 973-313-6211 291 F
javonda.asante@shu.edu
ASANTI, Rochelle .... 818-299-5526.. 73 K
ASARO, Linda .... 212-817-7490 302 B
intstu@gc.cuny.edu
ASATO, Susan .... 760-757-2121.. 52 F
sasato@miracosta.edu
ASAWA, Archibald, E .... 949-480-4006.. 64 D
asawa@soka.edu
ASAY, Meredith .... 307-766-2903 517 B
masay@uwyo.edu
ASBILL, Jonathan .... 918-444-2400 376 G
asbill01@nsuok.edu
ASBURY, Denise .... 423-652-4895 432 I
dasbury@king.edu
ASBURY, Jo-Ellen .... 718-951-5864 301 E
jo-ellen.asbury@brooklyn.cuny.edu
ASBURY, Sean .... 614-287-2525 360 C
sasbury@cscc.edu
ASCARELLI, Daniela, E .. 215-895-6280 394 C
daniela.elena.ascarelli@drexel.edu
ASCENCIO, Mario .... 626-396-2231.. 26 L
mario.ascencio@artcenter.edu
ASCH, Emily .... 651-690-6650 249 T
ejasch@stkate.edu
ASCHEMAN, SVD,
Thomas .... 563-876-3353 168 H
tascheman@dwci.edu
ASCHENBRENER, Matt .. 262-472-1570 512 C
aschenbm@uww.edu
ASCHER, Marie .... 914-594-4208 318 A
marie_ascher@nymc.edu
ASCHIM, Joan .... 541-463-5591 383 F
aschimj@lanecc.edu
ASCHLIMAN, David, A .. 260-422-5561 159 D
daaschliman@indianatech.edu
ASCIONE, Lou .... 619-388-7873.. 60 E
lascione@sdccd.edu
ASELTYNE, Dennis .... 707-468-3131.. 51 E
daseltyne@mendocino.edu
ASENCIO, Vimarie .... 787-753-6000 522 Q
ASENCIO-PINTO, Aida ... 708-209-3492 136 I
aida.asencio-pinto@cuchicago.edu
ASETTA, Eric .... 617-824-3075 214 E
eric_asetta@emerson.edu
ASGEIRSDOTTIR,
Aslaug .... 207-786-6066 198 E
aasgeirs@bates.edu
ASGHAR, Midhat .... 936-261-2156 458 F
miasghar@pvamu.edu
ASH, Beth .... 740-474-8896 367 E
bash@ohiochristian.edu
ASH, David, E .... 989-774-3094 228 E
ash1de@cmich.edu
ASH, Eric .... 907-375-4515 470 I
ash@wbu.edu
ASH, Hope .... 304-865-6015 502 C
hope.ash@ovu.edu
ASH, Kay .... 360-475-7500 496 F
kash@olympic.edu
ASH, Kenya, D .... 513-529-7157 365 I
ashkd@miamioh.edu

ASH, Michael .... 319-208-5050 173 G
mash@scciowa.edu
ASH, Steven .... 352-854-2322.. 97 C
ashs@cf.edu
ASHAOLU, John .... 724-480-3470 392 K
john.ashaolu@ccbc.edu
ASHBAUGH, Jackie, E ... 330-972-8973 371 D
jackie1@uakron.edu
ASHBURN, Beth, D .... 336-725-8344 348 C
ashburnb@piedmontu.edu
ASHBURN, Elyse .... 410-455-2065 208 A
eashburn@umbc.edu
ASHBURN, Maureen ...... 617-735-9838 214 F
ashburnm@emmanuel.edu
ASHBY, Brendan .... 651-846-1314 247 G
brendan.ashby@saintpaul.edu
ASHBY, Deborah .... 910-898-9651 345 A
ashbyd@montgomery.edu
ASHBY, Pamela .... 207-834-7516 201 E
pam.ashby@maine.edu
ASHBY, Patti .... 405-912-9017 379 A
pashby@ru.edu
ASHBY, Todd .... 843-863-7984 419 C
tashby@csuniv.edu
ASHBY, Valerie .... 919-684-4510 337 C
asdean@duke.edu
ASHCRAFT, Eric .... 859-846-5781 188 B
ewashcraft@midway.edu
ASHCRAFT, Matthew ...... 480-461-7215.. 13 I
matthew.aschcraft@mesacc.edu
ASHCROFT, Josh .... 509-359-2451 494 D
jashcroft@ewu.edu
ASHDOWN, Jane .... 516-877-4065 297 I
jashdown@adelphi.edu
ASHER, Bernadette .... 404-627-2681 116 E
bernadette.asher@beulah.edu
ASHER, Curt .... 661-654-3042.. 31 B
casher@csub.edu
ASHER, Joy .... 859-238-5284 184 C
joy.asher@centre.edu
ASHER, Pamala .... 816-268-5442 264 G
pjasher@nts.edu
ASHFORD, Bruce, R ...... 919-761-2435 349 C
bashford@sebts.edu
ASHFORD, Craig .... 541-346-3756 387 F
cashford@uoregon.edu
ASHFORD, Rebecca .... 423-697-4455 436 F
rebecca.ashford@chattanoogastate.edu
ASHFORD, Scott .... 541-737-1211 385 F
scott.ashford@oregonstate.edu
ASHLEY, Bill .... 601-276-3717 256 A
bashley@smcc.edu
ASHLEY, Corey .... 847-628-7099 142 B
corey.ashley@judsonu.edu
ASHLEY, Donna .... 646-717-9706 309 B
ashley@gts.edu
ASHLEY, Garrett, P .... 562-951-4625.. 30 J
gashley@calstate.edu
ASHLEY, Kimberly .... 903-877-5739 469 A
kimberly.ashley@uthct.edu
ASHLEY, Kurt .... 630-617-3262 138 C
kurt.ashley@elmhurst.edu
ASHLEY, Lance .... 704-669-4092 342 B
ashleyl@clevelandcc.edu
ASHLEY, Mark .... 909-621-8090.. 45 D
mark_ashley@hmc.edu
ASHLEY, Mary Ellen ...... 937-775-4271 374 B
maryellen.ashley@wright.edu
ASHLEY, Richard .... 704-272-5463 346 F
rashley@spcc.edu
ASHLEY, Tim, M .... 315-267-2222 328 A
ashleytm@potsdam.edu
ASHLEY, Traci, D .... 919-209-2563 344 C
tdashley@johnstoncc.edu
ASHLEY, Tracy .... 757-258-6674 489 G
ashleyt@tncc.edu
ASHLEY, SR.,
Willard W.C .... 732-247-5241 287 E
washley@nbts.edu
ASHLEY-PAULEY, Jonita 423-798-7830 439 C
jpauley@tusculum.edu
ASHLOCK, Benjamin ..... 415-351-3541.. 60 G
bashlock@sfai.edu
ASHMEN, Jeff .... 912-443-4155 125 D
jashmen@savannahtech.edu
ASHMON, Scott .... 949-214-3735.. 40 I
scott.ashmon@cui.edu
ASHMYAN, Ilya .... 201-360-4693 286 E
iashmyan@hccc.edu
ASHOUR, Cheryl .... 780-744-1150.. 55 K
cashour@palomar.edu
ASHPOLE, Steven .... 360-596-5240 498 G
sashpole@spscc.edu
ASHRAF, Ali .... 415-503-6280.. 60 H
security@sfcm.edu
ASHRAF, Tasneem .... 520-335-1883.. 11 R
ashraft@cochise.edu

ASHTON, Andrew .... 845-437-5785 333 A
anashton@vassar.edu
ASHTON, Loye .... 601-977-7944 256 B
lashton@tougaloo.edu
ASHTON, M. John .... 801-581-3055 472 P
john.ashton@alumni.utah.edu
ASHTON, Nadine .... 313-664-7673 228 H
nashton@collegeforcreativestudies.edu
ASHTON, Sharon .... 904-620-2115 110 E
sashton@unf.edu
ASHTON-MILLER,
James, A .... 734-764-7516 237 I
jaam@umich.edu
ASHTON-PRITTING,
Randi, L .... 860-768-4268.. 89 C
pritting@hartford.edu
ASHWORTH, Brett .... 806-742-0012 463 B
ASHWORTH, Dennis .... 706-355-5167 115 H
dashworth@athenstech.edu
ASHWORTH, Ken .... 202-806-6100.. 92 C
ASIFOA, Sereima .... 684-699-9155 519 F
s.asifoa@amsamoa.edu
ASITO, Pioria .... 680-488-3540 520 E
pasito1149@gmail.com
ASKA, Aaron .... 201-200-3035 287 F
aaska@njcu.edu
ASKELSON, Denise .... 218-935-0417 251 F
denise.askelson@wetcc.edu
ASKELSON, Mary, M ...... 503-788-6644 386 F
askelsom@reed.edu
ASKERLUND, Robert ..... 801-957-4101 474 B
robert.askerlund@slcc.edu
ASKEW, Consuella, A .... 973-353-5160 290 D
consuella.askew@rutgers.edu
ASKEW, George, R .... 864-656-3140 419 F
gaskew@clemson.edu
ASKEW, J. Alicia .... 864-833-8215 423 D
jaaskew@presby.edu
ASKEW, Joseph .... 731-989-6651 432 C
jaskew@fhu.edu
ASKEW, Susan, S .... 931-598-1710 436 A
saskew@sewanee.edu
ASKEW, Tara .... 706-649-1901 118 D
taskew@columbustech.edu
ASKEW-ROBINSON,
Jipaum .... 618-634-3360 151 G
jipaumr@shawneecc.edu
ASKEY, Angela .... 520-494-5485.. 11 P
angela.askey@centralaz.edu
ASKINS, Rana .... 903-813-2444 443 F
raskins@austincollege.edu
ASKREN, Mark .... 402-472-2311 277 G
maskren1@unl.edu
ASKREN, Mark, S .... 402-472-4242 277 E
mark.askren@unl.edu
ASLAM, Ersal .... 973-596-5303 288 A
ersal.aslam@njit.edu
ASMAN, Kevin .... 360-596-5283 498 G
kasman@spscc.edu
ASMUS, Colleen, M ...... 850-474-2642 111 D
casmus@uwf.edu
ASMUTH, Shawn .... 904-620-2730 110 E
shawn.asmuth@unf.edu
ASONEVICH, Walter, J .. 814-262-3820 405 A
wasonevich@pennhighlands.edu
ASONSO, Kristine .... 904-826-0084.. 71 I
kasonso@usa.edu
ASOODEH, Mike, M .... 985-549-2314 197 E
asoodeh@selu.edu
ASPAN, Paul .... 610-660-1865 409 H
paspan@sju.edu
ASPEGREN, Kevin .... 863-874-8514 109 E
ASPER, Kris .... 713-718-6858 450 D
kris.asper@hccs.edu
ASPERGER, Joseph .... 810-762-9749 232 C
jasperge@kettering.edu
ASPESLAGH, Kayla .... 614-235-4136 370 M
kaspeslagh@tlsohio.edu
ASPINALL, David .... 910-221-2224 338 A
daspinall@gcd.edu
ASPINALL, Robin, J ...... 909-621-8116.. 38 A
robin.aspinall@cmc.edu
ASPINWALL, Neil .... 337-421-6965 193 F
neil.aspinwall@sowela.edu
ASSA, Carolyn .... 508-373-9534 211 F
carolyn.assa@becker.edu
ASSAD, Arjang, A .... 412-648-1556 412 I
aassad@pitt.edu
ASSAEL, Leon .... 612-624-2424 250 E
assael@umn.edu
ASSAF, Michael .... 413-775-1318 219 F
assafm@gcc.mass.edu
ASSANIS, Dennis .... 302-831-2111.. 90 I
president@udel.edu
ASSELIN, Edward, E ...... 518-255-5215 328 C
asselie@cobleskill.edu
ASSERSON, Elizabeth .... 406-994-4531 272 A
basserson@montana.edu

AUSTIN, Robert, C .... 806-371-5024 442 D
rcaustin@actx.edu
AUSTIN, Scott .... 757-594-7053 479 H
baustin@cnu.edu
AUSTIN, Sheila .... 334-244-3425.... 4 E
saustin1@aum.edu
AUSTIN, Suzanne, E ...... 205-934-6290.... 8 B
seaustin@uab.edu
AUSTIN, Tiffany .... 914-323-5484 314 A
tiffany.austin@mville.edu
AUSTIN, Timothy, R ...... 412-396-6054 394 D
taustin@duq.edu
AUSTIN, Tracey, M .... 603-526-3886 280 H
taustin@colby-sawyer.edu
AUSTIN, Troy .... 434-395-2057 482 E
austints@longwood.edu
AUSTIN, William .... 908-689-7618 292 G
will@warren.edu
AUSTIN-BRUNS, Emily .. 978-665-3025 217 E
eaustinb@fitchburgstate.edu
AUTEN, Mike .... 402-844-7058 276 G
mike@northeast.edu
AUTERO, Esa .... 954-545-4500 108 A
academics@sfbc.edu
AUTIO, Wesley .... 413-545-2963 216 H
autio@umass.edu
AUTREY, Denny .... 713-634-0011 457 G
dautrey@swbts.edu
AUTRY, Dean .... 270-686-4464 186 F
dean.autry@kctcs.edu
AUTRY, Shanna .... 850-201-8918 112 C
autrys@tcc.fl.edu
AUVENSHINE, Donnie ... 325-649-8408 450 H
dauvenshine@hputx.edu
AUVIL, Joe .... 509-793-2016 492 I
joea@bigbend.edu
AVAKIAN, Satenik .... 510-925-4282.. 25 P
savakian@aua.am
AVALONE, Valarie, L ..... 585-292-3021 315 L
vavalone@monroecc.edu
AVALOS, Jesse .... 617-730-7111 223 B
jesse.avalos@newbury.edu
AVALOS, Juan .... 949-582-4566.. 64 J
javalos@saddleback.edu
AVALOS, Natalie .... 818-767-0888.. 75 C
natalie.avalos@woodbury.edu
AVALOS, Steven .... 909-794-1084.. 40 B
savalos@cccollege.edu
AVALOS-THOMPSON,
Marlena .... 708-656-8000 146 F
m.avalos-thompson@morton.edu
AVANT, Tamara .... 912-650-6233 125 H
tavant@southuniversity.edu
AVANT, Toni, D .... 662-915-7174 256 C
tavant@olemiss.edu
AVELINO, Melanie .... 336-633-0256 345 F
mlavelino@randolph.edu
AVELLA, Christine .... 760-547-1800.. 43 G
cavella@fst.edu
AVELLANEDA, Carolina . 617-236-8859 215 B
cavellaneda@fisher.edu
AVEN, Forrest, F .... 210-829-3190 465 E
aven@uiwtx.edu
AVENARIUS, Daniel, R .. 608-342-1468 511 D
avenarid@uwplatt.edu
AVENDANO, John .... 815-802-8110 142 C
president@kcc.edu
AVENT, Randy, K .... 813-874-8614 109 E
AVENT, Sherri, M .... 336-334-7973 350 C
avent@ncat.edu
AVERESCH, Brenda .... 419-783-2352 361 A
baveresch@defiance.edu
AVERILL, Leslie .... 802-651-5907 474 G
averill@champlain.edu
AVERILL, Sue .... 330-672-2220 363 I
saveril2@kent.edu
AVERSA, Jeanne .... 617-973-8460 224 I
javersa@suffolk.edu
AVERY, Barbara, J .... 810-762-3434 238 B
baravery@umflint.edu
AVERY, Donald .... 478-289-2015 118 H
davery@ega.edu
AVERY, Earl .... 781-891-2907 212 A
eavery@bentley.edu
AVERY, James .... 731-661-5329 439 D
javery@uu.edu
AVERY, Kathy .... 918-293-4988 378 B
kathy.avery@okstate.edu
AVERY, Kristine .... 207-893-7755 200 G
kavery@sjcme.edu
AVERY, Lisa .... 971-722-4357 386 C
lisa.avery@pcc.edu
AVERY, Martin, D .... 315-386-7222 329 A
averym@canton.edu
AVERY, Paula .... 310-303-7213.. 51 B
pavery@marymountcalifornia.edu
AVERY, Sarah, E .... 630-637-5861 147 E
seavery@nactrl.edu

AVERY, Sherri, M .... 781-736-3706 213 A
savery@brandeis.edu
AVILÉS, Yvonne .... 787-264-1912 524 D
y_aviles@intersg.edu
AVILA, Glenna .... 661-255-1050.. 29 F
gavila@calarts.edu
AVILA, Laura .... 623-845-4780.. 13 H
laura.avila@gccaz.edu
AVILA, Lauri .... 928-428-8915.. 12 I
lauri.avila@eac.edu
AVILA, Margaret .... 323-568-3304.. 36 H
margaretavila@cdrewu.edu
AVILA, Nitza .... 787-257-0099 527 H
nitza.avila@upr.edu
AVILA, Pedro .... 707-524-1647.. 62 H
pavila@santarosa.edu
AVILA, Susan .... 510-594-3661.. 28 K
savila@cca.edu
AVILA, Vince .... 785-864-4036 181 I
vavila1@ku.edu
AVILES, Angel .... 787-780-5134 525 D
aaviles@nuc.edu
AVILES, Gladys, M .... 248-204-4123 233 A
gaviles@ltu.edu
AVILES, Jose .... 225-578-1175 193 M
javiles1@lsu.edu
AVILES, Jose, R .... 787-786-3030 526 F
javiles@ucb.edu.pr
AVILES, Lucas, N .... 787-265-3869 528 C
lucas.aviles@uprm.edu
AVILES-FERRAN,
Jeanette .... 787-620-2040 520 F
javiles@aupr.edu
AVILEZ, Shawnice .... 773-995-2345 135 F
savilez@csu.edu
AVINGTON, Leroy .... 323-259-2599.. 54 E
lavington@oxy.edu
AVISSAR, Roni .... 305-421-4000 112 O
avissar@miami.edu
AVITIA, Amber .... 559-935-3221.. 74 A
amberavitia@whccd.edu
AVRUCH, Kevin .... 703-993-3607 481 B
kavruch@gmu.edu
AW, Fanta .... 202-885-3357.. 91 C
fanta@american.edu
AWADALLAH, Baha .... 773-602-5068 135 L
bawadallah@ccc.edu
AWADI, Ali .... 814-332-3355 388 F
aawadi@allegheny.edu
AWAI-WILLIAMS, Anika 734-487-1849 229 K
AWAN, Seher .... 619-388-3428.. 60 C
sawan@sdccd.edu
AWBREY, Susan, M ...... 248-370-4955 235 J
awbrey@oakland.edu
AWE, Jacqueline .... 912-358-3114 125 C
awej@savannahstate.edu
AWE, Jennifer .... 212-799-5000 312 B
AWN, Peter .... 212-854-1932 305 E
pja3@columbia.edu
AWONIYI, Beatrice .... 352-395-5513 107 E
bea.awoniyi@sfcollege.edu
AWOPETU, Lawrence ..... 870-575-8649.. 22 E
awopetul@uapb.edu
AWUAH, Agatha .... 315-498-2500 319 G
awuaha@sunyocc.edu
AWUAH, Emmanuel .... 309-694-8584 139 G
emmanuel.awuah@icc.edu
AWWAD, Elise .... 630-515-3105 137 D
eawwad@devry.edu
AXELROD, Margaret ...... 703-284-1498 483 A
paxelrod@marymount.edu
AXLUND, Martin .... 307-755-2169 517 G
martin.axlund@zenith.org
AXLUND MCBRIDE,
RaeLyn .... 360-752-8344 492 H
raelyn.axlund.mcbride@btc.edu
AXMACHER, Ray .... 718-429-6600 333 B
ray.axmacher@vaughn.edu
AXTELL, Denise .... 530-242-7771.. 63 I
daxtell@shastacollege.edu
AXTELL, Richard, D .... 859-238-5342 184 C
rick.axtell@centre.edu
AYALA, Adriana .... 408-270-6434.. 61 O
adriana.ayala@evc.edu
AYALA, Benjamin .... 787-864-2222 524 A
benjamin.ayala@guayama.inter.edu
AYALA, Carlos .... 707-664-2132.. 35 A
dean.education@sonoma.edu
AYALA, Carmen .... 787-761-0640 527 C
decanaacademica@utcpr.edu
AYALA, Caroline .... 787-264-1912 524 D
caroline_ayala@intersg.edu
AYALA, Eddie .... 787-279-1912 523 J
eayala@bayamon.inter.edu
AYALA, Gladys, M .... 914-594-4498 318 A
gladys_ayala@nymc.edu
AYALA, Hector .... 787-850-9187 528 B
hector.ayala5@upr.edu

AYALA, Israel .... 787-891-0925 523 G
iayala@aguadilla.inter.edu
AYALA, Javier .... 619-644-7158.. 45 A
javier.ayala@gcccd.edu
AYALA, Mary .... 575-562-2421 293 O
mary.ayala@enmu.edu
AYALA, Oliva .... 818-364-7795.. 49 C
sancheo@lamission.edu
AYALA, Paul .... 210-805-5863 465 E
peayala@uiwtx.edu
AYALA, Ramon .... 787-250-1912 524 B
rayala@intermetro.edu
AYALA, Shawn .... 617-588-1352 211 G
sayala@bfit.edu
AYALA-AUSTIN, Eliazer . 408-288-3772.. 61 P
eliazer.ayala-austin@sjcc.edu
AYARS, Daniel .... 937-328-6040 359 H
ayarsd@clarkstate.edu
AYBAR, Jose, M .... 773-838-7511 136 A
jaybar@ccc.edu
AYCOCK, Allan .... 706-542-9902 127 A
aaycock@uga.edu
AYCOCK, Greg .... 951-739-7802.. 58 G
greg.aycock@norcocollege.edu
AYCOCK, Jim .... 662-246-6330 254 C
jaycock@msdelta.edu
AYDIN, Nurdan .... 201-200-3003 287 F
naydin@njcu.edu
AYE, Devin .... 760-366-5292.. 41 B
daye@cmccd.edu
AYERS, Benjamin, C ..... 706-542-8100 127 A
busdean@uga.edu
AYERS, David, J .... 724-458-2025 396 D
djayers@gcc.edu
AYERS, Donna .... 818-364-7799.. 49 C
ayersdj@lamission.edu
AYERS, Holly .... 870-512-7841.. 18 D
holly_ayers@asun.edu
AYERS, James, P .... 716-880-2179 314 F
james.p.ayers@medaille.edu
AYERS, Keith .... 251-626-3303.... 7 G
kayers@ussa.edu
AYERS, Lee .... 541-552-6505 386 H
ayersl@sou.edu
AYERS, Mary .... 662-562-3438 255 C
AYERS, Michael .... 718-758-8127 301 E
mrayers@brooklyn.cuny.edu
AYERS, Michael, V .... 336-734-7478 343 C
mayers@forsythtech.edu
AYERS, Nancy, A .... 208-467-8542 132 F
naayers@nnu.edu
AYERS, Shari .... 419-358-3030 357 E
ayerss@bluffton.edu
AYERS, Sheli .... 209-954-5139.. 61 B
sayers@deltacollege.edu
AYERS, Steve .... 252-328-9527 349 I
ayerss@ecu.edu
AYERS, Susan .... 978-232-2066 214 G
sayers@endicott.edu
AYERS, Tom .... 810-762-9787 232 C
tayers@kettering.edu
AYERSMAN, David, J .... 304-256-0281 503 B
dayersman@newriver.edu
AYEWHO, Michael, E ..... 412-578-6004 391 G
meayewoh@carlow.edu
AYKROID, David .... 847-543-2259 136 E
daykroid@clcillinois.edu
AYLESBURY, Tom .... 626-568-8850.. 47 G
AYLESWORTH, Chris ..... 413-236-2107 219 B
caylesworth@berkshirecc.edu
AYLETT, Ashley .... 870-584-1125.. 22 F
aaylett@cccua.edu
AYLOR, Pete .... 864-587-4229 424 D
aylorp@smcsc.edu
AYLWARD, Nick .... 216-373-5329 367 A
naylward@ndc.edu
AYLWARD, Robert, R ..... 307-766-4860 517 B
raylward@uwyo.edu
AYMAT-SANTANA,
Noel, J .... 787-758-2525 527 D
rector.rcm@upr.edu
AYNES, Danny .... 541-917-4999 384 A
aynesd@linnbenton.edu
AYO-AKINYEMI,
Stephanie .... 818-785-2726.. 35 N
AYON, Carlos .... 714-992-7064.. 54 A
cayon@fullcoll.edu
AYON, Maria .... 626-571-8811.. 72 C
mariaa@uwest.edu
AYOTTE, Scott .... 616-331-2242 230 G
ayottesc@gvsu.edu
AYOUBI, Amjad .... 504-865-5107 196 D
aamjad@tulane.edu
AYOUCH, Karen .... 315-866-0300 310 A
ayouchka@herkimer.edu
AYRAVAINEN, Eija .... 212-772-4878 302 E
eija.ayravainen@hunter.cuny.edu

AYRE-BOGGS, Rebecca . 810-766-4044 227 F
rboggs01@baker.edu
AYRES, Amy .... 405-208-7910 377 D
aayres@okcu.edu
AYRES, Christina, M ..... 573-202-6959 259 L
christina.ayres@eastcentral.edu
AYRES, Christina, M ..... 417-268-1012 257 F
ayresc@evangel.edu
AYRES, Dana .... 214-768-2841 457 B
dwayres@smu.edu
AYRES, Deb .... 636-949-4477 261 I
dayres@lindenwood.edu
AYRES, Jessica .... 650-433-3824.. 55 I
jayres@paloaltou.edu
AYRES, Susan .... 706-864-1998 127 B
susan.ayres@ung.edu
AYRIM, Burcu .... 305-474-6048 107 B
bayrim@stu.edu
AYTCH, Keith .... 408-270-6471.. 61 O
keith.aytch@evc.edu
AYTES, Kregg .... 406-994-4423 272 A
kregg.aytes@montana.edu
AYYAR, Radhika .... 936-261-3311 458 F
rayyar@pvamu.edu
AZAMA, Anthony, J .... 314-935-5000 269 L
anthony.j.azama@wustl.edu
AZAR, Eve .... 908-835-2335 292 G
azar@warren.edu
AZAREKNO, Anita .... 541-737-0123 385 F
AZARI, Cynthia .... 805-678-5807.. 72 G
cazari@vcccd.edu
AZARI, Cynthia .... 805-678-5808.. 73 B
cazari@vcccd.edu
AZDELL, Grant, L .... 804-752-7266 484 C
gazdell@rmc.edu
AZEBEOKHAI,
Ignatius, C .... 501-569-3180.. 22 B
icazebeokhai@ualr.edu
AZEVEDO, Mario .... 601-979-7036 253 E
mario.j.azevedo@jsums.edu
AZEVEDO, Steve .... 480-461-7974.. 13 I
steve.azevedo@mesacc.edu
AZHAND, Hamid, U .... 909-537-5137.. 33 D
hazhand@csusb.edu
AZIZ, Jihad, N .... 804-828-6200 487 E
jnaziz@vcu.edu
AZIZ, Nadim .... 864-656-0542 419 F
aziz@clemson.edu
AZIZAN-GARDNER,
Noor .... 573-882-6282 268 C
azizan-gardnern@missouri.edu
AZKOUL, Emilie .... 616-222-1447 229 B
emilie.azkoul@cornerstone.edu
AZURE, Jackie .... 406-768-3213 271 B
jazure@fpcc.edu
AZURE, Lisa .... 701-255-3285 355 I
lazure@uttc.edu
AZURE, Melody .... 701-854-8020 355 F
melody.azure@sittingbull.edu
AZURE, Tracy .... 701-477-7862 355 H
tazure@tm.edu
AZZAM-GOMEZ, Shady . 631-451-4920 330 B
azzamgs@sunysuffolk.edu
AZZARA, Tom .... 631-420-2599 329 D
azzaratf@farmingdale.edu
AZZARELLO, Tony .... 419-227-3141 372 D
AZZIZ, Ricardo .... 518-320-1313 324 F
ricardo.azziz@suny.edu
A'SEE, Carlito, D .... 803-536-7485 423 G
cdasee@scsu.edu

B

BÉLANGER, Annie .... 616-331-2621 230 G
belange1@gvsu.edu
BAADE, K. Austin .... 262-691-5550 515 B
kbaade@wctc.edu
BAAR, Tricia .... 501-337-5000.. 19 C
tbaar@coto.edu
BAART, Aaron .... 712-722-6079 168 I
aaron.baart@dordt.edu
BAAS, John .... 712-722-6020 168 I
john.baas@dordt.edu
BAAS, Mark .... 507-332-5876 247 H
mark.baas@southcentral.edu
BABALIS, Eva .... 718-779-1430 320 C
ebabalis@mail.plazacollege.edu
BABASHANIAN,
Mark, R .... 757-446-6003 480 C
babashmr@evms.edu
BABB, Brian .... 386-506-4457.. 97 I
babbb@daytonastate.edu
BABB, Brian, T .... 386-506-4457.. 97 I
babbb@daytonastate.edu
BABB, Michael .... 614-287-2473 360 C
mbabb6@cscc.edu
BABB, Stephanie .... 559-325-5242.. 66 F
stephanie.babb@cloviscollege.edu

BAI, Kang .... 815-836-5640 143 E
kbai@lewisu.edu
BAI, Lynn .... 516-739-1545 317 D
admissions@nyctcm.edu
BAI, Monica .... 928-523-6514.. 14 K
monica.bai@nau.edu
BAI, Yifeng .... 973-748-9000 284 A
yifeng_bai@bloomfield.edu
BAIA, Larissa .... 603-524-3207 280 K
BAIA, Patricia .... 518-445-2366 297 K
pbaia@albanylaw.edu
BAICKER, Katherine .... 773-702-1234 153 F
kbaicker@uchicago.edu
BAIDA, Ana .... 470-578-6555 122 C
abaida@kennesaw.edu
BAIDOO,
Christopher, E .... 619-239-0391.. 35 C
cbaidoo@cwsl.edu
BAIDWAN, Surjeet .... 410-951-6449 208 F
sbaidwan@coppin.edu
BAIER, Henry, D .... 734-764-3402 237 I
hbaier@umich.edu
BAIER, Valerie, A .... 570-326-3761 404 T
vbaier@pct.edu
BAIERL, Hans .... 920-924-3112 514 D
hbaierl@morainepark.edu
BAIERL, Kenneth, W ...... 574-520-4560 160 F
kbaierl@iusb.edu
BAIGENT, Peter, M .... 631-632-6700 325 F
peter.baigent@stonybrook.edu
BAIK, Sam .... 626-448-0023.. 46 K
BAIK, Sang .... 213-763-7007.. 49 F
baiks@lattc.edu
BAILARD, Rhiannon ...... 310-506-4702.. 56 D
rhiannon.bailard@pepperdine.edu
BAILEY, Alison .... 309-438-2947 140 L
baileya@ilstu.edu
BAILEY, Amanda .... 470-639-0703 123 E
amanda.bailey@morehouse.edu
BAILEY, Ann .... 662-325-3555 254 E
housing@saffairs.msstate.edu
BAILEY, Anthony .... 213-740-2852.. 72 B
arbailey@usc.edu
BAILEY, Barbara .... 773-252-5311 149 I
barbara.bailey@resu.edu
BAILEY, Beth .... 706-419-1104 118 E
beth.bailey@covenant.edu
BAILEY, Bliss, N .... 334-844-4511.... 4 D
bailebn@auburn.edu
BAILEY, Brian .... 312-567-6937 140 I
bbailey4@iit.edu
BAILEY, Cassy .... 785-594-8484 174 J
cassy.bailey@bakeru.edu
BAILEY, Charla .... 830-372-8098 461 D
cbailey@tlu.edu
BAILEY, Chris, C .... 570-372-4149 410 H
baileycj@susqu.edu
BAILEY, Christopher ...... 401-254-3124 417 C
cjbailey@rwu.edu
BAILEY, Christopher, C . 360-442-2101 495 G
cbailey@lowercolumbia.edu
BAILEY, Christy .... 843-477-2166 421 L
christy.bailey@hgtc.edu
BAILEY, Clint .... 252-328-2606 349 I
baileyrc@ecu.edu
BAILEY, Dan .... 845-675-4402 319 C
dan.bailey@nyack.edu
BAILEY, Danya .... 254-298-8364 458 C
danya.bailey@templejc.edu
BAILEY, David .... 304-384-5290 503 P
counseling@concord.edu
BAILEY, David, C .... 574-631-1097 165 A
bailey.77@nd.edu
BAILEY, Denice .... 503-594-3002 382 D
denice.bailey@clackamas.edu
BAILEY, Denise .... 903-233-3100 452 A
denisebailey@letu.edu
BAILEY, Dennis .... 970-255-2634.. 77 K
bailey@coloradomesa.edu
BAILEY, Dennis, A .... 850-644-8136 110 A
dbailey@fsu.edu
BAILEY, Dexter .... 631-632-4490 325 F
dexter.bailey@stonybrook.edu
BAILEY, Dexter, A .... 631-632-4811 325 F
dexter.bailey@stonybrook.edu
BAILEY, Dixon .... 254-647-3234 454 L
dbailey@rangercollege.edu
BAILEY, Donald, R .... 401-865-1188 416 E
drbailey@providence.edu
BAILEY, Duane .... 516-686-1133 317 G
duane.bailey@nyit.edu
BAILEY, Duane .... 203-932-7020.. 89 D
dbailey@newhaven.edu
BAILEY, Ed .... 231-995-1215 235 B
ebailey@nmc.edu
BAILEY, Gary .... 616-538-2330 230 E
gbailey@gbcol.edu
BAILEY, Gregory, P .... 530-226-4605.. 64 B
gbailey@simpsonu.edu
BAILEY, Guy .... 956-665-2100 468 A
president@utrgv.edu
BAILEY, Helen .... 423-869-6387 433 C
helen.bailey@lmunet.edu
BAILEY, Jack .... 304-766-4109 505 A
jbaile19@wvstateu.edu
BAILEY, Janie .... 870-633-4480.. 19 E
jbailey@eacc.edu
BAILEY, Jaye .... 408-924-1177.. 34 D
jaye.bailey@sjsu.edu
BAILEY, Jeannie .... 775-753-2317 279 A
jeannie.bailey@gbcnv.edu
BAILEY, Jeff .... 870-972-3077.. 18 A
jbailey@astate.edu
BAILEY, Jessica, H .... 601-984-6300 256 D
jhbailey@umc.edu
BAILEY, Jessika .... 580-559-5252 375 I
jbailey@ecok.edu
BAILEY, Jodi .... 201-200-2116 287 F
jbailey2@njcu.edu
BAILEY, Joseph, A .... 585-345-6900 309 C
jabailey@genesee.edu
BAILEY, Julie .... 432-264-5030 450 G
jbailey@howardcollege.edu
BAILEY, Julie, A .... 774-353-0661 211 F
julie.bailey@becker.edu
BAILEY, Keith .... 304-293-6979 505 B
keith.bailey@mail.wvu.edu
BAILEY, Kelly .... 918-610-0027 375 F
kbailey@communitycarecollege.edu
BAILEY, Kelly .... 724-738-4223 407 C
kelly.bailey@sru.edu
BAILEY, Kevin .... 704-687-2206 351 C
baileyk@uncc.edu
BAILEY, Kieren .... 402-486-2514 277 C
kieren.bailey@ucollege.edu
BAILEY, Larry .... 731-424-3520 437 B
lbailey@jscc.edu
BAILEY, Lee .... 573-592-4381 270 D
lee.bailey@williamwoods.edu
BAILEY, Lisa .... 909-652-6532.. 36 E
lisa.bailey@chaffey.edu
BAILEY, Mara .... 515-961-1684 173 E
mara.bailey@simpson.edu
BAILEY, Mark .... 909-621-8219.. 57 C
mark_bailey@pitzer.edu
BAILEY, Mark .... 205-853-1200.... 2 F
mbailey@jeffersonstate.edu
BAILEY, Mark, L .... 214-887-5001 448 G
mbailey@dts.edu
BAILEY, Mary .... 620-331-8332 178 E
mbailey@indycc.edu
BAILEY, Mary Kaye .... 702-651-7437 278 N
marykaye.bailey@csn.edu
BAILEY, Michael, A .... 202-687-6021.. 92 B
baileyma@georgetown.edu
BAILEY, Michelle .... 563-441-4152 169 A
mmbailey@eicc.edu
BAILEY, Mike .... 309-341-5336 134 H
mbailey@sandburg.edu
BAILEY, Mike .... 608-663-2000 507 M
mbailey@mediainstitute.edu
BAILEY, Patrick .... 818-677-2393.. 33 B
patrick.bailey@csun.edu
BAILEY, Patrick, X .... 504-865-3434 194 G
pbailey@loyno.edu
BAILEY, Paul .... 678-466-4377 117 I
paulbailey@clayton.edu
BAILEY, Peter, A .... 302-295-1191.. 91 B
peter.a.bailey@wilmu.edu
BAILEY, Phillip .... 501-450-3262.. 23 I
phillipb@uca.edu
BAILEY, JR., Richard, J 505-747-2140 295 H
BAILEY, Rita .... 470-578-2364 122 C
rbaile62@kennesaw.edu
BAILEY, Robbie .... 540-261-8463 485 G
robbie.bailey@svu.edu
BAILEY, Robyn .... 847-635-1428 148 D
rbailey@oakton.edu
BAILEY, Sara .... 352-638-9814.. 95 H
sbailey@beaconcollege.edu
BAILEY, Sharon, M .... 361-570-4236 465 D
baileysm@uhv.edu
BAILEY, Shaun .... 559-934-2254.. 73 N
shaunbailey@whccd.edu
BAILEY, Steve .... 434-381-6110 485 P
sbailey@sbc.edu
BAILEY, Tammy .... 252-789-0253 344 E
tammy.bailey@martincc.edu
BAILEY, Teresa .... 757-825-2770 489 G
baileyt@tncc.edu
BAILEY, Terraine .... 470-639-0584 123 E
terrain.bailey@morehouse.edu
BAILEY, Terry .... 706-272-2611 118 F
tbailey@daltonstate.edu
BAILEY, Travis .... 304-696-3032 504 C
bailey53@marshall.edu
BAILEY, William .... 814-393-2323 405 H
wbailey@clarion.edu
BAILEY, William, C .... 309-298-2442 155 D
wc-bailey@wiu.edu
BAILEY-AYE, Regena ..... 785-654-2416 174 G
rbailey@allencc.edu
BAILEY-CHEN, Robin ..... 661-255-1050.. 29 F
rbaileychen@calarts.edu
BAILEY-HOFMANN,
Holly .... 310-287-4547.. 49 H
baileyhh@wlac.edu
BAILEY-OCHOA, Celia ... 409-772-8909 469 C
cebailey@utmb.edu
BAILEY PENROD,
Juliett .... 256-726-7457.... 6 E
jbpenrod@oakwood.edu
BAILIE, John .... 267-246-5891 397 K
johnbailie@iirp.edu
BAILIN, Debra, M .... 802-626-6210 477 D
debra.bailin@lyndonstate.edu
BAILLARGEON, Betty ..... 860-215-9207.. 86 F
bbaillargeon@trcc.commnet.edu
BAILLIE, Christopher ..... 701-255-3285 355 I
cbaillie@uttc.edu
BAILO, Carole Anne ...... 480-212-1704.. 16 B
BAILON, Kathy .... 213-624-1200.. 42 N
kbailon@fidm.edu
BAILY, Jessica .... 914-674-7611 314 I
jbaily@mercy.edu
BAILY, Scott .... 970-491-7655.. 78 N
scott.baily@colostate.edu
BAIMA, Thomas, A .... 847-970-4866 154 H
tbaima@usml.edu
BAIN, Jeff, N .... 931-363-9872 433 E
jbain@martinmethodist.edu
BAIN, Michael .... 404-669-2097 124 F
michael.bain@point.edu
BAIN-SELBO, Eric .... 765-453-2000 160 B
ebainsel@iu.edu
BAINE, Brad .... 870-759-4128.. 23 K
bbaine@wbcoll.edu
BAINES, Joel, D .... 225-578-9905 193 M
jbaines@lsu.edu
BAINTER, Bradley .... 309-298-1808 155 D
bl-bainter@wiu.edu
BAIR, Ava .... 719-336-1574.. 80 N
ava.bair@lamarcc.edu
BAIR, Ryan .... 309-677-2697 134 G
rbair@fsmail.bradley.edu
BAIR, Susanne, P .... 716-878-4324 326 E
bairsp@buffalostate.edu
BAIRD, Bridget, R .... 423-439-8222 431 H
bairdb@etsu.edu
BAIRD, David .... 860-685-2119.. 89 F
dbaird@wesleyan.edu
BAIRD, Davis .... 508-793-7673 213 C
dbaird@clarku.edu
BAIRD, Denise .... 317-738-8270 157 L
dbaird@franklincollege.edu
BAIRD, Denise, M .... 317-738-8270 157 L
dbaird@franklincollege.edu
BAIRD, Dion .... 503-594-0760 382 D
dion.baird@clackamas.edu
BAIRD, Karen .... 312-322-1720 152 F
kbaird@spertus.edu
BAIRD, Lynn, N .... 208-885-6534 132 I
lbaird@uidaho.edu
BAIRD, Phil .... 605-586-5880 428 A
phil.baird@sintegleska.edu
BAIRD, Stephanie .... 405-425-5200 377 B
stephanie.baird@oc.edu
BAIRD, Timothy, R .... 724-847-6490 395 J
trbaird@geneva.edu
BAIRD-JAMES, Allison .. 310-794-8686.. 69 B
abaird-james@finance.ucla.edu
BAISDEN, Emma, L .... 304-896-7402 503 D
emma.baisden@southernwv.edu
BAISEY, Michael .... 301-624-2892 203 H
mbaisey@frederick.edu
BAISLEY, David, M .... 412-268-7456 391 H
david@cmu.edu
BAITMAN, Clay, L .... 618-235-2700 152 E
clay.baitman@swic.edu
BAJANDAS, Ivette .... 305-629-2929 107 D
ibajandas@sanignaciocollege.edu
BAJCZYK, Jim .... 920-565-1521 507 K
bajczykja@lakeland.edu
BAJOR, William .... 570-422-3588 406 A
wbajor@esu.edu
BAK, Doug .... 719-846-5513.. 82 L
doug.bak@trinidadstate.edu
BAKANE, Samir .... 973-655-7773 287 D
bakanes@mail.montclair.edu
BAKAR, Senem .... 202-885-3352.. 91 C
bakar@american.edu
BAKARI, Sentwali .... 719-255-3159.. 83 C
sbakari@uccs.edu
BAKE, Mark, A .... 920-433-6626 506 C
mark.bake@bellincollege.edu
BAKEMEIER, Emily, P .... 203-432-4444.. 89 G
emily.bakemeier@yale.edu
BAKER, Adria .... 713-348-6095 455 F
abaker@rice.edu
BAKER, Alvin .... 606-326-2422 185 E
alvin.baker@kctcs.edu
BAKER, Amanda .... 607-871-2164 298 A
bakera@alfred.edu
BAKER, Amanda, L .... 304-929-6717 503 B
abaker@newriver.edu
BAKER, Amy .... 573-288-6493 259 E
abaker@culver.edu
BAKER, Andrew, R .... 301-447-5295 206 B
baker@msmary.edu
BAKER, Barry .... 407-823-2564 110 C
barry.baker@ucf.edu
BAKER, Barry, A .... 425-235-5839 497 E
bbaker@rtc.edu
BAKER, Betty .... 304-793-6873 504 F
bbaker@osteo.wvsom.edu
BAKER, Bonnie .... 928-523-9413.. 14 K
bonnie.baker@nau.edu
BAKER, Brent .... 817-598-6270 470 J
bbaker@wc.edu
BAKER, Brent .... 817-598-6275 470 J
bbaker@wc.edu
BAKER, Brian .... 812-749-1212 163 B
bbaker@oak.edu
BAKER, Brian, J .... 540-286-1302 486 D
bbaker@umw.edu
BAKER, Carey .... 870-235-4042.. 21 F
clbaker@saumag.edu
BAKER, Caroline .... 410-455-8171 208 A
cbaker@umbc.edu
BAKER, Cheryl .... 304-647-6201 504 F
cbaker@osteo.wvsom.edu
BAKER, Chris .... 619-388-3400.. 60 C
BAKER, Chuck, S .... 423-775-7136 430 G
cbaker0930@bryan.edu
BAKER, Connie .... 805-289-6400.. 73 C
cbaker@vcccd.edu
BAKER, Dave .... 717-728-2272 392 B
davebaker@centralpenn.edu
BAKER, David, A .... 541-737-3871 385 F
david.baker@oregonstate.edu
BAKER, Debbie .... 307-382-1611 517 C
dbaker@westernwyoming.edu
BAKER, Deborah .... 413-565-1000 211 C
dbaker@baypath.edu
BAKER, Debra .... 708-456-0300 153 E
debrabaker@triton.edu
BAKER, Debra .... 662-246-6301 254 C
dbaker@msdelta.edu
BAKER, Denice .... 978-837-5231 221 G
bakerde@merrimack.edu
BAKER, Diane .... 269-927-6287 232 G
baker@lakemichigancollege.edu
BAKER, Donna .... 816-584-6847 265 C
donna.baker@park.edu
BAKER, Dyann, J .... 860-701-5016.. 87 F
baker_dy@mitchell.edu
BAKER, Elizabeth .... 252-222-6216 341 F
bakere@carteret.edu
BAKER, Elizabeth, A ...... 312-942-2702 150 F
elizabeth_baker@rush.edu
BAKER, Emerson .... 978-542-7126 218 E
ebaker@salemstate.edu
BAKER, Emily .... 909-748-8047.. 71 H
emily_baker@redlands.edu
BAKER, Erinnae .... 803-981-7075 426 J
ebaker@yorktech.edu
BAKER, Erma .... 757-221-3954 479 I
eabaker01@wm.edu
BAKER, Erma, A .... 540-654-2043 486 D
ebaker@umw.edu
BAKER, Frankie .... 513-569-1453 359 G
frankie.baker@cincinnatistate.edu
BAKER, Gail, F .... 619-260-4553.. 71 J
provost@sandiego.edu
BAKER, Gary .... 941-752-5431 108 P
bakerg@scf.edu
BAKER, Gisella .... 319-296-4465 169 H
gisella.baker@hawkeyecollege.edu
BAKER, Gordon .... 678-466-4334 117 I
gordonbaker@clayton.edu
BAKER, Hilary .... 818-677-7750.. 33 B
hilary.baker@csun.edu
BAKER, James .... 973-300-2100 291 I
jbaker@sussex.edu
BAKER, James .... 210-999-8076 464 B
jbaker5@trinity.edu
BAKER, James, P .... 417-836-8501 263 H
jbaker@missouristate.edu

BALL, Drexel, B .... 803-535-5263 419 E
dball@claflin.edu
BALL, Gregory, F .... 301-405-1691 207 G
gball@umd.edu
BALL, James, D .... 410-386-8188 203 A
jball@carrollcc.edu
BALL, Jason .... 561-297-3440 109 B
jball@fau.edu
BALL, John .... 504-568-4500 194 C
jball@lsuhsc.edu
BALL, Joshua .... 606-886-3863 185 F
jball0079@kctcs.edu
BALL, Justin .... 309-677-3850 134 G
jball@bradley.edu
BALL, Karen .... 559-791-2420.. 47 C
kball@portervillecollege.edu
BALL, Kathy .... 304-384-6009 503 P
bonner@concord.edu
BALL, Kenneth .... 703-993-1497 481 B
vsdean@gmu.edu
BALL, Kevin .... 330-941-1560 374 E
keball@ysu.edu
BALL, Kevin, A .... 248-364-3562 235 J
kevinball@oakland.edu
BALL, Kevin, J .... 806-371-5225 442 D
k0364101@actx.edu
BALL, Kim .... 704-894-2521 337 B
kiball@davidson.edu
BALL, Kimberly .... 657-278-4968.. 32 B
kball@fullerton.edu
BALL, Margaret, T .... 718-817-3010 308 G
mball@fordham.edu
BALL, Michael .... 859-246-6512 185 G
michael.ball@kctcs.edu
BALL, Shelley .... 865-471-3235 430 H
sball@cn.edu
BALL, Thomas, G .... 724-458-2163 396 D
tgball@gcc.edu
BALL, Travis .... 903-886-5060 459 E
travis.ball@tamuc.edu
BALL, Williams, S .... 513-558-7333 371 E
william.s.ball@uc.edu
BALL-WILLIAMSON,
Carrie .... 662-862-8123 253 D
cbball@iccms.edu
BALLABAN, David, C .... 610-921-7256 388 E
dballaban@albright.edu
BALLAGH DE TOVAR,
Jane .... 913-621-8791 177 A
jane@donnelly.edu
BALLAM, Anne .... 901-272-5145 434 B
aballam@mca.edu
BALLANTINE, Clay .... 413-559-5590 215 F
cballantine@hampshire.edu
BALLANTYNE, Trina .... 201-216-5128 291 G
trina.ballantyne@stevens.edu
BALLARD, Beth .... 859-622-1283 184 F
beth.ballard@eku.edu
BALLARD, Carol .... 863-680-6236 100 D
cballard@flsouthern.edu
BALLARD, Chris .... 217-362-6414 145 J
cballard@millikin.edu
BALLARD, Debra .... 310-665-6921.. 54 I
dballard@otis.edu
BALLARD, Donna .... 662-476-5054 253 A
dballard@eastms.edu
BALLARD, Glenda .... 512-448-8655 455 I
gballard@stedwards.edu
BALLARD, Jennifer .... 870-512-7861.. 18 D
jennifer_ballard@asun.edu
BALLARD, Jennifer .... 503-883-2509 383 H
jballard@linfield.edu
BALLARD, Katie .... 270-686-4529 186 F
katie.ballard@kctcs.edu
BALLARD, Ken .... 757-822-1972 489 H
kballard@tcc.edu
BALLARD, Linda .... 713-313-7480 461 E
ballard_lc@tsu.edu
BALLARD, Lowell .... 432-552-2415 469 D
BALLARD, Patrice .... 210-486-1720 442 A
pballard4@alamo.edu
BALLARD, Paul .... 509-963-1410 492 L
pballard@cwu.edu
BALLARD, Steve .... 870-543-5910.. 21 E
sballard@seark.edu
BALLARD, Taylor .... 281-487-1170 460 G
tballard@txchiro.edu
BALLARD, Terri .... 412-536-1251 398 E
terri.ballard@laroche.edu
BALLARD, Toron .... 815-280-2701 142 A
tballard@jjc.edu
BALLARD, William .... 802-287-8236 475 B
ballardb@greenmtn.edu
BALLARD, William, H .... 419-772-2020 367 G
b-ballard@onu.edu
BALLARD, William, P .... 802-656-2240 476 E
william.ballard@uvm.edu

BALLARD-THROWER,
Rhea .... 202-806-6100.. 92 C
rballard@law.howard.edu
BALLARINI, John .... 262-554-6110 508 E
jaballarini@yahoo.com
BALLARO, Mollie, A .... 716-827-2418 331 K
ballarom@trocaire.edu
BALLATO, John, M .... 864-656-3642 419 F
jballat@clemson.edu
BALLEISEN, Edward .... 919-684-1964 337 C
eballeis@duke.edu
BALLENGEE, Greg .... 740-351-3574 369 L
gballengee@shawnee.edu
BALLENTINE, Angela .... 252-492-2061 347 C
ballentine@vgcc.edu
BALLENTINE, Brian .... 848-932-7454 290 A
brian.ballentine@rutgers.edu
BALLENTINE, Howard .... 540-665-4767 485 C
hballent@su.edu
BALLENTINE, Leslie .... 970-207-4550.. 80 P
leslieb@mckinleycollege.edu
BALLENTINE, Leslie .... 970-207-4500.. 84 C
leslieb@uscareerinstitute.edu
BALLESTEROS, Victor .... 817-515-6456 458 B
victor.ballesteros@tccd.edu
BALLEW, Frank .... 785-227-3380 175 E
ballewf@bethanylb.edu
BALLEW, Lavonne .... 360-676-2772 496 C
lcballew@nwic.edu
BALLEW, Marcy .... 903-875-7330 453 J
marcy.ballew@navarrocollege.edu
BALLEW, Pamela, H .... 252-451-8329 345 B
phballew947@nashcc.edu
BALLEW, Steve .... 601-266-4131 256 E
steve.ballew@usm.edu
BALLINGER, Andrea .... 225-578-5739 193 M
aballinger@lsu.edu
BALLINGER, Kevin, M ... 714-432-5015.. 38 H
kballinger@occ.cccd.edu
BALLINGER, Marcia, J .. 440-366-4050 364 F
BALLINGER, Philip .... 206-221-2305 499 D
philipba@uw.edu
BALLMAN, Terry .... 909-537-5800.. 33 D
tballman@csusb.edu
BALLOM, Kenneth .... 217-333-2121 154 B
ballom@illinois.edu
BALLOU, Bradley .... 910-962-7803 352 A
balloub@uncw.edu
BALLOU, Dawn .... 617-732-2077 221 E
dawn.ballou@mcphs.edu
BALLOU, Trenna .... 435-722-6900 472 L
trenna@ubtech.edu
BALOG, Scott .... 850-201-8632 112 C
balogs@tcc.fl.edu
BALOGA, Monica .... 321-674-8889.. 99 K
mbaloga@fit.edu
BALOUGH, Sandra, A ... 814-472-3151 409 G
sbalough@francis.edu
BALSAM, Carl, E .... 773-244-5710 147 F
cbalsam@northpark.edu
BALSAMO, Anne .... 972-883-7550 467 D
axb161831@utdallas.edu
BALSAMO, Michael .... 586-445-7141 233 B
balsamom@macomb.edu
BALSAMO, Robert .... 608-743-4525 513 D
rbalsamo@blackhawk.edu
BALSBAUGH, Kevin .... 717-947-6102 404 S
kebalsba@pacollege.edu
BALSDON, Edmund .... 619-594-2309.. 34 B
ebalsdon@mail.sdsu.edu
BALSEIRO, Wanda, I .... 787-878-5475 523 H
wbalseiro@arecibo.inter.edu
BALSER, Jeffrey, R .... 615-936-3030 440 D
jeff.balser@vanderbilt.edu
BALSIGER, Leslie .... 541-888-1673 387 A
leslie.balsiger@socc.edu
BALSTER, Heidi .... 307-674-6446 516 P
hbalster@sheridan.edu
BALTER-REITZ, Susan ... 406-657-2214 272 B
sbalter-reitz@msubillings.edu
BALTES, Erin .... 207-859-1327 200 H
baltese@thomas.edu
BALTES, Tim .... 417-447-2631 264 K
baltest@otc.edu
BALTHAZARD, Pierre .... 916-278-6578.. 33 C
balthazard@csus.edu
BALTHROP, David .... 270-809-6937 188 D
dbalthrop@murraystate.edu
BALTIMORE, Lester, B .. 516-877-3142 297 I
baltimore@adelphi.edu
BALTZIS, Basil .... 973-596-3619 288 A
basil.c.baltzis@njit.edu
BALZA, Stephen, J .... 507-354-8221 243 C
balzasj@mlc-wels.edu
BALZANO, Wanda .... 336-758-4455 353 A
balzanow@wfu.edu
BAMBARA, Cynthia, S .. 301-784-5000 202 B
cbambara@allegany.edu

BAMBERG, Gwendolyn .. 803-793-5100 420 G
bambergg@denmarktech.edu
BAMBERGER, Gregory ... 610-683-4095 406 D
gbamberg@kutztown.edu
BAMBHROLIA, Bhavesh 215-204-1131 411 B
bhavesh@temple.edu
BAMBHROLIA, Savita .... 609-586-4800 287 A
bambhros@mccc.edu
BAMFO, Alex .... 202-238-2666.. 92 C
alexander.bamfo@howard.edu
BAMFORD, Ryan .... 413-545-9652 216 H
rbamford@umass.edu
BAMONTE, Paul .... 718-409-7254 329 E
pbamonte@sunymaritime.edu
BANA, Mark .... 303-914-6220.. 82 B
mark.bana@rrcc.edu
BANACH, Michael .... 718-940-5584 322 G
mbanach@sjcny.edu
BANAIAN, King .... 320-308-4791 247 E
kbanaian@stcloudstate.edu
BANALES, Jose .... 512-245-8336 463 A
jb1478@txstate.edu
BANASZAK, Larry .... 614-823-1693 368 O
lbanaszak@otterbein.edu
BANAVAR, Jayanth .... 541-346-3186 387 F
provost@uoregon.edu
BANBURY, Doug .... 517-607-2327 231 C
dbanbury@hillsdale.edu
BANCHOFF, Thomas .... 202-687-5117.. 92 B
banchoff@georgetown.edu
BANDA, Magda .... 708-656-8000 146 F
magna.banda@morton.edu
BANDAS, Mark .... 615-322-6400 440 D
mark.bandas@vanderbilt.edu
BANDELIN, Janis, M .... 864-294-2191 421 I
janis.bandelin@furman.edu
BANDO, Patricia, A .... 617-552-3307 212 E
patricia.bando@bc.edu
BANDOPADHYAYA,
Arindam .... 617-287-7700 216 I
arindam.bandopadhyaya@umb.edu
BANDRE, Mark, A .... 785-833-4306 179 C
mark.bandre@kwu.edu
BANDURSKI, Steven .... 810-762-9517 232 C
sbandurski@kettering.edu
BANDY, JR., John, M ... 404-413-4600 121 A
jbandy@gsu.edu
BANDY, Kanoe .... 661-763-7779.. 67 A
kbandy@taftcollege.edu
BANDY, Kenneth .... 704-334-6882 336 I
kbandy@charlottechristian.edu
BANDY, Sam .... 815-394-4138 150 C
sbandy@rockford.edu
BANDY, Wendy .... 931-526-3660 431 J
wendy.bandy@fortisinstitute.edu
BANDY-NEAL, LaMel .... 615-327-6767 434 A
lbneal@mmc.edu
BANDYOPADHYAY,
Santanu .... 714-484-7330.. 53 M
sbandyopadhyay@cypresscollege.edu
BANE, Jason .... 217-206-7848 154 A
jabane@uillinois.edu
BANE, Susan .... 252-399-6514 335 I
smbane@barton.edu
BANERJEE, Manju .... 802-387-6807 475 C
manjubanerjee@landmark.edu
BANERJEE-STEVENS,
Juni .... 530-898-6345.. 31 D
dbanerjee-stevens@csuchico.edu
BANESS KING,
Deborah .... 708-456-0300 153 E
debbiebanessking@triton.edu
BANEY, Todd .... 704-922-6485 343 D
baney.todd@gaston.edu
BANG, Sam .... 626-584-5398.. 43 K
sbang@fuller.edu
BANGASSER, Karen .... 605-331-6684 429 D
karen.bangasser@usiouxfalls.edu
BANGASSER, Kathy .... 815-599-3448 139 F
kathy.bangasser@highland.edu
BANGASSER, Susan .... 909-384-8650.. 59 I
sbangasser@sbccd.cc.ca.us
BANGERA, Gita .... 425-564-2442 492 G
gita.bangera@bellevuecollege.edu
BANGERT, Stephanie ..... 510-869-6511.. 59 F
sbangert@samuelmerritt.edu
BANGERT-DROWNS,
Robert, L .... 518-442-4988 324 G
rbangert@albany.edu
BANGS, Joann .... 651-690-6500 249 T
jmbangs@stkate.edu
BANGSBERG, David .... 503-484-2257 385 D
sphacad@ohsu.edu
BANGSUND, Jenny .... 605-331-6765 429 D
jenny.bangsund@usiouxfalls.edu
BANIAK, Rick .... 314-516-2366 268 E
baniakr@umsl.edu

BANICK, Gabrielle, A .... 402-472-5208 277 E
gbanick@nebraska.edu
BANISTER, Stephen .... 701-858-3855 354 C
stephen.banister@minotstateu.edu
BANJAC, Joyce .... 216-373-6363 367 A
jbanjac@ndc.edu
BANKART, Charles .... 785-864-6161 181 I
cbankart@ku.edu
BANKER, Bonnie .... 859-858-3511 183 D
bonnie.banker@asbury.edu
BANKIRER, Marcia .... 626-529-4317.. 55 C
mbankirer@pacificoaks.edu
BANKIRER, Marcia .... 303-292-0015.. 79 F
BANKO, Matthew .... 336-506-4243 340 L
matthew.banko@alamancecc.edu
BANKOLE-MEDINA,
Katherine .... 410-951-3431 208 F
kbankole@coppin.edu
BANKS, Alexis .... 251-981-3771.... 5 A
alexis.banks@columbiasouthern.edu
BANKS, Brooke, F .... 530-898-5201.. 31 D
bfbanks@csuchico.edu
BANKS, Cara .... 309-779-7704 153 C
cara.banks@trinitycollegeqc.edu
BANKS, Cerri, A .... 518-580-5352 324 D
cbanks@skidmore.edu
BANKS, Christy .... 631-687-4596 322 G
cbanks@sjcny.edu
BANKS, Dacia, L .... 315-684-6289 329 F
banksdl@morrisville.edu
BANKS, Darrell .... 859-233-8287 189 H
dbanks@transy.edu
BANKS, James, W .... 631-548-2605 330 B
banksj@sunysuffolk.edu
BANKS, Jeff .... 402-449-2858 274 H
jbanks2725@graceu.edu
BANKS, Julie, M .... 937-229-3233 372 A
jbanks1@udayton.edu
BANKS, Kathryn, M .... 252-638-7367 342 E
banksk@cravencc.edu
BANKS, Kenneeth .... 408-498-5104.. 38 I
kbanks@cogswell.edu
BANKS, Kenneth .... 408-498-5104.. 38 I
kbanks@cogswell.edu
BANKS, Kevin .... 443-885-3527 206 A
kevin.banks@morgan.edu
BANKS, Lezlie .... 706-855-8233.. 93 B
BANKS, Lucretia .... 252-335-3228 350 A
lrbanks@ecsu.edu
BANKS, Lynne .... 814-472-3002 409 G
lbanks@francis.edu
BANKS, M. Katherine .... 979-845-7203 459 C
k-banks@tamu.edu
BANKS, Mary .... 239-590-1172 109 C
mbanks@fgcu.edu
BANKS, McRae .... 336-334-5338 351 D
mcbanks@uncg.edu
BANKS, Melissa .... 912-443-3388 125 D
mbanks@savannahtech.edu
BANKS, Michael .... 816-604-6544 262 G
michael.banks@mcckc.edu
BANKS, Nannette .... 773-947-6322 145 A
nbanks@mccormick.edu
BANKS, Pat .... 770-426-2823 122 F
pbanks@life.edu
BANKS, Roman .... 225-771-5930 195 K
roman_banks@subr.edu
BANKS, JR., Roman .... 225-771-2435 195 J
roman_banks@subr.edu
BANKS, Sharon, S .... 304-766-3078 505 A
banksss@wvstateu.edu
BANKS, Steve .... 615-794-4254 435 G
sbanks@omorecollege.edu
BANKS, Traci .... 201-692-7304 286 B
traci161_banks@fdu.edu
BANKS, Wayne .... 870-574-4493.. 21 G
wbanks@sautech.edu
BANKS, William .... 856-227-7200 284 E
wbanks@camdencc.edu
BANKS, Willie .... 812-237-8111 159 C
willie.banks@indstate.edu
BANKS-DEAVER,
Yolanda, E .... 919-530-6204 350 D
ybanks@nccu.edu
BANKS-SANTILLI, Linda 617-879-2371 226 A
lsantilli@wheelock.edu
BANKSTON, Patrick .... 219-980-6562 160 C
pbanks@iun.edu
BANNAN, Denise, A .... 810-766-4272 227 E
denise.bannan@baker.edu
BANNISTER, Darlene ..... 830-792-7357 456 D
bannistr@schreiner.edu
BANNISTER, Justin .... 575-646-5981 295 B
jbannist@nmsu.edu
BANNISTER, Mark .... 785-628-5339 177 D
markbannister@fhsu.edu
BANNON, Douglas, F .... 319-398-5517 171 F
doug.bannon@kirkwood.cc.ia.us

BARNARD, Cindy .... 865-573-4517 432 H
cbarnard@johnsonu.edu
BARNARD, DeeDee .... 828-286-3636 344 A
ddbarnard@isothermal.edu
BARNARD, Kathy .... 208-885-7372 132 I
kathybarnard@uidaho.edu
BARNARD, Laura .... 440-525-7096 364 D
lbarnard@lakelandcc.edu
BARNARD, Mimi .... 615-460-8397 430 D
mimi.barnard@belmont.edu
BARNARD, Susan .... 201-447-7938 283 I
sbarnard@bergen.edu
BARNDS, W. Kent .... 309-794-7314 133 G
wkentbarnds@augustana.edu
BARNES, Andre .... 415-239-3151.. 37 H
abarnes@ccsf.edu
BARNES, Andrew .... 850-973-1604 104 D
barnesa@nfcc.edu
BARNES, Andrew .... 718-636-3570 320 D
awbarnes@pratt.edu
BARNES, April .... 859-622-1515 184 F
april.barnes@eku.edu
BARNES, Bradley .... 205-934-4073.... 8 B
bbarnes1@uab.edu
BARNES, Brian, M .... 907-474-7649.. 10 B
bmbarnes@alaska.edu
BARNES, Cheryl .... 304-384-6303 503 P
cbarnes@concord.edu
BARNES, Cindy .... 480-732-7093.. 13 E
cindy.barnes@cgc.edu
BARNES, David .... 251-981-3771.... 5 A
david.barnes@columbiasouthern.edu
BARNES, Desiree .... 302-857-6001.. 90 B
dbarnes@desu.edu
BARNES, Dewayne .... 415-703-9573.. 28 K
dbarnes@cca.edu
BARNES, Donna .... 402-557-7184 273 E
dobarnes@bellevue.edu
BARNES, Elizabeth, A .... 248-689-8282 238 F
bbarnes@walshcollege.edu
BARNES, Emanuel .... 601-877-6385 251 G
ebarnes@alcorn.edu
BARNES, Fatima .... 202-884-1723.. 92 C
fatima.barnes@howard.edu
BARNES, III, James, H . 651-638-6230 240 J
j-barnes@bethel.edu
BARNES, Jeffrey .... 951-552-8639.. 28 G
jbarnes@calbaptist.edu
BARNES, Jimmy .... 575-624-8021 295 A
jimmyb@nmmi.edu
BARNES, Joanne .... 765-677-2090 161 C
joanne.barnes@indwes.edu
BARNES, John .... 831-459-2973.. 70 C
barnes@ucsc.edu
BARNES, Julianna .... 619-660-4221.. 44 L
julianna.barnes@gcccd.edu
BARNES, Karen .... 601-925-3241 254 B
misscoll@bkstr.com
BARNES, Katharine, T .... 401-863-1914 415 K
katharine_barnes@brown.edu
BARNES, Katherine .... 304-345-2820 505 D
kbarnes@wvjc.edu
BARNES, Kathleen .... 978-232-2292 214 G
kbarnes@endicott.edu
BARNES, Kelly .... 706-295-6842 120 C
kbarnes@gntc.edu
BARNES, Kenneth, J ...... 716-851-1157 307 I
barnesk@ecc.edu
BARNES, Kerry .... 413-205-3703 210 E
kerry.barnes@aic.edu
BARNES, Kimberly .... 989-386-6622 234 B
kbarnes@midmich.edu
BARNES, Lori .... 941-727-2273 112 B
lbarnes@schnursing.edu
BARNES, Lynn .... 979-458-0971 459 C
lbarnes@tamu.edu
BARNES, M. Craig .... 609-497-7800 288 E
president@ptsem.edu
BARNES, Marc .... 504-816-4359 191 E
mbarnes@dillard.edu
BARNES, Mark .... 217-443-8871 137 B
mbarnes@dacc.edu
BARNES, Melissa .... 757-823-8131 483 F
mbarnes@nsu.edu
BARNES, Melody, C .... 212-998-1212 318 D
melody.barnes@nyu.edu
BARNES, Nancy .... 909-667-4470.. 37 J
nbarnes@claremontlincoln.edu
BARNES, Nicolas .... 540-986-1800 182 K
nbarnes@national-college.edu
BARNES, Nicole .... 724-287-8711 390 J
nicole.barnes@bc3.edu
BARNES, Nicole .... 281-478-3628 455 L
nicole.barnes@sjcd.edu
BARNES, Randy .... 619-388-3489.. 60 C
rbarnes@sdccd.edu
BARNES, Rebecca .... 315-781-3341 310 C
barnes@hws.edu
BARNES, Rita .... 931-372-3797 438 F
ritabarnes@tntech.edu
BARNES, Robert .... 404-527-4520 117 C
BARNES, Russell .... 713-348-4350 455 F
rcb@rice.edu
BARNES, Saralyn .... 702-968-1611 280 B
sbarnes@roseman.edu
BARNES, Scott .... 541-737-0123 385 F
BARNES, Scott, F .... 724-847-6787 395 J
sfbarnes@geneva.edu
BARNES, Shelly .... 252-527-6223 344 D
swbarnes16@lenoircc.edu
BARNES, Solita, K .... 670-237-6812 520 D
solita.barnes@marianas.edu
BARNES, Susan .... 405-878-5620 379 G
sjbarnes@stgregorys.edu
BARNES, Ted .... 254-295-4678 466 A
tbarnes@umhb.edu
BARNES, Travis .... 218-755-3988 244 B
tbarnes@bemidjistate.edu
BARNES-RHOADES,
Dianne .... 252-536-7239 343 F
dbarnes-rhoades128@halifaxcc.edu
BARNES WHYTE, Susan 503-883-2517 383 H
swhyte@linfield.edu
BARNET, John .... 914-961-8313 323 H
jbarnet@svots.edu
BARNETT, Alan .... 660-359-3948 264 H
abarnett@mail.ncmissouri.edu
BARNETT, Alan .... 731-286-3259 437 A
barnett@dscc.edu
BARNETT, Amy .... 765-998-5565 164 C
ambarnett@tayloru.edu
BARNETT, Beth .... 201-684-7529 289 C
bbarnett@ramapo.edu
BARNETT, Brad .... 540-568-7820 481 I
barnetbd@jmu.edu
BARNETT, Brooke .... 336-278-5659 337 G
bbarnett@elon.edu
BARNETT, Bryant .... 828-227-7303 352 C
barnett@wcu.edu
BARNETT, Charles .... 662-246-6304 254 C
cbarnett@msdelta.edu
BARNETT, David .... 630-960-7927 137 D
dbarnett@devry.edu
BARNETT, David, L .... 770-531-3116 116 F
dlbarnett@brenau.edu
BARNETT, Dawn .... 610-902-1071 391 B
dawn.barnett@cabrini.edu
BARNETT, Erin .... 906-487-7324 230 B
erin.barnett@finlandia.edu
BARNETT, Gina .... 415-565-4614.. 68 I
barnettg@uchastings.edu
BARNETT, Holly .... 614-837-4088 373 C
barnetth@valorcollege.edu
BARNETT, Jahnae, H ...... 800-995-3159 270 D
jahnae.barnett@williamwoods.edu
BARNETT, Jeffrey .... 410-617-2608 205 A
jbarnett@loyola.edu
BARNETT, Jenifer .... 707-664-3102.. 35 A
jenifer.barnett@sonoma.edu
BARNETT, Kimberly .... 719-502-2012.. 81 H
kimberly.barnett@ppcc.edu
BARNETT, Kristine .... 413-565-1000 211 C
kbarnett@baypath.edu
BARNETT, LaVerne .... 256-726-8328.... 6 E
lbarnett@oakwood.edu
BARNETT, Lenice .... 954-486-7728 112 N
registrar@uftl.edu
BARNETT, Martha .... 731-881-7052 440 B
mbarne37@utm.edu
BARNETT, Mike .... 785-628-4251 177 D
mbarnett@fhsu.edu
BARNETT, Monica .... 918-444-2230 376 G
barnettm@nsuok.edu
BARNETT, Randy .... 580-774-6051 380 B
randy.barnett@swosu.edu
BARNETT, Robert .... 810-766-6878 238 B
rbarnett@umflint.edu
BARNETT-PARKER,
Janie .... 425-640-1787 494 E
jbarnett@edcc.edu
BARNETTE, Andrew .... 724-925-4047 414 E
barnettea@westmoreland.edu
BARNETTE, Jeffrey .... 270-686-4359 183 J
jeffrey.barnette@brescia.edu
BARNETTE, Randy .... 708-456-0300 153 E
randybarnette@triton.edu
BARNETTE, Todd .... 864-656-4926 419 F
tebarne@clemson.edu
BARNETTE, Vivian, D .... 336-334-7727 350 C
vdbarnet@ncat.edu
BARNEY, Matthew, S .... 518-255-5628 328 C
barneyms@cobleskill.edu
BARNEY, Patti .... 954-201-7520.. 96 A
pbarney@broward.edu
BARNEY, Rick .... 502-585-9911 189 B
rbarney@spalding.edu
BARNEY, Tammy .... 504-286-5343 195 L
tbarney@suno.edu
BARNHARDT,
Carmen, N .... 714-449-7423.. 51 A
cbarnhardt@ketchum.edu
BARNHARDT, Denise .... 326-249-8186 342 F
dsbarnh@davidsonccc.edu
BARNHARDT, Doryann .. 410-778-7214 210 A
dbarnhardt2@washcoll.edu
BARNHARDT, Wendy .... 704-216-3700 346 C
wendy.barnhardt@rccc.edu
BARNHART, Amy .... 336-744-0900 336 D
ccc@outfitters4.com
BARNHART, Amy .... 937-775-5721 374 B
amy.barnhart@wright.edu
BARNHART, Bruce .... 724-938-4407 405 F
barnhart@calu.edu
BARNHART, Cynthia ...... 617-253-9742 221 C
BARNHART, Mitch, S .... 859-257-8015 190 B
mbarn@email.uky.edu
BARNHART, Ross .... 719-549-3365.. 81 M
ross.barnhart@pueblocc.edu
BARNHART, Terry, L ..... 671-735-5571 519 H
terry.barnhart@guamcc.edu
BARNHART, Wendy .... 706-385-1000 124 F
wendy.barnhart@point.edu
BARNHILL, Anita .... 606-589-2145 187 B
anita.barnhill@kctcs.edu
BARNHILL, Carol .... 870-972-2028.. 18 A
cbarnhil@astate.edu
BARNHILL, John .... 850-644-1224 110 A
jbarnhill@admin.fsu.edu
BARNHILL, Rob, M .... 262-243-5700 507 C
rob.barnhill@cuw.edu
BARNHILL, Tapp .... 802-254-6370 477 B
stb08170@ccv.vsc.edu
BARNHOUSE, Richard ... 941-752-5301 108 P
barnhr@scf.edu
BARNUM,
Chrisopher, C .... 563-333-6157 173 A
barnumchristopherc@sau.edu
BARNUM, David, L .... 402-280-2307 274 D
davidbarnum@creighton.edu
BARNUM, Martin .... 847-970-4843 154 H
mbarnum@usml.edu
BARNWELL, James .... 912-358-3004 125 C
barnwellj@savannahstate.edu
BARNWELL, Jon .... 504-214-4098 196 D
jon@tulane.edu
BARNWELL, Michael ..... 716-286-8637 318 F
barnwell@niagara.edu
BARNWELL, Vollie .... 828-251-6700 351 A
vbarnwel@unca.edu
BARON, Adam .... 248-218-2040 236 C
BARON, Bruce .... 909-382-4091.. 59 G
bbaron@sbccd.cc.ca.us
BARON, Melissa, M .... 724-946-7927 414 C
baronmm@westminster.edu
BARON, Sara .... 412-396-6130 394 D
barons1@duq.edu
BARONAS, James .... 410-328-8792 207 H
jbaro001@umaryland.edu
BARONE, Ann, E .... 401-865-2105 416 E
aebarone@providence.edu
BARONE, OSF,
Ann Carmen .... 419-824-3703 364 G
acarmen@lourdes.edu
BARONE, Joseph .... 848-445-6814 290 C
jbarone@rci.rutgers.edu
BARONE, Matthew .... 802-257-4333 475 D
mbarone@marlboro.edu
BARONE, Nancy .... 956-296-1441 468 A
nancy.barone@utrgv.edu
BARONI, Samiah, E .... 301-243-2118 518 C
samiah.baroni@dodiis.mil
BARONIO, Lisa, B .... 319-273-2487 167 A
lisa.baronio@uni.edu
BAROODY, Fadi, N .... 843-349-2058 420 A
fadi@coastal.edu
BAROUDI, George .... 516-299-3790 313 C
george.baroudi@liu.edu
BARQUINERO,
James, M .... 203-365-4763.. 88 C
barquineroj@sacredheart.edu
BARR, Carol, A .... 413-545-6330 216 H
cbarr@provost.umass.edu
BARR, Chris .... 618-634-3349 151 G
chrisb@shawneecc.edu
BARR, Cindy .... 704-645-4584 336 G
clbarr14@catawba.edu
BARR, Elizabeth .... 352-588-8824 106 N
elizabeth.barr@saintleo.edu
BARR, Jared, M .... 813-988-5131.. 99 D
barrj@floridacollege.edu
BARR, Jason .... 803-536-8749 423 G
jbarr2@scsu.edu
BARR, K. Jill .... 410-455-1337 208 A
jbarr@umbc.edu
BARR, Kevin .... 812-237-3600 159 C
kevin.barr@indstate.edu
BARR, Krispin, W .... 336-721-2627 348 H
krispin.barr@salem.edu
BARR, Lisa .... 661-291-3411.. 29 F
lbarr@calarts.edu
BARR, Mary .... 765-285-1569 156 C
mbarr@bsu.edu
BARR, Michael, S .... 734-763-2258 237 I
BARR, Rick .... 903-886-5744 459 E
rick.barr@tamuc.edu
BARR, Robin .... 386-506-4473.. 97 I
barrr@daytonastate.edu
BARR, Sarah .... 402-465-2193 276 E
sbarr@nebrwesleyan.edu
BARR, Victor .... 865-974-2196 439 I
vbarr@utk.edu
BARR-GILLESPIE, Ann ... 503-352-7200 385 I
barr-gillespie@pacificu.edu
BARRACK, Keith, D .... 973-655-4213 287 D
barrackk@mail.montclair.edu
BARRACKS, Jana, T ...... 641-422-4269 172 C
barrajan@niacc.edu
BARRACLOUGH, Diana . 610-499-4153 414 F
dbarraclough@widener.edu
BARRACLOUGH,
Jessica .... 785-670-1723 182 D
jessica.barraclough@washburn.edu
BARRAL, Jose, M .... 409-747-2180 469 C
jmbarral@utmb.edu
BARRALE, Ralph .... 636-227-2100 262 A
BARRAR, Elena .... 610-558-5516 402 G
barrare@neumann.edu
BARRAS, Brittney .... 504-278-6427 193 B
bbarras@nunez.edu
BARRAS, Janet .... 678-359-5022 121 B
janetb@gordonstate.edu
BARRAZA, Ana Lilia .... 562-907-4912.. 75 A
abarraza@whittier.edu
BARREDO, Ronald .... 615-963-5924 438 E
rbarredo@tnstate.edu
BARREE, Zita, M .... 434-223-6265 481 D
zbarree@hsc.edu
BARRENTINE, Debra, A . 256-228-6001.... 3 B
barrentined@nacc.edu
BARRENTINE, Jim .... 719-502-2148.. 81 H
jim.barrentine@ppcc.edu
BARRENTINE, Roger, A . 636-481-3106 261 B
rbarrent@jeffco.edu
BARRERA, Adriana, D ... 213-891-2081.. 48 K
barrerad@email.laccd.edu
BARRERA, Rosa, M .... 316-284-5241 175 F
rbarrera@bethelks.edu
BARRESE, Anthony .... 201-216-8768 291 G
anthony.barrese@stevens.edu
BARRESI, JR., Joseph .. 401-598-1000 416 C
jbarresi@jwu.edu
BARRESI, Lisa .... 859-572-6145 188 E
barresi@nku.edu
BARRETO, Daniel .... 210-486-0335 442 A
dbarretoalderr@alamo.edu
BARRETO, Myriam .... 787-265-3863 528 C
aeconomica@uprm.edu
BARRETO, Wanda .... 787-758-2480 528 D
wanda.barreto@upr.edu
BARRETT, Audra .... 972-860-8261 447 H
audrabarrett@dcccd.edu
BARRETT, Brian, D .... 817-515-6960 458 B
brian.barrett@tccd.edu
BARRETT, Carolyn .... 904-256-7092 102 B
cbarret@ju.edu
BARRETT, David .... 714-816-0366.. 67 J
david.barrett@trident.edu
BARRETT, Dustin .... 912-650-6250 125 H
dbarrett@southuniversity.edu
BARRETT, Gayle .... 860-343-5897.. 86 A
gbarrett@mxcc.edu
BARRETT, Ian .... 409-772-8692 469 C
icbarret@utmb.edu
BARRETT, James .... 920-924-6431 514 D
jbarrett8@morainepark.edu
BARRETT, James, F .... 330-325-6274 366 F
jbarrett1@neomed.edu
BARRETT, Jeannie .... 706-754-7704 123 G
jbarrett@northgatech.edu
BARRETT, Jennifer .... 785-833-4398 179 C
jennifer.barrett@kwu.edu
BARRETT, Jim .... 715-346-2727 511 F
jimbarrett@uwsp.edu
BARRETT, Jim .... 715-346-4093 511 F
jbarrett@uwsp.edu
BARRETT, Joan .... 417-447-6914 264 K
barrettj@otc.edu
BARRETT, Karinda .... 850-201-6209 112 C
barrettk@tcc.fl.edu
BARRETT, Kimberly .... 920-832-7451 507 L
kimberly.a.barrett@lawrence.edu

BARUA, Susamma .... 657-278-3362 .. 32 B
sbarua@fullerton.edu
BARWICK, Daniel, W .... 620-331-4100 178 E
dbarwick@indycc.edu
BARWINCZAK, Lisa .... 315-568-3311 317 A
lbarwinczak@nycc.edu
BARZACCHINI, Mike .... 847-925-6510 139 B
mbarzacc@harpercollege.edu
BARZENSKY, Jon .... 570-348-6241 401 B
barzensky@marywood.edu
BASALA, Nissim .... 732-370-1560 283 G
BASCH, Hersch .... 718-438-1002 315 A
BASCO, Chris .... 405-224-3140 381 B
cbasco@usao.edu
BASCO, Jared .... 202-884-9504 .. 93 C
bascoj@trinitydc.edu
BASCOM, Shawn .... 208-282-5304 132 B
bascshaw@isu.edu
BASER, Ric .... 210-486-4908 441 E
rbaser@alamo.edu
BASER, Ric, N .... 210-486-4900 441 G
rbaser@alamo.edu
BASFORD, Jerry, L .... 801-581-7793 472 P
jbasford@sa.utah.edu
BASH, Cassaundra .... 574-936-8898 155 L
cassaundra.bash@ancilla.edu
BASH, Lee .... 641-784-5072 169 D
bash@graceland.edu
BASHANT, Wendy .... 619-239-0391 .. 35 C
wbashant@cwsl.edu
BASHARA, Teri .... 318-678-6000 192 C
tbashara@bpcc.edu
BASHAW, Ed .... 620-341-5274 177 B
ebashaw@emporia.edu
BASHET, Abuzafar, M .... 972-860-7158 447 I
azbashet@dcccd.edu
BASHWINER, Bruce .... 585-273-5798 332 E
bruce.bashwiner@rochester.edu
BASIE, John, D .... 864-379-8873 421 E
basie@erskine.edu
BASIL, Meredith .... 657-278-3341 .. 32 B
mbasil@fullerton.edu
BASILE, Carole .... 602-543-6352 .. 10 K
carole.basile@asu.edu
BASILE, Elizabeth .... 718-368-4539 303 A
ebasile@kbcc.cuny.edu
BASILEO, Paul .... 631-451-4854 330 C
basilep@sunysuffolk.edu
BASILIO, Shelle .... 315-781-3880 310 C
basilio@hws.edu
BASINGER, David .... 585-594-6550 321 C
basingerd@roberts.edu
BASINGER, Randall, G .. 717-796-5375 401 L
rbasinge@messiah.edu
BASINSKI, Judith, B .... 716-878-4611 326 E
basinsjb@buffalostate.edu
BASIRATMAND,
Mehran .... 561-297-0230 109 B
mehran@fau.edu
BASKARAN, Christiana .. 523-953-4000 .. 49 A
baskarc@lacitycollege.edu
BASKEL, Elise .... 719-598-0200 .. 79 B
ebaskel@coloradotech.edu
BASKER, Judy .... 541-956-7291 386 G
jbasker@roguecc.edu
BASKETTE, Shawna .... 562-860-2451 .. 36 A
sbaskette@cerritos.edu
BASKI, Alison .... 909-869-3600 .. 31 A
aabaski@cpp.edu
BASKIN, Richard .... 678-359-5018 121 B
rbaskin@gordonstate.edu
BASKO, Aaron, M .... 410-543-6161 209 B
ambasko@salisbury.edu
BASLER, Julie .... 303-369-5151 .. 81 L
julie.basler@plattcolorado.edu
BASLEY, Carolyn .... 312-935-4556 149 K
cbasley@robertmorris.edu
BASNEY, Janet .... 541-956-7097 386 G
jfiano@roguecc.edu
BASOM, Richard .... 717-361-4762 394 F
basomr@etown.edu
BASS, Ashley .... 334-222-6591 .... 2 H
abass@lbwcc.edu
BASS, Brenda, L .... 319-273-2221 167 A
brenda.bass@uni.edu
BASS, Charles .... 619-260-4819 .. 71 J
charlesb@sandiego.edu
BASS, Donna .... 334-222-6591 .... 2 H
dbass@lbwcc.edu
BASS, Gordon .... 904-357-8891 100 F
gbass@fscj.edu
BASS, Inga .... 601-484-8823 253 G
ibass@meridiancc.edu
BASS, Jimmy .... 910-962-4292 352 A
bassj@uncw.edu
BASS, John, R .... 773-298-3419 151 C
bass@sxu.edu
BASS, Leonard, C .... 407-582-2745 113 F
lbass11@valenciacollege.edu
BASS, Mary, T .... 252-823-5166 343 A
bassm@edgecombe.edu
BASS, Randall .... 202-687-6400 .. 92 B
bassr@georgetown.edu
BASS, Scott, A .... 202-885-2127 .. 91 C
provost@american.edu
BASS, Vanessa, L .... 336-322-2127 345 D
vanessa.bass@piedmontcc.edu
BASS KEER, Wendy .... 818-712-2619 .. 49 D
basskew@piercecollege.edu
BASSETT, Baylor .... 678-839-6582 127 F
bbassett@westga.edu
BASSETT, Claire, M .... 713-798-4710 444 A
bassett@bcm.edu
BASSETT, Heidi, M .... 972-860-7255 447 I
hbassett@dcccd.edu
BASSETT, Jill .... 305-877-1967 109 D
jill.bassett@fiu.edu
BASSETT, Jill .... 603-899-4178 281 D
bassettj@franklinpierce.edu
BASSETT, John .... 309-649-6303 152 G
john.bassett@src.edu
BASSETT, Matthew, D .... 315-445-4450 312 F
bassetmd@lemoyne.edu
BASSETT, Robert .... 714-997-6715 .. 36 G
bassett@chapman.edu
BASSETT, Susan .... 607-274-3209 311 D
sbassett@ithaca.edu
BASSETTE-FARONE,
Lynda, D .... 607-436-2407 325 E
lynda.bassette-farone@oneonta.edu
BASSETTI, Mimi .... 215-572-2941 389 D
bassetti@arcadia.edu
BASSHAM, Mia, W .... 570-740-0420 400 F
mbassham@luzerne.edu
BASSI-COOK, Teresa .... 724-838-4295 410 E
tbassicook@setonhill.edu
BASSO, Sharon .... 909-621-8485 .. 38 A
sharon.basso@cmc.edu
BAST, Carrie, L .... 330-325-6718 366 F
cbast@neomed.edu
BAST, EJ .... 269-488-4755 231 G
ebast@kvcc.edu
BASTECKI-PEREZ,
Victoria .... 215-641-6482 402 A
vbasteck@mc3.edu
BASTIAN, Joni .... 618-537-6555 145 C
jjbastian@mckendree.edu
BASTIAN, Kayla .... 605-773-3455 428 D
kayla.bastian@sdbor.edu
BASTIN, Judy .... 316-322-3235 175 I
jbastin@butlercc.edu
BASTINE, Michael .... 661-362-3111 .. 39 C
michael.bastine@canyons.edu
BASTON, Michael, A .... 845-574-4000 321 F
BASU, Andra, M .... 610-799-1186 400 A
abasu@lccc.edu
BASUALDO, Maria .... 607-778-5030 326 C
basualdomi@sunybroome.edu
BATA, Anthony .... 319-399-8000 167 F
abata@coe.edu
BATALAMA, Stella .... 561-297-3426 109 B
BATCHELDER, Chris .... 405-744-5368 377 F
chris.batchelder@okstate.edu
BATCHELDER, Joseph .... 518-255-5620 328 C
batchejb@cobleskill.edu
BATCHELDER, Kathy .... 330-972-8944 371 D
ksbatch@uakron.edu
BATCHELDER, Rick .... 518-562-4106 304 C
rick.batchelder@clinton.edu
BATCHELLER, Tamara .... 313-578-0346 237 F
batchets@udmercy.edu
BATCHELOR, Donna, L .. 252-451-8221 345 B
dlbatchelor965@nashcc.edu
BATCHELOR, Gerald .... 901-333-4673 438 B
gbatchelor@southwest.tn.edu
BATCHELOR, Grady .... 304-724-3700 501 D
gbatchelor@apus.edu
BATCHELOR, Susan .... 618-545-3033 142 D
sbatchelor@kaskaskia.edu
BATCHER, Shelly .... 770-426-2653 122 F
sbatcher@life.edu
BATE, Jeff, B .... 801-375-5125 472 F
jbate@rmuohp.edu
BATE, Jennifer .... 201-216-9901 285 F
jennifer.bate@eicollege.edu
BATE, Joel, C .... 208-732-6836 131 I
jbate@csi.edu
BATEMAN, Bradley, W .. 434-947-8140 484 B
bbateman@randolphcollege.edu
BATEMAN, David .... 870-230-5150 .. 19 H
batemad@hsu.edu
BATEMAN, Douglas, R .. 318-678-6000 192 C
rbateman@bpcc.edu
BATEMAN, Heather .... 517-787-0800 231 E
batemanheathera@jccmi.edu
BATEMAN, Jamie .... 863-784-7181 108 B
jamie.bateman@southflorida.edu
BATEMAN, Joyce .... 417-447-6973 264 K
batemanj@otc.edu
BATEMAN, Mathew .... 814-866-8148 399 C
mbateman@lecom.edu
BATEMAN, Scott .... 315-792-7100 330 A
sbateman@sunypoly.edu
BATES, Anthony .... 708-235-7431 138 H
abates99@govst.edu
BATES, Aryana .... 206-934-3615 497 H
aryana.bates@seattlecolleges.edu
BATES, Brent .... 660-596-7252 267 E
bbates@sfccmo.edu
BATES, Brian .... 408-924-6518 .. 34 D
brian.bates@sjsu.edu
BATES, Christin .... 989-275-5000 232 E
christin.bates@kirtland.edu
BATES, Damien .... 928-317-5892 .. 11 B
damien.bates@azwestern.edu
BATES, Doug .... 931-372-3408 438 F
dbates@tntech.edu
BATES, Jeffrey .... 301-736-3631 205 B
jbates@msbbcs.edu
BATES, Jennifer .... 606-218-5253 190 E
jenniferbates@upike.edu
BATES, Joan .... 423-478-6205 436 G
jbates@clevelandstatecc.edu
BATES, Julie .... 501-660-1002 .. 17 L
jbates@asusystem.edu
BATES, Kay .... 662-472-9023 253 C
kbates@holmescc.edu
BATES, Kristen .... 336-757-3396 343 C
kbates@forsythtech.edu
BATES, Larry .... 865-694-6404 437 F
lbates@pstcc.edu
BATES, Lynette .... 909-558-4561 .. 48 H
lbates@llu.edu
BATES, Lynette .... 719-846-5559 .. 82 L
lynette.bates@trinidadstaet.edu
BATES, Mary Lou, W .... 518-580-5588 324 D
mbates@skidmore.edu
BATES, Michael .... 847-925-6304 139 B
mbates@harpercollege.edu
BATES, Michele .... 575-624-8096 295 A
bates@nmmi.edu
BATES, Patrick, M .... 585-292-2820 315 L
pbates@monroecc.edu
BATES, Reid .... 225-578-2457 193 M
rbates@lsu.edu
BATES, Ren .... 859-246-4605 185 G
ren.bates@kctcs.edu
BATES, Starnell .... 803-822-3235 422 D
batess@midlandstech.edu
BATES, Suzanne .... 314-434-4044 259 B
suzanne.bates@covenantseminary.edu
BATES, Suzanne .... 330-263-2365 360 A
sbates@wooster.edu
BATES, Tierney, J .... 919-530-6303 350 D
tbates10@nccu.edu
BATES, Trevor .... 419-251-8968 365 C
trevor.bates@mercycollege.edu
BATES, Wendy .... 707-476-4140 .. 39 F
wendy-bates@redwoods.edu
BATES, Winfrey .... 270-858-6501 186 G
winfrey.bates@kctcs.edu
BATES MOCK, Diana .... 559-453-5505 .. 43 J
diana.mock@fresno.edu
BATES-REESE, Fannie .... 205-391-2331 .... 3 E
freese@sheltonstate.edu
BATESON, Carrie .... 918-595-7871 380 D
carrie.bateson@tulsacc.edu
BATH, Michael, J .... 906-227-2151 235 A
mbath@nmu.edu
BATIC, Marjorie .... 317-955-6150 162 R
mbatic@marian.edu
BATIE, Larry .... 205-929-1446 .... 6 D
lbatie@miles.edu
BATISTA, Adrian .... 440-775-8472 367 B
adrian.batista@oberlin.edu
BATISTA, Angela .... 802-860-2734 474 G
abatista@champlain.edu
BATISTA, Jorge .... 347-964-8600 299 L
jbatista@boricuacollege.edu
BATISTA, Mari .... 787-728-1515 529 B
mbatista@sagrado.edu
BATISTA-SANTIAGO,
Gerardo .... 787-993-8950 527 G
gerardo.batista@upr.edu
BATISTE, Tenesha .... 228-497-7800 254 D
tenesha.batiste@mgccc.edu
BATSON, Marie .... 251-442-2370 .... 8 D
mbatson@umobile.edu
BATSON, Rebecca .... 302-857-7887 .. 90 B
rbatson@desu.edu
BATSON, Robert .... 937-775-2869 374 B
robert.batson@wright.edu
BATSON, Trice .... 269-488-4794 231 G
tbatson@kvcc.edu
BATT, Marylou .... 617-349-8564 216 D
mbatt@lesley.edu
BATTAGLIA, Andrea .... 417-873-7353 259 G
abattaglia@drury.edu
BATTAGLIA, Janet, M .... 540-464-7213 490 E
battagliajm@vmi.edu
BATTAGLINO, JR.,
John .... 617-353-3511 212 G
jbattag@bu.edu
BATTAGLINO, Lisa .... 508-531-1347 217 D
lbattaglino@bridgew.edu
BATTELL, Victoria, L .... 518-438-3111 314 B
vbattell@mariacollege.edu
BATTEN, James .... 903-927-3211 471 B
jbatten@wileyc.edu
BATTEN, Melissa .... 843-349-5228 421 L
melissa.batten@hgtc.edu
BATTEN-MICKENS,
Melodye .... 301-546-0656 206 E
mbatte10373@pgcc.edu
BATTIATA, Russell .... 941-355-9080 .. 97 M
admissions@ewcollege.org
BATTIATA, Russell .... 941-355-9080 .. 97 M
rbattiata@ewcollege.org
BATTINKOFF, Robert .... 989-686-9145 229 J
robertbattinkoff@delta.edu
BATTISTA, Joe, N .... 407-582-6622 113 F
jbattista@valenciacollege.edu
BATTISTA, Marc .... 847-214-7959 138 B
mbattista@elgin.edu
BATTISTA, Vince .... 312-567-8625 140 I
vbattista@iit.edu
BATTISTE, Jacques .... 504-520-7490 198 D
jbattis2@xula.edu
BATTISTE, Leilani .... 415-241-2294 .. 37 H
lbattist@ccsf.edu
BATTISTELLA, Diane .... 630-829-6415 133 I
dbatistella@ben.edu
BATTISTI, Francis .... 607-778-5138 326 C
battistifl@sunybroome.edu
BATTLE, Bernadette .... 434-949-1063 489 E
bernadette.battle@southside.edu
BATTLE, Bruce .... 503-491-7055 384 D
bruce.battle@mhcc.edu
BATTLE, Donna .... 919-760-8346 339 H
battledo@meredith.edu
BATTLE, Lydée .... 301-891-4128 209 E
lbattle@wau.edu
BATTLE-BROWN,
LaToya .... 973-353-1374 290 D
lbbrown@rutgers.edu
BATTLES, Denise, A .... 585-245-5501 327 B
battles@geneseo.edu
BATTLES, Linnea .... 251-380-2240 .... 7 B
lbattles@shc.edu
BATTRAW, Danny .... 928-428-8605 .. 12 I
danny.battraw@eac.edu
BATTSON, Harry .... 254-968-1620 459 A
battson@tarleton.edu
BATTTLE, Kiana .... 708-608-4360 146 C
battlek@morainevalley.edu
BATTURS, Beth Anne .... 410-777-7352 202 D
babatturs@aacc.edu
BATTY, Philip .... 616-331-8650 230 G
battyp@gvsu.edu
BATTY-HERBERT,
Kimberly .... 928-226-4362 .. 12 B
kimberly.batty-herbert@coconino.edu
BATWAY, Jody .... 734-432-5744 233 C
jbatway@madonna.edu
BATZER, Caren .... 718-990-6366 322 F
batzerc@stjohns.edu
BAUCHER, Gery .... 252-638-7283 342 E
baucherg@cravencc.edu
BAUCOM, Ian .... 434-924-4611 486 H
ibb4n@virginia.edu
BAUDRY, Michel .... 909-706-8271 .. 74 G
mbaudry@westernu.edu
BAUDRY YOUNG,
Rebecca .... 513-529-3438 365 I
baudryrm@miamioh.edu
BAUER, Amanda .... 661-763-7853 .. 67 A
abauer@taftcollege.edu
BAUER, C. Jon .... 636-584-6501 259 L
jon.bauer@eastcentral.edu
BAUER, Cortney, A .... 402-280-3533 274 D
cortneybauer@creighton.edu
BAUER, Cynthia, M .... 414-288-7343 508 C
cindy.bauer@marquette.edu
BAUER, Daniel, C .... 314-367-8700 266 D
daniel.bauer@stlcop.edu
BAUER, Danny .... 724-738-2773 407 C
dan.bauer@sru.edu
BAUER, David .... 859-858-3581 183 C
BAUER, Denise .... 845-451-1345 306 D
denise.bauer@culinary.edu

BAUER, Jackie 320-308-5486 247 F jbauer@sctcc.edu
BAUER, James 863-680-4186 100 D jbauer@flsouthern.edu
BAUER, James, R 503-370-6112 388 D jbauer@willamette.edu
BAUER, Jason, K 515-263-2887 169 E jbauer@grandview.edu
BAUER, Jeff 740-351-3472 369 L jbauer@shawnee.edu
BAUER, Jeffrey, C 513-732-5209 371 G jeff.bauer@uc.edu
BAUER, Jeremi 203-596-8359 87 H jebauer@post.edu
BAUER, Jody 215-751-8060 393 A jbauer@ccp.edu
BAUER, Judy, A 605-642-6111 428 F judy.bauer@bhsu.edu
BAUER, Julie 662-562-3274 255 C
BAUER, Kara 619-594-0489 34 B kbauer@mail.sdsu.edu
BAUER, Kelli 620-252-7180 176 K bauer.kelli@coffeyville.edu
BAUER, Kent 970-542-3111 81 A kent.bauer@morgancc.edu
BAUER, Mark 518-580-5996 324 D mbauer@skidmore.edu
BAUER, Mark, D 507-354-8221 243 C bauermd@mlc-wels.edu
BAUER, Mary 718-405-3233 304 H mary.bauer@mountsaintvincent.edu
BAUER, Mary Claire 518-629-7309 310 G m.bauer@hvcc.edu
BAUER, Matt 919-735-5151 347 E mattb@waynecc.edu
BAUER, Nancy 617-627-4230 225 A nancy.bauer@tufts.edu
BAUER, Patrick 847-925-6827 139 B pbauer@harpercollege.edu
BAUER, Scott 951-222-8000 58 H scott.bauer@rcc.edu
BAUER, Stacy 605-229-8405 427 J stacy.bauer@presentation.edu
BAUER, Thomas, G 805-565-6043 74 I tbauer@westmont.edu
BAUER, Tom 650-358-6782 61 Q bauert@smccd.edu
BAUER, Warren, K 515-574-1120 170 C bauer@iowacentral.edu
BAUERLE, Cynthia 540-568-3508 481 I bauerlcm@jmu.edu
BAUGH, Anita, G 320-308-5936 247 F abaugh@sctcc.edu
BAUGH, Frank 601-318-6772 256 I frank.baugh@wmcarey.edu
BAUGH, Robbie 940-668-3338 453 L rbaugh@nctc.edu
BAUGH, Shirley, A 618-537-6533 145 C sabaugh@mckendree.edu
BAUGHER, Justin 308-367-5210 278 A justin.baugher@unl.edu
BAUGHER, Kathy 510-430-2376 52 E kbaugher@mills.edu
BAUGHMAN, Linda, M 651-962-6053 251 D lmbaughman@stthomas.edu
BAUGHMAN, Matthew 618-453-2341 152 B baughman@siu.edu
BAUGHMAN, Patricia 936-261-1944 458 F pabaughman@pvamu.edu
BAUGHMAN, Rebecca, L 512-471-2303 467 C rbaughman@austin.utexas.edu
BAUGUESS, Seth 937-912-0622 374 B seth.bauguess@wright.edu
BAUGUS, John 626-815-4622 26 U jbaugus@apu.edu
BAUHARD, Bill 402-449-2817 274 H bbauhard6793@graceu.edu
BAUM, Benjamin 410-626-2522 206 F benjamin.baum@sjc.edu
BAUM, Christina 203-392-5760 85 A baumc1@southernct.edu
BAUM, Courtney 724-805-2253 410 B courtney.baum@email.stvincent.edu
BAUM, Cynthia 714-620-3700 26 I
BAUM, Daniel, B 410-777-2011 202 D dbbaum@aacc.edu
BAUM, John 570-408-4465 414 H john.baum@wilkes.edu
BAUM, Richard 212-998-4365 318 D rich.baum@nyu.edu
BAUM, Robert 724-805-2590 410 B bob.baum@email.stvincent.edu
BAUM, Robin 914-594-4882 318 A robin_baum@nymc.edu
BAUMAN, Angie 912-583-2241 116 G abaughman@bpc.edu
BAUMAN, Angie 912-583-2241 116 G abauman@bpc.edu
BAUMAN, Curtis 570-945-8506 398 C curtis.bauman@keystone.edu
BAUMAN, Dallas 631-632-6974 325 F dallas.bauman@stonybrook.edu
BAUMAN, Jerry 312-996-7240 153 H jbauman@uic.edu
BAUMAN, Joel 386-822-7100 111 E jbauman@stetson.edu
BAUMAN, Ryan 308-367-5247 278 A rbauman2@unl.edu
BAUMANN, Erick 708-524-5054 137 F ebauman@dom.edu
BAUMANN, Lawra 513-569-1759 359 G lawra.baumann@cincinnatistate.edu
BAUMANN, Melissa, J 513-745-3837 374 D baumannm@xavier.edu
BAUMANN, Robert 913-684-2741 518 I robert.baumann@leavenworth.army.mil
BAUMBACH, Kirk 804-752-7263 484 C kirkbaumbach@rmc.edu
BAUMEISTER, Bo 503-493-6587 382 I bbaumeister@cu-portland.edu
BAUMEL, Robert 978-656-3244 220 C baumelr@middlesex.mass.edu
BAUMER, Brian 718-990-3292 322 F baumerb@stjohns.edu
BAUMET, Robert, L 716-878-5304 326 E baumetrl@buffalostate.edu
BAUMGARDNER, Brice, D 573-629-3279 260 G bbaumgardner@hlg.edu
BAUMGARDNER, Deidra 317-738-8189 157 L dbaumgardner@franklincollege.edu
BAUMGARDNER, Julie, M 606-474-3200 185 C jmbaumgardner@kcu.edu
BAUMGARDNER, Waylon 951-343-4876 28 G wbaumgardner@calbaptist.edu
BAUMGARDNER, William, B 606-474-3151 185 C wbbaumgardner@kcu.edu
BAUMGART, Reilly 618-262-8641 140 F baumgartr@iecc.edu
BAUMGARTEN, Bobbie 214-637-3530 470 H bbaumgarten@wadecollege.edu
BAUMGARTEN, Matthew, J 757-822-1780 489 H mbaumgarten@tcc.edu
BAUMGARTNER, Annmarie 419-772-2729 367 G a-baumgartner@onu.edu
BAUMGARTNER, Bruce 814-732-2776 406 B bbaumgartner@edinboro.edu
BAUMGARTNER, David, A 319-335-1023 166 G david-baumgartner@uiowa.edu
BAUMGARTNER, Eric 414-277-7300 509 A
BAUMGARTNER, Holly, L 419-772-2130 367 G h-baumgartner@onu.edu
BAUMGARTNER, Renee 408-554-5344 62 F rbaumgartner@scu.edu
BAUMGARTNER, Timothy, K 713-348-4867 455 F timothy.k.baumgartner@rice.edu
BAUMHOVER, Lynne 563-589-0300 174 D lbaumhover@wartburgseminary.edu
BAUMLER, Kim 563-589-3178 173 J
BAUN, Dan 507-537-6978 248 A dan.baun@smsu.edu
BAUN, Jeffrey, S 610-359-5315 393 E jbaun@dccc.edu
BAUR, Cathy 760-750-4400 33 E cbaur@csusm.edu
BAUR, John 309-438-2583 140 L jebaur@ilstu.edu
BAURA, Gail 773-508-8070 144 D gbaura@luc.edu
BAURAIN, Thomas 816-311-0110 257 M thomas.baurain@calvary.edu
BAUS, Amy 563-589-3132 173 J abaus@dbq.edu
BAUSANO, Carrie, J 719-333-9751 518 H
BAUSHKE, Ken 270-745-3056 190 F ken.baushke@wku.edu
BAUSINGER, Patricia, E 570-321-4049 400 G baus@lycoming.edu
BAUSMAN, Marvin 319-398-5516 171 F marvin.bausman@kirkwood.edu
BAUSMITH, Shirley 843-661-1487 421 H sbausmith@fmarion.edu
BAUSS, Celia, N 864-592-4754 424 C baussc@sccsc.edu
BAUTISTA MOLLER, Lydia, B 954-607-4344 112 L
BAVER, Chad 406-683-7382 271 H chad.baver@umwestern.edu
BAVIER, Anne 817-272-2776 467 B bavier@uta.edu
BAVISI, Lata 505-922-2886 294 B lata@eccu.edu
BAVISI, Sanjay 505-922-2886 294 B
BAWA, Opinder 415-422-2787 72 A osbawa@usfca.edu
BAWCOM, Amy 254-526-1472 445 L amy.bawcom@ctcd.edu
BAWOROWSKY, John 414-288-4976 508 C john.baworowsky@marquette.edu
BAX, John 573-681-5860 261 H baxj2@lincolnu.edu
BAXTER, Agnes 919-546-8212 348 I abaxter@shawu.edu
BAXTER, Aimee, F 318-257-2641 197 A abaxter@latech.edu
BAXTER, Charlene 706-880-8311 122 D cbaxter@lagrange.edu
BAXTER, Diana 310-287-4387 49 H baxterdl@wlac.edu
BAXTER, Hilary 617-327-6777 226 B
BAXTER, Keith 580-745-2250 379 J kbaxter@se.edu
BAXTER, Kristine 239-489-9205 100 E kbaxter2@fsw.edu
BAXTER, Melissa 315-568-3271 317 A mbaxter@nycc.edu
BAXTER, Pat 212-229-8947 316 E baxterp@newschool.edu
BAXTER, Patrick 727-873-4040 111 B pbaxter@usfsp.edu
BAXTER, Randy, A 662-720-7576 255 B rabaxter@nemcc.edu
BAXTER, Steven 360-417-6300 496 I sbaxter@pencol.edu
BAY, Willow, C 213-740-6180 72 B wbay@usc.edu
BAYARDELLE, Eddy 718-289-5185 301 D eddy.bayardelle@bcc.cuny.edu
BAYER, Deborah 989-358-7458 227 A bayerd@alpenacc.edu
BAYER, Deborah, A 248-232-4211 235 D dabayer@oaklandcc.edu
BAYER, Deborah, A 248-232-4311 235 D dabayer@oaklandcc.edu
BAYERL, Sue 320-308-2111 247 E sjbayerl@stcloudstate.edu
BAYLES, Kenneth 402-559-4945 277 H kbayles@unmc.edu
BAYLESS, Debi 573-518-1330 263 E dbayless@mineralarea.edu
BAYLESS, Laura 978-665-3215 217 E lbayless@fitchburgstate.edu
BAYLOR, Bridget 540-453-2358 487 G baylorb@brcc.edu
BAYLOR, Chiquita 401-341-2225 417 D chiquita.baylor@salve.edu
BAYLOR, Kara 262-551-5812 506 H kbaylor@carthage.edu
BAYNE, Deann 402-872-2226 276 C dbayne@peru.edu
BAYNE, Doug 509-527-4253 499 E doug.bayne@wwcc.edu
BAYNE, Sheila 617-627-2000 225 A sheila.bayne@tufts.edu
BAYNE, Suzanne 423-472-7141 436 G sbayne@clevelandstatecc.edu
BAYNES, Leonard, M 713-743-2478 465 A lbaynes@central.uh.edu
BAYOUMI, Magdy, A 337-482-6147 197 F mab@louisiana.edu
BAYTO, Tammy 478-274-7852 123 I tbayto@oftc.edu
BAZAN, Teresita 512-223-7950 443 G tbazan@austincc.edu
BAZAN, Yamilet 951-785-2100 47 F ybazan@lasierra.edu
BAZANT, Robert, S 724-222-5330 403 E rbazant@penncommercial.edu
BAZAR, Leon 361-593-2258 460 B kulgb000@tamuk.edu
BAZEMORE, Alisha 757-823-8462 483 F albazemore@nsu.edu
BAZEMORE, Dennis 910-893-1540 336 C bazemored@campbell.edu
BAZEMORE, Haywood, M 803-705-4321 418 G bazemoreh@benedict.edu
BAZIAN, Hatem 510-356-4760 76 B hbazian@zaytuna.edu
BAZIL, Ted 914-961-8313 323 H ted@svots.edu
BAZILE, Samantha 845-398-4102 323 G sbazile@stac.edu
BAZILE, Stanley 718-960-8241 302 C stanley.bazile@lehman.cuny.edu
BAZLEY, Lisa 210-829-3959 465 E lisa@uiwtx.edu
BAZLUKE, Francine, T 802-656-8585 476 E francine.bazluke@uvm.edu
BAZYLEWICZ, Terry, T 908-852-1400 284 G bazylewiczt@centenaryuniversity.edu
BAZZELL, Darrell 512-471-3434 467 C bazzell@austin.utexas.edu
BEA, David 520-206-4519 15 L dbea@pima.edu
BEACH, Bradley 330-244-4732 373 F bbeach@walsh.edu
BEACH, Cora 541-962-3368 383 B cbeach@eou.edu
BEACH, Nancy, S 540-365-4529 480 L nbeach@ferrum.edu
BEACH, Natalie 503-399-5105 382 C natalie.beach@chemeketa.edu
BEACH, Vincent 641-585-8133 174 B vince.beach@waldorf.edu
BEACH, Wendy 906-635-2213 232 J
BEACHAM, David, M 864-597-4206 426 I beachamdm@wofford.edu
BEACHAM, Ralph 620-724-0390 177 E ralphb@fortscott.edu
BEACHLER, Kelly 941-309-4022 106 H kbeachle@ringling.edu
BEACHNAU, Andrew 616-331-2120 230 G beachnaa@gvsu.edu
BEACHY, Benjamin, S 540-432-4478 480 A ben.beachy@emu.edu
BEACHY, Jeff 408-554-5360 62 F jdbeachy@scu.edu
BEACON, John 812-237-3560 159 C john.beacon@indstate.edu
BEADLES, Mary 706-245-7226 119 A mbeadles@ec.edu
BEAGHAN, John, W 248-370-2445 235 J beaghan@oakland.edu
BEAGLE, Donald 704-461-6740 335 J donaldbeagle@bac.edu
BEAGLE, Mike 541-552-6127 386 H beaglem@sou.edu
BEAHM, Mary, G 814-863-6188 403 F mgb12@psu.edu
BEAIL, Linda 619-849-2408 57 H lindabeail@pointloma.edu
BEAKMAN, Andrew, W 315-792-3111 332 H awbeakma@utica.edu
BEAL, Jason 801-957-4205 474 B jason.beal@slcc.edu
BEAL, Jean 413-572-8574 218 F jbeal@westfield.ma.edu
BEAL, Judy 617-521-2139 224 E judy.beal@simmons.edu
BEAL, Lee 828-835-4233 347 B lbeal@tricountycc.edu
BEAL, Paige 412-392-3954 408 F pbeal@pointpark.edu
BEAL, Stephen 510-594-3630 28 K sbeal@cca.edu
BEALE, Charles, L 302-831-8107 90 I cbeale@udel.edu
BEALE, Connie, L 973-761-9401 291 F concetta.beale@shu.edu
BEALE, Marjorie, A 626-395-6369 29 I mbeale@caltech.edu
BEALER, Mitchell 435-586-7723 473 A bealer@suu.edu
BEALES, Sharon 610-861-5451 403 B sbeales@northampton.edu
BEALL, David 773-508-2391 144 D dbeall@luc.edu
BEALS, Linda, M 937-327-6374 374 A lbeals@wittenberg.edu
BEALS, Michael, J 714-556-3610 72 F officeofthepresident@vanguard.edu
BEAM, Brian 309-438-8404 140 L babeam@ilstu.edu
BEAM, Jay 843-953-5088 419 D jbeam1@citadel.edu
BEAM, John 510-464-3474 56 H jbeam@peralta.edu
BEAM, Julie 574-807-7020 156 E julie.beam@bethelcollege.edu
BEAM, Ruthanne 865-573-4517 432 H rubeam@johnsonu.edu
BEAM, Tony 864-977-2008 422 I tony.beam@ngu.edu
BEAMAN, Cynthia, A 812-888-4125 165 E cbeaman@vinu.edu
BEAMAN, Patricia, L 716-839-8538 306 E pbeaman@daemen.edu
BEAMER, Janet 704-499-9200 93 B

BEAMON, Jefff 912-650-6206 125 H jbeamon@southuniversity.edu
BEAMON, Stanley 312-850-7038 136 C sbeamon3@ccc.edu
BEAN, Al 207-780-5588 201 H albean@maine.edu
BEAN, Brent 413-485-7362 218 F bbean@westfield.ma.edu
BEAN, Christopher, A 540-665-4553 485 C cbean@su.edu
BEAN, Debra 925-969-3302 46 L dbean@jfku.edu
BEAN, James, C 617-373-2170 223 D
BEAN, Joanne 207-893-7895 200 G jbean@sjcme.edu
BEAN, Kellie 607-431-4400 309 E bwank@hartwick.edu
BEAN, Miho 603-206-8101 280 L msbean@ccsnh.edu
BEAN, Paul 785-242-5200 180 H paul.bean@ottawa.edu
BEAN, Shirley 253-833-9111 495 C sbean@greenriver.edu
BEAN, Stacey 937-778-7844 361 E sbean@edisonohio.edu
BEAN, Steve 218-322-2351 245 B steve.bean@itascacc.edu
BEAN, Zach 214-333-2212 447 D zach@dbu.edu
BEANE, Michael 508-854-4334 220 G mbeane@qcc.mass.edu
BEANE-BOOSE, Linda 509-533-3567 494 A linda.beane-boose@sfcc.spokane.edu
BEANS, Jessica 937-298-3399 364 B jessica.beans@kc.edu
BEAR, Marca 813-257-3280 113 E mbear@ut.edu
BEARBOWER, Sarah 608-796-3860 512 R sbearbower@viterbo.edu
BEARCE, John 702-651-7454 278 N john.bearce@csn.edu
BEARD, Alison 828-726-2311 341 D abeard@cccti.edu
BEARD, Ashley 601-477-5454 253 F ashley.beard@jcjc.edu
BEARD, Audrey, W 919-530-5327 350 D awbeard@nccu.edu
BEARD, Brian, C 302-356-6989 91 B bcbeard@wilmu.edu
BEARD, Christopher 808-675-3368 128 K christopher.beard@byuh.edu
BEARD, Gerald 662-562-3319 255 C
BEARD, Jason 206-296-2499 498 D beardj@seattleu.edu
BEARD, Katie 205-652-3528 9 C kbeard@uwa.edu
BEARD, Richard, L 717-867-6363 399 J rbeard@lvc.edu
BEARD, Robert 918-495-6588 378 H rbeard@oru.edu
BEARD, Russell 425-564-4200 492 G russ.beard@bellevuecollege.edu
BEARD, Scott 304-876-5176 504 D sbeard@shepherd.edu
BEARD, Tanika 706-821-8103 124 C recordsofficestaff@paine.edu
BEARD, Timothy, L 727-816-3400 105 C beardt@phsc.edu
BEARD, Virginia 616-395-7544 231 D beard@hope.edu
BEARDMORE, Kevin 270-686-4504 186 F kevin.beardmore@kctcs.edu
BEARDMORE, Melissa, A 410-777-2532 202 D mabeardmore@aacc.edu
BEARDSALL, Christopher 210-486-2312 441 I cbeardsall@alamo.edu
BEARDSLEE, Gene 402-872-2270 276 C gbeardslee@peru.edu
BEARDSLEY, Kathleen 215-572-2838 389 D beardsley@arcadia.edu
BEARDSLEY, Scott, C 434-924-7481 486 H scb4v@virginia.edu
BEARE, Paul 559-278-0210 32 A pbeare@csufresno.edu
BEARMAN, Alan 785-670-1855 182 D alan.bearman@washburn.edu
BEARROWS, Thomas, R 312-996-7762 153 H bearrows@uillinois.edu
BEARROWS, Thomas, R 312-996-7762 153 G bearrows@uillinois.edu
BEARSS, Carrie 810-989-5501 236 G cbearss@sc4.edu
BEARY, Richard 407-823-5242 110 C richard.beary@ucf.edu
BEASCA, Jeff 714-533-3946 35 B jeffb@calums.edu
BEASCA, Jeffrey 714-533-3946 35 B jeffb@calums.edu
BEASIMER, Linda, M 845-431-8979 307 A beasimer@sunydutchess.edu
BEASLEY, Gerald, R 607-255-2000 306 B
BEASLEY, Joan 386-822-7251 111 E jlbeasle@stetson.edu
BEASLEY, Laura 507-433-0676 247 C laura.beasley@riverland.edu
BEASLEY, Marcia 330-263-2165 360 A mbeasley@wooster.edu
BEASLEY, Sarah 304-384-6298 503 P sbeasley@concord.edu
BEASLEY, Teresa 903-693-1117 454 E tbeasley@panola.edu
BEASLEY, Vanessa 615-322-4948 440 D vanessa.beasley@vanderbilt.edu
BEASON, Stephanie 417-667-8181 259 A sbeason@cottey.edu
BEASSIE, Rhonda 936-294-2424 462 F rbeassie@shsu.edu
BEATA, Tony 402-461-7733 274 I tbeata@hastings.edu
BEATON, Kim 903-923-1606 471 B kbeaton@wileyc.edu
BEATSON, Bonnie 808-235-7374 130 I beatson@hawaii.edu
BEATTIE, Martha, J 603-646-2258 281 C martha.j.beattie@dartmouth.edu
BEATTIE, Simona 503-699-6302 384 B sbeattie@marylhurst.edu
BEATTIE, Terry 610-436-3317 407 D tbeattie@wcupa.edu
BEATTY, Anthany 859-257-8200 190 B anthany.beatty@uky.edu
BEATTY, Bernadette 575-624-8001 295 A noriega@nmmi.edu
BEATTY, Brian 415-338-6833 34 C bjbeatty@sfsu.edu
BEATTY, Del 435-652-7514 473 B beatty@dixie.edu
BEATTY, Doug 503-538-8383 383 C dbeatty@georgefox.edu
BEATTY, Fran 707-668-5663 41 F fran@dellarte.com
BEATTY, Kimberly 816-604-1011 262 F kimberly.beatty@mcckc.edu
BEATTY, Kimberly 713-718-5040 450 D kimberly.beatty@hccs.edu
BEATTY, Lisa, L 563-588-8000 169 B lbeatty@emmaus.edu
BEATTY, Luke 217-245-3020 139 H luke.beatty@mail.ic.edu
BEATTY, Michael 415-338-1124 34 C mbeatty@sfsu.edu
BEATTY, Robert 239-590-7300 109 C rbeatty@fgcu.edu
BEATTY, Susan, W 518-244-2301 321 G beatts2@sage.edu
BEATTY, Tracy 269-965-3931 232 A beattyt@kellogg.edu
BEATY, Andrew 309-846-3544 146 B andrew.beaty@moody.edu
BEATY, Lori 254-968-9430 459 A lbeaty@tarleton.edu
BEATY, Michael 303-368-7462 81 I mbeaty@pmi.edu
BEAUBIEN, Richard 423-442-2001 432 E beauienri@hiwassee.edu
BEAUBOEUF, Tamara, M 765-658-4529 157 H tbeauboeuf@depauw.edu
BEAUCHAMP, Belinda 787-758-2525 528 D belinda.beauchamp@upr.edu
BEAUCHAMP, Cheryl, L 518-629-8177 310 G c.beauchamp@hvcc.edu
BEAUCHAMP, Darrell 575-492-2676 294 L dbeauchamp@nmjc.edu
BEAUCHAMP, Lance 904-588-2104 102 B lbeauch@ju.edu
BEAUCHAMP, Norman 616-234-2785 233 G beauch66@msu.edu
BEAUCHAMP, Robbin 617-989-4112 225 E beauchampr1@wit.edu
BEAUCHEMIN, Carole 603-513-1170 282 G carole.beauchemin@granite.edu
BEAUDET, Sebastien 312-935-4234 141 C sbeaudet@icsw.edu
BEAUDIN, Giselda 407-646-2466 106 J gbeaudin@rollins.edu
BEAUDIN, Paul 631-451-4089 330 B beaudip@sunysuffolk.edu
BEAUDOIN, Shikara 920-693-1139 513 H shikara.beaudoin@gotoltc.edu
BEAUDOIN, Susan 518-381-1327 323 L beaudose@sunysccc.edu
BEAUDRY, Matt 313-593-5070 238 A mdbeau@umich.edu
BEAUJON, Francis 530-257-6181 47 J fbeaujon@lassencollege.edu
BEAULIER, Scott 701-231-8804 354 D scott.beaulier@ndsu.edu
BEAULIEU, Adrian, G 401-865-2114 416 E abeaulie@providence.edu
BEAULIEU, Ellen 207-602-2334 202 A ebeaulieu@une.edu
BEAULIEU, Gary, R 317-940-9624 156 I gbeaulie@butler.edu
BEAULIEU, Sharen 207-602-2339 202 A sbeaulieu@une.edu
BEAUMONT, Lee 434-592-3315 482 D lbeaumont@liberty.edu
BEAUMONT, Patricia, L 412-578-8772 391 G plbeaumont@carlow.edu
BEAUMONT DOSS, Katherine 210-486-3338 441 H kbeaumont@alamo.edu
BEAUPRE, David, R 610-660-1320 409 H dbeaupre@sju.edu
BEAUPRE, Walter 302-736-2436 90 J walt.beaupre@wesley.edu
BEAUPREWHITE, Renee 802-468-1339 477 A renee.beauprewhite@castleton.edu
BEAUREGARD, Jill 320-589-6036 251 A beaureja@morris.umn.edu
BEAUREGARD, Kathy, B 269-387-3061 239 E kathy.beauregard@wmich.edu
BEAUREGARD, Stephen 508-565-1375 224 H sbeauregard@stonehill.edu
BEAUVAIS, Laura 401-874-4341 417 E lbeauvais@uri.edu
BEAVEN, Liz 415-575-6105 29 H ebeaven@ciis.edu
BEAVER, David 304-293-8450 505 B david.beaver@mail.wvu.edu
BEAVER, Jeff, S 864-388-8208 422 A jbeaver@lander.edu
BEAVER, John 979-209-7300 444 D john.beaver@blinn.edu
BEAVER, John 979-209-7300 444 D jbeaver@blinn.edu
BEAVER, Kevin 410-644-6400 202 G kevin.beaver@brightwood.edu
BEAVER, Nancy 770-533-7001 122 E nbeaver@laniertech.edu
BEAVER, Randy, L 843-953-6802 420 C beaverr@cofc.edu
BEAVER, Robert 651-779-5744 244 D robert.beaver@century.edu
BEAVERS, Gayonne 940-397-3298 453 C gayonne.beavers@mwsu.edu
BEAVERS, Judy 517-321-0242 231 A jbeavers@glcc.edu
BEAVERS, Kristy 714-289-2020 36 G kbeavers@chapman.edu
BEAVERS, Philip, E 517-321-0242 231 A pbeavers@glcc.edu
BEBBER, Glenda, H 704-233-8742 353 D gbebber@wingate.edu
BEBENSEE, Mark, A 843-953-5155 419 D mark.bebensee@citadel.edu
BECCARIA, Michael 518-327-6376 320 A mbeccaria@paulsmiths.edu
BECENTI, Tonilee 505-786-4151 294 I tbecenti@navajotech.edu
BECERRA, Cynthia 209-478-0800 45 J cbecerra@humphreys.edu
BECERRA, Gilberto 210-486-3930 441 H gbecerra8@alamo.edu
BECERRA, Irma 305-474-6027 107 B ibecerra@stu.edu
BECERRA, Mary 657-278-2850 32 B mbecerra@fullerton.edu
BECERRIL, Gina 323-259-2548 54 E gbecerril@oxy.edu
BECHARD, Deanna 603-646-9100 282 C d.bechard@snhu.edu
BECHARD, Jennifer 207-985-7976 199 G jenniferbechard@landingschool.edu
BECHARD, Matthew 785-243-1435 176 I mbechard@cloud.edu
BECHER, Amy 412-365-1139 392 C abecher@chatham.edu
BECHER, Dave 304-724-3700 501 D
BECHER, Gregory, J 805-525-4417 67 E gbecher@thomasaquinas.edu
BECHERER, Jeffery 212-431-2888 317 H jeff.becherer@nyls.edu
BECHTEL, Brian 816-604-3036 262 J brian.bechtel@mcckc.edu
BECHTOLD, Brad 864-294-3166 421 I brad.bechtold@furman.edu
BECHTOLD, John 973-642-7664 288 A john.bechtold@njit.edu
BECICKA, Kim 319-398-5525 171 F kim.becicka@kirkwood.edu
BECK, Alan 617-327-6777 226 B alan_beck@williamjames.edu
BECK, Anne, D 313-664-7473 228 H abeck@collegeforcreativestudies.edu
BECK, Barbara, E 518-580-5800 324 D bbeck@skidmore.edu
BECK, Carina 406-994-7627 272 A cbeck@montana.edu
BECK, Cathy 402-354-7263 275 P cathy.beck@methodistcollege.edu
BECK, Cherie 517-371-5140 239 F beckc@cooley.edu
BECK, Daniel 405-733-7459 379 F dbeck@rose.edu
BECK, Deborah 603-342-3042 281 B dbeck@ccsnh.edu
BECK, Deborah, C 803-777-3957 424 I dbeck@sc.edu
BECK, Erika, D 805-437-8410 31 C erika.beck@csuci.edu
BECK, Jeffrey 908-737-5900 286 F jbeck@exchange.kean.edu
BECK, Jen 512-245-2152 463 A jb32@txstate.edu
BECK, Jeneane 319-384-0005 166 G jeneane-beck@uiowa.edu
BECK, Jennifer, M 512-448-8516 455 I jbeck@stedwards.edu
BECK, Judy 803-641-3269 425 A judyb@usca.edu
BECK, Julie 417-268-6030 257 H jbeck@gobbc.edu
BECK, Kristen 716-731-8850 318 E kbeck@niagaracc.suny.edu
BECK, Leesa 805-893-4165 70 B leesa.beck@sa.ucsb.edu
BECK, Maryann, M 334-833-4443 5 M mbeck@hawks.huntingdon.edu
BECK, Michael, J 310-825-2411 69 B michaelbeck@ucla.edu
BECK, Mike 919-718-7426 341 H mbeck@cccc.edu
BECK, Richard 918-343-7615 379 C rbeck@rsu.edu
BECK, Robert, J 414-229-3713 511 A rjbeck@uwm.edu
BECK, Ronda 517-371-5140 239 F beckr@cooley.edu
BECK, Ronda, S 859-257-4759 190 B ronda.beck@uky.edu
BECK, Stacie 480-423-6536 14 C stacie.beck@scottsdalecc.edu
BECK, Tamara 336-757-3345 343 C tbeck@forsythtech.edu
BECK-DUDLEY, Caryn 408-554-4523 62 F cbeckdudley@scu.edu
BECKEMEYER, Wendy, C 412-397-5212 409 C beckemeyer@rmu.edu
BECKER, Amy 612-874-3799 243 F amy_naughton@mcad.edu
BECKER, Anat 610-660-1968 409 H abecker@sju.edu
BECKER, Carol 212-854-9847 305 E cbecker@columbia.edu
BECKER, Charles, P 304-384-5190 503 P beckerc@concord.edu
BECKER, Deborah 901-678-3538 439 E dabecker@memphis.edu
BECKER, Dennis, M 303-871-3897 83 E dbecker@du.edu
BECKER, Gerrie 505-224-4551 293 L gbecker1@cnm.edu
BECKER, James 812-855-4884 159 G jambecke@iu.edu
BECKER, Janine 570-945-8112 398 C janine.becker@keystone.edu
BECKER, Jessica 575-492-2130 297 G jbecker@usw.edu
BECKER, Joan 617-287-5862 216 I joan.becker@umb.edu
BECKER, Joe 503-768-7971 383 G jbecker@lclark.edu
BECKER, Jonathan 845-758-7378 298 I jbecker@bard.edu
BECKER, Joseph 516-773-5000 519 C beckerj@usmma.edu
BECKER, Joyce, K 443-352-4031 207 C jbecker@stevenson.edu
BECKER, Karen 815-802-8405 142 C kbecker@kcc.edu
BECKER, Karl, D 267-295-2307 409 B kbecker@walnuthillcollege.edu
BECKER, Keri 616-331-8800 230 G beckeker@gvsu.edu
BECKER, Kristen 928-428-8308 12 I kristen.becker@eac.edu

BECKER, Lois .... 312-341-3615 150 D lbecker05@roosevelt.edu
BECKER, Mark, P .... 404-413-1300 121 A mbecker@gsu.edu
BECKER, Maureen .... 718-982-3690 302 A schoolhealthscience@csi.cuny.edu
BECKER, Mike .... 925-473-7362.. 41 A mbecker@losmedanos.edu
BECKER, Milissa, M ...... 651-641-8268 241 L becker@csp.edu
BECKER, Pete, D .... 708-209-3092 136 I pete.becker@cuchicago.edu
BECKER, Richard, A ...... 561-868-3137 105 A beckerr@palmbeachstate.edu
BECKER, Ron .... 201-761-6415 291 D rbecker@saintpeters.edu
BECKER, S. Ann .... 321-674-8960.. 99 K abecker@fit.edu
BECKER, Scott .... 517-355-2070 233 G beckersc@msu.edu
BECKER, Sheila, R .... 563-556-5110 172 D beckers@nicc.edu
BECKER, Stefan .... 718-960-1120 302 C stefan.becker@lehman.cuny.edu
BECKER, Steven .... 973-278-5400 299 F steven-becker@berkeleycollege.edu
BECKER, Steven .... 973-278-5400 283 J steven-becker@berkeleycollege.edu
BECKER-LUTZ, Jill .... 303-797-5882.. 76 I jill.beckerlutz@arapahoe.edu
BECKER-RICHARDS, Joicy .... 609-497-7900 288 E joicy.becker@ptsem.edu
BECKERMANN, Corie .... 320-308-4848 247 E cabeckermann@stcloudstate.edu
BECKETT, Karen, J .... 305-284-5749 112 O kbeckett@miami.edu
BECKETT, Keith .... 330-263-2500 360 A kbeckett@wooster.edu
BECKETT, Roger .... 419-289-5414 356 L rbeckett@ashland.edu
BECKETT, Suzanne .... 817-515-1225 458 B suzanne.beckett@tccd.edu
BECKETT, Thomas, A ..... 203-432-1414.. 89 G thomas.beckett@yale.edu
BECKHAM, Tammy, R ... 785-532-5660 179 A trbeckham@vet.ksu.edu
BECKHAM, Tim .... 605-225-1634 427 J
BECKHORN, Roy .... 916-568-3190.. 50 E beckhor@losrios.edu
BECKLER, Larry .... 843-525-8282 424 E lbeckler@tcl.edu
BECKLEY, Clark .... 913-234-0609 176 H clark.beckley@cleveland.edu
BECKLEY, David, L .... 662-252-2491 255 F dlbeckley@rustcollege.edu
BECKLEY, Gemma .... 662-252-8000 255 F gbeckley@rustcollege.edu
BECKMAN, John .... 319-296-4307 169 H john.beckman@hawkeyecollege.edu
BECKMAN, John, H .... 212-998-6848 318 D john.beckman@nyu.edu
BECKMAN, Seth .... 412-396-6082 394 D beckmans@duq.edu
BECKNER, Christine .... 718-368-5051 303 A cbeckner@kbcc.cuny.edu
BECKS, Crystal .... 661-654-3012.. 31 B cbecks@csub.edu
BECKSTROM, Amy, D .... 303-492-6494.. 83 B amy.beckstrom@colorado.edu
BECKSTROM, Brian, A ... 319-352-8217 174 C brian.beckstrom@wartburg.edu
BECKVOLD, John .... 304-462-6181 504 B john.beckvold@glenville.edu
BECKWITH, LaSharnda .. 714-879-3901.. 45 I lbeckwith@hiu.edu
BECNKER, Scott .... 319-335-5026 166 G scott-beckner@uiowa.edu
BECTON, Bret .... 337-482-6491 197 F bret.becton@louisiana.edu
BEDA, Cheri .... 308-398-7437 273 G cheribeda@cccneb.edu
BEDA, Eric, A .... 517-750-1200 237 D ebeda@arbor.edu
BEDDALL, Tina .... 559-278-6111.. 32 A tinab@csufresno.edu
BEDEAU, Koren, A .... 215-895-2200 394 C koren.a.bedeau@drexel.edu
BEDELL, Honey .... 563-336-3302 168 K hbedell@eicc.edu
BEDELL, Michael, D ...... 773-442-6100 147 G m-bedell@neiu.edu
BEDELL, Michaela .... 207-509-7292 200 I mbedell@unity.edu
BEDERSON, Ben .... 301-405-3394 207 G bederson@umd.edu
BEDFORD, April .... 718-951-5214 301 E abedford@brooklyn.cuny.edu
BEDFORD, Carter .... 817-515-1193 458 B carter.bedford@tccd.edu
BEDFORD, John .... 405-208-5322 377 D jbedford@okcu.edu
BEDFORD, Laura .... 315-792-3179 332 H lbedford@utica.edu
BEDFORD, Norm .... 702-774-8000 279 D norm.bedford@unlv.edu
BEDFORD, Wayne .... 205-652-3687.... 9 C dbedford@uwa.edu
BEDI, Param, S .... 570-577-1557 390 H param.bedi@bucknell.edu
BEDINGFIELD, Sarah ..... 603-427-7631 280 J sbedingfield@ccsnh.edu
BEDNAR, Gerald, J .... 440-943-7600 369 J jerrybednar@juno.com
BEDNARZ, Bridgette ...... 254-968-9271 459 A bednarz@tarleton.edu
BEDNARZ, Jeffrey .... 413-205-3208 210 E jeffrey.bednarz@aic.edu
BEDNEY, Elynda, A .... 269-471-6040 227 B bedney@andrews.edu
BEDOYA, Eduardo .... 231-777-0332 234 G eduardo.bedoya@muskegoncc.edu
BEDOYA, Theresa .... 410-225-2434 205 C tbedoya@mica.edu
BEDRYK, Michael .... 516-726-5644 519 C bedrykm@usmma.edu
BEDSOLE, Blake .... 205-652-3581.... 9 C bbedsole@uwa.edu
BEDTKE, James .... 507-457-1458 250 B jbedtke@smumn.edu
BEDWELL, Pamela .... 478-471-2730 123 A pamela.bedwell@mga.edu
BEDWELL, Teresa, M .... 937-775-2313 374 B teresa.bedwell@wright.edu
BEE, Richard .... 562-944-0351.. 27 E richard.e.bee@biola.edu
BEE, Timothy, S .... 520-621-1737.. 16 J timbee@email.arizona.edu
BEEBE, Anthony, E .... 805-730-4011.. 62 E beebe@sbcc.edu
BEEBE, Barbara, R .... 325-574-6501 470 N bbeebe@wtc.edu
BEEBE, Gayle, D .... 805-565-6024.. 74 I president@westmont.edu
BEEBE, Norman .... 413-775-1333 219 F beebe@gcc.mass.edu
BEEBE, Robert, D .... 909-593-3511.. 70 E rbeebe@laverne.edu
BEEBE STEVENS, Heather .... 509-434-5123 493 H
BEEBE-STEVENS, Heather .... 509-434-5123 493 I heather.beebe-stevens@ccs.spokane.edu
BEEBY, James, M .... 812-464-1853 165 C jmbeeby@usi.edu
BEECH, Amanda .... 661-255-1050.. 29 F abeech@calarts.edu
BEECH, Bettina .... 601-984-1020 256 D bbeech@umc.edu
BEECH, Rachel, A .... 520-621-6123.. 16 J rabeech@email.arizona.edu
BEECH, Thomas .... 218-755-3964 244 B tbeech@bemidjistate.edu
BEECHER, Shan, L .... 515-574-1985 170 C beecher@iowacentral.edu
BEEHLER, Jeff .... 509-865-0446 495 D beehler_j@heritage.edu
BEEHLER, John, M .... 256-782-5881..... 6 B president@jsu.edu
BEEHNER, Janel .... 540-985-8491 482 A jlbeehner@jchs.edu
BEEKE, Joel, R .... 616-977-0599 236 B joel.beeke@prts.edu
BEEKE, Jonathon .... 616-977-0599 236 B jonathon.beeke@prts.edu
BEEKE, Jonathon, D ...... 616-432-3408 236 B jonathon.beeke@prts.edu
BEEKMAN, William, R ... 517-353-9818 233 G beekman@msu.edu
BEELEN, Joan .... 616-957-6027 228 C jrb44@calvinseminary.edu
BEELER, Jeremy .... 908-835-9222 292 G jbeeler@warren.edu
BEELER, Monique .... 415-338-1111.. 34 C mbeeler@sfsu.edu
BEELER, Sydney .... 724-925-4050 414 E beelers@westmoreland.edu
BEEMAN, Greg .... 845-675-4417 319 C greg.beeman@nyack.edu
BEEMER, Matthew .... 904-596-2473 112 F mbeemer@tbc.edu
BEEMER, Pamela .... 847-491-7505 148 C p-beemer@northwestern.edu
BEEN, Sharon, A .... 501-882-8836.. 17 M sabeen@asub.edu
BEER, Francisca .... 909-537-5058.. 33 D fbeer@csusb.edu
BEER, Laura .... 503-699-3361 384 B lbeer@maryhurst.edu
BEER, Patrick .... 478-387-4783 120 B pbeer@gmc.edu
BEER, Richard .... 360-486-8784 497 F jrbeer@stmartin.edu
BEERS, David .... 253-879-3902 499 C dbeers@pugetsound.edu
BEERS, Di .... 425-235-2426 497 E dbeers@rtc.edu
BEERS, Josh .... 717-560-8240 399 D jbeers@lbc.edu
BEERS, Maggie .... 415-338-3613.. 34 C mbeers@sfsu.edu
BEERS, Stephen, T .... 479-524-7252.. 20 B sbeers@jbu.edu
BEERT, Brian .... 563-386-3570 169 G bbeert@hamiltontechcollege.com
BEESLEY, Brad .... 918-781-7450 374 H beesleyb@bacone.edu
BEESON, Duane, L .... 712-707-7116 172 G beeson@nwciowa.edu
BEESON, Joseph .... 215-702-4498 391 C jbeeson@cairn.edu
BEESON, Patricia, E ...... 412-624-4223 412 I beeson@pitt.edu
BEETS, Shannon .... 775-831-1314 280 C sbeets@sierranevada.edu
BEEZHOLD, Philip, D .... 616-526-6481 228 B pdb2@calvin.edu
BEG, Christina .... 216-397-1998 363 H cbeg@jcu.edu
BEGANY, James .... 502-852-5555 190 C jim.begany@louisville.edu
BEGASHAW, Negash ..... 803-705-4322 418 G negash.begashaw@benedict.edu
BEGAY, Janice .... 785-749-8419 178 A janice.begay@bie.edu
BEGAY, Karen, F .... 520-626-9809.. 16 J kfbegay@email.arizona.edu
BEGG, Melissa, D .... 212-854-2691 305 E mdb3@columbia.edu
BEGGS, Crystal .... 701-788-4647 354 B crystal.beggs@mayvillestate.edu
BEGIN, Gene, P .... 508-286-3223 225 G begin_gene@wheatoncollege.edu
BEGLEY, Eric .... 580-349-1396 377 E ebegley@opsu.edu
BEGLEY, John, B .... 270-384-8505 187 H begleyj@lindsey.edu
BEGLEY, Mary Ann .... 415-338-3885.. 34 C begley@sfsu.edu
BEGLEY, Thomas .... 518-276-6802 321 A begley@rpi.edu
BEGLY, Mark, L .... 757-221-1009 479 I mlbegly@wm.edu
BEHAN, Lawrence, M .... 413-662-5245 218 C l.behans@mcla.edu
BEHAN, Peggy .... 304-326-1472 502 D peggy.behan@salemu.edu
BEHAN KRAUS, Carolyn, A .... 203-773-8521.. 84 G cbehan@albertus.edu
BEHAUNEK, Luke .... 515-961-1562 173 E luke.behaunek@simpson.edu
BEHEN, Joseph .... 312-499-4272 151 F jbehen@saic.edu
BEHM, Bonnie Lee .... 610-519-6456 413 K bonnie.behm@villanova.edu
BEHMAND, Mojgan .... 415-485-3276.. 41 J mojgan.behmand@dominican.edu
BEHMER, Scott .... 440-610-2240 125 H sbehmer@southuniversity.edu
BEHN, Julie .... 408-944-6121 172 H julie.behn@palmer.edu
BEHNEN, Bob .... 660-626-2395 257 A bbehnen@atsu.edu
BEHNEN, Erin .... 618-650-3639 152 C etimpe@siue.edu
BEHNKE, Laura .... 215-702-4521 391 C lbehnke@cairn.edu
BEHR, Eileen, W .... 215-571-3548 394 C eileen.w.behr@drexel.edu
BEHR, Fred, C .... 507-786-3636 250 C behr@stolaf.edu
BEHR, Julie .... 706-778-8500 124 E jbehr@piedmont.edu
BEHR, Kate, E .... 914-337-9300 305 F kate.behr@concordia-ny.edu
BEHR, Kevin .... 361-354-2338 445 S kevind@coastalbend.edu
BEHR, Michelle .... 320-589-6035 251 A
BEHR, Richard, A .... 239-590-7399 109 C rbehr@fgcu.edu
BEHRE, William .... 732-987-2314 286 D wbehre@georgian.edu
BEHRENDT, Todd .... 315-792-5679 315 I tbehrendt@mvcc.edu
BEHRENS, Christina ...... 407-708-4722 107 G
BEHRENS, Eric .... 610-499-1036 414 F ebehrens@widener.edu
BEHRENS, Kim .... 559-791-2322.. 47 C kbehrens@portervillecollege.edu
BEHRENS, Michael .... 217-351-2433 148 H mbehrens@parkland.edu
BEHRENS, Susanne .... 713-623-2040 443 C sbehrens@aii.edu
BEHRNS, Kevin .... 314-977-9803 266 J behrnske@slu.edu
BEHRS, David .... 415-451-2802.. 60 I dbehrs@sfts.edu
BEHRS, David .... 415-451-2800.. 60 I dbehrs@sfts.edu
BEHUNEK, Sarah .... 303-458-3535.. 82 D sbehunek@regis.edu
BEHUNIN, Robert .... 435-797-9693 473 C robert.behunin@usu.edu
BEIDLEMAN, David, C .. 717-361-1493 394 F beidlemand@etown.edu
BEIDLER, James .... 614-287-2646 360 C jbeidler@cscc.edu
BEIER, Jason .... 608-890-1066 512 D jason.beier@uwex.uwc.edu
BEIER, Nancy, A .... 410-777-2834 202 D nabeier@aacc.edu
BEIGHLEY, David .... 304-367-4726 503 C david.beighley@pierpont.edu
BEIGHTS, Chad .... 765-677-2497 161 C chad.beights@indwes.edu
BEIKIRCH, Dale .... 432-685-5539 453 B dbeikirch@midland.edu
BEIL, Cheryl .... 202-994-6712.. 92 A cbeil@gwu.edu
BEILOCK, Sian, L .... 212-854-2021 299 B beilock@barnard.edu
BEIMER, Connie .... 505-277-2498 296 H cbeimer@unm.edu
BEINING, Lauren .... 215-887-5511 414 D lbeining@wts.edu
BEINKE, Dayna .... 816-415-5902 270 C beinked@william.jewell.edu
BEIRNE, Chris .... 706-385-1120 124 F chris.beirne@point.edu
BEIRNE, Jay .... 800-838-2580 222 E jbeirne@ngs.edu
BEISE, Elizabeth, J .... 301-405-6836 207 G beise@umd.edu
BEISECKER, Mark .... 805-893-4071.. 70 B mark.beisecker@bookstore.ucsb.edu
BEISSNER, Katherine ..... 315-464-6560 326 B beissnek@upstate.edu
BEISWANGER, Chris ..... 719-255-8227.. 83 C
BEITEL, Leland, R .... 443-334-2064 207 C lbeitel@stevenson.edu
BEITEY, George .... 619-388-7860.. 60 E gbeitey@sdccd.edu
BEITLER, Sidney .... 561-868-3484 105 A beitlers@palmbeachstate.edu
BEITO, Linda .... 205-366-8946.... 7 C beito@stillman.edu
BEITZEL, Vernon, L .... 540-464-7211 490 E beitzelvl@vmi.edu
BEJAR, Elizabeth .... 305-348-2151 109 D elizabeth.bejar@fiu.edu
BEJARANO, Ricky .... 505-747-5050 295 H rick.bejarano@nnmc.edu
BEJNAROWICZ, Ewa ...... 312-553-3193 135 J ebejnarowicz@ccc.edu
BEJOU, David .... 518-587-2100 329 C david.bejou@esc.edu
BEJUNE, Matthew .... 508-929-8511 219 A mbejune@worcester.edu
BEKAS, Nicholas, J .... 407-582-1038 113 F nbekas@valenciacollege.edu
BEKCHIAN, Arina .... 510-925-4282.. 25 P abekchya@aua.am
BEKE-HARRIGAN, Heidi 330-490-7186 373 F hbekeharrigan@walsh.edu
BEKISZ, Pete .... 315-279-5484 312 D pbekisz@keuka.edu
BEKKER, Corne .... 757-352-4401 484 E clbekker@regent.edu
BELAND, Thomas .... 802-776-5279 474 H tom.beland@csj.edu
BELANGER, OFM, Brian, C .... 518-783-5047 324 C bbelanger@siena.edu
BELANGER, David, J ..... 413-585-2530 224 F dbelange@smith.edu
BELANGER, Kenneth ...... 315-228-7220 304 G kbelanger@colgate.edu
BELANGER, Lisa .... 860-768-4666.. 89 C belanger@hartford.edu

BELANGER, Marc .... 414-930-3119 509 B
belangem@mtmary.edu
BELANGER-HAAS,
Aimee .... 937-328-6038 359 H
haasa@clarkstate.edu
BELCASTRO, Richard ..... 678-331-4459 122 F
richard.belcastro@life.edu
BELCHER, Carol .... 843-574-6230 424 G
carol.belcher@tridenttech.edu
BELCHER, Chris .... 417-865-2815 260 B
belcherc@evangel.edu
BELCHER, Dana .... 580-559-5564 375 I
dbelcher@ecok.edu
BELCHER, David, O .... 828-227-7100 352 C
dbelcher@wcu.edu
BELCHER, Deana .... 618-545-3198 142 D
dbelcher@kaskaskia.edu
BELCHER, Elizabeth, M . 304-929-5464 503 B
ebelcher@newriver.edu
BELCHER, James .... 806-894-9611 456 F
jbelcher@southplainscollege.edu
BELCHER, Jim .... 866-323-0233.. 57 M
president@providencecc.edu
BELCHER, Lawrence ...... 317-788-2397 164 H
belcherl@uindy.edu
BELCHER, Michael .... 978-934-3929 217 B
michael_belcher@uml.edu
BELCHER, Michael .... 209-946-2537.. 70 F
mbelcher@pacific.edu
BELD, Jo, M .... 507-786-3632 250 C
beld@stolaf.edu
BELDEN, Eric .... 330-490-7337 373 F
ebelden@walsh.edu
BELDEN, William .... 360-992-2103 493 E
wbelden@clark.edu
BELDONA, Sam .... 415-458-3786.. 41 J
sriram.beldona@dominican.edu
BELETE, Yared .... 303-797-5092.. 76 I
yared.belete@arapahoe.edu
BELEW, Amy .... 731-881-7901 440 B
abelew@utm.edu
BELFIELD, Kevin, D .... 973-596-3676 288 A
kevin.d.belfield@njit.edu
BELFIELD, Lisa .... 267-341-3621 397 G
lbeldfield@holyfamily.edu
BELFIELD, Sherri .... 704-378-1032 338 I
sbelfield@jcsu.edu
BELFIORE, Michael .... 914-606-7895 333 H
michael.belfiore@sunywcc.edu
BELIN, Jacki .... 908-526-1200 289 D
jacki.belin@raritanval.edu
BELISLE, Andria .... 320-308-3117 247 E
ojzimpel@stcloudstate.edu
BELISLE, William, R ...... 504-284-5539 195 L
wbelisle@suno.edu
BELK, Peter .... 913-469-8500 178 F
pbelk@jccc.edu
BELKNAP, Cindy .... 570-577-3654 390 H
cindy.belknap@bucknell.edu
BELKNAP, Monica .... 928-776-2217.. 17 G
monica.belknap@yc.edu
BELKNAP, Peggy .... 928-536-6231.. 15 B
peggy.belknap@npc.edu
BELKO, Dawn .... 763-424-0715 246 E
dbelko@nhcc.edu
BELL, Aimee .... 330-569-5279 362 J
bella1@hiram.edu
BELL, Barbara .... 216-987-4851 360 E
barbara.bell@tri-c.edu
BELL, Brett .... 619-388-7815.. 60 E
bbell@sdccd.edu
BELL, Brooke .... 615-687-6906 429 F
bbell@abcnash.edu
BELL, Carmen .... 575-624-8080 295 A
carmen@nmmi.edu
BELL, Carol .... 307-754-6190 516 Q
carol.bell@nwc.edu
BELL, Christopher .... 207-768-9511 201 G
chris@maine.edu
BELL, Cindy .... 406-657-2363 272 B
cindy.bell@msubillings.edu
BELL, Corinne .... 802-387-6863 475 C
corinnebell@landmark.edu
BELL, Craig, D .... 801-524-8100 471 L
BELL, Cynthia, M .... 330-941-3101 374 E
cmbell02@ysu.edu
BELL, Damon .... 360-475-7474 496 F
dbell@olympic.edu
BELL, Dana .... 580-745-2132 379 J
dbell@se.edu
BELL, Danielle .... 803-321-5128 422 H
danielle.bell@newberry.edu
BELL, Darrell .... 585-594-6200 321 C
bell_darrell@roberts.edu
BELL, Darrell .... 585-594-6202 319 B
bell_darrell@roberts.edu
BELL, David .... 646-565-6000 331 F
adam.hammerman@touro.edu
BELL, David, D .... 614-823-1300 368 O
dbell@otterbein.edu
BELL, Dean .... 312-322-1791 152 F
dbell@spertus.edu
BELL, Deborah, H .... 662-915-6867 256 C
dbell@olemiss.edu
BELL, Denise .... 508-793-2397 213 D
dbell@holycross.edu
BELL, Denise .... 850-973-9481 104 D
belld@nfcc.edu
BELL, Dolores .... 678-359-5015 121 B
doloresb@gordonstate.edu
BELL, Geraldine .... 205-929-1715.... 6 D
gbell@mail.miles.edu
BELL, Gregory, J .... 570-321-4395 400 G
bell@lycoming.edu
BELL, Harold .... 404-270-5269 126 D
hbell@spelman.edu
BELL, Hershey .... 814-866-6641 399 C
hbell@lecom.edu
BELL, III, J. Edward ...... 843-377-2426 419 B
ebell@charlestonlaw.edu
BELL, Jacqueline, B .... 843-377-1327 419 B
jbell@charlestonlaw.edu
BELL, James, L .... 580-327-8590 376 K
jlbell@nwosu.edu
BELL, Jennifer .... 952-885-5390 249 F
jbell@nwhealth.edu
BELL, Jennifer .... 856-256-4410 289 H
bellj@rowan.edu
BELL, Jenny .... 205-665-6565.... 8 E
jbell8@montevallo.edu
BELL, John, D .... 808-675-3455 128 K
john.bell@byuh.edu
BELL, Jorge .... 415-920-6001.. 37 H
jbell@ccsf.edu
BELL, Julie .... 217-228-5432 149 B
bellju@quincy.edu
BELL, Juliette, B .... 410-651-6101 208 C
jbbell@umes.edu
BELL, Kati .... 415-482-2483.. 41 J
kathrina.bell@dominican.edu
BELL, Katrina .... 973-328-5064 285 B
kbell@ccm.edu
BELL, Kelly .... 864-662-6064 418 E
kbell@andersonuniversity.edu
BELL, Kimberly .... 256-216-5364.... 4 C
kimberly.bell@athens.edu
BELL, Laura, G .... 215-871-6609 407 G
laurab@pcom.edu
BELL, Lauren, C .... 804-752-7268 484 C
lbell@rmc.edu
BELL, Lauren, P .... 615-353-3604 437 D
lauren.bell@nscc.edu
BELL, Leslie, T .... 910-521-6760 351 E
leslie.bell@uncp.edu
BELL, Lillie, F .... 318-357-6171 197 D
belle@nsula.edu
BELL, Linda .... 610-372-4721 408 G
lbell@racc.edu
BELL, Linda .... 212-854-2708 299 B
labell@barnard.edu
BELL, Lisa, G .... 859-246-6564 185 G
lisag.bell@kctcs.edu
BELL, Lynn .... 334-556-2223.... 2 B
lbell@wallace.edu
BELL, Marty .... 217-228-5432 149 B
bellma@quincy.edu
BELL, Melanie .... 919-735-5151 347 E
mjbell@waynecc.edu
BELL, Melleta .... 432-837-8388 462 G
mbell@sulross.edu
BELL, Micah .... 210-690-9000 449 K
mbell@hallmarkuniversity.edu
BELL, Michael, S .... 202-685-8685 518 B
bellm@ndu.edu
BELL, Nikki .... 912-583-3287 116 G
nbell@bpc.edu
BELL, Norma, G .... 205-853-1200.... 2 F
ngbell@jeffersonstate.edu
BELL, Peter .... 434-592-6515 482 D
pabell2@liberty.edu
BELL, Rebecca .... 432-685-4556 453 B
rbell@midland.edu
BELL, Rhonda .... 281-998-6150 456 A
rhonda.bell@sjcd.edu
BELL, Richette .... 310-900-1600.. 40 C
rbell@elcamino.edu
BELL, Robert, H .... 626-585-7205.. 56 B
rhbell@pasadena.edu
BELL, Robin .... 229-931-2352 125 G
rbell@southgatech.edu
BELL, Scott .... 907-474-6265.. 10 B
svbell2@alaska.edu
BELL, Sheree .... 636-481-3119 261 B
sbell6@jeffco.edu
BELL, Shirley .... 201-216-9901 285 F
shirley.bell@eicollege.edu
BELL, Stephen .... 610-558-5549 402 G
bells@neumann.edu
BELL, Steven .... 410-626-2502 206 F
skbell@sjc.edu
BELL, Steven .... 757-683-4419 483 G
sdbell@odu.edu
BELL, Stuart, R .... 205-348-5100.... 8 A
stuart.bell@ua.edu
BELL, Tamra .... 360-442-2621 495 G
tbell@lowercolumbia.edu
BELL, Tom, J .... 828-884-8142 335 L
bellt@brevard.edu
BELL, Tommy .... 618-453-7250 152 B
tbell@siu.edu
BELL, Trudy .... 805-546-3206.. 41 C
tbell@cuesta.edu
BELL, Wylie .... 910-410-1826 345 G
wdbell@richmondcc.edu
BELL ADAMS, Sandra ... 718-262-2363 304 A
sadams@york.cuny.edu
BELL-JORDAN, Katrina .. 773-442-5711 147 G
k-bell1@neiu.edu
BELLA, Andres .... 510-763-7787.. 24 D
abella@acchs.edu
BELLACERO,
Cynthia, M .... 252-638-7328 342 E
bellaceroc@cravencc.edu
BELLAFIORE, April .... 508-678-2811 219 C
april.bellafiore@bristolcc.edu
BELLAH, Eric .... 865-981-8225 433 F
eric.bellah@maryvillecollege.edu
BELLALTA, Maria .... 617-262-5000 212 C
maria.bellalta@the-bac.edu
BELLAMKONDA, Ravi ..... 919-660-5389 337 C
ravi@duke.edu
BELLAMY, Antoinette, P 910-630-7257 340 A
abellamy@methodist.edu
BELLAMY, James .... 419-267-1267 366 G
jbellamy@northweststate.edu
BELLAMY, Johnnie, O ... 972-860-7619 447 I
johnniebellamy@dcccd.edu
BELLAMY, Reagan .... 509-682-6445 500 D
rbellamy@wvc.edu
BELLAMY, Sandra .... 212-694-1000 299 L
sbellamy@boricuacollege.edu
BELLAMY, Scott .... 304-357-6696 502 E
scottbellamy@ucwv.edu
BELLANCA, Rose .... 734-973-3491 238 G
rbellanca@wccnet.edu
BELLANI, Rajesh .... 740-587-5034 361 B
bellanir@denison.edu
BELLANTONI, Jeffrey ..... 803-323-2323 426 H
bellantonij@winthrop.edu
BELLAVANCE, Leslie ...... 616-451-2787 230 A
lesliebelavance@ferris.edu
BELLAVIA, Rand .... 716-829-7616 307 B
bellavia@dyc.edu
BELLE ISLE, Denell .... 651-213-4678 242 F
BELLEFEUILLLE,
Barbara, K .... 574-807-7255 156 E
barb.bellefeuille@bethelcollege.edu
BELLEMER, Jess .... 828-898-8770 339 B
bellemerj@lmc.edu
BELLENGER, Lauren ...... 713-221-8197 465 C
bellengerl@uhd.edu
BELLENGHI, Tami .... 503-228-6528 381 I
tbellenghi@aii.edu
BELLEW, Kevin .... 859-858-3511 183 D
kevin.bellew@asbury.edu
BELLICINI, Pierre, A ...... 814-866-8121 399 C
pbellicini@lecom.edu
BELLINA, Amy .... 732-571-3586 287 C
abellina@monmouth.edu
BELLING, Karen .... 630-752-5021 155 F
karen.belling@wheaton.edu
BELLINGER, Andrew ...... 315-792-7141 330 A
abellinger@sunypoly.edu
BELLINGER, Eunice .... 304-205-6613 502 K
eunice.bellinger@bridgevalley.edu
BELLINGER, Jesse .... 803-705-4326 418 G
bellingerj@benedict.edu
BELLINGS, Andy .... 563-588-6420 167 E
andy.bellings@clarke.edu
BELLINI, Michel .... 217-265-5297 154 B
bellini@illinois.edu
BELLINO, Maria .... 480-517-8220.. 14 B
maria.bellino@riosalado.edu
BELLIVEAU, Cynthia, L . 802-656-3890 476 E
cynthia.belliveau@uvm.edu
BELLO, Chippi .... 360-992-2260 493 E
cbello@clark.edu
BELLO, Diane .... 631-632-6179 325 F
diane.bello@stonybrook.edu
BELLO, Violeta .... 310-834-3065.. 67 L
BELLO-DECASTRO,
Leigh .... 973-877-3483 285 K
bellodecastro@essex.edu
BELLOMY, Chasley .... 256-228-6001.... 3 B
bellomyc@nacc.edu
BELLONA, Steven, J ...... 315-859-4502 309 D
sbellona@hamilton.edu
BELLONI, Francis, L ...... 914-594-4110 318 A
francis_belloni@nymc.edu
BELLOTTE, Paul .... 304-243-2081 505 H
pbellotte@wju.edu
BELLOWS, Alan .... 801-649-5230 471 M
BELLOWS, Charlene ...... 508-793-2514 213 D
cbellows@holycross.edu
BELLOWS, Darrin .... 615-966-7600 433 D
darrin.bellows@lipscomb.edu
BELLOWS, Laurie .... 402-472-3755 277 G
lbellows1@unl.edu
BELLUCCI, Debbie .... 413-755-4334 221 B
dbellucci@stcc.edu
BELLUCCI, Keith .... 617-732-2145 221 E
keith.bellucci@mcphs.edu
BELLUM, Kim .... 605-882-5284 427 D
bellumk@lakeareatech.edu
BELMAN, David .... 925-473-7423.. 41 A
dbelman@losmedanos.edu
BELMAR, Eric .... 602-429-4927.. 15 K
ebelmar@ps.edu
BELMAR, Ricardo .... 305-607-6123 104 F
belmar@nova.edu
BELMODIS, Cassie .... 503-399-5159 382 C
cassie.belmodis@chemeketa.edu
BELOBRAJDIC, Scott ..... 618-650-2298 152 C
sbelobr@siue.edu
BELONNI-ROSARIO,
Ruth-Aimée .... 712-290-8709 399 F
rabelonni-rosario@lancasterseminary.edu
BELOTE, Eve .... 757-789-1767 488 A
ebelote@es.vccs.edu
BELOTE, Faith, D .... 757-594-7618 479 H
faith.belote@cnu.edu
BELOTE, Michael, R ...... 478-301-2850 122 H
belote_mr@mercer.edu
BELOW, Debbie .... 573-986-6888 266 M
dbelow@semo.edu
BELROSE, Jacqueline .... 978-632-6600 220 D
j_belrose@mwcc.mass.edu
BELSHER, Judy .... 602-243-8200.. 14 D
judy.belsher@southmountaincc.edu
BELSKY, Jeff .... 412-809-5100 408 D
belsky.jeff@pti.edu
BELSKY, Marianne .... 202-651-5031.. 91 H
marianne.belsky@gallaudet.edu
BELSKY, Yisroel .... 718-941-8000 315 C
BELSTRA, James, E .... 708-239-4720 153 B
jim.belstra@trnty.edu
BELTER, Joe .... 541-888-7634 387 A
joseph.belter@socc.edu
BELTON, Ada, A .... 803-705-4327 418 G
beltona@benedict.edu
BELTON, Allan .... 253-535-7101 496 G
allan.belton@plu.edu
BELTON, Allan .... 253-535-7121 496 G
allan.belton@plu.edu
BELTON, Ann .... 803-536-8406 423 G
abelton3@scsu.edu
BELTON, Kenny, B .... 410-651-3087 208 C
kbbelton@umes.edu
BELTON, Ray .... 225-771-4680 195 K
ray_belton@sus.edu
BELTON, Ray, L .... 225-771-4680 195 J
ray_belton@sus.edu
BELTON, Victor .... 678-662-7989 305 F
victor.belton@concordia-ny.edu
BELTRAME, Grace, J ...... 617-928-4041 222 D
gbeltrame@mountida.edu
BELTRAN, Cherie .... 254-267-7038 454 L
cbeltran@rangercollege.edu
BELTRAN, JD .... 415-351-3530.. 60 G
jdbeltran@sfai.edu
BELTRAN, Philip .... 408-554-4161.. 62 F
pjbeltran@scu.edu
BELTRONE, Gail .... 212-854-6031 299 B
gbeltron@barnard.edu
BELTZ, Marah .... 386-481-2928.. 95 J
beltzm@cookman.edu
BEMIS, Scot, R .... 603-646-3768 281 C
scot.r.bemis@dartmouth.edu
BEMSKI, Peter .... 928-541-7777.. 54 B
pbemski@ncu.edu
BEN AROUS, Gerard, A 212-998-3108 318 D
gba1@nyu.edu
BENABESS, Najiba .... 217-424-6285 145 J
nbenabess@millikin.edu
BENAICHA, Hedi .... 617-349-8836 216 D
hbenaich@lesley.edu
BENANDER, Mark .... 413-565-1000 211 C
mbenander@baypath.edu
BENAVIDES, Elma, F ..... 512-863-1441 457 I
benavide@southwestern.edu

BENAVIDES, Julie .... 323-265-8779.. 48 L benavij@elac.edu
BENAVIDES, Leticia .... 956-665-2255 468 A letty.benavides@utrgv.edu
BENAVIDES, Lewis .... 940-898-3555 464 A lbenavides@twu.edu
BENAVIDES-DOMINGUEZ, Patricia .... 361-698-2474 448 H pbdominguez@delmar.edu
BENAVIDEZ, Max .... 909-607-0875.. 37 L max.benavidez@cgu.edu
BENBOW, Camilla, P .... 615-322-8407 440 D camilla.benbow@vanderbilt.edu
BENCHOFF, Bryan .... 225-578-3811 193 M contact@lsufoundation.org
BENDAPUDI, Neeli .... 785-864-4904 181 I neeli@ku.edu
BENDARSH, Joe .... 212-960-0110 334 P joe.bednarsh@yu.edu
BENDECK, Yvette .... 281-283-3022 465 B bendeck@uhcl.edu
BENDEL, Colleen .... 740-593-1642 368 G bendl@ohio.edu
BENDELE, Jennifer .... 419-227-3141 372 D jennifer@unoh.edu
BENDER, Dave .... 614-823-1876 368 O dbender@otterbein.edu
BENDER, David, L .... 989-837-4374 235 C bender@northwood.edu
BENDER, Don .... 509-335-5593 499 G bender@wsu.edu
BENDER, Donna .... 504-314-2148 196 D dbender@tulane.edu
BENDER, Jennie, M ...... 606-474-3226 185 C jbender@kcu.edu
BENDER, Jim .... 651-638-6400 240 J j-bender@bethel.edu
BENDER, Judy .... 585-475-4315 321 D jebpsn@rit.edu
BENDER, Karla .... 713-718-8247 450 D karla.bender@hccs.edu
BENDER, Kim .... 307-778-4337 516 N kbender@lccc.wy.edu
BENDER, Laurie .... 732-224-2059 284 B lbender@brookdalecc.edu
BENDER, Linda .... 307-855-2102 516 I lbender@cwc.edu
BENDER, Loren, J .... 407-582-3408 113 F lbender2@valenciacollege.edu
BENDER, Marian .... 814-472-3931 409 G mbender@francis.edu
BENDER, Michael .... 845-207-0330 298 F
BENDER, Rick .... 432-685-4529 453 B rbender@midland.edu
BENDER, Shane .... 817-274-4284 444 C sbender@bhcarroll.edu
BENDER, Starr, S .... 407-303-5765.. 94 H starr.bender@adu.edu
BENDER, Stephanie .... 410-337-6431 204 A stephanie.bender@goucher.edu
BENDER, Susan .... 208-885-2539 132 I benders@uidaho.edu
BENDER, IV, Thomas, B .... 504-866-7426 195 E librarian@nds.edu
BENDER, Virginia .... 201-761-6024 291 D vbender@saintpeters.edu
BENDER, Virginia, A ...... 201-761-6024 291 D vbender@saintpeters.edu
BENDER, Yaakov .... 718-868-2300 299 D
BENDICKSON, Alisa ...... 414-930-3578 509 B bendicka@mtmary.edu
BENDICKSON, Kimberly 941-487-4668 110 B kbendickson@ncf.edu
BENDICKSON, Mary ...... 813-253-7210 101 M mbendickson@hccfl.edu
BENEDETTI, Brian .... 253-864-3235 497 B bbenedetti@pierce.ctc.edu
BENEDETTI, Marco, F ... 716-888-2480 300 G benedet2@canisius.edu
BENEDETTO, Geri .... 908-737-7000 286 F gbenedet@kean.edu
BENEDICK, Ronald, W .. 614-235-4136 370 M rbenedick@tlsohio.edu
BENEDICT, Amy .... 607-436-2534 325 E amy.benedict@oneonta.edu
BENEDICT, Barbara .... 719-549-3039.. 81 M barbara.benedict@pueblocc.edu
BENEDICT, Christine ..... 608-663-2294 507 D cbenedict@edgewood.edu
BENEDICT, David .... 860-486-2725.. 88 G david.benedict@uconn.edu
BENEDICT, Dow .... 304-876-5393 504 D dbenedic@shepherd.edu
BENEDICT, Dwight .... 202-651-5064.. 91 H dwight.benedict@gallaudet.edu
BENEDICT, Jody, C .... 585-385-8322 322 E jbenedict@sjfc.edu
BENEDICT, Reeta .... 207-509-7273 200 I rbenedict@unity.edu
BENEDICT, Stacie .... 559-453-7195.. 43 J stacie.benedict@fresno.edu
BENEDIK, Michael .... 979-845-4016 459 C benedik@tamu.edu
BENEFIEL, Lori .... 541-383-7572 382 B lbenefiel@cocc.edu
BENEFIEL, Ron .... 619-849-2613.. 57 H ronbenefiel@pointloma.edu
BENEFIEL, Shannon .... 606-337-1072 184 D shannon.benefiel@ccbbc.edu
BENEKE, Thomas, J ...... 515-574-1050 170 C beneke@iowacentral.edu
BENESH, Gina .... 314-539-5355 266 E gbenesh@stlcc.edu
BENET, Suzeanne .... 616-331-2400 230 G benets@gvsu.edu
BENFANTI, William, J ... 716-878-5557 326 E benfanwj@buffalostate.edu
BENFER, Pamela, A .... 570-577-1561 390 H pam.benfer@bucknell.edu
BENFORD, Gladys .... 870-575-8405.. 22 E benfordg@uapb.edu
BENFORD, Jeffrey .... 925-473-7425.. 41 A jbenford@losmedanos.edu
BENFORD, Kacee .... 575-461-4413 294 E kaceeb@mesalands.edu
BENFORD, Michael .... 713-221-8129 465 C benfordm@uhd.edu
BENGE, Robert .... 423-236-2855 436 C rcbenge@southern.edu
BENGEL, Jo Ann .... 626-815-5003.. 26 U jbengel@apu.edu
BENGFORT, Joseph .... 415-353-4273.. 70 A joe.bengfort@ucsf.edu
BENGINIA, Francis, A ... 610-330-5090 399 B benginif@lafayette.edu
BENGTSON, Kathy .... 612-767-7051 240 B kathy.bengtson@alfredadler.edu
BENHAM, Maenette .... 808-689-2770 130 A mbenham@hawaii.edu
BENHAM-DEAL, Tami .... 307-766-4286 517 B benham@uwyo.edu
BENIGER, Joe .... 920-565-1000 507 K benigerjw@lakeland.edu
BENINGHOVE, Linda ..... 201-216-5412 291 G linda.beninghove@stevens.edu
BENISH, Amy, L .... 262-554-2010 508 E albenish@aol.com
BENITEZ, Hubert .... 816-936-8711 266 K hbenitez@saintlukescollege.edu
BENITEZ, Leyda, L .... 610-519-3976 413 K leyda.benitez@villanova.edu
BENITEZ, Michael .... 253-879-3929 499 C mbenitez@pugetsound.edu
BENITEZ-RAMIREZ, Solange .... 787-993-8863 527 G solange.benitez@upr.edu
BENITO, Agueda .... 312-752-2094 142 E agueda.benito@kendall.edu
BENJAMIN, Ashu .... 504-286-5279 195 L abenjamin@suno.edu
BENJAMIN, Bill .... 727-873-4199 111 B benjamin@mail.usf.edu
BENJAMIN, Eric, V .... 931-598-1241 436 A ebenjami@sewanee.edu
BENJAMIN, Finbar .... 256-726-7105.... 6 E fbenjamin@oakwood.edu
BENJAMIN, Guy .... 808-237-5144 129 B
BENJAMIN, Jack .... 803-641-3327 425 A jackb@usca.edu
BENJAMIN, Jodi .... 402-941-6102 275 J benjamin@midlandu.edu
BENJAMIN, Richardean . 757-683-4960 483 G rbenjami@odu.edu
BENJAMIN, Robert .... 269-471-3310 227 B robertb@andrews.edu
BENJAMIN, Robert .... 617-745-3595 214 D robert.j.benjamin@enc.edu
BENJAMIN, Shanna .... 641-269-4510 169 F benjamin@grinnell.edu
BENKE, Jack .... 573-592-5231 270 B jack.benke@westminster-mo.edu
BENKE, Robin, P .... 276-328-0151 487 A rpb@wise.edu
BENKESER, Kristina .... 724-738-2052 407 C kristina.benkeser@sru.edu
BENKO, Hope .... 512-472-4133 456 E hope.benko@ssw.edu
BENKO, Richard, A .... 724-287-8711 390 J richard.benko@bc3.edu
BENLOLO, Henri .... 352-854-2322.. 97 C benloloh@cf.edu
BENMAMOUN, Abbas ... 919-684-4997 337 C elabbas.benmamoun@duke.edu
BENN, Delores .... 704-403-3502 336 B delores.benn@carolinashealthcare.org
BENN, Sherri .... 512-245-2278 463 A sb17@txstate.edu
BENN, Valerie .... 919-718-7423 341 H vbenn159@cccc.edu
BENN-MARSHALL, Karen .... 256-726-7005.... 6 E kmarshall@oakwood.edu
BENNATTS, Denise .... 253-833-9111 495 C dbennatts@greenriver.edu
BENNE, Jennifer .... 573-681-5125 261 H bennej@lincolnu.edu
BENNECKE, Margie .... 847-233-7700 148 A mbennecke@nc.edu
BENNEIAN, Teresa .... 717-290-8748 399 F tbenneian@lancasterseminary.edu
BENNER, Brent, W .... 813-253-6211 113 E bbenner@ut.edu
BENNER, Mary .... 405-208-5270 377 D mbenner@okcu.edu
BENNER, Patrick, B .... 804-289-8930 486 G pbenner@richmond.edu
BENNER, Tracy .... 614-823-1580 368 O tbenner@otterbein.edu
BENNETT, Amy .... 317-955-6768 162 R abennett@marian.edu
BENNETT, Anthony, T ... 910-672-1314 350 B abennett@uncfsu.edu
BENNETT, Bo .... 828-448-6197 339 B bennettb@lmc.edu
BENNETT, Bradley .... 785-460-5403 176 L brad.bennett@colbycc.edu
BENNETT, Calvin .... 601-484-8894 253 G cbennett@meridiancc.edu
BENNETT, Cameron, D .. 253-535-7150 496 G bennetcd@plu.edu
BENNETT, Carolyn .... 516-876-3203 327 C bennettc@oldwestbury.edu
BENNETT, Cathryn .... 336-272-7201 338 B cathryn.bennett@greensboro.edu
BENNETT, Christopher .. 440-375-7000 364 C cbennett@lec.edu
BENNETT, Curtis .... 562-985-5559.. 32 C curtis.bennett@csulb.edu
BENNETT, Daniel .... 828-669-8012 340 I dbennett@montreat.edu
BENNETT, David, A .... 606-474-3256 185 C dbennett@kcu.edu
BENNETT, David, P .... 202-806-6100.. 92 C
BENNETT, Derwin .... 518-255-5836 328 C bennetdd@cobleskill.edu
BENNETT, Diane .... 715-425-3195 511 E diane.bennett@uwrf.edu
BENNETT, Dorine .... 605-256-5137 428 G dorine.bennett@dsu.edu
BENNETT, Doug, L .... 740-368-3148 368 N dlbennet@owu.edu
BENNETT, Douglas .... 714-432-0202.. 38 H
BENNETT, Douglas .... 714-432-5126.. 38 H dbennett@occ.cccd.edu
BENNETT, Drew, A .... 417-255-7900 263 I wpchancellor@missouristate.edu
BENNETT, Drew, A .... 417-255-7900 263 H drewbennett@missouristate.edu
BENNETT, Eddie .... 434-736-2055 489 E eddie.bennett@southside.edu
BENNETT, Elbert .... 870-575-8504.. 22 E bennette@uapb.edu
BENNETT, Elizabeth, C .. 949-824-7982.. 69 A bennette@uci.edu
BENNETT, Elizabeth, P .. 717-290-8713 399 F ebennett@lancasterseminary.edu
BENNETT, Ephraim .... 757-823-8214 483 F ejbennett@nsu.edu
BENNETT, Eric .... 212-659-7290 312 E ebennett@tkc.edu
BENNETT, Gene .... 870-780-1201.. 17 K gbennett@smail.anc.edu
BENNETT, George .... 509-527-2930 499 F george.bennett@wallawalla.edu
BENNETT, Gloria .... 706-821-8726 124 C gbennett@paine.edu
BENNETT, Heather .... 309-796-5301 134 C bennetth@bhc.edu
BENNETT, Herman .... 212-817-7540 302 B hbennett@gc.cuny.edu
BENNETT, Holly, L .... 561-207-5400 105 A bennetth@palmbeachstate.edu
BENNETT, Jabbar .... 847-467-7490 148 C jabbar@northwestern.edu
BENNETT, James .... 913-288-7259 178 H jbennett@kckcc.edu
BENNETT, Janice, G ...... 563-588-8000 169 B jbennett@emmaus.edu
BENNETT, Janis, A .... 304-766-3010 505 A bennetja@wvstateu.edu
BENNETT, Jeffrey, L ...... 570-321-4031 400 G bennett@lycoming.edu
BENNETT, Jeremy .... 580-559-5256 375 I jbennett@ecok.edu
BENNETT, Jim .... 408-551-1910.. 62 F jbbennett@scu.edu
BENNETT, Jim .... 406-265-3594 272 C james.bennett10@msun.edu
BENNETT, Joan, W .... 848-932-6223 290 A profmycogirl@yahoo.com
BENNETT, JoAnn .... 937-327-6185 374 A jbennett@wittenberg.edu
BENNETT, Josh .... 406-447-6932 271 I josh.bennett@umhelelna.edu
BENNETT, Kari .... 518-438-3111 314 B bennettk@mariacollege.edu
BENNETT, Katrina .... 352-365-3510 103 B bennettk@lssc.edu
BENNETT, Kevin .... 904-256-7585 102 B kbennet1@ju.edu
BENNETT, Kim .... 260-665-4438 164 E bennettk@trine.edu
BENNETT, Kristen .... 903-670-2664 464 C kristen.bennett@tvcc.edu
BENNETT, Laura .... 541-956-7136 386 G lbennett@roguecc.edu
BENNETT, Linda L, M .... 812-464-1756 165 C bennettl@usi.edu
BENNETT, Lisa .... 585-594-6804 319 B bennett_lisa@roberts.edu
BENNETT, Lori .... 559-325-5200.. 66 F
BENNETT, Marla .... 217-732-3168 143 F hr@lincolnchristian.edu
BENNETT, Matt .... 517-338-3014 228 G mbennett@cleary.edu
BENNETT, Maybelle, T .. 202-806-4771.. 92 C maybelle.bennett@howard.edu
BENNETT, Michael, J ..... 727-341-3012 107 A bennett.michael@spcollege.edu
BENNETT, Patricia .... 850-729-4901 104 E bennettp@nwfsc.edu
BENNETT, Patrick .... 623-245-4600.. 16 H pbennett@uti.edu
BENNETT, Patrick .... 614-947-6836 362 A patrick.bennett@franklin.edu
BENNETT, Rex .... 765-998-2751 164 C
BENNETT, II, Richard, E .... 518-629-7205 310 G r.bennett@hvcc.edu
BENNETT, Rick .... 408-855-5232.. 74 C rick.bennett@wvm.edu
BENNETT, Robert .... 518-327-6049 320 A bbennett@paulsmiths.edu
BENNETT, Rodney .... 301-846-2501 203 H rbennett@frederick.edu
BENNETT, Rodney, D .... 601-266-5001 256 E president@usm.edu
BENNETT, Sari, M .... 603-862-4285 282 F sari.bennett@unh.edu
BENNETT, Scott .... 904-620-2002 110 E sbennett@unf.edu
BENNETT, Scott .... 281-425-6396 451 I sbennett@lee.edu
BENNETT, Sherri .... 870-838-2945.. 17 K sbennett@smail.anc.edu
BENNETT, Stephen, R .... 507-933-7526 242 D sbennett@gustavus.edu
BENNETT, Tameika .... 718-429-6600 333 B tameika.bennett@vaughn.edu
BENNETT, Tanya .... 678-717-2292 127 B tanya.bennett@ung.edu
BENNETT, II, Thomas ... 304-766-3112 505 A tbennett3@wvstateu.edu
BENNETT, Todd .... 404-364-8329 124 A tbennett1@oglethorpe.edu
BENNETT, Toni .... 901-321-3297 431 A toni.bennett@cbu.edu
BENNETT, Valerie .... 309-677-3961 134 G vbennett@bradley.edu
BENNETT, Vernell .... 662-846-4150 252 H vbennett@deltastate.edu
BENNIE, Kevin, M .... 530-226-4978.. 64 B kbennie@simpsonu.edu
BENNIE, Roanna .... 925-424-1104.. 36 D rbennie@laspositascollege.edu
BENNIEFIELD, Marcus .. 619-702-9400.. 30 C marcus.benniefield@cibu.edu
BENNIGHOFF, James ..... 254-710-3601 444 B james_bennighoff@baylor.edu
BENNING, Tom .... 314-529-9304 262 B tbenning@maryville.edu
BENNINGTON, Cheryl, C .... 304-336-8049 504 E cbennington@westliberty.edu
BENNION, Paul .... 208-459-5841 131 H pbennion@collegeofidaho.edu
BENOIT, Andy .... 337-482-6474 197 F ajbenoit@louisiana.edu
BENOIT, Andy .... 864-388-8183 422 A abenoit@lander.edu

BENOIT, Anthony .... 617-588-1324 211 G abenoit@bfit.edu
BENOIT, Debra .... 985-493-2563 197 C debi.benoit@nicholls.edu
BENOIT, Doug .... 714-992-7033.. 54 A dbenoit@fullcoll.edu
BENOIT, Jennifer, D ...... 814-865-8753 403 F jdd41@psu.edu
BENOIT, Michele .... 541-888-7421 387 A mbenoit@socc.edu
BENOIT, Pam .... 205-934-0622.... 8 B benoit@uab.edu
BENOIT, Thomas .... 325-793-3869 452 F tbenoit@mcm.edu
BENOL, Christine .... 732-571-7516 287 C cbenol@monmouth.edu
BENOLKEN, Julie .... 651-450-3622 245 A jbenolk@inverhills.edu
BENRUD, Ann .... 612-874-3793 243 F abenrud@mcad.edu
BENSE, Kim .... 970-675-3335.. 78 H kim.bense@cncc.edu
BENSEL, Terry .... 814-332-3391 388 F tbensel@allegheny.edu
BENSINK, Michael .... 508-678-2811 219 C michael.bensink@bristolcc.edu
BENSON, Allen, C .... 401-841-3397 518 E
BENSON, Barry .... 217-244-1206 154 B bensonb@illinois.edu
BENSON, Becca .... 601-925-3830 254 B rbenson@mc.edu
BENSON, Bill .... 541-962-3241 383 B wbenson@eou.edu
BENSON, Brenda .... 310-434-4433.. 62 G benson_brenda@smc.edu
BENSON, Bruce, D .... 303-860-5600.. 83 A officeofthepresident@cu.edu
BENSON, Craig .... 434-924-3593 486 H chb4x@virginia.edu
BENSON, Daniel .... 507-389-6838 246 A daniel.benson@mnsu.edu
BENSON, Duane .... 712-274-5133 172 A bensond@morningside.edu
BENSON, Ella .... 252-398-6304 336 K bensone@chowan.edu
BENSON, Erin, V .... 207-768-9453 201 G erin.benson@maine.edu
BENSON, Gus .... 859-622-3636 184 F gus.benson@eku.edu
BENSON, Haley .... 847-259-1840 135 H
BENSON, Holly .... 334-244-3125.... 4 E hbenson@aum.edu
BENSON, Jason .... 701-483-2014 354 A jason.bensen@sodexo.com
BENSON, Jennifer .... 706-355-5124 115 H jbenson@athenstech.edu
BENSON, Kristin, R .... 971-722-7724 386 C kristin.benson@pcc.edu
BENSON, Mark .... 518-442-2562 324 G mabenson@albany.edu
BENSON, Megan .... 602-383-8228.. 16 I mbenson@uat.edu
BENSON, Melinda .... 307-766-5080 517 B
BENSON, Michael .... 859-622-2977 184 F michael.benson@eku.edu
BENSON, Mindy .... 435-586-7763 473 A benson@suu.edu
BENSON, Neal, L .... 304-462-6119 504 B neal.benson@glenville.edu
BENSON, Patricia .... 610-526-6142 396 H pbenson@harcum.edu
BENSON, Patrick .... 312-788-1133 154 I meca@vandercook.edu
BENSON, Paul, H .... 937-229-2245 372 A pbenson1@udayton.edu
BENSON, Peter .... 203-287-3017.. 87 G paier.admin@snet.net
BENSON, Richard .... 972-883-2201 467 D benson@utdallas.edu
BENSON, Robert, M .... 865-882-4553 438 A bensonrm@roanestate.edu
BENSON, Robin .... 918-647-1344 375 B rbenson@carlalbert.edu
BENSON, Samantha .... 910-879-5567 341 A sbenson@bladencc.edu
BENSON, Scott, A .... 308-865-8431 277 F bensonsa1@unk.edu
BENSON, Stephanie, G . 706-355-5112 115 H sbenson@athenstech.edu
BENSON, Stephen .... 254-299-8649 452 E sbenson@mclennan.edu
BENSON, Vaughn .... 402-375-7245 276 D vabenso1@wsc.edu
BENSON, Wade, M .... 706-379-3111 128 H wadeb@yhc.edu
BENSON-CLAYTON, Taffye .... 334-844-4184.... 4 D tbc0028@auburn.edu
BENSON-TYUS, Hasanna .... 202-462-2101.. 92 D benson@iwp.edu
BENSTON, Kimberly, W 610-896-1021 397 F kbenston@haverford.edu
BENT, Lauren .... 978-837-5250 221 G
BENTE, James .... 630-942-2409 136 D bentej@cod.edu
BENTLEY, Barry .... 606-218-5988 190 E barrybentley@upike.edu
BENTLEY, Cynthia .... 225-923-2331 173 K bentleyc@uiu.edu
BENTLEY, Erik .... 952-358-8274 246 D erik.bentley@normandale.edu
BENTLEY, Jane .... 708-974-5703 146 C jane.bentley@morainevalley.edu
BENTLEY, Jay .... 478-387-0660 120 B jbentley@gmc.edu
BENTLEY, Kelvin .... 817-515-5024 458 B kelvin.bentley@tccd.edu
BENTLEY, Marissa .... 406-496-4377 272 E mbentley2@mtech.edu
BENTLEY, Sue .... 612-343-4442 249 E slbentle@northcentral.edu
BENTLEY, Tiffanie, L ...... 207-741-5610 200 C tbentley@smccme.edu
BENTLEY, Tony .... 309-347-5448 134 H abentley@sandurg.edu
BENTLEY-COLTHART, Nicki .... 304-472-8488 505 G bentley-colthart@wvwc.edu
BENTLIN, Dave .... 309-438-5454 140 L dmbentl@ilstu.edu
BENTON, Andrew, K ...... 310-506-4451.. 56 D andrew.benton@pepperdine.edu
BENTON, Brandie .... 870-230-5203.. 19 H bentonb@hsu.edu
BENTON, Debra, M .... 740-593-4260 368 G bentond@ohio.edu
BENTON, Graham .... 707-654-1147.. 32 E gbenton@csum.edu
BENTON, James .... 828-659-0444 344 G jimbenton@mcdowelltech.edu
BENTON, Jerel .... 715-394-8015 512 B jbenton1@uwsuper.edu
BENTON, Lauren .... 615-322-2851 440 D lauren.benton@vanderbilt.edu
BENTON, Sherry .... 352-392-1575 110 D shbenton@ufl.edu
BENTON, William .... 717-815-1271 415 G wbenton@ycp.edu
BENTZ, Allyson .... 724-846-5100 395 J
BENTZ, David .... 406-496-4835 272 E dbentz@mtech.edu
BENTZ, Mandy .... 865-539-7203 437 F mdbentz@pstcc.edu
BENULIS, Joan, R .... 585-385-8010 322 E jbenulis@sjfc.edu
BENVENGER, Deborah, A .... 215-871-6711 407 G admissions@pcom.edu
BENVENUTTI, Mary Beth .... 510-748-2211.. 56 G mbenvenutti@peralta.edu
BENWAY, Elizabeth .... 508-830-5086 218 D ebenway@maritime.edu
BENWELL, Deirdre .... 509-527-2066 499 F deirdre.benwell@wallawalla.edu
BENYSHEK, Carolyn, A . 719-333-9751 518 H
BENZ, Abigail .... 417-447-2614 264 K benza@otc.edu
BENZ, Edward .... 631-451-4567 330 C benze@sunysuffolk.edu
BENZ, Kathleen .... 661-362-3032.. 39 C kathleen.benz@canyons.edu
BENZ, Leah .... 217-641-4102 141 F lbenz@jwcc.edu
BENITEZ-RAMIREZ, Solange .... 787-993-8874 527 G solange.benitez@upr.edu
BEOUGHER, David .... 610-683-4305 406 D beougher@kutztown.edu
BEQUETTE, Angela, L .... 919-866-5394 347 D albequette@waketech.edu
BEQUETTE, Lori .... 704-355-3920 336 F lori.bequette@carolinascollege.edu
BERALDI, JR., Thomas . 603-645-9695 282 C t.beraldi@snhu.edu
BERAN, Connie .... 512-313-3000 446 N connie.beran@concordia.edu
BERAN, Paul, B .... 479-788-7007.. 22 A paul.beran@uafs.edu
BERAN, Wayne, B .... 361-570-4811 465 D beranw@uhv.edu
BERARDI, Richard .... 732-987-2469 286 D rberardi@georgian.edu
BERARDI, William .... 508-678-2811 219 C william.berardi@bristolcc.edu
BERARDINELLI, Joseph . 954-776-4476 102 G josephb@keiseruniversity.edu
BERARDINELLI, Joseph . 888-772-6077.. 98 F
BERBERET, James, M ... 815-599-3406 139 F jim.berberet@highland.edu
BERBRIER, Mitch .... 256-824-6200.... 8 C berbrim@uah.edu
BERCAW, Lynne .... 530-898-6421.. 31 D
BERCEL, James .... 585-582-8231 307 C jamesbercel@elim.edu
BERCOT, Rex, A .... 260-399-7700 165 B rbercot@sf.edu
BERDANIER, Bruce .... 203-254-4000.. 87 A bberdanier@fairfield.edu
BERENBAUM, Asher ...... 917-645-0536 315 G phecht@thejnet.com
BERENBAUM, Devorah .. 718-645-0536 315 G mirrer@thejnet.com
BERENBAUM, Rachel ..... 718-645-0536 315 G mirrer@thejnet.com
BERENSON, Jennifer, K . 540-375-2204 484 H berenson@roanoke.edu
BERESFORD, Jack .... 619-388-6914.. 60 B jberesford@sdccd.edu
BEREZNIAK, Ronald ...... 941-756-0690 399 C rberezniak@lecom.edu
BERG, Allison, S .... 404-686-2980 119 B allison.berg@emory.edu
BERG, Amy .... 607-753-5942 327 A amy.berg@cortland.edu
BERG, Beth .... 413-585-2106 224 F bberg@smith.edu
BERG, Cyndi .... 612-330-1212 240 G bergc2@augsburg.edu
BERG, Cynthia .... 801-581-8620 472 P cynthia.berg@csbs.utah.edu
BERG, Dale .... 520-326-1600.. 15 U
BERG, Denise .... 717-871-7551 407 A denise.berg@millersville.edu
BERG, Emily .... 701-231-8263 354 D emily.berg@ndsu.edu
BERG, Gary .... 805-437-8580.. 31 C gary.berg@csuci.edu
BERG, Gerralynne .... 715-634-4790 507 J gberg@lco.edu
BERG, James .... 212-220-8323 301 C jberg@bmcc.cuny.edu
BERG, Jessica, W .... 216-368-3283 358 C jessica.berg@case.edu
BERG, Jill, M .... 414-326-2301 507 B jill.berg@ccon.edu
BERG, Jody .... 402-354-7034 275 P jody.berg@methodistcollege.edu
BERG, Joel, H .... 206-543-5980 499 D joelberg@uw.edu
BERG, Kara .... 970-339-6407.. 76 E kara.odell@aims.edu
BERG, Kevin .... 509-682-6815 500 D kberg@wvc.edu
BERG, Kevin, A .... 253-535-7890 496 G bergka@plu.edu
BERG, Roger .... 913-621-8744 177 A rberg@donnelly.edu
BERG, Shane, A .... 609-497-7803 288 E comm-pub@ptsem.edu
BERG, Shelton, G .... 305-284-2241 112 O sberg@miami.edu
BERG, Stacey, L .... 832-824-4588 444 A sberg@bcm.edu
BERG, Tamara .... 507-457-5460 248 C tberg@winona.edu
BERG, Thomas .... 914-968-6200 323 C ftb@fatherberg.com
BERGAMASCO, Carla, R 412-578-6174 391 G crbergamasco@carlow.edu
BERGAN, Maureen .... 251-380-3498.... 7 B mbergan@shc.edu
BERGANDI, Cherrie .... 715-833-6483 513 E cbergandi@cvtc.edu
BERGANDI, Cherrie .... 608-785-9106 515 C bergandic@westerntc.edu
BERGANT, Amy .... 417-447-8984 264 K berganta@otc.edu
BERGEN, Lori .... 303-492-5007.. 83 B lori.bergen@colorado.edu
BERGEN, Randy .... 651-635-8041 240 J r-bergen@bethel.edu
BERGEN, Victoria .... 517-607-2301 231 C vbergen@hillsdale.edu
BERGENGREN, Audrey .. 651-846-1305 247 G audrey.bergengren@saintpaul.edu
BERGER, Amy, C .... 818-677-2932.. 33 B amy.berger@csun.edu
BERGER, Andy .... 312-935-4100 149 K aberger@robertmorris.edu
BERGER, Aron .... 845-426-3276 334 B ydm@thejnet.com
BERGER, Darlene .... 828-232-4999 351 A dberger@unca.edu
BERGER, David .... 212-960-5253 334 P dberger@yu.edu
BERGER, Derek .... 317-921-4882 161 F berger@ivytech.edu
BERGER, Elliot .... 212-431-2151 317 H elliot.berger@nyls.edu
BERGER, Fran .... 617-928-4681 222 D fberger@mountida.edu
BERGER, John .... 901-572-2452 430 C john.berger@bchs.edu
BERGER, Joseph .... 617-287-7600 216 I joseph.berger@umb.edu
BERGER, Leslie .... 405-208-5348 377 D lberger@okcu.edu
BERGER, Lynn .... 518-255-5423 328 C bergerla@cobleskill.edu
BERGER, Lynn .... 518-255-5465 328 C bergerla@cobleskill.edu
BERGER, Mark .... 404-261-1441 124 A mberger@oglethorpe.edu
BERGER, Michael .... 602-639-7500.. 12 P
BERGER, Patrice .... 402-472-5425 277 G pberger1@unl.edu
BERGER, Scott .... 320-762-4475 243 J scottb@alextech.edu
BERGER, Sheri .... 818-710-2281.. 49 D bergersl@piercecollege.edu
BERGER, William .... 814-732-1107 406 B wberger@edinboro.edu
BERGER, Yaakov .... 845-393-4308 334 E admin@kessertorah.org
BERGER-SWEENEY, Joanne .... 860-297-2086.. 88 E president@trincoll.edu
BERGERON, Bette, S .... 315-267-2108 328 A bergerbs@potsdam.edu
BERGERON, Ian .... 413-662-5592 218 C ian.bergeron@mcla.edu
BERGERON, Iva .... 214-860-8735 448 B ibergeron@dcccd.edu
BERGERON, Katherine ... 860-447-1911.. 86 H katherine.bergeron@conncoll.edu
BERGERON, Mindy .... 925-969-3300.. 46 L mbergeron@jfku.edu
BERGES, Cherry, L .... 270-824-8677 186 D cherry.berges@kctcs.edu
BERGESON, Daniel .... 507-222-5992 241 C dbergeso@carleton.edu
BERGESON, Patricia ...... 312-369-7478 136 H pbergeson@colum.edu
BERGESON, Rachel .... 631-632-6740 325 F rachel.bergeson@stonybrook.edu
BERGESON, Terry, M .... 253-535-7656 496 G bergestm@plu.edu
BERGETZ, Carl .... 312-942-6886 150 F carl_bergetz@rush.edu
BERGGREN, Kent, E ...... 208-535-5373 131 G kent.berggren@my.eitc.edu
BERGHOFF, Carolyn ...... 312-788-1151 154 I cberghoff@vandercook.edu
BERGIN, Bonita, M .... 707-545-3647.. 27 B bonnie@berginu.edu
BERGKAMP, Sheila .... 620-227-9404 176 N sbergkamp@dc3.edu
BERGLER, Michael .... 949-214-3187.. 40 I michael.bergler@cui.edu
BERGLUND, Bruce .... 616-526-6194 228 B brb6@calvin.edu
BERGLUND, Carson .... 617-873-0299 213 B carson.berglund@cambridgecollege.edu
BERGLUND, Lars .... 916-703-9120.. 68 H lberglund@ucdavis.edu
BERGLUND, Lori .... 712-749-2444 167 C berglundl@bvu.edu
BERGMAN, Greg .... 218-855-8145 244 C gbergman@clcmn.edu
BERGMAN, Joe .... 309-694-5367 139 G joe.bergman@icc.edu
BERGMAN, John .... 907-852-1867.... 9 H john.bergman@ilisagvik.edu
BERGMAN, Matthew ...... 217-228-5432 149 B bergmma@quincy.edu
BERGMAN, Rebecca, M 507-933-7538 242 D president@gustavus.edu
BERGMAN, JR., William, T .... 215-204-7405 411 B william.bergman@temple.edu
BERGMANN, Michelle ... 541-440-4620 387 E michelle.bergmann@umpqua.edu
BERGMANN, Ronald ...... 718-960-8421 302 C ronald.bergmann@lehman.cuny.edu
BERGMANN, Tom .... 847-947-5516 146 G tbergmann@nl.edu
BERGQUIST, Viola .... 320-308-5177 247 F vbergquist@sctcc.edu

BERGREN, Rebecca, A .. 717-337-6866 396 A
rbergren@gettysburg.edu
BERGRUD, Erik .... 816-584-6412 265 C
erik.bergrud@park.edu
BERGS, Thomas .... 651-846-1676 247 G
thomas.bergs@saintpaul.edu
BERGSMA, Brad .... 785-890-3641 180 G
brad.bergsma@nwktc.edu
BERGSMARK, Beth .... 202-687-5883.. 92 B
bab@georgetown.edu
BERGSTROM, Chip .... 617-217-9070 211 D
cbergstrom@baystate.edu
BERGSTROM, Mary, C .. 843-953-0193 420 C
bergstromm@cofc.edu
BERGSTROM, Scott, J ... 208-496-1136 131 D
bergstroms@byui.edu
BERGSTROM, Tracey ..... 361-582-2535 470 A
tracey.bergstrom@victoriacollege.edu
BERGTRAUM, Judy .... 646-664-2603 301 A
judy.bergtraum@cuny.edu
BERGUM, Mike .... 765-983-1483 157 I
bergumi@earlham.edu
BERHE, Annette .... 901-435-1351 433 A
annette.berhe@loc.edu
BERISH, Dolores .... 513-875-3344 359 C
dolores.berish@chatfield.edu
BERK, Anne-Marie .... 309-341-7793 142 G
apberk@knox.edu
BERK, Steven, L .... 806-743-3000 463 E
steven.berk@ttuhsc.edu
BERKE, Deborah .... 203-432-2279.. 89 G
deborah.berke@yale.edu
BERKELEY, Sydney, C ... 843-355-4121 426 G
berkeleys@wiltech.edu
BERKENPAS, Barb .... 507-537-6215 248 A
barb.berkenpas@smsu.edu
BERKEY, Jessica .... 864-294-2267 421 I
jessica.berkey@furman.edu
BERKHALTER, Dara .... 765-998-5112 164 C
dara_berkhalter@taylor.edu
BERKHEIMER, Eric, J .... 410-677-6553 209 B
ejberkheimer@salisbury.edu
BERKHEIMER, Karen ..... 410-334-2915 210 C
kberkheimer@worwic.edu
BERKHOF, Robert, A ..... 616-526-6091 228 B
berk@calvin.edu
BERKLAS, Jennifer, L .... 909-607-7976.. 63 F
jberklas@scrippscollege.edu
BERKLEY, Shelley .... 702-777-1776.. 67 H
shelley.berkley@tun.touro.edu
BERKMAN, Ronald, M .. 216-687-3544 359 L
ronald.berkman@csuohio.edu
BERKNER, Paul, D .... 207-859-4460 198 H
pberkner@colby.edu
BERKOWITZ, Bobbie ..... 212-305-3582 305 E
bb2509@columbia.edu
BERKOWITZ, David .... 256-824-6952.... 8 C
david.berkowitz@uah.edu
BERKOWITZ, Irving .... 561-868-3218 105 A
berkowii@palmbeachstate.edu
BERKOWITZ, Justin .... 386-267-0565.. 97 H
director@daytonacollege.edu
BERKSTEINER, Ethel ...... 912-443-5894 125 D
eberksteiner@savannahtech.edu
BERLAND, Eti .... 847-982-2500 139 E
berland@htc.edu
BERLEY, Susan .... 820-652-0636 344 G
susanberley@mcdowelltech.edu
BERLEY, Susan, A .... 828-448-6125 347 F
sberley@wpcc.edu
BERLIN, Ingrid .... 531-622-2717 275 F
iberlin@mccneb.edu
BERLIN, Linda .... 231-995-2118 235 B
lberlin@nmc.edu
BERLINER, Donna .... 630-942-2475 136 D
berliner@cod.edu
BERLINER, Herman, A ... 516-463-5676 310 D
herman.a.berliner@hofstra.edu
BERLO, Josh .... 218-726-8168 250 F
jpberlo@d.umn.edu
BERMAN, Ari .... 212-960-5300 334 P
president@yu.edu
BERMAN, Art .... 651-290-7522 248 U
art.berman@mitchellhamline.edu
BERMAN, Audrey .... 510-869-6611.. 59 F
aberman@samuelmerritt.edu
BERMAN, Bruce .... 714-895-8315.. 38 G
bberman@gwc.cccd.edu
BERMAN, David .... 215-204-2044 411 B
david.berman@temple.edu
BERMAN, Harris .... 617-636-2177 225 A
harris.berman@tufts.edu
BERMAN, Ila .... 434-924-7019 486 H
ilb8r@virginia.edu
BERMAN, Joel .... 954-262-2130 104 F
jb@nsu.nova.edu
BERMAN, Larry, S .... 404-413-5570 121 A
larryberman@gsu.edu
BERMAN, Lou Ann .... 903-566-7052 468 C
lberman@uttyler.edu
BERMAN, Marc .... 619-961-4271.. 67 F
mberman@tjsl.edu
BERMAN, Mark, A .... 518-782-6957 324 C
mberman@siena.edu
BERMAN, Michael .... 805-437-2099.. 31 C
michael.berman@csuci.edu
BERMAN, Morris .... 508-373-5821 221 E
morris.berman@mcphs.edu
BERMAN, Paula .... 617-277-3915 212 F
bermanp@bgsp.edu
BERMAN, Richard .... 813-974-9694 111 A
rberman@usf.edu
BERMAN, Shawn .... 505-277-1792 296 H
mchale@unm.edu
BERMAN, Sheryl .... 562-902-3360.. 65 D
sherylberman@scuhs.edu
BERMAN, Stanley .... 617-327-6777 226 B
stanley_berman@williamjames.edu
BERMEA, Gilbert, S .... 830-758-4111 457 C
gbermea@swtjc.edu
BERMEL, Patricia .... 619-680-4430.. 29 A
patricia.bermel@cc-sd.edu
BERMINGHAM, Jack ..... 206-878-3710 495 E
jbermingham@highline.edu
BERMINGHAM, Jordan . 503-226-4391 385 H
jbermingham@pnca.edu
BERMUDEZ, Eliezer .... 453-879-4817 473 B
eliezer.bermudez@dixie.edu
BERMUDEZ,
Emilia (Lilly) .... 405-878-5152 379 G
elbermudez@stgregorys.edu
BERMUDEZ, Gregory ...... 787-757-1520 527 H
gregory.bermudez@upr.edu
BERMUDEZ, Pedro .... 787-786-3030 526 F
pbermudez@ucb.edu.pr
BERN, Beana .... 802-586-7711 476 D
bbern@sterlingcollege.edu
BERNA, Francis, J .... 215-951-1346 398 F
berna@lasalle.edu
BERNABE, Arnaldo .... 718-518-6888 302 D
abernabe@hostos.cuny.edu
BERNADELLE, Guary ..... 815-967-7300 150 B
bernadelle@rockfordcareercollege.edu
BERNADO, Daniel .... 509-335-5581 499 G
bernado@wsu.edu
BERNAHL, Joni .... 217-786-9627 144 B
joni.bernahl@llcc.edu
BERNAIX, Laura .... 618-650-3969 152 C
lbernai@siue.edu
BERNAL, Jesse, M .... 616-331-3296 230 G
bernalje@gvsu.edu
BERNAL, Omar .... 847-233-7700 148 A
obernal@nc.edu
BERNAL-OLSON,
Patricia .... 937-229-4211 372 A
pbernalolson1@udayton.edu
BERNARD, Barbara .... 781-239-2629 220 A
bbernard@massbay.edu
BERNARD, Bill .... 212-924-5900 330 G
wbernard@swedishinstitute.edu
BERNARD, Christopher . 570-577-3011 390 H
chris.bernard@bucknell.edu
BERNARD, David, K ...... 314-921-9290 269 D
dbernard@ugst.edu
BERNARD, Frances .... 518-438-3111 314 B
franb@mariacollege.edu
BERNARD, Kacey .... 610-341-1459 394 E
kbernard@eastern.edu
BERNARD, Kenneth .... 803-938-3840 425 F
bernarkd@uscsumter.edu
BERNARD, Michael .... 530-422-7927.. 73 F
BERNARD, Nancy, M .... 334-844-4744.... 4 D
bernanm@auburn.edu
BERNARD, Pamela .... 919-684-3955 337 C
pam.bernard@duke.edu
BERNARD, Philip .... 617-989-4162 225 E
bernardp@wit.edu
BERNARD, Renee .... 814-472-2766 409 G
rbernard@francis.edu
BERNARD, Richard .... 405-974-3493 380 J
rbernard1@uco.edu
BERNARD, Vicki .... 314-340-5112 260 H
bernardv@hssu.edu
BERNARD-DONALS,
Michael .... 608-262-5246 510 C
mfbernarddon@wisc.edu
BERNARDINE, Marie ..... 305-237-4049 103 L
mbernar1@mdc.edu
BERNARDINO, Maria .... 209-954-5065.. 61 B
mbernardino@deltacollege.edu
BERNARDIS, Tim .... 406-638-3113 271 C
tim@lbhc.edu
BERNARDO, Lisa, M ..... 209-667-3094.. 33 F
lbernardo@csustan.edu
BERNARDO, Peter, R .... 216-397-4217 363 H
pbernardo@jcu.edu
BERNARDO-SOUSA,
Marie .... 401-598-1754 416 C
marie.bernardo-sousa@jwu.edu
BERNAS, Judith, A .... 602-827-2017.. 16 J
jbernas@email.arizona.edu
BERNAUER, Edmund ...... 808-521-2288 129 E
dean@orientalmedicine.edu
BERNAUER, Jeanne .... 808-521-2288 129 E
BERNDT, Michael .... 651-779-3493 244 D
michael.berndt@century.edu
BERNE, Jennifer .... 847-925-6737 139 B
jberne@harpercollege.edu
BERNE, Robert .... 212-998-2283 318 D
robert.berne@nyu.edu
BERNECKER, Kim .... 972-825-4634 457 F
kbernecker@sagu.edu
BERNER, Erika .... 802-776-5248 474 H
erika.berner@csj.edu
BERNER, JR.,
Howard, E .... 314-275-3514 149 A
howard.berner@principia.edu
BERNER, Nancy .... 931-598-1101 436 A
nberner@sewanee.edu
BERNET, Kristin .... 928-541-7777.. 54 B
kbernet@ncu.edu
BERNEY, Jan .... 360-438-4513 497 F
jberney@stmartin.edu
BERNHARD, Mark, C .... 812-228-5098 165 C
mcbernhard@usi.edu
BERNHARD, Robert, J ... 574-631-3902 165 A
bernhard.9@nd.edu
BERNHARD, William ..... 217-333-6677 154 B
bernhard@illinois.edu
BERNHARDSON,
Bonnie .... 218-879-0828 244 F
bonnie@fdltcc.edu
BERNHARDSON, Mark .. 218-879-0703 244 F
mbernhar@fdltcc.edu
BERNHARDT, Jay, M .... 512-471-8100 467 C
jay.bernhardt@austin.utexas.edu
BERNHARDT, Kevin, J .. 608-342-1365 511 D
bernhark@uwplatt.edu
BERNHARDT, Regina ..... 215-248-7021 392 D
bernhardtr@chc.edu
BERNIER, Jessica .... 845-437-5320 333 A
jebernier@vassar.edu
BERNIER, Jose .... 386-822-7045 111 E
jbernier@stetson.edu
BERNOI, Verna .... 443-518-4773 204 E
vbernoi@howardcc.edu
BERNOTAS, Scott, C ..... 412-624-9510 412 I
bernotas@pitt.edu
BERNOTSKY,
R. Lorraine .... 610-436-6977 407 D
lbernotsky@wcupa.edu
BERNSTEIN, Aimee .... 718-409-5979 329 E
abernstein@sunymaritime.edu
BERNSTEIN, Alan .... 229-333-5860 127 H
abernste@valdosta.edu
BERNSTEIN, David .... 845-406-4308 334 E
BERNSTEIN, Melissa ..... 801-581-3386 472 P
melissa.bernstein@law.utah.edu
BERNSTEIN, Michael ..... 631-632-4360 325 F
michael.bernstein@stonybrook.edu
BERNSTEIN, Pamela ...... 603-880-8308 282 D
tmc@thomasmorecollege.edu
BERNSTEIN, Pamela ...... 603-880-8308 282 D
pbernstein@thomasmorecollege.edu
BERNSTEIN, Robin .... 402-557-7300 273 E
robin.bernstein@bellevue.edu
BERNSTEIN, Zeke .... 802-440-4594 474 F
zbernstein@bennington.edu
BERNTSON, Joan, L ...... 218-751-8670 249 G
joanberntson@oakhills.edu
BEROKOFF, Mark .... 405-912-9030 379 A
mberokoff@ru.edu
BEROL, Polly .... 610-341-1386 394 E
pberol@eastern.edu
BEROWSKI, Alfred .... 315-866-0300 310 A
berowskfj@herkimer.edu
BERQUAM, Lori .... 608-263-5700 510 C
viceprovost@studentlife.wisc.edu
BERQUE, David, A .... 765-658-6267 157 H
dberque@depauw.edu
BERQUIST, Gina .... 503-255-0332 384 E
ginab@multnomah.edu
BERRAHOU, Catherine .. 248-689-8282 238 F
cberraho@walshcollege.edu
BERREAU, Lisa .... 435-797-3509 473 C
lisa.berreau@usu.edu
BERRIDGE, Bob .... 773-256-0783 144 G
bberridg@lstc.edu
BERRIOS, Amy .... 610-353-7630 390 E
BERRIOS, Carmen .... 787-738-2161 528 A
carmen.berrios@upr.edu
BERRIOS, Iris .... 787-743-7979 526 A
ac_irberrios@suagm.edu
BERRIOS, Jonathan .... 787-738-2161 528 A
jonathan.berrios@upr.edu
BERRIOS, Marianne .... 787-852-1430 522 P
mberrios@hccpr.edu
BERRIOS, William .... 212-592-2043 324 A
wberrios@sva.edu
BERRMAN, Terri .... 815-455-8783 145 B
tberryman@mchenry.edu
BERRY, Anthony, T .... 860-297-2000.. 88 E
BERRY, Brian .... 870-777-5722.. 23 A
brian.berry@uacch.edu
BERRY, Carolynn .... 336-750-2110 352 D
berryc@wssu.edu
BERRY, Chad .... 859-985-3490 183 I
chad_berry@berea.edu
BERRY, Clay .... 870-508-6124.. 18 C
cberry@asumh.edu
BERRY, Donna .... 559-638-0300.. 66 H
donna.berry@reedleycollege.edu
BERRY, Elizabeth, D ...... 607-746-4573 329 B
berryee@delhi.edu
BERRY, Emily .... 513-529-9625 365 I
emily.berry@miamioh.edu
BERRY, Evan .... 772-462-7945 101 Q
eberry@irsc.edu
BERRY, Gayle .... 937-376-6018 358 I
gberry@centralstate.edu
BERRY, Gwennette, C .... 319-273-2820 167 A
gwenne.berry@uni.edu
BERRY, Jessica .... 207-778-7295 201 D
jess.berry@maine.edu
BERRY, Joan, E .... 610-566-1776 415 A
jberry@williamson.edu
BERRY, Joanne .... 603-427-7609 280 J
jberry@ccsnh.edu
BERRY, John .... 304-734-6603 502 K
john.berry@bridgevalley.edu
BERRY, John .... 865-981-8145 433 F
john.berry@maryvillecollege.edu
BERRY, Josh .... 785-442-6031 178 C
jberry@highlandcc.edu
BERRY, Joshua .... 203-582-8695.. 88 A
joshua.berry@quinnipiac.edu
BERRY, Keith .... 813-253-7714 101 M
kberry@hccfl.edu
BERRY, Kimberly, G ...... 518-629-8007 310 G
k.berry@hvcc.edu
BERRY, Larry .... 423-614-8086 432 L
lberry@leeuniversity.edu
BERRY, Laura .... 870-743-3000.. 20 E
lberry@northark.edu
BERRY, Laura Lea .... 802-586-7711 476 D
lberry@sterlingcollege.edu
BERRY, Linda, C .... 708-209-3209 136 I
linda.berry@cuchicago.edu
BERRY, Mario .... 404-270-5376 126 D
mjberry@spelman.edu
BERRY, Marion .... 314-340-3366 260 H
berrym@hssu.edu
BERRY, Mark .... 302-736-2567.. 90 J
mark.berry@wesley.edu
BERRY, Mark, A .... 213-621-2200.. 39 A
BERRY, Mark, E .... 843-953-7645 420 C
berrym@cofc.edu
BERRY, Mary .... 605-677-5370 428 E
mary.berry@usd.edu
BERRY, Molly .... 217-424-6335 145 J
mberry@millikin.edu
BERRY, Nicole .... 718-270-6413 303 C
nberry@mec.cuny.edu
BERRY, Richard .... 936-468-2807 458 A
rberry@sfasu.edu
BERRY, Ronald .... 318-342-1103 198 A
rberry@ulm.edu
BERRY, Scott, D .... 864-488-4525 422 B
sberry@limestone.edu
BERRY, Steve .... 530-541-4660.. 47 I
sberry@ltcc.edu
BERRY, Steve .... 919-365-7711 349 D
BERRY, Trey .... 870-235-4001.. 21 F
tcberry@saumag.edu
BERRY-GUERIN,
Daneen .... 509-793-2053 492 I
daneenb@bigbend.edu
BERRYHILL, Anthony ..... 901-448-5705 440 C
aberryh2@uthsc.edu
BERRYMAN, Daniel .... 520-206-4740.. 15 L
dberryman@pima.edu
BERRYMAN, Jennifer ..... 508-856-2900 217 C
jennifer.berryman@umassmed.edu
BERRYMAN, Joanne .... 502-585-9911 189 B
jberryman@spalding.edu
BERRYMAN, Terri .... 815-455-8783 145 B
tberryman@mchenry.edu
BERRÍOS, José, E .... 787-257-7373 525 Q
jberrios34@suagm.edu
BERRÍOS, Olga, L .... 787-850-9340 528 B
olga.berrios@upr.edu

BERSCHEIDT, Jim, P ..... 402-280-1272 274 D
jimberscheidt@creighton.edu
BERSHAD, Carolyn .... 607-753-4728 327 A
carolyn.bershad@cortland.edu
BERSON, Gail .... 413-538-2515 222 C
gberson@mtholyoke.edu
BERT, Daryl, W .... 540-432-4101 480 A
daryl.bert@emu.edu
BERT, Melissa .... 320-589-6017 251 A
mbert@morris.umn.edu
BERTCH, Dennis .... 269-488-4205 231 G
dbertch@kvcc.edu
BERTE, Hope .... 718-982-2676 302 A
hope.berte@csi.cuny.edu
BERTEAUX, Susan .... 508-830-5035 218 D
sberteaux@maritime.edu
BERTELSEN, Kevin .... 707-654-1726.. 32 E
kbertelsen@csum.edu
BERTHELOT, Yves .... 404-385-3383 120 A
yves.berthelot@provost.gatech.edu
BERTHELSEN, Michael .. 612-624-3557 250 E
berth004@umn.edu
BERTHIAUME, Joseph ... 262-595-2058 511 C
berthiau@uwp.edu
BERTHIAUME, Peter, L .. 603-526-3675 280 H
pberthia@colby-sawyer.edu
BERTHOUMIEUX,
Rachel .... 516-686-1140 317 G
rberthou@nyit.edu
BERTI, David, M .... 617-422-7209 222 J
dberti@nesl.edu
BERTINI, Kristine .... 207-780-5180 201 H
kristine.bertini@maine.edu
BERTOLINI, Len, A .... 630-829-6127 133 I
lbertolini@ben.edu
BERTOLINO, Joe .... 203-392-5250.. 85 A
BERTOLUCCI, Linda .... 619-644-7799.. 45 A
linda.bertolucci@gcccd.edu
BERTONAZZI, Laura ...... 781-768-7060 224 A
laura.bertonazzi@regiscollege.edu
BERTOT, John .... 301-405-4252 207 G
jbertot@umd.edu
BERTOZZI, Stefano .... 510-642-2082.. 68 G
sbertozzi@berkeley.edu
BERTRAM, Brian .... 517-264-7676 236 I
bbertram@sienaheights.edu
BERTRAN-PASARELL,
Lourdes .... 787-728-1515 529 B
lbertran@sagrado.edu
BERTSCH, Lynda .... 701-858-3360 354 C
lynda.bertsch@minotstateu.edu
BERTSCH, Tauna .... 254-968-9921 459 A
bertsch@tarleton.edu
BERTSCHE, Allen, P ...... 309-794-8283 133 G
allenbertsche@augustana.edu
BERTSCHINGER,
Edmund .... 617-253-1000 221 C
BERTSOS, Daniel .... 937-775-4172 374 B
dan.bertsos@wright.edu
BERUBE, Danelle .... 802-860-2702 474 G
dberube@champlain.edu
BERUBE, Patricia .... 413-572-5415 218 F
pberube@westfield.ma.edu
BERUMEN, Yvonne .... 909-621-8129.. 57 C
yvonne_berumen@pitzer.edu
BERWICK, Robert .... 386-822-7141 111 E
rberwick@stetson.edu
BESANA, GianMario ...... 312-362-5554 137 C
gbesana@depaul.edu
BESCH, Rick .... 903-510-3233 464 D
rbes@tjc.edu
BESEDA, Michael .... 415-422-4019.. 72 A
mbeseda@usfca.edu
BESEL, Karl .... 219-980-6554 160 C
kbesel@iun.edu
BESENYEI, Alicia .... 304-384-6313 503 P
abesenyei@concord.edu
BESHARA, Alexa .... 732-255-0400 288 B
abeshara@ocean.edu
BESHEARS, Brenda .... 217-228-5520 134 F
bbeshears@brcn.edu
BESIKOF, Rudolph .... 951-487-3404.. 52 J
rbesikof@msjc.edu
BESKID, Novella .... 803-777-0958 424 I
novella@sc.edu
BESNARD, Pamela .... 909-621-8192.. 57 I
pamela.besnard@pomona.edu
BESNETTE HAUSER,
Carrie .... 970-945-8691.. 77 M
BESONG, Jeffrey, D .... 412-392-3819 408 F
jbesong@pointpark.edu
BESPALEC, Dale, A .... 414-464-9777 513 B
bespalec.dale@wspp.edu
BESPALOV, Oleg .... 661-763-7944.. 67 A
obespalov@taftcollege.edu
BESPALOV, Oleg .... 818-710-4292.. 49 D
bespalo@piercecollege.edu
BESSESEN, Marit .... 619-594-6578.. 34 B
bessesen@mail.sdsu.edu
BESSETTE, Bill .... 301-934-4753 203 D
wbessett@csmd.edu
BESSETTE, James .... 740-245-7225 372 E
jbessette@rio.edu
BESSETTE, Jeanine .... 313-577-2116 239 C
jeanine.bessette@wayne.edu
BESSETTE, Mark .... 518-381-1353 323 L
bessetma@sunysccc.edu
BESSETTE, Ray .... 207-941-7785 199 B
bessetter@husson.edu
BESSETTE, Roger .... 413-755-4390 221 B
rbessette@stcc.edu
BESSLER, Joseph, A ...... 918-270-6448 378 I
joe.bessler@ptstulsa.edu
BESSLER, Timothy .... 210-431-4396 455 J
tbessler@stmarytx.edu
BEST, JR., A. Reginald . 313-317-1700 231 B
arbest1@hfcc.edu
BEST, Alana .... 719-846-5011.. 82 L
BEST, Kathy .... 919-635-2788 349 F
kbest@umo.edu
BEST, Matthew .... 716-270-5262 307 I
bestm@ecc.edu
BEST, Michael .... 516-299-2501 313 C
michael.best@liu.edu
BEST, Mickey .... 505-287-6624 295 B
mbest@nmsu.edu
BEST, Neil, A .... 724-847-6643 395 J
nabest@geneva.edu
BEST, Robert .... 864-455-9812 425 E
best@sc.edu
BEST, Roger, J .... 660-543-8597 268 A
best@ucmo.edu
BEST, Sandra, M .... 912-358-4194 125 C
bestsm@savannahstate.edu
BEST, Sara .... 701-349-5793 355 G
sarabest@trinitybiblecollege.edu
BEST, Sharon .... 386-752-1822.. 99 J
sharon.best@fgc.edu
BESTER, Christian .... 718-780-0352 300 A
chris.bester@brooklaw.edu
BESTUL, Lisa .... 218-262-6752 244 H
lisabestul@hibbing.edu
BESWICK, Patrick, T ...... 724-738-4855 407 C
patrick.beswick@sru.edu
BETACCHINI, Kayla, A ... 716-880-2351 314 F
kayla.a.betacchini@medaille.edu
BETANCOURT, Carmen .. 787-841-2000 525 J
carmen_betancourt@pucpr.edu
BETANCOURT, Gigi .... 760-547-1800.. 43 G
jbetancourt@fst.edu
BETANCOURT, Gladys ... 787-743-7979 526 A
ut-gbetancou@suagm.edu
BETANCOURT, Ivonne ... 678-916-2611 115 K
ibetancourt@johnmarshall.edu
BETANCOURT LOPEZ,
Ilder .... 623-845-3730.. 13 H
ilder.betancourt.lopez@gccaz.edu
BETANCOURT SANTIAGO,
Victor .... 703-284-1677 483 A
victor.betancourt@marymount.edu
BETANCOURT VELEZ,
Ismael, J .... 563-425-5832 173 K
betancourti@uiu.edu
BETCHER, Tom .... 937-766-7681 358 D
tbetcher@cedarville.edu
BETECK, Ellis .... 937-255-5894 517 H
ellis.beteck@afit.edu
BETHARDS, Troy .... 417-328-1757 267 A
tbethards@sbuniv.edu
BETHEA, Edward .... 843-661-8060 421 F
ed.bethea@fdtc.edu
BETHEL, Genna .... 903-813-3001 443 F
gbethel@austincollege.edu
BETHKE, Jeffrey .... 312-362-6695 137 C
jbethke@depaul.edu
BETHMAN, Brenda .... 816-235-1643 268 D
bethmanb@umkc.edu
BETHSCHEIDER, John ... 281-756-5601 442 C
jbethscheider@alvincollege.edu
BETHUNE, Andrew, J .... 989-964-4071 236 F
ajbethune@svsu.edu
BETKOWSKI, Teresa ...... 678-359-5837 121 B
t_betkowski@gordonstate.edu
BETSCHART, Joseph, V . 503-845-3335 384 C
joseph.betschart@mtangel.edu
BETSINGER, Alicia, M ... 603-646-1247 281 C
alicia.m.betsinger@dartmouth.edu
BETSKY, Aaron .... 480-860-2700.. 12 N
abetsky@taliesin.edu
BETTELYOUN, Kim .... 605-455-6093 427 I
kbettelyoun@olc.edu
BETTENCOURT, Patrick .. 209-575-6373.. 75 J
bettencourtp@mjc.edu
BETTERSWORTH,
Michael, A .... 512-647-8790 461 G
michael.bettersworth@tstc.edu
BETTING, Daniel .... 216-791-5000 359 K
daniel.betting@cim.edu
BETTINGER, Lewis .... 608-342-1221 511 D
bettingerl@uwplatt.edu
BETTS, Albert .... 856-256-4200 289 H
betts@rowan.edu
BETTS, Charles .... 903-875-7540 453 J
charles.betts@navarrocollege.edu
BETTS, Keith .... 203-837-8600.. 85 B
bettsk@wcsu.edu
BETTS, Russell .... 312-567-3800 140 I
betts@iit.edu
BETTS, Steve .... 405-789-6400 379 K
sbetts@snu.edu
BETZ, A. Lorris .... 801-581-7480 472 P
lorris.betz@hsc.utah.edu
BETZ, Bridgette, K .... 573-341-4282 269 A
berry@mst.edu
BETZ, Cheri .... 517-264-7100 236 I
cbetz@sienaheights.edu
BETZ, Don .... 405-974-2311 380 J
betz@uco.edu
BETZ, Jon .... 505-566-3505 296 A
betzj@sanjuancollege.edu
BETZ, Kimberly .... 507-222-4295 241 C
kbetz@carleton.edu
BETZ, Leslie .... 309-556-3161 141 B
registrar@iwu.edu
BETZ, Philip .... 570-372-4197 410 H
betz@susqu.edu
BETZ, Stacey, A .... 610-799-1737 400 A
sbetz1@lccc.edu
BETZIG, Kaylen, A .... 262-691-5198 515 B
kbetzig@wctc.edu
BEU, Pat .... 308-432-6231 276 B
pbeu@csc.edu
BEUCLER, Keith .... 817-202-6420 457 E
keithb@swau.edu
BEUKELMAN, Doug, D .. 712-707-7121 172 G
dougb@nwciowa.edu
BEUS, Ben .... 509-542-4811 493 G
bbeus@columbiabasin.edu
BEUSSMAN, Victoria ..... 507-786-3325 250 C
beussman@stolaf.edu
BEUTEL, Kate .... 419-517-8880 364 G
kbeutel@lourdes.edu
BEUTLER, Randy, L .... 580-774-3766 380 B
randy.beutler@swosu.edu
BEVACQUA, Maria .... 507-389-5717 246 A
maria.bevacqua@mnsu.edu
BEVAN, Thomas .... 570-586-2400 392 E
tbevan@clarkssummitu.edu
BEVERAGE, JR.,
Morris, W .... 440-525-7118 364 D
mbeverage@lakelandcc.edu
BEVERIDGE, Kim .... 800-869-7223 125 B
kbeverid@scad.edu
BEVERIDGE, Thomas ..... 805-565-6017.. 74 I
tbeverid@westmont.edu
BEVERLY, Jason .... 601-928-6267 254 D
jason.beverly@mgccc.edu
BEVERLY, Pearlie .... 254-710-4466 444 B
pearl_beverly@baylor.edu
BEVILACQUA, Linda ...... 305-899-3010.. 95 G
lbevilacqua@barry.edu
BEVILLE, Jill .... 336-334-4013 351 D
jmbevill@uncg.edu
BEVINS, P. Scott .... 276-376-1066 487 A
pb8q@uvawise.edu
BEWERSDORF, Marsha . 316-295-5679 177 F
marsha_bewersdorf@friends.edu
BEY, George, J .... 601-974-1385 254 A
beygj@millsaps.edu
BEY, Mohammed .... 920-498-6826 514 G
mohammed.bey@nwtc.edu
BEYDA-LORIE, Sandra ... 773-442-5583 147 G
s-beyda@neiu.edu
BEYDLER, Julie .... 970-542-3129.. 81 A
julie.beydler@morgancc.edu
BEYELER, Jodi .... 574-535-7572 158 A
jodihb@goshen.edu
BEYELER, Noah .... 760-872-2000.. 41 E
ndbeyeler@deepsprings.edu
BEYER, Bryan .... 803-754-4100 420 E
BEYER, Christian .... 814-824-2915 401 J
cbeyer@mercyhurst.edu
BEYER, Christopher .... 309-794-2686 133 G
christopherbeyer@augustana.edu
BEYER, David .... 425-388-9573 494 F
dbeyer@everettcc.edu
BEYER, Lori .... 952-829-2408 240 H
lori.beyer@bethfel.org
BEYER, Neil .... 406-657-1705 272 B
neil.beyer@msubillings.edu
BEYER, Paul, N .... 443-997-1000 204 F
pbeyer@jhu.edu
BEYER HOUPT, Julia ..... 740-587-6636 361 B
houpt@denison.edu
BEYL, Caula .... 865-974-7303 439 I
cbeyl@utk.edu
BEYROUTY, Craig .... 301-405-2012 207 G
beyrouty@umd.edu
BEZEK, Cory, M .... 716-673-3251 325 C
cory.bezek@fredonia.edu
BEZHANYAN, Anush ..... 510-925-4282.. 25 P
abezhanyan@aua.am
BHADA, Farokh .... 401-232-6005 416 A
fbhada@bryant.edu
BHADURY, Joyendu ...... 585-395-5537 326 D
jbhadury@brockport.edu
BHAGAVATULA,
Vijayakumar (Kumar) ... 412-268-2478 391 H
vk16@andrew.cmu.edu
BHAKTA, Analisa .... 575-624-7155 294 A
analisa.bhakta@roswell.enmu.edu
BHALLA, Deepak .... 313-577-3980 239 C
deepak.bhalla@wayne.edu
BHASIN, Rohit .... 978-681-0800 221 D
rbhasin@mslaw.edu
BHATI, Karni .... 864-294-3019 421 I
karni.bhati@furman.edu
BHATIA, Rupinder .... 310-434-4549.. 62 G
bhatia_rupinder@smc.edu
BHATTACHARYA,
Kaushik .... 626-395-6365.. 29 I
vpr@caltech.edu
BHAUMIK, Nila .... 646-313-8000 303 G
nila.bhaumik@guttman.cuny.edu
BIAFORA, Frank .... 727-873-4292 111 B
fbiafora@mail.usf.edu
BIAL, Henry .... 785-864-3661 181 I
hbial@ku.edu
BIALK, Kathy .... 304-696-2281 504 C
bialkk@marshall.edu
BIANCAMANO, John, J . 740-593-2626 368 G
biancama@ohio.edu
BIANCHETTO, Melody ... 434-982-2347 486 H
msb2p@virginia.edu
BIANCHI, Amy, M .... 617-333-2236 214 B
abianchi@curry.edu
BIANCHI, Ashley .... 610-330-5055 399 B
biancia@lafayette.edu
BIANCHI, Carrie, K .... 914-251-6011 328 B
carrie.bianchi@purchase.edu
BIANCHI, Gina .... 217-424-3967 145 J
gbianchi@millikin.edu
BIANCO, Amy .... 845-848-4065 306 G
amy.bianco@dc.edu
BIANCO, Annamarie ...... 202-687-0100.. 92 B
amb504@georgetown.edu
BIANCO, Jennifer .... 508-213-2340 223 C
jennifer.bianco@nichols.edu
BIANSKI, Marty .... 260-459-4590 161 D
mbianski@ibcfortwayne.edu
BIAS, Jeanine .... 936-294-3026 462 F
jrb023@shsu.edu
BIAS, Randolph .... 512-471-3821 467 C
rbias@ischool.utexas.edu
BIBB, Sandra .... 316-978-3600 182 F
sandra.bibb@wichita.edu
BIBBEE, Mistie .... 304-696-3152 504 C
bibbeem@marshall.edu
BIBBEE, Mistie .... 828-227-7303 352 C
bibbee@wcu.edu
BIBBENS, Matthew, G .... 909-607-8966.. 38 A
matthew.bibbens@cmc.edu
BIBBO, Chris .... 727-816-3261 105 C
bibboc@phsc.edu
BIBLE, Brice .... 716-645-7979 325 B
bible@buffalo.edu
BIBLE, Robert .... 918-549-2800 375 E
rbible@cmn.edu
BIBLE, Tennille .... 605-229-8536 427 J
tennille.bible@presentation.edu
BIBO, JR., Tim .... 410-704-4685 209 C
tbibo@towson.edu
BIBY, Catherine .... 704-991-0206 346 I
cbiby0719@stanly.edu
BICAK, Charles, J .... 308-865-8209 277 F
bicakc@unk.edu
BICCHINELLA, Josh .... 907-277-1000.... 9 G
joshua.bicchinella@chartercollege.edu
BICE, Patricia .... 914-251-6360 328 B
patricia.bice@purchase.edu
BICHEL, Rebecca .... 817-272-1413 467 B
rbichel@uta.edu
BICHELMEYER, Barbara . 816-235-1101 268 D
bichelmeyer@umkc.edu
BICHELMEYER, Barbara . 816-235-1107 268 D
bichelmeyer@umkc.edu
BICKEL, Kathy .... 541-737-2351 385 F
kathy.bickel@oregonstate.edu

BICKEL, Teri ... 301-846-2612 203 H tbickel@frederick.edu
BICKELL, Kris ... 203-576-4851 .. 88 F ubonline@bridgeport.edu
BICKERTON, Molly ... 912-871-1600 123 J mbickerton@ogeecheetech.edu
BICKERTON, Sally ... 661-255-1050 .. 29 F
BICKFORD, Deborah, J . 937-229-5360 372 A dbickford1@udayton.edu
BICKFORD, Ian ... 413-528-7239 211 B ibickford@simons-rock.edu
BICKFORD, Jeffrey ... 978-556-3745 220 F jbickford@necc.mass.edu
BICKING, Michael, D ... 610-436-3478 407 D mbicking@wcupa.edu
BICKLEY, Carol, A ... 803-321-5124 422 H carol.bickley@newberry.edu
BICKLEY, Craig ... 724-357-4874 406 C cbickley@iup.edu
BICKLEY, Sally ... 361-698-1931 448 H sbickley@delmar.edu
BICKNELL, Brian ... 603-206-8009 280 L bbicknell@ccsnh.edu
BICKNELL, Robert ... 325-649-8600 450 H rbicknell@hputx.edu
BICKNELL-HOLMES, Tracy ... 208-426-1234 131 C tracybicknell-holmes@boisestate.edu
BICKSLER, Leslie ... 304-647-6279 504 F lbicksler@osteo.wvsom.edu
BIDDINGS-MURO, Regina, D ... 219-989-2323 163 E reginab@pnw.edu
BIDDLE, Chris ... 615-226-3990 433 B cbiddle@lincolntech.edu
BIDDLE, Elizabeth, A ... 570-326-3761 404 T ebiddle@pct.edu
BIDDY, Scott ... 510-642-7374 .. 68 G fsb@berkeley.edu
BIDDY, Scott ... 510-642-3507 .. 68 G fsb@berkeley.edu
BIDEGAIN, Laurie ... 575-461-4413 294 E
BIDLACK, Allison ... 907-796-6289 .. 10 C albidlack@alaska.edu
BIDLACK, Beth ... 212-851-5611 332 C beth.bidlack@uts.columbia.edu
BIDWELL, Lorena, L ... 269-471-6124 227 B lorena@andrews.edu
BIEBER, Ann, D ... 610-799-1581 400 A abieber@lccc.edu
BIEBIGHAUSER, Victor, K ... 334-395-8800 125 H vbiebighauser@southuniversity.edu
BIEBUYCK, Bill ... 563-588-6405 167 E bill.biebuyck@clarke.edu
BIECHLER, Laura ... 617-236-5470 215 B lbiechler@fisher.edu
BIEDERMANN, Scott ... 209-946-2166 .. 70 F sbiedermann@pacific.edu
BIEDSCHEID, Thomas ... 970-491-6321 .. 78 N tom.biedscheid@colostate.edu
BIEGANOWSKI, Rene ... 231-348-6658 234 H rbieganowski@ncmich.edu
BIEGENZAHN, Nathan ... 919-497-3250 339 F nbiegenzahn@louisburg.edu
BIEHL, Alysha ... 708-524-6296 137 F acomstock@dom.edu
BIEHLS, Kelly ... 716-829-8485 307 B biehls@dyc.edu
BIEHN, Christopher ... 607-274-3115 311 D cbiehn@ithaca.edu
BIELAWSKI, Bill ... 312-329-8047 146 B bill.bielawski@moody.edu
BIELBY, Steve ... 864-977-1249 422 I steve.bielby@ngu.edu
BIELEN, Ken ... 765-677-1825 161 C ken.bielen@indwes.edu
BIELEN, Paul ... 707-524-1606 .. 62 H pbielen@santarosa.edu
BIELFELDT, Dennis ... 605-692-9337 427 B
BIELICKI, Shawn ... 434-582-3035 482 D smbielicki@liberty.edu
BIELMAN, Jess ... 503-517-1140 388 A jbielman@warnerpacific.edu
BIEN, Andrea ... 651-290-6322 248 U andrea.bien@mitchellhamline.edu
BIENERT, Bonnie ... 847-628-2083 142 B bbienert@judsonu.edu
BIENFANG, Kim ... 763-433-1483 243 K kim.bienfang@anokaramsey.edu
BIENKOWSKI, Kathleen . 404-727-0737 119 B kathleen.bienkowski@emory.edu
BIENVENUE, Scott ... 603-578-8900 280 M sbienvenue@ccsnh.edu
BIENZ, Richard, A ... 260-399-7700 165 B rbienz@sf.edu
BIER, Alice, G ... 718-951-5189 301 E abier@brooklyn.cuny.edu
BIER, Debbie ... 412-521-6200 409 D debbie.bier@rosedaletech.org
BIERBAUER, Charles ... 803-777-4105 424 I bierbauer@sc.edu
BIERLICH, Sue ... 714-432-5562 .. 38 H sbierlich@occ.cccd.edu
BIERLY, Robert ... 864-294-2217 421 I robert.bierly@furman.edu
BIERMAN, Cindy ... 909-621-8265 .. 37 L cindy.bierman@cgu.edu
BIERMAN, Derek ... 402-844-7060 276 G derek@northeast.edu
BIERMAN, Lindsay ... 336-770-3200 352 B biermanl@uncsa.edu
BIERMAN, Luke ... 336-279-9201 337 G lbierman@elon.edu
BIERMAN, Matthew, J ... 309-298-1800 155 D mj-bierman@wiu.edu
BIERMAN, Matthew, J ... 309-298-2005 155 D mj-bierman@wiu.edu
BIERMAN, Scott ... 402-557-7245 273 E scott.bierman@bellevue.edu
BIERMAN, Scott ... 608-363-2201 506 D biermans@beloit.edu
BIERMANN, Mark ... 219-464-5779 165 D mark.biermann@valpo.edu
BIERMANN, Matt ... 989-275-5000 232 E matt.biermann@kirtland.edu
BIERNBAUM, John ... 309-298-3320 155 D j-biernbaum@wiu.edu
BIERS, Lisa, M ... 260-422-5561 159 D lmbiers@indianatech.edu
BIERSCHBACH, Richard . 313-577-3933 239 C
BIES, James, B ... 605-274-4124 426 K jim.bies@augie.edu
BIES, Susan ... 605-274-5503 426 K susan.bies@augie.edu
BIESCHKE, Kathleen ... 814-865-9520 403 F kxb11@psu.edu
BIESECKER, James ... 717-337-6700 396 A jbieseck@gettysburg.edu
BIETELCHIES, Wade ... 517-265-5161 226 F wbietelchies@adrian.edu
BIG SPRING, Anita ... 406-275-4974 273 A anita_bigspring@skc.edu
BIGARD, Heather ... 352-365-3525 103 B bigardh@lssc.edu
BIGBY, Angela, D ... 702-968-2046 280 B abigby@roseman.edu
BIGBY, Cindy ... 918-540-6201 376 F cbigby@neo.edu
BIGCRANE, Michael ... 406-275-4789 273 A michael_bigcrane@skc.edu
BIGDA, Steven, J ... 508-373-1979 211 F steven.bigda@becker.edu
BIGDELI JAHED, Fariba 502-597-6604 187 E fariba.bigdelijahed@kysu.edu
BIGELOW, Gary ... 617-228-3474 219 D gbigelow@bhcc.mass.edu
BIGELOW, Lisa ... 860-832-0105 .. 84 J bigelow@ccsu.edu
BIGELOW, Shannon ... 317-632-5553 162 P
BIGELOW, Susan ... 307-674-6446 516 P sbigelow@sheridan.edu
BIGG, Dort ... 954-763-9840 .. 94 S executivedirector@atom.edu
BIGGANE, Michael, J ... 716-851-1416 307 I biggane@ecc.edu
BIGGER, Kimberly ... 870-248-4000 .. 18 J kim.bigger@blackrivertech.edu
BIGGER, Roberta, H ... 864-597-4040 426 I biggerrh@wofford.edu
BIGGERS, Carla, D ... 409-944-1200 449 F cbiggers@gc.edu
BIGGERS, Darlene ... 281-283-3000 465 B biggers@uhcl.edu
BIGGERS, Darlene ... 281-283-2574 465 B biggers@uhcl.edu
BIGGIN, Margot ... 617-627-3287 225 A margot.biggin@tufts.edu
BIGGIO, Nancy ... 205-726-4267 .... 6 G ncbiggio@samford.edu
BIGGS, Kristen ... 231-843-5875 239 D kmbiggs@westshore.edu
BIGGS, Michelle ... 985-549-2150 197 E michelle.biggs@selu.edu
BIGGS, Patsy ... 501-420-1201 .. 17 I patsy.biggs@arkansasbaptist.edu
BIGGS, Shirley, A ... 803-535-5268 419 E sbiggs@claflin.edu
BIGGS, Sue, A ... 325-670-1314 450 A sbiggs@hsutx.edu
BIGGS, Vicki ... 314-505-7266 258 I biggsv@csl.edu
BIGGS GARBUIO, Judith ... 509-313-4100 495 A biggsgarbuio@gonzaga.edu
BIGWOOD, Christine ... 401-232-6348 416 A cbigwood@bryant.edu
BIKIS, Jekabs ... 503-554-2827 383 C jbikis@georgefox.edu
BILACH, Bernadett ... 480-994-9244 .. 16 E bernadettb@swiha.edu
BILBRUCK, Tom ... 661-362-3235 .. 39 C tom.bilbruck@canyons.edu
BILCHAK, Karen ... 814-254-0471 392 F kbilchak@pa.gov
BILDERBACK, Rebecca .. 620-365-5116 174 G bilderback@allencc.edu
BILDERBACK, Ryan ... 620-365-5116 174 G rbilderback@allencc.edu
BILES, Brad ... 816-584-6888 265 C brad.biles@park.edu
BILES, Deron ... 817-923-1921 457 G dbiles@swbts.edu
BILGER, Audrey ... 909-621-8137 .. 57 I audrey.bilger@pomona.edu
BILGER, Bonnie ... 760-366-5285 .. 41 B bbilger@cmccd.edu
BILGER, Cindy, L ... 570-577-1631 390 H cbilger@bucknell.edu
BILGER, Jackie ... 570-321-4309 400 G bilger@lycoming.edu
BILICH, Dan ... 330-867-1996 366 D
BILL, Tim ... 309-268-8129 139 D tim.bill@heartland.edu
BILLARD, Trisha ... 516-876-3053 327 C billardt@oldwestbury.edu
BILLEAUDEAU, Kim, A .. 337-262-5300 197 F kimberlyb@louisiana.edu
BILLEAUX, David ... 361-825-2393 460 A david.billeaux@tamucc.edu
BILLECI, Celesta ... 805-893-3437 .. 70 B celesta.billeci@sa.ucsb.edu
BILLEN, Isabelle ... 405-733-7580 379 F ibillen@rose.edu
BILLEN, Lindsey ... 580-581-6740 375 A lbillen@cameron.edu
BILLEY, Terry, L ... 580-928-5533 380 B terry.billey@swosu.edu
BILLHARTZ, Scott, L ... 618-537-6869 145 C slbillhartz@mckendree.edu
BILLI, John, E ... 734-936-5214 237 I jbilli@umich.edu
BILLICK, Tammy, N ... 971-722-7800 386 C tbillick@pcc.edu
BILLIE, Marie, H ... 410-651-7502 208 C mhbillie@umes.edu
BILLINGHAM, Diana ... 352-365-3545 103 B billingd@lssc.edu
BILLINGS, Amanda ... 214-648-2344 469 E amanda.billings@utsouthwestern.edu
BILLINGS, Darron ... 731-424-3520 437 B dbillings@jscc.edu
BILLINGS, James ... 928-541-7777 .. 54 B jbillings@ncu.edu
BILLINGS, Maria ... 201-216-9901 285 F maria.billings@eicollege.edu
BILLINGS, Molly ... 402-280-4722 274 D mollybillings@creighton.edu
BILLINGS-BERG, Sarah . 802-728-1586 477 E sberg@vtc.edu
BILLINGSLEA, Aldo ... 408-554-5578 .. 62 F abillingslea@scu.edu
BILLINGSLEY, Anna, B .. 540-654-1055 486 D abilling@umw.edu
BILLINGSLEY, Dale, B ... 502-852-5209 190 C dbbill01@louisville.edu
BILLINGSLEY, Dale, B ... 502-852-6153 190 C dbbill01@louisville.edu
BILLINGSLEY, Jodie ... 806-742-2020 463 D jodie.billingsley@ttu.edu
BILLINGSLEY, Linda ... 318-487-7630 191 J linda.billingsley@lacollege.edu
BILLINGSLEY, Scott ... 910-521-6224 351 E scott.billingsley@uncp.edu
BILLINGSLEY, Tiffany ... 870-633-4480 .. 19 E tbillingsley@eacc.edu
BILLITIER, Rick ... 585-594-7777 321 C billitier_rick@roberts.edu
BILLMAN, Carol ... 724-838-4204 410 E billman@setonhill.edu
BILLMAN, Kathleen ... 773-256-0770 144 G kbillman@lstc.edu
BILLS, Andy ... 336-841-4538 338 E abills@highpoint.edu
BILLS, Joyce ... 918-465-1777 375 J jbills@eosc.edu
BILLS, Kimberly ... 253-589-5846 493 F kimberly.bills@cptc.edu
BILLS, Matt ... 262-646-6513 509 C mbills@nashotah.edu
BILLS-WINDT, Caryn, A 312-413-8145 153 H cabw@uic.edu
BILLUPS, Kyle ... 408-848-4901 .. 44 B kbillups@gavilan.edu
BILLUPS, Terry ... 440-646-8109 373 B terry.billups@ursuline.edu
BILLUPS, Vory ... 404-225-4474 115 J vbillups@atlantatech.edu
BILODEAU, Brent ... 262-472-1172 512 C
BILODEAU, Leta ... 207-859-1201 200 H bilodeaul@thomas.edu
BILONG, Danilo Philbert ... 671-735-5554 519 H danilophilbert.bilong@guamcc.edu
BILOTTA, Barbara, J ... 716-880-2265 314 F barbara.bilotta@medaille.edu
BILOTTA, Leone ... 610-917-1483 413 G l_bilotta@valleyforge.edu
BILSKY, Edward ... 207-602-2707 202 A ebilsky@une.edu
BILSKY, Edward ... 509-452-5100 496 H ebilsky@pnwu.edu
BIMER, Tammy, C ... 734-763-9954 237 I tammyc@umich.edu
BINA, Shawn ... 218-235-2170 248 B s.bina@vcc.edu
BINARD, Kris ... 303-404-5103 .. 79 K kris.binard@frontrange.edu
BINAU, Brad, A ... 614-235-4136 370 M bbinau@tlsohio.edu
BINDER, Arthur ... 575-528-7070 295 E abinder@nmsu.edu
BINDER, Holly ... 417-873-7654 259 G hbinder@drury.edu
BINDER, Maureen ... 407-823-2771 110 C maureen.binder@ucf.edu
BINDEWALD, Kurt ... 504-865-3226 194 G kjbindew@loyno.edu
BINESH, Behzad ... 714-744-7099 .. 36 G binesh@chapman.edu
BINETTE, Louise ... 802-447-6343 476 C lbinette@svc.edu
BING, Andrea ... 415-565-4733 .. 68 I wellesan@uchastings.edu
BING, Richard, N ... 212-998-2391 318 D richard.bing@nyu.edu
BING, Sarah ... 870-743-3000 .. 20 E sbing@northark.edu
BINGAMON, Cindy ... 314-837-6777 266 A cbingamon@stlchristian.edu
BINGEL, Amanda, J ... 518-388-6117 332 B bingela@union.edu
BINGER, Nancy ... 847-628-2510 142 B nbinger@judsonu.edu
BINGHAM, Charlotte ... 806-742-3627 463 E charlotte.bingham@ttu.edu
BINGHAM, Charlotte ... 806-742-3627 463 D charlotte.bingham@ttu.edu
BINGHAM, Douglas, A .. 858-784-8469 .. 63 G
BINGHAM, Janet ... 703-993-8756 481 B bingham@gmu.edu
BINGHAM, Jeffrey ... 817-923-1921 457 G jbingham@swbts.edu
BINGHAM, Jeri ... 773-252-5131 149 I jeri.bingham@resu.edu
BINGHAM, Rachel ... 801-524-8129 471 L rbingham@ldsbc.edu
BINGHAM, Tom ... 808-956-7166 129 J bingham@hawaii.edu
BINGHAM, Vicki, L ... 662-846-4268 252 H vbingham@deltastate.edu
BINION, Anthony ... 773-291-6536 135 M abinion4@ccc.edu
BINION, Lachelle, N ... 412-578-6274 391 G lnbinion@carlow.edu
BINK, Cynthia ... 718-260-5030 303 D cbink@citytech.cuny.edu
BINKERD, James ... 707-638-5883 .. 67 H jim.binkerd@tu.edu
BINKLEY, Julie ... 706-233-7236 125 E 1150mgr@follett.com
BINKLEY, Kristi ... 615-514-2787 435 F kbinkley@nossi.edu
BINKOWSKI, Marcella ... 215-637-7700 397 G smbinkowski@holyfamily.edu
BINN, Brian, A ... 719-333-9751 518 H
BINNEY, Craig ... 508-565-1107 224 H cbinney@stonehill.edu
BINNEY, Diane, M ... 626-395-6651 .. 29 I dbinney@caltech.edu
BINNICKER, Paul ... 816-833-0524 169 D binnicke@graceland.edu
BINNING, William, C ... 330-941-3436 374 E wcbinning@ysu.edu
BINNINGTON, Ian ... 814-332-2357 388 F ibinning@allegheny.edu
BINOTTO, Joseph ... 610-896-1106 397 F
BINSTOCK, Jonathan ... 585-276-8902 332 E jbinstock@mag.rochester.edu

BIONDO, Drew ... 631-451-4776 330 B
biondodr@sunysuffolk.edu
BIOTEAU, Cynthia, A ... 904-632-3222 100 F
cynthia.bioteau@fscj.edu
BIR, Chad ... 317-955-6040 162 R
cbir@marian.edu
BIRBERICK, Anne ... 815-753-0494 147 H
annie@niu.edu
BIRCH, Andrea, C ... 770-718-5325 116 F
abirch@brenau.edu
BIRCH, Bruce ... 202-885-8611.. 94 C
bbirch@wesleyseminary.edu
BIRCH, Esther ... 301-736-3631 205 B
esther.birch@msbbcs.edu
BIRCH, Laura, A ... 217-420-6661 145 J
lbirch@millikin.edu
BIRCH, Mikel ... 801-957-4041 474 B
mikel.birch@slcc.edu
BIRCHAK, Chris ... 713-221-8007 465 C
birchakc@uhd.edu
BIRCHARD, Michael ... 763-424-0850 246 E
mbirchard@nhcc.edu
BIRCHWOOD, Rachel ... 845-451-1459 306 D
rachel.birchwood@culinary.edu
BIRCKBICHLER,
Carrie, J ... 724-738-2150 407 C
carrie.birckbichler@sru.edu
BIRD, Barb ... 765-998-5526 164 C
brbird@taylor.edu
BIRD, Brandon ... 206-726-5024 494 B
bbird@cornish.edu
BIRD, Brian ... 608-342-6188 511 D
birdbr@uwplatt.edu
BIRD, Jennifer ... 304-345-2820 505 D
jbird@wvjc.edu
BIRD, Jill ... 315-279-5726 312 D
jbird1@keuka.edu
BIRD, Lee, E ... 405-744-5328 377 F
lee.bird@okstate.edu
BIRD, Sheila ... 620-278-4247 181 G
sbird@sterling.edu
BIRD, Su Ann ... 229-931-2110 125 G
sbird@southgatech.edu
BIRD, SuAnn ... 229-931-2110 125 G
sbird@southgatech.edu
BIRD, Veronica ... 610-917-1422 413 G
rabird@valleyforge.edu
BIRDINE, Phil ... 580-477-7700 381 G
phil.birdine@wosc.edu
BIRDSELL, David ... 646-660-6700 301 B
david.birdsell@baruch.cuny.edu
BIRDSELL, Rebecca ... 217-245-3035 139 H
becky.birdsell@mail.ic.edu
BIRDSONG, Jeff ... 918-540-6348 376 F
jbirdsong@neo.edu
BIRDWELL, Cindy, A ... 517-264-7194 236 I
cbirdwell@sienaheights.edu
BIRDWELL, Kim ... 940-521-0720 453 L
kbirdwell@nctc.edu
BIRDWHISTELL,
Terry, L ... 859-218-1871 190 B
terry.bird@uky.edu
BIRELINE, David ... 740-474-8896 367 E
dbireline@ohiochristian.edu
BIRGE, James, F ... 413-662-5201 218 C
james.birge@mcla.edu
BIRGE, Susan, N ... 203-254-4000.. 87 A
sbirge@fairfield.edu
BIRINGER, Bobbi ... 312-261-3550 146 G
bobbi.biringer@nl.edu
BIRK, Michelle, L ... 618-235-2700 152 E
michelle.birk@swic.edu
BIRKE, Richard ... 503-370-6046 388 D
rbirke@willamette.edu
BIRKEDAHL, Patrice ... 510-659-6208.. 54 F
pbirkedahl@ohlone.edu
BIRKES, R. Dennis ... 724-287-8711 390 J
dennis.birkes@bc3.edu
BIRKHEAD, Mary ... 610-282-1100 393 G
mary.birkhead@desales.edu
BIRKHEAD, Susan ... 518-268-5130 323 J
susan.birkhead@sphp.com
BIRKNER, Linda, M ... 501-977-2006.. 23 B
birkner@uaccm.edu
BIRKY, Ian, T ... 610-758-3880 400 B
itb0@lehigh.edu
BIRKY, Joshua ... 217-351-2376 148 H
jbirky@parkland.edu
BIRMINGHAM,
Stacy, G ... 724-458-3841 396 D
sgbirmingham@gcc.edu
BIRNBACH, David, J ... 305-284-2002 112 O
dbirnbach@miami.edu
BIRNER, David, C ... 262-243-5700 507 C
david.birner@cuw.edu
BIRNEY, John, W ... 864-597-4135 426 I
birneyjw@wofford.edu
BIRNEY, Tyler ... 605-698-3966 428 C
tbirney@swc.tc
BIRNIE, Christine, R ... 585-385-8430 322 E
cbirnie@sjfc.edu
BIRON, Jackie ... 510-780-4500.. 48 D
jbiron@lifewest.edu
BIRON, Louise ... 518-255-5623 328 C
bironl@cobleskill.edu
BIRON, Rebecca, E ... 603-646-3113 281 C
rebecca.e.biron@dartmouth.edu
BIROS, Demetra ... 425-739-8315 495 F
demetra.biros@lwtech.edu
BIRREN, Susan, J ... 781-736-3451 213 A
birren@brandeis.edu
BIRTWISTLE, Heidi ... 610-341-1738 394 E
hbirtwis@eastern.edu
BIRX, Donald, L ... 603-535-2210 283 B
dlbirx@plymouth.edu
BISBEE, Chester, A ... 404-413-2000 121 A
cbisbee@gsu.edu
BISBEE, Nina ... 610-526-7935 390 G
nbisbee@brynmawr.edu
BISBEE, Yolanda ... 208-885-2468 132 I
yobiz@uidaho.edu
BISCHOF, Gary, H ... 269-387-3713 239 E
gary.bischof@wmich.edu
BISCHOFF, Boyd ... 801-274-3280 474 D
boyd@wgu.edu
BISCHOFF, Jeannette ... 916-660-7000.. 63 K
jbischoff@sierracollege.edu
BISCHOFF, Margaretha .. 956-872-8310 456 G
etybuh@southtexascollege.edu
BISCHOFF, Richard, W .. 216-368-5445 358 C
richard.bischoff@case.edu
BISCOE, Belinda, P ... 405-325-0473 380 L
bpbiscoe@ou.edu
BISER, Bruce ... 651-793-1910 245 E
bruce.biser@metrostate.edu
BISESE, Stephen, D ... 804-289-8615 486 G
sbisese@richmond.edu
BISH, Courtney, D ... 315-386-7120 329 A
bish@canton.edu
BISH, Kevin ... 859-858-2272 183 C
BISHOF, SR.,
Edward, J ... 973-596-3124 288 A
edward.bishof@njit.edu
BISHOP, Brad ... 540-365-4250 480 L
bradbishop@ferrum.edu
BISHOP, Brandan ... 616-222-1954 229 B
brandan.bishop@cornerstone.edu
BISHOP, Carl ... 704-290-5235 346 F
cbishop@spcc.edu
BISHOP, Carla ... 785-532-1858 179 A
cbishop@ksu.edu
BISHOP, Carol, M ... 607-746-4582 329 B
bishopcm@delhi.edu
BISHOP, Colleen ... 804-828-9914 487 E
cbishop4@vcu.edu
BISHOP, David ... 806-785-9285 470 I
bishop@wbu.edu
BISHOP, Dennis ... 214-638-0484 451 E
dbishop@kdstudio.com
BISHOP, Donald, C ... 574-631-7505 165 A
dbishop1@nd.edu
BISHOP, Emily, A ... 601-979-3975 253 E
emily.a.bishop@jsums.edu
BISHOP, Jason ... 603-271-6484 280 N
jbishop@ccsnh.edu
BISHOP, Jeffrey ... 314-977-1060 266 J
jbisho12@slu.edu
BISHOP, Kaylee ... 405-789-7661 380 A
kaylee.bishop@swcu.edu
BISHOP, Kelley ... 301-314-7236 207 G
kbishop1@umd.edu
BISHOP, Kristy ... 724-925-4212 414 E
bishopkr@westmoreland.edu
BISHOP, Kyle, K ... 240-895-4289 206 G
kkbishop@smcm.edu
BISHOP, Laura ... 918-495-6151 378 H
lbishop@oru.edu
BISHOP, Mary Kay ... 585-389-2012 316 D
mbishop2@naz.edu
BISHOP, Mike ... 951-552-8759.. 28 G
mbishop@calbaptist.edu
BISHOP, Nancy ... 803-778-6638 419 A
bishopnw@cctech.edu
BISHOP, Nathaniel, L ... 540-985-8484 482 A
nlbishop@jchs.edu
BISHOP, Norman ... 606-368-6091 182 H
normbishop@alc.edu
BISHOP, Pamela ... 614-287-2437 360 C
pbishop2@cscc.edu
BISHOP, Paul ... 805-965-0581.. 62 E
pwbishop@sbcc.edu
BISHOP, Phil ... 206-876-6100 498 C
pbishop@theseattleschool.edu
BISHOP, Richard ... 860-832-2201.. 84 J
bishopr@ccsu.edu
BISHOP, Robert, H ... 813-974-3780 111 A
robertbishop@usf.edu
BISHOP, Sandy ... 715-365-4564 514 E
sbishop@nicoletcollege.edu
BISHOP, Sasha ... 843-470-8396 424 E
sbishop@tcl.edu
BISHOP, Stephanie ... 765-983-1628 157 I
bishost@earlham.edu
BISHOP, Steve ... 601-276-3701 256 A
bishop@smcc.edu
BISHOP, Stuart ... 928-536-6265.. 15 B
stuart.bishop@npc.edu
BISHOP, Todd ... 336-734-7313 343 C
tbishop@forsythtech.edu
BISHOP, Wesley, T ... 504-286-5325 195 L
wbishop@suno.edu
BISHOP, William ... 916-278-7469.. 33 C
william.bishop@csus.edu
BISHOP, Wilsie, S ... 423-439-4811 431 H
bishopws@etsu.edu
BISHOP-CLARK,
Catherine, U ... 513-529-6721 365 I
bishopcu@miamioh.edu
BISIGNANO, Chris ... 914-251-6530 328 B
chris.bisignanoi@purchase.edu
BISKUPIAK, Walter, H ... 406-447-5521 270 H
bbiskupi@carroll.edu
BISMARK, Jeanie ... 870-235-4078.. 21 F
mjbismark@saumag.edu
BISPING, Timothy ... 936-468-3101 458 A
bispingto@sfasu.edu
BISSELL, Michelle ... 304-205-6640 502 K
michelle.bissell@bridgevalley.edu
BISSELL, Monika ... 207-795-2846 199 I
bisselmo@mchp.edu
BISSELL, Sally ... 419-783-2366 361 A
sbissell@defiance.edu
BISSELL PAULSON,
Lisa ... 707-965-7362.. 55 F
lpaulson@puc.edu
BISSET, Matthew, S ... 727-864-8482.. 97 O
bissetms@eckerd.edu
BISSET, William, J ... 718-862-7200 313 L
william.bisset@manhattan.edu
BISSINGER, Mary ... 805-482-2755.. 58M
mbissinger@stjohnsem.edu
BISSONETTE, David ... 218-855-8178 244 C
dbissonette@clcmn.edu
BISSONETTE, Matt ... 507-379-3335 247 C
matt.bissonette@riverland.edu
BISWAS, Harun ... 678-466-4240 117 I
harunbiswas@clayton.edu
BITIKOFER, Scott ... 407-646-2137 106 J
sbitikofer@rollins.edu
BITNER, Justin ... 314-246-7464 269 N
justinbitner77@webster.edu
BITNER, Scott ... 410-706-3822 207 H
sbitner@umaryland.edu
BITNER, Teddy ... 816-322-0110 257M
teddy.bitner@calvary.edu
BITTER, Michael ... 808-932-7095 129 I
BITTERBAUM, Erik, J ... 607-753-2201 327 A
erik.bitterbaum@cortland.edu
BITTERMAN, Annette ... 716-839-8459 306 E
abitterm@daemen.edu
BITTINGER, Dale ... 410-455-2278 208 A
bittinger@umbc.edu
BITTINGER, Randall ... 301-387-3091 203 I
randall.bittinger@garrettcollege.edu
BITTINGER, SaraBeth ... 301-687-3130 209 A
sbittinger@frostburg.edu
BITTLE, Carolyn ... 910-410-1751 345 G
ctbittle@richmondcc.edu
BITTNER, David ... 713-525-3589 466 J
bittned@stthom.edu
BITTON, Yoram ... 513-824-2261 309 F
ybitton@huc.edu
BITTORF, David, C ... 240-500-2000 204 B
dcbittorf@hagerstowncc.edu
BITZ, Dwight, D ... 540-458-8105 491 G
dbitz@wlu.edu
BITZER, Michael ... 704-637-4410 336 G
jmbitzer@catawba.edu
BITZER, Michael ... 704-637-4466 336 G
jmbitzer@catawba.edu
BITZER, Michelle ... 715-682-1484 509 D
mbitzer@northland.edu
BITZER, Steve ... 715-682-4591 515 D
steve.bitzer@witc.edu
BIUNDO, Rachel ... 804-594-1479 488 D
rbiundo@jtcc.edu
BIVENS, Danielle ... 541-245-7991 386 G
dbivens@roguecc.edu
BIVENS, Marquiettia, D . 502-597-6242 187 E
marquettia.bivens@kysu.edu
BIVINS, Dallas ... 480-941-1993.. 44 A
dallasbivins@gs.edu
BIXBY, David, E ... 626-815-5334.. 26 U
dbixby@apu.edu
BIXBY, Gary ... 215-751-8800 393 A
hmoore@ccp.edu
BIXBY, John, L ... 305-284-2211 112 O
jbixby@miami.edu
BIXEL, Patricia ... 207-941-7144 199 B
bixelp@husson.edu
BIXLER, Kirk, J ... 317-738-8801 157 L
kbixler@franklincollege.edu
BIZON, Walter, G ... 248-204-3020 233 A
wbizon@ltu.edu
BIZOT, Caroline ... 985-867-2273 195 I
cbizot@sjasc.edu
BJARNSON, Corey ... 513-241-4338 356 I
corey.bjarnson@antonellicollege.edu
BJELLAND, David ... 320-762-4407 243 J
davidb@alextech.edu
BJERKE, Ian ... 701-788-4692 354 B
ian.bjerke@mayvillestate.edu
BJERKE, Keith ... 701-231-6825 354 D
keith@ndsualumni.com
BJERKLIE, Joseph, R ... 207-834-8621 201 E
joseph.bjerklie@maine.edu
BJERUM, Joanna ... 316-284-5326 175 F
jbjerum@bethelks.edu
BJOKNE, Daniel, H ... 515-964-0601 169 C
bjokned@faith.edu
BJORDAHL, Julia ... 509-313-6102 495 A
bjordahl@gonzaga.edu
BJORGAN, Heather ... 309-796-5340 134 C
bjorganh@bhc.edu
BJORK, Johanna ... 208-792-2395 132 C
jcbjork@lcsc.edu
BJORK, Ross ... 662-915-7546 256 C
rbjork@olemiss.edu
BJORKLUND, Robert, B 651-638-6396 240 J
robert-bjorklund@bethel.edu
BJORKLUND, Tarah ... 651-846-1415 247 G
tarah.bjorklund@saintpaul.edu
BJORKMAN, Karen ... 419-530-7842 372 F
karen.bjorkman@utoledo.edu
BJORN, Thorr, D ... 401-874-5245 417 E
tbjorn@uri.edu
BJUNE, Stephanie ... 979-458-6000 458 E
sbjune@tamus.edu
BLACHFORD, Charles ... 215-753-3664 392 D
blachfordc@chc.edu
BLACK, Adam ... 801-863-6378 473 D
blackad@uvu.edu
BLACK, Ann ... 505-428-1811 296 B
ann.black@sfcc.edu
BLACK, April ... 405-789-7661 380 A
april.black@swcu.edu
BLACK, Bernadette ... 619-644-7100.. 45 A
bernadette.black@gcccd.edu
BLACK, Bettye, R ... 405-466-3294 375 L
brblack@langston.edu
BLACK, Britt ... 630-752-5072 155 F
britt.black@wheaton.edu
BLACK, Chantel ... 509-533-7067 493 I
chantel.black@scc.spokane.edu
BLACK, Connie ... 208-562-3252 132 A
connieblack@cwidaho.cc
BLACK, David ... 920-565-1104 507 K
blackdr@lakeland.edu
BLACK, Diane ... 251-442-2209.... 8 D
dblack@umobile.edu
BLACK, Ellen ... 843-349-5211 421 L
ellen.black@hgtc.edu
BLACK, Ellita ... 904-256-7016 102 B
BLACK, Gary ... 440-826-2900 357 B
gblack@bw.edu
BLACK, Glenn ... 419-289-5480 356 L
gblack@ashland.edu
BLACK, Heather ... 412-365-1281 392 C
hblack@chatham.edu
BLACK, James ... 802-635-1298 477 C
james.black@jsc.edu
BLACK, Jane ... 740-695-9500 357 D
jblack@belmontcollege.edu
BLACK, Jared ... 602-489-5300.. 10 G
jared.black@arizonachristian.edu
BLACK, Jason ... 205-726-3673.... 6 G
jjblack@samford.edu
BLACK, John ... 248-689-8282 238 F
jblack@walshcollege.edu
BLACK, John Paul ... 252-527-6223 344 D
jblack@lenoircc.edu
BLACK, John Paul ... 252-527-6223 344 D
jpblack73@lenoircc.edu
BLACK, Joshua ... 864-941-8542 423 C
black.j@ptc.edu
BLACK, Joshua ... 423-614-8370 432 L
jblack@leeuniversity.edu
BLACK, Josiah ... 605-336-6588 428 B
jblack@sfseminary.edu

BLANCHARD, Scott .... 802-322-1640 475 A scott.blanchard@goddard.edu
BLANCHARD, Susan ..... 804-204-1218 478 F registrar@btsr.edu
BLANCHET, Robert, C ... 315-684-6046 329 F blanchrc@morrisville.edu
BLANCHETT, Russell ..... 972-882-7520 459 E russell.blanchett@tamuc.edu
BLANCHETT, Wanda, J .. 848-932-0747 290 C wanda.blanchett@gse.rutgers.edu
BLANCHETTE, Gary .... 413-748-3408 224 G gblanchette@springfieldcollege.edu
BLANCHETTE, Nick .... 715-675-3331 514 F blanchet@ntc.edu
BLANCHIER, Andree ...... 530-242-7511.. 63 I ablanchier@shastacollege.edu
BLANCO MASIAS, Eva .. 408-554-5251.. 62 F eblanco@scu.edu
BLAND, Bartholomew, F .... 718-960-8731 302 C bartholomew.bland@lehman.cuny.edu
BLAND, Byron .... 650-433-3814.. 55 I bbland@paloaltou.edu
BLAND, Carmen .... 360-676-2772 496 C cbland@nwic.edu
BLAND, Constance .... 662-254-3800 255 A cgbland@mvsu.edu
BLAND, Dorothy .... 940-367-4927 466 B dorothy.bland@unt.edu
BLAND, Glenda .... 256-378-2004.... 1 G gbland@cacc.edu
BLAND, James .... 937-393-3431 370 C jbland@sscc.edu
BLAND, Janet, L .... 740-376-4741 365 A janet.bland@marietta.edu
BLAND, Jeanie .... 314-921-9290 269 D jbland@ugst.edu
BLAND, John, D .... 704-687-5822 351 C jdbland@uncc.edu
BLAND, Marissa .... 816-415-5938 270 C blandm@william.jewell.edu
BLAND, Morgan, R .... 252-451-8258 345 B mrbland492@nashcc.edu
BLAND, Sharon .... 240-567-3080 205 F sharon.bland@montgomerycollege.edu
BLAND, Terry .... 662-862-8282 253 D tgbland@iccms.edu
BLAND, Toni .... 714-480-7333.. 57 N bland_toni@rscd.edu
BLAND, Wilson, T .... 202-806-6131.. 92 C wtbland@howard.edu
BLANDFORD, David, K . 989-463-7147 226 H blandford@alma.edu
BLANDFORD, Jonathan, W .... 502-272-7404 183 H jblandford@bellarmine.edu
BLANDFORD, Rob .... 804-289-6010 486 G smcinvest@richmond.edu
BLANDON, Darwin .... 423-648-2678 435 M dblandon@richmont.edu
BLANEY, Diana .... 219-464-7867 165 D diana.blaney@valpo.edu
BLANK, Dave, L .... 336-278-6705 337 G dblank@elon.edu
BLANK, James .... 330-672-3614 363 I jblank@kent.edu
BLANK, Natalia .... 802-485-2025 475 I nblank@norwich.edu
BLANK, Rebecca .... 608-262-9946 510 C chancellor@news.wisc.edu
BLANKE, Raymond .... 405-733-7306 379 F rblanke@rose.edu
BLANKENBAKER, Zarina .... 817-515-7750 458 B zarina.blankenbaker@tccd.edu
BLANKENBERGER, Robert .... 217-206-7413 154 A rblan2@uis.edu
BLANKENBUEHLER, Carla .... 304-205-6706 502 K carla.blankenbuehler@bridgevalley.edu
BLANKENHEIM, Kim ..... 319-368-6464 172 B kblankenheim@mtmercy.edu
BLANKENHORN, Stacie . 503-359-1082 385 I bookstore@pacificu.edu
BLANKENSHIP, Bruce, A .... 304-457-6213 501 A blankenshipba@ab.edu
BLANKENSHIP, Bruce, A .... 304-457-6340 501 A blankenshipba@ab.edu
BLANKENSHIP, Bryan, P .... 859-858-2228 183 C
BLANKENSHIP, Daniel .. 309-467-6301 138 E dblankenship@eureka.edu
BLANKENSHIP, Karen ... 281-476-1850 455 L karen.blankenship@sjcd.edu
BLANKENSHIP, Kevin .... 615-230-3428 438 C kevin.blankenship@volstate.edu
BLANKENSHIP, Lori ...... 517-355-6560 233 G blankens@msu.edu
BLANKENSHIP, Mark, V 859-280-1250 187 G mblankenship@lextheo.edu
BLANKENSHIP, Mike ..... 601-605-3315 253 C mblankenship@holmescc.edu
BLANKENSHIP, Paul ..... 859-256-3100 185 D paul.blankenship@kctcs.edu
BLANKENSHIP, Ruth ..... 276-326-4556 478 H lrblankenship@bluefield.edu
BLANKENSHIP, Ruth ..... 276-326-4556 478 H rblankenship@bluefield.edu
BLANKENSHIP, Vince .... 903-923-2002 448 J vblankenship@etbu.edu
BLANKINSHIP, Blair ...... 410-837-5714 209 D bblankinship@ubalt.edu
BLANKMEYER, Bonnie, L .... 210-567-2691 468 E blankmeyer@uthscsa.edu
BLANKS, Cecelia .... 619-660-4240.. 44 L ceclia.blanks@gcccd.edu
BLANKSON, Joana .... 404-297-9522 120 D blanksonj@gptc.edu
BLANTON, Angela .... 412-268-4925 391 H ablanton@andrew.cmu.edu
BLANTON, Carmen .... 910-755-7332 341 C blantonc@brunswickcc.edu
BLANTON, James .... 205-929-6317.... 2 G jblanton@lawsonstate.edu
BLANTON, Jason .... 606-783-9361 188 C j.blanton@moreheadstate.edu
BLANTON, Jay, D .... 859-257-6605 190 B jay.blanton@uky.edu
BLANTON, Julie .... 620-665-3510 178 D
BLANTON, Michael .... 213-740-4577.. 72 B michael.blanton@usc.edu
BLANTON, Patricia, L .... 843-792-3811 422 C blanton@musc.edu
BLANTON, Ryan .... 580-349-1550 377 E rblanton@opsu.edu
BLANTON, Sharon .... 808-543-8000 129 C sblanton@hpu.edu
BLANTON, Sharon .... 609-771-3353 284 I blantons@tcnj.edu
BLASCHKE, Jayme, L .... 512-245-2180 463 A jb71@txstate.edu
BLASDEL, Amy .... 618-537-6330 145 C bookstores@mckendree.edu
BLASE, Frances, R .... 610-896-1014 397 F fblase@haverford.edu
BLASE, Kristen .... 603-428-2226 281 F kblase@nec.edu
BLASI, Laura, N .... 407-582-3486 113 F lblasi@valenciacollege.edu
BLASIG, Jerry, A .... 402-557-7075 273 E jerry.blasig@bellevue.edu
BLASINGAME, David, T . 314-935-5850 269 L david_blasingame@wustl.edu
BLASINI, Ivelisse .... 787-850-9341 528 B ivelisse.blasini@upr.edu
BLASS, Tammy .... 323-226-6511.. 50 A tblass@dhs.lacounty.gov
BLASSINGAME, Susan .. 806-720-7602 452 D susan.blassingame@lcu.edu
BLASTING, Ralph .... 716-673-3174 325 C ralph.blasting@fredonia.edu
BLASZAK, Julie .... 616-632-2945 227 C jab008@aquinas.edu
BLASZKOWSKI, Remek . 561-732-4424 107 C rblaszkowski@svdp.edu
BLATCHFORD, Alicia ..... 305-284-5155 112 O awb49@miami.edu
BLATTNER, Alan .... 919-962-2211 351 B allan_blattner@unc.edu
BLATTNER, Carolyn .... 919-508-2048 353 C cmblattner@peace.edu
BLATTNER, Nancy .... 973-618-3217 284 D nblattner@caldwell.edu
BLAU, Diane .... 248-476-1122 233 F dblau@mispp.edu
BLAU, Phil .... 740-351-3137 369 L pblau@shawnee.edu
BLAUWKAMP, Christi ... 760-366-3791.. 41 B cblauwkamp@cmccd.edu
BLAYLOCK, Andrew .... 217-786-4533 144 B andrew.blaylock@llcc.edu
BLAYLOCK, Benny .... 318-342-1603 198 A blaylock@ulm.edu
BLAYLOCK, James .... 903-586-2501 443 M james.blaylock@bmats.edu
BLAYLOCK, John, V ...... 402-844-7124 276 G johnb@northeast.edu
BLAYLOCK, Stephen ...... 813-988-5131.. 99 D blaylocks@floridacollege.edu
BLAYLOCK, Terry .... 936-294-1049 462 F tab064@shsu.edu
BLAZAK, Joe .... 724-964-8811 403 A jblazak@ncstrades.edu
BLAZER, Jessica .... 805-922-6966.. 24 J jessica.blazer@hancockcollege.edu
BLAZEY, Jerry .... 815-753-1883 147 H gblazey@niu.edu
BLAZIS, Enoch .... 507-786-3002 250 C blazis@stolaf.edu
BLEA, Kimberly .... 505-454-3566 294 J kjvaldez@nmhu.edu
BLECHMAN, Mindy .... 215-635-7300 396 B
BLEDSOE, Angie .... 816-654-7709 261 D abledsoe@kcumb.edu
BLEDSOE, Chad, A .... 910-898-9601 345 A bledsoec@montgomery.edu
BLEDSOE, Christopher .. 212-998-2040 318 D christopher.bledsoe@nyu.edu
BLEDSOE, Lisa .... 971-722-5852 386 C lbledsoe@pcc.edu
BLEDSOE, Mary .... 817-515-6792 458 B mary.bledsoe@tccd.edu
BLEDSOE, Ruth .... 213-763-7189.. 49 F bledsoerj@lattc.edu
BLEDSOE, W. Craig .... 615-966-1789 433 D craig.bledsoe@lipscomb.edu
BLEE, Kathleen, M .... 412-624-6094 412 I kblee@pitt.edu
BLEIBERG, Erika .... 973-655-4334 287 D bleiberge@mail.montclair.edu
BLEICKEN, Linda, M ..... 912-344-2535 115 D linda.bleicken@armstrong.edu
BLEIFIELD, Elaina .... 763-576-4113 244 A ebleifileld@anokatech.edu
BLEIKAMP, Kerry .... 303-963-3350.. 77 I kbleikamp@ccu.edu
BLEMINGS, Kenneth, P . 304-293-2100 505 B ken.blemings@mail.wvu.edu
BLEMKE, Lenore .... 715-365-4637 514 E lblemke@nicoletcollege.edu
BLENIS, Brian .... 484-664-3631 402 F brianblenis@muhlenberg.edu
BLENKER, Shawn, A ..... 208-467-8950 132 F sablenker@nnu.edu
BLESKACHEK, Leslie ..... 651-385-6304 245 G lbleskachek@southeastmn.edu
BLESSO, Thomas .... 480-947-6644.. 15 I thomas.blesso@pennfoster.edu
BLEVINS, Anita, F .... 423-478-7021 435 I ablevins@ptseminary.edu
BLEVINS, Bob .... 601-318-6155 256 I bblevins@wmcarey.edu
BLEVINS, Elisabeth .... 336-838-6100 347 G
BLEVINS, Elizabeth .... 740-351-3112 369 L eblevins@shawnee.edu
BLEVINS, Karen .... 606-326-2063 185 E karen.blevins@kctcs.edu
BLEVINS, Keisha .... 313-593-5666 238 A kgipson@umich.edu
BLEVINS, Lori .... 336-249-8186 342 F lori_blevins@davidsonccc.edu
BLEVINS, Rick .... 785-442-6110 178 C rblevins@highlandcc.edu
BLEVINS, Robert .... 601-318-6155 256 I robert.blevins@wmcarey.edu
BLEVINS, Ryan .... 219-464-5413 165 D ryan.blevins@valpo.edu
BLEVINS, Scarlett .... 276-944-6229 480 J scblevins@ehc.edu
BLEW, Chad .... 405-744-6604 377 F chad.blew@okstate.edu
BLEW, Denise, M .... 610-758-3179 400 B dmb3@lehigh.edu
BLEWETT, Patrick, A ...... 530-226-4033.. 64 B pblewett@simpsonu.edu
BLEY, Wayne, A .... 480-245-7903.. 13 C wayne.bley@arrows.ibcs.edu
BLEZA, Michelle .... 760-674-7828.. 39 D mbleza@collegeofthedesert.edu
BLICKHAN, Lynn .... 217-641-4206 141 F lblickhan@jwcc.edu
BLIER, Helen .... 412-924-1346 408 E hblier@pts.edu
BLIGH, Michelle .... 909-621-8647.. 37 L michelle.bligh@cgu.edu
BLIMLINE, R. Dean .... 937-529-2201 371 B rdblimline@united.edu
BLINDAUER, Rochelle, L .... 920-832-6541 507 L rochelle.l.blindauer@lawrence.edu
BLINKA, Sonja .... 409-933-8474 446 H sblinka@com.edu
BLISS, Lucinda .... 603-623-0313 281 G lucindabliss@nhia.edu
BLISS, Patricia, J .... 315-445-4141 312 F blisspj@lemoyne.edu
BLISS, Shannon .... 831-755-6875.. 45 C sbliss@hartnell.edu
BLISS, Shawna .... 360-475-7100 496 F sbliss@olympic.edu
BLITZ, Y .... 248-968-3360 239 K
BLITZER, Donna, M ...... 831-459-3983.. 70 C dblitzer@ucsc.edu
BLIZZARD, Mary .... 304-205-6750 502 K mary.blizzard@bridgevalley.edu
BLOCHER, Larry .... 334-670-3869.... 7 E lblocher@troy.edu
BLOCK, Debbie .... 507-457-2412 248 C dblock@winona.edu
BLOCK, Derryl .... 815-753-6155 147 H dblock@niu.edu
BLOCK, Gene, D .... 310-825-2151.. 69 B chancellor@conet.ucla.edu
BLOCK, Jayme, E .... 410-543-6156 209 B jeblock@salisbury.edu
BLOCK, Jeff .... 406-447-6958 271 I jeff.block@umhelena.edu
BLOCK, Joel .... 212-686-9244 298 C
BLOCK, Kailey .... 970-339-6433.. 76 E kailey.block@aims.edu
BLOCK, Regina, M .... 815-740-5047 154 G rblock@stfrancis.edu
BLOCK, Steven .... 956-665-2175 468 A steven.block@utrgv.edu
BLOCKER, Bill .... 832-252-4604 446 A bill.blocker@cbshouston.edu
BLOCKER, Peggy, J .... 303-765-3114.. 80 G pblocker@iliff.edu
BLOCKER, Robert, L ...... 203-432-4160.. 89 G robert.blocker@yale.edu
BLOCKSIDGE, Katie .... 740-364-9513 358 E blocksidge.3@osu.edu
BLODGETT, Bruce, M .... 315-294-8544 300 H blodgett@cayuga-cc.edu
BLOEM, Russell, J .... 616-526-6651 228 B rjb42@calvin.edu
BLOEMENDAAL, Mark ... 712-707-7127 172 G markb@nwciowa.edu
BLOEMKER, Geraldine, A .... 610-499-4107 414 F gabloemker@widener.edu
BLOHM, David .... 415-575-6107.. 29 H dblohm@ciis.edu
BLOHM, John .... 337-482-0911 197 F jib@louisiana.edu
BLOM, Alyssa .... 616-988-3624 232 F ablom@kuyper.edu
BLOMBERG, Brock .... 610-409-3587 413 H brock@ursinus.edu
BLOMBERG, Thomas ..... 850-644-7380 110 A tblomber@fsu.edu
BLOME, Christian .... 812-482-3030 165 E cblome@vinu.edu
BLOME, Shelley .... 701-671-2191 355 B shelley.blome@ndscs.edu
BLOMGREN, Laura .... 610-892-1536 405 C lblomgren@pit.edu
BLOMGREN, Peter, A .... 417-625-9625 263 G blomgren-p@mssu.edu
BLOMGREN, Rebecca .... 336-272-7102 338 B blomgrenr@greensboro.edu
BLONDE, Mitchell .... 419-447-6442 370 K blondemp@tiffin.edu
BLONDIN, Jo, A .... 937-328-6001 359 H blondinj@clarkstate.edu
BLONDIN, Monica, M .... 508-831-5469 226 E mmlucey@wpi.edu
BLOODSAW, Marti .... 309-694-5593 139 G marti.bloodsaw@icc.edu
BLOOM, Claudia .... 661-255-1050.. 29 F
BLOOM, Joel .... 516-299-3567 313 C joel.bloom@liu.edu
BLOOM, Joel, S .... 973-596-3102 288 A joel.s.bloom@njit.edu
BLOOM, John, S .... 214-887-5591 448 G jbloom@dts.edu
BLOOM, Mariesa .... 937-294-0592 369 K mariesa@saa.edu
BLOOM, Ronald .... 914-606-6912 333 H ronald.bloom@sunywcc.edu
BLOOM, Steven .... 617-243-2440 216 C sbloom@lasell.edu
BLOOM, Sue .... 814-393-2045 405 H sbloom@clarion.edu
BLOOM, Vicki .... 574-520-4448 160 F vdbloom@iusb.edu
BLOOM, William .... 310-434-4871.. 62 G bloom_william@smc.edu
BLOOM, William .... 325-942-2246 463 C william.bloom@angelo.edu
BLOOM, Yvonne .... 314-539-5150 266 E yhelberg@stlcc.edu
BLOOMBERG, Laura ...... 612-625-0608 250 E bloom004@umn.edu
BLOOMBERG, Steven .... 405-682-7879 377 C sbloomberg@occc.edu

BOGARD, Karen 870-543-5907 21 E kbogard@seark.edu
BOGARD, Michele, K 402-280-2775 274 D bogard@creighton.edu
BOGART, Denise 229-333-5709 127 H dbogart@valdosta.edu
BOGART, Lisa 201-216-9901 285 F lisa.bogart@eicollege.edu
BOGART, Marti, S 630-637-5355 147 E msbogart@noctrl.edu
BOGART, William, T 865-981-8101 433 F tom.bogart@maryvillecollege.edu
BOGASH, Ross 770-454-9270 93 B
BOGATSKI, Anatole 510-780-4500 48 D abogatski@lifewest.edu
BOGDALEK, Steven, J 248-204-3925 233 A sbogdalek@ltu.edu
BOGDAN, Georgiann 336-272-7102 338 B georgiann.bogdan@greensboro.edu
BOGEN, David 410-225-2319 205 C dbogen@mica.edu
BOGEN, Janice 215-503-4335 411 E janice.bogen@jefferson.edu
BOGEN, Janice, M 215-503-4335 411 E janice.bogen@jefferson.edu
BOGER-HAWKINS, Caitlin 860-738-6441 86 C cboger-hawkins@nwcc.edu
BOGERT, Brian 570-408-4015 414 H brian.bogert@wilkes.edu
BOGERTMAN, Krista 617-745-3895 214 D krista.bogertman@enc.edu
BOGGAN, Laura, K 423-652-4707 432 I lkboggan@king.edu
BOGGESS, Carol 828-689-1237 339 G cboggess@mhu.edu
BOGGESS, Kendra 304-384-5224 503 P president@concord.edu
BOGGIE, Mark 520-515-5451 11 R boggiem@cochise.edu
BOGGIO, Pamela, J 508-213-2483 223 C pamela.boggio@nichols.edu
BOGGS, Beverly 931-221-6540 430 B boggsb@apsu.edu
BOGGS, Bonnie 734-384-4103 234 C bboggs@monroeccc.edu
BOGGS, Gretchen, M 410-250-1088 208 C contedoc@ezy.net
BOGGS, John 505-566-3693 296 A boggsj@sanjuancollege.edu
BOGGS, Paul, R 903-233-3981 452 A paulboggs@letu.edu
BOGGS, Rainie 859-253-3637 184 G rainie.boggs@frontier.edu
BOGGS, Sherri 419-251-1865 365 C sherri.boggs@mercycollege.edu
BOGGS, Steven, E 858-534-6882 69 E dean-ps@ucsd.edu
BOGH, Wayne 909-389-3309 59 H wbogh@craftonhills.edu
BOGHOSSIAN, Fikru 443-885-3160 206 A fikru.boghossian@morgan.edu
BOGLE, Barry, J 915-831-7116 449 A bbogle@epcc.edu
BOGLE, Brittany 408-498-5137 38 I bbogle@cogswell.edu
BOGLE, Christy 704-991-0370 346 I cbogle9678@stanly.edu
BOGLE, Yvonne 413-782-1594 225 F yvonne.bogle@wne.edu
BOGLE JUBINVILLE, Kimberly 603-626-9100 282 C k.boglejubinville@snhu.edu
BOGLEY, John, W 509-527-5979 500 G bogleyj@whitman.edu
BOGNER, Drew 516-323-3200 315 J dbogner@molloy.edu
BOGOMILSKY, Moshe 718-434-0784 300 K
BOGOSIAN, Deborah 212-229-5600 316 E deborah.bogosian@newschool.edu
BOGUE, Michelle 269-782-1486 237 B mbogue@swmich.edu
BOHACH, Gregory 662-325-3006 254 E gbohach@dafvm.msstate.edu
BOHACZ, Candy 269-467-9945 230 C cbohacz@glenoaks.edu
BOHAM, Kenneth, A 252-789-0222 344 E kenneth.boham@martincc.edu
BOHAM, Sandra 406-275-4974 273 A sandra_boham@skc.edu
BOHANNON, Jeremy 405-682-7872 377 C jeremy.l.bohannon@occc.edu
BOHANNON, Vicki 703-812-4757 482 B vbohannon@leland.edu
BOHASKA, Chris 410-225-2490 205 C cbohaska@mica.edu
BOHL, Kelsey 318-342-1033 198 A bohl@ulm.edu
BOHL, Kyle 616-538-2330 230 E kbohl@gbcol.edu
BOHLANDER, Brad 919-515-7373 350 E bcbohlan@ncsu.edu
BOHLEKE, Henry "Chuck" 708-456-0300 153 E henrybohleke@triton.edu
BOHLEN, Greg 303-273-3333 78 J gbohlen@imines.edu
BOHLENDER, Kristi 970-491-6533 78 N kristi.bohlender@colostate.edu
BOHM, Tiffany 913-288-7274 178 H tbohm@kckcc.edu
BOHMAN, Andreas 509-963-2499 492 L bohmana@cwu.edu
BOHN, Andrea 610-409-3562 413 H abohn@ursinus.edu
BOHN, Bill 541-506-6090 382 G bbohn@cgcc.edu
BOHN, Crystal, D 309-341-7200 142 G cdbohn@knox.edu
BOHN, Michael 513-556-0626 371 E bearcad@ucmail.uc.edu
BOHN, Nicole 415-405-3583 34 C nbohn@sfsu.edu
BOHNEN, Evan 803-323-2275 426 H bohnene@winthrop.edu
BOHNENBLUST, Delyna 620-421-6700 179 D delynab@labette.edu
BOHNETT, Sally 419-251-1866 365 C sally.bohnett@mercycollege.edu
BOHNSACK, Morgan 760-252-2411 27 A mbohnsack@barstow.edu
BOHNY, David 973-618-3440 284 D dbohny@caldwell.edu
BOHREN, Karen 231-591-2607 230 A karenbohren@ferris.edu
BOHRER, Joseph, S 610-330-3161 399 B bohrerj@lafayette.edu
BOHRER, Monty 605-995-2997 427 A mobohrer@dwu.edu
BOICE, Daniel 870-460-1080 22 D boice@uamont.edu
BOICE, Nor 253-752-2020 494 H nboice@faithseminary.edu
BOICE-PARDEE, Heath 585-475-2268 321 D hbpvsa@rit.edu
BOIES, Brandy 540-868-7161 488 E bboies@lfcc.edu
BOIES, Chris 540-868-7129 488 E cboies@lfcc.edu
BOIKE, Allan 216-916-7468 363 I aboike1@kent.edu
BOISE, Craig, M 315-443-3678 330 H cmboise@law.syr.edu
BOISELLE, Phillip 561-297-0113 109 B pboiselle@fau.edu
BOISEN, Beth 715-232-1695 512 A boisenb@uwstout.edu
BOISSELLE, Juliet 315-781-3952 310 C jhboiselle@hws.edu
BOISSELLE, Vincent 315-781-3549 310 C boisselle@hws.edu
BOISSONEAULT, Susan 508-678-2811 219 C susan.boissoneault@bristolcc.edu
BOISVERT, Craig 304-647-6363 504 F cboisvert@osteo.wvsom.edu
BOISVERT, David 717-262-2002 415 B david.boisvert@wilson.edu
BOIVIN, Janet 808-544-1187 129 C jboivin@hpu.edu
BOJONCA, Victoria 317-299-0333 164 D victoria.bojonca@tcmi.org
BOKOSKI, Leslie 610-647-4400 397 I lbokoski@immaculata.edu
BOKSAN, George 610-861-1421 402 D boksang@moravian.edu
BOKTOR, Monir 949-794-9090 66 B mboktor@stanbridge.edu
BOLA, William 207-206-2365 202 A wbola@une.edu
BOLA, William 207-602-2365 202 A wbola@une.edu
BOLAND, Carolyn 513-244-4717 366 A carolyn.boland@msj.edu
BOLAND, Kristine 419-783-2469 361 A kboland@defiance.edu
BOLAND, Mary, G 808-956-8522 129 J mgboland@hawaii.edu
BOLAND, Mary Kate 610-647-4400 397 I mboland@immaculata.edu
BOLAND-CHASE, Ann 570-961-4728 401 B chase@marywood.edu
BOLAS, Jon 253-680-7000 492 F jbolas@bates.ctc.edu
BOLDREY, Penny 989-358-7297 227 A boldreyp@alpenacc.edu
BOLDT, Bill 503-725-5037 386 D boldtb@psuf.org
BOLDT, Deborah 505-428-1704 296 B deborah.boldt@sfcc.edu
BOLDUC, Michael, C 561-237-7180 103 E mbolduc@lynn.edu
BOLEK, Catherine 410-651-6714 208 C csbolek@umes.edu
BOLEN, Tom 913-684-3097 518 I
BOLENBAUGH, Peter 406-657-1106 272 I peter.bolenbaugh@rocky.edu
BOLERATZ, David 606-693-5000 187 D dboleratz@kmbc.edu
BOLERATZ, Jonathan 814-332-5206 388 F jboleratz@allegheny.edu
BOLES, Susan 970-824-1151 78 H susan.boles@cncc.edu
BOLES, Vickie 423-697-3395 436 F vickie.boles@chattanoogastate.edu
BOLEY, Paula 419-995-8218 363 G boley.p@rhodesstate.edu
BOLGER, Eric 417-690-2278 258 E bolger@cofo.edu
BOLIN, Joseph 951-343-4714 28 G jbolin@calbaptist.edu
BOLIN, Mark 256-352-8102 3 I mark.bolin@wallacestate.edu
BOLIN, Mary, C 859-257-8701 190 B marychandler.bolin@uky.edu
BOLING, Cindy 405-974-2547 380 J cboling@uco.edu
BOLL, Julie 217-228-5432 149 B bollju@quincy.edu
BOLLANT, Gwen 423-775-6596 435 H gbollant@ogs.edu
BOLLENBACHER, Brian 773-252-6464 149 I brian.bollenbacher@resu.edu
BOLLHEIMER, Meredith 814-824-3363 401 J mbollheimer@mercyhurst.edu
BOLLHORST, Robin 217-875-7200 149 J rbollhorst@richland.edu
BOLLIER, John, H 203-432-6754 89 G john.bollier@yale.edu
BOLLING, Phyllis 973-596-3420 288 A phyllis.bolling@njit.edu
BOLLINGER, Aaron 412-392-8118 408 F abollinger@pointpark.edu
BOLLINGER, Bruce 701-231-6177 354 D bruce.bollinger@ndsu.edu
BOLLINGER, Jacque 608-785-8075 510 F jbollinger@uwlax.edu
BOLLINGER, Larry 617-745-3000 214 D larry.bollinger@enc.edu
BOLLINGER, Lee, C 212-854-9970 305 E bollinger@columbia.edu
BOLLMAN, Dan 517-355-3366 233 G dbollman@ipf.msu.edu
BOLLMAN-DALANSKY, Terri, L 814-641-3424 398 B bollmat@juniata.edu
BOLLMANN, Eric, D 865-539-7368 437 F edbollmann@pstcc.edu
BOLLMANN, Janice, A 314-286-4805 265 F jabollmann@ranken.edu
BOLMAN, Ann 605-718-2401 429 E ann.bolman@wdt.edu
BOLMAN, Dave 602-383-8228 16 I dbolman@uat.edu
BOLNET, Carolle 718-270-6202 303 C bolnet@mec.cuny.edu
BOLOGNA, Brynn 816-584-6714 265 C brynn.bologna@park.edu
BOLOGNONE, John (Buddy) 213-624-1200 42 N bbolognone@fidm.edu
BOLSINGER, Tod 626-304-3711 43 K bolsinger@fuller.edu
BOLSTER, Jeff 619-849-2480 57 H jeffbolster@pointloma.edu
BOLSTRIDGE, Ronald 207-755-5384 199 K rbolstridge@cmcc.edu
BOLT, Barb 814-868-9900 395 A barbb@erieit.edu
BOLT, Barbara 814-864-6666 396 C barbarab@glit.edu
BOLT, Corrine 606-218-5327 190 E corrinebolt@upike.edu
BOLT, Susan 574-284-4556 163 J sbolt@saintmarys.edu
BOLT, Tracy, L 443-334-2270 207 C tbolt@stevenson.edu
BOLTON, Adrienne 985-448-4091 197 C adrienne.bolton@nicholls.edu
BOLTON, David 417-328-1538 267 A dbolton@sbuniv.edu
BOLTON, G. Allen 205-934-5493 8 B abolton@uab.edu
BOLTON, Harry 707-654-1192 32 E hbolton@csum.edu
BOLTON, James 484-664-3400 402 F jimbolton@muhlenberg.edu
BOLTON, Janice 770-962-7580 121 G jbolton@gwinnetttech.edu
BOLTON, Lance 719-502-2200 81 H lance.bolton@ppcc.edu
BOLTON, Meghann 512-313-3000 446 N meghann.bolton@concordia.edu
BOLTON, Melanie 256-378-4900 1 G mbolton@cacc.edu
BOLTON, Robert, D 517-750-1200 237 D rbolton@arbor.edu
BOLTON, Sarah 330-263-2311 360 A sbolton@wooster.edu
BOLTON, Tonya, D 870-759-4130 23 K tbolton@wbcoll.edu
BOLYAI, Stephen 973-720-2233 292 I bolyais@wpunj.edu
BOLYARD, Adrienne, M 206-726-5021 494 B abolyard@cornish.edu
BOLYARD, Brian 304-205-6767 502 K brian.bolyard@bridgevalley.edu
BOLYARD, Melissa 404-727-0692 119 B mbolyar@emory.edu
BOMAN, Victoria 256-761-6175 7 D vboman@talladega.edu
BOMAR, Charles 715-232-4055 512 A bomarc@uwstout.edu
BOMAR, Jimmy 731-352-4034 430 E bomarj@bethelu.edu
BOMBACK, Larry 215-717-3171 393 C larry.bomback@curtis.edu
BOMBERY, Kathleen 912-443-5828 125 D kbombery@savannahtech.edu
BOMER, Dee 615-687-6907 429 F dbomer@abcnash.edu
BOMGAARS, Deb 712-722-6689 168 I deb.bomgaars@dordt.edu
BONA, Dennis 218-793-2465 246 F dennis.bona@northlandcollege.edu
BONACIC, Patricia 310-900-1600 40 C pbonacic@elcamino.edu
BONACK, Anne, E 715-365-4415 514 E abonack@nicoletcollege.edu
BONADIE, Heidi 909-599-5433 48 E hbonadie@lifepacific.edu
BONADUCE DE NIGRIS, Francesca 713-646-1811 456 H fbonaducedenigris@stcl.edu
BONAHUE, Edward 352-381-3822 107 E ed.bonahue@sfcollege.edu
BONANNO, Joseph 812-855-4440 159 H jbonanno@indiana.edu
BONANNO, Steve, C 304-293-6967 505 B steve.bonanno@mail.wvu.edu
BONAPARTE, Donna 781-239-6434 211 A dbonaparte@babson.edu
BONATH, Kyle, K 806-742-3931 463 D kyle.k.bonath@ttu.edu
BONATO, Frederick 201-761-6020 291 D fbonato@saintpeters.edu
BONAVIA, Jan 708-709-7844 148 I jbonavia@prairiestate.edu
BONCUORE, Cheryl 847-574-5159 143 A cboncuore@lfgsm.edu
BOND, Alicia 570-408-6024 414 H alicia.bond@wilkes.edu
BOND, Bill, E 406-756-3818 271 A bbond@fvcc.edu
BOND, Bradley 815-753-9403 147 H bbond@niu.edu
BOND, Cindy, R 208-732-6454 131 I cbond@csi.edu
BOND, Dawn 512-476-2772 443 H registrar@austingrad.edu
BOND, Dawn 512-476-2772 443 H admissions@austingrad.edu
BOND, Debra 540-674-3607 488 G dbond@nr.edu
BOND, Emma 601-426-6346 255 G ebond@southeasternbaptist.edu
BOND, Erin 212-431-2199 317 H erin.bond@nyls.edu
BOND, Helen 202-806-0870 92 C hbond@howard.edu
BOND, Inge 408-988-2200 74 C inge.bond@missioncollege.edu
BOND, Jan 912-478-6397 120 E jbond@georgiasouthern.edu
BOND, Kerri 434-381-6346 485 P kbond@sbc.edu
BOND, Melisa 910-898-9634 345 A bondm@montgomery.edu
BOND, Meredith, R 216-687-5580 359 L m.bond40@csuohio.edu

BOND, Michelle .... 334-386-7275.... 5 I
mbond@faulkner.edu
BOND, Mollie .... 312-329-4177 146 B
mollie.bond@moody.edu
BOND, Nola .... 660-562-1763 264 I
nbond@nwmissouri.edu
BOND, Susan, E .... 610-359-1222 393 E
sbond@dccc.edu
BOND-HUIE,
Stephanie, A .... 512-499-4798 467 A
shuie@utsystem.edu
BOND-MAUPIN, Lisa .... 707-826-4491.. 34 A
ljb20@humboldt.edu
BONDAD, Theresa .... 435-652-7502 473 B
theresa.bondad@dixie.edu
BONDAVALLI, Bonnie .... 815-836-5242 143 E
bondavbo@lewisu.edu
BONDAVALLI, Bruno ..... 773-878-3439 150 I
bbondavalli@staugustine.edu
BONDAVALLI, Bruno ..... 773-878-7502 150 I
bbondavalli@staugustine.edu
BONDEROFF, Mary, H .. 315-684-6981 329 F
bondermh@morrisville.edu
BONDS, Dorothea .... 214-648-7500 469 E
dorothea.bonds@utsouthwestern.edu
BONDS, Jess .... 209-478-0800.. 45 J
jbonds@humphreys.edu
BONDS, Nechell, T .... 417-836-5517 263 H
nbonds@missouristate.edu
BONDS, Nell .... 870-743-3000.. 20 E
nbonds@northark.edu
BONDS, Thomas .... 662-862-8130 253 D
tabonds@iccms.edu
BONDS-RAACKE,
Jennifer .... 785-628-4236 177 D
jmbondsraacke@fhsu.edu
BONDURANT, Derrith .... 903-877-5728 469 A
derrith.bondurant@uthct.edu
BONDURANT,
Glenda, P .... 252-246-1333 347 H
gbondurant@wilsoncc.edu
BONDY, Jeff .... 406-994-2661 272 A
jbondy@montana.edu
BONDY, Kaylyn .... 701-774-4585 355 C
kaylyn.bondy@willistonstate.edu
BONE, Andrew .... 503-399-6593 382 C
andrew.bone@chemeketa.edu
BONE, Robyn .... 817-531-6552 463 G
rbone@txwes.edu
BONE, Robyn .... 817-531-6595 463 G
rbone@txwes.edu
BONEBRIGHT, Terri .... 501-450-1273.. 19 I
bonebright@hendrix.edu
BONELLI, Vicky .... 618-544-8657 140 D
bonelliv@iecc.edu
BONEMERY, Anne .... 413-755-4297 221 B
bonemery@stcc.edu
BONES, Rafael .... 252-335-3785 350 A
rabones@ecsu.edu
BONEWALD, Karen, I .... 603-526-3748 280 H
kbonewald@colby-sawyer.edu
BONEZ, Allison .... 317-955-6080 162 R
abonez@marian.edu
BONFANTI, Phil .... 228-896-2507 254 D
phil.bonfanti@mgccc.edu
BONFIGLIO, Robert, A .. 585-245-5618 327 B
bonfig@geneseo.edu
BONGARTZ, Michael ..... 816-235-1515 268 D
bongartzm@umkc.edu
BONGIORNO, Laurel ..... 802-651-5978 474 G
bongiorno@champlain.edu
BONGIOVANNI, Lynne .. 718-405-3753 304 H
lynne.bongiovanni@mountsaintvincent.edu
BONHARD, Gary .... 520-322-6330.. 12 Q
gary@hanuniversity.edu
BONI, Bethyn .... 315-568-3252 317 A
bboni@nycc.edu
BONI, Sharon .... 304-367-0205 504 A
sharon.boni@fairmontstate.edu
BONIFAS, Angela .... 309-298-2010 155 D
aj-bonifas@wiu.edu
BONIFER, Duane .... 309-457-2321 146 A
dbonifer@monmouthcollege.edu
BONIFORTI, Alfredo, H . 561-237-7173 103 E
aboniforti@lynn.edu
BONIFORTI, Chris, G .... 561-237-7163 103 E
cboniforti@lynn.edu
BONILLA, Angelita .... 973-353-1494 290 D
bonillan@andromeda.rutgers.edu
BONILLA, Anie .... 954-492-5353.. 96 J
abonilla@citycollege.edu
BONILLA, Carlos .... 626-529-8403.. 55 C
cbonilla@pacificoaks.edu
BONILLA, David .... 406-771-4425 272 D
dbonilla@gfcmsu.edu
BONILLA, Dennis .... 602-557-3213.. 17 C
dennis.bonilla@phoenix.edu
BONILLA, Kathleen .... 559-489-2221.. 66 G
kathy.bonilla@fresnocitycollege.edu
BONILLA, Mary Kay ...... 406-771-5123 272 D
mbonilla@gfcmsu.edu
BONILLA, Matthew .... 212-463-0400 331 F
matthew.bonilla3@touro.edu
BONILLA, Ravel .... 787-832-6000 522 Q
rbonilla@icprjc.edu
BONILLA, Ray .... 979-458-6128 458 E
rbonilla@tamus.edu
BONILLA, Ruth .... 787-746-1400 522 O
rbonilla@huertas.edu
BONJIONE, Frank .... 407-708-2126 107 G
bonjionef@seminolestate.edu
BONK, Sharon, B .... 617-588-1356 211 G
sbonk@bfit.edu
BONKOWSKI, Janet .... 920-465-2527 510 E
bonkowsj@uwgb.edu
BONN, Brenda .... 719-255-3317.. 83 C
bbonn@uccs.edu
BONN, Cynthia, L .... 401-874-7100 417 E
cynthia_bonn@uri.edu
BONN, Robert, R .... 262-551-5931 506 H
rbonn@carthage.edu
BONNELL, Chris .... 801-274-3280 474 D
chris.bonnell@wgu.edu
BONNELL, Dawn, A .... 215-898-7236 412 G
vpr@pobox.upenn.edu
BONNER, A. Frank .... 704-406-4236 337 H
president@gardner-webb.edu
BONNER, Connie, C ..... 260-359-4006 159 B
cbonner@huntington.edu
BONNER, Davita .... 386-481-2143.. 95 J
bonnerd@cookman.edu
BONNER, Debera .... 804-524-5276 491 A
dbonner@vsu.edu
BONNER, Jo .... 205-348-6149.... 7 H
jo.bonner@uasystem.edu
BONNER, John, B .... 425-276-9520 494 F
jbonner@everettcc.edu
BONNER, Judy .... 662-325-3742 254 E
judy.bonner@provost.msstate.edu
BONNER, Julia .... 414-229-4716 511 A
jbonner@uwm.edu
BONNER, Kenyon, R ..... 412-648-1006 412 I
krb114@pitt.edu
BONNER, Lisa .... 212-229-5600 316 E
lisa.murray@newschool.edu
BONNER, Lyle .... 940-552-6291 469 F
lbonner@vernoncollege.edu
BONNER, Mason .... 205-366-8814.... 7 C
mbonner@stillman.edu
BONNER, Tommy .... 507-222-4199 241 C
tbonner@carleton.edu
BONNER, William .... 518-736-3622 309 A
bbonner@fmcc.edu
BONNET, Larissa, B ...... 307-674-6446 516 P
lbonnet@sheridan.edu
BONNETTE, J. Michael .. 434-544-8907 482 F
bonnette@lynchburg.edu
BONNETTE, Thomas ...... 802-860-2705 474 G
bonnette@champlain.edu
BONNEY, Curtis .... 206-934-4521 497 H
curtis.bonney@seattlecolleges.edu
BONNEY, Emily .... 657-278-2948.. 32 B
ebonney@fullerton.edu
BONNILLA, Matthew ..... 646-565-6000 331 F
matthew.bonnilla@touro.edu
BONNIN, Linda .... 205-348-4592.... 8 A
linda.bonnin@ua.edu
BONNSTETTER, Bret ...... 847-925-6224 139 B
bbonnste@harpercollege.edu
BONOMO, Nawal .... 570-389-4199 405 E
nbonomo@bloomu.edu
BONONES, Patrick .... 404-471-6396 114 H
pbonones@agnesscott.edu
BONSTEEL, Susan, H .... 443-334-2320 207 C
shbonsteel@stevenson.edu
BONTRAGER, Cindy, A . 785-532-6226 179 A
cab@ksu.edu
BONTRAGER, Jeremy .... 336-725-8344 348 C
bontragerj@piedmontu.edu
BONTRAGER, Katie .... 937-481-2280 373 I
katie_bontrager@wilmington.edu
BONUCHI, Molly, A .... 308-635-6112 278 B
bonuchim@wncc.edu
BONURA, Nancy .... 432-264-3752 450 G
nbonura@howardcollege.edu
BONURA, Rocky .... 310-660-3670.. 42 C
rbonura@elcamino.edu
BONURA, Stephen .... 914-337-9300 305 F
steve.bonura@concordia-ny.edu
BOOB, Cristene, N .... 814-865-0512 403 F
cnb1@psu.edu
BOOCKER, David, J .... 402-554-2338 277 I
dboocker@unomaha.edu
BOOG, Melissa, M .... 410-543-6330 209 B
mmboog@salisbury.edu
BOOHER, Doug .... 812-855-9529 159 H
dbooher@indiana.edu
BOOHER, Mark .... 805-922-6966.. 24 J
mbooher@pcpa.org
BOOK, Connie, L .... 843-953-5007 419 D
cbook1@citadel.edu
BOOKER, Alicia .... 216-987-3048 360 E
alicia.booker@tri-c.edu
BOOKER, Betty .... 301-736-3631 205 B
betty.booker@msbbcs.edu
BOOKER, Kevin .... 470-639-0309 123 E
kevin.booker@morehouse.edu
BOOKER, Latoya .... 616-632-2455 227 C
latoya.booker@aquinas.edu
BOOKER, Latrice .... 219-980-6547 160 C
lbooker@iun.edu
BOOKER, Lonnie .... 785-833-4360 179 C
lonnie.booker@kwu.edu
BOOKER, Marc .... 205-934-9847.... 8 B
mbooker@uab.edu
BOOKER, Mary, L .... 415-422-2620.. 72 A
mbooker@usfca.edu
BOOKER, Michael .... 636-481-3312 261 B
mbooker@jeffco.edu
BOOKER, Ndala .... 407-303-6413.. 94 H
ndala.booker@adu.edu
BOOKER, RhaeAnn .... 616-698-7111 229 D
rbooker@davenport.edu
BOOKER, Steve .... 407-646-2395 106 J
sbooker@rollins.edu
BOOKER, Suzy .... 865-981-8203 433 F
suzy.booker@maryvillecollege.edu
BOOKMAN, Christopher 740-753-6088 362 K
bookmanc27574@hocking.edu
BOOKMAN, Douglas ..... 919-573-5350 349 A
dbookman@vsu.edu
BOOKOUT, James .... 334-670-3617.... 7 E
jbookout@troy.edu
BOOKOUT, Jeff .... 870-358-8614.. 18 D
jeff_bookout@asun.edu
BOOKSTAVER, John .... 636-922-8356 265 J
jbookstaver@stchas.edu
BOOKWALTER, Robert ... 304-696-2350 504 C
bookwalt@marshall.edu
BOOM, Philip .... 563-588-8000 169 B
pboom@emmaus.edu
BOOMER, Holly .... 970-675-3258.. 78 H
holly.boomer@cncc.edu
BOOMGAARDEN,
Donald, R .... 718-940-5902 322 G
dboomgaarden@sjcny.edu
BOON, Rachel, L .... 515-281-3332 166 E
rachel.boon@iowaregents.edu
BOONE, Becky .... 843-349-5274 421 L
becky.boone@hgtc.edu
BOONE, Beth .... 352-392-1311 110 D
bboone@ufl.edu
BOONE, Cheryl, A .... 513-585-0032 359 D
cheryl.boone@thechristcollege.edu
BOONE, Christopher, G 480-965-2236.. 10 K
christopher.g.boone@asu.edu
BOONE, Dan .... 615-248-1251 439 B
dboone@trevecca.edu
BOONE, Debbie .... 334-291-4927.... 1 H
debbie.boone@cv.edu
BOONE, John, B .... 919-866-5923 347 D
jbboone@waketech.edu
BOONE, Kathleen, C ...... 716-839-8301 306 E
kboone@daemen.edu
BOONE, Nickolis .... 319-385-6239 170 J
nick.boone@iw.edu
BOONE, Rebecca .... 318-357-5621 197 D
booner@nsula.edu
BOONE, Richard .... 707-826-3256.. 34 A
richard.boone@humboldt.edu
BOONE, Steve, E .... 501-686-7348.. 22 C
seboone@uams.edu
BOONE, Terri .... 803-812-7354 425 D
booneter@mailbox.sc.edu
BOONE, Zak .... 541-383-7212 382 B
zboone@cocc.edu
BOONSTRA, Brenda .... 706-776-0103 124 E
bboonstra@piedmont.edu
BOOR, Kathryn, J .... 607-255-2241 306 B
kjb4@cornell.edu
BOOREN, Diane .... 303-457-2757.. 76 G
diane.booren@zenith.org
BOOROS, Deborah .... 610-282-1100 393 G
deborah.booros@desales.edu
BOOS, David .... 605-995-3065 427 E
david.boos@mitchelltech.edu
BOOS, Jean .... 843-355-4167 426 G
boosj@wiltech.edu
BOOSINGER,
Timothy, R .... 334-844-5771.... 4 D
provost@auburn.edu
BOOSKA, Karry .... 802-728-1320 477 E
kbooska@vtc.edu
BOOTE, Marlys .... 319-335-2043 166 G
marlys-boote@uiowa.edu
BOOTH, Derrick .... 916-484-8403.. 50 F
boothd@arc.losrios.edu
BOOTH, Edward, C .... 850-263-3261.. 95 F
ecbooth@baptistcollege.edu
BOOTH, Eric, W .... 770-720-9198 124 H
ewb@reinhardt.edu
BOOTH, H. Austin .... 716-645-0983 325 B
abooth@buffalo.edu
BOOTH, Jane, E .... 212-854-0286 305 E
jeb@gc.columbia.edu
BOOTH, Jennifer .... 803-754-4100 420 E
BOOTH, Margaret .... 419-372-7975 357 F
boothmz@bgsu.edu
BOOTH, Molly .... 205-391-3978.... 3 E
mbooth@sheltonstate.edu
BOOTH, Paige .... 512-448-8429 455 I
paigeb@stedwards.edu
BOOTH, Ronnie, L .... 864-646-1773 424 F
rlbooth@tctc.edu
BOOTH, Scott .... 336-734-7317 343 C
sbooth@forsythtech.edu
BOOTH, Shane .... 713-785-5995 446 A
BOOTH, Susan, A .... 573-629-3002 260 G
sbooth@hlg.edu
BOOTH, Susan, L .... 540-224-4640 482 A
slbooth1@jchs.edu
BOOTH, Terry, L .... 803-778-6640 419 A
boothtl@cctech.edu
BOOTH, Terry, L .... 803-778-6624 419 A
boothtl@cctech.edu
BOOTHE, Jason .... 435-652-7526 473 B
boothe@dixie.edu
BOOTHE, Shane .... 832-252-4646 446 A
shane.boothe@cbshouston.edu
BOOTHMAN,
Christopher .... 870-972-2031.. 18 A
cboothman@astate.edu
BOOTMAN, J, L .... 520-626-1657.. 16 J
bootman@email.arizona.edu
BOOTON, Katie .... 402-280-5833 274 D
kbooton@creighton.edu
BOOTS, Joshua, D .... 563-588-7329 171 H
joshua.boots@loras.edu
BOOZANG, Kathleen ..... 973-642-8750 291 F
kathleen.boozang@shu.edu
BOOZE, David .... 714-484-7432.. 53M
dbooze@cypresscollege.edu
BOPKO, Patricia .... 909-652-6152.. 36 E
patricia.bopko@chaffey.edu
BOPP, Jodi, L .... 740-368-3324 368 N
jlbopp@owu.edu
BOQUET, OSB,
Gregory, M .... 985-867-2232 195 I
rector@sjasc.edu
BORAH, Jeffrey .... 631-420-2661 329 D
borahj@farmingdale.edu
BORASI, Raffaella .... 585-275-0880 332 E
raffaella.borasi@rochester.edu
BORBOA-PETERSON,
Stacey .... 701-777-4362 353 G
stacey.peterson@und.edu
BORCHARDT, Missy ...... 314-371-0236 265 F
BORCHARDT, Naftoli ..... 718-234-6404 299 I
yrand77@hotmail.com
BORCHERDING, Alan ..... 314-505-7763 258 I
borcherdinga@csl.edu
BORCHERDING,
Matthew .... 218-736-1506 245 H
matthew.borcherding@minnesota.edu
BORCHERS, Brian .... 208-885-2076 132 I
bborcher@uidaho.edu
BORCHERS, Mary Ellen . 614-236-6814 358 A
mborchers@capital.edu
BORCHERS, Mitch .... 913-469-8500 178 F
mborchers@jccc.edu
BORCHERS, Tim .... 402-872-2222 276 C
tborchers@peru.edu
BORCHERT, Anne, M .... 216-368-0242 358 C
amb14@case.edu
BORCK, Pat .... 478-471-2865 123 A
pat.borck@mga.edu
BORDA, Christopher ..... 706-233-4065 116 D
cborda@berry.edu
BORDEAU, Topher .... 802-586-7711 476 D
tbordeau@sterlingcollege.edu
BORDEAUX, Debra .... 605-856-5880 428 A
debra.bordeaux@sintegleska.edu
BORDEAUX, Lionel .... 605-856-5880 428 A
lionel.bordeaux@sintegleska.edu
BORDELON, Deborah .... 708-534-8045 138 H
dbordelon@govst.edu
BORDEN, Donald .... 856-227-7200 284 E
dborden@camdencc.edu
BORDEN, Jeff .... 352-588-8310 106 N
jeff.borden@saintleo.edu

BORDEN, M. Paige .... 407-823-4765 110 C
paige.borden@ucf.edu
BORDEN, Robert .... 661-255-1050.. 29 F
rborden@calarts.edu
BORDEN, Scott .... 740-245-7974 372 E
sborden@rio.edu
BORDEN, Sue .... 207-947-4591 198 F
sborden@bealcollege.edu
BORDEN, Susan .... 410-626-2506 206 F
susan.borden@sjc.edu
BORDER, Debra .... 402-481-3804 273 F
deb.border@bryanhealthcollege.edu
BORDERS, Julianna, G .. 419-334-8400 370 J
jborders01@terra.edu
BORDERS, Marianne ..... 803-981-7320 426 J
borders@sctechsystem.edu
BORDIN, Cristina, L ..... 512-464-8893 455 I
cristinb@stedwards.edu
BORDNICK, Patrick ...... 504-865-5314 196 D
bordnick@tulane.edu
BORDONARO, Vilma ..... 914-594-4900 318 A
vilma_bordonaro@nymc.edu
BOREING, Vicki .... 307-778-1102 516 N
vboreing@lccc.wy.edu
BOREK, Jarrod .... 860-932-4079.. 86 E
jborek@qvcc.edu
BOREK, John .... 434-528-5276 491 D
BORELLI, Tricia, S .... 563-588-7085 171 H
tricia.borelli@loras.edu
BOREN, David, L .... 405-325-3916 380 L
dboren@ou.edu
BOREN, J. B .... 806-352-5207 470 I
borenjb@wbu.edu
BOREN, Laura .... 254-968-9085 459 A
lboren@tarleton.edu
BORER, Ralph (Sam), J 402-557-7355 273 E
sam.borer@bellevue.edu
BORES, Gerald .... 503-552-2007 384 F
gbores@nunm.edu
BORFITZ, Joanne .... 315-228-7120 304 G
jborfitz@colgate.edu
BORGEN, Beth .... 920-565-1023 507 K
borgembm@lakeland.edu
BORGER, Jennika .... 610-861-1583 402 D
borgerj@moravian.edu
BORGER, Patricia, A ..... 414-229-3013 511 A
pborger@uwm.edu
BORGES, Carmen, B ..... 814-863-0471 403 F
cbb1@psu.edu
BORGES, Daniel .... 619-482-6336.. 65 H
dborges@swccd.edu
BORGES, Donald .... 209-575-6198.. 75 J
borgesd@mjc.edu
BORGES, Norma .... 787-725-6500 521 C
nborges@albizu.edu
BORGESON, Barbara ..... 814-838-7673 395 D
bborgeson@fortisinstitute.edu
BORGIA, Daniel, J .... 716-888-2160 300 G
borgiad@canisius.edu
BORGIA, Tom .... 304-293-2521 505 B
aborgia@hsc.wvu.edu
BORGLUM,
Karen Marie .... 407-582-3455 113 F
kborglum@valenciacollege.edu
BORGMAN,
Cathleen, M .... 203-254-4081.. 87 A
cborgman@fairfield.edu
BORGMAN, Kenneth, L . 989-463-7314 226 H
borgman@alma.edu
BORGMANN-INGWERSEN,
Marian .... 402-465-2415 276 E
mborgman@nebrwesleyan.edu
BORGOGNONI, Mary, E 716-286-8352 318 F
meb@niagara.edu
BORGONAH, Darryl .... 512-245-2550 463 A
djb129@txstate.edu
BORGSMILLER,
Stephen .... 573-472-3210 266 M
sjborgsmiller@semo.edu
BORGSTROM,
Henrik, C .... 716-286-8342 318 F
hcb@niagara.edu
BORGUS, Donna .... 585-389-2471 316 D
dborgus8@naz.edu
BORIA, Selina, M .... 508-854-4368 220 G
sboria@qcc.mass.edu
BORING, David .... 231-348-6838 234 H
dboring@ncmich.edu
BORIS, Barbara, A .... 610-409-3605 413 H
bboris@ursinus.edu
BORIS, LuAnn .... 740-284-7214 361 L
lboris@franciscan.edu
BORISKIN, Ronnie .... 917-493-4583 313 M
rboriskin@msmnyc.edu
BORJORQUEZ, Lina ...... 213-738-6719.. 65 I
finaid@swlaw.edu
BORK, Eric .... 870-307-7242.. 20 C
eric.bork@lyon.edu

BORKAN, Christie .... 330-569-5214 362 J
borkance@hiram.edu
BORKOVICH, Bruce .... 231-591-5000 230 A
brucebork ovich@ferris.edu
BORKOWSKI,
Donald, V .... 207-725-3947 198 G
dborkows@bowdoin.edu
BORKOWSKI, Ellen, Y ... 518-388-6293 332 B
borkowse@union.edu
BORLAND, Denise .... 715-422-5502 514 B
denise.borland@mstc.edu
BORN, Lauren .... 610-917-1465 413 G
leborn@valleyforge.edu
BORN, Matthew .... 610-436-2231 407 D
mborn@wcupa.edu
BORNE, Jade .... 817-515-5636 458 B
jade.borne@tccd.edu
BORNEMANN, Jeffrey ... 414-955-8793 508 D
jbornema@mcw.edu
BORNER, John .... 518-562-4121 304 C
john.borner@clinton.edu
BORNHORST, Mary .... 937-778-7837 361 E
mbornhorst@edisonohio.edu
BORNSTEIN, Eva .... 718-960-8232 302 C
eva.bornstein@lehman.cuny.edu
BORNSTEIN, Leah, L ..... 970-339-6210.. 76 E
leah.bornstein@aims.edu
BORNSTEIN, Rachel ...... 802-225-3318 475 H
rachel.bornstein@neci.edu
BORNUS, Susan .... 651-523-2929 242 E
sbornus@hamline.edu
BOROFF, Karen, A .... 973-761-9655 291 F
karen.boroff@shu.edu
BOROFSKY, David .... 504-865-3034 194 G
borofsky@loyno.edu
BORONICO, Jess .... 516-686-7838 317 G
jboronic@nyit.edu
BORONKAS, Michele .... 908-526-1200 289 D
michele.boronkas@raritanval.edu
BOROS-KAZAI, Mary ..... 608-363-2640 506 D
boroskaz@beloit.edu
BOROUGHS, SJ,
Philip, L .... 508-793-2525 213 D
pborough@holycross.edu
BOROWICK, Matthew .... 973-378-9822 291 F
matthew.borowick@shu.edu
BOROWICK, Matthew .... 973-378-9847 291 F
matthew.borowick@shu.edu
BOROWICZ, Laurie .... 815-825-9333 142 F
laurie.borowicz@kishwaukeecollege.edu
BOROZAN, Susan .... 941-309-5455 106 H
sborozan@ringling.edu
BORR, Mike .... 701-231-9535 354 D
mike.borr@ndsu.edu
BORRAS, Belma .... 787-738-2161 528 A
belma.borras@upr.edu
BORREGARD, Andrea .... 270-686-4521 186 F
andrea.borregard@kctcs.edu
BORREGO, Paul .... 210-486-2194 441 I
pborrego4@alamo.edu
BORREGO, Susan, E ...... 810-762-3322 238 B
sborrego@umflint.edu
BORRELL, Anthony .... 813-757-2111 101 M
aborrell2@hccfl.edu
BORREN, Tammy .... 931-540-2553 436 H
tborren@columbiastate.edu
BORRERO, Alejandro ..... 787-850-9109 528 B
alejandro.borrero@upr.edu
BORRERO, Jennifer, S .. 718-982-2335 302 A
jennifer.borrero@csi.cuny.edu
BORRERO, Maranjani .... 787-780-0070 521 B
mborrero@caribbean.edu
BORSCH, Elva .... 832-813-6571 452 C
elva.borsch@lonestar.edu
BORSIG, Jim .... 662-329-7100 254 F
jbborsig@muw.edu
BORSKI, Brian .... 972-860-4116 447 G
bborski@dcccd.edu
BORSTING, Eric, J .... 714-449-7436.. 51 A
eborsting@ketchum.edu
BORSZ, Michael .... 315-498-2097 319 G
m.a.borsz@sunyocc.edu
BORTH, Adam .... 620-223-2700 177 E
adamb@fortscott.edu
BORTMAN, Lisa .... 310-506-4393.. 56 D
lisa.bortman@pepperdine.edu
BORTMAN, Walter, J ..... 818-364-7800.. 49 C
bortmawj@lamission.edu
BORTON, Jeffrey .... 734-462-4400 236 H
jborton@schoolcraft.edu
BORTUNK, Ayelet .... 305-653-8770 114 F
abortunk@lecfl.com
BORTZ, Carolyn .... 610-861-5434 403 B
cbortz@northampton.edu
BORUCKI, Jennifer, C ... 818-947-2433.. 49 G
fongjc@lavc.edu
BORUFF-JONES, Polly .. 765-455-9343 160 B
pboruffj@iuk.edu

BORUM, John .... 214-333-5973 447 D
johnb@dbu.edu
BORUSZEWSKI, Richard 517-371-5140 239 F
boruszer@cooley.edu
BORYSEWICZ, Cathy ..... 704-355-5970 336 F
cathy.borysewicz@carolinascollege.edu
BOS, James .... 712-722-6030 168 I
jim.bos@dordt.edu
BOSACK-KOSEK,
Carol, A .... 570-408-5963 414 H
carol.bosack@wilkes.edu
BOSCH, Agnes .... 787-767-4300 528 F
agnes.bosch@upr.edu
BOSCHINI, JR.,
Victor, J .... 817-257-7783 461 A
v.boschini@tcu.edu
BOSCHUNG, Milla .... 205-348-6250.... 8 A
mboschun@ches.ua.edu
BOSCO, Carol .... 518-629-7117 310 G
c.bosco@hvcc.edu
BOSCO, SJ, Mark .... 202-687-1395.. 92 B
mb2263@georgetown.edu
BOSCO, Pat, J .... 785-532-6237 179 A
bosco@ksu.edu
BOSE, Janet .... 602-286-8327.. 13 G
janet.bose@gatewaycc.edu
BOSE, Shantanu .... 630-829-0281 137 D
sbose@devry.edu
BOSEMAN, Shelby .... 817-272-2142 467 B
sboseman@uta.edu
BOSEN, Patricia .... 518-580-5550 324 D
pbosen@skidmore.edu
BOSHEARS, Shannon .... 501-812-2221.. 23 C
sboshears@pulaskitech.edu
BOSIO, Katherine .... 810-762-9537 232 C
kbosio@kettering.edu
BOSKET, David .... 570-586-2400 392 E
dbosket@clarkssummitu.edu
BOSKO, Ronna .... 585-245-5596 327 B
bosko@geneseo.edu
BOSLAND, Judy .... 575-646-1720 295 B
jbosland@nmsu.edu
BOSLEY, Amy, N .... 407-582-8255 113 F
abosley@valenciacollege.edu
BOSLEY, Barry .... 717-358-4663 395 G
barry.bosley@fandm.edu
BOSLEY, Gabriele, W .... 502-272-8476 183 H
gbosley@bellarmine.edu
BOSLEY, Mike .... 407-582-7007 113 F
mbosley@valenciacollege.edu
BOSMAN, Linda .... 920-565-1023 507 K
bosmanlr@lakeland.edu
BOSS, Diane .... 479-936-5172.. 20 F
dboss@nwacc.edu
BOSS, Ken .... 708-239-4830 153 B
ken.boss@trnty.edu
BOSS, Samuel, C .... 802-626-6446 477 D
samuel.boss@lyndonstate.edu
BOSS, Shannon .... 215-780-1318 410 D
sboss@salus.edu
BOSSA, Susan, G .... 617-984-1656 223 H
sbossa@quincycollege.edu
BOSSARD, Jennifer .... 402-826-8221 274 E
jennifer.bossard@doane.edu
BOSSE, Jeannine .... 207-859-1105 200 H
sfs@thomas.edu
BOSSERMAN,
Sharon, S .... 540-887-7026 482 G
sbosserman@marybaldwin.edu
BOSSERT,
Elizabeth (Becky) .... 909-558-4517.. 48 H
bbossert@llu.edu
BOST, Rachel, R .... 662-915-7448 256 C
rbost@olemiss.edu
BOST, Tim .... 704-216-7230 346 C
tim.bost@rccc.edu
BOSTANIC, George .... 909-599-5433.. 48 E
jbostanic@lifepacific.edu
BOSTANIC, George .... 423-614-6018 432 L
gbostanic@leeuniversity.edu
BOSTIAN, Susan .... 605-626-2520 428 H
susan.bostian@northern.edu
BOSTIC, Blake .... 704-991-0183 346 I
sbostic2222@stanly.edu
BOSTIC, Heather .... 314-340-3567 260 H
bostich@hssu.edu
BOSTIC, Heidi, L .... 603-862-2062 282 F
heidi.bostic@unh.edu
BOSTIC, James .... 843-355-4177 426 G
bosticj@wiltech.edu
BOSTIC, Melodie .... 314-505-7626 258 I
bosticm@csl.edu
BOSTIC, Renee .... 718-270-6071 303 C
rbostic@mec.cuny.edu
BOSTICK, Carrolyn, J .... 202-806-1222.. 92 C
carrolyn.bostick@howard.edu
BOSTICK, Sharon .... 312-567-3293 140 I
sbostick@iit.edu

BOSTON, Brett .... 909-469-5528.. 74 G
bboston@westernu.edu
BOSTON, Denise .... 415-575-6100.. 29 H
dboston@ciis.edu
BOSTON, Ed .... 478-825-6347 119 C
bostone@fvsu.edu
BOSTON, Genyne .... 850-599-3276 109 A
genyne.boston@famu.edu
BOSTON, Kay .... 318-678-6000 192 C
kboston@bpcc.edu
BOSTON, Melissa .... 914-323-5158 314 A
melissa.boston@mville.edu
BOSTON, Pamela, F ...... 757-823-2293 483 F
pfboston@nsu.edu
BOSTROM, Robert .... 617-984-5937 223 H
rbostrom@quincycollege.edu
BOSTROM, Steve .... 425-889-5584 496 E
steve.bostrom@northwestu.edu
BOSWELL, Chris .... 307-766-2238 517 B
chris.boswell@uwyo.edu
BOSWELL, Ellen .... 303-556-5047.. 80 Q
boswelle@msudenver.edu
BOSWELL, Erin .... 314-529-9333 262 B
eboswell@maryville.edu
BOSWELL, Katherine ..... 817-598-6216 470 J
kboswell@wc.edu
BOSWELL, Robert .... 303-735-1332.. 83 B
robert.boswell@colorado.edu
BOSWELL, Sarah, R ...... 540-985-8309 482 A
srboswell@jchs.edu
BOSWORTH, Blair .... 216-987-4899 360 E
blair.bosworth@tri-c.edu
BOSWORTH, Susan, L .. 757-221-3584 479 I
slbosw@wm.edu
BOSWORTH, Theresa .... 541-278-5957 382 A
tbosworth@bluecc.edu
BOTCHAN, Michael, R .. 510-642-5716.. 68 G
mbotchan@berkeley.edu
BOTELER, Trina .... 770-975-4000 117 G
BOTENGAN, Richard ...... 760-252-2411.. 27 A
rbotengan@barstow.edu
BOTERO, Cecilia .... 662-915-7092 256 C
cbotero@olemiss.edu
BOTERO, Nancy .... 954-201-7414.. 96 A
nbotero@broward.edu
BOTHE, Dan .... 619-849-2290.. 57 H
danbothe@pointloma.edu
BOTHMA, Inge .... 512-492-3005 442 J
ibothma@aoma.edu
BOTHMER, James .... 402-280-5120 274 D
jbothmer@creighotn.edu
BOTHNER, Peter, G .... 585-389-2196 316 D
pbothne4@naz.edu
BOTHOF, Ken .... 859-572-6639 188 E
bothofk1@nku.edu
BOTKIN, Sarah .... 605-626-3007 428 H
sarah.botkin@northern.edu
BOTMAN, Selma .... 212-960-5217 334 P
selma.botman@yu.edu
BOTSTEIN, Leon .... 845-758-7423 298 I
president@bard.edu
BOTSTEIN, Leon .... 914-758-7423 211 B
president@bard.edu
BOTT, Jennifer, P .... 765-285-5323 156 C
jpbott@bsu.edu
BOTT, Rebecca .... 605-688-6361 429 B
rebecca.bott@sdstate.edu
BOTT, Rosa .... 276-328-0312 487 A
grb5u@uvawise.edu
BOTT-LYONS, Tobe .... 505-747-5010 295 H
tobe.bottlyons@nnmc.edu
BOTTA, Michael .... 412-392-3833 408 F
mfbotta@pointpark.edu
BOTTELBERGHE, John .... 303-360-4718.. 79 C
john.bottelberghe@ccaurora.edu
BOTTEM, Lisa .... 218-683-8544 246 F
lisa.bottem@northlandcollege.edu
BOTTEMILLER, Sandi ..... 503-768-7183 383 G
sjb@lclark.edu
BOTTER, Mary .... 802-447-6347 476 C
mbotter@svc.edu
BOTTINELLI, Stasi .... 303-751-8700.. 77 C
bottinelli@bel-rea.com
BOTTO, Karin .... 315-445-4155 312 F
bottoka@lemoyne.edu
BOTTOMLEY, George ..... 401-598-1000 416 C
gbottomley@jwu.edu
BOTTOMS, Rebecca .... 336-725-8344 348 C
bottomsb@piedmontu.edu
BOTTONI, James, A .... 608-243-4552 514 A
jbottoni@madisoncollege.edu
BOTTORFF, Margaret, B 302-831-2101.. 90 I
bottorff@udel.edu
BOTTRELL, Cynthia .... 319-296-4470 169 H
cynthia.bottrell@hawkeyecollege.edu
BOTZMAN, Thomas, J ... 570-674-6215 401 M
tbotzman@misericordia.edu

BOWLER, John 435-652-7913 473 B
john.bowler@dixie.edu

BOWLER, Shaun 951-827-4302 69 D
shaun.bowler@ucr.edu

BOWLES, Anita, K 864-587-4221 424 D
bowlesa@smcsc.edu

BOWLES, Crystal 918-293-5274 378 B
crystal.bowles@okstate.edu

BOWLES, Diane 704-378-1202 338 I
dbowles@jcsu.edu

BOWLES, Donna, J 812-941-2204 161 A
dbowles@ius.edu

BOWLES, James, H 270-824-8588 186 D
james.bowles@kctcs.edu

BOWLES, K. Johnson 585-245-5626 327 B
bowles@geneseo.edu

BOWLES, Ron 214-333-5520 447 D
ronb@dbu.edu

BOWLES, Ryan, A 507-786-3965 250 C
bowles@stolaf.edu

BOWLES, Ulisa 910-672-1411 350 B
ubowles@uncfsu.edu

BOWLIN, Stephanie 909-469-5383 74 G
sbowlin@westernu.edu

BOWLING, Damon 918-836-6886 380 C
damon.bowling@spartan.edu

BOWLING, Dee 252-737-1133 349 I
bowlingde@ecu.edu

BOWLING, Doug 513-569-1752 359 G
doug.bowling@cincinnatistate.edu

BOWLING, John, C 815-939-5221 148 F
jbowling@olivet.edu

BOWLING, Shannon 304-327-4131 503 O
sbowling@bluefieldstate.edu

BOWLING, Thomas 301-687-4311 209 A
tbowling@frostburg.edu

BOWLUS, Robin 419-358-3453 357 E
bowlusr@bluffton.edu

BOWMAN, Alayne 865-981-8011 433 F
alayne.bowman@maryvillecollege.edu

BOWMAN, Benjamin 574-284-4552 163 J
bbowman@saintmarys.edu

BOWMAN, Christine, D 512-863-1200 457 I
bowmanc@southwestern.edu

BOWMAN, Corey, L 660-543-4114 268 A
bowman@ucmo.edu

BOWMAN, David 202-806-7540 92 C
david.bowman@howard.edu

BOWMAN, David 509-359-6244 494 D
dbowman@ewu.edu

BOWMAN, Elizabeth 805-965-0581 62 E
bowmane@sbcc.edu

BOWMAN, Gina 870-972-2250 18 A
gbowman@astate.edu

BOWMAN, Glen 252-335-3424 350 A
gcbowman@ecsu.edu

BOWMAN, Gregory, W 304-293-3199 505 B
gregory.bowman@mail.wvu.edu

BOWMAN, Heath 252-328-6072 349 I
bowmanhe15@ecu.edu

BOWMAN, Helen, Y 215-895-2803 394 C
helen.y.bowman@drexel.edu

BOWMAN, Jeff 740-427-5114 364 A
bowmanj@kenyon.edu

BOWMAN, John 301-687-4212 209 A
jbowman@frostburg.edu

BOWMAN, Judith, M 757-683-3260 483 G
jbowman@odu.edu

BOWMAN, Keith 415-338-1571 34 C
kjbowman@sfsu.edu

BOWMAN, Kevin 808-687-7032 129 C
kbowman@hpu.edu

BOWMAN, Kimberly 717-901-5173 397 E
kbowman@harrisburgu.edu

BOWMAN, Lisa 918-495-6888 378 H
lbowman@oru.edu

BOWMAN, Michael 510-659-6064 54 F
mbowman@ohlone.edu

BOWMAN, Pam 662-685-4771 252 D
pbowman@bmc.edu

BOWMAN, Pamela, L 309-298-1971 155 D
pl-bowman@wiu.edu

BOWMAN, JR.,
Ronald, L 330-972-2157 371 C
rbowman@uakron.edu

BOWMAN, Scott 612-874-3677 243 F
scott_bowman@mcad.edu

BOWMAN, Stacie 978-837-3448 221 G
bowmans@merrimack.edu

BOWMAN, Teri, A 660-543-4900 268 A
tbowman@ucmo.edu

BOWMAN, William 202-319-5290 91 D
bowmanw@cua.edu

BOWMANN, John 636-949-4678 261 I
jbowmann@lindenwood.edu

BOWNE, Kristine 626-396-2474 26 L
kristine.bowne@artcenter.edu

BOWNES, Kim, M 603-535-2771 283 B
kbownes@plymouth.edu

BOWNES-JOHNSON,
Beth 256-352-8190 3 I
beth.johnson@wallacestate.edu

BOWRIN, Anthony, R 989-964-6012 236 F
abowrin@svsu.edu

BOWRON, Steve 507-433-0695 247 C
steve.bowron@riverland.edu

BOWSER, Adam 814-443-2522 405 A
abowser@pennhighlands.edu

BOWSER, Chris 641-683-5159 169 I
chris.bowser@indianhills.edu

BOWSER, Steve 404-270-5326 126 D
sbowser@spelman.edu

BOWYER, Karen, A 731-286-3301 437 A
bowyer@dscc.edu

BOX, Jay 859-256-3132 185 D
president@kctcs.edu

BOX, Jean, A 205-726-2565 6 G
jabox@samford.edu

BOX, Jennifer 541-684-7241 384 H
jbox@nwcu.edu

BOXDORFER, Bill 573-288-6571 259 E
bboxdorfer@culver.edu

BOXWELL, George 304-647-6290 504 F
gboxwell@osteo.wvsom.edu

BOYAN, Barbara, D 804-828-0190 487 E
bboyan@vcu.edu

BOYCE, Brian, D 617-964-1100 210 G
brian.boyce@ants.edu

BOYCE, Eric 828-251-6951 351 A
eboyce@unca.edu

BOYCE, Greg 719-846-5530 82 L
greg.boyce@trinidadstate.edu

BOYCE, Mary, C 212-854-1123 305 E
boyce@columbia.edu

BOYCE, Richard, N 704-337-2450 486 A
rboyce@upsem.edu

BOYCE, Robert 301-687-4043 209 A
rjboyce@frostburg.edu

BOYCE, Susan 802-776-5239 474 H
susan.boyce@csj.edu

BOYD, Amanda 701-777-2219 353 G
amanda.boyd@und.edu

BOYD, Angela 757-727-5328 481 E
angela.boyd@hamptonu.edu

BOYD, Betsy, A 541-346-0946 387 F
eaboyd@uoregon.edu

BOYD, Bill 910-323-5614 336 E
billboyd@ccbs.edu

BOYD, Brandon 931-372-6285 438 F
bboyd@tntech.edu

BOYD, Brian 407-823-3016 110 C
brian.boyd@ucf.edu

BOYD, Carla 520-515-5337 11 R
boydc@cochise.edu

BOYD, Carla, L 218-726-8795 250 F
clboyd@d.umn.edu

BOYD, Carla, M 217-443-8753 137 B
cboyd@dacc.edu

BOYD, Carrie 540-887-7220 482 G
cboyd@marybaldwin.edu

BOYD, Chrispher 336-770-3322 352 B
boydc@uncsa.edu

BOYD, Clarence 918-495-7767 378 H
cboyd@oru.edu

BOYD, Cynthia 770-426-2756 122 F
cboyd@life.edu

BOYD, Cynthia, E 312-942-6915 150 F
cynthia_e_boyd@rush.edu

BOYD, Danielle 618-634-3298 151 G
danielleb@shawneecc.edu

BOYD, David 734-432-5380 233 C
daveboyd@madonna.edu

BOYD, David, L 714-850-4800 67 B
boyd@taftu.edu

BOYD, Deborah 615-966-5708 433 D
deborah.boyd@lipscomb.edu

BOYD, Debra, C 803-323-2220 426 H
boydd@winthrop.edu

BOYD, Diane, E 334-844-1266 4 D
deb0020@auburn.edu

BOYD, Elizabeth 276-328-0128 487 A
egb4d@uvawise.edu

BOYD, JR., Eulas 718-780-0395 300 A
eulas.boyd@brooklaw.edu

BOYD, Evan, E 717-334-6286 412 E

BOYD, Frank 336-316-2205 338 C
boydfa@guilford.edu

BOYD, Gary 304-357-4704 502 E
garyboyd@ucwv.edu

BOYD, Gerald, L 240-629-7840 203 H
gboyd@frederick.edu

BOYD, Heather 303-273-3221 78 J
hboyd@mines.edu

BOYD, JR., James, I 707-965-7203 55 F
jboyd@puc.edu

BOYD, Jeffrey, S 757-822-1180 489 H
jsboyd@tcc.edu

BOYD, John 405-682-7501 377 C
jboyd@occc.edu

BOYD, John, C 828-766-1270 344 F
jboyd@mayland.edu

BOYD, Karen, O 314-576-5923 268 E
boyd@umsl.edu

BOYD, Kathleen 401-341-2374 417 D
boydk@salve.edu

BOYD, Kim 918-495-7108 378 H
kboyd@oru.edu

BOYD, Linda, D 617-732-2800 221 E
linda.boyd@mcphs.edu

BOYD, Lonnie 620-229-6136 181 F
lonnie.boyd@sckans.edu

BOYD, Mamie 864-250-8114 421 K
mamie.boyd@gvltec.edu

BOYD, Manih 800-567-2344 506 I
mboyd@menominee.edu

BOYD, Martha 302-736-2455 90 J
martha.boyd@wesley.edu

BOYD, Mary 970-945-8691 77 M

BOYD, Mary, K 706-236-2216 116 D
mboyd@berry.edu

BOYD, Michael 706-754-7807 123 G
mboyd@northgatech.edu

BOYD, Michael 815-802-8360 142 C
mboyd@kcc.edu

BOYD, Michael, D 901-333-4318 438 B
mdboyd@southwest.tn.edu

BOYD, Monica 336-917-5579 348 H
monica.boyd@salem.edu

BOYD, Monique 301-314-8280 207 G
mboyd1@umd.edu

BOYD, Nick 530-283-0202 42 K
nboyd@frc.edu

BOYD, Rick 803-775-8727 425 F
boydrl@uscsumter.edu

BOYD, Robert 559-278-4480 32 A
robert_boyd@csufresno.edu

BOYD, Ruth 580-774-3177 380 B
ruth.boyd@swosu.edu

BOYD, Sharon, H 910-962-7769 352 A
boyds@uncw.edu

BOYD, Steve 970-945-8691 77 M

BOYD, Steven 916-558-2226 50 I
boyds@scc.losrios.edu

BOYD, Susan 586-445-7408 233 B
boyds@macomb.edu

BOYD, Susan 734-432-5578 233 C
sboyd@madonna.edu

BOYD, Thomas 303-273-3020 78 J
tboyd@mines.edu

BOYD, Todd, T 580-774-3782 380 B
todd.boyd@swosu.edu

BOYD MCELROY, Diana 816-604-2326 262 I
diana.mcelroy@mcckc.edu

BOYD-PUGH,
Jennifer, N 305-899-4057 95 G
jboydpugh@barry.edu

BOYDL, Loni 414-443-8702 513 A
loni.boyd@wlc.edu

BOYDSTUN, Morris 479-394-7622 23 D
mboydstun@uarichmountain.edu

BOYER, Annette 724-925-4101 414 E
boyera@westmoreland.edu

BOYER, Bruce 508-565-1380 224 H
bboyer@stonehill.edu

BOYER, Bruce, E 573-875-7251 258 F
beboyer@ccis.edu

BOYER, Charles 406-994-3681 272 A
cboyer@montana.edu

BOYER, Debra, A 617-228-2403 219 D
dboyer@bhcc.mass.edu

BOYER, Gayle 440-775-8140 367 B
gayle.boyer@oberlin.edu

BOYER, John, W 773-702-8576 153 F
jwboyer@uchicago.edu

BOYER, Kim, L 518-956-8241 324 G
kboyer3@albany.edu

BOYER, Mary 215-702-4541 391 C
mboyer@cairn.edu

BOYER, Mary Jo 610-359-5394 393 E
mjboyer@dccc.edu

BOYER, Mary Jo 610-450-6524 393 E
mboyer@dccc.edu

BOYER, Naomi 863-298-6854 105 F
nboyer@polk.edu

BOYER, Paul, J 413-597-4181 226 C
paul.j.boyer@williams.edu

BOYER, Suzanne, L 410-777-2045 202 D
slboyer1@aacc.edu

BOYER FERHAT,
Caroline 573-592-4570 270 D
caroline.boyerferhat@williamwoods.edu

BOYER-OWENS, Linda 210-485-0230 441 E
lboyer-owens@alamo.edu

BOYERS, Jayson 517-586-3012 228 G
jboyers@cleary.edu

BOYES, Jerry, S 716-878-6533 326 E
boyesjs@buffalostate.edu

BOYES, Monica 530-895-2936 28 E
boyesmo@butte.edu

BOYETT, Chad 912-287-5808 117 J
cboyett@coastalpines.edu

BOYETT, Chris 419-995-8357 363 G
boyett.c@rhodestate.edu

BOYETT, James, C 501-362-1125 17 M
jcboyett@hebersprings.asub.edu

BOYETT, Jennifer 870-230-5401 19 H
boyettj@hsu.edu

BOYETT, Patricia 504-865-7880 194 G

BOYETTE, Alan, J 336-334-5494 351 D
alan_boyette@uncg.edu

BOYETTE, Barbara, G 336-316-2825 338 C
boyettebg@guilford.edu

BOYETTE, Rick 903-823-3274 458 D
ricky.boyette@texarkanacollege.edu

BOYETTE, Susan 404-413-3456 121 A
staylor83@gsu.edu

BOYK, Linda 610-902-8131 391 B
linda.boyk@cabrini.edu

BOYKIN, Coretta 251-578-1313 3 D
cboykin@rstc.edu

BOYKIN, Gregory 252-985-5117 348 A
gboykin@ncwc.edu

BOYKIN, Karen 215-780-1420 410 D
kboykin@salus.edu

BOYKIN, Lashanna 619-680-4430 29 A
lashanna.boykin@cc-sd.edu

BOYKIN, Regena 601-635-2111 252 I
rboykin@eccc.edu

BOYKIN, Ted 570-586-2400 392 E
tboykin@clarkssummitu.edu

BOYKIN, Tiffany, F 410-777-2305 202 D
tfboykin@aacc.edu

BOYLAN, Ellen 718-862-7597 313 L
eboylan01@manhattan.edu

BOYLAN, Erin 607-753-2516 327 A
erin.boylan@cortland.edu

BOYLAN, Stanley, L 646-565-6000 331 F
stanley.boylan@touro.edu

BOYLE, Allison, J 410-576-6316 206 G
aboyle@oag.state.md.us

BOYLE, Amy 504-865-2445 194 G
aboyle@loyno.edu

BOYLE, Ann 480-219-6107 257 A
aboyle@atsu.edu

BOYLE, Antonio, M 903-927-3329 471 B
amboyle@wileyc.edu

BOYLE, Bethany 314-773-0083 257 J
bboyle@brookesbible.org

BOYLE, Carol Ann 516-877-3775 297 I
boyle@adelphi.edu

BOYLE, Christine 201-761-7390 291 D
cboyle@saintpeters.edu

BOYLE, Deborah 727-341-3153 107 A
boyle.deborah@spcollege.edu

BOYLE, Jeanne, E 848-932-7505 290 C
jeboyle@rulmail.rutgers.edu

BOYLE, Jeffery 864-592-4823 424 C
boylej@sccsc.edu

BOYLE, Kate 360-438-4333 497 F
kboyle@stmartin.edu

BOYLE, Kevin 973-618-3372 284 D
kboyle@caldwell.edu

BOYLE, Lori 619-239-0391 35 C
lboyle@cwsl.edu

BOYLE, Nigel 909-621-8218 57 C
dean_faculty@pitzer.edu

BOYLE, Nuala 585-389-2670 316 D
nboyle5@naz.edu

BOYLE, Patrick, M 773-508-7070 144 D
pboyle@luc.edu

BOYLE, Robert, J 904-620-4663 110 E
rboyle@unf.edu

BOYLE, Sarah 215-489-2450 393 F
sarah.boyle@delval.edu

BOYLE, Sharon, I 215-926-2200 411 B
sharon.boyle@temple.edu

BOYLE, Taggart 617-984-1771 223 H
tboyle@quincycollege.edu

BOYLE, Thomas, A 630-515-6166 145 I
tboyle@midwestern.edu

BOYLES, Elinda 740-351-3005 369 L
eboyles@shawnee.edu

BOYLES, Joel 662-562-3240 255 C
jboyles@northwestms.edu

BOYLES, Robert 253-879-3633 499 C
bboyles@pugetsound.edu

BOYLES, Shery 919-760-8581 339 H
boyless@meredith.edu

BOYMAN, Robert 626-529-8033 55 C
rboyman@pacificoaks.edu

BOYMELGREEN, Shaya 718-434-0784 300 K

BOYNE, Andrew 985-448-7928 192 I andrew.boyne@fletcher.edu
BOYNTON, Andrew, C 617-552-4107 212 E andy.boynton@bc.edu
BOYNTON, Antoine 706-583-2552 115 H aboynton@athenstech.edu
BOYS, Kevin, S 937-393-3431 370 C kboys@sscc.edu
BOYS, Mary, C 212-280-1550 332 C mboys@uts.columbia.edu
BOYSUN, Virginia 406-377-9404 270 J vboysun@dawson.edu
BOYUM, Ginny 507-280-5081 247 D ginny.boyum@rctc.edu
BOYUM-BREEN, Trenda 952-806-3910 249 I
BOZARTH, Diane 573-288-6473 259 E dbozarth@culver.edu
BOZARTH, Peggy, I 270-707-3844 186 B peggy.bozarth@kctcs.edu
BOZEMAN-EVANS, Pamela 773-244-5662 147 F pbozeman@northpark.edu
BOZINSKI, Glenn 570-674-6434 401 M gbozinsk@misericordia.edu
BOZZUTO, Victoria 203-285-2408 85 E vbozzuto@gwcc.commnet.edu
BRAATEN, Jennifer, L 540-365-4202 480 L president@ferrum.edu
BRAATEN, Pamela, K 701-788-4773 354 B pamela.braaten@mayvillestate.edu
BRAATZ, Brady, J 913-971-3452 179 H bbraatz@mnu.edu
BRAATZ, Jay 312-362-7561 137 C jbraatz@depaul.edu
BRABAZON, Jodi 215-574-9600 397 H jodi.brabazon@hussiancollege.edu
BRABHAM, Curtis 405-422-1449 379 B
BRABHAM, Sherry, F 212-217-4020 308 B sherry_brabham@fitnyc.edu
BRABHAM, Susan, S 803-938-3795 425 F brabhams@uscsumter.edu
BRACCIANO, Susan 816-271-4214 264 B braccian@missouriwestern.edu
BRACCO, Anthony 212-237-8613 302 F abracco@jjay.cuny.edu
BRACE, Karen, K 260-982-5050 162 Q kkbrace@manchester.edu
BRACELY, Kenesha 904-470-8445 98 B k.bracely@ewc.edu
BRACERO, Carmen, A 787-844-9231 528 E carmen.bracero@upr.edu
BRACEROS, Amy 909-537-3224 33 D abracero@csusb.edu
BRACEY, Carol 951-343-4456 28 G cbracey@calbaptist.edu
BRACEY, Christopher, A 202-994-6510 92 A cabracey@gwu.edu
BRACEY, David 714-772-3330 25 R
BRACEY, Gerald 228-897-7101 256 I jerry.bracey@wmcarey.edu
BRACEY, Matthew 615-675-5329 441 B mbracey@welch.edu
BRACK, Jonathan, M 215-572-3878 414 D jbrack@wts.edu
BRACKE, Paul, J 509-313-6533 495 A
BRACKEN, Damien, S 617-747-2221 212 B admissions@berklee.edu
BRACKEN, Diane 850-484-1175 105 E dbracken@pensacolastate.edu
BRACKEN, James 330-672-2962 363 I jbracke1@kent.edu
BRACKEN, Lisa 803-778-6652 419 A brackenlm@cctech.edu
BRACKEN, Steven 713-226-5276 465 C brackens@uhd.edu
BRACKENBURY, John 310-544-6461 59 E john.brackenbury@usw.salvationarmy.org
BRACKENBURY, Pamilla 310-544-6405 59 E pamilla.brackenbury@usw.salvationarmy.org
BRACKETT, Andrew 802-831-1260 476 G abrackett@vermontlaw.edu
BRACKETT, Chantelle 802-831-1308 476 G cbrackett@vermontlaw.edu
BRACKETT, Geoffrey, L 845-575-3000 314 C geoffrey.brackett@marist.edu
BRACKETT, Robert 708-563-1577 140 I rbrackett@iit.edu
BRACKETT, Stacey 828-328-7309 339 C stacey.brackett@lr.edu
BRACKETT, Suzanne 252-985-5101 348 A sbrackett@ncwc.edu
BRACKIN, Chad 225-578-4736 193 L cmb@lsu.edu
BRACKIN, Rebekah 325-942-2248 463 C rebekah.brackin@angelo.edu
BRACKLEY, Autumn 208-562-3225 132 A autumnbrackley@cwidaho.cc
BRACKLEY, Paul 312-329-4225 146 B paul.brackley@moody.edu
BRACKMANN, Sarah 512-863-1987 457 I brackmas@southwestern.edu
BRACKNELL, Ann 205-391-2958 3 E abracknell@sheltonstate.edu
BRACY, Judy 504-486-7411 198 D jbracy@xula.edu
BRACY, Marion 504-520-7507 198 D mbracy@xula.edu
BRACY KNIGHT, Becca 310-954-5080 28 C
BRADAC, John 607-844-8222 331 D jpb012@tompkinscortland.edu
BRADACH, Carmen 218-749-7743 248 B c.bradach@mr.mnscu.edu
BRADACH, Carmen 218-749-7743 245 D c.bradach@mesabirange.edu
BRADBERRY, J. Chris 402-280-2950 274 D jcbradberry@creighton.edu
BRADBERRY, Randall 662-476-5064 253 A tbradberry@eastms.edu
BRADBERRY, Richard 443-885-3488 206 A richard.bradberry@morgan.edu
BRADBURY, Jane 309-692-4092 145 F jbradbury@midstate.edu
BRADDER, Kelley, L 515-961-1621 173 E kelley.bradder@simpson.edu
BRADDIX, D'Andre 314-516-5205 268 E braddixd@umsl.edu
BRADDOCK, Glenn 518-608-8472 308 A gbraddock@excelsior.edu
BRADDOCK, Reb 850-644-0453 110 A rbraddock@admin.fsu.edu
BRADDY, Linda, S 817-515-6686 458 B linda.braddy@tccd.edu
BRADE-STENNIS, Kesslyn 410-951-3543 208 F kbradestennis@coppin.edu
BRADEEN, NJ 212-217-4370 308 B
BRADEN, Jeffery, P 919-515-2468 350 E jeff_braden@ncsu.edu
BRADEN, Kale 916-484-8050 50 F bradenc@arc.losrios.edu
BRADFIELD, Brett 605-331-6712 429 D brett.bradfield@usiouxfalls.edu
BRADFIELD, Carol 407-303-9585 94 H carol.bradfield@adu.edu
BRADFIELD, Jennifer, S 440-775-8400 367 B jennifer.bradfield@oberlin.edu
BRADFIELD, Tanisha 714-432-5509 38 H tbradfield@occ.cccd.edu
BRADFIELD, Terry 202-885-8631 94 C tbradfield@wesleyseminary.edu
BRADFORD, Brenda 314-434-1115 263 F bradfbd@mobap.edu
BRADFORD, SR., Corey, S 936-261-2150 458 F csbradford@pvamu.edu
BRADFORD, Frances, C 757-221-7802 479 I fcbrad@wm.edu
BRADFORD, Grethel 301-891-4139 209 E gbradford@wau.edu
BRADFORD, Jerry 256-233-8278 4 C jerry.bradford@athens.edu
BRADFORD, Joy 404-880-8049 117 H jbradford@cau.edu
BRADFORD, Julie 801-818-8900 472 E julie.bradford@provocollege.edu
BRADFORD, Katheryn 413-485-7355 218 F kbradford@westfield.ma.edu
BRADFORD, Lawrence 323-241-5280 49 E bradfoll@lasc.edu
BRADFORD, Linda 205-247-8001 7 C lbradford@stillman.edu
BRADFORD, Michael 434-832-7293 487 H bradfordm@cvcc.vccs.edu
BRADFORD, Michele 256-439-6822 2 A mbradford@gadsdenstate.edu
BRADFORD, Paul 805-565-6237 74 I pbradford@westmont.edu
BRADFORD, Peggy 618-634-3221 151 G bradfordp@shawneecc.edu
BRADFORD-PERRY, Emma 225-771-4990 195 K emma_perry@subr.edu
BRADFORD ROUSE, Teri 805-565-7255 74 I tbradfordrouse@westmont.edu
BRADIN, Bernice 617-349-8685 216 D bbradin@lesley.edu
BRADLEY, Akirah 303-492-8476 83 B akirah.bradley@colorado.edu
BRADLEY, Alex 616-538-2330 230 E abradley@gbcol.edu
BRADLEY, Alice 704-290-5832 346 F abradley@spcc.edu
BRADLEY, Alvin 318-274-3278 196 G bradleya@gram.edu
BRADLEY, Angela 228-897-3886 254 D angela.bradley@mgccc.edu
BRADLEY, Brenda 712-274-6400 174 E brenda.bradley@witcc.edu
BRADLEY, Cedric 228-497-7627 254 D cedric.bradley@mgccc.edu
BRADLEY, Dale, R 304-367-4692 503 C dale.bradley@pierpont.edu
BRADLEY, Daniel, J 812-237-4000 159 C president@indstate.edu
BRADLEY, David, M 713-221-8610 465 C bradleyd@uhd.edu
BRADLEY, DeMethra 651-696-6220 243 B dbradley@macalester.edu
BRADLEY, Dennis, J 814-732-1030 406 B bradley@edinboro.edu
BRADLEY, Devon 517-483-1426 232 K bradled@lcc.edu
BRADLEY, Earlhagi 765-983-1311 157 I
BRADLEY, Elizabeth 845-437-7200 333 A elbradley@vassar.edu
BRADLEY, Jane 319-296-4230 169 H jane.bradley@hawkeyecollege.edu
BRADLEY, Jennifer 319-398-4913 171 F jbradley@kirkwood.edu
BRADLEY, Jennifer 808-734-9890 130 C jbradley@hawaii.edu
BRADLEY, Joseph 410-617-5780 205 A jbradley@loyola.edu
BRADLEY, Julie, M 972-758-3821 446 I jbradley@collin.edu
BRADLEY, Kathy 717-337-6960 396 A kbradley@gettysburg.edu
BRADLEY, Katy 405-789-6400 379 K kbradley@snu.edu
BRADLEY, Kim, S 704-687-5700 351 C kim.bradley@uncc.edu
BRADLEY, Liz 402-557-7266 273 E crumly@bellevue.edu
BRADLEY, Marcy, K 607-871-2350 298 A bradlemk@alfred.edu
BRADLEY, Mark 360-882-2200 44 A markbradley@gs.edu
BRADLEY, Martha, S 801-585-9604 472 P martha.bradley@utah.edu
BRADLEY, Mary Jane 870-972-3057 18 A mbradley@astate.edu
BRADLEY, Monica 318-274-6118 196 G bradleym@gram.edu
BRADLEY, Nedra 601-484-8674 253 G nbradley@meridiancc.edu
BRADLEY, Patrick, J 660-543-4515 268 A pbradley@ucmo.edu
BRADLEY, Paul 937-769-1683 356 G pbradley@antioch.edu
BRADLEY, Paul, A 651-631-5592 251 C pabradley@unwsp.edu
BRADLEY, Roger 386-267-0565 97 H director@daytonacollege.edu
BRADLEY, Ryan 205-348-8327 8 A ryan.bradley@ua.edu
BRADLEY, Tanya, W 802-626-6218 477 D tanya.bradley@lyndonstate.edu
BRADLEY, Tashia 937-708-5648 373 H tbradley@wilberforce.edu
BRADLEY, Thomas, G 502-852-5295 190 C tgerard.bradley@louisville.edu
BRADLEY, Tina 870-508-6130 18 C tbradley@asumh.edu
BRADLEY, Tracey 865-539-7158 437 F tcbradley@pstcc.edu
BRADLEY, Vinson 251-580-4908 5 M vinson.bradley@hawks.huntingdon.edu
BRADLEY-DOPPES, Peg 303-871-3399 83 E pbd@du.edu
BRADLEY-HASTY, Barbara 252-536-3386 343 F bhasty399@halifaxcc.edu
BRADSHAW, Amanda 910-592-8081 346 D jbradshaw@sampsoncc.edu
BRADSHAW, Amelia, M 804-523-5867 488 C abradshaw@reynolds.edu
BRADSHAW, Bob 510-659-6191 54 F bbradshaw@ohlone.edu
BRADSHAW, Boyd, A 317-274-3880 160 E bobradsh@iupui.edu
BRADSHAW, Brent 972-279-6511 442 E bbradshaw@amberton.edu
BRADSHAW, Debra 816-268-5472 264 G dlbradshaw@nts.edu
BRADSHAW, Debra 336-744-0900 336 D debra.bradshaw@carolina.edu
BRADSHAW, Erin 505-224-4000 293 L ebradshaw3@cnm.edu
BRADSHAW, Geoffrey, W 608-246-6165 514 A gbradshaw@madisoncollege.edu
BRADSHAW, George 909-274-4419 52 I gbradshaw@mtsac.edu
BRADSHAW, Keifer 336-517-1589 335 K kbradshaw@bennett.edu
BRADSHAW, Kim 704-355-5584 336 F kim.bradshaw@carolinascollege.edu
BRADSHAW, Kim 704-355-5584 336 B kim.bradshaw@carolinashealthcare.org
BRADSHAW, Lelia 276-523-2400 488 F lbradshaw@mecc.edu
BRADSHAW, Marjorie 913-234-0607 176 H marjorie.bradshaw@cleveland.edu
BRADSHAW, Mary Ann 575-492-2149 297 G mbradshaw@usw.edu
BRADSHAW, Michael 601-477-4161 253 F michael.bradshaw@jcjc.edu
BRADSHAW, Phillip 757-569-6744 489 B pbradshaw@pdc.edu
BRADSHAW, Stephen 404-835-6136 435 M sbradshaw@richmont.edu
BRADSHAW, William 215-951-1425 398 F bradshaww69@lasalle.edu
BRADSHER, Carl 434-791-5646 478 E cbradshe@averett.edu
BRADSTREET, Wendy 207-768-2771 200 B wbradstreet@nmcc.edu
BRADT, Jeremy 815-599-3500 139 F jeremy.bradt@highland.edu
BRADWAY, Marshall 413-565-1000 211 C mbradway@baypath.edu
BRADY, Allison 706-886-6831 126 F abrady@tfc.edu
BRADY, Anne Marie 240-895-2103 206 G ambrady@smcm.edu
BRADY, Bridget 805-898-4003 43 A blbrady@fielding.edu
BRADY, Christopher, D 815-921-2151 150 A c.brady@rockvalleycollege.edu
BRADY, Claire 352-365-3608 103 B bradyc@lssc.edu
BRADY, Cliff 419-783-2503 361 A cbrady@defiance.edu
BRADY, David, M 203-576-4589 88 F dbrady@bridgeport.edu
BRADY, Diane 925-424-1630 36 D dbrady@laspositascollege.edu
BRADY, Douglas 716-375-2455 322 B dbrady@sbu.edu
BRADY, Greg, A 815-753-1000 147 H gbrady@niu.edu
BRADY, Henry, E 510-642-5116 68 G hbrady@econ.berkeley.edu
BRADY, James 509-533-3680 494 A jim.brady@sfcc.spokane.edu
BRADY, Jeanne, F 610-660-1000 409 H jebrady@sju.edu
BRADY, Kathleen 732-987-2415 286 D kbrady@georgian.edu
BRADY, Kathleen 864-503-5901 425 H kbrady@uscupstate.edu
BRADY, Kathleen, T 843-792-5205 422 C bradyk@musc.edu
BRADY, Lauren 480-245-7989 13 C lauren.brady@ibcs.edu
BRADY, Marilyn 843-574-6566 424 G marilyn.brady@tridenttech.edu
BRADY, Michael 718-429-6600 333 B michael.brady@vaughn.edu
BRADY, Michael 307-382-1696 517 C mbrady@westernwyoming.edu
BRADY, Michele 309-556-3861 141 B mbrady@iwu.edu
BRADY, Patrcia 808-255-1082 131 A pablaw808@gmail.com
BRADY, Scott 630-942-2219 136 D bradys310@cod.edu
BRADY, Steven 812-877-8784 163 G brady1@rose-hulman.edu
BRADY, Todd 731-661-6566 439 D tbrady@uu.edu
BRAENDEL, Carly 828-669-8012 340 I cbraendel@montreat.edu
BRAESCH, Melissa 920-693-1101 513 H melissa.braesch@gotoltc.edu
BRAEUTIGAM, Ronald, R 847-491-7040 148 C braeutigam@northwestern.edu
BRAGG, Chris 208-732-6775 131 I cbragg@csi.edu
BRAGG, Darcy 229-928-2378 120 F darcy.bragg@gsw.edu
BRAGG, David 804-524-5598 491 A dbragg@vsu.edu
BRAGG, Dawn, S 414-456-8734 508 D dbragg@mcw.edu

BRAGG, Elizabeth .... 503-760-3131 381 J
elizabeth@birthingway.edu
BRAGG, Kayce .... 662-685-4771 252 D
kbragg@bmc.edu
BRAGG, Melissa .... 254-295-4608 466 A
mbragg@umhb.edu
BRAGG, Michael, B .... 206-543-1829 499 D
mbragg@uw.edu
BRAGG, Robert, S .... 276-328-0129 487 A
rsb2e@uvawise.edu
BRAGG, Theresa .... 405-878-5422 379 G
tabragg@stgregorys.edu
BRAGIN, Marc .... 740-427-5228 364 A
braginm@kenyon.edu
BRAHAMS, Teri, T .... 865-694-6476 437 F
tbrahams@pstcc.edu
BRAHM, Gary .... 949-753-4774.. 27 F
chancellor@brandman.edu
BRAIDES, Cheryl .... 215-612-6600 390 B
cbraides@chicareers.com
BRAILER, James .... 410-516-8070 204 F
jbraile1@jhu.edu
BRAILEY, Crystal .... 803-793-5512 420 G
braileyc@denmarktech.edu
BRAIM, Barry .... 413-775-1311 219 F
braim@gcc.mass.edu
BRAINARD, Lisa, C .... 518-292-1959 321 G
brainl@sage.edu
BRAINARD, Nancy .... 918-495-7119 378 H
nbrainard@oru.edu
BRAINER, Charles .... 765-998-5271 164 C
chbrainer@taylor.edu
BRAINERD, Thomas ...... 208-882-1566 132 D
tbrainerd@nsa.edu
BRAIS, Nathan .... 714-546-7600.. 38 F
nbrais@coastline.edu
BRAISHER, Lyndsey ...... 405-912-9007 379 A
lbraisher@ru.edu
BRAISHER, Mark, H ..... 405-912-9013 379 A
mbraisher@ru.edu
BRAKEFIELD, Jean Ann 843-349-2846 420 A
jeanann@coastal.edu
BRAKER, Regina .... 541-962-3509 383 B
rbraker@eou.edu
BRALL, Catherine, M .... 412-924-1404 408 E
cbrall@pts.edu
BRALLEY, Shannon .... 254-526-1934 445 L
shannon.bralley@ctcd.edu
BRALY, JR., Cliff .... 336-272-7102 338 B
bralyc@greensboro.edu
BRAMANTE, Paula .... 617-603-6900 222 F
paula.bramante@necb.edu
BRAMBLETT, Sandra, J . 404-894-8874 120 A
sandi@gatech.edu
BRAME, Tracey .... 616-301-6800 239 F
bramet@cooley.edu
BRAMLAGE, Jenell .... 215-968-8058 390 I
jenell.bramlage@bucks.edu
BRAMLETT, Nancy .... 913-758-4372 182 B
nancy.bramlett@stmary.edu
BRAMLETTE, Jeff .... 706-291-2121 125 E
jbramlette@shorter.edu
BRAMLEY, Mary .... 703-323-3749 488 H
mbramley@nvcc.edu
BRAMMELL, Keith .... 606-326-2426 185 E
keith.brammell@kctcs.edu
BRAMMER, Erika .... 423-652-6301 432 I
ebrammer@king.edu
BRAMMER, Robyn .... 714-895-8125.. 38 G
rbrammer@gwc.cccd.edu
BRAMON, Margie .... 800-995-3159 270 D
margie.bramon@williamwoods.edu
BRAMUCCI, Robert, S .... 949-582-4960.. 64 H
rbramucci@socccd.edu
BRANAM, Patricia .... 615-904-8409 434 H
pat.branam@mtsu.edu
BRANCA, Mickey .... 415-241-2255.. 37 H
mbranca@ccsf.edu
BRANCART, Victor .... 805-756-7416.. 30 K
vbrancar@calpoly.edu
BRANCATO, Katie, M ..... 216-368-7577 358 C
katie.brancato@case.edu
BRANCAZIO, Helen .... 304-829-7131 501 F
hbrancazio@bethanywv.edu
BRANCH, Anna .... 413-545-6237 216 H
abranch@soc.umass.edu
BRANCH, Anne .... 707-256-7161.. 53 D
anne.branch@napavalley.edu
BRANCH, Carol .... 310-846-2554.. 54 I
ananse@otis.edu
BRANCH, Craig .... 540-891-3007 488 B
cbranch@germanna.edu
BRANCH, Gary .... 256-395-2211.... 3 G
gbranch@suscc.edu
BRANCH, Gary, L .... 251-580-2100.... 1 I
gary.branch@faulknerstate.edu
BRANCH, Rachel, U ...... 904-819-6294.. 98 I
rbranch@flagler.edu
BRANCH, Regina, L ...... 910-272-3231 346 A
rbranch@robeson.edu
BRANCHEAU, Ed .... 858-225-4301.. 29 G
ebrancheau@calarttech.edu
BRANCHICK, Vivian .... 323-226-6301.. 50 A
vbranchick@dhs.lacounty.gov
BRANCHINI, Ann, Z ...... 516-323-3008 315 J
office-of-academic-affairs@molloy.edu
BRANCOLINI, Kristine ... 310-338-4593.. 50 J
kbrancol@lmu.edu
BRAND, Amy .... 617-253-4078 221 C
BRAND, Amy .... 601-553-3455 253 G
abrand@meridiancc.edu
BRAND, Beth .... 302-831-3043.. 90 I
bgbrand@udel.edu
BRAND, Dan .... 620-241-0723 176 G
dan.brand@centralchristian.edu
BRAND, David .... 910-678-8307 343 B
brandd@faytechcc.edu
BRAND, Frederick .... 609-984-1588 292 B
fbrand@tesu.edu
BRAND, Jonathan .... 319-895-4324 167 G
jbrand@cornellcollege.edu
BRAND, Richard .... 423-968-4861 432 I
rjbrand@king.edu
BRANDAU-HYNEK, Ann 608-785-9585 515 C
brandauhyneka@westerntc.edu
BRANDAUER,
Samantha, C .... 717-245-8068 394 A
brandaus@dickinson.edu
BRANDEL, Scott .... 312-752-2104 142 E
scott.brandel@kendall.edu
BRANDELL, Jerrold .... 313-577-4447 239 C
aa4537@wayne.edu
BRANDENBURG,
Aurelia .... 859-985-3173 183 I
aurelia_brandenburg@berea.edu
BRANDENBURG,
Laura, C .... 806-291-1106 470 I
brandenburgl@wbu.edu
BRANDENBURG,
Mark, C .... 843-953-5252 419 D
mark.brandenburg@citadel.edu
BRANDER, Kenneth .... 212-960-5263 334 P
brander@yu.edu
BRANDES, David .... 610-861-1441 402 D
brandesd@moravian.edu
BRANDES, Derek, R .... 509-527-4274 499 E
derek.brandes@wwcc.edu
BRANDES, Rand .... 828-328-7077 339 C
rand.brandes@lr.edu
BRANDFORD-CALVO,
Dania .... 401-874-2018 417 E
brandford@uri.edu
BRANDI, Anne, E .... 516-572-7205 316 C
anne.brandi@ncc.edu
BRANDI, Erica .... 610-398-5300 400 C
ebrandi@lincolntech.edu
BRANDKAMP, Katelyn ... 660-263-4100 264 C
katelynb@macc.edu
BRANDON, Alonzo, C ... 757-683-5383 483 G
abrandon@odu.edu
BRANDON, Deborah, L . 909-869-3427.. 31 A
dlbrandon@cpp.edu
BRANDON, Elvis .... 615-230-3375 438 C
elvis.brandon@volstate.edu
BRANDON, Eric .... 828-328-7301 339 C
eric.brandon@lr.edu
BRANDON, Felicia .... 914-674-7718 314 I
fbrandon@mercy.edu
BRANDON, Kevin .... 708-209-3127 136 I
kevin.brandon@cuchicago.edu
BRANDON, Lisa, K .... 618-537-6865 145 C
lkbrandon@mckendree.edu
BRANDON, Mark, E .... 205-348-5117.... 8 A
mbrandon@law.ua.edu
BRANDON, Robert .... 423-478-6229 436 G
rbrandon01@clevelandstatecc.edu
BRANDON, Sonia .... 970-248-1884.. 77 K
sbrandon@coloradomesa.edu
BRANDON, Tracey, P .... 336-599-0032 345 D
tracey.brandon@piedmontcc.edu
BRANDSEN, Cheryl .... 616-526-6102 228 B
brac@calvin.edu
BRANDSTATER, Nate ..... 937-395-8618 364 B
nate.brandstater@kc.edu
BRANDT, Alexander ...... 910-521-6573 351 E
alexander.brandt@uncp.edu
BRANDT, Amy .... 607-778-5014 326 C
brandtac@sunybroome.edu
BRANDT, Deanna .... 405-974-2753 380 J
dbrandt@uco.edu
BRANDT, Elaine .... 573-897-5000 267 F
BRANDT, Eric .... 218-733-7600 245 C
eric.brandt@lsc.edu
BRANDT, John .... 540-261-8467 485 G
john.brandt@svu.edu
BRANDT, Lisa .... 402-461-5177 275 D
BRANDT, Martin .... 631-420-2333 329 D
martin.brandt@farmingdale.edu
BRANDT, Mary, L .... 713-798-3380 444 A
brandt@bcm.edu
BRANDT, Scott .... 831-459-2425.. 70 C
sbrandt@ucsc.edu
BRANDT, William .... 973-278-5400 283 J
wab@berkeleycollege.edu
BRANDT, William .... 973-278-5400 299 F
wab@berkeleycollege.edu
BRANDT-RAUF, Paul ..... 215-895-2215 394 C
paul.w.brandt-rauf@drexel.edu
BRANDVOLD, Kelli .... 808-734-9575 130 C
kellib@hawaii.edu
BRANGAITIS, David .... 845-758-6822 298 I
dbrangaitis@bard.edu
BRANGMAN, Alan .... 302-831-1110.. 90 I
brangman@udel.edu
BRANHAM, Celeste .... 207-778-7087 201 D
cbranham@maine.edu
BRANHAM, Holly, L ...... 307-532-8303 516 J
holly.branham@ewc.wy.edu
BRANHAM, Jim .... 410-626-2545 206 F
jmbranham@sjc.edu
BRANHAM, Keith .... 309-672-5916 145 E
kbranham@methodistcol.edu
BRANHAM, Lorraine ...... 315-443-3627 330 H
lbranham@syr.edu
BRANHAM, Rich, A .... 651-631-5285 251 C
rabranham@unwsp.edu
BRANICKY, Michael .... 785-864-3881 181 I
mbranicky@ku.edu
BRANIGAN, David, E ..... 814-863-9150 403 F
deb7@psu.edu
BRANKIN, Joe .... 630-844-6878 133 H
jbrankin@aurora.edu
BRANKLE, Steve .... 479-524-7209.. 20 B
sbrankle@jbu.edu
BRANN, Shawn .... 817-722-1700 451 G
shawn.brann@tku.edu
BRANNAN, Angie, R ..... 262-524-7335 506 G
abrannan@carrollu.edu
BRANNAN, Colleen, E .. 607-436-2748 325 E
colleen.brannan@oneonta.edu
BRANNAN, Sandra .... 409-944-1387 449 F
sbrannan@gc.edu
BRANNAN, Thomas, I ... 205-934-0177.... 8 B
tbrannan@uab.edu
BRANNEN, Andrew .... 908-737-7023 286 F
abrannen@kean.edu
BRANNEN, Tammy .... 912-443-4797 125 D
tbrannen@savannahtech.edu
BRANNER, Wade, H ...... 540-464-7253 490 E
brannerwh@vmi.edu
BRANNIGAN, Michael ... 518-485-3789 305 B
brannigm@strose.edu
BRANNIN, Brooke .... 615-460-6364 430 D
brooke.brannin@belmont.edu
BRANNON, Jennifer ...... 478-934-3352 123 A
jennifer.brannon@mga.edu
BRANNON, Kelly .... 401-841-2220 518 E
BRANNON, Mark .... 256-306-2500.... 1 F
mark.brannon@calhoun.edu
BRANNON, Porter .... 704-878-3203 344 H
pbrannon@mitchellcc.edu
BRANNON, Tony, L .... 270-809-3328 188 D
tbrannon@murraystate.edu
BRANON, Rovy .... 206-685-6313 499 D
rbranon@uw.edu
BRANSCOME, Tara .... 256-331-5438.... 3 C
tbranscome@nwscc.edu
BRANSCOME, Tara .... 256-331-5299.... 3 C
tbranscome@nwscc.edu
BRANSCUM, Cindy .... 417-455-5506 259 D
cindybranscum@crowder.edu
BRANSON, Angela .... 312-942-9523 150 F
angela_branson@rush.edu
BRANSON, Cathy .... 606-487-3550 185 J
cathy.branson@kctcs.edu
BRANSON, Mark .... 312-662-4121 133 A
mbranson@adler.edu
BRANSON, Salinda Jo .. 309-649-6217 152 G
jo.branson@src.edu
BRANSON, Walter, J ..... 573-341-4122 269 A
bransonwj@mst.edu
BRANSTETTER, Marie .... 913-288-7211 178 H
marie@kckcc.edu
BRANT, Christine .... 734-432-5620 233 C
cbrant@madonna.edu
BRANT, David .... 310-506-4349.. 56 D
david.brant@pepperdine.edu
BRANT, Jo-Ann .... 574-535-7503 158 A
joannab@goshen.edu
BRANT, Keith .... 831-459-2654.. 70 C
keithb@ucsc.edu
BRANT, Todd .... 405-789-6400 379 K
tbrant@snu.edu
BRANTLEY, Allison .... 205-652-3665.... 9 C
abrantley@uwa.edu
BRANTLEY, Brenda .... 318-678-6000 192 C
bbrantley@bpcc.edu
BRANTLEY, Kyle .... 601-925-7634 254 B
brantley@mc.edu
BRANTLEY, Linda .... 978-762-4000 220 E
lbrantley@northshore.edu
BRANTLEY, Michael ...... 972-860-7640 447 I
mbrantley@dcccd.edu
BRANTLEY, Will .... 405-585-5000 377 A
will.brantley@okbu.edu
BRANTON-HOUSLEY,
Mary .... 970-204-8121.. 79 K
mary.branton-housley@frontrange.edu
BRANUM, Scott .... 409-944-1216 449 F
tbranum@gc.edu
BRAS, Rafael .... 404-385-5700 120 A
provost@gatech.edu
BRASE, Don .... 503-399-5184 382 C
don.brase@chemeketa.edu
BRASE, Heather .... 314-744-5342 263 F
matlock@mobap.edu
BRASEL, Steve .... 312-329-4194 146 B
steve.brasel@moody.edu
BRASFIELD, Logan .... 870-633-4480.. 19 E
lbrasfield@eacc.edu
BRASHEAR, Kurth .... 402-643-7408 274 B
kurth.brashear@cune.edu
BRASHEARS, Randolph .. 978-934-2384 217 B
randolph_brashears@uml.edu
BRASHIER, Jason .... 731-989-6571 432 C
jbrashier@fhu.edu
BRASHIER, Samuel .... 864-231-2000 418 E
sbrashier@andersonuniversity.edu
BRASIER, Terry 828-398-7146 340M
terrygbrasier@abtech.edu
BRASKAMP, Corey .... 605-256-5227 428 G
corey.braskamp@dsu.edu
BRASSARD, Kevin, F ..... 508-213-2213 223 C
kevin.brassard@nichols.edu
BRASSIL, Kristoffer, W .. 617-358-7000 212 G
kbrassil@bu.edu
BRASSORD, James, D ... 413-542-2202 210 F
jdbrassord@amherst.edu
BRASTETER, Christina ... 856-256-5173 289 H
brasteter@rowan.edu
BRASURE, III, Ralph ..... 860-515-3873.. 84 H
BRASWELL, Cara Mia .... 334-244-3498.... 4 E
cbraswe2@aum.edu
BRASWELL, Frank .... 651-846-1490 247 G
frank.braswell@saintpaul.edu
BRASWELL, James .... 281-476-2771 455 L
james.braswell@sjcd.edu
BRASWELL, Jody .... 417-690-3372 258 E
braswell@cofo.edu
BRASWELL, Kevin .... 931-372-6092 438 F
kbraswell@tntech.edu
BRATHWAITE,
Cicely Horsham .... 212-220-8141 301 C
chorshambrathwaite@bmcc.cuny.edu
BRATHWAITE, Edward ... 909-607-8509.. 37 L
edward.brathwaite@sodexo.com
BRATHWAITE, Ormond .. 216-987-5008 360 E
ormond.brathwaite@tri-c.edu
BRATHWAITE, Renea, C 612-343-4166 249 E
rcbrathw@northcentral.edu
BRATSCH, John .... 559-730-3830.. 39 G
johnbr@cos.edu
BRATSCH-PRINCE,
Dawn .... 515-294-6410 166 F
deprince@iastate.edu
BRATT, Jonathan .... 585-594-6830 321 C
bratt_jonathan@roberts.edu
BRATTOLI, Tamara .... 815-280-2470 142 A
tbrattol@jjc.edu
BRATTON, Marissa .... 808-544-0249 129 C
mbratton@hpu.edu
BRATTON, Phyllis, K ..... 701-252-3467 355 J
pbratton@uj.edu
BRATULIN, Paul .... 909-384-8978.. 59 I
pbratulin@sbccd.cc.ca.us
BRATZ, Jennifer .... 406-657-1032 272 I
jen.bratz@rocky.edu
BRAUCHLE, Ken .... 812-237-2334 159 C
ken.brauchle@indstate.edu
BRAUCKMULLER, Lois .. 352-854-2322.. 97 C
brauckml@cf.edu
BRAUD, Terry .... 985-448-4017 197 C
terry.braud@nicholls.edu
BRAUER, Cynthia, A ..... 757-221-1693 479 I
cabra1@wm.edu
BRAUER, Douglas .... 217-875-7200 149 J
dbrauer@richland.edu
BRAUER, Jeanna .... 417-667-8181 259 A
jbrauer@cottey.edu
BRAUER, Katie .... 843-863-7194 419 C
kbrauer@csuniv.edu

BRAUER, William, L ... 757-594-7040 479 H wbrauer@cnu.edu
BRAULT, Kelly, N ... 248-370-4921 235 J brault@oakland.edu
BRAUN, Abraham ... 845-425-1370 319 F
BRAUN, Amanda ... 414-229-6599 511 A abraun25@uwm.edu
BRAUN, Bernie ... 225-578-1295 193 M bbraun@lsu.edu
BRAUN, Dale, K ... 715-425-3840 511 E dale.k.braun@uwrf.edu
BRAUN, Dennis ... 508-767-7541 210 I dbraun@assumption.edu
BRAUN, Eric ... 740-351-3542 369 L ebraun@shawnee.edu
BRAUN, Eric ... 740-351-3257 369 L ebraun@shawnee.edu
BRAUN, H. Elizabeth ... 610-328-8365 410 I lbraun1@swarthmore.edu
BRAUN, Keith ... 518-327-6072 320 A kbraun@paulsmiths.edu
BRAUN, Keith, V ... 727-816-3336 105 C braunk@phsc.edu
BRAUN, Lynn ... 419-783-2548 361 A lbraun@defiance.edu
BRAUN, Mark ... 515-281-6527 166 E mark.braun@iowaregents.edu
BRAUN, Mary, C ... 319-273-6144 167 A mary.braun@uni.edu
BRAUN, Neil, S ... 212-346-1962 319 J nbraun@pace.edu
BRAUN, Raymond ... 419-372-3411 357 F rwbraun@bgsu.edu
BRAUN, Robert, D ... 303-492-7006.. 83 B bobby.braun@colorado.edu
BRAUN, Ronald ... 620-947-3121 181 H ronb@tabor.edu
BRAUN, Thomas, W ... 412-648-1938 412 I twb3@pitt.edu
BRAUNGARD, Elizabeth (Liz), A ... 717-361-1525 394 F braungarde@etown.edu
BRAUNGARD, John ... 518-629-4507 310 G j.braungard@hvcc.edu
BRAUNINGER, Roy ... 504-280-6590 194 F rbraunin@uno.edu
BRAUNSCHWEIG, Jim ... 712-274-6400 174 E jim.braunschweig@witcc.edu
BRAVAIS-SLYMAN, Karine ... 312-777-8674 140 G kbravais-slyman@aii.edu
BRAVE, Jennifer ... 608-789-6248 515 C bravej@westerntc.edu
BRAVEMAN, Daan ... 585-389-2004 316 D dbravem7@naz.edu
BRAVER, Joel ... 845-782-1380 335 B
BRAVERMAN, Lisa ... 201-692-2671 286 B lbraverman@fdu.edu
BRAVMAN, John, C ... 570-577-1511 390 H john.bravman@bucknell.edu
BRAVO, Deyse ... 423-236-2008 436 C
BRAVO, Irene ... 305-592-1223 521 C
BRAWNER, Dan ... 615-383-4848 441 A dbrawner@watkins.edu
BRAXTON, Joanne, E ... 631-451-4160 330 B braxtoj@sunysuffolk.edu
BRAXTON, Marcelius ... 931-221-7120 430 B braxtonm@apsu.edu
BRAXTON, Nancy ... 413-369-4044 214 A braxton@csld.edu
BRAXTON, Pamela ... 610-519-4032 413 K pamela.braxton@villanova.edu
BRAXTON, Sallie, W ... 540-286-8016 486 D sbraxton@umw.edu
BRAXTON, Weldon ... 218-322-2380 245 B weldon.braxton@itascacc.edu
BRAY, Brian ... 207-859-4730 198 H brain.bray@colby.edu
BRAY, Holly ... 860-486-4241.. 88 G holly.bray@uconn.edu
BRAY, Jane, S ... 757-683-3938 483 G jsbray@odu.edu
BRAY, John ... 765-677-1771 161 C john.bray@indwes.edu
BRAY, Laura ... 414-297-6048 514 C braylm@matc.edu
BRAY, Paul ... 515-964-0601 169 C brayp@faith.edu
BRAY, Richard ... 979-209-7285 444 D richard.bray@blinn.edu
BRAY, Russell ... 740-392-6868 366 B russell.bray@mvnu.edu
BRAY, Sean ... 410-617-2838 205 A sbray@loyola.edu
BRAY, Tim ... 612-624-2095 250 E brayx010@umn.edu
BRAYSHAW, Laurie ... 505-424-2305 294 C llogan@iaia.edu
BRAYTON, Kelley ... 310-434-3465.. 62 G brayton_kelley@smc.edu
BRAZ, Meredith ... 603-646-2246 281 C meredith.braz@dartmouth.edu
BRAZA, Peter ... 719-255-4550.. 83 C pbraza@uccs.edu
BRAZAS, Tony, A ... 757-479-3706 487 C tbrazas@vbts.edu
BRAZDA, Sara Jane ... 978-837-5257 221 G brazdas@merrimack.edu
BRAZELL, Phil ... 626-815-6000.. 26 U pbrazell@apu.edu
BRAZELL, Phil ... 626-857-2423.. 26 U pbrazell@apu.edu
BRAZELTON, Kent ... 713-646-1889 456 H kbrazelton@stcl.edu
BRAZES, Spencer ... 503-552-2016 384 F sbrazes@nunm.edu
BRAZIER, Elise ... 512-313-3000 446 N elise.brazier@concordia.edu
BRAZZEL, Thomas ... 979-830-4041 444 D thomas.brazzel@blinn.edu
BRAZZIL, Nancy, A ... 512-471-1232 467 C nancy@po.utexas.edu
BRAZZLE, Reggie ... 903-983-8217 451 F rbrazzle@kilgore.edu
BREAU, Walter, C ... 413-265-2222 213 E breauw@elms.edu
BREAULT, Donna ... 419-289-5369 356 L dbreault@ashland.edu
BREAULT, Jody ... 802-776-5236 474 H jody.breaultr@csj.edu
BREAULT, Susan ... 860-932-4062.. 86 E sbreault@qvcc.edu
BREAUX, Aminta ... 301-860-3555 208 E president@bowiestate.edu
BREAUX, David ... 662-846-4100 252 H dbreaux@deltastate.edu
BREAUX, Jules ... 337-482-6471 197 F breaux@louisiana.edu
BREAUX, Megan ... 337-482-1394 197 F mbreaux@louisiana.edu
BREAZILE, Chad ... 816-279-7000 257 B chad@abtu.edu
BRECCIAROLI, TJ ... 256-824-6700.... 8 C thomas.brecciaroli@uah.edu
BRECHBILL, Ryan ... 614-823-1520 368 O rbrechbill@otterbein.edu
BRECHER, Sharon ... 305-534-7050 112 D sbrecher@talmudicu.edu
BRECKENRIDGE, James 650-433-3826.. 55 I jbreckenridge@paloaltou.edu
BRECKENRIDGE, Jim ... 717-245-4711 519 A
BRECKENRIDGE, Joyce . 412-237-3110 392 G jbreckenridge@ccac.edu
BREDIGER, Les ... 843-208-4107 425 B lbredige@uscb.edu
BREEDEN, Amy ... 804-763-6300.. 93 B
BREEDEN, Ann Lloyd ... 804-289-8732 486 G abreeden@richmond.edu
BREEDEN, Susan, D ... 804-289-8400 486 G sbreeden@richmond.edu
BREEDEN, Suzette ... 304-734-6640 502 K suzette.breeden@bridgevalley.edu
BREEDLOVE, Liz ... 309-854-1715 134 C breedlovel@bhc.edu
BREEDLOVE, Paul ... 541-880-2239 383 E breedlove@klamathcc.edu
BREEMS, Jennifer ... 712-722-6043 168 I jenni.breems@dordt.edu
BREEN, David, K ... 508-849-3416 210 H dbreen@annamaria.edu
BREEN, Dennis ... 740-284-5201 361 L dbreen@franciscan.edu
BREEN, Lorraine ... 301-295-3007 518 G lorraine.breen@usuhs.edu
BREEN, Patricia, A ... 626-529-8008.. 55 C pbreen@pacificoaks.edu
BREEN, Thomas ... 518-292-1926 321 G breent@sage.edu
BREER, Mary ... 217-234-5401 143 B mbreer@lakeland.cc.il.us
BREERWOOD, Adam, J . 601-403-1201 255 D abreerwood@prcc.edu
BREES, Chris ... 641-844-5679 170 I chris.brees@iavalley.edu
BREESE, Jeffrey, R ... 330-823-2690 372 C breesejr@mountunion.edu
BREESE, Steven ... 203-392-5468.. 85 A breeses1@southernct.edu
BREESE, Steven ... 516-299-2395 313 D steven.breese@liu.edu
BREESE, William, E ... 414-277-7401 509 A breese@msoe.edu
BREFFLE, Barbara ... 714-449-7448.. 51 A bbreffle@ketchum.edu
BREGE, Nicholas ... 989-358-7202 227 A bregen@alpenacc.edu
BREHENY, Marie ... 413-775-1397 219 F brehenym@gcc.mass.edu
BREHLER, Elizabeth ... 336-506-4138 340 L elizabeth.brehler@alamancecc.edu
BREHM, Leslie ... 845-938-6947 519 D 8drm@usma.edu
BREHMEYER, Michelle .. 928-692-3072.. 14 I mbrehmeyer@mohave.edu
BREIER, Barbara ... 512-245-2396 463 A blb137@txstate.edu
BREILAND, Chris ... 918-333-6151 378 F cbreiland@okwu.edu
BREILAND, Whitney ... 918-333-6151 378 F wbreiland@okwu.edu
BREINER, Fred, J ... 865-539-7144 437 F fjbreiner@pstcc.edu
BREINER, Ozzie ... 610-758-3500 400 B lb05@lehigh.edu
BREIT, Karen ... 715-634-4790 507 J kbreit@lco.edu
BREITBACH, William ... 530-242-7555.. 63 I wbreitbach@shastacollege.edu
BREITBARTH, Jonathan, S ... 651-641-8796 241 L breitbarth@csp.edu
BREITENBACH, Edward . 231-777-0526 234 G edward.breitenbach@muskegoncc.edu
BREITER, Randy ... 305-442-9223 104 B rbreiter@mrc.edu
BREITHAUPT, Jeff ... 917-493-4702 313 M jbreithaupt@msmnyc.edu
BREITHAUPT, Scott ... 706-232-5374 116 D
BREITHOLZ, Brian ... 216-523-7221 359 L b.breittholz@csuohio.edu
BREITMEYER, Chris ... 503-338-2425 382 E cbreitmeyer@clatsopcc.edu
BREITSPRECKER, Lisa ... 414-930-3131 509 B breitspl@mtmary.edu
BREJA, Lisa ... 641-844-5576 170 G lisa.breja@iavalley.edu
BREJC, Jessica ... 303-546-5291.. 81 B jbrejc@naropa.edu
BREKKE, Alice ... 701-777-3511 353 G alice.brekke@und.edu
BREKKE, Paul ... 701-858-3485 354 C paul.brekke@minostateu.edu
BREKKEN, Kathryn, C ... 702-651-7535 278 N kc.brekken@csn.edu
BRELAND, Byron ... 408-288-3725.. 61 P byron.breland@sjcc.edu
BRELAND, Garry, M ... 601-318-6101 256 I garry.breland@wmcarey.edu
BRELAND, Jason ... 601-528-8424 254 D jason.breland@mgccc.edu
BRELAND, Jennifer, R ... 205-934-3555.... 8 B jbreland@uab.edu
BRELAND, Phyllis ... 315-389-4399 309 D pbreland@hamilton.edu
BRELLIS, Matthew ... 631-687-4561 322 G mbrellis@sjcny.edu
BREMER, Cris, M ... 559-489-2220.. 66 G crism.bremer@fresnocitycollege.edu
BREMER, Melanie ... 901-321-4482 431 A mbremer@cbu.edu
BREMS, Christiane ... 503-352-7330 385 I cbrems@pacificu.edu
BRENCHER, Anastasia ... 315-684-6020 329 F brencha@morrisville.edu
BRENEMAN, Curt ... 518-276-6305 321 A brenec@rpi.edu
BRENEMAN, Matt ... 714-449-7480.. 51 A mbrenema@ketchum.edu
BRENER, Laura ... 503-883-2449 383 H lbrener@linfield.edu
BRENKMAN, Katie ... 360-417-6276 496 I kbrenkman@pencol.edu
BRENN, James, E ... 803-535-5326 419 E jbrenn@claflin.edu
BRENNAMAN, Michael, D ... 502-597-6878 187 E michael.brennaman@kysu.edu
BRENNAN, Blair ... 308-432-6044 276 B bbrennan@csc.edu
BRENNAN, Bridget, H ... 410-334-2653 207 C bbrennan@stevenson.edu
BRENNAN, Christopher, P ... 727-864-8122.. 97 O brennacp@eckerd.edu
BRENNAN, Deb ... 308-398-7305 273 G dbrennan@cccneb.edu
BRENNAN, Joanne ... 562-977-6053.. 43 H joanne.brennan@fremont.edu
BRENNAN, Jonathan ... 518-629-7311 310 G j.brennan@hvcc.edu
BRENNAN, Joseph, A ... 518-956-8150 324 G jabrennan@albany.edu
BRENNAN, Joyce ... 508-678-2811 219 C joyce.brennan@bristolcc.edu
BRENNAN, Kate ... 856-225-6577 290 B katecb@camden.rutgers.edu
BRENNAN, Kelly ... 734-487-8898 229 K kelly.brennan@emich.edu
BRENNAN, Kelly ... 212-217-3800 308 B kelly_brennan@fitnyc.edu
BRENNAN, Leah ... 860-701-5061.. 87 F brennan_l@mitchell.edu
BRENNAN, Lipa ... 718-438-2727 335 C rlb@novominsk.com
BRENNAN, Rick ... 708-974-5388 146 C brennan@morainevalley.edu
BRENNAN, Robert, J ... 301-447-7432 206 B brennan@msmary.edu
BRENNAN, Shanon ... 570-454-6172 401 H
BRENNAN, Susan ... 781-891-2061 212 A sbrennan@bentley.edu
BRENNAN, Terrence, P . 972-881-5734 446 I tbrennan@collin.edu
BRENNAN, Terry ... 630-953-3707 135 A tbrennan@chamberlain.edu
BRENNAN, Thomas, M . 302-225-6312.. 90 G brennan@gbc.edu
BRENNAN, William ... 671-405-5921 223 H wbrennan@quincycollege.edu
BRENNAN, William, J ... 207-326-2220 200 F bill.brennan@mma.edu
BRENNEMAN, Darnell ... 740-857-1311 369 I dbrenneman@rosedale.edu
BRENNEMAN, David ... 812-855-0608 159 H davabren@indiana.edu
BRENNEMAN, Joy, D ... 806-371-5124 442 D jdbrenneman@actx.edu
BRENNEMANN, Kyle ... 573-629-3007 260 G kbrennemann@hlg.edu
BRENNEN, David, A ... 859-257-1678 190 B david.brennen@uky.edu
BRENNER, Beth ... 530-754-2023.. 68 H blbrenner@ucdavis.edu
BRENNER, Christina ... 610-436-3511 407 D cbrenner@wcupa.edu
BRENNER, David, A ... 858-534-1501.. 69 E dbrenner@ucsd.edu
BRENNER-SCOTTI, Laura ... 609-984-1141 292 B lbrennerscotti@tesu.edu
BRENNIE, Matthew ... 845-688-6068 331 L brenniem@sunyulster.edu
BRENSINGER, Terry ... 559-453-2325.. 43 J terry.brensinger@fresno.edu
BRENT, Daniel ... 617-327-6777 226 B dan_brent@williamjames.edu
BRENT, Matthew ... 804-758-6771 489 D mbrent@rappahannock.edu
BRENTLEY, Tyler ... 814-824-2000 401 J tbrentley@mercyhurst.edu
BRENTLINGER, Ann, M . 605-394-1604 429 A ann.brentlinger@sdsmt.edu
BRENZING, Pam ... 616-331-3490 230 G brenzinp@gvsu.edu
BRESCIANI, Dean ... 701-231-7211 354 D dean.bresciani@ndsu.edu
BRESE, James ... 808-356-5272 129 C jbrese@hpu.edu
BRESEE, Mikel ... 313-664-1546 228 H mbresee@collegeforcreativestudies.edu
BRESEMAN, Mark, D ... 920-832-6519 507 L mark.d.breseman@lawrence.edu
BRESINGHAM, Ann ... 312-935-6710 149 K abresingham@robertmorris.edu
BRESLAUER, Kenneth, J 732-445-3956 290 A kjbdna@rci.rutgers.edu
BRESLAWSKI, Terry ... 724-357-3077 406 C terry.breslawski@iup.edu
BRESLIN, Beau ... 518-580-5705 324 D bbreslin@skidmore.edu
BRESLIN, Eileen, T ... 210-567-5800 468 E breslin@uthscsa.edu
BRESLIN, Kate ... 267-341-3352 397 G kbreslin@holyfamily.edu
BRESLIN, Kathleen, A ... 610-359-5131 393 E kbreslin@dccc.edu
BRESLIN, Lisa ... 410-857-2225 205 E lbreslin@mcdaniel.edu
BRESNAHAN, Nicole ... 202-885-2822.. 91 C nlbres@american.edu
BRESSETTE, Andrew ... 706-290-2166 116 D abressette@berry.edu
BRESSLER, Coleen ... 402-844-7006 276 G coleen@northeast.edu
BRESSLER, Rebecca, B .. 662-915-7735 256 C rbbressl@olemiss.edu
BRESSO, Michele ... 408-848-4760.. 44 B mbresso@gavilan.edu
BRETHERTON, Jeff ... 218-299-4434 241 K jbrether@cord.edu
BRETON, Gary ... 706-236-1756 116 D gbreton@berry.edu

BRETSCHER, David .... 217-786-2238 144 B
david.bretscher@llcc.edu

BRETT, Jennifer .... 203-576-4122.. 88 F
acup@bridgeport.edu

BRETT, Jessie .... 541-962-3740 383 B
jbrett@eou.edu

BRETTSCHNEIDER, Marla, B .... 603-862-1750 282 F
marla.brettschneider@unh.edu

BRETZ, Brenda, K .... 717-245-1587 394 A
bretz@dickinson.edu

BREUNIG, Donovan ...... 413-205-3972 210 E
donovan.breunig@aic.edu

BREUNINGER, Rebecca . 215-968-8114 390 I
rebecca.breuninger@bucks.edu

BREW, Alan .... 715-682-1329 509 D
abrew@northland.edu

BREWER, Andrew .... 315-268-4022 304 B
abrewer@clarkson.edu

BREWER, Athos .... 713-718-5115 450 D
athos.brewer@hccs.edu

BREWER, Brent .... 269-687-5642 237 B
bbrewer01@swmich.edu

BREWER, Carol, A .... 507-933-8809 242 D
cbrewer@gustavus.edu

BREWER, Chris .... 615-494-8803 434 H
chris.brewer@mtsu.edu

BREWER, Clay .... 618-985-3741 141 D
claybrewer@jalc.edu

BREWER, Dawn, M .... 812-888-4225 105 E
dbrewer@vinu.edu

BREWER, Deborah .... 716-614-6200 318 E

BREWER, Deborah .... 716-614-5911 318 E
dbrewer@niagaracc.suny.edu

BREWER, Dominic .... 212-998-5001 318 D
dominic.brewer@nyu.edu

BREWER, George .... 706-272-4456 118 F
gbrewer@daltonstate.edu

BREWER, Jane, T .... 803-812-7317 425 D
jtbrewer@mailbox.sc.edu

BREWER, Janet .... 765-641-4272 156 A
jlbrewer@anderson.edu

BREWER, Janet .... 501-760-4313.. 20 D
janet.brewer@np.edu

BREWER, Jay .... 401-841-7008 518 E

BREWER, Jerry, T .... 803-777-5783 424 I
jerry-brewer@sc.edu

BREWER, Jim .... 870-460-1274.. 22 D
brewer@uamont.edu

BREWER, John .... 801-863-8320 473 D
brewerjc@uvu.edu

BREWER, JR., John, B .. 301-447-5043 206 B
brewer@msmary.edu

BREWER, Judy .... 319-656-2447 173 C
registrar@shilohuniversity.edu

BREWER, Kristina .... 260-665-4161 164 E
brewerk@trine.edu

BREWER, Mondy .... 806-720-7803 452 D
mondy.brewer@lcu.edu

BREWER, Nancy, A .... 631-451-4064 330 B
brewern@sunysuffolk.edu

BREWER, Rebecca .... 615-794-4254 435 G
rbrewer@omorecollege.edu

BREWER, Regina, L .... 336-628-4554 345 F
rlbrewer@randolph.edu

BREWER, Rick .... 318-487-7400 191 J
rick.brewer@lacollege.edu

BREWER, Robert, W .... 336-272-7102 338 B
rbrewer@greensboro.edu

BREWER, Ryan .... 205-329-7865.... 5 C
ryan.brewer@ecacolleges.com

BREWER, Stacey .... 864-596-9050 420 F
stacey.brewer@converse.edu

BREWER, Tim .... 704-878-3205 344 H
tbrewer@mitchellcc.edu

BREWER, Timothy .... 310-825-9570.. 69 B
tbrewer@conet.ucla.edu

BREWINGTON, Donald, E .... 512-505-3054 451 A
debrewington@htu.edu

BREWINGTON, Holly .... 910-592-8084 346 D
hbrewington@sampsoncc.edu

BREWINGTON, Mark ..... 910-630-7149 340 A
sbrewington@methodist.edu

BREWINGTON, Teare .... 803-536-8775 423 G
tbrewing@scsu.edu

BREWS, Peter, J .... 803-777-3176 424 I
peter.brews@moore.sc.edu

BREWSTER, Carrie .... 925-631-4643.. 59 C
cbrewste@stmarys-ca.edu

BREWSTER, Geoffrey .... 918-610-8303 378 I
geoff.brewster@ptstulsa.edu

BREWSTER, LaRita .... 256-761-6119.... 7 D
lmbrewster@talladega.edu

BREWSTER, Stephen .... 305-273-4499.. 96 N
stephen.brewster@cbt.edu

BREWSTER, Tom .... 276-326-4240 478 H
tbrewster@bluefield.edu

BREZEL, Allan .... 678-916-2606 115 K
abrezel@johnmarshall.edu

BREZIL, Chris .... 212-229-5300 316 E
brezilc@newschool.edu

BREZINA, Jennifer .... 615-230-3214 438 C
jennifer.brezina@volstate.edu

BREZINSKI, Donald .... 603-645-3109 282 C
d.brezinski@snhu.edu

BRIAN, Robert, M .... 912-583-3107 116 G
rbrian@bpc.edu

BRIAN, Thomas, J .... 918-631-2200 381 C
thomas-brian@utulsa.edu

BRIAND, Simone .... 913-234-0810 176 H
simone.briand@cleveland.edu

BRIAR, Jennifer .... 760-591-3012.. 71 I
jbriar@usa.edu

BRIAR, Jennifer .... 312-752-2205 142 E
jennifer.briar@kendall.edu

BRIAR, John .... 559-325-3600.. 29 D
jbriar@chsu.org

BRICE, Diane .... 806-371-5028 442 D
kdbrice@actx.edu

BRICE, Eloise, D .... 713-743-8165 464 F
edstuhr@central.uh.edu

BRICE, Eloise, D .... 713-743-8165 465 A
edstuhr@central.uh.edu

BRICE, Ian .... 704-330-6593 342 A
ian.brice@cpcc.edu

BRICE, Ken .... 510-466-7269.. 56 I
kbrice@peralta.edu

BRICE, Tanya .... 803-705-4945 418 G
bricet@benedict.edu

BRICE, Tanya .... 803-705-4945 418 G
tanya.brice@benedict.edu

BRICELAND, Cynthia .... 724-503-1001 414 A
cbriceland@washjeff.edu

BRICHTA, William .... 215-780-1307 410 D
wbrichta@salus.edu

BRICK, George .... 575-624-8023 295 A
brick@nmmi.edu

BRICKER, J. Douglas .... 412-396-6377 394 D
bricker@duq.edu

BRICKER, Susan .... 626-585-7614.. 56 B
sbricker@pasadena.edu

BRICKHOUSE, Nancy .... 314-977-2193 266 J
brickhouse@slu.edu

BRICKHOUSE, Wendy, W .... 252-335-0821 342 D
wbrickhouse@albemarle.edu

BRICKLE, Colleen .... 952-358-8158 246 D
colleen.brickle@normandale.edu

BRICKNER-WOOD, Larry .... 603-862-1165 282 F
larry.brickner-wood@unh.edu

BRIDDES, Bill .... 610-902-8526 391 B
0290mgr@follett.com

BRIDEL, David .... 213-821-4035.. 72 B
bridel@usc.edu

BRIDGE, Holly .... 417-328-1806 267 A
hbridge@sbuniv.edu

BRIDGE, Louise .... 801-863-8689 473 D
bridgelo@uvu.edu

BRIDGEFORTH, Daniel .. 703-812-4757 482 B
dbridgeforth@leland.edu

BRIDGEFORTH, Valerie . 601-318-6188 256 I
vbridgeforth@wmcarey.edu

BRIDGEMAN, Curtis .... 503-370-6402 388 D
cbridgem@willamette.edu

BRIDGEMAN, Doris .... 601-977-7836 256 B
dbridgeman@tougaloo.edu

BRIDGEMAN, Gregory ... 270-707-3904 186 B
gbridgeman0001@kctcs.edu

BRIDGEMAN, Valerie .... 740-362-3482 365 D
jbridgeman@mtso.edu

BRIDGENS, Marc, E .... 570-326-3761 404 T
mbridgen@pct.edu

BRIDGER, Donald .... 303-458-4206.. 82 D
dbridger@regis.edu

BRIDGES, Antoinette ..... 815-753-6727 147 H
abridges3@niu.edu

BRIDGES, Ceil, L .... 870-235-4079.. 21 F
clbridges@saumag.edu

BRIDGES, Clarence, F ... 312-413-5946 153 H
cbridges@uic.edu

BRIDGES, Darryl .... 843-661-1295 421 H
dbridges@fmarion.edu

BRIDGES, David .... 229-391-5050 114 G
dbridges@abac.edu

BRIDGES, Edward .... 304-647-6439 504 F
ebridges@osteo.wvsom.edu

BRIDGES, George, S .... 360-867-6100 494 G
bridges@evergreen.edu

BRIDGES, Harold, A .... 310-338-2700.. 50 J

BRIDGES, J. Thomas .... 704-847-5600 349 E
jbridges@ses.edu

BRIDGES, Karl .... 208-282-4131 132 B
bridkarl@isu.edu

BRIDGES, Katie .... 202-462-2101.. 92 D
kbridges@iwp.edu

BRIDGES, Kermit, S .... 972-825-4652 457 F
president@sagu.edu

BRIDGES, Kristina .... 319-399-8100 167 F
kbridges@coe.edu

BRIDGES, LaDonna .... 508-626-4906 218 A
lbridges@framingham.edu

BRIDGES, Linda, M .... 804-204-1201 478 F
lmbridges@btsr.edu

BRIDGES, Martin .... 910-410-1818 345 G
mwbridges@richmondcc.edu

BRIDGES, Michael, W ... 412-396-1813 394 D
bridgesm@duq.edu

BRIDGES, Robert .... 417-334-6411 258 E
rbridges@cofo.edu

BRIDGES, Ruth .... 254-298-8309 458 C
ruth.bridges@templejc.edu

BRIDGES, Scott, D .... 618-453-6214 152 B
bridges@siu.edu

BRIDGES, Shelton .... 502-451-0815 189 F
sbridges@sullivan.edu

BRIDGES, Shelton .... 502-451-0815 189 E
sbridges@sullivan.edu

BRIDGES, Steven, J .... 812-464-1849 165 C
sjbridge@usi.edu

BRIDGES, Tharsteen .... 334-874-5700.... 5 B
tbridges@ccal.edu

BRIDGES, Vernon, D .... 818-947-2541.. 49 G
bridgevd@lavc.edu

BRIDGESMITH, Lance .... 310-506-4700.. 56 D
lance.bridgesmith@pepperdine.edu

BRIDGHAM, Bethany ..... 202-885-3285.. 91 C
lawyers@american.edu

BRIDGLALL, Beatrice ..... 201-879-3604 283 I
bbridglall@bergen.edu

BRIDGMAN, Christa, L . 828-298-3325 353 B
cbridgma@warren-wilson.edu

BRIDGMON, Phillip .... 918-444-3617 376 G
bridgmon@nsuok.edu

BRIDWELL, Chadd .... 817-531-4422 463 G
cbridwell@txwes.edu

BRIDWELL, Joy .... 406-395-4875 273 B
jbridwell@stonechild.edu

BRIDWELL, Virginia .... 425-564-2198 492 G
virginia.bridwell@bellevuecollege.edu

BRIELER, Robert .... 636-481-3337 261 B
rbrieler@jeffco.edu

BRIELL, Nicolle .... 641-784-5083 169 D
nbriell1@graceland.edu

BRIELL, Scott .... 641-784-5110 169 D
sbriell1@graceland.edu

BRIELMAIER, Michele ... 507-389-7385 247 H
michele.brielmaier@southcentral.edu

BRIEN, Jane .... 845-758-4294 298 I
brien@bard.edu

BRIGDON, Beth, P .... 706-721-9667 116 B
bbrigdon@augusta.edu

BRIGETY, Reuben, E .... 202-994-6240.. 92 A
rbrigety@gwu.edu

BRIGGANCE, Richard .... 615-963-5171 438 E
rbriggance@tnstate.edu

BRIGGER, Clark, V .... 814-863-4774 403 F
cvb12@psu.edu

BRIGGLE, Jennifer .... 970-207-4550.. 80 P
jenniferbr@mckinleycollege.edu

BRIGGS, Catherine, R ... 856-222-9311 289 F
cbriggs@rcbc.edu

BRIGGS, Chad .... 847-628-2018 142 B
chad.briggs@judsonu.edu

BRIGGS, Charlotte .... 413-565-1000 211 C
cbriggs@baypath.edu

BRIGGS, Darcy .... 303-797-5623.. 76 I
darcy.briggs@arapahoe.edu

BRIGGS, Douglas, S ..... 540-636-2900 479 G
dougb@christendom.edu

BRIGGS, Eddie .... 864-388-8222 422 A
ebriggs@lander.edu

BRIGGS, Jeff .... 785-628-4241 177 D
jdbriggs@fhsu.edu

BRIGGS, Jeff .... 859-344-3352 189 G
briggsj@thomasmore.edu

BRIGGS, Jennifer .... 812-488-2602 164 G
jb610@evansville.edu

BRIGGS, SR., Jerryl .... 662-254-3425 255 A
jerryl.briggs@mvsu.edu

BRIGGS, Julie, A .... 585-245-5616 327 B
briggsja@geneseo.edu

BRIGGS, Karen .... 619-260-2762.. 71 J
karenbriggs@sandiego.edu

BRIGGS, Kenneth .... 860-215-9259.. 86 F
kbriggs@trcc.commnet.edu

BRIGGS, Kristin .... 336-249-8186 342 F
kristin_briggs@davidsonccc.edu

BRIGGS, LaNae, R .... 803-786-3856 420 D
lrbriggs@columbiasc.edu

BRIGGS, Larry .... 208-769-3474 132 E
ljbriggs@nic.edu

BRIGGS, Mary, K .... 276-944-6836 480 J
mkbriggs@ehc.edu

BRIGGS, Phillip .... 805-289-6036.. 73 C
pbriggs@vcccd.edu

BRIGGS, Stephanie .... 909-384-8534.. 59 I
sbriggs@sbccd.cc.ca.us

BRIGGS, Stephen, R ..... 706-236-2281 116 D
sbriggs@berry.edu

BRIGGS, Susan .... 406-683-7031 271 H
susan.briggs@umwestern.edu

BRIGGS, Thyra .... 909-607-4408.. 45 D
thyra_briggs@hmc.edu

BRIGGS, Tonya, M .... 610-359-7349 393 E
tbriggs@dccc.edu

BRIGGS, Vicki .... 574-284-4602 163 J
vbriggs@saintmarys.edu

BRIGGS, William .... 406-477-6215 270 I

BRIGGS-PICKETT, Jodi .. 508-849-3298 210 H
jbriggspickett@annamaria.edu

BRIGHAM, Bettie Ann ... 610-341-5823 394 E
bbrigham@eastern.edu

BRIGHAM, Carol, A ..... 215-951-1286 398 F
brigham85@lasalle.edu

BRIGHAM, David, R ..... 215-972-2056 404 Q
dbrigham@pafa.org

BRIGHAM, Jim .... 256-782-5884.... 6 B
brigham@jsu.edu

BRIGHAM, R. Scott .... 907-773-4044 135 K
sbrigham@ccc.edu

BRIGHT, Brett .... 620-665-3579 178 D
brightb@hutchcc.edu

BRIGHT, Harry .... 641-472-1178 171 J
hbright@mum.edu

BRIGHT, James (Phillip) .... 731-881-7845 440 B
pbright@utm.edu

BRIGHT, Jessica .... 512-313-3000 446 N
jessica.bright@concordia.edu

BRIGHT, Marvin .... 727-712-5742 107 A
bright.marvin@spcollege.edu

BRIGHT, Sarah .... 636-481-3218 261 B
sbright@jeffco.edu

BRIGHT, Steve .... 434-544-8208 482 F
bright@lynchburg.edu

BRIGHTON, Robyn .... 407-582-3895 113 F
rbrighton1@valenciacollege.edu

BRIGNONI, Linda, M .... 818-677-2085.. 33 B
linda.brignoni@csun.edu

BRIJBASI, Monique .... 305-628-6648 107 B
mbrijbasi@stu.edu

BRILEY, Jana .... 912-478-1301 120 E
janawms@georgiasouthern.edu

BRILL, Ann .... 309-341-7130 142 G
abrill@knox.edu

BRILL, Ann, M .... 785-864-4755 181 I
abrill@ku.edu

BRILLER, Vladimir .... 718-636-4245 320 D
vbriller@pratt.edu

BRILLEY, Amy .... 217-362-6488 145 J
abrilley@millikin.edu

BRILLHART, David .... 740-366-9319 358 E
brillhart.5@osu.edu

BRILLON, Lisa .... 408-288-3725.. 61 P
lisa.brillon@sjccd.edu

BRIM, Catherlyn .... 865-573-4517 432 H
cbrim@johnsonu.edu

BRIMHALL, Carrie .... 218-736-1524 245 H
carrie.brimhall@minnesota.edu

BRIMHALL, Joseph .... 503-251-5712 387 I
jebrimhall@uws.edu

BRIMHALL-VARGAS, Mark .... 781-736-4411 213 A
mbv@brandeis.edu

BRIMMER, Diane, L .... 608-796-3801 512 R
dlbrimmer@viterbo.edu

BRIMMERMAN, Roger ... 620-242-0424 179 G
brimmerr@mcpherson.edu

BRINDLE, Denise .... 978-665-3454 217 E
dbrindl1@fitchburgstate.edu

BRINDLEY, Roger .... 813-974-1218 111 A
brindley@usf.edu

BRINDLEY, Roger .... 813-974-0349 111 A
brindley@usf.edu

BRINER, Clare .... 708-974-5376 146 C
brinerc@morainevalley.edu

BRINEY, Colleen, M .... 479-575-2551.. 21 I
cbriney@uark.edu

BRINGAZE, Tammy .... 413-572-5491 218 F
tbringaze@westfield.ma.edu

BRINGER, Michael .... 573-288-6528 259 E
mbringer@culver.edu

BRINGSJORD, Elizabeth 518-320-1251 324 F
elizabeth.bringsjord@suny.edu

BRINING, Patricia .... 215-968-8091 390 I
patricia.brining@bucks.edu

BRINK, Benita .... 719-587-7426.. 76 D
babrink@adams.edu

BRINK, Deana .... 913-253-5042 181 C
deana.brink@spst.edu
BRINK, Haley, T .... 256-765-4201.... 9 A
htbrink@una.edu
BRINK, Laura .... 617-521-2127 224 E
laura.brink@simmons.edu
BRINK, Stephanie .... 573-823-8594 258 B
sbrink@centralmethodist.edu
BRINK-DRESCHER,
Judith .... 516-323-3925 315 J
jdrescher@molloy.edu
BRINKER, Cynthia, S .... 812-464-1774 165 C
cbrinker@usi.edu
BRINKERHOFF, Robert .. 401-454-6183 417 B
rbrinker@risd.edu
BRINKLEY, David .... 270-745-6140 190 F
david.brinkley@wku.edu
BRINKLEY, Martin .... 919-962-4417 351 B
martin92@unc.edu
BRINKLEY, Tom .... 336-278-7452 337 G
tbrinkley@elon.edu
BRINKMAN, Matt .... 423-614-8395 432 L
mmbrinkman@leeuniversity.edu
BRINKMAN, Sue .... 920-403-3210 509 J
sue.brinkman@snc.edu
BRINKOETTER, Darbe .... 217-875-7200 149 J
dbrinkoetter@richland.edu
BRINN, Greg .... 610-989-1330 413 I
bgrinn@vfmac.edu
BRINNEMAN, Charlotte . 859-525-6510 182 K
cbrinneman@national-college.edu
BRINNER, Jonda .... 502-410-6200 184 H
jbrinner@galencollege.edu
BRINSON, Bruce .... 214-379-5573 454 H
bbrinson@pqc.edu
BRINSON, Donna .... 678-341-6607 122 E
dbrinson@laniertech.edu
BRINSON, Marla .... 732-906-2513 287 B
mbrinson@middlesexcc.edu
BRINSON, Reggie .... 904-620-2820 110 E
reggie.brinson@unf.edu
BRINSON, Willie, L .... 919-735-5151 347 E
wlbrinson@waynecc.edu
BRINSON-BROWN,
Angela .... 305-626-3139.. 99 M
angela.brinson-brown@fmuniv.edu
BRIONES, Eloisa, M ..... 650-738-4227.. 62 B
briones@smccd.edu
BRISACK, Al .... 608-663-3289 507 D
abrisack@edgewood.edu
BRISBON, T. Muriel ...... 610-896-1250 397 F
tbrisbon@haverford.edu
BRISCO, Thomas, V ...... 325-670-1211 450 A
tbrisco@hsutx.edu
BRISCOE, Chad .... 574-372-5100 158 B
chad.briscoe@grace.edu
BRISCOE, Connie .... 407-646-2194 106 J
cbriscoe@rollins.edu
BRISENO, Nancy, M ...... 361-698-1293 448 H
nbriseno3@delmar.edu
BRISKEY, Marvin .... 614-947-6002 362 A
marv.briskey@franklin.edu
BRISLIN, Shawn, P .... 607-746-4670 329 B
brislisp@delhi.edu
BRISOLARA, Sharon ...... 530-242-7625.. 63 I
sbrisolara@shastacollege.edu
BRISSON, Caitrin .... 617-603-6900 222 F
caitrin.brisson@necb.edu
BRISSON, E. Carson ..... 804-355-0671 486 A
cbrisson@upsem.edu
BRISSON, Michelle .... 973-408-3454 285 E
mbrisson@drew.edu
BRISSON-FARLEY,
Andree .... 785-628-4000 177 D
a_brisson@fhsu.edu
BRISTLE, Shawn .... 928-758-3926.. 14 I
sbristle@mohave.edu
BRISTOL, Amanda .... 423-461-8490 435 A
abristol@milligan.edu
BRISTOL, Cecelia, M ..... 815-226-4083 150 C
cbristol@rockford.edu
BRISTOL, Louis .... 860-738-6328.. 86 C
lbristol@nwcc.edu
BRISTOR, Valerie .... 561-297-3357 109 B
bristor@fau.edu
BRISTOW, Aimee .... 573-592-5364 270 B
aimee.bristow@westminster-mo.edu
BRISTOW, Cliff .... 405-912-9037 379 A
cbristow@ru.edu
BRISTOW, Jessica .... 248-218-2038 236 C
jbristow@rc.edu
BRISTOW, Troy .... 630-637-5559 147 E
tbbristow@noctrl.edu
BRITE, Chris .... 660-944-2863 258 G
cbrite@conception.edu
BRITIGAN, Bradley, E ... 402-599-8878 277 H
bradley.britigan@unmc.edu
BRITSCH, James .... 575-492-2873 294 L
jbritsch@nmjc.edu
BRITT, Anthony .... 252-328-9317 349 I
britta@ecu.edu
BRITT, Deanna .... 434-582-2521 482 D
dbritt@liberty.edu
BRITT, Denise .... 404-752-1500 123 F
dbritt@msm.edu
BRITT, Eddie .... 601-643-8628 252 G
eddie.britt@colin.edu
BRITT, Frank .... 480-947-6644.. 15 I
frank.britt@pennfoster.edu
BRITT, Jeanette .... 814-824-2247 401 J
jbritt@mercyhurst.edu
BRITT, Julianne .... 781-891-3456 212 A
jbritt@bentley.edu
BRITT, Kenith .... 317-955-6209 162 R
kbritt@marian.edu
BRITT, Kimberly .... 757-789-1748 488 A
kbritt@es.vccs.edu
BRITT, Tammy, T .... 704-233-8111 353 D
tbritt@wingate.edu
BRITTAIN, Lee .... 936-468-3206 458 A
lbrittain@sfasu.edu
BRITTAIN, Linda, D .... 717-264-4141 415 B
lbrittain@wilson.edu
BRITTAIN, Ross, A .... 304-457-6428 501 A
brittainra@ab.edu
BRITTAIN, Vicki, S .... 512-245-2121 463 A
vb01@txstate.edu
BRITTON, Bill .... 805-756-2190.. 30 K
bibritto@calpoly.edu
BRITTON, Brian, J .... 401-232-6051 416 A
bbritton@bryant.edu
BRITTON, Cathy .... 785-227-3380 175 E
brittoncd@bethanylb.edu
BRITTON, Dana, J .... 800-233-4220 401 L
dbritton@messiah.edu
BRITTON, Dianne .... 803-754-4100 420 E
BRITTON, Gwen .... 603-314-7529 282 C
g.britton@snhu.edu
BRITTON, Ida .... 240-567-5264 205 F
ida.britton@montgomerycollege.edu
BRITTON, Karen .... 781-239-3101 220 A
kbritton@massbay.edu
BRITTON, Keith, E .... 803-938-3882 425 F
kbritton@uscsumter.edu
BRITTON, Mark .... 316-295-5787 177 F
mark_britton@friends.edu
BRITTON, Sharon .... 617-573-8536 224 I
sbritton@suffolk.edu
BRITTON-SPEARS, Ona . 918-463-2931 375 G
ona.britton-spears@connorsstate.edu
BRITZ, Johannes .... 412-229-4501 511 A
britz@uwm.edu
BRIXEY, Shawn .... 804-828-0100 487 E
brixey@vcu.edu
BRIZIARELLI, Susan ...... 516-877-4118 297 I
sbriziarelli@adelphi.edu
BRNARDIC, Marisa .... 610-989-1279 413 I
mbrnardic@vfmac.edu
BRNGER, Anne .... 802-258-3117 476 B
anne.brnger@worldlearning.org
BROADBRIDGE,
Christine .... 203-392-5240.. 85 A
broadbridgec1@southernct.edu
BROADDUS, Henry, R ... 757-221-3987 479 I
hrbroa@wm.edu
BROADDUS, Matthew .... 865-573-4517 432 H
mbroaddus@johnsonu.edu
BROADDUS, Susan, S .. 804-758-6724 489 D
sbroaddus@rappahannock.edu
BROADHURST, Gary ...... 315-792-5573 315 I
gbroadhurst@mvcc.edu
BROADIE, II, Paul .... 203-285-2060.. 85 E
BROADIE, II, Paul .... 203-332-5224.. 85 F
pbroadie@hcc.commnet.edu
BROADUS, Alicia .... 330-972-8901 371 D
broadus@uakron.edu
BROADUS, Dionne, C ... 216-368-2331 358 C
dionne.broadus@case.edu
BROADWATER, Bonnie . 301-387-3050 203 I
bonnie.broadwater@garrettcollege.edu
BROADWATER, Larry .... 865-251-1800 436 B
lbroadw@southcollegetn.edu
BROADWAY, Shane .... 501-660-1001.. 17 L
sbroadway@asusystem.edu
BROADWELL, Jennifer ... 757-340-2121 479 D
finaid2cvab@centura.edu
BROADWELL, Phyllis .... 912-279-5816 118 A
pbroadwell@ccga.edu
BROADWIN, Megan .... 205-329-7900.... 5 C
megan.samuels@ecacolleges.com
BROCK, Donna .... 404-880-8337 117 H
dbrock@cau.edu
BROCK, Doug .... 319-363-1323 172 B
dbrock@mtmercy.edu
BROCK, Greg .... 541-684-7252 384 H
gbrock@nwcu.edu
BROCK, III, Harry, B .... 205-726-4071.... 6 G
bbrock@samford.edu
BROCK, Kathy .... 620-792-9233 175 C
brockk@bartonccc.edu
BROCK, Lynn, A .... 937-766-7846 358 D
brockl@cedarville.edu
BROCK, Marcius .... 507-389-1180 246 A
marcius.brock@mnsu.edu
BROCK, Michael, G .... 610-989-1246 413 I
mbrock@vfmac.edu
BROCK, Michelle .... 704-290-5357 346 F
mbrock@spcc.edu
BROCK, Nikki .... 336-917-5473 348 H
nikki.brock@salem.edu
BROCK, Sabra .... 212-742-8770 331 F
sabra.brock@touro.edu
BROCK, Sharia .... 601-925-7714 254 B
sbrock@mc.edu
BROCK, Summer .... 252-399-6383 335 I
sebrock@barton.edu
BROCK-SMITH, Cynthia . 202-806-2530.. 92 C
cynthia.brocksmith@howard.edu
BROCKBANK, Kevin ...... 801-957-5009 474 B
kevin.brockbank@slcc.edu
BROCKBANK, Kevin ...... 509-533-7042 493 I
kevin.brockbank@scc.spokane.edu
BROCKBANK, Kevin ...... 509-533-3844 494 A
kevin.brockbank@ccs.spokane.edu
BROCKEL, Sarah .... 406-657-2243 272 B
sbrockel@msubillings.edu
BROCKEL, Sarah .... 406-247-5780 272 B
sbrockel@msubillings.edu
BROCKENBROUGH,
Karl, B .... 301-860-3470 208 E
kbrockenbrough@bowiestate.edu
BROCKER, Catherine ..... 703-284-1610 483 A
catherine.brocker@marymount.edu
BROCKETT, Lori .... 760-750-4405.. 33 E
brockett@csusm.edu
BROCKGREITENS, Kathy 636-922-8229 265 J
kbrockgreitens@stchas.edu
BROCKHOFF, Jennifer ... 502-585-9911 189 B
jbrockhoff@spalding.edu
BROCKHOUSE, Sandy ... 605-342-0317 427 C
sbrockhouse@johnwitherspooncollege.org
BROCKIE, Clarena .... 406-353-2607 270 E
cbrockie@ancollege.edu
BROCKIE, Dixie .... 406-353-2607 270 E
dbrockie@ancollege.edu
BROCKIE, Kimberly .... 406-353-2607 270 E
kbrockie@ancollege.edu
BROCKIE, Michele .... 406-353-2607 270 E
mbrockie@ancollege.edu
BROCKINTON,
W. Joseph .... 864-644-5142 424 B
jbrockinton@swu.edu
BROCKLEHURST,
Stephanie .... 215-836-2222 389 C
finaid@antonelli.edu
BROCKMAN, Diane .... 660-596-7205 267 E
dbrockman@sfccmo.edu
BROCKMAN, Mark .... 513-745-4842 374 D
brockmanm1@xavier.edu
BROCKMAN, Tracy .... 614-985-2324 369 D
tbrockman@pcj.edu
BROCKMYER,
Richard, A .... 801-832-2516 474 E
rbrockmyer@westminstercollege.edu
BROD, Catherine .... 914-251-6014 328 B
catherine.brod@purchase.edu
BRODA, Joanna .... 212-346-1652 319 J
jbroda@pace.edu
BRODA, Mary .... 517-750-1200 237 D
mary.broda@arbor.edu
BRODERICK,
Christopher .... 503-725-3773 386 D
christopher.broderick@pdx.edu
BRODERICK, Deborah ... 212-998-6825 318 D
deborah.broderick@nyu.edu
BRODERICK, Jo .... 978-921-4242 222 B
jo.broderick@montserrat.edu
BRODERICK, John, R .... 757-683-3159 483 G
jbroderi@odu.edu
BRODERICK, Kimberley . 413-755-4490 221 B
kebroderick@stcc.edu
BRODERICK, Mac .... 603-513-1327 282 G
mac.broderick@granite.edu
BRODERICK, Mark, C ... 410-617-2713 205 A
mbroder@loyola.edu
BRODERICK, Marybeth .. 845-848-7824 306 G
marybeth.broderick@dc.edu
BRODERICK, Michael .... 860-515-3885.. 84 H
mbroderick@charteroak.edu
BRODERICK, Shelley ..... 202-274-7332.. 93 D
sbroderick@udc.edu
BRODERICK, Victor, K .. 217-786-2414 144 B
victor.broderick@llcc.edu
BRODERSEN COCHRAN,
Lyn .... 563-441-4173 169 A
BRODERSON,
Maureen, A .... 817-552-3700 451 G
mbroderson@tku.edu
BRODEUR, Lynne .... 508-678-2811 219 C
lynne.brodeur@bristolcc.edu
BRODEUR, Thomas .... 860-832-2531.. 84 J
brodeur@ccsu.edu
BRODIE, Marilyn .... 408-288-3729.. 61 P
marilyn.brodie@sjcc.edu
BRODIGAN, Rebecca, H 207-859-4692 198 H
becky.brodigan@colby.edu
BRODL, Mark .... 309-556-3101 141 B
provost@iwu.edu
BRODL, Mark .... 210-999-7246 464 B
mbrodl@trinity.edu
BRODLEY, Carla, E .... 617-373-2462 223 D
BRODMERKEL, Darcy .... 570-674-6466 401 M
dbrodmer@misericordia.edu
BRODMERKEL, Douglas 516-876-2787 327 C
brodmerkeld@oldwestbury.edu
BRODRICK, Jeff .... 616-538-2330 230 E
jbrodrick@gbcol.edu
BRODSKY, Aryeh .... 732-765-9126 292 L
BRODSKY, Mikhail .... 510-208-2803.. 48 F
rector@lincolnuca.edu
BRODSKY, Stephen .... 212-346-1274 319 J
sbrodksy@pace.edu
BRODT, Bonita .... 312-893-7161 138 D
bbrodt@erikson.edu
BRODY, Charmain .... 610-398-5300 400 C
cbrody@lincolntech.edu
BRODY, Matthew .... 919-962-4651 349 G
msbrody@northcarolina.edu
BRODY, Michael .... 503-777-7521 386 F
brodym@reed.edu
BRODZINSKI, James ..... 219-464-6758 165 D
jim.brodzinski@valpo.edu
BROEDER, Jennifer .... 314-246-7988 269 N
jbroeder@webster.edu
BROEKER, Camy .... 317-274-4511 160 E
cbroeker@iupui.edu
BROERING, Naomi .... 619-574-6909.. 55 B
nbroering@pacificcollege.edu
BROETJE, Whitney .... 206-281-2831 498 B
broetw@spu.edu
BROFFT, Jeremy .... 757-388-2862 485 B
jbrofft@sentara.edu
BROGAN, Jamey .... 304-243-2385 505 H
jbrogan@wju.edu
BROGAN, Michael, S .... 716-839-8227 306 E
mbrogan@daemen.edu
BROGDEN, Jeff, D .... 919-658-7171 349 F
jbrogden@umo.edu
BROGDON, Jarrod .... 229-333-2100 128 G
jarrod.brogdon@wiregrass.edu
BROGE, Jason .... 989-275-5000 232 E
jason.broge@kirtland.edu
BROGE, Jason .... 314-505-7092 258 I
brogej@csl.edu
BROGHAMMER,
Sean, M .... 970-351-2806.. 83 F
sean.broghammer@unco.edu
BROIL, D.C .... 913-288-7117 178 H
dcbroil@kckcc.edu
BROILES, Janet .... 870-575-8471.. 22 E
broilesj@uapb.edu
BROKAW, Tim .... 207-621-3300 201 C
timothy.brokaw@maine.edu
BROKENBURR, Shenita . 608-262-8299 510 B
sbrokenburr@uwsa.edu
BROKER, Patricia .... 218-335-4200 242 I
BROKKE, Dan .... 952-829-2470 240 H
dan.brokke@bethfel.org
BROKKE, Derek .... 952-829-1320 240 H
derek.brokke@bethfel.org
BROKKEN, Patricia .... 540-362-6016 481 F
brokkenpe@hollins.edu
BROKVIST, Randi .... 904-632-3301 100 F
r.brokvis@fscj.edu
BROLINSON, Gunnar .... 540-231-4981 480 I
gbrolinson@vcom.vt.edu
BROLLEY, Francis, R ..... 815-224-0466 141 A
fran_brolley@ivcc.edu
BROM, Don .... 215-637-7700 397 G
dbrom@holyfamily.edu
BROMAN, Erica .... 413-572-5244 218 F
ebroman@westfield.ma.edu
BROMANDER, Lowell .... 651-523-2225 242 E
lbromander@hamline.edu
BROMFIELD,
Christopher .... 305-626-0207.. 99 M
christopher.bromfield@fmuniv.edu
BROMFIELD, Elaine .... 334-727-8508.... 7 F
ebromfield@tuskegee.edu

BROMFIELD, Robert, L .. 415-422-2786.. 72 A
rlbromfield@usfca.edu
BROMLEY, Dennis .... 801-957-4322 474 B
dennis.bromley@slcc.edu
BROMM, Drew .... 252-334-2043 340 B
drew.bromm@macuniversity.edu
BROMSTRUP, Bryan, T . 812-877-8222 163 G
bromstru@rose-hulman.edu
BRONDER, James, S ..... 419-998-3138 372 D
jsbronde@unoh.edu
BRONET, Frances .... 312-567-3163 140 I
fbronet@iit.edu
BRONFMAN, Jane .... 860-906-5103.. 85 D
jbronfman@ccc.commnet.edu
BRONISZ, John .... 505-224-3730 293 L
jbronisz@cnm.edu
BRONKEMA, F. David ... 610-225-5068 394 E
dbronkem@eastern.edu
BRONNER, Gwethalyn ... 847-543-2685 136 E
gbronner@clcillinois.edu
BRONNER, Jennifer, L .. 740-826-8463 366 C
jbronner@muskingum.edu
BRONSDON, Chris .... 619-594-7985.. 34 B
cbronsdo@mail.sdsu.edu
BRONSON, Eric .... 401-254-3369 417 C
ebronson@rwu.edu
BRONSON, Matthew ...... 415-257-1345.. 41 J
matthew.bronson@dominican.edu
BRONSTEIN, Fred .... 410-234-4700 204 F
fred.bronstein@jhu.edu
BRONSTEIN, Ken .... 360-383-3359 500 F
kbronstein@whatcom.ctc.edu
BRONSTEIN, Laura .... 607-777-5572 325 A
lbronst@binghamton.edu
BRONSTEIN, Susan .... 239-489-9357 100 E
sbronstein@fsw.edu
BROOK, Ryan .... 949-582-4722.. 64 J
rbrook@saddleback.edu
BROOKBANK, Julie .... 605-995-7104 427 E
julie.brookbank@mitchelltech.edu
BROOKBANK, Maureen . 202-319-5598.. 91 D
brookbank@cua.edu
BROOKE, Judith .... 321-674-8053.. 99 K
jbrooke@fit.edu
BROOKE, Patrick .... 651-638-6879 240 J
pbrooke@bethel.edu
BROOKER, Sarah .... 717-564-4112 390 A
sarah.brooker@brightwood.edu
BROOKEY, Lauren, F ..... 918-595-7977 380 D
lauren.brookey@tulsacc.edu
BROOKING, David .... 662-329-7138 254 F
dmbrooking@muw.edu
BROOKINS, Laura .... 610-917-1451 413 G
ljbrookins@valleyforge.edu
BROOKMAN, Kim .... 413-236-1003 219 B
kbrookman@berkshirecc.edu
BROOKNER, Laurie .... 415-565-8813.. 68 I
brookner@uchastings.edu
BROOKOVER, Joe .... 515-643-6611 171 K
jbrookover@mercydesmoines.org
BROOKS, Aaron .... 662-243-2655 253 A
abrooks@eastms.edu
BROOKS, Ann .... 918-302-3617 375 J
abrooks@eosc.edu
BROOKS, Ann Marie ..... 614-234-5800 365 L
abrooks@mccn.edu
BROOKS, Anthony .... 919-719-1983 348 I
anthony.brooks@shawu.edu
BROOKS, Beth .... 253-566-5054 499 A
bbrooks@tacomacc.edu
BROOKS, Billie, K .... 304-710-3363 503 A
billie.brooks@mctc.edu
BROOKS, Blake .... 317-632-5553 162 P
bbrooks@lincolntech.edu
BROOKS, Browning .... 850-644-8343 110 A
bbrooks@fsu.edu
BROOKS, Carlton .... 719-502-2003.. 81 H
carlton.brooks@ppcc.edu
BROOKS, Carrie Allison 901-272-5160 434 B
cbrooks@mca.edu
BROOKS, Chad .... 931-221-7414 430 B
brooksc@apsu.edu
BROOKS, Charles, R ..... 973-596-2875 288 A
brooks@njit.edu
BROOKS, Christopher ... 734-207-9581 146 B
chris.brooks@moody.edu
BROOKS, Cindy, L .... 610-799-1121 400 A
cbrooks@lccc.edu
BROOKS, Constance ..... 702-889-8426 278 M
constance_brooks@nshe.nevada.edu
BROOKS, Cynthia .... 615-963-7411 438 E
cbrooks@tnstate.edu
BROOKS, Dana, D .... 304-293-0826 505 B
dbrooks@mail.wvu.edu
BROOKS, Danny, K .... 336-841-9131 338 E
dbrooks@highpoint.edu
BROOKS, Darlene, D ..... 901-843-3901 435 L
brooksd@rhodes.edu
BROOKS, Donnie .... 601-974-1190 254 A
brookda@millsaps.edu
BROOKS, II, Earl, D ..... 260-665-4101 164 E
brookse@trine.edu
BROOKS, Gene .... 402-643-7411 274 B
gene.brooks@cune.edu
BROOKS, II, H. Gordon 337-482-6224 197 F
gbrooks@louisiana.edu
BROOKS, Ian .... 510-883-2056.. 41 I
ibrooks@dspt.edu
BROOKS, Jacquelyne .... 706-817-6966 184 G
jacquelyne.brooks@frontier.edu
BROOKS, James, L .... 323-856-7600.. 25 L
jbrooks@afi.com
BROOKS, Jason .... 620-341-5481 177 B
jbrooks5@emporia.edu
BROOKS, Jason .... 304-327-4181 503 O
jbrooks@bluefieldstate.edu
BROOKS, Jessie .... 404-270-5323 126 D
jlbrooks@spelman.edu
BROOKS, Jim, J .... 541-346-6121 387 F
brooksja@uoregon.edu
BROOKS, John .... 540-831-5582 484 A
jbrooks64@radford.edu
BROOKS, John, I .... 910-672-1060 350 B
jibrooks@uncfsu.edu
BROOKS, Jonathan .... 713-221-8184 465 C
brooksjo@uhd.edu
BROOKS, Joseph .... 303-963-3463.. 77 I
jbrooks@ccu.edu
BROOKS, Juliette .... 201-692-7050 286 B
juliette_brooks@fdu.edu
BROOKS, Justin, P .... 619-239-0391.. 35 C
jbrooks@cwsl.edu
BROOKS, Karl .... 847-635-1739 148 D
kbrooks@oakton.edu
BROOKS, Katharine, S .. 615-875-8136 440 D
katharine.s.brooks@vanderbilt.edu
BROOKS, Kelly .... 575-527-7551 295 E
kbrooks@nmsu.edu
BROOKS, Kent .... 307-268-2703 516 H
kbrooks@caspercollege.edu
BROOKS, Krista .... 559-453-2289.. 43 J
krista.brooks@fresno.edu
BROOKS, L. Rayburn .... 864-941-8301 423 C
brooks.r@ptc.edu
BROOKS, Larry .... 701-228-5452 354 G
larry.brooks@dakotacollege.edu
BROOKS, Larry .... 701-228-5457 354 G
larry.brooks@dakotacollege.edu
BROOKS, LaShon, F ..... 662-254-3425 255 A
lfbrooks@mvsu.edu
BROOKS, Letha .... 317-921-4976 161 G
lbrooks29@ivytech.edu
BROOKS, Lisa .... 818-240-1000.. 44 D
lbrooks@glendale.edu
BROOKS, Lois .... 541-737-0739 385 F
lois.brooks@oregonstate.edu
BROOKS, Lyvette .... 215-751-8046 393 A
lbrooks@ccp.edu
BROOKS, Marilyn, A ..... 804-257-5846 491 C
mabrooks2@vuu.edu
BROOKS, Mark .... 229-931-2246 125 G
mbrooks@southgatech.edu
BROOKS, Mark, D .... 270-901-1117 187 A
mark.brooks@kctcs.edu
BROOKS, Michelle .... 252-328-2872 349 I
brooksm@ecu.edu
BROOKS, Monica .... 304-696-6474 504 C
brooks@marshall.edu
BROOKS, Patricia .... 972-825-4652 457 F
pabrooks@sagu.edu
BROOKS, Paul .... 972-825-4616 457 F
pbrooks@sagu.edu
BROOKS, Peter .... 215-574-9600 397 H
peter.brooks@hussiancollege.edu
BROOKS, Randy, M ...... 217-424-6205 145 J
rbrooks@millikin.edu
BROOKS, Roger, L .... 804-289-8491 486 G
rbrooks@richmond.edu
BROOKS, Ron .... 901-678-2077 439 E
rbrooks@memphis.edu
BROOKS, Sarah .... 509-542-4837 493 G
sbrooks@columbiabasin.edu
BROOKS, Shannon .... 864-644-5072 424 B
sbrooks@swu.edu
BROOKS, Sharon .... 802-258-3344 476 B
sharon.brooks@sit.edu
BROOKS, Steve .... 954-492-5353.. 96 J
sbrooks@citycollege.edu
BROOKS, Terence .... 864-250-8211 421 K
terence.brooks@gvltec.edu
BROOKS, Teresa .... 903-693-2060 454 E
trbrooks@panola.edu
BROOKS, Thom, R .... 828-339-4202 346 H
tbrooks@southwesterncc.edu
BROOKS, Thomas .... 641-472-7000 171 J
tbrooks@mum.edu
BROOKS, Tim, L .... 402-280-2202 274 D
timbrooks@creighton.edu
BROOKS, Todd .... 706-236-2260 116 D
tbrooks@berry.edu
BROOKS, Turner .... 314-423-1900 257 C
turnerb@stltrades.com
BROOKS, Tyrone .... 509-542-4408 493 G
tbrooks@columbiabasin.edu
BROOKS, Vanessa .... 734-973-3491 238 G
vbrooks@wccnet.edu
BROOKS, Vera .... 410-462-8500 202 F
vbrooks@bccc.edu
BROOKS, Wendy .... 989-358-7299 227 A
brooksw@alpenacc.edu
BROOKS, Wesley .... 319-385-6284 170 J
wesley.brooks@iw.edu
BROOKS BLAIR,
Sarah, D .... 937-529-2201 371 B
sblair@united.edu
BROOKSHER, Jamie ...... 620-235-4136 180 J
jbrooksher@pittstate.edu
BROOKSHIRE, David ..... 276-244-1211 477 M
dbrookshire@asl.edu
BROOKSHIRE, Kathy ..... 601-484-8612 253 G
kbrooksh@meridiancc.edu
BROOMALL, James, K .. 302-831-2795.. 90 I
jbroom@udel.edu
BROOME, Barbara .... 330-672-8799 363 I
bbroome1@kent.edu
BROOME, Marion .... 919-684-3786 337 C
marion.broome@duke.edu
BROOME, Melba .... 202-274-6118.. 93 D
mbroome@udc.edu
BROOMHEAD, Keiko ..... 617-989-4034 225 E
broomheadk@wit.edu
BROPHY, Ann .... 314-246-7422 269 N
annbrophy26@webster.edu
BROPHY, Dale, G .... 801-585-2677 472 P
dale.brophy@dps.utah.edu
BROPHY, Katharine .... 305-348-2560 109 D
katharine.brophy@fiu.edu
BROPHY, Michael, S .... 630-829-6004 133 I
mbrophy@ben.edu
BROPHY, Timothy, S .... 352-273-4476 110 D
tbrophy@aa.ufl.edu
BROPHY, JR.,
William, E .... 256-824-6144.... 8 C
william.brophy@uah.edu
BRORBY, Gregory .... 775-753-2260 279 A
gregory.brorby@gbcnv.edu
BROSHOUS, Robert, D .. 563-589-3199 173 J
bbroshou@dbq.edu
BROSKE, Kathleen, M ... 920-924-2139 514 D
kbroske@morainepark.edu
BROSKY, Lisa .... 520-206-4850.. 15 L
lbrosky@pima.edu
BROSKY, Tony .... 502-272-8375 183 H
jbrosky@bellarmine.edu
BROSNAN, JoAnna, M .. 607-746-4727 329 B
brosnajm@delhi.edu
BROSNAN, Mary .... 516-323-3468 315 J
mbrosnan@molloy.edu
BROSS, Scott .... 309-268-8385 139 D
scott.bross@heartland.edu
BROSS-FREGONARA,
Nanci .... 304-704-1162 501 H
brossfregonaran@dewv.edu
BROSSMANN,
William, D .... 517-321-0242 231 A
wbrossmann@glcc.edu
BROSTROM, Nathan, E .. 510-987-9029.. 68 F
nathan.brostrom@ucop.edu
BROTHERS, Gregory, A . 713-646-1888 456 H
gbrothers@stcl.edu
BROTHERS, James, F ..... 937-229-2829 372 A
jbrothers1@udayton.edu
BROTHERS, Tricia .... 620-947-3121 181 H
triciab@tabor.edu
BROTHERS, William .... 828-339-4366 346 H
w_brothers@southwesterncc.edu
BROTHERSON,
Carrie, P .... 540-261-8534 485 G
carrie.brotherson@svu.edu
BROTHERSON, Todd ..... 540-261-4095 485 G
todd.brotherson@svu.edu
BROTHERTON, Jeffrey ... 614-222-4014 360 B
jbrotherton@ccad.edu
BROTHERTON,
Thomas, S .... 712-852-5224 170 D
tbrotherton@iowalakes.edu
BROTZMAN, Kelly .... 508-531-2147 217 D
kbrotzman@bridgew.edu
BROUGH, Aimee, B ...... 717-736-4122 396 G
abbrough@hacc.edu
BROUGHMAN, Lisa .... 434-947-8481 484 B
llee@randolphcollege.edu
BROUGHTON, Nancy .... 218-879-0837 244 F
sam@fdltcc.edu
BROUHARD,
Nathanael, T .... 215-972-2015 404 Q
nbrouhard@pafa.edu
BROUILLET, Susan .... 603-230-3576 280 I
sbrouillet@ccsnh.edu
BROUILLETTE,
Domenick, R .... 816-604-1370 262 F
domenick.brouillette@mcckc.edu
BROUNK, Thomas, M ... 314-935-5955 269 L
tom_brounk@wustl.edu
BROUSSARD, Camille ... 212-431-2354 317 H
camille.broussard@nyls.edu
BROUSSARD, Michael ... 337-550-1292 194 B
mpbrouss@lsue.edu
BROUWER, Dustin, J .... 605-336-6588 428 B
dbrouwer@sfseminary.edu
BROUWER, Tom .... 800-280-0307 155 H
tom.brouwer@ace.edu
BROWDER, Kathy .... 706-737-1422 116 B
kbrowder@augusta.edu
BROWER, Beth .... 609-586-4800 287 A
browerb@mccc.edu
BROWER, Bill .... 315-445-5441 312 F
browewih@lemoyne.edu
BROWER, Bob .... 619-849-2216.. 57 H
bobbrower@pointloma.edu
BROWER, Jennifer .... 505-224-4669 293 L
jbrower@cnm.edu
BROWER, Keith .... 718-862-7345 313 L
keith.brower@manhattan.edu
BROWER, Laura .... 805-289-6102.. 73 C
lbrower@vcccd.edu
BROWER, Lynn .... 818-778-5749.. 49 G
browerl@lavc.edu
BROWER, Paul, O .... 508-213-2271 223 C
paul.brower@nichols.edu
BROWER, Pearl, K .... 907-852-3333..... 9 H
pearl.brower@ilisagvik.edu
BROWER, Roderick .... 910-695-3994 346 E
browerr@sandhills.edu
BROWN, Aaron .... 951-222-8789.. 58 E
aaron.brown@rccd.edu
BROWN, Alanka .... 301-624-2724 203 H
albrown@frederick.edu
BROWN, Albert .... 360-596-5268 498 G
abrown@spscc.edu
BROWN, Alesia .... 864-941-8611 423 C
brown.a@ptc.edu
BROWN, Alfreda .... 330-672-2442 363 I
abbrown@kent.edu
BROWN, Allen .... 512-313-3000 446 N
allen.brown@concordia.edu
BROWN, Amon .... 202-651-5007.. 91 H
amon.brown@gallaudet.edu
BROWN, Amy, L .... 607-746-4584 329 B
brownal@delhi.edu
BROWN, Andrea .... 435-652-7595 473 B
abrown@dixie.edu
BROWN, Andrew .... 651-696-6069 243 B
dabrown@macalester.edu
BROWN, Angela .... 315-312-4100 327 D
angela.brown@oswego.edu
BROWN, Angela, C .... 254-968-9128 459 A
abrown@tarleton.edu
BROWN, Angela, P .... 731-425-2347 437 B
abrown@jscc.edu
BROWN, Angelo .... 810-762-0500 234 F
angelo.brown@mcc.edu
BROWN, Ann .... 919-516-5083 348 G
abrown@st-aug.edu
BROWN, Anne .... 704-687-8622 351 C
abrow316@uncc.edu
BROWN, Anne .... 617-228-3267 219 D
abrown@bhcc.mass.edu
BROWN, Annette .... 410-334-2900 210 C
abrown@worwic.edu
BROWN, Ansel, E .... 919-530-7477 350 D
browna@nccu.edu
BROWN, Art .... 515-964-6394 168 A
acbrown9@dmacc.edu
BROWN, B, T .... 252-536-7245 343 F
btbrown920@halifaxcc.edu
BROWN, Barry .... 617-928-4502 222 D
barrybrown@mountida.edu
BROWN, Becki .... 513-875-3344 359 C
becki.brown@chatfield.edu
BROWN, Beverly .... 718-262-2238 304 A
bbrown@york.cuny.edu
BROWN, Bill .... 919-760-2367 339 H
brownw@meredith.edu
BROWN, Bill .... 863-638-7228 113 I
bill.brown@warner.edu
BROWN, Bill .... 757-455-5730 491 F
bbrown@vwu.edu
BROWN, Bob .... 940-565-2055 466 B
bob.brown@unt.edu
BROWN, Bobbie .... 806-742-3661 463 D
bobbie.brown@ttu.edu

BROWN, Bradd ... 405-208-5001 377 D
bradd.brown@okcu.edu
BROWN, Braden ... 405-382-9277 379 I
b.brown@sscok.edu
BROWN, Bradley ... 435-586-7871 473 A
brown@suu.edu
BROWN, Brenda ... 321-674-7420.. 99 K
brendabrown@fit.edu
BROWN, Brenda, L ... 478-218-3288 117 E
bbrown@centralgatech.edu
BROWN, Brent, K ... 801-581-3003 472 P
brent.brown@osp.utah.edu
BROWN, Brian ... 315-364-3207 333 G
bbrown@wells.edu
BROWN, JR., Buck, F ... 864-379-8805 421 E
brown@erskine.edu
BROWN, Calvin ... 404-880-6042 117 H
cbrown@cau.edu
BROWN, Calvin ... 205-348-5966.... 8 A
cbrown@alumni.ua.edu
BROWN, Carl ... 614-947-6080 362 A
carl.brown@franklin.edu
BROWN, Carmen ... 803-812-7318 425 D
cdbrown@mailbox.sc.edu
BROWN, Carmen, A ... 305-474-6034 107 B
cabrown@stu.edu
BROWN, Carol ... 559-791-2316.. 47 C
cbrown@portervillecollege.edu
BROWN, Carol, J ... 309-341-7980 142 G
cbrown@knox.edu
BROWN, Carolanne ... 561-803-2050 104 I
carolanne_brown@pba.edu
BROWN, Carrie ... 607-274-3846 311 D
brownc@ithaca.edu
BROWN, Catherine ... 716-614-5950 318 E
cbrown@niagaracc.suny.edu
BROWN, Chad ... 918-647-1375 375 B
cbrown@carlalbert.edu
BROWN, Chad, M ... 740-588-1201 374 G
cbrown@zanestate.edu
BROWN, Charles ... 502-456-6773 189 F
cbrown@sullivan.edu
BROWN, Charlotte ... 405-466-3217 375 L
cjbrown@langston.edu
BROWN, Chelsea ... 301-934-2251 203 D
cbrown1@csmd.edu
BROWN, Cheryl-Ann ... 321-674-7581.. 99 K
cbrown@fit.edu
BROWN, Chris ... 205-934-1294.... 8 B
csbrown@uab.edu
BROWN, Christopher ... 785-864-4904 181 I
jcbrown2@ku.edu
BROWN, Christopher ... 949-376-6000.. 47 H
cbrown@lcad.edu
BROWN, Christopher, L 212-854-2254 305 E
clb2140@columbia.edu
BROWN,
Christopher, M ... 336-334-7551 350 C
cmbrown7@ncat.edu
BROWN, Cindy ... 417-455-5540 259 D
cindybrown@crowder.edu
BROWN, Courtney, L ... 540-365-4201 480 L
cbrown@ferrum.edu
BROWN, Craig ... 208-562-3412 132 A
craigbrown@cwidaho.cc
BROWN, Curressia ... 662-254-3600 255 A
cbrown@mvsu.edu
BROWN, Cynthia ... 956-665-4025 468 A
cynthia.brown@utrgv.edu
BROWN, Cynthia ... 706-754-7714 123 G
cbrown@northgatech.edu
BROWN, Cynthia ... 901-381-3939 440 I
cynthia@visible.edu
BROWN, Cynthia, F ... 413-662-5242 218 C
c.brown@mcla.edu
BROWN, Cynthia, G ... 508-213-2065 223 C
cindy.brown@nichols.edu
BROWN, Dale ... 402-552-3470 273 K
browndale@clarksoncollege.edu
BROWN, Dana ... 601-979-3060 253 E
dana.a.brown@jsums.edu
BROWN, Danene ... 619-388-2803.. 60 D
dmbrown@sdccd.edu
BROWN, Daniel ... 512-245-3579 463 A
db70@txstate.edu
BROWN, Daniel ... 806-291-3575 470 I
brownd@wbu.edu
BROWN, Danielle ... 251-580-2178.... 1 I
danielle.brown@faulknerstate.edu
BROWN, Darlene ... 215-248-7158 392 D
brown@chc.edu
BROWN, Darrell ... 254-968-9083 459 A
dwbrown@tarleton.edu
BROWN, Darryl ... 301-295-3412 518 G
darryl.brown@usuhs.edu
BROWN, David ... 262-691-5346 515 B
dbrown@wctc.edu
BROWN, David ... 256-233-8187.... 4 C
david.brown@athens.edu
BROWN, David ... 352-638-9721.. 95 H
dbrown@beaconcollege.edu
BROWN, David ... 314-434-4044 259 B
david.brown@covenantseminary.edu
BROWN, Deanie ... 217-206-6222 154 A
brown.deanie@uis.edu
BROWN, Deanne ... 505-473-6676 296 C
deanne.brown@santafeuniversity.edu
BROWN, Deborah ... 417-659-9307 263 G
brown-deborah@mssu.edu
BROWN, Deborah ... 202-319-6915.. 91 D
browndl@cua.edu
BROWN, Deborah, R ... 757-446-5828 480 C
browndr@evms.edu
BROWN, Debra ... 610-917-3955 413 G
dlbrown@valleyforge.edu
BROWN, Dennis ... 281-425-6300 451 I
dbrown@lee.edu
BROWN, Derek ... 303-404-5492.. 79 K
derek.brown@frontrange.edu
BROWN, Diane, M ... 484-365-8055 400 E
dbrown@lincoln.edu
BROWN, Dolores, M ... 262-524-7133 506 G
docampo@carrollu.edu
BROWN, Donna ... 479-248-7236.. 19 F
registrar@ecollege.edu
BROWN, Donna, L ... 218-477-2721 246 B
donna.brown@mnstate.edu
BROWN, Douglas ... 508-588-9100 220 B
BROWN, Douglas, E ... 515-964-0601 169 C
brownd@faith.edu
BROWN, Ed ... 406-657-1746 272 B
edward.brown2@msubillings.edu
BROWN, Eric ... 530-221-4275.. 63 H
ebrown@shasta.edu
BROWN, Eric ... 207-778-7276 201 D
brown.eric@maine.edu
BROWN, Erica ... 205-226-4733.... 4 F
ebrown@bsc.edu
BROWN, Erik ... 218-726-8891 250 F
etbrown@d.umn.edu
BROWN, Erika ... 404-752-1723 123 F
ebrown@msm.edu
BROWN, Erin ... 405-789-7661 380 A
erin.brown@swcu.edu
BROWN, Erinn ... 308-345-8112 275 I
browne@mpcc.edu
BROWN, JR., Ermen ... 701-766-1342 353 E
ermen.brown@littlehoop.edu
BROWN, Ethel, M ... 404-413-1300 121 A
ebrown@gsu.edu
BROWN, Fran ... 248-476-1122 233 F
fbrown@mispp.edu
BROWN, Fred ... 850-872-3843 101 J
fbrown@gulfcoast.edu
BROWN, Gary ... 608-785-9167 515 C
browng@westerntc.edu
BROWN, Gary, L ... 919-530-6023 350 D
gbrown@nccu.edu
BROWN, Geeta, A ... 714-712-7900.. 46 G
BROWN, George, H ... 828-227-7028 352 C
ghbrown@wcu.edu
BROWN, George, H ... 215-572-2900 389 D
president@arcadia.edu
BROWN, Giles ... 903-463-8620 449 J
browng@grayson.edu
BROWN, Glenn ... 973-684-5402 288 C
gbrown@pccc.edu
BROWN, Glory ... 850-599-3531 109 A
glory.brown@famu.edu
BROWN, Gregory ... 707-864-7000.. 64 E
gregory.brown@solano.edu
BROWN, Gregory, N ... 610-328-8316 410 I
gbrown1@swarthmore.edu
BROWN, Guilbert ... 814-732-2585 406 B
gbrown@edinboro.edu
BROWN, H. David ... 816-271-4327 264 B
browndav@missouriwestern.edu
BROWN, Harold ... 415-452-5163.. 37 H
hbrown@ccsf.edu
BROWN, Heather ... 909-869-2717.. 31 A
heatherbrown@cpp.edu
BROWN, Heather ... 916-686-7400.. 30 H
BROWN, Ivey ... 336-750-2105 352 D
browniv@wssu.edu
BROWN, J. Steven ... 202-319-4738.. 91 D
brownj@cua.edu
BROWN, J. T ... 650-508-3521.. 54 D
jtbrown@ndnu.edu
BROWN, J.J ... 828-262-2060 349 H
brownjj@appstate.edu
BROWN, Jack ... 209-946-7352.. 70 F
jbrown2@pacific.edu
BROWN, Jackie ... 323-563-5985.. 36 H
jackiebrown@cdrewu.edu
BROWN, Jackie ... 803-705-4971 418 G
brrownjw@benedict.edu
BROWN, James ... 661-824-2977.. 53 G
jbrown@ntps.edu
BROWN, James ... 570-389-4410 405 E
jbrown@bloomu.edu
BROWN, Janice ... 301-846-2484 203 H
jbrown@frederick.edu
BROWN, Jared ... 610-436-3305 407 D
jbrown@wcupa.edu
BROWN, Jasmin, K ... 910-630-7034 340 A
jabrown@methodist.edu
BROWN, Jeff ... 801-832-2900 474 E
jbrown@westminstercollege.edu
BROWN, Jeff ... 610-647-4400 397 I
jbrown11@immaculata.edu
BROWN, Jeff ... 828-250-2350 351 A
jbrown@unca.edu
BROWN, Jeff ... 509-533-7373 493 I
jeff.brown@scc.spokane.edu
BROWN, Jeffery ... 573-629-3260 260 G
jbrown@hlg.edu
BROWN, Jeffrey ... 802-776-5216 474 H
jeffrey.brown@csj.edu
BROWN, Jeffrey ... 804-862-6100 484 F
jbrown@rbc.edu
BROWN, Jeffrey ... 217-333-2747 154 B
brownjr@illinois.edu
BROWN, Jennifer ... 203-582-3246.. 88 A
jennifer.brown@quinnipiac.edu
BROWN, Jennifer ... 785-738-9085 180 E
jbrown@ncktc.edu
BROWN, Jeremy ... 951-639-5420.. 52 J
jbrown@msjc.edu
BROWN, Jeremy ... 530-541-4660.. 47 I
jjbrown@ltcc.edu
BROWN, Jeremy ... 970-248-1962.. 77 K
jbrown@coloradomesa.edu
BROWN, Jerri ... 928-350-2113.. 15 V
jbrown@prescott.edu
BROWN, Jesse ... 765-998-5344 164 C
jesse_brown@taylor.edu
BROWN, Jesse, M ... 260-359-4028 159 B
jbrown@huntington.edu
BROWN, Jessyca ... 254-659-7504 450 B
jbrown@hillcollege.edu
BROWN, Jim ... 781-239-3175 220 A
jbrown@massbay.edu
BROWN, Jim ... 828-689-1185 339 G
jbrown@mhu.edu
BROWN, JoAnn ... 318-274-6238 196 G
brownj@gram.edu
BROWN, JoAnn ... 318-670-9651 196 A
jwarren@susla.edu
BROWN, Joanne ... 409-832-2956 462 B
jcbrown@lit.edu
BROWN, John ... 404-270-5227 126 D
jbrow109@spelman.edu
BROWN, Jonathan ... 206-592-3257 495 E
jbrown@highline.edu
BROWN, Joseph ... 910-246-4957 346 E
brownj@sandhills.edu
BROWN, Joseph ... 903-923-2270 448 J
jbrown@etbu.edu
BROWN, Joyce ... 443-885-3015 206 A
joyce.brown@morgan.edu
BROWN, Joyce, F ... 212-217-4000 308 B
joyce_brown@fitnyc.edu
BROWN, Julia ... 662-472-9011 253 C
jubrown@holmescc.edu
BROWN, June, E ... 918-631-2584 381 C
june-brown@utulsa.edu
BROWN, Justin, C ... 402-472-3484 277 G
justin.brown@unl.edu
BROWN, Kali ... 252-492-2061 347 C
brownk@vgcc.edu
BROWN, Karen, A ... 607-436-2524 325 E
karen.brown@oneonta.edu
BROWN, Karen, J ... 603-899-4280 281 D
brownkj@franklinpierce.edu
BROWN, Kathleen ... 641-844-5670 170 I
kathleen.brown@iavalley.edu
BROWN, Kathleen, M ... 574-284-4557 163 J
kbrown@saintmarys.edu
BROWN, Kathren ... 801-863-8517 473 D
kbrown@uvu.edu
BROWN, Kathryn, F ... 612-624-3533 250 E
brown059@umn.edu
BROWN, Katrina, M ... 307-674-6446 516 P
kbrown@sheridan.edu
BROWN, Keith ... 440-366-7692 364 F
BROWN, Keith, A ... 205-853-1200.... 2 F
kbrown@jeffersonstate.edu
BROWN, Kelli ... 478-445-4715 119 E
kelli.brown@gcsu.edu
BROWN, Kelly ... 405-224-3140 381 B
kbrown@usao.edu
BROWN, Kelvin ... 252-335-0821 342 D
kelvin_brown78@albemarle.edu
BROWN, Ken ... 620-278-4217 181 G
kbrown@sterling.edu
BROWN, Kendrick ... 909-748-8359.. 71 H
kendrick_brown@redlands.edu
BROWN, Kennard, D ... 901-448-4797 440 C
kbrown@uthsc.edu
BROWN, Kenneth ... 318-675-3395 194 D
kbrown@lsuhsc.edu
BROWN, Kenneth ... 509-777-4486 500 H
kbrown@whitworth.edu
BROWN, Kevin ... 843-349-5398 421 L
kevin.brown@hgtc.edu
BROWN, Kevin ... 641-784-5149 169 D
brown@graceland.edu
BROWN, Kevin ... 812-866-7040 158 C
brownk@hanover.edu
BROWN, Kevin ... 812-866-7061 158 C
brownk@hanover.edu
BROWN, Kevin ... 517-750-1200 237 D
kevin.brown@arbor.edu
BROWN, Kevin ... 218-477-2795 246 B
kevin.brown@mnstate.edu
BROWN, Kevin ... 423-236-2874 436 C
kbrown@southern.edu
BROWN, Kevin, A ... 919-866-5475 347 D
kabrown@waketech.edu
BROWN, Kevin, H ... 206-239-4500 493 D
khbrown@cityu.edu
BROWN, Kim ... 859-985-3912 183 I
kimberly_brown@berea.edu
BROWN, Kim, S ... 757-455-3275 491 F
kbrown@vwu.edu
BROWN, Kimberly ... 515-271-1462 168 G
kimberly.brown@dmu.edu
BROWN, Kimberly ... 205-726-4582.... 6 G
kbrown7@samford.edu
BROWN, Kristen, C ... 336-272-7102 338 B
kristen.brown@greensboro.edu
BROWN, Kristine, A ... 609-896-5192 289 E
kbrown@rider.edu
BROWN, Kyle ... 315-386-7164 329 A
brownk@canton.edu
BROWN, Kyle, A ... 315-267-7164 328 A
browkya@potsdam.edu
BROWN, Kyris ... 205-349-4240.... 7 C
kbrown@stillman.edu
BROWN, Larry ... 804-524-1162 491 A
lbrown@vsu.edu
BROWN, Laura ... 863-667-5041 108 G
BROWN, Laura ... 860-632-3010.. 87 D
admissions@holyapostles.edu
BROWN, Laura ... 847-925-6133 139 B
lbrown@harpercollege.edu
BROWN, Laura ... 508-270-4116 220 A
lbrown@massbay.edu
BROWN, Laura ... 413-662-5223 218 C
l.brown@mcla.edu
BROWN, LeAnn ... 651-213-4092 242 F
ltbrown@hazeldenbettyford.edu
BROWN, LeeAnn ... 304-473-8160 505 G
brown_l@wvwc.edu
BROWN, Lenice ... 936-261-1068 458 F
ldbrown@pvamu.edu
BROWN, JR.,
Leonard, E ... 240-895-4208 206 G
lebrown1@smcm.edu
BROWN, Levy ... 252-492-2061 347 C
brownl@vgcc.edu
BROWN, Levy ... 252-527-6223 344 D
ldbrown53@lenoircc.edu
BROWN, Lewis ... 605-688-4161 429 B
lewis.brown@sdstate.edu
BROWN, Linda ... 404-527-4525 117 C
lbrown@carver.edu
BROWN, Linda ... 660-359-3948 264 H
lbrown@mail.ncmissouri.edu
BROWN, Linda, J ... 218-299-4206 241 K
linbrown@cord.edu
BROWN, Lisa ... 405-682-7896 377 C
lbrown@occc.edu
BROWN, Lisa, M ... 202-687-6457.. 92 B
lbrown@georgetown.edu
BROWN, Lisa, M ... 216-397-4184 363 H
lmbrown@jcu.edu
BROWN, Lori, A ... 973-313-6132 291 F
lori.brown@shu.edu
BROWN, Lucille ... 203-285-2114.. 85 E
lbrown@gwcc.commnet.edu
BROWN, Lynne ... 212-998-2350 318 D
lynne.brown@nyu.edu
BROWN, II,
M. Christopher ... 502-597-6260 187 E
president@kysu.edu
BROWN, Mandy ... 641-844-5715 170 I
mandy.brown@iavalley.edu

BROWN, Marcia, W ...... 973-353-3709 290 D
mwbrown@andromeda.rutgers.edu
BROWN, Marcus .... 217-875-7200 149 J
mbrown@richland.edu
BROWN, Margo .... 904-819-6474.. 98 I
mbrown@flagler.edu
BROWN, Mark .... 712-324-5061 172 E
mbrown@nwicc.edu
BROWN, Martha .... 806-742-0012 463 B
BROWN, Martha .... 806-742-2120 463 D
martha.brown@ttu.edu
BROWN, Mary .... 573-875-7201 258 F
mbrown10@ccis.edu
BROWN, Mary, L .... 864-596-9094 420 F
mary.brown@converse.edu
BROWN, Mary Jo .... 217-814-5162 151 B
maryjobrown@
stjohnscollegespringfield.edu
BROWN, Matt .... 901-381-3939 440 I
matt@visible.edu
BROWN, Max .... 603-524-3207 280 K
BROWN, Melanie, A ...... 904-808-7410 106 M
melaniebrown@sjrstate.edu
BROWN, Melissa .... 314-652-0300 266 C
mbrown@slchcmail.com
BROWN, Melissa .... 412-809-5100 408 D
brown.melissa@pti.edu
BROWN, Melissa, S ...... 909-607-0109.. 38 C
melissa_brown@kgi.edu
BROWN, Merv, R .... 208-496-2010 131 D
brownme@byui.edu
BROWN, Michael .... 406-447-6947 271 I
michael.brown@umhelena.edu
BROWN, Michael .... 937-376-2946 369 C
mbrown@payne.edu
BROWN, II, Michael, A 336-334-7940 350 C
mabrown8@ncat.edu
BROWN, Michael, T ...... 805-893-2944.. 70 B
michael.brown@extension.ucsb.edu
BROWN, Michele .... 847-635-1981 148 D
mbrown@oakton.edu
BROWN, Michelle .... 706-310-6205 127 B
michelle.brown@ung.edu
BROWN, Michelle .... 435-283-7127 474 A
michelle.brown@snow.edu
BROWN, Mike .... 903-463-8772 449 J
mbrown@grayson.edu
BROWN, Mikell .... 804-594-1509 488 D
mbrown@jtcc.edu
BROWN, Monica, R ...... 240-567-4341 205 F
monica.brown@montgomerycollege.edu
BROWN, Morgan .... 310-846-2648.. 54 I
mbrown@otis.edu
BROWN, Naima .... 352-395-5648 107 E
naima.brown@sfcollege.edu
BROWN, Nancy .... 516-876-3275 327 C
brownn@oldwestbury.edu
BROWN, Narren .... 507-389-7462 247 H
narren.brown@southcentral.edu
BROWN, Natasha .... 404-270-5617 126 D
nbrown29@spelman.edu
BROWN, Nedra .... 901-369-0835.. 93 B
BROWN, Nicholas .... 303-410-2407.. 82 K
nicholas.brown@spartan.edu
BROWN, Nicole, R .... 417-625-3137 263 G
brown-n@mssu.edu
BROWN, Owen .... 718-270-5045 303 C
obrown@mec.cuny.edu
BROWN, Pamela .... 718-260-5008 303 D
pbrown@citytech.cuny.edu
BROWN, Pamela .... 510-987-9251.. 68 F
pamela.brown@ucop.edu
BROWN, Pamela .... 843-574-6246 424 G
pamela.brown@tridenttech.edu
BROWN, Patrick .... 217-245-3176 139 H
patrick.brown@mail.ic.edu
BROWN, Patrick .... 425-235-2352 497 E
pbrown@rtc.edu
BROWN, Patty .... 423-697-2437 436 F
patty.brown@chattanoogastate.edu
BROWN, Paul .... 254-659-7860 450 B
pbrown@hillcollege.edu
BROWN, Peter .... 304-724-5000 501 G
pbrown@cdu.edu
BROWN, Philip .... 219-989-2240 163 E
pbrown4@pnw.edu
BROWN, Phillip, J .... 410-864-3613 207 A
pbrown@stmarys.edu
BROWN, Phillip, M .... 618-650-3415 152 C
phbrown@siue.edu
BROWN, R. McKenna ... 804-828-8471 487 E
mbrown@vcu.edu
BROWN, R. Michael .... 724-357-5924 406 C
rmbrown@iup.edu
BROWN, Rachel, A .... 202-994-6495.. 92 A
rabrown@gwu.edu
BROWN, Randy .... 732-987-2254 286 D
rbrown@georgian.edu
BROWN, JR., Randy, D 404-413-1800 121 A
rdbrown@gsu.edu
BROWN, Rashayla .... 312-629-6869 151 F
maffai@saic.edu
BROWN, Raymond, A ... 610-527-0200 409 E
bbrown@rosemont.edu
BROWN, Rebecca .... 850-599-3090 109 A
rebecca.brown@famu.edu
BROWN, Rebekkah, L ... 484-664-3247 402 F
rebekkahbrown@muhlenberg.edu
BROWN, Renee, D .... 419-559-2367 370 J
rbrown@terra.edu
BROWN, Rhonda .... 323-259-2500.. 54 E
rbrown@oxy.edu
BROWN, Ricardo .... 601-979-8836 253 E
ricardo.a.brown@jsums.edu
BROWN, Richard .... 423-425-4393 440 A
richard-brown@utc.edu
BROWN, Richard, B .... 801-581-6912 472 P
brown@coe.utah.edu
BROWN, Rick .... 814-641-3311 398 B
brownri@juniata.edu
BROWN, Ricky .... 252-493-7259 345 E
rbrown@email.pittcc.edu
BROWN, Robert .... 859-622-1693 184 F
bob.brown@eku.edu
BROWN, Robert .... 310-342-5200.. 72 D
BROWN, Robert .... 410-386-8224 203 A
rbrown@carrollcc.edu
BROWN, Robert .... 570-321-4250 400 G
brownr@lycoming.edu
BROWN, Robert .... 864-596-9744 420 F
robert.brown@converse.edu
BROWN, Robert, A .... 617-353-2200 212 G
rabrown@bu.edu
BROWN, Robert, C .... 216-368-4306 358 C
robert.c.brown@case.edu
BROWN, Robert, D .... 909-389-3362.. 59 H
rdbrown@craftonhills.edu
BROWN, Robert, L .... 803-981-7375 426 J
rbrown@yorktech.edu
BROWN, Robert, M .... 251-460-6151.... 9 B
rbrown@southalabama.edu
BROWN, Roger, H .... 617-747-2316 212 B
ootp@berklee.edu
BROWN, Rolanda .... 662-621-4244 252 E
rbrown@coahomacc.edu
BROWN, Ron .... 254-295-4517 466 A
rbrown@umhb.edu
BROWN, Ronald, C .... 512-245-2205 463 A
rb04@txstate.edu
BROWN, Ronald, T .... 702-895-3693 279 D
ronald.brown@unlv.edu
BROWN, Rosann .... 814-641-3133 398 B
brownr@juniata.edu
BROWN, Roxanne .... 773-602-5016 135 L
rbrown262@ccc.edu
BROWN, Russ .... 772-462-6004 101 Q
rbrown@irsc.edu
BROWN, Sabrina .... 434-395-2021 482 E
browncs2@longwood.edu
BROWN, Samantha .... 425-352-8514 492 K
sbrown@cascadia.edu
BROWN, Sandra .... 858-534-3526.. 69 E
sandrabrown@ucsd.edu
BROWN, Sandra .... 605-668-1555 427 F
sbrown@mtmc.edu
BROWN, Sara .... 501-760-4129.. 20 D
sara.brown@np.edu
BROWN, Sarah .... 918-647-1471 375 B
sbrown@carlalbert.edu
BROWN, Scott .... 434-528-5276 491 D
BROWN, Scott, C .... 330-263-2011 360 A
scbrown@wooster.edu
BROWN, Shannon .... 267-341-3314 397 G
sbrown10@holyfamily.edu
BROWN, Shannon .... 214-768-4909 457 B
shannonbrown@smu.edu
BROWN, Shannon .... 603-668-2211 282 C
s.brown8@snhu.edu
BROWN, Shannon .... 828-726-2288 341 D
sbrown@cccti.edu
BROWN, Sharon .... 252-335-0821 342 D
sharon_brown@albemarle.edu
BROWN, Sheila .... 937-376-6349 358 I
sbrown@centralstate.edu
BROWN, Shelley .... 330-490-7134 373 F
sbrown@walsh.edu
BROWN, Shirley .... 615-329-8756 431 I
sbrown@fisk.edu
BROWN, Simon .... 215-751-8039 393 A
sbrown@ccp.edu
BROWN, Sondra .... 703-891-1787 485 I
dean@standardcollege.edu
BROWN, Stephanie .... 561-237-7784 103 E
scbrown@lynn.edu
BROWN, Stephanie .... 954-262-7456 104 F
browstep@nova.edu
BROWN, Stephen, G ...... 530-221-4275.. 63 H
sbrown@shasta.edu
BROWN, Stephen, R ...... 478-301-2683 122 H
brown_sr@mercer.edu
BROWN, Steve .... 712-274-6400 174 E
steve.brown@witcc.edu
BROWN, Steve .... 724-805-2534 410 B
steve.brown@email.stvincent.edu
BROWN, Steven .... 850-474-2222 111 D
sbrown4@uwf.edu
BROWN, Steven, D .... 906-227-1188 235 A
stebrown@nmu.edu
BROWN, Sue, C .... 309-655-2206 151 A
sue.c.brown@osfhealthcare.org
BROWN, Susan .... 956-665-2383 468 A
susan.brown@utrgv.edu
BROWN, Susan, M .... 859-233-8225 189 H
subrown@transy.edu
BROWN, Suzi .... 228-896-2503 254 D
suzi.brown@mgccc.edu
BROWN, Sylvia .... 252-744-6422 349 I
brownsy@ecu.edu
BROWN, T. Rhett .... 704-233-8111 353 D
r.brown@wingate.edu
BROWN, Takeish, N ...... 804-257-5888 491 C
tnbrown@vuu.edu
BROWN, Takeshia .... 912-478-5409 120 E
fbrown@georgiasouthern.edu
BROWN, Tamara, L .... 936-261-5205 458 F
tlbrown@pvamu.edu
BROWN, Tavonda .... 870-743-3000.. 20 E
tbrown@northark.edu
BROWN, Teisa .... 610-519-8881 413 K
teisa.brown@villanova.edu
BROWN, Teresa .... 404-225-4700 115 J
tbrown@atlantatech.edu
BROWN, Terrence .... 901-751-8453 434 E
tbrown@mabts.edu
BROWN, Terry .... 716-673-3335 325 C
terry.brown@fredonia.edu
BROWN, Terry .... 610-683-4120 406 D
tbrown@kutztown.edu
BROWN, Thomas .... 205-929-1061.... 6 D
tbrown@miles.edu
BROWN, Thomas .... 540-231-3787 490 F
tbrown@vt.edu
BROWN, Thomas, W ...... 507-933-7005 242 D
brownie@gustavus.edu
BROWN, Tim .... 843-574-6424 424 G
tim.brown@tridenttech.edu
BROWN, Timothy .... 616-392-8555 239 J
tim@westernsem.edu
BROWN, Tom .... 352-638-9762.. 95 H
tbrown@beaconcollege.edu
BROWN, Tom .... 310-660-3015.. 42 C
tbrown@elcamino.edu
BROWN, Tomeka, K .... 318-670-9319 196 A
tbrown@susla.edu
BROWN, Trachanda .... 215-242-7989 392 D
brownt@chc.edu
BROWN, Tracy, H .... 512-471-5974 467 C
tracy.brown@austin.utexas.edu
BROWN, Travis .... 503-491-7219 384 D
travis.brown@mhcc.edu
BROWN, Trevor, L .... 614-292-4533 367 H
brown.2296@osu.edu
BROWN, Venessa .... 618-650-5867 152 C
vbrown@siue.edu
BROWN, Veronica .... 334-876-9395.... 2 C
veronica.brown@wccs.edu
BROWN, Victor .... 201-879-7033 283 I
vmbrown@bergen.edu
BROWN, Victor .... 937-395-5604 364 B
victor.brown@kc.edu
BROWN, Vintress .... 864-503-5553 425 H
vbrown@uscupstate.edu
BROWN, JR., Walter, E 412-648-3185 412 I
walter.brown@ia.pitt.edu
BROWN, Wanda .... 336-750-2000 352 D
brownwa@wssu.edu
BROWN, Warren .... 206-934-3601 497 G
warren.brown@seattlecolleges.edu
BROWN, Warren, J .... 206-934-3601 497 H
warren.brown@seattlecolleges.edu
BROWN, Wayne .... 518-464-8675 308 A
wbrown@excelsior.edu
BROWN, Wheeler .... 601-979-2360 253 E
wheeler.brown@jsums.edu
BROWN, Wilfred, E .... 805-893-4155.. 70 B
willie.brown@auxiliary.ucsb.edu
BROWN, William .... 970-339-3563.. 76 E
bill.brown@aims.edu
BROWN, William .... 812-855-1822 159 H
brownwm@indiana.edu
BROWN, William .... 301-696-3402 204 D
brownw@hood.edu
BROWN, William .... 973-408-3976 285 E
wbrown1@drew.edu
BROWN, III, William, E 757-822-7701 489 H
wbrown@tcc.edu
BROWN, William, H .... 704-894-2143 337 B
wibrown@davidson.edu
BROWN, William, T .... 615-353-3326 437 D
william.brown@nscc.edu
BROWN, William Terry . 203-332-5060.. 85 F
wbrown@housatonic.edu
BROWN, Zachary .... 607-431-4547 309 E
brownz@hartwick.edu
BROWN-CORNELIUS,
Denise .... 502-272-8270 183 H
dbrowncornelius@bellarmine.edu
BROWN GORDAN,
Loria .... 601-979-2107 253 E
loria.c.brown@jsums.edu
BROWN-GUILLORY,
Elizabeth, A .... 713-313-1180 461 E
brown-guilloryе@tsu.edu
BROWN MARSDEN,
Margaret .... 940-397-4253 453 C
margaret.brownmarsden@mwsu.edu
BROWN MCCLURE,
Fran'Cee .... 404-270-5133 126 D
fbrownmc@spelman.edu
BROWN-SOW, Lynette ... 215-751-8859 393 A
lbrown@ccp.edu
BROWN-WELTY, Sharon 909-537-8101.. 33 D
sharonb@csusb.edu
BROWN WYATT, Donna 660-626-2790 257 A
dbrown@atsu.edu
BROWN YOUNG,
Danita .... 217-333-6677 154 B
BROWNE, Brian .... 718-990-2762 322 F
browneb@stjohns.edu
BROWNE, Doug .... 620-417-1201 181 E
doug.browne@sccc.edu
BROWNE, Jacob .... 727-864-8846.. 97 O
brownejh@eckerd.edu
BROWNE, Joan, M .... 202-806-7513.. 92 C
jmbrowne@howard.edu
BROWNE, Kathleen .... 740-587-8646 361 B
brownek@denison.edu
BROWNE, Kevin .... 312-413-3471 153 H
kbrowne@uic.edu
BROWNE, Marcus .... 718-522-9073 298 E
mbrowne@asa.edu
BROWNE, Patrick .... 503-256-3180 387 I
pbrowne@uws.edu
BROWNE, Paul .... 574-631-8696 165 A
pbrowne@nd.edu
BROWNE, Todd .... 845-446-1522 519 D
todd.browne@wpaog.org
BROWNE-BOATSWAIN,
Venoreen .... 763-422-6094 244 A
venoreen.browne-boatswain@
anokaramsey.edu
BROWNE-BOATSWAIN,
Venoreen .... 763-422-6094 243 K
venoreen.browne-boatswain@
anokaramsey.edu
BROWNELL, Claire .... 303-871-4876.. 83 E
claire.brownell@du.edu
BROWNELL, Jayne, E .... 513-529-4631 365 I
browneje@miamioh.edu
BROWNELL, Jennifer ...... 336-506-4140 340 L
jennifer.brownell@alamancecc.edu
BROWNELL, Kelly, D ..... 919-613-7309 337 C
kelly.brownell@duke.edu
BROWNELL, Scott .... 612-330-1644 240 G
brownell@augsburg.edu
BROWNER, Stephanie ... 212-229-5100 316 E
browners@newschool.edu
BROWNIE, Ronald .... 605-626-2568 428 H
ronald.brownie@northern.edu
BROWNING, Ashley .... 540-362-6210 481 F
abrowning@hollins.edu
BROWNING, David, A ... 252-399-6329 335 I
dabrowning@barton.edu
BROWNING, E.R. (Jay) . 513-556-6153 371 E
jay.browning@uc.edu
BROWNING, Eric .... 740-392-6868 366 B
eric.browning@mvnu.edu
BROWNING, Gari .... 510-659-6200.. 54 F
gbrowning@ohlone.edu
BROWNING, Janelle ...... 617-747-2358 212 B
jbrowning@berklee.edu
BROWNING, Jason .... 307-674-6446 516 P
jbrowning@sheridan.edu
BROWNING, Joann .... 210-458-7379 468 B
joann.browning@utsa.edu
BROWNING, Katherine .. 301-387-3097 203 I
katherine.browning@garrettcollege.edu
BROWNING, Kelly .... 715-425-3342 511 E
kelly.browning@uwrf.edu
BROWNING, Kimbrea .... 513-487-1173 371 A
kimbrea.browning@myunion.edu

BROWNING, LK ... 931-540-2841 436 H
lkbrowning1@columbiastate.edu
BROWNING, Midge ... 618-374-5776 149 A
midge.browning@principia.edu
BROWNING, Peter ... 417-873-7231 259 G
pbrowning@drury.edu
BROWNING, Reggie ... 864-592-4660 424 C
browningr@sccsc.edu
BROWNING, Roger ... 618-393-2982 140 B
browningr@iecc.edu
BROWNING, Shea ... 828-227-7116 352 C
BROWNING, Steve ... 870-235-4102.. 21 F
dsbrowning@saumag.edu
BROWNLEE, Candace ... 309-268-8041 139 D
candace.brownlee@heartland.edu
BROWNLEE, David, W .. 610-558-5628 402 G
dbrownle@neumann.edu
BROWNLEE, James, H .. 330-471-8382 364 H
jbrownlee@malone.edu
BROWNLEE, Mordecai .. 210-486-2252 441 I
mbrownlee3@alamo.edu
BROWNLEE, Reb ... 814-262-3842 405 A
rbrownlee@pennhighlands.edu
BROWNLEE,
Tamarah, D ... 260-481-6677 160 D
brownlet@ipfw.edu
BROWNLOW, Antonio ... 662-254-3411 255 A
abrownlow@mvsu.edu
BROWNSBERGER,
William ... 660-944-2914 258 G
wbrownsberger@conception.edu
BROWNSON, James ... 208-885-5369 132 I
jbrownson@uidaho.edu
BROWNSTEIN, Aaron ... 323-822-9700.. 67 G
aaron.brownstein@touro.edu
BROXSON, Thomas ... 253-840-8338 497 B
tbroxson@pierce.ctc.edu
BROYLES, Jennifer ... 848-445-5573 290 C
jbroyles@echo.rutgers.edu
BROYLES, Joy ... 540-863-2861 487 I
jbroyles@dslcc.edu
BROYLES, Ken ... 423-461-8734 435 A
kbroyles@milligan.edu
BROYLES, Wendy ... 334-983-6556.... 7 E
whuckabee@troy.edu
BROZ, Roger ... 612-659-6805 245 F
roger.broz@minneapolis.edu
BROZA, Dave ... 651-638-6459 240 J
d-broza@bethel.edu
BROZOVICH, Mary ... 303-458-4376.. 82 D
mbrozovi@regis.edu
BROZZO, Shirley, A ... 906-227-1000 235 A
sbrozzo@nmu.edu
BRUBACHER, Don ... 517-607-3130 231 C
dbrubacher@hillsdale.edu
BRUBAKER, David ... 585-567-9484 310 F
david.brubaker@houghton.edu
BRUBAKER, Donald, C . 817-552-3700 451 G
dbrubaker@tku.edu
BRUBAKER, Glenn, R ... 607-587-4750 328 F
brubakgr@alfredstate.edu
BRUBAKER, Joel, A ... 724-847-6503 395 J
jabrubak@geneva.edu
BRUBAKER, Karl ... 620-327-8216 178 B
karlb@hesston.edu
BRUBAKER, Kevin ... 503-375-7030 383 A
kbrubaker@corban.edu
BRUBAKER, Sam, R ... 208-496-9817 131 D
brubakers@byui.edu
BRUBAKER, Sara ... 620-242-0413 179 G
brubakes@mcpherson.edu
BRUBAKER-COLE,
Susie ... 541-737-3626 385 F
susie.brubaker-cole@oregonstate.edu
BRUCE, Aaron, I ... 619-594-3319.. 34 B
abruce@mail.sdsu.edu
BRUCE, Alex, M ... 931-598-1919 436 A
ambruce@sewanee.edu
BRUCE, Beth ... 870-612-2057.. 22 H
beth.bruce@uaccb.edu
BRUCE, Dean ... 307-754-6123 516 Q
dean.bruce@nwc.edu
BRUCE, Debra ... 509-542-4604 493 G
dbruce@columbiabasin.edu
BRUCE, Gonzalo ... 208-426-3652 131 C
gonzalobruce@boisestate.edu
BRUCE, J. Michael ... 812-866-7039 158 C
bruce@hanover.edu
BRUCE, Jimmie, D ... 740-264-5591 361 D
jbruce@egcc.edu
BRUCE, Karen ... 205-879-5588.... 5 I
kbruce@faulkner.edu
BRUCE, Kathy ... 847-925-6732 139 B
kbruce@harpercollege.edu
BRUCE, Lori ... 662-325-7400 254 E
lmb102@msstate.edu
BRUCE, Matthew ... 925-969-3300.. 46 L
mbruce@jfku.edu
BRUCE, Motice ... 601-977-4470 256 B
mbruce@tougaloo.edu
BRUCE, Philip ... 912-478-5197 120 E
pbruce@georgiasouthern.edu
BRUCE, Rob ... 919-962-2646 351 B
rob_bruce@unc.edu
BRUCE, Robert (Todd) .. 216-397-1600 363 H
rbruce@jcu.edu
BRUCE, Stanyell ... 410-455-2632 208 A
bruce@umbc.edu
BRUCE, Steve ... 574-520-4457 160 F
stbruce@iusb.edu
BRUCE, Terry ... 619-393-2982 140 B
brucet@iecc.edu
BRUCE, Will ... 805-922-6966.. 24 J
wbruce@hancockcollege.edu
BRUCE, William, P ... 615-327-3927 432 G
pbruce@guptoncollege.edu
BRUCH, John ... 262-595-2228 511 C
bruch@uwp.edu
BRUCKI, Mark, J ... 248-204-2310 233 A
mbrucki@ltu.edu
BRUCKLER, Michael, L . 240-895-2045 206 G
mlbruckler@smcm.edu
BRUCKMAN, Steve ... 415-452-5321.. 37 H
sbruckman@ccsf.edu
BRUCKSTEIN, Irving ... 610-799-1132 400 A
ibruckstein@lccc.edu
BRUDE, Jon ... 719-549-3340.. 81 M
jon.brude@pueblocc.edu
BRUDER, Edward, C ... 717-815-1314 415 G
ebruder@ycp.edu
BRUDNICKI, James ... 856-222-9311 289 F
jbrudnic@rcbc.edu
BRUDNOK, Celine ... 724-805-2720 410 C
celine.brudnok@stvincent.edu
BRUDNOK, Celine, R ... 724-805-2720 410 B
celine.brudnok@email.stvincent.edu
BRUDVIG, James ... 845-758-7429 298 I
brudvig@bard.edu
BRUE ENRIGHT, Jan ... 605-256-5205 428 G
jan.brueenright@dsu.edu
BRUECK, Joshua ... 217-641-4320 141 F
jbrueck@jwcc.edu
BRUEGGEMAN, Mary ... 206-533-6724 498 E
mbrueggeman@shoreline.edu
BRUEGGEMANN, Chuck 618-537-6873 145 C
cebrueggemann@mckendree.edu
BRUEHL, Allen, A ... 508-767-7311 210 I
abruehl@assumption.edu
BRUEN, Christina, M ... 508-910-6633 217 A
cbruen@umassd.edu
BRUESS, Brian ... 920-403-3165 509 J
brian.bruess@snc.edu
BRUGAL-MENA,
Yocasta ... 787-743-3038 525 M
ybrugal@sanjuanbautista.edu
BRUGGEMAN, Jared ... 417-625-9574 263 G
bruggeman-j@mssu.edu
BRUGGEMAN, John, H . 513-487-3269 309 F
jbruggeman@huc.edu
BRUGGEMAN, Michael . 313-664-1440 228 H
mikeb@collegeforcreativestudies.edu
BRUGH, Larry ... 814-262-3849 405 A
lbrugh@pennhighlands.edu
BRUGH, Suzanne ... 814-262-6463 405 A
sbrugh@pennhighlands.edu
BRUGMAN, Donna, M .. 617-984-1776 223 H
dbrugman@quincycollege.edu
BRUHN, Christian ... 360-623-8364 493 A
christian.bruhn@centralia.edu
BRUHN, Mark, S ... 812-855-0326 159 G
mbruhn@iu.edu
BRUHN, Sheila ... 218-793-2465 246 F
sheila.bruhn@northlandcollege.edu
BRUHN, Tobias ... 215-968-8223 390 I
tobi.bruhn@bucks.edu
BRUINSMA, Paul ... 618-842-3711 140 C
bruinsmap@iecc.edu
BRUKARDT, David ... 608-262-3905 510 B
BRUKARDT, Mary Jane . 715-836-2320 510 D
brukarmj@uwec.edu
BRUMAGIN, Ruth ... 570-288-8400 395 E
ruthb@marcogrp.com
BRUMBACH, Mary ... 214-378-1549 447 F
mbrumbach@dcccd.edu
BRUMBERG, Joshua ... 212-817-7215 302 B
jbrumberg@gc.cuny.edu
BRUMFIELD, Adele, C ... 858-534-3156.. 69 E
acbrumfield@ucsd.edu
BRUMFIELD, Robb, T ... 225-578-2855 193 M
robb@lsu.edu
BRUMITT, Jane ... 312-629-6184 151 F
jbrumitt@saic.edu
BRUMLEY, Jessica ... 954-262-8835 104 F
jw1263@nova.edu
BRUMLEY, Larry, D ... 478-301-5700 122 H
brumley_ld@mercer.edu
BRUMMEL, Joe ... 641-628-7648 167 D
brummelj@central.edu
BRUMMELS, Lin ... 402-375-7321 276 D
librumm1@wsc.edu
BRUMMER, James, M ... 651-962-6595 251 D
jbrummer@stthomas.edu
BRUMMER, Joni, M ... 480-732-7226.. 13 E
joni.brummer@cgc.edu
BRUMMETT, Ross ... 865-471-3235 430 H
rbrummett@cn.edu
BRUMMUND, Barry, T .. 520-621-0588.. 16 J
brummund@email.arizona.edu
BRUNDAGE, Christina ... 570-348-6247 401 B
careerservices@marywood.edu
BRUNDAGE, Isaac ... 575-538-6339 297 H
brundagei@wnmu.edu
BRUNDAGE, Kelly ... 850-474-3063 111 D
kbrundage@uwf.edu
BRUNDAGE, Ken ... 814-871-7551 395 H
brundage001@gannon.edu
BRUNDAGE, Tracy ... 570-945-8316 398 C
tracy.brundage@keystone.edu
BRUNDIDGE, Linda ... 847-317-7023 153 D
lbrundid@tiu.edu
BRUNDO SHARRAR,
Tricia, A ... 402-280-4076 274 D
sharrar@creighton.edu
BRUNE, Carolyn ... 847-574-5154 143 A
cbrune@lfgsm.edu
BRUNEAU, Patrice ... 803-323-2266 426 H
bruneaup@winthrop.edu
BRUNELLE, Christopher 909-652-6591.. 36 E
christopher.brunelle@chaffey.edu
BRUNELLI, Leslie, G ... 803-777-7427 424 I
lgbrunel@mailbox.sc.edu
BRUNEN, Meredith ... 850-474-2712 111 D
mbrunen@uwf.edu
BRUNEN, Meredith ... 864-503-7417 425 H
mbrunen@uscupstate.edu
BRUNER, Cassie ... 979-230-3308 444 E
cassie.bruner@brazosport.edu
BRUNER, Darl, L ... 208-467-8843 132 F
dlbruner@nnu.edu
BRUNER, Greg ... 815-939-5249 148 F
gbruner@olivet.edu
BRUNER, Jeremy ... 501-450-3183.. 23 I
jbruner@uca.edu
BRUNER, Joe, W ... 859-858-3511 183 D
joe.bruner@asbury.edu
BRUNER, Joshua ... 646-717-9765 309 B
bruner@gts.edu
BRUNER, Judith ... 858-246-1800.. 69 E
jbruner@ucsd.edu
BRUNER, Ted ... 828-689-1242 339 G
tbruner@mhu.edu
BRUNET EAGAN,
Kathleen ... 973-328-5052 285 B
keagan@ccm.edu
BRUNET-KOCH,
Cameron ... 231-348-6601 234 H
ckoch@ncmich.edu
BRUNETT, Emerald ... 541-888-7229 387 A
emerald.brunett@socc.edu
BRUNETTA, Stephanie ... 607-431-4000 309 E
brunetta@hartwick.edu
BRUNETTE, Thomas ... 903-877-7212 469 A
tom.brunette@uthct.edu
BRUNETTO, Jeffrey ... 201-200-2040 287 F
jbrunetto@njcu.edu
BRUNGARDT, Cherie ... 970-521-6787.. 81 F
cherie.brungardt@njc.edu
BRUNGARDT, Heather ... 970-521-6623.. 81 F
heather.brungardt@njc.edu
BRUNICORDI, Tim ... 740-753-6523 362 K
brunicordit@hocking.edu
BRUNING, Merribeth ... 765-641-4406 156 A
mdbruning@anderson.edu
BRUNJES, Jim ... 806-742-0012 463 B
BRUNK, Debbie ... 419-866-0291 370 I
djbrunk@stautzenberger.com
BRUNKEN, Monica ... 210-690-9000 449 K
mbrunken@hallmarkuniversity.edu
BRUNKOW, Alan ... 402-761-8259 276 K
abrunkow@southeast.edu
BRUNKOW, Kristine ... 530-422-7927.. 73 F
BRUNNEMER, David ... 360-650-7732 500 E
david.brunnemer@wwu.edu
BRUNNER, Diane ... 419-473-2700 360 J
dbrunner@daviscollege.edu
BRUNNER, Jon, L ... 239-590-7950 109 C
jbrunner@fgcu.edu
BRUNNER, Karen, L ... 865-882-4606 438 A
brunnerkl@roanestate.edu
BRUNNER, Lane ... 903-566-7168 468 C
lbruner@uttyler.edu
BRUNNER, Ludwig ... 716-375-7666 322 B
lbrunner@sbu.edu
BRUNNER, Marc ... 931-221-7887 430 B
brunnerm@apsu.edu
BRUNNER, Mark ... 573-876-2381 267 G
mbrunner@stephens.edu
BRUNNER, Marta ... 518-580-5506 324 D
BRUNNER, Mary, K ... 810-989-5512 236 G
mbrunner@sc4.edu
BRUNNER, Matthew ... 540-851-5271 484 A
msbrunner@radford.edu
BRUNNER, Tim ... 419-473-2700 360 J
tbrunner@daviscollege.edu
BRUNNER, Timothy ... 419-473-2700 360 J
tbrunner@daviscolleg.edu
BRUNO, Bonnie ... 336-278-6603 337 G
bbruno2@elon.edu
BRUNO, Christopher ... 470-578-5483 122 C
cbruno3@kennesaw.edu
BRUNO, Craig ... 412-536-1152 398 E
craig.bruno@laroche.edu
BRUNO, Gene ... 865-524-8079 432 F
gbruno@hchs.edu
BRUNO, Joanne, Z ... 570-422-3539 406 A
provost@esu.edu
BRUNO, Kimberly ... 504-568-4820 194 C
kbruno@lsuhsc.edu
BRUNO, Laura ... 718-281-5212 303 F
lbruno@qcc.cuny.edu
BRUNO, Michael ... 808-956-8447 129 J
mbruno2@hawaii.edu
BRUNO, Nick, J ... 318-342-1010 198 A
bruno@ulm.edu
BRUNO, Patricia ... 781-280-3200 220 C
BRUNO, SC, Teresa ... 973-957-0188 283 C
academicdean@acs350.org
BRUNOLD, Timothy ... 213-740-6753.. 72 B
admdean@usc.edu
BRUNS, Clara ... 802-322-1603 475 A
clara.bruns@goddard.edu
BRUNS, David ... 419-358-3314 357 E
brunsd@bluffton.edu
BRUNS, Lisa ... 631-420-2245 329 D
lisa.bruns@farmingdale.edu
BRUNS, Sandy ... 712-324-5061 172 E
sandy@nwicc.edu
BRUNSON, Chrysandra . 303-963-3337.. 77 I
cbrunson@ccu.edu
BRUNSON, Claude ... 601-984-1012 256 D
cbrunson@umc.edu
BRUNSON, Isaac ... 256-761-6315.... 7 D
isaacbrunson@talladega.edu
BRUNSON, Mary Nelle . 936-468-2707 458 A
mbrunson@sfasu.edu
BRUNSON, Rod ... 973-353-5870 290 D
rodbruns@andromeda.rutgers.edu
BRUNSTING, Diane ... 708-597-3000 153 B
BRUNT, Bonnie ... 509-533-3339 494 A
bonnie.brunt@sfcc.spokane.edu
BRUNTMYER, Eric, I ... 325-670-1227 450 A
ebruntmyer@hsutx.edu
BRUNTON, Mark ... 702-579-3528 278 H
mark.brunton@brightwood.edu
BRUNTZ, Crystal ... 816-501-3600 257 G
crystal.bruntz@avila.edu
BRUSATI, Gerianne ... 845-341-4020 319 H
gerianne.brusati@sunyorange.edu
BRUSCATO, Brandon ... 318-342-5314 198 A
bruscato@ulm.edu
BRUSH, Thomas ... 410-617-1466 205 A
tdbrush@loyola.edu
BRUSOE, Suzanne ... 651-423-8205 244 E
suzanne.brusoe@dctc.edu
BRUSOE, Suzanne ... 651-423-8205 244 E
suzie.brusoe@dctc.edu
BRUSOE, Suzie ... 651-450-3642 245 A
sbrusoe@inverhills.edu
BRUSTER, Bernadette, L 903-927-3374 471 B
blbruster@wileyc.edu
BRUSTKERN, Kari ... 406-447-5422 270 H
kbrustkern@carroll.edu
BRUSZEWSKI, Roger ... 717-871-4087 407 A
roger.bruszewski@millersville.edu
BRUXVOORT, Debra ... 641-628-7671 167 D
bruxvoortb@central.edu
BRY, Jay ... 978-665-3131 217 E
jbry@fitchburgstate.edu
BRYAN, Ben ... 803-754-4100 420 E
BRYAN, Brett ... 541-278-5900 382 A
bbryan@bluecc.edu
BRYAN, Charles "Hank" 989-386-6622 234 B
cbryan@midmich.edu
BRYAN, Christopher ... 206-239-4500 493 D
BRYAN, Doug ... 704-406-4398 337 H
dbryan@gardner-webb.edu
BRYAN, James ... 316-322-3232 175 I
jbryan8@butlercc.edu
BRYAN, Karla ... 903-675-6229 464 C
kbryan@tvcc.edu

BRYAN, Laura .... 859-233-8121 189 H lbryan@transy.edu
BRYAN, Mitzi .... 718-636-3430 320 D mbryan@pratt.edu
BRYAN, Neva .... 276-328-0126 487 A njd8r@uvawise.edu
BRYAN, JR., Norman, B .... 864-833-8757 423 D nbbryan@presby.edu
BRYAN, Paul .... 215-893-5252 393 C paul.bryan@curtis.edu
BRYAN, Robert .... 216-987-4684 360 E robert.bryan@tri-c.edu
BRYAN, Susan .... 417-865-2815 260 B bryans@evangel.edu
BRYAN, Terry .... 832-252-4676 446 A terry.bryan@cbshouston.edu
BRYAN, Timothy, A .... 330-471-8539 364 H tbryan@malone.edu
BRYAN, Warren, J .... 540-464-7287 490 E bbryan@vmiaa.org
BRYAN, Wes .... 714-895-8101.. 38 G wbryan@gwc.cccd.edu
BRYAN WILLIAMS, Pamela .... 314-529-9614 262 B pbryanwilliams@maryville.edu
BRYANT, JR., Alfred ..... 910-775-4009 351 E alfred.bryant@uncp.edu
BRYANT, Amanda .... 252-222-6225 341 F bryanta@carteret.edu
BRYANT, Angela, V .... 229-928-1378 120 F angela.bryant@gsw.edu
BRYANT, Angie .... 615-460-6407 430 D angie.bryant@belmont.edu
BRYANT, Bianca .... 405-466-2038 375 L bjbryant@langston.edu
BRYANT, Bruce .... 870-236-6901.. 19 D bbryant@crc.edu
BRYANT, Carlton, G ...... 800-782-2422.. 30 G cbryant@mail.cnuas.edu
BRYANT, Chip .... 865-974-9557 439 I bryant00@utk.edu
BRYANT, Chris .... 931-393-1663 437 C cbryant@mscc.edu
BRYANT, Clint .... 706-737-1626 116 B cbryant1@augusta.edu
BRYANT, Courtney .... 501-852-0804.. 23 I cmullen@uca.edu
BRYANT, Courtney .... 509-527-2222 499 F courtney.bryant@wallawalla.edu
BRYANT, Cynthia, D ..... 225-771-3631 195 K cynthia_bryant@subr.edu
BRYANT, David, A .... 407-303-9305.. 94 H david.bryant@adu.edu
BRYANT, Elisa .... 417-625-3039 263 G bryant-e@mssu.edu
BRYANT, Essie, L .... 662-254-3440 255 A elbryant@mvsu.edu
BRYANT, Felicia .... 856-227-7200 284 E fbryant@camdencc.edu
BRYANT, Gerard .... 646-781-5625 302 F gwbryant@jjay.cuny.edu
BRYANT, Jack .... 405-422-1260 379 B jack.bryant@redlandscc.edu
BRYANT, III, James, S . 803-535-1330 423 B bryantj@octech.edu
BRYANT, Jody .... 864-231-2000 418 E jbryant@andersonuniversity.edu
BRYANT, John .... 309-556-3449 141 B jbryant@iwu.edu
BRYANT, Jordan .... 847-317-7074 153 D jbryant@tiu.edu
BRYANT, Joy, L .... 864-644-5385 424 B jbryant@swu.edu
BRYANT, Kimberly .... 215-895-1121 413 E k.bryant@usciences.edu
BRYANT, Kimberly .... 336-734-7236 343 C kbryant@forsythtech.edu
BRYANT, Kinney .... 405-425-5155 377 B kinney.bryant@oc.edu
BRYANT, III, Lewis .... 434-832-7615 487 H bryantl@cvcc.vccs.edu
BRYANT, Marcean .... 510-522-7221.. 56 G mbryant@peralta.edu
BRYANT, Mark .... 661-722-6300.. 26 C mbryant6@avc.edu
BRYANT, Matthew .... 504-816-8077 195 D internetdeanasst@nobts.edu
BRYANT, Matthew, S .... 423-432-4236 255 E mbryant@rts.edu
BRYANT, Michael .... 843-863-7973 419 C mbryant@csuniv.edu
BRYANT, Morgan .... 601-925-3354 254 B mbryant@mc.edu
BRYANT, Nijah, E .... 912-358-4172 125 C bryantn@savannahstate.edu
BRYANT, Pam .... 325-649-8401 450 H pbryant@hputx.edu
BRYANT, Paul .... 318-274-2374 196 G bryantp@gram.edu
BRYANT, Paul .... 606-248-2001 187 B pbryant0006@kctcs.edu
BRYANT, Ronnie .... 910-755-7483 341 C bryantr@brunswickcc.edu
BRYANT, Rosalynn .... 314-362-9253 260 E rjr9245@bjc.org
BRYANT, Scott .... 903-923-2069 448 J sbryant@etbu.edu
BRYANT, Sheila, M .... 931-221-7178 430 B bryantsm@apsu.edu
BRYANT, Stephanie .... 417-836-4408 263 H stephaniebryant@missouristate.edu
BRYANT, Steven, P .... 734-487-1849 229 K
BRYANT, Susan .... 334-214-4847.... 1 H susan.bryant@cv.edu
BRYANT, Tahnee .... 304-236-7620 503 D tahnee.bryant@southernwv.edu
BRYANT, Theresa .... 412-788-7360 392 G tbryant@ccac.edu
BRYANT, Tim .... 513-244-4504 366 A tim.bryant@msj.edu
BRYANT, Toni .... 830-792-7229 456 D tlbryant@schreiner.edu
BRYANT, Valentino .... 919-546-8681 348 I vbryant@shawu.edu
BRYANT, Vickie .... 817-461-8741 442 L vbryant@abu.edu
BRYANT, Wayne, H .... 318-670-9230 196 A wbryant@ssla.edu
BRYANT-FRIEDRICH, Amanda .... 419-530-4968 372 F amanda.bryant-friedrich@utoledo.edu
BRYARS, Beth .... 251-580-2227.... 1 I beth.bryars@faulknerstate.edu
BRYCE, Jeanne .... 928-428-8261.. 12 I jeanne.bryce@eac.edu
BRYCE, Mark .... 928-428-8231.. 12 I mark.bryce@eac.edu
BRYDE, Beverly .... 610-902-8331 391 B beverly.reilly.bryde@cabrini.edu
BRYDEN, David, L .... 336-841-9101 338 E dbryden@highpoint.edu
BRYDON, Lucinda, C .... 607-746-4603 329 B brydonlm@delhi.edu
BRYDON, Marria .... 405-878-5416 379 G mbrydon@stgregorys.edu
BRYENTON, John .... 270-686-4615 186 F john.bryenton@kctcs.edu
BRYLINSKY, Jody .... 269-387-2314 239 E jody.brylinsky@wmich.edu
BRYMER, Allison .... 205-726-2762..... 6 G aplemons@samford.edu
BRYMER, Krystin .... 334-244-3758.... 4 E kbrymer@aum.edu
BRYNE, Dara .... 212-484-1347 302 F dbyrne@jjay.cuny.edu
BRYNES, Steve .... 314-977-7363 266 J sbrynes@slu.edu
BRYNGIL, Dave .... 201-761-7302 291 D dbryngil@saintpeters.edu
BRYS-WILSON, Jessica . 252-985-5186 348 A jbrys-wilson@ncwc.edu
BRYSON, Allison .... 541-880-2370 383 E bryson@klamathcc.edu
BRYSON, Barbara .... 520-621-5511.. 16 J bwbryson@email.arizona.edu
BRYSON, Cynthia .... 713-771-5336 121 J cbryson@ict.edu
BRYSON, Lance .... 717-477-1451 407 B jlbrys@ship.edu
BRYSON, Suzanne .... 828-251-6128 351 A sbryson@unca.edu
BRYSON, Terri .... 931-393-1688 437 C tbryson@mscc.edu
BRZEZINSKI, Karen .... 715-675-3331 514 F brzezinski@ntc.edu
BRZORAD, John .... 828-328-7606 339 C john.brzorad@lr.edu
BRZOZOWSKI, Eileen .... 321-433-5687.. 97 N brzozowskie@easternflorida.edu
BRZYCKI, Shelly .... 847-578-8355 150 E shelly.brzycki@rosalindfranklin.edu
BRZYTWA, MaryClare ... 415-503-6263.. 60 H mcbrzytwa@sfcm.edu
BUBB, Kevin .... 517-483-9764 232 K bubbk@lcc.edu
BUBB, Terry .... 615-230-3398 438 C terry.bubb@volstate.edu
BUBNOVA, Elena .... 775-673-8239 279 C ebubnova@tmcc.edu
BUCALOS, Anne .... 502-272-8405 183 H abucalos@bellarmine.edu
BUCARO, S. Ted .... 937-229-4122 372 A sbucaro1@udayton.edu
BUCCI, Taffie .... 412-392-3959 408 F tbucci@pointpark.edu
BUCCIARELLI, Roseann . 732-906-4681 287 B rbucciarelli@middlesexcc.edu
BUCCILLI, Michael .... 203-285-2626.. 85 E mbuccilli@gwcc.commnet.edu
BUCELL, Michael .... 814-732-2252 406 B bucell@edinboro.edu
BUCELLO, Glenn, R .... 716-878-4128 326 E bucellgr@buffalostate.edu
BUCHA, Edward, R .... 724-738-2183 407 C ebucha@srufoundation.org
BUCHAN, Kristina .... 208-535-5477 131 G kristina.buchan@my.eitc.edu
BUCHANAN, April .... 864-455-4145 425 E abuchanan@ghs.org
BUCHANAN, Eddie .... 828-766-1227 344 F ebuchanan@mayland.edu
BUCHANAN, Evelyn .... 317-738-8235 157 L ebuchanan@franklincollege.edu
BUCHANAN, Kelly .... 619-201-8702.. 60 A kelly.buchanan@sdcc.edu
BUCHANAN, Kent, L ..... 405-208-5287 377 D kbuchanan@okcu.edu
BUCHANAN, Lane .... 307-766-5272 517 B lane@uwyo.edu
BUCHANAN, Lauren, A . 724-772-5520 390 J lauren.buchanan@bc3.edu
BUCHANAN, Linda, R ... 229-732-5926 115 B lindabuchanan@andrewcollege.edu
BUCHANAN, Merilyn ..... 805-437-8579.. 31 C merilyn.buchanan@csuci.edu
BUCHANAN, Pamela ..... 828-227-7640 352 C pbuchanan@wcu.edu
BUCHANAN, Russell ..... 610-292-9852 408 I rbuchanan@reseminary.edu
BUCHANAN, Shane .... 931-668-7010 437 C sbuchanan@mscc.edu
BUCHANAN, Trey .... 512-313-3000 446 N trey.buchanan@concordia.edu
BUCHANAN, Wayne ...... 561-803-2000 104 I wayne_buchanan@pba.edu
BUCHE, Nathan .... 620-665-3569 178 D buchen@hutchcc.edu
BUCHELE, Ann .... 541-917-4211 384 A buchela@linnbenton.edu
BUCHELI, Hernan .... 925-631-4060.. 59 C hmb5@stmarys-ca.edu
BUCHER, Denise .... 303-404-5481.. 79 K denise.bucher@frontrange.edu
BUCHER, Jasmine, A .... 717-867-6036 399 J bucher@lvc.edu
BUCHER, Jennifer .... 570-372-4157 410 H bucherjennifer@susqu.edu
BUCHER, Karen, H .... 540-665-4621 485 C kbucher@su.edu
BUCHER, Mary .... 864-503-5197 425 H mbucher@uscupstate.edu
BUCHER, Oskar .... 541-684-7273 384 H obucher@nwcu.edu
BUCHHOLZ, Cindy .... 361-582-2587 470 A cindy.buchholz@victoriacollege.edu
BUCHHOLZ, Reyne, D .... 757-822-1754 489 H rbuchholz@tcc.edu
BUCHHOLZ, Richard ...... 405-422-6204 379 B richard.buchholz@redlandscc.edu
BUCHHOLZ, Robert .... 336-278-5500 337 G rbuchholz@elon.edu
BUCHHOLZ, Ron .... 262-472-1498 512 C buchholr@uww.edu
BUCHHOLZ, Thomas ..... 713-792-2121 469 B
BUCHKO, Lindsay .... 202-448-7037.. 91 H lindsay.buchko@gallaudet.edu
BUCHMAN, Ashley .... 870-512-7812.. 18 D ashley_buchman@asun.edu
BUCHMAN, Lorne, M .... 626-396-2301.. 26 L president@artcenter.edu
BUCHMANN, Teresa ...... 253-833-9111 495 C tbuchmann@greenriver.edu
BUCHWALD, Adam .... 503-768-7227 383 G buchwald@lclark.edu
BUCHWALD, Carrie .... 847-574-5164 143 A cbuchwald@lfgsm.edu
BUCHWALD, Rosalinda . 626-914-8897.. 37 G rbuchwald@citruscollege.edu
BUCHWALD, Staci .... 541-552-6998 386 H buchwalds@sou.edu
BUCHWALDER, Mary, P 937-229-3131 372 A mbuchwalder1@udayton.edu
BUCK, A. Scott .... 252-328-6910 349 I bucka@ecu.edu
BUCK, Charles .... 208-292-1737 132 I buck@uidaho.edu
BUCK, David .... 208-282-3111 132 B buckdavi@isu.edu
BUCK, James, E .... 937-393-3431 370 C jbuck@sscc.edu
BUCK, John .... 314-246-4463 269 N buckjh@webster.edu
BUCK, Joseph, E .... 610-758-4711 400 B job316@lehigh.edu
BUCK, Karen .... 979-209-7280 444 D karenbuck@blinn.edu
BUCK, Katherine .... 973-290-4203 285 A kbuck@cse.edu
BUCK, Kevan, C .... 918-631-3245 381 C kevan-buck@utulsa.edu
BUCK, Kimberly .... 434-797-8458 487 J kimberly.buck@dcc.vccs.edu
BUCK, Leah .... 207-768-2768 200 B lbuck@nmcc.edu
BUCK, Marilyn .... 765-285-1333 156 C mbuck@bsu.edu
BUCK, Ryan .... 512-245-7966 463 A r_b259@txstate.edu
BUCK, Sharon .... 360-452-9277 496 I sbuck@pencol.edu
BUCK, Sylvia, T .... 812-488-2724 164 G sb79@evansville.edu
BUCKALEW, Danielle ..... 205-652-3852.... 9 C bdbuckalew@uwa.edu
BUCKEL, Maria .... 314-889-4533 260 C mbuckel@fontbonne.edu
BUCKELS, Carol .... 386-738-6686 111 E cbuckels@stetson.edu
BUCKENMEYER, Janet ... 812-237-2919 159 C janet.buckenmeyer@indstate.edu
BUCKHAULTS, Tex .... 806-874-3571 445 R tex.buckhaults@clarendoncollege.edu
BUCKHAULTS, Tresea, L .... 318-342-5247 198 A buckhaults@ulm.edu
BUCKHEISTER, Lori .... 678-407-5362 119 F lbuckheister@ggc.edu
BUCKI, SJ, John, P ...... 315-445-4110 312 F buckijp@lemoyne.edu
BUCKINGHAM, Bob, S .. 304-457-6588 501 A buckinghamrs@ab.edu
BUCKINGHAM, Jane ..... 802-258-3367 476 B jane.buckingham@worldlearning.org
BUCKINGHAM, John ..... 319-656-2447 173 C
BUCKINGHAM, Judith, P .... 936-468-4048 458 A jpbuckingham@sfasu.edu
BUCKINGHAM, Richard . 617-573-8605 224 I rbuckingham@suffolk.edu
BUCKINGHAM, Stacy .... 618-985-3741 141 D stacybuckingham@jalc.edu
BUCKLAND, Steve .... 517-264-3109 226 F sbuckland@adrian.edu
BUCKLER, C. Adam .... 317-896-9324 164 F abuckler@ubca.org
BUCKLES, Beverly, J ..... 909-558-4528.. 48 H bbuckles@llu.edu
BUCKLES, Dale .... 270-706-8431 185 H dale.buckles@kctcs.edu
BUCKLES, Gregory, B ... 802-443-5161 475 G deanofadmissions@middlebury.edu
BUCKLES, Jennifer .... 423-425-4677 440 A jennifer-buckles@utc.edu
BUCKLEW, Andrea, J .... 304-457-6438 501 A bucklewaj@ab.edu
BUCKLEW, Kathy .... 863-297-1016 105 F kbucklew@polk.edu
BUCKLEY, Alison .... 443-518-4133 204 E abuckley@howardcc.edu
BUCKLEY, Anne .... 205-934-9518..... 8 B abuckley@uab.edu
BUCKLEY, Cynthia, S .... 405-466-3204 375 L csbuckley@langston.edu
BUCKLEY, David .... 530-898-6411.. 31 D dbuckley@csuchico.edu
BUCKLEY, Debi .... 479-619-4217.. 20 F dbuckley@nwacc.edu
BUCKLEY, Emily .... 913-621-8731 177 A ebuckley@donnelly.edu
BUCKLEY, Gerard .... 315-781-3701 310 C buckley@hws.edu
BUCKLEY, Gerard, J ...... 585-475-6317 321 D gbuckley@ntid.rit.edu
BUCKLEY, Irene .... 914-674-7308 314 I ibuckley@mercy.edu
BUCKLEY, Jennifer .... 630-844-6155 133 H jbuckley@aurora.edu
BUCKLEY, Jerry .... 661-362-3410.. 39 C jerry.buckley@canyons.edu
BUCKLEY, John, M .... 302-857-1200.. 90 F john.buckley@dtcc.edu
BUCKLEY, John, W .... 718-817-4000 308 G jbuckley@fordham.edu
BUCKLEY, Larry .... 530-251-8839.. 47 J lbuckley@lassencollege.edu
BUCKLEY, Laura .... 617-405-5958 223 H lbuckley@quincycollege.edu
BUCKLEY, Linda .... 209-946-2787.. 70 F lbuckley@pacific.edu

BUNYARD, Magen ... 325-649-8613 450 H mbunyard@hputx.edu
BUNYI, Beth ... 760-630-1555 .. 28 B
BUOL, Deborah, L ... 563-589-3223 173 J dbuol@dbq.edu
BUONO, Lisa ... 805-493-3663 .. 30 E llbuono@callutheran.edu
BUOSCIO, Amy ... 708-237-5050 148 A abuoscio@nc.edu
BURAK, Deborah ... 610-861-4137 403 B dburak@northampton.edu
BURAK, Marshall, J ... 510-628-8016 .. 48 F mburak@lincolnuca.edu
BURBA, Dave ... 530-541-4660 .. 47 I burba@ltcc.edu
BURBA, Randy ... 714-997-6763 .. 36 G burba@chapman.edu
BURBACK, Michael ... 202-884-9812 .. 93 C burbackm@trinitydc.edu
BURBANTE, Gilberto ... 985-448-4208 197 C gilberto.burbante@nicholls.edu
BURBEY, Denise ... 716-338-1250 311 F deniseburbey@mail.sunyjcc.edu
BURCAT, Dina ... 646-592-4486 334 P burcat@yu.edu
BURCH, Beth ... 503-253-3443 385 B bburch@ocom.edu
BURCH, Christopher, L . 240-895-3115 206 G clburch@smcm.edu
BURCH, Chuck, S ... 704-406-4342 337 H cburch@gardner-webb.edu
BURCH, Doug ... 801-622-1573 472 H doug.burch@stevenshenager.edu
BURCH, Doug ... 801-622-1573 472 H doug.burch@stevenhenager.edu
BURCH, Franki ... 704-406-3522 337 H fburch@gardner-webb.edu
BURCH, Jim ... 912-443-5874 125 D jburch@savannahtech.edu
BURCH, John ... 731-881-7070 440 B jburch5@utm.edu
BURCH, Rhonda ... 812-866-7014 158 C burch@hanover.edu
BURCH, Sam ... 404-962-3263 127 G sam.burch@usg.edu
BURCH, Stacie ... 410-777-1963 202 D sqburch@aacc.edu
BURCH, Susan ... 406-756-3839 271 A sburch@fvcc.edu
BURCH-SIMS, G. Pamela ... 615-963-7043 438 E psims@tnstate.edu
BURCHAM, Timothy ... 870-972-2085 .. 18 A tburcham@astate.edu
BURCHAM, CFRE, Timothy, R ... 859-256-3100 185 D tim.burcham@kctcs.edu
BURCHARD, Bob, P ... 573-875-7410 258 F rpburchard@ccis.edu
BURCHARD, Elizabeth, B ... 802-443-5201 475 G eboudah@middlebury.edu
BURCHARD, Eric ... 740-593-1804 368 G burchard@ohio.edu
BURCHELL, Chad ... 801-627-8388 472 D burchelc@owatc.edu
BURCHETT, Amy ... 432-264-5063 450 G aburchett@howardcollege.edu
BURCHETT, Bonnie, L ... 423-439-4446 431 H bonnie@etsu.edu
BURCHETT, Dick ... 501-812-2238 .. 23 C dburchett@pulaskitech.edu
BURCHETT, Jody ... 740-588-1277 374 G jburchett@zanestate.edu
BURCHETT, Kevin ... 734-423-2139 233 E
BURCHETT, Lance, E ... 501-686-5987 .. 22 C leburchett@uams.edu
BURCHFIELD, Doug ... 828-627-4632 343 G ddburchfield@haywood.edu
BURCHFIELD, Nettie, L . 985-549-2068 197 E nburchfield@selu.edu
BURCK, Renee ... 517-264-3999 226 F rburck@adrian.edu
BURCKEL, Daryl ... 337-475-5556 197 B dburckel@mcneese.edu
BURD, Gail, D ... 520-626-4099 .. 16 J gburd@email.arizona.edu
BURD, Randy, M ... 520-626-1863 .. 16 J rburd@u.arizona.edu
BURDA, Ed ... 304-457-6238 501 A burdaep@ab.edu
BURDEN, Kathlyn ... 770-229-3328 126 B kburden@sctech.edu
BURDEN, Matthew ... 630-637-5433 147 E mburden@noctrl.edu
BURDEN, Regina ... 334-724-4746 .... 7 F rburden@mytu.tuskegee.edu
BURDEN, Velma ... 912-478-5421 120 E vburden@georgiasouthern.edu
BURDETTE, David ... 270-809-6979 188 D dburdette@murraystate.edu
BURDETTE, Vinson ... 803-508-7244 418 C burdettv@atc.edu
BURDETTE, William ... 304-696-6523 504 C burdette@marshall.edu
BURDICK, Alexis ... 805-765-9307 .. 62 D alexisburdick@collegesoflaw.edu
BURDICK, Evelyn, P ... 708-209-3259 136 I evelyn.burdick@cuchicago.edu
BURDICK, Jonathan ... 585-275-6805 332 E jonathan.burdick@rochester.edu
BURDICK, Julie ... 614-251-4588 367 F burdickj@ohiodominican.edu
BURDICK, Kirsten, N ... 205-934-4319 .... 8 B knburdick@uab.edu
BURDICK, Mary Ellen ... 315-684-6461 329 F burdicme@morrisville.edu
BURDINE, Mike ... 208-459-5663 131 H mburdine@collegeofidaho.edu
BURDISS, Marc ... 928-523-6249 .. 14 K marc.burdiss@nau.edu
BURDSALL, Dawn, M ... 610-660-1333 409 H dburdsal@sju.edu
BURDUE, JoEllen ... 414-277-7117 509 A burdue@msoe.edu
BURDZINSKI, Donna, R 352-797-5001 105 C burdzid@phsc.edu
BURDZINSKI, Kenneth, R ... 727-816-3412 105 C burdzink@phsc.edu
BURFORD, Kristina ... 501-450-1362 .. 19 I burford@hendrix.edu
BURFORD, Kyla ... 618-252-5400 151 J kyla.burford@sic.edu
BURG, James ... 260-481-4146 160 D burgj@ipfw.edu
BURG, Jennifer, R ... 802-447-4007 476 C jburg@svc.edu
BURG, Mary, G ... 785-864-3131 181 I mburg@ku.edu
BURGARD, Bambi ... 816-802-3455 261 C bburgard@kcai.edu
BURGARD, Daniel ... 817-735-2589 466 D daniel.burgard@unthsc.edu
BURGAU, Tam ... 715-858-1377 513 E tburgau@cvtc.edu
BURGAY, Stephen, P ... 617-353-1168 212 G burgay@bu.edu
BURGE, Charles ... 954-771-0376 102 W cburge@knoxseminary.edu
BURGE, David ... 703-993-5487 481 B dburge@gmu.edu
BURGE, Jennifer, G ... 309-677-4939 134 G jgruening@bradley.edu
BURGENER, Kelly, T ... 208-496-1119 131 D burgenerk@byui.edu
BURGER, Arnold ... 615-329-8516 431 I aburger@fisk.edu
BURGER, Bill ... 802-443-5834 475 G bburger@middlebury.edu
BURGER, Cindy, L ... 717-796-1800 401 L cburger@messiah.edu
BURGER, Cory ... 701-845-7302 354 E cory.burger@vcsu.edu
BURGER, Crystal ... 870-733-6831 .. 18 B ccburger@asumidsouth.edu
BURGER, Edward, B ... 512-863-1454 457 I burger@southwestern.edu
BURGER, Lisa ... 701-777-4706 353 G lisa.burger@und.edu
BURGER, Mark ... 417-667-8181 259 A mburger@cottey.edu
BURGER, Michael ... 334-244-3380 .... 4 E mburger1@aum.edu
BURGER, Rosemary ... 570-348-6280 401 B burger@marywood.edu
BURGESS, Aaron ... 513-244-8148 359 E aaron.burgess@ccuniversity.edu
BURGESS, Brenda, K ... 580-774-3000 380 B brenda.burgess@swosu.edu
BURGESS, Douglas ... 513-556-9900 371 E douglas.burgess@uc.edu
BURGESS, Duncan ... 206-934-6882 497 J duncan.burgess@seattlecolleges.edu
BURGESS, Eric ... 573-681-5609 261 H burgesse@lincolnu.edu
BURGESS, Esther ... 252-985-5134 348 A eburgess@ncwc.edu
BURGESS, Frederick ... 607-255-2000 306 B
BURGESS, Jodi ... 540-863-2835 487 I jburgess@dslcc.edu
BURGESS, Kimberly ... 386-481-2668 .. 95 J burgessk@cookman.edu
BURGESS, Marcus ... 305-626-1443 .. 99 M marcus.burgess@fmuniv.edu
BURGESS, Norma ... 615-966-6146 433 D norma.burgess@lipscomb.edu
BURGESS, Shane, C ... 520-621-7621 .. 16 J shaneburgess@email.arizona.edu
BURGESS, Stacy ... 530-226-4961 .. 64 B sburgess@simpsonu.edu
BURGESS, Sylvia ... 580-581-2284 375 A sylviab@cameron.edu
BURGESS, Valerie ... 603-880-8308 282 D vburgess@thomasmorecollege.edu
BURGEST, Arisa ... 404-756-4442 115 I aburgest@atlm.edu
BURGETT, Paul, J ... 585-275-2758 332 E pburgett@admin.rochester.edu
BURGGRAFF, Lucy ... 919-573-5350 349 A
BURGHER, Louis, W ... 402-552-2586 273 K burgherlouis@clarksoncollege.edu
BURGIN, David ... 419-251-7331 365 C david.burgin@mercycollege.edu
BURGIN, Jeffery ... 615-460-6407 430 D jeffery.burgin@belmont.edu
BURGIN, Sheila ... 360-442-2132 495 G sburgin@lowercolumbia.edu
BURGMAYER, Sharon ... 610-526-5106 390 G sburmay@brynmawr.edu
BURGNER, Daniel ... 806-742-0502 463 D daniel.burgner@ttu.edu
BURGNER, Ryan, C ... 308-635-6798 278 B burgnerr@wncc.edu
BURGOS, Gerardo ... 787-279-1912 523 J gburgos@bayamon.inter.edu
BURGOS, Jorge, A ... 787-720-4476 527 A decanatoestudiantes@mizpa.edu
BURGOS, Kathy ... 562-860-2451 .. 36 A kburgos@cerritos.edu
BURGOS, Maida ... 305-821-3333 100 A mburgos@fnu.edu
BURGOYNE, Bonnie ... 870-512-7740 .. 18 D bonnie_burgoyne@asun.edu
BURIK, Larry ... 909-607-2226 .. 57 C larry_burik@pitzer.edu
BURILLO, Madeline ... 713-718-7748 450 D madeline.burillo@hccs.edu
BURISH, Thomas, G ... 574-631-6631 165 A burish.2@nd.edu
BURK, Ann, M ... 308-432-6311 276 B aburk@csc.edu
BURK, Thomas ... 973-328-5037 285 B tburk@ccm.edu
BURKE, Andrew ... 575-646-2431 295 B aburke@nmsu.edu
BURKE, Barbara ... 718-260-5173 303 D bburke@citytech.cuny.edu
BURKE, Belinda ... 302-736-2484 .. 90 J belinda.burke@wesley.edu
BURKE, Brenda ... 801-581-7466 472 P bburke@sa.utah.edu
BURKE, Brian, W ... 413-545-2204 216 H bwburke@external.umass.edu
BURKE, Bridget ... 307-766-2474 517 B
BURKE, Carson ... 330-923-9959 361 I cburke@fortiscollege.edu
BURKE, Cathleen, C ... 804-828-0179 487 E ccburke@vcu.edu
BURKE, Chelsey ... 828-251-6501 351 A cburke@unca.edu
BURKE, Christy ... 740-376-4708 365 A christy.burke@marietta.edu
BURKE, Clarence ... 919-572-1625 335 F cburke@apexsot.edu
BURKE, Colleen ... 215-572-2785 389 D burkec@arcadia.edu
BURKE, Courtney ... 518-262-9590 297 L burkec4@mail.amc.edu
BURKE, Dale ... 808-544-9394 129 C dburke@hpu.edu
BURKE, Derek, A ... 252-398-6369 336 K burked@chowan.edu
BURKE, Donald, S ... 412-624-3001 412 I donburke@pitt.edu
BURKE, Greg ... 812-749-1288 163 B gburke@oak.edu
BURKE, Greg ... 318-357-5251 197 D burkeg@nsula.edu
BURKE, Indy ... 203-432-5109 .. 89 G indy.burke@yale.edu
BURKE, James ... 216-397-4484 363 H burke@jcu.edu
BURKE, Jeanmarie, R ... 315-568-3869 317 A jburke@nycc.edu
BURKE, Joe ... 620-421-6700 179 D joeburke@labette.edu
BURKE, John ... 845-848-4079 306 G john.burke@dc.edu
BURKE, John ... 361-570-4840 465 D burkej@uhv.edu
BURKE, John, D ... 617-552-3387 212 E john.burke.7@bc.edu
BURKE, Jonathan ... 949-376-6000 .. 47 H jburke@lcad.edu
BURKE, Jonathan, L ... 816-604-6620 262 G jon.burke@mcckc.edu
BURKE, Joseph, D ... 256-228-6001 .... 3 B burkej@nacc.edu
BURKE, Joy ... 814-371-2090 411 H jburke@triangle-tech.edu
BURKE, Kathleen, F ... 818-719-6408 .. 49 D kburke@piercecollege.edu
BURKE, Kelly, J ... 336-334-5375 351 D kjburke@uncg.edu
BURKE, Keri ... 503-883-2269 383 H kburke@linfield.edu
BURKE, Kevin ... 717-358-3981 395 G kevin.burke@fandm.edu
BURKE, Kevin, F ... 303-458-4087 .. 82 D kburke@regis.edu
BURKE, Kimberly, G ... 601-974-1250 254 A burkekg@millsaps.edu
BURKE, Letitia ... 201-327-8877 285 J lburke@eastwick.edu
BURKE, Lillian ... 410-225-4219 205 C lburke@mica.edu
BURKE, Lisa ... 630-617-5197 138 C lisab@elmhurst.edu
BURKE, Marcilynn ... 541-346-1000 387 F
BURKE, Mary ... 301-405-7766 207 G mburke21@umd.edu
BURKE, Mary, E ... 617-984-1640 223 H mburke@quincycollege.edu
BURKE, Matthew ... 617-928-4500 222 D mburke@mountida.edu
BURKE, Melinda, W ... 520-621-3557 .. 16 J mwburke@email.arizona.edu
BURKE, Michael, L ... 951-222-8800 .. 58 E michael.burke@rccd.edu
BURKE, Neva ... 901-435-1601 433 A neva_burke@loc.edu
BURKE, Pamela, B ... 540-665-4925 485 C psmulovi@su.edu
BURKE, Peggy ... 773-325-4605 137 C pburke@depaul.edu
BURKE, Sandra ... 662-252-8000 255 F sburke@rustcollege.edu
BURKE, Scott ... 617-928-7337 222 D sburke@mountida.edu
BURKE, Scott, M ... 404-413-2088 121 A sburke@gsu.edu
BURKE, Seth ... 540-665-6257 485 C sburke@su.edu
BURKE, Sharon ... 432-552-2747 469 D burke_s@utpb.edu
BURKE, Stephen ... 570-348-6282 401 B burke@marywood.edu
BURKE, Ted ... 508-541-1774 214 C tburke@dean.edu
BURKE, Thomas ... 410-864-3602 207 A tburke@stmarys.edu
BURKE, Thomas ... 601-266-5020 256 E thomas.burke@usm.edu
BURKE, Thomas, J ... 661-336-5104 .. 46 O tburke@kccd.edu
BURKE, Tracie, L ... 901-321-3357 431 A tburke@cbu.edu
BURKE, Vic ... 912-443-5500 125 D vburke@savannahtech.edu
BURKE, William, R ... 570-941-7887 413 F william.burke@scranton.edu
BURKE-DOE, Annie ... 760-591-3012 .. 71 I aburkedoe@usa.edu
BURKE-SULLIVAN, Eileen, C ... 402-280-3285 274 D e_burkesullivan@creighton.edu
BURKEE, James ... 914-337-9300 305 F james.burkee@concordia-ny.edu
BURKERT, Amy, L ... 412-268-5865 391 H ak11@andrew.cmu.edu
BURKES, Kate ... 479-619-4299 .. 20 F kburkes@nwacc.edu
BURKET, Lisa ... 317-896-9324 164 F lburket@ubca.org
BURKETT, Holly, L ... 865-981-5302 437 F hlburkett@pstcc.edu
BURKETT, James ... 407-447-7300 101 B jburkett@ftccollege.edu
BURKETT, Kaia ... 510-587-7890 .. 56 I kburkett@peralta.edu
BURKETT, Nancy ... 610-328-8651 410 I nburket1@swarthmore.edu
BURKETT, Norvel ... 865-974-3181 439 I nburkett@utk.edu
BURKETT, Timothy ... 704-847-5600 349 E itadmin@ses.edu
BURKEY, Daniel, E ... 402-280-2131 274 D dburkey@creighton.edu

BURSZTYN, Jacob .... 732-367-1060 283 K
jbursztyn@bmg.edu
BURT, Andrea .... 517-264-3100 226 F
aburt@adrian.edu
BURT, Charles .... 617-745-3725 214 D
charles.burt@enc.edu
BURT, Mickey, G .... 563-884-5451 172 H
mickey.burt@palmer.edu
BURTI, Ellen .... 718-940-5852 322 G
eburti@sjcny.edu
BURTIS, Karen, B .... 307-674-6446 516 P
kburtis@sheridan.edu
BURTLE, Melissa .... 229-217-4210 126 C
mburtle@southernregional.edu
BURTLEY, Harold .... 219-980-6539 160 C
hburtley@iun.edu
BURTNETT, Jody .... 217-875-7211 149 J
jburtnett@richland.edu
BURTON, Adam .... 951-343-4286.. 28 G
aburton@calbaptist.edu
BURTON, Adrienne .... 714-895-5103.. 38 G
aburton@gwc.cccd.edu
BURTON, Alan .... 580-745-2731 379 J
aburton@se.edu
BURTON, Andre, L .... 330-325-6733 366 F
aburton@neomed.edu
BURTON, Barbara .... 309-694-8817 139 G
barbara.burton@icc.edu
BURTON, Becky .... 706-583-2818 115 H
bburton@athenstech.edu
BURTON, Ben .... 317-921-4712 161 F
bburton@ivytech.edu
BURTON, Carol .... 828-227-7495 352 C
burton@wcu.edu
BURTON, Carolyn .... 410-778-2800 210 A
cburton2@washcoll.edu
BURTON, Chet .... 775-445-4236 279 F
chester.burton@wnc.edu
BURTON, Clen .... 409-933-8261 446 H
clenburton@com.edu
BURTON, Deborah .... 800-856-9544 273 C
BURTON, Derrick .... 641-585-8671 174 B
derrick.burton@waldorf.edu
BURTON, Donald, N .... 602-648-5750.. 12 H
dburton@dunlap-stone.edu
BURTON, Elisabeth .... 610-399-2710 405 G
eburton@cheyney.edu
BURTON, Elizabeth .... 610-399-2427 405 G
eburton@cheyney.edu
BURTON, Gregory, A .... 973-761-9362 291 F
gregory.burton@shu.edu
BURTON, Heather .... 540-868-7201 488 E
hburton@lfcc.edu
BURTON, Hyacinth .... 256-726-7070.... 6 E
hburton@oakwood.edu
BURTON, Jan .... 801-627-8309 472 D
burtonj@owatc.edu
BURTON, Khalilah .... 251-981-3771.... 5 A
khalilah.burton@columbiasouthern.edu
BURTON, Larry .... 336-272-7102 338 B
lwburton@greensboro.edu
BURTON, Lonnie .... 806-291-3635 470 I
burtonl@wbu.edu
BURTON, Mel .... 770-426-2986 122 F
mel.burton@life.edu
BURTON, Melody .... 503-517-1369 388 A
mburton@warnerpacific.edu
BURTON, Nathan .... 304-766-4354 505 A
nburton2@wvstateu.edu
BURTON, Patrice .... 708-596-2000 151 H
pburton@ssc.edu
BURTON, Raymond, A .... 804-523-5374 488 C
rburton@reynolds.edu
BURTON, Robert .... 808-984-3245 130 H
reburton@hawaii.edu
BURTON, Sharon .... 270-831-9646 186 A
sharon.burton@kctcs.edu
BURTON, Stacy .... 775-784-1740 279 E
sburton@unr.edu
BURTON, Terrance .... 508-999-8664 217 A
tburton@umassd.edu
BURTON, Timothy, P .... 516-877-3385 297 I
burton@adelphi.edu
BURTON, Velmer, S .... 501-569-3204.. 22 B
vsburton@ualr.edu
BURTON, JR.,
Velmer, S .... 662-915-1081 256 C
vsburton@olemiss.edu
BURTON-GOSS, Sadie .... 781-239-6334 211 A
sburtongoss@babson.edu
BURTON-KRIEGER,
Meagan .... 317-940-9901 156 I
mburtonk@butler.edu
BURWASH, Laura .... 270-384-8065 187 H
burwashl@lindsey.edu
BURWELL, Elissia .... 903-593-8311 461 B
eburwell@texascollege.edu

BURWELL, Jessica .... 425-640-1654 494 E
jessica.e.burwell@edcc.edu
BURWELL, Sylvia, M .... 202-885-2121.. 91 C
president@american.edu
BURY, John .... 918-631-2602 381 C
john-bury@utulsa.edu
BURZACHECHI,
Nancilee .... 412-237-4684 392 G
nancilee@ccac.edu
BURZICHELLI,
Dominick .... 856-415-2292 289 G
dburzichelli@rcgc.edu
BURZINSKI, Jody .... 620-421-6700 179 D
jodyb@labette.edu
BUSALACCHI, Richard .... 414-297-6969 514 C
busalacr@matc.edu
BUSAM KLENOWSKI,
Leah .... 513-745-4879 374 D
busaml@xavier.edu
BUSBEE, Walter .... 803-508-7254 418 C
busbeew@atc.edu
BUSBY, Dwayne .... 281-283-2019 465 B
busby@uhcl.edu
BUSBY, Joshua .... 405-466-3445 375 L
jabusby@langston.edu
BUSBY, Katie .... 662-915-5026 256 C
kbusby@olemiss.edu
BUSBY, Laura .... 801-863-8456 473 D
lbusby@uvu.edu
BUSBY, Martha .... 404-835-6121 435 M
mbusby@richmont.edu
BUSBY, Teresa .... 601-446-1211 252 G
teresa.busby@colin.edu
BUSCEMI, Vince .... 410-857-2290 205 E
vbuscemi@mcdaniel.edu
BUSCENI, Paul .... 312-752-2430 142 E
paul.busceni@kendall.edu
BUSCH, Brian .... 252-789-0247 344 E
bbusch@martincc.edu
BUSCH, Caroline, C .... 804-752-3267 484 C
cbusch@rmc.edu
BUSCH, Nancy .... 402-472-2526 277 G
nbusch2@unl.edu
BUSCHART, W. David .... 303-762-6907.. 79 G
david.buschart@denverseminary.edu
BUSCHER, Frank .... 630-844-5252 133 H
fbuscher@aurora.edu
BUSCHER, Frank, M .... 630-844-5252 133 H
fbuscher@aurora.edu
BUSCHER, Kristin .... 402-872-2298 276 C
kbuscher@peru.edu
BUSCHMAN, John, E .... 973-761-9005 291 F
john.buschman@shu.edu
BUSE, Carol .... 806-371-5994 442 D
acbuse@actx.edu
BUSE, Jon .... 319-398-4977 171 F
jon.buse@kirkwood.edu
BUSE, Kathleen .... 973-618-3411 284 D
kbuse@caldwell.edu
BUSE, William .... 212-799-5000 312 B
BUSEL, Yaakov .... 732-985-6533 289 A
BUSENBARK, Susan .... 815-921-4644 150 A
s.busenbark@rockvalleycollege.edu
BUSER, Boyd, R .... 606-218-5411 190 E
boydbuser@upike.edu
BUSH, Catherine .... 440-525-7119 364 D
cbush@lakelandcc.edu
BUSH, Cathy .... 440-525-7112 364 D
cbush@lakelandcc.edu
BUSH, Cody .... 931-221-7561 430 B
bushc@apsu.edu
BUSH, Darren .... 657-278-7271.. 32 B
dlbush@fullerton.edu
BUSH, David .... 435-797-1012 473 C
david.bush@usu.edu
BUSH, Edward, C .... 916-691-7321.. 50 G
bushe@crc.losrios.edu
BUSH, Janis .... 301-387-3049 203 I
janis.bush@garrettcollege.edu
BUSH, Jeffrey .... 304-457-6484 501 A
bushjt@ab.edu
BUSH, Jim .... 509-865-8570 495 D
bush_j@heritage.edu
BUSH, Keith .... 218-751-8670 249 G
it@oakhills.edu
BUSH, Kristen .... 540-231-1796 490 F
khbush@vt.edu
BUSH, Lisa, F .... 828-398-7202 340 M
lbush@abtech.edu
BUSH, Lonica .... 409-933-8413 446 H
lbush@com.edu
BUSH, Michael .... 805-678-5813.. 73 B
mbush@vcccd.edu
BUSH, Mickie .... 503-494-7800 385 D
regohsu@ohsu.edu
BUSH, Polly .... 585-340-9500 304 F
pbush@crcds.edu

BUSH, Tyre .... 607-962-9540 306 C
tbush4@corning-cc.edu
BUSHEE, Toby .... 909-748-8133.. 71 H
toby_bushee@redlands.edu
BUSHEY, Jane, L .... 480-245-7930.. 13 C
jane.bushey@ibcs.edu
BUSHEY, Stephanie .... 516-463-6853 310 D
stephanie.bushey@hofstra.edu
BUSHMAN, David, W .... 540-828-5605 478 J
dbushman@bridgewater.edu
BUSHNELL, Lynn, M .... 203-582-8651.. 88 A
lynn.bushnell@quinnipiac.edu
BUSHNELL, Ryan .... 517-321-0242 231 A
rbushnell@glcc.edu
BUSHONG, Sara .... 419-372-2856 357 F
sbushon@bgsu.edu
BUSHWAY, Deborah .... 952-887-1392 249 F
dbushway@nwhealth.edu
BUSKIRK, Susan .... 410-706-4937 207 H
sbuskirk@umaryland.edu
BUSS, Brian .... 920-735-5792 513 F
buss@fvtc.edu
BUSS, James, J .... 410-546-6902 209 B
jjbuss@salisbury.edu
BUSS, Marney .... 508-213-2101 223 C
marney.buss@nichols.edu
BUSSARD, Patsy, G .... 276-964-7332 489 F
pat.bussard@sw.edu
BUSSE, Dan .... 850-484-1158 105 E
dbusse@pensacolastate.edu
BUSSE, Max .... 214-333-5104 447 D
maxwellb@dbu.edu
BUSSELL, Helena .... 817-531-4405 463 G
hbussell@txwes.edu
BUSSELL, Paige .... 903-468-3209 459 E
paige.bussell@tamuc.edu
BUSSELL, Rachelle .... 909-558-4544.. 48 H
rbussell@llu.edu
BUSSELL, Shawn .... 419-824-3785 364 G
sbussell@lourdes.edu
BUSSEY, Brenda .... 508-929-8455 219 A
bbussey@worcester.edu
BUSSEY, Kevin .... 217-228-5432 149 B
busske@quincy.edu
BUSSEY, Tosha .... 404-225-4596 115 J
tbussey@atlantatech.edu
BUSTAMANTE, Camilla .. 505-428-1388 296 B
camilla.bustamante@sfcc.edu
BUSTAMANTE, Chris .... 480-517-8118.. 14 B
chris.bustamante@riosalado.edu
BUSTARD, James .... 217-351-2211 148 H
jbustard@parkland.edu
BUSTER-WILLIAMS,
Kimberley .... 540-654-1618 486 D
kwilli23@umw.edu
BUSTINZA, Reggie .... 815-753-8821 147 H
rbustinza@niu.edu
BUSTOS, Phillip .... 505-224-4741 293 L
pbustos@cnm.edu
BUTALA, Doug .... 605-882-5284 427 D
doug.butala@lakeareatech.edu
BUTCARIS, Michael .... 203-857-7000.. 86 D
BUTCHER, Alva .... 253-879-3394 499 C
abutcher@pugetsound.edu
BUTCHER, Claudette .... 918-293-5256 378 B
claudette.butcher@okstate.edu
BUTCHER, Emily .... 716-664-5100 311 E
BUTCHER, Marilea .... 304-647-6367 504 F
mbutcher@osteo.wvsom.edu
BUTCHER, Melissa .... 712-749-2049 167 C
butcherm@bvu.edu
BUTCHER, Michael .... 912-279-5815 118 A
mbutcher@ccga.edu
BUTCHER, Phil .... 713-942-3409 466 J
butchep@stthom.edu
BUTCHER, Teri .... 248-218-2042 236 C
tbutcher@rc.edu
BUTCHER, Thomas, A .... 616-331-2067 230 G
butchert@gvsu.edu
BUTCHER, Tina .... 706-507-8951 118 C
butcher_tina@columbusstate.edu
BUTCHKO, Thomas .... 570-208-5928 398 D
thomasbutchko@kings.edu
BUTDORFF, Carla .... 419-747-5401 366 E
196mgr@fheg.follett.com
BUTERA, Peter .... 716-286-8060 318 F
pbutera@niagara.edu
BUTERA, Rae-Anne .... 781-292-2321 215 C
rae-anne.butera@olin.edu
BUTERA, Vince .... 847-578-8374 150 E
vince.butera@rosalindfranklin.edu
BUTIKOFER, Jason .... 435-865-8330 473 A
jasonbutikofer@suu.edu
BUTIN, Dan .... 978-837-5338 221 G
dan.butin@merrimack.edu
BUTKOVICH, Michelle .... 248-204-2111 233 A
mbutkovic@ltu.edu

BUTKUS, Bonnie .... 585-475-5498 321 D
bjbdar@rit.edu
BUTLER, Alison .... 805-893-2622.. 70 B
alison.butler@ucsb.edu
BUTLER, Allen, P .... 815-455-8999 145 B
abutler@mchenry.edu
BUTLER, Andra .... 606-546-1224 189 I
abutler@unionky.edu
BUTLER, Andrea .... 402-466-4774 274 E
andrea.butler@doane.edu
BUTLER, Andrew .... 508-831-6634 226 E
abutler@wpi.edu
BUTLER, Barry .... 386-226-6000.. 98 C
butlerb@erau.edu
BUTLER, Beatrice .... 210-486-2300 441 I
bbutler@alamo.edu
BUTLER, Blake .... 501-760-4176.. 20 D
blake.butler@np.edu
BUTLER, Brady .... 412-536-1300 398 E
brady.butler@laroche.edu
BUTLER, Bruce, D .... 713-500-3369 468 D
bruce.d.butler@uth.tmc.edu
BUTLER, Bryant .... 601-968-5930 252 C
bbutler@belhaven.edu
BUTLER, Connie .... 402-643-7332 274 B
connie.butler@cune.edu
BUTLER, Craig, J .... 304-457-6445 501 A
butlercj@ab.edu
BUTLER, Cynthia .... 214-378-1772 447 F
cbutler@dcccd.edu
BUTLER, David .... 615-898-2182 434 H
david.butler@mtsu.edu
BUTLER, Duan .... 540-374-4300.. 93 B
BUTLER, Eric .... 303-871-7016.. 83 E
eric.butler@du.edu
BUTLER, Greg .... 601-477-4113 253 F
greg.butler@jcjc.edu
BUTLER, Henry .... 703-993-8644 481 B
hnbutler@gmu.edu
BUTLER, Jack .... 931-372-3227 438 F
jbutler@tntech.edu
BUTLER, Janice, R .... 570-577-3973 390 H
janice.butler@bucknell.edu
BUTLER, Jennifer .... 325-674-2630 441 D
jab10a@acu.edu
BUTLER, John, L .... 773-442-4200 147 G
j-butler1@neiu.edu
BUTLER, S.J., John, T .. 617-552-6855 212 E
john.butler@bc.edu
BUTLER, Ken .... 484-664-3126 402 F
kenbutler@muhlenberg.edu
BUTLER, Kevin .... 702-992-2000 279 B
kevin.butler@nsc.edu
BUTLER, Kim, I .... 515-263-2841 169 E
maintenance@grandview.edu
BUTLER, Lee .... 817-598-6345 470 J
cbutler@wc.edu
BUTLER, LeRoy .... 815-836-5923 143 E
butlerle@lewisu.edu
BUTLER, Lisa .... 660-543-4001 268 A
ljbutler@ucmo.edu
BUTLER, Lynn .... 847-543-2974 136 E
lbutler@clcillinois.edu
BUTLER, Margie .... 504-282-4455 195 D
mbutler@nobts.edu
BUTLER, Mary Edith .... 630-466-7900 155 C
mbutler@waubonsee.edu
BUTLER, Michael .... 909-469-5534.. 74 G
mbutler@westernu.edu
BUTLER, Monique .... 510-594-3725.. 28 K
mbutler@cca.edu
BUTLER, Paul, C .... 856-225-6637 290 B
pbutler@camden.rutgers.edu
BUTLER, Rebecca .... 614-287-2180 360 C
rbutler17@cscc.edu
BUTLER, Rebekah .... 617-364-3510 212 D
rbutler@boston.edu
BUTLER, Rhett .... 334-833-4474.... 5 M
chaplain@hawks.huntingdon.edu
BUTLER, Sandy .... 404-364-8870 124 A
sbutler@oglethorpe.edu
BUTLER, Shai .... 518-337-2306 305 B
butlers@strose.edu
BUTLER, Sharon .... 517-884-0101 233 G
sbutler@msu.edu
BUTLER, Sheri .... 318-371-3035 193 A
BUTLER, Stephen, L .... 251-626-3303.... 7 G
sbutler@ussa.edu
BUTLER, Vicki .... 870-235-4026.. 21 F
vjbutler@saumag.edu
BUTLER, Walter .... 731-352-4000 430 E
butlerw@bethelu.edu
BUTLER-PURRY,
Karen, L .... 979-845-8585 459 C
klbutler@tamu.edu
BUTRON, Jo Anna .... 831-646-4099.. 52 G
jbutron@mpc.edu

CAFFARELLI, Joseph ..... 973-720-2714 292 I
caffarellij@wpunj.edu
CAFFERTY, Jack .... 208-459-5168 131 H
jcafferty@collegeofidaho.edu
CAFFEY, Kevin .... 903-923-2011 448 J
kcaffey@etbu.edu
CAFFEY, Rob .... 785-532-6520 179 A
caffey@ksu.edu
CAFFEY, Walter, F .... 203-932-7205.. 89 D
wcaffey@newhaven.edu
CAFFIE, Janique .... 973-328-5149 285 B
jcaffie@ccm.edu
CAFFO, David, C .... 302-356-2474.. 91 B
david.c.caffo@wilmu.edu
CAFILLIO, Nicole .... 312-935-6689 149 K
ncafillio@robertmorris.edu
CAFONCELLI, Kathy, L ... 610-921-7600 388 E
kcafoncelli@albright.edu
CAGE, Beverly .... 361-698-1279 448 H
bacage@delmar.edu
CAGE, John .... 931-540-2587 436 H
jcage2@columbiastate.edu
CAGE, Stephanie .... 636-481-3298 261 B
scage@jeffco.edu
CAGGIANO, Marion .... 973-655-3417 287 D
caggianom@mail.montclair.edu
CAGGIANO, Sarah .... 401-454-6200 417 B
scaggian@risd.edu
CAGIGAS, Marcia .... 323-415-5383.. 48 L
cagigamp@elac.edu
CAGLE, David .... 815-802-8128 142 C
dcagle@kcc.edu
CAGLE, DeVonne .... 903-510-2417 464 D
dcag@tjc.edu
CAGLE, Kathy .... 703-993-8627 481 B
kcagle@gmu.edu
CAGLE, Randy, L .... 218-477-2477 246 B
caglera@mnstate.edu
CAGLE, Sheri .... 815-802-8822 142 C
scagle@kcc.edu
CAGNET, Danny .... 248-218-2190 236 C
dcagnet@rc.edu
CAHALAN, Jodi .... 515-271-1369 168 G
jodi.cahalan@dmu.edu
CAHALAN, SJ,
Patrick, J .... 310-338-5921.. 50 J
pcahalan@lmu.edu
CAHALL, Perry, J .... 614-885-5585 369 D
pcahall@pcj.edu
CAHAN, Susan .... 215-777-9894 411 B
susan.cahan@temple.edu
CAHEN, Robert .... 440-525-7097 364 D
bcahen@lakelandcc.edu
CAHILL, Bridget .... 847-925-6849 139 B
bcahilli@harpercollege.edu
CAHILL, Diane .... 740-593-4330 368 G
cahilld@ohio.edu
CAHILL, Elizabeth .... 215-965-4037 402 C
ecahill@moore.edu
CAHILL, Elizabeth, J ...... 304-384-6003 503 P
lcahill@concord.edu
CAHILL, Holly .... 701-477-7862 355 H
hcahill@tm.edu
CAHILL, Margaret, D ..... 651-962-6131 251 D
mdcahill@stthomas.edu
CAHILL, Melissa, L .... 410-888-9048 205 D
mcahill@muih.edu
CAHILL, Michael, T .... 856-225-6191 290 B
michael.cahill@law.rutgers.edu
CAHILL, Richard .... 859-985-3451 183 I
richard_cahill@berea.edu
CAHILL, Ryan .... 313-883-8696 236 D
cahill.ryan@shms.edu
CAHILL, Tina .... 617-405-5942 223 H
tcahill@quincycollege.edu
CAHN, Judith .... 212-484-1193 302 F
jcahn@jjay.cuny.edu
CAHOON, Kirsten .... 507-786-3268 250 C
cahoon@stolaf.edu
CAI, Maoyi .... 512-444-8082 461 C
cai@thsu.edu
CAILLET, Barb .... 330-684-8935 371 D
naumoff@uakron.edu
CAILLET, Barb .... 330-684-8935 371 D
CAILLOUX, Laura .... 360-679-5333 498 F
laura.cailloux@skagit.edu
CAIN, Candace .... 334-386-7182.... 5 I
ccain@faulkner.edu
CAIN, Chad .... 806-291-3500 470 I
chad.cain@wbu.edu
CAIN, Cheryl .... 361-593-2138 460 B
cheryl.cain@tamuk.edu
CAIN, Christele, N .... 443-518-4148 204 E
ccain2@howardcc.edu
CAIN, Darrell .... 317-917-5702 161 G
dcain@ivytech.edu
CAIN, John .... 352-588-8200 106 N
john.cain@saintleo.edu
CAIN, Katherine .... 314-977-4180 266 J
caink@slu.edu
CAIN, Kevin, G .... 304-462-6201 504 B
kevin.cain@glenville.edu
CAIN, Marcus .... 816-802-3468 261 C
mcain@kcai.edu
CAIN, Michael .... 716-829-2100 325 B
vphs@buffalo.edu
CAIN, Michael, E .... 716-829-3955 325 B
mcain@buffalo.edu
CAIN, Rebekah .... 252-985-5266 348 A
rcain@ncwc.edu
CAIN, Ruth .... 816-235-6084 268 D
cainre@umkc.edu
CAIN, Sandra .... 508-541-1658 214 C
scain@dean.edu
CAIN, Sara Beth .... 619-388-2721.. 60 D
scain@sdccd.edu
CAIN, Stephen, D .... 240-567-1796 205 F
stephen.cain@montgomerycollege.edu
CAIN, Wingate .... 820-652-0632 344 G
wingatecain@mcdowelltech.edu
CAIRES, Matthew .... 406-994-2826 272 A
mcaires@montana.edu
CAIRNS, Charles, B .... 520-626-0998.. 16 J
cairnsc@email.arizona.edu
CAIRNS, Janet .... 918-631-3101 381 C
janet-cairns@utulsa.edu
CAIRNS, Jill .... 207-834-7602 201 E
jillb@maine.edu
CAIRNS, Mike .... 415-451-2817.. 60 I
mcairns@sfts.edu
CAIRO, Jim, R .... 504-568-4246 194 C
jcairo@lsuhsu.edu
CAIROL, Miguel .... 718-260-5600 303 D
mcairol@citytech.cuny.edu
CAIRY, Timothy, J .... 610-499-1193 414 F
tjcairy@widener.edu
CAISON, Anthony .... 919-866-6101 347 D
amcaison@waketech.edu
CAKMAK, Burak .... 212-229-8966 316 E
cakmakb@newschool.edu
CAL, John .... 305-348-4001 109 D
john.cal@fiu.edu
CAL, Mark .... 575-439-3622 295 C
mcal@nmsu.edu
CALA, Catherine .... 330-941-3119 374 E
cacala@ysu.edu
CALABRESE, John .... 586-498-4066 233 B
calabresej93@macomb.edu
CALABRESE, Nancy .... 410-626-2553 206 F
nancy.calabrese@sjc.edu
CALABRESE, Walter .... 252-444-0739 342 E
calabresew@cravencc.edu
CALABRIA, Patrick .... 631-420-2400 329 D
patrick.calabria@farmingdale.edu
CALAF, Jorge .... 787-279-1912 523 J
jcalaf@bayamon.inter.edu
CALAIS, Debra .... 337-482-6199 197 F
dcalais@louisiana.edu
CALAIS, Erica .... 225-342-6950 196 F
erica.calais@la.gov
CALAMAI, Anthony, G ... 828-262-3078 349 H
calamaiag@appstate.edu
CALAMAIO, Caprice .... 913-234-0733 176 H
caprice.calamaio@cleveland.edu
CALAMARE, Susan, S ... 617-422-7387 222 J
scalamare@nesl.edu
CALAMETTI, Jeffrey, D .. 251-442-2242.... 8 D
jcalametti@umobile.edu
CALAMIA, James .... 732-255-0400 288 B
jcalamia@ocean.edu
CALAMIA, John, J .... 504-865-3946 194 G
calamia@loyno.edu
CALANDRA, Viviana ...... 407-303-7894.. 94 H
viviana.calandra@adu.edu
CALARESO, Joe .... 305-595-9500.. 94 F
admissions@amcollege.edu
CALCADO, Antonio .... 848-445-2474 290 A
acalcado@facilities.rutgers.edu
CALDARELLO, Beth .... 660-359-3948 264 H
bcaldarello@mail.ncmissouri.edu
CALDERA, Nancy .... 509-527-2315 499 F
nancy.caldera@wallawalla.edu
CALDERO FIGUEROA,
Ana, J .... 407-582-1431 113 F
acalderofigueroa@valenciacollege.edu
CALDERON, Ann Marie . 615-230-3401 438 C
annmarie.calderon@volstate.edu
CALDERON, Christina ..... 760-252-2411.. 27 A
ccalderon@barstow.edu
CALDERON, Gerardo ..... 209-954-5052.. 61 B
gcalderon@deltacollege.edu
CALDERON, Hermes .... 787-780-0070 521 B
hcalderon@caribbean.edu
CALDERON, Janet .... 407-303-6108.. 94 H
janet.calderon@adu.edu
CALDERON, Nancy, T .... 408-554-4400.. 62 F
ntcalderon@scu.edu
CALDERON, Rosa .... 310-338-8839.. 50 J
rosa.calderon@lmu.edu
CALDERON, Sonny .... 818-333-3558.. 53 I
sonny.calderon@nyfa.edu
CALDERONE, Jackie ...... 508-541-1530 214 C
0558mgr@fheg.follett.com
CALDERSON, Carl .... 619-201-8780.. 60 A
carl.calderson@sdcc.edu
CALDWELL, Adonna ...... 901-572-2592 430 C
adonna.caldwell@bchs.edu
CALDWELL, Agnes .... 419-783-2402 361 A
acaldwell@defiance.edu
CALDWELL, Benjamin .... 903-233-3200 452 A
benjamincaldwell@letu.edu
CALDWELL, Brinda, W .. 828-398-7134 340 M
bcaldwell@abtech.edu
CALDWELL, Cary .... 704-406-3939 337 H
ccaldwell@gardner-webb.edu
CALDWELL, Catherine ... 313-993-1544 237 F
caldwecr@udmercy.edu
CALDWELL, Cheryl .... 417-255-7960 263 I
cherylcaldwell@missouristate.edu
CALDWELL, Craig .... 801-957-5180 474 B
craig.caldwell@slcc.edu
CALDWELL, Dallas .... 405-974-2631 380 J
dcaldwell@uco.edu
CALDWELL, Daniel .... 601-318-6115 256 I
daniel.caldwell@wmcarey.edu
CALDWELL, David .... 615-248-7790 439 B
dcaldwell@trevecca.edu
CALDWELL, David .... 617-745-3705 214 D
david.calwell@enc.edu
CALDWELL, Diana .... 574-936-8898 155 L
diana.caldwell@ancilla.edu
CALDWELL, Donna .... 706-864-1410 127 B
donna.caldwell@ung.edu
CALDWELL, Gail .... 256-726-7024.... 6 E
gcaldwell@oakwood.edu
CALDWELL, Getchel .... 404-880-6189 117 H
gcaldwell@cau.edu
CALDWELL, Getchel .... 910-672-1661 350 B
gcaldwel@uncfsu.edu
CALDWELL, Helen .... 704-378-1014 338 I
hcaldwell@jcsu.edu
CALDWELL, Hollie .... 303-369-5151.. 81 L
hollie.caldwell@plattcolorado.edu
CALDWELL,
Jacqueline, H .... 918-631-2691 381 C
jacqueline-caldwell@utulsa.edu
CALDWELL, James .... 215-780-1306 410 D
jcaldwell@salus.edu
CALDWELL, James .... 215-780-1311 410 D
jcaldwell@salus.edu
CALDWELL, James, O ..... 303-837-0825.. 76 K
caldwellj@aii.edu
CALDWELL, Janet .... 615-327-6851 434 A
jcaldwell@mmc.edu
CALDWELL, Jeff .... 405-733-7395 379 F
jcaldwell@rose.edu
CALDWELL, Jim .... 215-780-1313 410 D
jcaldwell@salus.edu
CALDWELL, Jodi, K .... 912-478-5541 120 E
jodic@georgiasouthern.edu
CALDWELL, Katrina, M .. 662-915-2934 256 C
kmcaldw1@olemiss.edu
CALDWELL, Kisha .... 423-697-3250 436 F
kisha.caldwell@chattanoogastate.edu
CALDWELL, Larry, W ..... 605-336-6588 428 B
lcaldwell@sfseminary.edu
CALDWELL, Nina .... 314-529-9485 262 B
ncaldwell@maryville.edu
CALDWELL, Pamela .... 434-381-6141 485 P
pcaldwell@sbc.edu
CALDWELL, Patrice .... 575-562-2315 293 O
patrice.caldwell@enmu.edu
CALDWELL, Richard ...... 402-898-1000 274 C
rich_c@creativecenter.edu
CALDWELL, Robert, M .. 802-865-6400 474 G
rcaldwell@champlain.edu
CALDWELL, Sandra .... 559-638-0300.. 66 H
sandra.caldwell@reedleycollege.edu
CALDWELL, Sheila .... 678-717-3592 127 B
sheila.caldwell@ung.edu
CALDWELL, OSB,
Teresio .... 503-845-3169 384 C
teresio.caldwell@mtangel.edu
CALDWELL, Timothy ...... 509-777-1000 500 H
tcaldwell@whitworth.edu
CALDWELL, Trish .... 916-484-8354.. 50 F
caldwet@arc.losrios.edu
CALDWELL, Troy .... 740-695-9500 357 D
tcaldwell@belmontcollege.edu
CALDWELL, Virgil .... 505-566-3490 296 A
caldwellv@sanjuancollege.edu
CALDWELL, Ward .... 336-770-3283 352 B
caldwellw@uncsa.edu
CALDWELL, IV,
William, B .... 478-387-4775 120 B
wcaldwell@gmc.edu
CALE, Benjamin .... 304-877-6428 501 E
admissions@abc.edu
CALEB, Peter .... 917-493-4507 313 M
library@msmnyc.edu
CALENDA, Marianne ...... 717-361-1196 394 F
calendam@etown.edu
CALERO, Teofilo .... 773-878-2998 150 I
tcalero@staugustine.edu
CALFAS, Karen, J .... 858-822-7552.. 69 E
kcalfas@ucsd.edu
CALHOUN, Barbara, S ... 470-578-6258 122 C
bcalhoun@kennesaw.edu
CALHOUN, Chantae .... 910-362-7722 341 E
ccalhoun@cfcc.edu
CALHOUN, Cheryl .... 352-395-5719 107 E
cheryl.calhoun@sfcollege.edu
CALHOUN, Deborah, C . 803-934-3216 422 G
dcalhoun@morris.edu
CALHOUN, Dominique .. 713-313-7640 461 E
dominique.calhoun@tsu.edu
CALHOUN, Elizabeth ..... 520-626-9921.. 16 J
ecalhoun@email.arizona.edu
CALHOUN, John .... 619-849-2784.. 57 H
johncalhoun@pointloma.edu
CALHOUN, Kirk, A .... 903-877-7750 469 A
kirk.calhoun@uthct.edu
CALHOUN, Larry .... 912-538-3101 126 A
lcalhoun@southeasterntech.edu
CALHOUN, Linda .... 270-686-4473 186 F
linda.calhoun@kctcs.edu
CALHOUN, Lozanne ...... 870-543-5952.. 21 E
lcalhoun@seark.edu
CALHOUN, M. Grace ..... 215-898-7215 412 G
athdir@pobox.upenn.edu
CALHOUN, Matthew ...... 601-276-3718 256 A
mattc@smcc.edu
CALHOUN, Mitch .... 325-574-7612 470 N
mcalhoun@wtc.edu
CALHOUN, Patrick .... 409-839-2014 462 B
pcalhoun@lit.edu
CALHOUN, Paul .... 518-580-5590 324 D
pcalhoun@skidmore.edu
CALHOUN, Paula, M ..... 330-471-8236 364 H
pcalhoun@malone.edu
CALHOUN, Ralph .... 901-435-1276 433 A
ralph_calhoun@loc.edu
CALHOUN, Rica .... 309-298-3070 155 D
rh-calhoun@wiu.edu
CALHOUN, Rochelle ...... 609-258-3056 288 F
rochelle.calhoun@princeton.edu
CALHOUN, Thomas .... 601-979-1611 253 E
thomas.c.calhoun@jsums.edu
CALHOUN, Thomas, J ... 502-597-5510 187 E
thomas.calhoun@kysu.edu
CALHOUN, Valerie .... 678-359-5021 121 B
valerie_c@gordonstate.edu
CALHOUN, Vaughn, A ... 508-373-9736 211 F
vaughn.calhoun@becker.edu
CALHOUN-BROWN,
Allison .... 404-413-2067 121 A
acalhounbrown@gsu.edu
CALHOUN-FRENCH,
Diane .... 502-213-2621 186 C
diane.calhoun-french@kctcs.edu
CALICA, Corinna .... 925-424-1575.. 36 D
ccalica@laspositascollege.edu
CALILAN, James (Kimo) 707-864-7264.. 64 E
CALISE, Lisa .... 617-287-7050 216 G
lcalise@umassp.edu
CALISE, Thomasina, L ... 203-857-7003.. 86 D
tcalise@norwalk.edu
CALISSI, Barbara .... 516-323-3035 315 J
bcalissi@molloy.edu
CALISTO, George, W ..... 312-553-3149 135 J
gcalisto@ccc.edu
CALIXTO, Grace .... 210-690-9000 449 K
gcalixto@hallmarkuniversity.edu
CALKINS, Gregory .... 513-529-3020 365 I
calkingp@miamioh.edu
CALL, Carolyne .... 717-290-8738 399 F
ccall@lancasterseminary.edu
CALL, Christopher, D .... 805-565-6023.. 74 I
ccall@westmont.edu
CALL, Diane .... 718-631-6222 303 F
dcall@qcc.cuny.edu
CALL, Kevin .... 276-944-6155 480 J
kcall@ehc.edu
CALL, Susan .... 989-386-6604 234 B
scall@midmich.edu
CALL, Tyler .... 801-627-8451 472 D
callt@owatc.edu
CALLAGHAN,
Aloysius, R .... 651-962-5777 251 D
arcallaghan@stthomas.edu

CALLAGHAN, Carolyn ... 717-477-1348 407 B cmcallaghan@ship.edu
CALLAGHAN, Karen, A .. 305-899-3401.. 95 G kcallaghan@barry.edu
CALLAGHAN, MaryEllen 914-633-2512 311 B mcallaghan@iona.edu
CALLAHAN, Amy .... 503-352-2838 385 I amy.callahan@pacificu.edu
CALLAHAN, Audra .... 508-999-8620 217 A acallahan@umassd.edu
CALLAHAN, Candice ..... 718-779-1499 320 C info@plazacollege.edu
CALLAHAN, Caroline ..... 718-779-1499 320 C cmc@plazacollege.edu
CALLAHAN, III, Charles, E .... 718-779-1499 320 C cec3@plazacollege.edu
CALLAHAN, IV, Charles, E .... 718-779-1499 320 C cec4@plazacollege.edu
CALLAHAN, Cheryl, M .. 336-334-5099 351 D cmcallah@uncg.edu
CALLAHAN, Christopher 602-496-5012.. 10 K christopher.callahan@asu.edu
CALLAHAN, Clara, A ..... 215-955-6983 411 E clara.callahan@jefferson.edu
CALLAHAN, Joy, T .... 919-209-2027 344 C jtcallahan@johnstoncc.edu
CALLAHAN, Julie .... 603-645-9611 282 C j.callahan@snhu.edu
CALLAHAN, Margaret, F 708-216-3223 144 D mcallahan@luc.edu
CALLAHAN, Mary .... 617-258-6432 221 C
CALLAHAN, Michael .... 805-289-6344.. 73 C mcallahan@vcccd.edu
CALLAHAN, Patricia ...... 978-762-4000 220 E tcallaha@northshore.edu
CALLAHAN, Patrick, F ... 914-251-6435 328 B patrick.callahan@purchase.edu
CALLAHAN, Phyllis .... 513-529-6721 365 I callahp@miamioh.edu
CALLAHAN, Robert .... 319-363-1323 172 B rcallahan@mtmercy.edu
CALLAHAN, Sean .... 678-872-8542 119 G scallaha@highlands.edu
CALLAHAN, Tristin .... 256-840-4219.... 3 F tcallahan@snead.edu
CALLAN, Pam .... 325-481-8300 450 G pcallan@howardcollege.edu
CALLANAN, Cara .... 978-921-4242 222 B cara.callanan@montserrat.edu
CALLAND, Dana .... 606-759-7141 186 E dana.calland@kctcs.edu
CALLAND, David .... 434-592-7336 482 D dcalland@liberty.edu
CALLANDRILLO, Traci ... 202-885-3500.. 91 C callandr@american.edu
CALLAWAY, Cynthia ...... 757-825-2725 489 G callawayc@tncc.edu
CALLAWAY, J. Lea .... 910-672-1661 350 B jcallaw1@uncfsu.edu
CALLAWAY, MaryKatherine .... 225-578-6144 193 M mkc@lsu.edu
CALLAWAY, Rhonda ...... 936-294-2394 462 F rlc005@shsu.edu
CALLEJO PEREZ, David, M .... 989-964-4296 236 F dmcallej@svsu.edu
CALLEN, Bruce .... 417-873-7546 259 G bcallen@drury.edu
CALLEN, Chad .... 304-296-8282 505 E ctcallen@wvjc.edu
CALLEN, Patricia .... 304-296-8282 505 E pcallen@wvjc.edu
CALLENDER, David, L .... 409-772-1902 469 C dcallender@utmb.edu
CALLICOTT, Robin .... 803-641-3342 425 A robinc@usca.edu
CALLIER, Theodore .... 504-816-4018 191 E tcallier@dillard.edu
CALLIES, Kathryn .... 605-256-5143 428 G kathy.callies@dsu.edu
CALLIHAM, Marty .... 512-444-8082 461 C mcalliham@thsu.edu
CALLIHAN, Dan .... 785-227-3380 175 E callihandp@bethanylb.edu
CALLINAN, Dennis .... 845-574-4481 321 F dcallina@sunyrockland.edu
CALLISTO, Anthony .... 315-443-5480 330 H acallist@syr.edu
CALLOW-WRIGHT, Katie 773-795-3361 153 F ccallow@uchicago.edu
CALLOWAY, Terence ...... 850-599-3256 109 A terence.calloway@famu.edu
CALLUZZO, Vincent .... 914-633-2601 311 B vcalluzzo@iona.edu
CALLUZZO, Vincent .... 914-633-2256 311 B vcalluzzo@iona.edu
CALLWOOD-BRATHWAITE, Denise .... 305-623-1415.. 99 M denise.callwood-brathwaite@fmuniv.edu
CALMESE, Carlotta, V ..... 608-243-4270 514 A ccalmese@madisoncollege.edu
CALMET, Carlos .... 305-223-4561 106 L ccalmet@sjvcs.edu
CALNAN, Kerry .... 508-213-2207 223 C kerry.calnan@nichols.edu
CALO, Andrew .... 617-322-3513 216 B andrew_calo@laboure.edu
CALOBRISI, Charlotte, M .... 703-323-3110 488 H ccalobrisi@nvcc.edu
CALOCA, Luis .... 208-562-3396 132 A luiscaloca@cwidaho.cc
CALOGRIDES, JR., Thomas, G .... 757-822-7330 489 H tcalogrides@tcc.edu
CALOVINI, Susan .... 336-721-2617 348 H susan.calovini@salem.edu
CALPIN, Fran .... 570-945-8170 398 C fran.calpin@keystone.edu
CALTABIANO, Ronald ..... 312-362-7256 137 C rcalt@depaul.edu
CALUS-MCLAIN, Martha 503-352-2764 385 I martha@pacificu.edu
CALUZA, Kimberly .... 206-296-6090 498 D caluzak@seattleu.edu
CALVELLI, Louis .... 718-862-7977 313 L lcalvelli01@manhattan.edu
CALVERT, Carolyn, A ..... 325-793-3808 452 F ccalvert@mcm.edu
CALVERT, Chandra .... 605-718-2419 429 E chandra.calvert@wdt.edu
CALVERT, Lisa .... 806-742-1780 463 D lisa.calvert@ttu.edu
CALVERT, Lisa, D .... 806-742-0012 463 B
CALVERT, Maxine .... 405-422-1466 379 B calvertm@redlandscc.edu
CALVERT, Mike .... 620-672-2700 180 K michaelc@prattcc.edu
CALVERT, Ned .... 903-923-2120 448 J ncalvert@etbu.edu
CALVERT, Raymond, J ... 727-816-3418 105 C calverr@phsc.edu
CALVIN, Brent .... 559-730-3755.. 39 G brentc@cos.edu
CALVIN, Dennis, D .... 814-865-4028 403 F ifa@psu.edu
CALVO, Dean .... 909-621-8211.. 63 F dcalvo@scrippscollege.edu
CALZADA, Maria .... 504-865-3244 194 G calzada@loyno.edu
CALZONETTI, Frank, J ... 419-530-6171 372 F frank.calzonetti@utoledo.edu
CAMACHO, Alberto, J ... 787-257-7373 525 Q ajcamacho@suagm.edu
CAMACHO, Anita, C ...... 670-237-6824 520 D anita.camacho@marianas.edu
CAMACHO, Carmen, S .. 805-922-6966.. 24 J ccamacho@hancockcollege.edu
CAMACHO, Delia, M ...... 787-250-0000 527 D delia.camacho@upr.edu
CAMACHO, Francisco, C .... 671-734-0540 519 H mis@guamcc.edu
CAMACHO, Helen, B ..... 670-237-6702 520 D helen.camacho@marianas.edu
CAMACHO, Luis .... 787-725-6500 521 C lcamacho@albizu.edu
CAMACHO, Martin .... 940-397-4274 453 C martin.camacho@mwsu.edu
CAMACHO, Mildred .... 787-264-1912 524 D milcama@intersg.edu
CAMACHO-MARON, Wanda .... 617-670-4429 215 B wcamacho-maron@fisher.edu
CAMACHO-MELENDEZ, Iris, M .... 787-751-1912 524 E icamacho@juris.inter.edu
CAMANIA, Sarah .... 504-762-3021 192 H scaman@dcc.edu
CAMARA, Nivia .... 718-933-6700 315 K ncamara@monroecollege.edu
CAMARA-MONTULL, Manuel, E .... 787-250-0000 527 D manuel.camara@upr.edu
CAMARENA, Phame, M . 989-774-3902 228 E camar1pm@cmich.edu
CAMARGO, Judy, V .... 210-486-4951 441 G jcamargo@alamo.edu
CAMARILLO, Jane .... 925-631-4235.. 59 C jc11@stmarys-ca.edu
CAMARILLO, Richard ..... 805-546-3100.. 41 C richard_camarillo@cuesta.edu
CAMBIA, Barbara .... 561-237-7360 103 E bcambia@lynn.edu
CAMBONE, Joseph .... 978-542-6266 218 E jcambone@salemstate.edu
CAMBRA, Dena .... 570-586-2400 392 E dcambra@clarkssummitu.edu
CAMBRAY, Joseph .... 805-969-3626.. 55 G jcambray@pacifica.edu
CAMBRE, Charles .... 985-549-2244 197 E charles.cambre@selu.edu
CAMBRIA, James .... 212-517-0685 314 D jcambria@mm.edu
CAMBRON, Margaret ..... 270-852-3302 187 F mcambron@kwc.edu
CAMELO, Kathleen, M ... 518-564-2187 327 E camelokm@plattsburgh.edu
CAMERLENGO, Renee ... 412-268-2075 391 H reneec@andrew.cmu.edu
CAMERON, JR., A. Neill .... 864-656-2123 419 F cameron@clemson.edu
CAMERON, Celia .... 610-902-8254 391 B celia.l.cameron@cabrini.edu
CAMERON, Charley .... 318-678-6000 192 C ccameron@bpcc.edu
CAMERON, Cheryl, A ..... 206-221-1405 499 D ccameron@uw.edu
CAMERON, Christopher . 213-738-6749.. 65 I academicaffairs@swlaw.edu
CAMERON, Helene .... 301-934-7567 203 D hcameron@csmd.edu
CAMERON, J. Scott .... 301-243-2118 518 C
CAMERON, Jamye .... 425-739-8155 495 F jamye.cameron@lwtech.edu
CAMERON, Kenneth ...... 508-373-9452 211 F kenneth.cameron@becker.edu
CAMERON, Matthew, R . 305-899-3875.. 95 G mcameron@barry.edu
CAMERON, Patrick .... 617-558-1788 223 A pcameron@nesa.edu
CAMERON, Richard, L ... 478-301-5500 122 H cameron_rl@mercer.edu
CAMERON, Ryan, M ...... 402-280-3434 274 D ryancameron@creighton.edu
CAMERON, Samantha .... 906-248-8429 227 P scameron@bmcc.edu
CAMERON, Spencer ...... 303-220-1200.. 77 D spencer.cameron@cffp.edu
CAMERON, Suzette .... 386-506-4506.. 97 I cameros@daytonastate.edu
CAMERON-THOMPSON, AnnMarie .... 816-960-2008 258 D billing@cityvision.edu
CAMFIELD, Peter .... 580-349-1514 377 E pcamfield@opsu.edu
CAMILLE, Marc, M .... 203-773-8529.. 84 G mcamille@albertus.edu
CAMILLE, Michael .... 318-342-1906 198 A camille@ulm.edu
CAMILLE, Milton .... 603-752-1113 281 B mcamille@ccsnh.edu
CAMILLERI, Michael ...... 507-284-9328 241 E camilleri.michael@mayo.edu
CAMILLO, Thomas, P .... 814-871-7413 395 H camillo001@gannon.edu
CAMISCIONI, John .... 361-593-3312 460 B john.camiscioni@tamuk.edu
CAMMACK, Cindy .... 402-872-2313 276 C ccammack@peru.edu
CAMMARATA, Maria ...... 510-430-3322.. 52 E mcammarata@mills.edu
CAMMARATA, Miki .... 973-720-2179 292 I cammaratamj@wpunj.edu
CAMMARATA, Rita .... 212-217-3820 308 B rita_cammarata@fitnyc.edu
CAMMISH, Peter .... 707-864-7278.. 64 E peter.cammish@solano.edu
CAMOU, Fernando .... 623-845-3677.. 13 H f.camou@gccaz.edu
CAMP, Andy .... 518-580-5745 324 D acamp@skidmore.edu
CAMP, Billy .... 334-386-7255.... 5 I bcamp@faulkner.edu
CAMP, Carol .... 251-442-2213.... 8 D ccamp@umobile.edu
CAMP, Cathryn .... 301-546-0412 206 E
CAMP, Jamie .... 804-862-6100 484 F jcamp@rbc.edu
CAMP, Jon, P .... 863-680-4192 100 D jcamp@flsouthern.edu
CAMP, Keith .... 864-424-8091 425 G ckcamp@mailbox.sc.edu
CAMP, Robert, C .... 724-357-7889 406 C bobcamp@iup.edu
CAMP, Skip .... 239-513-1122 101 O bcamp@hodges.edu
CAMP, Sue, C .... 704-406-4378 337 H scamp@gardner-webb.edu
CAMP, Susan .... 405-319-8570 375 A susanc@cameron.edu
CAMPA, Jeff .... 816-322-0110 257 M jeff.campa@calvary.edu
CAMPAGNA, Michele .... 973-655-5369 287 D campagnam@mail.montclair.edu
CAMPANA, Karen .... 630-829-6345 133 I kcampana@ben.edu
CAMPANA, Maryjo .... 570-484-2181 406 E drt831@lockhaven.edu
CAMPANELLI, Kenneth .. 718-482-5502 303 B kcampanelli@lagcc.cuny.edu
CAMPANINI, Albino, P .. 321-674-8434.. 99 K bcampanini@fit.edu
CAMPBELL, Aaron .... 661-255-1050.. 29 F
CAMPBELL, Abigail .... 334-874-5700.... 5 B acampbell@ccal.edu
CAMPBELL, Alan .... 563-336-3308 168 K acampbell@eicc.edu
CAMPBELL, Alec .... 425-564-2728 492 G alec.campbell@bellevuecollege.edu
CAMPBELL, Amanda .... 812-488-2241 164 G ac283@evansville.edu
CAMPBELL, Amy .... 609-258-8896 288 F amyc@princeton.edu
CAMPBELL, Amy .... 517-264-3910 226 F acampbell@adrian.edu
CAMPBELL, Andrea .... 315-279-5994 312 D acampbell@keuka.edu
CAMPBELL, Andrew, G .. 401-863-2532 415 K andrew_campbell@brown.edu
CAMPBELL, Ann, E .... 757-446-5255 480 C campbeae@evms.edu
CAMPBELL, Anthony ...... 773-298-3121 151 C campbell@sxu.edu
CAMPBELL, Barbara .... 606-759-7141 186 E barbara.campbell@kctcs.edu
CAMPBELL, Bill .... 412-365-1140 392 C bcampbell@chatham.edu
CAMPBELL, Bonnie, L ... 815-224-0408 141 A bonnie_campbell@ivcc.edu
CAMPBELL, Carol .... 936-261-2111 458 F ccampbell@pvamu.edu
CAMPBELL, Catherine, C .... 252-638-7271 342 E campbelc@cravencc.edu
CAMPBELL, Celia, K ...... 617-627-3313 225 A celia.campbell@tufts.edu
CAMPBELL, Charles .... 334-386-7528.... 5 I ccampbell@faulkner.edu
CAMPBELL, Charlie .... 859-985-3674 183 I campbellc@berea.edu
CAMPBELL, Christie ...... 512-233-1635 455 I christie@stedwards.edu
CAMPBELL, Claire .... 978-927-2300 215 D claire.campbell@gordon.edu
CAMPBELL, Clark, D ..... 562-903-4867.. 27 E clark.campbell@biola.edu
CAMPBELL, Connan ...... 509-533-7081 493 I connan.campbell@scc.spokane.edu
CAMPBELL, Conway ...... 508-767-7505 210 I ccampbel@assumption.edu
CAMPBELL, Cory .... 724-838-4260 410 E ccampbell@setonhill.edu
CAMPBELL, Curtis .... 503-838-8094 388 B campbellc@wou.edu
CAMPBELL, Dan .... 413-552-2705 219 G dcampbell@hcc.edu
CAMPBELL, Danny .... 432-264-3752 450 G dcampbell@howardcollege.edu
CAMPBELL, David .... 662-562-3231 255 C
CAMPBELL, Deanna .... 760-872-5301.. 47 B dcampbel@cerrocoso.edu
CAMPBELL, Debra .... 231-843-5819 239 D djcampbell@westshore.edu
CAMPBELL, Diane .... 609-586-4800 287 A campbeld@mccc.edu
CAMPBELL, Donald .... 415-422-5368.. 72 A dmcampbell2@usfca.edu
CAMPBELL, Donald .... 610-896-1100 397 F dcampbel@haverford.edu
CAMPBELL, Douane .... 212-343-1234 315 D dcampbellr@mcny.edu
CAMPBELL, Ellen .... 814-641-3150 398 B campbee@juniata.edu
CAMPBELL, Elmyra, D ... 501-370-5275.. 21 A ecampbell@philander.edu
CAMPBELL, Elreo .... 765-658-4190 157 H elreocampbell@depauw.edu
CAMPBELL, Evelyn, S .... 309-794-7533 133 G evelyncampbell@augustana.edu
CAMPBELL, Fran .... 937-766-7653 358 D campf@cedarville.edu
CAMPBELL, Gail .... 928-289-6530.. 15 B gail.campbell@npc.edu
CAMPBELL, Gail .... 423-697-5718 436 F gail.campbell@chattanoogastate.edu

CAMPBELL, George .... 207-780-4141 201 H george.campbell@maine.edu
CAMPBELL, George .... 207-780-4708 201 H george.campbell@maine.edu
CAMPBELL, Hannah .... 802-860-2747 474 G hcampbell@champlain.edu
CAMPBELL, Harrison ..... 812-749-1216 163 B hcampbell@oak.edu
CAMPBELL, J. David ..... 256-228-6001.... 3 B campbelld@nacc.edu
CAMPBELL, James, F .... 401-865-2676 416 E james.campbell@providence.edu
CAMPBELL, Jamie .... 562-903-4555.. 27 E jamie.campbell@biola.edu
CAMPBELL, Jamie, L ..... 920-433-6665 506 C jamie.campbell@bellincollege.edu
CAMPBELL, Jane .... 302-622-8000.. 90 A
CAMPBELL, Jane, S .... 712-362-7947 170 D jcampbell@iowalakes.edu
CAMPBELL, Janell .... 701-224-5431 354 F janell.i.campbell@bismarckstate.edu
CAMPBELL, Jenni, L ...... 321-682-4981 113 F jcampbell60@valenciacollege.edu
CAMPBELL, Jennifer ...... 607-274-3860 311 D jcampbell1@ithaca.edu
CAMPBELL, Jo .... 805-756-7990.. 30 K jcampb33@calpoly.edu
CAMPBELL, Joann, N .... 904-620-2002 110 E jcampbel@unf.edu
CAMPBELL, Joanne .... 479-248-7236.. 19 F jcampbell@ecollege.edu
CAMPBELL, Joeseph ...... 870-680-8725.. 18 D joe_campbell@asun.edu
CAMPBELL, John .... 530-752-1730.. 68 H jgcampbell@ucdavis.edu
CAMPBELL, John, B ...... 901-722-3372 436 D jbcampbell@sco.edu
CAMPBELL, John, P ...... 304-293-7119 505 B john.campbell@mail.wvu.edu
CAMPBELL, Jonathan .... 870-230-5098.. 19 H campbej@hsu.edu
CAMPBELL, Karen, D ..... 757-822-1447 489 H kcampbell@tcc.edu
CAMPBELL, Karen, M .... 608-822-2300 515 A kcampbell@swtc.edu
CAMPBELL, Keith, E ...... 404-413-4465 121 A kcampbell@gsu.edu
CAMPBELL, Kelly, D ...... 404-687-4547 118 B campbellk@ctsnet.edu
CAMPBELL, Keni .... 907-796-6509.. 10 C klcampbell4@alaska.edu
CAMPBELL, Kevin .... 325-674-2765 441 D kac96b@acu.edu
CAMPBELL, Kim .... 614-234-5144 365 L kcampbell@mccn.edu
CAMPBELL, Kimberly ..... 913-971-3584 179 H kjcampbell@mnu.edu
CAMPBELL, Kimberly ..... 405-491-6335 379 K kcampbel@snu.edu
CAMPBELL, Kirby, D ..... 318-342-5147 198 A kcampbell@ulm.edu
CAMPBELL, Kristi .... 870-543-5959.. 21 E kcampbell@seark.edu
CAMPBELL, Lauren .... 215-637-7700 397 G lcampbell@holyfamily.edu
CAMPBELL, Lea .... 713-221-5548 465 C campbellc@uhd.edu
CAMPBELL, Lenora .... 336-285-3508 350 C lrcampbell@ncat.edu
CAMPBELL, Lisa .... 714-992-7085.. 54 A lcampbell@fullcoll.edu
CAMPBELL, Lisa .... 775-623-4824 279 A lisa.campbell@gbcnv.edu
CAMPBELL, Lisa, M ...... 724-287-8711 390 J lisa.campbell@bc3.edu
CAMPBELL, Lori .... 423-585-6933 438 D lori.campbell@ws.edu
CAMPBELL, Lucy .... 619-684-8783.. 53 J lcampbell@newschoolarch.edu
CAMPBELL, Mark .... 415-749-4581.. 60 G mcampbell@sfai.edu
CAMPBELL, Marshall ..... 979-230-3474 444 E marshall.campbell@brazosport.edu
CAMPBELL, Mary, B ...... 314-935-3617 269 L marycampbell@wustl.edu
CAMPBELL, Mary, B ...... 864-488-8280 422 B mcampbell@limestone.edu
CAMPBELL, Mason .... 870-508-6168.. 18 C mcampbell@asumh.edu
CAMPBELL, Matthew ..... 253-840-8419 497 B mcampbell@pierce.ctc.edu
CAMPBELL, Melanie ...... 434-381-6332 485 P mhcampbell@sbc.edu
CAMPBELL, Michael ...... 760-384-6159.. 47 B michael.campbell@cerrocoso.edu
CAMPBELL, Michael ...... 816-279-7000 257 B michael.campbell@abtu.edu
CAMPBELL, Michael, A . 423-585-2682 438 D mike.campbell@ws.edu
CAMPBELL, Michelle ...... 425-235-2352 497 E mcampbell@rtc.edu
CAMPBELL, Mike .... 423-585-2682 438 D michael.campbell@ws.edu
CAMPBELL, Mitchell, L . 916-558-2426.. 50 I campbem@scc.losrios.edu
CAMPBELL, Nicole, J .... 405-325-1978 380 L njudice@ou.edu
CAMPBELL, Pam .... 760-384-6178.. 47 B pagodfre@cerrocoso.edu
CAMPBELL, Patricia .... 209-946-2424.. 70 F pcampbell@pacific.edu
CAMPBELL, Patricia .... 617-627-3331 225 A patricia.campbell@tufts.edu
CAMPBELL, Patricia, R .. 727-816-3325 105 C campbep@phsc.edu
CAMPBELL, Phyllis .... 731-352-4046 430 E campbellp@bethelu.edu
CAMPBELL, Randy .... 607-778-5196 326 C campbellrj@sunybroome.edu
CAMPBELL, Richard .... 630-829-6462 133 I rcampbell@ben.edu
CAMPBELL, Robert .... 859-246-6387 185 G robert.campbell@kctcs.edu
CAMPBELL, Robert .... 410-704-4862 209 C rcampbell@towson.edu
CAMPBELL, Robert, D ... 212-817-7300 302 B rcampbell@gc.cuny.edu
CAMPBELL, Robin .... 336-517-2229 335 K rcampbell@bennett.edu
CAMPBELL, Rosana .... 570-484-2723 406 E rcampbel@lockhaven.edu
CAMPBELL, Samerah ..... 559-244-5989.. 66 E samerah.campbell@scccd.edu
CAMPBELL, Sara .... 423-614-8525 432 L scampbell@leeuniversity.edu
CAMPBELL, Scott .... 773-834-3390 153 F scottcampbell@uchicago.edu
CAMPBELL, Sharon .... 919-760-8011 339 H sharonca@meredith.edu
CAMPBELL, Shoshanna, M .... 718-780-7501 300 A shoshanna.campbell@brooklaw.edu
CAMPBELL, Sierra .... 708-802-6181 138 F scampbell@foxcollege.edu
CAMPBELL, Stanley, R .. 859-238-5271 184 C stan.campbell@centre.edu
CAMPBELL, Stephanie ... 318-357-5351 197 D campbells@nsula.edu
CAMPBELL, Stephanie ... 904-470-8114.. 98 B s.campbell@ewc.edu
CAMPBELL, Stephen ...... 409-772-9751 469 C stepcamp@utmb.edu
CAMPBELL, Stephen, M 216-368-5555 358 C stephen.campbell@case.edu
CAMPBELL, Terri .... 402-399-2419 274 A tcampbell@csm.edu
CAMPBELL, Thomas, F .. 214-905-3001 467 D thomas.f.campbell@utdallas.edu
CAMPBELL, Thomas, L .. 610-282-1100 393 G thomas.campbell@desales.edu
CAMPBELL, Timothy, G . 859-858-3511 183 D tim.campbell@asbury.edu
CAMPBELL, Timothy, M 443-334-2838 207 C tmcampbell@stevenson.edu
CAMPBELL, Tish .... 912-525-5000 125 B lcampbel@scad.edu
CAMPBELL, SJ, William, R .... 508-793-2446 213 D wcampbel@holycross.edu
CAMPBELL-HOOPS, Toma .... 406-353-2607 270 E thoops@ancollege.edu
CAMPBELL JACKSON, Candace .... 315-443-8734 330 H candace1@syr.edu
CAMPE, Robert, J .... 603-526-3076 280 H bob.campe@colby-sawyer.edu
CAMPEAU, Tony .... 406-994-2604 272 A tcampeau@montana.edu
CAMPEN, Darrin .... 240-567-5030 205 F darren.campen@montgomerycollege.edu
CAMPER, Shannon .... 845-451-1352 306 D shannon.camper@culinary.edu
CAMPERI, Marcelo, F .... 415-422-5939.. 72 A camperi@usfca.edu
CAMPION, James, R ..... 518-828-4181 305 D campion@sunycgcc.edu
CAMPION, William, J ..... 254-647-3234 454 L bcampion@rangercollege.edu
CAMPLESE, Cole, W ...... 773-702-8034 153 F kathiek@uchicago.edu
CAMPO, Carlos .... 419-289-5050 356 L ccampo@ashland.edu
CAMPO, Juan, E .... 805-893-3945.. 70 B jcampo@religion.ucsb.edu
CAMPO, Regina, Z .... 717-337-6207 396 A rcampo@gettysburg.edu
CAMPOS, Becky .... 714-997-6779.. 36 G bcampos@chapman.edu
CAMPOS, Cesar .... 312-939-0111 137 G cesar@eastwest.edu
CAMPOS, Darcie, R .... 708-534-5000 138 H dcampos@govst.edu
CAMPOS, Diana .... 575-234-9227 295 D dcampos@nmsu.edu
CAMPOS, Javier .... 559-453-4600.. 43 J javier.campos@fresno.edu
CAMPOS, Jesus .... 956-872-8330 456 G jhcampos@southtexascollege.edu
CAMPOS, Lisa .... 928-523-5353.. 14 K lisa.campos@nau.edu
CAMPOS, Nicolette .... 910-521-6695 351 E nicolette.campos@uncp.edu
CAMPS, Manel .... 831-459-2411.. 70 C mcamps@ucsc.edu
CAMUTI, Alice .... 931-372-6006 438 F acamuti@tntech.edu
CANACARIS, Diana .... 865-981-8198 433 F diana.canacaris@maryvillecollege.edu
CANADA, Allison, M ...... 410-334-2918 210 C acanada@worwic.edu
CANADA, Britt .... 325-574-7671 470 N bcanada@wtc.edu
CANADA, Jeff, H .... 410-543-6056 209 B jhcanada@salisbury.edu
CANADA, Mark .... 765-455-9227 160 B canadam@iuk.edu
CANADA, Ruth .... 573-681-5975 261 H canadar@lincolnu.edu
CANADAY, Bruce .... 314-446-8184 266 D bruce.canaday@stlcop.edu
CANADAY, JR., John .... 719-384-6818.. 81 G john.canaday@ojc.edu
CANADAY, Joseph .... 215-596-7524 413 E j.canaday@usciences.edu
CANAL, Marcie .... 213-738-6800.. 65 I administrativeservices@swlaw.edu
CANALE, Brad .... 906-227-2610 235 A bcanale@nmu.edu
CANALE, Mary .... 315-312-5558 327 D mary.canale@oswego.edu
CANALES, Carmen, I ..... 336-758-3256 353 A ccanales@wfu.edu
CANALES, Jason, G .... 413-662-5413 218 C jason.canales@mcla.edu
CANALES, Jo Ann .... 361-825-3884 460 A joann.canales@tamucc.edu
CANALES, Leticia .... 559-675-4800.. 66 H leticia.canales@scccd.edu
CANALES, Luis .... 309-438-0287 140 L lacanal@ilstu.edu
CANALS, Alex .... 718-933-6700 315 K acanals@monroecollege.edu
CANAN, Michelle .... 918-293-5494 378 B michelle.canan@okstate.edu
CANARY, Sharnie .... 845-569-3548 316 B sharnie.canary@msmc.edu
CANAS, Carlos .... 305-626-3698.. 99 M carlos.canas@fmuniv.edu
CANATELLA, Holle .... 570-484-2178 406 E hcanatel@lockhaven.edu
CANAVAN, Jessie .... 330-823-2579 372 C canavajl@mountunion.edu
CANAVAN, Linda, T ...... 781-292-2341 215 C linda.canavan@olin.edu
CANAVAN, Terry .... 631-499-7100 313 B tcanavan@libi.edu
CANCEKO CHAN, Genevieve .... 360-491-4700 497 F gchan@stmartin.edu
CANCEL, Jimmy .... 787-250-1912 524 B jcancel@metro.inter.edu
CANCEL, Olga .... 787-754-8000 527 B ocancel@pupr.edu
CANCEL-PEREZ, Magda, A .... 787-620-2040 520 F mcancel@aupr.edu
CANCILLA, Devon .... 816-235-1107 268 D cancillad@umkc.edu
CANCILLA, Mike .... 256-549-8311.... 2 A mcancilla@gadsdenstate.edu
CANDEE, Kate .... 920-923-8727 508 B kcandee@marianuniversity.edu
CANDELA, Natalie .... 810-762-9832 232 C ncandela@kettering.edu
CANDELARIA, J. Randel 336-734-7216 343 C jcandelaria@forsythtech.edu
CANDIA-BAILEY, Antoinette .... 410-704-2516 209 C acandiabailey@towson.edu
CANDIDO, James .... 512-313-3000 446 N james.candido@concordia.edu
CANDLER, George, B .... 212-327-7801 321 E candler@rockefeller.edu
CANDLER, Marietta .... 870-612-2070.. 22 H marietta.candler@uaccb.edu
CANDREVA, Anne, M .... 412-578-6043 391 G candrevaam@carlow.edu
CANEIRO-LIVINGSTON, Graciela .... 402-465-2110 276 E gcaneiro@nebrwesleyan.edu
CANEPA, Janet, A .... 203-254-4280.. 87 A jcanepa@fairfield.edu
CANEPA, Thomas .... 513-556-2495 371 E tom.canepa@uc.edu
CANEPI, Karen .... 702-968-2033 280 B kcanepi@roseman.edu
CANER, Emir .... 706-865-2134 126 G ecaner@truett.edu
CANFIELD, Clarke .... 207-741-5575 200 C ccanfield@smccme.edu
CANFIELD, Joe .... 206-726-5004 494 B jcanfield@cornish.edu
CANFIELD, Kathleen ...... 847-925-6437 139 B kcanfiel@harpercollege.edu
CANFIELD, Kipton .... 309-341-5325 134 H kcanfield@sandburg.edu
CANGELIO, Paula, R ..... 304-293-5841 505 B pacongelio@hsc.wvu.edu
CANGELLARIS, Andreas, C .... 217-333-2150 154 B cangella@illinois.edu
CANGEMI, Livia .... 212-650-3868 302 E livia.cangemi@hunter.cuny.edu
CANHAM, Drew .... 254-299-8645 452 E dcanham@mclennan.edu
CANHAM, Raymond, P . 972-238-6248 448 D canham@dcccd.edu
CANIA, Lisa, M .... 315-229-5585 323 D lcania@stlawu.edu
CANIDA, II, Robert, L ... 910-522-5790 351 E canida@uncp.edu
CANIGLIA, Alan, S .... 717-358-3934 395 G alan.caniglia@fandm.edu
CANIGLIA, Jason, J ...... 303-458-4160.. 82 D jcaniglia@regis.edu
CANINE, Kim .... 402-486-2507 277 C kim.canine@ucollege.edu
CANINO, Cathy .... 864-503-5657 425 H ccanino@uscupstate.edu
CANN, Alison .... 864-592-4991 424 C canna@sccsc.edu
CANNADA, JR., Robert, C .... 601-923-1600 255 E rcannada@rts.edu
CANNADAY SAULNY, Helen .... 202-994-6710.. 92 A saulnyh@gwu.edu
CANNADY, Sharell .... 704-378-3572 338 I cannady@jcsu.edu
CANNADY-SMITH, Allison .... 253-879-3450 499 C acannadysmith@pugetsound.edu
CANNAN, Erin .... 845-758-7454 298 I cannan@bard.edu
CANNEY, Catherine .... 978-665-3653 217 E ccanney@fitchburgstate.edu
CANNEY, Crystal .... 207-615-5968 202 A ccanney1@une.edu
CANNICI, James, P .... 972-883-2575 467 D cannici@utdallas.edu
CANNIFF, James, F .... 617-228-2435 219 D jfcanniff@bhcc.mass.edu
CANNING, Allison .... 843-525-8210 424 E acanning@tcl.edu
CANNING, Elizabeth .... 401-825-1230 416 B ebcanning@ccri.edu
CANNING, John, B .... 401-232-6020 416 A jcanning@bryant.edu
CANNING, Kathleen .... 713-348-4810 455 F
CANNON, Amy .... 270-901-1012 187 A amy.cannon@kctcs.edu
CANNON, Barbie .... 318-797-5116 194 E barbie.cannon@lsus.edu
CANNON, Brenda .... 931-393-1546 437 C bcannon@mscc.edu
CANNON, Bruce .... 406-656-9950 273 D
CANNON, Bunnie .... 225-578-0302 193 M bcannon@lsu.edu
CANNON, Chris .... 251-460-6161.... 9 B ccannon@southalabama.edu
CANNON, Glen, D .... 770-962-7580 121 G gcannon@gwinnetttech.edu
CANNON, Gordon .... 601-266-5116 256 E gordon.cannon@usm.edu
CANNON, Gregory .... 845-575-3000 314 C greg.cannon@marist.edu

CANNON, Jason 256-840-4150 3 F
jcannon@snead.edu
CANNON, Katherine 508-793-7499 213 C
kcannon@clarku.edu
CANNON, Kathleen 503-847-2557 387 I
kcannon@uws.edu
CANNON, Mark, B 808-675-3803 128 K
mark.cannon@byuh.edu
CANNON, Rebecca 225-768-0810 191 G
rebecca.cannon@ololcollege.edu
CANNON, Sharon 432-703-5270 463 E
sharon.cannon@ttuhsc.edu
CANNON, Sharon 610-399-2057 405 G
scannon@cheyney.edu
CANNON, Sondra 732-224-2695 284 B
scannon@brookdalecc.edu
CANNON, Thomas 646-592-4327 334 P
thomas.cannon@yu.edu
CANNON, Tyrone, H 415-422-6167 72 A
cannont@usfca.edu
CANO, Mary 915-566-9621 470 L
mcano@westerntech.edu
CANO-MORALES,
Anna, M 401-456-8810 417 A
acanomorales@ric.edu
CANON, Susan 507-786-3647 250 C
canon@stolaf.edu
CANON, Sybil 662-560-1103 255 C
srcanon@northwestms.edu
CANONICA, James 856-227-7200 284 E
jcanonica@camdencc.edu
CANOUGH, Corrine, M 585-785-1469 308 D
corinne.canough@flcc.edu
CANOY, Eugenio 408-274-7900 61 O
eugenio.canoy@evc.edu
CANOY, Robert, W 704-406-4395 337 H
rcanoy@gardner-webb.edu
CANT, Alan, G 973-655-4304 287 D
canta@mail.montclair.edu
CANT, David 714-241-6224 38 F
dcant@coastline.edu
CANTALUPA, Kathy 617-603-6900 222 F
kathy.cantalupa@necb.edu
CANTANIO, Teri, T 215-702-4422 391 C
tcatanio@cairn.edu
CANTARERO, Maritza 408-741-2429 74 D
maritza.cantarero@westvalley.edu
CANTER, Bridget 270-534-3088 187 C
bridget.canter@kctcs.edu
CANTERBURY, Jay 419-434-4076 372 B
canterbury@findlay.edu
CANTERBURY, Jenni 304-929-6727 503 B
jcanterbury@newriver.edu
CANTERINO, Patti 610-647-4400 397 I
pcanterino@immaculata.edu
CANTEY, Andrew 903-510-2186 464 D
acan2@tjc.edu
CANTINE, Stephen 401-254-5231 417 C
scantine@rwu.edu
CANTOR, Nancy, E 973-353-5541 290 D
nancy.cantor@rutgers.edu
CANTOR, Nancy, E 973-353-5541 290 A
nancy.cantor@rutgers.edu
CANTOR, Ronald, G 207-741-5501 200 C
rcantor@smccme.edu
CANTRELL, Andra, R 817-598-6260 470 J
acantrell@wc.edu
CANTRELL, Betsy 678-717-3941 127 B
betsy.cantrell@ung.edu
CANTRELL, Chuck 423-425-4363 440 A
chuck-cantrell@utc.edu
CANTRELL, Danny, R 304-766-4183 505 A
dcantrel@wvstateu.edu
CANTRELL, Hampton 310-258-5485 50 J
hcantrell@lmu.edu
CANTRELL, Jill 770-533-6903 122 E
cantrell@laniertech.edu
CANTRELL, Mark 304-876-5063 504 D
mcantrel@shepherd.edu
CANTRELL, Paul 361-358-2838 445 S
pcantrell@coastalbend.edu
CANTRELL, Sharon 787-743-7979 526 A
scantrel@suagm.edu
CANTRELL, Sirena 662-329-7127 254 F
slcantrell@muw.edu
CANTRELL, Sonja, G 304-696-2258 504 C
cantrel1@marshall.edu
CANTRELL, Steve 215-489-2356 393 F
steve.cantrell@delval.edu
CANTRELL, Tiffany 334-386-7450 5 I
tcantrell@faulkner.edu
CANTU, Larry 830-895-7223 456 D
ljcantu@schreiner.edu
CANTU, Pedro 210-341-1366 454 B
pcantu@ost.edu
CANTUTI-CASTELVETRI,
Ippolita, A 617-627-6696 225 A
ippolita.cantuti_castelvetri@tufts.edu
CANTWELL, Kevin 478-929-6712 123 A
kevin.cantwell@mga.edu
CANTWELL, Linda 405-491-6324 379 K
lcantwel@snu.edu
CANTWELL, Matilda 413-585-4595 224 F
mcantwel@smith.edu
CANTY, Joan 972-721-5148 464 E
jcanty@udallas.edu
CANTY, John 336-838-6558 347 G
jecanty331@wilkescc.edu
CANUP, Karen 864-578-8770 423 F
kcanup@sherman.edu
CAO, Hai Tao 512-444-8082 461 C
tcao@thsu.edu
CAO, Jian 847-467-1032 148 C
jcao@northwestern.edu
CAO, Nina 773-907-4473 135 K
ncao@ccc.edu
CAPA, Joseph 603-314-7530 282 C
j.capa@snhu.edu
CAPALBO, Susan 541-737-0123 385 F
susan.capalbo@oregonstate.edu
CAPALBO, Tony 815-455-8569 145 B
tcapalbo@mchenry.edu
CAPE, Coleen 620-792-9136 175 C
capec@bartonccc.edu
CAPECI, James 417-625-9806 263 G
capeci-j@mssu.edu
CAPEHEART, Loretta 360-992-2757 493 E
lcapeheart@clark.edu
CAPELA, Michael 661-763-7768 67 A
mcapela@taftcollege.edu
CAPELES, Belkis 912-478-5555 120 E
bcapeles@georgiasouthern.edu
CAPELES-DELGADO,
Julio 815-479-7568 145 B
jcapeles-delgado@mchenry.edu
CAPELL, Carey, M 843-953-6847 419 D
carey.capell@citadel.edu
CAPELLAZZI, Mark 585-271-3657 322 A
admissions@stbernards.edu
CAPELLE, Jomi 692-625-3291 520 C
jcapelle@cmi.edu
CAPELO, Jenny 509-682-6662 500 D
jcapelo@wvc.edu
CAPENER, Don 904-256-7430 102 B
dcapene@ju.edu
CAPERS, Meggin 610-341-5902 394 E
mcapers@eastern.edu
CAPETZ, Paul 651-255-6130 250 D
pcapetz@uniteseminary.edu
CAPEZZA, Kristen 516-877-3021 297 I
kcapezza@adelphi.edu
CAPFER, Karen 530-226-4101 64 B
kcapfer@simpsonu.edu
CAPILOUTO, Eli, I 859-257-1701 190 B
elic@uky.edu
CAPISCIOLTO, Ken 616-222-3000 232 F
kcapisciolto@kuyper.edu
CAPLES, Gwen 601-979-2282 253 E
gwendolyn.caples@jsums.edu
CAPLES, Philip 318-487-7946 191 J
philip.caples@lacollege.edu
CAPLINGER, Chris 912-478-3939 120 E
caplinca@georgiasouthern.edu
CAPLOW, Stacy 718-780-7944 300 A
stacy.caplow@brooklaw.edu
CAPO, Jeremy 712-325-3402 170 K
jcapo@iwcc.edu
CAPO, Leslie, L 504-568-4806 194 C
lcapo@lsuhsc.edu
CAPOLUPO, Catherine 508-565-1801 224 H
ccapolupo@stonehill.edu
CAPONI, Kimberly 630-466-7900 155 C
kcaponi@waubonsee.edu
CAPORALE, Matthew 203-479-4858 89 D
mcaporale@newhaven.edu
CAPORUSCIO, Josie 718-636-3649 320 D
jcaporus@pratt.edu
CAPOTOSTA, Amelia 610-372-4721 408 G
acapotosta@racc.edu
CAPOZZOLI, John 410-287-1469 203 B
jcapozzoli@cecil.edu
CAPP, Maureen 561-868-3333 105 A
cappm@palmbeachstate.edu
CAPPELLERI,
Mary Anne 508-565-1067 224 H
mcappelleri@stonehill.edu
CAPPELLO, Phillip 516-572-7300 316 C
phillip.cappello@ncc.edu
CAPPELLOO, Rocco 315-786-6561 311 H
rcappello@sunyjefferson.edu
CAPPLEMAN, Amy 662-862-8028 253 D
accappleman@iccms.edu
CAPPS, John 434-832-7601 487 H
cappsj@cvcc.vccs.edu
CAPPS, Matthew 940-397-4138 453 C
matthew.capps@mwsu.edu
CAPPS, Patricia 314-371-0236 265 F
pacapps@ranken.edu
CAPPS, Steve 936-633-5281 442 I
scapps@angelina.edu
CAPPS, Tammy 618-634-3280 151 G
tammyc@shawneecc.edu
CAPPS, Vanessa 828-286-3636 344 A
CAPRARIO, Janet 619-849-2958 57 H
janetcaprario@pointloma.edu
CAPRILES, Jose, A 787-758-2525 528 D
jose.capriles@upr.edu
CAPRIO, Anthony, S 413-782-1243 225 F
anthony.caprio@wne.edu
CAPRIOGLIO, Helen 719-549-2207 78 P
helen.caprioglio@csupueblo.edu
CAPRON, Clara 360-650-3470 500 E
clara.capron@wwu.edu
CAPSOURAS, Barbara 973-328-5059 285 B
bcapsour@ccm.edu
CAPUANO, Christopher 201-692-7094 286 B
capuano@fdu.edu
CAPUANO, Rebecca 413-565-1000 211 C
rcapuano@baypath.edu
CAPUANO, Sharon, Q 401-341-2904 417 D
sharon.capuano@salve.edu
CAPUNO, Jayson 818-575-6800 67 I
jayson.capuno@tuw.edu
CAPUTO, Michael, P 843-792-6246 422 C
caputom@musc.edu
CAQUIAS, Karen 787-284-1912 524 C
kcaquias@ponce.inter.edu
CARA, Robert 704-366-5066 255 E
rcara@rts.edu
CARABALLO, Ada 787-863-2390 523 K
ada.caraballo@fajardo.inter.edu
CARABALLO, Darryl 702-651-2677 278 N
darryl.caraballo@csn.edu
CARABALLO, Frances 787-892-2315 524 D
frances_caraballo@intersg.edu
CARABALLO, Jose, N 787-841-2000 525 J
jose_caraballorios@pucpr.edu
CARABALLO,
Maria Judith 787-761-0640 527 C
oficialderegistroacademico@utcpr.edu
CARABALLO, Omayra 787-284-1912 524 C
ocarabal@ponce.inter.edu
CARABALLO, Omayra 787-284-1912 524 C
acarabal@ponce.inter.edu
CARABALLO, Pablo 787-264-1912 524 D
pablo_caraballo_rodriguez@intersg.edu
CARABALLO, Sherri 817-531-7511 463 G
scaraballo@txwes.edu
CARACCIOLI, Pamela 315-312-3699 327 D
pamela.caraccioli@oswego.edu
CARACOGLIA, Erica, S 252-940-6425 340 N
erica.schatz@beaufortccc.edu
CARAHER, Claudia 315-228-7444 304 G
ccaraher@colgate.edu
CARAHER, Susan 701-777-6796 353 G
susan.caraher@und.edu
CARANTO, Jillian 626-650-2306 44 H
CARAVAGGIO, Steve 570-321-4153 400 G
caravagg@lycoming.edu
CARAWAY, Tom 907-852-1852 9 H
tom.caraway@ilisagvik.edu
CARBAJAL, Brent 360-650-3480 500 E
brent.carbajal@wwu.edu
CARBALLO, Lauren 516-671-8355 333 E
lcarballo@webb.edu
CARBALLO, Manuel 440-775-8411 367 B
manuel.carballo@oberlin.edu
CARBAUGH, Terri 562-985-8707 32 C
terri.carbaugh@csulb.edu
CARBERRY, Joseph 203-285-2011 85 E
jcarberry@gwcc.commnet.edu
CARBERRY, Paul 781-891-2009 212 A
pcarberry@bentley.edu
CARBIS, Kathryn 406-791-5274 273 C
kathryn.carbis@ugf.edu
CARBO-PORTER, Laurie 518-464-8406 308 A
lporter@excelsior.edu
CARBONE, Linsey 714-556-3610 72 F
linsey.carbone@vanguard.edu
CARBONE, Michele 808-586-3010 129 J
mcarbone@hawaii.edu
CARBONELL, Ivette 787-720-1022 521 A
icarbonell@atlanticu.edu
CARBONELL, John 731-661-5081 439 D
jcarbone@uu.edu
CARBONI, Michelle, L 815-224-0417 141 A
michelle_carboni@ivcc.edu
CARCANAGUES, Amy 210-829-3912 465 E
amyc@uiwtx.edu
CARCOPA, Joshua 800-955-2527 177 H
jcarcopa@grantham.edu
CARD, Christopher, D 920-832-6596 507 L
christopher.card@lawrence.edu
CARD, Lewis 406-771-4412 272 D
lewis.card@gfcmsu.edu
CARD, Margaret 617-989-4192 225 E
cardm@wit.edu
CARD, Michael 605-677-6926 428 E
michael.card@usd.edu
CARD, Steven 360-650-3109 500 E
steven.card@wwu.edu
CARDA, Sarah 605-668-1541 427 F
scarda@mtmc.edu
CARDARELLI, William 860-231-5246 89 E
bcardarelli@usj.edu
CARDELLE, Alberto 978-665-3295 217 E
acardelle@fitchburgstate.edu
CARDEN, Monica, W 540-674-3600 488 G
mcarden@nr.edu
CARDENA, Sonia 860-297-4193 88 E
sonia.cardena@trincoll.edu
CARDENAS, Becki 414-382-6111 506 A
becki.cardenas@alverno.edu
CARDENAS, Elizabeth 773-878-3921 150 I
ecardenas@staugustine.edu
CARDENAS, Eric, D 813-253-6232 113 E
ecardenas@ut.edu
CARDENAS, Jennifer 520-494-5420 11 P
jenni.cardenas@centralaz.edu
CARDENAS, Kerstin 507-222-4068 241 C
kcardena@carleton.edu
CARDENAS, Miguel, A 619-934-0797 60 F
CARDENAS, JR.,
Miguel, A 619-934-0797 60 F
CARDENAS, Monique 248-689-8282 238 F
mcardena@walshcollege.edu
CARDENAS, Patricia 210-458-4101 468 B
patricia.cardenas@utsa.edu
CARDENAS, Raul 303-315-2109 83 D
raul.cardenas@ucdenver.edu
CARDENAS, Tony 904-256-1231 99 C
acardenas@fcsl.edu
CARDENAS-ADAME,
Patricia 623-935-8812 13 F
patricia.cardenas-adame@
estrellamountain.edu
CARDENAS-CLAGUE,
Adeline 909-593-3511 70 E
acardenas-clague@laverne.edu
CARDER, Rick 765-677-2110 161 C
rick.carder@indwes.edu
CARDERO, Agda 787-728-1515 529 B
acardero@sagrado.edu
CARDILLO, Charlie 323-259-2937 54 E
ccardillo@oxy.edu
CARDILLO, Rosaleen 845-437-5844 333 A
roecardillo@vassar.edu
CARDIN, Matt 585-385-8143 322 E
mcardin@sjfc.edu
CARDINAL, Jason 651-779-3469 244 D
jason.cardinal@century.edu
CARDINAL, Mark 218-733-2032 245 C
mark.cardinal@lsc.edu
CARDINE, Darla, S 630-466-7900 155 C
dcardine@waubonsee.edu
CARDONA, Felix 718-518-6664 302 D
fcardona@hostos.cuny.edu
CARDONA, Joe 856-256-4236 289 H
cardona@rowan.edu
CARDONA, Jose 787-758-2525 528 D
jose.cardona8@upr.edu
CARDONA, Nelida 787-262-5786 526 D
directora_camuy@unitecpr.net
CARDONA, Teresa 787-754-8000 527 B
tcardona@pupr.edu
CARDONE, Stephen 609-497-7730 288 E
housing@ptsem.edu
CARDOZA, Carla 915-831-2638 449 A
ccardoza@epcc.edu
CARDOZA, Lisa 916-278-7043 33 C
lisa.cardoza@csus.edu
CARDOZO, Vincent 718-270-4210 326 A
vincent.cardozo@downstate.edu
CARDUCCI, Vince 313-664-1488 228 H
vcarducci@collegeforcreativestudies.edu
CARDWELL, Becky 916-388-5188 35 G
bcardwell@carrington.edu
CARDWELL, Catherine 727-873-4400 111 B
ccardwell@nelson.usf.edu
CARDWELL, Thomas 402-228-3468 276 K
tcardwel@southeast.edu
CAREAGA, Andrew, P 573-341-4183 269 A
acareaga@mst.edu
CARELLA, Emily 704-463-3047 348 B
emily.carella@pfeiffer.edu
CARELLA, Terry 517-371-5140 239 F
carellat@cooley.edu
CARET, Robert, L 301-445-1901 207 F
rcaret@usmd.edu
CAREW, William 863-680-4305 100 D
wcarew@flsouthern.edu

CAREY, Alexa .... 616-632-2882 227 C ajc004@aquinas.edu
CAREY, Amy .... 316-295-5888 177 F abcarey@friends.edu
CAREY, Cathy, T .... 801-524-1958 471 L cathycarey@ldsbc.edu
CAREY, Elaine .... 219-989-2401 163 E
CAREY, Felicia .... 336-917-5558 348 H felicia.carey@salem.edu
CAREY, Jason .... 718-951-5882 301 E jcarey@brooklyn.cuny.edu
CAREY, Joe .... 317-896-9324 164 F jcarey@ubca.org
CAREY, Karen .... 907-796-6256.. 10 C ktcarey@alaska.edu
CAREY, Marita .... 404-876-1227 117 A marita.carey@bccr.edu
CAREY, Michael .... 718-862-8000 313 L michael.carey@manhattan.edu
CAREY, Michael .... 509-313-3550 495 A carey@gonzaga.edu
CAREY, Peter, M .... 716-878-6332 326 E careypm@buffalostate.edu
CAREY, Russell, C .... 401-863-9650 415 K russell_carey@brown.edu
CAREY, Seamus .... 859-233-8111 189 H president@transy.edu
CAREY, Tim .... 607-274-3225 311 D tcarey@ithaca.edu
CAREY, Tom .... 206-239-4500 493 D
CAREY, William .... 845-451-1300 306 D william.carey@culinary.edu
CAREY-BUTLER, Sylvia .. 920-424-0348 511 B careybus@uwosh.edu
CARFAGNA, Angelo .... 201-692-7025 286 B angelo@fdu.edu
CARFORA, John .... 310-338-6004.. 50 J jcarfora@lmu.edu
CARGUELLO, Brett, M ... 315-655-7150 300 I bcarguello@cazenovia.edu
CARHART, Tori .... 315-228-7676 304 G tcarhart@colgate.edu
CARIGLIO-DORRIS, Jenna .... 330-569-5134 362 J carigliojd@hiram.edu
CARIKER, Heath .... 903-983-8657 451 F hcariker@kilgore.edu
CARILLI, Vincent .... 865-974-7449 439 I vincent.carilli@tennessee.edu
CARIN, Lawrence .... 919-681-6438 337 C lcarin@duke.edu
CARIO, William .... 262-243-4263 229 A william.cario@cuw.edu
CARIO, William, R .... 262-243-5700 507 C william.cario@cuw.edu
CARISSIMI, Laura, K ..... 440-366-7788 364 F
CARITO, Phyllis .... 518-828-4181 305 D carito@sunycgcc.edu
CARL, Ashley .... 813-253-7158 101 M acarl@hccfl.edu
CARL, Cathy .... 845-431-8635 307 A cathy.carl@sunydutchess.edu
CARL, Diane .... 570-321-4101 400 G carl@lycoming.edu
CARL, Heidi, A .... 765-361-6375 166 B carlh@wabash.edu
CARL, Peggy .... 978-542-6517 218 E pcarl@salemstate.edu
CARL, Steven, B .... 508-767-7267 210 I sb.carl@assumption.edu
CARLAND, Tammy Rae . 510-594-3649.. 28 K tcarland@cca.edu
CARLBLOM, Shelia .... 765-677-2191 161 C sheila.carlblom@indwes.edu
CARLETON, Lauren .... 218-869-5748 191 C lcarleton@centenary.edu
CARLETON, Mary Ruth .. 619-594-4562.. 34 B mcarleto@mail.sdsu.edu
CARLETON, Taylor .... 830-372-8026 461 D tcarleton@tlu.edu
CARLEY, Michael .... 559-791-2275.. 47 C mcarley@portervillecollege.edu
CARLI, Gale .... 510-742-3102.. 54 F gcarli@ohlone.edu
CARLILE, Kimberly, L .... 806-371-5017 442 D k0153833@actx.edu
CARLIN, Angela .... 360-412-6152 497 F acarlin@stmartin.edu
CARLIN, Jane .... 253-879-3118 499 C jcarlin@pugetsound.edu
CARLIN, Laurence .... 920-424-7364 511 B carlin@uwosh.edu
CARLIN, Melanie .... 217-357-9117 149 K mcarlin@robertmorris.edu
CARLIN, Michael .... 704-687-5500 351 C mike.carlin@uncc.edu
CARLING SMITH, Malcolm .... 916-339-4371.. 53 B mcarlingsmith@mticollege.edu
CARLISEL, Siri .... 518-828-4181 305 D carlisle@sunycgcc.edu
CARLISLE, Beth .... 602-943-2311.. 17 F beth.carlisle@west.edu
CARLISLE, Brian .... 909-607-2821.. 57 C brian_carlisle@pitzer.edu
CARLISLE, David, M ...... 323-563-4987.. 36 H davidcarlisle@cdrewu.edu
CARLISLE, Elizabeth .... 812-749-1241 163 B lcarlisle@oak.edu
CARLISLE, Nadis .... 256-372-5555.... 1 A nadis.carlisle@aamu.edu
CARLISLE, Sandra .... 320-629-5100 246 H carlisles@pine.edu
CARLISLE, Susan .... 502-213-5200 186 C susan.carlisle@kctcs.edu
CARLO, Jennifer, A .... 412-578-6087 391 G jacarlo@carlow.edu
CARLOCK, Danielle .... 480-423-6653.. 14 C d.carlock@scottsdalecc.edu
CARLOCK, Jennifer .... 309-655-7100 151 A jennifer.carlock@osfhealthcare.org
CARLOCK, Myra .... 731-352-4090 430 E carlockm@bethelu.edu
CARLOCK, Ruth .... 402-363-5704 278 E rmcarlock@york.edu
CARLOS, Raymond .... 909-384-8253.. 59 I rcarlos@sbccd.cc.ca.us
CARLSEN, Paul .... 920-693-1123 513 H paul.carlsen@gotoltc.edu
CARLSON, Bob .... 630-682-6002 140 I carlson@iit.edu
CARLSON, Britt .... 978-867-4221 215 D britt.carlson@gordon.edu
CARLSON, Caroline .... 949-376-6000.. 47 H ccarlson@lcad.edu
CARLSON, Catherina ..... 781-891-2989 212 A ccarlson@bentley.edu
CARLSON, Catherine ..... 419-448-3436 370 K carlsonc@tiffin.edu
CARLSON, Cathy .... 507-222-4075 241 C ccarlson@carleton.edu
CARLSON, Chris .... 951-222-8044.. 58 E chris.carlson@rcc.edu
CARLSON, Christopher .. 978-927-2300 215 D chris.carlson@gordon.edu
CARLSON, Craig .... 203-857-3344.. 86 D ccarlson@norwalk.edu
CARLSON, David .... 540-362-6675 481 F dcarlson@hollins.edu
CARLSON, David, H .... 979-845-8160 459 C davidcarlson@tamu.edu
CARLSON, Deb .... 402-354-7000 275 P deb.carlson@methodistcollege.edu
CARLSON, Don .... 925-424-1322.. 36 D dcarlson@laspositascollege.edu
CARLSON, Douglas .... 415-476-4527.. 70 A doug.carlson@ucsf.edu
CARLSON, James .... 847-578-8805 150 E james.carlson@rosalindfrannklin.edu
CARLSON, Jeffrey .... 708-524-6813 137 F jcarlson@dom.edu
CARLSON, Jessica .... 406-586-3585 271 E jessica.carlson@montanabiblecollege.edu
CARLSON, Jim .... 985-545-1500 192 K
CARLSON, Julie .... 402-844-7142 276 G juliec@northeast.edu
CARLSON, Karen .... 413-565-6850 211 C kcarlson@baypath.edu
CARLSON, Kathleen .... 773-298-3305 151 C carlson@sxu.edu
CARLSON, Kathleen .... 574-284-4543 163 J kcarlson@saintmarys.edu
CARLSON, Kenna Lee .... 402-486-2032 277 C kennalee.carlson@ucollege.edu
CARLSON, Kenneth .... 701-777-2127 353 G kenneth.carlson@und.edu
CARLSON, Kevin .... 906-217-4023 228 A kevin.carlson@baycollege.edu
CARLSON, Laina .... 651-450-3654 245 A lcarlso@inverhills.edu
CARLSON, Laura .... 574-631-8052 165 A lcarlson@nd.edu
CARLSON, Malinda, L ... 217-245-3011 139 H mcarlson@mail.ic.edu
CARLSON, Mark .... 651-201-1827 243 I mark.carlson@so.mnscu.edu
CARLSON, Marta .... 508-767-7275 210 I mcarlson@assumption.edu
CARLSON, Mary .... 616-222-3000 232 F mcarlson@kuyper.edu
CARLSON, Melinda .... 314-977-2824 266 J mcarlson2@slu.edu
CARLSON, Neil .... 616-526-6420 228 B nec4@calvin.edu
CARLSON, Nicki .... 218-683-8546 246 F nicki.carlson@northlandcollege.edu
CARLSON, Nicole .... 763-493-0597 246 E ncarlson@nhcc.edu
CARLSON, Paul .... 815-802-8652 142 C pcarlson@kcc.edu
CARLSON, Paula, J .... 563-387-1001 171 I president@luther.edu
CARLSON, Ria, M .... 949-824-7911.. 69 A ria.carlson@uci.edu
CARLSON, Rich .... 402-486-2508 277 C rich.carlson@ucollege.edu
CARLSON, Robert .... 785-227-3380 175 E carlsonr@bethanylb.edu
CARLSON, Skye .... 360-779-9993 496 B scarlson@ncad.edu
CARLSON, Steve .... 937-298-3399 364 B steve.carlson@ketteringhealth.org
CARLSON, Steve .... 920-206-2342 508 A steve.carlson@mbu.edu
CARLSON, Steven, T ..... 574-372-5100 158 B carlsost@grace.edu
CARLSON, Susan .... 510-987-0728.. 68 F susan.carlson@ucop.edu
CARLSON, Tammy .... 309-438-8846 140 L tscarls@ilstu.edu
CARLSON ZINK, Deanna .... 701-777-2611 353 G deannac@undfoundation.org
CARLSTON, Gary, L .... 435-283-7010 474 A gary.carlston@snow.edu
CARLTON, Christopher .. 717-477-1481 407 B cocarlton@ship.edu
CARLTON, Edith .... 731-286-3300 437 A carlton@dscc.edu
CARLTON, Keitha .... 903-785-7661 454 F kcarlton@parisjc.edu
CARLTON, LeAnn, K ...... 816-654-7213 261 D lcarlton@kcumb.edu
CARLTON, William .... 912-279-5892 118 A wcarlton@ccga.edu
CARLTON-CAREW, Miranda .... 704-499-9200.. 93 B
CARMAN, Kevin .... 775-784-1740 279 E kcarman@unr.edu
CARMEL, Julie .... 508-929-8754 219 A jcarmel@worcester.edu
CARMEN, Kim .... 318-675-5207 194 D shvreg@lsuhsc.edu
CARMEY, Emily .... 989-328-1245 234 D emily.carmey@montcalm.edu
CARMICAL, Beth .... 910-272-3343 346 A bcarmical@robeson.edu
CARMICHAEL, Ann, C ... 803-812-7330 425 D anncar@mailbox.sc.edu
CARMICHAEL, Beverly, C .... 904-819-6290.. 98 I bcarmichael@flagler.edu
CARMICHAEL, Brenda ... 620-343-4600 177 C bcarmichael@fhtc.edu
CARMICHAEL, John .... 360-867-6100 494 G carmichj@evergreen.edu
CARMICHAEL, Matthew . 541-346-4127 387 F mecarmic@uoregon.edu
CARMICHAEL, Paul .... 860-343-5787.. 86 A pcarmichael@mxcc.commnet.edu
CARMICHAEL, Peggy ..... 304-214-8901 503 E pcarmichael@wvncc.edu
CARMICHAEL, Stacey .... 770-394-8300 115 E stacey.carmichael@cbre.com
CARMICHAEL, William .. 901-369-0835.. 93 B
CARMINE, Kevin .... 718-319-7965 302 D kcarmine@hostos.cuny.edu
CARMODY, Mark .... 508-678-2811 219 C mark.carmody@bristolcc.edu
CARMODY, Patricia .... 507-537-6206 248 A patricia.carmody@smsu.edu
CARNAGHI, Jan .... 317-955-6154 162 R jcarnaghi@marian.edu
CARNAHAN, Diane .... 209-468-9155.. 67 C dcarnahan@sjcoe.net
CARNAHAN, Scott .... 503-883-2229 383 H scarnah@linfield.edu
CARNAROLI, Craig .... 215-898-6693 412 G carnarol@upenn.edu
CARNATHAN, Janice ...... 575-234-9200 295 D jcarnath@nmsu.edu
CARNE, Kim .... 906-786-5802 228 A carnek@baycollege.edu
CARNE, Margaret, A ...... 920-748-8180 509 H carnem@ripon.edu
CARNES, Allen .... 336-770-3320 352 B carnesa@uncsa.edu
CARNES, Gregory, A ...... 256-765-4245.... 9 A gacarnes@una.edu
CARNES, Kathy, M .... 252-493-7220 345 E kcarnes@email.pittcc.edu
CARNES, Peter .... 508-565-1206 224 H pcarnes@stonehill.edu
CARNEVALE, David .... 562-907-4284.. 75 A dcarneva@whittier.edu
CARNEY, Diane, E .... 412-291-6250 389 F dcarney@aii.edu
CARNEY, Gary .... 610-861-7909 402 D carneyg@moravian.edu
CARNEY, John .... 615-460-6000 430 D
CARNEY, Margaret .... 202-319-5515.. 91 D carneym@cua.edu
CARNEY, Martin .... 216-421-7424 359 J mcarney@cia.edu
CARNEY, Michael, J ...... 715-836-4353 510 D carneymj@uwec.edu
CARNEY, Michelle .... 785-864-8975 181 I mmcarney@ku.edu
CARNEY, Paige .... 304-766-3313 505 A carney3@wvstateu.edu
CARNEY, Paul .... 405-878-5169 379 G pbcarney@stgregorys.edu
CARNEY, Sheila, A .... 412-578-6424 391 G carneysa@carlow.edu
CARNEY, Susie .... 620-278-4228 181 G susie.carney@sterling.edu
CARNEY, Timothy .... 202-319-5619.. 91 D carneyt@cua.edu
CARNEY, Timothy, D ..... 412-578-8712 391 G tdcarney@carlow.edu
CARNEY-DEBORD, Nan . 740-587-6428 361 B carneydebord@denison.edu
CARNEY-HALL, Karla ..... 309-556-3111 141 B dstudent@iwu.edu
CARNICOM, Scott .... 570-484-2204 406 E carnicom@lockhaven.edu
CARNIE, Andrew, H .... 520-621-3471.. 16 J carnie@email.arizona.edu
CARNS, Mary Lee .... 843-525-5692 424 E mcarns@tcl.edu
CARNZ, Scott .... 206-239-2320 492 D scarnz@aii.edu
CARO, M.J .... 386-226-6339.. 98 C carom1@erau.edu
CARO, Mary Ellen .... 609-984-1130 292 B mcaro@tesu.edu
CAROL, Steve .... 732-987-2414 286 D scarol@georgian.edu
CAROLINA, Kimberly ..... 203-575-8056.. 86 B kcarolina@nv.edu
CARON, Bob .... 817-552-3700 451 G bcaron@tku.edu
CARON, Lenn .... 410-455-3260 208 A carlen@umbc.edu
CARON, Linda .... 937-775-2225 374 B linda.caron@wright.edu
CARON, Paul .... 310-506-4621.. 56 D paul.caron@pepperdine.edu
CAROTHERS, Amy .... 775-784-6620 279 E acarothers@unr.edu
CAROTHERS, Cat .... 425-640-1112 494 E cat.carothers@edcc.edu
CAROTHERS, John .... 775-784-1394 279 E jcarothers@adv.unr.edu
CAROTHERS, Todd .... 608-342-1226 511 D carotherst@uwplatt.edu
CAROW, Ken .... 317-274-2481 160 E kcarow@iupui.edu
CARP, Ralph .... 215-637-7700 397 G rcarp@holyfamily.edu
CARP, Richard, M .... 925-631-4040.. 59 C rmc8@stmarys-ca.edu
CARPENTER, Ariel .... 909-607-0434.. 37 L ariel.carpenter@cgu.edu
CARPENTER, Barbara ..... 225-771-2613 195 K carp.subr@aol.com
CARPENTER, Barbara ..... 225-771-2016 195 J barbara_carpenter@subr.edu
CARPENTER, Brenda ...... 405-682-1611 377 C bcarpenter@occc.edu
CARPENTER, Carol .... 616-977-5520 229 B carol.carpenter@cornerstone.edu
CARPENTER, Carolyn, A 573-629-3116 260 G carolyn.carpenter@hlg.edu
CARPENTER, Courtney .. 757-221-2001 479 I cmcarp@wm.edu
CARPENTER, Dana .... 225-771-2394 195 K dana_carpenter@subr.edu
CARPENTER, David .... 913-722-0272 178 G david.carpenter@kansaschristian.edu
CARPENTER, Debra .... 281-283-2150 465 B carpenter@uhcl.edu
CARPENTER, Harold, V . 913-722-0272 178 G harold.carpenter@kansaschristian.edu
CARPENTER, Hedy, L .... 818-677-2138.. 33 B hcarpenter@csun.edu

CARSON, Jessica .... 212-237-8717 302 F
jcarson@jjay.cuny.edu
CARSON, Joyce .... 312-553-2500 135 I
jcarson5@ccc.edu
CARSON, Monica .... 800-280-0307 155 H
monica.carson@ace.edu
CARSON, Paula .... 417-625-9394 263 G
carson-p@mssu.edu
CARSON, Rebecca .... 310-506-4558.. 56 D
rebecca.carson@pepperdine.edu
CARSON, Robert .... 419-995-8302 363 G
carson.r@rhodesstate.edu
CARSON, Scott .... 601-426-6346 255 G
scarson@southeasternbaptist.edu
CARSON, Scott, C .... 601-426-6346 255 G
scarson@southeasternbaptist.edu
CARSON, Staci .... 801-832-2750 474 E
scarson@westminstercollege.edu
CARSON, Steve .... 815-394-5058 150 C
scarson@rockford.edu
CARSON, Tamika .... 312-850-7070 136 C
tdavenport13@ccc.edu
CARSON, Warren .... 864-503-5634 425 H
wcarson@uscupstate.edu
CARSTARPHEN, Minnie . 334-876-9345.... 2 C
mcarstarphen@wccs.edu
CARSTENS, Jeffrey .... 402-375-7213 276 D
jecarst1@wsc.edu
CARSTENS, Joel, B .... 603-862-3671 282 F
joel.carstens@unh.edu
CARSTENS, Lisa .... 503-352-3065 385 I
carstens@pacificu.edu
CARSTENS, Ryan .... 509-533-7042 493 H
ryan.carstens@scc.spokane.edu
CARSTENSEN, Lundie .... 619-201-8705.. 60 A
lundie.carstensen@sdcc.edu
CARSWELL, Justin .... 417-690-3446 258 E
carswell@cofo.edu
CARSWELL, Linda .... 828-448-3110 347 F
lcarswell@wpcc.edu
CARSWELL, Pamela .... 386-752-1822.. 99 J
pamela.carswell@fgc.edu
CARSWELL, William .... 843-383-8063 420 B
wcarswell@coker.edu
CART, J. Robert .... 973-655-7028 287 D
cartr@mail.montclair.edu
CARTABUKE,
Jacqueline .... 516-877-6004 297 I
jcartabuke@adelphi.edu
CARTAGENA, Carlos .... 520-515-5485.. 11 R
cartagec@cochise.edu
CARTAGENA, Milagros .. 787-704-1020 522 J
mcartagena@ediccollege.edu
CARTAGENA, Moises ..... 787-850-9390 528 B
moises.cartagena@upr.edu
CARTE, Mandy .... 216-368-2595 358 C
mmc111@case.edu
CARTEE, Dawn, H .... 706-542-3451 127 A
cartee@uga.edu
CARTER, Abby .... 229-227-3177 126 C
acarter@southernregional.edu
CARTER, Alfonza .... 919-546-8527 348 I
alcarter@shawu.edu
CARTER, Allison, A .... 906-487-2335 234 A
allison@mtu.edu
CARTER, Amber .... 859-442-1712 185 I
amber.carter@kctcs.edu
CARTER, Andy .... 701-858-3042 354 C
andy.carter@minotstateu.edu
CARTER, Angela, M .... 336-334-4822 343 E
amcarter@gtcc.edu
CARTER, Anthony .... 404-413-2400 121 A
acarter107@gsu.edu
CARTER, Ashlee .... 617-585-1792 222 H
ashlee.carter@necmusic.edu
CARTER, Ashley .... 770-534-6164 116 F
acarter@brenau.edu
CARTER, Bates .... 302-622-8000.. 90 A
bcarter@dcad.edu
CARTER, Bessie .... 405-945-3211 378 C
cartebm@osuokc.edu
CARTER, Beth .... 910-630-7425 340 A
bcarter@methodist.edu
CARTER, Bobbi Jo .... 802-635-1381 477 C
bobbijo.carter@jsc.edu
CARTER, Brenda, C .... 214-491-6271 446 I
bcarter@collin.edu
CARTER, Brett .... 607-778-5003 326 C
carterbd@sunybroome.edu
CARTER, Cameron, S .... 530-754-7764.. 68 H
cscarter@ucdavis.edu
CARTER, Carmen .... 936-261-3502 458 F
crcarter@pvamu.edu
CARTER, Christopher ..... 425-235-2352 497 E
ccarter@rtc.edu
CARTER, Cindy .... 641-585-8130 174 B
carterc@waldorf.edu
CARTER, Cindy .... 559-453-3447.. 43 J
cindy.carter@fresno.edu
CARTER, Clark .... 843-863-8008 419 C
ccarter@csuniv.edu
CARTER, Clay .... 252-940-6357 340 N
clay.carter@beaufortccc.edu
CARTER, Cynthia .... 229-931-2057 125 G
ccarter@southgatech.edu
CARTER, Danita .... 314-918-2625 260 A
dcarter@eden.edu
CARTER, Darryl .... 716-878-6522 326 E
carterdc@buffalostate.edu
CARTER, David .... 512-232-6400 467 C
david.carter@austin.utexas.edu
CARTER, Derek .... 410-951-3748 208 F
dcarter@coppin.edu
CARTER, Dione .... 310-434-4858.. 62 G
carter_dione@smc.edu
CARTER, Don .... 928-523-1605.. 14 K
don.carter@nau.edu
CARTER, Ed .... 256-331-5277.... 3 C
cartere@nwscc.edu
CARTER, Edythe, L .... 806-371-5335 442 D
elcarter@actx.edu
CARTER, Emery .... 281-487-1170 460 G
ecarter@txchiro.edu
CARTER, Emily .... 609-258-5391 288 F
eac@princeton.edu
CARTER, Evonne .... 252-335-0821 342 D
evonne_carter@albemarle.edu
CARTER, F. 'Thatcher' ... 509-527-5195 500 G
carterft@whitman.edu
CARTER, Fantina .... 615-329-8586 431 I
fcarter@fisk.edu
CARTER, FeRita .... 951-222-8073.. 58 H
ferita.carter@rcc.edu
CARTER, Gary, L .... 731-661-5204 439 D
gcarter@uu.edu
CARTER, Glenda, F .... 903-927-3336 471 B
gcarter@wileyc.edu
CARTER, Glenn .... 302-831-3358.. 90 I
gcarter@udel.edu
CARTER, Helene .... 706-821-8233 124 C
hcarter@paine.edu
CARTER, Holly .... 812-488-1040 164 G
hc110@evansville.edu
CARTER, Hope .... 601-974-1000 254 A
CARTER, Hugh .... 334-222-6591.... 2 H
hcarter@lbwcc.edu
CARTER, Jacque .... 402-826-8253 274 E
jacque.carter@doane.edu
CARTER, Jamail .... 951-487-3409.. 52 J
jcarter@msjc.edu
CARTER, JaPrince, L ..... 804-342-3895 491 C
jlcarter@vuu.edu
CARTER, Jeffrey .... 252-335-0821 342 D
jeffrey_carter@albemarle.edu
CARTER, Jeffrey, W .... 800-287-8822 156 D
president@bethanyseminary.edu
CARTER, Jennifer, L .... 724-847-6603 395 J
jlcarter@geneva.edu
CARTER, Jennings .... 618-545-3169 142 D
jcarter@kaskaskia.edu
CARTER, Jessica .... 276-656-0312 489 A
jcarter@patrickhenry.edu
CARTER, Joelle, D .... 336-322-2163 345 D
joelle.carter@piedmontcc.edu
CARTER, John .... 334-953-5159 517 I
john.carter@us.af.mil
CARTER, John, B .... 413-542-2771 210 F
jbcarter@amherst.edu
CARTER, IHM,
Joseph Marie .... 610-647-4400 397 I
jcarter@immaculata.edu
CARTER, Julien, C .... 617-627-3271 225 A
julien.carter@tufts.edu
CARTER, June .... 864-503-5881 425 H
jcarter@uscupstate.edu
CARTER, Kathleen .... 706-778-8500 124 E
kcarter@piedmont.edu
CARTER, Kim .... 712-325-3320 170 K
kcarter@iwcc.edu
CARTER, Kim, C .... 859-257-9420 190 B
kccarter.1@uky.edu
CARTER, Kimberly .... 229-430-4600 114 I
kimberly.carter@asurams.edu
CARTER, Lana .... 719-296-6108.. 81 M
lana.carter@pueblocc.edu
CARTER, Laurie, A .... 717-477-1301 407 B
lacarter@ship.edu
CARTER, Lawrence, E .... 470-639-0323 123 E
lawrence.carter@morehouse.edu
CARTER, Lawrence, L .... 517-321-0242 231 A
lcarter@glcc.edu
CARTER, Leslie .... 479-979-1304.. 23 J
lcarter@ozarks.edu
CARTER, Linda .... 606-539-4230 190 A
linda.carter@ucumberlands.edu
CARTER, Linda .... 816-604-3081 262 J
linda.carter@mcckc.edu
CARTER, Linnie, S .... 717-780-2321 396 G
lscarter@hacc.edu
CARTER, Luther, F .... 843-661-1210 421 H
lcarter@fmarion.edu
CARTER, Malinda .... 815-280-2515 142 A
mcarter@jjc.edu
CARTER, Martin .... 404-527-4520 117 C
mcarter@carver.edu
CARTER, Matt .... 505-277-3003 296 H
mdcarter@unm.edu
CARTER, Melanie .... 202-806-2550.. 92 C
melcarter@howard.edu
CARTER, Michael .... 270-789-5001 184 B
mvcarter@campbellsville.edu
CARTER, Michele .... 254-526-1331 445 L
michele.carter@ctcd.edu
CARTER, Mike .... 918-495-7150 378 H
mcarter@oru.edu
CARTER, Nick .... 510-841-1905.. 25 F
ncarter@absw.edu
CARTER, Ninette .... 580-581-2226 375 A
ncarter@cameron.edu
CARTER, Pam .... 215-751-8737 393 A
pcarter@ccp.edu
CARTER, Paula .... 831-582-3004.. 33 A
pcarter@csumb.edu
CARTER, Peggy .... 731-352-4096 430 E
carterp@bethelu.edu
CARTER, Phillip .... 615-547-1307 431 D
pcarter@cumberland.edu
CARTER, Phyllis .... 510-464-3232.. 56 H
pcarter@peralta.edu
CARTER, Prudence .... 510-643-6644.. 68 G
pcarter@berkeley.edu
CARTER, Quamina .... 909-621-8965.. 37 L
quamina.carter@cgu.edu
CARTER, R. Daphne .... 843-661-1188 421 H
rcarter@fmarion.edu
CARTER, Regina, W .... 501-569-3408.. 22 B
rswade@ualr.edu
CARTER, Richard .... 251-460-6283.... 9 B
rcarter@southalabama.edu
CARTER, Robin .... 916-278-7737.. 33 C
carterr@csus.edu
CARTER, Rodney .... 305-626-3168.. 99 M
rodney.carter@fmuniv.edu
CARTER, Ronald, L .... 909-558-7616.. 48 H
rcarter@llu.edu
CARTER, Ronald, L .... 704-378-1006 338 I
rcarter@jcsu.edu
CARTER, Saundra .... 202-274-6430.. 93 D
scarter@udc.edu
CARTER, Scott .... 620-278-4290 181 G
scarter@sterling.edu
CARTER, Seth, M .... 785-460-5400 176 L
seth.carter@colbycc.edu
CARTER, Shanel .... 602-286-8330.. 13 G
shanel.carter@gatewaycc.edu
CARTER, Sharon, L .... 714-879-3901.. 45 I
slcarter@hiu.edu
CARTER, Shawna, M ..... 608-246-6249 514 A
smcarter@madisoncollege.edu
CARTER, Sheila .... 312-369-7187 136 H
scarter@colum.edu
CARTER, Shree .... 714-556-3610.. 72 F
scarter@vanguard.edu
CARTER, Shree .... 714-556-3610.. 72 F
vutrustees@vanguard.edu
CARTER, Sonja .... 212-961-3337 298 H
scarter@bankstreet.edu
CARTER, Spencer, D .... 269-471-3395 227 B
scarter@andrews.edu
CARTER, Steven, J .... 215-887-5511 414 D
scarter@wts.edu
CARTER, Sue, V .... 434-223-6220 481 D
svcarter@hsc.edu
CARTER, Tay Sha .... 479-619-4396.. 20 F
tcarter@nwacc.edu
CARTER, Thomas, E .... 315-470-6691 328 D
tecarter@esf.edu
CARTER, Tina, P .... 919-866-5000 347 D
CARTER, Todd .... 316-322-3201 175 I
tcarter@butlercc.edu
CARTER, Todd .... 620-417-1012 181 E
todd.carter@sccc.edu
CARTER, Tom .... 256-331-5263.... 3 C
tom.carter@nwscc.edu
CARTER, Veronika .... 802-656-0589 476 E
vlcarter@uvm.edu
CARTER, JR., Walter, E . 410-293-1000 519 E
CARTER, William, E .... 713-718-8708 450 D
william.carter@hccs.edu
CARTER, William, M ..... 412-648-1401 412 I
wmc4@pitt.edu
CARTER, Zina .... 979-532-6417 471 A
zinac@wcjc.edu
CARTER-CHAPMAN,
Renee .... 907-786-6486.. 10 A
rmcarterchapman@alaska.edu
CARTER-COLEY, Stacey . 252-492-2061 347 C
cartercoley@vgcc.edu
CARTER-DOVE,
Bernadette .... 919-209-2025 344 C
bjcarterdove@johnstoncc.edu
CARTER-ELIZONDO,
Stacy .... 409-880-8379 462 C
stacy.carter-elizondo@lamar.edu
CARTER-HARBOUR,
Courtney .... 972-860-7335 447 I
courtneycarter@dcccd.edu
CARTER-STEVENS,
Marilyn .... 718-862-7958 313 L
marilyn.carter@manhattan.edu
CARTER-TELLISON,
Katrina .... 561-237-7210 103 E
kcarter-tellison@lynn.edu
CARTHELL, Sidney, G .... 270-809-6836 188 D
scarthell@murraystate.edu
CARTIER, Jennifer .... 207-509-7282 200 I
jcartier@unity.edu
CARTIER, Jolie, L .... 619-239-0391.. 35 C
jcartier@cwsl.edu
CARTIER, Missy, M .... 559-323-2100.. 61 A
mcartier@sjcl.edu
CARTLEDGE, Ernest .... 240-567-7991 205 F
ernest.cartledge@montgomerycollege.edu
CARTLEDGE, Maureen ... 210-486-2174 441 I
mcartledge@alamo.edu
CARTMILL, Mark .... 859-985-3922 183 I
cartmillm@berea.edu
CARTNAL, Ryan .... 805-546-3946.. 41 C
rcartnal@cuesta.edu
CARTNEY, Michael, D .... 605-882-5284 427 D
cartneym@lakeareatech.edu
CARTOLANO, Joseph .... 718-631-6231 303 F
jcartolano@qcc.cuny.edu
CARTRIGHT, Jonathan ... 573-882-2011 268 B
CARTWRIGHT,
Alexander .... 573-882-3387 268 C
chancellor@missouri.edu
CARTWRIGHT, Bill .... 415-422-5417.. 72 A
jcartwri@usfca.edu
CARTWRIGHT, Cathy ..... 206-592-3339 495 E
ccartwright@highline.edu
CARTWRIGHT, Kevin ..... 949-376-6000.. 47 H
kcartwright@lcad.edu
CARTWRIGHT,
Michael, G .... 317-788-3233 164 H
mcartwright@uindy.edu
CARTY, Cheryl .... 478-471-5235 123 A
cheryl.carty@mga.edu
CARTY, Karenann .... 718-933-6700 315 K
kcarty@monroecollege.edu
CARTY, Pamela .... 856-200-4575 285 C
pcarty@cccnj.edu
CARTY, Raymond, W ..... 573-629-3094 260 G
rcarty@hlg.edu
CARULLO, Susan, H ...... 843-792-2071 422 C
carullos@musc.edu
CARUOLO, Michael .... 401-341-2334 417 D
michael.caruolo@salve.edu
CARUSO, Anne-Marie .... 617-989-4174 225 E
carusoa@wit.edu
CARUSO, Britni .... 217-814-5440 151 B
britni.caruso@stjohnscollegespringfield.edu
CARUSO, Elizabeth, S ... 585-395-2414 326 D
lcaruso@brockport.edu
CARUSO, Janet .... 516-572-7599 316 C
janet.caruso@ncc.edu
CARUSO, Joseph .... 909-558-4683.. 48 H
jcaruso@llu.edu
CARUSO, Michael .... 401-739-5000 416 D
mcaruso@neit.edu
CARUSO, Michele, E ..... 985-448-4081 197 C
michele.caruso@nicholls.edu
CARUSO, Rob .... 954-492-5353.. 96 J
rcaruso@citycollege.edu
CARUTHERS, Janet .... 573-875-7372 258 F
jaocaruthers@ccis.edu
CARVAJAL, Augusto .... 787-780-0070 521 B
acarvajal@caribbean.edu
CARVAJAL, Richard .... 229-333-5952 127 H
rcarvajal@valdosta.edu
CARVALHO, Corrine .... 651-690-6722 249 T
clcarvalho944@stkate.edu
CARVALHO, Corrine, I ... 651-962-5826 251 D
clcarvalho@stthomas.edu
CARVALHO, Marco .... 321-674-8020.. 99 K
mcarvalho@fit.edu
CARVALHO, Susan .... 205-348-8280.... 8 A
secarvalho@ua.edu

CASTELLINI, Michael ..... 907-474-7229.. 10 B
macastellini@alaska.edu
CASTELLINO, Lisa .... 707-826-5339.. 34 A
lisa.castellino@humboldt.edu
CASTELLO, Donald .... 815-836-5425 143 E
casteldo@lewisu.edu
CASTELLO, Ellen, J .... 575-646-2090 295 B
castello@nmsu.edu
CASTELLOE, Stephen ...... 336-334-4822 343 E
srcastelloe@gtcc.edu
CASTELLUCCI, Paul .... 847-467-6072 148 C
pjcastel@northwestern.edu
CASTENEDA, Debbie ...... 970-542-3140.. 81 A
debbie.casteneda@morgancc.edu
CASTERTON, Deanna ..... 563-387-1038 171 I
castde01@luther.edu
CASTETE, Ralynn, F .... 337-475-5140 197 B
rcastete@mcneese.edu
CASTIGLIA, Beth .... 973-278-5400 299 F
beth-castigli@berkeleycollege.edu
CASTIGLIA, Beth .... 201-559-6140 286 C
castigliab@felician.edu
CASTIGLIA, Beth .... 973-278-5400 283 J
beth-castigli@berkeleycollege.edu
CASTIGLIONE,
Joseph, R .... 405-325-8208 380 L
jcastiglione@ou.edu
CASTIGLIONE, Patricia .. 616-632-2809 227 C
trish.castiglione@aquinas.edu
CASTIGLIONI, Randy ..... 713-348-5241 455 F
castigr@rice.edu
CASTILAW, Timothy .... 660-543-4113 268 A
castilaw@ucmo.edu
CASTILLA, Rafael .... 201-327-8877 285 J
rcastilla@eastwick.edu
CASTILLO, Arely .... 318-342-1295 198 A
castillo@ulm.edu
CASTILLO, Candace .... 972-273-3013 448 C
ccastillo@dcccd.edu
CASTILLO, Carlos .... 305-348-2103 109 D
carlos.castillo8@fiu.edu
CASTILLO, Dale .... 785-309-3108 181 D
dale.castillo@salinatech.edu
CASTILLO, David .... 559-934-2166.. 73 M
davidcastillo2@whccd.edu
CASTILLO, Diana .... 254-526-1348 445 L
diana.castillo@ctcd.edu
CASTILLO, Elisa .... 978-542-6410 218 E
elisa.castillo@salemstate.edu
CASTILLO, Evelyn .... 787-284-1912 524 C
ecastillo@ponce.inter.edu
CASTILLO, Henry .... 718-862-7249 313 L
bookstore@manhattan.edu
CASTILLO, Jay .... 510-436-1648.. 45 G
jcastillo@hnu.edu
CASTILLO, JR., Juan, J . 956-326-2380 459 B
jjcastillo@tamiu.edu
CASTILLO, Keith .... 951-552-8720.. 28 G
kcastillo@calbaptist.edu
CASTILLO, Lida .... 626-873-2139.. 53 A
lcastillo@mtsierra.edu
CASTILLO, Maggie .... 623-935-8839.. 13 F
maggie.castillo@estrellamountain.edu
CASTILLO, Mario .... 832-813-6508 452 C
mario.k.castillo@lonestar.edu
CASTILLO, Nicole .... 209-946-2496.. 70 F
ncastillo@pacific.edu
CASTILLO, Pio .... 818-364-7866.. 49 C
castilpg@lamission.edu
CASTILLO, Raul, V .... 818-947-2618.. 49 G
castilrv@lavc.edu
CASTILLO, Rosalinda ..... 773-442-5300 147 G
r-castillo2@neiu.edu
CASTILLO, Salvador ...... 541-737-8083 385 F
salvador.castillo@oregonstate.edu
CASTILLO, Santiago .... 432-837-8885 462 G
santiago.castillo@sulross.edu
CASTILLO, Saundra .... 575-527-7076 295 E
scastillo@nmsu.edu
CASTILLO-ALANIZ,
Jo Elda .... 361-593-3991 460 B
jo.alaniz@tamuk.edu
CASTILLO CLARK,
Evette .... 925-631-4238.. 59 C
ecc4@stmarys-ca.edu
CASTILLO-FRICK, Iliana . 305-237-0294 103 L
ifrick@mdc.edu
CASTILLO-GARRISON,
Estella .... 949-582-4646.. 64 J
egarrison@saddleback.edu
CASTILLO JOHNSON,
Grace .... 909-537-5241.. 33 D
CASTILLON, Nicole .... 307-382-1642 517 C
ncastillon@westernwyoming.edu
CASTLE, Ashley .... 757-382-9900.. 93 B
CASTLE, Ashley .... 757-493-6000.. 93 B
CASTLE, Carey .... 218-793-8612 246 F
carey.castle@northlandcollege.edu
CASTLE, Carey .... 218-683-8612 246 F
carey.castle@northlandcollege.edu
CASTLE, Clinton .... 218-683-8600 246 F
clinton.castle@northlandcollege.edu
CASTLE, Josh .... 802-322-1672 475 A
josh.castle@goddard.edu
CASTLE, Lyle, W .... 208-282-3099 132 B
castlyle@isu.edu
CASTLE, Ruthie .... 662-562-3213 255 C
rcastle@northwestms.edu
CASTLE, Sarah .... 218-935-0417 251 F
sarah.castle@wetcc.edu
CASTLE, Stephen .... 517-750-1200 237 D
stephen.castle@arbor.edu
CASTLE, Tom .... 319-363-1323 172 B
tcastle@mtmercy.edu
CASTLEBERRY, Annettee 870-307-7227.. 20 C
annette.castleberry@lyon.edu
CASTLEBERRY, Joseph .. 425-889-4202 496 E
joseph.castleberry@northwestu.edu
CASTLEBERRY, Rita, J ... 580-327-8540 376 K
rjcastleberry@nwosu.edu
CASTLEBURY, Lisa .... 812-357-6515 164 A
lcastlebury@saintmeinrad.edu
CASTLEMAN, Janet, L ... 401-865-2816 416 E
jcastlem@providence.edu
CASTLEMAN, Louanna ... 910-678-0141 343 B
castleml@faytechcc.edu
CASTON, Gay Lynn .... 601-857-3396 253 B
glcaston@hindscc.edu
CASTONGUAY, Sharon .. 860-685-3377.. 89 F
scastonguay@wesleyan.edu
CASTONGUAY, Suzette .. 937-769-1375 356 G
scastonguay@antioch.edu
CASTOR, Tamela .... 661-362-3516.. 39 C
tammy.castor@canyons.edu
CASTORENA, Christina .. 425-640-1668 494 E
christina.castorena@edcc.edu
CASTRO, Adam .... 973-748-9000 284 A
adam_castro@bloomfield.edu
CASTRO, Bernie .... 856-691-8600 285 C
bcastro@cccnj.edu
CASTRO, Cynthia .... 208-885-6307 132 I
cynthiacastro@uidaho.edu
CASTRO, Daisy .... 787-753-6335 522 Q
dcastro@icprjc.edu
CASTRO, Donna .... 505-747-2160 295 H
donna.castro@nnmc.edu
CASTRO, Evelyn .... 718-804-8805 303 C
ecastro@mec.cuny.edu
CASTRO, Francia, L .... 212-694-1000 299 L
fcastro@boricuacollege.edu
CASTRO, Ida, L .... 570-504-9647 395 I
icastro@tcmc.edu
CASTRO, Joseph, I .... 559-278-2324.. 32 A
josephcastro@csufresno.edu
CASTRO, Juan, C .... 787-850-9375 528 B
juan.castro@upr.edu
CASTRO, Juan, C .... 787-743-3038 525 M
jcastro@sanjuanbautista.edu
CASTRO, Juan, C .... 787-850-9367 528 B
juan.castro@upr.edu
CASTRO, Judy .... 925-969-3300.. 46 L
jcastro@jfku.edu
CASTRO, Kaye .... 239-687-5343.. 95 B
kcastro@avemarialaw.edu
CASTRO, Lorna .... 787-764-0000 528 F
lorna.castro@upr.edu
CASTRO, Louise, P .... 915-747-8820 467 E
lpcastro@utep.edu
CASTRO, Madelyn .... 813-253-6201 113 E
macastro@ut.edu
CASTRO, Manny .... 670-237-6772 520 D
manny.castro@marianas.edu
CASTRO, Melba .... 657-278-5579.. 32 B
melbacastro@fullerton.edu
CASTRO, Octavio .... 414-288-5629 508 C
octavio.castro@marquette.edu
CASTRO, Raul .... 787-738-2161 528 A
raul.castro@upr.edu
CASTRO, Roz .... 630-953-3681 135 A
rcastro@chamberlain.edu
CASTRO, Sarah .... 202-624-1426 499 D
smcastro@uw.edu
CASTRO, Toni .... 206-592-3351 495 E
tcastro@highline.edu
CASTRO-DUARTE, Betsy 915-747-5640 467 E
bcastro@utep.edu
CASTRO-QUIRINO,
Sonya .... 806-743-3949 463 E
sonya.castro@ttuhsc.edu
CASTRO-ROMAKER,
Judith .... 608-246-6678 514 A
jcastro-romaker@madisoncollege.edu
CASTROVERDE MOSKOLENKO,
Tania .... 312-431-2391 150 D
CASTRUITA, Javier .... 408-741-2042.. 74 B
javier_castruita@wvm.edu
CASUCCIO, Anthony ...... 716-896-0700 333 C
acasuccio@villa.edu
CASWELL, Roger .... 620-341-5372 177 B
rcaswekk@emporia.edu
CATALANA, Paul .... 864-455-8201 425 E
pcatalana@ghs.org
CATALANO, Francesca .. 815-802-8758 142 C
fcatalano@kcc.edu
CATALANO, John .... 864-424-8019 425 G
jcat@mailbox.sc.edu
CATALANO, Megan .... 573-288-6570 259 E
mcatalano@culver.edu
CATALANO, Mike .... 605-995-2669 427 A
micatala@dwu.edu
CATALANO, Steven .... 718-489-5309 322 D
scatalano@sfc.edu
CATALDI, Amy, E .... 405-208-5446 377 D
acataldi@okcu.edu
CATALDI, Jennifer .... 317-738-8256 157 L
jcataldi@franklincollege.edu
CATALDO, Adrienne .... 803-938-3906 425 F
cataldo@uscsumter.edu
CATALFAMO, Kevin .... 856-351-2701 291 E
kcatalfamo@salemcc.edu
CATALLOZZI, Lori, A ..... 617-228-2048 219 D
lacatallozzi@bhcc.mass.edu
CATALON, Linda, H .... 225-771-2520 195 J
linda_catalon@sus.edu
CATANZARO, Sam .... 309-438-7018 140 L
catanzar@ilstu.edu
CATARELLI, Rebecca ..... 802-258-9233 475 D
rcatarelli@marlboro.edu
CATAUDELLA,
Vincent, B .... 203-576-5616.. 88 D
vincent.cataudella@stvincentscollege.edu
CATCHINGS, Robert .... 202-806-6700.. 92 C
rcatchings@howard.edu
CATE, Fred .... 812-855-1161 159 G
fcate@iu.edu
CATE, Fred, H .... 812-856-2096 159 H
vpr@iu.edu
CATE, Richard, H .... 802-656-0219 476 E
richard.cate@uvm.edu
CATELLA, Rosanne .... 440-934-3101 367 D
rcatella@ohiobusinesscollege.edu
CATER, Lisa .... 870-460-1420.. 22 D
caterl@uamont.edu
CATES, Brenda, B .... 919-658-7853 349 F
bcates@umo.edu
CATES, Carl .... 870-972-3973.. 18 A
ccates@astate.edu
CATES, Chris .... 423-585-2618 438 D
chris.cates@ws.edu
CATES, Damon .... 312-915-7405 144 D
dcates1@luc.edu
CATES, Jared .... 417-255-7233 263 I
jaredcated@missouristate.edu
CATES, Jo .... 312-942-8735 150 F
jo_cates@rush.edu
CATES, John .... 256-824-6633.... 8 C
john.cates@uah.edu
CATH, Tom .... 219-464-5005 165 D
tom.cath@valpo.edu
CATHCART, Scott .... 760-744-1150.. 55 K
scathcart@palomar.edu
CATHELINE, Jim .... 724-964-8811 403 A
jcatheline@ncstrades.edu
CATHERMAN, David .... 504-398-2279 196 E
dcatherman@uhcno.edu
CATHERWOOD, Ryan ...... 434-395-4804 482 E
catherwoodrp@longwood.edu
CATHEY, Patrice, A .... 716-878-4055 326 E
catheypc@mail.buffalostate.edu
CATHEY, Ron .... 318-257-4336 197 A
rcathey@latech.edu
CATHIE, Julie .... 530-541-4660.. 47 I
cathie@ltcc.edu
CATLETT, Deborrah, L .... 859-246-6810 185 G
deborrah.catlett@kctcs.edu
CATLETT, Hilary .... 509-257-2542 499 F
hilary.catlett@wallawalla.edu
CATLETT, Jennifer .... 865-471-3530 430 H
jcatlett@cn.edu
CATO, Amie .... 903-785-7661 454 F
acato@parisjc.edu
CATO, Jim .... 937-766-7610 358 D
catoj@cedarville.edu
CATO, Michael .... 845-437-7605 333 A
micato@vassar.edu
CATON, Bonnie .... 410-857-2259 205 E
bcaton@mcdaniel.edu
CATON, Brock, E .... 207-778-7033 201 D
brock.caton@maine.edu
CATON, Claire .... 713-646-1799 456 H
ccaton@stcl.edu
CATON, Lisa .... 979-627-0286 444 D
lisa.caton@blinn.edu
CATON, Rebecca, A .... 630-515-6190 145 I
rcaton@midwestern.edu
CATON, Rhonda .... 479-788-7073.. 22 A
rhonda.caton@uafs.edu
CATON, Sheron .... 325-794-4530 445 Q
sheron.caton@cisco.edu
CATOTA, Claudia .... 661-654-2137.. 31 B
ccatota@csub.edu
CATRON, Jonathan .... 864-644-5663 424 B
jcatron@swu.edu
CATRON-WOOD,
Rhonda, K .... 276-223-4772 490 C
rcatronwood@wcc.vccs.edu
CATT, Helen .... 229-430-3506 114 J
hcatt@albanytech.edu
CATTANACH, John, R .... 315-516-4100 268 E
cattanachj@umsl.edu
CATTANI, Jessica .... 213-624-1200.. 42 N
jcattani@fidm.edu
CATTIER, Alan, R .... 603-646-1349 281 C
alan.r.cattier@dartmouth.edu
CATTOLICA, Carolee ...... 707-256-7161.. 53 D
ccattolica@napavalley.edu
CATTON, Heather .... 936-468-5597 458 A
hcatton@sfasu.edu
CATTOOR, Chad, A .... 314-505-7304 258 I
cattoorc@csl.edu
CATZ, Jason .... 541-552-7070 386 H
catzj@sou.edu
CAUBLE, Christie .... 828-884-8250 335 L
caublecl@brevard.edu
CAUCE, Ana Mari .... 206-543-5010 499 D
pres@uw.edu
CAUDA, Lisa .... 585-475-7721 321 D
lisa.cauda@rit.edu
CAUDILL, Helene .... 209-667-3407.. 33 F
hcaudill@csustan.edu
CAUDILL, Reggie, J .... 973-596-5856 288 A
reggie.j.caudill@njit.edu
CAUDILL, Whitney, A .... 260-982-2658 162 Q
wjcaudill@manchester.edu
CAUDLE, Mary Anne ..... 252-789-0280 344 E
maryanne.caudle@martincc.edu
CAUDLE, Patricia, M ..... 909-748-8171.. 71 H
pat_caudle@redlands.edu
CAUGHMAN, Gretchen .. 706-721-4014 116 B
gcaughma@augusta.edu
CAULEY, Phil .... 828-227-2923 352 C
cauley@wcu.edu
CAULEY, Thomas .... 215-368-5000 389 H
tcauley@biblical.edu
CAULFIELD, Jack .... 508-213-2398 223 C
jack.caulfield@nichols.edu
CAULFIELD, Richard ...... 907-796-6509.. 10 C
racaulfield@alaska.edu
CAULK, Jeffrey .... 206-934-6020 497 H
jeffrey.caulk@seattlecolleges.edu
CAUPP, Jeffrey, G .... 480-245-7979.. 13 C
jeff.caupp@ibcs.edu
CAUSBY, Cory .... 828-227-7218 352 C
causby@wcu.edu
CAUSEY, Bruce .... 256-306-2569.... 1 F
bruce.causey@calhoun.edu
CAUSEY, Jana .... 601-554-5506 255 D
jcausey@prcc.edu
CAUSEY, Katherine .... 901-435-1259 433 A
katherine_causey@loc.edu
CAUSEY, Mary Frances . 928-350-1112.. 15 V
mcausey@prescott.edu
CAUSLAND, Luann .... 678-407-5231 119 F
lcausland@ggc.edu
CAUTIN, Robin .... 203-396-8020.. 88 C
cautinr@sacredheart.edu
CAUWELS, Beth .... 805-565-6101.. 74 I
bcauwels@westmont.edu
CAVACO, Frank .... 617-964-1100 210 G
fcavaco@ants.edu
CAVALIER, Amy .... 617-873-0106 213 B
amy.cavalier30@go.cambridgecollege.edu
CAVALIER, Deborah .... 617-747-2147 212 B
advisors@berkleemusic.com
CAVALIER, Wayne .... 210-341-1366 454 B
wcavalier@ost.edu
CAVALIERI, Correne ...... 718-779-1499 320 C
ccavalieri@plazacollege.edu
CAVALIERI, Cristina, G . 215-503-9496 411 E
cristina.cavalieri@jefferson.edu
CAVALIERI, Thomas ...... 856-566-6995 289 H
cavalita@rowan.edu
CAVALLARO,
Gregory, M .... 540-464-7328 490 E
gcav@vmiaa.org
CAVALLARO, Ronald, A . 401-825-1000 416 B
rcavallaro@ccri.edu
CAVALLARO, Vito .... 212-938-5500 328 E
vito@sunyopt.edu

CAVALLERANO, Tony .... 617-587-5647 222 G cavalleranot@neco.edu
CAVALLO, Julia .... 724-805-2592 410 C julia.cavallo@stvincent.edu
CAVALLO, Julia .... 724-805-2372 410 B julia.cavallo@email.stvincent.edu
CAVALLUZZI, Marty .... 253-840-8421 497 B mcavalluzzi@pierce.ctc.edu
CAVALOVITCH, Renee, T .... 412-397-6061 409 C cavalovitch@rmu.edu
CAVANAGH, Debbie ...... 310-338-4493.. 50 J debbie.cavanagh@lmu.edu
CAVANAGH, Jon .... 765-998-4161 164 C jon.cavanagh@taylor.edu
CAVANAGH, Kelly .... 614-508-7277 363 E kcavanagh@hondros.edu
CAVANAGH, Kevin .... 914-654-5085 305 A kcavanagh@cnr.edu
CAVANAGH, Paul .... 631-348-3169 317 G pcavanag@nyit.edu
CAVANAGH, Stephen ...... 413-545-5093 216 H dean@nursing.umass.edu
CAVANAUGH, Amy .... 503-943-7201 387 H cavanaug@up.edu
CAVANAUGH, Brian ...... 716-829-7878 307 B cavanaub@dyc.edu
CAVANAUGH, SSJ, Cecelia .... 215-753-3623 392 D ccavanau@chc.edu
CAVANAUGH, Kyle .... 919-684-2826 337 C kyle.cavanaugh@duke.edu
CAVANAUGH, Mary .... 212-396-7549 302 E mary.cavanaugh@hunter.cuny.edu
CAVANAUGH, Michael .. 585-582-8201 307 C michaelcavanaugh@elim.edu
CAVANESS, Kerrie .... 509-574-4870 500 I kcavaness@yvcc.edu
CAVANUAGH, Rachel .... 910-362-7317 341 E rcavenaugh@cfcc.edu
CAVAZOS, Christopher .. 505-224-4000 293 L ccavazos@cnm.edu
CAVAZOS, Rebecca .... 956-664-4680 456 G beckyc@southtexascollege.edu
CAVE, Erin, L .... 503-943-7125 387 H cave@up.edu
CAVENAUGH, Andy .... 910-296-2480 344 B acavenaugh@jamessprunt.edu
CAVENAUGH, Jennifer ... 407-691-1268 106 J jcavenaugh@rollins.edu
CAVENER, Douglas, R ... 814-865-9591 403 F drc9@psu.edu
CAVENY-NOECKER, Deanna, M .... 843-953-5731 420 C cavenyd@cofc.edu
CAVERHILL, Wendy .... 207-768-2708 200 B wcaverhill@nmcc.edu
CAVERLEY, Darla .... 320-629-5118 246 H calverleyd@pine.edu
CAVI, Sandra .... 309-438-8489 140 L skcavi@ilstu.edu
CAVICCHI, Daniel .... 401-454-6134 417 B dcavicch@risd.edu
CAVIEUX, Lydia .... 617-603-6935 222 F lydia.cavieux@necb.edu
CAVIN, JR., Elmo, M .... 806-743-3080 463 E elmo.cavin@ttuhsc.edu
CAVIN, Glynn .... 334-670-3617.... 7 E gcavin@troy.edu
CAVIN, Wesley .... 318-255-7950 197 A wes@latechalumni.org
CAVINESS, Autumn .... 512-505-3040 451 A adcaviness@htu.edu
CAVINESS, Debbie, J ..... 315-470-6632 328 D dcavines@esf.edu
CAVINESS, Howard .... 318-274-6437 196 G cavinessh@gram.edu
CAVINS-TULL, Kathryn .. 817-257-7820 461 A k.cavins@tcu.edu
CAVITT, Deborah .... 817-531-4298 463 G dcavitt@txwes.edu
CAWLEY, Deborah .... 610-527-0200 409 E deborah.cawley@rosemont.edu
CAWLEY, Frank .... 805-756-5352.. 30 K fcawley@calpoly.edu
CAWLEY, Jennifer .... 716-614-5950 318 E jcawley@niagaracc.suny.edu
CAWLEY, Patrick, J .... 843-792-4000 422 C cawleypj@musc.edu
CAWLEY, Steve .... 305-284-3515 112 O s.cawley@miami.edu
CAWLFIELD, Jeffrey .... 573-341-4557 269 A jdc@mst.edu
CAWOOD, J. Scott .... 215-702-4216 391 C scawood@cairn.edu
CAWOOD, Patti .... 423-614-8316 432 L pcawood@leeuniversity.edu
CAWTHON, Elisabeth ..... 817-272-3291 467 B cawthon2@uta.edu
CAWTHORNE, Jon, E .... 304-293-7272 505 B jon.cawthorne@mail.wvu.edu
CAWTHORNE, Jon, G .... 313-577-4059 239 C
CAWYER, Carol, S .... 406-466-6012 375 L cscawyer@langston.edu
CAYEA, Cynthia .... 516-364-0808 317 B library@nycollege.edu
CAYLOR, Deborah, Z ..... 540-458-8730 491 G dcaylor@wlu.edu
CAYWOOD, Janet .... 620-278-4280 181 G jcaywood@sterling.edu
CAYWOOD, Steven .... 620-278-4240 181 G scaywood@sterling.edu
CAZALET, David .... 865-539-7350 437 F djcazalet@pstcc.edu
CAZARES, Becky .... 559-934-2159.. 73 M beckycazares@whccd.edu
CAZARES, Javier .... 559-934-2176.. 73 M javiercazares@whccd.edu
CAZZETTA, Vinnie .... 845-341-4726 319 H vinnie.cazzetta@sunyorange.edu
CAÑIZALES, Rafael .... 909-558-4528.. 48 H rcanizales@llu.edu
CEA, Jorge .... 925-473-7430.. 41 A jcea@losmedanos.edu
CEBINA, Jody .... 704-687-1283 351 C jcebina@uncc.edu
CEBRICK, Daniel, T .... 570-208-5870 398 D dtcebric@kings.edu
CEBRZYNSKI, Gerard, J 847-735-5104 142 H cebrzynski@lakeforest.edu
CEBULA, Thomas .... 330-490-7051 373 F tcebula@walsh.edu
CECALA, Dianna .... 843-349-5207 421 L dianna.cecala@hgtc.edu
CECCHI, Joseph .... 505-277-5500 296 H cecchi@unm.edu
CECCHINI, Bernard .... 315-568-3127 317 A bcecchini@nycc.edu
CECCHINI, Dan .... 541-383-7700 382 B dcecchini@cocc.edu
CECE, Heidi .... 757-352-4809 484 E hcece@regent.edu
CECERE, Mollie .... 304-829-7591 501 F mcecere@bethanywv.edu
CECH, John .... 406-444-0314 271 F jcech@montana.edu
CECH, John .... 406-444-0316 271 F jcech@montana.edu
CECIL, Dale .... 270-686-4239 183 J dale.cecil@brescia.edu
CECIL, Matt .... 507-389-1713 246 A matt.cecil@mnsu.edu
CECIL, Patrick, A .... 502-895-3411 188 A pcecil@lpts.edu
CECOLA, Philip .... 856-200-4704 285 C pcecola@cccnj.edu
CEDAR, Leslie .... 512-471-3800 467 C cedar@alumni.utexas.edu
CEDERBERG, Alisha ...... 269-488-4231 231 G acederberg@kvcc.edu
CEDERHOLM, Annette .... 256-840-4142.... 3 F acederholm@snead.edu
CEDILLO, Arnulfo .... 510-436-2478.. 56 I acedillo@peralta.edu
CEDRONE, David, C .... 617-994-6904 216 F dmcedrone@bhe.mass.edu
CELA, Suela .... 406-377-9419 270 J scela@dawson.edu
CELAYA, Aintzane .... 305-284-4969 112 O a.celaya@miami.edu
CELENZA, Christopher ... 202-687-4043.. 92 B ccelenza@georgetown.edu
CELENZA, John .... 617-353-2445 212 G celenza@bu.edu
CELESTIN, Rose .... 870-575-8000.. 22 E celestinr@uapb.edu
CELHAY, Lilia .... 510-748-2318.. 56 G lcelhay@peralta.edu
CELIAN, Doris, M .... 734-487-0324 229 K dcelian@emich.edu
CELIS, Maricel .... 303-282-3427.. 82 G
CELL, Paul, M .... 973-655-5123 287 D cellp@mail.montclair.edu
CELLA, Barbara .... 925-473-7322.. 41 A bcella@losmedanos.edu
CELLEMME, Patricia .... 518-292-1710 321 G cellep@sage.edu
CELLI, David, S .... 570-389-4882 405 E dcelli@bloomu.edu
CELLINI, Roger .... 909-748-8020.. 71 H roger_cellini@redlands.edu
CELLINI, Todd .... 912-201-8007 125 H tcellini@southuniversity.edu
CELNIK, Rachel .... 845-352-3431 334 M shaareitorah@optonline.net
CELTEK, Serkan .... 956-872-5577 456 G sbceltek@southtexascollege.edu
CEMAN, Jamie .... 920-424-2442 511 B cemanj@uwosh.edu
CENDANA, Trish .... 304-293-4686 505 B trish.cendana@mail.wvu.edu
CENINA, Angela .... 714-547-9625.. 28 J acenina@calcoast.edu
CENSOR, Yerachmiel ..... 845-371-2481 334 H
CENTENO, Ilsa .... 787-743-3484 525 M icenteno@sanjuanbautista.edu
CENTENO, Sophia .... 714-533-1495.. 64 F scenteno@southbaylo.edu
CENTER, Daniel .... 734-432-5762 233 C dcenters@madonna.edu
CENTER, Mark, R .... 210-434-6711 454 D mrcenter@lake.ollusa.edu
CENTOR, Josh .... 412-268-3894 391 H jcentor@andrew.cmu.edu
CEO, Ray, A .... 240-895-3000 206 G raceo@smcm.edu
CEPEDA, Adrian .... 312-935-6683 149 K acepeda@robertmorris.edu
CEPEDA, Charlotte, R .... 670-237-6751 520 D charlotte.cepeda@marianas.edu
CEPERO, Ana .... 787-761-0640 527 C desarrollo@utcpr.edu
CEPERO, Yedi .... 305-821-3333 100 A ycepero@fnu.edu
CEPHAS, Marcia .... 410-951-3812 208 F mcephas@coppin.edu
CEPPI, Matthew .... 760-750-4040.. 33 E mceppi@csusm.edu
CEPPOS, Jerry .... 225-578-9294 193 M jceppos@lsu.edu
CERAMI, Joseph .... 713-525-3884 466 J ceramij@stthom.edu
CERAVOLO, Suzanne ..... 973-408-3464 285 E sceravol@drew.edu
CERCONE, Suzanne .... 570-504-7954 399 A cercones@lackawanna.edu
CERDA, Manuel .... 626-585-7400.. 56 B mcerda4@pasadena.edu
CERERZO, Sabrina .... 718-951-5622 301 E scerezo@brooklyn.cuny.edu
CERES, Joanne, T .... 252-493-7320 345 E jceres@email.pittcc.edu
CERES, Sharon .... 252-493-7621 345 E sceres@email.pittcc.edu
CEREZO, Juan, E .... 718-862-7328 313 L juan.cerezo@manhattan.edu
CERILLI, Annette .... 401-232-6323 416 A acerilli@bryant.edu
CERINO, Michael, H ...... 864-488-4564 422 B mcerino@limestone.edu
CERIO, Thea .... 508-541-1565 214 C tcerio@dean.edu
CERNA, Stephanie, P .... 830-703-1580 457 C scerna@swtjc.edu
CERNERA, Anthony .... 570-504-9619 395 I acernera@tcmc.edu
CERNERO, Mark .... 610-917-1430 413 G mscernero@valleyforge.edu
CERNERO, Mark .... 610-292-9852 408 I mark.cernero@reseminary.edu
CERNETIC, Jeanette .... 602-243-8127.. 14 D jeanette.cernetic@southmountaincc.edu
CERNY, Glenn .... 734-462-4400 236 H gcerny@schoolcraft.edu
CERRA, Susan .... 845-848-7404 306 G susan.cerra@dc.edu
CERRENTANO, Cynthia .. 816-604-4003 262 K cynthia.cerrentano@mcckc.edu
CERSLEY, Tracy .... 434-961-5211 489 C tcersley@pvcc.edu
CERUTI, LaTorya .... 901-333-4462 438 B lceruti@southwest.tn.edu
CERVANTES, Art .... 713-266-6594 449 C acervantes@fortiscollege.edu
CERVANTES, George ...... 202-495-3828.. 92 F advance@dhs.edu
CERVANTES, Javier .... 541-917-4999 384 A cervanj@linnbenton.edu
CERVANTES, Juana .... 915-779-8031 470 E jcervantes@computercareercenter.com
CERVANTES, Leslie .... 575-646-3616 295 B leslie86@nmsu.edu
CERVANTES, Lynda .... 915-532-3737 470 L lcervantes@westerntech.edu
CERVANTES, Mike .... 361-592-9335 460 B mike.cervantes@tamuk.edu
CERVANTES, Rafael .... 651-690-6857 249 T rcervantes@stkate.edu
CERVANTES, Richard ..... 979-830-4123 444 D richard.cervantes@blinn.edu
CERVELLI, Janice, A ...... 520-621-6751.. 16 J jcervell@email.arizona.edu
CERVELLI, Janice, A ...... 574-284-4602 163 J jcervelli@saintmarys.edu
CERVENKA, Mark .... 713-221-8043 465 C cervenkam@uhd.edu
CERVENY, Terri, A .... 518-388-6180 332 B cervenyt@union.edu
CERVINI, John .... 517-607-2670 231 C jcervini@hillsdale.edu
CERZA, Donna .... 570-208-5868 398 D donnacerza@kings.edu
CESAR, Mary Evelyn ...... 312-329-4119 146 B maryevelyn.cesar@moody.edu
CESAR-BERRO, Marlene 305-821-3333 100 A mceasr@fnu.edu
CESARANO, Betty .... 505-473-6652 296 C betty.cesarano@santafeuniversity.edu
CESAREO, Francesco, C 508-767-7321 210 I fcesareo@assumption.edu
CESCA, Michele .... 657-278-4869.. 32 B mcesca@fullerton.edu
CESELSKI, Teresa .... 660-831-4139 264 A ceselskit@moval.edu
CESMEBASI, Erol .... 201-216-5576 291 G erol.cesmebasi@stevens.edu
CESSNA, Tammy .... 859-858-2306 183 C
CESTERO, Nicolle, M ..... 413-205-3800 210 E nicolle.cestero@aic.edu
CESTONE, Amy .... 302-292-6100.. 93 B
CESTONE, Amy .... 202-408-2400.. 93 B
CETTIN, Matthew .... 814-732-1304 406 B mcettin@edinboro.edu
CEVALLOS, F. Javier ...... 508-626-4575 218 A jcevallos@framingham.edu
CHA, Jason .... 805-565-6132.. 74 I jacha@westmont.edu
CHABOLLA, Edgar .... 213-477-2653.. 52 H echabolla@msmu.edu
CHABON, Shelly .... 503-725-3419 386 D chabonr@pdx.edu
CHABOT, Lisabeth .... 607-274-3182 311 D lchabot@ithaca.edu
CHABOT-WIEFERICH, Nicole .... 781-891-2700 212 A nchabotwieferich@bentley.edu
CHABOT-WIEFERICH, Rebecca .... 617-262-5000 212 C rebecca.chabot-wieferich@the-bac.edu
CHACIN, Meredith .... 972-580-7600 444 C mchacin@bhcarroll.edu
CHACKRAVARTHY, Swapna .... 813-974-7555 111 A schackra@health.usf.edu
CHACONA, Julie, A .... 814-732-1779 406 B jchacona@edinboro.edu
CHACONIS, Alexis .... 718-260-5250 303 D achaconis@citytech.cuny.edu
CHADDOCK, Nicole .... 901-843-3009 435 L chaddockn@rhodes.edu
CHADEN, Caryn .... 312-362-8885 137 C cchaden@depaul.edu
CHADOS, Stacey .... 239-590-1039 109 C schados@fgcu.edu
CHADWELL, Faye .... 541-737-3411 385 F faye.chadwell@oregonstate.edu
CHADWELL, Lindsey ...... 907-786-6190.. 10 A lnchadwell@alaska.edu
CHADWICK, Becky, J .... 313-317-1534 231 B bchadwick@hfcc.edu
CHADWICK, Gregory ..... 252-737-7030 349 I chadwickg@ecu.edu
CHADWICK, II, Robert, B .... 410-293-1000 519 E
CHAFEE, Julie .... 508-929-8770 219 A jchaffee1@worcester.edu
CHAFFEE, Brandy .... 218-281-8434 250 G brandy@umn.edu
CHAFFEE, Cynthia .... 312-567-3084 140 I cchaffee@iit.edu
CHAFFEE, Reta .... 603-513-1350 282 G reta.chaffee@granite.edu
CHAFFIN, Jason .... 910-362-7275 341 E jchaffin@cfcc.edu
CHAFFIN, John .... 937-258-8251 363 F john.chaffin@icb.edu
CHAFIN, Chris .... 336-334-4822 343 E cnchafin@gtcc.edu
CHAFIN, Kris, L .... 260-359-4290 159 B kchafin@huntington.edu
CHAFIN-EVANS, Karen, S .... 606-218-5606 190 E karenevans@upike.edu
CHAGNON, William .... 203-857-7090.. 86 D wchagnon@norwalk.edu
CHAGNON-BURKE, Veronique .... 212-355-1501 300 M vchagnon-burke@christies.edu
CHAHIN, T. Jaime .... 512-245-3333 463 A tc03@txstate.edu

CHAHINO, Michael .... 847-214-7161 138 B
mchahino@elgin.edu
CHAICHIAN,
Mohammad .... 319-363-1323 172 B
mchaichian@mtmercy.edu
CHAIKEN, Miriam .... 575-646-2005 295 B
mchaiken@nmsu.edu
CHAISSON, Rebecca ...... 504-286-5050 195 L
rchaisson@suno.edu
CHAIY, H. Clarissa .... 949-872-2224.. 30 A
CHAKA, Wendi .... 508-999-8711 217 A
wchaka@umassd.edu
CHAKRABARTI,
Amitabha .... 785-532-6900 179 A
amitc@ksu.edu
CHAKRABORTY, David .. 781-283-2474 225 D
dchakraborty@wellesley.edu
CHALENBURG, Mike ..... 501-279-4041.. 19 G
chalenburg@harding.edu
CHALEUNPHONH,
Seuth .... 812-941-2319 161 A
schaleun@ius.edu
CHALFONTE, Barb .... 413-755-4465 221 B
blchalfonte@stcc.edu
CHALK, Gregg .... 508-541-1668 214 C
gchalk@dean.edu
CHALLIS, Don .... 478-445-5800 119 E
don.challis@gcsu.edu
CHALLY, Pam .... 904-620-2810 110 E
pchally@unf.edu
CHALMERS, Debbie .... 580-559-5206 375 I
dchalmers@ecok.edu
CHALMERS, Scott .... 773-256-0727 144 G
schalmer@lstc.edu
CHALMIERS, Harry .... 651-291-0177 243 D
harry.chalmiers@mcnallysmith.edu
CHALOUX, Matthew, P .. 561-237-7699 103 E
mchaloux@lynn.edu
CHALTRON, Bonnie .... 231-843-5985 239 D
bchaltron@westshore.edu
CHALUPA, Leo, M .... 202-994-7315.. 92 A
lmchalupa@gwu.edu
CHALYKOFF, John .... 203-396-8084.. 88 C
chalykoffj@sacredheart.edu
CHAMANDY, Susan .... 617-730-7157 223 B
susan.chamandy@newbury.edu
CHAMBERLAIN, Daniel .. 323-259-2732.. 54 E
chamberlain@oxy.edu
CHAMBERLAIN,
Dennis, R .... 678-359-5056 121 B
dennisc@gordonstate.edu
CHAMBERLAIN, Enrique 972-273-3405 448 C
echamberlain@dcccd.edu
CHAMBERLAIN,
Jonathan .... 704-216-3765 346 C
jonathan.chamberlain@rccc.edu
CHAMBERLAIN,
LaShanda .... 228-497-7630 254 D
lashanda.chamberlain@mgccc.edu
CHAMBERLAIN,
Mary Ellen, M .... 518-327-6220 320 A
mchamberlain@paulsmiths.edu
CHAMBERLAIN, Tina ...... 206-726-5197 494 B
tchamberlain@cornish.edu
CHAMBERLAND, Greg ... 802-776-5255 474 H
gregory.chamberland@csj.edu
CHAMBERLIN,
Christopher .... 212-353-4099 306 A
c.m.chamberlin@gmail.com
CHAMBERLIN, Lisa .... 509-527-5145 499 E
lisa.chamberlin@wwcc.edu
CHAMBERLIN, Lyn .... 203-932-7419.. 89 D
lchamberlin@newhaven.edu
CHAMBERLIN, Mona ..... 918-631-2656 381 C
mona-chamberlin@utulsa.edu
CHAMBERS, Andy .... 314-392-2211 263 F
chambers@mobap.edu
CHAMBERS, Brittany ..... 315-279-5212 312 D
bchambers@keuka.edu
CHAMBERS, Daniel, P ... 607-436-2491 325 E
daniel.chambers@oneonta.edu
CHAMBERS, Eric .... 573-651-2249 266 M
CHAMBERS, Franklin, D 607-436-2513 325 E
franklin.chambers@oneonta.edu
CHAMBERS, Jason .... 828-835-4297 347 B
jchambers@tricountycc.edu
CHAMBERS, Jeffrey .... 903-434-8106 453 M
jchambers@ntcc.edu
CHAMBERS, Jennifer ..... 503-699-6252 384 B
jchambers@marylhurst.edu
CHAMBERS, Jessica ...... 301-934-7568 203 D
jchambers2@csmd.edu
CHAMBERS, John .... 561-237-7973 103 E
jchambers@lynn.edu
CHAMBERS, Kathleen .... 413-796-2080 225 F
kathleen.chambers@wne.edu
CHAMBERS, Kemba .... 334-420-4479..... 3 H
kchambers@trenholmstate.edu

CHAMBERS, Larry .... 585-475-5520 321 D
larry.chambers@rit.edu
CHAMBERS, Mark .... 515-271-1408 168 G
mark.chambers@dmu.edu
CHAMBERS, Martha ...... 865-471-4351 430 H
mchambers@cn.edu
CHAMBERS, Melody .... 660-785-4114 267 K
mchamber@truman.edu
CHAMBERS, Michael ..... 865-573-4517 432 H
mchambers@johnsonu.edu
CHAMBERS, Sarah .... 203-285-2132.. 85 E
schambers@gwcc.commnet.edu
CHAMBERS, Tony .... 608-663-2212 507 D
tchambers@edgewood.edu
CHAMBERS, Yohna .... 817-257-7790 461 A
askhr@tcu.edu
CHAMBLEE, Marquita .... 313-577-9193 239 C
mtchamblee@wayne.edu
CHAMBLEE, Tim .... 662-325-3920 254 E
t.chamblee@msstate.edu
CHAMBLESS, Greta .... 334-244-3750.... 4 E
gchamble@aum.edu
CHAMBLISS, Mary .... 256-233-8161.... 4 C
mary.chambliss@athens.edu
CHAMP, Monica .... 918-595-7000 380 D
CHAMPAGNE, Gerald ..... 734-462-4400 236 H
gchampag@schoolcraft.edu
CHAMPAGNE, Michael .. 225-752-4233 191 I
mchampagne@iticollege.edu
CHAMPION, Belinda ...... 931-393-1765 437 C
bchampion@mscc.edu
CHAMPION, Jason .... 918-293-5342 378 B
jason.champion@okstate.edu
CHAMPION, Laura .... 616-526-6678 228 B
ldc4@calvin.edu
CHAMPION, Thomas ..... 510-593-2923.. 63 A
tchampion@saybrook.edu
CHAMPION, Willie .... 903-593-8311 461 B
wchampion@texascollege.edu
CHAMPLIN, Sheila .... 843-792-2691 422 C
champlin@musc.edu
CHAMPOLI, John .... 207-941-7175 199 B
campolij@husson.edu
CHAMRA, Louay, M ...... 248-370-2217 235 J
chamra@oakland.edu
CHAMSAZ, Amir .... 410-706-3802 207 H
achamsaz@umaryland.edu
CHAN, Alan .... 626-917-9482.. 37 D
alanc@cesna.edu
CHAN, Amy .... 408-733-1878.. 70 D
CHAN, Andy .... 336-758-4662 353 A
achan@wfu.edu
CHAN, Bill .... 614-947-6054 362 A
bill.chan@franklin.edu
CHAN, Caleb, K .... 517-750-1200 237 D
cchan@arbor.edu
CHAN, Chuen .... 510-464-3221.. 56 H
cchan@peralta.edu
CHAN, Claudia .... 718-482-5005 303 B
clchan@lagcc.cuny.edu
CHAN, Emily .... 719-389-6679.. 77 J
echan@coloradocollege.edu
CHAN, Eva .... 718-270-6487 303 C
echan@mec.cuny.edu
CHAN, Gilen .... 718-260-4981 303 D
gchan@citytech.cuny.edu
CHAN, Kara .... 412-521-6200 409 D
kara.chan@rosedaletech.org
CHAN, Karen .... 650-289-3344.. 59 D
karen.chan@stpatricksseminary.org
CHAN, Larry .... 937-775-2475 374 B
larry.chan@wright.edu
CHAN, Michael, L .... 671-735-5573 519 H
michael.chan@guamcc.edu
CHAN, Paul, H .... 303-871-4646.. 83 E
phchan@du.edu
CHAN, Regina .... 212-517-0501 314 D
rchan@mmm.edu
CHANCE, Bill .... 207-221-4373 202 A
wchance@une.edu
CHANCE, Chelsea .... 318-797-5364 194 E
chelsea.chance@lsus.edu
CHANCE, Dayne .... 908-709-7089 292 C
chance@ucc.edu
CHANCE, Katie .... 256-551-5214.... 2 D
katie.chance@drakestate.edu
CHANCE, Kenneth, B ...... 216-368-3266 358 C
kenneth.b.chance@case.edu
CHANCE, Steve, L .... 806-371-5161 442 D
slchance@actx.edu
CHANCELLOR, Ashley .... 314-921-9290 269 D
achancellor@ugst.edu
CHANCELLOR, John ...... 979-830-4590 444 D
john.chancellor@blinn.edu
CHANCEY, Danny .... 251-442-2491.... 8 D
dbchancey@umobile.edu
CHANCEY, Debra, H .... 251-689-8951.... 8 D
dchancey@umobile.edu

CHANCEY, Janna, L .... 903-510-3325 464 D
jcha@tjc.edu
CHANDA, Partha, P .... 240-895-2056 206 G
ppchanda@smcm.edu
CHANDI, Balbir .... 661-362-5416.. 39 C
balbir.chandi@canyons.edu
CHANDLER, Andrew ...... 408-741-2074.. 74 D
andrew.chandler@westvalley.edu
CHANDLER, Brandon ..... 856-225-6473 290 B
brandonc@rutgers.edu
CHANDLER, Chris .... 540-365-4287 480 L
cchandler@ferrum.edu
CHANDLER, Cullen, J ... 570-321-4173 400 G
chandler@lycoming.edu
CHANDLER, Debbie .... 318-675-4016 194 D
dchan3@lsuhsc.edu
CHANDLER, Derrall .... 619-388-3537.. 60 C
dchandle@sdccd.edu
CHANDLER, G. Thomas 803-777-5032 424 I
tchandler@sc.edu
CHANDLER, Kevin .... 586-263-6266 233 B
chandlerk85@macomb.edu
CHANDLER, Kim .... 651-696-6366 243 B
kchandle@macalester.edu
CHANDLER,
Kimberly, K .... 972-860-8388 447 I
kimchandler@dcccd.edu
CHANDLER, Kirk .... 336-334-4822 343 E
kdchandler@gtcc.edu
CHANDLER, Legail, P .... 314-362-4930 269 L
legail_chandler@wustl.edu
CHANDLER, Linda .... 910-695-3961 346 E
chandlerl@sandhills.edu
CHANDLER, Lucinda ..... 937-481-2346 373 I
lucinda_chandler@wilmington.edu
CHANDLER, Margaret .... 843-355-4133 426 G
chandlerm@wiltech.edu
CHANDLER, Maria .... 803-641-3317 425 A
mariac@usca.edu
CHANDLER, Marissa ..... 931-221-6851 430 B
chandlerm@apsu.edu
CHANDLER, Mary .... 315-445-4300 312 F
richermm@lemoyne.edu
CHANDLER, Norma .... 602-787-7073.. 13 J
norma.chandler@paradisevalley.edu
CHANDLER, Prentice ..... 931-221-7511 430 B
chandlerp@apsu.edu
CHANDLER, Rebecca ..... 310-338-2723.. 50 J
rchandler@lmu.edu
CHANDLER, Roger .... 303-963-3341.. 77 I
rchandler@ccu.edu
CHANDLER, Ronnette .... 831-479-6306.. 28 F
rochandl@cabrillo.edu
CHANDLER, Sabrina, J .. 914-606-6880 333 H
sabrina.johnson.chandler@sunywcc.edu
CHANDLER, Sean .... 406-353-2607 270 E
schandler@ancollege.edu
CHANDLER, Shelly .... 352-638-9710.. 95 H
schandler@beaconcollege.edu
CHANDLER, Tess .... 650-949-6149.. 43 E
chandlertess@fhda.edu
CHANDLER, Timothy ...... 410-704-2131 209 C
tchandler@towson.edu
CHANDLER, Vernita .... 256-469-7333.... 6 A
librn@hbc1.edu
CHANDLER KNIGHT,
Nelleen .... 617-873-0125 213 B
nelleen.knight@cambridgecollege.edu
CHANDO, Kristen .... 610-499-4142 414 F
kmchando@widener.edu
CHANDO, Michael .... 856-415-2282 289 G
mchando@rcgc.edu
CHANDRAKASAN,
Anantha .... 617-253-3291 221 C
CHANDRASEKAR,
Edwin .... 847-635-1876 148 D
echandra@oakton.edu
CHANEY, Bill .... 425-739-8119 495 F
bill.chaney@lwtech.edu
CHANEY, Carmela .... 323-856-7698.. 25 L
cchaney@afi.com
CHANEY, Jayn .... 641-269-3200 169 F
chaneyj@grinnell.edu
CHANEY, Josh .... 740-826-8024 366 C
jchaney@muskingum.edu
CHANEY, Kelly, A .... 920-923-7177 508 B
kachaney01@marianuniversity.edu
CHANEY, Kevin .... 740-392-6868 366 B
kevin.chaney@mvnu.edu
CHANEY, Matthew .... 231-591-2617 230 A
matthewchaney@ferris.edu
CHANEY, Rob .... 850-201-6085 112 C
chaneyr@tcc.fl.edu
CHANEY, Steve .... 916-367-4786.. 60 A
steve.chaney@sdcc.edu
CHANEY, Susan .... 505-438-8884 296 D
susan@acupuncturecollege.edu

CHANG, Charles .... 312-893-7245 138 D
cchang@erikson.edu
CHANG, Chaw-ye .... 610-436-3043 407 D
cchang@wcupa.edu
CHANG, Chiu-An .... 520-322-6330.. 12 Q
chiuan@hanuniversity.edu
CHANG, Christopher ..... 845-687-5096 331 L
changc@sunyulster.edu
CHANG, Cindy .... 818-719-6425.. 49 D
changck@piercecollege.edu
CHANG, Dean .... 301-314-8121 207 G
deanc@umd.edu
CHANG, Diane, E .... 808-956-0391 129 H
dianec@hawaii.edu
CHANG, Eun-Woo .... 419-289-5051 356 L
echang@ashland.edu
CHANG, Frank .... 213-740-4623.. 72 B
fjc@usc.edu
CHANG, George .... 908-737-3600 286 F
gchang@kean.edu
CHANG, Gilbert .... 239-513-1135 114 D
gchang@wolford.edu
CHANG, Jerry .... 808-932-7339 129 I
jerry7@hawaii.edu
CHANG, Jimmy .... 727-341-4305 107 A
chang.jimmy@spcollege.edu
CHANG, Jin .... 626-395-2908.. 29 I
jin.chang@caltech.edu
CHANG, Julian .... 520-795-0787.. 10 J
academicdean@asaom.edu
CHANG, Ling Ling .... 516-739-1545 317 D
library@nyctcm.edu
CHANG, Lvshao .... 408-433-2280.. 37 E
CHANG, Ly .... 425-235-2352 497 E
lchang@rtc.edu
CHANG, Mari .... 808-934-2526 130 D
changm@hawaii.edu
CHANG, Nancy, H .... 817-515-5222 458 B
nancy.chang@tccd.edu
CHANG, Peter, M .... 703-333-5904 491 H
mchang@wuv.edu
CHANG, Sheng-Chung .. 626-571-5110.. 48 G
shengchung@les.edu
CHANG, Wendy .... 305-237-0244 103 L
wchang1@mdc.edu
CHAO, Gloria .... 212-220-8304 301 C
gchao@bmcc.cuny.edu
CHAO-BUSHOVEN,
Karin .... 559-453-2058.. 43 J
karin.chao-bushoven@fresno.edu
CHAPA, Paul .... 210-999-8328 464 B
paul.chapa@trinity.edu
CHAPARRO, Luis .... 915-831-2132 449 A
lchapa13@epcc.edu
CHAPDELAINE,
Andrea, E .... 301-696-3855 204 D
chapdelaine@hood.edu
CHAPIN, Timothy .... 850-644-8515 110 A
tchapin@fsu.edu
CHAPIN, Wesley .... 715-425-0629 511 E
wes.chapin@uwrf.edu
CHAPMAN, Ana .... 201-360-4244 286 E
achapman@hccc.edu
CHAPMAN, Angela .... 203-575-8208.. 86 B
achapman@nv.edu
CHAPMAN, April .... 707-836-2904.. 62 H
achapman@santarosa.edu
CHAPMAN, Brenda, J .... 404-413-3505 121 A
bchapman@gsu.edu
CHAPMAN, Bryce .... 314-744-7631 263 F
chapmanb@mobap.edu
CHAPMAN, Dale, T .... 618-468-2001 143 D
dchapman@lc.edu
CHAPMAN, Daniel, W ... 774-354-0679 211 F
daniel.chapman@becker.edu
CHAPMAN, Dominique .. 413-572-5295 218 F
dchapman@westfield.ma.edu
CHAPMAN, Elaine .... 626-585-7608.. 56 B
efchapman@pasadena.edu
CHAPMAN, Eric .... 301-405-7136 207 G
echapman@umd.edu
CHAPMAN, J. Quincy .... 715-836-3630 510 D
chapmajq@uwec.edu
CHAPMAN, Jolene .... 419-559-2147 370 J
jmeyers@terra.edu
CHAPMAN, Katrina .... 615-248-1268 439 B
klchapman@trevecca.edu
CHAPMAN, Lenora .... 210-458-4071 468 B
lenora.chapman@utsa.edu
CHAPMAN, Linda .... 618-468-4000 143 D
lchapman@lc.edu
CHAPMAN, Lisa .... 919-807-7096 340 K
chapmanl@nccommunitycolleges.edu
CHAPMAN, Lorna .... 706-754-7789 123 G
lchapman@northgatech.edu
CHAPMAN, Matt .... 707-668-5663.. 41 F
CHAPMAN, Merv .... 816-414-3700 263 D
mchapman@mbts.edu

CHAPMAN, Michelle ..... 770-412-4005 126 B
michelle.chapman@sctech.edu
CHAPMAN, Nick .... 706-355-5048 115 H
nchapman@athenstech.edu
CHAPMAN, Richard, L .. 615-898-2988 434 H
richard.chapman@mtsu.edu
CHAPMAN, Robbin .... 781-283-3511 225 D
rchapman@wellesley.edu
CHAPMAN, Ronald, K ... 801-422-8157 471 E
ron_chapman@byu.edu
CHAPMAN, Sharon, H ... 803-938-3810 425 F
hamptons@uscsumter.edu
CHAPP, Belena .... 215-568-4010 402 C
bchapp@moore.edu
CHAPPEL, Jessica .... 802-225-3220 475 H
jessica.chappel@neci.edu
CHAPPELL, Cindy .... 619-849-2531.. 57 H
cindychappell@pointloma.edu
CHAPPELL, Dorothy, F .. 630-752-5627 155 F
dorothy.chappell@wheaton.edu
CHAPPELL, Jean .... 434-961-5446 489 C
jchappell@pvcc.edu
CHAPPELL, Joy, G .... 336-342-4261 346 B
chappellj@rockinghamcc.edu
CHAPPELL, Paul .... 661-946-2274.. 73 G
CHAPPELL, Susan .... 318-342-5424 198 A
chappell@ulm.edu
CHAPPELL-WILLIAMS,
Lynette .... 607-255-3976 306 B
lc75@cornell.edu
CHAPPLE, Tarana .... 816-604-4332 262 K
tarana.chapple@mcckc.edu
CHAPPY, Sharon, L .... 262-243-5700 507 C
sharon.chappy@cuw.edu
CHAPUT, Barbara .... 413-662-5596 218 C
barbara.chaput@mcla.edu
CHAPUT, JR., Maury, L 410-777-2324 202 D
mlchaput@aacc.edu
CHARBONNEAU, Bryan . 619-684-8774.. 53 J
bcharbonneau@newschoolarch.edu
CHARBONNEAU, Leticia 832-813-6246 452 C
leticia.t.charbonneau@lonestar.edu
CHARD, David .... 617-879-2211 226 A
dchard@wheelock.edu
CHARETTE, Ace .... 701-477-7862 355 H
acharette1@tm.edu
CHARETTE, Martin .... 860-932-4157.. 86 E
mcharette@qvcc.edu
CHARETTE, Melodie .... 406-657-1022 272 I
melodie.charette@rocky.edu
CHARETTE, Reno .... 406-657-2144 272 B
rcharette@msubillings.edu
CHARGIN, Jan .... 408-848-4724.. 44 B
jbchargin@gavilan.edu
CHARITY, Sherika .... 804-758-6737 489 D
scharity@rappahannock.edu
CHARLES, Amy .... 608-822-2324 515 A
acharles@swtc.edu
CHARLES, Claudia .... 314-889-1434 260 C
ccharles@fontbonne.edu
CHARLES, Cynthia .... 504-816-4263 191 E
ccharles@dillard.edu
CHARLES, D. Maurice ... 315-781-3671 310 C
charles@hws.edu
CHARLES, Harvey .... 518-591-8183 324 G
hcharles@albany.edu
CHARLES, Jeffrey, R ...... 408-554-4607.. 62 F
jcharles@scu.edu
CHARLES, John .... 217-545-8080 152 A
jcharles@siu.edu
CHARLES, John .... 617-253-3292 221 C
CHARLES, Kevin, E .... 603-862-1098 282 F
kevin.charles@unh.edu
CHARLES, Kristin .... 415-239-3303.. 37 H
CHARLES, Madonna .... 718-951-5133 301 E
mcharles@brooklyn.cuny.edu
CHARLES, Mitch .... 916-388-2800.. 35 F
mpcharles@carrington.edu
CHARLES, Olivier .... 334-347-2623.... 1 J
ocharles@escc.edu
CHARLES, Renee .... 309-677-3260 134 G
rcharles@fsmail.bradley.edu
CHARLES, Robiaun, R ... 404-471-6000 114 H
rcharles@agnesscott.edu
CHARLES, Shawn, M ..... 504-286-5348 195 L
scharles@suno.edu
CHARLEY, Susan .... 731-286-3226 437 A
charley@dscc.edu
CHARLIER, Hara, D .... 218-855-8053 244 C
hcharlier@clcmn.edu
CHARLTON, Nick .... 570-586-2400 392 E
ncharlton@clarkssummitu.edu
CHARLTON, Parker .... 412-291-6315 389 F
pcharlton@aii.edu
CHARLTON, Patricia, A . 702-651-5667 278 N
patty.charlton@csn.edu
CHARLTON, Wade .... 774-261-1500 224 D
CHARNAY, Richard .... 405-682-1611 377 C
richard.j.charnay@occc.edu
CHARNEY, Dennis, S ..... 212-241-5674 311 A
CHARNEY, Len .... 617-262-5000 212 C
len.charney@the-bac.edu
CHARNOW, Rebecca ..... 917-493-4404 313 M
rcharnow@msmnyc.edu
CHAROENSIRI, Kanitta .. 540-231-5313 490 F
charkx@vt.edu
CHARPENTIER, Jennifer . 262-564-2866 513 G
charpentierj@gtc.edu
CHARPENTIER, Paul ...... 207-741-5503 200 C
pcharpentier@smccme.edu
CHARRIEZ, Ivette .... 787-878-6000 522 Q
icharriez@icprjc.edu
CHARRON, Michael .... 507-457-1606 250 B
mcharron@smumn.edu
CHARTON, Jacques .... 415-485-3227.. 41 J
charton@dominican.edu
CHASE, Anne .... 859-985-3266 183 I
anne_chase@berea.edu
CHASE, Christy .... 203-582-8738.. 88 A
christy.chase@quinnipiac.edu
CHASE, Del .... 719-336-1514.. 80 N
del.chase@frontrange.edu
CHASE, Diane .... 702-895-3301 279 D
diane.chase@unlv.edu
CHASE, Geoffrey .... 805-437-8441.. 31 C
geoffrey.chase@csuci.edu
CHASE, Gregory, M .... 336-734-7246 343 C
gchase@forsythtech.edu
CHASE, Horace, W .... 731-425-2610 437 B
hchase@jscc.edu
CHASE, Julie .... 207-741-5874 200 C
jchase@smccme.edu
CHASE, Marilyn, O .... 317-788-2192 164 H
chase@uindy.edu
CHASE, Mary, E .... 402-280-2703 274 D
marychase@creighton.edu
CHASE, MaryEtta .... 801-957-4799 474 B
maryetta.chase@slcc.edu
CHASE, Michael .... 309-647-7030 143 B
mchase@lakeland.cc.il.us
CHASE, Norris .... 309-677-2648 134 G
nchase@fsmail.bradley.edu
CHASE, Patricia, A .... 304-293-5101 505 B
pachase@hsc.wvu.edu
CHASE-LANSDALE,
Lindsay .... 847-491-8543 148 C
lcl@northwestern.edu
CHASNOV, Robert .... 937-766-7683 358 D
chasnovr@cedarville.edu
CHASON, Myra .... 310-289-5123.. 73 H
CHASSAPIS, Constantin . 201-216-5564 291 G
constantin.chassapis@stevens.edu
CHASTAIN, Celina .... 864-225-7653 421 G
celinachastain@forrestcollege.edu
CHASTAIN, Donna .... 541-737-0123 385 F
donna.chastain@oregonstate.edu
CHASTAIN, Melissa .... 502-585-9911 189 B
mchastain@spalding.edu
CHASTAIN, Roger .... 904-596-2416 112 F
rchastain@tbc.edu
CHASTAIN, Tricia .... 404-962-3240 127 G
tricia.chastain@usg.edu
CHASTANT, Jane .... 713-623-2040 443 C
jchastant@aii.edu
CHASTEEN, Denny .... 678-839-5560 127 F
dchasteen@westga.edu
CHATAS, Geoffrey .... 614-292-9232 367 H
chatas.1@osu.edu
CHATFIELD, Brenda, L .. 785-890-3641 180 G
brenda.chatfield@nwktc.edu
CHATHAM, David, W ..... 864-833-7028 423 D
dchatham@presby.edu
CHATMAN, Anthony ...... 706-233-7315 125 E
achatman@shorter.edu
CHATMAN, Cheryl, T ..... 651-603-6151 241 L
chatman@csp.edu
CHATMAN, Jesse .... 901-435-1470 433 A
jesse_chatman@loc.edu
CHATMAN, Patricia .... 313-317-6603 231 B
pchatman@hfcc.edu
CHATMAN, Rodney .... 937-229-2131 372 A
rchatman1@udayton.edu
CHATMON, Angelo, V ... 804-257-5856 491 C
achatmon@vuu.edu
CHATMON, Anthony ...... 706-233-7315 125 E
achatmon@shorter.edu
CHATMON, Catherine ..... 336-725-8344 348 C
chatmonc@piedmontu.edu
CHATRIAND, Craig .... 509-777-3208 500 H
cchatriand@whitworth.edu
CHATTERJEE-SUTTON,
Eva .... 724-503-1001 414 A
echatterjeesutton@washjeff.edu
CHATTIN, Duane, H .... 812-888-4164 165 E
dchattin@vinu.edu
CHAU, Lindy .... 805-378-1437.. 73 A
lchau@vcccd.edu
CHAUDHERY, Mitali ...... 313-927-1548 233 D
mchaudhe@marygrove.edu
CHAUDRI, Aamer .... 734-973-3408 238 G
elmontague@wccnet.edu
CHAUDRY, Aliya .... 405-466-3565 375 L
achaudry@langston.edu
CHAUFFEE, Gary .... 832-230-5555 453 K
gchaffee@na.edu
CHAULK, Amanda .... 802-728-1527 477 E
achaulk@vtc.edu
CHAURET, Christian ...... 765-455-9371 160 B
cchauret@iuk.edu
CHAUVIN, Marc .... 985-545-1500 192 K
CHAVES, William .... 509-359-2347 494 D
wchaves@ewu.edu
CHAVEZ, Antonio, T ...... 512-428-1246 455 I
tonyc@stedwards.edu
CHAVEZ, April .... 575-769-4061 293 M
april.chavez@clovis.edu
CHAVEZ, Augustine .... 916-691-7418.. 50 G
CHAVEZ, Christine .... 310-568-6691.. 50 J
cchavez@lmu.edu
CHAVEZ, Consuelo, E ... 575-461-4413 294 E
conniec@mesalands.edu
CHAVEZ, Dennis, J .... 607-777-2428 325 A
dchavez@binghamton.edu
CHAVEZ, Diana .... 415-703-9575.. 28 K
dchavez@cca.edu
CHAVEZ, Gloriann .... 909-384-8665.. 59 I
gchavez@sbccd.cc.ca.us
CHAVEZ, Gloriann .... 909-389-3248.. 59 H
gchavez@sbccd.cc.ca.us
CHAVEZ, Israel .... 563-588-8000 169 B
ichavez@emmaus.edu
CHAVEZ, Lisa, M .... 323-343-3500.. 32 D
lchavez@calstatela.edu
CHAVEZ, Mary .... 719-549-3353.. 81 M
mary.chavez@pueblocc.edu
CHAVEZ, Matilda .... 602-243-8231.. 14 D
matilda.chavez@southmountaincc.edu
CHAVEZ, Michael .... 661-654-3181.. 31 B
mchavez14@csub.edu
CHAVEZ, Miguel .... 330-490-7341 373 F
mchavez@walsh.edu
CHAVEZ, Olga .... 915-831-3322 449 A
ochave30@epcc.edu
CHAVEZ, Patricia .... 201-684-7622 289 C
pchavez@ramapo.edu
CHAVEZ, Robert .... 215-576-0800 408 H
rchavez@rrc.edu
CHAVEZ, Robert .... 615-460-6670 430 D
robert.chavez@belmont.edu
CHAVEZ, Robert .... 210-829-6030 465 E
rgchavez@uiwtx.edu
CHAVEZ, Susan .... 505-425-7511 294 J
CHAVEZ, Todd .... 813-974-1642 111 A
tchavez@usf.edu
CHAVEZ-SILVA, Monica 641-269-3900 169 F
chavezsm@grinnell.edu
CHAVIRA, Rejoice .... 909-389-3456.. 59 H
rchavira@craftonhills.edu
CHAVIS, Donna .... 843-921-6907 423 A
dchavis@netc.edu
CHAVIS, Gordon .... 407-823-3004 110 C
gordon.chavis@ucf.edu
CHAVIS, Keesha .... 973-655-7632 287 D
chavisk@mail.montclair.edu
CHAVIS, Kimberly .... 847-925-6507 139 B
kchavis@harpercollege.edu
CHAVIS, JR., Mack .... 731-571-3147 432 J
mchavis@lanecollege.edu
CHAVIS, Sharon, M .... 919-516-4203 348 G
smlipscomb@st-aug.edu
CHAVIS, Tim .... 248-204-3700 233 A
tchavis@ltu.edu
CHAVOUS, Warren .... 803-812-7345 425 D
chavousg@mailbox.sc.edu
CHAW, Debbie .... 510-885-3803.. 31 F
debbie.chaw@csueastbay.edu
CHAYA, Patricia .... 585-343-0055 309 C
pechaya@genesee.edu
CHAYKIN, Rachelle .... 610-892-1528 405 C
rchaykin@pit.edu
CHE, Jacqueline .... 670-237-6834 520 D
jacqueline.che@marianas.edu
CHEAGLE, Dorothy, S .... 803-934-3227 422 G
dcheagle@morris.edu
CHEAL, Sheryl .... 617-732-2880 221 E
sheryl.cheal@mcphs.edu
CHEATEM, Michelle ...... 410-617-5171 205 A
micheatem@loyola.edu
CHEATHAM,
Christopher .... 713-221-8518 465 C
cheathamc@uhd.edu
CHEATHAM, Judy, B ..... 931-363-9823 433 E
jcheatham@martinmethodist.edu
CHEATHAM, Kelly .... 214-887-5370 448 G
kcheatham@dts.edu
CHECA, Lorena .... 760-750-4056.. 33 E
lcheca@csusm.edu
CHECCI, Peg .... 802-793-0728 475 H
peg.checci@neci.edu
CHECCIO, Albert, R .... 213-740-2211.. 72 B
checcio@usc.edu
CHECK, Andrea, G .... 260-422-5561 159 D
agcheck@indianatech.edu
CHECKOVICH, Peter, G . 304-260-4380 502 J
pcheckov@blueridgectc.edu
CHECOV, Elissa .... 770-962-7580 121 G
echecov@gwinnetttech.edu
CHEEK, Annesa .... 937-512-4115 370 A
annesa.cheek@sinclair.edu
CHEEK, Debbie, Q .... 843-921-6945 423 A
dcheek@netc.edu
CHEEK, Lee .... 478-289-2048 118 H
lcheek@ega.edu
CHEEK, Philip .... 360-239-5639 497 F
philip.cheek@stmartin.edu
CHEEKS, Roger .... 757-352-4486 484 E
rogeche@regent.edu
CHEERS, Karen .... 276-739-2561 490 A
kcheers@vhcc.edu
CHEERS, Marcia .... 918-781-7225 374 H
cheersm@bacone.edu
CHEESEBRO, Deborah ... 757-221-1144 479 I
dcheesbro@wm.edu
CHEETHAM, William, C . 315-445-4400 312 F
cheethwc@lemoyne.edu
CHEEVER, Rex .... 620-665-3382 178 D
cheeverr@hutchcc.edu
CHEFFER, Sandra .... 479-667-2950.. 18 G
scheffer@atu.edu
CHEGE, Peter .... 661-722-6300.. 26 C
pchege@avc.edu
CHEIN, Zalman .... 718-774-5050 331 B
CHEKWA, Emmanuel ...... 205-929-1410.... 6 D
echekwa@miles.edu
CHELBERG, Gene .... 415-405-3728.. 34 C
chelberg@sfsu.edu
CHELL, Travis, L .... 423-652-6368 432 I
tlchell@king.edu
CHELLMAN, Laura, G .... 715-836-5954 510 D
chellmlg@uwec.edu
CHELNICK, Robert .... 773-975-1295 508 E
krisbob1@cs.com
CHELSEN, Paul, O .... 630-752-5026 155 F
paul.chelsen@wheaton.edu
CHEMASK, Stephen .... 704-461-6859 335 J
stephenchemask@bac.edu
CHEMBARS, Joanie .... 706-864-1838 127 B
joanie.chembars@ung.edu
CHEMERINSKY, Erwin .... 510-642-6483.. 68 G
echemerinsky@law.berkeley.edu
CHEN, Allan .... 484-664-3464 402 F
allenchen@muhlenberg.edu
CHEN, Bill .... 626-571-8811.. 72 C
billchen@uwest.edu
CHEN, Chau-Kuang .... 615-327-6848 434 A
ckchen@mmc.edu
CHEN, Chunju .... 978-542-2046 218 E
chunju.chen@salemstate.edu
CHEN, Deborah .... 214-648-2898 469 E
deborah.chen@utsouthwestern.edu
CHEN, Ekron .... 626-571-5110.. 48 G
ekron@les.edu
CHEN, Hang .... 704-378-1049 338 I
hchen@jcsu.edu
CHEN, Huapei .... 859-985-3538 183 I
huapei_chen@berea.edu
CHEN, Hui-Ling .... 603-222-4203 282 A
hchen@anselm.edu
CHEN, Jack .... 516-877-3334 297 I
jchen@adelphi.edu
CHEN, Jane .... 212-472-1500 318 B
jchen@nysid.edu
CHEN, Jie .... 540-568-6131 481 I
chen9jx@jmu.edu
CHEN, Jie-Qi .... 312-893-7132 138 D
jchen@erikson.edu
CHEN, Judy .... 718-990-1428 322 F
chenr@stjohns.edu
CHEN, Julie .... 978-934-2226 217 B
julie_chen@uml.edu
CHEN, Liana .... 408-345-2633.. 43 C
accountant@fivebranches.edu
CHEN, Liana .... 408-260-0208.. 43 B
accounting@fivebranches.edu
CHEN, Linda .... 574-520-4338 160 F
lchen@iusb.edu
CHEN, Lisa .... 401-874-4638 417 E
lchen@uri.edu
CHEN, Luke .... 626-289-7719.. 24 I
lchen@amu.edu

CHEN, Meghan ... 909-274-5658 52 I
mchen@mtsac.edu

CHEN, SVD, Paul ... 563-876-3353 168 H
zchen@dwci.edu

CHEN, Qi ... 219-473-4375 157 A
qchen@ccsj.edu

CHEN, JR., Ronald, K ... 973-353-5561 290 D
ronald.chen@rutgers.edu

CHEN, Rong ... 909-537-5024 33 D
rchen@csusb.edu

CHEN, Steve ... 509-434-5425 493 H
steve.chen@ccs.spokane.edu

CHEN, Steve ... 509-434-5427 493 I
steve.chen@ccs.spokane.edu

CHEN, Steve ... 509-434-5425 494 A
steve.chen@ccs.spokane.edu

CHEN, Tonnie ... 212-659-7209 312 E
tchen@tkc.edu

CHEN, Wei ... 405-974-5198 380 J
wchen@uco.edu

CHEN, Xiangming ... 860-297-5170 88 E
xiangming.chen@trincoll.edu

CHEN, Yanping ... 703-516-0035 486 C
yanping.chen@umtweb.edu

CHEN, Yemeng ... 516-739-1545 317 D
president@nyctcm.edu

CHEN-MENICHINI,
Desiree ... 630-617-3033 138 C
chend@elmhurst.edu

CHENAIL, Ronald ... 954-262-3019 104 F
ron@nova.edu

CHENAULT, Venida ... 785-830-2770 178 A
president@haskell.edu

CHENETTE, Jonathan ... 845-437-5300 333 A
jochenette@vassar.edu

CHENEVERT, Layne ... 318-670-6377 196 A
lchenevert@susla.edu

CHENEVERT, Peter, S ... 207-859-5530 198 H
pschenev@colby.edu

CHENEY, Gail ... 907-796-6473 10 C
gcheney@alaska.edu

CHENEY, John ... 413-542-2331 210 F
jycheney@amherst.edu

CHENEY, Victor ... 904-819-6213 98 I
vcheney@flagler.edu

CHENG, Alex ... 662-915-7407 256 C
acheng@olemiss.edu

CHENG, Judy ... 714-895-8382 38 G
jcheng@gwc.cccd.edu

CHENG, Kevin ... 408-435-8989 64 A

CHENG, Rita ... 928-523-3232 14 K
rita.cheng@nau.edu

CHENG, Terrence ... 203-251-8510 88 G
terrence.cheng@uconn.edu

CHENG, Wayne ... 714-533-1495 64 F
waynecheng@southbaylo.edu

CHENG, Weili ... 203-432-1940 89 G
weili.cheng@yale.edu

CHENG, Yan ... 954-763-9840 94 S
dean@atom.edu

CHENG-LEVINE, Jia-Yi ... 661-362-5806 39 C
jia-yi.cheng-levine@canyons.edu

CHENIER, Terese ... 413-782-3111 225 F
terese.chenier@law.wne.edu

CHENOWETH,
Candace, A ... 262-472-1592 512 C
chenowec@uww.edu

CHENOWETH, Gregg, A ... 574-807-7210 156 E
gregg.chenoweth@bethelcollege.edu

CHENOWETH, John ... 262-472-1592 512 C
chenowej@uww.edu

CHEONG-CHOO, Tae ... 703-323-5690 491 E

CHERAGHI, S. Hossein ... 413-782-1272 225 F
cheraghi@wne.edu

CHERENEGAR, Jessica ... 605-331-6671 429 D
jessica.cherenegar@usiouxfalls.edu

CHEREPON, Joseph ... 860-465-5778 84 K
chereponjo@easternct.edu

CHERETTA, Robson ... 718-405-3200 304 H
cheretta.robson@mountsaintvincent.edu

CHEREWICK, Daniel, P ... 248-341-2011 235 D
dpcherew@oaklandcc.edu

CHERLAND, Ryan, M ... 949-824-4521 69 A
ryan.cherland@uci.edu

CHERMAK, Heather, A ... 208-885-2020 132 I
hchermak@uidaho.edu

CHERN, James ... 973-655-7240 287 D
chernj@mail.montclair.edu

CHERNOBILSKY, Ellina ... 973-618-3951 284 D
echernobilsky@caldwell.edu

CHERNOW, Barbara, D ... 401-863-9400 415 K
barbara_chernow@brown.edu

CHERRIN, Bruce, E ... 505-277-1740 296 H
cherrin@unm.edu

CHERRY, David ... 509-777-4408 500 H
dcherry@whitworth.edu

CHERRY, Evonne ... 254-267-7042 454 L
echerry@rangercollege.edu

CHERRY, Jennifer ... 252-789-0316 344 E
jennifer.cherry@martincc.edu

CHERRY, Jewel, B ... 336-734-7297 343 C
jcherry@forsythtech.edu

CHERRY, Luke ... 661-362-2603 51 C
lcherry@masters.edu

CHERRY, Mark ... 321-433-7031 97 N
cherrym@easternflorida.edu

CHERRY, Mary Jo ... 440-646-8147 373 B
mcherry@ursuline.edu

CHERRY, Michelle ... 305-809-3278 99 L
michelle.cherry@fkcc.edu

CHERRY, Norman ... 252-794-4861 344 E
norman.cherry@martincc.edu

CHERRY, Paul ... 501-205-8805 19 B
pcherry@cbc.edu

CHERRY, Shirley ... 870-575-8461 22 E
cherrys@uapb.edu

CHERRY, Stephanie ... 319-296-2320 169 H
stephanie.cherry@hawkeyecollege.edu

CHERUBIN, Dan ... 860-685-2570 89 F
dcherubin@wesleyan.edu

CHERUBINI, Angela ... 914-395-2567 323 K
acherubini@sarahlawrence.edu

CHERUBINO, Thomas ... 908-709-7546 292 C
cherubino@ucc.edu

CHESBROUGH,
Ronald, D ... 315-655-7128 300 I
rdchesbrough@cazenovia.edu

CHESHIRE, Hall ... 540-654-1379 486 D
hcheshir@umw.edu

CHESLER, Barbara ... 973-618-3212 284 D
bchesler@caldwell.edu

CHESLEY, Laurie ... 616-234-3920 230 F
lchesley@grcc.edu

CHESNEY, Linda, H ... 718-262-5119 304 A
chesney@york.cuny.edu

CHESNEY, Thom, D ... 972-860-4809 447 G

CHESNUT, Renae ... 515-271-1814 168 J
renae.chesnut@drake.edu

CHESNUT, Robert, W ... 217-581-2125 138 A
rwchesnut@eiu.edu

CHESNUT, Veronica ... 334-876-9411 2 C
veronica.chesnut@wccs.edu

CHESSER, Tim ... 859-442-4129 185 I
tim.chesser@kctcs.edu

CHESSUM, Gary ... 858-646-3126 62 C
gchessum@sbpdiscovery.org

CHESTER, Ann, L ... 304-293-1026 505 B
achester@hsc.wvu.edu

CHESTER, Brandi ... 870-248-4000 18 J
brandic@blackrivertech.edu

CHESTER, Cathie ... 914-251-5976 328 B
cathie.chester@purchase.edu

CHESTER, Detrenyona ... 770-426-2730 122 F
detrenyona.chester@life.edu

CHESTER, Kate ... 971-722-8233 386 C
kate.chester@pcc.edu

CHESTER, Rosalind ... 504-394-7744 196 E
rchester@uhcno.edu

CHESTER, Steven ... 860-343-5864 86 A
schester@mxcc.commnet.edu

CHESTER, Thomas, P ... 609-652-4384 291 H
thomas.chester@stockton.edu

CHESTER, Timothy, M ... 706-542-3145 127 A
tchester@uga.edu

CHESTERTON, Susan ... 610-399-2080 405 G
schesterton@cheyney.edu

CHESTNUT, SR.,
Coley, C ... 334-874-5700 5 B
cchestnut@ccal.edu

CHESTNUT, Emmanuel ... 757-822-1421 489 H
echestnut@tcc.edu

CHESTNUTT, Larry ... 248-204-2409 233 A
lchestnutt@ltu.edu

CHEU, Susan ... 408-864-8976 43 E
cheususan@deanza.edu

CHEUNG, Alvin ... 916-686-8883 30 H

CHEVALIER, David ... 478-289-2370 118 H
dchevalier@ega.edu

CHEVALIER, Jason ... 909-652-6904 36 E
jason.chevalier@chaffey.edu

CHEVALIER, JR.,
Joseph ... 404-756-5773 123 F
jchevalier@msm.edu

CHEVALIER, Lizette ... 618-453-7653 152 B
apap@siu.edu

CHEVERTON, Holly ... 518-783-2341 324 C
hcheverton@siena.edu

CHEVES, Brad, E ... 214-768-2667 457 B
bcheves@smu.edu

CHEVRETTE, II,
Joseph, M ... 315-733-2307 332 F
jchevrette@uscny.edu

CHEW, Elaine ... 254-968-9611 459 A
chew@tarleton.edu

CHEW, Kenneth ... 812-237-3939 159 C
kenneth.chew@indstate.edu

CHEYNE, Larry ... 503-399-5210 382 C
larry.cheyne@chemeketa.edu

CHEZUM, Kelly, O ... 315-268-4483 304 B
kchezum@clarkson.edu

CHI, Wenjun ... 610-660-1204 409 H
wchi@sju.edu

CHIA, Samuel ... 214-887-5121 448 G
schia@dts.edu

CHIAPPA, Jonathan ... 603-646-0343 281 C
jonathan.chiappa@dartmouth.edu

CHIAPPETTA, Anthony ... 202-319-5623 91 D
chiappetta@cua.edu

CHIAPPINI, Thomas, A ... 330-494-6170 370 G
tchiappini@starkstate.edu

CHIARELLA, Stephanie ... 802-831-1237 476 G
schiarella@vermontlaw.edu

CHIAVELLI, James ... 978-837-5509 221 G
chiavellij@merrimack.edu

CHICHESTER, Susan, E ... 585-245-5577 327 B
sue@geneseo.edu

CHICK, Brian ... 603-206-8158 280 L
bchick@ccsnh.edu

CHICKERING,
F. William ... 609-896-5111 289 E
wchickering@rider.edu

CHICKERING, Fran ... 603-427-7629 280 J
fchickering@ccsnh.edu

CHICO HURST, Karen ... 518-442-5540 324 G
kchicohurst@albany.edu

CHICOINE, David ... 307-766-4194 517 B

CHIDDICK, Troy ... 610-527-0200 409 E
tchiddick@rosemont.edu

CHIDIAC, George ... 626-585-7424 56 B
gchidiac@pasadena.edu

CHIELLI, Jack, J ... 301-447-5366 206 B
j.j.chielli@msmary.edu

CHIEVES, Kevin ... 912-443-5491 125 D
kchieves@savannahtech.edu

CHIGAS, Diana ... 617-627-5870 225 A
diano.chigas@tufts.edu

CHIGAWA, Steven ... 808-235-7457 130 I
chigawa@hawaii.edu

CHIGAZOLA, Deborah ... 707-527-4525 62 H
dchigazola@santarosa.edu

CHIGOS, Lisa ... 619-961-4326 67 F
lchigos@tjsl.edu

CHIH, Lo-Li ... 808-974-7595 129 I
loli@hawaii.edu

CHIKWINYA, Mary ... 253-566-5100 499 A
mchikwinya@tacomacc.edu

CHIKWINYA, Mary ... 253-566-5127 499 A
mchikwinya@tacomacc.edu

CHIKWINYA, Micki ... 253-833-9111 495 C
mchikwinya@greenriver.edu

CHILCOAT, Cynthia, A ... 928-523-6120 14 K
cindy.chilcoat@nau.edu

CHILDERS, Amber ... 501-337-5000 19 C
amber@coto.edu

CHILDERS, Camille ... 316-978-3620 182 F
camille.childers@wichita.edu

CHILDERS, Chance ... 734-995-7311 229 A
chance.childers@cuaa.edu

CHILDERS, Christopher ... 773-244-5750 147 F
cchilders@northpark.edu

CHILDERS, Henry, A ... 520-626-6779 16 J
hankc@email.arizona.edu

CHILDERS, Jana ... 415-451-2859 60 I
jchilders@sfts.edu

CHILDERS, Karen ... 909-384-8987 59 I
kchilder@sbccd.cc.ca.us

CHILDERS, Mark ... 254-710-2211 444 B
mark_childers@baylor.edu

CHILDERS, JR.,
William, A ... 304-336-5100 504 E
bill.childers@westliberty.edu

CHILDRES, Donna ... 706-236-1714 116 D
dchildres@berry.edu

CHILDRESS, Amanda ... 256-840-4210 3 F
achildress@snead.edu

CHILDRESS, Jamie ... 919-718-7239 341 H
jchildress@cccc.edu

CHILDRESS, Marc ... 913-344-1236 174 J
marc.childress@bakeru.edu

CHILDREY, Cynthia, A ... 928-523-6838 14 K
cynthia.childrey@nau.edu

CHILDREY, Lauren, T ... 336-272-7102 338 B
lauren.childrey@greensboro.edu

CHILDS, Brittany ... 903-566-7444 468 C
bchilds@uttyler.edu

CHILDS, Cindy ... 410-778-7700 210 A
cchilds2@washcoll.edu

CHILDS, David, E ... 304-877-6428 501 E
david.childs@abc.edu

CHILDS, Gladys ... 817-531-4444 463 G
gchilds@txwes.edu

CHILDS, K. Paige ... 864-941-8688 423 C
childs.p@ptc.edu

CHILDS, Kimberly, M ... 936-468-2805 458 A
kchilds@sfasu.edu

CHILDS, Linda, J ... 304-877-6428 501 E
linda.childs@abc.edu

CHILDS, M. Dee ... 979-845-9999 459 C
mdeechilds@tamu.edu

CHILDS, Richard, G ... 410-864-4274 207 A
rchilds@stmarys.edu

CHILDS, Shannon ... 541-880-2210 383 E
childs@klamathcc.edu

CHILDS, Sidney, R ... 989-964-2932 236 F
schilds@svsu.edu

CHILES, Kristie ... 702-579-3530 278 H
kristie.chiles@brightwood.edu

CHILES, Rebecca ... 503-838-8481 388 B
chilesr@wou.edu

CHILES, Thomas ... 617-552-0840 212 E
thomas.chiles@bc.edu

CHILICKI, Stacy ... 207-216-4312 200 E
schilicki@yccc.edu

CHILLO, Joseph, L ... 617-730-7035 223 B
joseph.chillo@newbury.edu

CHILSTRON, Brian ... 714-662-4402 55 A
bchilstron@pacific-college.edu

CHILTON, Bette ... 815-825-9308 142 F
bette.chilton@kishwaukeecollege.edu

CHILTON, Elizabeth ... 607-777-2145 325 A
chilton@binghamton.edu

CHILTON, Lisa ... 434-832-6689 487 H
chiltonl@cvcc.vccs.edu

CHIMENTI, Vito, R ... 215-670-9297 403 D
vrchimenti@peirce.edu

CHIMIENTI, Sonia ... 508-856-2300 217 C
sonia.chimienti@umassmed.edu

CHIN, Andrew ... 850-599-3244 109 A
andrew.chin@famu.edu

CHIN, Brady ... 310-577-3000 75 G
bchin@yosan.edu

CHIN, Christine ... 202-885-6365 91 C
cchin@american.edu

CHIN, Jean, E ... 706-542-8715 127 A
jchin@uga.edu

CHIN, Julie ... 818-299-5500 73 K
jchin@westcoastuniversity.edu

CHIN, Penny, J ... 516-876-3137 327 C
chinp@oldwestbury.edu

CHINERY, Mary ... 732-987-2341 286 D
mchinery@georgian.edu

CHING, Eric ... 864-294-3347 421 I
eric.chingr@furman.edu

CHING, Warren ... 691-320-2480 519 G
chiefsecurity@comfsm.fm

CHINN, Derek ... 503-255-0332 384 E
dchinn@multnomah.edu

CHINN, Jeffrey ... 619-961-4235 67 F
jchinn@tjsl.edu

CHINNIAH, Nim, S ... 847-491-5534 148 C
nim.chinniah@northwestern.edu

CHINNOCK PETROSKI,
Mary, J ... 308-865-8655 277 F
petroskimj@unk.edu

CHINWAH, Lovette ... 937-376-6631 358 I
lchinwah@centralstate.edu

CHIOCHIOS, Tim ... 650-543-3722 51 F
tim.chiochios@menlo.edu

CHIODO, Brian ... 724-222-5330 403 E
bchiodo@penncommercial.edu

CHIPMAN, Nelson ... 412-392-4306 408 F
nchipman@pointpark.edu

CHIPMAN, Stephanie ... 217-245-3030 139 H
stephanie.chipman@mail.ic.edu

CHIPMAN, Wayne ... 417-873-7258 259 G
wchipman@drury.edu

CHIPPS, Michael, R ... 402-844-7054 276 G
michaelc@northeast.edu

CHIQUITO, Yug Fon ... 626-529-8246 55 C
ychiquito@pacificoaks.edu

CHIRICO, Donna ... 718-262-2804 304 A
dchirico@york.cuny.edu

CHISCHILLY, Ann Marie ... 928-523-9651 14 K
ann-marie.chischilly@nau.edu

CHISEM, Lori ... 205-929-3409 2 G
lchisem@lawsonstate.edu

CHISHA, Mwata ... 800-567-2344 506 I
mchisha@menominee.edu

CHISHOLM, Barbara ... 334-727-8535 7 F
chisholm@mytu.tuskegee.edu

CHISHOLM, Brendan, H ... 508-856-4031 217 C
brendan.chisholm@umassmed.edu

CHISHOLM, Bruce, T ... 336-322-2146 345 D
bruce.chisholm@piedmontcc.edu

CHISHOLM,
Douglas, W ... 937-766-7992 358 D
chisd@cedarville.edu

CHISHOLM, Kelly ... 603-206-8004 280 L
kchisholm@ccsnh.edu

CHISHOLM, Laura ... 610-647-4400 397 I
lchisholm@immaculata.edu

CHRISTOPHER, John, J . 732-571-3598 287 C
jochrist@monmouth.edu
CHRISTOPHER, Kasker .. 845-938-3808 519 D
christopher.kasker@usma.edu
CHRISTOPHER,
Kimberly .... 508-999-8586 217 A
kchristopher@umassd.edu
CHRISTOPHER, Marv ..... 707-654-1050.. 32 E
mchristopher@csum.edu
CHRISTOPHER, Robert .. 563-333-6260 173 A
christopherrobert@sau.edu
CHRISTOPHER, Sundar . 256-824-6606.... 8 C
christs@uah.edu
CHRISTOPHERSON,
Karen .... 707-468-3091.. 51 E
kchristo@mendocino.edu
CHRISTOPHERSON,
Michelle .... 218-281-8679 250 G
mchristo@umn.edu
CHRISTOPHERSON,
Neal, J .... 509-527-5056 500 G
christnj@whitman.edu
CHRISTY, Benjamin, C .. 716-878-6326 326 E
christy@buffalostate.edu
CHRISTY, David .... 646-660-6500 301 B
david.christy@baruch.cuny.edu
CHRISTY, Dick .... 910-521-6560 351 E
dick.christy@uncp.edu
CHRISTY, Gaye .... 731-661-5202 439 D
gchristy@uu.edu
CHRISTY, Gregory, E ..... 712-707-7100 172 G
president@nwciowa.edu
CHRISTY, John, R .... 256-961-7763.... 8 C
john.christy@uah.edu
CHRISTY, Jon, A .... 563-387-1016 171 I
chrijo01@luther.edu
CHRISTY, Kathleen .... 716-829-7801 307 B
christyk@dyc.edu
CHRISTY, Kathy .... 417-447-6963 264 K
christyk@otc.edu
CHRISTY, Michelle, D ... 617-324-9022 221 C
CHRITE, Brent .... 303-871-6858.. 83 E
brent.chrite@du.edu
CHRONISTER, Eric .... 702-895-3487 279 D
eric.chronister@unlv.edu
CHRONISTER, Lynne ...... 251-460-6333.... 9 B
lchronister@southalabama.edu
CHRUSCIEL, Don .... 661-395-4011.. 47 A
CHRUSZCZYK,
Cynthia, A .... 305-899-3125.. 95 G
cchruszczyk@barry.edu
CHRYSANTHOU,
Juanita .... 702-651-7374 278 N
juanita.chrysanthou@csn.edu
CHRZASTEK, OP, Brian . 202-495-3842.. 92 F
bchrzastek@dhs.edu
CHU, Helen, Y .... 541-346-1235 387 F
helenc@uoregon.edu
CHU, Zduy .... 229-333-5920 127 H
zchu@valdosta.edu
CHUA, Nate .... 641-844-5473 170 I
nate.chua@iavalley.edu
CHUAH, Iris .... 707-965-6231.. 55 F
ichuah@puc.edu
CHUANG, Paiyi .... 626-917-9482.. 37 D
paiyic@cesna.edu
CHUBB, Andrew, M ...... 989-964-4144 236 F
achubb@svsu.edu
CHUBICK, Rita .... 205-552-1214.... 5 C
rita.chubick@ecacolleges.com
CHUCHIAK, John, F ...... 417-836-5425 263 H
johnchuchiak@missouristate.edu
CHUDAKOFF, Kathy, L .. 330-325-6375 366 F
kchudakoff@neomed.edu
CHUDY-SZCZUR,
Beverly .... 716-926-8940 310 B
bchudy@hilbert.edu
CHUGUNOVA, Marina ..... 909-607-9489.. 37 L
marina.chugunova@cgu.edu
CHUI, Kevin .... 503-352-7377 385 I
chui5115@pacificu.edu
CHUKS, Samuel .... 251-405-7015.... 1 E
schuks@bishop.edu
CHULVICK, Charles, E ... 908-526-1200 289 D
chuck.chulvick@raritanval.edu
CHUMBLER, Neale, R ..... 270-745-7003 190 F
neale.chumbler@wku.edu
CHUN, Marvin .... 203-432-2900.. 89 G
marvin.chun@yale.edu
CHUN, Patrick .... 561-297-4434 109 B
pchun@fau.edu
CHUN, Victoria .... 315-228-7611 304 G
vchun@colgate.edu
CHUNG, Christina .... 661-362-3127.. 39 C
christina.chung@canyons.edu
CHUNG, Lucy .... 847-866-3877 138 G
lucy.chung@garrett.edu
CHUNG, Norm .... 502-897-4209 189 A
nchung@sbts.edu
CHUNG, Peggy .... 718-779-1499 320 C
pchung@plazacollege.edu
CHUNG, Russell .... 614-688-1698 367 H
chung.592@osu.edu
CHUNG, Sandy, S .... 503-943-8484 387 H
chung@up.edu
CHUNG, Silvan .... 808-845-9404 130 E
silvan@hawaii.edu
CHUNG, Tony .... 619-594-5211.. 34 B
tchung@mail.sdsu.edu
CHUNG, Wing-Kit .... 503-517-1813 388 C
wchung@westernseminary.edu
CHUNG-HOON, Tanise .. 801-422-4403 471 E
tanise@byu.edu
CHUNN, Robert .... 813-253-7260 101 M
rchunn@hccfl.edu
CHUPP, Tim .... 616-222-3000 232 F
tchupp@kuyper.edu
CHURCH, Cathy .... 928-350-4100.. 15 V
cchurch@prescott.edu
CHURCH, David, B .... 206-281-2602 498 B
dchurch@spu.edu
CHURCH, David, M .... 719-884-5000 180 B
dmchurch@nbc.edu
CHURCH, Donna .... 828-726-2211 341 D
dchurch@cccti.edu
CHURCH, John, C .... 610-989-1203 413 I
jchurch@vfmac.edu
CHURCH, Kelly .... 336-838-6175 347 G
kachurch667@wilkescc.edu
CHURCH, Linda .... 660-596-7222 267 E
lchurch@sfccmo.edu
CHURCH, Marjorie, R .... 336-841-4692 338 E
mchurch@highpoint.edu
CHURCHILL,
Clifford, W .... 772-546-5534 101 N
cliffchurchill@hsbc.edu
CHURCHILL, David .... 405-682-1611 377 C
dchurchill@occc.edu
CHURCHILL, Sally, J ..... 734-763-5553 237 I
sjc@umich.edu
CHURCHILL, Tim .... 509-434-5165 493 H
timothy.churchill@ccs.spokane.edu
CHURLA, Josita .... 267-341-3469 397 G
jchurla@holyfaily.edu
CHUSID, Eileen .... 212-410-8127 317 C
echusid@nycpm.edu
CHUTE, Mary .... 609-292-6201 292 B
mchute@njstatelib.org
CHUTE, Pat .... 706-272-4420 118 F
pchute@daltonstate.edu
CHVAL, Kathryn, B .... 573-882-8524 268 C
chvalkb@missouri.edu
CHYCINSKI, Jodi .... 616-331-2025 230 G
chycinsj@gvsu.edu
CHYKA, Robert, D .... 716-880-2343 314 F
robert.d.chyka@medaille.edu
CHYR, Fred, A .... 909-593-3511.. 70 E
fchyr@laverne.edu
CHYTKA, Evelyn, J .... 307-766-2398 517 B
jchytka@uwyo.edu
CIABOCCHI, Elizabeth .... 718-990-6113 322 F
ciabocce@stjohns.edu
CIACCIO, Dolores .... 631-420-2411 329 D
dolores.ciaccio@farmingdale.edu
CIANCHETTA, Susan, A . 410-827-5811 203 C
scianchetta@chesapeake.edu
CIANCI, Christine .... 724-589-2195 411 D
ccianci@thiel.edu
CIANCI, Karen .... 559-453-2273.. 43 J
karen.cianci@fresno.edu
CIARAMITARO, Barbara . 248-689-8282 238 F
bciara2@walshcollege.edu
CIARDULLI, Lisa .... 352-395-5817 107 E
lisa.ciardulli@sfcollege.edu
CIBUZAR, Jean .... 202-651-5282.. 91 H
jean.cibuzar@gallaudet.edu
CICALA, RSM,
Joseph, J .... 610-796-8211 389 A
joe.cicala@alvernia.edu
CICALA, Mary Ann .... 512-223-7109 443 G
mary.cicala@austincc.edu
CICCARELLI, Andrea ...... 812-855-3550 159 H
aciccare@indiana.edu
CICCHELLI, Cindy .... 734-462-4400 236 H
ccicchel@schoolcraft.edu
CICCI, Cindy .... 307-754-6058 516 Q
cindy.cicci@nwc.edu
CICHOCKI, David .... 617-984-1773 223 H
ccichocki@quincycollege.edu
CICHOCKI, Eileen .... 707-468-3068.. 51 E
ecichock@mendocino.edu
CICHOMSKA, Grace, J ... 708-524-6288 137 F
gcichomska@dom.edu
CICHON, Jeff .... 715-675-3331 514 F
cichon@ntc.edu
CICHOSZ, Chris .... 507-453-2741 245 G
ccichosz@southeastmn.edu
CICHOSZ, Christopher ... 507-457-5555 248 C
ccichosz@winona.edu
CID, Carmen, R .... 860-465-5295.. 84 K
cid@easternct.edu
CID, Rolando .... 787-738-2161 528 A
rolando.cid@upr.edu
CIEJKA, Patricia, A .... 409-772-8745 469 C
pciejka@utmb.edu
CIENSKI, John, P .... 631-451-4080 330 C
cienskj@sunysuffolk.edu
CIEPLY, Kevin .... 239-687-5305.. 95 B
kcieply@avemarialaw.edu
CIESEMIER, Krisin .... 815-280-2862 142 A
kciesemi@jjc.edu
CIESLA, Carolyn .... 708-709-2949 148 I
cciesla@prairiestate.edu
CIESLINSKI, Mike .... 810-232-8153 234 F
mike.cieslinski@mcc.edu
CIEZ-VOLZ, Kathleen ..... 904-361-6257 100 F
kathleen.ciez.volz@fscj.edu
CIFRA, Jason, S .... 510-981-2820.. 56 F
jcifra@peralta.edu
CIFUENTES, Luis .... 361-825-2577 460 A
luis.cifuentes@tamucc.edu
CIHA, Lisa .... 319-399-8669 167 F
lciha@coe.edu
CIHAK, Michael .... 320-589-6154 251 A
cihakmw@morris.umn.edu
CILENTO, Eugene, V ...... 304-293-4157 505 B
gene.cilento@mail.wvu.edu
CILLAY, David .... 509-335-5454 499 G
dcillay@wsu.edu
CIMA, Cara .... 863-680-4390 100 D
ccima@flsouthern.edu
CIMALORE, Ann .... 205-853-1200.... 2 F
acimalore@jeffersonstate.edu
CIMAROSSA, Valerie ...... 602-383-8228.. 16 I
vcimarossa@uat.edu
CIMINELLI, Mary .... 972-273-3130 448 C
marygciminelli@dcccd.edu
CIMINELLI, Thomas, E .. 716-888-2250 300 G
ciminel1@canisius.edu
CIMINO, Chris .... 865-974-9880 439 I
cimino@utk.edu
CIMITILE, Maria, C .... 616-331-2400 230 G
cimitilm@gvsu.edu
CIMORELLI, Nick .... 843-863-7581 419 C
ncimorel@csuniv.edu
CIMPL, Linda .... 605-995-2896 427 A
licimpl@dwu.edu
CINGEL, Pamela .... 305-474-6866 107 B
pcingel@stu.edu
CINSON, Michael .... 330-490-4969 373 F
mcinson@walsh.edu
CINTORINO, Salvatore .. 860-832-1889.. 84 J
cintorino@ccsu.edu
CINTRÓN, Myriam .... 787-850-9302 528 B
myriam.cintron1@upr.edu
CINTRON, Arnaldo .... 787-864-2222 524 A
arnaldo.cintron@guayama.inter.edu
CINTRON, Edgardo .... 787-857-3600 523 I
ecintron@br.inter.edu
CINTRON, Filomena .... 787-857-3600 523 I
fcintron@br.inter.edu
CINTRON, José, R .... 787-766-1717 526 B
jrcintron@suagm.edu
CINTRON, Nancy, A .... 718-960-8366 302 C
nancy.cintron@lehman.cuny.edu
CINTRON-OTERO,
Carmen .... 787-993-8922 527 G
carmen.cintron2@upr.edu
CIOCCO, Ronalee .... 724-503-1001 414 A
rciocco@washjeff.edu
CIOCE, Michael .... 856-222-9311 289 F
mcioce@rcbc.edu
CIOFFI, Laura .... 212-752-1530 312 G
laura.cioffi@limcollege.edu
CIOLFI, Michael, A .... 203-576-4278.. 88 F
mciolfi@bridgeport.edu
CIORRA, Anthony .... 203-371-7912.. 88 C
ciorraa@sacredheart.edu
CIOSEK, Edward .... 413-748-3108 224 G
eciosek@springfieldcollege.edu
CIOTOLI, Carlo .... 212-443-1297 318 D
carlo.ciotoli@nyu.edu
CIPFL, Joseph, J .... 618-537-6462 145 C
jjcipfl@mckendree.edu
CIPOLLA, Anthony .... 845-848-7814 306 G
anthony.cipolla@dc.edu
CIPOLLA, Robert, D .... 401-825-2221 416 B
rcipolla@ccri.edu
CIPRES, Elizabeth .... 949-451-5410.. 64 I
ecipres@ivc.edu
CIPRIANI, Colleen .... 614-234-5828 365 L
ccipriani@mccn.edu
CIPRIANO, Matt, J .... 215-968-8255 390 I
cipriano@bucks.edu
CIPRIANO, Michael .... 978-934-2654 217 B
michael_cipriano@uml.edu
CIRAULO, Paul .... 212-517-0531 314 D
pciraulo@mmm.edu
CIRCE, Scott .... 305-223-4561 106 L
scirce@sjvcs.edu
CIRCE, Shana .... 845-257-3231 325 D
circes@newpaltz.edu
CIRCELLI, William, A ..... 518-564-5022 327 E
circelwa@plattsburgh.edu
CIRCLE, Kelly .... 303-914-6213.. 82 B
kelly.circle@rrcc.edu
CIRELLI, Joyce .... 724-480-3474 392 K
joyce.cirelli@ccbc.edu
CIRELLI, Rachel .... 718-862-7308 313 L
rcirelli01@manhattan.edu
CIRI, Michael .... 907-796-6534.. 10 C
maciri@alaska.edu
CIRI, Michael .... 907-796-6452.. 10 C
maciri@alaska.edu
CIRILLO, Laureen .... 413-565-1006 211 C
lcirillo@baypath.edu
CIRILLO, Robert .... 914-606-6981 333 H
robert.cirillo@sunywcc.edu
CIRIONI, Frank .... 714-895-8700.. 38 G
fcirioni@gwc.cccd.edu
CIRKS, Julie .... 563-588-6436 167 E
julie.cirks@clarke.edu
CIRRINCIONE,
AnnaMaria .... 607-753-2336 327 A
annamaria.cirrincione@cortland.edu
CISLER, Ronald, A .... 414-229-5663 511 A
rac@uwm.edu
CISLER, Valerie .... 715-346-4920 511 F
vcisler@uwsp.edu
CISNA, Shawn .... 309-796-5000 134 C
cisnas@bhc.edu
CISNEROS, Maria .... 504-671-5603 192 H
mcisne@dcc.edu
CISNEROS, Teo .... 210-924-4338 443 N
teo.cisneros@bua.edu
CISSELL, Jason, A .... 502-272-8329 183 H
jcissell@bellarmine.edu
CITARELLA, Alberto .... 802-656-3244 476 E
alberto.citarella@uvm.edu
CITRON, Chaim .... 323-937-3763.. 75 F
ccitron@yoec.edu
CITTI, Lori, A .... 410-516-6760 204 F
lcitti1@jhu.edu
CIUFFO, Patricia .... 646-565-6000 331 F
patricia.ciuffo@touro.edu
CIULLO, Carol .... 304-724-5000 501 G
cciullo@cdu.edu
CLAASSEN, Bjoern, A .... 901-321-3234 431 A
bclaasse@cbu.edu
CLABBY, William, J .... 512-448-8704 455 I
bclabby@stedwards.edu
CLACK, Olivia .... 870-574-4481.. 21 G
oclack@sautech.edu
CLAERBOUT, Libby .... 701-858-4155 354 C
libby.claerbout@minotstateu.edu
CLAERHOUT, Cathryn .... 231-995-1034 235 B
cclaerhout@nmc.edu
CLAEYS, Aimee, K .... 515-281-6456 166 E
aimee.claeys@iowaregents.edu
CLAFFEY, JR.,
George, F .... 860-515-3777.. 84 H
gclaffey@charteroak.edu
CLAFFEY, Marian, A ...... 773-508-7473 144 D
mclaffe@luc.edu
CLAGETT, Craig, A .... 410-386-8163 203 A
cclagett@carrollcc.edu
CLAGHORN, Patricia ..... 856-415-5504 289 G
pclaghorn@rcgc.edu
CLAGUE, Roger .... 530-749-3804.. 75 K
rclague@yccd.edu
CLAIRE, Michael .... 650-574-6222.. 62 A
clairem@smccd.edu
CLANCY, Amanda .... 303-678-3736.. 79 K
amanda.clancy@frontrange.edu
CLANCY, Gerard .... 918-631-3244 381 C
gerard-clancy@utulsa.edu
CLANCY, Patricia .... 718-390-3422 333 D
patricia.clancy@wagner.edu
CLANCY, SJ, Tim, R ...... 509-313-6701 495 A
clancy@gonzaga.edu
CLANTON, Andre .... 770-426-2708 122 F
andre.clanton@life.edu
CLANTON, Ann .... 251-405-7055.... 1 E
aclanton@bishop.edu
CLANTON, Janet .... 573-897-5000 267 F
CLANTON, Karen .... 256-824-6013.... 8 C
karen.clanton@uah.edu
CLANTON, Tammi .... 830-792-7206 456 D
tkclanton@schreiner.edu

CLAPHAM LAVIN, Theresa ... 303-352-6625.. 79 D
CLAPP, Kenneth, W ... 704-637-4446 336 G kclapp@catawba.edu
CLAPP, Marlene ... 508-830-5069 218 D mclapp@maritime.edu
CLAPP, Shay ... 918-540-6188 376 F shay.clapp@neo.edu
CLAPP, Stacey ... 609-343-5632 283 D sclapp@atlantic.edu
CLAPPER, Mark, A ... 717-361-1499 394 F clapperm@etown.edu
CLAPPER-DEWELL, Theophylact ... 315-858-3914 310 E frtheophylact@jordanville.org
CLARDY, Betsy, B ... 409-772-8789 469 C bbclardy@utmb.edu
CLARDY, JR., Mike ... 334-844-9996.... 4 D clardch@auburn.edu
CLARENSAU, Michael ... 972-825-4827 457 F mclarensau@sagu.edu
CLARK, Adon ... 478-374-6407 123 A adon.clark@mga.edu
CLARK, Adrian, R ... 816-654-7095 261 D arclark@kcumb.edu
CLARK, Alice ... 662-915-7583 256 C amclark@olemiss.edu
CLARK, Amanda ... 979-830-4743 444 D amanda.clark@blinn.edu
CLARK, Amanda ... 509-777-4482 500 H amandaclark@whitworth.edu
CLARK, Amy ... 503-838-8187 388 B clarkaj@wou.edu
CLARK, Ann, B ... 860-727-6761.. 87 B aclark@goodwin.edu
CLARK, Annette, C ... 206-398-4000 498 D annclark@seattleu.edu
CLARK, Benita, I ... 919-866-7894 347 D biclark@waketech.edu
CLARK, Beverly ... 228-896-2512 254 D beverly.clark@mgccc.edu
CLARK, Bill ... 626-584-5588.. 43 K billclark@fuller.edu
CLARK, Bob ... 310-506-4798.. 56 D bob.clark@pepperdine.edu
CLARK, Brandi ... 520-494-5577.. 11 P brandi.clark@centralaz.edu
CLARK, Brian ... 401-427-6920 417 B bclark@risd.edu
CLARK, Brian, J ... 207-859-4604 198 H bjclark@colby.edu
CLARK, Brock ... 228-497-7634 254 D brock.clark@mgccc.edu
CLARK, Bryon ... 580-745-2064 379 J bclark@se.edu
CLARK, Carol ... 931-221-7570 430 B clarkc@apsu.edu
CLARK, Carol, D ... 931-221-7570 430 B clarkc@apsu.edu
CLARK, Charles, E ... 920-683-4710 512 D charles.clark@uwc.edu
CLARK, Charles, L ... 309-341-7399 142 G clclark@knox.edu
CLARK, Cheryl ... 318-487-7602 191 J cheryl.clark@lacollege.edu
CLARK, Chris ... 618-634-3233 151 G chrisc@shawneecc.edu
CLARK, Christina ... 703-284-1560 483 A christina.clark@marymount.edu
CLARK, Courtney ... 216-987-5504 360 E courtney.clark@tri-c.edu
CLARK, Curtis ... 860-701-7708.. 87 F clark_c@mitchell.edu
CLARK, Cynthia, A ... 860-628-4751.. 87 E cclark@lincolncollegene.edu
CLARK, Dallas, B ... 540-464-7321 490 E clarkdb@vmi.edu
CLARK, Dan ... 503-838-8483 388 B clarkd@wou.edu
CLARK, Dana ... 810-766-4028 227 F dlclark07@baker.edu
CLARK, Dana ... 810-766-4028 227 E dana.clark@baker.edu
CLARK, Daniel ... 616-234-4354 230 F dbclark@grcc.edu
CLARK, Daniel ... 630-752-5593 155 F daniel.clark@wheaton.edu
CLARK, Dave ... 701-224-5434 354 F david.clark@bismarckstate.edu
CLARK, David ... 651-638-6553 240 J d-clark@bethel.edu
CLARK, David ... 301-736-3631 205 B david.clark@msbbcs.edu
CLARK, David ... 301-736-3631 205 B dclarkmel@msn.com
CLARK, David ... 559-638-0300.. 66 H david.clark@reedleycollege.edu
CLARK, David ... 414-375-0457 511 A dclark@uwm.edu
CLARK, Dean ... 620-229-6000 181 F dean.clark@sckans.edu
CLARK, Debra ... 865-694-6602 437 F dclark@pstcc.edu
CLARK, Denise ... 301-405-4282 207 G djclark@umd.edu
CLARK, Deron ... 575-392-4510 294 L
CLARK, Dewey ... 252-985-5140 348 A dclark@ncwc.edu
CLARK, Dianne ... 318-371-3035 193 A
CLARK, Donald ... 207-602-2274 202 A dclark@une.edu
CLARK, Donna ... 254-442-5001 445 Q donna.clark@cisco.edu
CLARK, Douglas ... 610-341-5810 394 E dclark1@eastern.edu
CLARK, Douglas, R ... 951-785-2244.. 47 F dclark@lasierra.edu
CLARK, Douglas, S ... 510-642-4192.. 68 G cocdean@berkeley.edu
CLARK, Duwon ... 573-681-5477 261 H clarkd@lincolnu.edu
CLARK, Edgar ... 305-626-3713.. 99 M edgar.clark@fmuniv.edu
CLARK, Edmond ... 570-577-2000 390 H
CLARK, Edmund, U ... 651-962-6266 251 D clar7281@stthomas.edu
CLARK, Ehrin ... 570-945-8119 398 C ehrin.clark@keystone.edu
CLARK, Elaine ... 801-581-8221 472 P eclark@utah.edu
CLARK, Elizabeth ... 660-785-7200 267 K eclark@truman.edu
CLARK, Eric ... 617-984-1741 223 H eclark@quincycollege.edu
CLARK, Eric ... 937-258-8251 363 F eric.clark@icb.edu
CLARK, Erica ... 620-343-4600 177 C
CLARK, Frederick ... 508-531-1201 217 D fred.clark@bridgew.edu
CLARK, Gary, A ... 310-825-5108.. 69 B gclark@admission.ucla.edu
CLARK, Gary, C ... 405-744-6384 377 F gary.clark@okstate.edu
CLARK, Gaye ... 910-410-1804 345 G agclark@richmondcc.edu
CLARK, Ginger ... 813-253-7051 101 M gclark@hccfl.edu
CLARK, Glenn ... 401-341-2400 417 D glenn.clark@salve.edu
CLARK, Jacqueline ... 256-549-8695.... 2 A jclark@gadsdenstate.edu
CLARK, Jacqueline ... 718-270-6994 303 C jaclark@mec.cuny.edu
CLARK, James ... 314-773-0083 257 J james.clark@calvary.edu
CLARK, James ... 252-399-6450 335 I jclark@barton.edu
CLARK, James ... 513-556-4615 371 E clark2j9@ucmail.uc.edu
CLARK, James, A ... 334-844-4765.... 4 D clarkj3@auburn.edu
CLARK, James, E ... 803-536-7013 423 G jclark@scsu.edu
CLARK, James, T ... 304-336-8043 504 E clarkj@westliberty.edu
CLARK, Jamie, K ... 740-588-1222 374 G jclark@zanestate.edu
CLARK, Janet ... 812-535-5182 163 I jclark@smwc.edu
CLARK, Jeanian ... 540-868-7122 488 E jclark@lfcc.edu
CLARK, Jennifer ... 724-589-2858 411 D jclark@thiel.edu
CLARK, Jennifer, M ... 210-567-6536 468 E clarkjm@uthscsa.edu
CLARK, Jennifer, R ... 312-915-7819 144 D jclark7@luc.edu
CLARK, Jesse ... 970-351-1785.. 83 F jesse.clark@unco.edu
CLARK, Jill ... 712-325-3285 170 K jclark@iwcc.edu
CLARK, Jimmy ... 479-979-1484.. 23 J jclark@ozarks.edu
CLARK, Joan ... 304-357-4750 502 E joanclark@ucwv.edu
CLARK, John, B ... 203-837-8300.. 85 B clarkj@wcsu.edu
CLARK, John, S ... 865-694-6601 437 F jclark@pstcc.edu
CLARK, Joy ... 334-244-3600.... 4 E jclark@aum.edu
CLARK, Kacey ... 617-603-6928 222 F kacey.clark@necb.edu
CLARK, Karen ... 765-973-8242 160 A krclark@iue.edu
CLARK, Karen ... 254-299-8689 452 E kclark@mclennan.edu
CLARK, Karen, M ... 708-344-4700 144 A kclark@lincolntech.edu
CLARK, Karisa, A ... 304-877-6428 501 E publicrelations@abc.edu
CLARK, Kathy ... 630-844-5443 133 H kclark@aurora.edu
CLARK, Kimberlee ... 425-352-8204 492 K kclark@cascadia.edu
CLARK, Kimberley ... 717-334-6286 412 E
CLARK, Kimberly, M ... 336-342-4261 346 B clarkk@rockinghamcc.edu
CLARK, Kirstie ... 704-355-8894 336 F kirstie.clark@carolinashealthcare.org
CLARK, Kristin ... 559-925-3217.. 74 A kristinclark@whccd.edu
CLARK, Kyle ... 850-644-4242 110 A kyle@fsu.edu
CLARK, Kym ... 432-264-5144 450 G kclark@howardcollege.edu
CLARK, L. Nathan, N ... 775-856-2266 278 I nclark@ccnn4u.com
CLARK, Lanette ... 406-758-6328 271 B lclark@fpcc.edu
CLARK, Laron ... 757-728-5357 481 E laron.clark@hamptonu.edu
CLARK, Larry ... 253-589-5602 493 F larry.clark@cptc.edu
CLARK, Laura ... 870-777-5722.. 23 A laura.clark@uacch.edu
CLARK, Laurie ... 979-830-4336 444 D laurie.clark@blinn.edu
CLARK, Lawrence, S ... 318-797-5234 194 E larry.clark@lsus.edu
CLARK, Leanna ... 303-315-7734.. 83 D leanna.clark@ucdenver.edu
CLARK, Lesa, C ... 757-683-4406 483 G lclark@odu.edu
CLARK, Letitia ... 714-438-4606.. 38 E lclark35@cccd.edu
CLARK, Linda ... 662-332-8750 254 C liclark@msdelta.edu
CLARK, Linda, J ... 360-442-2100 495 G lclark@lowercolumbia.edu
CLARK, Lisa ... 910-642-7141 346 G lisa.clark@sccnc.edu
CLARK, Margie ... 517-483-1461 232 K clarkm@lcc.edu
CLARK, Mark ... 515-964-6213 168 A maclark@dmacc.edu
CLARK, Marla ... 269-927-8762 232 G mclark@lakemichigancollege.edu
CLARK, Martha ... 760-872-2000.. 41 E mclark@deepsprings.edu
CLARK, Mary ... 657-278-4717.. 32 B maryclark@fullerton.edu
CLARK, Mary ... 501-977-2011.. 23 B clark@uaccm.edu
CLARK, Mary ... 252-222-6190 341 F clarkm@carteret.edu
CLARK, Mary, L ... 202-885-2155.. 91 C mlclark@american.edu
CLARK, Matthew ... 612-626-4734 250 E mclark@umn.edu
CLARK, OSB, Matthew .. 985-867-2245 195 I mrclark@sjasc.edu
CLARK, Melinda ... 813-226-4858 106 N melinda.clark@saintleo.edu
CLARK, Melody, A ... 513-558-9154 371 E melody.clark@uc.edu
CLARK, MelodyAnn ... 219-844-0100 156 F melodyann.clark@brightwood.edu
CLARK, Michael ... 910-521-6815 351 E michael.clark@uncp.edu
CLARK, Michael ... 570-321-4249 400 G clark@lycoming.edu
CLARK, Michelle ... 859-858-3511 183 D michelle.clark@asbury.edu
CLARK, Murray, B ... 859-323-5220 190 B mbclar2@email.uky.edu
CLARK, Nigel, N ... 304-293-4813 505 B nigel.clark@mail.wvu.edu
CLARK, Nuriyah ... 716-851-1205 307 I clarkn@ecc.edu
CLARK, Pam ... 989-686-9225 229 J pamelaclark@delta.edu
CLARK, Patricia ... 910-272-3505 346 A pclark@robeson.edu
CLARK, Paul, E ... 610-921-7708 388 E pclark@albright.edu
CLARK, Randall ... 714-432-5898.. 38 H rclark@occ.cccd.edu
CLARK, Rebecca ... 304-865-6085 502 C rebecca.clark@ovu.edu
CLARK, Richard ... 702-895-1469 279 D richard.clark@unlv.edu
CLARK, Richard ... 404-894-4154 120 A rick.clark@admission.gatech.edu
CLARK, Richard ... 865-573-4517 432 H rclark@johnsonu.edu
CLARK, Rob ... 585-275-5931 332 E rclark@rochester.edu
CLARK, Robert ... 404-880-6623 117 H rclark@cau.edu
CLARK, Robert, A ... 207-941-7138 199 B clarkr@husson.edu
CLARK, Robert, E ... 757-683-3018 483 G reclark@odu.edu
CLARK, II, Robert, E ... 302-736-2508.. 90 J robert.clark@wesley.edu
CLARK, Robert, K ... 856-691-8600 285 C rclark@cccnj.edu
CLARK, Rodney ... 508-678-2811 219 C rodney.clark@bristolcc.edu
CLARK, Ron, M ... 972-238-6277 448 D rclark@dcccd.edu
CLARK, Ryan ... 503-699-6268 384 B rclark@marylhurst.edu
CLARK, Ryan ... 503-699-3316 384 B rclark@marylhurst.edu
CLARK, Sandra ... 410-857-2217 205 E sgclark@mcdaniel.edu
CLARK, Sara, M ... 417-836-6105 263 H saraclark@missouristate.edu
CLARK, Sarah ... 406-657-1007 272 I sarah.clark@rocky.edu
CLARK, Sarah, E ... 863-667-5463 108 G seclark@seu.edu
CLARK, Scott ... 415-451-2833.. 60 I sclark@sfts.edu
CLARK, Scott, D ... 716-888-8357 300 G clarks@canisius.edu
CLARK, Sharon, L ... 813-988-5131.. 99 D clarks@floridacollege.edu
CLARK, Sherri ... 606-248-2224 187 B sherril.clark@kctcs.edu
CLARK, Steve ... 541-737-4875 385 F steve.clark@oregonstate.edu
CLARK, Susan ... 517-629-0798 226 G sclark@albion.edu
CLARK, Tammy, L ... 813-258-7522 113 E tclark@ut.edu
CLARK, Tarryl ... 651-450-3618 245 A tclark@inverhills.edu
CLARK, Terry ... 618-453-7960 152 B tclark@business.siu.edu
CLARK, Thomas ... 919-582-3750 348 I tomclark@shawu.edu
CLARK, Todd ... 404-526-7366 125 A t.clark@sae.edu
CLARK, Todd ... 909-469-5473.. 74 G tclark@westernu.edu
CLARK, Todd, A ... 336-316-2133 338 C clarkta@guilford.edu
CLARK, Tracie ... 704-330-6022 342 A tracie.clark@cpcc.edu
CLARK, Tracy ... 218-935-0417 251 F tracy.clark@wetcc.edu
CLARK, Tyler ... 502-897-4203 189 A tclark@sbts.edu
CLARK, Vernon, A ... 940-565-2453 466 B allen.clark@unt.edu
CLARK, Victoria ... 425-822-8266 496 E victoria.clark@northwestu.edu
CLARK, Vincent, W ... 718-960-8539 302 C vincent.clark@lehman.cuny.edu
CLARK, Walter ... 715-346-2320 511 F walter.clark@uwsp.edu
CLARK, Wayne, N ... 208-496-2510 131 D clarkw@byui.edu
CLARK, William ... 856-351-2602 291 E clark@salemcc.edu
CLARK, William ... 330-972-8772 371 D bclark3@uakron.edu
CLARK, William (Bill) ... 740-376-4601 365 A wbc001@marietta.edu
CLARK, Yvette ... 603-645-9623 282 C y.clark@snhu.edu
CLARK, Yvette ... 931-372-3004 438 F yclark@tntech.edu
CLARK-BETANCOURT, Tammy, L ... 217-443-8778 137 B tbetancourt@dacc.edu
CLARK-EVANS, Barbara . 913-288-7504 178 H bclark@kckcc.edu
CLARK-GOFF, Kylah ... 325-649-8148 450 H kclarkgoff@hputx.edu
CLARK-TALLEY, Christine ... 703-993-8757 481 B cclarkta@gmu.edu
CLARK-WHITE, Patricia . 949-585-2987.. 27 F pwhite@brandman.edu
CLARKBERG, Marin, E .. 607-255-9101 306 B mec30@cornell.edu

CLARKE, Anthony .... 910-642-7141 346 G
anthony.clarke@sccnc.edu
CLARKE, Calaundra .... 225-771-2552 196 B
cclarke@sulc.edu
CLARKE, Cara .... 606-759-7141 186 E
cara.clarke@kctcs.edu
CLARKE, Chris .... 760-252-2411.. 27 A
cclarke@barstow.edu
CLARKE, Christopher ..... 212-431-2871 317 H
christopher.clarke@nyls.edu
CLARKE, Cyril, R .... 540-231-7910 490 F
clarkecr@vt.edu
CLARKE, Damian, A ...... 803-536-8480 423 G
dclarke5@scsu.edu
CLARKE, David .... 518-694-7252 297 J
david.clarke@acphs.edu
CLARKE, Edmond .... 610-409-3206 413 H
eclarke@ursinus.edu
CLARKE, Germel .... 202-884-9000.. 93 C
clarkeg@trinitydc.edu
CLARKE, Ivan .... 310-233-4436.. 49 B
clarkein@lahc.edu
CLARKE, Jaime .... 503-594-3220 382 D
jaimec@clackamas.edu
CLARKE, Karen .... 808-853-1040 129 F
karenclarke@pacrim.edu
CLARKE, Karen .... 330-672-8533 363 I
kclarke8@kent.edu
CLARKE, Kathy .... 916-348-4689.. 42 F
kclarke@epic.edu
CLARKE, Kenneth, I .... 607-255-6002 306 B
kic2@cornell.edu
CLARKE, Kevin .... 516-773-5000 519 C
clarkek@usmma.edu
CLARKE, Malanie .... 212-621-4101 302 F
maclarke@jjay.cuny.edu
CLARKE, Mark .... 713-743-9854 465 A
mclarke@uh.edu
CLARKE, Megan .... 906-248-8435 227 P
mclarke@bmcc.edu
CLARKE, Patrick .... 435-586-5479 473 A
clarke@suu.edu
CLARKE, Rachelle .... 480-517-8544.. 14 B
rachelle.clark@riosalado.edu
CLARKE, Robert .... 503-493-6555 382 I
rclarke@cu-portland.edu
CLARKE, Ryan .... 601-635-2111 252 I
rclarke@eccc.edu
CLARKE, Sonia .... 985-858-5861 192 I
sonia.clarke@fletcher.edu
CLARKE, Ursala .... 754-312-2898 102 V
uclarke@keycollege.edu
CLARKE-ANDERSON,
Shannon .... 718-270-5143 303 C
shannon@mec.cuny.edu
CLARKE-GLOVER,
Jazzmine .... 718-390-3280 333 D
j.clarke-glover@wagner.edu
CLARKE-TURNER, Kay ... 973-596-3140 288 A
kay.turner@njit.edu
CLARKSON, Kris .... 208-282-2794 132 B
clarkri3@isu.edu
CLARKSON, Sallie .... 843-349-2448 420 A
sallie@coastal.edu
CLARKSON, William ...... 610-917-1477 413 G
wmclarkson@valleyforge.edu
CLARKSTON, Bobbie ..... 423-636-7300 439 C
bclarkston@tusculum.edu
CLARO, Aida .... 305-899-3674.. 95 G
aclaro@barry.edu
CLARY, Bruce .... 620-242-0506 179 G
claryb@mcpherson.edu
CLARY, Dean .... 309-649-6316 152 G
dean.clary@src.edu
CLARY, Donnie, O .... 252-398-6250 336 K
claryd@chowan.edu
CLARY, Ernest .... 484-646-5933 406 D
clary@kutztown.edu
CLARY, Gail .... 229-931-2318 125 G
gclary@southgatech.edu
CLARY, Henry .... 276-326-4471 478 H
hclary@bluefield.edu
CLARY, Joshua, R .... 270-686-4332 183 J
josh.clary@brescia.edu
CLARY, Stephanie .... 270-686-9550 183 J
stephanie.clary@brescia.edu
CLASS, Richard, T .... 212-472-1500 318 B
rclass@nysid.edu
CLAUSEN, Dave .... 530-251-8826.. 47 J
dclausen@lassencollege.edu
CLAUSEN, Doris .... 201-216-5016 291 G
doris.clausen@stevens.edu
CLAUSEN, Janice .... 661-654-3360.. 31 B
jclausen@csub.edu
CLAUSEN, Terry .... 870-850-8606.. 21 E
tclausen@seark.edu
CLAUSON, Kevin, L .... 423-775-7324 430 G
kclauson4864@bryan.edu
CLAUSON BASH,
Kathleen, M .... 641-784-5064 169 D
clauson@graceland.edu
CLAUSS, Daniel .... 949-582-4547.. 64 J
dclauss@saddleback.edu
CLAUSS, Karl .... 610-690-5707 410 I
kclauss1@swarthmore.edu
CLAUSS, Sandy .... 210-366-2701 454 K
CLAUSSEN, Linda, C ..... 540-674-3614 488 G
lclaussen@nr.edu
CLAUSSEN, Nicole .... 605-256-5744 428 G
nicole.claussen@dsu.edu
CLAVELLE, Martha .... 619-644-7000.. 45 A
martha.clavelle@gcccd.edu
CLAVERIE, Mark .... 518-587-2100 329 C
mark.claverie@esc.edu
CLAVIER, Cheri .... 423-439-7483 431 H
clavier@etsu.edu
CLAVIJO, Manuel .... 508-849-3280 210 H
mclavijo@annamaria.edu
CLAVILLE, Michelle .... 757-727-5239 481 E
michelle.claville@hamptonu.edu
CLAWSON, Dana .... 318-677-3100 197 D
roed@nsula.edu
CLAWSON, David .... 215-955-5001 411 E
david.clawson@jefferson.edu
CLAWSON, Michelle .... 757-727-5474 481 E
michelle.clawson@hamptonu.edu
CLAXTON, Brenda .... 432-264-5160 450 G
bclaxton@howardcollege.edu
CLAXTON, Patricia .... 325-574-7607 470 N
pclaxton@wtc.edu
CLAXTON, Stephanie, L 315-267-2154 328 A
claxtosc@potsdam.edu
CLAY, Aileen .... 603-206-8175 280 L
aclay@ccsnh.edu
CLAY, Antoinette, M ...... 732-255-0400 288 B
aclay@ocean.edu
CLAY, Brian .... 501-370-5336.. 21 A
bclay@philander.edu
CLAY, Daniel .... 319-335-5380 166 G
daniel-clay@uiowa.edu
CLAY, Doreen .... 818-710-2510.. 49 D
claydj@piercecollege.edu
CLAY, George, W .... 864-656-0723 419 F
gclay@clemson.edu
CLAY, Gladys .... 904-470-8087.. 98 B
gladys.clay@ewc.edu
CLAY, John, L .... 256-469-7333.... 6 A
president@hbc1.edu
CLAY, Karen .... 662-329-7104 254 F
kgclay@muw.edu
CLAY, Karen .... 541-962-3792 383 B
karen.clay@eou.edu
CLAY, Lauren .... 662-476-5060 253 A
lclay@eastms.edu
CLAY, Maggie .... 310-393-0411.. 56 A
mclay@rand.org
CLAY, Martyn .... 813-757-2110 101 M
mclay6@hccfl.edu
CLAY, Melanie, N .... 678-839-0627 127 F
melaniec@westga.edu
CLAY, Mercedes .... 419-783-2362 361 A
mclay@defiance.edu
CLAY, Patricia .... 610-282-1100 393 G
patricia.clay@desales.edu
CLAY, Philip, N .... 508-831-5201 226 E
pclay@wpi.edu
CLAY, Rex .... 704-922-6243 343 D
clay.rex@gaston.edu
CLAY, Rodney .... 803-938-3850 425 F
clay2@uscsumter.edu
CLAY, Rosetta .... 650-543-3732.. 51 F
rosetta.clay@menlo.edu
CLAY, Sandra .... 903-586-2518 451 C
sclay@jacksonville-college.edu
CLAY, Sharon .... 913-758-6108 182 B
sharon.clay@stmary.edu
CLAY, Trish .... 304-558-2104 503 N
patricia.clay@wvhepc.edu
CLAY-ROOKS, Saskia ..... 703-993-3738 481 B
sclayroo@gmu.edu
CLAYBAUGH, Tracy, L .. 603-535-2550 283 B
tlclaybaugh@plymouth.edu
CLAYBON, John .... 405-682-1611 377 C
jclaybon@occc.edu
CLAYBORN, Eleanor ...... 662-252-8000 255 F
eclayborn@rustcollege.edu
CLAYBORNE, Hannah ..... 419-289-5324 356 L
hclaybor@ashland.edu
CLAYBORNE, Staci, G ... 618-235-2700 152 E
staci.clayborne@swic.edu
CLAYBROOK,
Jennifer, D .... 706-880-8032 122 D
jclaybrook@lagrange.edu
CLAYBURN, Justina .... 269-471-6553 227 B
justina@andrews.edu
CLAYCOMB, Ann .... 304-293-9919 505 B
ann.claycomb@mail.wvu.edu
CLAYPOOL, Joe .... 859-323-5445 190 B
joseph.claypool@uky.edu
CLAYPOOLE, Jack .... 803-777-4113 424 I
jclaypoole@mycarolina.org
CLAYTER, Seth .... 207-699-5032 199 H
sclayter@meca.edu
CLAYTON, Carrie .... 903-566-7184 468 C
cclayton@uttyler.edu
CLAYTON, Dana .... 812-488-2500 164 G
dc26@evansville.edu
CLAYTON, Ellen .... 443-334-2558 207 C
eclayton@stevenson.edu
CLAYTON, Jack, A .... 304-842-8269 504 A
jclayton@fairmontstate.edu
CLAYTON, Jan, L .... 918-595-7901 380 D
jan.clayton@tulsacc.edu
CLAYTON, Janet, S .... 803-934-3246 422 G
jclayton@morris.edu
CLAYTON, Jay .... 412-338-4770 390 D
jay.clayton@brightwoodcareer.edu
CLAYTON, Jeffrey .... 954-492-5353.. 96 J
jclayton@citycollege.edu
CLAYTON, Kirk .... 757-490-1241 477 F
kclayton@auto.edu
CLAYTON, Kori .... 501-337-5000.. 19 C
kclayon@coto.edu
CLAYTON, Michael .... 214-818-1350 447 A
mclayton@criswell.edu
CLAYTON, Patricia, I ..... 336-322-2105 345 D
patti.clayton@piedmontcc.edu
CLAYTON, Tiffany .... 610-921-6619 388 E
tclayton@albright.edu
CLAYTON, Tonya, M ...... 989-386-6601 234 B
tmclayton@midmich.edu
CLAYTON, Yvette .... 256-372-5690.... 1 A
yvette.clayton@aamu.edu
CLEANTHES, Jeff .... 901-843-3456 435 L
cleanthesj@rhodes.edu
CLEARFIELD, Michael .... 707-638-5982.. 67 H
michael.clearfield@tu.edu
CLEARWATER, Bonnie ... 954-262-0225 104 F
bclearwater@moafl.org
CLEARY, Anita .... 509-452-5100 496 H
acleary@pnwu.edu
CLEARY, Brian .... 860-512-2613.. 85 G
bcleary@manchestercc.edu
CLEARY, Charles .... 860-773-3403.. 86 G
ccleary@txcc.commnet.edu
CLEARY, Delores .... 509-963-2152 492 L
delores.cleary@cwu.edu
CLEARY, Kathleen .... 937-512-3159 370 A
kathleen.cleary@sinclair.edu
CLEARY, Keelan .... 503-534-4051 384 B
kcleary@marylhurst.edu
CLEARY, Kelly .... 610-896-1181 397 F
kcleary@haverford.edu
CLEARY, Lynn .... 315-464-3921 326 B
clearyl@upstate.edu
CLEARY, Lynn .... 315-464-5387 326 B
clearyl@upstate.edu
CLEARY, Sally .... 973-290-4449 285 A
scleary@cse.edu
CLEARY, Thomas .... 210-485-0500 441 E
tcleary1@alamo.edu
CLEARY, Thomas, R ...... 619-260-4297.. 71 J
tcleary@sandiego.edu
CLEARY, Valerie .... 503-725-9744 386 D
vcleary@pdx.edu
CLEAVER, Richard, G .... 340-693-1042 529 C
richard.cleaver@uvi.edu
CLEAVES, Wandamae .... 207-947-4591 198 F
bookstore@bealcollege.edu
CLEBSCH, Bill .... 650-725-0056.. 66 C
clebsch@stanford.edu
CLECKNER, Lisa .... 315-781-4381 310 C
cleckner@hws.edu
CLEEK, Stu .... 805-565-6029.. 74 I
scleek@westmont.edu
CLEGG, Cynthia, B .... 405-325-2910 380 L
cclegg@hsc.net.ou.edu
CLEGG, Neill .... 336-272-7102 338 B
cleggn@greensboro.edu
CLEM, Amy .... 903-566-7480 468 C
aclem@uttyler.edu
CLEM, Monica .... 814-732-1460 406 B
mclem@edinboro.edu
CLEM, Randy .... 916-558-2424.. 50 I
clemrj@scc.losrios.edu
CLEMENCE, Patrick .... 319-398-1274 171 F
patrick.clemence@kirkwood.edu
CLEMENS, Bonnie .... 909-607-3679.. 37 K
bonnie_clemens@cuc.claremont.edu
CLEMENS, Jacob, E .... 419-372-9623 357 F
clemenj@bgsu.edu
CLEMENT,
Christopher, D .... 603-862-3081 282 F
christopher.clement@unh.edu
CLEMENT, Fred .... 512-472-4133 456 E
fred.clement@ssw.edu
CLEMENT, Gregory .... 978-632-6600 220 D
g_clement@mwcc.mass.edu
CLEMENT, James, A ...... 205-726-2395.... 6 G
jaclemen@samford.edu
CLEMENT, Jane .... 901-678-2068 439 E
jclement@memphis.edu
CLEMENT, Julia .... 617-327-6777 226 B
CLEMENT, Linda, M .... 301-314-8430 207 G
lclement@umd.edu
CLEMENT, Lynnette .... 215-991-3682 398 F
clementl@lasalle.edu
CLEMENT, Mercedes ..... 386-506-3440.. 97 I
clemenm@daytonastate.edu
CLEMENT, Nancy .... 985-448-7915 192 I
nancy.clement@fletcher.edu
CLEMENT, Richard .... 505-277-4241 296 H
riclement@unm.edu
CLEMENT, William .... 757-822-7373 489 H
wclement@tcc.edu
CLEMENT CORNIES,
Dawn .... 901-843-3745 435 L
corniesd@rhodes.edu
CLEMENTS, Angela .... 512-313-3000 446 N
angela.clements@concordia.edu
CLEMENTS, Blayne .... 931-221-7466 430 B
clementsb@apsu.edu
CLEMENTS, Brandi .... 931-221-7841 430 B
clementsbr@apsu.edu
CLEMENTS, Carole .... 303-546-3584.. 81 B
carole@naropa.edu
CLEMENTS, DeAnnia ...... 229-468-2031 128 G
deannia.clements@wiregrass.edu
CLEMENTS, Gary .... 252-527-6223 344 D
gclements@lenoircc.edu
CLEMENTS, Geri .... 478-553-2066 123 H
gclements@oftc.edu
CLEMENTS, James, P .... 864-656-3413 419 F
president@clemson.edu
CLEMENTS, Kieran .... 706-886-6831 126 F
clements@tfc.edu
CLEMENTS, Mari, L .... 626-584-5501.. 43 K
clements@fuller.edu
CLEMENTS, Michelle ..... 206-296-5870 498 D
hr@seattleu.edu
CLEMENTS, Stephen, K . 859-858-3511 183 D
steve.clements@asbury.edu
CLEMENTS, Tommy .... 276-523-7431 488 F
tclements@mecc.edu
CLEMENTS, Vickie .... 814-864-6666 396 C
vickiec@glit.edu
CLEMENTS, William .... 802-485-2370 475 I
bclements@norwich.edu
CLEMETSEN, Bruce .... 541-917-4806 384 A
clemetb@linnbenton.edu
CLEMMER, Kristi .... 432-335-6865 454 C
kclemmer@odessa.edu
CLEMMER, Margaret ...... 202-885-2141.. 91 C
megc@american.edu
CLEMMONS, Brian .... 732-906-2509 287 B
bclemmons@middlesexcc.edu
CLEMMONS, Fran .... 865-688-9422 432 B
CLEMMONS, Raechelle .. 704-894-3246 337 B
raclemmons@davidson.edu
CLEMMONS, Sarah .... 850-718-2288.. 96 H
clemmonss@chipola.edu
CLEMMONS, Val .... 910-362-7373 341 E
vclemmons@cfcc.edu
CLEMO, Lorrie .... 716-829-7673 307 B
clemo@dyc.edu
CLEMONS, Benjamin, P 507-354-8221 243 C
clemonbp@mlc-wels.edu
CLEMONS, Brian .... 816-415-7802 270 C
clemonsb@william.jewell.edu
CLEMONS, Cassie .... 912-287-5834 117 J
cclemons@coastalpines.edu
CLEMONS, Cheryl .... 270-686-4250 183 J
cheryl.clemons@brescia.edu
CLEMONS, Chuck .... 352-395-5202 107 E
chuck.clemons@sfcollege.edu
CLEMONS, Neil .... 386-506-3813.. 97 I
clemonn@daytonastate.edu
CLEMONS, Rita .... 909-635-0250 213 B
rita.clemons@cambridgecollege.edu
CLEMONS, Teresa, G ..... 806-345-5548 442 D
t0155151@actx.edu
CLENDENEN, Holly .... 608-822-2362 515 A
hclendenen@swtc.edu
CLENDENEN, Mike .... 252-493-7608 345 E
mclendenen@email.pittcc.edu
CLERE, Ray, R .... 859-257-1987 190 B
ray.clere@uky.edu
CLERIE, Carole .... 478-825-6301 119 C
cleriec@fvsu.edu

COCHRAN, Connie, L .... 713-313-7606 461 E cochrancl@tsu.edu
COCHRAN, Douglas .... 541-737-4085 385 F career.services@oregonstate.edu
COCHRAN, Gerardine, K .... 727-816-3190 105 C cochran@phsc.edu
COCHRAN, Glenn .... 508-626-4636 218 A gcochran@framingham.edu
COCHRAN, Jeanne .... 619-849-2513.. 57 H jeannecochran@pointloma.edu
COCHRAN, Linda .... 601-923-1661 255 E lcochran@rts.edu
COCHRAN, Mark, J .... 501-686-2540.. 21 H mjcochran@uasys.edu
COCHRAN, Michelle ...... 203-773-8535.. 84 G mcochran@albertus.edu
COCHRAN, Monica, J ... 304-367-4711 504 A monica.cochran@fairmontstate.edu
COCHRAN, Nancy .... 303-871-6986.. 83 E nancy.cochran@du.edu
COCHRAN, Nathan .... 501-370-5317.. 21 A ncochran@philander.edu
COCHRAN, Raylene .... 850-478-8496 105 D rcochran@pcci.edu
COCHRAN, Rodney .... 423-869-7101 433 C rodney.cochran@lmunet.edu
COCHRAN, III, Sam, V . 319-335-7294 166 G sam-cochran@uiowa.edu
COCHRAN, Stuart .... 646-313-8000 303 G stuart.cochran@guttman.cuny.edu
COCHRAN, Susan, E ..... 207-778-7200 201 D cochran@maine.edu
COCHRAN, Teri .... 918-444-3410 376 G cochrant@nsuok.edu
COCHRAN, Thomas .... 901-321-3381 431 A tcochran@cbu.edu
COCHRAN, W. Scott ...... 864-587-4236 424 D cochranc@smcsc.edu
COCHRANE, Ashley .... 859-985-3605 183 I cochranea@berea.edu
COCHRANE, Lori .... 401-254-5480 417 C lcochrane@rwu.edu
COCHRANE, Paul .... 207-228-8598 201 H paul.cochrane@maine.edu
COCKE, Paul .... 360-650-3350 500 E paul.cocke@wwu.edu
COCKERELL, K.T .... 210-341-1366 454 B ktcockerell@ost.edu
COCKERHAM, Anne .... 703-675-9437 184 G anne.cockerham@frontier.edu
COCKERHAM, Becky ...... 301-934-2251 203 D beckyc@csmd.edu
COCKERHAM, Richard ... 318-678-6000 192 C rcockerham@bpcc.edu
COCKETT, Noelle, E .... 435-797-7172 473 C noelle.cockett@usu.edu
COCKLIN, Joel .... 419-434-4250 373 K jcocklin@winebrenner.edu
COCKRELL, Grant .... 205-391-2384.... 3 E gcockrell@sheltonstate.edu
COCKRELL, Matt .... 864-379-6670 421 E cockrell@erskine.edu
COCKRELL, Phillip .... 419-530-7963 372 F phillip.cockrell@utoledo.edu
COCKRELL, Todd .... 281-649-3417 450 C tcockrell@hbu.edu
COCKRIEL, Torie .... 270-745-5394 190 F torie.cockriel@wku.edu
COCKRUM, Colton .... 901-678-2156 439 E ccockrum@memphis.edu
COCKRUM, Dave .... 361-570-4321 465 D cockrumd@uhv.edu
COCKRUM, Larry, L ...... 606-539-4201 190 A presoff@ucumberlands.edu
COCLANIS-LODING, Chris .... 815-479-8713 145 B ccoclanis-loding@mchenry.edu
COCO, Karen .... 318-670-9324 196 A kcoco@susla.edu
COCOLA, Elizabeth .... 860-231-5272.. 89 E ecocola@usj.edu
COCOZZA, Christopher, R .... 610-282-1100 393 G christopher.cocozza@desales.edu
COCOZZOLI, Gary, R ..... 248-204-3006 233 A gcocozzol@ltu.edu
CODD, John .... 201-692-7071 286 B johncodd@fdu.edu
CODD, Justin .... 410-225-2290 205 C jcodd@mica.edu
CODDINGTON, Andrew . 315-228-6921 304 G acoddington@colgate.edu
CODERKO, Charles .... 217-206-7375 154 A ccode2@uis.edu
CODINA, Julie .... 619-684-8778.. 53 J jcodina@newschoolarch.edu
CODJOE, Henry, M .... 706-272-4406 118 F hcodjoe@daltonstate.edu
CODNER, Jackie .... 580-745-2810 379 J jcodner@se.edu
CODNER, Kolton .... 724-480-3460 392 K kolton.codner@ccbc.edu
CODNER, Renee .... 760-630-1555.. 28 B renee.codner@brightwood.edu
CODY, Ginnie .... 662-476-5728 253 A mcody@eastms.edu
CODY, Kenneth .... 781-891-2887 212 A kcody@bentley.edu
CODY, Mary Ellen .... 203-285-2296.. 85 E mcody@gwcc.commnet.edu
CODY, William .... 207-454-1011 200 D wcody@wccc.me.edu
COE, Bonnie, L .... 740-364-9509 358 E bcoe@cotc.edu
COE, Cheri .... 978-921-4242 222 B cheri.coe@montserrat.edu
COE, Desiree .... 602-682-6821.. 11 A dcoe@azsummitlaw.edu
COE, Douglas, A .... 406-496-4207 272 E dcoe@mtech.edu
COE, Erica .... 360-475-7263 496 F ecoe@olympic.edu
COE, Lea .... 229-931-2381 125 G lcoe@southgatech.edu
COE, Richard .... 941-487-4380 110 B coe@ncf.edu
COEHOORN, Joel .... 402-363-5603 278 E jcoehoorn@york.edu
COELHO, Marty .... 707-476-4358.. 39 F marty-coelho@redwoods.edu
COES, Alvie .... 706-355-5175 115 H acoes@athenstech.edu
COFER, Carol .... 304-327-4144 503 O ccofer@bluefieldstate.edu
COFER, Dagmar .... 909-469-5203.. 74 G dcofer@westernu.edu
COFER, Mildred .... 973-877-3468 285 K cofer@essex.edu
COFER, Stacy .... 316-323-6729 175 I scofer@butlercc.edu
COFFEE, Laura, F .... 336-342-4261 346 B coffeel@rockinghamcc.edu
COFFEE, Michael, P ...... 936-468-1257 458 A coffeemp@sfasu.edu
COFFEY, Amanda, A ...... 717-796-1800 401 L acoffey@messiah.edu
COFFEY, Ben .... 620-242-0488 179 G coffeyb@mcpherson.edu
COFFEY, Jaime .... 941-309-1178 106 H jcoffey@ringling.edu
COFFEY, Paul .... 312-899-5176 151 F pcoffey@saic.edu
COFFEY, Peter .... 312-362-8610 137 C pcoffey2@depaul.edu
COFFEY, Ron, L .... 260-359-4029 159 B rcoffey@huntington.edu
COFFEY, Suzanne, R ..... 413-542-2337 210 F studentaffairs@amherst.edu
COFFIA, Betsy .... 231-995-2825 235 B bcoffia@nmc.edu
COFFIN, Deb .... 303-492-8477.. 83 B deb.coffin@colorado.edu
COFFIN, Gordie .... 402-465-2544 276 E gcoffin@nebrwesleyan.edu
COFFIN, Lee .... 603-646-2604 281 C lee.coffin@dartmouth.edu
COFFIN, Ruth .... 509-793-2065 492 I ruthc@bigbend.edu
COFFIN, William .... 410-293-2809 519 E coffin@usna.edu
COFFMAN, Benjamin, S 989-774-3581 228 E coffm1bs@cmich.edu
COFFMAN, Curt .... 812-888-5131 165 E ccoffman@vinu.edu
COFFMAN, Kathryn, D ... 317-738-8063 157 L kcoffman@franklincollege.edu
COFFMAN, Marie, E ...... 724-852-3399 414 B mcoffman@waynesburg.edu
COFFMAN, Renee .... 702-968-2020 280 B rcoffman@roseman.edu
COFIELD, Bridgette, N ... 412-578-8897 391 G bncofield@carlow.edu
COFONE, Albin .... 631-451-4335 330 C cofonea@sunysuffolk.edu
COGBURN, Wendy, L .... 205-348-0537.... 8 A wcogburn@ctl.ua.edu
COGDELL, Edith .... 210-829-6037 465 E cogdell@uiwtx.edu
COGDILL, Rex .... 307-532-8257 516 J rex.cogdill@ewc.wy.edu
COGER, Robin, N .... 336-285-2640 350 C rncoger@ncat.edu
COGGIN, Rod .... 662-720-7306 255 B rcoggin@nemcc.edu
COGGIN, Rod .... 662-720-7306 255 B rbcoggin@nemcc.edu
COGGINS, Patrick .... 940-397-4239 453 C patrick.coggins@mwsu.edu
COGGINS VIENTOS, Sonja .... 615-327-6223 434 A svientos@mmc.edu
COGHILL, Karen .... 760-366-3791.. 41 B kcoghill@cmccd.edu
COGHLAN, Cathan .... 817-257-7475 461 A c.coghlan@tcu.edu
COGHLAN, Laura .... 360-867-6676 494 G coghlanl@evergreen.edu
COGLIANO, Herb .... 305-694-2401 112 A
COGSHELL, Nickyia .... 651-201-1812 243 I nickyia.cogshell@so.mnscu.edu
COGSWELL, Bob .... 910-893-1217 336 C cogswell@campbell.edu
COGSWELL, Katherine ... 315-445-6124 312 F cogswek@lemoyne.edu
COHALL, Kirkpatrick, G . 212-870-1208 318 C kcohall@nyts.edu
COHEA, Melissa .... 707-654-1789.. 32 E mcohea@csum.edu
COHEN, Alise .... 845-848-4036 306 G alise.cohen@dc.edu
COHEN, Bernadette .... 404-270-5091 126 D bcohen@spelman.edu
COHEN, Brad .... 740-593-1220 368 G cohenb@ohio.edu
COHEN, Brian .... 646-664-2004 301 A brian.cohen@cuny.edu
COHEN, Dan .... 617-373-5001 223 D
COHEN, David .... 631-656-2157 308 F david.cohen@ftc.edu
COHEN, David .... 800-371-6105.. 14 J david@nationalparalegal.edu
COHEN, Henry .... 707-638-5221 331 F henry.cohen@touro.edu
COHEN, Herbert .... 732-224-2215 284 B hcohen@brookdalecc.edu
COHEN, Ilene .... 732-255-0400 288 B icohen@ocean.edu
COHEN, Jason .... 413-755-4438 221 B jlcohen@stcc.edu
COHEN, Jennifer .... 206-543-2212 499 D huskyad@uw.edu
COHEN, Joan .... 207-741-5559 200 C jcohen@smccme.edu
COHEN, John .... 662-325-8082 254 E jcohen@athletics.msstate.edu
COHEN, Jonah .... 203-285-2289.. 85 E jcohen@gwcc.commnet.edu
COHEN, Kathleen, L ...... 607-735-1728 307 G kcohen@elmira.edu
COHEN, Kristin, E .... 919-508-2206 353 C kris.cohen@peace.edu
COHEN, Laurie .... 480-423-6511.. 14 C laurie.cohen@scottsdalecc.edu
COHEN, Lee .... 662-915-7178 256 C leecohen@olemiss.edu
COHEN, Lizabeth .... 617-495-8602 215 G lizabeth_cohen@radcliffe.harvard.edu
COHEN, Mark, J .... 202-687-7610.. 92 B cohenm@georgetown.edu
COHEN, Megan, S .... 617-353-2200 212 G mseiler@bu.edu
COHEN, Melissa .... 717-796-5220 401 L mcohen@messiah.edu
COHEN, Michael, E .... 772-466-4822.. 95 D m.cohen@aviator.edu
COHEN, Michelle .... 808-739-4674 129 A michelle.cohen@chaminade.edu
COHEN, Michelle, E ...... 215-596-8540 413 E m.cohen@usciences.edu
COHEN, Neil .... 864-578-8770 423 F ncohen@sherman.edu
COHEN, Paul, R .... 412-624-5139 412 I prcohen@pitt.edu
COHEN, Paula .... 215-895-1266 394 C paula.marantz.cohen@drexel.edu
COHEN, Peter .... 602-557-3211.. 17 C peter.cohen@phoenix.edu
COHEN, Peter .... 718-368-5563 303 A pcohen@kbcc.cuny.edu
COHEN, Pinchas .... 213-740-1354.. 72 B hassy@usc.edu
COHEN, Richard .... 215-985-2500 415 D rjc@phmc.org
COHEN, Richard, L .... 847-735-5555 142 H cohen@lakeforest.edu
COHEN, Ronald, A .... 570-372-4103 410 H cohen@susqu.edu
COHEN, Scott .... 731-425-2615 437 B scohen@jscc.edu
COHEN, Shaya .... 347-619-9074 335 A
COHEN, Susan, J .... 215-574-9600 397 H susan.cohen@hussiancollege.edu
COHEN, Tamara .... 352-392-1261 110 D tamararc@dso.ufl.edu
COHEN, Todd .... 303-964-6404.. 82 D tcohen@regis.edu
COHEN, Vicki .... 201-692-2132 286 B cohen@fdu.edu
COHEN, William, A .... 626-350-1500.. 29 E
COHEN, William, A .... 301-405-9354 207 G wcohen@umd.edu
COHEN, Yehuda .... 347-619-9074 335 A
COHEN, Zoe .... 978-837-5121 221 G cohenz@merrimack.edu
COHEN-ROSE, Amy .... 617-277-3915 212 F cohenrose@bgsp.edu
COHENOUR, LeeDel ...... 303-360-4914.. 79 C leedel.cohenour@ccaurora.edu
COHICK, Lynn, H .... 630-752-5069 155 F lynn.cohick@wheaton.edu
COHN, Stephen, A .... 919-687-3606 337 C stevec@acpub.duke.edu
COHRS, Daniel, L .... 303-963-3352.. 77 I dcohrs@ccu.edu
COHUNE, Ellen .... 805-756-2527.. 30 K ecohune@calpoly.edu
COKE, Kim .... 573-875-7420 258 F kjcoke@ccis.edu
COKER, Alan .... 208-885-5541 132 I alanc@uidaho.edu
COKER, Amber .... 850-913-3293 101 J acoker@gulfcoast.edu
COKER, Bryan, F .... 410-337-6150 204 A bryan.coker@goucher.edu
COKER, Dawn .... 706-880-8267 122 D dcoker@lagrange.edu
COKER, Jeff .... 540-665-4587 485 C jcoker2@su.edu
COKER, Jeffrey, S .... 724-946-7123 414 C cokerjs@westminster.edu
COKER, Keller .... 212-229-5896 316 E cokerk@newschool.edu
COKER, Kim .... 870-574-4533.. 21 G kcoker@sautech.edu
COKER, Melissa, A .... 843-355-4117 426 G cokerm@wiltech.edu
COKER, Renee .... 646-592-4336 334 P renee.coker@yu.edu
COKER, Scott, A .... 309-298-1834 155 D sa-coker@wiu.edu
COKER, Sherry .... 417-447-8884 264 K cokers@otc.edu
COKER-KOLO, Doyin ..... 812-941-2385 161 A ecokerko@ius.edu
COKKINOS, Michael ...... 212-217-4476 308 B michael_cokkinos@fitnyc.edu
COLÓN, Ingrid, Y .... 787-884-3838 520 G icolon@atenascollege.edu
COLÓN, Jesús, I .... 787-850-9335 528 B jesus.colon1@upr.edu
COLÓN, Maria, J .... 787-250-1912 524 B mjcolon@intermetro.com
COLADARCI, Richard ...... 603-230-3512 280 I rcoladarci@ccsnh.edu
COLADARCI, Ted, T .... 207-581-1415 201 B theo@maine.edu
COLAGROSS, Glenda ..... 256-331-5275.... 3 C colg@nwscc.edu
COLAGROSS, Glenda ..... 256-395-2211.... 3 G gcolagross@suscc.edu
COLAHAN, Michael .... 610-896-1350 397 F mcolahan@haverford.edu
COLANANNI, Terri .... 501-337-5000.. 19 C terric@coto.edu
COLANER, Kevin, T .... 909-869-3365.. 31 A ktcolaner@cpp.edu
COLANGELO, Carmon ... 314-935-9300 269 L colangelo@wustl.edu
COLAPIETRO, Cathy, L .. 913-971-3298 179 H ccolapietro@mnu.edu
COLARIC, Susan .... 727-497-5051 107 A colaric.susan@spcollege.edu
COLARULLI, Guy, C ...... 860-768-4749.. 89 C colarulli@hartford.edu
COLASURDO, Giuseppe, N .... 713-500-3000 468 D giuseppe.n.colasurdo@uth.tmc.edu
COLATCH, John, P .... 570-577-1592 390 H john.colatch@bucknell.edu
COLBAN, Tom .... 201-360-4393 286 E tcolban@follett.com
COLBECK, Ellen .... 217-875-7200 149 J ecolbeck@richland.edu
COLBERT, Carly, J .... 315-445-4312 312 F colbercj@lemoyne.edu
COLBERT, Claudia .... 718-997-3009 303 E claudia.colbert@qc.cuny.edu
COLBERT, Debbie .... 541-737-0123 385 F
COLBERT, Mary, J .... 410-857-2214 205 E mcolbert@mcdaniel.edu

COLLETON, Chelsi .... 803-323-2376 426 H
colletonc@winthrop.edu

COLLETT, Howard, M .... 801-524-8174 471 L
howardc@ldsbc.edu

COLLEY, Debra .... 716-286-8317 318 F
dcolley@niagara.edu

COLLEY, Karen .... 312-413-2548 153 H
karenc@uic.edu

COLLEY, Kenna .... 540-831-5439 484 A
kcolley@radford.edu

COLLIE, Cynthia .... 336-506-4410 340 L
cynthia.collie@alamancecc.edu

COLLIE, Susan, A .... 501-882-8967.. 17 M
sacollie@asub.edu

COLLIER, Barry, S .... 317-940-8421 156 I
bcollier@butler.edu

COLLIER, Carolyn .... 318-274-6265 196 G
collierc@gram.edu

COLLIER, Cindy .... 661-395-4281.. 47 A
ccollier@bakersfieldcollege.edu

COLLIER, Douglas .... 253-752-2020 494 H
accounting@faithseminary.edu

COLLIER, Gail .... 432-837-8243 462 G
gcollier@sulross.edu

COLLIER, Jackie .... 859-985-3110 183 I
collierj@berea.edu

COLLIER, Jay .... 402-375-7325 276 D
jacolli1@wsc.edu

COLLIER, Kristen, L ...... 937-327-7523 374 A
kcollier@wittenberg.edu

COLLIER, Li .... 707-524-1797.. 62 H
lcollier@santarosa.edu

COLLIER, Lisa .... 217-786-2446 144 B
lisa.collier@llcc.edu

COLLIER, Roger .... 918-444-2900 376 G
collier@nsuok.edu

COLLIER, Sam .... 859-442-1146 185 I
sam.collier@kctcs.edu

COLLIER, Scott .... 704-290-5872 346 F
scollier@spcc.edu

COLLIER, Sharon .... 870-633-4480.. 19 E
scollier@eacc.edu

COLLIER, Veronica .... 409-880-8185 462 B
vcollier@lit.edu

COLLIER, Yeman .... 210-567-7052 468 E
colliery@uthscsa.edu

COLLIGAN, Amanda ...... 617-984-1709 223 H
acolligan@quincycollege.edu

COLLING, Lynnde .... 307-268-2247 516 H
lcolling@caspercollege.edu

COLLINGWOOD, Brian .. 814-871-7681 395 H
collingw001@gannon.edu

COLLINGWOOD, Marlin 603-535-2475 283 B
mcollingwood@plymouth.edu

COLLINGWOOD, Tracy .. 716-673-3327 325 C
tracy.collingwood@fredonia.edu

COLLINS, Alyssa, D ...... 417-255-7265 263 I
alyssacollins@missouristate.edu

COLLINS, Anthony, G .... 315-268-6444 304 B
president@clarkson.edu

COLLINS, Aristide, J .... 202-994-6500.. 92 A
aristide@gwu.edu

COLLINS, Ashley .... 703-729-8800.. 93 B

COLLINS, Berkeley .... 202-885-6074.. 94 C
bcollins@wesleyseminary.edu

COLLINS, Berkeley .... 202-885-8644.. 94 C
bcollins@wesleyseminary.edu

COLLINS, Bob .... 801-274-3280 474 D
robert.collins@wgu.edu

COLLINS, Bryan .... 256-830-2626.... 5 I
bcollins@faulkner.edu

COLLINS, Buddy .... 662-862-8271 253 D
bacollins@iccms.edu

COLLINS, Candy .... 301-423-3600.. 93 B

COLLINS, Carrie .... 215-871-6154 407 G
carrieco@pcom.edu

COLLINS, Celeste .... 212-472-1500 318 B
ccollins@nysid.edu

COLLINS, Charles .... 207-741-5737 200 C
ccollins2@smccme.edu

COLLINS, Christina .... 317-921-4544 161 G
ccollins18@ivytech.edu

COLLINS, Christine .... 337-421-6969 193 F
christine.collins@sowela.edu

COLLINS, SJ,
Christopher .... 314-977-7075 266 J
ccolli11@slu.edu

COLLINS, Claire .... 828-227-7100 352 C

COLLINS, Cole .... 575-624-7127 294 A
cole.collins@roswell.enmu.edu

COLLINS, Dana .... 580-349-1574 377 E
dcollins@opsu.edu

COLLINS, Darron .... 207-801-5601 199 A
dcollins@coa.edu

COLLINS, Dave .... 937-512-2522 370 A
dave.collins@sinclair.edu

COLLINS, David .... 501-279-4291.. 19 G
dcollins@harding.edu

COLLINS, Dawn, M .... 773-508-3802 144 D
dcollins4@luc.edu

COLLINS, Dean, C .... 706-385-1094 124 F
dean.collins@point.edu

COLLINS, Deanne .... 770-533-6924 122 E
dcollins@laniertech.edu

COLLINS, Deborah .... 870-230-5640.. 19 H
collind@hsu.edu

COLLINS, Derrick, K ...... 773-995-3505 135 F
dcollins@csu.edu

COLLINS, Dorothy .... 740-264-5591 361 D
dcollins@egcc.edu

COLLINS, Elaine, C .... 802-626-6404 477 D
elaine.collins@lyndonstate.edu

COLLINS, Elaine, C .... 802-635-1240 477 C
cecilia.north@jsc.edu

COLLINS, Elizabeth .... 303-860-5600.. 83 A
elizabeth.collins@cu.edu

COLLINS, Ellen .... 402-552-6140 273 K
collins@clarksoncollege.edu

COLLINS, Ellen .... 617-323-6662 226 B
ellen_collins@williamjes.edu

COLLINS, Ernest .... 215-635-7300 396 B
ecollins@gratz.edu

COLLINS, Fuji .... 209-228-4331.. 69 C
fcollins@ucmerced.edu

COLLINS, Gary .... 478-301-2970 122 H
collins_g@mercer.edu

COLLINS, Gregory .... 530-251-8889.. 47 J
gcollins@lassencollege.edu

COLLINS,
Jacqueline, M .... 410-651-6407 208 C
jmcollins@umes.edu

COLLINS, James .... 916-558-2279.. 50 I
collins@scc.losrios.edu

COLLINS, James, E .... 508-793-7443 213 C
jcollins@clarku.edu

COLLINS, James, E .... 563-588-7103 171 H
jim.collins@loras.edu

COLLINS, Jennifer, M .... 214-768-8999 457 B
jmc@smu.edu

COLLINS, Jerry .... 602-242-6265.. 11 G
jerry.collins@brooklinecollege.edu

COLLINS, Jim .... 256-766-6610.... 5 K
jcollins@hcu.edu

COLLINS, Jodi .... 912-478-5519 120 E
jcollins@georgiasouthern.edu

COLLINS, Jodie .... 360-475-7682 496 F
jcollins@olympic.edu

COLLINS, John .... 707-965-6311.. 55 F
jcollins@puc.edu

COLLINS, John .... 812-866-6837 158 C
collins@hanover.edu

COLLINS, John, D .... 727-816-3310 105 C
collinj@phsc.edu

COLLINS, Joseph .... 763-424-0964 246 E
jcollins@nhcc.edu

COLLINS, Justin .... 580-349-1522 377 E
jkcollins@opsu.edu

COLLINS, Kamari .... 413-755-4558 221 B
kacollins@stcc.edu

COLLINS, Kathy .... 713-348-5147 455 F
kcollins@rice.edu

COLLINS, Kathy, M .... 401-874-2427 417 E
kmcollins@uri.edu

COLLINS, Ken .... 440-366-7738 364 F

COLLINS, Kevin .... 407-278-8824 255 E
kcollins@rts.edu

COLLINS, Kevin .... 239-590-7966 109 C
kcollins@fgcu.edu

COLLINS, Kevin .... 443-518-4690 204 E
kcollins@howardcc.edu

COLLINS, Kim .... 706-419-1439 118 E
kim.collins@covenant.edu

COLLINS, Kimberley .... 585-292-2105 315 L
kcollins@monroecc.edu

COLLINS, Kristine .... 208-426-2484 131 C
kcollin@boisestate.edu

COLLINS, Kristy .... 310-506-4116.. 56 D
kristy.collins@pepperdine.edu

COLLINS, Kyle, T .... 563-562-3263 172 D
collinsk@nicc.edu

COLLINS, Lance, R .... 607-255-9679 306 B
lc246@cornell.edu

COLLINS, Laurene, E ..... 804-257-5667 491 C
lecollins@vuu.edu

COLLINS, Laverne .... 412-536-1059 398 E
laverne.collins@laroche.edu

COLLINS, Leigh Ann ..... 979-532-6520 471 A
lacollins@wcjc.edu

COLLINS, Lorraine .... 407-447-7300 101 B
lcollins@ftccollege.edu

COLLINS, III, Love .... 901-448-7218 440 C
lcollins@utfi.org

COLLINS, Marie .... 239-489-9214 100 E
marie.collins@fsw.edu

COLLINS, Mark .... 425-352-8260 492 K
mcollins@cascadia.edu

COLLINS, Mark .... 978-837-5131 221 G
collinsma@merrimack.edu

COLLINS, Mary .... 724-805-2564 410 B
mary.collins@email.stvincent.edu

COLLINS, Mary, K .... 315-445-4791 312 F
collinsm@lemoyne.edu

COLLINS,
Mary Elizabeth .... 253-879-3237 499 C
lcollins@pugetsound.edu

COLLINS, Matthew .... 502-895-3411 188 A
mcollins@lpts.edu

COLLINS, Michael .... 641-673-1393 174 F
collinsm@wmpenn.edu

COLLINS, Michael .... 714-564-6981.. 58 A
collins_michaelt@sac.edu

COLLINS, Michael .... 805-525-4417.. 67 E
mcollins@thomasaquinas.edu

COLLINS, Michael .... 269-488-4255 231 G
mcollins@kvcc.edu

COLLINS, Michael, F ..... 508-856-8100 217 C
michael.collins@umassmed.edu

COLLINS, Mildred, D ..... 615-327-6413 434 A
mcollins@mmc.edu

COLLINS, Miranda .... 740-376-4458 365 A
miranda.collins@marietta.edu

COLLINS, Monique .... 850-484-1630 105 E
mcollins@pensacolastate.edu

COLLINS, Patrick .... 617-627-4173 225 A
patrick.collins@tufts.edu

COLLINS, Patty .... 409-882-3343 462 D
patty.collins@lsco.edu

COLLINS, Paul .... 312-662-4448 133 A
pcollins@adler.edu

COLLINS, Ray .... 404-527-4520 117 C
rcollins@carver.edu

COLLINS, SR.,
Ronnie, L .... 410-951-3392 208 F
rcollins@coppin.edu

COLLINS, Sarah .... 402-826-8501 274 E
sarah.collins@doane.edu

COLLINS, Scott .... 518-736-3622 309 A
scollins@fmcc.suny.edu

COLLINS, Sean .... 617-521-2296 224 E
sean.collins@simmons.edu

COLLINS, Sean .... 828-898-3193 339 B
collinss@lmc.edu

COLLINS, Sheila .... 773-995-3973 135 F
scolli25@csu.edu

COLLINS,
Sibrina Nichelle .... 248-204-2227 233 A
scollins@ltu.edu

COLLINS, Steve .... 870-612-2026.. 22 H
steve.collins@uaccb.edu

COLLINS, Tana .... 205-387-0511.... 1 D
tana.collins@bscc.edu

COLLINS, Trudy .... 406-657-1680 272 B
tcollins@msubillings.edu

COLLINS, Valerie, H ...... 516-572-7664 316 C
valerie.collins@ncc.edu

COLLINS, Walter .... 415-451-2822.. 60 I
wcollins@sfts.edu

COLLINS, Wanda .... 404-727-7450 119 B
wanda.collins@emory.edu

COLLINS, Wanda .... 919-660-1024 337 C
wanda.collins@duke.edu

COLLINS, II, William ..... 716-888-8208 300 G
collinsw@canisius.edu

COLLINS, Yadigar .... 740-587-6530 361 B
collinsy@denison.edu

COLLINS-HALL, Lori .... 937-319-0069 356 F
lcollinshall@antiochcollege.edu

COLLINS JUDD, Cristle . 914-395-2201 323 K
president@sarahlawrence.edu

COLLINWOOD, Nancy .... 801-626-6569 473 E
ncollinwood@weber.edu

COLLIS, Jennifer .... 440-375-7175 364 C
jcollis@lec.edu

COLLMIER, Robert .... 973-748-9000 284 A
robert_collmier@bloomfield.edu

COLLOGAN, Jessica ...... 904-256-7269 102 B
jcollog@ju.edu

COLLUM, Tammy .... 770-975-4125 117 G
tcollum@chattahoocheetech.edu

COLLUMBIEN, Bill, S ..... 651-696-6686 243 B
wcollumb@macalester.edu

COLMAN, Avrohom .... 732-367-1060 283 K

COLMAN, Gabriela .... 254-710-8300 444 B
gabriela_colman@baylor.edu

COLMENERO,
Jacinto (JC) .... 361-354-2559 445 S
jcolmenero@coastalbend.edu

COLMERAUER, Joanne .. 716-270-2826 307 I
colmerauer@ecc.edu

COLOM, Albert, N .... 904-620-2881 110 E
colom@unf.edu

COLOMBAT, Andre .... 410-617-2910 205 A
acp@loyola.edu

COLON,
Adabel-Vanessa .... 787-250-1912 524 B
avcolon@metro.inter.edu

COLON, Ana Isabel .... 787-857-3600 523 I
acolon@br.inter.edu

COLON, Angie .... 787-863-2390 523 K
angie.colon@fajardo.inter.edu

COLON, Brenda .... 787-765-4210 521 G
bcolon@cempr.edu

COLON, Diana, M .... 787-257-7373 525 Q
dmcolon@suagm.edu

COLON, Eddie .... 816-279-7000 257 B
eddie.colon@abtu.edu

COLON, Hector, W .... 787-284-1912 524 C
hwcolon@ponce.inter.edu

COLON, Iris .... 787-746-1400 522 O
icolon@huertas.edu

COLON, Isaac .... 787-844-8991 528 E
isaaccolondegro@upr.edu

COLON, Jaime .... 787-279-1912 523 J
jcolon@bayamon.inter.edu

COLON, Leandro .... 787-841-2000 525 J
leandro_colon@pucpr.edu

COLON, Lesbia .... 787-844-8181 528 E
lesbia.colon@upr.edu

COLON, Luis .... 787-761-0640 527 C
lcolon@utcpr.edu

COLON, Luis .... 787-815-0000 527 F
luis.colon19@upr.edu

COLON, Maggie .... 787-763-1912 523 F
mcolon@inter.edu

COLON, Michelle .... 407-888-8689.. 99 F
mcolon@fcim.edu

COLON, Mirta .... 787-754-8000 527 B
mcolon@pupr.edu

COLON, Myrna .... 787-834-9595 526 E
mcolon@uaa.edu

COLON, Nidia .... 787-786-3030 526 F
ncolon@ucb.edu.pr

COLON, Victor .... 787-786-3030 526 F
vcolon@ucb.edu.pr

COLON, Victor .... 515-289-9200 170 B
vcolon@inste.edu

COLON, Vilma, E .... 787-284-1912 524 C
vcolon@ponce.inter.edu

COLON-CANALES,
Wanda .... 301-891-4093 209 E
wcanales@wau.edu

COLON COSME,
Edwin, J .... 787-744-1060 525 A
edwincolon@mechtech.edu

COLON-GUASP,
Wilfredo .... 787-288-1118 525 P

COLON NEGRON,
Edgar .... 787-758-2525 528 D
edgar.colon2@upr.edu

COLONNO, Daniel, J ..... 413-662-5281 218 C
d.colonno@mcla.edu

COLORADO, Ana .... 787-725-8120 522 M
acolorado0013@eap.edu

COLSON, Darrel, D .... 319-352-8450 174 C
president@wartburg.edu

COLSON, Jessica .... 413-265-2454 213 E
colsonj@elms.edu

COLSON, John .... 951-639-5201.. 52 J
jcolson@msjc.edu

COLSON, Matthew .... 631-632-4932 325 F
matthew.colson@stonybrook.edu

COLTER, Scott .... 817-923-1921 457 G
scolter@swbts.edu

COLTER-BRABHAM,
Constance .... 803-780-1189 426 F
cbrabham@voorhees.edu

COLTHARP, Duane .... 210-999-8201 464 B
dcolthar@trinity.edu

COLTHARP, Glenn .... 417-455-5740 259 D
glenncoltharp@crowder.edu

COLTMAN, Heather .... 540-568-3429 481 I
coltmahj@jmu.edu

COLUCCI, David .... 718-779-1499 320 C
dcolluci@plazacollege.edu

COLUCCI, Rita .... 508-626-4993 218 A
rcolucci@framingham.edu

COLUMBUS, Kristi .... 319-895-4153 167 G
kcolumbus@cornellcollege.edu

COLUSSY-ESTES, Kate ... 404-471-6437 114 H
kcolussyestes@agnesscott.edu

COLVEY, Kirsten, S .... 909-389-3327.. 59 H
kcolvey@craftonhills.edu

COLVILLE, John .... 903-988-3747 451 F
jcolville@kilgore.edu

COLVIN, Christopher ..... 508-213-2368 223 C
christopher.colvin@nichols.edu

COLVIN, Gail, B .... 719-333-9751 518 H

COLVIN, Jenna .... 706-867-4518 127 B
jenna.colvin@ung.edu

COLVSON, W. Mark ...... 845-257-3719 325 D
colvsonm@newpaltz.edu

CONNIRY, JR., Charles, J .... 503-554-6152 383 C cconniry@georgefox.edu
CONNOLLY, Adam .... 843-383-8050 420 B aconnolly@coker.edu
CONNOLLY, Ann Marie . 313-883-8500 236 D connolly.annmarie@shms.edu
CONNOLLY, Barbara ...... 845-569-3202 316 B barbara.connolly@msmc.edu
CONNOLLY, Dan .... 920-686-6209 510 A dan.connolly@sl.edu
CONNOLLY, Daniel .... 515-271-2872 168 J daniel.connolly@drake.edu
CONNOLLY, Derry .... 858-653-6740.. 46 M dconnolly@jpcatholic.com
CONNOLLY, James .... 203-332-5088.. 85 F jconnolly@hcc.commnet.edu
CONNOLLY, James, D ... 203-332-5090.. 85 F jconnolly@hcc.commnet.edu
CONNOLLY, Jon, H .... 973-300-2120 291 I jconnolly@sussex.edu
CONNOLLY, Joy .... 212-817-7200 302 B provost@gc.cuny.edu
CONNOLLY, Justin .... 256-766-6610.... 5 K jconnolly@hcu.edu
CONNOLLY, Laura .... 970-351-2707.. 83 F laura.connolly@unco.edu
CONNOLLY, Lidy .... 858-653-6740.. 46 M lconnolly@jpcatholic.com
CONNOLLY, Meg .... 314-977-7121 266 J burnesmm@slu.edu
CONNOLLY, Melissa, A . 516-463-4160 310 D melissa.a.connolly@hofstra.edu
CONNOLLY, Michael ..... 320-363-3512 250 A mconnolly@csbsju.edu
CONNOLLY, Patricia, A . 412-536-1243 398 E patricia.connolly@laroche.edu
CONNOLLY, Paula .... 978-837-5128 221 G connollyp@merrimack.edu
CONNOLLY, Robert .... 404-894-2500 120 A robert.connolly@police.gatech.edu
CONNOLLY, Shawn, M . 973-655-5427 287 D connollys@mail.montclair.edu
CONNOLLY, Tara .... 515-964-6447 168 A tkconnolly@dmacc.edu
CONNOR, Beth .... 402-898-1000 274 C beth_c@creativecenter.edu
CONNOR, Cassandra ..... 228-897-7137 256 I cconnor@wmcarey.edu
CONNOR, Francis, P ..... 260-399-7700 165 B fconnor@sf.edu
CONNOR, Gary .... 704-216-3723 346 C gary.connor@rccc.edu
CONNOR, Joanne, M .... 856-256-4102 289 H connorj@rowan.edu
CONNOR, Lorri, B .... 704-403-3207 336 B lorri.connor@carolinashealthcare.org
CONNOR, Pat .... 812-855-0973 159 G connorp@indiana.edu
CONNOR, Pat .... 812-855-0973 159 H connorp@indiana.edu
CONNOR, Rianne .... 707-476-4151.. 39 F rianne-connor@redwoods.edu
CONNOR, Rianne .... 707-476-4183.. 39 F rianne-connor@redwoods.edu
CONNOR, Roger .... 203-837-9301.. 85 B connorr@wcsu.edu
CONNOR, Rosie .... 435-283-7160 474 A rosie.connor@snow.edu
CONNOR, Shane .... 216-687-2084 359 L s.c.connor@csuohio.edu
CONNOR, Terry, D .... 859-344-3308 189 G connort@thomasmore.edu
CONNORS, Anne .... 207-453-5126 200 A aconnors@kvcc.me.edu
CONNORS, Chalese .... 940-898-2373 464 A cconnors@twu.edu
CONNORS, Cheryl, C .... 401-739-5000 416 D cconnors@neit.edu
CONNORS, David .... 323-343-4004.. 32 D david.connors@calstatela.edu
CONNORS, John .... 215-596-8973 413 E j.connors@usciences.edu
CONNORS, Michael, W . 773-371-5484 134 J mconnors@ctu.edu
CONNORS, Nancy .... 631-420-2142 329 D nancy.connors@farmingdale.edu
CONNORS, Natalie .... 219-989-2600 163 E natalie.connors@pnw.edu
CONNUCK, Wendy .... 215-489-2921 393 F wendy.connuck@delval.edu
CONOLEY, Jane, C .... 562-985-4121.. 32 C csulb-president@csulb.edu
CONOLLY, Brian .... 413-528-7217 211 B bconolly@simons-rock.edu
CONOLLY, Charlene ...... 410-287-1910 203 B cconolly@cecil.edu
CONOVER, David .... 541-346-2090 387 F dconover@uoregon.edu
CONOVER, Dustin .... 307-382-1644 517 C dconover@westernwyoming.edu
CONOVER, Melanie .... 801-524-1927 471 L conoverm@ldsbc.edu
CONOVER, Phillip .... 217-228-5432 149 B conoverp@quincy.edu
CONOVER, Ross, P .... 240-895-4304 206 G rpconover@smcm.edu
CONQUE, Chasse, S ..... 501-569-3167.. 22 B csconque@ualr.edu
CONRAD, Deb .... 775-445-4236 279 F deb.conrad@wnc.edu
CONRAD, Jacqueline ..... 617-873-0621 213 B jacqueline.conrad@cambridgecollege.edu
CONRAD, James, A .... 509-535-4051 146 B jim.conrad@moody.edu
CONRAD, Jeffrey .... 617-236-8831 215 B jconrad@fisher.edu
CONRAD, Jon, B .... 610-861-1526 402 D conradj@moravian.edu
CONRAD, Kari, M .... 570-577-1217 390 H kari.conrad@bucknell.edu
CONRAD, Kelley .... 231-777-0321 234 G kelley.conrad@muskegoncc.edu
CONRAD, Kristin .... 434-582-7602 482 D klconrad@liberty.edu
CONRAD, Lara .... 614-251-4718 367 F conradl@ohiodominican.edu
CONRAD, Rebecca .... 207-699-5017 199 H bconrad@meca.edu
CONRAD, Rhonda .... 641-683-5115 169 I rhonda.conrad@indianhills.edu
CONRAD, Robert .... 410-857-2250 205 E rconrad@mcdaniel.edu
CONRAD, Scott .... 707-524-1553.. 62 H sconrad@santarosa.edu
CONRAD, Valarie .... 312-949-7304 140 A vconrad@ico.edu
CONRAD WEISMAN, Sarah .... 315-312-3557 327 D sarah.weisman@oswego.edu
CONRADSEN, Susan ..... 706-236-5494 116 D sconradsen@berry.edu
CONREY, Meredith .... 936-294-3602 462 F meredithconrey@shsu.edu
CONROE, Nicole .... 716-829-7645 307 B conroen@dyc.edu
CONROY, Kevin .... 802-224-3000 476 H kevin.conroy@vsc.edu
CONROY, Kristen .... 617-735-9980 214 F conroyk@emmanuel.edu
CONROY, Nina .... 646-313-8000 303 G nina.conroy@guttman.cuny.edu
CONROY, Shelley, F ...... 214-820-3361 444 B shelley_conroy@baylor.edu
CONROY, Terry .... 254-867-3058 461 G terry.conroy@tstc.edu
CONROY, Timothy .... 207-974-4682 199 L tconroy@emcc.edu
CONROY-RANDALL, Britta .... 415-575-6176.. 29 H bcrandall@ciis.edu
CONSIDINE, Marilynn, S .... 503-552-1504 384 F mconsidine@nunm.edu
CONSIDINE-FONTES, Lisa, M .... 401-825-2444 416 B lfontes@ccri.edu
CONSTABLE, Jean .... 830-372-8090 461 D jconstable@tlu.edu
CONSTABLE, Peter .... 217-333-2760 154 B constabl@illinois.edu
CONSTANCE, Eric, F ...... 315-786-2252 311 H econstance@sunyjefferson.edu
CONSTANINOU, Constantia .... 631-632-7100 325 F constantia.constantinou@stonybrook.edu
CONSTANTINE, Carol .... 508-678-2811 219 C carol.constantine@bristolcc.edu
CONSTANTINE, Christopher .... 870-508-6104.. 18 C cconstantine@asumh.edu
CONSTANTINE, OSB, Cyprian, G .... 724-805-2332 410 C cyprian.constantine@stvincent.edu
CONSTANTINE, Doris, F 512-448-8525 455 I dorisc@stedwards.edu
CONSTANTINO, Cynthia 310-660-3111.. 42 C cconstan@elcamino.edu
CONSTANTINO, John .... 808-245-8245 130 F johncons@hawaii.edu
CONSTANTINO, Patricia 617-745-3724 214 D patricia.constantino@enc.edu
CONSTANTINO, Rocco .. 805-965-0581.. 62 E rfconstantino@sbcc.edu
CONSTON, Marcia .... 704-330-6647 342 A marcia.conston@cpcc.edu
CONTARDI, Heather .... 570-558-1818 395 F hcontardi@fortisinstitute.edu
CONTARINO, Sue .... 847-925-6200 139 B scontari@harpercollege.edu
CONTE, Andrew .... 412-392-8055 408 F aconte@pointpark.edu
CONTE, John .... 214-637-3530 470 H jconte@wadecollege.edu
CONTE, Millie .... 718-631-6222 303 F mconte@qcc.cuny.edu
CONTINO-CONNER, Cheryl .... 828-339-4245 346 H cheryl@southwesterncc.edu
CONTOMANOLIS, Emanuel .... 585-475-5464 321 D emcoce@rit.edu
CONTOMANOLIS, Laurel .... 585-275-3166 332 E laurel.contomanolis@rochester.edu
CONTRERAS, David .... 619-684-8769.. 53 J dcontreras@newschoolarch.edu
CONTRERAS, Eduardo, R .... 503-943-8266 387 H contrera@up.edu
CONTRERAS, Gilbert ...... 714-992-7074.. 54 A gcontreras@fullcoll.edu
CONTRERAS, Lisa .... 312-935-6620 149 K lcontreras@robertmorris.edu
CONTRERAS, Maribel .... 787-746-1400 522 O mcontreras@huertas.edu
CONTRERAS, Raquel, J . 864-656-2451 419 F rcontre@clemson.edu
CONTRERAS, JR., Sebastian .... 847-635-1756 148 D scontrer@oakton.edu
CONTRERAS, Sylvia .... 608-663-3278 507 D scontreras@edgewood.edu
CONVER, Kathleen .... 309-677-2242 134 G mkc@fsmail.bradley.edu
CONVERSE, Kenneth, L . 712-749-2101 167 C conversek@bvu.edu
CONVERSE, Sharon, K .. 248-341-2154 235 D skconver@oaklandcc.edu
CONVERSE, Wayne .... 563-425-5507 173 K cookc30@uiu.edu
CONVERTINO, Gary .... 508-541-1681 214 C gconvertino@dean.edu
CONWAY, Andrew .... 909-607-9406.. 37 L andrew.conway@cgu.edu
CONWAY, Danielle .... 207-780-4344 201 H dconway@maine.edu
CONWAY, Francine .... 848-445-2325 290 C francine.conway@rutgers.edu
CONWAY, Heidi .... 443-997-8113 204 F hconway3@jhu.edu
CONWAY, Jean, L .... 972-860-7001 447 I jconway@dcccd.edu
CONWAY, John .... 601-974-1138 254 A john.conway@millsaps.edu
CONWAY, Jordyn .... 518-445-3207 297 K jconw@albanylaw.edu
CONWAY, Karen .... 901-321-3536 431 A kconway@cbu.edu
CONWAY, Katie .... 212-678-6625 331 C conway@tc.edu
CONWAY, Morrie .... 402-878-3309 275 C mconway@littlepriest.edu
CONWAY, Pete .... 701-255-3285 355 I pconway@uttc.edu
CONWAY, Sharon .... 301-891-4005 209 E sconway@wau.edu
CONWAY, Teresa .... 509-359-6489 494 D tconway@ewu.edu
CONWAY, JR., Thomas . 252-335-3228 350 A chancellor@ecsu.edu
CONWAY-TURNER, Katherine, S .... 716-878-4101 326 E conwayks@buffalostate.edu
CONWELL, James, C ..... 812-877-8006 163 G conwell@rose-hulman.edu
CONYERS, Gregory .... 718-270-7416 326 A greg.conyers@downstate.edu
CONYERS, Lance .... 270-831-9632 186 A lance.conyers@kctcs.edu
CONYERS, Rhyan, M ..... 859-233-8500 189 H rconyers@transy.edu
CONZATTI, Maria, P ...... 516-572-7600 316 C maria.conzatti@ncc.edu
CONZELMAN, Karen ...... 623-845-3612.. 13 H karen.ann.conzelman@gccaz.edu
CONZEN, Christopher ... 212-752-1530 312 G christopher.conzen@limcollege.edu
COOGAN, Jay .... 612-874-3737 243 F president@mcad.edu
COOK, Aaron .... 303-546-5284.. 81 B acook@naropa.edu
COOK, Alicia .... 973-748-9000 284 A alicia_cook@bloomfield.edu
COOK, Allen, P .... 203-576-4206.. 88 F acook@bridgeport.edu
COOK, Amber .... 814-871-7421 395 H cook0692@gannon.edu
COOK, Andrea, P .... 503-517-1212 388 A acook@warnerpacific.edu
COOK, Angela .... 336-734-7618 343 C acook@forsythtech.edu
COOK, Anita .... 914-606-6745 333 H anita.cook@sunywcc.edu
COOK, Barbara Jo .... 770-467-6038 126 B bcook@sctech.edu
COOK, Bradley .... 435-586-7704 473 A bradcook@suu.edu
COOK, Brett .... 208-496-2710 131 D cookb@byui.edu
COOK, Brian .... 440-525-7084 364 D bcook@lakelandcc.edu
COOK, Bruce .... 386-506-4417.. 97 I cookb@daytonastate.edu
COOK, Carey, W .... 208-467-8643 132 F cwcook@nnu.edu
COOK, Chaney .... 303-458-3529.. 82 D cgivens@regis.edu
COOK, Charles .... 512-223-7612 443 G charles.cook@austincc.edu
COOK, Chris .... 806-742-2136 463 D chris.cook@ttu.edu
COOK, Christopher .... 208-885-6739 132 I chrisco@uidaho.edu
COOK, Cindy .... 281-283-2595 465 B cookc@uhcl.edu
COOK, Corey .... 208-426-1368 131 C coreydcook@boisestate.edu
COOK, Courtney .... 207-699-5060 199 H ccook@meca.edu
COOK, Craig, A .... 530-226-4188.. 64 B ccook@simpsonu.edu
COOK, Craig, A .... 518-276-3777 321 A cookc5@rpi.edu
COOK, Darrell .... 202-885-3546.. 91 C dcook@american.edu
COOK, David .... 309-694-8551 139 G dcook@icc.edu
COOK, David .... 913-897-8400 181 I davidcook@ku.edu
COOK, David, E .... 218-722-4000 242 B davidc@dbumn.edu
COOK, Debra .... 918-335-6264 378 F dcook@okwu.edu
COOK, Don .... 954-201-7538.. 96 A dcook@broward.edu
COOK, Donalda .... 410-617-2842 205 A dcook@loyola.edu
COOK, Donelda .... 410-617-5171 205 A dcook@loyola.edu
COOK, Donna, L .... 575-439-3699 295 C donnac@nmsu.edu
COOK, Donna, M .... 401-341-2435 417 D donna.cook@salve.edu
COOK, Douglas .... 757-352-4331 484 E dougcoo@regent.edu
COOK, Edith .... 724-830-1014 410 E ecook@setonhill.edu
COOK, Edward .... 401-232-6320 416 A ecook4@bryant.edu
COOK, Ellen, D .... 337-482-6306 197 F edcook@louisiana.edu
COOK, Elsie .... 510-567-6174.. 66 I drcook@sum.edu
COOK, Gary .... 214-333-5130 447 D chancellor@dbu.edu
COOK, Greg .... 262-472-1077 512 C cookg@uww.edu
COOK, Holly .... 970-207-4500.. 84 C hollyc@uscareerinstitute.edu
COOK, Holly .... 970-207-4550.. 80 P hollyc@mckinleycollege.edu
COOK, Howard, M .... 864-488-8344 422 B hcook@limestone.edu
COOK, James .... 336-734-7311 343 C jcook@forsythtech.edu
COOK, Janelle .... 907-796-6255.. 10 C jmcook3@alaska.edu
COOK, Jason, D .... 254-710-1412 444 B jason_cook@baylor.edu
COOK, Jeffrey .... 657-278-4475.. 32 B jcook@fullerton.edu
COOK, Jeffrey .... 513-569-1579 359 G jeffrey.cook@cincinnatistate.edu
COOK, Jerry .... 936-294-3620 462 F bio_jlc@shsu.edu
COOK, Jessica .... 302-736-2435.. 90 J jessica.cook@wesley.edu

COOPER, Sandy .... 918-595-7856 380 D
sandy.cooper@tulsacc.edu
COOPER, Shaina .... 202-274-5410.. 93 D
shaina.cooper@udc.edu
COOPER, Shannon .... 916-691-7738.. 50 G
coopers@crc.losrios.edu
COOPER, Stephanie .... 973-300-2161 291 I
scooper@sussex.edu
COOPER, Stewart, E ...... 219-464-5002 165 D
stewart.cooper@valpo.edu
COOPER, Susan .... 412-323-4000 389 I
scooper@mcg-btc.org
COOPER, Tana .... 620-792-9241 175 C
coopert@bartonccc.edu
COOPER, Tara, L .... 606-546-1241 189 I
tcooper@unionky.edu
COOPER, Toya .... 805-565-6832.. 74 I
tcooper@westmont.edu
COOPER, Tracey, L .... 440-525-7230 364 D
tcooper@lakelandcc.edu
COOPER, Tuesday .... 860-512-3000.. 85 G
tcooper@manchestercc.edu
COOROUGH, Randall .... 262-691-5168 515 B
rcoorough@wctc.edu
COOTE, Samra .... 404-752-5223 123 F
scoote@msm.edu
COOTER, Robert, B .... 502-272-7992 183 H
rcooter@bellarmine.edu
COOTS, Kevin .... 610-372-4721 408 G
kcoots@racc.edu
COP, Kenneth, B .... 732-932-7211 290 A
kcop@aps.rutgers.edu
COP, Kenneth, B .... 732-932-7211 290 C
kcop@aps.rutgers.edu
COPAS, Tyra .... 423-354-5259 437 E
tlcopas@northeaststate.edu
COPASS, Ron .... 239-489-9129 100 E
rlcopass@fsw.edu
COPE, Jill .... 509-453-0374 497 A
jill.cope@perrytech.edu
COPE, Marla .... 913-234-0687 176 H
marla.cope@cleveland.edu
COPE, Michael .... 310-506-4270.. 56 D
mike.cope@pepperdine.edu
COPELAND, Angela .... 903-566-7080 468 C
jcopeland@uttyler.edu
COPELAND, Boyd .... 636-922-8238 265 J
bcopeland@stchas.edu
COPELAND, Brian .... 616-331-2831 230 G
copelabr@gvsu.edu
COPELAND, Cathy .... 425-739-8156 495 F
cathy.copeland@lwtech.edu
COPELAND, David, L ..... 540-464-7218 490 E
copelanddl@vmi.edu
COPELAND, Gayle .... 530-226-4133.. 64 B
gcopeland@simpsonu.edu
COPELAND, Jeff .... 813-253-7016 101 M
hcopeland4@hccfl.edu
COPELAND, John, C ..... 754-312-2898 102 V
jcopeland@keycollege.edu
COPELAND, Judson ...... 405-425-5129 377 B
judson.copeland@oc.edu
COPELAND, Kate .... 503-226-4391 385 H
kcopeland@pnca.edu
COPELAND, Kenneth ..... 434-395-2016 482 E
copelandpk@longwood.edu
COPELAND, Kristopher .. 972-273-3000 448 C
COPELAND, Leigh .... 843-525-8231 424 E
lcopeland@tcl.edu
COPELAND, Maura .... 912-478-7481 120 E
mconley@georgiasouthern.edu
COPELAND, Michele ..... 612-659-6248 245 F
michele.copeland@minneapolis.edu
COPELAND, Paul .... 302-736-2538.. 90 J
paul.copeland@wesley.edu
COPELAND, JR.,
Robert, M .... 803-327-7402 419 G
rcopeland@clintoncollege.edu
COPELAND, Shannon .... 409-880-8922 462 C
shannon.copeland@lamar.edu
COPELAND, Wanda .... 610-796-8437 389 A
wanda.copeland@alvernia.edu
COPELAND-MORGAN,
Youlonda .... 310-825-2665.. 69 B
ycopeland-morgan@saonet.ucla.edu
COPELIN, Laylan .... 979-458-6425 458 E
lcopelin@tamus.edu
COPELY, Pat .... 937-376-2946 369 C
pcopely@payne.edu
COPENHAVER, Bonny .... 715-394-6677 515 D
bonny.copenhaver@witc.edu
COPENHAVER, Martin ... 617-964-1100 210 G
mcopenhaver@ants.edu
COPENHAVER, Michael . 619-644-7000.. 45 A
michael.coppenhaver@gcccd.edu
COPLAN, Jan .... 802-387-7175 475 C
jancoplan@landmark.edu
COPLAND, Katherine ..... 917-493-4030 313 M
kcopland@msmnyc.edu
COPLIN, Kimberly, A ..... 740-587-6243 361 B
coplin@denison.edu
COPLIN, Louis .... 518-629-7348 310 G
l.coplin@hvcc.edu
COPLIN, Wendell .... 318-397-6144 192 J
COPONITI, Laura, I .... 405-224-3140 381 B
lcoponiti@usao.edu
COPONITI, Mike .... 405-224-3140 381 B
mcoponiti@usao.edu
COPONITI, Mike, D .... 405-224-3140 381 B
mcoponiti@usao.edu
COPP, Crista .... 310-338-1745.. 50 J
crista.copp@lmu.edu
COPP, Destini .... 404-432-3475 125 H
acopp@southuniversity.edu
COPPEDGE, Robin .... 580-387-7000 376 D
rcoppedge@mscok.edu
COPPER, Christine .... 419-755-4753 366 E
ccopper@ncstatecollege.edu
COPPER GLENZ, Becky . 978-665-3564 217 E
bcopperg@fitchburgstate.edu
COPPERSMITH, Clifford . 406-247-3009 272 B
ccoppersmith@msubillings.edu
COPPLE, Chad .... 618-437-5321 149 H
copplec@rlc.edu
COPPLE, James (Dean) . 865-694-6536 437 F
jdcopple@pstcc.edu
COPPOLA, David, L .... 570-945-8500 398 C
david.coppola@keystone.edu
COPPOLA, Stephen, A ... 704-687-5965 351 C
scoppola@uncc.edu
COPPOLA, William .... 817-515-3001 458 B
william.coppola@tccd.edu
COQUELLIN, Janet .... 806-743-2865 463 E
janet.coquellin@ttuhsc.edu
COQUEREL, Phoebe ...... 404-225-4529 115 J
pcoquerel@atlantatech.edu
CORA, Gladys .... 787-766-1717 526 B
um_gcora@suagm.edu
CORA, Jesus .... 787-250-1912 524 B
jacora@metro.inter.edu
CORA-IZQUIERDO,
Gladys .... 787-288-1118 525 P
CORAZZA, Anthony .... 718-368-5124 303 A
acorazza@kbcc.cuny.edu
CORBA, David .... 586-286-2058 233 B
corbad@macomb.edu
CORBAT, Carol .... 318-473-6431 194 A
ccorbat@lsua.edu
CORBETT, Ann .... 207-621-3145 201 C
annie@maine.edu
CORBETT, Carrie .... 901-272-5111 434 B
ccorbett@mca.edu
CORBETT, Christopher ... 912-525-5000 125 B
ccorbett@scad.edu
CORBETT, Diane .... 614-292-8595 367 H
corbett.168@osu.edu
CORBETT, Faith .... 718-260-5564 303 D
fcorbett@citytech.cuny.edu
CORBETT, Heather .... 860-768-2409.. 89 C
hcorbett@hartford.edu
CORBETT, Idna .... 859-572-5379 188 E
corbetti1@nku.edu
CORBETT, Marcus .... 803-793-5289 420 G
corbettm@denmarktech.edu
CORBETT, Martin .... 315-781-3656 310 C
corbett@hws.edu
CORBETT, Mickey .... 432-837-8059 462 G
mcorbett@sulross.edu
CORBIN, Chuck .... 317-931-3324 157 D
ccorbin@cts.edu
CORBIN, Edith .... 856-222-9311 289 F
ecorbin@rcbc.edu
CORBIN, Nancy .... 360-650-3000 500 E
nancy.corbin@wwu.edu
CORBIN, Russ .... 315-498-2831 319 G
corbinr@sunyocc.edu
CORBIN, Thomas .... 802-443-5504 475 G
corbin@middlebury.edu
CORBIN, Ty .... 804-523-5726 488 C
tcorbin@reynolds.edu
CORBITT, Sandra, K ...... 540-338-1776 483 H
slife@phc.edu
CORBITT, Timothy .... 315-229-5392 323 D
tcorbitt@stlawu.edu
CORBITT, Zach .... 864-596-9215 420 F
zach.corbitt@converse.edu
CORCORAN, Heather, A 314-935-9292 269 L
hcorcoran@wustl.edu
CORCORAN, Jerry, M .... 815-224-0404 141 A
jerry_corcoran@ivcc.edu
CORCORAN, Kevin, J .... 248-370-2140 235 J
corcoran@oakland.edu
CORCORAN, Mary .... 617-928-4596 222 D
mcorcoran@mountida.edu
CORCORAN, Mike .... 757-490-1241 477 F
mcorcoran@auto.edu
CORCORAN, Paul .... 507-389-2267 246 A
paul.corcoran@mnsu.edu
CORCORAN, Tim .... 619-644-7572.. 44 K
tim.corcoran@gcccd.edu
CORCORAN, William ..... 201-612-5234 283 I
wcorcoran@bergen.edu
CORCORAN,
William, M .... 570-208-5846 398 D
wmcorcor@kings.edu
CORDANO, Mark .... 978-837-5407 221 G
cordanom@merrimack.edu
CORDANO,
Roberta (Bobbi) .... 202-651-5005.. 91 H
roberta.cordano@gallaudet.edu
CORDEIRO, Wayne .... 808-853-1040 129 F
waynecordeiro@pacrim.edu
CORDEIRO, Wayne .... 541-485-1780 384 G
waynecordeiro@newhope.edu
CORDEIRO, William ...... 805-437-8860.. 31 C
william.cordeiro@csuci.edu
CORDELL, David .... 425-640-1412 494 E
dcordell@edcc.edu
CORDELL, Janice, K ...... 563-387-1018 171 I
cordellj@luther.edu
CORDELL, Joyce, Y .... 915-831-6530 449 A
jyamasak@epcc.edu
CORDELL, Michelle .... 479-619-4361.. 20 F
mcordell@nwacc.edu
CORDELL, Peggy .... 706-295-6959 120 C
pcordell@gntc.edu
CORDELL, Penny .... 706-272-4498 118 F
pcordell@daltonstate.edu
CORDER, Colleen .... 503-552-1702 384 F
ccorder@nunm.edu
CORDER, Lauren .... 239-513-1135 114 D
CORDERO, Carlos, O .... 787-850-9303 528 B
carlos.cordero1@upr.edu
CORDERO, Edwin .... 864-578-8770 423 F
ecordero@sherman.edu
CORDERO, Heather .... 847-317-7071 153 D
hcordero@tiu.edu
CORDERO, Irma, L .... 787-740-1611 526 G
irma.cordero@uccaribe.edu
CORDERO, Pilar .... 787-815-0000 527 F
pilar.cordero@upr.edu
CORDERO, Zain .... 787-882-2065 526 D
mis@unitecpr.net
CORDERY, Simon .... 706-864-1819 127 B
simon.cordery@ung.edu
CORDES, Mark .... 815-753-0380 147 H
mcordes@niu.edu
CORDIA, Judith .... 775-445-3295 279 F
judith.cordia@wnc.edu
CORDISCO, Shelli .... 607-778-5222 326 C
cordiscosl@sunybroome.edu
CORDLE, David .... 620-341-5171 177 B
dcordle@emporia.edu
CORDLE, Robbie, L .... 301-687-4403 209 A
rcordle@frostburg.edu
CORDOVA, Denise .... 775-682-6708 279 E
dcordova@unr.edu
CORDOVA, Francie .... 505-277-5251 296 H
fcordova3@unm.edu
CORDOVA, John .... 661-362-5586.. 39 C
john.cordova@canyons.edu
CORDOVA, Jose, A .... 787-704-1020 522 J
jcordova@ediccollege.edu
CORDOVA, Kelly .... 757-455-5709 491 F
kcordova@vwu.edu
CORDOVA, Matthew ...... 505-454-2559 294 D
mcordova@luna.edu
CORDOVA, Mitchell .... 239-590-7074 109 C
mcordova@fgcu.edu
CORDOVA, Ryan .... 505-747-2288 295 H
rcordova@nnmc.edu
CORDOVA QUERO,
Hugo .... 510-549-4705.. 66 D
hquero@sksm.edu
CORDRAY, Ethan .... 573-681-5507 261 H
cordraye@lincolnu.edu
CORDRAY, Mary .... 843-208-8139 425 B
marymac@uscb.edu
CORDRAY, Mitch .... 417-455-5712 259 D
mitchcordray@crowder.edu
CORDULACK, John .... 217-875-7211 149 J
jcordulack@richland.edu
CORDULACK, Tricia .... 217-875-7211 149 J
tcordulack@richland.edu
CORENO, Kendra .... 440-449-5368 373 B
kcoreno@follett.com
COREY, Barry, H .... 562-903-4701.. 27 E
president@biola.edu
COREY, Frederick, C ..... 602-496-0624.. 10 K
frederick.corey@asu.edu
COREY, George, A .... 413-577-5211 216 H
gcorey@uhs.umass.edu
COREY, M, J .... 304-637-1344 501 H
coreym@dewv.edu
COREY, Steven .... 312-369-7844 136 H
scorey@colum.edu
COREY, Steven, M .... 269-749-7642 236 A
scorey@olivetcollege.edu
CORIA, Elizabeth .... 415-239-3382.. 37 H
ecoria@ccsf.edu
CORIALE, Mary .... 585-785-1442 308 D
mary.coriale@flcc.edu
CORINO, Mark, A .... 973-618-3412 284 D
mcorino@caldwell.edu
CORKILL, Jim, R .... 805-893-5882.. 70 B
jim.corkill@bfs.ucsb.edu
CORKRAN, Ken .... 508-541-1700 214 C
kcorkran@dean.edu
CORKRUM, Dalia, L ...... 509-527-5193 500 G
corkrum@whitman.edu
CORKUM, David .... 617-552-4500 212 E
david.corkum@bc.edu
CORLE, Trish .... 814-262-3841 405 A
tcorle@pennhighlands.edu
CORLEW, Amy .... 931-221-6131 430 B
corlewa@apsu.edu
CORLEY, David .... 530-257-6181.. 47 J
dcorley@lassencollege.edu
CORLEY, Raymond .... 803-327-7402 419 G
rcorley@clintoncollege.edu
CORLEY, Scott .... 615-460-5547 430 D
scott.corley@belmont.edu
CORLEY, Stacey .... 941-359-7674 106 H
scorley@ringling.edu
CORLEY, Thomas .... 785-242-5200 180 H
thomas.corley@ottawa.edu
CORLISS, Bruce .... 401-874-6222 417 E
bruce.corliss@gso.uri.edu
CORLISS, Carolyn .... 251-442-2276.... 8 D
ccorliss@umobile.edu
CORLISS, Jon .... 205-975-6092.... 8 B
joncorliss@uab.edu
CORMACK, Alastair .... 607-871-2422 298 A
cormack@alfred.edu
CORMACK, Jody .... 562-985-4128.. 32 C
jody.cormack@csulb.edu
CORMAN, RJ .... 828-398-7286 340 M
richardjcorman@abtech.edu
CORMICAN, Beverly ...... 864-242-5100 418 H
CORMIER, Cathy .... 318-473-6459 194 A
ccormier@lsua.edu
CORMIER, Garth .... 207-941-7626 199 B
cormierg@husson.edu
CORMIER, Matthew .... 508-362-2131 219 E
mcormier@capecod.edu
CORN, Melanie .... 614-222-3220 360 B
mcorn@ccad.edu
CORNACCHIA,
Eugene, J .... 201-761-6010 291 D
ecornacchia@saintpeters.edu
CORNEA, Sheila .... 423-614-8630 432 L
scornea@leeuniversity.edu
CORNEJO, Silvia .... 619-216-6755.. 65 H
scornejo@swccd.edu
CORNELIUS, Adrian, R .. 301-314-8249 207 G
adrianc@umd.edu
CORNELIUS, Barbara .... 903-813-2536 443 F
bcornelius@austincollege.edu
CORNELIUS, Ken .... 334-244-3232.... 4 E
kcornelius@aum.edu
CORNELIUS, Michael .... 480-423-6573.. 14 C
michael.cornelius@scottsdalecc.edu
CORNELIUS, Tim .... 479-619-3117.. 20 F
tcornelius@nwacc.edu
CORNELL, Andrew .... 703-822-6515 488 H
acornell@nvcc.edu
CORNELL, Brian .... 607-735-1720 307 G
bcornell@elmira.edu
CORNELL, Craig .... 740-597-3280 368 G
cornellc@ohio.edu
CORNELL, Dennis .... 213-740-2111.. 72 B
dcornell@president.usc.edu
CORNELL, Dona, H .... 832-842-0949 464 F
dhcornell@uh.edu
CORNELL, Dona, H .... 713-743-0949 465 A
dhcornell@uh.edu
CORNELL, Ken .... 425-889-7800 496 E
ken.cornell@northwestu.edu
CORNELL-SCOTT,
Andrea .... 540-887-7270 482 G
ascott@marybaldwin.edu
CORNELL-SWANSON,
LaVonne .... 320-308-4785 247 E
lcornellswanson@stcloudstate.edu
CORNELY, Joe .... 513-244-4955 366 A
joseph.cornely@msjl.edu
CORNER, Kimberly .... 402-465-7783 276 E
kcorner@nebrwesleyan.edu
CORNER, William, T ...... 616-526-6451 228 B
wtc2@calvin.edu

COTTON, Beverly 940-565-4098 466 B
beverly.cotton@unt.edu
COTTON, SR., George 850-599-3491 109 A
george.cotton@famu.edu
COTTON, Gregory 319-895-4454 167 G
gcotton@cornellcollege.edu
COTTON, Michael 336-517-2299 335 K
mcotton@bennett.edu
COTTON, Patricia 334-229-4712 4 A
pcotton@alasu.edu
COTTON, Sabrina 256-726-7408 6 E
cotton@oakwood.edu
COTTON, Todd 205-726-4144 6 G
tcotton@samford.edu
COTTON, Trae 336-750-3200 352 D
cottontt@wssu.edu
COTTON KELLY,
Montique 860-486-2240 88 G
montique.cotton.kelly@uconn.edu
COTTONE, John 607-753-2701 327 A
john.cottone@cortland.edu
COTTONHAM, Patricia 337-482-6266 197 F
patcottonham@louisiana.edu
COTTRELL, Alan 210-486-5000 441 F
COTTRELL, Debbie 830-372-8002 461 D
dcottrell@tlu.edu
COTTRELL, Debbie 254-295-5059 466 A
dcottrell@umhb.edu
COTTRELL, Janet 802-865-6492 474 G
cottrell@champlain.edu
COTTRELL, Liesl 773-252-5114 149 I
liesl.cottrell@resu.edu
COTTRELL, Terrance, L 815-740-5041 154 G
tcottrell@stfrancis.edu
COTTRILL, Chad 503-883-2506 383 H
ccottril@linfield.edu
COTTRILL, F. Layton 304-696-6295 504 C
cottrill@marshall.edu
COTY, Mark 941-782-5980 399 C
mcoty@lecom.edu
COUCH, Alisha, M 740-368-3099 368 N
amcouch@owu.edu
COUCH, Brian 239-280-1695 95 C
brian.couch@avemaria.edu
COUCH, Charlie 970-351-2231 83 F
charlie.couch@unco.edu
COUCH, JR., Gene, C 276-739-2421 490 A
gcouch@vhcc.edu
COUCH, Laurie, L 606-783-2434 188 C
l.couch@moreheadstate.edu
COUCH, Lisa 760-384-6230 47 B
lcouch@cerrocoso.edu
COUCH, Valerie 405-208-5440 377 D
vcouch@okcu.edu
COUCHEY, Evangeline 845-675-4733 319 C
evangeline.couchey@nyack.edu
COUGHENAIR, Russ 813-974-9718 111 A
COUGHENOUR, Kevin 703-539-6890 485 J
kcoughenour@stratford.edu
COUGHLIN, Cass 620-341-5264 177 B
ccoughli@emporia.edu
COUGHLIN, OFM,
F. Edward 518-783-2302 324 C
ecoughlin@siena.edu
COUGHLIN, John 248-370-4618 235 J
jcoughli@oakland.edu
COUGHLIN, Kathleen 210-829-6012 465 E
coughlin@uiwtx.edu
COUGHLIN, Kevin 305-348-2320 109 D
kevin.coughlinjr@fiu.edu
COUGHLIN, Mary Ann 413-748-3959 224 G
mcoughlin@springfieldcollege.edu
COUGHLIN, Meredith 772-462-7304 101 Q
mcoughli@irsc.edu
COUGHLIN, Robert, D 860-685-2543 89 F
rdcoughlin@wesleyan.edu
COUILLARD, Michael 719-502-3352 81 H
mike.couillard@ppcc.edu
COULBY, Susan 302-622-8000 90 A
COULIER, Laura 616-988-1000 228 I
laura.c@compass.edu
COULING, Mike 972-660-5701 452 B
mcouling@lincolntech.com
COULLIETTE, Holly 904-808-7441 106 M
hollycoulliette@sjrstate.edu
COULOMBE, Jennifer, B 336-734-7723 343 C
jcoulombe@forsythtech.edu
COULON, Richard 949-824-6510 69 A
rcoulon@uci.edu
COULOTTE, Clifford 718-997-5100 303 E
clifford.coulotte@qc.cuny.edu
COULS, Lauren 803-641-2837 425 A
laurenc@usca.edu
COULSTON, Susan 269-782-1396 237 B
scoulston@swmich.edu
COULTER, Ann 641-782-1340 173 I
coulter@swcciowa.edu
COULTER, Chris 719-389-6568 77 J
chris.coulter@coloradocollege.edu
COULTER, Cindy 828-327-7000 341 G
ccoulter@cvcc.edu
COULTER, Denise 609-343-5007 283 D
dcoulter@atlantic.edu
COULTER, Laurie 903-813-2900 443 F
lcoulter@austincollege.edu
COULTER, Lisa 610-683-4072 406 D
coulter@kutztown.edu
COULTER, Martha 802-468-1314 477 A
martha.coulter@castleton.edu
COULTER, Megan, L 540-985-8481 482 A
mlcoulter@jchs.edu
COULTER, Seana 443-885-3110 206 A
seana.coulter@morgan.edu
COUNCIL, Juanette 910-672-1208 350 B
jcouncil@uncfsu.edu
COUNCIL, Mark 910-362-7009 341 E
mcouncil@cfcc.edu
COUNCIL, Tim 909-607-7811 37 L
tim.council@cgu.edu
COUNSIL, Brian 620-365-5116 174 G
counsil@allencc.edu
COUNTEE, Jerome 559-324-6475 66 E
COUNTS, LaNeta 404-471-6483 114 H
lcounts@agnesscott.edu
COUPE, Maria 845-398-4038 323 G
mcoupe@stac.edu
COURANT, Paul, N 734-764-9292 237 I
provost@umich.edu
COURCHAINE, Jeff 714-892-7711 38 G
jcourchaine@gwc.cccd.edu
COURET, Esther 845-431-8673 307 A
esther.couret@sunydutchess.edu
COUREY, Scott 616-394-4287 229 B
scott.courey@cornerstone.edu
COURMIER, Curtis 781-239-2432 220 A
ccormier@massbay.edu
COURNOYER, Jeff 617-287-7377 216 G
jcournoyer@umassp.edu
COURNOYER, Jennifer 860-932-4131 86 E
jcournoyer@qvcc.edu
COURS, Deborah, A 818-677-2455 33 B
dcours@csun.edu
COURSEY, Greg 706-437-6808 116 A
gcoursey@augustatech.edu
COURTEMANCHE, Brian 978-927-2278 214 G
bcourtem@endicott.edu
COURTEY, Susan 818-240-1000 44 D
scourtey@glendale.edu
COURTLEY-TODD,
Laura, J 305-628-6677 107 B
lcourtle@stu.edu
COURTNEY, Bonnie 717-262-2017 415 B
bonnie.courtney@wilson.edu
COURTNEY, Justin, F 419-772-2145 367 G
j-courtney@onu.edu
COURTNEY, Matthew, B 859-846-5309 188 B
mcourtney@midway.edu
COURTNEY, Nycole 307-766-3296 517 B
nf@uwyo.edu
COURTNEY, Sharon, P 504-988-3390 196 D
sharonc@tulane.edu
COURTNEY, Susan 410-516-8894 204 F
courtney@jhu.edu
COURTNEY-BIEDRZYCKI,
Caitlin 978-816-7627 214 G
ccourtne@endicott.edu
COURTRIGHT, Amy 209-954-5151 61 B
acourtright@deltacollege.edu
COURTRIGHT, Caren 509-793-2038 492 I
carenc@bigbend.edu
COUSINS, Amirah 718-289-5155 301 D
amirah.cousins@bcc.cuny.edu
COUSINS, Kathryn 212-484-1156 302 F
kcousins@jjay.cuny.edu
COUTILISH,
Theodore, G 734-487-2483 229 K
ted.coutilish@emich.edu
COUTS, LeeAnn 740-392-6868 366 B
leeann.couts@mvnu.edu
COUTS, Suzann 325-793-4608 452 F
couts.suzann@mcm.edu
COUTTS, Christopher 540-351-1513 488 E
ccoutts@lfcc.edu
COUTTS, Greg 773-298-3090 151 C
coutts@sxu.edu
COUTURE, Daniel, R 802-654-3243 476 A
dcouture@smcvt.edu
COUTURIER, OFM,
David 716-375-2160 322 B
dcouturi@sbu.edu
COVAL, Scott 610-282-1100 393 G
scott.coval@desales.edu
COVAR, Tom 864-388-8305 422 A
tcovar@lander.edu
COVAULT, Pamela 785-242-2067 180 C
pcovault@neosho.edu
COVE, Lorraine, D 617-573-8160 224 I
lcove@acad.suffolk.edu
COVER, Michael, S 570-577-3348 390 H
mike.cover@bucknell.edu
COVERS, Beth, A 810-762-9925 232 C
bcovers@kettering.edu
COVERT, Sarah 706-542-9389 127 A
covert@uga.edu
COVERT, Sheree, S 319-352-8272 174 C
sheree.covert@wartburg.edu
COVEY, Angie, E 540-674-3655 488 G
acovey@nr.edu
COVEY, Bruce 404-727-6223 119 B
bcovey@emory.edu
COVEY, David 518-861-2560 314 B
dcovey@mariacollege.edu
COVEY, Douglass, F 404-413-1500 121 A
dcovey@gsu.edu
COVILL, Mesa 715-232-1151 512 A
covillm@uwstout.edu
COVILLE, Jan 603-447-3970 282 G
jan.coville@granite.edu
COVINGTON,
Adrienne, S 252-451-8236 345 B
ascovington197@nashcc.edu
COVINGTON, Chatonda 919-530-7517 350 D
cbcovington@nccu.edu
COVINGTON, Dan 606-546-1285 189 I
dcovin@unionky.edu
COVINGTON, Dave, R 208-467-8060 132 F
dcovington@nnu.edu
COVINGTON, Gayle, J 434-395-2210 482 E
covingtogj@longwood.edu
COVINGTON, Janet 713-348-6312 455 F
jcov@rice.edu
COVINGTON, Mary 919-966-9176 351 B
mary_covington@unc.edu
COVINGTON, Robert, D 501-450-5202 23 I
dcovington@uca.edu
COVINGTON, Sim 315-792-7165 330 A
sim.covington@sunyit.edu
COVINGTON, Sirena 312-788-1146 154 I
scovington@vandercook.edu
COVINGTON, Troy 757-823-9540 483 F
tjcovington@nsu.edu
COVINO, Nicholas 617-327-6777 226 B
nicholas_covino@williamjames.edu
COVINO, Paul, F 508-767-7057 210 I
pf.covino@assumption.edu
COVINO, William, A 323-343-3030 32 D
bill.covino@calstatela.edu
COVITZ, Bobby 513-487-3259 309 F
rcovitz@huc.edu
COVONE, Michael 305-899-3551 95 G
mcovone@barry.edu
COWAN, Anthony 901-435-1470 433 A
anthony_cowan@loc.edu
COWAN, Cindy 864-977-2058 422 I
cindy.cowan@ngu.edu
COWAN, Cristina 816-501-3756 257 G
COWAN, David 507-389-2267 246 A
david.cowan@mnsu.edu
COWAN, Judith 803-327-7402 419 G
jcowan@clintoncollege.edu
COWAN, Kenneth, H 402-559-4238 277 H
kcowan@unmc.edu
COWAN, Michelle 901-435-1386 433 A
michelle_cowan@loc.edu
COWAN, Patricia 501-686-8493 22 C
pacowan@uams.edu
COWAN, Theresa 954-201-7554 96 A
tcowan@broward.edu
COWAN, Vickie, M 718-862-7398 313 L
vickie.cowan@manhattan.edu
COWART, Lisa 803-323-2273 426 H
cowartl@winthrop.edu
COWDEN, Belle 812-465-1061 165 C
bcowden@usi.edu
COWDEN, Clint 831-755-6960 45 C
ccowden@hartnell.edu
COWDEN, Clint 559-934-2701 73 N
clintcowden@whccd.edu
COWDERY, Aaron 740-376-4452 365 A
aaron.cowdery@marietta.edu
COWDIN, Terry 503-251-5727 387 I
tcowdin@uws.edu
COWDREY, Scott 410-778-7894 210 A
scowdrey2@washcoll.edu
COWELL, Elizabeth 831-459-2076 70 C
mcowell@ucsc.edu
COWELL, JR.,
James, W 626-395-4464 29 I
jcowell@caltech.edu
COWELL, John, K 706-721-0570 116 B
jcowell@augusta.edu
COWELL, Karen 803-778-7825 419 A
cowellkw@cctech.edu
COWELL, Leslie 334-386-7106 5 I
lcowell@faulkner.edu
COWELL-OATES, June 314-454-8694 260 E
jcowell-oates@bjc.org
COWEN, Rahmel 334-244-3668 4 E
rcowen@aum.edu
COWEN, Will 805-289-6347 73 C
wcowen@vcccd.edu
COWGER, John 701-594-8192 355 A
john.cowger@lrsc.edu
COWGER, Melinda, K 303-722-5724 80 O
mcowger@lincolntech.edu
COWGER, Tiffany 618-262-8641 140 F
cowgert@iecc.edu
COWHERD, Mark 256-824-6480 8 C
mark.cowherd@uah.edu
COWHEY, Peter 858-534-2230 69 E
evc@ucsd.edu
COWING, Michelle 503-493-6392 382 I
mcowing@cu-portland.edu
COWLES, John 616-234-3673 230 F
jcowles@grcc.edu
COWLEY, Dave 435-797-1146 473 C
dave.cowley@usu.edu
COWLEY, Julie, A 512-863-1720 457 I
cowleyj@southwestern.edu
COWLEY, Rod 425-352-8223 492 K
rcowley@cascadia.edu
COWLIN, Lynn 815-455-8688 145 B
lcowlin@mchenry.edu
COWLING, Richard 630-353-8802 134 K
rcowling@chamberlain.edu
COWSER, Erin, K 985-549-5861 197 E
erin.moore@selu.edu
COX, Amber 407-708-4722 107 G
COX, Ann 212-875-4416 298 H
acox@bankstreet.edu
COX, Anthony 706-778-8500 124 E
acox@piedmont.edu
COX, Barbara 850-599-3796 109 A
barbara.cox@famu.edu
COX, Brandy, A 479-575-2801 21 I
brandyac@uark.edu
COX, Brant, M 757-446-5800 480 C
coxbm@evms.edu
COX, Cameron 253-964-6598 497 B
cmcox@pierce.ctc.edu
COX, Carolyn 304-384-5323 503 P
ccox@concord.edu
COX, Cathy 478-301-2602 122 H
COX, Cathy 707-476-4264 39 F
cathy-cox@redwoods.edu
COX, Charlene 219-464-5093 165 D
charlene.cox@valpo.edu
COX, Cheryl 864-592-4613 424 C
coxc@sccsc.edu
COX, Christen 910-755-7300 341 C
coxc@brunswickcc.edu
COX, Christopher, N 319-273-2737 167 A
chris.cox@uni.edu
COX, Christopher, P 419-372-8932 357 F
cpcox@bgsu.edu
COX, Christy 252-639-7340 349 F
ccox@umo.edu
COX, Colleen 978-656-3284 220 C
COX, Curtis 406-275-4820 273 A
curtis_cox@skc.edu
COX, Dave 217-234-5376 143 B
dcox5612@lakeland.cc.il.us
COX, Dave 509-533-7179 493 I
dave.cox@scc.spokane.edu
COX, David 575-835-5615 294 K
david.cox@nmt.edu
COX, David, W 716-878-5336 326 E
coxdw@buffalostate.edu
COX, Dennis 949-214-3182 40 I
dennis.cox@cui.edu
COX, Dennis 727-376-6911 112 G
dcox@trinitycollege.edu
COX, Donna 870-543-5968 21 E
dcox@seark.edu
COX, Ed 845-431-8071 307 A
ecox@sunydutchess.edu
COX, Erika, M 210-458-4859 468 B
erika.cox@utsa.edu
COX, Fran 662-472-9035 253 C
fcox@holmescc.edu
COX, G. Paul 216-987-2701 360 E
g.cox@tri-c.edu
COX, Gregg 561-237-7210 103 E
gcox@lynn.edu
COX, Helen 808-245-8210 130 F
helencox@hawaii.edu
COX, J. Ben 254-710-2414 444 B
ben_cox@baylor.edu

COX, Jamie, S .... 256-766-6610.... 5 K jcox@hcu.edu
COX, Jana .... 707-524-1579.. 62 H jcox@santarosa.edu
COX, Janet .... 513-244-4466 366 A janet.cox@msj.edu
COX, Jeff, A .... 336-838-6112 347 G jacox302@wilkescc.edu
COX, Jeffrey, W .... 585-475-7433 321 D jwccst@rit.edu
COX, Jennifer .... 503-228-6528 381 I jcox@aii.edu
COX, Jennifer .... 580-559-5714 375 I jcox@ecok.edu
COX, Jesse .... 313-927-1404 233 D jcox@marygrove.edu
COX, John, L .... 508-362-2131 219 E jcox@capecod.edu
COX, Kenneth .... 540-831-7600 484 A kcox3@radford.edu
COX, Kevin .... 214-887-5233 448 G kcox@dts.edu
COX, Lady, D .... 334-844-5672.... 4 D ldc0006@auburn.edu
COX, LaShanta' .... 770-962-7580 121 G lcox@gwinnetttech.edu
COX, Leah .... 410-704-2000 209 C lcox@towson.edu
COX, Leah .... 540-654-1263 486 D lcox@umw.edu
COX, Leana .... 970-675-3334.. 78 H leana.cox@cncc.edu
COX, Lindsay .... 802-387-7121 475 C registrar@landmark.edu
COX, Lisa, B .... 423-869-6722 433 C lisa.cox@lmunet.edu
COX, Lori .... 618-252-5400 151 J lori.cox@sic.edu
COX, Lynn .... 606-589-3073 187 B lynn.cox@kctcs.edu
COX, Mary .... 724-830-1027 410 E cox@setonhill.edu
COX, Matthew .... 719-255-3375.. 83 C mcox4@uccs.edu
COX, Michele, D .... 804-289-8838 486 G mcox@richmond.edu
COX, Miekka, M .... 812-465-7175 165 C mmcox1@usi.edu
COX, Monte .... 501-279-4808.. 19 G mcox@harding.edu
COX, Nancy, M .... 859-257-4772 190 B ncox@email.uky.edu
COX, Nathan .... 864-231-2000 418 E ncox@andersonuniversity.edu
COX, Paul .... 305-428-5700 104 A pmcox@aii.edu
COX, Randall .... 903-785-7661 454 F rcox@parisjc.edu
COX, Robert .... 360-623-8385 493 A robert.cox@centralia.edu
COX, Robert .... 212-220-8041 301 C rcox@bmcc.cuny.edu
COX, Ross .... 229-225-4098 126 C rcox@southernregional.edu
COX, Ryan .... 916-568-3101.. 50 E coxr@losrios.edu
COX, Sam .... 405-945-6789 378 C coxjs@osuokc.edu
COX, Sandra .... 936-633-5211 442 I scox@angelina.edu
COX, Sandy .... 309-796-5635 134 C coxs@bhc.edu
COX, Sandy .... 920-424-2061 511 B coxs@uwosh.edu
COX, Sherry, P .... 336-838-6422 347 G spcox072@wilkescc.edu
COX, Steve .... 318-767-2603 194 A scox@lsua.edu
COX, Steven .... 918-595-7866 380 D steven.cox@tulsacc.edu
COX, Steven, W .... 903-877-7841 469 A steven.cox@uthct.edu
COX, Susan .... 559-453-2026.. 43 J sue.cox@fresno.edu
COX, Susan, S .... 610-606-4609 392 A sue@cedarcrest.edu
COX, Sylvia .... 910-642-7141 346 G scox@sccnc.edu
COX, Terry .... 425-640-1489 494 E terry.cox@edcc.edu
COX, Tiffa .... 615-963-7494 438 E tcox9@tnstate.edu
COX, Tyler .... 931-424-2015 433 E tcox@martinmethodist.edu
COX, Virgil .... 704-922-6295 343 D cox.virgil@gaston.edu
COX, Wayne .... 864-231-2000 418 E wcox@andersonuniversity.edu
COX-KELLEY, Shannon .. 903-434-8359 453 M scoxkelley@ntcc.edu
COX-LANYON, Victoria .. 508-793-7258 213 C vcoxlanyon@clarku.edu
COX TINDOL, Judith ..... 575-234-9208 295 D jcox@nmsu.edu
COXWELL, Amy .... 423-648-2407 435 M acoxwell@richmont.edu
COY, Daniella .... 561-732-4424 107 C dcoy@svdp.edu
COY, Katherine .... 847-925-6955 139 B kcoy@harpercollege.edu
COY-OGAN, Lynne .... 207-973-1077 199 B coyoganl@my.husson.edu
COYKENDALL, John, W 785-833-4349 179 C john.coykendall@kwu.edu
COYLE, Brendan .... 805-267-1690.. 48 B
COYLE, James .... 714-997-7074.. 36 G coyle@chapman.edu
COYLE, Jennifer .... 503-352-2770 385 I coylej@pacificu.edu
COYLE, John .... 814-886-6465 402 E jcoyle@mtaloy.edu
COYLE, Mark .... 612-624-4497 250 E mcoyle@umn.edu
COYNE, Ann, C .... 617-573-8239 224 I aecoyne@suffolk.edu
COYNE, Colin, M .... 205-726-4037.... 6 G ccoyne@samford.edu
COYNE, John, B .... 330-569-5284 362 J coynejb@hiram.edu
COYNE, John, M .... 724-264-1328 396 D jmcoyne@gcc.edu
COYNE, Matthew .... 802-828-8600 476 F
COYNE, Michael .... 570-372-4128 410 H coyne@susqu.edu
COYNE, Michael .... 928-681-0800 221 D coyne@mslaw.edu
COYNE, Michael .... 978-681-0800 221 D mcoyne@mslaw.edu
COYNE, Mildred .... 954-201-7811.. 96 A mcoyne@broward.edu
COZART, Wayne .... 434-243-9041 486 H wdc9q@virginia.edu
COZZENS, David .... 817-257-7926 461 A d.s.cozzens@tcu.edu
COZZENS, Glenn .... 417-268-6022 257 H gcozzens@gobbc.edu
COZZENS, Susan .... 404-894-5054 120 A susan.cozzens@iac.gatech.edu
COZZOCREA, Rebecca .. 518-736-3622 309 A rebecca.cozzocrea@fmcc.suny.edu
CRABB, Ann .... 208-467-8593 132 F atcrabb@nnu.edu
CRABB, Jenna, S .... 505-277-2531 296 H jennas@unm.edu
CRABB, John .... 407-923-1618 255 E jcrabb@rts.edu
CRABBE, Kim .... 518-580-5790 324 D kcrabbe@skidmore.edu
CRABILL, Casey .... 315-498-2211 319 G president@sunyocc.edu
CRABREE, Troy .... 206-239-4500 493 D troy.crabtree@cityu.edu
CRABTREE, Aaron, T ..... 574-372-5100 158 B crabtrat@grace.edu
CRABTREE, April .... 415-422-5287.. 72 A acrabtree@usfca.edu
CRABTREE, Brian .... 678-547-6306 122 H
CRABTREE, Diane .... 503-883-2507 383 H dcrabtre@linfield.edu
CRABTREE, Gina, D .... 316-978-3672 182 F gina.crabtree@wichita.edu
CRABTREE, Gordon, L ... 801-581-7480 472 P gordon.crabtree@hsc.utah.edu
CRABTREE, James .... 612-343-4773 249 E jmcrabtr@northcentral.edu
CRABTREE, Jenna .... 217-228-5520 134 F crabtreej@brcn.edu
CRABTREE, Jerry .... 256-233-8222.... 4 C jerry.crabtree@athens.edu
CRABTREE, Kacy .... 541-440-4682 387 E kacy.crabtree@umpqua.edu
CRABTREE, Kay .... 402-481-8847 273 F kay.crabtree@bryanhealthcollege.edu
CRABTREE, Peter .... 510-464-3218.. 56 H pcrabtree@peralta.edu
CRABTREE, Robbin, D ... 310-338-2716.. 50 J robbin.crabtree@lmu.edu
CRABTREE, Shane .... 801-957-4571 474 B shane.crabtree@slcc.edu
CRACCO, Elizabeth .... 860-486-4705.. 88 G elizabeth.cracco@uconn.edu
CRACE, Robert, K .... 757-221-1236 479 I rkcrac@wm.edu
CRACKENBERG, Peter .... 503-554-2138 383 C pcrackenberg@georgefox.edu
CRADDOCK, Alden .... 314-529-6687 262 B acraddock@maryville.edu
CRADDOCK, Amanda, E 843-349-2979 420 A acraddoc@coastal.edu
CRADDOCK, Chris .... 903-983-8181 451 F ccraddock@kilgore.edu
CRADDOCK, Jackie .... 510-594-3612.. 28 K jcraddock@cca.edu
CRADY, Thomas .... 406-243-5225 271 G thomas.crady@umontana.edu
CRAFT, Edwin .... 662-846-4760 252 H ecraft@deltastate.edu
CRAFT, Jonathan .... 256-216-3310.... 4 C jonathan.craft@athens.edu
CRAFT, Linda .... 214-638-0484 451 E linda@kdstudio.com
CRAFT, Shonda, M .... 320-308-4894 247 E smcraft@stcloudstate.edu
CRAFT, Stephen .... 205-665-6540.... 8 E scraft@montevallo.edu
CRAFT, Tonya .... 601-974-1200 254 A craftte@millsaps.edu
CRAFT, William, J .... 218-299-3000 241 K president@cord.edu
CRAFTON, Linda .... 262-595-2341 511 C crafton@uwp.edu
CRAFTON, Michael .... 678-839-4875 127 F mcrafton@westga.edu
CRAFTON, Teresa .... 478-274-7833 123 I tcrafton@oftc.edu
CRAFTS, Deborah .... 617-236-5451 215 B dcrafts@fisher.edu
CRAGAR, Beth .... 931-598-1312 436 A bcragar@sewanee.edu
CRAGER, Cindy .... 609-626-3658 291 H cindy.crager@stockton.edu
CRAGLE, Deb .... 570-586-2400 392 E dcragle@clarkssummitu.edu
CRAGLE, Rachael, C ...... 865-539-7219 437 F rccragle@pstcc.edu
CRAGO, David, C .... 419-772-2205 367 G d-crago@onu.edu
CRAHEN, Sherri, A .... 216-397-3010 363 H scrahen@jcu.edu
CRAIG, Barbara .... 269-927-8147 232 G craig@lakemichigancollege.edu
CRAIG, Carrick .... 269-387-1900 239 E carrick.craig@wmich.edu
CRAIG, Catharine .... 641-784-5029 169 D ceelliot@graceland.edu
CRAIG, Christopher, J ... 417-836-5215 263 H chriscraig@missouristate.edu
CRAIG, David .... 573-882-9570 268 C davidcr@missouri.edu
CRAIG, David .... 406-657-2209 272 B david.craig2@msubillings.edu
CRAIG, Dennis .... 914-251-5985 328 B dennis.craig@purchase.edu
CRAIG, Erin .... 315-866-0300 310 A
CRAIG, James .... 520-206-6916.. 15 L jcraig7@pima.edu
CRAIG, Jayne .... 575-769-4039 293 M jayne.craig@clovis.edu
CRAIG, John .... 610-436-3133 407 D jcraig@wcupa.edu
CRAIG, Johnny .... 414-297-6279 514 C craigjl@matc.edu
CRAIG, Kim .... 651-603-6223 241 L craig@csp.edu
CRAIG, La Saundra .... 513-569-1532 359 G lasaundra.craig@cincinnatistate.edu
CRAIG, Mardi, P .... 865-981-8167 433 F mardi.craig@maryvillecollege.edu
CRAIG, Marva .... 212-220-8131 301 C mcraig@bmcc.cuny.edu
CRAIG, Michael .... 816-501-4065 265 I michael.craig@rockhurst.edu
CRAIG, Osubi .... 804-524-5247 491 A ocraig@vsu.edu
CRAIG, Paige .... 708-209-3509 136 I paige.craig@cuchicago.edu
CRAIG, Raymond .... 419-372-2340 357 F racraig@bgsu.edu
CRAIG, Sandy .... 618-262-8641 140 F craigs@iecc.edu
CRAIG, Stephanie, A ..... 814-371-2090 411 H scraig@triangle-tech.edu
CRAIG, Stephen .... 801-422-3013 131 D stephen_craig@byu.edu
CRAIG, Tammy .... 314-918-2624 260 A tcraig@eden.edu
CRAIG, Terese .... 608-757-7704 513 D tcraig@blackhawk.edu
CRAIG, Thomas .... 903-877-7442 469 A tom.craig@uthct.edu
CRAIG, Todd .... 404-261-1441 124 A institutionalresearch@oglethorpe.edu
CRAIG, William, G .... 732-571-3427 287 C craig@monmouth.edu
CRAIG KUNG, Pang-Jen .... 919-301-6500.. 93 B
CRAIG-MARIUS, Renee .. 559-638-0300.. 66 H renee.craig-marius@reedleycollege.edu
CRAIG-TAYLOR, Phyliss, V .... 919-530-6112 350 D pcraigtaylor@nccu.edu
CRAIGG, Dorenda .... 336-315-7800.. 93 B
CRAIGMILES, Jan .... 859-858-3511 183 D jan.craigmiles@asbury.edu
CRAIK, Rebecca, L .... 215-572-2143 389 D craikr@arcadia.edu
CRAIN, Betty .... 940-898-3505 464 A bcrain@twu.edu
CRAIN, John, L .... 985-549-2280 197 E jcrain@selu.edu
CRAIN, Rick .... 678-717-3623 127 B rick.crain@ung.edu
CRAIN, Terry .... 618-985-3741 141 D terrycrain@jalc.edu
CRAINER, Bryan, E .... 989-964-4091 236 F becraine@svsu.edu
CRAKES, Aileen .... 619-388-2896.. 60 D acrakes@sdccd.edu
CRAM-RAHLF, Shelly ..... 563-288-6011 168 M scramrahlf@eicc.edu
CRAMB, Alan .... 312-567-3106 140 I president@iit.edu
CRAMER, Alicia .... 713-646-1808 456 H acramer@stcl.edu
CRAMER, Gregory, D .... 630-889-6536 147 D gcramer@nuhs.edu
CRAMER, Janet .... 303-546-3588.. 81 B jcramer@naropa.edu
CRAMER, Joel .... 317-738-8197 157 L jcramer@franklincollege.edu
CRAMER, Judy .... 978-542-6139 218 E judy.cramer@salemstate.edu
CRAMER, Paul .... 610-921-7260 388 E pcramer@albright.edu
CRAMER, Steven, M ...... 608-262-5246 510 C steven.cramer@wisc.edu
CRAMER, Walter .... 203-837-8547.. 85 B cramerw@wcsu.edu
CRAMPTON, Anne-Marie .... 719-336-1520.. 80 N anne-marie.crampton@lamarcc.edu
CRAMPTON, Laraine ...... 310-577-3000.. 75 G lcrampton@yosan.edu
CRAMPTON, Scott .... 719-336-1681.. 80 N scott.crampton@lamarcc.edu
CRAMPTON, Tom .... 810-762-0506 234 F thomas.crampto@mcc.edu
CRAMPTON, Troy, D ..... 515-574-1114 170 C crampton@iowacentral.edu
CRAMSEY, Rachel .... 217-228-5520 134 F rcramsey@brcn.edu
CRANCE, Gina-Lyn .... 610-921-7611 388 E gcrance@albright.edu
CRANDALL, Donald, W . 479-524-7150.. 20 B dcrandal@jbu.edu
CRANDALL, James .... 530-242-7989.. 63 I jcrandall@shastacollege.edu
CRANDALL, Jordan .... 918-495-6010 378 H jcrandall@oru.edu
CRANDALL, Julie .... 800-486-7049 371 A julie.crandall@myunion.edu
CRANDALL, Laura .... 315-470-4865 328 D ldcranda@esf.edu
CRANDALL, Lynne .... 239-489-1000 100 E lcrandall1@fsw.edu
CRANDALL, Paige .... 914-395-2575 323 K pcrandall@sarahlawrence.edu
CRANDALL, Stephen, S . 607-871-2987 298 A fcrandall@alfred.edu
CRANDELL, Gale, M ...... 989-386-6664 234 B gcrandell@midmich.edu
CRANDELL, Jackie .... 614-882-2551 361 K jcrandell@fortiscollege.edu
CRANE, Amanda .... 972-580-7600 444 C acrane@bhcarroll.edu
CRANE, Anne .... 316-295-5610 177 F annec@friends.edu
CRANE, Daniel, R .... 651-631-5100 251 C drcrane@unwsp.edu
CRANE, David .... 508-531-6145 217 D dcrane@bridgew.edu
CRANE, Jeff .... 270-384-8150 187 H cranej@lindsey.edu
CRANE, Jeff .... 360-438-4564 497 F jcrane@stmartin.edu
CRANE, Paul .... 810-762-9887 232 C pcrane@kettering.edu
CRANE, Rob, M .... 913-288-7283 178 H rcrane@kckcc.edu

CRANE, Ron 972-825-4818 457 F rcrane@sagu.edu
CRANE, Steven 415-561-6555 57 K steven.crane@presidio.edu
CRANE, Susan 914-337-9300 305 F susan.crane@concordia-ny.edu
CRANE, Susan, L 989-964-4350 236 F scrane@svsu.edu
CRANFORD, Bill 601-925-3283 254 B cranford@mc.edu
CRANFORD, Maria 801-649-5230 471 M clinicaldean@midwifery.edu
CRANFORD, Shannon 580-628-6229 376 J shannon.cranford@noc.edu
CRANFORD, Timothy 510-869-1508 59 F tcranford@samuelmerritt.edu
CRANHAM, John, B 919-508-2336 353 C jbcranham@peace.edu
CRANK, Robert 816-322-0110 257 M bob.crank@calvary.edu
CRANMER, Wendy 585-395-2126 326 D wcranmer@brockport.edu
CRANMORE, Jill, A 217-443-8756 137 B jcranmore@dacc.edu
CRANSTON, Amy 215-951-1081 398 F cranston@lasalle.edu
CRANSTON, Carolyn 412-924-1375 408 E ccranston@pts.edu
CRANWELL, Mary 732-987-2285 286 D mcranwell@georgian.edu
CRAPANZANO, Vincent 845-398-4019 323 G vcrapanz@stac.edu
CRAREY, II, Patrick 301-891-4481 209 E pcrarey@wau.edu
CRARY, Kami 718-997-5541 303 E kami.crary@qc.cuny.edu
CRARY-STACHOWIAK, Sage 413-205-3521 210 E sage.stachowiak@aic.edu
CRATER, Lucas 217-545-9362 152 A lcrater@siumed.edu
CRATERFIELD, Mollye 309-341-5230 134 H mcraterfield@sandburg.edu
CRATTY, Frederic, W 203-837-8665 85 B crattyf@wcsu.edu
CRAVEN, Bryan, C 850-718-2375 96 H cravenb@chipola.edu
CRAVEN, Heather 973-328-5281 285 B hcraven@ccm.edu
CRAVEN, Katherine 781-239-5955 211 A kcraven@babson.edu
CRAVEN, Nora 715-365-4576 514 E ncraven@nicoletcollege.edu
CRAVEN, Randy 423-236-2732 436 C rlcraven@southern.edu
CRAVENS, Joshua 513-721-7944 362 D jcravens@gbs.edu
CRAVENS, Michael 419-824-3620 364 G mcravens@sistersosf.org
CRAVER, Ken 903-510-2591 464 D kcra@tjc.edu
CRAVER, Robert 303-369-5151 81 L robert.craver@plattcolorado.edu
CRAVER, III, William 678-225-7509 407 G williamcr@pcom.edu
CRAVO, Ana, M 201-761-6104 291 D acravo@saintpeters.edu
CRAWFORD, Andrew 216-987-2202 360 E andrew.crawford@tri-c.edu
CRAWFORD, Andrew, B 757-594-7663 479 H andrew.crawford@cnu.edu
CRAWFORD, Anna 304-260-4380 502 J acrawfor@blueridgectc.edu
CRAWFORD, Arminda 614-985-2241 369 D acrawford@pcj.edu
CRAWFORD, Audrey 205-665-6030 8 E acrawford@montevallo.edu
CRAWFORD, Brian, L 304-336-8004 504 E brian.crawford@westliberty.edu
CRAWFORD, Brittany 334-683-2382 3 A bcrawford@marionmilitary.edu
CRAWFORD, Bruce 205-929-6312 2 G bcrawford@lawsonstate.edu
CRAWFORD, Bryan 719-562-7002 81 M bryan.crawford@pueblocc.edu
CRAWFORD, Cardon, B 843-953-6966 419 D cardon.crawford@citadel.edu
CRAWFORD, Charlie 425-640-1557 494 E charlie.crawford@edcc.edu
CRAWFORD, Chemene, L 214-860-2170 448 A chemene.crawford@dcccd.edu
CRAWFORD, Chris 903-923-2223 448 J chrisc@etbu.edu
CRAWFORD, Chris 605-642-6262 428 F chris.crawford@bhsu.edu
CRAWFORD, Clinton 718-270-5140 303 C crawford@mec.cuny.edu
CRAWFORD, Cynthia 909-537-5315 33 D ccrawfor@csusb.edu
CRAWFORD, David 303-797-5762 76 I david.crawford@arapahoe.edu
CRAWFORD, David 773-947-6307 145 A dcrawford@mccormick.edu
CRAWFORD, David 773-947-6250 145 A dcrawford@mccormick.edu
CRAWFORD, David, S 202-526-3799 93 A dcrawford@johnpaulii.edu
CRAWFORD, Debbie 970-945-8691 77 M
CRAWFORD, Deborah 703-993-2268 481 B dcrawfo7@gmu.edu
CRAWFORD, Deena 601-266-4829 256 E deena.crawford@usm.edu
CRAWFORD, Eboni 973-803-5000 288 D ecrawford@pillar.edu
CRAWFORD, Galen 415-351-3509 60 G gcrawford@sfai.edu
CRAWFORD, Gregory 513-529-2345 365 I president@miamioh.edu
CRAWFORD, Holly 585-275-2800 332 E hcrawford@admin.rochester.edu
CRAWFORD, Isiaah 253-879-3201 499 C president@pugetsound.edu
CRAWFORD, James 336-517-1818 335 K jcrawford@bennett.edu
CRAWFORD, Jenny 410-777-1204 202 D jlcrawford1@aacc.edu
CRAWFORD, John 330-672-2760 363 I jcrawfor1@kent.edu
CRAWFORD, John, D 229-333-5939 127 H jdcrawford@valdosta.edu
CRAWFORD, John, P 716-880-2879 314 F jpc334@medaille.edu
CRAWFORD, Jonas 805-678-5870 73 B jcrawford@vcccd.edu
CRAWFORD, Kevin 240-500-2000 204 B klcrawford@hagerstowncc.edu
CRAWFORD, Kevin 803-641-3495 425 A kevincr@usca.edu
CRAWFORD, Malinda 406-756-3828 271 A mcrawfor@fvcc.edu
CRAWFORD, Matthew 612-659-6701 245 F matthew.crawford@minneapolis.edu
CRAWFORD, Michael 773-838-7500 136 A mcrawford34@ccc.edu
CRAWFORD, Mike 863-680-6211 100 D mcrawford@flsouthern.edu
CRAWFORD, Peg 617-732-2132 221 E peg.crawford@mcphs.edu
CRAWFORD, Ray Scott 318-678-6000 192 C rcrawford@bpcc.edu
CRAWFORD, Rhia, M 828-448-6048 347 F rcrawford@wpcc.edu
CRAWFORD, Stacey, L 240-500-2000 204 B slcrawford@hagerstowncc.edu
CRAWFORD, Teresa 863-784-7061 108 B teresa.crawford@southflorida.edu
CRAWFORD, Teri 281-998-6151 455 K teri.crawford@sjcd.edu
CRAWFORD, Thomas, P 412-624-5822 412 I tom.crawford@ia.pitt.edu
CRAWFORD, Tim 254-295-4180 466 A tcrawford@umhb.edu
CRAWFORD, Valerie 309-268-8150 139 D val.crawford@heartland.edu
CRAWFORD, Wendy 870-733-6711 18 B wcrawford@asumidsouth.edu
CRAWFORD, III, William, H 480-732-7309 13 E bill.crawford.iii@cgc.edu
CRAWFORD-FOWLER, Sally 620-341-5221 177 B scrowfo4@emporia.edu
CRAWLEY, Cathy 478-445-5149 119 E cathy.crawley@gcsu.edu
CRAWLEY, William 850-474-2077 111 D wcrawley@uwf.edu
CRAWMER, Martha 989-686-9291 229 J marthacrawmer@delta.edu
CRAWSHAW, Taylor 620-331-4100 178 E tcrawshaw@indycc.edu
CRAYS, Linda, L 713-500-2080 468 D linda.l.crays@uth.tmc.edu
CRAYTON, DiOnetta 617-253-5010 221 C
CRAZY THUNDER, Susan 715-365-4434 514 E scrazythunder@nicoletcollege.edu
CREAGER, Carol 540-887-7310 482 G ccreager@marybaldwin.edu
CREAGH, CM, Kevin 716-286-8400 318 F kcreagh@niagara.edu
CREAHAN, Patricia, H 716-888-2616 300 G creahan@canisius.edu
CREAMER, Barry 214-818-1300 447 A bcreamer@criswell.edu
CREAMER, David 513-529-4225 365 I creamerd@miamioh.edu
CREAMER, Jenni 864-646-1615 424 F jevans12@tctc.edu
CREAMER, Julie 507-222-4280 241 C jcreamer@carleton.edu
CREAMER, Kelli 205-853-1200 2 F kcreamer@jeffersonstate.edu
CREAMER, Stephen 978-762-4000 220 E screamer@northshore.edu
CREARY, Ferne 305-237-2222 103 L fcreary@mdc.edu
CREASMAN, Alice 304-473-8440 505 G creasman_aj@wvwc.edu
CREASMAN, Boyd 304-473-8042 505 G creasman@wvwc.edu
CREASON, Paul 562-938-4171 48 I pcreason@lbcc.edu
CREASON, Rita, A 270-789-5233 184 B racreason@campbellsville.edu
CREASY, Rick 423-472-7141 436 G rcreasy@clevelandstatecc.edu
CREDE, Brad 573-897-5000 267 F
CREDILLE, John 417-328-1606 267 A jcredille@sbuniv.edu
CREDLE, Sid, H 757-727-5361 481 E sid.credle@hamptonu.edu
CREE, Robert, A 315-364-3408 333 G rcree@wells.edu
CREECH, Bill 918-595-7000 380 D bill.creech@tulsacc.edu
CREECH, Jennifer, M 937-229-4141 372 A jcreech1@udayton.edu
CREECH, Karlton, W 207-581-1052 201 B karlton.creech@maine.edu
CREECH, Pat 918-540-6294 376 F pcreech@neo.edu
CREECH, Tom 810-762-9616 232 C tcreech@kettering.edu
CREECY, Scott 870-762-3159 17 K screecy@smail.anc.edu
CREED, J. Bradley 910-893-1205 336 C creed@campbell.edu
CREED-DIKEOGU, Gloria 785-242-5200 180 H creeddikeogu@ottawa.edu
CREEGER, Joan 704-216-3602 346 C joan.creeger@rccc.edu
CREEHAN, Dennis, W 304-457-6404 501 A creehandw@ab.edu
CREEK, Frederick 541-552-6910 386 H creekf@sou.edu
CREEKMORE, Crystal 256-233-8174 4 C crystal.creekmore@athens.edu
CREEKMORE, Paul, R 630-515-7217 145 I rcreek@midwestern.edu
CREEL, Angie 928-344-7776 11 B angela.creel-erb@azwestern.edu
CREEL, Laura 864-294-3031 421 I laura.creel@furman.edu
CREEL, Rickey 256-215-4321 1 G rcreel@cacc.edu
CREEL, Ronnie 334-670-3496 7 E rcreel@troy.edu
CREEL, Shane 361-593-2237 460 B randolph.creel@tamuk.edu
CREELY, Hilliary, E 724-357-2655 406 C hcreely@iup.edu
CREER, Andrew 801-863-8608 473 D andrew.creer@uvu.edu
CREFT, Dawn, H 407-303-9706 94 H dawn.creft@adu.edu
CREGER, LeAnn 517-607-2305 231 C lcreger@hillsdale.edu
CREGGER, Crystal, Y 276-233-4762 490 C ccregger@wcc.vccs.edu
CREIGHTON, Grace 914-674-7369 314 I gcreighton@mercy.edu
CREIGHTON, Joslyn 816-559-5622 265 C joslyn.creighton@park.edu
CREIGHTON, Shannon, B 864-488-4371 422 B screighton@limestone.edu
CREMER, Douglas 818-767-0888 75 C douglas.cremer@woodbury.edu
CRENSHAW, Chris 601-266-4414 256 E christopher.crenshaw@usm.edu
CRENSHAW, Christine 405-744-5358 377 F christine.crenshaw@okstate.edu
CRENSHAW, Pamela 714-556-3610 72 F pcrenshaw@vanguard.edu
CREQUE, Rachael 563-425-5170 173 K crequer74@uiu.edu
CRESPIE, Nancie 301-891-4147 209 E ncrespie@wau.edu
CRESPINO, Curt, J 816-235-1105 268 D crespinocj@umkc.edu
CRESPO, Jorge 787-751-0178 525 O ac_jcrespo@suagm.edu
CRESPO, Jorge, L 787-751-0178 525 O ac_jcrespo@suagm.edu
CRESPO, Lyliana 787-863-2390 523 K lyliana.crespo@fajardo.inter.edu
CRESPO, Natalie 410-386-8229 203 A ncrespo@carrollcc.edu
CRESPO, Ricardo 787-751-1912 524 E rcnevarez@juris.inter.edu
CRESPO-LOPEZ, Sylvia 212-237-8897 302 F sylopez@jjay.cuny.edu
CRESPO-MARTINEZ, María, I 787-993-8886 527 G maria.crespo@upr.edu
CRESPY, Charles, T 989-774-2481 228 E cresp1ct@cmich.edu
CRESS, Pam 509-527-2421 499 F pam.cress@wallawalla.edu
CRESSWELL, Timothy 860-297-2144 88 E timothy.cresswell@trincoll.edu
CREVISTON, Thomas, E 913-684-3097 518 I
CREW, Rudolph, F 718-270-5000 303 C rcrew@mec.cuny.edu
CREWE, Sandra 202-806-7300 92 C screwe@howard.edu
CREWELL, Don 626-395-6280 29 I dcrewell@caltech.edu
CREWS, Amy 256-765-4437 9 A aecrews@una.edu
CREWS, Angie 301-891-4134 209 E acrews@wau.edu
CREWS, Annie 301-546-0916 206 E crewsad@pgcc.edu
CREWS, Bradford 216-368-4303 358 C bradford.crews@case.edu
CREWS, Chris 812-941-2000 161 A cmcrews@ius.edu
CREWS, Denise 217-875-7200 149 J dcrews@richland.edu
CREWS, Kimberly 202-274-5857 93 D kcrews@udc.edu
CREWS, LaJada 336-744-0900 336 D frontoffice@carolina.edu
CREWS, Micah, R 423-652-4773 432 I mrcrews@king.edu
CREWS, Michele 617-879-2114 226 A mcrews@wheelock.edu
CREWS, Patricia, S 850-484-1700 105 E pcrews@pensacolastate.edu
CREWS, Sharon 205-929-6307 2 G sharon.crews@lawsonstate.edu
CREWS, Tena 803-777-6727 424 I tcrews@mailbox.sc.edu
CREWS, William, O 360-882-2120 44 A bcrews@nwbaptist.org
CRIBBS, Christopher, D 502-597-6822 187 E christopher.cribbs@kysu.edu
CRICK, James 502-451-0815 189 E jcrick@sullivan.edu
CRICKARD, Valerie 704-687-1862 351 C vcrickar@uncc.edu
CRICKENBERGER, Leslie 931-372-3034 438 F lcrickenberger@tntech.edu
CRICKENBERGER, Leslie 931-372-3888 438 F lcrickenberger@tntech.edu
CRICKETTE, Grace 262-472-1918 512 C
CRICKMER, Janet 276-944-6658 480 J jcrickme@ehc.edu
CRIDER, Kevin, L 518-580-5929 324 D kcrider@skidmore.edu
CRIDER, Kyle 559-934-2129 73 M kylecrider@whccd.edu
CRIDER, Scott 972-721-5218 464 E crider@udallas.edu
CRIDER, Wayne 706-245-7226 119 A wcrider@ec.edu
CRIGLER, Jeremy, T 203-716-8470 196 D jcrigler@tulane.edu
CRILL-HORNSBY, Cherylyn 559-324-6465 66 E cherylyn.crill-hornsby@scccd.edu
CRILLEY, Bonnie 814-866-8144 399 C bcrilley@lecom.edu
CRIMMIN, Nancy, P 508-373-1900 211 F nancy.crimmin@becker.edu
CRIMMINS, Cindy 717-815-1216 415 G ccrimmins@ycp.edu
CRIMMINS, Kate 410-837-6135 209 D kcrimmins@ubalt.edu
CRIMMINS LECHOWICZ, Catherine 860-685-2841 89 F ccrimmins@wesleyan.edu
CRINO, Sally, E 563-333-6080 173 A crinosallye@sau.edu

CRIPE, Stephen, A .... 989-837-4387 235 C cripe@northwood.edu
CRIPPIN-HAAKE, Tracy, L .... 515-574-1192 170 C crippin@iowacentral.edu
CRIPPS, Kimberly .... 205-726-4180.... 6 G kcripps@samford.edu
CRISAFULLI, Susan .... 317-738-8240 157 L scrisafulli@franklincollege.edu
CRISCI, David .... 781-768-7843 224 A david.crisci@regiscollege.edu
CRISER, III, Marshall, M .... 850-245-0466 108 Q chancellor@flbog.edu
CRISLER, Patricia .... 531-622-2759 275 F pcrisler@mccneb.edu
CRISLIP, Ann .... 518-262-9550 297 L crislia@mail.amc.edu
CRISLIP-TACY, Carolyn .. 304-367-4241 504 A crisliptacy@fairmontstate.edu
CRISMAN, Matthew .... 870-307-7250.. 20 C matthew.crisman@lyon.edu
CRISMAN, Matthew .... 276-944-6491 480 J mcrisman@ehc.edu
CRISMON, M. Lynn .... 512-471-3718 467 C lynn.crismon@austin.utexas.edu
CRISP, Brad .... 325-674-2503 441 D cbc06d@acu.edu
CRISP, JR., Delmas, S .. 910-630-7031 340 A dcrisp@methodist.edu
CRISP, Kathryn .... 615-898-2088 434 H kathy.crisp@mtsu.edu
CRISP, Michael, D .... 864-833-8308 423 D mdcrisp@presby.edu
CRISP, Whitney .... 229-931-2299 125 G wcrisp@southgatech.edu
CRISP, Winston, B .... 919-966-4045 351 B wbcrisp@email.unc.edu
CRISPELL, Brian, L .... 813-988-5131.. 99 D crispellb@floridacollege.edu
CRISS, Paul .... 901-888-3343 252 C pcriss@belhaven.edu
CRISS, Sarah .... 661-763-7711.. 67 A scriss@taftcollege.edu
CRISSINGER, Amy, S .... 605-256-5139 428 G amy.crissinger@dsu.edu
CRIST, Mike .... 330-941-3001 374 E
CRIST, William, J .... 337-482-2001 197 F wjc4092@louisiana.edu
CRISTANCHO MERCADO, Oscar, J .... 407-582-3306 113 F ocristanchomercad@valenciacollege.edu
CRISTE, Vince .... 800-877-5456 479 G alumni@christendom.edu
CRISTELLO, Justin .... 859-846-5304 188 B jcristello@midway.edu
CRISTINI, Angela .... 201-684-7724 289 C acristin@ramapo.edu
CRISTOBAL, Remy, B .... 671-735-2218 520 B remybc@triton.uog.edu
CRISTOFARO, Theresa, R .... 856-225-6053 290 B terri.cristofaro@rutgers.edu
CRISWELL, Chantal, C .... 386-226-6202.. 98 C criswelm@erau.edu
CRITES, Randall .... 304-473-8030 505 G crites@wvwc.edu
CRITES, Stephen .... 915-747-7018 467 E scrites@utep.edu
CRITES, Tammy .... 304-473-8186 505 G crites_t@wvwc.edu
CRITTENDEN, Barbara, J .... 641-782-1425 173 I crittenden@swcciowa.edu
CRITTENDEN, Steve .... 763-433-1982 243 K steve.crittenden@anokaramsey.edu
CROCHET, Monique .... 985-448-4110 197 C monique.crochet@nicholls.edu
CROCITTO, Peter .... 954-776-4476 102 G peterc@keiseruniversity.edu
CROCKEM, Rajanel .... 713-313-1066 461 E crockemr@tsu.edu
CROCKER, Daniel .... 207-974-4623 199 L dcrocker@emcc.edu
CROCKER, Harold .... 201-684-7091 289 C hcrocker@ramapo.edu
CROCKER, Heidi .... 323-731-2383.. 55 E hcrocker@psuca.edu
CROCKER, Jack .... 575-538-6318 297 H jack.crocker@wnmu.edu
CROCKER, Jane, S .... 856-415-2250 289 G jcrocker@rcgc.edu
CROCKER, Marjorie .... 706-419-1544 118 E crocker@covenant.edu
CROCKER, Phyllis .... 313-596-0210 237 F pcrocker@udmercy.edu
CROCKETT, Bennie, R ... 601-318-6116 256 I crockett@wmcarey.edu
CROCKETT, Charles, E ... 936-261-2653 458 F cecrockett@pvamu.edu
CROCKETT, Daniel, E .... 304-558-4618 503 N daniel.crockett@wvhepc.edu
CROCKETT, Deborah .... 207-947-4591 198 F dcrockett@bealcollege.edu
CROCKETT, Michael .... 928-428-8215.. 12 I mike.crockett@eac.edu
CROCKETT, Nathan .... 864-242-5100 418 H
CROCKETT, Suzonne .... 409-882-3062 462 D suzonne.crockett@lsco.edu
CROCKETT, Vivian .... 239-304-7344.. 95 C vivian.crockett@avemaria.edu
CROCKETT, William, P .. 410-706-3902 207 H bcrocket@umaryland.edu
CROCKETT-RAY, Sharon 210-486-2886 441 I scrockett-ray@alamo.edu
CROCKETT-RAY, Sharon 210-486-2887 441 I scrockett-ray@alamo.edu
CROCQUET, Marc .... 954-262-8842 104 F crocquet@nsu.nova.edu
CROFCHICK, Frank .... 570-662-4342 406 F fcrofchi@mansfield.edu
CROFF, Troy .... 503-581-8600 383 A tcroff@corban.edu
CROFT, Lucy, S .... 904-620-2525 110 E lcroft@unf.edu
CROFT, Maureen, G .... 832-842-8703 465 A mgcroft@uh.edu
CROFT, Roger .... 670-237-6769 520 D roger.croft@marianas.edu
CROFTON, Michael .... 513-569-6577 362 E michael.crofton@email.gscollege.edu
CROFTON, Stephanie, O 336-841-4569 338 E scrofton@highpoint.edu
CROGAN, Evelyn .... 760-795-6610.. 52 F ecrogan@miracosta.edu
CROGHAN, Chris, M .... 605-336-6588 428 B croghan@augie.edu
CROGHAN, David .... 301-846-2708 203 H dcroghan@frederick.edu
CROGHAN, John .... 315-859-4129 309 D jcroghan@hamilton.edu
CROKE, Ryan .... 217-206-7795 154 A rcroke@uis.edu
CROMARTIE, Anthony ... 973-877-1873 285 K cromartie@essex.edu
CROMARTIE, Fred .... 251-626-3303.... 7 G fcromartie@ussa.edu
CROMATIE, Stanley .... 904-470-8277.. 98 B stanley.cromatie@ewc.edu
CROMBIE, Stephanie ..... 860-628-4751.. 87 E scrombie@lincolncollegene.edu
CROMIE, Carol .... 409-772-9795 469 C cacromie@utmb.edu
CROMLEY, Brenda .... 570-389-4674 405 E bcromley@bloomu.edu
CROMLEY, Robert .... 903-877-7455 469 A robert.cromley@uthct.edu
CROMWELL, Jim .... 808-689-2918 130 A cromwell@hawaii.edu
CROMWELL, Michelle .... 802-257-7751 476 B michelle.cromwell@sit.edu
CRONAN, David .... 708-709-3585 148 I dcronan@prairiestate.edu
CRONAUER, OSB, Patrick, T .... 724-805-2324 410 C patrick.cronauer@stvincent.edu
CRONE, Darren .... 972-883-4826 467 D darren.crone@utdallas.edu
CRONE, Kimberly .... 860-231-5360.. 89 E kcrone@usj.edu
CRONE, Marilyn .... 206-296-5841 498 D cronem@seattleu.edu
CRONIC, Sue .... 770-533-7007 122 E scronic@laniertech.edu
CRONIN, Charles .... 610-526-1458 389 B tip.cronin@theamericancollege.edu
CRONIN, Corey .... 978-542-7517 218 E corey.cronin@salemstate.edu
CRONIN, Marta .... 772-462-7215 101 Q mcronin@irsc.edu
CRONIN, Mary, A .... 713-348-4070 455 F cronin@rice.edu
CRONIN, Rachel .... 323-259-2500.. 54 E rcronin@oxy.edu
CRONIN, Shawn .... 978-762-4000 220 E scronin@northshore.edu
CRONIN, Trish .... 508-793-7160 213 C tcronin@clarku.edu
CRONK, Keith .... 501-279-5700.. 19 G kcronk@harding.edu
CRONK, Nancy, L .... 765-285-1722 156 C ncronk@bsu.edu
CRONLEY, Maria, L .... 419-772-2034 367 G m-cronley@onu.edu
CRONMILLER, Janelle ... 610-647-4400 397 I jcronmiller@immaculata.edu
CROOK, Brady .... 516-877-6890 297 I bcrook@adelphi.edu
CROOK, Chris .... 785-864-9331 181 I ccrook@ku.edu
CROOK, David .... 646-664-8102 301 A david.crook@cuny.edu
CROOK, Evonne .... 423-236-2830 436 C ercrook@southern.edu
CROOK, Linda .... 303-914-6256.. 82 B linda.crook@rrcc.edu
CROOK, Marcus .... 231-845-3329 239 D mcrook@westshore.edu
CROOK, Patricia .... 615-963-5280 438 E pcrook@tnstate.edu
CROOK, Rebecca .... 321-674-8099.. 99 K bcrook@fit.edu
CROOKENDALE, Humphrey .... 212-343-1234 315 D hcrookendale@mcny.edu
CROOKER, Benjamin ..... 718-817-3048 308 G crooker@fordham.edu
CROOKS, John, R .... 440-366-7793 364 F
CROONQUIST, Matt .... 641-673-2123 174 F croonquistm@wmpenn.edu
CROOP, Patricia .... 518-464-8642 308 A pcroop@excelsior.edu
CROOT, Rick .... 360-417-6553 496 I rcroot@pencol.edu
CROPPER, USMS, Thomas, A .... 707-654-1011.. 32 E tacropper@csum.edu
CROPSEY, Jeffrey .... 800-955-2527 177 H jcropsey@grantham.edu
CROSBIE, Jeff .... 435-797-1042 473 C jeff.crosbie@usu.edu
CROSBY, Anita, L .... 334-387-3877.... 4 B anitacrosby@amridgeuniversity.edu
CROSBY, Cheryl .... 352-854-2322.. 97 C crosbyc@cf.edu
CROSBY, Devin .... 561-237-7213 103 E dcrosby@lynn.edu
CROSBY, Faye .... 831-459-5031.. 70 C fjcrosby@ucsc.edu
CROSBY, Gary .... 256-372-8164.... 1 A gary.crosby@aamu.edu
CROSBY, James .... 307-778-1340 516 N jcrosby@lccc.wy.edu
CROSBY, Jean .... 765-285-7057 156 C jkcrosby@bsu.edu
CROSBY, Jesse .... 207-947-4591 198 F jcrosby@bealcollege.edu
CROSBY, John .... 740-284-5349 361 L jcrosby@franciscan.edu
CROSBY, Kim .... 870-307-7275.. 20 C kim.crosby@lyon.edu
CROSBY, Lynne .... 931-221-6240 430 B crosbyl@apsu.edu
CROSBY, Mark .... 207-859-5500 198 H mcrosby@colby.edu
CROSBY, Pamela .... 863-667-5279 108 G pscrosby@seu.edu
CROSBY, Stephanie .... 559-442-8237.. 66 G stephanie.crosby@fresnocitycollege.edu
CROSBY, Susan, E .... 540-453-2363 487 G crosbys@brcc.edu
CROSBY LEHMANN, Carl .... 507-786-3894 250 C lehmann@stolaf.edu
CROSEN, Rachel .... 517-355-6675 233 G crosenra@msu.edu
CROSKERY, Patrick, T ... 419-772-2197 367 G p-croskery@onu.edu
CROSLIN, Joey .... 405-208-5075 377 D jcroslin@okcu.edu
CROSS, Berri, V .... 336-334-4822 343 E bvcross@gtcc.edu
CROSS, Charles, E .... 415-422-6522.. 72 A cross@usfca.edu
CROSS, Colette .... 281-649-3475 450 C ccross@hbu.edu
CROSS, David .... 713-718-8636 450 D david.cross@hccs.edu
CROSS, David .... 603-862-2090 282 F counseling.center@unh.edu
CROSS, Dennis, W .... 540-458-8232 491 G dcross@wlu.edu
CROSS, Dwight .... 802-225-6324 475 H dwight.cross@neci.edu
CROSS, Dwight .... 802-728-1250 477 E dcross@vtc.edu
CROSS, Jeffrey .... 248-476-1122 233 F jcross@mispp.edu
CROSS, Jeffrey, F .... 217-581-2121 138 A jfcross@eiu.edu
CROSS, Jesse .... 336-334-4822 343 E jlcross@gtcc.edu
CROSS, Joe .... 858-653-6740.. 46M jcross@jpcatholic.com
CROSS, Kris .... 937-393-3431 370 C kcross@sscc.edu
CROSS, Kristen .... 870-612-2011.. 22 H kristen.cross@uaccb.edu
CROSS, Kristie .... 660-359-3948 264 H kcross@mail.ncmissouri.edu
CROSS, Mary, M .... 615-353-3301 437 D mary.cross@nscc.edu
CROSS, Myrna, J .... 580-477-7712 381 G myrna.cross@wosc.edu
CROSS, Penny .... 828-652-0645 344 G penncyc@mcdowelltech.edu
CROSS, Ray, W .... 608-262-2321 510 B rcross@uwsa.edu
CROSS, Roberta .... 724-503-1001 414 A rcross@washjeff.edu
CROSS, Solomon .... 972-860-8120 447 H scross@dcccd.edu
CROSS, Stephanie .... 540-545-7245 485 C scross92@su.edu
CROSS, Stephen .... 404-894-8885 120 A cross@gatech.edu
CROSS, Teresa .... 660-359-3948 264 H tcross@mail.ncmissouri.edu
CROSS, Terry .... 423-614-8140 432 L tcross@leeuniversity.edu
CROSS, Tim, L .... 865-974-7114 439 I tlcross@utk.edu
CROSS, Timothy .... 617-349-8698 216 D timothy.cross@lesley.edu
CROSS, Timothy .... 740-826-6121 366 C tcross@muskingum.edu
CROSS, Tomeka .... 256-551-7264.... 2 D tomeka.cross@drakestate.edu
CROSSLAND, Elisa .... 713-226-5519 465 C crosslande@uhd.edu
CROSSLAND, George ..... 409-944-1356 449 F gcrossla@gc.edu
CROSSLAND, Martin ...... 913-971-3514 179 H mcrossland@mnu.edu
CROSSLEY, John, L .... 315-733-2307 332 F jcrossley@uscny.edu
CROSSMAN, Raymond, E .... 312-662-4001 133 A rec@adler.edu
CROSSON, Elaine .... 718-817-3111 308 G ecrosson@fordham.edu
CROTHERS, Tammy .... 309-467-6309 138 E tcrothers@eureka.edu
CROUCH, Alicia .... 859-256-3100 185 D alicia.crouch@kctcs.edu
CROUCH, Frank .... 610-861-1516 402 D crouchf@moravian.edu
CROUCH, Julia .... 918-335-6212 378 F jcrouch@okwu.edu
CROUCH, Michael, A .... 205-726-2820.... 6 G mcrouch@samford.edu
CROUCH, Mike .... 620-343-4600 177 C mcrouch@fhtc.edu
CROUCH, Nancy .... 910-775-4355 351 E nancy.crouch@uncp.edu
CROUCH, Peter .... 817-272-2571 467 B peter.crouch@uta.edu
CROUCH, Tony .... 405-789-7661 380 A tony.crouch@swcu.edu
CROUCHET, Cristeen ..... 253-589-5895 493 F cristeen.crouchet@cptc.edu
CROUGHAN, Mary, S .... 702-895-1828 279 D mary.croughan@unlv.edu
CROUNSE, Cheryl .... 978-542-7527 218 E cheryl.crounse@salemstate.edu
CROUSE, Chase .... 858-653-6740.. 46M ccrouse@jpcatholic.com
CROUSE, Donald .... 956-295-3515 461 F donald.crouse@tsc.edu
CROUSE, JR., Francis, C .... 814-886-6383 402 E fcrouse@mtaloy.edu
CROUSE, Jen .... 307-674-6446 516 P jcrouse@sheridan.edu
CROUSE, Matt .... 575-646-3202 295 B mcrouse@nmsu.edu
CROUSE, Robert .... 573-592-5019 270 B rob.crouse@westminster-mo.edu
CROUSE, Steve .... 864-977-7016 422 I steve.crouse@ngu.edu
CROUTER, Ann, C .... 814-865-1420 403 F ac1@psu.edu
CROW, Angela .... 479-968-0271.. 18 G acrow@atu.edu
CROW, C. Robert .... 616-526-6165 228 B rcrow@calvin.edu
CROW, Carla .... 561-803-2155 104 I carla_crow@pba.edu
CROW, Donna, E .... 435-797-3588 473 C donna.crow@usu.edu
CROW, Len .... 909-652-6508.. 36 E leonard.crow@chaffey.edu

CROW, Macey .... 208-467-8523 132 F
maceycrow@nnu.edu
CROW, Mandy .... 615-248-7782 439 B
mmcrow@trevecca.edu
CROW, Mariesa, L .... 573-341-4154 269 A
crow@mst.edu
CROW, Michael, M .... 480-965-8972.. 10 K
michael.crow@asu.edu
CROW, Scott .... 916-484-8647.. 50 F
crows@arc.losrios.edu
CROW, Scott .... 419-824-3938 364 G
scrow@lourdes.edu
CROW, Steven, L .... 831-646-4040.. 52 G
scrow@mpc.edu
CROW, Tony, L .... 303-458-4161.. 82 D
tcrow@regis.edu
CROWDER, Darren .... 417-328-1797 267 A
dcrowder@sbuniv.edu
CROWDER, Jenn .... 208-562-2106 132 A
jenncrowder@cwidaho.cc
CROWDER, Mike .... 806-743-7865 463 E
mike.crowder@ttuhsc.edu
CROWDER, Teresa .... 816-584-6252 265 C
teresa.crowder@park.edu
CROWDER, Vickie .... 304-473-8032 505 G
crowder_v@wvwc.edu
CROWE, Aliesha, R .... 715-833-6277 513 E
acrowe3@cvtc.edu
CROWE, Carl .... 410-778-7235 210 A
ccrowe2@washcoll.edu
CROWE, Gregg .... 503-228-6528 381 I
gcrowe@aii.edu
CROWE, Jason .... 314-454-7770 260 E
jcrowe@bjc.org
CROWE, Kathryn, M ...... 336-334-5880 351 D
kathy_crowe@uncg.edu
CROWE, Ken .... 706-864-1499 127 B
ken.crowe@ung.edu
CROWE, Lindsey .... 270-852-3118 187 F
lcrowe@kwc.edu
CROWE, Mary, L .... 863-680-4181 100 D
mcrowe@flsouthern.edu
CROWE, Richard .... 818-343-2890.. 40 A
rcrowe@columbiacollege.edu
CROWE, Sharon .... 414-847-3216 508 G
sharoncrowe@miad.edu
CROWE, Stephanie .... 406-496-4568 272 E
scrowe@mtech.edu
CROWE, Thomas .... 847-543-2473 136 E
tcrowe@clcillinois.edu
CROWELL, Anthony .... 212-431-2840 317 H
anthony.crowell@nyls.edu
CROWELL, Heidi .... 603-897-8630 281 I
hcrowell@rivier.edu
CROWELL, Scott .... 507-537-6844 248 A
scott.crowell@smsu.edu
CROWETIPTON, Vaughn 864-294-2138 421 I
vaughn.crowetipton@furman.edu
CROWL, Rebecca, R .... 330-363-6347 357 A
rebecca.crowl@aultman.com
CROWL, Ronald .... 330-829-2756 372 C
crowlrl@mountunion.edu
CROWLEY, Cara, J .... 806-345-5518 442 D
cjcrowley@actx.edu
CROWLEY, Janelle .... 608-342-1176 511 D
crowleyja@uwplatt.edu
CROWLEY, Kimberly, A . 806-354-6087 442 D
kacrowley@actx.edu
CROWLEY, Merritt .... 508-286-3464 225 G
crowley_merritt@wheatoncollege.edu
CROWLEY, Michael .... 617-573-8646 224 I
mcrowley2@suffolk.edu
CROWLEY, Rachel .... 605-331-6661 429 D
rachel.crowley@usiouxfalls.edu
CROWLEY, Tanya .... 978-665-4789 217 E
tcrowle7@fitchburgstate.edu
CROWLEY, Timothy, D .. 207-768-2811 200 B
tcrowley@nmcc.edu
CROWN, Deborah, F ..... 407-646-2405 106 J
dcrown@rollins.edu
CROWSON, Allan .... 615-675-5277 441 B
acrowson@welch.edu
CROWSON, Dennis .... 979-830-4456 444 D
dennis.crowson@blinn.edu
CROWTHER, Cameron ... 540-261-8528 485 G
cameron.crowther@svu.edu
CROWTHER,
Cameron, T .... 540-261-8483 485 G
cameron.crowther@svu.edu
CROWTHER, Edward ...... 719-587-7811.. 76 D
ercrowth@adams.edu
CROWTHER,
Elizabeth, H .... 804-758-6701 489 D
ecrowther@rappahannock.edu
CROWTHER, Lori .... 620-792-9216 175 C
crowtherl@bartonccc.edu
CROWTHER, Steven .... 910-221-2224 338 A
scrowther@gcd.edu

CROY, Jason .... 706-245-7226 119 A
jcroy@ec.edu
CROY, Kyle .... 541-888-7316 387 A
kcroy@socc.edu
CROYLE, Kristin .... 956-665-3671 468 A
kristin.croyle@utrgv.edu
CROYLE, Mary .... 806-743-2143 463 E
mary.croyle@ttuhsc.edu
CRUCITTI, Thomas .... 203-837-9090.. 85 B
crucittit@wcsu.edu
CRUICKSHANK,
Cameron .... 734-432-5495 233 C
ccruickshank@madonna.edu
CRUICKSHANK, Laura ... 860-486-2086.. 88 G
laura.cruickshank@uconn.edu
CRUIKSHANK, Alexis ..... 206-281-2752 498 B
acruikshank@spu.edu
CRUIKSHANK, Nancy, L 724-738-4831 407 C
nancy.cruikshank@sru.edu
CRUISE, Rodney, J .... 386-226-7303.. 98 C
cruiser@erau.edu
CRULL, Matthew .... 815-825-9433 142 F
matt.crull@kishwaukeecollege.edu
CRUM, Claude .... 606-368-6061 182 H
claudecrum@alc.edu
CRUM, Denny .... 502-852-0841 190 C
denny.crum@louisville.edu
CRUM, Lyndsey .... 970-351-2551.. 83 F
lyndsey.crum@unco.edu
CRUM, Michael, R .... 515-294-8105 166 F
mcrum@iastate.edu
CRUMBAKER, Chad .... 304-424-8242 505 C
chad.crumbaker@wvup.edu
CRUME, Gene .... 847-628-2002 142 B
gene.crume@judsonu.edu
CRUMEDY, Ron, C .... 409-944-1237 449 F
rcrumedy@gc.edu
CRUMIT-HANCOCK,
Lisa .... 419-783-2332 361 A
lcrumithancock@defiance.edu
CRUMLEY, Christopher .. 281-476-1810 455 L
christopher.crumley@sjcd.edu
CRUMLEY, Kristie .... 410-386-8408 203 A
kcrumley@carrollcc.edu
CRUMLEY, Terri .... 319-363-1323 172 B
tcrumley@mtmercy.edu
CRUMMIE, Robert, W .... 404-527-4520 117 C
rcrummie@carver.edu
CRUMP, D'adra .... 718-940-5869 322 G
dcrump@sjcny.edu
CRUMP, Tammy .... 704-991-0267 346 I
tcrump5648@stanly.edu
CRUMP-PHILLIPS,
Maureen .... 256-761-6100.... 7 D
CRUMRIN, Robin .... 812-237-3700 159 C
robin.crumrin@indstate.edu
CRUMRINE, Stephen ..... 208-562-3172 132 A
stephencrumrine@cwidaho.cc
CRUSCIEL, Robert .... 814-472-3021 409 G
rcrusciel@francis.edu
CRUSE, David .... 517-265-5161 226 F
dcruse@adrian.edu
CRUSE, Michele .... 971-722-5307 386 C
michele.cruse@pcc.edu
CRUSE, Susan .... 404-727-6061 119 B
scruse2@emory.edu
CRUSE, Terry .... 601-484-0220 254 E
tdcruse@meridian.msstate.edu
CRUSER, Kevin .... 940-898-2000 464 A
kcruser@twu.edu
CRUSTO-WAY,
Kathy, M .... 817-515-3065 458 B
kathy.crusto-way@tccd.edu
CRUTCHER, Caicey .... 620-792-9386 175 C
crutcherc@bartonccc.edu
CRUTCHER, Ronald, A ... 804-289-8100 486 G
ronald.crutcher@richmond.edu
CRUTCHER, Terri .... 615-230-3343 438 C
terri.crutcher@volstate.edu
CRUTCHFIELD, Carla ..... 501-337-5000.. 19 C
ccrutchfield@coto.edu
CRUTCHFIELD, Russell .. 678-839-6442 127 F
rcrutchf@westga.edu
CRUTE, Ashley .... 434-395-2064 482 E
crutean@longwood.edu
CRUTSINGER, Bob .... 785-670-1745 182 D
bob.crutsinger@washburn.edu
CRUTSINGER, Christy .... 940-565-2550 466 B
christy.crutsinger@unt.edu
CRUZ, Anthony .... 314-539-5000 266 E
acruz@stlcc.edu
CRUZ, Beatriz .... 718-429-6600 333 B
beatriz.cruz@vaughn.edu
CRUZ, Elizabeth .... 787-780-5134 525 D
ecruz@nuc.edu
CRUZ, Erin .... 559-791-2332.. 47 C
ecruz@portervillecollege.edu

CRUZ, Esteban .... 217-786-2200 144 B
esteban.cruz@llcc.edu
CRUZ, Evelyn .... 787-850-9203 528 B
evelyn.cruz1@upr.edu
CRUZ, Felicita .... 787-834-9595 526 E
fcruz@uaa.edu
CRUZ, Heather, A .... 716-851-1621 307 I
cruzh@ecc.edu
CRUZ, Hilda .... 787-264-1912 524 D
hmcruz@intersg.edu
CRUZ, Irma del Pilar ..... 787-828-1319 526 B
um_idelpilar@suagm.edu
CRUZ, Israel .... 787-264-1912 524 D
icruz@intersg.edu
CRUZ, Jackie .... 831-755-6810.. 45 C
jcruz@hartnell.edu
CRUZ, Jaime .... 787-738-2161 528 A
jaime.cruz3@upr.edu
CRUZ, Jairo .... 305-325-9090 112 I
CRUZ, Jessica .... 310-233-4112.. 49 B
cruzj@lahc.edu
CRUZ, Jessica .... 906-227-2000 235 A
jecruz@nmu.edu
CRUZ, Jose, L .... 718-960-8111 302 C
president.cruz@lehman.cuny.edu
CRUZ, Jose, M .... 787-279-1912 523 J
jcruz@bayamon.inter.edu
CRUZ, Lambert .... 602-386-4160.. 10 G
lambert.cruz@arizonachristian.edu
CRUZ, Lourdes .... 203-575-8091.. 86 B
lcruz@nv.edu
CRUZ, Madeline .... 787-834-9595 526 E
mcruz@uaa.edu
CRUZ, Marcia .... 787-758-2525 528 D
marcia.cruz1@upr.edu
CRUZ, Marco Antonio ... 909-607-7283.. 57 C
marcoantonio_cruz@pitzer.edu
CRUZ, Mariela .... 787-884-6000 522 Q
CRUZ, Mayra .... 787-751-0178 525 O
mcruz@suagm.edu
CRUZ, Nathaniel .... 718-518-4253 302 D
ncruz@hostos.cuny.edu
CRUZ, Octavio .... 408-270-6423.. 61 O
octavio.cruz@evc.edu
CRUZ, Odalis .... 352-335-2332.. 94 D
odalis.cruz@acupuncturist.edu
CRUZ, Oscar .... 787-250-1912 524 B
ocruz@metro.inter.edu
CRUZ, Rosa, E .... 787-848-1589 525 H
rcruz@popac.edu
CRUZ, Rosalia .... 212-694-1000 299 L
rcruz@boricuacollege.edu
CRUZ, Roxanna .... 305-899-7826.. 95 G
rpcruz@barry.edu
CRUZ, Villan .... 718-933-6700 315 K
vcrux@monroecollege.edu
CRUZ, Wanda .... 787-738-2161 528 A
wanda.cruz3@upr.edu
CRUZ, Xauel .... 787-848-1589 525 H
xcruz@popac.edu
CRUZ-GONZALEZ,
Carlos, R .... 719-333-9751 518 H
CRUZ-JOHNSON, Celia . 408-288-3719.. 61 P
celia.cruz-johnson@sjcc.edu
CRUZ-PABÓN, Olga, I ... 787-751-1912 524 E
oicruz@juris.inter.edu
CRUZ PAUL, Theresa .... 828-227-3812 352 C
tcpaul@wcu.edu
CRUZ-SOTO, Thomas ..... 909-869-3306.. 31 A
tacruzsoto@cpp.edu
CRUZ-URIBE, Kathryn ... 765-973-8201 160 A
kathcruz@iue.edu
CRUZADO, Waded .... 406-994-2341 272 A
president_cruzado@montana.edu
CRUZVERGARA,
Christine .... 781-283-2492 225 D
ccruzver@wellesley.edu
CRYER, Byron, L .... 214-648-2590 469 E
byron.cryer@utsouthwestern.edu
CRYER, Danielle, N .... 253-535-7493 496 G
cryerdn@plu.edu
CRYSTAL, Jonathan .... 718-817-0136 308 G
crystal@fordham.edu
CRYSTAL, Maureen .... 718-270-1976 326 A
maureen.crystal@downstate.edu
CSELLAR, Maralee, B .... 202-994-7564.. 92 A
csellar@gwu.edu
CSOMAN, Kati, R .... 814-641-3184 398 B
csomank@juniata.edu
CUBARRUBIA,
Archieval .... 305-237-7450 103 L
acubarru@mdc.edu
CUBBA, Stephanie .... 213-477-2766.. 52 H
scubba@msmu.edu
CUBBAGE, Alan, K .... 847-491-4886 148 C
a-cubbage@northwestern.edu

CUBBERLEY,
Frances, M .... 610-359-5141 393 E
fcubberl@dccc.edu
CUBBINS, Elaine .... 520-383-8401.. 16 G
ecubbins@tocc.edu
CUBELIC, Chuck .... 412-809-5100 408 D
cubelic.chuck@pti.edu
CUBERO, Chris .... 724-738-4267 407 C
chris.cubero@sru.edu
CUBILLOS, Sergio .... 786-331-1000 104 C
CUBIT, James, R .... 847-735-5054 142 H
cubit@lakeforest.edu
CUBRIEL, III, Robert ..... 361-572-6406 470 A
robert.cubriel@victoriacollege.edu
CUCARESE, Lisa .... 304-829-7831 501 F
lcucarese@bethanywv.edu
CUCCIA, Christopher ..... 973-761-7554 291 F
christopher.cuccia@shu.edu
CUCCO, Jeremy, L .... 253-879-2710 499 C
jcucco@pugetsound.edu
CUCCURULLO, Suzanne 781-891-2741 212 A
scuccurullo@bentley.edu
CUCHENS, Pat .... 281-283-3065 465 B
cuchens@uhcl.edu
CUCKSEY, Elli 615-384-4641 370M
ecucksey@tlsohio.edu
CUCURELLA-ADORNO,
Ana, E .... 787-780-0070 521 B
acucurella@caribbean.edu
CUDD, Ann .... 617-353-2401 212 G
acudd@bu.edu
CUELLAR, Leana .... 847-635-1655 148 D
lcuellar@oakton.edu
CUELLAR, Toni .... 254-298-8808 458 C
toni.cuellar@templejc.edu
CUETO, Jose .... 787-769-0007 521 B
jcueto@caribbean.edu
CUETO, Jose, M .... 787-780-0070 521 B
jcueto@caribbean.edu
CUEVA, Patricia .... 360-676-2772 496 C
pcueva@nwic.edu
CUEVAS, Carmen .... 312-935-6445 149 K
ccuevas@robertmorris.edu
CUEVAS, Frank .... 865-974-2571 439 I
fcuevas@utk.edu
CUEVAS, Jessica .... 213-477-2570.. 52 H
jcuevas@msmu.edu
CUEVAS, Monica .... 559-442-4600.. 66 G
monica.cuevas@fresnocitycollege.edu
CUEVAS, Patricia .... 312-553-6029 135 J
pcuevas@ccc.edu
CUFF, Michael .... 508-830-5037 218 D
mcuff@maritime.edu
CUKANNA, Paul-James . 412-396-6207 394 D
cukanna@duq.edu
CUKROWSKI, Ken, R ..... 325-674-3700 441 D
cukrowskik@acu.edu
CULBERSON, Pamela .... 912-344-2518 115 D
pam.culberson@armstrong.edu
CULBERSON, Roy .... 940-498-6282 453 L
rculberson@nctc.edu
CULBERT, John .... 773-325-7954 137 C
jculbert@depaul.edu
CULBERTSON,
Charles, R .... 540-828-5720 478 J
cculbert@bridgewater.edu
CULBREATH, Jahan .... 937-376-6373 358 I
jculbreath@centralstate.edu
CULHAN, Timothy, P .... 859-238-5360 184 C
tim.culhan@centre.edu
CULLARS, Kyle .... 478-445-1976 119 E
kyle.cullars@gcsu.edu
CULLEN, Andrew .... 303-871-3740.. 83 E
andrew.a.cullen@du.edu
CULLEN, Ann .... 843-525-8247 424 E
acullen@tcl.edu
CULLEN, Cathleen, R ..... 508-767-7533 210 I
ccullen@assumption.edu
CULLEN, Daryl .... 408-260-0208.. 43 B
sjfinaid@fivebranches.edu
CULLEN, Jim .... 570-961-7864 399 A
cullenj@lakcawanna.edu
CULLEN, Kathleen .... 608-266-9399 513 C
kathleen.cullen@wtcsystem.edu
CULLEN, Laura .... 734-462-4400 236 H
lcullen@schoolcraft.edu
CULLEN, Sharon .... 703-993-8700 481 B
scullen1@gmu.edu
CULLENEN, Rachel .... 607-274-3306 311 D
rcullenen@ithaca.edu
CULLENS, Linda .... 831-477-3222.. 28 F
liculllen@cabrillo.edu
CULLER, Angela .... 336-758-4010 353 A
culleraa@wfu.edu
CULLER, Kevin, J .... 313-845-9755 231 B
kjculler@hfcc.edu
CULLER, Lori, L .... 260-359-4213 159 B
lculler@huntington.edu

CURRIE, John .... 865-974-1224 439 I jcurrie@utk.edu
CURRIE, Lauren .... 518-562-4122 304 C lauren.currie@clinton.edu
CURRIE, Madison .... 661-362-2209.. 51 C mcurrie@masters.edu
CURRIE, Madison .... 661-259-3540.. 51 C
CURRIE, Sarah .... 704-406-4373 337 H scurrie@gardner-webb.edu
CURRIE, Wayne .... 603-222-4282 282 A wcurrie@anselm.edu
CURRIER, Camile .... 318-342-5215 198 A currier@ulm.edu
CURRIER, Chuck .... 630-942-2790 136 D currier@cod.edu
CURRIER, Nicole .... 301-891-4146 209 E ncurrier@wau.edu
CURRIN, Alicia .... 903-886-5034 459 E alicia.currin@tamuc.edu
CURRIN, Bruce, A .... 402-472-3105 277 G bcurrin1@unl.edu
CURRIN, Thomas .... 678-915-7482 122 C tcurrin@kennesaw.edu
CURRISTINE, Eileen .... 609-343-6810 283 D ecurrist@atlantic.edu
CURRIVAN, Megan, D ... 617-322-3500 216 B
CURRY, Anne .... 205-226-4904.... 4 F acurry@bsc.edu
CURRY, Carolyn, S .... 240-895-4282 206 G cscurry@smcm.edu
CURRY, Chris .... 731-989-6349 432 C ccurry@fhu.edu
CURRY, JR., Chuck .... 336-316-2104 338 C curryrc@guilford.edu
CURRY, Cynthia .... 305-626-3619.. 99 M cynthia.curry@fmuniv.edu
CURRY, Cynthia, S .... 304-367-4386 504 A cindy.curry@fairmontstate.edu
CURRY, Dean, C .... 717-796-1800 401 L dcurry@messiah.edu
CURRY, Deborah .... 256-549-8321.... 2 A dcurry@gadsdenstate.edu
CURRY, Elizabeth, A ...... 904-620-2615 110 E e.curry@unf.edu
CURRY, Evan .... 215-702-4461 391 C ecurry@cairn.edu
CURRY, Georgette .... 706-225-5300.. 93 B
CURRY, Gina .... 916-278-5992.. 33 C curryg@skymail.csus.edu
CURRY, James .... 402-844-7063 276 G jamesc@northeast.edu
CURRY, James .... 212-346-1200 319 J
CURRY, Janel .... 978-867-4063 215 D janel.curry@gordon.edu
CURRY, Jason .... 615-329-8582 431 I jcurry@fisk.edu
CURRY, Jason, R .... 615-329-8697 431 I jcurry@fisk.edu
CURRY, Keith .... 310-900-1600.. 40 C kcurry@elcamino.edu
CURRY, Melissa .... 937-294-6155 357 I melissa.curry@brightwood.edu
CURRY, Mike .... 352-395-5204 107 E michael.curry@sfcollege.edu
CURRY, Milton, S .... 213-740-2723.. 72 B archdean@usc.edu
CURRY, Molly .... 919-747-0007 347 D mpcurry@waketech.edu
CURRY, Ralph .... 906-786-5802 228 A curryr@baycollege.edu
CURRY, Reva .... 989-686-9298 229 J revacurry@delta.edu
CURRY, Robert .... 662-252-8000 255 F rcurry@rustcollege.edu
CURRY, Robert .... 805-922-6966.. 24 J rcurry@hancockcollege.edu
CURRY, Susan .... 618-514-3110 149 A susan.curry@principia.edu
CURRY, Susan .... 319-384-5452 166 G sue-curry@uiowa.edu
CURRY, Susan .... 601-318-6773 256 I scurry@wmcarey.edu
CURRY, Susan, J .... 319-335-3565 166 G sue-curry@uiowa.edu
CURRY, Terri, A .... 712-274-5259 172 A currytе@morningside.edu
CURRY, II, Theodore, H .... 517-353-5300 233 G thcurry@msu.edu
CURRY, Tim .... 606-546-1682 189 I tcurry@unionky.edu
CURRY, William, N .... 601-318-6103 256 I bill.curry@wmcarey.edu
CURRY, Yewston .... 706-821-8292 124 C ycurry@paine.edu
CURRY-ROBERTS, April, E .... 615-327-6453 434 A acurry@mmc.edu
CURTIN, Jason, E .... 410-546-6938 209 B jecurtin@salisbury.edu
CURTIN, Maria .... 508-565-1311 224 H mcurtin@stonehill.edu
CURTIN, Shawn, P .... 717-867-6207 399 J curtin@lvc.edu
CURTIN, Valerie .... 406-447-6913 271 I valerie.curtin@umhelena.edu
CURTIN, William .... 773-508-8851 144 D wcurtin@luc.edu
CURTIS, Amy .... 207-879-8757 199 C acurtis@idsva.org
CURTIS, Ardys, E .... 253-535-7149 496 G acurtis@plu.edu
CURTIS, Carolyn, G .... 518-629-7204 310 G c.curtis@hvcc.edu
CURTIS, Charles .... 903-813-2088 443 F ccurtis@austincollege.edu
CURTIS, Chris .... 912-344-2919 115 D chris.curtis@armstrong.edu
CURTIS, Christine .... 256-824-6335.... 8 C provost@uah.edu
CURTIS, Danielle .... 828-898-3478 339 B curtisd@lmc.edu
CURTIS, Deborah .... 716-286-8711 318 F dcurtis@niagara.edu
CURTIS, Deborah, J ...... 660-543-4116 268 A curtis@ucmo.edu
CURTIS, Elaine .... 931-540-2534 436 H bcurtis@columbiastate.edu
CURTIS, III, Guy, E ...... 540-868-4079 488 E gcurtis@lfcc.edu
CURTIS, Jason .... 805-546-3125.. 41 C jason_curtis@cuesta.edu
CURTIS, Jeanne, F .... 215-898-6300 412 G curtis@isc.upenn.edu
CURTIS, Jena .... 607-753-2979 327 A jena.curtis@cortland.edu
CURTIS, Jennifer .... 760-384-6212.. 47 B jennifer.curtis@cerrocoso.edu
CURTIS, Jerri .... 301-295-3638 518 G jerri.curtis@usuhs.edu
CURTIS, K. Tyler .... 620-341-5440 177 B kcurtis2@emporia.edu
CURTIS, Kelly, T .... 864-488-4601 422 B kcurtis@limestone.edu
CURTIS, Linda, H .... 919-516-4297 348 G lrhubbard@st-aug.edu
CURTIS, Marvin .... 574-520-4170 160 F mcurtis@iusb.edu
CURTIS, Matt .... 914-831-0313 305 C mcurtis@cw.edu
CURTIS, Michael .... 978-927-2300 215 D michael.curtis@gordon.edu
CURTIS, Michael, T .... 304-704-9111 501 H curtism@dewv.edu
CURTIS, Regina .... 413-775-1426 219 F curtis@gcc.mass.edu
CURTIS, Rick .... 406-243-2122 271 G richard.curtis@umontana.edu
CURTIS, Roxie .... 816-802-3437 261 C rcurtis@kcai.edu
CURTIS, Shannon .... 508-767-7248 210 I sj.curtis@assumption.edu
CURTIS, Tashana, M ...... 315-684-6520 329 F curtistm@morrisville.edu
CURTIS, Timothy .... 928-428-8220.. 12 I tim.curtis@eac.edu
CURTIS, Trina .... 828-726-2303 341 D tcurtis@cccti.edu
CURTIS-DIERKS, Erin .... 785-594-7890 174 J erin.curtis-dierks@bakeru.edu
CURTIS POWELL, Melissa .... 614-235-4136 370 M mcpowell@tlsohio.edu
CURTO, Stephen, A .... 732-224-2593 284 B scurto@brookdalecc.edu
CURTRIGHT, Jonathan, W .... 573-884-8738 268 C curtrightj@health.missouri.edu
CUSACK, Emma .... 949-794-9090.. 66 B ecusack@stanbridge.edu
CUSACK, Jacqueline, L . 973-596-6445 288 A jacqueline.l.cusack@njit.edu
CUSACK, Kristen .... 303-360-4701.. 79 C kristen.cusack@ccaurora.edu
CUSACK, Mary .... 810-762-0474 234 F
CUSATO, Brian .... 859-238-5205 184 C b.cusato@centre.edu
CUSEO, Amanda .... 915-779-8031 470 E acuseo@computercareercenter.com
CUSEO, Vincent .... 323-259-2700.. 54 E vcuseo@oxy.edu
CUSHENBERRY, Shalither .... 225-743-8500 193 C scushenberry@rpcc.edu
CUSHING, Katie .... 508-213-2111 223 C katie.cushing@nichols.edu
CUSHING, Mark .... 865-545-5330 433 C mark.cushing@lmunet.edu
CUSHING, Ryan .... 815-394-5047 150 C rcushing@rockford.edu
CUSHMAN, Brooke .... 208-792-2675 132 C blcushman@lcsc.edu
CUSHMAN, Robert .... 585-395-2032 326 D rcushman@brockport.edu
CUSHMAN, JR., Robert, A .... 707-965-6311.. 55 F president@puc.edu
CUSICK, Dianna .... 612-659-6319 245 F dianna.cusick@minneapolis.edu
CUSICK, Sherry .... 563-589-3721 173 J scusick@dbq.edu
CUSICK, Susan .... 773-896-2400 135 G scusick@ctschicago.edu
CUSSEN, Susan .... 845-451-1471 306 D susan.cussen@culinary.edu
CUSTER, Carole, A .... 515-294-9624 166 F cacuste@iastate.edu
CUSTER, Laura .... 859-344-3314 189 G custerl@thomasmore.edu
CUSTODIA-LORA, Noemi .... 978-738-7401 220 F ncustodialora@necc.mass.edu
CUTCHENS, Melinda ...... 229-333-5952 127 H cutchens@valdosta.edu
CUTCHIN, Jeff .... 618-393-2982 140 B cutchinj@iecc.edu
CUTCHINS, Cathy .... 757-569-6712 489 B ccutchins@pdc.edu
CUTHRELL, Patrick .... 252-335-0821 342 D patrick_cuthrell@albemarle.edu
CUTIETTA, Robert, A .... 213-740-5389.. 72 B musicdean@thornton.usc.edu
CUTLER, Amy .... 509-777-4733 500 H acutler@whitworth.edu
CUTLER, Brooke .... 310-506-4246.. 56 D brooke.cutler@pepperdine.edu
CUTLER, Chris .... 315-268-6745 304 B ccutler@clarkson.edu
CUTLER, Jerry .... 212-229-5671 316 E cutlerjm@newschool.edu
CUTLER, Nancy .... 408-554-4915.. 62 F ncutler@scu.edu
CUTLER, Stephen, J ...... 803-777-8310 424 I ashley@sccp.sc.edu
CUTONE, Joan .... 412-536-1079 398 E joan.cutone@laroche.edu
CUTRELL, Kathy .... 336-821-2470 338 G kcutrell@johnwesley.edu
CUTRELL, Lori .... 615-230-4834 438 C lori.cutrell@volstate.edu
CUTRI, David .... 419-530-6294 372 F david.cutri@utoledo.edu
CUTSHALL, Heather .... 620-223-2700 177 E heatherc@fortscott.edu
CUTSHAW, Kathleen, D . 808-956-9190 129 J cutshaw@hawaii.edu
CUTSHAW, Kyle .... 276-944-6528 480 J kcutshaw@ehc.edu
CUTSHAW, Oliver .... 213-615-7211.. 37 B ocutshaw@thechicagoschool.edu
CUTSPEC, John .... 828-251-6868 351 A jcutspec@unca.edu
CUTTING, Jeff .... 617-928-4573 222 D jcutting@mountida.edu
CUTTING, Judith .... 831-646-4000.. 52 G jcutting@mpc.edu
CUTTINO, Robert, E .... 770-538-4749 116 F rcuttino@brenau.edu
CUZYDLO, Karen .... 517-787-0800 231 E cuzydlokareni@jccmi.edu
CUZZOLINO, Robert, G . 215-871-6770 407 G bob@pcom.edu
CVETIC, Diane .... 925-969-3300.. 46 L dcvetic@jfku.edu
CVETIC, Mike .... 412-237-4146 392 G mcvetic@ccac.edu
CVITKOVIC, Vicky .... 847-543-6504 136 E vcvitkovic@clcillinois.edu
CWYK, Alysson .... 215-965-4050 402 C acwyk@moore.edu
CYGAN, Brian, L .... 570-326-3761 404 T brian.cygan@pct.edu
CYPHERS, Russell .... 276-523-7473 488 F rcyphers@mecc.edu
CYPRESS, Sharen .... 731-989-6986 432 C scypress@fhu.edu
CYR, Cheryl, A .... 860-253-3050.. 85 C ccyr@asnuntuck.edu
CYREE, Kendall, B .... 662-915-1103 256 C kbcyree@olemiss.edu
CYRUS, Cynthia, J .... 615-322-4474 440 D cynthia.j.cyrus@vanderbilt.edu
CYRUS, Kasundra .... 225-771-4660 195 K kasundra_cyrus@subr.edu
CZAJKA, Darcy .... 518-388-6101 332 B czajkad@union.edu
CZAPAR, George .... 217-333-5900 154 B gfc@illinois.edu
CZARAPATA, Paul .... 859-256-3100 185 D paul.czarapata@kctcs.edu
CZARDA, Lawrence, D ... 336-217-7221 338 B lczarda@greensboro.edu
CZARNECKI, John .... 716-926-8800 310 B jczarnecki@hilbet.edu
CZEKANSKI, Kathleen .... 215-951-1432 398 F czekanski@lasalle.edu
CZERWINSKI, Rick .... 540-887-7336 482 G rczerwin@marybaldwin.edu
CZOP-BARTLEY, Amy ..... 215-884-8942 415 C librarian@woninstitute.edu
CZUCHRY, Michael .... 830-372-6047 461 D mczuchry@tlu.edu
CZUPRYNSKI, Denise .... 406-791-5306 273 C denise.czuprynski@ugf.edu

D

DA GRACA, John .... 956-968-2132 460 B j-dagraca@tamuk.edu
DA SILVA, Jose .... 509-527-4300 499 E jose.dasilva@wwcc.edu
DAAR, Judith .... 714-444-4141.. 75 A jdaar@law.whittier.edu
DAAR, Karen .... 818-947-2378.. 49 G daarkl@lavc.edu
DAAS, Mahesh .... 785-864-3114 181 I mahesh@ku.edu
DABIDAT, Mike .... 212-812-4040 317 E mdabidat@nycda.edu
DABIRIAN, Amir .... 657-278-5000.. 32 B adabirian@fullerton.edu
DABNEY, Emily, C .... 662-846-4052 252 H edabney@deltastate.edu
DABNEY, Jerome .... 773-602-5252 135 L jdabney@ccc.edu
DABOLL-LAVOIE, Kathleen .... 585-389-2591 316 D kdaboll9@naz.edu
DABROWSKI, Jan .... 503-699-6275 384 B jdabrowski@marylhurst.edu
DACAL, Anita, S .... 412-578-6343 391 G dacalas@carlow.edu
DACE, Karen, L .... 317-278-3820 160 E kdace@iupui.edu
DACEY, Joe .... 508-565-1804 224 H jdacey@stonehill.edu
DACEY, Susan .... 973-748-9000 284 A susan_dacey@bloomfield.edu
DACHELET, Derek .... 608-822-2417 515 A ddachelet@swtc.edu
DACHILLE, Nancy .... 215-248-7048 392 D ndachill@chc.edu
DACOSTA, Dennis .... 718-960-8559 302 C dennis.dacosta@lehman.cuny.edu
DACOSTA, Herbert .... 309-694-5754 139 G herbert.dacosta@icc.edu
DACOSTA, Tracy, M .... 401-254-3541 417 C tdacosta@rwu.edu
DACUS, Kent .... 951-343-4687.. 28 G kdacus@calbaptist.edu
DADABHOY, Khushnur, Z .... 760-252-2411.. 27 A kdadabhoy@barstow.edu
DADABHOY, Zavareh .... 661-395-4204.. 47 A zav.dadabhoy@bakersfieldcollege.edu
DADARRIA, Nikki .... 908-835-9222 292 G ndadarria@warren.edu
DADEY, Cheryl .... 702-254-7577 279 G cheryl.dadey@northwestcareercollege.edu
DADEZ, Edward .... 352-588-8206 106 N ed.dadez@saintleo.edu
DADIAN PEREZ, Sara ... 603-623-0313 281 G saradadian@nhia.edu
DAFFER, Steve .... 405-733-7424 379 F sdaffer@rose.edu
DAFFRON, Jeanne .... 816-271-4234 264 B daffron@missouriwestern.edu
DAFLER, James, E .... 724-946-7313 414 C daflerje@westminster.edu
DAGANAAR, Mark .... 913-469-8500 178 F mdaganaar@jccc.edu
DAGG, Joey .... 304-876-5395 504 D jdagg@shepherd.edu
DAGGETT, Michael .... 518-243-4473 299 E daggettm@ellismedicine.org
DAGGETT, Natalie .... 575-769-4956 293 M natalie.daggett@clovis.edu
DAGGETT, Natalie .... 575-769-4115 293 M natalie.daggett@clovis.edu
DAGGETT, Paula .... 210-486-0224 442 A pdaggett@alamo.edu

DAGHER, Lisa, M .... 773-947-6320 145 A ldagher@mccormick.edu
DAGLEY, Stephen .... 978-927-2300 215 D stephen.dagley@gordon.edu
DAGUE, Saralyn .... 304-829-7835 501 F sdague@bethanywv.edu
DAHER, Michael .... 313-845-6460 231 B mdaher@hfcc.edu
DAHILL, Rosemary .... 914-395-2202 323 K rdahill@sarahlawrence.edu
DAHIYA, Rakesh .... 214-768-2802 457 B rdahiya@smu.edu
DAHL, Barbara, A .... 219-981-4235 160 C badahl@iun.edu
DAHL, Bonnie, L .... 701-355-8245 355 K bldahl@umary.edu
DAHL, Katie .... 303-369-5151.. 81 L katie.dahl@plattcolorado.edu
DAHL, Mark .... 503-768-7339 383 G dahl@lclark.edu
DAHL, Noel .... 415-703-9537.. 28 K ndahl@cca.edu
DAHL, Tracy .... 360-623-8388 493 A tracy.dahl@centralia.edu
DAHLBERG, Albert, A .... 401-863-1885 415 K albert_a_dahlberg@brown.edu
DAHLBERG, James .... 715-468-2815 515 D jim.dahlberg@witc.edu
DAHLBERG, Margaret .... 701-845-7200 354 E margaret.dahlberg@vcsu.edu
DAHLBERG, Steve .... 218-935-0417 251 F sdahlberg@wetcc.edu
DAHLBERG, Teresa .... 315-443-4341 330 H dahlberg@syr.edu
DAHLE, Tammi .... 205-665-6262.... 8 E dahlet@montevallo.edu
DAHLEN, David, L .... 507-284-4839 241 F dahlen.david@mayo.edu
DAHLEN, David, L .... 507-284-2749 241 E dahlen.david@mayo.edu
DAHLER, Nathan .... 513-721-7944 362 D ndahler@gbs.edu
DAHLGREN, Donna, J ... 812-941-2682 161 A ddahlgre@ius.edu
DAHLGREN, Jean .... 518-292-1704 321 G scadean@sage.edu
DAHLGREN, Jerod, T .... 716-878-5569 326 E dahlgrjt@buffalostate.edu
DAHLINGER MEANS, Gretchen .... 213-740-5086.. 72 B gdahlinger@hr.usc.edu
DAHLOR, Cara .... 816-415-5223 270 C dahlorc@william.jewell.edu
DAHLQUIST, Kent, R ..... 610-683-4027 406 D dahlquis@kutztown.edu
DAHLQUIST, Sally .... 651-450-3567 245 A sdahlqu@inverhills.edu
DAHLSTROM, Duane ..... 320-308-5026 247 F ddahlstrom@sctcc.edu
DAHLSTROM, Joe, F ..... 361-570-4150 465 D dahlstromj@uhv.edu
DAHLSTROM, Joe, F ..... 361-570-4150 470 A joe.dahlstrom@victoriacollege.edu
DAHLSTROM, Thomas, A .... 610-341-5898 394 E tdahlstr@eastern.edu
DAHLVANG, Donna, R .. 715-394-8393 512 B ddahlva1@uwsuper.edu
DAHMES, Victoria .... 504-398-2237 196 E vdahmes@uhcno.edu
DAHMS, David, W .... 563-562-3263 172 D dahmsd@nicc.edu
DAHNERT, Stephen .... 845-437-5500 333 A stdahnert@vassar.edu
DAHULICH, Michael ...... 570-561-1818 410 A bishop.michael@stots.edu
DAI, Hai-Lung .... 215-204-9570 411 B hai-lung.dai@temple.edu
DAICHENDT, Jim .... 619-849-2412.. 57 H jimdaichendt@pointloma.edu
DAIEK, Deborah .... 734-462-4400 236 H ddaiek@schoolcraft.edu
DAIG, Bart .... 810-766-4280 227 E bart.daig@baker.edu
DAIGLE, Anna .... 337-421-6954 193 F anna.daigle@sowela.edu
DAIGLE, Claire .... 415-351-3573.. 60 G cdaigle@sfai.edu
DAIGLE, David .... 207-216-4410 200 E ddaigle@yccc.edu
DAIGLE, Dick .... 757-490-1241 477 F ddaigle@auto.edu
DAIGLER, David .... 207-629-4000 199 J ddaigler@mccs.me.edu
DAILEY, Bracken, J .... 951-827-3427.. 69 D bracken.dailey@ucr.edu
DAILEY, Brian .... 910-962-3711 352 A daileyb@uncw.edu
DAILEY, David .... 218-749-7772 245 D d.dailey@mesabirange.edu
DAILEY, Deborah .... 215-489-2915 393 F deborah.dailey@delval.edu
DAILEY, Janine .... 617-731-7623 223 F jdailey@pmc.edu
DAILEY, Kathlyn, C .... 512-245-2208 463 A kd01@txstate.edu
DAILEY, Samantha .... 815-825-9324 142 F samantha.dailey@kishwaukeecollege.edu
DAILEY, Tim .... 541-888-7439 387 A tdailey@socc.edu
DAILY, Daniel, R .... 605-677-5371 428 E daniel.daily@usd.edu
DAILY, Hall, P .... 626-395-6256.. 29 I hdaily@caltech.edu
DAIN, Benny .... 580-349-1560 377 E bdain@opsu.edu
DAIN, Claudette, E .... 626-914-8886.. 37 G cdain@citruscollege.edu
DAIRE, Andrew, P .... 804-827-2670 487 E apdaire@vcu.edu
DAIS, Olga .... 646-312-3320 301 B olga.dais@baruch.cuny.edu
DAISEY, Mary Beth, B .. 856-225-2825 290 B daisey@camden.rutgers.edu
DAISY, Jennifer .... 620-431-2820 180 C jdaisy@neosho.edu
DAISY, Joseph, M .... 691-320-2480 519 G jdaisy@comfsm.fm
DAITCH, Jonathan .... 562-977-6013.. 43 H jonathan.daitch@fremont.edu
DAKOTA, Cherie .... 906-524-8403 232 D cdakota@kbocc.edu
DAKWAR, Mohammad .. 414-297-8087 514 C dakwarmm@matc.edu
DALBEY, Mark .... 314-434-4044 259 B shannon.hathaway@covenantseminary.edu
DALBOW, Dawn, S .... 540-828-5310 478 J ddalbow@bridgewater.edu
DALE, Alan .... 405-682-1611 377 C alan.dale@occc.edu
DALE, Amie, G .... 757-594-7672 479 H amie.dale@cnu.edu
DALE, Cheryl .... 601-318-6199 256 I cheryl.dale@wmcarey.edu
DALE, Dianna, C .... 610-361-2448 402 G daled@neumann.edu
DALE, Elizabeth .... 215-503-5138 411 E elizabeth.dale@jefferson.edu
DALE, Karen .... 520-452-2621.. 11 R dalek@cochise.edu
DALE, Kimberly .... 954-776-4476 102 G kdale@keiseruniversity.edu
DALE, Kory, J .... 479-524-7116.. 20 B kdale@jbu.edu
DALE, Lynn, F .... 864-592-4833 424 C dalel@sccsc.edu
DALE, Marc .... 630-466-7900 155 C mdale@waubonsee.edu
DALE, Paul .... 480-731-8101.. 13 D paul.dale@domail.maricopa.edu
DALE, Paul .... 602-787-6610.. 13 J paul.dale@paradisevalley.edu
DALE, Valjean .... 510-723-6716.. 36 C vdale@chabotcollege.edu
DALE-CARTER, April ...... 909-384-8922.. 59 I acarter@sbccd.cc.ca.us
DALE-CARTER, April ...... 909-794-2161.. 59 H
DALEKE, David .... 812-855-6902 159 H daleked@indiana.edu
DALENE, Jack .... 435-283-7130 474 A jack.dalene@snow.edu
DALES, Sandra .... 910-695-3789 346 E daless@sandhills.edu
DALEY, Ben .... 619-398-4902.. 45 F bdaley@hightechhigh.org
DALEY, Carol .... 540-338-2700 501 G cdaley@cdu.edu
DALEY, Elizabeth, M ...... 213-740-2804.. 72 B edaley@cinema.usc.edu
DALEY, George, Q .... 617-495-1000 215 G
DALEY, Karen .... 616-698-7111 229 D kdaley@davenport.edu
DALEY, Ken .... 641-472-1163 171 J kdaley@mum.edu
DALEY, Maggie .... 617-746-1990 216 A maggie.daley@hult.edu
DALEY, Michael, D .... 716-673-3434 325 C michael.daley@fredonia.edu
DALEY, Suzanne, L .... 518-564-2080 327 E daleysl@plattsburgh.edu
DALGLISH, Lucy, A .... 301-405-2383 207 G dalglish@umd.edu
DALLAM, Colleen, C ..... 410-334-2864 210 C cdallam@worwic.edu
DALLAS, Derek .... 217-403-4599 148 H ddallas@parkland.edu
DALLAVALLE, Nancy ...... 203-254-4000.. 87 A ndallavalle@fairfield.edu
DALLAVALLE, Til .... 732-906-2602 287 B tdallavalle@middlesexcc.edu
DALLENBACH, Dave ...... 610-917-1402 413 G d_dallenbach@valleyforge.edu
DALLY, Brenda .... 580-581-2230 375 A brendad@cameon.edu
DALLY, Tammy .... 619-201-8670.. 60 A tammy.dally@sdcc.edu
DALMAGE, Sharon .... 818-710-2523.. 49 D dalmagsc@piercecollege.edu
DALONZO, Beth, A .... 740-826-8041 366 C bdalonzo@muskingum.edu
DALPES, Paulette .... 303-360-4824.. 79 C paulette.dalpes@ccaurora.edu
DALRYMPLE, Jim .... 417-626-1234 264 J dalrymple.jim@occ.edu
DALRYMPLE, Scott .... 573-875-7200 258 F sdalrymple@ccis.edu
DALSING, Deirdre, L ..... 608-342-1865 511 D dalsingd@uwplatt.edu
DALSKE, James .... 707-654-1070.. 32 E jdalske@csum.edu
DALTON, Amy .... 937-327-7457 374 A daltona@wittenberg.edu
DALTON, Brenda .... 404-270-5245 126 D bdalton@spelman.edu
DALTON, Brenda .... 972-860-4677 447 G bdalton@dcccd.edu
DALTON, Brett, A .... 864-656-2444 419 F dbrett@clemson.edu
DALTON, Brian .... 607-871-2406 298 A dalton@alfred.edu
DALTON, Dana .... 910-672-1811 350 B ddalton4@uncfsu.edu
DALTON, Dixie .... 434-736-2085 489 E dixie.dalton@southside.edu
DALTON, Dori .... 419-559-2342 370 J ddalton@terra.edu
DALTON, Jaime .... 620-235-4101 180 J jdalton@pittstate.edu
DALTON, James .... 845-938-2050 519 D 8ord@usma.edu
DALTON, James, T .... 734-764-7312 237 I daltonjt@umich.edu
DALTON, Jill .... 207-699-5018 199 H jdalton@meca.edu
DALTON, John .... 765-973-8450 160 A jodalton@iue.edu
DALTON, Judith .... 215-572-4088 389 D daltonj@arcadia.edu
DALTON, Thomas .... 518-464-8632 308 A tdalton@excelsior.edu
DALTON, Valerie .... 404-215-2666 123 E valerie.dalton@morehouse.edu
DALTON, Walter, H .... 828-395-1300 344 A wdalton@isothermal.edu
DALTON-RUSSELL, Belinda .... 270-534-3081 187 C belinda.dalton-russell@kctcs.edu
DALY, Adrian .... 213-621-2200.. 39 A
DALY, Brian .... 619-239-0391.. 35 C bdaly@cwsl.edu
DALY, Cory .... 307-855-2186 516 I cdaly@cwc.edu
DALY, Dion .... 716-829-8176 307 B dalyd@dyc.edu
DALY, Erin .... 952-358-8834 246 D erin.daly@normandale.edu
DALY, Jacqueline .... 908-835-2309 292 G jdaly@warren.edu
DALY, Jerry .... 909-558-4581.. 48 H jdaly@llu.edu
DALY, Jillian .... 209-575-6159.. 75 J dalyj@mjc.edu
DALY, Jon .... 860-628-4751.. 87 E jdaly@lincolncollegene.edu
DALY, Jonathan, P .... 805-525-4417.. 67 E jdaly@thomasaquinas.edu
DALY, Kathleen .... 850-644-1000 110 A kdaly@fsu.edu
DALY, Kelly .... 714-432-0202.. 38 H kdaly@occ.cccd.edu
DALY, Lois, K .... 518-783-2306 324 C daly@siena.edu
DALY, Mark .... 620-341-6522 177 B mdaly@emporia.edu
DALY, Melissa .... 856-227-7200 284 E mdaly@camdencc.edu
DALY, Rebecca .... 906-487-7253 230 B rebecca.daly@finlandia.edu
DALY, Ross .... 914-251-6550 328 B ross.daly@purchase.edu
DALY EIMER, Anne, M . 856-691-8600 285 C adaly@cccnj.edu
DALZELL, Douglas .... 410-951-3826 208 F ddalzell@coppin.edu
DALZIEL, Murray .... 410-837-4955 209 D mdalziel@ubalt.edu
DAM, Stacy .... 402-481-8698 273 F stacy.dam@bryanhealthcollege.edu
DAMARI, David .... 231-591-3706 230 A daviddamari@ferris.edu
DAMAS, Tammi, L .... 202-806-4859.. 92 C tammi.damas@howard.edu
DAMAZO, Dennis, E ...... 724-847-5678 395 J dedamazo@geneva.edu
DAMES, Christopher ...... 314-516-6473 268 E cdames@umsl.edu
DAMES, Jeanine .... 203-432-0800.. 89 G jeanine.dames@yale.edu
DAMEWOOD, Tony, M .. 402-552-6109 273 K damewood@clarksoncollege.edu
DAMIANI, Glenn .... 505-224-3223 293 L gdamiani@cnm.edu
DAMIANI, Joel, J .... 716-851-1405 307 I damiani@ecc.edu
DAMIANI, Susan, M ...... 718-990-7562 322 F damianis@stjohns.edu
DAMIANO, Fred .... 315-781-3955 310 C damiano@hws.edu
DAMICI, Lindsay .... 802-654-2000 476 A
DAMICO, Debra, L .... 718-862-7213 313 L debra.damico@manhattan.edu
DAMICO, Paul .... 252-638-0156 342 E damicop@cravencc.edu
DAMINSKI, Sara, M ...... 314-286-3658 265 F smdaninski@ranken.edu
DAMM, Richard, T .... 920-748-8322 509 H dammr@ripon.edu
DAMMER, Bob .... 310-434-4397.. 62 G dammer_bob@smc.edu
DAMMERS, Rick .... 856-256-4551 289 H
DAMMON, Robert .... 412-268-3696 391 H rd19@andrew.cmu.edu
DAMON, Jud .... 904-819-6252.. 98 I jdamon@flagler.edu
DAMPEER, Angela .... 817-531-4444 463 G adampeer@txwes.edu
DAMPHOUSSE, Kelly ..... 870-972-3030.. 18 A kdamp@astate.edu
DAMPIER, Paul .... 212-346-1200 319 J
DAMPIER, Paula .... 770-297-5896 116 F pland@brenau.edu
DAMRAUER, Robert .... 303-315-2131.. 83 D robert.damrauer@ucdenver.edu
DAMRON, Karla .... 214-860-2473 448 A kdamron@dcccd.edu
DAMRON, Laura .... 606-218-5272 190 E lauradamron@upike.edu
DAMRON, Nancy .... 913-971-3533 179 H nldamron@mnu.edu
DAMRON, Ronald .... 606-218-5276 190 E ronalddamron@upike.edu
DAMRON, Steve .... 254-968-9227 459 A sdamron@tarleton.edu
DAMRON, Toni .... 325-649-8097 450 H tdamron@hputx.edu
DAMROSE-MAHLMANN, Christine .... 757-822-1298 489 H cmahlmann@tcc.edu
DAMROW, Bobbi .... 715-422-5421 514 B bobbi.damrow@mstc.edu
DAMROW, Bobbi .... 715-675-3331 514 F damrow@ntc.edu
DAMS, Scott .... 610-861-1601 402 D damss@moravian.edu
DAMSCHRODER, Matthew .... 814-641-3151 398 B damschm@juniata.edu
DAN, Chong .... 704-216-6035 339 E cdan@livingstone.edu
DANA, Robert, Q .... 207-581-1405 201 B rdana@maine.edu
DANA, Samantha .... 413-755-5337 221 B sidana@stcc.edu
DANAHAR, David .... 337-482-6454 197 F david.danahar@louisiana.edu
DANAJOVITS, Joseph .... 860-738-6368.. 86 C jdanajovits@nwcc.edu
DANCE, Andrea .... 252-335-0821 342 D andrea_dance@albemarle.edu
DANCER, Erin .... 770-426-2974 122 F erin.dancer@life.edu
DANCKAERT, Seraphim . 570-561-1818 410 A seraphim.danckaert@stots.edu
DANCY, Gerlinde .... 963-638-2941 114 A dancygl@webber.edu
DANCY, Regina, M .... 704-636-6454 338 F rdancy@hoodseminary.edu
DANDELAKE, George .... 904-470-8150.. 98 B g.dandelake@ewc.edu

DANDO, Mary 303-492-2975 83 B mary.dando@colorado.edu

DANDORPH, Michael 312-942-5756 150 F michael_dandorph@rush.edu

DANDRIDGE, Horace 313-927-1555 233 D hdandridge@marygrove.edu

DANE, Jane, H 757-683-6702 483 G jhdane@odu.edu

DANEAU, Nancy, S 212-998-2015 318 D nancy.daneau@nyu.edu

DANEIL, Chris 813-974-2628 111 A cldaniel@usf.edu

DANEN, Todd 920-403-3943 509 J todd.danen@snc.edu

DANES, Mark 515-271-1661 168 G mark.danes@dmu.edu

DANFORD, Richard, K 740-376-4736 365 A richard.danford@marietta.edu

DANFORD, Thomas 916-568-3018 50 E danfort@losrios.edu

DANFORTH, Dave 218-281-8490 250 G danfo002@umn.edu

DANFORTH, Elizabeth 406-994-3836 272 A danforth@montana.edu

DANG, Hung, D 805-437-8918 31 C hung.dang@csuci.edu

DANG-WILLIAMS, Thao 314-246-8757 269 N thaodangwilliams@webster.edu

DANGERFIELD, Deneen 410-462-8311 202 F dedangerfield@bccc.edu

DANHAUSER, Susan 770-537-5353 128 F susan.danhauser@westgatech.edu

DANHEISER, Priscilla, R 478-301-2084 122 H danheiser_p@mercer.edu

DANICA, Kathleen 518-244-4552 321 G bouchk2@sage.edu

DANIEL, Andrea, D 706-355-5111 115 H adaniel@athenstech.edu

DANIEL, Brett 903-675-6393 464 C bdaniel@tvcc.edu

DANIEL, Chris 606-886-3863 185 F chris.daniel@kctcs.edu

DANIEL, David, E 512-499-4201 467 A ddaniel@utsystem.edu

DANIEL, Dean 940-855-4322 470 I danield@wbu.edu

DANIEL, Eileen 585-395-5505 326 D edaniel@brockport.edu

DANIEL, Juliet 828-225-3993 337 A admissions@daoisttraditions.edu

DANIEL, Kathleen 305-809-3248 99 L kathleen.daniel@fkcc.edu

DANIEL, Kevin, S 719-587-7741 76 D ksdaniel@adams.edu

DANIEL, Larry 843-953-5097 419 D ldaniel@citadel.edu

DANIEL, Meredith 864-941-8442 423 C meredith.d@ptc.edu

DANIEL, Mick 864-977-7160 422 I mick.daniel@ngu.edu

DANIEL, Nancy 828-448-3160 347 F ndaniel@wpcc.edu

DANIEL, Nancy, C 617-449-7068 225 C nancy.daniel@urbancollege.edu

DANIEL, Robin, L 336-272-7102 338 B rdaniel@greensboro.edu

DANIEL, Sharlene 423-775-6596 435 H sdaniel@ogs.edu

DANIEL, Sherman 680-488-2471 520 E shermand1961@yahoo.com

DANIEL, Steve, G 678-664-0530 128 F steve.daniel@westgatech.edu

DANIEL, Tamara 731-286-3322 437 A tdaniel@dscc.edu

DANIEL, W. John 205-934-3474 8 B wdaniel@uab.edu

DANIEL-ROBINSON, Kim 973-720-3678 292 I danielrobinsonk@wpunj.edu

DANIELL, Steven 817-531-4405 463 G sdaniell@txwes.edu

DANIELS, Andrea 910-410-1724 345 G asdaniels@richmondcc.edu

DANIELS, C. Wess 336-316-2445 338 C danielscw@guilford.edu

DANIELS, Christy 252-328-6212 349 I danielsc@ecu.edu

DANIELS, Clayton 706-379-3111 128 H cpdaniels@yhc.edu

DANIELS, Cordelia 503-821-8881 385 H cdaniels@pnca.edu

DANIELS, Debra 661-763-7710 67 A ddaniels@taftcollege.edu

DANIELS, Delika 212-772-4804 302 E

DANIELS, Dennis, E 936-261-3085 458 F dedaniels@pvamu.edu

DANIELS, Eric 732-255-0400 288 B edaniels@ocean.edu

DANIELS, George, T 919-572-1625 335 F gdaniels14@apexsot.edu

DANIELS, Gerri, L 906-227-2650 235 A gdaniels@nmu.edu

DANIELS, Heather, M 608-263-1011 510 C soas@soas.wisc.edu

DANIELS, III, Jack, E 608-246-6676 514 A jdanielsiii@madisoncollege.edu

DANIELS, Jim 508-678-2811 219 C jim.daniels@bristolcc.edu

DANIELS, Julie 601-974-1443 254 A julie.daniels@millsaps.edu

DANIELS, LaMetrius 615-248-1521 439 B ldaniels@trevecca.edu

DANIELS, Linda 601-977-4462 256 B ldaniels@tougaloo.edu

DANIELS, Lisa 518-608-8398 308 A ldaniels@excelsior.edu

DANIELS, Mark 425-235-2352 497 E mdaniels@rtc.edu

DANIELS, Martin, C 518-276-6813 321 A daniem@rpi.edu

DANIELS, Matt 641-844-5708 170 I matt.daniels@iavalley.edu

DANIELS, Michael 617-585-0200 212 C michael.daniels@the-bac.edu

DANIELS, Michael 828-448-3564 347 F mdaniels@wpcc.edu

DANIELS, JR., Mitchell, E 765-494-4600 163 C

DANIELS, Orangel, J 910-362-7129 341 E odaniels@cfcc.edu

DANIELS, Patti, J 618-537-6936 145 C pjdaniels@mckendree.edu

DANIELS, Randell, W 734-384-4224 234 C rdaniels@monroeccc.edu

DANIELS, Rick 815-921-4284 150 A s.daniels@rockvalleycollege.edu

DANIELS, Ronald, J 410-516-4170 204 F president@jhu.edu

DANIELS, Rowena 229-430-2799 114 I rowena.daniels@asurams.edu

DANIELS, Terri, G 407-582-6801 113 F tdaniels31@valenciacollege.edu

DANIELS, Ursula 201-612-5355 283 I udaniels@bergen.edu

DANIELSEN, Randy 480-219-6009 257 A rdanielsen@atsu.edu

DANIELSON, Eric 301-447-5505 206 B danielson@msmary.edu

DANIELSON, Lisa, M 920-424-3007 511 B danielsn@uwosh.edu

DANIELSON, Marsha 507-389-7426 247 H marsha.danielson@southcentral.edu

DANIELSON, Mary Ann 402-280-2535 274 D maddam@creighton.edu

DANIELSON, Michelle 507-285-7180 247 D michelle.danielson@rctc.edu

DANIELSON, Timothy 414-229-4463 511 A danieltj@uwm.edu

DANIEU, Paul, F 716-851-1856 307 I danieu@ecc.edu

DANIK, Steve 410-951-3575 208 F sdanik@coppin.edu

DANILOWICZ, Bret 405-744-5663 377 F bret.danilowicz@okstate.edu

DANKEL, Richard 401-232-6117 416 A rdankel@bryant.edu

DANKO, James 413-755-4812 221 B jdanko@stcc.edu

DANKO, James, M 317-940-9900 156 I president@butler.edu

DANLEY, Charrita, D 757-727-5231 481 E charrita.danley@hamptonu.edu

DANLEY, Stacy 803-533-3743 423 G sdanley@scsu.edu

DANNA, Debra 504-864-7550 194 G danna@loyno.edu

DANNA, John 716-851-1360 307 I danna@ecc.edu

DANNA, Stephen 518-792-5425 327 E dann1253@plattsburgh.edu

DANNECKER, Ronald 716-829-7600 307 B dannecrh@dyc.edu

DANNEMILLER, Stanley, D 330-325-6558 366 F sdannemiller@neomed.edu

DANNEN, Troy 504-865-5500 196 D tdannen@tulane.edu

DANNENBAUM, Martha, C 979-458-8300 459 C mdannenbaum@tamu.edu

DANNENBERG, Dave 907-786-4447 10 A ddannenberg@alaska.edu

DANNER, Deborah 509-359-2383 494 D ddanner2@ewu.edu

DANNER, John, P 210-458-4105 468 B john.danner@utsa.edu

DANNER, Megan 512-863-1056 457 I davidsom@southwestern.edu

DANOWITZ, Mary Ann 919-515-5900 350 E mdanowi@ncsu.edu

DANSBY, Bob 334-291-4965 1 H bob.dansby@cv.edu

DANSER, Dolores, A 717-245-1589 394 A danserd@dickinson.edu

DANTLEY, Michael 513-529-6317 365 I dantleme@miamioh.edu

DANUFF, Allan 352-854-2322 97 C danuffa@cf.edu

DANZI, SJ, Rocco 201-761-6014 291 D rdanzi@saintpeters.edu

DANZY, Jamia 585-292-3010 315 L jdanzy1@monroecc.edu

DAO, Chau 909-274-4450 52 I cdao@mtsac.edu

DAOAS, Doman 691-320-2480 519 G daoas@comfsm.fm

DAOOD, Christopher 262-691-5314 515 B cdaood@wctc.edu

DAOUST, Carolyn 989-358-7211 227 A daoust@alpenacc.edu

DAPICE-WONG, Stephanie 631-665-1600 331 F stephanie.wong@touro.edu

DAPP, Kelly 661-362-3983 39 C kelly.dapp@canyons.edu

DAPRA, Joe 816-322-0110 257 M joe.dapra@calvary.edu

DAQUILA, August 609-343-5116 283 D adaquila@atlantic.edu

DARABI, Rachelle 417-836-8346 263 H rachelledarabi@missouristate.edu

DARAFSHI, Gloria 650-306-3479 61 R darafshi@smccd.edu

DARBANDI, Shiva 207-699-5090 199 H sdarbandi@meca.edu

DARBEAU, Ron 479-788-7611 22 A ron.darbeau@uafs.edu

DARBONE, Davidson 337-421-6940 193 F david.darbone@sowela.edu

DARBUT, Jeff 480-461-7382 13 I jeffrey.darbut@mesacc.edu

DARBY, Kadia 212-616-7263 309 G kadia.darby@helenefuld.edu

DARBY, Shani 212-431-2896 317 H shani.darby@nyls.edu

DARCANGELO, Robin 562-938-4387 48 I rdarcangelo@lbcc.edu

DARCY, Kip 810-762-7331 232 C kdarcy@kettering.edu

DARDEN, Alyssa 614-947-6685 362 A alyssa.darden@franklin.edu

DARDEN, Elbert 816-501-4275 265 I elbert.darden@rockhurst.edu

DARDEN, Joanna 901-572-2448 430 C joanna.darden@bchs.edu

DARDEN-BEAUFORD, Yulonda 404-225-4488 115 J ybeauford@atlantatech.edu

DARDIS, Greg 503-675-3969 384 B gdardis@marylhurst.edu

DARGA, Richard 773-995-2378 135 F rdarga@csu.edu

DARIAROW, Esmail 239-939-4766 108 H edariarow@southerntech.edu

DARIN, Jessica 805-756-6000 30 K darin@calpoly.edu

DARK, Shawna 562-985-8115 32 C shawna.dark@csulb.edu

DARLACK, James 978-468-7111 215 E jdarlack@gordonconwell.edu

DARLAND, Suzanne 270-706-8460 185 H suzanne.darland@kctcs.edu

DARLAND, Zane 606-693-5000 187 D zdarland@kmbc.edu

DARLEY, Maria 706-729-2306 116 B mdarley@augusta.edu

DARLING, Candida 801-957-4186 474 B candida.darling@slcc.edu

DARLING, Diane 215-612-6600 390 B ddarling@chicareers.com

DARLING, Douglas, D 701-662-1506 355 A doug.darling@lrsc.edu

DARLING, Hilary 661-253-7724 29 F hdarling@calarts.edu

DARLINGTON, Carol 989-386-6625 234 B cdarlington@midmich.edu

DARMODY, Brian, P 301-405-1990 207 G bdarmody@umd.edu

DARMON, Robin 619-260-4654 71 J rdarmon@sandiego.edu

DARMSTAEDTER, Nicholous 901-272-5177 434 B ndarmstaedter@mca.edu

DARNALL, Teresa 828-898-8752 339 B darnallt@lmc.edu

DARNALL BURKE, Randi 707-826-3361 34 A darnall@humboldt.edu

DARNELL, Charles 435-797-1952 473 C charles.darnell@usu.edu

DARNELL, Darrell, L 202-994-1000 92 A ddarnell@gwu.edu

DARR, Eric, D 717-901-5111 397 E edarr@harrisburgu.edu

DARR, Kristi 515-294-6458 166 F kdarr@iastate.edu

DARR, Roy (Alan) 330-684-8916 371 D adarr@uakron.edu

DARR, Steven 863-638-7230 113 I steven.darr@warner.edu

DARRAH, Thom 541-885-1600 385 E thom.darrah@oit.edu

DARRELL, Bart 270-852-3104 187 F bdarrell@kwc.edu

DARROCH, Jenny 909-607-3811 37 L jenny.darroch@cgu.edu

DARROUZET, Hunter 563-588-8192 167 E hunter.darrouzet@clarke.edu

DARROW, Denny 765-494-7395 163 C

DARROW, Louis 330-490-7373 373 F ldarrow@walsh.edu

DARST, Valerie 660-263-4100 264 C valeried@macc.edu

DART, Lucas 308-698-5270 277 F ldart@nufoundation.org

DARTY, Roxanne 210-690-9000 449 K rdarty@hallmarkuniversity.edu

DARWIN, John, W 402-280-3994 274 D johndarwin@creighton.edu

DARWIN, Mike 205-726-4241 6 G mdarwin@samford.edu

DAS, A. Andrew 630-617-3541 138 C adas@elmhurst.edu

DAS, Pradeep, K 404-627-2681 116 E pradeep.das@beulah.edu

DASBURG, Deanne 828-884-8129 335 L dasburg@brevard.edu

DASCHBACH, Hugh 210-999-8490 464 B hdaschba@trinity.edu

DASEY-MORALES, Maureen 316-978-3440 182 F maureen.dasey-morales@wichita.edu

DASGUPTA, Nandini 510-869-6597 59 F ndasgupta@samuelmerritt.edu

DASHE, Alejandra 952-888-4777 249 F adashe@nwhealth.edu

DASHER, Leah 912-538-3186 126 A ldasher@southeasterntech.edu

DASHIELD, Richeleen 908-526-1200 289 D richeleen.dashield@raritanval.edu

DASHIELL, Christian 620-278-4341 181 G cdashiell@sterling.edu

DASIGI, Venu 419-372-8719 357 F vdasigi@bgsu.edu

DASILVA, Jose 940-872-4002 453 L jdasilva@nctc.edu

DASILVA, Joseph 413-755-4889 221 B jdasilva@stcc.edu

DASILVA, Kirsten 201-684-7621 289 C kdasilv1@ramapo.edu

DASILVA, Yvonne 713-348-2697 455 F

DASINGER, Royce 334-670-3365 7 E rdansinger@troy.edu

DASTMOZD, Rassoul 651-846-1335 247 G rassoul.dastmozd@saintpaul.edu

DATCHER, Dwight 617-879-2238 226 A ddatcher@wheelock.edu

DATEMA, Betsy 574-232-2408 163 F bdatema@rtuvt.com

DATHER, Julie 605-668-1525 427 F jdather@mtmc.edu

DATTA, Sumana 979-845-6774 459 C sumad@tamu.edu

DATTAGUPTA, Satya 504-865-5731 196 D dattagupta@tulane.edu

DATUIN, Bonnie Mae, M 671-735-5616 519 H bonniemae.datuin@guamcc.edu

DAU, Kristen 907-442-3400 10 B krdau@alaska.edu

DAUBENMIRE, Jeff 740-753-6122 362 K daubenmirej@hocking.edu

DAUBERMAN, Barbara, A 804-752-7300 484 C bdauberman@rmc.edu

DAUBERT, Christopher, R 573-882-0368 268 C daubertc@missouri.edu

DAVIS, Cheryl .... 270-745-6733 190 F
cheryl.davis@wku.edu
DAVIS, Chris .... 706-385-1041 124 F
chris.davis@point.edu
DAVIS, Chris .... 501-450-3321.. 23 I
cdavis@uca.edu
DAVIS, Christine .... 479-619-3156.. 20 F
cdavis22@nwacc.edu
DAVIS, Christine .... 239-433-6950 100 E
christine.davis@fsw.edu
DAVIS, Christopher .... 602-943-2311.. 17 F
christopher.davis@west.edu
DAVIS, Christopher, A .. 410-293-6381 519 E
cdavis@usna.edu
DAVIS, Chuck .... 206-934-4340 497 I
chuck.davis@seattlecolleges.edu
DAVIS, Cliff .... 708-344-4700 144 A
cdavis@lincolntech.edu
DAVIS, Cliff .... 417-447-2652 264 K
davisc@otc.edu
DAVIS, Colin .... 309-649-6395 152 G
colin.davis@src.edu
DAVIS, Connie .... 985-549-2094 197 E
cdavis@selu.edu
DAVIS, D. Scott .... 478-301-2110 122 H
davis_ds@mercer.edu
DAVIS, Dan .... 701-228-5451 354 G
danny.davis@dakotacollege.edu
DAVIS, Dana .... 478-445-2301 117 D
ddavis@centralgatech.edu
DAVIS, Daniel .... 212-854-6939 299 B
ddavis@barnard.edu
DAVIS, Daniel .... 817-722-1614 451 G
daniel.davis@tku.edu
DAVIS, Danny .... 413-748-3532 224 G
ddavis@springfieldcollege.edu
DAVIS, Daryl, J .... 407-582-1255 113 F
djdavis@valenciacollege.edu
DAVIS, David, H .... 828-694-1845 341 B
daviddav@blueridge.edu
DAVIS, Deborah .... 804-828-0100 487 E
deborah.davis@vcuhealth.org
DAVIS, Debra, C .... 251-445-9404.... 9 B
ddavis@southalabama.edu
DAVIS, Deidra .... 207-326-2138 200 F
deidra.davis@mma.edu
DAVIS, Denise .... 314-264-1000 269 G
denise.davis@vatterott.edu
DAVIS, Denise, L .... 804-862-6100 484 F
ddavis@rbc.edu
DAVIS, Derrick .... 301-860-3427 208 E
dldavis@bowiestate.edu
DAVIS, Diana .... 513-244-4301 366 A
diana.davis@msj.edu
DAVIS, Dirk .... 951-343-3905.. 28 G
ddavis@calbaptist.edu
DAVIS, Don .... 626-815-3828.. 26 U
ddavis@apu.edu
DAVIS, Donald, L .... 972-883-6176 467 D
don.davis@utdallas.edu
DAVIS, Donna .... 760-757-2121.. 52 F
ddavis@miracosta.edu
DAVIS, Donna .... 636-922-8300 265 J
ddavis@stchas.edu
DAVIS, Donna, J .... 415-422-6822.. 72 A
davisdj@usfca.edu
DAVIS, Dwayne, L .... 719-333-9751 518 H
DAVIS, Ed, L .... 404-880-8475 117 H
edavis@cau.edu
DAVIS, Eddie .... 972-825-4686 457 F
edavis@sagu.edu
DAVIS, Elizabeth .... 410-871-3376 205 E
emdavis@mcdaniel.edu
DAVIS, Elizabeth .... 864-294-2100 421 I
elizabeth.davis@furman.edu
DAVIS, Elizabeth, B .... 415-422-2508.. 72 A
ebdavis@usfca.edu
DAVIS, Ellen .... 254-298-8591 458 C
ellen.davis@templejc.edu
DAVIS, Eric .... 505-424-2351 294 C
eric.davis@iaia.edu
DAVIS, Erik .... 805-969-3626.. 55 G
edavis@pacifica.edu
DAVIS, Erika .... 610-558-5613 402 G
davise@neumann.edu
DAVIS, Erin .... 319-895-4296 167 G
edavis@cornellcollege.edu
DAVIS, Evelyn .... 423-624-0077 430 I
evelynd@chattanoogacollege.edu
DAVIS, Evett .... 706-771-4027 116 A
edavis@augustatech.edu
DAVIS, Felicia .... 773-291-6313 135 M
fdavis@ccc.edu
DAVIS, Fontaine .... 386-481-2005.. 95 J
davisf@cookman.edu
DAVIS, Frances .... 478-471-2472 123 A
frances.davis@mga.edu

DAVIS, G. Todd .... 559-638-0300.. 66 H
todd.davis@reedleycollege.edu
DAVIS, G. William .... 443-518-3209 204 E
gdavis@howardcc.edu
DAVIS, George .... 717-866-5775 395 C
george.davis@evangelical.edu
DAVIS, Gilda .... 504-286-5176 195 L
gdavis@suno.edu
DAVIS, Glenda .... 214-379-5526 454 H
gdavis@pqc.edu
DAVIS, Glenn .... 212-463-0400 331 F
glenn.davis2@touro.edu
DAVIS, Glenn .... 320-308-5272 247 E
gmdavis@stcloudstate.edu
DAVIS, Grant .... 610-647-4400 397 I
gdavis@immaculata.edu
DAVIS, Greg .... 360-438-8772 497 F
gdavis@stmartin.edu
DAVIS, Gregory .... 920-465-2334 510 E
davisg@uwgb.edu
DAVIS, Guy .... 423-697-4466 436 F
guy.davis@chattanoogastate.edu
DAVIS, Harriet, F .... 919-530-6151 350 D
hfdavis@nccu.edu
DAVIS, Hazel .... 480-517-8273.. 14 B
hazel.davis@riosalado.edu
DAVIS, Heather .... 336-750-3350 352 D
davish@wssu.edu
DAVIS, Heidi, L .... 504-865-3086 194 G
heidi@loyno.edu
DAVIS, Herbert, R .... 919-572-1625 335 F
hdavis@apexsot.edu
DAVIS, Hope .... 574-520-4339 160 F
DAVIS, Houston, D .... 501-450-5286.. 23 I
hdavis@uca.edu
DAVIS, Howard .... 805-378-4133.. 73 A
hdavis@vcccd.edu
DAVIS, Howard .... 248-204-2316 233 A
hdavis@ltu.edu
DAVIS, Jack .... 540-231-6416 490 F
davisa@vt.edu
DAVIS, Jackie .... 712-707-7114 172 G
jackie.davis@nwciowa.edu
DAVIS, Jake .... 270-686-2111 183 J
jake.davis@brescia.edu
DAVIS, James .... 310-206-0011.. 69 B
jdavis@conet.ucla.edu
DAVIS, James .... 804-819-4995 487 F
jdavis@vccs.edu
DAVIS, James, F .... 308-865-8517 277 F
davisjf@unk.edu
DAVIS, James, J .... 202-806-6700.. 92 C
jdavis@howard.edu
DAVIS, Jamie .... 912-443-4162 125 D
jdavis@savannahtech.edu
DAVIS, Janis .... 949-794-9090.. 66 B
jdavis@stanbridge.edu
DAVIS, Jarred .... 214-860-8680 448 B
DAVIS, Jason .... 218-726-8782 250 F
jdavis@d.umn.edu
DAVIS, Jean .... 314-362-9180 260 E
jean.davis@bjc.org
DAVIS, Jeff .... 706-802-5105 119 G
jdavis@highlands.edu
DAVIS, Jeff .... 912-871-1640 123 J
jdavis@ogeecheetech.edu
DAVIS, Jeff .... 541-757-8944 384 A
jeff.davis@linnbenton.edu
DAVIS, Jeffrey .... 662-325-3444 254 E
jdavis@alumni.msstate.edu
DAVIS, Jenna .... 719-336-1589.. 80 N
jenna.davis@lamarcc.edu
DAVIS, Jennifer .... 216-987-4236 360 E
jennifer.davis@tri-c.edu
DAVIS, Jennifer (J.J.) .... 703-993-8750 481 B
jjdavis@gmu.edu
DAVIS, Jerold .... 212-592-2829 324 A
jdavis8@sva.edu
DAVIS, Jerome .... 212-854-5017 305 E
jd2145@columbia.edu
DAVIS, Jerry, C .... 417-690-2470 258 E
pres@cofo.edu
DAVIS, Jerry, W .... 260-356-6000 159 B
jdavis@huntington.edu
DAVIS, Jim, L .... 701-477-7862 355 H
jdavis@tm.edu
DAVIS, Joan, Y .... 504-671-5420 192 H
jydavis@dcc.edu
DAVIS, Joan, Y .... 504-762-3000 192 H
jydavis@dcc.edu
DAVIS, Joe, D .... 641-422-4121 172 C
davisjoe@niacc.edu
DAVIS, John .... 603-641-7770 282 A
jdavis@anselm.edu
DAVIS, John .... 920-206-2371 508 A
john.davis@mbu.edu
DAVIS, John .... 870-460-1189.. 22 D
davisjc@uamont.edu

DAVIS, John .... 910-843-5304 340 J
DAVIS, John .... 920-206-2332 508 A
john.davis@mbu.edu
DAVIS, John .... 870-460-1189.. 22 D
davisjc@uamont.edu
DAVIS, John .... 307-766-6225 517 B
jdavis71@uwyo.edu
DAVIS, John, M .... 540-423-9179 488 B
jdavis@germanna.edu
DAVIS, Jon .... 360-676-2772 496 C
jdavis@nwic.edu
DAVIS, Jon .... 843-863-7218 419 C
jdavis@csuniv.edu
DAVIS, Jonathan .... 704-669-4124 342 B
davisj@clevelandcc.edu
DAVIS, Jonathan, M ...... 802-626-6418 477 C
jonathan.davis@lsc.vsc.edu
DAVIS, Jonathan, M ...... 802-626-6419 477 D
jonathan.davis@lyndonstate.edu
DAVIS, Jordan .... 214-333-6830 447 D
jordan@dbu.edu
DAVIS, Josephine .... 478-825-6472 119 C
davisj@fvsu.edu
DAVIS, Joy .... 970-207-4550.. 80 P
joyd@mckinleycollege.edu
DAVIS, Joyce, E .... 404-270-5571 126 D
jdavis44@spelman.edu
DAVIS, Julia, T .... 478-301-2644 122 H
davis_jt@mercer.edu
DAVIS, Julie .... 478-934-3518 123 A
julie.davis3@mga.edu
DAVIS, Julie .... 630-752-5079 155 F
julie.davis@wheaton.edu
DAVIS, Julie .... 315-268-6713 304 B
davisju@clarkson.edu
DAVIS, Julie, A .... 207-778-7264 201 D
jadavis@maine.edu
DAVIS, June .... 910-296-2424 344 B
jdavis@jamessprunt.edu
DAVIS, Karan, P .... 850-718-2205.. 96 H
davisk@chipola.edu
DAVIS, Karen .... 805-493-3164.. 30 E
kdavis@callutheran.edu
DAVIS, Kathleen, B .... 716-888-2500 300 G
daviskb@canisius.edu
DAVIS, Kathryn .... 501-370-5234.. 21 A
kdavis@philander.edu
DAVIS, Kathy .... 207-602-2373 202 A
kdavis17@une.edu
DAVIS, Katie .... 478-274-7775 123 I
kdavis@oftc.edu
DAVIS, Kelly .... 479-968-0242.. 18 G
kdavis@atu.edu
DAVIS, Kelly .... 817-272-2194 467 B
kdavis@uta.edu
DAVIS, Kelvin .... 662-846-4698 252 H
kddavis@deltastate.edu
DAVIS, Kelvin .... 803-376-5700 418 D
kdavis@allenuniversity.edu
DAVIS, Ken .... 803-536-7017 423 G
ken.davis@scsu.edu
DAVIS, Kenneth, L .... 212-659-9003 311 A
DAVIS, JR.,
Kenneth, M .... 919-658-2502 349 F
kdavis@umo.edu
DAVIS, Kenny .... 910-272-3500 346 A
kdavis@robeson.edu
DAVIS, Kery .... 202-806-7141.. 92 C
kery.davis@howard.edu
DAVIS, Kevin, L .... 936-468-2011 458 A
DAVIS, Kim .... 843-661-1210 421 H
kdavis@fmarion.edu
DAVIS, Kristy .... 479-968-0329.. 18 G
kdavis51@atu.edu
DAVIS, Larry, D .... 501-977-2013.. 23 B
davis@uaccm.edu
DAVIS, Larry, E .... 412-624-6337 412 I
ledavis@pitt.edu
DAVIS, Larry, J .... 314-516-5606 268 E
ldavis@umsl.edu
DAVIS, LaTricia .... 870-235-4001.. 21 F
ldavis@saumag.edu
DAVIS, Leana .... 815-479-7661 145 B
ldavis@mchenry.edu
DAVIS, Leander .... 310-287-4314.. 49 H
davisl@wlac.edu
DAVIS, Lee .... 912-344-2535 115 D
lee.davis@armstrong.edu
DAVIS, LeeAnn .... 386-506-3404.. 97 I
davisl@daytonastate.edu
DAVIS, Len, L .... 516-876-3191 327 C
davisl@oldwestbury.edu
DAVIS, Linda .... 573-592-4382 270 D
linda.davis@williamwoods.edu
DAVIS, Linda .... 810-989-5765 236 G
ldavis@sc4.edu
DAVIS, Linda .... 617-879-2341 226 A
ldavis@wheelock.edu

DAVIS, Linda, P .... 386-822-7710 111 E
ldavis@stetson.edu
DAVIS, Lois .... 503-725-2320 386 D
loisd@pdx.edu
DAVIS, Loren .... 253-589-5771 493 F
loren.davis@cptc.edu
DAVIS, Lori .... 859-622-2933 184 F
lori.davis@eku.edu
DAVIS, Lorna .... 559-934-2203.. 73 N
lornadavis@whccd.edu
DAVIS, Louis .... 706-855-8233.. 93 B
DAVIS, Lowell, K .... 828-227-7495 352 C
lkdavis@wcu.edu
DAVIS, LuAnn .... 402-486-2503 277 C
luann.davis@ucollege.edu
DAVIS, Lynne .... 508-270-4021 220 A
ldavis@massbay.edu
DAVIS, M. Andrew .... 919-572-1625 335 F
madavis@gmail.com
DAVIS, MacArthur .... 336-744-0900 336 D
macarthur.davis@carolina.edu
DAVIS, Maggie .... 513-244-4630 366 A
maggie.davis@msj.edu
DAVIS, Malcolm .... 832-842-4719 465 A
mdavis@uh.edu
DAVIS, Margie .... 614-251-4567 367 F
davism8@ohiodominican.edu
DAVIS, Maria .... 269-749-7643 236 A
mdavis@olivetcollege.edu
DAVIS, Marilyn, S .... 217-424-6379 145 J
mdavis@millikin.edu
DAVIS, Marilynn .... 404-880-8550 117 H
mdavis@cau.edu
DAVIS, Marissa .... 814-506-8318 405 A
mdavis@pennhighlands.edu
DAVIS, Marjorie .... 509-533-4152 494 A
marjorie.davis@sfcc.spokane.edu
DAVIS, Mark .... 706-880-8060 122 D
mdavis@lagrange.edu
DAVIS, Mark .... 205-652-3570.... 9 C
mdavis@uwa.edu
DAVIS, Mark .... 205-652-5456.... 9 C
mdavis@uwa.edu
DAVIS, Mark, L .... 515-964-0601 169 C
davism@faith.edu
DAVIS, Marsha .... 845-758-7433 298 I
davis@bard.edu
DAVIS, Marty .... 678-839-6614 127 F
gdavis@westga.edu
DAVIS, Mary .... 212-217-4300 308 B
mary_davis@fitnyc.edu
DAVIS, Mary .... 828-298-3325 353 B
mdavis@warren-wilson.edu
DAVIS, Matt .... 505-984-6000 295 K
DAVIS, Matthew .... 402-557-7232 273 E
matthew.davis@bellevue.edu
DAVIS, Matthew .... 920-206-2310 508 A
matthew.davis@mbu.edu
DAVIS, Matthew, D .... 812-877-8421 163 G
matthew.davis@rose-hulman.edu
DAVIS, Matthew, H .... 302-356-2491.. 91 B
matthew.h.davis@wilmu.edu
DAVIS, Maureen .... 760-921-5524.. 55 J
maureen.davis@paloverde.edu
DAVIS, Meadow .... 207-725-3037 198 G
mdavis1@bowdoin.edu
DAVIS, Meagon .... 478-757-3803 128 E
mdavis@wesleyancollege.edu
DAVIS, Megan .... 304-724-5000 501 G
mdavis@cdu.edu
DAVIS, Megan, W .... 603-862-3894 282 F
megan.davis@unh.edu
DAVIS, Melissa .... 281-873-0262 446 J
library@commonwealth.edu
DAVIS, Melvin .... 601-979-1400 253 E
melvin.davis@jsums.edu
DAVIS, Melvin, D .... 256-765-4821.... 9 A
mdavis2@una.edu
DAVIS, Michael .... 318-342-5171 198 A
mdavis@ulm.edu
DAVIS, Michael .... 770-381-7200 121 D
DAVIS, Michael .... 770-457-2021 121 F
DAVIS, Michael .... 770-859-9779 121 E
mdavis@medtech.edu
DAVIS, Michael .... 661-362-2845.. 51 C
mdavis@masters.edu
DAVIS, Michael .... 617-373-2121 223 D
DAVIS, Michelle .... 404-527-7793 122 B
lmdavis@itc.edu
DAVIS, Michelle .... 781-292-2251 215 C
michelle.davis@olin.edu
DAVIS, Michelle .... 701-228-5670 354 G
michelle.r.davis@dakotacollege.edu
DAVIS, Mike .... 580-745-2392 379 J
mdavis@se.edu
DAVIS, Mike .... 386-752-1822.. 99 J
mike.davis@fgc.edu

DAY-PERROOTS, Susan, D .... 304-293-3733 505 B sue.day-perroots@mail.wvu.edu
DAYAL, Ravinder .... 916-388-2814.. 35 F rdayal@carrington.edu
DAYHOFF, Brenda .... 301-846-2481 203 H bdayhoff@frederick.edu
DAYHOFF, Sharon, S .... 717-337-6276 396 A sdayhoff@gettysburg.edu
DAYLEY, Newell .... 801-863-7359 473 D newell.dayley@uvu.edu
DAYMON, Cynthia .... 215-368-5000 389 H cdaymon@biblical.edu
DAYNES, Gary .... 252-399-6343 335 I gdaynes@barton.edu
DAYOUB, Missy, H .... 770-720-5522 124 H mhd1@reinhardt.edu
DAYTON, Kay .... 615-230-3675 438 C kay.dayton@volstate.edu
DAYTON, Lynne .... 334-222-6591.... 2 H ldayton@lbwcc.edu
DAYTON-JOHNSON, Jeffrey .... 831-647-4647 475 G jdaytonjohnson@miis.edu
DAYZIE, Meryl .... 928-724-6950.. 12 G mdayzie@dinecollege.edu
DE ANGELIS, John .... 212-678-3012 331 C deangelis@tc.edu
DE ANGULO, Bonnie .... 305-223-4561 106 L deangulo@sjvcs.edu
DE AQUINO, Carlos ...... 727-736-5082 107 F cdeaquino@schiller.edu
DE BAEZ SNYDER, Tracey .... 724-830-1125 410 E snyderdebaez@setonhill.edu
DE BERLY, Geraldine, N .... 413-545-2111 216 H gdeberly@cpe.umass.edu
DE BOER, David .... 616-451-3511 229 D ddeboer@davenport.edu
DE BONO, Chad .... 719-336-1517.. 80 N chad.debono@lamarcc.edu
DE BOTTON, Leonard ... 973-278-5400 299 F len@berkeleycollege.edu
DE BOTTON, Leonard ... 973-278-5400 283 J len@berkeleycollege.edu
DE CHANT, Richard ...... 216-987-3193 360 E richard.dechant@tri-c.edu
DE COLA, John .... 239-304-7901.. 95 C john.decola@avemaria.edu
DE DIOS, Paul .... 714-484-7335.. 53 M pdedios@cypresscollege.edu
DE DIOS UNANUE, Teresa .... 787-720-0596 521 A
DE FALUSSY, George, H .... 607-735-1978 307 G gdefalussy@elmira.edu
DE FATIMA LIMA, Maria .... 615-327-6533 434 A mflima@mmc.edu
DE FAZIO, Alice .... 201-200-3317 287 F adefazio@njcu.edu
DE FILIPPIS, Daisy Cocco .... 203-575-8044.. 86 B ddefilippis@nv.edu
DE FREITAS, Lisa, H ..... 864-597-4203 426 I defreitaslh@wofford.edu
DE FRIES, Carol .... 215-496-6122 393 A cdefries@ccp.edu
DE GROAT, II, Arthur, S .... 785-532-0369 179 A degroata@ksu.edu
DE GROAT, Jaycee .... 845-436-4890 330 F jdegroat@sunysullivan.edu
DE GUZMAN, Maria, I .. 787-257-7373 525 Q ac_mguzman@suagm.edu
DE HAAS PHILLIPS, Sylvia .... 413-565-1000 211 C sdphillips@baypath.edu
DE HARO, Oscar .... 707-256-7365.. 53 D odeharo@napavalley.edu
DE HART, Megan .... 757-340-2121 479 D stuadvcvab@centura.edu
DE JESUS, Eigna .... 787-257-7373 525 Q eidejesus@suagm.edu
DE JESUS, Norma .... 312-369-7465 136 H ndejesus@colum.edu
DE JESUS, Ramon .... 787-878-5475 523 H rdjesus@arecibo.inter.edu
DE JESUS, Victoria .... 787-751-0178 525 O ac_vdejesus@suagm.edu
DE JESUS-ALICEA, Angela .... 787-864-2222 524 A angela.dejesus@guayama.inter.edu
DE JESUS, Marcos .... 787-993-8953 527 G marcos.dejesus@upr.edu
DE JONG, Sven .... 304-829-7281 501 F sdejong@bethanywv.edu
DE LA CERDA, Paul ...... 323-267-3724.. 48 L delacep@elac.edu
DE LA GARZA, Ana ...... 956-295-3622 461 F ana.delagarza@tsc.edu
DE LA GARZA, Marco .. 818-947-2324.. 49 G delagamj@lavc.edu
DE LA GARZA, Ricardo 956-872-3714 456 G rickdlg@southtexascollege.edu
DE LA GUARDIA, Teresa, S .... 305-284-2928 112 O tdelaguardia@miami.edu
DE LA LAMA, Carlos .... 619-388-3520.. 60 C
DE LA PAZ, Gloria .... 914-606-6744 333 H gloria.delapaz@sunywcc.edu
DE LA ROSA, Casar ...... 301-369-2800 202 J
DE LA ROSA, Shirley .... 684-699-9155 519 F s.delarosa@amsamoa.edu
DE LA TORRE, Jorge .... 425-640-1233 494 E jorge.delatorre@edcc.edu
DE LA TORRE, Marisela .... 213-356-5376.. 65 A marisela_delatorre@sciarc.edu
DE LA TORRE, Susana . 510-436-2598.. 56 I sdelatorre@peralta.edu
DE LA VEGA, Gabriela .. 415-442-7297.. 44 E gdelavega@ggu.edu
DE LA VEGA, Kristina ... 818-677-2118.. 33 B kristina.delavega@csun.edu
DE LACEY, Lora .... 630-844-5510 133 H ldelacey@aurora.edu
DE LATORRE, Adela, I .. 530-752-2613.. 68 H vcstudentaffairs@ucdavis.edu
DE LEÓN, Beatriz .... 787-743-3038 525 M bdeleon@sanjuanbautista.edu
DE LEON, Daniel .... 956-872-5558 456 G ddeleon@southtexascollege.edu
DE LEON, Lee .... 325-674-2353 441 D ldeleon5@acu.edu
DE LEONARDIS, David, J .... 614-885-5585 369 D ddeleon@pcj.edu
DE LONG, Linda .... 909-593-3511.. 70 E ldelong@laverne.edu
DE LOS REYES, Jose .... 415-749-4519.. 60 G jdelosreyes@sfai.edu
DE LUCA, Anne .... 510-642-2261.. 68 G adeluca@berkeley.edu
DE LUCA, James, P .... 843-953-6861 419 D jdeluca@citadel.edu
DE MARCO, Thomas ..... 610-519-4155 413 K thomas.demarco@villanova.edu
DE MELLO, Duilia .... 202-319-5244.. 91 D demello@cua.edu
DE NOBLE, Timothy ...... 785-532-5950 179 A tdenoble@ksu.edu
DE NULLY, Jasmine, A . 212-998-2775 318 D jasmine.denully@nyu.edu
DE OLIVEIRA, Glenisson .... 940-565-3305 466 B glenisson.deoliveira@unt.edu
DE P. MENDEZ, Maria . 787-284-1912 524 C mpmendez@ponce.inter.edu
DE PAULA, Anna .... 201-761-7450 291 D adepaula@saintpeters.edu
DE PRATER, Victoria, L 209-468-9155.. 67 C vdeprater@sjcoe.net
DE ROSE, John .... 203-287-3034.. 87 G paier.fad@snet.net
DE ROSSI, Scott, S .... 919-537-3236 351 B scott_derossi@unc.edu
DE RUBERTIS, Andrew .. 414-410-4221 506 F aderubertis@stritch.edu
DE SANTIAGO, Mildred 787-892-5131 524 D mdesanti@intersg.edu
DE SPAIN, Donna .... 630-844-3840 133 H ddespain@aurora.edu
DE VELASCO, Joanna .... 305-284-3441 112 O jdevelasco@miami.edu
DE VEYGA, Guillermo ... 201-200-3003 287 F gdeveyga@njcu.edu
DE YAMPERT, Fredi ...... 906-487-7301 230 B fredi.deyampert@finlandia.edu
DE YOUNG, Brian .... 336-316-2410 338 C deyoungbk@guilford.edu
DE YOUNG, Gene .... 541-684-7219 384 H gdeyoung@nwcu.edu
DEACON, Charles, A ..... 202-687-3600.. 92 B deacon@georgetown.edu
DEACY, Deborah, S .... 909-593-3511.. 70 E ddeacy@laverne.edu
DEAHL, Anne, D .... 414-288-6786 508 C anne.deahl@marquette.edu
DEAHL, Kathy, S .... 208-732-6201 131 I kdeahl@csi.edu
DEAL, Charley, T .... 731-881-7610 440 B cdeal@utm.edu
DEAL, David .... 276-656-0258 489 A ddeal@patrickhenry.edu
DEAL, Kelley, P .... 252-451-8235 345 B kpdeal870@nashcc.edu
DEAL, Lisa .... 352-392-1331 110 D lsd@ufl.edu
DEAL, Megan .... 972-860-5262 447 H rdeal@dcccd.edu
DEAL, Pamela .... 912-478-8748 120 E pdeal@georgiasouthern.edu
DEAL, Shannon .... 731-881-7750 440 B sdeal@utm.edu
DEAL, Todd .... 912-478-1435 120 E stdeal@georgiasouthern.edu
DEAN, Adam, S .... 417-667-8181 259 A adean@cottey.edu
DEAN, Anthony .... 334-386-7508.... 5 I tdean@faulkner.edu
DEAN, Barbara .... 502-942-8503 189 F bsdean@sullivan.edu
DEAN, Bill .... 806-742-3641 463 D bill.dean@ttu.edu
DEAN, Brian .... 626-914-8597.. 37 G bdean@citruscollege.edu
DEAN, Clay .... 470-578-4737 122 C cdean15@kennesaw.edu
DEAN, Denis, J .... 972-883-6852 467 D denis.dean@utdallas.edu
DEAN, Don .... 914-323-5219 314 A donald.dean@mville.edu
DEAN, Donald .... 614-323-5219 314 A donald.dean@mville.edu
DEAN, Gayle .... 505-566-3204 296 A deang@sanjuancollege.edu
DEAN, James, H .... 941-359-7524 106 H jdean@ringling.edu
DEAN, James, S .... 412-531-4433 393 D info@deantech.edu
DEAN, Jeffrey .... 502-272-8014 183 H jdean@bellarmine.edu
DEAN, Jeffrey, L .... 856-225-2747 290 B jldean@camden.rutgers.edu
DEAN, Jennifer .... 313-993-1090 237 F deanjl@udmercy.edu
DEAN, Jerome .... 617-928-4500 222 D jdean@mountida.edu
DEAN, Johnie .... 859-846-5779 188 B jdean@midway.edu
DEAN, Jonathan, E .... 828-339-4614 346 H j_dean@southwesterncc.edu
DEAN, Justin .... 740-389-4636 365 B deanj@mtc.edu
DEAN, Karol .... 914-674-7517 314 I kdean@mercy.edu
DEAN, Kathy, L .... 251-442-2215.... 8 D kdean@umobile.edu
DEAN, Kayla .... 501-882-8867.. 17 M kidean@asub.edu
DEAN, Kevin .... 610-436-2996 407 D kdean@wcupa.edu
DEAN, Kristina .... 410-888-9048 205 D kdean@muih.edu
DEAN, LeAnn .... 320-589-6173 251 A deanl@morris.umn.edu
DEAN, Lynne .... 210-486-4135 441 G ldean12@alamo.edu
DEAN, Marcus .... 334-727-8989.... 7 F
DEAN, Mark .... 620-792-9235 175 C deanm@bartonccc.edu
DEAN, Matt .... 864-681-1457 425 G mcdean@mailbox.sc.edu
DEAN, Miles .... 410-287-1147 203 B mdean@cecil.edu
DEAN, Paul, M .... 603-862-1427 282 F paul.dean@unh.edu
DEAN, Rachel .... 406-265-3720 272 C rachel.dean1@msun.edu
DEAN, Ron .... 415-451-2864.. 60 I rdean@sfts.edu
DEAN, Samuel, J .... 614-985-2226 369 D sdean@pcj.edu
DEAN, Sheryl, L .... 810-766-4062 227 E sheryl.dean@baker.edu
DEAN, Takeem .... 704-378-1132 338 I tdean@jcsu.edu
DEAN, Thomas, K .... 319-335-1995 166 G thomas-k-dean@uiowa.edu
DEAN, Tony .... 303-273-3643.. 78 J amdean@mines.edu
DEAN, Tonya .... 972-524-3341 457 H
DEAN, Troy .... 541-684-7293 384 H tdean@nwcu.edu
DEAN, Wendy .... 909-667-4420.. 37 J wdean@claremontlincoln.edu
DEAN, Willow .... 316-322-3124 175 I wdean@butlercc.edu
DEAN-BAAR, Susan ...... 314-516-6066 268 E deanbaar@umsl.edu
DEANE, Lynne, P .... 804-289-8064 486 G ldeane@richmond.edu
DEANE, Martin .... 718-270-3199 326 A martin.deane@downstate.edu
DEANER, Kathy .... 718-429-6600 333 B kathy.deaner@vaughn.edu
DEANGELIS, Beth .... 518-782-6109 324 C bdeangelis@siena.edu
DEANGELIS, Gennaro .... 860-253-3048.. 85 C gdeangelis@asnuntuck.edu
DEANGELIS, Peter .... 215-955-4773 411 E peter.deangelis@jefferson.edu
DEANGELO, Jane .... 530-221-4275.. 63 H jdeangelo@shasta.edu
DEANGELO, OFM CONV, Jude .... 202-319-5575.. 91 D deangelo@cua.edu
DEANNA, Linda .... 312-996-4857 153 H ldeanna@uic.edu
DEANS, Beverly .... 919-735-5151 347 E bdeans@waynecc.edu
DEANS, Greg .... 252-451-8275 345 B gddeans098@nashcc.edu
DEAR, Carley .... 601-857-3357 253 B carley.dear@hindscc.edu
DEAR, Michael .... 760-757-2121.. 52 F mdear@miracosta.edu
DEARAUJO-RIVERA, Izabel, D .... 401-333-7151 416 B iddearaujo@ccri.edu
DEARBORN, Heidi .... 360-596-5358 498 G hdearborn@spscc.edu
DEARBORN, Philip, E ... 717-560-8233 399 D pdearborn@lbc.edu
DEARCORN, Casey .... 307-754-6084 516 Q casey.dearcorn@nwc.edu
DEARDORFF, Lori .... 405-878-5488 379 G lkdeardorff@stgregorys.edu
DEARDURFF, Mindy, J .. 651-696-6143 243 B mdeardur@macalester.edu
DEARSTYNE, Kenneth .... 610-607-6265 408 G kdearstyne@racc.edu
DEARTH, Christopher .... 302-736-2529.. 90 J christopher.dearth@wesley.edu
DEAS, Deborah .... 951-827-4564.. 69 D deborah.deas@medsch.ucr.edu
DEASE, Dennis, J .... 651-962-8520 251 D djdease@stthomas.edu
DEASE, Mary Ann .... 203-837-8248.. 85 B deasem@wcsu.edu
DEASIS, Mark .... 951-372-7014.. 58 G mark.deasis@norcocollege.edu
DEASON, Michael .... 972-860-4670 447 G mdeason@dcccd.edu
DEATER, Kate .... 814-472-3222 409 G kdeater@francis.edu
DEATHERAGE, Eric .... 417-455-5610 259 D ericdeatherage@crowder.edu
DEATHERIDGE, Janet .... 312-915-6512 144 D jdeathe@luc.edu
DEATLEY, Carry .... 256-215-4311.... 1 G cdeatley@cacc.edu
DEATON, Andrea, D ...... 405-325-1646 380 L adeaton@ou.edu
DEATON, Benjamin .... 864-231-2000 418 E bdeaton@andersonuniversity.edu
DEATON, Judy .... 949-675-4451.. 46 H judy@idi.edu
DEATON, Vicki .... 901-678-2125 439 E vddeaton@memphis.edu
DEATS, Jacqueline .... 714-997-6851.. 36 G deats@chapman.edu
DEATS, John .... 432-685-4726 453 B jdeats@midland.edu
DEAVER, Rhonda .... 252-527-6223 344 D rgdeaver10@lenoircc.edu
DEAVER, Robin .... 910-678-8484 343 B deaverr@faytechcc.edu
DEBARI, Serge .... 508-849-3447 210 H sdibari@annamaria.edu
DEBARTOLO, Peggy .... 210-436-3727 455 J pdebartolo@stmarytx.edu
DEBASIO, Nancy .... 816-995-2810 265 I nancy.debasio@researchcollege.edu
DEBELA, Kenesa .... 773-256-0716 144 G kdebela@lstc.edu
DEBELL, Gail .... 206-281-2853 498 B gdebell@spu.edu
DEBENEDETTI, Pablo ..... 609-258-5480 288 F pdebene@princeton.edu
DEBENEDICTIS, Katie .... 419-530-5660 372 F katie.debenedictis@utoledo.edu
DEBENEDICTS, Elissa .... 217-757-1190 298 D edebenedicts@funeraleducation.org
DEBERNARDI, Maureen 617-779-4369 224 B admissionsandrecords@sjs.edu
DEBERRY, Jacqueline ... 731-352-4298 430 E deberryj@bethelu.edu
DEBERRY, Marilyn .... 803-376-5827 418 D myoung@allenuniversity.edu

DEBERRY, Ron .... 757-826-1883 478 G
execvp@bcva.edu
DEBIAS, Patti .... 773-256-0728 144 G
pdebias@lstc.edu
DEBIASE, Paul .... 212-217-3750 308 B
paul_debiase@fitnyc.edu
DEBLOIS, Nicole .... 207-795-2270 199 I
debloini@mchp.edu
DEBLOIS, Yvonne .... 717-871-7083 407 A
yvonne.deblois@millersville.edu
DEBOARD, John .... 580-581-2237 375 A
jdeboard@cameron.edu
DEBOBES, Erin .... 508-531-2744 217 D
erin.debobes@bridgew.edu
DEBOCK, Devin .... 918-293-4944 378 B
devin.debock@okstate.edu
DEBOEF, Cindy, S .... 231-777-0303 234 G
cindy.deboef@muskegoncc.edu
DEBOEF, Ryan .... 417-836-8500 263 H
ryandeboef@missouristate.edu
DEBOER, Aaron .... 641-844-5767 170 I
aaron.deboer@iavalley.edu
DEBOER, Eileen .... 318-487-7222 191 J
eileen.deboer@lacollege.edu
DEBOER, Fredrik .... 718-951-5000 301 E
fredrik.deboer@brooklyn.cuny.edu
DEBOER, Jeffrey .... 219-864-2400 162 U
jdeboer@midamerica.edu
DEBOER, Keith .... 616-222-1247 229 B
keith.deboer@cornerstone.edu
DEBOLT, Ken .... 315-781-3146 310 C
debolt@hws.edu
DEBOLT, Peg .... 260-359-4068 159 B
pdebolt@huntington.edu
DEBONI, Toni .... 805-437-8962.. 31 C
toni.deboni@csuci.edu
DEBORD, Bonnie, H .... 770-720-5502 124 H
bhd@reinhardt.edu
DEBORD, Cris .... 304-293-2545 505 B
cris.debord@mail.wvu.edu
DEBOWER, Lore .... 508-362-2131 219 E
ldebower@capecod.edu
DEBRAGA, Angie .... 775-775-2231 279 A
angie.debraga@gbcnv.edu
DEBRAGGIO,
Michael, J .... 315-859-4654 309 D
mdebragg@hamilton.edu
DEBRIZZI, JR.,
Thomas, A .... 203-576-4690.. 8C F
tdebriz@bridgeport.edu
DEBRO, Angela .... 256-372-5230.... 1 A
angela.debro@aamu.edu
DEBRUM, David .... 692-625-6416 520 C
ddebrum@cmi.edu
DEBRUM, Emil .... 692-625-3291 520 C
edebrum@cmi.edu
DEBURE, Olivier .... 727-864-8366.. 97 O
debureoc@eckerd.edu
DEBURRO, Jennifer .... 207-602-2132 202 A
jdeburro@une.edu
DEBUS, Casey .... 307-532-8311 516 J
casey.debus@ewc.wy.edu
DEC, Lynda .... 207-973-3370 201 A
lynda.dec@maine.edu
DEC, Ted .... 631-687-5155 322 G
tdec@sjcny.edu
DECAEN, Christopher .... 805-525-4417.. 67 E
cdecaen@thomasaquinas.edu
DECAIRE, Maryann .... 847-578-3217 150 E
maryann.decaire@rosalindfranklin.edu
DECALO, Ruth .... 212-678-8915 312 A
rudecalo@jtsa.edu
DECAMILLIS, Susan .... 231-995-1014 235 B
sdecamillis@nmc.edu
DECANDIA, Salvatore .... 718-780-7982 300 A
salvatore.decandia@brooklaw.edu
DECAPRIO, Nicholas ..... 518-244-4551 321 G
decapn@sage.edu
DECAPUA, Lynn .... 732-987-2729 286 D
ldecapua@georgian.edu
DECARIE, Linette, A ...... 617-353-7118 212 G
decarie@bu.edu
DECARLO, Robert, L ...... 516-877-3184 297 I
decarlo@adelphi.edu
DECARO, Louis .... 646-378-6174 319 C
louis.decaro@nyack.edu
DECAROLIS, Crystal ...... 845-905-4632 306 D
crystal.decarolis@culinary.edu
DECAROLIS, Donna, M . 215-895-1795 394 C
donna.marie.decarolis@drexel.edu
DECARVALHO,
Fatima, M .... 976-655-7818 287 D
decarvalhf@mail.montclair.edu
DECARVALHO,
Meghan, M .... 401-341-2348 417 D
meghan.decarvalho@salve.edu
DECASTRO-SALLIS,
Kishma .... 412-397-6238 409 C
sallis@rmu.edu
DECATUR, Jane .... 508-626-4585 218 A
jdecatur@framingham.edu
DECATUR, Sean .... 740-427-5111 364 A
decatur@kenyon.edu
DECATUR, William .... 313-577-5580 239 C
william.decatur@wayne.edu
DECAY, Jarlene .... 972-860-0800 447 H
jdecay@dcccd.edu
DECELLE, Jerry, L .... 518-564-2082 327 E
decellejl@plattsburgh.edu
DECELLE, Michael, P ..... 603-641-4107 282 F
mike.decelle@unh.edu
DECELLES, Katherine ..... 617-558-1788 223 A
kdecelles@nesa.edu
DECENA, Peter .... 408-924-2222.. 34 D
peter.decena@sjsu.edu
DECENT, Bridgette .... 901-678-5502 439 E
bdecent@memphis.edu
DECENT,
Christopher, M .... 904-620-2131 110 E
c.decent@unf.edu
DECENZO, David, A ...... 843-349-2001 420 A
ddecenzo@coastal.edu
DECHAMBEAU,
Aimee, L .... 330-972-7488 371 C
aimee@uakron.edu
DECHANT, Margaret ...... 361-825-5951 460 A
margaret.dechant@tamucc.edu
DECHARINTE, Janeen .... 815-836-5263 143 E
decharja@lewisu.edu
DECHARIO, Douglas, C 785-864-9525 181 I
d325d867@ku.edu
DECHIARO, Thomas ...... 215-895-1434 394 C
tdechiaro@drexel.edu
DECHILLO, Neal .... 978-542-6630 218 E
ndechillo@salemstate.edu
DECICCO, Stephanie 773-291-6100 135M
sdecicco@ccc.edu
DECK, Amanda .... 617-405-5967 223 H
adeck@quincycollege.edu
DECKER, Allison .... 217-479-7000 144 I
DECKER, Amber .... 859-442-1147 185 I
amber.decker@kctcs.edu
DECKER, Ann .... 772-462-7240 101 Q
adecker@irsc.edu
DECKER, Barbara, Q ..... 515-643-6601 171 K
bdecker@mercydesmoines.org
DECKER, Christy .... 518-828-4181 305 D
christy.decker@sunycgcc.edu
DECKER, Craig .... 719-255-4338.. 83 C
cdecker@uccs.edu
DECKER, David, R .... 614-947-6017 362 A
david.decker@franklin.edu
DECKER, Douglas .... 724-983-0700 399 I
ddecker@laurel.edu
DECKER, Douglas, S ..... 724-439-4900 399 H
ddecker@laurel.edu
DECKER, Jarron, P .... 518-276-6216 321 A
deckej3@rpi.edu
DECKER, John .... 989-964-4612 236 F
jdecker1@svsu.edu
DECKER, John .... 417-268-6002 257 H
jdecker@gobbc.edu
DECKER, Nancy .... 724-983-0700 399 I
ndecker@laurel.edu
DECKER, Nancy, M ...... 724-439-4900 399 H
ndecker@laurel.edu
DECKER, Randy .... 903-586-2518 451 C
rdecker@jacksonville-college.edu
DECKER, Stephanie ...... 973-684-6868 288 C
sdecker@pccc.edu
DECKER, Steven .... 715-468-2815 515 D
steven.decker@witc.edu
DECKER, Susan .... 812-535-5138 163 I
sdecker@smwc.edu
DECKER, Timothy .... 845-298-0755 307 A
tdecker@sunydutchess.edu
DECKER, William, C ...... 501-569-3302.. 22 B
wcdecker@ualr.edu
DECKERT, Glenn .... 978-867-4736 215 D
glenn.deckert@gordon.edu
DECKINGA, Mike .... 219-864-2400 162 U
mdeckinga@midamerica.edu
DECLEENE, Catherine .... 317-738-8090 157 L
cdecleene@franklincollege.edu
DECMAN, Mike .... 815-740-3427 154 G
mdecman@stfrancis.edu
DECOCINIS, Anthony ..... 215-972-2007 404 Q
adecocinis@pafa.edu
DECOCK, Murray, L ...... 315-228-7489 304 G
mdecock@colgate.edu
DECONCILLIS, Pat .... 724-222-5330 403 E
pdeconcillis@penncommercial.edu
DECONINCK, Lori .... 603-668-2211 282 C
l.deconinck@snhu.edu
DECONNO, David .... 518-580-5719 324 D
ddeconno@skidmore.edu
DECOOKE, Peggy .... 914-251-6485 328 B
peggy.decooke@purchase.edu
DECOOKE, Peggy .... 914-251-6750 328 B
peggy.decooke@purchase.edu
DECORDOVA, Endia ...... 860-701-5162.. 87 F
decordova_e@mitchell.edu
DECOSTER, Daisy .... 201-761-6465 291 D
ddecoster@saintpeters.edu
DECOTEAU, Katina .... 701-255-3285 355 I
kdecoteau@uttc.edu
DECOURSEY, Paul, A .... 515-574-1055 170 C
decoursey@iowacentral.edu
DECOUTEAU, Jolene ...... 701-255-3285 355 I
jolene.decouteau@uttc.edu
DECRISTO, James .... 336-734-2862 352 B
decristoj@uncsa.edu
DECRISTOFORO,
Joseph, R .... 210-458-7070 468 B
joe.decristoforo@utsa.edu
DECUIR, Bobbie .... 337-482-1000 197 F
bobbie@louisiana.edu
DECUIR, Karla .... 281-396-3792 465 D
decuirk@uhv.edu
DEDDO, Gary .... 626-650-2306.. 44 H
DEDEAUX, Vanessa ...... 601-928-6230 254 D
vanessa.dedeaux@mgccc.edu
DEDEO, Patrick .... 973-720-2224 292 I
dedeop@wpunj.edu
DEDIEMAR, Jeanette ..... 317-788-3298 164 H
dediemarj@uindy.edu
DEDOMINICI, Peter ...... 703-330-8400.. 93 B
DEDONATO, Joy .... 516-572-7943 316 C
joy.dedonato@ncc.edu
DEDWYLER, Jason .... 601-477-4075 253 F
jason.dedwyler@jcjc.edu
DEE, Edward .... 718-779-1499 320 C
edee@plazacollege.edu
DEE, Kay, C .... 812-877-8502 163 G
dee@rose-hulman.edu
DEE, Shawn, G .... 336-334-4822 343 E
sgdee@gtcc.edu
DEE, Tina .... 231-777-0660 234 G
tina.dee@muskegoncc.edu
DEEB, Bassam, M .... 716-826-1200 331 K
deebb@trocaire.edu
DEEB, Tiffni .... 612-659-6600 245 F
tiffni.deeb@minneapolis.edu
DEEDRICK, Gary, A ...... 864-242-5100 418 H
DEEDS, Brad .... 530-541-4660.. 47 I
deeds@ltcc.edu
DEEDS, Cher .... 330-684-8952 371 D
cher@uakron.edu
DEEDS, Sarene .... 417-873-7869 259 G
sdeeds@drury.edu
DEEDS, William, C .... 712-274-5103 172 A
deeds@morningside.edu
DEEG, Richard .... 215-204-7443 411 B
DEEGAN, Christopher .... 312-413-7662 153 H
deegan@uic.edu
DEEGEN, Lynn .... 601-928-6212 254 D
lynn.deegen@mgccc.edu
DEEHR, Marylouise ...... 440-449-4202 373 B
mdeehr@ursuline.edu
DEEK, Fadi, P .... 973-596-3220 288 A
fadi.deek@njit.edu
DEEL, Connie .... 785-594-8362 174 J
connie.deel@bakeru.edu
DEEL, Michael .... 276-498-5237 477 L
mdeel@acp.edu
DEEL, Susan, M .... 989-463-7176 226 H
deel@alma.edu
DEELY, Pamela .... 630-829-6047 133 I
pdeely@ben.edu
DEEM, Marie .... 412-536-1128 398 E
marie.deem@laroche.edu
DEEN, Michael .... 903-813-2306 443 F
mdeen@austincollege.edu
DEEN, Robert .... 720-279-8990.. 80 C
bdeen@holmesinstitute.edu
DEER, Joe, W .... 308-635-6145 278 B
deerj234@wncc.edu
DEER, Susan .... 845-574-4280 321 F
sdeer@sunyrockland.edu
DEES, Charles .... 973-596-3400 288 A
charles.dees@njit.edu
DEES, Margaret .... 904-256-7020 102 B
mdees@ju.edu
DEES-BURNETT,
Keichanda .... 816-235-5628 268 D
deesk@umkc.edu
DEESE, Phyllis .... 903-823-3355 458 D
phyllis.deese@texarkanacollege.edu
DEESS, Eugene, P .... 973-596-3110 288 A
deess@njit.edu
DEETER, Daniel, P .... 864-597-4232 426 I
deeterdp@wofford.edu
DEETZ, Kristi, R .... 812-888-4141 165 E
kdeetz@vinu.edu
DEFALCO, Ron, E .... 713-718-7586 450 D
ron.defalco@hccs.edu
DEFATTA, Jerry .... 601-266-5013 256 E
jerry.defatta@usm.edu
DEFAUW, Nikki, J .... 563-333-6345 173 A
defauwnikkij@sau.edu
DEFAZIO, Jeannie .... 330-490-7332 373 F
jdefazio@walsh.edu
DEFAZIO, Robert .... 716-375-2190 322 B
DEFEDE, Kathryn .... 559-925-3145.. 73M
kathryndefede@whccd.edu
DEFEIS, Evelyn .... 973-684-5900 288 C
edefeis@pccc.edu
DEFELICE, Robert .... 781-891-2256 212 A
rdefelice@bentley.edu
DEFELICE, Stacey .... 516-876-3009 327 C
defelices@oldwestbury.edu
DEFEO, Gregory .... 412-809-5100 408 D
defeo.greg@pti.edu
DEFFENBACHER, Mark .. 559-453-2239.. 43 J
mark.deffenbacher@fresno.edu
DEFFENBAUGH,
Cynthia, B .... 804-289-8438 486 G
cdeffenb@richmond.edu
DEFILIPPIS, Brian, J ..... 410-704-2358 209 C
bdefilippis@towson.edu
DEFLORIO, Melody .... 802-831-1037 476 G
mdeflorio@vermontlaw.edu
DEFOOR, Keith .... 706-379-3111 128 H
kdefoor@yhc.edu
DEFORD, Victoria .... 763-424-0955 246 E
vdeford@nhcc.edu
DEFORE, Jody .... 678-359-5990 121 B
jody@gordonstate.edu
DEFORE, Matt .... 205-726-4021.... 6 G
mdefore@samford.edu
DEFOREST, Kristin, A .... 607-746-4590 329 B
deforeka@delhi.edu
DEFRANCIS, Robert .... 304-214-8820 503 E
rdefrancis@wvncc.edu
DEFRANCO, Jeff .... 530-541-4660.. 47 I
defranco@ltcc.edu
DEFRATES, Bruce .... 509-359-2314 494 D
bdefrates@ewu.edu
DEFREECE, Michele, T .. 607-746-4652 329 B
defreemt@delhi.edu
DEFREITAS, Jack .... 660-263-3900 258 A
jackdefreitas@cccb.edu
DEFRIES, Robert .... 320-762-4637 243 J
bobd@alextech.edu
DEGAIN, Sabrina .... 336-506-4161 340 L
sabrina.degain@alamancecc.edu
DEGAISH, Ann .... 361-825-2612 460 A
ann.degaish@tamucc.edu
DEGARMO, David, L ..... 417-862-9533 260 D
ddegarmo@globaluniversity.edu
DEGARMO, Kristin .... 417-862-9533 260 D
kdegarmo@globaluniversity.edu
DEGAZON, Karen .... 212-938-5654 328 E
kdegazon@sunyopt.edu
DEGEARE, Christopher .. 636-481-3467 261 B
cdegear1@jeffco.edu
DEGENHARDT, Brian ..... 660-626-2397 257 A
bdegenhardt@atsu.edu
DEGENHART,
Mary Louise .... 314-367-8700 266 D
mary.degenhart@stlcop.edu
DEGEORGE,
Christine, C .... 941-359-7645 106 H
ccarnegi@ringling.edu
DEGER, Coquina, L .... 425-602-3006 492 E
cdeger@bastyr.edu
DEGERMAN, Roger .... 336-316-2123 338 C
degermanre@guilford.edu
DEGEUS, Marilyn, J ...... 816-654-7262 261 D
mdegeus@kcumb.edu
DEGIACINTO, Jennifer ... 808-455-0595 130 G
jdigiaci@hawaii.edu
DEGIOIA,
John (Jack), J .... 202-687-4134.. 92 B
president@georgetown.edu
DEGIOVANNI, Kim .... 301-387-3040 203 I
kim.degiovanni@garrettcollege.edu
DEGIULIO, Jules .... 541-440-7648 387 E
jules.degiulio@umpqua.edu
DEGN, Jason .... 479-619-4337.. 20 F
jdegn@nwacc.edu
DEGNER, Katie .... 352-424-1719 106 N
katie.degner@saintleo.edu
DEGRAAF, Donald .... 616-526-6225 228 B
ddegraaf@calvin.edu
DEGRAFFENREID,
Pamela .... 828-227-7346 352 C
degraffen@wcu.edu
DEGRANGE, Karen, A .... 812-877-8285 163 G
degrange@rose-hulman.edu

DEGRAW, Heather .... 425-739-8200 495 F heather.degraw@lwtech.edu
DEGRAW, Julie .... 419-358-3248 357 E degrawj@bluffton.edu
DEGROAT, Kevin .... 718-405-3400 304 H kevin.degroat@mountsaintvincent.edu
DEGROFT, Michael .... 717-391-3506 411 C degroft@stevenscollege.edu
DEGWECK, Benjamin, J 205-358-1452.... 5 C ben.degweck@ecacolleges.com
DEHAEMERS, Jennifer ... 816-235-1143 268 D dehaemersj@umkc.edu
DEHART, Carrick .... 805-375-8919.. 31 C carrick.dehart@csuci.edu
DEHART, Doris .... 323-226-4911.. 50 A ddehart@dhs.lacounty.gov
DEHART, Jennifer .... 207-509-7100 200 I jdehart@unity.edu
DEHART, Joe .... 515-791-1721 168 A jcdehart@dmacc.edu
DEHART, Katy .... 301-369-2800 202 J kdehart@captechu.edu
DEHAVEN, Barbara .... 201-216-8762 291 G barbara.dehaven@stevens.edu
DEHAY, Galen .... 864-646-2037 424 F gdehay@tctc.edu
DEHAYES, Donald, H .... 401-874-4410 417 E donald_dehayes@uri.edu
DEHEN, Regina .... 503-552-1966 384 F rdehen@nunm.edu
DEHGHANI, Mo .... 201-216-8911 291 G mo.dehghani@stevens.edu
DEHMER, Mackenzie ..... 402-449-2882 274 H mdehmer8729@graceu.edu
DEHN, Paula .... 270-852-3117 187 F pdehn@kwc.edu
DEHNE, Nathan, D .... 414-410-4060 506 F nddehne@stritch.edu
DEHOOGH-KLIEWER, Michelle .... 605-331-6619 429 D michelle.dehoogh-kliewer@usiouxfalls.edu
DEHORN, Thomas .... 574-239-8383 158 M tdehorn@hcc-nd.edu
DEHOYOS, Diane, N ..... 915-747-5601 467 E dndehoyos@utep.edu
DEI, Michael .... 281-649-3406 450 C mdei@hbu.edu
DEIBERT, Glenn .... 912-287-5827 117 J gdeibert@coastalpines.edu
DEIBERT, Renee .... 706-439-6314 123 G rdeibert@northgatech.edu
DEIBLER, Lauren, C ...... 717-361-1164 394 F deiblerl@etown.edu
DEICHEN, Michael, G .... 407-823-2094 110 C michael.deichen@ucf.edu
DEIFELL, Hope .... 828-669-8012 340 I hdeifell@montreat.edu
DEIGHTON, Joseph .... 314-889-1410 260 C jdeighton@fontbonne.edu
DEIGNAN, Kathleen .... 609-258-5431 288 F kdeignan@princeton.edu
DEIKE, Randall, C .... 215-895-2901 394 C rcd58@drexel.edu
DEIKE, Terri .... 903-233-3769 452 A terrideike@letu.edu
DEIMAN-THORNTON, Ann .... 651-450-3753 245 A adeiman@inverhills.edu
DEINNOCENTIIS, Maria . 212-517-0482 314 D mdeinnocentiis@mmm.edu
DEITCH, Elaine, C .... 610-861-1340 402 D deitche@moravian.edu
DEITCH, Marissa .... 215-572-2972 389 D deitchm@arcadia.edu
DEITCHMAN, Jay .... 518-629-7567 310 G j.deitchman@hvcc.edu
DEITEMEYER, Kandi, W . 704-330-6566 342 A kandi.deitemeyer@cpcc.edu
DEITRICH, Ross, D .... 610-566-1776 415 A rdeitrich@williamson.edu
DEITRICK, Becky .... 570-372-4015 410 H deitrick@susqu.edu
DEJAGER, Brad .... 218-751-8670 249 G braddejager@oakhills.edu
DEJAYNES, Lana .... 660-596-7295 267 E ldejaynes@sfccmo.edu
DEJEAN, Preston .... 516-726-5836 519 C dejeanp@usmma.edu
DEJESUS, Jorge .... 212-650-3165 302 E jd1339@hunter.cuny.edu
DEJESUS, Marian .... 787-765-3560 522 K mjesus@edpuniversity.edu
DEJESUS-AVILES, Desire .... 212-924-5900 330 G ddejesusaviles@swedishinstitute.edu
DEJESUS-RUEFF, Richard .... 585-385-8229 322 E rdejesus-rueff@sjfc.edu
DEJI, Deborah .... 312-939-0111 137 G deborah@eastwest.edu
DEJOICE, Mary Jo .... 304-637-1359 501 H dejoicem@dewv.edu
DEJONG, Carol .... 616-395-7760 231 D cdejong@hope.edu
DEJONG, David, N .... 412-624-4228 412 I dejong@pitt.edu
DEJONG, Debbie .... 516-299-3438 313 D debbie.dejong@liu.edu
DEJONG, E. Shawn .... 413-755-4260 221 B esdejong@stcc.edu
DEJOY, Jennifer .... 207-326-2256 200 F jennifer.dejoy@mma.edu
DEJTHAI, Eddie .... 239-280-2507.. 95 C eddie.dejthai@avemaria.edu
DEKAN, Doug, D .... 715-833-6238 513 E ddekan@cvtc.edu
DEKAY, Amy .... 716-880-2177 314 F adekay@medaille.edu
DEKAY, Amy, M .... 716-880-2224 314 F amy.marie.dekay@medaille.edu
DEKAY, Todd .... 575-624-7059 294 A todd.dekay@roswell.enmu.edu
DEKAY, Todd .... 717-358-6021 395 G todd.dekay@fandm.edu
DEKETELAERE, Vicki ...... 517-483-1478 232 K deketelv@lcc.edu
DEKEYSER, Georgia .... 907-786-4048.. 10 A gkdekeyser@alaska.edu
DEKKER NETTLEMAN, Mary .... 605-357-1309 428 E med@usd.edu
DEKLOTZ, Steve .... 503-493-6286 382 I sdeklotz@cu-portland.edu
DEKOVEN, Aram .... 860-701-6930 519 B aram.dekoven@uscg.mil
DEKREY, Susan .... 845-437-7400 333 A sudekrey@vassar.edu
DEKRUIF, Kimberly .... 909-469-5342.. 74 G kdekruif@westernu.edu
DEL BALZO, Mary Beth 914-831-0343 305 C mbdelbalzo@cw.edu
DEL BELLO, Wendy .... 281-756-3600 442 C wdelbello@alvincollege.edu
DEL BELLO, Wendy .... 281-756-3600 442 C wdebello@alvincollege.edu
DEL BELLO, Wendy .... 281-756-3600 442 C wdelbello@alvincollege.edu
DEL C. RODRIGUEZ, Maria .... 787-727-1515 529 B mrodriguez@sagrado.edu
DEL CASINO, Vincent, J .... 520-621-6688.. 16 J vdelcasino@email.arizona.edu
DEL CONTE, Christopher .... 817-257-7710 461 A c.delconte@tcu.edu
DEL GIUDICE, Dante, T 401-456-8091 417 A ddelgiudice@ric.edu
DEL GIUDICE, Michale . 303-724-0731.. 83 D michael.delguidice@ucdenver.edu
DEL GIUDICE, Tristan, S .... 814-641-3390 398 B delgiut@juniata.edu
DEL MAR APONTE, Maria .... 812-877-8935 163 G aponte@rose-hulman.edu
DEL PILAR BONNIN OROZCO, Maria .... 787-848-5739 526 C
DEL PINO KLOQUES, David .... 409-772-8423 469 C dadelpin@utmb.edu
DEL RIO, Esteban .... 619-260-7455.. 71 J edelrio@sandiego.edu
DEL RIO-MORALES, Ricardo .... 787-725-6500 521 C consejoactivo@gmail.com
DEL ROSARIO, Dativa ... 510-434-3891.. 56 I ddelrosario@peralta.edu
DEL ROSARIO, Diana .... 216-987-2296 360 E diana.del-rosario@tri-c.edu
DEL TONDO, Bruce .... 719-587-7227.. 76 D bdeltond@adams.edu
DEL TORO, Debra .... 210-829-6001 465 E ddeltoro@uiwtx.edu
DEL TORO, Edgar .... 787-894-2828 529 A edgar.deltoro@upr.edu
DEL VACCHIO, Andrea .. 610-558-5532 402 G vanhorna@neumann.edu
DEL VALLE, Nilkaliz .... 787-852-1430 522 P n.delvalle.f@hccpr.edu
DEL VALLE, Wilfredo ..... 787-863-2390 523 K wilfredo.delvalle@fajardo.inter.edu
DELA ROSA, Chris .... 510-659-6514.. 54 F cdelarosa@ohlone.edu
DELA TEJA, Magdalena . 817-515-6203 458 B magdalena.delateja@tccd.edu
DELABY, Lisa .... 530-895-2937.. 28 E delabyli@butte.edu
DELACH, Ruth .... 412-809-5100 408 D delach.ruth@pti.edu
DELACRUZ, Marisa .... 646-312-1000 301 B marisa.delacruz@baruch.cuny.edu
DELAET, Lee .... 314-889-4539 260 C ldelaet@fontbonne.edu
DELAFONTAINE, Patrice 573-884-9080 268 C delafontaine@missouri.edu
DELAGUERRA, Christy .. 201-327-8877 285 J cdelaguerra@eastwick.edu
DELAHOYDE, Theresa ... 402-481-8843 273 F theresa.delahoyde@bryanhealthcollege.edu
DELAHUNT, III, Thomas, F .... 215-951-1024 398 F delahunt@lasalle.edu
DELAIN, Cindy .... 559-737-6265.. 39 G cindyd@cos.edu
DELAMATER, Thomas, R .... 972-599-3144 446 I tdelamater@collin.edu
DELAND, Robert .... 312-788-1142 154 I rdeland@vandercook.edu
DELANDSHEER, Alyson . 906-487-7339 230 B alyson.delandsheer@finlandia.edu
DELANEY, Anne Marie .. 781-239-6481 211 A delaneya@babson.edu
DELANEY, Christopher .. 717-337-6235 396 A cdelaney@gettysburg.edu
DELANEY, Connie, J ..... 612-624-1410 250 E delan108@umn.edu
DELANEY, John, A .... 904-620-2500 110 E jdelaney@unf.edu
DELANEY, John, T .... 202-885-1985.. 91 C jdelamey@american.edu
DELANEY, Kevin, J .... 215-204-3745 411 B kevin.delaney@temple.edu
DELANEY, Kristine .... 315-470-7380 299 K kristinedelaney@crouse.org
DELANEY, Marymichele 617-243-2176 216 C mdelaney@lasell.edu
DELANEY, Matthew .... 610-683-4778 406 D mdelaney@kutztown.edu
DELANEY, Maura .... 413-236-2101 219 B mdelaney@berkshirecc.edu
DELANEY, Meredith .... 513-936-1734 371 F meredith.delaney@uc.edu
DELANEY, Peggy .... 831-459-4317.. 70 C pdelaney@ucsc.edu
DELANEY, Sean .... 410-532-5371 206 D sdelaney@ndm.edu
DELANEY, Stephanie ..... 206-934-5819 497 J stephanie.delaney@seattlecolleges.edu
DELANEY, Timothy, J .... 740-284-5210 361 L tdelaney@franciscan.edu
DELANEY, Ute .... 845-752-3000 332 A registrar@uts.edu
DELANOY, Debra .... 845-687-5088 331 L delanoyd@sunyulster.edu
DELANTER, Jennifer ...... 281-649-3321 450 C jdelsanter@hbu.edu
DELANY, Michelle .... 860-465-5244.. 84 K delanym@easternct.edu
DELAP, Joseph .... 256-233-8203.... 4 C joe.delap@athens.edu
DELAPP, Jan .... 916-484-8633.. 50 F delappj@arc.losrios.edu
DELARGE, Kimberly, F .. 585-685-6191 315 L kdelarge@monroecc.edu
DELARGY, Deborah .... 714-966-8500.. 73 D ddelargy@ves.edu
DELAROSBY, Hal, R ...... 253-535-8259 496 G delarosby@plu.edu
DELAROSSA, Arnie .... 860-215-9236.. 86 F adelarossa@trcc.commnet.edu
DELASHMIT, Margaret ... 662-252-8000 255 F mdelashmit@rustcollege.edu
DELASHMUTT, Michael . 646-717-9781 309 B delashmutt@gts.edu
DELATE, John .... 973-655-7477 287 D delatej@mail.montclair.edu
DELAUDER, Saundra ...... 302-857-6001.. 90 B
DELAVALLADE, Tonjia ... 937-376-6028 358 I tdelavallade@ceentralstate.edu
DELAVAN, Katharine ...... 440-375-7389 364 C kdelavan@lec.edu
DELAWALLA, Noorali .... 562-860-2451.. 36 A ndelawalla@cerritos.edu
DELAY, Mary, G .... 210-567-2010 468 E delay@uthscsa.edu
DELBELSO, Debra .... 518-783-2339 324 C ddelbelso@siena.edu
DELBERT, August, C ..... 412-578-6471 391 G acdelbert@carlow.edu
DELBRIDGE, Kristina ..... 518-587-2100 329 C kristina.delbridge@esc.edu
DELCAMBRE, Ken .... 409-944-1314 449 F kdelcamb@gc.edu
DELCOURE, Natalya .... 361-593-3801 460 B natalya.delcoure@tamuk.edu
DELCOURT, Carrie .... 309-796-5318 134 C delcourtc@bhc.edu
DELEEUW, Jamie .... 734-384-4237 234 C jdeleeuw@monroeccc.edu
DELEON, Carolyn .... 619-201-8700.. 60 A
DELEON, Daniel .... 956-295-3805 461 F daniel.deleon@tsc.edu
DELEON, Daniel .... 956-380-8187 455 G ddeleon@riogrande.edu
DELEON, Delia .... 575-646-3121 295 B ddeleon@nmsu.edu
DELEON, Esteban .... 202-464-6636 476 B esteban.deleon@worldlearning.org
DELEON, Hilda .... 713-798-4612 444 A hildad@bcm.edu
DELEON, Rocio .... 310-954-4025.. 52 H rdeleon@msmu.edu
DELEON, Rolando .... 262-691-5175 515 B rdeleon5@wctc.edu
DELEON, Zelma .... 940-565-3901 466 B zelma.deleon@unt.edu
DELEON GUERRERA, Neda, C .... 670-234-5498 520 D neda.dlguerrero@marianas.edu
DELFFS, Erin .... 512-448-8768 455 I edelffs@stedwards.edu
DELFORTE, Joseph, L ... 585-785-1227 308 D joseph.delforte@flcc.edu
DELGADILLO, Carlos ..... 509-527-4282 499 E carlos.delgadillo@wwcc.edu
DELGADILLO, Carlos, E 509-527-4282 499 E carlos.delgadillo@wwcc.edu
DELGADO, Carlos, M .... 787-766-1717 526 B um_cfuentes@suagm.edu
DELGADO, Christina ..... 949-451-5693.. 64 I cdelgado@ivc.edu
DELGADO, Christopher . 210-486-3000 441 H cdelgado@alamo.edu
DELGADO, Chryssa .... 210-784-1355 460 C chryssa.delgado@tamusa.edu
DELGADO, Fernando ..... 218-726-7104 250 F vcaa@d.umn.edu
DELGADO, Heyda .... 787-622-8000 527 B hdelgado@pupr.edu
DELGADO, Irene, R .... 718-289-5869 301 D irene.delgado@bcc.cuny.edu
DELGADO, Junior .... 413-572-5546 218 F jdelgado@westfield.ma.edu
DELGADO, Luis, J .... 787-780-0070 521 B jdelgado@caribbean.edu
DELGADO, Ricardo .... 636-949-4735 261 I rdelgado@lindenwood.edu
DELGADO, Steve .... 562-907-4219.. 75 A sdelgado@whittier.edu
DELGADO, Vivian .... 218-755-2528 244 B vdelgado@bemidjistate.edu
DELGADO RODRIGUEZ, Wanda .... 787-815-0000 527 F wanda.delgado@upr.edu
DELGAUDIO, Rose .... 562-938-4397.. 48 I rdelgaudio@lbcc.edu
DELGIORNO, Christopher, M .... 845-575-3000 314 C christopher.delgiorno@marist.edu
DELGRECO, Michael ...... 978-837-5292 221 G delgrecom@merrimack.edu
DELHOUSAYE, Darryl, L 602-429-4932.. 15 K ddelhousaye@ps.edu
DELICH, Jeremy .... 914-251-5982 328 B jeremy.delich@purchase.edu
DELISA, Kenneth, J ...... 860-465-5269.. 84 K delisak@easternct.edu
DELISA, Monica .... 478-445-5768 119 E monica.delisa@gcsu.edu
DELISIO, Therese .... 773-380-6787 134 B tdelisio@bexleyseabury.edu
DELISLE, David, W .... 315-268-6666 304 B ddelisle@clarkson.edu
DELISLE, Joseph .... 781-239-2577 220 A jdelisle@massbay.edu
DELITTO, Anthony .... 412-383-6560 412 I delitto@pitt.edu
DELIZIO, Carissa .... 401-456-8126 417 A cdelizio@ric.edu
DELL, Troy .... 301-687-4471 209 A tadell@frostburg.edu
DELLA COLETTA, Cristina .... 858-534-6270.. 69 E cdellacoletta@ucsd.edu

DENNING, CSC, John, F .... 508-565-1301 224 H
jdenning@stonehill.edu
DENNING, Pamela .... 919-719-8889 348 I
pdenning@shawu.edu
DENNING, Rusty .... 864-941-8417 423 C
denning.r@ptc.edu
DENNING, William .... 919-466-4400.. 93 B
DENNIS, Anne .... 515-643-6640 171 K
adennis@mercydesmoines.org
DENNIS, Christina, M ... 610-399-2369 405 G
passhe-cdennis@cheyney.edu
DENNIS, Christine .... 310-338-2775.. 50 J
christine.dennis@lmu.edu
DENNIS, Dave .... 319-363-1323 172 B
ddennis@mtmercy.edu
DENNIS, Diana .... 815-753-2111 147 H
ddennis@niu.edu
DENNIS, James, M .... 618-537-6936 145 C
jdennis@mckendree.edu
DENNIS, Janet .... 412-536-1092 398 E
janet.dennis@laroche.edu
DENNIS, Jeff .... 864-250-8987 421 K
jeff.dennis@gvltec.edu
DENNIS, Jennifer .... 541-737-4881 385 F
DENNIS, Larry .... 850-644-5804 110 A
larry.dennis@cci.fsu.edu
DENNIS, Lynn, M .... 863-680-4107 100 D
ldennis@flsouthern.edu
DENNIS, Marie .... 215-567-7080 389 E
mdennis@edmc.edu
DENNIS, Peggy .... 419-372-8495 357 F
fayed@bgsu.edu
DENNIS, Raymond .... 310-338-5994.. 50 J
raymond.dennis@lmu.edu
DENNIS, Roger, J .... 215-571-4755 394 C
rjd45@drexel.edu
DENNIS, Suzanne .... 718-780-0314 300 A
suzanne.dennis@brooklaw.edu
DENNIS, Terry .... 863-680-4148 100 D
vdennis@flsouthern.edu
DENNIS, Vicki .... 318-678-6000 192 C
vdennis@bpcc.edu
DENNIS, Yolanda .... 508-588-9100 220 B
DENNISON, Anne .... 207-699-5054 199 H
adennison@meca.edu
DENNISON, Corley .... 304-558-0261 503 N
corley.dennison@wvhepc.edu
DENNISON, Lori, R .... 315-859-4412 309 D
ldenniso@hamilton.edu
DENNISON, Sondra, R .. 724-357-2696 406 C
sondra.dennison@iup.edu
DENNISON, Wayne .... 812-877-8858 163 G
dennison@rose-hulman.edu
DENNISTON, Marsha .... 605-331-6633 429 D
marsha.denniston@usiouxfalls.edu
DENNISTON, Terry .... 423-425-4203 440 A
terry-denniston@utc.edu
DENNY, Bryan .... 918-465-1818 375 J
bdenny@eosc.edu
DENNY, Bryan .... 918-465-2361 375 J
bdenny@eosc.edu
DENNY, David .... 503-699-6313 384 B
ddenny@marylhurst.edu
DENON, Gregory .... 978-934-2418 217 B
gregory_denon@uml.edu
DENOR, Kathy .... 800-567-2344 506 I
kdenor@menominee.edu
DENSBERGER, Derek ..... 714-556-3610.. 72 F
ddensberger@vanguard.edu
DENSE, Angela .... 417-865-2815 260 B
densea@evangel.edu
DENSLOW, Kathy .... 325-793-4903 452 F
kdenslow@mcm.edu
DENSMORE, Timothy .... 607-844-8222 331 D
tad@tompkinscortland.edu
DENSON, John .... 205-665-6235.... 8 E
jdenson1@montevallo.edu
DENSON, Michael .... 415-476-1414.. 70 A
mike.denson@ucsf.edu
DENSON, Rob .... 515-964-6638 168 A
rjdenson@dmacc.edu
DENT, Deborah, F .... 601-979-4299 253 E
deborah.f.dent@jsums.edu
DENT, Valeda, F .... 718-990-6559 322 F
dentv@stjohns.edu
DENTE, Michael .... 802-626-6456 477 C
michael.dente@lyndonstate.edu
DENTE, Michael, A .... 802-626-6375 477 D
michael.dente@lyndonstate.edu
DENTINO, Daniel .... 304-243-2237 505 H
ddentino@wju.edu
DENTLER, James .... 330-337-6403 356 B
registrar@awc.edu
DENTON, Andrew .... 612-343-4745 249 E
adenton@northcentral.edu
DENTON, Brian .... 620-341-6374 177 B
bdenton1@emporia.edu
DENTON, Carol .... 704-922-6484 343 D
denton.carol@gaston.edu
DENTON, Christine .... 808-739-8597 129 A
christine.denton@chaminade.edu
DENTON, David .... 931-221-6380 430 B
dentond@apsu.edu
DENTON, Melissa .... 913-234-0750 176 H
melissa.denton@cleveland.edu
DENVER, Genae .... 785-539-3571 179 F
gdenver@mccks.edu
DENYS, Mark .... 215-204-7500 411 B
mark.denys@temple.edu
DENZINE, Gypsy, M ...... 304-293-5704 505 B
gypsy.denzine@mail.wvu.edu
DEOCAMPO, Erlinda, N . 323-415-4163.. 48 L
deocamen@elac.edu
DEOLALIKAR, Anil .... 951-827-1575.. 69 D
anil.deolalikar@ucr.edu
DEOLIVEIRA, Shushawna .... 718-270-4744 326 A
shushawna.deoliveira@downstate.edu
DEORIO, Frank, A .... 718-817-4910 308 G
deorio@fordham.edu
DEPACE, Paul .... 401-874-2725 417 E
pauldepace@uri.edu
DEPAOLA, John .... 518-262-6008 297 L
depaolj@mail.amc.edu
DEPAOLA, Natacha .... 312-567-3009 140 I
depaola@iit.edu
DEPAOLIS, Cheryl .... 412-924-1384 408 E
cdepaolis@pts.edu
DEPAS, Jacob .... 920-465-2000 510 E
depasj@uwgb.edu
DEPASS, Michelle .... 212-229-5400 316 E
michelle.depass@newschool.edu
DEPAULL, Mark .... 607-753-2111 327 A
mark.depaull@cortland.edu
DEPAUW, Karen, P .... 540-231-7581 490 F
kpdepauw@vt.edu
DEPEDER, Suzanne .... 312-362-8648 137 C
sdepeder@depaul.edu
DEPERRO, Dennis, R .... 315-445-4685 312 F
deperrdr@lemoyne.edu
DEPERRO, Dennis, R .... 716-375-2222 322 B
drdeperro@sbu.edu
DEPEW, Chris .... 845-434-5750 330 F
cdepew@sullivan.suny.edu
DEPEW, Dennis, R .... 423-439-4289 431 H
depewd@etsu.edu
DEPEW, Elizabeth .... 219-785-5239 163 E
ebabcock@pnw.edu
DEPEW, Sally .... 231-591-3823 230 A
sallydepew@ferris.edu
DEPIETRO, Laura, A ...... 724-847-6590 395 J
ladepiet@geneva.edu
DEPINHO, Ronald .... 713-792-6000 469 B
DEPINTO, Michael .... 908-526-1200 289 D
michael.depinto@raritanval.edu
DEPOO, Tilokie .... 212-343-1234 315 D
tdepoo@mcny.edu
DEPOUTOT, Al .... 727-376-6911 112 G
adepoutot@trinitycollege.edu
DEPOY, Bryan .... 440-375-7028 364 C
bdepoy@lec.edu
DEPPERT, Phillip .... 831-242-5200 517 K
DEPPONG, Greg .... 517-355-5020 233 G
deppong@msu.edu
DEPREY, Linda .... 207-834-7800 201 E
lindad@maine.edu
DEPUTY, Meghan .... 386-312-4169 106 M
meghandeputy@sjrstate.edu
DEPUTY, Paul .... 907-786-4413.. 10 A
pdeputy@alaska.edu
DEPUY, Rebecca .... 817-598-6388 470 J
rdepuy@wc.edu
DER, Brenda .... 410-837-4813 209 D
bder@ubalt.edu
DER KIUREGHIAN, Armen .... 510-925-4282.. 25 P
adk@aua.am
DER SIMONIAN, Raffi ... 207-699-5010 199 H
rdersimonian@meca.edu
DERAMUS, Danny .... 501-279-4339.. 19 G
dderamus@harding.edu
DERANEK, Suzanne .... 507-457-1729 250 B
sderanek@smumn.edu
DERAVI, Fariba, S .... 334-244-3249.... 4 E
fderavi@aum.edu
DERBY, Dustin, C .... 563-884-5682 172 H
dustin.derby@palmer.edu
DERBYSHIRE, Lynne ..... 401-874-4732 417 E
derbyshire@uri.edu
DERDEN, Wade .... 501-760-6390.. 20 D
wade.derden@np.edu
DERDERIAN, Todd .... 508-767-7392 210 I
tderderi@assumption.edu
DEREBERY, Britanny ...... 903-813-2423 443 F
bderebery@austincollege.edu
DEREMER, Dennis .... 970-204-8255.. 79 K
dennis.deremer@frontrange.edu
DERICO, Amanda .... 513-244-8149 359 E
amanda.derico@ccuniversity.edu
DERIEUX, Anne .... 206-726-5171 494 B
aderieux@cornish.edu
DERIGGI, Nancy .... 914-923-2699 319 J
DERING, Allison .... 337-421-6955 193 F
allison.dering@sowela.edu
DERK, Malcolm .... 570-372-4571 410 H
derk@susqu.edu
DERMISHYAN, Sima ..... 916-877-7977.. 58 J
sima@sui.edu
DERMODY, Sean, B ...... 518-564-2539 327 E
dermodsb@plattsburgh.edu
DEROCHE, Jessica .... 972-899-8402 453 L
jderoche@nctc.edu
DEROCHI, Jack .... 803-323-2204 426 H
derochij@winthrop.edu
DEROEUN, Sheila, D ..... 225-771-5808 195 J
sheila_duplechain@subr.edu
DEROSA, John .... 203-837-9806.. 85 B
derosaj@wcsu.edu
DEROSA, Michael .... 510-869-8821.. 59 F
mderosa@samuelmerritt.edu
DEROSE, Angela .... 203-287-3032.. 87 G
paier.admin@snet.net
DEROSE, Angela .... 203-287-3033.. 87 G
paier.admin@snet.net
DEROSE, Michelle .... 616-632-2826 227 C
derosmic@aquinas.edu
DEROSE, Paul .... 602-285-7517.. 14 A
paul.derose@phoenixcollege.edu
DEROSE, Rae .... 312-777-8646 140 G
rderose@aii.edu
DEROSIER, Stephen ...... 603-752-1113 281 B
sderosier@ccsnh.edu
DEROUIN, Karen .... 413-552-2248 219 G
kderouin@hcc.edu
DERR, Colleen .... 765-677-3467 161 C
colleen.derr@indwes.edu
DERR, Debra .... 503-491-7211 384 D
debra.derr@mhcc.edu
DERR, Ed .... 417-873-7418 259 G
ederr@drury.edu
DERR, Gary, L .... 802-656-2212 476 E
gary.derr@uvm.edu
DERR, Matthew .... 802-586-7711 476 D
mderr@sterlingcollege.edu
DERRICK, Brandi, M ..... 903-434-8103 453 M
bderrick@ntcc.edu
DERRICK, Damon .... 936-468-4305 458 A
derrickdc@sfasu.edu
DERRICK, Diahann .... 541-881-5827 387 D
dderrick@tvcc.cc
DERRICK, Gwen .... 918-270-6424 378 I
gwen.derrick@ptstulsa.edu
DERRICK, Joey .... 803-777-3205 424 I
jcderric@mailbox.sc.edu
DERRICO, Cindy .... 805-437-3340.. 31 C
cindy.derrico@csuci.edu
DERRITT, Shawn .... 913-288-7437 178 H
sderritt@kckcc.edu
DERRIVAN, Kevin .... 617-850-1222 215 I
kderrivan@hchc.edu
DERRY, John, L .... 714-879-3901.. 45 I
jderry@hiu.edu
DERSCH, Denise .... 856-351-2682 291 E
ddersch@salemcc.edu
DERSTINE, Andria .... 440-775-8665 367 B
andria.derstine@oberlin.edu
DERUBBO, Jeff .... 724-938-4415 405 F
derubbo@calu.edu
DERUE, Scott .... 734-764-1363 237 I
DERUSSO, Katherine, E . 585-292-2320 315 L
kderusso@monroecc.edu
DERVIN, Alice .... 618-374-5106 149 A
alice.dervin@principia.edu
DERVISEVIC, Ajisa .... 516-686-7441 317 G
ajisad@nyit.edu
DERYCZ-KESSLER, Diana .... 323-464-5200.. 50 B
DESAI, Anand .... 316-978-3200 182 F
anand.desai@wichita.edu
DESALLES, Albert .... 310-434-4831.. 62 G
desalles_albert@smc.edu
DESALVO, Dianne, S ..... 989-774-4308 228 E
desal1ds@cmich.edu
DESANCTIS, Francesca .. 207-974-4810 199 L
fdesanctis@emcc.edu
DESANCTIS, Greg .... 908-526-1200 289 D
greg.desanctis@raritanval.edu
DESANCTIS, Marielena .. 954-201-6511.. 96 A
mdesanct@broward.edu
DESANTIS, Charles, E ... 202-687-1787.. 92 B
ced33@georgetown.edu
DESANTIS, Linda .... 609-343-5093 283 D
desantis@atlantic.edu
DESANTIS, Matthew, K .. 863-680-5055 100 D
mdesantis@flsouthern.edu
DESANTIS, Melanie, A .. 717-871-4950 407 A
melanie.desantis@millersville.edu
DESANTIS, Melissa .... 303-724-1748.. 83 D
melissa.desantis@ucdenver.edu
DESANTIS, Victor .... 717-871-7619 407 A
victor.desantis@millersville.edu
DESANTO, William .... 610-917-1438 413 G
wfdesanto@valleyforge.edu
DESANTOS, Cynthia ...... 409-747-9323 469 C
cydesant@utmb.edu
DESAUTELS-POLIQUIN, Lisa .... 207-859-1243 200 H
desautelsl@thomas.edu
DESBROW, Susan .... 850-484-1605 105 E
sdesbrow@pensacolastate.edu
DESCHAMPS, Eric .... 928-523-8334.. 14 K
eric.deschamps@nau.edu
DESCHENES, Molly .... 508-286-3458 225 G
deschenes_molly@wheatoncollege.edu
DESCUTNER, David .... 740-593-2600 368 G
descutne@ohio.edu
DESHIELDS, Richard ..... 509-963-1515 492 L
richard.deshields@cwu.edu
DESHLER, Kirsten .... 805-893-4588.. 70 B
kirsten.deshler@ia.ucsb.edu
DESHPANDE, Satish ...... 269-387-5067 239 E
satish.deshpande@wmich.edu
DESIDERIO, Lauren .... 212-353-4252 306 A
laurdesi@cooper.edu
DESIMONE, Albert, J ..... 269-337-7292 231 F
al.desimone@kzoo.edu
DESIMONE, Barbara ...... 716-614-6220 318 E
murphy@niagaracc.suny.edu
DESIR, Chantal .... 954-532-9614 101 P
DESJARDINS, Karla .... 860-932-4000.. 86 E
kdesjardins@qvcc.edu
DESJARDINS, Linda ...... 413-775-1105 219 F
desjardins@gcc.mass.edu
DESJEANS, Karen .... 413-552-2221 219 G
kdesjeans@hcc.edu
DESLATTE, Daniel .... 903-877-5077 469 A
daniel.deslatte@uthct.edu
DESMARAIS, Ethel, M ... 610-526-5245 390 G
edesmara@brynmawr.edu
DESMARAIS, Rachel, M 336-734-7175 343 C
rdesmarais@forsythtech.edu
DESMARTEAU, Doug ..... 620-365-5116 174 G
desmarteau@allencc.edu
DESMET, Erin .... 517-265-5161 226 F
edesmet@adrian.edu
DESMITH, Kristin .... 907-786-1263.. 10 A
kadesmith@alaska.edu
DESMOND, Bill .... 309-796-5437 134 C
desmondw@bhc.edu
DESMOND, Jill .... 414-382-6067 506 A
jill.desmond@alverno.edu
DESMOND, Nell .... 540-887-7225 482 G
hdesmond@marybaldwin.edu
DESOUZA, Priscila .... 650-543-3786.. 51 F
priscila.desouza@menlo.edu
DESPAIN, Trenton .... 540-261-8453 485 G
trenton.despain@svu.edu
DESPATHY, Carol .... 603-206-8136 280 L
cdespathy@ccsnh.edu
DESPLAS, Edward .... 505-566-3253 296 A
desplase@sanjuancollege.edu
DESROCHES, Reginal ..... 713-348-4009 455 F
rdr@rice.edu
DESSELLIER, Roberta, M .... 906-487-2200 234 A
rmdessel@mtu.edu
DESTEFANO, Joanne, M .... 607-255-4242 306 B
jmd11@cornell.edu
DESTEIGUER, John .... 405-425-5100 377 B
john.desteiguer@oc.edu
DESTEPHANO, Andrew .. 212-986-4343 299 F
afd@berkeleycollege.edu
DESTEPHANO, Andrew .. 212-986-4343 283 J
afd@berkeleycollege.edu
DESTER, Lisa .... 518-743-2232 328 G
desterl@sunyacc.edu
DESVIGNE, LaVora .... 718-482-5114 303 B
ldesvigne@lagcc.cuny.edu
DESWERT, Lisa .... 541-506-6058 382 G
ldeswert@cgcc.edu
DETAMPEL, SuAnn .... 920-465-2302 510 E
detampes@uwgb.edu
DETAR, Dave .... 412-521-6200 409 D
dave.detar@rosedaletech.org
DETAR, Eric .... 315-279-5378 312 D
edetar@keuka.edu
DETEMPLE, Jon Jay .... 610-526-6119 396 H
jdetemple@harcum.edu
DETER, Daniel .... 434-592-4172 482 D
ddeter@liberty.edu

DIAZ, Glenda .... 787-863-2390 523 K
glenda.diaz@fajardo.inter.edu
DIAZ, Jillian .... 203-591-5619.. 87 H
jdiaz@post.edu
DIAZ, Joel .... 805-678-5810.. 73 B
jdiaz@vcccd.edu
DIAZ, Jorge, L .... 787-786-3030 526 F
jdiaz@ucb.edu.pr
DIAZ, Kris .... 440-826-2900 357 B
kdiaz@bw.edu
DIAZ, Leticia, M .... 321-206-5602.. 95 G
ldiaz@barry.edu
DIAZ, Luis, R .... 787-751-0160 522 B
lrdiaz@cmpr.pr.gov
DIAZ, Maria, S .... 787-257-7373 525 Q
ue_mdiaz@suagm.edu
DIAZ, Mario .... 312-850-7492 136 C
mdiaz103@ccc.edu
DIAZ, Mauro .... 818-767-0888.. 75 C
DIAZ, Mayra, E .... 787-725-8120 522 M
mediaz@eap.edu
DIAZ, Minerva .... 787-738-2161 528 A
minerva.diaz@upr.edu
DIAZ, Mischelle, R .... 512-448-8404 455 I
mischeld@stedwards.edu
DIAZ, Ramonita .... 787-878-5475 523 H
rdiaz@arecibo.inter.edu
DIAZ, Robert .... 212-220-8305 301 C
rdiaz@bmcc.cuny.edu
DIAZ, Roberto .... 215-717-3107 393 C
roberto.diaz@curtis.edu
DIAZ, Russell .... 845-848-4048 306 G
russell.diaz@dc.edu
DIAZ, Sam .... 570-504-9069 395 I
sdiaz@tcmc.edu
DIAZ, Santos .... 830-591-7342 457 C
sdiaz2@swtjc.edu
DIAZ, Sharon, C .... 510-869-6512.. 59 F
sdiaz@samuelmerritt.edu
DIAZ, Sonia .... 787-728-1515 529 B
sdiaz@sagrado.edu
DIAZ, Sylvia .... 631-451-4486 330 B
diazs@sunysuffolk.edu
DIAZ, Veronica .... 310-434-4224.. 62 G
diaz_veronica@smc.edu
DIAZ, Walter .... 860-465-5247.. 84 K
diazw@easternct.edu
DIAZ, Walter .... 956-665-3553 468 A
walter.diaz@utrgv.edu
DIAZ, Yenny .... 305-348-2621 109 D
yenny.diaz@fiu.edu
DIAZ, Zaida .... 787-257-0199 527 H
zaida.diaz@upr.edu
DIAZ ALONSO, Herman 213-613-2200.. 65 A
directors_office@sciarc.edu
DIAZ BONACQUISTI,
Judi .... 303-352-3074.. 79 D
judi.diazbonacquisti@ccd.edu
DIAZ-HERRERA,
Jorge, L .... 315-279-5201 312 D
jdiazh@keuka.edu
DIAZ-RIOS, Erika .... 787-250-0000 527 D
erika.diaz1@upr.edu
DIAZ-RODRIGUEZ,
Nereida .... 787-798-6732 526 G
nereida.diaz@uccaribe.edu
DIAZ-RODRIGUEZ,
Victor .... 787-250-0000 527 D
victor.diaz@upr.edu
DIAZ SEMPRIT,
Ruth, M .... 787-763-6700 522 N
rmdiaz@se-pr.edu
DIAZ-TORRES, Marie ..... 973-353-5089 290 D
mdtorres@newark.rutgers.edu
DIAZ WREST, Alicia ...... 559-323-2100.. 61 A
awrest@sjcl.edu
DIAZPINEIRO, Odalys ... 718-997-5646 303 E
odalys.diazpineiro@qc.edu
DIBARTOLO, Adraina ..... 845-437-5315 333 A
adbartolo@vassar.edu
DIBARTOLO, Gerard, R . 410-548-3503 209 B
grdibartolo@salisbury.edu
DIBARTOLO, Patricia ..... 413-585-3913 224 F
pdibarto@smith.edu
DIBARTOLOMEO,
Michael .... 973-720-2903 292 I
dibartolomeom@wpunj.edu
DIBB, Andrew M, T ...... 267-502-2582 390 F
andrew.dibb@brynathyn.edu
DIBBERT, Douglas, S .... 919-962-7050 351 B
doug_dibbert@unc.edu
DIBBINI, Murad .... 909-447-6321.. 38 B
mdibbini@cst.edu
DIBBLE, Deborah, A ...... 716-673-3131 325 C
deborah.dibble@fredonia.edu
DIBBLE, Rita .... 651-793-1805 245 E
rita.dibble@metrostate.edu

DIBELLA, Jeannette .... 603-206-8006 280 L
jdibella@ccsnh.edu
DIBELLA, Sue .... 702-895-4317 279 D
sue.dibella@unlv.edu
DIBENEDETTO,
Eileen, M .... 212-854-7732 299 B
edibened@barnard.edu
DIBERT, Cregg .... 814-262-3837 405 A
cdibert@pennhighlands.edu
DIBIASIO, Daniel, A ...... 419-772-2030 367 G
d-dibiasio@onu.edu
DIBISCEGLIE, Lisa .... 732-255-0400 288 B
ldibisceglie@ocean.edu
DIBLEY, Paula .... 704-216-3467 346 C
paula.dibley@rccc.edu
DIBONA, Brian .... 815-479-7510 145 B
bdibona@mchenry.edu
DIBRIGIDA, Vladimir .... 303-329-6355.. 78 L
director@cstcm.edu
DIBRITO, Kyle, J .... 717-736-4117 396 G
kjdibrit@hacc.edu
DICAPRIO, Deborah, A .. 845-575-3000 314 C
deborah.dicaprio@marist.edu
DICARLO, Joseph .... 508-929-8090 219 A
jdicarlo1@worcester.edu
DICARO, David .... 585-385-8025 322 E
ddicaro@sjfc.edu
DICARO, Kim .... 313-496-2625 238 H
kdicaro1@wcccd.edu
DICCE, Lisa .... 718-951-5065 301 E
lisa.dicce@brooklyn.cuny.edu
DICE, Douglas .... 989-463-7162 226 H
dice@alma.edu
DICENZO, Robert .... 540-665-1280 485 C
dicenzo@su.edu
DICESARE, Deborah, A .. 818-778-5522.. 49 G
dicesad@lavc.edu
DICGEL, James .... 202-865-6660.. 92 C
DICHELE, Anne, M .... 203-582-3463.. 88 A
anne.dichele@quinnipiac.edu
DICHRISTINA, Joseph ... 860-297-2156.. 88 E
joseph.dichristina@trincoll.edu
DICK, Denise .... 516-299-2522 313 C
denise.dick@liu.edu
DICK, Melissa, L .... 724-357-2550 406 C
m.l.dick@iup.edu
DICKENS, Anne .... 281-459-7634 456 A
anne.dickens@sjcd.edu
DICKENS, Brian .... 607-274-8000 311 D
bdickens@ithaca.edu
DICKENS, Linda, N .... 512-232-2646 467 C
linda.dickens@austin.utexas.edu
DICKENS, Margaret, A .. 715-833-6419 513 E
mdickens@cvtc.edu
DICKENS, Reginald .... 704-216-6025 339 E
rdickens@livingstone.edu
DICKENS, Robert, L .... 210-458-4065 468 B
robert.dickens@utsa.edu
DICKENS, Ross, N .... 731-881-7225 440 B
rdicken2@utm.edu
DICKENSON, Henry, H .. 940-565-2662 466 B
hank.dickenson@unt.edu
DICKERMAN, Robert .... 413-755-4606 221 B
dickerman@stcc.edu
DICKERSON, Aerial .... 912-279-4514 118 A
adickerson@ccga.edu
DICKERSON, Beverly ..... 870-245-5299.. 20 G
dickersonb@obu.edu
DICKERSON, Charlene .. 803-793-5134 420 G
dickersonc@denmarktech.edu
DICKERSON, Charles ..... 864-622-6001 418 E
cdickerson@andersonuniversity.edu
DICKERSON, Darby .... 313-427-2737 141 E
ddickerson@jmls.edu
DICKERSON, Dee Ann ... 918-647-1307 375 B
ddickerson@carlalbert.edu
DICKERSON, Hannah .... 704-233-8291 353 D
h.dickerson@wingate.edu
DICKERSON, John .... 662-325-2663 254 E
jdickerson@registrar.msstate.edu
DICKERSON, John, R .... 662-325-2663 254 E
jdickerson@registrar.msstate.edu
DICKERSON, Kenny .... 252-985-5438 348 A
kdickerson@ncwc.edu
DICKERSON, Larry .... 816-802-3363 261 C
ldickerson@kcai.edu
DICKERSON, Leslie .... 406-496-4879 272 E
ldickerson@mtech.edu
DICKERSON,
Maniphore .... 408-288-3117.. 61 P
maniphore.dickerson@sjcc.edu
DICKERSON, Mark .... 626-387-5763.. 26 U
mdickerson@apu.edu
DICKERSON, Mary Ann . 913-469-8500 178 F
mdkerson@jccc.edu
DICKERSON, Michelle ... 219-980-6618 160 C
mtdicker@iun.edu

DICKERSON, Rochelle ... 973-290-4478 285 A
rdickerson@cse.edu
DICKERSON, Shirley ..... 936-468-4109 458 A
sdickerson@sfasu.edu
DICKERT, Gerry .... 409-984-6342 462 E
dickertgl@lamarpa.edu
DICKES, David .... 605-668-4020 427 F
david.dickes@mtmc.edu
DICKEY, Daryl .... 678-839-6534 127 F
ddickey@westga.edu
DICKEY, JP .... 417-455-5466 259 D
jamesdickey@crowder.edu
DICKEY, M. Thaxter ...... 813-988-5131.. 99 D
dickeyt@floridacollege.edu
DICKEY, Marilyn .... 850-201-6652 112 C
dickeym@tcc.fl.edu
DICKEY, Matt .... 417-626-1234 264 J
dickey.matt@occ.edu
DICKEY, Todd, R .... 213-740-8184.. 72 B
svpadmin@usc.edu
DICKEY, Wanda .... 813-988-5131.. 99 D
library@floridacollege.edu
DICKEY, Wyman .... 904-269-7086 101 D
wdickey@fortiscollege.edu
DICKIE, George .... 406-874-6196 271 D
dickieg@milescc.edu
DICKINSON, Deborah .... 252-862-1287 345 H
ddoakey6906@roanokechowan.edu
DICKINSON, J. Barry .... 267-341-3373 397 G
bdickinson@holyfamily.edu
DICKINSON,
Marjorie, M .... 530-752-2619.. 68 H
mmdickinson@ucdavis.edu
DICKINSON, Maureen ... 309-796-5052 134 C
dickinsonm@bhc.edu
DICKINSON, Robyn .... 570-941-4178 413 F
robyn.dickinson@scranton.edu
DICKINSON, Rosie, A .... 956-326-2202 459 B
rosie@tamiu.edu
DICKMAN, Brent .... 212-280-1402 332 C
bdickman@uts.columbia.edu
DICKMAN, Daina .... 503-760-3131 381 J
daina@birthingway.edu
DICKMAN, Tom .... 301-696-3494 204 D
dickman@hood.edu
DICKMEYER, Lou .... 507-389-1268 246 A
louise.dickmeyer@mnsu.edu
DICKS, Karin .... 512-448-8405 455 I
karind@stedwards.edu
DICKS, Nikasha .... 803-508-7477 418 C
DICKSON, Angela .... 415-955-2100.. 24 K
adickson@alliant.edu
DICKSON, Brook, E .... 540-362-6287 481 F
bdickson@hollins.edu
DICKSON, Carol .... 802-586-7711 476 D
cdickson@sterlingcollege.edu
DICKSON, Chris, M .... 260-422-5561 159 D
cmdickson@indianatech.edu
DICKSON, John .... 727-873-4350 111 B
jdickson@mail.usf.edu
DICKSON, Kari .... 806-743-2946 463 E
kari.dickson@ttuhsc.edu
DICKSON, Kristopher .... 760-384-6148.. 47 B
kristopher.dickson@cerrocoso.edu
DICKSON, Laura, M ...... 515-281-3939 166 E
laura.dickson@iowaregents.edu
DICKSON, Laurie .... 928-523-6771.. 14 K
laurie.dickson@nau.edu
DICKSON, Risa, E .... 808-956-6897 129 H
risad@hawaii.edu
DICKSON, Shondra .... 202-448-7294.. 91 H
shondra.dickson@gallaudet.edu
DICKSON, Zach .... 405-789-7661 380 A
zach.dickson@swcu.edu
DICKSTEIN, Gary .... 937-775-2808 374 B
gary.dickstein@wright.edu
DICOLA, Rose Ann .... 412-237-6517 392 G
rdicola@ccac.edu
DICORLETO, Paul, E ...... 330-672-1733 363 I
dicorlp@kent.edu
DICOSTANZO, Elina ...... 910-755-8517 341 C
dicostanzoe@brunswickcc.edu
DIDDAMS, Margaret ...... 630-752-5004 155 F
margaret.diddams@wheaton.edu
DIDIER, Kim .... 515-965-7064 168 A
kmdidier@dmacc.edu
DIDIER, Meredith .... 919-962-1591 349 G
mbdidier@northcarolina.edu
DIDION, Catherine .... 781-292-2300 215 C
catherine.didion@olin.edu
DIDION, Judy, A .... 248-364-8787 235 J
jdidion@oakland.edu
DIDLAKE, Ralph, H .... 601-984-5009 256 D
rdidlake@umc.edu
DIEBOLD, Alain .... 315-792-7100 330 A
adiebold@sunypoly.edu
DIEBOLD, Ann .... 610-519-4560 413 K
ann.diebold@villanova.edu

DIECKMAN, Stacy .... 402-844-7288 276 G
stacyd@northeast.edu
DIECKMEYER, Diane ...... 760-757-2121.. 52 F
ddieckmeyer@miracosta.edu
DIEFENDORF, Wendy .... 518-244-2443 321 G
diefew@sage.edu
DIEGO, Elizabeth, A ...... 671-735-5506 519 H
elizabeth.diego@guamcc.edu
DIEHL, Amy .... 717-477-7447 407 B
DIEHL, Beatrice .... 518-454-2142 305 B
diehlb@strose.edu
DIEHL, Bert .... 440-525-7140 364 D
rdiehl@lakelandcc.edu
DIEHL, Dave .... 301-696-3800 204 D
diehld@hood.edu
DIEHL, David .... 615-248-1291 439 B
ddiehl@trevecca.edu
DIEHL, David, W .... 630-844-4933 133 H
ddiehl@aurora.edu
DIEHL, Hope, L .... 610-359-5333 393 E
hdiehl@dccc.edu
DIEHL, Joan .... 570-348-6248 401 B
1226mgr@fheg.follett.com
DIEHL, Melissa, M .... 570-577-3776 390 H
melissa.diehl@bucknell.edu
DIEHL, Michele .... 215-646-7300 396 E
diehl.m@gmercyu.edu
DIEHL, Randy, L .... 512-471-4141 467 C
diehl@austin.utexas.edu
DIEHL, Shanda .... 360-992-2421 493 E
sdiehl@clark.edu
DIEHL, Timothy .... 207-725-3716 198 G
tdiehl@bowdoin.edu
DIEHM, Perry .... 405-789-6400 379 K
pdiehm@snu.edu
DIEKER, R. Joseph .... 319-895-4210 167 G
jdieker@cornellcollege.edu
DIEKMAN, Larry .... 269-467-9945 230 C
ldiekman@glenoaks.edu
DIEKMAN, Mary Jo .... 440-775-5302 367 B
mdiekman@oberlin.edu
DIEKMANN, Beth .... 507-285-7259 247 D
beth.diekmann@rctc.edu
DIEL-HUNT, Sarah .... 309-268-8593 139 D
sarah.dielhunt@heartland.edu
DIEM, Carol .... 206-543-6285 499 D
cdiem@uw.edu
DIEM, Richard, A .... 210-458-6463 468 B
richard.diem@utsa.edu
DIEMER, Gregory, M ..... 715-346-2641 511 F
gdiemer@uwsp.edu
DIEMER, Robert .... 352-588-8974 106 N
robert.diemer@saintleo.edu
DIENGER, Rebecca, J .... 715-836-4423 510 D
diengerj@uwec.edu
DIENST, Tom .... 907-796-6497.. 10 C
trdienst@alaska.edu
DIERENFIELD, Bruce, J . 716-888-2683 300 G
derenfb@canisius.edu
DIERINGER, Deanna, L . 907-474-6629.. 10 B
dldieringer@alaska.edu
DIERKS, David, R .... 319-335-3305 166 G
david-dierks@uiowa.edu
DIERMEIER, Daniel, D ... 773-702-9623 153 F
ddiermeier@uchicago.edu
DIES, Andrew .... 912-344-2514 115 D
andrew.dies@armstrong.edu
DIESNER, Michael, R .... 717-867-6231 399 J
diesner@lvc.edu
DIETERICH, Scott .... 718-409-7204 329 E
sdieterich@sunymaritime.edu
DIETERLY, Catherine ..... 510-567-6174.. 66 I
cdieterly@sum.edu
DIETIKER, Kristen .... 650-543-3889.. 51 F
kdietiker@menlo.edu
DIETRICH, Julie .... 610-499-4190 414 F
jdietrich@mail.widener.edu
DIETRICH, Kim, E .... 260-399-7700 165 B
kdietrich@sf.edu
DIETRICH, Robb .... 570-321-4401 400 G
dietrich@lycoming.edu
DIETRICH, Robert .... 617-373-4827 223 D
DIETRICH, Robin .... 540-887-7025 482 G
rdietrich@marybaldwin.edu
DIETRICH, Sandra, L ..... 919-866-5674 347 D
sldietrich@waketech.edu
DIETZ, Carol, P .... 216-397-4314 363 H
cdietz@jcu.edu
DIETZ, Connie, R .... 316-978-6988 182 F
connie.dietz@wichita.edu
DIETZ, Fred, K .... 270-809-2684 188 D
fdietz@murraystate.edu
DIETZ, Jonathan .... 620-792-9281 175 C
dietzj@bartonccc.edu
DIETZ, Kelley .... 919-508-2220 353 C
kelley.dietz@peace.edu
DIETZ, Kenneth .... 502-852-6176 190 C
kenneth.dietz@louisville.edu

DIRCKS, Curt .... 718-405-3223 304 H
curt.dircks@mountsaintvincent.edu
DIRE, James .... 808-245-8229 130 F
dire@hawaii.edu
DIRICO, Rocco .... 617-627-3780 225 A
rocco.dirico@tufts.edu
DIRIKER, Veronique, L .. 410-651-8142 208 C
vdiriker@umes.edu
DIRINGER, Lissie .... 212-824-2212 309 F
ldiringer@huc.edu
DIRK, Brian .... 440-375-7220 364 C
bdirk@lec.edu
DIRKS, Kathleen, M ...... 815-835-6386 151 E
kathleen.m.dirks@svcc.edu
DIRKS, Randy .... 952-829-1388 240 H
randy.dirks@bethfel.org
DIRKSCHNEIDER, Carla 402-552-6295 273 K
dirkschneider@clarksoncollege.edu
DIRKSE, John .... 661-654-6181.. 31 B
jdirkse@csub.edu
DIRKSEN, Dawn .... 866-323-0233.. 57 M
admin@providencecc.edu
DISABATINO, Gail .... 617-287-5800 216 I
gail.disabatino@umb.edu
DISALVIO, Philip .... 617-287-7925 216 I
philip.disalvio@umb.edu
DISALVO, Anthony .... 909-652-6257.. 36 E
anthony.disalvo@chaffey.edu
DISALVO, Stephen .... 314-529-9521 262 B
sdisalvo@maryville.edu
DISALVO, Steven, R ...... 603-641-7010 282 A
sdisalvo@anselm.edu
DISANO, Maria .... 401-874-7078 417 E
mdisano@uri.edu
DISANTE, Nancy .... 303-861-1151.. 79 E
ndisante@concorde.edu
DISANTI, Francis, J ...... 610-660-1506 409 H
disanti@sju.edu
DISBROW, Lynn .... 470-578-3550 122 C
ldisbrow@kennesaw.edu
DISCALA, Anthony .... 480-517-8411.. 14 B
anthony.discala@riosalado.edu
DISCELLO, Michael .... 724-337-1000 391 D
mdiscello@careerta.edu
DISCENZA, Tobias .... 239-489-9329 100 E
tjdiscenza@fsw.edu
DISCHINO, Maureen ..... 617-989-4009 225 E
dischinom@wit.edu
DISHMAN, Leslie, B ...... 985-448-4415 197 C
leslie.dishman@nicholls.edu
DISHMAN, Marcie .... 919-718-7491 341 H
mdishman@cccc.edu
DISHMAN, Melissa .... 307-778-1372 516 N
mdishman@lccc.wy.edu
DISHMAN, Mike .... 470-578-7588 122 C
mdishma2@kennesaw.edu
DISION, Maria .... 691-320-2480 519 G
mdison@comfsm.fm
DISKIN, Alan .... 702-651-7924 278 N
alan.diskin@csn.edu
DISKIN, Becca, L .... 417-659-5422 263 G
diskin-b@mssu.edu
DISLER, Heather .... 727-344-8065 107 A
disler.heather@spcollege.edu
DISMUKES, David .... 225-578-4400 193 M
dismukes@lsu.edu
DISNEW, Carolyn .... 212-752-1530 312 G
carolyn.disnew@limcollege.edu
DISORBO, Brenda .... 301-696-3413 204 D
disorbo@hood.edu
DISPIGNO, OFM,
Francis, J .... 716-375-2142 322 B
fdispigno@sbu.edu
DISQUE, Carol .... 336-506-4138 340 L
carol.disque@alamancecc.edu
DISTASI, Vincent, F .... 724-458-2116 396 D
vfdistasi@gcc.edu
DISTEFANO, Ann, L ...... 570-577-3200 390 H
ann.distefano@bucknell.edu
DISTEFANO, Augustine . 215-596-8800 413 E
DISTEFANO, Leslie .... 315-786-2234 311 H
ldistefano@sunyjefferson.edu
DISTEFANO, Phillip, P .. 303-492-8908.. 83 B
phil.distefano@colorado.edu
DITLEFSEN, Ed .... 208-732-6847 131 I
editlefsen@csi.edu
DITMAN, Mark .... 713-348-5441 455 F
mditman@rice.edu
DITOMMSO, Anthony .... 412-237-4413 392 G
adtommaso@ccac.edu
DITORO, Tim .... 936-633-5204 442 I
tditoro@angelina.edu
DITTEMORE, Nancy .... 951-785-2300.. 47 F
ndittemo@lasierra.edu
DITTMAN, Jeff, L .... 605-256-5229 428 G
jeff.dittman@dsu.edu
DITTMAN, Judy .... 605-256-5673 428 G
judy.dittman@dsu.edu
DITTMAN, Scott .... 540-458-8455 491 G
sdittman@wlu.edu
DITTMAR, Amy .... 734-763-1282 237 I
DITTMER, Amy .... 573-592-4313 270 D
amy.dittmer@williamwoods.edu
DITTMER, Michael .... 513-244-4619 366 A
michael.dittmer@msj.edu
DITTO, John .... 979-230-3157 444 E
john.ditto@brazosport.edu
DITTO, Liz .... 419-434-4510 372 B
dittoe@findlay.edu
DITTO, Therese .... 815-288-5511 151 E
DITTO, William .... 919-515-7277 350 E
william_ditto@ncsu.edu
DITTRICH, Linda .... 315-786-2323 311 H
ldittrich@sunyjefferson.edu
DITULIO, James, E .... 309-298-2453 155 D
je-ditulio@wiu.edu
DITULLIO, Daniel, F ...... 508-767-7321 210 I
df.ditullio@assumption.edu
DITZLER, Mauri, A .... 517-629-0210 226 G
mditzler@albion.edu
DIVALERIO, Thomas, J . 856-225-6050 290 B
tdivaler@camden.rutgers.edu
DIVELY, Mary Jo .... 412-268-9519 391 H
mjdively@andrew.cmu.edu
DIVEN-BROWN, Laura ... 662-915-7175 256 C
ldivenbr@olemiss.edu
DIVENS, Gary .... 856-338-1817 284 E
gdivens@camdencc.edu
DIVER, Theresa .... 603-626-9100 282 C
theresa.diver@snhu.edu
DIVINCENZO, Mark .... 617-452-2082 221 C
DIVINE, Darren, D .... 307-268-2548 516 H
darrendivine@caspercollege.edu
DIVINO, Claudio, F .... 252-334-2049 340 B
claudio.divino@macuniversity.edu
DIVITO, Catherine .... 501-812-2206.. 23 C
cdivito@pulaskitech.edu
DIVJAK, Robert .... 203-575-8235.. 86 B
rdivjak@nv.edu
DIWARA, Patrica .... 719-502-2037.. 81 H
patricia.diawar@ppcc.edu
DIX, Julie .... 508-849-3401 210 H
jdix@annamaria.edu
DIXEY, Mary .... 413-552-2261 219 G
mdixey@hcc.edu
DIXIE, Wendy, D .... 502-597-7000 187 E
wendy.dixie@kysu.edu
DIXON, Brad .... 660-248-6267 258 B
bdixon@centralmethodist.edu
DIXON, Brian .... 509-335-9711 499 G
DIXON, Bruce, W .... 606-474-3215 185 C
bdixon@kcu.edu
DIXON, Carol .... 757-352-4013 484 E
carodix@regent.edu
DIXON, Cassie .... 704-403-1798 336 B
cassie.dixon@carolinashealthcare.org
DIXON, Catherine .... 509-359-4863 494 D
cdixon@ewu.edu
DIXON, Catherine .... 410-626-2548 206 F
cathy.dixon@sjc.edu
DIXON, Clay-Edward .... 510-649-2540.. 44 J
cedixon@gtu.edu
DIXON, David .... 216-649-8700 363 I
ddixon@kent.edu
DIXON, Dawn, S .... 919-464-2373 344 C
dsdixon@johnstoncc.edu
DIXON, Jacqueline .... 727-553-3369 111 A
jdixon@usf.edu
DIXON, Janet .... 701-224-5739 354 F
janet.dixon@bismarckstate.edu
DIXON, Jenny .... 928-681-5656.. 14 I
jdixon@mohave.edu
DIXON, Jeri, L .... 630-801-7900 155 C
jdixon@waubonsee.edu
DIXON, Jesse .... 618-482-8326 152 C
jessdix@siue.edu
DIXON, John .... 843-661-1335 421 H
jdixon@fmarion.edu
DIXON, Joyce, A .... 662-254-3308 255 A
jadixon@mvsu.edu
DIXON, Karrie .... 919-843-5008 349 G
kdixon@northcarolina.edu
DIXON, Kathy .... 541-888-7408 387 A
kathy.dixon@socc.edu
DIXON, Kenn .... 256-726-8205.... 6 E
kdixon@oakwood.edu
DIXON, Kristin .... 503-375-7080 383 A
kdixon@corban.edu
DIXON, Lloyd, E .... 662-254-3335 255 A
ldixon@mvsu.edu
DIXON, Lynn .... 512-223-1222 443 G
cdixon@austincc.edu
DIXON, Margaret .... 662-621-4670 252 E
mdixon@coahomacc.edu
DIXON, Melanie .... 916-608-6713.. 50 H
dixonm@flc.losrios.edu
DIXON, Michael, G .... 260-982-5276 162 Q
mgdixon@manchester.edu
DIXON, Patrick .... 870-972-2042.. 18 A
pdixon@astate.edu
DIXON, Ramona .... 610-399-2220 405 G
rdixon@cheyney.edu
DIXON, Robert .... 312-413-1878 153 H
robd@uic.edu
DIXON, Robert .... 405-744-6512 377 F
robert.dixon@okstate.edu
DIXON, Roger .... 478-471-2720 123 A
roger.dixon@mga.edu
DIXON, Samuel .... 678-466-4200 117 I
samdixon@clayton.edu
DIXON, Sean .... 602-212-0501.. 11 F
sean.dixon@brightoncollege.edu
DIXON, Sean .... 602-212-0501.. 15 H
DIXON, Terrance .... 404-954-6520 123 E
terrance.dixon@morehouse.edu
DIXON, Tiffany .... 312-850-7013 136 C
tdixon10@ccc.edu
DIXON, Todd .... 386-312-4190 106 M
todddixon@sjrstate.edu
DIXON, William .... 270-831-9650 186 A
bill.dixon@kctcs.edu
DIXON, Willie .... 334-229-4200.... 4 A
wdixon@alasu.edu
DIXON-PETERS, Earic .... 818-710-2911.. 49 D
peterseb@piercecollege.edu
DIZAZZO, Laura .... 206-934-5492 497 I
laura.dizazzo@seattlecolleges.edu
DIZON, Michael, M ...... 773-442-4226 147 G
m-dizon@neiu.edu
DJALALI, Chaden .... 319-335-2610 166 G
chaden-djalali@uiowa.edu
DJEUKENG, Benji, N ..... 804-627-5306 478 I
benjamin_djeukeng@bshsi.org
DJUKIC, Stevan .... 918-876-2529 378 F
sdjukic@okwu.edu
DJUNAIDI, Harjanto ...... 931-540-2523 436 H
hdjunaidi@columbiastate.edu
DJURIC, Teresa, A .... 540-887-7243 482 G
tdjuric@marybaldwin.edu
DLUGOS, James, S .... 207-893-7711 200 G
jdlugos@sjcme.edu
DLUGOS, Joseph .... 252-399-6366 335 I
jadlugos@barton.edu
DLUGOS, OSA,
Raymond .... 978-837-5130 221 G
dlugosr@merrimack.edu
DMITROVSKY, Ethan ..... 713-792-2121 469 B
DO, Dao .... 714-484-7316.. 53 M
ddo@cypresscollege.edu
DO, Teresa .... 312-427-2737 141 E
tdo@jmls.edu
DOAK, Bryan, E .... 928-344-7617.. 11 B
bryan.doak@azwestern.edu
DOAK, Joshua, M .... 417-659-4460 263 G
doak-j@mssu.edu
DOAK, Robert .... 773-380-6783 134 B
bdoak@bexleyseabury.edu
DOAN, Kathleen .... 207-741-5805 200 C
kdoan@smccme.edu
DOAN, Linh .... 714-903-2762.. 68 A
DOAN, Viet .... 701-231-5143 354 D
viet.doan@ndsu.edu
DOANE, Amy .... 620-947-3121 181 H
amydoane@tabor.edu
DOANE, Christopher ..... 502-852-6907 190 C
doane@louisville.edu
DOANE, Dudley, J .... 434-982-3013 486 H
djd4j@virginia.edu
DOANE, Dudley, J .... 434-924-3371 486 H
djd4j@virginia.edu
DOANE, Paulann .... 307-268-2256 516 H
pdoane@caspercollege.edu
DOBBELAERE,
Arthur, G .... 630-515-7305 145 I
adobbe@midwestern.edu
DOBBELMANN, Duncan 802-440-4400 474 F
duncand@bennington.edu
DOBBERSTEIN, Trina ..... 440-826-2111 357 B
tdobbers@bw.edu
DOBBINS, Kenneth .... 336-506-4126 340 L
kenneth.dobbins@alamancecc.edu
DOBBS, Brian .... 208-732-6266 131 I
bdobbs@csi.edu
DOBBS, Gwen .... 479-636-9222.. 20 F
gdobbs@nwacc.edu
DOBBS, Lynn .... 662-329-7231 254 F
rldobbs@muw.edu
DOBBS, Ricky .... 903-468-8707 459 E
ricky.dobbs@tamuc.edu
DOBBS, Trish .... 315-268-4443 304 B
tdobbs@clarkson.edu
DOBELL, Dan .... 315-255-1743 300 H
DOBI, Hanko, H .... 203-932-7191.. 89 D
hdobi@newhaven.edu
DOBIAS, Dale .... 651-255-6144 250 D
ddobias@unitedseminary.edu
DOBIE, Elizabeth, A ...... 607-871-2171 298 A
dobie@alfred.edu
DOBIES, Anne Marie ..... 716-888-3749 300 G
dobies@canisius.edu
DOBIS, David .... 805-756-1104.. 30 K
ddobis@calpoly.edu
DOBISH, Rodney, W ..... 412-396-4781 394 D
dobish@duq.edu
DOBIYANSKI, Victoria ... 850-644-2428 110 A
vdobiyanski@admin.fsu.edu
DOBKIN, Bethami .... 925-631-4408.. 59 C
bethami.dobkin4@stmarys-ca.edu
DOBMEYER, Ann .... 413-565-1000 211 C
dobmeyer@baypath.edu
DOBRANSKY, Mary .... 402-557-7160 273 E
mary.dobransky@bellevue.edu
DOBRINSKY,
Herbert, C .... 212-960-0850 334 P
dobrinsk@yu.edu
DOBROTA, Joseph .... 757-221-2420 479 I
jdobrota@wm.edu
DOBROWSKI, Pauline ... 508-565-1363 224 H
pdobrowski@stonehill.edu
DOBSON, Alyssa .... 724-738-2220 407 C
alyssa.dobson@sru.edu
DOBSON, Catherine ...... 417-208-0636 261 D
cdobson@kcumb.edu
DOBSON, Cheryl .... 417-625-9389 263 G
dobson-c@mssu.edu
DOBSON, Cheryl .... 914-323-5177 314 A
cheryl.dobson@mville.edu
DOBSON, Christopher ... 814-472-3391 409 G
cdobson@francis.edu
DOBSON, Lark, T .... 301-546-0616 206 E
dobsonlt@pgcc.edu
DOBSON, Laura .... 828-328-7028 339 C
laura.dobson@lr.edu
DOBSON, Van .... 757-221-2255 479 I
vdobson@wm.edu
DOBSON-HOPKINS,
Nina .... 443-885-3130 206 A
nina.hopkins@morgan.edu
DOCHTERMAN, Cliff ...... 831-459-4524.. 70 C
bananaslugdoc@ucsc.edu
DOCKENDORF, Amy, L . 605-256-5130 428 G
amy.dockendorf@dsu.edu
DOCKERY, David, S ...... 847-317-8001 153 D
dsdockery@tiu.edu
DOCKERY, DeAnn .... 620-229-6210 181 F
deann.dockery@sckans.edu
DOCKERY, Jonathan ...... 847-317-7083 153 D
jsdockery@tiu.edu
DOCKERY, Kirbie .... 910-630-7167 340 A
kdockery@methodist.edu
DOCKERY, Rachael, M .. 417-836-8507 263 H
rmdockery@missouristate.edu
DOCKING, Jeffrey, R ..... 517-265-5161 226 F
jdocking@adrian.edu
DOCKINS, Waynna .... 870-612-2009.. 22 H
waynna.dockins@uaccb.edu
DOCTOR, John .... 650-738-4166.. 62 B
doctorj@smccd.edu
DOCTOR, OFM, John .... 218-228-5432 149 B
doctojo@quincy.edu
DOCTOR, OFM, John .... 217-228-5432 149 B
docotjo@quincy.edu
DODD, Daran .... 828-694-1832 341 B
d_dodd@blueridge.edu
DODD, David .... 502-456-6504 189 F
dhdodd@sullivan.edu
DODD, David .... 201-216-5491 291 G
david.dodd@stevens.edu
DODD, Linda, M .... 724-287-8711 390 J
linda.dodd@bc3.edu
DODD, Paul .... 530-754-7806.. 68 H
pdodd@ucdavis.edu
DODD, Shelley .... 307-766-4273 517 B
shelley@uwyo.edu
DODD, William .... 832-813-6564 452 C
william.m.dodd@lonestar.edu
DODDS, Cheryl .... 800-431-8488.. 26 F
DODDS, Michel .... 816-322-0110 257 M
mike.dodds@calvary.edu
DODDY, Lori .... 214-860-8680 448 B
DODGE, Barbara .... 920-693-1386 513 H
barbara.dodge@gotoltc.edu
DODGE, Brian, R .... 607-871-2154 298 A
dodgeb@alfred.edu
DODGE, Cabot, W .... 978-468-7111 215 E
cdodge@gcts.edu
DODGE, Darla .... 775-445-4224 279 F
darla.dodge@wnc.edu
DODGE, Gail .... 757-683-3277 483 G
gdodge@odu.edu
DODGE, Georgina .... 319-335-3565 166 G
georgina-dodge@uiowa.edu

DODGE, Georgina 570-577-2000 390 H
DODGE, Kevin 301-387-3328 203 I kevin.dodge@garrettcollege.edu
DODGE, Marvin 435-586-7721 473 A marvindodge@suu.edu
DODGE, Michelle 503-847-2560 387 I mdodge@uws.edu
DODGE, Norma Jean 620-417-1171 181 E normajean.dodge@sccc.edu
DODGE, Rhonda, M 727-816-3401 105 C dodger@phsc.edu
DODGE, Richard 954-262-3651 104 F dodge@nova.edu
DODGE, William, W 210-567-3160 468 E dodge@uthscsa.edu
DODGE-REYOME, Nancy, M 315-267-2131 328 A dodgenm@potsdam.edu
DODRILL, Laura 623-845-3528 13 H laura.dodrill@gccaz.edu
DODRILL, Stella 304-647-6310 504 F sdodrill@osteo.wvsom.edu
DODSON, André 941-377-4880 103 K
DODSON, Don, C 408-554-2145 62 F ddodson@scu.edu
DODSON, Jennifer 269-467-9945 230 C jdodson@glenoaks.edu
DODSON, Jerry 254-442-5152 445 Q jerry.dodson@cisco.edu
DODSON, Phyllis 317-789-8255 157 G pdidson@crossroads.edu
DODSON, Shelley 765-973-8332 160 A midodson@iue.edu
DODSON, Wendy, B 910-246-2868 346 E dodsonw@sandhills.edu
DOEBLE, Gina 239-489-9029 100 E gdoeble@fsw.edu
DOELL, Margaret 719-587-8383 76 D mjdoell@adams.edu
DOEPKER, Joel 636-584-6527 259 L joel.doepker@eastcentral.edu
DOERFER, Carol 518-828-4181 305 D doerfer@sunycgcc.edu
DOERGE, Rebecca, w 412-268-5124 391 H rwdoerge@andrew.cmu.edu
DOERING, Dionne 952-358-8271 246 D dionne.doering@normandale.edu
DOERING, Douglas 207-699-5082 199 H doug@meca.edu
DOERING, Laura, J 515-294-0760 166 F ljdoeri@iastate.edu
DOERMANN, Thomas 319-363-1323 172 B tdoermann@mtmercy.edu
DOERNEMAN, Randy, B 405-325-1206 380 L rdoerneman@ou.edu
DOERNER, Kinchel 605-688-5642 429 B kinchel.doerner@sdstate.edu
DOERNER, Kinchel 605-688-4181 429 B kinchel.doerner@sdstate.edu
DOERPINGHAUS, Helen 803-777-2808 424 I doerpihi@mailbox.sc.edu
DOERR, Gail 410-888-9048 205 D gdoerr@muih.edu
DOGBEVIA, Moses 402-461-7466 274 I mdogbevia@hastings.edu
DOGGETT, Jeffrey 978-837-5207 221 G doggettj@merrimack.edu
DOGGETT, Kelly 512-492-3014 442 J businessofficer@aoma.edu
DOGONNIUCK, Theodore 516-773-5000 519 C dogonniuck@usmma.edu
DOHE, Brian 509-527-4928 500 G dohe@whitman.edu
DOHENY, Sarah 207-581-1372 201 B sarah.doheny@maine.edu
DOHERTY, Brian 941-487-4300 110 B bdoherty@ncf.edu
DOHERTY, Brian, E 413-265-2372 213 E dohertyb@elms.edu
DOHERTY, Cynthia, A 717-736-4279 396 G cadohert@hacc.edu
DOHERTY, Eileen 773-298-5060 151 C edoherty@sxu.edu
DOHERTY, Frank, J 540-568-6830 481 I dohertfj@jmu.edu
DOHERTY, Jennifer 818-836-5038 143 E dohert@lewisu.edu
DOHERTY, Kathleen, T 717-780-2496 396 G ktdohert@hacc.edu
DOHERTY, Kathryn 410-532-5316 206 D kdoherty@ndm.edu
DOHERTY, Kenneth 313-577-3756 239 C ken-doherty@wayne.edu
DOHERTY, Kevin 620-421-6700 179 D kevind@labette.edu
DOHERTY, Kristal 864-646-1795 424 F kdoherty@tctc.edu
DOHERTY, Leanna, J 620-421-6700 179 D leannan@labette.edu
DOHERTY, Paula 360-417-6275 496 I pdoherty@pencol.edu
DOHERTY, Perry 617-585-1295 222 H perry.doherty@necmusic.edu
DOHERTY, Sharon 651-690-6783 249 T sldoherty@stkate.edu
DOHERTY, Steve 269-488-4442 231 G sdoherty@kvcc.edu
DOHERTY, Tiffany 603-513-1328 282 G tiffany.doherty@granite.edu
DOHNALIK, Judith 254-298-8600 458 C j.dohnalik@templejc.edu
DOIRON, Gail, M 978-665-3101 217 E gdoiron@fitchburgstate.edu
DOKTOR, Caryn, G 212-799-5000 312 B
DOLAK, James 970-491-4752 78 N jim.dolak@colostate.edu
DOLAK, Lisa, A 315-443-1860 330 H ladolak@syr.edu
DOLAMORE, Joan 617-243-2485 216 C jdolamore@lasell.edu
DOLAN, Abby 714-816-0366 67 J abby.dolan@trident.edu
DOLAN, Daniel 212-237-8900 302 F ddolan@jjay.cuny.edu
DOLAN, Gayle 617-277-3915 212 F dolang@bgsp.edu
DOLAN, James, E 317-381-6028 165 E jdolan@vinu.edu
DOLAN, Jill, S 609-258-3040 288 F jsdolan@princeton.edu
DOLAN, Jo Ann 410-617-2131 205 A jdolan@loyola.edu
DOLAN, John, F 617-521-2670 224 E john.dolan@simmons.edu
DOLAN, Julie, L 508-793-7443 213 C jdolan@clarku.edu
DOLAN, Kevin 617-732-2144 221 E kevin.dolan@mcphs.edu
DOLAN, Kevin 215-951-1010 398 F dolank@lasalle.edu
DOLAN, Linda 320-762-4439 243 J lindad@alextech.edu
DOLAN, Mary, K 315-267-4816 328 A dolanmk@potsdam.edu
DOLAN, Scott 614-234-1788 365 L sdolan@mccn.edu
DOLAN, Stacey, L 312-788-1147 154 I sdolan@vandercook.edu
DOLAN, Stephen 610-785-6216 409 F sdolan@scs.edu
DOLAN, Tammy 701-328-4116 353 F tammy.dolan@ndus.edu
DOLAN, Tina, M 781-283-3501 225 D cdolan@wellesley.edu
DOLAN WINTER, Elizabeth 801-585-7002 472 P liz.winter@legal.utah.edu
DOLBERRY, Carol 870-460-1034 22 D dolberryc@uamont.edu
DOLCI, Elizabeth 802-635-1482 477 C elizabeth.dolci@jsc.edu
DOLDER-ZIEKE, Beth, D 608-796-3828 512 R bdzieke@viterbo.edu
DOLEN, Tom 408-864-8764 43 E dolentom@deanza.edu
DOLHEIMER, Mary, E 717-815-1274 415 G mdolheim@ycp.edu
DOLINAR, Jon 216-987-4354 360 E jon.dolinar@tri-c.edu
DOLIVE, Mark 817-515-2113 458 B mark.dolive@tccd.edu
DOLL, Caroline 805-437-3232 31 C caroline.doll@csuci.edu
DOLL, Cheryl, A 610-799-1087 400 A cdoll@lccc.edu
DOLL, Christopher 740-366-9383 358 E doll.4@cotc.edu
DOLL, DeAnne 641-673-2118 174 F dollde@wmpenn.edu
DOLL, Nicole 859-344-3309 189 G dolln@thomasmore.edu
DOLLA, Marie 718-779-1499 320 C mdolla@plazacollege.edu
DOLLAR, Marek 513-529-4036 365 I dollarm@miamioh.edu
DOLLARD, Catherine, L 740-587-6238 361 B dollard@denison.edu
DOLLARD, Heidi 413-545-6133 216 H heidi.dollard@umass.edu
DOLLARD, Pam 715-346-3975 511 F pam.dollard@uwsp.edu
DOLLARD, Vincent 404-727-3366 119 B vdollar@emory.edu
DOLLING, David 202-994-6080 92 A dolling@gwu.edu
DOLLING, Lisa 914-323-5262 314 A lisa.dolling@mville.edu
DOLLINS, David 814-393-2306 405 H ddollins@clarion.edu
DOLLYHITE, Ronald 336-838-6149 347 G radollyhite367@wilkescc.edu
DOLPHIN, Jen 712-274-5110 172 A dolphinj@morningside.edu
DOLS, Kenn 218-855-8132 244 C kdols@clcmn.edu
DOLSEN, David, H 620-229-6298 181 F david.dolsen@sckans.edu
DOLTER, Kathryn 319-398-5630 171 F kathryn.dolter@kirkwood.edu
DOMACHOWSKI, Andrea 419-824-3704 364 G adomachowski@lourdes.edu
DOMACK, Alicia 414-277-7351 509 A domack@msoe.edu
DOMAN, Dakota 501-370-5295 21 A ddoman@philander.edu
DOMAN-FLYGARE, Sarah 763-424-0755 246 E sdoman-flygare@nhcc.edu
DOMANN, Moira 503-768-7680 383 G clb@lclark.edu
DOMAS, Matthew, S 662-562-3235 255 C gmdomas@northwestms.edu
DOMBROSKI, Mike 417-667-8181 259 A mdombroski@cottey.edu
DOMBROWSKI, Michael 716-614-5980 318 E mdombrowski@niagaracc.suny.edu
DOMBROWSKI, Teresa, A 630-515-6479 145 I tdombr@midwestern.edu
DOMECK, Craig 561-803-2302 104 I craig_domeck@pba.edu
DOMENE, Douglas, S 714-879-3901 45 I dsdomene@hiu.edu
DOMENECH, Manuel, A 512-394-9766 71 I mdomenech@usa.edu
DOMENECH, Roxanna, D 787-766-1717 526 B rdomenech1@suagm.edu
DOMENITZ, Linda 860-906-5153 85 D ldomenitz@ccc.commnet.edu
DOMES, Chris, E 610-558-5501 402 G cdomes@neumann.edu
DOMEYER, Janelle 402-399-2457 274 A jdomeyer@csm.edu
DOMIANO, Sam 985-549-2282 197 E sdomiano@selu.edu
DOMICK, Timothy 908-852-1400 284 G library@centenaryuniversity.edu
DOMIJAN, Alex 956-665-3510 468 A alexander.domijan@utrgv.edu
DOMINE, Karen 541-888-7212 387 A khelland@socc.edu
DOMINGO, Courtney, N 808-956-6486 129 H cmnd@hawaii.edu
DOMINGO, Junior 310-900-1600 40 C
DOMINGUEZ, Aaron 202-319-5115 91 D dominguez@cua.edu
DOMINGUEZ, Carmen 661-362-3116 39 C carmen.dominguez@canyons.edu
DOMINGUEZ, Dolores 859-371-9393 183 G ddominguez@beckfield.edu
DOMINGUEZ, Israel 949-582-4777 64 J idominguez@saddleback.edu
DOMINGUEZ, Leo 432-837-8596 462 G leodo@sulross.edu
DOMINGUEZ, Leo, G 432-837-8033 462 G leodo@sulross.edu
DOMINGUEZ, Mary 831-755-6714 45 C mdomingu@hartnell.edu
DOMINGUEZ, Nora 909-593-3511 70 E ndominguez@laverne.edu
DOMINGUEZ, Norberto 787-296-0453 523 F dominguez@inter.edu
DOMINGUEZ, Randy, G 918-595-8999 380 D randy.dominguez@tulsacc.edu
DOMINICIS, Erick 305-237-6583 103 L edominic@mdc.edu
DOMINICK, Ann 281-487-1170 460 G adominick@txchiro.edu
DOMINICK, Jay 609-258-5601 288 F jdominick@princeton.edu
DOMINO, Derek 920-686-6135 510 A derek.domino@sl.edu
DOMINY, Robert 478-757-3579 117 D rdominy@centralgatech.edu
DOMKE-DAMONTE, Darla, J 843-349-2129 420 A ddamonte@coastal.edu
DOMMER, David 919-658-7854 349 F ddommer@umo.edu
DOMPE, Rudy 818-719-6440 49 D domperf@piercecollege.edu
DOMPIERRE, Michael, B 636-922-8355 265 J mdompierre@stchas.edu
DOMZALSKI, Jim 570-740-0342 400 F jdomzalski@luzerne.edu
DONA, David 541-383-7222 382 B ddona@cocc.edu
DONAGHUE, Jennifer, H 202-994-4477 92 A iso@gwu.edu
DONAHOE, Frances 570-389-4652 405 E fdonahoe@bloomu.edu
DONAHOO, David 434-592-5868 482 D ddonahoo@liberty.edu
DONAHOO, Lori 270-831-9737 186 A lori.donahoo@kctcs.edu
DONAHUE, Amy 860-486-4037 88 G amy.donahue@uconn.edu
DONAHUE, Bob 614-947-6010 362 A robert.donahue@franklin.edu
DONAHUE, Colin 818-677-2333 33 B colin.donahue@csun.edu
DONAHUE, David, A 802-443-3060 475 G ddonahue@middlebury.edu
DONAHUE, Eileen, B 203-432-5850 89 G eileen.donahue@yale.edu
DONAHUE, James, A 925-631-4203 59 C president@stmarys-ca.edu
DONAHUE, James, P 423-652-6002 432 I jpd@king.edu
DONAHUE, Janice, M 423-585-6921 438 D janice.donahue@ws.edu
DONAHUE, Joseph 610-526-1867 396 H jdonahue@harcum.edu
DONAHUE, Linda, V 802-654-2563 476 A ldonahue@smcvt.edu
DONAHUE, Lorraine 814-262-3822 405 A ldonahue@pennhighlands.edu
DONAHUE, Nancy 865-694-6541 437 F ndonahue@pstcc.edu
DONAHUE, Neil 516-463-5400 310 D neil.h.donahue@hofstra.edu
DONAHUE, Patrick 812-855-3207 159 H donahued@indiana.edu
DONAHUE, Robert 617-353-9515 212 G rdonahue@bu.edu
DONAHUE, Sean 772-462-7751 101 Q sdonahue@irsc.edu
DONALD, Rebecca 847-317-4004 153 D rmiller@tiu.edu
DONALD, Ryan, J 330-471-8195 364 H rdonald@malone.edu
DONALDSON, Adam 334-386-7254 5 I adonaldson@faulkner.edu
DONALDSON, Anthony 951-343-4841 28 G adonaldson@calbaptist.edu
DONALDSON, Aura 951-552-8865 28 G audonaldson@calbaptist.edu
DONALDSON, Devlin 847-628-2087 142 B devlin.donaldson@judsonu.edu
DONALDSON, Janice, W 904-620-2476 110 E jdonalds@unf.edu
DONALDSON, Jody 319-398-7186 171 F jdonald@kirkwood.edu
DONALDSON, Paul 985-545-1500 192 K
DONALDSON, Scott 510-780-4500 48 D sdonaldson@lifewest.edu
DONALDSON, Tracey 732-255-0400 288 B tdonaldson@ocean.edu
DONAT, Kim 920-424-3377 511 B donatk@uwosh.edu
DONATH, Ben 712-749-2181 167 C donath@bvu.edu
DONATHAN, David 859-336-1743 185 H david.donathan@kctcs.edu
DONATI, Dana 724-480-3608 392 K dana.donati@ccbc.edu
DONATO, CSC, John, J 503-943-8532 387 H donato@up.edu
DONATO, Milagros 787-863-2390 523 K milagros.donato@fajardo.inter.edu
DONAVANT, Brian 731-881-3510 440 B bdonavant@utm.edu
DONAVANT, Lori, A 731-881-7815 440 B ldonavant@utm.edu
DONAVON, Annette 716-375-2234 322 B amcgraw@sbu.edu
DONCEVIC, John, G 724-847-6692 395 J jgdoncev@geneva.edu
DONCITS, Diane 651-641-3472 242 J ddoncits@luthersem.edu
DONCSECZ, Joseph, J 814-865-1355 403 F jjd7@psu.edu

DONDERO, Susan .... 414-326-1797 507 B
susan.dondero@ascension.org
DONE, Karen .... 662-621-4153 252 E
kwdone@coahomacc.edu
DONE, Kenneth .... 662-254-3624 255 A
kenneth.done@mvsu.edu
DONEGAN, Helen .... 407-235-3935 110 C
helen.donegan@ucf.edu
DONEGAN, John, P ...... 734-487-3591 229 K
jdonega1@emich.edu
DONELAN, Pam .... 605-229-8401 427 J
pam.donelan@presentation.edu
DONELSON, Felecia ...... 901-334-5823 434 C
fdonelson@memphisseminary.edu
DONELSON, Rollin .... 336-334-5963 351 D
rollin_donelson@uncg.edu
DONES, Abraham .... 919-536-7200 342 G
donesa@durhamtech.edu
DONEZ, Norma, C .... 787-751-0178 526 A
nodonez@suagm.edu
DONG, Jianyu (June) .... 323-343-4510.. 32 D
jdong2@calstatela.edu
DONG, Suhua .... 717-337-6487 396 A
sdong@gettysburg.edu
DONHAM, Brent .... 903-886-5390 459 E
brent.donham@tamuc.edu
DONHAM, Marilyn .... 734-973-3630 238 G
mdonham@wccnet.edu
DONINI, Joseph .... 845-398-4040 323 G
jdonini@stac.edu
DONIUS, Mary Alice ..... 203-365-4508.. 88 C
doniusm@sacredheart.edu
DONKERSLOOT,
Norman .... 616-392-8555 239 J
norman@westernsem.edu
DONLAN, Michael, J ...... 757-446-5890 480 C
donlanmj@evms.edu
DONLEY, Kathy .... 304-865-6004 502 C
kathy.donley@ovu.edu
DONLEY, Michael .... 903-566-7284 468 C
mdonley@uttyler.edu
DONLEY, Victoria .... 440-934-3101 367 D
vdonley@ohiobusinesscollege.edu
DONLIN, Mary .... 507-453-1479 245 G
mdonlin@southeastmn.edu
DONLON, Pam .... 513-618-1926 359 F
pdonlon@ccms.edu
DONNA, Jerry .... 863-784-7108 108 B
jerry.donna@southflorida.edu
DONNAY, Brent .... 320-308-3039 247 E
btdonnay@stcloudstate.edu
DONNELL, Ramsey .... 312-427-2737 141 E
rdonnell@jmls.edu
DONNELL, Richard .... 731-410-6716 432 J
rdonnell@lanecollege.edu
DONNELL, Robert .... 314-264-1000 269 G
robert.donnell@vatterott.edu
DONNELL, Shauna, H .... 479-968-0343.. 18 G
sdonnell@atu.edu
DONNELLI, Amber .... 775-753-2135 279 A
amber.donnelli@gbcnv.edu
DONNELLY, Cynthia ...... 401-341-3160 417 D
cynthia.donnelly@salve.edu
DONNELLY, David .... 914-654-5321 305 A
ddonnelly@cnr.edu
DONNELLY, Eileen, G .... 302-356-6812.. 91 B
eileen.g.donnelly@wilmu.edu
DONNELLY, Jeffrey .... 732-987-2427 286 D
jdonnelly@georgian.edu
DONNELLY, Jilian .... 610-361-5261 402 G
donnellj@neumann.edu
DONNELLY, John .... 434-961-5205 489 C
jdonnelly@pvcc.edu
DONNELLY, JR.,
Joseph .... 617-373-2520 223 D
DONNELLY, Sarah .... 908-526-1200 289 D
sarah.donnelly@raritanval.edu
DONNELLY, Sharon .... 215-489-2317 393 F
sharon.donnelly@delval.edu
DONNELLY, Sherri .... 518-445-2396 297 K
sdonn@albanylaw.edu
DONNELLY HAMILTON,
Ann, E .... 419-772-1022 367 G
a-donnelly@onu.edu
DONNER, Nancy .... 212-261-1572 317 G
nancy.donner@nyit.edu
DONNHAUSER, Marc .... 951-639-5670.. 52 J
mdonnhauser@msjc.edu
DONNITHORNE, Jeffrey 334-953-5613 517 I
jeffrey.donnithorne@us.af.mil
DONOFF, R. Bruce .... 617-432-1401 215 G
DONOFF, Susan .... 305-474-6062 107 B
sdonoff@stu.edu
DONOFRIO, Jason .... 480-860-2700.. 12 N
jdonofrio@taliesin.edu
DONOFRIO, Joseph ...... 864-578-8770 423 F
jdonofrio@sherman.edu
DONOGHUE, Daniel, J .. 858-822-5155.. 69 E
ddonoghue@ucsd.edu
DONOGHUE, Karen, A .. 203-254-4000.. 87 A
kdonoghue@fairfield.edu
DONOHOE, Janet .... 678-839-6636 127 F
jdonohoe@westga.edu
DONOHOE, Kerry .... 978-934-2542 217 B
kerry_donohoe@uml.edu
DONOHOE, Nancy .... 312-935-4804 149 K
ndonohoe@robertmorris.edu
DONOHOO, Daniel .... 650-325-5621.. 59 D
daniel.donohoo@stpatricksseminary.org
DONOHUE, Beth .... 315-568-3115 317 A
bdonohue@nycc.edu
DONOHUE, John .... 609-771-2393 284 I
jdonohue@tcnj.edu
DONOHUE, Mary .... 518-736-3622 309 A
mdonohue@fmcc.suny.edu
DONOHUE, Michael, T .. 212-752-1530 312 G
michael.donohue@limcollege.edu
DONOHUE, Michelle ...... 831-479-6525.. 28 F
midonohu@cabrillo.edu
DONOHUE, Patrick, R ... 570-941-4072 413 F
patrick.donohue@scranton.edu
DONOHUE, OSA,
Peter, M .... 610-519-8881 413 K
peter.donohue@villanova.edu
DONOHUE, Terry .... 631-656-2121 308 F
theresa.donahue@ftc.edu
DONOHUE-GONZALEZ,
Kristen .... 914-323-7534 314 A
kristen.donohue-gonzalez@mville.edu
DONOTO, Chris .... 847-317-8113 153 D
cdonoto@tiu.edu
DONOVAN, Amy .... 617-868-9600 216 D
DONOVAN, SND, Anne . 617-735-9822 214 F
donovan@emmanuel.edu
DONOVAN, Anthony ...... 615-460-5802 430 D
anthony.donovan@belmont.edu
DONOVAN, Celeste .... 620-417-1016 181 E
celeste.donovan@sccc.edu
DONOVAN, Eileen .... 802-728-1325 477 E
ecd04180@vtc.edu
DONOVAN, Gary, L .... 320-589-6065 251 A
donovang@morris.umn.edu
DONOVAN, James .... 657-278-2777.. 32 B
jdonovan@fullerton.edu
DONOVAN, Joan .... 607-844-8222 331 D
donovaj@tompkinscortland.edu
DONOVAN, Joseph .... 978-542-6119 218 E
jdonovan@salemstate.edu
DONOVAN, Kevin .... 716-896-0700 333 C
kdonovan@villa.edu
DONOVAN, Michael .... 617-353-8630 212 G
donovanm@bu.edu
DONOVAN, R. Nowell ... 817-257-7101 461 A
r.donovan@tcu.edu
DONOVAN, Steve .... 860-297-2281.. 88 E
steve.donovan@trincoll.edu
DONOVAN, Susan, M .... 502-272-8234 183 H
sdonovan@bellarmine.edu
DONOVAN, Veronica ..... 913-758-4372 182 B
veronica.donovan@stmary.edu
DONOWAY, Troy .... 301-687-7003 209 A
dtdonoway@frostburg.edu
DONSBACH, Dave .... 217-351-2393 148 H
ddonsbach@parkland.edu
DONSBACH, James .... 585-343-0055 309 C
jadonsbach@genesee.edu
DONSKY, Aaron .... 408-435-8989.. 64 A
DONTES, Arnim .... 214-648-3572 469 E
arnim.dontes@utsouthwestern.edu
DOODY, Josh .... 650-508-3685.. 54 D
jdoody@ndnu.edu
DOODY, Kevin .... 909-593-3511.. 70 E
DOOLEN, Toni .... 541-737-6400 385 F
toni.doolen@oregonstate.edu
DOOLEN, Toni .... 541-737-0123 385 F
toni.doolen@oregonstate.edu
DOOLEY, Chris .... 912-583-3221 116 G
cdooley@bpc.edu
DOOLEY, Dan .... 765-973-8348 160 A
dadooley@iue.edu
DOOLEY, David, M .... 401-874-2444 417 E
davedooley@uri.edu
DOOLEY, Dawn .... 907-786-1214.. 10 A
dpdooley@alaska.edu
DOOLEY, Donna .... 603-271-6484 280 N
ddooley@ccsnh.edu
DOOLEY, Elizabeth, A .... 407-823-2373 110 C
elizabeth.dooley@ucf.edu
DOOLEY, Frank, J .... 765-494-0615 163 C
dooleyf@purdue.edu
DOOLEY, John, E .... 540-231-2265 490 F
jdooley@vt.edu
DOOLEY, Jon .... 336-278-7220 337 G
jdooley4@elon.edu
DOOLEY, Joseph, M ..... 203-392-5375.. 85 A
dooleyj1@southernct.edu
DOOLEY,
Kathleen A, M .... 630-515-6078 145 I
kdoole@midwestern.edu
DOOLEY, Larry .... 864-656-3200 419 F
dooley@clemson.edu
DOOLEY, Lisa .... 701-858-3447 354 C
lisa.dooley@minotstateu.edu
DOOLEY, Marella .... 754-312-2898 102 V
mdooley@keycollege.edu
DOOLEY, Margaret .... 520-494-5215.. 11 P
margaret.dooley1@centralaz.edu
DOOLEY, Marietta .... 215-780-1260 410 D
mdooley@salus.edu
DOOLEY, Robert .... 423-425-4313 440 A
robert-dooley@utc.edu
DOOLEY, Ron .... 754-312-2898 102 V
admissions@keycollege.edu
DOOLEY, Ronald, H ...... 754-312-2898 102 V
rdooley@keycollege.edu
DOOLEY, Sue .... 831-656-3023 518 D
sgdooley@nps.edu
DOOLITTLE, Eric .... 630-637-5104 147 E
edoolittle@noctrl.edu
DOOLOS, Robert, K .... 225-578-1686 193 M
rdoolos@lsu.edu
DOORN, Dawn .... 760-480-8474.. 74 H
ddoorn@wscal.edu
DOPMAN, Kelly .... 573-592-5327 270 B
kelly.dopman@westminster-mo.edu
DOPP, Amy .... 413-552-2747 219 G
adopp@hcc.edu
DOPP, Kristi .... 206-592-3504 495 E
kdopp@highline.edu
DOPP, Mary Jane .... 219-989-2915 163 E
dopp@pnw.edu
DOPSON, Brian .... 386-752-1822.. 99 J
brian.dopson@fgc.edu
DOPSON, Lea, R .... 909-869-3464.. 31 A
lrdopson@cpp.edu
DORADO, Luis .... 310-233-4031.. 49 B
doradol@lahc.edu
DORAN, Andrea .... 775-445-4265 279 F
andrea.doran@wnc.edu
DORAN, Brenda .... 401-232-6106 416 A
bdoran@bryant.edu
DORAN, Christine, M ..... 315-267-3354 328 A
dorancm@potsdam.edu
DORAN, Douglas .... 772-462-7159 101 Q
ddoran@irsc.edu
DORAN, Dru, A .... 810-762-3000 238 B
drudoran@umflint.edu
DORAN, Marcia .... 203-285-2389.. 85 E
mdoran@gwcc.commnet.edu
DORAN, Pam .... 803-777-2752 424 I
pdoran@mailbox.sc.edu
DORAN, Stacy .... 920-735-5698 513 F
doran@fvtc.edu
DORANTES, Andrew, R . 909-621-8126.. 45 D
andrew_dorantes@hmc.edu
DORCEY, Penny, R .... 734-384-4311 234 C
pdorcey@monroeccc.edu
DORCHEUS, Greg .... 503-338-2489 382 E
gdorcheus@clatsopcc.edu
DORCHEUS, Stephanie .. 503-338-2425 382 E
sdorcheus@clatsopcc.edu
DORDICK, Jonathan, S . 518-276-4873 321 A
dordick@rpi.edu
DORE, David .... 520-206-7100.. 15 L
ddore@pima.edu
DORE, David .... 520-206-2111.. 15 L
ddore@pima.edu
DORF, Laurie .... 718-997-3920 303 E
laurie.dorf@qc.cuny.edu
DORFF, Robert .... 470-578-6124 122 C
rdorff@kennesaw.edu
DORFMAN, Laura .... 310-377-5501.. 51 B
ldorfman@marymountcalifornia.edu
DORGAN, Mark, W .... 802-656-0518 476 E
mark.dorgan@uvm.edu
DORGAN, Sheila .... 508-910-6527 217 A
sdorgan@umassd.edu
DORHOUT, Peter, K ...... 785-532-5110 179 A
dorhout@ksu.edu
DORIA, Joseph .... 201-761-6195 291 D
jdoria@saintpeters.edu
DORIANI, Daniel, M ..... 314-434-4044 259 B
dan.doriani@covenantseminary.edu
DORIS, Eugene, P .... 203-254-4000.. 87 A
edoris@fairfield.edu
DORITY, Nancy .... 657-278-2350.. 32 B
ndority@fullerton.edu
DORMAN, Jay, A .... 334-833-4406.... 5 M
jdorman@hawks.huntingdon.edu
DORMAN, Jeremy .... 903-693-2009 454 E
jdorman@panola.edu
DORMAN, Jesse .... 402-872-2246 276 C
jdorman@peru.edu
DORMAN, Laura .... 217-206-6005 154 A
dorman.laura@uis.edu
DORMAN, Peter .... 434-832-7837 487 H
dormanp@cvcc.vccs.edu
DORMAN, Steve, M .... 478-445-4444 119 E
steve.dorman@gcsu.edu
DORMINY, Bill .... 706-385-1466 124 F
bill.dorminy@point.edu
DORMINY, Sally .... 229-245-2462 128 G
sally.dorminy@wiregrass.edu
DORN, Charles .... 207-725-3290 198 G
cdorn@bowdoin.edu
DORN, Paul .... 916-608-6820.. 50 H
paul.dorn@harrisctr.net
DORN, Sara .... 314-421-0949 267 H
sdorn@siba.edu
DORNE, Clifford .... 989-964-7072 236 F
cdorne@svsu.edu
DORNER, Michael, H .... 651-641-8811 241 L
dorner@csp.edu
DORNES, Delfina .... 618-468-5200 143 D
ddornes@lc.edu
DORNES, Stephanie ...... 909-607-7894.. 37 K
stephanie_dornes@cuc.claremont.edu
DORPH, Martin .... 212-992-8282 318 D
martin.dorph@nyu.edu
DORR, Aimee .... 510-987-9020.. 68 F
aimee.dorr@ucop.edu
DORR, Jodi, L .... 810-762-7996 232 C
jdorr@kettering.edu
DORR, Mary, I .... 913-288-7145 178 H
mdorr@kckcc.edu
DORRANCE, Lindsay ..... 410-225-2321 205 C
ldorrance@mica.edu
DORRELL, Martha .... 803-321-5373 422 H
martha.dorrell@newberry.edu
DORRELL, Natalie .... 760-384-6260.. 47 B
ndorrell@cerrocoso.edu
DORRIAN, John .... 843-953-6779 419 D
DORRILL, Lauri .... 334-670-3276.... 7 E
ldorrill@troy.edu
DORSA, Daniel .... 503-494-1084 385 D
research@ohsu.edu
DORSCHEL, Matt .... 208-885-7209 132 I
mdorschel@uidaho.edu
DORSETT, Alvin, J .... 410-651-6174 208 C
ajdorsett@umes.edu
DORSETT, James .... 517-353-1720 233 G
jdorsett@msu.edu
DORSEY, Alan, T .... 706-542-1561 127 A
atdorsey@uga.edu
DORSEY, Andrew, R ...... 303-404-5481.. 79 K
andy.dorsey@frontrange.edu
DORSEY, Brynnmarie ..... 484-664-3199 402 F
brynnmariedorsey@muhlenberg.edu
DORSEY, Christopher .... 860-465-4398.. 84 K
dorseyc@easternct.edu
DORSEY, David, F .... 440-775-5191 367 B
david.dorsey@oberlin.edu
DORSEY, Judith .... 718-270-1867 326 A
judtih.dorsey@downstate.edu
DORSEY, Lynn .... 203-576-4743.. 88 F
ldorsey@bridgeport.edu
DORSEY, Melanie .... 917-493-4588 313 M
mdorsey@msmnyc.edu
DORSEY, Michael, W ..... 508-831-5609 226 E
mwdorsey@wpi.edu
DORSEY, Peter .... 301-447-7435 206 B
dorsey@msmary.edu
DORSEY, Stuart, B .... 830-372-8001 461 D
sdorsey@tlu.edu
DORSEY, Tamara .... 301-548-5500.. 93 B
DORSEY, Tara .... 407-831-9816.. 96 I
tdorsey@citycollege.edu
DORSEY, Tim .... 216-987-5027 360 E
tim.dorsey@tri-c.edu
DORSEY-ROBINSON,
Sylvia .... 559-925-3331.. 74 A
sylviadorseyrobinson@whccd.edu
DORTCH, Derrick .... 202-462-2101.. 92 D
ddortch@iwp.edu
DORTH, Kari .... 415-561-6555.. 57 K
kari.dorth@presidio.edu
DORTON, Alicia .... 678-359-5585 121 B
aliciad@gordonstate.edu
DORTON, Kim .... 276-523-2400 488 F
kdorton@mecc.edu
DORTON, Lynn .... 615-244-5848 435 N
l.dorton@sae.edu
DORY, Ondrea .... 641-784-5447 169 D
dory@graceland.edu
DOS SANTOS, Linda ..... 212-960-5300 334 P
linda.dossantos@yu.edu
DOSAL, Paul, J .... 813-974-5118 111 A
pdosal@usf.edu

DOWNING, Rossann ..... 816-604-4071 262 K
rossann.downing@mcckc.edu
DOWNING, Sherry .... 828-884-8437 335 L
downinsc@brevard.edu
DOWNING, Stacy, L ...... 302-857-6300.. 90 B
sdowning@desu.edu
DOWNING, Steve .... 317-955-6351 162 R
sdowning@marian.edu
DOWNS, Amy .... 717-815-1781 415 G
adowns@ycp.edu
DOWNS, Jesse, G 225-578-7180 193M
jdowns@lsu.edu
DOWNS, Mary .... 920-735-5695 513 F
downsm@fvtc.edu
DOWNS, Nate .... 580-774-3700 380 B
nate.downs@swosu.edu
DOWNS, Timothy .... 605-626-2521 428 H
president@northern.edu
DOWNS, Wil .... 812-237-4114 159 C
wil.downs@indstate.edu
DOWNS, William .... 252-328-6249 349 I
downsw14@ecu.edu
DOWNS-BURNS, Kim .... 802-443-5158 475 G
kdowns@middlebury.edu
DOWTY, Dean .... 310-233-4216.. 49 B
dowtydl@lahc.edu
DOWTY, Janet .... 317-738-8100 157 L
jdowty@franklincollege.edu
DOXEY, Tia, M .... 919-530-7269 350 D
tdoxey@nccu.edu
DOYLE, Adrian .... 310-338-1973.. 50 J
adrian.doyle@lmu.edu
DOYLE, Amanda .... 337-482-6730 197 F
amandad@louisiana.edu
DOYLE, Anne .... 617-663-7054 216 C
adoyle@lasell.edu
DOYLE, Barbara .... 805-765-9300.. 62 D
DOYLE, Catherine .... 585-389-2123 316 D
cdoyle0@naz.edu
DOYLE, Cathleen, H ...... 410-777-2902 202 D
chdoyle@aacc.edu
DOYLE, Christy .... 208-769-3481 132 E
cadoyle@nic.edu
DOYLE, Creig .... 904-819-6200.. 98 I
DOYLE, Denise .... 210-283-6827 465 E
ddoyle@uiwtx.edu
DOYLE, Diana, M .... 303-797-5701.. 76 I
diana.doyle@arapahoe.edu
DOYLE, Eileen .... 914-633-2483 311 B
edoyle@iona.edu
DOYLE, Fiona, M .... 510-642-5472.. 68 G
graddean@berkeley.edu
DOYLE, Francis, J .... 617-495-1000 215 G
DOYLE, Fred .... 518-956-7942 324 G
fddoyle@albany.edu
DOYLE, Gerald .... 312-567-5203 140 I
doyle@iit.edu
DOYLE, J. Griffin .... 706-542-8096 127 A
gdoyle@uga.edu
DOYLE, Jamie .... 858-225-4301.. 29 G
info@calarttech.edu
DOYLE, Janice, B .... 301-445-1901 207 F
jdoyle@usmd.edu
DOYLE, Jeff .... 254-710-3100 444 B
jeff_doyle@baylor.edu
DOYLE, Jillian .... 323-469-3300.. 25 D
jdoyle@amda.edu
DOYLE, John .... 734-432-5737 233 C
jdoyle@madonna.edu
DOYLE, Joy, E .... 724-847-6636 395 J
jedoyle@geneva.edu
DOYLE, Leslie .... 314-889-4503 260 C
ldoyle@fontbonne.edu
DOYLE, Lori, N .... 215-895-2613 394 C
lori.n.doyle@drexel.edu
DOYLE, Maria .... 678-839-4780 127 F
mdoyle@westga.edu
DOYLE, Mary .... 831-459-4906.. 70 C
mdoyle1@ucsc.edu
DOYLE, Michael, H .... 563-588-7823 171 H
mike.doyle@loras.edu
DOYLE, Oliver, J .... 406-791-5263 273 C
oliver.doyle@ugf.edu
DOYLE, Pam .... 316-677-9400 182 E
pdoyle@watc.edu
DOYLE, Sean .... 304-243-2641 505 H
sdoyle@wju.edu
DOYLE, Sheila .... 607-777-3844 325 A
sdoyle@binghamton.edu
DOYLE, Susan .... 205-726-2375.... 6 G
sdoyle@samford.edu
DOYLE, Timothy .... 901-321-3548 431 A
tdoyle1@cbu.edu
DOYLE, William .... 804-758-6700 489 D
wdoyle@rappahannock.edu
DOYLEN, Michael .... 414-229-4781 511 A
doylenm@uwm.edu

DOZIER, Cheryl .... 912-358-4000 125 C
ssupresident@savannahstate.edu
DOZIER, John .... 803-777-9943 424 I
jdozier@mailbox.sc.edu
DOZIER, Ken .... 252-399-6596 335 I
kdozier@barton.edu
DOZIER, Luann, D .... 504-865-5794 196 D
ldozier@tulane.edu
DOZIER, Rodney .... 620-276-9603 177 G
rodney.dozier@gcccks.edu
DRABIK, Daniel .... 954-545-4500 108 A
ddrabik@sfbc.edu
DRABIK, Joshua .... 954-545-4500 108 A
webmaster@sfbc.edu
DRABIK, Mary, A .... 954-545-4500 108 A
mdrabik@sfbc.edu
DRACHMAN, Annette, R 843-792-4063 422 C
drachmar@musc.edu
DRAEGER, James .... 262-691-5323 515 B
jdraeger5@wctc.edu
DRAEMEL, Ian .... 785-738-9031 180 E
idraemel@ncktc.edu
DRAGAN, Kimberly .... 860-738-6418.. 86 C
kdragan@nwcc.edu
DRAGON, Emily .... 207-602-2451 202 A
edragon@une.edu
DRAGOUN, Mary Beth .. 805-581-1233.. 42 G
mdragoun@eternitybiblecollege.com
DRAGUSHANSKAYA,
Ludmilla .... 718-522-9073 298 E
mdragush@asa.edu
DRAIN, Cecil, B .... 804-828-7247 487 E
cbdrain@vcu.edu
DRAIN, Jerome .... 713-718-7746 450 D
jerome.drain@hccs.edu
DRAIN, Timothy, S .... 903-510-2458 464 D
tdra@tjc.edu
DRAKE, Brent .... 702-895-3011 279 D
brent.drake@unlv.edu
DRAKE, Brian .... 713-221-2765 465 C
drakeb@uhd.edu
DRAKE, Brittney .... 714-816-0366.. 67 J
brittney.drake@trident.edu
DRAKE, David .... 706-865-2134 126 G
ddrake@truett.edu
DRAKE, Dawn, M .... 608-342-1468 511 D
drake@uwplatt.edu
DRAKE, Edna .... 601-977-7876 256 B
edrake@tougaloo.edu
DRAKE, George .... 717-871-7333 407 A
george.drake@millersville.edu
DRAKE, Howard .... 863-669-2321 105 F
hdrake@polk.edu
DRAKE, James .... 214-648-2088 469 E
james.drake@utsouthwestern.edu
DRAKE, Jennifer .... 360-867-6400 494 G
DRAKE, Jennifer .... 704-847-5600 349 E
jdrake@ses.edu
DRAKE, Kay, L .... 859-238-5467 184 C
kay.drake@centre.edu
DRAKE, Kourtney .... 816-279-7000 257 B
registrar@abtu.edu
DRAKE, Lynette .... 217-581-3221 138 A
ldrake@eiu.edu
DRAKE, Michael, V .... 614-292-2424 367 H
drake.379@osu.edu
DRAKE, Paul .... 671-734-1812 520 A
pdrake@piu.edu
DRAKE, Peter .... 212-842-5970 316 F
pdrake@nyaa.edu
DRAKE, Roger, D .... 660-248-6221 258 B
rdrake@centralmethodist.edu
DRAKE, Steve .... 618-283-4170 143 B
DRAKE, Steven .... 207-509-7200 200 I
sdrake@unity.edu
DRAKE, Susan, K .... 217-245-3041 139 H
sdrake@mail.ic.edu
DRAKE, Tom .... 207-581-1677 201 F
thomas.s.drake@maine.edu
DRAKE, Tom 575-769-4994 293M
tom.drake@clovis.edu
DRAKE, Tonya .... 425-640-1559 494 E
tonya.drake@edcc.edu
DRAKE, Tyler .... 480-212-1704.. 16 B
DRAKE-DEESE, Kent ...... 603-358-2346 283 A
kdrakedeese@keene.edu
DRAKEFORD,
Constance, M .... 803-786-3612 420 D
cmdrakeford@columbiasc.edu
DRAKSLER, Vicki .... 309-692-4092 145 F
vdraksler@midstate.edu
DRAMMEH, Lamin .... 205-349-4240.... 7 C
ldrammeh@stillman.edu
DRANKA, Scott .... 413-748-3110 224 G
sdranka@springfieldcollege.edu
DRANSFIELD, Scott .... 540-261-4122 485 G
scott.dransfield@svu.edu

DRAPEAU, Guy .... 860-297-4210.. 88 E
guy.drapeau@trincoll.edu
DRAPER, David .... 310-377-5501.. 51 B
ddraper@marymountcalifornia.edu
DRAPER, Dennis .... 310-338-7504.. 50 J
dennis.draper@lmu.edu
DRAPER, Diana, M .... 203-254-4125.. 87 A
ddraper@fairfield.edu
DRAPER, Frances .... 303-492-7531.. 83 B
frances.draper@colorado.edu
DRAPER, Jeri .... 215-751-8199 393 A
jdraper@ccp.edu
DRAPER, Mark .... 717-866-5775 395 C
mdraper@evangelical.edu
DRAPER, Nancy, J .... 405-912-9024 379 A
ndraper@ru.edu
DRAPER, Sherry .... 785-670-2312 182 D
sherry.draper@washburn.edu
DRASGOW, Fritz .... 217-333-1480 154 B
fdrasgow@illinois.edu
DRASS, Mike .... 302-736-2545.. 90 J
michael.drass@wesley.edu
DRAUD, Matthew .... 517-264-7667 236 I
mdraud@sienaheights.edu
DRAUDE, Barbara, J ..... 615-904-8383 434 H
barbara.draude@mtsu.edu
DRAUGHON,
Katherine, A .... 812-465-1630 165 C
kdraughon@usi.edu
DRAVES, Patricia, H ...... 641-784-5111 169 D
pat.draves@graceland.edu
DRAWDY, Lester, W ...... 770-720-5927 124 H
lwd@reinhardt.edu
DRAYER, Judy .... 602-274-1885.. 15 J
jdrayer@pihma.edu
DRAYFAHL, Perry, M .... 610-499-1291 414 F
pmdrayfahl@widener.edu
DRAYNA, Jonathan .... 414-425-8300 509 I
jdrayna@shsst.edu
DRAYTON, Lakenya .... 229-732-5952 115 B
lakenyadrayton@andrewcollege.edu
DRAYTON, Paul .... 856-222-9311 289 F
DRAYTON, Ronald .... 803-738-7606 422 D
draytonr@midlandstech.edu
DREBIN, Diane .... 541-278-5796 382 A
ddrebin@bluecc.edu
DREES, John .... 502-852-6739 190 C
jddree01@exchange.louisville.edu
DREES, Lynn .... 941-752-5428 108 P
dreesl@scf.edu
DREESE, Dawn .... 610-989-1307 413 I
ddreese@vfmac.edu
DREESSEN, Angela .... 309-694-5353 139 G
angela.dreessen@icc.edu
DREFFS, Daryl .... 603-668-2211 282 C
d.dreffs@snhu.edu
DREGER, Barb .... 920-735-4776 513 F
dreger@fvtc.edu
DREGIER, Denise, M ..... 443-412-2428 204 C
ddregier@harford.edu
DREHER, Karolina .... 610-796-8218 389 A
karolina.dreher@alvernia.edu
DREIER, Alexander .... 203-432-4949.. 89 G
alexander.dreier@yale.edu
DREILICH, Tom .... 661-824-2977.. 53 G
tdreilich@ntps.edu
DREIS, Marilyn .... 509-359-2371 494 D
mdreis@ewu.edu
DREISBACH, Joseph, H . 570-941-4760 413 F
joseph.dreisbach@scranton.edu
DREITH, Michael .... 314-422-2250 266 E
mdreith@stlcc.edu
DREITLEIN, Matthew ..... 315-279-5734 312 D
mdreitlein@keuka.edu
DRELL, Persis .... 650-724-4074.. 66 C
provost@stanford.edu
DRENKOW, Daniel, D ... 605-274-5251 426 K
dan.drenkow@augie.edu
DRENNEN, Rebecca, J .. 973-278-5400 283 J
rjd@berkeleycollege.edu
DRENNEN, Rebecca, J .. 212-986-4343 299 F
rjd@berkeleycollege.edu
DRENNING, Caleb .... 814-472-3035 409 G
cdrenning@francis.edu
DRESCHER, Greg .... 916-416-6476 306 D
greg.drescher@culinary.edu
DRESCHER, Kurt, W ...... 978-468-7111 215 E
kdrescher@gcts.edu
DRESS, Jennifer .... 410-455-2868 208 A
dress@umbc.edu
DRESSEN, Dan .... 507-786-3420 250 C
dressen@stolaf.edu
DRESSER, Charles .... 607-729-1581 306 F
cdresser@davisny.edu
DRESSER, Kathy .... 914-337-9300 305 F
kathy.dresser@concordia-ny.edu

DRESSER-RECKTENWALD,
Wendy .... 607-587-4025 328 F
dressews@alfredstate.edu
DREVON, Charles 574-239-8392 158M
cdrevon@hcc-nd.edu
DREVS, John .... 312-915-6941 144 D
jdrevs@luc.edu
DREW, Daniel, J .... 716-888-2569 300 G
drewd@canisius.edu
DREW, Phil .... 405-425-1842 377 B
philip.drew@oc.edu
DREWELOW, Lonna .... 319-363-1323 172 B
ldrewelow@mtmercy.edu
DREWENSKI, Shirley ..... 708-596-2000 151 H
sdrewenski@ssc.edu
DREWS, David .... 517-265-5161 226 F
ddrews@adrian.edu
DREXEL, Penny, M .... 814-332-4311 388 F
pdrexel@allegheny.edu
DREXLER, Brad .... 610-861-5475 403 B
bdrexler@northampton.edu
DREXLER, Jim .... 706-419-1427 118 E
jim.drexler@covenant.edu
DREXLER, Julie .... 229-333-2100 128 G
julie.drexler@wiregrass.edu
DREXLER-HINES,
Elizabeth .... 508-767-7343 210 I
ea.drexlerhines@assumption.edu
DREYER, Allen, R .... 570-586-2400 392 E
adreyer@clarkssummitu.edu
DREYER, John, M .... 260-452-3139 157 F
john.dreyer@ctsfw.edu
DREYER, Thomas .... 978-934-4801 217 B
thomas_dreyer@uml.edu
DREYFUS, Mark, B .... 757-671-7171 480 D
president@ecpi.edu
DREYFUSS, Shannon ..... 303-963-3411.. 77 I
sdreyfuss@ccu.edu
DREYFUSS, Simeon .... 503-699-3961 384 B
sdreyfuss@marylhurst.edu
DREYFUSS, Teresa .... 562-908-3403.. 58 D
tdreyfuss@riohondo.edu
DRIEDGER, Derek .... 605-995-2635 427 A
dedriedg@dwu.edu
DRIER, Tracy, M .... 715-833-6498 513 E
tdrier@cvtc.edu
DRIES, Kelly, J .... 414-410-4390 506 F
kjdries@stritch.edu
DRIESSEN, Daniel .... 701-662-1508 355 A
daniel.driessen@lrsc.edu
DRIESSNER, Johnnie ..... 503-493-6549 382 I
jdriessner@cu-portland.edu
DRIGGERS, Jon .... 828-898-8797 339 B
driggersj@lmc.edu
DRIGGERS, Randy .... 504-282-4455 195 D
rdriggers@nobts.edu
DRIGGS, Bethany .... 207-509-7169 200 I
bdriggs@unity.edu
DRINAN, Helen, G .... 617-521-2070 224 E
helen.drinan@simmons.edu
DRINDAK, Desiree .... 518-587-2100 329 C
desiree.drindak@esc.edu
DRINKARD, Gretchen .... 314-454-7055 260 E
gdrinkard@bjc.org
DRISCOLL, Debbie .... 434-544-8125 482 F
driscoll@lynchburg.edu
DRISCOLL, Diane, H ...... 603-526-3673 280 H
ddriscoll@colby-sawyer.edu
DRISCOLL, Frederick ..... 617-989-4135 225 E
driscollf@wit.edu
DRISCOLL, Laura .... 307-268-2733 516 H
ldriscoll@caspercollege.edu
DRISCOLL, Lori .... 850-769-1551 101 J
ldriscoll@gulfcoast.edu
DRISCOLL, Marcy, P ..... 850-644-6885 110 A
mdriscoll@fsu.edu
DRISCOLL, Mary .... 803-641-3448 425 A
maryc@usca.edu
DRISCOLL, Mary, E .... 212-650-5697 301 F
mdriscoll@ccny.cuny.edu
DRISCOLL, Michael .... 757-789-1754 488 A
mdriscoll@es.vccs.edu
DRISCOLL, Michael, A .. 724-357-2200 406 C
michael.driscoll@iup.edu
DRISCOLL, Micheline .... 718-368-5436 303 A
mdriscoll@kbcc.cuny.edu
DRISCOLL, Michelle .... 816-501-3608 257 G
michelle.driscoll@avila.edu
DRISCOLL, Robert, G .... 401-865-2090 416 E
rdriscol@providence.edu
DRISKELL, Chad .... 601-266-6525 256 E
chad.driskell@usm.edu
DRISKELL, Robyn, L ...... 254-710-3555 444 B
robyn_driskell@baylor.edu
DRISKILL, Bob .... 434-544-8100 482 F
driskill.b@lynchburg.edu
DRISKILL, Owen .... 865-481-2000 438 A
driskillo@roanestate.edu

DUFFY, Susan .... 781-239-6425 211 A
sduffy@babson.edu
DUFFY, II, William, R ... 563-425-5221 173 K
duffyw@uiu.edu
DUFNER, Jessie .... 406-874-6226 271 D
dufnerj@milescc.edu
DUFORT, Linda .... 630-279-4100 138 C
DUFOUR, Graciela .... 815-836-5270 143 E
dufourgr@lewisu.edu
DUFOUR, Jeff .... 518-694-7395 297 J
jeff.dufour@acphs.edu
DUFRENE, Uric .... 812-941-2208 161 A
udufrene@ius.edu
DUFRESNE-REYES,
Alice .... 408-848-4791.. 44 B
adufresnereyes@gavilan.edu
DUGAN, James .... 816-654-7219 261 D
jdugan@kcumb.edu
DUGAN, Mary .... 775-784-3941 279 E
mdugan@unr.edu
DUGAN, Melinda, E ...... 215-887-5511 414 D
mdugan@wts.edu
DUGAN, Robert .... 850-474-2492 111 D
rdugan@uwf.edu
DUGAN-WOOD, Joyce .. 205-929-1458.... 6 D
jduganwood@miles.edu
DUGATKIN, David .... 845-257-3802 325 D
dugatkind@newpaltz.edu
DUGGAN, Christina .... 781-768-7228 224 A
christina.duggan@regiscollege.edu
DUGGAN, Kuris .... 937-327-6471 374 A
duggank@wittenberg.edu
DUGGAN, Michael .... 617-824-8268 214 E
michael_duggar@emerson.edu
DUGGAN, Sean .... 806-742-2661 463 D
s.duggan@ttu.edu
DUGGAN GOLD, Lori ... 212-817-7170 302 B
lduggangold@gc.cuny.edu
DUGGER, Neil .... 214-333-5202 447 D
neil@dbu.edu
DUGGIN, Josh .... 731-286-3338 437 A
duggin@dscc.edu
DUGUID, Iain .... 215-887-5511 414 D
iduguid@wts.edu
DUGUID, James .... 864-231-2000 418 E
jduguid@andersonuniversity.edu
DUGUID, Stephanie ...... 601-643-5101 252 G
DUHL, Greg .... 651-290-6409 248 U
gregory.duhl@mitchellhamline.edu
DUHON, Gail .... 616-222-1431 229 B
gail.duhon@cornerstone.edu
DUHON, Stacey, D .... 318-274-6174 196 G
duhons@gram.edu
DUIN, Diane .... 406-896-5841 272 B
dduin@msubillings.edu
DUIN, Diane .... 406-657-1651 272 B
dduin@msubillings.edu
DUIN, Diane .... 406-896-5841 272 B
dduin@msubillings.edu
DUITCH, Suri .... 504-865-5555 196 D
sduitch@tulane.edu
DUKAKIS, Mary .... 603-668-2211 282 C
m.dukakis@snhu.edu
DUKE, Christopher .... 615-329-8505 431 I
cduke@fisk.edu
DUKE, Del, G .... 870-235-4171.. 21 F
dgduke@saumag.edu
DUKE, Lynda .... 309-556-3255 141 B
lduke@iwu.edu
DUKE, Robert .... 626-815-5441.. 26 U
rrduke@apu.edu
DUKE, Russell .... 626-650-2306.. 44 H
DUKE, Shalamon .... 310-287-4423.. 49 H
dukesa@wlac.edu
DUKE, Stacey .... 479-524-7371.. 20 B
sduke@jbu.edu
DUKE, Steven .... 336-758-5938 353 A
dukest@wfu.edu
DUKE, Steven, T .... 402-472-8845 277 E
sduke@nebraska.edu
DUKE, Todd .... 765-973-8611 160 A
mtduke@iue.edu
DUKERICH, Janet, M ..... 512-232-3310 467 C
janet.dukerich@austin.utexas.edu
DUKES, Charlene, M ..... 301-546-0400 206 E
dukescm@pgcc.edu
DUKES, Gary .... 503-838-8221 388 B
dukesg@wou.edu
DUKES, Jimmy .... 504-816-8092 195 D
jdukes@nobts.edu
DULABAUM, Mary .... 847-628-2089 142 B
mdulabaum@judsonu.edu
DULANEY, Wes .... 931-540-2617 436 H
wdulaney@columbiastate.edu
DULANY, Ann .... 740-284-5254 361 L
adulany@franciscan.edu
DULAY, Sarah .... 708-237-5050 148 A
sdulay@nc.edu
DULEPSKI, Deborah, L .. 203-576-2388.. 88 F
ddulepsk@bridgeport.edu
DULGAR, Laura .... 623-935-8808.. 13 F
laura.dulgar@estrellamountain.edu
DULLEA, Kora .... 651-793-1856 245 E
kora.dullea@metrostate.edu
DULLEA, Robert .... 206-296-2590 498 D
dullea@seattleu.edu
DULSKI-BUCHOLZ,
Andi, L .... 701-788-4833 354 B
andrea.dulskibucholz@mayvillestate.edu
DUMANCELA, Fanny ...... 718-518-4434 302 D
fdumancela@hostos.cuny.edu
DUMAS, Brandon .... 225-771-3922 195 K
brandon_dumas@subr.edu
DUMAS, Doris .... 847-735-5039 142 H
dumas@lakeforest.edu
DUMAS, Kathryn .... 610-647-4400 397 I
kdumas@immaculata.edu
DUMAS, Maureen .... 401-598-2350 416 C
mdumas@jwu.edu
DUMAS SERFES,
Pamela .... 860-439-5226.. 86 H
pamela.dumasserfes@conncoll.edu
DUMAUAL, Roberto ...... 718-522-9073 298 E
rdumaual@asa.edu
DUMAY, Harry, E .... 413-265-2293 213 E
hdumay@elms.edu
DUMBLETON, Eric .... 415-565-4616.. 68 I
dumbletoneric@uchastings.edu
DUMDEI, Mike .... 903-823-3107 458 D
michael.dumdei@texarkanacollege.edu
DUMIRE, William .... 724-852-3382 414 B
wdumire@waynesburg.edu
DUMM, Pamela .... 502-213-2109 186 C
pamela.dumm@kctcs.edu
DUMMER, Robin, K .... 530-226-4130.. 64 B
rdummer@simpsonu.edu
DUMONT, Betsy .... 209-228-2969.. 69 C
edumont@ucmerced.edu
DUMONT, Elizabeth, R .. 413-545-2554 216 H
edumont@umass.edu
DUMONT, Judith, C ...... 972-860-7026 447 I
jdumont@dcccd.edu
DUMONT, Sara, E .... 202-885-1321.. 91 C
dumont@american.edu
DUMONT-SMITH,
Cheryl .... 860-343-5869.. 86 A
cdumont-smith@mxcc.edu
DUMONTELLE, Janine ... 714-997-6553.. 36 G
jpdumont@chapman.edu
DUMPSON,
Kimberly, C .... 410-651-7686 208 C
kdumpson@umes.edu
DUNAGAN, Pam .... 706-368-6397 116 D
pdunagan@berry.edu
DUNAVIN, Callie .... 870-733-6840.. 18 B
cdunavin@asumidsouth.edu
DUNAWAY, Greg, A ...... 804-594-1430 488 D
gdunaway@jtcc.edu
DUNAWAY, Gregory ...... 304-293-4611 505 B
gregory.dunaway@mail.wvu.edu
DUNBAR, Deirdre, M .... 262-554-2010 508 E
midwestcollege@aol.com
DUNBAR, Dorlena .... 516-572-7759 316 C
dorlena.dunbar@ncc.edu
DUNBAR, Joan .... 313-577-5542 239 C
aj0824@wayne.edu
DUNBAR, Melanie .... 814-866-8160 399 C
mdunbar@lecom.edu
DUNBAR, Michelle .... 323-343-2730.. 32 D
mdunbar3@calstatela.edu
DUNBAR, Nathan .... 503-517-1206 388 A
ndunbar@warnerpacific.edu
DUNBAR, Nelia .... 575-835-7625 294 K
nelia.dunbar@nmt.edu
DUNBAR, William, J ..... 262-554-2010 508 E
dunbarphd@yahoo.com
DUNBAR-JACOB,
Jacqueline .... 412-624-2400 412 I
dunbar@pitt.edu
DUNCAN, Angela .... 336-316-2144 338 C
duncanav@guilford.edu
DUNCAN, C. Michael .... 413-782-1240 225 F
cmichael.duncan@wne.edu
DUNCAN, Carolyn, W ... 704-216-6195 339 E
cduncan@livingstone.edu
DUNCAN, Charles .... 919-508-2395 353 C
cduncan@peace.edu
DUNCAN, Christopher ... 314-977-2244 266 J
cmduncan@slu.edu
DUNCAN, Claudia .... 252-399-6521 335 I
cduncan@barton.edu
DUNCAN, Darrell .... 615-966-6166 433 D
darrell.duncan@lipscomb.edu
DUNCAN, Dennis, L ...... 574-372-5100 158 B
duncandl@grace.edu
DUNCAN, JR., Eugene .. 717-299-7782 411 C
duncan@stevenscollege.edu
DUNCAN, Issac .... 270-686-4324 183 J
issac.duncan@brescia.edu
DUNCAN, J. Ligon .... 601-923-1600 255 E
lduncan@rts.edu
DUNCAN, Jane .... 954-262-5382 104 F
janedunc@nova.edu
DUNCAN, Jay, R .... 770-720-5543 124 H
jrd@reinhardt.edu
DUNCAN, Jenny .... 918-293-5488 378 B
jenny.duncan@okstate.edu
DUNCAN, Jerelyn .... 501-420-1237.. 17 I
jerelyn.duncan@arkansasbaptist.edu
DUNCAN, Jerelyn, L ...... 501-420-1237.. 17 I
jerelyn.duncan@arkansasbaptist.edu
DUNCAN, Jim .... 901-843-3850 435 L
duncanjb@rhodes.edu
DUNCAN, Joan .... 470-578-3051 122 C
jduncan@kennesaw.edu
DUNCAN, John .... 740-377-2520 370 L
john.duncan@tsbc.edu
DUNCAN, John .... 313-883-8599 236 D
duncan.john@shms.edu
DUNCAN, John .... 864-231-2000 418 E
jduncan@andersonuniversity.edu
DUNCAN, K. Michael ..... 843-953-6356 420 C
duncanm@cofc.edu
DUNCAN, Kelly .... 605-626-2415 428 H
kelly.duncan@northern.edu
DUNCAN, Kristen .... 541-552-8019 386 H
kastk@sou.edu
DUNCAN, Laura, H .... 334-833-4069.... 5 M
lduncan@hawks.huntingdon.edu
DUNCAN, Lewis, M ...... 401-841-7004 518 E
DUNCAN, Linda .... 773-244-5697 147 F
lduncan@northpark.edu
DUNCAN, Martina .... 207-725-3358 198 G
mduncan@bowdoin.edu
DUNCAN, Matthew .... 408-554-4583.. 62 F
mduncan@scu.edu
DUNCAN, Michael, W ... 724-847-6528 395 J
mwduncan@geneva.edu
DUNCAN, Nancy .... 503-399-2530 382 C
nancy.duncan@chemeketa.edu
DUNCAN, Randy .... 704-687-7323 351 C
rduncan@uncc.edu
DUNCAN, Renae, D .... 270-809-3744 188 D
rduncan@murraystate.edu
DUNCAN, Robert, L ...... 806-742-0012 463 B
DUNCAN, Robert, L ...... 806-742-0012 463 D
chancellor@ttu.edu
DUNCAN, Steve .... 252-328-6105 349 I
duncans@ecu.edu
DUNCAN, Susan .... 502-852-6373 190 C
shdunc01@louisville.edu
DUNCAN, Suzanne .... 757-388-3693 485 B
sxduncan@sentara.com
DUNCAN, Teresa, S ...... 865-882-4648 438 A
duncants@roanestate.edu
DUNCAN, Tim .... 678-466-4672 117 I
timduncan@clayton.edu
DUNCAN, Todd .... 513-556-6445 371 E
todd.duncan@uc.edu
DUNCAN, Tracey .... 931-372-6091 438 F
tduncan@tntech.edu
DUNCAN, Wendy .... 559-325-3600.. 29 D
wduncan@chsu.org
DUNCAN, William, H ..... 916-660-7000.. 63 K
president@sierracollege.edu
DUNCAN, William, R .... 423-439-6000 431 H
duncanw@etsu.edu
DUNCAN-HERRING,
Chevene .... 270-534-3209 187 C
chevene.duncan-herring@kctcs.edu
DUNCAN-POITIER,
Johanna .... 518-320-1303 324 F
johanna.duncan-poitier@suny.edu
DUNCAN RAINES, Lisa . 757-594-7846 479 H
duncanl@cnu.edu
DUNCKLEE, Mary .... 508-565-3360 224 H
stonehillbkstr@fheg.follett.com
DUNCOMBE, Kemmoree 269-927-8183 232 G
kduncombe@lakemichigancollege.edu
DUNDAS, Robert, G ...... 559-278-3936.. 32 A
rdundas@csufresno.edu
DUNEK, Susan .... 319-208-5193 173 G
sdunek@scciowa.edu
DUNGAN, Bonnie, J ..... 607-871-2612 298 A
dunganbj@alfred.edu
DUNGAN, Lynley .... 817-735-2000 466 D
lynley.dungan@unthsc.edu
DUNGEY, Deborah, J .... 936-361-1000 458 F
djdungey@pvamu.edu
DUNHAM, Andrew .... 517-629-0216 226 G
adunham@albion.edu
DUNHAM, Andrew, M ... 517-629-0477 226 G
ddunham@albion.edu
DUNHAM, Anne .... 276-739-2456 490 A
adunham@vhcc.edu
DUNHAM, David .... 209-228-4264.. 69 C
ddunham@ucmerced.edu
DUNHAM, Dennis .... 405-974-2374 380 J
ddunham1@uco.edu
DUNHAM, Douglas, N .. 816-501-4617 265 I
douglas.dunham@rockhurst.edu
DUNHAM, Elizabeth ...... 802-447-4631 476 C
bdunham@svc.edu
DUNHAM, Mark, E .... 660-263-3900 258 A
markdunham@cccb.edu
DUNHAM, Rhonda, J .... 660-263-3900 258 A
rhondadunham@cccb.edu
DUNHAM, Stephen, S ... 814-867-4088 403 F
ssd13@psu.edu
DUNHAM, Thomas .... 773-907-4477 135 K
tdunham@ccc.edu
DUNHAM HOWIE,
Jules .... 937-376-2946 369 C
juleshouse@payne.edu
DUNHAM STRAND,
Amy .... 616-632-8900 227 C
stranamy@aquinas.edu
DUNIVAN, Daniel .... 812-749-1239 163 B
ddunivan@oak.edu
DUNIVAN, Daniel .... 812-749-1386 163 B
ddunivan@oak.edu
DUNIWAY, Robert .... 206-296-2105 498 D
rduniway@seattleu.edu
DUNKEL, Aaron .... 805-525-4417.. 67 E
adunkel@thomasaquinas.edu
DUNKEL, Norbert, W ..... 352-392-2171 110 D
norbd@housing.ufl.edu
DUNKELMAN, James ...... 562-907-4205.. 75 A
jdunkelman@whittier.edu
DUNKER, Eric .... 303-797-5859.. 76 I
eric.dunker@arapahoe.edu
DUNKERTON, David, W 304-877-6428 501 E
david.dunkerton@abc.edu
DUNKLE, David .... 850-973-9440 104 D
dunkled@nfcc.edu
DUNKLE, John, H .... 847-491-2151 148 C
j-dunkle@northwestern.edu
DUNKLE, Kurt .... 646-717-9740 309 B
dunkle@gts.edu
DUNKLE, Mike .... 402-471-2505 276 A
mdunkle@nscs.edu
DUNKLEBERGER,
Kay, E .... 570-326-3761 404 T
kdunkleb@pct.edu
DUNKLEBERGER,
Robert, L .... 570-321-4278 400 G
dunkleberger@lycoming.edu
DUNKLEY, Eugene .... 618-664-6543 139 A
eugene.dunkley@greenville.edu
DUNKLIN, Ashley .... 251-380-3470.... 7 B
adunklin@shc.edu
DUNKLIN, Kendrick ...... 251-380-4000.... 7 B
kdunklin@shc.edu
DUNLAP, Doug .... 620-365-5116 174 G
ddunlap@allencc.edu
DUNLAP, James, H .... 517-355-2223 233 G
dunlap@msu.edu
DUNLAP, Kelli .... 239-432-7387 100 E
kdunlap2@fsw.edu
DUNLAP, Marilyn .... 808-956-6151 129 J
mdunlap@hawaii.edu
DUNLAP, Scott .... 973-720-3232 292 I
dunlaps@wpunj.edu
DUNLAP, Susan, L .... 516-726-5816 519 C
dunlaps@usmma.edu
DUNLAVEY, Patrick .... 440-826-2900 357 B
DUNLAVY, Dustin .... 740-366-1351 358 E
ddunlavy@cotc.edu
DUNLAY, Robert, W ...... 402-280-2600 274 D
robertdunlay@creighton.edu
DUNLEAVY, Aidan .... 316-295-5214 177 F
aidan_dunleavy@friends.edu
DUNLEAVY, Ginnie .... 401-427-6978 417 B
vdunleav@risd.edu
DUNLEAVY, James, F ... 610-861-5463 403 B
jdunleavy@northampton.edu
DUNLEAVY, Lindsey ...... 614-222-3268 360 B
ldunleavy@ccad.edu
DUNLEAVY, Patricia, E .. 570-348-6220 401 B
dunleavy@marywood.edu
DUNLEVY, Elizabeth ...... 630-353-8702 134 K
edunlevy@chamberlain.edu
DUNMAN, ReNee, S ...... 757-683-3141 483 G
rdunman@odu.edu
DUNN, Amy .... 651-793-1303 245 E
amy.dunn@metrostate.edu
DUNN, Andrew .... 714-438-4611.. 38 E
adunn@mail.cccd.edu
DUNN, Ashley .... 818-778-5518.. 49 G
dunnae@lavc.edu

DUNN, Barry, H .... 605-688-4111 429 B
barry.dunn@sdstate.edu
DUNN, Becky .... 573-897-5000 267 F
DUNN, Billie .... 440-375-7506 364 C
bdunn@lec.edu
DUNN, Billie .... 440-375-7000 364 C
bdunn@lec.edu
DUNN, Brad .... 512-863-1944 457 I
dunnb@southwestern.edu
DUNN, Christopher .... 617-482-3103 216 H
cdunn@admin.umass.edu
DUNN, Claire, B .... 315-470-6650 328 D
cbdunn@esf.edu
DUNN, Corey .... 404-471-6176 114 H
cdunn@agnesscott.edu
DUNN, Dana, L .... 336-334-5494 351 D
dldunn@uncg.edu
DUNN, Daniel .... 312-329-4451 146 B
daniel.dunn@moody.edu
DUNN, Darren .... 970-351-2362.. 83 F
darren.dunn@unco.edu
DUNN, Deborah .... 734-432-5457 233 C
ddunn@madonna.edu
DUNN, Denise, A .... 319-296-4267 169 H
denise.dunn@hawkeyecollege.edu
DUNN, Elizabeth, E .... 574-520-4322 160 F
elizdunn@iusb.edu
DUNN, Erin .... 727-873-4547 111 B
edunn1@mail.usf.edu
DUNN, Florence .... 559-325-3600.. 29 D
fdunn@chsu.org
DUNN, Galen .... 618-842-3711 140 C
dunng@iecc.edu
DUNN, Gary .... 831-459-2628.. 70 C
gmdunn@ucsc.edu
DUNN, Jaime .... 410-626-2500 206 F
jaime.dunn@sjc.edu
DUNN, James .... 470-578-6675 122 C
DUNN, James .... 610-989-1301 413 I
jdunn@vfmac.edu
DUNN, James, J .... 336-758-4240 353 A
jdunn@vergercapital.com
DUNN, Jeanette, R .... 864-587-4271 424 D
dunnj@smcsc.edu
DUNN, Jimmy .... 559-325-3600.. 29 D
jdunn@chsu.org
DUNN, John .... 206-592-3455 495 E
jdunn@highline.edu
DUNN, John, B .... 617-552-3350 212 E
jack.dunn@bc.edu
DUNN, Joshua .... 972-923-5493 457 F
jdunn@sagu.edu
DUNN, Judi, B .... 402-552-6123 273 K
dunn@clarksoncollege.edu
DUNN, Julie, A .... 563-588-7136 171 H
julie.dunn@loras.edu
DUNN, Keith .... 601-974-1010 254 A
keith.dunn@millsaps.edu
DUNN, Kelly .... 715-682-1351 509 D
kdunn@northland.edu
DUNN, Kevin .... 617-627-2816 225 A
kevin.dunn@tufts.edu
DUNN, Kevin .... 859-246-6716 185 G
kevin.dunn@kctcs.edu
DUNN, Kristin .... 405-382-9525 379 I
k.dunn@sscok.edu
DUNN, Leah .... 828-251-6545 351 A
dunn@unca.edu
DUNN, Leoma .... 859-344-3524 189 G
dunnl@thomasmore.edu
DUNN, Lisa .... 602-274-1885.. 15 J
ldunn@pihma.edu
DUNN, Margaret .... 937-775-2933 374 B
margaret.dunn@wright.edu
DUNN, Mary .... 978-542-6202 218 E
mary.dunn@salemstate.edu
DUNN, Meg .... 212-757-1190 298 D
mdunn@funeraleducation.org
DUNN, Michael, K .... 240-895-4105 206 G
mkdunn@smcm.edu
DUNN, Michele .... 201-684-7701 289 C
mdunn@ramapo.edu
DUNN, Paul .... 860-701-7739.. 87 F
dunn_p@mitchell.edu
DUNN, Paul .... 360-650-3472 500 E
paul.dunn@wwu.edu
DUNN, Randy .... 706-379-3111 128 H
rjdunn@yhc.edu
DUNN, Randy, J .... 618-536-3471 152 A
rdunn@siu.edu
DUNN, Robin .... 410-626-2540 206 F
robin.dunn@sjc.edu
DUNN, Rodney .... 317-931-2318 157 D
rdunn@cts.edu
DUNN, Rose Ellen .... 609-497-7817 288 E
rose.ellen.dunn@ptsem.edu
DUNN, Scott .... 229-243-6992 116 C
sdunn@bainbridge.edu
DUNN, Shari .... 704-687-5723 351 C
shari.dunn@uncc.edu
DUNN, Stanley .... 518-276-8433 321 A
dunns6@rpi.edu
DUNN, T. Michael .... 334-833-4495.... 5 M
mdunn@hawks.huntingdon.edu
DUNN, Tara .... 662-562-3305 255 C
DUNN, Tim .... 520-795-0787.. 10 J
admissions@asaom.edu
DUNN, W. Brent .... 417-836-6666 263 H
brentdunn@missouristate.edu
DUNN, Wendy, L .... 319-399-8710 167 F
wdunn@coe.edu
DUNN BOGGS, Debbie . 614-234-5681 365 L
dboggs@mccn.edu
DUNN-RAMSAY, Sheri .. 910-410-1907 345 G
srdunn-ramsay@richmondcc.edu
DUNNAGAN, Tim .... 208-426-3917 131 C
timdunnagan@boisestate.edu
DUNNE, Jennifer .... 617-333-2271 214 B
jdunne1213@curry.edu
DUNNE, Martha, L .... 212-998-2115 318 D
marti.dunne@nyu.edu
DUNNE, Michele, A ...... 515-263-2853 169 E
mdunne@grandview.edu
DUNNE, Nicole .... 831-646-3007.. 52 G
ndunne@mpc.edu
DUNNE, Thomas, A ...... 718-817-0180 308 G
tdunne@fordham.edu
DUNNE, Timothy .... 207-741-5506 200 C
tdunne@smccme.edu
DUNNE, Will .... 386-506-4486.. 97 I
dunnew@daytonastate.edu
DUNNE-CASCIO,
Colleen .... 541-962-3476 383 B
ccascio@eou.edu
DUNNELL, Scott .... 330-569-5288 362 J
dunnellsp@hiram.edu
DUNNETT, Stephen, C .. 716-645-2368 325 B
dunnett@buffalo.edu
DUNNING, Arthur, N .... 229-430-4605 114 I
art.dunning@asurams.edu
DUNNING, Elaura .... 503-760-3131 381 J
elaura@birthingway.edu
DUNNING, Jim .... 805-756-5551.. 30 K
jdunning@calpoly.edu
DUNNING, John .... 402-375-7286 276 D
jodunni1@wsc.edu
DUNNING, Sue .... 863-638-2937 114 A
dunnings@webber.edu
DUNNINGS, Lance .... 404-880-8051 117 H
ldunning@cau.edu
DUNNINGTON,
Sandra, F .... 301-546-0406 206 E
dunninsf@pgcc.edu
DUNNIVANT, Stephen ... 850-201-6038 112 C
dunnivas@tcc.fl.edu
DUNNUCK, John .... 954-201-7405.. 96 A
jdunnuck@broward.edu
DUNPHE, Beth .... 212-343-1234 315 D
bdunphe@mcny.edu
DUNPHY, Michael .... 330-490-7201 373 F
mdunphy@walsh.edu
DUNPHY-CULP, Bryan ... 215-646-7300 396 E
dunphy-culp.b@gmercyu.edu
DUNSEATH, Jennifer ..... 401-254-3275 417 C
jdunseath@rwu.edu
DUNSON, Kenneth .... 972-238-6171 448 D
kdunson@dcccd.edu
DUNSTON, Karen .... 503-352-2218 385 I
dunstonk@pacificu.edu
DUNSTON, Rita .... 540-654-1063 486 D
rdunston@umw.edu
DUNSTON, Stephani ...... 706-225-5300.. 93 B
DUNSWORTH, April ...... 405-878-5308 379 G
addunsworth@stgregorys.edu
DUNSWORTH, Emily ..... 651-290-6476 248 U
emily.dunsworth@mitchellhamline.edu
DUNSWORTH,
Richard, L .... 479-979-1242.. 23 J
rdunsworth@ozarks.edu
DUNTLEY, Mark .... 503-768-7082 383 G
duntley@lclark.edu
DUNTON, Renee .... 207-947-4591 198 F
rdunton@bealcollege.edu
DUNTON, Susan, B .... 603-271-6484 280 N
sdunton@ccsnh.edu
DUNWORTH, David .... 312-487-4743 153 A
david.dunworth@tribecaflashpoint.edu
DUPAUL, Stephanie ...... 804-287-6442 486 G
sdupaul@richmond.edu
DUPAY, Abbie .... 812-941-2115 161 A
aedupay@ius.edu
DUPEE, Daniel .... 315-786-2401 311 H
ddupee@sunyjefferson.edu
DUPELL, Linda .... 978-665-4342 217 E
ldupell@fitchburgstate.edu
DUPES, Steven .... 717-720-4118 405 D
sdupes@passhe.edu
DUPIER, Charles .... 606-539-4316 190 A
chuck.dupier@ucumberlands.edu
DUPIER, Jo .... 606-539-4208 190 A
jo.dupier@ucumberlands.edu
DUPLESSIS, Julie .... 319-385-6208 170 J
julie.duplessis@iw.edu
DUPLESSIS, Tamika .... 504-941-8500 192 H
tduple@dcc.edu
DUPONT, Joseph .... 617-552-3430 212 E
joseph.dupont@bc.edu
DUPONT, Michael .... 817-515-3584 458 B
michael.dupont@tccd.edu
DUPONT, Richard .... 203-332-5991.. 85 F
rdupont@hcc.commnet.edu
DUPRA, JoAnn .... 870-543-5993.. 21 E
jdupra@seark.edu
DUPRE, Kim .... 804-862-6100 484 F
kdupre@rbc.edu
DUPRE, Sean .... 405-878-5420 379 G
sdupre@stgregorys.edu
DUPRE, Tara .... 985-549-2001 197 E
tara.dupre@selu.edu
DUPRE, Terry, G .... 985-448-4031 197 C
terry.dupre@nicholls.edu
DUPREE, Carol .... 325-794-4401 445 Q
carol.dupree@cisco.edu
DUPREE, Cathy, P .... 252-823-5166 343 A
dupreec@edgecombe.edu
DUPREE, David .... 504-280-6235 194 F
ddupree@uno.edu
DUPREE, Jason, M .... 580-774-7081 380 B
jason.dupree@swosu.edu
DUPREE, Jeffrey .... 918-781-7218 374 H
dupreej@bacone.edu
DUPREE, Kathy .... 281-212-1610 465 B
dupree@uhcl.edu
DUPREE, Leslie, M .... 309-794-7626 133 G
lesliedupree@augustana.edu
DUPREE, Paul, J .... 859-858-3511 183 D
pdupree@asbury.edu
DUPREY, Lorey .... 207-509-7264 200 I
lduprey@unity.edu
DUPREY, Wayne, A .... 518-564-2033 327 E
dupreywa@plattsburgh.edu
DUPRE', Carolyn .... 601-877-4701 251 G
cdupre@alcorn.edu
DUPRIEST, Barclay, F ... 804-752-7371 484 C
bdupries@rmc.edu
DUPUIS, Kellie, J .... 518-320-3264 324 F
kellie.dupuis@suny.edu
DUPUIS, Martin .... 407-823-5948 110 C
martin.dupuis@ucf.edu
DUPUIS, Mishelle .... 910-938-6251 342 C
dupuism@coastalcarolina.edu
DUQUE, Jessica .... 828-627-4521 343 G
jlduque@haywood.edu
DURAJ, Jonathan .... 937-327-7817 374 A
jduraj@wittenberg.edu
DURAN, Adrianna .... 915-779-8031 470 E
aduran@computercareercenter.com
DURAN, Armando .... 626-585-7148.. 56 B
axduran@pasadena.edu
DURAN, Dorothy .... 507-453-2721 245 G
dduran@southeastmn.edu
DURAN, Kelly .... 716-839-8290 306 E
kduran@daemen.edu
DURAN, Laura .... 580-349-1590 377 E
lduran@opsu.edu
DURAN, Lydia .... 575-646-2035 295 B
lbduran@nmsu.edu
DURAN, Margret .... 806-743-2300 463 E
margret.duran@ttuhsc.edu
DURAN, Michael .... 505-984-6000 295 K
DURAN, Michelle .... 361-593-5501 460 B
michelle.duran@tamuk.edu
DURAN, Veronica .... 520-494-5260.. 11 P
veronica.duran@centralaz.edu
DURAN-CERDA,
Dolores .... 520-206-4999.. 15 L
dcerda@pima.edu
DURAND, Bonita, R ...... 716-878-4102 326 E
durandbr@buffalostate.edu
DURAND, Gene .... 562-938-4095.. 48 I
gdurand@lbcc.edu
DURAND, Scott .... 603-626-9100 282 C
s.durand@snhu.edu
DURAND, Stefanie .... 509-452-5100 496 H
sdurand@pnwu.edu
DURANT, Benjamin .... 919-530-7425 350 D
benjamin.durant@nccu.edu
DURANT, Brian, M .... 315-255-1743 300 H
brian.durant@cayuga-cc.edu
DURANT, Joseph, M ..... 843-792-2252 422 C
durantjm@musc.edu
DURANT, Joyce, M .... 843-661-1300 421 H
jdurant@fmarion.edu
DURANT, Leroy, A .... 803-535-5341 419 E
ldurant@claflin.edu
DURANT, Linda, S .... 610-499-4123 414 F
lsdurant@widener.edu
DURANT, Natalie .... 860-768-5565.. 89 C
ndurant@hartford.edu
DURANT, Tamara .... 518-783-2307 324 C
tdurant@siena.edu
DURANT JONES, Lisa ... 585-389-2775 316 D
ldurant4@naz.edu
DURBAK, Andres .... 773-907-4708 135 K
adurbak@ccc.edu
DURBEN, Katherine .... 414-288-5470 508 C
katherine.durben@marquette.edu
DURBIN, Bryce .... 706-236-2282 116 D
bdurbin@berry.edu
DURBIN, Rachel .... 503-494-7800 385 D
finaid@ohsu.edu
DURDEN, Lori, S .... 912-871-1638 123 J
ldurden@ogeecheetech.edu
DURDEN, Tracey .... 734-432-5673 233 C
tdurden@madonna.edu
DUREE, Christopher ...... 641-844-5720 170 G
christopher.duree@iavalley.edu
DUREE, Christopher, A . 641-844-5720 170 I
christopher.duree@iavalley.edu
DUREN, Marion .... 608-249-6611 507 F
careers@msn.herzing.edu
DURETTE, Kristi .... 603-645-9780 282 C
k.durette@snhu.edu
DURFEE, Carissa .... 617-989-4086 225 E
durfeec@wit.edu
DURFEE, Jeffrey, A .... 904-620-2820 110 E
jdurfee@unf.edu
DURGIN, William .... 315-792-7200 330 A
william.durgin@sunyit.edu
DURGLO, Dan .... 406-275-4972 273 A
dan_durglo@skc.edu
DURHAM, Bree .... 850-729-6458 104 E
durhamb@nwfsc.edu
DURHAM, Danielle .... 660-831-4172 264 A
durhamd@moval.edu
DURHAM, David, L .... 304-293-8220 505 B
david.durham@mail.wvu.edu
DURHAM, Dawn, W ...... 864-833-8477 423 D
dwdurham@presby.edu
DURHAM, Ed .... 410-287-1010 203 B
edurham@cecil.edu
DURHAM, Gesele .... 414-229-3305 511 A
gedurham@uwm.edu
DURHAM, Jerry .... 319-226-2015 166 C
jerry.durham@allencollege.edu
DURHAM, John, R .... 610-519-7164 413 K
john.durham@villanova.edu
DURHAM, Kathy, F .... 828-448-3102 347 F
kdurham@wpcc.edu
DURHAM, Kimberly ...... 954-262-8730 104 F
durham@nova.edu
DURHAM, Lovely .... 305-626-3711.. 99 M
lovely.durham@fmuniv.edu
DURHAM, Lynn .... 404-894-8261 120 A
lynn.durham@carnegie.gatech.edu
DURHAM, Monica .... 419-755-4896 366 E
mdurham@ncstatecollege.edu
DURHAM, Rhonda .... 501-882-4442.. 17 M
rsdurham@asub.edu
DURHAM, Tammara ...... 785-864-4060 181 I
tdurham@ku.edu
DURHAM, Teresa .... 269-965-3931 232 A
durhamt@kellogg.edu
DURHAM, William, H ... 704-233-8219 353 D
durham@wingate.edu
DURHAM DECESARO,
Genevieve .... 806-742-3601 463 D
genevieve.durham@ttu.edu
DURIAN-GAMBELL,
Angella .... 641-673-1076 174 F
gambella@wmpenn.edu
DURICK, Brian .... 949-480-4018.. 64 D
bdurick@soka.edu
DURKEE, Gene .... 603-428-2358 281 F
edurkee@nec.edu
DURKEE, Robert, K .... 609-258-6428 288 F
durkee@princeton.edu
DURKIN, Karen .... 856-415-2284 289 G
kdurkin@rcgc.edu
DURKIN, Mary .... 718-429-6600 333 B
mary.durkin@vaughn.edu
DURKIN, Rebecca .... 847-578-8351 150 E
rebecca.durkin@rosalindfranklin.edu
DURKLE, Robert, F .... 937-229-4411 372 A
rdurkle1@udayton.edu
DURMOWICZ, Meredith 443-334-2414 207 C
mdurmowicz@stevenson.edu
DURNFORD, Ronald, R . 504-520-5031 198 D
rdurnfor@xula.edu
DURNIN, Ellen .... 203-392-5356.. 85 A
durnine1@southernct.edu

DUROCHER, Becky, L ... 985-448-4510 197 C
becky.durocher@nicholls.edu
DUROSS, Frank .... 315-792-5526 315 I
fduross@mvcc.edu
DURR, Elaine .... 336-278-5229 337 G
edurr@elon.edu
DURR, Jeanne .... 307-766-5600 517 B
edurr@uwyo.edu
DURR, Kimberly, H .... 618-650-2475 152 C
kdurr@siue.edu
DURRETT, Duane .... 817-598-6222 470 J
ddurrett@wc.edu
DURSI, Joseph, F .... 914-594-4487 318 A
joseph_dursi@nymc.edu
DURSI, Joseph, F .... 914-594-4234 318 A
joseph_dursi@nymc.edu
DURSO, Mary .... 215-568-9215 415 D
mdurso@phmc.org
DURSO, Thomas, W ...... 610-921-7526 388 E
tdurso@albright.edu
DURST, Devoiry .... 732-414-2834 293 E
yeshivatoraschaim@gmail.com
DURST, Ellen .... 415-575-6153.. 29 H
edurst@ciis.edu
DURST, Lisa .... 440-525-7721 364 D
ldurst@lakelandcc.edu
DURST, Steve .... 231-591-2254 230 A
stephendurst@ferris.edu
DURYEA, David .... 607-753-2211 327 A
david.duryea@cortland.edu
DUSDIEKER, Carol .... 419-448-2080 362 G
cdusdiek@heidelberg.edu
DUSEK, Craig .... 620-417-1204 181 E
craig.dusek@sccc.edu
DUSENBURY, Renata ...... 919-546-8252 348 I
rdusenbury@shawu.edu
DUSING, Roger .... 816-584-6386 265 C
roger.dusing@park.edu
DUSSEAU, Daniel .... 703-425-5369 488 H
ddusseau@nvcc.edu
DUSSERT, Alain .... 805-969-3626.. 55 G
adussert@pacifica.edu
DUSSOURD, Ellen, A .... 716-645-2258 325 B
dussourd@buffalo.edu
DUSTIN, Kevin, M .... 801-957-4083 474 B
kevin.dustin@slcc.edu
DUSZYNSKI, Aaron .... 920-686-6179 510 A
aaron.duszynski@sl.edu
DUTCH, Jennifer .... 402-363-5719 278 E
jdutch@york.edu
DUTCHER, Debra .... 518-327-6082 320 A
ddutcher@paulsmiths.edu
DUTCHER, Donald .... 315-866-0300 310 A
dutcherdm@herkimer.edu
DUTCHER, James .... 518-255-5337 328 C
dutchejm@cobleskill.edu
DUTCHER, Victoria, J .... 603-862-4979 282 F
victoria.dutcher@unh.edu
DUTKIEWICZ, Jennifer .. 814-393-2352 405 H
jdutkiewicz@clarion.edu
DUTKO, Teresa .... 513-618-1928 359 F
tdutko@ccms.edu
DUTLER, Sue .... 312-935-2210 149 K
sdutler@robertmorris.edu
DUTMER, Brendan, C .... 815-599-3493 139 F
brendan.dutmer@highland.edu
DUTRA, Bruce .... 973-328-5400 285 B
bdutra@ccm.edu
DUTREMBLE, Kathy .... 850-484-2076 105 E
kdutremble@pensacolastate.edu
DUTRISAC, Gordon .... 425-352-8288 492 K
gdutrisac@cascadia.edu
DUTSCHKE, Jeremy, D .. 870-759-4120.. 23 K
jdutschke@wbcoll.edu
DUTTA, Debasish .... 765-494-9709 163 C
DUTTA, Debasish .... 848-932-7821 290 A
deba.dutta@rutgers.edu
DUTTA, Debasish .... 848-932-7821 290 C
deba.dutta@rutgers.edu
DUTTA, Mitra .... 312-996-6174 153 H
dutta@uic.edu
DUTTA, Soumitra .... 607-255-8791 306 B
soumitra.dutta@cornell.edu
DUTTON, Ashley .... 860-231-5245.. 89 E
adutton@usj.edu
DUTTON, Colleen .... 972-883-2130 467 D
colleen.dutton@utdallas.edu
DUTTON, Dennis .... 620-278-4364 181 G
ddutton@sterling.edu
DUTTON, Timothy .... 937-752-2189 364 B
timothy.dutton@ketteringhealth.org
DUTTON COX, Deborah 603-862-1627 282 F
debbie.dutton@unh.edu
DUUS, Martin .... 212-280-1426 332 C
mduus@uts.columbia.edu
DUVAL, Amanda, L .... 920-923-8082 508 B
alduval92@marianuniversity.edu
DUVAL, Derethia .... 415-338-2208.. 34 C
derethia@sfsu.edu
DUVAL, Madonna .... 513-562-8752 356 J
madonna.duval@artacademy.edu
DUVALL, Staci .... 501-977-2087.. 23 B
duvall@uaccm.edu
DUVALL, Steve .... 740-389-4636 365 B
duvalls@mtc.edu
DUVALL, William .... 864-231-2144 418 E
wduvall@andersonuniversity.edu
DUVLL, Kathleen .... 509-793-2050 492 I
kathleend@bigbend.edu
DUXBURY, Rebecca ...... 724-838-4215 410 E
rduxbury@setonhill.edu
DUXBURY-EDWARDS,
Chris .... 303-329-6355.. 78 L
recruiting@cstcm.edu
DVORACSEK, Joe .... 727-341-6108 107 A
dvoracsek.joe@spcollege.edu
DVORAK, Jerome .... 570-389-4995 405 E
jdvorak@bloomufdn.org
DVORAK, Leah, M .... 262-243-5700 507 C
leah.dvorak@cuw.edu
DVORAK, Robert .... 909-687-1560.. 44 A
robertdvorak@gs.edu
DVORAK, Sarah .... 574-284-4587 163 J
sdvorak@saintmarys.edu
DVORAK, Susan .... 414-464-9777 513 B
dvorak.susan@wspp.edu
DVORKIN, Ariel .... 212-431-7959 317 H
ariel.dvorkin@nyls.edu
DWIGHT, Beverly, J ...... 413-796-2210 225 F
beverly.dwight@wne.edu
DWIRE, Steven, W .... 518-337-4915 305 B
dwires@strose.edu
DWORACZYK, Bill .... 214-768-3140 457 B
billd@smu.edu
DWORKIN, Aaron, P ...... 734-764-0584 237 I
aaronpau@umich.edu
DWORKIS, Paul, S .... 301-405-2584 207 G
pdworkis@umd.edu
DWORSCHAK, Mark .... 520-206-4558.. 15 L
mdworschak@pima.edu
DWYER, James, P .... 989-964-4209 236 F
jdwyer@svsu.edu
DWYER, Jeff .... 517-355-2308 233 G
dwyerje@msu.edu
DWYER, Johanna .... 360-596-5234 498 G
jdwyer@spscc.edu
DWYER, Katelyn .... 617-322-3524 216 B
katelyn_dwyer@laboure.edu
DWYER, Kathleen .... 502-410-6200 184 H
kdwyer@galencollege.edu
DWYER, Ken .... 508-854-4579 220 G
krd@qcc.mass.edu
DWYER, Susan, J .... 301-405-1102 207 G
dwyer@umd.edu
DWYER, Thomas .... 502-410-6200 184 H
tdwyer@galencollege.edu
DWYER, Thomas, L .... 401-598-1000 416 C
tom.dwyer@jwu.edu
DWYER, Thomas, P ...... 804-752-7244 484 C
tdwyer@rmc.edu
DYBA, Chris .... 252-328-9565 349 I
dyba@ecu.edu
DYBA, Christopher .... 252-328-9565 349 I
dybac@ecu.edu
DYBWAD, Peter .... 510-841-9230.. 75 E
pdybwad@wi.edu
DYCK-LAUMANN,
Rebecca .... 901-678-2814 439 E
rlaumann@memphis.edu
DYCKMAN, Gayle .... 585-245-5501 327 B
dyckman@geneseo.edu
DYCZKO, Moira .... 574-520-4383 160 F
mdyczko@iusb.edu
DYE, Christine .... 910-755-7304 341 C
dyec@brunswickcc.edu
DYE, David .... 480-994-9244.. 16 E
davidd@swiha.edu
DYE, James .... 276-964-7278 489 F
james.dye@sw.edu
DYE, Jane .... 423-545-9572 432 E
dyejane@hiwassee.edu
DYE, Joanna .... 309-796-5442 134 C
dyej@bhc.edu
DYE, John .... 330-337-6403 356 B
college@awc.edu
DYE, Larry .... 580-628-6217 376 J
larry.dye@noc.edu
DYE, Lisa .... 618-252-5400 151 J
lisa.dye@sic.edu
DYE, Melissa .... 815-835-6253 151 E
melissa.m.dye@svcc.edu
DYE, Ronald .... 256-761-0949.... 7 D
rdye@talladega.edu
DYE, Ryan, D .... 563-333-6389 173 A
dyeryand@sau.edu
DYE, Sheila .... 806-720-7233 452 D
sheila.dye@lcu.edu
DYER, Cheryl, A .... 414-955-8225 508 D
cdyer@mcw.edu
DYER, Cynthia, M .... 515-961-1519 173 E
cyd.dyer@simpson.edu
DYER, Esther, L .... 865-971-5216 437 F
eldyer@pstcc.edu
DYER, Jennifer .... 213-821-5002.. 72 B
jennifer.dyer@stevens.usc.edu
DYER, John, C .... 214-887-5141 448 G
jdyer@dts.edu
DYER, Karen .... 812-535-5101 163 I
kdyer@smwc.edu
DYER, Kent .... 484-664-3140 402 F
kentdyer@muhlenberg.edu
DYER, Kristyn, M .... 508-793-2418 213 D
kdyer@holycross.edu
DYER, Robin .... 704-669-4128 342 B
dyer@clevelandcc.edu
DYER, Ruth .... 785-532-6224 179 A
rdyer@ksu.edu
DYER, Tricia .... 207-621-3390 201 C
triciad@maine.edu
DYER, Una .... 340-693-1002 529 C
udyer@uvi.edu
DYER, Wayne, R .... 973-803-5000 288 D
wdyer@pillar.edu
DYERLY, Kevin, M .... 909-748-8026.. 71 H
kevin_dyerly@redlands.edu
DYESS, Hubert .... 601-426-6346 255 G
hdyess@southeasternbaptist.edu
DYKE, Gary .... 281-649-3335 450 C
gdyke@hbu.edu
DYKEMA, Ann, C .... 616-977-0599 236 B
ann.dykema@prts.edu
DYKES, Alllison, K .... 404-727-9895 119 B
allison.dykes@emory.edu
DYKES, Donald, E .... 860-444-8213 519 B
donald.e.dykes@uscga.edu
DYKES, Stephanie .... 206-934-3655 497 H
stephanie.dykes@seattlecolleges.edu
DYKES-ANDERSON,
Michelle .... 606-589-3049 187 B
michelle.dykes-anderson@kctcs.edu
DYKSHOORN, Sharon ... 712-274-6400 174 E
sharon.dykshoorn@witcc.edu
DYKSTRA, Arlen, R .... 314-392-2201 263 F
adykstra@mobap.edu
DYKSTRA, Doug .... 808-235-7402 130 I
dykstra@hawaii.edu
DYKSTRA, Frank .... 520-515-5311.. 11 R
poncho@cochise.edu
DYKSTRA, Gail .... 972-708-7340 449 I
gail_dykstra@gial.edu
DYKSTRA, Joel .... 575-624-8203 295 A
dykstra@nmmi.edu
DYKSTRA, Karen .... 406-243-5211 271 G
karen.dykstra@umontana.edu
DYKSTRA, Kurt, D .... 708-239-4791 153 B
kurt.dykstra@trnty.edu
DYKSTRA, Philip .... 714-484-7311.. 53 M
pdykstra@cypresscollege.edu
DYLAK, Sandy .... 914-251-6953 328 B
sandy.dylak@purchase.edu
DYMENT, Christine .... 508-588-9100 220 B
DYMOWSKI, Tom .... 210-829-3131 465 E
dymowski@uiwtx.edu
DYMSKI, M, L .... 617-349-8208 216 D
mld@lesley.edu
DYNAN-DOBBERTIEN,
Lisa .... 904-620-2900 110 E
n00914995@unf.edu
DYRUD, Lars .... 218-683-8616 246 F
lars.dyrud@northlandcollege.edu
DYSARD, Nancy, J .... 443-412-2408 204 C
ndysard@harford.edu
DYSART, Charles .... 334-876-9248.... 2 C
charles.dysart@wccs.edu
DYSART, Sarah .... 773-508-7476 144 D
sdysart@luc.edu
DYSON, Carolyn .... 941-359-4200 111 C
DYSON, Greg .... 937-766-3330 358 D
gdyson@cedarville.edu
DYSON, Keisha .... 708-534-4044 138 H
kdyson@govst.edu
DYSON, Melissa, J .... 217-245-3080 139 H
mdyson@mail.ic.edu
DZAPO, Kyle .... 309-677-2596 134 G
kdzapo@bradley.edu
DZIEDZIAK, Michael ..... 610-341-1376 394 E
mdziedzi@eastern.edu
DZIEKAN, Rebecca .... 585-343-0055 309 C
rldziekan@genesee.edu
DZIELSKI, Mark .... 716-851-1073 307 I
dzielski@ecc.edu
DZIESINSKI, Lori .... 989-356-9021 227 A
dziesinl@alpenacc.edu
DZIEWATKOSKI,
Julius, J .... 740-264-5591 361 D
jdziewatkoski@egcc.edu
DZINANKA, John, S ...... 631-420-2017 329 D
john.dzinanka@farmingdale.edu
DZUREC, Laura, C .... 610-499-4214 414 F
lcdzurec@widener.edu
DZWONKOWSKI,
David, R .... 315-470-6626 328 D
drdzwonk@esf.edu
DÍAZ, Ángel .... 787-764-0000 528 F
angel.diaz10@upr.edu
DÍAZ, Tania .... 787-720-1022 521 A
recursos@atlanticu.edu
DÍAZ, Valerie .... 787-844-8181 528 E
valerie.diaz3@upr.edu
DÍAZ URBINA, Gloria ... 787-764-0000 528 F
gloria.diaz5@upr.edu
D'ABROSCO, Lou .... 401-598-4621 416 C
louis.d'abrosca@jwu.edu
D'ADAMO-WEINSTEIN,
Lisa .... 518-587-2100 329 C
lisa.dadamo-weinstein@esc.edu
D'AGATI, Michael .... 973-684-5920 288 C
mdagati@pccc.edu
D'AGOSTINO, Alexa ...... 914-674-7698 314 I
adagostino4@mercy.edu
D'AGOSTINO, Darrin ..... 816-654-7338 261 D
ddagostino@kcumb.edu
D'AGOSTINO, Erica .... 610-330-5080 399 B
dagostie@lafayette.edu
D'AGOSTINO, Jennifer .. 518-587-2100 329 C
jennifer.d'agostino@esc.edu
D'AGOSTINO, Jo Beth .. 773-508-7063 144 D
jdagost@luc.edu
D'AGOSTINO, Julie .... 847-925-6523 139 B
jdagosti@harpercollege.edu
D'AGOSTINO, Laura ...... 518-244-6857 321 G
dagosl1@sage.edu
D'AGOSTINO, Thomas .. 315-781-3307 310 C
tdagostino@hws.edu
D'AGOSTINO, Toni, J ... 409-772-2138 469 C
todagost@utmb.edu
D'ALESSANDRO,
Colleen .... 404-364-8319 124 A
cdalessandro@oglethorpe.edu
D'ALESSANDRO,
Enrico, L .... 315-684-6410 329 F
dalessel@morrisville.edu
D'ALLEVA, Anne .... 860-486-3016.. 88 G
anne.dalleva@uconn.edu
D'ALOISIO, Sally .... 732-906-7700 287 B
sdaloisio@middlesexcc.edu
D'AMATO, Anthony .... 312-567-8821 140 I
damato@iit.edu
D'AMATO, Christina ...... 516-323-4835 315 J
cdamato@molloy.edu
D'AMATO, Salvatore ..... 716-829-8377 307 B
damatos@dyc.edu
D'AMBRA, Diane .... 401-598-1854 416 C
ddambra@jwu.edu
D'AMBROSE, Martin ..... 312-987-2396 141 E
6dambrose@jmls.edu
D'AMBROSIO, Arnold ... 313-993-1025 237 F
dambroaa1@udmercy.edu
D'AMBROSIO,
Christopher .... 914-337-9300 305 F
christopher.dambrosio@concordia-ny.edu
D'AMBROSIO, Rose ...... 201-692-2706 286 B
rose_dambrosio@fdu.edu
D'AMBROSIO, Steve ..... 856-227-7200 284 E
sdambrosio@camdencc.edu
D'AMBROSIO, Vincent .. 352-588-8432 106 N
vincent.dambrosio@saintleo.edu
D'AMICO, Doreen .... 212-410-8054 317 C
ddamico@nycpm.edu
D'AMICO, Gabrielle ...... 570-408-4510 414 H
gabrielle.damico@wilkes.edu
D'AMICO, Janna .... 517-265-5161 226 F
jdamico@adrian.edu
D'AMORE, Jonathan, L . 802-654-2347 476 A
jdamore@smcvt.edu
D'AMOUR, Angela, L .... 805-565-6125.. 74 I
adamour@westmont.edu
D'ANDREA, William ...... 864-231-2000 418 E
bdandrea@andersonuniversity.edu
D'ANGELO, Frank .... 928-771-4885.. 17 G
frank.dangelo@yc.edu
D'ANGELO, Kathryn, P . 215-204-6545 411 B
kathryn.dangelo@temple.edu
D'ANGELO, Louann .... 413-572-5622 218 F
ldangelo@westfield.ma.edu
D'ANNA, Debora .... 828-884-8391 335 L
debora.danna@brevard.edu
D'APOLITO, Maria .... 614-222-6175 360 B
mdapolito@ccad.edu

E

EBY, Tim, J ... 314-516-6765 268 E ebyt@umsl.edu
ECABERT, Gayle ... 859-371-9393 183 G gecabert@beckfield.edu
ECCLES, Tom ... 845-758-7598 298 I ccs@bard.edu
ECHAMBADI, Raj ... 617-373-3232 223 D
ECHEANDIA, Manuel ... 787-786-3030 526 F mecheandia@ucb.edu.pr
ECHEGARAY, Luis ... 787-725-6500 521 C lechegaray@albizu.edu
ECHEVARRI, Richard ... 215-780-1410 410 D rech@salus.edu
ECHEVARRIA, Agustin ... 787-763-5845 523 F aecheva@inter.edu
ECHEVARRÍA, Ángel ... 787-764-0000 528 F angel.echevarria4@upr.edu
ECHOLS, Darren ... 423-614-8519 432 L dechols@leeuniversity.edu
ECHOLS, Steven, F ... 912-583-2241 116 G sechols@bpc.edu
ECHOLS TOBE, Dorothy 201-684-7008 289 C dechols@ramapo.edu
ECK, Jim ... 770-531-3129 116 F jeck@brenau.edu
ECK, Kristi ... 315-312-2212 327 D kristi.eck@oswego.edu
ECK, Stephen ... 405-425-5118 377 B stephen.eck@oc.edu
ECK, Stephen, M ... 973-596-3306 288 A steven.eck@njit.edu
ECK, Tim ... 801-626-6352 473 E teck@weber.edu
ECKARDT, Chip, P ... 715-836-2381 510 D eckardpp@uwec.edu
ECKARDT, Jill ... 940-898-3676 464 A jeckardt@twu.edu
ECKEL, Todd ... 909-593-3511.. 70 E teckel@laverne.edu
ECKENRODE, Jeanine ... 315-498-2237 319 G j.a.eckenrode@sunyocc.edu
ECKER, Brian ... 717-262-2017 415 B brian.ecker@wilson.edu
ECKERT, Amber ... 858-635-4535.. 24 L aeckert@alliant.edu
ECKERT, Jason, C ... 937-229-2045 372 A jeckert1@udayton.edu
ECKERT, Lisa ... 906-227-1828 235 A leckert@nmu.edu
ECKERT, Robin ... 610-372-4721 408 G reckert@racc.edu
ECKERT, Steve ... 928-314-9475.. 11 B steve.eckert@azwestern.edu
ECKERT, Wendy ... 423-439-6052 431 H research@etsu.edu
ECKLES, Blaine ... 208-885-6757 132 I beckles@uidaho.edu
ECKLES, Robert ... 212-410-8480 317 C reckles@nycpm.edu
ECKLEY, Amy ... 920-686-6131 510 A amy.eckley@sl.edu
ECKLEY, Catherine ... 304-357-4925 502 E catherineeckley@ucwv.edu
ECKLUND, Joe ... 402-280-5531 274 D josephecklund@creighton.edu
ECKLUND, Todd ... 719-549-3175.. 81 M todd.ecklund@pueblocc.edu
ECKMAN, Angela ... 715-738-3852 513 E aeckman@cvtc.edu
ECKMAN, Charles ... 305-284-1959 112 O ceckman@miami.edu
ECKMAN, Steven, W ... 402-363-5621 278 E seckman@york.edu
ECKRICH, Steve, E ... 541-737-4323 385 F stevee@osubookstore.com
ECKSTEIN, Mark ... 716-829-8349 307 B eckstein@dyc.edu
ECKSTEIN, Melanie ... 704-461-6877 335 J melanieeckstein@bac.edu
EDAMALA, Charles ... 309-438-3618 140 L cmedama@ilstu.edu
EDBURG, Lisa ... 573-518-2294 263 E lisae@mineralarea.edu
EDDINGER, Pam, Y ... 617-228-2400 219 D peddinger@bhcc.mass.edu
EDDINGTON, Natalie, D 410-706-2176 207 H neddingt@rx.umaryland.edu
EDDINS, Trevell ... 815-280-2884 142 A teddins@jjc.edu
EDDS-ELLIS, Stacy ... 270-686-4573 186 F stacy.edds@kctcs.edu
EDDY, Brant ... 360-867-6358 494 G eddyb@evergreen.edu
EDDY, James, M ... 336-315-7388 351 D jmeddy@uncg.edu
EDDY, Rick ... 309-341-5234 134 H reddy@sandburg.edu
EDDY, Shayna ... 508-626-4506 218 A seddy@framingham.edu
EDDY, Tiana ... 719-384-6842.. 81 G tiana.eddy@ojc.edu
EDEL, Logan ... 515-961-1579 173 E logan.edel@simpson.edu
EDELBROCK, Craig ... 205-348-6331.... 8 A cedelbrock@ccs.ua.edu
EDELEN, Charles ... 812-941-2400 161 A cedelen@ius.edu
EDELMAN, Adam ... 406-994-5091 272 A aedelman@montana.edu
EDELMAN, Daniel ... 972-338-1400 466 C daniel.edelman@untdallas.edu
EDELMAN, Debbie ... 618-468-2010 143 D dedelman@lc.edu
EDELSON, Jeffrey ... 510-642-5039.. 68 G swdean@berkeley.edu
EDELSON, Maurice, F ... 212-799-5000 312 B
EDELSTEIN, Ronald, A ... 323-563-4980.. 36 H ronaldedelstein@cdrewu.edu
EDEN, Bradford, L ... 219-464-5099 165 D brad.eden@valpo.edu
EDEN, Gene, F ... 610-799-1146 400 A geden@lccc.edu
EDEN, James, R ... 920-924-3317 514 D jeden@morainepark.edu
EDEN, Peter, A ... 802-387-6730 475 C petereden@landmark.edu
EDEN, SM, Tim ... 210-436-3786 455 J teden@stmarytx.edu
EDENS, Ashley ... 423-585-6813 438 D ashley.edens@ws.edu
EDENS, Barb ... 423-236-2587 436 C barbedens@southern.edu
EDENS, Byron ... 423-308-9652 348 C edensb@piedmontu.edu
EDENS, Gary ... 915-747-7471 467 E gedens@utep.edu
EDENS, Mike ... 903-693-2021 454 E medens@panola.edu
EDER, Jeff ... 847-628-2023 142 B jeffrey.eder@judsonu.edu
EDER, Robert ... 773-256-0784 144 G reder@lstc.edu
EDGAR, Kimberly, S ... 615-898-5825 434 H kimberly.edgar@mtsu.edu
EDGAR, Richard, J ... 240-895-3206 206 G rjedgar@smcm.edu
EDGAR-SMITH, Susan ... 610-341-4379 394 E sedgarsm@eastern.edu
EDGE, LaJill ... 920-565-1000 507 K edgely@lakeland.edu
EDGECOMBE, Nydia ... 718-518-4180 302 D nedgecombe@hostos.cuny.edu
EDGELL, Robert ... 315-792-7116 330 A robert.edgell@sunyit.edu
EDGENS, Jeff ... 307-268-2713 517 B jedgens@uwyo.edu
EDGERTON, Teresa ... 402-486-2067 277 C teresa.edgerton@ucollege.edu
EDGEWORTH, Lori ... 419-251-1614 365 C lori.edgeworth@mercycollege.edu
EDGHILL-WALDEN, Vernese ... 815-753-2638 147 H vedghillwalden@niu.edu
EDGINGTON, Kyle ... 972-883-6527 467 D kyle.edgington@utdallas.edu
EDGINGTON, Rick ... 580-628-6220 376 J rick.edgington@noc.edu
EDGINGTON, Steve ... 714-879-3901.. 45 I sedgington@hiu.edu
EDGINGTON, Thomas, J ... 574-372-5100 158 B edging@grace.edu
EDGMON, Angie ... 615-675-5278 441 B finaid@welch.edu
EDGREN, JR., Gerald ... 618-842-3711 140 C edgreng@iecc.edu
EDICK, Nancy ... 402-554-2719 277 I nedick@unomaha.edu
EDINGTON, Julie ... 870-248-4000.. 18 J julie.edington@blackrivertech.edu
EDINGTON, Maurice ... 850-599-8316 109 A maurice.edington@famu.edu
EDINGTON, Pamela, R ... 845-431-8980 307 A pamela.edington@sunydutchess.edu
EDIZEL, Gerar ... 607-871-2412 298 A fedizel@alfred.edu
EDKINS, Charles ... 570-674-6294 401 M cedkins@misericordia.edu
EDLUND, Erin ... 651-423-8233 244 E erin.edlund@dctc.edu
EDLUND, Matthew ... 651-361-3450 243 D medlund@mcnallysmith.edu
EDMAN, Neal, A ... 724-946-7110 414 C nedman@westminster.edu
EDMAN, Patricia ... 612-374-5800 242 C pedman@dunwoody.edu
EDMAN, Sally ... 712-707-7321 172 G sedman@nwciowa.edu
EDMINSTER, David ... 303-546-3514.. 81 B davee@naropa.edu
EDMINSTER, Warren ... 270-809-3166 188 D wedminster@murraystate.edu
EDMOND, Betty ... 512-492-3006 442 J president@aoma.edu
EDMOND, Beverly ... 406-243-4689 271 G beverly.edmond@umontana.edu
EDMOND, Cara ... 512-454-7001 442 J cedmond@aoma.edu
EDMOND, Steven ... 312-505-6472 451 A ssedmond@htu.edu
EDMONDS, Charles, W . 570-321-4347 400 G edmonds@lycoming.edu
EDMONDS, Christopher 808-734-9124 130 C cme33@hawaii.edu
EDMONDS, Heather ... 617-587-5579 222 G edmondsh@neco.edu
EDMONDS, Jane ... 781-239-4998 211 A jedmonds@babson.edu
EDMONDS, John ... 540-785-5440 487 B johnedmonds@vbc.edu
EDMONDS, Kerry ... 540-362-6630 481 F kedmonds@hollins.edu
EDMONDS, Lawson ... 205-652-3545.... 9 C ledmonds@uwa.edu
EDMONDS, Lawson, C .. 205-652-3545.... 9 C ledmonds@uwa.edu
EDMONDS, Lorna Jean . 740-593-1889 368 G edmonds@ohio.edu
EDMONDS, Mabel ... 253-589-5510 493 F mabel.edmonds@cptc.edu
EDMONDS, Melody ... 931-393-1698 437 C medmonds@mscc.edu
EDMONDS, Michelle ... 434-949-1006 489 E michelle.edmonds@southside.edu
EDMONDS, Michelle, K 434-949-1006 489 E michelle.edmonds@southside.edu
EDMONDS, Mike ... 719-389-6684.. 77 J medmonds@coloradocollege.edu
EDMONDS, William ... 814-732-2761 406 B eup_admissions@edinboro.edu
EDMONDSON, Charles (Ricks) ... 817-515-7726 458 B charles.edmondson@tccd.edu
EDMONDSON, Jackie ... 256-549-8224.... 2 A jedmondson@gadsdenstate.edu
EDMONDSON, Lauren ... 417-873-7569 259 G ledmondson@drury.edu
EDMONDSON, Melanie, M ... 443-334-2272 207 C medmondson@stevenson.edu
EDMONDSON, Steve ... 563-588-8000 169 B sedmondson@emmaus.edu
EDMONDSON, William .. 814-871-7298 395 H edmondso002@gannon.edu
EDMONSON, Stacey ... 936-294-1101 462 F edu_sle01@shsu.edu
EDMUND, Devon ... 866-492-5336 251 E devon.edmund@mail.waldenu.edu
EDMUNDSON, John ... 928-314-9500.. 11 B john.edmundson@azwestern.edu
EDONICK, Jessica ... 717-396-7833 404 R jedonick@pcad.edu
EDRICH, Terri ... 972-860-4825 447 G tedrich@dcccd.edu
EDSALL, Denese ... 954-201-7502.. 96 A dedsall@broward.edu
EDSALL, Paul ... 724-838-4236 410 E edsall@setonhill.edu
EDSCORN, Steven ... 918-444-3211 376 G edscorn@nsuok.edu
EDSON, Brenda ... 434-947-4287 484 B bedson@randolphcollege.edu
EDSTROM, Julie ... 406-791-5271 273 C julie.edstrom@ugf.edu
EDUARDO, Marcelo ... 601-925-3214 254 B eduardo@mc.edu
EDWALDS-GILBERT, Gretchen ... 909-607-9100.. 63 F gedwalds@scrippscollege.edu
EDWARD, Alexander ... 229-430-0664 114 J ealexander@albanytech.edu
EDWARDS, Allen, G ... 865-539-7375 437 F aedwards@pstcc.edu
EDWARDS, Amanda ... 816-331-5700 265 D aedwards@pcitraining.edu
EDWARDS, Amanda ... 828-398-7176 340 M
EDWARDS, Amy ... 217-333-3551 154 B aledward@illinois.edu
EDWARDS, Anne ... 856-222-9311 289 F aedwards@rcbc.edu
EDWARDS, Annette ... 757-789-1768 488 A aedwards@es.vccs.edu
EDWARDS, April ... 630-617-3063 138 C april.edwards@elmhurst.edu
EDWARDS, Bahola ... 432-685-4520 453 B bahola@midland.edu
EDWARDS, Bambi ... 252-638-7317 342 E edwardsb@cravencc.edu
EDWARDS, Betty ... 334-420-4321.... 3 H bedwards@trenholmstate.edu
EDWARDS, Brad ... 479-524-7212.. 20 B bedwards@jbu.edu
EDWARDS, Brad ... 703-993-3212 481 B bedwards@gmu.edu
EDWARDS, Brian ... 252-335-0821 342 D brian_edwards@albemarle.edu
EDWARDS, Bruce ... 808-356-5256 129 C bedwards@hpu.edu
EDWARDS, Byron ... 615-514-2787 435 F dredwards@nossi.edu
EDWARDS, Candace ... 410-386-8505 203 A cedwards@carrollcc.edu
EDWARDS, Carlton, G ... 804-257-5851 491 C cgedwards@vuu.edu
EDWARDS, Carmen ... 432-685-4589 453 B cedwards@midland.edu
EDWARDS, Cathy ... 214-860-8685 448 B cedwards@dcccd.edu
EDWARDS, Chris ... 601-481-1316 253 G cedwards@meridiancc.edu
EDWARDS, Cody ... 703-993-4564 481 B cedward7@gmu.edu
EDWARDS, Connie ... 724-738-2226 407 C constance.edwards@sru.edu
EDWARDS, Cynthia ... 404-297-9522 120 D edwardsc@gptc.edu
EDWARDS, Dave ... 657-278-7739.. 32 B daveedwards@fullerton.edu
EDWARDS, David ... 609-586-4800 287 A edwardsd@mccc.edu
EDWARDS, David ... 330-941-3394 374 E dwedwards@ysu.edu
EDWARDS, Delyssa ... 740-245-7431 372 E dedwards@rio.edu
EDWARDS, Donald ... 828-689-1246 339 G dedwards@mhu.edu
EDWARDS, Doreen ... 585-475-2146 321 D ddeen@rit.edu
EDWARDS, Earl, W ... 858-534-8750.. 69 E ewedwards@ucsd.edu
EDWARDS, Edra ... 832-230-5188 453 K registrar@na.edu
EDWARDS, Elizabeth ... 662-862-8265 253 D etedwards@iccms.edu
EDWARDS, Ellen ... 207-947-4591 198 F eedwards@bealcollege.edu
EDWARDS, Emory ... 201-761-6108 291 D eedwards@saintpeters.edu
EDWARDS, Eugene ... 503-375-7010 383 A eedwards@corban.edu
EDWARDS, Frank ... 404-880-8672 117 H fedwards@cau.edu
EDWARDS, Gary ... 661-362-2291.. 51 C gedwards@masters.edu
EDWARDS, Geoffrey, M 812-488-1102 164 G ge21@evansville.edu
EDWARDS, Hazel ... 202-806-6100.. 92 C
EDWARDS, Hollly ... 325-670-1026 450 A holly.edwards@hsutx.edu
EDWARDS, Holly ... 252-493-7206 345 E hedwards@email.pittcc.edu
EDWARDS, Ian, C ... 412-396-6204 394 D edwards181@duq.edu
EDWARDS, Ishmell, H ... 662-252-8000 255 F iedwards@rustcollege.edu
EDWARDS, James ... 252-492-2061 347 C edwardsj@vgcc.edu
EDWARDS, James, E ... 757-822-5121 489 H jeedwards@tcc.edu
EDWARDS, Jamie ... 276-223-4829 490 C jedwards@wcc.vccs.edu
EDWARDS, Jan ... 719-227-8294.. 77 J jan.edwards@coloradocollege.edu
EDWARDS, Jane ... 203-432-8680.. 89 G jane.edwards@yale.edu
EDWARDS, Jason ... 252-985-5102 348 A jedwards@ncwc.edu
EDWARDS, Jeff ... 337-439-5765 191 D jeff@deltatech.edu
EDWARDS, Jennifer, T .. 254-968-9480 459 A jtedwards@tarleton.edu
EDWARDS, John ... 212-343-1234 315 D
EDWARDS, Jon ... 508-270-4102 220 A jedwards@massbay.edu
EDWARDS, Jonathan, P 843-661-1181 421 H jedwards@fmarion.edu
EDWARDS, Joyce, P ... 336-334-7755 350 C edwardsj@ncat.edu
EDWARDS, Judson ... 334-670-3989.... 7 E jcedwards@troy.edu

EDWARDS, Karen .... 251-460-7092.... 9 B
cedwards@southalabama.edu
EDWARDS, Karen .... 281-756-3639 442 C
kedwards@alvincollege.edu
EDWARDS, Karen, K ..... 641-269-3703 169 F
edwardsk@grinnell.edu
EDWARDS, Karin .... 971-722-5302 386 C
karin.edwards@pcc.edu
EDWARDS, Kendra .... 816-604-5249 262 F
kendra.edwards@mcckc.edu
EDWARDS, Keston .... 708-344-4700 144 A
kedwards@lincolntech.edu
EDWARDS, Kevin .... 740-474-8896 367 E
kedwards@ohiochristian.edu
EDWARDS, Kimberly ..... 909-447-2592.. 38 B
kedwards@cst.edu
EDWARDS, Laurie, L ..... 712-324-5061 172 E
ledwards@nwicc.edu
EDWARDS, Lendozia ..... 615-871-2260.. 93 B
EDWARDS, Lisa .... 646-660-6036 301 B
lisa.edwards@baruch.cuny.edu
EDWARDS, Lola .... 229-430-1702 114 J
ledwards@albanytech.edu
EDWARDS, Louis, W ..... 713-313-6747 461 E
edwards_lw@tsu.edu
EDWARDS, Mark .... 605-256-5680 428 G
mark.edwards@dsu.edu
EDWARDS, Mark, H ...... 315-655-7334 300 I
medwards@cazenovia.edu
EDWARDS, Mary, A ...... 304-336-8000 504 E
edwardsm@westliberty.edu
EDWARDS, Matthew ...... 864-646-1474 424 F
medward3@tctc.edu
EDWARDS, Michael .... 641-673-2120 174 F
edwardsml@wmpenn.edu
EDWARDS, Michelle ...... 337-439-5765 191 D
michelle@deltatech.edu
EDWARDS, Mike .... 615-675-5333 441 B
mike.edwards@welch.edu
EDWARDS, Nigel .... 850-599-3183 109 A
nigel.edwards@famu.edu
EDWARDS, Paul .... 978-927-2300 215 D
paul.edwards@gordon.edu
EDWARDS, JR.,
Quinton, T .... 662-915-3784 256 C
qtedward@olemiss.edu
EDWARDS, Randy .... 828-262-2090 349 H
edwardsk@appstate.edu
EDWARDS, Richard .... 518-629-7356 310 G
r.edwards@hvcc.edu
EDWARDS, Rick .... 828-395-1676 344 A
redwards@isothermal.edu
EDWARDS, Rosie .... 334-514-5063.... 2 E
rosie.edwards@istc.edu
EDWARDS, Sabrina .... 904-470-8952.. 98 B
sabrina.edwards@ewc.edu
EDWARDS, Sarah .... 270-706-8447 185 H
sarah.edwards@kctcs.edu
EDWARDS, Shawn .... 843-953-6989 419 D
shawn.edwards@citadel.edu
EDWARDS, Sheryl .... 870-235-5090.. 21 F
saedwards@saumag.edu
EDWARDS, Stacia .... 740-203-8011 360 C
sedward1@cscc.edu
EDWARDS, Stephanie .... 619-201-8713.. 60 A
stephanie.edwards@sdcc.edu
EDWARDS, Steve .... 912-583-3218 116 G
sedwards@bpc.edu
EDWARDS, Tania .... 816-322-0110 257 M
tania.edwards@calvary.edu
EDWARDS, TerCraig, D . 336-734-7953 343 C
tedwards@forsythtech.edu
EDWARDS, Thomas .... 207-859-1362 200 H
edwardst@thomas.edu
EDWARDS, Tim .... 205-652-3531.... 9 C
tedwards@uwa.edu
EDWARDS, Tim .... 205-652-3457.... 9 C
tedwards@uwa.edu
EDWARDS, Timothy ...... 907-786-1381.... 9 I
tmedwards202@alaska.edu
EDWARDS, Timothy ...... 208-882-1566 132 D
timedwards@nsa.edu
EDWARDS, Tracy .... 405-945-3376 378 C
tracyle@osuokc.edu
EDWARDS, Tyler .... 605-256-5318 428 G
tyler.edwards@dsu.edu
EDWARDS, Ulrica, S ..... 318-274-7297 196 G
edwardsu@gram.edu
EDWARDS, Wanda .... 910-296-1812 344 B
wedwards@jamessprunt.edu
EDWARDS, Wayne .... 516-876-3175 327 C
edwardsw@oldwestbury.edu
EDWARDS-EVANS,
Nicole .... 601-979-2244 253 E
nicole.e.evans@jsums.edu
EDWARDS LANGE,
Sheila .... 206-934-4144 497 G
sheila.edwardslange@seattlecolleges.edu
EDWARDS LANGE,
Sheila .... 206-934-4144 497 I
sheila.edwardslange@seattlecolleges.edu
EDYTHE, Abdullah, E .... 904-620-5408 110 E
e.abdullah@unf.edu
EELLS, Rachel .... 708-209-3255 136 I
rachel.eells@cuchicago.edu
EFFLANDT, Scott .... 913-684-3443 518 I
EFFORD, Lelia .... 305-626-3180.. 99 M
lefford@fmuniv.edu
EFTHIMIOU, Chris .... 718-289-5169 301 D
chris.efthimiou@bcc.cuny.edu
EFTHYMIOU,
Lampeto (Betty) .... 718-631-6611 303 F
lefthymiou@qcc.cuny.edu
EGAN, Beth-Anne .... 860-253-3030.. 85 C
began@asnuntuck.edu
EGAN, Brian .... 973-684-5999 288 C
began@pccc.edu
EGAN, Carolyn .... 850-644-4440 110 A
cegan@fsu.edu
EGAN, Eric .... 760-921-5520.. 55 J
eegan@paloverde.edu
EGAN, Jonathon .... 562-947-8755.. 65 D
jonathonegan@scuhs.edu
EGAN, Kristen .... 847-628-2017 142 B
kristen.egan@judsonu.edu
EGAN, Maryan .... 239-590-1234 109 C
megan@fgcu.edu
EGAN, Russi .... 530-541-4660.. 47 I
egan@ltcc.edu
EGAN, Thomas .... 215-572-2900 389 D
egant@arcadia.edu
EGBE, Daniel .... 501-370-5259.. 21 A
degbe@philander.edu
EGBE, Daniel .... 501-370-5268.. 21 A
degbe@philander.edu
EGBE, Emmanuel .... 718-270-5170 303 C
egbe@mec.cuny.edu
EGBE, Odey, P .... 478-289-2039 118 H
oegbe@ega.edu
EGBERT, Jeb .... 949-783-4800.. 73 K
jegbert@westcoastuniversity.edu
EGBERT, Jessica, D .... 801-375-5125 472 F
jegbert@rmuohp.edu
EGDORF, Randall .... 217-641-4973 141 F
regdorf@jwcc.edu
EGE, Daryle .... 309-467-6394 138 E
dege@eureka.edu
EGELER, William, G .... 207-768-2792 200 B
wegeler@nmcc.edu
EGENESS, Cynthia .... 651-690-6864 249 T
cnegeness@stkate.edu
EGENREIDER, Mike .... 765-674-6901 161 C
mike.egenreider@indwes.edu
EGERSON, Veronica, V .. 414-464-9777 513 B
egerson.veronica@wspp.edu
EGERSTROM, Sarah .... 715-425-3500 511 E
sarah.r.egerstrom@uwrf.edu
EGGEN, Tyler .... 907-564-8311.... 9 F
teegen@alaskapacific.edu
EGGENSPERGER,
Martin .... 870-508-6102.. 18 C
meggensperger@asumh.edu
EGGERS, Daniel, W .... 512-245-1555 463 A
dwe16@txstate.edu
EGGERS, John, M .... 320-308-0121 247 E
jmeggers@stcloudstate.edu
EGGERS, Marilyn .... 909-558-7658.. 48 H
meggers@llu.edu
EGGERS, Ron .... 252-399-6417 335 I
reggers@barton.edu
EGGERS, Troy .... 212-854-5939 305 E
te99@columbia.edu
EGGERSTEDT, Jane .... 318-675-6124 194 D
jegger@lsuhsc.edu
EGGERT, Mary .... 414-847-3211 508 G
maryeggert@miad.edu
EGGLESTON, Joseph ...... 562-947-8755.. 65 D
josepheggleston@scuhs.edu
EGGLESTON, Kathryn, K 972-238-6364 448 D
keggleston@dcccd.edu
EGGLESTON, Meghan .... 276-656-0285 489 A
meggleston@patrickhenry.edu
EGGLESTON, Tami .... 618-537-6926 145 C
teggleston@mckendree.edu
EGGLESTON WILLIAMS,
Latrice, E .... 773-995-2548 135 F
egglest@csu.edu
EGIEBOR, Nosa .... 315-470-6510 328 D
noegiebo@esf.edu
EGLE, Don .... 903-233-3290 452 A
donegle@letu.edu
EGLI, Ryan .... 215-368-5000 389 H
regli@biblical.edu
EGLSAER, Richard .... 936-294-1001 462 F
eglsaer@shsu.edu
EGRESI, Chad .... 410-888-9048 205 D
cegresi@muih.edu
EGUARAS, Agnes .... 818-240-1000.. 44 D
aeguaras@glendale.edu
EGUCHI, Amy .... 973-748-9000 284 A
amy_eguchi@bloomfield.edu
EGUEZ GUEVARA, Pilar 925-969-3300.. 46 L
pguevara@jfku.edu
EHASZ, Maribeth .... 407-823-4372 110 C
maribeth.ehasz@ucf.edu
EHLER, Gina, M .... 262-524-7247 506 G
gehler@carrollu.edu
EHLERS, Chris .... 918-781-7233 374 H
ehlersc@bacone.edu
EHLERS, Nancy, M .... 716-652-8900 300 L
nehlers@cks.edu
EHLERS, Pam .... 405-744-2122 377 F
pam.ehlers@okstate.edu
EHLERT, Alycia .... 386-506-3769.. 97 I
alycia.ehlert@daytonastate.edu
EHLERT, Kim .... 262-691-5594 515 B
kehlert@wctc.edu
EHLING, William .... 252-328-6387 349 I
ehlingw16@ecu.edu
EHMAN, Amanda .... 740-245-7443 372 E
amandae@rio.edu
EHMANN, William .... 703-284-1550 483 A
william.ehmann@marymount.edu
EHMEN, Stacy, L .... 217-443-8746 137 B
stacy@dacc.edu
EHRENREICH, Yaakov ... 718-941-8000 315 C
EHRESMAN, Terry .... 620-278-4264 181 G
tehresman@sterling.edu
EHRHARDT, Tom .... 312-261-3165 146 G
tom.ehrhardt@nl.edu
EHRIE, Ryan .... 570-662-4636 406 F
rehrie@mansfield.edu
EHRLICH, Anne, R .... 309-341-7221 142 G
arehrlich@knox.edu
EHRLICH, Brian .... 321-674-8202.. 99 K
behrlich@fit.edu
EHRLICH, Robert .... 660-626-2297 257 A
rehrlich@atsu.edu
EHRLICH, Sam .... 830-372-8155 461 D
sehrlich@tlu.edu
EHRMAN, James, E .... 717-866-5775 395 C
james.ehrman@evangelical.edu
EHRMAN, Sheryl .... 408-924-3800.. 34 D
EHRMANTRAUT,
Dominic .... 901-321-3286 431 A
dehrmant@cbu.edu
EHST, Suzanne .... 574-535-7839 158 A
sehst@goshen.edu
EIBECK, Pamela, A .... 209-946-2222.. 70 F
president@pacific.edu
EICHELBERGER, Lisa ...... 678-466-4900 117 I
lisaeichelberger@clayton.edu
EICHELROTH, Kathleen .. 508-929-8098 219 A
keichelroth@worcester.edu
EICHENBERGER, Julie ... 620-223-2700 177 E
juliee@fortscott.edu
EICHENLAUB, Mark, P .. 618-235-2700 152 E
mark.eichenlaub@swic.edu
EICHENSTEIN, Joseph ... 732-985-6533 289 A
EICHER, Michael .... 614-292-9858 367 H
eicher@osu.edu
EICHFIELD, Tara .... 912-287-5809 117 J
teichfield@coastalpines.edu
EICHHORN, Gregory, E . 203-582-8906.. 88 A
gregory.eichhorn@quinnipiac.edu
EICHHORN, Kristen, C .. 315-312-3152 327 D
kristen.eichhorn@oswego.edu
EICHHORST, Amy .... 301-405-2102 207 G
aeich@umd.edu
EICHHORST, Carly .... 507-786-3357 250 C
eichho1@stolaf.edu
EICHLER, Richard .... 212-854-2878 305 E
re1@columbia.edu
EICHNER, John .... 716-614-6430 318 E
jeichner@niagaracc.suny.edu
EICHNER, Kevin .... 785-242-5200 180 H
kevin.eichner@ottawa.edu
EICHOLTZ, Kristin .... 610-282-1100 393 G
kristin.eicholtz@desales.edu
EICHORST, Christopher . 509-777-4780 500 H
ceichorst@whitworth.edu
EICHORST, Shawn .... 402-472-3011 277 G
seichorst@huskers.com
EICHTEN, Jonathan .... 320-308-5580 247 F
jeichten@sctcc.edu
EICK, Christine, L .... 334-844-4870.... 4 D
eickchr@auburn.edu
EICKEN, Hajo .... 907-474-7331.. 10 B
heicken@alaska.edu
EICKHOFF, Chad .... 928-523-7141.. 14 K
chad.eickhoff@nau.edu
EICKHOFF, Jeffrey .... 402-643-4052 276 I
sggs@sggs.edu
EICKHOLT, Marcia .... 419-227-3141 372 D
marcia@unoh.edu
EICKHORST, Lindsay ..... 309-268-8031 139 D
lindsay.eickhorst@heartland.edu
EICKMEIER, Valerie .... 317-920-2403 160 E
veickmei@iupui.edu
EID, Haithum .... 504-286-5010 195 L
heid@suno.edu
EIDE, Greg .... 503-375-7021 383 A
geide@corban.edu
EIDENBERG, Julia .... 503-517-1816 388 C
jeidenberg@westernseminary.edu
EIDSON, Kristi .... 270-686-4216 183 J
kristi.eidson@brescia.edu
EIDSON, Paul .... 714-841-6252 270 F
dreidson@apollosuniversity.edu
EIDSON, Rebecca, W .... 864-646-1507 424 F
reidson@tctc.edu
EIDSON, Scott .... 406-799-1515 270 F
seidson@apollosuniversity.edu
EIERMANN, Jason .... 985-448-4521 197 C
jason.eiermann@nicholls.edu
EIFERT, Robert .... 217-824-4004 143 B
reifert@lakeland.cc.il.us
EIGENBRODE, Jill .... 410-532-5152 206 D
jeigenbrode@ndm.edu
EIGENBROOD, Rick .... 206-281-2710 498 B
eigend@spu.edu
EIGHMY, Sunny .... 641-628-5272 167 D
eighmys@central.edu
EIGHMY, T. Tyler .... 210-458-4101 468 B
EIKE, Claire .... 312-629-9379 151 F
ceike@saic.edu
EIKENBERRY, Michael ... 317-940-8940 156 I
meikenbe@butler.edu
EIKENS, Anita .... 414-382-6343 506 A
anita.eikens@alverno.edu
EIKNER, Megan, E .... 806-335-4352 442 D
meeikner@actx.edu
EILAND, Victoria .... 229-430-4637 114 I
victoria.eiland@asurams.edu
EILERING, Susan .... 217-479-7106 144 I
susan.eilering@mac.edu
EIMER, Greg, A .... 217-732-3155 143 G
geimer@lincolncollege.edu
EIMERS, Mardy, T .... 573-882-3412 268 C
eimersm@missouri.edu
EINESMAN, Floralynn ..... 619-239-0391.. 35 C
fle@cwsl.edu
EINFELD, Aaron .... 616-957-7035 228 C
aaron@calvinseminary.edu
EINHELLIG, Frank, E ...... 417-836-5119 263 H
frankeinhellig@missouristate.edu
EINOLF, Karl, W .... 260-422-5561 159 D
kweinolf@indianatech.edu
EINSPAHR, Kent .... 402-643-7315 274 B
kent.einspahr@cune.edu
EINSTEIN, Heath, A .... 817-257-7490 461 A
h.einstein@tcu.edu
EIOLA, William, T .... 419-772-2261 367 G
w-eiola@onu.edu
EIS, Linda .... 417-625-3797 263 G
eis-l@mssu.edu
EISBACH, Sebastian ...... 515-271-1471 168 G
sebastian.eisbach@dmu.edu
EISEMAN, Margaret .... 412-396-6061 394 D
eiseman@duq.edu
EISEN, Arnold, M .... 212-678-8072 312 A
areisen@jtsa.edu
EISEN, Jeffrey, M .... 919-658-7759 349 F
jeisen@umo.edu
EISEN, Karen .... 718-780-0343 300 A
karen.eisen@brooklaw.edu
EISENBACH, Regina .... 760-750-4253.. 33 E
regina@csusm.edu
EISENBACH, Theresa ..... 203-332-5013.. 85 F
teisenbach@hcc.commnet.edu
EISENBARTH, Jeffrey ..... 407-646-2117 106 J
jeisenbarth@rollins.edu
EISENBARTH,
Kathryn, L .... 503-352-2705 385 I
eisenbak@pacificu.edu
EISENBEISER, Colleen ... 410-777-1249 202 D
ckeisenbeiser@aacc.edu
EISENBERG, Eric .... 813-974-2804 111 A
eisenberg@usf.edu
EISENBERG, Larry, A ..... 314-516-6469 268 E
eisenbergl@umsl.edu
EISENBERGER, Israel ..... 845-362-3053 299 C
EISENHART, Pamela ...... 717-337-6010 396 A
peisenha@gettysburg.edu
EISENHAUER, Jay .... 304-829-7465 501 F
jeisenhauer@bethanywv.edu

EISENHAUER, Joseph .... 313-993-1204 237 F
eisenhjg@udmercy.edu
EISENHAUER, Thomas .. 816-415-5990 270 C
eisenhauer@william.jewell.edu
EISENHAUER, Walt .... 570-484-2168 406 E
weisenha@lockhaven.edu
EISENHOUR, Lyn .... 425-352-8548 492 K
leisenhour@cascadia.edu
EISENHUTH, Wayne ...... 507-222-4427 241 C
weisenhu@carleton.edu
EISENMAN, Ann .... 563-244-7040 168 L
aeisenman@eicc.edu
EISENMAN, Elaine .... 781-239-4355 211 A
eeisenman@babson.edu
EISENMENGER, Paul ..... 847-317-7087 153 D
peisenme@tiu.edu
EISENSTEIN, Laya .... 718-268-4700 320 K
EISENSTEIN, Paul .... 614-823-1609 368 O
peisenstein@otterbein.edu
EISENTRAGER, Pete ...... 816-235-2665 268 D
eisentragerp@umkc.edu
EISGRUBER,
Cristopher, L .... 609-258-3026 288 F
eisgrube@princeton.edu
EISINGER, David, W ..... 920-923-8576 508 B
dweisinger@marianuniversity.edu
EISLER, David, L .... 231-591-2500 230 A
davideisler@ferris.edu
EISNAUGLE, Eva .... 704-978-1344 344 H
eeisnaugle@mitchellcc.edu
EISNER, SND, Janet ...... 617-735-9825 214 F
president@emmanuel.edu
EITEL, Keith .... 817-923-1921 457 G
keitel@swbts.edu
EITEL, Norine .... 660-626-2391 257 A
neitel@atsu.edu
EJIGIRI, Damien .... 225-771-3092 195 K
dejigiri@yahoo.com
EKARIUS, John .... 215-503-5017 411 E
john.ekarius@jefferson.edu
EKKER, David, A .... 757-822-7198 489 H
dekker@tcc.edu
EKNESS, Ray .... 406-243-4088 271 G
ray.ekness@umontana.edu
EKOUE-TOTOU, Patrick . 415-883-2211.. 39 E
pekouetotou@marin.edu
EKPO, NseAbasi .... 937-376-6411 358 I
nekpo@centralstate.edu
EKSTROM, Rodney .... 603-535-2217 283 B
raekstrom@plymouth.edu
EL-AMIN, Aisha .... 312-413-3450 153 H
aelami2@uic.edu
EL FATTAL, David .... 805-652-5536.. 72 G
delfattal@vcccd.edu
EL-HAGGAN, Ahmed ..... 410-951-3850 208 F
elhaggan@coppin.edu
EL-KHOURY, Rodolphe . 305-284-9092 112 O
rxe66@miami.edu
EL-REWINI, Hesham ...... 701-777-4138 353 G
hesham.el-rewini@und.edu
EL-REWINI, Hesham ...... 701-777-3412 353 G
rewini@engr.und.edu
ELAM, Demar .... 334-387-3877.... 4 B
demarelam@amridgeuniversity.edu
ELAM, Harry, J .... 650-723-2300.. 66 C
helam@stanford.edu
ELAM, Michael, A .... 252-536-7217 343 F
ELAM, Terry .... 434-592-3966 482 D
tlelam@liberty.edu
ELAM, Terry, D .... 706-771-4005 116 A
telam@augustatech.edu
ELAND, Tom .... 612-659-6286 245 F
thomas.eland@minneapolis.edu
ELARDE, Chris .... 914-923-2804 319 J
ELBASSIOUNY, Samir ... 908-835-9222 292 G
selbassiouny@warren.edu
ELBE, Michael .... 217-641-4101 141 F
melbe@jwcc.edu
ELCHANANI, Matanya ... 203-576-4322.. 88 F
matanya@btidgeport.edu
ELDAYRIE, Elias, G .... 352-273-1788 110 D
eldayrie@ufl.edu
ELDEMIRE, Flavia .... 803-255-4742 418 D
feldemire@allenuniversity.edu
ELDER, Britni .... 501-205-8923.. 19 B
belder@cbc.edu
ELDER, Dana .... 509-359-6305 494 D
delder@ewu.edu
ELDER, Darla .... 814-732-2743 406 B
delder@edinboro.edu
ELDER, Gregory .... 386-481-2906.. 95 J
elderg@cookman.edu
ELDER, Jackie .... 903-223-3110 460 D
jackie.elder@tamut.edu
ELDER, Jill .... 605-718-2411 429 E
jill.elder@wdt.edu
ELDER, Keith .... 205-726-4655..... 6 G
kelder@samford.edu

ELDER, Kelly .... 412-268-8977 391 H
kelder@andrew.cmu.edu
ELDER, Matthew .... 502-585-9911 189 B
melder@spalding.edu
ELDER, Paul .... 269-471-3284 227 B
elderp@andrews.edu
ELDER, Shelia .... 404-962-3002 127 G
shelia.elder@usg.edu
ELDER, Steve .... 501-205-8893.. 19 B
selder@cbc.edu
ELDER, Thomas .... 903-510-3038 464 D
teld@tjc.edu
ELDER, Vivian .... 417-447-8114 264 K
elderv@otc.edu
ELDERS, Candice .... 269-927-8198 232 G
cedlers@lakemichigancollege.edu
ELDRIDGE, Amy .... 312-935-4240 141 C
aeldridge@icsw.edu
ELDRIDGE, Audrey .... 208-562-3509 132 A
audreyeldridge@cwidaho.cc
ELDRIDGE, Connie .... 847-574-5264 143 A
celdridge@lfgsm.edu
ELDRIDGE, Daryl .... 866-931-4300 265 H
daryl.eldridge@rockbridge.edu
ELDRIDGE, Jonathan ..... 415-485-9619.. 39 E
jeldridge@marin.edu
ELDRIDGE, Karen .... 865-981-8207 433 F
karen.eldridge@maryvillecollege.edu
ELDRIDGE, Kim .... 202-884-9053.. 93 C
mortonk@trinitydc.edu
ELDRIDGE, Marie .... 931-598-1111 436 A
police@sewanee.edu
ELDRIDGE, Randy .... 610-527-0200 409 E
reldridge@rosemont.edu
ELDRIDGE, Ray .... 615-966-5946 433 D
ray.eldridge@lipscomb.edu
ELEBARIO, Jessica .... 575-461-4413 294 E
jessicae@mesalands.edu
ELEFF, Zev .... 847-982-2500 139 E
eleff@htc.edu
ELENICH, Richard .... 906-487-2763 234 A
rjelenic@mtu.edu
ELENWO, Elizabeth .... 619-549-3974.. 65 C
elizabeth.elenwo@socalsem.edu
ELEY, Greg .... 765-998-5224 164 C
greley@taylor.edu
ELFRINK, Stephanie ...... 314-529-9370 262 B
selfrink@maryville.edu
ELGARICO, Michael .... 805-493-3049.. 30 E
elgarico@callutheran.edu
ELGREN, Timothy .... 440-775-8410 367 B
tim.elgren@oberlin.edu
ELHINDI, Mohamed .... 608-785-8309 510 F
melhindi@uwlax.edu
ELI, Lauren .... 303-300-8740.. 77 F
lauren.eli@collegeamerica.com
ELI, Lisa, G .... 407-582-6649 113 F
leli@valenciacollege.edu
ELIA, Anthony .... 317-937-2365 157 D
aelia@cts.edu
ELIADI, Carol .... 617-373-5680 221 E
carol.eliadi@mcphs.edu
ELIAS, Benjamin .... 888-775-1514.. 68 D
belias@unitekcollege.edu
ELIAS, Charles .... 718-482-5052 303 B
celias@lagcc.cuny.edu
ELIAS, Jack .... 401-863-3330 415 K
jack_elias@brown.edu
ELIAS, Janelle .... 480-517-8767.. 14 B
janelle.elias@riosalado.edu
ELIAS, Michael .... 610-896-1228 397 F
melias@haverford.edu
ELIAS, Stephanny, J ...... 617-333-2010 214 B
selias0104@curry.edu
ELIAS, Steven, M .... 970-247-7010.. 79 J
selias@fortlewis.edu
ELIAS BLOOMER,
Michelle .... 617-228-2465 219 D
mveliasbl@bhcc.mass.edu
ELIASON, Eric, J .... 218-299-3001 241 K
vpaa@cord.edu
ELIASSON-CREEK, Fia ... 253-833-9111 495 C
feliasson-creek@greenriver.edu
ELIAV, Eli .... 585-275-5688 332 E
eli_eliav@urmc.rochester.edu
ELICK, Cynthia, M .... 260-481-6204 160 D
elick@ipfw.edu
ELICKER, Beth .... 207-699-5045 199 H
belicker@meca.edu
ELIPTICO, Frankie, M .... 670-237-6781 520 D
frankie.eliptico@marianas.edu
ELIQUE, Jose .... 702-895-3668 279 D
chiefofpolice@unlv.edu
ELISH-PIPER, Laurie ...... 815-753-9055 147 H
laurieep@niu.edu
ELIZA, Lourdes .... 787-852-1430 522 P
leliza@hccpr.edu

ELIZANDRO, John .... 516-686-7605 317 G
jelizand@nyit.edu
ELIZONDO, Laura, M .... 956-326-2213 459 B
laura@tamiu.edu
ELIZONDO, Maria, G .... 956-872-3558 456 G
melizondo@southtexascollege.edu
ELKESHK, Abed .... 718-405-3300 304 H
abed.elkeshk@mountsaintvincent.edu
ELKINS, Germaine .... 910-695-3706 346 E
elkinsg@sandhills.edu
ELKINS, Julie, B .... 617-228-2436 219 D
jelkins@bhcc.mass.edu
ELKINS, Leah, C .... 513-241-4338 356 I
leah.elkins@antonellicollege.edu
ELKINS, Mark .... 904-596-2445 112 F
melkins@tbc.edu
ELKINS, Mary Jane .... 434-949-1051 489 E
mary.elkins@southside.edu
ELKINS, Mary Jane .... 434-949-1000 489 E
mary.elkins@southside.edu
ELKINS, Mary Jane .... 434-949-1051 489 E
mary.elkins@southside.edu
ELKINS, Paula, S .... 706-886-6831 126 F
pelkins@tfc.edu
ELKINS, Penny, L .... 478-301-2120 122 H
elkins_pl@mercer.edu
ELKINS, Susan .... 803-777-7695 424 I
selkins@mailbox.sc.edu
ELKS, Martha .... 404-752-1881 123 F
melks@msm.edu
ELLARD, Katherine .... 662-472-9134 253 C
kellard@holmescc.edu
ELLARD, Mark .... 334-291-4981.... 1 H
mark.ellard@cv.edu
ELLARD, Owen, H .... 210-567-2413 468 E
ellard@uthscsa.edu
ELLENBERG, George, B . 850-474-2035 111 D
gellenberg@uwf.edu
ELLENBERG, Todd, M ... 305-284-6047 112 O
tellenberg@miami.edu
ELLENBERGER, Amy ...... 818-333-3558.. 53 I
amy.ellenberger@nyfa.edu
ELLENBURG, Aaron .... 434-200-7033 478 N
aaron.ellenburg@centrahealth.com
ELLENBURG, Phil .... 615-966-1000 433 D
ELLENS, Timothy, L .... 616-526-6475 228 B
tje6@calvin.edu
ELLER, Greg .... 901-321-3307 431 A
geller@cbu.edu
ELLER, Greg .... 850-729-5332 104 E
eller@nwfsc.edu
ELLERBE, Laverne .... 757-822-1994 489 H
lellerbe@tcc.edu
ELLERKER, Charla .... 863-784-7176 108 B
charla.ellerker@southflorida.edu
ELLERMAN, Brittany ...... 217-228-5432 149 B
ellerbr@quincy.edu
ELLERSON, Patricia .... 760-245-4271.. 73 E
patricia.ellerson@vvc.edu
ELLERTSON, Chris .... 847-735-5011 142 H
ellertson@lakeforest.edu
ELLERTSON, Shari .... 208-426-1614 131 C
shariellerston@boisestate.edu
ELLIBEE, Margaret .... 501-812-2216.. 23 C
mellibee@pulaskitech.edu
ELLIE, Beth .... 715-675-3331 514 F
ellie@ntc.edu
ELLIFF POUND, Lee ...... 417-625-9355 263 G
pound-l@mssu.edu
ELLIG, Tracy .... 406-994-5607 272 A
tellig@montana.edu
ELLIMAN, Don .... 303-315-7682.. 83 D
chancellor@ucdenver.edu
ELLINGER, Amanda, M . 540-985-8206 482 A
amellinger@jchs.edu
ELLINGER, John, M ...... 419-372-2006 357 F
johne@bgsu.edu
ELLINGER, Paul .... 217-333-5503 154 B
pellinge@illinois.edu
ELLINGHUYSEN, Scott .. 507-457-5696 248 C
sellinghuysen@winona.edu
ELLINGSON, Mike .... 701-231-7307 354 D
michael.ellingson@ndsu.edu
ELLINGTON, Dyan .... 575-624-7157 294 A
dyan.ellington@roswell.enmu.edu
ELLINGTON, Keri .... 317-738-8086 157 L
kellington@franklincollege.edu
ELLINGTON, Michael, A 304-293-2702 505 B
michael.ellington@mail.wvu.edu
ELLINGTON, Ross .... 850-645-6900 110 A
wellington@fsu.edu
ELLINOR, Ben .... 941-359-4200 111 C
ELLINWOOD, Dawn, M . 802-654-2566 476 A
dellinwood@smcvt.edu
ELLIOT, Robert .... 646-717-9764 309 B
elliot@gts.edu

ELLIOT BROWN,
Karin, A .... 323-343-3820.. 32 D
kbrown5@calstatela.edu
ELLIOTT, Barbara .... 717-396-7833 404 R
belliott@pcad.edu
ELLIOTT, Brian .... 503-588-9207 383 A
belliott@corban.edu
ELLIOTT, Charles .... 304-384-5334 503 P
celliott@concord.edu
ELLIOTT, Clara .... 413-552-2219 219 G
celliott@hcc.edu
ELLIOTT, Clifton, R .... 843-355-4138 426 G
elliottr@wiltech.edu
ELLIOTT, Deborah, M .... 315-786-2416 311 H
delliott@sunyjefferson.edu
ELLIOTT, Erin .... 212-517-3929 324 E
e.elliott@sothebysinstitute.com
ELLIOTT, Fatina .... 318-670-9315 196 A
felliott@susla.edu
ELLIOTT, Jacquelyn .... 520-494-5200.. 11 P
jackie.elliott@centralaz.edu
ELLIOTT, James .... 312-329-4166 146 B
jim.elliott@moody.edu
ELLIOTT, Jeffrey .... 402-885-8228 277 H
jeffrey.elliott@unmc.edu
ELLIOTT, John .... 860-486-1361.. 88 G
john.elliott@uconn.edu
ELLIOTT, John, P .... 412-624-6127 412 I
jelliott@cfo.pitt.edu
ELLIOTT, SC, Karen .... 513-244-4844 366 A
karen.elliott@msj.edu
ELLIOTT, Kathy .... 405-744-4188 377 F
kathy.elliott@okstate.edu
ELLIOTT, Ken .... 601-709-0966 252 C
kelliott@belhaven.edu
ELLIOTT, Ken .... 828-327-7000 341 G
kelliott@cvcc.edu
ELLIOTT, Kenneth .... 337-550-1302 194 B
kelliott@lsue.edu
ELLIOTT, Kiersten .... 310-434-4173.. 62 G
elliott_kiersten@smc.edu
ELLIOTT, Marilyn .... 859-858-2033 183 C
ELLIOTT, Mark .... 615-248-1271 439 B
melliott@trevecca.edu
ELLIOTT, Marvin, L .... 606-474-3253 185 C
melliott@kcu.edu
ELLIOTT, Melissa, J ...... 940-552-6291 469 F
mjelliott@vernoncollege.edu
ELLIOTT, Michael .... 860-297-2000.. 88 E
michael.elliott@trincoll.edu
ELLIOTT, Michael, A ...... 404-727-6817 119 B
mellio2@emory.edu
ELLIOTT, Michael, S ...... 870-297-4261.. 88 E
michael.elliott@trincoll.edu
ELLIOTT, Myra .... 606-886-3863 185 F
myrat.elliott@kctcs.edu
ELLIOTT, Patrick .... 443-412-2345 204 C
pelliott@harford.edu
ELLIOTT, Patrick .... 607-777-2043 325 A
pelliott@binghamton.edu
ELLIOTT, Peter .... 863-297-1081 105 F
pelliott@polk.edu
ELLIOTT, Rennae .... 256-726-7533.... 6 E
elliott@oakwood.edu
ELLIOTT, Rita .... 815-226-3374 150 C
relliott@rockford.edu
ELLIOTT, Rob .... 715-675-3331 514 F
elliottr@ntc.edu
ELLIOTT, Sally .... 336-593-5402 343 C
selliott@forsythtech.edu
ELLIOTT, Scott .... 618-985-3741 141 D
scottelliott@jalc.edu
ELLIOTT, Scott, D .... 601-484-8619 253 G
selliott@meridiancc.edu
ELLIOTT, Sherman .... 602-639-7500.. 12 P
ELLIOTT, Stanley .... 919-719-1898 348 I
selliott@shawu.edu
ELLIOTT, Steven .... 402-375-7208 276 D
stellio1@wsc.edu
ELLIOTT, Tracy .... 408-808-2022.. 34 D
tracy.elliott@sjsu.edu
ELLIOTT CAIN, Pam .... 515-294-6218 166 F
pelliott@iastate.edu
ELLIOTT-NELSON, Linda 928-344-7516.. 11 B
linda.elliott-nelson@azwestern.edu
ELLIS, Brent .... 517-750-1200 237 D
bellis@arbor.edu
ELLIS, Bret .... 801-626-7660 473 E
bretellis@weber.edu
ELLIS, Brian, F .... 405-325-6211 380 L
be@ou.edu
ELLIS, Cheryl .... 580-327-8530 376 K
clellis@nwosu.edu
ELLIS, Christi .... 417-667-8181 259 A
cellis@cottey.edu
ELLIS, Christine .... 260-459-4501 161 D
cellis@ibcfortwayne.edu

ENDRESS, Wendy .... 360-867-6296 494 G
endressw@evergreen.edu
ENDRIJONAS, Erika, A .. 818-947-2321.. 49 G
endrijea@lavc.edu
ENDSLEY, Douglas .... 210-829-6004 465 E
douge@uiwtx.edu
ENDSLEY, Kara .... 919-530-5597 350 D
kendsley@nccu.edu
ENDY, Michael .... 817-598-6211 470 J
mendy@wc.edu
ENEA, Marie, L .... 610-330-5200 399 B
eneam@lafayette.edu
ENER, Sarah .... 970-339-6366.. 76 E
sarah.ener@aims.edu
ENG, Dave .... 845-398-4084 323 G
deng@stac.edu
ENG, Edwin .... 559-244-5910.. 66 E
ed.eng@scccd.edu
ENGBROCK, M. Jeff ...... 409-944-1215 449 F
mengbroc@gc.edu
ENGEBRETSON, Pam ..... 651-779-3994 244 D
pam.engebretson@century.edu
ENGEL, Amy .... 631-687-5149 322 G
aengel@sjcny.edu
ENGEL, Angela .... 309-438-3305 140 L
akengel@ilstu.edu
ENGEL, Deidre .... 712-279-5448 167 B
deidre.engel@briarcliff.edu
ENGEL, Heather .... 585-475-2627 321 D
hcedar@rit.edu
ENGEL, Jennifer .... 773-508-3899 144 D
jengel2@luc.edu
ENGEL, Michelle .... 414-382-6037 506 A
michelle.engel@alverno.edu
ENGEL, Renata, S .... 814-863-6726 403 F
rse1@psu.edu
ENGEL, Richard, R .... 530-752-9960.. 68 H
rrengel@ucdavis.edu
ENGEL, Steven .... 912-478-0357 120 E
sengel@georgiasouthern.edu
ENGELBACH, Karl, M ..... 530-754-7237.. 68 H
kmengelbach@ucdavis.edu
ENGELBOURG, Karen ..... 617-638-4560 212 G
engelbou@bu.edu
ENGELBRECHT, Laci ...... 217-479-7043 144 I
laci.engelbrecht@mac.edu
ENGELBRIDE, Ed .... 518-956-8140 324 G
eengelbride@albany.edu
ENGELDINGER, Lyle .... 760-252-2511.. 27 A
lengeldinger@barstow.edu
ENGELHARDT, Kelli .... 406-791-5237 273 C
kelli.engelhardt@ugf.edu
ENGELHART, Brian, W .. 260-422-5561 159 D
bwengelhart@indianatech.edu
ENGELHART, Rene .... 916-646-2774.. 59 F
rengelhart@samuelmerritt.edu
ENGELHART, Rene .... 919-646-2774.. 59 F
rengelhart@samuelmerritt.edu
ENGELKEMIER, John ...... 312-329-2145 146 B
john.engelkemier@moody.edu
ENGELKING, Heather ..... 407-708-2103 107 G
engelkingh@seminolestate.edu
ENGELLANT, Roxanne ... 406-683-7305 271 H
roxanne.engellant@umwestern.edu
ENGELLS, Thomas .... 409-772-1503 469 C
tengells@utmb.edu
ENGELMAN, Laura .... 507-285-7206 247 D
laura.engelman@rctc.edu
ENGELMEYER, Renee ..... 507-285-7183 247 D
renee.engelmeyer@rctc.edu
ENGELSCHALL,
Emily, D .... 951-827-3986.. 69 D
emily.engelschall@ucr.edu
ENGELSMA, Chris .... 616-432-3406 236 B
chris.engelsma@prts.edu
ENGEN, Stuart .... 701-671-2446 355 B
stuart.engen@ndscs.edu
ENGER, Lee .... 217-228-5432 149 B
engerle@quincy.edu
ENGERMAN, Kimarie ...... 340-692-4110 529 C
kengerman@uvi.edu
ENGFER, Tom .... 323-860-4349.. 53 C
tengfer@mi.edu
ENGH, SJ, Michael, E ... 408-554-4100.. 62 F
mengh@scu.edu
ENGLAND, A, W .... 313-593-5290 238 A
england@umich.edu
ENGLAND, Amy .... 918-631-3288 381 C
amy-england@utulsa.edu
ENGLAND, David .... 860-773-1401.. 86 G
dengland@txcc.commnet.edu
ENGLAND, David .... 615-966-6210 433 D
david.england@lipscomb.edu
ENGLAND, Jerry .... 615-547-1240 431 D
jengland@cumberland.edu
ENGLAND, Kelly .... 657-278-5254.. 32 B
kengland@fullerton.edu
ENGLAND, Kenneth .... 607-962-9334 306 C
kengland@corning-cc.edu
ENGLAND, Richard .... 217-581-2017 138 A
rengland@eiu.edu
ENGLAND, Robert .... 606-693-5000 187 D
bengland@kmbc.edu
ENGLAR, Samantha .... 618-537-6548 145 C
smenglar@mckendree.edu
ENGLE, Chris .... 810-762-0242 234 F
chris.engle@mcc.edu
ENGLE, Diane .... 620-792-9271 175 C
engled@bartonccc.edu
ENGLE, Jason .... 509-544-4935 493 G
jengle@columbiabasin.edu
ENGLE, Kevin, E .... 330-972-8948 371 D
kengle@uakron.edu
ENGLE, Marcia, J .... 540-432-4148 480 A
marcy.engle@emu.edu
ENGLE, Patricia, A .... 248-370-2160 235 J
pengle@oakland.edu
ENGLEHARDT,
Richard, E .... 606-693-5000 187 D
registrar@kmbc.edu
ENGLEHART, Kathy .... 207-453-5117 200 A
kenglehart@kvcc.me.edu
ENGLERT, Anne .... 210-458-7228 468 B
anne.englert@utsa.edu
ENGLERT, Jeannine .... 212-960-5274 334 P
englert@yu.edu
ENGLERT, Mark, G .... 307-686-0254 516 P
menglert@sheridan.edu
ENGLERT, Patrick .... 502-272-8323 183 H
penglert@bellarmine.edu
ENGLERT, Richard, M ... 215-204-7405 411 B
president@temple.edu
ENGLESTATTER, Pauline 301-447-5600 206 B
englesta@msmary.edu
ENGLIN, Peter, D .... 515-294-5636 166 F
penglin@iastate.edu
ENGLISH, Ana .... 928-317-6092.. 11 B
ana.english@azwestern.edu
ENGLISH, Anderson ...... 412-291-6301 389 F
aenglish@aii.edu
ENGLISH, Andy .... 515-961-1547 173 E
andy.english@simpson.edu
ENGLISH, Anna .... 404-756-4002 115 I
aenglish@atlm.edu
ENGLISH, Anna .... 770-537-5721 128 F
anna.english@westgatech.edu
ENGLISH, Ashley .... 334-808-6539.... 7 E
englisha@troy.edu
ENGLISH, Chris .... 828-694-1728 341 B
chrise@blueridge.edu
ENGLISH, Claude .... 816-584-6492 265 C
claude.english@park.edu
ENGLISH, Cyndy .... 504-865-5738 196 D
cenglish@tulane.edu
ENGLISH, David .... 336-770-3262 352 B
englishd@uncsa.edu
ENGLISH, David, A .... 740-587-6262 361 B
englishda@denison.edu
ENGLISH, Eva .... 406-353-2607 270 E
eenglish@ancollege.edu
ENGLISH, John .... 479-575-3054.. 21 I
jre@uark.edu
ENGLISH, Kim .... 864-388-8350 422 A
kenglish@lander.edu
ENGLISH, Lindsay .... 216-987-3610 360 E
lindsay.english@tri-c.edu
ENGLISH, Mattie .... 918-463-2931 375 G
mattie.english@connorsstate.edu
ENGLISH, Mechelle .... 850-412-6605 109 A
mechelle.english@famu.edu
ENGLISH, Sarah, H .... 845-575-3000 314 C
sarah.english@marist.edu
ENGLISH, Susan .... 757-825-2952 489 G
englishs@tncc.edu
ENGLISH, Suzanne .... 724-805-2660 410 C
suzanne.english@stvincent.edu
ENGLISH, Suzanne .... 724-805-2660 410 B
suzanne.english@email.stvincent.edu
ENGLOT, Peter, T .... 973-353-5541 290 A
peter.englot@rutgers.edu
ENGLOT, Peter, T .... 973-353-5541 290 D
peter.englot@rutgers.edu
ENGLUND, Tim .... 509-963-1866 492 L
tim.englund@cwu.edu
ENGSTROM, Dan, M ...... 724-938-1523 405 F
engstrom@calu.edu
ENGSTROM, Larry .... 775-682-8803 279 E
engstrom@unr.edu
ENGSTROM, Rick .... 425-889-6397 496 E
rick.engstrom@northwestu.edu
ENICKS, Charles .... 706-721-9660 116 B
cenicks@augusta.edu
ENKE, Kathryn .... 320-363-5070 241 I
kenke@csbsju.edu
ENLOE, Donald .... 303-871-2463.. 83 E
denloe@du.edu
ENLOW, Grady .... 229-226-1621 126 E
genlow@thomasu.edu
ENNEKING, Thomas ...... 317-955-6014 162 R
tenneking@marian.edu
ENNELLO-BUTLER,
Deanna .... 518-694-7305 297 J
deanna.ennello-butler@acphs.edu
ENNIS, Daniel .... 843-349-2746 420 A
dennis@coastal.edu
ENNIS, Daniel, G .... 410-516-2373 204 F
danielgennis@jhu.edu
ENNIS, Jackie .... 252-399-6571 335 I
jennis@barton.edu
ENNIS, Kim .... 205-387-0511.... 1 D
kim.ennis@bscc.edu
ENNIS, Matt .... 941-752-5574 108 P
ennism@scf.edu
ENNIS, Theresa .... 931-372-6124 438 F
tennis@tntech.edu
ENNIST, Phyllis .... 937-529-2201 371 B
pjennist@united.edu
ENNS-REMPEL, Kevin .... 559-453-2300.. 43 J
kevin.enns.rempel@fresno.edu
ENO, Alisha .... 303-765-3102.. 80 G
aeno@iliff.edu
ENOKAWA, Jerilyn .... 808-734-9899 130 C
jilorenz@hawaii.edu
ENOMA, Benjamin .... 212-463-0400 331 F
benjamin.enoma@touro.edu
ENOS, Chris .... 785-670-1153 182 D
chris.enos@washburn.edu
ENRIGHT, John .... 213-613-2200.. 65 A
john_enright@sciarc.edu
ENRIGHT, Patrick .... 973-328-5700 285 B
penright@ccm.edu
ENRIGHT, Sara .... 401-825-1084 416 B
senright@ccri.edu
ENRIQUEZ, Anita, B ...... 671-735-2994 520 B
abe@triton.uog.edu
ENRIQUEZ, Igrí .... 787-765-3560 522 K
enriquez@edpuniversity.edu
ENRIQUEZ FIELD,
Diana .... 650-508-3761.. 54 D
denriquezfield@ndnu.edu
ENS, Terry .... 620-947-3121 181 H
terryens@tabor.edu
ENSER, Jason .... 518-743-2277 328 G
enserj@sunyacc.edu
ENSIGN, Margee, M ...... 717-245-1322 394 A
ensignm@dickinson.edu
ENSING, Kim .... 805-922-6966.. 24 J
kensing@hancockcollege.edu
ENSLEY, Cynthia .... 252-638-7201 342 E
ensleyc@cravencc.edu
ENSLEY, Dana .... 706-379-3111 128 H
ddensley@yhc.edu
ENSLEY, Kevin .... 817-923-1921 457 G
kensley@swbts.edu
ENSLIN, Jonathan .... 262-472-1482 512 C
enslinj@uww.edu
ENSMAN, Richard .... 585-343-0055 309 C
rgensman@genesee.edu
ENSMAN, JR.,
Richard, G .... 585-345-6809 309 C
rgensman@genesee.edu
ENSMINGER, Michelle .. 806-743-9196 463 E
michelle.ensminger@ttuhsc.edu
ENSOR, Pat .... 713-221-8011 465 C
ensorp@uhd.edu
ENSTE, Joe .... 301-447-7436 206 B
enste@msmary.edu
ENTERANTE, Anthony .... 504-280-6159 194 F
aentera1@uno.edu
ENTERS, David, T .... 262-243-5700 507 C
dave.enters@cuw.edu
ENTESSARI, Abbass .... 305-623-1441.. 99 M
abbass.entessari@fmuniv.edu
ENTIN, Pauline .... 928-523-1580.. 14 K
pauline.entin@nau.edu
ENTINGER, Julienne, N . 651-628-3380 251 C
jnentinger@unwsp.edu
ENTREKIN, Cindy .... 256-215-4246.... 1 G
centrekin@cacc.edu
ENTRINGER, Chris, E .... 563-556-5110 172 D
entringc@nicc.edu
ENTZEROTH, Lyn .... 918-631-2400 381 C
lyn-entzeroth@utulsa.edu
ENWEMEKA,
Chukuka, S .... 619-594-6881.. 34 B
enwemeka@mail.sdsu.edu
ENWRIGHT, Kelly .... 513-562-8743 356 J
kenwright@artacademy.edu
ENYEDI, Alex .... 707-826-3722.. 34 A
alex.enyedi@humboldt.edu
ENZ, Jeff .... 760-355-6577.. 46 B
jeff.enz@imperial.edu
ENZ FINKEN, Kathleen . 805-756-2186.. 30 K
kenzfink@calpoly.edu
ENZOR, Sharon, B .... 662-685-4771 252 D
senzor@bmc.edu
ENZWEILER,
Raymond, N .... 614-885-5585 369 D
renzweiler@pcj.edu
EOFF, Shirley .... 325-942-2722 463 C
shirley.eoff@angleo.edu
EPLION, David .... 812-941-2269 161 A
deplion@ius.edu
EPP, Adam .... 425-889-5263 496 E
adam.epp@northwestu.edu
EPP, Michelle .... 651-696-6062 243 B
mepp@macalester.edu
EPPEHIMER, Trevor .... 704-636-6743 338 F
teppehimer@hoodseminary.edu
EPPER, Rhonda .... 303-556-3595.. 79 D
EPPERLY, Dustin .... 740-474-8896 367 E
depperly@ohiochristian.edu
EPPERSON, Annissa ...... 913-758-6172 182 B
eppersona@stmary.edu
EPPERSON, Brenda .... 214-860-8678 448 B
bepperson@dcccd.edu
EPPERSON, Brian .... 918-335-6207 378 F
bepperson@okwu.edu
EPPERSON, Douglas ..... 805-756-2706.. 30 K
dleppers@calpoly.edu
EPPERSON, Shonte .... 903-927-3260 471 B
sepperson@wileyc.edu
EPPERSON, Steve .... 360-416-7714 498 F
steve.epperson@skagit.edu
EPPES, Tom .... 252-328-6481 349 I
eppest17@ecu.edu
EPPICH, David .... 505-566-3318 296 A
eppichd@sanjuancollege.edu
EPPINETTE, Chance, W . 318-342-5021 198 A
eppinette@ulm.edu
EPPINGER, Beth .... 479-788-7334.. 22 A
beth.eppinger@uafs.edu
EPPLER, Michelle .... 402-557-7010 273 E
michelle.eppler@bellevue.edu
EPPLEY, Douglas .... 724-537-4555 410 B
douglas.eppley@stvincent.edu
EPPLEY, Douglas .... 724-532-5034 410 C
douglas.eppley@stvincent.edu
EPPLING, Chris .... 706-865-2134 126 G
ceppling@truett.edu
EPPLING, Marcie, T ...... 256-824-6443.... 8 C
marcie.eppling@uah.edu
EPPS, Bruce .... 614-236-6461 358 A
bepps@capital.edu
EPPS, Charmica, D .... 804-524-5595 491 A
cepps@vsu.edu
EPPS, Eric, L .... 815-288-5511 151 E
EPPS, JoAnne, A .... 215-204-4775 411 B
provost@temple.edu
EPPS, Lynn .... 910-898-9603 345 A
eppsl@montgomery.edu
EPPS, Patricia .... 717-358-4107 395 G
patty.epps@fandm.edu
EPPS, William, D .... 318-345-9000 192 J
EPSTEIN, Adam .... 314-965-8363 263 A
EPSTEIN, Bonnie .... 212-678-8997 312 A
boepstein@jtsa.edu
EPSTEIN, Catherine, A ... 413-542-2334 210 F
cepstein@amherst.edu
EPSTEIN, Joanne .... 352-335-2332.. 94 D
jeanne.epstein@acupuncturist.edu
EPSTEIN, Keith .... 860-723-0062.. 84 I
epsteink@ct.edu
EPSTEIN, Scott .... 616-554-5691 229 D
sepstein1@davenport.edu
EPSTEIN, Shlomo, Z ...... 718-438-1002 315 A
EPSTEIN, Warren .... 719-502-2666.. 81 H
warren.epstein@ppcc.edu
EQUINOA, Kim .... 805-893-3858.. 70 B
kim.equinoa@sa.ucsb.edu
ERARDI, Lauren .... 203-582-3686.. 88 A
lauren.erardi@quinnipiac.edu
ERARIO, Vince .... 678-264-8808 122 F
vince.erario@life.edu
ERATO, Michael, J .... 414-425-8300 509 I
merato@shsst.edu
ERB, Brian, I .... 706-236-2234 116 D
berb@berry.edu
ERB, Daniel, E .... 336-841-4595 338 E
derb@highpoint.edu
ERB, Jennifer, L .... 610-799-1034 400 A
0617mgr@sheg.follett.com
ERBELE, Cindy .... 706-865-2134 126 G
cerbele@truett.edu
ERBES, Paul, K .... 563-589-0221 174 D
perbes@wartburgseminary.edu
ERCKERT, Joseph .... 215-489-2397 393 F
joseph.erckert@delval.edu
ERDEI, Diane .... 415-955-2100.. 24 K
derdei@alliant.edu

ESPOSITO, James .... 212-678-8095 312 A
jaesposito@jtsa.edu
ESPOSITO, Juliana .... 508-854-4276 220 G
jesposito@qcc.mass.edu
ESPOSITO, Mark .... 309-796-5427 134 C
espositom@bhc.edu
ESPOSITO, Richard, C ... 412-396-6607 394 D
esposito@duq.edu
ESPOSITO, Samantha .... 304-296-8282 505 E
sesposito@wvjc.edu
ESPOSITO, Scott .... 203-254-4000.. 87 A
sesposito@fairfield.edu
ESPOSITO-NOY, Celia ... 707-864-7112.. 64 E
celia.esposito-noy@solano.edu
ESPY, Kimberly, A .... 520-621-3513.. 16 J
kespy@email.arizona.edu
ESPY, Tracy, Y .... 704-463-3440 348 B
tracy.espy@pfeiffer.edu
ESQUEDA, Angie .... 805-730-4011.. 62 E
esqueda@sbcc.edu
ESQUIBEL, Jamie .... 877-442-0505.. 84 B
jamie.esquibel@rockies.edu
ESQUILIN, Luis .... 787-758-6260 523 F
esquilin@inter.edu
ESQUITH, Stephen, L ..... 517-355-0212 233 G
esquith@msu.edu
ESQUIVEL, Carlos .... 212-875-4615 298 H
cesquivel@bankstreet.edu
ESQUIVEL, Ruben, E ..... 214-648-0448 469 E
ruben.esquivel@utsouthwestern.edu
ESQUIVEL, Tammy .... 858-279-4500.. 28 A
ESRY, Kip .... 800-955-2527 177 H
kesry@grantham.edu
ESSEL, Albert .... 573-681-5550 261 H
essela@lincolnu.edu
ESSENBURG, Curt .... 616-222-3000 232 F
cessenburg@kuyper.edu
ESSER, Kurt .... 407-708-2148 107 G
esserk@seminolestate.edu
ESSES, Levi .... 316-942-4291 180 D
essesl@newmanu.edu
ESSEX, Don .... 301-891-4222 209 E
dessex@wau.edu
ESSIG, Mary .... 304-647-6213 504 F
messig@osteo.wvsom.edu
ESSL, Mike .... 212-353-4207 306 A
essl@cooper.edu
ESTABROOK,
Madeleine, A .... 617-373-2772 223 D
ESTEBAN, A. Gabriel ...... 312-362-8850 137 C
president@depaul.edu
ESTELLA, Marlon .... 909-599-5433.. 48 E
mestella@lifepacific.edu
ESTENSON, Chad .... 701-662-1521 355 A
chad.estenson@lrsc.edu
ESTENSON, Marlene ...... 513-244-8337 359 E
marlene.estenson@ccuniversity.edu
ESTEP, Alison .... 206-378-5056 498 B
estep@spu.edu
ESTEP, Randy .... 864-379-8869 421 E
estep@erskine.edu
ESTEPP, J. Mark .... 276-964-7315 489 F
mark.estepp@sw.edu
ESTEPP, Stella .... 304-896-7382 503 D
stella.estepp@southernwv.edu
ESTER, Joyce, C .... 952-358-8150 246 D
joyce.ester@normandale.edu
ESTERBERG, Kristin, G .. 315-267-2100 328 A
president@potsdam.edu
ESTERHUIZEN, Amy .... 814-393-2337 405 H
aesterhuizen@clarion.edu
ESTERLINE, David, V ..... 412-924-1366 408 E
desterline@pts.edu
ESTERS, Randy .... 870-743-3000.. 20 E
randy.esters@northark.edu
ESTES, Ashley .... 713-646-1793 456 H
aestes@stcl.edu
ESTES, Chris .... 615-329-8690 431 I
cestes@fisk.edu
ESTES, IV, Edward, R ..... 757-479-3706 487 C
eestes@vbts.edu
ESTES, Eric, S .... 401-863-1800 415 K
eric_estes@brown.edu
ESTES, James .... 202-885-8696.. 94 C
jestes@wesleyseminary.edu
ESTES, Jessica .... 405-878-5102 379 G
jaestes@stgregorys.edu
ESTES, Kelly .... 865-573-4517 432 H
kestes@johnsonu.edu
ESTES, Lane .... 205-226-4640.... 4 F
lestes@bsc.edu
ESTES, Michael, T .... 757-822-1784 489 H
mestes@tcc.edu
ESTES, Wendy .... 678-717-3845 127 B
wendy.estes@ung.edu
ESTES, William .... 423-614-8175 432 L
bestes@leeuniversity.edu

ESTEVEZ, Edwin .... 618-664-7021 139 A
edwin.estevez@greenville.edu
ESTEVEZ, Francisco, A .. 860-701-6728 519 B
fransisco.a.estevez@uscg.mil
ESTEY, Alicia .... 208-426-1249 131 C
aliciaestey@boisestate.edu
ESTILL, Donna .... 256-306-2756.... 1 F
donna.estill@calhoun.edu
ESTILL, Sandi, L .... 606-759-7141 186 E
sandi.estill@kctcs.edu
ESTLACK, Ashlee .... 806-874-3571 445 R
ashlee.estlack@clarendoncollege.edu
ESTLACK, Scarlet .... 806-874-3571 445 R
scarlet.estlack@clarendoncollege.edu
ESTLACK, Tom .... 412-809-5100 408 D
estlack.tom@pti.edu
ESTOCK, Steven .... 575-562-2632 293 O
steven.estock@enmu.edu
ESTRADA, Donna .... 985-448-7954 192 I
donna.estrada@fletcher.edu
ESTRADA, Ella Mae .... 212-431-2827 317 H
ellamae.estrada@nyls.edu
ESTRADA, EllaMae .... 212-431-2827 317 H
ellamae.estrada@nyls.edu
ESTRADA, George .... 203-576-4330.. 88 F
gestrada@bridgeport.edu
ESTRADA, George .... 530-242-7929.. 63 I
gestrada@shastacollege.edu
ESTRADA, Jeri .... 970-521-6730.. 81 F
jeri.estrada@njc.edu
ESTRADA, Maria .... 787-780-5134 525 D
mestrada@nuc.edu
ESTRADA, Rebecca .... 505-428-1604 296 B
rebecca.estrada@sfcc.edu
ESTRADA, Robert .... 925-473-7540.. 41 A
restrada@losmedanos.edu
ESTRADA-HAMBY, Lisa . 940-397-4076 453 C
lisa.hamby@mwsu.edu
ESTRADA TORRES,
Omar .... 516-876-3067 327 C
estradatorreso@oldwestbury.edu
ESTRELLA, Luz .... 787-882-2065 526 D
recursoshumanos@unitecpr.net
ESTRELLA, Luz .... 787-882-2065 526 D
colocaciones@unitecpr.net
ESTREMERA, Luis .... 787-758-2525 528 D
luis.estremera@upr.edu
ESTRIN, David .... 718-522-9073 298 E
david@asa.edu
ETE, Sonia .... 310-360-8888.. 27 D
ETE, Thierry .... 310-360-8888.. 27 D
ETHERIDGE, Joey .... 479-213-0022.. 23 J
jetheridge@ozarks.edu
ETHERTON, Scott .... 503-370-6707 388 D
swetherton@willamette.edu
ETHIER, Richard .... 802-224-3000 476 H
richard.ethier@vsc.edu
ETHINGTON, Caroline ..... 810-762-9917 232 C
cethingt@kettering.edu
ETHINGTON, Robert ...... 707-527-4573.. 62 H
rethington@santarosa.edu
ETIENNE, Guy .... 754-312-2898 102 V
registrar@keycollege.edu
ETIENNE, Sabrina .... 301-891-4177 209 E
setienne@wau.edu
ETSCHMAIER, Gale .... 619-594-1643.. 34 B
gale.etschmaier@sdsu.edu
ETTARO, Barbara .... 814-863-1030 403 F
bxm7@psu.edu
ETTENSOHN, Clare .... 973-290-4240 285 A
cettensohn@cse.edu
ETTER, Patricia .... 314-889-1419 260 C
petter@fontbonne.edu
ETTINGER, Sherri .... 617-521-2451 224 E
sherri.ettinger@simmons.edu
ETTLE, Violeta .... 202-885-2720.. 91 C
vi@american.edu
ETTLICH, Sherry .... 541-552-6576 386 H
ettlich@sou.edu
ETTLING, John .... 518-564-2010 327 E
president_office@plattsburgh.edu
ETTORE, JD .... 567-661-7974 369 A
johndavid_ettore@owens.edu
ETUALE, Mikaele .... 684-699-9155 519 F
m.etuale@amsamoa.edu
ETZEL, Brent .... 479-968-0417.. 18 G
betzel@atu.edu
ETZEL, Gabriel .... 434-582-7707 482 D
gbetzel@liberty.edu
EUBANK, Charlotte .... 573-840-9105 267 J
ceubank@trcc.edu
EUBANK, Chelsea .... 352-638-9747.. 95 H
ceubank@beaconcollege.edu
EUBANK, Jeff .... 215-702-4202 391 C
jeubank@cairn.edu
EUBANKS, David .... 864-294-2000 421 I
david.eubanks@furman.edu

EUBANKS, Gail .... 912-443-5443 125 D
geubanks@savannahtech.edu
EUBANKS, Jamie .... 252-399-6368 335 I
jceubanks@barton.edu
EUBANKS, Karen .... 904-256-1121.. 99 C
keubanks@fcsl.edu
EUBANKS, Karla .... 912-427-5899 117 J
keubanks@coastalpines.edu
EUBANKS, Kathleen, L .. 508-999-8086 217 A
keubanks@umassd.edu
EUBANKS, Nekita .... 704-216-3778 346 C
nekita.eubanks@rccc.edu
EUCLIDE, Holly .... 920-693-1860 513 H
holly.euclide@gotoltc.edu
EUGENE, Nicholas .... 410-951-3462 208 F
neugene@coppin.edu
EULE, Ann .... 603-578-8900 280 M
aeule@ccsnh.edu
EUNICE, E, E .... 850-201-7000 112 C
eunicee@tcc.fl.edu
EURE, Darius .... 252-335-8530 350 A
ddeure@ecsu.edu
EURICH, David .... 610-526-1171 389 B
dave.eurich@theamericancollege.edu
EURY, Brian .... 610-902-8734 391 B
brian.eury@cabrini.edu
EUSTROM, Jim .... 503-399-5144 382 C
jim.eustrom@chemeketa.edu
EVAN, Joseph .... 570-208-5895 398 D
josephevan@kings.edu
EVANGELISTA,
Joleen, M .... 671-735-5540 519 H
materialsmanagement@guamcc.edu
EVANGELISTA, Nancy ..... 607-871-2649 298 A
fevangel@alfred.edu
EVANOSKY, Sonya .... 630-353-8708 134 K
sevanosky@chamberlain.edu
EVANOVICH, Dolan .... 315-443-4263 330 H
dolane@syr.edu
EVANS, Alice .... 314-434-4044 259 B
alice.evans@covenantseminary.edu
EVANS, Amy .... 903-463-8628 449 J
evansa@grayson.edu
EVANS, Andrea .... 708-534-8396 138 H
aevans6@govst.edu
EVANS, Angela .... 269-782-1323 237 B
aevans14@swmich.edu
EVANS, Angela .... 512-471-8947 467 C
dean.a.evans@austin.utexas.edu
EVANS, Angela, J .... 470-578-6300 122 C
aevans@kennesaw.edu
EVANS, Annette .... 706-542-7066 127 A
amevans@uga.edu
EVANS, April .... 765-998-4625 164 C
apevans@taylor.edu
EVANS, Barry .... 903-923-2148 448 J
bevans@etbu.edu
EVANS, Barry, W .... 806-291-1028 470 I
evansb@wbu.edu
EVANS, Belinda .... 304-647-6401 504 F
bevans@osteo.wvsom.edu
EVANS, Beverly, A .... 717-815-1228 415 G
behinger@ycp.edu
EVANS, Brenda .... 978-934-5021 217 B
brenda_evans@uml.edu
EVANS, Brian .... 502-863-8223 184 I
brian_evans@georgetowncollege.edu
EVANS, Brian .... 651-641-8766 241 L
bevans@csp.edu
EVANS, Brian .... 423-697-2417 436 F
brian.evans@chattanoogastate.edu
EVANS, Brian, K .... 801-422-3760 471 E
brian_evans@byu.edu
EVANS, Carolyn, L .... 601-977-7764 256 B
cevans@tougaloo.edu
EVANS, Charlotte .... 402-554-2772 277 I
cevans@unomaha.edu
EVANS, Chas .... 601-635-2111 252 I
cevans@eccc.edu
EVANS, Cheryl .... 580-628-6201 376 J
cheryl.evans@noc.edu
EVANS, Cheryl, O .... 585-385-8015 322 E
cevans@sjfc.edu
EVANS, Chris .... 713-831-7863 466 J
evanscp@stthom.edu
EVANS, Chuck .... 205-226-4625.... 4 F
cwevans@bsc.edu
EVANS, Craig, S .... 315-364-3200 333 G
craig.evans@wells.edu
EVANS, Damian .... 262-595-2540 511 C
damian.evans@uwp.edu
EVANS, Damien .... 262-595-2540 511 C
damian.evans@uwp.edu
EVANS, Dana .... 601-718-5900.. 93 B
EVANS, David .... 229-391-2609 126 C
devans@southernregional.edu
EVANS, David .... 209-667-3153.. 33 F
devans@csustan.edu

EVANS, David .... 406-756-3872 271 A
devans@fvcc.edu
EVANS, David .... 972-273-3561 448 C
devans@dcccd.edu
EVANS, David, R .... 802-447-6319 476 C
devans@svc.edu
EVANS, Diane, T .... 936-261-2202 458 F
dtevans@pvamu.edu
EVANS, Doreen .... 928-213-6060.. 12 D
doreen.evans@collegeamerica.edu
EVANS, Edward .... 361-825-2693 460 A
edward.evans@tamucc.edu
EVANS, Elizabeth .... 662-254-3800 255 A
edevans@mvsu.edu
EVANS, Emily .... 859-846-5815 188 B
eeevans@midway.edu
EVANS, Eric .... 440-375-7000 364 C
EVANS, Eric, D .... 781-981-7000 221 C
EVANS, Erik .... 570-389-4047 405 E
eevans@bloomu.edu
EVANS, Ernest .... 573-288-6375 259 E
eevans@culver.edu
EVANS, Faye .... 404-225-4526 115 J
fevans@atlantatech.edu
EVANS, Frederick M, G . 803-536-7133 423 G
fevans3@scsu.edu
EVANS, Gail .... 909-469-3796.. 74 G
devans@westernu.edu
EVANS, Gary .... 607-753-2302 327 A
gary.evans@cortland.edu
EVANS, George .... 618-545-3030 142 D
gevans@kaskaskia.edu
EVANS, JR., Gilbert, L .. 386-312-4127 106 M
gilbertevans@sjrstate.edu
EVANS, Ivan .... 858-534-2247.. 69 E
ercprovost@ucsd.edu
EVANS, J. David .... 470-578-6194 122 C
devans@kennesaw.edu
EVANS, Jack .... 706-721-3964 116 B
jaevans@augusta.edu
EVANS, JR., Jack .... 972-524-3341 457 H
EVANS, SR., Jack .... 972-524-3341 457 H
EVANS, Jacquie .... 757-481-5005 492 A
EVANS, Janet, D .... 412-392-3824 408 F
jevans@pointpark.edu
EVANS, Janie .... 802-287-8203 475 B
evansj@greenmtn.edu
EVANS, Jeannette, H ...... 315-684-6067 329 F
evansjh@morrisville.edu
EVANS, Jeffrey, L .... 313-593-5110 238 A
jlevan@umich.edu
EVANS, Jennifer, M .... 717-867-6271 399 J
jevans@lvc.edu
EVANS, Jessica .... 254-968-9682 459 A
jevans@tarleton.edu
EVANS, Jill .... 208-496-9812 131 D
evansj@byui.edu
EVANS, Joseph .... 410-706-8501 207 H
jevans@umaryland.edu
EVANS, Joy .... 231-995-1084 235 B
jevans@nmc.edu
EVANS, Kamira .... 610-892-1504 405 C
kevans@pit.edu
EVANS, Karen, V .... 610-921-7630 388 E
kevans@albright.edu
EVANS, Karyn .... 937-393-3431 370 C
kevans@sscc.edu
EVANS, Katherine .... 973-761-9500 291 F
katherine.evans@shu.edu
EVANS, Kathleen .... 315-312-2240 327 D
kathleen.evans@oswego.edu
EVANS, Kenne .... 817-515-3055 458 B
kenneth.evans@tccd.edu
EVANS, Kenneth, R .... 409-880-8405 462 C
kenneth.evans@lamar.edu
EVANS, Kimberly .... 802-831-1225 476 G
kevans@vermontlaw.edu
EVANS, Laurie .... 313-664-1501 228 H
levans@collegeforcreativestudies.edu
EVANS, Layna .... 214-333-5275 447 D
layna@dbu.edu
EVANS, Liz .... 412-392-5945 408 F
eevans@pointpark.edu
EVANS, III, Louis, D ..... 713-221-2766 465 C
evansl@uhd.edu
EVANS, Maggie .... 757-221-4314 479 I
living@wm.edu
EVANS, Marcheta .... 210-434-6711 454 D
mevans@lake.ollusa.edu
EVANS, Marisa, L .... 814-886-6336 402 E
mevans@mtaloy.edu
EVANS, Mark .... 330-672-2972 363 I
mevans@kent.edu
EVANS, Mark .... 845-938-5502 519 D
mark.evans@usma.edu
EVANS, Maya .... 847-635-1973 148 D
mevans@oakton.edu

FAIMON, Peg .... 812-855-2561 159 H
pfaimon@indiana.edu
FAIN, Carol .... 704-403-3511 336 B
carol.fain@carolinashealthcare.org
FAIN, Juanita .... 702-895-4387 279 D
juanita.fain@unlv.edu
FAIN, Richard, D .... 305-284-4025 112 O
FAIN, Starr .... 334-387-3877 .... 4 B
starrfain@amridgeuniversity.edu
FAIR, George, W .... 972-883-2350 467 D
gwfair@utdallas.edu
FAIR, George, W .... 972-883-4566 467 D
gwfair@utdallas.edu
FAIR, Kathy .... 903-983-8236 451 F
kfair@kilgore.edu
FAIR, Terry .... 404-894-9396 120 A
terry.fair@business.gatech.edu
FAIR, Vickie .... 202-994-9633 .. 92 A
vvfair14@gwu.edu
FAIR-SZOFRAN, Nancy .. 509-434-5060 493 H
nancy.szofran@ccs.spokane.edu
FAIR-SZOFRAN, Nancy .. 509-434-5060 493 I
nancy.szofran@ccs.spokane.edu
FAIRBAIRN, Katie .... 707-468-3164 .. 51 E
kfairbairn@mendocino.edu
FAIRBANKS, Daniel .... 801-863-6440 473 D
daniel.fairbanks@uvu.edu
FAIRBANKS, Kathleen ... 716-926-8923 310 B
kfairbanks@hilbert.edu
FAIRBANKS, Kenneth, E 276-223-4868 490 C
kfairbanks@wcc.vccs.edu
FAIRBANKS, Warren ...... 508-626-4590 218 A
wfairbanks@framingham.edu
FAIRBANKS LAWSON,
Diana .... 231-995-1019 235 B
dfairbanks@nmc.edu
FAIRCHILD, Diana .... 208-426-1540 131 C
dfairchild@boisestate.edu
FAIRCHILD, Joseph, J ... 757-822-7208 489 H
jfairchild@tcc.edu
FAIRCHILD, Thomas ...... 817-735-5497 466 D
thomas.fairchild@unthsc.edu
FAIRCHILDS, Angela ..... 209-588-5115 .. 75 I
fairchildsa@yosemite.edu
FAIRCLOTH, Brad .... 828-669-8012 340 I
bfaircloth@montreat.edu
FAIRCLOTH, Jimmy .... 478-218-3385 117 E
jfaircloth@centralgatech.edu
FAIRCLOTH, Jimmy .... 478-218-3385 117 D
jfaircloth@centralgatech.edu
FAIRFAX, Kathleen .... 605-688-4156 429 B
kathleen.fairfax@sdstate.edu
FAIRLESS, Michael, J .... 330-471-8100 364 H
mfairless@malone.edu
FAIRLEY, Danny .... 913-360-7256 175 D
dfairley@benedictine.edu
FAIRMAN, Jerilyn .... 315-786-6542 311 H
jfairman@sunyjefferson.edu
FAIRWEATHER, Alisa ..... 503-847-2550 387 I
afairweather@uws.edu
FAISON, Brian .... 701-777-2234 353 G
brian.faison@und.edu
FAISON, Frederick .... 484-365-8075 400 E
ffaison@lincoln.edu
FAISON, Nicole .... 973-748-9000 284 A
nicole_faison@bloomfield.edu
FAITH, Helen .... 541-463-5266 383 F
faithh@lanecc.edu
FAITHFUL, Mark .... 252-493-7428 345 E
mfaithful@email.pittcc.edu
FAJACK, Matthew, W .... 919-962-2211 351 B
mfajack@unc.edu
FAKHIR, Bazra .... 304-205-6630 502 K
bazra.fakhir@bridgevalley.edu
FALA, Gregory .... 215-951-1907 398 F
fala@lasalle.edu
FALABELLA, Deneb .... 410-888-9048 205 D
dfalabella@muih.edu
FALANCE, Melissa .... 856-691-8600 285 C
mfalance@cccnj.edu
FALASTER, Marilyn .... 618-985-3741 141 D
marilynfalaster@jalc.edu
FALAVOLITO, Stephen ... 412-531-4433 393 D
info@deantech.edu
FALCHER, Rosanna .... 315-792-3015 332 H
refalche@utica.edu
FALCIANI-WHITE,
Nancy, K .... 804-752-7256 484 C
nancyfalcianiwhite@rmc.edu
FALCK, Brian, G .... 717-245-1686 394 A
falckb@dickinson.edu
FALCK, Larry, B .... 843-661-1251 421 H
lfalck@fmarion.edu
FALCK-YI, Suzanne .... 641-585-8225 174 B
falckyis@waldorf.edu
FALCO, James .... 608-524-7825 514 A
jsfalco@madisoncollege.edu

FALCO, Kathleen, P .... 207-778-7280 201 D
kathleen.falco@maine.edu
FALCON, Kim .... 918-495-6928 378 H
kfalcon@oru.edu
FALCON, Luis .... 978-934-3843 217 B
luis_falcon@uml.edu
FALCON-CHANDLER,
Carole .... 406-353-2607 270 E
cfalconchan@hotmail.com
FALCONE, Alice, A .... 978-867-4208 215 D
alice.falcone@gordon.edu
FALCONER, John .... 308-865-8702 277 F
falconerj@unk.edu
FALCONETTI, Angela ..... 863-297-1098 105 F
agarciafalconetti@polk.edu
FALDER, Mike .... 765-998-5538 164 C
mcfalder@taylor.edu
FALDUTO, Ellen .... 330-263-2230 360 A
efalduto@wooster.edu
FALDUTO, Matt .... 319-398-1274 171 F
matt.falduto@kirkwood.edu
FALE, Tauvela .... 684-699-9155 519 F
t.fale@amsamoa.edu
FALES, Julia .... 269-749-7595 236 A
jfales@olivetcollege.edu
FALES, Michael, F .... 269-749-7624 236 A
mfales@olivetcollege.edu
FALESE, Joseph .... 815-836-5275 143 E
falesejo@lewisu.edu
FALEY, Heather .... 802-440-4423 474 F
hfaley@bennington.edu
FALK, Adam, F .... 413-597-4233 226 C
adam.f.falk@williams.edu
FALK, Anne .... 814-234-7755 410 G
afalk@southhills.edu
FALK, Barry, L .... 804-828-1803 487 E
blfalk@vcu.edu
FALK, Dan .... 620-229-6267 181 F
dan.falk@sckans.edu
FALK, Israel .... 845-371-2481 334 H
FALK, Randy .... 541-917-4999 384 A
falkr@linnbenton.edu
FALK, Stephanie, A .... 717-867-6696 399 J
falk@lvc.edu
FALKE, Steve, J .... 814-863-0205 403 F
sjf7@psu.edu
FALKENBERG, Janice .... 414-297-8718 514 C
falkenjm@matc.edu
FALKENHAGEN, Kim ..... 715-682-1868 509 D
kfalkenhagen@northland.edu
FALKIEWICZ, Linda, K .. 313-577-3550 239 C
lfalkiewicz@wayne.edu
FALKNER, Jay .... 918-647-1210 375 B
jfalkner@carlalbert.edu
FALKNER, Tina .... 612-626-0302 250 E
rovic001@umn.edu
FALKS, Delisa, F .... 979-458-5311 459 C
delisa@tamu.edu
FALL, Matt .... 517-483-1953 232 K
fallm@lcc.edu
FALL, Stephany .... 850-599-3203 109 A
stephany.fall@famu.edu
FALLACARO, Anthony .... 603-645-9604 282 C
a.fallacaro@snhu.edu
FALLAH ASL,
Mohammad .... 703-993-5424 481 B
mfallaha@gmu.edu
FALLAVOLLITA, John ..... 603-623-0313 281 G
johnfallavollita@nhia.edu
FALLDINE, Cory .... 620-341-5297 177 B
cfalldin@emporia.edu
FALLEN, Melissa .... 804-204-1210 478 F
mfallen@btsr.edu
FALLERT, Danelle .... 323-265-8797 .. 48 L
fallerdj@elac.edu
FALLETA, David, A .... 304-457-6213 501 A
falletada@ab.edu
FALLETTA, Eva, R .... 480-732-7231 .. 13 E
eva.falletta@cgc.edu
FALLING, Cary .... 405-425-5290 377 B
cary.falling@oc.edu
FALLING, Sali, K .... 765-285-5162 156 C
sfalling@bsu.edu
FALLIS, Drew .... 210-292-6258 518 G
drew.fallis@us.af.mil
FALLON, Anne Marie ..... 508-830-6485 218 D
afallon@maritime.edu
FALLON, Greg .... 973-684-5895 288 C
gfallon@pccc.edu
FALLON, Kevin, C .... 410-543-6075 209 B
kcfallon@salisbury.edu
FALLON-KORB,
Melissa, A .... 607-436-3368 325 E
melissa.fallon@oneonta.edu
FALLONE, Deborah, A ... 914-323-5224 314 A
deborah.fallone@mville.edu
FALLOWS, John .... 215-335-0800 400 D
jfallows@lincolntech.edu

FALLOWS, Noel .... 706-542-2202 127 A
nfallows@uga.edu
FALLS, Meda .... 731-925-5722 437 B
mfalls@jscc.edu
FALLS, William, A .... 802-656-3166 476 E
william.falls@uvm.edu
FALOTICO, Michael .... 312-467-2328 .. 37 B
mfalotico@thechicagoschool.edu
FALTER, James .... 330-494-6170 370 G
jfalter@starkstate.edu
FALTER, Jim .... 712-749-2415 167 C
falterj@bvu.edu
FALTYN, Tim .... 580-349-1302 377 E
faltyn@opsu.edu
FALVO, Amy .... 904-819-6305 .. 98 I
afalvo@flagler.edu
FALWELL, JR., Jerry ...... 434-582-2950 482 D
jlfjr@liberty.edu
FALWELL, Tyler .... 434-592-3095 482 D
tylerfalwell@liberty.edu
FALZERANO,
Christine, E .... 203-576-4566 .. 88 F
cfalzera@bridgeport.edu
FALZERANO, Jennifer .... 541-463-3413 383 F
falzeranoj@lanecc.edu
FALZONE, Kris .... 219-989-2217 163 E
kris.falzone@pnw.edu
FAMA, Melissa .... 978-632-6600 220 D
m_fama@mwcc.mass.edu
FAMBLE, JR., Freddie ... 325-793-4906 452 F
ffamble@mcm.edu
FAMULARE, Marybeth ... 717-264-4141 415 B
marybeth.famulare@wilson.edu
FAMULARE, Nick .... 518-388-6175 332 B
famularn@union.edu
FAN, C. Cindy .... 310-825-4921 .. 69 B
cfan@international.ucla.edu
FAN, Jing .... 512-492-3051 442 J
jfan@aoma.edu
FAN, Lori .... 417-836-5654 263 H
lfan@missouristate.edu
FANCHER, Janet .... 620-223-2700 177 E
janetf@fortscott.edu
FANCHER, Karen .... 503-255-0332 384 E
kfancher@multnomah.edu
FANCHER, Sarah .... 417-447-8171 264 K
fanchers@otc.edu
FANDOZZI, Melissa ...... 518-828-4181 305 D
melissa.fandozzi@sunycgcc.edu
FANEUFF, Ken .... 706-379-3111 128 H
kfaneuff@yhc.edu
FANG, John .... 213-487-0110 .. 41 K
dean@dula.edu
FANGMEYER, Len, J ..... 308-865-8555 277 F
fangmeyerlj@unk.edu
FANKLAND, Dinelle .... 904-264-2172 106 I
FANN, Erin .... 843-921-6916 423 A
efann@netc.edu
FANNAN, Lisa, L .... 816-604-2314 262 I
lisa.fannan@mcckc.edu
FANNIN, Larry .... 801-878-1053 280 B
lfannin@roseman.edu
FANNIN, Larry .... 702-968-5944 280 B
lfannin@roseman.edu
FANNIN, Nichole .... 678-839-5035 127 F
nfannin@westga.edu
FANNIN, Toni .... 925-969-2347 .. 40 L
tfannin@dvc.edu
FANNING, Daniel .... 218-733-6945 245 C
daniel.fanning@lsc.edu
FANNING, Lucas .... 570-484-2838 406 E
laf1158@lockhaven.edu
FANNING, Vivian .... 276-223-4777 490 C
vfanning@wcc.vccs.edu
FANSHAW, Charles .... 202-685-3929 518 B
fanshawc@ndu.edu
FANSLAU, Michelle .... 863-674-6003 100 E
michelle.fanslau@fsw.edu
FANSLER, A. Gigi .... 217-732-3155 143 G
gfansler@lincolncollege.edu
FANT, JR., Gene, C ...... 864-977-7018 422 I
gene.fant@ngu.edu
FANT, Greg .... 575-646-2127 295 B
gfant@nmsu.edu
FANT, Joshua, W .... 860-701-6727 519 B
joshua.w.fant@uscg.mil
FANTASIA, Bethany .... 617-262-5000 212 C
bethany.fantasia@the-bac.edu
FANTER, Jeff .... 317-921-4502 161 F
jfanter@ivytech.edu
FANTINI, Maria .... 856-351-2601 291 E
mfantini@salemcc.edu
FANTOZZI, Joseph .... 212-650-7865 301 F
jfantozzi@ccny.cuny.edu
FANUZZI, Robert .... 718-390-4266 322 F
fanuzzir@stjohns.edu
FAOUR, Sheila .... 318-675-6001 194 D
sfaour@lsuhsc.edu

FAOUR, William, G .... 423-624-0077 430 I
billf@chattanoogacollege.edu
FARA, Tejinder .... 334-727-8164 .... 7 F
tfara@mytu.tuskegee.edu
FARABEE, Lars, C .... 336-841-9604 338 E
lfarabee@highpoint.edu
FARAGALLA, Sameh .... 973-661-0600 285 I
sfaragalla@eastwick.edu
FARAHANI, Gohar .... 301-846-2451 203 H
gfarahani@frederick.edu
FARAHI, Dawood .... 908-737-7000 286 F
dfarahi@kean.edu
FARANDA, Nicholas ...... 914-261-9758 316 E
farandan@newschool.edu
FARARA, Joseph .... 802-635-1272 477 C
joseph.farara@jsc.edu
FARBANIEC, David .... 845-257-3196 325 D
farbanid@newpaltz.edu
FARE, Bridget, M .... 412-396-6052 394 D
fareb@duq.edu
FARES, Ted .... 575-562-2511 293 O
ted.fares@enmu.edu
FARFAN, Erika, M .... 740-427-5571 364 A
farfane@kenyon.edu
FARHA, Darron .... 219-464-6702 165 D
darron.farha@valpo.edu
FARHA, Darron, C .... 219-464-6702 165 D
darron.farha@valpo.edu
FARIA, Geraldine .... 718-951-3706 301 E
gfaria@brooklyn.cuny.edu
FARIA, Pamela .... 617-243-2221 216 C
pfaria@lasell.edu
FARIAS, Antonio .... 860-685-3927 .. 89 F
afarias@wesleyan.edu
FARIAS, Isidro .... 707-654-1127 .. 32 E
ifarias@csum.edu
FARIAS, Jaime .... 915-831-7724 449 A
jfarias@epcc.edu
FARIAS, Richard .... 210-486-0373 442 A
rfarias14@alamo.edu
FARIDIAN, Fred .... 650-685-6616 .. 45 B
ffaridian@gurnick.edu
FARINA, Matthew, R ..... 212-592-2126 324 A
mfarina@sva.edu
FARINA-HESS, Nadra .... 619-644-7390 .. 45 A
nadra.farina-hess@gcccd.edu
FARINELLI, Rob .... 301-934-7539 203 D
rfarinelli@csmd.edu
FARINO, Patricia .... 617-585-0200 212 C
patricia.farino@the-bac.edu
FARIS, Debbie .... 434-381-6324 485 P
dfaris@sbc.edu
FARIS, Mickie .... 213-283-4218 .. 37 B
mfaris@thechicagoschool.edu
FARISH, Christina .... 662-846-4009 252 H
cfarish@deltastate.edu
FARISH, Donald, J .... 401-254-3201 417 C
dfarish@rwu.edu
FARISH, Guy, E .... 440-826-2478 357 B
gfarish@bw.edu
FARISH, Jennifer .... 662-846-4675 252 H
jfarish@deltastate.edu
FARKAS, Abraham .... 707-524-1508 .. 62 H
afarkas@santarosa.edu
FARKAS, John .... 201-559-1433 286 C
FARLAND, Lisa .... 310-338-7896 .. 50 J
lisa.farland@lmu.edu
FARLESS, John, A .... 812-228-5157 165 C
jafarless@usi.edu
FARLEY, Barbara, A .... 217-245-3001 139 H
barbara.farley@mail.ic.edu
FARLEY, Christy .... 602-872-2555 .. 14 K
christy.farley@nau.edu
FARLEY, Dottie .... 972-241-3371 447 E
dfarley@dallas.edu
FARLEY, Dwayne .... 617-879-7805 218 B
dfarley@massart.edu
FARLEY, Emy .... 507-222-4289 241 C
efarley@carleton.edu
FARLEY, Erik, S .... 745-587-6605 361 B
farleye@denison.edu
FARLEY, Greg .... 785-628-4215 177 D
gfarley@fhsu.edu
FARLEY, Jeff .... 330-569-5109 362 J
farleyja@hiram.edu
FARLEY, Jerry, B .... 785-670-1556 182 D
jerry.farley@washburn.edu
FARLEY, Karen .... 563-336-3323 168 K
kfarley@eicc.edu
FARLEY, Kim .... 307-382-1616 517 C
kfarley@westernwyoming.edu
FARLEY, Margaret .... 307-624-7010 516 J
margaret.farley@ewc.wy.edu
FARLEY, Mark .... 661-255-1050 .. 29 F
FARLEY, Patrick .... 301-891-4551 209 E
pfarley@wau.edu
FARLEY, Penelope, L .... 410-778-7224 210 A
pfarley2@washcoll.edu

FAY, Derek, R 208-496-7310 131 D
fayd@byui.edu
FAY, Laurie 518-783-2307 324 C
fay@siena.edu
FAY, Patrick 303-556-5714 80 Q
pfay1@msudenver.edu
FAY-REILLY, Tara 914-674-7762 314 I
tfreilly@mercy.edu
FAYAD, Barbara, H 864-938-3722 423 D
bfayad@presby.edu
FAYEK, Moaty 408-864-8896 43 E
fayekmoaty@deanza.edu
FAYLOR, David, L 256-469-7333 6 A
deaninst@hbc1.edu
FAYMONVILLE, Carmen 920-424-0890 511 B
faymonvc@uwosh.edu
FAYNE, Harriet 718-960-8222 302 C
harriet.fayne@lehman.cuny.edu
FAYNE, Mauri 815-802-3454 261 C
mfayne@kcai.edu
FAYOYIN, MaryJo 912-358-4329 125 C
fayoyinm@savannahstate.edu
FAYTAK, Shelley 814-838-7673 395 D
sfaytak@fortisinstitute.edu
FAZ, Isaac 214-378-1793 447 F
isaac.faz@dcccd.edu
FAZAL, Shana 312-662-4000 133 A
sfazal@adler.edu
FAZALARE, Amie 304-367-4015 504 A
amie.fazalare@fairmontstate.edu
FAZALARE, Amie, M 304-367-4867 504 A
amie.fazalare@fairmontstate.edu
FAZEKAS, Evelyn 315-792-3002 332 H
efazekas@utica.ucsu.edu
FAZEKAS, Jennifer 203-932-7274 89 D
jfazekas@newhaven.edu
FAZIO, James, I 619-201-8978 65 C
jfazio@socalsem.edu
FAZIO, Jamie 585-389-2308 316 D
jfazio1@naz.edu
FAZIO, Jennifer 732-255-0400 288 B
jfazio@ocean.edu
FAZIO, Kari 610-526-5160 390 G
kfazio@brynmawr.edu
FAZIO, Patricia 860-486-5634 88 G
patricia.fazio@uconn.edu
FAZIOLI, Mark 802-287-8319 475 B
mark.fazioli@greenmtn.edu
FAZZANO FICANO,
Adriana 954-201-7518 96 A
afazzano@broward.edu
FEAGANS, Frank 972-883-6900 467 D
frank.feagans@utdallas.edu
FEAGIN, Susan, K 212-851-7999 305 E
skf17@columbia.edu
FEALY, Robert 513-556-6703 371 E
fealyrl@ucmail.uc.edu
FEAN, Judith 574-284-4886 163 J
jfean@saintmarys.edu
FEAR, Kevin, G 724-653-2222 394 B
kfear@dec.edu
FEARN, Odell 865-882-4679 438 A
fearnao@roanestate.edu
FEASEL, Brenda 740-389-4636 365 B
feaselb@mtc.edu
FEASEL, Edward, M 949-480-4133 64 D
feasel@soka.edu
FEASEL, Edward, M 949-480-4133 64 D
efeasel@soka.edu
FEASTER, Blanton 903-586-2518 451 C
FEASTER, Glenn 865-573-4517 432 H
gfeaster@johnsonu.edu
FEATHERLY, Elise 281-487-1170 460 G
efeatherly@txchiro.edu
FEATHERSTON, Guy 903-875-7585 453 J
guy.featherston@navarrocollege.edu
FEATHERSTONE, John 415-476-1323 70 A
jdbf@ucsf.edu
FEATHERSTONE,
Richard 435-652-7651 473 B
featherstone@dixie.edu
FEAVER, John, H 405-224-3140 381 B
jfeaver@usao.edu
FECHNER, Mary 575-439-3696 295 C
mfechner@nmsu.edu
FECHO, Susan 252-399-6480 335 I
sfecho@barton.edu
FECHTER, Sharon 240-567-7563 205 F
sharon.fechter@montgomerycollege.edu
FEDDEMA, Lana, L 320-308-1595 247 F
lfeddema@sctcc.edu
FEDELE, Dominick 205-329-7900 5 C
dominick.fedele@ecacolleges.com
FEDELE, Jennifer, J 724-357-4820 406 C
j.j.fedele@iup.edu
FEDER, Mary, M 631-451-4256 330 B
federm@sunysuffolk.edu

FEDERER, Gina 972-273-3006 448 C
gfederer@dcccd.edu
FEDERLINE, Pamela 252-335-0821 342 D
pamela_federline60@albemarle.edu
FEDERMAN, Robin 310-824-1586 24 B
robinfederman@hotmail.com
FEDEROFF, Alyssa 304-829-7064 501 F
afederoff@bethanywv.edu
FEDEROFF, Howard 949-824-5926 69 A
federoff@uci.edu
FEDEROWICZ, Jane 610-527-0200 409 E
jfederowicz@rosemont.edu
FEDIN, Audrey 408-498-5151 38 I
afedin@cogswell.edu
FEDJE, Jay 563-588-6468 167 E
jay.fedje@clarke.edu
FEDLER, Kyle 863-680-4124 100 D
kfedler@flsouthern.edu
FEDORCHAK, David 410-704-3974 209 C
dfedorchak@towson.edu
FEDORCHAK, Lynn 607-778-5319 326 C
fedorchaklm@sunybroome.edu
FEDORKO, Kathleen, C 215-968-8220 390 I
fedorkok@bucks.edu
FEDRIZZI-WILLIAMS,
Linda 717-728-2219 392 B
lindafedrizzi@centralpenn.edu
FEE, Andy 562-985-7976 32 C
andy.fee@csulb.edu
FEE, Richard 714-484-7152 53 M
rfee@cypresscollege.edu
FEE, T. Joshua 859-858-3511 183 D
josh.fee@asbury.edu
FEE, William 928-524-7482 15 B
william.fee@npc.edu
FEELER, William 432-685-4626 453 B
bfeeler@midland.edu
FEELEY, Brian 336-278-7446 337 G
bfeeley@elon.edu
FEELEY, John 970-204-8131 79 K
john.feeley@frontrange.edu
FEELEY, Maria 860-768-4275 89 C
feeley@hartford.edu
FEELY, SND, Katherine 216-397-1966 363 H
kfeely@jcu.edu
FEENEY, David, F 508-678-2811 219 C
david.feeney@bristolcc.edu
FEENEY, Gregory 859-246-6329 185 G
greg.feeney@kctcs.edu
FEENEY, John, J 530-898-6541 31 D
jfeeney@csuchico.edu
FEENSTRA, Ronald, J 616-957-7193 228 C
feenro@calvinseminary.edu
FEERER, Pam 620-252-7355 176 K
feerer.pam@coffeyville.edu
FEEZELL, Travis 402-461-7326 274 I
tfeezell@hastings.edu
FEGAN, Kevin, G 972-293-5449 235 C
fegan@northwood.edu
FEGETT, Greg 217-443-8888 137 B
gfegett@dacc.edu
FEGLEY, Bryan 252-399-6544 335 I
bsfegley@barton.edu
FEGLEY, Danielle 541-383-7219 382 B
dfegley@cocc.edu
FEHLAU, Fred 626-396-2290 26 L
fred.fehlau@artcenter.edu
FEHLBERG, Mark 773-702-3321 153 F
mafehl@uchicago.edu
FEHN, Heather 609-771-2101 284 I
hfehn@tcnj.edu
FEHNRICH, Jennifer 567-661-7101 369 A
jennifer_fehnrich@owens.edu
FEHR, Joy 951-785-2982 47 F
jfehr@lasierra.edu
FEHRENBACHER,
Richard 206-220-8280 498 D
fehrenbacher@seattleu.edu
FEHRENBACHER, Rick 206-220-8269 498 D
fehrenbacher@seattleu.edu
FEIBEL, Ann 718-482-5642 303 B
afeibel@lagcc.cuny.edu
FEICHTER, Kathryn 330-966-5452 370 G
kfeichter@starkstate.edu
FEIER, Julie 970-943-3017 84 E
jfeier@western.edu
FEIEREISEL, Mark 312-915-7625 144 D
mfeiere@luc.edu
FEIERMAN, Michael 212-678-3438 331 C
mf192@tc.columbia.edu
FEIERTAG, Jason 484-664-3140 402 F
jasonfeiertag@muhlenberg.edu
FEIGELSTOCK, Yitzchok 516-225-4700 320 H
rcli@mlb.edu
FEIGENBAUM, Peter 718-817-2243 308 G
pfeigenbaum@fordham.edu
FEIGENSON, Neal, R 203-582-3213 88 A
neal.feigenson@quinnipiac.edu

FEIGERT, James, M 949-582-4342 64 J
jfeigert@saddleback.edu
FEIGERT, Kendra, M 717-867-6126 399 J
feigert@lvc.edu
FEIGH, Kim 847-735-6008 142 H
weidnerfeigh@lakeforest.edu
FEIL, Hallie 308-635-6032 278 B
feilh@wncc.edu
FEILEN, Bryan 317-632-5553 162 P
bfeilen@lincolntech.edu
FEIN, Cheryl 212-217-4700 308 B
cheryl_fein@fitnyc.edu
FEIN, Gene 718-817-3900 308 G
fein@fordham.edu
FEIN, Jason 973-408-3648 285 E
jfein@drew.edu
FEIN, Jason 207-786-6341 198 E
jfein@bates.edu
FEIN, Michael, T 434-832-7751 487 H
feinm@cvcc.vccs.edu
FEINBERG, Diane 405-974-2658 380 J
dfeinberg@uco.edu
FEINBERG, Elisha 718-268-4700 320 K
FEINGOLD, Ruth, P 503-370-6285 388 D
feingold@willamette.edu
FEINMAN, Shannon, V 434-949-1005 489 E
shannon.feinman@southside.edu
FEINSTEIN, Andrew 408-924-2400 34 D
FEINSTEIN, David 212-964-2830 315 B
FEINSTEIN, Lee 812-856-7900 159 H
lafeinst@indiana.edu
FEINSTEIN, Sheryl, J 308-865-8265 277 F
feinsteinsg@unk.edu
FEIST, K. Cameron 315-859-4413 309 D
cfeist@hamilton.edu
FEIST-PRICE, Sonja, M 859-257-9293 190 B
sonja.feist-price@uky.edu
FEISTHAMEL, Kevin, P 330-569-5952 362 J
FEISTRITZER, Richard 844-283-2246 91 G
FEITZ, David, A 801-321-7211 472 O
dfeitz@ushe.edu
FEKE, Donald, L 216-368-4389 358 C
dlf4@case.edu
FEKETE, Bettina 808-675-3701 128 K
feketeb@go.byuh.edu
FEKETE, Michael 815-836-5549 143 E
feketemi@lewisu.edu
FEKULA, Michael 803-641-3340 425 A
mickf@usca.edu
FELCH, Katrina 715-675-3331 514 F
felch@ntc.edu
FELD, Rachel, M 507-354-8221 243 C
feldrm@mlc-wels.edu
FELDBLUM, Miriam 909-621-8017 57 I
miriam.feldblum@pomona.edu
FELDER, Andrea 202-885-6000 91 C
FELDER, Bruce, B 304-696-3983 504 C
felder1@marshall.edu
FELDER, JR., E. Lee 605-677-5671 428 E
lee.felder@usd.edu
FELDER, Luther 706-821-8295 124 C
lfelder@paine.edu
FELDER-DEAS,
Altoya, A 803-934-3167 422 G
afdeas@morris.edu
FELDHAUS, ESQ,
Joseph, H 513-745-3908 374 D
feldhausjl@xavier.edu
FELDHEGE, Zach 916-649-8168 27 L
zach.feldhege@brightwood.edu
FELDHUES, Nicole 412-396-6644 394 D
feldhuesn@duq.edu
FELDMAN, Aharon 410-484-7200 206 C
raf@nirc.edu
FELDMAN, Andrew 509-533-3538 494 A
andrew.feldman@sfcc.spokane.edu
FELDMAN, Andrew 509-434-5107 493 H
andrew.feldman@sfcc.spokane.edu
FELDMAN, Barbara 941-487-4200 110 B
bfeldman@ncf.edu
FELDMAN, Dan 781-736-8405 213 A
feldman@brandeis.edu
FELDMAN, Harriet, R 212-346-1200 319 J
hfeldman@pace.edu
FELDMAN, James 518-225-5631 328 C
feldmajs@cobleskill.edu
FELDMAN, Leonard, C 848-445-4524 290 A
l.c.feldman@rutgers.edu
FELDMAN, Lori 219-989-2608 163 E
feldman@pnw.edu
FELDMAN, Mary Jane 716-614-5926 318 E
feldman@niagaracc.suny.edu
FELDMAN, Rachelle 510-642-7117 68 G
FELDMAN, Richard 212-799-5000 312 B
FELDMANN, Dorothy 781-891-2782 212 A
dfeldmann@bentley.edu

FELDMANN,
Raymond, C 410-704-4672 209 C
rfeldmann@towson.edu
FELDNER, Lisa 701-328-2960 353 F
lisa.feldner@ndus.edu
FELDSTEIN, Andrew 785-628-4788 177 D
apfeldstein@fhsu.edu
FELDSTEIN, Jay, S 215-871-6800 407 G
jfeldstein@pcom.edu
FELDT, Tina 318-869-5424 191 C
tfeldt@centenary.edu
FELIBERTY, Victor, A 787-284-1912 524 C
vfeliber@ponce.inter.edu
FELICE, Susan 708-656-8000 146 F
susan.felice@morton.edu
FELICIANO, Betania 787-832-6000 522 Q
FELICIANO, Danilo 413-565-1000 211 C
dfeliciano@baypath.edu
FELICIANO, Nydia, I 787-279-1912 523 J
nfeliciano@bayamon.inter.edu
FELICIANO, Patsy 813-974-3827 111 A
pfelicia@admin.usf.edu
FELICIANO, Yelitza 787-783-0039 522 C
yelitza.feliciano@dewey.edu
FELIO, John, R 518-783-2328 324 C
jfelio@siena.edu
FELIU, Julio 787-841-2000 525 J
jfeliu@pucpr.edu
FELIX, Jovany 850-561-2106 109 A
jovany.felix@famu.edu
FELIX-MATA, Bertha 559-934-2217 73 N
berthafelixmata@whccd.edu
FELKER, Sharon, M 303-963-3369 77 I
sfelker@ccu.edu
FELKER, Steven 757-825-2716 489 G
felkers@tncc.edu
FELL, Janet 732-923-4645 287 C
jfell@monmouth.edu
FELL, Katherine, R 419-434-4510 372 B
fell@findlay.edu
FELLEGY, Anna 218-879-0878 244 F
afellegy@fdltcc.edu
FELLER, David, C 414-955-8424 508 D
dfeller@mcw.edu
FELLER, Scott 765-361-6224 166 B
fellers@wabash.edu
FELLINGER, Jennifer 616-395-7860 231 D
fellinger@hope.edu
FELLOWS, Gail 610-436-3333 407 D
gfellows@wcupa.edu
FELLOWS, Maureen, O 315-470-6621 328 D
mfellows@esf.edu
FELPS, Jennifer 903-334-6752 460 D
jfelps@tamut.edu
FELSER, Francis, J 716-250-7500 300 B
fjfelser@bryantstratton.edu
FELSKE, Eileen 973-618-3419 284 D
efelske@caldwell.edu
FELTES, Carol 212-327-8909 321 E
cfeltes@rockvax.rockefeller.edu
FELTHOUSEN, Mat 216-421-7384 359 J
mfelthousen@cia.edu
FELTHOUSEN, Robert 541-956-7147 386 G
rfelthousen@roguecc.edu
FELTMAN, Richard 718-951-5693 301 E
rfeltman@brooklyn.cuny.edu
FELTNER, Michael, E 310-506-4280 56 D
michael.feltner@pepperdine.edu
FELTON, David, A 601-984-6000 256 D
dafelton@umc.edu
FELTON, Herman, J 937-708-5704 373 H
hfelton@wilberforce.edu
FELTON, Jennifer 712-749-2120 167 C
feltonj@bvu.edu
FELTON, Pamela 312-322-1734 152 F
pfelton@spertus.edu
FELTON, Rob 503-554-2129 383 C
rfelton@georgefox.edu
FELTON, Shawn 607-255-5241 306 B
admissions@cornell.edu
FELTON, Terence 630-466-7900 155 C
tfelton@waubonsee.edu
FELTS, Renee 757-569-6760 489 B
rfelts@pdc.edu
FELTS, Ronald 661-726-1911 68 E
ron.felts@uav.edu
FELTY, Darren 843-958-5813 424 G
darren.felty@tridenttech.edu
FELTY, Donna, H 423-652-4752 432 I
dhfelty@king.edu
FEMINO, Charles 978-232-2221 214 G
cfemino@endicott.edu
FEMINO, Donny 978-232-5201 214 G
dfemino@endicott.edu
FENCSIK, Alissa 510-204-0727 37 F
afencsik@cdsp.edu
FENDER, Samantha 828-689-1126 339 G
sfender@mhu.edu

FENDERS, Nancy 207-941-7153 199 B fendersn@husson.edu
FENDRICH, Chris 719-549-2611 78 P chris.fendrich@csupueblo.edu
FENG, Phoenix 617-449-7067 225 C phoenix.feng@urbancollege.edu
FENG, Xiaodong 916-686-8066 30 H
FENLASON, Julie 320-762-4531 243 J julief@alextech.edu
FENLASON, Laurie 413-585-2170 224 F lfenlaso@smith.edu
FENN, Janice 812-877-8786 163 G fenn@rose-hulman.edu
FENN, Patricia 732-255-0400 288 B pfenn@ocean.edu
FENNELL, Angelia 903-593-8311 461 B afennell@texascollege.edu
FENNELL, Barbara 432-686-4250 453 B bfennell@midland.edu
FENNELL, Catherine 610-527-0200 409 E fennell@roesmont.edu
FENNELL, Catherine 610-896-1221 397 F cfennell@haverford.edu
FENNELL, Dwight 903-593-8311 461 B dfennell@texascollege.edu
FENNELL, Sabrina 716-839-8228 306 E sfennell@daemen.edu
FENNER, Felicia 706-821-8320 124 C ffenner@paine.edu
FENNER, Richard 315-792-3112 332 H rfenner@utica.edu
FENNERN, Nicole 507-457-1638 250 B nfennern@smumn.edu
FENNING, Amy, E 731-881-7340 440 B
FENNING, Julie 218-793-2463 246 F julie.fenning@northlandcollege.edu
FENSKE, Cynthia 734-995-7443 229 A cindy.fenske@cuaa.edu
FENSKE, Susanne 814-393-2351 405 H sfenske@clarion.edu
FENTON, James 863-680-4277 100 D jfenton@flsouthern.edu
FENTON, Kimberly 716-286-8566 318 F kfenton@niagara.edu
FENTON, Lisa 708-802-6582 138 F lfenton@foxcollege.edu
FENTON, Patrick 408-741-2056 74 D pat.fenton@westvalley.edu
FENTON, William, E 502-272-8059 183 H wfenton@bellarmine.edu
FENTRESS, Craig, M 240-500-2000 204 B cmfentress@hagerstowncc.edu
FENVES, Gregory, L 512-471-1232 467 C president@utexas.edu
FENWICK, Garland 540-423-9046 488 B gfenwick@germanna.edu
FENWICK, Jim 818-947-2508 49 G fenwicjl@lavc.edu
FERALDI, Corey 803-641-3280 425 A coreyf@usca.edu
FERALDI, Patricia, A 716-673-3553 325 C patricia.feraldi@fredonia.edu
FERBER, Anna 212-431-2808 317 H anna.ferber@nyls.edu
FERBER, David 402-399-2319 274 A dferber@csm.edu
FERBER, Moshe 718-601-3523 334 O mosheferber@ytariverdale.org
FERBER, Stephen, M 412-624-8166 412 I smf200@pitt.edu
FERBRACHE, Jeanne 402-559-3937 277 H jferbrache@unmc.edu
FERCH, John 907-745-3201 9 D jferch@akbible.edu
FERDAUS, Riaz 225-490-1662 191 G riaz.ferdaus@ololcollege.edu
FERDINAND, Jason 256-726-7277 6 E jferdinand@oakwood.edu
FERDOLAGE, Traci 707-826-4111 34 A traci.ferdolage@humboldt.edu
FEREBEE, Cheryl 678-916-2615 115 K cferebee@johnmarshall.edu
FEREBEE, Ryan 804-524-5297 491 A rferebee@vsu.edu
FEREBEE, Ryan, A 757-594-7033 479 H ryan.ferebee@cnu.edu
FEREDE, Mulugeta 512-475-6600 467 C mferede@utexas.edu
FEREIRA, James 864-231-2000 418 E jfereira@andersonuniversity.edu
FERGUS, Roy 516-299-2277 313 D roy.fergus@liu.edu
FERGUSON, Barclay 414-955-8740 508 D bferguson@mcw.edu
FERGUSON, Benny 709-379-3111 128 H bferguson1@yhc.edu
FERGUSON, Brandi 620-225-0186 176 N bferguson@dc3.edu
FERGUSON, Brooke 540-857-6323 490 B bferguson@virginiawestern.edu
FERGUSON, Bruce 310-665-6860 54 I bferguson@otis.edu
FERGUSON, Buddy 864-379-8727 421 E ferguson@erskine.edu
FERGUSON, Charity, F 270-384-8100 187 H fergusonc@lindsey.edu
FERGUSON, Christy 716-286-8345 318 F clf@niagara.edu
FERGUSON, Colin 276-656-0349 489 A cferguson@patrickhenry.edu
FERGUSON, Cristie 903-693-2005 454 E cferguson@panola.edu
FERGUSON, Darla 321-433-7080 97 N fergusond@easternflorida.edu
FERGUSON, Derek 630-829-1101 133 I dferguson@ben.edu
FERGUSON, Devin 972-825-4700 457 F dferguson@sagu.edu
FERGUSON, Douglas, J 610-359-7399 393 E dferguson@dccc.edu
FERGUSON, Glenda 478-757-5241 128 E gferguson@wesleyancollege.edu
FERGUSON, Hege 850-644-1389 110 A hferguson@admin.fsu.edu
FERGUSON, Jennifer 757-822-1913 489 H jferguson@tcc.edu
FERGUSON, Jessame, E 410-857-2741 205 E jferguson@mcdaniel.edu
FERGUSON, Julie 570-941-4330 413 F julie.ferguson@scranton.edu
FERGUSON, Keith 256-233-8215 4 C keith.ferguson@athens.edu
FERGUSON, Kenlanna 269-337-7191 231 F kenlanna.feguson@kzoo.edu
FERGUSON, Kenneth, H 540-636-2900 479 G kferguson@christendom.edu
FERGUSON, Kevin 708-344-4700 144 A kferguson@lincolntech.edu
FERGUSON, Kimberly 814-332-4356 388 F kferguson@allegheny.edu
FERGUSON, Lee 903-923-2048 448 J lferguson@etbu.edu
FERGUSON, Leonard 605-455-6057 427 I lferguson@olc.edu
FERGUSON, Lisa 270-789-5109 184 B lgferguson@campbellsville.edu
FERGUSON, Lisa, M 740-283-6450 361 L lferguson@franciscan.edu
FERGUSON, Lori 580-349-1566 377 E lorif@opsu.edu
FERGUSON, Mark 973-290-4238 285 A mferguson@cse.edu
FERGUSON, Michael 304-243-2389 505 H mferguson@wju.edu
FERGUSON, Noreen 248-204-3106 233 A nferguson@ltu.edu
FERGUSON, Pam 309-672-5513 145 E pferguson@methodistcol.edu
FERGUSON, Pamela 973-720-2615 292 I fergusonp4@wpunj.edu
FERGUSON, Paul 562-903-4732 27 E paul.ferguson@biola.edu
FERGUSON, Randy 276-656-0229 489 A rferguson@patrickhenry.edu
FERGUSON, Rhonda 903-886-5014 459 E rhonda.ferguson@tamuc.edu
FERGUSON, Rose, A 815-599-3402 139 F rose.ferguson@highland.edu
FERGUSON, JR., Roy, W 540-828-5307 478 J rferguso@bridgewater.edu
FERGUSON, Sam 325-793-4631 452 F ferguson.sam@mcm.edu
FERGUSON, Sarah 972-860-4854 447 G sferguson@dcccd.edu
FERGUSON, Sarah 612-728-5112 250 B sferguso@smumn.edu
FERGUSON, Scott 419-448-3300 370 K fergusonscl@tiffin.edu
FERGUSON, Stephanie 417-455-5566 259 D sferguso@crowder.edu
FERGUSON, Teresa 864-587-4002 424 D fergusont@smcsc.edu
FERGUSON, Teresa, D 864-587-4003 424 D fergusont@smcsc.edu
FERGUSON, Thomas, C 614-231-3095 134 B tferguson@bexleyseabury.edu
FERGUSON, Timothy 859-572-7770 188 E fergusont2@nku.edu
FERGUSON, Vicki 510-215-3921 40 K vferguson@contracosta.edu
FERGUSON, Vicky 254-519-5720 459 D vferguson@tamuct.edu
FERGUSON, William, L 864-379-8881 421 E ferguson@erskine.edu
FERKEL, Greta 312-662-4409 133 A gferkel@adler.edu
FERLAND, Chris 478-445-3350 119 E chris.ferland@gcsu.edu
FERLAND, Leanda 617-824-8610 214 E leanda_ferland@emerson.edu
FERLAND, William, R 401-333-7131 416 B wferland@ccri.edu
FERLEGER, Naomi, A 845-575-3000 314 C naomi.ferleger@marist.edu
FERLIC, Joseph, E 304-326-1304 502 D jferlic@salemu.edu
FERME, Valerio 928-523-8632 14 K valerio.ferme@nau.edu
FERNÁNDEZ RODRÍGUEZ, José, R 787-880-6577 527 F jose.fernandez1@upr.edu
FERNÓS, Manuel, J 787-766-1912 524 E mfernos@inter.edu
FERN, Kathy, T 314-286-4895 265 F ktfern@ranken.edu
FERNALD, Julian, L 831-459-4341 70 C jfernald@ucsc.edu
FERNANDER, Kevin, A 561-868-3143 105 A fernandk@palmbeachstate.edu
FERNANDES, Brian 845-848-7807 306 G brian.fernandes@dc.edu
FERNANDES, Jane, K 336-316-2146 338 C fernandesjk@guilford.edu
FERNANDES, Kim 816-604-1418 262 F kim.fernandes@mcckc.edu
FERNANDES, Rick 724-805-2274 410 B rick.fernandes@stvincent.edu
FERNANDES, Sidney 813-974-1780 111 A sfernand@health.usf.edu
FERNANDEZ, Carmen 670-237-6700 520 D carmen.fernandez@marianas.edu
FERNANDEZ, Diana 413-559-6253 215 F dfpr@hampshire.edu
FERNANDEZ, Edith 702-992-2358 279 B edith.fernandez@nsc.edu
FERNANDEZ, Eva 718-997-2867 303 E eva.fernandez@qc.cuny.edu
FERNANDEZ, Fabian 727-736-5082 107 F ffernandez@schiller.edu
FERNANDEZ, Frank 614-236-6504 358 A ffernand@capital.edu
FERNANDEZ, Henry, B 954-486-7728 112 N hfpresident@uftl.edu
FERNANDEZ, Hilda 305-623-2355 107 B hfernandez@stu.edu
FERNANDEZ, J. Anthony 208-792-2216 132 C tfernandez@lcsc.edu
FERNANDEZ, Jazmine 954-776-4476 102 G jazminef@keiseruniversity.edu
FERNANDEZ, Jeffrey 508-289-2325 226 D jfernandez@whoi.edu
FERNANDEZ, John 787-725-6500 521 C jfernandez@albizu.edu
FERNANDEZ, John 787-832-4040 527 D rector.uprm@upr.edu
FERNANDEZ, Jose 973-684-6107 288 C jfernandez@pccc.edu
FERNANDEZ, Jose, A 407-582-1701 113 F jfernandez145@valenciacollege.edu
FERNANDEZ, Jose Luis 818-710-6406 49 D fernanjl@piercecollege.edu
FERNANDEZ, Luis 830-591-7276 457 C lmfernandez@swtjc.edu
FERNANDEZ, Maria, I 787-832-4040 528 C ossoa@uprm.edu
FERNANDEZ, Mayra 509-453-0374 497 A mayra.fernandez@perrytech.edu
FERNANDEZ, Rodolfo, J 305-284-4085 112 O rudyfernandez@miami.edu
FERNANDEZ, Ruby 863-638-2947 114 A fernandezrm@webber.edu
FERNANDEZ, Sam 602-212-0501 15 H sfernandez@brightoncollege.edu
FERNANDEZ, Vivian 848-932-3020 290 A vpfsr@hr.rutgers.edu
FERNANDEZ, Wayne 808-236-3597 129 C wfernandez@hpu.edu
FERNANDEZ, Yaniris 413-559-5781 215 F ymfpr@hampshire.edu
FERNANDEZ VAN CLEVE, John 787-265-3878 528 C rector.uprm@upr.edu
FERNANDEZ-ZAVALA, Margarita 787-993-0000 527 D rectoria.uprb@upr.edu
FERNANDO, Gihan 202-885-1829 91 C gihan@american.edu
FERNANDO, Shane 910-362-7890 341 E sfernando@cfcc.edu
FERNE, Mark 801-832-2233 474 E mferne@westminstercollege.edu
FERNENDEZ, Sam 602-212-0501 11 F sam.fernendez@brightoncollege.edu
FERNETTE, Eric 713-500-3110 468 D eric.fernette@uth.tmc.edu
FERNHALL, Bo 312-996-6695 153 H fernhall@uic.edu
FERNIANY, Will 205-975-5362 8 B ferniany@uab.edu
FERNOS, Manuel, J 787-766-1912 524 A mfernos@inter.edu
FERNOS, Manuel, L 787-763-4203 523 F mfernos@inter.edu
FERO, Laura 828-898-8769 339 B ferol@lmc.edu
FEROE, John 845-437-5742 333 A feroe@vassar.edu
FERRAN, Mayra, M 787-257-7373 525 Q mferran@suagm.edu
FERRAN, Peggy 315-781-3311 310 C ferran@hws.edu
FERRANTE, John 516-918-2787 333 E jferrante@webb.edu
FERRANTE, Regina 860-512-3633 85 G rferrante@manchestercc.edu
FERRAO DELGADO, Luis, A 787-763-3930 528 F rectoria.rrp@upr.edu
FERRARA, Anthony, A 901-448-5523 440 C aferrar1@uthsc.edu
FERRARA, Brandi 315-781-3517 310 C bferrara@hws.edu
FERRARA, Brendan 912-443-5783 125 D bferrara@savannahtech.edu
FERRARA, Hania 201-692-2381 286 B ferrara@fdu.edu
FERRARA, Joseph 202-687-4134 92 B jaf@georgetown.edu
FERRARA, Maria 201-447-7236 283 I mferrara@bergen.edu
FERRARA, Michael 603-862-1178 282 F mike.ferrara@unh.edu
FERRARA, Victoria 914-674-3094 314 I vferrara@mercy.edu
FERRARI, Ahniwa 360-538-4051 495 B ahniwa.ferrari@ghc.edu
FERRARI, Bernard 410-234-9214 204 F bferrari@jhu.edu
FERRARI, Cynthia 724-830-4639 410 E ferrari@setonhill.edu
FERRARI, John 305-821-3333 100 A jferrari@fnu.edu
FERRARI, Loretta 212-229-5860 316 E ferraril@newschool.edu
FERRARI, Susan 641-269-4983 169 F ferraris@grinnell.edu
FERRARO, Johnathan 419-434-4749 372 B ferraro@findlay.edu
FERRARO, Roger 860-906-5259 85 D rferraro@ccc.commnet.edu
FERRATO, Christy 505-566-3299 296 A ferratoc@sanjuancollege.edu
FERRAUILO-DAVIS, Mary-Jo 518-736-3622 309 A mary-jo.ferrauilo-davis@fmcc.suny.edu
FERRE, Loren 785-670-1794 182 D loren.ferre@washburn.edu
FERREIRA, Debora, D 413-545-3464 216 H ferreira@admin.umass.edu
FERREIRA, Kenneth 603-899-4186 281 D ferreirak@franklinpierce.edu
FERREIRA, Lisa 619-961-4202 67 F lisaf@tjsl.edu
FERREIRA, Maritza 678-466-4467 117 I maritzaferreira@clayton.edu
FERREIRA, Milagros 954-763-9840 94 S registrar@atom.edu
FERREIRA, Paul 207-326-2418 200 F paul.ferreira@mma.edu
FERREIRA, Robert 401-865-2407 416 E rferreir@providence.edu
FERREL, Kathleen 715-365-4416 514 E kferrel@nicoletcollege.edu
FERRELL, Amber 910-296-2400 344 B aferrell@jamessprunt.edu
FERRELL, Lottie 919-516-4351 348 G lferrell@st-aug.edu
FERRELL, Martin 336-631-1561 352 B ferrellm@uncsa.edu
FERRENCE, Steve 315-792-7100 330 A sferrence@sunypoly.edu
FERRENTINO, Robert, C 989-328-1221 234 D bobf@montcalm.edu
FERRER, Brunilda 787-264-1912 524 D bferrer@intersg.edu
FERRER, Jose 787-832-4040 528 C decep@uprm.edu

FERRER, Laura 787-864-2222 524 A laura.ferrer@guayama.inter.edu

FERRER, Mercedes 787-265-3877 528 C director.oiip@upr.edu

FERRER, Yolanda 787-834-9595 526 E yferrer@uaa.edu

FERRER MEDINA, Sonia, N 787-884-3838 520 G sferrer@atenascollege.edu

FERRER-MUNIZ, Karen 518-629-7234 310 G k.ferrermuniz@hvcc.edu

FERRERO, JR., Ray 954-262-7575 104 F ferrero@nova.edu

FERRES, Steven 845-574-4770 321 F sferres@sunyrockland.edu

FERRETTI, Anthony, J 941-756-0690 399 C aferretti@lecom.edu

FERRETTI, Bruce, S 610-330-5375 399 B ferrettb@lafayette.edu

FERRETTI, John, M 814-866-6641 399 C hmckenzie@lecom.edu

FERRETTI, Kenneth, M 215-965-4007 402 C kferretti@moore.edu

FERRETTI, Richard 814-666-6641 399 C rferretti@lecom.edu

FERRETTI, Silvia, M 814-866-6641 399 C ckonnerth@lecom.edu

FERRETTI, Stephanie 215-871-6486 407 G stephanief@pcom.edu

FERRICK, Courtney 914-633-2336 311 B kferrick@iona.edu

FERRIER, Douglas, M 956-326-2400 459 B douglas.ferrier@tamiu.edu

FERRIER, Katy 717-871-5702 407 A katy.ferrier@millersville.edu

FERRIS, Adriann 510-780-4500 48 D aferris@lifewest.edu

FERRIS, Bill 206-543-9004 499 D bferris@uw.edu

FERRIS, Christian 361-593-2132 460 B christian.farris@tamuk.edu

FERRIS, Diane, L 727-864-7761 97 O ferrisdl@eckerd.edu

FERRIS, Jo 760-757-2121 52 F jferris@miracosta.edu

FERRIS, John 619-594-4967 34 B jferris@mail.sdsu.edu

FERRIS, Mary 805-893-2251 70 B mary.ferris@sa.ucsb.edu

FERRO, David 801-626-6303 473 E dferro@weber.edu

FERRO, Deanna 315-731-5797 315 I dferro@mvcc.edu

FERRO, Jennifer 310-450-4613 62 G ferro_jennifer@smc.edu

FERRO, Lynn, P 717-815-1558 415 G lferro@ycp.edu

FERRO, Robert 617-989-4557 225 E ferrob@wit.edu

FERRUCCI, Rosemary 516-686-1081 317 G rferrucc@nyit.edu

FERRUOLO, Stephen, C 619-260-4527 71 J lawdean@sandiego.edu

FERRY, Catherine, T 717-358-3962 395 G cathie.ferry@fandm.edu

FERRY, Marylou 909-607-0283 57 I marylou.ferry@pomona.edu

FERRY, Michael, H 212-752-1530 312 G michael.ferry@limcollege.edu

FERRY, Patrick 734-995-7300 229 A patrick.ferry@cuw.edu

FERRY, Patrick, T 262-243-5700 507 C patrick.ferry@cuw.edu

FERRY, Richard, E 610-921-7825 388 E rferry@albright.edu

FERRY, Tamara, R 262-243-5700 507 C tamara.ferry@cuw.edu

FERULLO, Tony 978-232-2384 214 G aferullo@endicott.edu

FERUS, Kenneth, S 401-456-8033 417 A kferus@ric.edu

FERZELY, Eliza 402-941-6141 275 J ferzely@midlandu.edu

FESCOE, Michael 973-290-4498 285 A mfescoe@cse.edu

FESER, Ed 541-737-2111 385 F osu.provost@oregonstate.edu

FESER, Neil 504-468-2900 196 C neil@southwest.edu

FESKE, Brent 912-344-2596 115 D brent.feske@armstrong.edu

FESKO, John 760-480-8474 74 H jvfesko@wscal.edu

FESSENBECKER, Denise 310-377-5501 51 B dfessenbecker@marymountcalifornia.edu

FESSENDEN, June, S 623-845-3406 13 H june.fessenden@gccaz.edu

FESSLER, Brent 210-690-9000 449 K bfessler@hallmarkuniversity.edu

FESSLER, Cale 816-271-4226 264 B cfessler@missouriwestern.edu

FESSLER, Karen, P 570-326-3761 404 T kfessler@pct.edu

FESSLER, Matthew 201-360-4131 286 E mfessler@hccc.edu

FETICK, Fay 314-529-9673 262 B ffetick@maryville.edu

FETROW, Aaron, L 540-375-2592 484 H fetrow@roanoke.edu

FETROW, Jacquelyn, S 610-921-7600 388 E jfetrow@albright.edu

FETSCH, Cindy 701-777-4156 353 G cynthia.fetsch@und.edu

FETTER, Bridget 863-669-2843 105 F bfetter@polk.edu

FETTER, Steve 301-405-5793 207 G sfetter@umd.edu

FETTER, Wayne, R 337-475-5433 197 B wfetter@mcneese.edu

FETTERMAN, Les 814-871-5678 395 H

FETTEROLF, Bernadette, M 785-354-5853 174 J bfetterolf@stormontvail.org

FEUCHT-HAVIAR, Joyce, A 818-677-4711 33 B joyce.feucht-haviar@csun.edu

FEUDO, John 978-934-4814 217 B john_feudo@uml.edu

FEUER, Avraham 732-367-1060 283 K afeuer@bmg.edu

FEUER, Michael, J 202-994-6160 92 A mjfeuer@gwu.edu

FEUERBORN, Eric 405-224-3140 381 B efeuerborn@usao.edu

FEUERBORN, Matt 815-825-9381 142 F matthew.feuerborn@kishwaukeecollege.edu

FEUERSTEIN, Christian 802-586-7711 476 D cfeuerstein@sterlingcollege.edu

FEULING, Michael 503-838-8449 388 B feulingm@wou.edu

FEUSTEL, Paul 518-262-5339 297 L feustep@mail.amc.edu

FEUSTLE, Judith 443-352-4292 207 C jfeustle@stevenson.edu

FEVIG, David 219-464-5304 165 D david.fevig@valpo.edu

FEVOLA, Christopher, N 516-299-3149 313 C christopher.fevola@liu.edu

FEW, Tamaria 417-836-6616 263 H tammyfew@missouristate.edu

FEWOX, Keli 706-355-5081 115 H kfewox@athenstech.edu

FEY, Charles, J 973-596-5642 288 A cfey@njit.edu

FEY, Charles, J 973-596-6476 288 A cfey@njit.edu

FEY, Jo 660-263-4100 264 C jof@macc.edu

FEY-YENSAN, Nancy 704-687-8374 351 C nfeyyens@uncc.edu

FEYEN, Deanna 979-532-6304 471 A deannaf@wcjc.edu

FEYEN, Mike 979-532-6358 471 A mikef@wcjc.edu

FEYERHERM, Dianne, E 254-299-8843 452 E dfeyerherm@mclennan.edu

FEYERHERM, Sarah 410-778-7752 210 A sfeyerherm2@washcoll.edu

FEYTEN, Carine 940-898-3201 464 A cfeyten@twu.edu

FEZIO, Beth 864-644-5216 424 B bfezio@swu.edu

FIALA, Bill 626-815-2109 26 U bfiala@apu.edu

FIALA, Deborah 702-463-2122 280 F

FIALA, Kelly, A 410-543-6335 209 B kafiala@salisbury.edu

FICK, Steve 512-313-3000 446 N steve.fick@concordia.edu

FICK, Verlyn 520-515-5414 11 R fickv@cochise.edu

FICKE, Joan, C 973-655-4368 287 D fickej@mail.montclair.edu

FICKEN, Roger 970-675-3275 78 H roger.ficken@cncc.edu

FICKENSCHER, II, Carl, C 260-452-2131 157 F carl.fickenscher@ctsfw.edu

FICKLER, Debra 610-519-7857 413 K debra.fickler@villanova.edu

FIDATI, Brian 484-664-3110 402 F brianfidati@muhlenberg.edu

FIDELI, Baycan 631-451-4212 330 B fidelib@sunysuffok.edu

FIDLER, Jane, P 617-333-2355 214 B jfidler0803@curry.edu

FIDLER-SHEPPARD, Rebecca 856-227-7200 284 E rsheppard@camdencc.edu

FIEBELKORN, Donna 906-635-2728 232 J dfiebelkorn@lssu.edu

FIEBIG, Andrea 847-925-6371 139 B afiebig@harpercollege.edu

FIEDLER, Peter 617-353-6500 212 G pfiedler@bu.edu

FIEDLER, Scott 417-447-6903 264 K fiedlers@otc.edu

FIEDLER, Thomas 617-353-3488 212 G tfiedler@bu.edu

FIEF, Gary 559-442-8277 66 G gary.fief@fresnocitycollege.edu

FIEGE, William 804-594-1406 488 D bfiege@jtcc.edu

FIEGEL, Gregg 805-756-7029 30 K gfiegel@calpoly.edu

FIELD, Betty Ann 702-992-8554 11 C bafield@aii.edu

FIELD, Jay 415-239-3993 37 H jfield@ccsf.edu

FIELD, Stephen, G 585-594-6150 321 C fields@roberts.edu

FIELDER, Kala 931-221-1121 434 J kala.fielder@miller-motte.com

FIELDER, Marsha 517-265-5161 226 F mfielder@adrian.edu

FIELDHOUSE, Susan 615-898-5814 434 H susan.fieldhouse@mtsu.edu

FIELDING, Julie 607-735-1830 307 G jfielding@elmira.edu

FIELDING, Ruby 803-376-5727 418 D rfielding@allenuniversity.edu

FIELDING, William 256-782-5773 6 B fielding@jsu.edu

FIELDS, Andy 530-529-8980 63 I afields@shastacollege.edu

FIELDS, Anika 850-599-3145 109 A anika.fields@famu.edu

FIELDS, Ann, Z 901-722-3230 436 D annfields@sco.edu

FIELDS, Bamby 509-359-6564 494 D bfields@ewu.edu

FIELDS, Beverly 806-457-4200 449 D bfields@fpctx.edu

FIELDS, Chad 479-394-7622 23 D cfields@uarichmountain.edu

FIELDS, Cheryl 505-428-1238 296 B cheryl.fields@sfcc.edu

FIELDS, Christine 276-739-2426 490 A cfields@vhcc.edu

FIELDS, Darin 419-434-4553 372 B fieldsd2@findlay.edu

FIELDS, Fonda 931-221-6279 430 B fieldsf@apsu.edu

FIELDS, Gene 337-482-9246 197 F gene.fields@louisiana.edu

FIELDS, Joe 864-488-8347 422 B jfields@limestone.edu

FIELDS, John 229-430-4711 114 I john.fields@asurams.edu

FIELDS, John 608-663-3407 507 D jfields@edgewood.edu

FIELDS, L. Paige 785-864-7573 181 I paige.fields@ku.edu

FIELDS, LaVern 816-802-3399 261 C lfields@kcai.edu

FIELDS, Lee, M 252-334-2080 340 B lee.fields@macuniversity.edu

FIELDS, Michael 707-668-5663 41 F

FIELDS, Michael 713-221-8179 465 C fieldsm@uhd.edu

FIELDS, Mitch 315-312-6600 327 D mitch.fields@oswego.edu

FIELDS, Petra 704-991-0231 346 I pfields7679@stanly.edu

FIELDS, Richard 704-669-4243 342 B fieldsr198@clevelandcc.edu

FIELDS, Russell 775-784-6987 279 E rfields@unr.edu

FIELDS, Shawn 860-628-4751 87 E sfields@lincolncollegene.edu

FIELDS, Sheldon 516-686-3939 317 G sheldon.fields@nyit.edu

FIELDS, Stanley 708-656-8000 146 F stanley.fields@morton.edu

FIELDS, Todd, E 972-881-5174 446 I tfields@collin.edu

FIELDS, W. Bradley 859-238-5485 184 C brad.fields@centre.edu

FIELER, Vickie, K 603-594-2567 282 B vfieler@sjhnh.org

FIENE, Jay 909-537-5600 33 D jfiene@csusb.edu

FIER, Luke 540-671-6981 479 G luke.fier@christendom.edu

FIER, Sara 507-537-7150 248 A sara.fier@smsu.edu

FIERKE, Carol, A 734-764-4401 237 I

FIERKE, Carol, A 979-845-4016 459 C provost@tamu.edu

FIERKE, Kimberly 607-431-4000 309 E fierkek@hartwick.edu

FIERO, Diane 661-362-3424 39 C diane.fiero@canyons.edu

FIERRO, Jose, L 562-860-2451 36 A jfierro@cerritos.edu

FIESE, Richard 325-646-2502 450 H rfiese@hputx.edu

FIEZ, Terri 303-492-7401 83 B terri.fiez@colorado.edu

FIFE, Dustin 970-943-2053 84 E dfife@western.edu

FIFE, Linda, L 443-412-2377 204 C lfife@harford.edu

FIFER, Susan 217-641-4201 141 F sfifer@jwcc.edu

FIFER, Tom 660-831-4219 264 A fifert@moval.edu

FIFRICK, Heather 608-822-2366 515 A hfifrick@swtc.edu

FIGARI, Charles, A 713-500-8400 468 D charles.a.figari@uth.tmc.edu

FIGGS, Joel 620-241-0723 176 G joel.figgs@centralchristian.edu

FIGLER, Daniel 910-642-7141 346 G daniel.figler@sccnc.edu

FIGLER, Daniel, J 304-710-3495 503 A figler@mctc.edu

FIGLIO, David, N 847-491-3828 148 C figlio@northwestern.edu

FIGUEIREDO, Marianne 617-521-2270 224 E marianne.figueiredo@simmons.edu

FIGUEORA JIMENEZ, Carmen 787-751-7410 528 F carmen.figueroajimenez@upr.edu

FIGUERA, Lilia 787-758-2525 528 D ayudante-rector@upr.edu

FIGUEREDO, Ann, W 610-896-1142 397 F afiguere@haverford.edu

FIGUEREDO, Fernando 305-348-3829 109 D figueref@fiu.edu

FIGUEROA, Arturo 787-728-1515 529 B afigueroa@sagrado.edu

FIGUEROA, Aurea 787-884-3838 520 G dir_rh@atenascollege.edu

FIGUEROA, Benjamin 831-755-6995 45 C bfigueroa@hartnell.edu

FIGUEROA, Carlos, O 787-850-9320 528 B carlos.figueroa7@upr.edu

FIGUEROA, Carolina 781-891-2855 212 A cfigueroa@bentley.edu

FIGUEROA, Eduardo 787-882-2065 526 D technoloa_industrial@unitecpr.net

FIGUEROA, Fernando 859-442-1175 185 I fernando.figueroa@kctcs.edu

FIGUEROA, Gema 787-738-2161 528 A gema.figueroa@upr.edu

FIGUEROA, Ivan 802-447-4692 476 C ifigueroa@svc.edu

FIGUEROA, Jennifer, E 570-577-1028 390 H j.figueroa@bucknell.edu

FIGUEROA, Julio 787-257-7373 525 Q ue_jfigueroa@suagm.edu

FIGUEROA, Maria, V 787-743-7979 526 A ut_mfigueroa@suagm.edu

FIGUEROA, Marilyn 787-728-1515 529 B mfr@sagrado.edu

FIGUEROA, Mark 503-768-7676 383 G figueroa@lclark.edu

FIGUEROA, Vitaliano 619-594-3557 34 B vfigueroa@mail.sdsu.edu

FIGUEROA, William 787-758-2525 528 D william.figueroa2@upr.edu

FIJAL, Amanda 773-702-7659 153 F afijal@uchicago.edu

FIKE, David, J 415-442-7059 44 E dfike@ggu.edu

FIKE, Janet 304-214-8837 503 E jfike@wvncc.edu

FIKE-CURRY, Esther 407-831-9816 96 I efike@citycollege.edu

FIKE-CURRY, Esther 954-492-5353 96 J efike@citycollege.edu

FIKES, Gloria 713-942-9505 450 E gfikes@hgst.edu

FIKSE, Peggy 209-575-7707 75 J fiksep@mjc.edu

FILAN, Sonia 480-461-7446 13 I sonia.filan@mesacc.edu

FILARDI, Salvatore 203-582-8800 88 A salvatore.filardi@quinnipiac.edu

FISHEL, Teresa .... 651-696-6343 243 B
fishel@macalester.edu
FISHER, Andrew .... 507-222-4300 241 C
afisher@carleton.edu
FISHER, Andrew .... 940-668-4234 453 L
afisher@nctc.edu
FISHER, Ann .... 313-993-1582 237 F
fisheram@udmercy.edu
FISHER, Anne, E .... 941-487-4254 110 B
fisher@ncf.edu
FISHER, Anthony .... 912-525-5000 125 B
afisher@scad.edu
FISHER, Barrett .... 651-638-6083 240 J
fisbar@bethel.edu
FISHER, Barry .... 620-450-2179 180 K
barryf@prattcc.edu
FISHER, Beth .... 901-722-3200 436 D
bfisher@sco.edu
FISHER, Brian .... 239-590-1786 109 C
bfisher@fgcu.edu
FISHER, Brock .... 815-455-8561 145 B
bfisher@mchenry.edu
FISHER, Bryan .... 479-968-0674.. 18 G
pfisher1@atu.edu
FISHER, Courtney .... 870-762-3105.. 17 K
cfisher@smail.anc.edu
FISHER, Craig .... 325-674-2622 441 D
craig.fisher@acu.edu
FISHER, David .... 918-540-6233 376 F
dfisher@neo.edu
FISHER, David, A .... 864-242-5100 418 H
FISHER, Dawn .... 940-397-4787 453 C
dawn.fisher@mwsu.edu
FISHER, Dianna, L .... 657-278-2586.. 32 B
difisher@fullerton.edu
FISHER, Donna, M .... 620-417-1111 181 E
donna.fisher@sccc.edu
FISHER, Edward .... 714-872-5692.. 51 A
efisher@ketchum.edu
FISHER, Elise .... 816-415-7641 270 C
fishere@william.jewell.edu
FISHER, Elizabeth, A ..... 205-934-2974.... 8 B
efisher@uab.edu
FISHER, Ellen .... 212-472-1500 318 B
efisher@nysid.edu
FISHER, Glenn, R .... 570-577-1921 390 H
glenn.fisher@bucknell.edu
FISHER, Gloria .... 817-515-5777 458 B
gloria.fisher@tccd.edu
FISHER, Hilry .... 212-817-7523 302 B
hfisher@gc.cuny.edu
FISHER, Howard .... 903-927-0183 471 B
hlfisher@wileyc.edu
FISHER, James, R .... 585-785-1207 308 D
james.fisher@flcc.edu
FISHER, Jane .... 516-877-3220 297 I
fisher2@adelphi.edu
FISHER, Jay .... 931-598-1142 436 A
jafisher@sewanee.edu
FISHER, Jeffrey .... 614-222-3277 360 B
jfisher@ccad.edu
FISHER, Jennifer, L .... 304-293-8531 505 B
jennifer.fisher@mail.wvu.edu
FISHER, Jeremy, M .... 402-280-3819 274 D
jfisher@creighton.edu
FISHER, Jim, J .... 843-792-4275 422 C
fisherj@musc.edu
FISHER, Joseph, B .... 210-690-9000 449 K
jfisher@hallmarkuniversity.edu
FISHER, Joy .... 310-233-4033.. 49 B
fisherjp@lahc.edu
FISHER, Judith .... 269-471-3470 227 B
jfisher@andrews.edu
FISHER, Julie .... 773-896-2400 135 G
julie.fisher@ctschicago.edu
FISHER, Katie .... 828-328-7247 339 C
katie.fisher@lr.edu
FISHER, Kelly .... 978-232-2328 214 G
kfisher@endicott.edu
FISHER, Kevin .... 859-233-8889 189 H
kfisher@transy.edu
FISHER, L. Dean .... 607-962-9264 306 C
lfisher6@corning-cc.edu
FISHER, Laurie .... 406-243-6989 271 G
laurie.fisher@umontana.edu
FISHER, Lee .... 216-687-2300 359 L
l.fisher@law.csuohio.edu
FISHER, Linda .... 916-660-7605.. 63 K
lfisher@sierracollege.edu
FISHER, Marc .... 805-893-3132.. 70 B
marc.fisher@vcadmin.ucsb.edu
FISHER, Mark .... 417-873-7294 259 G
mfisher005@drury.edu
FISHER, Maurissa .... 503-330-5012 384 C
maurissa.fisher@mtangel.edu
FISHER, Michael .... 541-383-7238 382 B
mfisher@cocc.edu
FISHER, Michael .... 858-785-1458 308 D
michael.fisher@flcc.edu
FISHER, Myra .... 619-849-2388.. 57 H
myrafisher@pointloma.edu
FISHER, Nevan .... 585-389-2370 316 D
nfisher2@naz.edu
FISHER, Nicole .... 213-356-5327.. 65 A
nicole_fisher@sciarc.edu
FISHER, Ocie .... 903-593-8311 461 B
ofisher@texascollege.edu
FISHER, P. Brian .... 843-953-7532 420 C
fisherb@cofc.edu
FISHER, Patti, J .... 574-807-7625 156 E
patti.fisher@bethelcollege.edu
FISHER, Rebecca .... 877-248-6724.. 13 A
rfisher@hmu.edu
FISHER, Robert .... 507-457-6658 250 B
rfisher@smumn.edu
FISHER, Robert, C .... 615-460-6793 430 D
bob.fisher@belmont.edu
FISHER, Robert, H .... 773-298-3031 151 C
fisher@sxu.edu
FISHER, Scheiby, C ...... 956-326-2780 459 B
sfisher@tamiu.edu
FISHER, Stephanie .... 252-823-5166 343 A
FISHER, Susan .... 814-262-3833 405 A
sfisher@pennhighlands.edu
FISHER, Thomas .... 574-520-4207 160 F
fishert@iu.edu
FISHER, Tiffany .... 574-936-8898 155 L
tiffany.fisher@ancilla.edu
FISHER, Timothy .... 860-570-5127.. 88 G
timothy.fisher@uconn.edu
FISHER, Tom .... 505-323-9282 470 I
twfisher@wbu.edu
FISHER, William .... 508-793-7676 213 C
wfisher@clarku.edu
FISHER, Witney .... 864-596-9139 420 F
witney.fisher@converse.edu
FISHER-WILLIAMS, Nan 386-481-2098.. 95 J
williamsnan@cookman.edu
FISHMAN, David .... 845-406-4308 334 E
FISHMAN, Joan .... 212-431-2876 317 H
joan.fishman@nyls.edu
FISHMAN, Joan, R .... 212-431-2850 317 H
joan.fishman@nyls.edu
FISHMAN, Robert .... 734-764-1315 237 I
fishmanr@umich.edu
FISHMAN, Yisroel .... 718-645-0536 315 G
FISHNER, Carrie, J .... 607-746-4635 329 B
fishnecj@delhi.edu
FISHSTEIN, Janet .... 781-239-5840 211 A
jfishstein@babson.edu
FISK, Cheryl .... 952-446-4172 242 A
fiskc@crown.edu
FISK, Francine, J .... 918-631-2495 381 C
francine-fisk@utulsa.edu
FISK, Robert .... 304-647-6361 504 F
rfisk@osteo.wvsom.edu
FISKAA, Evelyn .... 845-848-4032 306 G
evelyn.fiskaa@dc.edu
FISKE, Jason .... 619-961-4217.. 67 F
jfiske@tjsl.edu
FISKE, Joshua, A .... 315-268-6718 304 B
jfiske@clarkson.edu
FISNE, Katherine .... 570-961-7810 399 A
fisnek@lackawanna.edu
FISSINGER, Matthew, X 310-338-2750.. 50 J
mfissing@lmu.edu
FISTER, Cherie .... 314-529-9563 262 B
cfister@maryville.edu
FISTER, K. Renee .... 270-809-3763 188 D
kfister@murraystate.edu
FISTLER, Amy .... 651-255-6111 250 D
afistler@unitedseminary.edu
FITCH, CD .... 620-862-5252 175 B
cd.fitch@barclaycollege.edu
FITCH, Elizabeth .... 615-220-7800 437 C
efitch@mscc.edu
FITCH, Gene .... 972-883-6236 467 D
gene.fitch@utdallas.edu
FITCH, James .... 814-332-2381 388 F
jfitch@allegheny.edu
FITCH, James .... 940-668-4271 453 L
jfitch@nctc.edu
FITCH, Jerome, H .... 803-535-5549 419 E
jfitch@claflin.edu
FITCH, Megan .... 610-896-2958 397 F
mfitch@haverford.edu
FITCH, Michelle .... 712-279-3503 173 B
michelle.fitch@stlukescollege.edu
FITCH, Peggy .... 641-628-5249 167 D
fitchp@central.edu
FITCH, Poppy .... 858-513-9240.. 26 T
poppy.fitch@ashford.edu
FITE-MORGAN, Amber .. 256-765-4487.... 9 A
afitemorgan@una.edu
FITHIAN, David, B .... 773-702-2305 153 F
fithian@uchicago.edu
FITSIMMONS, Gary, N .. 423-775-7196 430 G
gary.fitsimmons@bryan.edu
FITTA, Kevin, J .... 401-456-9885 417 A
kfitta@ric.edu
FITTS, Alex .... 907-474-7980.. 10 B
affitts@alaska.edu
FITTS, Bev .... 503-517-1031 388 A
bfitts@warnerpacific.edu
FITTS, Michael, A .... 504-865-5201 196 D
maf@tulane.edu
FITZ, Craig, R .... 610-359-5288 393 E
cfitz@dccc.edu
FITZ, Franzetta .... 850-599-3460 109 A
franzetta.fitz@famu.edu
FITZ, Gregory .... 214-648-8712 469 E
greg.fitz@utsouthwestern.edu
FITZ, SM, James, F .... 937-229-2899 372 A
jfitz1@udayton.edu
FITZ-GERALD, Jim .... 251-580-2194.... 1 I
jim.fitz-gerald@faulknerstate.edu
FITZGERALD, Barrie, D . 229-333-7836 127 H
bdfitzgerald@valdosta.edu
FITZGERALD, Ed .... 618-252-5400 151 J
eddie.fitzgerald@sic.edu
FITZGERALD, Ed .... 765-973-8422 160 A
efitzger@iue.edu
FITZGERALD, Erin .... 860-723-0013.. 84 I
fitzgeralde@ct.edu
FITZGERALD, Erin .... 401-341-3108 417 D
erin.fitzgerald@salve.edu
FITZGERALD, Faith, M .. 757-823-8407 483 F
fmfitzgerald@nsu.edu
FITZGERALD,
Francis, X .... 718-951-5504 301 E
fxfitzgerald@brooklyn.cuny.edu
FITZGERALD, Frank .... 540-231-1216 490 F
fitzgera@vt.edu
FITZGERALD, Glynis, A . 860-832-2364.. 84 J
fitzgeraldg@ccsu.edu
FITZGERALD, Gregory ... 410-532-5109 206 D
gfitzgerald@ndm.edu
FITZGERALD, Hiram, E .. 517-353-8977 233 G
fitzger9@msu.edu
FITZGERALD, Ione .... 312-461-0600 133 C
ifitzgerald@aaart.edu
FITZGERALD, Jessica .... 314-744-5301 263 F
fitzgerald@mobap.edu
FITZGERALD, Joanne .... 585-389-2070 316 D
jfitzge0@naz.edu
FITZGERALD, Kate .... 330-941-3582 374 E
kafitzgerald@ysu.edu
FITZGERALD, Larry, L ... 434-924-5426 486 H
llf2n@virginia.edu
FITZGERALD,
Lorraine, G .... 312-915-6411 144 D
lsnyde2@luc.edu
FITZGERALD, Marcia ..... 518-828-4181 305 D
fitzgerald@sunycgcc.edu
FITZGERALD, Margaret .. 701-231-8211 354 D
margaret.fitzgerald@ndsu.edu
FITZGERALD, Paul .... 814-868-9900 395 A
paulf@erieit.edu
FITZGERALD, SJ,
Paul, J .... 415-422-6762.. 72 A
pjfitzgerald@usfca.edu
FITZGERALD, Robert, F . 401-863-2500 415 K
robert_fitzgerald@brown.edu
FITZGERALD, Ryan .... 806-716-2175 456 F
rfitzgerald@southplainscollege.edu
FITZGERALD, Scott .... 614-823-0113 368 O
sfitzgerald@otterbein.edu
FITZGERALD, Sean, P ... 419-372-0464 357 F
sfitzge@bgsu.edu
FITZGERALD, Susan ...... 860-768-4011.. 89 C
fitzgeral@hartford.edu
FITZGERALD, Teresa ..... 786-331-1000 104 C
tfitzgerald@maufl.edu
FITZGERALD MILLER,
Judith .... 573-882-0278 268 C
millerjud@missouri.edu
FITZGIBBON, Cecelia .... 215-965-4000 402 C
cfitzgibbon@moore.edu
FITZGIBBON, James ...... 510-231-5000.. 46 N
james.x.fitzgibbon@kp.org
FITZGIBBON, John .... 831-582-3000.. 33 A
jfitzgibbon@csumb.edu
FITZGIBBONS,
Courtney .... 212-431-2859 317 H
courtney.fitzgibbons@nyls.edu
FITZGIBBONS, SJ,
John, P .... 303-458-4190.. 82 D
president@regis.edu
FITZHUGH, Keena .... 215-785-0111 404 P
FITZMAURICE, Patricia .. 212-752-1530 312 G
patricia.fitzmaurice@limcollege.edu
FITZPATRICK, Angela .... 574-239-8357 158 M
afitzpatrick@hcc-nd.edu
FITZPATRICK,
Christiana .... 706-419-1279 118 E
christiana.fitzpatrick@covenant.edu
FITZPATRICK, Christine . 317-274-4417 160 E
cfitzpat@iupui.edu
FITZPATRICK, Colleen ... 802-443-3177 475 G
cfitzpatrick@middlebury.edu
FITZPATRICK, Craig ...... 303-722-5724.. 80 O
cfitzpatrick@lincolntech.edu
FITZPATRICK, Daniel ..... 304-384-5276 503 P
dfitzpatrick@concord.edu
FITZPATRICK, Holly .... 413-775-1813 219 F
fitzpatrickh@gcc.mass.edu
FITZPATRICK, James, D 203-254-4000.. 87 A
jfitzpatrick@fairfield.edu
FITZPATRICK, Jane .... 606-783-2053 188 C
j.fitzpatrick@moreheadstate.edu
FITZPATRICK, Laura ...... 432-264-5009 450 G
lfitzpatrick@howardcollege.edu
FITZPATRICK,
M. Louise .... 610-519-4909 413 K
louise.fitzpatrick@villanova.edu
FITZPATRICK, SC,
Margaret, M .... 845-398-4013 323 G
mfitzpat@stac.edu
FITZPATRICK, Mark .... 212-229-5300 316 E
fitzpame@newschool.edu
FITZPATRICK,
Mary Anne .... 803-777-4621 424 I
fitzpatm@mailbox.sc.edu
FITZPATRICK, Michael .. 620-450-2175 180 K
michaelf@prattcc.edu
FITZPATRICK, Pat .... 718-390-3131 333 D
pfitzpat@wagner.edu
FITZPATRICK, Sharon .... 405-945-3292 378 C
shfitzp@osuokc.edu
FITZPATRICK, Susan ..... 906-635-2831 232 J
sfitzpatrick@lssu.edu
FITZPATRICK,
Timothy, J .... 352-273-1325 110 D
timf@ufl.edu
FITZPATRICK,
Timothy, M .... 860-444-8603 519 B
timothy.m.fitzpatrick@uscga.edu
FITZPATRICK, Tracy ...... 914-251-6105 328 B
tracy.fitzpatrick@purchase.edu
FITZSIMMONS, Joanne . 518-445-2324 297 K
jfitz@albanylaw.edu
FITZSIMMONS, Katie ..... 701-328-4109 353 F
katie.fitzsimmons@ndus.edu
FITZSIMMONS, Linda .... 207-454-1033 200 D
lwinchester@wccc.me.edu
FITZSIMMONS, Lynda ... 303-282-3427.. 82 G
FITZSIMMONS, Peter ..... 408-531-6130.. 61 N
peter.fitzsimmons@sjeccd.org
FITZSIMMONS,
Stephanie .... 732-224-2369 284 B
sfitzsimmons@brookdalecc.edu
FITZSIMMONS, Tracy .... 540-665-4505 485 C
tfitzsim@su.edu
FITZSIMMONS,
Verna, M .... 785-826-2601 179 A
vfitzsimmons@ksu.edu
FITZSIMONS, Debra ...... 949-582-4840.. 64 H
dfitzsimons@socccd.edu
FIVECOAT, Frederick ...... 610-892-1519 405 C
ffivecoat@pit.edu
FIXEN, Randall .... 701-662-1518 355 A
randy.fixen@lrsc.edu
FJORTOFT, Nancy, F ..... 630-515-6072 145 I
nfjort@midwestern.edu
FLAA, Carol .... 701-224-5519 354 F
carol.flaa@bismarckstate.edu
FLABIANO, Heather .... 314-446-8179 266 D
heather.flabiano@stlcop.edu
FLACK, Anna .... 631-451-4008 330 B
flacka@sunysuffolk.edu
FLACK, Felecia, J .... 906-227-1272 235 A
fflack@nmu.edu
FLACK, Lisa .... 217-228-5432 149 B
flackli@quincy.edu
FLACK, Tamala .... 315-228-7014 304 G
tflack@colgate.edu
FLACK, Toney .... 316-978-3919 182 F
toney.flack@wichita.edu
FLACK, Wayne, R .... 218-299-3362 241 K
flack@cord.edu
FLAD-JESION, Ann .... 950-565-1000 507 K
flad-jesionad@lakeland.edu
FLADELAND, Diane .... 701-355-8140 355 K
dflade@umary.edu
FLADELAND, Sara .... 208-769-7750 132 E
sara_fladeland@nic.edu
FLADRY, Robert .... 303-753-6046.. 82 E
rfladry@rmcad.edu

FLORES, Harold .... 305-821-3333 100 A
hflores@fnu.edu
FLORES, Hector .... 409-880-8305 462 C
hector.flores@lamar.edu
FLORES, Jaime .... 860-343-5757.. 86 A
jflores@mxcc.edu
FLORES, Javier .... 325-942-2047 463 C
javier.flores@angelo.edu
FLORES, Jayne, T .... 671-735-5638 519 H
pio@guamcc.edu
FLORES, Jennifer, L ...... 520-626-9443.. 16 J
jenniferflores@email.arizona.edu
FLORES, John .... 214-637-3530 470 H
jflores@wadecollege.edu
FLORES, Juanita .... 830-591-7252 457 C
jsflores2@swtjc.edu
FLORES, Kelly .... 206-239-4500 493 D
FLORES, Laureano .... 661-722-6300.. 26 C
lflores@avc.edu
FLORES, Lucinda .... 210-297-9638 443 K
lgflores@baptisthealthsystem.com
FLORES, Maria, E .... 787-743-7979 526 A
ut_mflores@suagm.edu
FLORES, Marilyn .... 714-628-4880.. 58 B
flores_marilyn@sccollege.edu
FLORES, Mary .... 208-792-2325 132 C
mflores@lcsc.edu
FLORES, Matt .... 512-245-2922 463 A
mgf20@txstate.edu
FLORES, Michael .... 210-486-3963 441 E
rflores@alamo.edu
FLORES, Michael .... 702-651-7336 278 N
michael.flores@csn.edu
FLORES, Mike .... 210-486-3960 441 H
rflores@alamo.edu
FLORES, Mildred .... 787-780-0070 521 B
mflores@caribbean.edu
FLORES, Minerva .... 707-468-3011.. 51 E
mflores@mendocino.edu
FLORES, Ricardo .... 787-701-5100 522 J
riflores@ediccollege.edu
FLORES, Robert, E .... 863-453-6661 108 B
robert.flores@southflorida.edu
FLORES, Rolando .... 575-646-3748 295 B
rolflo@nmsu.edu
FLORES, Waleska .... 787-184-1912 524 C
waflores@ponce.inter.edu
FLORES-CHURCH,
Adriana .... 562-860-2451.. 36 A
achurch@cerritos.edu
FLORES GRIFFITH, Lisa 909-607-1887.. 37 L
lisa.griffith@cgu.edu
FLORES-LOPEZ, Brenda . 423-236-2276 436 C
bfloreslopez@southern.edu
FLORES-MEDINA,
Donna .... 505-454-5328 294 D
dflores@luna.edu
FLORES-SANTOS,
Mayra, M .... 787-250-0000 527 D
mayra.flores@upr.edu
FLORESCA, Ann .... 270-745-6463 190 F
ann.floresca@wku.edu
FLOREY, Nancy .... 717-947-6098 404 S
neflorey@pacollege.edu
FLOREZ, Cristina .... 305-237-3350 103 L
cflorez1@mdc.edu
FLOREZ-NEVAREZ, Tina 254-519-8015 459 D
t.flores@tamuct.edu
FLORIAN, Greg, E .... 217-875-7200 149 J
gflorian@richland.edu
FLORIAN, James, S .... 520-621-3680.. 16 J
florianj@email.arizona.edu
FLORIAN, Kelley .... 804-627-5300 478 I
kelley_florian@bshsi.org
FLORIO, Laura, L .... 712-274-5381 172 A
floriol@morningside.edu
FLOROS, John .... 785-532-6147 179 A
floros@ksu.edu
FLORY, Julie, A .... 314-935-5408 269 L
julie.flory@wustl.edu
FLORY, Nathan .... 903-923-2137 448 J
nflory@etbu.edu
FLOT, Rob .... 323-259-2500.. 54 E
rflot@oxy.edu
FLOTTE, Terence, R .... 508-856-8000 217 C
terry.flotte@umassmed.edu
FLOUHOUSE, Steve .... 606-326-2055 185 E
steve.flouhouse@kctcs.edu
FLOURNOY, Eric .... 706-385-1459 124 F
FLOURNOY, Jacob, W .. 501-686-2901.. 21 H
jwflournoy@uasys.edu
FLOWER, Hannah .... 912-525-5000 125 B
hcrocket@scad.edu
FLOWER, Mark .... 212-621-3789 302 F
mflower@jjay.cuny.edu
FLOWER KIM, Laura ..... 626-395-6330.. 29 I
laura.flowerkim@caltech.edu

FLOWERS, Alisa .... 657-278-2998.. 32 B
aflowers@fullerton.edu
FLOWERS, Carol, A ...... 404-727-0833 119 B
caflowe@emory.edu
FLOWERS, Damon .... 734-677-5322 238 G
dflowers@wccnet.edu
FLOWERS, Daniel .... 574-284-4574 163 J
dflowers@saintmarys.edu
FLOWERS, Eric .... 870-230-5420.. 19 H
flowers@hsu.edu
FLOWERS, Gayle .... 318-678-6000 192 C
gflowers@bpcc.edu
FLOWERS, Geni .... 843-521-4122 425 B
meflower@uscb.edu
FLOWERS, George .... 334-844-4700.... 4 D
flowegt@auburn.edu
FLOWERS, Kathleen .... 315-781-3825 310 C
kflowers@hws.edu
FLOWERS, Ken .... 269-927-4103 232 G
flowers@lakemichigancollege.edu
FLOWERS, Laura .... 615-550-3168 441 C
laura@williamsoncc.edu
FLOWERS, Marshall .... 276-326-4355 478 H
mflowers@bluefield.edu
FLOWERS, Patricia, J .... 850-644-0415 110 A
pjflowers@fsu.edu
FLOWERS, Robert .... 315-781-3827 310 C
flowers@hws.edu
FLOYD, Andrew .... 229-430-3983 114 I
andrew.floyd@asurams.edu
FLOYD, Arlene .... 330-941-2333 374 E
afloyd@ysu.edu
FLOYD, Barbara .... 419-530-8549 372 F
barbara.floyd@utoledo.edu
FLOYD, Brian .... 304-367-4786 503 C
brian.floyd@pierpont.edu
FLOYD, David .... 225-765-2437 193 M
dfloyd@lsu.edu
FLOYD, Dawn .... 828-328-7040 339 C
dawn.floyd@lr.edu
FLOYD, Deborah .... 561-297-4358 109 B
dfloyd@fau.edu
FLOYD, India .... 215-612-6600 390 B
ifloyd@chicareers.com
FLOYD, James, J .... 909-621-8351.. 38 A
james.floyd@cmc.edu
FLOYD, Linda .... 706-233-7357 125 E
lfloyd@shorter.edu
FLOYD, Morris .... 316-942-4291 180 D
floydm@newmanu.edu
FLOYD, Polly, K .... 850-263-3261.. 95 F
pkfloyd@baptistcollege.edu
FLOYD, Shawnda .... 972-273-3590 448 C
shawndafloyd@dcccd.edu
FLOYD, Steven .... 405-585-5132 377 A
steven.floyd@okbu.edu
FLOYD, Stuart .... 864-977-7669 422 I
stuart.floyd@ngu.edu
FLOYD, Tony .... 843-383-8175 420 B
tfloyd@coker.edu
FLOYD, Wesley .... 662-720-7594 255 B
wcfloyd@nemcc.edu
FLOYD-SMITH, Tamara .. 334-727-8953.... 7 F
tfloyd@mytu.tuskegee.edu
FLUCKEY, Kari .... 402-461-7300 274 I
kfluckey@hastings.edu
FLUEGEMAN, Tere .... 949-582-4920.. 64 H
tfluegeman@socccd.edu
FLUET, Gregoire, J .... 845-569-3154 316 B
gregoire.fluet@msmc.edu
FLUGSTAD, Bjorn .... 928-523-4240.. 14 K
bjorn.flugstad@nau.edu
FLUGUM, Deborah .... 818-677-2301.. 33 B
deborah.flugum@csun.edu
FLUHARTY, Steven, J .... 215-898-7320 412 G
sasdean@sas.upenn.edu
FLUKE, Donald, W .... 574-372-5100 158 B
dwfluke@grace.edu
FLUKE, Lauri, A .... 405-585-5131 377 A
lauri.fluke@okbu.edu
FLUKER, Marcus .... 256-761-6100.... 7 D
mfluker@talladega.edu
FLUKER, Zillah .... 334-229-5679.... 4 A
zfluker@alasu.edu
FLUNKER, Thomas, G ... 507-933-7449 242 D
tflunker@gustavus.edu
FLUSCHE, Sara .... 940-668-3351 453 L
sflusche@nctc.edu
FLY, Chris .... 405-878-5142 379 G
cafly@stgregorys.edu
FLY, Pam .... 918-444-2060 376 G
fly@nsuok.edu
FLYNN, JR., Charles, L 718-405-3232 304 H
charles.flynn@mountsaintvincent.edu
FLYNN, Chris .... 540-231-6557 490 F
flynnc@vt.edu
FLYNN, Christie .... 253-964-6553 497 B
cflynn@pierce.ctc.edu

FLYNN, Clif .... 864-503-5635 425 H
cflynn@uscupstate.edu
FLYNN, Daniel .... 561-297-0268 109 B
flynnd@fau.edu
FLYNN, Eric, F .... 203-285-2371.. 85 E
eflynn@gwcc.commnet.edu
FLYNN, Erin .... 503-725-8490 386 D
erin.flynn@pdx.edu
FLYNN, Gary .... 262-564-3218 513 G
flynng@gtc.edu
FLYNN, Jackie .... 412-391-7021 413 J
admissions@vettechinstitute.edu
FLYNN, Jay .... 205-726-2732.... 6 G
jflynn@samford.edu
FLYNN, Jeff .... 208-562-3220 132 A
jeffflynn@cwidaho.cc
FLYNN, Joan .... 410-617-5161 205 A
jflynn@loyola.edu
FLYNN, John, J .... 212-769-5055 321 B
FLYNN, Karen .... 203-932-7317.. 89 D
kflynn@newhaven.edu
FLYNN, Kathy, A .... 319-296-4218 169 H
kathleen.flynn@hawkeyecollege.edu
FLYNN, Mari .... 570-945-8335 398 C
mari.flynn@keystone.edu
FLYNN, Marilyn, L .... 213-740-8311.. 72 B
mflynn@usc.edu
FLYNN, Mark .... 706-568-2080 118 C
flynn_mark@columbusstate.edu
FLYNN, Maura .... 716-926-8822 310 B
mflynn@hilbert.edu
FLYNN, Michael .... 716-685-9631 317 A
mflynn@nycc.edu
FLYNN, Molly .... 716-829-8313 307 B
flynnm@dyc.edu
FLYNN, Seth, M .... 414-955-4780 508 D
sflynn@mcw.edu
FLYNN, Stuart, D .... 602-827-2066.. 16 J
flynns@email.arizona.edu
FLYNN, Thomas, F .... 610-796-8203 389 A
tom.flynn@alvernia.edu
FLYNN, Thomas, V .... 505-565-1413 224 H
tflynn@stonehill.edu
FOBBS, Shelia .... 318-274-3350 196 G
fobbshe@gram.edu
FOCARETO, Nicole .... 704-461-6665 335 J
nicolefocareto@bac.edu
FOCKLER, Debra .... 509-359-6348 494 D
dfockler@ewu.edu
FODNESS, Kacie .... 605-256-5100 428 G
kacie.fodness@dsu.edu
FOECKLER, Michael, S .. 540-636-2900 479 G
foeckler@christendom.edu
FOEHL, Brooks, L .... 413-597-4408 226 C
brooks.l.foehl@williams.edu
FOELSCH, Joseph .... 212-772-4540 302 E
jf1128@hunter.cuny.edu
FOERSTER, Amy .... 570-577-1954 390 H
amy.foerster@bucknell.edu
FOERSTER, Amy, C .... 570-577-1954 390 H
amy.foerster@bucknell.edu
FOGARTY, John .... 850-644-1346 110 A
john.fogarty@med.fsu.edu
FOGARTY, Raymond ...... 401-232-6407 416 A
rfogarty@bryant.edu
FOGARTY, Timothy, P ... 814-393-2235 405 H
tfogarty@clarion.edu
FOGARTY, William .... 413-552-2800 219 G
bfogarty@hcc.edu
FOGEL, Henry .... 312-341-3782 150 D
hfogel@roosevelt.edu
FOGEL, Kim .... 864-592-4600 424 C
FOGERTY, Jennifer .... 215-503-6335 411 E
jennifer.fogerty@jefferson.edu
FOGG, Davina, K .... 509-527-4201 499 E
davina.fogg@wwcc.edu
FOGG, Richard .... 785-320-4557 179 E
richardfogg@manhattantech.edu
FOGGS, Ranodore, M .... 618-537-6911 145 C
rmfoggs@mckendree.edu
FOGLE, Laura .... 803-793-5129 420 G
foglel@denmarktech.edu
FOGLE, Leann .... 906-487-7276 230 B
leann.fogle@finlandia.edu
FOGLE, Shanda .... 803-780-1360 426 F
sruffin@voorhees.edu
FOGLEMAN, David .... 318-670-9590 196 A
dfogleman@susla.edu
FOGLIASSO, John .... 316-942-4291 180 D
fogliassoj@newmanu.edu
FOGT, James .... 314-340-3541 260 H
fogtj@hssu.edu
FOHL, Dana .... 859-622-6973 184 F
dana.fohl@eku.edu
FOHRMAN, Jonathan .... 760-757-2121.. 52 F
jfohrman@miracosta.edu
FOIL WHITE, Quincy ..... 704-330-6863 342 A
quincy.foil@cpcc.edu

FOISY, Brian, R .... 208-885-6174 132 I
brianfoisy@uidaho.edu
FOK, Kristie .... 602-286-8062.. 13 G
kristie.fok@gatewaycc.edu
FOLADARE, Joshua .... 315-781-3700 310 C
foladare@hws.edu
FOLBERG, Robert .... 248-370-3634 235 J
rfolberg@oakland.edu
FOLDA, Joe .... 719-549-2730.. 78 P
joe.folda@csupueblo.edu
FOLDARE, Joshua .... 585-385-8198 322 E
jfoldare@sjfc.edu
FOLDEN, Tracey .... 812-488-2509 164 G
tf91@evansville.edu
FOLDS-BENNETT,
Trisha, H .... 843-953-5084 420 C
foldsbennettt@cofc.edu
FOLEY, Anne .... 312-369-7477 136 H
afoley@colum.edu
FOLEY, Beth .... 435-797-1437 473 C
beth.foley@usu.edu
FOLEY, Brad .... 541-346-5661 387 F
bfoley@uoregon.edu
FOLEY, Chris .... 844-948-4863 159 H
cfoley@iu.edu
FOLEY, Chris, J .... 844-948-4863 159 G
cfoley@iu.edu
FOLEY, Erin .... 410-532-3586 206 D
efoley@ndm.edu
FOLEY, Erin .... 541-885-1013 385 E
erin.foley@oit.edu
FOLEY, Francis, P .... 410-293-1104 519 E
ffoley@usna.edu
FOLEY, Hank .... 516-686-7650 317 G
president@nyit.edu
FOLEY, Janice, A .... 336-841-9506 338 E
jfoley@highpoint.edu
FOLEY, Jeremy, N .... 352-375-4683 110 D
jeremy@gators.uaa.ufl.edu
FOLEY, John .... 508-793-7444 213 C
jfoley@clarku.edu
FOLEY, Kathleen .... 570-674-6403 401 M
kfoley@misericordia.edu
FOLEY, Kevin .... 631-451-4380 330 B
foleyk@sunysuffolk.edu
FOLEY, Lee .... 859-371-9393 183 G
lfoley@beckfield.edu
FOLEY, Linda .... 402-354-7050 275 P
linda.foley@methodistcollege.edu
FOLEY, Marie .... 973-761-9015 291 F
marie.foleyll@shu.edu
FOLEY, Mary .... 620-792-9278 175 C
foleym@bartonccc.edu
FOLEY, Nick .... 816-331-5700 265 D
nfoley@pcitraining.edu
FOLEY, Paul, J .... 563-333-6025 173 A
foleypaulj@sau.edu
FOLEY, Phyllis .... 615-230-4828 438 C
phyllis.foley@volstate.edu
FOLEY, Richard, T .... 304-457-6260 501 A
foleyrt@ab.edu
FOLEY, Rob .... 303-357-5838.. 79 G
rob.foley@denverseminary.edu
FOLEY, Robert .... 516-572-7677 316 C
robert.foley@ncc.edu
FOLEY, Ryan .... 912-688-6061 123 J
rfoley@ogeecheetech.edu
FOLEY, Susan .... 248-689-8282 238 F
sfoley@walshcollege.edu
FOLEY, Thomas .... 413-265-2494 213 E
foleyt@elms.edu
FOLEY, Thomas, P .... 814-886-6411 402 E
tfoley@mtaloy.edu
FOLGER, Pamela, M ...... 217-424-6294 145 J
pmfolger@millikin.edu
FOLK, Kevin .... 417-862-9533 260 D
kfolk@globaluniversity.edu
FOLKESTAD, William ..... 719-549-2865.. 78 P
william.folkestad@csupueblo.edu
FOLKS, Liesl .... 716-645-2771 325 B
seasdean@eng.buffalo.edu
FOLKS, Lonnie .... 609-652-4877 291 H
lonnie.folks@stockton.edu
FOLLICK, David .... 516-572-7210 316 C
david.follick@ncc.edu
FOLLICK, Edwin .... 714-533-1495.. 64 F
edfollick@southbaylo.edu
FOLLOWELL, Coleen ..... 562-985-4121.. 32 C
coleen.followell@csulb.edu
FOLLOWELL, Wendell .... 859-256-3100 185 D
wendell.followell@kctcs.edu
FOLSE, Dick .... 309-556-3058 141 B
dfolse@iwu.edu
FOLSE, Victoria .... 309-556-3051 141 B
nursing@iwu.edu
FOLSOM, Michele .... 716-888-8367 300 G
folsom@canisius.edu

FORRY, Jennifer .... 617-713-5901 223 B
jennifer.forry@newbury.edu
FORS, Brian .... 507-280-2816 247 D
brian.fors@rctc.edu
FORSDICK, Emily .... 901-321-3461 431 A
emathis@cbu.edu
FORSETH, Eric, A .... 712-722-6004 168 I
eric.forseth@dordt.edu
FORSHEY, Jennifer .... 906-932-4231 230 D
jenniferf@gogebic.edu
FORSSTROM, Janice, M 978-762-4000 220 E
jforsstr@northshore.edu
FORSTER, Dan .... 413-572-5365 218 F
dforster@westfield.ma.edu
FORSTER, Jerry .... 304-929-1478 502 E
jerryforster@ucwv.edu
FORSTER, Kathy .... 716-673-3341 325 C
kathy.forster@fredonia.edu
FORSTER, Sarah .... 507-222-4206 241 C
sforster@carleton.edu
FORSTMAN, Valerie .... 817-257-7513 445 H
v.forstman@tcu.edu
FORSYTH, Anne, S .... 805-525-4417.. 67 E
aforsyth@thomasaquinas.edu
FORSYTH, Nate .... 641-648-4611 170 H
nate.forsyth@iavalley.edu
FORSYTHE, Marty .... 251-405-7070.... 1 E
mforsythe@bishop.edu
FORSYTHE, Micah .... 406-586-3585 271 E
micah.forsythe@montanabiblecollege.edu
FORSYTHE, Robert, E .... 313-577-4501 239 C
robert.forsythe@wayne.edu
FORSYTHE, Ryan .... 508-929-8498 219 A
rforsythe@worcester.edu
FORT, Gregg .... 607-431-4026 309 E
fortg@hartwick.edu
FORT, Rebecca, L .... 330-471-8313 364 H
rfort@malone.edu
FORTE, Joe .... 603-456-2656 281 H
jforte@northeastcatholic.edu
FORTE, Mario .... 831-582-4796.. 33 A
mforte@csumb.edu
FORTE, Paul, D .... 828-262-2030 349 H
fortepd@appstate.edu
FORTE, Teresa (Terrie) .. 413-747-0204 213 B
teresa.forte@cambridgecollege.edu
FORTGANG, William ..... 631-656-3189 308 F
william.fortgang@ftc.edu
FORTHMAN, Emily .... 618-634-3223 151 G
emilyf@shawneecc.edu
FORTHOFER, Scott .... 406-496-4500 272 E
sforthofer@mtech.edu
FORTI, Kevin .... 401-454-6651 417 B
kforti@risd.edu
FORTIN, Barbara .... 530-898-4113.. 31 D
bfortin@csuchico.edu
FORTIN, Maurice, G ...... 325-942-2222 463 C
maurice.fortin@angelo.edu
FORTIN-WAVRA,
Marion .... 402-554-4800 277 I
mfortin-wavra@unomaha.edu
FORTINI, Mary-Ellen ..... 408-554-4806.. 62 F
mfortini@scu.edu
FORTINO, Matthew .... 212-924-5900 330 G
mfortino@swedishinstitute.edu
FORTMAN, Brian, J .... 864-833-8287 423 D
bjfortman@presby.edu
FORTMAN, Susan .... 516-323-4311 315 J
sfortman@molloy.edu
FORTNER, Beverly .... 785-832-6659 178 A
beverly.fortner@bie.edu
FORTNER, Everette .... 434-924-8900 486 H
ewf5db@virginia.edu
FORTNER, James .... 404-894-7894 120 A
james.fortner@business.gatech.edu
FORTNER, Martin .... 318-670-9322 196 A
mfortner@susla.edu
FORTNER, Melissa .... 706-865-2134 126 G
mfortner@truett.edu
FORTRESS, Marty .... 517-750-1200 237 D
marty.fortress@arbor.edu
FORTSCH, Peggy .... 319-226-2031 166 C
peggy.fortsch@allencollege.edu
FORTSON, Carolyn .... 803-793-5213 420 G
fortsonc@denmarktech.edu
FORTSON, Daniel .... 415-442-7000.. 44 E
dfortson@ggu.edu
FORTSON, Jill .... 325-674-2653 441 D
jill.fortson@acu.edu
FORTUNATO, Frank .... 904-264-2172 106 I
frank.fortunato@om.org
FORTUNE, Diana .... 518-891-2915 319 A
dfortune@nccc.edu
FORTUNE, Lydell .... 716-842-2770 307 I
FOSCHIA, Christine .... 724-805-2524 410 B
chris.foschia@stvincent.edu
FOSCHIA, Christine, L ... 724-805-2524 410 C
christine.foschia@stvincent.edu
FOSDYCK, Rick .... 641-683-5117 169 I
rick.fosdyck@indianhills.edu
FOSHANG, Trevor .... 952-885-5462 249 F
tfoshang@nwhealth.edu
FOSHEE, Brian, E .... 901-843-3870 435 L
foshee@rhodes.edu
FOSHEE, Kenneth, H ..... 205-348-2857..... 8 A
ken.foshee@ua.edu
FOSKEY, Becky .... 478-289-2104 118 H
bfoskey@ega.edu
FOSS, Ben .... 941-487-4777 110 B
bfoss@ncf.edu
FOSS, Erica .... 620-278-4213 181 G
efoss@sterling.edu
FOSS, Heather .... 206-934-6616 497 J
heather.foss@seattlecolleges.edu
FOSS, Jennifer, J .... 757-683-3132 483 G
jfoss@odu.edu
FOSS, Lisa .... 320-308-4028 247 E
lhfoss@stcloudstate.edu
FOSSEN, Linda .... 360-752-8440 492 H
lfossen@btc.edu
FOSSEN, Sarah .... 612-330-1565 240 G
fossen@augsburg.edu
FOSSUM, Dallas .... 701-671-2314 355 B
dallas.fossum@ndscs.edu
FOSSUM, Michael, E ..... 409-740-4408 459 C
fossum@tamu.edu
FOSSUM, Scott .... 605-995-7178 427 E
scott.fossum@mitchelltech.edu
FOSSUM, Theresa, W .... 630-515-7663 145 I
tfossum@midwestern.edu
FOSTER, Alan .... 918-781-7285 374 H
fostera@bacone.edu
FOSTER, Andrew .... 203-773-8542.. 84 G
afoster@albertus.edu
FOSTER, Anne .... 513-569-1898 359 G
anne.foster@cincinnatistate.edu
FOSTER, Ben .... 972-524-3341 457 H
FOSTER, Cherie, A .... 248-341-2117 235 D
cafoster@oaklandcc.edu
FOSTER, Clark, M .... 518-564-3601 327 E
fostercm@plattsburgh.edu
FOSTER, Claybourne ..... 901-435-1307 433 A
claybourne_foster@loc.edu
FOSTER, Colleen .... 575-835-5525 294 K
colleen.foster@nmt.edu
FOSTER, Connie .... 270-745-2904 190 F
connie.foster@wku.edu
FOSTER, Delbert, T .... 803-536-8191 423 G
dfoster@scsu.edu
FOSTER, Diane .... 610-359-5100 393 E
dfoster@dccc.edu
FOSTER, Donna .... 864-941-8430 423 C
foster.d@ptc.edu
FOSTER, Doug .... 803-777-0707 424 I
drdofster@mailbox.sc.edu
FOSTER, Dyrell .... 951-571-6384.. 58 F
dyrell.foster@mvc.edu
FOSTER, Gretchen, K ..... 308-635-6183 278 B
fosterg2@wncc.edu
FOSTER, Isaac .... 646-378-6125 319 C
isaac.foster@nyack.edu
FOSTER, Jackie .... 910-362-7019 341 E
jfoster@cfcc.edu
FOSTER, James, E .... 503-554-2144 383 C
jfoster@georgefox.edu
FOSTER, Janet .... 562-985-5459.. 32 C
janet.foster@csulb.edu
FOSTER, John .... 843-383-8136 420 B
jfoster@coker.edu
FOSTER, Joseph .... 703-284-1646 483 A
joseph.foster@marymount.edu
FOSTER, Karen .... 318-342-5236 198 A
kfoster@ulm.edu
FOSTER, Karen .... 208-535-5343 131 G
karen.foster@my.eitc.edu
FOSTER, Kathryn, A .... 207-778-7256 201 D
kfoster@maine.edu
FOSTER, Kathryn, V .... 512-232-3316 467 C
k.foster@austin.utexas.edu
FOSTER, Kevin .... 212-650-6201 301 F
kfoster@ccny.cuny.edu
FOSTER, Kristen .... 559-730-3921.. 39 G
kristenf@cos.edu
FOSTER, Lauren .... 828-898-2496 339 B
fosterlm@lmc.edu
FOSTER, Linda .... 904-470-8012.. 98 B
lefoster@ewc.edu
FOSTER, Marieo .... 202-274-5050.. 93 D
marieo.foster@udc.edu
FOSTER, Mary Louise ... 402-844-7129 276 G
marylouise@northeast.edu
FOSTER, Meezie .... 302-225-6235.. 90 G
fosterm@gbc.edu
FOSTER, Meichele .... 573-876-7110 267 G
mfoster@stephens.edu
FOSTER, Michelle, R ..... 407-582-2008 113 F
mrfoster@valenciacollege.edu
FOSTER, Mike .... 207-941-7063 199 B
fostermi@husson.edu
FOSTER, Mike .... 641-673-1058 174 F
fostermik@wmpenn.edu
FOSTER, Morris, W .... 757-683-3460 483 G
mfoster@odu.edu
FOSTER, Nicola .... 212-346-1949 319 J
nfoster@pace.edu
FOSTER, Pam .... 785-670-1509 182 D
pam.foster@washburn.edu
FOSTER, Paul .... 406-657-1705 272 B
paul.foster4@msubillings.edu
FOSTER, Paul, C .... 513-558-9021 371 E
paul.foster@uc.edu
FOSTER, Robert, W .... 304-647-6285 504 F
rfoster@osteo.wvsom.edu
FOSTER, Scot .... 510-869-8921.. 59 F
sfoster@samuelmerritt.edu
FOSTER, Shelby .... 510-659-7369.. 54 F
sfoster@ohlone.edu
FOSTER, Stacey .... 314-539-5185 266 E
sfoster@stlcc.edu
FOSTER, Stephanie .... 703-993-5106 481 B
sfoste21@gmu.edu
FOSTER, Steve .... 281-998-6075 460 G
sfoster@txchiro.edu
FOSTER, Tim .... 559-730-3902.. 39 G
timf@cos.edu
FOSTER, Tim .... 970-248-1498.. 77 K
tfoster@coloradomesa.edu
FOSTER, Timothy .... 717-757-1100 415 J
tim.foster@yti.edu
FOSTER, Timothy, J ...... 309-341-7814 142 G
tfoster@knox.edu
FOSTER, Timothy, W ..... 207-725-3228 198 G
tfoster@bowdoin.edu
FOSTER, Todd .... 803-705-4565 418 G
todd.foster@benedict.edu
FOSTER, Traci, L .... 334-683-5190.... 6 C
tfoster@judson.edu
FOSTER, Tracy .... 920-206-2388 508 A
tracy.foster@mbu.edu
FOSTER, Vicki .... 828-898-8785 339 B
fosterv@lmc.edu
FOSTER ZSIGA, Erin ..... 207-786-6215 198 E
efoster@bates.edu
FOSTNER, Jay, J .... 920-403-3169 509 J
jay.fostner@snc.edu
FOTH, Rod .... 336-334-4822 343 E
rsfoth@gtcc.edu
FOTI, Bill .... 603-526-3613 280 H
wfoti@colby-sawyer.edu
FOTIOO, Jamie .... 501-450-1373.. 19 I
fotioo@hendrix.edu
FOTOUHI, Farshad .... 313-577-3776 239 C
fotouhi@wayne.edu
FOUBERG, Andi .... 605-697-5198 429 B
andi.fouberg@statealum.com
FOUBERG, Erin .... 605-626-3456 428 H
erin.fouberg@northern.edu
FOUCART, Steve .... 417-836-4563 263 H
stevefoucart@missouristate.edu
FOUCHT, Craig .... 919-735-5151 347 E
cfoucht@waynecc.edu
FOUGERE, John .... 573-882-0601 268 B
fougerej@umsystem.edu
FOUGERES, Michel .... 727-864-7987.. 97 O
fougermw@eckerd.edu
FOUGHT, Rick .... 901-448-5694 440 C
rfought1@uthsc.edu
FOUGHT, Wendy .... 231-439-6349 234 H
wfought@ncmich.edu
FOULKROD,
Marianna, K .... 317-788-3302 164 H
mfoulkrod@uindy.edu
FOUNTAIN, Cheryl, A ... 904-620-2496 110 E
fountain@unf.edu
FOUNTAIN, Jennifer ...... 541-552-6234 386 H
fountainj@sou.edu
FOUNTAIN, Wesley .... 910-672-1685 350 B
wtfountain01@uncfsu.edu
FOUNTAINE, Cynthia ..... 618-453-8761 152 B
fountaine@siu.edu
FOURMAN, Elizabeth ..... 574-284-4584 163 J
efourman@saintmarys.edu
FOURMY CUTRER,
Emily .... 903-223-3001 460 D
emily.cutrer@tamut.edu
FOURNIER, Eric .... 205-726-2113.... 6 G
ejfourni@samford.edu
FOURNIER, Jody .... 614-236-6445 358 A
jfournier@capital.edu
FOURNIER, Nicole .... 207-768-9589 201 G
nicole.l.fournier@maine.edu
FOURNIER, Robert .... 313-577-4280 239 C
ai5611@wayne.edu
FOURNIER, Timothy, J .. 848-932-9955 290 A
timothy.fournier@rutgers.edu
FOUST, Amanda .... 785-309-3114 181 D
amanda.foust@salinatech.edu
FOUST, Dane, R .... 410-543-6080 209 B
drfoust@salisbury.edu
FOUST, David .... 901-751-8453 434 E
dfoust@mabts.edu
FOUST, Jasper .... 706-646-6302 126 B
jfoust@sctech.edu
FOUST, John .... 585-785-1599 308 D
john.foust@flcc.edu
FOUST, Julia .... 708-239-4608 153 B
julia.foust@trnty.edu
FOUST, Kevin .... 540-231-6512 490 F
foustk@vt.edu
FOUTS, Susan .... 828-227-7397 352 C
sfouts@wcu.edu
FOUTY, Dennis .... 832-842-4603 464 F
dfouty@uh.edu
FOUTY, Dennis .... 832-842-4603 465 A
dfouty@uh.edu
FOUTZ, Jason .... 928-536-7440.. 15 B
jason.foutz@npc.edu
FOWL, Steve .... 410-617-2327 205 A
sfowl@loyola.edu
FOWLE, Marilyn .... 940-397-4117 453 C
marilyn.fowle@mwsu.edu
FOWLER, Bill .... 870-864-7146.. 21 D
bfowler@southark.edu
FOWLER, Carlton .... 816-604-4101 262 K
carlton.fowler@mcckc.edu
FOWLER, Christopher .... 419-358-3409 357 E
fowlerc@bluffton.edu
FOWLER, Craig .... 828-227-7282 352 C
cfowler@wcu.edu
FOWLER, Craig .... 715-234-7082 515 D
craig.fowler@witc.edu
FOWLER, George, J .... 757-683-4141 483 G
gfowler@odu.edu
FOWLER, Gregory .... 603-626-9100 282 C
g.fowler@snhu.edu
FOWLER, Heather, L ...... 570-577-1188 390 H
h.fowler@bucknell.edu
FOWLER, James, R .... 401-341-2908 417 D
jim.fowler@salve.edu
FOWLER, Jason .... 919-761-2252 349 C
jfowler@sebts.edu
FOWLER, Jeffrey .... 314-977-2849 266 J
fowlerjl@slu.edu
FOWLER, Julie, H .... 903-983-8281 451 F
jfowler@kilgore.edu
FOWLER, Justin .... 503-552-1517 384 F
jfowler@nunm.edu
FOWLER, Kelly .... 559-325-5214.. 66 F
kelly.fowler@cloviscollege.edu
FOWLER, Lee .... 864-503-5140 425 H
lfowler2@uscupstate.edu
FOWLER, Liesl, A .... 309-794-7211 133 G
lieslfowler@augustana.edu
FOWLER, Lisa .... 303-914-6302.. 82 B
lisa.fowler@rrcc.edu
FOWLER, Logan .... 208-792-2200 132 C
ljfowler@lcsc.edu
FOWLER, Marc .... 616-222-1443 229 B
marc.fowler@cornerstone.edu
FOWLER, Mary .... 770-533-6918 122 E
mfowler@laniertech.edu
FOWLER, Matt .... 618-262-8641 140 F
fowlerm@iecc.edu
FOWLER, Matthew .... 913-288-7326 178 H
ffowler@kckcc.edu
FOWLER, Mike .... 502-451-0815 189 F
mfowler@sullivan.edu
FOWLER, Pamela, W ..... 734-763-4119 237 I
pfowler@umich.edu
FOWLER, Paul .... 404-727-0512 119 B
pgfowle@emory.edu
FOWLER, Paul .... 337-550-1433 194 B
pfowler@lsue.edu
FOWLER, Perphelia .... 505-786-4100 294 I
FOWLER, Peter .... 617-989-4082 225 E
fowlerp@wit.edu
FOWLER, Ramsey .... 512-448-8736 455 I
ramseyf@stedwards.edu
FOWLER, Robert .... 315-866-0300 310 A
fowlerrc@herkimer.edu
FOWLER, S. Kevin .... 903-510-2307 464 D
kfow@tjc.edu
FOWLER, Sandra .... 229-931-2237 120 F
sandra.fowler@gsw.edu
FOWLER, Sandy .... 530-674-9199.. 35 D
sfowler@cambridge.edu
FOWLER, Sky .... 618-252-5400 151 J
sky.fowler@sic.edu

FRANKLIN, Cathy .... 803-705-4781 418 G cathy.franklin@benedict.edu
FRANKLIN, Celeste .... 215-972-7600 404 Q
FRANKLIN, David .... 202-274-5706.. 93 D david.franklin@udc.edu
FRANKLIN, Greta .... 309-556-3412 141 B gfrankli@iwu.edu
FRANKLIN, Janice .... 334-229-4106.... 4 A franklin@alasu.edu
FRANKLIN, Joseph .... 575-835-5964 294 K joe.franklin@nmt.edu
FRANKLIN, Julie .... 801-422-2810 471 E julie_franklin@byu.edu
FRANKLIN, Karen .... 575-624-7138 294 A karen.franklin@roswell.enmu.edu
FRANKLIN, Kathy, C ..... 434-528-5276 491 D kfranklin@vul.edu
FRANKLIN, Katrina, V ... 434-528-5276 491 D tfranklin@vul.edu
FRANKLIN, Laura, A ..... 608-342-1817 511 D franklinl@uwplatt.edu
FRANKLIN, Laurie .... 425-388-9035 494 F lfranklin@everettcc.edu
FRANKLIN, Marshall, E . 864-242-5100 418 H
FRANKLIN, Milton, S .... 540-828-5761 478 J mfranklin@bridgewater.edu
FRANKLIN, Mona .... 785-749-8448 178 A mona.franklin@bie.edu
FRANKLIN, Randall .... 434-832-7617 487 H franklinr@cvcc.vccs.edu
FRANKLIN, Roschoune . 323-856-7621.. 25 L rfranklin@afi.com
FRANKLIN, Shannon ...... 541-278-5951 382 A sfranklin@bluecc.edu
FRANKLIN, Somer .... 936-294-1009 462 F somer@shsu.edu
FRANKLIN, Susan .... 402-461-7410 274 I sfranklin@hastings.edu
FRANKLIN, Timothy, V . 973-596-5515 288 A timothy.v.franklin@njit.edu
FRANKLIN, Truitt .... 706-865-2134 126 G tfranklin@truett.edu
FRANKLIN, William .... 310-243-3784.. 31 E wfranklin@csudh.edu
FRANKMAN, Tom .... 573-592-1166 270 D tom.frankman@williamwoods.edu
FRANKO, Debra .... 617-373-5454 223 D
FRANKOVICH, Lauren .... 917-493-4543 313 M lfrankovich@msmnyc.edu
FRANKOWSKI, Brian ..... 215-991-3736 398 F frankowskib1@lasalle.edu
FRANKS, Billie .... 606-589-3029 187 B billie.franks@kctcs.edu
FRANKS, Brian .... 817-531-4452 463 G bfranks@txwes.edu
FRANKS, Debra, J .... 864-388-8749 422 A jfranks@lander.edu
FRANKS, Dennis .... 336-278-5555 337 G dfranks3@elon.edu
FRANKS, Mark .... 920-498-6269 514 G mark.franks@nwtc.edu
FRANKS, Rita .... 318-257-2577 197 A rfranks@latech.edu
FRANKS, Tammy .... 228-497-7700 254 D tammy.franks@mgccc.edu
FRANKS, Tiffany, M ...... 434-791-5670 478 E tfranks@averett.edu
FRANKS-HELWICH, Stephanie, L .... 724-938-4301 405 F franks@calu.edu
FRANKY, Jason .... 845-569-3394 316 B jason.franky@msmc.edu
FRANKZEN, Rhonda ...... 307-268-2025 516 H rhonda.franzen@caspercollege.edu
FRANQUI, Alicia .... 718-262-2137 304 A afranqui@york.cuny.edu
FRANSON, Terry .... 626-812-3061.. 26 U tfranson@apu.edu
FRANTZ, Jane .... 859-442-1175 185 I jane.frantz@kctcs.edu
FRANTZ, Meg .... 609-633-9658 292 B mfrantz@tesu.edu
FRANTZ, Michael .... 712-749-2140 167 C frantzm@bvu.edu
FRANZ, Brad .... 580-327-8632 376 K bmfranz@nwosu.edu
FRANZ, Chris .... 303-953-3415.. 77 I cfranz@ccu.edu
FRANZ, Janet .... 509-682-6400 500 D jfranz@wvc.edu
FRANZ, Jennifer .... 920-748-8108 509 H franzj@ripon.edu
FRANZ, Mark .... 314-889-1488 260 C mfranz@fontbonne.edu
FRANZ, Matt .... 937-328-6045 359 H franzm@clarkstate.edu
FRANZ, Michelle .... 407-708-2396 107 G franzm@seminolstate.edu
FRANZ, Sandra .... 802-626-4865 477 C sandra.franz@lyndonstate.edu
FRANZ, Sandra, L .... 802-626-4865 477 D sandra.franz@lyndonstate.edu
FRANZ, Scott .... 620-947-3121 181 H scottf@tabor.edu
FRANZ, William, T .... 804-752-7268 484 C wfranz@rmc.edu
FRANZA, Richard, M ..... 706-737-1418 116 B rfranza@augusta.edu
FRANZA, Thomas .... 443-412-2489 204 C tfranza@harford.edu
FRANZEN, Kristine .... 563-387-1330 171 I frankr03@luther.edu
FRANZEO, Linda .... 903-813-2468 443 F bookstore@austincollege.edu
FRASCA, Melissa Sue ... 617-873-0474 213 B melissasue.frasca@cambridgecollege.edu
FRASCIELLO, Michael .... 315-443-5502 330 H mfrascie@syr.edu
FRASCO, Mark .... 970-542-3174.. 81 A mark.frasco@morgancc.edu
FRASER, Bruce .... 772-462-7691 101 Q bfraser@irsc.edu
FRASER, Cathryn .... 507-284-9024 241 F fraser.cathryn@mayo.edu
FRASER, Cathy .... 507-266-7095 241 E cathy.fraser@mayo.edu
FRASER, Dori .... 919-735-5151 347 E dori@waynecc.edu
FRASER, Greg .... 313-664-7660 228 H gfraser@collegeforcreativestudies.edu
FRASER, Heather .... 207-795-7166 199 I fraserhe@mchp.edu
FRASER, Jeanmarie .... 508-362-2131 219 E jfraser@capecod.edu
FRASER, Lynne .... 401-865-1534 416 E lfraser1@providence.edu
FRASER, Morrison .... 217-854-5550 134 E morrison.fraser@blackburn.edu
FRASER, Robin .... 845-368-7241 323 I robin.fraser@use.salvationarmy.org
FRASER, Sheri .... 207-621-3136 201 C fraser@maine.edu
FRASER, Sherry, J .... 914-337-9300 305 F sherry.fraser@concordia-ny.edu
FRASER, Wayne .... 603-366-5266 280 K wfraser@ccsnh.edu
FRASHER, Kristy .... 765-973-8275 160 A sm628@bncollege.com
FRASIER, George .... 253-833-9111 495 C gfrasier@geenriver.edu
FRASSINELLI, David, W 203-254-4254.. 87 A dfrassinelli@fairfield.edu
FRATELLA, Janet .... 541-552-6127 386 H fratellaj@sou.edu
FRATER, Joel, L .... 585-685-6001 315 L jfrater@monroecc.edu
FRATO-SWEENEY, Ed .... 330-569-5239 362 J sweeneyea@hiram.edu
FRAUSTO, Lissa .... 956-295-3771 461 F lissa.frausto@tsc.edu
FRAWLEY, Maria, H ...... 202-242-6817.. 92 A mfrawley@gwu.edu
FRAZE, Steve .... 806-742-2808 463 D steven.fraze@ttu.edu
FRAZEE, David .... 336-506-4135 340 L david.frazee@alamancecc.edu
FRAZEE, Sally, M .... 215-204-8611 411 B sally.frazee@temple.edu
FRAZELL, Mary .... 740-587-5717 361 B frazellm@denison.edu
FRAZER, Christopher, A 978-934-4331 217 B christopher_frazer@uml.edu
FRAZER, Elmo .... 510-654-2934.. 58 K efrazer@expression.edu
FRAZER, Gael .... 850-484-1759 105 E gfrazer@pensacolastate.edu
FRAZER, Gregory .... 251-445-9254..... 9 B rfrazer@southalabama.edu
FRAZER, Thomas, K ...... 352-392-9230 110 D frazer@ufl.edu
FRAZIER, Al .... 501-279-4240.. 19 G afrazier@harding.edu
FRAZIER, III, Arthur, E . 404-270-5436 126 D aefrazier@spelman.edu
FRAZIER, Bryan .... 276-326-4272 478 H bfrazier@bluefield.edu
FRAZIER, Connie .... 701-777-4251 353 G connie.frazier@und.edu
FRAZIER, David .... 918-540-6113 376 F david.frazier@neo.edu
FRAZIER, Deborah .... 360-417-6202 496 I dfrazier@pencol.edu
FRAZIER, Deborah, J .... 870-612-2001.. 22 H debbie.frazier@uaccb.edu
FRAZIER, DeWayne .... 319-385-6205 170 J dewayne.frazier@iw.edu
FRAZIER, Doug .... 912-344-2818 115 D doug.frazier@armstrong.edu
FRAZIER, JR., Ernest, T 504-278-6421 193 B cfrazier@nunez.edu
FRAZIER, Fred .... 801-627-8471 472 D frazierf@owatc.edu
FRAZIER, Herb .... 620-862-5252 175 B herb.frazier@barclaycollege.edu
FRAZIER, John .... 330-823-2243 372 C fraziejl@mountunion.edu
FRAZIER, Julie .... 731-286-3204 437 A frazier@dscc.edu
FRAZIER, Larry .... 903-233-3951 452 A larryfrazier@letu.edu
FRAZIER, Lisa .... 775-753-2147 279 A lisa.frazier@gbcnv.edu
FRAZIER, Lorraine .... 713-500-2001 468 D lorraine.frazier@uth.tmc.edu
FRAZIER, Melissa .... 914-395-2303 323 K mfrazier@sarahlawrence.edu
FRAZIER, Mitsu .... 801-274-3280 474 D mitsu.frazier@wgu.edu
FRAZIER, Renae .... 864-941-8357 423 C frazier.r@ptc.edu
FRAZIER, Royce .... 620-862-5252 175 B president@barclaycollege.edu
FRAZIER, Sean .... 815-753-1000 147 H sfrazier@niu.edu
FRAZIER, Shanelle .... 662-621-4674 252 E sfrazier@coahomacc.edu
FRAZIER, Stephen, L ..... 309-298-4500 155 D sl-frazier@wiu.edu
FRAZIER, Steven, R .... 860-738-6409.. 86 C sfrazier@nwcc.edu
FRAZIER-HELD, Jamie ... 912-650-5672 125 H jfrazier-held@southuniversity.edu
FRAZOR, Diane .... 210-826-7595 470 I frazord@wbu.edu
FRAZZA, Christian .... 406-447-4344 270 H cfrazza@carroll.edu
FREAD, Marilyn .... 630-889-6661 147 D mfread@nuhs.edu
FRECHETTE, Carri .... 207-699-5073 199 H cfrechette@meca.edu
FRECHETTE, Michael, T . 253-535-7164 496 G frechemt@plu.edu
FRED, Leota .... 406-586-3585 271 E leota.fred@montanabiblecollege.edu
FREDA, Kristin .... 212-875-4450 298 H kfreda@bankstreet.edu
FREDEEN, DonnaJean, A .... 609-896-5010 289 E dfredeen@rider.edu
FREDENBURGH, III, Paul, H .... 202-685-4342 518 B paul.h.fredenburgh@ndu.edu
FREDERICK, Brian .... 337-482-6480 197 F jdh7220@louisiana.edu
FREDERICK, David .... 513-721-7944 362 D dfrederick@gbs.edu
FREDERICK, Debra .... 605-274-5514 426 K deb.frederick@augie.edu
FREDERICK, G. Marcille, H .... 540-432-4170 480 A marci.frederick@emu.edu
FREDERICK, Heidi .... 615-248-1529 439 B hrfrederick@trevecca.edu
FREDERICK, Jeff .... 910-521-6439 351 E jeff.frederick@uncp.edu
FREDERICK, Julia .... 337-482-6700 197 F jcg0624@louisiana.edu
FREDERICK, Lesley, J .... 217-786-2597 144 B lesley.frederick@llcc.edu
FREDERICK, Linda, D .... 504-286-5106 195 L lfrederick@suno.edu
FREDERICK, Michelle .... 202-885-2689.. 91 C afrederi@american.edu
FREDERICK, Pam .... 540-423-9125 488 B pfrederick@germanna.edu
FREDERICK, Richard .... 662-252-8000 255 F rfrederick@rustcollege.edu
FREDERICK, Robert .... 256-824-7200.... 8 C robert.frederick@uah.edu
FREDERICK, Robert, J .... 319-273-6857 167 A robert.frederick@uni.edu
FREDERICK, Steven, G .. 518-562-4195 304 C steven.frederick@clinton.edu
FREDERICK, Todd .... 805-546-3118.. 41 C tfrederi@cuesta.edu
FREDERICK, Wayne .... 202-806-2500.. 92 C wfrederick@howard.edu
FREDERICK-RITZ, Misty 814-234-7755 410 G mfrederickritz@southhills.edu
FREDERICKS, Dan .... 601-968-5977 252 C dfredericks@belhaven.edu
FREDERICKS, Kimberly .. 518-292-1782 321 G fredek1@sage.edu
FREDERICKSON, Joel .... 651-638-6317 240 J frejoe@bethel.edu
FREDERIKSEN, Jens ...... 615-329-8762 431 I jfrederiksen@fisk.edu
FREDETTE, Emile .... 802-728-1292 477 E efredett@vtc.edu
FREDRICH, Dolores .... 516-463-1800 310 D dolores.fredrich@hofstra.edu
FREDRICK, Kay .... 605-626-2518 428 H kay.fredrick@northern.edu
FREDRICKSON, Angela .. 402-375-7220 276 D anfredr1@wsc.edu
FREDRICKSON, Kurt ...... 626-584-5654.. 43 K kurtf@fuller.edu
FREDRIKSON, Dawn ...... 708-974-5202 146 C fredrikson@morainevalley.edu
FREDS, Anthony .... 989-317-4602 234 B afreds@midmich.edu
FREDSON, Janice .... 509-682-6505 500 D jfredson@wvc.edu
FREE, Carolyn, G .... 803-536-8402 423 G cfree@scsu.edu
FREE, Rhona, C .... 860-231-5221.. 89 E rfree@usj.edu
FREE, Rikky, L .... 501-882-4445.. 17 M rlfree@asub.edu
FREEBOURN, Randal ..... 937-327-7009 374 A freebournr@wittenberg.edu
FREEBURGH, Charles .... 225-216-8162 192 B freeburghc@mybrcc.edu
FREED, Carol .... 507-389-7211 247 H carol.freed@southcentral.edu
FREED, Curt .... 970-542-3105.. 81 A curt.freed@morgancc.edu
FREED, Linda .... 817-257-7516 461 A linda.freed@tcu.edu
FREED, Suzanne, K .... 518-242-6046 324 G sfreed@albany.edu
FREED, Ty .... 812-888-4447 165 E tfreed@vinu.edu
FREEDLAND, Gregory .... 717-871-5874 407 A gregory.freedland@millersville.edu
FREEDMAN, Cheryl .... 215-468-8800 397 L admissions@culinaryarts.edu
FREEDMAN, Daniel .... 845-257-3728 325 D freedmad@newpaltz.edu
FREEDMAN, Kimberly ... 617-588-1367 211 G kfreedman@bfit.edu
FREEDMAN, Michael ..... 301-985-7200 208 D michael.freedman@umuc.edu
FREEDMAN, Phyllis, D .. 304-326-1390 502 D pfreedman@salemu.edu
FREEDMAN, Stephen ..... 718-817-3040 308 G sfreedman@fordham.edu
FREEDMAN, Victoria ..... 212-430-3179 334 P vfreedman@aecom.yu.edu
FREEDMAN, Wendy, A .. 845-437-5700 333 A wefreedman@vassar.edu
FREEED, Rusty .... 254-968-9746 459 A freed@tarleton.edu
FREEH, Mary Beth .... 610-606-4605 392 A mafreeh@cedarcrest.edu
FREEL, Lisa .... 301-846-2468 203 H lfreel@frederick.edu
FREELAND, Brian .... 304-724-3700 501 D bfreeland@apus.edu
FREELAND, Melissa, A .. 843-792-4364 422 C freelan@musc.edu
FREELANDER, Chichi .... 405-491-6396 379 K cfreelan@snu.edu
FREELS, Cindy .... 573-288-6511 259 E cfreels@culver.edu
FREELS, Ean .... 515-964-6514 168 A enfreels@dmacc.edu
FREEMAN, Abby .... 313-943-4000 238 H afreema2@wcccd.edu
FREEMAN, Abby .... 402-472-7211 277 G
FREEMAN, Alston .... 803-934-3179 422 G afreeman@morris.edu
FREEMAN, Andrew .... 740-753-6290 362 K freemana@hocking.edu
FREEMAN, Angela .... 315-781-3339 310 C freeman@hws.edu
FREEMAN, Angela .... 404-752-1657 123 F afreeman@msm.edu
FREEMAN, Annie .... 704-406-4491 337 H akfreeman@gardner-webb.edu
FREEMAN, Bobby .... 828-298-3325 353 B purchasing@warren-wilson.edu
FREEMAN, Carol Ann .... 845-675-4794 319 C carol_ann.freeman@nyack.edu
FREEMAN, Catharine ..... 319-296-4041 169 H catharine.freeman@hawkeyecollege.edu
FREEMAN, Cecily .... 901-722-3200 436 D cfreeman@sco.edu

FRIERSON, Tobe .... 912-344-2503 115 D
tobe.frierson@armstrong.edu
FRIERSON, Tobe, R .... 864-379-6687 421 E
frierson@erskine.edu
FRIES, Jane .... 970-542-3106.. 81 A
jane.fries@morgancc.edu
FRIES, Katherine .... 203-857-7105.. 86 D
kfries@norwalk.edu
FRIESEMA, Nathan .... 607-735-1821 307 G
nfriesema@elmira.edu
FRIESEN, Joshua .... 864-250-8994 421 K
joshua.friesen@gvltec.edu
FRIESEN, Wilbert .... 847-628-1001 142 B
will.friesen@judsonu.edu
FRIGGE, Maria .... 334-670-3736.... 7 E
lfrigge@troy.edu
FRINK, Brian .... 920-565-1000 507 K
brinkbt@lakeland.edu
FRINK, Dorothy .... 219-980-6994 160 C
defrink@iun.edu
FRINK, Kandy .... 307-382-1602 517 C
kfrink@westernwyoming.edu
FRIONA, Joseph, M ...... 260-399-7700 165 B
jfriona@sf.edu
FRISBEE, Sean .... 304-293-4731 505 B
sean.frisbee@mail.wvu.edu
FRISBEE, Stephen .... 315-792-5399 315 I
sfrisbee@mvcc.edu
FRISBIE, Kathy .... 970-542-3240.. 81 A
kathy.frisbie@morgancc.edu
FRISBY, Anthony .... 215-503-4990 411 E
anthony.frisby@jefferson.edu
FRISBY, Bernard .... 703-212-7410 481 C
FRISCH, Connie .... 320-629-5166 246 H
frisch@pine.edu
FRISCH, Kim .... 303-458-4909.. 82 D
kfrisch@regis.edu
FRISCH, Randy, C .... 206-239-4500 493 D
president@cityu.edu
FRISCIA, Jim .... 503-256-3180 387 I
jfriscia@uws.edu
FRISENDA, Louis .... 703-247-8341 483 A
louis.frisenda@marymount.edu
FRISHMAN, Niki .... 760-872-2000.. 41 E
nikif@deepsprings.edu
FRISINA, Warren .... 516-463-4783 310 D
warren.frisina@hofstra.edu
FRISKICS, Scott .... 406-353-2607 270 E
friskics@hotmail.com
FRISKNEY, Paul .... 513-244-8128 359 E
paul.friskney@ccuniversity.edu
FRISQUE, Megan .... 512-863-1584 457 I
frisquem@southwestern.edu
FRIST, Matthew, J .... 412-396-6063 394 D
frist@duq.edu
FRITCH, John, E .... 319-273-2725 167 A
john.fritch@uni.edu
FRITCH, Margie .... 760-744-1150.. 55 K
mfritch@palomar.edu
FRITCHLE, Anthony .... 706-867-3166 127 B
anthony.frichtle@ung.edu
FRITH, Cary .... 740-593-2723 368 G
frith@ohio.edu
FRITSCH, Denise .... 859-442-4162 185 I
denise.fritsch@kctcs.edu
FRITSCHE, Teresa .... 570-422-3422 406 A
tfritsche@esu.edu
FRITSKY, Wren .... 570-389-4070 405 E
wfritsky@bloomu.edu
FRITTON, Sandra .... 540-654-1266 486 D
sfritton@umw.edu
FRITTS, Jack .... 630-829-6060 133 I
jfritts@ben.edu
FRITTS, Mary Lou, A ..... 816-235-1107 268 D
frittsml@umkc.edu
FRITZ, John .... 410-455-6596 208 A
fritz@umbc.edu
FRITZ, Sarah .... 608-246-6559 514 A
fritz@madisoncollege.edu
FRITZ, Stephen, J .... 651-962-5901 251 D
sjfritz@stthomas.edu
FRITZ, Susan, M .... 402-472-5242 277 E
smfritz@nebraska.edu
FRITZ, Ted, P .... 412-624-0072 412 I
tfritz@pitt.edu
FRITZ, Thomas, R .... 814-472-3006 409 G
tfritz@francis.edu
FRITZ, William, J .... 718-982-2400 302 A
president@csi.cuny.edu
FRITZE, Barbara, B .... 717-337-6582 396 A
bfritze@gettysburg.edu
FRITZE, Ronald .... 256-216-5524.... 4 C
ron.fritze@athens.edu
FRITZMAN, D. Jason ...... 304-243-2043 505 H
jfritzman@wju.edu
FRIZZA-POMPA, Julio ... 619-265-0107.. 57 G
jfrizza@platt.edu

FRIZZELL, Douglas .... 412-396-3234 394 D
frizzelld@duq.edu
FROCK, Gemma .... 803-508-7277 418 C
frockg@atc.edu
FROEHLE, Mary .... 561-723-4424 107 C
mfroehle@svdp.edu
FROEHLICH-MUELLER,
Kerry .... 715-422-5493 514 B
kerry.froehlichmueller@mstc.edu
FROHARDT, Russell .... 210-486-4136 441 G
rfrohardt@alamo.edu
FROHOFF, Katherine ..... 816-501-4151 265 I
katherine.frohoff@rockhurst.edu
FROHRIB, Patti .... 920-735-5611 513 F
frohrib@fvtc.edu
FROLE, Angelo .... 614-287-5020 360 C
afrole@cscc.edu
FROMBGEN, Elizabeth ... 724-589-2200 411 D
efrombgen@thiel.edu
FROMING, William .... 650-433-3830.. 55 I
bfroming@paloaltou.edu
FROMMELT, Steve .... 309-796-5933 134 C
frommelts@bhc.edu
FRONCEK, Maureen ...... 312-341-4167 150 D
mfroncek@roosevelt.edu
FRONCZEK, Andrew, F .. 216-397-4275 363 H
afronczek@jcu.edu
FRONCZEK, Walter .... 708-974-5372 146 C
fronczek@morainevalley.edu
FRONHEISER, Joey .... 405-945-3250 378 C
fronhei@osuokc.edu
FRONK, Peter .... 608-363-2375 506 D
fronkp@beloit.edu
FRONK, Suzette .... 828-898-8809 339 B
fronks@lmc.edu
FRONMUELLER,
Michael .... 715-425-3335 511 E
michael.fronmueller@uwrf.edu
FRONRATH, Scott .... 727-341-4495 107 A
fronrath.scott@spcollege.edu
FRONTERA, Daniel .... 716-851-1832 307 I
vafrontera@ecc.edu
FRONTERA, Jose, A ...... 787-841-2000 525 J
jose_frontera@pucpr.edu
FRONTIERA, Charlene ... 650-574-6268.. 62 A
frontierac@smccd.edu
FRONTIERA, Patrick ...... 310-338-4489.. 50 J
pfrontiera@lmu.edu
FRONZONI, Susan .... 570-674-6249 401 M
sfronzon@misericordia.edu
FROSCH, Jeff .... 512-313-3000 446 N
jeff.frosch@concordia.edu
FROSLID JONES,
Karen, L .... 202-885-6155.. 91 C
kfroslid@american.edu
FROSSARD, RET.,
Margaret O'Mara .... 312-427-2737 141 E
mfrossar@jmls.edu
FROST, Catherine .... 510-215-3928.. 40 K
cfrost@contracosta.edu
FROST, Christopher .... 210-436-3737 455 J
cfrost@stmarytx.edu
FROST, Dana, L .... 864-644-5004 424 B
dfrost@swu.edu
FROST, Eric .... 315-464-4393 326 B
froste@upstate.edu
FROST, James .... 830-303-0404 461 D
frost@frostlawoffice.com
FROST, Judith .... 207-755-5265 199 K
jfrost@cmcc.edu
FROST, Julia, H .... 479-979-1401.. 23 J
jfrost@ozarks.edu
FROST, Leanne .... 406-771-4372 272 D
leanne.frost@gfcmsu.edu
FROST, Linda .... 423-425-5922 440 A
linda-frost@utc.edu
FROST, Mark .... 518-783-4100 324 C
mfrost@siena.edu
FROST, Mary .... 563-884-5664 172 H
mary.frost@palmer.edu
FROST, Meghan .... 602-827-2646.. 14 K
meghan.frost@nau.edu
FROST, Mike .... 406-243-4711 271 G
mike.frost@umontana.edu
FROST, Pamela .... 614-825-6255 356 C
pfrost@aiam.edu
FROST, Richard, A .... 616-395-7800 231 D
frost@hope.edu
FROST, Stacy .... 507-537-6483 248 A
stacy.frost@smsu.edu
FROST, Vivian .... 620-252-7199 176 K
frost.vivian@coffeyville.edu
FROUDE, Bill .... 859-572-5112 188 E
froudew1@nku.edu
FRUCHTHANDLER,
Abraham, H .... 718-377-0777 320 E
FRUEAN, Evelyn, V .... 684-699-9155 519 F
e.fruean@amsamoa.edu

FRUEH, Elizabeth .... 715-425-4192 511 E
elizabeth.frueh@uwrf.edu
FRUITTICHER, Lee .... 706-721-7928 116 B
lfruitticher@augusta.edu
FRUM, Jennifer, L .... 706-542-6126 127 A
jfrum@uga.edu
FRUMKIN, Jeffery, R ...... 734-763-4551 237 I
jfrumkin@umich.edu
FRUMKIN, Michael .... 407-823-6424 110 C
michael.frumkin@ucf.edu
FRUMKIN, Steven .... 212-217-4330 308 B
steven_frumkin@fitnyc.edu
FRUTCHEY, Shelby .... 512-516-8703 125 H
sfrutchey@southuniversity.edu
FRY, Angela .... 870-574-4523.. 21 G
afry@sautech.edu
FRY, Bobbye, G .... 210-829-6006 465 E
fry@uiwtx.edu
FRY, Donna .... 810-237-6503 238 B
donnafry@umflint.edu
FRY, John .... 708-239-4863 153 B
john.fry@trnty.edu
FRY, John, A .... 215-895-2100 394 C
jaf@drexel.edu
FRY, Pamela .... 405-744-5627 377 F
pamela.fry@okstate.edu
FRYDA, Kathleen .... 920-498-6288 514 G
kathleen.fryda@nwtc.edu
FRYE, Brandon .... 850-474-2384 111 D
bfrye@uwf.edu
FRYE, Harland .... 252-789-0225 344 E
harlan.frye@martincc.edu
FRYE, Holly .... 304-876-5402 504 D
hfrye@shepherd.edu
FRYE, Jeffrey .... 419-434-4501 372 B
frye@findlay.edu
FRYE, Karen .... 910-898-9620 345 A
fryek@montgomery.edu
FRYE, Keener .... 307-766-4166 517 B
hfry1@uwyo.edu
FRYE, Lela .... 352-395-5420 107 E
lela.frye@sfcollege.edu
FRYE, Todd .... 913-971-3617 179 H
tmfrye@mnu.edu
FRYER, Robert .... 570-484-2344 406 E
rcf138@lockhaven.edu
FRYKBERG, Jay .... 310-342-5200.. 72 D
FRYLING, Michelle, S ... 724-357-2302 406 C
mfryling@iup.edu
FRYNS, Jennifer .... 352-854-2322.. 97 C
frynsj@cf.edu
FRYSON, David, M .... 304-293-3431 505 B
david.fryson@mail.wvu.edu
FU, Di .... 954-763-9840.. 94 S
fudi@atom.edu
FUCHS, Catherine .... 615-327-7264 440 D
catherine.fuchs@vanderbilt.edu
FUCHS, Kyle .... 937-328-6006 359 H
fuchsk@clarkstate.edu
FUCHS, Lisa .... 402-354-7065 275 P
lisa.fuchs@methodistcollege.edu
FUCHS, Monique .... 617-989-4513 225 E
fuchsm@wit.edu
FUCHS, Tina, M .... 503-838-8220 388 B
fuchst@wou.edu
FUCHS, W. Kent .... 352-392-1311 110 D
president@ufl.edu
FUCHSER, Kathy .... 402-562-1267 273 G
kathyfuchser@cccneb.edu
FUDALLY, Steve .... 218-733-7600 245 C
steve.fudally@lsc.edu
FUDGE, Denise, G .... 270-384-8203 187 H
fudged@lindsey.edu
FUDGE, Sara .... 513-244-8445 359 E
sara.fudge@ccuniversity.edu
FUENTES, Alán .... 718-289-5197 301 D
alan.fuentes@bcc.cuny.edu
FUENTES, Angeles .... 831-582-4136.. 33 A
afuentes@csumb.edu
FUENTES, Angelica, M .. 956-295-3383 461 F
angelica.fuentes@tsc.edu
FUENTES, Jose, A .... 787-279-1912 523 J
jfuentes@bayamon.inter.edu
FUENTES, Monserrat .... 804-828-1674 487 E
mfuentes@vcu.edu
FUENTES, Ramonita .... 787-751-0178 525 O
ac_rfuentes@suagm.edu
FUENTES, Trisha, D .... 973-290-4130 285 A
tfuentes@cse.edu
FUENTES, Vilma .... 352-395-5030 107 E
vilma.fuentes@sfcollege.edu
FUENTES-AFFLICK,
Elena .... 415-476-1977.. 70 A
elena.fuentes-afflick@ucsf.edu
FUENTEZ, Tammy .... 620-421-6700 179 D
tammyf@labette.edu
FUERST, Nathan .... 860-486-3137.. 88 G
nathan.fuerst@uconn.edu

FUERY, Patrick .... 714-997-6947.. 36 G
fuery@chapman.edu
FUEST, Melissa .... 201-216-3346 291 G
melissa.fuest@stevens.edu
FUGALE, Stephen .... 610-519-4400 413 K
stephen.fugale@villanova.edu
FUGATE, Amy .... 810-762-0237 234 F
amy.fugate@mcc.edu
FUGATE, Megan, A .... 620-421-6700 179 D
meganf@labette.edu
FUGATE, Stu .... 606-487-3196 185 J
stu.fugate@kctcs.edu
FUGATE, Wesley .... 434-947-8000 484 B
wfugate@randolphcollege.edu
FUGATE-ROBERTS,
Kimberly .... 352-395-5510 107 E
kimberly.fugate-roberts@sfcollege.edu
FUGAZZOTTO, Sam .... 212-678-4055 331 C
fugazzotto@tc.edu
FUGIEL, Lisa .... 413-755-4786 221 B
lfugiel@stcc.edu
FUGITT, Gilbert .... 949-214-3057.. 40 I
gilbert.fugitt@cui.edu
FUHLER, Justin .... 217-479-7153 144 I
justin.fuhler@mac.edu
FUHRMAN, Hillary .... 330-941-2453 374 E
hlfuhrman@ysu.edu
FUHRMAN, JR.,
L. Clifton .... 864-938-3907 423 D
lcfuhrman@presby.edu
FUHRMAN, Susan, H ..... 212-678-3131 331 C
susanf@tc.columbia.edu
FUHRMAN, Tim .... 509-793-2351 492 I
timf@bigbend.edu
FUHRMANN, Dave .... 805-652-5577.. 72 G
dfuhrmann@vcccd.edu
FUHRMANN, Donald, J . 814-824-2104 401 J
dfuhrmann@mercyhurst.edu
FUHS, Kristen .... 818-767-0888.. 75 C
FUITH, Leanne .... 651-290-7526 248 U
leanne.fuith@mitchellhamline.edu
FUJII, Marnie .... 952-829-4192 240 H
marnie.fujii@bethfel.org
FUJII, Stephanie .... 480-423-6300.. 14 C
stephanie.fujii@scottsdalecc.edu
FUJIMOTO, Kell .... 408-924-5910.. 34 D
kell.fujimoto@sjsu.edu
FUJIWARA, Mariko .... 206-592-4319 495 E
mfujiwara@highline.edu
FUJIYOSHI, Lois, M ...... 808-932-7664 129 I
lfujiyos@hawaii.edu
FULBRIGHT, Kyle .... 423-746-5327 439 A
kfulbright@twcnet.edu
FULCHER, Kerry .... 619-849-2651.. 57 H
kerryfulcher@pointloma.edu
FULCOMER, Eric, W ...... 815-226-4010 150 C
efulcomer@rockford.edu
FULFORD, David .... 602-275-7133.. 16 A
david.fulford@rsiaz.edu
FULFORD, Leroy .... 740-377-2520 370 L
leroy.fulford@tsbc.edu
FULFORD, Lynda .... 805-493-3839.. 30 E
fulford@callutheran.edu
FULFORD, William, J .... 251-460-7277.... 9 B
hfulford@southalabama.edu
FULGINITI, John .... 928-541-7777.. 54 B
jfulginiti@ncu.edu
FULIGNI, Paul .... 618-650-2560 152 C
pfulign@siue.edu
FULIGNI, Paul .... 515-294-2631 166 F
pfuligni@iastate.edu
FULK, Scott .... 219-980-6792 160 C
sfulk@iun.edu
FULK, Sheryl, E .... 812-877-8514 163 G
fulk1@rose-hulman.edu
FULKERSON, Cathy .... 775-445-3219 279 F
cathy.fulkerson@wnc.edu
FULKERSON, Cathy .... 775-753-2108 279 A
cathy.fulkerson@gbcnv.edu
FULKERSON,
Christopher, D .... 336-278-5055 337 G
fulkers@elon.edu
FULKERSON, Diane .... 941-359-4316 111 C
dfulkerson@sar.usf.edu
FULL, Karen .... 239-304-7371.. 95 C
karen.full@avemaria.edu
FULLAM, Deborah .... 610-896-1000 397 F
dfullam@haverford.edu
FULLAN, Jesse .... 563-588-8000 169 B
jfullan@emmaus.edu
FULLANA, Yaremis, P .... 407-582-1463 113 F
yfullana@valenciacollege.edu
FULLBRIGHT, Marshall . 559-730-3735.. 39 G
marshallf@cos.edu
FULLEM, Wendy .... 973-300-2120 291 I
wfullem@sussex.edu
FULLER, Belinda .... 304-766-3387 505 A
bfuller@wvstateu.edu

G

GAFFIN, John 859-572-6611 188 E gaffinj@nku.edu
GAFFNER, Lori 618-664-7120 139 A lori.gaffner@greenville.edu
GAFFNEY, Eva 508-531-1337 217 D egaffney@bridgew.edu
GAFFNEY, Kathryn 860-215-9266.. 86 F kgaffney@trcc.commnet.edu
GAFFNEY, Kevin 775-445-4223 279 F kevin.gaffney@wnc.edu
GAFFNEY, Lorita 920-686-6200 510 A lorita.gaffney@sl.edu
GAFFNEY, Michelle 330-823-2496 372 C gaffnemi@mountunion.edu
GAFFNEY, Phillip 706-204-2201 119 G pgaffney@highlands.edu
GAFFNEY, Tiffany, D 401-865-2191 416 E tgaffne1@providence.edu
GAFFORD, Brian 931-393-1576 437 C bgafford@mscc.edu
GAGAN, Kelly 585-389-2411 316 D kgagan8@naz.edu
GAGE, Adrian 508-929-8563 219 A agage@worcester.edu
GAGE, Brent 319-335-1548 166 G brent-gage@uiowa.edu
GAGE, Chris 812-866-7028 158 C gage@hanover.edu
GAGE, David 315-781-3734 310 C gage@hws.edu
GAGE, J. Scott 978-837-5468 221 G j.scott.gage@merrimack.edu
GAGE, Jeannie 361-825-2332 460 A jeannie.gage@tamucc.edu
GAGE, Julia 401-841-6535 518 E julia.gage@usnwc.edu
GAGER, Sarah 203-575-8034.. 86 B sgager@nv.edu
GAGLIANO, Patricia 772-462-7565 101 Q pgaglian@irsc.edu
GAGLINI, Louis, V 617-358-5732 212 G lgaglini@bu.edu
GAGNE PENDLETON, Lori 860-515-3858.. 84 H lpendleton@charteroak.edu
GAGNON, Craig, L 920-832-6587 507 L craig.l.gagnon@lawrence.edu
GAGNON, Karen 712-274-5159 172 A gagnon@morningside.edu
GAGNON, Nicole 701-477-7862 355 H ngagnon@tm.edu
GAGNON, Paula 207-216-4318 200 E pgagnon@yccc.edu
GAGNON, Pauline 678-839-5450 127 F pgagnon@westga.edu
GAGNON, Roberta 269-965-3931 232 A gagnonr@kellogg.edu
GAGNOW, Robin, W 440-826-8153 357 B rgagnow@bw.edu
GAHAGAN, Nicole 262-691-5240 515 B ngahagan@wctc.edu
GAHAGANS, Steve 479-575-6626.. 21 I steveg@uark.edu
GAHN, Sandra, W 515-294-5389 166 F sgahn@iastate.edu
GAIA, Celeste 276-944-6917 480 J cgaia@ehc.edu
GAIER, Mary 937-512-2163 370 A mary.gaier@sinclair.edu
GAIK, Molly 773-298-3000 151 C gaik@sxu.edu
GAIKO, Sylvia 270-745-8985 190 F sylvia.gaiko@wku.edu
GAIL, Keli, A 413-597-4233 226 C kg8@williams.edu
GAILEY, Andrew 706-865-2134 126 G agailey@truett.edu
GAILEY, Kim 970-943-3140.. 84 E kgailey@western.edu
GAILLAT, Ana 508-678-2811 219 C ana.gaillat@bristolcc.edu
GAILOR, Kathleen 845-451-1302 306 D kathy.gailor@culinary.edu
GAIMARO, Amy 516-323-4415 315 J agaimaro@molloy.edu
GAINER, Nancy 610-436-4164 407 D ngainer@wcupa.edu
GAINES, Adrienne, S 334-833-4480.... 5 M againes@hawks.huntingdon.edu
GAINES, Angela 225-771-2552 196 B againes@sulc.edu
GAINES, Anne 212-229-8908 316 E gainesa@newschool.edu
GAINES, Chad 660-248-6197 258 B cgaines@centralmethodist.edu
GAINES, Cliff 254-501-3101 445 L cgaines@ctcd.edu
GAINES, Gina 914-606-7612 333 H gina.gaines@sunywcc.edu
GAINES, Glynnis 254-299-8306 452 E ggaines@mclennan.edu
GAINES, John 615-936-2811 440 D john.gaines@vanderbilt.edu
GAINES, Justin 706-867-2781 127 B justin.gaines@ung.edu
GAINES, Kim 256-306-2592.... 1 F kim.gaines@calhoun.edu
GAINES, JR., Larry, R 856-225-6174 290 B gaines@camden.rutgers.edu
GAINES, JR., Larry, R 856-225-6174 290 A gaines@camden.rutgers.edu
GAINES, Michael 336-334-5946 351 D registrar@uncg.edu
GAINES, Michael 937-376-6031 358 I mgaines@centralstate.edu
GAINES, Randy 208-282-2872 132 B gainrand@isu.edu
GAINES, Shawna 615-248-1378 439 B ssgaines@trevecca.edu
GAINES, Shivaun, P 973-655-7648 287 D gainess@mail.montclair.edu
GAINES, Steven, D 805-893-7363.. 70 B gaines@ucsb.edu
GAINES-OLLIE, Brenda 901-435-1526 433 A brenda_gaines-ollie@loc.edu
GAINEY, Karen, W 864-488-4504 422 B kgainey@limestone.edu
GAISER, J. Christopher 503-883-2308 383 H cgaiser@linfield.edu
GAISSER, Josh 828-898-3311 339 B gaisserj@lmc.edu
GAISSERT, John 706-355-5039 115 H jgaissert@athenstech.edu
GAITAN, Deborah 210-486-4454 441 G dgaitan@alamo.edu
GAITAN, Susie 361-354-2714 445 S mgaitan@coastalbend.edu
GAITERS-JORDAN, Jacquelyn 719-502-3078.. 81 H jacquelyn.gaiters-jordan@ppcc.edu
GAITHER, Kimberly 573-288-6340 259 E kgaither@culver.edu
GAITHER, Sarah 704-216-6111 339 E
GAITHER, Sonya 678-359-5078 121 B sgaither@gordonstate.edu
GAITO, Madalyn 828-652-0630 344 G madalyng@mcdowelltech.edu
GAJDARDZISKA-JOSIFOVSKA, Marija 414-229-5520 511 A mgj@uwm.edu
GAJDOSIK, Olga 262-554-2010 508 E olga6542@yahoo.com
GAJEWSKI, Linda 219-473-4217 157 A lgajewski@ccsj.edu
GAJRIA, Meenakshi 845-398-4154 323 G mgajria@stac.edu
GALADIMA, Bulus 562-903-4844.. 27 E bulus.galadima@biola.edu
GALAN, Julia 904-819-6603.. 98 I jgalan@flagler.edu
GALANES, Gloria 417-836-5247 263 H gloriagalanes@missouristate.edu
GALANO, Hector 714-879-3901.. 45 I hgalano@hiu.edu
GALANSKI, Kay, A 724-946-7218 414 C galanska@westminster.edu
GALANSKY, Galia 212-772-4511 302 E galia.galansky@hunter.cuny.edu
GALARDI, Karen 215-504-2000 397 G kgalardi@holyfamily.edu
GALATOLO, Ron, D 650-574-6550.. 61 Q galatolo@smccd.edu
GALAVIZ, Gina 541-962-3496 383 B ggalaviz@eou.edu
GALBARY, Tiffany 406-395-4875 273 B
GALBIATI, Jacquelyn 856-227-7200 284 E jgalbiati@camdencc.edu
GALBIERZ, Todd 636-922-8359 265 J tgalbierz@stchas.edu
GALBRAITH, II, Jay, R 407-582-3420 113 F jgalbraith1@valenciacollege.edu
GALBRAITH, Jennifer 909-274-4600.. 52 I jgalbraith@mtsac.edu
GALBRAITH, Mark 619-849-2489.. 57 H markgalbraith@pointloma.edu
GALBRAITH, Richard, A 802-656-2918 476 E richard.galbraith@uvm.edu
GALBRAITH, Thomas, J 530-226-4185.. 64 B tgalbraith@simpsonu.edu
GALBREATH, Dodd 615-966-1771 433 D dodd.galbreath@lipscomb.edu
GALBREATH, Susan, C 615-966-5952 433 D susan.galbreath@lipscomb.edu
GALCHINSKY, Michael 404-413-2000 121 A mgalchinsky@gsu.edu
GALDIERI, Virginia 908-852-1440 284 G galdieriv@centenaryuniversity.edu
GALE, Andrea 909-607-1236.. 38 A andrea.gale@cmc.edu
GALE, Jason 615-297-7545 429 H galej@aquinascollege.edu
GALE, Jennifer 610-917-1488 413 G jdgale@valleyforge.edu
GALE, Mary 952-885-5437 249 F mgale@nwhealth.edu
GALE, Nicole, L 410-651-6458 208 C nlgale@umes.edu
GALEA, Sandro 617-638-4644 212 G sgalea@bu.edu
GALECKE, Robert, M 972-721-5203 464 E galecke@udallas.edu
GALELEI, Scott 607-729-8915 307 E sgalelei@ebi-college.com
GALER, Scott, W 208-496-4310 131 D galers@byui.edu
GALEY, Frank, D 307-766-4133 517 B fgaley@uwyo.edu
GALEY, Julie 716-652-8900 300 L jgaley@cks.edu
GALICK, Rob 815-280-6647 142 A rgalick@jjc.edu
GALIK, Barbara 309-677-2850 134 G barbara@bradley.edu
GALIL, Zvi 404-894-8357 120 A galil@gatech.edu
GALINDO, Emily 530-752-0339.. 68 H ecgalindo@ucdavis.edu
GALINDO, Gabriel 520-287-5583.. 11 R galindog@cochise.edu
GALINDO, Israel 404-687-4558 118 B galindol@ctsnet.edu
GALINSKI, Bonnie 978-542-2532 218 E bgalinski@salemstate.edu
GALIPAULT, Margaret 740-587-6287 361 B galipaultm@denison.edu
GALIPEAU-KONATE, Bethany 540-542-6285 485 C bgalipea@su.edu
GALKIN, Daphne 914-831-0413 305 C dgalkin@cw.edu
GALL, Connie 405-692-3258 376 C cgall@macu.edu
GALL, George 386-481-2043.. 95 J gallg@cookman.edu
GALL, Jen 510-849-8241.. 55 D jgall@psr.edu
GALL, Rob 707-765-1836.. 52 A
GALL RITCHIE, Amy, S 800-287-8822 156 D ritcham@bethanyseminary.edu
GALLAGAN, Marilynn 978-656-3300 220 C gallaganm@middlesex.mass.edu
GALLAGHER, Abisola 201-200-3165 287 F agallagher@njcu.edu
GALLAGHER, Amber 949-582-4860.. 64 J agallagher4@saddleback.edu
GALLAGHER, Amie 908-526-1200 289 D amie.gallagher@raritanval.edu
GALLAGHER, Beth, E 805-756-2236.. 30 K begallag@calpoly.edu
GALLAGHER, AA, Dennis, M 508-767-7033 210 I dgallagh@assumption.edu
GALLAGHER, Ed 256-766-6610.... 5 K egallagher@hcu.edu
GALLAGHER, Elizabeth 925-631-4223.. 59 C egallagh@stmarys-ca.edu
GALLAGHER, Geraldine M, P 407-582-3155 113 F ggallagher@valenciacollege.edu
GALLAGHER, CSC, James, T 503-943-8011 387 H gallaghe@up.edu
GALLAGHER, Joanna 215-572-2187 389 D gallagher@arcadia.edu
GALLAGHER, John 573-341-4286 269 A gallagherjo@mst.edu
GALLAGHER, Judith 817-515-7702 458 B judith.gallagher@tccd.edu
GALLAGHER, Karen 607-753-4717 327 A karen.gallagher@cortland.edu
GALLAGHER, Karen, S 213-740-5756.. 72 B rsoedean@usc.edu
GALLAGHER, Kathleen 215-503-6959 411 E kathleen.gallagher@jefferson.edu
GALLAGHER, Leslie, D 281-425-6301 451 I lgallagher@lee.edu
GALLAGHER, Lori 713-525-3592 466 J irishstudies@stthom.edu
GALLAGHER, Mary 213-763-7040.. 49 F mgallagh@lattc.edu
GALLAGHER, Mary 213-763-7227.. 49 F mgallagh@lattc.edu
GALLAGHER, Mary Beth 314-719-3554 260 C mbgallagher@fontbonne.edu
GALLAGHER, Mary Beth 276-223-4765 490 C mgallagher@wcc.vccs.edu
GALLAGHER, Matthew 310-665-6819.. 54 I mgallagher@otis.edu
GALLAGHER, Maureen 914-395-2385 323 K mgallagh@sarahlawrence.edu
GALLAGHER, Megan 717-396-7833 404 R mgallagher@pcad.edu
GALLAGHER, Miles 717-871-7210 407 A miles.gallagher@millersville.edu
GALLAGHER, Patricia 781-292-2416 215 C patricia.gallagher@olin.edu
GALLAGHER, Patrick 908-709-7045 292 C gallagher@ucc.edu
GALLAGHER, Patrick 412-624-4200 412 I pdg@pitt.edu
GALLAGHER, Richard 914-968-6200 323 C richard.gallagher@archny.org
GALLAGHER, Scott 573-592-4337 270 D scott.gallagher@williamwoods.edu
GALLAGHER, Steve 336-631-1217 352 B gallaghers@uncsa.edu
GALLAGHER, Susan 503-312-5424 384 C susan.gallagher@mtangel.edu
GALLAGHER, Susan, P 518-629-8138 310 G s.gallagher@hvcc.edu
GALLAGHER, Terri 724-480-3427 392 K terri.gallagher@ccbc.edu
GALLAGHER-LEPAK, Susan 920-465-2034 510 E galaghs@uwgb.edu
GALLANT, Danny, R 936-468-2203 458 A dgallant@sfasu.edu
GALLARDO, Ignacio 805-893-4412.. 70 B ignacio.gallardo@ucsb.edu
GALLARDO, Mark 573-341-4981 269 A gallardom@mst.edu
GALLARDO, Ruben, C 915-831-6306 449 A rgalla16@epcc.edu
GALLART, Stephen 845-687-5187 331 L gallarts@sunyulster.edu
GALLATIN, Cynthia 203-582-8521.. 88 A cynthia.gallatin@quinnipiac.edu
GALLEGLY, Carolyn 628-985-3741 141 D carolyngallegly@jalc.edu
GALLEGLY, Michael 973-300-2306 291 I mgallegly@sussex.edu
GALLEGO, Hector, F 919-516-4929 348 G hfgallego@st-aug.edu
GALLEGOS, Jeremy 316-295-5871 177 F jeremy_gallegos@friends.edu
GALLEGOS, Joel, A 704-687-7755 351 C jagalleg@uncc.edu
GALLEGOS, John 916-348-4689.. 42 F jgallegos@epic.edu
GALLEGOS, Jose Alfred 323-242-5511.. 49 E gallegja@lasc.edu
GALLEN, Peter, C 864-592-4680 424 C gallenp@sccsc.edu
GALLENBERG, Dale 715-425-3841 511 E dale.gallenberg@uwrf.edu
GALLENTINE, Jerry, L 605-721-5225 427 G jgallentine@national.edu
GALLEY, Amy 307-382-1645 517 C agalley@westernwyoming.edu
GALLIANETTI, David, D 920-565-1119 507 K gallianettidd@lakeland.edu
GALLIE, Alain 770-220-7908 119 D agallie@gcuniv.edu
GALLIGAN, Chad 623-935-8075.. 13 F chad.galligan@estrellamountain.edu
GALLIGAN, Chris 860-832-1764.. 84 J galliganc@ccsu.edu
GALLIGAN, Gina 718-289-5562 301 D gina.galligan@bcc.cuny.edu
GALLIGAN, Meghan 907-852-1763.... 9 H registration@ilisagvik.edu
GALLIHUGH, Joel 313-993-1235 237 F gallihja@udmercy.edu
GALLIMORE, Alec, D 734-647-7008 237 I
GALLIMORE, Anna 336-721-2852 348 H anna.gallimore@ssalem.edu
GALLIMORE, Rebecca 269-965-3931 232 A gallimorer@kellogg.edu
GALLIMORE, Sarah 717-815-6470 415 G sgallimo@ycp.edu
GALLINGER, Dawn 406-447-5179 270 H dgallinger@carroll.edu
GALLION, Melanie 843-525-8224 424 E mgallion@tcl.edu
GALLIPEAU, Jean, B 315-443-3765 330 H jbgallip@syr.edu
GALLISATH, Glenda 847-578-8787 150 E glenda.gallisath@rosalindfranklin.edu

GARCIA, Gilda .... 512-245-2539 463 A
gg18@txstate.edu
GARCIA, Gladys .... 661-654-3485.. 31 B
ggarcia32@csub.edu
GARCIA, Heather .... 305-809-3178.. 99 L
heather.garcia@fkcc.edu
GARCIA, Helen .... 915-566-9621 470 L
hgarcia@westerntech.edu
GARCIA, Herminia, C .... 561-732-4424 107 C
hgarcia@svdp.edu
GARCIA, Irene .... 830-372-6309 461 D
igarcia@tlu.edu
GARCIA, Irma .... 718-489-5490 322 D
igarcia@sfc.edu
GARCIA, Isabel .... 352-723-5800 110 D
agarcia2@dental.ufl.edu
GARCIA, Jennifer .... 530-752-3113.. 68 H
jlroth@ucdavis.edu
GARCIA, Jessica .... 325-670-1448 450 A
jessica.garcia@hsutx.edu
GARCIA, Joann .... 760-252-2411.. 27 A
jgarcia@barstow.edu
GARCIA, Joe .... 520-626-1197.. 16 J
skipgarcia@email.arizona.edu
GARCIA, Joseph .... 518-587-2100 329 C
joseph.garcia@esc.edu
GARCIA, Joyce .... 323-265-8732.. 48 L
garciajb@elac.edu
GARCIA, JR., Juan, G .... 956-326-2468 459 B
jgarcia@tamiu.edu
GARCIA, Julia .... 830-569-4222 445 S
jgarcia@coastalbend.edu
GARCIA, Katrina .... 361-698-1270 448 H
krodriguez@delmar.edu
GARCIA, Kellie .... 661-654-3206.. 31 B
kgarcia@csub.edu
GARCIA, Kim, L .... 408-223-6704.. 61 N
kim.garcia@sjeccd.org
GARCIA, Lily .... 202-408-2400.. 93 B
GARCIA, Luis .... 787-890-2681 527 E
luis.garcia23@upr.edu
GARCIA, Luis, A .... 802-656-3390 476 E
luis.garcia@uvm.edu
GARCIA, Lupe .... 805-893-4089.. 70 B
lupe.garcia@sa.ucsb.edu
GARCIA, Margaret .... 323-343-3830.. 32 D
mgarcia2@calstatela.edu
GARCIA, Maria .... 305-595-9500.. 94 F
registrar@amcollege.edu
GARCIA, Maria .... 210-341-1366 454 B
mgarcia@ost.edu
GARCIA, Maria .... 409-882-3319 462 D
maria.garcia@lsco.edu
GARCIA, Mark .... 661-259-7800.. 39 C
mark.garcia@canyons.edu
GARCIA, Mark, S .... 972-599-3185 446 I
mgarcia@collin.edu
GARCIA, Martha .... 760-355-6136.. 46 B
martha.garcia@imperial.edu
GARCIA, Melody .... 212-659-7299 312 E
mgarcia@tkc.edu
GARCIA, Michael .... 973-761-9731 291 F
michael.garcia@shu.edu
GARCIA, Mildred .... 657-278-3456.. 32 B
presidentgarcia@fullerton.edu
GARCIA, Oscar, S .... 830-591-7330 457 C
osgarcia@swtjc.edu
GARCIA, Patricia .... 580-774-3021 380 B
patricia.garcia@swosu.edu
GARCIA, Penny, A .... 575-562-2443 293 O
penny.a.garcia@enmu.edu
GARCIA, Pete .... 305-348-0504 109 D
pete.garcia@fiu.edu
GARCIA, Phil .... 916-278-8758.. 33 C
garciap@csus.edu
GARCIA, Racquel .... 212-247-3434 313 K
GARCIA, Ramona .... 915-595-1935 444 K
ramona.garcia@brightwood.edu
GARCIA, Raul .... 254-526-1903 445 L
rgarcia@ctcd.edu
GARCIA, Rodrigo .... 714-992-7018.. 54 A
rgarcia1@fullcoll.edu
GARCIA, Rolando .... 954-201-8800.. 96 A
rgarcia4@broward.edu
GARCIA, Rolando .... 787-743-7979 526 A
GARCIA, Ron .... 505-454-3251 294 J
garcia_rs@nmhu.edu
GARCIA, Rosalinda .... 210-434-6711 454 D
rgarcia@lake.ollusa.edu
GARCIA, Rosella .... 212-678-3004 331 C
garcia@tc.columbia.edu
GARCIA, Rosemarie, M . 505-428-1201 296 B
rosemarie.garcia@sfcc.edu
GARCIA, Rosie .... 210-829-6013 465 E
rosiep@uiwtx.edu
GARCIA, Sarah .... 208-769-3341 132 E
sarah_garcia@nic.edu
GARCIA, Stephen, R ...... 760-245-4271.. 73 E
steve.garcia@vvc.edu
GARCIA, Steve .... 909-748-8477.. 71 H
steve_garcia@redlands.edu
GARCIA, Sunshine .... 805-437-3776.. 31 C
sunshine.garcia@csuci.edu
GARCIA, Tania .... 805-437-8452.. 31 C
tania.garcia@csuci.edu
GARCIA, Tara .... 657-278-5312.. 32 B
tgarcia@fullerton.edu
GARCIA, Teresa .... 319-208-5249 173 G
tgarcia@scciowa.edu
GARCIA, Teresa .... 956-872-2114 456 G
tgarci80@southtexascollege.edu
GARCIA, Tina .... 303-352-3199.. 79 D
GARCIA, Tony .... 608-663-2256 507 D
tgarcia@edgewood.edu
GARCIA, Valentin .... 559-791-2218.. 47 C
val.garcia@portervillecollege.edu
GARCIA, Valeria .... 813-974-6987 111 A
vgarcia@usf.edu
GARCIA, Veronica .... 210-486-5425 441 E
vgarcia2@alamo.edu
GARCIA, Veronica .... 210-486-5000 441 F
GARCIA, Viviana .... 760-750-4040.. 33 E
vivigarcia@csusm.edu
GARCIA, Vladimir .... 787-725-8120 522 M
vgarcia0068@eap.edu
GARCIA, William .... 973-596-5320 288 A
william.garcia@njit.edu
GARCIA, William, L .... 925-424-1405.. 36 D
wgarcia@laspositascollege.edu
GARCIA, Yolanda .... 707-527-4671.. 62 H
ygarcia2@santarosa.edu
GARCIA, Zahira .... 787-620-2040 520 F
zgarcia@aupr.edu
GARCIA-ACOSTA,
Amarillys .... 787-746-1400 522 O
agarcia@huertas.edu
GARCIA-GARIBAY,
Miguel .... 310-825-1042.. 69 B
mgarciagaribay@college.ucla.edu
GARCIA-GUZMAN,
Yessica .... 732-255-0400 288 B
ygarcia-guzman@ocean.edu
GARCIA-HILLS,
Rosemarie .... 708-209-3257 136 I
rosemarie.garcia@cuchicago.edu
GARCIA-LEON, Jose ...... 212-799-5000 312 B
GARCIA-MCMILLIAN,
Darilis .... 971-722-4486 386 C
darilis.garciamcmillian@pcc.edu
GARCIA-MILLER, Maria . 209-478-0800.. 45 J
mgarcia@humphreys.edu
GARCIA-REYES, Ana, I .. 718-518-4313 302 D
agreyes@hostos.cuny.edu
GARCIA RIVERA, Doris . 787-763-6700 522 N
drdgarcia@se-pr.edu
GARCÍA, Katherine .... 787-766-1717 526 B
garciak1@suagm.edu
GARCÍA, Tary .... 787-264-1912 524 D
tdgarcia@intersg.edu
GARD, Daniel .... 708-209-3004 136 I
daniel.gard@cuchicago.edu
GARD, Evelyn .... 203-285-2065.. 85 E
egard@gwcc.commnet.edu
GARD, Julee, A .... 815-740-3372 154 G
jgard@stfrancis.edu
GARDE, Shekhar .... 518-276-6298 321 A
gardes@rpi.edu
GARDEA, Oscar, M .... 415-338-2897.. 34 C
omgardea@sfsu.edu
GARDELLA, Patrick .... 859-858-2130 183 C
GARDI, Kerri .... 610-683-4647 406 D
gardi@kutztown.edu
GARDIAL, Sarah .... 319-335-0866 166 G
sarah-gardial@uiowa.edu
GARDIER PATERSON,
Mary, T .... 570-340-6018 401 B
paterson@marywood.edu
GARDIN, Carey, C .... 920-923-7617 508 B
cgardin@marianuniversity.edu
GARDINA, Jackie .... 805-765-9300.. 62 D
GARDINA, Susan .... 717-947-6094 404 S
sgardina2@pacollege.edu
GARDINER, Duane .... 361-593-2170 460 B
duane.gardiner@tamuk.edu
GARDINER, Lori .... 801-422-7079 471 E
lori@byu.edu
GARDNER, Amanda .... 276-944-6922 480 J
agardner@ehc.edu
GARDNER, FNP, Amy ... 607-431-4120 309 E
gardnera@hartwick.edu
GARDNER, Andy .... 704-669-4041 342 B
gardnera@clevelandcc.edu
GARDNER, Beth .... 304-252-9547 502 F
bgardner@valley.edu
GARDNER, Betina .... 859-622-1778 184 F
betina.gardner@eku.edu
GARDNER, Bonnie .... 636-584-6502 259 L
bonnie.gardner@eastcentral.edu
GARDNER, Bonnie, S .... 636-584-6502 259 L
bonnie.gardner@eastcentral.edu
GARDNER, Brian .... 314-529-9387 262 B
bgardner@maryville.edu
GARDNER, Butch .... 501-279-4454.. 19 G
bgardner@harding.edu
GARDNER, Candice, L .. 801-863-3000 473 D
candice.gardner@uvu.edu
GARDNER, Catherine .... 508-999-8253 217 A
cgardner@umassd.edu
GARDNER, Chris .... 910-410-1731 345 G
csgardner@richmondcc.edu
GARDNER, Chris, L .... 864-597-4236 426 I
gardnercl@wofford.edu
GARDNER, Christina ...... 619-849-2246.. 57 H
christinagardner@pointloma.edu
GARDNER, Clinton .... 202-274-2303.. 94 B
president@potomac.edu
GARDNER, Craig .... 801-957-4601 474 B
craig.gardner@slcc.edu
GARDNER, Daniel .... 207-255-1248 201 F
daniel.j.gardner@maine.edu
GARDNER, David .... 207-326-2485 200 F
david.gardner@mma.edu
GARDNER, David, M ...... 785-864-0229 181 I
gardner@ku.edu
GARDNER, Della .... 406-657-1005 272 I
della.gardner@rocky.edu
GARDNER, Denise .... 865-974-4373 439 I
d.gardner@utk.edu
GARDNER, Dinelia .... 201-559-6154 286 C
gardnerd@felician.edu
GARDNER, Donna .... 816-415-7622 270 C
gardnerd@william.jewell.edu
GARDNER, Dudley .... 928-226-4224.. 12 B
dudley.garnder@coconino.edu
GARDNER, Greg .... 405-682-7546 377 C
ggardner@occc.edu
GARDNER, Iva, L .... 803-516-4616 423 G
igardner@scsu.edu
GARDNER, Jared, L ...... 208-535-5313 131 G
jared.gardner@my.eitc.edu
GARDNER, Kari .... 928-317-6050.. 11 B
kari.gardner@azwestern.edu
GARDNER, Katherine, B 919-658-7746 349 F
kgardner@umo.edu
GARDNER, Kathleen ...... 989-774-3112 228 E
gardn2k@cmich.edu
GARDNER, Kelly .... 818-333-3558.. 53 I
kelly.gardner@nyfa.edu
GARDNER, Laurie, A ..... 207-778-7272 201 D
lgardner@main.edu
GARDNER, Lisa .... 208-426-1698 131 C
lisagardner@boisestate.edu
GARDNER, Marie .... 785-242-2067 180 C
mgardner@neosho.edu
GARDNER, Marilyn .... 617-322-3500 216 B
GARDNER, Mary .... 610-341-5961 394 E
mgardner@eastern.edu
GARDNER, Melissa .... 330-823-6092 372 C
gardnemf@mountunion.edu
GARDNER, Michael, D .. 931-598-1890 436 A
mdgardne@sewanee.edu
GARDNER, Pamela, K ... 802-656-3450 476 E
pamela.k.gardner@uvm.edu
GARDNER, Phil .... 517-355-9510 233 G
GARDNER, Phil .... 864-977-7014 422 I
phil.gardner@ngu.edu
GARDNER, Reginald, J . 615-353-3486 437 D
reginald.gardner@nscc.edu
GARDNER, Richard .... 212-924-5900 330 G
rgardner@swedishinstitute.edu
GARDNER, Richard .... 540-261-8596 485 G
richard.gardner@svu.edu
GARDNER, Ron .... 559-297-4500.. 46 E
GARDNER, Sarah .... 415-485-3239.. 41 J
sarah.gardner@dominican.edu
GARDNER, Sidney .... 973-655-7130 287 D
gardnersi@mail.montclair.edu
GARDNER,
Stephanie, F .... 501-686-5572.. 22 C
sfgardner@uams.edu
GARDNER, Suzanne ...... 727-341-3160 107 A
gardner.suzanne@spcollege.edu
GARDNER, Tracy .... 937-294-0592 369 K
tracy@saa.edu
GARDNER, Vicki .... 815-802-8123 142 C
vgardner@kcc.edu
GARDNER-BRIM,
Cynthia .... 212-870-1244 318 C
cgardnerbrim@nyts.edu
GARDOSKI, Sharon .... 570-586-2400 392 E
sgardoski@clarkssummitu.edu
GARDZINA, Matthew, K 570-577-3159 390 H
matt.gardzina@bucknell.edu
GAREWSKI, Jeffrey, A ... 860-465-4521.. 84 K
garewskij@easternct.edu
GAREY, Cheri .... 704-534-4128 138 H
cgarey@govst.edu
GAREY, Kelly .... 503-552-1603 384 F
kgarey@nunm.edu
GAREY, Stephen, P .... 443-412-2156 204 C
sgarey@harford.edu
GARFINKEL, Stephen .... 212-678-8050 312 A
stgarfinkel@jtsa.edu
GARFOOT, John .... 716-829-7636 307 B
garfootj@dyc.edu
GARFUNKEL, Eric, L ..... 848-932-2747 290 A
egarf@rutgers.edu
GARFUNKLE, Eric .... 848-445-2747 290 C
egarf@rutgers.edu
GARGANI, Lauren .... 207-326-2260 200 F
lauren.gargani@mma.edu
GARGANO, JR.,
Michael .... 203-576-5277.. 88 D
michael.gargano@stvincentscollege.edu
GARGIULO, Kimberly .... 914-337-9300 305 F
kim.gargiulo@concordia-ny.edu
GARGIULO, Kimberly .... 914-337-9300 305 F
kimberly.gargiulo@concordia-ny.edu
GARGIULO, Leslie .... 949-359-0045.. 30 B
GARGUILE, Mary .... 360-475-7400 496 F
mgarguile@olympic.edu
GARIBALDI, Antoine, M 313-993-1455 237 F
garibaldi@udmercy.edu
GARIEPY, David .... 574-284-5000 163 J
dgariepy@saintmarys.edu
GARII, Barb .... 718-940-5846 322 G
bgarii@sjcny.edu
GARISS, Julie .... 417-626-1234 264 J
gariss.julie@occ.edu
GARISS, Randy .... 417-626-1234 264 J
gariss.randy@occ.edu
GARLAND, Anita, H .... 434-223-6120 481 D
agarland@hsc.edu
GARLAND, Colleen, C ... 740-368-3015 368 N
ccgarland@owu.edu
GARLAND, Daniel .... 412-291-6240 389 F
dgarland@aii.edu
GARLAND, Elizabeth ...... 503-370-6209 388 D
ecarson@willamette.edu
GARLAND, Jeffrey, W .... 302-831-2113.. 90 I
jgarland@udel.edu
GARLAND, Jonathan ..... 907-745-3201.... 9 D
jgarland@akbible.edu
GARLAND, Peter, H .... 717-720-4010 405 D
pgarland@passhe.edu
GARLAND, Philip .... 619-260-4724.. 71 J
pgarland@sandiego.edu
GARLAND, Rebecca, R .. 815-740-3648 154 G
rgarland@stfrancis.edu
GARLAND, Robert, R ..... 330-823-3847 372 C
garlanrr@mountunion.edu
GARLAND, Sheila .... 325-671-2357 452 F
GARLAND, Zanne .... 828-298-3325 353 B
zgarland@warren-wilson.edu
GARLICK, Rebecca .... 979-743-5222 444 D
bgarlick@blinn.edu
GARLICK, Stella .... 304-263-6262 502 A
sgarlick@martinsburginstitute.edu
GARMAN, Deanna .... 423-585-6897 438 D
deanna.garman@ws.edu
GARMAN, Gregory, C ... 804-828-1574 487 E
ggarman@vcu.edu
GARN, Gregg, A .... 405-325-1267 380 L
garn@ou.edu
GARNAR, Martin .... 719-255-3115.. 83 C
mgarnar@uccs.edu
GARNER, Amber .... 662-720-7256 255 B
acgarner@nemcc.edu
GARNER, Ann .... 410-516-8056 204 F
agarner7@jhu.edu
GARNER, Ann, M .... 703-993-2368 481 B
agarner3@gmu.edu
GARNER, April .... 843-349-7870 421 L
april.garner@hgtc.edu
GARNER, Cindy .... 901-722-3223 436 D
cgarner@sco.edu
GARNER, David .... 215-887-5511 414 D
dgarner@wts.edu
GARNER, Graham .... 315-684-6041 329 F
garnerg@morrisville.edu
GARNER, Kim .... 209-228-6305.. 69 C
kgarner@ucmerced.edu
GARNER, Larry .... 254-519-5725 459 D
lgarner@tamuct.edu
GARNER, Latonya .... 662-254-3421 255 A
lcgarner@mvsu.edu
GARNER, Lyn .... 281-998-6150 456 A
lyn.garner@sjcd.edu
GARNER, Mark .... 610-353-7630 390 E

GARNER, Mary Ann ...... 229-468-2018 128 G
maryann.garner@wiregrass.edu
GARNER, MaryAnne ...... 202-462-2101.. 92 D
garner@iwp.edu
GARNER, Porter .... 979-845-7514 459 C
porter-garner@tamu.edu
GARNER, Ray .... 256-824-4688.... 8 C
ray.garner@uah.edu
GARNER, Regina .... 214-860-8553 448 B
rgarner@dcccd.edu
GARNER, Richard .... 516-877-3800 297 I
garner@adelphi.edu
GARNER, Sam .... 402-363-5620 278 E
sgarner@york.edu
GARNER, Sissy .... 931-363-9815 433 E
sgarner@martinmethodist.edu
GARNER, Tim .... 256-782-8220.... 6 B
tgarner@jsu.edu
GARNETT, Heather .... 434-544-8431 482 F
garnett.h@lynchburg.edu
GARNETT, Sherman, W . 517-353-6753 233 G
garnetts@msu.edu
GARNICK, Renee .... 302-622-8000.. 90 A
rgarnick@dcad.edu
GARNO, Art .... 315-386-7197 329 A
garnoa@canton.edu
GAROFALO, Jorge, H .... 787-743-7979 526 A
ut_jgarofalo@suagm.edu
GAROFALO, Marise .... 570-504-7000 395 I
mgarofalo@tcmc.edu
GAROFALO, Teresa .... 605-229-8434 427 J
teresa.garofalo@presentation.edu
GAROFANO, John .... 401-841-1812 518 E
GAROFFOLO, Gary .... 580-581-2221 375 A
ggaroffo@cameron.edu
GARON, Jon .... 954-262-6101 104 F
garon@nova.edu
GARR, Bethany .... 864-596-9595 420 F
healthservices@converse.edu
GARRABRANTS, Nancy . 413-545-4764 216 H
n.garrabrants@cns.umass.edu
GARRANT, Ines .... 617-358-0513 212 G
igarrant@bu.edu
GARRELL, Robin, L .... 310-825-4383.. 69 B
rgarrell@gdnet.ucla.edu
GARREN, Cynthia .... 863-784-7177 108 B
cynthia.garren@southflorida.edu
GARREN, Kenneth, R .... 434-544-8200 482 F
president@lynchburg.edu
GARREN, Mary Ann ...... 870-762-3168.. 17 K
mgarren@smail.anc.edu
GARREN, Steve .... 217-234-5459 143 B
sgarren@lakeland.cc.il.us
GARRETSON, Angela, R 973-596-3101 288 A
angela.r.garretson@njit.edu
GARRETSON, Charlie .... 601-477-4249 253 F
charlie.garretson@jcjc.edu
GARRETT, Allison .... 620-341-5551 177 B
agarrett@emporia.edu
GARRETT, Bonnie, J ...... 410-777-2503 202 D
bjgarrett@aacc.edu
GARRETT, Charlotte ...... 785-833-4419 179 C
charlotte.garrett@kwu.edu
GARRETT, Craig .... 402-844-7046 276 G
craigg@northeast.edu
GARRETT, Dan, T .... 325-674-2508 441 D
garrettd@acu.edu
GARRETT, Deborah, A ... 501-882-8986.. 17 M
dagarrett@asub.edu
GARRETT, Don .... 325-674-2213 441 D
dlg09a@acu.edu
GARRETT, G. Nimai .... 803-376-5704 418 D
ggarrett@allenuniversity.edu
GARRETT, Geoffrey .... 215-898-4715 412 G
ggarrett@wharton.upenn.edu
GARRETT, Gina .... 870-307-7557.. 20 C
gina.garrett@lyon.edu
GARRETT, Glenda .... 214-860-8666 448 B
ghall@dcccd.edu
GARRETT, Heather .... 845-368-7220 323 I
GARRETT, Helen .... 206-685-2553 499 D
helenbg@uw.edu
GARRETT, James .... 412-268-5090 391 H
garrett@cmu.edu
GARRETT, Jason .... 731-661-5365 439 D
jgarrett@uu.edu
GARRETT, Jinnie .... 540-365-4370 480 L
jmgarrett@ferrum.edu
GARRETT, Jonathan .... 513-244-1728 359 E
jonathan.garrett@ccuniversity.edu
GARRETT, Kelly .... 713-623-2040 443 C
kgarrett@aii.edu
GARRETT, Kevin .... 304-384-5340 503 P
garrettad@concord.edu
GARRETT, LaCharlotte ... 504-284-5435 195 L
lgarrett@suno.edu
GARRETT, Larry .... 361-485-6803 470 A
larry.garrett@victoriacollege.edu

GARRETT, Leonard .... 214-860-3697 448 B
lgarrett@dcccd.edu
GARRETT, Lynn .... 407-404-6060 107 G
garrettl@seminolestate.edu
GARRETT, Mark .... 270-901-1065 187 A
mark.garrett@kctcs.edu
GARRETT, Natasha .... 412-536-1296 398 E
natasha.garrett@laroche.edu
GARRETT, Nicole, L .... 919-658-7896 349 F
ngarrett@umo.edu
GARRETT, P, B .... 202-994-0108.. 92 A
pgarrett@gwu.edu
GARRETT, Paul .... 864-977-7035 422 I
paul.garrett@ngu.edu
GARRETT, Paula, K .... 828-298-3325 353 B
pgarrett@warren-wilson.edu
GARRETT, Rachele .... 936-468-2403 458 A
nixonhr@sfasu.edu
GARRETT, Rick .... 765-641-4156 156 A
ragarrett@anderson.edu
GARRETT, Rob, J .... 208-496-1124 131 D
garrettr@byui.edu
GARRETT, Robin .... 254-526-1733 445 L
robin.garrett@ctcd.edu
GARRETT, Sarah .... 301-387-3157 203 I
sarah.garrett@garrettcollege.edu
GARRETT, Schnell, R ..... 443-518-4766 204 E
sgarrett@howardcc.edu
GARRETT, Stacey .... 615-238-6350 431 I
sgarrett@bonelaw.com
GARRETT, Stephanie ...... 864-225-7653 421 G
stephaniegarrett@forrestcollege.edu
GARRETT, Susan, R .... 502-895-3411 188 A
sgarrett@lpts.edu
GARRETT, Todd, L .... 913-971-3278 179 H
tgarrett@mnu.edu
GARRETT FINSTER,
Susan .... 619-239-0391.. 35 C
sgf@cwsl.edu
GARRICK DUHANEY,
Laurel .... 845-257-3561 325 D
duhaneyl@newpaltz.edu
GARRIOCH, Shay .... 845-451-4365 306 D
shay.garrioch@culinary.edu
GARRIS, Daffie, H .... 336-633-0290 345 F
dhgarris@randolph.edu
GARRIS, Eric, L .... 843-661-1160 421 H
egarris@fmarion.edu
GARRIS, Rick .... 303-963-3290.. 77 I
rgarris@ccu.edu
GARRISON, Amy .... 828-689-1295 339 G
agarrison@mhu.edu
GARRISON, Cindy .... 931-526-3660 431 J
cynthia.stephenson@fortisinstitute.edu
GARRISON, Deborah ..... 309-672-5583 145 E
dgarrison@methodistcol.edu
GARRISON, Helene .... 949-376-6000.. 47 H
hgarrison@lcad.edu
GARRISON, James .... 913-971-3626 179 H
jgarriso@mnu.edu
GARRISON, James, R ... 913-971-3296 179 H
jgarriso@mnu.edu
GARRISON, Joseph, L .. 989-774-5251 228 E
garri2jl@cmich.edu
GARRISON, Julie, A ...... 269-387-5202 239 E
julie.garrison@wmich.edu
GARRISON, Lorie .... 580-581-2612 375 A
loriebg@cameron.edu
GARRISON, Mark .... 443-885-3185 206 A
mark.garrison@morgan.edu
GARRISON, Michael, J . 651-962-5187 251 D
mjgarrison@stthomas.edu
GARRISON, Phil .... 315-568-3268 317 A
pgarrison@nycc.edu
GARRISON, Rebecca ..... 314-539-5154 266 E
rgarrison@stlcc.edu
GARRISON, Ryan .... 828-652-6021 344 G
rgarrison@mcdowelltech.edu
GARRISON, Scott .... 231-591-3729 230 A
scottgarrison@ferris.edu
GARRISON, Shane .... 270-789-5541 184 B
msgarrison@campbellsville.edu
GARRISON, Tom .... 208-792-2247 132 C
tgarrison@lcsc.edu
GARRITY, Christopher ... 413-205-3366 210 E
christopher.garrity@aic.edu
GARRITY, Collette .... 212-343-1234 315 D
cgarrity@mcny.edu
GARRITY, Geraldine ...... 928-724-6814.. 12 G
ggarrity@dinecollege.edu
GARRITY, Janet .... 610-647-4400 397 I
jgarrity@immaculata.edu
GARRITY, Kathleen, E ... 608-822-2471 515 A
kgarrity@swtc.edu
GARRITY, Michael .... 708-456-0300 153 E
michaelgarrity@triton.edu
GARRITY, Mitch .... 505-277-0111 296 H
mgarrity@unm.edu

GARRITY, Patricia .... 608-897-8514 281 I
pgarrity@rivier.edu
GARROW, Joy .... 517-264-7123 236 I
jgarrow@sienaheights.edu
GARRY, Kirby .... 831-582-3534.. 33 A
kgarry@csumb.edu
GARSTECKI, Marcus ...... 605-256-5124 428 G
marcus.garstecki@dsu.edu
GARTEN, Ann .... 310-660-3406.. 42 C
agarten@elcamino.edu
GARTEN, Ann, M .... 310-660-3670.. 42 C
agarten@elcamino.edu
GARTENMAYER,
Charles .... 913-360-7583 175 D
cgartenmayer@benedictine.edu
GARTHOFF, Jerry .... 207-621-3067 201 C
garthoff@maine.edu
GARTHWAITE, Jonathan 603-271-6484 280 N
jgarthwaite@ccsnh.edu
GARTI, Elizabeth .... 914-773-3813 319 J
GARTIN, Stanton .... 970-521-6650.. 81 F
stanton.gartin@njc.edu
GARTNER, Lia .... 212-229-5192 316 E
gartnerl@newschool.edu
GARTNER, Maggie .... 979-845-4427 459 C
molona@tamu.edu
GARTON, Jilda .... 404-894-4819 120 A
jilda.garton@gtrc.gatech.edu
GARTRELL, William .... 626-396-2316.. 26 L
bill.gartrell@artcenter.edu
GARUS, Marcella Marie 716-896-0700 333 C
smgarus@villa.edu
GARVER, Beth .... 617-585-0200 212 C
beth.garver@the-bac.edu
GARVER, Robert, A .... 419-866-0261 370 I
ragarver@stautzenberger.com
GARVEY, Ann, L .... 612-330-1168 240 G
garvey@augsburg.edu
GARVEY, Carol .... 712-274-5178 172 A
garvey@morningside.edu
GARVEY, James .... 618-453-4550 152 B
jgarvey@siu.edu
GARVEY, James .... 215-637-7700 397 G
jgarvey@holyfamily.edu
GARVEY, John, H .... 202-319-5100.. 91 D
cua-president@cua.edu
GARVEY, Judy .... 714-241-6230.. 38 F
jgarvey@coastline.edu
GARVEY, Kathleen, M ... 508-373-9455 211 F
kathleen.garvey@becker.edu
GARVEY, Kevin .... 908-737-5018 286 F
kgarvey@kean.edu
GARVILLA, Johnny .... 706-865-2134 126 G
jgarvilla@truett.edu
GARVIN, Maureen .... 912-525-5000 125 B
mgarvin@scad.edu
GARVIN, Natara .... 615-329-8635 431 I
ngarvin@fisk.edu
GARVIN, William .... 417-873-7482 259 G
wgarvin@drury.edu
GARVIN AQUILINO,
Rose .... 240-567-4249 205 F
rose.garvinaquilino@
montgomerycollege.edu
GARVIN-LEIGHTON,
Timothy .... 706-778-8500 124 E
tleighton@piedmont.edu
GARY, Aaron .... 201-216-5240 291 G
aaron.gary@stevens.edu
GARY, Carole .... 865-539-7025 437 F
cgary2@pstcc.edu
GARY, Cynthia .... 405-682-1611 377 C
cynthia.d.gary@occc.edu
GARY, Kevin .... 610-527-0200 409 E
kevin.gary@rosemont.edu
GARY, Linda .... 903-510-3515 464 D
lgar@tjc.edu
GARY, Marc .... 212-678-8080 312 A
magary@jtsa.edu
GARY, Michael .... 305-626-3722.. 99 M
michael.gary@fmuniv.edu
GARY, William .... 216-987-3110 360 E
william.gary@tri-c.edu
GARZA, Ana Lisa .... 512-245-2780 463 A
ag02@txstate.edu
GARZA, Cynthia .... 713-718-7049 450 D
cynthia.garza3@hccs.edu
GARZA, Edwardo .... 773-838-7500 136 A
egarza20@ccc.edu
GARZA, Felipe .... 361-593-2611 460 B
felipe.garza@tamuk.edu
GARZA, Javier .... 254-968-9104 459 A
garza@tarleton.edu
GARZA, Jon .... 713-221-8950 465 C
garzaj@uhd.edu
GARZA, Kim .... 509-793-2010 492 I
kimg@bigbend.edu

GARZA, Lisa .... 940-898-2950 464 A
lgarza10@twu.edu
GARZA, Mary Jane .... 361-825-5749 460 A
maryjane.garza@tamucc.edu
GARZA, Noemi .... 956-872-2681 456 G
ngarza24@southtexascollege.edu
GARZA, Nora, R .... 956-721-5868 451 H
nrgarza@laredo.edu
GARZA, Rebecca, J .... 214-860-2618 448 A
rgarza@dcccd.edu
GARZA, Richie .... 806-371-5022 442 D
rrgarza@actx.edu
GARZA, Robert .... 214-860-8700 448 B
robertgarza@dcccd.edu
GARZA, Roberto .... 305-223-4561 106 L
rgarza@sjvcs.edu
GARZA, Roberto, A .... 956-326-2325 459 B
facil@tamiu.edu
GARZA, JR., Victor ...... 408-274-7900.. 61 O
victor.garza@evc.edu
GARZA-RODERICK,
Jessie .... 209-833-7900.. 61 B
jgarza-roderick@deltacollege.edu
GARZARELLI, Todd .... 262-472-1918 512 C
GASAWAY, Debbie .... 870-460-1622.. 22 D
gasaway@uamont.edu
GASAWAY, Rapheael ..... 202-274-6069.. 93 D
rapheael.gasaway@udc.edu
GASBARRO, Dennis ...... 716-614-5982 318 E
dgasbarro@niagaracc.suny.edu
GASCHE, Currie .... 847-574-5158 143 A
cgasche@lfgsm.edu
GASCHK, Kenneth, K ..... 262-243-5700 507 C
ken.gaschk@cuw.edu
GASCOIGNE, Carolyn .... 325-942-2162 463 C
carolyn.gascoigne@angelo.edu
GASE, Chris .... 740-389-4636 365 B
gasec@mtc.edu
GASH, Bill .... 678-717-2357 127 B
william.gash@ung.edu
GASH, Justin .... 317-738-8092 157 L
jgash@franklincollege.edu
GASIOROWSKI, John .... 312-553-2500 135 I
jgasiorowski@ccc.edu
GASKELL, Carolyn .... 509-527-2133 499 F
carolyn.gaskell@wallawalla.edu
GASKELL, Debbie .... 910-378-8212 349 F
dgaskell@umo.edu
GASKELL, Millicent .... 610-519-6371 413 K
millicent.gaskell@villanova.edu
GASKIN, Elizabeth .... 772-462-5604 101 Q
egaskin@irsc.edu
GASKIN, Keith .... 901-334-5811 434 C
kgaskin@memphisseminary.edu
GASKINS, Leebrian, E ... 956-326-2310 459 B
lgaskins@tamiu.edu
GASOSKE, Betsy .... 314-434-4044 259 B
registrar@covenantseminary.edu
GASPAR, Roger .... 732-743-3800.. 93 B
GASPARD, Harold .... 504-671-6247 192 H
hgaspa@dcc.edu
GASPARIAN, Albert .... 714-895-8334.. 38 G
agasparian@gwc.cccd.edu
GASPARICH, Gail .... 978-542-6265 218 E
ggasparich@salemstate.edu
GASPARRO, Paul .... 740-699-3037 357 D
pgasparro@belmontcollege.edu
GASPER, Joseph .... 570-740-0372 400 F
jgasper@luzerne.edu
GASQUE, Tarlough .... 240-567-7588 205 F
tarlough.gasque@montgomerycollege.edu
GASS, Melanie .... 704-403-1613 336 B
melanie.gass@carolinashealthcare.org
GASS, Michael .... 828-232-5118 351 A
mgass@unca.edu
GASSMAN, Chad .... 847-628-1579 142 B
chad.gassman@judsonu.edu
GASSNER, Sheila .... 573-681-5084 261 H
gassners@lincolnu.edu
GAST, Brad .... 715-675-3331 514 F
gast@ntc.edu
GAST, Tracy .... 716-270-5612 307 I
gast@ecc.edu
GASTON, David .... 212-517-3929 324 E
d.gaston@sothebysinstitute.com
GASTON, David .... 785-864-3624 181 I
adgaston@ku.edu
GASTON, Della, J .... 336-342-4261 346 B
gastond@rockinghamcc.edu
GASTON, H. Neely .... 704-527-9909 215 E
ngaston@gordonconwell.edu
GASTON, H. Neely .... 704-527-9909 215 E
ngaston@gcts.edu
GASTON, Kenneth .... 410-651-7550 208 C
klgaston@umes.edu
GASTON, Lori .... 704-894-2208 337 B
logaston@davidson.edu

GASTON, Patricia .... 518-629-7292 310 G
p.gaston@hvcc.edu
GASWICK, Kari .... 308-432-6487 276 B
kgaswick@csc.edu
GATCH, Denise, D .... 941-752-5325 108 P
gatchd@scf.edu
GATCH, Maura .... 406-265-3536 272 C
maura.gatch@msun.edu
GATCHELL, Michael, D .. 864-294-2475 421 I
mike.gatchell@furman.edu
GATELY, Kevin .... 603-897-8232 281 I
kgately@rivier.edu
GATELY, Paul .... 401-841-7531 518 E
GATES, Cynthia, K .... 405-585-5255 377 A
cynthia.gates@okbu.edu
GATES, David .... 503-594-6000 382 D
davidg@clackamas.edu
GATES, Debra .... 315-279-5273 312 D
dgates@keuka.edu
GATES, Dennis .... 513-751-1206 356 A
dennis@aic-arts.edu
GATES, Glenn .... 973-618-3259 284 D
ggates@caldwell.edu
GATES, James .... 607-729-1581 306 F
jgates@davisny.edu
GATES, Jane McBride ... 860-723-0058.. 84 I
gatesj@ct.edu
GATES, Jeffrey .... 315-792-3006 332 H
jtgates@utica.edu
GATES, Joan .... 859-572-5588 188 E
gatesj4@nku.edu
GATES, Kathryn, F .... 662-915-7206 256 C
kfg@olemiss.edu
GATES, Pamela, S .... 989-774-3342 228 E
gates1ps@cmich.edu
GATES, Reginald .... 817-515-5001 458 B
reginald.gates@tccd.edu
GATES, Victor .... 254-526-1168 445 L
victor.gates@ctcd.edu
GATES, William, R .... 831-656-2754 518 D
bgates@nps.edu
GATES BLACK, L. Joy ... 610-359-5100 393 E
jgatesblack@dccc.edu
GATESMAN, Robert .... 814-393-2578 405 H
rgatesman@clarion.edu
GATEWOOD, Algie, C .... 336-506-4150 340 L
algie.gatewood@alamancecc.edu
GATEWOOD, David .... 714-895-8156.. 38 G
dgatewood@gwc.cccd.edu
GATEWOOD, Dawn .... 434-381-6202 485 P
dgatewood@sbc.edu
GATEWOOD, Jace .... 678-916-2639 115 K
jgatewood@johnmarshall.edu
GATHERCOLE, Karen ..... 321-674-7229.. 99 K
kgathercole@fit.edu
GATHERS, Avis .... 803-793-5241 420 G
gathersa@denmarktech.edu
GATHINGS, Cedric .... 304-696-4347 504 C
studentaffairs@marshall.edu
GATHJE, Peter .... 901-334-5830 434 C
GATLIN, Alan .... 989-463-7143 226 H
gatlina@alma.edu
GATLIN, Greg .... 617-573-8428 224 I
ggatlin@suffolk.edu
GATLIN, Kenda .... 206-281-2569 498 B
kgatlin@spu.edu
GATLING, Sharron .... 757-221-2617 479 I
sggatl@wm.edu
GATO, Stacy .... 434-791-7110 478 E
sgato@averett.edu
GATRELL, Jay, D .... 217-581-2121 138 A
jgatrell@eiu.edu
GATTAS, Jeffrey, P .... 858-822-6914.. 69 E
jgattas@ucsd.edu
GATTAS, Joyce, M .... 619-594-1343.. 34 B
gattas@mail.sdsu.edu
GATTI, Robert, M .... 614-823-1250 368 O
rgatti@otterbein.edu
GATTIS, Tom .... 614-222-3237 360 B
tgattis@ccad.edu
GATTO, John .... 606-546-1728 189 I
jgatto@unionky.edu
GATTO, Joseph, C .... 716-652-8900 300 L
jgatto@cks.edu
GATTON, Pam .... 903-983-8207 451 F
pgatton@kilgore.edu
GATZA, Camille .... 360-752-8549 492 H
cgatza@btc.edu
GAU, Michael .... 608-342-1468 511 D
gaum@uwplatt.edu
GAUBATZ, Noreen .... 803-323-3707 426 H
gaubatzn@winthrop.edu
GAUD, Angela .... 305-443-9170 106 K
GAUDIN, Wendy .... 504-520-7469 198 D
wgaudin@xula.edu
GAUDINO, James, L ...... 509-963-2111 492 L
gaudino@cwu.edu

GAUDREAU, Alison, K .. 248-364-6117 235 J
agaudreau@oakland.edu
GAUGER, John .... 434-582-8946 482 D
jmgauger@liberty.edu
GAUGH, Sherri .... 505-566-4007 296 A
gaughs@sanjuancollege.edu
GAUGHAN, Cheryl .... 619-849-2499.. 57 H
cherylgaughan@pointloma.edu
GAUL, Julie, M .... 412-578-6042 391 G
jmgaul@carlow.edu
GAUL, Volker .... 715-344-3063 514 B
volker.gaul@mstc.edu
GAULDEN, Susan .... 973-877-3533 285 K
gaulden@essex.edu
GAULT, Brian, C .... 601-923-1686 255 E
bgault@rts.edu
GAUMER, Richard, K ..... 276-944-6966 480 J
rgaumer@ehc.edu
GAUNCE, Lori .... 606-759-7141 186 E
lori.gaunce@kctcs.edu
GAUNDER, Alisa .... 512-863-1418 457 I
gaundera@southwestern.edu
GAUNT, Victoria, F .... 410-864-4234 207 A
vgaunt@stmarys.edu
GAURMER, Terry .... 303-458-1629.. 82 D
tgaurmer@regis.edu
GAUS, Gregory, J .... 630-515-7307 145 I
ggausx@midwestern.edu
GAUSE, Genell .... 843-661-8351 421 F
genell.gause@fdtc.edu
GAUTAM, Mridul .... 775-327-2363 279 E
mgautam@unr.edu
GAUTHIER, Chad .... 318-473-6497 194 A
cgauthier@lsua.edu
GAUTHIER, Laureen ...... 802-225-3205 475 H
laureen.gauthier@neci.edu
GAUTHIER, Theresa ...... 585-785-1304 308 D
theresa.gauthier@flcc.edu
GAUTNEY, Michael, B ... 256-765-4274.... 9 A
mbgautney@una.edu
GAUVIN, Charles .... 508-289-2449 226 D
cgauvin@whoi.edu
GAUVIN, Keith, R .... 203-837-9202.. 85 B
gauvink@wcsu.edu
GAVALETZ, Tami .... 618-374-5187 149 A
tami.gavaletz@principia.edu
GAVARRA-OH,
Mary Anne .... 818-710-2234.. 49 D
gavarrm@piercecollege.edu
GAVENTA, Sarah .... 512-404-4885 443 I
sgaventa@austinseminary.edu
GAVER, Bob .... 402-363-5721 278 E
bagaver@york.edu
GAVIGAN, Lisa .... 508-286-3799 225 G
gavigan_lisa@wheatoncollege.edu
GAVIN, Andrew .... 262-595-2485 511 C
gavin@uwp.edu
GAVIN, Carrie .... 850-599-3076 109 A
carrie.gavin@famu.edu
GAVIN, Jack .... 732-571-3536 287 C
gavin@monmouth.edu
GAVIN, M. F. Chip .... 207-621-3173 201 A
chip.gavin@maine.edu
GAVIN, Michael .... 414-297-6760 514 C
gavinmj@matc.edu
GAVIN, Michael, H .... 410-777-2332 202 D
mhgavin@aacc.edu
GAVIN, Mike .... 828-395-1295 344 A
mgavin@isothermal.edu
GAVIN, Paul .... 319-363-1323 172 B
pgavin@mtmercy.edu
GAVIN, Paula .... 386-752-1822.. 99 J
paula.gavin@fgc.edu
GAVIT, Carolyn, S .... 910-962-4103 352 A
gavitc@uncw.edu
GAVLICK, Christopher ... 718-636-3579 320 D
cgavlick@pratt.edu
GAVLIK, Deborah .... 937-512-3999 370 A
deborah.gavlik@sinclair.edu
GAW, Kevin .... 401-232-6090 416 A
kgaw@bryant.edu
GAWEL, Matthew .... 207-893-6601 200 G
mgawel@sjcme.edu
GAWELEK, Mary Ann .... 419-824-3809 364 G
mgawelek@lourdes.edu
GAWENDA, Matt .... 312-922-1884 144 H
mgawenda@maccormac.edu
GAWRONSKI, JR.,
Michael .... 845-341-4284 319 H
michael.gawronski@sunyorange.edu
GAWTHROP, Larry .... 810-762-0235 234 F
larry.gawthrop@mcc.edu
GAXIOLA, Thomas .... 559-443-8612.. 66 G
thom.gaxiola@fresnocitycollege.edu
GAXIOLA GAXIOLA,
Tannya, R .... 520-621-4130.. 16 J
tannya@email.arizona.edu

GAY, Bill .... 760-427-2314.. 46 B
bill.gay@imperial.edu
GAY, Bob .... 304-724-3700 501 D
rgay@apus.edu
GAY, Cliff .... 478-289-2025 118 H
cgay@ega.edu
GAY, Gloria .... 919-536-7200 342 G
gayg@durhamtech.edu
GAY, Jeff .... 315-684-6053 329 F
gayjl@morrisville.edu
GAY, John .... 410-386-8434 203 A
jgay@carrollcc.edu
GAY, Judith .... 215-751-8351 393 A
jgay@ccp.edu
GAY, Michelle .... 704-403-1758 336 B
michelle.gay@carolinashealthcare.org
GAY, Shirley .... 252-862-1307 345 H
swgay6885@roanokechowan.edu
GAYER, Richard, H .... 622-229-9929.. 47 E
GAYESKI, Diane .... 607-274-3895 311 D
gayeski@ithaca.edu
GAYLARD, Cindy, M ..... 850-973-1618 104 D
gaylardc@nfcc.edu
GAYLE, Ruth, R .... 215-965-4002 402 C
rgayle@moore.edu
GAYLEN, Nancy .... 708-974-5349 146 C
gaylenn@morainevalley.edu
GAYLOR, IV, Charles .... 919-735-5151 347 E
cpgaylor@waynecc.edu
GAYMER, Dawn, M .... 269-387-4207 239 E
dawn.gaymer@wmich.edu
GAYMON, Denise .... 256-551-1710.... 2 D
denise.gaymon@drakestate.edu
GAYMON, Joffery .... 850-474-3386 111 D
jgaymon@uwf.edu
GAYNOR, Dona, E .... 321-674-8102.. 99 K
dgaynor@fit.edu
GAYNOR, Julie .... 940-397-4353 453 C
julie.gaynor@mwsu.edu
GAYNOR, Michael, M ... 610-519-4000 413 K
michael.gaynor@villanova.edu
GAYNOR, Suzanne .... 607-431-4670 309 E
gaynors@hartwick.edu
GAYS, Elizabeth .... 931-372-3034 438 F
egays@tntech.edu
GAYTON, Jeffrey .... 541-552-6833 386 H
gaytonj@sou.edu
GAYTON, Linda .... 973-684-6104 288 C
lgayton@pccc.edu
GAZAILLE, Jerri .... 325-793-3803 452 F
jgazaille@mcm.edu
GAZAL, Mary .... 724-805-2627 410 B
mary.gazal@stvincent.edu
GAZAL, Mary .... 724-805-2555 410 C
mary.gazal@stvincent.edu
GAZZALE, Bob .... 323-856-7600.. 25 L
bgazzale@afi.com
GAZZARA HESS,
Margaret .... 508-588-9100 220 B
GAZZILLO, Sara .... 201-684-7610 289 C
sgazzill@ramapo.edu
GEAGHAN, Tom .... 216-687-4745 359 L
t.geaghan@csuohio.edu
GEALT, Michael, A .... 989-774-3931 228 E
gealt1ma@cmich.edu
GEANES, Stephanie, B .. 252-451-8257 345 B
sbgeanes925@nashcc.edu
GEAR, Jackie .... 215-968-8416 390 I
jaclyn.gear@bucks.edu
GEAR, Lisa, L .... 213-738-6834.. 65 I
admissions@swlaw.edu
GEARAN, Dan .... 603-428-2372 281 F
dgearan@nec.edu
GEARHART, Gregory, L . 717-691-6007 401 L
gearhart@messiah.edu
GEARHART TURNER,
Patti .... 817-531-5820 463 G
pturner@txwes.edu
GEARIN, Christopher, A 314-434-2212 261 A
cgearin@hickeycollege.edu
GEARY, Colette .... 218-723-6033 241 J
president@css.edu
GEARY, Gregg .... 562-903-4834.. 27 E
gregg.geary@biola.edu
GEARY, Jason .... 301-405-5554 207 G
geary@umd.edu
GEARY, Leslie, H .... 203-576-4625.. 88 F
lgeary@bridgeport.edu
GEARY, Melanie .... 303-534-6290.. 78 M
melanie.geary@colostate.edu
GEARY, Parrish .... 916-484-8172.. 50 F
gearyp@arc.losrios.edu
GEARY, Tracy .... 860-701-7784.. 87 F
geary_t@mitchell.edu
GEASEY, David, W .... 607-436-3314 325 E
david.geasey@oneonta.edu
GEBEL, Karen .... 319-296-2320 169 H
karen.gebel@hawkeyecollege.edu

GEBEL, Linda .... 563-425-5225 173 K
gebell@uiu.edu
GEBEL, Vicky .... 607-871-2186 298 A
gebel@alfred.edu
GEBER, David .... 917-493-4516 313 M
dgeber@msmnyc.edu
GEBERT, Gordon .... 212-650-7284 301 F
ggebert@ccny.cuny.edu
GEBHARDT, Michael, B 215-204-6542 411 B
michael.gebhardt@temple.edu
GEBHARDT, Virginia ...... 660-263-4100 264 C
virginig@macc.edu
GEBHART, Jennifer, L ... 937-775-5611 374 B
jennifer.gebhart@wright.edu
GEBHART, Patrick .... 281-756-3584 442 C
pgebhart@alvincollege.edu
GEBO, Kelly .... 410-516-5985 204 F
kgebo@jhmi.edu
GEBRU, Amanuel .... 805-378-1400.. 73 A
agebru@vcccd.edu
GEDDINGS, Scarlet .... 803-535-1243 423 B
geddingss@octech.edu
GEDDIS, Catherine .... 212-854-2551 299 B
cgeddis@barnard.edu
GEDDIS, Janet .... 610-358-4254 402 G
geddisj@neumann.edu
GEDLINSKE, Paul .... 920-424-0404 511 B
gedlinsk@uwosh.edu
GEDNALSKE, Julie .... 605-331-6683 429 D
julie.gednalske@usiouxfalls.edu
GEDRO, Julie .... 585-224-3222 329 C
julie.gedro@esc.edu
GEE, Brad .... 715-425-3224 511 E
brad.gee@uwrf.edu
GEE, David .... 909-537-7195.. 33 D
david.gee@csusb.edu
GEE, E. Gordon .... 304-293-5531 505 B
gordon.gee@mail.wvu.edu
GEE, Henry .... 562-908-3489.. 58 D
hgee@riohondo.edu
GEE, Karen, L .... 804-257-5854 491 C
klgee@vuu.edu
GEE, Rodney .... 314-340-3340 260 H
geer@hssu.edu
GEE, Terry .... 619-594-2853.. 34 B
tgee@mail.sdsu.edu
GEEHAN, Margaret .... 518-629-7151 310 G
m.geehan@hvcc.edu
GEEL, Donna .... 207-454-1013 200 D
dgeel@wccc.me.edu
GEER, John, G .... 615-322-2809 440 D
john.geer@vanderbilt.edu
GEER, Nathan .... 503-375-7010 383 A
ngeer@corban.edu
GEETER, Andy .... 229-732-5934 115 B
andygeeter@andrewcollege.edu
GEETER, Candy .... 248-341-2138 235 D
crgeeter@oaklandcc.edu
GEETTER, Erika .... 617-353-2326 212 G
egeetter@bu.edu
GEFELL, Michele, D ...... 315-786-2271 311 H
mgefell@sunyjefferson.edu
GEFFERT, Bryn .... 413-542-2212 210 F
bgeffert@amherst.edu
GEGENHEIMER BALDASSARO,
Sarah .... 202-994-5152.. 92 A
sarahgb@gwu.edu
GEGG-LAPLUME,
Tamara .... 314-968-6982 269 N
laplume@webster.edu
GEGGIE, Steven .... 847-317-8178 153 D
sgeggie@tiu.edu
GEHBAUER, Daryl .... 636-481-3120 261 B
dgehbaue@jeffco.edu
GEHEBER, Leah .... 225-768-1746 191 G
lgeheber@ololcollege.edu
GEHLER, Jan, L .... 480-423-6310.. 14 C
jan.gehler@scottsdalecc.edu
GEHLERT, Sarah .... 803-777-5292 424 I
sgehlert@mailbox.sc.edu
GEHLHAUSEN, Keith ..... 812-488-2943 164 G
kg77@evansville.edu
GEHRET, Steve .... 423-636-5096 439 C
sgehret@tusculum.edu
GEHRICH, Michael, D ... 317-381-6000 165 E
mgehrich@vinu.edu
GEHRIG, Stacy .... 309-694-5512 139 G
sgehrig@icc.edu
GEHRING, Suzanne .... 859-858-3511 183 D
suzanne.gehring@asbury.edu
GEHRINGER, Steve .... 610-409-3000 413 H
GEHRKE, Deb .... 651-793-1278 245 E
deb.gehrke@metrostate.edu
GEHRKE, Sean .... 425-388-9392 494 F
sgehrke@everettcc.edu
GEHRKE, Shelly .... 620-341-5421 177 B
rgehrke@emporia.edu

GERGER, Daniel ... 212-217-3315 308 B daniel_gerger@fitnyc.edu
GERGER, Rick ... 314-246-8708 269 N rickgerger06@webster.edu
GERGES, Marilia ... 931-540-2618 436 H mgerges@columbiastate.edu
GERHARDT, Cassie ... 701-777-4200 353 G cassie.gerhardt@und.edu
GERHARDT, Cassie ... 701-777-3667 353 G
GERHARDT, Mark ... 605-256-5008 428 G mark.gerhardt@dsu.edu
GERHARDT, Winifred ... 440-826-8002 357 B wgerhard@bw.edu
GERHART, Robert ... 229-391-4850 114 G rgerhart@abac.edu
GERHOFF, Sondra ... 866-251-3244 104 G
GERIA, Kellyann, R ... 215-699-5700 399 G kgeria@lsb.edu
GERICS, Aron ... 810-762-0200 234 F aron.gerics@mcc.edu
GERIG, Jill ... 912-478-5367 120 E jgerig@georgiasouthern.edu
GERIGUIS, David ... 951-785-2002 .. 47 F dgerigui@lasierra.edu
GERIK, Debbie ... 254-659-7704 450 B debgerik@hillcollege.edu
GERIN, Jean-Louis ... 802-225-3356 475 H jean-louis.gerin@neci.edu
GERING, Carol ... 907-455-2071 .. 10 B csgering@alaska.edu
GERINGER, Sandra ... 251-626-3303 .... 7 G sgeringer@ussa.edu
GERISCH, Carl ... 541-888-7707 387 A carl.gerisch@socc.edu
GERITY, Patrick, E ... 724-925-4219 414 E gerityk@wccc.edu
GERKEN, Heather ... 203-432-1660 .. 89 G heather.gerken@yale.edu
GERKEN, Stacey ... 715-346-3553 511 F sgerken@uwsp.edu
GERKIN, Jeffrey, G ... 865-974-3131 439 I jgerkin@utk.edu
GERL, Beth, R ... 410-857-2244 205 E bgerl@mcdaniel.edu
GERLACH, Alysa ... 617-373-5144 223 D
GERLACH, David, M ... 217-732-3155 143 G dgerlach@lincolncollege.edu
GERLACH, Karen ... 202-884-9203 .. 93 C gerlachk@trinitydc.edu
GERLACH, Matthew ... 313-883-8541 236 D gerlach.matthew@shms.edu
GERLACH, Peter ... 319-399-8843 167 F pgerlachi@coe.edu
GERLICH, Bella ... 806-742-2261 463 D bella.gerlich@ttu.edu
GERMAN, Deborah ... 407-266-1000 110 C deborah.german@ucf.edu
GERMAN, James, D ... 973-655-4382 287 D germanj@mail.montclair.edu
GERMAN, Lisa ... 256-352-8306 .... 3 I lisa.german@wallacestate.edu
GERMAN, Lisa, A ... 713-743-0291 465 A lagerman@uh.edu
GERMANO, William ... 516-796-4800 317 A wgermano@nycc.edu
GERMANY, Carole, H ... 601-635-6201 252 I cgermany@eccc.edu
GERMANY, Debbie ... 803-754-4100 420 E
GERMERAAD, Stephanie ... 310-954-5080 .. 28 C
GERMIC, Stephen, A ... 406-657-1020 272 I stephen.germic@rocky.edu
GERNER, Steven, W ... 262-243-5700 507 C steven.gerner@cuw.edu
GERNES, Todd, S ... 508-565-1946 224 H tgernes@stonehill.edu
GERODIMOS, Ashley ... 219-989-2414 163 E ashley.geriodimos@pnw.edu
GEROW, Gary ... 207-941-7907 199 B gerowg@husson.edu
GERRAIN, Dawn ... 518-608-8271 308 A dgerrain@excelsior.edu
GERRETSEN, Amy, L ... 920-748-8353 509 H gerretsena@ripon.edu
GERRIETS, Carla ... 402-399-2391 274 A cgerriets@csm.edu
GERRISH, James ... 973-290-4479 285 A jgerrish@cse.edu
GERRY, Bobbi, J ... 208-885-6111 132 I bgerry@uidaho.edu
GERSH, Sheila ... 914-674-7339 314 I sgersh@mercy.edu
GERSHEN, Jay, A ... 330-325-6263 366 F president@neomed.edu
GERSHMAN, Richard ... 615-383-4848 441 A rgershman@watkins.edu
GERSICH, Frank ... 309-457-2119 146 A fgersich@monmouthcollege.edu

GERST, Bernard ... 410-704-2505 209 C bgerst@towson.edu
GERST, Matthew ... 314-529-9300 262 B
GERSTENBERGER, Julie 806-716-2019 456 F jgerstenberger@southplainscollege.edu
GERSTENBERGER, Shawn ... 702-895-1565 279 D shawn.gerstenberger@unlv.edu
GERSTL-PEPIN, Cynthia 413-545-0111 216 H cgerstlp@umass.edu
GERSTMAYR, Andrew ... 973-748-9000 284 A andrew_gerstmayr@bloomfield.edu
GERTH, Daniel ... 314-516-7197 268 E gerthd@umsl.edu
GERTNER, Kimberly, A .. 843-953-5758 420 C gertnerka@cofc.edu
GERTSON, Katherine ... 212-799-5000 312 B
GERTZ, Genie ... 202-651-5653 .. 91 H genie.gertz@gallaudet.edu
GERVAIS, Shayne ... 304-367-4658 504 A sgervais@fairmontstate.edu
GERVASI, Robert ... 614-251-4690 367 F robert.gervasi@ohiodominican.edu
GERZINA, Gretchen ... 413-577-3902 216 H dean@honors.umass.edu
GERZINA, Holly, A ... 330-325-6740 366 F hgerzina@neomed.edu
GESELE, Scott ... 757-594-7863 479 H scott.gesele@cnu.edu
GESING, Amanda ... 716-338-1056 311 F amandagesing@mail.sunyjcc.edu
GESO, Cristina ... 215-955-8164 411 E cristina.geso@jefferson.edu
GESSLER, Klaus ... 845-431-8939 307 A gessler@sunydutchess.edu
GESSNER, Bob, F ... 407-582-1321 113 F rgessner@valenciacollege.edu
GESSNER, James, R ... 218-722-4000 242 B jimg@dbumn.edu
GESSNER, Michael ... 270-706-8727 185 H bkselizabethtown@bncollege.com
GESTOSO, Lloyd ... 215-702-4275 391 C lgestoso@cairn.edu
GESTRING, Sheila ... 605-677-5255 428 E sheila.gestring@usd.edu
GETCHELL, JR., Charles, M ... 603-641-7320 282 A cgetchell@anselm.edu
GETCHELL, Stephanie, L ... 919-530-7824 350 D getchells@nccu.edu
GETMAN, Meghan ... 315-792-7264 330 A meghan.getman@sunyit.edu
GETSINGER, Joseph ... 856-415-6209 289 G jgetsinger@rcgc.edu
GETTINGS, Michael ... 540-362-6414 481 F mgettings@hollins.edu
GETTY, Marc, D ... 304-326-1258 502 D mgetty@salemu.edu
GETZ, Karen ... 724-266-3838 412 D kgetz@tsm.edu
GETZ, Kathleen ... 410-617-2301 205 A kgetz@loyola.edu
GETZ, Rob ... 610-902-8147 391 B rag44@cabrini.edu
GETZ, Roger ... 207-768-9595 201 G roger.getz@maine.edu
GEU, Thomas ... 605-677-5443 428 E thomas.geu@usd.edu
GEUDER, Maridith ... 662-329-7119 254 F mgeuder@muw.edu
GEVITZ, Norman ... 660-626-2371 257 A ngevitz@atsu.edu
GEYE, Trina ... 254-968-9400 459 A geye@tarleton.edu
GEYER, Dennis ... 916-278-3625 .. 33 C dgeyer@csus.edu
GEYER, Enid ... 518-262-6008 297 L geyere@mail.amc.edu
GEYER, Jon ... 614-236-6955 358 A jgeyer@capital.edu
GEYER, Mariann, K ... 412-392-3805 408 F mgeyer@pointpark.edu
GFELLER, Josh ... 785-320-4530 179 E joshgfeller@manhattantech.edu
GHAHRAMANI, Saeed ... 413-782-1218 225 F sghahram@wne.edu
GHALI, Ghali, E ... 318-675-5240 194 D gghali@lsuhsc.edu
GHAMMACHI, Gabe ... 502-456-6504 189 F gghammachi@sullivan.edu
GHAN, Mark ... 775-445-4468 279 F mark.ghan@wnc.edu
GHANEM, Salma ... 312-362-8610 137 C sghanem@depaul.edu
GHANNADIAN, F. Frank ... 813-253-6221 113 E fghannadian@ut.edu

GHAZARIAN, Esther, A . 781-768-7280 224 A esther.ghazarian@regiscollege.edu
GHAZARYAN, Ashot ... 510-925-4282 .. 25 P ashot.ghazaryan@aua.am
GHEBREYSUS, Ghirmay . 225-771-5262 195 K ghirmay_ghebreysus@subr.edu
GHEE, Harry ... 910-323-5614 336 E dean@ccbs.edu
GHERBI, Naima ... 860-439-2411 .. 86 H nghe@conncoll.edu
GHERKE, Amy ... 304-865-6034 502 C amy.gherke@ovu.edu
GHILANI, Mary ... 570-740-0456 400 F mghilani@luzerne.edu
GHILONI, Adam ... 864-646-1583 424 F aghiloni@tctc.edu
GHIO, Frederick, W ... 401-456-8201 417 A fghio@ric.edu
GHOLSON, Robert, D ... 601-266-4466 256 E robert.gholson@usm.edu
GHOLSON, Shari ... 270-534-3372 187 C shari.gholson@kctcs.edu
GHORAYEB, Samir ... 409-984-6484 462 E samir.ghorayeb@lamarpa.edu
GHORI, Zaid ... 650-738-7088 .. 62 B ghoriz@smccd.edu
GHORMOZ, Jacquelyn .. 570-504-9073 395 I jghormoz@tcmc.edu
GHORPADE, Anuja ... 817-735-2055 466 D anuja.ghorpade@unthsc.edu
GHOSAL, Bobby ... 601-928-6213 254 D bobby.ghosal@mgccc.edu
GHOSH, Guru ... 540-231-3205 490 F gghosh@vt.edu
GHOSH, Jayati ... 610-499-4300 414 F jghosh@widener.edu
GHOSH, Monica ... 808-956-7205 129 J monicag@hawaii.edu
GHOSH, Sibdas ... 914-633-2207 311 B sghosh@iona.edu
GIACOMINI, Mike ... 626-300-5444 .. 57 D
GIAMBRA, Leonard, M . 860-701-6679 519 B leonard.m.giambra@uscg.mil
GIAMPAOLI, Michael, J 203-576-4168 .. 88 F gmichael@bridgeport.edu
GIAMPIETRO, Michael .. 413-565-1000 211 C mgiampietro@baypath.edu
GIANETTI, Margaret ... 541-276-1260 382 A
GIANNELLIS, Emmanuel, P ... 607-255-2000 306 B
GIANNESCHI, Matt ... 970-945-8691 .. 77 M mgianneschi@coloradomtn.edu
GIANNET, Stanley, M ... 727-816-3490 105 C giannes@phsc.edu
GIANNINI, Gaetan ... 610-606-4666 392 A gtgianni@cedarcrest.edu
GIANNINI, Gaetan ... 215-641-6303 402 A ggiannini@mc3.edu
GIANNINI, Tula ... 718-636-3702 320 D tgiannin@pratt.edu
GIANNIOS, Paivi ... 816-501-4075 265 I paivi.giannios@rockhurst.edu
GIANNOTTI, Louis, J ... 410-293-1400 519 E giannott@usna.edu
GIANOTTI, Margaret ... 541-278-5775 382 A mgianotti@bluecc.edu
GIANOUSSOPOULOS, Denise ... 626-396-2298 .. 26 L dgianou@artcenter.edu
GIANOUSSOPOULOS, Denise ... 909-537-5250 .. 33 D denise.gianoussopoulos@csusb.edu
GIANTISCO, Alison ... 215-965-8569 402 C agiantisco@moore.edu
GIANTURCO, Deborah ... 716-839-8210 306 E dgiantur@daemen.edu
GIARDULLO, Kelly ... 781-891-2014 212 A kgiardullo@bentley.edu
GIARRUSSO, John ... 518-956-8090 324 G jgiarrusso@albany.edu
GIAUQUE, Margie, T ... 218-755-2038 244 B mgiauque@bemidjistate.edu
GIBB, Deborah ... 212-229-5667 316 E gibbd@newschool.edu
GIBB, Julie ... 309-341-5242 134 H jgibb@sandburg.edu
GIBB, Katharine ... 864-503-5444 425 H kgibb@uscupstate.edu
GIBB, Randy ... 602-639-7500 .. 12 P
GIBBEL, Mark ... 212-229-5662 316 E gibbelm@newschool.edu
GIBBENS, Charlie, E ... 915-747-5352 467 E cegibbens@utep.edu
GIBBISON, Godfrey ... 843-953-3596 420 C gibbisonga@lowcountrygraduatecenter.org
GIBBONS, Arthur ... 845-758-7442 298 I gibbons@bard.edu

GIBBONS, Dennis ... 315-792-5361 315 I dgibbons@mvcc.edu
GIBBONS, Earl, F ... 360-650-3308 500 E earl.gibbons@wwu.edu
GIBBONS, Kristie ... 540-261-4100 485 G kristie.gibbons@svu.edu
GIBBONS, Michael ... 540-261-8400 485 G michael.gibbons@svu.edu
GIBBONS, Michael ... 540-261-8472 485 G michael.gibbons@svu.edu
GIBBONS, Michael ... 478-471-2430 123 A michael.gibbons@mga.edu
GIBBONS, Susan ... 203-432-1810 .. 89 G susan.gibbons@yale.edu
GIBBONS, Thomas, F ... 312-503-3011 148 C tgibbons@northwestern.edu
GIBBS, Beth, B ... 207-859-1130 200 H gibbs@thomas.edu
GIBBS, Brian ... 503-494-5657 385 D cedma@ohsu.edu
GIBBS, Charles ... 202-238-2446 .. 92 C charles.gibbs@howard.edu
GIBBS, Danny ... 615-366-4400 436 E
GIBBS, Donna ... 314-514-3101 149 A donna.gibbs@principia.edu
GIBBS, Donna, L ... 253-535-6023 496 G gibbsdl@plu.edu
GIBBS, Doug ... 314-514-3104 149 A doug.gibbs@principia.edu
GIBBS, Hilary ... 229-333-5797 127 H hhgibbs@valdosta.edu
GIBBS, Hilary, H ... 229-259-5503 127 H hhgibbs@valdosta.edu
GIBBS, J. D ... 252-527-6223 344 D jdgibbs27@lenoircc.edu
GIBBS, Jamie ... 252-249-1851 345 C jgibbs@pamlicocc.edu
GIBBS, Jeremiah ... 317-788-2058 164 H gibbsj@uindy.edu
GIBBS, Jim ... 806-651-3289 460 E jgibbs@mail.wtamu.edu
GIBBS, Nicole ... 919-530-6096 350 D ngibbs2@nccu.edu
GIBBS, Patricia, M ... 478-757-5166 128 E pgibbs@wesleyancollege.edu
GIBBS, Patty ... 478-757-5260 128 E pgibbs@wesleyancollege.edu
GIBBS, Raymond ... 802-773-5900 474 H raymond.gibbs@csj.edu
GIBBS, Renisha, L ... 850-644-8082 110 A rgibbs@admin.fsu.edu
GIBBS, Ryan ... 806-716-2207 456 F rgibbs@southplainscollege.edu
GIBBS, Sarah ... 919-209-2086 344 C sfgibbs@johnstoncc.edu
GIBBS, Sarah, E ... 724-458-2183 396 D segibbs@gcc.edu
GIBBS, Tricia ... 603-623-0313 281 G patriciagibbs@nhia.edu
GIBBS DRAYTON, Marilyn ... 803-535-5309 419 E mgibbs@claflin.edu
GIBELLINO, Pamela ... 937-778-7856 361 E pgibellino@edisonohio.edu
GIBERT, Lisa ... 360-992-2677 493 E lgibert@clark.edu
GIBLER, Linda ... 210-341-1366 454 B lgibler@ost.edu
GIBLER, Rhonda ... 573-882-2094 268 C giblerr@missouri.edu
GIBLIN, Frank ... 248-370-2395 235 J giblin@oakland.edu
GIBLIN, Patrick ... 314-246-7174 269 N patrickgiblin61@webster.edu
GIBLIN, Tara ... 714-432-5093 .. 38 H tgiblin@occ.cccd.edu
GIBNEY, Glenn ... 912-344-2563 115 D glenn.gibney@armstrong.edu
GIBRALTER, Jonathan ... 315-364-3265 333 G president@wells.edu
GIBSON, Amy, B ... 630-515-7198 145 I agibso@midwestern.edu
GIBSON, Bernard ... 916-608-6780 .. 50 H gibsonb@flc.losrios.edu
GIBSON, Brenda ... 503-255-0332 384 E bgibson@multnomah.edu
GIBSON, Cedrick ... 904-779-4045 100 F cegibson@fscj.edu
GIBSON, Christine ... 814-641-3707 398 B gibsonc@juniata.edu
GIBSON, Chyvonne ... 708-209-3007 136 I chyvonne.gibson@cuchicago.edu
GIBSON, Clayton ... 256-372-5221 .... 1 A clayton.gibson@aamu.edu
GIBSON, Corinne, J ... 724-738-2700 407 C corinne.gibson@sru.edu
GIBSON, Dan ... 214-333-5340 447 D danielg@dbu.edu

GIBSON, Danielle .... 888-947-2684 177 H
dgibson5@grantham.edu
GIBSON, David .... 413-559-6623 215 F
djgcm@hampshire.edu
GIBSON, David, W .... 432-837-8702 462 G
dgibson@sulross.edu
GIBSON, Dennis .... 301-387-3051 203 I
dennis.gibson@garrettcollege.edu
GIBSON, Diana .... 304-327-4195 503 O
dgibson@bluefieldstate.edu
GIBSON, Donald, E .... 203-254-4070.. 87 A
dgibson@fairfield.edu
GIBSON, Donna, S .... 212-639-2109 313 I
gibsond@mskcc.org
GIBSON, Edie, B .... 731-881-7508 440 B
edgibson@utm.edu
GIBSON, Ginger .... 352-395-5211 107 E
ginger.gibson@sfcollege.edu
GIBSON, Gloria .... 443-885-3350 206 A
gloria.gibson@morgan.edu
GIBSON, J. Murray .... 850-410-6161 109 A
jm.gibson@famu.edu
GIBSON, Jacqueline ...... 662-254-3636 255 A
jacqueline.gibson@mvsu.edu
GIBSON, James .... 662-476-5078 253 A
jgibson@eastms.edu
GIBSON, Janae .... 214-333-7240 447 D
janae@dbu.edu
GIBSON, Jane .... 901-375-4400 434 F
janegibson@midsouthchristian.edu
GIBSON, Janell, E .... 972-438-6932 454 G
jgibson@parker.edu
GIBSON, Jeff .... 417-625-9727 263 G
gibson-j@mssu.edu
GIBSON, Jeff .... 319-895-4357 167 G
jgibson@cornellcollege.edu
GIBSON, Jeffrey .... 302-736-2420.. 90 J
jeffrey.gibson@wesley.edu
GIBSON, Jencie .... 276-656-0202 489 A
jgibson@patrickhenry.edu
GIBSON, Jeremy .... 978-837-5306 221 G
gibsonj@merrimack.edu
GIBSON, John .... 918-595-7724 380 D
john.gibson@tulsacc.edu
GIBSON, Joseph .... 843-574-6311 424 G
joe.gibson@tridenttech.edu
GIBSON, Joyce .... 207-753-6594 201 H
jgibson@maine.edu
GIBSON, Keith, E .... 540-464-7334 490 E
gibsonke@vmi.edu
GIBSON, Kelly .... 913-971-3392 179 H
krgibson@mnu.edu
GIBSON, Kirk .... 541-956-7186 386 G
kgibson@roguecc.edu
GIBSON, Kody .... 502-897-4617 189 A
kgibson@sbts.edu
GIBSON, Lloyd, G .... 203-576-4385.. 88 F
llgibson@bridgeport.edu
GIBSON, Lynn .... 662-685-4771 252 D
lgibson@bmc.edu
GIBSON, Mandi .... 713-646-1702 456 H
mgibson@stcl.edu
GIBSON, Marc .... 318-675-4928 194 D
mgibso@lsuhsc.edu
GIBSON, Mark, T .... 919-866-5404 347 D
mtgibson@waketech.edu
GIBSON, Michael .... 256-840-4124.... 3 F
mgibson@snead.edu
GIBSON, Michael, A ...... 434-924-8837 486 H
mag3u@virginia.edu
GIBSON, Murray .... 850-410-6161 110 A
jmgibson@fsu.edu
GIBSON, Nathan .... 719-255-3075.. 83 C
ngibson@uccs.edu
GIBSON, Nola, R .... 601-974-1132 254 A
gibsonk@millsaps.edu
GIBSON, Pamela .... 910-486-3930 343 B
gibsonp@faytechcc.edu
GIBSON, Rhonda .... 978-468-7111 215 E
rgibson@gordonconwell.edu
GIBSON, Rick .... 310-506-4125.. 56 D
rick.gibson@pepperdine.edu
GIBSON, Rob .... 620-341-6694 177 B
rgibson1@emporia.edu
GIBSON, Ryan .... 606-368-6130 182 H
ryangibson@alc.edu
GIBSON, Sally .... 816-271-4369 264 B
sgibson14@missouriwestern.edu
GIBSON, Sandra, S .... 803-934-3419 422 G
sangibson@morris.edu
GIBSON, Shanan .... 903-886-5178 459 E
shanan.gibson@tamuc.edu
GIBSON, Shonda .... 903-886-5743 459 E
shonda.gibson@tamuc.edu
GIBSON, Stacey .... 208-282-3973 132 B
gibssta2@isu.edu
GIBSON, Susan .... 404-880-8757 117 H
sgibson@cau.edu
GIBSON, Sylvia .... 520-494-5573.. 11 P
sylvia.gibson@centralaz.edu
GIBSON, Tammy .... 706-379-3111 128 H
tgibson@yhc.edu
GIBSON, Terry .... 972-923-6406 453 J
terry.gibson@navarrocollege.edu
GIBSON, Tim .... 618-985-3741 141 D
timgibson@jalc.edu
GIBSON, Tim .... 304-642-9997 501 H
gibsont@dewv.edu
GIBSON, Todd, D .... 724-458-2147 396 D
tdgibson@gcc.edu
GIBSON, Tom .... 419-372-2299 357 F
tjgibso@bgsu.edu
GIBSON, Yolanda .... 703-284-1697 483 A
yolanda.gibson@marymount.edu
GIBSON SHEFFIELD,
Gail .... 802-387-6797 475 C
gailsheffield@landmark.edu
GIBSON-SHREVE, Lada . 330-494-6170 370 G
lshreve@starkstate.edu
GIDDENS, Jean .... 804-828-5174 487 E
jgiddens@vcu.edu
GIDDINGS, Andrew .... 480-461-7802.. 13 I
andrew.giddings@mesacc.edu
GIDDINGS, Geoffrey, J . 937-376-6464 358 I
ggiddings@centralstate.edu
GIDDINGS, Meg, H .... 229-245-6490 127 H
mhgiddin@valdosta.edu
GIDDIS, Rayanne .... 352-854-2322.. 97 C
giddisr@cf.edu
GIDDY, Shawn .... 256-782-5299.... 6 B
sgiddy@jsu.edu
GIDEON, Amy, C .... 615-868-6503 434 G
amy@mtsa.edu
GIDLEY, James, S .... 724-847-6719 395 J
jsgidley@geneva.edu
GIE, Lori .... 504-520-5730 198 D
lgie@xula.edu
GIELOW, Bob .... 617-559-8610 215 H
bgielow@hebrewcollege.edu
GIELOW, Curt .... 734-995-7331 229 A
curt.gielow@cuw.edu
GIERI, Joe .... 505-425-7511 294 J
GIERING, Mike .... 503-517-1220 388 A
mgiering@warnerpacific.edu
GIEROK, Ed .... 503-554-2090 383 C
egierok@georgefox.edu
GIES, Jason .... 814-254-0564 392 F
jgies@pa.gov
GIESCHEN, Charles, A .. 260-452-2104 157 F
charles.gieschen@ctsfw.edu
GIESE, Martin .... 218-751-8670 249 G
martingiese@oakhills.edu
GIESE, Melissa .... 816-604-1492 262 F
melissa.giese@mcckc.edu
GIESE, Ralph .... 719-255-4327.. 83 C
rgiese@uccs.edu
GIESECKE, Marian, K .... 806-651-2055 460 E
mgiesecke@mail.wtamu.edu
GIESEKE, Amy .... 515-961-1615 173 E
amy.gieseke@simpson.edu
GIESEKE, Melinda .... 630-617-3010 138 C
melinda.gieseke@elmhurst.edu
GIESELMAN, Tammy ..... 812-488-2260 164 G
tg85@evansville.edu
GIESEMAN, Mark .... 913-758-6526 182 B
giesemanm@stmary.edu
GIESSMAN, Michelle ..... 636-949-4975 261 I
mgiessman@lindenwood.edu
GIFFIN, Thomas .... 678-466-4474 117 I
thomasgiffin@clayton.edu
GIFFORD, Darcy .... 734-487-5375 229 K
dgiffor2@emich.edu
GIFFORD, Denise, D ..... 610-499-1265 414 F
ddgifford@widener.edu
GIFFORD, Rachel .... 870-838-2902.. 17 K
rgifford@smail.anc.edu
GIFFORD, Rhonda .... 724-938-4413 405 F
gifford@calu.edu
GIFFROW, Tammy .... 281-756-3598 442 C
tgiffrow@alvincollege.edu
GIGER, Chris .... 662-846-4760 252 H
cgiger@deltastate.edu
GIGER, Keith .... 615-297-7545 429 H
gigerk@aquinascollege.edu
GIGER, Lisa .... 662-846-4035 252 H
lgiger@deltastate.edu
GIGLIO, Elizabeth .... 845-758-7177 298 I
giglio@bard.edu
GIGLIOTTI, Chandra, M 410-827-5812 203 C
cgigliotti@chesapeake.edu
GIGLIOTTI, Lori .... 402-354-7044 275 P
lori.gigliotti@methodistcollege.edu
GIGOT, Jeremy .... 620-276-9570 177 G
jeremy.gigot@gcccks.edu
GIGUERE, Marlene .... 770-538-4722 116 F
mgiguere@brenau.edu
GIGUETTE, Marguerite ... 504-520-7525 198 D
mgiguett@xula.edu
GIL, Andres .... 305-348-2494 109 D
andres.gil@fiu.edu
GIL, Betty .... 401-874-2310 417 E
bettyg@uri.edu
GILBERT, Aerin .... 410-923-4585.. 93 B
GILBERT, Alan .... 718-951-5102 301 E
agilbert@brooklyn.cuny.edu
GILBERT, Bryan .... 512-313-3000 446 N
bryan.gilbert@concordia.edu
GILBERT, Carl .... 580-559-5410 375 I
cgilbert@ecok.edu
GILBERT, Charlene .... 419-530-2413 372 F
charlene.gilbert@utoledo.edu
GILBERT, Cherryl .... 770-229-3409 126 B
cgilbert@sctech.edu
GILBERT, Corynn .... 541-684-7222 384 H
cgilbert@nwcu.edu
GILBERT, David, H .... 414-906-4670 511 A
dhg@uwm.edu
GILBERT, Dianna .... 225-771-7827 195 J
dianna_gilbert@subr.edu
GILBERT, Elinor .... 213-615-2700.. 37 B
egilbert@thechicagoschool.edu
GILBERT, Emily, R .... 806-371-5403 442 D
e0400185@actx.edu
GILBERT, Faye .... 601-266-4659 256 E
faye.gilbert@usm.edu
GILBERT, Fred .... 928-757-0854.. 14 I
fgilbert@mohave.edu
GILBERT, Gail .... 630-617-6130 138 C
gail.gilbert@elmhurst.edu
GILBERT, Glen, G .... 252-328-0038 349 I
gilbertg@ecu.edu
GILBERT, Glenn .... 574-535-7351 158 A
ggilbert@goshen.edu
GILBERT, Jan .... 308-367-5252 278 A
jgilbert3@unl.edu
GILBERT, Jerome, A ...... 304-696-3977 504 C
gilbert@marshall.edu
GILBERT, Joey .... 276-739-2473 490 A
jgilbert@vhcc.edu
GILBERT, Jon .... 601-266-1000 256 E
jon.gilbert@usm.edu
GILBERT, Karen .... 404-471-6435 114 H
kgilbert@agnesscott.edu
GILBERT, Larry .... 940-498-6282 453 L
lgilbert@nctc.edu
GILBERT, Lynda .... 205-348-4530.... 8 A
lgilbert@fa.ua.edu
GILBERT, Lynne .... 660-562-1110 264 I
lynneg@nwmissouri.edu
GILBERT, Michael .... 213-624-1200.. 42 N
mgilbert@fidm.edu
GILBERT, Michael .... 860-486-6137.. 88 G
michael.gilbert@uconn.edu
GILBERT, Mindy .... 615-514-2787 435 F
mgilbert@nossi.edu
GILBERT, Nancy .... 419-448-3413 370 K
ngilbert@tiffin.edu
GILBERT, Peter, J .... 920-832-7353 507 L
peter.j.gilbert@lawrence.edu
GILBERT, Regina .... 615-383-4848 441 A
rgilbert@watkins.edu
GILBERT, Rhonda .... 319-226-2011 166 C
rhonda.gilbert@allencollege.edu
GILBERT, Rowdy, C .... 405-325-1703 380 L
rowdy@ou.edu
GILBERT, Sharon .... 603-542-7744 281 A
sgilbert@ccsnh.edu
GILBERT, Susan, P .... 678-547-6438 122 H
gilbert_sp@mercer.edu
GILBERT, Teresa .... 423-478-7702 435 I
tgilbert@ptseminary.edu
GILBERT, Trent .... 309-457-2210 146 A
tgilbert@monmouthcollege.edu
GILBERTSON, Sandi .... 701-671-2904 355 B
sandi.gilbertson@ndscs.edu
GILBES, Fernando .... 787-265-3828 528 C
decano.arci@uprm.edu
GILCHRIST, Cheryl, B .... 502-852-8139 190 C
cbgilc01@louisville.edu
GILCHRIST, Debra .... 253-964-6584 497 B
dgilchrist@pierce.ctc.edu
GILCHRIST, Graham ...... 386-481-2097.. 95 J
gilchrisstg@cookman.edu
GILCHRIST, James, A .... 269-387-2382 239 E
james.gilchrist@wmich.edu
GILCHRIST, Lou Ann ..... 660-785-4111 267 K
lcg@truman.edu
GILCREASE, Kathy .... 936-294-1012 462 F
gilcrease@shsu.edu
GILCREAST, Emily .... 401-598-1000 416 C
egilcreast@jwu.edu
GILDAWIE, Janice .... 413-528-7698 211 B
jgildawie@simons-rock.edu
GILDEN, Bruce, F .... 858-499-0202.. 39 B
bgilden@coleman.edu
GILDERSLEEVE,
Elizabeth .... 781-283-2376 225 D
egilders@wellesley.edu
GILDERSLEEVE,
Elizabeth, T .... 781-283-2376 225 D
egilders@wellesley.edu
GILDERSLEEVE,
Susan, M .... 402-472-3886 277 G
sgildersleeve1@unl.edu
GILDNER, Dan .... 937-529-2201 371 B
dgildner@united.edu
GILDNER, Justin .... 828-298-3325 353 B
jgildner@warren-wilson.edu
GILE, Jason .... 630-620-2105 147 I
jgile@faculty.seminary.edu
GILE, Joseph .... 316-942-4291 180 D
gilej@newmanu.edu
GILES, Daniel .... 330-337-6403 356 B
bookstore@awc.edu
GILES, Francis .... 716-614-6407 318 E
fgiles@niagaracc.suny.edu
GILES, Gordon .... 513-875-3344 359 C
gordon.giles@chatfield.edu
GILES, JR., Henry, C ..... 864-592-4616 424 C
gilesh@sccsc.edu
GILES, Pam .... 276-523-2400 488 F
pgiles@mecc.edu
GILES, Robert .... 662-627-2571 252 E
GILES, Roger, W .... 870-235-4008.. 21 F
rwgiles@saumag.edu
GILES, Wayne .... 312-996-5939 153 H
wgiles@uic.edu
GILFERT, Christy .... 941-637-5678 100 E
cgilfert@fsw.edu
GILFILLAN, Margaret ..... 412-392-3994 408 F
mgilfillan@pointpark.edu
GILGALLON, James .... 570-208-8103 398 D
jamesgilgallon@kings.edu
GILGOUR, Joe .... 660-596-7393 267 E
jgilgour@sfccmo.edu
GILKER, Bill .... 817-760-5504 450 B
wmgilker@hillcollege.edu
GILKERSON, Tammeil .... 510-464-3236.. 56 H
tgilkerson@peralta.edu
GILL, Allison .... 978-837-5175 221 G
gilla@merrimack.edu
GILL, Barbara, A .... 301-314-8350 207 G
bgill@umd.edu
GILL, Barbara, J .... 850-201-6570 112 C
gillb@tcc.fl.edu
GILL, Casey .... 937-327-7801 374 A
gillc@wittenberg.edu
GILL, Chris .... 515-271-3918 168 J
chris.gill@drake.edu
GILL, D. Christopher ...... 573-288-6322 259 E
cgill@culver.edu
GILL, Dennis .... 541-881-5915 387 D
dgill@tvcc.cc
GILL, Elizabeth, A .... 716-888-2150 300 G
gille@canisius.edu
GILL, Jackie .... 816-604-5250 262 H
jackie.gill@mcckc.edu
GILL, Janet .... 712-274-6400 174 E
janet.gill@witcc.edu
GILL, Janet .... 303-333-4224.. 76 L
GILL, Jason .... 847-866-3987 138 G
jason.gill@garrett.edu
GILL, Jeffery, A .... 574-372-5100 158 B
gillja@grace.edu
GILL, Lanae .... 313-993-1230 237 F
gillla@udmercy.edu
GILL, Lee, A .... 864-656-4238 419 F
lagill@clemson.edu
GILL, Mark .... 970-491-6211.. 78 N
mark.gill@colostate.edu
GILL, Michele .... 402-844-7748 276 G
micheleg@northeast.edu
GILL, Nancy .... 805-437-8456.. 31 C
nancy.gill@csuci.edu
GILL, Nicholas .... 207-216-4467 200 E
ngill@yccc.edu
GILL, Paula .... 615-460-8637 430 D
paula.gill@belmont.edu
GILL, Ruth .... 410-334-2928 210 C
rgill@worwic.edu
GILL, Sandra .... 630-829-6216 133 I
sgill@ben.edu
GILL, Sean .... 951-827-6063.. 69 D
sean.gill@ucr.edu
GILL, Stacey .... 256-551-5211.... 2 D
stacey.gill@drakestate.edu
GILL, Steven .... 609-258-3466 288 F
sgill@princeton.edu
GILLAHAN, Sheila .... 731-286-3316 437 A
gillahan@dscc.edu

GILLAM WEIR, Linda .... 501-420-1200.. 17 I linda.gillam@arkansasbaptist.edu

GILLAN, Darlene ... 617-879-7050 218 B sgillan@massart.edu

GILLAN, Maria ... 973-684-5904 288 C mgillan@pccc.edu

GILLAND, Laura ... 704-637-4410 336 G lgwimpey@catawba.edu

GILLARD, Natalie ... 575-461-4413 294 E natalieg@mesalands.edu

GILLARD, Natalie ... 443-352-4489 207 C ngillard@stevenson.edu

GILLARDI, Michael ... 401-598-1450 416 C mgillardi@jwu.edu

GILLASPIE, Breanda ... 972-241-3371 447 E bgillaspie@dallas.edu

GILLASPIE, Ray ... 270-824-8592 186 D ray.gillaspie@kctcs.edu

GILLE, Chaudron ... 706-864-1840 127 B chaudron.gille@ung.edu

GILLECE, Nancy, E ... 301-696-3710 204 D gillece@hood.edu

GILLEN, Dan ... 319-296-4268 169 H daniel.gillen@hawkeyecollege.edu

GILLENWATER, Jody ... 502-213-8803 189 E jgillenwater@sullivan.edu

GILLERLAIN, Kelly ... 757-822-5159 489 H kgillerlain@tcc.edu

GILLES, Barbara, L ... 412-578-6123 391 G gillesbl@carlow.edu

GILLESPIE, Adrienne, G 801-626-7243 473 E adrienneandrews@weber.edu

GILLESPIE, Andrew, R ... 334-844-5009.... 4 D arg0014@auburn.edu

GILLESPIE, Anne Marie . 740-351-3251 369 L agillespie@shawnee.edu

GILLESPIE, Barbara ... 276-326-4237 478 H bgillespie@bluefield.edu

GILLESPIE, Bart ... 678-839-6582 127 F bgillesp@westga.edu

GILLESPIE, Christine ... 201-612-7488 283 I cgillespie@bergen.edu

GILLESPIE, Dave ... 402-941-6545 275 J gillespie@midlandu.edu

GILLESPIE, Denise ... 662-620-5368 253 D dlgillespie@iccms.edu

GILLESPIE, Greg ... 805-652-5502.. 72 G ggillespie@vcccd.edu

GILLESPIE, Greg ... 805-289-6460.. 73 C ggillespie@vcccd.edu

GILLESPIE, Griffin ... 701-777-2103 353 G 1120mgr@follett.com

GILLESPIE, Jon ... 210-829-3971 465 E jong@uiwtx.edu

GILLESPIE, Mary Ellen .. 860-768-4989.. 89 C ad@hartford.edu

GILLESPIE, Melanie ... 864-644-5504 424 B mlgillespie@swu.edu

GILLESPIE, Michele, K .. 336-758-5000 353 A gillesmk@wfu.edu

GILLESPIE, Teresa ... 425-889-5290 496 E teresa.gillespie@northwestu.edu

GILLESS, J. Keith ... 510-642-7171.. 68 G gilless@berkeley.edu

GILLETT, Charisse, L ... 859-280-1230 187 G cgillett@lextheo.edu

GILLETTE, Donna ... 207-947-4591 198 F dgillette@bealcollege.edu

GILLETTE, Jack ... 617-349-8401 216 D jgillett@lesley.edu

GILLETTE, John ... 509-533-8378 493 H john.gillette@ccs.spokane.edu

GILLETTE, John ... 509-533-8378 494 A john.gillette@ccs.spokane.edu

GILLETTE, John ... 406-657-1714 272 B john.gillette2@msubillings.edu

GILLETTE, Kimberly ... 218-282-8442 250 G gillette@umn.edu

GILLETTE, Lynn ... 985-448-4011 197 C lynn.gillette@nicholls.edu

GILLETTE, Maureen ... 973-275-2725 291 F

GILLETTE, Susan ... 410-706-5353 207 H sgillett@umaryland.edu

GILLEY, Michael ... 276-523-2400 488 F mgilley@mecc.edu

GILLEY, Ryan ... 513-529-2107 365 I gilleyrl@miamioh.edu

GILLIAM, Dara ... 405-695-5533 375 K dgilliam@familyoffaith.edu

GILLIAM, Dara ... 405-273-5331 375 K dgilliam@familyoffaith.edu

GILLIAM, Franklin, D ... 336-334-5266 351 D fgilliam@uncg.edu

GILLIAM, Keshia ... 864-596-9029 420 F nikeshiajackson.gilliam@converse.edu

GILLIAM, Kevin ... 616-222-3000 232 F kgilliam@kuyper.edu

GILLIAM, Melissa ... 773-834-0840 153 F mgilliam@babies.bsd.uchicago.edu

GILLIAM, Rebecca ... 318-670-9353 196 A rgilliam@susla.edu

GILLIAM, Thomas, J ... 850-484-1500 105 E tgilliam@pensacolastate.edu

GILLIAM, Tom ... 850-484-1500 105 E tgilliam@pensacolastate.edu

GILLIAM PHILLIPS, Ruth ... 919-530-7908 350 D ruth.gilliam.phillips@nccu.edu

GILLICK, SJ, Lawrence .. 402-280-2664 274 D igillick@creighton.edu

GILLIE, Esther ... 757-352-4182 484 E egillie@regent.edu

GILLIE, Lynn, L ... 607-735-1804 307 G lgillie@elmira.edu

GILLIES, Cheryl ... 626-396-2278.. 26 L cheryl.gillies@artcenter.edu

GILLIGAN, Thomas ... 650-723-1198.. 66 C

GILLIGAN, William ... 617-824-8190 214 E william_gilligan@emerson.edu

GILLIHAN, Crystal ... 870-512-7747.. 18 D crystal_gillihan@asun.edu

GILLILAND, Brandon ... 845-434-5750 330 F bgilliland@sullivan.suny.edu

GILLILAND, Christie ... 253-833-9111 495 C cgilliland@greenriver.edu

GILLILAND, Drew ... 541-552-6319 386 H gilliland@sou.edu

GILLILAND, Jane, A ... 607-587-3979 328 F gillilja@alfredstate.edu

GILLILAND, Mary, K ... 520-494-5210.. 11 P marykay.gilliland@centralaz.edu

GILLILAND, William ... 301-295-9845 518 G william.gilliland@usuhs.edu

GILLIN, Douglas, P ... 828-262-7781 349 H gillindp@appstate.edu

GILLINGS, Alison ... 800-280-0307 155 H alison.gillings@ace.edu

GILLIS, Arthur ... 225-743-8500 193 C agillis@rpcc.edu

GILLIS, Dawn ... 914-606-6844 333 H dawn.gillis@sunywcc.edu

GILLIS, Graham ... 501-450-3181.. 23 I ggillis@uca.edu

GILLIS, James ... 240-567-7348 205 F james.gillis@montgomerycollege.edu

GILLIS, Lynette ... 512-313-3000 446 N lynette.gillis@concordia.edu

GILLIS-OLION, Marion .. 910-672-1265 350 B molion@uncfsu.edu

GILLISPIE, Billy ... 254-267-7059 454 L bgillispie@rangercollege.edu

GILLISPIE, James ... 540-868-7042 488 E jgillispie@lfcc.edu

GILLISS, Buster ... 701-224-5512 354 F buster.gilliss@bismarckstate.edu

GILLITZER, Nadia ... 319-363-1323 172 B ngillitzer@mtmercy.edu

GILLLILAN, Kevin, L ... 256-765-4357.... 9 A kgillilan@una.edu

GILLMAN, Howard, A ... 949-824-5111.. 69 A chancellor@uci.edu

GILLMAN, Rick ... 219-464-6718 165 D rick.gillman@valpo.edu

GILLMAN, Sally ... 605-688-4151 429 B sally.gillman@sdstate.edu

GILLMING, Kenneth, D . 617-364-3510 212 D kgillming@boston.edu

GILLOOLY, Jeffrey ... 508-793-7512 213 C jgillooly@clarku.edu

GILLS, Twyla ... 214-379-5460 454 H tgills@pqc.edu

GILLUM, Deborah ... 574-807-7015 156 E gillumd@bethelcollege.edu

GILLUS, Raynaldo ... 662-254-3636 255 A raynaldo.hall@mvsu.edu

GILMAN, Isaac ... 503-352-1401 385 I gilmani@pacificu.edu

GILMAN, James ... 860-701-5182.. 87 F gilman_j@mitchell.edu

GILMAN, Jean ... 314-977-3415 266 J jgilman2@slu.edu

GILMAN, Sharon ... 520-515-5382.. 11 R gilmans@cochise.edu

GILMAN, Wendy ... 518-255-5520 328 C gilmanwc@cobleskill.edu

GILMARTIN, Anne ... 914-674-7337 314 I agilmartin@mercy.edu

GILMARTIN, Kevin, M ... 626-395-6351.. 29 I kmg@hss.caltech.edu

GILMER, Chris ... 601-629-3568 251 G cgilmer@alcorn.edu

GILMER, Elizabeth ... 478-289-2037 118 H egilmer@ega.edu

GILMER, Garrett ... 419-372-2081 357 F ggilmer@bgsu.edu

GILMER, Ray ... 240-567-7970 205 F ray.gilmer@montgomerycollege.edu

GILMER, Stephanie ... 540-261-8480 485 G stephanie.gilmer@svu.edu

GILMORE, Calvin, L ... 336-272-7102 338 B gilmorec@greensboro.edu

GILMORE, Dan ... 856-256-4684 289 H gilmore@rowan.edu

GILMORE, Darwin ... 850-718-2270.. 96 H gilmored@chipola.edu

GILMORE, David ... 617-989-4328 225 E gilmored@wit.edu

GILMORE, Denise ... 620-431-2820 180 C dgilmore@neosho.edu

GILMORE, Derrick, C ... 502-597-5787 187 E derrick.gilmore@kysu.edu

GILMORE, Don ... 661-362-2811.. 51 C dgilmore@masters.edu

GILMORE, Eric, J ... 402-280-2100 274 D ericgilmore@creighton.edu

GILMORE, Grover, C ... 216-368-2270 358 C gcg@case.edu

GILMORE, Jennifer, D ... 812-888-5332 165 E jgilmore@vinu.edu

GILMORE, John, W ... 609-497-7705 288 E john.gilmore@ptsem.edu

GILMORE, Malinda ... 256-372-5230.... 1 A malinda.gilmore@aamu.edu

GILMORE, Robert ... 914-323-5357 314 A robert.gilmore@mville.edu

GILMORE, Wilson ... 505-786-4104 294 I wgilmorei@navajotech.edu

GILMORE ENGLISH, Jessica ... 425-235-2463 497 E jgilmoreenglishl@rtc.edu

GILMOUR, Davie, J ... 570-320-8010 403 F djg120@psu.edu

GILMOUR, Davie Jane .. 570-326-3761 404 T dgilmour@pct.edu

GILORMINI, Dominique 787-766-1912 524 E dgilormini@inter.edu

GILORMINI-DE GRACIA, Dominique ... 787-763-4203 523 F dgilormini@inter.edu

GILREATH, Scott ... 765-677-6515 161 C scott.gilreath@indwes.edu

GILREATH, Scott, A ... 812-488-2492 164 G sg157@evansville.edu

GILROY, Janice ... 914-606-6610 333 H janice.gilroy@sunywcc.edu

GILROY, Maryellen ... 518-783-2328 324 C mgilroy@siena.edu

GILROY, Matt ... 541-888-7259 387 A matt.gilroy@socc.edu

GILSON, David ... 216-791-5000 359 K david.gilson@cim.edu

GILSON, Jannie ... 508-588-9100 220 B

GILSON, Ken ... 562-903-4870.. 27 E ken.gilson@biola.edu

GILSTRAP, Donald ... 205-348-7561.... 8 A dlgilstrap@ua.edu

GILSTRAP, Linda ... 619-216-6614.. 65 H lgilstrap@swccd.edu

GILTNER, Greg ... 405-425-5501 377 B greg.giltner@oc.edu

GIMA, Wesley, T ... 671-735-3025 519 H wesley.gima@guamcc.edu

GIMBEL-JAGGERS, Rachel ... 502-447-1000 189 D rgimbel@spencerian.edu

GIMNESS, Erik ... 253-964-6529 497 B egimness@pierce.ctc.edu

GINDER, Greg ... 317-955-6018 162 R gginder@marian.edu

GINDER, Terry ... 212-217-4260 308 B terry_ginder@fitnyc.edu

GINDER, Zachary ... 760-366-5294.. 41 B zginder@cmccd.edu

GINDRO, Leslie ... 781-768-7068 224 A leslie.gindro@regiscollege.edu

GINES, Joan ... 801-585-9144 472 P joan.gines@utah.edu

GINES, Scott ... 361-593-2411 460 B david.gines@tamuk.edu

GINEVAN, Douglas, W .. 207-786-6093 198 E dginevan@bates.edu

GINGERELLA, David, A . 401-456-8200 417 A dgingerella@ric.edu

GINGERICH, Jeffrey ... 610-902-8301 391 B jeffrey.p.gingerich@cabrini.edu

GINGERICH, Samuel ... 907-786-1437.. 10 A chancellor@alaska.edu

GINGERICH, Willard, P . 973-655-4382 287 D gingerichw@mail.montclair.edu

GINGRAS, Gregory ... 510-869-1588.. 59 F ggingras@samuelmerritt.edu

GINGRICH, Nicole ... 610-282-1100 393 G nicole.gingrich@desales.edu

GINN, Bryan ... 678-225-7500 407 G bginn@pcom.edu

GINN, Julie ... 781-239-2734 220 A jginn@massbay.edu

GINNETTI, Jennifer ... 215-646-7300 396 E ginnetti.j@gmercyu.edu

GINSBERG, Mark, R ... 703-993-2004 481 B mginsber@gmu.edu

GINSBERG, Rick ... 785-864-4297 181 I ginsberg@ku.edu

GINSBURG, Charles, M 214-648-8597 469 E charles.ginsburg@utsouthwestern.edu

GINTER, Judy ... 859-985-3000 183 I

GINTER, Matthew ... 419-434-5624 372 B ginterm@findlay.edu

GINTY, Kevin ... 773-508-2204 144 D kginty@luc.edu

GIOGLIO, Tom ... 570-484-2102 406 E tmg252@lockhaven.edu

GIORDANI, Robert ... 410-704-3508 209 C rgiordani@towson.edu

GIORDANO, Amy ... 567-661-7883 369 A amy_giordano@owens.edu

GIORDANO, Christopher ... 718-982-2335 302 A christopher.giordano@csi.cuny.edu

GIORDANO, George ... 315-268-7722 304 B ggiordan@clarkson.edu

GIORDANO, Matthew .... 716-896-0700 333 C giordano@villa.edu

GIORDANO, Nicholas, J ... 334-844-5737.... 4 D njg0003@auburn.edu

GIOVANNELLI, Joseph .. 718-951-5116 301 E jgiovannelli@brooklyn.cuny.edu

GIOVANNELLI, Tony ... 724-964-8811 403 A tgiovannelli@ncstrades.edu

GIOVANNINI, Eugene, V ... 817-515-5201 458 B chancellors.office@tccd.edu

GIPSON, Amy ... 386-822-7220 111 E agipson@stetson.edu

GIPSON, Andre ... 770-216-2960 121 J agipson@ict.edu

GIPSON, Cory ... 903-730-4890 451 D cgipson@jarvis.edu

GIPSON, Macklin ... 731-426-7547 432 J mgipson@lanecollege.edu

GIPSON, Maurice ... 870-972-3081.. 18 A mgipson@astate.edu

GIPSON, Patrick ... 773-602-5524 135 L pgipson2@ccc.edu

GIPSON, Tim ... 760-872-2000.. 41 E tgipson@deepsprings.edu

GIPSON, William ... 215-898-0809 412 G wgipson@exchange.upenn.edu

GIRALDO, Luis ... 805-965-0581.. 62 E lggiraldo@sbcc.edu

GIRARD, Angie ... 509-452-5100 496 H agirard@pnwu.edu

GIRARD, Don ... 310-434-4287.. 62 G girard_donald@smc.edu

GIRARD, Jerry ... 406-683-7181 271 H jerry.girard@umwestern.edu

GIRARD, Preble ... 337-475-5243 197 B preble@mcneese.edu

GIRARD-MALLEY, Jenny ... 510-436-1081.. 45 G girard-malley@hnu.edu

GIRARDELLI, Dawn ... 650-949-6952.. 43 F girardellidawn@foothill.edu

GIRAUD, Gerald ... 307-754-6235 516 Q gerald.giraud@nwc.edu

GIRDWOOD, Anna ... 636-949-4654 261 I agirdwood@lindenwood.edu

GIRELLI, Carl, A ... 434-947-8126 484 B cgirelli@randolphcollege.edu

GIRKINS, Margaret, L ... 406-756-3884 271 A mgirkins@fvcc.edu

GIROD, Carlos ... 214-648-8960 469 E carlos.girod@utsouthwestern.edu

GIROD, Douglas, A ... 785-864-3131 181 I dgirod@ku.edu

GIROD, Mark ... 503-838-8471 388 B girodm@wou.edu

GIRON, Jenny ... 915-831-6571 449 A jgiron6@epcc.edu

GIROUX, Jenifer ... 401-456-8990 417 A jgiroux@ric.edu

GISH, Jennifer ... 518-337-5694 305 B gishj@strose.edu

GISH, Joanne ... 805-565-6066.. 74 I jgish@westmont.edu

GISSENDANNER, Cindy, H ... 410-704-5456 209 C cgissendanner@towson.edu

GISSY, Cynthia ... 304-424-8259 505 C cindy.gissy@wvup.edu

GLOTZBACH, Philip, A .. 518-580-5700 324 D pglotzba@skidmore.edu
GLOVER, Brandi ... 660-263-4100 264 C brandiglover@macc.edu
GLOVER, David ... 501-812-2318.. 23 C dglover@pulaskitech.edu
GLOVER, David ... 757-727-5259 481 E david.glover@hamptonu.edu
GLOVER, Fanchon ... 757-221-7940 479 I wfglov@wm.edu
GLOVER, Gail ... 585-245-5536 327 B glover@geneseo.edu
GLOVER, Glenda ... 615-963-7401 438 E president@tnstate.edu
GLOVER, Jennifer ... 804-425-5797 479 F jglover@ccc-va.com
GLOVER, Joseph ... 352-392-2404 110 D jglover@aa.ufl.edu
GLOVER, Joseph, M ... 812-941-2028 161 A joglover@ius.edu
GLOVER, Katie ... 703-370-6600 483 I
GLOVER, Kerri ... 828-254-1921 340 M kerriaglover@abtech.edu
GLOVER, Kofi ... 813-974-2010 111 A glover@usf.edu
GLOVER, Larry ... 615-329-8826 431 I lglover@fisk.edu
GLOVER, Laura ... 906-227-2244 235 A lglover@nmu.edu
GLOVER, Nathaniel ... 904-470-8012.. 98 B n.glover@ewc.edu
GLOVER, Oveta ... 803-376-5700 418 D oglover@allenuniversity.edu
GLOVER, Paula ... 660-263-4100 264 C paulag@macc.edu
GLOVER, Shirley ... 478-988-6890 117 E sglover@centralgatech.edu
GLOWKA, Arthur, W ... 770-720-5628 124 H awg@reinhardt.edu
GLUCKOWSKY, Moshe, M ... 718-774-3430 300 K
GLYER-CULVER, Betty ... 916-568-3068.. 50 E glyercb@losrios.edu
GLYNN, Carol ... 248-689-8282 238 F cglynn@walshcollege.edu
GLYNN, Graham ... 540-831-5404 484 A geglynn@radford.edu
GLYNN, John, B ... 414-410-4313 506 F jbglynn@stritch.edu
GLYNN, Terry, S ... 858-499-0202.. 39 B tglynn@coleman.edu
GLYNN TOTH, Liz ... 717-243-5121 394 A
GMEINER, Rebecca ... 678-466-4145 117 I rebeccagmeiner@clayton.edu
GNADINGER, Cindy ... 262-524-7246 506 G cgnadinger@carrollu.edu
GNAGE, Marie, F ... 904-632-5094 100 F marie.gnage@fscj.edu
GNAN, Peter, D ... 708-209-3192 136 I pete.gnan@cuchicago.edu
GNANDT, Brian ... 805-756-1400.. 30 K bgnandt@calpoly.edu
GNECCO, Donald ... 706-776-0117 124 E dgnecco@piedmont.edu
GOAD, Philip ... 256-766-6610.... 5 K pgoad@hcu.edu
GOAD, William ... 405-425-5180 377 B bill.goad@oc.edu
GOALDER, Tiffany ... 573-876-7207 267 G tgoalder@stephens.edu
GOBEN, Allen ... 817-515-6200 458 B allen.goben@tccd.edu
GOBEN, Jason ... 606-693-5000 187 D jgoben@kmbc.edu
GOBER, Chris, G ... 636-922-8211 265 J cgober@stchas.edu
GOBER, T. Kale ... 501-450-3197.. 23 I kgober@uca.edu
GOBERISH, John, S ... 724-480-3450 392 K john.goberish@ccbc.edu
GOBLE, Allison ... 606-326-2432 185 E allison.goble@kctcs.edu
GOBLE, Bryen ... 606-886-3863 185 F bryen.goble@kctcs.edu
GOBLE, David, S ... 843-953-1267 419 D dgoble@citadel.edu
GOBLET, Lois ... 518-255-5524 328 C gobletle@cobleskill.edu
GOCHENAUR, Heather, K ... 260-982-5873 162 Q hkgochenaur@manchester.edu
GOCHIS, Cheryl ... 254-710-2000 444 B cheryl_gochis@baylor.edu
GOCHIS, Sue ... 530-541-4660.. 47 I gochis@ltcc.edu
GOCHIS, Suzanne ... 831-479-6527.. 28 F sugochis@cabrillo.edu
GOCIAL, Tammy ... 314-529-6893 262 B tgocial@maryville.edu
GOCKLEY, Daniel, L ... 214-458-6200 468 B daniel.gockley@utsa.edu
GODARD, Mike ... 660-543-4811 268 A godard@ucmo.edu
GODDARD, Amy ... 405-224-3140 381 B agoddard@usao.edu
GODDARD, Courtney ... 816-584-6559 265 C courtney.goddard@park.edu
GODDARD, Deanna ... 507-457-2493 248 C dgoddard@winona.edu
GODDARD, Diane, H ... 785-864-4904 181 I dgoddard@ku.edu
GODDARD, Jerry ... 661-946-2274.. 73 G
GODDARD, Robert ... 802-776-5248 474 H robert.goddard@csj.edu
GODDARD, Scott, D ... 304-637-1352 501 H goddards@dewv.edu
GODDARD, Steve ... 402-472-3123 277 G goddard@unl.edu
GODDARD MCGUIRK, Lisa ... 814-871-7664 395 H
GODDEN, Barb ... 712-325-3230 170 K bgodden@iwcc.edu
GODDEN, Consuelo ... 404-297-9522 120 D goddenc@gptc.edu
GODDING, Jesse ... 972-825-4811 457 F jgodding@sagu.edu
GODEK, Jim ... 949-376-6000.. 47 H jgodek@lcad.edu
GODEL-GENGENBACH, Kay ... 303-384-2120.. 78 J kgengenb@mines.edu
GODES, Iris ... 508-541-1547 214 C igodes@dean.edu
GODFREY, Christian ... 208-535-5387 131 G christian.godfrey@my.eitc.edu
GODFREY, JoAnn ... 315-684-6044 329 F godfrej@morrisville.edu
GODFREY, Kevin ... 805-482-2755.. 58 M registrar-sjs@stjohnsem.edu
GODFREY, Lisa ... 919-777-7784 341 H lgodfrey@cccc.edu
GODFREY, Rodney ... 662-241-7636 254 F ragodfrey@muw.edu
GODFREY, SJ, Timothy, S ... 415-422-6272.. 72 A tgodfrey@usfca.edu
GODFREY-DAWSON, Angela, R ... 252-335-0821 342 D adawson@albemarle.edu
GODFRIAUX, Colleen ... 608-265-9807 512 D colleen.godfriaux@uwc.edu
GODIN, Patricia, A ... 919-866-5170 347 D pagodin@waketech.edu
GODLESKI, Kasha ... 315-445-4772 312 F godleska@lemoyne.edu
GODLESKI, Mark, G ... 315-445-4520 312 F godlesmg@lemoyne.edu
GODMAN, Anne ... 217-479-7141 144 I anne.godman@mac.edu
GODO, James ... 630-637-5809 147 E jwgodo@noctrl.edu
GODREAU, Susan, E ... 315-267-2162 328 A godrease@potsdam.edu
GODSEY, R. Kirby ... 478-330-5609 122 H godsey_rk@mercer.edu
GODWIN, Angeline, D .. 276-656-0201 489 A agodwin@patrickhenry.edu
GODWIN, Deena ... 360-992-2932 493 E dgodson@clark.edu
GODWIN, Donald, R ... 619-260-4588.. 71 J donald.godwin@sandiego.edu
GODWIN, John ... 202-685-4242 518 B john.godwin@ndu.edu
GODWIN, Mandy ... 251-578-1313.... 3 D mgodwin@rstc.edu
GODWIN, Wendell ... 580-559-5274 375 I wgodwin@ecok.edu
GODWIN-HANSON, Lucy, P ... 919-530-5063 350 D lpgodwin@nccu.edu
GODZWA, Alicia ... 540-362-6660 481 F agodzwa@hollins.edu
GOEBEL, Dan ... 928-523-3657.. 14 K
GOEBEL, Jeffrey, D ... 218-477-2069 246 B goebelj@mnstate.edu
GOECKER, James, A ... 812-877-8894 163 G goecker@rose-hulman.edu
GOEDDE, Tony, G ... 419-434-4556 372 B goedde@findlay.edu
GOEKE, Victoria ... 702-651-5946 278 N victoria.goeke@csn.edu
GOEL, Meeta ... 661-722-6300.. 26 C mgoel@avc.edu
GOELDNER, Jason ... 715-365-4534 514 E jgoeldner@nicoletcollege.edu
GOELLNER, Marilyn ... 814-732-1778 406 B mgoellner@edinboro.edu
GOELZHAUSER, Michael, J ... 812-465-1649 165 C mjgoelzh@usi.edu
GOEN, Brandon ... 806-720-7313 452 D brandon.goen@lcu.edu
GOEN, Jennifer ... 239-590-1020 109 C jgoen@fgcu.edu
GOEPPINGER, Kathleen, H ... 630-515-7300 145 I drgoeppinger@midwestern.edu
GOERING, Doug ... 907-474-7730.. 10 B djgoering@alaska.edu
GOERING, Wynn, M ... 505-277-7601 296 H wgoering@unm.edu
GOERLITZ, Ryan, J ... 414-955-8125 508 D rgoerlit@mcw.edu
GOERTEMILLER, Paul, M ... 972-860-7091 447 I paulgoertemiller@dcccd.edu
GOERTZ, Christine ... 563-884-5159 172 H christine.goertz@palmer.edu
GOERTZEN, Leroy ... 503-375-7103 383 A lgoertzen@corban.edu
GOERZEN, Les ... 316-284-5261 175 F lgoerzen@bethelks.edu
GOETCHIUS, Stephen, H ... 860-215-9002.. 86 F sgoetchius@trcc.commnet.edu
GOETHE, Corey ... 989-386-6622 234 B cgoethe@midmich.edu
GOETSCH, John ... 661-946-2274.. 73 G
GOETSCH, Lori, A ... 785-532-7402 179 A lgoetsch@ksu.edu
GOETSCH, Steven, A ... 603-358-2058 283 A steven.goetsch@keene.edu
GOETSCHIUS, Susan ... 607-871-2170 298 A goetschius@alfred.edu
GOETTSCH, Gay ... 575-769-4043 293 M gay.goettsch@clovis.edu
GOETZ, Amy ... 304-793-6845 504 F agoetz@osteo.wvsom.edu
GOETZ, Julie, K ... 260-359-4127 159 B jgoetz@huntington.edu
GOETZ, Michael, A ... 414-847-3305 508 G mikegoetz@miad.edu
GOETZ, Michele ... 619-594-1862.. 34 B mgoetz@foundation.sdsu.edu
GOETZ, Stephen ... 907-474-6215.. 10 B sfgoetz@alaska.edu
GOEWERT, Ed ... 618-374-5109 149 A ed.goewert@principia.edu
GOFF, Anton ... 718-990-6173 322 F goffa@stjohns.edu
GOFF, David ... 303-724-7304.. 83 D david.goff@ucdenver.edu
GOFF, David, W ... 870-236-6901.. 19 D dgoff@crc.edu
GOFF, Jamie ... 325-674-2751 441 D jdb99a@acu.edu
GOFF, Jay ... 314-977-3733 266 J goffjw@slu.edu
GOFF, Karen ... 404-471-6391 114 H kgoff@agnesscott.edu
GOFF, Kim ... 916-558-2054.. 50 I goffk@scc.losrios.edu
GOFF, Michelle ... 478-289-2095 118 H mgoff@ega.edu
GOFF, Patricia, A ... 401-865-1031 416 E pgoff@providence.edu
GOFF, Sue ... 503-594-3110 382 D sue.goff@clackamas.edu
GOFF, Tiffanie ... 419-448-3509 370 K gofftn@tiffin.edu
GOFF-CREWS, Kimberly 203-432-6602.. 89 G kimberly.goff-crews@yale.edu
GOFFE-RUSH, Lorraine, A ... 617-253-6512 221 C
GOFORTH, Cheri, D ... 501-686-5850.. 22 C goforthcherid@uams.edu
GOFORTH, Chris ... 864-294-2024 421 I chris.goforth@furman.edu
GOGA, Nedzad ... 718-636-3599 320 D ngoga@pratt.edu
GOGA, Robert, D ... 412-624-6609 412 I rgoga@cfo.pitt.edu
GOGGIN, Trudi ... 708-524-6824 137 F tgoggin@dom.edu
GOGNAT, Timothy ... 859-622-2696 184 F timothy.gognat@eku.edu
GOH, Michael ... 612-624-2590 250 E mgoh@umn.edu
GOH, Sumheda ... 408-260-0208.. 43 C sjextension@fivebranches.edu
GOHEEN, Peter ... 207-551-5765 200 B pgoheen@nmcc.edu
GOHLKE, Brian, B ... 608-757-7773 513 D bgohlke@blackhawk.edu
GOHMANN, Jennifer ... 502-585-9911 189 B jgohmann@spalding.edu
GOHSMAN, JR., John, L ... 314-935-7391 269 L jgohsman@wustl.edu
GOIN, JR., Randy ... 717-720-4423 405 D rgoin@passhe.edu
GOINES, Janice ... 979-230-3395 444 E janice.goines@brazosport.edu
GOINGS, Eric ... 918-335-6257 378 F egoings@okwu.edu
GOINS, David ... 409-882-3367 462 D david.goins@lsco.edu
GOINS, Jen ... 765-285-5555 156 C jgoins@bsu.edu
GOINS, Jennifer ... 804-627-5300 478 I jennifer_goins@bshsi.org
GOINS, Jessica, D ... 864-488-4590 422 B jgoins@limestone.edu
GOINS, LaKeya ... 205-366-8150.... 7 C lgoins@stillman.edu
GOINS, Rick ... 479-788-7026.. 22 A rick.goins@uafs.edu
GOINS, Scott, E ... 337-475-5456 197 B sgoins@mcneese.edu
GOINS, Suzanne ... 251-460-6111.... 9 B sgoins@southalabama.edu
GOITIA PADILLA, Francisco, J ... 787-763-6700 522 N javiergoitia@aol.com
GOKCEK, Gigi ... 415-482-2427.. 41 J gigi.gokcek@dominican.edu
GOKE-PARIOLA, Abiodun ... 630-637-5356 147 E agokepariola@noctrl.edu
GOLABEK, Sue ... 843-208-8144 425 B sgolabek@uscb.edu
GOLAN, Jay ... 212-817-7130 302 B jgolan@gc.cuny.edu
GOLAND, Lois ... 518-782-6673 324 C lgoland@siena.edu
GOLATO, Andrea ... 512-245-2581 463 A a_g554@txstate.edu
GOLBA, Gina ... 816-802-3397 261 C ggolba@kcai.edu
GOLD, Cheryl ... 727-864-8058.. 97 O goldcc@eckerd.edu
GOLD, E ... 212-964-2830 315 B egold@mtj.edu
GOLD, Ellen ... 734-487-1107 229 K ellen.gold@emich.edu
GOLD, Harriet, B ... 270-384-8017 187 H goldh@lindsey.edu
GOLD, Jeffery, P ... 402-559-4000 277 H
GOLD, Jeffrey, P ... 402-554-2419 277 I jeffrey.gold@unomaha.edu
GOLD, Jered ... 626-396-2251.. 26 L jered.gold@artcenter.edu
GOLD, Kathleen, E ... 802-626-4860 477 D kathleen.gold@lyndonstate.edu
GOLD, Kenneth ... 718-982-3720 302 A education@csi.cuny.edu
GOLD, Kimberly ... 910-272-3230 346 A kgold@robeson.edu
GOLD, Mark ... 718-951-5861 301 E mark@brooklyn.cuny.edu
GOLDAMMER, Diana ... 605-995-2160 427 A digoldam@dwu.edu
GOLDBART, Paul ... 404-894-3300 120 A paul.goldbart@cos.gatech.edu
GOLDBERG, Brian ... 401-709-8579 417 B bgoldber@risd.edu
GOLDBERG, Carole, E ... 310-206-9345.. 69 B cgoldberg@conet.ucla.edu
GOLDBERG, David ... 440-943-5300 369 G dgoldberg@telsheyeshiva.edu
GOLDBERG, Elaine ... 646-565-6000 331 F elaine.goldberg@touro.edu
GOLDBERG, Jane, F ... 360-538-4005 495 B jgoldber@ghc.edu
GOLDBERG, Jeffrey, B ... 520-621-6594.. 16 J jgoldberg@arizona.edu
GOLDBERG, Rageshwar 661-255-1050.. 29 F rgoldberg@calarts.edu
GOLDBERG, Robert ... 212-854-2003 299 B rgoldber@barnard.edu
GOLDBERG, Suzanne, B ... 212-854-0411 305 E sgoldb1@law.columbia.edu
GOLDBERG, Yisroel ... 973-267-9404 289 B financialaid@rca.edu
GOLDBERGBELLE, Jonathan ... 217-206-8319 154 A goldbergbelle.jonathan@uis.edu
GOLDBERGER, David ... 845-783-9901 332 G

GOLDBERGER, Jo ... 212-229-5192 316 E
jogo@newschool.edu
GOLDBLUM, Tom ... 610-989-1329 413 I
tgoldblum@vfmac.edu
GOLDEN, Andrew, K ... 609-258-4136 288 F
agolden@princeton.edu
GOLDEN, Beverley ... 903-566-7303 468 C
bgolden@uttyler.edu
GOLDEN, Carolyn ... 334-244-3369.... 4 E
cgolden2@aum.edu
GOLDEN, Cheryl ... 316-942-4291 180 D
goldenc@newmanu.edu
GOLDEN, Chris ... 423-614-8020 432 L
cgolden@leeuniversity.edu
GOLDEN, Cynthia ... 412-624-3335 412 I
goldenc@pitt.edu
GOLDEN, David ... 865-974-0782 439 H
dgolden@tennessee.edu
GOLDEN, Denise ... 814-871-7663 395 H
golden007@gannon.edu
GOLDEN, Frederick ... 803-516-4561 423 G
fgolden@scsu.edu
GOLDEN, Jay ... 252-328-9479 349 I
goldenj17@ecu.edu
GOLDEN, Jill ... 864-294-2180 421 I
jill.golden@furman.edu
GOLDEN, Kendra, J ... 509-527-4952 500 G
golden@whitman.edu
GOLDEN, Marthe ... 713-348-4428 455 F
marthe.golden@rice.edu
GOLDEN, Paul ... 570-586-2400 392 E
pgolden@clarkssummitu.edu
GOLDEN, Robert, N ... 608-263-4910 510 C
rngolden@wisc.edu
GOLDENBERG,
David, H ... 860-768-4100.. 89 C
goldenberg@hartford.edu
GOLDENBERG,
David, H ... 860-768-4055.. 89 C
goldenber@hartford.edu
GOLDENBERG, Isabel ... 202-741-2656.. 92 A
iag@gwu.edu
GOLDENBERG, Jay ... 646-216-2862 317 E
jgoldenberg@nycda.edu
GOLDENBERG, Mary ... 847-491-2005 148 C
m-goldenberg@northwestern.edu
GOLDENSON, Jeff ... 781-292-2389 215 C
jeff.goldenson@olin.edu
GOLDEY, Ellen ... 561-799-8579 109 B
egoldey@fau.edu
GOLDFEIZ, Emanuel ... 410-653-0433 206 C
GOLDGEIER, Eileen ... 919-515-3932 350 E
eileen_goldgeier@ncsu.edu
GOLDHABER, Yochanan 718-232-7800 334 G
GOLDHAHN, Anna ... 513-244-4273 366 A
anna.goldhahn@msj.edu
GOLDIN, Michael, M ... 248-232-4412 235 D
mmgoldin@oaklandcc.edu
GOLDING, Sharale ... 860-512-2703.. 85 G
sgolding@manchestercc.edu
GOLDING, Stephen ... 740-597-5221 368 G
golding@ohio.edu
GOLDING, Stephen, M . 214-887-5191 448 G
sgolding@dts.edu
GOLDING, Tena ... 985-549-2316 197 E
tgolding@selu.edu
GOLDMAN, Gregg ... 520-621-5977.. 16 J
ggoldman@email.arizona.edu
GOLDMAN, Larry ... 908-709-7130 292 C
goldman@ucc.edu
GOLDMAN, Lee ... 212-305-2752 305 E
lg2379@columbia.edu
GOLDMAN, Lynn, R ... 202-994-1000.. 92 A
GOLDMAN, Zvi ... 203-591-5651.. 87 H
zgoldman@post.edu
GOLDMON, Moses ... 731-426-1722 432 J
mgoldmon@lanecollege.edu
GOLDNER, Lauren ... 310-824-1586.. 24 B
lgoldner@ajrca.edu
GOLDSBERRY,
Kimberlie ... 262-551-5721 506 H
kgoldsberry@carthage.edu
GOLDSBERRY, Mark ... 402-554-3083 277 I
mgoldsberry@unomaha.edu
GOLDSBY, Michael ... 765-285-9002 156 C
mgoldsby@bsu.edu
GOLDSCHMID, Steven ... 520-626-4555.. 16 J
sgoldsch@email.arizona.edu
GOLDSCHMIDT, Erik ... 251-380-3499.... 7 B
egoldschmidt@shc.edu
GOLDSCHMIDT, Robert . 646-565-6000 331 F
robertgo@touro.edu
GOLDSMITH, Carole ... 559-489-2212.. 66 G
carole.goldsmith@fresnocitycollege.edu
GOLDSMITH, Carolee ... 970-204-5363.. 79 K
carolee.goldsmith@frontrange.edu
GOLDSMITH, Diane ... 401-874-4128 417 E
dgoldsmith@uri.edu
GOLDSMITH, Glenn ... 574-269-5344 158 B
goldsmga@grace.edu
GOLDSMITH, Gordon ... 303-404-5799.. 79 K
gordon.goldsmith@frontrange.edu
GOLDSMITH, Kristie ... 901-678-1782 439 E
kgldsmth@memphis.edu
GOLDSMITH, Rae ... 618-453-2518 152 B
rae.goldsmith@siu.edu
GOLDSMITH, Steve ... 903-813-2342 443 F
sgoldsmith@austincollege.edu
GOLDSTEIN, Adam ... 336-758-5226 353 A
GOLDSTEIN, Benjamin .. 213-763-3683.. 49 F
goldstbd@lattc.edu
GOLDSTEIN, Bill ... 641-472-7000 171 J
bgoldstein@mum.edu
GOLDSTEIN, Brian, A ... 215-951-1015 398 F
goldstein@lasalle.edu
GOLDSTEIN, Cheryl ... 212-517-0683 314 D
cgoldstein@mmm.edu
GOLDSTEIN, Chip, B ... 415-575-6100.. 29 H
cgoldstein@ciis.edu
GOLDSTEIN, Jeffrey, E .. 610-330-5001 399 B
goldstej@lafayette.edu
GOLDSTEIN, Jody ... 978-934-4574 217 B
jody_goldstein@uml.edu
GOLDSTEIN, Joel ... 336-315-7800.. 93 B
GOLDSTEIN, Leonard ... 480-219-6017 257 A
lgoldstein@atsu.edu
GOLDSTEIN, Mary Ellen 704-463-1360 348 B
mary.goldstein@pfeiffer.edu
GOLDSTEIN, Matthias ... 410-704-2466 209 C
mgoldstein@towson.edu
GOLDSTEIN, Robert, S .. 502-852-6169 190 C
rsgold03@louisville.edu
GOLDSTEIN, Serge, J ... 609-258-6059 288 F
serge@princeton.edu
GOLDSTEIN, Sharon ... 973-684-6919 288 C
sgoldstein@pccc.edu
GOLDSTEIN, Sheri, E ... 561-862-4310 105 A
goldstse@palmbeachstate.edu
GOLDSTEIN, Steve ... 708-216-3223 144 D
sgoldstrin3@lumc.edu
GOLDSTEIN, Stuart ... 973-720-2110 292 I
goldsteins@wpunj.edu
GOLDSTON, David ... 202-789-1828 221 C
GOLDWATER,
Joanne, A ... 240-895-4207 206 G
jagoldwater@smcm.edu
GOLEMBESKI,
Richard, M ... 804-752-3288 484 C
richardgolembesi@rmc.edu
GOLEN, Harriet, S ... 215-670-9328 403 D
hsgolen@peirce.edu
GOLETZ, JR.,
Gregory, J ... 610-799-1172 400 A
ggoletz@lccc.edu
GOLEY, Julie ... 706-737-1604 116 B
jgoley@augusta.edu
GOLIAS, David, P ... 651-286-7446 251 C
dpgolias@unwsp.edu
GOLICH, Vicki ... 303-556-5382.. 80 Q
vgolich@msudenver.edu
GOLIN, Dana ... 212-616-7264 309 G
dana.golin@helenefuld.edu
GOLIS, Kim ... 623-845-3562.. 13 H
kim.golis@gccaz.edu
GOLLAHALLI, Anil, V ... 405-325-4124 380 L
agollahalli@ou.edu
GOLLBERG, Linda ... 208-885-4074 132 I
lstrong@uidaho.edu
GOLLENBERG, Gary ... 914-337-9300 305 F
gary.gollenberg@concordia-ny.edu
GOLLETTE, Tonya ... 251-442-2917.... 8 D
tgollette@umobile.edu
GOLLING, Werner, M ... 316-978-3030 182 F
werner.golling@wichita.edu
GOLLNICK, Donna, A ... 844-283-2246.. 91 G
GOLSHANI, Forouzan ... 562-985-1512.. 32 C
forouzan.golshani@csulb.edu
GOLTERMANN, Michael 310-287-4579.. 49 H
golterjm@wlac.edu
GOLTSER, Zhanna ... 410-857-2234 205 E
zgoltser@mcdaniel.edu
GOLTZ, Jeff, W ... 407-582-8265 113 F
jgoltz@valenciacollege.edu
GOLUB, Andrew ... 207-602-2319 202 A
agolub@une.edu
GOLUBOFF, Risa, L ... 434-924-7343 486 H
rlg3b@virginia.edu
GOMBAR, Sarah ... 734-432-5755 233 C
sgombar@madonna.edu
GOMBERG, Barry, G ... 801-626-6240 473 E
bgomberg@weber.edu
GOMES, Antoinette ... 401-456-8791 417 A
agomes@ric.edu
GOMES, David ... 508-999-8192 217 A
dgomes3@umassd.edu
GOMES, Farrah-Marie ... 808-932-7445 129 I
GOMES, Farrahmarie ... 808-974-7664 129 I
fmgomes@hawaii.edu
GOMES, Lyle ... 661-632-6105 325 F
lyle.gomes@stonybrook.edu
GOMES, Roxanne ... 401-874-2442 417 E
rgomes@uri.edu
GOMES, Stacy ... 619-574-6909.. 55 B
sgomes@pacificcollege.edu
GOMEZ, Alicia ... 956-872-5529 456 G
agomez@southtexascollege.edu
GOMEZ, Bellegran ... 562-860-2451.. 36 A
bgomez@cerritos.edu
GOMEZ, Beth ... 951-487-3011.. 52 J
bgomez@msjc.edu
GOMEZ, Carlos, J ... 850-644-2003 110 A
cjgomez@fsu.edu
GOMEZ, Christina ... 312-899-7479 151 F
cgomez3@saic.edu
GOMEZ, David ... 718-518-4300 302 D
dgomez@hostos.cuny.edu
GOMEZ, Dax ... 615-514-2787 435 F
dgomez@nossi.edu
GOMEZ, Doris ... 757-352-4686 484 E
dorirop@regent.edu
GOMEZ, Elba ... 559-244-5973.. 66 E
elba.gomez@scccd.edu
GOMEZ, Elizabeth ... 213-252-5100.. 24 A
egomez@alu.edu
GOMEZ, Eva, C ... 805-437-3271.. 31 C
eva.gomez@csuci.edu
GOMEZ, Fernando, C ... 512-463-1808 462 A
fernando.gomez@tsus.edu
GOMEZ, Gabe ... 505-984-6102 295 K
gabe.gomez@sjc.edu
GOMEZ, Jaime, A ... 619-260-4886.. 71 J
jagomez@sandiego.edu
GOMEZ, Johanna ... 718-518-6556 302 D
jgomez@hostos.cuny.edu
GOMEZ, Jose, A ... 323-343-3030.. 32 D
jose.gomez@calstatela.edu
GOMEZ, Jose, D ... 787-834-9595 526 E
jgomez@uaa.edu
GOMEZ, Liz ... 850-484-1702 105 E
lgomez@pensacolastate.edu
GOMEZ, Magda ... 216-987-0204 360 E
magna.gomez@tri-c.edu
GOMEZ, Mary ... 336-342-4261 346 B
gomezm@rockinghamcc.edu
GOMEZ, Petra ... 805-922-6966.. 24 J
petra.gomez@hancockcollege.edu
GOMEZ, Rebecca ... 714-484-7285.. 53 M
rgomez@cypresscollege.edu
GOMEZ, Rebecca ... 312-915-8725 144 D
rgomez1@luc.edu
GOMEZ, Rowena ... 650-433-3823.. 55 I
rgomez@paloaltou.edu
GOMEZ-ARIAS, Thomas 209-667-3288.. 33 F
GOMEZ-HEITZEBERG,
Nan ... 661-395-4305.. 47 A
ngomez@bakersfieldcollege.edu
GOMEZ-PALACIO, Dan .. 573-875-7421 258 F
edgomez@ccis.edu
GOMEZ-TAYLOR, Sara ... 425-352-8284 492 K
sgtaylor@cascadia.edu
GOMIS, Melissa ... 402-826-8565 274 E
melissa.gomis@doane.edu
GONE, Jeremy ... 402-878-2380 275 C
GONG, Ann, M ... 212-752-1530 312 G
annmarie.gong@limcollege.edu
GONG, Changzhen ... 651-631-0204 240 C
tcmhealth@aol.com
GONG, Harry, S ... 716-286-8716 318 F
hgong@niagara.edu
GONNELLA, Chris ... 701-788-4807 354 B
christine.gonnella@mayvillestate.edu
GONSALVES, Michael ... 404-364-8535 124 A
mgonsalves@oglethorpe.edu
GONSALVES-MCCABE,
Kristi ... 303-458-4153.. 82 D
kgonsalv@regis.edu
GONSIOR, Maura ... 575-538-6328 297 H
gonsiorm@wnmu.edu
GONSOULIN, Sid ... 601-266-5767 256 E
sidney.gonsoulin@usm.edu
GONTHIER, Gary ... 603-271-6484 280 N
ggonthier@ccsnh.edu
GONTHIER, Sheri ... 603-271-6484 280 N
sgonthier@ccsnh.edu
GONYEA, David ... 207-755-5251 199 K
dgonyea@cmcc.edu
GONYEA, Jennifer ... 252-246-1228 347 H
jgonyea@wilsoncc.edu
GONYEA, Judith, G ... 617-353-3760 212 G
jgonyea@bu.edu
GONYEA, Nathan ... 518-587-2100 329 C
nathan.gonyea@esc.edu
GONZÁLEZ, Carlos ... 787-765-9695 528 F
carlos.gonzalez55@upr.edu
GONZÁLEZ, Celia ... 787-844-8181 528 E
celia.gonzalez@upr.edu
GONZÁLEZ, Héctor ... 787-834-9595 526 E
hgonzalez@uaa.edu
GONZÁLEZ, Marisol ... 787-264-1912 524 D
mgonzalez@intersg.edu
GONZÁLEZ, Terestella ... 787-257-7373 525 Q
tergonzalez@suagm.edu
GONZÁLEZ, Widalys ... 787-884-3838 520 G
wgonzalez@atenascollege.edu
GONZÁLEZ DE RESENDE,
María, A ... 787-993-8872 527 G
maria.gonzalez34@upr.edu
GONZALES, Adrian ... 760-744-1150.. 55 K
adriangonzales@palomar.edu
GONZALES, Al ... 623-845-3035.. 13 H
al.gonzales@gccaz.edu
GONZALES, Alberto ... 615-460-8259 430 D
alberto.gonzales@belmont.edu
GONZALES, Ana ... 210-829-3937 465 E
anagonza@uiwtx.edu
GONZALES, Benito ... 575-562-2115 293 O
benito.gonzales@enmu.edu
GONZALES, Casey ... 817-272-2099 467 B
gonzales@uta.edu
GONZALES, Christina ... 303-492-8476.. 83 B
christina.gonzales@colorado.edu
GONZALES, Damon, P .. 616-732-1156 229 D
damon.gonzales@davenport.edu
GONZALES, Deanna ... 408-924-2013.. 34 D
deanna.gonzales@sjsu.edu
GONZALES, Frank ... 808-373-2849 131 A
GONZALES, Hector ... 830-591-7281 457 C
hegonzales@swtjc.edu
GONZALES, JR.,
Joseph, M ... 312-329-4202 146 B
joe.gonzales@moody.edu
GONZALES, Junius ... 919-843-8347 349 G
jjgonzales@northcarolina.edu
GONZALES, Leticia ... 432-837-8193 462 G
lgonzales@sulross.edu
GONZALES, Louis ... 432-335-6848 454 C
lgonzales@odessa.edu
GONZALES, Lucinda, A . 972-860-7668 447 I
lucindagonzales@dcccd.edu
GONZALES, Mario ... 559-638-0300.. 66 H
mario.gonzales@reedleycollege.edu
GONZALES, Mark ... 408-270-6450.. 61 O
mark.gonzales@evc.edu
GONZALES, Mark ... 408-274-7900.. 61 O
mark.gonzales@evc.edu
GONZALES, Mary Jo ... 509-335-2355 499 G
mj_gonzales@wsu.edu
GONZALES, Patrick ... 956-665-3110 468 A
patrick.gonzales@utrgv.edu
GONZALES, Philip ... 505-277-1092 296 H
gonzales@unm.edu
GONZALES, Rhonda ... 719-549-2315.. 78 P
rhonda.gonzales@csupueblo.edu
GONZALES, Richard ... 970-947-8428.. 77 M
rgonzales4@coloradomtn.edu
GONZALES, Robert ... 719-549-2943.. 78 P
robert.gonzales@csupueblo.edu
GONZALES, Roxanne ... 505-425-7511 294 J
GONZALES, Samuel ... 210-458-4136 468 B
sam.gonzales@utsa.edu
GONZALES, Sonia ... 303-404-5558.. 79 K
sonia.gonzales@frontrange.edu
GONZALES, Veronica ... 956-665-7495 468 A
veronica.gonzales@utrgv.edu
GONZALES-TAPIA,
Sarah ... 626-914-8556.. 37 G
sgonzales-tapia@citruscollege.edu
GONZALEZ, Alex ... 505-277-4792 296 H
agonzale@unm.edu
GONZALEZ, Amilcar ... 939-292-2223 529 A
amilcar.gonzalez2@upr.edu
GONZALEZ, Anna ... 503-768-7110 383 G
annag@lclark.edu
GONZALEZ, Antonio ... 212-854-3362 299 B
agonzale@barnard.edu
GONZALEZ, Arturo ... 202-646-1337.. 92 E
GONZALEZ, Beatriz ... 909-593-3511.. 70 E
bgonzalez@laverne.edu
GONZALEZ, Benjamin ... 915-747-8550 467 E
bgonzalez22@utep.edu
GONZALEZ, Blanca, M .. 787-250-1912 524 B
bmgonzalez@metro.inter.edu
GONZALEZ, Carla ... 313-664-7431 228 H
cgonzalez@collegeforcreativestudies.
edu
GONZALEZ, Carlos, J ... 787-622-8000 527 B
gonzalez@pupr.edu
GONZALEZ, Carlos, R ... 818-364-7778.. 49 C
gonzalcr@lamission.edu
GONZALEZ, Caroline ... 787-786-3030 526 F
cagonzalez@ucb.edu.pr

GONZALEZ, Cheryl, N ... 904-620-2507 110 E cheryl.gonzalez@unf.edu
GONZALEZ, Claudia ...... 305-348-2111 109 D clgonzal@fiu.edu
GONZALEZ, Deena .... 310-338-1958.. 50 J dgonzale@lmu.edu
GONZALEZ, Edith .... 212-817-7520 302 B egonzalez@gc.cuny.edu
GONZALEZ, Eladio .... 787-664-0353 529 A eladio.gonzalez1@upr.edu
GONZALEZ, Eliseo .... 805-678-5930.. 73 B
GONZALEZ, Elma, D ..... 936-261-2124 458 F edgonzalez@pvamu.edu
GONZALEZ, Fernando ... 787-743-3484 525 M fgonzalez@sanjuanbautista.edu
GONZALEZ, Fernando ... 787-884-6000 522 Q fgonzalez@icprjc.edu
GONZALEZ, Francisco .... 918-333-6151 378 F francisco@gonzalezfirm.com
GONZALEZ, George .... 281-998-6177 455 K george.gonzalez@sjcd.edu
GONZALEZ, Gina, D ...... 956-326-2206 459 B gina@tamiu.edu
GONZALEZ, Griselda ..... 212-217-4000 308 B griselda_gonzalez@fitnyc.edu
GONZALEZ, Herman ...... 602-787-6601.. 13 J herman.gonzalez@paradisevalley.edu
GONZALEZ, Iris .... 787-878-5475 523 H ibgonzalez@arecibo.inter.edu
GONZALEZ, Jaime .... 787-620-2958 520 F jgonzalez@aupr.edu
GONZALEZ, Jaime .... 787-620-2040 520 F carroyo@aupr.edu
GONZALEZ, Jean .... 714-867-5009.. 64 G jgonzalez@southcoastcollege.com
GONZALEZ, Jenny .... 773-577-8100 137 A
GONZALEZ, Jeremy .... 312-553-5641 135 J
GONZALEZ, Jorge, G .... 269-337-7220 231 F jorge.gonzalez@kzoo.edu
GONZALEZ, Jose, N ...... 787-850-9419 528 B jose.gonzalez48@upr.edu
GONZALEZ, Juan, C ..... 858-534-4370.. 69 E vcsa@ucsd.edu
GONZALEZ, Juan, C ..... 956-665-2124 468 A juan.gonzalez@utrgv.edu
GONZALEZ, Juan, R ...... 787-264-1912 524 D juan_gonzalez_mendoza@intersg.edu
GONZALEZ, Karen .... 787-766-1717 526 B um_kgonzalez@suagm.edu
GONZALEZ, Kelly .... 214-648-3519 469 E kelly.gonzalez@utsouthwestern.edu
GONZALEZ, Lissette, V . 787-265-3883 528 C lissette.gonzalez1@upr.edu
GONZALEZ, Lizbeth .... 603-578-8900 280 M lgonzalez@ccsnh.edu
GONZALEZ, Lori .... 901-448-4930 440 C lsgonz01@uthsc.edu
GONZALEZ, Luis .... 512-542-7848 460 B luis.gonzalez@tamus.edu
GONZALEZ, Luis, J .... 724-357-2330 406 C luis.gonzalez@iup.edu
GONZALEZ, Mari, G ...... 787-743-7979 526 A mggonzalez@suagm.edu
GONZALEZ, Maria .... 951-372-7137.. 58 G maria.gonzalez@norcocollege.edu
GONZALEZ, Marilyn ...... 787-882-2065 526 D secretaria_ejecutiva@unitecpr.net
GONZALEZ, Martha, O .. 956-326-2361 459 B marthao.gonzalez@tamiu.edu
GONZALEZ, Mary .... 361-593-2494 460 B kamlp00@tamuk.edu
GONZALEZ, Mauricio .... 904-620-2600 110 E mgonzale@unf.edu
GONZALEZ, Megan .... 850-474-2658 111 D megang@uwf.edu
GONZALEZ, Melissa ...... 713-718-5053 450 D melissa.gonzalez@hccs.edu
GONZALEZ, Monica, D . 787-723-4481 521 H mgonzalez@ceaprc.edu
GONZALEZ, Nichole ...... 716-375-2572 322 B
GONZALEZ, Nicolas ...... 956-872-2133 456 G ngon@southtexascollege.edu
GONZALEZ, Noelia .... 209-667-3070.. 33 F ngonzalez4@csustan.edu
GONZALEZ, Norberto .... 787-250-0000 527 D norberto.gonzalez4@upr.edu
GONZALEZ, Patricia ...... 787-250-1912 524 B pgonzalez@metro.inter.edu
GONZALEZ, Patricia ...... 661-255-1050.. 29 F gonzalez@calarts.edu
GONZALEZ, Paulette, B . 718-990-6521 322 F gonzalep@stjohns.edu
GONZALEZ, Ramon, F .. 787-758-2525 528 D ramon.gonzalez5@upr.edu
GONZALEZ, Raymond ... 718-289-5154 301 D raymond.gonzalez@bcc.cuny.edu
GONZALEZ, Reinaldo .... 787-744-8519 522 J rgonzalez@ediccollege.edu
GONZALEZ, Richard ...... 239-992-4624 103 H
GONZALEZ, Rick .... 424-207-3727.. 54 I rgonzalez@otis.edu
GONZALEZ, Roberto, O . 310-287-4333.. 49 H gonzalro@wlac.edu
GONZALEZ, Rocelia, T .. 904-620-2870 110 E rrgonz@unf.edu
GONZALEZ, Ruth .... 860-738-6315.. 86 C rgonzalez@nwcc.edu
GONZALEZ, Samantha .. 860-512-2674.. 85 G sgonzalez@manchestercc.edu
GONZALEZ, Samuel ...... 787-738-2161 528 A samuel.gomzalez10@upr.edu
GONZALEZ, Sandra .... 787-882-2065 526 D administracion_empresas@unitecpr.net
GONZALEZ, Sandra .... 323-563-9375.. 36 H sandragonzalez@cdrewu.edu
GONZALEZ, Saraliz .... 787-857-3600 523 I sgonzalez@br.inter.edu
GONZALEZ, Sergio .... 401-863-1000 415 K
GONZALEZ, Sophia .... 210-486-2247 441 I fklein@alamo.edu
GONZALEZ, Stacy .... 518-244-4557 321 G gonzas@sage.edu
GONZALEZ, Steven .... 602-286-8008.. 13 G steven.gonzalez@gatewaycc.edu
GONZALEZ, Ted .... 254-526-1668 445 L ted.gonzalez@ctcd.edu
GONZALEZ, Thomasa .... 609-652-4724 291 H t.gonzalez@stockton.edu
GONZALEZ, Tina .... 212-799-5000 312 B
GONZALEZ, Victor .... 956-872-2336 456 G vgonzalez99@southtexascollege.edu
GONZALEZ, Yadira .... 541-278-5753 382 A ygonzalez@bluecc.edu
GONZALEZ, Yaitzaenid .. 787-765-3560 522 K ygonzalez@edpuniversity.edu
GONZALEZ-CORTES, Otilio .... 787-815-0000 527 D otilio.gonzalez@upr.edu
GONZALEZ-GARCIA, Evelyn, E .... 787-890-2681 527 E evelyn.gonzalez4@upr.edu
GONZALEZ-GUERRA, Migdalia .... 787-890-2681 527 E migdalia.gonzalez2@upr.edu
GONZALEZ MEDINA, CMF, Ruben, A .... 787-848-5265 525 J ruben_gonzalez@pucpr.edu
GONZALEZ SMITH, Ericka .... 336-285-4509 350 C egonzalezsmtih@ncat.edu
GONZALEZ TORRES, Ali .... 413-528-7647 211 B agonzaleztorres@simons-rock.edu
GOOCH, Cynthia .... 531-622-2649 275 F cgooch@mccneb.edu
GOOCH, Darlene .... 919-962-4388 351 B darlene_gooch@unc.edu
GOOCH, Ellen .... 518-327-6225 320 A egooch@paulsmiths.edu
GOOCH, Jackie .... 256-233-8211.... 4 C jackie.gooch@athens.edu
GOOCH, Janet .... 660-785-4383 267 K jquinzer@truman.edu
GOOCH, Janet .... 660-785-4105 267 K jquinzer@truman.edu
GOOCH, Josh .... 620-665-3594 178 D goochj@hutchcc.edu
GOOCH, Zanetta .... 615-963-7401 438 E zgooch@tnstate.edu
GOOD, Claire .... 207-621-3000 201 C claire.good@maine.edu
GOOD, Darrin .... 562-907-4204.. 75 A dgood@whittier.edu
GOOD, Gayle, A .... 402-363-5621 278 E gagood@york.edu
GOOD, Glenn .... 352-392-3261 110 D ggood@coe.ufl.edu
GOOD, Jennifer .... 251-380-2278.... 7 B jgood@shc.edu
GOOD, Julie .... 541-463-5547 383 F goodj@lanecc.edu
GOOD, Kristin .... 734-973-3722 238 G kgood@wccnet.edu
GOOD, Larry .... 402-363-5718 278 E lbgood@york.edu
GOOD, Lee Anna .... 432-552-2800 469 D good_l@utpb.edu
GOOD, Megan, R .... 334-844-6844.... 4 D mrg0030@auburn.edu
GOOD, Michael, L .... 352-273-7500 110 D mgood@ufl.edu
GOOD, Rhonda .... 717-337-6015 396 A rgood@gettysburg.edu
GOOD, RT .... 561-237-7458 103 E rgood@lynn.edu
GOOD LUCK, Aldean .... 406-638-3118 271 C goodluckav@lbhc.edu
GOODALE, Brian .... 518-587-2100 329 C brian.goodale@esc.edu
GOODARZI, Shirin, M .. 410-777-2148 202 D smgoodarzi@aacc.edu
GOODBURN, Amy .... 402-472-3751 277 G agoodburn1@unl.edu
GOODCUFF, Esther .... 516-877-3681 297 I goodcuff@adelphi.edu
GOODE, Abreeta .... 210-829-3932 465 E agoode@uiwtx.edu
GOODE, Diana .... 313-577-5426 239 C diana.goode@wayne.edu
GOODE, Greg, J .... 812-237-7778 159 C greg.goode@indstate.edu
GOODE, Jess .... 312-567-3970 140 I jgoode1@iit.edu
GOODE, Jodi .... 325-646-2502 450 H jgoode@hputx.edu
GOODE, Kendra .... 205-453-6300.. 93 B
GOODE, Kevin .... 814-866-8406 399 C kgoode@lecom.edu
GOODE, Tammy .... 423-585-6845 438 D tammy.goode@ws.edu
GOODE, Tressman .... 217-479-7059 144 I tressman.goode@mac.edu
GOODE, Tyler .... 828-339-4394 346 H t_goode@southwesterncc.edu
GOODELL-LACKEY, Shirley, J .... 802-654-2586 476 A sgoodell-lackey@smcvt.edu
GOODEN, Kimberly, L ... 313-927-1552 233 D kgooden@marygrove.edu
GOODFELLOW, Sandy ... 615-675-5280 441 B alex@welch.edu
GOODFELLOW, Tim ...... 503-554-2585 383 C tgoodfellow@georgefox.edu
GOODFRIEND, Kimberly .... 972-883-2201 467 D kimberly.goodfriend@utdallas.edu
GOODGAME, Henry .... 470-639-0400 123 E henry.goodgame@morehouse.edu
GOODGE, Marshall, M .. 570-561-1818 410 A mgoodge@stots.edu
GOODGE, Samuel .... 304-829-7905 501 F sgoodge@bethanywv.edu
GOODHEART, Marc .... 617-496-9480 215 G marc_goodheart@harvard.edu
GOODHUE LYNCH, Mary .... 508-588-9100 220 B
GOODING, Betsy .... 903-434-8137 453 M bgooding@ntcc.edu
GOODING, Samuel .... 512-568-3300.. 93 B
GOODING, Samuel .... 210-202-3700.. 93 B
GOODLETT, Sean .... 978-665-3832 217 E sgoodlett@fitchburgstate.edu
GOODLING, Barry, G .... 717-796-5064 401 L bgoodlin@messiah.edu
GOODLING, Eileen, J .... 716-338-1025 311 F eileengoodling@mail.sunyjcc.edu
GOODMAN, Andrew .... 212-824-2260 309 F andrew.goodman@huc.edu
GOODMAN, Brent .... 619-849-2371.. 57 H brentgoodman@pointloma.edu
GOODMAN, Carl .... 850-599-3276 109 A carl.goodman@famu.edu
GOODMAN, Catie .... 850-201-8281 112 C goodmanc@tcc.fl.edu
GOODMAN, Charlie .... 606-337-1148 184 D charlie.goodman@ccbbc.edu
GOODMAN, Danica .... 206-934-5338 497 J danica.goodman@seattlecolleges.edu
GOODMAN, Debbie .... 229-225-3978 126 C dgoodman@southernregional.edu
GOODMAN, Dennis, S .. 573-341-4284 269 A dgoodman@mst.edu
GOODMAN, Grayson ..... 407-303-1631.. 94 H grayson.goodman@adu.edu
GOODMAN, Guy .... 602-243-8000.. 14 D guy.goodman@southmountaincc.edu
GOODMAN, Hunter, P .. 937-229-4915 372 A hgoodman1@udayton.edu
GOODMAN, J. Andy ..... 314-516-7133 268 E goodmanjam@umsl.edu
GOODMAN, Jacque .... 641-844-5640 170 G jacque.goodman@iavalley.edu
GOODMAN, Jacque .... 641-844-7106 170 I jacque.goodman@iavalley.edu
GOODMAN, James .... 808-455-0664 130 G goodmanj@hawaii.edu
GOODMAN, Jeremy ...... 781-292-2373 215 C jeremy.goodman@olin.edu
GOODMAN, Jerry, C ..... 713-798-7234 444 A jgoodman@bcm.edu
GOODMAN, Larry, J ..... 312-942-7073 150 F larry_j_goodman@rush.edu
GOODMAN, Lena, C ..... 920-433-6638 506 C lena.goodman@bellincollege.edu
GOODMAN, Marc, P ..... 310-506-4607.. 56 D marc.goodman@pepperdine.edu
GOODMAN, Mark .... 646-565-6000 331 F mark.goodman@touro.edu
GOODMAN, Maxine .... 713-646-1868 456 H mgoodman@stcl.edu
GOODMAN, Michael ...... 504-865-5725 196 D mgoodman@tulane.edu
GOODMAN, Pete .... 619-201-8694.. 60 A pete.goodman@sdcc.edu
GOODMAN, Richard, H . 503-494-5078 385 D goodmanr@ohsu.edu
GOODMAN, Robert, M .. 848-932-3600 290 C execdean@aesop.rutgers.edu
GOODMAN, Shannon, M .... 940-565-2000 466 B shannon.goodman@unt.edu
GOODMAN, Sharon .... 910-410-1734 345 G sbgoodman@richmondcc.edu
GOODMAN, Steven, R .. 901-448-7125 440 C sgoodma5@uthsc.edu
GOODMAN, Willie, F .... 404-527-5735 122 B wgoodman@itc.edu
GOODNESS, Gail, C ...... 603-646-3011 281 C gail.c.goodness@dartmouth.edu
GOODNOUGH, Doug ..... 517-264-7141 236 I dgoodnou@sienaheights.edu
GOODNOW, Jean .... 989-686-9200 229 J jeangoodnow@delta.edu
GOODRICH, Bill .... 858-695-8587 159 A bgoodrich@horizonuniversity.edu
GOODRICH, Deborah, J 607-587-3946 328 F goodridj@alfredstate.edu
GOODRICH, James .... 503-352-2814 385 I jgoodrich@pacificu.edu
GOODRICH, Joy, P .... 804-257-5606 491 C jgoodrich@vuu.edu
GOODRICH, Joy, P .... 804-354-5210 491 C jgoodrich@vuu.edu
GOODRICH, Mark .... 707-654-1563.. 32 E mgoodrich@csum.edu
GOODRICH, Shannon ... 208-769-3303 132 E sgoodrich@nic.edu
GOODRICH PELLETIER, Monica .... 508-213-2108 223 C monica.goodrich-pelletier@nichols.edu
GOODRIDGE, Ellengold 256-726-7093.... 6 E egoodridge@oakwood.edu
GOODSON, Alyn .... 252-335-2972 350 A agoodson@ecsu.edu
GOODSON, Drew .... 919-718-7287 341 H dgoodson@cccc.edu
GOODSON, Kenneth ...... 903-434-8260 453 M kgoodson@ntcc.edu
GOODSON, Leigh .... 918-595-7868 380 D leigh.goodson@tulsacc.edu
GOODSON, Linda .... 334-699-2266.... 1 B
GOODSON, Michael .... 507-786-3294 250 C goodson@stolaf.edu
GOODSPEED, Seth .... 612-874-3745 243 F agoodspeed@mcad.edu
GOODSTEIN, Eban .... 845-758-7067 298 I ebangood@bard.edu
GOODSTEIN, Richard, E 864-656-3084 419 F regst@clemson.edu
GOODSTONE, Michael .. 631-420-2337 329 D michael.goodstone@farmingdale.edu
GOODWILL, Caitlin .... 509-574-4775 500 I cgoodwill@yvcc.edu
GOODWIN, Amanda .... 215-489-2926 393 F amanda.goodwin@delval.edu
GOODWIN, Ann, E .... 859-238-5760 184 C ann.goodwin@centre.edu
GOODWIN, Cheryl .... 978-556-3854 220 F cgoodwin@necc.mass.edu
GOODWIN, Cheryl .... 206-876-6100 498 C cgoodwin@theseattleschool.edu
GOODWIN, Christine, M .... 718-990-1993 322 F goodwinc@stjohns.edu
GOODWIN, Christy .... 251-578-1313.... 3 D cbulger@rstc.edu
GOODWIN, Cindi, J ...... 336-633-4475 345 F cjgoodwin@randolph.edu
GOODWIN, Darrell .... 206-296-6060 498 D goodwind@seattleu.edu
GOODWIN, Eric .... 503-297-5544 385 A egoodwin@ocac.edu
GOODWIN, Erika, A ...... 937-481-2241 373 I erika_goodwin@wilmington.edu
GOODWIN, Jerome .... 919-530-6739 350 D jgoodwin@nccu.edu
GOODWIN, Kristine, C .. 401-865-2144 416 E kgoodwi2@providence.edu
GOODWIN, Laura .... 303-315-2105.. 83 D laura.goodwin@ucdenver.edu

GOODWIN, Lisa .... 503-883-2492 383 H lgoodwin@linfield.edu

GOODWIN, LouAnn ...... 989-386-6622 234 B lrgoodwin@midmich.edu

GOODWIN, Mary Ann ... 509-533-3820 494 A maryann.goodwin@ccs.spokane.edu

GOODWIN, Michelle ...... 301-934-7635 203 D michellg@csmd.edu

GOODWIN, Mike .... 541-737-3288 385 F mike.goodwin@oregonstate.edu

GOODWIN, Naomi .... 310-243-3750.. 31 E ngoodwin@csudh.edu

GOODWIN, Peter .... 410-228-9250 208 B

GOODWIN, Virginia ...... 317-543-4796 162 S vgoodwin@martin.edu

GOODWIN, Wendell, B . 919-866-5148 347 D wbgoodwin@waketech.edu

GOODWIN, Whittington 281-649-3238 450 C wgoodwin@hbu.edu

GOODYEAR, Anne .... 207-798-4352 198 G agoodyea@bowdoin.edu

GOODYEAR, Frank .... 207-725-3673 198 G fgoodyea@bowdoin.edu

GOODYEAR, Jack .... 214-333-5595 447 D jackg@dbu.edu

GOOKIN, Karen .... 207-454-1054 200 D kgookin@wccc.me.edu

GOOLSBY, Edwin, G ..... 727-816-3264 105 C goolsbe@phsc.edu

GOON, Arthur .... 215-489-2491 393 F arthur.goon@delval.edu

GOON, Dean .... 740-392-6868 366 B dean.goon@mvnu.edu

GOOR, Mark .... 909-593-3511.. 70 E mgoor@laverne.edu

GOORIS, Daniel .... 773-244-5222 147 F dgooris@northpark.edu

GOPLEN, Joanna .... 315-312-3234 327 D joanna.goplen@oswego.edu

GOPLIN, Scott .... 260-665-4365 164 E goplins@trine.edu

GOPP, Jeff .... 408-848-4705.. 44 B jgopp@gavilan.edu

GORAB, Beth .... 973-618-3204 284 D bgorab@caldwell.edu

GORBANDT, Melissa ..... 859-572-5744 188 E gorbandt@nku.edu

GORBEA-DÍAZ, Maribel . 787-993-8852 527 G maribel.gorbea@upr.edu

GORCZYCA, Matthew ..... 716-926-8884 310 B mgorczyca@hilbert.edu

GORDEN, JR., Monroe . 310-825-1514.. 69 B mgorden@saonet.ucla.edu

GORDER, Corey .... 701-228-5673 354 G corey.gorder@dakotacollege.edu

GORDIEN CASE, Lori, K .... 909-593-3511.. 70 E lgordien@laverne.edu

GORDLEY, Matthew, E .. 412-578-6262 391 G megordley@carlow.edu

GORDON, Allen .... 765-285-2983 156 C agordon@bsu.edu

GORDON, Andrew .... 904-470-8244.. 98 B andrew.gordon@ewc.edu

GORDON, Andrew .... 315-443-5459 330 H agordon@syr.edu

GORDON, Carin, M .... 407-582-2556 113 F cgordon15@valenciacollege.edu

GORDON, Carl .... 409-933-8246 446 H cgordon@com.edu

GORDON, Casey .... 320-363-5620 241 I cgordon@csbsju.edu

GORDON, Casey .... 320-363-5620 250 A cgordon@csbsju.edu

GORDON, David, E .... 804-257-5783 491 C degordon@vuu.edu

GORDON, Debra .... 404-297-9522 120 D gordond@gptc.edu

GORDON, Dennis .... 949-451-5483.. 64 I dgordon@ivc.edu

GORDON, Donny .... 707-654-1175.. 32 E dgordon@csum.edu

GORDON, Eloisa .... 787-257-7373 525 Q elgordon@suagm.edu

GORDON, Eloísa .... 787-727-7880 529 B egordon@sagrado.edu

GORDON, Eric .... 207-992-4925 199 B gordoner@husson.edu

GORDON, Evelyn .... 765-973-8232 160 A evgordon@iue.edu

GORDON, Glenda .... 541-684-7225 384 H ggordon@nwcu.edu

GORDON, Greg .... 781-239-6278 211 A ggordon@babson.edu

GORDON, Howard .... 315-312-2213 327 D howard.gordon@oswego.edu

GORDON, III, James, D .... 801-422-4919 471 E jim_gordon@byu.edu

GORDON, Jan, M .... 502-447-1000 189 D jgordon@spencerian.edu

GORDON, Jeffrey .... 518-262-5486 297 L gordonj@mail.amc.edu

GORDON, Joan .... 917-493-4584 313M joangordon@msmnyc.edu

GORDON, John .... 202-274-5998.. 93 D john.gordon@udc.edu

GORDON, Joyce .... 270-809-7070 188 D jgordon@murraystate.edu

GORDON, Julie .... 608-262-5316 510 B jgordon@uwsa.edu

GORDON, Kelly .... 512-313-3000 446 N kelly.gordon@concordia.edu

GORDON, Kevin .... 727-344-8062 107 A gordon.kevin@spcollege.edu

GORDON, Kim .... 312-280-3500 140 G

GORDON, Lori .... 801-375-5125 472 F lgordon@rmuohp.edu

GORDON, Lynne .... 312-935-4242 141 C lgordon@icsw.edu

GORDON, Mark .... 651-290-6310 248 U mark.gordon@mitchellhamline.edu

GORDON, Mark, B .... 248-370-3000 235 J gordon@oakland.edu

GORDON, Matthew .... 707-468-3165.. 51 E mgordon@mendocino.edu

GORDON, Melissa .... 770-229-3327 126 B mgordon@sctech.edu

GORDON, Monica .... 692-625-3291 520 C mgordon@cmi.edu

GORDON, Nanci .... 802-773-5900 474 H nanci.gordon@csj.edu

GORDON, Patti .... 662-560-1105 255 C

GORDON, Paul .... 660-831-4176 264 A gordonp@moval.edu

GORDON, Rebecca, J ... 205-975-6149.... 8 B rjgordon@uab.edu

GORDON, River .... 612-874-3727 243 F rgordon182@mcad.edu

GORDON, Ronald .... 937-328-6095 359 H gordonr@clarkstate.edu

GORDON, Sally .... 814-886-6395 402 E sgordon@mtaloy.edu

GORDON, Samantha ..... 954-308-2218.. 94 P sagordon@aii.edu

GORDON, Sandra .... 718-473-8701 303 D sgordon@citytech.cuny.edu

GORDON, Saundra, E ... 812-941-2394 161 A gordonse@ius.edu

GORDON, Scott .... 509-359-7900 494 D sgordon@ewu.edu

GORDON, Stephanie ..... 304-829-7115 501 F sgordon@bethanywv.edu

GORDON, T. Scott .... 724-458-3352 396 D tsgordon@gcc.edu

GORDON, Timothy .... 414-229-4632 511 A gordont@uwm.edu

GORDON, Tom .... 914-632-5400 315 K tgordon@monroecollege.edu

GORDON, Tonia, J .... 814-886-6390 402 E tgordon@mtaloy.edu

GORDON, Wade .... 218-733-7656 245 C w.gordon@lsc.edu

GORDON, Wes .... 662-325-9129 254 E wgordon@foundation.msstate.edu

GORDON, Yolanda .... 334-872-2533.... 6 H yolandagordon176@yahoo.com

GORDY, Mary .... 303-300-8740.. 77 F mary.gordy@collegeamerica.com

GORDY, Reggie .... 334-291-4947.... 1 H reggie.gordy@cv.edu

GORE, Chris .... 903-988-7446 451 F cgore@kilgore.edu

GORE, Frederick, S .... 863-667-5729 108 G fsgore@seu.edu

GORE, Paul .... 256-264-5060.... 3 F pgore@snead.edu

GORE, Paul .... 513-745-3119 374 D gorep@xavier.edu

GORE, Scott .... 410-386-8467 203 A sgore@carrollcc.edu

GORE, Shana .... 850-474-2398 111 D sgore1@uwf.edu

GORE, Sonya .... 405-682-1611 377 C sonya.d.gore@occc.edu

GORE, Vennie .... 517-355-7457 233 G gore@msu.edu

GORE, Vikki .... 509-452-5100 496 H vgore@pnwu.edu

GORES, Connie, J .... 507-537-6272 248 A president@smsu.edu

GORES, Greg .... 507-538-5027 241 E gores.greg@mayo.edu

GORES, Julie, C .... 608-246-6633 514 A jgores@madisoncollege.edu

GORETSKY, Andrew .... 215-572-2900 389 D

GORETZKY, Andrew ...... 215-572-2934 389 D goretskya@arcadia.edu

GORGA, Joe .... 925-969-4229.. 40 L jgorga@dvc.edu

GORHAM, Chad .... 256-228-6001.... 3 B gorhamchad@nacc.edu

GORHAM, Faust .... 661-654-3425.. 31 B fgorham@csub.edu

GORHAM, Jayne .... 321-433-5282.. 97 N gorhamj@easternflorida.edu

GORHAM, Jonathan ...... 617-243-2315 216 C jgorham@lasell.edu

GORINI, Cathy .... 641-472-1161 171 J dof@mum.edu

GORINI, Cathy .... 641-472-1107 171 J cgorini@mum.edu

GORINSHTEYN, Dasha .. 718-368-4975 303 A dasha.gorinshteyn@kbcc.cuny.edu

GORKA, Gary .... 415-257-1301.. 41 J gary.gorka@dominican.edu

GORMAN, Bonnie, B ..... 906-487-2212 234 A bbgorman@mtu.edu

GORMAN, Deb .... 920-996-2813 513 F gorman@fvtc.edu

GORMAN, June .... 610-647-4400 397 I jgorman@immaculata.edu

GORMAN, Keith .... 856-200-4638 285 C kgorman@cccnj.edu

GORMAN, Kimberly ...... 828-227-7469 352 C ksgorman@wcu.edu

GORMAN, Leah .... 903-988-7521 451 F lgorman@kilgore.edu

GORMAN, Luke .... 603-526-3797 280 H luke.gorman@colby-sawyer.edu

GORMAN, Mary .... 646-312-3315 301 B mary.gorman@baruch.cuny.edu

GORMAN, Michael .... 856-351-2601 291 E mgorman@salemcc.edu

GORMAN, Robin, A ...... 724-357-2410 406 C rgorman@iup.edu

GORMAN, Susan, L ...... 617-558-1788 223 A sgorman@nesa.edu

GORMAN, Susan, T ...... 443-334-2205 207 C sgorman@stevenson.edu

GORMAN, Wendy .... 715-682-1322 509 D wgorman@northland.edu

GORMAN, Wil .... 573-651-2297 266M wgorman@semo.edu

GORMAN, William, P .... 617-989-4147 225 E gormanb@wit.edu

GORMAN, Zach .... 309-677-3100 134 G zgorman@bradley.edu

GORMAN-SMITH, Deborah .... 773-702-1234 153 F debgs@uchicago.edu

GORMLEY, Christina, L . 717-337-6611 396 A cgormley@gettysburg.edu

GORMLEY, Kenneth, G .. 412-396-6060 394 D president@duq.edu

GORMLEY, Melissa, E ... 608-342-1151 511 D gormleym@uwplatt.edu

GORNEAULT, Gregg ...... 860-906-5127.. 85 D ggorneault@ccc.commnet.edu

GORR, Nathan .... 612-330-1390 240 G gorr@augsburg.edu

GORRELL, Cathy .... 303-458-4117.. 82 D cgorrell@regis.edu

GORRELL, Cathy .... 303-458-4100.. 82 D cgorrell@regis.edu

GORRELL, John .... 304-424-8269 505 C john.gorrell@wvup.edu

GORRELL, Renee .... 314-454-8171 260 E rgorrell@bjc.org

GORSKI, Holly .... 253-964-6519 497 B hgorski@pierce.ctc.edu

GORSLINE, Denise, M .. 218-477-4654 246 B gorsline@mnstate.edu

GORSLINE, Michael ...... 847-317-8145 153 D mgorsline@tiu.edu

GORT, Amy .... 651-793-1920 245 E amy.gort@metrostate.edu

GORTI, Anantha .... 703-284-1488 483 A anantha.gorti@marymount.edu

GORTNER, Jessica .... 319-363-1323 172 B jgortner@mtmercy.edu

GORTON, Holly, J .... 231-995-1012 235 B hgorton@nmc.edu

GOSA, Polly .... 520-515-8750.. 11 R gosap@cochise.edu

GOSCH, Judy .... 865-539-7233 437 F jagosch@pstcc.edu

GOSE, Becca .... 541-737-2474 385 F

GOSHORN, Mark .... 859-344-3513 189 G goshorm@thomasmore.edu

GOSIER, Michelle .... 585-385-8064 322 E mgosier@sjfc.edu

GOSLIN, Elle .... 860-932-4000.. 86 E egoslin@qvcc.edu

GOSNELL, Kelly, S .... 859-846-5788 188 B ksgosnell@midway.edu

GOSNELL, Victor .... 434-947-8138 484 B vgosnell@randolphcollege.edu

GOSNEY, Sue .... 213-356-5330.. 65 A sue_gosney@sciarc.edu

GOSS, Barbara .... 205-853-1200.... 2 F bgoss@jeffersonstate.edu

GOSS, Jonathan, D .... 315-268-2290 304 B jgoss@clarkson.edu

GOSS, Nathan, R .... 770-534-6162 116 F ngoss@brenau.edu

GOSS, Peter .... 971-722-4490 386 C

GOSS, Ronald .... 541-956-7119 386 G rgoss@roguecc.edu

GOSSARD, Sheryl, R ..... 615-353-3305 437 D sheryl.gossard@nscc.edu

GOSSELIN, Grant .... 508-286-3780 225 G gosselin_grant@wheatoncollege.edu

GOSSELIN, Karen .... 603-623-0313 281 G karengosselin@nhia.edu

GOSSEN, Douglas .... 920-693-1221 513 H doug.gossen@gotoltc.edu

GOSSEN, Ronald, H ...... 314-516-5776 268 E ron@umsl.edu

GOSSEN, Tim .... 507-457-1597 250 B tgossen@smumn.edu

GOSSETT, Betty .... 716-673-3321 325 C betty.gossett@fredonia.edu

GOSSETT, John .... 828-652-6021 344 G johngossett@mcdowelltech.edu

GOSSFELD-BENZING, Sara .... 715-675-3331 514 F gossfeld-benzing@ntc.edu

GOSWAMI, Jaya .... 361-593-3290 460 B jaya.goswami@tamuk.edu

GOSWAMI, Jaya .... 361-593-4411 460 B jaya.goswami@tamuk.edu

GOSWAMI, Utpal, K ...... 816-604-3044 262 J utpal.goswami@mcckc.edu

GOSZ, Mike .... 312-567-3198 140 I gosz@iit.edu

GOTANDA, John .... 808-544-0201 129 C jgotanda@hpu.edu

GOTAY, Susanne .... 787-725-8120 522M consejerasusanne@eap.edu

GOTCHER, David .... 615-904-8042 434 H david.gotcher@mtsu.edu

GOTCHER, Mike .... 931-372-3366 438 F mgotcher@tntech.edu

GOTHAM, Kerry .... 585-395-2068 326 D kgotham@brockport.edu

GOTHARD, Mathew, J ... 303-963-3223.. 77 I mgothard@ccu.edu

GOTSCH, Kenneth .... 847-543-2631 136 E kgotsch@clcillinois.edu

GOTSCH, Sarah, A .... 574-631-3903 165 A sgotsch@nd.edu

GOTSCHALL, Matt .... 402-562-1211 273 G mgotschall@cccneb.edu

GOTSHALL, Kathy .... 812-535-5162 163 I kgotshal@smwc.edu

GOTSMAN, Craig .... 973-596-5488 288 A craig.gotsman@njit.edu

GOTT, Jared .... 731-989-6649 432 C jgott@fhu.edu

GOTTARDY, John .... 716-645-2450 325 B johngott@buffalo.edu

GOTTDIENER, Yitzchok .. 718-941-8000 315 C

GOTTFRIED, Matt .... 719-389-6381.. 77 J mgottfried@coloradocollege.edu

GOTTLIEB, Jane .... 212-799-5000 312 B

GOTTLIEB, Rachelle .... 904-620-2903 110 E r.gottlieb@unf.edu

GOTTLIEB, Tracy, T .... 973-761-9074 291 F tracy.gottlieb@shu.edu

GOTTSCHALK, Glenn, F . 410-293-1911 519 E gotts@usna.edu

GOTTSCHALK, Katherine 765-983-1267 157 I gottska@earlham.edu

GOTTSCHALK, Sandy ..... 785-623-6150 180 E sgottschalk@ncktc.edu

GOTTSHALL, Lori .... 954-771-0376 102W lgottshall@knoxseminary.edu

GOTTULA, Todd .... 308-865-8454 277 F gottulatm@unk.edu

GOTZON, Mary, A .... 610-282-1100 393 G mary.gotzon@desales.edu

GOUCH, Shawn .... 724-805-2895 410 B shawn.gouch@stvincent.edu

GOUCH, Shawn .... 724-805-2894 410 C shawn.guch@stvincent.edu

GOUDEAU, Arthur .... 281-487-1170 460 G agoudeau@txchiro.edu

GOUDEAU, LaTasha ...... 713-221-8162 465 C
goudeaul@uhd.edu
GOUGH, Allison .... 808-544-1109 129 C
agough@hpu.edu
GOUGH, Annette .... 732-571-3402 287 C
gough@monmouth.edu
GOUGH, Christopher .... 203-332-5022.. 85 F
cgough@hcc.commnet.edu
GOUGH, Darby .... 816-501-3660 257 G
darby.gough@avila.edu
GOUGH, Richard, J ...... 843-525-8247 424 E
rgough@tcl.edu
GOUKER, Toby .... 301-654-7267 207 B
GOULD, Amanda .... 413-565-1000 211 C
agould@baypath.edu
GOULD, Cassie .... 212-517-0687 314 D
cgould@mmm.edu
GOULD, Dean, J .... 702-889-8426 278 M
dean_gould@nshe.nevada.edu
GOULD, Kenneth .... 718-951-3136 301 E
kgould@brooklyn.cuny.edu
GOULD, Kimberley .... 802-447-6333 476 C
kgould@svc.edu
GOULD, Kyle .... 765-998-4635 164 C
kygould@taylor.edu
GOULD, Mark .... 978-837-5072 221 G
gouldm@merrimack.edu
GOULD, Robert, J .... 724-503-1001 414 A
rgould@washjeff.edu
GOULD, Shari .... 814-732-1294 406 B
sgould@edinboro.edu
GOULD, Shelby .... 903-510-3158 464 D
sgou@tjc.edu
GOULD, Terri .... 989-686-9081 229 J
tlgould@delta.edu
GOULD, Thomas .... 252-493-7406 345 E
tgould@email.pittcc.edu
GOULD, Trent .... 601-266-4568 256 E
trent.gould@usm.edu
GOULD, Trent .... 601-266-5253 256 E
trent.gould@usm.edu
GOULDING, Laurel .... 701-662-1513 355 A
laurel.goulding@lrsc.edu
GOULDING, Ruth .... 619-239-0391.. 35 C
rgoulding@cwsl.edu
GOULET, Bonnie .... 203-576-8752.. 86 B
bgoulet@nv.edu
GOULET, Caroline .... 210-283-6924 465 E
goulet@uiwtx.edu
GOULET, Stephen, P ..... 508-793-7598 213 C
sgoulet@clarku.edu
GOUNARD, Jean, F .... 716-878-5331 326 E
gounarjf@buffalostate.edu
GOURD, David .... 206-934-4349 497 I
david.gourd@seattlecolleges.edu
GOURDINE, Raji .... 334-876-9292.... 2 C
rgourdine@wccs.edu
GOURJI, Konstantin ...... 650-685-6616.. 45 B
kgourji@gurnick.edu
GOURLAY, Charles .... 910-630-7156 340 A
sgourley@methodist.edu
GOURLEY, Kristin .... 865-981-8215 433 F
kristin.gourley@maryvillecollege.edu
GOURLEY, Pamela, L .... 276-944-6122 480 J
pgourley@ehc.edu
GOURNEAU, Haven .... 406-768-6300 271 B
hgourneau@fpcc.edu
GOURNEAU, William ..... 701-255-3285 355 I
wgourneau@uttc.edu
GOUSE, Richard, I .... 401-739-5000 416 D
rgouse@neit.edu
GOUVEA, Nicole, R .... 208-426-4362 131 C
nicolegouvea@boisestate.edu
GOUVEIA, Jan, N .... 808-956-6405 129 H
jgouveia@hawaii.edu
GOUVEIA, Neil .... 718-429-6600 333 B
neil.gouveia@vaughn.edu
GOUVIN, Eric, J .... 413-796-2201 225 F
eric.gouvin@law.wne.edu
GOVAN, JR., Tom .... 708-596-2000 151 H
tgovan@ssc.edu
GOVEA, Sam .... 972-860-4216 447 G
sgovea@dcccd.edu
GOVENDER, Yogani ...... 787-250-1912 524 B
ygovender@intermetro.onmicrosoft.com
GOVER, Bruce .... 606-679-8501 186 G
bruce.gover@kctcs.edu
GOVER, Kristie .... 904-256-7070 102 B
kgover1@ju.edu
GOVINDARAJU, Venu ... 716-645-3321 325 B
vpr@buffalo.edu
GOVITZ, Leanne .... 989-686-9490 229 J
leannegovitz@delta.edu
GOVITZ, Scott .... 989-386-6624 234 B
sgovitz@midmich.edu
GOW, Joe .... 608-785-8004 510 F
jgow@uwlax.edu
GOWAN, Mary .... 540-568-3254 481 I
gowanma@jmu.edu
GOWANS, Faye .... 803-822-3251 422 D
gowansf@midlandstech.edu
GOWDY, Stephen .... 616-538-2330 230 E
sgowdy@gbcol.edu
GOWENS, Krystal .... 714-556-3610.. 72 F
krystal.gowens@vanguard.edu
GOWER, Donna .... 405-224-3140 381 B
dgower@usao.edu
GOWER, John, M .... 848-932-4300 290 A
michael.gower@rutgers.edu
GOWER, Paula .... 405-585-5410 377 A
paula.gower@okbu.edu
GOWER, Ryan .... 618-544-8657 140 D
gowerry@iecc.edu
GOWER, Stephanie .... 678-422-4100.. 93 B
GOYAL, Arun .... 951-222-8000.. 58 H
arun.goyal@rcc.edu
GOYETTE, John .... 805-525-4417.. 67 E
jgoyette@thomasaquinas.edu
GOYETTE, Sylvain .... 815-836-5974 143 E
goyettsy@lewisu.edu
GOYUNYAN, Gevorg ..... 510-925-4282.. 25 P
gevorg@aua.am
GOZIK, Nick .... 617-552-3827 212 E
nick.gozik@bc.edu
GOZUM, Allan .... 937-769-1304 356 G
agozum@antioch.edu
GRABE, William .... 928-523-4340.. 14 K
william.grabe@nau.edu
GRABER, David .... 402-375-7257 276 D
dagrabe1@wsc.edu
GRABER, Linda .... 866-931-4300 265 H
linda.graber@rockbridge.edu
GRABER, Thomas .... 570-208-5900 398 D
thomasgraber@kings.edu
GRABOWSKA, Lynette ... 605-367-6122 429 C
lynette.grabowska@southeasttech.edu
GRABOWSKI, Janice, T . 724-925-4123 414 E
grabowskij@westmoreland.edu
GRABOWSKI, John, F ... 410-777-2231 202 D
jfgrabowski@aacc.edu
GRABOWSKI, Lisa .... 303-797-5746.. 76 I
lisa.grabowski@arapahoe.edu
GRABOWSKI, Mark .... 417-328-1556 267 A
mgrabowski@sbuniv.edu
GRACA, Michael .... 508-286-3503 225 G
graca_michael@wheatoncollege.edu
GRACE, Anna .... 503-253-3443 385 B
anna.grace@ocom.edu
GRACE, Coy, F .... 870-633-4480.. 19 E
cgrace@eacc.edu
GRACE, Danielle .... 301-447-5330 206 B
grace@msmary.edu
GRACE, Dennis .... 239-304-7093.. 95 C
dennis.grace@avemaria.edu
GRACE, Glenda .... 718-997-5725 303 E
glenda.grace@qc.cuny.edu
GRACE, John .... 517-264-7198 236 I
jgrace@sienaheights.edu
GRACE, Lynn .... 734-973-3507 238 G
lgmartin@wccnet.edu
GRACE, Melissa, H .... 850-474-3423 111 D
mgrace@uwf.edu
GRACE, Michelle, M ..... 847-543-2274 136 E
mgrace@clcillinois.edu
GRACE, Nabil, F .... 248-204-2500 233 A
ngrace@ltu.edu
GRACE, Selena .... 208-373-1874 132 B
gracsele@isu.edu
GRACE, Sherie .... 256-228-6001.... 3 B
graces@nacc.edu
GRACE, Ted, W .... 618-453-4485 152 B
tgrace@siu.edu
GRACIA, Jessica, L .... 508-565-1301 224 H
jlgracia@stonehill.edu
GRACIAS, Vincente, H ... 732-235-6300 290 A
vincente.gracia@rutgers.edu
GRACYALNY, David .... 410-225-2220 205 C
dgracyal@mica.edu
GRACYK, June .... 440-684-6083 373 B
jgracyk@ursuline.edu
GRADDY, Elizabeth .... 213-740-6715.. 72 B
graddy@usc.edu
GRADOWSKI, Charles ... 484-365-7404 400 E
cgradowski@lincoln.edu
GRADY, Amber, N .... 870-759-4188.. 23 K
agrady@wbcoll.edu
GRADY, David, L .... 205-348-6681.... 8 A
david.grady@ua.edu
GRADY, Helene .... 443-997-3359 204 F
hgrady1@jhu.edu
GRADY, Jonathan .... 810-762-3085 238 B
jrgrady@umflint.edu
GRADY, Lynne .... 706-379-3111 128 H
lbgrady@yhc.edu
GRADY, Meghan .... 610-606-4612 392 A
megrady@cedarcrest.edu
GRADY, Sara .... 508-929-8130 219 A
sara.grady@worcester.edu
GRADY, Sarah .... 718-409-7262 329 E
sgrady@sunymaritime.edu
GRAEBERT, James, K .... 414-288-3048 508 C
james.graebert@marquette.edu
GRAEM, David .... 903-675-6364 464 C
dgraem@tvcc.edu
GRAETHER, Anna .... 816-654-7122 261 D
agraether@kcumb.edu
GRAF, Bob .... 651-696-6280 243 B
rgraf@macalester.edu
GRAF, Katie, M .... 716-839-8364 306 E
kgraf@daemen.edu
GRAF, Megan .... 713-646-2968 456 H
mgraf@stcl.edu
GRAF, Mel .... 401-598-4949 416 C
mgraf@jwu.edu
GRAFER, Maggie .... 516-877-3844 297 I
yoon@adelphi.edu
GRAFF, Eric, S .... 614-885-5585 369 D
egraff@pcj.edu
GRAFF, Irene .... 310-660-3515.. 42 C
igraff@elcamino.edu
GRAFF, Irene .... 310-660-3670.. 42 C
igraff@elcamino.edu
GRAFF, Jenna .... 920-424-0775 511 B
graff@uwosh.edu
GRAFF, Jonathan, K ...... 575-624-8400 295 A
graff@nmmi.edu
GRAFF, Michael .... 440-525-7060 364 D
mgraff@laeklandcc.edu
GRAFF, Nadja .... 212-463-0400 331 F
nadja.graff@touro.edu
GRAFFIUS, Jeff .... 740-753-6336 362 K
graffiusj@hocking.edu
GRAFIUS, Brandon .... 313-831-5200 229 L
bgrafius@etseminary.edu
GRAFTON, Anthony .... 870-307-7315.. 20 C
anthony.grafton@lyon.edu
GRAFTON, Donald .... 541-485-1780 384 G
donaldgrafton@newhope.edu
GRAFTON, Ken .... 701-231-7655 354 D
k.grafton@ndsu.edu
GRAFTON, Phillip .... 937-766-7834 358 D
graftonp@cedarville.edu
GRAFTON, Steve, C .... 734-763-9730 237 I
sgrafton@umich.edu
GRAGG, Derrick .... 918-631-2181 381 C
derrick-gragg@utulsa.edu
GRAGG, J.D .... 660-543-4290 268 A
gragg@ucmo.edu
GRAGG, Matt .... 909-748-8108.. 71 H
matt_gragg@redlands.edu
GRAGG, Philip, T .... 619-239-0391.. 35 C
pgragg@cwsl.edu
GRAHAM, Amy .... 315-470-7858 299 K
amygraham@crouse.org
GRAHAM, Angela .... 540-863-2806 487 I
agraham@dslcc.edu
GRAHAM, Annette .... 845-451-1610 306 D
annette.graham@culinary.edu
GRAHAM, Anthony .... 336-334-7757 350 C
agraham@ncat.edu
GRAHAM, April .... 661-362-3248.. 39 C
april.graham@canyons.edu
GRAHAM, Archie .... 414-297-6870 514 C
grahama@matc.edu
GRAHAM, Carlos .... 573-681-5912 261 H
grahamc@lincolnu.edu
GRAHAM, Carole .... 540-857-6696 490 B
cgraham@virginiawestern.edu
GRAHAM, Christy .... 423-869-6314 433 C
christy.graham@lmunet.edu
GRAHAM, Chuck .... 352-335-2332.. 94 D
chuck.graham@acupuncturist.edu
GRAHAM, Cynthia .... 919-546-8333 348 I
cgraham@shawu.edu
GRAHAM, Darren .... 641-683-4273 169 I
darren.graham@indianhills.edu
GRAHAM, Doug .... 612-343-4798 249 E
dmgraham@northcentral.edu
GRAHAM, Earl .... 203-332-5290.. 85 F
egraham@housatonic.edu
GRAHAM, Eva .... 661-255-1050.. 29 F
egraham@calarts.edu
GRAHAM, Greg .... 321-674-7707.. 99 K
ggraham@fit.edu
GRAHAM, Gwen .... 219-464-5115 165 D
gwen.graham@valpo.edu
GRAHAM, James, F ...... 660-543-4279 268 A
graham@ucmo.edu
GRAHAM, Jean .... 251-580-2293.... 1 I
jean.graham@faulknerstate.edu
GRAHAM, Jeanne .... 906-932-4231 230 D
jeanneg@gogebic.edu
GRAHAM, Jeff .... 301-687-4311 209 A
jlgraham@frostburg.edu
GRAHAM, Jeffrey .... 956-665-2751 468 A
jeff.graham@utrgv.edu
GRAHAM, Jennifer .... 254-298-8592 458 C
jennifer.graham@templejc.edu
GRAHAM, Joan, E .... 585-475-6079 321 D
jegirp@rit.edu
GRAHAM, Joe .... 419-720-6670 369 F
jgraham@proskills.edu
GRAHAM, John .... 845-938-5868 519 D
john.graham@usma.edu
GRAHAM, John, D .... 812-855-1432 159 H
grahamjd@indiana.edu
GRAHAM, John, M .... 512-471-4716 467 C
john.graham@athletics.utexas.edu
GRAHAM, John-Bauer ... 256-782-5255.... 6 B
jgraham@jsu.edu
GRAHAM, Jonathan .... 765-983-1295 157 I
grahajo@earlham.edu
GRAHAM, Kathleen .... 570-577-3607 390 H
kathy.graham@bucknell.edu
GRAHAM, Keith .... 901-375-4400 434 F
keithgraham@midsouthchristian.edu
GRAHAM, Keith .... 570-740-0302 400 F
kgraham@luzerne.edu
GRAHAM, Kerwin .... 336-750-2078 352 D
grahamkw@wssu.edu
GRAHAM, Kevin .... 321-674-8111.. 99 K
kgraham@fit.edu
GRAHAM, Kevin, C .... 217-424-6360 145 J
kgraham@millikin.edu
GRAHAM, LeRoy .... 802-443-5669 475 G
leroyg@middlebury.edu
GRAHAM, JR.,
Lewis, P .... 803-934-3404 422 G
lgraham@morris.edu
GRAHAM, Lindsey .... 978-556-3621 220 F
lgraham@necc.mass.edu
GRAHAM, Lori .... 910-755-7325 341 C
grahaml@brunswickcc.edu
GRAHAM, JR.,
Louis, W .... 617-253-2808 221 C
GRAHAM, Mark, R .... 276-944-6104 480 J
mgraham@ehc.edu
GRAHAM, Mary, S .... 601-928-6280 254 D
mary.graham@mgccc.edu
GRAHAM, Michael .... 847-947-5333 146 G
michael.graham@nl.edu
GRAHAM, SJ,
Michael, J .... 513-745-3502 374 D
GRAHAM, Paula .... 914-964-4282 304 D
pgraham@riversidehealth.org
GRAHAM, Randy .... 713-525-3813 466 J
grahamra@stthom.edu
GRAHAM, Robbie .... 907-786-1190.... 9 I
rlgraham3@alaska.edu
GRAHAM, Robert .... 773-602-5265 135 L
rgraham24@ccc.edu
GRAHAM, Robert, J ...... 724-458-2187 396 D
rjgraham@gcc.edu
GRAHAM, Robin .... 406-444-0360 271 F
rgraham@montana.edu
GRAHAM, Robin .... 914-282-6087 332 A
r.graham@uts.edu
GRAHAM, Rosmari .... 814-732-1246 406 B
rgraham@edinboro.edu
GRAHAM, Roy .... 803-934-3298 422 G
roygraham@morris.edu
GRAHAM, Sharon, D ..... 785-864-4790 181 I
sgraham@ku.edu
GRAHAM, Shelci .... 212-217-3600 308 B
shelci_graham@fitnyc.edu
GRAHAM, Stephanie ...... 909-607-6722.. 45 D
stephanie_graham@hmc.edu
GRAHAM, Stephen, A ... 973-761-9011 291 F
stephen.graham@shu.edu
GRAHAM, Steve .... 252-492-2061 347 C
grahams@vgcc.edu
GRAHAM, Steven, W ..... 573-884-3360 268 B
grahams@umsystem.edu
GRAHAM, Tamara, K ..... 401-841-2245 518 E
tamara.graham@usnwc.edu
GRAHAM, Toby .... 706-542-0621 127 A
tgraham@uga.edu
GRAHAM, Van .... 903-233-3900 452 A
vangraham@letu.edu
GRAHAM, Whitney .... 580-477-7784 381 G
whitney.graham@newmoodle.wosc.edu
GRAHAM, William, H ..... 502-597-5865 187 E
william.graham@kysu.edu
GRAHAM-ROY, Anita ..... 808-954-4935 129 B
GRAHN, Lance .... 330-675-8820 363 I
lgrahn@kent.edu
GRAMELSPACHER,
Dave .... 812-357-8429 164 A
dgramelspacher@saintmeinrad.edu

GRAY, Karol .... 804-828-6116 487 E
kgray@vcu.edu
GRAY, Kathleen .... 718-489-5340 322 D
kgray4@sfc.edu
GRAY, Kelly .... 575-769-4179 293 M
kelly.gray@clovis.edu
GRAY, Kelly .... 419-755-4823 366 E
kgray@ncstatecollege.edu
GRAY, Kilen .... 502-895-3411 188 A
kgray@lpts.edu
GRAY, Kristen .... 706-778-0100 124 E
kgray@piedmont.edu
GRAY, Kristen .... 616-395-7945 231 D
gray@hope.edu
GRAY, Leslie .... 510-594-3705.. 28 K
lgray@cca.edu
GRAY, Lisa, G .... 410-546-6390 209 B
lggray@salisbury.edu
GRAY, Lloyd .... 601-974-1000 254 A
lloyd.gray@millsaps.edu
GRAY, Lydia, E .... 718-862-7231 313 L
lydia.gray@manhattan.edu
GRAY, Marisa .... 913-288-7284 178 H
mcgray@kckcc.edu
GRAY, Maryann, J .... 310-825-5573.. 69 B
mgray@conet.ucla.edu
GRAY, Michaelle .... 580-387-7131 376 D
mgray@mscok.edu
GRAY, Michaelle .... 580-387-7000 376 D
mgray@mscok.edu
GRAY, Monita, M .... 920-832-6697 507 L
monita.m.gray@lawrence.edu
GRAY, Nancy .... 970-339-6392.. 76 E
nancy.gray@aims.edu
GRAY, Rebecca .... 254-968-9473 459 A
rgray@tarleton.edu
GRAY, Robert, R .... 804-257-5842 491 C
rrgray@vuu.edu
GRAY, Robin, L .... 334-727-8503.... 7 F
rgray@tuskegee.edu
GRAY, Sandra, C .... 859-858-3511 183 D
president@asbury.edu
GRAY, Sarah .... 309-649-6265 152 G
sarah.gray@src.edu
GRAY, Sean .... 319-385-6271 170 J
sean.gray@iw.edu
GRAY, Seneca .... 503-768-6781 383 G
seneca@lclark.edu
GRAY, Shashuna .... 540-891-3046 488 B
dgray@germanna.edu
GRAY, Shaun .... 207-741-5580 200 C
sgray@smccme.edu
GRAY, Shawn .... 409-880-8466 462 C
shawn.gray@lamar.edu
GRAY, Sheryl .... 865-471-3240 430 H
sgray@cn.edu
GRAY, Shonda .... 443-885-3430 206 A
shonda.gray@morgan.edu
GRAY, Simon .... 716-285-1212 318 F
sgray@niagara.edu
GRAY, Susan .... 207-602-2248 202 A
sgray@une.edu
GRAY, Susan .... 478-289-2028 118 H
sgray@ega.edu
GRAY, Thomas, J .... 718-270-1122 326 A
thomas.gray@downstate.edu
GRAY, Tiffany .... 206-296-6070 498 D
grayt@seattleu.edu
GRAY, Tim .... 303-937-4420.. 77 B
tim.gray@augustineinstitute.org
GRAY, Timothy, R .... 309-341-7203 142 G
trgray@knox.edu
GRAY, Toni, B .... 806-371-2912 442 D
tbgray@actx.edu
GRAY, Tracy .... 858-695-8587 159 A
tgray@horizonuniversity.edu
GRAY, Tuesday, A .... 225-216-8403 192 B
grayt@mybrcc.edu
GRAY, Vance .... 404-756-4033 115 I
vgray@atlm.edu
GRAY, Velma .... 901-435-1676 433 A
velma_gray@loc.edu
GRAY, Warren, S .... 401-865-1602 416 E
wgray@providence.edu
GRAY, Whitney .... 913-971-3374 179 H
wbgray@mnu.edu
GRAY-DEVINE, Sherry ... 580-387-7212 376 D
sgray@mscok.edu
GRAY KOGEN,
Elizabeth .... 212-472-1500 318 B
giving@nysid.edu
GRAY PAYTON, Pamela 619-260-4681.. 71 J
grayp@sandiego.edu
GRAY-VICKREY, Peg ..... 254-519-5447 459 D
gray-vickrey@tamuct.edu
GRAY WILSON,
Stephanie .... 614-236-6894 358 A
honors@capital.edu

GRAYBILL, Jody, D .... 570-577-3351 390 H
jody.graybill@bucknell.edu
GRAYBOYS, James .... 334-229-4401.... 4 A
jgrayboys@alasu.edu
GRAYLEE, Laleh .... 657-278-4228.. 32 B
lgraylee@fullerton.edu
GRAYS, Rodney .... 301-447-7411 206 B
grays@msmary.edu
GRAYS, Shantay .... 713-718-7497 450 D
shanty.grays@hccs.edu
GRAYSON, Chinester .... 334-874-5700.... 5 B
cgrayson@ccal.edu
GRAYSON, Denise, R .... 605-256-5152 428 G
denise.grayson@dsu.edu
GRAYSON, Lorenzo .... 251-405-7170.... 1 E
lgrayson@bishop.edu
GRAZIANO, Joanne .... 516-299-2999 313 D
joanne.graziano@liu.edu
GRAZIANO, Judith .... 651-793-1368 245 E
judith.graziano@metrostate.edu
GRAZIANO, Lisa .... 716-851-1499 307 I
grazianol@ecc.edu
GRAZIANO, Vincent, S . 412-391-6710 389 J
vgraziano@bradfordpittsburgh.edu
GRAZZINI-OLSON,
Nancy .... 952-851-0066 240 A
GREANEY, Bryan .... 917-493-4477 313 M
bgreaney@msmnyc.edu
GREANEY, KC .... 707-778-4188.. 62 H
kgreaney@santarosa.edu
GREASON, Jessica .... 816-584-6329 265 C
jessica.greason@park.edu
GREASON, Walter .... 732-263-5423 287 C
wgreason@monmouth.edu
GREATHOUSE, Jo .... 979-230-3234 444 E
jo.greathouse@brazosport.edu
GREAVES, Joyce, M ...... 210-690-9000 449 K
jgreaves@hallmarkuniversity.edu
GREAVES, Matthew, C ... 202-687-3488.. 92 B
mcg3@georgetown.edu
GREAVES, Valerie .... 734-973-3345 238 G
vgreaves@wccnet.edu
GREBEL, David, A .... 817-257-7130 461 A
d.grebel@tcu.edu
GREBIN, Kevin .... 605-331-6772 429 D
kevin.grebin@usiouxfalls.edu
GREBING, Karen .... 239-513-1122 101 O
kgrebing@hodges.edu
GREBINOSKI, Jeff .... 920-498-7193 514 G
jeffrey.grebinoski@nwtc.edu
GRECO, Adrianna .... 845-431-3700 307 A
adrianna.greco@sunydutchess.edu
GRECO, Anne .... 215-751-8217 393 A
agreco@ccp.edu
GRECO, Frank, M .... 412-365-1133 392 C
greco@chatham.edu
GRECO, Juneann .... 570-340-6004 401 B
greco@marywood.edu
GRECO, Michelle .... 504-671-6001 192 H
mgreco@dcc.edu
GRECO, Peter .... 925-631-4747.. 59 C
plg2@stmarys-ca.edu
GREDEN, Leigh .... 734-487-8676 229 K
lgreden@emich.edu
GREDER, Darcy, L .... 309-556-3541 141 B
dgreder@iwu.edu
GREEAR, Amy .... 276-523-7480 488 F
agreear@mecc.edu
GREEN, Adam .... 304-558-0655 503 N
adam.green@wvhepc.edu
GREEN, Allen .... 914-395-2527 323 K
agreen@sarahlawrence.edu
GREEN, Andy .... 256-782-5268.... 6 B
agreen@jsu.edu
GREEN, Anita .... 313-593-5190 238 A
ujima@umich.edu
GREEN, Ann, F .... 828-694-1709 341 B
anng@blueridge.edu
GREEN, Anne-Marie ...... 815-825-9443 142 F
anne-marie.green@kishwaukeecollege.edu
GREEN, Ashley .... 817-722-1656 451 G
ashley.green@tku.edu
GREEN, Ashley .... 817-722-1612 451 G
ashley.green@tku.edu
GREEN, Audrey .... 661-362-3424.. 39 C
audrey.green@canyons.edu
GREEN, Becky .... 806-874-3571 445 R
becky.green@clarendoncollege.edu
GREEN, Bevley, W .... 251-460-6188.... 9 B
bwgreen@southalabama.edu
GREEN, Bichevia .... 803-535-1249 423 B
greenb@octech.edu
GREEN, Brenda .... 561-586-0121 101 K
bgreen@hci.edu
GREEN, Brenda, F .... 615-327-5770 434 A
bgreen@mmc.edu

GREEN, Charlotte .... 601-318-6495 256 I
cgreen@wmcarey.edu
GREEN, Cheryl .... 920-424-4000 511 B
green@uwosh.edu
GREEN, Cheryl .... 703-526-6978 483 A
cheryl.green@marymount.edu
GREEN, Chris .... 805-546-3902.. 41 C
cgreen@cuesta.edu
GREEN, Chris .... 859-985-3727 183 I
greenchr@berea.edu
GREEN, Cindy .... 334-222-6591.... 2 H
cgreen@lbwcc.edu
GREEN, Cindy .... 314-539-5227 266 E
cgreen2@stlcc.edu
GREEN, Clarence .... 660-562-1254 264 I
cgreen@nwmissouri.edu
GREEN, Constance, C ... 503-842-8222 387 C
conniegreen@tillamookbaycc.edu
GREEN, Danette .... 504-816-4026 191 E
dgreen@dillard.edu
GREEN, Danny .... 717-815-1924 415 G
greend@ycp.edu
GREEN, David, A .... 217-786-2406 144 B
david.green@llcc.edu
GREEN, David, M .... 818-947-2679.. 49 G
greendm@lavc.edu
GREEN, Denise .... 334-670-3712.... 7 E
mbgreen@troy.edu
GREEN, Dennis .... 603-644-3194 282 C
d.green@snhu.edu
GREEN, Donald .... 217-732-3168 143 F
pres@lincolnchristian.edu
GREEN, Donald, J .... 706-295-6328 119 G
dgreen@highlands.edu
GREEN, Donna .... 562-985-5468.. 32 C
donna.green@csulb.edu
GREEN, Dwayne .... 320-629-5159 246 H
greend@pine.edu
GREEN, Elaine .... 215-248-7063 392 D
greene@chc.edu
GREEN, Eleanor, M .... 979-845-5051 459 C
emgreen@tamu.edu
GREEN, Elna, C .... 706-737-1738 116 B
elngreen@augusta.edu
GREEN, Eric, J .... 606-337-4521 184 D
eric.green@ccbbc.edu
GREEN, Gary, M .... 336-734-7200 343 C
ggreen@forsythtech.edu
GREEN, Geoff .... 805-965-0581.. 62 E
green@sbccfoundation.org
GREEN, Haley .... 425-352-8258 492 K
hgreen@cascadia.edu
GREEN, James "Dub" .... 843-574-6774 424 G
james.green@tridenttech.edu
GREEN, James .... 314-340-3502 260 H
greenj@hssu.edu
GREEN, Janel .... 504-816-4447 191 E
jegreen@dillard.edu
GREEN, Jean .... 217-228-5432 149 B
greenje@quincy.edu
GREEN, Jeffrey .... 312-662-4401 133 A
jgreen@adler.edu
GREEN, Jennifer .... 909-621-8000.. 45 D
jgreen@hmc.edu
GREEN, Jennifer .... 860-932-4140.. 86 E
jgreen@qvcc.edu
GREEN, Jennifer .... 212-854-3953 299 B
jengreen@barnard.edu
GREEN, Jennifer .... 865-524-8079 432 F
jgreen@hchs.edu
GREEN, Jennifer, K .... 434-395-2944 482 E
greenjk@longwood.edu
GREEN, Jerry .... 718-817-4170 308 G
jgreen@fordham.edu
GREEN, Joel, B .... 626-584-5205.. 43 K
provost@fuller.edu
GREEN, Joel, B .... 626-584-5304.. 43 K
jbgreen@fuller.edu
GREEN, John .... 620-276-9595 177 G
john.green@gcccks.edu
GREEN, John .... 252-222-6273 341 F
greenj@carteret.edu
GREEN, John, C .... 330-972-1901 371 C
green@uakron.edu
GREEN, Jonathan .... 570-372-4130 410 H
supres@susqu.edu
GREEN, Judith .... 201-684-7523 289 C
jgreen2@ramapo.edu
GREEN, Julie .... 207-941-7129 199 B
greenj@husson.edu
GREEN, Karen .... 610-526-6008 396 H
kgreen@harcum.edu
GREEN, Kelly .... 360-596-5214 498 G
kgreen@spscc.edu
GREEN, Kerri .... 607-431-4162 309 E
greenk2@hartwick.edu
GREEN, Latrelle, A .... 804-257-5662 491 C
lagreen@vuu.edu

GREEN, Lillie, F .... 757-727-5057 481 E
lillie.green@hamptonu.edu
GREEN, Lisa .... 315-792-3736 332 H
lcgreen@utica.edu
GREEN, Lorry .... 864-977-7124 422 I
lorry.green@ngu.edu
GREEN, Lynette .... 920-403-3235 509 J
lynette.green@snc.edu
GREEN, Mariah .... 970-943-7122.. 84 E
mgreen@western.edu
GREEN, Mark .... 812-237-2304 159 C
mark.green@indstate.edu
GREEN, Mary .... 269-965-3931 232 A
greenm@kellogg.edu
GREEN, Matthew .... 845-688-1568 331 L
greenm@sunyulster.edu
GREEN, Matthew .... 805-546-3924.. 41 C
mgreen@cuesta.edu
GREEN, Matthew .... 423-869-6241 433 C
matthew.green@lmunet.edu
GREEN, Maureen .... 252-789-0297 344 E
maureen.green@martincc.edu
GREEN, Melanie, H .... 804-627-5300 478 I
melanie_green@bshsi.org
GREEN, Melissa .... 530-938-5374.. 39 H
mgreen8@siskiyous.edu
GREEN, III, Melvin .... 229-333-5954 127 H
GREEN, Michael, R .... 717-867-6208 399 J
mgreen@lvc.edu
GREEN, Michael, S .... 518-629-4554 310 G
m.green@hvcc.edu
GREEN, Mike .... 615-966-6000 433 D
mike.green@lipscomb.edu
GREEN, Mike .... 541-737-2447 385 F
GREEN, Mike .... 541-737-9275 385 F
GREEN, Moishe .... 845-352-5852 334 B
GREEN, Monica .... 951-372-7877.. 58 G
monica.green@norcocollege.edu
GREEN, Myrtes, D .... 205-929-6305.... 2 G
mdgreen@lawsonstate.edu
GREEN, Nancy .... 704-403-3599 336 B
nancy.green@carolinashealthcare.org
GREEN, Nicole .... 310-825-0768.. 69 B
ngreen@caps.ucla.edu
GREEN, O. Jerome .... 501-374-6305.. 21 C
GREEN, Patrick .... 918-595-7440 380 D
patrick.green@tulsacc.edu
GREEN, Paul .... 785-833-4387 179 C
green@kwu.edu
GREEN, Rachel .... 570-662-4815 406 F
rgreen@mansfield.edu
GREEN, Ragan .... 478-275-7865 123 I
rgreen@oftc.edu
GREEN, Ramona .... 903-223-3058 460 D
ramona.green@tamut.edu
GREEN, Ray .... 903-468-3005 459 E
raymond.green@tamuc.edu
GREEN, Rebecca .... 760-355-6499.. 46 B
becky.green@imperial.edu
GREEN, Richard .... 317-789-8271 157 G
rgreen@crossroads.edu
GREEN, Ronnie, D .... 402-472-2116 277 G
rgreen@unl.edu
GREEN, Rosalyn .... 405-744-9153 377 F
rosalyn.green@okstate.edu
GREEN, Ruvain .... 845-352-5852 334 B
GREEN, Samantha .... 973-720-2107 292 I
greens19@wpunj.edu
GREEN, Sandy, B .... 864-488-8348 422 B
sgreen@limestone.edu
GREEN, Satasha .... 773-995-3586 135 F
sgreen34@csu.edu
GREEN, Saytra .... 518-580-8418 324 D
sgreen3@skidmore.edu
GREEN, Staci .... 701-483-2562 354 A
staci.green@dickinsonstate.edu
GREEN, Stacy .... 207-974-4679 199 L
sgreen@emcc.edu
GREEN, Susan .... 734-432-5595 233 C
sgreen@madonna.edu
GREEN, Susan .... 802-635-1308 477 C
susan.green@jsc.edu
GREEN, Tamekia, S .... 706-396-8118 124 C
tgreen@paine.edu
GREEN, Teresa .... 806-716-2205 456 F
tgreen@southplainscollege.edu
GREEN, Tica, D .... 336-272-7102 338 B
tica.green@greensboro.edu
GREEN, Tiffany .... 256-539-8161.... 2 D
GREEN, Tim .... 256-549-8601.... 2 A
tgreen@gadsdenstate.edu
GREEN, Timothy, M .... 615-248-1378 439 B
tgreen@trevecca.edu
GREEN, Tom .... 216-421-7491 359 J
tgreen@cia.edu
GREEN, Tracie .... 209-384-6000.. 51 G
tracie.green@mccd.edu
GREEN, Tracy, A .... 440-366-4073 364 F

GREEN, Tracy, S 804-523-5789 488 C tgreen@reynolds.edu
GREEN, Vannessa 718-951-5712 301 E vgreen@brooklyn.cuny.edu
GREEN, Walter 678-359-5733 121 B walterg@gordonstate.edu
GREEN, Wayne 334-974-5700 5 B wgreen@ccal.edu
GREEN, Wayne, A 845-938-3419 519 D 8sgs@usma.edu
GREEN, William 423-614-8240 432 L wgreen@leeuniversity.edu.edu
GREEN, William, S 305-284-2006 112 O wgreen@miami.edu
GREEN COWLES, Maria 610-647-4400 397 I mcowles@immaculata.edu
GREEN-DAVIS, Brittany 662-621-4157 252 E bdavis@coahomacc.edu
GREEN-FULLER, Shonda 256-469-7333 6 A reg@hbc1.edu
GREEN-HAMANN, Matthew 207-992-4951 199 B green-hamannm@husson.edu
GREEN-POWELL, Patricia 850-561-2989 109 A patricia.greenpowell@famu.edu
GREEN-QUARLES, Ryanne 916-361-5114 35 G rgreen@carrington.edu
GREENAN, Jennie 309-692-4092 145 F jgreenan@midstate.edu
GREENBAUN, Yvonne 856-415-2138 289 G ygreenbaun@rcgc.edu
GREENBERG, Aaron 561-237-7915 103 E agreenberg@lynn.edu
GREENBERG, Bryce 801-375-5125 472 F bgreenberg@rmuohp.edu
GREENBERG, David 212-854-4446 305 E david.greenberg@columbia.edu
GREENBERG, Judith 617-422-7245 222 J jgreenberg@nesl.edu
GREENBERG, Mark 360-650-3051 500 E mark.greenberg@wwu.edu
GREENBERG, Michael, R 848-932-5475 290 C mrg@rci.rutgers.edu
GREENBERG, Raymond, S 512-499-4201 467 A rgreenberg@utsystem.edu
GREENBERG, Roberta 718-933-6700 315 K rgreenbe@monroecollege.edu
GREENBERG, Scott, B 508-626-4550 218 A sgreenberg@framingham.edu
GREENBERG, Yeshaya 305-534-7050 112 D
GREENBLATT, Austria Jazmin 718-522-9073 298 E agreenblatt@asa.edu
GREENE, Allen 716-645-3454 325 B ub-athleticdirector@buffalo.edu
GREENE, Andrew, S 717-867-6200 399 J greene@lvc.edu
GREENE, Brenda 718-270-4949 303 C bgreene@mec.cuny.edu
GREENE, Cary 910-695-3781 346 E greenec@sandhills.edu
GREENE, Christina 910-362-7074 341 E cgreene@cfcc.edu
GREENE, Clark, M 401-456-8440 417 A cgreene@ric.edu
GREENE, Dale 706-542-4741 127 A wdgreene@uga.edu
GREENE, David, A 207-859-4604 198 H david.greene@colby.edu
GREENE, Debra 573-681-5074 261 H greened@lincolnu.edu
GREENE, Doug 641-782-1324 173 I greene@swcciowa.edu
GREENE, Dwaine 502-863-8030 184 I president@georgetowncollege.edu
GREENE, Eric 269-965-3931 232 A greenee@kellogg.edu
GREENE, Gayle 919-866-5143 347 D dggreene@waketech.edu
GREENE, Gloria 256-824-6000 8 C gloria.green@uah.edu
GREENE, Jason 256-824-6736 8 C jason.greene@uah.edu
GREENE, Jeff, W 606-474-3298 185 C jgreene@kcu.edu
GREENE, Jessica, A 617-552-3111 212 E jessica.greene.2@bc.edu
GREENE, Joseph, J 401-598-1038 416 C jgreene@jwu.edu
GREENE, Julia 860-512-3372 85 G jgreene@manchestercc.edu
GREENE, Karen, L 614-234-5685 365 L kgreene@mccn.edu
GREENE, Kelly 337-521-8959 193 E kelly.greene@solacc.edu
GREENE, Ken, S 252-334-2019 340 B ken.greene@macuniversity.edu
GREENE, Kimberly 714-556-3610 72 F kimberly.greene@vanguard.edu
GREENE, Kimberly, A 816-604-2322 262 I kim.greene@mcckc.edu
GREENE, Lori 317-940-6086 156 I lgreene@butler.edu
GREENE, Michael 480-732-7146 13 E mike.greene@cgc.edu
GREENE, Michael 870-248-4000 18 J mike.greene@blackrivertech.edu
GREENE, Michaelyn 936-633-5215 442 I mgreene@angelina.edu
GREENE, Patricia 843-521-4117 425 B pagreene@uscb.edu
GREENE, Peggy 503-399-6031 382 C peggy.greene@chemeketa.edu
GREENE, Perry 516-877-4041 297 I greene@adelphi.edu
GREENE, Richard 504-278-6418 193 B rgreene@nunez.edu
GREENE, Ryan 478-757-2511 123 A ryan.greene@mga.edu
GREENE, Ryan 206-296-6260 498 D greener@seattleu.edu
GREENE, Sarah, E 717-867-6985 399 J sgreene@lvc.edu
GREENE, Shelley, W 336-633-0174 345 F swgreene@randolph.edu
GREENE, Tawana 870-460-1026 22 D jonesta@uamont.edu
GREENE, Thomas 718-636-3784 320 D tgreene@pratt.edu
GREENE, Thomas, G 916-484-8211 50 F greenet@arc.losrios.edu
GREENE, Thomas, G 503-943-7105 387 H greene@up.edu
GREENE, Thomas Christopher 802-828-8613 476 F thomas.greene@vcfa.edu
GREENE, Tim 828-766-1220 344 F tgreene@mayland.edu
GREENE, Timothy, D 315-655-7377 300 I tdgreene@cazenovia.edu
GREENE, Timothy, J 269-387-2378 239 E tim.greene@wmich.edu
GREENE, Tracy 605-688-5248 429 B tracy.greene@sdstate.edu
GREENE, Travis 661-255-1050 29 F tgreene@calarts.edu
GREENE, Vanessa 616-395-7800 231 D greene@hope.edu
GREENE POROCHNIAK, Chanel 570-408-3845 414 H chanel.greene@wilkes.edu
GREENE-RAINEY, Velva 484-365-7335 400 E vgrainey@lincoln.edu
GREENER, Kellie 906-635-2693 232 J kgreener@lssu.edu
GREENFELD, Solomon 718-782-7070 332 D sgreenfeld@utsny.edu
GREENFIELD, Brenda, T 315-470-6683 328 D bgreenfield@esf.edu
GREENFIELD, Helga 404-270-6425 126 D hgreenfield@spelman.edu
GREENFIELD, Ilene 973-278-5400 299 F igl@berkeleycollege.edu
GREENFIELD, Ilene 973-278-5400 283 J igl@berkeleycollege.edu
GREENFIELD, OSFS, James, J 610-282-1100 393 G james.greenfield@desales.edu
GREENFIELD, Meg 504-278-6424 193 B mgreenfield@nunez.edu
GREENFIELD, Steve 240-567-2583 205 F steve.greenfield@montgomerycollege.edu
GREENGART, Eli 410-484-7200 206 C egreengart@nirc.edu
GREENHALGH, Jill 651-779-3338 244 D jill.greenhalgh@century.edu
GREENHALGH, Mark 714-992-7042 54 A mgreenhalgh@fullcoll.edu
GREENHAW, David, M 314-918-2620 260 A dgreenhaw@eden.edu
GREENHAW, Eric 479-524-7285 20 B egreenhaw@jbu.edu
GREENHOUSE, Jeremy 413-755-4524 221 B jgreenhouse@stcc.edu
GREENING, Kris 870-743-3000 20 E kgreening@northark.edu
GREENING, RK 920-686-6238 510 A rk.greening@sl.edu
GREENLAND, Nicole 510-436-1462 45 G greenland@hnu.edu
GREENLAND, William 773-702-7433 153 F greenland@uchicago.edu
GREENLEAF, Maxine 662-254-3577 255 A max.greenleaf@mvsu.edu
GREENLEE, Carmen, M 207-725-3286 198 G cgreenle@bowdoin.edu
GREENLEE, Lisa 580-477-7702 381 G lisa.greenlee@wosc.edu
GREENLEE, Pam 815-939-5211 148 F pgreenl@olivet.edu
GREENLEE, Zach 314-744-7639 263 F greenleez@mobap.edu
GREENO, Darren 360-416-7729 498 F darren.greeno@skagit.edu
GREENO, Jimmie 215-972-2303 404 Q jgreeno@pafa.edu
GREENO, John, G 412-396-5103 394 D greenoj@duq.edu
GREENSLADE, Ernestine 978-556-3862 220 F egreenslade@necc.mass.edu
GREENSLADE-SMITH, Toni 614-292-8266 367 H greenslade-smith.1@osu.edu
GREENSTEIN, Benjamin 401-254-3043 417 C bgreenstein@rwu.edu
GREENSTEIN, Kerry 352-787-7660 95 H kgreenstein@beaconcollege.edu
GREENSTREET, Robert, C 414-229-4016 511 A bobg@uwm.edu
GREENTHAL, Joseph, T 607-587-3938 328 F greentjt@alfredstate.edu
GREENUP, Troy 562-907-4287 75 A greenup@whittier.edu
GREENWALD, J. Patrick 716-888-8216 300 G greenwal@canisius.edu
GREENWALD, Lorraine 631-420-2479 329 D lorraine.greenwald@farmingdale.edu
GREENWALD, Nicole 206-876-6100 498 C ngreenwald@theseattleschool.edu
GREENWALD, Reesa 973-275-2828 291 F reesa.greenwald@shu.edu
GREENWALD, Richard 203-254-4000 87 A rgreenwald@fairfield.edu
GREENWALT, Riane, B 618-650-2852 152 C rgreenw@siue.edu
GREENWAY, Adam 502-897-4043 189 A agreenway@sbts.edu
GREENWAY, Doug 605-995-3056 427 E doug.greenway@mitchelltech.edu
GREENWAY, Janet 605-995-7194 427 E janet.greenway@mitchelltech.edu
GREENWAY, Lidell 229-468-2240 128 G lidell.greenway@wiregrass.edu
GREENWELL, Brian 330-490-7282 373 F bgreenwell@walsh.edu
GREENWELL, Joseph, D 510-642-6770 68 G deanofstudents@berkeley.edu
GREENWOOD, Gail 423-472-7141 436 G ggreenwood@clevelandstatecc.edu
GREENWOOD, Jennifer 731-881-7380 440 B jgreenwood@utm.edu
GREENWOOD, Kevin 614-947-6095 362 A kevin.greenwood@franklin.edu
GREENWOOD, Marisol 972-773-8300 93 B
GREENWOOD, Marisol 972-535-3700 93 B
GREENWOOD, Marisol 469-454-3400 93 B
GREENWOOD, Marisol 214-429-3900 93 B
GREENWOOD, Nichole 801-832-2027 474 E nhg@westminstercollege.edu
GREENWOOD, Paul 813-257-3095 113 E
GREENWOOD-BLACKSHEAR, Sheila 410-706-2281 207 H sheila.blackshear@umaryland.edu
GREENY, Eric 818-767-0888 75 C
GREER, Bobby, T 864-488-8251 422 B bgreer@limestone.edu
GREER, Charles 951-827-3093 69 D charles.greer@ucr.edu
GREER, Chelsea 251-380-4195 7 B cgreer@shc.edu
GREER, Christine, G 906-227-1700 235 A cgreer@nmu.edu
GREER, Colleen 218-755-2989 244 B cgreer@bemidjistate.edu
GREER, James 325-793-4882 452 F jgreer@mcm.edu
GREER, Jennifer 205-348-4890 8 A jdgreer@ua.edu
GREER, Jody 260-665-4105 164 E greerj@trine.edu
GREER, Karla, J 972-860-7173 447 I kgreer@dcccd.edu
GREER, Kevin 417-626-1234 264 J greer.kevin@occ.edu
GREER, Kimberly 209-667-3203 33 F kgreer@csustan.edu
GREER, M. Bradley 864-424-8039 425 G greerm@mailbox.sc.edu
GREER, Melodie 267-502-2407 390 F melodie.greer@brynathyn.edu
GREER, Michael 203-591-5641 87 H mgreer@post.edu
GREER, Rebecca 914-361-6220 316 A rgreer@montefiore.org
GREER, Sheree 606-474-3186 185 C sgreer@kcu.edu
GREER, Sherman, D 901-333-4101 438 B sdgreer@southwest.tn.edu
GREER, T. Richard 585-594-6160 321 C greerr@roberts.edu
GREER, Todd 251-442-2701 8 D tgreer@umobile.edu
GREER, William, B 423-461-8710 435 A bgreer@milligan.edu
GREGERSEN, Denise 707-545-3647 27 B denise@berginu.edu
GREGERSON, Robert (Bob) 239-590-7156 109 C rgregerson@fgcu.edu
GREGG, Carla 712-274-5463 172 A gregg@morningside.edu
GREGG, Claire 864-455-8209 425 E cgregg@ghs.org
GREGG, Cody 956-872-2528 456 G cgregg@southtexascollege.edu
GREGG, Ellen 970-351-2877 83 F ellen.gregg@unco.edu
GREGG, Gerald, A 503-943-7161 387 H gregg@up.edu
GREGG, Karla 417-447-6966 264 K greggk@otc.edu
GREGG, Kelly 954-262-4335 104 F kgregg1@nova.edu
GREGG, Kori 620-441-5245 176 M kori.gregg@cowley.edu
GREGG, Michael, J 817-552-3700 451 G lpyun@tku.edu
GREGG, Phyllis 312-362-8850 137 C pgregg@depaul.edu
GREGG, Robert, S 609-652-4542 291 H robert.gregg@stockton.edu
GREGG, Virginia 518-276-6426 321 A greggv@rpi.edu
GREGGS, Rob 405-682-7877 377 C rgreggs@occc.edu
GREGOIRE, David, P 518-564-2090 327 E gregoidp@plattsburgh.edu
GREGOIRE, JR., Paul, E 504-282-4455 195 D pgregoire@nobts.edu
GREGOIRE, Tom 614-292-9426 367 H gregoire.5@osu.edu
GREGOR, Lynn, D 860-253-3163 85 C lgregor@asnuntuck.edu
GREGORI-GAHAN, Heidi, M 812-465-1248 165 C gahan@usi.edu
GREGORIO, Kyle 918-293-5210 378 B kylelg@okstate.edu
GREGOROWICZ, Stephen 609-586-4800 287 A gregoros@mccc.edu
GREGORY, Alison 570-321-4082 400 G gregory@lycoming.edu
GREGORY, Anne 260-982-5285 162 Q aggregory@manchester.edu
GREGORY, Anne 219-989-2335 163 E
GREGORY, Brent 662-246-6302 254 C bgregory@msdelta.edu
GREGORY, Carolyn 216-368-5276 358 C carolyn.gregory@case.edu
GREGORY, Charles, J 207-741-5643 200 C cgregory@smccme.edu
GREGORY, Christine 212-517-0562 314 D cgregory@mmm.edu
GREGORY, Christopher 508-626-4510 218 A cgregory@framingham.edu
GREGORY, Dan 320-308-4909 247 E ddgregory@stcloudstate.edu
GREGORY, Dan 512-313-3000 446 N daniel.gregory@concordia.edu
GREGORY, David 617-747-2558 212 B dgregory@berklee.edu
GREGORY, David, B 615-366-4430 436 E david.gregory@tbr.edu
GREGORY, David, L 606-783-5100 188 C d.gregory@moreheadstate.edu
GREGORY, Denise 205-726-2725 6 G djgregor@samford.edu
GREGORY, Derek 570-961-7839 399 A gregoryd@lackawanna.edu
GREGORY, Ellen, D 859-846-6046 188 B egregory@midway.edu

GREGORY, Jeffery .... 570-961-7868 399 A
gregoryj@lackawanna.edu
GREGORY, Katherine .... 515-294-6162 166 F
gregoryk@iastate.edu
GREGORY, Lisa .... 217-875-7200 149 J
lgregory@richland.edu
GREGORY, Matthew .... 617-322-3500 216 B
GREGORY, Melissa .... 240-567-5036 205 F
melissa.gregory@montgomerycollege.edu
GREGORY, Miraglia .... 707-654-4528.. 53 D
mgregory@napavalley.edu
GREGORY, Patrick .... 334-386-7259.... 5 I
pgregory@faulkner.edu
GREGORY, Paula .... 417-208-0632 261 D
pgregory@kcumb.edu
GREGORY, Peggy .... 802-287-8376 475 B
peggy.gregory@greenmtn.edu
GREGORY, Rhonda .... 615-230-3668 438 C
rhonda.gregory@volstate.edu
GREGORY, Rich .... 818-909-5517.. 51 C
rgregory@tms.edu
GREGORY, Steve .... 906-635-2182 232 J
sgregory@lssu.edu
GREGORY, Tom, F .... 570-326-3761 404 T
tgregory@pct.edu
GREGORY, Tony .... 864-424-8000 425 G
gregorga@mailbox.sc.edu
GREGORY, Travis .... 760-750-4954.. 33 E
tgregory@csusm.edu
GREGORY, Trisha .... 301-687-4201 209 A
tgregory@frostburg.edu
GREGORYK, Kerry .... 515-271-1665 168 G
kerry.gregoryk@dmu.edu
GREGORYK, Kerry .... 701-845-7480 354 E
kerry.gregoryk@vcsu.edu
GREGORYK, Michael, D 909-274-4230.. 52 I
mgregoryk@mtsac.edu
GREGSON,
Donald (Jay) .... 210-690-9000 449 K
dgregson@hallmarkuniversity.edu
GREGSON, Joanna .... 253-531-6900 496 G
GREIFE, Alice, L .... 660-543-4450 268 A
greife@ucmo.edu
GREIFFENDORF, OP,
Mary Agnes .... 615-297-7545 429 H
srmagnes@aquinascollege.edu
GREIG, Carl .... 903-223-3062 460 D
carl.greig@tamut.edu
GREIG, Judith, M .... 650-508-3503.. 54 D
jgreig@ndnu.edu
GREIL, Stan .... 405-733-7488 379 F
sgreil@rose.edu
GREIMAN, Judith .... 631-632-4418 325 F
judith.greiman@stonybrook.edu
GREIMAN, Judith .... 631-632-6265 325 F
judith.greiman@stonybrook.edu
GREINER, Cathleen .... 949-451-5565.. 64 I
cgreiner@ivc.edu
GREINER, Mary .... 641-269-4818 169 F
greinerm@grinnell.edu
GREINER, Stephanie .... 515-271-1386 168 G
stephanie.greiner@dmu.edu
GREINER, Stephen, G .... 304-336-8000 504 E
stephen.greiner@westliberty.edu
GREINER, Susan, L .... 336-322-2245 345 D
sue.greiner@piedmontcc.edu
GREMILLION, Henry .... 504-619-8500 194 C
hgremi@lsuhsc.edu
GREMMELS,
Gillian (Jill), S .... 704-894-2160 337 B
jigremmels@davidson.edu
GRENDER, Teresa .... 606-368-6044 182 H
teresagrender@alc.edu
GRENIER, Kyle .... 617-236-4446 215 B
kgrenier@fisher.edu
GRENIER, Tina .... 701-671-2612 355 B
tina.grenier@ndscs.edu
GRENNAN, Jon .... 845-451-1323 306 D
jon.grennan@culinary.edu
GRENUS, Steven .... 785-670-1574 182 D
steven.grenus@washburn.edu
GRENZ, Jonathan .... 561-803-2543 104 I
jon_grenz@pba.edu
GRENZOW, Kelly .... 715-425-3531 511 E
kelly.grenzow@uwrf.edu
GRESCH, Mary .... 206-685-3710 499 D
mgresch@uw.edu
GRESH, Colleen .... 860-701-5030.. 87 F
gresh_c@mitchell.edu
GRESHAM, Jonathan .... 423-636-7300 439 C
jgresham@tusculum.edu
GRESHAM, Kathryn .... 828-884-8328 335 L
greshakb@brevard.edu
GRESHAM, Susan .... 812-535-5121 163 I
sgresham@smwc.edu
GRESS, Michael .... 812-888-4176 165 E
mgress@vinu.edu
GRESS, Vicky .... 217-333-4493 154 B
gress@illinois.edu
GRESSLEY, Jerry, A .... 260-359-4052 159 B
jgressley@huntington.edu
GRETCH, Jim .... 406-791-5320 273 C
jim.gretch@ugf.edu
GRETCHENUK, Phyllis ... 206-934-5479 497 I
phyllis.gretchenuk@seattlecolleges.edu
GRETINA, Lauren .... 718-518-4284 302 D
lgretina@hostos.cuny.edu
GRETZ, Dan .... 715-634-4790 507 J
dgretz@lco.edu
GREUFE, Sandra .... 641-648-4611 170 H
sandra.greufe@iavalley.edu
GREVE, Debbie .... 620-235-4206 180 J
dgreve@pittstate.edu
GREVE, Jennifer .... 402-844-7062 276 G
jenniferg@northeast.edu
GREVESEN, Chris .... 973-278-5400 283 J
chris-grevesen@berkeleycollege.edu
GREVI, Laura .... 914-337-9300 305 F
laura.grevi@concordia-ny.edu
GREVING, John .... 402-465-2486 276 E
jgreving@nebrwesleyan.edu
GREW-GILLEN, Cheryl .... 701-777-4200 353 G
cheryl.grewgillen@und.edu
GREWAL, Daman .... 707-654-1727.. 32 E
dgrewal@csum.edu
GREWAL, Parwinder .... 956-882-6701 468 A
parwinder.grewal@utrgv.edu
GREY, Erin .... 307-382-1647 517 C
egrey@westernwyoming.edu
GREY, Gregory, D .... 410-334-2933 210 C
ggrey@worwic.edu
GREY, Jeanette .... 303-458-4231.. 82 D
jgrey@regis.edu
GREY, Kimberly .... 314-392-2241 263 F
grey@mobap.edu
GREY, Marge .... 209-946-2311.. 70 F
mgrey@pacific.edu
GREY, Pam .... 408-864-8209.. 43 E
greypam@deanza.edu
GREY, Thomasina .... 505-786-4186 294 I
tgrey@navajotech.edu
GREYDANUS, John .... 541-737-9099 385 F
john.greydanus@oregonstate.edu
GREYWATER, Brigitte .... 701-662-1546 355 A
brigitte.greywater@lrsc.edu
GRIBB, Molly .... 608-342-1561 511 D
gribbm@uwplatt.edu
GRIBBEN, Les .... 212-817-7470 302 B
lgribben@gc.cuny.edu
GRIBBIN, David .... 478-289-2047 118 H
dgribbin@ega.edu
GRIBBLE, Kari .... 608-663-2305 507 D
kgribble@edgewood.edu
GRIBBLE, Scott .... 308-632-6933 277 B
GRIBBLE, Shannon, L .... 301-687-7588 209 A
slgribble@frostburg.edu
GRIBBONS, Barry .... 661-362-5500.. 39 C
barry.gribbons@canyons.edu
GRIBLIN, Diana .... 316-942-4291 180 D
griblind@newmanu.edu
GRICE, Brittany .... 805-437-3608.. 31 C
brittany.grice@csuci.edu
GRICE, Ronnie, D .... 785-532-1131 179 A
raker@ksu.edu
GRICE, Vivian, D .... 803-641-3550 425 A
viviang@usca.edu
GRIECO, Stephen .... 215-885-2360 401 A
sgrieco@manor.edu
GRIEGER, Mary .... 414-425-8300 509 I
mgrieger@shsst.edu
GRIEGO, Orlando .... 815-740-3452 154 G
ogriego@stfrancis.edu
GRIER, Douglas, L .... 630-466-7900 155 C
dgrier@waubonsee.edu
GRIER, Ed .... 804-828-1062 487 E
egrier@vcu.edu
GRIER, Frank, O .... 334-833-4005.... 5 M
fgrier@hawks.huntingdon.edu
GRIER, Judith .... 757-789-1753 488 A
jgrier@es.vccs.edu
GRIER, Lauri .... 909-748-8390.. 71 H
lauri_grier@redlands.edu
GRIESBACH, Scott .... 715-232-1334 512 A
griesbachs@uwstout.edu
GRIESHEIMER, Tina .... 303-797-5901.. 76 I
tina.griesheimer@arapahoe.edu
GRIESSE, Sarah .... 612-330-1489 240 G
griesse@augsburg.edu
GRIEVE, Cathy .... 303-871-2397.. 83 E
cgrieve@du.edu
GRIEVE, Kimberly .... 605-677-5331 428 E
kimberly.grieve@usd.edu
GRIEVE, Robyn .... 408-260-0208.. 43 B
daom@fivebranches.edu
GRIFFEL, Michael, M .... 541-346-2667 387 F
mgriffel@uoregon.edu
GRIFFEN, Emily .... 413-542-2265 210 F
egriffen@amherst.edu
GRIFFETH, Jennifer .... 706-355-5025 115 H
jgriffeth@athenstech.edu
GRIFFIN, Bert .... 502-585-9911 189 B
bgriffin@spalding.edu
GRIFFIN, Bruce .... 650-358-6722.. 61 Q
griffinb@smccd.edu
GRIFFIN, Bryan .... 989-774-7112 228 E
griff3bl@cmich.edu
GRIFFIN, Catherine .... 734-432-5460 233 C
kgriffin@madonna.edu
GRIFFIN, Cathy .... 908-526-1200 289 D
cathy.griffin@raritanval.edu
GRIFFIN, Clifton, P .... 410-548-3894 209 B
cpgriffin@salisbury.edu
GRIFFIN, Courtney .... 334-229-4302.... 4 A
cgriffin@alasu.edu
GRIFFIN, Dale, M .... 405-585-5700 377 A
dale.griffin@okbu.edu
GRIFFIN, Dan .... 731-661-5120 439 D
dgriffin@uu.edu
GRIFFIN, Daniel .... 315-312-2250 327 D
daniel.griffin@oswego.edu
GRIFFIN, David .... 617-824-8500 214 E
david_griffin@emerson.edu
GRIFFIN, Deborah .... 510-659-6151.. 54 F
dgriffin@ohlone.edu
GRIFFIN, Donitha .... 334-876-9302.... 2 C
donitha.griffin@wccs.edu
GRIFFIN, Elaine .... 615-966-5818 433 D
elaine.griffin@lipscomb.edu
GRIFFIN, Ellen .... 973-655-3123 287 D
griffinel@mail.montclair.edu
GRIFFIN, Greg .... 315-786-2291 311 H
ggriffin@sunyjefferson.edu
GRIFFIN, Hayden .... 252-737-1026 349 I
griffino@ecu.edu
GRIFFIN, Heather .... 502-895-3411 188 A
hgriffin@lpts.edu
GRIFFIN, Jacquelyn, H . 864-977-7081 422 I
jackie.griffin@ngu.edu
GRIFFIN, Janie .... 503-491-6701 384 D
janie.griffin@mhcc.edu
GRIFFIN, Jason .... 567-661-2692 369 A
jason_griffin@owens.edu
GRIFFIN, Jeff .... 765-455-9339 160 B
griffon0@purdue.edu
GRIFFIN, Jeff, D .... 504-816-8018 195 D
jgriffin@nobts.edu
GRIFFIN, Joe .... 765-973-8633 160 A
joegrif@iue.edu
GRIFFIN, Jonathan .... 602-429-4912.. 15 K
jgriffin@ps.edu
GRIFFIN, Karen .... 813-253-7002 101 M
kgriffin@hccfl.edu
GRIFFIN, Karen .... 636-584-6575 259 L
karen.griffin@eastcentral.edu
GRIFFIN, Kate .... 757-233-8785 491 F
agriffine@vwu.edu
GRIFFIN, Larry .... 252-399-6331 335 I
lcgriffin@barton.edu
GRIFFIN, Larry .... 901-375-4400 434 F
larrygriffin@midsouthchristian.edu
GRIFFIN, Leslie .... 662-846-4400 252 H
lgriffin@deltastate.edu
GRIFFIN, Lisa .... 229-217-4144 126 C
lgriffin@southernregional.edu
GRIFFIN, Lonnie .... 912-408-3024 125 D
lfgriffin@savannahtech.edu
GRIFFIN, Lori .... 253-912-3633 497 B
lgriffin@pierce.ctc.edu
GRIFFIN, Lynn .... 843-383-8071 420 B
lgriffin@coker.edu
GRIFFIN, Mark .... 785-628-4026 177 D
magriffin2@fhsu.edu
GRIFFIN, Mark .... 973-353-1458 290 D
markg@andromeda.rutgers.edu
GRIFFIN, Michael .... 212-636-6520 308 G
mgriffin19@fordham.edu
GRIFFIN, Michael .... 574-239-8400 158 M
GRIFFIN, Nancy, D .... 207-780-4547 201 H
nancy.d.griffin@maine.edu
GRIFFIN, Neil .... 864-592-4897 424 C
griffinn@sccsc.edu
GRIFFIN, Patricia, L .... 785-628-5377 177 D
pgriffin@fhsu.edu
GRIFFIN, Patrick .... 845-431-8924 307 A
griffin@sunydutchess.edu
GRIFFIN, CM,
Patrick, J .... 718-990-6311 322 F
griffinp@stjohns.edu
GRIFFIN, Paul, F .... 315-684-6081 329 F
griffipf@morrisville.edu
GRIFFIN, Ragan, K .... 724-357-2218 406 C
rgriffin@iup.edu
GRIFFIN, Robert .... 901-375-4400 434 F
robertgriffin@midsouthchristian.edu
GRIFFIN, Sallie .... 601-877-6377 251 G
sgriffin@alcorn.edu
GRIFFIN, Stephen, L .... 651-962-6855 251 D
stephen.griffin@stthomas.edu
GRIFFIN, Tamara .... 870-612-2022.. 22 H
tamara.griffin@uaccb.edu
GRIFFIN, Thomas, H .... 919-515-5036 350 E
thgriffi@ncsu.edu
GRIFFIN, Tim .... 602-639-7500.. 12 P
GRIFFIN, Tim .... 303-914-6516.. 82 B
tim.griffin@rrcc.edu
GRIFFIN, Timothy .... 202-408-2400.. 93 B
GRIFFIN, Timothy .... 201-216-5107 291 G
timothy.griffin@stevens.edu
GRIFFIN, Walt, R .... 864-488-4616 422 B
wgriffin@limestone.edu
GRIFFIN CALKINS,
Nancy .... 336-334-4822 343 E
nfgriffincalkins@gtcc.edu
GRIFFIN-SOBEL, Joyce .. 509-324-7332 499 G
joyce.griffin-sobel@wsu.edu
GRIFFIS, Teresa .... 912-525-5000 125 B
tgriffis@scad.edu
GRIFFITH, Abby .... 607-871-2082 298 A
griffitha@alfred.edu
GRIFFITH, Ashley .... 714-484-7425.. 53 M
agriffith@cypresscollege.edu
GRIFFITH, Bradley .... 618-985-3741 141 D
bradleygriffith@jalc.edu
GRIFFITH, Celeste .... 212-686-9040 333 I
cgriffith@woodtobecoburn.edu
GRIFFITH, Cynthia .... 281-756-3601 442 C
cgriffith@alvincollege.edu
GRIFFITH, David .... 903-813-2587 443 F
dgriffith@austincollege.edu
GRIFFITH, Denise .... 618-634-3277 151 G
deniseg@shawneecc.edu
GRIFFITH, Jimmie .... 828-726-2225 341 D
jgriffith@cccti.edu
GRIFFITH, Jolene .... 641-782-1456 173 I
griffith@swcciowa.edu
GRIFFITH, Julie, K .... 765-494-6838 163 C
jgriff@purdue.edu
GRIFFITH, Kathy .... 740-392-6868 366 B
kathy.griffity@mvnu.edu
GRIFFITH, Kevin .... 574-520-4879 160 F
kevgriff@iusb.edu
GRIFFITH, Larry, K .... 724-847-6585 395 J
lkgriffith@geneva.edu
GRIFFITH, Launey, P .... 337-550-1390 194 B
lgriffit@lsue.edu
GRIFFITH, Lauren .... 904-680-7700.. 99 C
GRIFFITH, Margo .... 907-474-6600.. 10 B
margo.griffith@alaska.edu
GRIFFITH, Maxine, F .... 212-854-6524 305 E
mfg30@columbia.edu
GRIFFITH, Raymont .... 502-597-6678 187 E
ray.griffith@kysu.edu
GRIFFITH,
Rebecca (Becki) .... 817-515-7778 458 B
rebecca.griffith@tccd.edu
GRIFFITH, Roger, D .... 304-647-6563 503 B
rgriffith@newriver.edu
GRIFFITH, Ross .... 336-414-1715 317 B
rgriffith@nycollege.edu
GRIFFITH, Ryan .... 209-946-2090.. 70 F
rgriffith@pacific.edu
GRIFFITH, Sarah .... 360-442-2520 495 G
sgriffith@lowercolumbia.edu
GRIFFITH, Trevor .... 513-244-4370 366 A
trevor.griffith@msj.edu
GRIFFITH-GREEN,
Nicole .... 606-326-2000 185 E
nicole.griffithgreen@kctcs.edu
GRIFFITH-KLINE,
Cheryl .... 704-687-7077 351 C
GRIFFITHS, Andy .... 207-801-5605 199 A
agriffiths@coa.edu
GRIFFITHS,
José -Marie .... 605-256-5112 428 G
presidentsoffice@dsu.edu
GRIFFITHS, Kelly .... 360-417-6201 496 I
kgriffiths@pencol.edu
GRIFFUS, Randall .... 706-272-4440 118 F
rgriffus@daltonstate.edu
GRIFFY, Loretta .... 931-221-7634 430 B
griffyl@apsu.edu
GRIGAR, Mary .... 312-341-3548 150 D
mgrigar@roosevelt.edu
GRIGG, Dan .... 636-949-4939 261 I
dgrigg@lindenwood.edu
GRIGG, Eddie, G .... 704-334-6882 336 I
egrigg@charlottechristian.edu
GRIGG, Lauralynn, M ... 608-258-2401 514 A
lmgrigg@madisoncollege.edu

GRIGGS, Brandon ... 254-519-5748 459 D
griggs@tamuct.edu
GRIGGS, Donald, R ... 843-953-5420 420 C
griggsd@cofc.edu
GRIGGS, Gary, B ... 831-459-2464.. 70 C
griggs@es.ucsc.edu
GRIGGS, LaSonya ... 607-844-8222 331 D
lag@tompkinscortland.edu
GRIGGS, Robert, J ... 605-367-8355 429 C
robert.griggs@southeasttech.edu
GRIGGS, Ron ... 402-461-7337 274 I
ron.griggs@hastings.edu
GRIGGS, Ronald, K ... 740-427-5632 364 A
griggs@kenyon.edu
GRIGNON, Rose, L ... 518-244-2311 321 G
grignr@sage.edu
GRIGSBY, Bryon, L ... 610-861-1364 402 D
grigsbyb@moravian.edu
GRIGSBY, Delores ... 301-696-3440 204 D
grigsby@hood.edu
GRIGSBY, Gwen, W ... 512-232-1781 467 C
gwen.grigsby@austin.utexas.edu
GRIGSBY, Mark ... 918-540-6275 376 F
mgrigsby@neo.edu
GRIGSBY, Rebekah ... 903-923-2212 448 J
rgrigsby@etbu.edu
GRIJALVA, Norma ... 575-646-6030 295 B
norma@nmsu.edu
GRIJALVA, Sara ... 575-835-5133 294 K
sara.jgrijalva@nmt.edu
GRILL, Joshua, L ... 570-577-3223 390 H
josh.grill@bucknell.edu
GRILL, Stephen, A ... 574-372-5100 158 B
grillsa@grace.edu
GRILLO, Robert ... 305-348-2738 109 D
robert.grillo@fiu.edu
GRILLOT, Suzette, R ... 405-325-6003 380 L
sgrillot@ou.edu
GRILLOT, Tina ... 620-441-5376 176 M
tina.grillot@cowley.edu
GRIMALDI, Matthew ... 570-945-8231 398 C
matthew.grimaldi@keystone.edu
GRIMES, Brittany ... 309-341-5221 134 H
bgrimes@sandburg.edu
GRIMES, Carolyn ... 803-793-5174 420 G
grimesc@denmarktech.edu
GRIMES, Charles, R ... 330-471-8438 364 H
cgrimes@malone.edu
GRIMES, Daniel ... 574-296-6266 155 K
dgrimes@ambs.edu
GRIMES, Deborah ... 252-527-6223 344 D
dgrimes@lenoircc.edu
GRIMES, Donnie ... 606-539-4197 190 A
donnie.grimes@ucumberlands.edu
GRIMES, Elizabeth ... 910-962-3274 352 A
grimese@uncw.edu
GRIMES, Hubert ... 386-481-2752.. 95 J
grimesh@cookman.edu
GRIMES, Hubert, L ... 386-481-2001.. 95 J
grimesh@cookman.edu
GRIMES, Jana, L ... 765-658-6697 157 H
janagrimes@depauw.edu
GRIMES, Judith ... 816-271-5991 264 B
grimes@missouriwestern.edu
GRIMES, Kathleen ... 570-577-1554 390 H
kathleen.grimes@bucknell.edu
GRIMES, Kendra, S ... 804-752-7374 484 C
kendragrimes@rmc.edu
GRIMES, Kristen ... 951-487-3002.. 52 J
kgrimes@msjc.edu
GRIMES, Larry ... 304-829-7420 501 F
lgrimes@bethanywv.edu
GRIMES, Paul ... 620-235-4598 180 J
paul.grimes@pittstate.edu
GRIMES, SJ, Robert ... 212-636-6300 308 G
rgrimes@fordham.edu
GRIMES,
Robert (Bud), D ... 731-881-7615 440 B
bgrimes@utm.edu
GRIMES, Sheila ... 530-938-5200.. 39 H
grimes@siskiyous.edu
GRIMES, Sidney ... 212-217-4040 308 B
sidney_grimes@fitnyc.edu
GRIMES, Steve ... 918-540-6226 376 F
sgrimes@neo.edu
GRIMES, Terri, A ... 815-599-3514 139 F
terri.grimes@highland.edu
GRIMES, Tresmaine ... 973-748-9000 284 A
tresmaine_grimes@bloomfield.edu
GRIMES-HILLMAN,
Michelle ... 562-938-4932.. 48 I
mhillman@lbcc.edu
GRIMLEY, Lee Ann ... 319-895-4378 167 G
lgrimley@cornellcollege.edu
GRIMM, Barbara, M ... 919-516-4128 348 G
bmgrimm@st-aug.edu
GRIMM, Gary ... 503-370-6814 388 D
ggrimm@willamette.edu
GRIMM, Lyndsay, L ... 724-450-4045 396 D
llgrimm@gcc.edu
GRIMM, Randy ... 816-322-0110 257 M
randy.grimm@calvary.edu
GRIMM, Rich ... 847-317-7055 153 D
ragrimm@tiu.edu
GRIMM, Roger ... 903-510-2389 464 D
rgri2@tjc.edu
GRIMM, Tonya ... 660-626-2076 257 A
tgrimm@atsu.edu
GRIMMER, Karen, D ... 618-374-5152 149 A
karen.grimmer@principia.edu
GRIMMER, Kevin, M ... 315-792-7520 330 A
grimmek@sunyit.edu
GRIMMETT, Branden ... 310-258-8779.. 50 J
branden.grimmett@lmu.edu
GRIMSLEY, Deloris ... 973-877-3056 285 K
dgrimsle@essex.edu
GRIMSLEY, Kim ... 719-384-6988.. 81 G
kim.grimsley@ojc.edu
GRIMSON, W. Eric, L ... 617-253-5415 221 C
GRINDBERG, Tony ... 701-231-6914 355 B
tony.grindberg@ndscs.edu
GRINDELL, Monique ... 503-352-1566 385 I
grindelm@pacificu.edu
GRINDLEY, Krystle ... 318-670-9472 196 A
kbeauchamp@susla.edu
GRINER, Andrea ... 478-757-3551 117 E
agriner@centralgatech.edu
GRINER, Andrea ... 478-757-3551 117 D
agriner@centralgatech.edu
GRINNAGER, Donn ... 605-274-4498 426 K
donn.grinnager@augie.edu
GRINNAN, Susan ... 804-706-5016 488 D
sgrinnan@jtcc.edu
GRINNAN, Susan ... 804-706-5035 488 D
sgrinnan@jtcc.edu
GRIPENSTRAW,
Suzanne ... 530-879-4078.. 28 E
gripenstrawsu@butte.edu
GRIPP, Kristine ... 216-791-5000 359 K
kristine.gripp@cim.edu
GRIPPO, Anne ... 870-972-3079.. 18 A
agrippo@astate.edu
GRISCOM, William, E ... 717-299-7722 411 C
griscom@stevenscollege.edu
GRISHAM, Bob ... 360-438-4372 497 F
bgrisham@stmartin.edu
GRISHAM, Erin ... 928-523-6990.. 14 K
erin.grisham@nau.edu
GRISHAM, Linda ... 781-239-3147 220 A
lgrisham@massbay.edu
GRISI, Mark, P ... 315-684-6465 329 F
grisimp@morrisville.edu
GRISNIK, Kelly ... 913-758-4359 182 B
kelly.grisnik@stmary.edu
GRISSETT, Jendia ... 334-386-7422.... 5 I
jgrissett@faulkner.edu
GRISSOM, Cytha, D ... 717-477-1444 407 B
cdgris@ship.edu
GRISSOM, Randy, W ... 505-428-1201 296 B
randy.grissom@sfcc.edu
GRISWOLD, Al ... 253-680-7204 492 F
agriswold@bates.ctc.edu
GRISWOLD, Anna, M ... 814-863-0507 403 F
amg5@psu.edu
GRISWOLD, Bill ... 334-290-3254.... 2 E
bill.griswold@istc.edu
GRISWOLD, Catherine ... 716-827-2407 331 K
griswoldc@trocaire.edu
GRISWOLD, Emmett ... 229-430-3396 114 J
egriswold@albanytech.edu
GRISWOLD, Richard, M 617-262-5000 212 C
richard.griswold@the-bac.edu
GRISWOLD, Robyn ... 603-578-8900 280 M
GRITTON, Mark ... 559-934-2455.. 73 N
markgritton@whccd.edu
GRIZ, William ... 239-513-1122 101 O
bgriz@hodges.edu
GRIZANTI, Robert ... 716-896-0700 333 C
bgrizanti@villa.edu
GRIZZELL, Kyle ... 513-562-6262 356 J
kgrizzell@artacademy.edu
GRIZZLE, Debra, F ... 706-245-7226 119 A
dgrizzle@ec.edu
GRIZZLE, Jerry, W ... 575-624-8001 295 A
supt@nmmi.edu
GRIZZLE, Oniffe ... 765-973-8474 160 A
ogrizzle@iue.edu
GROAT, Gary ... 909-687-1701.. 44 A
garygroat@gs.edu
GROBE, Jennifer ... 815-599-3688 139 F
jennifer.grobe@highland.edu
GROBER, Max ... 903-813-2361 443 F
mgrober@austincollege.edu
GROCE, Jeanetta ... 903-875-7619 459 E
jeanetta.groce@tamuc.edu
GRODE-HANKS, Carol ... 605-995-3023 427 E
carol.grode-hanks@mitchelltech.edu
GRODSKY, Jennifer ... 202-393-7272 212 G
jgrodsky@bu.edu
GROELING, Jeff ... 765-998-5246 164 C
jfgroeling@taylor.edu
GROENENDYK, Peter ... 910-962-3241 352 A
groenendykp@uncw.edu
GROENER, Michael ... 510-436-1250.. 45 G
groener@hnu.edu
GROENEVELD, Bill ... 805-565-6849.. 74 I
procurement@westmont.edu
GROENEWOLD, Theresa 208-535-5411 131 G
theresa.groenewold@my.eitc.edu
GROENINGER, Sandra ... 847-543-2345 136 E
sgroeninger@clcillinois.edu
GROENNERT, Harvey ... 618-394-2200 143 B
hgroennert@lakeland.cc.i.us
GROENWALD, Susan ... 888-556-8226 134 K
sgroenwald@chamberlain.edu
GROESSER, Bradley ... 712-325-3310 170 K
bgroesser@iwcc.edu
GROETSCH, Laura ... 262-646-6514 509 C
lgroetsch@nashotah.edu
GROFF, Susan, L ... 302-831-3666.. 90 I
groff@udel.edu
GROGAN, Angela ... 573-592-5245 270 B
angela.grogan@westminster-mo.edu
GROGAN,
Jacqueline, H ... 718-990-6176 322 F
groganj@stjohns.edu
GROGAN, Margaret ... 714-516-5968.. 36 G
grogan@chapman.edu
GROGAN, Rita ... 559-934-2128.. 73 M
ritagrogan@whccd.edu
GROGG, Pete ... 812-855-6511 159 H
pgrogg@indiana.edu
GROGG, Sam, L ... 516-877-3167 297 I
grogg@adelphi.edu
GROGRAN, Torie ... 573-986-6191 266 M
tgrogran@semo.edu
GROH, Sara ... 315-228-6134 304 G
sgroh@colgate.edu
GROLEAU, Dan ... 715-365-4450 514 E
dgroleau@nicoletcollege.edu
GROLEAU, Ron, W ... 815-224-0482 141 A
ron_groleau@ivcc.edu
GROMAN, Elizabeth, A .. 260-399-7700 165 B
bgroman@sf.edu
GROMATZKY, Steven ... 913-360-7511 175 D
sgromatzky@benedictine.edu
GROMIS, Jeffrey ... 610-341-1775 394 E
jgromis@eastern.edu
GRONA, Marion ... 940-552-6291 469 F
mgrona@vernoncollege.edu
GROND, Greta ... 712-707-7248 172 G
ggrond@nwciowa.edu
GRONDAHL, Mary, M ... 518-454-5150 305 B
grondahm@strose.edu
GRONEFELD,
Joseph, W ... 502-597-6339 187 E
joseph.gronefeld@kysu.edu
GRONEWALD, Kate ... 903-233-3291 452 A
kategronewald@letu.edu
GRONNIGER, Eileen, C . 785-442-6010 178 C
egronniger@highlandcc.edu
GRONO, Anthony ... 718-817-4943 308 G
grono@fordham.edu
GRONSKY, Jennifer ... 215-503-8189 411 E
jennifer.gronsky@jefferson.edu
GRONSKY, Jennifer, M . 215-503-8189 411 E
jennifer.gronsky@jefferson.edu
GROOM, Ruth ... 513-529-9210 365 I
groomra@miamioh.edu
GROOME, Jean, M ... 336-734-7292 343 C
jgroome@forsythtech.edu
GROOMS, Catherine ... 661-362-5151.. 39 C
catherine.grooms@canyons.edu
GROOMS, Craig ... 606-546-1709 189 I
cgrooms@unionky.edu
GROOMS, David ... 808-984-3376 130 H
grooms@hawaii.edu
GROOT, Joycelyn ... 714-241-6323.. 38 F
jgroot@coastline.edu
GROPACK, Stacy ... 516-299-2486 313 D
stacy.gropack@liu.edu
GROPEN, Laura ... 760-744-1150.. 55 K
lgropen@palomar.edu
GROPP, Jonathan ... 864-231-2000 418 E
jgropp@andersonuniversity.edu
GROPPER, Daniel ... 561-297-3629 109 B
dgropper@fau.edu
GRORUD, Kelley ... 608-663-2200 507 D
kgrorud@edgewood.edu
GROS, Kathy, R ... 504-865-3237 194 G
kgros@loyno.edu
GROSBY, Karen ... 954-262-5885 104 F
grosby@nsu.nova.edu
GROSE, Kay ... 304-865-6230 502 C
kay.grose@ovu.edu
GROSOVSKY, Andrew ... 617-287-5775 216 I
andrew.grosovsky@umb.edu
GROSPITCH, Eric ... 785-670-2100 182 D
eric.grospitch@washburn.edu
GROSS, Anne ... 303-871-3382.. 83 E
agross@du.edu
GROSS, Bryan, J ... 413-782-1233 225 F
bryan.gross@wne.edu
GROSS, Candace ... 870-512-7716.. 18 D
candace_gross@asun.edu
GROSS, Carla, E ... 717-796-1800 401 L
cgross@messiah.edu
GROSS, Charles ... 406-447-5480 270 H
cgross@carroll.edu
GROSS, Cynthia, A ... 240-895-4382 206 G
cagross@smcm.edu
GROSS, Dana ... 507-786-3624 250 C
grossd@stolaf.edu
GROSS, Daryl, J ... 323-343-3080.. 32 D
dgross4@calstatela.edu
GROSS, Dolores ... 915-831-6484 449 A
dgross2@epcc.edu
GROSS, Erik ... 603-862-1584 282 F
erik.gross@unh.edu
GROSS, Heidi ... 307-686-0254 516 P
hgross@sheridan.edu
GROSS, Kristina ... 608-663-2000 507 M
kgross@mediainstitute.edu
GROSS, Laura ... 518-255-5626 328 C
grossll@cobleskill.edu
GROSS, Mendel ... 718-854-8700 331 A
GROSS, Michael ... 732-987-2373 286 D
mgross@georgian.edu
GROSS, Michael ... 508-362-2131 219 E
mgross@capecod.edu
GROSS, Michael, L ... 610-921-7672 388 E
mgross@albright.edu
GROSS, Monika ... 301-860-4091 208 E
mgross@bowiestate.edu
GROSS, Natalie ... 914-337-0700 323 K
ngross@sarahlawrence.edu
GROSS, Scott ... 606-487-3528 185 J
scott.gross@kctcs.edu
GROSS, Susan ... 201-216-8142 291 G
susan.gross@stevens.edu
GROSS, Tim ... 770-426-2658 122 F
tgross@life.edu
GROSS-GRAY,
Shelley, J ... 615-353-3259 437 D
shelley.gross-gray@nscc.edu
GROSS-KINZY, Terri ... 848-445-8418 290 A
kinzytg@rutgers.edu
GROSS METHNER,
Sara, E ... 651-962-6901 251 D
gros6968@stthomas.edu
GROSSE, Kerry, J ... 414-955-8874 508 D
kegrosse@mcw.edu
GROSSE, Mike ... 502-451-0815 189 F
mgrosse@sullivan.edu
GROSSI, OSB, Anthony . 724-537-4554 410 B
anthony.grossi@email.stvincent.edu
GROSSI, Deann ... 312-777-8665 140 G
dgrossi@aii.edu
GROSSKOPF, John ... 850-973-1601 104 D
grosskopfj@nfcc.edu
GROSSMAN, David ... 714-992-7046.. 54 A
dgrossman@fullcoll.edu
GROSSMAN, LuAnn ... 605-331-6738 429 D
luann.grossman@usiouxfalls.edu
GROSSMAN, Michal ... 732-414-2834 293 E
ytcbks@gmail.com
GROSSMAN, Miriam ... 845-425-1370 319 F
GROSSMAN, Pam ... 215-898-7014 412 G
grossman@gse.upenn.edu
GROSSMAN, Richard, G 603-535-2425 283 B
rggrossman@plymouth.edu
GROSSO, Andrew ... 262-646-6510 509 C
agrosso@nashotah.edu
GROSSO, Michael ... 626-571-8811.. 72 C
michaelg@uwest.edu
GROSSO, Michael ... 360-486-8868 497 F
michael.grosso@stmartin.edu
GROSVENOR, Ari ... 978-921-4242 222 B
ari.grosvenor@montserrat.edu
GROSZ, Tanya, L ... 651-286-7453 251 C
tlgrosz@unwsp.edu
GROTE, Lisa ... 605-626-2521 428 H
lisa.grote@northern.edu
GROTH, Clayton ... 608-249-6611 507 F
cgroth@herzing.edu
GROTH, Dennis ... 812-855-8783 159 H
vpue@indiana.edu
GROTH, Kathy ... 219-464-5114 165 D
kathy.groth@valpo.edu
GROTRIAN, Jim ... 402-557-7860 273 E
jgrotrian@bellevue.edu

GROTTON, Nancy 503-253-3443 385 B
ngrotton@ocom.edu
GROTZINGER, John, P 626-395-6005 29 I
grotz@gps.caltech.edu
GROUNDS, Cynthia 785-749-8418 178 A
cynthia.grounds@bie.edu
GROVE, Amber 208-376-7731 131 B
agrove@boisebible.edu
GROVE, Dana 817-515-4506 458 B
dana.grove@tccd.edu
GROVE, Daryl 563-425-5311 173 K
groved@uiu.edu
GROVE, Doug 949-214-3434 40 I
doug.grove@cui.edu
GROVE, Kathy, M 641-422-4382 172 C
grovekat@niacc.edu
GROVE, Laurie 717-396-7188 411 C
grove@stevenscollege.edu
GROVE, Luke, J 515-574-1062 170 C
grove@iowacentral.edu
GROVE, Melinda 330-972-7140 371 C
mgrove@uakron.edu
GROVE, Shannon, D 814-886-6391 402 E
sgrove@mtaloy.edu
GROVENSTEIN,
Elizabeth 919-807-7070 340 K
GROVER, Arthur 610-660-1164 409 H
agrover@sju.edu
GROVER, Barbara 801-957-4434 474 B
barbara.grover@slcc.edu
GROVER, Carol, N 315-279-5252 312 D
cgrover@keuka.edu
GROVER, Rajiv 901-678-3633 439 E
rgrover@memphis.edu
GROVER-BISKER, Edna 573-341-4292 269 A
egroverb@mst.edu
GROVER-ROOSA,
Janice 307-382-1701 517 C
jgrover@westernwyoming.edu
GROVES, Allen, W 434-924-7429 486 H
awg8vd@virginia.edu
GROVES, Devany 904-620-2506 110 E
dgroves@unf.edu
GROVES, Doris 309-438-7304 140 L
dfgrove@ilstu.edu
GROVES, Jason 325-674-2646 441 D
jason.groves@acu.edu
GROVES, John 215-572-2940 389 D
grovesj@arcadia.edu
GROVES, Kathleen, H 585-395-2317 326 D
kgroves@brockport.edu
GROVES, Kathy 573-592-1106 270 D
kathy.groves@williamwoods.edu
GROVES, Loren 307-686-0254 516 P
lgroves@sheridan.edu
GROVES, Robert 517-884-1008 233 G
grovesr@msu.edu
GROVES, Robert, M 202-687-6400 92 B
provost@georgetown.edu
GROVES, Suzanne 817-515-1541 458 B
suzanne.groves@tccd.edu
GROVES, William 937-769-1345 356 G
bgroves@antioch.edu
GROVES-SCOTT,
Victoria 501-450-3175 23 I
vickigs@uca.edu
GROW, David 801-274-3280 474 D
dgrow@wgu.edu
GROW, Tamara, J 660-562-1146 264 I
tammi@nwmissouri.edu
GROWNS, Richard, O 501-977-2024 23 B
growns@uaccm.edu
GROZA, Adam 909-687-1450 44 A
adamgroza@gs.edu
GRUBB, Dan 910-592-8081 346 D
dgrubb@sampsoncc.edu
GRUBB, Derek 970-542-3158 81 A
derek.grubb@morgancc.edu
GRUBB, Geoffrey, J 419-824-3818 364 G
ggrubb@lourdes.edu
GRUBB, Hannah 212-659-3604 312 E
hgrubb@tkc.edu
GRUBB, John 423-354-5144 437 E
jmgrubb@northeaststate.edu
GRUBB, Josh 276-326-4208 478 H
jgrubb@bluefield.edu
GRUBB, Kevin 610-519-4060 413 K
kevin.c.grubb@villanova.edu
GRUBB, Lillie 620-223-2700 177 E
lillieg@fortscott.edu
GRUBBS, Jeff 970-675-2261 78 H
GRUBE, M. Marshall 423-439-4219 431 H
grube@etsu.edu
GRUBE, Sean 816-235-8719 268 D
grubes@umkc.edu
GRUBER, Carol 215-646-7300 396 E
gruber.c@gmercyu.edu
GRUBER,
Christopher, J 704-894-2710 337 B
chgruber@davidson.edu
GRUBER, Darlene 610-917-1414 413 G
d_gruber@valleyforge.edu
GRUBER, Elizabeth 570-484-2858 406 E
egruber@lockhaven.edu
GRUBER, Jay 202-687-7014 92 B
jg1502@georgetown.edu
GRUBER, Thomas 504-671-6480 192 H
tgrube@dcc.edu
GRUBMAN, Joshua 617-928-4026 222 D
sgrubmanr@mountida.edu
GRUDZINSKI, Shanelle 402-844-7692 276 G
shanelle@northeast.edu
GRUEGER, Andrea 217-228-5432 149 B
gruegan@quincy.edu
GRUEN, Kris 802-322-1721 475 A
kris.gruen@goddard.edu
GRUENDLER, Donny 323-462-1384 53 C
donnyg@mi.edu
GRUENIG, Gwendolyn 907-450-8190 9 I
gdgruenig@alaska.edu
GRUENING, Kyle 715-365-4446 514 E
gruening@nicoletcollege.edu
GRUESER, Suzanna 213-624-1200 42 N
sgrueser@fidm.edu
GRUHLER, Sarah 360-992-2406 493 E
sgruhler@clark.edu
GRUICHICH, Dawn 480-732-7050 13 E
dawn.gruichich@cgc.edu
GRULKE, Kimmi 928-226-4343 12 B
kimmi.grulke@coconino.edu
GRUNBLATT, Akiva 718-268-4700 320 K
GRUND, Faye 419-520-2602 356 L
fgrund@ashland.edu
GRUNDEN, Cynthia 312-369-7125 136 H
cgrunden@colum.edu
GRUNDER, Mark 989-358-7317 227 A
grunderm@alpenacc.edu
GRUNDIG, John 863-680-6212 100 D
jgrundig@flsouthern.edu
GRUNDY, Jeffrey, W 973-596-2451 288 A
jeffrey.w.grundy@njit.edu
GRUNDY, Marc, A 423-236-2875 436 C
magrundy@southern.edu
GRUNINGER, Sandra 212-686-9040 333 I
sgruninger@woodtobecoburn.edu
GRUNKLEE, David 319-296-4042 169 H
david.grunklee@hawkeyecollege.edu
GRUNLOH, Jean Anne 217-234-5329 143 B
jgrunloh@lakeland.cc.il.us
GRUNOW, Tamie, L 513-556-1015 371 E
grunowtl@ucmail.uc.edu
GRUNWALD, Gerald 215-503-8982 411 E
gerald.grunwald@jefferson.edu
GRUS, Shannon, M 636-584-6505 259 L
shannon.grus@eastcentral.edu
GRUSHINSKI, Alberta 570-945-8373 398 C
alberta.grushinski@keystone.edu
GRUSKA, Julie 320-363-3395 250 A
jgruska@csbsju.edu
GRUSKA, Julie, E 320-363-3395 241 I
jgruska@csbsju.edu
GRUSKOS, Cynthia 732-224-2204 284 B
cgruskos@brookdalecc.edu
GRUSZKA, Bill 678-466-4351 117 I
billgruska@clayton.edu
GRUTKOWSKI, Marc 814-838-7673 395 D
mgrutkowski@fortisinstitute.edu
GRUTZKUHN, Bill 301-846-2452 203 H
wgrutzkuhn@frederick.edu
GRUYS, Melissa 260-481-6461 160 D
gruysm@ipfw.edu
GRZESIAK, Michael, P 724-503-1001 414 A
mgrzesiak@washjeff.edu
GRZYBOWSKI, Mark, J 815-224-0393 141 A
mark_grzybowski@ivcc.edu
GRZYWACZ,
Norberto, M 202-687-5603 92 B
norberto@georgetown.edu
GSTALDER, Steven 203-773-0129 84 G
sgstalder@albertus.edu
GUADALUPE, Raúl 787-993-8867 527 G
raul.guadalupe@upr.edu
GUADALUPE, Sarahi 787-276-0130 527 H
sarahi.guadalupe@upr.edu
GUADALUPE, Yvonne 787-766-1717 526 B
yguadalupe@suagm.edu
GUAH, Matthew 803-536-8152 423 G
mguah@scsu.edu
GUAJARDO, George 210-486-3736 441 H
gguajardo41@alamo.edu
GUAJARDO, Nicole, R 757-594-8069 479 H
nguajard@cnu.edu
GUALTIERI, Kelly 207-326-2207 200 F
kelly.gualtieri@mma.edu
GUAMAN, Luis 203-857-7025 86 D
lguaman@norwalk.edu
GUAN, Sharon 773-325-7726 137 C
xguan@depaul.edu
GUARASCI, Richard 718-390-3131 333 D
guarasci@wagner.edu
GUARD, Louis 315-781-3309 310 C
guard@hws.edu
GUARIGLIA, Carolyn, L 315-255-1743 300 H
guarigliac@cayuga-cc.edu
GUARIGLIA, Daniel, M 716-286-8431 318 F
dmg@niagara.edu
GUARIN-KLEIN, Natalia 718-951-5696 301 E
nataliag@brooklyn.cuny.edu
GUARINO, Mindy 708-344-4700 144 A
mguarino@lincolntech.edu
GUASCONI, Joseph 973-378-2643 291 F
joseph.guasconi@shu.edu
GUAY, Sheila 401-323-6324 416 A
sguay@bryant.edu
GUBAN, Philip 440-943-7676 369 J
pguban@dioceseofcleveland.org
GUBAN, Philip 440-943-7600 369 J
pguban@dioceseofcleveland.org
GUBBINS, Jean, E 216-368-5557 358 C
jeg2@case.edu
GUBLER, Seth 435-652-7571 473 B
sgubler@dixie.edu
GUBSER, Kristin 602-286-8000 13 G
GUCKAVAN, Joseph 215-489-2361 393 F
joseph.guckavan@delval.edu
GUCKERT, Donald, J 319-335-1201 166 G
don-guckert@uiowa.edu
GUDELUNAS, David 813-253-6100 113 E
GUDUR, Jaganmohan 303-458-4050 82 D
jgudur@regis.edu
GUDVANGEN, John, E 303-871-4857 83 E
john.gudvangen@du.edu
GUECO, Allan 818-766-8151 40 F
agueco@concorde.edu
GUEGOLD, Tina 614-236-6242 358 A
tguegold@capital.edu
GUELDA, Debbie 218-755-2786 244 B
dguelda@bemidjistate.edu
GUELICH, Julie 952-358-8156 246 D
julie.guelich@normandale.edu
GUENARD, Erik, M 906-932-4231 230 D
erikg@gogebic.edu
GUENARD, Hayward 434-544-8168 482 F
guenard_h@lynchburg.edu
GUENGERICH, Alison 773-907-4445 135 K
aguengerich1@ccc.edu
GUENTER-SCHLESINGER,
Sue 360-650-3307 500 E
sue.guenter-schlesinger@wwu.edu
GUENTHER, Thomas 847-543-2264 136 E
tguenther@clcillinois.edu
GUENZLER-STEVENS,
Marsha, A 301-314-8505 207 G
mguenzle@umd.edu
GUERIN, Donna 215-885-2360 401 A
dguerin@manor.edu
GUERIN, Thomas, B 513-556-2389 371 E
tom.guerin@uc.edu
GUERRA, Blanca 210-567-2621 468 E
guerrabe@uthscsa.edu
GUERRA, Deborah 475-210-5337 88 D
dguerra@ascension.org
GUERRA, Elizabeth 909-469-5418 74 G
guerra@westernu.edu
GUERRA, JR., Juan, M 214-648-2400 469 E
juan.guerra@utsouthwestern.edu
GUERRA, Laura 563-588-8000 169 B
lguerra@emmaus.edu
GUERRA, Luis 510-436-1516 45 G
guerra@hnu.edu
GUERRA, Manuel 503-399-5076 382 C
manuel.guerra@chemeketa.edu
GUERRA, Michael 510-628-8031 48 F
mguerra@lincolnuca.edu
GUERRA, Nancy 949-824-6094 69 A
nguerra1@uci.edu
GUERRA, Sabra 254-968-9770 459 A
sguerra@tarleton.edu
GUERRA, Yvonne 210-486-4339 441 G
yguerra6@alamo.edu
GUERRA GAIER, Norma 512-245-2645 463 A
ng14@txstate.edu
GUERRERO, Bertha, M 671-735-5638 519 H
boardoftrustees@guamcc.edu
GUERRERO, Daniel, G 310-206-6382 69 B
dguerrero@athletics.ucla.edu
GUERRERO, Dolores 361-593-2717 460 B
dolores.guerrero@tamuk.edu
GUERRERO, Jennifer 609-984-1588 292 B
jguerrero@tesu.edu
GUERRERO, Larry 575-492-2107 297 G
lguerrero@usw.edu
GUERRERO, Omar 787-857-3600 523 I
oguerrero@br.inter.edu
GUERRERO, Philip, C 671-735-5640 519 H
philip.guerrero2@guamcc.edu
GUERRERO, Rico 559-324-6481 66 E
rico.guerrero@scccd.edu
GUERRERO, Roberto 210-509-8080 461 C
rguerrero@thsu.edu
GUERRERO, Tammy 219-989-2675 163 E
tsguerre@pnw.edu
GUERRERO, Tim 303-410-2429 82 K
tim.guerrero@spartan.edu
GUERRETTE, Leslie 207-741-5715 200 C
lguerrette@smccme.edu
GUERRIERO, William 480-732-7012 13 E
william.guerriero@cgc.edu
GUESS, Cynthia 573-341-4215 269 A
cguess@mst.edu
GUESS, Melissa 310-660-3492 42 C
mguess@elcamino.edu
GUEST, Charles 251-460-6261 9 B
cguest@southalabama.edu
GUEST, Denise 540-891-3040 488 B
dguest@germanna.edu
GUEST, James 402-472-7488 277 G
jguest2@unl.edu
GUEST, Stephany 816-415-5929 270 C
sguest@william.jewell.edu
GUEST, Susan 870-633-4480 19 E
sguest@eacc.edu
GUETTI, Joan 973-761-9018 291 F
joan.guetti@shu.edu
GUEVARA, Antonio 956-295-3715 461 F
antonio.guevara@tsc.edu
GUEVARA, Christine 505-473-6404 296 C
christine.guevara@santafeuniversity.edu
GUEVERRA, Jonathan 305-809-3204 99 L
jonathan.gueverra@fkcc.edu
GUEVIN, Todd 610-917-1493 413 G
tgguevin@valleyforge.edu
GUEZMIR, Jean 651-690-6533 249 T
jmguezmir254@stkate.edu
GUFFEY, Larry, D 256-228-6001 3 B
ldguffey@nacc.edu
GUFFEY, Patti 828-669-8012 340 I
pguffey@montreat.edu
GUFFY, Ted 361-825-2722 460 A
ted.guffy@tamucc.edu
GUGELCHUK, Gary 909-469-5381 74 G
gugelchuk@westernu.edu
GUGENHEIMER,
Yirmiya 718-853-8500 331 E
GUGLIELMO, B. Joseph 415-476-8010 70 A
guglielmoj@pharmacy.ucsf.edu
GUGLIELMONI, Mark, J 203-254-4080 87 A
mguglielmoni@fairfield.edu
GUICE, Leslie, K 318-257-3785 197 A
guice@latech.edu
GUIDA, Amedeo 239-304-7905 95 C
fr.guida@avemaria.edu
GUIDALI, Francesca 619-684-8828 53 J
fguidali@newschoolarch.edu
GUIDO, Deana, L 252-451-8244 345 B
dguido744@nashcc.edu
GUIDO, Diane 626-812-3034 26 U
dguido@apu.edu
GUILARTE, Tomas 305-348-2000 109 D
tomas.guilarte@fiu.edu
GUILBEAU, OP,
Aquinas 202-495-3853 92 F
aguilbeau@dhs.edu
GUILBEAULT, Nancy, G 612-330-1169 240 G
guilbeau@augsburg.edu
GUILER, Douglas 352-365-3526 103 B
guilerd@lssc.edu
GUILES, Serena 802-287-8376 475 B
serena.guiles@greenmtn.edu
GUILFOILE, Patrick 715-232-2421 512 A
guilfoilep@uwstout.edu
GUILFORD, Renate, H 703-993-2299 481 B
rguilfor@gmu.edu
GUILFOYLE, Michael, K 508-767-7331 210 I
mk.guilfoyle@assumption.edu
GUILLEN, Christian 707-826-3739 34 A
cg36@humboldt.edu
GUILLEN, George 281-283-3950 465 B
guillen@uhcl.edu
GUILLEN, Oscar 510-659-6105 54 F
oguillen@ohlone.edu
GUILLEN, Patrick, J 808-932-7348 129 I
GUILLETTE, Natalie, L 802-656-4183 476 E
natalie.guillette@uvm.edu
GUILLIANI, Melissa 787-766-1717 526 B
mguilliani@suagm.edu
GUILLIOM, Allison 313-577-2230 239 C
dy9063@wayne.edu
GUILLORY, Abby 337-482-5811 197 F
abby@louisiana.edu

GUY, Georgina .... 949-582-4738.. 64 J
gguy@saddleback.edu

GUY, Kristen .... 650-433-3878.. 55 I
kguy@paloaltou.edu

GUY, Shawn .... 336-517-2209 335 K
sguy@bennett.edu

GUY, Stephanie .... 206-934-7935 497 J
stephanie.guy@seattlecolleges.edu

GUY-ANDERSON,
Adrian .... 504-816-4325 191 E
aguy@dillard.edu

GUY-SHEFTALL, Beverly 404-270-5624 126 D
bsheftall@spelman.edu

GUYER, Kim .... 402-898-1000 274 C
kim_g@creativecenter.edu

GUYETTE, Daniel .... 269-387-5810 239 E
daniel.guyette@wmich.edu

GUYETTE, Randy .... 828-835-4253 347 B
rguyette@tricountycc.edu

GUYNES, Del .... 972-923-5437 457 F
dguynes@sagu.edu

GUYOL, Kate .... 314-792-7435 261 E
guyol@kenrick.edu

GUYTON, Deirdre .... 304-327-4569 503 O
dguyton@bluefieldstate.edu

GUYTON, Don .... 713-743-8000 464 F
dguyton@uh.edu

GUYTON, Sondra .... 910-879-5634 341 A
sguyton@bladencc.edu

GUYTON-MCCLENDON,
Nicole .... 256-761-6211.... 7 D
nguyton@talladega.edu

GUZAUSKAS, Lauren ..... 206-934-5484 497 I
lauren.guzauskas@seattlecolleges.edu

GUZDAR, Farida, P .... 443-518-3823 204 E
fguzdar@howardcc.edu

GUZELIMIAN, Ara .... 212-799-5000 312 B

GUZICK, David, S .... 352-733-1700 110 D
dguzick@ufl.edu

GUZMAN, Alejandro ...... 818-523-9026.. 49 C
guzmana4@lamission.edu

GUZMAN, Andrew .... 213-740-7331.. 72 B
andrewgu@usc.edu

GUZMAN, Angelica .... 209-575-6471.. 75 J

GUZMAN, Ariel .... 787-751-0160 522 B
aguzman@cmpr.pr.gov

GUZMAN, Debora .... 210-434-6711 454 D
daguzman@lake.ollusa.edu

GUZMAN, Gregory .... 419-434-4207 373 K
gregory.guzman@winebrenner.edu

GUZMAN, John .... 718-782-2200 299 L
jguzman@boricuacollege.edu

GUZMAN, Juan .... 308-865-8127 277 F
guzmanj@unk.edu

GUZMAN,
Juan Johnny, C .... 830-591-7264 457 C
jcguzman@swtjc.edu

GUZMAN, Leslie Ann .... 787-746-1400 522 O
lguzman@huertas.edu

GUZMAN, Margo .... 209-588-5222.. 75 I
guzmanm@yosemite.edu

GUZMAN, Maricela .... 818-401-1030.. 40 A
mguzman@columbiacollege.edu

GUZMAN, Ruben .... 949-451-5220.. 64 I
rguzman@ivc.edu

GUZMAN, Tobias .... 970-351-1944.. 83 F
tobias.guzman@unco.edu

GUZMAN-LOPEZ,
Evelyn .... 787-480-2410 521 J
eguzman@sanjuanciudadpatria.com

GUZOFSKY, Rosalie .... 215-635-7300 396 B
rguzofsky@gratz.edu

GUZZARDO, Joseph ...... 609-777-3083 292 B
jguzzardo@tesu.edu

GUZZI, Martin .... 607-778-5245 326 C
guzzimj@sunybroome.edu

GUZZI, Michael, A .... 530-898-4336.. 31 D
maguzzi@csuchico.edu

GUZZO, Linda .... 860-906-5132.. 85 D
lguzzo@ccc.commnet.edu

GWALTNEY, Darrell .... 615-460-5552 430 D
darrell.gwaltney@belmont.edu

GWARTNEY, Kurt .... 918-270-6470 378 I
kurt.gwartney@ptstulsa.edu

GWATNEY, Bradley .... 432-837-8190 462 G
bradley.gwatney@sulross.edu

GWAZDA, Edward .... 609-586-4800 287 A
gwazdae@mccc.edu

GWINN, Janice .... 304-357-4383 502 E
janicegwinn@ucwv.edu

GWINNER, Kevin, P ...... 785-532-7227 179 A
kgwinner@ksu.edu

GYAPONG, Samuel .... 478-825-6732 119 C
gyapongs@fvsu.edu

GYERTSON, David .... 859-858-2335 183 C

GYLLIN, John .... 407-708-4722 107 G
gyllinj@seminolestate.edu

GYMZIAK, Paul .... 603-623-0313 281 G
paulgymziak@nhia.edu

GYORKE, Allan .... 305-284-6101 112 O
a.gyorke@miami.edu

H

HA, Kevin .... 760-328-5554.. 51 D

HA, Viet, X .... 864-833-8193 423 D
vxha@presby.edu

HAACK, Julie, A .... 563-333-6314 173 A
haackjuliea@sau.edu

HAACK, Kristen .... 617-521-2917 224 E
kristen.haack@simmons.edu

HAAG, Brandon .... 678-717-3885 127 B
brandon.haag@ung.edu

HAAG, Kelly .... 414-229-6589 511 A
kajohnso@uwm.edu

HAAKE, Anne .... 585-475-4786 321 D
arhics@rit.edu

HAAKONSEN, Alexis ..... 203-392-5644.. 85 A
haakonsena1@southernct.edu

HAAN, Andrea .... 563-884-5447 172 H
andrea.haan@palmer.edu

HAAN, Fred .... 712-722-6050 168 I
fred.haan@dordt.edu

HAAR, Annemarie .... 510-594-3657.. 28 K
ahaar@cca.edu

HAAR, Jean .... 507-389-5445 246 A
jean.haar@mnsu.edu

HAAR, Scott .... 417-862-5700 257 L
shaar@bryancolleges.edu

HAARSMA, Jill .... 712-707-7100 172 G
jhaarsma@nwciowa.edu

HAAS, Bob .... 740-389-4636 365 B
haasr@mtc.edu

HAAS, Evelyn .... 612-767-7044 240 B
ev@alfredadler.edu

HAAS, Jesse .... 575-528-7548 295 E
jhaas@nmsu.edu

HAAS, Mark .... 517-355-5014 233 G
hass@finance.msu.edu

HAAS, Mary Ann .... 207-992-4900 199 B
haasm@husson.edu

HAAS, Mitch .... 503-251-5728 387 I
mhaas@uws.edu

HAAS, Nate .... 970-351-1763.. 83 F
nate.haas@unco.edu

HAAS, Nicole .... 718-951-5671 301 E
nicole@brooklyn.cuny.edu

HAAS, Ocki .... 417-865-2815 260 B
haaso@evangel.edu

HAAS, Sarah .... 573-518-2307 263 E
shaas@mineralarea.edu

HAAS, Sarah .... 563-588-6307 167 E
sarah.haas@clarke.edu

HAAS, Stephen .... 800-371-6105.. 14 J
shaas@nationalparalegal.edu

HAAS, Sue .... 434-961-5229 489 C
shaas@pvcc.edu

HAAS, Thomas, J .... 616-331-2100 230 G
president@gvsu.edu

HAASE, Ryan .... 620-862-5252 175 B
rhaase@barclaycollege.edu

HAATVEDT, Chad .... 218-322-2444 245 B
chad.haatvedt@itascacc.edu

HABA, Jerry .... 972-721-5018 464 E
dhaba@udallas.edu

HABEGER, Christian, M 864-379-8813 421 E
habeger@erskine.edu

HABEGGER, Thomas .... 614-287-5422 360 C
thabegge@cscc.edu

HABEGGER, Toni .... 509-359-6373 494 D
thabegger@ewu.edu

HABEL, Leah .... 406-771-4327 272 D
lhabel@gfcmsu.edu

HABER, Carole .... 504-865-5225 196 D
chaber@tulane.edu

HABER, Jessica .... 914-674-7457 314 I
jhaber@mercy.edu

HABER, Melanie .... 860-512-2803.. 85 G
mhaber@manchestercc.edu

HABERER, Ronald, J ..... 716-888-8527 300 G
habererr@canisius.edu

HABERLE, Charles, J .... 401-865-1154 416 E
chaberle@providence.edu

HABERSTICH, Laura ...... 559-297-4500.. 46 E

HABETZ, Pauline, M ..... 713-500-8425 468 D
pauline.m.habetz@uth.tmc.edu

HABIB, Bob .... 757-352-4840 484 E
robehab@regent.edu

HABIB, Claudia .... 559-675-4800.. 66 H
claudia.habib@scccd.edu

HABICH, Maegan .... 704-463-3409 348 B
maegan.habich@pfeiffer.edu

HABROCK, Marty .... 402-554-3408 277 I
mhabrock@unomaha.edu

HABSCHMIDT, Cathy ..... 765-983-1772 157 I
habscca@earlham.edu

HABUCHMAI, Joseph .... 691-320-2480 519 G
jhabuchmai@comfsm.fm

HABUKI, Daniel, Y .... 949-480-4005.. 64 D
habuki@soka.edu

HABURSKY, Mary Jo .... 304-243-2233 505 H
maryjoh@wju.edu

HABURSKY, Stephen ..... 304-243-4453 505 H
habursky@wju.edu

HACHE, Jason .... 952-829-2405 240 H
jason.hache@bethfel.org

HACK, Mary, C .... 609-984-1661 292 B
mhack@tesu.edu

HACKBARTH, Wade .... 608-785-9123 515 C
hackbarthw@westerntc.edu

HACKE, Keith .... 314-539-5000 266 E
khacke@stlcc.edu

HACKEMER, Kurt .... 605-677-5221 428 E
kurt.hackemer@usd.edu

HACKER, Cheryl .... 740-351-3283 369 L
chacker@shawnee.edu

HACKER, Eugene .... 540-365-4268 480 L
ehacker@ferrum.edu

HACKERT, Marvin, L ..... 512-232-3604 467 C
m.hackert@austin.utexas.edu

HACKET, JR.,
William, C .... 863-667-5004 108 G
wchacket@seu.edu

HACKETT, Amy, E .... 253-879-3140 499 C
ahackett@pugetsound.edu

HACKETT, Gail .... 804-828-1345 487 E
ghackett@vcu.edu

HACKETT, Keith .... 907-786-1250.. 10 A
khackett2@alaska.edu

HACKETT, Keith .... 319-895-4230 167 G
khackett@cornellcollege.edu

HACKETT, Lelia .... 254-526-1293 445 L
lelia.hackett@ctcd.edu

HACKETT, Mary .... 707-826-3311.. 34 A
mary.hackett@humboldt.edu

HACKETT, Matthew .... 859-572-5198 188 E
hackettm2@nku.edu

HACKETT, Royce .... 229-931-2074 120 F
royce.hackett@gsw.edu

HACKETT, Timothy .... 510-436-2464.. 56 I
thackett@peralta.edu

HACKLE, Dale .... 850-973-1616 104 D
hackled@nfcc.edu

HACKLER, Gwen .... 405-789-6400 379 K
ghackler@snu.edu

HACKLER, Yolanda .... 316-322-3104 175 I
yhackler@butlercc.edu

HACKMAN, Erika .... 845-341-4768 319 H
erika.hackman@sunyorange.edu

HACKNEY, James .... 617-373-2101 223 D

HADAWAY, Maura .... 307-778-1204 516 N
mhadaway@lccc.wy.edu

HADDAD, Abdallah .... 843-349-2938 420 A
abdallah@coastal.edu

HADDAD, Emily, A .... 207-581-1954 201 B
emily.haddad@maine.edu

HADDAD, Kamel .... 760-750-8034.. 33 E
khaddad@csusm.edu

HADDELAND, Patricia ... 503-883-2259 383 H
phaddel@linfield.edu

HADDOCK, Gregory .... 660-562-1145 264 I
haddock@nwmissouri.edu

HADDOCK, Jennifer ...... 870-743-3000.. 20 E
jhaddock@northark.edu

HADDON, Phoebe, A .... 856-225-6095 290 A
chancellor@camden.rutgers.edu

HADDON, Phoebe, A .... 856-225-6095 290 B
chancellor@camden.rutgers.edu

HADDOW, Deborah, E .. 607-733-2307 332 F
dhaddow@uscny.edu

HADDOW, Donna .... 719-846-5541.. 82 L
donna.haddow@trinidadstate.edu

HADENFELDT, Sharon .... 402-481-8606 273 F
sharon.hadenfeldt@bryanhealthcollege.edu

HADERTHAUER, Janine . 787-264-1912 524 D
janine@intersg.edu

HADJEZ, Claudia .... 305-899-3970.. 95 G
chadjez@barry.edu

HADLEY, Amy .... 716-338-1189 311 F
amyhadley@mail.sunyjcc.edu

HADLEY, Craig .... 207-992-1953 199 B
hadleyc@husson.edu

HADLEY, H. Roger .... 909-558-4481.. 48 H
rhadley@llu.edu

HADLEY, Jeremy .... 505-473-6411 296 C
jeremy.hadley@santafeuniversity.edu

HADLEY, June, M .... 817-552-3700 451 G
jhadley@tku.edu

HADLEY, Kim .... 479-524-7117.. 20 B
khadley@jbu.edu

HADLEY, Linda .... 706-568-2044 118 C
hadley_linda@columbusstate.edu

HADLEY, Pamela .... 610-399-2260 405 G
phadley@cheyney.edu

HADLEY, Richard .... 508-588-9100 220 B

HADLEY, Robyn, S .... 314-935-7192 269 L
robyn.hadley@wustl.edu

HADLEY-SHAKYA,
Kara, M .... 319-273-2281 167 A
kara.hadleyshakya@uni.edu

HADLOCK, Heather .... 903-923-2319 448 J
hhadlock@etbu.edu

HADSELL, Heidi .... 860-509-9502.. 87 C
hadsell@hartsem.edu

HADSELL, Krissta .... 740-397-9000 366 B
krissta.hadsell@mvnu.edu

HADVINA, Shellie .... 818-677-5541.. 33 B
shellie.hadvina@csun.edu

HADWIN, Julie .... 803-812-7304 425 D
jhadwin@mailbox.sc.edu

HAEBERLE, Kathleen ..... 559-325-3600.. 29 D
khaeberle@chsu.org

HAECKER, Ryan .... 512-444-8082 461 C
library@thsu.edu

HAEFNER, Brenda .... 319-363-1323 172 B
bhaefner@mtmercy.edu

HAEFNER, Jeremy, A .... 585-475-6399 321 D
jahpro@rit.edu

HAEGER, Loredana, C ... 901-572-2772 430 C
loredana.haeger@bchs.edu

HAELEN, Robert .... 518-320-1502 324 F
bob.haelen@suny.edu

HAENSEL, Angela .... 513-569-4845 359 G
angela.haensel@cincinnatistate.edu

HAERENS, Joy .... 909-652-6840.. 36 E
joy.haerens@chaffey.edu

HAESLOOP, Mary .... 650-508-3651.. 54 D
mhaesloop@ndnu.edu

HAFFAR, Warren .... 215-572-4094 389 D
haffarw@arcadia.edu

HAFFEY, Jim .... 662-472-9013 253 C
jhaffey@holmescc.edu

HAFFORD, Patrick .... 617-989-4870 225 E
haffordp@wit.edu

HAFT, Jennifer .... 210-784-1612 460 C
jennifer.haft@tamusa.edu

HAFT, Tami .... 208-769-7729 132 E
tami_haft@nic.edu

HAGA-DUFFY, Laura ..... 541-956-7158 386 G
lduffy@roguecc.edu

HAGAER, Timi .... 941-359-4200 111 C

HAGAN, Abdalla, F .... 903-927-3343 471 B
afhagan@wileyc.edu

HAGAN, Alise .... 337-482-9029 197 F
alise@louisiana.edu

HAGAN, Bruce .... 949-451-5254.. 64 I
bhagan@ivc.edu

HAGAN, Dara .... 763-488-2465 244 G
dara.hagan@hennepintech.edu

HAGAN, Eric .... 610-282-1100 393 G
eric.hagan@desales.edu

HAGAN, Joanna .... 480-858-9100.. 16 D
j.hagan@scnm.edu

HAGAN, Kacy .... 570-662-4054 406 F
khagan@mansfield.edu

HAGAN, Khalli .... 225-743-8500 193 C
khagan@rpcc.edu

HAGAN, Lauren .... 312-915-7676 144 D
lhagan@luc.edu

HAGAN, Scott, A .... 612-343-4741 249 E
sahagan@northcentral.edu

HAGAN, Waldon .... 201-879-1577 283 I
whagan@bergen.edu

HAGAN, Willie, J .... 310-243-3301.. 31 E
presidenthagan@csudh.edu

HAGAN, Winifred, M ..... 617-994-6912 216 F
whagan@bhe.mass.edu

HAGANDER, Sonja .... 612-330-1435 240 G
hagander@augsburg.edu

HAGANS, Lori, R .... 405-878-2708 377 A
lori.hagans@okbu.edu

HAGARA, Kimberly, K ... 409-747-3277 469 C
kkhagara@utmb.edu

HAGARTY, Michael .... 507-457-6695 250 B
mhagarty@smumn.edu

HAGE, Gloria .... 734-487-3246 229 K
ghage@emich.edu

HAGEDONR, Andy .... 812-357-6520 164 A
ahagedorn@saintmeinrad.edu

HAGEDORN, Andy .... 812-357-6520 164 A
ahagedorn@saintmeinrad.edu

HAGEDORN, Valerie, A . 412-531-4433 393 D
info@deantech.edu

HAGELIN, John .... 641-472-8194 171 J
president@mum.edu

HAGEMAN, Kristin .... 651-773-1780 244 D
kristin.hageman@century.edu

HALIEMUN, Cynthia ...... 217-228-5432 149 B
haliecy@quincy.edu
HALKIAS, Carlesha .... 717-477-1161 407 B
cghalkias@ship.edu
HALL, Allyson .... 860-465-5283.. 84 K
hallall@easternct.edu
HALL, Amber, L .... 501-450-3663.. 23 I
amberh@uca.edu
HALL, Amy .... 225-214-6979 191 G
amy.hall@ololcollege.edu
HALL, Amy, J .... 540-674-3600 488 G
ahall@nr.edu
HALL, Anders, W .... 615-322-2451 440 D
anders.hall@vanderbilt.edu
HALL, Andy .... 425-889-5212 496 E
andy.hall@northwestu.edu
HALL, Andy .... 423-585-6801 438 D
robert.hall@ws.edu
HALL, Andy .... 423-585-6801 438 D
andy.hall@ws.edu
HALL, Ann .... 989-463-7411 226 H
hall@alma.edu
HALL, Aubrey .... 312-567-5792 140 I
hall@iit.edu
HALL, Becky .... 404-364-8469 124 A
bhall1@oglethorpe.edu
HALL, Benjamin .... 740-362-3448 365 D
bhall@mtso.edu
HALL, Betty .... 864-592-4942 424 C
hallb@sccsc.edu
HALL, Bobbie .... 404-527-5264 122 B
bhall@itc.edu
HALL, Bobby, L .... 806-291-3401 470 I
hallb@wbu.edu
HALL, Brad, R .... 406-338-5441 270 G
brad@bfcc.edu
HALL, C. Rick .... 706-771-4020 116 A
chall@augustatech.edu
HALL, Carol .... 860-515-3880.. 84 H
chall@charteroak.edu
HALL, Carol .... 860-515-3889.. 84 H
chall@charteroak.edu
HALL, Carrie .... 510-430-2050.. 52 E
cmilliga@mills.edu
HALL, Cassie .... 406-447-4572 270 H
chall@carroll.edu
HALL, Cathy .... 605-229-8453 427 J
cathy.hall@presentation.edu
HALL, Charles .... 252-335-3961 350 A
crhall@ecsu.edu
HALL, Charles, F .... 310-506-4532.. 56 D
charles.hall@pepperdine.edu
HALL, Chaundra .... 501-686-2921.. 21 H
chall@uasys.edu
HALL, Cheryl .... 985-549-5312 197 E
chall@selu.edu
HALL, Chris .... 618-537-6833 145 C
chall@mckendree.edu
HALL, Christopher .... 803-793-5101 420 G
hallch@denmarktech.edu
HALL, Cynthia .... 530-283-0202.. 42 K
chall@frc.edu
HALL, Daniel .... 502-852-6026 190 C
daniel.hall@louisville.edu
HALL, Daniel, B .... 323-241-5467.. 49 E
halldb@lasc.edu
HALL, David .... 340-693-1000 529 C
dhall@uvi.edu
HALL, Deborah, P .... 828-884-8262 335 L
dphall@brevard.edu
HALL, Delinda .... 617-745-3869 214 D
delinda.hall@enc.edu
HALL, Delores .... 216-421-7423 359 J
dhall@cia.edu
HALL, Dennis .... 817-531-4872 463 G
dhall@txwes.edu
HALL, Derek .... 906-227-2716 235 A
halld@nmu.edu
HALL, Don .... 508-854-4515 220 G
dhall@qcc.mass.edu
HALL, Donald, E .... 610-758-4570 400 B
deh211@lehigh.edu
HALL, Douglas, L .... 336-841-9338 338 E
dhall1@highpoint.edu
HALL, Elizabeth .... 856-415-2228 289 G
ehall@rcgc.edu
HALL, Ellis, F .... 317-738-8080 157 L
ehall@franklincollege.edu
HALL, Eric .... 978-232-2294 214 G
ehall@endicott.edu
HALL, Frank, A .... 989-964-4144 236 F
frhall@svsu.edu
HALL, Genevieve .... 937-708-3425 373 H
ghall@wilberforce.edu
HALL, George .... 859-442-4188 185 I
george.hall@kctcs.edu
HALL, Gregory .... 860-444-8624 519 B
gregory.hall@uscga.edu
HALL, Gwen .... 304-724-3700 501 D
ghall@apus.edu
HALL, Haley .... 803-535-1262 423 B
hallht@octech.edu
HALL, Hollie, M .... 607-587-4200 328 F
hallhm@alfredstate.edu
HALL, Jack, C .... 386-312-4293 106 M
jackhall@sjrstate.edu
HALL, Jackie .... 606-487-3180 185 J
jackie.hall@kctcs.edu
HALL, James .... 251-381-3491.... 7 B
jhall@shc.edu
HALL, James .... 520-515-5329.. 11 R
bohall@cochise.edu
HALL, James, R .... 864-597-4351 426 I
halljr@wofford.edu
HALL, Jami .... 706-272-4428 118 F
jhall@daltonstate.edu
HALL, Jason .... 910-893-1291 336 C
hallj@campbell.edu
HALL, Jean .... 785-227-3380 175 E
hallje@bethanylb.edu
HALL, Jeffrey, B .... 706-419-1121 118 E
hall@covenant.edu
HALL, Jennifer .... 330-829-6644 372 C
halljene@mountunion.edu
HALL, Jessica .... 614-251-4372 367 F
hallj@ohiodominican.edu
HALL, Jessica .... 478-934-3458 123 A
jessica.hall@mga.edu
HALL, Jill .... 863-297-1072 105 F
jhall@polk.edu
HALL, Jim .... 479-619-4182.. 20 F
jhall@nwacc.edu
HALL, Jim .... 631-420-2457 329 D
jim.hall@farmingdale.edu
HALL, III, Jim .... 405-325-1700 380 L
tripp@ou.edu
HALL, Jody .... 580-745-2526 379 J
jhall@se.edu
HALL, John, A .... 214-768-3518 457 B
jhall@smu.edu
HALL, John, D .... 817-272-2102 467 B
jhall@uta.edu
HALL, Jon Mark .... 812-464-1846 165 C
jmhall@usi.edu
HALL, Joseph, C .... 757-823-8675 483 F
jchall@nsu.edu
HALL, Joy Lin .... 918-343-7541 379 C
jhall@rsu.edu
HALL, Juanita .... 805-493-3951.. 30 E
jahall@callutheran.edu
HALL, Karla .... 502-213-2507 186 C
karla.hall@kctcs.edu
HALL, Karyn .... 936-468-3806 458 A
khall@sfasu.edu
HALL, Kathleen .... 937-255-6234 517 H
kathleen.hall@afit.edu
HALL, Kathleen, K .... 937-255-6234 517 H
kathleen.hall@afit.edu
HALL, Kathy .... 319-398-7650 171 F
khall@kirkwood.edu
HALL, Katie .... 614-292-2424 367 H
hall.738@osu.edu
HALL, Kelli .... 606-886-3863 185 F
kelli.hall@kctcs.edu
HALL, Kellie .... 701-477-7862 355 H
kmhall@tm.edu
HALL, Kenneth .... 570-484-2598 406 E
khall@lockhaven.edu
HALL, Kevin .... 706-886-6831 126 F
khall@tfc.edu
HALL, Kevin .... 651-603-6165 241 L
khall@csp.edu
HALL, Kevin, A .... 585-292-2904 315 L
khall006@monroecc.edu
HALL, Kim .... 360-416-7601 498 F
kim.hall@skagit.edu
HALL, Kim, B .... 865-251-1800 436 B
khall@southcollegetn.edu
HALL, Kimberly .... 614-287-2408 360 C
khall46@cscc.edu
HALL, Kristen .... 413-644-4400 211 B
HALL, Kristin, E .... 845-758-7531 298 I
hall@bard.edu
HALL, Kristy .... 276-523-2400 488 F
khall@mecc.edu
HALL, Lareese .... 401-709-5909 417 B
lhall@risd.edu
HALL, Larretta .... 701-255-3285 355 I
lhall@uttc.edu
HALL, Larry .... 828-328-7112 339 C
larry.hall@lr.edu
HALL, Lataria .... 559-925-3338.. 74 A
latariahall@whccd.edu
HALL, Lawrence .... 860-832-2298.. 84 J
halllaw@ccsu.edu
HALL, JR., Lawrence ..... 615-327-5732 434 A
lhall@mmc.edu
HALL, Les .... 803-545-5048 424 I
les.hall@uscmed.sc.edu
HALL, Leslie .... 503-338-2450 382 E
lhall@clatsopcc.edu
HALL, Linda .... 434-544-8126 482 F
hall.l@lynchburg.edu
HALL, Linda, M .... 585-292-2103 315 L
lhall38@monroecc.edu
HALL, Lisa .... 423-236-2900 436 C
lhwoodcock@southern.edu
HALL, Lori .... 503-594-3162 382 D
lori.hall@clackamas.edu
HALL, Lori .... 207-741-5501 200 C
lhall@smccme.edu
HALL, Lydia .... 936-294-3608 462 F
lth003@shsu.edu
HALL, Lyndon .... 252-257-1900 347 C
halll@vgcc.edu
HALL, Lynn .... 812-866-7385 158 C
hall@hanover.edu
HALL, Mark .... 615-297-7545 429 H
hallm@aquinascollege.edu
HALL, Mark .... 919-545-8043 341 H
mhall@cccc.edu
HALL, Mark .... 734-384-4261 234 C
mhall@monroeccc.edu
HALL, Mark .... 918-495-7742 378 H
mhall@oru.edu
HALL, Marlon, R .... 530-251-8820.. 47 J
mhall@lassencollege.edu
HALL, Mary .... 828-232-5109 351 A
mhall7@unca.edu
HALL, Mary Theresa ..... 724-589-2154 411 D
mthall@thiel.edu
HALL, Matthew .... 805-893-8989.. 70 B
matthall@ucsb.edu
HALL, Matthew .... 502-897-4043 189 A
mhall@sbts.edu
HALL, Matthew .... 502-897-4555 189 A
mhall@sbts.edu
HALL, Michael .... 302-736-2483.. 90 J
j.michael.hall@wesley.edu
HALL, Michael, R .... 336-841-9235 338 E
mhall@highpoint.edu
HALL, Michael, W .... 540-654-1025 486 D
mhall2@umw.edu
HALL, Micheal .... 770-426-2829 122 F
micheal.hall@life.edu
HALL, Michelle .... 404-364-8418 124 A
mhall@oglethorpe.edu
HALL, Michelle .... 620-278-4211 181 G
mhall@sterling.edu
HALL, Michelle .... 985-549-2077 197 E
mhall@selu.edu
HALL, Nicole .... 312-629-6100 151 F
nhall1@saic.edu
HALL, Nicole .... 336-334-4174 351 D
nrhall@uncg.edu
HALL, Norma .... 317-788-3206 164 H
hallne@uindy.edu
HALL, Norman, D .... 618-664-7119 139 A
norm.hall@greenville.edu
HALL, Pam .... 623-845-3825.. 13 H
pam.hall@gccaz.edu
HALL, Pamela .... 313-845-6410 231 B
phall@hfcc.edu
HALL, Patricia .... 479-394-7622.. 23 D
phall@uarichmountain.edu
HALL, Patty .... 402-465-2237 276 E
phall@nebrwesleyan.edu
HALL, Paulakay .... 423-775-7308 430 G
phall7036@bryan.edu
HALL, Persephone .... 860-439-2646.. 86 H
phall3@conncoll.edu
HALL, Philip, D .... 843-792-8979 422 C
hallpd@musc.edu
HALL, Qiana, M .... 502-597-5759 187 E
qiana.hall@kysu.edu
HALL, Randolph, W .... 213-740-6709.. 72 B
rwhall@usc.edu
HALL, Raymond, D .... 810-762-3335 238 B
raydhall@umflint.edu
HALL, Ricardo .... 610-758-3890 400 B
rih217@lehigh.edu
HALL, Richard .... 307-674-6446 516 P
rhall@sheridan.edu
HALL, Rickey .... 206-685-0518 499 D
vpomad@uw.edu
HALL, Robert .... 716-829-7657 307 B
hallrm@dyc.edu
HALL, Rodney .... 804-524-2954 491 A
rhall@vsu.edu
HALL, Ron .... 865-251-1800 436 B
rhall@southcollegetn.edu
HALL, Ryan .... 513-921-9856 359 C
ryan.hall@chatfield.edu
HALL, Sandy .... 325-674-2273 441 D
halls@acu.edu
HALL, Sherlynn .... 501-420-1260.. 17 I
sherlynn.hall@arkansasbaptist.edu
HALL, Steven .... 501-212-6608.. 19 B
shall@cbc.edu
HALL, Steven .... 309-341-7823 142 G
shall@knox.edu
HALL, Steven, A .... 617-358-0476 212 G
sahall@bu.edu
HALL, Susan .... 214-378-1609 447 F
shall@dcccd.edu
HALL, Susan .... 856-415-2185 289 G
shall@rcgc.edu
HALL, Tami .... 870-307-7203.. 20 C
tami.hall@lyon.edu
HALL, Tammy .... 501-279-4018.. 19 G
thall@harding.edu
HALL, Teri .... 316-978-3021 182 F
teri.hall@wichita.edu
HALL, Terry .... 225-771-2552 196 B
thall@sulc.edu
HALL, Terry .... 415-561-1908.. 37 H
thall@ccsf.edu
HALL, Tim .... 410-455-2207 208 A
halltw@umbc.edu
HALL, Tim .... 205-726-2771.... 6 G
thall5@samford.edu
HALL, Tim .... 308-535-3612 275 I
hallt@mpcc.edu
HALL, Timothy .... 914-674-7307 314 I
thall@mercy.edu
HALL, Timothy .... 239-513-1122 101 O
thall@hodges.edu
HALL, Tom .... 904-256-7715 102 B
thall5@ju.edu
HALL, Tracy .... 360-867-6205 494 G
hallt@evergreen.edu
HALL, Tracy, A .... 336-316-2349 338 C
thall@guilford.edu
HALL, Tracy, D .... 901-333-4200 438 B
tdhall@southwest.tn.edu
HALL, Tyson .... 423-236-2912 436 C
HALL, Wayne .... 502-852-6111 190 C
whall@louisville.edu
HALL, Welling .... 765-983-1318 157 I
wellingh@earlham.edu
HALL, Wendy .... 360-442-2491 495 G
whall@lowercolumbia.edu
HALL, William .... 714-997-6891.. 36 G
whall@chapman.edu
HALL, William .... 603-862-1287 282 F
bill.hall@unh.edu
HALL, JR., William .... 859-858-3511 183 D
bill.hall@asbury.edu
HALL, William, B .... 401-341-2132 417 D
hallb@salve.edu
HALL, William, C .... 617-984-1760 223 H
whall@quincycollege.edu
HALL, William, M .... 256-824-2302.... 8 C
william.hall@uah.edu
HALL, Wilson .... 707-664-2880.. 35 A
hallwi@sonoma.edu
HALL-JONES, Jenny ...... 740-593-1800 368 G
hallj1@ohio.edu
HALL SMITH, Willa .... 202-797-3670.... 7 F
HALL WATKINS, Angela 512-505-3070 451 A
ahwatkins@htu.edu
HALL-YATES, Joyce .... 419-448-3049 370 K
hallyatesjc@tiffin.edu
HALLADAY, Choi .... 253-964-6506 497 B
challaday@pierce.ctc.edu
HALLADAY, Chris .... 610-758-3900 400 B
pch214@lehigh.edu
HALLAHAN, Scott .... 415-581-8873.. 68 I
hallahan@uchastings.edu
HALLANGER, Nathan ...... 612-330-1674 240 G
hallange@augsburg.edu
HALLBERG, Robert .... 773-298-3109 151 C
hallberg@sxu.edu
HALLE, Kevin .... 402-375-7234 276 D
kehalle1@wsc.edu
HALLEEN, Jan .... 952-888-4777 249 F
jhalleen@nwhealth.edu
HALLER, Amy .... 815-455-8768 145 B
ahaller@mchenry.edu
HALLER, Bryan .... 212-220-8013 301 C
bhaller@bmcc.cuny.edu
HALLER, John, G .... 305-284-3970 112 O
jgh22@miami.edu
HALLER, Pam .... 715-833-6397 513 E
phaller1@cvtc.edu
HALLERAN, Donna .... 608-265-3443 510 C
dhalleran@vc.wisc.edu
HALLERAN, Michael .... 757-221-1993 479 I
halleran@wm.edu
HALLETT, Tom .... 708-209-3350 136 I
tom.hallett@cuchicago.edu

HAMLIN, Lyn .... 201-200-3525 287 F
lhamlin@njcu.edu
HAMLIN, Toby .... 518-608-8218 308 A
thamlin@excelsior.edu
HAMM, Bernard, C .... 804-828-1233 487 E
bchamm2@vcu.edu
HAMM, Bradley, J .... 847-491-5439 148 C
bradely.hamm@northwestern.edu
HAMM, Darryl .... 559-278-4240.. 32 A
dhamm@csufresno.edu
HAMM, Harlisha .... 212-817-7150 302 B
hhamm@gc.cuny.edu
HAMM, Jennifer .... 828-327-7000 341 G
jhamm@cvcc.edu
HAMM, Jolene .... 434-961-5301 489 C
jhamm@pvcc.edu
HAMM, K. Joy .... 941-487-5000 110 B
jhamm@ncf.edu
HAMM, L, L .... 504-988-5462 196 D
lhamm@tulane.edu
HAMM, Leonard .... 410-951-3906 208 F
lhamm@coppin.edu
HAMM, Rod .... 620-947-3121 181 H
rodneyhamm@tabor.edu
HAMM, Tammy, S .... 423-439-4457 431 H
hammt@etsu.edu
HAMMACK, Becky .... 325-674-2265 441 D
rsh12a@acu.edu
HAMMACK, Mike .... 325-670-1278 450 A
mhammack@hsutx.edu
HAMMAN, John .... 240-567-7794 205 F
john.hamman@montgomerycollege.edu
HAMMAR, Matt .... 503-554-2162 383 C
mhammar@georgefox.edu
HAMME, Gary .... 321-674-8832.. 99 K
gary@fit.edu
HAMMEKE, Curtis .... 785-628-4050 177 D
chammeke@fhsu.edu
HAMMEL, Nicole .... 484-664-3163 402 F
nicolehammel@muhlenberg.edu
HAMMEL, Rachel .... 330-490-7452 373 F
rhammel@walsh.edu
HAMMELL, Rebecca, J .. 717-245-1858 394 A
hammellr@dickinson.edu
HAMMER, Adam .... 320-308-3151 247 E
aehammer@stcloudstate.edu
HAMMER, Amanda .... 575-461-4413 294 E
amandah@mesalands.edu
HAMMER, Bradley, C .... 419-434-6922 372 B
hammer@findlay.edu
HAMMER, Kimberley, A 412-578-6294 391 G
kahammer@carlow.edu
HAMMER, Kimberley, A 412-397-6413 409 C
hammerk@rmu.edu
HAMMER, Larry .... 828-227-7232 352 C
hammer@wcu.edu
HAMMER, Lila, D .... 260-982-5234 162 Q
ldhammer@manchester.edu
HAMMERMAN,
Adam, D .... 914-594-4570 318 A
adam_hammerman@nymc.edu
HAMMERSEN, Frederick 301-243-2123 518 C
frederick.hammersen@dodiis.mil
HAMMES, Meg .... 563-387-1375 171 I
hammma01@luther.edu
HAMMETT, Amy, S .... 216-368-4318 358 C
registrar@case.edu
HAMMETT, Becky .... 870-460-1050.. 22 D
hammettb@uamont.edu
HAMMETT, Fred .... 404-225-4016 115 J
fhammett@atlantatech.edu
HAMMETT, Maria, A ...... 478-301-2226 122 H
hammett_ma@mercer.edu
HAMMILL, Graham, L ... 716-645-3786 325 B
ghammill@buffalo.edu
HAMMILL, Viv .... 406-444-0325 271 F
vhammill@montana.edu
HAMMITT, Stephanie ..... 218-879-0810 244 F
shammitt@fdltcc.edu
HAMMOCK, Susan .... 478-240-5162 123 H
shammock@oftc.edu
HAMMON, Darrel, L ...... 801-863-7353 473 D
darrel.hammon@uvu.edu
HAMMON, Kyle .... 360-442-2551 495 G
khammon@lowercolumbia.edu
HAMMOND, Anna .... 904-470-8004.. 98 B
anna.hammond@ewc.edu
HAMMOND, Ben .... 781-283-2305 225 D
HAMMOND, Brad .... 307-754-6400 516 Q
brad.hammond@nwc.edu
HAMMOND, Brian .... 301-934-7853 203 D
bhammond@csmd.edu
HAMMOND, Caroline .... 870-864-7102.. 21 D
chammond@southark.edu
HAMMOND, Charles ...... 646-378-6131 319 C
charles.hammond@nyack.edu
HAMMOND, Charles, A 302-225-6352.. 90 G
hammond@gbc.edu
HAMMOND,
Christine, M .... 989-386-6602 234 B
chammond@midmich.edu
HAMMOND, Dale .... 509-777-3730 500 H
dhammond@whitworth.edu
HAMMOND, Debbie .... 843-953-5507 420 C
hammonddd@cofc.edu
HAMMOND, Denise .... 870-584-1118.. 22 F
dhammond@cccua.edu
HAMMOND, Dianne ...... 352-245-4119 112 E
HAMMOND,
Elizabeth, D .... 478-301-2960 122 H
hammond_bd@mercer.edu
HAMMOND, Erin .... 314-256-8808 257 D
hammond@ai.edu
HAMMOND, Jamie .... 203-575-8022.. 86 B
jhammond@nv.edu
HAMMOND, Jeff .... 601-266-5001 256 E
jeff.hammond@usm.edu
HAMMOND, Jeremy ...... 909-748-8273.. 71 H
jeremy_hammond@redlands.edu
HAMMOND, Jerome .... 423-614-8310 432 L
jhammond@leeuniveristy.edu
HAMMOND, Karen, S ... 240-500-2000 204 B
kshammond@hagerstowncc.edu
HAMMOND, Ken .... 573-876-7299 267 G
khammond@stephens.edu
HAMMOND, Kim .... 512-505-3021 451 A
kim.hammond@thompsonfacilities.com
HAMMOND, Mark .... 910-893-1211 336 C
hammond@campbell.edu
HAMMOND, Michael ..... 765-998-5204 164 C
mchammond@taylor.edu
HAMMOND, Michelle .... 620-341-5208 177 B
mhammon2@emporia.edu
HAMMOND, Mike .... 641-628-5379 167 D
hammondm@central.edu
HAMMOND, Mike .... 803-535-1267 423 B
hammondm@octech.edu
HAMMOND, Paul, D ..... 848-932-8404 290 C
paul.hammond@rutgers.edu
HAMMOND, Randy .... 717-477-1256 407 B
rphamm@ship.edu
HAMMOND, Russell ...... 845-341-4007 319 H
russell.hammond@sunyorange.edu
HAMMOND, Troy, D ..... 630-637-5454 147 E
tdhammond@noctrl.edu
HAMMOND, Vanessa .... 423-614-8511 432 L
vhammond@leeuniversity.edu
HAMMOND NASS,
Holly .... 207-602-2306 202 A
hnass@une.edu
HAMMONDS, David ...... 936-294-2709 462 F
david.hammonds@shsu.edu
HAMMONDS, Diane, M 610-526-1407 389 B
diane.hammonds@theamericancollege.edu
HAMMONDS, Jennifer ... 740-351-3207 369 L
jhammonds@shawnee.edu
HAMMONDS, Luke .... 601-477-4058 253 F
luke.hammonds@jcjc.edu
HAMMONDS, MarTeze .. 479-880-4358.. 18 G
mhammonds2@atu.edu
HAMMONS, Jamirae ..... 606-539-4201 190 A
jamirae.hammons@ucumberlands.edu
HAMMONS, Stacy .... 765-677-3061 161 C
stacy.hammons@indwes.edu
HAMMONS, Steve .... 606-679-8501 186 G
steve.hammons@kctcs.edu
HAMMONTREE, Tonya .. 501-205-8809.. 19 B
thammontree@cbc.edu
HAMMS, Gavin .... 318-247-6328 196 G
hammsg@gram.edu
HAMNER, Elise .... 541-888-7211 387 A
elise.hamner@socc.edu
HAMNER, Mark, S .... 940-898-3013 464 A
mhamner@twu.edu
HAMP, Herlisa .... 408-741-4616.. 74 D
herlisa.hamp@westvalley.edu
HAMPSON, Bill .... 816-995-2818 265 G
bill.hampson@researchcollege.edu
HAMPSON, Nancy .... 970-207-4550.. 80 P
nancyh@mckinleycollege.edu
HAMPTON, Audrey .... 661-255-1050.. 29 F
HAMPTON, Brian .... 580-559-5225 375 I
bridham@ecok.edu
HAMPTON, Diane .... 870-733-6880.. 18 B
dhampton@asumidsouth.edu
HAMPTON, Franki .... 540-453-2285 487 G
hamptonf@brcc.edu
HAMPTON, Iyisha .... 334-244-3674.... 4 E
ihampton@aum.edu
HAMPTON, Jarvis, D ..... 806-651-3451 460 E
jhampton@mail.wtamu.edu
HAMPTON, Jennifer .... 630-752-5327 155 F
jennifer.hampton@wheaton.edu
HAMPTON, Joyce .... 413-265-2423 213 E
hamptonj@elms.edu
HAMPTON, Julie .... 309-649-6201 152 G
julie.hampton@src.edu
HAMPTON, Kay, S .... 912-279-5960 118 A
khampton@ccga.edu
HAMPTON, Lacy .... 210-486-2178 441 I
lhampton14@alamo.edu
HAMPTON, Lee .... 517-787-0800 231 E
hamptonleem@jccmi.edu
HAMPTON, Logan, C .... 731-426-7595 432 J
lhampton@lanecollege.edu
HAMPTON, Mark .... 516-686-7517 317 G
mark.hampton@nyit.edu
HAMPTON, Michael ...... 503-883-2442 383 H
mhampton@linfield.edu
HAMPTON, Mike .... 305-919-4018 109 D
mike.hampton@fiu.edu
HAMPTON, Renee .... 417-667-8181 259 A
rhampton@cottey.edu
HAMPTON, Tabatha .... 870-762-3121.. 17 K
thampton@smail.anc.edu
HAMPTON, Terri .... 951-222-8589.. 58 E
terri.hampton@rccd.edu
HAMPTON, Valerie, J .... 607-777-4775 325 A
vhampton@binghamton.edu
HAMPTON, Victoria .... 860-768-4296.. 89 C
vhampton@hartford.edu
HAMPTON, Wayne .... 219-844-0100 156 F
wayne.hampton@brightwood.edu
HAMPTON VANSANT,
Gwendolyn .... 413-528-7273 211 B
ghamptonvansant@simons-rock.edu
HAMRICK, David, S ...... 512-232-7604 467 C
dhamrick@utpress.utexas.edu
HAMRICK, Howard, I ..... 281-756-3700 442 C
hhamrick@alvincollege.edu
HAMRICK, James .... 410-857-2202 205 E
jhamrick@mcdaniel.edu
HAMRICK, Jeff .... 415-422-6136.. 72 A
jhamrick@usfca.edu
HAMRICK, Mike .... 304-696-5408 504 C
hamrickm@marshall.edu
HAMRICK, Patricia, L .... 719-333-9751 518 H
HAMRICK, Robin, G ...... 704-406-3996 337 H
rhamrick@gardner-webb.edu
HAMRICK, Sarah .... 202-651-5214.. 91 H
sarah.hamrick@gallaudet.edu
HAMSTRA, Brent .... 423-236-2203 436 C
bhamstra@southern.edu
HAMSTRA, Pete .... 602-386-4114.. 10 G
pete.hamstra@arizonachristian.edu
HAMZAVI, Maria .... 858-499-0202.. 39 B
mhamzavi@coleman.edu
HAMZE, Cathrine .... 510-356-4760.. 76 B
HAN, David, S .... 423-478-7524 435 I
dhan@ptseminary.edu
HAN, Jenjen .... 407-888-8689.. 99 F
jhan@fcim.edu
HAN, Jin .... 714-995-9988.. 47 D
HAN, Joseph .... 509-963-2197 492 L
joseph.han@cwu.edu
HAN, Joseph .... 216-687-5343 359 L
joseph.han@csuohio.edu
HAN, Ki Won .... 714-527-0691.. 42 H
HAN, Luoheng .... 205-348-4890.... 8 A
luoheng.han@ua.edu
HAN, Peter .... 303-273-3131.. 78 J
phan@mines.edu
HAN, Seung Goo .... 213-386-0080.. 52 C
HAN, Woojin .... 714-533-3946.. 35 B
woojin.han@calums.edu
HAN, Yuan-Yuan .... 407-888-8689.. 99 F
y2han@fcim.edu
HANADA, Karen .... 808-984-3527 130 H
tkhanada@hawaii.edu
HANADA,
Tamone Karen .... 808-984-3527 130 H
tkhanada@hawaii.edu
HANAK, Lesley .... 912-525-5000 125 B
lhanak@scad.edu
HANASSAB, Shideh .... 310-825-1681.. 69 B
shanassa@saonet.ucla.edu
HANAVAN, Laura .... 816-415-7804 270 C
hanavanl@william.jewell.edu
HANBURY, II,
George, L .... 954-262-7575 104 F
hanbury@nsu.nova.edu
HANBURY, John .... 276-656-0205 489 A
jhanbury@patrickhenry.edu
HANCE, JR., James, H . 401-598-1000 416 C
HANCKEL, Julianne .... 512-505-3072 451 A
jphanckel@htu.edu
HANCKS, Jeffrey .... 309-298-1929 155 D
jl-hancks@wiu.edu
HANCOCK, Anthony .... 713-718-6283 450 D
anthony.hancock@hccs.edu
HANCOCK, Barry .... 618-985-3741 141 D
barryhancock@jalc.edu
HANCOCK, JR., Ben, E . 910-630-7000 340 A
bhancock@methodist.edu
HANCOCK, Blair .... 336-838-6128 347 G
bmhancock168@wilkescc.edu
HANCOCK, Heather .... 918-595-7842 380 D
heather.hancock@tulsacc.edu
HANCOCK, John .... 713-500-2401 468 D
john.hancock@uth.tmc.edu
HANCOCK, John .... 503-768-7160 383 G
hancock@lclark.edu
HANCOCK, Jory, L .... 520-626-8030.. 16 J
jory@email.arizona.edu
HANCOCK, Lua .... 386-822-7343 111 E
lhancock@stetson.edu
HANCOCK, Mara .... 510-594-5080.. 28 K
mhancock@cca.edu
HANCOCK, Merodie .... 518-587-2100 329 C
president@esc.edu
HANCOCK, Sean .... 760-921-5428.. 55 J
sean.hancock@paloverde.edu
HANCOCK, Wanda .... 229-225-5089 126 C
whancock@southernregional.edu
HANCOX, Robert, E .... 610-892-1578 405 C
rhancox@pit.edu
HAND, Christie .... 304-358-2000 501 I
christie@future.edu
HAND, Jeffrey .... 856-256-5186 289 H
handj@rowan.edu
HAND, Kelli .... 704-637-4416 336 G
kmhand@catawba.edu
HAND, Mary .... 518-743-2248 328 G
handm@sunyacc.edu
HAND, Natalie .... 484-664-3804 402 F
nataliehand@muhlenberg.edu
HAND, Theresa .... 518-244-4590 321 G
handt@sage.edu
HANDCOX, Jenelle .... 910-521-6255 351 E
jenelle.handcox@uncp.edu
HANDEL, Greg .... 318-357-4522 197 D
handelg@nsula.edu
HANDEL, Greg .... 318-357-4330 197 D
handelg@nsula.edu
HANDFIELD, Sandy .... 321-433-5502.. 97 N
handfields@easternflorida.edu
HANDFORD, Ann .... 262-524-7211 506 G
ahandfor@carrollu.edu
HANDLER, Janet .... 319-363-1323 172 B
jhandler@mtmercy.edu
HANDLER, Jeffrey .... 201-761-7101 291 D
jhandler@saintpeters.edu
HANDLER, Lisa, M .... 414-410-4207 506 F
lmhandler@stritch.edu
HANDLEY, Robert, L ..... 785-670-1878 182 D
bob.handley@washburn.edu
HANDOJO, Jeanne .... 626-584-5366.. 43 K
jeanne@fuller.edu
HANDS, Ashanti .... 619-388-2678.. 60 D
ahands@sdccd.edu
HANDS, Colette .... 847-635-2604 148 D
chands@oakton.edu
HANDS, Melanie .... 620-276-9638 177 G
melanie.hands@gcccks.edu
HANDWERK, Phil .... 336-758-5244 353 A
handwepg@wfu.edu
HANDWORK, David .... 870-972-2066.. 18 A
dhandwork@astate.edu
HANDY, Beth .... 410-888-9048 205 D
bhandy@muih.edu
HANDY, Cromwell .... 334-229-4309.... 4 A
chandy@alasu.edu
HANDY, Cynthia, H .... 404-752-1654 123 F
cynthia@msm.edu
HANDY, Linda, B .... 317-788-3349 164 H
handy@uindy.edu
HANDY, Maisha .... 404-527-7705 122 B
mhandy@itc.edu
HANDY, Ty, J .... 502-213-2121 186 C
ty.handy@kctcs.edu
HANDYSIDE, David .... 920-206-2341 508 A
david.handyside@mbu.edu
HANDZLIK, Diane, M .... 716-896-0700 333 C
dianeh@villa.edu
HANE, Jennifer .... 719-255-3180.. 83 C
jhane@uccs.edu
HANEBUTTE, Shema ...... 253-566-6006 499 A
shanebutte@tacomacc.edu
HANEFIELD, Robert .... 580-581-2417 375 A
rhanefield@cameron.edu
HANELLY, William .... 570-484-2002 406 E
whanelly@lockhaven.edu
HANES, Barbara .... 484-840-4604 402 G
hanesb@neumann.edu
HANES, Billie .... 919-530-5086 350 D
bhanes@nccu.edu
HANES, Carol .... 903-875-7594 453 J
carol.hanes@navarrocollege.edu
HANES, Madlyn, L .... 814-863-0327 403 F
mqh3@psu.edu

HANES, Rick ... 937-778-8600 361 E
rhanes@edisonohio.edu
HANES-GOODLANDER,
Lisa ... 651-846-1383 247 G
lisa.hanes@saintpaul.edu
HANEY, Cindy, M ... 610-799-1122 400 A
chaney1@lccc.edu
HANEY, Daniel ... 870-307-7226.. 20 C
daniel.haney@lyon.edu
HANEY, David ... 908-852-1400 284 G
haneyd@centenaryuniversity.edu
HANEY, Frank ... 913-234-0788 176 H
frank.haney@cleveland.edu
HANEY, Jay ... 432-552-2764 469 D
haney_j@utpb.edu
HANEY, Kent ... 661-362-2844.. 51 C
khaney@masters.edu
HANEY, Lee Anna ... 828-694-1885 341 B
leeannah@blueridge.edu
HANEY, Michele ... 303-914-6215.. 82 B
michele.haney@rrcc.edu
HANEY, Pamela ... 708-974-5204 146 C
haney@morainevalley.edu
HANEY, Regina ... 806-457-4200 449 D
rhaney@fpctx.edu
HANEY, Richard, J ... 847-543-2200 136 E
rhaney@clcillinois.edu
HANF, Stuart, J ... 302-327-4894.. 91 B
stuart.j.hanf@wilmu.edu
HANFORD, Thomas ... 607-753-4702 327 A
thomas.hanford@cortland.edu
HANG, Foua ... 920-693-1387 513 H
foua.hang@gotoltc.edu
HANG, Phillip ... 734-432-5662 233 C
phang@madonna.edu
HANGEN, Susan ... 201-684-7407 289 C
shangen@ramapo.edu
HANIFIN, Martin ... 518-327-6226 320 A
mhanifin@paulsmiths.edu
HANIFIN, Sheila ... 413-782-1628 225 F
shanifin@wne.edu
HANINCIK, Amanda ... 610-921-7529 388 E
ahanincik@albright.edu
HANK, Jack, L ... 210-434-6711 454 D
jlhank@lake.ollusa.edu
HANKE, Robert ... 401-454-6599 417 B
rhanke@risd.edu
HANKERSON, Brian ... 954-486-7728 112 N
bhankersoncfo@uftl.edu
HANKERSON, Reggie ... 662-621-4231 252 E
rhankerson@coahomacc.edu
HANKES, Doug ... 334-844-5123.... 4 D
hankedm@auburn.edu
HANKINS, Jeff ... 501-660-1004.. 17 L
jhankins@asusystem.edu
HANKINS, Kim ... 815-455-8778 145 B
khankins@mchenry.edu
HANKINS, Lori ... 904-826-0084.. 71 I
lhankins@usa.edu
HANKINS, Orlando, E ... 919-516-4860 348 G
oehankins@st-aug.edu
HANKINS, Paul ... 479-788-7431.. 22 A
paul.hankins@uafs.edu
HANKS, Sharon ... 928-757-0879.. 14 I
shanks@mohave.edu
HANLE, Donald ... 301-243-2183 518 C
donald.hanle@dodiis.mil
HANLEY, Darla, S ... 617-747-2664 212 B
dhanley@berklee.edu
HANLEY, Donna ... 417-873-7201 259 G
dhanley@drury.edu
HANLEY, Madalyn ... 718-489-5468 322 D
mhanley@sfc.edu
HANLEY, Paula ... 847-925-6337 139 B
phanley@harpercollege.edu
HANLEY, Peggy ... 318-274-6546 196 G
peggy@gram.edu
HANLEY, Rodney, S ... 615-329-8614 431 I
rshanley@fisk.edu
HANLEY, Theodore ... 713-718-8566 450 D
theodore.hanley@hccs.edu
HANLEY, William Lee ... 212-659-3604 312 E
wlhanley@tkc.edu
HANLEY-MAXWELL,
Cheryl ... 217-333-6677 154 B
cherylhm@illinois.edu
HANLIN, Shawn ... 541-888-1546 387 A
shanlin@socc.edu
HANLON, Christopher ... 610-921-7264 388 E
chanlon@albright.edu
HANLON, Erin ... 617-322-3552 216 B
erin_hanlon@laboure.edu
HANLON, Joyce ... 617-730-7074 223 B
joyce.hanlon@newbury.edu
HANLON, Philip, J ... 603-646-2223 281 C
philip.j.hanlon@dartmouth.edu
HANNA, Aaron ... 210-431-3335 455 J
ahanna1@stmarytx.edu
HANNA, Bashar, W ... 570-389-4526 405 E
bhanna@bloomu.edu
HANNA, C. Phil ... 270-384-8102 187 H
hannap@lindsey.edu
HANNA, Chris ... 616-432-3407 236 B
chris.hanna@prts.edu
HANNA, Dorothy ... 785-833-4468 179 C
dahanna@kwu.edu
HANNA, Kimberly ... 575-461-4413 294 E
kimberlyh@mesalands.edu
HANNA, Mae ... 513-732-5332 371 G
mae.hanna@uc.edu
HANNA, Michael ... 315-781-3574 310 C
hanna@hws.edu
HANNA, Patricia ... 610-861-7874 402 D
hannap@moravian.edu
HANNA, Randy ... 850-770-2102 110 A
rhanna@fsu.edu
HANNA, Sean ... 585-275-2354 332 E
sean.hanna@rochester.edu
HANNA, Tara ... 419-517-8908 364 G
thanna@lourdes.edu
HANNABAS, Liz ... 817-272-0777 467 B
hannabas@uta.edu
HANNABURY,
Stephen, P ... 781-292-2401 215 C
stephen.hannabury@olin.edu
HANNAFIN, Robert ... 203-254-4250.. 87 A
rhannafin@fairfield.edu
HANNAFORD, Bo, S ... 580-327-8406 376 K
bshannaford@nwosu.edu
HANNAH, Marcus ... 334-876-9360.... 2 C
marcus.hannah@wccs.edu
HANNAH, Russ ... 870-972-3303.. 18 A
rhannah@astate.edu
HANNAN, Christopher .. 319-291-2705 169 H
christopher.hannan@hawkeyecollege.
edu
HANNAN, Michael ... 814-732-2729 406 B
hannan@edinboro.edu
HANNAN, Steven, M ... 419-289-5007 356 L
shannan@ashland.edu
HANNAR, Christine ... 636-949-4965 261 I
channar@lindenwood.edu
HANNE, Benjamin, C ... 620-229-6371 181 F
ben.hanne@sckans.edu
HANNEMAN, Richard ... 531-622-2739 275 F
rhanneman@mccneb.edu
HANNES, Sarah ... 307-778-1178 516 N
shannes@lccc.wy.edu
HANNIGAN, Joseph ... 214-860-2232 448 A
joseph.hannigan@dcccd.edu
HANNIGAN, Robyn ... 617-287-4857 216 I
robyn.hannigan@umb.edu
HANNING, Chris ... 610-430-4178 407 D
channing@wcupa.edu
HANNO, Dennis ... 508-286-8244 225 G
hanno_dennis@wheatoncollege.edu
HANNON, Bernard, M ... 765-285-1033 156 C
bmhannon@bsu.edu
HANNON, Jim, M ... 563-333-6359 173 A
hannonjamesm@ambrose.sau.edu
HANNON, Kristin ... 330-823-6555 372 C
hannonkr@mountunion.edu
HANNON, Lauretta ... 404-225-4604 115 J
lhannon@atlantatech.edu
HANNON, Ron ... 408-848-4895.. 44 B
rhannon@gavilan.edu
HANNUM, Natalie ... 925-473-7403.. 41 A
nhannum@losmedanos.edu
HANOFEE, Rose ... 845-434-5750 330 F
rhanofee@sullivan.suny.edu
HANOLD, John, W ... 814-863-0768 403 F
jhh6@psu.edu
HANRAHAN, Chelsea ... 603-428-2291 281 F
chanrahan@nec.edu
HANRAHAN, Mark ... 740-284-5247 361 L
mhanrahan@franciscan.edu
HANRAHAN, Neil, S ... 212-998-4581 318 D
nsh2@nyu.edu
HANRAHAN, Susan, N .. 870-972-3112.. 18 A
hanrahan@astate.edu
HANRAHAN, Thomas ... 718-399-4308 320 D
hanrahan@pratt.edu
HANRAHAN,
Thomas, M ... 717-867-6030 399 J
hanrahan@lvc.edu
HANRAHAN, Tim ... 573-592-1107 270 D
tim.hanrahan@williamwoods.edu
HANSARD, Jamie ... 806-742-1480 463 D
jamie.hansard@ttu.edu
HANSBARGER, Tom ... 845-938-2715 519 D
tom.hansbarger@usma.edu
HANSBURG, David ... 303-273-3300.. 78 J
hansburg@mines.edu
HANSCOM, Marcus ... 401-254-3345 417 C
mhanscom@rwu.edu
HANSEL, Marie, C ... 708-709-3542 148 I
mhansel@prairiestate.edu
HANSEN, Anne, W ... 518-564-2090 327 E
hansenaw@plattsburgh.edu
HANSEN, Blaine, J ... 828-898-8838 339 B
hansenb@lmc.edu
HANSEN, Carl, F ... 707-826-3731.. 34 A
ch1@humboldt.edu
HANSEN, Chelsea ... 954-486-7728 112 N
chansen@uftl.edu
HANSEN, Cheryl ... 402-494-2311 275 M
HANSEN, Chris ... 423-236-2915 436 C
chansen@southern.edu
HANSEN, Christian ... 207-453-5128 200 A
chansen@kvcc.me.edu
HANSEN, Corinne ... 605-642-6215 428 F
corinne.hansen@bhsu.edu
HANSEN, Craig ... 651-793-1300 245 E
craig.hansen@metrostate.edu
HANSEN, David ... 843-574-6021 424 G
david.hansen@tridenttech.edu
HANSEN, David ... 605-367-7568 428 D
dave.hansen@sdbor.edu
HANSEN, David ... 435-797-1645 473 C
david.hansen@usu.edu
HANSEN, Dean ... 415-451-2806.. 60 I
maintenance@sfts.edu
HANSEN, Douglas ... 801-957-4084 474 B
douglas.hansen@slcc.edu
HANSEN, Eric ... 619-594-2941.. 34 B
ehansen@mail.sdsu.edu
HANSEN, Eric ... 432-264-5046 450 G
ehansen@howardcollege.edu
HANSEN, Gregg ... 978-468-7111 215 E
ghansen@gcts.edu
HANSEN, Jennifer ... 315-229-5441 323 D
jhansen@stlawu.edu
HANSEN, Jessica ... 302-736-2444.. 90 J
jessica.warner@wesley.edu
HANSEN, Jill ... 815-825-9517 142 F
jill.hansen@kishwaukeecollege.edu
HANSEN, John ... 307-532-8304 516 J
john.hansen@ewc.wy.edu
HANSEN, Jon ... 308-432-6231 276 B
jhansen@csc.edu
HANSEN, Jory ... 605-995-2151 427 A
johansen@dwu.edu
HANSEN, Julie ... 641-673-1096 174 F
hansenj@wmpenn.edu
HANSEN, Kathy ... 320-363-5307 241 I
kghansen@csbsju.edu
HANSEN, Kaylyn, L ... 580-327-8418 376 K
klhansen@nwosu.edu
HANSEN, Kenneth ... 402-559-5301 277 H
hansenkl@unmc.edu
HANSEN, Kent, A ... 909-558-2644.. 48 H
khansen@claysonlaw.com
HANSEN, Kevin ... 319-398-5625 171 F
kevin.hansen@kirkwood.edu
HANSEN, Kristine ... 651-793-1300 245 E
kristine.hansen@metrostate.edu
HANSEN, Linda, L ... 406-768-6351 271 B
lhansen@fpcc.edu
HANSEN, Lynn ... 407-823-2362 110 C
lynn.hansen@ucf.edu
HANSEN, Mandy ... 719-255-7528.. 83 C
mhansen2@uccs.edu
HANSEN, Marie ... 207-973-1081 199 B
hansenm@my.husson.edu
HANSEN, Matt, B ... 563-333-6258 173 A
hansenmattb@sau.edu
HANSEN, Michele, J ... 317-278-2618 160 E
mjhansen@iupui.edu
HANSEN, Noah ... 619-594-4808.. 34 B
nhansen@mail.sdsu.edu
HANSEN, Patricia ... 417-865-2815 260 B
hansenp@evangel.edu
HANSEN, Peter ... 210-436-3324 455 J
phansen@stmarytx.edu
HANSEN, Richard ... 617-349-8518 216 D
richard.hansen@lesley.edu
HANSEN, Richard ... 913-971-3381 179 H
rdhanson@mnu.edu
HANSEN, Richard, A ... 334-844-8348.... 4 D
rah0019@auburn.edu
HANSEN, Shelley ... 530-541-4660.. 47 I
hansen@ltcc.edu
HANSEN, Sherri ... 435-283-7251 474 A
sherri.hansen@snow.edu
HANSEN, Steven ... 405-974-3773 380 J
shansen8@uco.edu
HANSEN, Susan ... 860-727-6782.. 87 B
shansen@goodwin.edu
HANSEN, Terry ... 432-264-5600 450 G
thansen@howardcollege.edu
HANSEN, Terry ... 432-264-5040 450 G
thansen@howardcollege.edu
HANSEN-KIEFFER,
Kristin, M ... 717-796-5234 401 L
khansen@messiah.edu
HANSHAW, Mark ... 817-531-4444 463 G
mhanshaw@txwes.edu
HANSHER, Lesley, A ... 719-884-5000 180 B
lahansher@nbc.edu
HANSHEW, Daniel, S ... 304-877-6428 501 E
dan.hanshew@abc.edu
HANSHUMAKER, David . 978-478-3400 223 E
dhanshumaker@northpoint.edu
HANSON, Andrew ... 208-792-2218 132 C
ahanson@lcsc.edu
HANSON, Andrew ... 845-938-2022 519 D
8gc@usma.edu
HANSON, Brenda ... 406-756-3812 271 A
bhanson@fvcc.edu
HANSON, Brent ... 540-261-8575 485 G
brent.hanson@svu.edu
HANSON, Casey ... 208-885-7053 132 I
caseyh@uidaho.edu
HANSON, Catherine ... 979-230-3632 444 E
cathie.hanson@brazosport.edu
HANSON, Charlene ... 401-841-6541 518 E
HANSON, Charles, D ... 810-762-7812 232 C
chanson@kettering.edu
HANSON, Cheryl ... 208-282-2533 132 B
hanscher@isu.edu
HANSON, Christina, R .. 717-796-1800 401 L
chanson@messiah.edu
HANSON, Daniel ... 215-641-6642 402 A
dhanson@mc3.edu
HANSON, Daniel ... 402-872-2239 276 C
dhanson@peru.edu
HANSON, Danielle ... 312-915-7510 144 D
dhanson@luc.edu
HANSON, Denise ... 319-226-2012 166 C
denise.hanson@allencollege.edu
HANSON, Gary, A ... 310-506-4405.. 56 D
gary.hanson@pepperdine.edu
HANSON, Gordon ... 858-822-7523.. 69 E
ghanson@ucsd.edu
HANSON, Janet, K ... 507-786-3018 250 C
jhanson@stolaf.edu
HANSON, Janna ... 605-688-6304 429 B
jana.hanson@sdstate.edu
HANSON, Karen ... 612-625-0051 250 E
karhan@umn.edu
HANSON, Kent ... 763-433-1179 243 K
kent.hanson@anokaramsey.edu
HANSON, Kent ... 763-576-4700 244 A
HANSON, Kirk, O ... 408-554-7898.. 62 F
kohanson@scu.edu
HANSON, Kristina ... 281-487-1170 460 G
khanson@txchiro.edu
HANSON, Linda ... 641-844-5731 170 I
linda.hanson@iavalley.edu
HANSON, Lisa ... 309-341-5212 134 H
lhanson@sandburg.edu
HANSON, Mark ... 920-206-2373 508 A
mark.hanson@mbu.edu
HANSON, Megan ... 810-762-9781 232 C
mhanson@kettering.edu
HANSON, Nina ... 425-889-5235 496 E
nina.hanson@northwestu.edu
HANSON, Patricia ... 701-777-4228 353 G
pat.hanson@und.edu
HANSON, Patti ... 641-422-1521 172 C
patti.hanson@iwd.iowa.gov
HANSON, Paula ... 903-886-5890 459 E
paula.hanson@tamuc.edu
HANSON, Peter ... 513-875-3344 359 C
peter.hanson@chatfield.edu
HANSON, Rhoda ... 503-842-8222 387 C
rhodahanson@tillamookbaycc.edu
HANSON, Richard ... 605-256-5111 428 G
richard.hanson@dsu.edu
HANSON, Sara ... 402-399-2350 274 A
shanson@csm.edu
HANSON, Sara ... 608-663-2329 507 D
sarahanson@edgewood.edu
HANSON, Shirley, M ... 701-788-4767 354 B
shirley.m.hanson@mayvillestate.edu
HANSON, Stephen, E ... 757-221-3590 479 I
sehanson@wm.edu
HANSON, Steven, D ... 517-355-2352 233 G
ispdean@msu.edu
HANSON, Susan ... 909-469-5329.. 74 G
shanson@westernu.edu
HANSON, Tonya ... 952-358-8213 246 D
tonya.hanson@normandale.edu
HANSON, Travis ... 906-487-7234 230 B
travis.hanson@finlandia.edu
HANSON, Virginia ... 773-577-8100 137 A
HANSS, Patrick, G ... 315-386-7222 329 A
hanssp@canton.edu
HANSTAD, Kari ... 701-483-2326 354 A
kari.hanstad@dickinsonstate.edu

HANSTEIN, Andrea ... 650-949-7645 .. 43 F
hansteinandrea@foothill.edu
HANTEN, Joan ... 360-475-7305 496 F
jhanten@olympic.edu
HANTL, Bill ... 216-881-1700 368 F
bhantl@ohiotech.edu
HANTLA, Bryce, F ... 832-252-4615 446 A
bryce.hantla@cbshouston.edu
HANTZ, Joan ... 406-477-6215 270 I
jhantz@cdkc.edu
HANTZSCHEL, Linda, J . 516-463-6903 310 D
linda.j.hantzschel@hofstra.edu
HANUSA, Matt ... 206-239-4500 493 D
HANUSCIN, R. Douglas 419-755-4871 366 E
dhanusci@ncstatecollege.edu
HANYCZ, Colleen, M ... 215-951-1010 398 F
president@lasalle.edu
HANYPSIAK, Krista, L ... 716-645-3020 325 B
klh5@buffalo.edu
HANZLIK, Gilbert ... 804-524-3698 491 A
ghanzik@vsu.edu
HANZLIK, Jodie, R ... 970-491-6817 .. 78 N
jodie.hanzlik@colostate.edu
HAO, Lan ... 626-914-8521 .. 37 G
lhao@citruscollege.edu
HAPGOOD-WHITE,
Jennifer ... 617-253-2811 221 C
HAPPE, Doyle ... 713-529-2778 445 K
happe@paralegal.edu
HAPPEL, Harriet ... 661-362-3653 .. 39 C
harriet.happel@canyons.edu
HAPSMITH, Linda, M ... 907-474-1849 .. 10 B
lhapsmith@alaska.edu
HARA, Lou ... 785-749-8440 178 A
lhara@haskell.edu
HARA, Michael ... 651-690-6845 249 T
mehara140@stkate.edu
HARADA, Margaret ... 425-564-2064 492 G
maggie.harada@bellevuecollege.edu
HARARI-RAFUL, Joseph 347-394-1036 299 G
rjraful@ateret.net
HARBACH, Barbara ... 314-516-7776 268 E
bharbach@umsl.edu
HARBAUGH, Martha ... 314-529-9360 262 B
mharbaugh@maryville.edu
HARBAUGH, Melinda ... 360-442-2662 495 G
mharbaugh@lowercolumbia.edu
HARBER, Dan ... 507-433-0609 247 C
dharber@riverland.edu
HARBER, Linda ... 703-993-2602 481 B
lharber@gmu.edu
HARBER, Zachery ... 870-612-2081 .. 22 H
zach.harber@uaccb.edu
HARBERT, Robert, E ... 706-419-1116 118 E
harbert@covenant.edu
HARBIN, Averl ... 716-286-8406 318 F
aharbin@niagara.edu
HARBIN, Suzanne ... 256-352-8144 .... 3 I
suzanne.harbin@wallacestate.edu
HARBISON, Amanda ... 205-391-5878 .... 3 E
aharbison@sheltonstate.edu
HARBOUK, Joseph ... 303-404-5546 .. 79 K
joseph.harbouk@frontrange.edu
HARBOUR, Petra ... 952-829-2470 240 H
petra.harbour@bethfel.org
HARBOURT, Ellen, K ... 740-427-5121 364 A
harbourte@kenyon.edu
HARDASH, Peter ... 714-564-6000 .. 58 A
hardash_peter@rsccd.edu
HARDASH, Peter ... 714-480-7340 .. 57 N
hardash_peter@rsccd.edu
HARDAWAY, Pat ... 563-884-5866 172 H
pat.hardaway@palmer.edu
HARDAWAY, Rex ... 404-727-4332 119 B
rex.hardaway@emory.edu
HARDAWAY, Thelria ... 615-963-5137 438 E
thardaway@tnstate.edu
HARDCASTLE, Ben ... 918-444-2017 376 G
harrdcast@nsuok.edu
HARDCASTLE, Bob ... 610-359-5182 393 E
bhardcastle@dccc.edu
HARDCASTLE, Louis, B . 770-484-1204 122 G
lutherrice@lutherrice.edu
HARDEE, Jerry, L ... 706-821-8230 124 C
jhardee@paine.edu
HARDEE, John ... 870-230-5320 .. 19 H
hardee@hsu.edu
HARDEE, Teresa ... 302-857-6200 .. 90 B
thardee@desu.edu
HARDEE, Terrence ... 856-776-2370 285 C
thardee@cccnj.edu
HARDEMON, Rhonda ... 312-850-7894 136 C
rhardemon@ccc.edu
HARDEN, Daniel ... 916-348-4689 .. 42 F
dharden@epic.edu
HARDEN, Derrick ... 847-543-2225 136 E
dharden@clcillinois.edu

HARDEN, Erica ... 478-553-2068 123 H
eharden@oftc.edu
HARDEN, Jim ... 906-487-7307 230 B
jim.harden@finlandia.edu
HARDEN, Kelly ... 731-661-5946 439 D
kharden@uu.edu
HARDEN, Kennith ... 360-596-5360 498 G
kharden@spscc.edu
HARDEN, Mark ... 419-289-5160 356 L
mharden@ashland.edu
HARDEN, Michelle ... 614-508-7219 363 E
mharden@hondros.edu
HARDEN, Robert ... 972-825-4814 457 F
rharden@sagu.edu
HARDEN, Ronald, W ... 916-348-4689 .. 42 F
rharden@epic.edu
HARDEN, Siegfried ... 334-670-3660 .... 7 E
sbharden@troy.edu
HARDEN, Yoshiko ... 206-934-3842 497 I
yoshiko.harden@seattlecolleges.edu
HARDER, James, M ... 419-358-3324 357 E
harderj@bluffton.edu
HARDER, Kenette ... 816-414-3730 263 D
kharder@mbts.edu
HARDER, Maria ... 402-465-2117 276 E
mharder@nebrwesleyan.edu
HARDER, Matthew ... 304-336-8006 504 E
mharder@westliberty.edu
HARDER, Natalie ... 337-521-8959 193 E
natalie.harder@solacc.edu
HARDERS, Michael ... 419-530-8425 372 F
michael.harders@utoledo.edu
HARDESKI, Grace, L ... 215-955-6618 411 E
grace.hardeski@jefferson.edu
HARDESTY, Amy ... 806-720-7178 452 D
amy.hardesty@lcu.edu
HARDESTY, Chris, C ... 386-226-6512 .. 98 C
chris.hardesty@erau.edu
HARDESTY, Jon, H ... 972-548-6803 446 I
jhardesty@collin.edu
HARDESTY, Karla ... 719-587-8124 .. 76 D
karla_hardesty@adams.edu
HARDESTY, Larry, E ... 724-458-2700 396 D
lehardesty@gcc.edu
HARDGRAVE, Bill ... 334-844-4030 .... 4 D
bch0014@auburn.edu
HARDGROVE, David ... 201-360-4361 286 E
dhardgrove@hccc.edu
HARDGROVE, Mark ... 404-627-2681 116 E
mark.hardgrove@beulah.edu
HARDIE, Susan ... 909-652-6531 .. 36 E
susan.hardie@chaffey.edu
HARDIN, Abbey ... 217-854-5562 134 E
abbey.hardin@blackburn.edu
HARDIN, Carol ... 434-544-8321 482 F
hardin@lynchburg.edu
HARDIN, Dan ... 575-492-2771 294 L
dhardin@nmjc.edu
HARDIN, David, M ... 910-362-7020 341 E
dhardin@cfcc.edu
HARDIN, Elizabeth, A ... 704-687-5750 351 C
eahardin@uncc.edu
HARDIN, Fred ... 864-388-8340 422 A
fhardin@lander.edu
HARDIN, Marie ... 814-863-1484 403 F
mch208@psu.edu
HARDIN, Michael ... 205-726-2718 .... 6 G
mhardin@samford.edu
HARDIN, Mike, W ... 704-406-4280 337 H
mhardin@gardner-webb.edu
HARDIN, Pam ... 828-627-4544 343 G
pahardin@haywood.edu
HARDIN, Phil ... 870-245-5400 .. 20 G
hardinp@obu.edu
HARDIN, Philip, W ... 870-245-5400 .. 20 G
hardinp@obu.edu
HARDIN, Richard, H ... 636-481-3130 261 B
rhardin@jeffco.edu
HARDIN, Sally, B ... 619-260-4550 .. 71 J
shardin@sandiego.edu
HARDIN, Sandy ... 575-492-4735 294 L
shardin@nmjc.edu
HARDIN, Walter, A ... 803-323-2261 426 H
hardinw@winthrop.edu
HARDIN, Wille ... 501-420-1252 .. 17 I
willie.hardin@arkansasbaptist.edu
HARDING, Benjamin ... 215-702-4321 391 C
bharding@cairn.edu
HARDING, Blane ... 775-784-4936 279 E
bharding@unr.edu
HARDING, James ... 802-287-8393 475 B
hardingj@greenmtn.edu
HARDING, Kelly ... 660-263-3900 258 A
bookstore@cccb.edu
HARDING, Marc, L ... 412-624-7175 412 I
mharding@pitt.edu
HARDING, Millicent ... 606-759-7141 186 E
millicent.harding@kctcs.edu

HARDING, Sally ... 212-431-2319 317 H
sally.harding@nyls.edu
HARDING, Sam ... 217-854-5617 134 E
sam.harding@blackburn.edu
HARDING, Sarah ... 612-874-3737 243 F
sharding@mcad.edu
HARDING, Shannan ... 218-235-2153 248 B
s.harding@vcc.edu
HARDING, JR., Tayloe .. 803-777-4336 424 I
tharding@mozart.sc.edu
HARDING, Teresa ... 701-766-1309 353 E
teresa.harding@littlehoop.edu
HARDING, Terry, M ... 716-878-6112 326 E
hardintm@buffalostate.edu
HARDING, Timothy ... 813-258-7281 113 E
tharding@ut.edu
HARDISON, Al ... 910-893-1441 336 C
hardison@campbell.edu
HARDISON, John ... 910-296-2433 344 B
jhardison@jamessprunt.edu
HARDISON, R. Karol ... 270-809-4388 188 D
rhardison@murraystate.edu
HARDLEY, Michelle, M . 805-565-7263 .. 74 I
mhardley@westmont.edu
HARDMAN,
Alton (Tony) ... 580-349-1542 377 E
ahardman@opsu.edu
HARDMAN, John ... 870-245-5189 .. 20 G
hardmanj@obu.edu
HARDMAN, Michael, L . 801-587-8889 472 P
michael.hardman@utah.edu
HARDMAN, II,
Robert, O ... 304-637-1331 501 H
hardmanr@dewv.edu
HARDMON,
Tamecka, C ... 401-456-8213 417 A
thardmon@ric.edu
HARDRICK, Jaffus ... 305-348-2190 109 D
jaffus.hardrick@fiu.edu
HARDT, Jim ... 412-392-6186 408 F
jhardt@pointpark.edu
HARDT, John ... 708-327-9213 144 D
jhardt@lumc.edu
HARDT, John, P ... 570-577-1232 390 H
john.hardt@bucknell.edu
HARDT, William, M ... 609-258-3379 288 F
whardt@princeton.edu
HARDWICK, James ... 813-253-6209 113 E
jhardwick@ut.edu
HARDWICK, James, D .. 406-447-4530 270 H
jhardwic@carroll.edu
HARDWICK, Karen, M ... 202-274-5400 .. 93 D
karen.hardwick@udc.edu
HARDWICK, Monica ... 719-549-3024 .. 81 M
monica.hardwick@pueblocc.edu
HARDWOOD-ROM,
Melissa ... 479-575-5004 .. 21 I
mhardwood@uark.edu
HARDY, Angelic ... 570-484-2628 406 E
anh1227@lockhaven.edu
HARDY, Anthony ... 334-556-2447 .... 2 B
ahardy@wallace.edu
HARDY, Beatriz, B ... 410-543-6133 209 B
bbhardy@salisbury.edu
HARDY, Catherine ... 203-575-8080 .. 86 B
chardy@nv.edu
HARDY, Charles ... 910-962-3460 352 A
hardyc@uncw.edu
HARDY, Christina ... 330-941-3511 374 E
chardy@ysu.edu
HARDY, SR., Daniel, R . 330-337-6403 356 B
president@awc.edu
HARDY, Deborah, L ... 440-525-7446 364 D
dhardy@lakelandcc.edu
HARDY, Deborah, L ... 440-525-7828 364 D
dhardy@lakelandcc.edu
HARDY, Faye, B ... 803-705-4653 418 G
faye.hardy@benedict.edu
HARDY, Kacee ... 731-286-3238 437 A
hardy@dscc.edu
HARDY, Karin, S ... 801-585-6220 472 P
karin.hardy@utah.edu
HARDY, Kevin ... 207-947-4591 198 F
khardy@bealcollege.edu
HARDY, Lonza ... 870-575-8471 .. 22 E
hardyl@uapb.edu
HARDY, Mark, G ... 615-963-5301 438 E
mhardy@tnstate.edu
HARDY, Pollye ... 205-348-3952 .... 8 A
phardy@fa.ua.edu
HARDY, Randall ... 757-727-5640 481 E
randall.hardy@hamptonu.edu
HARDY, Rebekah, L ... 410-778-7865 210 A
rhardy2@washcoll.edu
HARDY, Richard, J ... 309-298-2228 155 D
rj-hardy@wiu.edu
HARDY, Robert, M ... 203-396-8390 .. 88 C
hardyr@sacredheart.edu

HARDY, Stacia ... 225-216-8247 192 B
hardys@mybrcc.edu
HARDY, Stacy ... 706-233-7358 125 E
shardy@shorter.edu
HARDY, Stephanie, K ... 540-261-4088 485 G
stephanie.hardy@svu.edu
HARDY, Steven ... 973-684-6036 288 C
shardy@pccc.edu
HARDY, Thomas, P ... 312-996-3772 153 G
hardyt@uillinois.edu
HARDY, Tyrrell ... 505-786-4183 294 I
thardy@navajotech.edu
HARDY, Virginia ... 252-328-6541 349 I
hardyv@ecu.edu
HARDY-LUCAS, Faye ... 757-727-5233 481 E
faye.hardy-lucas@hamptonu.edu
HARE, Angela ... 717-796-5360 401 L
ahare@messiah.edu
HARE, Emily ... 919-718-7230 341 H
ehare@cccc.edu
HARE, Erica ... 802-828-8545 476 F
erica.hare@vcfa.edu
HARE, Michelle ... 803-323-2189 426 H
harem@winthrop.edu
HARE, Randolph ... 540-458-8496 491 G
rhare@wlu.edu
HARE, Sara ... 605-256-7321 428 G
sara.hare@dsu.edu
HARE, Terri ... 309-298-2446 155 D
ta-hare@wiu.edu
HAREWOOD, Anita ... 410-837-4533 209 D
aharewood@ubalt.edu
HAREWOOD,
Gwendolyn ... 718-262-5299 304 A
gharewood@york.cuny.edu
HAREWOOD, Wayne, H 718-368-5681 303 A
wharewood@kbcc.cuny.edu
HAREZA, Dennis, F ... 216-397-1886 363 H
dhareza@jcu.edu
HARF, James ... 314-529-6851 262 B
jharf@maryville.edu
HARFORD, Ellen ... 207-216-4435 200 E
eharford@yccc.edu
HARFST, Terri ... 618-453-4613 152 B
terriw@siu.edu
HARGER, Kate ... 815-455-8695 145 B
kharger@mchenry.edu
HARGETT, Jack ... 901-321-3231 431 A
jhargett@cbu.edu
HARGIS, Joe ... 507-222-4327 241 C
jhargis@carleton.edu
HARGIS, Kenton ... 812-488-2142 164 G
kh88@evansville.edu
HARGIS, Michael ... 501-450-3106 .. 23 I
mhargis@uca.edu
HARGIS, Randall ... 318-487-7129 191 J
randall.hargis@lacollege.edu
HARGIS, V. Burns ... 405-744-6384 377 F
osupres@okstate.edu
HARGRAVE, Alan ... 765-285-8011 156 C
ahargrave@bsu.edu
HARGRAVE, Gary ... 319-656-2447 173 C
HARGRAVE, Jaime ... 713-500-3476 468 D
jaime.n.hargrave@uth.tmc.edu
HARGRAVE, Stephanie .. 336-316-2499 338 C
hargravesj@gulford.edu
HARGRAVE MEISLAHN,
Nancy ... 860-685-2269 .. 89 F
nmeislahn@wesleyan.edu
HARGRAVES,
Christopher ... 949-582-4213 .. 64 J
chargraves@saddleback.edu
HARGRAVES, Darla ... 517-338-3323 228 G
dhargraves@cleary.edu
HARGRAVES, J. Stanley 804-278-4379 486 A
shargraves@upsem.edu
HARGREAVES, Ken ... 626-395-8115 .. 29 I
ken.hargreaves@caltech.edu
HARGROVE, Debra ... 717-245-1901 394 A
hargrove@dickinson.edu
HARGROVE, Demond ... 201-200-3507 287 F
dhargrove@njcu.edu
HARGROVE, Kristi ... 615-383-4848 441 A
khargrove@watkins.edu
HARGROVE, Kristy ... 615-383-4848 441 A
khargrove@watkins.edu
HARGROVE, S. Keith ... 615-963-5451 438 E
skhargrove@tnstate.edu
HARGROVE, Tony ... 870-584-1165 .. 22 F
thargrove@cccua.edu
HARGUST, Zenobia ... 610-328-8398 410 I
zhargus1@swarthmore.edu
HARICHANDRAN,
Ronald ... 203-932-7167 .. 89 D
rharichandran@newhaven.edu
HARICOMBE,
Lorraine, J ... 512-495-4350 467 C
ljharic@austin.utexas.edu

HARING, Gayle ... 239-513-1122 101 O
gharing@hodges.edu
HARING, Peter ... 402-399-2332 274 A
pharing@csm.edu
HARKAVY, Ira ... 215-898-5351 412 G
harkavy@upenn.edu
HARKENRIDER, Tom ... 949-480-4091.. 64 D
harkenrider@soka.edu
HARKER, Alan, R ... 801-422-5995 471 E
alan_harker@byu.edu
HARKER, Heather ... 202-651-5005.. 91 H
heather.harker@gallaudet.edu
HARKER, Perry, L ... 252-222-6205 341 F
harkerp@carteret.edu
HARKER, Phillip ... 802-225-3201 475 H
phillip.harker@neci.edu
HARKEY, Betsy ... 940-552-6291 469 F
bharkey@vernoncollege.edu
HARKINS, Anita ... 402-826-8586 274 E
anita.harkins@doane.edu
HARKINS, Brenda ... 405-422-1410 379 B
harkinsb@redlandscc.edu
HARKINS, Dennis ... 714-432-5712.. 38 H
dharkins@occ.cccd.edu
HARKINS,
Gerald (Bob), R ... 512-471-5767 467 C
bharkins@austin.utexas.edu
HARKINS, Vincent ... 202-885-3704.. 91 C
vharkins@american.edu
HARKNESS, Charles ... 440-826-2426 357 B
charkness@bw.edu
HARKNESS, M. Frances 610-902-8546 391 B
mfrances.harkness@cabrini.edu
HARKNESS, Sarah, E ... 423-439-8304 431 H
bradfors@etsu.edu
HARLACHER, Paul ... 850-644-0170 110 A
pharlacher@fsu.edu
HARLAN, Brian ... 661-255-1050.. 29 F
bharlan@calarts.edu
HARLAN, Cathy ... 954-262-5366 104 F
charlan@nova.edu
HARLAN, Mark ... 813-974-1442 111 A
markharlan@usf.edu
HARLAN, Sabrina ... 617-873-0118 213 B
sabrina.harlan@cambridgecollege.edu
HARLAND, Teresa, L ... 218-299-3733 241 K
harland@cord.edu
HARLAND-WHITE,
Faith, A ... 410-777-2961 202 D
faharlandwhite@aacc.edu
HARLANDER, Heidi ... 320-363-2724 241 I
hharlander@csbsju.edu
HARLANDER, Heidi ... 320-363-2724 250 A
hharlander@csbsju.edu
HARLEMAN, Kathleen ... 217-333-6677 154 B
harleman@illinois.edu
HARLESS, Cleta, M ... 304-357-4736 502 E
cletaharless@ucwv.edu
HARLESS, Debra ... 651-638-6371 240 J
d-harless@bethel.edu
HARLESS, Donna ... 704-403-1558 336 B
donna.harless@carolinashealthcare.org
HARLESS, Roberta ... 336-838-6146 347 G
rjharless610@wilkescc.edu
HARLEY, Jay ... 214-333-6812 447 D
jay@dbu.edu
HARLEY, Jeffrey, A ... 401-841-3089 518 E
HARLEY, Joyce, W ... 973-877-4347 285 K
harley@essex.edu
HARLOW, Angie, D ... 770-720-5603 124 H
adh@reinhardt.edu
HARLOW, Debra, B ... 336-322-2157 345 D
debra.harlow@piedmontcc.edu
HARLOW, Renee ... 603-358-2493 283 A
rharlow@keene.edu
HARMAN, Elizabeth ... 619-260-4682.. 71 J
harman@sandiego.edu
HARMAN, Holli ... 276-498-5231 477 L
hharman@acp.edu
HARMAN, Jacob ... 212-960-5241 334 P
jharman@yu.edu
HARMAN, Joany ... 916-608-6622.. 50 H
harmanj@flc.losrios.edu
HARMAN, John ... 504-568-5135 194 C
jharman@lsuhsc.edu
HARMAN, John ... 225-578-2111 193 L
HARMAN, Lisa, F ... 574-372-5100 158 B
harmanlf@grace.edu
HARMAN, William ... 801-878-1403 280 B
wharman@roseman.edu
HARMELINK, Harlan ... 712-722-6082 168 I
harlan.harmelink@dordt.edu
HARMENING, Todd ... 651-201-1856 243 I
todd.harmening@so.mnscu.edu
HARMON, Alison ... 406-994-4133 272 A
harmon@montana.edu
HARMON, Amy ... 619-594-0133.. 34 B
aharmon@mail.sdsu.edu
HARMON, Carolyn, L ... 252-399-6357 335 I
clharmon@barton.edu
HARMON, Cindy, S ... 573-882-2388 268 B
harmonc@umsystem.edu
HARMON, Debra, J ... 217-732-3155 143 G
dharmon@lincolncollege.edu
HARMON, Erica ... 802-447-6319 476 C
eharmon@svc.edu
HARMON, Jason, M ... 920-923-8599 508 B
jmharmon@marianuniversity.edu
HARMON, Jeff ... 208-732-6210 131 I
jharmon@csi.edu
HARMON, Jeff ... 573-651-5910 266 M
jharmon@semo.edu
HARMON, Jeff, S ... 732-255-0400 288 B
jharmon@ocean.edu
HARMON, Justin ... 212-854-7580 299 B
jharmon@barnard.edu
HARMON, Kara ... 801-689-2160 472 C
kharmon@nightingale.edu
HARMON, Kate ... 503-244-0726 381 H
kateharmon@achs.edu
HARMON, Kevin ... 701-858-3299 354 C
kevin.harmon@minotstateu.edu
HARMON, Ladelle ... 828-652-0626 344 G
ladelleh@mcdoweltech.edu
HARMON, LaVerne, T ... 302-356-6818.. 91 B
donna.m.quinn@wilmu.edu
HARMON, Martino ... 515-294-0754 166 F
mharmon@iastate.edu
HARMON, Martino ... 515-294-4420 166 F
mharmon@iastate.edu
HARMON, Melanie, B ... 260-982-5211 162 Q
mbharmon@manchester.edu
HARMON, Monique ... 740-351-3010 369 L
mharmon@shawnee.edu
HARMON, Nathaniel, S . 417-268-6007 257 H
nharmon@gobbc.edu
HARMON, Patricia ... 304-929-5460 503 B
pharmon@newriver.edu
HARMON, Sammi ... 352-338-1193.. 98 G
HARMON, Shirley, K ... 972-758-3800 446 I
sharmon@collin.edu
HARMON, Steve, K ... 956-326-2180 459 B
harmon@tamiu.edu
HARMON, Travis ... 256-766-6610.... 5 K
tharmon@hcu.edu
HARMON, W. Ken ... 470-578-6023 122 C
wharmon3@kennesaw.edu
HARMON FERRY,
Debbie ... 503-883-2607 383 H
dharmon@linfield.edu
HARMON-FRANCIS,
Barbara ... 201-684-7543 289 C
bharmonf@ramapo.edu
HARMS, Brenda ... 715-394-8155 512 B
bharms1@uwsuper.edu
HARMS, Cory, L ... 515-294-8757 166 F
clharms@iastate.edu
HARMS, Dennis ... 708-239-4816 153 B
dennis.harms@trnty.edu
HARMS, Kelli ... 641-585-8143 174 B
kelli.harms@waldorf.edu
HARMS, Mason ... 641-585-8137 174 B
harmsm@waldorf.edu
HARMSEN, Mark ... 254-526-1365 445 L
mark.harmsen@ctcd.edu
HARN, William ... 409-880-8229 462 C
william.harn@lamar.edu
HARNACKE, Jacob ... 217-732-3155 143 G
jharnacke@lincolncollege.edu
HARNDEN, Greg ... 501-279-4305.. 19 G
gharnden@harding.edu
HARNE, George, A ... 603-456-2656 281 H
administration@northeastcatholic.edu
HARNER, Holly ... 215-951-1865 398 F
harner@lasalle.edu
HARNER, Kristy ... 423-614-8110 432 L
kharner@leeuniversity.edu
HARNER, Mike ... 517-607-2303 231 C
mharner@hillsdale.edu
HARNEY, Jake, P ... 770-720-9102 124 H
jph@reinhardt.edu
HARNEY, Malea ... 217-773-4441 143 B
mharney@lakeland.cc.il.us
HARNISH, Eric ... 661-259-7800.. 39 C
eric.harnish@canyons.edu
HARNUM, Donald, P ... 609-896-5054 289 E
harnum@rider.edu
HAROLD, Martin ... 858-653-6740.. 46 M
mharold@jpcatholic.com
HARP, Debbie ... 606-539-4259 190 A
debbie.harp@ucumberlands.edu
HARP, Dillon ... 660-831-4157 264 A
harpd@moval.edu
HARP, Elizabeth, R ... 815-282-7900 150 H
bethharp@sacn.edu
HARP, Jeff ... 405-974-2800 380 J
jharp@uco.edu
HARP, John, W ... 319-895-4234 167 G
jharp@cornellcollege.edu
HARP, Randy ... 903-886-5351 459 E
randy.harp@tamuc.edu
HARP-STEPHENS,
Becky ... 859-246-6498 185 G
becky.harp@kctcs.edu
HARPE, J. Michael ... 410-651-6587 208 C
jmharpe@umes.edu
HARPER, Amy ... 828-286-3636 344 A
aharper@isothermal.edu
HARPER, Betty, J ... 814-863-8721 403 F
bjh17@psu.edu
HARPER, David ... 410-822-5400 203 C
dharper@chesapeake.edu
HARPER, David ... 412-396-5589 394 D
harperd1@duq.edu
HARPER, Deborah ... 607-274-3136 311 D
dharper@ithaca.edu
HARPER, Donna, L ... 540-568-3705 481 I
harperdl@jmu.edu
HARPER, Doreen, C ... 205-934-5360.... 8 B
dcharper@uab.edu
HARPER, E. Royster ... 734-764-5132 237 I
harperer@umich.edu
HARPER, Elizabeth ... 703-323-3459 488 H
eharper@nvcc.edu
HARPER, Heather ... 615-230-3519 438 C
heather.harper@volstate.edu
HARPER, Jimmy ... 423-614-8420 432 L
jharper@leeuniversity.edu
HARPER, Jimmy ... 912-260-4317 125 F
jimmy.harper@sgsc.edu
HARPER, Jimmy ... 912-260-4314 125 F
jimmy.harper@sgsc.edu
HARPER, Joann ... 706-245-7226 119 A
jharper@ec.edu
HARPER, Jonathan ... 617-730-7091 223 B
jonathan.harper@newbury.edu
HARPER, Josh ... 503-255-0332 384 E
jharper@multnomah.edu
HARPER, Karla ... 937-376-6444 358 I
kharper@centralstate.edu
HARPER, Kerry ... 814-641-3353 398 B
harperk@juniata.edu
HARPER, Kimberly, P ... 540-828-5393 478 J
kharper@bridgewater.edu
HARPER, Kristin ... 205-226-4720.... 4 F
kharper@bsc.edu
HARPER, Kyle ... 405-325-3221 380 L
kyleharper@ou.edu
HARPER, Lisa ... 405-974-2553 380 J
lharper@uco.edu
HARPER, Lisa, D ... 859-858-3511 183 D
lisa.harper@asbury.edu
HARPER, Lisa, M ... 903-510-2147 464 D
lhar@tjc.edu
HARPER, Marjoree ... 318-678-6000 192 C
mharper@bpcc.edu
HARPER, Mary, J ... 812-465-1026 165 C
mjharper@usi.edu
HARPER, Norma ... 706-233-7268 125 E
nharper@shorter.edu
HARPER, Pam ... 270-706-8434 185 H
pamela.harper@kctcs.edu
HARPER, Patricia ... 816-654-7162 261 D
pharper@kcumb.edu
HARPER, Randy ... 870-574-4590.. 21 G
rharper@sautech.edu
HARPER, Robert ... 559-278-2482.. 32 A
roberth@csufresno.edu
HARPER, Robert, C ... 972-860-8324 447 I
robertharper@dcccd.edu
HARPER, Rosie ... 601-977-7818 256 B
rharper@tougaloo.edu
HARPER, Sandra ... 325-793-3800 452 F
harper.sandra@mcm.edu
HARPER, Stephany ... 304-462-6171 504 B
stephany.harper@glenville.edu
HARPER, Tameka ... 501-420-1253.. 17 I
tameka.harper@arkansasbaptist.edu
HARPER, Teresa, B ... 502-213-2121 186 C
teresa.harper@kctcs.edu
HARPER, Terry ... 307-778-1185 516 N
tharper@lccc.wy.edu
HARPER, Vernon ... 661-654-3420.. 31 B
vharper@csub.edu
HARPER-MARINICK,
Maria ... 480-731-8100.. 13 D
maria.harper@domail.maricopa.edu
HARPHAM, Edward ... 972-883-6729 467 D
harpham@utdallas.edu
HARPHAM, Jennifer, E ... 330-972-5860 371 C
jharpham@uakron.edu
HARPHAM, Jennifer, E ... 757-822-1360 489 H
jharpham@tcc.edu
HARPIN, Kimberlee ... 815-802-8472 142 C
kharpin@kcc.edu
HARPINE, Annette ... 910-938-6789 342 C
harpinea@coastalcarolina.edu
HARPOLE, Jessica ... 662-329-7352 254 F
jjharpole@muw.edu
HARPOLE, Theresa ... 662-476-5274 253 A
tharpole@eastms.edu
HARPOOL, David ... 928-541-7777.. 54 B
dharpool@ncu.edu
HARPS, Juanita ... 706-821-8339 124 C
jharps@paine.edu
HARPS, Trynette Lottie .. 231-777-0559 234 G
trynette.lottie-harps@muskegoncc.edu
HARPST, Steve ... 845-341-4230 319 H
steve.harpst@sunyorange.edu
HARR, Lois ... 718-862-7142 313 L
lois.harr@manhattan.edu
HARR, Shannon, L ... 606-783-2529 188 C
s.harr@moreheadstate.edu
HARRA, Alice ... 503-517-7421 386 F
harraa@reed.edu
HARRAL, Judy ... 361-825-2495 460 A
judy.harral@tamucc.edu
HARRAL, Kevin ... 650-949-7223.. 43 F
harralkevin@foothill.edu
HARRAL, Nicole, D ... 928-344-7600.. 11 B
nicole.harral@azwestern.edu
HARRELD, Bruce ... 319-335-3549 166 G
HARRELL, III, Alfred, E . 225-771-3911 195 J
alfred_harrell@sus.edu
HARRELL, Autumn ... 941-487-4505 110 B
aharrell@ncf.edu
HARRELL, Brian ... 478-934-3027 123 A
brian.harrell@mga.edu
HARRELL, Bryant, L ... 860-727-6756.. 87 B
bharrell@goodwin.edu
HARRELL, Chalisa ... 252-536-7220 343 F
HARRELL, Evelyn ... 504-286-5234 195 L
eharrell@suno.edu
HARRELL, Frank (Doug) 504-865-5352 196 D
fharrel@tulane.edu
HARRELL, Ivan ... 404-297-9522 120 D
harrelli@gptc.edu
HARRELL, Jerry, H ... 317-921-4447 161 G
jeharrel@ivytech.edu
HARRELL, Jessica ... 336-506-4113 340 L
jessica.harrell@alamancecc.edu
HARRELL, Johnna, C ... 757-822-1191 489 H
jcharrell@tcc.edu
HARRELL, Jonathan ... 757-352-4453 484 E
jonahar@regent.edu
HARRELL, Joseph, H ... 513-558-4635 371 E
joseph.harrell@uc.edu
HARRELL, Kimberly ... 916-691-7390.. 50 G
harrelk@crc.losrios.edu
HARRELL, Lauren ... 229-243-6077 116 C
lauren.harrell@bainbridge.edu
HARRELL, Lee ... 941-359-7532 106 H
lharrell@ringling.edu
HARRELL, Michael ... 718-270-1490 326 A
michael.harrell@downstate.edu
HARRELL, P. Randy ... 252-398-6209 336 K
harrer@chowan.edu
HARRELL, Pamela, J ... 919-209-2048 344 C
pjharrell@johnstoncc.edu
HARRELL, Rex ... 252-398-6273 336 K
rharre@chowan.edu
HARRELL, Shereada ... 850-599-3700 109 A
shereada.harrell@famu.edu
HARRELL, Wanda ... 423-585-6976 438 D
wanda.harrell@ws.edu
HARRELSON, Chris ... 505-566-3284 296 A
harrelsonc@sanjuancollege.edu
HARRELSON, Joshua ... 678-481-8072 124 F
joshua.harrelson@point.edu
HARREYS, M. Seamus .. 617-373-4095 223 D
HARRI, Ed ... 360-383-3230 500 F
eharri@whatcom.ctc.edu
HARRI, Robert ... 563-387-2103 171 I
harrro01@luther.edu
HARRIEL, Mary ... 770-689-4965 115 E
mharriel@aii.edu
HARRIER, Briana, K ... 515-964-0601 169 C
harrierb@faith.edu
HARRIES, Peter, J ... 919-515-1989 350 E
pjharrie@ncsu.edu
HARRIGAN, Tammy ... 401-598-1012 416 C
tharrigan@jwu.edu
HARRIGER, Christine ... 434-947-8344 484 B
charriger@randolphcollege.edu
HARRIGER, Sherill ... 863-638-7235 113 I
sherill.harriger@warner.edu
HARRILL, Thad ... 828-395-1624 344 A
tharrill@isothermal.edu
HARRING, Christopher .. 410-225-2255 205 C
charring@mica.edu

HARRING, Kathleen .... 484-664-3134 402 F
provost's_office@muhlenberg.edu
HARRING-HENDON, Janice, M .... 773-442-4046 147 G
j-harringhendon@neiu.edu
HARRINGTON, Angela .. 973-278-5400 299 F
angela-harringt@berkeleycollege.edu
HARRINGTON, Angela .. 973-278-5400 283 J
angela-harringt@berkeleycollege.edu
HARRINGTON, Anne, E . 603-641-7465 282 A
aharrington@anselm.edu
HARRINGTON, Billie ..... 864-578-8770 423 F
bharrington@sherman.edu
HARRINGTON, Bonnie .. 215-751-8253 393 A
bharrington@ccp.edu
HARRINGTON, Caroline 323-469-3300.. 25 D
charrington@amda.edu
HARRINGTON, Christopher .... 410-651-6083 208 C
cjharrington@umes.edu
HARRINGTON, Daniel, P .... 540-526-2559 491 B
HARRINGTON, David ... 603-641-7020 282 A
dharrington@anselm.edu
HARRINGTON, Donna ... 505-467-6831 296 F
donnaharrington@swc.edu
HARRINGTON, Kim .... 404-894-2499 120 A
kim.harrington@ohr.gatech.edu
HARRINGTON, Kimberly .... 704-216-6151 339 E
kharrington@livingstone.edu
HARRINGTON, L. Katharine .... 213-740-7849.. 72 B
vpap@usc.edu
HARRINGTON, Lynn ..... 708-974-5704 146 C
harrington@morainevalley.edu
HARRINGTON, Melinda 620-276-9514 177 G
melinda.harrington@gcccks.edu
HARRINGTON, Michael . 631-420-2053 329 D
michael.harrington@farmingdale.edu
HARRINGTON, Michael, J .... 415-422-2790.. 72 A
harrington@usfca.edu
HARRINGTON, Robert ... 417-625-3191 263 G
harrington-r@mssu.edu
HARRINGTON, Sean, P . 540-464-7132 490 E
harringtonsp@vmi.edu
HARRINGTON, Shawn, M .... 860-231-5314.. 89 E
sharrington@usj.edu
HARRINGTON, Sherre Lee .... 706-236-2285 116 D
sharrington@berry.edu
HARRINGTON, Thomas . 504-280-1154 194 F
trharrin@uno.edu
HARRINGTON-MARTIN, Angela .... 317-543-3250 162 S
aharrington@martin.edu
HARRIOTT, Danielle ...... 815-965-8616 150 B
dharriot@rockfordcareercollege.edu
HARRIS, Aaron .... 952-829-2411 240 H
aaron.harris@bethfel.org
HARRIS, Alex .... 610-604-7700.. 93 B
HARRIS, Alex .... 208-769-7156 132 E
afharris@nic.edu
HARRIS, Alice .... 304-424-8224 505 C
alice.harris@wvup.edu
HARRIS, Allatia .... 281-459-7140 455 K
allatia.harris@sjcd.edu
HARRIS, Alvin .... 501-370-5284.. 21 A
aharris@philander.edu
HARRIS, Amelia, J .... 276-376-4557 487 A
ajh7a@uvawise.edu
HARRIS, Amy .... 863-667-5060 108 G
ajharris@seu.edu
HARRIS, Andrew .... 415-338-7692.. 34 C
a1harris@sfsu.edu
HARRIS, Angie .... 717-245-1556 394 A
harrisa@dickinson.edu
HARRIS, Anjour .... 804-828-2021 487 E
abharris@vcu.edu
HARRIS, Anna-Lize .... 201-216-5208 291 G
anna-lize.harris@stevens.edu
HARRIS, Anne .... 415-338-6598.. 34 C
aharris@sfsu.edu
HARRIS, Anne .... 765-658-4359 157 H
aharris@depauw.edu
HARRIS, April .... 714-556-3610.. 72 F
april.harris@vanguard.edu
HARRIS, Bennie, L .... 404-752-1955 123 F
bharris@msm.edu
HARRIS, Beryl .... 410-951-6280 208 F
bharris@coppin.edu
HARRIS, Beth .... 203-287-3023.. 87 G
paierartlibrary@snet.net
HARRIS, Bethany, W ..... 434-949-1007 489 E
bethany.harris@southside.edu
HARRIS, Betsy, A .... 207-768-2791 200 B
bharris@nmcc.edu
HARRIS, Beverly .... 620-331-4100 178 E
bharris@indycc.edu
HARRIS, Beverly .... 757-823-2409 483 F
bbharris@nsu.edu
HARRIS, Brent .... 254-295-8642 466 A
bharris@umhb.edu
HARRIS, Brett .... 662-915-1537 256 C
beharris@olemiss.edu
HARRIS, Bruce .... 435-879-4638 473 B
bruce.harris@dixie.edu
HARRIS, JR., Calvin ..... 410-209-6049 202 F
charris@bccc.edu
HARRIS, Carol .... 605-342-0317 427 C
charris@johnwitherspooncollege.org
HARRIS, Carolyn .... 559-325-3600.. 29 D
charris@chsu.org
HARRIS, Charles .... 334-420-4232.... 3 H
charris@trenholmstate.edu
HARRIS, Charles, S ...... 434-791-5701 478 E
csharris@averett.edu
HARRIS, Chelsy .... 719-502-3034.. 81 H
chelsy.harris@ppcc.edu
HARRIS, Chonnea .... 661-726-1911.. 68 E
chonnea.harris@uav.edu
HARRIS, Chris .... 949-214-3169.. 40 I
chris.harris@cui.edu
HARRIS, Chris .... 601-635-2111 252 I
charris@eccc.edu
HARRIS, Christopher ..... 419-434-4347 372 B
harrisc1@findlay.edu
HARRIS, Clarissa .... 828-771-3816 353 B
charris@warren-wilson.edu
HARRIS, Clark .... 307-778-1103 516 N
charris@lccc.wy.edu
HARRIS, Clayton .... 216-987-4425 360 E
clayton.harris@tri-c.edu
HARRIS, Cliff .... 313-664-7403 228 H
charris@collegeforcreativestudies.edu
HARRIS, Craig .... 716-839-8212 306 E
charris@daemen.edu
HARRIS, Craig .... 540-857-7797 490 B
charris@virginiawestern.edu
HARRIS, Darrell, A .... 904-264-2172 106 I
dharris@iws.edu
HARRIS, David .... 805-756-1211.. 30 K
harris@calpoly.edu
HARRIS, David .... 320-308-4866 247 E
djharris@stcloudstate.edu
HARRIS, David .... 718-268-4700 320 K
HARRIS, David .... 843-574-6411 424 G
david.harris@tridenttech.edu
HARRIS, David, P .... 909-558-7600.. 48 H
dpharris@llu.edu
HARRIS, David, R .... 617-627-3310 225 A
david.harris@tufts.edu
HARRIS, David, W .... 505-277-7520 296 H
dwharris@unm.edu
HARRIS, David, W .... 319-273-2470 167 A
david.harris@uni.edu
HARRIS, Debbie .... 804-751-9191 479 F
dharris@ccc-va.com
HARRIS, Delana .... 601-403-1197 255 D
dharris@prcc.edu
HARRIS, Delphia .... 901-435-1380 433 A
delphia_harris@loc.edu
HARRIS, Denise .... 716-926-8727 310 B
dharris@hilbert.edu
HARRIS, Dennis .... 405-422-1283 379 B
harrisd@redlandscc.edu
HARRIS, Derrell .... 912-287-5855 117 J
dharris@coastalpines.edu
HARRIS, Dianne .... 801-581-8816 472 P
dianne.harris@hum.utah.edu
HARRIS, Dina .... 574-520-4131 160 F
dlharris@iusb.edu
HARRIS, Donald .... 303-871-2267.. 83 E
don.harris@du.edu
HARRIS, Elizabeth .... 714-816-0366.. 67 J
elizabeth.harris@trident.edu
HARRIS, Erica .... 606-539-4250 190 A
erica.harris@ucumberlands.edu
HARRIS, Eugenia .... 615-248-1306 439 B
eharris@trevecca.edu
HARRIS, Felicia .... 937-376-6611 358 I
fharris@centralstate.edu
HARRIS, SR., Forrest, E 615-256-1463 429 F
officeofthepresident@abcnash.edu
HARRIS, Fred .... 408-848-4715.. 44 B
fharris@gavilan.edu
HARRIS, G. Duncan .... 860-512-3203.. 85 G
gharris@manchestercc.edu
HARRIS, Gail .... 423-746-5208 439 A
gharris@tnwesleyan.edu
HARRIS, Gary, L .... 202-806-2550.. 92 C
gharris@howard.edu
HARRIS, Gary, L .... 202-806-6800.. 92 C
gharris@howard.edu
HARRIS, Gheretta .... 231-591-3947 230 A
gherettaharris@ferris.edu
HARRIS, Greg .... 770-426-2836 122 F
gharris@life.edu
HARRIS, Greg .... 602-275-7133.. 16 A
greg.harris@rsiaz.edu
HARRIS, Greg .... 503-584-7153 382 C
greg.harris@chemeketa.edu
HARRIS, Helen .... 225-216-8287 192 B
harrish@mybrcc.edu
HARRIS, Hubert, D .... 804-524-1085 491 A
hharris@vsu.edu
HARRIS, Jacob .... 251-981-3771.... 5 A
jacob.harris@columbiasouthern.edu
HARRIS, Jacqueline .... 860-832-1945.. 84 J
jharris@ccsu.edu
HARRIS, James .... 731-352-4200 430 E
harrisj@bethelu.edu
HARRIS, James .... 903-593-8311 461 B
jharris@texascollege.edu
HARRIS, James, T .... 619-260-4520.. 71 J
president@sandiego.edu
HARRIS, Janette .... 530-938-5500.. 39 H
jharris6@siskiyous.edu
HARRIS, Jean .... 941-487-4570 110 B
jharris@ncf.edu
HARRIS, Jennifer, K ...... 802-626-6458 477 D
jennifer.harris@lyndonstate.edu
HARRIS, Jesse .... 208-459-5222 131 H
jharris@collegeofidaho.edu
HARRIS, Jesse .... 864-225-7653 421 G
jesseharris@forrestcollege.edu
HARRIS, Jewell .... 601-979-1773 253 E
jewell.e.harris@jsums.edu
HARRIS, Jim, C .... 770-216-2960 121 J
jharris@ict.edu
HARRIS, John .... 515-961-1626 173 E
john.harris@simpson.edu
HARRIS, John .... 601-635-2111 252 I
jharris@eccc.edu
HARRIS, John .... 518-244-4582 321 G
harrisj8@sage.edu
HARRIS, John .... 903-923-2181 448 J
jharris@etbu.edu
HARRIS, Joshua .... 252-246-1257 347 H
jharris@wilsoncc.edu
HARRIS, Judy .... 760-744-1150.. 55 K
jharris@palomar.edu
HARRIS, Kandace .... 919-546-8334 348 I
kharris@shawu.edu
HARRIS, Kara .... 812-237-3166 159 C
kara.harris@indstate.edu
HARRIS, Kathleen .... 636-481-3488 261 B
kharri14@jeffco.edu
HARRIS, Kelly .... 904-680-7700.. 99 C
HARRIS, Kendall, T .... 936-261-9900 458 F
ktharris@pvamu.edu
HARRIS, Kim .... 662-720-7193 255 B
kkharris@nemcc.edu
HARRIS, Kim .... 865-882-4695 438 A
harriskb@roanestate.edu
HARRIS, Kip, B .... 208-496-9200 131 D
harrisk@byui.edu
HARRIS, Kristi .... 660-357-6203 264 H
kharris@mail.ncmissouri.edu
HARRIS, Kristin .... 940-855-2203 469 F
kharris@vernoncollege.edu
HARRIS, Lakeisha, L ..... 410-651-6507 208 C
llharris@umes.edu
HARRIS, Lamel .... 408-288-3736.. 61 P
lamel.harris@sjcc.edu
HARRIS, Liesl, W .... 205-853-1200.... 2 F
lwharris@jeffersonstate.edu
HARRIS, Lisa .... 763-433-1292 243 K
lisa.harris@anokaramsey.edu
HARRIS, Lori .... 757-233-8786 491 F
lharris@vwu.edu
HARRIS, Marc .... 717-867-6077 399 J
harris@lvc.edu
HARRIS, Mark .... 609-586-4800 287 A
harrisma@mccc.edu
HARRIS, Mark .... 336-454-1126 343 E
meharris@gtcc.edu
HARRIS, Mark, T .... 414-229-8417 511 A
mtharris@uwm.edu
HARRIS, Martha .... 785-594-8338 174 J
martha.harris@bakeru.edu
HARRIS, Marty .... 626-968-1328.. 48 A
HARRIS, Mary .... 317-931-4440 157 D
mharris@cts.edu
HARRIS, Mary, E .... 512-223-7705 443 G
mharris3@austincc.edu
HARRIS, Matthew .... 417-447-8290 264 K
harrism@otc.edu
HARRIS, Maurice, A ...... 315-443-4734 330 H
maharr17@syr.edu
HARRIS, Mel .... 703-812-4757 482 B
mharris@leland.edu
HARRIS, Melissa, D ...... 716-880-3368 314 F
melissa.d.harris@medaille.edu
HARRIS, Melvin .... 256-726-7374.... 6 E
mharris@oakwood.edu
HARRIS, Michael .... 715-425-3774 511 E
michael.harris@uwrf.edu
HARRIS, Molly .... 903-463-8700 449 J
harrism@grayson.edu
HARRIS, Nancy .... 323-856-7600.. 25 L
nharris@afi.com
HARRIS, Nick, L .... 504-816-4704 191 E
nharris@dillard.edu
HARRIS, Nykkia .... 405-466-3257 375 L
nlharris@langston.edu
HARRIS, Patricia .... 662-252-8000 255 F
pharris@rustcollege.edu
HARRIS, Patricia .... 616-988-3624 232 F
pharris@kuyper.edu
HARRIS, Patrick .... 406-447-4380 270 H
pharris@carroll.edu
HARRIS, Patty .... 651-290-6358 248 U
patty.harris@mitchellhamline.edu
HARRIS, Paul .... 585-475-4992 321 D
pahdar@rit.edu
HARRIS, Paul, C .... 757-727-6165 481 E
paul.harris@hamptonu.edu
HARRIS, Perry .... 205-853-1200.... 2 F
pharris3@jeffersonstate.edu
HARRIS, Peter .... 860-512-3213.. 85 G
pharris@manchestercc.edu
HARRIS, Philip, L .... 847-467-6270 148 C
phil.harris@northwestern.edu
HARRIS, Randall .... 601-857-3363 253 B
randall.harris@hindscc.edu
HARRIS, Randy .... 814-866-8416 399 C
rharris@lecom.edu
HARRIS, Renard .... 843-953-5079 420 C
harrisr@cofc.edu
HARRIS, Rhonda, L .... 757-683-4007 483 G
rlharris@odu.edu
HARRIS, Richard .... 479-508-3310.. 18 G
rharris1@atu.edu
HARRIS, Richard, C ...... 516-671-2215 333 E
rharris@webb.edu
HARRIS, Rob .... 417-328-1827 267 A
rharris@sbuniv.edu
HARRIS, Robin .... 252-335-0821 342 D
robin_harris@albemarle.edu
HARRIS, Rotesha .... 404-880-6917 117 H
rharris@cau.edu
HARRIS, Sandra .... 734-995-7309 229 A
sandra.harris@cuaa.edu
HARRIS, Scott .... 309-298-1949 155 D
sd-harris@wiu.edu
HARRIS, Sedwick .... 610-861-4558 403 B
sharris@northampton.edu
HARRIS, Shanel .... 702-579-3527 278 H
shanel.harris@brightwood.edu
HARRIS, Shari .... 217-641-4532 141 F
sharris@jwcc.edu
HARRIS, Sharlene, J ..... 340-693-1361 529 C
sharris@uvi.edu
HARRIS, Skip .... 802-651-5961 474 G
sharris@champlain.edu
HARRIS, Stephen, A ...... 615-248-1245 439 B
sharris@trevecca.edu
HARRIS, Steve .... 301-548-5500.. 93 B
HARRIS, Steven .... 814-393-2225 405 H
harris@clarion.edu
HARRIS, Susan, G .... 434-924-7120 486 H
sgh4c@virginia.edu
HARRIS, Suzann .... 615-248-1201 439 B
sharris3@trevecca.edu
HARRIS, Tara .... 864-941-8525 423 C
harris.t@ptc.edu
HARRIS, Terral .... 912-279-5726 118 A
tharris@ccga.edu
HARRIS, Terrance .... 805-756-2767.. 30 K
tharris@calpoly.edu
HARRIS, Terrance .... 936-294-1325 462 F
tjharris@shsu.edu
HARRIS, Terrence .... 315-786-2238 311 H
tharris@sunyjefferson.edu
HARRIS, Thomas, W ...... 859-257-1933 190 B
tom.harris@uky.edu
HARRIS, Tieka .... 201-360-4180 286 E
tharris@hccc.edu
HARRIS, Todd, D .... 910-630-7155 340 A
toharris@methodist.edu
HARRIS, Tonya .... 870-838-2913.. 17 K
tharris@smail.anc.edu
HARRIS, Tosca .... 620-365-5116 174 G
harris@allencc.edu
HARRIS, Tracy .... 240-725-5300 203 D
tracy.harris@csmd.edu

HARRIS, Travaris .... 847-925-6673 139 B tharris@harpercollege.edu
HARRIS, Tretha .... 214-429-3900.. 93 B
HARRIS, Tretha .... 972-773-8300.. 93 B
HARRIS, Tretha .... 972-535-3700.. 93 B
HARRIS, Wayne .... 757-727-5071 481 E wayne.harris@hamptonu.edu
HARRIS, Wendy .... 410-462-7407 202 F wharris@bccc.edu
HARRIS, Wesley .... 314-516-7192 268 E harriswr@umsl.edu
HARRIS, Wilma, K .... 479-979-1215.. 23 J wkharris@ozarks.edu
HARRIS, Yolanda .... 719-502-4689.. 81 H yolanda.harris@ppcc.edu
HARRIS-BRACKETT, Betsy .... 770-962-7580 121 G bharris@gwinnetttech.edu
HARRIS-CALDWELL, Jeanne .... 949-582-4607.. 64 J jharriscaldwell@saddleback.edu
HARRIS COHEN, David .. 626-264-8880.. 71 A
HARRIS-DUFF, Joanne .. 540-828-5749 478 J jharris-duff@bridgewater.edu
HARRIS-JOLLY, Stephanie .... 229-903-3610 114 I stephanie.harris-jolly@asurams.edu
HARRIS KISUNZU, Cheryl .... 301-891-4116 209 E charris@wau.edu
HARRIS-MATHEWS, Colette .... 916-691-7170.. 50 G harriscl@crc.losrios.edu
HARRIS PAOLILLO, Linda .... 212-752-1530 312 G linda.harris@limcollege.edu
HARRIS-RANSOM, Lori . 732-255-0400 288 B lharris-ransom@ocean.edu
HARRIS-SNYDER, April . 570-459-1573 399 A snydera@lackawanna.edu
HARRISON, Andolyn ..... 318-274-2549 196 G harrisonan@gram.edu
HARRISON, Angela .... 757-823-2037 483 F sm505@bncollege.com
HARRISON, Antione ...... 518-381-1449 323 L harrisaw@sunysccc.edu
HARRISON, B. Timothy . 618-537-6962 145 C btharrison@mckendree.edu
HARRISON, Bob .... 526-947-8755.. 65 D bobharrison@scuhs.edu
HARRISON, Brian .... 334-683-2313.... 3 A bharrison@marionmilitary.edu
HARRISON, Carol .... 301-934-7552 203 D carolh@csmd.edu
HARRISON, Charles ...... 918-825-4678 378 B charles.harrison10@okstate.edu
HARRISON, Cheryl .... 718-862-7862 313 L cheryl.harrison@manhattan.edu
HARRISON, Chris .... 615-230-3352 438 C christopher.harrison@volstate.edu
HARRISON, Christopher 252-940-6444 340 N chris.harrison@beaufortccc.edu
HARRISON, Crystal .... 920-498-5541 514 G crystal.harrison@nwtc.edu
HARRISON, Cynthia, F .. 914-968-6200 323 C
HARRISON, David .... 336-770-3273 352 B harrisondl@uncsa.edu
HARRISON, David, T ..... 614-287-2402 360 C dth@cscc.edu
HARRISON, Debra .... 304-326-1559 502 D debra.harrison@salemu.edu
HARRISON, Dianne, F ... 818-677-2121.. 33 B dianne.harrison@csun.edu
HARRISON, Earnestine .. 480-517-8381.. 14 B earnestine.harrison@riosalado.edu
HARRISON, Elise .... 617-824-8595 214 E elise_harrison@emerson.edu
HARRISON, Faimous .... 209-513-9403.. 33 F fharrison@csustan.edu
HARRISON, Fiona .... 626-395-6601.. 29 I fiona@srl.caltech.edu
HARRISON, Hope, A ..... 717-780-2547 396 G haharris@hacc.edu
HARRISON, Janice .... 508-565-1096 224 H jharrison@stonehill.edu
HARRISON, Jim .... 478-553-2108 123 H jharrison@oftc.edu
HARRISON, Jim, H .... 920-206-2327 508 A jim.harrison@mbu.edu
HARRISON, Justin .... 858-513-9240.. 26 T justin.harrison@ashford.edu
HARRISON, Kathy, L ..... 417-268-1026 257 F harrisonk@evangel.edu
HARRISON, Kelly, G ..... 904-620-1707 110 E n00874366@unf.edu
HARRISON, Kenneth ..... 334-291-4963.... 1 H kenneth.harrison@cv.edu
HARRISON, Kim, W ...... 931-363-9876 433 E kharrison@martinmethodist.edu
HARRISON, Lee .... 423-461-8719 435 A lharrison@milligan.edu
HARRISON, Lonnie .... 575-492-2168 297 G lharrison@usw.edu
HARRISON, M. Blake .... 270-852-3460 187 F bharrison@kwc.edu
HARRISON, Malou .... 305-237-1152 103 L mharriso@mdc.edu
HARRISON, Mark .... 360-475-7700 496 F mharrison@olympic.edu
HARRISON, Melissa ...... 903-434-8122 453 M mharrison@ntcc.edu
HARRISON, Melvin .... 225-743-8500 193 C mharrison@rpcc.edu
HARRISON, Merrell, J ... 606-783-2035 188 C m.harrison@moreheadstate.edu
HARRISON, Merrilou ..... 509-865-0712 495 D harrison_m@heritage.edu
HARRISON, Michael, C . 517-321-0242 231 A mharrison@glcc.edu
HARRISON, Nancy .... 530-541-4660.. 47 I harrison@ltcc.edu
HARRISON, Rodney, A .. 816-414-3700 263 D rharrison@mbts.edu
HARRISON, Ryan .... 313-664-7678 228 H rharrison@collegeforcreativestudies.edu
HARRISON, Sandra .... 310-506-6500.. 56 D sandra.k.harrison@pepperdine.edu
HARRISON, Sara .... 937-229-2641 372 A sharrison1@udayton.edu
HARRISON, Scot .... 360-438-8808 497 F sharrison@stmartin.edu
HARRISON, Scott .... 219-464-5335 165 D scott.harrison@valpo.edu
HARRISON, Shannon .... 516-877-3486 297 I sharrison@adelphi.edu
HARRISON, Shawn .... 240-567-4292 205 F shawn.harrison@montgomerycollege.edu
HARRISON, Steve .... 843-349-6405 420 A harrison@coastal.edu
HARRISON, Suzan .... 727-864-8212.. 97 O harrisms@eckerd.edu
HARRISON, Tammiko .... 601-979-2345 253 E tammiko.l.harrison@jsums.edu
HARRISON, Teresa .... 256-331-5215.... 3 C teresah@nwscc.edu
HARRISON, Teresa .... 757-925-6782 489 B tharrison@pdc.edu
HARRISON, Tim .... 805-289-6121.. 73 C tharrison@vcccd.edu
HARRISON, Tracey .... 601-925-3239 254 B tharriso@mc.edu
HARRISON, W. Darryl ... 706-385-1098 124 F darryl.harrison@point.edu
HARRISON, Wendy .... 757-569-6792 489 B wharrison@pdc.edu
HARRISON-MERCER, Sheryl, E .... 678-916-2681 115 K sharrison@johnmarshall.edu
HARRISON-TAYLOR, Tiffany .... 503-760-3131 381 J tiffany@birthingway.edu
HARRISS, Frankie .... 691-320-2480 519 G frankieh@comfsm.fm
HARROD, Joseph, C ..... 502-897-4215 189 A jharrod@sbts.edu
HARROLD, Cindy .... 620-429-3896 176 K harrold.cindy@coffeyville.edu
HARROLD, Frank .... 801-626-6232 473 E frankharrold@weber.edu
HARROZ, JR., Joseph .. 405-325-4702 380 L jharroz@ou.edu
HARSHBARGER, Beth .... 612-343-4464 249 E bharshbarger@northcentral.edu
HARSHBARGER, Bruce .. 478-445-5169 119 E bruce.harshbarger@gcsu.edu
HARSHBARGER, John ... 440-775-8470 367 B john.harshbarger@oberlin.edu
HARSHMAN, Cheryl, R . 304-336-8035 504 E harshmac@westliberty.edu
HARSHMAN, Cris .... 828-254-1921 340 M charshman@abtech.edu
HART, Aaron .... 317-274-7200 160 E aarohart@iupui.edu
HART, Anne .... 239-280-1669.. 95 C anne.hart@avemaria.edu
HART, Brad .... 912-538-3121 126 A brhart@southeasterntech.edu
HART, Charlene .... 775-784-4040 279 E crhart@unr.edu
HART, Charles .... 601-643-8358 252 G charles.hart@colin.edu
HART, Chris .... 502-585-9911 189 B chart@spalding.edu
HART, Chris .... 410-837-5739 209 D chart@ubalt.edu
HART, Christi .... 503-491-6961 384 D christi.hart@mhcc.edu
HART, Christina .... 772-462-4702 101 Q chart@irsc.edu
HART, Christopher .... 207-255-1403 201 F christopher.hart1@maine.edu
HART, Craig, H .... 801-422-3567 471 E craig_hart@byu.edu
HART, Deanna .... 562-860-2451.. 36 A dhart@cerritos.edu
HART, Debra .... 304-696-2597 504 C hart70@marshall.edu
HART, Emily .... 518-243-4381 299 E harte@ellismedicine.org
HART, Erick .... 585-395-2579 326 D ehart@brockport.edu
HART, Eyvonne .... 912-486-7784 123 J ehart@ogeecheetech.edu
HART, George .... 978-934-4556 217 B george_hart@uml.edu
HART, James, R .... 904-264-2172 106 I president@iws.edu
HART, James, T .... 804-862-6100 484 F jhart@rbc.edu
HART, Jan .... 501-686-6751.. 22 C hartjank@uams.edu
HART, Jeni .... 573-884-1402 268 C hartjl@missouri.edu
HART, Jennifer, L .... 717-871-7001 407 A jennifer.hart@millersville.edu
HART, Jill .... 914-674-7362 314 I jhart2@mercy.edu
HART, Jimmy, W .... 615-898-5131 434 H jimmy.hart@mtsu.edu
HART, John .... 937-766-4898 358 D johnhart@cedarville.edu
HART, Jon .... 605-995-2152 427 A johart1@dwu.edu
HART, Joy .... 502-852-6976 190 C jlhart01@louisville.edu
HART, Julie .... 315-498-2214 319 G hartj@sunyocc.edu
HART, Karen .... 248-218-2011 236 C khart@rc.edu
HART, Kathleen .... 209-954-5018.. 61 B khart@deltacollege.edu
HART, Kathy .... 660-562-1192 264 I juliah@nwmissouri.edu
HART, Kelly .... 413-572-8519 218 F khart@westfield.ma.edu
HART, Kristin .... 718-409-7236 329 E khart@sunymaritime.edu
HART, Kristy .... 916-608-6993.. 50 H hartk@flc.losrios.edu
HART, LaToya .... 601-877-2336 251 G lhart@alcorn.edu
HART, Mary Ann .... 973-761-9365 291 F maryann.hart@shu.edu
HART, Michael .... 207-741-5500 200 C mhart@smccme.edu
HART, Mickey .... 614-222-3294 360 B mhart@ccad.edu
HART, Peter, L .... 978-232-2058 214 G lehart@endicott.edu
HART, Richard, H .... 909-558-4540.. 48 H rhart@llu.edu
HART, Richard, L .... 214-768-4301 457 B rlhart@smu.edu
HART, Sara .... 724-805-2064 410 B sara.hart@stvincent.edu
HART, Susan .... 615-343-2388 440 D susan.hart@vanderbilt.edu
HART, Thomas .... 412-396-6002 394 D hartt1@duq.edu
HART, Tim .... 316-978-6192 182 F tim.hart@wichita.edu
HART, Trois, K .... 260-399-7700 165 B thart@sf.edu
HART RUTHENBECK, Robin .... 740-427-5136 364 A hartruthenbeck1@kenyon.edu
HART-STEFFES, Jeanne, S .... 413-782-1282 225 F jeanne.hart-steffes@wne.edu
HART-THORE, Dawn ...... 504-278-6332 193 B dhart@nunez.edu
HARTE WEYANT, Meghan .... 407-646-2599 106 J mweyant@rollins.edu
HARTENBURG, Gary ...... 281-649-3630 450 C ghartenburg@hbu.edu
HARTER, Christina .... 425-739-8225 495 F chris.harter@lwtech.edu
HARTER, Donald, L .... 315-792-3191 332 H dharter@utica.edu
HARTER, Jill .... 314-367-8700 266 D jill.harter@stlcop.edu
HARTER, Kris .... 937-298-3399 364 B kris.harter@kc.edu
HARTER, Michelle .... 912-583-3245 116 G mharter@bpc.edu
HARTER, Seth .... 802-258-9293 475 D sharter@marlboro.edu
HARTFORD, Darren, E ... 202-685-4337 518 B darren.hartford@ndu.edu
HARTFORD, Paul .... 952-829-4180 240 H paul.hartford@bethfel.org
HARTFORD, Sharon, M . 509-527-4323 499 E sharon.hartford@wwcc.edu
HARTFORD, Stephanie .. 608-985-2828 141 D stephaniehartford@jalc.edu
HARTFORD, Theresa ..... 952-829-4189 240 H theresa.hartford@bethfel.org
HARTGE, Gary .... 352-395-5835 107 E gary.hartge@sfcollege.edu
HARTGRAVES, Stan .... 949-398-2358.. 73 K shartgraves@westcoastuniversity.edu
HARTHORN, Karen, M .. 651-962-6353 251 D kmharthorn@stthomas.edu
HARTIG, Elizabeth .... 734-995-7314 229 A elizabeth.hartig@cuaa.edu
HARTIGAN, William, J .. 401-865-2166 416 E hartigan@providence.edu
HARTING, Troy, R .... 719-333-9751 518 H
HARTING, William .... 317-955-6016 162 R bharting@marian.edu
HARTING, William .... 317-955-6015 162 R bharting@marian.edu
HARTKE, Emily .... 217-234-5430 143 B ehartke@lakeland.cc.il.us
HARTL, Derek .... 563-387-1433 171 I hartde01@luther.edu
HARTL, Renae .... 563-387-1244 171 I hartre01@luther.edu
HARTLAUB, Mark .... 361-825-2659 460 A mark.hartlaub@tamucc.edu
HARTLESS, Megan .... 540-453-2209 487 G hartlessm@brcc.edu
HARTLEY, Brian .... 618-664-6821 139 A brian.hartley@greenville.edu
HARTLEY, Christina .... 401-454-6794 417 B chartley@risd.edu
HARTLEY, Dale .... 304-424-8253 505 C dale.hartley@wvup.edu
HARTLEY, Greg, L .... 916-348-4689.. 42 F ghartley@epic.edu
HARTLEY, Kelley .... 260-481-6643 160 D hartleyk@ipfw.edu
HARTLEY, Laura .... 503-554-2143 383 C lhartley@georgefox.edu
HARTLEY, Lorraine .... 216-987-2424 360 E lorraine.hartley@tri-c.edu
HARTLEY, Rick .... 262-646-6547 509 C rhartley@nashotah.edu
HARTLEY, Roger .... 410-837-5210 209 D rhartley@ubalt.edu
HARTLEY, Toni, R .... 724-439-4900 399 H thartley@laurel.edu
HARTLINE, Beverly .... 406-496-4456 272 E bhartline@mtech.edu
HARTLINE, Michael .... 850-644-4405 110 A mhartline@cob.fsu.edu
HARTMAN, Alexander, M .... 508-373-9435 211 F alexander.hartman@becker.edu
HARTMAN, Barbara, A .. 570-577-3218 390 H barbara.hartman@bucknell.edu
HARTMAN, Brandi, P .... 864-488-4604 422 B bhartman@limestone.edu
HARTMAN, Brian .... 509-525-2694 499 F brian.hartman@wallawalla.edu
HARTMAN, Bryan, G ..... 518-564-2280 327 E hartmabg@plattsburgh.edu
HARTMAN, Cathy .... 940-565-3025 466 B cathy.hartman@unt.edu
HARTMAN, Chris, T ...... 215-885-2360 401 A chartman@manor.edu
HARTMAN, Christine .... 717-796-1800 401 L chartman@messiah.edu
HARTMAN, Cynthia .... 740-389-4636 365 B hartmanc@mtc.edu
HARTMAN, Dean, A ...... 706-880-8246 122 D dhartman@lagrange.edu
HARTMAN, Eric .... 931-598-1443 436 A ehartman@sewanee.edu
HARTMAN, Fritz .... 574-535-7423 158 A fritzdh@goshen.edu
HARTMAN, Jackie, L ..... 785-532-6221 179 A jlh1980@ksu.edu
HARTMAN, Joel, L .... 407-823-6778 110 C joel.hartman@ucf.edu
HARTMAN, Joseph .... 978-934-2576 217 B joseph_hartman@uml.edu

HARTMAN, Joseph .... 972-825-4774 457 F
jhartman@sagu.edu
HARTMAN, Karen .... 949-794-9090.. 66 B
khartman@stanbridge.edu
HARTMAN, Kimberly ..... 727-712-5876 107 A
hartman.kimberly@spcollege.edu
HARTMAN, Laurie .... 315-792-7400 330 A
laurie.hartman@sunyit.edu
HARTMAN, Nathan .... 859-344-3602 189 G
nathan.hartman@thomasmore.edu
HARTMAN, Phil .... 817-257-7727 461 A
p.hartman@tcu.edu
HARTMAN, Rob .... 803-754-4100 420 E
HARTMAN, Robin .... 714-879-3901.. 45 I
rhartman@hiu.edu
HARTMAN, Sherry, L .... 208-467-8588 132 F
slhartman@nnu.edu
HARTMAN, Stephanie ... 304-358-2000 501 I
stephanie@future.edu
HARTMAN, Thomas ...... 336-506-4201 340 L
thomas.hartman@alamancecc.edu
HARTMAN, Tracy .... 804-204-1214 478 F
thartman@btsr.edu
HARTMAN, Virginia .... 215-368-5000 389 H
vhartman@biblical.edu
HARTMANN, Angela ...... 361-570-4374 465 D
hartmanna@uhv.edu
HARTMANN, Bruce .... 630-466-7900 155 C
bhartmann@waubonsee.edu
HARTMANN,
Gretchen, L .... 605-336-6588 428 B
ghartmann@sfseminary.edu
HARTMANN, Marc .... 203-285-2622.. 85 E
mhartmann@gwcc.commnet.edu
HARTMANN, Patricia ..... 414-382-6072 506 A
pat.hartmann@alverno.edu
HARTMANN, Richard .... 714-992-7044.. 54 A
rhartmann@fullcoll.edu
HARTMANN, Wendy ...... 636-584-6712 259 L
wendy.hartmann@eastcentral.edu
HARTMANN-TURNER,
Donna .... 425-235-2352 497 E
dhartmann-turner@rtc.edu
HARTNETT, David .... 231-348-6603 234 H
dhartnett@ncmich.edu
HARTNETT, Erin .... 716-888-2711 300 G
hartnete@canisius.edu
HARTNETT, Ryan .... 716-896-0700 333 C
hartnettr@villa.edu
HARTO, Diana, L .... 304-336-8139 504 E
diana.harto@westliberty.edu
HARTOG, John .... 712-324-5066 172 E
jhartog@nwicc.edu
HARTOG, Paul, A .... 515-964-0601 169 C
hartogp@faith.edu
HARTON, Mary Kay ...... 928-344-7580.. 11 B
marykay.harton@azwestern.edu
HARTS, Melissa, L .... 727-816-3466 105 C
hartsm@phsc.edu
HARTS, Stanley, H .... 910-962-3057 352 A
hartss@uncw.edu
HARTSELL, Angela .... 239-489-9427 100 E
ahartsell1@fsw.edu
HARTSELL, Skip .... 501-450-1348.. 19 I
hartsell@hendrix.edu
HARTSHORN, Tricia .... 620-242-0441 179 G
hartshot@mcpherson.edu
HARTSOCK, Michael ...... 217-424-6265 145 J
mhartsock@millikin.edu
HARTSOE, Janice .... 864-644-5538 424 B
jhartsoe@swu.edu
HARTSON, Michelle ...... 931-431-9700 435 E
mhartson@nci.edu
HARTUNG, Jason .... 661-362-2207.. 51 C
jhartung@masters.edu
HARTUNIAN, Sharon ..... 413-528-7350 211 B
shartunian@simons-rock.edu
HARTWELL, John .... 435-797-2060 473 C
john.hartwell@usu.edu
HARTWELL, Stephanie ... 617-287-6529 216 I
stephanie.hartwell@umb.edu
HARTZ, James .... 270-686-4630 186 F
jim.hartz@kctcs.edu
HARTZ, Jason .... 517-264-7149 236 I
jhartz@sienaheights.edu
HARTZ, Ronald, G .... 671-735-5555 519 H
ronald.hartz@guamcc.edu
HARTZEL, Ruth Ann ...... 724-847-5673 395 J
rhartzel@geneva.edu
HARTZELL, Jay, C .... 512-471-5058 467 C
dean.hartzell@mccombs.utexas.edu
HARTZLER, Christi .... 407-823-4663 110 C
christi.hartzler@ucf.edu
HARTZLER, Murray, G ... 843-661-1237 421 H
mhartzler@fmarion.edu
HARVEL, Kathryn .... 816-654-7285 261 D
kharvel@kcumb.edu

HARVEY, Addie .... 901-435-1704 433 A
addie_harvey@loc.edu
HARVEY, Amy, R .... 718-990-5076 322 F
goodmana@stjohns.edu
HARVEY, Barron, H .... 202-806-1500.. 92 C
bharvey@howard.edu
HARVEY, Bev .... 402-437-2554 276 K
bharvey@southeast.edu
HARVEY, Binti .... 909-607-9665.. 63 F
bharvey@scrippscollege.edu
HARVEY, Bryan, C .... 413-545-6238 216 H
harvey@chancellor.umass.edu
HARVEY, Cameron .... 901-381-3939 440 I
cameron@visible.edu
HARVEY, Chad .... 605-995-2830 427 A
chharvey@dwu.edu
HARVEY, Diana .... 510-642-6436.. 68 G
dharvey@berkeley.edu
HARVEY, Diana .... 801-957-4278 474 B
diana.harvey@slcc.edu
HARVEY, George .... 919-761-2203 349 C
harvey@sebts.edu
HARVEY, John .... 870-460-1058.. 22 D
harveyj@uamont.edu
HARVEY, John .... 803-754-4100 420 E
HARVEY, Katie .... 304-345-2820 505 D
kharvey@wvjc.edu
HARVEY, Kem .... 864-592-4795 424 C
harveyk@sccsc.edu
HARVEY, Kimberly .... 585-245-5571 327 B
harvey@geneseo.edu
HARVEY, Kimberly .... 636-481-3200 261 B
kharvey@jeffco.edu
HARVEY, Laurie .... 516-686-7711 317 G
lharve05@nyit.edu
HARVEY, Linda .... 718-780-0382 300 A
linda.harvey@brooklaw.edu
HARVEY, Lydia .... 907-564-8218.... 9 F
lydiah@alaskapacific.edu
HARVEY, Marcus .... 816-604-4121 262 K
marcus.harvey@mcckc.edu
HARVEY, Melissa .... 715-682-1674 509 D
mharvey@northland.edu
HARVEY, Monica .... 712-279-3112 173 B
monica.harvey@stlukescollege.edu
HARVEY, Peter, W .... 509-527-5145 500 G
harvey@whitman.edu
HARVEY, Richard, C ...... 304-367-4395 504 A
richard.harvey@fairmontstate.edu
HARVEY, Roberta .... 856-256-5140 289 H
harvey@rowan.edu
HARVEY, Ryan, D .... 740-826-8051 366 C
harvey@muskingum.edu
HARVEY, Sally .... 480-858-9100.. 16 D
s.harvey@scnm.edu
HARVEY, Sarah, J .... 260-359-4010 159 B
sharvey@huntington.edu
HARVEY, Scott .... 864-646-1556 424 F
sharvey@tctc.edu
HARVEY, Shannon, S .... 717-339-3503 396 G
ssharvey@hacc.edu
HARVEY, Stephen .... 212-731-3419 311 A
stephen.harvey@mssm.edu
HARVEY, Stewart, A .... 207-581-2668 201 B
stewarth@maine.edu
HARVEY, Stu .... 405-682-7849 377 C
sharvey@occc.edu
HARVEY, William, R ...... 757-727-5231 481 E
presidentsoffice@hamptonu.edu
HARVEY-LIVINGSTON,
Kim .... 903-566-7197 468 C
klivingston@uttyler.edu
HARVEY-SAHAK,
Judy, B .... 909-621-8973.. 63 F
judy.sahak@scrippscollege.edu
HARVEY-SMITH, Alicia .. 832-813-6648 452 C
alicia.harvey-smith@lonestar.edu
HARVILLE, Beth .... 417-873-4085 259 G
bharville@drury.edu
HARVIN, Lillian .... 510-869-8785.. 59 F
lharvin@samuelmerritt.edu
HARVIN, Peter .... 864-231-2000 418 E
pharvin@andersonuniversity.edu
HARVISON,
Mary Catherine .... 318-795-2400 194 E
mary.harvison@lsus.edu
HARWARD, Brian .... 814-332-3027 388 F
bharward@allegheny.edu
HARWARD, Sherry .... 801-863-6813 473 D
sherry.harward@uvu.edu
HARWELL, Neal .... 870-248-4000.. 18 J
neal.harwell@blackrivertech.edu
HARWOOD, Gina .... 718-960-8245 302 C
gina.harwood@lehman.cuny.edu
HARWOOD, Melissa .... 802-831-1339 476 G
mharwood@vermontlaw.edu
HARWOOD, Mike .... 541-346-8267 387 F
maharwoo@uoregon.edu

HARWOOD, Scott .... 518-891-2915 319 A
sharwood@nccc.edu
HASAN, Abul .... 918-293-4809 378 B
abul.hasan@okstate.edu
HASAN, Nash .... 704-461-6257 335 J
nashhasan@bac.edu
HASAN, Zia .... 803-535-5219 419 E
hasan@claflin.edu
HASELDEN, Gregory, W 864-379-8812 421 E
haselden@erskine.edu
HASELHORST, Christina 620-227-9541 176 N
chaselhorst@dc3.edu
HASELOFF, Gregory, K .. 859-858-3511 183 D
greg.haseloff@asbury.edu
HASENKAMP,
Mindy-Kate .... 503-255-0332 384 E
mhasenkamp@multnomah.edu
HASENPFLUG, Cathy ..... 406-994-4284 272 A
catherine.hasenpflug@montana.edu
HASH, Jennifer .... 303-722-5724.. 80 O
jhash@lincolntech.edu
HASH, Joseph .... 707-476-4213.. 39 F
joe-hash@redwoods.edu
HASHEMI-BOZARTH,
Monica .... 316-295-8701 177 F
monica_hashemi@friends.edu
HASHIM, Sharief .... 802-447-4658 476 C
shashim@svc.edu
HASHIM, Susanne .... 937-319-0163 356 F
shashim@antiochcollege.edu
HASINGER, Guenther .... 808-956-8566 129 J
hasinger@hawaii.edu
HASKAMP, Misty .... 573-875-7582 258 F
mrhaskamp@ccis.edu
HASKETT, Tammy .... 828-227-7222 352 C
haskett@wcu.edu
HASKEY, Glennita .... 928-724-6736.. 12 G
ghaskey@dinecollege.edu
HASKINS, Brenda .... 985-448-4518 197 C
brenda.haskins@nicholls.edu
HASKINS, Eileen, T .... 401-598-1035 416 C
ehaskins@jwu.edu
HASKINS, Jamie .... 573-592-5262 270 B
jamie.haskins@westminster-mo.edu
HASKINS, Michael .... 251-460-6211.... 9 B
mhaskins@southalabama.edu
HASLAG, Daniel .... 573-592-5240 270 B
dan.haslag@westminster-mo.edu
HASLAM, Kent .... 406-243-5348 271 G
kent.haslam@umontana.edu
HASLAM STRAUGHAN,
Hope .... 617-879-2330 226 A
hstraughan@wheelock.edu
HASLER, Paul .... 715-346-3059 511 F
phasler@uwsp.edu
HASLER, Susan .... 410-617-1619 205 A
sahasler@loyola.edu
HASNAIN, Syed .... 850-729-6448 104 E
hasnains@nwfsc.edu
HASS, Amy, M .... 352-392-1358 110 D
amhass@ufl.edu
HASS, Marjorie .... 901-843-3730 435 L
hassm@rhodes.edu
HASS, Martha .... 518-694-7238 297 J
martha.hass@acphs.edu
HASS, Moshe .... 845-425-1370 319 F
HASSAN, Nidia .... 903-510-2883 464 D
nhas@tjc.edu
HASSANPOUR, Zinat ..... 704-403-1698 336 B
zinat.hassanpour@carolinashealthcare.org
HASSEL, George, E .... 610-499-4182 414 F
gehassel.sr@widener.edu
HASSELL, Keith .... 203-576-4466.. 88 F
khassell@bridgeport.edu
HASSELL, Rusty .... 706-385-1503 124 F
rusty.hassell@point.edu
HASSEN, Marjorie .... 207-725-3281 198 G
mhassen@bowdoin.edu
HASSENZAHL,
David, M .... 530-898-6121.. 31 D
dhassenzahl@csuchico.edu
HASSENZAHL, Roger ..... 765-285-1532 156 C
rahassenzahl@bsu.edu
HASSETT, Danny .... 214-333-5118 447 D
dannyh@dbu.edu
HASSEVOORT, Darrin .... 423-697-3383 436 F
darrin.hassevoort@chattanoogastate.edu
HASSIG, Kathleen, A ..... 530-898-5201.. 31 D
khassig@csuchico.edu
HASSINGER, Steven ...... 717-728-2262 392 B
stevehassinger@centralpenn.edu
HASSLER, Daniel, M ..... 312-329-8913 146 B
daniel.hassler@moody.edu
HASSON, Amy, S .... 410-548-3316 209 B
ashasson@salisbury.edu

HASSON, Monalisa .... 805-965-0581.. 62 E
mhasson@sbcc.edu
HASSUMANI, Sabrina .... 713-743-2755 465 A
shassumani@uh.edu
HASTED, Grigor .... 517-607-2620 231 C
ghasted@hillsdale.edu
HASTINGS, Adam .... 434-961-5348 489 C
ahastings@pvcc.edu
HASTINGS, Brian .... 402-458-1100 277 G
bhastings@nufoundation.org
HASTINGS, Dana, M ..... 785-532-6221 179 A
dhasting@ksu.edu
HASTINGS, Jan .... 818-401-1298.. 40 A
jhastings@columbiacollege.edu
HASTINGS, Judeann ...... 574-239-8372 158 M
jhastings@hcc-nd.edu
HASTINGS, Michael, M . 207-581-1484 201 B
mhastings@maine.edu
HASTINGS, Michelle ...... 314-367-8700 266 D
michelle.hastings@stlcop.edu
HASTINGS, Nancy .... 312-329-4415 146 B
nancy.hastings@moody.edu
HASTINGS, Peter .... 978-837-5357 221 G
HASTINGS, Ron .... 909-384-8542.. 59 I
rhastings@sbccd.cc.ca.us
HASTY, Taylor .... 423-775-7568 430 G
jhasty6628@bryan.edu
HASZ, Dave .... 952-829-1896 240 H
dave.hasz@bethfel.org
HATANAKA, Janice .... 562-985-7878.. 32 C
janice.hatanaka@csulb.edu
HATCH, David .... 910-521-6679 351 E
david.hatch@uncp.edu
HATCH, Donna, M .... 972-548-6884 446 I
dhatch@collin.edu
HATCH, SHCJ,
Jeanne Marie .... 610-527-0200 409 E
jhatch@rosemont.edu
HATCH, Mark .... 719-389-6805.. 77 J
mhatch@coloradocollege.edu
HATCH, Mary .... 847-214-7421 138 B
mhatch@elgin.edu
HATCH, Melanie .... 478-471-2730 123 A
melanie.hatch@mga.edu
HATCH, Nathan, O .... 336-758-5211 353 A
hatch@wfu.edu
HATCHEL, Doni, S .... 910-898-9613 345 A
codyd@montgomery.edu
HATCHER, Betty, K .... 252-638-3745 342 E
hatcherb@cravencc.edu
HATCHER, Brian .... 410-617-5026 205 A
bhatcher@loyola.edu
HATCHER, Doreen .... 909-537-5037.. 33 D
dhatcher@csusb.edu
HATCHER, Genetta, Y .... 313-831-5200 229 L
ghatcher@etseminary.edu
HATCHER, Lewis, A .... 612-343-4450 249 E
lahatche@northcentral.edu
HATCHER, Oeida .... 434-544-8344 482 F
hatcher@lynchburg.edu
HATCHER, Pam .... 859-246-6788 185 G
pam.hatcher@kctcs.edu
HATCHER, Robert .... 212-817-7020 302 B
rhatcher@gc.cuny.edu
HATCHETT, Steven .... 512-505-3041 451 A
HATCHETT, Timothy, L .. 202-274-5102.. 93 D
timothy.hatchett@udc.edu
HATEGEKIMANA,
Claver .... 360-416-6655 186 C
claver.hategekimana@kctcs.edu
HATFIELD, Amy .... 360-475-7555 496 F
ahatfield@olympic.edu
HATFIELD, Barbara, S ... 318-473-6446 194 A
bhatfield@lsua.edu
HATFIELD, Chad .... 914-961-8313 323 H
hatfield@svots.edu
HATFIELD, Jenna .... 252-335-0821 342 D
jenna_hatfield@albemarle.edu
HATFIELD, Jennifer .... 606-546-1521 189 I
jhatfield@unionky.edu
HATFIELD, Karen .... 352-588-8460 106 N
karen.hatfield@saintleo.edu
HATFIELD, Mark .... 662-720-7270 255 B
mahatfield@nemcc.edu
HATFIELD, Misty .... 803-938-3728 425 F
hatfielm@uscsumter.edu
HATHAWAY, Brent, A .... 702-895-3362 279 D
brent.hathaway@unlv.edu
HATHAWAY, Charles, B 914-594-4480 318 A
charles_hathaway@nymc.edu
HATHAWAY,
Gretchel, L .... 518-388-8327 332 B
hathawag@union.edu
HATHAWAY, Jeffrey ...... 516-463-6750 310 D
jeffrey.hathaway@hofstra.edu
HATHAWAY, Joel .... 314-434-4044 259 B
joel.hathaway@covenantseminary.edu

HATHAWAY, Kathleen 425-564-2630 492 G kathleen.hathaway@bellevuecollege.edu

HATHAWAY, Nicholas, S 405-325-3916 380 L nhathaway@ou.edu

HATHAWAY, William 757-352-4294 484 E willhat@regent.edu

HATHAWAY-CLARK, Bill 303-458-4162 82 D whathawa@regis.edu

HATHCOCK, Michele 828-398-7203 340 M mhathcock@abtech.edu

HATHMAN, Laurie, E 816-501-4144 265 I laurie.hathman@rockhurst.edu

HATHORN, Janine, M 540-458-8671 491 G jhathorn@wlu.edu

HATHORN, Pamela 918-444-3800 376 G hathorn@nsuok.edu

HATLEN, Mary, J 920-923-7161 508 B mhatlen@marianuniversity.edu

HATRAK, Gregory 914-961-8313 323 H ghatrak@svots.edu

HATTAWAY, Trey 903-983-8218 451 F thattaway@kilgore.edu

HATTEBERG, Gregory, A 214-887-5101 448 G alumni@dts.edu

HATTEN, Angie 309-692-4092 145 F ahatten@midstate.edu

HATTEN, Gerrie 805-756-5878 30 K ghatten@calpoly.edu

HATTENDORF, Lori 513-244-4230 366 A lori.hattendorf@msj.edu

HATTO, Susan 989-328-1254 234 D susanh@montcalm.edu

HATTON, Alan 802-681-2878 476 C ahatton@svc.edu

HATTON, Jay 703-784-2105 518 A jay.hatton@usmc.mil

HATTON, John 314-577-8353 266 J hattonjf@slu.edu

HATTON, Karl 618-664-7130 139 A karl.hatton@greenville.edu

HATTON, Martin 662-329-7231 254 F mlhatton@muw.edu

HATTON, Nora 620-235-4276 180 J nhatton@pittstate.edu

HATTON-FICKLIN, Brenda 501-370-5271 21 A

HATTORI-UCHIMA, Margaret 671-735-2653 520 B muchima@triton.uog.edu

HAUB, Elaine 812-941-2284 161 A ehaub@ius.edu

HAUBENREISER, Jenny 541-737-9355 385 F

HAUBER, Mark, E 646-664-8910 301 A mark.hauber@cuny.edu

HAUBOLD, Glen 575-646-2101 295 B ghaubold@nmsu.edu

HAUCK, Nancy 435-652-7844 473 B hauck@dixie.edu

HAUCK, Sadie 570-389-4208 405 E shauck@bloomu.edu

HAUCK, Steven 605-882-5284 427 D haucks@lakeareatech.edu

HAUDE, Erica 620-947-3121 181 H ericah@tabor.edu

HAUER, Donna 651-690-6827 249 T dmhauer@stkate.edu

HAUF, Todd 701-483-2570 354 A todd.hauf@dickinsonstate.edu

HAUFF, Brian 417-865-2815 260 B hauffb@evangel.edu

HAUFF, Joel, S 520-621-0964 16 J hauff@email.arizona.edu

HAUG, Christopher, T 503-943-7205 387 H haug@up.edu

HAUG, Marsha, L 610-436-3411 407 D mhaug@wcupa.edu

HAUGABROOK, Adrian, K 617-879-2008 226 A ahaugabrook@wheelock.edu

HAUGABROOK, Brian 229-245-4357 127 H bahaugab@valdosta.edu

HAUGE, Todd, W 410-293-1600 519 E hauge@usna.edu

HAUGEN, Daniel 612-861-7554 240 B haugen@alfredadler.edu

HAUGEN, Dolores 253-566-6090 499 A dhaugen@tacomacc.edu

HAUGEN, Donna, M 516-572-7809 316 C donna.haugen@ncc.edu

HAUGEN, Doris 847-628-1510 142 B dhaugen@judsonu.edu

HAUGEN, Doug 530-938-5295 39 H haugen@siskiyous.edu

HAUGEN, Jay 314-977-2269 266 J haugenjp@slu.edu

HAUGEN, Regina 270-384-8300 187 H haugenr@lindsey.edu

HAUGH, Kevin 610-902-8258 391 B kevin.o.haugh@cabrini.edu

HAUGHEY, Caitlin 617-305-1999 224 I chaughley@suffolk.edu

HAUGHIE, Jennifer, A 717-477-1235 407 B jahaughie@ship.edu

HAUGHT, Kenneth 701-483-2149 354 A ken.haught@dickinsonstate.edu

HAUGHT, Paul 901-321-3230 431 A phaught@cbu.edu

HAUGO, Gary 218-477-2948 246 B gary.haugo@mnstate.edu

HAUK, Gary, S 404-727-6021 119 B gary.hauk@emory.edu

HAUK, Matthew 406-791-5224 273 C matthew.hauk@ugf.edu

HAUNERT, Bryan 410-617-5131 205 A bthaunert@loyola.edu

HAUPERT, Vincent, D 260-359-4089 159 B vhaupert@huntington.edu

HAUPT, Benjamin 314-505-7040 258 I hauptb@csl.edu

HAUPTMAN, Catherine, M 308-367-5200 278 A chauptman4@unl.edu

HAUS, David 207-941-7124 199 B haussd@husson.edu

HAUS, Teri 970-943-2196 84 E thaus@western.edu

HAUSCARRIAGUE, Elizabeth 925-969-2085 40 L ehauscarriague@dvc.edu

HAUSCHILD, Karen 843-953-5404 420 C hauschildkb@cofc.edu

HAUSCHILDT, James 513-862-3799 362 E james.hauschildt@email.gscollege.edu

HAUSE, Jeffrey, P 402-280-3581 274 D jeffreyhause@creighton.edu

HAUSER, Carrie 248-476-1122 233 F chauser@mispp.edu

HAUSER, Dan 336-841-9057 338 E dhauser@highpoint.edu

HAUSER, John, D 252-222-6140 341 F hauserj@carteret.edu

HAUSER, Joseph, H 901-722-3228 436 D jhauser@sco.edu

HAUSER, LuAnn 620-431-2820 180 C lhauser@neosho.edu

HAUSER, Stephen, C 608-246-2101 514 A shauser@madisoncollege.edu

HAUSFELD, Patricia 631-691-8733 311 C hausfeldp@idti.edu

HAUSINGER, Shannon 281-290-2832 452 C shannon.hausinger@lonestar.edu

HAUSMAN, Kristan, R 740-587-6271 361 B hausmank@denison.edu

HAUTANEN, David, L 240-895-5000 206 G dlhautanen@smcm.edu

HAUVER, Dottie 508-793-2327 213 D dhauver@holycross.edu

HAVARD, Mary, G 409-772-8779 469 C mghavard@utmb.edu

HAVARD, Patty 559-325-3600 29 D phavard@chsu.org

HAVEARD, Melanie, J 850-474-2540 111 D mhaveard@uwf.edu

HAVELY, Candace 319-296-4229 169 H candace.havely@hawkeyecollege.edu

HAVENS, Bruce 417-862-9533 260 D bhavens@globaluniversity.edu

HAVENS, Dan 303-373-2008 82 F dhavens@rvu.edu

HAVENS, Debra 254-526-1214 445 L debra.havens@ctcd.edu

HAVENS, Luisa 540-231-4623 490 F

HAVERKAMPF, Kelly 715-365-4917 514 E khaverkampf@nicoletcollege.edu

HAVERLY, Mark 660-596-7407 267 E mhaverly@sfccmo.edu

HAVERSTIC, Margaret 417-667-8181 259 A mhaverstic@cottey.edu

HAVERTY, April 414-955-4844 508 D ahaverty@mcw.edu

HAVHOLM, Karen, G 715-836-3405 510 D havholkg@uwec.edu

HAVIG, Dee 307-754-6412 516 Q dee.havig@nwc.edu

HAVIGHORST, Deborah, S 708-709-7918 148 I dhavighorst@prairiestate.edu

HAVILAND, Bobbie 620-365-5116 174 G haviland@allencc.edu

HAVIS, Joseph 314-889-1478 260 C jhavis@fontbonne.edu

HAVRON, Tom 620-223-2700 177 E tomha@fortscott.edu

HAWES, Heather 404-270-5068 126 D hhawes@spelman.edu

HAWES, Jeffrey 309-854-1835 134 C hawesj@bhc.edu

HAWES, Matthew 315-866-0300 310 A hawesmr@herkimer.edu

HAWGOOD, Samuel 415-476-6582 70 A sam.hawgood@ucsf.edu

HAWK, Brian, L 417-865-2815 257 F hawkb@evangel.edu

HAWKEN, Christopher 559-925-3304 74 A christopherhawken@whccd.edu

HAWKES, Jennifer 610-527-0200 409 E jennifer.hawkes@rosemont.edu

HAWKES, Mark 605-256-5274 428 G mark.hawkes@dsu.edu

HAWKES, Nicole 617-353-2230 212 G nhawkes@bu.edu

HAWKES, Peter 570-422-3494 406 A phawkes@esu.edu

HAWKINS, Amanda, B 253-535-7667 496 G hawkinab@plu.edu

HAWKINS, Andre 772-462-7100 101 Q ahawkins@irsc.edu

HAWKINS, Audrey 903-675-6357 464 C ahawkins@tvcc.edu

HAWKINS, Beth 501-977-2028 23 B hawkins@uaccm.edu

HAWKINS, Billy, C 256-761-6212 7 D bhawkins@talladega.edu

HAWKINS, Brandy 325-942-2259 463 C brandy.hawkins@angelo.edu

HAWKINS, Brian 619-702-9400 30 C brian.hawkins@cibu.edu

HAWKINS, Cheryl 734-462-4400 236 H chawkins@schoolcraft.edu

HAWKINS, Christie 405-744-4244 377 F christie.hawkins@okstate.edu

HAWKINS, Christy 757-258-6531 489 G hawkinsc@tncc.edu

HAWKINS, Darien 757-728-6544 481 E darien.hawkins@hamptonu.edu

HAWKINS, Daryl 610-341-5822 394 E dhawkins@eastern.edu

HAWKINS, Dean 806-651-2563 460 E dhawkins@mail.wtamu.edu

HAWKINS, Eileen 646-237-8905 312 E ehawkins@tkc.edu

HAWKINS, Eileen 410-209-6037 202 F ehawkins@bccc.edu

HAWKINS, Evan 317-955-6254 162 R ehawkins@marian.edu

HAWKINS, Greg 904-819-6322 98 I ghawkins@flagler.edu

HAWKINS, Greg 901-986-5969 252 C stlife@belhaven.edu

HAWKINS, Irene 302-857-6261 90 B ihawkins@desu.edu

HAWKINS, J. Barney 703-370-6600 483 I

HAWKINS, JR., Jack 334-670-3200 7 E jhawkins@troy.edu

HAWKINS, Jacqueline 270-706-8538 185 H jhawkins0045@kctcs.edu

HAWKINS, Jeffrey 717-720-4070 407 A jhawkins@passhe.edu

HAWKINS, Jodi 401-874-2141 417 E jhawkins@uri.edu

HAWKINS, John 302-622-8000 90 A

HAWKINS, Julia, L 606-783-5189 188 C j.hawkins@moreheadstate.edu

HAWKINS, Katherine 540-831-5149 484 A khawkins3@radford.edu

HAWKINS, Marcia 606-546-1625 189 I mhawkins@unionky.edu

HAWKINS, Marcy, T 260-359-4097 159 B mhawkins@huntington.edu

HAWKINS, Margaret, E 941-752-5307 108 P hawkinm@scf.edu

HAWKINS, Mary, B 402-557-7005 273 E mary.hawkins@bellevue.edu

HAWKINS, MaryAnn 765-641-4535 156 A mahawkins@anderson.edu

HAWKINS, Michele 561-297-3069 109 B mhawkins@fau.edu

HAWKINS, Mike 816-414-3700 263 D registrar@mbts.edu

HAWKINS, Paul, M 386-312-4134 106 M mikehawkins@sjrstate.edu

HAWKINS, Reynani 559-325-5295 66 F reynani.hawkins@cloviscollege.edu

HAWKINS, Robin 773-995-3755 135 F rhawkins@csu.edu

HAWKINS, Ronald, E 434-592-4030 482 D rehawkin@liberty.edu

HAWKINS, Tony 301-846-2491 203 H thawkins@frederick.edu

HAWKINS, Vernon, L 922-860-4221 447 G vhawkins@dcccd.edu

HAWKINS, Wesley, E 561-297-4168 109 B whawkins@fau.edu

HAWKINS, William 860-231-5405 89 E bhawkins@usj.edu

HAWKINSON, Kenneth, S 610-683-4102 406 D hawkinson@kutztown.edu

HAWKS, Brenda 617-735-9920 214 F hawksb@emmanuel.edu

HAWKS, Matt 407-646-2104 106 J mhawks@rollins.edu

HAWLEY, Eric 435-797-8146 473 C eric.hawley@usu.edu

HAWLEY, Harold 843-349-5279 421 L harold.hawley@hgtc.edu

HAWLEY, Katie 802-865-6424 474 G hawley@champlain.edu

HAWLEY, Michael, E 314-286-4846 265 F mehawley@ranken.edu

HAWLEY, Michelle 207-755-5370 199 K mhawley@cmcc.edu

HAWLEY, Michelle 323-343-3830 32 D mhawley@calstatela.edu

HAWLEY, Pamela 410-455-2832 208 A mcinnis@umbc.edu

HAWLEY, Peter 312-487-4743 153 A peter.hawley@tribecaflashpoint.edu

HAWLEY, Stephanie 512-223-7637 443 G shawley@austincc.edu

HAWLEY, Thomas, A 231-843-5803 239 D tahawley@westshore.edu

HAWORTH, John 423-697-2692 436 F john.haworth@chattanoogastate.edu

HAWORTH, Karen 847-947-5246 146 G khaworth@nl.edu

HAWORTH, Timothy 310-568-7191 50 J thaworth@lmu.edu

HAWTIN, Mary, L 810-989-5546 236 G mhawtin@sc4.edu

HAWTON, Noelle 651-201-1801 243 I noelle.hawton@so.mnscu.edu

HAWXHURST, Joan, C 269-337-7384 231 F joan.hawxhurst@kzoo.edu

HAXTON, Lori 660-626-2236 257 A lhaxton@atsu.edu

HAY, April 812-237-2020 159 C april.hay@indstate.edu

HAY, David 859-858-3511 183 D david.hay@asbury.edu

HAY, Judy 307-778-1217 516 N jhay@lccc.wy.edu

HAY, Kuni 408-741-2052 74 D kuni.hay@westvalley.edu

HAY, Laura 912-583-3202 116 G lhay@bpc.edu

HAY, Mary 828-298-3325 353 B mhay@warren-wilson.edu

HAY, Rod 310-243-3301 31 E rhay@csudh.edu

HAY, Sharon, L 401-865-2750 416 E sharhay@providence.edu

HAYASHI, Lori Lei 808-455-0657 130 G lhayashi@hawaii.edu

HAYASHI, Nobi 312-362-6962 137 C nhayashi@depaul.edu

HAYASHI-PETERSEN, Elaine 360-867-5195 494 G peach@evergreen.edu

HAYASHIDA, Peter, A 951-827-5203 69 D peter.hayashida@ucr.edu

HAYDEN, Cathy, C 601-857-3322 253 B cchayden@hindscc.edu

HAYDEN, Jacob 913-758-6146 182 B jacob.hayden@stmary.edu

HAYDEN, John, D 215-836-2222 389 C john.hayden@antonelli.edu

HAYDEN, Kevin 315-470-6500 328 D kmhayden@esf.edu

HAYDEN, Ruby 425-739-8208 495 F ruby.hayden@lwtech.edu

HAYDEN-ROY, Patrick 402-465-2440 276 E phr@nebrwesleyan.edu

HAYDON, Darrell 209-667-3077 33 F dhaydon@csustan.edu

HAYE, Erin 207-216-4311 200 E ehaye@yccc.edu

HAYE, Jack 540-338-1776 483 H president@phc.edu

HAYE, Melissa 304-327-4145 503 O mhaye@bluefieldstate.edu

HAYEK, John 512-463-7281 462 A joh.hayek@tsus.edu

HAYEN, Christopher, M 518-388-6358 332 B hayenc@union.edu

HAYEN, Janet 605-995-2648 427 A jahayen@dwu.edu

HAYES, Alastair 802-828-8600 476 F

HAYES, Ann, C .... 717-867-6416 399 J
hayes@lvc.edu
HAYES, Ann, K .... 573-651-2552 266 M
ahayes@semo.edu
HAYES, Anne .... 434-949-1000 489 E
anne.hayes@southside.edu
HAYES, B. Grant .... 252-328-1000 349 I
hayesb15@ecu.edu
HAYES, Blair .... 301-985-7940 208 D
blair.hayes@umuc.edu
HAYES, Charles .... 734-462-4400 236 H
chayes@schoolcraft.edu
HAYES, Chris .... 806-720-7156 452 D
chris.hayes@lcu.edu
HAYES, Clint .... 606-679-8501 186 G
clint.hayes@kctcs.edu
HAYES, Dale .... 772-462-7809 101 Q
lhayes@irsc.edu
HAYES, Dan .... 434-791-7252 478 E
dhayes@averett.edu
HAYES, Daniel, J .... 315-267-2147 328 A
hayesdj@potsdam.edu
HAYES, David .... 337-421-6960 193 F
david.hayes@sowela.edu
HAYES, David .... 319-399-8555 167 F
dhayes@coe.edu
HAYES, Denise .... 909-621-8355.. 37 K
denise_hayes@cuc.claremont.edu
HAYES, Emily .... 618-937-2127 146 E
ehayes@morthland.edu
HAYES, Eric .... 773-602-5062 135 L
ehayes@ccc.edu
HAYES, Erik, Z .... 812-877-8230 163 G
hayesez@rose-hulman.edu
HAYES, Gaye .... 229-928-1273 120 F
gaye.hayes@gsw.edu
HAYES, Gaynelle .... 409-944-1205 449 F
ghayes@gc.edu
HAYES, George .... 212-431-2837 317 H
george.hayes@nyls.edu
HAYES, Ginny .... 970-943-2130.. 84 E
ghayes@western.edu
HAYES, Hannah .... 503-517-1833 388 C
hhayes@westernseminary.edu
HAYES, Ingrid .... 404-270-5186 126 D
ihayes1@spelman.edu
HAYES, Jack .... 401-863-2972 415 K
jack_hayes@brown.edu
HAYES, Janet .... 229-430-3525 114 J
jhayes@albanytech.edu
HAYES, Jeff .... 678-359-5008 121 B
jeff@gordonstate.edu
HAYES, Jerry .... 216-373-5211 367 A
jhayes@ndc.edu
HAYES, John .... 970-491-6675.. 78 N
john.hayes@colostate.edu
HAYES, John, J .... 508-856-3507 217 C
john.hayes@umassmed.edu
HAYES, Josh .... 317-788-3219 164 H
hayesje@uindy.edu
HAYES, Joshua .... 270-745-5121 190 F
joshua.hayes@wku.edu
HAYES, Julie, C .... 413-545-4169 216 H
jhayes@hfa.umass.edu
HAYES, Katheryn .... 773-602-5000 135 L
khayes@ccc.edu
HAYES, Kellee .... 815-802-8828 142 C
khayes@kcc.edu
HAYES, Lance, R .... 512-448-8750 455 I
lanceh@stedwards.edu
HAYES, LaTonya .... 501-370-5341.. 21 A
lhayes@philander.edu
HAYES, Libby .... 937-481-2282 373 I
libby_hayes@wilmington.edu
HAYES, Linda .... 513-862-3571 362 E
linda.hayes@email.gscollege.edu
HAYES, Maggie .... 406-994-2343 272 A
maggie.hammett@montana.edu
HAYES, Margaret .... 928-314-9515.. 11 B
peggy.hayes@azwestern.edu
HAYES, Marion .... 888-488-4968.. 46 J
HAYES, Mary Jo .... 208-562-3329 132 A
maryjohayes@cwidaho.cc
HAYES, Matthew, D .... 304-696-2523 504 C
hayes2@marshall.edu
HAYES, Michael .... 508-999-8058 217 A
mhayes@umassd.edu
HAYES, JR., Michael, F 716-888-2420 300 G
hayes28@canisius.edu
HAYES, Michelle .... 312-935-4106 149 K
mhayes@robertmorri.edu
HAYES, Michelle .... 847-578-7124 149 K
mhayes@robertmorris.edu
HAYES, Mike .... 423-614-8406 432 L
mhayes@leeuniversity.edu
HAYES, Ray .... 205-348-4840.... 7 H
crhayes@uasystem.edu
HAYES, Rebecca, L .... 330-325-6498 366 F
rlhayes@neomed.edu
HAYES, Rhonda .... 252-335-3103 350 A
rmhayes@ecsu.edu
HAYES, Robin, A .... 501-882-8936.. 17 M
rahayes@asub.edu
HAYES, Scott .... 434-582-2777 482 D
smhayes@liberty.edu
HAYES, Susan .... 973-618-3553 284 D
shayes@caldwell.edu
HAYES, Terri .... 928-523-6608.. 14 K
terri.hayes@nau.edu
HAYES, Thomas .... 513-745-3528 374 D
hayes@xavier.edu
HAYES, Trent .... 937-529-2201 371 B
tdhayes@united.edu
HAYES, Valerie .... 609-652-4693 291 H
valerie.hayes@stockton.edu
HAYES, Wendy .... 937-376-6332 358 I
whayes@centralstate.edu
HAYES-MARTIN,
Melville .... 510-204-0705.. 37 F
mhayesmartin@cdsp.edu
HAYES-MORRISON,
Ruth .... 352-371-2833.. 97 L
admissions@dragonrises.edu
HAYGOOD, Courtney .... 870-574-4458.. 21 G
chaygood@sautech.edu
HAYGOOD, Jennifer ...... 919-807-7021 340 K
haygoodj@nccommunitycolleges.edu
HAYGOOD, Jennifer ...... 919-807-6951 340 K
haygoodj@nccommunitycolleges.edu
HAYLER, David, E .... 828-262-6276 349 H
haylerd@appstate.edu
HAYMAN, Jerry .... 207-974-4685 199 L
jhayman@emcc.edu
HAYMOND, Jeffrey .... 937-766-4442 358 D
jhaymond@cedarville.edu
HAYMORE, Teresa .... 706-865-2134 126 G
thaymore@truett.edu
HAYNER, Kate .... 510-869-6511.. 59 F
khayner@samuelmerritt.edu
HAYNER, Leon .... 407-646-2649 106 J
lhayner@rollins.edu
HAYNES, Amy, M .... 330-684-8932 371 D
hamy@uakron.edu
HAYNES, Anthony .... 615-741-8220 439 H
anthony.haynes@tennessee.edu
HAYNES, Brian, L .... 909-537-5185.. 33 D
bhaynes@csusb.edu
HAYNES, Carolyn, A ..... 513-529-6722 365 I
haynesca@miamioh.edu
HAYNES, Courtney .... 478-757-5167 128 E
chaynes@wesleyancollege.edu
HAYNES, David, A .... 540-985-4020 482 A
dahaynes@jchs.edu
HAYNES, Dawna .... 509-793-2077 492 I
dawnah@bigbend.edu
HAYNES, Derrick .... 303-360-4721.. 79 C
derrick.haynes@ccaurora.edu
HAYNES, Douglas, M .... 949-824-1540.. 69 A
dhaynes@uci.edu
HAYNES, Hal .... 715-682-1230 509 D
hhaynes@northland.edu
HAYNES, James .... 585-395-2651 326 D
jhaynes@brockport.edu
HAYNES, Jerry .... 301-846-2459 203 H
jhaynes@frederick.edu
HAYNES, John, G .... 806-743-7387 463 E
john.g.haynes@ttuhsc.edu
HAYNES, Karen, S .... 760-750-4040.. 33 E
pres@csusm.edu
HAYNES, Lamar .... 918-836-6886 380 C
lamar.haynes@spartan.edu
HAYNES, Leticia .... 413-597-4376 226 C
lseh1@williams.edu
HAYNES, Lisa .... 616-331-7204 230 G
haynesl@gvsu.edu
HAYNES, Mike .... 254-968-9354 459 A
rhaynes@tarleton.edu
HAYNES, Pamela, J .... 336-888-9055 338 E
phaynes@highpoint.edu
HAYNES, Patricia, A ...... 636-922-8427 265 J
phaynes@stchas.edu
HAYNES, Penny, A .... 518-381-1374 323 L
haynespa@sunysccc.edu
HAYNES, Ryan .... 916-577-2200.. 75 B
dgluck@jessup.edu
HAYNES, Sandra .... 303-556-2978.. 80 Q
hayness@msudenver.edu
HAYNES, Scot .... 912-201-8000 125 H
HAYNES, Stephanie, C .. 304-637-1335 501 H
hayness@dewv.edu
HAYNES, Tiffany .... 559-791-2447.. 47 C
tduke@portervillecollege.edu
HAYNES, Victoria .... 913-971-3833 179 H
vmhaynes@mnu.edu
HAYNIE, Glenda, D .... 804-333-6719 489 D
ghaynie@rappahannock.edu
HAYNIE, Janice .... 910-672-1211 350 B
jhaynie@uncfsu.edu
HAYNIE, Michael .... 315-443-0149 330 H
jmhaynie@syr.edu
HAYNIE, Nadja .... 985-380-2957 193 D
nadjahaynie@scl.edu
HAYNIE, Stacia .... 225-578-8274 193 M
pohayn@lsu.edu
HAYNIE, Todd .... 928-428-8320.. 12 I
todd.haynie@eac.edu
HAYS, Antoinette, M ..... 781-768-7122 224 A
antoinette.hays@regiscollege.edu
HAYS, Carrie .... 713-221-8001 465 C
haysc@uhd.edu
HAYS, Danny .... 870-245-5526.. 20 G
haysd@obu.edu
HAYS, Eric .... 785-594-8384 174 J
eric.hays@bakeru.edu
HAYS, Kristi .... 785-227-3380 175 E
hayskl@bethanylb.edu
HAYS, Mark .... 214-378-1821 447 F
mhays@dcccd.edu
HAYS, Rex .... 913-469-8500 178 F
rhays@jccc.edu
HAYS, Ryan .... 513-556-2201 371 E
ryan.hays@uc.edu
HAYS, Stacie .... 712-274-5254 172 A
hays@morningside.edu
HAYS, Victoria .... 800-856-9544 273 C
victoria.hays@ugf.edu
HAYS, Wm. Randy .... 859-238-5471 184 C
randy.hays@centre.edu
HAYSBERT, JoAnn, W ... 757-727-5693 481 E
joann.haysbert@hamptonu.edu
HAYTAS, Debra .... 304-263-6262 502 A
dhaytas@martinsburginstitute.edu
HAYTER, Christopher, A 614-823-1348 368 O
chayter@otterbein.edu
HAYTER, Richard .... 972-721-5227 464 E
rhayter@udallas.edu
HAYTER, Sonya .... 417-269-3469 259 C
sonya.hayter@coxcollege.edu
HAYTON, Heather .... 336-316-2397 338 C
hhayton@guilford.edu
HAYTON, James, C .... 848-445-4616 290 C
james.hayton@rutgers.edu
HAYWARD, Albert, G .... 803-516-4541 423 G
ahayward@scsu.edu
HAYWARD, Dawn .... 215-646-7300 396 E
hayward.d@gmercyu.edu
HAYWARD, Georgeann . 302-857-6001.. 90 B
ghayward@desu.edu
HAYWARD, Jennifer .... 541-463-5132 383 F
haywardj@lanecc.edu
HAYWARD, Lisa .... 603-526-3761 280 H
lisa.hayward@colby-sawyer.edu
HAYWARD, Maysa .... 732-255-0400 288 B
mhayward@ocean.edu
HAYWARD, Milian .... 540-857-6076 490 B
mhayward@virginiawestern.edu
HAYWARD, William, C . 312-996-3254 153 H
whaywa2@uic.edu
HAYWOOD, Ben .... 903-233-3561 452 A
benhaywood@letu.edu
HAYWOOD, Chanta .... 478-825-6118 119 C
haywoodc@fvsu.edu
HAYWOOD, Davida .... 334-229-4241.... 4 A
dhaywood@alasu.edu
HAYWOOD, Michele .... 910-898-9604 345 A
haywoodm@montgomery.edu
HAYWOOD, Zina .... 262-564-3104 513 G
haywoodz@gtc.edu
HAYWORTH,
Kimberly, K .... 517-750-1200 237 D
kimh@arbor.edu
HAZAM, Bruce .... 207-801-5645 199 A
bhazam@coa.edu
HAZARD, Laurie, L .... 401-232-6746 416 A
lhazard@bryant.edu
HAZARD, Victor, A .... 859-257-3754 190 B
vahaz@uky.edu
HAZEL, Julie .... 719-502-3005.. 81 H
julie.hazel@ppcc.edu
HAZELBAKER, Chato ..... 360-992-2921 493 E
chazelbaker@clark.edu
HAZELBAKER, Nicole ..... 406-683-7900 271 H
nicole.hazelbaker@umwestern.edu
HAZELTON, Janet .... 802-468-1208 477 A
janet.hazelton@castleton.edu
HAZELTON, Rahneeka .... 817-202-6733 457 E
rahneeka@swau.edu
HAZEN, Ian .... 315-268-7122 304 B
ihazen@clarkson.edu
HAZEN, Meghan .... 217-333-2034 154 B
registrar@illinois.edu
HAZLETT, Brian .... 717-871-5714 407 A
brian.hazlett@millersville.edu
HAZLETT, Laura .... 510-594-3688.. 28 K
lhazlett@cca.edu
HAZLETT, Margaret .... 717-358-5816 395 G
margaret.hazlett@fandm.edu
HAZLETT, Mia .... 774-330-4301 219 E
mhazlett@capecod.edu
HAZZARD, Mike .... 270-706-8686 185 H
mikew.hazzard@kctcs.edu
HAZZARD, Terry .... 251-405-7087.... 1 E
thazzard@bishop.edu
HA'O, Melanie .... 401-841-7367 518 E
HE, Joyce .... 408-260-8868.. 43 B
sjclinic@fivebranches.edu
HE, Phil .... 617-373-6817 223 D
HE, Yuxin .... 512-454-1188 442 J
info@aoma.edu
HEABERLIN, Robert .... 770-254-7280 127 F
rheaber@westga.edu
HEACOCK, Maureen ...... 937-769-1846 356 G
mheacock@antioch.edu
HEAD, Carolyn .... 901-321-3256 431 A
chead1@cbu.edu
HEAD, John .... 678-839-6423 127 F
jhead@westg.edu
HEAD, Judith .... 214-638-0484 451 E
jhead@kdstudio.com
HEAD, Rachel .... 610-328-8362 410 I
rhead1@swarthmore.edu
HEAD, Stephen .... 832-813-6515 452 C
steve.head@lonestar.edu
HEAD, Sue .... 417-690-2241 258 E
shead@cofo.edu
HEAD, Susan .... 315-792-7342 330 A
susan.head@sunyit.edu
HEADING-GRANT,
Wanda .... 802-656-3131 476 E
HEADING-GRANT,
Wanda, R .... 802-656-8426 476 E
wanda.heading-grant@uvm.edu
HEADINGS, Ron .... 801-832-2206 474 E
rheadings@westminstercollege.edu
HEADLEY, Cory, L .... 605-394-2336 429 A
michael.keegan@sdsmt.edu
HEADLEY, Scot .... 503-554-2836 383 C
sheadley@georgefox.edu
HEADRICK, Dennis .... 402-323-3427 276 K
dheadric@southeast.edu
HEADRICK, Robert .... 479-248-7236.. 19 F
bheadrick@ecollege.edu
HEAFNER, Lori .... 843-349-7871 421 L
lori.heafner@hgtc.edu
HEAGLE, Leanne .... 937-255-6565 517 H
leanne.heagle@afit.edu
HEALD, Donna, N .... 563-588-7107 171 H
donna.heald@loras.edu
HEALEY, Dale .... 952-888-4777 249 F
dhealey@nwhealth.edu
HEALEY, Erin .... 828-898-8944 339 B
healeye@lmc.edu
HEALEY, Stephen, E ...... 203-576-4668.. 88 F
healey@bridgeport.edu
HEALTON, Edward, B .... 202-877-1504.. 92 B
ebh4@georgetown.edu
HEALTON, Edward, B .... 202-687-4600.. 92 B
ebh4@georgetown.edu
HEALY, Amy .... 518-255-5118 328 C
healyak@cobleskill.edu
HEALY, David .... 904-256-7024 102 B
dhealy1@ju.edu
HEALY, Gayle .... 518-629-7326 310 G
g.healy@hvcc.edu
HEALY, Heidi .... 847-214-7006 138 B
hhealy@elgin.edu
HEALY, John (Jack) .... 218-477-2581 246 B
jack.healy@mnstate.edu
HEALY, Robert .... 716-286-8341 318 F
rhealy@niagara.edu
HEALY, Rose Mary .... 973-278-5400 299 F
rmh@berkeleycollege.edu
HEALY, Rose Mary .... 973-278-5400 283 J
rmh@berkeleycollege.edu
HEALY, Sally, J .... 302-356-6993.. 91 B
sally.j.healy@wilmu.edu
HEALY, William, L .... 863-680-4140 100 D
whealy@flsouthern.edu
HEAMES, Joyce .... 706-236-2233 116 D
jheames@berry.edu
HEANEY, Kevin, B .... 609-258-4488 288 F
kjheaney@princeton.edu
HEANEY, Nicole .... 508-678-2811 219 C
nicole.heaney@bristolcc.edu
HEAP, Jeffrey .... 815-280-2401 142 A
jheap@jjc.edu
HEARASINGH, Chelsea . 719-384-6976.. 81 G
chelsea.herasingh@ojc.edu

HEARD, Allison .... 815-740-5025 154 G
aheard@stfrancis.edu
HEARD, Anissa .... 949-451-5364.. 64 I
aheard@ivc.edu
HEARD, Frederick .... 713-718-7757 450 D
frederick.heard@hccs.edu
HEARD, John .... 660-626-2397 257 A
jheard@atsu.edu
HEARD, Katrina .... 337-521-8900 193 E
katrina.heard@solacc.edu
HEARD, Michael .... 229-217-4207 126 C
mheard@southernregional.edu
HEARD, Michael .... 404-756-4443 115 I
mheard@atlm.edu
HEARIN, Rick .... 848-932-0185 290 A
rick.hearin@rutgers.edu
HEARN, Deyna .... 310-434-4435.. 62 G
hearn_deyna@smc.edu
HEARN, Greg, K .... 706-245-7226 119 A
ghearn@lifesprings.net
HEARN, Jessica .... 502-863-8437 184 I
jessica_hearn@georgetowncollege.edu
HEARN, Maribeth .... 815-740-3384 154 G
mhearn@stfrancis.edu
HEARN, Sabrina, B .... 205-934-9176.... 7 H
shearn@uasystem.edu
HEARNE, Chad .... 501-450-5015.. 23 I
chearne@uca.edu
HEARRING, April .... 410-386-8444 203 A
aherring@carrollcc.edu
HEARTLEIN, Karrie .... 309-341-7340 142 G
kheartle@knox.edu
HEARTS-GLASS, Angela . 312-850-7168 136 C
aheartsglass@ccc.edu
HEASLEY, Kristin .... 215-951-1013 398 F
heasley@lasalle.edu
HEASTON, Amy .... 912-344-2505 115 D
amy.heaston@armstrong.edu
HEATH, Aaron .... 816-322-0110 257 M
aaron.heath@calvary.edu
HEATH, Bob .... 417-626-1234 264 J
heath.bob@occ.edu
HEATH, Cantey .... 803-777-3106 424 I
canteyh@mailbox.sc.edu
HEATH, Cassandra, A ... 530-226-4608.. 64 B
cheath@simpsonu.edu
HEATH, Cheryl, A .... 307-674-6446 516 P
cheath@sheridan.edu
HEATH, David, A .... 212-938-5650 328 E
dheath@sunyopt.edu
HEATH, Donna, R .... 336-334-5092 351 D
drheath@uncg.edu
HEATH, Elaine .... 919-660-3434 337 C
eheath@div.duke.edu
HEATH, Hildy .... 415-405-4256.. 34 C
hheath@sfsu.edu
HEATH, Janie, H .... 859-257-9000 190 B
jheath@uky.edu
HEATH, Janine .... 573-840-9698 267 J
jheath@trcc.edu
HEATH, Jason .... 502-897-4106 189 A
jheath@sbts.edu
HEATH, Joan, L .... 512-245-2133 463 A
jh06@txstate.edu
HEATH, Judy .... 410-777-1177 202 D
jheath@aacc.edu
HEATH, Kathy .... 207-326-2339 200 F
kathy.heath@mma.edu
HEATH, Marie .... 904-470-8933.. 98 B
m.heath@ewc.edu
HEATH, Mary-Teresa ..... 518-828-4181 305 D
mary-teresa.heath@sunycgcc.edu
HEATH, Rebekah, A .... 563-333-6447 173 A
heathrebekaha@sau.edu
HEATH, Richard, C .... 410-777-2204 202 D
rcheath@aacc.edu
HEATH, Robert .... 205-366-8851.... 7 C
rheath@stillman.edu
HEATH, Savannah .... 910-898-9617 345 A
heaths@montgomery.edu
HEATHERLY, David, L .... 910-938-6211 342 C
heatherlyd@coastalcarolina.edu
HEATLIE, Pamela .... 734-763-0235 237 I
HEATON, Dennis .... 641-470-1399 171 J
dheaton@mum.edu
HEATON, Haidee .... 573-288-6434 259 E
hheaton@culver.edu
HEATON, Karick .... 801-302-2879 472 A
karick.heaton@neumont.edu
HEATON, Mandy .... 503-777-7289 386 F
heatonm@reed.edu
HEATON, Scott .... 209-946-2541.. 70 F
sheaton@pacific.edu
HEATON, Tim .... 605-688-5117 429 B
tim.heaton@sdstate.edu
HEATOR, Martin .... 734-462-4400 236 H
mheator@schoolcraft.edu
HEATWOLE, Deirdre ...... 617-287-5324 216 G
dheatwole@umassp.edu
HEAVENER, Mac .... 904-596-2400 112 F
macheavener@tbc.edu
HEAVENER, Matthew ..... 904-596-2420 112 F
mheavener@tbc.org
HEAVEY, Chris .... 702-895-0186 279 D
chris.heavey@unlv.edu
HEAVREN, Brian .... 860-297-2279.. 88 E
brian.heavren@trincoll.edu
HEAVY RUNNER, Joely . 701-255-3285 355 I
jheavyrunner@uttc.edu
HEBARD, John .... 907-474-6831.. 10 B
jahebard@alaska.edu
HEBARD, Natalie, J .... 208-535-5398 131 G
natalie.hebard@my.eitc.edu
HEBBARD, Matthew ...... 956-872-2147 456 G
mshebbar@southtexascollege.edu
HEBERLE, Julia, F .... 610-921-7581 388 E
jheberle@albright.edu
HEBERT, Carolyn .... 860-515-3880.. 84 H
chebert@charteroak.edu
HEBERT, Deborrah .... 409-984-6156 462 E
hebertda@lamarpa.edu
HEBERT, Gurdeep .... 559-325-5378.. 66 F
gurdeep.hebert@cloviscollege.edu
HEBERT, Jaimie .... 912-478-5211 120 E
jhebert@georgiasouthern.edu
HEBERT, Joseph .... 281-998-6150 456 B
joseph.hebert@sjcd.edu
HEBERT, Katie .... 508-626-4575 218 A
khebert@framingham.edu
HEBERT, Mark .... 502-852-3133 190 C
mark.hebert@louisville.edu
HEBERT, Richard .... 203-576-4804.. 88 F
rhebert@bridgeport.edu
HEBERT, Rudolph .... 413-572-5699 218 F
rudy@westfield.ma.edu
HEBERT, Shawn .... 575-624-8480 295 A
hebert@nmmi.edu
HEBERT-JOHNSON,
Melissa .... 309-796-5465 134 C
herbertm@bhc.edu
HEBMANN, Rigel .... 661-824-2977.. 53 G
rhebmann@ntps.edu
HEBNER, Chad .... 478-822-1042 119 C
hebnerc@fvsu.edu
HEBRA, Jada .... 603-665-7173 282 C
j.hebra@snhu.edu
HECHT, Amy .... 609-771-2201 284 I
amyhecht@tcnj.edu
HECHT, Amy .... 850-644-5590 110 A
ahecht@fsu.edu
HECHT, Boruch .... 973-267-9404 289 B
boruch.hecht@gmail.com
HECHT, Donald .... 714-882-7800.. 30 I
dhecht@calsouthern.edu
HECHT, Pinchas .... 718-645-0536 315 G
phecht@thejnet.com
HECK, Annie .... 541-737-0790 385 F
annie.heck@oregonstate.edu
HECK, Barbara, H .... 410-778-7805 210 A
bheck2@washcoll.edu
HECK, Catherine, J .... 740-283-6498 361 L
check@franciscan.edu
HECK, Melissa .... 918-335-6334 378 F
HECK, Paul .... 773-878-3194 150 I
pheck@staugustine.edu
HECK, Rafael .... 847-628-1546 142 B
rafael.heck@judsonu.edu
HECK, Thomas, R .... 701-252-3467 355 J
theck@uj.edu
HECK, Traci .... 918-595-3411 380 D
traci.heck@tulsacc.edu
HECKAMAN, Daniel, A .. 218-477-2300 246 B
daniel.heckaman@mnstate.edu
HECKAMAN, Judith, M . 717-560-8278 399 D
jheckaman@lbc.edu
HECKARD-FARMER,
Bonnie .... 734-462-4400 236 H
bheckard@schoolcraft.edu
HECKENLAIBLE, Anna ... 605-331-6651 429 D
anna.heckenlaible@usiouxfalls.edu
HECKER, Barbara .... 650-493-4430.. 64 C
barbara.hecker@sofia.edu
HECKER, Jeffrey, E .... 207-581-1547 201 B
hecker@maine.edu
HECKLER, Mark, A .... 219-464-5115 165 D
mark.heckler@valpo.edu
HECKLER, Pamela .... 410-706-5631 207 H
pheckler@umaryland.edu
HECKMAN, Jeffrey .... 315-279-5328 312 D
jheckman@keuka.edu
HECKMAN, Mary Ellen .. 610-372-4721 408 G
mheckman@racc.edu
HECKMAN, Richard, A .. 717-245-1308 394 A
heckman@dickinson.edu
HECKMANN, John .... 815-753-2900 147 H
jheckmann@niu.edu
HECKSTALL, Jaime, P ... 252-862-1255 345 H
jheckstall6664@roanokechowan.edu
HECT, Daniel .... 740-587-5789 361 B
hectd@denison.edu
HECTOR, Gerald .... 607-255-6243 306 B
glh82@cornell.edu
HEDAYAT, Nasser .... 407-582-3326 113 F
nhedayat@valenciacollege.edu
HEDBERG, Rick .... 701-858-3000 354 C
rick.hedberg@minotstateu.edu
HEDBERG, William, B .... 518-956-8030 324 G
whedberg@albany.edu
HEDDEN, Alli .... 410-837-6149 209 D
ahedden@ubalt.edu
HEDDERICK,
Malgorzata .... 617-324-7239 221 C
HEDDLESTON, George .. 423-425-4363 440 A
george-heddleston@utc.edu
HEDDLESTON,
Patrick, D .... 330-823-6599 372 C
heddlepd@mountunion.edu
HEDEEN, Deborah .... 406-683-7115 271 H
deborah.hedeen@umwestern.edu
HEDEEN, Paul .... 734-384-4152 234 C
phedeen@monroeccc.edu
HEDEGARD, Heidi .... 603-862-0967 282 E
heidi.hedegard@usnh.edu
HEDGE, Dennis .... 605-688-4173 429 B
dennis.hedge@sdstate.edu
HEDGEPATH, Donna ..... 270-789-5231 184 B
drhedgepath@campbellsville.edu
HEDGES, Denise, C .... 417-667-8181 259 A
dhedges@cottey.edu
HEDGES, Don .... 847-317-7141 153 D
dhedges@tiu.edu
HEDGES, Douglas .... 609-343-4911 283 D
hedges@atlantic.edu
HEDGES, Jerris, R .... 808-692-0899 129 J
jerris@hawaii.edu
HEDGES, Tammy .... 901-678-2843 439 E
thedges@memphis.edu
HEDGPETH, Ruth .... 704-330-6729 342 A
ruth.hedgpeth@cpcc.edu
HEDIN, Norma .... 214-333-5599 447 D
norma@dbu.edu
HEDLAND HANSEN,
Katherine .... 425-235-2356 497 E
khedlandhansen@rtc.edu
HEDLUN, Randy, J .... 417-862-9533 260 D
rhedlun@globaluniversity.edu
HEDLUND, Paul .... 785-833-4446 179 C
paul.hedlund@kwu.edu
HEDLUND, Wayne .... 585-582-8250 307 C
waynehedlund@elim.edu
HEDMAN, Shawn .... 507-537-6292 248 A
shawn.hedman@smsu.edu
HEDRICK, Van .... 940-668-7347 453 L
vhedrick@nctc.edu
HEDWALL, Angela .... 206-239-2299 492 D
ahedwall@aii.edu
HEEL, Michael, A .... 585-292-2564 315 L
mheel@monroecc.edu
HEEMSTRA, John .... 605-995-7204 427 E
john.heemstra@mitchelltech.edu
HEERDINK, Joe .... 270-831-9615 186 A
joe.heerdink@kctcs.edu
HEEREN, Diana .... 210-999-7163 464 B
dheeren@trinity.edu
HEEREN, Matthew .... 660-626-2064 257 A
mheeren@atsu.edu
HEERMAN, Heather, L ... 508-565-1301 224 H
hheerman@stonehill.edu
HEERMANN, Keith .... 417-862-9533 260 D
kheermann@globaluniversity.edu
HEERSINK, Heather .... 719-587-7759.. 76 D
heather_heersink@adams.edu
HEERSINK, Jordan .... 303-963-3388.. 77 I
joheersink@ccu.edu
HEESACKER-SMITH,
Angela .... 402-354-7256 275 P
angela.heesackersmith@
methodistcollege.edu
HEETER-BASS, Janet ...... 740-826-8083 366 C
jheeter@muskingum.edu
HEETLAND, David, L ..... 847-866-3970 138 G
david.heetland@garrett.edu
HEFFER, David .... 410-337-6112 204 A
david.heffer@goucher.edu
HEFFERIN, Cathy, D ...... 336-633-0208 345 F
cdhefferin@randolph.edu
HEFFERNAN, Erika .... 305-809-3261.. 99 L
erika.heffernan@fkcc.edu
HEFFERNAN, Robert, J .. 848-932-7305 290 A
heffernan@irap.rutgers.edu
HEFFERNAN, Robert, J .. 848-932-7305 290 C
heffernan@instlres.rutgers.edu
HEFFERNAN,
Thomas, J .... 561-237-7270 103 E
theffernan@lynn.edu
HEFLEY, Jacqueline, D .. 512-404-4826 443 I
jhefley@austinseminary.edu
HEFLIN, David .... 903-586-2518 451 C
dheflin@jacksonville-college.edu
HEFLIN, David .... 270-534-3388 187 C
david.heflin@kctcs.edu
HEFLIN, Michael, A .... 716-878-3000 326 E
heflinma@buffalostate.edu
HEFLIN, Sherry .... 717-815-1257 415 G
sheflin@ycp.edu
HEFNER, Alana .... 254-968-9078 459 A
hefner@tarleton.edu
HEFNER, David .... 404-752-1725 123 F
dhefner@msm.edu
HEGAB, Hisham .... 318-257-4647 197 A
hhegab@latech.edu
HEGARTY, James .... 618-374-5157 149 A
james.hegarty@principia.edu
HEGARTY, Kevin, P .... 734-764-7272 237 I
officeofevpcfo@umich.edu
HEGEDUS, Mary Ellen ... 574-239-8391 158 M
mhegedus@hcc-nd.edu
HEGEDUS, Stephen .... 203-392-5900.. 85 A
schoolofeducation@southernct.edu
HEGEL, Barbara .... 907-796-6457.. 10 C
bahegel@alaska.edu
HEGEMAN, Jay .... 301-687-4738 209 A
jhegeman@frostburg.edu
HEGEMEYER, Betty .... 979-830-4188 444 D
bj.hegemeyer@blinn.edu
HEGENBARTH, Chris ..... 218-235-2164 248 B
c.hegenbarth@vcc.edu
HEGER, Laura .... 570-389-4179 405 E
lheger@bloomu.edu
HEGGEMEYER, Terri ...... 402-844-7263 276 G
terrih@northeast.edu
HEGGOY, Liv .... 540-868-4091 488 E
lheggoy@lfcc.edu
HEGLAND, Paul, R .... 262-551-5858 506 H
paul@carthage.edu
HEGLAND, Paul, R .... 262-551-5708 506 H
paul@carthage.edu
HEGLAND, Suzanne ...... 617-585-1313 222 H
suzanne.hegland@necmusic.edu
HEGMAN, John, P .... 404-471-6109 114 H
jhegman@agnesscott.edu
HEIDA, Debbie .... 706-236-2207 116 D
dheida@berry.edu
HEIDBREDER, Kay, K .... 540-231-6293 490 F
heidbred@vt.edu
HEIDE, Gale .... 406-586-3585 271 E
gale.heide@montanabiblecollege.edu
HEIDEMAN, Carl, E .... 616-395-7670 231 D
heideman@hope.edu
HEIDEMAN, Greg .... 859-846-5417 188 B
gheideman.ca@midway.edu
HEIDEMANN, Molly ...... 513-529-8600 365 I
mheidemann@miamioh.edu
HEIDENREICH, Kari ...... 262-472-1921 512 C
heidenreka12@uww.edu
HEIDER, Donald, B .... 312-915-6548 144 D
dheider@luc.edu
HEIDER, Mary Jane .... 585-345-6813 309 C
mjheider@genesee.edu
HEIDERSBACH, Annie ... 440-826-3530 357 B
aheiders@bw.edu
HEIDICK, Venesa, A ...... 979-845-1059 459 C
vheidick@tamu.edu
HEIDINGSFIELD,
Michael, J .... 512-499-4688 467 A
mheidingsfield@utsystem.edu
HEIDKE, Stephen .... 314-392-2372 263 F
heidkesj@mobap.edu
HEIDLE, Wayne .... 714-463-7589.. 51 A
wheidle@ketchum.edu
HEIDORF, Marc .... 414-930-3219 509 B
heidorfm@mtmary.edu
HEIDRICH, Mark .... 208-459-5199 131 H
mheidrich@collegeofidaho.edu
HEIDRICK, Judy .... 785-738-9058 180 E
jheidrick@ncktc.edu
HEIDT, Loretta, A .... 701-483-2418 354 A
loretta.heidt@dickinsonstate.edu
HEIDT, Mason .... 276-244-1226 477 M
mheidt@asl.edu
HEIDT, Matthew .... 716-926-8792 310 B
mheidt@hilbert.edu
HEIDTKE, Staci, L .... 715-836-5358 510 D
heidtksl@uwec.edu
HEIER, Greg .... 605-229-8587 427 J
greg.heier@presentation.edu
HEIFNER, Bryan .... 432-335-6512 454 C
bheifner@odessa.edu
HEIGHES, Robert .... 734-487-1222 229 K
rheighes@emich.edu

HEIGHT, Linda, L .... 248-204-2159 233 A
lheight@ltu.edu
HEIKEL, Karen .... 715-394-8055 512 B
kheikel@uwsuper.edu
HEIKKILA, Christina ...... 910-362-7313 341 E
cheikkila@cfcc.edu
HEIL, Elissa .... 717-262-2018 415 B
elissa.heil@wilson.edu
HEIL, Mark .... 208-426-1200 131 C
markheil@boisestate.edu
HEIL, Mary Colleen .... 717-396-7833 404 R
mcheil@pcad.edu
HEILAND, Donna .... 718-636-3744 320 D
dheiland@pratt.edu
HEILAND, Joyce .... 916-361-6340.. 50 H
heilanj@flc.losrios.edu
HEILBRON, Shawn, R ... 631-632-7205 325 F
shawn.heilbron@stonybrook.edu
HEILEMAN, Greg .... 859-257-9000 190 B
greg.heileman@uky.edu
HEILES, Kenneth, A .... 479-308-2200.. 17 J
HEILGEIST, Pete .... 360-650-3127 500 E
pete.heilgeist@wwu.edu
HEILLE, Gregory .... 314-256-8881 257 D
heille@ai.edu
HEILMAN, Carl, R .... 620-792-9301 175 C
heilmanc@bartonccc.edu
HEILMAN, Todd, E .... 212-346-1200 319 J
HEILMAN, Valerie .... 701-228-5437 354 G
valerie.heilman@dakotacollege.edu
HEILMANN, Ray .... 217-228-5432 149 B
heilmra@quincy.edu
HEIM, Edward .... 610-796-2838 389 A
edward.heim@alvernia.edu
HEIM, Peggy, M .... 610-799-1532 400 A
pheim@lccc.edu
HEIM, William .... 626-395-4701.. 29 I
william.heim@caltech.edu
HEIMAN, Kelly, J .... 262-524-7695 506 G
kheiman@carrollu.edu
HEIMAN, Scott, R .... 608-243-4890 514 A
sheiman@madisoncollege.edu
HEIMAN, Suzette, T ...... 573-882-6861 268 C
heimans@umsystem.edu
HEIMBACH, Celeste ...... 671-734-1812 520 A
cheimbach@piu.edu
HEIMBAUGH, Sharon .... 773-442-5805 147 G
s-heimbaugh@neiu.edu
HEIMBURGER, David .... 314-977-3139 266 J
dheimbu1@slu.edu
HEIMMERMANN, Dan ... 432-552-2110 469 D
heimmermann_d@utpb.edu
HEIMOVITZ, Issac .... 718-438-1002 315 A
HEIN, Anna .... 386-481-2894.. 95 J
heina@cookman.edu
HEIN, Beth .... 651-779-3438 244 D
beth.hein@century.edu
HEIN, Denise .... 517-265-5161 226 F
dhein@adrian.edu
HEIN, Holly .... 207-509-7244 200 I
hhein@unity.edu
HEIN, Steven, M .... 912-478-0831 120 E
shein@georgiasouthern.edu
HEINBUCH, Danielle ..... 714-895-8970.. 38 G
dheinbuch@gwc.cccd.edu
HEINDEL, Patricia .... 973-290-4102 285 A
pheindel@cse.edu
HEINDL, Michael, J ...... 601-928-6234 254 D
michael.heindl@mgccc.edu
HEINE, Greg .... 605-668-1500 427 F
greg.heine@mtmc.edu
HEINECKE-KRUMHUS,
Leah .... 773-442-5416 147 G
l-heinecke-krumhus@neiu.edu
HEINEMAN, Pete .... 402-557-7146 273 E
pete.heineman@bellevue.edu
HEINEMAN, William ...... 978-556-3327 220 F
wheineman@necc.mass.edu
HEINEMANN, Brian .... 760-366-5278.. 41 B
bheinemann@cmccd.edu
HEINEMANN, Karen ...... 904-632-5167 100 F
HEINEMANN, Karen ...... 903-875-7355 453 J
karen.heinemann@navarrocollege.edu
HEINEN, Jack .... 828-669-8012 340 I
jheinen@montreat.edu
HEINEN, Jim .... 847-970-4809 154 H
jheinen@usml.edu
HEINEN, Terry .... 615-230-3227 438 C
terry.heinen@volstate.edu
HEINERICHS, Scott .... 610-436-2733 407 D
sheinerichs@wcupa.edu
HEINLE, Sharon .... 703-726-1087.. 92 A
sheinle@gwu.edu
HEINRICH, Matt, W .... 816-501-4064 265 I
matt.heinrich@rockhurst.edu
HEINRICH, Peggy .... 847-214-7635 138 B
pheinrich@elgin.edu

HEINRICH, Robert, R .... 609-626-6039 291 H
robert.heinrich@stockton.edu
HEINRICHS, Abigail .... 262-551-2450 506 H
aheinrichs@carthage.edu
HEINSELMAN, Gregg ..... 715-425-4444 511 E
gregg.heinselman@uwrf.edu
HEINSELMAN,
Gregg, M .... 715-425-4444 511 E
gregg.heinselman@uwrf.edu
HEINTZ, Douglas .... 210-690-9000 449 K
dheintz@hallmarkuniversity.edu
HEINTZ, Jill .... 315-792-5584 315 I
jheintz@mvcc.edu
HEINTZ, Nicholas .... 319-363-1323 172 B
nheintz@mtmercy.edu
HEINZ, Kartha .... 206-876-6100 498 C
kheinz@theseattleschool.edu
HEINZEKEHR, Justin ..... 574-535-7000 158 A
justinbh@goshen.edu
HEINZEKEHR, Justin ..... 574-535-7110 158 A
justinbh@goshen.edu
HEINZELMAN, Wendi ..... 585-275-4151 332 E
wendi.heinzelman@rochester.edu
HEINZMAN, Mary, B ..... 563-333-6241 173 A
heinzmanmarymaryb@sau.edu
HEISER, Andy .... 360-416-7745 498 F
andy.heiser@skagit.edu
HEISER, Donna .... 239-687-5402.. 95 B
dheiser@avemarialaw.edu
HEISER, Gregory, M ...... 405-325-8679 380 L
gheiser@ou.edu
HEISEY, Jennifer .... 513-556-4344 371 E
heiseyj@ucmail.uc.edu
HEISS, Beth, L .... 517-265-5161 226 F
bheiss@adrian.edu
HEISSERER, Nick .... 218-855-8038 244 C
nheisserer@clcmn.edu
HEIST, Daniel, P .... 814-865-1359 403 F
dph3@psu.edu
HEISTAD, Deirdre, A ..... 319-273-2633 167 A
d.heistad@uni.edu
HEITHAUS, Michael ...... 305-348-2866 109 D
michael.heithaus@fiu.edu
HEITKAMP, Andrew .... 701-858-4002 354 C
andy.heitkamp@minotstateu.edu
HEITKAMP, Mike .... 701-252-3467 355 J
mike.heitkamp@uj.edu
HEITKEMPER, Mary .... 509-313-4231 495 A
heitkemper@gonzaga.edu
HEITMAN, Dave .... 916-577-2200.. 75 B
dheitman@jessup.edu
HEITMANN, Damen .... 402-461-7397 274 I
dheitmann@hastings.edu
HEITZ, Cheryl .... 928-523-3711.. 14 K
cheryl.heitz@nau.edu
HEITZENRATER, Kim, D 931-598-1121 436 A
kheitzen@sewanee.edu
HEITZINGER, Karen .... 716-375-2328 322 B
kheitzin@sbu.edu
HEIZER NEWQUIST,
Leslie .... 425-564-2191 492 G
leslie.newquist@bellevuecollege.edu
HEJL, Cindy .... 303-556-4029.. 80 Q
hejlc@msudenver.edu
HELBIG, Suzanne, C ..... 949-824-7366.. 69 A
shelbig@uci.edu
HELBIG, Tuesdi .... 270-745-3250 190 F
tuesdi.helbig@wku.edu
HELBLE, Joseph .... 603-646-2238 281 C
joseph.helble@dartmouth.edu
HELBLING, Brenda .... 208-885-9191 132 I
brendah@uidaho.edu
HELD, II, John .... 573-341-6533 269 A
heldjohn@mst.edu
HELD, Joshua .... 847-945-8800 153 D
jrheld@tiu.edu
HELDEROP, Sue .... 248-364-6135 235 J
helderop@oakland.edu
HELDMAN, Lou .... 316-978-7114 182 F
lou.heldman@wichita.edu
HELDT, Paula .... 812-488-2479 164 G
ph28@evansville.edu
HELEKAR, Andrea, D ..... 213-624-1200.. 42 N
ahelekar@fidm.edu
HELENS, Joyce .... 775-753-2265 279 A
joyce.helens@gbcnv.edu
HELFRICH, Lori .... 314-719-3663 260 C
lhelfrich@fontbonne.edu
HELGE, Kristyn, S .... 817-515-7463 458 B
kristyn.helge@tccd.edu
HELGESEN, Paul .... 978-867-4730 215 D
paul.helgesen@gordon.edu
HELGESEN, Pete .... 913-360-7476 175 D
phelgesen@benedictine.edu
HELGESON, Grant .... 808-455-0645 130 G
helgeson@hawaii.edu
HELGESON, Richard ...... 731-881-7010 440 B
helgeson@utm.edu

HELGESON, Stuart .... 610-989-1276 413 I
shelgeson@vfmac.edu
HELGESTAD, Chris .... 612-861-7554 240 B
chris.helgestad@alfredadler.edu
HELIEISAR, Jennifer ...... 691-320-2480 519 G
jenniferh@comfsm.fm
HELIS, James, A .... 516-726-5815 519 C
helisj@usmma.edu
HELITZER, Deborah .... 602-496-0789.. 10 K
deborah.helitzer@asu.edu
HELLA, Lori, L .... 989-774-7194 228 E
hella1ll@cmich.edu
HELLDOBLER,
Richard, J .... 773-442-5400 147 G
r-helldobler@neiu.edu
HELLEMAN, Kathryn ...... 419-434-4256 373 K
khelleman@winebrenner.edu
HELLER, Adam .... 623-245-4600.. 16 H
aheller@uti.edu
HELLER, Donald .... 415-422-6136.. 72 A
deheller@usfca.edu
HELLER, James .... 262-595-2455 511 C
james.heller@uwp.edu
HELLER, Joshua, J .... 212-752-1530 312 G
joshua.heller@limcollege.edu
HELLER, Joshua, W ...... 585-785-1335 308 D
joshua.heller@flcc.edu
HELLER, Lauren .... 706-290-2688 116 D
lheller@berry.edu
HELLER, Laurent .... 608-263-2467 510 C
lheller@wisc.edu
HELLER, Mary .... 406-265-4198 272 C
mary.heller@msun.edu
HELLER, Mary .... 610-989-1345 413 I
mheller@vfmac.edu
HELLER, Matthew, D ..... 607-587-3992 328 F
hellermd@alfredstate.edu
HELLER, Tracy .... 858-635-4772.. 24 L
theller@alliant.edu
HELLER, Tracy .... 858-635-4535.. 24 K
theller@alliant.edu
HELLER DE MESSER,
Kirk .... 414-930-3221 509 B
hellerk@mtmary.edu
HELLER-ROSS, Holly, B . 518-564-5180 327 E
hellerhb@plattsburgh.edu
HELLER ROSS, Holly, B 518-564-5192 327 E
hellerhb@plattsburgh.edu
HELLERMANN, David ..... 651-290-6457 248 U
david.hellermann@mitchellhamline.edu
HELLERSTEIN, Laurel .... 978-232-2153 214 G
lhellers@endicott.edu
HELLERUD, Nancy .... 314-246-7440 269 N
nancyhellerud@webster.edu
HELLIE, Thomas .... 503-883-2408 383 H
thellie@linfield.edu
HELLING, Mary Kay ...... 605-688-4153 429 B
mary.helling@sdstate.edu
HELLING, Mary Kay ...... 605-688-4173 429 B
mary.helling@sdstate.edu
HELLING, Nathan, M ..... 605-336-6588 428 B
nhelling@sfseminary.edu
HELLMAN, Frances .... 510-642-5872.. 68 G
fhellman@berkeley.edu
HELLMAN, Joel .... 202-687-0100.. 92 B
jhellman@georgetown.edu
HELLMANN, Emily .... 859-344-3386 189 G
hellmae@thomasmore.edu
HELLMICH, David, M ..... 815-835-6303 151 E
david.m.hellmich@svcc.edu
HELLRUNG, Scott, A ..... 414-410-4697 506 F
shellrung@stritch.edu
HELLUMS, Duane .... 502-410-6200 184 H
dhellums@galencollege.edu
HELLUMS, Paula .... 337-421-6965 193 F
paula.hellums@sowela.edu
HELLWIG, Beth, A .... 715-836-5992 510 D
hellwiba@uwec.edu
HELLWIG, Brant, J .... 540-458-5352 491 G
hellwig@wlu.edu
HELLYER, Brenda .... 281-998-6100 455 K
brenda.hellyer@sjcd.edu
HELM, Hunt, C .... 502-272-8046 183 H
hhelm@bellarmine.edu
HELM, Jonathan, C .... 254-710-1181 444 B
jonathan_helm@baylor.edu
HELM, Lloyd .... 503-594-6793 382 D
lloyd.helm@clackamas.edu
HELM, Peyton .... 508-999-8004 217 A
chancellor@umassd.edu
HELM, Scott .... 641-782-1481 173 I
helm@swcciowa.edu
HELM, Steven .... 540-831-5471 484 A
shelm@radford.edu
HELMBRECHT, Alex .... 308-432-6212 276 B
ahlembrecht@csc.edu
HELMER, Robert, C .... 440-826-2424 357 B
rhelmer@bw.edu

HELMER, Shannon .... 610-799-1857 400 A
shelmer@lccc.edu
HELMICK, Mary .... 540-231-6221 490 F
mhelmick@vt.edu
HELMICK, Michael, S .... 828-448-3102 347 F
mhelmick@wpcc.edu
HELMICK, Tom .... 724-852-3210 414 B
thelmick@waynesburg.edu
HELMINCK, Aloysius ..... 808-956-6451 129 J
helminck@hawaii.edu
HELMING, Jay .... 202-685-3909 518 B
jay.helming@ndu.edu
HELMREICH, Anne .... 817-257-2787 461 A
a.helmreich@tcu.edu
HELMS, Carol .... 509-453-0374 497 A
carol.helms@perrytech.edu
HELMS, Chris .... 828-766-1291 344 F
chelms@mayland.edu
HELMS, Clint .... 706-233-7265 125 E
HELMS, Joel .... 715-232-2639 512 A
helmsj@uwstout.edu
HELMS, Lance .... 912-538-3207 126 A
lhelms@southeasterntech.edu
HELMS, Mark .... 704-330-6127 342 A
mark.helms@cpcc.edu
HELMS, Michael .... 334-347-2623.... 1 J
mhelms@escc.edu
HELMS, Sherrie .... 478-289-2360 118 H
shelms@ega.edu
HELMS, Steve .... 334-222-6591.... 2 H
shelms@lbwcc.edu
HELMS, Wanda .... 505-224-4000 293 L
whelms@cnm.edu
HELMSING, Debra, F .... 260-665-4240 164 E
helmsingd@trine.edu
HELMSTETTER, Ashley ... 419-448-2231 362 G
ahelmste@heidelberg.edu
HELMUS, Aimee .... 910-362-7012 341 E
ahelmus@cfcc.edu
HELMUS, Mark .... 765-285-5555 156 C
dmhelmus@bsu.edu
HELOU, Ibrahim (Abe) .. 909-593-3511.. 70 E
ihelou@laverne.edu
HELSPER, Nancy .... 320-589-6012 251 A
helsper@morris.umn.edu
HELSTON, Stephanie ..... 212-757-1190 298 D
shelston@funeraleducation.org
HELTON, Karen .... 903-927-3369 471 B
khelton@wileyc.edu
HELTON, Patricia .... 727-873-4882 111 B
phelton@mail.usf.edu
HELTON, Tom .... 706-507-8909 118 C
helton_tom@columbusstate.edu
HELVERING, Christal ..... 765-641-4205 156 A
crhelvering@anderson.edu
HELVESTON, David .... 225-308-4420 192 A
davidhelveston@lctcs.edu
HELWIG, Anna .... 708-596-2000 151 H
ahelwig@ssc.edu
HELWIG, Christine, A ... 518-629-7343 310 G
c.helwig@hvcc.edu
HELWIG, Daniel .... 717-867-6220 399 J
helwig@lvc.edu
HELWIG, Susan, M .... 570-674-6368 401 M
shelwig@misericordia.edu
HELYER, Kella .... 503-838-8684 388 B
helyerk@wou.edu
HEMANN, Patty .... 507-433-0816 247 C
patty.hemann@riverland.edu
HEMANS, Peter .... 828-694-1723 341 B
peterh@blueridge.edu
HEMBREE, Jennifer .... 707-654-1780.. 32 E
jhembree@csum.edu
HEMBREE, Lois, D .... 620-421-6700 179 D
loish@labette.edu
HEMENWAY, Jessica ..... 920-693-1118 513 H
jessica.hemenway@gotoltc.edu
HEMENWAY, Michael ..... 303-765-3173.. 80 G
mhemenway@iliff.edu
HEMESATH, Michael ..... 320-363-2882 250 A
sjpresident@csbsju.edu
HEMINGWAY, Wen .... 810-766-4105 227 F
whemin01@baker.edu
HEMKER, Judy .... 618-545-3105 142 D
jhemker@kaskaskia.edu
HEMLICK, Lisa, M .... 610-341-5830 394 E
lhemlick@eastern.edu
HEMMASI, Harriette ...... 401-863-2162 415 K
harriette_hemmasi@brown.edu
HEMMENBACH, Jimmi .. 808-543-8083 129 C
jhemmenbach@hpu.edu
HEMMER, Katie .... 212-842-5962 316 F
khemmer@nyaa.edu
HEMMER, Laura .... 314-505-7203 258 I
hemmerl@csl.edu
HEMMER, Michelle .... 919-508-2260 353 C
michelle.hemmer@peace.edu

HEMMESCH, Michael .... 320-363-2595 250 A
mhemmesch@csbsju.edu
HEMMESCH, Michael .... 320-363-2595 241 I
mhemmesch@csbsju.edu
HEMMILA, Deanna .... 906-227-2637 235 A
dhemmila@nmu.edu
HEMMINGSEN, Jens ..... 614-236-6105 358 A
jhemming@capital.edu
HEMMINWAY, Robin ..... 612-238-4542 250 B
rhemenwa@smumn.edu
HEMPEL, Lamont, C ...... 909-748-8589.. 71 H
monty_hempel@redlands.edu
HEMPEN, Laurie .... 319-208-5063 173 G
lhempen@scciowa.edu
HEMPHILL, Brian, O ..... 540-831-5401 484 A
president@radford.edu
HEMPHILL, F. Bruce ..... 337-475-5563 197 B
bhemphill@mcneese.edu
HEMPHILL, Teale .... 719-336-1591.. 80 N
teale.hemphill@lamarcc.edu
HEMPILL, Geoffrey .... 718-420-4269 333 D
geoffrey.hempill@wagner.edu
HEMPSEY, John Paul ..... 928-524-7418.. 15 B
paul.hempsey@npc.edu
HEMPTON, David, N ..... 617-496-8026 215 G
dhempton@hds.harvard.edu
HEMRIC, Cheryl .... 910-296-2070 344 B
chemric@jamessprunt.edu
HEMRICK, Robert, D ..... 731-425-2636 437 B
dhemrick@jscc.edu
HEMWAY, Joseph .... 718-399-4293 320 D
jhemway@pratt.edu
HENAHAN, David .... 518-587-2100 329 C
david.henahan@esc.edu
HENAN, Carmen .... 505-424-2336 294 C
chenan@iaia.edu
HENARD, Kevin .... 254-298-8425 458 C
kevin.henard@templejc.edu
HENCHEY, Russell .... 740-245-7231 372 E
rhenchey@rio.edu
HENCHY, Alexandra ...... 859-858-2049 183 C
HENCHY, Dolores .... 201-355-1133 286 C
henchyd@felician.edu
HENCK, Anita .... 626-815-5348.. 26 U
ahenck@apu.edu
HENDERSHOT, Debra .... 256-306-2581.... 1 F
debi.hendershot@calhoun.edu
HENDERSHOT, Jason .... 814-393-2111 405 H
jhendershot@clarion.edu
HENDERSHOT,
Stephanie, N .... 412-262-6251 409 C
hendershot@rmu.edu
HENDERSON, Aaron .... 559-453-2207.. 43 J
aaron.henderson@fresno.edu
HENDERSON, Aimee ...... 662-846-4391 252 H
ahenderson@deltastate.edu
HENDERSON, Allan, D .. 314-773-0083 257 J
ahenderson@brookesbible.org
HENDERSON, Allen .... 817-531-4405 463 G
ahenderson@txwes.edu
HENDERSON, Andrea .... 309-298-1977 155 D
ad-henderson@wiu.edu
HENDERSON, Angela .... 773-995-2411 135 F
ahende22@csu.edu
HENDERSON, Brad .... 620-331-4100 178 E
bhenderson@indycc.edu
HENDERSON, Brad .... 806-291-3616 470 I
brad.henderson@wbu.edu
HENDERSON, Brian .... 276-656-0313 489 A
bhenderson@patrickhenry.edu
HENDERSON, Carol .... 315-364-3356 333 G
chenderson@wells.edu
HENDERSON, Carol, E .. 302-831-3919.. 90 I
ceh@udel.edu
HENDERSON, Carrie ..... 904-632-3307 100 F
carrie.henderson@fscj.edu
HENDERSON,
Chiquita, A .... 727-816-3205 105 C
henderc@phsc.edu
HENDERSON, Christina . 515-271-1501 168 G
christina.henderson@dmu.edu
HENDERSON, Christine . 773-371-5450 134 J
chenderson@ctu.edu
HENDERSON, Cori .... 859-572-6534 188 E
hendersonc5@nku.edu
HENDERSON, Cynthia ... 903-223-3053 460 D
cynthia.henderson@tamut.edu
HENDERSON, Danny ...... 405-682-7890 377 C
danny.m.henderson@occc.edu
HENDERSON, Darren ..... 219-473-4346 157 A
dhenderson@ccsj.edu
HENDERSON,
Darwin, C .... 505-786-4300 294 I
chenderson@navajotech.edu
HENDERSON, Dave .... 541-917-4331 384 A
henderd@linnbenton.edu
HENDERSON, Debbie .... 417-690-2222 258 E
henderson@cofo.edu
HENDERSON, Dee .... 731-424-3520 437 B
dhenderson@jscc.edu
HENDERSON, Donna ..... 757-822-1898 489 H
dhenderson@tcc.edu
HENDERSON, Eddie, W 806-651-2600 460 E
ehenderson@mail.wtamu.edu
HENDERSON, George .... 704-330-4806 342 A
george.henderson@cpcc.edu
HENDERSON, Howard ... 580-349-1380 377 E
howardh@opsu.edu
HENDERSON, Idell .... 404-527-6356 122 B
ihenderson@itc.edu
HENDERSON, James ..... 856-256-4175 289 H
henderson@rowan.edu
HENDERSON, James, B 225-342-6950 196 F
jim.henderson@la.gov
HENDERSON, James, P 608-262-3826 510 B
jhenderson@uwsa.edu
HENDERSON, Janice ..... 850-729-5392 104 E
hendersonj@nwfsc.edu
HENDERSON, Joe, T ..... 731-881-3506 440 B
jhende33@utm.edu
HENDERSON, John .... 217-581-8396 138 A
jghenderson@eiu.edu
HENDERSON, Julie .... 510-987-9195.. 68 F
julie.henderson@ucop.edu
HENDERSON, Kathy ...... 408-855-5113.. 74 C
kathy.henderson@missioncollege.edu
HENDERSON, Keli .... 724-938-5985 405 F
henderson_k@calu.edu
HENDERSON, Kenneth .. 617-373-5089 223 D
HENDERSON, Kyle, W .. 740-427-5729 364 A
hendersonk@kenyon.edu
HENDERSON, Lisle .... 718-636-3664 320 D
lhenders@pratt.edu
HENDERSON, Mantra .... 662-254-3495 255 A
mlhenderson@mvsu.edu
HENDERSON, Mark .... 217-244-6227 154 B
mhenders@illinois.edu
HENDERSON, Mark .... 713-525-3155 466 J
hendermk@stthom.edu
HENDERSON, Michelle . 760-252-2411.. 27 A
mhenderson@barstow.edu
HENDERSON, Mitchell .. 718-482-5534 303 B
mhenderson@lagcc.cuny.edu
HENDERSON, Nancy ..... 319-296-4448 169 H
nancy.henderson@hawkeyecollege.edu
HENDERSON, Necedah . 256-233-8151.... 4 C
necedah.henderson@athens.edu
HENDERSON, Nicole ..... 215-641-6545 402 A
nhenders@mc3.edu
HENDERSON, Pamela ... 251-460-6133.... 9 B
phenderson@southalabama.edu
HENDERSON, Paul .... 207-602-2302 202 A
phenderson@une.edu
HENDERSON, Peter .... 410-455-3263 208 A
phenders@umbc.edu
HENDERSON, Ron, R .... 618-235-2700 152 E
ronald.henderson@swic.edu
HENDERSON, Sandra .... 205-929-6333.... 2 G
shenderson@lawsonstate.edu
HENDERSON, Sean .... 559-442-8295.. 66 G
sean.henderson@fresnocitycollege.edu
HENDERSON, Sharon .... 334-833-4482.... 5 M
0377mgr@fheg.follett.com
HENDERSON, Sue .... 201-200-3111 287 F
shenderson@njcu.edu
HENDERSON, Susan ..... 843-383-8264 420 B
shenderson@coker.edu
HENDERSON, Tammy .... 850-484-1766 105 E
thenderson@pensacolastate.edu
HENDERSON, Toni .... 910-296-2438 344 B
thenderson@jamessprunt.edu
HENDERSON, Tony, C .. 313-831-5200 229 L
thenderson@etseminary.edu
HENDERSON, Trennis ... 870-245-5206.. 20 G
hendersont@obu.edu
HENDERSON, Virginia ... 601-968-5903 252 C
vhenderson@belhaven.edu
HENDERSON, Zandra .... 713-718-6202 450 D
zandra.henderson@hccs.edu
HENDERSON-GASSER,
Ellen .... 217-357-3129 134 H
ehenderson@sandburg.edu
HENDLER, Gail .... 708-216-9192 144 D
ghendler@lumc.edu
HENDREY, Elizabeth ...... 718-997-5900 303 E
elizabeth.hendrey@qc.cuny.edu
HENDRICK, Ronald .... 517-355-0232 233 G
hendric6@msu.edu
HENDRICK, Sarah .... 661-654-3370.. 31 B
shendrick@csub.edu
HENDRICK, Sarah .... 860-932-4096.. 86 E
shendrick@qvcc.edu
HENDRICKS, Barbara .... 612-359-6496 240 G
hendricb@augsburg.edu
HENDRICKS, Bill .... 214-887-5252 448 G
bhendricks@dts.edu
HENDRICKS, Cynthia, L 651-696-6145 243 B
chendric@macalester.edu
HENDRICKS, Dawn .... 570-321-4022 400 G
henddawn@lycoming.edu
HENDRICKS, Francis, L 570-662-4046 406 F
fhendricks@mansfield.edu
HENDRICKS, Jeff .... 270-852-8977 186 F
jhendricks0008@kctcs.edu
HENDRICKS, Jeff .... 336-278-5580 337 G
jhendrick4@elon.edu
HENDRICKS, Joan, C .... 215-898-8841 412 G
vetdean@vet.upenn.edu
HENDRICKS, Laurie, M . 515-574-1145 170 C
hendricks@iowacentral.edu
HENDRICKS, JR., Lynn . 305-348-3661 109 D
llynn.hendricks@fiu.edu
HENDRICKS, Michael .... 864-294-2000 421 I
michael.hendricks@furman.edu
HENDRICKS,
Michelle, M .... 570-577-2404 390 H
michelle.jones@bucknell.edu
HENDRICKS, Richard, J 708-974-5203 146 C
HENDRICKS, Ron .... 202-274-2303.. 94 B
marketing@potomac.edu
HENDRICKS, Sylvia .... 520-383-8401.. 16 G
shendricks@tocc.edu
HENDRICKS, Tom, M .... 248-233-2814 235 D
tmhendri@oaklandcc.edu
HENDRICKS HARIG,
Linda .... 865-974-8170 439 H
linda.hendricks@tennessee.edu
HENDRICKSON,
Anthony, R .... 402-280-2852 274 D
anthonyhendrickson@creighton.edu
HENDRICKSON, SJ,
Daniel, S .... 402-280-2770 274 D
president@creighton.edu
HENDRICKSON, Karen ... 701-231-8356 354 D
karen.hendrickson@ndsu.edu
HENDRICKSON, Ken ..... 936-294-1031 462 F
his_keh@shsu.edu
HENDRICKSON,
Kristine .... 401-341-2148 417 D
hendrick@salve.edu
HENDRICKSON, Philip .. 402-643-7358 274 B
philip.hendrickson@cune.edu
HENDRICKSON,
Ryan, C .... 217-581-2220 138 A
rchendrickson@eiu.edu
HENDRICKSON, Sandy .. 425-889-5232 496 E
sandy.hendrickson@northwestu.edu
HENDRICKSON, Tracy ... 218-335-4200 242 I
HENDRICKSON,
Vicki, A .... 918-631-2526 381 C
vicki-hendrickson@utulsa.edu
HENDRIKSMA, Jane, E . 616-526-6116 228 B
jhendrik@calvin.edu
HENDRIX, Andrew .... 803-641-3490 425 A
andrewh@usca.edu
HENDRIX, Dean, D .... 210-458-4889 468 B
dean.hendrix@utsa.edu
HENDRIX, Frances .... 405-733-7394 379 F
fhendrix@rose.edu
HENDRIX, Grace .... 208-882-1566 132 D
ghendrix@nsa.edu
HENDRIX, Joan .... 601-766-6425 254 D
joan.hendrix@mgccc.edu
HENDRIX, Kristie, F ...... 336-734-7051 343 C
khendrix@forsythtech.edu
HENDRIX, Mary .... 304-876-5107 504 D
mhendrix@shepherd.edu
HENDRIX, Pat .... 931-393-1629 437 C
phendrix@mscc.edu
HENDRY, Christopher ... 978-665-4933 217 E
chendry@fitchburgstate.edu
HENDRY, David .... 727-873-4475 111 B
dhendry@usf.edu
HENDRYX, Julie, A .... 260-422-5561 159 D
jahendryx@indianatech.edu
HENEGAR, Kellie .... 618-545-3025 142 D
khenegar@kaskaskia.edu
HENGSTERMAN, Stacey 518-320-1148 324 F
stacey.hengsterman@suny.edu
HENICK, Steven, T .... 410-777-2429 202 D
sthenick@aacc.edu
HENIK, John .... 319-398-5518 171 F
jhenik@kirkwood.edu
HENK, William, A .... 414-288-7376 508 C
william.henk@marquette.edu
HENKARO, Daniel .... 334-874-5700.... 5 B
dhenkaro@ccal.edu
HENKE, Corrine .... 208-426-4045 131 C
chenke@boisestate.edu
HENKE, Holger .... 908-737-5326 286 F
hhenke@wku.edu
HENKELMAN, Amy .... 415-257-1304.. 41 J
amy.henkelman@dominican.edu
HENLEY, Antonio .... 704-330-1320 338 I
ahenley@jcsu.edu
HENLEY, Blair .... 423-636-7300 439 C
bhenley@tusculum.edu
HENLEY, Brian, L .... 423-439-4213 431 H
henleybl@etsu.edu
HENLEY, Charles .... 936-294-4719 462 F
ceh071@shsu.edu
HENLEY, Dolly .... 870-777-5722.. 23 A
dolly.henley@uacch.edu
HENLEY, Keldon .... 870-245-4188.. 20 G
henleyk@obu.edu
HENLEY, Kyle .... 541-346-2329 387 F
henley@uoregon.edu
HENLEY, Marilynn, D .... 602-614-2337.. 10 E
HENLEY, Marsia .... 215-751-8902 393 A
mhenley@ccp.edu
HENNES, Doug, E .... 651-962-6402 251 D
dehennes@stthomas.edu
HENNESSEY, Brendan ... 575-562-2424 293 O
brendan.hennessey@enmu.edu
HENNESSEY, David .... 617-243-2478 216 C
dhennessey@lasell.edu
HENNESSEY, Judith .... 530-898-6189.. 31 D
jehennessey@csuchico.edu
HENNESSEY, Patrick ...... 914-606-6638 333 H
patrick.hennessey@sunywcc.edu
HENNESSEY, Richard .... 203-332-5079.. 85 F
rhennessey@hcc.commnet.edu
HENNESSY, Cari Lynn ... 773-907-4456 135 K
chennessy4@ccc.edu
HENNESSY, Catherine ... 516-463-6820 310 D
catherine.hennessy@hofstra.edu
HENNESSY, John, L .... 650-723-2300.. 66 C
HENNESSY, Lynne, M ... 203-773-8529.. 84 G
lhennessy@albertus.edu
HENNESSY, Michael ...... 512-245-2317 463 A
mh17@txstate.edu
HENNIG, Kathy .... 415-487-2413.. 37 H
khenning@ccsf.edu
HENNIGAN, Ed .... 570-740-0399 400 F
ehennigan@luzerne.edu
HENNIGAN, Paul .... 412-392-3990 408 F
phennigan@pointpark.edu
HENNIGES, Amy .... 920-465-2380 510 E
hennigea@uwgb.edu
HENNING, Amy .... 215-572-2900 389 D
henninga@arcadia.edu
HENNING, John .... 732-571-4484 287 C
jhenning@monmouth.edu
HENNING, Kent, L .... 515-263-2802 169 E
khenning@grandview.edu
HENNING, Patricia .... 505-277-6128 296 H
henning@unm.edu
HENNING, Patricia .... 269-548-3217 231 G
phenning@kvcc.edu
HENNING, Stefanie .... 617-747-2246 212 B
careercenter@berklee.edu
HENNING, Stephanie ..... 641-628-5343 167 D
hennings@central.edu
HENNING, William .... 715-833-6670 513 E
whenning@cvtc.edu
HENNINGER, Betty .... 503-883-2568 383 H
behennin@linfield.edu
HENNINGER,
Edward, A .... 570-326-3761 404 T
ehenning@pct.edu
HENNINGSEN,
James, D .... 352-873-5835.. 97 C
jim.henningsen@cf.edu
HENNIS, Anne, R .... 336-386-3451 347 A
hennisa@surry.edu
HENRICH, IHM, Mary .... 610-647-4400 397 I
mhenrich@immaculata.edu
HENRICH, William, L ...... 210-567-2050 468 E
henrich@uthscsa.edu
HENRICHS, Susan, M .... 907-474-7096.. 10 B
smhenrichs@alaska.edu
HENRICHSEN, Courtney 636-584-6583 259 L
courtney.henrichsen@eastcentral.edu
HENRICKSON, Jay, A .... 701-788-4899 354 B
jay.henrickson@mayvillestate.edu
HENRIE, Kimberly .... 801-321-7104 472 O
khenrie@ushe.edu
HENRIE, M. Elaine .... 620-341-5211 177 B
ehenrie@emporia.edu
HENRIE, M. Elaine .... 620-341-5457 177 B
ehenrie@emporia.edu
HENRIKSEN, Deb .... 605-642-6581 428 F
deb.henriksen@bhsu.edu
HENRIKSEN, J.L .... 509-533-7295 493 I
jl.henriksen@scc.spokane.edu
HENRIKSEN, Melanie ..... 503-552-1848 384 F
mhenriksen@nunm.edu
HENRIKSEN, Smokey ..... 406-338-5441 270 G
smokeyh@bfcc.edu
HENRIQUES, Richard .... 402-486-2511 277 C
richard.henriqes@ucollege.edu

HENRIQUES, Shilo .... 508-588-9100 220 B
HENRIQUEZ, Ernesto .... 607-436-3592 325 E
ernesto.henriquez@oneonta.edu
HENRIS, Dan .... 989-463-7144 226 H
henris@alma.edu
HENRIS, Shawn .... 716-827-2522 331 K
henriss@trocaire.edu
HENRY, Alison .... 609-652-4831 291 H
alison.henry@stockton.edu
HENRY, Amy .... 404-894-7475 120 A
amy.henry@oie.gatech.edu
HENRY, Barbara, L .... 419-372-4825 357 F
bhenry@bgsu.edu
HENRY, Carolyn, J .... 573-882-7821 268 C
henryc@missouri.edu
HENRY, Charles, E .... 713-313-4343 461 E
henryce@tsu.edu
HENRY, Dale .... 731-352-4239 430 E
henryd@bethelu.edu
HENRY, David .... 813-974-4150 111 A
dlhenry@usf.edu
HENRY, Debbie .... 832-842-5786 465 A
daherman@central.uh.edu
HENRY, Deena, H .... 919-209-2017 344 C
dhhenry@johnstoncc.edu
HENRY, Donna, P .... 276-328-0122 487 A
dhenry@uvawise.edu
HENRY, Earl .... 256-726-8308.... 6 E
ehenry@oakwood.edu
HENRY, Ed .... 941-752-5323 108 P
henrye@scf.edu
HENRY, Etta, A .... 757-683-5889 483 G
ehenry@odu.edu
HENRY, Geneva .... 202-994-6455.. 92 A
genevahenry@gwu.edu
HENRY, Glenn .... 706-355-5033 115 H
ghenry@athenstech.edu
HENRY, Jamie .... 618-544-8657 140 D
henryj@iecc.edu
HENRY, Jennifer .... 314-529-9552 262 B
jhenry@maryville.edu
HENRY, Jerlynn .... 505-786-4180 294 I
jhenry@navajotech.edu
HENRY, Jerry, W .... 361-698-2178 448 H
jhenry12@delmar.edu
HENRY, Jonathan .... 207-941-7720 199 B
henryj@husson.edu
HENRY, Karl .... 251-665-4099.... 1 E
khenry@bishop.edu
HENRY, Kelly .... 716-884-9120 300 C
kkhenry@bryantstratton.edu
HENRY, Kevin, C .... 717-866-5775 395 C
khenry@evangelical.edu
HENRY, Kimberly .... 712-325-3207 170 K
khenry@iwcc.edu
HENRY, Kyonna .... 920-748-8190 509 H
henryk@ripon.edu
HENRY, LaTonya .... 830-372-8178 461 D
lhenry@tlu.edu
HENRY, Linda .... 913-360-7500 175 D
lhenry@benedictine.edu
HENRY, Marci .... 970-521-6617.. 81 F
marci.henry@njc.edu
HENRY, Matthew .... 903-233-3510 452 A
matthewhenry@letu.edu
HENRY, Melanie .... 985-380-2483 193 D
melaniehenry@scl.edu
HENRY, Melody .... 903-434-8148 453 M
mhenry@ntcc.edu
HENRY, Nick .... 706-272-4435 118 F
nhenry@daltonstate.edu
HENRY, Peter, B .... 212-998-0909 318 D
pbhenry@nyu.edu
HENRY, Rachel .... 402-471-2505 276 A
rhenry@nscs.edu
HENRY, Robert .... 413-572-5205 218 F
rhenry@westfield.ma.edu
HENRY, Robert, H .... 405-208-5032 377 D
rhenry@okcu.edu
HENRY, Ronald .... 850-599-3560 109 A
ronald.henry@famu.edu
HENRY, Ryan .... 806-743-9855 463 E
ryan.henry@ttuhsc.edu
HENRY, Sandra .... 334-983-6556.... 7 E
shenry@troy.edu
HENRY, Shannon, B ...... 336-750-2020 352 D
henrysb@wssu.edu
HENRY, Veronica .... 631-420-2622 329 D
veronica.henry@farmingdale.edu
HENRY, William .... 559-791-2315.. 47 C
bhenry@portervillecollege.edu
HENRY, Winfield .... 336-506-4136 340 L
winfield.henry@almanancecc.edu
HENRY POWELL, Jonita 704-379-6800.. 93 B
HENRY-QUINN, Barbara 877-442-0505.. 84 B
barbara.henry-quinn@rockies.edu

HENRY ROBINSON,
Shanelle .... 914-773-3775 319 J
shenryrobinson@pace.edu
HENSEL, Chad .... 740-389-4636 365 B
henselc@mtc.edu
HENSEL, Desiree .... 812-855-7089 159 H
dehensel@indiana.edu
HENSEL, Wendy .... 404-413-9040 121 A
whensel@gsu.edu
HENSGEN, Brian, C .... 217-442-3044 137 B
bhensgen@dacc.edu
HENSHAW, Debbie .... 706-649-1888 118 D
dhenshaw@columbustech.edu
HENSHAW, Rodney, N .. 515-271-3993 168 J
rod.henshaw@drake.edu
HENSLER, Brandon .... 954-262-5385 104 F
bh623@nova.edu
HENSLEY, Alec .... 812-749-1421 163 B
ahensley@oak.edu
HENSLEY, Chiara .... 734-487-0074 229 K
emu_ombuds@emich.edu
HENSLEY, Lige .... 317-921-4882 161 F
lhensley@ivytech.edu
HENSLEY, Linda .... 619-388-2797.. 60 D
lhensley@sdccd.edu
HENSLEY, Mary .... 979-830-4112 444 D
chancellor@blinn.edu
HENSLEY, Michele, R .... 540-432-4139 480 A
michele.hensley@emu.edu
HENSLEY, Ron .... 417-255-7268 263 I
ronhensley@missouristate.edu
HENSLEY, Steve, L .... 864-242-5100 418 H
HENSON, Alexander, L .. 804-828-0138 487 E
alhenson@vcu.edu
HENSON, Don .... 901-722-4719 436 D
dhenson@sco.edu
HENSON, Gregory, J ..... 605-336-6588 428 B
ghenson@sfseminary.edu
HENSON, John, H .... 717-245-1434 394 A
henson@dickinson.edu
HENSON, Kevin .... 714-432-5796.. 38 H
khenson@occ.cccd.edu
HENSON, Michael, C .... 606-783-9080 188 C
m.henson@moreheadstate.edu
HENSON, Nicholas .... 937-395-8112 364 B
nicholas.henson@kc.edu
HENSON, Pamella, A .... 314-935-5277 269 L
hensonp@wustl.edu
HENSON, Perry .... 864-597-4000 426 I
hensonpv@wofford.edu
HENSON, Richard .... 408-498-0100.. 38 I
rhenson@cogswell.edu
HENSON, Travis .... 618-545-3177 142 D
thenson@kaskaskia.edu
HENSRUD, Faith .... 218-333-6600 246 G
fhensrud@bemidjistate.edu
HENSRUD, Faith, C .... 218-755-2011 244 B
fhensrud@bemidjistate.edu
HENTHORN, Becky .... 580-387-7000 376 D
bhenthorn@mscok.edu
HENTIES, Brian, B .... 407-582-3337 113 F
mhenties@valenciacollege.edu
HENTON, June, M .... 334-844-4790.... 4 D
hentoju@auburn.edu
HENTSCHEL, Alain, R .... 386-312-4302 106 M
alainhentschel@sjrstate.edu
HENTZ, Paula .... 386-822-7012 111 E
phentz@stetson.edu
HENZE, George .... 920-693-1733 513 H
george.henze@gotoltc.edu
HENZEL, JR., John, R .. 706-245-7226 119 A
jhenzel@ec.edu
HEOS, Pamela .... 517-371-5140 239 F
heosp@cooley.edu
HEPBURN, Deborah, G . 814-371-2090 412 B
dhepburn@triangle-tech.edu
HEPBURN, Deborah, G . 412-359-1000 412 C
dhepburn@triangle-tech.edu
HEPBURN, Deborah, G . 814-371-2090 412 C
dhepburn@triangle-tech.edu
HEPERI, Vernon, L .... 801-422-7254 471 E
vernon_heperi@byu.edu
HEPHNER LABANC,
Brandi .... 662-915-7705 256 C
bhl@olemiss.edu
HEPLER, Lisa, L .... 814-393-2229 405 H
lhepler@clarion.edu
HEPNER, Kevin .... 617-708-3501 221 A
khepner@rcc.mass.edu
HEPPERT, Joseph .... 806-742-3904 463 D
joseph.heppert@ttu.edu
HEPPNER, Angela .... 817-554-5950 452 G
aheppner@messengercollege.edu
HEPPNER, Erich .... 218-855-8000 244 C
HEPPNER, Harold, H ...... 406-353-2607 270 E
hheppner@ancollege.edu
HER, Chou .... 209-228-7865.. 69 C
cher@ucmerced.edu

HERALD, John .... 606-886-3863 185 F
john.herald@kctcs.edu
HERAN, Dieter .... 734-995-7502 229 A
security@cuaa.edu
HERATH, Ludmi .... 361-570-4109 465 D
herathl@uhv.edu
HERB, Amanda .... 740-374-8716 373 G
aherb@wscc.edu
HERB, Amanda, K .... 740-374-8716 373 G
aherb@wscc.edu
HERB, Martha .... 202-646-1337.. 92 E
HERBERT, Eileen, C ...... 716-888-2791 300 G
herberte@canisius.edu
HERBERT, George, E ..... 319-335-3179 166 G
george-herbert@uiowa.edu
HERBERT, James .... 207-602-2306 202 A
HERBERT, Jane .... 212-817-7100 302 B
jherbert@gc.cuny.edu
HERBERT, Jennifer, J .... 304-724-3700 501 D
jherbert@apus.edu
HERBERT, Julie .... 440-375-7000 364 C
jherbert@lec.edu
HERBERT, Loren .... 215-968-8638 390 I
loren.herbert@bucks.edu
HERBERT, Mike .... 541-888-7208 387 A
mherbert@socc.edu
HERBERT, Tom .... 513-529-4029 365 I
herbertw@miamioh.edu
HERBERT-ASHTON,
Marilyn, J .... 540-857-6372 490 B
mherbert-ashton@virginiawestern.edu
HERBOLD, Kirk .... 830-372-8150 461 D
kherbold@tlu.edu
HERBRAND, Laurie .... 209-228-2741.. 69 C
lherbrand@ucmerced.edu
HERBST, Adam .... 320-363-3819 250 A
aherbst@csbsju.edu
HERBST, Daniel .... 480-732-7120.. 13 E
daniel.herbst@cgc.edu
HERBST, Joel .... 561-297-3970 109 B
jherbst1@fau.edu
HERBST, John, H .... 859-257-5781 190 B
herbst@uky.edu
HERBST, Shea, A .... 563-556-5110 172 D
herbsts@nicc.edu
HERBST, Susan .... 860-486-2337.. 88 G
president@uconn.edu
HERBSTER, David .... 605-677-5309 428 E
david.herbster@usd.edu
HERBSTER, Jessica .... 334-347-2623.... 1 J
jherbster@escc.edu
HERBURGER, Lida .... 541-463-3142 383 F
herburgerl@lanecc.edu
HERCOD, Laura, H .... 603-646-0574 281 C
laura.h.hercod@dartmouth.edu
HERDLICK, Mike .... 419-448-3421 370 K
herdlickm@tiffin.edu
HEREDIA, Maria .... 619-398-4902.. 45 F
mheredia@hightechhigh.org
HERENDEEN, Steve, A .. 260-422-5561 159 D
saherendeen@indianatech.edu
HERESHKO, David .... 570-784-3123 405 E
hereshko@bloomu.edu
HERFEL, Amy .... 608-249-6611 507 F
amyherfel@herzing.edu
HERGAN, Mark, J .... 443-352-4400 207 C
mhergan@stevenson.edu
HERGERT, Travis, J .... 641-422-4990 172 C
hergetra@niacc.edu
HERIGON, Amber .... 406-791-5248 273 C
amber.herigon@ugf.edu
HERINGER, David .... 325-793-4700 452 F
heringer.david@mcm.edu
HERLETH, Sally .... 660-785-4031 267 K
sallydet@truman.edu
HERLEY, Wade .... 402-844-7299 276 G
wade@northeast.edu
HERLIHY, Jim .... 803-641-3406 425 A
HERLIHY, Joseph, M .... 617-552-2855 212 E
joseph.herlihy@bc.edu
HERLOCKER, Linda, K ... 407-582-1511 113 F
lherlocker@valenciacollege.edu
HERMAN, Alyssa .... 212-960-0863 334 P
alyssa.herman@yu.edu
HERMAN, Amber .... 336-838-6292 347 G
adherman130@wilkescc.edu
HERMAN, Anne .... 503-352-2777 385 I
hermana@pacificu.edu
HERMAN, Barbara, B ..... 817-257-7855 461 A
b.herman@tcu.edu
HERMAN, Bruce .... 410-455-2460 208 A
bherman@umbc.edu
HERMAN, Bruce .... 410-455-2472 208 A
bherman@umbc.edu
HERMAN, Deborah .... 860-512-2872.. 85 G
dherman@manchestercc.edu
HERMAN, Harry .... 516-323-3503 315 J
hherman@molloy.edu

HERMAN, Jack .... 605-856-5880 428 A
jack.herman@sintegleska.edu
HERMAN, Jeanne .... 330-941-2264 374 E
jmherman@ysu.edu
HERMAN, Jeff .... 828-726-2294 341 D
jherman@cccti.edu
HERMAN, Jeffrey .... 619-849-2534.. 57 H
jeffreyherman@pointloma.edu
HERMAN, Nick .... 703-993-9515 481 B
nherman@gmu.edu
HERMAN, Rachel .... 608-342-1891 511 D
hermanra@uwplatt.edu
HERMAN, Sharon .... 919-278-2669 348 I
sharon.herman@shawu.edu
HERMAN, Stacie .... 330-490-7365 373 F
sherman@walsh.edu
HERMAN, Vanessa, J .... 212-346-1025 319 J
vherman@pace.edu
HERMAN-BARLOW,
Janet .... 440-366-7105 364 F
HERMANN, David .... 815-802-8524 142 C
dhermann@kcc.edu
HERMANN, Michael .... 785-833-4410 179 C
mike.hermann@kwu.edu
HERMANN, Paula .... 785-833-4337 179 C
paula.hermann@kwu.edu
HERMANN-ARTIM,
Diane .... 802-388-5371 477 B
dmh01060@ccv.vsc.edu
HERMANO, Mara .... 401-454-6336 417 B
mhermano@risd.edu
HERMANSEN, Beckie ..... 435-283-7346 474 A
beckie.hermansen@snow.edu
HERMANSEN,
Noreen, M .... 319-273-6078 167 A
noreen.hermansen@uni.edu
HERMANSTON, Fran ...... 509-335-3942 499 G
HERMES, Chuck .... 920-424-3466 511 B
hermes@uwosh.edu
HERMES, John .... 405-425-1815 377 B
john.hermes@oc.edu
HERMES, Joseph .... 312-996-3490 153 H
jhermes@uic.edu
HERMES, Wayne, J .... 970-247-7432.. 79 J
hermes_w@fortlewis.edu
HERMON, Vada .... 620-227-9213 176 N
vhermon@dc3.edu
HERMS, Ron .... 559-453-2075.. 43 J
ron.herms@fresno.edu
HERMSEN, Cindy, L .... 248-370-3370 235 J
hermsen@oakland.edu
HERNÁNDEZ, Olga .... 787-834-5151 525 J
olgan_hernandez@pucpr.edu
HERNÁNDEZ, Walitza .... 787-884-3838 520 G
dir_registra@atenascollege.edu
HERNÁNDEZ NÚÑEZ,
Maria, L .... 787-884-3838 520 G
presidenta@atenascollege.edu
HERN, Marcia, J .... 502-852-8300 190 C
m.hern@louisville.edu
HERN, Marsha, L .... 716-338-1060 311 F
marshahern@mail.sunyjcc.edu
HERNANDEZ, Albert ...... 303-765-3183.. 80 G
ahernandez@iliff.edu
HERNANDEZ, Alex .... 915-831-6383 449 A
aherna78@epcc.edu
HERNANDEZ, Alfredo .... 561-732-4424 107 C
ahernandez@svdp.edu
HERNANDEZ, Alina .... 504-816-4024 191 E
ahernandez@dillard.edu
HERNANDEZ, Ana .... 813-974-4262 111 A
ahernandez@usf.edu
HERNANDEZ,
Aracely, C .... 956-326-2232 459 B
achernandez@tamiu.edu
HERNANDEZ, Arnold ...... 208-459-5868 131 H
ahernandez@collegeofidaho.edu
HERNANDEZ, Axel, N ... 858-499-0202.. 39 B
ahernandez@coleman.edu
HERNANDEZ, Ayana, D . 919-530-7266 350 D
ahernandez@nccu.edu
HERNANDEZ, Brian .... 787-284-1912 524 C
bhernand@ponce.inter.edu
HERNANDEZ, Caridad ... 305-821-3333 100 A
csanchez@fnu.edu
HERNANDEZ, Carlos ..... 936-294-2686 462 F
jch060@shsu.edu
HERNANDEZ, Carol .... 415-485-9506.. 39 E
chernandez@marin.edu
HERNANDEZ, Cathy ...... 602-286-8028.. 13 G
cathleen.hernandez@gwmail.maricopa.edu
HERNANDEZ, Christine . 916-558-2438.. 50 I
hernanc@scc.losrios.edu
HERNANDEZ, David .... 805-565-6164.. 74 I
dhernand@westmont.edu
HERNANDEZ, Deanne ... 713-500-3192 468 D
deanne.m.hernandez@uth.tmc.edu

HERTZ, Adam .... 610-328-8325 410 I
ahertz1@swarthmore.edu
HERTZ, Amy .... 828-884-8124 335 L
hertzae@brevard.edu
HERTZ, Elisa .... 646-313-8000 303 G
elisa.hertz@guttman.cuny.edu
HERTZ, Kara .... 509-313-5981 495 A
hertzk@gonzaga.edu
HERTZOG, Janet .... 607-778-5203 326 C
hertzogjm@sunybroome.edu
HERTZOG, Laura .... 212-772-4220 302 E
lschacht@hunter.cuny.edu
HERVEY, Brian, T .... 949-824-8941.. 69 A
bhervey@uci.edu
HERVEY, Lloyd .... 501-370-5237.. 21 A
lhervey@philander.edu
HERZ, Denise .... 323-343-4737.. 32 D
dherz@calstatela.edu
HERZBERG, Tina .... 864-503-5572 425 H
therzberg@uscupstate.edu
HERZBERGER,
Sharon, D .... 562-907-4201.. 75 A
president@whittier.edu
HERZEK, Farley .... 718-368-5109 303 A
president@kbcc.cuny.edu
HERZIG, Brenda, H .... 218-726-8794 250 F
bherzig@d.umn.edu
HERZING, Renee .... 608-249-6611 507 F
rherzing@herzing.edu
HERZOG, Jennifer .... 925-631-4108.. 59 C
jgh3@stmarys-ca.edu
HERZOG, Robert .... 608-249-6611 507 F
rherzog@herzing.edu
HERZOG, Serge .... 775-784-4546 279 E
serge@unr.edu
HESCH, Kim .... 701-845-7403 354 E
kim.hesch@vcsu.edu
HESCHT, Sonya .... 304-865-6113 502 C
sonya.hescht@ovu.edu
HESELIUS, Helen, S ...... 757-446-6065 480 C
heselihs@evms.edu
HESHEL, Alan .... 213-427-2200.. 35 O
HESKEL, Mitch .... 310-434-3414.. 62 G
heskel_mitch@smc.edu
HESKIN, Russel .... 909-469-5230.. 74 G
rheskin@westernu.edu
HESLEP, Debbie, S .... 662-846-4020 252 H
dheslep@deltastate.edu
HESLEPH, Jack .... 801-957-4013 474 B
jack.hesleph@slcc.edu
HESS, Allison, B .... 801-626-7948 473 E
ahess@weber.edu
HESS, Ann .... 928-536-6257.. 15 B
ann.hess@npc.edu
HESS, Cynthia .... 918-595-7980 380 D
cindy.hess@tulsacc.edu
HESS, Cynthia .... 254-968-9125 459 A
hess@tarleton.edu
HESS, Danielle .... 509-335-2636 499 G
danielleh@wsu.edu
HESS, Darrell .... 619-594-5639.. 34 B
dhess@sdsu.edu
HESS, David .... 706-721-2231 116 B
dhess@augusta.edu
HESS, Diana .... 608-262-1763 510 C
dhess@wisc.edu
HESS, E. Clayton .... 423-869-6391 433 C
clayton.hess@lmunet.edu
HESS, Gregory, D .... 765-361-6221 166 B
hessg@wabash.edu
HESS, Jay .... 317-278-0318 159 G
jayhess@iu.edu
HESS, Jay, L .... 317-278-0318 159 H
davis219@iu.edu
HESS, Jay, L .... 317-274-8157 160 E
jayhess@iu.edu
HESS, Kathleen .... 978-542-7316 218 E
khess@salemstate.edu
HESS, Kimberly, L .... 802-656-1467 476 E
kimberly.hess@uvm.edu
HESS, Maren .... 910-893-1200 336 C
hess@campbell.edu
HESS, Mitchell, R .... 314-516-6608 268 E
hessmr@umsl.edu
HESS, Pam .... 440-375-8005 364 C
phess@lec.edu
HESS, Patrice .... 309-694-5295 139 G
phess@icc.edu
HESS, Resa .... 760-384-6259.. 47 B
rhess@cerrocoso.edu
HESS, Richard .... 858-566-1200.. 41 G
rhess@disd.edu
HESS, Shimon .... 718-259-2525 299 I
HESS, Shivon .... 559-638-0300.. 66 H
shivon.hess@reedleycollege.edu
HESS, Stephen .... 801-581-3100 472 P
stephen.hess@utah.edu
HESS, Steve .... 866-687-2258.. 30 B

HESS, Thomas, R .... 606-218-5475 190 E
thomashess@upike.edu
HESS, Tim .... 765-285-1736 156 C
trhess@bsu.edu
HESS, William .... 510-628-8013.. 48 F
whess@lincolnuca.edu
HESS MOLL, Sandra ...... 815-455-8987 145 B
smoll@mchenry.edu
HESS SALISBURY, Kelly 508-531-1816 217 D
kelly.hess@bridgew.edu
HESSBERG, Lee .... 518-262-3828 297 L
hessbel@mail.amc.edu
HESSE, Amellia .... 641-472-7000 171 J
amhesse@mum.edu
HESSE, Aster .... 641-472-1110 171 J
aster@mum.edu
HESSE, Carla .... 510-642-5195.. 68 G
chesse@berkeley.edu
HESSE, Cindy .... 303-360-4752.. 79 C
cindy.hesse@ccaurora.edu
HESSE, Manyu .... 641-472-1190 171 J
mhesse@mum.edu
HESSEL, Skip .... 816-322-0110 257 M
skip.hessel@calvary.edu
HESSELMAN, James ...... 812-941-2227 161 A
jhesselm@ius.edu
HESSEN, David .... 610-372-4721 408 G
dhessen@racc.edu
HESSION, Katie .... 312-915-7781 144 D
khessio@luc.edu
HESTAND, Doug .... 419-755-4727 366 E
dhestand@ncstatecollege.edu
HESTAND, Phil .... 870-972-2318.. 18 A
phestand@astate.edu
HESTER, Amanda .... 228-497-7649 254 D
amanda.hester@mgccc.edu
HESTER, Barry, C .... 318-670-9407 196 A
bhester@susla.edu
HESTER, Dana .... 626-914-8870.. 37 G
dhester@citruscollege.edu
HESTER, Jean .... 614-222-3263 360 B
jhester@ccad.edu
HESTER, Kevin .... 615-675-5322 441 B
khester@welch.edu
HESTER, Mary .... 620-242-0487 179 G
hesterm@mcpherson.edu
HESTER, Melissa .... 910-879-5502 341 A
mhester@bladencc.edu
HESTER, Ranan .... 501-279-4331.. 19 G
rhester@harding.edu
HESTER, Rebeckah .... 765-973-8585 160 A
rrieder@iue.edu
HESTER, Richard .... 205-652-3581.... 9 C
rth@uwa.edu
HESTON, Chris .... 443-518-4603 204 E
cheston@howardcc.edu
HESTON, Grant .... 407-823-5988 110 C
grant.heston@ucf.edu
HESTON, Michele .... 863-784-7227 108 B
michele.heston@southflorida.edu
HETH, Justin .... 630-752-5022 155 F
justin.heth@wheaton.edu
HETHERINGTON,
Kathleen, B .... 443-518-1820 204 E
khetherington@howardcc.edu
HETHERINGTON,
Rhonda .... 208-376-7731 131 B
rhetherington@boisebible.edu
HETHERINGTON,
Stephen .... 856-227-7200 284 E
shetherington@camdencc.edu
HETHERINGTON,
Vincent, J .... 216-707-8004 363 I
vhetheri@kent.edu
HETHORN, Janet .... 989-774-1885 228 E
hetho1j@cmich.edu
HETRICK, Fran .... 719-502-3261.. 81 H
fran.hetrick@ppcc.edu
HETRICK, Janice .... 215-637-7700 397 G
jhetrick@holyfamily.edu
HETRICK, Jarred .... 814-371-2090 411 H
jhetrick@triangle-tech.edu
HETRICK, Lori .... 864-587-4208 424 D
hetrickl@smcsc.edu
HETTES, Stacey .... 864-597-4659 426 I
hettessr@wofford.edu
HETTLEMAN, Thomas .... 410-617-1120 205 A
tdhettleman@loyola.edu
HETTRICK, Allyson .... 828-298-3325 353 B
ahettrick@warren-wilson.edu
HETZEL, Bob .... 608-785-6491 510 F
bhetzel@uwlax.edu
HETZEL, June .... 562-903-6000.. 27 E
june.hetzel@bioloa.edu
HETZEL, Lisa .... 815-226-3398 150 C
lhetzel@rockford.edu
HETZLER, Mark .... 816-501-4843 265 I
mark.hetzler@rockhurst.edu

HEUBLER, Deborah, T ... 808-956-2980 129 J
dhuebler@hawaii.edu
HEUER, John, J .... 215-898-6884 412 G
heuer@upenn.edu
HEUER, Timothy .... 773-508-3254 144 D
theuer@luc.edu
HEUETT, Brian .... 406-265-3520 272 C
brian.heuett@msun.edu
HEUGEL, Jim .... 425-889-4098 496 E
jim.heugel@northwestu.edu
HEULITT, Ken .... 312-329-2070 146 B
ken.heulitt@moody.edu
HEUPEL, Dick .... 765-285-2894 156 C
dheupel@bsu.edu
HEURING, Curt .... 609-771-3269 284 I
heuring@tcnj.edu
HEUSER, Jacob .... 309-677-3159 134 G
jheuser@fsmail.bradley.edu
HEUSER, Kimberly .... 732-224-2268 284 B
kheuser@brookdalecc.edu
HEUSER, Roger .... 714-556-3610.. 72 F
HEUSNER, Nadine .... 386-481-2170.. 95 J
heusnern@cookman.edu
HEUSNER, Nadine .... 386-481-2272.. 95 J
heusnern@cookman.edu
HEUSNER, Scott .... 734-462-4400 236 H
sheusner@schoolcraft.edu
HEUSNER, Warren .... 386-481-2933.. 95 J
heusnerw@cookman.edu
HEUTON, Mary Ellen ..... 205-665-6010.... 8 E
mheuton@montevallo.edu
HEWERDINE, Kevin, L .. 812-877-8184 163 G
hewerdin@rose-hulman.edu
HEWES, Randy .... 405-325-3811 380 L
hewes@ou.edu
HEWETT, James, E .... 712-749-2248 167 C
hewettj@bvu.edu
HEWETT, Kelly .... 410-334-2908 210 C
khewett@worwic.edu
HEWETT, Lamar .... 843-782-8608 425 D
dlhewett@mailbox.sc.edu
HEWITT, Bradley, L .... 618-650-2871 152 C
bhewitt@siue.edu
HEWITT, David .... 361-593-3963 460 B
david.hewitt@tamuk.edu
HEWITT, Dawn .... 718-262-2060 304 A
hewittd@york.cuny.edu
HEWITT, Emma .... 712-274-6400 174 E
emma.hewitt@witcc.edu
HEWITT, Gordon, J .... 315-859-4084 309 D
ghewitt@hamilton.edu
HEWITT, JR.,
Harold, W .... 714-997-6717.. 36 G
hewitt@chapman.edu
HEWITT, Kasona .... 914-337-9300 305 F
kasona.hewitt@concordia-ny.edu
HEWITT, Kimberly .... 410-516-8075 204 F
khewitt4@jhu.edu
HEWITT, Mark, S .... 781-736-2010 213 A
mhewitt@brandeis.edu
HEWITT, Michael .... 718-951-5131 301 E
mhewitt@brooklyn.cuny.edu
HEWITT, Michele .... 518-831-8810 299 E
hewittm@ellismedicine.org
HEWITT, Russ .... 402-826-8295 274 E
russ.hewitt@doane.edu
HEWITT, Stephany .... 843-574-6922 424 G
stephany.hewitt@tridenttech.edu
HEWITT-CLARKE,
Gail-Selina .... 301-295-1667 518 G
gail-selina.hewitt-clarke@usuhs.edu
HEWITT WATKINS,
Sharon .... 718-990-3369 322 F
hewittws@stjohns.edu
HEXTER, Ralph, J .... 530-752-4964.. 68 H
provost@ucdavis.edu
HEY, Jeanne .... 207-602-2371 202 A
jhey@une.edu
HEYDARI, Shahryar .... 706-778-8500 124 E
sheydari@piedmont.edu
HEYDUK, David .... 607-431-4459 309 E
heydukd0@hartwick.edu
HEYE, Nick .... 858-653-6740.. 46 M
nheye@jpcatholic.com
HEYER, Cary, R .... 608-246-6443 514 A
cheyer@madisoncollege.edu
HEYER, Doreen, E .... 213-738-6801.. 65 I
academicadmin@swlaw.edu
HEYING, Leslie .... 712-279-5405 167 B
leslie.heying@briarcliff.edu
HEYING, Lori .... 319-363-1323 172 B
lheying@mtmercy.edu
HEYING, Steve .... 210-829-6023 465 E
lindaw@uiwtx.edu
HEYMAN, George, P ..... 585-271-3657 322 A
george.heyman@stbernards.edu
HEYMAN, Jeffrey .... 510-466-7369.. 56 I
jheyman@peralta.edu

HEYMAN, Jeffrey .... 510-466-7200.. 56 E
jheyman@peralta.edu
HEYMAN, Jeffrey .... 510-466-7369.. 56 F
jheyman@peralta.edu
HEYMANN, Jody .... 310-825-6381.. 69 B
jody.heymann@ph.ucla.edu
HEYNDERICKX, Roy, F .. 360-438-4307 497 F
president@stmartin.edu
HEYNING, Katharina, E . 262-472-1101 512 C
heyningk@uww.edu
HEYWARD, Kerry, L ...... 404-413-0500 121 A
kheyward@gsu.edu
HEYWARD, Loretta .... 912-358-3049 125 C
heywardl@savannahstate.edu
HEYWARD, Toyia .... 610-683-4102 406 D
heyward@kutztown.edu
HIATT, Aaron .... 415-689-5705.. 56 C
ahiatt@patten.edu
HIATT, Edwin, L .... 229-333-5886 127 H
elhiatt@valdosta.edu
HIATT, Elaine .... 614-825-6255 356 C
ehiatt@aiam.edu
HIATT, Jim .... 615-248-1613 439 B
jhiatt@trevecca.edu
HIATT, Jon .... 605-331-6636 429 D
jon.hiatt@usiouxfalls.edu
HIBBARD, David .... 910-775-4520 351 E
david.hibbard@uncp.edu
HIBBARD, J. Todd .... 313-993-1088 237 F
hibbarja@udmercy.edu
HIBBARD, James .... 608-342-1668 511 D
hibbardj@uwplatt.edu
HIBBARD, Josh .... 509-963-3087 492 L
josh.hibbard@cwu.edu
HIBBARD, Steven, V ...... 262-243-5700 507 C
steve.hibbard@cuw.edu
HIBBERD, Charles .... 402-472-2966 277 G
hibberd@unl.edu
HIBBERT, Mary .... 405-491-6365 379 K
mhibbert@snu.edu
HIBBS, Randy .... 920-206-2318 508 A
randy.hibbs@mbu.edu
HIBBS, Roz .... 618-374-5153 149 A
roz.hibbs@principia.edu
HIBBS, Thomas, S .... 254-710-7689 444 B
thomas_hibbs@baylor.edu
HIBLER, Dirk .... 904-819-6336.. 98 I
dhibler@flagler.edu
HIBNER, Lisa .... 225-216-8244 192 B
hibnerl@mybrcc.edu
HICE, Muriel .... 269-488-4410 231 G
mhice@kvcc.edu
HICHWA, Richard, D ..... 319-335-2106 166 G
richard-hichwa@uiowa.edu
HICKE, Linda, A .... 512-471-3285 467 C
cnsdean@austin.utexas.edu
HICKEL, Sabrina .... 314-434-4044 259 B
sabrina.hickel@covenantseminary.edu
HICKENLOOPER, Brian .. 208-282-3540 132 B
hickbria@isu.edu
HICKERSON, Jim .... 812-866-6741 158 C
hickerson@hanover.edu
HICKERSON, Keith, E .... 610-526-1000 389 B
keith.hickerson@theamericancollege.
edu
HICKEY, Beverly .... 662-685-4771 252 D
bhickey@bmc.edu
HICKEY, Dean .... 617-243-2190 216 C
dhickey@lasell.edu
HICKEY, James, E .... 401-841-3499 518 E
HICKEY, Jane .... 410-455-1517 208 A
jchickey@umbc.edu
HICKEY, John, M .... 253-879-3203 499 C
hickey@pugetsound.edu
HICKEY, Lynn .... 210-458-4161 468 B
lynn.hickey@utsa.edu
HICKEY, Melissa .... 845-675-4424 319 C
melissa.hickey@nyack.edu
HICKEY, Michael, J .... 518-783-2355 324 C
mjhickey@siena.edu
HICKEY, JR., Robert, E . 937-775-3326 374 B
robert.hickey@wright.edu
HICKMAN, Carla .... 314-889-1416 260 C
chickman@fontbonne.edu
HICKMAN, Gaby .... 803-786-3770 420 D
gahickman@columbiasc.edu
HICKMAN, George .... 518-262-8006 297 L
hickmag@mail.amc.edu
HICKMAN, Joseph .... 406-243-2412 271 G
joseph.hickman@umontana.edu
HICKMAN, Randall .... 586-445-7866 233 B
hickmanr@macomb.edu
HICKMAN, Saeedah .... 718-960-8357 302 C
saeedah.hickman@lehman.cuny.edu
HICKMAN,
Shannon Regan .... 310-983-3525.. 69 B
shickman@volunteer.ucla.edu

HICKMAN, Tanner .... 901-751-8453 434 E tannerh@mabts.edu
HICKMAN, Tim .... 909-558-4532.. 48 H thickman@llu.edu
HICKMAN, Tom .... 701-671-2354 355 B tom.hickman@ndscs.edu
HICKMAN, Wesley .... 803-777-7440 424 I whickman@mailbox.sc.edu
HICKMAN, Wesley, T .... 803-777-7440 424 I whickman@mailbox.sc.edu
HICKMAN, Yoouhenky .. 407-303-1878.. 94 H yoouhenk.hickman@adu.edu
HICKMAN HOLLAND, Heather .... 415-749-4540.. 60 G hhickman@sfai.edu
HICKOX, Chad .... 406-447-6928 271 I chad.hickox@umhelena.edu
HICKOX, Tracey .... 217-351-2200 148 H thickox@parkland.edu
HICKS, OSB, Boniface, N .... 724-532-6662 410 C boniface.hicks@stvincent.edu
HICKS, Brenda, D .... 620-229-6387 181 F brenda.hicks@sckans.edu
HICKS, Brian, A .... 336-734-7191 343 C bhicks@forsythtech.edu
HICKS, Bruce .... 310-287-4307.. 49 H hicksbr@wlac.edu
HICKS, Bruno .... 978-665-3530 217 E bhicks5@fitchburgstate.edu
HICKS, Bryan .... 256-372-4014.... 1 A byran.hicks@aamu.edu
HICKS, JR., Cecil .... 402-554-2321 277 I clhicks@unomaha.edu
HICKS, Cheryl .... 913-621-8765 177 A clhicks@donnelly.edu
HICKS, Cliff .... 360-442-2441 495 G chicks@lowercolumbia.edu
HICKS, David, L .... 610-292-9852 408 I bishophicks@comcast.net
HICKS, Deanita .... 870-762-3146.. 17 K dhicks@smail.anc.edu
HICKS, Debbie, L .... 757-455-3338 491 F dlhicks@vwu.edu
HICKS, Dennis .... 765-973-8456 160 A dehicks@iue.edu
HICKS, Diana .... 916-484-8654.. 50 F hicksd@arc.losrios.edu
HICKS, Doajo .... 435-652-4242 473 B doajo.hicks@dixie.edu
HICKS, Douglas, A .... 404-784-8300 119 B douglas.hicks@emory.edu
HICKS, Ed .... 334-386-7309.... 5 I ehicks@faulkner.edu
HICKS, Elena, D .... 214-768-4115 457 B ehicks@smu.edu
HICKS, Erica .... 352-588-8307 106 N erica.hicks@saintleo.edu
HICKS, Howard .... 570-586-2400 392 E hhicks@clarkssummitu.edu
HICKS, J. David .... 423-652-4782 432 I jdhicks@king.edu
HICKS, Janet, K .... 570-586-2400 392 E jhicks@clarkssummitu.edu
HICKS, Jeffrey, T .... 606-886-3863 185 F jeffrey.hicks@kctcs.edu
HICKS, Jim .... 423-425-4246 440 A jim-hicks@utc.edu
HICKS, Juanita .... 678-839-6424 127 F jhicks@westga.edu
HICKS, Jud .... 806-457-4200 449 D jhicks@fpctx.edu
HICKS, Julia .... 860-685-2100.. 89 F jhicks@wesleyan.edu
HICKS, Julie .... 252-492-2061 347 C hicksj@vgcc.edu
HICKS, Kathy .... 423-636-7320 439 C khicks@tusculum.edu
HICKS, Kelly .... 918-343-7573 379 C kellyhicks@rsu.edu
HICKS, Kristen .... 605-668-1270 427 F kristen.hicks@mtmc.edu
HICKS, LaTanya, O .... 510-593-2991.. 63 A lhicks@saybrook.edu
HICKS, Marcus .... 404-297-9522 120 D hicksm@gptc.edu
HICKS, Megan .... 319-895-4828 167 G mhicks@cornellcollege.edu
HICKS, Michael, R .... 817-735-2000 466 D michael.hicks@unthsc.edu
HICKS, Minora .... 803-327-7402 419 G mhicks@clintoncollege.edu
HICKS, Mona, L .... 561-803-2174 104 I mona_hicks@pba.edu
HICKS, Ramona .... 314-977-1572 266 J rhicks4@slu.edu
HICKS, Renee, G .... 985-493-2556 197 C renee.hicks@nicholls.edu
HICKS, Scott .... 434-582-7707 482 D smhicks@liberty.edu
HICKS, Shawn .... 415-422-5380.. 72 A srhicks2@usfca.edu
HICKS, Stacey .... 209-384-6100.. 51 G
HICKS, Stephanie .... 334-833-4571.... 5 M stephanie.hicks@hawks.huntingdon.edu
HICKS, Terri .... 205-226-4611.... 4 F thicks@bsc.edu
HICKS, Timothy, J .... 315-859-4790 309 D thicks@hamilton.edu
HICKS, Tom .... 319-399-8741 167 F thicks@coe.edu
HICKS, Virginia .... 304-876-5712 504 D vhicks@shepherd.edu
HICKS, Willie .... 501-420-1232.. 17 I willie.hicks@arkansasbaptist.edu
HICKSON, Darleen .... 949-794-9090.. 66 B dhickson@stanbridge.edu
HICSWA, Stefani .... 307-754-6200 516 Q stefani.hicswa@nwc.edu
HIDALGO, Lisa .... 985-448-7939 192 I lisa.hidalgo@fletcher.edu
HIEBERT, Theodore .... 773-947-6341 145 A
HIEDEMAN, Ann .... 218-477-2066 246 B ann.hiedeman@mnstate.edu
HIELEMA, Leslie .... 407-629-7259.. 99 K lhielema@fit.edu
HIEMENZ, Karen, A .... 320-308-5017 247 F khiemenz@sctcc.edu
HIEMER, Linda .... 802-831-1623 476 G lheimer@vermontlaw.edu
HIERHOLZER, Kathleen . 804-627-5300 478 I kathleen_hierholzer@bshsi.org
HIERS, Richard .... 314-434-4044 259 B richard.hiers@covenantseminary.edu
HIESIGER, Linda .... 413-585-2231 224 F lhiesige@smith.edu
HIETALA, Robert .... 406-994-5523 272 A robert.hietala@montana.edu
HIETAPELTO, Amy .... 218-726-7281 250 F lsbe@d.umn.edu
HIETSCH, Stephen, C .... 717-245-1891 394 A hietschs@dickinson.edu
HIGA, Pat .... 949-582-4585.. 64 J phiga@saddleback.edu
HIGASHI, Lori .... 541-485-1780 384 G lorihigashi@enewhope.edu
HIGBEE, Isabelle .... 601-974-1220 254 A higbeie@millsaps.edu
HIGDEM, Julie .... 763-488-2453 244 G julie.higdem@hennepintech.edu
HIGDON, Hal, L .... 417-447-2602 264 K higdonh@otc.edu
HIGDON, Jo Ann .... 310-660-3107.. 42 C jhigdon@elcamino.edu
HIGDON, Jo Ann .... 310-660-3670.. 42 C jhigdon@elcamino.edu
HIGDON, Troy .... 706-385-1066 124 F troy.higdon@point.edu
HIGGINBOTHAM, Amanda .... 610-921-7636 388 E ahigginbotham@albright.edu
HIGGINBOTHAM, Debra 940-397-4120 453 C debra.higginbotham@mwsu.edu
HIGGINBOTHAM, Helen 201-684-7540 289 C hhigginb@ramapo.edu
HIGGINBOTHAM, Karen 212-472-1500 318 B khigginbotham@nysid.edu
HIGGINBOTHAM, Ray ... 931-393-1737 437 C rhigginbotham@mscc.edu
HIGGINBOTHAM, Rocky .... 662-476-5014 253 A rhigginbotham@eastms.edu
HIGGINBOTHOM, Julie . 618-544-8657 140 D higginbothomj@iecc.edu
HIGGINS, Bonnie .... 218-755-3790 244 B bhiggins@bemidjistate.edu
HIGGINS, Brandon .... 903-823-3024 458 D brandon.higgins@texarkanacollege.edu
HIGGINS, Brenda .... 660-785-4562 267 K bhiggins@truman.edu
HIGGINS, Carla .... 419-783-2571 361 A chiggins@defiance.edu
HIGGINS, Chelious .... 312-939-0111 137 G chelious@eastwest.edu
HIGGINS, Colette .... 808-235-7339 130 I chiggins@hawaii.edu
HIGGINS, Dalton .... 918-335-6865 378 F dhiggins@okwu.edu
HIGGINS, Dawn .... 603-271-6484 280 N dhiggins@ccsnh.edu
HIGGINS, Diana .... 309-341-5341 134 H dhiggins@sandburg.edu
HIGGINS, Elizabeth .... 207-780-4632 201 H bhiggins@maine.edu
HIGGINS, Kacey .... 325-670-1368 450 A kacey.higgins@hsutx.edu
HIGGINS, Kerena .... 360-650-2040 500 E kerena.higgins@wwu.edu
HIGGINS, Linda, A .... 803-641-3444 425 A lindahi@usca.edu
HIGGINS, Mark .... 314-977-3833 266 J markhiggins@slu.edu
HIGGINS, Mark .... 802-387-1678 475 C mhiggins@landmark.edu
HIGGINS, Michael .... 314-434-4044 259 B mike.higgins@covenantseminary.edu
HIGGINS, TOR, Michael, J .... 760-547-1800.. 43 G mjhiggins@fst.edu
HIGGINS, Peter, J .... 678-359-5156 121 B phiggins@gordonstate.edu
HIGGINS, Ronnell, A ..... 203-432-9455.. 89 G ronnell.higgins@yale.edu
HIGGINS, Sandra .... 718-260-5700 303 D shiggins@citytech.cuny.edu
HIGGINS, Shana .... 909-748-8097.. 71 H shana_higgins@redlands.edu
HIGGINS, Shannon .... 909-448-4901.. 70 E shiggins@laverne.edu
HIGGINS, Sharon .... 410-617-5025 205 A sbhiggins@loyola.edu
HIGGINS, Tammy .... 620-235-4240 180 J thiggins@pittstate.edu
HIGGINS, Terri .... 641-782-1431 173 I thiggins@swcciowa.edu
HIGGINS, Thomas, J .... 518-564-3013 327 E higgintj@plattsburgh.edu
HIGGINS, Tony .... 405-585-4427 377 A tony.higgins@okbu.edu
HIGGINS, Wendy .... 707-654-1194.. 32 E whiggins@csum.edu
HIGGS, David .... 601-643-8376 252 G david.higgs@colin.edu
HIGGS, Fred .... 713-348-5923 455 F higgs@rice.edu
HIGGS, Jessica .... 309-677-2700 134 G jhiggs@bradley.edu
HIGGS, Jessica .... 309-677-2700 134 G bradleyhealthservices@fsmail.bradley.edu
HIGGS, John .... 724-480-3558 392 K john.higgs@ccbc.edu
HIGGS, Ronnie .... 831-582-4363.. 33 A rhiggs@csumb.edu
HIGGS, Toni .... 904-256-7184 102 B thiggs@ju.edu
HIGH, Jennifer .... 252-399-6397 335 I jmhigh@barton.edu
HIGH, Katherine, N .... 865-974-3843 439 H khigh@tennessee.edu
HIGHAM, Pamela, S ..... 814-332-3576 388 F phigham@allegheny.edu
HIGHERS, Cami .... 918-444-4200 376 G highersc@nsuok.edu
HIGHLEY, Melinda, C ... 606-783-2033 188 C m.highley@moreheadstate.edu
HIGHSMITH, Stephen .... 610-902-1070 391 B smh395@cabrini.edu
HIGHTOWER, Damara ... 803-705-4438 418 G hightowerd@benedict.edu
HIGHTOWER, Darlene ... 405-744-3555 377 F darlene.hightower@okstate.edu
HIGHTOWER, Tabitha .... 773-947-6309 145 A thightower@mccormick.edu
HIGINBOTHAM, Lynn, E .... 212-998-4444 318 D lynn.higinbotham@nyu.edu
HIGLE, Robin .... 978-468-7111 215 E rhigle@gcts.edu
HIGLEY, Tony .... 509-434-5123 494 A tony.higley@ccs.spokane.edu
HIGLEY, William, J .... 570-586-2400 392 E whigley@clarkssummitu.edu
HIJLEH, Mark .... 212-659-7200 312 E mhijleh@tkc.edu
HILARIO, Francis .... 787-704-1020 522 J fhilario@ediccollege.edu
HILBERT, Diane .... 972-238-6250 448 D dhilbert@dcccd.edu
HILBERT, Pamela .... 703-323-3222 488 H philbert@nvcc.edu
HILBERT, Stephen .... 216-987-3501 360 E stephen.hilbert@tri-c.edu
HILBORN, David .... 216-381-1680 367 A dhilborn@ndc.edu
HILBY, Jim .... 414-382-6327 506 A jim.hilby@alverno.edu
HILDAGO, Rommel .... 671-735-2645 520 B rhildago@triton.uog.edu
HILDEBRAND, Carol ...... 415-485-9306.. 39 E childebrand@marin.edu
HILDEBRAND, Lisa .... 212-812-4041 317 E lhildebrand@nycda.edu
HILDEN, Scott .... 734-677-5306 238 G sjhilden@wccnet.edu
HILDERBRAND, Barbara 407-708-2114 107 G hilderbrandb@seminolestate.edu
HILDERBRAND, Carey ... 801-274-3280 474 D carey.hilderbrand@wgu.edu
HILDRETH, James E.K .. 615-327-6904 434 A jhildreth@mmc.edu
HILEMAN, Jeffrey .... 814-732-1333 406 B jhileman@edinboro.edu
HILEMAN, Sharon .... 432-837-8015 462 G shileman@sulross.edu
HILER, Cathy, A .... 540-985-8245 482 A cahiler@jchs.edu
HILES, Jason .... 602-639-7500.. 12 P
HILES, Tom .... 573-882-7703 268 C hilest@missouri.edu
HILGENBRINK, Robert, J .... 618-235-2700 152 E robert.hilgenbrink@swic.edu
HILGERSOM, Karin .... 775-673-7000 279 C
HILKE, David .... 805-493-3960.. 30 E dhilke@callutheran.edu
HILKE, Jurgen .... 301-846-2401 203 H jhilke@frederic.edu
HILL, Alan .... 765-658-4199 157 H alanhill@depauw.edu
HILL, Alan, P .... 765-658-4199 157 H alanhill@depauw.edu
HILL, JR., Allen .... 281-283-2222 465 B hilljr@uhcl.edu
HILL, Amber .... 928-524-7484.. 15 B amber.hill@npc.edu
HILL, Angela .... 707-476-4177.. 39 F angela-hill@redwoods.edu
HILL, Angela .... 304-336-5635 504 E angie.hill@westliberty.edu
HILL, B. Scott .... 540-985-4693 482 A bshill@jchs.edu
HILL, Ben .... 319-384-3400 166 G benjamin-hill-1@uiowa.edu
HILL, Brandi .... 931-372-3317 438 F bhill@tntech.edu
HILL, Brandon .... 765-677-2200 161 C brandon.hill@indwes.edu
HILL, Brian .... 412-268-1939 391 H brianhill@cmu.edu
HILL, Brian, W .... 540-231-5107 480 I bhill@vcom.vt.edu
HILL, Calvin, R .... 413-748-3552 224 G chill@springfieldcollege.edu
HILL, Caroline .... 406-756-3806 271 A cahill@fvcc.edu
HILL, Charles .... 920-424-1255 511 B hill@uwosh.edu
HILL, Chris .... 801-581-5605 472 P chill@huntsman.utah.edu
HILL, Chris .... 760-797-2121.. 52 F chill@miracosta.edu
HILL, Christine .... 614-222-6178 360 B chill@ccad.edu
HILL, Christopher, D ...... 404-413-2574 121 A chill@gsu.edu
HILL, Christopher, J ...... 412-392-4707 408 F chill@pointpark.edu
HILL, Christopher, R ...... 303-871-2539.. 83 E christopher.r.hill@du.edu
HILL, Craig, C .... 214-768-2534 457 B craighill@smu.edu
HILL, Craig, R .... 352-392-1336 110 D craighill@ufl.edu
HILL, Curtis .... 435-865-8621 473 A hillc@suu.edu
HILL, Dachea .... 269-387-2000 239 E dachea.hill@wmich.edu
HILL, Deana .... 570-484-2014 406 E dhill@lockhaven.edu
HILL, Deborah .... 843-746-5100.. 93 B
HILL, Deborah .... 972-279-6511 442 E dhill@amberton.edu
HILL, Deidra .... 610-796-8376 389 A deidra.hill@alvernia.edu
HILL, Dennis .... 479-394-7622.. 23 D dhill@uarichmountain.edu
HILL, Diane .... 973-353-1630 290 D dianeh@andromeda.rutgers.edu
HILL, Dometrius .... 903-510-2353 464 D dhil2@tjc.edu
HILL, Doree .... 252-222-6282 341 F hilld@carteret.edu
HILL, Doris .... 763-488-0129 246 E dhill@nhcc.edu
HILL, Edith .... 815-965-8616 150 B ehill@rockfordcareercollege.edu
HILL, Edward .... 254-501-5837 459 D edward.hill@tamuct.edu
HILL, Eileen .... 831-479-6458.. 28 F eihill@cabrillo.edu

HILL, Eugene ... 760-921-5421 .. 55 J
gene.hill@paloverde.edu
HILL, Flo ... 229-430-4879 114 I
flo.hill@asurams.edu
HILL, G. Richard ... 801-626-7313 473 E
grhill@weber.edu
HILL, Gary ... 573-681-5496 261 H
hillg@lincolnu.edu
HILL, George, C ... 615-343-3112 440 D
george.c.hill@vanderbilt.edu
HILL, Gladys ... 205-391-2457 .... 3 E
ghill@sheltonstate.edu
HILL, Holly, L ... 904-826-8636 .. 98 I
hhill@flagler.edu
HILL, James ... 414-229-1122 511 A
jimhill@uwm.edu
HILL, Jamie ... 309-796-5284 134 C
hillj@bhc.edu
HILL, Janeen ... 714-628-7223 .. 36 G
jhill@chapman.edu
HILL, Janice ... 973-290-4468 285 A
jhill01@cse.edu
HILL, Jennifer ... 256-352-8032 .... 3 I
jennifer.hill@wallacestate.edu
HILL, Jessica ... 413-755-4320 221 B
jehill@stcc.edu
HILL, Jessica ... 937-395-8006 364 B
jessica.hill@ketteringhealth.org
HILL, Jody ... 662-658-4771 252 D
jhill@bmc.edu
HILL, John, T ... 562-907-4241 .. 75 A
jthill@whittier.edu
HILL, Jonathan, H ... 212-346-1810 319 J
HILL, Joseph ... 215-503-0033 411 E
joseph.hill@jefferson.edu
HILL, Joslyn ... 405-425-5476 377 B
joslyn.hill@oc.edu
HILL, Katrina ... 937-298-3399 364 B
katrina.hill@kc.edu
HILL, Kelli ... 309-268-8100 139 D
kelli.hill@heartland.edu
HILL, Kelly ... 352-588-7560 106 N
kelly.hill02@saintleo.edu
HILL, Ken ... 207-801-5630 199 A
khill@coa.edu
HILL, Kimberly ... 650-725-5582 .. 55 I
khill@paloaltou.edu
HILL, Kimberly ... 252-527-6223 344 D
HILL, Larry ... 773-702-2060 153 F
lhill@uchicago.edu
HILL, Lauretta ... 214-378-1853 447 F
lauretta.hill@dcccd.edu
HILL, Leia ... 662-476-5346 253 A
lhill@eastms.edu
HILL, Lisa ... 252-940-6223 340 N
lisa.hill@beaufortccc.edu
HILL, Manda ... 907-564-8299 .... 9 F
mhill@alaskapacific.edu
HILL, Marie ... 617-587-5678 222 G
hillm@neco.edu
HILL, Mark ... 651-641-8223 241 L
hill@csp.edu
HILL, Mark, J ... 315-470-6670 328 D
mjhill@esf.edu
HILL, Mary ... 202-806-6100 .. 92 C
HILL, Mary, M ... 989-774-3331 228 E
hill1mm@cmich.edu
HILL, Mathew, B ... 651-631-5362 251 C
mbhill@unwsp.edu
HILL, Melissa ... 509-865-0411 495 D
hill_m@heritage.edu
HILL, Melissa, D ... 812-941-2359 161 A
mhill02@ius.edu
HILL, Michael ... 610-328-8067 410 I
mhill1@swarthmore.edu
HILL, Michelle ... 225-771-2350 195 J
michelle_hill@sus.edu
HILL, Michelle, D ... 757-823-8135 483 F
mdhill@nsu.edu
HILL, Miriam ... 651-638-6415 240 J
m-hill@bethel.edu
HILL, Molly ... 605-229-8390 427 J
molly.hill@presentation.edu
HILL, Nicole, R ... 717-477-1373 407 B
nrhill@ship.edu
HILL, Paul, L ... 304-558-0699 503 N
paul.hill@wvhepc.edu
HILL, Reggie ... 479-979-1203 .. 23 J
rhill@ozarks.edu
HILL, Reinhold, R ... 812-348-7226 160 E
reihill@iupuc.edu
HILL, Renee ... 514-287-5299 360 C
rhill39@cscc.edu
HILL, Rick ... 252-222-6153 341 F
hillr@carteret.edu
HILL, Robert ... 818-240-1000 .. 44 D
rhill@glendale.edu
HILL, Robert, A ... 617-353-3560 212 G
rahill@bu.edu
HILL, Robert, W ... 936-468-3501 458 A
rhill@sfasu.edu
HILL, Sam ... 850-729-5277 104 E
hills@nwfsc.edu
HILL, Sam ... 703-878-5778 488 H
shill@nvcc.edu
HILL, Sean ... 618-468-6000 143 D
shill@lc.edu
HILL, Shannon ... 805-546-3279 .. 41 C
shannon_hill@cuesta.edu
HILL, Shantey ... 631-687-1445 322 G
shill4@sjcny.edu
HILL, Sharon ... 781-891-2108 212 A
shill@bentley.edu
HILL, Sharon ... 770-229-3454 126 B
sirby@sctech.edu
HILL, Sheila, M ... 706-771-4840 116 A
shill@augustatech.edu
HILL, Sherri ... 203-837-8200 .. 85 B
HILL, Shirley ... 901-435-1450 433 A
shirley_hill@loc.edu
HILL, Soni ... 513-569-4215 359 G
soni.hill@cincinnatistate.edu
HILL, Stacey ... 509-777-3842 500 H
shill@whitworth.edu
HILL, Stephanie ... 937-376-6591 358 I
shill2@centralstate.edu
HILL, Steven, E ... 801-422-8153 471 E
steve_hill@byu.edu
HILL, Tina ... 434-947-8537 484 B
thill@randolphcollege.edu
HILL, Travis, R ... 315-859-4023 309 D
thill@hamilton.edu
HILL, W. Timothy ... 801-422-7011 471 E
wthill@byu.edu
HILL, Walter, A ... 334-727-8157 .... 7 F
hillwa@mytu.tuskegee.edu
HILL, Wayne, R ... 330-972-2148 371 C
whill@uakron.edu
HILL, Wes ... 252-246-1339 347 H
whill@wilsoncc.edu
HILL, William ... 732-571-3580 287 C
hill@monmouth.edu
HILL, William ... 713-646-1764 456 H
whill@kennedywilson.com
HILL, II, William, L ... 215-965-4022 402 C
whill@moore.edu
HILL, JR., Willie, L ... 413-545-3517 216 H
drwhill@aol.com
HILL, Wynn, N ... 208-496-9200 131 D
hillw@byui.edu
HILL-CHEATOM, Petrina 716-851-1120 307 I
cheatom@ecc.edu
HILL-CLARKE, Kandi ... 901-678-5495 439 E
kyhill@memphis.edu
HILL HART, Erin ... 336-334-7965 350 C
ehhart@ncat.edu
HILL-HUBBARD,
Marion ... 214-333-5261 447 D
marion@dbu.edu
HILLARD, Cecilia, J ... 414-955-8493 508 D
chillard@mcw.edu
HILLBERRY, Andrew ... 860-768-5574 .. 89 C
hillberry@hartford.edu
HILLE, Jim ... 817-257-7031 461 A
j.hille@tcu.edu
HILLEBRAND, Kayli ... 714-556-3610 .. 72 F
kayli.hillebrand@vanguard.edu
HILLEMEIER, A. Craig ... 717-531-8323 403 F
ach10@psu.edu
HILLER, Renee ... 906-487-2280 234 A
rlhiller@mtu.edu
HILLER-FREUND,
Darby, L ... 937-327-7930 374 A
hillerd@wittenberg.edu
HILLERMAN, Donnie ... 660-359-3948 264 H
dhillerman@mail.ncmissouri.edu
HILLERY, Barbara ... 516-876-3915 327 C
hilleryb@oldwestbury.edu
HILLES, Sharon ... 909-869-3261 .. 31 A
shilles@cpp.edu
HILLESLAND, Michelle .. 253-589-5586 493 F
michelle.hillesland@cptc.edu
HILLIAR, Mara, M ... 804-594-1570 488 D
mhilliar@jtcc.edu
HILLIARD, Aaron ... 425-564-2445 492 G
aaron.hilliard@bellevuecollege.edu
HILLIARD, Beth ... 859-256-3100 185 D
beth.hilliard@kctcs.edu
HILLIARD, Colette ... 903-675-6306 464 C
chilliard@tvcc.edu
HILLIARD, Dianne ... 775-445-3288 279 F
dianne.hilliard@wnc.edu
HILLIARD, Kristin ... 407-926-2000 .. 93 B
HILLIARD, Kristina ... 904-538-1000 .. 93 B
HILLIARD, Rob ... 866-492-5336 251 E
robert.hilliard@laureate.net
HILLIS, Ed ... 512-863-1066 457 I
hillise@southwestern.edu
HILLIS, Greg ... 575-439-3624 295 C
ghillis@nmsu.edu
HILLIS, Michael ... 805-493-3422 .. 30 E
mhillis@callutheran.edu
HILLMAN, Amy ... 480-965-3402 .. 10 K
amy.hillman@asu.edu
HILLMAN, Ashia ... 580-559-5891 375 I
ashnhil@ecok.edu
HILLMAN, Elizabeth, L .. 510-430-2094 .. 52 E
bhillman@mills.edu
HILLMAN, George ... 214-887-5261 448 G
ghillman@dts.edu
HILLMAN, Gracia ... 202-806-2530 .. 92 C
gracia.hillman@howard.edu
HILLMAN BARRERA,
Darrel ... 787-759-6061 528 F
presidente.upr@upr.edu
HILLMER, Paul ... 651-641-8215 241 L
hillmer@csp.edu
HILLS, Amy ... 616-988-1000 228 I
amy.h@compass.edu
HILLS, Fred ... 254-299-8602 452 E
fhills@mclennan.edu
HILLS, Fred ... 254-299-8661 452 E
fhills@mclennan.edu
HILLS, Megan ... 319-385-6391 170 J
megan.hills@iw.edu
HILLS, Michael, S ... 740-587-6627 361 B
hills@denison.edu
HILLS, Warren, L ... 269-387-3895 239 E
warren.l.hills@wmich.edu
HILLSTROM, Maury ... 310-377-5501 .. 51 B
mhillstrom@marymountcalifornia.edu
HILLYER, Rebecca ... 503-399-8677 382 C
rebecca.hillyer@chemeketa.edu
HILMEY, David ... 716-375-2603 322 B
dhilmey@sbu.edu
HILSABECK, Alison ... 312-261-3149 146 G
ahilsabeck@nl.edu
HILT, Elizabeth ... 650-433-3818 .. 55 I
ehilt@paloaltou.edu
HILT, Michael ... 402-554-2232 277 I
mhilt@unomaha.edu
HILTEN, Stephanie ... 309-341-5327 134 H
shilten@sandburg.edu
HILTERBRAN, Stephen .. 870-543-5907 .. 21 E
shilterbran@seark.edu
HILTON, Carol ... 949-582-4872 .. 64 J
chilton@saddleback.edu
HILTON, Don ... 254-267-7007 454 L
dhilton@rangercollege.edu
HILTON, III, Earl, M ... 336-334-7686 350 C
hiltone@ncat.edu
HILTON, James, L ... 734-764-9358 237 I
hilton@umich.edu
HILTON, Mark ... 803-786-3966 420 D
mhilton@columbiasc.edu
HILTON, Richard, H ... 315-697-2307 332 F
rhilton@uscny.edu
HILTON, Stacey ... 928-717-7775 .. 17 G
stacey.hilton@yc.edu
HILTON, Warren ... 610-683-4327 406 D
hilton@kutztown.edu
HILTON-MORROW,
Wendy, S ... 309-794-7282 133 G
wendyhilton-morrow@augustana.edu
HILTS, Deb, B ... 607-431-4171 309 E
hiltsd@hartwick.edu
HILVO, Wendy ... 414-326-2337 507 B
wendy.hilvo@ccon.edu
HILYER, Billy, D ... 334-386-7414 .... 5 I
bhilyer@faulkner.edu
HIMBEAULT-TAYLOR,
Simone ... 734-764-5132 237 I
shtaylor@umich.edu
HIMBER, Richard ... 985-549-2064 197 E
HIMELFARB, Igor ... 510-250-6113 .. 48 F
ihimelfarb@lincolnuca.edu
HIMES, A.C. (Buddy) ... 936-468-2801 458 A
himesac@sfasu.edu
HIMES, Christine ... 312-567-3933 140 I
chimes@iit.edu
HIMLEY, Margaret, R ... 315-443-1137 330 H
mrhimley@syr.edu
HIMMELBERGER,
Stacey, J ... 315-859-4416 309 D
shimmelb@hamilton.edu
HIMMELREICH, Ellen ... 607-735-1855 307 G
ehimmelreich@elmira.edu
HIMMELSTEIN, Amos ... 323-259-1347 .. 54 E
himmelstein@oxy.edu
HIMSEL, Christian, R ... 262-243-5700 507 C
christian.himsel@cuw.edu
HINCH, Virginia (Gini) .. 509-359-2329 494 D
vhinch@ewu.edu
HINCHMAN, Mary ... 760-750-4520 .. 33 E
mhinchmn@csusm.edu
HINCKLEY, Alicia, A ... 253-535-7447 496 G
hincklaa@plu.edu
HINCKLEY, Richard ... 702-651-7488 278 N
richard.hinckley@csn.edu
HINCKLEY, Shane ... 979-845-4621 459 C
shane.hinckley@tamu.edu
HINCY, Charles, J ... 334-242-2688 .... 4 D
cjh0033@auburn.edu
HIND, Jonathan, T ... 315-859-4116 309 D
jhind@hamilton.edu
HINDE, RJ ... 865-974-0684 439 I
rhinde@utk.edu
HINDES, Victoria ... 408-741-2020 .. 74 D
victoria.hindes@westvalley.edu
HINDS, David ... 361-582-2560 470 A
david.hinds@victoriacollege.edu
HINDS, Thomas ... 412-924-1369 408 E
thinds@pts.edu
HINDSON, Ed ... 434-592-7365 482 D
ehindson@liberty.edu
HINE, Christopher ... 661-336-5040 .. 46 O
christopher.hine@kccd.edu
HINE, James ... 415-502-3037 .. 70 A
jhine@finance.ucsf.edu
HINE, Laura ... 901-272-5115 434 B
lhine@mca.edu
HINE, Mark, L ... 434-592-3240 482 D
mhine@liberty.edu
HINE, Melissa ... 540-362-6281 481 F
hinemd@hollins.edu
HINE, Terry ... 203-576-5072 .. 88 D
thine@stvincentscollege.edu
HINEMAN, Sheri ... 712-274-5335 172 A
hineman@morningside.edu
HINERMAN, Nate ... 415-442-6510 .. 44 E
nhinerman@ggu.edu
HINES, Alexander ... 507-457-5597 248 C
ahines@winona.edu
HINES, Chantell ... 832-813-6841 452 C
chantell.hines@lonestar.edu
HINES, CharMaine ... 313-469-2720 238 H
chines1@wcccd.edu
HINES, Cory ... 214-333-5628 447 D
coryh@dbu.edu
HINES, Craig ... 312-662-4111 133 A
chines@adler.edu
HINES, Florence, W ... 410-857-2273 205 E
fhines@mcdaniel.edu
HINES, Jean, C ... 804-289-8181 486 G
jhines@richmond.edu
HINES, Jillian ... 619-200-8993 .. 65 C
jillian.hines@socalsem.edu
HINES, Joseph ... 908-497-4317 292 C
joseph.hines@ucc.edu
HINES, Joseph, D ... 724-847-6518 395 J
jdh@geneva.edu
HINES, Kenneth, D ... 919-658-7755 349 F
dhines@umo.edu
HINES, Lara ... 314-392-2242 263 F
robeyl@mobap.edu
HINES, Melvin ... 334-229-4505 .... 4 A
mhines@alasu.edu
HINES, Nancy ... 509-777-4638 500 H
nhines@whitworth.edu
HINES, Nancy, A ... 563-333-6377 173 A
hinesnancya@sau.edu
HINES, Patrick ... 919-536-7200 342 G
hinesp@durhamtech.edu
HINES, Patti ... 619-574-6909 .. 55 B
phines@pacificcollege.edu
HINES, Resche ... 386-822-7257 111 E
rhines@stetson.edu
HINES, Ruth ... 617-427-0600 221 A
rhines@rcc.mass.edu
HINES, Sam ... 305-626-3631 .. 99 M
sam.hines@fmuniv.edu
HINES, Scott ... 650-433-3855 .. 55 I
shines@paloaltou.edu
HINES, Shanna ... 207-786-8388 198 E
shines@bates.edu
HINES, Susan ... 434-395-2921 482 E
hinessr@longwood.edu
HINES, Teresa ... 919-658-7720 349 F
thines@umo.edu
HINES, Wendy ... 828-565-4069 343 G
whines@haywood.edu
HINEY, Delaine, S ... 712-362-0428 170 D
dhiney@iowalakes.edu
HINGA, Beth, D ... 308-865-8208 277 F
hingabd@unk.edu
HINGA, Gilbert ... 308-865-8528 277 F
hingag2@unk.edu
HINGELBERG, Julie ... 313-664-7494 228 H
julieh@collegeforcreativestudies.edu

HINGORANI, Kamal 334-229-4123 4 A
khingorani@alasu.edu
HINGSTON, Mariko 415-338-1761 34 C
mtodd@sfsu.edu
HINKEL, Nate 501-686-2951 21 H
nhinkel@uasys.edu
HINKES, Madeleine 619-388-2320 60 D
mhinkes@sdccd.edu
HINKLE, Adrian 405-789-7661 380 A
adrian.hinkle@swcu.edu
HINKLE, Barbara 724-838-4206 410 E
hinkle@setonhill.edu
HINKLE, Barbara, C 724-838-4218 410 E
hinkle@setonhill.edu
HINKLE, Bernadette 479-968-0300 18 G
bhinkle@atu.edu
HINKLE, Christina 949-582-4605 64 J
chinkle@saddleback.edu
HINKLE, Craig 214-890-3837 448 D
chinkle@dcccd.edu
HINKLE, Jason 661-362-3420 39 C
jason.hinkle@canyons.edu
HINKLE, Keith 310-506-4898 56 D
keith.hinkle@pepperdine.edu
HINKLE, Lance 405-744-5237 377 F
lance.hinkle@okstate.edu
HINKLE, Robin 502-585-9911 189 B
rhinkle@spalding.edu
HINKLE, Sandy, L 573-651-2250 266 M
shinkle@semo.edu
HINKLE, Sara 610-436-3511 407 D
shinkle@wcupa.edu
HINKLEY, Lisa 847-735-5235 142 H
hinkley@lakeforest.edu
HINKLEY, Richard 434-592-3077 482 D
rdhinkle@liberty.edu
HINKS, David 919-515-6500 350 E
dhinks@ncsu.edu
HINKSON, Avis 212-854-3075 299 B
ahinkson@barnard.edu
HINNANT, Lori 704-233-8979 353 D
l.hinnant@wingate.edu
HINNERS, Gordon 828-689-1208 339 G
ghinners@mhu.edu
HINOJOSA, Felix 915-831-2623 449 A
fhinojo3@epcc.edu
HINOJOSA, Maggie 956-665-2321 468 A
maggie.hinojosa@utrgv.edu
HINOJOSA, Maria 210-486-2379 441 I
mhinojosa@alamo.edu
HINSHAW, Dana 620-665-3322 178 D
hinshawd@hutchcc.edu
HINSHAW, Garrett, D 828-327-7000 341 G
ghinshaw@cvcc.edu
HINSHAW, Lynn 828-898-3473 339 B
hinshaw@lmc.edu
HINSHAW, Stephanie 800-280-0307 155 H
stephanie.hinshaw@ace.edu
HINSON, Bobby 850-201-6071 112 C
hinsonb@tcc.fl.edu
HINSON, David, J 417-873-6887 259 G
dhinson@drury.edu
HINSON, Scott 870-512-7827 18 D
scott_hinson@asun.edu
HINSON, Stacey 850-718-2362 96 H
hinsons@chipola.edu
HINTERSTOISSER, Tanja 802-651-5896 474 G
thinterstoisser@champlain.edu
HINTON, Amy, E 601-426-6346 255 G
ahinton@southeasternbaptist.edu
HINTON, Billy, C 713-500-8444 468 D
william.c.hinton@uth.tmc.edu
HINTON, Jeff 903-223-3087 460 D
jhinton@tamut.edu
HINTON, John, A 252-398-6376 336 K
hintoj@chowan.edu
HINTON, Marie 410-209-6072 202 F
mhinton@bccc.edu
HINTON, Mary 320-363-5505 241 I
csbpres@csbsju.edu
HINTON, Pat 919-497-3217 339 F
phinton@louisburg.edu
HINTON, Richard 701-255-7500 355 K
rmhinton@umary.edu
HINTON, Tim 205-391-2979 3 E
thinton@sheltonstate.edu
HINTON, Toby, R 770-534-6257 116 F
thinton@brenau.edu
HINTON, Wendy 570-955-1456 399 A
hintonw@lackawanna.edu
HINTY, Danny 614-222-3224 360 B
dhinty@ccad.edu
HINTZ, Carol 816-235-1621 268 D
hintzc@umkc.edu
HINTZ, Debra 231-843-5850 239 D
dhintz@westshore.edu
HINTZ, Lynn 863-784-7105 108 B
lynn.hintz@southflorida.edu

HINTZ, Nancy, L 920-748-8346 509 H
hintzn@ripon.edu
HINTZ, Sharon 908-835-2356 292 G
hintz@warren.edu
HINTZE, Nate 207-725-3536 198 G
nhintze@bowdoin.edu
HINZE, Jodey 281-649-3130 450 C
jhinze@hbu.edu
HINZMAN, Larry 907-474-5837 10 B
ldhinzman@alaska.edu
HIONIDES, David 214-887-5201 448 G
dhionides@dts.edu
HIOTT, Connie 912-279-5965 118 A
chiott@ccga.edu
HIPES, Barrett 212-799-5000 312 B
HIPOLITO, Veronica 928-226-4334 12 B
veronica.hipolito@coconino.edu
HIPP, Joye, G 803-786-3178 420 D
joyehipp@columbiasc.edu
HIPPEN, Kristi 309-457-2327 146 A
khippen@monmouthcollege.edu
HIPPLER, Stanley 337-562-4290 197 B
stan@mcneese.edu
HIPPOLITE WRIGHT,
Debbie 808-675-3799 128 K
debbie.hippolite.wright@byuh.edu
HIPPS, OSB,
Norman, W 724-805-2271 410 B
norman.hipps@email.stvincent.edu
HIPPS, Suzanne 602-243-8153 14 D
suzanne.hipps@smcmail.maricopa.edu
HIPWELL, Jody 870-762-3191 17 K
jhipwell@smail.anc.edu
HIRAK, Joe 802-728-1238 477 E
jhirak@vtc.edu
HIRALDO, Rafael 787-863-2390 523 K
rafael.hiraldo@fajardo.inter.edu
HIRAMOTO, Patti 831-582-3366 33 A
phiramoto@csumb.edu
HIRASE-STACEY,
Joanne 208-282-3934 132 B
hirajoan@isu.edu
HIRATA, Heather 808-932-7369 129 I
hiratah@hawaii.edu
HIRD, Andrew 802-485-2460 475 I
ahird@norwich.edu
HIRD, Lon 605-367-7284 429 C
lon.hird@southeasttech.edu
HIRDLER, Joy, L 707-965-6232 55 F
jhirdler@puc.edu
HIRNEISEN, Deborah 610-917-2003 413 G
dghirneisen@valleyforge.edu
HIRNER, Leo, J 816-604-4501 262 F
leo.hirner@mcckc.edu
HIRONAKA-JUTEAU,
Jody 559-278-4004 32 A
jhironak@csufresno.edu
HIRSCH, Andrew 570-577-3698 390 H
andy.hirsch@bucknell.edu
HIRSCH, Glenn 612-624-4390 250 E
ghirsch@umn.edu
HIRSCH, Linda, R 563-333-6296 173 A
hirschlindar@sau.edu
HIRSCH, Michael 512-505-3125 451 A
mlhirsch@htu.edu
HIRSCH, Samuel 215-751-8160 393 A
shirsch@ccp.edu
HIRSCHBECK,
Denise, R 314-935-5320 269 L
dhirschbeck@wustl.edu
HIRSCHY, Margaret 419-434-4260 373 K
hirschym@findlay.edu
HIRSH, Erin 215-635-7300 396 B
HIRSH, Erin 215-635-7300 396 B
ehirsh@gratz.edu
HIRSHLER, Dave 740-474-8896 367 E
dhirshler@ohiochristian.edu
HIRSHMAN, Elliot 410-486-7000 207 C
HIRSHON, Arnold 216-368-5292 358 C
arnold.hirshon@case.edu
HIRST, Martha, K 718-817-3120 308 G
mhirst1@fordham.edu
HIRT, Amy 615-794-4254 435 G
ahirt@omorecollege.edu
HIRT, Sonia 301-405-9421 207 G
shirt@umd.edu
HIRTLE, Christopher 413-572-5455 218 F
chris@westfield.ma.edu
HIRTZ, Jared 717-262-2006 415 B
jared.hirtz@wilson.edu
HISCANO, Lisa 908-965-6091 292 C
hiscano@ucc.edu
HISCANO, Lisa 908-965-2358 292 C
hiscano@ucc.edu
HISE, Jeremy 580-628-6345 376 J
jeremy.hise@noc.edu
HISE, Paul 806-720-7279 452 D
paul.hise@lcu.edu

HISER, Larry, R 740-376-4665 365 A
larry.hiser@marietta.edu
HISEY, Richard, M 617-747-2018 212 B
rhisey@berklee.edu
HISKES, Anne 616-331-8655 230 G
hiskesa@gvsu.edu
HISLE, W. Lee 860-439-2650 86 H
wlhis@conncoll.edu
HISRICH, Matt 765-983-1523 157 I
hisrima@earlham.edu
HISS, Nancy 503-699-6242 384 B
nhiss@marylhurst.edu
HISSONG, Wesley 315-786-6517 311 H
whissong@sunyjefferson.edu
HITCH, Elizabeth, J 801-321-7122 472 O
ehitch@ushe.edu
HITCHCOCK, Cheryl, Y 443-885-3535 206 A
cheryl.hitchcock@morgan.edu
HITCHCOCK, Claude, E 443-885-3938 206 A
claude.hitchcock@morgan.edu
HITCHCOCK, Susan 607-255-9043 306 B
sh54@cornell.edu
HITCHELL, Dan 860-297-4224 88 E
dan.hitchell@trincoll.edu
HITE, Griffin 256-765-4400 9 A
una@bkstr.com
HITE, Joe 940-552-6291 469 F
jhite@vernoncollege.edu
HITE, Trudy, E 302-356-6965 91 B
trudy.e.hite@wilmu.edu
HITES, Michael, H 214-768-3805 457 B
hites@smu.edu
HITESMAN, Bill 402-461-2400 273 G
bhitesman@cccneb.edu
HITT, Jennifer 901-321-3465 431 A
jhitt@cbu.edu
HITT, John, C 407-823-1823 110 C
john.hitt@ucf.edu
HITT, Richard, J 863-784-7036 108 B
richard.hitt@southflorida.edu
HITTLE, Ann 509-452-5100 496 H
ahittle@pnwu.edu
HITTLE, Ben 509-452-5100 496 H
bhittle@pnwu.edu
HITZEMAN, Adam 312-922-1884 144 H
ahitzeman@maccormac.edu
HIVELY, Karla, R 304-457-6317 501 A
hivelykr@ab.edu
HIX, Karla 402-375-7000 276 D
HIX, Patty 803-754-4100 420 E
HIXON, Carla 701-224-5580 354 F
carla.hixson@bismarckstate.edu
HIXON, Sharon 706-272-4594 118 F
shixon@daltonstate.edu
HIXSON, Carol 561-297-3165 109 B
hixson@fau.edu
HIXSON, John 479-619-4341 20 F
jhixson@nwacc.edu
HIXSON, Tom 909-687-1500 44 A
tomhixson@gs.edu
HIXSON-WALLACE,
Julie 501-279-5205 19 G
jahixson@harding.edu
HIYANE-BROWN, Kathi 360-383-3330 500 F
presoffice@whatcom.ctc.edu
HJALTALIN, Lisa 509-434-5275 493 H
lisa.hjaltalin@ccs.spokane.edu
HJALTALIN, Lisa 509-434-5210 493 I
lisa.hjaltalin@ccs.spokane.edu
HJALTALIN, Lisa 509-434-5210 494 A
lisa.hjaltalin@ccs.spokane.edu
HJELLUM, Wilma 531-622-2723 275 F
whjellum@mccneb.edu
HJERPE, Karen 724-938-4351 405 F
hjerpe@calu.edu
HLADEK, Thomas 718-482-5510 303 B
tomhl@lagcc.cuny.edu
HLADIS, Jirka 303-245-4702 81 B
jirka@naropa.edu
HLASNY, Robert, G 603-535-2461 283 B
rhlasny@plymouth.edu
HLAVENKA, Lawrence 201-689-7057 283 I
lhlavenka@bergen.edu
HLAVIN, Karen 847-543-2384 136 E
khlavin@clcillinois.edu
HLEBOWITSH, Peter 205-348-6052 8 A
peter.hleb@ua.edu
HLINAK, Matthew, J 708-714-9056 137 F
mhlinak@dom.edu
HLINKA, Karen 270-534-3236 187 C
karen.hlinka@kctcs.edu
HLUBB, Emma 931-424-7366 433 E
ehlubb@martinmethodist.edu
HLUBB, James, R 931-424-7379 433 E
jhlubb@martinmethodist.edu
HLUCH, Dale, A 330-325-6191 366 F
dhluch@neomed.edu
HLUSKA, David, J 719-333-9751 518 H

HMIELESKI, Kristin 413-265-2340 213 E
hmieleskik@elms.edu
HMIELEWSKI,
Christopher 507-537-7984 248 A
christopher.hmielewski@smsu.edu
HO, Co 714-992-7021 54 A
cho@fullcoll.edu
HO, Deanna 312-935-4860 149 K
dho@robertmorris.edu
HO, Katy 808-845-9158 130 E
katyho@hawaii.edu
HO, Katy, W 971-722-4005 386 C
kho@pcc.edu
HO, Nan 925-424-1182 36 D
nho@laspositascollege.edu
HO, Sam 408-223-6798 61 N
sam.ho@sjeccd.org
HO, Sandra 603-427-7614 280 J
sho@ccsnh.edu
HO, Victor 415-565-4624 68 I
hov@uchastings.edu
HOAG, David, A 863-638-7209 113 I
david.hoag@warner.edu
HOAG, Jamie, D 508-793-2011 213 D
jhoag@holycross.edu
HOAG, William 617-541-5357 221 A
whoag@rcc.mass.edu
HOAGLAND,
Christopher 215-955-1861 411 E
christopher.hoagland@jefferson.edu
HOAGLAND, Steven 740-699-9500 357 D
HOANG, Andy 562-985-8201 32 C
andy.hoang@csulb.edu
HOANG, Minh-Ha 619-260-4506 71 J
hoangm@sandiego.edu
HOANG POE, Linh 808-734-9570 130 C
lhoang@hawaii.edu
HOAR, Robert 406-657-2367 272 B
rhoar@msubillings.edu
HOARD, Phil 317-896-9324 164 F
phoard@ubca.org
HOATSON, John 954-776-4476 102 G
jhoatson@keiseruniversity.edu
HOBAN, Elizabeth 973-328-5160 285 B
ehoban@ccm.edu
HOBAN, Kristi, M 817-257-7803 461 A
k.hoban@tcu.edu
HOBAN, Patricia, K 503-375-5477 388 D
phoban@willamette.edu
HOBART, Will 361-825-2616 460 A
will.hobart@tamucc.edu
HOBBS, Clinton, G 478-757-5161 128 E
chobbs@wesleyancollege.edu
HOBBS, Jeanie 817-598-6267 470 J
hobbs@wc.edu
HOBBS, Jeremy 415-351-3536 60 G
jhobbs@sfai.edu
HOBBS, Lynn 410-626-2504 206 F
lynn.hobbs@sjc.edu
HOBBS, Marcia, B 270-809-2193 188 D
mhobbs4@murraystate.edu
HOBBS, Nancy, A 734-764-7270 237 I
hobbsn@umich.edu
HOBBS, Pamelia, C 336-322-2120 345 D
pam.hobbs@piedmontcc.edu
HOBBS, Patrick 732-445-8610 290 A
ad@scarletknights.com
HOBBS, Patrick, E 732-445-7839 290 C
patrick.hobbs@rutgers.edu
HOBBS, Phillip, M 205-853-1200 2 F
mhobbs@jeffersonstate.edu
HOBBS, Rick 408-855-5325 74 C
rick.hobbs@missioncollege.edu
HOBBS, Tommy 205-929-3521 2 G
thobbs@lawsonstate.edu
HOBBY, Angela 229-333-2100 128 G
angela.hobby@wiregrass.edu
HOBBY, Brett 713-221-5075 465 C
hobbyb@uhd.edu
HOBBY-MEARS,
Michelle 949-480-4134 64 D
mhobby@soka.edu
HOBELMAN, Greg 317-896-9324 164 F
ghobelman@ubca.org
HOBERMAN, Chaim 516-225-4700 320 H
HOBIN, Caron, T 413-565-1333 211 C
chobin@baypath.edu
HOBLER, Dean 419-998-3103 372 D
dahobler@unoh.edu
HOBLET, Kent, H 662-325-1418 254 E
hoblet@cvm.msstate.edu
HOBSON, Elizabeth 847-214-6945 138 B
ehobson@elgin.edu
HOBSON, Lynn, M 620-341-5267 177 B
lhobson@emporia.edu
HOBSON, Paula, L 603-535-2212 283 B
phobson@plymouth.edu

HOBSON, Sheila .... 301-860-3451 208 E
shobson@bowiestate.edu
HOBSON, Tricia .... 405-422-1263 379 B
hobsont@redlandscc.edu
HOBSON-PAPE, Karri .... 706-542-8083 127 A
karri@uga.edu
HOBY, Lori, L .... 503-370-6546 388 D
lhoby@willamette.edu
HOBYAK, Michael, S .... 215-785-0111 404 P
HOCH, Cathy .... 515-961-1398 173 E
cathy.hoch@simpson.edu
HOCHANADEL, Gery ..... 913-234-0758 176 H
gary.hochanadel@cleveland.edu
HOCHMAN, Alex .... 415-422-2437.. 72 A
ahochman@usfca.edu
HOCHSTEIN, Dale .... 212-774-0748 314 D
phochstein@mmm.edu
HOCHSTEIN, Jessica ..... 402-399-2664 274 A
jhochstein@csm.edu
HOCK, Amy .... 402-471-2505 276 A
ahock@nscs.edu
HOCK, Joan .... 215-489-2975 393 F
joan.hock@delval.edu
HOCK, Nathan .... 802-828-2800 477 B
nxh08030@ccv.vsc.edu
HOCKENBERRY,
Frederick .... 301-846-2544 203 H
fhockenberry@frederick.edu
HOCKENHULL, Ben .... 440-775-6727 367 B
ben.hockenhull@oberlin.edu
HOCKEY, Chris .... 315-498-2579 319 G
c.l.hockey@sunyocc.edu
HOCKMAN, Joan .... 814-371-2090 411 H
jhockman@triangle-tech.edu
HOCOY, Dan .... 716-842-2770 307 I
HOCUTT, Kirby .... 806-742-3355 463 D
kirby.hocutt@ttu.edu
HODA-KEARSE,
Rebecca .... 315-498-2119 319 G
r.a.hoda-kearse@sunyocc.edu
HODEL, Laura .... 607-778-5028 326 C
hodellj@sunybroome.edu
HODES, Max .... 510-845-5373.. 30 D
max@cjc.edu
HODGDEN, Jessica .... 401-454-6764 417 B
jhodgden@risd.edu
HODGE, Andrea .... 213-740-4225.. 72 B
ahodge@usc.edu
HODGE, Brad, K .... 215-670-9206 403 D
bhodge@peirce.edu
HODGE, Brian .... 561-297-2774 109 B
bhodge@fau.edu
HODGE, David .... 334-291-4928.... 1 H
david.hodge@cv.edu
HODGE, Dena, S .... 864-379-8833 421 E
hodge@erskine.edu
HODGE, Duane .... 937-328-6054 359 H
hodged@clarkstate.edu
HODGE, Evelyn .... 334-229-4139.... 4 A
ehodge@alasu.edu
HODGE, Gary, B .... 972-548-6677 446 I
ghodge@collin.edu
HODGE, Jeremy .... 334-229-4156.... 4 A
jhodge@alasu.edu
HODGE, Jimmer .... 218-262-6705 244 H
jimmerhodge@hibbing.edu
HODGE, Johnesa .... 313-496-2796 238 H
jdimick1@wcccd.edu
HODGE, Margaret .... 706-385-1069 124 F
margaret.hodge@point.edu
HODGE, Marilyn, R .... 757-822-7245 489 H
mhodge@tcc.edu
HODGE, Michael .... 470-639-0801 123 E
michael.hodge@morehouse.edu
HODGE, Michel .... 718-631-6351 303 F
mhodge@qcc.cuny.edu
HODGE, Mildred .... 860-215-9252.. 86 F
mhodge@trcc.commnet.edu
HODGE, Paula .... 661-362-5108.. 39 C
paula.hodge@canyons.edu
HODGE, Rick .... 323-242-5388.. 49 E
hodgerl@lasc.edu
HODGE, Sandra .... 601-979-2282 253 E
sandra.hodge@jsums.edu
HODGE, Sheryl .... 620-327-8231 178 B
sherylh@hesston.edu
HODGE, Terrell, L .... 269-387-6000 239 E
terrell.hodge@wmich.edu
HODGE, Tiffani .... 404-523-8520 126 D
thodge3@spelman.edu
HODGEN, Danielle .... 509-527-4301 499 E
danielle.hodgen@wwcc.edu
HODGES, Bridget .... 716-827-2425 331 K
hodgesb@trocaire.edu
HODGES, Caryl .... 650-508-3621.. 54 D
chodges@ndnu.edu
HODGES, Christopher ... 215-717-3117 393 C
christopher.hodges@curtis.edu

HODGES, Courtney .... 434-395-2823 482 E
hodgesmc@longwood.edu
HODGES, Dawn .... 770-229-3293 126 B
dhodges@sctech.edu
HODGES, Elizabeth, R ... 787-850-9337 528 B
elizabeth.hodges@upr.edu
HODGES, Greg .... 276-656-0315 489 A
ghodges@patrickhenry.edu
HODGES, Jame'l .... 804-524-3662 491 A
jhodges@vsu.edu
HODGES, Jeff .... 540-362-6503 481 F
jhodges@hollins.edu
HODGES, Jill .... 906-487-3310 234 A
jhodges@mtu.edu
HODGES, Jimmy .... 256-352-8229.... 3 I
jimmy.hodges@wallacestate.edu
HODGES, Kristen .... 312-752-2268 142 E
kristen.hodges@kendall.edu
HODGES, Lorraine .... 973-803-5000 288 D
lhodges@pillar.edu
HODGES, Mike .... 423-472-7141 436 G
mhodges@clevelandstatecc.edu
HODGES, Mindy .... 859-371-9393 183 G
mhodges@beckfield.edu
HODGES, Omega .... 828-298-3325 353 B
ohodges@warren-wilson.edu
HODGES, Rhonda .... 276-656-0256 489 A
rhodges@patrickhenry.edu
HODGES, Richard .... 757-825-2868 489 G
hodgesr@tncc.edu
HODGES, Ricky, C .... 336-734-7272 343 C
rhodges@forsythtech.edu
HODGES, Ruth, A .... 803-536-8638 423 G
rhodges@scsu.edu
HODGES, Stephen, J ..... 617-746-1990 216 A
stephen.hodges@hult.edu
HODGES, Tim .... 785-594-8365 174 J
tim.hodges@bakeru.edu
HODGES, Tina .... 731-352-4032 430 E
hodgest@bethelu.edu
HODGES, YLonne .... 912-688-6922 123 J
yhodges@ogeecheetech.edu
HODGES, Zachary .... 713-718-5721 450 D
zachary.hodges@hccs.edu
HODGES MOORE, Sue .. 859-572-5349 188 E
moores4@nku.edu
HODGINS, Diane, W ..... 850-729-6485 104 E
hodginsd@nwfsc.edu
HODGINS, Ewart .... 919-573-5350 349 A
HODGKISS, William, S . 858-534-3131.. 69 E
hodgkissavc@ucsd.edu
HODGSON, Bev .... 218-755-4214 244 B
bhodgson@bemidjistate.edu
HODGSON, Matt .... 707-826-3321.. 34 A
matthodson@humboldt.edu
HODGSON, Robert .... 217-641-4349 141 F
rhodgson@jwcc.edu
HODNETT, James .... 478-387-4715 120 B
jhodnett@gmc.edu
HODNETT, Martin .... 256-726-7052.... 6 E
mhodnett@oakwood.edu
HODO, Tammy .... 904-256-1234.. 99 C
thodo@fcsl.edu
HODOWANEC,
Mary Kate .... 609-835-6000.. 93 B
HODOWANEC,
Mary Kate .... 856-482-4200.. 93 B
HODOWANEC, Michael . 610-372-4721 408 G
mhodowanec@racc.edu
HODSDON, Roger .... 626-815-5080.. 26 U
rhodsdon@apu.edu
HODSON, April .... 860-215-9007.. 86 F
ahodson@trcc.commnet.edu
HODSON, Brad .... 417-625-3072 263 G
hodson-b@mssu.edu
HODSON, Luke .... 859-985-3503 183 I
hodsonl@berea.edu
HOEBEE, John .... 602-386-4810.. 10 G
john.hoebee@arizonachristian.edu
HOEBELHEINRICH,
Holly .... 605-394-4800 427 G
hhoebelheinrich@national.edu
HOEBER, Mark, S .... 716-851-1413 307 I
hoeber@ecc.edu
HOEF, Ted .... 314-968-6980 269 N
hoeftl@webster.edu
HOEFFNER, Denise, R ... 785-309-3110 181 D
denise.hoeffner@salinatech.edu
HOEFFNER, Lori .... 516-877-3232 297 I
hoeffner@adelphi.edu
HOEFT, Jeanne .... 913-253-5019 181 C
jeanne.hoeft@spst.edu
HOEG, Portia .... 814-332-3350 388 F
phoeg@allegheny.edu
HOEH, Susan .... 407-888-8689.. 99 F
shoeh@fcim.edu
HOEHN, Alex, J .... 718-990-2998 322 F
hoehna@stjohns.edu

HOEHNKE, Diane .... 414-443-8627 513 A
diane.hoehnke@wlc.edu
HOEKSEMA, Jim .... 641-673-1107 174 F
hoeksemaj@wmpenn.edu
HOEKSTRA, Erik .... 712-722-6002 168 I
erik.hoekstra@dordt.edu
HOEKSTRA, Jack .... 803-732-6716 422 D
hoekstraj@midlandstech.edu
HOEKSTRA, Jonathan .... 254-867-4892 461 G
jonathan.hoekstra@tstc.edu
HOEL, Aaron .... 301-687-3101 209 A
ahoel@frostburg.edu
HOEL, Monica, S .... 276-944-6109 480 J
mshoel@ehc.edu
HOELLEN, Kathy, L .... 803-981-7150 426 J
khoellen@yorktech.edu
HOELSCHER, Ronda ...... 325-793-4857 452 F
hoelscher.ronda@mcm.edu
HOERITZ, Kim .... 412-396-6213 394 D
hoeritzk@duq.edu
HOESING, Kristin .... 402-562-1296 273 G
khoesing@cccneb.edu
HOESING, Paul .... 314-792-6136 261 E
hoesing@kenrick.edu
HOESL, Tina .... 513-244-4465 366 A
tina.hoesl@msj.edu
HOETING, Mark .... 404-894-9044 120 A
mark.hoeting@oit.gatech.edu
HOEY, John .... 508-999-8071 217 A
jhoey@umassd.edu
HOFER, Glenn .... 651-638-6069 240 J
glenn-hofer@bethel.edu
HOFER, Jared .... 605-995-3022 427 E
jared.hofer@mitchelltech.edu
HOFER, Jeanie, H .... 573-341-6425 269 A
jeanie@mst.edu
HOFER, Leslie, A .... 815-224-0230 141 A
leslie_hofer@ivcc.edu
HOFER, Sean .... 512-568-3300.. 93 B
HOFER, Sean .... 210-202-3700.. 93 B
HOFF, Brad .... 507-786-3310 250 C
hoff@stolaf.edu
HOFF, Craig .... 810-762-9856 232 C
choff@kettering.edu
HOFF, Dianne .... 678-839-6570 127 F
dhoff@westga.edu
HOFF, Julie .... 361-825-2649 460 A
julie.hoff@tamucc.edu
HOFF, Kevin .... 541-956-7925 386 G
khoff@roguecc.edu
HOFF, Michael, B .... 423-439-6593 431 H
hoffmb@etsu.edu
HOFFELT, Dana .... 775-831-1314 280 C
dhoffelt@sierranevada.edu
HOFFHINES, Kristen ...... 847-925-6522 139 B
khoffhin@harpercollege.edu
HOFFLAND, Scott .... 414-229-4146 511 A
scotth@uwm.edu
HOFFMAN, A, P .... 334-556-2225.... 2 B
ahoffman@wallace.edu
HOFFMAN, Barbara .... 319-399-8540 167 F
bhoffman@coe.edu
HOFFMAN, Bart .... 714-564-6800.. 58 A
hoffman_bart@sac.edu
HOFFMAN, Beth .... 301-687-4101 209 A
bhoffman@frostburg.edu
HOFFMAN, Charles, E ... 314-516-6280 268 E
hoffmance@umsl.edu
HOFFMAN, Chelsea ...... 251-981-3771.... 5 A
chelsea.hoffman@columbiasouthern.edu
HOFFMAN, Cierra .... 678-331-4331 122 F
cierra.hoffman@life.edu
HOFFMAN, Cindy .... 724-805-2573 410 C
cindy.hoffman@stvincent.edu
HOFFMAN, Darin .... 507-529-2724 247 D
darin.hoffman@rctc.edu
HOFFMAN, Erin .... 847-735-5200 142 H
hoffman@lakeforest.edu
HOFFMAN, Heather .... 770-426-2780 122 F
hhoffman@life.edu
HOFFMAN, Jaime .... 323-259-2500.. 54 E
jhoffman@oxy.edu
HOFFMAN, James .... 575-646-4083 295 B
jhoffman@nmsu.edu
HOFFMAN, Jeffrey, L .... 315-255-1743 300 H
foundation@cayuga-cc.edu
HOFFMAN, Jo .... 508-531-1899 217 D
j2hoffman@bridgew.edu
HOFFMAN, Joeseph ...... 718-409-3147 329 E
jhoffman@sunymaritime.edu
HOFFMAN, John .... 215-572-2900 389 D
hoffmanj@arcadia.edu
HOFFMAN, John, J .... 848-932-7697 290 A
jjh241@rutgers.edu
HOFFMAN, Joseph, M .. 301-687-4120 209 A
jhoffman@frostburg.edu

HOFFMAN, Karissa .... 620-241-0723 176 G
karissa.shultis@centralchristian.edu
HOFFMAN, Kurt .... 301-784-5000 202 B
khoffman@allegany.edu
HOFFMAN, Larry .... 914-395-2384 323 K
lhoffman@sarahlawrence.edu
HOFFMAN, Laura .... 941-359-4237 111 C
hoffman@sar.usf.edu
HOFFMAN, Lawrence .... 703-284-5716 483 A
lhoffman@marymount.edu
HOFFMAN, Louis .... 410-484-7200 206 C
lhoffman@nirc.edu
HOFFMAN, Maria .... 305-821-3333 100 A
mhoffman@fnu.edu
HOFFMAN, Marion, S ... 850-488-2447 110 D
marionh@ufl.edu
HOFFMAN, Mark .... 610-341-5935 394 E
hoffman@eastern.edu
HOFFMAN, SR.,
Martin, A .... 856-222-9311 289 F
mhoffman@rcbc.edu
HOFFMAN, Mary, F .... 715-836-4353 510 D
hoffmamf@uwec.edu
HOFFMAN, Matthew ...... 814-262-3826 405 A
mhoffman@pennhighlands.edu
HOFFMAN, Michael ...... 716-375-2530 322 B
mhoffman@sbu.edu
HOFFMAN, Michael ...... 515-965-7130 168 A
mjhoffman@dmacc.edu
HOFFMAN, Michael, D . 414-410-4057 506 F
mdhoffman@stritch.edu
HOFFMAN, Molly .... 740-362-3373 365 D
mhoffman@mtso.edu
HOFFMAN, Patricia .... 410-706-7355 207 H
phoffman@umaryland.edu
HOFFMAN, Peter .... 912-344-2576 115 D
peter.hoffman@armstrong.edu
HOFFMAN, Phyllis .... 510-642-6000.. 68 G
phoffman@berkeley.edu
HOFFMAN, Robyn .... 859-344-3344 189 G
hoffmanr@thomasmore.edu
HOFFMAN, Sandra .... 856-415-2220 289 G
shoffma2@rcgc.edu
HOFFMAN, Sharon, L ... 802-287-8215 475 B
hoffmans@greenmtn.edu
HOFFMAN, Sharon, L ... 802-287-8216 475 B
hoffmans2@greenmtn.edu
HOFFMAN, Sonia .... 336-272-7102 338 B
sonia.hoffman@greensboro.edu
HOFFMAN, Steve .... 765-361-6236 166 B
hoffmans@wabash.edu
HOFFMAN, Steven, A .... 859-236-6688 184 C
steven.hoffman@centre.edu
HOFFMAN, Thomas .... 507-453-2770 245 G
thoffman@southeastmn.edu
HOFFMANN, Donna ...... 909-389-3333.. 59 H
dhoffman@sbccd.edu
HOFFMANN, Maria .... 718-818-6470 323 F
mhoffmann@edaff.com
HOFFMANN, Mark .... 701-777-2492 353 G
mark.hoffmann@und.edu
HOFFMANN, Pauline ..... 716-375-2578 322 B
hoffmann@sbu.edu
HOFFMANN, Stephanie . 314-367-8700 266 D
stephanie.hoffmann@stlcop.edu
HOFFMANN, Susie .... 785-670-1643 182 D
susie.hoffmann@washburn.edu
HOFFMANN HARDING,
Erin .... 574-631-7394 165 A
eharding@nd.edu
HOFFMANS, Kim .... 805-289-6406.. 73 C
khoffmans@vcccd.edu
HOFFMEISTER, Chelsey 952-829-1479 240 H
chelsey.hoffmeister@bethfel.org
HOFFMEYER, Tom .... 254-710-1561 444 B
tom_hoffmeyer@baylor.edu
HOFFPAUIR, Stephanie . 513-721-7944 362 D
shoffpauir@gbs.edu
HOFHERR, Michael .... 614-292-6553 367 H
hofherr3@osu.edu
HOFMANN, John .... 650-508-3500.. 54 D
jmhofmann@ndnu.edu
HOFMANN, Karen .... 407-823-2811 110 C
karen.hofmann@ucf.edu
HOFMANN, Paul .... 916-278-6686.. 33 C
paul.hofmann@csus.edu
HOFMEISTER, David ...... 316-295-5682 177 F
david_hofmeister@friends.edu
HOFMEISTER, Gretchen . 507-222-4301 241 C
ghofmeis@carleton.edu
HOFMEYER, Karna .... 712-324-5061 172 E
khofmeyer@nwicc.edu
HOFRENNING, Ilene ...... 508-626-4900 218 A
ihofrenning@framingham.edu
HOFSTEDT, Petra .... 715-682-1983 509 D
phofstedt@northland.edu
HOFSTETTER, Dale .... 513-745-8308 371 F
hofsteda@uc.edu

HOFSTETTER, Shirley ..... 573-518-2190 263 E shofstetter@mineralarea.edu
HOFSTETTER, Thomas ... 410-706-2069 207 H thofs001@umaryland.edu
HOFSTROM, Hillary, E .. 570-326-3761 404 T heh1@pct.edu
HOFTIEZER, David .... 609-984-1164 292 B dhoftiezer@tesu.edu
HOGAN, Aaron .... 479-968-0376.. 18 G ahogan@atu.edu
HOGAN, Amy .... 785-242-5200 180 H amy.hogan@ottawa.edu
HOGAN, Andrea .... 203-582-5215.. 88 A andrea.hogan@quinnipiac.edu
HOGAN, Anne .... 901-678-2350 439 E anne.hogan@memphis.edu
HOGAN, Barbara .... 215-248-7120 392 D hoganb@chc.edu
HOGAN, Beverly, W ...... 601-977-7730 256 B bhogan@tougaloo.edu
HOGAN, Bill .... 206-296-5451 498 D hoganw@seattleu.edu
HOGAN, Brenda .... 478-471-6684 123 A brenda.hogan@mga.edu
HOGAN, Carrie .... 518-783-2554 324 C chogan@siena.edu
HOGAN, Cheryl .... 231-843-5864 239 D clhogan@westshore.edu
HOGAN, Eileen .... 605-642-6341 428 F eileen.hogan@bhsu.edu
HOGAN, James .... 704-878-4321 344 H jhogan@mitchellcc.edu
HOGAN, Joan, P .... 828-448-6041 347 F jhogan@wpcc.edu
HOGAN, John .... 501-760-4200.. 20 D john.hogan@np.edu
HOGAN, Judith .... 781-280-3816 220 C hoganj@middlesex.mass.edu
HOGAN, Kay .... 850-973-1605 104 D hogank@nfcc.edu
HOGAN, Kimberly .... 860-343-5731.. 86 A khogan@mxcc.edu
HOGAN, Lesley .... 425-235-7872 497 E lhogan@rtc.edu
HOGAN, Martha, A .... 972-238-6210 448 D mhogan@dcccd.edu
HOGAN, Meaghan .... 215-204-4315 411 B meagan.hogan@temple.edu
HOGAN, Melissa .... 847-330-4503 150 D mhogan03@roosevelt.edu
HOGAN, Pashia .... 423-354-2425 437 E phhogan@northeaststate.edu
HOGAN, Pat .... 910-362-7003 341 E phogan@cfcc.edu
HOGAN, Patrick, D .... 434-924-3252 486 H pdh9t@virginia.edu
HOGAN, Patrick, N .... 301-445-1927 207 F phogan@usmd.edu
HOGAN, Paul .... 603-271-6484 280 N phogan@ccsnh.edu
HOGAN, Robert .... 908-709-7151 292 C robert.hogan@ucc.edu
HOGAN, Ron .... 318-342-1017 198 A hogan@ulm.edu
HOGAN, Sean .... 847-543-2419 136 E shogan@clcillinois.edu
HOGAN, Sharon .... 503-943-8677 387 H hogans@up.edu
HOGAN, Susan, S .... 413-597-4204 226 C susan.s.hogan@williams.edu
HOGAN, Terrance, E ..... 305-474-6018 107 B thogan@stu.edu
HOGAN, William .... 907-786-4407.. 10 A whhogan@alaska.edu
HOGANS, Karen .... 352-435-6358 103 B hogansk@lssc.edu
HOGENCAMP, Kelly ...... 909-607-2981.. 63 F khogenca@scrippscollege.edu
HOGENSON, Liz .... 763-424-0902 246 E lhogenson@nhcc.edu
HOGGARD, Justin .... 573-840-9689 267 J jhoggard@trcc.edu
HOGGE, Jane .... 717-815-1410 415 G jhogge@ycp.edu
HOGLE, Paul .... 216-791-5000 359 K paul.hogle@cim.edu
HOGSETT, Denise .... 304-696-2370 504 C hogsettd@marshall.edu
HOGSGAARD, Soren ..... 412-392-4201 408 F shogsgaard@pointpark.edu
HOGUE, Belinda .... 334-727-8763.... 7 F bahoque@mytu.tuskegee.edu
HOGUE, Dale, A .... 719-333-9751 518 H
HOGUE, Eileen .... 719-502-2419.. 81 H eileen.hogue@ppcc.edu
HOGUE, Eric .... 916-577-2200.. 75 B ehogue@jessup.edu
HOGUE, Jarrod .... 503-491-7019 384 D jarrod.hogue@mhcc.edu
HOGUE, Jason .... 402-872-2429 276 C jhogue@peru.edu
HOGUE, Julie .... 815-224-0481 141 A julie_hogue@ivcc.edu
HOGUE, Laurel .... 660-543-4984 268 A lhogue@ucmo.edu
HOGUE, Matthew, L ...... 843-349-2813 420 A dhogue@coastal.edu
HOGUE, Stacey .... 501-812-2299.. 23 C shogue@pulaskitech.edu
HOGYA, Tiffany .... 330-823-2072 372 C hogyata@mountunion.edu
HOHBERG, Tonian .... 213-624-1200.. 42 N thohberg@fidm.edu
HOHENSTEIN, Janet, M 218-477-2956 246 B hohenst@mnstate.edu
HOHERTZ, Cherie, L ..... 972-721-5040 464 E chohertz@udallas.edu
HOHIEMER, Victoria ...... 270-686-4512 186 F vickie.hohiemer@kctcs.edu
HOHL, Kathleen, M .... 414-410-4202 506 F kghohl@stritch.edu
HOHMAN, Adam, R ...... 260-982-5228 162 Q arhohman@manchester.edu
HOHN, Daniel .... 303-797-5753.. 76 I daniel.hohn@arapahoe.edu
HOI, Samuel .... 410-225-2237 205 C president@mica.edu
HOIDA, Will .... 775-881-1314 280 C whoida@sierranevada.edu
HOILAND, Erin .... 360-412-6149 497 F ehoiland@stmartin.edu
HOILE, Linda .... 209-575-6498.. 75 J hoilel@yosemite.edu
HOILMAN, Sandra, K .... 828-448-6025 347 F shoilman@wpcc.edu
HOIT, Marc, I .... 919-515-0141 350 E mark_hoit@ncsu.edu
HOJAN, Elizabeth, M .... 262-554-2010 508 E mwcfinancialaid@aol.com
HOJAN-CLARK, Jane ..... 212-853-0469 305 E jh3574@columbia.edu
HOJSACK, Dana .... 619-849-2678.. 57 H danahojsack@pointloma.edu
HOKE, Chris .... 701-252-3467 355 J choke@uj.edu
HOKE, Cynthia .... 229-430-4605 114 I cynthia.hoke@asurams.edu
HOKE, Mary .... 210-829-3982 465 E mhoke@uiwtx.edu
HOKE, Rick .... 818-243-1131.. 44 C
HOKOANA, Lui .... 808-984-3636 130 H lhokoana@hawaii.edu
HOLAHAN, Barbara .... 516-686-7533 317 G bholahan@nyit.edu
HOLAK, Susan, L .... 718-982-2920 302 A schoolofbusiness@csi.cuny.edu
HOLAWAY, Rick .... 615-966-6133 433 D rick.holaway@lipscomb.edu
HOLBERG, Connie .... 315-786-2402 311 H cholberg@sunyjefferson.edu
HOLBERG, John .... 706-419-1565 118 E john.holberg@covenant.edu
HOLBERT, Jennifer, A ... 412-578-8725 391 G jaholbert@carlow.edu
HOLBROOK, Carl .... 334-347-2623.... 1 J cholbrook@escc.edu
HOLBROOK, Catherine, B .... 413-662-5231 218 C catherine.holbrook@mcla.edu
HOLBROOK, Christine ... 413-552-2319 219 G cholbrook@hcc.edu
HOLBROOK, Eddie .... 704-669-4223 342 B holbrook@clevelandcc.edu
HOLBROOK, Jennifer ..... 870-230-5275.. 19 H holbroj@hsu.edu
HOLBROOK, Kate .... 719-389-7986.. 77 J kate.holbrook@coloradocollege.edu
HOLBROOK, Peter .... 419-448-5864 370 K holbrookpj@tiffin.edu
HOLBROOKS, Johnnie, L .... 432-837-8100 462 G johnnieh@sulross.edu
HOLCOMB, David .... 254-295-4184 466 A dholcomb@umhb.edu
HOLCOMB, Gay .... 859-858-3511 183 D gay.holcomb@asbury.edu
HOLCOMB, Glen .... 405-789-6400 379 K gholcomb@snu.edu
HOLCOMB, Mark .... 815-939-5236 148 F mholcomb@olivet.edu
HOLCOMB, Robert .... 707-527-4615.. 62 H rholcomb@santarosa.edu
HOLCOMB, Todd, R .... 308-635-6101 278 B holcombt@wncc.edu
HOLCOMB-MCCOY, Cheryl .... 202-885-3720.. 91 C cholcomb@american.edu
HOLCOMBE, Annalisa ..... 801-832-2551 474 E asteggell@westminstercollege.edu
HOLCOMBE, Robert .... 864-424-8024 425 G reholcom@mailbox.sc.edu
HOLDA, Heather .... 860-509-9502.. 87 C hholda@hartsem.edu
HOLDEMAN, David .... 940-565-2497 466 B david.holdeman@unt.edu
HOLDEMAN, Lisa, K ..... 713-743-8408 464 F lkholdeman@uh.edu
HOLDEMAN, Lisa, K ..... 713-743-0945 465 A lkholdeman@uh.edu
HOLDEN, Brad .... 541-278-5783 382 A bholden@bluecc.edu
HOLDEN, Cheryl .... 509-542-4761 493 G cholden@columbiabasin.edu
HOLDEN, Dave .... 618-664-6750 139 A dave.holden@greenville.edu
HOLDEN, Elaine, P .... 704-637-4402 336 G epholden@catawba.edu
HOLDEN, Ginger .... 209-954-5040.. 61 B gholden@deltacollege.edu
HOLDEN, Joan .... 773-508-2530 144 D jholde1@luc.edu
HOLDEN, John .... 973-408-3226 285 E jholden@drew.edu
HOLDEN, Joseph, M ..... 714-966-8500.. 73 D info@ves.edu
HOLDEN, Kimberly .... 706-771-4019 116 A kholden@augustatech.edu
HOLDEN, Larry .... 615-327-6339 434 A lholden@mmc.edu
HOLDEN, Nina .... 313-664-7864 228 H nholden@collegeforcreativestudies.edu
HOLDEN, Randy .... 540-231-3171 490 F rholden@vt.edu
HOLDEN, Ronald .... 330-823-2138 372 C holdenrf@mountunion.edu
HOLDEN, Scott, A .... 212-799-5000 312 B
HOLDEN, Teresa .... 618-664-6844 139 A teresa.holden@greenville.edu
HOLDEN, Wesley .... 772-546-5534 101 N wesleyholden@hsbc.edu
HOLDEN-DUFFY, Cheryl .... 410-651-6460 208 C clduffy@umes.edu
HOLDER, Ann .... 936-294-1613 462 F lib_ahh@shsu.edu
HOLDER, Beth .... 336-841-9279 338 E bholder@highpoint.edu
HOLDER, Candace .... 336-386-3382 347 A holderc@surry.edu
HOLDER, Cheryl .... 618-842-3711 140 C holderc@iecc.edu
HOLDER, Dinelly .... 718-429-6600 333 B dinelly.holder@vaughn.edu
HOLDER, Gerald, D .... 412-624-9811 412 I holder@engr.pitt.edu
HOLDER, Jayne .... 423-425-4785 440 A jayne-holder@utc.edu
HOLDER, Karen .... 212-924-5900 330 G registrar@swedishinstitute.edu
HOLDER, Karen, G .... 214-887-5221 448 G kholder@dts.edu
HOLDER, Mike .... 405-744-7231 377 F mike.holder@okstate.edu
HOLDERBY, Kindle .... 918-781-7340 374 H holderbyk@bacone.edu
HOLDING, Frederick ..... 910-962-1123 352 A holdingf@uncw.edu
HOLDNAK, John, R .... 850-872-3800 101 J jholdnak@gulfcoast.edu
HOLDREN, Chris .... 503-375-7173 383 A choldren@corban.edu
HOLDSWORTH, Madeleine .... 312-893-7114 138 D mholdsworth@erikson.edu
HOLECHECK, Sarah .... 989-275-5000 232 E sarah.holecheck@kirtland.edu
HOLEHOUSE, Fonda ...... 304-357-4766 502 E fondaholehouse@ucwv.edu
HOLEMAN, Doris .... 334-727-8382.... 7 F dholeman@mytu.tuskegee.edu
HOLEMAN, Gary .... 304-896-7436 503 D gary.holeman@southernwv.edu
HOLESTINE, Dan .... 800-280-0307 155 H dan.holestine@ace.edu
HOLFORD, Chris .... 219-989-2468 163 E cholford@pnw.edu
HOLGER, David, K .... 515-294-7184 166 F holger@iastate.edu
HOLGUIN, Emilsen .... 518-608-8356 308 A eholguin@excelsior.edu
HOLIFIELD, Brenda .... 870-780-1227.. 17 K bholifield@smail.anc.edu
HOLIGROCKI, Rick .... 805-493-3528.. 30 E rholigrocki@callutheran.edu
HOLL, Lynn .... 609-586-4800 287 A holll@mccc.edu
HOLLAAR, Jean .... 218-477-2070 246 B jean.hollaar@mnstate.edu
HOLLADAY, Allison .... 570-321-4220 400 G holladay@lycoming.edu
HOLLADAY, Clare, M .... 563-333-6346 173 A holladayclarem@sau.edu
HOLLADAY, Kelly .... 575-492-2801 294 L kholladay@nmjc.edu
HOLLAND, Alex .... 520-322-6330.. 12 Q alex@hanuniversity.edu
HOLLAND, Alex .... 520-795-0787.. 10 J president@asaom.edu
HOLLAND, Alex .... 520-322-6330.. 12 Q info@hanuniversity.edu
HOLLAND, Alice .... 610-328-8058 410 I ahollan3@swarthmore.edu
HOLLAND, Ann, T .... 270-707-3724 186 B ann.holland@kctcs.edu
HOLLAND, Bill .... 573-651-2332 266M bholland@semo.edu
HOLLAND, Christopher . 904-632-3131 100 F chris.holland@fscj.edu
HOLLAND, Colleen .... 417-455-5588 259 D colleenholland@crowder.edu
HOLLAND, Demario .... 405-466-3370 375 L luchief@langston.edu
HOLLAND, Diana, M ..... 845-938-3103 519 D 8uscc@usma.edu
HOLLAND, Don .... 574-936-8898 155 L don.holland@ancilla.edu
HOLLAND, Ellen, S .... 214-768-2083 457 B esholland@smu.edu
HOLLAND, Jeff .... 304-424-8229 505 C jeff.holland@wvup.edu
HOLLAND, Kevin .... 940-552-6291 469 F kholland@vernoncollege.edu
HOLLAND, Kimberly .... 334-727-8881.... 7 F kholland@tuskegee.edu
HOLLAND, Kristine .... 567-661-7172 369 A kristine_holland@owens.edu
HOLLAND, LaTonya .... 301-546-0007 206 E hollanlt@pgcc.edu
HOLLAND, Leslie .... 901-722-3238 436 D lholland@sco.edu
HOLLAND, Linda .... 501-354-7565.. 23 B holland@uaccm.edu
HOLLAND, Matthew, S .. 801-863-3000 473 D president.holland@uvu.edu
HOLLAND, Melinda .... 919-658-7702 349 F mholland@umo.edu
HOLLAND, Michelle .... 904-819-6223.. 98 I mholland@flagler.edu
HOLLAND, Nicole .... 866-492-5336 251 E nicole.holland@mail.waldenu.edu
HOLLAND, Peter .... 212-851-2033 305 E ph2118@columbia.edu
HOLLAND, Rolanda, J ... 919-572-1625 335 F rholland@apexsot.edu
HOLLAND, Sam .... 214-768-2880 457 B sholland@smu.edu
HOLLAND, Scott .... 800-287-8822 156 D hollasc@bethanyseminary.edu
HOLLAND, Sharon .... 301-295-3578 518 G sharon.holland@usuhs.edu
HOLLAND, Steven, C ..... 520-621-1556.. 16 J sholland@email.arizona.edu
HOLLAND, Tina .... 225-768-1710 191 G tina.holland@ololcollege.edu
HOLLAND, Tony .... 334-556-2214.... 2 B tholland@wallace.edu
HOLLAND, Tracey .... 845-437-5620 333 A trholland@vassar.edu
HOLLANDER, Lisa .... 219-464-6882 165 D lisa.hollander@valpo.edu
HOLLANDER, Teri .... 301-445-1909 207 F tholland@usmd.edu
HOLLANDSWORTH, Heather .... 540-365-4282 480 L hhollandsworth@ferrum.edu
HOLLAWAY, Jamie .... 319-352-8521 174 C jamie.hollaway@wartburg.edu
HOLLDORF, Barry .... 206-878-3710 495 E bholldorf@highline.edu
HOLLENBAUGH, David . 724-805-2590 410 C david.hollenbaugh@stvincent.edu
HOLLENBECK, Dean ...... 620-343-4600 177 C dhollenbeck@fhtc.edu
HOLLENBECK, Peter ...... 765-494-4185 163 C phollenb@purdue.edu
HOLLENHORST, Steven . 360-650-3521 500 E steve.hollenhorst@wwu.edu
HOLLER, Juanita .... 805-756-2100.. 30 K jmholler@calpoly.edu

HOLLER, Richard, G ...... 724-925-4129 414 E
hollerr@westmoreland.edu
HOLLER, Stacy .... 301-387-3045 203 I
stacy.holler@garrettcollege.edu
HOLLER, Steve .... 503-255-0332 384 E
sholler@multnomah.edu
HOLLERAN, Meghan ..... 660-263-4100 264 C
meghanh@macc.edu
HOLLERAN, Theresa ...... 614-251-4730 367 F
hollerat@ohiodominican.edu
HOLLERICH, Mary .... 612-330-1000 240 G
HOLLERN, Denny .... 740-366-9301 358 E
dhollern@cotc.edu
HOLLEY, Debra .... 434-797-8410 487 J
dholley@dcc.vccs.edu
HOLLEY, Earle .... 843-208-8143 425 B
eholley@uscb.edu
HOLLEY, Joey .... 334-347-2623.... 1 J
jholley@escc.edu
HOLLEY, Steven .... 325-674-6552 441 D
steven.holley@acu.edu
HOLLEY, Tracy, S .... 540-365-4216 480 L
tholley@ferrum.edu
HOLLEY-WALKER,
Danielle, R .... 202-806-8000.. 92 C
danielle.holley-walker@howard.edu
HOLLIDAY, Chrissy .... 719-549-2997.. 78 P
chrissy.holliday@csupueblo.edu
HOLLIDAY, Deann .... 425-352-8324 492 K
dholliday@cascadia.edu
HOLLIDAY, Jill .... 304-256-0262 503 B
jholliday@newriver.edu
HOLLIDAY, Lisa, C .... 503-370-6574 388 D
lcjones@willamette.edu
HOLLIDAY, Matthew ...... 239-489-9052 100 E
mholliday@fsw.edu
HOLLIDAY, Paul .... 213-356-5348.. 65 A
paul_holliday@sciarc.edu
HOLLIDAY, Shawn, P ..... 580-327-8410 376 K
spholliday@nwosu.edu
HOLLIDAY, Theresa .... 913-288-7110 178 H
tholliday@kckcc.edu
HOLLIER, Larry, H .... 504-568-4800 194 C
lhholl@lsuhsc.edu
HOLLIFIELD, Jim .... 901-722-3264 436 D
jhollifield@sco.edu
HOLLIMAN, Stephanie .. 641-683-5751 169 I
stephanie.holliman@indianhills.edu
HOLLINGER, Dennis ...... 978-468-7111 215 E
dhollinger@gcts.edu
HOLLINGSHEAD,
Brad, E .... 863-680-4970 100 D
bhollingshead@flsouthern.edu
HOLLINGSWORTH,
Gabe .... 704-233-8368 353 D
g.hollingsworth@wingate.edu
HOLLINGSWORTH,
Jeffrey, K .... 301-405-7700 207 G
hollings@umd.edu
HOLLINGSWORTH,
Kimberly .... 312-850-7048 136 C
khollingsworth@ccc.edu
HOLLINGSWORTH,
Patricia .... 812-856-2511 159 H
pwhollin@indiana.edu
HOLLINGSWORTH,
Rusty .... 270-789-5009 184 B
rhollingsworth@campbellsville.edu
HOLLINGSWORTH,
Stacey .... 601-635-6406 252 I
sholling@eccc.edu
HOLLINS, Cary .... 225-771-5662 195 K
cary_hollins@subr.edu
HOLLINS, Cassandra ..... 205-929-2091.... 2 G
creneehollins@lawsonstate.edu
HOLLINS, Emily .... 540-665-4914 485 C
ehollins2@su.edu
HOLLINS, JR.,
Thomas, N .... 804-523-5296 488 C
thollins@reynolds.edu
HOLLIS, Debra .... 704-378-1128 338 I
dhollis@jcsu.edu
HOLLIS, Denson .... 662-915-5092 256 C
dhollis@olemiss.edu
HOLLIS, Erika, M .... 303-964-5387.. 82 D
ehollis@regis.edu
HOLLIS, John .... 870-777-5722.. 23 A
john.hollis@uacch.edu
HOLLIS, Keith .... 978-837-5356 221 G
hollisk@merrimack.edu
HOLLIS, Mark .... 440-943-7600 369 J
mhollis@dioceseofcleveland.org
HOLLIS, Mark, J .... 517-355-1623 233 G
hollis@msu.edu
HOLLIS, Quintress .... 478-757-5175 128 E
qhollis@wesleyancollege.edu
HOLLISTER, Ryan .... 215-780-1235 410 D
HOLLISTER, Thomas ..... 617-496-2650 215 G
thomas_hollister@harvard.edu
HOLLMAN-STANCIL,
Cynthia .... 903-730-4890 451 D
chollman-stancil@jarvis.edu
HOLLOMAN, Darryl, B .. 404-413-1500 121 A
dholloman@gsu.edu
HOLLOMAN, Mike .... 919-497-3249 339 F
mholloman@louisburg.edu
HOLLOW, Jeffrey .... 414-297-6663 514 C
hollowj4@matc.edu
HOLLOWAY, Amy .... 478-757-3510 117 D
aholloway@centralgatech.edu
HOLLOWAY, Amy, L ..... 478-757-3510 117 E
aholloway@centralgatech.edu
HOLLOWAY, Antonio ..... 512-444-8082 461 C
faid@thsu.edu
HOLLOWAY, Betsy, B .... 205-726-4109.... 6 G
bbhollow@samford.edu
HOLLOWAY, C. Allen .... 501-977-2031.. 23 B
holloway@uaccm.edu
HOLLOWAY, Charles ..... 606-783-2022 188 C
c.holloway@moreheadstate.edu
HOLLOWAY, David, J .... 304-877-6428 501 E
dave.holloway@abc.edu
HOLLOWAY, Denise, W 478-757-5211 128 E
dholloway@wesleyancollege.edu
HOLLOWAY, James, P .. 734-763-0395 237 I
hagar@umich.edu
HOLLOWAY, Jerry, R .... 918-631-2539 381 C
jerry-holloway@utulsa.edu
HOLLOWAY, Jessica ..... 479-968-0269.. 18 G
jholloway@atu.edu
HOLLOWAY, Jessica ..... 312-850-7152 136 C
jholloway@ccc.edu
HOLLOWAY,
Jonathan, S .... 847-491-5117 148 C
nu-provost@northwestern.edu
HOLLOWAY, Larry .... 859-257-1687 190 B
larry.holloway@uky.edu
HOLLOWAY, Leslie .... 314-340-3390 260 H
hollowal@hssu.edu
HOLLOWAY, Linda .... 940-565-2239 466 B
linda.holloway@unt.edu
HOLLOWAY, Linda, C ... 217-581-2979 138 A
lcholloway@eiu.edu
HOLLOWAY, Lorretta ..... 508-626-4926 218 A
lholloway@framingham.edu
HOLLOWAY, Michelle ... 386-752-1822.. 99 J
michelle.holloway@fgc.edu
HOLLOWAY, Rachel, L .. 540-231-4167 490 F
rholloway@vt.edu
HOLLOWAY, Saletta ...... 615-327-6869 434 A
sholloway@mmc.edu
HOLLOWAY, Stacy .... 618-985-3741 141 D
stacyholloway@jalc.edu
HOLLOWAY, Thadeus .... 912-423-0498 116 G
thadeusholloway@rts.hush.com
HOLLOWELL, James ...... 701-228-5678 354 G
james.hollowell@dakotacollege.edu
HOLLOWELL, Lorna .... 218-281-8580 250 G
lholl0we@umn.edu
HOLLOWELL,
Meghan, E .... 513-585-4841 359 D
meghan.hollowell@thechristcollege.edu
HOLLY, Gordon, K .... 330-972-8740 371 D
gholly@uakron.edu
HOLLY, Jackie .... 920-693-1128 513 H
jackie.holly@gotoltc.edu
HOLLY, Julie .... 205-226-4761.... 4 F
jbholly@bsc.edu
HOLLY, Shelly .... 918-631-2550 381 C
shelly-holly@utulsa.edu
HOLM, Cyndi .... 507-537-7854 248 A
cyndi.holm@smsu.edu
HOLM, Janet .... 253-589-5545 493 F
janet.holm@cptc.edu
HOLMAN, Dena .... 828-726-2737 341 D
dnholman@cccti.edu
HOLMAN, Fred, B .... 775-784-4853 279 E
fholman@unr.edu
HOLMAN, George .... 308-865-8519 277 F
holmangp@unk.edu
HOLMAN, James .... 414-443-8566 513 A
james.holman@wlc.edu
HOLMAN, Jill .... 706-867-2532 127 B
jill.holman@ung.edu
HOLMAN, John .... 606-218-5194 190 E
johnholman@upike.edu
HOLMAN, Keisha .... 254-526-1106 445 L
keisha.holman@ctcd.edu
HOLMAN, Lucy .... 410-837-4333 209 D
lholman@ubalt.edu
HOLMAN, Mark .... 701-854-8024 355 F
mark.holman@sittingbull.edu
HOLMAN, Neil .... 847-574-5230 143 A
nholman@lfgsm.edu
HOLMAN, Pat .... 505-984-6144 295 K
pat.holman@sjc.edu
HOLMAN, Sara, C .... 920-832-6583 507 L
sara.b.holman@lawrence.edu
HOLMAN, Steve, L .... 618-235-2700 152 E
steven.holman@swic.edu
HOLMAN-BROOKS,
Leslie .... 803-793-5287 420 G
holmanbrooksl@denmarktech.edu
HOLMANS, Jim .... 325-674-4974 441 D
holmansj@acu.edu
HOLMBOE, Janelle .... 828-298-3325 353 B
jholmboe@warren-wilson.edu
HOLME, Susan, H .... 509-527-5790 500 G
holmesl@whitman.edu
HOLMES, JR.,
Archie, L .... 434-982-2016 486 H
ah7sj@virginia.edu
HOLMES, Barbara, J ...... 202-274-6156.. 93 D
bholmes@udc.edu
HOLMES, Betsy .... 603-623-0313 281 G
betsyholmes@nhia.edu
HOLMES, Beverly .... 309-341-7755 142 G
bholmes@knox.edu
HOLMES, Carlos .... 302-857-6062.. 90 B
cholmes@desu.edu
HOLMES, Cassandra ..... 941-752-5389 108 P
holmesc@scf.edu
HOLMES, Cayce .... 910-410-1721 345 G
ccholmes@richmondcc.edu
HOLMES, Charley .... 903-586-2501 443 M
charley.holmes@bmats.edu
HOLMES, Chris .... 617-746-1990 216 A
chris.holmes@hult.edu
HOLMES, Christine, L ... 508-849-3418 210 H
cholmes@annamaria.edu
HOLMES,
Christopher, W .... 254-710-3821 444 B
christopher_holmes@baylor.edu
HOLMES, Crystal, M ..... 864-597-4014 426 I
holmescm@wofford.edu
HOLMES, Debra .... 912-279-5787 118 A
dholmes@ccga.edu
HOLMES, Edward, J ...... 716-851-1016 307 I
holmese@ecc.edu
HOLMES, Ella .... 601-979-6858 253 E
ella.b.holmes@jsums.edu
HOLMES, Emily .... 336-272-7102 338 B
emily.holmes@greensboro.edu
HOLMES, Emily .... 570-702-8956 398 A
eholmes@johnson.edu
HOLMES, Erin .... 907-786-1544.. 10 A
ejholmes@alaska.edu
HOLMES, Frank .... 936-294-3625 462 F
holmes@shsu.edu
HOLMES, Gilbert .... 909-460-2000.. 70 E
gholmes@laverne.edu
HOLMES, Greg .... 541-463-5516 383 F
holmesg@lanecc.edu
HOLMES, Heather, W .... 410-677-4865 209 B
hwholmes@salisbury.edu
HOLMES, Joan .... 813-253-7043 101 M
jholmes16@hccfl.edu
HOLMES, John, D .... 402-449-2809 274 H
jholmes@graceu.edu
HOLMES, Judy .... 785-825-5422 175 G
jholmes@brownmackie.edu
HOLMES, Julia .... 417-447-8188 264 K
holmesju@otc.edu
HOLMES, Kathryn .... 801-832-2565 474 E
kholmes@westminstercollege.edu
HOLMES, Kenneth, M ... 202-806-2100.. 92 C
kenneth.holmes@howard.edu
HOLMES, Kristen .... 256-352-8118.... 3 I
kristen.holmes@wallacestate.edu
HOLMES, Leasa, O .... 919-735-5151 347 E
loh@waynecc.edu
HOLMES, Leslie .... 864-379-6571 421 E
lholmes@erskine.edu
HOLMES, Lisa .... 760-252-2411.. 27 A
lholmes@barstow.edu
HOLMES, Lloyd, A .... 585-292-2120 315 L
lholmes20@monroecc.edu
HOLMES, Lucina .... 508-362-2131 219 E
lholmes@capecod.edu
HOLMES, Malcolm .... 540-654-1617 486 D
mholmes3@umw.edu
HOLMES, Megan .... 314-529-6852 262 B
mholmes3@maryville.edu
HOLMES, Michelle, M ... 510-841-1905.. 25 F
mmholmes@absw.edu
HOLMES, O'Neal .... 334-683-2350.... 3 A
oholmes@marionmilitary.edu
HOLMES, Paige .... 207-992-1939 199 B
holmesp@husson.edu
HOLMES, Phillip, M ...... 478-387-4905 120 B
mholmes@gmc.edu
HOLMES, Radonna .... 972-825-4762 457 F
rholmes@sagu.edu
HOLMES, IV, Richard .... 805-493-3586.. 30 E
holmes@callutheran.edu
HOLMES, Robert .... 602-243-8062.. 14 D
bear.holmes@southmountaincc.edu
HOLMES, Rodney .... 480-461-7325.. 13 I
rodney.holmes@mesacc.edu
HOLMES, Ryan, C .... 305-284-5353 112 O
rch88@miami.edu
HOLMES, Shandria .... 773-602-5517 135 L
sholmes65@ccc.edu
HOLMES, Stephanie ...... 309-694-8420 139 G
stephanie.holmes@icc.edu
HOLMES, Terrell .... 302-857-6375.. 90 B
tholmes@desu.edu
HOLMES, Tiffany .... 850-561-2888 109 A
tiffany.holmes@famu.edu
HOLMES, Tiffany .... 312-759-1671 151 F
tholmes@saic.edu
HOLMES, Valerie .... 252-335-3271 350 A
vlholmes@ecsu.edu
HOLMES, Wendy .... 845-341-4662 319 H
wendy.holmes@sunyorange.edu
HOLMES, William, A ..... 989-774-4308 228 E
holme1wa@cmich.edu
HOLMES-BUTLER,
Layna .... 610-399-2461 405 G
laynaholmes@cheyney.edu
HOLMES-LEOPOLD, RJ . 319-895-4445 167 G
rholmes-leopold@cornellcollege.edu
HOLMGREN, Richard, A 814-332-2898 388 F
rholmgre@allegheny.edu
HOLMOE, Tom .... 801-422-7649 471 E
tom_holmoe@byu.edu
HOLMQUEST, Kate .... 312-645-8300 516 F
kate@wrightgrad.edu
HOLMQUIST, Jake .... 718-862-7449 313 L
jake.holmquist@manhattan.edu
HOLMQUIST, Loren .... 619-644-7653.. 45 A
loren.holmquist@gcccd.edu
HOLOHAN-MOYER,
Irene .... 716-839-8214 306 E
imoyer@daemen.edu
HOLOMAN, Christopher 318-869-5101 191 C
president@centenary.edu
HOLOWICKI, Linda .... 708-209-3170 136 I
linda.holowicki@cuchicago.edu
HOLS, Eric .... 703-284-1601 483 A
eric.hols@marymount.edu
HOLSAPPLE, Dawn .... 518-828-4181 305 D
holsapple@sunycgcc.edu
HOLSAPPLE, Matthew ... 301-696-3569 204 D
holsapple@hood.edu
HOLSCLAW, Sheila, K ... 859-846-5310 188 B
sholsclaw@midway.edu
HOLSENBECK, Daniel .... 407-823-2387 110 C
daniel.holsenbeck@ucf.edu
HOLSER, Derek, P .... 757-481-5005 492 A
HOLSINGER, Kent .... 860-486-2182.. 88 G
kent.holsinger@uconn.edu
HOLSINGER-FUCHS,
Pamela .... 360-688-2101 497 F
pholsingerfuchs@stmartin.edu
HOLSOPPLE, Lee .... 202-885-3409.. 91 C
lee.holsopple@american.edu
HOLST, Barry .... 651-635-8500 240 J
barry-holst@bethel.edu
HOLSTAD, Deb .... 320-308-3277 247 F
dholstad@sctcc.edu
HOLSTAD, Deb, A .... 320-308-3227 247 F
dholstad@sctcc.edu
HOLSTEGE, Christopher 434-924-5185 486 H
ch2fx@virginia.edu
HOLSTEIN, Michael, L .. 317-788-3214 164 H
mholstein@uindy.edu
HOLSTEN, Robert .... 252-246-1254 347 H
rholsten@wilsoncc.edu
HOLSTER, Melissa .... 617-228-2271 219 D
mholster@bhcc.mass.edu
HOLSTON, J.B .... 303-871-3773.. 83 E
jb.holston@du.edu
HOLSTON, Jo-Ann, M ... 334-833-4410.... 5 M
jholston@hawks.huntingdon.edu
HOLSTON, Tavarez .... 770-533-6921 122 E
tholston@laniertech.edu
HOLSTON, William .... 336-841-9221 338 E
bookstor@highpoint.edu
HOLT, Anthony .... 313-577-2062 239 C
aa6479@wayne.edu
HOLT, Barbara .... 337-439-5765 191 D
barbara@deltatech.edu
HOLT, Brooke .... 479-619-4298.. 20 F
bholt@nwacc.edu
HOLT, Bruce .... 865-981-8035 433 F
bruce.holt@maryvillecollege.edu
HOLT, Christine, J .... 573-882-0829 268 C
holtcj@missouri.edu

HOPKINS, Bruce .... 229-430-2837 114 J
bhopkins@albanytech.edu
HOPKINS, Carolyn .... 760-366-3791.. 41 B
chopkins@cmccd.edu
HOPKINS, Christi .... 620-242-0414 179 G
hopkinsc@mcpherson.edu
HOPKINS, Darlene .... 910-630-7150 340 A
dhopkins@methodist.edu
HOPKINS, Dennis .... 828-726-2750 341 D
dhopkins@cccti.edu
HOPKINS, Drew, W .... 609-984-3430 292 B
dhopkins@tesu.edu
HOPKINS, Elijah .... 406-768-6371 271 B
ehopkins@fpcc.edu
HOPKINS, Gena .... 260-459-4500 161 D
ghopkins@ibcfortwayne.edu
HOPKINS, John .... 330-263-2082 360 A
jhopkins@wooster.edu
HOPKINS, John, L .... 203-596-4652.. 87 H
jhopkins@post.edu
HOPKINS, Joseph .... 205-726-2778.... 6 G
jhopkins@samford.edu
HOPKINS, Kathryn .... 260-481-6710 160 D
hopkinsk@ipfw.edu
HOPKINS, Kent .... 480-965-2408.. 10 K
kent.hopkins@asu.edu
HOPKINS, Kevin .... 785-594-8553 174 J
kevin.hopkins@bakeru.edu
HOPKINS, Laura .... 206-934-7798 497 H
laura.hopkins@seattlecolleges.edu
HOPKINS, OP, Maggie . 608-663-3388 507 D
mhopkins@edgewood.edu
HOPKINS, Marilyn .... 707-638-5276.. 67 H
marilyn.hopkins@tu.edu
HOPKINS, Mark .... 706-236-2231 116 D
mhopkins@berry.edu
HOPKINS, Melissa .... 573-518-2177 263 E
mhopkins@mineralarea.edu
HOPKINS, Michael .... 773-702-1234 153 F
HOPKINS, Paulette .... 619-388-7350.. 60 E
phopkins@sdccd.edu
HOPKINS, Randy .... 816-501-4659 265 I
randy.hopkins@rockhurst.edu
HOPKINS, Rebecca .... 507-457-6620 250 B
rhopkins@smumn.edu
HOPKINS, Robert, P ..... 212-353-4350 306 A
bob@cooper.edu
HOPKINS, Ronnie .... 803-780-1179 426 F
rhopkins@voorhees.edu
HOPKINS, Sara .... 615-248-1653 439 B
shopkins@trevecca.edu
HOPKINS, Sarah .... 707-527-4831.. 62 H
shopkins@santarosa.edu
HOPKINS, Shirley, L ..... 804-523-5896 488 C
shopkins@reynolds.edu
HOPKINS, Stacy .... 724-357-2230 406 C
stacy.hopkins@iup.edu
HOPKINS, T. Hampton .. 704-355-5316 336 F
hampton.hopkins@carolinascollege.edu
HOPKINS, Thomas, F .... 540-464-7228 490 E
hopkinstf@vmi.edu
HOPKINS, Tony .... 502-585-9911 189 B
thopkins@spalding.edu
HOPKINS, Wille .... 718-951-3166 301 E
whopkins@brooklyn.cuny.edu
HOPKINS-GROSS, Anne 518-255-5214 328 C
hopkinam@cobleskill.edu
HOPKINS-JENKINS,
Amber .... 212-938-5607 328 E
aehopkinsjenkins@sunyopt.edu
HOPKINS-POSELLE,
Denise .... 914-637-2757 311 B
dhopkins@iona.edu
HOPMANS, Jan .... 530-752-7172.. 68 H
jwhopmans@ucdavis.edu
HOPP, Lisa .... 219-989-2818 163 E
ljhopp@pnw.edu
HOPP, Melissa .... 443-840-3176 203 E
mhopp@ccbcmd.edu
HOPP, Susan .... 503-883-2278 383 H
shopp@linfield.edu
HOPPE, Daniel .... 843-349-5357 421 L
daniel.hoppe@hgtc.edu
HOPPE, Elizabeth .... 909-706-3497.. 74 G
shoppe@westernu.edu
HOPPE, Heather .... 843-349-5238 421 L
heather.hoppe@hgtc.edu
HOPPE, James .... 617-824-8640 214 E
james_hoppe@emerson.edu
HOPPE, Ken .... 870-236-6901.. 19 D
khoppe@crc.edu
HOPPE, Marianne .... 406-265-3765 272 C
hoppe@msun.edu
HOPPE, Terry .... 706-416-0200 124 F
HOPPER, Carrie .... 270-534-3412 187 C
carrie.hopper@kctcs.edu
HOPPER, Darla .... 812-535-5110 163 I
dhopper@smwc.edu
HOPPER, George, M ..... 662-325-2953 254 E
ghopper@cfr.msstate.edu
HOPPER, Jeffrey .... 501-279-4478.. 19 G
hopper@harding.edu
HOPPER, Lisa .... 501-760-4241.. 20 D
lisa.hopper@np.edu
HOPPER, Lorrie .... 559-325-5246.. 66 F
lorrie.hopper@cloviscollege.edu
HOPPER, Richard .... 207-453-5129 200 A
president@kvcc.me.edu
HOPPER, Rosita .... 401-598-1000 416 C
rhopper@jwu.edu
HOPPER, Susan .... 731-661-5078 439 D
shopper@uu.edu
HOPPER, William, E ...... 305-626-3701.. 99 M
william.hopper@fmuniv.edu
HOPPER, JR.,
William, E .... 305-626-3701.. 99 M
william.hopper@fmuniv.edu
HOPPLE, Marcella .... 574-936-8898 155 L
marcella.hopple@ancilla.edu
HOPSON, April .... 706-649-1858 118 D
ahopson@columbustech.edu
HOPSON, JR.,
George, A .... 864-977-2194 422 I
george.hopson@ngu.edu
HOPSON, Pamela, F ..... 812-465-7188 165 C
pfhopson@usi.edu
HOPWOOD, Dennis, T .. 509-527-5172 500 G
hopwoodt@whitman.edu
HOPWOOD, Julie .... 765-285-1104 156 C
jhopwood@bsu.edu
HORACE, David .... 678-872-8133 119 G
dhorace@highlands.edu
HORACE, Herny .... 773-602-5340 135 L
HORACEK, Mark .... 801-375-5125 472 F
mhoracek@rmuohp.edu
HORADAN, Lloyd .... 478-553-2060 123 H
lhoradan@oftc.edu
HORADAN, Lloyd .... 478-553-2060 123 I
lhoradan@oftc.edu
HORAK, Janice .... 254-968-9890 459 A
jhorak@tarleton.edu
HORAK, Maureen .... 413-662-5205 218 C
m.horak@mcla.edu
HORAN, Kevin .... 925-473-7401.. 41 A
khoran@losmedanos.edu
HORAN, Michael, D .... 312-567-3000 140 I
HORAN, Thomas .... 909-748-8748.. 71 H
thomas_horan@redlands.edu
HORBACEWICZ, Jill .... 212-463-0400 331 F
jillh@touro.edu
HORBACK, Sachi .... 253-964-6531 497 B
shorback@pierce.ctc.edu
HORCH, Scott .... 574-936-8898 155 L
scott.horch@ancilla.edu
HORD, Lisa .... 937-393-3431 370 C
lhord@sscc.edu
HOREJES, Thomas .... 202-448-7036.. 91 H
thomas.horejes@gallaudet.edu
HORELL, Eric .... 814-472-3904 409 G
ehorell@francis.edu
HORGAN, Elizabeth .... 508-213-2289 223 C
elizabeth.horgan@nichols.edu
HORGAN, Joan .... 518-454-5296 305 B
horganj@strose.edu
HORGAN, Lynne .... 828-251-6417 351 A
lhorgan@unca.edu
HORGAN, Ralph, R .... 412-268-6156 391 H
rh44@andrew.cmu.edu
HORINEK, Charity .... 620-417-1133 181 E
charity.horinek@sccc.edu
HORINEK, Jon .... 415-485-9414.. 39 E
jhorinek@marin.edu
HORISSIAN, Kevork, T .. 570-577-3623 390 H
kevork.horissian@bucknell.edu
HORN, Allison .... 503-883-2323 383 H
ahorn@linfield.edu
HORN, Brian, S .... 727-816-3458 105 C
hornb@phsc.edu
HORN, Cindy .... 231-591-5309 230 A
cindyhorn@ferris.edu
HORN, Jamie .... 334-386-7168.... 5 I
jhorn@faulkner.edu
HORN, Jason .... 504-520-7330 198 D
jhorn1@xula.edu
HORN, Jay .... 817-272-2355 467 B
horn@uta.edu
HORN, John .... 608-890-0158 510 C
horn1@recsports.wisc.edu
HORN, John, F .... 215-898-7593 412 G
horn3@upenn.edu
HORN, Michael .... 704-330-5963 342 A
michael.horn@cpcc.edu
HORN, Paul, M .... 212-998-3228 318 D
paul.horn@nyu.edu
HORN, Phillip .... 606-546-1726 189 I
phillip.horn@unionky.edu
HORN, Randolph .... 205-726-2179.... 6 G
rchorn@samford.edu
HORN, Sameul, E .... 864-242-5100 418 H
HORN, Samuel, E .... 864-242-5100 418 H
HORN, Vincent .... 215-596-7532 413 E
v.horn@usciences.edu
HORN BUNK, Sheri .... 661-763-7936.. 67 A
shornbunk@taftcollege.edu
HORNBACHER, Noel ..... 313-593-5410 238 A
noelhorn@umich.edu
HORNBECK, Billi .... 605-455-6037 427 I
bhornbeck@olc.edu
HORNBERGER, Lois ...... 503-352-2240 385 I
lhornberger@pacificu.edu
HORNBERGER, Rob .... 417-836-6444 263 H
robhornberger@missouristate.edu
HORNBUCKLE, Jami, M 606-783-2372 188 C
j.hornbuckle@moreheadstate.edu
HORNE, Bart .... 502-863-8182 184 I
bart_horne@georgetowncollege.edu
HORNE, Cathy .... 704-272-5337 346 F
chorne@spcc.edu
HORNE, David .... 410-704-4236 209 C
dhorne@towson.edu
HORNE, Derek .... 601-877-6500 251 G
djhorne@alcorn.edu
HORNE, Greg .... 419-772-2521 367 G
g-horne@onu.edu
HORNE, Hadie, C .... 252-246-1221 347 H
hhorne@wilsoncc.edu
HORNE, LynnDee .... 910-521-6202 351 E
lynndee.horne@uncp.edu
HORNE, Megan .... 606-326-2074 185 E
mhorne0001@kctcs.edu
HORNE, Nicole .... 603-444-3439 282 G
nicole.horne@granite.edu
HORNE, Valerie .... 601-403-1211 255 D
vhorne@prcc.edu
HORNER, Andrew, E ..... 937-229-3736 372 A
ahorner1@udayton.edu
HORNER, Donnie .... 904-256-7031 102 B
dhorner3@ju.edu
HORNER, Doug .... 925-485-5277.. 36 B
dhorner@clpccd.org
HORNER, Ed .... 213-621-2200.. 39 A
HORNER, Jeffrey, T ...... 423-798-7952 438 D
jeff.horner@ws.edu
HORNER, Jennifer .... 860-465-5775.. 84 K
hornerje@easternct.edu
HORNER, Jody .... 402-941-6000 275 J
president@midlandu.edu
HORNER, Kristin .... 620-251-7700 176 K
horner.kristin@coffeyville.edu
HORNER, Pat .... 701-845-7702 354 E
HORNER, Stacy .... 269-782-1220 237 B
shorner@swmich.edu
HORNER, Theresa .... 716-827-2485 331 K
hornert@trocaire.edu
HORNICK, Robert .... 510-567-6174.. 66 I
bhornick@sum.edu
HORNING, Kirsten .... 503-338-2341 382 E
khorning@clatsopcc.edu
HORNOR, Tara, F .... 843-953-5336 419 D
tara.mcnealy@citadel.edu
HORNS, Phyllis, N .... 252-744-2265 349 I
hornsp@ecu.edu
HORNSBY, Jake .... 415-518-5396.. 68 I
hornsbyj@uchastings.edu
HORNSBY, Jake .... 510-885-7617.. 31 F
jake.hornsby@csueastbay.edu
HORNSBY, Leigh .... 423-354-5255 437 E
mlhornsby@northeaststate.edu
HOROWITZ, Avery .... 718-252-7800 331 F
averymh@touro.edu
HOROWITZ,
Boruch Avrohom .... 718-438-2018 320 G
rcby26@aol.com
HOROWITZ, Elias .... 845-783-0833 332 G
HOROWITZ, Judy .... 716-673-3335 325 C
judy.horowitz@fredonia.edu
HOROWITZ, Samuel, L . 904-264-2172 106 I
shorowitz@iws.edu
HOROWITZ, Sara .... 212-678-8838 312 A
sahorowitz@jtsa.edu
HORSCH, Ellen, S .... 906-487-1737 234 A
eshorsch@mtu.edu
HORSEY, Dwight, G .... 717-871-5100 407 A
dwight.horsey@millersville.edu
HORSMAN, Steve .... 317-931-2378 157 D
HORSTEAD, Jenease ..... 706-821-8392 124 C
jhorstead@paine.edu
HORSWELL, Michael ...... 561-297-3803 109 B
horswell@fau.edu
HORTMAN-FOWLER,
Kristen .... 716-829-7557 307 B
hortmank@dyc.edu
HORTON, Becky .... 478-825-6226 119 C
hortonb@fvsu.edu
HORTON, C, R .... 864-488-4586 422 B
chorton@limestone.edu
HORTON, Claudia .... 816-833-0524 169 D
horton@graceland.edu
HORTON, Connie .... 310-506-4472.. 56 D
connie.horton@pepperdine.edu
HORTON, Connie .... 310-506-4210.. 56 D
connie.horton@pepperdine.edu
HORTON, Dolly .... 828-395-1663 344 A
dhorton@isothermal.edu
HORTON, Howard, E ..... 617-603-6900 222 F
howard.horton@necb.edu
HORTON, Jane, T .... 540-458-8401 491 G
jhorton@wlu.edu
HORTON, Jeff .... 270-707-3721 186 B
jeff.horton@kctcs.edu
HORTON, Jennifer .... 434-544-8432 482 F
horton.jl@lynchburg.edu
HORTON, Johnna .... 507-389-7223 247 H
johnna.horton@southcentral.edu
HORTON, Joseph, M .... 603-641-7600 282 A
jhorton@anselm.edu
HORTON, Julian, K .... 240-500-2000 204 B
jkhorton@hagerstowncc.edu
HORTON, Kelley, R .... 910-775-4403 351 E
kelley.horton@uncp.edu
HORTON, Kimberly .... 937-778-7806 361 E
khorton@edisonohio.edu
HORTON, Leslie .... 508-854-2798 220 G
lhorton@qcc.mass.edu
HORTON, Monique .... 773-995-4424 135 F
m-horton@csu.edu
HORTON, Paul .... 772-462-7520 101 Q
phorton@irsc.edu
HORTON, Ray .... 513-244-8420 359 E
ray.horton@ccuniversity.edu
HORTON, Rose .... 573-341-7685 269 A
hortonrm@mst.edu
HORTON, Susan .... 845-434-5750 330 F
shorton@sullivan.suny.edu
HORTON, Walter, E .... 512-245-2314 463 A
weh21@txstate.edu
HORTON-MACK, Phyllis 770-689-5026 115 E
phorton@aii.edu
HORVATH, Fran .... 831-582-3878.. 33 A
fhorvath@csumb.edu
HORVATH, Karl .... 215-951-1860 398 F
horvathk@lasalle.edu
HORVATH, Virginia, S ... 716-673-3456 325 C
virginia.horvath@fredonia.edu
HORVATH-PLYMAN,
Melissa .... 201-684-7081 289 C
mhorvath@ramapo.edu
HORWITZ, Gayle .... 646-664-9006 301 A
gayle.horwitz@cuny.edu
HORWITZ, Julie, R .... 401-456-8170 417 A
jhorwitz@ric.edu
HORWITZ, Pam .... 314-529-9401 262 B
phorwitz@maryville.edu
HOSACK, Susan, E .... 314-935-5567 269 L
sue.hosack@wustl.edu
HOSCH, Braden, J .... 631-632-6210 325 F
braden.hosch@stonybrook.edu
HOSCH, Jason .... 504-278-6281 193 B
jhosch@nunez.edu
HOSEA, Walter .... 865-251-1800 436 B
whosea@southcollegetn.edu
HOSEI, Huan .... 671-735-5558 519 H
huan.hosei@guamcc.edu
HOSELTON, Steven, A ... 312-341-2442 150 D
shoselton@roosevelt.edu
HOSENEY, Jason .... 360-538-4066 495 B
HOSEY, Heidi .... 814-824-2336 401 J
hhosey@mercyhurst.edu
HOSHIKO, Carol .... 808-734-9568 130 C
hoshiko@hawaii.edu
HOSKEN, Dan .... 818-677-2246.. 33 B
dan.hosken@csun.edu
HOSKEY, Lisa .... 607-274-3011 311 D
HOSKIN, Brittany .... 205-366-8885.... 7 C
bhoskin@stillman.edu
HOSKING, Amanda .... 215-567-7080 389 E
ahosking@aii.edu
HOSKINS, Jamieta .... 312-922-1884 144 H
ahoskins@maccormac.edu
HOSKINS, Sheila .... 252-823-5166 343 A
hoskinss@edgecombe.edu
HOSKINS, Steve .... 606-546-4151 189 I
shoskins@unionky.edu
HOSKINSON, Heidi .... 918-343-7852 379 C
hhoskinson@rsu.edu
HOSKOVEC, Victoria ...... 402-399-2431 274 A
vhoskovec@csm.edu
HOSLET, Charles .... 608-265-2822 510 C
charles.hoslet@wisc.edu
HOSMER, Kerri .... 706-295-6554 120 C
khosmer@gntc.edu

HOWARD, Stefanie .... 310-393-0411.. 56 A
stefanie_howard@rand.org
HOWARD, Steven .... 619-596-2766.. 24 H
showard@advancedtraining.edu
HOWARD, Susan .... 603-283-2367 356 G
showard@antioch.edu
HOWARD, Trish .... 801-863-8440 473 D
howardpa@uvu.edu
HOWARD, Valerie, M .... 412-397-6802 409 C
howardv@rmu.edu
HOWARD, Vikki .... 218-335-4255 242 I
vikki.howard@lltc.edu
HOWARD, Will .... 253-566-5344 499 A
whoward@tacomacc.edu
HOWARD, Yaffa .... 215-635-7300 396 B
yhoward@gratz.edu
HOWARD, Yelitza, M .... 956-326-2171 459 B
yelitza.howard@tamiu.edu
HOWARD-VITAL,
Michelle .... 305-626-3600.. 99 M
mhoward-vital@fmuniv.edu
HOWARD-VITAL,
Michelle .... 305-626-3186.. 99 M
mhoward-vital@fmuniv.edu
HOWARTH, James, R ..... 860-465-4418.. 84 K
howarthj@easternct.edu
HOWATT-NAB, Summer 805-893-5752.. 70 B
showatt-nab@ltsc.ucsb.edu
HOWDEN, Norman .... 214-860-2176 448 A
norman@dcccd.edu
HOWDEN, Tonya .... 269-467-9945 230 C
thowden@glenoaks.edu
HOWDYSHELL,
Cynthia, K .... 540-828-5314 478 J
chowdysh@bridgewater.edu
HOWE, Amanda .... 215-204-5578 411 B
amanda.howe@temple.edu
HOWE, Brian .... 620-792-9254 175 C
howeb@bartonccc.edu
HOWE, Deborah .... 503-253-3443 385 B
president@ocom.edu
HOWE, Derek .... 617-353-6540 212 G
dhowe@bu.edu
HOWE, Jennifer, L .... 937-229-2973 372 A
jhowe1@udayton.edu
HOWE, Jodi, L .... 607-871-2325 298 A
howe@alfred.edu
HOWE, Joseph .... 757-388-2604 485 B
jhowe@sentara.edu
HOWE, Ken, D .... 985-549-2240 197 E
khowe@selu.edu
HOWE, Mark .... 951-343-4299.. 28 G
mhowe@calbaptist.edu
HOWE, Mark .... 518-464-8508 308 A
mhowe@excelsior.edu
HOWE, Melissa .... 617-747-2316 212 B
ootp@berklee.edu
HOWE, Mic .... 503-352-2214 385 I
mic.howe@pacificu.edu
HOWE, Mike .... 507-433-0621 247 C
mike.howe@riverland.edu
HOWE, Nanci .... 650-725-3104.. 66 C
nanhowe@stanford.edu
HOWE, Terri .... 361-825-2629 460 A
terri.howe@tamucc.edu
HOWE, Tiffany .... 605-718-2905 429 E
tiffany.howe@wdt.edu
HOWELL, Aaron .... 434-791-5651 478 E
ahowell@averett.edu
HOWELL, Allan .... 516-299-4225 313 C
allan.howell@liu.edu
HOWELL, Ann .... 208-282-7893 132 B
howeanna@isu.edu
HOWELL, Ann .... 208-282-7893 132 B
howeanna@iau.edu
HOWELL, Candace .... 843-349-7132 421 L
candace.howell@hgtc.edu
HOWELL, Candice .... 402-465-2401 276 E
chowell@nebrwesleyan.edu
HOWELL, Charles .... 330-941-3265 374 E
clhowell01@ysu.edu
HOWELL, Daniel .... 978-478-3400 223 E
dhowell@northpoint.edu
HOWELL, David, B .... 540-365-4413 480 L
dhowell@ferrum.edu
HOWELL, Dianne, B ...... 318-797-5190 194 E
dianne.howell@lsus.edu
HOWELL, Dustin .... 501-279-5776.. 19 G
dhowell@harding.edu
HOWELL, Ed .... 785-628-5304 177 D
ehowell@fhsu.edu
HOWELL, Elizabeth .... 520-206-4778.. 15 L
ehowell1@pima.edu
HOWELL, Hayes .... 870-759-4143.. 23 K
howell@wbcoll.edu
HOWELL, Helen .... 208-882-1566 132 D
hhowell@nsa.edu
HOWELL, James .... 806-716-2369 456 F
jhowell@southplainscollege.edu
HOWELL, James, R .... 252-398-6313 336 K
howelj@chowan.edu
HOWELL, Jay .... 409-747-9082 469 C
jhowell@utmb.edu
HOWELL, Jessica .... 904-826-8620.. 98 I
jhowell@flagler.edu
HOWELL, Jonathan .... 860-701-5161.. 87 F
howell_j@mitchell.edu
HOWELL, Karen .... 904-826-0084.. 71 I
khowell@usa.edu
HOWELL, Kathryn .... 414-410-4003 506 F
khowell@stritch.edu
HOWELL, Kevin, A .... 813-257-7777 113 E
khowell@ut.edu
HOWELL, La Donna ...... 918-465-1753 375 J
lhowell@eosc.edu
HOWELL, Laura .... 662-846-4624 252 H
lhowell@deltastate.edu
HOWELL, Laurence, A ... 973-596-3686 288 A
laurence.a.howell@njit.edu
HOWELL, LaVerne, B .... 864-977-7013 422 I
laverne.howell@ngu.edu
HOWELL, Lisa .... 760-773-2511.. 39 D
lhowell@collegeofthedesert.edu
HOWELL, Liz .... 501-279-4276.. 19 G
lhowell@harding.edu
HOWELL, Marie .... 803-535-1207 423 B
howellm@octech.edu
HOWELL, Martie .... 716-286-8300 318 F
meh@niagara.edu
HOWELL, Marya, L .... 704-894-2642 337 B
mahowell@davidson.edu
HOWELL, Maurice .... 410-462-8539 202 F
mhowell@bccc.edu
HOWELL, Rohan .... 718-409-2220 329 E
rhowell@sunymaritime.edu
HOWELL, Ronshetta ...... 863-297-1004 105 F
rhowell@polk.edu
HOWELL, Shirley .... 773-252-5125 149 I
shirley.howell@resu.edu
HOWELL, Stephen, C .... 419-289-5944 356 L
showell@ashland.edu
HOWELL, Steven .... 209-946-3066.. 70 F
showell@pacific.edu
HOWELL, Verna, G .... 864-656-5444 419 F
howell@clemson.edu
HOWELL, Wendy .... 229-430-3816 114 J
whowell@albanytech.edu
HOWELLS, Jeffrey, D ..... 318-675-8152 194 D
jhowel1@lsuhsc.edu
HOWERTER, Wendy, L .. 217-786-2283 144 B
wendy.howerter@llcc.edu
HOWERTON, Cheryl, L .. 217-424-6317 145 J
chowerton@millikin.edu
HOWERTON, Lisa, A ..... 270-824-8582 186 D
lisa.howerton@kctcs.edu
HOWES, Jennifer .... 626-395-8331.. 29 I
jhowes@caltech.edu
HOWES, Meg .... 630-617-3781 138 C
howesm@elmhurst.edu
HOWEY, Debbie .... 573-334-6825 266 L
dhowey@sehealth.org
HOWIE, Dennis .... 313-927-1200 233 D
HOWIE, Douglas .... 972-524-3341 457 H
HOWIE, Michael .... 402-461-7743 274 I
mhowie@hastings.edu
HOWILER, Robert, W .... 864-833-8324 423 D
rhowiler@presby.edu
HOWLAND, Bonnie, J ... 413-662-5210 218 C
bonnie.howland@mcla.edu
HOWLAND, Jerri .... 315-312-3378 327 D
jerri.howland@oswego.edu
HOWLAND, Susan .... 775-445-3249 279 F
susan.howland@wnc.edu
HOWLE, Jonathan .... 718-779-1499 320 C
jhowle@plazacollege.edu
HOWLE, Meg .... 843-574-6356 424 G
meg.howle@tridenttech.edu
HOWLETT, Bernadette .... 503-251-2812 387 I
bhowlett@uws.edu
HOWLETT, Beth .... 503-253-3443 385 B
bhowlett@ocom.edu
HOWLETT, Jeffrey .... 919-760-8828 339 H
howlettj@meredith.edu
HOWLETT, Lucy, J .... 540-674-3619 488 G
lhowlett@nr.edu
HOWLETT, Sophia .... 802-258-3359 476 B
sophia.howlett@sit.edu
HOWLEY, James .... 773-481-8460 136 B
jhowley@ccc.edu
HOWLEY, Kathleen .... 717-720-4200 405 D
khowley@passhe.edu
HOWLEY, Nicholas .... 410-888-9048 205 D
nhowley@muih.edu
HOWORTH, Aidan .... 773-244-6208 147 F
ahoworth@northpark.edu
HOWRIGAN, Penny .... 802-635-1219 477 C
penny.howrigan@jsc.edu
HOWSARE, Anne .... 515-248-7206 168 A
amhowsare@dmacc.edu
HOWSER, Tamyra .... 253-566-6050 499 A
thowser@tacomacc.edu
HOXIE, David, E .... 304-457-6306 501 A
hoxiede@ab.edu
HOXIE, Hal .... 620-241-0723 176 G
hal.hoxie@centralchristian.edu
HOXIE, Saundra, E .... 304-457-6278 501 A
hoxiese@ab.edu
HOXSIE, Patti, D .... 706-880-8327 122 D
phoxsie@lagrange.edu
HOXTER, Laney .... 410-287-1043 203 B
lhoxter@cecil.edu
HOY, Cliff .... 423-636-7307 439 C
choy@tusculum.edu
HOY, Leah .... 817-272-2185 467 B
hoy@uta.edu
HOY, Linda .... 575-538-6317 297 H
hoyl@wnmu.edu
HOY, Murray, K .... 410-334-2810 210 C
rhoy@worwic.edu
HOYACK, Chuck .... 520-417-4060.. 11 R
hoyackc@cochise.edu
HOYER, Gary .... 214-887-5031 448 G
ghoyer@dts.edu
HOYERT, Mark .... 219-980-6731 160 C
mhoyert@iun.edu
HOYLE, Gary .... 412-346-2100 408 B
ghoyle@pia.edu
HOYLE, Ken, R .... 919-718-7436 341 H
khoyle@cccc.edu
HOYLE, Michael .... 617-243-2100 216 C
mhoyle@lasell.edu
HOYOS, Angel .... 787-758-2525 528 D
angel.hoyos@upr.edu
HOYOS, Denise .... 520-417-4148.. 11 R
hoyosd@cochise.edu
HOYT, Angela .... 831-479-6324.. 28 F
anhoyt@cabrillo.edu
HOYT, Bill .... 717-764-9550 393 B
bhoyt@csb.edu
HOYT, Brad .... 217-641-4975 141 F
bhoyt@jwcc.edu
HOYT, Dana, G .... 936-294-1013 462 F
dghoyt@shsu.edu
HOYT, David, R .... 972-599-3133 446 I
dhoyt@collin.edu
HOYT, Debra .... 404-880-8773 117 H
dhoyt@cau.edu
HOYT, Jeffery .... 561-297-2719 109 B
hoytj@fau.edu
HOYT, Justin .... 518-629-7328 310 G
j.hoyt@hvcc.edu
HOYT, Lisa .... 973-655-5333 287 D
hoytl@mail.montclair.edu
HOYT, Patricia .... 301-846-2660 203 H
phoyt@frerick.edu
HOZDIK, Elaine .... 239-590-7931 109 C
ehozdik@fgcu.edu
HRABEC, Erika, J .... 734-764-6270 237 I
erikah@umich.edu
HRABOSKY, James, A ... 724-287-8711 390 J
james.hrabosky@bc3.edu
HRABOWSKI,
Freeman, A .... 410-455-3880 208 A
hrabowski@umbc.edu
HRACZO, Rebecca .... 704-463-3368 348 B
rebecca.hraczo@pfeiffer.edu
HRADSKY, Robert .... 202-885-3318.. 91 C
hradsky@american.edu
HRDLICKA, Rick .... 909-384-8656.. 59 I
rhrdlicka@sbccd.cc.ca.us
HRIBAR, Frank, J .... 517-265-5161 226 F
fhribar@adrian.edu
HRISHENKO,
Michael, S .... 330-941-3520 374 E
mshrishenko@ysu.edu
HRISTIS, Emilia .... 516-562-3405 307 D
ehristis@northwell.edu
HRITZAK, Susan, A .... 570-408-4850 414 H
susan.hritzak@wilkes.edu
HRNCIR, Charlie .... 979-458-7155 458 E
chrncir@tamus.edu
HRNCIR, Duane .... 907-786-1050.. 10 A
provost@alaska.edu
HROMCO, John .... 503-493-6243 382 I
jhromco@cu-portland.edu
HROMISIN, Ronald, S .... 570-674-6312 401 M
rhromisi@misericordia.edu
HRON, Stacey .... 218-683-8584 246 F
stacey.hron@northlandcollege.edu
HRPCEK, Jean .... 262-595-2211 511 C
hrpcek@uwp.edu
HRUBY, Nick .... 303-861-1151.. 79 E
nhruby@concorde.edu
HRUSKA, Amanda .... 920-565-1000 507 K
hurskaaj@lakeland.edu
HRUTKA, Mary Ellen ..... 410-888-9048 205 D
mhrutka@muih.edu
HSIAO, Terence .... 425-352-8196 492 K
thsiao@cascadia.edu
HSIEH, Chialin .... 925-473-7309.. 41 A
chsieh@losmedanos.edu
HSIEH, Patricia .... 619-388-7834.. 60 E
phsieh@sdccd.edu
HSIEH, Peter .... 510-592-9688.. 54 C
phsieh@npu.edu
HSIEH, Rosalia .... 622-229-9929.. 47 E
HSU, Andrew .... 419-530-2739 372 F
andrew.hsu@utoledo.edu
HSU, Andy .... 213-413-9500.. 65 E
registrar@scusoma.edu
HSU, Kwei .... 979-532-6350 471 A
kweih@wcjc.edu
HSU, Lily .... 401-598-1000 416 C
lhsu@jwu.edu
HSU, Raymond .... 626-917-9482.. 37 D
raymondh@cesna.edu
HSU, Stephen .... 517-355-0306 233 G
hsu@msu.edu
HU, Alex .... 408-260-0208.. 43 B
es@fivebranches.edu
HU, Feng Sheng .... 217-333-1350 154 B
fshu@illinois.edu
HU, Johnny .... 206-934-5300 497 J
johnny.hu@seattlecolleges.edu
HU, Jonathan .... 520-795-0787.. 10 J
manager@asaom.edu
HU, Mi .... 847-214-7137 138 B
mhu@elgin.edu
HU, S. Jack .... 734-764-1185 237 I
jackhu@umich.edu
HUA, Henry .... 714-484-7217.. 53 M
hhua@cypresscollege.edu
HUA, Maggie .... 510-628-8029.. 48 F
maggiehua@lincolnuca.edu
HUA, Susan .... 818-677-2077.. 33 B
susan.hua@csun.edu
HUANG, Che-Tsao .... 718-262-2750 304 A
huang@york.cuny.edu
HUANG, Christopher ..... 708-534-4503 138 H
chuang@govst.edu
HUANG, Gina .... 408-260-0208.. 43 B
sjstudentservices@fivebranches.edu
HUANG, Gina .... 408-260-0208.. 43 C
sjstudentservices@fivebranches.edu
HUANG, Guiyou .... 318-473-6444 194 A
chancellor@lsua.edu
HUANG, Jefferson .... 909-621-8114.. 38 A
jefferson.huang@cmc.edu
HUANG, Jerry .... 818-364-7836.. 49 C
huangjc@lamission.edu
HUANG, Lixin .... 415-575-6100.. 29 H
lhuang@ciis.edu
HUANG, Roger, D .... 574-631-1691 165 A
huang.31@nd.edu
HUANG, Tracy .... 650-306-3198.. 61 R
huangt@smccd.edu
HUANG, Wen .... 713-780-9777 442 F
info@acaom.edu
HUARD, Jenny .... 660-944-2823 258 G
communications@conception.edu
HUARD, Ruth .... 408-924-2670.. 34 D
ruth.huard@sjsu.edu
HUARD, Susan, D .... 603-206-8002 280 L
shuard@ccsnh.edu
HUBAND, David, E .... 757-446-8474 480 C
hubandde@evms.edu
HUBBARD, Ann .... 772-462-7544 101 Q
ahubbard@irsc.edu
HUBBARD, Betty .... 334-874-5700.... 5 B
b.hubbard@ccal.edu
HUBBARD, Daren .... 313-577-9489 239 C
daren@wayne.edu
HUBBARD, James .... 309-268-8452 139 D
jim.hubbard@heartland.edu
HUBBARD, Jeannette ..... 726-946-7179 414 C
hubbarj@westminster.edu
HUBBARD, Joan .... 801-626-6403 473 E
jhubbard@weber.edu
HUBBARD, Laura, E .... 716-645-5124 325 B
laurahub@buffalo.edu
HUBBARD, Michael .... 513-745-3741 374 D
0565mgr@fheg.follett.com
HUBBARD, R. Glenn ...... 212-854-2888 305 E
rgh1@columbia.edu
HUBBARD, Ruth .... 443-334-2331 207 C
rhubbard@stevenson.edu
HUBBARD, Sandie .... 303-991-1575.. 76 H
sandie.hubbard@americansentinel.edu
HUBBARD, Steven .... 440-366-7239 364 F
HUBBARD, William .... 920-465-2510 510 E
hubbardw@uwgb.edu

HUGHES, Cynthia .... 212-616-7200 309 G
HUGHES, David .... 501-760-4311.. 20 D
david.hughes@np.edu
HUGHES, David .... 435-586-7735 473 A
hughes@suu.edu
HUGHES, Deborah .... 786-279-2643 298 E
dhughes@asa.edu
HUGHES, DeVetta .... 843-574-6199 424 G
devetta.hughes@tridenttech.edu
HUGHES, Donna, D ...... 717-245-1577 394 A
hughsdo@dickinson.edu
HUGHES, Dorothy .... 631-420-2166 329 D
hughesd@farmingdale.edu
HUGHES, Erinn .... 281-649-3213 450 C
erhughes@hbu.edu
HUGHES, Ernie .... 404-752-1734 123 F
ehughes@msm.edu
HUGHES, Frank .... 605-274-4325 426 K
frank.hughes@augie.edu
HUGHES, Gary .... 215-780-1402 410 D
HUGHES, George .... 805-756-6650.. 30 K
grhughes@calpoly.edu
HUGHES, Gerunda, B .... 202-865-0207.. 92 C
ghughes@howard.edu
HUGHES, Glyn .... 804-484-1656 486 G
ghughes@richmond.edu
HUGHES, Greg .... 301-369-2800 202 J
ghughes@captechu.edu
HUGHES, Jacqueline ..... 909-537-5029.. 33 D
jacqueline.hughes@csusb.edu
HUGHES, James, J .... 860-297-2376.. 88 E
james.hughes@trincoll.edu
HUGHES, James, J .... 617-287-5420 216 I
jamesj.hughes@umb.edu
HUGHES, James, L .... 410-706-1935 207 H
jhughes@umaryland.edu
HUGHES, Jason .... 970-351-1273.. 83 F
jason.hughes@unco.edu
HUGHES, Jay .... 870-460-1022.. 22 D
hughesj@uamont.edu
HUGHES, Jeanell .... 502-852-7591 190 C
jnhugh02@exchange.louisville.edu
HUGHES, Jennifer .... 650-574-6118.. 62 A
hughesj@smccd.edu
HUGHES, Jennifer .... 903-586-2518 451 C
jguerra@jacksonville-college.edu
HUGHES, Jerry, M .... 660-543-4250 268 A
hughes@ucmo.edu
HUGHES, Jim .... 620-235-4154 180 J
jhughes@pittstate.edu
HUGHES, John .... 661-362-2223.. 51 C
jhughes@masters.edu
HUGHES, John .... 208-732-6549 131 I
jhughes@csi.edu
HUGHES, John .... 404-835-6120 435 M
jhughes@richmont.edu
HUGHES, Joseph .... 479-979-1228.. 23 J
jhughes@ozarks.edu
HUGHES, Joshua, A ...... 419-289-5034 356 L
jhughe11@ashland.edu
HUGHES, Karla .... 870-460-1020.. 22 D
hughesk@uamont.edu
HUGHES, Kevin, M .... 757-594-7160 479 H
kmhughes@cnu.edu
HUGHES, Kristin .... 413-585-2701 224 F
khughes@smith.edu
HUGHES, Laura .... 870-460-1454.. 22 D
hughesl@uamont.edu
HUGHES, Laura .... 208-792-2224 132 C
lhughes@lcsc.edu
HUGHES, LeAnn .... 309-556-3031 141 B
lhughes@iwu.edu
HUGHES, Lecia .... 325-793-4998 452 F
hughes.lecia@mcm.edu
HUGHES, Leslie .... 601-635-2111 252 I
lhughes@eccc.edu
HUGHES, Linda .... 402-354-7049 275 P
linda.hughes@methodistcollege.edu
HUGHES, Louise .... 870-612-2013.. 22 H
louise.hughes@uaccb.edu
HUGHES, Lucie .... 410-827-5879 203 C
lhughes@chesapeake.edu
HUGHES, Mark .... 301-925-3800 254 B
rmhughes@mc.edu
HUGHES, Mark .... 512-245-2501 463 A
mh66@txstate.edu
HUGHES, Marshall .... 617-427-0600 221 A
mhughes@rcc.mass.edu
HUGHES, Matthew .... 850-718-2344.. 96 H
hughesm@chipola.edu
HUGHES, Matthew .... 773-252-5310 149 I
matthew.hughes@resu.edu
HUGHES, Meghan .... 401-825-2188 416 B
meghanhughes@ccri.edu
HUGHES, Melany .... 308-432-6415 276 B
mhughes@csc.edu
HUGHES, Melissa .... 318-257-4205 197 A
mhughes@latech.edu
HUGHES, Michael .... 415-422-2465.. 72 A
hughesm@usfca.edu
HUGHES, Michelle .... 508-588-9100 220 B
HUGHES, Mike .... 231-591-2924 230 A
mikehughes@ferris.edu
HUGHES, Mike, C .... 817-923-1921 457 G
mhughes@swbts.edu
HUGHES, Nancy .... 405-224-3140 381 B
nhughes@usao.edu
HUGHES, Pennie, D ...... 864-488-4544 422 B
phughes@limestone.edu
HUGHES, Perry .... 276-223-4757 490 C
phughes@wcc.vccs.edu
HUGHES, Randy .... 361-593-3209 460 B
j.hughes@tamuk.edu
HUGHES, Robert .... 626-914-8811.. 37 G
rhughes@citruscollege.edu
HUGHES, Robert, A .... 402-572-3654 273 J
robert.hughes@alegent.org
HUGHES, Robin, L .... 317-274-6862 160 E
roblhugh@indiana.edu
HUGHES, Romana .... 817-257-7434 461 A
r.hughes@tcu.edu
HUGHES, Samantha ...... 740-427-5820 364 A
hughess@kenyon.edu
HUGHES, Sandra .... 281-487-1170 460 G
shughes@txchiro.edu
HUGHES, Sandra .... 843-863-7933 419 C
shughes@csuniv.edu
HUGHES, Sheila .... 925-631-4585.. 59 C
smh21@stmarys-ca.edu
HUGHES, Stephen .... 315-228-7130 304 G
shughes1@colgate.edu
HUGHES, Todd .... 508-588-9100 220 B
HUGHES, Tom .... 928-776-2205.. 17 G
tom.hughes@yc.edu
HUGHES, Wendy .... 864-941-8317 423 C
whughes@ptc.edu
HUGHES HARRIS,
Cynthia .... 850-599-3818 109 A
cynthia.hugheshartis@famu.edu
HUGHEY, Andrew, C ..... 713-313-7470 461 E
hugheyac@tsu.edu
HUGHEY, Richard .... 831-459-1993.. 70 C
vpdue@ucsc.edu
HUGHEY, Willie, R .... 615-329-8663 431 I
whughey@fisk.edu
HUGINE, JR., Andrew ... 256-372-5230.... 1 A
andrew.hugine@aamu.edu
HUGLE, Shelbie .... 859-246-6216 185 G
shelbie.hugle@kctcs.edu
HUGUENARD, Alex .... 731-661-5316 439 D
ahuguenard@uu.edu
HUGUENIN, Sanders ..... 276-328-0120 487 A
jsh4ew@uvawise.edu
HUGUET, Marie-Pierre .. 802-387-1682 475 C
mariepierrehuguet@landmark.edu
HUGULEY, Wendy .... 706-864-1545 127 B
wendy.huguley@ung.edu
HUH, Dong Hyun .... 714-525-0088.. 44 I
sd@gm.edu
HUHTA, Keith .... 480-245-7903.. 13 C
khuhta@mgmi.org
HUI, Andrew .... 215-702-4203 391 C
ahui@cairn.edu
HUI, Timothy, K .... 215-702-4377 391 C
thui@cairn.edu
HUINDA, Jeff .... 417-865-2815 260 B
huindaj@evangel.edu
HUINER, Leslie .... 760-245-4271.. 73 E
leslie.huiner@vvc.edu
HUISH, David .... 928-524-7888.. 15 B
david.huish@npc.edu
HUISMAN, Brandon ...... 712-722-6028 168 I
brandon.huisman@dordt.edu
HUISMAN, Karen .... 231-591-2505 230 A
karenhuisman@ferris.edu
HUISMAN, Rhonda .... 320-308-2022 247 E
HUISMAN, Rhonda .... 317-955-6223 162 R
rhuisman@marian.edu
HUKE, Theresa .... 610-361-5249 402 G
huket@neumann.edu
HUKILL, Lezlie .... 806-291-3446 470 I
hukill@wbu.edu
HUKOWICZ, Elizabeth ... 413-265-2459 213 E
hukowicze@elms.edu
HULET, David .... 661-362-2832.. 51 C
dhulet@masters.edu
HULETT, Kevin .... 918-293-5476 378 B
kevin.hulett@okstate.edu
HULETT, Matt .... 505-277-0385 296 H
mhulett@unm.edu
HULETT, Tom .... 816-604-3063 262 J
tom.hulett@mcckc.edu
HULIN, Alicia .... 337-521-8920 193 E
alicia.hulin@solacc.edu
HULIN, Christopher, P .. 615-868-6503 434 G
chris.hulin@mtsa.edu
HULKE, Carla, J .... 507-354-8221 243 C
hulkecj@mlc-wels.edu
HULL, Anne .... 904-826-0084.. 71 I
ahull@usa.edu
HULL, Brian .... 479-979-1211.. 23 J
bhull@ozarks.edu
HULL, Brooks .... 318-257-0211 197 A
bhull@latech.edu
HULL, Edward, C .... 413-545-1964 216 H
ehull@umass.edu
HULL, Hsiawen .... 661-362-3666.. 39 C
hsiawen.hull@canyons.edu
HULL, Jim .... 217-234-5225 143 B
jhull17327@lakeland.cc.il.us
HULL, Judy, M .... 931-372-3491 438 F
jmhull@tntech.edu
HULL, Justin .... 973-684-6741 288 C
jhull@pccc.edu
HULL, Lynne .... 614-947-6046 362 A
lynne.hull@franklin.edu
HULL, Nathan .... 509-453-0374 497 A
nathan.hull@perrytech.edu
HULL, Robert .... 815-928-5429 148 F
rehull@olivet.edu
HULL, Shawn .... 573-592-4220 270 D
shawn.hull@williamwoods.edu
HULL, Stephen .... 863-297-1026 105 F
shull@polk.edu
HULL, Teresa .... 909-652-7653.. 36 E
teresa.hull@chaffey.edu
HULL, William .... 269-749-7535 236 A
bjhull@olivetcollege.edu
HULL, Yvonne .... 620-251-7700 176 K
HULLETT, Lisa .... 256-352-8267.... 3 I
lisa.hullett@wallacestate.edu
HULON, Jane .... 601-643-8310 252 G
jane.hulon@colin.edu
HULS, Jack .... 360-417-6246 496 I
jhuls@pencol.edu
HULS, Sean .... 218-726-8711 250 F
shuls@d.umn.edu
HULSE, Debra .... 325-793-4761 452 F
hulse.debra@mcm.edu
HULSEBUS, John .... 269-927-6846 232 G
jhulsebus@lakemichigancollege.edu
HULSEY, Amy .... 706-754-7852 123 G
ahulsey@northgatech.edu
HULSEY, Janet .... 706-419-1262 118 E
hulsey@covenant.edu
HULSEY, Tara .... 304-293-6521 505 B
thulsey@hsc.wvu.edu
HULST, Mary .... 616-526-7617 228 B
msh4@calvin.edu
HULSTINE, Thomas .... 717-947-6095 404 S
tjhulsti@pacollege.edu
HULT, Lori .... 219-757-6132 163 H
lori.hult@franciscanalliance.org
HULT, Nicole .... 719-590-6708.. 79 B
nhult@coloradotech.edu
HULTBERG, Jane .... 207-801-5660 199 A
jhultberg@coa.edu
HULTBERG, Larry .... 503-375-7035 383 A
lhutlberg@corban.edu
HULVEY, Dale, B .... 540-568-7063 481 I
hulveydb@jmu.edu
HUMBERGER, Laura ...... 406-994-4361 272 A
lhumberger@montana.edu
HUMBERT, Mark .... 315-312-2248 327 D
mark.humbert@oswego.edu
HUMBLE, James .... 610-785-6275 409 F
jhumble@scs.edu
HUME, Samantha .... 808-983-4100 129 D
HUME, Wyatt .... 801-587-1208 472 P
rory.hume@hsc.utah.edu
HUMERICK,
Rosalind, M .... 386-312-4212 106 M
rosalindhumerick@sjrstate.edu
HUMES, Cynthia .... 909-607-8713.. 38 A
cynthia.humes@cmc.edu
HUMISTON, Dolores ..... 509-777-4320 500 H
dhumiston@whitworth.edu
HUMKE, Amy .... 815-479-7518 145 B
ahumke@mchenry.edu
HUMMEL, Amanda .... 419-448-3422 370 K
hummelas@tiffin.edu
HUMMEL, Beth .... 207-768-2739 200 B
bhummel@nmcc.edu
HUMMEL, Heather .... 580-774-3233 380 B
heather.hummel@swosu.edu
HUMMEL, Kate .... 570-321-4246 400 G
hummel@lycoming.edu
HUMMEL, Mary .... 301-314-8428 207 G
mlhummel@umd.edu
HUMMEL, Sarah .... 757-481-5005 492 A
HUMMEL, Scott .... 601-318-6497 256 I
shummel@wmcarey.edu
HUMMEL, Scott, R .... 610-330-5403 399 B
hummels@lafayette.edu
HUMMER, Alissa .... 805-893-4091.. 70 B
alissa.hummer@planning.ucsb.edu
HUMMER, John .... 575-647-2266 293 J
HUMMINGBIRD,
Edward .... 505-922-6506 296 G
edward.hummingbird@bie.edu
HUMMONS, Tina .... 937-512-3120 370 A
tina.hummons@sinclair.edu
HUMPHERYS, Bryce ...... 509-793-2055 492 I
bryceh@bigbend.edu
HUMPHREY, Bonnie ...... 660-831-4108 264 A
humphreyb@moval.edu
HUMPHREY, Dana, N .... 207-581-2217 201 B
danah@maine.edu
HUMPHREY, David .... 541-552-6522 386 H
humphred2@sou.edu
HUMPHREY, George ..... 617-732-2874 221 E
george.humphrey@mcphs.edu
HUMPHREY, George, D 520-626-7301.. 16 J
ghumphre@email.arizona.edu
HUMPHREY, J. Timothy 217-786-2240 144 B
tim.humphrey@llcc.edu
HUMPHREY, IV,
James, E .... 704-687-5732 351 C
jesh.humphrey@uncc.edu
HUMPHREY, Julie .... 919-536-7211 342 G
humphreyj@durhamtech.edu
HUMPHREY, Kathy, W .. 412-624-4200 412 I
kathyh@pitt.edu
HUMPHREY, Keith .... 805-756-1521.. 30 K
humphrey@calpoly.edu
HUMPHREY, Kim .... 919-761-2224 349 C
khumphrey@sebts.edu
HUMPHREY, Lesley .... 949-582-4272.. 64 J
lhumphrey@saddleback.edu
HUMPHREY, Marie .... 719-549-2919.. 78 P
marie.humphrey@csupueblo.edu
HUMPHREY, Reed .... 460-243-2417 271 G
reed.humphrey@umontana.edu
HUMPHREY, Roger .... 307-532-8261 516 J
roger.humphrey@ewc.wy.edu
HUMPHREY, Scott .... 315-792-3835 332 H
shumphrey@utica.edu
HUMPHREY, Shawn .... 717-728-2419 392 B
shawnhumphrey@centralpenn.edu
HUMPHREY, Twila .... 719-502-2052.. 81 H
twila.humphrey@ppcc.edu
HUMPHREYS, Carol, R . 510-593-2920.. 63 A
chumphreys@saybrook.edu
HUMPHREYS, Jennifer .. 918-647-1270 375 B
jmhumphreys@carlalbert.edu
HUMPHREYS, Joe .... 361-485-4485 465 D
humphreysj@uhv.edu
HUMPHREYS, John .... 903-886-5514 459 E
john.humphreys@tamuc.edu
HUMPHREYS, Katie .... 702-895-0892 279 D
katie.humphreys@unlv.edu
HUMPHREYS, JR.,
Robert, G .... 209-478-0800.. 45 J
bhumphreys@humphreys.edu
HUMPHRIES, Brian, L .... 651-286-7620 251 C
blhumphries@unwsp.edu
HUMPHRIES, Corey ...... 706-233-7231 125 E
chumphries@shorter.edu
HUMPHRIES,
Gregory, G .... 704-406-4647 337 H
ghumphries@gardner-webb.edu
HUMPHRIES, Karl .... 903-875-7600 453 J
karl.humphries@navarrocollege.edu
HUMPHRIES, Tara .... 919-735-5151 347 E
tarah@waynecc.edu
HUNDLEY, Christina ..... 602-787-6622.. 13 J
christina.hundley@paradisevalley.edu
HUNDLEY, Patrick .... 662-846-4704 252 H
phundley@deltastate.edu
HUNDLEY, Stephen .... 317-274-4111 160 E
shundley@iupui.edu
HUNE, Raymond .... 573-592-1638 270 D
raymond.hune@williamwoods.edu
HUNEYCUTT, Richy .... 252-527-6223 344 D
rhuneycutt@lenoircc.edu
HUNG, Alex .... 626-571-5110.. 48 G
alexhung@les.edu
HUNGER, Suzanne .... 406-265-3568 272 C
suzanne.hunger@msun.edu
HUNGERFORD, Dan .... 601-974-1000 254 A
HUNHOFF, Christian ...... 605-668-5126 427 F
christian.hunhoff@mtmc.edu
HUNKER, Kurt .... 619-684-8787.. 53 J
khunker@newschoolarch.edu
HUNN, Martha, S .... 843-349-2962 420 A
mhunn@coastal.edu
HUNN, II, Marvin, T ..... 214-887-5281 448 G
mhunn@dts.edu
HUNNEWELL, Lila .... 617-358-5220 212 G
lilawell@bu.edu

HUNNICUTT, Christopher 540-365-4450 480 L chunnicutt@ferrum.edu
HUNNICUTT, Marianne 630-942-4306 136 D hunnicutt@cod.edu
HUNSADER, Tricia 423-636-7300 439 C thunsader@tusculum.edu
HUNSAKER, Charles 660-785-4133 267 K hunsaker@truman.edu
HUNSAKER, Deanna 660-626-2356 257 A dhunsaker@atsu.edu
HUNSAKER, Wayne 801-622-1573 472 H wayne.hunsaker@stevenhenager.edu
HUNSBERGER, Jill 734-481-2324 229 K jhunsberg1@emich.edu
HUNSICKER, Donald 617-262-5000 212 C don.hunsicker@the-bac.edu
HUNSINGER PATTEN, Rachael 518-743-2243 328 G pattenr@sunyacc.edu
HUNSINGER PATTEN, Rachael 518-743-2255 328 G pattenr@sunyacc.edu
HUNSUCKER, Scott, E 704-233-8221 353 D scotth@wingate.edu
HUNT, Alice 773-896-2400 135 G ahunt@ctschicago.edu
HUNT, Ana 501-202-6200 18 I
HUNT, Ana 501-760-4213 20 D ana.hunt@np.edu
HUNT, Bill (William) 918-495-7750 378 H whunt@oru.edu
HUNT, Brittany 919-497-3338 339 F bhunt@louisburg.edu
HUNT, Cammie 910-521-6515 351 E cammie.hunt@uncp.edu
HUNT, Daphne 254-968-1852 459 A djhunt@tarleton.edu
HUNT, Darnell 310-267-4304 69 B dhunt@soc.ucla.edu
HUNT, Denise 760-921-5510 55 J dhunt@paloverde.edu
HUNT, Edward, L 212-870-1227 318 C ehunt@nyts.edu
HUNT, Emily 806-651-5330 460 E ehunt@mail.wtamu.edu
HUNT, Gerry 405-208-5582 377 D ghunt@okcu.edu
HUNT, Gordon 407-265-8383 96 C
HUNT, Hallie 657-278-2011 32 B
HUNT, Jamer 212-229-8950 316 E huntj@newschool.edu
HUNT, James 850-644-4041 110 A jhunt@fsu.edu
HUNT, James 325-793-3806 452 F hunt.james@mcm.edu
HUNT, Jamie 336-750-3148 352 D huntj@wssu.edu
HUNT, Janet 501-337-5000 19 C jhunt@coto.edu
HUNT, Janette 727-341-3229 107 A hunt.janette@spcollege.edu
HUNT, Jeff 303-963-3254 77 I jhunt@ccu.edu
HUNT, Jeff 864-592-4727 424 C huntj@sccsc.edu
HUNT, Jeffrey 808-235-7442 130 I jwhunt@hawaii.edu
HUNT, Jill 270-809-3763 188 D thunt2@murraystate.edu
HUNT, Judith, L 973-655-4301 287 D huntjl@mail.montclair.edu
HUNT, Karen 937-327-6377 374 A khunt@wittenberg.edu
HUNT, Kathy 206-546-4741 498 E khunt@shoreline.edu
HUNT, Lawrence 413-585-2260 224 F lhunt@smith.edu
HUNT, Lori 509-533-7378 493 I lori.hunt@scc.spokane.edu
HUNT, Louis, D 919-515-1428 350 E ldhunt@ncsu.edu
HUNT, Mark 334-386-7140 5 I mhunt@faulkner.edu
HUNT, Morgan 910-521-6533 351 E morgan.hunt@uncp.edu
HUNT, Patrick, G 240-895-4307 206 G pghunt@smcm.edu
HUNT, Paul, M 517-432-4499 233 G pmhunt@msu.edu
HUNT, Philip 605-394-2497 429 A philip.hunt@sdsmt.edu
HUNT, Roe, B 803-535-5471 419 E rhunt@claflin.edu
HUNT, Rusty 252-527-6223 344 D
HUNT, Sellestine 936-633-5290 442 I shunt@angelina.edu
HUNT, Skyler 304-357-4741 502 E skylerhunt@ucwv.edu
HUNT, Steve 828-327-7000 341 G shunt@cvcc.edu
HUNT, Steve 503-375-7591 383 A shunt@corban.edu
HUNT, Terry, L 541-346-8905 387 F thunt@uoregon.edu
HUNT, Thomas 626-815-3004 26 U thunt@apu.edu
HUNT, Tolif, R 319-273-3217 167 A tolif.hunt@uni.edu
HUNT-BULL, Nicholas 518-327-6247 320 A nhuntbull@paulsmiths.edu
HUNTER, Amelia 615-329-8537 431 I ahunter@fisk.edu
HUNTER, Barbara 904-361-6352 100 F barbara.hunter@fscj.edu
HUNTER, Bill 850-973-9448 104 D hunterb@nfcc.edu
HUNTER, Bonnie, L 219-464-5411 165 D bonnie.hunter@valpo.edu
HUNTER, Carolyn, A 513-585-2068 359 D carolyn.hunter@thechristcollege.edu
HUNTER, Chip 509-335-3596 499 G chip.hunter@wsu.edu
HUNTER, Donna, L 304-766-4146 505 A hunterdl@wvstateu.edu
HUNTER, Gary 970-247-7224 79 J ghunter@fortlewis.edu
HUNTER, Gayle 386-752-1822 99 J gayle.hunter@fgc.edu
HUNTER, Gerald, E 757-823-8011 483 F gehunter@nsu.edu
HUNTER, JR., Jairy, C 843-863-7502 419 C jhunter@csuniv.edu
HUNTER, James 270-707-3713 186 B
HUNTER, Janet 563-387-2229 171 I hunterja@luther.edu
HUNTER, Jim 928-645-6681 12 B jim.hunter@coconino.edu
HUNTER, John 417-626-1234 264 J library@occ.edu
HUNTER, John, G 503-494-8220 385 D somdeansoffice@ohsu.edu
HUNTER, Kim 513-244-4248 366 A kim.hunter@msj.edu
HUNTER, Kymm 803-705-4519 418 G hunterk@benedict.edu
HUNTER, Lai-Monte 603-428-2298 281 F lhunter@nec.edu
HUNTER, Larry, T 614-236-6641 358 A lhunter2@capital.edu
HUNTER, LeAnn 509-452-5100 496 H lhunter@pnwu.edu
HUNTER, Lisa 716-673-3717 325 C lisa.hunter@fredonia.edu
HUNTER, Lorna 208-459-5319 131 H lhunter@collegeofidaho.edu
HUNTER, Lynn 781-239-3111 220 A lhunter@massbay.edu
HUNTER, Maggie 510-430-3220 52 E mhunter@mills.edu
HUNTER, Marc 405-382-9950 379 I m.hunter@sscok.edu
HUNTER, Melissa 931-221-7315 430 B hunterm@apsu.edu
HUNTER, Pam 760-773-2508 39 D phunter@collegeofthedesert.edu
HUNTER, Patricia 425-739-8361 495 F patricia.hunter@lwtech.edu
HUNTER, Patti 805-565-7262 74 I phunter@westmont.edu
HUNTER, Rathenia 847-947-5887 146 G rhunter@nl.edu
HUNTER, Rebecca 508-793-7561 213 C rhunter@clarku.edu
HUNTER, Rebecca 212-229-5620 316 E hunterr@newschool.edu
HUNTER, Richie, C 518-276-2800 321 A hunter3@rpi.edu
HUNTER, Steve 360-867-6310 494 G hunters@evergreen.edu
HUNTER, Susan, J 207-581-1717 201 F hunter@maine.edu
HUNTER, Susan, J 207-581-1512 201 B president@umaine.edu
HUNTER, Susan, S 804-523-5375 488 C shunter@reynolds.edu
HUNTER, Teressa 405-466-3274 375 L thunter@langston.edu
HUNTER, Tim, W 814-332-2755 388 F thunter@allegheny.edu
HUNTER, Tracie 281-290-2722 452 C tracie.n.hunter@lonestar.edu
HUNTER, Valerie 201-684-7502 289 C vhunter@ramapo.edu
HUNTER, W. Bingham 602-429-4431 15 K bhunter@ps.edu
HUNTER, William 670-237-6719 520 D william.hunter@marianas.edu
HUNTER-CEVERA, Jenny 301-447-5218 206 B hunterce@msmary.edu
HUNTER-GOLDSWORTHY, Heidi 540-654-2468 486 D hhunterg@umw.edu
HUNTER HAYES, Tracy 732-247-5241 287 E thunterhayes@nbts.edu
HUNTER-MCKINNEY, Shaunna, E 434-223-6193 481 D shunter@hsc.edu
HUNTER-RAINEY, Sharron 918-877-8151 375 L srainey@langston.edu
HUNTINGTON, Liz 415-451-2841 60 I lhuntington@sfts.edu
HUNTINGTON, Robert 419-448-2202 362 G president@heidelberg.edu
HUNTLEY, Deborah, R 989-964-4296 236 F huntley@svsu.edu
HUNTLEY, Julie 918-495-7040 378 H jhuntley@oru.edu
HUNTLEY, Kristy 203-479-4559 89 D khuntley@newhaven.edu
HUNTLEY, Richard 972-721-4142 464 E rhuntley@udallas.edu
HUNTLEY, Steve, E 904-264-2172 106 I steve.huntley@iws.edu
HUNTON, Ladonna, L 270-745-6867 190 F ladonna.hunton@wku.edu
HUNTOON, Ivan 785-594-8396 174 J ivan.huntoon@bakeru.edu
HUNTOON, Jacqueline, E 906-487-2440 234 A jeh@mtu.edu
HUNTSINGER, Trish 828-395-1297 344 A thuntsing@isothermal.edu
HUNTSMAN, Deborah, C 330-672-3237 363 I dhuntsm1@kent.edu
HUNZER, Kathleen 715-425-3843 511 E kathleen.hunzer@uwrf.edu
HUNZIGER, Lucas 913-367-6204 178 C lhunziger@highlandcc.edu
HUO, Xiaoming (Sharon) 931-372-3463 438 F xhuo@tntech.edu
HUOPPI, Jennifer 860-465-4357 84 K huoppij@easternct.edu
HUOPPI, Margie 860-932-4098 86 E mhuoppi@qvcc.edu
HUPFER, Mary, A 812-464-1627 165 C mhupfer@usi.edu
HUPKE, Doug 415-405-3824 34 C dhupke@sfsu.edu
HUPP, Mark 419-755-5665 366 E mhupp@ncstatecollege.edu
HUPP, Stephen 304-424-8273 505 C stephen.hupp@wvup.edu
HUPPE, Alicia, L 972-377-1749 446 I ahuppe@collin.edu
HUPPERT, Susan 515-271-1384 168 G susan.huppert@dmu.edu
HUPPON, Dana 561-433-2330 108 F
HURD, Anne, J 336-272-7102 338 B anne.hurd@greensboro.edu
HURD, Brian, K 216-397-1974 363 H bhurd@jcu.edu
HURD, Catherine 704-463-3112 348 B catherine.hurd@pfeiffer.edu
HURD, James, R 850-474-2214 111 D jhurd@uwf.edu
HURD, Roy 707-546-4000 42 E rhurd@empcol.edu
HURD, Sherie 707-546-4000 42 E shurd@empcol.edu
HURD-CRANK, Cathy 606-886-3863 185 F cathy.hurdcrank@kctcs.edu
HURDLE, Terri 513-244-4467 366 A terri.hurdle@msj.edu
HURDLE-WINSLOW, Lynn 252-335-0821 342 D lynnhw@albermarle.edu
HURDT, Emily 704-669-4321 342 B hurdte@clevelandcc.edu
HURLBURT, Linda 856-415-2106 289 G lhurlbu2@rcgc.edu
HURLBURT, Rob 716-375-2622 322 B rhurl@sbu.edu
HURLBUT, Jeffrey 949-451-5546 64 I jhurlbut@ivc.edu
HURLBUT, L, E 540-464-7292 490 E hurlbutle@vmi.edu
HURLE, Ron 928-226-4285 12 B ron.hurle@coconino.edu
HURLEY, Charles, T 574-631-7495 165 A hurley.32@nd.edu
HURLEY, Deanne 440-646-8108 373 B dhurley@ursuline.edu
HURLEY, Deanne 440-646-8320 373 B dhurley@ursuline.edu
HURLEY, Elizabeth 212-799-5000 312 B
HURLEY, James 423-869-6254 433 C james.hurley@lmunet.edu
HURLEY, James 423-869-6298 433 C james.hurley@lmunet.edu
HURLEY, James, B 601-923-1630 255 E jhurley@rts.edu
HURLEY, John 360-867-6500 494 G hurleyj@evergreen.edu
HURLEY, John, J 716-888-2100 300 G hurleyj@canisius.edu
HURLEY, Kristin 301-447-5372 206 B k.hurley@msmary.edu
HURLEY, Leah, A 214-648-7986 469 E leah.hurley@utsouthwestern.edu
HURLEY, Patricia 818-240-1000 44 D phurley@glendale.edu
HURLEY, Rachel 937-529-2201 371 B rehurley@united.edu
HURLEY, Ronald 201-200-3127 287 F rhurley@njcu.edu
HURLEY, Sam 903-928-3288 464 C shurley@tvcc.edu
HURLEY, Scott 217-732-3168 143 F shurley@lincolnchristian.edu
HURLEY, Tracy 210-784-2300 460 C thurley@tamusa.edu
HURLEY, Wanda 601-635-2111 252 I whurley@eccc.edu
HURN, Jeffrey 785-442-6077 178 C jhurn@highlandcc.edu
HURN, Patricia, D 734-764-7185 237 I
HURNS, Kimberly 734-973-3488 238 G khurns@wccnet.edu
HURRELL, Rockie 719-502-2007 81 H rockie.hurrell@ppcc.edu
HURSON, Abigail, S 443-352-4920 207 C hurson@stevenson.edu
HURSSEY, Elizabeth 662-254-3531 255 A ejhurssey@mvsu.edu
HURSSEY, Terrence 662-254-3584 255 A terrence.hurssey@mvsu.edu
HURST, Andrew 719-590-6797 79 B ahurst@coloradotech.edu
HURST, Angela 334-420-4483 3 H alhurst@trenholmstate.edu
HURST, Jamie 303-556-8452 80 Q jhurst7@msudenver.edu
HURST, Jason 205-391-5880 3 E jhurst@sheltonstate.edu
HURST, Jeffrey, J 801-626-7256 473 E jhurst@weber.edu
HURST, Kevin 740-588-1342 374 G khurst@zanestate.edu
HURST, Larry 661-362-3875 39 C larry.hurst@canyons.edu
HURST, Laura 610-660-1175 409 H lannhurs@sju.edu
HURST, Mark 423-585-6876 438 D mark.hurst@ws.edu
HURST, Richard, S 773-508-7465 144 D rhurst@luc.edu
HURST, Roy 432-552-2120 469 D
HURST, Susan 870-245-5567 20 G hursts@obu.edu
HURT, Aaron 620-235-4093 180 J ahurt@pittstate.edu
HURT, Amelia 405-208-5181 377 D aehurt@okcu.edu
HURT, Chandra 773-777-4220 148 A churt@nc.edu
HURT, Matt 217-351-2582 148 H mhurt@parkland.edu
HURTADO, Christina 785-628-4470 177 D cmhurtado@fhsu.edu
HURTADO, David 215-324-0746 394 E dhurtado@eastern.edu
HURTADO, Geoffrey 414-229-5390 511 A ghurtado@uwm.edu
HURTIG, Juliet, K 419-772-2032 367 G j-hurtig@onu.edu
HURWITCH, Stacie 518-354-5282 319 A shurwitch@nccc.edu
HUSAIN, Naveed 212-678-3955 331 C husain@tc.columbia.edu
HUSAK, William 310-338-5940 50 J whusak@lmu.edu
HUSBAND, Eileen, K 248-341-2184 235 D ekhusban@oaklandcc.edu

HUSBAND-ARDOIN, Madeline .... 337-482-6826 197 F msh9748@louisiana.edu
HUSCHLE, Brian .... 218-793-2592 246 F brian.huschle@northlandcollege.edu
HUSEIN, Lori .... 909-607-9192.. 37 K lori_husein@cuc.claremont.edu
HUSELTON, Ken .... 412-323-4000 389 I khuselton@mcg-btc.org
HUSHON, Kate .... 814-868-9900 395 A kateh@erieit.edu
HUSK, Mark, A .... 317-921-4723 161 F mhusk@ivytech.edu
HUSKEY, Jeff .... 805-893-2181.. 70 B jeff.huskey@recreation.ucsb.edu
HUSKEY, Jeffrey .... 605-688-6415 429 B jeffrey.huskey@sdstate.edu
HUSKEY, Melynda .... 360-650-3839 500 E melynda.huskey@wwu.edu
HUSLIG, Lorie .... 940-898-3201 464 A lhuslig@twu.edu
HUSMANN, Calvin, D ... 920-832-6517 507 L calvin.d.husmann@lawrence.edu
HUSMANN, Mike .... 712-274-5310 172 A husmann@morningside.edu
HUSON, Lisa .... 309-438-8999 140 L lhuson@ilstu.edu
HUSPENI, Todd .... 715-346-4446 511 F todd.huspeni@uwsp.edu
HUSS, David .... 731-352-4001 430 E hussd@bethelu.edu
HUSS, Fenwick .... 646-312-3030 301 B fenwick.huss@baruch.cuny.edu
HUSS, Julie .... 360-623-8474 493 A julie.huss@centralia.edu
HUSSAIN, Asif .... 718-368-6674 303 A ahussain@kbcc.cuny.edu
HUSSAIN, Nayyer .... 845-574-4242 321 F rondell@sunyrockland.edu
HUSSEY, Heather .... 928-541-7777.. 54 B hhussey@ncu.edu
HUSSEY, Leigh Ann ...... 678-839-6421 127 F lhussey@westga.edu
HUSSEY, Mark, A .... 979-862-4384 459 C mhussey@tamu.edu
HUSSEY, Michael .... 207-786-6103 198 E mhussey@bates.edu
HUSSON, James, J .... 617-552-3441 212 E james.husson@bc.edu
HUST, Ashley .... 928-350-4506.. 15 V ahust@prescott.edu
HUSTED, Jean, L .... 203-582-8645.. 88 A jean.husted@quinnipiac.edu
HUSTEDDE, Stephen ..... 602-305-5605.. 14 D stephen.hustedde@southmountaincc.edu
HUSTON, R. Patrick ...... 434-971-3301 517 N
HUSTON, Robin, E .... 405-325-1974 380 L rhuston@ou.edu
HUSTON, Susan, A .... 716-645-5300 325 B huston@buffalo.edu
HUSTON, Tracey, D ...... 814-865-7600 403 F tdh7@psu.edu
HUSUM, Jennifer .... 303-797-5674.. 76 I jennifer.husum@arapahoe.edu
HUTCHCRAFT, Joy, D .... 309-438-8041 140 L jdhutch@ilstu.edu
HUTCHENS, David .... 606-218-5282 190 E davidhutchens@upike.edu
HUTCHENS, James .... 954-262-4648 104 F jamesh@nsu.nova.edu
HUTCHENS, Sue .... 937-481-2214 373 I sue_hutchens@wilmington.edu
HUTCHERSON, Annette . 863-297-1039 105 F ahutcherson@polk.edu
HUTCHERSON, Cecil, L . 864-592-4693 424 C hutchersonc@sccsc.edu
HUTCHERSON, James ... 910-642-7141 346 G james.hutcherson@sccnc.edu
HUTCHERSON, Patricia, J .... 318-274-3242 196 G jenkinsp@gram.edu
HUTCHESON, Philip ...... 615-966-5850 433 D philip.hutcheson@lipscomb.edu
HUTCHINGS, Hayden .... 843-383-8081 420 B hhutchings@coker.edu
HUTCHINGS, James ...... 309-341-5317 134 H jhutchings@sandburg.edu
HUTCHINGS, Jessica ..... 337-475-5512 197 B jhutchings@mcneese.edu
HUTCHINGS, Rachel ...... 918-595-7846 380 D rachel.hutchings@tulsacc.edu
HUTCHINS, Carin .... 713-718-8430 450 D carin.hutchins@hccs.edu
HUTCHINS, Donald .... 870-307-7233.. 20 C donald.hutchins@lyon.edu
HUTCHINS, Frankie .... 334-872-2533.... 6 H frankie.hutchins@yahoo.com
HUTCHINS, Jim .... 937-327-7307 374 A hutchinsj@wittenberg.edu
HUTCHINS, Paul, C .... 910-592-8081 346 D phutchins@sampsoncc.edu
HUTCHINS, Robin .... 918-444-2000 376 G hutchinr@nsuok.edu
HUTCHINS, Ronald .... 906-635-2446 232 J rhutchins@lssu.edu
HUTCHINS, Ronald, R ... 434-924-1255 486 H rrh8z@virginia.edu
HUTCHINS, Thomas ...... 931-221-7456 430 B hutchinst@apsu.edu
HUTCHINS, Wesley, D .. 336-757-3053 343 C whutchins@forsythtech.edu
HUTCHINSON, Adriane . 815-479-7829 145 B ahutchinson@mchenry.edu
HUTCHINSON, Alison ... 717-871-5005 407 A alison.hutchinson@millersville.edu
HUTCHINSON, Andre ..... 503-943-7306 387 H hutchina@up.edu
HUTCHINSON, Brian, A 606-783-2088 188 C b.hutchinson@moreheadstate.edu
HUTCHINSON, Dana ..... 802-860-2721 474 G dhutchinson@champlain.edu
HUTCHINSON, Doug ..... 714-556-3610.. 72 F doug.hutchinson@vanguard.edu
HUTCHINSON, Erica ..... 207-509-7145 200 I ehutchinson@unity.edu
HUTCHINSON, Gayle, E 530-898-5201.. 31 D ghutchinson@csuchico.edu
HUTCHINSON, John, S . 713-348-4996 455 F hutchinson@rice.edu
HUTCHINSON, Kathryn, T .... 718-990-6820 322 F hutchink@stjohns.edu
HUTCHINSON, Laura ..... 800-747-2687 146 A
HUTCHINSON, Natalie ... 515-271-1430 168 G natalie.hutchinson@dmu.edu
HUTCHINSON, Natalie ... 503-760-3131 381 J natalie@birthingway.edu
HUTCHINSON, Paulette . 610-527-0200 409 E phutchinson@rosemont.edu
HUTCHINSON, Ryan ...... 919-761-2100 349 C rhutchinson@sebts.edu
HUTCHINSON, Tom .... 601-266-6407 256 E thomas.hutchinson@usm.edu
HUTCHINSON BELL, Robin .... 614-234-1372 365 L rhutchinsonbell@mccn.edu
HUTCHISON, Adam, C .. 254-867-4834 461 G achutchison@tstc.edu
HUTCHISON, Chris .... 714-628-7321.. 36 G hutchiso@chapman.edu
HUTCHISON, David .... 660-248-6260 258 B drhutchi@centralmethodist.edu
HUTCHISON, Donna .... 217-732-3155 143 G dhutchison@lincolncollege.edu
HUTCHISON, Frances ..... 409-747-2148 469 C fbhutchi@utmb.edu
HUTCHISON, James, R . 928-344-7704.. 11 B james.hutchison@azwestern.edu
HUTCHISON, Karen .... 717-396-7833 404 R khutchison@pcad.edu
HUTCHISON, Kathleen ... 601-925-3870 254 B khutchis@mc.edu
HUTCHISON, Michael, V .... 479-968-0400.. 18 G mhutchison@atu.edu
HUTCHISON, Sadie .... 928-523-7010.. 14 K sadie.hutchison@nau.edu
HUTCHISON, Theresa, R .... 817-598-6271 470 J thutchison@wc.edu
HUTCHISON-CARAVEO, Shannon .... 619-849-2549.. 57 H shannonhutchison@pointloma.edu
HUTCHISONS, Wendy ..... 503-654-8000 386 A whutchisons@pioneerpacific.edu
HUTH, F. Robert .... 386-822-7015 111 E fhuth@stetson.edu
HUTLEY, Mike .... 352-395-4177 107 E michael.hutley@sfcollege.edu
HUTSELL, Emily .... 574-936-8898 155 L emily.hutsell@ancilla.edu
HUTSON, Jerome .... 610-436-3273 407 D jhutson@wcupa.edu
HUTSON, Mary Pope, M .... 434-381-6272 485 P mpmhutson@sbc.edu
HUTTENLOCHER, Daniel, S .... 212-255-8587 306 B huttenlocher@cornell.edu
HUTTER, Jeffrey, W .... 617-638-4780 212 G jhutter@bu.edu
HUTTI, Deb .... 217-234-5273 143 B dhutti@lakeland.cc.il.us
HUTTNER, Trinity .... 425-558-0299 494 C thuttner@digipen.edu
HUTTO, Dena .... 503-777-7572 386 F dhutto@reed.edu
HUTTO, J. Laurence ...... 843-953-7696 419 D huttoj1@citadel.edu
HUTTO, Jimmy .... 334-493-3573.... 2 H jhutto@lbwcc.edu
HUTTO, Kenneth .... 678-359-5010 121 B kennyh@gordonstate.edu
HUTTO, Kim .... 304-876-5157 504 D khutto@shepherd.edu
HUTTO-HARRIS, LaShanda .... 864-578-8770 423 F lhutto@sherman.edu
HUTTON, Debra .... 313-593-5430 238 A dghutton@umich.edu
HUTTON, James, D .... 317-447-6200 158 H james.hutton@harrison.edu
HUTTON, Tom .... 719-255-3439.. 83 C thutton@uccs.edu
HUTTON-LOPEZ, Karen . 909-469-5650.. 74 G klopez@westernu.edu
HUTTON SISTARE, Sallie .... 843-792-3433 422 C hutton@musc.edu
HUTTON SISTARE, Sallie .... 704-687-7787 351 C ssistare@uncc.edu
HUTZLEY, Brian, G .... 859-238-5458 184 C brian.hutzley@centre.edu
HUVAL, Barbara .... 409-984-6330 462 E barbara.huval@lamarpa.edu
HUVAL, Scott .... 251-442-2390.... 8 D shuval@umobile.edu
HUX, Victor .... 541-485-1780 384 G victorhux@newhope.edu
HUXFORD, Wye .... 706-385-1012 124 F wye.huxford@point.edu
HUYBRECHT, Melissa ... 612-874-3764 243 F mhubrecht@mcad.edu
HUYCK, Kristen .... 760-795-2121.. 52 F khuyck@miracosta.edu
HUYKE, Gretchen .... 787-832-6772 528 C asesorialegal@uprm.edu
HVEEM, David .... 661-654-6459.. 31 B hveem-david@aramark.com
HWANG, Amy .... 617-745-3855 214 D amy.hwang@enc.edu
HWANG, Delphine .... 415-749-4535.. 60 G registrar@sfai.edu
HWANG, Leo .... 413-775-1221 219 F hwang@gcc.mass.edu
HWU, Alex .... 707-826-3731.. 34 A sh1911@humboldt.edu
HYATT, Danny .... 903-463-8622 449 J hyattdan@grayson.edu
HYATT, Garey .... 410-951-3366 208 F ghyatt@coppin.edu
HYATT, Katherine, E ...... 770-720-5591 124 H keh@reinhardt.edu
HYATT, Regina .... 662-325-3045 254 E rhyatt@saffairs.msstate.edu
HYBL, Andrew .... 510-204-0716.. 37 F ahybl@cdsp.edu
HYDE, Clyanne .... 828-339-4000 346 H c_hyde@southwesterncc.edu
HYDE, Gerald .... 704-878-3200 344 H ghyde@mitchellcc.edu
HYDE, Holly .... 828-835-4219 347 B hhyde@tricountycc.edu
HYDE, John .... 516-686-7527 317 G jmhyde@nyit.edu
HYDE, Katrina, A .... 304-336-8510 504 E katrina.hyde@westliberty.edu
HYDE, Maria .... 916-691-7361.. 50 G hydem@crc.losrios.edu
HYDE, Matthew .... 610-330-5100 399 B hydem@lafayette.edu
HYDE, Richard, D .... 979-532-6346 471 A richardh@wcjc.edu
HYDE, Truell .... 254-710-3435 444 B truell_hyde@baylor.edu
HYDEN, John, P .... 330-941-3235 374 E jphyden@ysu.edu
HYDER, Bret .... 651-638-6242 240 J bret-hyder@bethel.edu
HYDER, Mark .... 423-236-2155 436 C markhyder@southern.edu
HYDRO, Susan .... 609-771-2997 284 I berksus@tcnj.edu
HYELER, Maral .... 310-434-3551.. 62 G hyeler_maral@smc.edu
HYER, Cindy, T .... 727-376-6911 112 G cindy.hyer@trinitycollege.edu
HYER, Joel .... 308-432-6359 276 B jhyer@csc.edu
HYLAND, Cheryl .... 615-220-7801 437 C chyland@mscc.edu
HYLAND, David .... 814-725-7079 401 J dhyland@mercyhurst.edu
HYLTON, Gary .... 304-384-5233 503 P ghylton@concord.edu
HYLTON, Katelin .... 606-368-6055 182 H katelinhylton@alc.edu
HYMAN, Cindy .... 303-871-2234.. 83 E cynthia.hyman@du.edu
HYMAN, Susan .... 410-704-2097 209 C shyman@towson.edu
HYMANS, Diane, J .... 614-235-4136 370 M dhymans@tlsohio.edu
HYMON-PARKER, Shirley .... 336-334-7979 350 C sjhymonp@ncat.edu
HYNDMAN, Maggie .... 603-513-1319 282 G maggie.hyndman@granite.edu
HYNDMAN, Steve .... 502-410-6200 184 H shyndman@galencollege.edu
HYNDMAN, III, William 850-599-3295 109 A william.hyndman@famu.edu
HYNDS, Andy .... 217-875-7200 149 J ahynds@richland.edu
HYNDS, Steve .... 417-873-7406 259 G shynds@drury.edu
HYNEK, Mary, T .... 913-360-7431 175 D mhynek@benedictine.edu
HYNES, Jeff .... 623-845-3899.. 13 H jeff.hynes@gccaz.edu
HYNES, Jeff .... 708-209-3444 136 I jeff.hynes@cuchicago.edu
HYNES, Kevin, P .... 630-515-6073 145 I khynes@midwestern.edu
HYNES, Peter .... 973-684-6602 288 C phynes@pccc.edu
HYNES, Robert .... 978-665-3152 217 E rhynes@fitchburgstate.edu
HYNES, Tim .... 678-466-4300 117 I thomashynes@clayton.edu
HYNICK, Karen .... 978-762-4000 220 E khynick@northshore.edu
HYNSON, Cassandra ..... 302-736-2428.. 90 J cassandra.hynson@wesley.edu
HYPOLITE, Renee .... 949-794-9090.. 66 B rhypolite@stanbridge.edu
HYRUP MADSEN, Anne 619-702-9400.. 30 C
HYSELL, Deborah .... 419-755-4894 366 E dhysell@ncstatecollege.edu
HYUN, Eunsook .... 239-590-7791 109 C ehyun@fgcu.edu
HYUN, Timothy .... 253-752-2020 494 H librarian@faithseminary.edu

I

IACAMPO, Beth .... 860-297-2273.. 88 E beth.iacampo@trincoll.edu
IACOBUCCI, Richard, M 617-541-5394 221 A riacobucci@rcc.mass.edu
IACONO, Anthony, J ..... 973-328-5031 285 B tiacono@ccm.edu
IACOVELLI, John .... 609-652-4833 291 H john.iacovelli@stockton.edu
IACOVOU, Charles .... 336-758-5110 353 A iacovou@wfu.edu
IACUESSA, Michelle, A . 845-569-3217 316 B michelle.iacuessa@msmc.edu
IACULLO, Gerald .... 973-642-3888 283 J gji@berkeleycollege.edu
IACULLO, Gerald .... 973-642-3888 299 F gji@berkeleycollege.edu
IADEVAIA, Norma .... 310-506-4149.. 56 D norma.iadevaia@pepperdine.edu
IALENTI, Vincent .... 978-632-6600 220 D v_ialenti@mwcc.mass.edu
IAMUNNO, Janine .... 910-962-2445 352 A iamunnoj@uncw.edu
IANELLO, Lisa, A .... 305-684-6020 329 F iannella@morrisville.edu
IANETTA, Catalina .... 617-585-0100 212 C catalina.ianetta@the-bac.edu
IANNACE, John-Paul ...... 914-606-8501 333 H john-paul.iannace@sunywcc.edu
IANNAZZI, Michael, L .. 203-371-7899.. 88 C iannazzim@sacredheart.edu
IANNELLI, Clare .... 281-998-1357 455 K clare.iannelli@sjcd.edu
IANNELLI, Clare .... 281-998-6150 456 B clare.iannelli@sjcd.edu
IANNELLI, Clare .... 281-998-6150 456 A clare.iannelli@sjcd.edu
IANNELLI, Clare .... 281-998-6150 455 L clare.iannelli@sjcd.edu
IANNELLI, Richard .... 615-343-2717 440 D richard.iannelli@vanderbilt.edu
IANNELLI, Robert .... 610-647-4400 397 I riannelli@immaculata.edu

IPACH, Nichole ... 805-437-8893.. 31 C
nichole.ipach@csuci.edu
IPPOLITO, Andrew ... 201-692-2531 286 B
andrew_ippolito@fdu.edu
IRANI, Daraius ... 410-704-3780 209 C
dirani@towson.edu
IRBY, Adam, W ... 336-322-2253 345 D
adam.irby@piedmontcc.edu
IRBY, Bernice ... 803-934-3408 422 G
birby@morris.edu
IRBY, Michele ... 573-651-5120 266 M
mirby@semo.edu
IRELAND, Alan ... 336-750-2935 352 D
irelandag@wssu.edu
IRELAND, Ashley ... 270-809-5604 188 D
aireland@murraystate.edu
IRELAND, Jim ... 620-792-9339 175 C
irelandj@bartonccc.edu
IRELAND, Timothy ... 716-286-8342 318 F
toi@niagara.edu
IREY, Sayumi ... 425-564-2300 492 G
sayumi.irey@bellevuecollege.edu
IRIS, Michael ... 973-278-5400 283 J
mki@berkeleycollege.edu
IRIS, Michael ... 212-986-4343 299 F
mki@berkeleycollege.edu
IRISH, Allyson ... 617-521-2324 224 E
allyson.irish@simmons.edu
IRIZARRY, Eliel, B ... 787-766-1717 526 B
eirizarry21@suagm.edu
IRIZARRY, Rolando ... 410-778-7268 210 A
ririzarry2@washcoll.edu
IRLA-CHESNEY, Kathy ... 603-862-3409 282 F
kathy.irla-chesney@unh.edu
IRLAND, Kim ... 518-891-2915 319 A
kirland@nccc.edu
IRMSCHER, Christoph ... 812-855-9491 159 H
cirmsche@indiana.edu
IROFF, Jayson ... 954-201-7423.. 96 A
jiroff@broward.edu
IRONS, Warren ... 615-329-8604 431 I
wirons@fisk.edu
IRSIK, Sherry ... 252-527-6223 344 D
skirsik87@lenoircc.edu
IRUDAYAM, Irene ... 508-849-3410 210 H
iirudayam@annamaria.edu
IRVIN, Dale, T ... 212-870-1223 318 C
dirvin@nyts.edu
IRVIN, Dave ... 865-974-2178 439 I
irvin@utk.edu
IRVIN, Howard ... 323-241-5328.. 49 E
irvinhj@lasc.edu
IRVIN, Kim ... 903-434-8132 453 M
kirvin@ntcc.edu
IRVIN, L. Dexter ... 702-651-3008 278 N
dexter.irvin@csn.edu
IRVIN, Roger ... 828-327-7000 341 G
rirvin@cvcc.edu
IRVIN, ValaRay ... 225-771-2480 195 J
valaray_irvin@subr.edu
IRVIN, ValaRay ... 225-771-2480 195 K
valaray_irvin@subr.edu
IRVIN, Zoe, A ... 443-518-4742 204 E
zirvin@howardcc.edu
IRVINE, Angela ... 802-654-2396 476 A
airvine@smcvt.edu
IRVINE, Colin ... 406-447-4404 270 H
cirvine@carroll.edu
IRVINE, David ... 518-262-5251 297 L
irvined@mail.amc.edu
IRVINE, Lesley ... 909-621-8016.. 57 I
lesley.irvine@pomona.edu
IRVINE, Shelly ... 540-887-7367 482 G
sirvine@marybaldwin.edu
IRVING, Jacqueline ... 610-341-5872 394 E
jirving@eastern.edu
IRVING, JR., Merrill ... 763-488-2414 244 G
merrill.irving@hennepintech.edu
IRVING, Tim ... 503-552-1814 384 F
tirving@nunm.edu
IRWIN, Bonnie ... 831-582-4401.. 33 A
birwin@csumb.edu
IRWIN, Dennis ... 740-593-1479 368 G
irwind@ohio.edu
IRWIN, Holly ... 619-849-2706.. 57 H
hollyirwin@pointloma.edu
IRWIN, Jim ... 909-607-3183.. 37 L
jim.irwin@cgu.edu
IRWIN, Joseph ... 404-894-0771 120 A
joe.irwin@alumni.gatech.edu
IRWIN, Kris ... 434-947-8144 484 B
kirwin@randolphcollege.edu
IRWIN, Kristy ... 610-519-6288 413 K
kristy.irwin@villanova.edu
IRWIN, Lorry ... 845-434-5750 330 F
lirwin@sullivan.suny.edu
IRWIN, Richard ... 901-678-5014 439 E
rirwin@memphis.edu
IRWIN, Robert ... 864-578-8770 423 F
rirwin@sherman.edu
IRWIN, Suzy ... 903-823-3095 458 D
suzanne.irwin@texarkanacollege.edu
ISAAC, Donna ... 559-934-2102.. 73 M
donnaisaac@whccd.edu
ISAAC, Mark ... 559-453-5516.. 43 J
mark.isaac@fresno.edu
ISAAC, Nancy ... 620-431-2820 180 C
nisaac@neosho.edu
ISAAC, Susan ... 478-387-4746 120 B
sisaac@gmc.edu
ISAAC, Wolde-Ab ... 951-222-8000.. 58 E
wolde-ab.isaac@rcc.edu
ISAAC, Wolde-Ab ... 951-222-8155.. 58 H
wolde-ab.isaac@rcc.edu
ISAAC-SAVAGE,
Paulette, E ... 314-516-5303 268 E
episaac@umsl.edu
ISAACK, Kyle ... 513-231-2223 356 M
kisaack@athenaeum.edu
ISAACS, Becky ... 580-559-5243 375 I
bisaacs@ecok.edu
ISAACS, Eric, D ... 773-702-8825 153 F
isaacs@uchicago.edu
ISAACS, Tanya ... 718-270-6910 303 C
tisaacs@mec.cuny.edu
ISAACS, Yolanda ... 815-280-6691 142 A
yisaacs@jjc.edu
ISAACSON, Christy ... 206-934-3706 497 H
christy.isaacson@seattlecolleges.edu
ISAACSON, Emily ... 419-448-2184 362 G
eisaacso@heidelberg.edu
ISAACSON, Lyn, R ... 641-628-5266 167 D
isaacsonl@central.edu
ISAACSON, Marcia ... 847-467-6171 148 C
marcia.isaacson@northwestern.edu
ISAACSON, Michael, L ... 605-642-6788 428 F
michael.isaacson@bhsu.edu
ISABELLE, Callista, S ... 484-664-3120 402 F
callistaisabelle@muhlenberg.edu
ISABELLE, Geoffrey, S ... 315-684-6070 329 F
isabelgs@morrisville.edu
ISACKMAN, Brigid, K ... 215-596-8701 413 E
b.isackman@usciences.edu
ISACKSON, Ann ... 616-234-4031 230 F
aisackson@grcc.edu
ISACSON, Barbara ... 973-748-9000 284 A
barbara_isacson@bloomfield.edu
ISAK, Misty ... 609-984-1588 292 B
misak@tesu.edu
ISAKOFF, Louis, A ... 757-352-2794 484 E
isakoff@regent.edu
ISBELL, Corey ... 785-738-9055 180 E
cisbell@ncktc.edu
ISBELL, Dwayne ... 303-722-5724.. 80 O
disbell@lincolntech.edu
ISBELL, Keith ... 931-540-2533 436 H
kisbell2@columbiastate.edu
ISBELL, Monica ... 336-506-4130 340 L
monica.isbell@alamancecc.edu
ISBELL, Teresa, S ... 214-860-2017 448 A
tisbell@dcccd.edu
ISCH, Larry, A ... 479-979-1420.. 23 J
laisch@ozarks.edu
ISEKENEGBE, Thomas ... 718-289-5155 301 D
thomas.isekenegbe@bcc.cuny.edu
ISELI, Madeline ... 937-512-2510 370 A
madeline.iseli@sinclair.edu
ISEMINGER, Andrea ... 515-965-7137 168 A
aliseminger1@dmacc.edu
ISEMINGER, Ernie ... 909-607-8252.. 37 L
ernie.iseminger@cgu.edu
ISENBECK, Jennifer ... 813-253-6227 113 E
jisenbeck@ut.edu
ISENBERG, Laurie ... 510-780-4500.. 48 D
lisenberg@lifewest.edu
ISENHOUR, John, L ... 470-578-6109 122 C
jisenhou@kennesaw.edu
ISH, Cheryl, J ... 570-208-5855 398 D
cjish@kings.edu
ISH-HURVITZ, Rami ... 626-264-8880.. 71 A
ISHA, Julie ... 202-319-5022.. 91 D
isha@cua.edu
ISHEE, Jimmy ... 501-450-3122.. 23 I
jishee@uca.edu
ISHIDA, Kevin ... 808-689-2500 130 A
kevini@hawaii.edu
ISHIDA, Yoshiharu ... 808-946-3773 128 J
ISHIHARA, Kulamanu ... 808-984-3272 130 H
vorhies@hawaii.edu
ISHII, Susan ... 562-903-4049.. 27 E
susan.ishii@biola.edu
ISHIKAWA, Jayne ... 310-660-3593.. 42 C
jishikawa@elcamino.edu
ISHIKAWA, Mark ... 707-965-6312.. 55 F
mishikawa@puc.edu
ISHIYAMA, Howard, J ... 412-536-1282 398 E
howard.ishiyama@laroche.edu
ISHMAEL, Amy ... 918-540-6212 376 F
aishmael@neo.edu
ISHMAN, Scott ... 618-453-7984 152 B
sishman@siu.edu
ISHOOF, Saif ... 305-348-2000 109 D
sishoof@fiu.edu
ISHOP, Kendra ... 734-763-5837 237 I
ISLE, Wendy ... 620-331-4100 178 E
wisle@indycc.edu
ISLEY, MD ... 515-965-7120 168 A
mdisley@dmacc.edu
ISMAIL, Amid ... 215-707-2799 411 B
amid.ismail@temple.edu
ISMAIL, Lizah ... 864-488-4610 422 B
lismail@limestone.edu
ISMAIL, Shaik ... 503-883-2228 383 H
sismail@linfield.edu
ISMAILI, Karim ... 508-531-1295 217 D
kismaili@bridgew.edu
ISOM, Andy ... 501-882-4428.. 17 M
adisom@asub.edu
ISOM, Darryl ... 470-639-0334 123 E
darryl.isom@morehouse.edu
ISOMOTO, Robert, G ... 310-434-4201.. 62 G
isomoto_robert@smc.edu
ISOZAKI, Peggy ... 415-883-2211.. 39 E
pisozaki@marin.edu
ISSA, Yasser ... 661-362-3438.. 39 C
yasser.issa@canyons.edu
ISSACSON, Ron ... 435-652-7515 473 B
isaacson@dixie.edu
ISSELMANN, Sandy ... 920-686-6180 510 A
sandy.isselmann@sl.edu
ISSOD, Cheryl ... 410-225-2310 205 C
cissod@mica.edu
ISTRE, Kourtney ... 337-475-5148 197 B
kistre1@mcneese.edu
ITALIANO, Christina ... 414-326-2306 507 B
christina.italiano@ccon.edu
ITALIANO, Elise ... 202-319-5600.. 91 D
italiano@cua.edu
ITANO, Joanne, K ... 808-956-9404 129 H
itano@hawaii.edu
ITTLEMAN, Leona, R ... 413-755-4055 221 B
ittleman@stcc.edu
ITTOOP, Alphonsa ... 212-616-7282 309 G
alphonsa.ittoop@helenefuld.edu
IUDICELLO, Kathleen ... 623-935-8055.. 13 F
kathleen.iudicello@estrellamountain.edu
IULIANO, Robert ... 617-496-6109 215 G
robert_iuliano@harvard.edu
IUSO, Kenneth, J ... 848-445-2620 290 A
iuso@rci.rutgers.edu
IUSO, Kenneth, J ... 848-445-2620 290 C
iuso@rci.rutgers.edu
IVAN, Courtney ... 269-467-9945 230 C
civan@glenoaks.edu
IVAN, Elaine, R ... 719-365-8291.. 82 N
elaine.ivan@uchealth.org
IVANKOVIC, John ... 845-341-4190 319 H
john.ivankovic@sunyorange.edu
IVANKOVIC, Judith ... 845-575-3000 314 C
judith.ivankovic@marist.edu
IVELISSE, Brenda ... 808-734-9456 130 C
ivelisse@hawaii.edu
IVERSEN, Jerre ... 903-566-7110 468 C
jiversen@uttyler.edu
IVERSON, Amy ... 386-506-3240.. 97 I
iversoa@daytonastate.edu
IVERSON, Brent, L ... 512-475-7000 467 C
iversonb@austin.utexas.edu
IVERSON, Cort ... 319-398-7116 171 F
cort.iverson@kirkwood.edu
IVERSON, Daryl, A ... 864-231-2005 418 E
diverson@andersonuniversity.edu
IVERSON, Jeremy ... 509-793-2031 492 I
jeremyi@bigbend.edu
IVERSON, Robert ... 626-914-8888.. 37 G
riverson@citruscollege.edu
IVERSON, Scott ... 219-989-4150 163 E
siverson@pnw.edu
IVERSON, Terrie ... 406-657-2155 272 B
tiverson@msubillings.edu
IVERSON, Veda ... 605-331-6726 429 D
veda.iverson@usiouxfalls.edu
IVERSON, William ... 817-202-6229 457 E
wiverson@swau.edu
IVERY, Curtis, L ... 313-496-2510 238 H
civery1@wcccd.edu
IVES, Emily ... 518-458-5441 305 B
ivese@strose.edu
IVES, John ... 716-896-0700 333 C
jives@villa.edu
IVES, Kathy ... 716-896-0700 333 C
kathyi@villa.edu
IVES, Richard ... 518-783-3285 324 C
rives@siena.edu
IVES, Richard ... 269-488-4865 231 G
rives@kvcc.edu
IVES, Stephanie ... 215-204-7188 411 B
stephanie.ives@temple.edu
IVES, Suong ... 315-268-7791 304 B
sives@clarkson.edu
IVESTER, Kathie ... 706-754-7750 123 G
kivester@northgatech.edu
IVESTER, Mark ... 706-754-7701 123 G
mivester@northgatech.edu
IVESTER, Steve ... 630-752-5088 155 F
steve.ivester@wheaton.edu
IVEY, Connie ... 910-272-3305 346 A
civey@robeson.edu
IVEY, Michelle ... 334-683-2359.... 3 A
mivey@marionmilitary.edu
IVEY, Ryan ... 931-221-7904 430 B
iveyr@apsu.edu
IVEY, Tracey ... 919-735-5151 347 E
ivey@waynecc.edu
IVIE, Jennifer ... 918-595-7925 380 D
jennifer.ivie@tulsacc.edu
IVIE, Wendy ... 541-885-1539 385 E
wendy.ivie@oit.edu
IVIS, Dan ... 515-965-7029 168 A
drivis@dmacc.edu
IVORY, Audrey ... 919-516-4201 348 G
laivory@st-aug.edu
IVRY, Patricia ... 203-837-9500.. 85 B
ivryp@wcsu.edu
IVY, Bill ... 918-595-7868 380 D
bill.ivy@tulsacc.edu
IWAMA, Kenichi ... 718-982-2400 302 A
kenichi.iwama@csi.cuny.edu
IWAMOTO, Dawn ... 866-621-0124.. 84 B
dawn.iwamoto@rockies.edu
IWAMURA, Jane ... 626-571-8811.. 72 C
janei@uwest.edu
IWANE, David ... 213-615-7268.. 37 B
diwane@thechicagoschool.edu
IWANENKO, JR.,
Walter ... 814-871-7401 395 H
iwanenko001@gannon.edu
IWANKOW, Thomas ... 518-861-2574 314 B
tiwankow@mariacollege.edu
IWANOWICZ, Sue ... 518-694-7217 297 J
susan.iwanowicz@acphs.edu
IWASA, Mark ... 916-278-6851.. 33 C
miwasa@csus.edu
IWATA, Chris ... 916-558-2552.. 50 I
iwatac@scc.losrios.edu
IYENGAR, Sundararaj ... 305-348-3549 109 D
undararaj.iyengar@fiu.edu
IYER, Chitra ... 727-873-4873 111 B
ciyer@usf.edu
IYER, Nalini ... 206-296-6161 498 D
niyer@seattleu.edu
IYER, Sandhya, L ... 603-646-0101 281 C
sandhya.l.iyer@dartmouth.edu
IYER, Savitri, V ... 585-245-5952 327 B
iyer@geneseo.edu
IZADI, Mahyar ... 217-581-3526 138 A
mizadi@eiu.edu
IZADIAN, Ali ... 657-278-2122.. 32 B
izadian@fullerton.edu
IZBRAND, Joe ... 210-458-8754 468 B
joe.izbrand@utsa.edu
IZIENICKI, Kylie ... 303-369-5151.. 81 L
kylie.izienicki@plattcolorado.edu
IZMIRIAN, Dayanne ... 619-260-4777.. 71 J
dizmirian@sandiego.edu
IZUMI, Yoshiko ... 714-867-5009.. 64 G
yizumi@southcoastcollege.com
IZVONAR, Ivana ... 650-543-3787.. 51 F
iizvonar@menlo.edu
IZZI, Lou ... 603-428-2292 281 F
lizzi@nec.edu
IZZI, Michael, A ... 949-824-6932.. 69 A
mizzi@uci.edu

J

JABAR, Abdul ... 212-346-1521 319 J
ajabar@pace.edu
JABBOUR, Alice ... 804-862-6100 484 F
ajabbour@rbc.edu
JABLONSKI, Anna ... 661-255-1050.. 29 F
ajablonski@calarts.edu
JABLONSKI, John ... 518-743-2236 328 G
jablonski@sunyacc.edu
JABLONSKI, Margaret ... 508-531-1276 217 D
margaret.jablonski@bridgew.edu
JABLONSKI, Suzanne ... 212-678-4084 331 C
jablonski@tc.columbia.edu
JABLONSKY, Carol ... 516-686-1014 317 G
cjablons@nyit.edu

JACKSON, Tanise .... 850-412-5246 109 A
tanise.jackson@famu.edu
JACKSON, Tekesha .... 229-732-5962 115 B
tekeshajackson@andrewcollege.edu
JACKSON, Teresa .... 314-652-0300 266 C
tjackson@slchcmail.com
JACKSON, Terilyn .... 949-214-3039.. 40 I
terilyn.jackson@cui.edu
JACKSON, Terrence .... 334-872-2533.... 6 H
tejack3@gmail.com
JACKSON, Theron .... 318-670-6000 196 A
tjackson@susla.edu
JACKSON, Tiffany .... 941-359-4340 111 C
tjackson5@sar.usf.edu
JACKSON, Tim .... 512-448-8575 455 I
seubookstore@texasbook.com
JACKSON, Tom .... 918-444-2220 376 G
jacks009@nsuok.edu
JACKSON, JR., Tom .... 605-642-6111 428 F
tom.jackson@bhsu.edu
JACKSON, Tondaleya .... 803-705-4479 418 G
jacksont@benedict.edu
JACKSON, Tonya .... 470-639-0525 123 E
tonya.jackson@morehouse.edu
JACKSON, Tracey .... 317-543-3235 162 S
JACKSON, Twana .... 304-929-6716 503 B
tjackson@newriver.edu
JACKSON, Tyrone .... 601-857-3232 253 B
tyrone.jackson@hindscc.edu
JACKSON, Victor .... 214-649-4060 449 I
vic_jackson@gial.edu
JACKSON, Vincent .... 213-763-7035.. 49 F
vjackson@lattc.edu
JACKSON, Wanda .... 205-932-3221.... 1 D
wanda.jackson@bscc.edu
JACKSON, Wayne .... 407-823-2716 110 C
wayne.jackson@ucf.edu
JACKSON, Weldon .... 301-860-3460 208 E
wjackson@bowiestate.edu
JACKSON, Wendy .... 704-216-6158 339 E
wjackso@livingstone.edu
JACKSON, William .... 301-891-4475 209 E
wjackson@wau.edu
JACKSON, William .... 217-234-5296 143 B
wjackson60312@lakeland.cc.il.us
JACKSON, Wilma .... 402-826-8620 274 E
wilma.jackson@doane.edu
JACKSON, Zena .... 817-515-3010 458 B
zena.jackson@tccd.edu
JACKSON-DAVIS,
Dorothy, G .... 601-877-6460 251 G
djdavis@alcorn.edu
JACKSON-ELMOORE,
Cynthia .... 517-355-2326 233 G
jacks174@msu.edu
JACKSON-HAMMOND,
Cynthia .... 937-376-6332 358 I
chammond@centralstate.edu
JACKSON-LEE, Sophia ... 318-670-9355 196 A
slee@susla.edu
JACKSON-RICHARDSON,
Georanda .... 205-366-8877.... 7 C
gvjackson@stillman.edu
JACKSON-WILLIAMS,
Loretta .... 601-984-5006 256 D
ljackson@umc.edu
JACOB, Shirley .... 985-549-2217 197 E
shirley.jacob@selu.edu
JACOBOWITZ, Chanie ... 732-367-1060 283 K
cjacobowitz@bmg.edu
JACOBOWITZ, Moses .... 845-782-1380 335 B
JACOBS, Aaron .... 605-718-3061 429 E
aaron.jacobs@wdt.edu
JACOBS, Andrew .... 334-386-7657.... 5 I
ajacobs@faulkner.edu
JACOBS, Andrew, C ...... 207-834-7671 201 E
andrew.jacobs@maine.edu
JACOBS, Bernadette ...... 505-428-1778 296 B
bernadette.jacobs@sfcc.edu
JACOBS, Bonita .... 706-864-1993 127 B
president@ung.edu
JACOBS, Brandi, D .... 304-696-3328 504 C
jacobs2@marshall.edu
JACOBS, Bret .... 504-865-3979 194 G
bljacobs@loyno.edu
JACOBS, Carmela .... 785-587-2800 179 E
carmelajacobs@manhattantech.edu
JACOBS, Cathleen .... 412-536-1033 398 E
cathleen.jacobs@laroche.edu
JACOBS, Chris .... 360-992-2268 493 E
cjacobs@clark.edu
JACOBS, Craig, M .... 610-892-1509 405 C
cjacobs@pit.edu
JACOBS, Danny, O .... 409-772-4793 469 C
djacobs@utmb.edu
JACOBS, Dawn Ellen ..... 951-343-4275.. 28 G
djacobs@calbaptist.edu

JACOBS, Dennis .... 408-554-4533.. 62 F
dcjacobs@scu.edu
JACOBS, Derya, A .... 412-397-6307 409 C
jacobs@rmu.edu
JACOBS, Diane .... 412-237-3184 392 G
djacobs@ccac.edu
JACOBS, Diane .... 412-237-3064 392 G
djacobs@ccac.edu
JACOBS, Francois .... 303-404-5022.. 79 K
francois.jacobs@frontrange.edu
JACOBS, Gina .... 619-594-4563.. 34 B
gina.jacobs@mail.sdsu.edu
JACOBS, Holly, A .... 330-941-2340 374 E
hajacobs@ysu.edu
JACOBS, Jeanne .... 305-237-5006 103 L
jfjacobs@mdc.edu
JACOBS, Jeff .... 701-231-7537 354 D
jeffrey.jacobs@ndsu.edu
JACOBS, Jennifer .... 573-897-5000 267 F
JACOBS, Jessica .... 978-232-2458 214 G
jjacob@endicott.edu
JACOBS, Jo-Ann .... 718-270-6024 303 C
jo-ann@mec.cuny.edu
JACOBS, JR., John, O .. 334-844-9891.... 4 D
jacobjo@auburn.edu
JACOBS, Joshua .... 312-942-5450 150 F
JACOBS, Joshua .... 660-248-6214 258 B
jejacobs@centralmethodist.edu
JACOBS, Judy .... 620-792-9349 175 C
jacobsj@bartonccc.edu
JACOBS, Ken .... 785-628-4259 177 D
kjacobs@fhsu.edu
JACOBS, Kevin .... 303-315-2727.. 83 D
kevin.jacobs@ucdenver.edu
JACOBS, Lacie .... 910-879-5505 341 A
ljacobs@bladencc.edu
JACOBS, Laura .... 479-575-5555.. 21 I
laura@uark.edu
JACOBS, Laura .... 715-394-8233 512 B
ljacobs@uwsuper.edu
JACOBS, Linda .... 517-265-5161 226 F
ljacobs@adrian.edu
JACOBS, Maria .... 603-456-2656 281 H
mjacobs@northeastcatholic.edu
JACOBS, Mark .... 480-965-2354.. 10 K
mark.jacobs@asu.edu
JACOBS, Mary, R .... 513-875-3344 359 C
mary.jacobs@chatfield.edu
JACOBS, Michael .... 585-292-3369 315 L
JACOBS, Michael .... 419-267-1330 366 G
mjacobs@northweststate.edu
JACOBS, Nicole .... 410-617-2271 205 A
nmjacobs@loyola.edu
JACOBS, Pat .... 661-654-2483.. 31 B
pjacobs@csub.edu
JACOBS, Ralph .... 719-549-2256.. 78 P
ralph.jacobs@csupueblo.edu
JACOBS, Shelle .... 573-897-5000 267 F
JACOBS, Steve .... 303-458-3560.. 82 D
jjacobs@regis.edu
JACOBS, Tina .... 405-422-1454 379 B
tina.jacobs@redlandscc.edu
JACOBS, OFS, Vicki, L .. 260-399-7700 165 B
vjacobs@sf.edu
JACOBS, Walt .... 408-924-5300.. 34 D
walt.jacobs@sjsu.edu
JACOBS, Warren .... 323-343-3440.. 32 D
warren.jacobs@calstatela.edu
JACOBS ANDERSON,
Laura .... 503-370-6206 388 D
ljacobsa@willamette.edu
JACOBS-BECK, Kim .... 513-732-5217 371 G
kimberly.jacobs@uc.edu
JACOBS ELSON, Claire . 609-258-4131 288 F
celson@princeton.edu
JACOBS-WILKE,
Alexandra, M .... 315-267-2918 328 A
jacobsam@potsdam.edu
JACOBSEN, Brandy .... 318-670-9371 196 A
bjacobsen@susla.edu
JACOBSEN, Christie ...... 610-625-7797 402 D
jacobsen@moravian.edu
JACOBSEN, Gabe .... 206-281-2043 498 B
jacobseng@spu.edu
JACOBSEN, James .... 605-367-4875 429 C
james.jacobsen@southeasttech.edu
JACOBSEN, Jon .... 909-621-8000.. 45 D
jacobsen@hmc.edu
JACOBSEN, Joyce .... 860-685-2010.. 89 F
jjacobsen@wesleyan.edu
JACOBSEN, Laura .... 540-831-5431 484 A
ljacobsen@radford.edu
JACOBSEN, Ruth .... 206-281-2114 498 B
rjacobsen@spu.edu
JACOBSEN, Stan .... 828-884-8381 335 L
jacobssf@brevard.edu
JACOBSMA, Kelly, G ..... 616-395-7790 231 D
jacobsma@hope.edu

JACOBSOHN, Stephen ... 917-493-4487 313 M
sjacobsohn@msmnyc.edu
JACOBSON, Adela .... 619-388-7313.. 60 E
ajacobso@sdccd.edu
JACOBSON, Bob .... 510-642-6000.. 68 G
JACOBSON, Bryan .... 701-349-5771 355 G
bjacobson@trinitybiblecollege.edu
JACOBSON, Cynthia .... 620-365-5116 174 G
jacobson@allencc.edu
JACOBSON, Dan .... 808-488-8570 470 I
dan.jacobson@wbu.edu
JACOBSON, Dan .... 715-675-3331 514 F
jacobson@ntc.edu
JACOBSON, David .... 323-822-9700.. 67 G
JACOBSON, Gloria .... 773-298-3706 151 C
jacobson@sxu.edu
JACOBSON, Jean .... 610-902-8231 391 B
jean.jacobson@cabrini.edu
JACOBSON, Jennifer ..... 218-846-3769 245 H
jennifer.jacobson@minnesota.edu
JACOBSON, Karin .... 620-431-2800 180 C
kjacobson@neosho.edu
JACOBSON, Kinga .... 920-686-6260 510 A
kinga.jacobson@sl.edu
JACOBSON, Mark .... 414-416-9503 511 A
markj@uwm.edu
JACOBSON, Mary .... 763-433-1315 244 A
mary.jacobson@anokaramsey.edu
JACOBSON, Mary .... 763-433-1315 243 K
mary.jacobson@anokaramsey.edu
JACOBSON, Renee, R .... 231-995-1256 235 B
jacobsr@nmc.edu
JACOBSON, Ron .... 718-817-1000 308 G
rjacobson@fordham.edu
JACOBSON, Shane .... 802-656-6626 476 E
shane.jacobson@uvm.edu
JACOBSON, Terra .... 708-974-5467 146 C
jacobsont6@morainevalley.edu
JACOBSON, Tim .... 952-995-1471 244 G
tim.jacobson@hennepintech.edu
JACOBSON, Timothy, K 262-691-5221 515 B
tjacobson9@wctc.edu
JACOBSON-SCHULTE,
Patrick .... 651-450-3000 245 A
pjacobs@inverhills.edu
JACOBSON-SCHULTE,
Patrick .... 651-450-3522 245 A
pjacobs@inverhills.edu
JACOBY, Robin, M .... 214-648-2288 469 E
robin.jacoby@utsouthwestern.edu
JACOBY, Susan .... 202-651-5005.. 91 H
susan.jacoby@gallaudet.edu
JACOT, Jaclyn .... 509-279-6212 493 I
jaclyn.jacot@scc.spokane.edu
JACQUE, Mark .... 410-837-6875 209 D
mjacque@ubalt.edu
JACQUES, Ed .... 617-879-2446 226 A
ejacques@wheelock.edu
JACQUES, Kathleen, C .. 207-795-2858 199 I
jacqueka@mchp.edu
JACQUES, Theresa, K .... 906-487-2936 234 A
tjacques@mtu.edu
JACQUEZ, Elvira, E .... 210-458-4101 468 B
elvira.jacquez@utsa.edu
JACQUEZ, Ricardo .... 530-898-5963.. 31 D
rjacquez@csuchico.edu
JACSO, Jeff .... 812-237-3525 159 C
jeff.jacso@indstate.edu
JACZYNSKI, Linda .... 610-519-4080 413 K
linda.jaczynski@villanova.edu
JADALLAH, Edward .... 843-349-2773 420 A
ejadalla@coastal.edu
JADHAV, Esther .... 859-858-3511 183 D
esther.jadhav@asbury.edu
JADLOS, Melissa .... 585-385-8164 322 E
mjadlos@sjfc.edu
JADUSHLEVER, Renee ... 510-430-2033.. 52 E
reneejad@mills.edu
JAECKEL, Andrea .... 928-350-4006.. 15 V
andrea.jaeckel@prescott.edu
JAEGER, David .... 239-590-2315 109 C
djaeger@fgcu.edu
JAEGER, Nattalie .... 515-239-9002 324 B
JAEGER, Timothy, J .... 949-214-3179.. 40 I
tim.jaeger@cui.edu
JAEHNIG, Adrea .... 207-699-5035 199 H
ajaehnig@meca.edu
JAEN, Ulysses .... 239-687-5501.. 95 B
ujaen@avemarialaw.edu
JAFERIAN, Warren .... 978-232-2272 214 G
wjaferia@endicott.edu
JAFFE, Daniel .... 512-471-2877 467 C
vp-research-sr@austin.utexas.edu
JAFFE, David, L .... 561-237-7099 103 E
djaffe@lynn.edu
JAFFE, Judith, A .... 781-736-2104 213 A
jjaffe@brandeis.edu

JAFFE, Steven, R .... 562-902-3384.. 65 D
stevenjaffee@scuhs.edu
JAFFE, Susan .... 336-770-3207 352 B
jaffes@uncsa.edu
JAFFE, Victoria .... 602-206-8115 280 L
vjaffe@ccsnh.edu
JAFFE, Yaakov .... 347-619-9074 335 A
JAFFEE, Victoria .... 949-214-3042.. 40 I
victori.jaffe@cui.edu
JAFFRAY, Shelly .... 714-564-6500.. 58 A
jaffray_shelly@sac.edu
JAGANATHAN,
Sivakumar .... 713-348-4293 455 F
JAGARD, John .... 516-463-6613 310 D
john.jagard@hofstra.edu
JAGENDORF, Susan .... 518-255-5558 328 C
jagends@cobleskill.edu
JAGER, Ben .... 859-572-5172 188 E
jagerbl@nku.edu
JAGER, Tim .... 712-274-5313 172 A
jager@morningside.edu
JAGGARS, Damon, E ..... 614-292-4241 367 H
jaggars.1@osu.edu
JAGGARS, Jess .... 802-485-2824 475 I
jjaggars@norwich.edu
JAGGER, Kathleen .... 859-344-3578 189 G
jaggerk@thomasmore.edu
JAGODZINSKI, Paul ...... 928-523-2408.. 14 K
paul.jagodzinski@nau.edu
JAGORD, Mary-Jo .... 716-878-6001 326 E
jagordmj@buffalostate.edu
JAH, Cassaundra .... 575-758-8914 294 H
cassaundraj@midwiferycollege.edu
JAHAGIRDAR, Vaishali .. 518-694-7223 297 J
vaishali.jahagirdar@acphs.edu
JAHAN, Mina .... 408-855-5360.. 74 C
mina.jahan@wvm.edu
JAHANGIR, Rashed .... 312-939-0111 137 G
rashed@eastwest.edu
JAHANIAN, Farnam .... 412-268-2201 391 H
president@andrew.cmu.edu
JAHNKE, Eileen .... 920-403-3251 509 J
eileen.jahnke@snc.edu
JAHNKE, Tamera, S .... 417-836-5249 263 H
tamerajahnke@missouristate.edu
JAHR, Helen .... 507-433-0527 247 C
helen.jahr@riverland.edu
JAIME, Andres .... 210-434-6711 454 D
aijaime@lake.ollusa.edu
JAIME, Victor .... 760-355-6219.. 46 B
victor.jaime@imperial.edu
JAIN, Anil .... 323-953-4000.. 49 A
jainak@lacitycollege.edu
JAIN, Anjani .... 203-432-6035.. 89 G
anjani.jain@yale.edu
JAIN, Arun .... 713-743-1422 465 A
ajain@uh.edu
JAIN, Madhu .... 312-939-0111 137 G
madhu@eastwest.edu
JAINI, Yolanda .... 714-533-1495.. 64 F
ymjaini@southbaylo.edu
JAKIEL DIULUS,
Lindsey .... 504-278-6421 193 B
ljakiel@nunez.edu
JAKO, Robert .... 925-969-3300.. 46 L
rjako@jfku.edu
JAKUBOW, Sandra .... 561-297-3534 109 B
sjakubow@fau.edu
JAKUBOWSKI, Jason ..... 716-286-8405 318 F
jjakubowski@niagara.edu
JAKUBOWSKI, Laura ...... 802-468-6072 477 A
laura.jakubowski@castleton.edu
JAKUBS, Deborah .... 919-660-5800 337 C
deborah.jakubs@duke.edu
JAKUPS, Steve .... 920-403-1346 509 J
steve.jakups@snc.edu
JAKWAY, Julie .... 941-752-5326 108 P
jakwayj@scf.edu
JALOMO, Romero .... 831-755-6822.. 45 C
rjalomo@hartnell.edu
JALOWIEC, Tammi .... 218-935-0417 251 F
tammi.jalowiec@wetcc.edu
JALSEVAC, Paul .... 540-636-2900 479 G
pjalsevac@christendom.edu
JAMERSON, James .... 606-546-2553 189 I
jjamerson@unionky.edu
JAMERSON, JR.,
Londell .... 816-604-1453 262 F
londell.jamerson@mcckc.edu
JAMERSON, Sun Kyong 440-366-7569 364 F
JAMES, JR.,
Advergus, D .... 334-727-8088.... 7 F
jamesad@mytu.tuskegee.edu
JAMES, Angel .... 216-373-5238 367 A
ajames@ndc.edu
JAMES, Anisa .... 606-546-1704 189 I
ajames@unionky.edu

JAMES, Arthur .... 972-860-4417 448 C
ajames@dcccd.edu
JAMES, Barbara .... 423-236-2942 436 C
bjames@southern.edu
JAMES, Blake .... 305-284-6381 112 O
bjames@miami.edu
JAMES, Bruce .... 501-370-5234.. 21 A
bjames@philander.edu
JAMES, Catherine .... 269-965-3931 232 A
jamesc@kellogg.edu
JAMES, Cheryl .... 850-973-9416 104 D
jamesc@nfcc.edu
JAMES, Clark .... 850-644-4752 110 A
jclark5@fsu.edu
JAMES, Deborah .... 804-862-6100 484 F
djames@rbc.edu
JAMES, Denise .... 708-209-3337 136 I
denise.james@cuchicago.edu
JAMES, Donna .... 701-845-7276 354 E
donna.james@vcsu.edu
JAMES, Erika .... 404-727-6377 119 B
erika.james@emory.edu
JAMES, III, Frank .... 215-368-5000 389 H
fjames@biblical.edu
JAMES, Glenn .... 210-829-3940 465 E
gjames@uiwtx.edu
JAMES, Glenn, W .... 931-372-6144 438 F
gjames@tntech.edu
JAMES, Gloria, P .... 903-927-3208 471 B
gpjames@wileyc.edu
JAMES, Gwendolyn .... 509-533-8090 493 I
gwendolyn.james@scc.spokane.edu
JAMES, Henry, D .... 704-687-8454 351 C
hjames1@uncc.edu
JAMES, Hollis .... 423-236-2002 436 C
hjames@southern.edu
JAMES, Holly .... 502-863-7094 184 I
holly_james@georgetowncollege.edu
JAMES, Jacqueline .... 404-270-5111 126 D
jjames@spelman.edu
JAMES, Jamie .... 603-626-9100 282 C
j.james@snhu.edu
JAMES, Janet, C .... 972-238-6974 448 D
jjames@dcccd.edu
JAMES, Jennifer .... 718-270-5083 303 C
jenjames@mec.cuny.edu
JAMES, Jeremy .... 334-556-2361.... 2 B
jjames@wallace.edu
JAMES, Jesse, L .... 563-589-3214 173 J
jjames@dbq.edu
JAMES, Jill .... 856-351-2910 291 E
jjames@salemcc.edu
JAMES, Jim .... 404-962-3155 127 G
jim.james@usg.edu
JAMES, Joy, L .... 804-706-5214 488 D
jjames@jtcc.edu
JAMES, Kamille .... 718-780-7505 300 A
kamille.james@brooklaw.edu
JAMES, Karen .... 336-517-1565 335 K
kjames@bennett.edu
JAMES, Kathy .... 325-649-8409 450 H
kjames@hputx.edu
JAMES, Kelly .... 785-890-3641 180 G
kelly.james@nwktc.edu
JAMES, Kelly .... 815-394-5045 150 C
kjames@rockford.edu
JAMES, Kesha .... 205-929-6450.... 2 G
kjames@lawsonstate.edu
JAMES, Lacrecia .... 504-486-7411 198 D
ljames6@xula.edu
JAMES, Lance .... 360-538-4120 495 B
ljames@ghc.edu
JAMES, Leroy "Lee" .... 410-516-4612 204 F
ljames10@jhu.edu
JAMES, Lisa .... 256-726-7270.... 6 E
ljames@oakwood.edu
JAMES, Lisa .... 719-502-2056.. 81 H
lisa.james@ppcc.edu
JAMES, Mary, B .... 503-777-7250 386 F
mjames@reed.edu
JAMES, Matricia .... 716-375-2000 322 B
mjames@sbu.edu
JAMES, Michael .... 360-676-2772 496 C
mjames@nwic.edu
JAMES, Michelle .... 412-536-1139 398 E
michelle.james@laroche.edu
JAMES, Mike .... 501-279-4529.. 19 G
james@harding.edu
JAMES, Mike .... 956-665-2451 468 A
mike.james@utrgv.edu
JAMES, Novia .... 520-383-8401.. 16 G
njames@tocc.edu
JAMES, Patrick .... 256-824-6942.... 8 C
patrick.james@uah.edu
JAMES, Patrick .... 312-629-6600 151 F
pjames@saic.edu
JAMES, Peggy .... 262-595-2101 511 C
james@uwp.edu
JAMES, Penny .... 402-354-7225 275 P
penny.james@methodistcollege.edu
JAMES, Ron .... 575-538-6715 297 H
ron.james@wnmu.edu
JAMES, Ruben .... 310-900-1600.. 40 C
rjames@elcamino.edu
JAMES, Ruby, F .... 217-420-6029 145 J
rjames@millikin.edu
JAMES, Sarah, R .... 812-941-2020 161 A
jamessr@ius.edu
JAMES, Scott .... 978-542-6243 218 E
sjames@salemstate.edu
JAMES, Shauna .... 256-765-4279.... 9 A
sljames@una.edu
JAMES, Skip .... 850-973-9477 104 D
jamess@nfcc.edu
JAMES, Stephen .... 865-251-1800 436 B
sjames1@southcollegetn.edu
JAMES, Susan, M .... 757-822-1084 489 H
sjames@tcc.edu
JAMES, Sylvia .... 253-964-6715 497 B
JAMES, Tessa .... 800-567-2344 506 I
tjames@menominee.edu
JAMES, Thomas .... 212-678-3050 331 C
james@tc.edu
JAMES, Timmy .... 256-331-6281.... 3 C
timmy.james@nwscc.edu
JAMES, Timothy .... 419-372-2346 357 F
timsj@bgsu.edu
JAMES, Tracy .... 636-481-3187 261 B
tjames@jeffco.edu
JAMES, Ursla .... 386-481-2975.. 95 J
jamesu@cookman.edu
JAMES, Vernon .... 706-880-8979 122 D
vjames@lagrange.edu
JAMES, W. Brian .... 706-245-7226 119 A
bjames@ec.edu
JAMES, Wayne .... 219-980-7222 160 C
wljames@iun.edu
JAMES-BATTELLE, Brice 870-733-6790.. 18 B
bjames-battelle@asumidsouth.edu
JAMES BLACKWELL,
Leanna .... 413-565-1000 211 C
ljamesblackwell@baypath.edu
JAMES-MOORE, Annette 901-272-5153 434 B
amoore@mca.edu
JAMES WALKER,
Cherena .... 323-259-2623.. 54 E
cwalker2@oxy.edu
JAMESON, Dennis .... 916-577-2200.. 75 B
djameson@jessup.edu
JAMESON, Gretchen, M 262-243-5700 507 C
gretchen.jameson@cuw.edu
JAMESON, J, L .... 215-898-6796 412 G
ljameson@mail.med.upenn.edu
JAMESON, Kim .... 405-682-7534 377 C
kjameson@occc.edu
JAMESON, Maisha .... 510-464-3236.. 56 H
mjameson@peralta.edu
JAMESON, Sean .... 914-395-2494 323 K
sjameson@sarahlawrence.edu
JAMESON, Stacey .... 212-924-5900 330 G
sjameson@swedishinstitute.edu
JAMESON DUBOW,
Emily .... 509-453-0374 497 A
emily.jameson@perrytech.edu
JAMIESON, Michelle, E . 724-287-8711 390 J
michelle.jamieson@bc3.edu
JAMIESON, Richard, J .. 216-368-3720 358 C
rjj@case.edu
JAMIESON-DRAKE,
David .... 919-684-0736 337 C
david.jamieson.drake@duke.edu
JAMISON, Ann, M .... 814-393-2220 405 H
ajamison@clarion.edu
JAMISON, Calvin, D ..... 972-883-2213 467 D
cjamison@utdallas.edu
JAMISON, Charles .... 610-409-3607 413 H
cjamison@ursinus.edu
JAMISON, David, L .... 412-397-6226 409 C
jamison@rmu.edu
JAMISON, Kristin, E ...... 217-245-3046 139 H
kristin.jamison@mail.ic.edu
JAMISON, Larry, W .... 814-393-1926 405 H
ljamison@cuf-inc.org
JAMISON, Leslie .... 609-343-5004 283 D
ljamison@atlantic.edu
JAMISON, Lucretzia ...... 773-451-3798 135 L
ljamison@ccc.edu
JAMISON, Matt .... 303-678-3845.. 79 K
matt.jamison@frontrange.edu
JAMISON, Todd, M .... 740-587-5712 361 B
jamisont@denison.edu
JAMISON, Wayne .... 803-786-3343 420 D
wjamison@columbiasc.edu
JAMOUS, Danielly .... 401-739-5000 416 D
djamous@neit.edu
JAMROS, Brian .... 503-280-8554 382 I
bjamros@cu-portland.edu
JANAK, Bickram .... 443-885-3144 206 A
bickram.janak@morgan.edu
JANARO, Walter, A .... 540-636-2900 479 G
walter@christendom.edu
JANCHENKO, Michael ... 312-329-4495 146 B
michael.janchenko@moody.edu
JANDA, Kenneth, C .... 949-824-6022.. 69 A
kcjanda@uci.edu
JANDHYALA, Vikram ..... 206-543-0905 499 D
vj@uw.edu
JANDRIS, Thomas .... 708-209-3597 136 I
thomas.jandris@cuchicago.edu
JANE, Jennifer .... 808-675-3211 128 K
jennifer.lane@byuh.edu
JANELLE, Sherri .... 304-876-5043 504 D
sjanelle@shepherd.edu
JANELLE, William, P ..... 603-862-2650 282 F
william.janelle@unh.edu
JANES, Jennifer .... 315-364-3483 333 G
jjanes@wells.edu
JANES, Kristin .... 828-669-8012 340 I
kjanes@montreat.edu
JANES, Michael, G .... 215-596-8697 413 E
m.janes@usciences.edu
JANESCH, Cynthia, D .... 570-577-3763 390 H
cindy.janesch@bucknell.edu
JANG, Michelle .... 714-533-1495.. 64 F
michelle@southbaylo.edu
JANIK, Mary Mark .... 716-896-0700 333 C
janik@villa.edu
JANIS, Robert, J .... 312-362-8762 137 C
bjanis@depaul.edu
JANIS, Roger, D .... 530-226-4758.. 64 B
rjanis@simpsonu.edu
JANIS, Sofia, A .... 412-359-1000 412 C
sjanis@triangle-tech.edu
JANITZ, Suzanne .... 607-431-4244 309 E
janitzs@hartwick.edu
JANKE, Louise, L .... 608-785-8604 510 F
ljanke@uwlax.edu
JANKO, Karen .... 312-777-8666 140 G
kjanko@aii.edu
JANKOWSKI, Cheryl ..... 440-934-3101 367 D
cjankowski@ohiobusinesscollege.edu
JANKOWSKI, Mark .... 518-587-2100 329 C
mark.jankowski@esc.edu
JANKOWSKI NIEMCZURA,
Leslie .... 614-222-3225 360 B
ljankowski@ccad.edu
JANNEY, Cindy .... 507-389-1011 246 A
cynthia.janney@mnsu.edu
JANNEY, Dell Ann .... 573-288-6388 259 E
djanney@culver.edu
JANNEY, Justin .... 229-243-6030 116 C
JANNEY, Suzanne .... 941-487-4110 110 B
janney@ncf.edu
JANOSKY, Janine .... 313-593-5090 238 A
jjanosky@umich.edu
JANOW, Merit, E .... 212-854-4604 305 E
mj60@columbia.edu
JANOWSKI, Barbara ...... 832-584-5122 125 H
bjanowski@southuniversity.edu
JANOWSKI, Lori .... 212-650-3133 302 E
lori.janowski@hunter.cuny.edu
JANOYAN, Kerop .... 315-268-6506 304 B
kjanoyan@clarkson.edu
JANS, Roger .... 201-684-7231 289 C
rjans@ramapo.edu
JANSE, Korey .... 661-255-1050.. 29 F
JANSEN, James, S .... 402-280-1804 274 D
jimjansen@creighton.edu
JANSEN, Jennifer .... 510-594-3763.. 28 K
jjansen@cca.edu
JANSEN, Mark .... 815-599-3455 139 F
mark.jansen@highland.edu
JANSEN, Sandy .... 865-974-6611 439 H
sjansen@utk.edu
JANSEN, Shelley .... 970-943-2101.. 84 E
sjansen@western.edu
JANSMA, Dana .... 269-337-7210 231 F
dana.jansma@kzoo.edu
JANSMA, Pamela .... 303-556-2557.. 83 D
pamela.jansma@ucdenver.edu
JANSSEN, Jessica .... 402-941-6523 275 J
janssen@midlandu.edu
JANSSEN, Jill, M .... 815-599-3412 139 F
jill.janssen@highland.edu
JANSSEN, Michelle, L ... 765-361-6365 166 B
janssenm@wabash.edu
JANSSEN, William .... 631-656-2157 308 F
JANSSEN-ROBINSON,
Aimee .... 812-535-5219 163 I
a.janssen-robinson@smwc.edu
JANSSON, Hilary .... 401-825-2425 416 B
hjansson@ccri.edu
JANSSON, Jimilea .... 580-628-6771 376 J
jimilea.jansson@noc.edu
JANUSCH, Barry .... 360-475-7458 496 F
bjanusch@olympic.edu
JANUTIS, Rachel .... 614-236-6383 358 A
rjanutis@law.capital.edu
JANZ, Curtis .... 479-788-7591.. 22 A
curtis.janz@uafs.edu
JANZ, Jeff .... 414-288-7206 508 C
jeff.janz@marquette.edu
JANZ, Kenneth .... 507-457-2299 248 C
kjanz@winona.edu
JANZ, Mary .... 414-288-7208 508 C
mary.janz@marquette.edu
JANZEN, Amy .... 405-425-5907 377 B
amy.janzen@oc.edu
JANZEN, Scott .... 574-296-6213 155 K
registrar@ambs.edu
JAQUES, Kate .... 916-484-8406.. 50 F
jaquesk@arc.losrios.edu
JAQUES, Richard .... 703-784-2105 518 A
richard.jaques@usmc.mil
JAQUES-ANGLIN,
Kristie .... 617-537-6547 145 C
kljaques-anglin@mckendree.edu
JAQUILLARD, Jenny ...... 800-869-7223 125 B
jjaquill@scad.edu
JARACZEWSKI, John ..... 262-595-2591 511 C
john.jaraczewski@uwp.edu
JARAMILLO, Brooke ...... 229-333-2100 128 G
brooke.jaramillo@wiregrass.edu
JARAMILLO, Ed .... 360-416-7719 498 F
ed.jaramillo@skagit.edu
JARAMILLO, Jessica ..... 505-454-3593 294 J
jessica@nmhu.edu
JARAMILLO, John .... 949-582-4311.. 64 J
jjaramillo@saddleback.edu
JARAMILLO, Justin .... 303-315-1845.. 83 D
justin.jaramillo@ucdenver.edu
JARAMILLO, Luis .... 212-229-5611 316 E
jaramillo@newschool.edu
JARAMILLO FLEMING,
Melissa .... 575-835-5880 294 K
melissa.jaramillo@nmt.edu
JARANSKI, Ann .... 330-941-3737 374 E
atjaronski@ysu.edu
JARBOE, Dan .... 870-245-5591.. 20 G
jarboed@obu.edu
JARBOE, Marlena .... 540-453-2260 487 G
jarboem@brcc.edu
JARBOE, Shannon, K .... 240-895-4309 206 G
skjarboe@smcm.edu
JARDINE, Daniel, D ...... 607-587-4036 328 F
jardindd@alfredstate.edu
JARDINE, David .... 269-471-3965 227 B
djardine@andrews.edu
JARETT, Sadie .... 334-874-5700.... 5 B
sjarett@ccal.edu
JARICH, Amy .... 510-642-3175.. 68 G
awjarich@berkeley.edu
JARKOWSKI,
Melissa, M .... 585-292-2279 315 L
mjarkowski@monroecc.edu
JARLEY, Paul .... 407-823-2181 110 C
pjarley@bus.ucf.edu
JARMAN, James .... 928-757-0827.. 14 I
jjarman@mohave.edu
JARMIN MILLER
Catherine .... 503-883-2494 383 H
cjarmin@linfield.edu
JARMOND, Martin .... 617-552-4680 212 E
martin.jarmond@bc.edu
JARMUL, Eileen .... 252-789-0219 344 E
eileen.jarmul@martincc.edu
JARMULOWICZ,
Linda, D .... 901-678-5800 439 E
ljrmlwcz@memphis.edu
JARNAGIN, Lea, M .... 909-869-3310.. 31 A
lmjarnagin@cpp.edu
JARNAGIN, Missy .... 805-437-3282.. 31 C
missy.jarnagin@csuci.edu
JARNIGAN, Renee .... 423-585-6960 438 D
renee.jarnigan@ws.edu
JARONSKI, Ann .... 813-974-3598 111 A
atj1@usf.edu
JAROT, Lisa .... 847-628-1572 142 B
ljarot@judsonu.edu
JARR, William .... 770-426-2632 122 F
wdjarr@life.edu
JARRELL, Bruce, E .... 410-706-2304 207 H
bjarrell@umaryland.edu
JARRELL, James .... 443-997-6393 204 F
jjarrell@jhu.edu
JARRELL, Lacey .... 541-880-2285 383 E
jarrell@klamathcc.edu
JARRELL, Paul .... 805-965-0581.. 62 E
pejarrell@sbcc.edu

JARRELL, Sasha .... 850-729-5363 104 E
jarrells@nwfsc.edu
JARRELL, Sheila .... 928-776-2188.. 17 G
sheila.jarrell@yc.edu
JARRET, Ronald .... 508-793-2541 213 D
rjarret@holycross.edu
JARRETT, Amy .... 864-644-5011 424 B
ajarrett@swu.edu
JARRETT, Courtney .... 540-535-3461 485 C
cjarrett1@su.edu
JARRETT, James .... 863-680-4459 100 D
jjarrett@flsouthern.edu
JARRETT, Juan .... 706-542-2621 127 A
jarrettj@uga.edu
JARRETT, Katrina .... 937-708-5760 373 H
kjarrett@wilbeforce.edu
JARRETT BROMBERG,
Shelly .... 513-529-7135 365 I
jarretam@miamioh.edu
JARRY, Timothy .... 508-793-2515 213 D
tjarry@holycross.edu
JARSTFER, Amiel .... 423-869-6364 433 C
amiel.jarstfer@lmunet.edu
JARSTFER, Amiel .... 423-869-6203 433 C
amiel.jarstfer@lmunet.edu
JARUSZEWICZ,
Candace, L .... 843-953-5606 420 C
jaruszewiczc@cofc.edu
JARVIS, Anne .... 609-258-3170 288 F
ajarvis@princeton.edu
JARVIS, Cliff .... 573-875-7300 258 F
csjarvis@email.ccis.edu
JARVIS, Emily .... 478-757-4023 128 E
ejarvis@wesleyancollege.edu
JARVIS, Frances, H .... 617-228-2400 219 D
fjarvis@bhcc.mass.edu
JARVIS, Jeffrey, A .... 419-227-3141 372 D
jjarvis@unoh.edu
JARVIS, Keith .... 307-532-8255 516 J
keith.jarvis@ewc.wy.edu
JARVIS, Michelle .... 317-940-8056 156 I
mjarvis@butler.edu
JARZABSKI, Kerri, P ..... 413-782-1312 225 F
kerri.jarzabski@wne.edu
JARZYNA, Dave .... 260-665-4270 164 E
jarzynad@trine.edu
JASCOR, Barb .... 715-422-5476 514 B
barb.jascor@mstc.edu
JASEK, Michael, D .... 575-646-1722 295 B
mjasek@nmsu.edu
JASHINSKI, Michelle, L 814-371-2090 411 H
mjashinski@triangle-tech.edu
JASHO, Gay-linn .... 404-880-8892 117 H
gjasho@cau.edu
JASINSKI, John .... 660-562-1110 264 I
johnj@nwmissouri.edu
JASKA, Jamie .... 254-659-7730 450 B
jjaska@hillcollege.edu
JASKEN, Julia .... 410-857-2247 205 E
jjasken@mcdaniel.edu
JASMAN, Troy .... 712-274-6400 174 E
troy.jasman@witcc.edu
JASMIN, Reba .... 256-372-8692.... 1 A
reba.jasmin@aamu.edu
JASON, Caldwell .... 336-887-3000 338 G
JASON, Hoerr, U .... 610-921-7221 388 E
jhoerr@albright.edu
JASON, Karen, W .... 508-531-2750 217 D
kjason@bridgew.edu
JASPERSON, Steve .... 909-706-8661.. 74 G
sjasperson@westernu.edu
JASS, Lori, K .... 503-517-1320 388 A
ljass@warnerpacific.edu
JASSO, Sonia .... 210-805-5814 465 E
sjasso@uiwtx.edu
JASTORFF, Mark, A .... 970-247-7074.. 79 J
majastorff@fortlewis.edu
JASTORFF, Michael .... 605-642-6279 428 F
michael.jastorff@bhsu.edu
JASUR, Angela .... 631-420-2717 329 D
angela.jasur@farmingdale.edu
JASWAL, Faisal .... 425-564-6151 492 G
fjaswal@bellevuecollege.edu
JASZKA, Michael, S ...... 716-286-8343 318 F
msj@niagara.edu
JATTKOWSKI-HUDSON,
Anna, J .... 815-226-3392 150 C
ajattkowski-hudson@rockford.edu
JAUDON, Jon .... 706-529-7623 118 F
jjaudon@daltonstate.edu
JAUNARAJS, Imants ...... 740-593-2909 368 G
jaunaraj@ohio.edu
JAURON, Lester .... 530-895-2266.. 28 E
jauronle@butte.edu
JAVAHERIPOUR, G. H .... 530-741-6707.. 76 A
gjavaher@yccd.edu
JAVARIZ, Gerardo .... 787-890-2681 527 E
gerardo.javariz@upr.edu
JAVDEKAR, Chitra .... 781-239-2585 220 A
cjavdekar@massbay.edu
JAVIER, Byron, A .... 312-850-7126 136 C
bjavier@ccc.edu
JAVOR, Seta .... 818-767-0888.. 75 C
seta.javor@woodbury.edu
JAVOROSKI, Alan .... 715-422-5402 514 B
al.javoroski@mstc.edu
JAWAHAR, Jim .... 309-438-7018 140 L
jimoham@ilstu.edu
JAY, Andrea .... 305-348-1105 109 D
andrea.jay@fiu.edu
JAY, Jodye .... 903-586-2518 451 C
jjay@jacksonville-college.edu
JAYARAMAN, Ruki .... 224-293-5746 133 D
rjayaraman@aiuonline.edu
JAYASURIYA, Kumara ... 304-766-3146 505 A
kjayasuriya@wvstateu.edu
JAYAWICKREMA,
Arosha .... 860-768-4276.. 89 C
jaya@hartford.edu
JAYE, Marilyn .... 617-559-8642 215 H
mjaye@hebrewcollege.edu
JAYNE, Delaina .... 570-945-8130 398 C
delaina.jayne@keystone.edu
JAYNE, Joann .... 718-429-6600 333 B
joann.jayne@vaughn.edu
JAYNES, Tom .... 919-536-7200 342 G
jaynest@durhamtech.edu
JAZDZEWSKI, Rich, L ... 920-832-6574 507 L
richard.l.jazdzewski@lawrence.edu
JAZWIECKI,
Gabrielle, E .... 203-837-8281.. 85 B
jazwieckig@wcsu.edu
JAZZABI, Monica .... 323-343-3342.. 32 D
mjazzabi@cslanet.calstatela.edu
JBARA, Craig .... 269-353-1263 231 G
cjbara@kvcc.edu
JEAN, Libby .... 269-749-7655 236 A
ljean@olivetcollege.edu
JEAN, Marc .... 201-216-9901 285 F
marc.jean@eicollege.edu
JEAN, Martin, D .... 203-432-9681.. 89 G
martin.jean@yale.edu
JEAN, Paul .... 508-531-2660 217 D
paul.jean@bridgew.edu
JEAN-JACQUES, Tanya .. 617-541-5308 221 A
tjean-jacques@rcc.mass.edu
JEAN-LOUIS, Patrick ..... 617-541-5388 221 A
pjeanlouis@rcc.mass.edu
JEAN-MARIE, Cherisna . 903-730-4890 451 D
cjeanmarie@jarvis.edu
JEAN-MARIE, Gadtane ... 319-273-2717 167 A
gaetane.jean-marie@uni.edu
JEAN MARIE, Vivaldi .... 718-270-5031 303 C
vjean-marie@mec.cuny.edu
JEAN - MICHEL, Jean ... 718-270-6417 303 C
jjean-michel@mec.cuny.edu
JEANCAKE, Chris .... 912-427-1958 117 J
cjeancake@coastalpines.edu
JEANFREAU,
Jennifer, N .... 504-865-2282 194 G
jnjeanfr@loyno.edu
JEBALI, Lisa .... 978-837-5109 221 G
jebalil@merrimack.edu
JEBB, Cindy .... 845-938-2000 519 D
8dean@usma.edu
JECH, Sue .... 507-433-0610 247 C
sue.jech@riverland.edu
JECHURA, Kacey .... 303-300-8740.. 77 F
kacey.jechura@collegeamerica.com
JEDNAK, P. Michael ...... 860-486-4741.. 88 G
michael.jednak@uconn.edu
JEDYNAK-BELL,
Corinne .... 210-283-6430 465 E
jedynakb@uiwtx.edu
JEELANI, Shaik .... 334-727-8970.... 7 F
jeelanis@mytu.tuskegee.edu
JEFFCOAT, Holly .... 860-486-0497.. 88 G
JEFFERIES, Yvette .... 973-877-3006 285 K
jefferies@essex.edu
JEFFERIES-JACKSON,
Tamara .... 803-536-8103 423 G
thughes@scsu.edu
JEFFERS, Carrie .... 586-286-2187 233 B
jeffersc@macomb.edu
JEFFERS, Karen .... 918-595-7441 380 D
karen.jeffers@tulsacc.edu
JEFFERS, Linda .... 209-946-2125.. 70 F
ljeffers@pacific.edu
JEFFERSON, Adriene ..... 772-462-7156 101 Q
ajeffers@irsc.edu
JEFFERSON, Barbie, F ... 864-597-4237 426 I
jeffersonbf@wofford.edu
JEFFERSON, Donald ...... 334-874-5700.... 5 B
djefferson@ccal.edu
JEFFERSON, Doug .... 817-598-6247 470 J
djefferson@wc.edu
JEFFERSON, Joy, L .... 757-683-3097 483 G
jljeffer@odu.edu
JEFFERSON, Lynda .... 803-780-1279 426 F
jefferson@voorhees.edu
JEFFERSON, Mara .... 919-890-7500.. 93 B
JEFFERSON, Michael ...... 707-965-7080.. 55 F
mjeffereson@puc.edu
JEFFERSON, Shirley ...... 802-831-1333 476 G
sjefferson@vermontlaw.edu
JEFFERSON, Venessa, F 803-934-3175 422 G
vjefferson@morris.edu
JEFFERSON, Willie .... 803-780-1049 426 F
williej@voorhees.edu
JEFFERSON-GOMEZ,
Anita, R .... 937-708-5520 373 H
ajefferson-gomez@wilberforce.edu
JEFFERY, Charles .... 623-845-3692.. 13 H
charles.jeffery@gccaz.edu
JEFFERY, John, A .... 610-660-1062 409 H
jjeffery@sju.edu
JEFFERY, Kathryn, E ...... 310-434-4200.. 62 G
jeffery_kathryn@smc.edu
JEFFRESS, Conway, A ... 734-462-4400 236 H
jeffress@schoolcraft.edu
JEFFREY, Don .... 334-983-6556.... 7 E
djeffr@troy.edu
JEFFREY, Douglas .... 517-607-2518 231 C
djeffrey@hillsdale.edu
JEFFREY, Kim .... 806-874-3571 445 R
kim.jeffrey@clarendoncollege.edu
JEFFREY, Russell .... 512-313-3000 446 N
russell.jeffrey@concordia.edu
JEFFRIES, Christopher ... 504-816-4662 191 E
cjeffries@dillard.edu
JEFFRIES, Frankie .... 901-435-1530 433 A
frankie_jeffries@loc.edu
JEFFRIES, Michael .... 660-543-8203 268 A
jeffries@ucmo.edu
JEFFRIES, Pamela, R ..... 202-994-8429.. 92 A
pjeffries@gwu.edu
JEFFRIES, Rick .... 863-669-2840 105 F
rjeffries@polk.edu
JEFFRIES, Sandy .... 949-451-5210.. 64 I
sjeffries@ivc.edu
JEFFRIES, Scott .... 214-333-5211 447 D
scottj@dbu.edu
JEFFRIES, Shellie .... 616-632-2130 227 C
jeffrmic@aquinas.edu
JEFFRIES, Susan, K .... 580-327-8570 376 K
skjeffries@nwosu.edu
JEFREMOW, George ...... 212-217-4420 308 B
george_jefremow@fitnyc.edu
JEKA, Mary, R .... 617-627-4220 225 A
mary.jeka@tufts.edu
JELINEK, John, A .... 312-329-4185 146 B
john.jelinek@moody.edu
JELINKOVA, Klara .... 713-348-2211 455 F
klara.jelinkova@rice.edu
JELLEMA, Kate .... 802-451-7510 475 D
katej@gradschool.marlboro.edu
JELLERSON, George ...... 804-862-6100 484 F
gjellerson@rbc.edu
JELLISON, Rebecca .... 269-782-1241 237 B
rjellison@swmich.edu
JEMIOLA, Richard .... 757-352-4028 484 E
richjem@regent.edu
JEMISON, Jan .... 415-565-4723.. 68 I
jemisonj@uchastings.edu
JEMISON, William .... 315-268-6509 304 B
wjemison@clarkson.edu
JENCKS, Doyle .... 580-477-7736 381 G
doyle.jencks@wosc.edu
JENDRASZAK, Stephen . 612-330-1182 240 G
jendra@augsburg.edu
JENE, Beverly .... 802-322-1650 475 A
beverly.jene@goddard.edu
JENEFSKY, Cyd .... 209-946-2300.. 70 F
cjenefsky@pacific.edu
JENEMANN, David .... 802-656-8209 476 E
david.jenemann@uvm.edu
JENERETTE, Kim .... 937-766-7866 358 D
kimjenerette@cedarville.edu
JENIK, Jeff .... 803-641-3258 425 A
jeffj@usca.edu
JENIOUS, Anita .... 615-322-4705 440 D
anita.jenious@vanderbilt.edu
JENKINS, Adam .... 620-229-6091 181 F
adam.jenkins@sckans.edu
JENKINS, Allen .... 718-933-6700 315 K
ajenkins@monroecollege.edu
JENKINS, Amelia .... 504-520-7541 198 D
ajenki10@xula.edu
JENKINS, Anthony, L ..... 304-766-3112 505 A
anthony.jenkins@wvstateu.edu
JENKINS, Bethany .... 212-659-7284 312 E
bjenkins@tkc.edu
JENKINS, Betty, A .... 803-705-4808 418 G
jenkinsb@benedict.edu
JENKINS, Brandon .... 919-735-5151 347 E
bmjenkins@waynecc.edu
JENKINS, Brandon .... 919-739-6841 347 E
bmjenkins@waynecc.edu
JENKINS, Briar .... 580-477-7700 381 G
briar.jenkins@wosc.edu
JENKINS, Bryan .... 919-807-7147 340 K
jenkinsb@nccommunitycolleges.edu
JENKINS, Cara .... 610-436-3513 407 D
cjenkins@wcupa.edu
JENKINS, Carri, P .... 801-422-1166 471 E
carri_jenkins@byu.edu
JENKINS, Cheryl, S .... 919-760-8338 339 H
jenkinsc@meredith.edu
JENKINS, Daniel .... 334-874-5700.... 5 B
djenkins@ccal.edu
JENKINS, David, A .... 502-852-7997 190 C
d.jenkins@louisville.edu
JENKINS, Deborah, D ... 410-334-2904 210 C
djenkins@worwic.edu
JENKINS, Doug .... 417-865-2815 260 B
jenkinsd@evangel.edu
JENKINS, Freddie .... 229-732-5919 115 B
freddiejenkins@andrewcollege.edu
JENKINS, G. Scott .... 336-334-7977 350 C
gsjenkin@ncat.edu
JENKINS, Garry .... 612-625-4841 250 E
JENKINS, Geraldine, M . 440-646-8322 373 B
gerri.jenkins@ursuline.edu
JENKINS, Glendon .... 479-979-1447.. 23 J
gjenkins@ozarks.edu
JENKINS, Gloria .... 574-284-4723 163 J
gjenkins@saintmarys.edu
JENKINS, H. E .... 713-942-5079 466 J
jenkinhe@stthom.edu
JENKINS, J. Marshall .... 706-236-2259 116 D
mjenkins@berry.edu
JENKINS,
Jacqueline, M .... 212-752-1530 312 G
jacqueline.jenkins@limcollege.edu
JENKINS, Jade .... 803-780-1019 426 F
jade@voorhees.edu
JENKINS, Jan .... 479-968-0456.. 18 G
ejenkins@atu.edu
JENKINS, Jeffrey, L .... 812-877-8209 163 G
jenkins@rose-hulman.edu
JENKINS, SR.,
Jimmy, R .... 704-216-6098 339 E
jjenkins@livingstone.edu
JENKINS, Jo Ann .... 708-608-4199 146 C
jenkinsj52@morainevalley.edu
JENKINS, John, A .... 404-527-4520 117 C
jjenkins@carver.edu
JENKINS, CSC, John, I .. 574-631-3903 165 A
jenkins.1@nd.edu
JENKINS, Juanita, M ..... 570-422-3961 406 A
jjenkins20@esu.edu
JENKINS, Kara .... 540-535-3572 485 C
kjenkins@su.edu
JENKINS, Katrina .... 407-646-2115 106 J
kejenkins@rollins.edu
JENKINS, Keith .... 585-475-7404 321 D
kbjgpt@rit.edu
JENKINS, Keith .... 936-294-1759 462 F
rca_kej@shsu.edu
JENKINS, Kevin .... 870-307-7220.. 20 C
kevin.jenkins@lyon.edu
JENKINS, Lucy 603-578-8900 280M
ljenkins@ccsnh.edu
JENKINS, Malia .... 619-201-8728.. 60 A
malia.jenkins@sdcc.edu
JENKINS, Matt .... 304-263-0979 502 F
mjenkins@valley.edu
JENKINS, Melanie .... 617-573-8160 224 I
mjenkins@suffolk.edu
JENKINS, Melanie .... 804-484-1581 486 G
mjenkin3@richmond.edu
JENKINS, Mike .... 903-983-8189 451 F
mjenkins@kilgore.edu
JENKINS, Morris 573-651-2178 266M
mjenkins@semo.edu
JENKINS, Nichelle .... 212-280-1317 332 C
njenkins@uts.columbia.edu
JENKINS, Nick .... 828-328-7356 339 C
nick.jenkins@lr.edu
JENKINS, Patsy .... 318-473-6474 194 A
pjenkins@lsua.edu
JENKINS, Rebecca .... 419-434-5692 372 B
jenkinsr1@findlay.edu
JENKINS, Ricky .... 405-466-3623 375 L
rjjenkins@langston.edu
JENKINS, Robert .... 909-384-8662.. 59 I
rjenkins@sbccd.cc.ca.us
JENKINS, Robert .... 713-500-3334 468 D
robert.jenkins@uth.tmc.edu
JENKINS, Robert .... 903-877-7777 469 A
robert.jenkins@uth.tmc.edu

JENKINS, Rod .... 972-708-7369 449 I
rod_jenkins@gial.edu
JENKINS, Rodney .... 928-445-7300.. 17 G
rodney.jenkins@yc.edu
JENKINS, Ronny .... 202-319-5492.. 91 D
jenkinsr@cua.edu
JENKINS, Sam .... 770-537-6012 128 F
sam.jenkins@westgatech.edu
JENKINS, Scott .... 402-643-7482 274 B
finaid@cune.edu
JENKINS, Shantelle .... 610-225-5457 394 E
shantelle.jenkins@eastern.edu
JENKINS, Sharon .... 575-439-3806 295 C
djenkins@nmsu.edu
JENKINS, Sonja .... 478-988-6800 117 E
sjenkins@centralgatech.edu
JENKINS, Sonja .... 478-218-3308 117 D
sjenkins@centralgatech.edu
JENKINS, Stephen .... 678-466-4143 117 I
stephenjenkins@clayton.edu
JENKINS, Steve .... 619-201-8720.. 60 A
steve.jenkins@sdcc.edu
JENKINS, Steven .... 740-392-6868 366 B
steven.jenkins@mvnu.edu
JENKINS, Sylvia .... 708-974-5201 146 C
president@morainevalley.edu
JENKINS, Tara, F .... 508-854-4249 220 G
tjenkins@qcc.mass.edu
JENKINS, Timothy, S .... 219-464-5411 165 D
tim.jenkins@valpo.edu
JENKINS, Vanessa, C .... 757-823-8173 483 F
vcjenkins@nsu.edu
JENKS, Ann, M .... 269-337-7297 231 F
ann.jenks@kzoo.edu
JENKS, Catherine .... 678-839-6449 127 F
cjenks@westga.edu
JENKS, Dean .... 503-517-1093 388 A
djenks@warnerpacific.edu
JENKS, Salli .... 402-486-2529 277 C
salli.jenks@ucollege.edu
JENKS, Wayne .... 919-761-2277 349 C
wjenks@sebts.edu
JENNEMAN, Eugene, A . 231-995-1572 235 B
ejenneman@nmc.edu
JENNETTE, Judy .... 252-789-0310 344 E
judy.jennette@martincc.edu
JENNETTEN, Tory .... 309-677-2259 134 G
tory@fsmail.bradley.edu
JENNINGS, Amani .... 732-987-2601 286 D
ajennings@georgian.edu
JENNINGS, Arbolina, L . 713-313-7661 461 E
jennings_al@tsu.edu
JENNINGS, Barbara .... 641-844-5522 170 G
barb.jennings@iavalley.edu
JENNINGS, Bill .... 541-880-2247 383 E
jenningsb@klamathcc.edu
JENNINGS, Bret .... 256-765-4658.... 9 A
nmjennings@una.edu
JENNINGS, Carlette .... 404-876-1227 117 A
carlette.jennings@bccr.edu
JENNINGS, Charla .... 870-743-3000.. 20 E
charlam@northark.edu
JENNINGS, Chris .... 626-387-5763.. 26 U
cjennings@apu.edu
JENNINGS, Chris .... 213-624-1200.. 42 N
cjennings@fidm.edu
JENNINGS, Christal .... 610-225-5102 394 E
cjenning@eastern.edu
JENNINGS, Clarence ..... 734-677-5003 238 G
cjennings@wccnet.edu
JENNINGS, David, C ...... 845-675-4616 319 C
david.jennings@nyack.edu
JENNINGS, Eli .... 808-853-1040 129 F
elijennings@pacrim.edu
JENNINGS, Hope .... 937-775-4818 374 B
hope.jennings@wright.edu
JENNINGS, Jamie .... 541-880-2228 383 E
jennings@klamathcc.edu
JENNINGS, Lisa .... 603-645-9770 282 C
l.jennings@snhu.edu
JENNINGS, Liz .... 651-361-3411 243 D
liz.jennings@mcnallysmith.edu
JENNINGS, Lynn .... 252-335-0821 342 D
lynn_jennings@albemarle.edu
JENNINGS, Patricia .... 203-596-4693.. 87 H
pjennings@post.edu
JENNINGS, Sarah, E ..... 870-235-4040.. 21 F
sejennings@saumag.edu
JENNINGS, Susan .... 423-697-2576 436 F
susan.jennings@chattanoogastate.edu
JENNINGS, Thomas, W . 850-645-9655 110 A
tjennings@fsu.edu
JENNINGS, Todd .... 909-537-5655.. 33 D
tjennin@csusb.edu
JENNISON, Barry .... 423-697-2614 436 F
barry.jennison@chattanoogastate.edu
JENNUM, Joe .... 909-274-4630.. 52 I
jjennum@mtsac.edu
JENOURE, Rita .... 202-651-5005.. 91 H
rita.jenoure@gallaudet.edu
JENSEN, Al .... 360-752-8571 492 H
ajensen@btc.edu
JENSEN, Brenda .... 808-236-3533 129 C
bjensen@hpu.edu
JENSEN, Brian, C .... 724-847-6134 395 J
bcjensen@geneva.edu
JENSEN, Christopher ..... 270-745-5065 190 F
christopher.jensen@wku.edu
JENSEN, Chuck .... 970-339-6509.. 76 E
chuck.jensen@aims.edu
JENSEN, Dale .... 417-865-2815 260 B
jensend@evangel.edu
JENSEN, Dan .... 712-279-3734 173 B
dan.jensen@stlukescollege.edu
JENSEN, Dan .... 817-735-2500 466 D
danny.jensen@unthsc.edu
JENSEN, David, H .... 512-404-4821 443 I
djensen@austinseminary.edu
JENSEN, Doug .... 661-722-6300.. 26 C
djensen@avc.edu
JENSEN, Douglas, J ...... 815-921-4001 150 A
d.jensen@rockvalleycollege.edu
JENSEN, Eric, R .... 309-556-3151 141 B
president@iwu.edu
JENSEN, Gail, M .... 402-280-3727 274 D
gailjensen@creighton.edu
JENSEN, Jed .... 307-686-0254 516 P
jjensen@sheridan.edu
JENSEN, Jennifer, M ..... 610-758-3705 400 B
jmj313@lehigh.edu
JENSEN, John, A .... 540-458-8604 491 G
jensenj@wlu.edu
JENSEN, Joshua .... 509-527-5768 500 G
jensenj@whitman.edu
JENSEN, Kae .... 208-562-3336 132 A
kaejensen@cwidaho.cc
JENSEN, Katie .... 425-388-9581 494 F
JENSEN, Kevin .... 607-436-2158 325 E
kevin.jensen@oneonta.edu
JENSEN, Kim .... 303-494-7988.. 77 A
JENSEN, Larry .... 802-776-5236 474 H
larry.jensen@csj.edu
JENSEN, Laura .... 970-491-5939.. 78 N
l.jensen@colostate.edu
JENSEN, Laura .... 239-590-1155 109 C
ljensen@fgcu.edu
JENSEN, Laurie .... 218-723-2380 245 C
laurie.jensen@lsc.edu
JENSEN, Megan .... 509-574-4635 500 I
mjensen@yvcc.edu
JENSEN, Melissa .... 208-426-1093 131 C
melissajensen@boisestate.edu
JENSEN, Melissa .... 319-398-5491 171 F
melissa.jensen@kirkwood.edu
JENSEN, Michael, E .... 801-422-4327 471 E
jensen@byu.edu
JENSEN, Nathan .... 714-432-5909.. 38 H
njensen@occ.cccd.edu
JENSEN, Patricia .... 414-382-6321 506 A
JENSEN, Paul .... 708-456-0300 153 E
pauljensen@triton.edu
JENSEN, Paul, E .... 215-895-2122 394 C
paul.eric.jensen@drexel.edu
JENSEN, Peter, E .... 605-677-5341 428 E
pete.jensen@usd.edu
JENSEN, Riki .... 989-328-1220 234 D
riki.jensen@montcalm.edu
JENSEN, Robert .... 619-201-8698.. 60 A
robert.jensen@sdcc.edu
JENSEN, Sandra .... 319-234-5748 169 H
sandra.jensen@hawkeyecollege.edu
JENSEN, Scott .... 316-978-3693 182 F
scott.jensen@wichita.edu
JENSEN, Sol .... 815-753-2253 147 H
sjensen1@niu.edu
JENSEN, Stanley, C .... 313-845-9650 231 B
sjensen@hfcc.edu
JENSEN, Steve, M .... 563-588-8000 169 B
smjensen@emmaus.edu
JENSEN, Steven .... 713-831-7864 466 J
jensensj@stthom.edu
JENSEN, Steven, M .... 330-471-8521 364 H
jensen@malone.edu
JENSEN, Tom, P .... 618-537-6959 145 C
tpjensen@mckendree.edu
JENSEN, Tyler .... 307-674-6446 516 P
tjensen@sheridan.edu
JENSEN, Valerie .... 707-468-3280.. 51 E
vjensen@mendocino.edu
JENSON, Hal, B .... 269-337-4400 239 I
JENSON, Hal, B .... 269-337-4500 239 E
hal.jenson@med.wmich.edu
JENSON, Jody .... 406-477-6215 270 I
JENSON, John .... 671-735-2694 520 B
jjenson@triton.uog.edu
JENSON, Linda .... 817-515-4521 458 B
linda.jenson@tccd.edu
JENT, Laura .... 931-393-1544 437 C
ljent@mscc.edu
JEONG, Inho .... 213-386-0080.. 52 C
JEONG, Peter .... 973-748-9000 284 A
peter_jeong@bloomfield.edu
JEONG, Wooseob .... 620-341-5203 177 B
wjeong1@emporia.edu
JEPSON, Darla .... 815-802-8832 142 C
djepson@kcc.edu
JEPSON, Lyle .... 802-770-7061 477 A
lyle.jepson@castleton.edu
JERABEK, Megan .... 610-436-2205 407 D
mjerabek@wcupa.edu
JERALDS, Jeri Ann .... 314-837-6777 266 A
jjeralds@stlchristian.edu
JERDAN, David .... 215-968-8184 390 I
david.jerdan@bucks.edu
JERDINE, Kimberly .... 248-204-3943 233 A
kosantows@ltu.edu
JEREBKO, Peter, J .... 716-851-1221 307 I
jerebko@ecc.edu
JEREMIAH, David .... 619-201-8995.. 65 C
david.jeremiah@socalsem.edu
JERGOVIC, Diana .... 626-395-6214.. 29 I
jergovic@caltech.edu
JERIES, John .... 630-829-6584 133 I
jeries@ben.edu
JERMAN, Willa, H .... 919-866-5701 347 D
whjerman@waketech.edu
JERMAN LIGUORI,
Denise .... 201-447-7480 283 I
djerman@bergen.edu
JERMIER, James .... 563-387-1506 171 I
jermja01@luther.edu
JERNBERG, Beth .... 605-331-6644 429 D
beth.jernberg@usiouxfalls.edu
JERNBERG, Leslie .... 208-535-5353 131 G
leslie.jernberg@my.eitc.edu
JERNIEAN, Denise .... 615-361-7555 431 G
djerniean@daymarinstitute.edu
JERNIGAN, Julie .... 972-721-4127 464 E
jjernigan@udallas.edu
JERNIGAN, Justin .... 678-407-5879 119 F
jjerniga@ggc.edu
JERNIGAN, Ron .... 505-566-3035 296 A
jerniganr@sanjuancollege.edu
JERNIGAN, Tony .... 301-934-7715 203 D
tjernigan@csmd.edu
JEROME, Allison .... 808-735-4852 129 A
ajerome@chaminade.edu
JEROME, Denny .... 641-585-8183 174 B
jeromed@waldorf.edu
JEROME, Etido, S .... 504-520-7593 198 D
ejerome@xula.edu
JEROME, Leslie .... 914-632-5400 315 K
ljerome@monroecollege.edu
JEROME, Marc, M .... 718-933-6700 315 K
mjerome@monroecollege.edu
JEROME, Priya .... 619-482-6557.. 65 H
pjerome@swccd.edu
JERRY, Lisa .... 516-726-5799 519 C
jerryl@usmma.edu
JERSKY, Brian .... 562-985-4128.. 32 C
brian.jersky@csulb.edu
JERUE, James, M .... 401-456-8262 417 A
jjerue@ric.edu
JERZAK, Page, A .... 407-582-3865 113 F
pjerzak@valenciacollege.edu
JESENSKY, Danielle .... 432-552-2100 469 D
jesensky_d@utpb.edu
JESIONOWSKI,
Rosemary, K .... 540-654-2037 486 D
rjesiono@umw.edu
JESME, Shannon .... 218-683-8577 246 F
shannon.jesme@northlandcollege.edu
JESPERSEN,
Christopher .... 706-864-1771 127 B
christopher.jespersen@ung.edu
JESSE, III, John, J .... 402-280-3835 274 D
johnjesse@creighton.edu
JESSEE, Pamela .... 815-836-5691 143 E
jesseepa@lewisu.edu
JESSELL, Kenneth .... 305-348-2101 109 D
kenneth.jessell@fiu.edu
JESSIE, Jason .... 334-222-6591.... 2 H
jjessie@lbwcc.edu
JESSOGNE, Cheryl .... 312-499-4186 151 F
cjessogne@saic.edu
JESSON, Andrew, R .... 530-226-4142.. 64 B
ajesson@simpsonu.edu
JESSOP, Craig .... 435-797-3046 473 C
craig.jessop@usu.edu
JESSUP, Anita, R .... 909-869-4426.. 31 A
arjessup@cpp.edu
JESSUP, Jim .... 916-577-2200.. 75 B
jjessup@jessup.edu
JESSUP, Len .... 702-895-3201 279 D
len.jessup@unlv.edu
JESSUP, Rhonda, E .... 919-658-7754 349 F
rjessup@umo.edu
JESSUP, Tracy, C .... 704-406-4279 337 H
tjessup@gardner-webb.edu
JESTER, Christopher ...... 302-736-2468.. 90 J
christopher.jester@wesley.edu
JESUS CESAREO,
Lourdes .... 787-763-6700 522 N
ldjesus@se-pr.edu
JETER, Everett .... 704-922-6226 343 D
jeter.everett@gaston.edu
JETER, Jeff .... 817-272-2101 467 B
jeter@uta.edu
JETER, Pamela .... 253-589-6085 493 F
pamela.jeter@cptc.edu
JETER-TWILLEY,
Rhonda .... 301-860-3132 208 E
rjeter@bowiestate.edu
JETT, Andy .... 913-344-1247 174 J
andy.jett@bakeru.edu
JETT, Melissa .... 417-255-7955 263 I
melissajett@missouristate.edu
JETT, Susan, P .... 864-424-8027 425 G
jettsp@mailbox.sc.edu
JETT, Wendy .... 541-463-5803 383 F
jettw@lanecc.edu
JETTE, Tracey .... 406-265-3708 272 C
tracey.jette@msun.edu
JETTON, Kent .... 731-286-3250 437 A
jetton@dscc.edu
JEW, Carl .... 415-561-1875.. 37 H
cjew@ccsf.edu
JEWELL, Christy .... 916-577-2200.. 75 B
cjewell@jessup.edu
JEWELL, David .... 307-766-5760 517 B
david.jewell@uwyo.edu
JEWELL, Kirk .... 405-385-5100 377 F
kjewell@osugiving.com
JEWELL, Nikki .... 269-965-3931 232 A
jewelln@kellogg.edu
JEWELL, Scott .... 617-349-8714 216 D
sjewell@lesley.edu
JEWELL, Shelley .... 615-460-6643 430 D
shelley.jewell@elmont.edu
JEWETT, Darla .... 207-741-5584 200 C
djewett@smccme.edu
JEWETT, John .... 386-752-1822.. 99 J
john.jewett@fgc.edu
JEWSBURY, Evan .... 417-625-9805 263 G
jewsbury-e@mssu.edu
JEZAK, Patricia .... 567-661-2650 369 A
patricia_jezak@owens.edu
JEZEK, Kenda .... 918-495-6198 378 H
kjezek@oru.edu
JEZEK-TAUSSIG,
Jennifer .... 314-516-5428 268 E
jezektaussig@umsl.edu
JEZIORSKI, Jennifer ...... 847-735-5242 142 H
jeziorski@lakeforest.edu
JHA, Mona .... 646-312-4542 301 B
mona.jha@baruch.cuny.edu
JHAJ, Sukhwant, S .... 503-725-2277 386 D
jhaj@pdx.edu
JHANJI, Andy, A .... 850-644-4747 110 A
ajhanji@foundation.fsu.edu
JHASHI, Tamara .... 914-674-7803 314 I
tjhashi@mercy.edu
JI, Zhe .... 812-888-5886 165 E
zji@vinu.edu
JI, Zhe .... 812-888-4156 165 E
zji@vinu.edu
JIA, Ning .... 413-565-1000 211 C
njia@baypath.edu
JIAMBALVO, Jim .... 206-543-9132 499 D
jjiambal@uw.edu
JIANG, Shaojie .... 608-796-3172 512 R
sjiang@viterbo.edu
JIE, Yiyun .... 334-229-6859.... 4 A
yjiek@alasu.edu
JIGA, Anthony .... 212-998-2278 318 D
anthony.jiga@nyu.edu
JILES, Michael .... 678-664-0534 128 F
michael.jiles@westgatech.edu
JIMÉNEZ, Mayra .... 787-250-8581 528 F
mayra.jimenez@upr.edu
JIMÉNEZ-PÉREZ, Nancy 787-993-8877 527 G
nancy.jimenez1@upr.edu
JIMENEZ, Allison .... 248-218-2268 236 C
ajimenez@rc.edu
JIMENEZ, Amanda .... 304-865-6003 502 C
amanda.jimenez@ovu.edu
JIMENEZ, Andre .... 707-654-1186.. 32 E
bookstore@csum.edu
JIMENEZ, Annie, A .... 480-732-7391.. 13 E
a.jimenez@cgc.edu

JIMENEZ, Araceli .... 661-726-1911.. 68 E
araceli.jimenez@uav.edu

JIMENEZ, Asdrubal .... 787-891-0925 523 G
ajimenez@aguadilla.inter.edu

JIMENEZ, Audra .... 706-754-7766 123 G
ajimenez@northgatech.edu

JIMENEZ, Camilo .... 315-733-2307 332 F
cjimenez@uscny.edu

JIMENEZ, Carlos .... 719-389-7153.. 77 J
cjimenez@coloradocollege.edu

JIMENEZ, Carlos .... 787-890-2681 527 E
c.jimenez@upr.edu

JIMENEZ, Elena .... 773-896-2400 135 G
ejimenez@ctschicago.edu

JIMENEZ, Eva .... 530-242-7565.. 63 I
ejimenez@shastacollege.edu

JIMENEZ, Irma .... 787-878-6000 522 Q
ijimenez@icprjc.edu

JIMENEZ, Julie .... 719-549-3222.. 81 M
julie.jimenez@pueblocc.edu

JIMENEZ, Louis, E .... 512-245-3562 463 A
lej27@txstate.edu

JIMENEZ, Misael .... 787-834-9595 526 E
mjimenez@uaa.edu

JIMENEZ, Obed .... 787-834-9595 526 E
ojimenez@uaa.edu

JIMENEZ, Rachel .... 909-607-9226.. 37 L
rachel.jimenez@cgu.edu

JIMENEZ, Silverio .... 787-882-2065 526 D
dispensario@unitecpr.net

JIMENEZ, Tomas .... 787-766-1912 524 A
tjimenez@inter.edu

JIMENEZ, Whitney .... 765-641-4131 156 A
wmjimenez@anderson.edu

JIMENEZ, Zoe .... 787-850-9354 528 B
zoe.jimenez@upr.edu

JIMENEZ CHAFEY,
Maria .... 787-764-0000 528 F
maria.jimenez16@upr.edu

JIMENEZ-SANDOVAL,
Saul .... 559-278-3056.. 32 A
ssandoval@csufresno.edu

JIMINEZ, Laura .... 408-848-4743.. 44 B
0282mgr@fheg.follett.com

JIMISON, Nancy, M .... 804-706-5024 488 D
njiminson@jtcc.edu

JIMMERSON, Judy .... 229-430-3514 114 J
jjimmerson@albanytech.edu

JIN, David-Xudong .... 410-462-8215 202 F
djin@bccc.edu

JIN, Elizabeth .... 626-289-7719.. 24 I
ejin@amu.edu

JIN, Steve .... 916-577-2200.. 75 B
sjin@jessup.edu

JIN, Young Chung .... 213-381-0081.. 46 I
yjin@irus.edu

JINGOZIAN, Sunshine .. 407-264-9400.. 93 B

JINGOZIAN, Sunshine .. 407-618-5900.. 93 B

JINGOZIAN, Sunshine .. 407-926-2000.. 93 B

JINKINS, Michael .... 502-895-3411 188 A
mjinkins@lpts.edu

JINRIGHT, Dwight .... 205-358-8543.... 8 E
jinrightd@montevallo.edu

JIRAK, Randy .... 785-227-3380 175 E
jirakr@bethanylb.edu

JIRON, Bill .... 541-956-7188 386 G
bjiron@roguecc.edu

JIROUSEK, Nancy .... 440-826-2298 357 B
njirouse@bw.edu

JIROVEC, Kelly .... 402-826-8265 274 E
kelly.jirovec@doane.edu

JIRU, Mintesinot .... 410-951-4139 208 F
mjiru@coppin.edu

JIWANI, Nazleen .... 713-646-1869 456 H
njiwani@stcl.edu

JLAGER, Joan .... 269-806-8688 184 G
joan.jlager@frontier.edu

JO, Hyun Seok .... 770-220-7918 119 D
chs@gcuniv.edu

JOACHIM KITZMAN,
Patricia .... 641-628-5271 167 D
kitzmanp@central.edu

JOANIS, Jessica, L .... 920-748-8164 509 H
joanisj@ripon.edu

JOANIS, Pierre, D .... 570-577-1631 390 H
p.joanis@bucknell.edu

JOBE, Jarrett .... 405-974-2626 380 J
jjobe@uco.edu

JOBE, Nicholas .... 513-231-2223 356 M
njobe@athenaeum.edu

JOBE, Steve .... 812-866-7005 158 C
jobe@hanover.edu

JOBSON, John, E .... 616-395-7800 231 D
jobson@hope.edu

JOBSON, Sarah .... 425-889-5597 496 E
sarah.jobson@northwestu.edu

JOBST, Ken, B .... 502-776-1443 188 F
kjobst@simmonscollegeky.edu

JOCHEMS, Jeff .... 417-447-7932 264 K
jochemsj@otc.edu

JODIS, Stephen, M .... 724-805-2358 410 B
stephen.jodis@email.stvincent.edu

JODOIN, Elizabeth .... 864-503-5195 425 H
ejodoin@uscupstate.edu

JOEL PEREZ, Joel .... 562-907-4233.. 75 A
jperez@whittier.edu

JOENS, Angela .... 530-752-9328.. 68 H
amjoens@ucdavis.edu

JOENSEN, William, M ... 563-588-7104 171 H
william.joensen@loras.edu

JOERSCHKE, Bonnie, C . 706-542-8208 127 A
bonniej@uga.edu

JOFEN, Moshe .... 718-269-4080 300 J

JOHANNES, Cheri .... 406-657-2158 272 B
cjohannes@msubillings.edu

JOHANNES, Stephen ..... 706-886-6831 126 F
sjohannes@tfc.edu

JOHANNESEN,
Christine .... 518-255-5522 328 C
johanncm@cobleskill.edu

JOHANNSEN, Danelle .... 712-279-3377 173 B
danelle.johannsen@stlukescollege.edu

JOHANNSEN,
Danelle, D .... 712-279-3377 173 B
danelle.johannsen@stlukescollege.edu

JOHANSEN, Bob, L .... 626-815-4603.. 26 U
bjohansen@apu.edu

JOHANSEN, Jane .... 843-349-2227 420 A

JOHANSEN, Misty .... 312-362-7324 137 C
mjohans1@depaul.edu

JOHANSEN, Paul .... 219-785-5344 163 E
johansen@pnw.edu

JOHANSON, Rod .... 503-517-1010 388 A
rjohanson@warnerpacific.edu

JOHANSSON,
Theresa, C .... 540-231-8205 490 F
theresaj@vt.edu

JOHN, Adam .... 620-227-9359 176 N
ajohn@dc3.edu

JOHN, Daphne .... 440-775-8410 367 B
djohn@oberlin.edu

JOHN, III, David, R ...... 704-366-4853 255 E
djohn@rts.edu

JOHN, Jeremy .... 540-261-8598 485 G
jeremy.john@svu.edu

JOHN, Kristi .... 405-224-3140 381 B

JOHN, JR., Leon, S ...... 570-422-3659 406 A
ljohn2@esu.edu

JOHN, Mary .... 818-947-2313.. 49 G
johnms@lavc.edu

JOHN, Rebecca .... 612-330-1482 240 G
rjohn@augsburg.edu

JOHN, Rowan .... 219-989-2255 163 E
rowan@pnw.edu

JOHN, Samuel .... 201-447-7868 283 I
sjohn@bergen.edu

JOHN, Stephen, S .... 806-716-2217 456 F
sjohn@southplainscollege.edu

JOHNDROW, David, A .. 570-674-6762 401 M
djohndro@misericordia.edu

JOHNOSON, April .... 301-860-3831 208 E
aljohnson@bowiestate.edu

JOHNS, Chris .... 334-229-4382.... 4 A
cjohns@alasu.edu

JOHNS, David .... 606-546-4151 189 I
djohns@unionky.edu

JOHNS, Greg .... 417-865-2815 260 B
johnsg@evangel.edu

JOHNS, Jeffrey .... 662-846-4155 252 H
jjohns@deltastate.edu

JOHNS, Krista .... 925-485-5244.. 36 B
kjohns@clpccd.org

JOHNS, Patrick .... 218-733-7600 245 C
p.johns@lsc.edu

JOHNS, Priscilla, C .... 671-735-5517 519 H
priscilla.johns@guamcc.edu

JOHNS, Sean .... 763-433-1124 244 A
sean.johns@anokaramsey.edu

JOHNS, Sheila, R .... 308-635-6366 278 B
johnss23@wncc.edu

JOHNS, Timothy .... 920-206-2332 508 A
timothy.johns@mbu.edu

JOHNS, Xenia .... 770-228-7348 126 B
xjohns@sctech.edu

JOHNS-HINES,
Stephani .... 785-309-3103 181 D
stephani.johnshines@salinatech.edu

JOHNSEN, David, C .... 319-335-7144 166 G
david-johnsen@uiowa.edu

JOHNSEN, James, R ..... 907-450-8000.... 9 I
ua.president@alaska.edu

JOHNSEN, John .... 315-792-3122 332 H
jjohnsen@utica.edu

JOHNSON, Aaron .... 303-762-6933.. 79 G
aaron.johnson@denverseminary.edu

JOHNSON, Abe .... 972-377-1551 446 I
ajohnson@collin.edu

JOHNSON, Adam .... 651-846-1782 247 G
adam.johnson@saintpaul.edu

JOHNSON, Adam .... 405-974-2385 380 J
adjohnson@uco.edu

JOHNSON, Alan .... 662-329-7411 254 F
alan.johnson@sodexo.com

JOHNSON, JR.,
Albert, D .... 580-581-2999 375 A
aljohnson@cameron.edu

JOHNSON, Alesa .... 606-451-6693 186 G
alesa.johnson@kctcs.edu

JOHNSON, Alex .... 617-726-2947 222 A

JOHNSON, Alex .... 216-987-4853 360 E
alex.johnson@tri-c.edu

JOHNSON, Alton .... 937-376-6276 358 I
ajohnson@centralstate.edu

JOHNSON, Amy .... 509-359-2292 494 D
amyjohns@ewu.edu

JOHNSON, Amy .... 731-286-3398 437 A
ajohnson@dscc.edu

JOHNSON, Andrea .... 206-934-3628 497 H
andrea.johnson@seattlecolleges.edu

JOHNSON, Andrea .... 870-236-6901.. 19 D
ajohnson@crc.edu

JOHNSON, Andrew .... 610-799-1155 400 A
ajohnson23@lccc.edu

JOHNSON, Andrew, W .. 316-284-5230 175 F
ajohnson@bethelks.edu

JOHNSON, Angela .... 502-213-2141 186 C
angela.johnson@kctcs.edu

JOHNSON, Angela .... 334-808-6261.... 7 E
ajohnson@troy.edu

JOHNSON, Angela .... 216-987-4213 360 E
angela.johnson@tri-c.edu

JOHNSON, Anna .... 740-753-6553 362 K
johnsona@hocking.edu

JOHNSON, Anthony ...... 401-454-6638 417 B
ajohnson@risd.edu

JOHNSON, Antoinette .... 757-925-6340 489 B
ajohnson@pdc.edu

JOHNSON, April .... 334-670-3402.... 7 E
acjohnson@troy.edu

JOHNSON, Arlene .... 256-726-7287.... 6 E
ajohnson@oakwood.edu

JOHNSON, Arvid, C .... 815-740-3369 154 G
ajohnson@stfrancis.edu

JOHNSON, Ashlee .... 314-392-2305 263 F
johnsona@mobap.edu

JOHNSON, Barbara .... 609-777-4351 292 B
bjohnson@tesu.edu

JOHNSON, Barbara .... 570-372-4404 410 H
johnsonbarbara@susqu.edu

JOHNSON, Barry .... 408-864-5678.. 43 E
johnsonbarry@deanza.edu

JOHNSON, Barry .... 704-406-4440 337 H
bjohnson@gardner-webb.edu

JOHNSON, Bart .... 218-322-2388 245 B
bart.johnson@itascacc.edu

JOHNSON, Bart .... 218-322-2401 245 B
bart.johnson@itascacc.edu

JOHNSON, Becky .... 903-983-8223 451 F
rjohnson@kilgore.edu

JOHNSON, Betsy .... 419-372-2651 357 F
betsyj@bgsu.edu

JOHNSON, Bill .... 209-932-2824.. 70 F
bjohnson3@pacific.edu

JOHNSON, Billy .... 404-627-2681 116 E
billy.johnson@beulah.edu

JOHNSON, Bonnie .... 641-673-1036 174 F
johnsonb@wmpenn.edu

JOHNSON, Brad .... 859-858-3511 183 D
bjohnson@asbury.edu

JOHNSON, Brad .... 417-328-1805 267 A
bjohnson@sbuniv.edu

JOHNSON, Brad .... 360-650-6400 500 E
brad.johnson@wwu.edu

JOHNSON, Brad, W .... 903-434-8102 453 M
bjohnson@ntcc.edu

JOHNSON, Bradley .... 239-304-7098.. 95 C
bradley.johnson@avemaria.edu

JOHNSON, Brandi .... 978-232-3096 214 G
bjohnson@endicott.edu

JOHNSON, Brandon .... 816-501-2400 257 G
brandon.johnson@avila.edu

JOHNSON, Brenda .... 510-780-4500.. 48 D
bjohnson@lifewest.edu

JOHNSON, Brenda .... 773-702-8743 153 F
brendajohnson@uchicago.edu

JOHNSON, Brenda .... 510-981-2830.. 56 F
bjohnson@peralta.edu

JOHNSON, Brian .... 504-314-2486 196 D
johnson@tulane.edu

JOHNSON, Brian, D .... 208-885-6246 132 I
johnsonb@uidaho.edu

JOHNSON, Brian, T .... 219-464-6732 165 D
brian.johnson1@valpo.edu

JOHNSON, Brooke .... 608-757-7654 513 D
bjohnson97@blackhawk.edu

JOHNSON, Bryan .... 610-526-1582 389 B
bryan.johnson@theamericancollege.edu

JOHNSON, Bryan, M ..... 205-726-4036.... 6 G
bmjohnso@samford.edu

JOHNSON, C. Lynn .... 320-222-5208 247 B
lynn.johnson@ridgewater.edu

JOHNSON, Calvin, M .... 334-844-4546.... 4 D
johncal@auburn.edu

JOHNSON, Carl .... 847-317-7005 153 D
cjohnson@tiu.edu

JOHNSON, Carl .... 303-871-3111.. 83 E
cdjohnson@du.edu

JOHNSON, Carl .... 817-461-8741 442 L
cjohnson@abu.edu

JOHNSON, Carley .... 215-717-6380 412 F
cajohnson@uarts.edu

JOHNSON, Carol .... 404-880-6992 117 H
cjohnson@cau.edu

JOHNSON, Carol .... 704-878-3225 344 H
cjohnson@mitchellcc.edu

JOHNSON, Casie .... 507-453-2663 245 G
cjohnson@southeastmn.edu

JOHNSON, Cass .... 312-362-5596 137 C
cjohn161@depaul.edu

JOHNSON,
Cassandra, M .... 903-927-3336 471 B
cmjohnson@wileyc.edu

JOHNSON, Catherine ..... 207-780-4141 201 H
catherine.johnson@maine.edu

JOHNSON, Catherine ..... 585-785-1212 308 D
catherine.johnson@flcc.edu

JOHNSON,
Catherine, W .... 336-506-4237 340 L
cathy.johnson@alamancecc.edu

JOHNSON, Chad .... 952-888-4777 249 F
cgjohnson@nwhealth.edu

JOHNSON, Charles, R ... 812-888-4208 165 E
president@vinu.edu

JOHNSON, Charlie .... 405-974-2315 380 J
chjohnson@uco.edu

JOHNSON, Charlotte ..... 909-621-8277.. 63 F
deanofstudentsoffice@scrippscollege.edu

JOHNSON, Charlotte ..... 870-584-1115.. 22 F
cjohnson@cccua.edu

JOHNSON, Cheryl .... 707-826-4503.. 34 A
cheryl.johnson@humboldt.edu

JOHNSON, Cheryl, L .... 412-624-8030 412 I
clj@pitt.edu

JOHNSON, Cheryll, A ... 734-432-5315 233 C
cjohnson@madonna.edu

JOHNSON, Chris .... 303-762-6924.. 79 G
chris.johnson@denverseminary.edu

JOHNSON, Chris .... 251-580-2222.... 1 I
chris.johnson@faulknerstate.edu

JOHNSON, Chris .... 434-592-3015 482 D
cjohnson@liberty.edu

JOHNSON, Christine ..... 509-434-5006 493 H
cjohnson@ccs.spokane.edu

JOHNSON, Christine ..... 509-434-5006 493 I
christine.johnson@ccs.spokane.edu

JOHNSON, Christine, L 859-858-2176 183 C

JOHNSON, Christol .... 214-860-2627 448 A
christoljohnson@dcccd.edu

JOHNSON, Christopher . 209-239-4500 493 D

JOHNSON, Christopher . 805-965-0581.. 62 E
ckjohnson2@sbcc.edu

JOHNSON, Christopher . 217-732-3155 143 G
cjohnson@lincolncollege.edu

JOHNSON, Christopher . 315-792-3340 332 H
cmjohnson@utica.edu

JOHNSON, Christopher . 940-898-3206 464 A
cjohnson44@twu.edu

JOHNSON, Cindi Beth .. 651-255-6137 250 D
cbjohnson@unitedseminary.edu

JOHNSON, Cindy .... 620-235-4185 180 J
cynthia.johnson@pittstate.edu

JOHNSON, Cindy, K ..... 816-604-1011 262 F
cindy.johnson@mcckc.edu

JOHNSON, JR., Clyde .. 443-552-1659 205 C
cjohnson01@mica.edu

JOHNSON, Connie .... 719-598-0200.. 79 B
cjohnson@coloradotech.edu

JOHNSON, Cornelius ..... 214-860-2496 448 A
cjohnson@dcccd.edu

JOHNSON, Courtney ..... 610-341-5840 394 E
cjohns26@eastern.edu

JOHNSON, Craig .... 870-972-2852.. 18 A
crjohnso@astate.edu

JOHNSON, Craig .... 773-244-5637 147 F
crjohnson@northpark.edu

JOHNSON, Croslena ..... 864-646-1568 424 F
cjohnso5@tctc.edu

JOHNSON, Curtis .... 501-420-1211.. 17 I
curtis.johnson@arkansasbaptist.edu

JOHNSON, Cuthrell .... 336-750-2230 352 D
johnsonc@wssu.edu

JOHNSON, Cydney, M .. 315-684-6036 329 F
johnsocm@morrisville.edu

JOHNSON, Cynda Ann . 540-526-2559 491 B
cajohnson@vt.edu

JOHNSON, Cyndy .... 512-448-8657 455 I
cjohns12@stedwards.edu

JOHNSON, Cynthia .... 360-486-8131 497 F
cjohnson@stmartin.edu

JOHNSON, D. Nichole .. 614-236-6945 358 A
njohnson@capital.edu

JOHNSON, Dacia .... 218-736-1512 245 H
dacia.johnson@minnesota.edu

JOHNSON, Dale .... 510-780-4500.. 48 D
djohnson@lifewest.edu

JOHNSON, Damon .... 512-505-3060 451 A

JOHNSON, Danae .... 229-226-1621 126 E
djohnson@thomasu.edu

JOHNSON, Danette .... 604-274-1252 311 D
djohnson@ithaca.edu

JOHNSON, Danette .... 804-524-5070 491 A
dljohnson@vsu.edu

JOHNSON, Daniel .... 701-662-1515 355 A
dan.johnson@lrsc.edu

JOHNSON, Daniel .... 918-444-4211 376 G
johnso89@nsuok.edu

JOHNSON, Daniel .... 206-934-6709 497 J
daniel.johnson@seattlecolleges.edu

JOHNSON, Daniel .... 803-812-7353 425 D
johns943@mailbox.sc.edu

JOHNSON, Daniel, R .. 203-582-8930.. 88 A
dan.johnson@quinnipiac.edu

JOHNSON, Daniel, W ... 414-443-8952 513 A
daniel.johnson@wlc.edu

JOHNSON, Danny .... 406-586-3585 271 E
djohnson@montanabiblecollege.edu

JOHNSON, Darryl .... 336-517-2358 335 K
djohnson@bennett.edu

JOHNSON, Darryl .... 206-934-3646 497 H
darryl.johnson@seattlecolleges.edu

JOHNSON, Daryl .... 651-793-1227 245 E
daryl.johnson@metrostate.edu

JOHNSON, David .... 716-338-1002 311 F
davejohnson@mail.sunyjcc.edu

JOHNSON, David .... 812-855-8908 159 H
vpem@indiana.edu

JOHNSON, David .... 606-368-6031 182 H
davidjohnson@alc.edu

JOHNSON, David .... 256-824-6288.... 8 C
david.johnson@uah.edu

JOHNSON, David, B ..... 812-855-8908 159 G
vpem@indiana.edu

JOHNSON, David, J ...... 513-745-3202 374 D
johnsond8@xavier.edu

JOHNSON, David, M ..... 650-306-3298.. 61 R
johnsond@smccd.edu

JOHNSON, David, N ..... 919-209-2050 344 C
dnjohnson@johnstoncc.edu

JOHNSON, Deadre .... 202-885-2721.. 91 C
deadrej@american.edu

JOHNSON, Dean, L .... 906-487-2668 234 A
dean@mtu.edu

JOHNSON, Debbie .... 218-733-6904 245 C
debra.johnson@lsc.edu

JOHNSON, Deborah ...... 806-457-4200 449 D
djohnson@fpctx.edu

JOHNSON, Deborah ...... 618-634-3374 151 G
deborahj@shawneecc.edu

JOHNSON, Deborah ...... 419-251-1821 365 C
deborah.johnson@mercycollege.edu

JOHNSON, Deborah ...... 484-365-7429 400 E
dejohnson@lincoln.edu

JOHNSON, Debra, J ...... 540-985-8492 482 A
djjohnson@jchs.edu

JOHNSON, Deirdra, G ... 410-334-2902 210 C
djohnson@worwic.edu

JOHNSON, Demetrius ... 703-284-5960 483 A
demetrius.johnson@marymount.edu

JOHNSON, Dennis .... 719-549-3035.. 81 M
dennis.johnson@pueblocc.edu

JOHNSON, Derek .... 608-663-2324 507 D
derekjohnson@edgewood.edu

JOHNSON, Derrick .... 252-335-3291 350 A
dajohnson2@ecsu.edu

JOHNSON, Deshawn ..... 248-204-2117 233 A
djohnson@ltu.edu

JOHNSON, DeWayne .... 909-915-1121.. 40 G

JOHNSON, Dexter .... 425-564-4261 492 G
dexter.johnson@bellevuecollege.edu

JOHNSON, Diana .... 508-373-9468 211 F
diana.johnson@becker.edu

JOHNSON, Diana .... 479-725-4681.. 20 F
djohnson@nwacc.edu

JOHNSON, Diane .... 518-828-4181 305 D
diane.johnson@sunycgcc.edu

JOHNSON, Diane .... 801-883-8336 472 B
djohnson@new.edu

JOHNSON, Donielle, R . 972-860-7372 447 I
doniellejohnson@dcccd.edu

JOHNSON, Donnie .... 309-672-5513 145 E
djohnson@methodistcol.edu

JOHNSON, Dorianne ..... 937-708-5777 373 H
djohnson@wilberforce.edu

JOHNSON, Doris .... 213-487-0150.. 41 K
omcdirector@dula.edu

JOHNSON, Doris .... 972-524-3341 457 H

JOHNSON, Doug .... 785-460-5411 176 L
doug.johnson@colbycc.edu

JOHNSON, Douglas, P . 207-581-1392 201 B
douglasj@maine.edu

JOHNSON, Dreand, R ... 515-574-1149 170 C
djohnson@iowacentral.edu

JOHNSON, Duane .... 701-224-5789 354 F
duane.johnson.1@bismarckstate.edu

JOHNSON, Dustin .... 715-394-8122 512 B
djohns75@uwsuper.edu

JOHNSON, Earl .... 918-631-3142 381 C
earl-johnson@utulsa.edu

JOHNSON, Eartha .... 504-816-4723 191 E
ejohnson@dillard.edu

JOHNSON, Edward .... 716-827-2456 331 K
johnsone@trocaire.edu

JOHNSON, Elise .... 586-498-4119 233 B
johnsonem@macomb.edu

JOHNSON, Elizabeth ..... 203-596-4638.. 87 H
ejohnson@post.edu

JOHNSON, Elizabeth ..... 813-253-7449 101 M
bjohnson@hccfl.edu

JOHNSON, Ellen .... 617-521-2515 224 E
ellen.johnson3@simmons.edu

JOHNSON, Eric .... 402-844-7236 276 G
eric@northeast.edu

JOHNSON, Eric .... 813-253-7560 101 M
ejohnson71@hccfl.edu

JOHNSON, Eric .... 219-464-5085 165 D
eric.johnson@valpo.edu

JOHNSON, Eric .... 309-692-4092 145 F
eajohnson@midstate.edu

JOHNSON, Eric, C .... 617-627-5484 225 A
eric.johnson@tufts.edu

JOHNSON, Eric, P .... 218-299-3447 241 K
johnson@cord.edu

JOHNSON, Eric, S .... 207-859-4460 198 H
eric.johnson@colby.edu

JOHNSON, Eric, W .... 985-549-3860 197 E
ejohnson@selu.edu

JOHNSON, Fatima, R ..... 585-245-5620 327 B
johnsonf@geneseo.edu

JOHNSON, Fengling, M 651-628-3372 251 C
fmjohnson@unwsp.edu

JOHNSON, Frank .... 404-756-4013 115 I
frankjohnson@atlm.edu

JOHNSON, Frank .... 620-947-3121 181 H
frankj@tabor.edu

JOHNSON, Frank .... 503-517-1374 388 A
fjjohnson@warnerpacific.edu

JOHNSON, G. David ..... 251-460-6261.... 9 B
djohnson@southalabama.edu

JOHNSON, Gail .... 903-593-8311 461 B
gjohnson@texascollege.edu

JOHNSON, Gail .... 540-863-2819 487 I
gjohnson@dslcc.edu

JOHNSON, Gary .... 515-271-3133 168 J
gary.johnson@drake.edu

JOHNSON, Gary, C .... 402-461-7407 274 I
gcjohnson@hastings.edu

JOHNSON, George .... 210-486-2640 441 I
gjohnson@alamo.edu

JOHNSON, George, W .. 803-535-5077 419 E
geojohnson@claflin.edu

JOHNSON, Glen .... 205-391-2327.... 3 E
gjohnson@sheltonstate.edu

JOHNSON, Glen .... 281-649-3801 450 C
glenjohnson@hbu.edu

JOHNSON, Glen .... 276-739-2467 490 A
gjohnson@vhcc.edu

JOHNSON, Glenn .... 304-929-1495 502 E
glennjohnson@ucwv.edu

JOHNSON, Gloria, C ..... 615-963-7518 438 E
gjohnson@tnstate.edu

JOHNSON, Gloria, R ..... 302-356-6845.. 91 B
gloria.r.johnson@wilmu.edu

JOHNSON, Gordon, L ... 270-745-2243 190 F
gordon.johnson@wku.edu

JOHNSON, Greg, L .... 612-343-3545 249 E

JOHNSON, Gregg .... 412-392-3898 408 F
gjohnson@pointpark.edu

JOHNSON, Gretchen ..... 212-650-5471 301 F
gjohnson@ccny.cuny.edu

JOHNSON, H. Wayne .... 847-317-8085 153 D
wjohnson@tiu.edu

JOHNSON, H. Wilson ... 716-888-2301 300 G
johns273@canisius.edu

JOHNSON, Haley .... 615-269-8300 430 F

JOHNSON, Harper .... 719-255-3594.. 83 C
hjohnson@uccs.edu

JOHNSON, Harriet .... 802-224-3001 476 H
harriet.johnson@vsc.edu

JOHNSON, Heidi .... 217-333-1676 154 B
johnso19@illinois.edu

JOHNSON, Henry .... 336-517-2137 335 K
hjohnson@bennett.edu

JOHNSON, Holly .... 319-296-4283 169 H
holly.johnson@hawkeyecollege.edu

JOHNSON, J. Lee .... 517-264-7108 236 I
ljohnson@sienaheights.edu

JOHNSON, James, F ..... 215-898-2173 412 G
johnsonj@isc.upenn.edu

JOHNSON, Janet, L .... 812-464-1924 165 C
jljohnson@usi.edu

JOHNSON, Janett .... 575-769-4910 293 M
janett.johnson@clovis.edu

JOHNSON, Jason .... 423-869-6028 433 C
jason.johnson02@lmunet.edu

JOHNSON, Jason .... 303-534-6270.. 78 M
jason.johnson@colostate.edu

JOHNSON, Jason .... 580-628-6240 376 J
jason.johnson@noc.edu

JOHNSON, Jason, L ...... 970-491-6270.. 78 N
jason.johnson@colostate.edu

JOHNSON, Jay .... 314-889-1423 260 C
jjohnson@fontbonne.edu

JOHNSON, Jean .... 773-838-7544 136 A
jjohnson2@ccc.edu

JOHNSON, Jeff .... 303-292-0015.. 79 F

JOHNSON, Jeff .... 318-628-4342 192 G

JOHNSON, Jeff .... 214-333-5759 447 D
jeff@dbu.edu

JOHNSON, Jeffrey .... 850-718-2237.. 96 H
johnsonj@chipola.edu

JOHNSON, Jeffrey, A .... 757-446-6100 480 C
johnsonja@evms.edu

JOHNSON, Jeffrey, C .... 561-237-7333 103 E
jjohnson@lynn.edu

JOHNSON, Jeffrey, W ... 515-294-6561 166 F
jjohnsn@iastate.edu

JOHNSON, Jennifer .... 559-442-8281.. 66 G
jennifer.johnson@fresnocitycollege.edu

JOHNSON, Jennifer .... 503-768-6626 383 G
jjj@lclark.edu

JOHNSON, Jenny .... 731-989-6378 432 C
jjohnson@fhu.edu

JOHNSON, Jerry .... 713-221-2720 465 C
johnsonj@uhd.edu

JOHNSON, Jessica .... 213-738-6705.. 65 I
registrar@swlaw.edu

JOHNSON, Jessica .... 918-335-6829 378 F
jjohnson@okwu.edu

JOHNSON, Jessica, R ... 800-747-2687 146 A

JOHNSON, Jill .... 515-961-1595 173 E
jill.johnson@simpson.edu

JOHNSON, Jill .... 309-341-5320 134 H
jjohnson@sandburg.edu

JOHNSON, Jill .... 803-321-5136 422 H
jill.johnson@newberry.edu

JOHNSON, Jill, K .... 904-632-5016 100 F
jill.johnson@fscj.edu

JOHNSON, Jill, R .... 864-587-4232 424 D
johnsoj@smcsc.edu

JOHNSON, Jim .... 620-235-4389 180 J
jjohnson@pittstate.edu

JOHNSON, Jim, K .... 651-286-7773 251 C
jkjohnson2@unwsp.edu

JOHNSON, Jo Ann .... 580-559-5246 375 I
jajohnsn@ecok.edu

JOHNSON, Jodi, S .... 706-272-4475 118 F
jjohnson@daltonstate.edu

JOHNSON, John, J .... 361-698-1269 448 H
jjohnson@delmar.edu

JOHNSON, JR.,
John, R .... 704-406-4303 337 H
jrjohnson@gardner-webb.edu

JOHNSON, Joseph .... 619-594-1424.. 34 B
jjohnson@mail.sdsu.edu

JOHNSON, Joseph, F ..... 804-257-5835 491 C
jfjohnson@vuu.edu

JOHNSON, Joyce .... 229-430-4792 114 I
joyce.johnson@asurams.edu

JOHNSON, Joyce .... 951-639-5439.. 52 J
jajohnso@msjc.edu

JOHNSON, Joycelyn ...... 225-771-2770 195 J
joycelyn_johnson@subr.edu

JOHNSON, Juanita .... 850-599-3491 109 A
juanita.johnson@famu.edu

JOHNSON, Judith .... 212-961-3399 298 H
jjohnson@bankstreet.edu

JOHNSON, Judy .... 309-438-7611 140 L
jjohns4@ilstu.edu

JOHNSON, Julia .... 760-750-4195.. 33 E
jjohnson@csusm.edu

JOHNSON, Julia .... 360-623-8451 493 A
julia.johnson@centralia.edu

JOHNSON, Julie .... 209-667-3351.. 33 F
jjohnson34@csustan.edu

JOHNSON, Julie .... 309-556-3134 141 B
jjohns11@iwu.edu

JOHNSON, Julie .... 605-455-6011 427 I
jjohnson@olc.edu

JOHNSON, Julie, A .... 209-667-3351.. 33 F
jjohnson34@csustan.edu

JOHNSON, Julie, A .... 352-273-6309 110 D
johnson@cop.ufl.edu

JOHNSON, Julie, H .... 920-748-8772 509 H
johnsonj@ripon.edu

JOHNSON, Juliet .... 615-329-8503 431 I
jjohnson@fisk.edu

JOHNSON, Karen .... 480-423-6597.. 14 C
karen.johnson@scottsdalecc.edu

JOHNSON, Karen .... 507-457-5300 248 C
kjohnson@winona.edu

JOHNSON, Karen .... 402-354-7038 275 P
karen.johnson@methodistcollege.edu

JOHNSON, Karen .... 918-495-7371 378 H
kjohnson@oru.edu

JOHNSON, Karen, A ...... 574-284-4571 163 J
kjohnson@saintmarys.edu

JOHNSON, Karen, D ...... 630-515-7268 145 I
kjohns@midwestern.edu

JOHNSON, Karen, L .... 607-735-1827 307 G
kajohnson@elmira.edu

JOHNSON, Katharine ..... 602-787-7106.. 13 J
katharine.johnson@paradisevalley.edu

JOHNSON, Kathryn, B .. 315-268-5515 304 B
kjohnson@clarkson.edu

JOHNSON, Kathy .... 269-488-4223 231 G
kjohnson@kvcc.edu

JOHNSON, Kathy, E .... 317-274-4500 160 E
kjohnso@iupui.edu

JOHNSON, Kathy, J .... 605-642-6512 428 F
kathy.johnson@bhsu.edu

JOHNSON, Kay .... 936-468-2206 458 A

JOHNSON, Keesha .... 501-337-5000.. 19 C
kjohnson@coto.edu

JOHNSON, Keith .... 205-453-6300.. 93 B

JOHNSON, Keith .... 785-242-5200 180 H
keith.johnson@ottawa.edu

JOHNSON, Keith .... 408-855-5457.. 74 C
keith.johnson@wvm.edu

JOHNSON, Keith .... 701-671-2218 355 B
keith.johnson@ndscs.edu

JOHNSON, Kellye .... 405-789-7661 380 A
kellye.johnson@swcu.edu

JOHNSON, Kenneth .... 740-593-2247 368 G
johnsok9@ohio.edu

JOHNSON, Kenneth .... 850-644-9396 110 A
ken.johnson@fsu.edu

JOHNSON, Kent, M .... 319-273-2122 167 A
kent.johnson@uni.edu

JOHNSON, Kerry .... 562-985-4128.. 32 C
kerry.johnson@csulb.edu

JOHNSON, Kevin .... 620-341-5667 177 B
kjohnson@emporia.edu

JOHNSON, Kevin, R .... 530-752-7225.. 68 H
krjohnson@ucdavis.edu

JOHNSON, Kim .... 714-556-3610.. 72 F
officevpem@vanguard.edu

JOHNSON, Kim, M .... 773-896-2400 135 G
kjohnson@ctschicago.edu

JOHNSON, Kimberlee ... 215-769-3128 394 E
kjohnso2@eastern.edu

JOHNSON, Kimberly ..... 765-361-6209 166 B
johnsonk@wabash.edu

JOHNSON, Kinte .... 707-476-4293.. 39 F
kinte-johnson@redwoods.edu

JOHNSON, Kit .... 512-913-4371 455 I
kitj@stedwards.edu

JOHNSON, Kristen .... 719-502-3363.. 81 H
kristen.johnson@ppcc.edu

JOHNSON, Kristina .... 518-320-1355 324 F
chancellor@suny.edu

JOHNSON, Kristy .... 319-385-6241 170 J
kristy.johnson@iw.edu

JOHNSON, Kyle .... 808-739-8552 129 A
kyle.johnson@chaminade.edu

JOHNSON, LaKenya ...... 229-931-2057 125 G
ljohnson@southgatech.edu

JOHNSON, Lakesia .... 641-269-9801 169 F
johnsola@grinnell.edu

JOHNSON, Lamont .... 803-750-2510.. 93 B

JOHNSON, Larry .... 706-272-4571 118 F
ljohnson@daltonstate.edu

JOHNSON, Larry .... 870-236-6901.. 19 D
ljohnson@crc.edu

JOHNSON, Larry .... 202-685-2128 518 B
johnsonl@ndu.edu

JOHNSON, Latesha .... 757-822-1054 489 H
ldjohnson@tcc.edu

JOHNSON, Laura .... 870-574-4513.. 21 G
ljohnson@sautech.edu

JOHNSON, Laura ... 502-863-7969 184 I
laura_johnson@georgetowncollege.edu

JOHNSON, Laura ... 906-217-4022 228 A
lauralee.johnson@baycollege.edu

JOHNSON, Laura ... 704-216-6029 339 E
ljohnson@livingstone.edu

JOHNSON, Laura, T ... 520-621-3175.. 16 J
ltj@email.arizona.edu

JOHNSON, Laurie ... 605-995-2901 427 A
lajohnso@dwu.edu

JOHNSON, Lawrence, J 513-556-2322 371 E
lawrence.johnson@uc.edu

JOHNSON, Lawrence, P 413-572-8485 218 F
ljohnson@westfield.ma.edu

JOHNSON, Le Keisha ... 210-567-2651 468 E
johnsonld@uthscsa.edu

JOHNSON, Lea, A ... 617-322-3500 216 B

JOHNSON, Leda ... 623-935-8868.. 13 F
leda.johnson@estrellamountain.edu

JOHNSON, Lee Ann ... 229-333-5666 127 H
1493mgr@follett.com

JOHNSON, Lennor ... 760-355-6153.. 46 B
lennor.johnson@imperial.edu

JOHNSON, Leon ... 718-270-6961 303 C
ljohnson@mec.cuny.edu

JOHNSON, Les ... 218-281-8345 250 G
ljohnson@umn.edu

JOHNSON, Leslie ... 706-872-8072 119 G
ljohnson@highlands.edu

JOHNSON, Leslie ... 626-396-2200.. 26 L
leslie.johnson@artcenter.edu

JOHNSON, Leslie ... 937-769-1345 356 G
lbates@antioch.edu

JOHNSON, Leslie, R ... 217-786-2848 144 B
leslie.johnson@llcc.edu

JOHNSON, Levester ... 309-438-5451 140 L
ljohn13@ilstu.edu

JOHNSON, Lewis ... 850-599-8316 109 A
lewis.johnson@famu.edu

JOHNSON, Lillian ... 410-337-6040 204 A
lillian.johnson@goucher.edu

JOHNSON, Lindsay ... 618-833-3399 151 G
lindsayj@shawneecc.edu

JOHNSON, Linsay ... 402-280-2703 274 D
lindsayjohnson@creighton.edu

JOHNSON, Lisa ... 701-858-3494 353 F
lisa.a.johnson@ndus.edu

JOHNSON, Lisa ... 407-646-2391 106 J
adjohnson@rollins.edu

JOHNSON, Lisa ... 201-684-6259 289 C
ljohnso5@ramapo.edu

JOHNSON, Lisa ... 423-636-7305 439 C
ljohnson@tusculum.edu

JOHNSON, Lisa ... 617-287-6020 216 I
lisa.johnson@umb.edu

JOHNSON, Lisa ... 804-862-6100 484 F
lsjohnson@rbc.edu

JOHNSON, Lisa, A ... 252-335-0821 342 D
lajohnson@albemarle.edu

JOHNSON, Lois, M ... 717-720-4122 405 D
ljohnson@passhe.edu

JOHNSON, Louise, N ... 563-589-0201 174 D
ljohnson@wartburgseminary.edu

JOHNSON, Lucia ... 972-860-2924 447 H
ljohnson@dcccd.edu

JOHNSON, Lynda, K ... 470-578-6033 122 C
ljohnson@kennesaw.edu

JOHNSON, Lynn ... 303-534-6290.. 78 M
lynn.johnson@colostate.edu

JOHNSON, Lynn ... 970-491-1550.. 78 N
lynn.johnson@colostate.edu

JOHNSON, Lynn ... 631-632-6151 325 F
lynn.johnson@stonybrook.edu

JOHNSON, Lynn ... 218-755-2068 244 B
ljohnson@bemidjistate.edu

JOHNSON, Lynn ... 541-440-7690 387 E
lynn.johnson@umpqua.edu

JOHNSON, Lynne ... 907-796-6416.. 10 C
lejohnson@alaska.edu

JOHNSON, M. Eric ... 615-322-2534 440 D
eric.johnson@vanderbilt.edu

JOHNSON, Maggie, A ... 972-708-7573 449 I
admissions@gial.edu

JOHNSON, Malonda ... 740-351-3398 369 L
mjohnson@shawnee.edu

JOHNSON, Marc ... 775-784-4805 279 E
marc.johnson@unr.edu

JOHNSON, Marco ... 661-726-1911.. 68 E
marco.johnson@uav.edu

JOHNSON, Marcus ... 702-651-4148 278 N
marcus.johnson@csn.edu

JOHNSON, Marcus ... 914-632-5400 315 K
mjohnson@monroecollege.edu

JOHNSON, Maren, A ... 701-788-4743 354 B
allison.johnson.3@mayvillestate.edu

JOHNSON, Margaret ... 972-708-7616 449 I
financial-aid@gial.edu

JOHNSON, Marguerite .. 617-274-3377 221 E
peg.johnson@mcphs.edu

JOHNSON, Maria ... 909-748-8333.. 71 H
maria_johnson@redlands.edu

JOHNSON,
Marianne, H ... 215-699-5700 399 G
mjohnson@lsb.edu

JOHNSON, Marie ... 657-278-2638.. 32 B
mariejohnson@fullerton.edu

JOHNSON, Marie, D ... 802-656-5700 476 E
marie.johnson@uvm.edu

JOHNSON, Mark ... 281-459-7106 456 A
mark.johnson@sjcd.edu

JOHNSON, Mark ... 507-389-2555 246 A
mark.johnson@mnsu.edu

JOHNSON, Mark ... 248-218-2080 236 C
mjohnson@rc.edu

JOHNSON, Mark ... 651-690-6824 249 T
majohnson6@stkate.edu

JOHNSON, Mark ... 314-889-1467 260 C
mjohnson@fontbonne.edu

JOHNSON, Mark ... 425-235-2352 497 E
mark.johnson@rtc.edu

JOHNSON, Mark, R ... 919-735-5151 347 E
mrjohnson@waynecc.edu

JOHNSON, Mary ... 919-760-8535 339 H
mbjohnson@meredith.edu

JOHNSON, Mary ... 507-453-2745 245 G
mjohnson@southeastmn.edu

JOHNSON, Mary ... 402-494-2311 275 M
mjohnson@thenicc.edu

JOHNSON, Mary ... 334-291-4973.... 1 H
mary.johnson@cv.edu

JOHNSON, Mary Jean .. 419-358-3272 357 E
johnsonmj@bluffton.edu

JOHNSON, Mary Jo ... 307-674-6446 516 P
mjjohnson@sheridan.edu

JOHNSON, Matt ... 906-217-4134 228 A
matt.c.johnson@baycollege.edu

JOHNSON, Matthew ... 413-205-3532 210 E
matthew.johnson@aic.edu

JOHNSON, Megan ... 302-622-8000.. 90 A

JOHNSON, Melissa ... 701-671-2520 355 B
melissa.j.johnson@ndscs.edu

JOHNSON, Melvina ... 866-492-5336 251 E
melvina.johnson@laureate.net

JOHNSON, Meredith, G 404-814-8813 127 A
mgurley@uga.edu

JOHNSON, Michael ... 615-248-7735 439 B
mjohnson@trevecca.edu

JOHNSON, Michael ... 660-562-1248 264 I
mikej@nwmissouri.edu

JOHNSON, Michael ... 256-372-5601.... 1 A
michael.johnson@aamu.edu

JOHNSON, Michael ... 502-456-6504 189 F
mkjohnson@sullivan.edu

JOHNSON, Michael ... 713-743-8859 464 F
cmj@uh.edu

JOHNSON, Michael, C .. 214-860-2167 448 A
mcjohnson@dcccd.edu

JOHNSON, Michael, D .. 781-239-4428 211 A
mjohnson8@babson.edu

JOHNSON, Michael, D .. 407-823-1911 110 C
michael.johnson@ucf.edu

JOHNSON, Michael, L .. 270-824-8567 186 D
michael.johnson@kctcs.edu

JOHNSON, Michele ... 973-720-2397 292 I
johnsonm73j@wpunj.edu

JOHNSON, Michele ... 253-864-3100 497 B
mjohnson@pierce.ctc.edu

JOHNSON, Michelle ... 626-969-3434.. 26 U
mmjohnson@apu.edu

JOHNSON, Michelle ... 631-420-2369 329 D
michelle.johnson@farmingdale.edu

JOHNSON, Michelle ... 605-688-4128 429 B
michelle.johnson@sdstate.edu

JOHNSON, Michelle ... 626-815-4550.. 26 U
mmjohnson@apu.edu

JOHNSON, Michelle ... 309-341-5258 134 H
mljohnson@sandburg.edu

JOHNSON, Michelle ... 414-229-6444 511 A
john3453@uwm.edu

JOHNSON, Mike ... 713-743-8859 465 A
cmj@uh.edu

JOHNSON, Mike ... 479-575-6601.. 21 I
mrj03@uark.edu

JOHNSON, Mike ... 405-585-5130 377 A
mike.johnson@okbu.edu

JOHNSON, Mikki ... 559-442-4600.. 66 G
mikki.johnson@fresnocitycollege.edu

JOHNSON, Mildred ... 540-231-6267 490 F
mildredj@vt.edu

JOHNSON, Mimi ... 334-420-4243.... 3 H
mjohnson@trenholmstate.edu

JOHNSON, Mitchell ... 336-334-4822 343 E
mjohnson@gtcc.edu

JOHNSON, Monika, L ... 901-333-5065 438 B
mljohnson@southwest.tn.edu

JOHNSON, Monty ... 218-631-7812 245 H
monty.johnson@minnesota.edu

JOHNSON, Nancy ... 607-962-9345 306 C

JOHNSON, Nancy ... 952-885-5428 249 F
njohnson@nwhealth.edu

JOHNSON, Nancy ... 307-382-1757 517 C
njohnson@westernwyoming.edu

JOHNSON, Nancy, A ... 309-794-7475 133 G
nancyjohnson@augustana.edu

JOHNSON, Nancy, N ... 713-646-1751 456 H
njohnson@stcl.edu

JOHNSON, Nathan ... 616-538-2330 230 E
njohnson@gbcol.edu

JOHNSON, Neil, A ... 303-867-1155.. 84 F
johnson@taft.edu

JOHNSON, Nina ... 218-755-3760 244 B
njjohnson@bemidjistate.edu

JOHNSON, P. Brandon . 239-590-7347 109 C
pbjohnson@fgcu.edu

JOHNSON, Pam ... 708-524-6562 137 F
pjohnson@dom.edu

JOHNSON, Pam ... 256-835-5456.... 2 A
pjohnson@gadsdenstate.edu

JOHNSON, Pamela ... 610-989-1328 413 I
pjohnson@vfmac.edu

JOHNSON, Pamela, D ... 937-766-7765 358 D
johnsonp@cedarville.edu

JOHNSON, Patricia ... 202-274-5946.. 93 D
mblanchard@udc.edu

JOHNSON, Patricia, A ... 610-758-3178 400 B
paj214@lehigh.edu

JOHNSON, Patrick ... 240-567-5288 205 F
patrick.johnson@montgomerycollege.
edu

JOHNSON, Patrick, H ... 615-327-6061 434 A
pjohnson@mmc.edu

JOHNSON, Paul ... 404-727-7727 119 B
rpaul.johnson@emory.edu

JOHNSON, Paul, C ... 303-273-3280.. 78 J
presoffice@mines.edu

JOHNSON, Paula, A ... 781-283-2237 225 D
pjohnson@wellesley.edu

JOHNSON, CRM,
Paula, J ... 858-534-2552.. 69 E
pjjohnson@ucsd.edu

JOHNSON, Paulette ... 256-726-7250.... 6 E
pjohnson@oakwood.edu

JOHNSON, Peg ... 505-428-1352 296 B
peg.johnson@sfcc.edu

JOHNSON, Peggy, A ... 814-865-2631 403 F
paj6@psu.edu

JOHNSON, Phil ... 334-244-3202.... 4 E
pjohns23@aum.edu

JOHNSON, Philip ... 906-487-7201 230 B
philip.johnson@finlandia.edu

JOHNSON, Philip, M ... 503-255-0332 384 E
pjohnson@multnomah.edu

JOHNSON, Phillip ... 205-391-2665.... 3 E
pjohnson@sheltonstate.edu

JOHNSON, Quentin ... 363-334-4822 343 E
qrjohnson@gtcc.edu

JOHNSON, Ralph ... 470-639-0427 123 E
ralph.johnson@morehouse.edu

JOHNSON, Ralph ... 301-891-4028 209 E
rejohnson@wau.edu

JOHNSON, Ralph ... 864-977-2077 422 I
ralph.johnson@ngu.edu

JOHNSON, Ralph, F ... 706-542-7369 127 A
rfj@uga.edu

JOHNSON, Ralph, W ... 504-762-3005 192 H
rjohns3@dcc.edu

JOHNSON, Rana ... 207-509-7140 200 I
rjohnson@unity.edu

JOHNSON, Randolph ... 864-644-5220 424 B
rjohnson@swu.edu

JOHNSON, Raniyah ... 408-223-6768.. 61 O
raniyah.johnson@evc.edu

JOHNSON, Rebecca ... 770-467-6037 126 B
rajohnson@sctech.edu

JOHNSON, Rebecca ... 541-322-3100 385 F
rebecca.johnson@osucascades.edu

JOHNSON, Rebecca ... 414-930-3242 509 B
johnsonr@mtmary.edu

JOHNSON, Rebecca, D . 203-932-7176.. 89 D
rjohnson@newhaven.edu

JOHNSON, Rhea ... 925-969-3300.. 46 L
rjohnson1@jfku.edu

JOHNSON, Richard ... 870-236-6901.. 19 D
rjohnson@crc.edu

JOHNSON, Richard, A .. 864-597-4090 426 I
johnsonra@wofford.edu

JOHNSON, Rick ... 919-684-3737 337 C
rick.johnson@duke.edu

JOHNSON, Rick ... 239-590-7072 109 C
rjohnson@wgcu.edu

JOHNSON, Rick ... 307-778-1135 516 N
rjohnson@lccc.wy.edu

JOHNSON, Rita ... 828-328-7235 339 C
rita.johnson@lr.edu

JOHNSON, Robert, E ... 913-667-5715 176 F
rjohnson@cbts.edu

JOHNSON, Robert, E ... 704-687-8242 351 C
robejohn@uncc.edu

JOHNSON, JR.,
Robert, M ... 901-843-3745 435 L
johnsonb@rhodes.edu

JOHNSON, Robert, R ... 610-526-1301 389 B
bob.johnson@theamericancollege.edu

JOHNSON, Roberta, L ... 515-294-0109 166 F
rljohns@iastate.edu

JOHNSON, Rod ... 503-699-6266 384 B
rjohnson@marylhurst.edu

JOHNSON, Rodney ... 937-766-4114 358 D
johnsonr@cedarville.edu

JOHNSON, Ronald ... 714-432-5605.. 38 H
rgjohnson@occ.cccd.edu

JOHNSON, Ronald, A ... 404-880-8566 117 H
rjohnson@cau.edu

JOHNSON, Ronald, W ... 310-206-0401.. 69 B
rojohnso@saonet.ucla.edu

JOHNSON, Ronnie, J ... 903-586-2501 443 M

JOHNSON, Rory ... 707-465-2300.. 39 F
rory-johnson@redwoods.edu

JOHNSON, Ruben ... 972-860-8161 447 H
rjohnson@dcccd.edu

JOHNSON, Russell, R ... 207-859-4776 198 H
margaret.mcfadden@colby.edu

JOHNSON, Ryan ... 501-205-8815.. 19 B
rjohnson@cbc.edu

JOHNSON, Ryan ... 254-442-5173 445 Q
ryan.johnson@cisco.edu

JOHNSON, Sabrina, C .. 540-654-1046 486 D
sjohnson@umw.edu

JOHNSON, Sandra ... 661-726-1911.. 68 E
sandra.johnson@uav.edu

JOHNSON, Sandra, S ... 585-475-2267 321 D
ssjvsa@rit.edu

JOHNSON, Sara ... 315-265-9260 304 B
clarkson@bkstr.com

JOHNSON, Sarah ... 419-448-3039 370 K
depughst@tiffin.edu

JOHNSON, Scott ... 831-479-5663.. 28 F
scjohnso@cabrillo.edu

JOHNSON, Scott ... 810-762-3160 238 B
scotjohn@umflint.edu

JOHNSON, Scott ... 336-838-6141 347 G
sajohnson366@wilkescc.edu

JOHNSON, Sean ... 707-664-4032.. 35 A
sean.johnson@sonoma.edu

JOHNSON, Sean ... 701-252-3467 355 J
sean.johnson@uj.edu

JOHNSON, Seth ... 716-375-2382 322 B
sjohnson@sbu.edu

JOHNSON, Sharon ... 314-516-6817 268 E
sharon_johnson@umsl.edu

JOHNSON, Sharon ... 262-564-3164 513 G
johnsonsh@gtc.edu

JOHNSON, Sheila, G ... 405-744-6321 377 F
sheila.johnson@okstate.edu

JOHNSON, Shelia ... 304-327-4040 503 O
sjohnson@bluefieldstate.edu

JOHNSON, Sherie ... 410-951-3846 208 F
shejohnson@coppin.edu

JOHNSON, Sherrick, L .. 706-771-4008 116 A
sjohnson@augustatech.edu

JOHNSON, Sonia ... 870-236-6901.. 19 D
sjohnson@crc.edu

JOHNSON, Stacey ... 718-368-1193 313 B
sjohnson@libi.edu

JOHNSON, Stacey, R ... 407-582-2822 113 F
srjohnson@valenciacollege.edu

JOHNSON, Stacy ... 248-689-8282 238 F
sjohnso6@walshcollege.edu

JOHNSON, Stephanie ... 573-875-7357 258 F
sgjohnson@ccis.edu

JOHNSON, Stephanie ... 704-379-6800.. 93 B

JOHNSON, Stephen ... 626-812-3020.. 26 U
sjohnson@apu.edu

JOHNSON, Stephen ... 560-860-2451.. 36 A
sjohnson@cerritos.edu

JOHNSON, Stephen ... 325-674-2751 441 D
scj98d@acu.edu

JOHNSON, Steve ... 504-280-6303 194 F
sgjohnso@uno.edu

JOHNSON, Steve ... 913-360-7415 175 D
stevej@benedictine.edu

JOHNSON, Steve ... 602-429-4975.. 15 K
sjohnson@ps.edu

JOHNSON, Steven ... 334-874-5700.... 5 B
sjohnson@ccal.edu

JOHNSON, Steven ... 603-626-9100 282 C
s.johnson5@snhu.edu

JOHNSON, Steven, D ... 816-604-6563 262 G
steven.johnson@mcckc.edu

JONES, Brenda .... 414-847-3231 508 G brendajones@miad.edu
JONES, Brian .... 310-544-6442.. 59 E brian.jones@usw.salvationarmy.org
JONES, Brian .... 704-378-1238 338 I bjones@jcsu.edu
JONES, Brian .... 507-389-2422 246 A brian.jones@mnsu.edu
JONES, Brian, W .... 202-419-0400.. 93 B
JONES, Britt, E .... 325-670-1317 450 A brittj@hsutx.edu
JONES, Bruce, A .... 713-743-2490 465 A bajones@uh.edu
JONES, Bryan, H .... 206-281-2405 498 B bryan@spu.edu
JONES, Byron .... 602-557-9322.. 17 C byron.jones@phoenix.edu
JONES, C. Darryl .... 510-231-5000.. 46 N darryl.jones@kp.org
JONES, Candice .... 404-297-9522 120 D jonesc@gptc.edu
JONES, Carl .... 318-357-4254 197 D jonesc@nsula.edu
JONES, Carnell .... 401-874-9500 417 E carnell@uri.edu
JONES, Carol .... 478-218-3700 117 D cjones@centralgatech.edu
JONES, Carol .... 706-272-4545 118 F cjones@daltonstate.edu
JONES, Carol, F .... 478-988-6800 117 E cjones@centralgatech.edu
JONES, Cassandra .... 706-419-1117 118 E cassandra.jones@covenant.edu
JONES, Cassandra .... 240-567-4248 205 F cassandra.jones@montgomerycollege.edu
JONES, Cassie .... 434-791-5684 478 E cwjones@averett.edu
JONES, Cathy .... 704-330-1461 338 I cjones2@jcsu.edu
JONES, Cecelia .... 903-730-4890 451 D cjones@jarvis.edu
JONES, Charles .... 478-825-6156 119 C jonesc02@fvsu.edu
JONES, Cheri .... 502-852-4494 190 C cjjone01@louisville.edu
JONES, Chris .... 641-472-1219 171 J cjones@mum.edu
JONES, Chris .... 641-472-1105 171 J cjones@mum.edu
JONES, Chris .... 405-585-4120 377 A chris.jones@okbu.edu
JONES, Christa, K .... 972-860-7033 447 I christaj@dcccd.edu
JONES, Christopher .... 978-867-4500 215 D chris.jones@gordon.edu
JONES, Christopher .... 309-677-2380 134 G cmjones@fsmail.bradley.edu
JONES, Cindy .... 805-289-6410.. 73 C cjones_1@vcccd.edu
JONES, Cindy, M .... 417-873-7330 259 G cjones@drury.edu
JONES, Clayton, H .... 662-915-1999 256 C chj1@olemiss.edu
JONES, Cliff .... 870-733-6731.. 18 B cejones@asumidsouth.edu
JONES, Clifton .... 254-519-5424 459 D cwjones@tamuct.edu
JONES, Clifton .... 325-942-2337 463 C clifton.jones@angelo.edu
JONES, Cody .... 205-665-6130.... 8 E ccjones@montevallo.edu
JONES, Courtney .... 405-382-9204 379 I c.jones@sscok.edu
JONES, Cravor .... 304-327-4016 503 O cjones@bluefieldstate.edu
JONES, Cristen .... 410-923-4500.. 93 B
JONES, Curtis .... 912-201-6123 125 H cejones@southuniversity.edu
JONES, Dan .... 714-546-7600.. 38 F djones@coastline.edu
JONES, Dan, L .... 828-262-3180 349 H jonesdl@appstate.edu
JONES, Dan, L .... 423-439-4841 431 H jonesdl4@etsu.edu
JONES, Darci .... 814-824-2233 401 J djones@mercyhurst.edu
JONES, Darnell .... 816-501-4117 265 I darnell.jones@rockhurst.edu
JONES, Darrell, C .... 714-879-3901.. 45 I dcjones@hiu.edu
JONES, Darren .... 501-977-2191.. 23 B jones@uaccm.edu
JONES, Darren .... 301-736-3631 205 B darren.jones@msbbcs.edu
JONES, Darrin .... 360-538-4234 495 B djones@ghc.edu
JONES, Darryl, E .... 717-801-3211 396 G dejones@hacc.edu
JONES, David .... 706-542-8131 127 A dsjones@uga.edu
JONES, David .... 931-363-9816 433 E djones@martinmethodist.edu
JONES, David .... 573-592-5288 270 B david.jones@westminster-mo.edu
JONES, David .... 507-389-2121 246 A david.jones@mnsu.edu
JONES, David .... 715-836-4490 510 D jonesm@uwec.edu
JONES, David .... 307-766-6556 517 B dljones@uwyo.edu
JONES, David, R .... 301-784-5000 202 B djones@allegany.edu
JONES, Dawn .... 903-927-3203 471 B dijones@wileyc.edu
JONES, Debra .... 618-374-5162 149 A debra.jones@principia.edu
JONES, Debra .... 229-430-3605 114 J djones@albanytech.edu
JONES, Debra, A .... 804-257-5712 491 C dajones@vuu.edu
JONES, Deneese .... 210-999-8201 464 B djones2@trinity.edu
JONES, Diana .... 641-784-5412 169 D dianaj@gracelend.edu
JONES, Dianna .... 781-768-7291 224 A dianna.jones@regiscollege.edu
JONES, Don .... 312-341-2296 150 D djones74@roosevelt.edu
JONES, Donald .... 860-768-4751.. 89 C djones@hartford.edu
JONES, Donald, A .... 502-371-8330 183 E djones@ata.edu
JONES, Donald, E .... 803-754-4100 420 E
JONES, Doug .... 423-636-7300 439 C djones@tusculum.edu
JONES, Douglas, W ...... 805-565-6048.. 74 I vpfinance@westmont.edu
JONES, Eddie, V .... 989-964-4228 236 F evjones@svsu.edu
JONES, Edward .... 312-329-4354 146 B edward.jones@moody.edu
JONES, JR., Edward ...... 202-274-7441.. 93 D ejones@udc.edu
JONES, Eli .... 479-575-5949.. 21 I ejones@walton.uark.edu
JONES, Eli .... 979-845-4712 459 C elijones@tamu.edu
JONES, Elizabeth, R ...... 404-413-3003 121 A bethjones@gsu.edu
JONES, Elliot .... 318-247-3811 196 G
JONES, Elliot .... 248-218-2036 236 C ejones@rc.edu
JONES, Elwin .... 251-981-3771.... 5 A elwin.jones@columbiasouthern.edu
JONES, Emily, M .... 413-542-2267 210 F ejones@amherst.edu
JONES, Eric .... 641-628-5420 167 D jonese@central.edu
JONES, Ericka .... 512-505-3035 451 A edjones@htu.edu
JONES, Eugene, G .... 407-582-1635 113 F ejones102@valenciacollege.edu
JONES, Faye, M .... 615-353-3556 437 D faye.jones@nscc.edu
JONES, Garry .... 407-679-0100 101 F gjones@fullsail.com
JONES, Garry .... 662-243-2643 253 A gjones@eastms.edu
JONES, Gary .... 618-252-5400 151 J gary.jones@sic.edu
JONES, Gary .... 405-425-5904 377 B gary.jones@oc.edu
JONES, Gayle .... 352-395-5226 107 E gayle.jones@sfcollege.edu
JONES, Gerald .... 334-386-7600.... 5 I gjones@faulkner.edu
JONES, Geraldine .... 724-938-4400 405 F jones_gm@calu.edu
JONES, Gina .... 612-330-1051 240 G jonesg@augsburg.edu
JONES, Gina, G .... 803-323-2194 426 H jonesgg@winthrop.edu
JONES, Glendell .... 870-230-5091.. 19 H president@hsu.edu
JONES, Glenn .... 973-720-2950 292 I jonesg13@wpunj.edu
JONES, Gloria .... 803-323-3900 426 H jonesg@winthrop.edu
JONES, Gordon .... 208-426-2975 131 C gojones@boisestate.edu
JONES, Grady .... 812-749-1228 163 B gjones@oak.edu
JONES, Gwen .... 262-595-2151 511 C gaines@uwp.edu
JONES, Harold .... 903-675-6256 464 C hjones@tvcc.edu
JONES, Harold, P .... 205-934-5149.... 8 B jonesh@uab.edu
JONES, Hollie .... 718-270-4989 303 C hjones@mec.cuny.edu
JONES, Holly .... 319-385-6220 170 J holly.jones@iw.edu
JONES, J. Pernell .... 610-341-5948 394 E pjones1@eastern.edu
JONES, J. Preston .... 954-262-5127 104 F prestonj@nova.edu
JONES, James .... 575-461-4413 294 E jimj@mesalands.edu
JONES, Jane, M .... 423-439-4211 431 H jonesj@etsu.edu
JONES, Janet .... 256-331-5310.... 3 C janetj@nwscc.edu
JONES, Janice .... 270-707-3707 186 B jjones0004@kctcs.edu
JONES, Jeff .... 407-823-1582 110 C jeffrey.jones@ucf.edu
JONES, Jeff .... 928-226-4297.. 12 B jeff.jones@coconino.edu
JONES, Jeff .... 909-687-1750.. 44 A jeffjones@gs.edu
JONES, Jeffrey .... 484-646-4144 406 D jjones@kutztown.edu
JONES, Jen .... 254-295-8645 466 A jen.jones@umhb.edu
JONES, Jennifer .... 815-455-8770 145 B jjones@mchenry.edu
JONES, Jennifer .... 201-200-3005 287 F jjones@njcu.edu
JONES, Jennifer .... 920-465-2111 510 E jonesj@uwgb.edu
JONES, Jennifer .... 252-536-7254 343 F
JONES, Jenny .... 858-499-0202.. 39 B jjones@coleman.edu
JONES, Jenny, L .... 404-880-8549 117 H jjones@cau.edu
JONES, Jeremy .... 541-962-3553 383 B jdjones1@eou.edu
JONES, Jerry .... 254-519-5446 459 D jerry.jones@tamuct.edu
JONES, Jessica, S .... 252-246-1216 347 H jjones@wilsoncc.edu
JONES, Jessie .... 406-395-4875 273 B
JONES, Jill .... 309-438-3135 140 L jajones2@ilstu.edu
JONES, Jill, D .... 208-467-8521 132 F jdjones@nnu.edu
JONES, Jim .... 517-787-0800 231 E jonesjamesl@jccmi.edu
JONES, Jim .... 325-670-1207 450 A jjones@hsutx.edu
JONES, John .... 316-978-7751 182 F john.jones@wichita.edu
JONES, John .... 904-596-2304 112 F jjones@tbc.edu
JONES, John .... 765-677-2387 161 C john.jones@indwes.edu
JONES, John .... 479-788-7456.. 22 A john.jones@uafs.edu
JONES, John, D .... 870-307-7326.. 20 C john.jones@lyon.edu
JONES, John, P .... 520-621-1112.. 16 J jpjones@email.arizona.edu
JONES, III, John, R ...... 205-996-0132.... 8 B jrjones3@uab.edu
JONES, John, S .... 772-546-5534 101 N johnjones@hsbc.edu
JONES, Jon .... 417-268-6049 257 H jjones@gobbc.edu
JONES, Joree .... 334-291-4913.... 1 H joree.jones@cv.edu
JONES, Joseph .... 501-420-1202.. 17 I joseph.jones@arkansasbaptist.edu
JONES, Joseph .... 559-453-2010.. 43 J fpupres@fresno.edu
JONES, Joshua .... 309-677-1000 134 G jejones@bradley.edu
JONES, Joshua .... 303-837-0825.. 76 K jejones@aii.edu
JONES, Joshua .... 864-503-5093 425 H jjones3@uscupstate.edu
JONES, Joy .... 304-865-6102 502 C joy.jones@ovu.edu
JONES, Joye .... 205-391-2283.... 3 E jjones1@sheltonstate.edu
JONES, Judy .... 979-532-6561 471 A judyj@wcjc.edu
JONES, Julia, A .... 801-581-5701 472 P julia.jones@utah.edu
JONES, Justin, K .... 801-524-1921 471 L jkjones@ldsbc.edu
JONES, Karen .... 803-323-3708 426 H jonesk@winthrop.edu
JONES, Karen .... 928-776-2307.. 17 G karen.jones@yc.edu
JONES, Karen .... 419-448-2130 362 G kjones9@heidelberg.edu
JONES, Karen, S .... 478-289-2012 118 H kjones@ega.edu
JONES, Kate .... 952-446-4166 242 A joneska@crown.edu
JONES, Kathleen .... 815-825-1709 142 F kathleen.jones@kishwaukeecollege.edu
JONES, Kathy .... 713-348-5460 455 F kjones@rice.edu
JONES, Katie, P .... 864-488-4597 422 B kjones@limestone.edu
JONES, Kayla .... 361-354-2532 445 S kdjones@coastalbend.edu
JONES, Keisha .... 336-249-8186 342 F keisha_jones@davidsonccc.edu
JONES, Kelly .... 802-586-7711 476 D kjones@sterlingcollege.edu
JONES, Kenneth .... 706-778-8500 124 E kjones@piedmont.edu
JONES, JR., Kenneth .... 404-727-4144 119 B kenneth.jones@emory.edu
JONES, Kenneth, E .... 252-335-3294 350 A kejones@ecsu.edu
JONES, Kent .... 256-228-6001.... 3 B jonesk@nacc.edu
JONES, Kevin .... 863-638-7297 113 I kevin.jones@warner.edu
JONES, Kevin .... 863-297-1000 105 F kjones@polk.edu
JONES, Kevin .... 518-736-3622 309 A kevin.jones@fmcc.suny.edu
JONES, Kim .... 530-895-2298.. 28 E joneski@butte.edu
JONES, Kim .... 903-823-3004 458 D kimberly.jones@texarkanacollege.edu
JONES, Kim .... 361-593-2187 460 B krkdy00@tamuk.edu
JONES, Kimberly .... 904-256-7642 102 B kmarian@ju.edu
JONES, Kimberly, B ...... 334-670-3113.... 7 E kbrink@troy.edu
JONES, Kitty .... 360-867-6851 494 G jonesk@evergreen.edu
JONES, Kona .... 217-875-7211 149 J kona@richland.edu
JONES, Kristen .... 206-934-3701 497 H kristen.jones@seattlecolleges.edu
JONES, Lance .... 307-268-2672 516 H ljones@caspercollege.edu
JONES, Landon .... 816-415-6335 270 C jonesl@william.jewell.edu
JONES, Laura .... 928-523-9084.. 14 K laura.jones@nau.edu
JONES, Laura, B .... 734-764-7423 237 I laurabj@umich.edu
JONES, Laurel .... 831-479-6306.. 28 F lajones@cabrillo.edu
JONES, Laurene .... 609-586-4800 287 A jonesl@mccc.edu
JONES, Laurie, S .... 706-568-2005 118 C jones_laurie@columbusstate.edu
JONES, Lenroy .... 419-289-5067 356 L ljones31@ashland.edu
JONES, Leonard .... 360-650-2953 500 E leonard.jones@wwu.edu
JONES, Leslie .... 985-448-4325 197 C leslie.jones@nicholls.edu
JONES, Lester .... 909-706-3509.. 74 G ljones@westernu.edu
JONES, Lewis .... 802-322-1676 475 A
JONES, Linda, E .... 413-782-1247 225 F linda.jones@wne.edu
JONES, Linda, T .... 240-895-3246 206 G ltjones1@smcm.edu
JONES, Lirse .... 973-720-2101 292 I jonesl@wpunj.edu
JONES, Lisa .... 801-832-2237 474 E ljones@westminstercollege.edu
JONES, Lisa .... 912-358-4000 125 C jonesl@savannahstate.edu
JONES, Lisa .... 845-257-3216 325 D jonesl@newpaltz.edu
JONES, Lisa .... 252-335-0821 342 D lisa_jones@albemarle.edu
JONES, Loree, D .... 856-885-6095 290 B loree.jones@rutgers.edu
JONES, Marcia .... 678-466-4250 117 I marciajones@clayton.edu
JONES, Marcus .... 318-357-5701 197 D marcusj@nsula.edu
JONES, Marcy .... 217-479-7028 144 I marcy.jones@mac.edu
JONES, Margaret .... 914-422-4043 319 J mjones@pace.edu

JONES, Marian ... 704-378-1074 338 I
myjones@jcsu.edu
JONES, Marie ... 828-884-8248 335 L
jonesmf@brevard.edu
JONES, Marie ... 334-876-9284 ... 2 C
marie.jones@wccs.edu
JONES, Mark ... 352-588-8367 106 N
mark.jones@saintleo.edu
JONES, Marleen ... 918-495-7163 378 H
mjones@oru.edu
JONES, Marlon ... 662-252-8000 255 F
mjones2@rustcollege.edu
JONES, Marvin, L ... 410-651-6144 208 C
mljones@umes.edu
JONES, Mary ... 805-289-6346 .. 73 C
mjones@vcccd.edu
JONES, Mary ... 913-971-3393 179 H
maryjones@mnu.edu
JONES, Mary, O ... 845-575-3000 314 C
mary.jones@marist.edu
JONES, Matteel ... 864-250-8177 421 K
matteel.jones@gvltec.edu
JONES, Mautra ... 405-466-2937 375 L
mjones@langston.edu
JONES, Melanie, E ... 803-327-8012 426 J
mjones@yorktech.edu
JONES, Melinda, L ... 901-678-2690 439 E
mljones6@memphis.edu
JONES, Melissa ... 864-622-6011 418 E
melissajones@andersonuniversity.edu
JONES, Melissa ... 217-854-5514 134 E
melissa.k.jones@blackburn.edu
JONES, Melissa, A ... 910-678-8474 343 B
jonesma@faytechcc.edu
JONES, Melvin ... 304-766-3061 505 A
mjones55@wvstateu.edu
JONES, Meredith ... 580-559-5668 375 I
mjones@ecok.edu
JONES, Michael ... 909-607-8585 .. 38 C
michael_jones@kgi.edu
JONES, Michael ... 412-578-6378 391 G
mbjones@carlow.edu
JONES, Mike ... 601-925-3819 254 B
jones01@mc.edu
JONES, Mike ... 434-544-8538 482 F
jones.mj@lynchburg.edu
JONES, Molly ... 513-618-1933 359 F
mjones@ccms.edu
JONES, Monica ... 859-985-3795 183 I
jonesmo@berea.edu
JONES, Monterrio ... 803-780-1209 426 F
mjones@voorhees.edu
JONES, Nancy ... 714-241-6209 .. 38 F
njones@coastline.edu
JONES, Natalie ... 207-780-4141 201 H
natalie.jones@maine.edu
JONES, Nathaniel ... 951-571-6341 .. 58 F
nathaniel.jones@mvc.edu
JONES, Ned, J ... 518-783-2423 324 C
jones@siena.edu
JONES, Nicholas, P ... 814-865-2505 403 F
npj1@psu.edu
JONES, Nicole ... 619-660-4302 .. 44 L
nicole.jones@gcccd.edu
JONES, Nina ... 662-915-7690 256 C
nina@olemiss.edu
JONES, Nolan ... 972-825-7970 457 F
nojones@sagu.edu
JONES, Norm ... 316-942-4291 180 D
jonesn@newmanu.edu
JONES, Norman ... 256-372-8653 ... 1 A
norman.jones@aamu.edu
JONES, Olivia ... 919-530-7713 350 D
ojones@nccu.edu
JONES, Orion ... 419-448-3368 370 K
jonesov@tiffin.edu
JONES, Pam ... 909-621-8130 .. 57 C
pam_jones@pitzer.edu
JONES, Pam ... 501-882-8956 .. 17 M
pljones@asub.edu
JONES, Para, M ... 330-494-6170 370 G
pjones@starkstate.edu
JONES, Parago ... 303-329-6355 .. 78 L
clinicdirector@cstcm.edu
JONES, Patricia ... 301-736-3631 205 B
patricia.jones@msbbcs.edu
JONES, Patricia ... 864-592-4634 424 C
jonesp@sccsc.edu
JONES, Patrick ... 904-256-7502 102 B
pjones15@ju.edu
JONES, Paul ... 478-825-6315 119 C
jonesp@fvsu.edu
JONES, Paulette ... 405-912-9020 379 A
pjones@ru.edu
JONES, Peter ... 415-575-6100 .. 29 H
pjones@ciis.edu
JONES, Phil ... 772-546-5534 101 N
philjones@hsbc.edu
JONES, Philip ... 717-245-1509 394 A
jonesph@dickinson.edu
JONES, JR., Philip, M .. 704-687-0514 351 C
pmjones@uncc.edu
JONES, R. Channing ... 910-272-3600 346 A
cjones@robeson.edu
JONES, Rachel ... 870-245-5593 .. 20 G
jonesrm@obu.edu
JONES, Randy ... 805-565-7048 .. 74 I
rjones@westmont.edu
JONES, Randy ... 304-384-5385 503 P
rjones@concord.edu
JONES, Randy, P ... 214-768-2146 457 B
rpjones@smu.edu
JONES, Rauchelle ... 281-283-2536 465 B
jonesrau@uhcl.edu
JONES, Rene ... 870-733-6769 .. 18 B
rjones@asumidsouth.edu
JONES, Renee ... 615-547-1359 431 D
rjones@cumberland.edu
JONES, Richard ... 856-256-4040 289 H
jonesri@rowan.edu
JONES, Robert ... 303-762-6913 .. 79 G
robert.jones@denverseminary.edu
JONES, Robert ... 239-732-3720 100 E
rrjones@fsw.edu
JONES, Robert ... 903-823-3154 458 D
robert.jones@texarkanacollege.edu
JONES, Robert ... 401-232-6027 416 A
rjones10@bryant.edu
JONES, Robert, A ... 317-788-3304 164 H
rjones@uindy.edu
JONES, Robert, H ... 864-656-3940 419 F
provost@clemson.edu
JONES, Robert, J ... 217-333-6290 153 G
rjjones@illinois.edu
JONES, Robert, J ... 217-333-6677 154 B
JONES, Robert, P ... 915-831-3112 449 A
rjones35@epcc.edu
JONES, Robin ... 575-769-4921 293 M
robin.jones@clovis.edu
JONES, Robyn ... 503-534-4023 384 B
rjones@marylhurst.edu
JONES, Rockwell, F ... 740-368-3000 368 N
rfjones@owu.edu
JONES, Roger ... 310-377-5501 .. 51 B
rjones@marymountcalifornia.edu
JONES, Roger ... 434-544-8444 482 F
jones@lynchburg.edu
JONES, Ronald, L ... 901-272-5145 434 B
rjones@mca.edu
JONES, Rose ... 256-331-5313 ... 3 C
jonesr@nwscc.edu
JONES, Rosemary ... 206-726-5169 494 B
rjones@cornish.edu
JONES, Rythee ... 301-891-4542 209 E
eljones@wau.edu
JONES, Sam ... 850-729-4929 104 E
joness@nwfsc.edu
JONES, Sam ... 601-477-4038 253 F
sam.jones@jcjc.edu
JONES,
Samantha Major ... 828-835-4203 347 B
sjones@tricountycc.edu
JONES, Samuel ... 601-979-2260 253 E
samuel.jones@jsums.edu
JONES, Samuel, B ... 843-953-6367 420 C
jonessa@cofc.edu
JONES, Samuel, E ... 757-221-2565 479 I
sejone@wm.edu
JONES, Sarah, L ... 540-464-7667 490 E
jonessl10@vmi.edu
JONES, Scott ... 765-455-9388 160 B
scotjone@iuk.edu
JONES, Serene ... 212-280-1403 332 C
sjones@uts.columbia.edu
JONES, Sha-Ron, E ... 410-951-3610 208 F
shajones@coppin.edu
JONES, Shaniqua ... 708-239-4560 153 B
shaniqua.jones@trnty.edu
JONES, Shannon ... 843-792-8839 422 C
joneshan@musc.edu
JONES, Sharon, A ... 503-943-8168 387 H
joness@up.edu
JONES, Shawn ... 870-230-5072 .. 19 H
jonessh@hsu.edu
JONES, Shealeigh ... 940-552-6291 469 F
sjones@vernoncollege.edu
JONES, Sheba ... 312-662-4131 133 A
sjones@adler.edu
JONES, Sheila ... 706-295-6366 119 G
shjones@highlands.edu
JONES, Sheila Dove ... 570-389-4027 405 E
sjones@bloomu.edu
JONES, Sheri ... 858-513-9240 .. 26 T
sheri.jones@ashford.edu
JONES, Sherry ... 781-762-1211 215 A
sjones@fmc.edu
JONES, Sherry ... 214-860-2202 448 A
sljones@dcccd.edu
JONES, Stacey ... 479-788-7302 .. 22 A
stacey.jones@uafs.edu
JONES, Stacey, F ... 757-823-8408 483 F
provost@nsu.edu
JONES, Stanley ... 229-333-5732 127 H
sjones@valdosta.edu
JONES, Stephanie ... 313-993-1549 237 F
landerss@udmercy.edu
JONES, Stephen ... 903-593-8311 461 B
sjones@texascollege.edu
JONES, Stephen, B ... 304-367-4151 504 A
steve.jones@fairmontstate.edu
JONES, Steven, K ... 719-333-9751 518 H
JONES, Steven, L ... 765-361-6450 166 B
joness@wabash.edu
JONES, Stuart ... 413-748-3757 224 G
sdjones@springfieldcollege.edu
JONES, Stuart ... 435-586-7775 473 A
jones@suu.edu
JONES, Sue ... 936-633-5291 442 I
sjones@angelina.edu
JONES, Susan ... 334-683-5171 ... 6 C
sjones@judson.edu
JONES, Susan, M ... 864-250-8191 421 K
susan.m.jones@gvltec.edu
JONES, Teresa, A ... 225-216-8071 192 B
jonest@mybrcc.edu
JONES, Thomas, H ... 704-406-4369 337 H
tjones@gardner-webb.edu
JONES, Tiffane ... 708-596-2000 151 H
tjones@ssc.edu
JONES, Tiffany, S ... 336-256-0863 350 C
tsjones@ncat.edu
JONES, Tim ... 334-493-3573 ... 2 H
twjones@lbwcc.edu
JONES, Tim ... 410-827-5704 203 C
tjones@chesapeake.edu
JONES, Tim ... 501-812-2760 .. 23 C
thjones@pulaskitech.edu
JONES, Tim ... 870-230-5117 .. 19 H
jonest@hsu.edu
JONES, Tim ... 850-245-0466 108 Q
tim.jones@flbog.edu
JONES, Tim ... 608-363-2137 506 D
jonestp@beloit.edu
JONES, Timothy Paul ... 502-897-4347 189 A
tjones@sbts.edu
JONES, Tina, N ... 205-652-3497 ... 9 C
tnj@uwa.edu
JONES, Todd ... 515-964-6242 168 A
tgjones@dmacc.edu
JONES, Todd ... 706-295-6335 119 G
tjones@highlands.edu
JONES, Todd ... 215-751-8167 393 A
tjones@ccp.edu
JONES, Tom, O ... 870-759-4101 .. 23 K
tjones@wbcoll.edu
JONES, Tony ... 816-802-3422 261 C
tonyjones@kcai.edu
JONES, Tony ... 804-706-5235 488 D
tjones@jtcc.edu
JONES, Tracy, A ... 605-336-6588 428 B
tjones@sfseminary.edu
JONES, Trevor, H ... 410-334-2828 210 C
tjones@worwic.edu
JONES, Trina ... 757-569-6720 489 B
tjones@pdc.edu
JONES, Trish ... 859-846-5784 188 B
tjones@midway.edu
JONES, Tristan ... 785-242-2067 180 C
tjones@neosho.edu
JONES, Tyron ... 843-661-8324 421 F
tyron.jones@fdtc.edu
JONES, Ursula ... 802-383-6679 474 G
ujones@champlain.edu
JONES, Valerie ... 432-335-6477 454 C
vjones@odessa.edu
JONES, Valerie ... 740-474-8896 367 E
vjones3@ohiochristian.edu
JONES, Valon ... 620-331-4100 178 E
vjones@indycc.edu
JONES, Virginia ... 804-333-6781 489 D
vrjones@rappahannock.edu
JONES, Walter ... 310-287-4244 .. 49 H
joneswc@wlac.edu
JONES, Wayne ... 405-733-7450 379 F
wzjones@rose.edu
JONES, JR., Wayne ... 603-862-1234 282 F
wayne.jones@unh.edu
JONES, Wendy ... 325-674-2359 441 D
jonesw@acu.edu
JONES, William ... 785-227-3380 175 E
president@bethanylb.edu
JONES, William, T ... 315-386-7063 329 A
joneswt@canton.edu
JONES, Willie ... 504-284-5520 195 L
wijones@suno.edu
JONES, Wilma ... 718-982-4001 302 A
wilma.jones@csi.cuny.edu
JONES, Yasemin ... 212-217-4052 308 B
yasemin_jones@fitnyc.edu
JONES, Yolanda ... 622-254-3528 255 A
yjones@mvsu.edu
JONES, Zantrell, Y ... 803-323-2273 426 H
jonesz@winthrop.edu
JONES-HALL,
Jennifer, L ... 618-453-4846 152 B
jennifer.jones-hall@siu.edu
JONES-JAMES,
Kimberly ... 225-490-1645 191 G
kimberly.jones-james@ololcollege.edu
JONES-JOHNSON,
Michelle ... 508-831-5473 226 E
mjonesjohnson@wpi.edu
JONES-MALONE,
Dionne ... 219-473-4305 157 A
djonesmalone@ccsj.edu
JONES-POPPE, Erin ... 802-443-2759 475 G
ejonespoppe@middlebury.edu
JONES-SCHENK, Jan ... 801-274-3280 474 D
jjonesschenk@wgu.edu
JONES SCHWEITZER,
Sharon ... 210-999-8406 464 B
sjones@trinity.edu
JONES-TINTLE,
Pamela, A ... 909-607-8684 .. 57 C
pam_jones@pitzer.edu
JONES-VARNELL,
Karla (Page) ... 252-638-7266 342 E
jonesp@cravencc.edu
JONES WATKINS,
Brenda ... 708-456-0300 153 E
brendawatkins@triton.edu
JONES-WILKINS,
Brenda ... 979-209-7264 444 D
brendawilkins@blinn.edu
JONG PARK, Tae ... 703-354-3533 482 C
JONSON, Adam ... 318-473-6571 194 A
adamj@lsua.edu
JONTE-PACE, Diane, E .. 408-554-4751 .. 62 F
djontepace@scu.edu
JOOF, Henan ... 213-763-7207 .. 49 F
joofh@lattc.edu
JOPLIN, David ... 918-444-2885 376 G
joplind@nsuok.edu
JOPLING, James ... 318-345-9266 192 J
jamesjopling@ladelta.edu
JORDAHL, Ronald, I ... 704-847-5600 349 E
rjordahl@ses.edu
JORDAN, A. Dane ... 704-233-8026 353 D
djordan@wingate.edu
JORDAN, Amber ... 706-295-6768 120 C
ajordan@gntc.edu
JORDAN, Andy ... 803-508-7241 418 C
jordana@atc.edu
JORDAN, Angela ... 312-935-2002 149 K
ajordan@robertmorris.edu
JORDAN, Angelnique ... 229-420-7030 114 I
angelnique.jordan@asurams.edu
JORDAN, Antonio ... 336-249-8186 342 F
antonio_jordan@davidsonccc.edu
JORDAN, Augustus ... 802-443-5141 475 G
jordan@middlebury.edu
JORDAN, Belva Brown .. 909-447-2527 .. 38 B
bjordan@cst.edu
JORDAN, Ben ... 256-395-2211 ... 3 G
benjordan@suscc.edu
JORDAN, Bill ... 715-346-2441 511 F
bjordan@uwsp.edu
JORDAN, Brett ... 734-432-5672 233 C
bjordan@madonna.edu
JORDAN, Brian ... 718-489-5493 322 D
bjordan@sfc.edu
JORDAN, C. Greer ... 414-955-8685 508 D
gjordan@mcw.edu
JORDAN, Chuck ... 870-777-5722 .. 23 A
JORDAN, Colin ... 941-487-4218 110 B
cjordan@ncf.edu
JORDAN, Cordell ... 405-682-1611 377 C
cjordan@occc.edu
JORDAN, Corey ... 315-386-7319 329 A
jordanc@canton.edu
JORDAN, Cyrenthia ... 507-389-2986 246 A
cyrenthia.jordan@mnsu.edu
JORDAN, Dave ... 443-518-3801 204 E
djordan@howardcc.edu
JORDAN, David, M ... 404-712-8096 119 B
david.m.jordan@emory.edu
JORDAN, Diane ... 573-334-9181 262 C
djordan_mbc@yahoo.com
JORDAN, Donald, K ... 212-650-7278 301 F
djordan@ccnyalumni.org

JORDAN, Edward, K ... 386-312-4151 106 M
edwardjordan@sjrstate.edu
JORDAN, Elizabeth, P ... 302-295-1186 .. 91 B
elizabeth.p.jordan@wilmu.edu
JORDAN, Eunice ... 802-225-3317 475 H
eunice.jordan@neci.edu
JORDAN, Heather ... 605-626-2550 428 H
heather.jordan@northern.edu
JORDAN, Holly ... 254-526-1128 445 L
holly.jordan@ctcd.edu
JORDAN, Jeffrey, C ... 206-281-2123 498 B
jordaj2@spu.edu
JORDAN, Jessica ... 415-422-5455 .. 72 A
jgjordan@usfca.edu
JORDAN, John ... 425-889-7788 496 E
john.jordan@northwestu.edu
JORDAN, Judy, G ... 615-547-1249 431 D
jjordan@cumberland.edu
JORDAN, Kindra, K ... 503-370-6055 388 D
kjordan@willamette.edu
JORDAN, Lashanda ... 601-979-2477 253 E
lashanda.w.jordan@jsums.edu
JORDAN, Laurie ... 802-443-5626 475 G
ljordan@middlebury.edu
JORDAN, Leo ... 931-431-9700 435 E
JORDAN, Lisa ... 919-684-2424 337 C
lisa.jordan@duke.edu
JORDAN, Lisa ... 619-239-0391 .. 35 C
ljordan@cwsl.edu
JORDAN, Loretta ... 714-628-4933 .. 58 B
jordan_lorrie@sccollege.edu
JORDAN, Lucille, A ... 603-578-8900 280 M
ljordan@ccsnh.edu
JORDAN, Marilyn, L ... 619-239-0391 .. 35 C
mjordan@cwsl.edu
JORDAN, Mary, V ... 423-439-4445 431 H
jordanm@etsu.edu
JORDAN, Matthew ... 818-947-2316 .. 49 G
jordanmt@lavc.edu
JORDAN, Megan, K ... 781-283-3795 225 D
mjordan@wellesley.edu
JORDAN, Michael ... 914-633-2206 311 B
mjordan@iona.edu
JORDAN, Michael ... 585-567-9228 310 F
michael.jordan@houghton.edu
JORDAN, Michael, J ... 252-823-5166 343 A
jordanm@edgecombe.edu
JORDAN, Myron ... 510-748-2301 .. 56 G
mjordan@peralta.edu
JORDAN, Myron ... 510-748-2234 .. 56 G
mjordan@peralta.edu
JORDAN, Nancy ... 603-623-0313 281 G
nancyjordan@nhia.edu
JORDAN, Nancy ... 903-223-3166 460 D
njordan@tamut.edu
JORDAN, Percy ... 409-984-6335 462 E
jordanpj@lamarpa.edu
JORDAN, Peter ... 817-515-4501 458 B
peter.jordan@tccd.edu
JORDAN, Richard ... 806-414-9648 463 E
richard.jordan@ttuhsc.edu
JORDAN, Ronald ... 714-516-5486 .. 36 G
rpjordan@chapman.edu
JORDAN, Sandra ... 803-641-3434 425 A
sandraj@usca.edu
JORDAN, Scott ... 860-486-3455 .. 88 G
scott.jordan@uconn.edu
JORDAN, Shannon ... 724-532-6740 410 C
shannon.jordan@stvincent.edu
JORDAN, Stacy ... 501-205-8817 .. 19 B
sjordan@cbc.edu
JORDAN, Susan ... 870-862-8131 .. 21 D
sjordan@southark.edu
JORDAN, Tuajuanda, C . 240-895-4410 206 G
tcjordan@smcm.edu
JORDAN, Vivian, R ... 240-895-2039 206 G
vrjordan@smcm.edu
JORDAN-GOODEN,
Joyce ... 601-979-1591 253 E
joyce.m.jordan-gooden@jsums.edu
JORDAN-SMITH,
Barbara ... 518-445-3398 297 K
bjord@albanylaw.edu
JORDANO, Mark ... 814-871-7438 395 H
jordan001@gannon.edu
JORDEN, Rhonda ... 501-603-1401 .. 22 C
jordenrhondal@uams.edu
JORDEN, Steven ... 660-626-2529 257 A
sjorden@atsu.edu
JORDON, Christina ... 863-638-2944 114 A
cmjordon@webber.edu
JORDON, Renee ... 617-603-6900 222 F
renee.jordon@necb.edu
JORDRE, Todd ... 605-626-3005 428 H
todd.jordre@northern.edu
JORE, Katie ... 715-346-3710 511 F
kjore@uwsp.edu

JORGENS, Amy, G ... 402-323-3414 276 K
ajorgens@southeast.edu
JORGENSEN, Harlan, R . 712-707-7333 172 G
harlan@nwciowa.edu
JORGENSEN, Jerry ... 605-274-4045 426 K
jerry.jorgensen@augie.edu
JORGENSEN, Laurie ... 630-942-2755 136 D
jorgensenl@cod.edu
JORGENSEN, Michael ... 435-283-7262 474 A
michael.jorgensen@snow.edu
JORGENSEN, Patti ... 920-735-5649 513 F
jorgensp@fvtc.edu
JORGENSEN, Ronald, A 712-274-5128 172 A
jorgensenr@morningside.edu
JORGENSON, Evelyn, E 479-619-4191 .. 20 F
ejorgenson@nwacc.edu
JORGENSON, Jan ... 509-452-5100 496 H
jjorgenson@pnwu.edu
JORISSEN, Shari ... 866-492-5336 251 E
shari.jorissen@mail.waldenu.edu
JOR'DAN, Jamilah ... 773-995-2076 135 F
jjordan@csu.edu
JOSAY ZULLO, Ashley .. 724-838-7832 410 E
josay@setonhill.edu
JOSCHKO, Brian ... 309-677-1002 134 G
bjoschko@bradley.edu
JOSE, Juana Clare ... 520-383-8401 .. 16 G
jjose@tocc.edu
JOSE, Robert ... 617-373-7515 223 D
JOSEPH, Beatriz ... 210-486-3936 441 H
ijospeh@alamo.edu
JOSEPH, Bel ... 213-615-7236 .. 37 B
njoseph@thechicagoschool.edu
JOSEPH, Cynthia ... 562-907-4830 .. 75 A
cjoseph@whittier.edu
JOSEPH, Daniel, P ... 410-951-3549 208 F
djoseph@coppin.edu
JOSEPH, Darnell ... 713-313-1826 461 E
djoseph@tsu.edu
JOSEPH, Elizabeth ... 708-534-5000 138 H
ejoseph@govst.edu
JOSEPH, Eric ... 405-692-3106 376 C
ejoseph@macu.edu
JOSEPH, James, E ... 315-445-4279 312 F
josepjae@lemoyne.edu
JOSEPH, Jann ... 574-520-4183 160 F
jljoseph@iusb.edu
JOSEPH, Jerry ... 217-206-6003 154 A
gjose1@uis.edu
JOSEPH, Joanne ... 315-792-7326 330 A
joanne.joseph@sunyit.edu
JOSEPH, John ... 810-766-4103 227 F
jjosep08@baker.edu
JOSEPH, Josh ... 212-960-0083 334 P
josh.joseph@yu.edu
JOSEPH, Laura ... 631-420-2003 329 D
laura.joseph@farmingdale.edu
JOSEPH, Laurel ... 281-756-3513 442 C
ljoseph@alvincollege.edu
JOSEPH, Mark ... 740-284-5870 361 L
mjoseph@franciscan.edu
JOSEPH, Mary Ann ... 617-873-0227 213 B
maryann.joseph@cambridgecollege.edu
JOSEPH, Michael ... 219-464-6896 165 D
michael.joseph@valpo.edu
JOSEPH, Michiko ... 808-689-2710 130 A
msjoseph@hawaii.edu
JOSEPH, Noson ... 718-601-3523 334 O
njoseph@ytariverdale.org
JOSEPH, Patricia ... 484-365-7659 400 E
joseph@lincoln.edu
JOSEPH, Sonya, F ... 407-582-7734 113 F
sjoseph@valenciacollege.edu
JOSEPH, Stephen, M ... 724-287-8711 390 J
steve.joseph@bc3.edu
JOSEPH, Susan ... 423-697-3136 436 F
susan.joseph@chattanoogastate.edu
JOSEPH, Wendy ... 253-589-5822 493 F
wendy.joseph@cptc.edu
JOSEPH-SILVERSTEIN,
Jackie ... 920-459-6610 512 D
jackie.josephsilvers@uwc.edu
JOSEPHSON, David ... 973-655-6956 287 D
josephsond@mail.montclair.edu
JOSEY, Peige ... 334-222-6591 .... 2 H
pjosey@lbwcc.edu
JOSHEE, Jeet ... 562-985-4106 .. 32 C
jeet.joshee@csulb.edu
JOSHEE, Jeet ... 562-985-8330 .. 32 C
jeet.joshee@csulb.edu
JOSHI, Maulin ... 973-618-3519 284 D
mjoshi@caldwell.edu
JOSLIN, Dennis, A ... 402-354-7257 275 P
dennis.joslin@methodistcollege.edu
JOSLIN, Michael ... 661-362-3260 .. 39 C
michael.joslin@canyons.edu
JOSLIN, Monica ... 413-662-5242 218 C
m.joslin@mcla.edu

JOSLIN, Randy ... 530-541-4660 .. 47 I
joslin@ltcc.edu
JOSS, Jamie ... 304-637-1342 501 H
jossj@dewv.edu
JOSS, Liz ... 317-931-2316 157 D
ljoss@cts.edu
JOSSELL, Steven ... 662-621-4304 252 E
sjossell@coahomacc.edu
JOST, Muktha, B ... 336-285-2496 350 C
mjost@ncat.edu
JOST, Steve, A ... 301-860-4212 208 E
sjost@bowiestate.edu
JOTHEN, Karen ... 651-690-6666 249 T
kgjothen@stkate.edu
JOUGHIN, Sarah ... 207-581-3437 201 B
JOURDAN, Lee Ann ... 765-658-4036 157 H
leeannjourdan@depauw.edu
JOVANOVICH, Donna ... 804-594-1576 488 D
djovanovich@jtcc.edu
JOVELL, Kristi ... 802-865-5728 474 G
kjovell@champlain.edu
JOVEN, Robert ... 203-582-3468 .. 88 A
robert.joven@quinnipiac.edu
JOWERS, Angel ... 205-652-3547 .... 9 C
ajowers@uwa.edu
JOY, Alonzo, F ... 202-806-6100 .. 92 C
JOY, Darrell ... 225-248-1015 191 F
djoy@fortis.edu
JOY, John ... 937-393-3431 370 C
jjoy@sscc.edu
JOY, Steaven ... 731-426-7531 432 J
sjoy@lanecollege.edu
JOYAUX, Aimee ... 804-862-6100 484 F
ajoyaux@rbc.edu
JOYCE, Colman ... 503-206-3205 387 I
cjoyce@uws.edu
JOYCE, Dan ... 610-660-3291 409 H
djoyce@sju.edu
JOYCE, Daniel ... 215-951-1539 398 F
joyced@lasalle.edu
JOYCE, David, C ... 828-884-8264 335 L
president@brevard.edu
JOYCE, Gerard ... 610-282-1100 393 G
gerard.joyce@desales.edu
JOYCE, Jane ... 617-349-8785 216 D
ajoyce5@lesley.edu
JOYCE, Jeff ... 828-884-8202 335 L
joycejj@brevard.edu
JOYCE, Kelly ... 812-866-7160 158 C
joyce@hanover.edu
JOYCE, Kevin ... 914-674-7775 314 I
kjoyce@mercy.edu
JOYCE, Kimberly ... 410-287-1022 203 B
kjoyce@cecil.edu
JOYCE, Maureen ... 617-588-1363 211 G
mjoyce@bfit.edu
JOYE, Teresa ... 510-649-2410 .. 44 J
tjoye@gtu.edu
JOYNER, Barry ... 912-478-5322 120 E
joyner@georgiasouthern.edu
JOYNER, Caroline ... 912-623-2400 118 H
ccjoyner@ega.edu
JOYNER, Chartarra ... 336-334-7631 350 C
cmjoyne2@ncat.edu
JOYNER, Jill ... 704-847-5600 349 E
jjoyner@ses.edu
JOYNER, Joseph, G ... 904-819-6288 .. 98 I
jjoyner@flagler.edu
JOYNER, Kathy ... 415-485-9502 .. 39 E
k.joyner@marin.edu
JOYNER, Laurie, M ... 773-298-3000 151 C
joyner@sxu.edu
JOYNER, Mark ... 919-497-3204 339 F
mjoyner@louisburg.edu
JOYNER, Scott ... 803-321-5617 422 H
scott.joyner@newberry.edu
JOYNER, SR., Stephen .. 704-330-1406 338 I
sjoyner@jcsu.edu
JOYNER, Wendell ... 718-289-5910 301 D
wendell.joyner@bcc.cuny.edu
JOYNER-GRAHAM,
JoAnn ... 718-270-4832 303 C
jjoyner@mec.cuny.edu
JOYNER-KEENE, Faye ... 618-524-3003 151 G
fayej@shawneecc.edu
JOZAITIS, Judy ... 217-786-2200 144 B
judy.jozaitis@llcc.edu
JOZWIAK, Jeff ... 574-239-8377 158 M
jjozwiak@hcc-nd.edu
JROSKI, Linda, L ... 610-330-5017 399 B
jroskil@lafayette.edu
JUARBE, Lorraine ... 787-763-6425 523 F
ljuarbe@inter.edu
JUARBE, Myriam ... 787-720-4476 527 A
asistenciaeconomica@mizpa.edu
JUAREZ, Elisa ... 520-494-5426 .. 11 P
elisa.juarez@centralaz.edu

JUAREZ, Reina ... 858-534-3755 .. 69 E
rjuarez@ucsd.edu
JUCKIEWICZ, Robert, W 516-463-6900 310 D
robert.w.juckiewicz@hofstra.edu
JUDD, Kimberly ... 802-387-6723 475 C
kjudd@landmark.edu
JUDD, Matthew ... 909-274-4425 .. 52 I
mjudd@mtsac.edu
JUDD, Summer ... 731-989-6662 432 C
sjudd@fhu.edu
JUDD, Tim ... 270-789-5027 184 B
tmjudd@campbellsville.edu
JUDE, China ... 718-997-2795 303 E
china.jude@qc.cuny.edu
JUDE, Willie ... 573-681-5506 261 H
judew@lincolnu.edu
JUDGE, Anne Marie ... 518-445-3219 297 K
ajudg@albanylaw.edu
JUDGE, Charlie, N ... 412-578-6069 391 G
ncjudge@carlow.edu
JUDGE, Jeffrey ... 952-358-8585 246 D
jeff.judge@normandale.edu
JUDGE, John ... 202-319-5160 .. 91 D
judge@cua.edu
JUDGE, Kristin, O ... 215-572-2928 389 D
judgek@arcadia.edu
JUDGE, Linda ... 925-631-4686 .. 59 C
ljudge@stmarys-ca.edu
JUDGE, Rebecca ... 507-786-3358 250 C
judge@stolaf.edu
JUDGE, Sheila ... 504-816-4370 191 E
sjudge@dillard.edu
JUDKINS, Jason ... 760-245-4271 .. 73 E
jason.judkins@vvc.edu
JUDKINS, Leslie ... 229-243-6852 116 C
leslie.judkins@bainbridge.edu
JUDSON, Frank ... 570-586-2400 392 E
fjudson@clarkssummitu.edu
JUDY, Allison ... 308-635-6081 278 B
judya2@wncc.edu
JUDY, Joyce, M ... 802-828-2800 477 B
jmj10300@ccv.vsc.edu
JUEDES, Scott ... 781-283-2360 225 D
sjuedes@wellesley.edu
JUEHNE, Elizabeth ... 618-537-6529 145 C
bjuehne@mckendree.edu
JUELE, Lilia ... 845-574-4480 321 F
ljuele@sunyrockland.edu
JUERGENS, Valorie ... 269-467-9945 230 C
vjuergens@glenoaks.edu
JUGOVICH, Shelly ... 218-748-2416 247 A
shelly.jugovich@mesabirange.edu
JUHL, Lavonne ... 501-812-2293 .. 23 C
ljuhl@pulaskitech.edu
JUHLIN, Eric ... 801-281-7603 .. 29 A
eric.juhlin@collegeamerica.edu
JUHLIN, Eric ... 800-972-5149 471 K
JUKANOVICH, Jennifer . 978-867-4263 215 D
jennifer.jukanovich@gordon.edu
JUKKALA, Clint, A ... 215-972-7623 404 Q
cjukkala@pafa.edu
JUKOSKI, Mary Ellen ... 860-215-9001 .. 86 F
mjukoski@trcc.commnet.edu
JULIA, Jake ... 847-491-2912 148 C
jjulia@northwestern.edu
JULIAN, Augusta, A ... 859-246-6501 185 G
augusta.julian@kctcs.edu
JULIAN, Betsy ... 541-383-7530 382 B
bjulian@cocc.edu
JULIAN, Charity ... 812-749-1235 163 B
cjulian@oak.edu
JULIAN, Elizabeth, A ... 706-771-4049 116 A
ejulian@augustatech.edu
JULIAN, James ... 617-287-7050 216 G
jjulian@umassp.edu
JULIAN, Janelle ... 314-719-8057 260 C
jjulian@fontbonne.edu
JULIAN, Karen, M ... 651-962-6176 251 D
kmjulian@stthomas.edu
JULIAN, Kris, N ... 336-629-2758 345 F
knjulian@randolph.edu
JULIAN, Leisa ... 785-864-4868 181 I
ljulian@ku.edu
JULIAN, Tijuana, S ... 417-873-7215 259 G
tjulian@drury.edu
JULIAN, Tracey ... 423-636-7300 439 C
tjulian@tusculum.edu
JULIAN BOWDEN,
Kimberly ... 404-727-8782 119 B
kjulian@emory.edu
JULIANO, Ben ... 530-898-5623 .. 31 D
bjuliano@csuchico.edu
JULIANO, Joseph, P ... 212-998-8015 318 D
joe.juliano@nyu.edu
JULIANO, Roland ... 908-852-1400 284 G
julianor@centenaryuniversity.edu
JULIEN, Earlye, A ... 563-884-5476 172 H
earlye.julien@palmer.edu

K

KALITA, Tish .... 260-982-5083 162 Q
lnkalita@manchester.edu
KALK, Jonathan .... 808-245-8272 130 F
kalk@hawaii.edu
KALKA, Alicia .... 304-367-4917 504 A
alicia.kalka@fairmontstate.edu
KALKBRENNER,
Suzanne, K .... 518-629-4530 310 G
s.kalkbrenner@hvcc.edu
KALLERGIS, Sophia, D .. 440-826-2180 357 B
skallerg@bw.edu
KALLIERIS, Nick, C .... 847-543-2476 136 E
nkallieris@clcillinois.edu
KALLIN, Robert .... 717-337-6301 396 A
rkallin@gettysburg.edu
KALLIO, Kenneth .... 585-245-5531 327 B
kallio@geneseo.edu
KALLMEYER, Adam .... 513-862-3723 362 E
adam.kallmeyer@email.gscollege.edu
KALLUSKY, Barbara .... 651-290-7678 248 U
barbara.kallusky@mitchellhamline.edu
KALM, Stephen .... 406-243-4970 271 G
stephen.kalm@umontana.edu
KALMANOWITZ, Osher . 718-645-0536 315 G
phecht@thejnet.com
KALMANSON, Dan, P ... 973-378-9856 291 F
daniel.kalmanson@shu.edu
KALMEY, Jon .... 814-866-8147 399 C
jkalmey@lecom.edu
KALOGIANNIS, Natalie .. 707-664-2874.. 35 A
natalie.kalogiannis@sonoma.edu
KALOOSTIAN, Damita .... 602-243-8021.. 14 D
damita.kaloostian@smcmail.maricopa.edu
KALSBEEK, David, H ..... 312-362-8706 137 C
dkalsbee@depaul.edu
KALSCHEUR, S.J.,
Gregory .... 617-552-2393 212 E
gregory.kalscheur@bc.edu
KALTCHEV, Matey .... 414-277-7300 509 A
kaltchev@msoe.edu
KALTCHEV, Matey .... 414-277-7544 509 A
kaltchev@msoe.edu
KALTENECKER, Mike ..... 208-459-5187 131 H
mkaltenecker@collegeofidaho.edu
KALTENMARK, Michael . 317-940-9672 156 I
mkaltenm@butler.edu
KALTHOFF, Theodore, J 501-882-8830.. 17 M
tjkalthoff@asub.edu
KALU, Mma .... 919-546-8350 348 I
mkalu@shawu.edu
KALUARACHCHI, Jagath 435-797-2776 473 C
jagath.kaluarachchi@usu.edu
KALUSH, Paul .... 213-738-6818.. 65 I
accounting@swlaw.edu
KALWEIT, Clayton .... 847-970-4811 154 H
ckalweit@usml.edu
KALYAYEVA, Julia .... 510-845-0752.. 75 E
jkalyayeva@wi.edu
KALYN, Andrea .... 440-775-8200 367 B
andrea.kalyn@oberlin.edu
KALYNOVSKYI, Serhii ... 707-965-6218.. 55 F
skalynovskyi@puc.edu
KAM, Moshe .... 973-596-6506 288 A
moshe.kam@njit.edu
KAMAHELE, Ron .... 907-786-1419.. 10 A
rckamahale@alaska.edu
KAMARA, Sheku .... 414-277-7416 509 A
kamara@msoe.edu
KAMAT, Deborah .... 440-484-7027 373 B
deborah.kamat@ursuline.edu
KAMATH, Kiran .... 831-646-4034.. 52 G
kkamath@mpc.edu
KAMENETSKY, Shmuel .. 215-473-1212 411 A
talmudicalyeshiva@yahoo.com
KAMENETSKY, Sholom . 215-477-1000 411 A
talmudicalyeshvia@yahoo.com
KAMERON, Katherine .... 425-352-8388 492 K
kkameron@cascadia.edu
KAMIAB, Jane .... 336-770-3297 352 B
kamiabj@uncsa.edu
KAMICKER, Anfrea .... 724-846-5100 395 J
KAMIENIECKI, Sheldon . 831-459-2919.. 70 C
sk1@ucsc.edu
KAMINSKI, Crystal .... 312-752-2122 142 E
crystal.kaminski@kendall.edu
KAMINSKI, Janice, M ... 724-480-3423 392 K
jan.kaminski@ccbc.edu
KAMINSKI, Linda .... 509-574-4635 500 I
lkaminski@yvcc.edu
KAMINSKI, Marie .... 414-847-3334 508 G
mkaminski@miad.edu
KAMINSKI, Michael ...... 213-624-1200.. 42 N
mkaminski@fidm.edu
KAMINSKY, Paul, A ...... 615-353-3615 437 D
paul.kaminsky@nscc.edu
KAMITSUKA, David .... 440-775-8410 367 B
david.kamitsuka@oberlin.edu
KAMLET, Lee .... 203-582-3641.. 88 A
lee.kamlet@quinnipiac.edu
KAMMER, Dan .... 573-876-7273 267 G
dkammer@stephens.edu
KAMMER, Roy .... 651-213-4863 242 F
rkammer@hazeldenbettyford.edu
KAMMERER, Andy, A .... 402-280-4273 274 D
andykammerer@creighton.edu
KAMMERER, Joe .... 417-255-7240 263 I
joekammerer@missouristate.edu
KAMMERMAN, Amy ...... 615-383-4848 441 A
akammerman@watkins.edu
KAMMERZELL, Joan ...... 360-752-8436 492 H
jkammerzell@btc.edu
KAMOCHE, Njambi .... 847-925-6764 139 B
nkamoche@harpercollege.edu
KAMP, Cyndi .... 317-955-6103 162 R
ckamp@marian.edu
KAMPA, Michelle .... 414-847-3262 508 G
michellekampa@miad.edu
KAMPE, Brent, S .... 626-584-5423.. 43 K
brentkampe@fuller.edu
KAMPF, Stephen .... 419-372-7485 357 F
skampf@bgsu.edu
KAMPFSCHULTE, Darcy . 616-632-2894 227 C
kampfdar@aquinas.edu
KAMPHAUS, Lisa .... 412-536-1526 398 E
lisa.kamphaus@laroche.edu
KAMPHAUS, Randy, W . 541-346-1601 387 F
randyk@uoregon.edu
KAMPS, Anne .... 920-498-6367 514 G
anne.kamps@nwtc.edu
KAMPS, Larissa .... 866-323-0233.. 57 M
admissions@providencecc.edu
KAMWITHI, Gina .... 419-755-4711 366 E
gkamwithi@ncstatecollege.edu
KANACH, Nancy, A .... 609-258-5524 288 F
nkanach@princeton.edu
KANAK, Daniel .... 610-359-5135 393 E
dkanak@dccc.edu
KANAKIS, Chris .... 312-942-2831 150 F
chris_kanakis@rush.edu
KANALIS, Mike .... 724-938-4409 405 F
kanalis@calu.edu
KANARAS, Elizabeth ...... 610-902-8283 391 B
KANAREK, Berel .... 914-736-1500 319 E
KANAREK, E .... 914-736-1500 319 E
KANAWADA, Christine .. 518-694-7357 297 J
christine.kanawada@acphs.edu
KANBAR, Hiam .... 831-242-5618 517 K
hiam.n.kanbar@dliflc.edu
KANDUS-FISHER,
Christopher .... 617-747-2231 212 B
studentaffairs@berklee.edu
KANE, Andrew .... 609-258-3469 288 F
kane@princeton.edu
KANE, Barry, S .... 212-854-1458 305 E
barry@columbia.edu
KANE, Brian .... 610-785-6265 409 F
bkane@scs.edu
KANE, Candice .... 704-233-8631 353 D
c.kane@wingate.edu
KANE, Christopher .... 215-951-1585 398 F
kanec@lasalle.edu
KANE, Colleen .... 715-422-5510 514 B
colleen.kane@mstc.edu
KANE, Daniel, C .... 207-768-9475 201 G
daniel.c.kane@maine.edu
KANE, Elizabeth .... 201-761-6046 291 D
ekane@saintpeters.edu
KANE, Jessie .... 478-825-6291 119 C
kanej@fvsu.edu
KANE, Katherine, J .... 864-938-3913 423 D
kjkane@presby.edu
KANE, Kathleen .... 856-227-7200 284 E
kkane@camdencc.edu
KANE, Kerri .... 413-755-4115 221 B
kpkane@stcc.edu
KANE, Kevin, M .... 610-660-3025 409 H
kkane@sju.edu
KANE, Kim .... 707-638-5280.. 67 H
kim.kane@tu.edu
KANE, Luanne .... 763-433-1297 243 K
luanne.kane@anokaramsey.edu
KANE, Michael .... 760-384-6258.. 47 B
michael.kane@cerrocoso.edu
KANE, Michael .... 859-858-3511 183 D
mike.kane@asbury.edu
KANE, Michael .... 281-476-1858 455 L
michael.kane@sjcd.edu
KANE, Molly .... 847-290-6425 147 J
mkane@nwsc.edu
KANE, Robert .... 215-567-7080 389 E
rkane@aii.edu
KANE, Robert, C .... 202-685-3927 518 B
galen.r.kane.mil@ndu.edu
KANE, Ryan, D .... 407-582-3421 113 F
rkane8@valenciacollege.edu
KANE, Sara, F .... 863-638-7602 113 I
sara.kane@warner.edu
KANE, Scott .... 401-456-8061 417 A
skane@ric.edu
KANE, Sylvia .... 714-556-3610.. 72 F
KANE, Terrence .... 607-777-5014 325 A
tkane@binghamton.edu
KANE, Terrence .... 607-777-2131 325 A
tkane@binghamton.edu
KANE, Thomas .... 781-891-2340 212 A
tkane@bentley.edu
KANE, Thomas, F .... 570-674-6223 401 M
tkane@misericordia.edu
KANE, Vicki .... 814-944-5643 415 H
vicki.kane@yti.edu
KANELOS, Gwen, E .... 708-209-3101 136 I
gwen.kanelos@cuchicago.edu
KANELOS, Peter .... 410-626-2510 206 F
pkanelos@sjc.edu
KANEVSKAYA, Svetlana . 212-752-1530 312 G
svetlana.kanevskaya@limcollege.edu
KANG, Angela .... 218-262-6746 244 H
angela.kang@hibbing.edu
KANG, David .... 303-492-4212.. 83 B
david.kang@colorado.edu
KANG, Hyo Jeong .... 714-535-3886.. 64 F
hjkang@southbaylo.edu
KANG, Jerry .... 310-825-3935.. 69 B
jkang@equity.ucla.edu
KANG, Mia .... 770-220-7906 119 D
academic@gcuniv.edu
KANG, Min .... 714-525-0088.. 44 I
gmu@gm.edu
KANG, Soohae .... 714-527-0691.. 42 H
KANG, Woo Joong .... 562-926-1023.. 57 J
wookang78@ptsa.edu
KANGAS, Michelle .... 218-855-8034 244 C
mkangas@clcmn.edu
KANGAS, Richard .... 218-322-2319 245 B
richard.kangas@itascacc.edu
KANIA, Edward, A .... 704-894-2125 337 B
edkania@davidson.edu
KANICH, Amy .... 814-886-6483 402 E
akanich@mtaloy.edu
KANIKKEBERG,
Dee Dee .... 208-885-6571 132 I
deedeek@uidaho.edu
KANIS, David .... 773-995-2497 135 F
dkanis@csu.edu
KANISS, John .... 253-589-5529 493 F
john.kaniss@cptc.edu
KANLIOGLU, Osman ..... 832-230-5555 453 K
osman@na.edu
KANN, Andrea .... 212-824-2208 309 F
akann@huc.edu
KANN, Stephanie, J ...... 847-808-8444 155 G
skann@worshamcollege.com
KANNAN, Gavindarajan . 478-825-6320 119 C
kannang@fvsu.edu
KANNE, Lynn .... 206-934-4072 497 I
lynn.kanne@seattlecolleges.edu
KANNENBERG, Gregory 920-465-2239 510 E
kannenbg@uwgb.edu
KANNENWISCHER,
Susan, E .... 614-236-6511 358 A
skannenwischer@capital.edu
KANOY, David .... 910-362-7695 341 E
dkanoy@cfcc.edu
KANPOL, Barry .... 616-331-6820 230 G
kanpolb@gvsu.edu
KANT, Sudarson .... 314-340-3317 260 H
kants@hssu.edu
KANTARDJIEFF,
Katherine .... 760-750-7204.. 33 E
kkantard@csusm.edu
KANTER, Connie .... 206-296-6148 498 D
kanterc@seattleu.edu
KANTER, Steven .... 816-235-1803 268 D
kantersl@umkc.edu
KANTNER, Joanne .... 815-825-9450 142 F
joanne.kantner@kishwaukeecollege.edu
KANTNER, John .... 904-620-1360 110 E
j.kantner@unf.edu
KANTNER, John .... 904-620-2455 110 E
j.kantner@unf.edu
KANTNER, Michael .... 856-256-4566 289 H
kantner@rowan.edu
KANTO, Kind .... 691-330-2620 519 G
kank@comfsm.fm
KANTOR, Ali .... 617-521-1038 224 E
ali.kantor@simmons.edu
KANTOR, Rebecca .... 303-315-6343.. 83 D
rebecca.kantor@ucdenver.edu
KANU, Andrew .... 804-524-5930 491 A
akanu@vsu.edu
KANZ, Maryellen .... 507-453-2673 245 G
mkanz@southeastmn.edu
KAO, Chi-Chang .... 650-723-2300.. 66 C
KAO, Teresa .... 626-571-5110.. 48 G
teresakao@les.edu
KAOPUIKI, Ryon .... 317-447-6126 158 H
ryon.kaopuiki@harrison.edu
KAOUDIS, Kathy .... 303-914-6341.. 82 B
kathy.koaudis@rrcc.edu
KAPCSOS, Kathy .... 610-861-5499 403 B
kkapcsos@northampton.edu
KAPFHAMMER, Sean .... 410-777-2836 202 D
srkapfhammer@aacc.edu
KAPILESHWARI,
Sameer .... 850-599-8033 109 A
sameer.kapileshwari@famu.edu
KAPIN, Kim .... 928-776-2067.. 17 G
kim.kapin@yc.edu
KAPLA, Dale, P .... 906-227-2920 235 A
dkapla@nmu.edu
KAPLAN, Anita, S .... 561-868-4102 105 A
kaplana1@palmbeachstate.edu
KAPLAN, Anne, C .... 815-753-9503 147 H
akaplan@niu.edu
KAPLAN, Beth .... 617-879-2250 226 A
bkaplan@wheelock.edu
KAPLAN, John .... 208-426-3221 131 C
johnkaplan@boisestate.edu
KAPLAN, Jonathan, A ... 866-492-5336 251 E
jonathan.kaplan@mail.waldenu.edu
KAPLAN, Judith .... 216-987-4497 360 E
judith.kaplan@tri-c.edu
KAPLAN, Leonard, I ...... 973-596-3638 288 A
leonard.i.kaplan@njit.edu
KAPLAN, Richard .... 617-732-2808 221 E
richard.kaplan@mcphs.edu
KAPLAN, Ronald, S .... 847-578-8840 150 E
ronald.kaplan@rosalindfranklin.edu
KAPLAN, Steven, H .... 203-932-7276.. 89 D
skaplan@newhaven.edu
KAPLAN, Thomas .... 937-327-7040 374 A
tkaplan@wittenberg.edu
KAPLINSKY, Yoheved ..... 212-799-5000 312 B
KAPLOWITZ, Craig .... 847-628-1126 142 B
ckaplowitz@judsonu.edu
KAPOCIUS, Andrew .... 219-980-6841 160 C
ajkapoci@iun.edu
KAPOUN, Jim .... 717-815-1353 415 G
jkapoun@ycp.edu
KAPP, Alisha .... 217-854-5110 134 E
alisha.kapp@blackburn.edu
KAPP, Elizabeth .... 701-252-3467 355 J
elizabeth.kapp@uj.edu
KAPPANADZE,
Margaret .... 607-735-1867 307 G
mkappanadze@elmira.edu
KAPPAUF, Linda .... 704-290-5215 346 F
lkappauf@spcc.edu
KAPPEL, Rachel .... 518-828-4181 305 D
rachel.kappel@sunycgcc.edu
KAPPEL, Stephanie .... 304-214-8801 503 E
skappel@wvncc.edu
KAPPELER, Victor .... 859-622-3565 184 F
victor.kappeler@eku.edu
KAPPENMAN, Angi .... 605-256-5134 428 G
angi.kappenman@dsu.edu
KAPPES, Christiaan .... 412-321-8383 391 A
dean@bcs.edu
KAPRAL, Jami .... 920-693-1159 513 H
jami.kapral@gotoltc.edu
KAPRIVE, Mark .... 561-803-2542 104 I
mark_kaprive@pba.edu
KAPSAL, Sean .... 859-344-3600 189 G
kapsals@thomasmore.edu
KAPTAIN, Laurence .... 303-352-3559.. 83 D
laurence.kaptain@ucdenver.edu
KAPTIK, Michael, W ..... 808-956-8177 129 J
kaptik@hawaii.edu
KAPUR, Anup .... 609-771-2859 284 I
kapura@tcnj.edu
KAPURCH, Jason .... 508-929-8045 219 A
jkapurch@worcester.edu
KARABETSOS,
Michael, L .... 517-264-7109 236 I
mkarabet@sienaheights.edu
KARACAL, Cem .... 618-650-2861 152 C
skaraca@siue.edu
KARAFA, Andy .... 716-673-3173 325 C
andy.karafa@fredonia.edu
KARAFIN, Diana .... 212-998-4426 318 D
diana.karafin@nyu.edu
KARAFIN, Diana, L .... 212-998-4426 318 D
diana.karafin@nyu.edu
KARAGEZIAN, Vardan ... 818-240-6900.. 25 O
KARAGOZIAN, Ann, R .. 310-825-5653.. 69 B
akaragozian@conet.ucla.edu
KARAHADIAN, Milton ... 619-849-2649.. 57 H
miltonkarahadian@pointloma.edu
KARAM, Robert .... 318-342-5014 198 A
karam@ulm.edu

KAUSHAL, Janice .... 708-709-3595 148 I
jkaushal@prairiestate.edu
KAUSHANSKY, Kenneth 631-444-9011 325 F
kenneth.kashansky@stonybrook.edu
KAUSHIK, Suresh, C ..... 334-420-4244.... 3 H
skaushik@trenholmstate.edu
KAUSS, Bruce .... 541-278-5763 382 A
bkauss@bluecc.edu
KAUTZ, III, John .... 561-803-2084 104 I
john_kautz@pba.edu
KAUTZ, Kathy .... 203-932-7338.. 89 D
kkautz@newhaven.edu
KAUTZ, Rebecca .... 308-635-6062 278 B
kautzb2@wncc.edu
KAUTZMAN, Amy .... 916-278-5679.. 33 C
kautzman@csus.edu
KAVALIER, Barbara .... 636-922-8380 265 J
KAVALIERATOS,
Gerasimos (Jerry) .... 480-860-2700.. 12 N
gkavalieratos@taliesin.edu
KAVANAGH, Kathy, J .... 914-594-4487 318 A
kathy_johnston@nymc.edu
KAVANAGH, Kenneth .... 239-590-7007 109 C
kavanagh@fgcu.edu
KAVANAUGH, Gerard .... 508-999-8002 217 A
gkavanaugh@umassd.edu
KAVANAUGH, Maria, A . 508-565-1331 224 H
mkavanaugh@stonehill.edu
KAVANAUGH, Steven ..... 610-896-1141 397 F
skavanau@haverford.edu
KAVASCH, Kris .... 903-877-7752 469 A
kris.kavasch@uthct.edu
KAVCSAK, Lynn, E .... 919-866-5696 347 D
lekavcsak@waketech.edu
KAVENEY, Shannon .... 562-860-2451.. 36 A
skaveney@cerritos.edu
KAVOURIS, John .... 312-369-8646 136 H
jkavouris@colum.edu
KAVRAN, Elizabeth .... 440-646-8107 373 B
ekavran@ursuline.edu
KAWAHARA, Colleen .... 503-370-6031 388 D
kawahara@willamette.edu
KAWAI`AE`A, Keiki .... 808-932-7360 129 I
keiki@hawaii.edu
KAWALL, Scott .... 815-825-9837 142 F
scott.kawall@kishwaukeecollege.edu
KAWANNA, JR.,
Ronald .... 708-596-2000 151 H
rkawanna@ssc.edu
KAWAR, Ferris .... 310-434-3911.. 62 G
kawar_ferris@smc.edu
KAWAUCHI, John .... 970-943-2266.. 84 E
jkawauchi@western.edu
KAY, Carol .... 915-831-6725 449 A
ckay@epcc.edu
KAY, Catherine .... 313-577-8423 239 C
catherine.kay@wayne.edu
KAY, Gwen .... 518-320-1376 324 F
gwen.kay@suny.edu
KAY, James, F .... 609-497-7815 288 E
academic.dean@ptsem.edu
KAY, Sabrina .... 213-355-7777.. 43 H
sabrina.kay@fremont.edu
KAY-WONG, Chelsea ...... 808-932-7442 129 I
ckwong@hawaii.edu
KAYALAR, Dee .... 718-940-5566 322 G
dkayalar@sjcny.edu
KAYE, Johanna .... 503-554-2235 383 C
kayej@georgefox.edu
KAYE, Joyce .... 212-592-2011 324 A
jkaye3@sva.edu
KAYE, Karen .... 440-826-2168 357 B
kkaye@bw.edu
KAYLOR, Alice, J .... 724-537-4566 410 B
alice.kaylor@email.stvincent.edu
KAYLOR, Debbie .... 208-426-4351 131 C
debbiekaylor@boisestate.edu
KAYLOR, Sean, P .... 845-575-3000 314 C
sean.kaylor@marist.edu
KAYNAMA, Shohreh, A . 410-704-3342 209 C
skaynama@towson.edu
KAYNARD, Meryl .... 718-982-2355 302 A
meryl.kaynard@csi.cuny.edu
KAYS, Brenda, S .... 903-983-8100 451 F
bkays@kilgore.edu
KAYSEN-LUZBETAK,
Angie .... 815-280-6679 142 A
akaysen@jjc.edu
KAZAMA, Susan .... 808-734-9519 130 C
smurata@hawaii.edu
KAZANECKI-KEMPTER,
Diane .... 631-420-2065 329 D
diane.kazanecki-kempter@farmingdale.edu
KAZARIAN, Julie .... 508-929-8077 219 A
jkazarian@worcester.edu
KAZDA, Kathleen .... 262-691-5464 515 B
kkazda@wctc.edu
KAZEE, Thomas, A .... 812-488-2151 164 G
president@evansville.edu
KAZEN, James, D .... 210-567-0390 468 E
kazen@uthscsa.edu
KAZEN, Tom .... 708-239-4866 153 B
thomas.kazen@trnty.edu
KAZER, Meredith, W ...... 203-254-4150.. 87 A
mkazer@fairfield.edu
KAZEROUNIAN, Kazem . 860-486-2221.. 88 G
kazem.kazerounian@uconn.edu
KAZMAN, Nelly .... 909-593-3511.. 70 E
nkazman@laverne.edu
KAZMI, Saba .... 909-652-6193.. 36 E
saba.kazmi@chaffey.edu
KAZMIR, Darin .... 361-582-2417 470 A
darin.kazmir@victoriacollege.edu
KAZUMA, Clement .... 680-488-2471 520 E
KAZYAKA, Carrie .... 619-961-4324.. 67 F
ckazyaka@tjsl.edu
KEA, Gwen .... 919-546-8223 348 I
gkea@shawu.edu
KEADY, Thomas, J .... 617-552-6795 212 E
thomas.keady@bc.edu
KEAIRNS, Kathy .... 303-871-4156.. 83 E
kathy.keairns@du.edu
KEAL, Aaron, J .... 620-421-6700 179 D
aaronk@labette.edu
KEALA, David .... 808-675-3572 128 K
david.keala@byuh.edu
KEAN, Linda .... 781-239-4284 211 A
kean@babson.edu
KEANE, Christopher ...... 509-335-3574 499 G
chris.keane@vetmed.wsu.edu
KEANE, JR., Donald ...... 602-872-7795.. 13 E
donald.keane@cgc.edu
KEANE, James .... 610-896-1023 397 F
jkeane@haverford.edu
KEANE, Nancyellen .... 434-381-6506 485 P
nkeane@sbc.edu
KEANE, Timothy .... 303-458-1844.. 82 D
keane@regis.edu
KEARLEY, Mark .... 850-644-1841 110 A
mkearley@fsu.edu
KEARN, Tim .... 559-297-4500.. 46 E
KEARNEY, Anne, E .... 315-445-4195 312 F
kearneae@lemoyne.edu
KEARNEY, Janice .... 870-575-8000.. 22 E
kearneyj@uapb.edu
KEARNEY,
Jeannie (Carol) .... 507-433-0571 247 C
jeannie.kearney@riverland.edu
KEARNEY, Joseph, D .... 414-288-1955 508 C
joseph.kearney@marquette.edu
KEARNEY, Kate .... 610-647-4400 397 I
kkearney@immaculata.edu
KEARNEY, Kimberly ...... 540-261-8542 485 G
kim.kearney@svu.edu
KEARNEY, Margaret ...... 585-275-9093 332 E
margaret.kearney@rochester.edu
KEARNEY, Matthew .... 314-889-4686 260 C
mkearney@fontbonne.edu
KEARNEY, Stephen .... 617-984-1734 223 H
skearney@quincycollege.edu
KEARNS, Chris .... 406-994-2828 272 A
chris.kearns@montana.edu
KEARNS, Gayle .... 405-470-2636 380 A
gayle.kearns@swcu.edu
KEARNS, Jane .... 802-728-1231 477 E
jkearns@vtc.edu
KEARNS, Jennifer .... 619-388-2759.. 60 D
jkearns@sdccd.edu
KEARNS, Joanne .... 973-328-5044 285 B
jkearns@ccm.edu
KEARNS, Kevin .... 716-673-3758 325 C
kevin.kearns@fredonia.edu
KEARNS, Lorna, R .... 412-624-6786 412 I
lrkearns@pitt.edu
KEARNS, Michael .... 928-757-0801.. 14 I
mkearns@mohave.edu
KEARNS, Michelle .... 801-863-8976 473 D
michelle.kearns@uvu.edu
KEARNS, Richard .... 918-631-2150 381 C
richard-kearns@utulsa.edu
KEARNS, Susan, L .... 512-475-7368 467 C
susan.kearns@austin.utexas.edu
KEARNS, Tom .... 765-983-1465 157 I
kearnto@earlham.edu
KEARNS-BARRETT,
Marybeth .... 508-793-2448 213 D
mkearns@holycross.edu
KEARNY,
Wowek (Sean) .... 210-784-2500 460 C
wowek.kearney@tamusa.edu
KEARY, Chris .... 785-864-5900 181 I
ckeary@ku.edu
KEAS, Lenora .... 361-698-1207 448 H
lkeas@delmar.edu
KEASLER, Robert, L .... 540-665-4533 485 C
rkeasler@su.edu
KEASLING, Diane .... 423-461-8968 435 A
dlkeasling@milligan.edu
KEAST, Cindy .... 620-665-3565 178 D
keastc@hutchcc.edu
KEATHLEY, Gwynne ...... 410-225-5242 205 C
gkeathley@mica.edu
KEATING, Andrew .... 406-657-1104 272 I
andrew.keating@rocky.edu
KEATING, Brendan .... 312-915-6147 144 D
bkeating@luc.edu
KEATING, Frederick .... 856-415-2100 289 G
fkeating@rcgc.edu
KEATING, Jeff .... 909-469-5205.. 74 G
jkeating@westernu.edu
KEATING, Joseph .... 740-588-1242 374 G
jkeating@zanestate.edu
KEATING, Kathy .... 616-234-4953 230 F
kkeating@grcc.edu
KEATING, Lisa .... 518-454-2833 305 B
keatingl@strose.edu
KEATING, Richard, S .... 413-782-1473 225 F
richard.keating@wne.edu
KEATON, Alicia .... 407-823-2827 110 C
alicia.keaton@ucf.edu
KEATY, Anthony .... 781-899-5500 223 G
akeaty@psjs.edu
KEBABIAN, Helen .... 315-228-7451 304 G
hkebabian@colgate.edu
KEBISEK, Kris .... 503-297-5544 385 A
kkebisek@ocac.edu
KEBREAB, Ermia .... 530-754-9707.. 68 H
ekebreab@ucdavis.edu
KECHICHIAN,
Avedis (Avo) .... 909-593-3511.. 70 E
akechichian2@laverne.edu
KECK, Kathleen, A .... 518-327-6223 320 A
kkeck@paulsmiths.edu
KECK, Kay .... 269-965-3931 232 A
keckk@kellogg.edu
KECK, III, Ray, M .... 903-886-5011 459 E
ray.keck@tamuc.edu
KECKLEY, Kim .... 540-665-4841 485 C
kkeckley@su.edu
KECSKÉS, Gary .... 630-466-7900 155 C
gkecskes@waubonsee.edu
KEDROSKI, Cristie .... 850-729-5357 104 E
kedroskc@nwfsc.edu
KEDROWSKI, Karen .... 218-748-2418 244 H
kkedrowski@nhed.edu
KEDROWSKI, Karen .... 218-748-2418 245 B
kkedrowski@nhed.edu
KEDROWSKI, Karen .... 218-748-2418 245 D
kkedrowski@mesabirange.edu
KEDROWSKI, Karen, M . 803-323-2160 426 H
kedrowskik@winthrop.edu
KEDSKI, Cathy .... 508-830-5042 218 D
ckedski@maritime.edu
KEE, Josh .... 870-235-4321.. 21 F
jrkee@saumag.edu
KEEBLER, David .... 805-289-6114.. 72 G
dkeebler@vcccd.edu
KEEBLER, David .... 805-289-6354.. 73 C
dkeebler@vcccd.edu
KEECH, Brian, T .... 215-895-2244 394 C
brian.keech@drexel.edu
KEECH, Renee .... 860-465-4596.. 84 K
keechr@easternct.edu
KEEDY, Thomas, E .... 765-361-6227 166 B
keedyt@wabash.edu
KEEFE, Maureen .... 617-879-7705 218 B
mkeefe@massart.edu
KEEFE, Phil .... 914-674-7782 314 I
pkeefe@mercy.edu
KEEFE, Sarah .... 603-641-7371 282 A
skeefe@anselm.edu
KEEFE, Terri, K .... 610-799-1580 400 A
tkeefe@lccc.edu
KEEFE, Thomas, W .... 972-721-5203 464 E
KEEFER, Charles .... 620-450-2120 180 K
KEEFER, Elizabeth, J ..... 216-368-4286 358 C
elizabeth.keefer@case.edu
KEEFER, Elizabeth, J ..... 216-368-5555 358 C
elizabeth.keefer@case.edu
KEEFER, Matthew, W ..... 618-453-7313 152 B
keefer@siu.edu
KEEFER, Maureen, H ..... 412-397-6484 409 C
keefer@rmu.edu
KEEFER, Michael, R ...... 814-393-1610 405 H
mkeefer@cuf-inc.org
KEEGAN, Beth .... 309-556-3127 141 B
bkeegan@iwu.edu
KEEGAN, Bridget, M ..... 402-280-4015 274 D
bmkeegan@creighton.edu
KEEGAN, George .... 574-284-4017 163 J
gkeegan@saintmarys.edu
KEEGAN, Joe .... 518-891-2915 319 A
jkeegan@nccc.edu
KEEGAN, Kim .... 603-206-8005 280 L
kkeegan@ccsnh.edu
KEEGAN, Thomas .... 360-416-7997 498 F
thomas.keegan@skagit.edu
KEEGAN, Vicki .... 608-262-3786 512 D
vicki.keegan@uwc.edu
KEEHLWETTER,
F. Stanley .... 724-458-2142 396 D
fskeehlwetter@gcc.edu
KEEHN, Jay .... 305-653-7141 371 A
jay.keehn@myunion.edu
KEEL, Brooks, A .... 706-721-2301 116 B
president@augusta.edu
KEEL, Darla .... 901-678-5755 439 E
darkeel@memphis.edu
KEEL, Dave .... 804-758-6731 489 D
dkeel@rappahannock.edu
KEELER, Anne, B .... 540-828-5470 478 J
akeeler@bridgewater.edu
KEELER, Bruce .... 714-241-6257.. 38 F
bkeeler@coastline.edu
KEELER, John, T .... 412-624-7605 412 I
keeler@pitt.edu
KEELER, Karen .... 603-206-8002 280 L
kkeeler@ccsnh.edu
KEELER-STROM,
Michela .... 402-844-7122 276 G
michela@northeast.edu
KEELEY, Brian .... 360-383-3375 500 F
bkeeley@whatcom.ctc.edu
KEELEY, Dan .... 845-574-4452 321 F
dkeeley@sunyrockand.edu
KEELEY, Edward, J .... 608-663-2223 507 D
ekeeley@edgewood.edu
KEELEY, Eileen, M .... 704-894-2422 337 B
eikeeley@davidson.edu
KEELEY, Gloria .... 312-996-2860 153 H
gkeeley@uic.edu
KEELEY, Louise Carroll . 508-767-7312 210 I
lkeeley@assumption.edu
KEELS, Carl .... 301-736-3631 205 B
genekeels@aol.com
KEEN, Cathy .... 352-395-5829 107 E
cathy.keen@sfcollege.edu
KEEN, James .... 504-821-5881 191 B
jkeen@cameroncollege.com
KEEN, Jim .... 617-559-8600 215 H
KEEN, Larry .... 910-678-8321 343 B
keenl@faytechcc.edu
KEEN, Meghan .... 989-386-6622 234 B
mckeen@midmich.edu
KEEN, Michael .... 802-681-2848 476 C
mkeen@svc.edu
KEEN, Ralph .... 312-413-2267 153 H
rkeen01@uic.edu
KEEN, Russell .... 706-721-2301 116 B
rukeen@augusta.edu
KEEN, Suzanne, P .... 540-458-8746 491 G
keens@wlu.edu
KEEN, W. Hubert .... 516-572-7205 316 C
hubert.keen@ncc.edu
KEENAN, Claudine .... 609-652-3593 291 H
claudine.keenan@stockton.edu
KEENAN, SJ, James, F . 617-552-3880 212 E
james.keenan.2@bc.edu
KEENAN, John .... 978-542-6400 218 E
jkeenan@salemstate.edu
KEENAN, Kathleen .... 617-879-7065 218 B
kkeenan@massart.edu
KEENAN, Laurie .... 518-464-8575 308 A
laurie@excelsior.edu
KEENAN, Mary .... 218-726-7009 250 F
mkeenan@d.umn.edu
KEENAN, Maura .... 215-780-1266 410 D
mkeenan@salus.edu
KEENAN, Ruth .... 281-998-6368 455 K
ruth.keenan@sjcd.edu
KEENAN, Timothy .... 920-924-3420 514 D
tkeenan@morainepark.edu
KEENE, David .... 859-276-4357 189 F
dkeene@sullivan.edu
KEENE, Joanne .... 928-523-7478.. 14 K
joanne.keene@nau.edu
KEENE, Vickie .... 276-498-5230 477 L
vkeene@acp.edu
KEENER, Andrea .... 305-899-3310.. 95 G
akeener@barry.edu
KEENER, Barb .... 419-755-4539 366 E
bkeener@ncstatecollege.edu
KEENER, Dauthan .... 734-995-7461 229 A
dauthan.keener@cuaa.edu
KEENER, Dave .... 209-588-5366.. 75 I
keenerd@yosemite.cc.ca.us
KEENER, Donna .... 813-974-5705 111 A
dlkeener@usf.edu

KEENER, Dorie .... 609-343-4920 283 D dkeener@atlantic.edu
KEENER, Gary, S .... 540-863-2900 487 I gkeener@dslcc.edu
KEENER, John, F .... 434-947-8367 484 B jkeener@randolphcollege.edu
KEENEY, Hunter .... 409-882-3312 462 D hunter.keeney@lsco.edu
KEENEY, Jeffrey .... 918-335-6847 378 F jkeeney@okwu.edu
KEENEY, Madonna .... 815-599-3449 139 F madonna.keeney@highland.edu
KEENEY, Mary Ellen, R . 518-587-2100 329 C maryellen.keeney@esc.edu
KEENUM, Mark, E .... 662-325-3221 254 E president@msstate.edu
KEENUM, Nancy .... 256-306-2850.... 1 F nancy.keenum@calhoun.edu
KEEP, William .... 609-771-3255 284 I keep@tcnj.edu
KEESE, Russelle .... 919-546-8565 348 I rkeese@shawu.edu
KEESEY, Aiza .... 661-255-1050.. 29 F
KEESLING, Donna .... 765-993-1341 157 I keesldo@earlham.edu
KEETER, Brian, C .... 334-844-4650.... 4 D bck0001@auburn.edu
KEETER, Howell, W .... 417-690-2370 258 E hkeeter@cofo.edu
KEETER, Tara .... 252-536-7223 343 F tkeeter618@halifaxcc.edu
KEETON, Kristi .... 913-971-3544 179 H kkeeton@mnu.edu
KEETON, Tim .... 913-971-3607 179 H tkeeton@mnu.edu
KEFAUVER, Lucy .... 304-336-8432 504 E
KEFERL, Joseph, E .... 937-775-2821 374 B joseph.keferl@wright.edu
KEFFER, Shari, B .... 618-537-6981 145 C sbkeffer@mckendree.edu
KEGEL, Gregory, D .... 406-265-3720 272 C kegel@msun.edu
KEGELMAN, Nancy .... 732-224-2221 284 B nkegelman@brookdalecc.edu
KEGLEY, Jacquelyn .... 661-654-2249.. 31 B jkegley@csub.edu
KEHL, Glen .... 573-592-5979 270 B glen.kehl@westminster-mo.edu
KEHL, Maria .... 760-922-8714.. 55 J mkehl@paloverde.edu
KEHL, Susan .... 501-279-4941.. 19 G skehl@harding.edu
KEHNEMOUYI, Muhammad .... 240-567-4406 205 F muhammad.kehnemouyi@montgomerycollege.edu
KEHOE, Sharon, A .... 208-882-2536 132 I skehoe@uidaho.edu
KEHRES, Larry, T .... 330-823-4880 372 C kehreslt@mountunion.edu
KEHRING, Justin .... 262-564-3072 513 G kehringj@gtc.edu
KEHRLI, Katherine .... 206-934-4386 497 I kathrine.kehrli@seattlecolleges.edu
KEIGHER, Craig .... 815-802-8402 142 C ckeigher@kcc.edu
KEIL, Virginia .... 419-530-5402 372 F virginia.keil@utoledo.edu
KEILEN, Sean .... 831-459-3700.. 70 C keilen@ucsc.edu
KEILERS, Vikki .... 903-233-4141 452 A vikkikeilers@letu.edu
KEILLOR, Robin .... 503-352-2081 385 I keillor@pacificu.edu
KEILTY, Andrea .... 860-486-5519.. 88 G andrea.keilty@uconn.edu
KEIM, Anita .... 505-473-6638 296 C anita.keim@santafeuniversity.edu
KEINATH, Barbara .... 218-281-8340 250 G bkeinath@umn.edu
KEINO, Leah .... 403-375-7112 276 D lekeino1@wsc.edu
KEIRN, Christy, C .... 870-508-6107.. 18 C ckeirn@asumh.edu
KEIRSTEAD, Carol, A .... 864-242-5100 418 H
KEIS, Karen .... 518-783-2330 324 C kkeis@siena.edu
KEISER, Arthur .... 954-776-4476 102 G artk@keiseruniversity.edu
KEISER, Belinda .... 954-776-4476 102 G belindak@keiseruniversity.edu
KEISER, Pamela, G .... 570-577-1238 390 H pamela.keiser@bucknell.edu
KEISER, Sue, T .... 662-915-7111 256 C stkeiser@olemiss.edu
KEISTER, Brian .... 267-502-6034 390 F brian.keister@brynathyn.edu
KEISTER, Shaun, B .... 530-754-8616.. 68 H sbkeister@ucdavis.edu
KEITA, Alma, G .... 229-931-2708 120 F alma.keita@gsw.edu
KEITES, Jim .... 352-395-5536 107 E jim.keites@sfcollege.edu
KEITH, Barry .... 704-463-3439 348 B barry.keith@pfeiffer.edu
KEITH, C. David .... 478-301-5639 122 H keith_cd@mercer.edu
KEITH, Caleb .... 479-979-1351.. 23 J ckeith@ozarks.edu
KEITH, Dana .... 205-348-4745.... 7 H
KEITH, Elizabeth .... 808-983-4100 129 D
KEITH, Heather .... 908-709-7514 292 C keith@ucc.edu
KEITH, Jason .... 662-325-2480 254 E keith@che.msstate.edu
KEITH, Jeffrey .... 813-663-0100.. 93 B jeffrey.keith@strayer.edu
KEITH, Jeffrey .... 813-882-0100.. 93 B
KEITH, Joe .... 704-825-6272 343 D keith.joe@gaston.edu
KEITH, Kent .... 808-853-1040 129 F kentkeith@pacrim.edu
KEITH, Michael .... 818-722-1635 451 G michael.keith@tku.edu
KEITH, Nancy .... 806-291-3766 470 I keithn@wbu.edu
KEITH, Paul .... 832-252-4673 446 A paul.keith@cbshouston.edu
KEITH, Paul .... 713-785-5995 446 A
KEITH, Paula, S .... 618-536-3471 152 A pkeith@siu.edu
KEITH, Shelby, C .... 318-797-5221 194 E shelby.keith@lsus.edu
KEITH, Shelley .... 540-654-2266 486 D tkeith@umw.edu
KEITH, Susan .... 325-942-2169 463 C susan.keith@angelo.edu
KEITH, Thomas, W .... 270-852-3142 187 F tkeith@kwc.edu
KEIZS, Marcia, V .... 718-262-2350 304 A mkeizs@york.cuny.edu
KELAHER, James, E ...... 713-798-7880 444 A jkelaher@bcm.edu
KELCH, Nick .... 706-729-2246 118 H nkelch@ega.edu
KELCHNER, Dana .... 660-596-7250 267 E dkelchner@sfccmo.edu
KELCHNER, Mark .... 660-596-7402 267 E mkelchner@sfccmo.edu
KELDERMAN, Mark .... 616-977-0599 236 B mark.kelderman@prts.edu
KELEHEAR, Zach .... 706-737-1499 116 B zkelehear@augusta.edu
KELEHER-HUGHES, Jacqueline .... 518-381-1240 323 L kelehejs@sunysccc.edu
KELEJIAN, Carol .... 804-862-6100 484 F ckelejian@rbc.edu
KELEMEN, Frank .... 517-629-0236 226 G fkelemen@albion.edu
KELEMEN, Paul .... 972-273-3590 448 C pkelemen@dcccd.edu
KELEN, Sarah, A .... 402-465-2113 276 E sak@nebrwesleyan.edu
KELL, Christine .... 814-866-8169 399 C ckell@lecom.edu
KELLAM, James .... 864-596-9019 420 F james.kellam@converse.edu
KELLAND, Chad .... 540-261-8470 485 G chad.kelland@svu.edu
KELLAR, Deborah .... 303-762-6893.. 79 G debbie.kellar@denverseminary.edu
KELLAR, Doug .... 419-448-2000 362 G dkellar@heidelberg.edu
KELLAR, Michelle .... 641-628-5431 167 D kellarm@central.edu
KELLE, Janet .... 207-941-7131 199 B kellej@husson.edu
KELLEHER, Alyssa .... 860-486-3802.. 88 G alyssa.kelleher@uconn.edu
KELLEHER, Audrey .... 877-804-1424 252 C akelleher@belhaven.edu
KELLEHER, Erin, C .... 978-665-3150 217 E ekelleher@fitchburgstate.edu
KELLEHER, William, J ... 413-782-1288 225 F william.kelleher@wne.edu
KELLEN, Vince .... 858-534-3396.. 69 E vkellen@ucsd.edu
KELLEPOURIS, Nikos .... 913-971-3687 179 H nskellepouris@mnu.edu
KELLER, Barbara .... 906-635-2267 232 J bkeller@lssu.edu
KELLER, Bruce .... 215-572-2922 389 D kellerb@arcadia.edu
KELLER, Chaim, D .... 773-463-7738 152 J cdkeller@telshe.edu
KELLER, Christine .... 314-889-4579 260 C ckeller@fontbonne.edu
KELLER, Christopher, J . 336-256-0452 351 D cjkeller@uncg.edu
KELLER, Cindy .... 276-656-0337 489 A ckeller@patrickhenry.edu
KELLER, Deborah .... 517-264-7100 236 I dkeller@sienaheights.edu
KELLER, Diane .... 570-340-6047 401 B keller@marywood.edu
KELLER, Harrison, A ..... 512-232-8277 467 C harrison.keller@austin.utexas.edu
KELLER, SJ, Herbert, R . 570-941-7500 413 F
KELLER, Ida .... 214-860-2010 448 A ikeller@dcccd.edu
KELLER, Jason .... 781-762-1211 215 A jkeller@fmc.edu
KELLER, Jean .... 940-565-4961 466 B jean.keller@unt.edu
KELLER, Joe .... 661-362-2226.. 51 C jkeller@masters.edu
KELLER, John, C .... 319-335-2142 166 G john-keller@uiowa.edu
KELLER, Jonathan .... 617-994-6941 216 F jkeller@bhe.mass.edu
KELLER, Kerri, D .... 785-532-6506 179 A kdkeller@ksu.edu
KELLER, Kristina .... 320-308-5538 247 F kkeller@sctcc.edu
KELLER, Linda .... 619-961-4282.. 67 F lkeller@tjsl.edu
KELLER, Linda, B .... 270-852-3110 187 F lkeller@kwc.edu
KELLER, Lori .... 509-682-6705 500 D lkeller@wvc.edu
KELLER, Mae .... 734-995-7378 229 A mae.keller@cuaa.edu
KELLER, Margaret .... 985-732-6640 192 K
KELLER, Marlon, D .... 215-699-5700 399 G mkeller@lsb.edu
KELLER, Michael, A ...... 650-723-5553.. 66 C michael.keller@stanford.edu
KELLER, Mike .... 904-276-6826 106 M mikekeller@sjrstate.edu
KELLER, Rebecca .... 518-262-8105 297 L kellere@mail.amc.edu
KELLER, Richard .... 518-262-6008 297 L kellerr@mail.amc.edu
KELLER, Rod .... 541-888-7292 387 A rod.keller@socc.edu
KELLER, Scott .... 201-761-6028 291 D skeller@saintpeters.edu
KELLER, Scott .... 815-280-2775 142 A skeller@jjc.edu
KELLER, Tammy, S .... 270-686-4246 183 J tammy.keller@brescia.edu
KELLER, Terry .... 419-824-3535 364 G tkeller@lourdes.edu
KELLER, Travis .... 740-392-6868 366 B travis.keller@mvnu.edu
KELLER, William .... 718-997-5557 303 E william.keller@qc.cuny.edu
KELLER, William .... 484-664-3230 402 F williamkeller@muhlenberg.edu
KELLER FLANERY, Hannah .... 870-612-2016.. 22 H hannah.keller@uaccb.edu
KELLERMANN, Arthur .... 301-295-3017 518 G arthur.kellermann@usuhs.edu
KELLERSBERGER, Gail ... 713-221-8150 465 C kellersbergerg@uhd.edu
KELLETT, Lucas, C .... 207-778-7096 201 D luke.kellett@maine.edu
KELLETT, Maria .... 609-463-3670 283 D mkellett@atlantic.edu
KELLEWAY, Kelly .... 215-968-8152 390 I kelly.kelleway@bucks.edu
KELLEY, Ann .... 334-347-2623.... 1 J akelley@escc.edu
KELLEY, Betty .... 863-667-5249 108 G bkelley@seu.edu
KELLEY, Bev .... 620-241-0723 176 G bev.kelley@centralchristian.edu
KELLEY, JR., Charles, S .... 504-282-4455 195 D ckelley@nobts.edu
KELLEY, Cynthia, S .... 270-824-8562 186 D cindy.kelley@kctcs.edu
KELLEY, Dale .... 731-352-6428 430 E kelleyd@bethelu.edu
KELLEY, Danny, R .... 926-261-3180 458 F drkelley@pvamu.edu
KELLEY, David .... 313-883-8760 236 D kelley.david@shms.edu
KELLEY, Dennis .... 575-492-2530 294 L dkelley@nmjc.edu
KELLEY, Ed .... 405-325-4410 380 L ekelley@ou.edu
KELLEY, Gary, F .... 978-232-2048 214 G gkelley@endicott.edu
KELLEY, Gloria .... 704-330-6441 342 A gloria.kelley@cpcc.edu
KELLEY, Jane .... 518-736-3622 309 A jkelley@fmcc.suny.edu
KELLEY, Janet .... 918-444-2228 376 G kelleyje@nsuok.edu
KELLEY, Janet, L .... 541-485-1780 384 G jankelley@newhope.edu
KELLEY, Janine .... 570-740-0462 400 F jkelley@luzerne.edu
KELLEY, Jeanne .... 617-353-3565 212 G jkelley@bu.edu
KELLEY, Joni .... 641-683-5251 169 I joni.kelley@indianhills.edu
KELLEY, Katherine, M ... 423-439-4224 431 H kelleyk@etsu.edu
KELLEY, Kelvin, J .... 325-670-5898 450 A kjkelley@hsutx.edu
KELLEY, Kevin .... 417-328-1536 267 A kkelley@sbuniv.edu
KELLEY, Kevin, M .... 530-898-5700.. 31 D kmkelley@csuchico.edu
KELLEY, Kimberly .... 240-567-5010 205 F kimberly.kelley@montgomerycollege.edu
KELLEY, Kimberly .... 309-268-8410 139 D kim.kelley@heartland.edu
KELLEY, Kimberly .... 770-533-7017 122 E kkelley@laniertech.edu
KELLEY, Kirk .... 918-465-2361 375 J kkelley@eosc.edu
KELLEY, Kris .... 336-917-5460 348 H kris.kelley@salem.edu
KELLEY, Larry, H .... 252-985-5138 348 A lkelley@ncwc.edu
KELLEY, Lawrence .... 419-530-1448 372 F lawrence.kelley@utoledo.edu
KELLEY, Mark .... 541-485-1780 384 G markkelley@newhope.edu
KELLEY, Michael .... 336-770-3214 352 B kelleym@uncsa.edu
KELLEY, Michelle .... 608-663-3256 507 D registrar@edgewood.edu
KELLEY, Mimi .... 918-465-1769 375 J mkelley@eosc.edu
KELLEY, Ritch .... 570-586-2400 392 E rkelley@clarkssummitu.edu
KELLEY, Rosa .... 646-312-2050 301 B rosa.kelley@baruch.cuny.edu
KELLEY, Scott, C .... 512-499-4560 467 A skelley@utsystem.edu
KELLEY, Teresa .... 706-379-3111 128 H teresak@yhc.edu
KELLEY, Teresa .... 785-242-5200 180 H teresa.kelley@ottawa.edu
KELLEY, Thomas .... 508-626-4614 218 A tkelley@framingham.edu
KELLEY, Warren .... 301-314-8436 207 G wkelley@umd.edu
KELLIE, Shawn .... 270-706-8549 185 H shawn.kellie@kctcs.edu
KELLIHER, Marsha .... 248-689-8282 238 F mkellihe@walshcollege.edu
KELLISON, Dennis .... 540-678-7324 485 C dkelliso@su.edu
KELLISON, Karen .... 540-868-7190 488 E kkellison@lfcc.edu
KELLMAN, Jordan .... 337-482-6219 197 F kellman@louisiana.edu
KELLOG, Kelly .... 918-647-1407 375 B krkellogl@carlalbert.edu
KELLOG, Torri .... 954-492-5353.. 96 J tkellog@citycollege.edu
KELLOGG, Gary .... 530-221-4275.. 63 H gkellogg@shasta.edu
KELLOGG, Isaiah .... 636-584-6685 259 L isaiah.kellogg@eastcentral.edu
KELLOGG, John .... 612-625-3387 250 E j-kell@umn.edu
KELLOGG, Leslie .... 269-927-6748 232 G lkellogg@lakemichigancollege.edu
KELLOGG, Magdalen ..... 315-568-3067 317 A mkellogg@nycc.edu
KELLOGG, Sandi .... 503-399-5041 382 C sandi.kellogg@chemeketa.edu
KELLOGG, Tonia .... 405-585-5802 377 A tonia.kellogg@okbu.edu
KELLY, Alan, J .... 516-463-5027 310 D alan.j.kelly@hofstra.edu
KELLY, Amber .... 662-246-6263 254 C akelly@msdelta.edu
KELLY, Amy .... 360-596-5349 498 G akelly1@spscc.edu

KELLY, Anna 401-739-5000 416 D akelly@neit.edu
KELLY, Audrey 908-737-7000 286 F vzajda@kean.edu
KELLY, Audrey 908-737-7000 286 F aukelly@kean.edu
KELLY, Barbara 334-386-7299 5 I bkelly@faulkner.edu
KELLY, Benji 270-789-5211 184 B jbkelly@campbellsville.edu
KELLY, Blaine 513-732-5301 371 G blaine.kelley@uc.edu
KELLY, Bonnie 229-468-2091 128 G bonnie.kelly@wiregrass.edu
KELLY, Brenda, S 507-933-7541 242 D bkelly@gustavus.edu
KELLY, Brendan 864-503-5200 425 H bkelly@uscupstate.edu
KELLY, Brian 508-541-1622 214 C bkelly@dean.edu
KELLY, Brian 541-463-5310 383 F kellyb@lanecc.edu
KELLY, Bryan 866-687-2258 30 B
KELLY, Calvin, A 512-448-8538 455 I ckelly1@stedwards.edu
KELLY, Carrie 928-692-3085 14 I ckelly@mohave.edu
KELLY, Chassie 662-720-7239 255 B cmkelly@nemcc.edu
KELLY, Chris 620-235-4122 180 J ckelly@pittstate.edu
KELLY, Christine 909-621-8177 37 L christine.kelly@cgu.edu
KELLY, Daniel 734-487-2031 229 K dkelly20@emich.edu
KELLY, Darin 215-717-3108 393 C darin.kelly@curtis.edu
KELLY, OSB, David 724-805-2644 410 B david.kelly@email.stvincent.edu
KELLY, OSB, David 724-805-2644 410 C david.kelly@stvincent.edu
KELLY, Debra 609-771-2161 284 I dkelly@tcnj.edu
KELLY, Dennis 937-481-2555 373 I dennis_kelly@wilmington.edu
KELLY, Drew 610-526-6669 396 H dkelly@harcum.edu
KELLY, Edward, J 423-439-8550 431 H kellye@etsu.edu
KELLY, Francis, E 845-575-3000 314 C francis.kelly@marist.edu
KELLY, George, N 615-327-6800 434 A gkelly@mmc.edu
KELLY, Grayson 864-646-8361 424 F
KELLY, Hank 740-474-8896 367 E hkelly@ohiochristian.edu
KELLY, Heather, A 302-831-2021 90 I hkelly@udel.edu
KELLY, Inesha 773-481-8103 136 B ikelly1@ccc.edu
KELLY, Jack 717-262-2013 415 B jkelly@wilson.edu
KELLY, Jack 617-732-2143 221 E jack.kelly@mcphs.edu
KELLY, James 401-841-3674 518 E
KELLY, Janet, H 478-988-6800 117 E jkelly@centralgatech.edu
KELLY, Jeffrey, M 443-352-4012 207 C jkelly@stevenson.edu
KELLY, Jeffrey, M 443-352-4306 207 C jkelly@stevenson.edu
KELLY, Jeneen 914-323-5337 314 A jeneen.kelly@mville.edu
KELLY, Jennifer 412-338-4770 390 D jkelly@brightwoodcareer.edu
KELLY, John 617-735-9710 214 F kellyjo@emmanuel.edu
KELLY, John 561-297-3450 109 B president@fau.edu
KELLY, Julie, A 860-444-8508 519 B julie.a.kelly@uscg.mil
KELLY, Kara 574-284-4601 163 J kkelly@saintmarys.edu
KELLY, Karen 334-291-4938 1 H karen.kelly@cv.edu
KELLY, Kathleen 617-585-1154 222 H kathleen.kelly@necmusic.edu
KELLY, Kathy 513-244-4418 366 A kathy.kelly@msj.edu
KELLY, Kelly 608-822-2305 515 A kkelly@swtc.edu
KELLY, Kevin, P 410-269-5087 207 H kkelly@umaryland.edu
KELLY, Kevin, R 937-229-3557 372 A kellyker@udayton.edu
KELLY, Kieran 617-254-2610 224 B kieran.kelly@sjs.edu
KELLY, Kirk 503-725-6246 386 D kkelly@pdx.edu
KELLY, Laura 315-312-3151 327 D laura.kelly@oswego.edu
KELLY, Lauren, E 407-582-8125 113 F lkelly22@valenciacollege.edu
KELLY, Lee 718-997-4455 303 E lee.kelly@qc.cuny.edu
KELLY, Leslie, E 207-834-7522 201 E lesliek@maine.edu
KELLY, Lori 305-809-3504 99 L lori.kelly@fkcc.edu
KELLY, Lyn 585-475-2946 321 D lyn.kelly@rit.edu
KELLY, Lynn 229-226-1621 126 E lkelly@thomasu.edu
KELLY, Margaret, S 215-637-7700 397 G mkelly@holyfamily.edu
KELLY, Marisa 617-573-8000 224 I mjkelly@suffolk.edu
KELLY, Mark 269-927-8100 232 G kelly@lakemichigancollege.edu
KELLY, Matthew 740-364-9644 358 E mkelly@cotc.edu
KELLY, Maureen 708-235-7556 138 H mkelly7@govst.edu
KELLY, Mitch 252-398-6246 336 K
KELLY, Paul 202-651-5075 91 H paul.kelly@gallaudet.edu
KELLY, SCJ, Paul 414-425-8300 509 I pkelly@shsst.edu
KELLY, Renee 518-608-8464 308 A rkelly@excelsior.edu
KELLY, Richard 201-559-3510 286 C kellyr@felician.edu
KELLY, Rob 410-617-2842 205 A rkelly1@loyola.edu
KELLY, Robert 620-665-3417 178 D kellyr@hutchcc.edu
KELLY, Rosemary 910-678-8325 343 B kellyr@faytechcc.edu
KELLY, Roxanne 218-285-2202 247 A
KELLY, Sandra 803-777-2808 424 I sjkelly@mailbox.sc.edu
KELLY, Sara 585-395-2122 326 D skelly@brockport.edu
KELLY, Sarah, M 802-654-3000 476 A skelly@smcvt.edu
KELLY, Scott, A 979-458-6120 459 C s-kelly@tamus.edu
KELLY, Sean Ann 570-702-8963 398 A skelly@johnson.edu
KELLY, Stephanie 317-788-6099 164 H spkelly@uindy.edu
KELLY, Stephen 212-220-8261 301 C skelly@bmcc.cuny.edu
KELLY, Steve 757-481-5005 492 A
KELLY, Susan 617-287-7050 216 G skelly@umassp.edu
KELLY, T. Liisa 910-843-5304 340 J
KELLY, Tami 281-459-7653 456 A tami.kelly@sjcd.edu
KELLY, Thomas 607-431-4111 309 E kellyt2@hartwick.edu
KELLY, Thomas, M 312-915-6400 144 D tkelly4@luc.edu
KELLY, Todd 719-549-2380 78 P todd.kelly@csupueblo.edu
KELLY, Tracy 716-338-1042 311 F tracykelly@mail.sunyjcc.edu
KELLY, William 605-642-6371 428 F william.kelly@bhsu.edu
KELLY, Yvan, J 904-819-6392 98 I kellyyj@flagler.edu
KELLY-ALBERTSON, Lynn, C 269-387-2745 239 E lynn.kelly-albertson@wmich.edu
KELLY BATES, Martha 847-578-8582 150 E martha.bates@rosalindfranklin.edu
KELLY-BOWRY, Tanya 303-831-6192 83 A tanya.kellybowry@cu.edu
KELLY KLEESE, Christine 919-536-7200 342 G kleesec@durhamtech.edu
KELLY-VERGONA, Barbara 973-957-0188 283 C registrar@acs350.org
KELNHOFER, Jack 732-255-0400 288 B jkelnhofer@ocean.edu
KELSCH, Anne 701-777-3325 353 G anne.kelsch@und.edu
KELSCH, Tyler 303-546-3569 81 B tkelsch@naropa.edu
KELSER, Sandra, B 334-833-4409 5 M skelser@hawks.huntingdon.edu
KELSEY, Anita 765-285-8101 156 C akelsey@bsu.edu
KELSEY, Jane 217-854-5511 134 E jane.kelsey@blackburn.edu
KELSEY, Katie, M 402-280-1715 274 D katiekelsey@creighton.edu
KELSEY, Madelaine 203-596-4624 87 H mkelsey@post.edu
KELSEY, Ross 281-998-6150 456 B ross.kelsey@sjcd.edu
KELSO, Anne-Marie 541-881-5838 387 D akelso@tvcc.cc
KELSO, William 912-344-2541 115 D william.kelso@armstrong.edu
KELSOE, Amanda 919-684-2174 337 C amanda.kelso@duke.edu
KELTER, Paul 701-231-8692 354 D paul.kelter@ndsu.edu
KELTON, Emily 303-273-3148 78 J ekelton@mines.edu
KELTY, Ed 480-731-8246 13 D edward.kelty@domail.maricopa.edu
KEM, John 717-245-4400 519 A
KEMBEL, Trisha 970-542-3126 81 A trisha.kembel@morgancc.edu
KEMERER, John, J 740-593-0465 368 G kemerer@ohio.edu
KEMKER, Brett 504-280-6220 194 F bkemker@uno.edu
KEMMERER, Kristel 845-431-8952 307 A kristel.kemmerer@sunydutchess.edu
KEMMY, David 401-254-3428 417 C dkemmy@rwu.edu
KEMNITZ, Marcie 308-398-7400 273 G mkemnitz@cccneb.edu
KEMP, Arnold 312-899-1294 151 F akemp@saic.edu
KEMP, Cathy 662-243-2623 253 A ckemp@eastms.edu
KEMP, Dale, A 630-752-5085 155 F dale.kemp@wheaton.edu
KEMP, Danny 540-831-7167 484 A dmkemp@radford.edu
KEMP, Dawn 317-632-5553 162 P dkemp@lincolntech.edu
KEMP, Gloria 501-686-6728 22 C kempgloriad@uams.edu
KEMP, Jerylle 212-237-8964 302 F jkemp@jjay.cuny.edu
KEMP, John 864-294-3717 421 I john.kemp@furman.edu
KEMP, Josh 870-307-7398 20 C josh.kemp@lyon.edu
KEMP, Katie 847-317-8177 153 D katiek@tiu.edu
KEMP, Lisa 703-993-2483 481 B lkemp@gmu.edu
KEMP, Rick 480-517-8508 14 B rick.kemp@riosalado.edu
KEMP, Sheron 256-331-5368 3 C skemp@nwscc.edu
KEMP, Shirley 304-829-7485 501 F skemp@bethanywv.edu
KEMP, Stephen 515-292-9694 166 D stephen.kemp@antiochschool.edu
KEMP, Steve 760-366-5283 41 B skemp@cmccd.edu
KEMPA, Richard 307-382-1731 517 C rkempa@westernwyoming.edu
KEMPE, Michael, A 330-325-6481 366 F mkempe@neomed.edu
KEMPEL, Leo 517-355-5114 233 G kempel@egr.msu.edu
KEMPER, James 740-588-1209 374 G jkemper@zanestate.edu
KEMPER, Kenneth, B 616-538-2330 230 E preskemper@gbcol.edu
KEMPER, Terry 262-695-3459 515 B tkemper1@wctc.edu
KEMPER-PELLE, Cathy 541-956-7000 386 G ckemperpelle@roguecc.edu
KEMPF, Emily, J 816-501-3571 265 I emily.kempf@rockhurst.edu
KEMPF, Gary 620-278-4469 181 G gkempf@sterling.edu
KEMPF-LEONARD, Kimberly 502-852-2234 190 C asdean@louisville.edu
KEMPSON, Dorothy 912-877-1906 115 D dorothy.kempson@armstrong.edu
KEMPTON, Daniel 740-283-6228 361 L dkempton@franciscan.edu
KENAUSIS, Veronica 203-837-9109 85 B kenausisv@wcsu.edu
KENBER, Tammy 707-664-3100 35 A kenber@sonoma.edu
KENCH, Brian 203-932-7115 89 D bkench@newhaven.edu
KENDALL, Chris 507-457-1640 250 B ckendall@smumn.edu
KENDALL, Curtis, L 540-828-5476 478 J ckendall@bridgewater.edu
KENDALL, Deborah 408-554-2717 62 F dkendall@scu.edu
KENDALL, Donna 781-891-3441 212 A dkendall@bentley.edu
KENDALL, Elizabeth 845-574-4269 321 F ekendall@sunyrockland.edu
KENDALL, Justin 620-862-5252 175 B justin.kendall@barclaycollege.edu
KENDALL, Kenny 315-470-7749 299 K kennethkendall@crouse.org
KENDALL, Matt 740-695-9500 357 D mkendall@belmontcollege.edu
KENDALL, Peter 828-328-7100 339 C peter.kendall@lr.edu
KENDALL, Rex 812-514-8446 159 C rkendall@indstatefoundation.org
KENDALL, Stephanie 978-837-5321 221 G kendalls@merrimack.edu
KENDALL-DOMNICK, Meitaka 692-625-3394 520 C mkendall@cmi.edu
KENDERDINE, Linda 410-706-5036 207 H lcassard@umaryland.edu
KENDIG, P. Tysen 860-486-6713 88 G tysen.kendig@uconn.edu
KENDJORIA, Barrett 864-656-2354 419 F bkendjo@clemson.edu
KENDREX, Bradley, S 480-732-7379 13 E bradley.kendrex@cgc.edu
KENDRICK, Bethany 620-421-6700 179 D bethanyk@labette.edu
KENDRICK, Catherine 978-934-2495 217 B catherine_kendrick@uml.edu
KENDRICK, Curtis 607-777-4550 325 A kendrick@binghamton.edu
KENDRICK, Haley 704-406-3957 337 H hkendrick@gardner-webb.edu
KENDRICK, Lacy 804-204-1235 478 F lkendrick@btsr.edu
KENDRICK, R. Ryan 716-286-8708 318 F rkendrick@niagara.edu
KENDZIERSKI, Christian 410-532-3191 206 D ckendzierski@ndm.edu
KENERSON, Laura 401-874-5271 417 E lkenerson@uri.edu
KENERSON, Murle 615-963-5203 438 E mkenerson@tnstate.edu
KENESSON, Alexander 253-680-7150 492 F akenesson@bates.ctc.edu
KENESSON, Summer, S 253-535-8145 496 G kenessss@plu.edu
KENIMER, Ann 979-845-3210 459 C a-kenimer@tamu.edu
KENISTON, Joseph, C 315-229-1858 323 D jkeniston@stlawu.edu
KENISTON, Leonda 434-961-5380 489 C lkeniston@pvcc.edu
KENKEL, Kevin 605-995-2617 427 A kekenkel@dwu.edu
KENKEL, Mary Beth 321-674-8142 99 K mkenkel@fit.edu
KENMILLE, Cleo 406-275-4864 273 A cleo_kenmille@skc.edu
KENNA-SCHENK, Becca 360-951-3733 500 E becca.kenna-schenk@wwu.edu
KENNAMER, Mike 256-228-6001 3 B kennamerm@nacc.edu
KENNARD, Douglas 304-876-5330 504 D dkennard@shepherd.edu
KENNARD, Janet 713-942-9505 450 E jkennard@hgst.edu
KENNEDAY, Mark, A 501-686-5674 22 C kennedaymark@uams.edu
KENNEDY, Aaron 575-461-4413 294 E aaronk@mesalands.edu
KENNEDY, Alexis 708-534-7096 138 H akennedy@govst.edu
KENNEDY, Andrea 336-841-9283 338 E akennedy@highpoint.edu
KENNEDY, Barbara 606-539-4214 190 A barbara.kennedy@ucumberlands.edu
KENNEDY, Barbara 724-222-5330 403 E bkennedy@penncommercial.edu
KENNEDY, Bill 406-657-2011 272 B foundation@msubillings.edu
KENNEDY, Brenda, J 251-580-2185 1 I brenda.kennedy@faulknerstate.edu
KENNEDY, Brett, E 706-236-2215 116 D bkennedy@berry.edu
KENNEDY, Brianne 619-388-3513 60 C bkennedy@sdccd.edu
KENNEDY, Bridget 906-786-5802 228 A bridget.kennedy@baycollege.edu
KENNEDY, Carol, M 570-577-1511 390 H carol.kennedy@bucknell.edu

KERRY, Susan .... 218-723-6083 241 J
skerry@css.edu
KERSCHNER, Joseph, E 414-955-8213 508 D
jkerschner@mcw.edu
KERSENBROCK,
Angela, M .... 407-708-2483 107 G
kersenbrocka@seminolestate.edu
KERSEY, Elizabeth, A ..... 757-683-3152 483 G
ekersey@odu.edu
KERSEY, Pam .... 619-660-4453.. 44 L
pam.kersey@gcccd.edu
KERSEY, Shakeyia .... 610-902-8594 391 B
shakeyia.n.kersey@cabrini.edu
KERSH, Rogan .... 336-758-3128 353 A
kersh@wfu.edu
KERSHNER, Marcy .... 843-383-8045 420 B
mkershner@coker.edu
KERSHNER, Scott, M ..... 570-372-4220 410 H
kershner@susqu.edu
KERSTEN, Andrew .... 208-885-7885 132 I
andrewkersten@uidaho.edu
KERSTEN, Belen .... 559-730-3794.. 39 G
belenk@cos.edu
KERSTEN, David, W ...... 773-244-6235 147 F
dwkersten@northpark.edu
KERSTEN, James, B ...... 515-574-1132 170 C
kersten@iowacentral.edu
KERSTETTER, Philip, P .. 919-658-7746 349 F
pkerstetter@umo.edu
KERTAMUS, Lorisa .... 804-527-1000.. 93 B
KERTULIS-TARTAR,
Gina .... 706-272-4516 118 F
gkertulistartar@daltonstate.edu
KERTZ, Nancy .... 515-643-6615 171 K
nkertz@mercydesmoines.org
KERWIN, Courtney .... 315-792-7419 330 A
courtney.kerwin@sunyit.edu
KERWIN, Linda .... 716-827-2454 331 K
kerwinl@trocaire.edu
KERWIN, William .... 949-282-2718.. 64 I
wkerwin@ivc.edu
KERWITZ, Ann .... 815-921-4001 150 A
a.kerwitz@rockvalleycollege.edu
KERYLOW, Tiffany .... 802-387-6725 475 C
tiffanykerylow@landmark.edu
KESARIS, Thomas, L ..... 610-660-1836 409 H
tkesaris@sju.edu
KESERAUSKIS, Beth ...... 314-446-8207 266 D
beth.keserauskis@stlcop.edu
KESHNER, Larry .... 708-344-4700 144 A
lkeshner@lincolntech.edu
KESHVALA, Seelpa .... 281-290-3940 452 C
seelpa.h.keshvala@lonestar.edu
KESICKI, Michael .... 814-871-5873 395 H
kesicki001@gannon.edu
KESKULA, Douglas, R ... 828-227-7271 352 C
drkeskula@wcu.edu
KESLER, Michael, W ..... 802-776-5219 474 H
michael.kesler@csj.edu
KESNER, Idalene, F .... 812-855-8489 159 H
ikesner@indiana.edu
KESNER, Idalene, F .... 812-855-8489 159 G
ikesner@indiana.edu
KESSEL, Christine .... 309-779-7708 153 C
christine.kessel@trinitycollegeqc.edu
KESSEL, Joyce .... 716-896-0700 333 C
jkessel@villa.edu
KESSELMAN, Harvey ..... 609-652-4521 291 H
harvey.kesselman@stockton.edu
KESSIE, Michael .... 941-487-4212 110 B
mkessie@ncf.edu
KESSINGER, David .... 618-664-7109 139 A
david.kessinger@greenville.edu
KESSINGER, Steve .... 276-326-4603 478 H
skessinger@bluefield.edu
KESSLER, Brian .... 423-869-7077 433 C
brian.kessler@lmunet.edu
KESSLER, Gene .... 219-473-4299 157 A
gkessler@ccsj.edu
KESSLER, Jeffrey, A .... 516-877-3660 297 I
kessler@adelphi.edu
KESSLER, Kathleen .... 802-839-8317 475 H
kathleen.kessler@neci.edu
KESSLER, Lisa .... 909-869-2203.. 31 A
lakessler@cpp.edu
KESSLER, Lisa .... 512-313-3000 446 N
lisa.kessler@concordia.edu
KESSLER, Mary .... 812-488-2569 164 G
mk43@evansville.edu
KESSLER, Nevin, E .... 848-932-7890 290 A
nkessler@winants.rutgers.edu
KESSLER, Richard .... 212-580-0210 316 E
kesslerr@newschool.edu
KESSLER, Sheryl .... 215-972-7600 404 Q
skessler@pafa.org
KESSLER, Susan, B .... 386-312-4021 106 M
susankessler@sjrstate.edu
KESSLER, Suzanne .... 914-251-6600 328 B
suzanne.kessler@purchase.edu
KESSLER-CLEARY,
Timothy .... 973-618-3484 284 D
tcleary@caldwell.edu
KESTEN, Philip, R .... 408-554-4311.. 62 F
pkesten@scu.edu
KESTENBAUM, Yoel ...... 845-782-1380 335 B
KESTER, Jennifer .... 623-845-3377.. 13 H
jennifer.kester@gccaz.edu
KESTER, John .... 910-410-1778 345 G
jikester@richmondcc.edu
KESTER, Kelly .... 360-383-3245 500 F
kkester@whatcom.ctc.edu
KESTER, Kris .... 406-791-5291 273 C
kris.kester@ugf.edu
KESTER, Lori .... 303-352-4498.. 80 Q
lkester@msudenver.edu
KESTERSON, Donald ..... 863-784-7132 108 B
donald.kesterson@southflorida.edu
KESTERSON, Ronald, L . 865-694-6608 437 F
rkesterson@pstcc.edu
KESTNER-RICKETTS,
Laura, F .... 414-288-7424 508 C
laura.kestner@marquette.edu
KETCHEN, John .... 865-573-4517 432 H
jketchen@johnsonu.edu
KETCHESON, Kathi, A ... 503-725-3425 386 D
ketchesonk@pdx.edu
KETELS, Margo .... 563-589-3765 173 J
mketels@dbq.edu
KETELSEN, Scott, A .... 319-273-2761 167 A
scott.ketelsen@uni.edu
KETJEN, William .... 330-823-2293 372 C
ketjenwl@mountunion.edu
KETNER, Annette .... 619-260-2925.. 71 J
aketner@sandiego.edu
KETO, Stephen, W .... 218-726-7101 250 F
vcfo@d.umn.edu
KETTEMAN, P. Greg ...... 615-675-5312 441 B
gketteman@welch.edu
KETTEN, Michelle .... 570-504-8094 399 A
kettenm@lackawanna.edu
KETTENBEIL, Kenneth .... 313-593-5140 238 A
kketten@umich.edu
KETTERER, Patricia .... 212-772-4475 302 E
patricia.ketterer@hunter.cuny.edu
KETTERING, Juliane ...... 801-627-8389 472 D
ketterij@owatc.edu
KETTERING, Rocky .... 706-507-8954 118 C
kettering_rocky@columbusstate.edu
KETTERING-LANE,
Denise .... 800-287-8822 156 D
kettede@bethanyseminary.edu
KETTERLING, Jayme ...... 208-732-6552 131 I
jketterling@csi.edu
KETTERMAN, Beth .... 252-744-2212 349 I
kettermane@ecu.edu
KETTING-WELLER,
Ginger .... 951-785-2266.. 47 F
gketting@lasierra.edu
KETTINGER, Kevin .... 585-567-9350 310 F
kevin.kettinger@houghton.edu
KETTINGER, Kirk .... 585-594-6415 321 C
kettinger_kirk@roberts.edu
KETTLEWELL, Kelly .... 570-577-1604 390 H
kelly.kettlewell@bucknell.edu
KETTNER, Valrey, V .... 701-231-9608 354 D
val.kettner@ndsu.edu
KEUFFEL, Elizabeth .... 603-641-7203 282 A
ekeuffel@anselm.edu
KEUSS, Theresa .... 314-516-4602 268 E
keusst@umsl.edu
KEVARI, Jacob .... 760-366-5279.. 41 B
jkevari@cmccd.edu
KEVIL, Chris .... 318-675-4102 194 D
ckevil@lsuhsc.edu
KEVIL, Tim .... 903-875-7443 453 J
tim.kevil@navarrocollege.edu
KEVORKIAN, Chris .... 206-726-5000 494 B
ckevorkian@cornish.edu
KEY, Charles .... 865-471-3447 430 H
ckey@cn.edu
KEY, Dan .... 641-844-5741 170 I
dan.key@iavalley.edu
KEY, Dillon .... 864-977-7122 422 I
dillon.key@ngu.edu
KEY, Roby, V .... 817-257-7706 461 A
r.key@tcu.edu
KEY, Shelly .... 361-593-5991 460 B
shelly.key@tamuk.edu
KEY, Stacy .... 479-979-1360.. 23 J
skey@ozarks.edu
KEY, Stan, R .... 859-257-8907 190 B
stan.key@uky.edu
KEYES, Adam .... 508-793-7453 213 C
akeyes@clarku.edu
KEYES, Beth, H .... 937-229-3766 372 A
bkeyes@udayton.edu
KEYES, Pat .... 401-841-3089 518 E
KEYS, James, A .... 910-843-5304 340 J
KEYS, Margo, A .... 715-858-1825 513 E
mkeys@cvtc.edu
KEYS, Marina .... 503-845-3550 384 C
marina.keys@mtangel.edu
KEYS, Staci .... 417-667-8181 259 A
skeys@cottey.edu
KEYS, Terrance .... 585-292-3432 315 L
tkeys@monroecc.edu
KHACHATRYAN, Davit ... 949-451-5326.. 64 I
dkhachatryan@ivc.edu
KHACHIKIAN, Crist .... 818-677-2138.. 33 B
crist.khachikian@csun.edu
KHADANGA, Dave .... 334-386-7113.... 5 I
dkhadanga@faulkner.edu
KHADEM, Farnaz .... 626-395-2240.. 29 I
fkhadem@caltech.edu
KHADKA, Chandni .... 256-782-8304.... 6 B
ckhadka@jsu.edu
KHALDEN, Jeff .... 817-598-6485 470 J
jkhalden@wc.edu
KHALEDI, Morteza .... 817-272-3491 467 B
morteza.khaledi@uta.edu
KHALSA, Barbara .... 480-517-8778.. 14 B
barbara.khalsa@riosalado.edu
KHAMIS, Hanan .... 508-999-8845 217 A
admissions@umassd.edu
KHAMOUNA, Mo .... 308-367-5213 278 A
mkhamouna1@unl.edu
KHAMSAMRAN, Anna ... 575-758-8914 294 H
annak@midwiferycollege.edu
KHAN, Adil .... 636-227-2100 262 A
KHAN, Ali .... 402-559-4950 277 H
ali.khan@unmc.edu
KHAN, Feroze .... 703-539-6890 485 J
fkhan@stratford.edu
KHAN, M. Wasiullah ..... 312-939-0111 137 G
chancellor@eastwest.edu
KHAN, Raza .... 410-386-8222 203 A
rkhan@carrollcc.edu
KHAN, Robert .... 201-360-4033 286 E
rkhan@hccc.edu
KHAN, Sadya .... 708-974-5283 146 C
khans46@morainevalley.edu
KHAN, Unab, I .... 401-863-3953 415 K
unab_khan@brown.edu
KHAN-MARCUS,
Zaveeni .... 805-893-8411.. 70 B
zaveeni.khan-marcus@sa.ucsb.edu
KHANEJA, Gurvinder ...... 201-684-7766 289 C
gkhaneja@ramapo.edu
KHANI, Anthony .... 646-717-9743 309 B
khani@gts.edu
KHANNA, Pradeep .... 217-333-9525 154 B
pkhanna@illinois.edu
KHANOYAN, Gayane ..... 818-988-2300.. 53 E
KHARGONEKAR,
Pramod .... 949-824-5796.. 69 A
pkhargon@uci.edu
KHARKOVYY, Andriy ..... 269-471-3591 227 B
alumni@andrews.edu
KHARTABIL, Basim .... 312-935-3036 149 K
bkhartabil@robertmorris.edu
KHATOR, Renu .... 713-743-8820 464 F
rkhator@uh.edu
KHATOR, Renu .... 713-743-8820 465 A
rkhator@uh.edu
KHATRI, Achal .... 617-873-0235 213 B
achal.khatri@cambridgecollege.edu
KHAVARI, Jenn .... 207-974-4673 199 L
jkhavari@emcc.edu
KHAWAR, Mariam .... 607-735-1932 307 G
mkhawar@elmira.edu
KHAYUM, Mohammed .. 812-465-1681 165 C
mkhayum@usi.edu
KHEHRA, Harry .... 281-290-6576 452 C
harry.khehra@lonestar.edu
KHOJA, Faiza .... 713-221-8218 465 C
khojafai@uhd.edu
KHOO, Poh Lin .... 651-793-1828 245 E
pohlin.khoo@metrostate.edu
KHOSLA, Pradeep, K ..... 858-534-3135.. 69 E
chancellor@ucsd.edu
KHOSRAVANI, Mariam .. 714-241-6159.. 38 F
mkhosravani@coastline.edu
KHOSROWPANAH,
Shahram .... 671-735-2694 520 B
khosrow@triton.uog.edu
KHOURY, Melik Peter .... 207-509-7221 200 I
mkhoury@unity.edu
KHOURY, Philip, S .... 617-253-0887 221 C
KHURANA, Nikki .... 909-607-2626.. 63 F
nkhurana@scrippscollege.edu
KHURANA, Rakesh .... 617-495-4137 215 G
rkhurana@fas.harvard.edu
KIA, Norman .... 575-769-4074 293 M
norman.kia@clovis.edu
KIAMAN, Matthew .... 626-585-3200.. 56 B
mxkiaman@pasadena.edu
KIAN, David .... 561-297-3007 109 B
dkian@fau.edu
KIBER, Matthew .... 410-778-7207 210 A
mkiber2@washcoll.edu
KIBLER, Bill .... 432-837-8000 462 G
president@sulross.edu
KIBLER, David .... 864-941-8475 423 C
kibler.d@ptc.edu
KIBLER, Michele .... 614-222-4009 360 B
mkibler@ccad.edu
KICHA, Grace .... 626-448-0023.. 46 K
KICKHAM-SAMY, Mary . 313-927-1540 233 D
mkickham@marygrove.edu
KICKLITER, Holly .... 727-873-4455 111 B
hkicklit@mail.usf.edu
KICKNER, Bob .... 253-833-9111 495 C
bkickner@greenriver.edu
KIDD, Anessa .... 334-876-9303.... 2 C
anessa.kidd@wccs.edu
KIDD, Beth Ann .... 903-675-6223 464 C
bkidd@tvcc.edu
KIDD, Jane .... 706-369-6833 124 E
jkidd@piedmont.edu
KIDD, Kevin .... 617-989-9095 225 E
kiddk@wit.edu
KIDD, Mary .... 615-514-2787 435 F
financialaid@nossi.edu
KIDD, Quentin .... 757-594-8499 479 H
qkidd@cnu.edu
KIDD, Twyla .... 704-463-3067 348 B
twyla.kidd@pfeiffer.edu
KIDD, Windy .... 859-280-1237 187 G
wkidd@lextheo.edu
KIDDER, Paulette .... 206-296-5405 498 D
pwkidder@seattleu.edu
KIDDIE, Thomas .... 304-766-4116 505 A
tkiddie@wvstateu.edu
KIDDOO, Sandy .... 715-422-5525 514 B
sandy.kiddoo@mstc.edu
KIDESS LUCEY, Tamie .. 413-748-3161 224 G
tkidessl@springfieldcollege.edu
KIDWELL, Debra .... 573-681-5418 261 H
purchasing@lincolnu.edu
KIDWELL, Eric, A .... 334-833-4420.... 5 M
ekidwell@hawks.huntingdon.edu
KIDWELL, John .... 870-460-1083.. 22 D
kidwell@uamont.edu
KIDWELL, Kim .... 217-333-0460 154 B
kkidwell@illinois.edu
KIDWELL, Martin .... 503-253-3443 385 B
mkidwell@ocom.edu
KIEBA-TOLKSDORF,
Helen, C .... 248-689-8282 238 F
hkieba@walshcollege.edu
KIEC, Michael .... 216-373-5227 367 A
mkiec@ndc.edu
KIEC, Michele .... 610-683-4500 406 D
kiec@kutztown.edu
KIECKHAFER, David, S . 608-342-1321 511 D
kieckhaferd@uwplatt.edu
KIEDA, David, B .... 801-581-8796 472 P
dave.kieda@utah.edu
KIEF, Bob .... 253-879-2820 499 C
bkief@pugetsound.edu
KIEFER, Cindy .... 406-756-3843 271 A
ckiefer@fvcc.edu
KIEFER, David, E .... 626-584-5409.. 43 K
dkiefer@fuller.edu
KIEFER, Irene .... 800-567-2344 506 I
ikiefer@menominee.edu
KIEFER, Mike .... 941-752-5000 108 P
KIEFER, William .... 412-809-5100 408 D
kiefer.william@pti.edu
KIEFFER, Barb .... 920-735-5734 513 F
kieffer@fvtc.edu
KIEFFER, Don .... 212-986-4343 299 F
dmk@berkeleycollege.edu
KIEFFER, Don .... 212-986-4343 283 J
dmk@berkeleycollege.edu
KIEFFER, Linda .... 509-359-6345 494 D
lkieffer@ewu.edu
KIEFFER, Rebecca .... 585-385-8280 322 E
rkieffer@sjfc.edu
KIEFFER, Shelly .... 318-473-6508 194 A
skieffer@lsua.edu
KIEFNER, Vincent .... 908-737-4869 286 F
vkiefner@kean.edu
KIEFT, Beth Anne .... 386-822-7151 111 E
bkieft@stetson.edu
KIEFT, Thom .... 352-536-2150 103 B
kieftt@lssc.edu
KIEHL, Ermalynn .... 850-474-2405 111 D
ekiehl@uwf.edu

KIMMELMAN, Eric ... 518-736-3622 309 A
ekimmelm@fmcc.suny.edu
KIMMELMAN, Scott ... 772-462-7760 101 Q
skimmelm@irsc.edu
KIMMENS, Randy ... 480-731-8202 .. 13 D
randy.kimmens@domail.maricopa.edu
KIMMINS, William, P ... 516-876-3179 327 C
kimminsw@oldwestbury.edu
KIMREY, Phil ... 205-726-2736 .... 6 G
ppkimrey@samford.edu
KIMSEY, Phillip ... 706-204-2283 119 G
pkimsey@highlands.edu
KIMURA, Melissa ... 562-947-8755 .. 65 D
melissakimura@scuhs.edu
KIN, Amanda, E ... 205-853-1200 .... 2 F
akin@jeffersonstate.edu
KINANE, Denis, F ... 215-898-1038 412 G
dfkinane@dental.upenn.edu
KINANE, Michael, G ... 516-876-3162 327 C
kinanem@oldwestbury.edu
KINANE, Michael, G ... 516-876-3212 327 C
kinanem@oldwestbury.edu
KINARD, Mary ... 205-387-0511 .... 1 D
mary.kinard@bscc.edu
KINARD, Sylvia ... 718-270-6936 303 C
skinard@mec.cuny.edu
KINARD, Sylvia, G ... 718-270-6136 303 C
sthompson@mec.cuny.edu
KINARD, Trent ... 803-812-7468 425 D
tkinard@mailbox.sc.edu
KINARD, Zeolean, F ... 864-941-8688 423 C
kinard.z@ptc.edu
KINCADE, Luis ... 432-264-5092 450 G
wkincade@howardcollege.edu
KINCAID, Brenda, L ... 615-297-7545 429 H
kincaid@aquinascollege.edu
KINCAID, David, N ... 719-333-9751 518 H
KINCAID, Heather ... 740-374-8716 373 G
hkincaid@wscc.edu
KINCAID, Rachel ... 225-342-6950 196 F
rachel.kincaid@la.gov
KINCAID, William ... 317-931-2303 157 D
bkincaid@cts.edu
KINCAID, William ... 317-931-2330 157 D
bkincaid@cts.edu
KINCANNON, Mary ... 817-257-7237 461 A
m.kincannon@tcu.edu
KINCART, Joel ... 605-394-2436 429 A
joel.kincart@sdsmt.edu
KINCHEN, Thomas, A ... 850-263-3261 .. 95 F
takinchen@baptistcollege.edu
KINCHENS, Eulish ... 229-931-2249 125 G
ekinchens@southgatech.edu
KINCHERLOW-MARTIN,
Janet ... 256-306-2561 .... 1 F
janet.martin@calhoun.edu
KIND, Jule ... 765-677-2980 161 C
jule.kind@indwes.edu
KIND-KEPPEL, Heather .. 262-595-2239 511 C
kindkepp@uwp.edu
KINDEL, Roger ... 973-443-8972 286 B
roger_p_kindel@fdu.edu
KINDER, Angie, M ... 304-260-4380 502 J
akinder@blueridgectc.edu
KINDER, Chad, L ... 580-774-3790 380 B
chad.kinder@swosu.edu
KINDERS, Mark ... 405-974-5560 380 J
mkinders@uco.edu
KINDL, Christine ... 724-938-5492 405 F
kindl@calu.edu
KINDLE, Derek ... 608-262-3060 510 C
derek.kindle@wisc.edu
KINDLE, Joan ... 563-336-3488 168 K
jkindle@eicc.edu
KINDLER, Andreas ... 309-677-3107 134 G
akindler@bradley.edu
KINDLER, Lisa ... 704-406-3923 337 H
lkindler@gardner-webb.edu
KINDON, Victoria ... 434-395-2001 482 E
kindonv@longwood.edu
KINEAVY, Jacqueline ... 973-684-6300 288 C
jkineavy@pccc.edu
KINEL, Janine, S ... 860-297-2255 .. 88 E
janine.kinel@trincoll.edu
KINERNEY, Donna ... 240-567-8827 205 F
donna.kinerney@montgomerycollege.edu
KINERSON, Sara ... 802-635-1257 477 C
sara.kinerson@jsc.edu
KINES, James ... 864-231-2177 418 E
jkines@andersonuniversity.edu
KINES, Teresa ... 336-249-8186 342 F
tkines@davidsonccc.edu
KING, Adolf ... 865-354-3000 438 A
kingaa@roanestate.edu
KING, Adrienne ... 270-809-4894 188 D
aking20@murraystate.edu
KING, Ahyana ... 716-926-8835 310 B
aking@hilbert.edu
KING, Albert ... 419-289-5959 356 L
aking@ashland.edu
KING, Alicia, M ... 956-665-2118 468 A
alicia.king@utrgv.edu
KING, Alissa ... 601-318-6474 256 I
aking@wmcarey.edu
KING, Allyson ... 229-732-5956 115 B
allysonking@andrewcollege.edu
KING, Amy, L ... 304-457-6354 501 A
kingal@ab.edu
KING, Andrew ... 207-780-5670 201 H
andrew.king@maine.edu
KING, Andrew, B ... 904-620-2602 110 E
a.king@unf.edu
KING, Angella ... 859-246-6696 185 G
angie.king@kctcs.edu
KING, Anthony ... 937-255-6565 517 H
anthony.king@afit.edu
KING, Art ... 646-312-4570 301 B
art.king@baruch.cuny.edu
KING, B, J ... 423-439-4414 431 H
kingbj@etsu.edu
KING, B, J ... 423-439-5884 431 H
kingbj@etsu.edu
KING, Barabara ... 903-533-5468 464 D
bkin2@tjc.edu
KING, Bayard ... 212-217-4020 308 B
bayard_king@fitnyc.edu
KING, Becky, L ... 254-710-2711 444 B
becky_king@baylor.edu
KING, Bob ... 210-999-7011 464 B
bob.king@trinity.edu
KING, Brenda, M ... 304-336-8076 504 E
kingbren@westliberty.edu
KING, Brian ... 916-568-3021 .. 50 E
kingb@losrios.edu
KING, Brian ... 814-866-6641 399 C
bking@lecom.edu
KING, Bruce ... 510-235-7800 .. 40 K
bking@contracosta.edu
KING, Bruce ... 507-786-3334 250 C
kingb@stolaf.edu
KING, Bryan ... 760-252-2411 .. 27 A
bking1@barstow.edu
KING, Carolee ... 409-772-1904 469 C
caaking@utmb.edu
KING, Charles ... 409-933-8404 446 H
cking@com.edu
KING, Charles, W ... 540-568-6434 481 I
kingcw@jmu.edu
KING, Christopher ... 956-665-2222 468 A
chris.king@utrgv.edu
KING, Corey ... 561-297-3988 109 B
cking14@fau.edu
KING, Corinna ... 515-263-2802 169 E
cking@grandview.edu
KING, Craig ... 212-870-1238 318 C
cking@nyts.edu
KING, Curt ... 978-542-6446 218 E
cking@salemstate.edu
KING, Cynthia, L ... 610-861-5510 403 B
cking@northampton.edu
KING, D. Wayne ... 859-238-5550 184 C
wayne.king@centre.edu
KING, Daniel, P ... 334-844-4810 .... 4 D
dpk0002@auburn.edu
KING, David, A ... 540-432-4440 480 A
david.king@emu.edu
KING, David, A ... 330-471-8121 364 H
dking@malone.edu
KING, David, A ... 541-737-2676 385 F
ecampus@oregonstate.edu
KING, David, W ... 805-565-6036 .. 74 I
dking@westmont.edu
KING, Deborah ... 870-338-6474 .. 22 G
KING, Del ... 404-727-7567 119 B
dking2@emory.edu
KING, Denise ... 423-472-7141 436 G
dking05@clevelandstatecc.edu
KING, Dennis ... 785-628-4276 177 D
dking@fhsu.edu
KING, Dennis ... 828-398-7112 340 M
dennisfking@abtech.edu
KING, Donald ... 508-999-8575 217 A
dking@umassd.edu
KING, JR., Donald ... 765-285-1478 156 C
jking@bsu.edu
KING, Donna ... 903-463-8735 449 J
donnaking@grayson.edu
KING, Dottie ... 812-535-5296 163 I
president@smwc.edu
KING, Duane ... 918-596-2710 381 C
duane-king@utulsa.edu
KING, Ebony ... 712-749-2379 167 C
kinge@bvu.edu
KING, Eddie ... 843-208-8135 425 B
eking@uscb.edu
KING, Elizabeth, H ... 316-978-3510 182 F
elizabeth.king@wichita.edu
KING, Eric ... 316-978-3106 182 F
eric.king@wichita.edu
KING, Fleurette ... 970-351-3012 .. 83 F
fleurette.king@unco.edu
KING, Frances ... 704-463-3037 348 B
frances.king@pfeiffer.edu
KING, Fred, L ... 304-293-3449 505 B
fred.king@mail.wvu.edu
KING, Garrett ... 580-774-3267 380 B
garrett.king@swosu.edu
KING, Glenda ... 662-252-8000 255 F
gking@rustcollege.edu
KING, Gordon, B ... 617-557-1520 224 I
gking@suffolk.edu
KING, Greg ... 304-384-6305 503 P
gking@concord.edu
KING, Greg ... 309-556-3031 141 B
gking@iwu.edu
KING, Greg ... 423-236-2983 436 C
gking@southern.edu
KING, Gregory ... 330-823-2282 372 C
kinggl@mountunion.edu
KING, JR., H. Lee ... 434-223-7258 481 D
lking@hsc.edu
KING, Henry, D ... 260-422-5561 159 D
hdking@indianatech.edu
KING, Herbert ... 651-793-1508 245 E
herbert.king@metrostate.edu
KING, Irene ... 610-519-4080 413 K
irene.king@villanova.edu
KING, Jackie, E ... 585-275-9900 332 E
jking@admin.rochester.edu
KING, James ... 202-651-5000 .. 91 H
james.king@gallaudet.edu
KING, James ... 615-336-4460 436 E
james.king@tbr.edu
KING, James ... 423-323-0201 437 E
KING, Janice ... 775-753-2361 279 A
janice.king@gbcnv.edu
KING, Jean ... 508-856-4979 217 C
jean.king@umassmed.edu
KING, Jennifer ... 413-559-5427 215 F
KING, Jeremy, R ... 864-656-4275 419 F
jking2@clemson.edu
KING, Jerry ... 903-675-6211 464 C
jking@tvcc.edu
KING, Jim, M ... 318-257-2445 197 A
king@latech.edu
KING, Joan ... 509-335-9681 499 G
joank@wsu.edu
KING, Jodie ... 215-248-7004 392 D
kingj@chc.edu
KING, Joel ... 308-398-7315 273 G
joelking@cccneb.edu
KING, John ... 541-552-6261 386 H
kingjo@sou.edu
KING, John, J ... 401-254-3042 417 C
jjking@rwu.edu
KING, John, M ... 617-552-4445 212 E
john.king.2@bc.edu
KING, Jonathan ... 619-482-6379 .. 65 H
jking@swccd.edu
KING, Jovanna, J ... 864-656-0663 419 F
jovanna@clemson.edu
KING, Julie, A ... 803-786-3871 420 D
juking@columbiasc.edu
KING, Karen, D ... 423-439-5654 431 H
kingk@etsu.edu
KING, Katherine ... 949-480-4161 .. 64 D
kking@soka.edu
KING, Katie ... 405-491-6350 379 K
kking@snu.edu
KING, Kenneth ... 801-878-1419 280 B
kking@roseman.edu
KING, Khristian, J ... 716-673-3398 325 C
khristian.king@fredonia.edu
KING, Kimberly ... 239-280-2484 .. 95 C
kimberly.king@avemaria.edu
KING, Kwanna ... 918-463-2931 375 G
kwanna.king@connorsstate.edu
KING, Laura ... 870-512-7850 .. 18 D
laura_king@asun.edu
KING, Laura ... 651-846-1316 247 G
laura.king@saintpaul.edu
KING, Laura, M ... 651-201-1732 243 I
laura.king@so.mnscu.edu
KING, Leslie ... 718-518-4377 302 D
lking@hostos.cuny.edu
KING, Leslie ... 770-426-2713 122 F
lesliek@life.edu
KING, Libby ... 423-869-6358 433 C
libby.king@lmunet.edu
KING, Linda ... 864-231-2000 418 E
dking@andersonuniversity.edu
KING, Linda ... 903-886-5013 459 E
linda.king@tamuc.edu
KING, Lorene ... 386-506-3658 .. 97 I
lorene.king@daytonastate.edu
KING, Lynn ... 910-879-5520 341 A
lking@bladencc.edu
KING, Marsha, M ... 260-399-7700 165 B
mking@sf.edu
KING, Martha ... 708-216-3354 144 D
mking17@luc.edu
KING, Mary ... 940-552-6291 469 F
mking@vernoncollege.edu
KING, Mary, B ... 336-734-7901 343 C
mking@forsythtech.edu
KING, Mary Jo ... 270-706-8530 185 H
maryjo.king@kctcs.edu
KING, Melinda ... 706-368-7748 119 G
mewers@highlands.edu
KING, Melinda ... 205-348-4904 .... 8 A
mjking@ua.edu
KING, Michael ... 913-360-7633 175 D
mking@benedictine.edu
KING, Michael ... 706-754-7711 123 G
mking@northgatech.edu
KING, Michael ... 301-955-1264 207 G
mking8@umd.edu
KING, Michelle ... 310-434-3323 .. 62 G
king_michelle@smc.edu
KING, Mike ... 617-747-2363 212 B
enrollment@berklee.edu
KING, Mike ... 812-535-5273 163 I
mking2@smwc.edu
KING, Mindy ... 715-346-2321 511 F
mking@uwsp.edu
KING, Natalie ... 831-582-3609 .. 33 A
nmking@csumb.edu
KING, Natasha ... 912-287-5827 117 J
nking@coastalpines.edu
KING, Nathaniel ... 702-992-2806 279 B
nathaniel.king@nsc.edu
KING, Patricia, J ... 918-687-3299 374 H
kingp@bacone.edu
KING, Paula Kay ... 765-973-8331 160 A
pkayking@iue.edu
KING, Peggy ... 630-752-5246 155 F
peggy.king@wheaton.edu
KING, Peter, D ... 843-661-1281 421 H
pking@fmarion.edu
KING, Phillip ... 650-306-3236 .. 61 R
kingp@smccd.edu
KING, Phyllis ... 414-229-6175 511 A
pking@wm.edu
KING, Queen ... 661-654-2251 .. 31 B
qking@csub.edu
KING, Rhonda ... 504-671-5051 192 H
rking1@dcc.edu
KING, Rhonda ... 717-796-1800 401 L
rking@messiah.edu
KING, Robert ... 707-654-1245 .. 32 E
rking@csum.edu
KING, Rodmon, C ... 859-238-5267 184 C
rodmon.king@centre.edu
KING, Ronan ... 276-944-6125 480 J
rking@ehc.edu
KING, Ryan ... 207-326-0136 200 F
ryan.king@mma.edu
KING, S. Bruce ... 336-758-5774 353 A
kingsb@wfu.edu
KING, Samuel ... 901-435-1509 433 A
samuel_king@loc.edu
KING, Samuel ... 206-239-2234 492 D
sjking@aii.edu
KING, Sasha ... 310-434-3404 .. 62 G
king_sasha@smc.edu
KING, Scott ... 916-649-8168 .. 27 L
scott.king@brightwood.edu
KING, Shawn ... 509-359-6878 494 D
sking@ewu.edu
KING, Sheila, D ... 310-506-4151 .. 56 D
sheila.king@pepperdine.edu
KING, Shelly ... 816-415-5963 270 C
kings@william.jewell.edu
KING, Stephanie ... 716-851-1999 307 I
kings@ecc.edu
KING, Stephanie ... 413-565-1000 211 C
sking@baypath.edu
KING, Steven ... 413-662-5410 218 C
steven.king@mcla.edu
KING, Sue ... 816-501-3759 257 G
sue.king@avila.edu
KING, Susan, L ... 207-780-4681 201 H
susank@maine.edu
KING, Susan, R ... 919-962-1204 351 B
susanking@unc.edu
KING, JR.,
Talmadge, E ... 415-476-2342 .. 70 A
talmadge.king@ucsf.edu

KIRSTEN, Jan .... 732-255-0400 288 B
jkirsten@ocean.edu
KIRTLEY, Adam, M .... 509-522-4449 500 G
kirtleam@whitman.edu
KIRTMAN, Janet .... 212-346-1700 319 J
jkirtman@pace.edu
KIRTMAN, Lisa .... 657-278-5901.. 32 B
lkirtman@fullerton.edu
KIRVES, Carol .... 270-707-3751 186 B
carol.kirves@kctcs.edu
KIRWIN, Luanne .... 617-373-2520 223 D
KISELYUK, Ella .... 212-817-7700 302 B
ekiselyuk@gc.cuny.edu
KISER, Dan .... 828-328-7154 339 C
dan.kiser@lr.edu
KISER, Joseph, B .... 276-328-0143 487 A
jbk5b@uvawise.edu
KISER, Kristy .... 276-328-0220 487 A
kej5c@uvawise.edu
KISER, Lee .... 828-448-6707 347 F
lkiser@wpcc.edu
KISER, Lyda .... 540-869-0623 488 E
lkiser@lfcc.edu
KISER, Ronnie .... 276-964-7603 489 F
ronnie.kiser@sw.edu
KISER-MILLER, Kathy .... 970-945-8691.. 77 M
KISH, Anne .... 406-683-7492 271 H
anne.kish@umwestern.edu
KISH, Deborah .... 970-339-6459.. 76 E
deb.kish@aims.edu
KISH, Joy .... 828-689-1140 339 G
jkish@mhu.edu
KISH-GOODLING,
Donna, M .... 484-664-3479 402 F
donnakish-goodling@muhlenberg.edu
KISHBAUGH, Amanda ... 570-389-4297 405 E
akishba2@bloomu.edu
KISHEN, Ron .... 480-557-2000.. 17 C
ron.kishen@phoenix.edu
KISLER, Jeffrey .... 215-717-6415 412 F
jkisler@uarts.edu
KISLING, Reid .... 503-517-1820 388 C
rkisling@westernseminary.edu
KISNER, Adrienne .... 617-879-1156 226 A
akisner@wheelock.edu
KISONGO, Ibuchwa .... 763-424-0806 246 E
ikisongo@nhcc.edu
KISPERT, Craig, G .... 206-281-2536 498 B
ckispert@spu.edu
KISPERT, John, J .... 843-661-1110 421 H
jkispert@fmarion.edu
KISS, Elizabeth .... 404-471-6280 114 H
president@agnesscott.edu
KISS, John, Z .... 336-334-5607 351 D
kzkiss@uncg.edu
KISSAL, Carol .... 404-727-2827 119 B
carol.dillon.kissal@emory.edu
KISSEBERTH, Sara .... 419-358-3484 357 E
kisseberths@bluffton.edu
KISSEL, Karen .... 630-617-3012 138 C
karen.kissel@elmhurst.edu
KISSELL, Joseph .... 570-389-4263 405 E
jkissell@bloomu.edu
KISSICK, Sharon .... 919-508-2311 353 C
sharon.kissick@peace.edu
KISSINGER, John .... 937-298-3399 364 B
john.kissinger@kc.edu
KISSINGER, Kurt, A .... 814-865-6574 403 F
kak47@psu.edu
KISSINGER, Sue .... 715-346-3361 511 F
skissing@uwsp.edu
KISTNER, Angie .... 618-437-5321 149 H
kistner@rlc.edu
KISTNER, Frances .... 508-373-5749 221 E
KISTNER, Janet .... 850-644-7836 110 A
jkistner@fsu.edu
KISTNER, Ken .... 305-273-4499.. 96 N
ken@cbt.edu
KISTNER, Warren .... 309-556-3071 141 B
wkistner@iwu.edu
KISTULENTZ, Steven ..... 352-588-7218 106 N
steven.kistulentz@saintleo.edu
KITAGAWA, Susan .... 831-646-4014.. 52 G
skitagawa@mpc.edu
KITCH, Rhonda .... 701-231-7987 354 D
rhonda.k.kitch@ndsu.edu
KITCHEN, Augusta .... 803-780-1159 426 F
akitchen@voorhees.edu
KITCHEN, Barbara .... 859-846-5725 188 B
bkitchen@midway.edu
KITCHEN, Herbert .... 510-466-7374.. 56 I
hkitchen@peralta.edu
KITCHEN, Mark .... 307-754-6405 516 Q
mark.kitchen@nwc.edu
KITCHEN, Steve .... 650-949-6150.. 43 D
kitchensteve@fhda.edu
KITCHEN, Todd .... 479-619-4232.. 20 F
tkitchen@nwacc.edu
KITCHENS, Elizabeth ..... 605-999-7136 427 E
elizabeth.kitchens@mitchelltech.edu
KITCHENS, Joann .... 701-662-1502 355 A
joann.kitchens@lrsc.edu
KITCHENS, Joseph, H ... 770-720-5966 124 H
jhk@reinhardt.edu
KITCHENS, Penny .... 478-553-2060 123 H
pkitchens@oftc.edu
KITCHENS, Ronnie .... 601-426-6346 255 G
rkitchens@southeasternbaptist.edu
KITCHENS, Tempie .... 770-233-6170 126 B
tkitchens@sctech.edu
KITCHIN, Lindy .... 252-985-5369 348 A
lkitchin@ncwc.edu
KITCHIN, Steven, H .... 401-739-5000 416 D
skitchin@neit.edu
KITCHINGS, Maribeth .... 601-974-1002 254 A
kitchme@millsaps.edu
KITE, Joy, A .... 608-822-2319 515 A
jkite@swtc.edu
KITE, Michelle .... 269-782-1302 237 B
mkite@swmich.edu
KITE, Terry .... 636-481-3273 261 B
tkite@jeffco.edu
KITEI, Susan, C .... 610-758-3870 400 B
sck0@lehigh.edu
KITHCART, Jane .... 845-687-5111 331 L
kithcarj@sunyulster.edu
KITLEY, Barry, S .... 336-841-9363 338 E
bkitley@highpoint.edu
KITSON, Anna .... 502-410-6200 184 H
akitson@galencollege.edu
KITTINGER, Fred .... 407-823-1208 110 C
fred.kittinger@ucf.edu
KITTLE, Daniel .... 319-352-8745 174 C
daniel.kittle@wartburg.edu
KITTLE, Paul .... 336-841-9107 338 E
pkittle@highpoint.edu
KITTNER, Missy .... 254-299-8514 452 E
mkittner@mclennan.edu
KITTO, Kathleen .... 360-650-5929 500 E
kathleen.kitto@wwu.edu
KITTREDGE,
Cynthia Briggs .... 512-472-4133 456 E
cynthia.kittredge@ssw.edu
KITTRELL-MIKELL,
Deborah .... 478-289-2161 118 H
dkittrell@ega.edu
KITTS, Justin .... 606-546-1232 189 I
jkitts@unionky.edu
KITTS, Kenneth .... 256-765-4211.... 9 A
kkitts@una.edu
KITZINGER, Denis .... 603-880-8308 282 D
dkitzinger@thomasmorecollege.edu
KITZINGER, Sara .... 603-566-5017 282 D
skitzinger@thomasmorecollege.edu
KIVLIGHAN, Mia .... 540-432-4211 480 A
mia.kivlighan@emu.edu
KIWUS, Christopher ...... 540-231-6291 490 F
chkiwus@vt.edu
KIYOSAKI, Donna, F ..... 808-956-7616 129 H
donnafay@hawaii.edu
KIYOSHI, Joaquin .... 670-237-6858 520 D
jack.kiyoshi@marianas.edu
KJELLEREN, Donald, J .. 413-597-2312 226 C
donald.f.kjelleren@williams.edu
KLAAS, Brian .... 816-235-1333 268 D
klaasb@umkc.edu
KLAAS, Carlene .... 312-362-8146 137 C
cklaas@depaul.edu
KLAAS, Daniel .... 412-291-6286 389 F
dklaas@aii.edu
KLAASSEN, Sara .... 816-322-0110 257 M
sara.klaassen@calvary.edu
KLABE, Kimberly .... 301-447-5377 206 B
klabe@msmary.edu
KLADIVKO, Deborah ..... 803-641-3577 425 A
debk@usca.edu
KLAEHN, Scott .... 651-450-3000 245 A
sklaehn@inverhills.edu
KLAFFKE, David .... 360-383-3016 500 F
dklaffke@whatcom.ctc.edu
KLAG, Michael, J .... 410-955-3540 204 F
michaelj.klag@jhu.edu
KLAIBER, Beverly, G ..... 530-226-4179.. 64 B
bklaiber@simpsonu.edu
KLAIBER, James, S .... 440-775-5603 367 B
jim.klaiber@oberlin.edu
KLAMEN, David .... 508-999-8010 217 A
dklamen@umassd.edu
KLAPATAUSKAS,
Kyle, J .... 563-588-7829 171 H
kyle.klapatauskas@loras.edu
KLAPPER, Robert .... 770-729-8400 115 F
KLARUP, Doug .... 217-581-6227 138 A
dgklarup@eiu.edu
KLASEK, Angie .... 402-466-4774 274 E
angie.klasek@doane.edu
KLASEN, James .... 617-588-1344 211 G
jklasen@bfit.edu
KLASKO, Stephen, K ..... 215-955-6617 411 E
stephen.klasko@jefferson.edu
KLASS, Marissa .... 412-291-6620 389 F
mklass@aii.edu
KLASS, Stephen, P .... 413-597-3118 226 C
stephen.p.klass@williams.edu
KLASSY, Garrett .... 312-996-2695 153 H
gklassy@uic.edu
KLATT, Sara .... 712-274-6400 174 E
sara.klatt@witcc.edu
KLAUBER, James, S ...... 256-306-2555.... 1 F
jim.klauber@calhoun.edu
KLAUDER, Mark, J .... 802-447-6322 476 C
mklauder@svc.edu
KLAUS, Chad, L .... 609-258-5498 288 F
klaus@princeton.edu
KLAUS, Dennis .... 801-957-4250 474 B
dennis.klaus@slcc.edu
KLAUSMEYER, Robert ... 573-875-7304 258 F
rklausmeyer@ccis.edu
KLAVER, Lenny .... 660-359-3948 264 H
lklaver@mail.ncmissouri.edu
KLAWE, Maria, M .... 909-921-8120.. 45 D
klawe@hmc.edu
KLAWITTER, Christina ... 608-363-2660 506 D
klawitterc@beloit.edu
KLAWUNN, Margaret .... 805-893-3651.. 70 B
margaret.klawunn@sa.ucsb.edu
KLAY, Kathy, A .... 937-328-6085 359 H
klayk@clarkstate.edu
KLEBE, Kelli .... 719-255-3779.. 83 C
kklebe@uccs.edu
KLEBESADEL, Shirley .... 715-232-2190 512 A
klebesadels@uwstout.edu
KLECKNER, Joan .... 610-902-8201 391 B
joan.d.kleckner@cabrini.edu
KLEDZIK, Eric .... 321-674-8107.. 99 K
ekledzik@fit.edu
KLEEMAN, Amy .... 407-582-1238 113 F
akleeman@valenciacollege.edu
KLEFFMAN, Terry, L ...... 806-371-5111 442 D
tlkleffman@actx.edu
KLEICH, Tammie .... 308-635-6072 278 B
kleicht@wncc.edu
KLEIMAN, Adriana .... 213-615-7295.. 37 B
akleiman@thechicagoschool.edu
KLEIN, Andrew, O .... 508-849-3313 210 H
aklein@annamaria.edu
KLEIN, Andrew, R .... 317-274-2581 160 E
anrklein@iupui.edu
KLEIN, Barb .... 641-648-4611 170 H
barb.klein@iavalley.edu
KLEIN, Cynthia .... 412-809-5100 408 D
klein.cynthia@pti.edu
KLEIN, Erica .... 516-877-3744 297 I
eklein@adelphi.edu
KLEIN, Erick, P .... 651-631-5141 251 C
epklein@unwsp.edu
KLEIN, Erin .... 701-252-3467 355 J
eklein@uj.edu
KLEIN, Gary .... 608-663-6713 507 D
garyklein@edgewood.edu
KLEIN, Jacob .... 248-689-8282 238 F
jklein@walshcollege.edu
KLEIN, Jacqueline .... 518-454-2851 305 B
kleinj@strose.edu
KLEIN, Janie .... 925-631-4916.. 59 C
mminguil@stmarys-ca.edu
KLEIN, Jeff .... 909-652-6317.. 36 E
jeff.klein@chaffey.edu
KLEIN, Jennifer .... 949-582-4565.. 64 J
jklein26@saddleback.edu
KLEIN, Jim .... 502-456-6508 189 F
jklein@sullivan.edu
KLEIN, Judy .... 267-341-3615 397 G
jklein@holyfamily.edu
KLEIN, June .... 650-433-3849.. 55 I
jklein@paloaltou.edu
KLEIN, Karen .... 580-774-3268 380 B
karen.klein@swosu.edu
KLEIN, Leslie, G .... 410-358-3144 210 B
KLEIN, Lori .... 907-796-6036.. 10 C
laklein@alaska.edu
KLEIN, Marjorie, S .... 814-332-5910 388 F
mklein@allegheny.edu
KLEIN, Mendel .... 718-384-5460 334 J
KLEIN, Michael .... 718-368-5087 303 A
mklein@kbcc.cuny.edu
KLEIN, Michael .... 215-204-1927 411 B
mike.klein@temple.edu
KLEIN, Michelle, W .... 504-866-7426 195 E
finance@nds.edu
KLEIN, Patti .... 651-523-2421 242 E
pklein01@hamline.edu
KLEIN, Ray .... 812-941-2457 161 A
rayklein@ius.edu
KLEIN, Sara .... 201-216-3543 291 G
sara.klein@stevens.edu
KLEIN, Sheryn .... 415-451-2812.. 60 I
sklein@sfts.edu
KLEIN, Steve .... 503-352-2822 385 I
kleinsk@pacificu.edu
KLEIN, Steven .... 517-629-0321 226 G
sklein@albion.edu
KLEIN, Stuart .... 212-431-2170 317 H
stuart.klein@nyls.edu
KLEIN, Terry .... 715-468-2815 515 D
terry.klein@witc.edu
KLEINBERG, David .... 630-829-6304 133 I
dkleinberg@ben.edu
KLEINDL, Brad .... 816-584-6308 265 C
brad.kleindl@park.edu
KLEINE, Patricia, A .... 715-836-2320 510 D
kleinepa@uwec.edu
KLEINER, Zev .... 347-394-1036 299 G
zkleiner@ateret.net
KLEINHANS, Randy .... 574-372-5100 158 B
kleinhrp@grace.edu
KLEINKAUFMAN, Dovid 718-327-7600 334 C
info@yofr.org
KLEINKOPF, Karl .... 208-732-6201 131 I
csitrustees@csi.edu
KLEINLEIN, Tom .... 912-478-5047 120 E
tkleinlein@georgiasouthern.edu
KLEINMAN, Daniel, L .... 617-353-2230 212 G
dlklein@bu.edu
KLEINMAN, Kent .... 607-255-9110 306 B
aapdean@cornell.edu
KLEINMAN, Kim .... 314-246-7768 269 N
kleinman@webster.edu
KLEINMAN, Yisroel .... 718-853-8500 331 E
KLEINSCHMIDT, Robert . 609-586-4800 287 A
kleinscr@mccc.edu
KLEINWORTH, Tom .... 713-798-6498 444 A
tklein@bcm.edu
KLEISER, Richele .... 559-325-3600.. 29 D
rkleiser@chsu.org
KLEMANN, M. Adam ...... 330-471-8308 364 H
aklemann@malone.edu
KLEMENS, Kristina .... 262-595-2004 511 C
klemens@uwp.edu
KLEMENT, Emily .... 940-872-4002 453 L
eklement@nctc.edu
KLEMENT, Emily .... 910-668-3331 453 L
eklement@nctc.edu
KLEMIUK, Christy .... 903-463-8650 449 J
klemiukc@grayson.edu
KLEMM, Dave .... 217-732-3155 143 G
dklemm@lincolncollege.edu
KLEMM, Jotisa .... 817-515-3083 458 B
jotisa.klemm@tccd.edu
KLEMPNER, Mark, D ..... 617-474-3250 217 C
mark.klempner@umassmed.edu
KLEN, Joseph, R .... 765-361-6052 166 B
klenj@wabash.edu
KLENIEWSKI, Nancy ...... 607-436-2500 325 E
nancy.kleniewski@oneonta.edu
KLENKE, James, W .... 618-650-2020 152 C
jklenke@siue.edu
KLEPFER, Jennifer .... 352-854-2322.. 97 C
klepferj@cf.edu
KLEPITSCH, Heather, A . 815-282-7900 150 H
heatherklepitsch@sacn.edu
KLEPONIS, Stephen .... 610-526-6017 396 H
skleponis@harcum.edu
KLEPPER, Scott .... 405-789-7661 380 A
scott.klepper@swcu.edu
KLESCHICK, Paul .... 413-205-3212 210 E
paul.kleschick@aic.edu
KLESNER, Joe, L .... 740-427-5114 364 A
klesner@kenyon.edu
KLESS, Teresa, M .... 401-825-2003 416 B
tkless@ccri.edu
KLETT, Breanna .... 562-903-4751.. 27 E
breanna.klett@biola.edu
KLEVA, Barbara .... 609-984-1124 292 B
bkleva@tesu.edu
KLEVEN, Daniel .... 612-455-3420 241 A
daniel.kleven@bcsmn.edu
KLEVENO, Robert .... 951-222-8000.. 58 H
robert.kleveno@rcc.edu
KLEVER, Sunny .... 503-338-2306 382 E
sklever@clatsopcc.edu
KLEYN, Henk .... 616-977-0599 236 B
henk.kleyn@prts.edu
KLIER, Jody .... 701-845-7297 354 E
jody.klier@vcsu.edu
KLIEVER, Amanda .... 541-917-4204 384 A
klievea@linnbenton.edu
KLIEWER, Wayne .... 620-947-3121 181 H
waynekliewer@tabor.edu
KLIEWONEIT, Chris .... 989-386-6652 234 B
ckliewon@midmich.edu

KLIGMAN, Linda, B .... 267-975-2254 397 K lindakligman@iirp.edu
KLIMCZYK, Karen .... 219-464-5015 165 D karen.klimczyk@valpo.edu
KLIMKOWSKI, Ann Francis .... 419-885-3211 364 G aklimkowski@lourdes.edu
KLIMOFF, Dodi .... 215-635-7300 396 B dklimoff@gratz.edu
KLIMPT, Kelly .... 281-756-3539 442 C kklimpt@alvincollege.edu
KLINE, Amy .... 212-875-4504 298 H akline@bankstreet.edu
KLINE, J .... 615-383-4848 441 A jkline@watkins.edu
KLINE, John .... 847-585-0014 133 D jkline@aiuonline.edu
KLINE, Julie .... 909-593-3511.. 70 E jkline@laverne.edu
KLINE, Julie, C .... 507-933-6075 242 D jkline@gustavus.edu
KLINE, Loni, N .... 570-326-3761 404 T lnk6@pct.edu
KLINE, Mae .... 407-328-2096 107 G kline@seminolestate.edu
KLINE, Rebecca .... 573-876-7111 267 G rkline@stephens.edu
KLINE, Richard .... 440-375-7512 364 C rkline@lec.edu
KLINE, Ronald, J .... 610-861-1510 402 D kliner@moravian.edu
KLINE, Sharon .... 360-475-7778 496 F skline@olympic.edu
KLINE, Thomas .... 262-551-6036 506 H tkline@carthage.edu
KLINE, William .... 978-837-5134 221 G klinew@merrimack.edu
KLINE, William .... 812-877-8136 163 G kline@rose-hulman.edu
KLINEPETER, Pamela ..... 606-326-2254 185 E pamela.klinepeter@kctcs.edu
KLINESMITH, Jerry .... 740-264-5591 361 D jklinesmith@egcc.edu
KLING, Lenda .... 850-201-8660 112 C klingl@tcc.fl.edu
KLING, Rory .... 785-890-3641 180 G rory.kling@nwktc.edu
KLINGBEIL, Nathan, W . 937-775-5007 374 B nathan.klingbeil@wright.edu
KLINGBERG, Jessica ...... 708-209-3505 136 I jessica.klingberg@cuchicago.edu
KLINGENBERG, Erin ...... 701-845-7424 354 E erin.klingenberg@vcsu.edu
KLINGENSMITH, Lynn ... 610-436-2513 407 D lklingensmith@wcupa.edu
KLINGER, Joe .... 708-456-0300 153 E joeklinger@triton.edu
KLINGER, John .... 314-505-7384 258 I klingerj@csl.edu
KLINGER, Michelle .... 602-285-7842.. 14 A michelle.klinger@phoenixcollege.edu
KLINGLER, Thomas, G .. 330-325-6606 366 F tklingler@neomed.edu
KLINGSHIRN, Connie .... 419-267-1329 366 G cklingshirn@northweststate.edu
KLINGSMITH, Libby ...... 970-339-6237.. 76 E libby.klingsmith@aims.edu
KLINK, Charles, J .... 804-828-7525 487 E cjklink@vcu.edu
KLINK, Marian .... 239-513-1122 101 O mklink@hodges.edu
KLINKENBERG, Laurel .. 217-641-4500 141 F lklinkenberg@jwcc.edu
KLINKNER, Melvin .... 262-595-2076 511 C klinkner@uwp.edu
KLIPP, Todd L, C .... 617-353-9550 212 G tklipp@bu.edu
KLIPPENSTEIN, Stacy .... 406-874-6165 271 D president@milescc.edu
KLIPPER, Frances .... 800-.95-5.25.. 177 H fklipper@grantham.edu
KLOBERDANZ, Jennifer . 815-280-2414 142 A jkloberd@jjc.edu
KLOBERDANZ, Mark ..... 515-271-4526 168 J mark.kloberdanz@drake.edu
KLOBY, Kathryn .... 732-263-5892 287 C kkloby@monmouth.edu
KLOCEK, David .... 276-376-3445 487 A dmk8e@uvawise.edu
KLOCHKOVA, Olga .... 503-251-5773 387 I oklochkova@uws.edu
KLOCKO, Timothy .... 434-381-6208 485 P tklocko@sbc.edu
KLOCKO, Timothy .... 573-876-7210 267 G tklocko@stephens.edu
KLOEHN, Steven .... 412-268-6449 391 H skloehn@andrew.cmu.edu
KLOEPPEL, Beverly .... 505-277-3432 296 H bkloeppe@unm.edu
KLOEPPEL, Brian .... 828-227-7398 352 C bkloeppel@wcu.edu
KLOFT, Craig .... 563-589-3251 173 J ckloft@dbq.edu
KLOHA, Jeffrey .... 314-505-7566 258 I klohaj@csl.edu
KLOKE, Rafeeka .... 360-383-3330 500 F rkloke@whatcom.ctc.edu
KLONOFF, Elizabeth ...... 407-823-5538 110 C elizabeth.klonoff@ucf.edu
KLONOSKI, Edward .... 860-515-3888.. 84 H eklonoski@charteroak.edu
KLOOS, Lori .... 320-308-5017 247 F lkloos@sctcc.edu
KLOPFER, Jerome, J ..... 575-624-8380 295 A klopfer@nmmi.edu
KLOPPENBERG, Lisa ..... 408-554-4362.. 62 F lkloppenberg@scu.edu
KLOPSCH, Vicki, P .... 909-621-8180.. 63 F vklopsch@scrippscollege.edu
KLOS, Elizabeth .... 313-664-7861 228 H eklos@collegeforcreativestudies.edu
KLOS, Hank, M .... 608-785-5092 510 F hklos@uwlax.edu
KLOS, Laura .... 314-446-8325 266 D laura.klos@stlcop.edu
KLOS, Ryan .... 815-455-8562 145 B rklos@mchenry.edu
KLOSE, Kathryn .... 240-684-2476 208 D kathryn.klose@umuc.edu
KLOSS, Michael, P .... 404-727-1984 119 B mkloss@emory.edu
KLOSS, Michelle .... 410-386-8411 203 A mkloss@carrollcc.edu
KLOSTERMAN, Timothy . 805-482-2755.. 58 M tklosterman@stjohnsem.edu
KLOSTERMANN, Jill ...... 618-545-3081 142 D jklostermann@kaskaskia.edu
KLOTMAN, Mary, E .... 919-684-2455 337 C mary.klotman@duke.edu
KLOTMAN, Paul .... 713-798-4800 444 A president@bcm.edu
KLOTT, Stacie .... 870-743-3000.. 20 E sklott@northark.edu
KLOTZBACH, Daniel, P . 309-556-3527 141 B dklotzba@iwu.edu
KLOTZBIER, Ed .... 209-228-4038.. 69 C eklotzbier@ucmerced.edu
KLUBERT, Kelly .... 304-243-8165 505 H kklubert@wju.edu
KLUCK, Linda .... 512-223-7503 443 G lkluck@austincc.edu
KLUCK, Ron .... 402-562-1253 273 G rkluck@cccneb.edu
KLUCK, Wesley .... 870-245-5220.. 20 G kluckw@obu.edu
KLUCKING, Joel .... 509-963-2323 492 L joel.klucking@cwu.edu
KLUDING, Tom .... 419-755-5659 366 E tkluding@ncstatecollege.edu
KLUEVER, Al .... 507-389-7412 247 H al.kluever@southcentral.edu
KLUG, Jane .... 605-642-6080 428 F jane.klug@bhsu.edu
KLUG, Jeff .... 909-384-8286.. 59 I jklug@sbccd.cc.ca.us
KLUG-WESSERL, Tia ...... 808-373-2849 131 A tiankaiwei@icloud.com
KLUGE, Cindy .... 414-229-4586 511 A ckluge@uwm.edu
KLUGH, Elgin .... 410-951-3044 208 F eklugh@coppin.edu
KLUIN, Richard .... 605-367-5692 429 C rich.kluin@southeasttech.edu
KLUKAS, Christopher, M .... 724-266-3838 412 D cklukas@tsm.edu
KLUMP, J. Val .... 414-382-1700 511 A vklump@uwm.edu
KLUNDT, Matthew .... 319-385-6262 170 J matthew.klundt@iw.edu
KLUTE, Paul .... 706-425-3183 127 A pklute@uga.edu
KLUTH, David .... 503-493-6538 382 I ckunert@cu-portland.edu
KLUTTZ-LEACH, Camille 336-750-2046 352 D leachck@wssu.edu
KLUVER, Erica, L .... 515-263-2816 169 E ekluver@grandview.edu
KLUVER, Kirk, R .... 319-335-1494 166 G kirk-kluver@uiowa.edu
KLUZA, Margaret .... 773-481-8183 136 B mkluza@ccc.edu
KLYMENKO, Anthony ..... 201-559-6100 286 C klymenkoa@felician.edu
KLYMENKO, Priscilla .... 201-559-6037 286 C klymenkop@felician.edu
KMIECH, Joseph .... 715-425-3658 511 E joseph.kmiech@uwrf.edu
KNAAPEN, Laura .... 920-424-2368 511 B knaapen@uwosh.edu
KNABE, Alexis .... 907-474-2600.. 10 B asknabe@alaska.edu
KNAFF, Mary .... 423-697-3371 436 F mary.knaff@chattanoogastate.edu
KNAGGS, Randy .... 802-257-4333 475 D rlknaggs@marlboro.edu
KNAPP, Brian .... 314-744-7695 263 F knappb@mobap.edu
KNAPP, Clair, W .... 260-982-5245 162 Q cwknapp@manchester.edu
KNAPP, Jeffrey .... 518-454-5374 305 B knappj@strose.edu
KNAPP, John .... 724-503-1001 414 A jknapp@washjeff.edu
KNAPP, Jolene .... 313-927-1373 233 D jknapp@marygrove.edu
KNAPP, Katherine .... 713-221-5055 465 C knappk@uhd.edu
KNAPP, Lori .... 516-299-4030 313 D lori.knapp@liu.edu
KNAPP, Peter .... 651-290-6423 248 U peter.knapp@mitchellhamline.edu
KNAPP, Scott, E .... 207-755-5230 199 K sknapp@cmcc.edu
KNAPP, William .... 860-297-2366.. 88 E william.knapp@trincoll.edu
KNAPPENBERGER, Ron . 864-455-8149 425 E ronk@ghs.org
KNAPPER, Logan .... 918-463-2931 375 G logan.knapper@connorsstate.edu
KNAPPER, William, D ... 308-635-6102 278 B knapperw@wncc.edu
KNARR, James .... 757-481-5005 492 A
KNARR, Rob .... 513-936-1724 371 F robert.knarr@uc.edu
KNAUER, Christopher, B .... 704-687-5703 351 C cknauer@uncc.edu
KNAUS, Kathy .... 720-890-8922.. 80 I finance@itea.edu
KNAUS, Kelli .... 440-646-8316 373 B kknaus@ursuline.edu
KNEALING, Todd .... 712-279-5402 167 B todd.knealing@briarcliff.edu
KNECHT, James .... 405-744-9650 377 F james.knecht@okstate.edu
KNECHT, Mike, W .... 270-831-9760 186 A mike.knecht@kctcs.edu
KNEEBONE, Elaine .... 870-230-5820.. 19 H kneebone@hsu.edu
KNEFEL, Mary Anne ...... 563-589-3215 173 J mknefel@dbq.edu
KNELLY, Kennith .... 518-564-3622 327 E kknel001@plattsburgh.edu
KNEPP, Marcia .... 301-387-3056 203 I marcia.knepp@garrettcollege.edu
KNERR, Amanda .... 812-237-3993 159 C amanda.knerr@indstate.edu
KNERR, Douglas .... 810-762-3177 238 B dknerr@umflint.edu
KNESAL, Amanda .... 228-377-0090 256 I amanda.knesal@wmcarey.edu
KNESER, Greg .... 507-786-3503 250 C kneser@stolaf.edu
KNETL, Brian .... 847-925-6738 139 B bknetl@harpercollege.edu
KNETTER, Michael, M ... 608-265-9953 510 C mike.knetter@supportuw.org
KNEWMAN, Liv .... 504-865-2011 194 G lknewman@loyno.edu
KNICELEY, Allen .... 704-669-4037 342 B kniceleya@clevelandcc.edu
KNICKERBOCKER, Troy . 210-805-5818 465 E troyk@uiwtx.edu
KNIER, Carey, A .... 920-565-1527 507 K knierca@lakeland.edu
KNIERING, John .... 860-768-4288.. 89 C kniering@hartford.edu
KNIFE, Christopher .... 352-854-2322.. 97 C knifec@cf.edu
KNIFFEN, Chad .... 832-252-0712 446 A chad.kniffen@cbshouston.edu
KNIFFEN, Robyn .... 402-399-2435 274 A rkniffen@csm.edu
KNIGHT, Aaron .... 713-718-2445 450 D aaron.knight@hccs.edu
KNIGHT, Allison, P .... 757-446-5244 480 C knightap@evms.edu
KNIGHT, Antonia .... 716-286-8204 318 F abk@niagara.edu
KNIGHT, Arlinda .... 334-420-4235.... 3 H aknight@trenholmstate.edu
KNIGHT, Aubrey, L .... 815-740-5047 154 G aknight@stfrancis.edu
KNIGHT, Brenda .... 850-201-6055 112 C knightbr@tcc.fl.edu
KNIGHT, Brent .... 517-483-1851 232 K knightb4@lcc.edu
KNIGHT, Cindi .... 304-647-6299 504 F cknight@osteo.wvsom.edu
KNIGHT, Darryl .... 847-925-6675 139 B dknight@harpercollege.edu
KNIGHT, David .... 256-726-7389.... 6 E dknight@oakwood.edu
KNIGHT, Debra, L .... 217-443-8865 137 B dknight@dacc.edu
KNIGHT, Derric .... 906-635-6244 232 J
KNIGHT, Gary, E .... 803-705-4559 418 G knightg@benedict.edu
KNIGHT, Gayle .... 601-318-6197 256 I gayle.knight@wmcarey.edu
KNIGHT, Holly .... 508-830-5029 218 D hknight@maritime.edu
KNIGHT, Jacob, E .... 317-738-8080 157 L jknight@franklincollege.edu
KNIGHT, Jaime .... 508-531-2337 217 D j2knight@bridgew.edu
KNIGHT, Jeff .... 904-819-6423.. 98 I jknight1@flagler.edu
KNIGHT, Jennifer, A ...... 240-500-2000 204 B jaknight1@hagerstowncc.edu
KNIGHT, John, C .... 423-585-6882 438 D john.knight@ws.edu
KNIGHT, Lance .... 404-364-8543 124 A lknight@oglethorpe.edu
KNIGHT, Leonard .... 760-245-4271.. 73 E leonard.knight@vvc.edu
KNIGHT, Lora .... 540-261-8538 485 G lora.knight@svu.edu
KNIGHT, Mary .... 847-635-1718 148 D mknight@oakton.edu
KNIGHT, Mary, E .... 512-471-3727 467 C bd.knightme@austin.utexas.edu
KNIGHT, Mary Beth .... 864-597-4215 426 I knightmb@wofford.edu
KNIGHT, Melvin .... 973-877-3301 285 K knight@essex.edu
KNIGHT, Robert .... 360-992-2101 493 E rknight@clark.edu
KNIGHT, Robert, M .... 530-898-5351.. 31 D rmknight@csuchico.edu
KNIGHT, Robin .... 478-387-4890 120 B roknight@gmc.edu
KNIGHT, Roger, A .... 601-403-1206 255 D rknight@prcc.edu
KNIGHT, Sherry, S .... 989-774-6107 228 E knigh1s@cmich.edu
KNIGHT, Stephanie, L .... 214-768-4242 457 B slknight@smu.edu
KNIGHT, Tamara .... 804-751-9191 479 F tknight@ccc-va.com
KNIGHT, Tim .... 870-245-5528.. 20 G knightt@obu.edu
KNIGHT, Wendy, S .... 563-556-5110 172 D knightw@nicc.edu
KNIGHT, William .... 765-285-5974 156 C wknight@bsu.edu
KNIGHT, Xavier .... 218-723-5966 241 J xknight@css.edu
KNIGHTON, Denise .... 662-915-7792 256 C denisek@olemiss.edu
KNIGHTON, Diana .... 205-929-1439.... 6 D dknighton@miles.edu
KNIGHTON, Edmund ..... 916-961-8727.. 58 I
KNIGHTON, Jeffery .... 678-359-5018 121 B jknighton@gordonstate.edu
KNIGHTON, Joy .... 229-430-3602 114 J jknighton@albanytech.edu
KNIGHTS, John, E .... 407-582-5197 113 F jknights@valenciacollege.edu
KNIGHTS, Susan .... 208-562-2159 132 A susanknights@cwidaho.cc
KNILEY, Mary Lynne ..... 585-582-8317 307 C marykniley@elim.edu
KNIPFEL, Shirley, J .... 515-294-1781 166 F sknipfel@iastate.edu
KNIPPEL, Dianne .... 661-722-6300.. 26 C dknippel@avc.edu
KNISELY, Bertie .... 610-861-1345 402 D kniselyb@moravian.edu
KNISELY, Bridget .... 612-343-4741 249 E bknisel@northcentral.edu
KNISLEY, Patrick .... 212-217-4320 308 B patrick_knisley@fitnyc.edu
KNISLEY, Sharon .... 513-244-8443 359 E sharon.knisley@ccuniversity.edu
KNISPEL, Todd .... 620-431-2820 180 C tknispel@neosho.edu
KNISS, Fred, L .... 540-432-4105 480 A fred.kniss@emu.edu

KNITIG, Sherri .... 785-890-3641 180 G
sherri.knitig@nwktc.edu
KNITTER, Mike .... 773-702-2039 153 F
mknitter@uchicago.edu
KNOBEL, David .... 954-535-8820.. 98 O
dknobel@careercollege.edu
KNOBEL, Jennifer .... 816-501-4890 265 I
jennifer.knobel@rockhurst.edu
KNOBLAUCH, Laura ...... 309-438-8658 140 L
lmknobl@ilstu.edu
KNOBLICH, Julie .... 620-792-9275 175 C
knoblichj@bartonccc.edu
KNOCH, Dan .... 517-607-2401 231 C
dknoch@hillsdale.edu
KNOCHE, Charlotte, M .. 651-641-8240 241 L
knoche@csp.edu
KNODEL, Becky .... 701-252-3467 355 J
bknodel@uj.edu
KNODLE-BRAGIEL, Lisa 503-883-2214 383 H
lbragiel@linfield.edu
KNOEBEL, Ann, G .... 210-999-7601 464 B
aknoebel@trinity.edu
KNOEBEL, Thomas, L ... 414-425-8300 509 I
rector@shsst.edu
KNOELL, Karen .... 605-995-2647 427 A
kaknoell@dwu.edu
KNOETTGEN, Amber ...... 785-243-1435 176 I
aknoettgen@cloud.edu
KNOETTGEN, Suzi .... 785-243-1435 176 I
sknoettgen@cloud.edu
KNOLL, Eric .... 314-446-8375 266 D
eric.knoll@stlcop.edu
KNOLL, Joseph .... 617-824-8112 214 E
joseph_knoll@emerson.edu
KNOLL, Molly, H .... 641-422-4404 172 C
knollmol@niacc.edu
KNOLL-FINN, MJ .... 212-998-4553 318 D
mjknollfinn@nyu.edu
KNOLLE, Jon .... 831-646-3030.. 52 G
jknolle@mpc.edu
KNOLLMAN, Paul, L ..... 734-384-4282 234 C
pknollman@monroeccc.edu
KNOOR, Robert .... 616-957-6039 228 C
rknoor@calvinseminary.edu
KNOP, Joachim, W .... 202-994-6506.. 92 A
knop@gwu.edu
KNOPF, Leigh, E .... 860-773-1356.. 86 G
lknopf@txcc.commnet.edu
KNOPP, David .... 423-473-2390 436 G
dknopp@clevelandstatecc.edu
KNORR, Dan .... 570-389-4655 405 E
dknorr@bloomu.edu
KNORR, Stephen, C ...... 573-882-2726 268 B
knorrs@umsystem.edu
KNORR, Walter .... 312-413-9097 153 G
wknorr@uillinois.edu
KNOST, Julie .... 812-855-7559 159 G
knost@indiana.edu
KNOST, Julie .... 812-855-7559 159 H
affirm@indiana.edu
KNOTHE, Thomas, E ...... 608-796-3376 512 R
teknothe@viterbo.edu
KNOTT, Allan .... 214-860-8531 448 B
aknott@dcccd.edu
KNOTT, Blythe .... 503-768-7296 383 G
blythe@lclark.edu
KNOTT, Catherine .... 812-866-7087 158 C
knott@hanover.edu
KNOTT, Gail .... 308-535-3605 275 I
knottg@mpcc.edu
KNOTT, Gregory .... 860-486-6135.. 88 G
gknott@foundation.uconn.edu
KNOTT, Jack, H .... 213-740-0350.. 72 B
jhknott@usc.edu
KNOTT, Kevin .... 217-351-2239 148 H
kknott@parkland.edu
KNOTT, Theresa .... 716-827-1480 331 K
knottt@trocaire.edu
KNOTTS, Brad .... 812-749-1215 163 B
bknotts@oak.edu
KNOTTS, Cecil .... 318-357-5965 197 D
knottsc@nsula.edu
KNOTTS, Debby .... 505-277-5765 296 H
debby@unm.edu
KNOUSE, Christine .... 717-262-2016 415 B
cknouse@wilson.edu
KNOWLES, Bill .... 405-382-9272 379 I
b.knowles@sscok.edu
KNOWLES, Harley .... 423-746-5201 439 A
hknowles@tnwesleyan.edu
KNOWLES, James, M .... 409-984-6432 462 E
knowlejm@lamarpa.edu
KNOWLES, Melody, D .... 703-370-6600 483 I
KNOWLES, Monica .... 360-992-2904 493 E
mknowles@clark.edu
KNOWLES, Susan .... 315-268-6633 304 B
sknowles@clarkson.edu

KNOWLTON, Eloise .... 508-767-7487 210 I
eknowlton@assumption.edu
KNOWLTON, James, A .. 719-333-9751 518 H
KNOX, Ashley .... 845-569-3798 316 B
ashley.knox@msmc.edu
KNOX, Chrisanne .... 925-969-2048.. 40 L
cknox@dvc.edu
KNOX, Craig .... 850-201-8660 112 C
KNOX, Darby .... 503-821-8927 385 H
dknox@pnca.edu
KNOX, Gordon .... 415-749-4549.. 60 G
gknox@sfai.edu
KNOX, Linda, B .... 219-989-3169 163 E
lbknox@pnw.edu
KNOX, Lindsay .... 503-554-2242 383 C
lknox@georgefox.edu
KNOX, Michael, J .... 806-651-2050 460 E
mknox@wtamu.edu
KNOX, Ramon .... 562-938-4362.. 48 I
rknox@lbcc.edu
KNOX, Ryan .... 309-248-8189 139 D
ryan.knox@heartland.edu
KNOX, Tracey .... 970-521-6643.. 81 F
tracey.knox@njc.edu
KNOX, Wayne .... 512-505-3003 451 A
wknox@htu.edu
KNOX, Yvette .... 630-829-6004 133 I
yknox@ben.edu
KNUCKLES, Leator .... 410-238-9000.. 93 B
KNUDSEN, Alice, B .... 510-430-2350.. 52 E
aknudsen@mills.edu
KNUDSEN, J. Todd .... 315-568-3146 317 A
dodiorne@nycc.edu
KNUDSEN, Ross .... 208-376-7731 131 B
rknudsen@boisebible.edu
KNUDSON, Dan .... 218-299-6521 245 H
dan.knudson@minnesota.edu
KNUDSON, Edward, T ... 661-722-6300.. 26 C
eknudson@avc.edu
KNUDSON, Kari .... 701-224-5604 354 F
kari.l.knudson@bismarckstate.edu
KNUDSON, Paula, M ..... 319-273-2332 167 A
paula.knudson@uni.edu
KNUDSON-CARL, Tara .. 402-399-2449 274 A
tknudsoncarl@csm.edu
KNUPPEL, Lisa .... 714-432-5575.. 38 H
lknuppel@occ.cccd.edu
KNUST, Alyse .... 217-424-3769 145 J
aknust@millikin.edu
KNUTEL, Phillip .... 781-239-4225 211 A
pknutel@babson.edu
KNUTH, Barbara, A .... 607-255-5864 306 B
bak3@cornell.edu
KNUTH, Doug .... 775-784-6900 279 E
dknuth@unr.edu
KNUTSEN, Mark .... 423-697-4785 436 F
mark.knutsen@chattanoogastate.edu
KNUTSON, Jennifer .... 605-331-6611 429 D
jennifer.knutson@usiouxfalls.edu
KNUTSON, Kailani .... 559-791-2294.. 47 C
kknutson@portervillecollege.edu
KNUTSON, Karen .... 320-363-5922 241 I
kknutson@csbsju.edu
KNUTSON, Karen, G ...... 320-363-5922 250 A
kknutson@csbsju.edu
KNUTSON, Ryan .... 605-688-4988 429 B
ryan.knutson@sdstate.edu
KNUTSON, Sherry .... 415-749-4571.. 60 G
sknutson@sfai.edu
KNUTSON, Todd .... 605-331-6813 429 D
todd.knutson@usiouxfalls.edu
KNUTSON-KOLODZNE,
Jim .... 320-308-5447 247 E
jkolodzne@stcloudstate.edu
KNUTSON-MILLER, Kari 657-278-7511.. 32 B
kkmiller@fullerton.edu
KO, Isaac .... 714-517-1945.. 27 C
financialaid@buc.edu
KO, Jeanne .... 212-472-1500 318 B
jko@nysid.edu
KO, Shinsaeng .... 404-727-0825 119 B
shinsaeng.ko@emory.edu
KO, Yoo, K .... 571-730-4750 263 C
wdc@midwest.edu
KOAN, Mark .... 602-285-7855.. 14 A
mark.koan@phoenixcollege.edu
KOBALLA, Thomas .... 912-478-5648 120 E
tkoballa@georgiasouthern.edu
KOBAN, Nicolas .... 207-778-7430 201 D
nicholas.koban@maine.edu
KOBAYASHI, Frank .... 916-484-8202.. 50 F
kobayaf@arc.losrios.edu
KOBAYASHI, Leigh .... 808-544-0272 129 C
lkobayashi@hpu.edu
KOBERNUSZ, Bob .... 605-995-7128 427 E
bob.kobernusz@mitchelltech.edu
KOBES, Patricia .... 845-574-4280 321 F
pkobes@sunyrockland.edu

KOBLER, Soheila .... 973-618-3724 284 D
skobler@caldwell.edu
KOBLER, Wendy .... 937-327-6405 374 A
koblerw@wittenberg.edu
KOBMAN, Lisa .... 513-244-4979 366 A
lisa.kobman@msj.edu
KOBOLAKIS, Evan .... 516-876-3379 327 C
kobolakise@oldwestbury.edu
KOBRIN, Jennifer .... 212-817-7209 302 B
jkobrin@gc.cuny.edu
KOBRYN, Danielle .... 845-398-4016 323 G
dkobryn@stac.edu
KOBUS, Gloria .... 330-941-3142 374 E
gjkobus@ysu.edu
KOBYLSKI, Gerald .... 845-938-5608 519 D
gerald.kobylski@usma.edu
KOBYLSKI, Janet .... 570-408-4501 414 H
janet.kobylski@wilkes.edu
KOCAR, Deb .... 617-349-8800 216 D
ugadm@lesley.edu
KOCER, Ken .... 605-668-1589 427 F
kkocer@mtmc.edu
KOCH, Bill .... 252-328-6166 349 I
kochb@ecu.edu
KOCH, Bradley .... 610-902-8571 391 B
bradley.r.koch@cabrini.edu
KOCH, Don .... 618-634-3289 151 G
donk@shawneecc.edu
KOCH, Erec .... 212-650-8166 301 F
ekoch1@ccny.cuny.edu
KOCH, Geraldine .... 201-559-3515 286 C
kochg@felician.edu
KOCH, Greg .... 770-960-1298 121 J
gkoch@ict.edu
KOCH, Kelly .... 989-386-6639 234 B
kkoch@midmich.edu
KOCH, Kenneth .... 303-492-7311.. 83 B
kenneth.koch@colorado.edu
KOCH, Kevin .... 781-762-1211 215 A
kkoch@fmc.edu
KOCH, Malcolm .... 731-881-1017 440 B
mkoch@utm.edu
KOCH, Paul .... 831-459-2931.. 70 C
plkoch@ucsc.edu
KOCH, Paul .... 563-333-6212 173 A
kochpaulc@sau.edu
KOCH, Susan .... 217-206-6634 154 A
koch@uis.edu
KOCH, Susan .... 217-206-6634 153 G
koch@uis.edu
KOCH, Thomas, L .... 520-621-2448.. 16 J
tlkoch@email.arizona.edu
KOCH, Virginia, A .... 334-844-3466.... 4 D
vak0001@auburn.edu
KOCHAN, Julie .... 518-454-5145 305 B
kochanj@strose.edu
KOCHAN, Roman .... 562-985-4047.. 32 C
roman.kochan@csulb.edu
KOCHANEK, Lea .... 210-341-1366 454 B
lkochanek@ost.edu
KOCHARD, Lawrence, E 434-924-8976 486 H
lek8e@virginia.edu
KOCHARYAN, Armine .... 916-877-7977.. 58 J
armine@sui.edu
KOCHER, Andy, M .... 317-788-3493 164 H
akocher@uindy.edu
KOCHER, Becky .... 419-372-2424 357 F
rkocher@bgsu.edu
KOCHER, Craig, T .... 804-289-8500 486 G
ckocher@richmond.edu
KOCHERA, Melissah .... 203-596-4652.. 87 H
mkochera@post.edu
KOCHEVAR, Brenda .... 218-749-0314 245 D
b.kochevar@mesabirange.edu
KOCHEVAR, Deborah ...... 508-887-4700 225 A
deborah.kochevar@tufts.edu
KOCHIS, Stephen, J ...... 845-575-3000 314 C
stephen.kochis@marist.edu
KOCHUBA, Sara .... 724-503-1001 414 A
skochuba@washjeff.edu
KOCIAN, Bryce .... 979-532-6315 471 A
brycek@wcjc.edu
KOCIAN, Justin .... 402-494-2311 275 M
jkocian@thenicc.edu
KOCIK, Piotr .... 718-518-6610 302 D
pkocik@hostos.cuny.edu
KOCIOLEK, Patrick .... 303-492-8464.. 83 B
patrick.kociolek@colorado.edu
KOCK, Timothy .... 670-237-6849 520 D
tim.kock@marianas.edu
KOCOUR, Bruce .... 865-471-3240 430 H
bkocour@cn.edu
KOCSIS, Katie, L .... 716-286-8669 318 F
kkocsis@niagara.edu
KODAMA, Be-Jay .... 808-739-8526 129 A
bkodama@chaminade.edu
KODAT, Catherine .... 920-832-6528 507 L
catherine.g.kodat@lawrence.edu

KOEBEL, Dave .... 531-622-2391 275 F
dkoebel@mccneb.edu
KOEBEL, Derek .... 336-309-5814 125 H
KOEGLER, Jason, W ...... 304-336-8302 504 E
jkoegler@westliberty.edu
KOEHLER, Al .... 636-922-8452 265 J
alkoehler@stchas.edu
KOEHLER, David .... 308-635-6021 278 B
koehlerd@wncc.edu
KOEHLER, David .... 541-881-5583 387 D
dkoehler@tvcc.cc
KOEHLER, David, C .... 212-998-6995 318 D
david.koehler@nyu.edu
KOEHLER, Donna .... 253-589-5588 493 F
donna.koehler@cptc.edu
KOEHLER, John .... 406-791-5330 273 C
john.koehler@ugf.edu
KOEHLER, Laurie .... 202-994-1529.. 92 A
koehler@gwu.edu
KOEHLER, Lori .... 617-984-1695 223 H
lkoehler@quincycollege.edu
KOEHLER, Martha Kaye 813-253-7007 101 M
mkoehler@hccfl.edu
KOEHLER, R. Brien .... 262-646-6545 509 C
rkoehler@nashotah.edu
KOEHLER, Randy .... 513-244-8449 359 E
randy.koehler@ccuniversity.edu
KOEHLER, Randy .... 513-244-1726 359 E
hr@ccuniversity.edu
KOEHN, Effie .... 406-243-5580 271 G
effie.koehn@umontana.edu
KOEHN, Jack .... 224-293-5961.. 79 B
KOEHN, Michelle .... 316-226-2002 166 C
michelle.koehn@allencollege.edu
KOEHN, Sara .... 620-276-9574 177 G
sara.koehn@gcccks.edu
KOEHNEKE, Mary, A ...... 716-888-2300 300 G
mkoehneke@canisius.edu
KOEHNKE, Paul .... 704-330-6121 342 A
paul.koehnke@cpcc.edu
KOELKER, June .... 817-257-7106 461 A
j.koelker@tcu.edu
KOELLER, Martin, E ...... 973-761-9782 291 F
martin.koeller@shu.edu
KOELTZOW, Dawn .... 309-677-2510 134 G
dkoeltzow@fsmail.bradley.edu
KOENECKE, David .... 660-626-2410 257 A
dkoenecke@atsu.edu
KOENIG, Gigi .... 715-394-8014 512 B
gkoenig1@uwsuper.edu
KOENIG, Jason, T .... 864-833-8490 423 D
jtkoenig@presby.edu
KOENIG, Jerry, L .... 317-921-4491 161 G
jkoenig@ivytech.edu
KOENIG, Linda .... 740-351-3539 369 L
lkoenig@shawnee.edu
KOEPKE, Mark .... 701-252-3467 355 J
mkoepke@uj.edu
KOEPPEL, Edmund .... 516-572-7126 316 C
edmund.koeppel@ncc.edu
KOEPPEN, Bruce .... 203-582-5301.. 88 A
bruce.koeppen@quinnipiac.edu
KOEPPLINGER, Janet .... 419-267-1258 366 G
jkoepplinger@northweststate.edu
KOERBER, Brent .... 614-236-7167 358 A
bkoerber@capital.edu
KOERNER, Melissa .... 801-832-2601 474 E
mkoerner@westminstercollege.edu
KOERNERT, Andrew, H . 757-594-8480 479 H
andrew.koernert@cnu.edu
KOERSELMAN, Corky ..... 712-707-7000 172 G
corky.koerselman@nwciowa.edu
KOERT, Carol Ann .... 973-290-4208 285 A
ckoert@cse.edu
KOERWER, V. Scott .... 570-504-7000 395 I
vkoerwer@tcmc.edu
KOESER, Bryan .... 920-693-1731 513 H
bryan.koeser@gotoltc.edu
KOESTER, Craig .... 651-641-3471 242 J
ckoester@luthersem.edu
KOETTING, Sandy .... 573-681-5071 261 H
koettings@lincolnu.edu
KOETZNER, John .... 707-468-3000.. 51 E
jkoetzne@mendocino.edu
KOEVEN, Gary, J .... 435-652-7770 473 B
koeven@dixie.edu
KOFF, Gordon, D .... 603-646-2451 281 C
gordon.d.koff@dartmouth.edu
KOFFLER, Jeromy, A ..... 503-943-7470 387 H
koffler@up.edu
KOGA, Laura, A .... 815-740-3392 154 G
lkoga@stfrancis.edu
KOGAN, Alexander .... 212-327-8001 321 E
kogana@rockefeller.edu
KOGAN, Lilly .... 212-517-3929 324 E
l.kogan@sothebysinstitute.com
KOH, Alex .... 978-468-7111 215 E
akoh@gordonconwell.edu

KOH, Lee 781-239-2637 220 A
lkoh@massbay.edu
KOHL, Bunny 856-227-7200 284 E
bkohl@camdencc.edu
KOHL, Erin 608-243-4052 514 A
ekohl@madisoncollege.edu
KOHL, James 978-934-2108 217 B
james_kohl@uml.edu
KOHL, Marie 315-792-5340 315 I
mkohl@mvcc.edu
KOHL, Troy 920-735-5766 513 F
kohlt@fvtc.edu
KOHLER, Dave 360-867-6451 494 G
kohlerd@evergreen.edu
KOHLER, David 806-651-2116 460 E
dkohler@mail.wtamu.edu
KOHLER, Donald 712-325-3262 170 K
dkohler@iwcc.edu
KOHLER, Elizabeth 734-462-4400 236 H
bkohler@schoolcraft.edu
KOHLER, Patti 435-797-0174 473 C
patti.kohler@usu.edu
KOHLES, Paula, S 402-280-2731 274 D
paulakohles@creighton.edu
KOHLHEPP, William, C 203-582-5226 88 A
william.kohlhepp@quinnipiac.edu
KOHLI, Cathy, L 419-995-8060 363 G
kohli.c@rhodesstate.edu
KOHLMAN, Bradley 316-284-5251 175 F
bkohlman@bethelks.edu
KOHLMAN, Mark 740-427-5000 364 A
kohlmanm@kenyon.edu
KOHLMEYER, Bill 503-399-6505 382 C
bill.kohlmeyer@chemeketa.edu
KOHN, David 845-341-4388 319 H
david.kohn@sunyorange.edu
KOHN, Edward 802-485-2410 475 I
ekohn@norwich.edu
KOHN, Gary 608-757-7769 513 D
gkohn@blackhawk.edu
KOHN, Melissa 920-236-6100 513 F
kohn@fvtc.edu
KOHN, Paul 404-385-3708 120 A
paul.kohn@ssc.gatech.edu
KOHN, Rebecca 215-572-4009 389 D
KOHN, Selina 706-821-8467 124 C
skohn@paine.edu
KOHN, Shayeh 718-327-7600 334 C
skohn@yofr.org
KOHNKE, Maria 805-493-3105 30 E
kohnke@callutheran.edu
KOHR, Lesa 585-594-6220 319 B
kohrl@roberts.edu
KOHR, Lesa, J 585-594-6966 321 C
kohrl@roberts.edu
KOHRMAN, Elaine 606-451-6918 186 G
elaine.kohrman@kctcs.edu
KOHRN, Lynn 203-932-7131 89 D
lkohrn@newhaven.edu
KOHRS, Becky 402-471-2505 276 A
bkohrs@nscs.edu
KOIRALA-AZAD,
Shabnam 415-422-6525 72 A
skoirala@usfca.edu
KOKAJKO, Hillary, C 336-841-9118 338 E
hkokajko@highpoint.edu
KOKER, John 920-424-2220 511 B
koker@uwosh.edu
KOKER, Michelle 612-624-2941 250 E
koker@umn.edu
KOKILEPERSAUD,
Premdat 443-885-3177 206 A
prem.kokilepersaud@morgan.edu
KOKINOVA,
Margarita, D 330-325-6333 366 F
mkokinov@neomed.edu
KOKKALA, Irene 706-864-1862 127 B
irene.kokkala@ung.edu
KOKOLUS, Cait 610-785-6280 409 F
ckokolus@scs.edu
KOKOLUS, John 717-361-1291 394 F
kokolusj@etown.edu
KOKONAS, Georgios 914-961-8313 323 H
gkokonas@svots.edu
KOKX-TEMPLET, Ann 281-998-6103 455 K
ann.kokx-templet@sjcd.edu
KOLACINSKI, John 213-484-8850 28 D
KOLANDER, John, D 414-443-8816 513 A
john.kolander@wlc.edu
KOLB, Christine 630-620-2101 147 I
ckolb@seminary.edu
KOLB, Daniel 812-357-6566 164 A
dkolb@saintmeinrad.edu
KOLB, Edward, W 773-702-7950 153 F
rocky.kolb@uchicago.edu
KOLB, George, R 610-519-4580 413 K
george.kolb@villanova.edu
KOLB, John, E 518-276-2122 321 A
kolbj@rpi.edu
KOLBE, Rick 574-520-4346 160 F
rkolbe@iusb.edu
KOLCHARNO, Julia 570-504-9614 395 I
jkolcharno@tcmc.edu
KOLDIN, Hillary 518-608-8382 308 A
hkoldin@excelsior.edu
KOLENBRANDER,
Kirk, D 617-253-3365 221 C
KOLENDA, Richard 315-312-2246 327 D
richard.kolenda@oswego.edu
KOLENOVIC, Zeke 212-472-1500 318 B
zkolenovic@nysid.edu
KOLIMAGA, Karen 978-632-6600 220 D
k_kolimaga@mwcc.mass.edu
KOLISON, Stephen 317-788-3212 164 H
kolisons@uindy.edu
KOLISZ, Karin 219-757-6132 163 H
karin.kolisz@franciscanalliance.org
KOLK-CONNER,
Theresa 740-588-1221 374 G
tkolk@zanestate.edu
KOLL, Nancy 773-481-8663 136 B
nkoll@ccc.edu
KOLLAR, Kristen 216-791-5000 359 K
KOLLAR, Kristen 216-791-5000 359 K
kristen.kollar@cim.edu
KOLLAR, Lisa, S 386-226-7068 98 C
lisa.kollar@erau.edu
KOLLAR, OSB, Rene 724-805-2343 410 B
rene.kollar@email.stvincent.edu
KOLLATH, Carissa 402-844-7159 276 G
carissa@northeast.edu
KOLLBAUM, Kristin, E 712-324-5061 172 E
kkollbaum@nwicc.edu
KOLLER, Craig, A 610-799-1073 400 A
ckoller@lccc.edu
KOLLER, Rebecca, H 402-472-3917 277 E
rkoller@nebraska.edu
KOLLER, Tim 303-762-6944 79 G
tim.koller@denverseminary.edu
KOLLIEN, Mike 989-358-7339 227 A
kollienm@alpenacc.edu
KOLLIGIAN, John 609-258-3285 288 F
jkjr@princeton.edu
KOLLMAN, Willy 330-972-2575 371 C
wrk1@uakron.edu
KOLLMEYER, Will 662-685-4771 252 D
wkollmeyer@bmc.edu
KOLLMORGEN, Terry 918-495-6175 378 H
tmk@oru.edu
KOLLROSS, Crystal 626-585-7759 56 B
cakollross@pasadena.edu
KOLLS, Mary Ann 815-825-9426 142 F
maryann.kolls@kishwaukeecollege.edu
KOLLURU, Ramesh 337-482-6541 197 F
rxk6962@louisiana.edu
KOLMODIN, Jane 510-549-4702 66 D
jkolmodin@sksm.edu
KOLODZIEJSKI,
Gwynne 610-796-8325 389 A
gwynne.kolodziejski@alvernia.edu
KOLOMITZ, Kara 781-768-7055 224 A
kara.kolomitz@regiscollege.edu
KOLSTAD, Michael 417-865-2815 260 B
kolstadm@evangel.edu
KOLVOORD, Robert 540-568-2752 481 I
kolvoora@jmu.edu
KOLWINSKA,
Jeremy, W 651-631-5100 251 C
jwkolwinska@unwsp.edu
KOM, Sheila 208-792-2288 132 C
sheilak@lcsc.edu
KOMACEK, Stan 724-938-1589 405 F
komacek@calu.edu
KOMACEK, Stan 724-938-4187 405 F
komacek@calu.edu
KOMANECKI, William 309-655-2180 151 A
william.g.komanecki@osfhealthcare.org
KOMARINSKI, Cindy 724-925-4251 414 E
komarinskic@westmoreland.edu
KOMARRAJU, Meera 618-453-2466 152 B
meerak@siu.edu
KOMDAT, Mark 404-297-9522 120 D
komdatm@gptc.edu
KOMORA, Melissa 518-244-2325 321 G
komorm@sage.edu
KOMOTO, Cary 952-358-9007 246 D
cary.komoto@normandale.edu
KOMP, Chuck 715-365-4537 514 E
ckomp@nicoletcollege.edu
KOMPELIEN, Ken 701-671-2297 355 B
ken.kompelien@ndscs.edu
KONA, Mijana 215-335-0800 400 D
mkona@lincolntech.edu
KONAN, Denise, E 808-956-6570 129 J
konan@hawaii.edu
KONAN, LaCretia 815-825-9791 142 F
lacretia.konan@kishwaukeecollege.edu
KONCZAL, Timothy, J 330-672-9192 363 I
tkonczal@kent.edu
KONDA, Kevin, J 316-978-7022 182 F
kevin.konda@wichita.edu
KONDRACH, Carol, S 609-895-5196 289 E
kondrach@rider.edu
KONDRAK, Mark 651-523-2512 242 E
mkondrak01@hamline.edu
KONDROT, Jacquelyn 814-332-4356 388 F
jkondrot@allegheny.edu
KONDZIELAWA, Eric 804-862-6100 484 F
ekondzielawa@rbc.edu
KONE, Drissa 212-563-6647 332 A
d.kone@uts.edu
KONEN, Judee, L 402-461-7434 274 I
jkonen@hastings.edu
KONG, Xiangping 609-626-6025 291 H
xiangping.kong@stockton.edu
KONIECZKA, Jeanette 312-752-2382 142 E
jeanette.konieczka@kendall.edu
KONING, Amy 616-234-4226 230 F
akoning@grcc.edu
KONING, Shawnn 951-343-4224 28 G
skoning@calbaptist.edu
KONISIEWICZ, Richard 440-646-8355 373 B
richard.konisiewicz@ursuline.edu
KONKLE, Patricia, A 812-888-4208 165 E
pkonkle@vinu.edu
KONKOLESKI, RJ 740-695-9500 357 D
rkonkoleski@belmontcollege.edu
KONKOTH, Shanthi 718-522-9073 298 E
skonkoth@asa.edu
KONNY, Sharon 847-214-7367 138 B
skonny@elgin.edu
KONOPA AIGOTTI,
Claire 317-940-9900 156 I
caigotti@butler.edu
KONOPELSKI, Joseph 831-459-4676 70 C
joek@ucsc.edu
KONOPKA, Daniel 914-633-2069 311 B
dkonopka@iona.edu
KONOPKA, Joseph 732-255-0521 288 B
jkonopka@ocean.edu
KONOPSKI, Michael, J 570-321-4126 400 G
konopski@lycoming.edu
KONRAD, Jim 847-491-8121 148 C
j-konrad@northwestern.edu
KONSCHAK, Norma 952-358-8243 246 D
KONSTALID, Daniel, T 717-337-6200 396 A
dkonstal@gettysburg.edu
KONUWA, Alfred, B 530-661-5712 75 L
akonuwa@yccd.edu
KONWERSKI, Peter, A 202-994-7210 92 A
peterk@gwu.edu
KONYA, Jeffrey, F 248-370-2669 235 J
konya@oakland.edu
KONYAOLE, Cederic 504-816-4872 191 E
ckonyaole@dillard.edu
KONZ, Jeff 828-251-6570 351 A
jkonz@unca.edu
KONZELMAN, Leanne 425-889-5208 496 E
leanne.konzelman@northwestu.edu
KOO, James 714-525-0088 44 I
administration@gm.edu
KOO, Jason 571-633-9651 486 E
jason.koo@uona.edu
KOO, Kyung Mo 562-926-1023 57 J
kmkoo@ptsa.edu
KOOB, Sondra 215-785-0111 404 P
KOOCHER, Gerald, P 773-325-8475 137 C
gkoocher@depaul.edu
KOOHANG, Alex 478-471-2801 123 A
alex.koohang@mga.edu
KOOI, Jana 904-997-2649 100 F
jana.kooi@fscj.edu
KOOI, Janeen, W 260-982-5202 162 Q
jwkooi@manchester.edu
KOOK, Grace 213-381-0081 46 I
gracekook@gmail.com
KOOK, Kathleen 510-649-2464 44 J
kkook@gtu.edu
KOOMER, Ajoy 714-872-5695 51 A
akoomer@ketchum.edu
KOON, Chi 718-270-6107 303 C
chi@mec.cuny.edu
KOONCE, JR.,
George, E 920-923-7676 508 B
gkoonce@marianuniversity.edu
KOONG, Kai 334-727-8811 7 F
kkoong@tuskegee.edu
KOONSE, Cyndi 573-592-4358 270 D
cyndi.koonse@williamwoods.edu
KOONTS, Christine 703-591-7042 490 D
ckoonts@viu.edu
KOONTZ, David 562-903-4760 27 E
dave.koontz@biola.edu
KOOP, Stuart 207-893-7750 200 G
skoop@sjcme.edu
KOOPMANS, Ken 517-607-2609 231 C
kkoopmans@hillsdale.edu
KOOREN, Lisa 209-478-0800 45 J
lkooren@humphreys.edu
KOOS, Agnes 530-283-0202 42 K
akoos@frc.edu
KOOTI, John 717-477-1435 407 B
jgkooti@ship.edu
KOOTTUNGAL, Yvette 305-899-3600 95 G
ybrown@barry.edu
KOPACH,
Christopher, M 520-241-6482 16 J
ckopach@email.arizona.edu
KOPAS, Michael 973-408-3609 285 E
mkopas@drew.edu
KOPAS, Michael 914-251-6916 328 B
michael.kopas@purchase.edu
KOPAS, William 954-262-4412 104 F
wk128@nsu.nova.edu
KOPECKY, Lisa 657-278-2194 32 B
ljkopecky@fullerton.edu
KOPECKY, Lisa 508-362-2131 219 E
lkopecky@capecod.edu
KOPERA, Ken 864-646-1770 424 F
kkopera@tctc.edu
KOPERA, Kerry 630-515-5400 137 D
kkopera@devry.edu
KOPERSKI, Kate 716-286-8288 318 F
kjk@niagara.edu
KOPERSKI, Mike 415-442-7082 44 E
mkoperski@ggu.edu
KOPICKO, Ronald, L 517-750-1200 237 D
rkopicko@arbor.edu
KOPIT, Niccole 800-955-2527 177 H
nkopit@grantham.edu
KOPONEN, Glenn 845-675-4691 319 C
glenn.koponen@nyack.edu
KOPP, Courtney, A 515-574-1020 170 C
kopp@iowacentral.edu
KOPP, Jason 952-995-1626 244 G
jason.kopp@hennepintech.edu
KOPP, Sacha 631-632-6976 325 F
sacha.kopp@stonybrook.edu
KOPP, Will, E 740-368-3108 368 N
wekopp@owu.edu
KOPP-MILLER, Barbara 419-530-4488 372 F
barbara.kopp-miller@utoledo.edu
KOPPEL, Michael 202-885-8610 94 C
mkoppel@wesleyseminary.edu
KOPPELL, Jonathan 602-496-0402 10 K
koppel@asu.edu
KOPPEN, Jason 928-774-3890 13 B
KOPPER, Beverly, A 262-472-1918 512 C
kopperb@uww.edu
KOPPI, Stefan 508-831-5260 226 E
skoppi@wpi.edu
KOPPI, Susan, W 518-580-5468 324 D
skoppi@skidmore.edu
KOPPITZ, Michelle 630-829-6098 133 I
mkoppitz@ben.edu
KOPS, Christopher 414-955-8703 508 D
ckops@mcw.edu
KOPSTAIN, Eric 615-875-8617 440 D
eric.kopstain@vanderbilt.edu
KOPYAR, Joseph 607-778-5407 326 C
1303mgr@fheg.follett.com
KORALESKY, Barron 413-597-3072 226 C
barron.koralesky@williams.edu
KORANGY, Amir 323-463-2500 67 D
korangya@toa.edu
KORB-NICE, Jobe, S 206-281-2564 498 B
jobe@spu.edu
KORBEL, Linda 847-635-1952 148 D
lkorbel@oakton.edu
KORD, JoLanna 620-341-6829 177 B
jkord@emporia.edu
KORELLIS, Peggy 773-907-4321 135 K
pkorellis@ccc.edu
KOREN, Christina 814-886-6407 402 E
ckoren@mtaloy.edu
KORETOFF, Lisa, A 336-334-4822 343 E
lakoretoff@gtcc.edu
KORETSKY, Carla, M 269-387-4360 239 E
carla.koretsky@wmich.edu
KORETZKY, Gary 212-746-1363 306 B
gak2008@med.cornell.edu
KORF, Abraham 305-673-5664 114 F
rabbikorf@hotmail.com
KORF, Benche 305-528-4108 114 F
bckorf@lecfl.com
KORF, Benzion 305-653-8770 114 F
bkorf@lecfl.com
KORGAN, Christos 760-471-1316 59 A
ckorgan@skcca.edu
KORINEK, Clare, M 312-915-7235 144 D
ckorine@luc.edu

KORINKE, Kim .... 805-378-1463.. 73 A
kkorinke@vcccd.edu
KORITARI, Andi .... 312-261-3317 146 G
andi.koritari@nl.edu
KORKLAN, Michael .... 816-604-1000 262 K
michael.korklan@mcckc.edu
KORMAN, Thomas, P ... 517-750-1200 237 D
tkorman@arbor.edu
KORMANAK, Steve .... 608-757-7766 513 D
skormanak@blackhawk.edu
KORN, Jane .... 509-313-3700 495 A
jkorn@lawschool.gonzaga.edu
KORN, Judy .... 320-589-6011 251 A
kornjr@morris.umn.edu
KORN, Timothy .... 716-829-7640 307 B
kornt@dyc.edu
KORNAHRENS, Chris ..... 650-508-3640.. 54 D
ckornahrens@ndnu.edu
KORNBERG, Judith .... 212-986-4343 299 F
jdk@berkeleycollege.edu
KORNBERG, Judith .... 212-986-4343 283 J
jdk@berkeleycollege.edu
KORNBERG, Mindy .... 206-685-4730 499 D
mindyk@uw.edu
KORNBLUH, Mark, L ..... 859-257-1375 190 B
kornbluh@uky.edu
KORNBLUH, Rebecca .... 909-621-8000.. 57 C
rebecca_kornbluh@cucmail.claremont.edu
KORNBLUTH, Sally .... 919-684-2631 337 C
sally.kornbluth@duke.edu
KORNEGAY, Barbara, R 919-658-7756 349 F
bkornegay@umo.edu
KORNEGAY, Jeffrey .... 910-879-5574 341 A
jkornegay@bladencc.edu
KORNEGAY, Joy .... 919-735-5151 347 E
jkornegay@waynecc.edu
KORNER, Barbara, O ..... 814-865-2591 403 F
bok2@psu.edu
KORNKVEN, Kelly, J ..... 701-788-4816 354 B
kelly.kornkven@mayvillestate.edu
KORNMILLER,
Brenda, L .... 740-374-8716 373 G
bkornmiller@wscc.edu
KORNWEIBEL, Karen, R 423-439-7881 431 H
kornweib@etsu.edu
KOROIVULAONO,
Theresa, B .... 692-625-3394 520 C
tkoroivulaono@cmi.edu
KOROLISHIN, Michael .. 215-517-2383 389 D
korolism@arcadia.edu
KOROMA, Joseph .... 510-464-3414.. 56 H
jkoroma@peralta.edu
KORONKIEWICZ, Talia .. 615-230-3477 438 C
talia.koronkiewicz@volstate.edu
KOROSEC, Ronnie .... 407-823-0676 110 C
ronnie@ucf.edu
KORPELA, Doreen .... 906-487-7201 230 B
doreen.korpela@finlandia.edu
KORPI, Jeff .... 906-227-2620 235 A
jkorpi@nmu.edu
KORR, Wynne, S .... 217-333-2261 154 B
wkorr@illinois.edu
KORSAKOV, Stephan ..... 212-966-0300 316 F
skorsakov@nyaa.edu
KORSCHINOWSKI,
Claire .... 253-589-5516 493 F
claire.korschinowski@cptc.edu
KORSHORK, Lori .... 206-726-5151 494 B
lkorshork@cornish.edu
KORSTAD, Donna .... 509-542-4401 493 G
dkorstad@columbiabasin.edu
KORSTAD, John .... 918-495-6942 378 H
jkorstad@oru.edu
KORT, J. Thomas .... 609-497-7782 288 E
j.thomas.kort@ptsem.edu
KORTA, Allison .... 716-614-6231 318 E
akorta@niagaracc.suny.edu
KORTE, Andrea .... 910-695-3767 346 E
kortea@sandhills.edu
KORTICS, Wayne .... 937-433-3410 361 H
wkortics@edaff.com
KORUS, Daniel .... 361-698-1065 448 H
dkorus@delmar.edu
KORVAS, Ronald .... 617-824-8544 214 E
ronald_korvas@emerson.edu
KORVER, Bill .... 910-323-5614 336 E
president@ccbs.edu
KORZENDORFER, Kate .. 781-768-7340 224 A
kate.korzendorfer@regiscollege.edu
KORZINEK, Sue .... 616-331-2035 230 G
korzines@gvsu.edu
KOSANKA, Nanci .... 419-559-2465 370 J
nkosanka@terra.edu
KOSARUE, Lori .... 517-264-7132 236 I
lshearer@sienaheights.edu
KOSBOTH, Michele .... 617-243-2227 216 C
mkosboth@lasell.edu
KOSCHMEDER,
Douglas, D .... 319-352-8761 174 C
doug.koschmeder@wartburg.edu
KOSER, Ashley .... 570-484-2128 406 E
ashley.koser@lhufoundation.org
KOSH, Jamie .... 814-472-3372 409 G
jkosh@francis.edu
KOSH, Kelvin .... 662-252-8094 255 F
KOSHMIDER, III,
John, W .... 330-471-8326 364 H
jkoshmider@malone.edu
KOSHUT, Thomas, M .... 256-824-6100.... 8 C
tom.koshut@uah.edu
KOSIEK, Timothy, J ...... 708-709-3702 148 I
tkosiek@prairiestate.edu
KOSINSKI, Mark .... 203-285-2077.. 85 E
mkosinski@gwcc.commnet.edu
KOSINSKY, James, A .... 708-209-3519 136 I
jim.kosinsky@cuchicago.edu
KOSKI, Janet .... 906-227-2420 235 A
jakoski@nmu.edu
KOSKI, Lynne, D .... 402-844-7036 276 G
lynne@northeast.edu
KOSKY, Kristy .... 740-695-9500 357 D
kkosky@belmontcollege.edu
KOSLOW MARTIN, Jodi 773-244-5740 147 F
jkoslow@northpark.edu
KOSMICKI, Frank .... 618-453-5371 152 B
kosmicki@siu.edu
KOSMOSKI, Kathleen .... 912-486-7409 123 J
kkosmoski@ogeecheetech.edu
KOSOBUCKI, Dave .... 858-695-8587 159 A
dkosobucki@horizonuniversity.edu
KOSOWSKY, Vicki .... 812-535-5216 163 I
vkosowsk@smwc.edu
KOSS, Kim .... 706-721-0140 116 B
kkoss@augusta.edu
KOSS, Michelle .... 586-286-2172 233 B
kossm26@macomb.edu
KOSSE, Glenn, F .... 502-272-8328 183 H
gkosse@bellarmine.edu
KOSSO, Cynthia .... 610-861-1348 402 D
kossoc@moravian.edu
KOSSUTH, Joanne .... 860-701-5155.. 87 F
kossuth_j@mitchell.edu
KOST, Patricia, L .... 216-368-2165 358 C
patricia.kost@case.edu
KOSTELL, Stacey .... 802-656-1394 476 E
stacey.kostell@uvm.edu
KOSTELL, Stacey, R .... 802-656-1394 476 E
stacey.kostell@uvm.edu
KOSTELNIK, Marjorie .... 402-472-2913 277 G
mkostelnik2@unl.edu
KOSTELNIK, Marjorie .... 402-472-8636 277 E
mkostelnik@nebraska.edu
KOSTEN, Linda .... 303-871-7922.. 83 E
linda.kosten@du.edu
KOSTER, Ed .... 402-761-8224 276 K
ekoster@southeast.edu
KOSTIHOVA, Marcela .... 651-523-2252 242 E
mkostihova01@hamline.edu
KOSTRZEWA, Waldemar 203-575-8297.. 86 B
wkostrzewa@nv.edu
KOSTRZEWSKI, Diana ... 303-292-0015.. 79 F
KOSTYUKOV, Victoria ... 718-522-9073 298 E
victoria_kostyukov@asa.edu
KOTAJARVI, Kathleen .... 920-693-1163 513 H
kathleen.kotajarvi@gotoltc.edu
KOTCAMP, Butch .... 740-351-3429 369 L
bkotcamp@shawnee.edu
KOTECKI, Kathy .... 406-657-2087 272 B
kkotecki@msubillings.edu
KOTH, Jason .... 212-592-2259 324 A
jkoth@sva.edu
KOTH, Kent .... 206-296-2329 498 D
kothk@seattleu.edu
KOTLAS, Maureen .... 301-405-3960 207 G
mkotlas@umd.edu
KOTLER, A. Malkiel .... 732-367-1060 283 K
KOTLER, Aaron .... 732-367-1060 283 K
akotler@bmg.edu
KOTLER, Yitzchok, S ..... 732-367-1060 283 K
KOTLIKOFF, Michael, I . 607-255-2364 306 B
provost@cornell.edu
KOTLINSKI, Michael, J . 717-337-6363 396 A
mkotlinski@gettysburg.edu
KOTOISUVA, Agnes .... 692-625-3394 520 C
KOTORI, Chiaki .... 570-321-4029 400 G
kotori@lycoming.edu
KOTOWICZ, Keith, A ..... 414-847-3301 508 G
keithkotowicz@miad.edu
KOTOWSKI, Jenni .... 352-365-3571 103 B
kotoskj@lssc.edu
KOTOWSKI, Kelli .... 740-597-1819 368 G
kotowskk@ohio.edu
KOTRBA, Darla .... 605-995-3023 427 E
darla.kotrba@mitchelltech.edu
KOTT, Micheal .... 708-656-8000 146 F
micheal.kott@morton.edu
KOTTAS, Kathy .... 620-792-9355 175 C
kottask@bartonccc.edu
KOTTER, David .... 303-963-3336.. 77 I
dkotter@ccu.edu
KOTTICH, Sarah .... 402-399-2427 274 A
skottich@csm.edu
KOTTKE, Dawn .... 719-474-8556.. 76 F
dawn.kottke@zenith.org
KOTTON, Stevenson ...... 692-625-3394 520 C
KOTTON, Stevenson ...... 692-625-4931 520 C
skotton@cmi.edu
KOTTOYIL, Joseph .... 305-223-4561 106 L
josephpothen@hotmail.com
KOTWICKI, Lee .... 941-363-7218 108 P
kotwicl@scf.edu
KOUA, Deb .... 515-965-7025 168 A
dkkoua@dmacc.edu
KOUANCHAO, Ketmani . 626-585-7560.. 56 B
kkouanchao@pasadena.edu
KOUBEK, Richard .... 225-578-8863 193 M
rkoubek@lsu.edu
KOUBEK, Richard, J ...... 225-578-2111 193 L
KOUCOS, Brianna .... 801-832-2592 474 E
bkoucos@westminstercollege.edu
KOUCOUMARIS,
John, S .... 740-695-9500 357 D
jkoucoumaris@belmontcollege.edu
KOUDELIK-JONES,
Rachelle .... 540-857-6187 490 B
rkoudelikjones@virginiawestern.edu
KOUDOU, Nick .... 816-559-6182 265 C
nick.koudou@park.edu
KOUGH, Katherine .... 717-262-2006 415 B
kkough@wilson.edu
KOUKARI, Ray .... 262-619-6712 513 G
koukarir@gtc.edu
KOUKOL, June .... 617-333-2091 214 B
jkoukol@curry.edu
KOULIK, Chet .... 845-451-1347 306 D
chet.koulik@culinary.edu
KOULOS, Elleni, R .... 909-593-3511.. 70 E
ekoulos@laverne.edu
KOUMAS, Sokratis .... 508-999-8859 217 A
skoumas@umassd.edu
KOURIS, Demitris .... 605-394-2256 429 A
demitris.kouris@sdsmt.edu
KOURY, Kevin, A .... 724-938-4125 405 F
koury@calu.edu
KOUTOUZOS, Elena .... 252-985-5291 348 A
ekoutouzos@ncwc.edu
KOUTSIDIS, Anastasia ... 646-313-8000 303 G
anastasia.koutsidis@guttman.cuny.edu
KOVAC, Matt .... 724-287-8711 390 J
matt.kovac@bc3.edu
KOVACH-ALLEN,
Katharina, E .... 585-345-6831 309 C
kekovachallen@genesee.edu
KOVACICH, Christine, L 330-325-6551 366 F
ckovacich@neomed.edu
KOVACS, Anita .... 904-632-3217 100 F
anita.kovacs@fscj.edu
KOVACS, Charles .... 941-359-7650 106 H
ckovacs@ringling.edu
KOVACS, Gene .... 850-245-0466 108 Q
gene.kovacs@flbog.edu
KOVACS, Mark, C .... 315-792-3025 332 H
mkovacs@utica.edu
KOVAL, Volga .... 707-826-4143.. 34 A
volga.koval@humboldt.edu
KOVALCHICK, Ann .... 209-228-4899.. 69 C
akovalchick@ucmerced.edu
KOVALCHICK, Eugene ... 267-341-3545 397 G
gkovalchick@holyfamily.edu
KOVALCHICK, Mary .... 610-799-1957 400 A
mkovalchick@lccc.edu
KOVANES, Tera, D .... 540-654-1042 486 D
tkovanes@umw.edu
KOVATCH, Julie .... 503-338-2429 382 E
jkovatch@clatsopcc.edu
KOVATCH, Richard, A .... 434-982-5166 486 H
rak3e@virginia.edu
KOVOLSKI, Chris .... 610-519-7450 413 K
chris.kovolski@villanova.edu
KOWAL, Donna, M .... 585-395-5400 326 D
dkowal@brockport.edu
KOWAL, John .... 518-438-3111 314 B
jkowal@mariacollege.edu
KOWALESKI, Curt .... 920-403-3117 509 J
curt.kowaleski@snc.edu
KOWALESKI, Mary, A ... 989-964-4041 236 F
makowale@svsu.edu
KOWALEWSKI, John, L . 801-626-7212 473 E
jkowalewski@weber.edu
KOWALEWSKY, Lyn ...... 989-358-7280 227 A
kowalewl@alpenacc.edu
KOWALIK, Margaret ...... 315-781-3695 310 C
kowalik@hws.edu
KOWALIK, Thomas .... 607-777-2792 325 A
kowalik@binghamton.edu
KOWALSKI, David .... 215-641-6674 402 A
dkowalsi@mc3.edu
KOWALSKI, Gerard, J ... 706-542-8318 127 A
kowalski@uga.edu
KOWALSKI, Joann .... 607-735-1825 307 G
jkowalski@elmira.edu
KOWALSKI, JR.,
Jonathan, V .... 414-277-4510 509 A
kowalski@msoe.edu
KOWALSKI, Karl .... 907-450-8383.. 10 B
karl.kowalski@alaska.edu
KOWALSKI, Karl .... 907-450-8383.... 9 I
karl.kowalski@alaska.edu
KOWALSKI, Marion .... 212-961-3370 298 H
mkowalski@bankstreet.edu
KOWALSKI, Melanie ...... 570-504-1583 399 A
kowalskim@lackawanna.edu
KOWALSKI, Patrick, A ... 513-556-1299 371 E
patrick.kowalski@uc.edu
KOWALSKI, Timothy, J . 864-327-9800 480 I
tkowalski@vcom.vt.edu
KOWALSKI-BRAUN,
Marlene .... 616-331-3585 230 G
kowalskm@gvsu.edu
KOWALSKY, Margaret ... 570-208-5986 398 D
margaretkowalsky@kings.edu
KOWARSCH, Jason .... 817-202-6270 457 E
jasonk@swau.edu
KOWCHECK, Tyler .... 724-503-1001 414 A
tkowcheck@washjeff.edu
KOWEEK, Joan .... 518-828-4181 305 D
joan.koweek@sunycgcc.edu
KOWERT, Baylee, L .... 903-813-3000 443 F
bkowert@austincollege.edu
KOWICH, Colleen .... 816-271-5650 264 B
ckowich@missouriwestern.edu
KOWNACKI, James .... 570-484-2460 406 E
jkownack@lockhaven.edu
KOWTA, Mayumi .... 805-437-3107.. 31 C
mayumi.kowta@csuci.edu
KOYZIS, Pamela .... 626-395-8075.. 29 I
pamela.koyzis@caltech.edu
KOZACHYN, Karen .... 610-359-5362 393 E
kkozachy@dccc.edu
KOZAK, Gregory .... 847-574-5194 143 A
gkozak@lfgsm.edu
KOZAK, Laura, A .... 410-706-8138 207 H
lkozak@umaryland.edu
KOZARIK, Greg .... 216-881-1700 368 F
gkozarik@ohiotech.edu
KOZDEMBA, Kathy .... 412-536-1047 398 E
kozdemba@verizon.net
KOZIATEK, Caroline .... 203-932-7479.. 89 D
ckoziatek@newhaven.edu
KOZIL, Cindy, T .... 508-541-1552 214 C
ckozil@dean.edu
KOZIMOR, Renee .... 847-635-1761 148 D
rkozimor@oakton.edu
KOZINSKI, Thaddeus .... 307-332-2930 517 F
tkozinski@wyomingcatholiccollege.com
KOZIOL, Nicholas, J ..... 716-880-2207 314 F
nicholas.j.koziol@medaille.edu
KOZISEK, Chelsea .... 239-304-7096.. 95 C
chelsea.kozisek@avemaria.edu
KOZISEK, Kelly, L .... 541-737-4261 385 F
kelly.kozisek@oregonstate.edu
KOZISEK, Sue .... 402-421-7410 275 K
KOZLOWSKI, Michael ... 860-723-0261.. 84 I
kozlowskim@ct.edu
KOZLOWSKI, Michelle .. 559-934-2240.. 73 M
michellekozlowski@whccd.edu
KOZOJED, Bob, J .... 701-788-4872 354 B
bob.kozojed@mayvillestate.edu
KOZUMA, Hikaru .... 215-898-6081 412 G
kozuma@upenn.edu
KRABBENHOFT, Alan .... 765-455-9275 160 B
agkrabbe@iupui.edu
KRAEMER, David .... 212-678-8075 312 A
dakraemer@jtsa.edu
KRAEMER, Laurence ...... 516-465-8099 307 D
lkraemer@nshs.edu
KRAEMER, Ronald, D .... 574-631-9700 165 A
kraemer.5@nd.edu
KRAFT, Damon .... 785-833-4371 179 C
kraft@kwu.edu
KRAFT, Deborah .... 443-334-2337 207 C
dkraft@stevenson.edu
KRAFT, Deborah .... 281-756-3509 442 C
dkraft@alvincollege.edu
KRAFT, Erin .... 847-851-5468.. 79 B
ekraft@coloradotech.edu
KRAFT, Gary, L .... 402-472-3609 277 G
gary.kraft@unl.edu

KRIETE, Jennie .... 321-433-7408.. 97 N
krietej@easternflorida.edu
KRIGEL, Belinda .... 256-233-8100.... 4 C
belinda.krigel@athens.edu
KRIGEL, Belinda .... 256-233-8104.... 4 C
belinda.krigel@athens.edu
KRIKAU, Paul .... 920-923-7666 508 B
pwkrikau25@marianuniversity.edu
KRIKORIAN,
Gregory, H .... 717-867-6238 399 J
krikoria@lvc.edu
KRILEY, Taylor .... 785-628-5826 177 D
tkriley@fhsu.edu
KRIMPELBEIN, Kristi ..... 715-232-2441 512 A
krimpelbeink@uwstout.edu
KRINGEL, Dawny .... 575-492-2114 297 G
dkringel@usw.edu
KRISAK, Wendy .... 610-282-1100 393 G
wendy.krisak@desales.edu
KRISHNAIAH, Raghu ..... 816-943-9600.. 17 C
raghu.krishnaiah@phoenix.edu
KRISHNAMOORTI,
Ramanan .... 713-743-4307 465 A
rkrishna@central.uh.edu
KRISHNAMURTHY,
Sushma .... 318-342-1041 198 A
krishnamurthy@ulm.edu
KRISHNAN, G, V .... 713-221-8478 465 C
krishnang@uhd.edu
KRISHNAN, Ramayya .... 412-268-2159 391 H
rk2x@andrew.cmu.edu
KRISHNAN, Ranga .... 312-563-2033 150 F
ranga_krishnan@rush.edu
KRISHNASWAMY,
Vidya .... 972-860-8152 447 H
vkrishnaswamy@dcccd.edu
KRISNAN, Kris .... 661-654-2124.. 31 B
skrishnan@csub.edu
KRISS, Cindi .... 785-460-4678 176 L
cindi.kriss@colbycc.edu
KRISS, George .... 618-537-6425 145 C
gnkriss@mckendree.edu
KRISS, OSF, M. Elise .... 260-399-7700 165 B
ekriss@sf.edu
KRISSOFF BOEHM,
Lisa .... 508-531-2809 217 D
lkrissoffboehm@bridgew.edu
KRIST, Paula, S .... 619-260-7878.. 71 J
pkrist@sandiego.edu
KRISTENSEN,
Douglas, A .... 308-865-8208 277 F
kristensend@unk.edu
KRISTOFF-RAMPATA,
Tricia .... 904-819-6311.. 98 I
tkristoff@flagler.edu
KRITSCHER, Matthew .... 510-723-6743.. 36 C
mkritscher@chabotcollege.edu
KRITSCHER, Matthew .... 510-723-6600.. 36 C
mkritscher@chabotcollege.edu
KRITSKY, Gene .... 513-244-4401 366 A
gene.kritsky@msj.edu
KRIVESTI, Robin .... 740-593-2665 368 G
krivesti@ohio.edu
KRIVOSKI, James, F ..... 610-330-5200 399 B
krivoskj@lafayette.edu
KRIZ, Christine .... 540-868-7094 488 E
ckriz@lfcc.edu
KROB, Jay, C .... 785-833-4440 179 C
jayk@kwu.edu
KROBER, Kent .... 618-664-6410 139 A
kent.krober@greenville.edu
KROBOTH, Patricia, D ... 412-624-3270 412 I
pkroboth@pitt.edu
KROEGER, Brian .... 573-288-6450 259 E
bkroeger@culver.edu
KROEGER, Matthew, D .. 319-273-2347 167 A
matthew.kroeger@uni.edu
KROEKER, Cheyenne ...... 620-241-0723 176 G
cheyenne.kroeker@centralchristian.edu
KROEKER, Dean .... 620-241-0723 176 G
dean.kroeker@centralchristian.edu
KROENING, Mike .... 507-453-2752 245 G
mkroening@southeastmn.edu
KROENKE, Paul .... 309-677-2325 134 G
pkroenke@bradley.edu
KROGER, John .... 503-777-7500 386 F
krogerj@reed.edu
KROGH, Mary Anne ...... 605-362-0100 427 F
mary.krogh@mtmc.edu
KROGH-DUREE, Brenda 641-673-1064 174 F
kroghdureeb@wmpenn.edu
KROH, Lynne .... 417-862-9533 260 D
enroll@globaluniversity.edu
KROHN, Lisa .... 712-274-5100 172 A
krohn@morningside.edu
KROHN, Paul .... 630-617-3142 138 C
paulk@elmhurst.edu
KROL, Naz .... 814-866-8152 399 C
nkrol@lecom.edu
KROLAK, Steven .... 812-941-2470 161 A
skrolak@ius.edu
KROLL, Jason .... 732-571-3411 287 C
jkroll@monmouth.edu
KROLL, John, R .... 773-702-1941 153 F
xjrk@uchicago.edu
KROLL, Mark .... 956-882-5803 468 A
mark.kroll@utrgv.edu
KRONEMAN, Ann .... 517-483-1604 232 K
kronemaa@lcc.edu
KRONENFIELD, Michael 480-219-6091 257 A
mkronenfield@atsu.edu
KRONISER, Maria .... 412-365-1862 392 C
mkroniser@chatham.edu
KROOT, Irwin .... 212-229-5671 316 E
krooti@newschool.edu
KROPF, Kevin .... 417-873-7524 259 G
kkropf@drury.edu
KROPF, Nancy, P .... 404-413-2000 121 A
nkropf@gsu.edu
KROPFF, Robert .... 330-972-7048 371 C
bobk@uakron.edu
KROPIEWNICKI, Mary ... 912-358-4100 125 C
sote@savannahstate.edu
KROSCH, Brandon .... 651-255-6136 250 D
bkrosch@unitedseminary.edu
KROTSENG, Marsha, V . 304-327-4000 503 O
mkrotseng@bluefieldstate.edu
KROTZER, Mary, J .... 205-247-8164.... 7 C
mkrotzer@stillman.edu
KROUSE, Alisa .... 713-963-8979 125 H
akrouse@southuniversity.edu
KROUSE, John .... 956-296-1445 468 A
john.krouse@utrgv.edu
KROUSEL-WOOD,
M. A. 'Tonette' .... 504-865-5261 196 D
mawood@tulane.edu
KROVI, Ravi .... 330-972-7442 371 C
krovi@uakron.edu
KRSTIC, Miroslav .... 858-534-5556.. 69 E
mkrstic@ucsd.edu
KRTINIC, Marina .... 708-709-7921 148 I
mkrtinic@prairiestate.edu
KRUCKEBERG, Tara .... 626-395-8661.. 29 I
tkruckeb@caltech.edu
KRUCKENBERG, Erica ... 785-227-3380 175 E
kruckenberges@bethanylb.edu
KRUCZEK, Thomas .... 216-373-5238 367 A
tkruczek@ndc.edu
KRUEGER, Beth .... 520-515-5380.. 11 R
kruegerbeth@cochise.edu
KRUEGER, Bryon, D ...... 651-631-5392 251 C
bdkrueger@unwsp.edu
KRUEGER, Carr .... 801-422-3760 471 E
carr@byu.edu
KRUEGER, Christopher .. 410-626-2558 206 F
chris.krueger@sjc.edu
KRUEGER, Clancy .... 617-217-9054 211 D
ckrueger@baystate.edu
KRUEGER, Conrad .... 210-486-0915 442 A
ckrueger@alamo.edu
KRUEGER, Jill .... 914-633-2004 311 B
jkrueger@iona.edu
KRUEGER, Joni .... 605-274-4015 426 K
joni.krueger@augie.edu
KRUEGER, Justin .... 815-226-4006 150 C
jkrueger@rockford.edu
KRUEGER, Kurt, J .... 949-214-3194.. 40 I
kurt.krueger@cui.edu
KRUEGER, Laura .... 480-423-6133.. 14 C
laura.krueger@scottsdalecc.edu
KRUEGER, Mablene .... 312-935-6645 149 K
mkrueger@robertmorris.edu
KRUEGER, Mary, M .... 419-372-8034 357 F
mkruege@bgsu.edu
KRUEGER, Michelle .... 941-359-4200 111 C
KRUEMMLING, Brooke .. 215-780-1364 410 D
KRUG, Anita .... 206-543-2586 499 D
lawdean@uw.edu
KRUG, Anna .... 312-427-2737 141 E
akrug@jmls.edu
KRUG, Cherie .... 301-387-3100 203 I
cherie.krug@garrettcollege.edu
KRUG, Jeffrey .... 570-389-4745 405 E
jakrug@bloomu.edu
KRUG, Sheila, R .... 620-229-6368 181 F
sheila.krug@sckans.edu
KRUG, Stefan .... 617-521-3929 224 E
stefan.krug@simmons.edu
KRUGER, Darrell, P .... 828-262-2070 349 H
krugerdp@appstate.edu
KRUGER, Jenny .... 712-325-3326 170 K
jkruger@iwcc.edu
KRUGER, Michael, J ...... 704-366-5066 255 E
mkruger@rts.edu
KRUGER, Severa .... 920-923-7600 508 B
KRUHLY, Leslie, L .... 215-898-7005 412 G
kruhly@upenn.edu
KRUKONES, James, H .. 216-397-4762 363 H
jkrukones@jcu.edu
KRULL, Kimberly .... 316-322-3100 175 I
kim.krull@butlercc.edu
KRULL, Lucille .... 503-251-6115 499 F
lucy.krull@wallawalla.edu
KRUMER, Walter .... 718-522-9073 298 E
vkrumer@asa.edu
KRUMHANSL, Ezra .... 502-585-9911 189 B
ekrumhansl@spalding.edu
KRUML, Susan .... 402-941-6200 275 J
kruml@midlandu.edu
KRUMM, Beth .... 314-516-6604 268 E
krumme@umsl.edu
KRUMM, Brenda, L .... 620-431-2820 180 C
bkrumm@neosho.edu
KRUMM, Javier .... 951-785-2295.. 47 F
jkrumm@lasierra.edu
KRUMMEN SCHRAVEN,
Ginger, B .... 920-433-6631 506 C
ginger.krummen@bellincollege.edu
KRUMPE, Keith .... 828-250-3880 351 A
kkrumpe@unca.edu
KRUPICA, Suzanne .... 217-854-5761 134 E
suzanne.krupica@blackburn.edu
KRUPIN, Maria .... 845-451-1385 306 D
maria.krupin@culinary.edu
KRUPKA, Ben .... 413-528-7413 211 B
benkrupk@simons-rock.edu
KRUPKA, Moshe .... 646-565-6000 331 F
moshe.krupka@touro.edu
KRUPNICK, Kayla .... 415-442-7228.. 44 E
kkrupnick@ggu.edu
KRUPNIK,
Malka Bracha .... 718-252-6333 334 N
KRUPP, Jason .... 727-341-3339 107 A
krupp.jason@spcollege.edu
KRUPP, Robert, A .... 503-517-1838 388 C
rakrupp@westernseminary.edu
KRUPPS, Gina .... 309-341-5264 134 H
gkrupps@sandburg.edu
KRUPPSTADT, Tom .... 877-476-8674 449 H
KRUPSKI, Eric, A .... 617-422-7298 222 J
ekrupski@nesl.edu
KRUSE, Amy .... 320-629-5129 246 H
krusea@pine.edu
KRUSE, Beckie .... 262-243-5700 507 C
beckie.kruse@cuw.edu
KRUSE, Heather .... 602-285-7229.. 14 A
heather.kruse@phoenixcollege.edu
KRUSE, Janetta .... 817-598-6391 470 J
jkruse@wc.edu
KRUSE, Jerry, E .... 217-545-0200 152 B
jkruse@siumed.edu
KRUSE, Mary .... 517-264-7112 236 I
mkruse@sienaheights.edu
KRUSE, Schoen .... 816-654-7641 261 D
skruse@kcumb.edu
KRUSE, Thomas, D .... 563-588-4948 171 H
tom.kruse@loras.edu
KRUSE, Tracy, L .... 402-844-7056 276 G
tracyk@northeast.edu
KRUSEMARK, Diane .... 651-638-6043 240 J
d-krusemark@bethel.edu
KRUSEMARK, Stacy, L .. 605-256-5127 428 G
stacy.krusemark@dsu.edu
KRUSEMARK,
Stephanie .... 928-350-2230.. 15 V
stephanie.krusemark@prescott.edu
KRUSEMARK,
Stephanie, L .... 202-884-9401.. 93 C
krusemarks@trinitydc.edu
KRUSLING, James .... 415-442-7248.. 44 E
jkrusling@ggu.edu
KRUSNIAK, Bryan .... 660-626-2364 257 A
bkrusniak@atsu.edu
KRUTKY, Judith, B .... 440-826-2257 357 B
jkrutky@bw.edu
KRUTZ, Ellen .... 610-519-4237 413 K
ellen.krutz@villanova.edu
KRUZANSKY, Charles ... 518-434-4157 306 B
albany_office@cornell.edu
KRYCKA, Kevin .... 206-296-5398 498 D
krycka@seattleu.edu
KRYCZKA, Susan .... 518-608-8150 308 A
skryczka@excelsior.edu
KRYLOWICZ, Brian .... 413-748-3345 224 G
bkrylowicz@springfieldcollege.edu
KRYSIEWSKI, Ron .... 570-702-8953 398 A
rkrysiewski@johnson.edu
KRYZHANOVSKAYA,
Tatyana .... 718-522-9073 298 E
tkryzhanovskaya@asa.edu
KRZAK, Chris .... 209-946-2211.. 70 F
ckrzak@pacific.edu
KRZANIK, Jacki .... 413-662-5421 218 C
j.krzanik@mcla.edu
KRZYWICKI, James .... 440-684-6119 373 B
jkrzywicki@ursuline.edu
KTUL, Kathy .... 252-492-2061 347 C
ktul@vgcc.edu
KUAN, Christine .... 212-517-3929 324 E
c.kuan@sothebysinstitute.com
KUAN, Jeffrey .... 909-447-2552.. 38 B
jkuan@cst.edu
KUANG, Connie .... 213-615-7269.. 37 B
ckuang@thechicagoschool.edu
KUBA, Jodie, M .... 808-956-7251 129 J
jodiek@hawaii.edu
KUBA, Shawn .... 304-473-8560 505 G
kuba_s@wvwc.edu
KUBACAK, James .... 254-299-8608 452 E
jkubacak@mclennan.edu
KUBAJAK, Jacob .... 660-944-2832 258 G
jacob@conception.edu
KUBASEK, Stephen .... 352-588-8355 106 N
stephen.kubasek@saintleo.edu
KUBAT, Robert, A .... 814-863-3681 403 F
rak28@psu.edu
KUBATZKE, Trevor, A .... 269-927-8600 232 G
tkubatzke@lakemichigancollege.edu
KUBEJA, Judy .... 814-732-1372 406 B
kubeja@edinboro.edu
KUBEK, Ron .... 717-560-8274 399 D
rkubek@lbc.edu
KUBERSKI, Chris .... 815-599-3417 139 F
chris.kuberski@highland.edu
KUBIAK, Cathy .... 616-234-3971 230 F
ckubiak@grcc.edu
KUBICA, Richard .... 401-874-4599 417 E
richard_kubica@uri.edu
KUBICZ, Vicky .... 740-284-5244 361 L
vkubicz@franciscan.edu
KUBIK, Rachel .... 714-432-5834.. 38 H
rkubik@occ.cccd.edu
KUBILUS, Norbert, J ..... 858-499-0202.. 39 B
nkubilus@coleman.edu
KUBINAK, Lois, A .... 610-921-7612 388 E
lkubinak@albright.edu
KUBIT, Michael, J .... 814-865-3540 403 F
mjk469@psu.edu
KUBO, Takeo .... 408-288-3733.. 61 P
takeo.kubo@sjcc.edu
KUBOW, Stephen .... 732-255-0356 286 F
skubow@kean.edu
KUCER, Peter .... 860-632-3001.. 87 D
pkucer@holyapostles.edu
KUCERA, Kevin .... 734-487-2390 229 K
kkucera@emich.edu
KUCERA, Victoria .... 402-461-2414 273 G
vkucera@cccneb.edu
KUCIA, John, F .... 513-745-3997 374 D
kucia@xavier.edu
KUCIC, Terry .... 814-371-2090 412 C
tkucic@triangle-tech.edu
KUCIK, Maggie .... 317-955-6213 162 R
mkucik@marian.edu
KUCINSKI, Nancy .... 325-670-1298 450 A
nkicinski@hsutx.edu
KUCKER, Patricia .... 215-717-6388 412 F
pkucker@uarts.edu
KUCKO, Jane .... 918-631-3225 381 C
jane-kucko@utulsa.edu
KUDRAVETZ, Douglas ... 202-885-3283.. 91 C
doug@american.edu
KUE, Mailee .... 401-232-6448 416 A
mkue@bryant.edu
KUEBEL-HERNANDEZ,
Jan .... 323-473-5673.. 73 K
KUEBLER, Alan, S .... 314-935-5727 269 L
alan_kuebler@wustl.edu
KUECKER, Aaron .... 708-239-4839 153 B
aaron.kuecker@trnty.edu
KUEHLER, Robert .... 303-837-2112.. 83 A
robert.kuehler@cu.edu
KUEHN, Martha .... 218-855-8221 244 C
mkuehn@clcmn.edu
KUEHN, Paul .... 808-455-0268 130 G
pkuehn@hawaii.edu
KUEHNER, Holly .... 850-872-3804 101 J
hkuehner@gulfcoast.edu
KUEHNER, Megan, R .... 904-620-2523 110 E
mkuehner@unf.edu
KUEHNL, Kody .... 614-947-6104 362 A
kody.kuehnl@franklin.edu
KUENNEN, Connie .... 563-562-3263 172 D
kuennenc@nicc.edu
KUENTZEL, Jeffrey .... 313-577-2840 239 C
jkuentzel@wayne.edu
KUENZLI, David, P .... 719-333-9751 518 H
KUERZI, Kenneth .... 856-256-4138 289 H
kuerzi@rowan.edu

KUESTER, Vickie 715-232-2132 512 A kuesterv@uwstout.edu
KUETER, Jeanne 847-574-5224 143 A jkueter@lfgsm.edu
KUETHER, Eva 414-297-6897 514 C kuethere@matc.edu
KUFFEL, Lorne 205-348-7204 8 A lkuffel@ua.edu
KUFFREY, Casey, W 770-484-1204 122 G casey.kuffrey@lutherrice.edu
KUFUOR, Edward 718-522-9073 298 E ekufuor@asa.edu
KUGLER, Angela 425-558-0299 494 C akugler@digipen.edu
KUGLER, Anne 216-397-4770 363 H akugler@jcu.edu
KUGLER, Sharon 203-432-1128 89 G sharon.kugler@yale.edu
KUHAJDA, Kimberlee, A 440-826-2251 357 B kkuhajda@bw.edu
KUHAR, Marilyn 617-228-3290 219 D mkkuhar@bhcc.mass.edu
KUHAR, MJ 541-278-5811 382 A mjkuhar@bluecc.edu
KUHL, Ryan 207-326-2479 200 F ryan.kuhl@mma.edu
KUHL, Sara 262-472-1194 512 C kuhls@uww.edu
KUHL, Susan 918-960-5255 380 I sue.kuhl@twsweld.com
KUHLHORST, Michelle, L 260-399-7700 165 B mkuhlhorst@sf.edu
KUHLMAN, Ann 203-432-2305 89 G ann.kuhlman@yale.edu
KUHLMAN, Gregory 718-951-5174 301 E kuhlman@brooklyn.cuny.edu
KUHLMANN, Diana, E 620-341-5173 177 B dkuhlman@emporia.edu
KUHLMEIER, Sylvia 417-255-7949 263 I sylviakuhlmeier@missouristate.edu
KUHN, Bill 952-446-4162 242 A kuhnb@crown.edu
KUHN, Charles 301-447-5244 206 B ckuhn@msmary.edu
KUHN, Esther 817-722-1745 451 G esther.kuhn@tku.edu
KUHN, Helen 217-245-3013 139 H registrar@mail.ic.edu
KUHN, Jens-Uwe 805-965-0581 62 E jkuhn@sbcc.edu
KUHN, Karen 630-942-2698 136 D kuhnk36@cod.edu
KUHN, Kathryn, A 414-955-8217 508 D kkuhn@mcw.edu
KUHN, Kevin 601-477-4108 253 F kevin.kuhn@jcjc.edu
KUHN, Lisa 410-386-8032 203 A lkuhn@carrollcc.edu
KUHN, Paul 732-247-5241 287 E pkuhn@nbts.edu
KUHN, Sean 937-294-6155 357 I sean.kuhn@brightwood.edu
KUHN, Sheila Jane 928-523-7732 14 K jane.kuhn@nau.edu
KUHN, Shelly 262-691-5450 515 B skuhn4@wctc.edu
KUHN, Stephen 262-524-7132 506 G skuhn@carrollu.edu
KUHN-SCHNELL, Tamara 217-786-2353 144 B tammy.schnell@llcc.edu
KUHNLENZ, Fritz 617-747-2012 212 B alumniaffairs@berklee.edu
KUHR, Brittanie 419-517-8990 364 G bkuhr@lourdes.edu
KUIPERS, David 229-931-2004 125 G dkuipers@southgatech.edu
KUJAT, Marilee 989-386-6622 234 B mkujat@midmich.edu
KUJAWA, Lisa, R 248-204-2403 233 A lkujawa@ltu.edu
KUJAWA, Thomas 920-465-2300 510 E kujawat@uwgb.edu
KUJAWA, Tricia, A 217-786-2211 144 B tricia.kujawa@llcc.edu
KUJAWA-HOLBROOK, Sheryl 909-447-2521 38 B skujawa-holbrook@cst.edu
KUKAINIS, Maris 856-227-7200 284 E mkukainis@camdencc.edu
KUKAY, Mike 406-496-4673 272 E mkukay@mtech.edu
KUKER, Ronald 513-244-4711 366 A ronald.kuker@msj.edu
KUKOR, Jerome, J 848-932-7275 290 C kukor@aesop.rutgers.edu
KUKREJA, Anil 504-520-7652 198 D akukreja@xula.edu
KUKREJA, Sunil 253-879-3207 499 C skukreja@pugetsound.edu
KUKUK, Carley, a 715-836-5171 510 D kukukca@uwec.edu
KUKULIES, Emily Ann 808-845-9219 130 E kukulies@hawaii.edu
KULAGA, Jon 740-474-8896 367 E
KULAGA, Jon, S 859-858-3511 183 D jon.kulaga@asbury.edu
KULECK, Gary 541-885-1000 385 E gary.kuleck@oit.edu
KULESZA, Darrell 508-541-1864 214 C dkulesza@dean.edu
KULESZA, Randy 814-866-8423 399 C rkulsza@lecom.edu
KULICK, Steven, W 315-445-4560 312 F kulicksw@lemoyne.edu
KULIK, Dmitry 202-462-2101 92 D kulik@iwp.edu
KULIS, Carol 858-653-3000 30 F ckulis@calmu.edu
KULKARNI, Sanjeev 609-258-3035 288 F kulkarni@princeton.edu
KULL, F. Jon 603-646-1552 281 C f.jon.kull@dartmouth.edu
KULL, Michael 219-989-2231 163 E mjkull@pnw.edu
KULL, Sherry 610-341-1576 394 E skull@eastern.edu
KULL, Stephen 989-774-1028 228 E kull2sl@cmich.edu
KULOW, Beth 641-782-1413 173 I kulow@swcciowa.edu
KULPA, Brian 734-487-2390 229 K bkulpa@emich.edu
KUMAR, Coleen 718-818-6470 323 F ckumar@edaff.com
KUMAR, Mukul 617-746-1990 216 A mukul.kumar@hult.edu
KUMAR, Neeraj 312-341-3587 150 D neeraj.kumar@roosevelt.edu
KUMAR, Neeraj 432-703-5257 463 E neeraj.kumar@ttuhsc.edu
KUMAR, Nikhil 914-323-5129 314 A nikhil.kumar@mville.edu
KUMAR, Senthil 617-217-9733 211 D skumar@baystate.edu
KUMAR, Sunil 410-516-3355 204 F provost@jhu.edu
KUMAR, Thulasi 703-993-5883 481 B traghura@gmu.edu
KUMAR, Vijay 215-898-7244 412 G kumar@seas.upenn.edu
KUMARASAMY, Sundar 617-373-4810 223 D
KUMLER, Kurt 412-268-2922 391 H kkumler@andrew.cmu.edu
KUMM, David 402-643-7222 274 B david.kumm@cune.edu
KUMMER, Maryann, S 313-927-1373 233 D mkummer@marygrove.edu
KUMMERMAN, Howard 562-908-3476 58 D foundation@riohondo.edu
KUMMERMAN, Howard 562-908-3412 58 D howard.kummerman@riohondo.edu
KUMP, Jessica 304-876-5378 504 D jkump@shepherd.edu
KUMP, Lee 814-863-1274 403 F lrk4@psu.edu
KUMP, Melissa 406-496-4108 272 E mkump@mtech.edu
KUMPF, Dan 805-289-6285 73 C dkumpf@vcccd.edu
KUNA, Gerri 701-858-3497 354 C gerri.kuna@minotstateu.edu
KUNCE, Kim, M 708-709-3684 148 I kkunce@prairiestate.edu
KUNCL, Ralph, W 909-748-8390 71 H ralph_kuncl@redlands.edu
KUNDELL, Ken, F 410-543-6043 209 B kfkundell@salisblury.edu
KUNDINGER, Amy 920-403-4223 509 J amy.kundinger@snc.edu
KUNE, Natacha, F 206-543-1240 499 D fookune@uw.edu
KUNERT, Erin 219-464-5333 165 D erin.kunert@valpo.edu
KUNIYOSHI, Tammy 808-956-3028 129 J tammyk@hawaii.edu
KUNKA, Jennifer 843-661-1362 421 H jkunka@fmarion.edu
KUNKEL, Adam 970-521-6952 81 F adam.kunkel@njc.edu
KUNKEL, Bruce 619-849-2571 57 H brucekunkel@pointloma.edu
KUNKEL, Karl 573-651-2063 266 M kkunkel@semo.edu
KUNKEL, Roberta 559-325-5356 66 F roberta.kunkel@cloviscollege.edu
KUNKO, Bill 575-492-2501 294 L bkunko@nmjc.edu
KUNKO, Christina 575-492-2782 294 L ckunko@nmjc.edu
KUNO, Phyllis 701-349-5407 355 G phylliskuno@trinitybiblecollege.edu
KUNSELMAN, Scott, G 248-370-4039 235 J skunselman@oakland.edu
KUNST, John 919-658-7742 349 F jkunst@umo.edu
KUNTZ, Daniel 805-493-3855 30 E kuntz@callutheran.edu
KUNTZ, David 216-987-4790 360 E david.kuntz@tri-c.edu
KUNTZ, F. Douglas 570-321-4116 400 G kuntz@lycoming.edu
KUNTZ, Jason 717-391-7322 411 C kuntz@stevenscollege.edu
KUNTZ, John 973-300-2231 291 I jkuntz@sussex.edu
KUNTZ, Lisa, M 610-398-5300 400 C lkuntz@lincolntech.edu
KUNTZ, Twyla 701-349-5438 355 G twyla@trinitybiblecollege.edu
KUNTZ, Wayne 228-897-4361 254 D wayne.kuntz@mgccc.edu
KUNZ, Katherine 415-485-3242 41 J katherine.kunz@dominican.edu
KUNZ, Kent 208-334-4781 132 B kunzkent@isu.edu
KUNZ, Leonard 908-852-1400 284 G kunzl01@centenaryuniversity.edu
KUNZE, Joel 563-425-5259 173 K kunzej@uiu.edu
KUNZELMAN, Ryan 248-689-8282 238 F rkunzelm@walshcollege.edu
KUO, David 215-871-7128 407 G davidku@pcom.edu
KUO, David 215-871-6690 407 G davidku@pcom.edu
KUO, Elaine 650-949-6198 43 F kuoelaine@foothill.edu
KUO, Kent 541-737-3525 385 F kent.kuo@oregonstate.edu
KUO, Ling Ling 626-571-8811 72 C linglingk@uwest.edu
KUO, Wai Lan 512-444-8082 461 C wkuo@thsu.edu
KUPCZYNSKI, Bonnie, L 218-722-4000 242 B bonniek@dbumn.edu
KUPERMAN, Eli 732-367-1060 283 K ekuperman@bmg.edu
KUPERSMITH, Peter, A 215-489-2254 393 F peter.kupersmith@delval.edu
KUPPER, Jodi 402-471-2505 276 A jkupper@nscs.edu
KUPPINGER, Karen 585-389-2100 316 D kkuppin9@naz.edu
KURAI, Mark 925-969-3300 46 L mkurai@jfku.edu
KURAPATI, Raaj 361-593-2410 460 B raajkumar.kurapati@tamuk.edu
KURIMAY, Mary Beth 610-436-6931 407 D mkurimay@wcupa.edu
KURKER-STEWART, Nicole 860-768-5101 89 C kurkerste@hartford.edu
KURN, Seth 401-739-5000 416 D skurn@neit.edu
KUROKAWA, Linda 760-757-2121 52 F lkorokawa@miracosta.edu
KUROPAS, Michael 217-420-6765 145 J mkuropas@millikin.edu
KUROWSKI, Kristy 904-819-6489 98 I kkurowski@flagler.edu
KURPIUS, David, D 573-882-6686 268 C kurpius@missouri.edu
KURTENBACH, Jim 515-294-0323 166 F jmk@iastate.edu
KURTH, Ann 203-785-2393 89 G ann.kurth@yale.edu
KURTH, Christine 614-251-4513 367 F kurthc@ohiodominican.edu
KURTINITIS, Sandra, L 443-840-1015 203 E skurtinitis@ccbcmd.edu
KURTYKA, Steve 973-761-9454 291 F steve.kurtyka@shu.edu
KURTZ, Andrew 419-372-0623 357 F kurtz@bgsu.edu
KURTZ, Charles 816-322-0110 257 M charles.kurtz@calvary.edu
KURTZ, Diane, L 517-750-1200 237 D dkurtz@arbor.edu
KURTZ, Josef 617-735-9979 214 F kurtzj@emmanuel.edu
KURTZ, Karna 218-726-7912 250 F kurtz@d.umn.edu
KURTZ, Rebecca 740-695-9500 357 D bkurtz@belmontcollege.edu
KURTZ, Rick 740-351-3208 369 L rkurtz@shawnee.edu
KURTZ, Steve 573-518-2146 263 E skurtz@mineralarea.edu
KURTZ, Terri 361-572-6463 470 A terri.kurtz@victoriacollege.edu
KURTZ, Terry, J 440-826-3170 357 B tkurtz@bw.edu
KURTZ HOFFMAN, Linda, A 330-471-8145 364 H lhoffman@malone.edu
KURTZ-SHAW, Brad 208-467-8419 132 F bradshaw@nnu.edu
KURTZ-SHAW, Georgann 618-664-6602 139 A georgann.kurtz-shaw@greenville.edu
KURZ, Jane 215-951-3730 398 F kurz@lasalle.edu
KURZU, Laura 504-861-5881 194 G lfkurzu@loyno.edu
KUSANO, Ellen, I 808-932-7365 129 I ekusano@hawaii.edu
KUSCH, Bruce, C 801-524-8100 471 L
KUSER, Janet 617-236-5458 215 B jkuser@fisher.edu
KUSH, Lynn 215-619-7419 402 A lkush@mc3.edu
KUSHMIDER, Kristin 303-724-8488 83 D kristin.kushmider@ucdenver.edu
KUSHNER, Cynthia 440-366-7610 364 F
KUSHNER, Melissa 610-647-4400 397 I mkushner@immaculata.edu
KUSHNER, Mikhel, A 410-706-1852 207 H mikhel.kushner@umaryland.edu
KUSHNER, Tiffany 908-852-1400 284 G kushnert@centenaryuniversity.edu
KUSKOWSKI, David 864-656-5463 419 F dkuskow@clemson.edu
KUSNIERZ, Zbigniew 773-252-5316 149 I zbigniew.kusnierz@resu.edu
KUSPA, Adam 713-798-4032 444 A akuspa@bcm.edu
KUSPA, Adam 713-798-1060 444 A akuspa@bcm.edu
KUSSE, Debra 585-475-3947 321 D dskpur@rit.edu
KUSTER, Brian 270-745-2791 190 F brian.kuster@wku.edu
KUSTER, Frank 860-231-5214 89 E fkuster@usj.edu
KUSTER-DALE, Kim 308-635-6103 278 B kusterdk@wncc.edu
KUSTRA, Robert, W 208-426-1491 131 C bobkustra@boisestate.edu
KUSZYNSKI, Lawrence, J 352-854-2322 97 C larry.kuszynski@cf.edu
KUTATELADZE, Andrei 303-871-2693 83 E akutatel@du.edu
KUTCHER, Kevin 856-351-2612 291 E kkutcher@salemcc.edu
KUTHY, Anna 270-686-4277 183 J anna.kuthy@brescia.edu
KUTI, Morakinyo 937-376-6547 358 I mkuti@centralstate.edu
KUTLENIOS, Rose, M 304-336-8108 504 E rose.kutlenios@westliberty.edu
KUTNER, Sender 847-982-2500 139 E kutner@htc.edu
KUTSHIED, Mandy 828-298-3325 353 B mkutshied@warren-wilson.edu
KUTSKO, Jim 505-438-8884 296 D
KUTTENKULER, Scott 870-850-4826 21 E skuttenkuler@seark.edu
KUTZKE, Mike 320-222-5218 247 B mike.kutzke@ridgewater.edu
KUWASAKI, L. Michelle 206-592-3693 495 E mkuwasaki@highline.edu
KUWITZKY, Chris 405-325-5161 380 L ckuwitzky@ou.edu
KUYKENDALL, John 870-575-8498 22 E kuykendallj@uapb.edu
KUYKENDALL, Randy 915-532-3737 470 L rkuykendall@westerntech.edu
KUYKENDALL, Robin 575-769-4916 293 M robin.kuykendall@clovis.edu
KUYKENDALL, Todd 575-769-4919 293 M todd.kuykendall@clovis.edu
KUZMA, Marta 203-432-2606 89 G marta.kuzma@yale.edu
KUZMESKI, David 413-205-3337 210 E david.kuzmeski@aic.edu
KUZMICK, Branden 713-221-8682 465 C kuzmickb@uhd.edu

KVAAL, Kimberly .... 512-448-8413 455 I
kimkvaal@stedwards.edu
KVAM, Robert, A .... 765-285-5495 156 C
rkvam@bsu.edu
KVIGNE, Eric .... 530-752-1247.. 68 H
epkvigne@ucdavis.edu
KVINLAUG, Josh .... 515-271-7875 168 G
joshua.kvinlaug@dmu.edu
KVISTAD, Gregg, O .... 303-871-2966.. 83 E
gkvistad@du.edu
KWAN, Billy .... 212-472-1500 318 B
bkwan@nysid.edu
KWANBUNBUMPEN,
Ada .... 204-286-5244 195 L
akwanbunbumpen@suno.edu
KWAPONG, Sam .... 619-849-2524.. 57 H
samkwapong@pointloma.edu
KWASIGROH, Catherine 731-661-5281 439 D
ckwasigroh@uu.edu
KWASIKPUI, Tremaine .. 713-221-8563 465 C
kwasikpuit@uhd.edu
KWASITSU, Lishi .... 503-517-1023 388 A
lkwasitsu@warnerpacific.edu
KWAST, Steven, L .... 334-953-2044 517 I
KWENDA, Maxwell .... 509-313-6948 495 A
kwenda@gonzaga.edu
KWESKIN, Amy, B .... 314-935-9842 269 L
amy.b.kweskin@wustl.edu
KWIATKOWSKI, Amy .... 415-955-2100.. 24 K
akwiatkowski@alliant.edu
KWIATKOWSKI,
Anthony .... 773-907-4830 135 K
akwiatkowski@ccc.edu
KWILINSKI, Kathie .... 206-934-7965 497 J
kathie.kwilinski@seattlecolleges.edu
KWIST, Sabrina, T .... 925-473-7314.. 41 A
skwist@losmedanos.edu
KWOK, Borree .... 910-893-1460 336 C
kwokb@campbell.edu
KWOLEK, Katherine .... 617-262-5000 212 C
katherine.kwolek@the-bac.edu
KWOLEK-FOLLAND,
Angel .... 352-392-4792 110 D
akf@aa.ufl.edu
KWONG ABAZIA,
Larissa .... 609-497-7785 288 E
larissa.kwong@ptsem.edu
KWONG-SITO, Winny .... 617-585-0200 212 C
winny.kwong-sito@the-bac.edu
KYLE, James, R .... 619-596-2766.. 24 H
jkyle@advancedtraining.edu
KYLE, Jean .... 507-433-0568 247 C
jean.kyle@riverland.edu
KYLE, Michael .... 507-786-3025 250 C
kylem@stolaf.edu
KYLE, Paul .... 913-469-8500 178 F
pkyle@jccc.edu
KYLE, Roberta .... 508-929-8811 219 A
rkyle@worcester.edu
KYNERD, Emily .... 615-794-4254 435 G
ekynerd@omorecollege.edu
KYNOR, James .... 303-352-3221.. 79 D
KYPRIOS, Linda, A .... 972-881-5726 446 I
lkyprios@collin.edu
KYRIAKIDES, Michelle .. 516-463-6060 310 D
michelle.kyriakides@hofstra.edu
KYRKANIDES,
Stephanos .... 859-323-1884 190 B
stephanos@uky.edu
KYSOR, Darwin, V .... 814-641-3351 398 B
kysord@juniata.edu
KYTE, Richard, L .... 608-796-3704 512 R
rlkyte@viterbo.edu
KYZER, Melany .... 405-491-6600 379 K
mkyzer@snu.edu

L

LÓPEZ, Brunilda .... 787-850-9342 528 B
brunilda.lopez@upr.edu
LÓPEZ, Israel .... 787-743-3038 525 M
ilopezgomez@sanjuanbautista.edu
LA BARBERA,
Christopher .... 781-239-2463 220 A
clabarbera@massbay.edu
LA BRANCHE, Mark, D . 931-363-9802 433 E
mlabranche@martinmethodist.edu
LA CHAPELLE,
Jacqueline .... 337-550-1282 194 B
jlachape@lsue.edu
LA LUZ, Maribel .... 860-723-0617.. 84 I
laluzm@ct.edu
LA MAZZA, Bernadette .. 480-732-7019.. 13 E
bernadette.la.mazza@cgc.edu
LA MOE, Jeffrey, P .... 913-684-2905 518 I
LA PERLA-MORALES,
Joann .... 732-906-2517 287 B
jlaperla@middlesexcc.edu
LA PIERRE, Mary .... 518-562-4125 304 C
mary.lapierre@clinton.edu
LA POINT, Kristine, L ... 773-975-1295 508 E
krisbob1@cs.com
LA RUE, Lacie .... 541-737-4218 385 F
lacie.larue@oregonstate.edu
LA TORRA, Grace .... 206-876-6100 498 C
glatorra@theseattleschool.edu
LA VENTURE, Kelly .... 218-755-4404 244 B
klaventure@bemidjistate.edu
LA VOY, Sharon, A .... 301-405-5590 207 G
slavoy@umd.edu
LAACK, Kevin .... 909-593-3511.. 70 E
klaack@laverne.edu
LAACKMAN, Donald, J .. 802-860-2734 474 G
dlaackman@champlain.edu
LAAGER, Melinda .... 912-427-5835 117 J
mlaager@coastalpines.edu
LABADIE, Shawn .... 757-826-1883 478 G
registrar@bcva.edu
LABAN, Danielle .... 312-261-3162 146 G
dlaban@nl.edu
LABARBERA, Mark .... 219-464-6894 165 D
mark.labarbera@valpo.edu
LABARBERA, Paul .... 845-758-7819 298 I
labarbera@bard.edu
LABAT, Nichole .... 985-545-1500 192 K
LABAT, Tony .... 415-351-3574.. 60 G
tlabat@sfai.edu
LABATE, Ken .... 702-776-5268 474 H
ken.labate@csj.edu
LABATE, William .... 310-206-7323.. 69 B
labate@idre.ucla.edu
LABAUGH, Amy, R .... 208-496-1155 131 D
labaugha@byui.edu
LABBE, Shirley .... 504-520-7515 198 D
slabbe@xula.edu
LABBERTON, Mark, A ... 626-584-5201.. 43 K
LABE, Geoffey .... 610-896-1806 397 F
glabe@haverford.edu
LABEFF, Toni .... 903-434-8105 453 M
tlabeff@ntcc.edu
LABELL, Yitzi .... 301-649-7077 210 D
ylabell@yeshiva.edu
LABENSKI, Paula .... 570-740-0388 400 F
plabenski@luzerne.edu
LABINE, Nancy .... 423-478-6227 436 G
nlabine@clevelandstatecc.edu
LABKOWSKI, Zalman .... 718-434-0784 300 K
LABOE, Mark .... 773-325-4004 137 C
mlaboe@depaul.edu
LABOE, Timothy .... 313-883-8556 236 D
laboe.timothy@shms.edu
LABONTE, Gene, R .... 978-542-6542 218 E
glabonte@salemstate.edu
LABONTE, Jason .... 631-656-2113 308 F
jason.labonte@ftc.edu
LABONTE, Kim .... 618-650-2789 152 A
klabont@siue.edu
LABONTE, Robert .... 978-632-6600 220 D
r_labonte@mwcc.mass.edu
LABOR, Jennifer .... 918-465-1814 375 J
jlabor@eosc.edu
LABORDE, Bridget .... 985-543-4120 192 K
LABOSKY, John .... 218-723-6460 241 J
llabosky1@css.edu
LABOY, Gloryber .... 787-751-0160 522 B
glaboy@cmpr.pr.gov
LABOY, Rafael .... 787-720-4476 527 A
relacionespublicas@mizpa.edu
LABRADOR, Victoria .... 510-666-8248.. 24 E
faofficer@aimc.edu
LABRANCHE, Michael ... 504-398-2241 196 E
mlabranche@uhcno.edu
LABREC, Ronald, A .... 860-444-8286 519 B
ronald.a.labrec@uscg.mil
LABRIE, John .... 617-373-2000 223 D
j.labrie@northeastern.edu
LABRIE, Lori, A .... 713-313-7040 461 E
labrie_la@tsu.edu
LABRIOLA, Elisabeth, S 860-439-2064.. 86 H
elisabeth.labriola@conncoll.edu
LABRON, Wendy .... 617-735-9778 214 F
labronw@emmanuel.edu
LABROSSE, Tonya, B .... 603-899-4097 281 D
labrosset@franklinpierce.edu
LABRY, Daniel .... 877-476-8674 449 H
LABS, Jeff .... 715-365-4406 514 E
jlabs@nicoletcollege.edu
LABYAK, Gregory .... 618-545-3015 142 D
glabyak@kaskaskia.edu
LACASCIO, Joe .... 508-286-3405 225 G
lacascio_joe@wheatoncollege.edu
LACEY, Aaron .... 314-264-1802 155 B
aaron.lacey@vatterott-college.edu
LACEY, Kasi .... 573-592-5269 270 B
kasi.lacey@westminster-mo.edu
LACEY, Kristin .... 864-455-7981 425 E
klacey@ghs.org
LACEY, Mark .... 904-632-3319 100 F
mark.lacey@fscj.edu
LACEY, Pete .... 810-989-5561 236 G
placey@sc4.edu
LACEY, R. Alton .... 314-392-2355 263 F
president@mobap.edu
LACEY, Sherry Leigh .... 334-833-4562.... 5 M
internships@hawks.huntingdon.edu
LACH, Carolyn .... 773-244-5506 147 F
clach@northpark.edu
LACHANCE, Andrea .... 607-753-5430 327 A
andrea.lachance@cortland.edu
LACHANCE, Beatrice .... 615-547-1222 431 D
blachance@cumberland.edu
LACHANCE, Elizabeth, A 585-385-8410 322 E
llachance@sjfc.edu
LACHANCE, Laurie, G .... 207-859-1201 200 H
president@thomas.edu
LACHAPELL, Tara, A .... 920-748-8713 509 H
lachapellt@ripon.edu
LACHAPELLE,
Andrea, M .... 401-825-2100 416 B
amlachapelle@ccri.edu
LACHAPELLE, Laurie .... 978-762-4000 220 E
llachape@northshore.edu
LACHENBRUCH, Mary ... 406-444-0330 271 F
LACHICA-CHAVEZ,
Cassandra, M .... 915-831-2580 449 A
clachica@epcc.edu
LACHNEY, Kent .... 318-473-6414 194 A
klachney@lsua.edu
LACIO, Erin .... 620-450-2218 180 K
erinl@prattcc.edu
LACKEY, Chad .... 704-878-3250 344 H
clackey@mitchellcc.edu
LACKEY, David, A .... 570-586-2400 392 E
dlackey@clarkssummitu.edu
LACKEY, Grant .... 916-686-7300.. 30 H
LACKEY, Laura, W .... 478-301-4106 122 H
lackey_l@mercer.edu
LACKEY, Miles .... 515-294-2220 166 F
mlackey@iastate.edu
LACKEY, Polly, R .... 806-291-3702 470 I
lackeyp@wbu.edu
LACKEY, Russell, L .... 515-263-6004 169 E
rlackey@grandview.edu
LACKIE, Mary .... 479-788-7021.. 22 A
mary.lackie@uafs.edu
LACKLAND, Jonathan .... 309-438-5677 140 L
jwlackl@ilstu.edu
LACKNER, Elisabeth .... 718-631-6279 303 F
elackner@qcc.cuny.edu
LACKNER, Sandra .... 828-395-1429 344 A
slackner@isothermal.edu
LACLAIR, Bethaney .... 802-258-3357 476 B
bethaney.laclair@worldlearning.org
LACOLA, Chris .... 803-786-3933 420 D
clacola@columbiasc.edu
LACOMBA, A.J .... 570-326-3761 404 T
ajlacomba@pct.edu
LACOMBA, AJ .... 518-587-2100 329 C
aj.lacomba@esc.edu
LACOSTE-CAPUTO,
Jenny .... 512-499-4363 467 A
jcaputo@utsystem.edu
LACOURSE, Michael .... 435-652-7506 473 B
lacourse@dixie.edu
LACOURSE, Peter, W .... 231-995-1198 235 B
placourse@nmc.edu
LACOURSE, William .... 410-455-2598 208 A
lacourse@umbc.edu
LACOVARA, Vincent, A .. 202-319-6735.. 91 D
lacovara@cua.edu
LACRETA, James .... 781-736-2231 213 A
jlacreta@brandeis.edu
LACRO, Erika .... 808-845-9225 130 E
lacro@hawaii.edu
LACROIX, Mike .... 419-755-4048 366 E
lacroix.12@osu.edu
LACROIX, Nicole .... 303-914-6400.. 82 B
nicole.lacroix@rrcc.edu
LACROIX, Roland, J .... 207-581-4053 201 B
roland.j.lacroix@maine.edu
LACUEVA, Graciela .... 216-397-4625 363 H
glacueva@jcu.edu
LACY, Alan .... 309-438-8864 140 L
aclacy@ilstu.edu
LACY, Charles, F .... 702-968-2016 280 B
clacy@roseman.edu
LACY, Melanie .... 908-621-8198.. 57 C
melanie_lacy@pitzer.edu
LACY, Sherea .... 616-538-2330 230 E
slacy@gbcol.edu
LACY, Shim .... 209-946-2223.. 70 F
slacy@pacific.edu
LADAGE, Marcia .... 816-936-8716 266 K
mladage@saintlukescollege.edu
LADANY, Nicholas .... 619-260-4540.. 71 J
nladany@sandiego.edu
LADAS, Katie .... 651-696-6315 243 B
kladas@macalester.edu
LADD, Cindy .... 952-358-8223 246 D
cindy.ladd@normandale.edu
LADD, Susan, K .... 515-271-3048 168 J
susan.ladd@drake.edu
LADDEN, Kevin .... 215-489-2472 393 F
kevin.ladden@delval.edu
LADE, Becky .... 515-271-1485 168 G
becky.lade@dmu.edu
LADENBURGER, Ed .... 252-222-6179 341 F
ladenburgerj@carteret.edu
LADER, Donald .... 816-279-7000 257 B
don.lader@abtu.edu
LADINO, Pedro .... 310-377-5501.. 51 B
pladino@marymountcalifornia.edu
LADITKA, Doug .... 330-263-2310 360 A
dladitka@wooster.edu
LADNER, Bobby .... 903-730-4890 451 D
bladner@jarvis.edu
LADNER, Hilda .... 320-589-6095 251 A
hladner@morris.umn.edu
LADORE, Frank .... 203-392-5367.. 85 A
ladoref1@southernct.edu
LADUCER, Wanda .... 701-477-7862 355 H
wladucer@tm.edu
LADUE, Chad .... 518-891-2915 319 A
cladue@nccc.edu
LADUSAW, William .... 831-459-2115.. 70 C
artsdean@ucsc.edu
LADWIG, Laura .... 616-977-0599 236 B
laura.ladwig@prts.edu
LADWIG, Steven .... 707-826-6221.. 34 A
ladwig@humboldt.edu
LAENEN, Carol .... 231-348-6839 234 H
claenen@ncmich.edu
LAESSLE, Jamie .... 313-664-1460 228 H
jlaessle@collegeforcreativestudies.edu
LAFARGE, Vicki .... 781-891-2089 212 A
vlafarge@bentley.edu
LAFATA, Sandi .... 314-918-2691 260 A
slafata@eden.edu
LAFATA-JOHNSON,
Paulette .... 219-980-6769 160 C
plafataj@iun.edu
LAFAVE, Alan .... 605-626-2524 428 H
alan.lafave@northern.edu
LAFAVE, Joshua, J .... 315-267-2165 328 A
lafavejj@potsdam.edu
LAFAYETTE, Jack .... 610-921-6652 388 E
jlafayette@albright.edu
LAFERLA, Chris .... 712-325-3288 170 K
claferla@iwcc.edu
LAFERLA, Frank .... 949-824-5315.. 69 A
laferla@uci.edu
LAFEVOR, Kimberly .... 256-216-5359.... 4 C
kim.lafevor@athens.edu
LAFFELY, Andrew, J .... 719-333-9751 518 H
LAFFERTY, T. Kevin .... 813-258-7456 113 E
klafferty@ut.edu
LAFFERTY, William, J .... 717-337-6912 396 A
wlaffert@gettysburg.edu
LAFFITTE, Ron .... 704-463-3401 348 B
ron.laffitte@pfeiffer.edu
LAFLAMME, Jacques .... 401-739-5000 416 D
jlaflamme@neit.edu
LAFLAMME, Martha .... 603-752-1113 281 B
mlaflamme@ccsnh.edu
LAFLASH, Debra, A .... 508-854-4551 220 G
dal@qcc.mass.edu
LAFOND, Leon, A .... 340-639-1111 529 C
llafond@live.uvi.edu
LAFONTAINE, Joni .... 701-477-7862 355 H
jlafontaine@tm.edu
LAFONTANA, Kathryn .... 440-646-8101 373 B
kathryn.lafontana@ursuline.edu
LAFORGE,
William (Bill) .... 662-846-4000 252 H
wlaforge@deltastate.edu
LAFRANCE, Dawn .... 315-228-7385 304 G
dlafrance@colgate.edu
LAFRANCE, George .... 505-786-4311 294 I
glefrance@navajotech.edu
LAFROMEOISE, Tanya .... 605-698-3966 428 C
tlafromeoise@swc.tc
LAGAL, Billy .... 361-570-4865 465 D
lagalb@uhv.edu
LAGANA, Brandon, T .... 815-753-4405 147 H
blagana@niu.edu
LAGATTA, Regina .... 518-629-7736 310 G
r.lagatta@hvcc.edu
LAGEORGE, Lisa .... 661-362-2205.. 51 C
llageorge@masters.edu

LAGESON, David ... 541-962-3114 383 B
dlageson@eou.edu
LAGO, Baldomero ... 801-863-7301 473 D
lagoba@uvu.edu
LAGORIO, Grant ... 541-245-7873 386 G
glagorio@roguecc.edu
LAGRANGE, Teresa ... 216-687-4700 359 L
t.lagrange@csuohio.edu
LAGRASSA, Michael ... 508-999-9180 217 A
mlagrassa@umassd.edu
LAGUARDIA COOPER,
Beth ... 304-724-3700 501 D
blaguardia@apus.edu
LAGUE, Lorna ... 218-935-0417 251 F
lorna.lague@wetcc.edu
LAGUERRE, Jowel ... 510-466-7202.. 56 I
jlaguerre@peralta.edu
LAGUERRE, Jowel, C ... 510-466-7202.. 56 E
jlaguerre@peralta.edu
LAGUERRE-BROWN,
Caroline ... 202-994-2360.. 92 A
clbrown@gwu.edu
LAGUNA, Robert ... 512-492-3010 442 J
rlaguna@aoma.edu
LAHAIE, Ute ... 330-490-7453 373 F
ulahaie@walsh.edu
LAHART, Edward ... 570-504-9668 395 I
elahart@tcmc.edu
LAHER, Ron ... 307-532-8218 516 J
ron.laher@ewc.wy.edu
LAHEY, John, L ... 203-582-8700.. 88 A
john.lahey@quinnipiac.edu
LAHM, Chris ... 417-626-1234 264 J
lahm.chris@occ.edu
LAHM, Terry, D ... 614-236-6108 358 A
tlahm@capital.edu
LAHODA, Anne, L ... 412-397-5235 409 C
lahoda@rmu.edu
LAHR, Sheri, K ... 580-327-8550 376 K
sklahr@nwosu.edu
LAHTI, Michele ... 209-667-3131.. 33 F
mlahti@csustan.edu
LAHURD, Jennifer ... 941-752-5000 108 P
lahurdj@scf.edu
LAI, Chun ... 215-887-5511 414 D
clai@wts.edu
LAI, James ... 386-481-2306.. 95 J
laij@cookman.edu
LAI, Mary, M ... 516-299-2502 313 C
mary.lai@liu.edu
LAI HING, Kenneth ... 256-726-7112.... 6 E
laihing@oakwood.edu
LAIDACKER, Crystal ... 972-241-3371 447 E
claidacker@dallas.edu
LAIDLAW, Katharine ... 336-770-3293 352 B
laidlawk@uncsa.edu
LAIN, Jill ... 214-860-8680 448 B
LAINE, Vance ... 309-268-4355 143 G
vlaine@lincolncollege.edu
LAINO, Nicholas ... 315-866-0300 310 A
lainonf@herkimer.edu
LAIR, Patrick ... 651-423-8399 244 E
patrick.lair@dctc.edu
LAIRD, Allan ... 208-459-5454 131 H
alaird@collegeofidaho.edu
LAIRD, Kenneth ... 831-755-6888.. 45 C
klaird@hartnell.edu
LAIRD, Nicole ... 870-230-5076.. 19 H
lairdn@hsu.edu
LAIRD, Richard ... 321-433-7090.. 97 N
lairdr@easternflorida.edu
LAIRD, Stephen ... 509-452-5100 496 H
slaird@pnwu.edu
LAIRMORE, Michael, D . 530-752-1361.. 68 H
mdlairmore@ucdavis.edu
LAJEUNESSE, Deb ... 419-824-3733 364 G
dlajeunesse@lourdes.edu
LAJINESS, Kim ... 912-583-3255 116 G
klajiness@bpc.edu
LAJINESS, Todd ... 313-883-8501 236 D
lajiness.todd@shms.edu
LAJUBUTU, Oyebanjo ... 573-341-4954 269 A
lajubutuo@mst.edu
LAKE, Claude ... 205-391-2328.... 3 E
clake@sheltonstate.edu
LAKE, Claude ... 205-391-2996.... 3 E
clake@sheltonstate.edu
LAKE, Diana ... 360-475-7831 496 F
dlake@olympic.edu
LAKE, Doris, J ... 270-831-9617 186 A
doris.lake@kctcs.edu
LAKE, Erinn ... 814-732-2856 406 B
lakee@edinboro.edu
LAKE, Erinn ... 814-732-2724 406 B
lakee@edinboro.edu
LAKE, Kathryn ... 740-427-5113 364 A
lakek@kenyon.edu
LAKE, Kathy ... 231-591-2113 230 A
kathylake@ferris.edu
LAKE, Kathy ... 414-382-6084 506 A
kathy.lake@alverno.edu
LAKE, Kendra ... 810-989-5642 236 G
kklake@sc4.edu
LAKE, Lyndon, J ... 315-267-2573 328 A
lakelj@potsdam.edu
LAKE, Michael, P ... 850-644-2478 110 A
mlake@admin.fsu.edu
LAKE, Patti ... 406-683-7031 271 H
patricia.lake@umwestern.edu
LAKE, Rebecca ... 847-925-6633 139 B
rlake@harpercollege.edu
LAKE, Rebecca ... 361-570-4835 465 D
laker@uhv.edu
LAKE, Stephanie, S ... 919-866-5927 347 D
sslake@waketech.edu
LAKE, Todd ... 615-460-6628 430 D
todd.lake@belmont.edu
LAKE-KING, Shirley, L .. 340-693-1400 529 C
sking@uvi.edu
LAKEN, Michael, J ... 630-515-6148 145 I
mlaken@midwestern.edu
LAKER, Craig ... 260-203-2914 164 E
lakerc@trine.edu
LAKETA, Dave ... 815-740-3464 154 G
dlaketa@stfrancis.edu
LAKEY, David, L ... 903-877-8894 469 A
david.lakey@uthct.edu
LAKHANI, Vikash ... 661-654-2161.. 31 B
vlakhani@csub.edu
LAKHAVANI, F. Meena . 716-851-1977 307 I
lakhavani@ecc.edu
LAKHAVANI, Kumar ... 336-322-2215 345 D
kumar.lakhavani@piedmontcc.edu
LAKHLANI, Himesh ... 713-425-3100 446 C
hlakhlani@chcp.edu
LAKIS, James ... 570-321-4141 400 G
lakis@lycoming.edu
LAKOSIL, Jennifer ... 520-515-8750.. 11 R
lakosilj@cochise.edu
LAKSHMINARAYANAN,
Sambhavi ... 718-270-5122 303 C
slakshminarayanan@mec.cuny.edu
LALA, Andrea ... 518-608-8153 308 A
alala@excelsior.edu
LALANDE, Emmanuel ... 314-340-5112 260 H
lalandee@hssu.edu
LALANNE, Bob ... 510-643-7384.. 68 G
vcre@berkeley.edu
LALCHANDANI, Atam ... 775-831-1314 280 C
kyoung@sierranevada.edu
LALIBERTE, Michael, R . 607-746-4090 329 B
lalibemr@delhi.edu
LALJIANI, Karen ... 972-860-5295 447 H
laljiani@dcccd.edu
LALLY, Jay ... 321-674-8225.. 99 K
jlally@fit.edu
LALLY, Kim, B ... 937-229-3902 372 A
klally1@udayton.edu
LALLY, Mary ... 617-573-8430 224 I
mlally@suffolk.edu
LALLY, Shiela ... 617-236-4422 215 B
slally@fisher.edu
LALLY-GREEN, Maureen 412-396-6280 394 D
lallygreen@duq.edu
LALOVIC-HAND, Mira ... 856-256-4146 289 H
lalovic-hand@rowan.edu
LALUZERNE, Joseph ... 651-638-6879 240 J
j-laluzerne@bethel.edu
LALUZERNE,
Shannon, S ... 920-923-7661 508 B
slaluzerne@marianuniversity.edu
LAM, Edward ... 888-488-4968.. 46 J
edlam@itu.edu
LAM, Felix ... 212-650-8173 301 F
flam@ccny.cuny.edu
LAM, Hazzan Nathan ... 310-824-1586.. 24 B
hlam@ajrca.edu
LAM, Kenneth ... 212-217-4126 308 B
kenneth_lam@fitnyc.edu
LAM, Simon, Y ... 415-338-2541.. 34 C
slam@sfsu.edu
LAM YUEN, Peteru, K ... 684-699-9155 519 F
p.lamyuen@amsamoa.edu
LAMADRID, Edward ... 773-477-4822.. 55 B
elamadrid@pacificcollege.edu
LAMADRID, Lucas ... 310-377-5501.. 51 B
llamadrid@marymountcalifornia.edu
LAMAGNA, Dan ... 570-961-1579 399 A
lamagnad@lackawanna.edu
LAMANNA, John ... 239-280-1595.. 95 C
john.lamanna@avemaria.edu
LAMANNA, Paul, A ... 716-851-1469 307 I
lamanna@ecc.edu
LAMANNA, Richard ... 718-289-5355 301 D
richard.lamanna@bcc.cuny.edu
LAMANQUE, Andrew ... 650-949-7179.. 43 F
lamanqueandrew@foothill.edu
LAMAR, Kimberly ... 630-353-8711 134 K
klamar@chamberlain.edu
LAMAR, Melissa ... 860-773-1407.. 86 G
mlamar@txcc.commnet.edu
LAMAR, Sharmaine ... 610-690-5675 410 I
slamar1@swarthmore.edu
LAMARAND, Donita, M . 757-446-6009 480 C
lamaradm@evms.edu
LAMARCH, Jessica ... 906-217-4086 228 A
jessica.lamarch@baycollege.edu
LAMARCHE, Gilles ... 770-426-2674 122 F
gilles.lamarche@life.edu
LAMARCHE, Paul ... 609-258-4999 288 F
lamarche@princeton.edu
LAMARSH, Karen ... 678-466-5115 117 I
karenlamarsh@clayton.edu
LAMAS, Frank ... 559-278-2541.. 32 A
flamas@csufresno.edu
LAMASCUS, Scott ... 405-425-5469 377 B
scott.lamascus@oc.edu
LAMB, Bill ... 319-398-5509 171 F
blamb@kirkwood.edu
LAMB, Colin ... 620-276-9595 177 G
colin.lamb@gcccks.edu
LAMB, Craig ... 585-345-6969 309 C
crlamb@genesee.edu
LAMB, Craig ... 704-216-3500 346 C
craig.lamb@rccc.edu
LAMB, Curtis, S ... 864-488-8354 422 B
clamb@limestone.edu
LAMB, David ... 716-829-7652 307 B
kavinokytheater@dyc.edu
LAMB, David ... 215-368-5000 389 H
dlamb@biblical.edu
LAMB, Duane ... 205-348-8092.... 8 A
dlamb@fa.ua.edu
LAMB, Ernest ... 218-477-2764 246 B
ernest.lamb@mnstate.edu
LAMB, Jason ... 540-261-8509 485 G
jason.lamb@svu.edu
LAMB, Jeffrey ... 510-436-2411.. 56 I
jlamb@peralta.edu
LAMB, Jennifer ... 276-326-4397 478 H
jlamb@bluefield.edu
LAMB, Jon ... 734-462-4400 236 H
jlamb@schoolcraft.edu
LAMB, Keith ... 815-825-9398 142 F
keith.lamb@kishwaukeecollege.edu
LAMB, Keith ... 940-397-4291 453 C
keith.lamb@mwsu.edu
LAMB, Ken ... 513-861-6400 371 A
ken.lamb@myunion.edu
LAMB, Kevin, D ... 859-238-5367 184 C
kevin.lamb@centre.edu
LAMB, Kyle ... 731-989-6020 432 C
klamb@fhu.edu
LAMB, Linda ... 315-866-0300 310 A
lamblc@herkimer.edu
LAMB, Margaret ... 619-388-6957.. 60 B
mlamb@sdccd.edu
LAMB, Mark ... 618-664-6801 139 A
mark.lamb@greenville.edu
LAMB, Mary ... 707-468-3071.. 51 E
mlamb@mendocino.edu
LAMB, Marybeth ... 508-531-1353 217 D
marybeth.lamb@bridgew.edu
LAMB, Melissa ... 912-427-5840 117 J
mlamb@coastalpines.edu
LAMB, Michael ... 316-978-3804 182 F
mike.lamb@wichita.edu
LAMB, Rosemary ... 662-246-6256 254 C
rlamb@msdelta.edu
LAMB, Will ... 781-239-5237 211 A
wlamb@babson.edu
LAMB, Will ... 415-749-4532.. 60 G
wlamb@sfai.edu
LAMB, William, B ... 914-633-2558 311 B
wlamb@iona.edu
LAMBA, Sandy ... 707-864-7000.. 64 E
sandy.lamba@solano.edu
LAMBDIN, Brandon ... 423-746-5337 439 A
bslambdin@tnwewsleyan.edu
LAMBE, Joan ... 212-772-5462 302 E
joan.lambe@hunter.cuny.edu
LAMBERT, Angela ... 304-327-4161 503 O
alambert@bluefieldstate.edu
LAMBERT, Angela ... 304-327-4480 503 O
alambert@bluefieldstate.edu
LAMBERT, Anne ... 713-525-2160 466 J
lambera@stthom.edu
LAMBERT, Barry ... 254-968-9104 459 A
blambert@tarleton.edu
LAMBERT, Bill ... 909-274-4215.. 52 I
wlambert@mtsac.edu
LAMBERT, Cindy ... 630-829-6688 133 I
clambert@ben.edu
LAMBERT, David ... 740-377-2520 370 L
LAMBERT, Dewayne ... 985-732-6640 192 K
LAMBERT, Edward ... 617-287-5300 216 I
edward.lambert@umb.edu
LAMBERT, Elizabeth ... 315-279-5412 312 D
elambertt@keuka.edu
LAMBERT, Ginger ... 281-998-6183 455 K
ginger.lambert@sjcd.edu
LAMBERT,
Huntington, D ... 617-495-1000 215 G
lambert@fas.harvard.edu
LAMBERT, James ... 802-776-5290 474 H
james.lambert@csj.edu
LAMBERT, James ... 419-372-9970 357 F
jlamber@bgsu.edu
LAMBERT, Jason ... 828-339-4218 346 H
j_lambert@southwesterncc.edu
LAMBERT, Jay ... 361-570-4290 465 D
lambertj1@uhv.edu
LAMBERT, Kim, D ... 315-792-3341 332 H
klambert@utica.edu
LAMBERT, III, Lake ... 812-866-7056 158 C
lambert@hanover.edu
LAMBERT, Lee, D ... 520-206-4747.. 15 L
llambert@pima.edu
LAMBERT, Leo, M ... 336-278-7900 337 G
lambert@elon.edu
LAMBERT, Lori, A ... 513-745-3203 374 D
lambert@xavier.edu
LAMBERT, Mark, A ... 540-985-9031 482 A
malambert@jchs.edu
LAMBERT, Martha ... 617-427-0060 221 A
mlambert@rcc.mass.edu
LAMBERT, Matthew, T ... 757-221-1001 479 I
mtlambert@wm.edu
LAMBERT, Patrick ... 845-398-4396 323 G
plambert@stac.edu
LAMBERT, Rebecca ... 479-524-7493.. 20 B
blambert@jbu.edu
LAMBERT, Steven ... 732-987-2745 286 D
slambert@georgian.edu
LAMBERT, Tamatha ... 229-391-4993 114 G
tlambert@abac.edu
LAMBERT, Toni ... 434-949-1017 489 E
toni.lambert@southside.edu
LAMBERT-GIBSON,
Micheline ... 903-730-4890 451 D
mlambert@jarvis.edu
LAMBERT-THOMAS,
Kim ... 708-235-7421 138 H
kthomas13@govst.edu
LAMBERTH, John ... 817-760-5831 450 B
jlamberth@hillcollege.edu
LAMBERTON, Ryan ... 925-631-4015.. 59 C
rml4@stmarys-ca.edu
LAMBERTSON,
Nathaniel ... 989-775-4123 236 E
nlambertson@sagchip.edu
LAMBETH, Gregory ... 208-885-6716 132 I
lambeth@uidaho.edu
LAMBLA, Kenneth, A ... 704-687-0090 351 C
kalambla@uncc.edu
LAMBORN, John, E ... 765-361-6327 166 B
lambornj@wabash.edu
LAMBOY, Camille ... 787-743-7979 526 A
calamboy@suagm.edu
LAMBOY, Maritza ... 787-834-9595 526 E
mlamboy@uaa.edu
LAMBRAKIS, Christine .. 602-286-8227.. 13 G
christine.lambrakis@gwmail.maricopa.edu
LAMBRECHT, Anne, K ... 989-463-7225 226 H
lambrechtak@alma.edu
LAMBRECHT, Jessica ... 920-565-1043 507 K
lambrechtjn@lakeland.edu
LAMBRECHT, John ... 708-456-0300 153 E
johnlambrecht@triton.edu
LAMBRECHTSEN, Karen . 916-577-2200.. 75 B
klambrechtsen@jessup.edu
LAMBRIGHT, Jonathan .. 912-358-3267 125 C
lambrij@savannahstate.edu
LAMBSON, Leah ... 252-398-6259 336 K
lambsl@chowan.edu
LAMELZA, George ... 417-447-2664 264 K
lamelzag@otc.edu
LAMENDOLA, Nicholas . 585-389-2072 316 D
nlamend7@naz.edu
LAMERS, Chet ... 920-498-5723 514 G
chet.lamers@nwtc.edu
LAMERSON, Samuel ... 954-771-0376 102 W
slamerson@knoxseminary.edu
LAMICA, Victoria ... 925-485-5287.. 36 C
vlamica@clpccd.cc.ca.us
LAMIMAN, Lynne, M ... 972-708-7536 449 I
LAMIQUIZ, Jason ... 509-453-0374 497 A
jason.lamiquiz@perrytech.edu
LAMKIN, Fletcher ... 304-424-8200 505 C
president@wvup.edu

LAMM, Deborah, L .... 252-823-5166 343 A
lammd@edgecombe.edu
LAMM, Edward .... 920-403-3007 509 J
edward.lamm@snc.edu
LAMM, Gary .... 254-295-4545 466 A
glamm@umhb.edu
LAMMERS, Amanda .... 770-534-6108 116 F
alammers@brenau.edu
LAMMERS, Kimberly ...... 419-289-5306 356 L
klammers@ashland.edu
LAMMONS, Anthony ..... 951-343-4217.. 28 G
alammons@calbaptist.edu
LAMONACA, Stephanie . 415-451-2824.. 60 I
slamonaca@sfts.edu
LAMONTAGNE, Ramona 815-836-5291 143 E
lamontra@lewisu.edu
LAMONTAGNE, Susan ... 413-572-5425 218 F
slamontagne@westfield.ma.edu
LAMORA, Sharley .... 503-343-2715 384 C
sharley.lamora@mtangel.edu
LAMORTE, Debra, A ...... 212-998-6411 318 D
debra.lamorte@nyu.edu
LAMOTHE, Stan .... 641-472-1194 171 J
hrdirector@mum.edu
LAMOTT, Eric, E .... 651-641-8729 241 L
lamott@csp.edu
LAMOUREUX, Wayne .... 617-243-2291 216 C
wlamoureux@lasell.edu
LAMPARSKI, Mary Jo ... 312-662-4031 133 A
mlamparski@adler.edu
LAMPE, Gregory, P .... 608-263-1794 512 D
greg.lampe@uwc.edu
LAMPE, Lawrence, P ..... 513-556-2201 371 E
lampelp@ucmail.uc.edu
LAMPE, Paul .... 636-584-6581 259 L
paul.lampe@eastcentral.edu
LAMPHERE, Susan, M .. 330-325-6398 366 F
slamphere@neomed.edu
LAMPING, Patrick .... 859-442-4175 185 I
patrick.lamping@kctcs.edu
LAMPKIN, Alison .... 706-368-7772 119 G
alampkin@highlands.edu
LAMPKIN, Patricia, M ... 434-924-7984 486 H
pml@virginia.edu
LAMPKIN-WILLIAMS,
Ann .... 313-593-5321 238 A
lampkin@umich.edu
LAMPLEY, Katie .... 781-891-2243 212 A
klampley@bentley.edu
LAMPO, Jane .... 816-654-7282 261 D
jlampo@kcumb.edu
LAMPSHIRE, Cassie ...... 617-603-6900 222 F
cassie.lampshire@necb.edu
LAMPSON, Dawayne ..... 715-682-1399 509 D
dlampson@northland.edu
LAMSMA, Matt .... 509-313-4100 495 A
lamsma@gonzaga.edu
LAMSON, Patty .... 765-983-1424 157 I
pattyo@earlham.edu
LAMURAGLIA, Rose ...... 619-388-3488.. 60 C
rlamurag@sdccd.edu
LAMUTH, Jim .... 435-722-6900 472 L
LAMY, Melissa .... 425-739-8251 495 F
melissa.lamy@lwtech.edu
LAMY, Patrick, J .... 973-748-9000 284 A
patrick_lamy@bloomfield.edu
LAN, Stan .... 206-378-5094 498 B
lans@spu.edu
LANA, Peter .... 585-389-2344 316 D
plana0@naz.edu
LANAGAN, Keni .... 865-981-8308 433 F
keni.lanagan@maryvillecollege.edu
LANAHAN, Richard .... 570-208-6069 398 D
richardlanahan@kings.edu
LANCASTER, Adrianna ... 580-559-5204 375 I
alancaster@ecok.edu
LANCASTER, Adrianna ... 580-559-5368 375 I
alancaster@ecok.edu
LANCASTER, Amy, E ...... 864-597-4026 426 I
lancasterae@wofford.edu
LANCASTER, Andrea ...... 425-235-2352 497 E
alancaster@rtc.edu
LANCASTER, Beth .... 864-596-9704 420 F
beth.lancaster@converse.edu
LANCASTER, Brad .... 717-337-6377 396 A
blancast@gettysburg.edu
LANCASTER, David .... 304-424-8346 505 C
david.lancaster@wvup.edu
LANCASTER, Dennis ...... 417-255-7272 263 I
dennislancaster@missouristate.edu
LANCASTER, James .... 626-852-6403.. 37 G
jlancaster@citruscollege.edu
LANCASTER, Jennifer ..... 718-489-5323 322 D
jlancaster@sfc.edu
LANCASTER, Loren .... 406-874-6171 271 D
lancastral@milescc.edu
LANCASTER, Mark, A .... 800-287-8822 156 D
lancama@bethanyseminary.edu

LANCASTER, Robin .... 501-882-4547.. 17 M
rglancaster@asub.edu
LANCE, Ann, H .... 507-284-2915 241 F
lance.ann@mayo.edu
LAND, Christopher .... 508-289-2900 226 D
cland@whoi.edu
LAND, Mark, D .... 864-656-4233 419 F
mdland@clemson.edu
LAND, Matt .... 260-665-4143 164 E
landm@trine.edu
LAND, Richard, D .... 704-847-5600 349 E
cwoodside@ses.edu
LAND, Roderic .... 801-957-4228 474 B
roderic.land@slcc.edu
LAND, Sabrina .... 773-821-4976 135 F
sland20@csu.edu
LAND, Tiffany .... 912-344-2689 115 D
tiffany.land@armstrong.edu
LANDAETA,
Maria Carolina .... 305-629-2929 107 D
mlandaeta@sanignaciocollege.edu
LANDAU, Joshua .... 717-815-6632 415 G
jlandau@ycp.edu
LANDAU, Yehuda, L ..... 732-942-1811 293 A
LANDEK, Michael .... 312-413-1227 153 H
mlandek@uic.edu
LANDEN, Jenny .... 505-428-1837 296 B
jenny.landen@sfcc.edu
LANDEN, Marcia .... 601-266-4119 256 E
marcia.landen@usm.edu
LANDEN, Robyn .... 307-268-2362 516 H
rlanden@caspercollege.edu
LANDENBERGER,
Rebecca .... 906-217-4266 228 A
becky.landenberger@baycollege.edu
LANDENBURGER,
Marguerite .... 540-665-4618 485 C
mlandenb@su.edu
LANDER, Laura .... 903-927-3300 471 B
llander@wileyc.edu
LANDER, Maria .... 704-290-5267 346 F
mlander@spcc.edu
LANDER, Sharon .... 615-550-3166 441 C
sharon@williamsoncc.edu
LANDERS, Joanne .... 423-746-5279 439 A
jlanders@tnwesleyan.edu
LANDERS, Mary, G .... 336-334-2014 351 D
mglander@uncg.edu
LANDERS, Richard .... 212-280-1373 332 C
rlanders@uts.columbia.edu
LANDERS, Thomas, L ... 405-325-2621 380 L
landers@ou.edu
LANDERS, Timothy, M .. 585-343-0055 309 C
tmlanders@genesee.edu
LANDES, Marie, C .... 540-665-4516 485 C
mlandes@su.edu
LANDES, Mark .... 620-327-8219 178 B
markl@hesston.edu
LANDEY, Sena .... 765-983-1468 157 I
landse@earlham.edu
LANDGAARD, Jodi .... 507-372-3403 246 C
jodi.landgaard@mnwest.edu
LANDGRAF, Kurt, M ..... 410-778-7201 210 A
LANDGRAF, Tanya .... 712-749-2212 167 C
landgraft@bvu.edu
LANDGREBE, Jessica ..... 217-424-3965 145 J
jlandgrebe@millikin.edu
LANDGREN, Peter, E ..... 513-556-2588 371 E
provost@uc.edu
LANDHERR, Ashlyn .... 517-607-2625 231 C
alandherr@hillsdale.edu
LANDING, Haydee .... 787-725-8120 522 M
hlandiing0030@eap.edu
LANDIS, David .... 620-278-4235 181 G
dlandis@sterling.edu
LANDIS, Jean, W .... 215-951-1020 398 F
landis@lasalle.edu
LANDIS, SCC,
Marie Cecelia .... 973-957-0188 283 C
criss@acs350.org
LANDIS, Sarah .... 540-828-5334 478 J
slandis@bridgewater.edu
LANDPHAIR, Juliette ..... 540-654-1062 486 D
jlandpha@umw.edu
LANDRAU-ESPINOSA,
Barbara .... 787-993-8856 527 G
barbara.landrau@upr.edu
LANDREBE, Robert, S ... 859-858-2192 183 C
LANDREMAN, Lisa .... 401-254-3032 417 C
llandreman@rwu.edu
LANDRETH, Paige .... 405-682-7503 377 C
plandreth@occc.edu
LANDRITH, James .... 864-231-2000 418 E
wlandrith@andersonuniversity.edu
LANDRUM, Beverly, J ... 843-349-2399 420 A
blandrum@coastal.edu
LANDRUM, Kay .... 817-598-6499 470 J
klandrum@wc.edu

LANDRUM, Kay .... 616-222-1402 229 B
kay.landrum@cornerstone.edu
LANDRUM, Treina .... 318-342-1004 198 A
landrum@ulm.edu
LANDRUM, Zalika .... 773-602-5116 135 L
zlandrum@ccc.edu
LANDRUM-SIMS,
Alonzetta .... 334-347-2623.... 1 J
alandrum-sims@escc.edu
LANDRY, Abbie .... 318-357-4403 197 D
landry@nsula.edu
LANDRY, Bill .... 843-574-6745 424 G
bill.landry@tridenttech.edu
LANDRY, Brett .... 972-721-4067 464 E
rlandry@udallas.edu
LANDRY, David, M .... 504-398-2109 196 E
dlandry@uhcno.edu
LANDRY, Debbie .... 918-444-3700 376 G
landry@nsuok.edu
LANDRY, Debborah .... 918-444-2060 376 G
landryd@nsuok.edu
LANDRY, Fred .... 318-869-5136 191 C
flandry@centenary.edu
LANDRY, Karen .... 425-267-0153 494 F
klandry@everettcc.edu
LANDRY, Lisa, C .... 337-482-5430 197 F
ldlandry@louisiana.edu
LANDRY, Patrick .... 337-482-6402 197 F
pml@louisiana.edu
LANDRY, Sandra .... 704-878-3325 344 H
slandry@mitchellcc.edu
LANDRY, Shawntel, D ... 800-280-0307 155 H
shawntel.landry@ace.edu
LANDRY, Stephen .... 973-275-2299 291 F
stephen.landry@shu.edu
LANDSAW, Christy .... 918-444-2192 376 G
landsaw@nsuok.edu
LANDSTROM, Corey ...... 563-387-1020 171 I
clandstrom@luther.edu
LANDWER, Allan, J .... 325-670-2222 450 A
alandwer@hsutx.edu
LANDWERMEYER,
Elizabeth .... 817-515-3049 458 B
elizabeth.landwermeyer@tccd.edu
LANE, Austin, A .... 713-313-1179 461 E
austin.lane@tsu.edu
LANE, Barbara .... 573-329-5160 261 H
laneb@lincolnu.edu
LANE, Bradley .... 206-934-5481 497 I
bradley.lane@seattlecolleges.edu
LANE, Brian .... 904-256-7326 102 B
wlane@ju.edu
LANE, Charles, E .... 352-392-9122 110 D
charlielane@ufl.edu
LANE, Dean .... 202-462-2101.. 92 D
dlane@iwp.edu
LANE, Deborah .... 405-744-6384 377 F
debbie.lane@okstate.edu
LANE, Deborah .... 865-573-4517 432 H
dlane@johnsonu.edu
LANE, Diane, L .... 217-362-6416 145 J
dlane@millikin.edu
LANE, Edwin, H .... 816-415-7587 270 C
lanee@william.jewell.edu
LANE, Greg .... 619-574-6909.. 55 B
glane@pacificcollege.edu
LANE, Jeremy .... 405-466-3428 375 L
jlane@langston.edu
LANE, Jill, L .... 678-466-4100 117 I
jilllane@clayton.edu
LANE, John .... 713-221-8292 465 C
lanej@uhd.edu
LANE, Jolene, A .... 330-972-6237 371 C
jolenealane@uakron.edu
LANE, Jon .... 940-397-4241 453 C
jon.lane@mwsu.edu
LANE, Joseph .... 304-829-7311 501 F
jlane@bethanywv.edu
LANE, Kim .... 909-607-3778.. 37 K
kiml@cuc.claremont.edu
LANE, Kimberly, A .... 864-833-8379 423 D
kalane@presby.edu
LANE, Kristi .... 218-683-8631 246 F
kristi.lane@northlandcollege.edu
LANE, Laura .... 248-476-1122 233 F
llane@mispp.edu
LANE, Marguerite .... 516-323-4014 315 J
mlane@molloy.edu
LANE, Mark .... 808-455-0213 130 G
marklane@hawaii.edu
LANE, Mark .... 214-648-3404 469 E
mark.lane@utsouthwestern.edu
LANE, Michael .... 516-686-7723 317 G
mlane@nyit.edu
LANE, Mike .... 816-271-4476 264 B
lane@missouriwestern.edu
LANE, Natalie .... 307-382-1673 517 C
nlane@westernwyoming.edu

LANE, Nathan .... 561-803-2754 104 I
nathan_lane@pba.edu
LANE, Nicole .... 559-278-2364.. 32 A
nlane@csufresno.edu
LANE, Phillip .... 618-985-2828 141 D
philliplane@jalc.edu
LANE, Robert, J .... 515-961-1417 173 E
bob.lane@simpson.edu
LANE, Ron .... 910-246-4109 346 E
laner@sandhills.edu
LANE, Scott .... 603-428-2411 281 F
slane@nec.edu
LANE, Shelese .... 404-270-5110 126 D
sjlane@spelman.edu
LANE, Stephanie .... 707-826-3132.. 34 A
sml19@humboldt.edu
LANE, Tracey, R .... 817-722-1621 451 G
tracey.lane@tku.edu
LANE-MARTIN, Tanya .... 585-345-6800 309 C
tmlanemartin@genesee.edu
LANEAR, John .... 928-541-7777.. 54 B
jlanear@ncu.edu
LANESSKOG, Stig .... 909-621-8026.. 37 K
stig_lanesskog@cuc.claremont.edu
LANEY, Brenda .... 816-501-4122 265 I
brenda.laney@rockhurst.edu
LANEY, Candy .... 406-874-6165 271 D
laneyc@milescc.edu
LANEY, Mary, A .... 386-312-4069 106 M
maryannelaney@sjrstate.edu
LANFEAR, Jeffery .... 773-325-8308 137 C
jlanfear@depaul.edu
LANG, Ashley .... 319-352-8486 174 C
ashley.lang@wartburg.edu
LANG, Christine .... 843-574-6162 424 G
chris.lang@tridenttech.edu
LANG, Christopher .... 304-865-6107 502 C
christopher.lang@ovu.edu
LANG, Cyndi .... 574-520-4490 160 F
clang@iusb.edu
LANG, JR., George, E ... 410-293-1568 519 E
glang@usna.edu
LANG, Heather .... 971-722-4532 386 C
heather.lang@pcc.edu
LANG, Jennifer, R .... 718-780-0679 300 A
jennifer.lang@brooklaw.edu
LANG, Katherine .... 580-559-5471 375 I
klang@ecok.edu
LANG, Kathy, J .... 414-288-1782 508 C
kathy.lang@marquette.edu
LANG, Krystal, P .... 314-516-6940 268 E
langk@umsl.edu
LANG, Mandy .... 715-422-5446 514 B
mandy.lang@mstc.edu
LANG, Marjorie .... 313-993-1802 237 F
langma@udmercy.edu
LANG, Melissa, W .... 757-446-6054 480 C
langmw@evms.edu
LANG, Michelle .... 503-517-1190 388 A
mlang@warnerpacific.edu
LANG, Milton .... 530-752-8787.. 68 H
lmlang@ucdavis.edu
LANG, Mindy .... 212-353-4212 306 A
lang@cooper.edu
LANG, Natasha .... 925-424-1634.. 36 D
nlang@laspositascollege.edu
LANG, Sandra .... 618-664-2800 139 A
sandy.lang@greenville.edu
LANG, Stephen, W .... 432-837-8061 462 G
slang@sulross.edu
LANG, Stuart .... 612-374-5800 242 C
slang@dunwoody.edu
LANGAN, Nicole .... 570-945-8274 398 C
nicole.langan@keystone.edu
LANGAN, Rikki .... 217-479-7030 144 I
rikki.langan@mac.edu
LANGDON, Dawn .... 585-785-1277 308 D
dawn.langdon@flcc.edu
LANGDON, Deb .... 740-389-4636 365 B
langdond@mtc.edu
LANGDON, Heather, H .. 828-262-2093 349 H
langdonhh@appstate.edu
LANGDON, Rita .... 516-299-2334 313 D
rita.langdon@liu.edu
LANGE, Amy .... 785-243-1435 176 I
alange@cloud.edu
LANGE, Andrea, G .... 410-778-7776 210 A
alange2@washcoll.edu
LANGE, Douglas .... 843-661-8300 421 F
douglas.lange@fdtc.edu
LANGE, Janet .... 309-677-2523 134 G
lange@bradley.edu
LANGE, Janet .... 309-677-2374 134 G
lange@fsmail.bradley.edu
LANGE, Jean .... 203-582-8444.. 88 A
jean.lange@quinnipiac.edu
LANGE, Karen, M .... 651-962-6120 251 D
kmlange@stthomas.edu

LANGE, Robert, J 757-594-7015 479 H
robert.lange@cnu.edu
LANGE, Steven 320-629-5155 246 H
langes@pine.edu
LANGE, Tom, J 715-831-7285 513 E
tlange8@cvtc.edu
LANGE, Tyana 570-484-2087 406 E
tsl400@lockhaven.edu
LANGE, Tyler 206-616-5631 499 D
langet2@uw.edu
LANGEMAK, Elizabeth 215-951-1145 398 F
langemak@lasalle.edu
LANGEN, Jill 810-766-4374 227 E
jill.langen@baker.edu
LANGENDORGER,
Stephen, J 419-372-7234 357 F
slangen@bgsu.edu
LANGER, Manfred 740-377-2520 370 L
manfred.langer@tsbc.edu
LANGER, Patricia, M 651-696-6562 243 B
planger@macalester.edu
LANGER, Peter 617-287-5611 216 I
peter.langer@umb.edu
LANGERBEIN, Helmut 870-235-4200.. 21 F
helmetlangerbein@saumag.edu
LANGERUD, Steve 641-472-1110 171 J
slangerud@mum.edu
LANGEVIN, Duetta 909-274-4230.. 52 I
dlangevin@mtsac.edu
LANGEVIN, John 207-602-2549 202 A
jlangevin@une.edu
LANGFORD, Allison 417-328-2093 267 A
alangford@sbuniv.edu
LANGFORD, David 201-692-9867 286 B
david_langford@fdu.edu
LANGFORD, Debra 304-876-5216 504 D
dlangfor@shepherd.edu
LANGFORD, Gabriel, J 863-680-4316 100 D
glangford@flsouthern.edu
LANGFORD, Joel, C 770-720-5585 124 H
jcl@reinhardt.edu
LANGFORD, Pamela 909-537-7454.. 33 D
plangfor@csusb.edu
LANGFORD, Russ 417-862-9533 260 D
rlangford@globaluniversity.edu
LANGHAM, Gay 601-643-8307 252 G
gay.langham@colin.edu
LANGHAM, Julie 706-595-0166 116 A
jlangham@augustatech.edu
LANGHAM, Lynda 936-468-2503 458 A
llangham@sfasu.edu
LANGHAM, Pam 850-474-3419 111 D
plangham@uwf.edu
LANGHAMMER, Paul 401-874-9500 417 E
langhammer@uri.edu
LANGHAUSER, Derek 207-629-4000 199 J
dlanghauser@mccs.me.edu
LANGHOUT, Regina 831-459-2769.. 70 C
langhout@ucsc.edu
LANGKILDE, Jared 480-461-7396.. 13 I
jared.langkilde@mesacc.edu
LANGLAND, Meg 573-592-5381 270 B
meg.langland@westminster-mo.edu
LANGLEY, Amy 256-840-4185.... 3 F
alangley@snead.edu
LANGLEY, Goldie 614-947-6509 362 A
goldie.langley@franklin.edu
LANGLEY, Jesse 252-985-5177 348 A
jlangley@ncwc.edu
LANGLEY, Maia 502-418-5638 186 C
maia.langley@kctcs.edu
LANGLEY, Pamela 603-271-6484 280 N
plangley@ccsnh.edu
LANGLEY-TURNBAUGH,
Samantha 859-572-7528 188 E
langleys1@nku.edu
LANGLOIS, OP, John 202-495-3831.. 92 F
president@dhs.edu
LANGLOIS, Mary Ann 716-888-2103 300 G
langloim@canisius.edu
LANGOLF, Judi 810-762-9585 232 C
jlangolf@kettering.edu
LANGOLF, Judi 810-766-8756 227 F
jlango01@baker.edu
LANGONI, Kerri 505-566-3515 296 A
langonik@sanjuancollege.edu
LANGREHR, Andrew 314-539-5364 266 E
andrewlangrehr@stlcc.edu
LANGRELL, Ron 253-680-7103 492 F
rlangrell@bates.ctc.edu
LANGRIDGE, Nick 540-568-3197 481 I
langrinl@jmu.edu
LANGSETH, Kay 319-895-4242 167 G
klangseth@cornellcollege.edu
LANGSTON, Aaron 903-875-7328 453 J
aaron.langston@navarrocollege.edu
LANGSTON, II, Bill, C 863-680-4209 100 D
blangston@flsouthern.edu
LANGSTON, Carol 903-334-6628 460 D
carol.langston@tamut.edu
LANGSTON, Emily 410-972-3303 206 F
emily.langston@sjc.edu
LANGSTON, Ginna, V 918-631-2641 381 C
ruth-langston@utulsa.edu
LANGSTON, Katie 651-255-6166 250 D
klangston@unitedseminary.edu
LANGSTON, Louanne 601-857-3749 253 B
louanne.langston@hindscc.edu
LANGSTRAAT, Jim 971-722-4200 386 C
jim.langstraat@pcc.edu
LANGSTRAAT, Nate 360-383-3350 500 F
nlangstraat@whatcom.ctc.edu
LANGUTH, Christine 860-215-9260.. 86 F
clanguth@trcc.commnet.edu
LANHAM, Chuck 360-650-3917 500 E
chuck.lanham@wwu.edu
LANHAM, Heather 937-778-7803 361 E
hlanham@edisonohio.edu
LANHAM, Jeff 740-245-7485 372 E
jlanham@rio.edu
LANHAM, Terri 270-686-4548 186 F
terri.lanham@kctcs.edu
LANIER, Anna 316-978-3001 182 F
anna.weyers@wichita.edu
LANIER, Annette 503-768-7685 383 G
annette@lclark.edu
LANIER, Carolyn, D 330-325-6259 366 F
clanier@neomed.edu
LANIER, Charity 281-201-3800.. 93 B
LANIER, Charity 281-949-1800.. 93 B
LANIER, Ginger 540-261-8469 485 G
ginger.lanier@svu.edu
LANIER, Greg 850-474-3160 111 D
glanier@uwf.edu
LANIER, John 706-385-1065 124 F
john.lanier@point.edu
LANIER, Lisa 912-871-1606 123 J
llanier@ogeecheetech.edu
LANIER, Mandy 334-556-2235.... 2 B
mlanier@wallace.edu
LANIER, Mark 910-962-3030 352 A
lanierm@uncw.edu
LANIER, Percy 205-929-1663.... 6 D
plani@mail.miles.edu
LANIER, Stephen, M 313-577-5600 239 C
stephen.lanier@wayne.edu
LANIER, Walter 414-297-7710 514 C
lanierw@matc.edu
LANIGAN, John 440-826-3566 357 B
jlanigan@bw.edu
LANINGA, Brad 708-239-4804 153 B
brad.laninga@trnty.edu
LANK, Kristy 207-985-7976 199 G
kristy@landingschool.edu
LANKES, Susan 716-652-8900 300 L
slankes@buffalodiocese.org
LANKFORD, Lisa 828-398-7540 340 M
lisahlankford@abtech.edu
LANN, Jennifer 802-387-6764 475 C
jlann@landmark.edu
LANNERT, Mary 406-447-6944 271 I
mary.lannert@umhelena.edu
LANNING, Brek 828-565-4027 343 G
bwlanning@haywood.edu
LANNING, Crystal 715-425-3246 511 E
crystal.lanning@uwrf.edu
LANNING, Gale 507-453-1443 245 G
glanning@southeastmn.edu
LANNING, Paul 408-924-1120.. 34 D
paul.lanning@sjsu.edu
LANNING, Stephanie 620-227-9370 176 N
slg@dc3.edu
LANOUE, David 870-235-4004.. 21 F
davidlanoue@saumag.edu
LANOUETTE,
P. Michael 407-831-9816.. 96 I
mlanouette@citycollege.edu
LANPHER, Jim 803-754-4100 420 E
LANSING, Sean, T 414-410-4583 506 F
stlansing@stritch.edu
LANSIQUOT,
Beverley, A 340-692-4117 529 C
beverley.lansiquot@uvi.edu
LANTER, Jennifer 920-924-3163 514 D
jlanter@morainepark.edu
LANTHIER, Eric 617-243-2433 216 C
elanthier@lasell.edu
LANTING, Mark 815-825-9453 142 F
mark.lanting@kishwaukeecollege.edu
LANTIS, Glenda 541-318-3753 382 B
glantis@cocc.edu
LANTZ, David 301-387-3011 203 I
david.lantz@garrettcollege.edu
LANTZ, Dona 614-222-6171 360 B
dlantz@ccad.edu
LANTZ, Mary Jan 409-944-1281 449 F
mlantz@gc.edu
LANTZ, Susan 570-372-4415 410 H
lantzs@susqu.edu
LANTZKY-EATON,
Kristina 716-926-8854 310 B
klantzky@hilbert.edu
LANYON, Scott 612-625-2809 250 E
slanyon@umn.edu
LANZA-GALINDO,
Oscar 610-499-4087 414 F
olanzagalindo@widener.edu
LANZI, Lesley 518-736-3622 309 A
lesley.lanzi@fmcc.suny.edu
LAOUTARIS, Kathy 914-337-9300 305 F
kathy.laoutaris@concordia-ny.edu
LAP, James 718-260-5565 303 D
jlap@citytech.cuny.edu
LAPALOMBARA,
Catherine 301-546-0414 206 E
lapalocx@pgcc.edu
LAPAYOVER, Alan 215-576-0800 408 H
alapayover@rrc.edu
LAPENTA, Thomas 302-831-2171.. 90 I
lapenta@udel.edu
LAPERA, Rita 570-702-8995 398 A
rlapera@johnson.edu
LAPERLE, Kimberly 508-856-8992 217 C
kimberlymuri.laperle@umassmed.edu
LAPETINO, Kelly 708-709-3795 148 I
klapetino@prairiestate.edu
LAPHAM, Steve 301-891-4161 209 E
slapham@wau.edu
LAPIANA, William, P 212-431-2840 317 H
william.lapiana@nyls.edu
LAPIDUS, Chaim, D 410-484-7200 206 C
cdl@nirc.edu
LAPIDUS, Richard, S 978-665-3101 217 E
rlapidus@fitchburgstate.edu
LAPIER, Terrance 407-265-8383.. 96 C
LAPIER, Terry 561-381-4990.. 96 B
LAPIERRE, Jonathan 617-879-2427 226 A
jlapierre@wheelock.edu
LAPIKAS, Ken 814-724-0700 399 H
klapikas@laurel.edu
LAPIKAS, Sonya, L 724-589-2172 411 D
slapikas@thiel.edu
LAPIN, Lisa, A 650-723-2300.. 66 C
LAPINSKI, Scott 903-566-7181 468 C
slapinski@uttyler.edu
LAPLACA, Spencer 909-607-8740.. 38 C
spencer_laplaca@kgi.edu
LAPLANT, James, T 229-333-5694 127 H
jtlaplant@valdosta.edu
LAPLANTE, Brian 518-445-2381 297 K
blapl@albanylaw.edu
LAPLANTE, Kim 920-498-5487 514 G
kim.laplante@nwtc.edu
LAPLANTE, Melissa 603-342-3086 281 B
mlaplante@ccsnh.edu
LAPOINTE, Laurence 860-465-5113.. 84 K
lapointel@easternct.edu
LAPOINTE, Matthew 202-884-9135.. 93 C
lapointem@trinitydc.edu
LAPOINTE, Michael 219-980-7106 160 C
mslapoin@iun.edu
LAPOMARDO, Elaine 413-775-1804 219 F
lapomardoe@gcc.mass.edu
LAPORTA, Jennifer 570-941-6645 413 F
jennifer.laporta@scranton.edu
LAPORTE, Laura 518-736-3622 309 A
llaporte@fmcc.suny.edu
LAPORTE, Sandra 312-567-5199 140 I
laporte@iit.edu
LAPOS, Christopher 570-389-4740 405 E
clapos@bloomu.edu
LAPP, Ian 781-239-5700 211 A
ilapp@babson.edu
LAPP, Katherine, N 617-495-9877 215 G
katie_lapp@harvard.edu
LAPPIN, Julie, M 909-537-5002.. 33 D
jlappin@csusb.edu
LAPPLE, James, H 212-327-8371 321 E
james.lapple@rockefeller.edu
LAPRADE, Kimberly 602-639-7500.. 12 P
LAPRAY, Kim 208-732-6299 131 I
klapray@csi.edu
LAPREY, Amy 508-286-3522 225 G
laprey_amy@wheatoncollege.edu
LAPREZIOSA, Mark 215-572-2900 389 D
laprezim@arcadia.edu
LAPRISE, John 423-585-2336 438 D
john.laprise@ws.edu
LAPUMA, Stephanie 402-354-7000 275 P
stephanie.lapuma@methodistcollege.edu
LAQUEY, Karen 806-291-3526 470 I
laqueyk@wbu.edu
LARA, Ernest 623-935-8014.. 13 F
ernie.lara@estrellamountain.edu
LARA, Javier 210-805-3572 465 E
jdlara@uiwtx.edu
LARA, Jessika 214-379-5494 454 H
jlara@pqc.edu
LARA, Larry 714-992-7025.. 54 A
llara@fullcoll.edu
LARA,
María de Lourdes 787-850-9204 528 B
maria.lara1@upr.edu
LARA, Matthew 575-538-6001 297 H
laram@wnmu.edu
LARACUENTE, Luis 787-815-0000 527 F
luis.laracuente1@upr.edu
LARACUENTE-QUIÑONES,
Jaime 787-993-8881 527 G
jaime.laracuente1@upr.edu
LARANGE, Shannon 413-775-1410 219 F
larange@gcc.mass.edu
LARAQUE-ARENA,
Danielle, L 315-464-5540 326 B
laraqued@upstate.edu
LARCOM, Geoffrey 734-487-4401 229 K
glarcom@emich.edu
LARDIZABAL, Alana 541-552-8110 386 H
lardizaba@sou.edu
LARDNER, Emily 360-538-4009 495 B
emily.lardner@ghc.edu
LARDNER, Patrick 803-777-2036 424 I
lardnerp@mailbox.sc.edu
LAREAU, Martin 708-596-2000 151 H
mlareau@ssc.edu
LAREY, Keith, L 903-813-2431 443 F
klarey@austincollege.edu
LARGE, JR., Donald, L 334-844-4650.... 4 D
largedl@auburn.edu
LARGE, Kandice 703-284-1614 483 A
bstore@marymount.edu
LARGE, Ron 509-313-6767 495 A
large@gonzaga.edu
LARGEN, Kristin 717-334-6286 412 E
klargen@ltsg.edu
LARGEN, Kristin 717-337-6280 396 A
klargen@gettysburg.edu
LARGENT, Trudy 510-466-7252.. 56 I
tlargent@peralta.edu
LARGENT, Trudy 510-466-7252.. 56 F
tlargent@peralta.edu
LARIC, Katie 303-762-6948.. 79 G
katie.laric@denverseminary.edu
LARICK, Duane, K 919-515-2196 350 E
duane_larick@ncsu.edu
LARIOS, Jose 828-669-8012 340 I
jose.larios@montreat.edu
LARIOS, Liza 718-631-6356 303 F
llarios@qcc.cuny.edu
LARIVE, Cynthia 951-827-1129.. 69 D
provost@ucr.edu
LARK, Catherine 603-646-2442 281 C
catherine.lark@dartmouth.edu
LARKAN-SKINNER,
Kara 210-434-6711 454 D
klarkan-skinner@lake.ollusa.edu
LARKIN, Conal 203-575-8173.. 86 B
clarkin@nv.edu
LARKIN, Josh 802-828-2835 477 B
jsl11010@ccv.vsc.edu
LARKIN, SSJ,
Mary Josephine 215-248-7055 392 D
mjlarkin@chc.edu
LARKIN, Michael 406-447-4495 270 H
mlarkin@carroll.edu
LARKIN, Patti 619-482-6325.. 65 H
plarkin@swccd.edu
LARKIN, Thomas, F 413-748-3458 224 G
tlarkin@springfieldcollege.edu
LARKIN-BEENE,
Bridgett 815-280-2476 142 A
blarkin@jjc.edu
LARKINS, Mike 870-574-4516.. 21 G
mlarkins@sautech.edu
LARKINS, Tammy 870-574-4564.. 21 G
tlarkins@sautech.edu
LARMON, Natalie 661-255-1050.. 29 F
LARNER, Eve 914-606-6562 333 H
eve.larner@sunywcc.edu
LAROBINA, Michael, D 203-371-7859.. 88 C
larobinam@sacredheart.edu
LAROCCA, Sandy 402-898-1000 274 C
sandy_l@creativecenter.edu
LAROCHELLE, Josee 518-564-2130 327 E
jlaro007@plattsburgh.edu
LAROCQUE, Edward, A 260-399-7700 165 B
elarocque@sf.edu
LAROCQUE,
Monique, M 207-581-3143 201 B
mlarocque@maine.edu

LAROCQUE, Sandra .... 701-477-7862 355 H
salrocqu@tm.edu
LAROSA, John .... 352-588-8325 106 N
john.larosa@saintleo.edu
LAROSEE, Howie .... 617-879-7938 218 B
hlarosee@massart.edu
LARRABEE, Ashley .... 361-825-3020 460 A
ashley.larrabee@tamucc.edu
LARRAT, Paul .... 401-874-5011 417 E
larrat@uri.edu
LARRIVEE, Linda .... 508-929-8333 219 A
llarrivee@worcester.edu
LARRY, Latasha .... 773-291-6210 135 M
llarry4@ccc.edu
LARSCHEID, Slade .... 605-274-4316 426 K
slade.larscheid@augie.edu
LARSEN, Carl .... 423-636-7313 439 C
clarsen@tusculum.edu
LARSEN, Cheryl .... 847-866-3995 138 G
cheryl.larsen@garrett.edu
LARSEN, Curt .... 801-957-4186 474 B
curt.larsen@slcc.edu
LARSEN, Cynde .... 608-822-2642 515 A
clarsen@swtc.edu
LARSEN, Daniel .... 630-466-7900 155 C
dlarsen@waubonsee.edu
LARSEN, David .... 253-833-9111 495 C
dlarsen@greenriver.edu
LARSEN, Erik .... 909-748-8035.. 71 H
erik_larsen@redlands.edu
LARSEN, Geri .... 610-647-4400 397 I
hr@immaculata.edu
LARSEN, Jennifer .... 402-559-4837 277 H
jlarsen@unmc.edu
LARSEN, Jon-Erik .... 503-352-7221 385 I
larsenj@pacificu.edu
LARSEN, Katrina .... 715-425-4891 511 E
katrina.larsen@uwrf.edu
LARSEN, Kerstin .... 609-258-9289 288 F
klarsen@princeton.edu
LARSEN, Kevin, W .... 252-334-2009 340 B
kevin.larsen@macuniversity.edu
LARSEN, Kevin, W .... 252-334-2044 340 B
kevin.larsen@macuniversity.edu
LARSEN, Marci .... 435-283-7013 474 A
marci.larsen@snow.edu
LARSEN, Matt .... 701-231-5614 354 D
matt.larsen@ndsu.edu
LARSEN, Ron .... 406-657-2300 272 B
LARSEN, Ron .... 406-994-4371 272 A
ronl@montana.edu
LARSEN, Susan .... 575-562-2211 293 O
susan.larsen@enmu.edu
LARSEN, Whitney, M .... 540-261-8530 485 G
whitney.larsen@svu.edu
LARSON, Ann .... 502-852-6044 190 C
ann.larson@louisville.edu
LARSON, Barb .... 308-398-7359 273 G
blarson@cccneb.edu
LARSON, Barbara .... 913-469-8500 178 F
blarson@jccc.edu
LARSON, Brittany .... 262-650-4887 506 G
blarson@carrollu.edu
LARSON, Cate .... 651-631-0204 240 C
clarson@aaaom.edu
LARSON, Craig .... 763-424-0733 246 E
clarson@nhcc.edu
LARSON, Dale, C .... 214-887-5021 448 G
dlarson@dts.edu
LARSON, Dan .... 541-737-4771 385 F
dan.larson@oregonstate.edu
LARSON, Dan .... 541-737-8748 385 F
deanofstudents@oregonstate.edu
LARSON, David .... 864-231-2000 418 E
dlarson@andersonuniversity.edu
LARSON, Debra .... 618-537-6816 145 C
dlarson@mckendree.edu
LARSON, Debra .... 530-898-6101.. 31 D
dslarson@csuchico.edu
LARSON, Donna .... 503-594-3440 382 D
donnal@clackamas.edu
LARSON, Doreen .... 937-778-7801 361 E
LARSON, Gary, N .... 630-752-5990 155 F
gary.larson@wheaton.edu
LARSON, Gayle .... 651-423-8307 244 E
gayle.larson@dctc.edu
LARSON, Gloria, C .... 781-891-2101 212 A
glarson@bentley.edu
LARSON, Heidi .... 701-252-3467 355 J
hlarson@uj.edu
LARSON, Jennifer .... 701-845-7401 354 E
jennifer.larson@vcsu.edu
LARSON, Jon, H .... 732-255-0330 288 B
jlarson@ocean.edu
LARSON, Kelly .... 815-280-2218 142 A
klarson@jjc.edu
LARSON, Kristin .... 906-635-2453 232 J
klarsen1@lssu.edu
LARSON, Lawrence, E ... 401-863-1422 415 K
lawrence_larson@brown.edu
LARSON, Lesley .... 570-321-4456 400 G
larsonl@lycoming.edu
LARSON, Lisa .... 207-974-4691 199 L
llarson@emcc.edu
LARSON, Lois .... 651-793-1411 245 E
lois.larson@metrostate.edu
LARSON, Matthew .... 860-486-2616.. 88 G
matthew.larson@uconn.edu
LARSON, Melinda .... 616-395-7070 231 D
larson@hope.edu
LARSON, Paul, V .... 805-565-6286.. 74 I
plarson@westmont.edu
LARSON, Peter .... 848-445-5012 290 A
peter.larson@rutgers.edu
LARSON, Rebecca .... 630-752-5566 155 F
rebecca.a.larson@wheaton.edu
LARSON, Rick .... 952-446-4190 242 A
larsonr@crown.edu
LARSON, Rodney .... 207-941-7122 199 B
larsonr@husson.edu
LARSON, Ruth .... 315-470-4716 328 D
rlarson@esf.edu
LARSON, Sandra .... 847-578-3400 150 E
sandra.larson@rosalindfranklin.edu
LARSON, Sandy .... 229-931-2450 125 G
slarson@southgatech.edu
LARSON, Shane .... 970-945-8691.. 77 M
LARSON, Shane .... 620-441-5246 176 M
shane.larson@cowley.edu
LARSON, Steve .... 406-756-3821 271 A
slarson@fvcc.edu
LARSON, Thomas .... 309-694-5225 139 G
thomas.larson@icc.edu
LARSON, Thomas, R ..... 423-652-4765 432 I
trlarson@king.edu
LARSON, Trudy .... 775-784-7103 279 E
tlarson@unr.edu
LARSON, Vernon, C ...... 607-436-3369 325 E
vernon.larson@oneonta.edu
LARSON-COONEY, Kim . 303-797-5723.. 76 I
kim.larson-cooney@arapahoe.edu
LARSSON, E. Axel .... 973-408-3048 285 E
elarsson@drew.edu
LARTEY, Charles, R .... 330-471-8469 364 H
clartey@malone.edu
LARUE, Clint .... 405-425-5191 377 B
clint.larue@oc.edu
LARUE, Rita, E .... 215-895-1534 394 C
larue@drexel.edu
LARUE, Shanda .... 270-686-4252 183 J
shanda.larue@brescia.edu
LARUSSO,
Christopher, P .... 716-880-2377 314 F
christopher.p.larusso@medaille.edu
LARVICK, Steve .... 541-552-6594 386 H
larvick@sou.edu
LASAKOW, Paul, H .... 757-822-1452 489 H
plasakow@tcc.edu
LASALA, Kathleen .... 540-678-4381 485 C
klasala@su.edu
LASALDE-DOMINICCI,
Jose, A .... 787-250-0000 527 D
jose.lasalde@upr.edu
LASALLE, Jody .... 619-961-4359.. 67 F
jlasalle@tjsl.edu
LASANEN, Raymond, E . 906-487-2510 234 A
relasane@mtu.edu
LASCANO, Rey .... 432-552-2108 469 D
lascano_r@utpb.edu
LASCEK, Natalie .... 717-396-7833 404 R
nlascek@pcad.edu
LASCH, Chris .... 480-860-2700.. 12 N
clasch@taliesin.edu
LASCH, Jackie, D .... 407-582-3302 113 F
jlasch@valenciacollege.edu
LASECKI, Matthew .... 410-706-3950 207 H
matthew.lasecki@umaryland.edu
LASER KIGER, Amy .... 540-453-2211 487 G
kigera@brcc.edu
LASEY, Brian .... 479-968-0261.. 18 G
blasey@atu.edu
LASH, Jonathan .... 413-559-5521 215 F
president@hampshire.edu
LASH, Julie .... 317-274-2548 160 E
jlash@iupui.edu
LASHBROOK, Jeffrey, T 585-395-5028 326 D
jlashbro@brockport.edu
LASHER, Katherine, M .. 989-774-3253 228 E
lashe1km@cmich.edu
LASHER, Marie .... 603-456-2656 281 H
mlasher@northeastcatholic.edu
LASHER, Robert, W .... 603-646-3095 281 C
robert.w.lasher@dartmouth.edu
LASHLEY, Bob .... 405-425-5120 377 B
bob.lashley@oc.edu
LASHLEY, Brian, R .... 860-465-5306.. 84 K
lashleyb@easternct.edu
LASHLEY, Edwin, L .... 410-543-6222 209 B
ellashley@salisbury.edu
LASHLEY, Heather .... 212-616-7292 309 G
heather.lashley@helenefuld.edu
LASHLEY, Jeffery .... 660-263-4100 264 C
jeffl@macc.edu
LASHLEY, Kent .... 405-733-7306 379 F
klashley@rose.edu
LASHLEY, Lynn .... 205-652-3417.... 9 C
lsl@uwa.edu
LASHLEY, Marsha .... 660-831-4115 264 A
lashleym@moval.edu
LASHLEY, Sarah, E .... 859-238-5573 184 C
sarah.lashley@centre.edu
LASHURE, Faith .... 630-466-7900 155 C
flashure@waubonsee.edu
LASICH, Deb .... 303-273-3097.. 78 J
dlasich@mines.edu
LASIEWSKI, Doreen .... 401-739-5000 416 D
dlasiewski@neit.edu
LASITER, Paul, B .... 310-506-4497.. 56 D
paul.lasiter@pepperdine.edu
LASKARIS, Theodore ..... 802-860-2757 474 G
tlaskaris@champlain.edu
LASKE, Lori, L .... 719-587-7867.. 76 D
lllaske@adams.edu
LASKER, Y. Mayer .... 718-377-0777 320 E
LASKIN, Emily .... 626-396-2455.. 26 L
emily.laskin@artcenter.edu
LASKOFSKI, Mike .... 703-993-4573 481 B
mlaskofs@gmu.edu
LASKY, Melodee, S .... 848-932-9064 290 A
mlasky@echo.rutgers.edu
LASLEY, Steven, T .... 615-460-6404 430 D
steve.lasley@belmont.edu
LASSEN, Gregg .... 504-280-6207 194 F
glassen@uno.edu
LASSETTER, Jerry .... 919-761-2266 349 C
jlassetter@sebts.edu
LASSIAL, Erin .... 315-386-7608 329 A
lassiale@canton.edu
LASSITER, Catherine ...... 252-222-6290 341 F
lassiterc@carteret.edu
LASSITER, Colleen .... 706-233-7337 125 E
classiter@shorter.edu
LASSITER, Donald, L ..... 910-630-7081 340 A
lassiter@methodist.edu
LASSITER, Elbert, J ...... 336-633-0217 345 F
ejlassiter@randolph.edu
LASSITER, John .... 706-295-6511 120 C
jlassiter@gntc.edu
LASSITER, Joshua .... 252-335-3665 350 A
jllassiter@ecsu.edu
LASSITER, Lisabeth .... 972-883-4059 467 D
lisabeth.lassiter@utdallas.edu
LASSITER, Timothy .... 252-862-1351 345 H
tmlassiter6983@roanokechowan.edu
LASSNER, David .... 808-956-7651 129 J
david@hawaii.edu
LASSNER, David, K .... 808-956-8207 129 H
david@hawaii.edu
LASSNER, Jennifer .... 319-335-2123 166 G
jennifer-lassner@uiowa.edu
LAST, Brad .... 435-652-7858 473 B
blast@dixie.edu
LAST, Brett, I .... 610-861-5460 403 B
blast@northampton.edu
LASTER, Katherine .... 229-430-3848 114 I
katherine.laster@asurams.edu
LASTER, Leslie .... 920-565-1000 507 K
lasterlg@lakeland.edu
LASTINGER, Michael ..... 304-293-6955 505 B
michael.lastinger@mail.wvu.edu
LASTORIA, Cindy .... 585-567-9526 310 F
cindy.lastoria@houghton.edu
LASTRA, Sarai .... 787-743-7979 526 A
ut_slastra@suagm.edu
LATA, Fran .... 303-373-2008.. 82 F
flata@rvu.edu
LATANE, Jane .... 520-383-8401.. 16 G
jlatane@tocc.edu
LATCHAW HIRSH,
Sharon .... 610-527-0200 409 E
shirsh@rosemont.edu
LATCHUM, Lucy, L .... 757-594-7702 479 H
llatchum@cnu.edu
LATCOVICH, Mark, A ..... 440-943-7600 369 J
mal@dioceseofcleveland.org
LATESSA, Kenneth .... 804-862-6100 484 F
klatessa@rbc.edu
LATHAM, Adrienne .... 615-329-8632 431 I
alatham@fisk.edu
LATHAM, Amy .... 662-562-3201 255 C
a_latham@northwestms.edu
LATHAM, Brenda .... 209-381-6410.. 51 G
latham.b@mccd.edu
LATHAM, Clara .... 940-397-4757 453 C
clara.latham@mwsu.edu
LATHAM, Heather .... 410-626-2511 206 F
heather.latham@sjc.edu
LATHAM, Linda .... 336-734-7412 343 C
llatham@forsythtech.edu
LATHAM, Linda, H .... 334-734-7582 343 C
llatham@forsythtech.edu
LATHAM, Mark .... 912-260-4300 125 F
mark.latham@sgsc.edu
LATHAM, Michael .... 641-269-3100 169 F
latham@grinnell.edu
LATHAM, Mike .... 252-451-8327 345 B
dmlatham118@nashcc.edu
LATHAM, Paula, J .... 606-679-8501 186 G
paula.latham@kctcs.edu
LATHAM, Sarah .... 831-459-3778.. 70 C
sclatham@ucsc.edu
LATHAM, Scott .... 978-934-2832 217 B
scott_latham@uml.edu
LATHAM, Sheila .... 701-858-4145 354 C
sheila.latham@minotstateu.edu
LATHAM, Tricia .... 580-477-7725 381 G
tricia.latham@wosc.edu
LATHAM, William .... 202-274-5210.. 93 D
william.latham@udc.edu
LATHEM, Lindsay, S ...... 336-272-7102 338 B
lindsay.lathem@greensboro.edu
LATHROP, Sam .... 217-228-5432 149 B
lathrsa@quincy.edu
LATIF, Niaz .... 219-989-3251 163 E
nlatif@pnw.edu
LATIMER, Dewana .... 731-425-2624 437 B
dlatimer@jscc.edu
LATIMER, Margaret .... 240-567-7711 205 F
margaret.latimer@montgomerycollege.
edu
LATIMER, Tanisha .... 864-250-8107 421 K
tanisha.latimer@gvltec.edu
LATIMER, William .... 718-960-7306 302 C
william.latimer@lehman.cuny.edu
LATIN, Quintin .... 617-322-3500 216 B
LATINI, Theresa, F .... 717-334-6286 412 E
LATIOLAIS, Scott .... 425-235-2409 497 E
slatiolais@rtc.edu
LATIOLAIS, Scott .... 253-589-5546 493 F
scott.latiolais@cptc.edu
LATORELLA, Jacqueline . 813-253-6219 113 E
jlatorella@ut.edu
LATORRACA, Dominic ... 732-224-2301 284 B
dlatorraca@brookdalecc.edu
LATORRE, Daria .... 610-796-8481 389 A
daria.latorre@alvernia.edu
LATOUF, Christina .... 646-660-6114 301 B
christina.latouf@baruch.cuny.edu
LATOUR, Bill .... 217-641-4290 141 F
blatour@jwcc.edu
LATOUR, Mickey, A ...... 618-453-2469 152 B
mlatour@siu.edu
LATOUR, Terry, S .... 814-393-2343 405 H
tlatour@clarion.edu
LATSHAW, Todd, M ...... 717-867-6330 399 J
latshaw@lvc.edu
LATTA, Bruce, J .... 410-293-1801 519 E
latta@usna.edu
LATTA, Mark, A .... 402-280-5061 274 D
marklatta@creighton.edu
LATTA, Michael .... 812-877-8975 163 G
mlatta@rose-hulman.edu
LATTA KIRBY, Dawn ..... 239-590-1094 109 C
dkirby@fgcu.edu
LATTER, Deborah .... 863-784-7251 108 B
latterd@southflorida.edu
LATTER, George .... 619-849-2317.. 57 H
georgelatter@pointloma.edu
LATTIMORE, Dan, L ...... 901-678-2991 439 E
dlattimr@memphis.edu
LATTIMORE, Glenda .... 601-979-2227 253 E
glenda.s.lattimore@jsums.edu
LATTIMORE, John .... 704-669-4020 342 B
lattimorej@clevelandcc.edu
LATTIMORE, Mark .... 478-825-6296 119 C
lattimorem@fvsu.edu
LATTIMORE, Vergel, L ... 704-636-6823 338 F
vlattimore@hoodseminary.edu
LATTING, John .... 404-727-6036 119 B
john.latting@emory.edu
LATTY, Erika .... 207-509-7297 200 I
elatty@unity.edu
LATVIS, Mike .... 313-436-9152 238 A
latvism@umich.edu
LATZ, Gil .... 317-278-1265 160 E
glatz@iupui.edu
LAU, Bradley, A .... 503-554-2312 383 C
blau@georgefox.edu
LAU, John .... 760-355-6235.. 46 B
john.lau@imperial.edu

LAU, Lawrence ... 310-577-3000 .. 75 G
lau@yosan.edu
LAU, Margaret ... 805-922-6966 .. 24 J
mlau@hancockcollege.edu
LAU, Pam ... 217-351-2542 148 H
plau@parkland.edu
LAU, Stuart ... 808-956-8010 129 J
stuartl@hawaii.edu
LAUB, Jeffrey, W ... 434-832-7707 487 H
laubj@cvcc.vccs.edu
LAUB, Joe ... 212-484-1108 302 F
jlaub@jjay.cuny.edu
LAUBAUCH, Harold ... 954-262-1303 104 F
harold@nsu.nova.edu
LAUBE, Philip ... 740-826-8101 366 C
plaube@muskingum.edu
LAUBER, Jeremy ... 516-918-3628 299 M
jlauber@bcl.edu
LAUBER, Ray ... 620-341-5077 177 B
rlauber@emporia.edu
LAUCHNER, Kathy ... 512-313-3000 446 N
kathy.lauchner@concordia.edu
LAUCHNER, Kerri ... 805-493-3225 .. 30 E
klauchne@callutheran.edu
LAUDE, David, A ... 512-471-4363 467 C
dalaude@austin.utexas.edu
LAUDENSLAGER,
Kristin ... 610-282-1100 393 G
kristin.laudenslager@desales.edu
LAUDER, Frank ... 617-873-0137 213 B
finaid@cambridgecollege.edu
LAUDER, Sue, M ... 978-665-3313 217 E
slauder@fitchburgstate.edu
LAUDERBACK, Cindy ... 360-417-6341 496 I
clauderback@pencol.edu
LAUDERDALE, Wendy ... 985-549-5544 197 E
wlauderdale@selu.edu
LAUER, Andrew, J ... 212-960-0051 334 P
andrewlauer@yu.edu
LAUER, Bonnie ... 570-740-0734 400 F
blauer@luzerne.edu
LAUER, Brenda ... 719-502-2403 .. 81 H
brenda.lauer@ppcc.edu
LAUER, Heather ... 304-205-6697 502 K
heather.lauer@bridgevalley.edu
LAUER, John ... 719-389-6200 .. 77 J
jlauer@coloradocollege.edu
LAUER, Jonathan, D ... 717-691-6006 401 L
jlauer@messiah.edu
LAUER, Karla ... 941-752-5694 108 P
lauerk@scf.edu
LAUER, Theresa ... 909-607-2760 .. 45 D
theresa_lauer@hmc.edu
LAUFER, Marilyn ... 334-844-1486 .... 4 D
laufema@auburn.edu
LAUG, Adam ... 641-269-3200 169 F
laugadam@grinnell.edu
LAUGHEAD, Ross ... 210-485-0060 441 E
rlaughead@alamo.edu
LAUGHHUNN, Seirra ... 217-234-5222 143 B
slaughhunn42647@lakeland.cc.il.us
LAUGHLIN,
Frederick, L ... 231-995-1197 235 B
flaughlin@nmc.edu
LAUGHLIN, Karen, L ... 850-644-2740 110 A
klaughlin@admin.fsu.edu
LAUGHLIN, Lynn ... 217-732-3168 143 F
llaughli@lincolnchristian.edu
LAUGHLIN, Michelle, E 712-274-5493 172 A
laughlinm@morningside.edu
LAUGHLIN, Ronda ... 360-752-8334 492 H
rlaughlin@btc.edu
LAUGHLIN, Russ ... 817-202-6462 457 E
laughlinr@swau.edu
LAUGHRAN, Patrick ... 508-626-4357 218 A
plaughran@framingham.edu
LAUNDERVILLE, OSB,
Dale ... 320-363-3389 250 A
dlaunderville@csbsju.edu
LAUNEY, Lisa ... 225-752-4233 191 I
llauney@iticollege.edu
LAUNIUS, Katy ... 918-343-7707 379 C
klaunius@rsu.edu
LAUR, Dave ... 906-786-5802 228 A
dave.laur@baycollege.edu
LAURANZON,
Anne Marie ... 804-752-7317 484 C
alauranz@rmc.edu
LAUREDO, Luis ... 305-629-2929 107 D
llauredo@sanignaciocollege.edu
LAURENCE, David ... 928-776-7666 .. 17 G
david.laurence@yc.edu
LAURENCEAU-MEDINA,
Jean-Pierre ... 410-810-8465 210 A
jlaurenceaumedina2@washcoll.edu
LAURENT, Dianna ... 985-867-2415 195 I
dlaurent@sjasc.edu
LAURENZ, Jamie ... 575-562-2312 293 O
jamie.laurenz@enmu.edu
LAURENZI, Kellie, L ... 412-397-5201 409 C
laurenzi@rmu.edu
LAURIA, James ... 412-809-5100 408 D
lauria.james@pti.edu
LAURIE, Sean ... 516-323-4820 315 J
slaurie@molloy.edu
LAURINE, Robert ... 404-962-3300 127 G
bobby.laurine@usg.edu
LAURITA, Brandi ... 419-434-4663 372 B
ankney@findlay.edu
LAURITSEN, Jessica ... 763-488-2605 244 G
jessica.lauritsen@hennepintech.edu
LAURO, Reno ... 609-497-7948 288 E
reno.lauro@ptsem.edu
LAUSCH, Mark, C ... 608-243-4508 514 A
mlausch@madisoncollege.edu
LAUSELL, Ana, C ... 787-891-0925 523 G
amelon@aguadilla.inter.edu
LAUSIER, Patrick ... 864-578-8770 423 F
plausier@sherman.edu
LAUZON, Minnie ... 607-274-3111 311 D
mlauzon@ithaca.edu
LAUZON CLABO,
Laurie ... 313-577-4082 239 C
laurie.lauzon.clabo@wayne.edu
LAVACK, Krista, M ... 315-267-2779 328 A
lavackkm@potsdam.edu
LAVALLÉE-WELCH,
Catherine ... 608-785-8805 510 F
clavallee-welch@uwlax.edu
LAVALLEY, Ken ... 603-862-4343 282 F
ken.lavalley@unh.edu
LAVALLIERE, Pamela ... 608-663-3317 507 D
plavalliere@edgewood.edu
LAVARIEGA MONFORTI,
Jessica ... 805-493-3555 .. 30 E
jlavariega@callutheran.edu
LAVELLI, Lucinda ... 352-392-0207 110 D
llavelli@arts.ufl.edu
LAVENDER, Bernadette .. 770-426-2633 122 F
bernadette.lavender@life.edu
LAVENDER, Julie ... 989-275-5000 232 E
julie.lavender@kirtland.edu
LAVENDER, Martha, G .. 256-549-8221 .... 2 A
mlavender@gadsdenstate.edu
LAVENDER, Melissa ... 850-747-3211 101 J
mlavender@gulfcoast.edu
LAVENDER, Michael, K . 828-652-0681 344 G
michaell@mcdowelltech.edu
LAVENDER, Randall ... 310-665-6963 .. 54 I
rlavender@otis.edu
LAVERDURE, Andrea ... 701-477-7862 355 H
LAVERGNE, Paul ... 718-429-6600 333 B
paul.lavergne@vaughn.edu
LAVERNIA, Enrique, J ... 949-824-5801 .. 69 A
provost@uci.edu
LAVERY, Hugh, J ... 215-955-6834 411 E
hugh.lavery@jefferson.edu
LAVERY, Roger ... 765-285-6000 156 C
rlavery@bsu.edu
LAVES, Beth ... 270-745-1900 190 F
beth.laves@wku.edu
LAVIAL, Pierre ... 772-466-4822 .. 95 D
pierre.lavial@aviator.edu
LAVIGNA, Lisa ... 518-608-8252 308 A
llavigna@excelsior.edu
LAVIGNE, Robert, W ... 508-213-2217 223 C
robert.lavigne@nichols.edu
LAVIN, Gabrielle ... 215-965-4027 402 C
glavin@moore.edu
LAVINDER,
Katherine, W ... 610-758-4159 400 B
kwl211@lehigh.edu
LAVINE, Danielle ... 860-509-9511 .. 87 C
dlavine@hartsem.edu
LAVIOLETTE, Marc ... 239-590-7891 109 C
mlaviole@fgcu.edu
LAVIT, Daniel, A ... 270-809-2160 188 D
dlavit@murraystate.edu
LAVOIE, Chuck ... 802-468-1250 477 A
chuck.lavoie@castleton.edu
LAVOIE, Lisa ... 860-255-3786 .. 86 G
llavoie@txcc.commnet.edu
LAVORATA,
Christina, M ... 304-367-4101 504 A
chris.lavorata@fairmontstate.edu
LAVORGNA, Briana ... 304-434-8000 502 L
briana.lavorgna@easternwv.edu
LAW, Amir ... 925-424-1275 .. 36 D
alaw@laspositascollege.edu
LAW, Christy ... 516-918-3650 299 M
claw@bcl.edu
LAW, Danielle ... 503-552-1668 384 F
dlaw@nunm.edu
LAW, John ... 413-236-3001 219 B
jlaw@berkshirecc.edu
LAW, Nancy ... 903-983-8101 451 F
nlaw@kilgore.edu
LAW, Scott ... 515-271-3860 168 J
scott.law@drake.edu
LAW, Shirley ... 646-313-8000 303 G
shirley.law@guttman.cuny.edu
LAW, Theresa ... 505-454-3198 294 J
tlaw@nmhu.edu
LAWDERMILT, Sherry ... 701-777-6373 353 G
sherry.lawdermilt@und.edu
LAWERENCE, Gail ... 325-235-7333 461 G
gail.lawerence@tstc.edu
LAWHORN, Harry ... 937-778-7871 361 E
hlawhorn@edisonohio.edu
LAWHORN, Janice ... 928-428-8509 .. 12 I
janice.lawhorn@eac.edu
LAWHORN, Paul ... 423-775-6596 435 H
registrar@ogs.edu
LAWHORN, Paul ... 423-775-6596 435 H
plawhorn@ogs.edu
LAWHORNE, Angela ... 757-569-6064 489 B
alawhorne@pdc.edu
LAWHORNE, Jeffrey, L .. 540-464-7215 490 E
lawhornejl@vmi.edu
LAWHORNE, Lectra ... 470-578-3644 122 C
llawhorn@kennesaw.edu
LAWLER, Brigid ... 802-258-9261 475 D
blawler@marlboro.edu
LAWLER, Hannah ... 310-434-3472 .. 62 G
lawler_hannah@smc.edu
LAWLER, Marsha ... 915-566-9621 470 L
mlawler@westerntech.edu
LAWLER, Whitney ... 303-964-4052 .. 82 D
wfranker@regis.edu
LAWLER-SAGARIN,
Kimberly ... 630-617-3202 138 C
ksagarin@elmhurst.edu
LAWLESS, Daniel, M ... 843-349-2021 420 A
dan@coastal.edu
LAWLESS, J. Alan ... 918-343-7715 379 C
alawless@rsu.edu
LAWLESS, John ... 315-460-3161 329 C
john.lawless@esc.edu
LAWLESS, Richard ... 516-572-7317 316 C
richard.lawless@ncc.edu
LAWLOR, Andrew ... 410-857-2762 205 E
alawlor@mcdaniel.edu
LAWLOR, David ... 414-288-4714 508 C
dave.lawlor@marquette.edu
LAWLOR, Kevin, P ... 203-254-4000 .. 87 A
klawlor@fairfield.edu
LAWLOR, Sarah ... 406-447-4515 270 H
slawlor@carroll.edu
LAWLOR, Susan ... 415-451-2853 .. 60 I
slawlor@sfts.edu
LAWRENCE, Alfred, C ... 915-831-4463 449 A
alawren4@epcc.edu
LAWRENCE, Alicia ... 212-854-5561 299 B
alawrenc@barnard.edu
LAWRENCE, Amanda ... 616-949-5300 229 B
amanda.lawrence@cornerstone.edu
LAWRENCE, Barbara ... 336-316-2196 338 C
blawrenc@guilford.edu
LAWRENCE, Charles ... 206-296-6384 498 D
lawrence@seattleu.edu
LAWRENCE, Craig, D ... 205-929-3427 .... 2 G
clawrence@lawsonstate.edu
LAWRENCE, Dan ... 303-360-4740 .. 79 C
dan.lawrence@ccaurora.edu
LAWRENCE, Deborah ... 317-955-6208 162 R
dlawrence@marian.edu
LAWRENCE, Deborah ... 518-244-2466 321 G
lawred@sage.edu
LAWRENCE, Derrick ... 605-698-3966 428 C
dlawrence@swc.tc
LAWRENCE, Diana ... 502-456-6506 189 F
dlawrence@sullivan.edu
LAWRENCE, Frank ... 518-255-5317 328 C
lawrenfj@cobleskill.edu
LAWRENCE, Gary ... 805-893-3781 .. 70 B
gary@ucen.ucsb.edu
LAWRENCE, Jason ... 870-368-2058 .. 20 H
jason.lawrence@ozarka.edu
LAWRENCE, Jaye ... 507-222-4438 241 C
jlawrenc@carleton.edu
LAWRENCE, Jennifer ... 318-678-6000 192 C
jelawrence@bpcc.edu
LAWRENCE, John, D ... 515-294-5390 166 F
jdlaw@iastate.edu
LAWRENCE, Karl ... 518-608-8198 308 A
klawrence@excelsior.edu
LAWRENCE, Kevin ... 757-388-2862 485 B
klawrence@sentara.edu
LAWRENCE, Lara ... 660-263-3900 258 A
laralawrence@cccb.edu
LAWRENCE, Larry, D ... 501-450-3196 .. 23 I
larryl@pplant.uca.edu
LAWRENCE, Laura ... 870-368-2010 .. 20 H
llawrence@ozarka.edu
LAWRENCE, Leigh-Anne 434-961-6574 489 C
llawrence@pvcc.edu
LAWRENCE, Lesa ... 218-755-4142 244 B
llawrence@bemidjistate.edu
LAWRENCE, Leslie ... 518-276-6287 321 A
lawrel@rpi.edu
LAWRENCE, Maureen ... 732-906-2505 287 B
mlawrence@middlesexcc.edu
LAWRENCE, Melissa ... 770-533-7009 122 E
mlawrence@laniertech.edu
LAWRENCE, Melody, L .. 828-339-4224 346 H
mlawrence@southwesterncc.edu
LAWRENCE, Pareena, G 309-794-7000 133 G
pareenalawrence@augustana.edu
LAWRENCE, Pareena, G 540-362-6321 481 F
presoffc@hollins.edu
LAWRENCE, Paul ... 212-241-7892 311 A
paul.lawrence@mssm.edu
LAWRENCE, Randall, K . 817-554-5950 452 G
rlawrence@messengercollege.edu
LAWRENCE, Robin, P ... 864-388-8234 422 A
rlawrence@lander.edu
LAWRENCE, JR.,
Roosevelt ... 313-927-1511 233 D
rlawrence2535@marygrove.edu
LAWRENCE, Ross ... 406-874-6172 271 D
lawrencer@milescc.edu
LAWRENCE, Sarah ... 212-229-8916 316 E
lawrence@newschool.edu
LAWRENCE, Sharee ... 478-825-6282 119 C
lawrencs@fvsu.edu
LAWRENCE, Stephanie .. 229-430-4650 114 I
stephanie.lawrence@asurams.edu
LAWRENCE, Stevie ... 478-822-1018 119 C
lawrences@fvsu.edu
LAWRENCE, Tena ... 701-252-3467 355 J
tlawrenc@uj.edu
LAWRENCE KEANE,
Loretta ... 212-217-4700 308 B
loretta_keane@fitnyc.edu
LAWRENCE-PHILLIPS,
Teresa ... 615-963-1545 438 E
tphillips@tnstate.edu
LAWRENCE-RAMAEKER,
Janice ... 715-232-2114 512 A
ramaekerj@uwstout.edu
LAWRENSON, Lisa ... 916-484-8411 .. 50 F
lawrenl@arc.losrios.edu
LAWRENZ, Frances ... 612-625-2048 250 E
lawrenz@umn.edu
LAWRY, Kathleen ... 419-448-5859 370 K
lawrykm@tiffin.edu
LAWS, Michaele, D ... 423-439-8245 431 H
lawsm@etsu.edu
LAWS, Mishelle ... 562-985-8356 .. 32 C
mishelle.laws@csulb.edu
LAWS, Page ... 757-823-8208 483 F
prlaws@nsu.edu
LAWS, Paige ... 870-633-4480 .. 19 E
plaws@eacc.edu
LAWSON, Andrea ... 608-265-5600 510 C
ajlawson@uhs.wisc.edu
LAWSON, Christopher ... 617-333-2929 214 B
clawson0307@curry.edu
LAWSON, Dan ... 419-289-5244 356 L
dlawson@ashland.edu
LAWSON, Daniel, L ... 415-422-4222 .. 72 A
lawson@usfca.edu
LAWSON, Danny, L ... 423-323-0234 437 E
dllawson@northeaststate.edu
LAWSON, Darren, P ... 864-242-5100 418 H
LAWSON, Deneen ... 864-242-5100 418 H
LAWSON, Diana ... 616-331-7100 230 G
lawsond1@gvsu.edu
LAWSON, Donald ... 864-424-8040 425 G
lawsondr@mailbox.sc.edu
LAWSON, Earl ... 831-582-3062 .. 33 A
elawson@csumb.edu
LAWSON, Ekaterina ... 212-799-5000 312 B
LAWSON, Elizabeth ... 212-686-9244 298 C
blawson@aada.edu
LAWSON, Joanne ... 870-633-4480 .. 19 E
jlawson@eacc.edu
LAWSON, Kelvin ... 904-281-9800 109 A
kelvin.lawson@famu.edu
LAWSON, Kenneth ... 360-416-7732 498 F
kenneth.lawson@skagit.edu
LAWSON, Melanie ... 713-313-7762 461 E
lawson_mw@tsu.edu
LAWSON, Melanie, E ... 260-982-5052 162 Q
melawson@manchester.edu
LAWSON, Patricia ... 312-893-7120 138 D
plawson@erikson.edu
LAWSON, Patricia, P ... 540-868-7098 488 E
plawson@lfcc.edu
LAWSON, Paul ... 912-921-2900 93 B

LAWSON, Paul 678-323-7700 93 B
LAWSON, Raymond 815-479-7573 145 B
rlawson@mchenry.edu
LAWSON, Rebecca, L 843-661-1841 421 H
rlawson@fmarion.edu
LAWSON, Regina, G 336-758-6066 353 A
lawsonrg@wfu.edu
LAWSON, Richie 662-562-3494 255 C
LAWSON, Robert 229-430-4702 114 I
robert.lawson@asurams.edu
LAWSON, Scott 276-328-0211 487 A
msl6r@uvawise.edu
LAWSON, Sheeler 336-770-3264 352 B
lawsons@uncsa.edu
LAWSON, Steve 859-985-3050 183 I
steve_lawson@berea.edu
LAWSON, Thomas 661-255-1050 29 F
tlawson@calarts.edu
LAWSON, Valerie 276-376-4528 487 A
vas7k@uvawise.edu
LAWSON, Victoria 206-221-6075 499 D
lawson@uw.edu
LAWSON, Von 714-628-4883 58 B
lawson_von@sccollege.edu
LAWSON-BORDERS, Gracie 202-806-7694 92 C
gracie.lawsonborders@howard.edu
LAWTER, JR., Vernon 352-746-6721 97 C
lawterv@cf.edu
LAWTON, Jennifer, G 413-559-5484 215 F
LAWTON, Kenneth, B 570-662-4913 406 F
klawton@mansfield.edu
LAWTON, Margaret, M 843-377-2423 419 B
mlawton@charlestonlaw.edu
LAWVER, Miranda 906-932-4231 230 D
mirandal@gogebic.edu
LAWYER, Becky 952-888-4777 249 F
blawyer@nwhealth.edu
LAWYER, Mary, K 518-783-4288 324 C
mlawyer@siena.edu
LAWYER, Scott 901-321-3104 431 A
mlawyer@cbu.edu
LAX, William 802-254-0152 371 A
bill.lax@myunion.edu
LAXMI, Priti 210-297-9634 443 K
pxlaxmi@baptisthealthsystem.com
LAY, Barbara, A 740-587-6551 361 B
layb@denison.edu
LAY, Bethany 931-540-2837 436 H
blay@columbiastate.edu
LAY, Brian, K 734-384-4188 234 C
blay@monroeccc.edu
LAY, John 617-739-1700 222 I
jlay@aii.edu
LAY, Kim 620-252-7135 176 K
lay.kim@coffeyville.edu
LAY, Robert, S 617-552-2371 212 E
robert.lay@bc.edu
LAY, Robin 423-636-7300 439 C
rlay@tusculum.edu
LAYER, Paul 907-474-7608 10 B
pwlayer@alaska.edu
LAYISH, Michael, D 781-239-4022 211 A
mlayish@babson.edu
LAYMAN, Susan 918-631-3244 381 C
susan-layman@utulsa.edu
LAYMON, Denise 218-846-3720 245 H
denise.laymon@minnesota.edu
LAYMON, Steven, E 434-982-5206 486 H
sel5v@virginia.edu
LAYNE, Candace 304-357-4862 502 E
candacelayne@ucwv.edu
LAYNE, Preston 276-523-7491 488 F
playne@mecc.edu
LAYNE, Rosemary 321-674-8137 99 K
rlayne@fit.edu
LAYSER, Gaia 541-245-7549 386 G
glayser@roguecc.edu
LAYTHAM, D. Brent 410-864-4202 207 A
blaytham@stmarys.edu
LAYTON, Becky 601-947-4201 254 D
becky.layton@mgccc.edu
LAYTON, Bruce 847-491-5680 148 C
b-layton@northwestern.edu
LAYTON, Christopher 281-873-0262 446 J
c.layton@commonwealth.edu
LAYTON, David, B 724-847-6508 395 J
dblayton@geneva.edu
LAYTON, Susan 303-458-1638 82 D
slayton@regis.edu
LAYTON, III, William, C 207-859-4342 198 H
bill.layton@colby.edu
LAYZELL, Daniel 225-578-4342 193 M
dlayzell@lsu.edu
LAZAR, Kathleen 716-880-2362 314 F
kathleen.lazar@medaille.edu
LAZARAKIS, Pam 978-867-4275 215 D
pam.lazarakis@gordon.edu
LAZARSKI, Derek 773-907-4790 135 K
dlazarski@ccc.edu
LAZENBY, Paul 805-525-4417 67 E
plazenby@thomasaquinas.edu
LAZOWSKI, Stephen 740-376-4600 365 A
stephen.lazowski@marietta.edu
LAZROE, Tony 732-571-4491 287 C
alazroe@monmouth.edu
LAZU, Carlos 787-850-9804 528 B
carlos.lazu@upr.edu
LAZZARI, John (JW) 775-445-3259 279 F
john.lazzari@wnc.edu
LAZZELL, Greg 928-350-4302 15 V
glazzell@prescott.edu
LE, Hung, V 310-506-4307 56 D
hung.le@pepperdine.edu
LE, Joey Alan 510-567-6174 66 I
jle@sum.edu
LE, Tam 713-718-2648 450 D
tam.le@hccs.edu
LE CLAIR, Denise, Y 402-280-2166 274 D
leclair@creighton.edu
LE COUP COLLIER, Bridget 773-702-5671 153 F
bcollier@uchicago.edu
LE MASTERS, Philip 325-793-3898 452 F
plemasters@mcm.edu
LE ROY, Michael, K 616-526-6100 228 B
president@calvin.edu
LE SAUX, Catherine 812-866-7399 158 C
lesaux@hanover.edu
LE SHANA, Jim 620-862-5252 175 B
jim.leshana@barclaycollege.edu
LEA, Brette, E 512-223-7611 443 G
blea@austincc.edu
LEA, Deborah 225-216-8361 192 B
lead@mybrcc.edu
LEA, Jernice 484-365-7250 400 E
jlea@lincoln.edu
LEA, Kizzy 704-216-7235 346 C
kizzy.lea@rccc.edu
LEACH, Adria 978-542-7524 218 E
adria.leach@salemstate.edu
LEACH, Brittany 502-213-8201 189 E
bleach@sctd.edu
LEACH, James, B 919-530-5157 350 D
jleach@nccu.edu
LEACH, John 404-727-6039 119 B
john.blanchard.leach@emory.edu
LEACH, Karen, L 315-859-4524 309 D
kleach@hamilton.edu
LEACH, Karla, N 307-382-1602 517 C
kleach@westernwyoming.edu
LEACH, Lawrence 603-899-4316 281 D
leachla@franklinpierce.edu
LEACH, Les 610-957-6060 410 I
lleach1@swarthmore.edu
LEACH, Monica, T 919-530-6682 350 D
monica.leach@nccu.edu
LEACH, R. Gavin 906-227-2200 235 A
gleach@nmu.edu
LEACH, Robin 719-549-3310 81 M
robin.leach@pueblocc.edu
LEACH, Stephen, E 304-367-4692 503 C
stephen.leach@pierpont.edu
LEACH, Steven 214-645-5439 469 E
steven.leach@utsouthwestern.edu
LEACH, Timothy 207-326-2276 200 F
tim.leach@mma.edu
LEACH, Todd, A 409-747-3811 469 C
tleach@utmb.edu
LEACH, Todd, J 603-862-0918 282 E
todd.leach@usnh.edu
LEADBETER, Marci 410-532-5390 206 D
mleadbeter@ndm.edu
LEADER, Jeanne 425-388-9502 494 F
jleader@everettcc.edu
LEADLEY, Robert 734-462-4400 236 H
rleadley@schoolcraft.edu
LEAFGREEN, Melet 214-648-6335 469 E
melet.leafgreen@utsouthwestern.edu
LEAGUE, Timothy 410-386-8052 203 A
tleague@carrollcc.edu
LEAHEY, Christine 310-846-2640 54 I
cleahey@otis.edu
LEAHEY, James, P 859-238-5224 184 C
jamey.leahey@centre.edu
LEAHY, Daniel 781-768-7559 224 A
daniel.leahy@regiscollege.edu
LEAHY, Debra 617-603-6900 222 F
debra.leahy@necb.edu
LEAHY, Kevin 760-245-4271 73 E
kevin.leahy@vvc.edu
LEAHY, Mindy, S 563-884-5647 172 H
mindy.leahy@palmer.edu
LEAHY, Patrick, F 570-408-4000 414 H
patrick.leahy@wilkes.edu
LEAHY, Thomas 515-643-6621 171 K
tleahy@mercydesmoines.org
LEAHY, Timothy, J 334-953-5613 517 I
timothy.leahy@us.af.mil
LEAHY, S.J., William, P 617-552-3250 212 E
william.leahy@bc.edu
LEAK, Arthur 765-641-4162 156 A
ajleak@anderson.edu
LEAK, Monica 703-812-4757 482 B
mleak@leland.edu
LEAKER, Catherine 646-230-1214 329 C
catherine.leaker@esc.edu
LEAKS, Ileka, L 864-488-4557 422 B
ileaks@limestone.edu
LEAL, Abe 510-594-3781 28 K
abe@cca.edu
LEAL-SOTELO, Margaret 310-267-5439 69 B
mlealsotelo@conet.ucla.edu
LEAMAN, David, E 715-836-2542 510 D
leamande@uwec.edu
LEAMAN, Douglas, W 937-775-2611 374 B
douglas.leaman@wright.edu
LEAMY, Michael, B 978-665-4783 217 E
mleamy1@fitchburgstate.edu
LEAR, Doug 603-899-4123 281 D
leard@franklinpierce.edu
LEAR, Shelly 315-781-3388 310 C
lear@hws.edu
LEARNARD, Kim 678-664-0515 128 F
kim.learnard@westgatech.edu
LEARNED, Betsy, P 401-254-3625 417 C
blearned@rwu.edu
LEARY, Carol, A 413-565-1000 211 C
cleary@baypath.edu
LEARY, Claudine 740-363-1146 365 D
cleary@mtso.edu
LEARY, James 508-856-8200 217 C
james.leary@umassmed.edu
LEARY, John 434-947-8109 484 B
jleary@randolphcollege.edu
LEARY, Karen 413-748-3516 224 G
kleary@springfieldcollege.edu
LEARY, Mary 252-862-1302 345 H
meleary3157@roanokechowan.edu
LEARY, Russell, J 920-433-6635 506 C
russell.leary@bellincollege.edu
LEARY, Sharon 214-648-0100 469 E
sharon.leary@utsouthwestern.edu
LEARY, Thomas, P 570-740-0388 400 F
tleary@luzerne.edu
LEARY, Timothy 206-296-6160 498 D
tleary@seattleu.edu
LEAS, Terry 509-793-2001 492 I
terryl@bigbend.edu
LEASE, Sharon 405-692-3190 376 C
slease@macu.edu
LEASE BUTTS, Jennifer 860-486-4223 88 G
jennifer.lease@uconn.edu
LEAT, Denise 714-432-5670 38 H
dleat@occ.cccd.edu
LEATH, Steven 334-844-4650 4 D
president@auburn.edu
LEATHERMAN, W. Dale 870-759-4124 23 K
dleatherman@wbcoll.edu
LEATHERS, Barb 309-268-8130 139 D
barb.leathers@heartland.edu
LEATHERS, Debra, L 213-738-6814 65 I
advancement@swlaw.edu
LEATHERS, Evelyn 336-517-1761 335 K
evelyn.leathers@bennett.edu
LEATHERS, Mardy 636-584-6530 259 L
mardy.leathers@eastcentral.edu
LEATHERWOOD, Laura, B 828-694-1706 341 B
lbleatherwood@blueridge.edu
LEAVER, Betty Lou 831-242-5291 517 K
betty.lou.leaver@dliflc.edu
LEAVER, Walt 615-966-7653 433 D
walt.leaver@lipscomb.edu
LEAVITT, Andrew, J 920-424-0200 511 B
leavitt@uwosh.edu
LEAVITT, Cindy 215-204-7077 411 B
cindy.leavitt@temple.edu
LEAVITT, David 617-228-3287 219 D
djleavit@bhcc.mass.edu
LEAVITT, David 650-433-3839 55 I
support@paloaltou.edu
LEAVITT, Gabriel 503-517-7696 386 F
leavittg@reed.edu
LEAVITT, Stephen, C 518-388-6116 332 B
leavitts@union.edu
LEBAIL, Carolyn 802-387-6814 475 C
carolynlebail@landmark.edu
LEBAR, Peter, M 814-332-5369 388 F
plebar@allegheny.edu
LEBARRON, Lynne 203-837-8188 85 B
lebarronl@wcsu.edu
LEBBY, Kimberly 803-376-5700 418 D
klebby@allenuniversity.edu
LEBEAU, Bryan 913-758-6115 182 B
lebeau87@stmary.edu
LEBEAU, Mandie, A 617-422-7499 222 J
mlebeau@nesl.edu
LEBEAU, Michael 205-226-4719 4 F
mlebeau@bsc.edu
LEBEDEFF, Alex 510-659-6263 54 F
alebedeff@ohlone.edu
LEBER, Frank, W 312-329-4388 146 B
frank.leber@moody.edu
LEBER, Sally, S 740-368-3080 368 N
ssleber@owu.edu
LEBERT, Jeff 918-335-6842 378 F
jlebert@okwu.edu
LEBESCH, Anna, M 904-276-6783 106 M
annalebesch@sjrstate.edu
LEBESCO, Kathleen 212-517-0522 314 D
klebesco@mmm.edu
LEBIODA, Ed 805-437-8547 31 C
ed.lebioda@csuci.edu
LEBLANC, Ann 757-352-4222 484 E
aleblanc@regent.edu
LEBLANC, AnnMarie, M 412-397-6460 409 C
leblanc@rmu.edu
LEBLANC, Corlin 225-216-8605 192 B
leblancc@mybrcc.edu
LEBLANC, David 601-635-2111 252 I
dleblanc@eccc.edu
LEBLANC, Elva, C 817-515-5250 458 B
elva.leblanc@tccd.edu
LEBLANC, Erica 310-434-4227 62 G
leblanc_erica@smc.edu
LEBLANC, George, J 848-445-4636 290 A
george.leblanc@rutgers.edu
LEBLANC, Jacqueline 212-752-1530 312 G
jacqueline.leblanc@limcollege.edu
LEBLANC, Jerry, L 337-482-6235 197 F
jerrylukeleblanc@louisiana.edu
LEBLANC, Paul 603-645-9631 282 C
p.leblanc@snhu.edu
LEBLANC, Thomas, J 202-994-6500 92 A
leblanc@gwu.edu
LEBLEU BURNS, Michele 408-864-8218 43 E
lebleuburnsmichele@deanza.edu
LEBO, Maggie 717-728-2406 392 B
margeretlebo@centralpenn.edu
LEBO, Russ 559-734-9000 61 C
russl@sjvc.edu
LEBRECHT, Amanda 714-556-3610 72 F
amanda.lebrecht@vanguard.edu
LEBRECK, Paul 847-925-6647 139 B
plebreck@harpercollege.edu
LEBRETON, Ryan 570-577-3122 390 H
ryan.lebreton@bucknell.edu
LEBRON, Mayra 787-850-9392 528 B
mayra.lebron@upr.edu
LEBRON, Nestor, A 787-864-2222 524 A
nestor.lebron@guayama.inter.edu
LEBRUN, Kathy 512-472-4133 456 E
kathy.lebrun@ssw.edu
LECATO, William 757-789-1797 488 A
wlecato@es.vccs.edu
LECH, Jennifer 602-639-7500 12 P
LECHE, Adriane 252-536-7260 343 F
aleche096@halifaxcc.edu
LECHLER, Terry 254-299-8652 452 E
tlechler@mclennan.edu
LECHNER, David, E 402-472-2191 277 E
dlechner@nebraska.edu
LECHNER, JR., Jack, E 513-761-2020 359 F
jlechner@ccms.edu
LECHOWSKI, Piotr 773-929-8500 137 E
plechowski@devry.edu
LECHTENBERG, Melanie 217-641-4310 141 F
mlechtenberg@jwcc.edu
LECKONBY, Larry, W 704-637-4474 336 G
lleckonb14@catawba.edu
LECKRONE, Michael, J 260-982-5004 162 Q
mjleckrone@manchester.edu
LECLAIR, Mary 315-781-3697 310 C
leclair@hws.edu
LECLERC, Robin 248-204-2203 233 A
rleclerc@ltu.edu
LECLERC-DICKLER, Florence 212-229-5676 316 E
leclercf@newschool.edu
LECOUNT, Heidi 919-760-8633 339 H
lecounth@meredith.edu
LECOURT, Nancy 707-965-6234 55 F
nlecourt@puc.edu
LECRONE, Jeffrey, L 570-321-4112 400 G
lecrone@lycoming.edu

LECRONE, Timothy 207-509-7283 200 I tlecrone@unity.edu
LEDBETTER, Beverly, E 401-863-9900 415 K beverly_ledbetter@brown.edu
LEDBETTER, Brad 828-652-0674 344 G bradl@mcdowelltech.edu
LEDBETTER, Bronson 602-387-4307 17 C bronson.ledbetter@phoenix.edu
LEDBETTER, Cathy 706-204-2390 119 G cledbett@highlands.edu
LEDBETTER, Kim, M 828-652-0602 344 G kims@mcdowelltech.edu
LEDBETTER, Lisa 704-216-3620 346 C lisa.ledbetter@rccc.edu
LEDBETTER, Mary, L 828-659-6001 344 G maryl@mcdowelltech.edu
LEDBETTER, Neal 251-442-2429 8 D nledbetter@umobile.edu
LEDBETTER, Sheri 714-289-3143 36 G sledbett@chapman.edu
LEDBETTER, Sislena 202-274-5373 93 D sledbetter@udc.edu
LEDDY, Michael 401-341-2195 417 D mike.leddy@salve.edu
LEDER, Harold 225-578-6801 193 M hleder@lsu.edu
LEDERER, John 206-934-6075 497 H john.lederer@seattlecolleges.edu
LEDERER, Stephanie 941-309-4110 106 H slederer@ringling.edu
LEDERMAN, Bill 269-467-9945 230 C blederman@glenoaks.edu
LEDERMAN, Evin 845-451-1205 306 D evin.lederman@culinary.edu
LEDERMANN, Sarah 518-255-5516 328 C lederms@cobleskill.edu
LEDERMANN, Stacy, A 585-385-8142 322 E sledermann@sjfc.edu
LEDESMA, Amadeo 575-527-7531 295 E amadeol@nmsu.edu
LEDESMA, Mark 206-726-5028 494 B mledesma@cornish.edu
LEDESMA, Rosalie 408-223-6782 61 N rosalie.ledesma@sjeccd.org
LEDEZMA, Rosabla 336-750-2855 352 D ledezmara@wssu.edu
LEDFORD, Catherine, M 858-534-3391 69 E cledford@ucsd.edu
LEDFORD, Howard 770-535-6275 122 E hledford@laniertech.edu
LEDFORD, Julia 270-686-4627 186 F julia.ledford@kctcs.edu
LEDFORD, Laura 217-362-6499 145 J lledford@millikin.edu
LEDFORD, Patrick 706-754-7728 123 G pledford@northgatech.edu
LEDFORD, Randy 828-766-1280 344 F rledford@mayland.edu
LEDFORD, Terry 864-941-8568 423 C ledford.t@ptc.edu
LEDFORD, Tommy, R 828-766-1190 344 F tledford@mayland.edu
LEDING, Albert 479-979-1207 23 J aleding@ozarks.edu
LEDLOW, Susan, E 407-582-3423 113 F sledlow@valenciacollege.edu
LEDNICKY, Margaret 916-558-2544 50 I lednicm@scc.losrios.edu
LEDONNE, Peter 201-447-7159 283 I pledonne@bergen.edu
LEDOUX, Debra 320-762-4482 243 J debral@alextech.edu
LEDUC, Don 517-371-5140 239 F leducd@cooley.edu
LEDUC, Laura 517-371-5140 239 F leducl@cooley.edu
LEDUFF, Kimberly 850-474-2600 111 D kleduff@uwf.edu
LEDVINA, Anne 205-226-7722 4 F aledvina@bsc.edu
LEE, Abby 541-881-5582 387 D alee@tvcc.cc
LEE, Adriana 760-744-1150 55 K alee@palomar.edu
LEE, Allisha 270-707-3958 186 B allisha.lee@kctcs.edu
LEE, Amanda 910-362-7555 341 E alee@cfcc.edu
LEE, Amy 510-748-2288 56 G ahlee@peralta.edu
LEE, Amy 207-741-5644 200 C alee@smccme.edu
LEE, Amy 781-280-3200 220 C
LEE, IHM, Andrea, J 414-382-6064 506 A andrea.lee@alverno.edu
LEE, Annette 516-562-1108 307 D alee@northwell.edu
LEE, Anthony 888-491-8686 74 E alee@westcliff.edu
LEE, April 610-660-1329 409 H alee@sju.edu
LEE, Asa 202-885-8614 94 C alee@wesleyseminary.edu
LEE, Barbara, A 848-932-2600 290 A blee@oldqueens.rutgers.edu
LEE, Bill 415-442-7058 44 E blee@ggu.edu
LEE, Brandon, W 361-485-4400 465 D leebw@uhv.edu
LEE, Brenda 419-530-7730 372 F brenda.lee@utoledo.edu
LEE, Brian 310-577-3000 75 G blee@yosan.edu
LEE, Brian, K 626-395-6307 29 I brian.lee@caltech.edu
LEE, Catherine 334-844-1350 4 D leecath@auburn.edu
LEE, Catherine 910-362-7033 341 E clee@cfcc.edu
LEE, Charley 714-527-0691 42 H
LEE, Chris 501-882-8887 17 M cllee@asub.edu
LEE, Chris 270-706-8622 185 H chris.lee@kctcs.edu
LEE, Christine 863-297-1000 105 F clee@polk.edu
LEE, Christopher 920-832-7694 507 L christopher.lee@lawrence.edu
LEE, Christopher 804-819-4685 487 F clee@vccs.edu
LEE, Chul 812-488-2155 164 G cl162@evansville.edu
LEE, Chung-Shing 253-535-7251 496 G clee@plu.edu
LEE, Cindy 352-588-8869 106 N cindy.lee@saintleo.edu
LEE, Claudia 714-895-8130 38 G clee@gwc.cccd.edu
LEE, Craig 949-480-4235 64 D clee@soka.edu
LEE, Curtis 253-964-6595 497 B clee@pierce.ctc.edu
LEE, Cynthia 713-313-7523 461 E lee_cl@tsu.edu
LEE, Daniel, J 253-535-7177 496 G daniel.lee@plu.edu
LEE, Darriona 985-732-6640 192 K
LEE, David 270-745-2297 190 F david.lee@wku.edu
LEE, David 626-289-7719 24 I dlee@amu.edu
LEE, David 303-273-3155 78 J dlee@mines.edu
LEE, David, C 706-542-5969 127 A dclee@uga.edu
LEE, David, S 609-258-9548 288 F davidlee@princeton.edu
LEE, David, Y 703-333-5904 491 H dylee@wuv.edu
LEE, David Chang, S 714-525-0088 44 I cfo@gm.edu
LEE, Deborah 949-214-3433 40 I deborah.lee@cui.edu
LEE, Debra, A 330-471-8406 364 H dlee@malone.edu
LEE, Delores 310-243-3189 31 E dslee@csudh.edu
LEE, Dennis 229-227-2414 126 C dlee@southernregional.edu
LEE, Dewain 812-866-7078 158 C lee@hanover.edu
LEE, Diane, M 410-455-2859 208 A dlee@umbc.edu
LEE, Don 662-246-6441 254 C dlee@msdelta.edu
LEE, Donna 651-696-6220 243 B donnalee@macalester.edu
LEE, Donny 501-279-4187 19 G dlee@harding.edu
LEE, Donzell 601-877-6142 251 G dlee@alcorn.edu
LEE, Doug 724-852-3212 414 B dlee@waynesburg.edu
LEE, Douglas 319-335-0444 166 G douglas-lee@uiowa.edu
LEE, D'Andrea, J 225-771-2552 196 B djlee@sulc.edu
LEE, Ed 715-346-3612 511 F ed.lee@uwsp.edu
LEE, Eliot 562-926-1023 57 J eliotlee@ptsa.edu
LEE, Elizabeth 503-943-7485 387 H leeel@up.edu
LEE, Elwyn, C 832-842-5090 465 A eclee@uh.edu
LEE, Eun Moo 770-220-7929 119 D emlee@gcuniv.edu
LEE, Gloria 203-392-5200 85 A leeg1@southernct.edu
LEE, Grace 415-442-7859 44 E glee@ggu.edu
LEE, Grayce 504-468-2900 196 C drlee@southwest.edu
LEE, Hannah 213-381-0081 46 I library@irus.edu
LEE, Harlan 425-564-4042 492 G harlan.lee@bellevuecollege.edu
LEE, Hee, C 636-327-4645 263 C hclee@midwest.edu
LEE, Helen Elaine 617-253-2642 221 C
LEE, Herbert 831-459-1349 70 C vpaa@ucsc.edu
LEE, Ho Woo 770-279-0507 119 D howlee21@gcuniv.edu
LEE, Holly 580-628-6274 376 J holly.lee@noc.edu
LEE, Howoo 770-220-7920 119 D howlee21@gcuniv.edu
LEE, Hubert 610-361-2499 402 G leeh@neumann.edu
LEE, Humphrey 256-331-5214 3 C hlee@nwscc.edu
LEE, Ilses-Mari 406-994-4689 272 A ilselee@montana.edu
LEE, J. Brent 843-355-4144 426 G leeb@wiltech.edu
LEE, James 760-252-2411 27 A jlee@barstow.edu
LEE, James 617-873-0236 213 B james.lee@cambridgecollege.edu
LEE, James, D 808-675-3289 128 K james.lee@byuh.edu
LEE, James, S 626-448-0023 46 K president@itsla.edu
LEE, Janet 303-458-3552 82 D jlee@regis.edu
LEE, Jason 937-766-7674 358 D jasonlee@cedarville.edu
LEE, Jay 970-521-6607 81 F jay.lee@njc.edu
LEE, Jay 507-537-7285 248 A jay.lee@smsu.edu
LEE, Jeffrey 973-877-3000 285 K
LEE, Jin 323-643-0301 25 K
LEE, Joanne, C 714-995-9988 47 D
LEE, Joe 207-581-1619 201 B
LEE, John 651-255-6156 250 D jlee@unitedseminary.edu
LEE, John 703-812-4757 482 B jlee@leland.edu
LEE, JR., John, M 252-335-3223 350 A jmleejr@ecsu.edu
LEE, Jonathan 310-233-4471 49 B leej@lahc.edu
LEE, Jonathan 508-626-4697 218 A jlee8@framingham.edu
LEE, Jonathan, E 540-375-2237 484 H jelee@roanoke.edu
LEE, Joni, C 501-569-3186 22 B jclee@ualr.edu
LEE, Judy 718-818-6470 323 F jlee@edaff.com
LEE, Karen 619-849-2535 57 H karenlee@pointloma.edu
LEE, Kathleen, F 317-917-5935 161 G klee@ivytech.edu
LEE, Katrina, K 919-658-2502 349 F klee@umo.edu
LEE, Kenya, N 646-312-3322 301 B kenya.lee@baruch.cuny.edu
LEE, Kiama 601-923-1681 255 E klee@rts.edu
LEE, Kimberly 229-420-1284 114 J klee@albanytech.edu
LEE, Kwang Hoon 213-381-0081 46 I khlee@irus.edu
LEE, Kyu, H 253-752-2020 494 H klee@faithseminary.edu
LEE, Kyuboem 215-368-5000 389 H klee@biblical.edu
LEE, Lenetta 484-365-7253 400 E llee@lincoln.edu
LEE, Lily 240-567-5272 205 F lily.lee@montgomerycollege.edu
LEE, Linda, S 657-725-7789 66 C lslee@stanford.edu
LEE, Lisa 212-410-8007 317 C llee@nycpm.edu
LEE, Malisa 559-278-2061 32 A malisa_lee@csufresno.edu
LEE, Marsha 662-246-6314 254 C mlee@msdelta.edu
LEE, Martin 707-524-1649 62 H mlee@santarosa.edu
LEE, SSJ, Mary Esther 215-248-7062 392 D leem@chc.edu
LEE, Mary Margaret 802-860-2721 474 G mlee@champlain.edu
LEE, Mary W, L 630-515-7311 145 I mleexx@midwestern.edu
LEE, Maryke 407-582-2309 113 F mllee@valenciacollege.edu
LEE, Matt 225-578-7155 193 M mlee@lsu.edu
LEE, Matthew 913-722-0272 178 G matt.lee@kansaschristian.edu
LEE, Mei-Lin 210-436-3414 455 J mlee@stmarytx.edu
LEE, Melissa 863-784-7123 108 B melissa.lee@southflorida.edu
LEE, Mi Hee 770-220-7905 119 D admissions@gcuniv.edu
LEE, Miae 888-777-7675 494 H mlee@faithseminary.edu
LEE, Michael 213-386-0080 52 C
LEE, Michael 678-225-7340 407 G michaellee@pcom.edu
LEE, Michael, D 229-226-1621 126 E mlee@thomasu.edu
LEE, Michele 864-424-8038 425 G michele@mailbox.sc.edu
LEE, Michelle 910-362-7733 341 E mlee@cfcc.edu
LEE, Mike, C 818-947-2336 49 G leemc@lavc.edu
LEE, Mimi 323-643-0301 25 K
LEE, Ming-Tung (Mike) 916-278-6241 33 C mikelee@csus.edu
LEE, Norman 315-294-8412 300 H norman.lee@cayuga-cc.edu
LEE, Ok-Hee 218-477-2095 246 B okheelee@mnstate.edu
LEE, Otto 310-233-4010 49 B leeow@lahc.edu
LEE, Patricia, A 843-355-4127 426 G leepa@wiltech.edu
LEE, SJ, Patrick 800-986-9585 495 A leep@gonzaga.edu
LEE, Peter 651-255-6113 250 D plee@unitedseminary.edu
LEE, Quinneka 402-375-7318 276 D qulee1@wsc.edu
LEE, Raeann 614-416-6239 357 H rlee@bradfordschoolcolumbus.edu
LEE, Randall 601-635-6375 252 I rlee@eccc.edu
LEE, Randolph 860-297-2413 88 E randolph.lee@trincoll.edu
LEE, Richard 607-436-2520 325 E richard.lee@oneonta.edu
LEE, Robert, W 260-399-7700 165 B rlee@sf.edu
LEE, Sam 951-372-7199 58 G samuel.lee@norcocollege.edu
LEE, Samuel 323-643-0301 25 K kyoung317@gmail.com
LEE, Samuel, Y 714-995-9988 47 D
LEE, Sang Meyng 562-926-1023 57 J sangmeynglee@msn.com
LEE, Sara 251-626-3303 7 G registrar@ussa.edu
LEE, Sean 802-831-1078 476 G slee@vermontlaw.edu
LEE, Seong Joo 213-386-0080 52 C
LEE, Seung Deok 213-487-0110 41 K president@dula.edu
LEE, Shad 760-921-5431 55 J shad.lee@paloverde.edu
LEE, Sondra 916-608-6572 50 H lees@flc.losrios.edu
LEE, Soo Young 714-527-0691 42 H
LEE, Staci 760-921-5512 55 J staci.lee@paloverde.edu
LEE, Stephen 304-293-0141 505 B stephen.lee@mail.wvu.edu
LEE, Steven 757-446-5221 480 C leect@evms.edu
LEE, Susan 808-956-5852 130 B susanlee@hawaii.edu
LEE, Suzanne 773-298-3191 151 C slee@sxu.edu
LEE, Suzanne 773-298-3020 151 C lee@sxu.edu
LEE, Tamara 334-229-4475 4 A tlee@alasu.edu
LEE, Tenpao 716-286-8050 318 F tlee@niagara.edu
LEE, Teresa 785-670-1538 182 D teresa.lee@washburn.edu

LEE, Terri, S .... 919-209-2125 344 C
tslee@johnstoncc.edu
LEE, Theresa .... 865-974-4337 439 I
artscidean@utk.edu
LEE, Tiffany .... 562-944-0351.. 27 E
tiffany.lee@biola.edu
LEE, Tiffany .... 484-365-7842 400 E
tlee@lincoln.edu
LEE, Timothy .... 773-995-2002 135 F
tlee27@csu.edu
LEE, Timothy .... 518-956-8219 324 G
tmlee@albany.edu
LEE, Torian .... 504-486-7411 198 D
tllee@xula.edu
LEE, Traci .... 480-314-2102.. 16 C
LEE, Treva, A .... 504-520-7566 198 D
tlee@xula.edu
LEE, Tyjaun .... 816-604-4203 262 K
tyjaun.lee@mcckc.edu
LEE, Vina .... 845-672-0550 308 C
LEE, Wendy .... 415-257-1354.. 41 J
wendy.lee@dominican.edu
LEE, Wes .... 405-491-6455 379 K
wlee@snu.edu
LEE, Y. Ben .... 260-422-5561 159 D
yblee@indianatech.edu
LEE, Youn .... 703-425-4143 481 H
LEE, Yueh-Ting .... 618-453-4527 152 B
leey@siu.edu
LEE, Yuet .... 909-621-8243.. 57 C
yuet_lee@pitzer.edu
LEE, Yung Jae .... 925-631-4610.. 59 C
ylee@stmarys-ca.edu
LEE, Zelda .... 803-535-5348 419 E
zlee@claflin.edu
LEE-BARBER, Jill .... 404-413-1640 121 A
jleebarber@gsu.edu
LEE-COLLICK, Valescia .. 866-492-5336 251 E
valescia.lee-collick@mail.waldenu.edu
LEE ISBARA, Jiseon ...... 503-297-5544 385 A
jlee@ocac.edu
LEE-LEWIS, Sherri .... 310-434-4419.. 62 G
lee-lewis_sherri@smc.edu
LEE-OPERARIO, Tam ..... 510-436-1348.. 45 G
lee-operario@hnu.edu
LEE SANG, Brian .... 202-885-6108.. 91 C
leesang@american.edu
LEE-YUAN, Mona .... 516-739-1545 317 D
clinicdirector@nyctcm.edu
LEEBRON, David, W ...... 713-348-5050 455 F
president@rice.edu
LEEBRON TUTELMAN,
Elizabeth .... 215-204-8660 411 B
elizabeth.leebron@temple.edu
LEECH, Jackie .... 870-733-6741.. 18 B
jleech@asumidsouth.edu
LEECY, Melissa .... 804-752-3205 484 C
melissaleecy@rmc.edu
LEEDER, Mike .... 229-931-2222 120 F
mike.leeder@gsw.edu
LEEDS, Elke .... 470-578-7550 122 C
eleeds@kennesaw.edu
LEEDS, Mark .... 817-923-1921 457 G
mleeds@swbts.edu
LEEDS, Stacy .... 479-575-4504.. 21 I
sleeds@uark.edu
LEEDS CARSON, Ben .... 831-459-4512.. 70 C
blc@ucsc.edu
LEEDY, David .... 212-659-0741 312 E
dleedy@tkc.edu
LEEDY, Debbie .... 623-845-4770.. 13 H
debbie.leedy@gccaz.edu
LEEK, Linda .... 859-985-3205 183 I
leekl@berea.edu
LEEK, Marilyn, J .... 515-961-1675 173 E
marilyn.leek@simpson.edu
LEEMON, Donna .... 334-683-2362.... 3 A
dleemon@marionmilitary.edu
LEENEY-PANAGROSSI,
Anne .... 203-773-8595.. 84 G
panagrossi@albertus.edu
LEENHOUTS, David .... 979-532-6905 471 A
leenhoutsd@wcjc.edu
LEEPER, Greg .... 612-343-4457 249 E
gjleeper@northcentral.edu
LEEPER, Karla .... 706-721-7406 116 B
kleeper@augusta.edu
LEES, Melissa .... 410-617-6769 205 A
mklees@loyola.edu
LEESE, Mike .... 254-968-9081 459 A
leese@tarleton.edu
LEETH, Blake .... 256-840-4170.... 3 F
bleeth@snead.edu
LEETHAM, Lorlie .... 805-756-1131.. 30 K
lleetham@calpoly.edu
LEFAUVE, Linda, M .... 704-894-2124 337 B
lilefauve@davidson.edu

LEFEBVRE, Carol .... 706-721-8611 116 B
clefebvr@augusta.edu
LEFEBVRE, Raymond ..... 508-531-2247 217 D
raymond.lefebvre@bridgew.edu
LEFELD, Amanda, L .... 740-587-6647 361 B
lefelda@denison.edu
LEFEVER-DAVIS, Shirley 316-978-3301 182 F
shirley.lefever-davis@wichita.edu
LEFEVRE, Lisa .... 970-521-6615.. 81 F
lisa.lefevre@njc.edu
LEFEW, Susan .... 304-357-4713 502 E
susanlefew@ucwv.edu
LEFFARD, Mary Ellen .... 770-426-2971 122 F
maryellen.leffard@life.edu
LEFFEL, Lisa .... 414-443-8796 513 A
lisa.leffel@wlc.edu
LEFFELMAN, Jeremy ...... 218-755-4222 244 B
jleffelman@bemidjistate.edu
LEFFLER, Danielle .... 812-941-2274 161 A
lefflerd@ius.edu
LEFFLER, Emily .... 713-221-5845 465 C
lefflere@uhd.edu
LEFFLER, Ernest .... 781-891-2552 212 A
eleffler@bentley.edu
LEFFLER, Lyvier .... 817-515-3015 458 B
lyvier.leffler@tccd.edu
LEFKOFF, Jeff .... 949-824-7335.. 69 A
jlefkoff@uci.edu
LEFLER, Jennifer .... 952-358-8200 246 D
jennifer.lefler@normandale.edu
LEFLER, Mike .... 402-826-8589 274 E
mike.lefler@doane.edu
LEFLER, Rochelle, L ...... 813-932-1710 103 I
LEFLORE, Larry .... 940-898-3415 464 A
llflore@twu.edu
LEFOE, Grant .... 704-290-5269 346 F
glefoe@spcc.edu
LEFORT, Donna, P .... 256-765-4252.... 9 A
dpjacobs@una.edu
LEFRANCOIS, Paul, R .... 864-488-4527 422 B
plefrancois@limestone.edu
LEFSTIN, Jeffrey .... 415-565-4682.. 68 I
lefstinj@uchastings.edu
LEFTHAND, Frederica .... 406-638-3131 271 C
lefthandfv@lbhc.edu
LEFTWICH, Shawn, B .... 630-752-5011 155 F
shawn.leftwich@wheaton.edu
LEGASPI, Lorenze .... 619-644-7141.. 45 A
lorenze.legaspi@gcccd.edu
LEGASPI, Lorenzo .... 925-485-5203.. 36 B
llegaspi@clpccd.org
LEGAULT, Greg .... 785-227-3380 175 E
legaultg@bethanylb.edu
LEGERE, Paul .... 301-243-2157 518 C
paul.legere@dodiis.mil
LEGG, David .... 865-573-4517 432 H
dlegg@johnsonu.edu
LEGG, Hal, S .... 607-436-2748 325 E
hal.legg@oneonta.edu
LEGG, Jamie, W .... 910-630-7028 340 A
jlegg@methodist.edu
LEGG, Margaret, A .... 423-775-7201 430 G
leggma@bryan.edu
LEGGE, Allison .... 919-843-6155 351 B
alegge@unc.edu
LEGGE, Karen .... 570-961-7886 399 A
leggek@lackawanna.edu
LEGGETT, Susan .... 413-572-8580 218 F
sleggett@westfield.ma.edu
LEGGETT, Terri .... 252-789-0204 344 E
terri.leggett@martincc.edu
LEGGETT, Vi .... 330-363-6183 357 A
vi.leggett@aultman.com
LEGGETTE, Priscilla .... 315-386-7315 329 A
leggettep@canton.edu
LEGGITT, Dan .... 618-544-8657 140 D
leggittd@iecc.edu
LEGRANDE, Tomikia, P . 713-221-8100 465 C
legrandet@uhd.edu
LEGREID, Ann, M .... 304-876-5011 504 D
alegreid@shepherd.edu
LEGRO, Jeffrey .... 804-289-8153 486 G
jlegro@richmond.edu
LEGRO, Jeffrey, W .... 434-924-6835 486 H
legro@virginia.edu
LEGURIA, Gina .... 209-575-6507.. 75 H
leguriag@yosemite.edu
LEHFELDT, Elizabeth ...... 216-687-5559 359 L
e.lehfeldt@csuohio.edu
LEHKER, Michael .... 956-665-2291 468 A
michael.lehker@utrgv.edu
LEHMAN, Andrew .... 717-720-4030 405 D
alehman@passhe.edu
LEHMAN, Ann .... 716-375-2435 322 B
alehman@sbu.edu
LEHMAN, Criquett .... 940-552-6291 469 F
cslehman@vernoncollege.edu

LEHMAN, DeWayne .... 617-287-5302 216 I
dewayne.lehman@umb.edu
LEHMAN, Douglas, K .... 937-327-7016 374 A
dlehman@wittenberg.edu
LEHMAN, Ed .... 540-432-4390 480 A
lehmanem@emu.edu
LEHMAN, John, B .... 906-487-1832 234 A
jblehman@mtu.edu
LEHMAN, Joseph .... 814-472-3054 409 G
jlehman@francis.edu
LEHMAN, Kathryn .... 352-395-5496 107 E
kathryn.lehman@sfcollege.edu
LEHMAN, Theresa .... 317-738-8176 157 L
tlehman@franklincollege.edu
LEHMAN, Tracey, A .... 541-885-1291 385 E
tracey.lehman@oit.edu
LEHMAN, William, H ..... 262-554-2010 508 E
lehmannw@yahoo.com
LEHMAN-FELTS, Juliana 940-397-4193 453 C
juliana.felts@mwsu.edu
LEHMANN, Craig .... 631-444-2253 325 F
craig.lehmann@stonybrook.edu
LEHMANN, Daniel .... 617-559-8773 215 H
dlehmann@hebrewcollege.edu
LEHMANN, Michael .... 608-263-2467 510 C
michael.lehman@wisc.edu
LEHMKKUHL, James ..... 937-778-8600 361 E
jlehmkkuhl@edisonohio.edu
LEHMPUHL, David .... 719-549-2340.. 78 P
david.lehmpuhl@csupueblo.edu
LEHN, Patricia .... 920-924-6326 514 D
plehn@morainepark.edu
LEHNER, Eric, J .... 757-479-3706 487 C
elehner@vbts.edu
LEHNERTZ, Rod .... 319-335-3500 166 G
rodney-lehnertz@uiowa.edu
LEHOCKY, John, F .... 847-970-4810 154 H
jlehocky@usml.edu
LEHOTAK, Ed .... 402-557-7050 273 E
ed.lehotak@bellevue.edu
LEHR, David .... 434-395-4952 482 E
lehrdl@longwood.edu
LEHR, Kirk, A .... 989-317-4611 234 B
klehr@midmich.edu
LEHRE, Elaine .... 906-248-8422 227 P
elehre@bmcc.edu
LEHRIAN, Amanda .... 863-674-6010 100 E
amanda.lehrian@fsw.edu
LEHRLING, Tony .... 580-745-2186 379 J
tlehrling@se.edu
LEHRMAN, Susan .... 856-256-5225 289 H
lehrman@rowan.edu
LEHTONEN, Rona .... 856-225-2309 290 B
rlehtonen@facilities.rutgers.edu
LEHWALD, Annie .... 816-501-4276 265 I
anne.lehwald@rockhurst.edu
LEI, Lei .... 848-445-3600 290 C
llei@business.rutgers.edu
LEI, Lei .... 973-353-1604 290 D
llei@business.rutgers.edu
LEIBLE, Art .... 310-660-3539.. 42 C
aleible@elcamino.edu
LEIBOLD, Susanne .... 563-588-6580 167 E
susanne.leibold@clarke.edu
LEICHLITER, Kirk .... 970-351-2446.. 83 F
kirk.leichliter@unco.edu
LEICHTNAM, Marky .... 614-985-2212 369 D
mleichtnam@pcj.edu
LEICHTY, Jeff, S .... 260-422-5561 159 D
jsleichty@indianatech.edu
LEIDERMAN, Roni .... 954-262-6930 104 F
roni@nova.edu
LEIDIG, Julie .... 703-450-2517 488 H
jleidig@nvcc.edu
LEIDIG, Mary, B .... 770-720-9150 124 H
mbl@reinhardt.edu
LEIDINGER, Angie .... 864-656-5615 419 F
angiel@clemson.edu
LEIFELD, Martin, F .... 314-516-4151 268 E
leifeldm@umsl.edu
LEIFELD, Robert, A .... 712-362-0439 170 D
rleifeld@iowalakes.edu
LEIGH, Anthony, J .... 334-833-4528.... 5 M
aleigh@hawks.huntingdon.edu
LEIGH, Bradley, K .... 419-372-2238 357 F
bleigh@bgsu.edu
LEIGH, Nathan .... 907-796-6496.. 10 C
nleigh1@alaska.edu
LEIGH, Susan .... 562-985-5471.. 32 C
susan.leigh@csulb.edu
LEIGH, Thomas .... 719-590-6774.. 79 B
tleigh@coloradotech.edu
LEIGHTON, Corey .... 207-947-4591 198 F
cleighton@bealcollege.edu
LEIGHTON, Dennis .... 207-221-4665 202 A
dleighton@une.edu
LEIGHTON, Jackie .... 609-258-5006 288 F
jleighto@princeton.edu

LEIGHTON, Robyn .... 207-454-1024 200 D
rleighton@wccc.me.edu
LEIJA, Shirley .... 210-486-3608 441 H
sleija@alamo.edu
LEIKER, Jeff .... 620-252-7147 176 K
leiker.jeff@coffeyville.edu
LEIKER, Meg .... 619-265-0107.. 57 G
mleiker@platt.edu
LEIKER, Robert, D .... 619-265-0107.. 57 G
rleiker@platt.edu
LEILER, Dina .... 773-481-8612 136 B
dleiler@ccc.edu
LEIMBACH, Bill .... 410-337-6298 204 A
bleimbach@goucher.edu
LEIMBEK, Melissa .... 763-424-0713 246 E
mleimbek@nhcc.edu
LEIMER, Christina .... 415-485-9545.. 39 E
cleimer@marin.edu
LEIMER, Jennifer .... 601-928-6211 254 D
jennifer.leimer@mgccc.edu
LEINAWEAVER, Justin ... 417-873-7167 259 G
jleinaweaver@drury.edu
LEINBERRY, Beth .... 401-841-4448 518 E
LEINEN, Jared .... 402-363-5675 278 E
jaleinen@york.edu
LEINEN, Margaret .... 858-534-2827.. 69 E
mleinen@ucsd.edu
LEINGANG, Dan .... 701-224-5525 354 F
daniel.leingang@bismarckstate.edu
LEININGER, Jeffrey .... 708-209-3470 136 I
jeff.leininger@cuchicago.edu
LEINWALL, Checka .... 605-626-2530 428 H
checka.leinwall@northern.edu
LEIPOLD, Bil .... 973-353-5500 290 D
bil.leipold@rutgers.edu
LEISCH, Dawn .... 512-505-3044 451 A
dleisch@htu.edu
LEISETH, Jon .... 218-299-3448 241 K
leiseth@cord.edu
LEISINGER, Scott, C ..... 319-352-8495 174 C
scott.leisinger@wartburg.edu
LEIST, Terry .... 406-994-4361 272 A
tleist@montana.edu
LEISTIKOW, Claudia, M 920-748-8742 509 H
leistikowc@ripon.edu
LEITE, Pedro .... 913-621-8700 177 A
pleite@donnelly.edu
LEITE, Randy .... 740-593-9336 368 G
leite@ohio.edu
LEITER, Dena .... 908-709-7622 292 C
leiter@ucc.edu
LEITERMAN, Gene .... 918-293-5026 378 B
gene.leiterman@okstate.edu
LEITGEB, Robert .... 757-455-3114 491 F
rletgeib@vwc.edu
LEITHNER STAUFFER,
Andrea, C .... 570-577-1331 390 H
andrea.leithner.stauffer@bucknell.edu
LEITSON, Cynthia .... 216-987-4702 360 E
cynthia.leitson@tri-c.edu
LEITZEL, Thomas, C .... 863-784-7110 108 B
leitzelt@southflorida.edu
LEIVA, Laurie .... 504-861-5419 194 G
laleiva@loyno.edu
LEJTER, Nelly .... 603-428-2217 281 F
nlejter@nec.edu
LEJUEZ, Carl, W .... 785-864-3661 181 I
clejuez@ku.edu
LELAND, Chris .... 405-733-7350 379 F
cleland@rose.edu
LELAND, Dorothy .... 209-228-4417.. 69 C
chancellor@ucmerced.edu
LELAND, John, E .... 937-229-2114 372 A
john.leland@udri.udayton.edu
LELAND, Melinda, T .... 276-739-2548 490 A
mleland@vhcc.edu
LELAND, Ted .... 209-946-2392.. 70 F
tleland@pacific.edu
LELCHOOK, Heather ...... 970-667-4611.. 76 E
heather.lelchook@aims.edu
LELE, Pradeep .... 281-618-7123 452 C
pradeep.m.lele@lonestar.edu
LELFER, John .... 704-463-3039 348 B
john.lefler@pfeiffer.edu
LELIAERT, Deborah, S ... 940-565-2108 466 B
deborah.leliaert@unt.edu
LELIK, Mary, K .... 919-515-6434 350 E
mklelik@ncsu.edu
LELONG, Kristine, D ...... 504-865-3858 194 G
klelong@loyno.edu
LELOUDIS, James, L ..... 919-966-5110 351 B
leloudis@unc.edu
LEMAHIEU, Dan .... 847-735-5083 142 H
lemahieu@lakeforest.edu
LEMAHIEU, Keith .... 219-864-2400 162 U
klemahieu@midamerica.edu
LEMAIRE, Renee .... 334-222-6591.... 2 H
rlemaire@lbwcc.edu

LEMAR, Darrell 617-228-2416 219 D dwlemar@bhcc.mass.edu
LEMARBE, Thomas, P 248-370-2445 235 J lemarbe@oakland.edu
LEMASTER, Charles 254-267-7060 454 L clemaster@rangercollege.edu
LEMASTER, J. Michael 937-258-8251 363 F
LEMASTER, Mary 540-665-4513 485 C mlesmate@su.edu
LEMASTERS, Michael, W 724-357-2696 406 C michael.lemasters@iup.edu
LEMAY, Elaine 510-869-6739 59 F elemay@samuelmerritt.edu
LEMAY, Jerret 315-312-2237 327 D jerret.lemay@oswego.edu
LEMAY, Tandra 985-448-7950 192 I tandra.lemay@fletcher.edu
LEMBKE, Roberta 507-786-3097 250 C lembke@stolaf.edu
LEMBURG, Mary 713-718-8505 450 D mary.lemburg@hccs.edu
LEMCOE, Diane 908-526-1200 289 D diane.lemcoe@raritanval.edu
LEMELLE, Erica 757-352-4778 484 E ericlem@regent.edu
LEMERE, Brian, J 864-597-4068 426 I lemerebj@wofford.edu
LEMEROND, James 920-693-1840 513 H james.lemerond@gotoltc.edu
LEMERY, Cynthia 518-327-6399 320 A clemery@paulsmiths.edu
LEMEUNIER, Jennifer 337-482-0900 197 F jlemeunier@louisiana.edu
LEMIEN, Laura 603-366-5221 280 K llemien@ccsnh.edu
LEMING, Crystal 785-670-1470 182 D crystal.leming@washburn.edu
LEMING, Heidi 615-366-3948 436 E heidi.leming@tbr.edu
LEMIRE, Joseph 414-229-4627 511 A lemire@uwm.edu
LEMIRE, Mark 315-792-7100 330 A mark.lemire@sunypoly.edu
LEMISCH, Jamie 215-780-1391 410 D jlemisch@salus.edu
LEMKE, Chris 616-222-1360 229 B chris.lemke@cornerstone.edu
LEMLER, Brad 325-649-8704 450 H blemler@hputx.edu
LEMME, Daryl 605-718-2953 429 E daryl.lemme@wdt.edu
LEMME, Gary, D 334-844-4444 4 D gdl0003@aces.edu
LEMMON, John 650-508-3494 54 D jlemmon@ndnu.edu
LEMMON, John 650-508-3605 54 D jlemmon@ndnu.edu
LEMOINE, Lynn 651-290-7668 248 U lynn.lemoine@mitchellhamline.edu
LEMOINE, Patrice, A 860-297-2086 88 E patrice.lemoine@trincoll.edu
LEMOINE, Sandra, M 318-342-1235 198 A slemoine@ulm.edu
LEMON, Deborah, A 812-856-3731 159 G dalemon@iu.edu
LEMON, Deborah, A 812-855-6783 159 H dalemon@iu.edu
LEMON, Jason 619-260-4585 71 J jasonlemon@sandiego.edu
LEMON, Ronald, E 304-896-7425 503 D ronald.lemon@southernwv.edu
LEMON, William, J 314-516-4702 268 E lemonj@umsl.edu
LEMONIS, Samuel 601-857-3204 253 B splemonis@hindscc.edu
LEMONIUS, Garfield 412-392-6112 408 F glemonius@pointpark.edu
LEMONS, James 434-832-7680 487 H lemonsj@cvcc.vccs.edu
LEMUEL, Robert, L 989-964-4393 236 F lemuel@svsu.edu
LEMURA, Linda, M 315-445-4120 312 F president14@lemoyne.edu
LEMUS, Maria De Jesus 773-371-5453 134 J mlemus@ctu.edu
LENA, III, Hugh, F 401-865-2155 416 E hlena@providence.edu
LENAHAN, Robert 631-632-6350 325 F robert.lenahan@stonybrook.edu
LENCKE, Scott 901-381-3939 440 I scott@visible.edu
LENCZOWSKI, John 202-462-2101 92 D lenczowski@iwp.edu
LENEZ, Nicole 540-365-4456 480 L nlenez@ferrum.edu
LENFEST, Richard 413-572-5405 218 F rlenfest@westfield.ma.edu
LENGSFELD, Corinne 303-871-4843 83 E clengsfe@du.edu
LENHARDT, Andrew, R 812-465-7115 165 C alenhardt@usi.edu
LENHART, Brian, L 972-881-5801 446 I blenhard@collin.edu
LENHART, Jeff 704-847-5600 349 E jlenhart@ses.edu
LENHARTH, Donna 417-667-8181 259 A dlenharth@cottey.edu
LENIG, Joni 931-540-2517 436 H jlenig@columbiastate.edu
LENIG, Joni, L 931-540-2752 436 H jlenig@columbiastate.edu
LENIHAN, Bernard 908-709-7605 292 C lenihan@ucc.edu
LENIHAN, David 787-840-2575 525 I dlenihan@psm.edu
LENIO, Jim 866-492-5336 251 E jim.lenio@mail.waldenu.edu
LENITNI, James, P 248-370-2193 235 J jlentini@oakland.edu
LENK, Robert 405-789-7661 380 A robert.lenk@swcu.edu
LENN, Michael 608-262-1234 510 C mlenn@wisc.edu
LENNEMAN, Marc 406-447-4869 270 H mlenneman@carroll.edu
LENNERTON, Mark 718-289-5655 301 D mark.lennerton@bcc.cuny.edu
LENNERTZ, Reid 239-590-7960 109 C rlennert@fgcu.edu
LENNEY, Raina 202-885-5936 91 C lenney@american.edu
LENNO, Chip 831-582-3000 33 A
LENNON, John 845-848-4061 306 G john.lennon@dc.edu
LENNOX, JR., William, J 352-588-8242 106 N bill.lennox@saintleo.edu
LENO, Melissa 218-733-5903 245 C m.leno@lsc.edu
LENO, Tom 701-224-5497 354 F thomas.leno@bismarckstate.edu
LENOIR, Nina 714-997-6622 36 G lenoir@chapman.edu
LENON, Fe, L 773-442-5143 147 G f-lenon@neiu.edu
LENORE-JENKINS, Shani 314-529-9350 262 B slenore@maryville.edu
LENOX, Richard 806-742-3671 463 D richard.lenox@ttu.edu
LENROW, Jon 215-670-9359 403 D jlenrow@peirce.edu
LENSER, Leslie, A 615-460-6456 430 D
LENSING, Peggy 563-387-1015 171 I lensinpe@luther.edu
LENSING TATE, Amy 414-229-3844 511 A lensing@uwm.edu
LENT, Tina 209-954-5151 61 B tlent@deltacollege.edu
LENTINO, Nicholas 860-727-6765 87 B nlentino@goodwin.edu
LENTZ, Brannon 334-514-8607 2 E brannon.lentz@istc.edu
LENTZ, Heather 605-995-7227 427 E heather.lentz@mitchelltech.edu
LENTZ, Kristi, L 701-788-4772 354 B kristi.lentz@mayvillestate.edu
LENTZ, Sherry 904-596-2443 112 F slentz@tbc.edu
LENTZ, Victoria, A 410-543-6262 209 B valentz@salisbury.edu
LENWAY, Stefanie, A 651-962-4201 251 D lenw0002@stthomas.edu
LENZ, Christopher 323-343-3237 32 D clenz@cslanet.calstatela.edu
LENZ, Craig, J 334-699-2266 1 B
LENZ, Joseph 515-271-4028 168 J joseph.lenz@drake.edu
LENZ, Mary 320-762-4648 243 J maryl@alextech.edu
LENZ, Patrick, J 510-987-9101 68 F patrick.lenz@ucop.edu
LENZER, Julie 301-405-2960 207 G jlenzer@umd.edu
LENZI, Patrick 610-436-1048 407 D plenzi@wcupa.edu
LEO, Donald 706-542-1653 127 A donleo@engr.uga.edu
LEO, Grace, D 787-279-1912 523 J gdileo@bayamon.inter.edu
LEO, Jonathan 423-869-7094 433 C jonathan.leo@lmunet.edu
LEO, Laurie 585-594-6861 321 C leo_laurie@roberts.edu
LEO, Laurie 585-594-6861 319 B leo_laurie@roberts.edu
LEO, Sydney, R 607-431-4320 309 E leos@hartwick.edu
LEOMITI, Sonny, J 684-699-9155 519 F s.leomiti@amsamoa.edu
LEON, Carmen, L 787-894-2828 529 A carmen.leon@upr.edu
LEON, Christine 714-564-6230 58 A leon_christine@sac.edu
LEON, Juan, C 787-844-8812 528 E juan.leon1@upr.edu
LEON, Kelly 513-745-3877 374 D leon@xavier.edu
LEON, Linda, J 330-471-8442 364 H lleon2@malone.edu
LEON, Nelson 212-752-1530 312 G nelson.leon@limcollege.edu
LEON, Orlando 559-278-3923 32 A oleon@csufresno.edu
LEON, Tony 559-297-4500 46 E
LEON, Way 415-422-2868 72 A leon@usfca.edu
LEON GUERRERO, Ann S, A 671-735-2941 520 B annsalg@triton.uog.edu
LEON GUERRERO, Barbara, B 671-735-5519 519 H csi@guamcc.edu
LEON GUERRERO, Deborah, D 671-735-2585 520 B deborah@triton.uog.edu
LEON-JORDAN, Jordania 262-595-2010 511 C leonjord@uwp.edu
LEON-VICKS, Lilly 775-445-3324 279 F lilly.leon-vicks@wnc.edu
LEONARD, Alan 315-228-7474 304 G pleonard@colgate.edu
LEONARD, Alice 414-276-5200 157 E alice.leonard@ccr.edu
LEONARD, Andy 704-461-6200 335 J andyleonard@bac.edu
LEONARD, Bethany 262-695-6520 515 B bleonard3@wctc.edu
LEONARD, Bob 765-658-4161 157 H bobleonard@depauw.edu
LEONARD, Brenda 704-330-6626 342 A brenda.leonard@cpcc.edu
LEONARD, Bryan 217-245-3048 139 H bryan.leonard@mail.ic.edu
LEONARD, Courtney 563-588-6585 167 E courtney.leonard@clarke.edu
LEONARD, David, M 540-458-8752 491 G dleonard@wlu.edu
LEONARD, Debbie 305-809-3203 99 L debbie.leonard@fkcc.edu
LEONARD, Dennis 402-461-7477 274 I dleonard@hastings.edu
LEONARD, J. Rich 919-865-5878 336 C leonardjr@campbell.edu
LEONARD, Jason 423-420-1211 432 E leonarja@hiwassee.edu
LEONARD, Jesse, W 814-641-3162 398 B leonarj@juniata.edu
LEONARD, John 804-758-6764 489 D jleonard@rappahannock.edu
LEONARD, Katie 570-702-8925 398 A kleonard@johnson.edu
LEONARD, Marjolie 631-632-6280 325 F marjolie.leonard@stonybrook.edu
LEONARD, Mary Kathleen 814-871-7430 395 H leonard010@gannon.edu
LEONARD, Pam 229-391-5050 114 G pleonard@abac.edu
LEONARD, Patricia, L 910-962-3117 352 A leonard@uncw.edu
LEONARD, Raychelle 928-724-6671 12 G rleonard@dinecollege.edu
LEONARD, Robert 256-824-2233 8 C robert.leonard@uah.edu
LEONARD, Roberta 724-589-2842 411 D rleonard@thiel.edu
LEONARD, Steve 317-738-8316 157 L sleonard@franklincollege.edu
LEONARD, Thomas, C 510-642-3773 68 G toml@berkeley.edu
LEONARD, Timothy 410-704-3936 209 C tleonard@towson.edu
LEONARD, Vee 239-590-1101 109 C vleonard@fgcu.edu
LEONARD, William 617-735-9883 214 F leonard@emmanuel.edu
LEONARD, William 610-361-5217 402 G leonardw@neumann.edu
LEONARD-MARTIN, Peg 615-460-6856 430 D peg.leonardmartin@belmont.edu
LEONE, Charles 215-204-7900 411 B charles.leone@temple.edu
LEONE, Deanna 657-278-2097 32 B dleone@fullerton.edu
LEONE, John 518-828-4181 305 D john.leone@sunycgcc.edu
LEONE, Loida 620-278-4202 181 G lleone@sterling.edu
LEONETTI, Marc 401-254-3843 417 C mleonetti@rwu.edu
LEONG, Nori 808-544-0292 129 C nleong@hpu.edu
LEONI, Amy 740-695-9500 357 D aleoni@belmontcollege.edu
LEONOR, JR., Samuel, E 951-785-2090 47 F sleonor@lasierra.edu
LEOPALDI-ALEMAN, Daniela 312-752-2198 142 E daniela.leopaldi@kendall.edu
LEOPARD, Tim 205-348-8157 8 A tleopard@fa.ua.edu
LEOPOLD, Emily 617-588-1347 211 G eleopold@bfit.edu
LEOPOLD, Joseph 727-341-3719 107 A
LEOPOLD, Lillian 619-482-6564 65 H lleopold@swccd.edu
LEOS, Jonathan, S 323-856-7742 25 L jleos@afi.com
LEOUSIS, Kim 251-442-2290 8 D kleousis@umobile.edu
LEPAGE, Sharon 808-440-4263 129 A slepage@chaminade.edu
LEPERA, John 410-323-6211 203 F admissions@fts.edu
LEPHART, Scott, M 859-323-1100 190 B scott.lephart@uky.edu
LEPLEY, Pamela, D 804-828-6057 487 E pdlepley@vcu.edu
LEPPANEN, Hannu 906-487-7285 230 B hannu.leppanen@finlandia.edu
LEPPELLERE, Terry 312-777-8594 140 G tleppellere@aii.edu
LEPPER, Charles 801-957-4285 474 B charles.lepper@slcc.edu
LEPPERT, Glenn, W 620-862-5252 175 B registrar@barclaycollege.edu
LEPRE, Dave 575-835-5091 294 K dave.lepre@nmt.edu
LERBINGER, Jan 617-585-1284 222 H jan.lerbinger@necmusic.edu
LERCH, Derek 530-283-0202 42 K dlerch@frc.edu
LERCH, Maureen, T 330-972-8951 371 D mlerch@uakron.edu
LERER, Nava 516-877-3236 297 I lerer@adelphi.edu
LERMA, Raul, H 915-831-2229 449 A rlerma23@epcc.edu
LERMAN, Linda 203-857-7211 86 D llerman@norwalk.edu
LERMAN, Steven, R 831-656-2371 518 D slerman@nps.edu
LERNER, Babrara 940-898-2000 464 A
LERNER, Sharon 212-817-7400 302 B slerner@gc.cuny.edu
LEROSEN, Genene, D 804-523-5550 488 C glerosen@reynolds.edu
LEROY, Antonio 229-430-3635 114 I antonio.leroy@asurams.edu
LEROY, Francois 859-572-7976 188 E leroy@nku.edu
LEROY, Glen, S 617-262-5000 212 C glen.leroy@the-bac.edu
LEROY, Lindsay 910-962-2684 352 A leroyl@uncw.edu
LEROY, Thomas 315-470-6667 328 D tjleroy@esf.edu
LESAGE, Jasper 316-295-5881 177 F jasper_lesage@friends.edu
LESAN, Thomas, L 641-782-1443 173 I lesan@swcciowa.edu
LESANE, II, Cornell 814-332-2102 388 F clesane@allegheny.edu
LESAVOY, Barbara 585-395-5700 326 D blesavoy@brockport.edu
LESCAULT, JR., Maurice, A 434-971-3291 517 N moe.lescault.mil@mail.mil
LESCH, William, J 563-333-6266 173 A leschwilliam@sau.edu
LESCHES, Elchonon 718-363-2034 331 B bmotzal@gmail.com
LESCINSKI, CSJ, Joan 563-333-6213 173 A officeofthepresident@sau.edu

LESCZINSKI, Michael .... 518-608-8450 308 A mlesczinski@excelsior.edu
LESEN, Beth .... 916-278-6060.. 33 C beth.lesen@csus.edu
LESESNE, David, L .... 804-752-7305 484 C davidlesesne@rmc.edu
LESH, Aja .... 626-815-6000.. 26 U alesh@apu.edu
LESHAN, Tim, E .... 617-373-8528 223 D
LESHIN, Laurie .... 508-831-5200 226 E president@wpi.edu
LESHINSKIE, Eric .... 623-845-3155.. 13 H eric.leshinskie@gccaz.edu
LESHKEVICH, Peter ...... 734-973-3729 238 G pleshkev@wccnet.edu
LESHOK, Paul .... 414-930-3305 509 B leshokp@mtmary.edu
LESIAK, Erin .... 308-398-7406 273 G erinlesiak@cccneb.edu
LESKO, Kathleen .... 518-454-5154 305 B leskok@strose.edu
LESLEY, Kimberly ...... 215-965-8582 402 C klesley@moore.edu
LESLIE, Benjamin, C ..... 704-406-4239 337 H bleslie@gardner-webb.edu
LESLIE, Bruce .... 210-485-0020 441 E bleslie@alamo.edu
LESLIE, Donald .... 434-528-5276 491 D dleslie@vul.edu
LESLIE, Frances, M .... 949-824-6351.. 69 A fmleslie@uci.edu
LESLIE, Howard .... 973-278-5400 299 F hdl@berkeleycollege.edu
LESLIE, Howard .... 973-278-5400 283 J hdl@berkeleycollege.edu
LESLIE, Julie .... 419-251-1598 365 C julie.leslie@mercycollege.edu
LESLIE, Ken .... 802-635-1315 477 C ken.leslie@jsc.edu
LESLIE, Paul, L .... 336-272-7102 338 B lesliep@greensboro.edu
LESLIE, Robert .... 864-592-4910 424 C leslier@sccsc.edu
LESLIE, Robin .... 864-596-9056 420 F robin.leslie@converse.edu
LESLIE, Steve .... 512-322-3789 467 A sleslie@utsystem.edu
LESSANE JENKINS, Wanda .... 910-672-1145 350 B wljenkins@uncfsu.edu
LESSARD, Richard, J ..... 617-732-2149 221 E richard.lessard@mcphs.edu
LESSEIG, Lisa .... 912-279-5737 118 A llesseig@ccga.edu
LESSEM, Louis, A .... 313-577-2268 239 C louis.lessem@wayne.edu
LESSER, Cheryl, A .... 518-562-4110 304 C cheryl.lesser@clinton.edu
LESSER, Edward, R .... 617-585-1211 222 H ed.lesser@necmusic.edu
LESSER, Mary .... 828-328-7078 339 C mary.lesser@lr.edu
LESSITER, Julie .... 318-795-4238 194 E julie.lessiter@lsus.edu
LESSNER, Kimberly .... 903-510-2383 464 D kles@tjc.edu
LESTAGE, Richard .... 617-746-1990 216 A richard.lestage@hult.edu
LESTER, Cancee .... 936-591-9075 454 E clester@panola.edu
LESTER, Dyan, E .... 276-964-7677 489 F dyan.lester@sw.edu
LESTER, Gillian .... 212-854-2675 305 E glester@law.columbia.edu
LESTER, Jason .... 281-649-3339 450 C jlester@hbu.edu
LESTER, John .... 706-507-8720 118 C lester_john@columbusstate.edu
LESTER, John .... 334-670-3923.... 7 E jlester@troy.edu
LESTER, Karen, K .... 218-477-2062 246 B lesterka@mnstate.edu
LESTER, Mike .... 507-285-7254 247 D mike.lester@rctc.edu
LESTER, Richard, K .... 617-253-7704 221 C
LESTER, Ron .... 405-491-6356 379 K rlester@snu.edu
LESTER, Steve .... 404-880-8985 117 H steven.lester@dtz.com
LESTER, Tammy .... 252-451-8371 345 B ttlester342@nashcc.edu
LESTER, Thomas .... 276-964-7683 489 F thomas.lester@sw.edu
LESTER, Wanda .... 919-530-6458 350 D wanda.lester@nccu.edu
LESWICK, Brenda .... 909-607-1403.. 37 L brenda.leswick@cgu.edu
LETCHER, Owen .... 408-270-6401.. 61 N owen.letcher@sjeccd.org
LETCHWORTH, Deemie .. 601-643-8403 252 G deemie.letchworth@colin.edu
LETCHWORTH, Megan ... 928-350-1006.. 15 V megan.letchworth@prescott.edu
LETENDRE, Donald, E ... 319-335-8794 166 G donald-letendre@uiowa.edu
LETH-STEENSEN, Ted .... 413-565-1000 211 C tlethsteensen@baypath.edu
LETIZIA, Katelyn .... 716-926-8942 310 B kletizia@hilbert.edu
LETLOW, Julia .... 318-342-5447 198 A letlow@ulm.edu
LETO, Leah .... 201-761-6102 291 D lleto@saintpeters.edu
LETO, Michael, A .... 413-545-4200 216 H mleto@admin.umass.edu
LETONEK, Stefan .... 330-337-6403 356 B college@awc.edu
LETSCHE, Mary Ellen ..... 305-899-3011.. 95 G mletsche@barry.edu
LETSOU, Peter, V .... 901-678-2421 439 E pvletsou@memphis.edu
LETT, Vivian .... 770-689-4808 115 E vlett@edmc.edu
LETTIERE, Barbara .... 610-647-4400 397 I blettiere@immaculata.edu
LETTING, III, Al .... 877-476-8674 449 H
LETTINI, Gabriella .... 510-549-4714.. 66 D glettini@sksm.edu
LETTINI, Pat .... 516-876-3191 327 C lettinip@oldwestbury.edu
LETTKO, James .... 518-464-8500 308 A jlettko@excelsior.edu
LETZRING, Tim .... 903-886-5181 459 E tim.letzring@tamuc.edu
LEU, Tom .... 815-965-8616 150 B tomleu@rockfordcareercollege.edu
LEUENBERGER, Deniz ... 508-531-1201 217 D dleuenberger@bridgew.edu
LEUENBERGER, Derek ... 508-531-1715 217 D d1leuenberger@bridgew.edu
LEUKEN, Joel .... 605-394-2643 429 A joel.leuken@sdsmt.edu
LEUMA, Elizabeth .... 684-699-9155 519 F e.leuma@amsamoa.edu
LEUNER, Jean .... 334-244-3658.... 4 E jleuner@aum.edu
LEUNG, Katheryn .... 626-917-9482.. 37 D kleung@cesna.edu
LEUPP, Stephanie .... 918-335-6286 378 F sleupp@okwu.edu
LEUSCH, Lucy .... 404-364-8309 124 A lleusch@oglethorpe.edu
LEUTZINGER, Eugene .... 319-296-4457 169 H eugene.leutzinger@hawkeyecollege.edu
LEVA, Gennaro, J .... 215-204-2452 411 B levagj@temple.edu
LEVAN, Gretchen .... 610-917-1478 413 G gllevan@valleyforge.edu
LEVAN, Kent, G .... 314-977-7143 266 J levankg@slu.edu
LEVANDER, Caroline ..... 717-348-4228 455 F clevande@rice.edu
LEVANDOSKI, Mark .... 641-269-4544 169 F levandos@grinnell.edu
LEVAO, Richard, A .... 973-748-9000 284 A rlevao@bloomfield.edu
LEVARIO GUTIERREZ, Estela .... 775-337-5647 279 C elevario@tmcc.edu
LEVAS, Frances .... 617-731-3500 215 I flevas@hchc.edu
LEVATO, Peggy, S .... 315-379-3871 329 A levatop@canton.edu
LEVAULT, Nancy .... 618-797-7311 152 E nancy.levault@swic.edu
LEVEILLE, Rick .... 678-664-0533 128 F rick.leveille@westgatech.edu
LEVEN, Carol .... 212-217-4700 308 B carol_leven@fitnyc.edu
LEVEN, Scott .... 417-447-6985 264 K levens@otc.edu
LEVENS, Michael .... 248-689-8282 238 F mlevens@walshcollege.edu
LEVENSON, Josh .... 818-763-2563.. 27 J
LEVENSON, Stephanie .... 630-617-3354 138 C slevenson@elmhurst.edu
LEVEQUE, Rod .... 909-593-3511.. 70 E rleveque@laverne.edu
LEVERENZ, Jeffrey .... 262-691-5301 515 B jleverenz@wctc.edu
LEVERETTE, Valerie .... 410-462-8054 202 F vleverette@bccc.edu
LEVERGOOD, Bill, J .... 417-268-6043 257 H blevergoodl@gobbc.edu
LEVERING, E, H .... 305-237-0777 103 L eleverin@mdc.edu
LEVERS, David, W .... 718-289-5157 301 D david.levers@bcc.cuny.edu
LEVERSEE, Gordon .... 603-358-2545 283 A gleverse@keene.edu
LEVERTON, Kathryn .... 609-771-2881 284 I leverton@tcnj.edu
LEVESQUE, Andrew .... 860-231-5238.. 89 E ajlevesque@usj.edu
LEVESQUE, Jacqueline .. 713-798-3356 444 A levesque@bcm.edu
LEVESQUE, Jeanne .... 617-552-4787 212 E jeanne.levesque@bc.edu
LEVESQUE, Maurice ...... 336-278-6455 337 G levesque@elon.edu
LEVESQUE, Neil .... 603-222-4109 282 A nlevesque@anselm.edu
LEVETT, Kerry .... 541-463-5315 383 F levettk@lanecc.edu
LEVETZOW, Megan .... 563-333-6070 173 A levetzowmegan@sau.edu
LEVEY, Lynn .... 508-793-7194 213 C llevey@clarku.edu
LEVEY, Steve .... 713-718-5261 450 D stephen.levey@hccs.edu
LEVI, David, F .... 919-613-7001 337 C david.levi@law.duke.edu
LEVICKI, Glenn .... 843-525-8276 424 E glevicki@tcl.edu
LEVIN, Avrohom, C .... 773-463-7738 152 J aclevin@telshe.edu
LEVIN, Gary, M .... 305-760-7500 103 C
LEVIN, Jason .... 801-274-3280 474 D jason.levin@wgu.edu
LEVIN, Jeffrey, L .... 903-877-5884 469 A jeffrey.levin@uthct.edu
LEVIN, Jonathan .... 650-723-2300.. 66 C jdlevin@stanford.edu
LEVIN, Jonathan .... 540-654-1241 486 D jlevin@umw.edu
LEVIN, Lubbe .... 310-794-0810.. 69 B llevin@chr.ucla.edu
LEVIN, Marc .... 410-888-9048 205 D mlevin@muih.edu
LEVIN, Rob .... 207-801-5623 199 A rlevin@coa.edu
LEVIN, Yitzchok .... 773-463-7738 152 J yzlevin@telshe.edu
LEVINE, Al .... 612-624-5054 250 E aslevine@umn.edu
LEVINE, Arthur, S .... 412-648-8975 412 I alevine@pitt.edu
LEVINE, Berinthia .... 216-523-7275 359 L berinthia.levine@csuohio.edu
LEVINE, Beth, F .... 718-951-2023 301 E bflevine@brooklyn.cuny.edu
LEVINE, Heidi .... 515-961-1617 173 E heidi.levine@simpson.edu
LEVINE, Helen .... 727-873-4744 111 B hlevine@mail.usf.edu
LEVINE, Isaac .... 732-367-1060 283 K ilevine@bmg.edu
LEVINE, Joel .... 619-482-6349.. 65 H jlevine@swccd.edu
LEVINE, Laurie .... 561-237-7181 103 E llevine@lynn.edu
LEVINE, Lawrence, M .... 303-492-4691.. 83 B larry.levine@colorado.edu
LEVINE, Louis, L .... 212-410-8023 317 C llevine@nycpm.edu
LEVINE, Martin, L .... 213-740-2101.. 72 B levine@usc.edu
LEVINE, Michael, F .... 716-878-4311 326 E levinemf@buffalostate.edu
LEVINE, Shana .... 503-768-7548 383 G slevine@lclark.edu
LEVINE, Susan .... 212-875-4657 298 H slevine@bankstreet.edu
LEVINE, Vikki .... 607-274-3075 311 D vlevine@ithaca.edu
LEVINE, Virginia .... 607-753-2201 327 A virginia.levine@cortland.edu
LEVINE, Yasemin .... 212-217-4923 308 B yasemin_levine@fitnyc.edu
LEVINE-CLARK, Michael 303-871-3413.. 83 E miclark@du.edu
LEVINE LAUFGRABEN, Jodi .... 215-204-7423 411 B jodi.levine@temple.edu
LEVINESS, Peter, O .... 804-289-8119 486 G plevines@richmond.edu
LEVINO, Evelyn .... 614-947-6765 362 A evelyn.levino@franklin.edu
LEVINS, Pat .... 973-618-3604 284 D plevins@caldwell.edu
LEVINSKY, Robert .... 757-455-3415 491 F rlevinsky@vwu.edu
LEVINSON, David .... 203-857-7024.. 84 I dlevinson@ncc.commnet.edu
LEVINSON, David, L ...... 203-857-7024.. 86 D dlevinson@norwalk.edu
LEVINSON, Karen .... 215-596-8709 413 E k.levins@usciences.edu
LEVINSTEIN, Edward ..... 585-343-0055 309 C ejlevenstein@genesee.edu
LEVIS, Joseph .... 718-405-3329 304 H joseph.levis@mountsaintvincent.edu
LEVISEUR, Jacquelyn .... 330-941-2136 374 E jmleviseur@ysu.edu
LEVISTER, JR., Joseph, W .... 910-678-8327 343 B levistej@faytechcc.edu
LEVITT, Bart .... 412-809-5100 408 D levitt.bart@pti.edu
LEVITTE, Yael .... 607-255-6867 306 B yael.levitte@cornell.edu
LEVITZKE, Shannon .... 334-222-6591.... 2 H slevitzke@lbwcc.edu
LEVY, Ben .... 201-684-7533 289 C blevy1@ramapo.edu
LEVY, Carly .... 617-735-1014 221 E carly.levy@mcphs.edu
LEVY, Daisy .... 802-447-6387 476 C dlevy@svc.edu
LEVY, Dennis, P .... 610-861-7925 402 D levyd@moravian.edu
LEVY, Douglas .... 586-445-7535 233 B levyd@macomb.edu
LEVY, Gary .... 410-704-2124 209 C glevy@towson.edu
LEVY, Laura .... 504-988-3291 196 D llevy@tulane.edu
LEVY, Margaree .... 651-255-6118 250 D mlevy@unitedseminary.edu
LEVY, Mitchell .... 609-343-5087 283 D mlevy@atlantic.edu
LEVY, Morgan .... 585-275-7814 332 E morgan.levy@rochester.edu
LEVY, Odelia .... 212-220-1236 301 C
LEVY CRUZ, Madeline ... 570-558-1818 395 F mlevycruz@fortisinstitute.edu
LEW, Gary, B .... 716-888-2255 300 G lew@canisius.edu
LEW, John .... 336-278-5560 337 G jlew@elon.edu
LEW YAN VOON, Lok ... 678-839-5190 127 F lokl@westga.edu
LEWALLEN, Willard .... 831-755-6900.. 45 C wlewallen@hartnell.edu
LEWANDOWSKI, Joseph, D .... 660-543-4633 268 A lewandowski@ucmo.edu
LEWANDOWSKI, Linda .. 906-786-5802 228 A lewandol@baycollege.edu
LEWANDOWSKI, Linda .. 419-383-5858 372 F linda.lewandowski@utoledo.edu
LEWELLEN, Randy .... 903-983-8130 451 F rlewellen@kilgore.edu
LEWICKI, Denise .... 860-628-4751.. 87 E dlewicki@lincolncollegene.edu
LEWIN, Jonathan, S ...... 404-778-4432 119 B jon.lewin@emory.edu
LEWIN, Lisa, M .... 414-410-4230 506 F lmlewin@stritch.edu
LEWIN, Luis .... 817-735-5097 466 B luis.lewin@untsystem.edu
LEWIN, Ross, D .... 301-405-8535 207 G rdlewin@umd.edu
LEWIS, Alana .... 706-821-8361 124 C alewis@paine.edu
LEWIS, Albert .... 425-564-2265 492 G albert.lewis@bellevuecollege.edu
LEWIS, Alicia .... 415-351-3556.. 60 G alewis@sfai.edu
LEWIS, Andre .... 831-582-3044.. 33 A alewis@csumb.edu
LEWIS, Andrew .... 304-829-7645 501 F alewis@bethanywv.edu
LEWIS, Ann .... 208-769-7812 132 E ann_lewis@nic.edu
LEWIS, Barbara .... 360-676-2772 496 C bjlewis@nwic.edu
LEWIS, Beth .... 361-698-1205 448 H bethlewis@delmar.edu
LEWIS, Beverly, N .... 336-734-7512 343 C blewis@forsythtech.edu
LEWIS, Bill .... 505-566-3339 296 A lewisb@sanjuancollege.edu
LEWIS, Blaine, D .... 330-823-7365 372 C lewisbd@mountunion.edu
LEWIS, Bo .... 928-724-6679.. 12 G blewis@dinecollege.edu
LEWIS, Brenda .... 863-680-6285 100 D blewis@flsouthern.edu

LIBERATOSCIOLI, Daniel .... 267-295-2316 409 B
president@walnuthillcollege.edu
LIBERATOSCIOLI, Peggy .... 267-295-2315 409 B
pl@walnuthillcollege.edu
LIBERMAN, Ira .... 718-438-1002 315 A
yliberman@yeshivanet.com
LIBERTELLI, Joseph .... 202-274-7338.. 93 D
jlibertelli@udc.edu
LIBERTO, Terri .... 412-536-1813 398 E
terri.liberto@laroche.edu
LIBERTY, Bob .... 254-526-1310 445 L
bob.liberty@ctcd.edu
LIBERTY, Cynthia .... 336-770-3333 352 B
libertyc@uncsa.edu
LIBERTY, Paul .... 703-993-8860 481 B
pliberty@gmu.edu
LIBET, Alice, Q .... 843-792-4930 422 C
libeta@musc.edu
LIBHART, Bonnie .... 256-652-3752 435 H
drbonnie@me.com
LIBUNAO, Arte .... 949-783-4800.. 73 K
LIBUTTI, Dean .... 401-874-4408 417 E
dean@uri.edu
LIBUTTI, Ken .... 561-868-3239 105 A
libuttik@palmbeachstate.edu
LIBUTTI, Steven, K .... 732-235-8064 290 A
sl1442@rutgers.edu
LICARI, Frank .... 702-990-4433 280 B
flicari@roseman.edu
LICARI, Michael, J .... 812-237-2309 159 C
mike.licari@indstate.edu
LICATA, Betty Jo .... 330-941-3064 374 E
bjlicata@ysu.edu
LICATA, Christine, M .... 585-475-2953 321 D
cmlnbt@rit.edu
LICHT, Daniel .... 914-395-2301 323 K
dlicht@sarahlawrence.edu
LICHT, Jodi, N .... 212-752-1530 312 G
jodi.licht@limcollege.edu
LICHT, William .... 920-206-2320 508 A
william.licht@mbu.edu
LICHTBLAU, Jobey .... 710-231-7672 354 D
jobey.lichtblau@ndsu.edu
LICHTENBERG, Anne, V .... 859-257-5068 190 B
anne.lichtenberg@uky.edu
LICHTENBERGER, Lynn .... 856-691-8600 285 C
llichtenberger@cccnj.edu
LICHTENSTEIN, Mark .... 315-470-4748 328 D
malichte@esf.edu
LICHTSINN, Jill .... 260-982-5015 162 Q
jslichtsinn@manchester.edu
LICINIO, Julio .... 315-464-9720 326 B
licinioj@upstate.edu
LICITRA, Danielle .... 617-879-7750 218 B
dlicitra@massart.edu
LIDDELL, Alan, C .... 908-526-1200 289 D
alan.liddell@raritanval.edu
LIDDELL, Peter, E .... 315-294-8861 300 H
liddell@cayuga-cc.edu
LIDDELL, Tammy .... 206-296-6052 498 D
liddellt@seattleu.edu
LIDDICOAT, Al .... 805-756-2844.. 30 K
aliddico@calpoly.edu
LIDDICOAT, Blair .... 480-517-8108.. 14 B
blair.liddicoat@riosalado.edu
LIDDLE, Ken .... 713-348-2287 455 F
kliddle@rice.edu
LIDDLE, Trevor, C .... 956-326-2380 459 B
tliddle@tamiu.edu
LIDDY, Colette .... 973-618-3209 284 D
cliddy@caldwell.edu
LIDDY, Elizabeth, D .... 315-443-2879 330 H
liddy@syr.edu
LIDERS, Gunta .... 585-275-5373 332 E
gliders@orpa.rochester.edu
LIDGUS, Jonathan, A .... 314-516-5537 268 E
lidgusj@umsl.edu
LIDH, Todd .... 828-898-8712 339 B
lidht@lmc.edu
LIDSKY, Lyrissa .... 573-882-3246 268 C
lidskyl@missouri.edu
LIDSTONE, Rhonda, W .... 478-301-2005 122 H
lidstone_rw@mercer.edu
LIDSTONE, Sheila .... 409-772-9866 469 C
shlidsto@utmb.edu
LIDSTROM, Mary, E .... 206-685-1751 499 D
lidstrom@uw.edu
LIDY, Paul .... 217-362-6410 145 J
plidy@millikin.edu
LIEBAU, Linda, B .... 513-244-4593 366 A
linda.liebau@msj.edu
LIEBENGOOD, Kelly .... 903-233-3372 452 A
kellyliebengood@letu.edu
LIEBER, Barbara .... 217-641-4535 141 F
blieber@jwcc.edu
LIEBER, Steve .... 480-461-7066.. 13 I
steven.lieber@mesacc.edu
LIEBERMAN, Devorah, A .... 909-593-3511.. 70 E
dlieberman@laverne.edu
LIEBERMAN, Ilene .... 610-499-4275 414 F
idlieberman@widener.edu
LIEBERT, Jane .... 913-758-6126 182 B
jane.liebert@stmary.edu
LIEBERTHAL, Susan .... 631-451-4539 330 C
liebers@sunysuffolk.edu
LIEBESKIND, Lanny, S .... 404-727-6604 119 B
cheml1@emory.edu
LIEBHABER, Karen .... 870-248-4000.. 18 J
karenl@blackrivertech.edu
LIEBLING, Mark .... 231-995-1342 235 B
mliebling@nmc.edu
LIEBOWITZ, Ronald, D .... 781-736-2000 213 A
president@brandeis.edu
LIEBRECHT, Alan .... 510-436-1198.. 45 G
liebrecht@hnu.edu
LIEBROCK, Lorie .... 575-835-5481 294 K
lorie.liebrock@nmt.edu
LIEBSCHER, Kim, K .... 580-774-3776 380 B
kim.liebscher@swosu.edu
LIEBST, Anne .... 479-788-7205.. 22 A
anne.liebst@uafs.edu
LIEBURN, Scott .... 920-924-6459 514 D
slieburn@morainepark.edu
LIECHTY, Dan .... 574-535-7563 158 A
dankl@goshen.edu
LIECHTY, Jeanne, M .... 574-535-7401 158 A
jeannem@goshen.edu
LIEDERBACH, Mark .... 919-761-2100 349 C
mliederbach@sebts.edu
LIEDTKA, Theresa .... 423-425-4506 440 A
theresa-liedtka@utc.edu
LIEDTKE, Richard, W .... 785-670-1812 182 D
richard.liedtke@washburn.edu
LIEF, Charles, G .... 303-245-4804.. 81 B
president@naropa.edu
LIEF, Nathan, P .... 651-696-6140 243 B
nlief@macalester.edu
LIEHR, Michael .... 518-956-8685 330 A
mliehr@sunypoly.edu
LIEN, Joelle .... 605-626-2558 428 H
joelle.lien@northern.edu
LIEN, Joelle .... 605-626-7958 428 H
joelle.lien@northern.edu
LIERK, Kyle, C .... 402-280-2591 274 D
kylelierk@creighton.edu
LIERLEY, Mark .... 480-858-9100.. 16 D
m.lierley@scnm.edu
LIERZ, Rachel .... 913-469-8500 178 F
rachellierz@jccc.edu
LIES, CSC, William, M .... 574-631-9800 165 A
lies.7@nd.edu
LIESEN, Joseph .... 573-288-6480 259 E
jliesen@culver.edu
LIESEN, Kristen .... 217-228-5432 149 B
liesekr@quincy.edu
LIESKE, Barb .... 219-464-6717 165 D
barb.lieske@valpo.edu
LIESKE, Brian .... 510-666-8248.. 24 E
blieske@aimc.edu
LIESMAN, Laura .... 732-987-2685 286 D
lliesman@georgian.edu
LIESTMAN, Daniel .... 509-865-8500 495 D
LIETO, Mary .... 914-923-2690 319 J
mlieto@pace.edu
LIEU, Mark .... 510-659-6173.. 54 F
mlieu@ohlone.edu
LIEURANCE, Lorissa .... 515-271-3781 168 J
lorissa.lieurance@drake.edu
LIEVANOS, Destry .... 760-630-1555.. 28 B
destry.lievanos@brightwood.edu
LIEWER, Chris .... 402-554-2200 277 I
cliewer@unomaha.edu
LIFKA, David .... 607-254-8621 306 B
lifka@cornell.edu
LIFSEY, Britt .... 678-359-5108 121 B
brittl@gordonstate.edu
LIFTON, Richard, P .... 212-327-8080 321 E
rickl@rockefeller.edu
LIGEIKIS, David .... 607-778-5575 326 C
ligeikisd@sunybroome.edu
LIGEIKIS, Kelli, H .... 607-746-4540 329 B
ligeikkh@delhi.edu
LIGHT, Brad .... 336-334-4355 351 D
uncg@bkstore.com
LIGHT, Cathy .... 412-268-5345 391 H
calight@andrew.cmu.edu
LIGHT, Cathy, A .... 412-268-5345 391 H
calight@andrew.cmu.edu
LIGHT, Kathleen .... 210-829-3943 465 E
light@uiwtx.edu
LIGHT, Margaret .... 717-262-2010 415 B
margaret.light@wilson.edu
LIGHT, Michael .... 860-297-2046.. 88 E
michael.light@trincoll.edu
LIGHT, Steve .... 701-777-2135 353 G
steven.light@und.edu
LIGHT, Wesley .... 717-477-1121 407 B
wwlight@ship.edu
LIGHTCAP, Lisa .... 610-282-1100 393 G
lisa.lightcap@desales.edu
LIGHTCAP, Rhonda .... 516-671-0379 333 E
rlightcap@webb.edu
LIGHTCAP, Stephen .... 215-717-6375 412 F
slightcap@uarts.edu
LIGHTFIELD, Nancy, R .... 608-757-7750 513 D
nlightfield@blackhawk.edu
LIGHTFOOT, Carolyn, A .... 281-425-6455 451 I
clightfo@lee.edu
LIGHTFOOT, David .... 434-832-7643 487 H
lightfootd@cvcc.vccs.edu
LIGHTHILL, M. Joyce .... 641-784-5222 169 D
lighthil@graceland.edu
LIGHTLY, Rachael .... 505-473-6440 296 C
rachael.lightly@santafeuniversity.edu
LIGHTNER, Michael .... 303-860-5726.. 83 A
lightner@cu.edu
LIGHTNER, Robin .... 513-745-5660 371 F
robin.lightner@uc.edu
LIGHTY, JoAnn .... 208-426-2688 131 C
joannlighty@boisestate.edu
LIGHTY, Rachael .... 619-684-8775.. 53 J
rlighty@newschoolarch.edu
LIGIOSO, Yulian .... 562-463-7099.. 58 D
yligioso@riohondo.edu
LIGIOSO, Yulian .... 707-864-7000.. 64 E
yulian.ligioso@solano.edu
LIGMAN, Scott .... 509-527-2395 499 F
scott.ligman@wallawalla.edu
LIGNOWSKI, Beth .... 201-559-6027 286 C
0267mgr@sheg.follett.com
LIGON, Eric .... 940-565-4003 466 B
eric.ligon@unt.edu
LIGON, Theresa .... 713-780-9777 442 F
LIKENS, Erin .... 601-643-8316 252 G
erin.likens@colin.edu
LIKES, Wendy, M .... 901-448-6135 440 C
wlikes@uthsc.edu
LIKNESS, Tabitha .... 605-668-1566 427 F
tabitha.likness@mtmc.edu
LILES, Elaine .... 407-646-2296 106 J
eliles@rollins.edu
LILES, Kevin .... 803-641-3319 425 A
kevinl@usca.edu
LILES, Tammy .... 859-246-6449 185 G
tammy.liles@kctcs.edu
LILFORD, Grant .... 912-583-2241 116 G
glilford@bpc.edu
LILIENTHAL, Ronda .... 615-248-1245 439 B
rlilienthal@trevecca.edu
LILJEGREN, Donna .... 630-947-8914 133 H
dliljegren@aurora.edu
LILJEGREN, Lisa .... 262-243-5700 507 C
lisa.liljegren@cuw.edu
LILLBACK, Peter, A .... 215-572-3811 414 D
plillback@wts.edu
LILLEBO, Troy .... 816-235-6585 268 D
lillebot@umkc.edu
LILLEHAUGEN, Sandi .... 701-662-1543 355 A
sandra.lillehaugen@lrsc.edu
LILLES, Anthony .... 805-482-2755.. 58 M
alilles@stjohnsem.edu
LILLESTON, Judith .... 914-831-0369 305 C
jlilleston@cw.edu
LILLEY, Ben .... 252-985-5113 348 A
blilley@ncwc.edu
LILLEY, Richard .... 443-840-4698 203 E
rlilley@ccbcmd.edu
LILLIE, Deb .... 319-385-6210 170 J
deb.lillie@iw.edu
LILLIE, Sandra .... 720-890-8922.. 80 I
president@itea.edu
LILLIS, John, R .... 574-372-5100 158 B
lillisjr@grace.edu
LILLQUIST, Erik .... 973-275-4811 291 F
erik.lillquist@shu.edu
LILLQUIST, Mark .... 863-297-1083 105 F
mlilquist@polk.edu
LILLY, Bill .... 304-462-6052 504 B
bill.lilly@glenville.edu
LILLY, Flavius, R .... 410-706-7767 207 H
flilly@umaryland.edu
LILLY, Kenneth, E .... 304-877-6428 501 E
ken.lilly@abc.edu
LILYARD-MITCHELL, Corrine .... 757-822-1889 489 H
cmitchell@tcc.edu
LIM, Adriene, I .... 541-346-3056 387 F
alim@uoregon.edu
LIM, Choong .... 808-735-4708 129 A
clim@chaminade.edu
LIM, Dan .... 407-303-9473.. 94 H
dan.lim@adu.edu
LIM, David .... 213-386-0080.. 52 C
mtsa1996@gmail.com
LIM, Gim .... 215-751-8275 393 A
glim@ccp.edu
LIM, Jung Ho .... 213-385-2322.. 75 D
LIM, Rosy .... 323-731-2383.. 55 E
rosylim@psuca.edu
LIM, Sung Jin .... 213-385-2322.. 75 D
sunglim@wmu.edu
LIM, Teik .... 817-272-2103 467 B
teik.lim@uta.edu
LIM, Xieng .... 425-739-8264 495 F
xieng.lim@lwtech.edu
LIM-THOMPSON, Soo-Yin .... 218-281-8248 250 G
slimthom@umn.edu
LIMA, Brad .... 508-830-5012 218 D
blima@maritime.edu
LIMA, Judy, E .... 205-329-7904.... 5 C
judy.lima@ecacolleges.com
LIMAS, Celestino .... 509-865-8580 495 D
limas_c@heritage.edu
LIMAYEM, Moez .... 813-974-3229 111 A
mlimayem@usf.edu
LIMBACH, Patrick, A .... 513-558-0026 371 E
pat.limbach@uc.edu
LIMBAUGH, James, M .... 310-287-4325.. 49 H
limbaujm@wlac.edu
LIMBO, Alesha .... 605-342-0317 427 C
studentservices@johnwitherspooncollege.org
LIMONCELLI, Jerry .... 516-686-7815 317 G
jlimonce@nyit.edu
LIMPER, Leslie .... 503-352-2871 385 I
limp5635@pacificu.edu
LIMTUATCO, Edwin, E .... 671-735-5560 519 H
edwin.limtuatco@guamcc.edu
LIN, Anne .... 410-532-5545 206 D
alin@ndm.edu
LIN, Chia-Yen .... 619-260-4598.. 71 J
linc@sandiego.edu
LIN, Frank .... 909-537-5787.. 33 D
flin@csusb.edu
LIN, Janice .... 219-464-5333 165 D
janice.lin@valpo.edu
LIN, Kathleen .... 626-571-5110.. 48 G
kathleenlin@les.edu
LIN, Kuo-Liang .... 626-571-5110.. 48 G
klin@les.edu
LIN, Lin .... 860-343-5763.. 86 A
llin@mxcc.edu
LIN, Lisa (Ping-Hui) .... 512-444-8082 461 C
lisalin@thsu.edu
LIN, Paul .... 512-444-8082 461 C
thsu@thsu.edu
LIN, Susan, X .... 808-956-7161 129 H
slin@hawaii.edu
LIN, Yi-Chun Tricia .... 203-392-6864.. 85 A
lyny4@southernct.edu
LIN-COOK, Wendy .... 973-596-3309 288 A
wendy.w.lin-cook@njit.edu
LINAKER, Kathleen .... 315-792-5376 315 I
klinaker@mvcc.edu
LINAM, Gail .... 214-333-5372 447 D
gaill@dbu.edu
LINAMEN, Larry .... 951-552-8744.. 28 G
llinamen@calbaptist.edu
LINBACK, John .... 574-936-8898 155 L
john.linback@ancilla.edu
LINC, Linda .... 330-490-7250 373 F
llinc@walsh.edu
LINCKE, James .... 610-353-7630 390 E
LINCOLN, Holly .... 636-481-3230 261 B
hlincoln@jeffco.edu
LINCOLN, Jonathan .... 973-720-2580 292 I
lincolnj@wpunj.edu
LINCOLN, Judy .... 314-837-6777 266 A
jlincoln@stlchristian.edu
LINCOLN, Michael .... 973-278-5400 283 J
mil@berkeleycollege.edu
LINCOLN, Timothy .... 512-404-4873 443 I
tlincoln@austinseminary.edu
LIND, James, F .... 757-451-6200 480 C
lindjf@evms.edu
LIND, Joshua .... 715-232-2121 512 A
lindj@uwstout.edu
LIND, Joy .... 605-575-2063 429 D
joy.lind@usiouxfalls.edu
LIND, Kristen .... 218-322-2403 245 B
kristen.lind@itascacc.edu
LIND, Kristen .... 651-793-1889 245 E
kristen.lind@metrostate.edu
LIND, Steven .... 415-442-6622.. 44 E
slind@ggu.edu
LIND, William .... 843-953-5011 419 D
wlind@citadel.edu

LIPPERT, Robert .... 559-453-2189.. 43 J
robert.lippert@fresno.edu
LIPPIELLO, Steve .... 724-925-4071 414 E
lippiellos@westmoreland.edu
LIPPMAN, Fred .... 954-262-1508 104 F
flippman@nsu.nova.edu
LIPPMAN, Stuart .... 646-565-6000 331 F
stuartl@touro.edu
LIPPS, Mark .... 231-843-5886 239 D
malipps@westshore.edu
LIPSCHUTZ, Ronnie .... 831-459-3275.. 70 C
rligsch@ucsc.edu
LIPSCOMB, Benjamin ..... 585-567-9374 310 F
benjamin.lipscomb@houghton.edu
LIPSCOMB, Natasha ...... 704-216-3622 346 C
natasha.lipscomb@rccc.edu
LIPSCOMB, Rodney .... 940-498-6445 453 L
rlipscomb@nctc.edu
LIPSCOMB, Sharyon ...... 225-578-8833 193 L
slipsc1@lsu.edu
LIPSCOMB, Tamra .... 540-863-2905 487 I
tlipscomb@dslcc.edu
LIPSCOMB, Victoria, D .. 915-831-6458 449 A
vbills@epcc.edu
LIPSETT, Teresa .... 787-743-7979 526 A
ut_tlipsett@suagm.edu
LIPSHITZ, Rita .... 773-973-0241 139 E
lipshitz@htc.edu
LIPSKIER, Hershel .... 973-267-9404 289 B
info@rca.edu
LIPSTREU, Tiffany .... 614-823-1414 368 O
tlipstreu@otterbein.edu
LIPTON, Mitchell .... 212-353-4126 306 A
lipton@cooper.edu
LIQUORI, Gary .... 401-874-9330 417 E
gliguori@uri.edu
LIRA, Ken .... 949-451-5435.. 64 I
klira@ivc.edu
LIRLEY, Sean .... 719-336-1543.. 80 N
sean.lirley@lamarcc.edu
LISCHIN, Renee .... 973-408-3955 285 E
rlischin@drew.edu
LISCHWE, Sheila, T .... 864-656-1661 419 F
slischw@clemson.edu
LISCIO, Gina .... 315-792-7288 330 A
gina.liscio@sunyit.edu
LISENBY, Sadie .... 901-321-3527 431 A
slisenby@cbu.edu
LISI, Claire .... 631-420-2239 329 D
claire.lisi@farmingdale.edu
LISI, Peter .... 860-768-2446.. 89 C
lisi@hartford.edu
LISK, Patti .... 540-423-9824 488 B
plisk@germanna.edu
LISKER, Donna .... 413-585-4900 224 F
dlisker@smith.edu
LISLE, Kristy .... 650-949-7209.. 43 F
lislekristy@foothill.edu
LISNER, Lydia .... 804-627-5300 478 I
lydia_lisner@bshsi.org
LISS, Donna .... 660-785-4163 267 K
dliss@truman.edu
LISS, Josha .... 267-341-3100 397 G
jliss@holyfamily.edu
LISS, Julia, E .... 909-607-3541.. 63 F
julia.liss@scrippscollege.edu
LISS, Ron .... 928-717-7778.. 17 G
ron.liss@yc.edu
LISS, Tony .... 212-650-7947 301 F
tliss@ccny.cuny.edu
LISSY, Barbara, G .... 215-576-0800 408 H
blissy@rrc.edu
LIST, Allison .... 631-687-5198 322 G
alist@sjcny.edu
LIST, Ryon .... 906-932-4231 230 D
ryonl@gogebic.edu
LISTAU, Michael .... 850-484-2586 105 E
mlistau@pensacolastate.edu
LISTER, Basil .... 816-604-6748 262 G
basil.lister@mcckc.edu
LISTER, Charlotte, T ...... 302-857-1290.. 90 F
clister@dtcc.edu
LISTER, Kevin .... 314-367-8700 266 D
kevin.lister@stlcop.edu
LISTER, Tommy .... 626-584-5338.. 43 K
tommylister@fuller.edu
LISTI, Garnette .... 504-762-3032 192 H
glisti@dcc.edu
LISTON, Brenda .... 614-947-6532 362 A
brenda.liston@franklin.edu
LISTWAK, Jeffrey, A ...... 412-397-5263 409 C
listwak@rmu.edu
LISZKA, Justin .... 336-272-7102 338 B
justin.liszka@greensboro.edu
LITCH, Mary .... 714-628-2753.. 36 G
litch@chapman.edu
LITCHFIELD, Jamie .... 413-565-1000 211 C
jlitchfield@baypath.edu
LITCHMAN, Jennifer, B . 410-706-3477 207 H
jlitchman@umaryland.edu
LITHERLAND, Steve, E .. 757-822-1944 489 H
slitherland@tcc.edu
LITKE, Russ .... 419-995-8342 363 G
litke.r@rhodeesstate.edu
LITMAN, Kay .... 610-372-4721 408 G
klitman@racc.edu
LITOLFF, Edwin .... 225-342-6950 196 F
edwin.litolff@la.gov
LITT, Eleni .... 212-229-8947 316 E
litte@newschool.edu
LITT, Jacquelyn, S .... 573-882-0647 268 C
littj@missouri.edu
LITT, Jacquelyn, S .... 848-932-2900 290 C
jacquelyn.litt@rutgers.edu
LITTERAL, Samuel, M .... 304-896-7426 503 D
samuel.litteral@southernwv.edu
LITTLE, Albert .... 904-632-5167 100 F
al.little@fscj.edu
LITTLE, Andrew, P .... 410-777-2227 202 D
aplittle1@aacc.edu
LITTLE, Chris .... 530-895-4047.. 28 E
littlech@butte.edu
LITTLE, Daniel .... 313-593-5500 238 A
delittle@umich.edu
LITTLE, Glenn, W .... 863-784-7218 108 B
glenn.little@southflorida.edu
LITTLE, Gloria .... 212-787-5300 298 B
LITTLE, Jennifer .... 864-592-4808 424 C
littlej@sccsc.edu
LITTLE, Joe .... 404-880-8812 117 H
jlittle@cau.edu
LITTLE, Kendall, G .... 601-977-7870 256 B
klittle@tougaloo.edu
LITTLE, Kevin, K .... 831-656-2508 518 D
kllittle@nps.edu
LITTLE, Lara .... 704-463-3353 348 B
lara.little@pfeiffer.edu
LITTLE, Nicole .... 302-622-8000.. 90 A
nlittle@dcad.edu
LITTLE, Pamela .... 256-551-1711.... 2 D
pamela.little@drakestate.edu
LITTLE, Rebecca, K .... 812-888-4220 165 E
rlittle@vinu.edu
LITTLE, Scott .... 601-968-5956 252 C
slittle@belhaven.edu
LITTLE, Shanon .... 415-257-1350.. 41 J
shanon.little@dominican.edu
LITTLE, Sylvester .... 863-292-3762 105 F
slittle@polk.edu
LITTLE, William .... 607-962-9458 306 C
wlittle@corning-cc.edu
LITTLE-BERRY, Teri .... 352-854-2322.. 97 C
berryt@cf.edu
LITTLE WHITEMAN,
Iona .... 701-627-4738 355 D
ilittl@nhsc.edu
LITTLEBEAR, Richard ..... 406-477-6215 270 I
rlbear@cdkc.edu
LITTLEFIELD,
Elizabeth, S .... 804-523-5181 488 C
blittlefield@reynolds.edu
LITTLEFIELD, Julie .... 979-230-3576 444 E
julie.littlefield@brazosport.edu
LITTLEJOHN, Sylvia .... 803-738-7764 422 D
littlejohns@midlandstech.edu
LITTLEPAGE, Craig, K .... 434-982-5100 486 H
ckl9e@virginia.edu
LITTLETON, Denise .... 757-823-8701 483 F
dlittleton@nsu.edu
LITTLETON, Judith .... 510-567-6174.. 66 I
jlittleton@sum.edu
LITTLETON, Robert, A .... 423-652-6022 432 I
ralittle@king.edu
LITTLETON-STEIB,
Larissa .... 225-216-8403 192 B
chancellorsoffice@mybrcc.edu
LITTMAN, Cheryl .... 718-997-2805 303 E
cheryl.littman@qc.cuny.edu
LITTMAN, Jared, E .... 718-990-2920 322 F
littmanj@stjohns.edu
LITTON, Freddie .... 361-570-4261 465 D
littonf@uhv.edu
LITTREL, Darla .... 972-923-6440 453 J
darla.littrel@navarrocollege.edu
LITTRELL, Beth .... 402-461-7372 274 I
blittrell@hastings.edu
LITTRELL, Johnny .... 931-540-2840 436 H
jlittrell@columbiastate.edu
LITTRELL, Meghann .... 513-244-4524 366 A
meghann.littrell@msj.edu
LITVINOV, Dimitri .... 713-743-4168 465 A
litvinov@central.uh.edu
LITWACK, Kim .... 414-229-4189 511 A
litwack@uwm.edu
LITWIN, Daveen, H .... 603-646-3780 281 C
daveen.h.litwin@dartmouth.edu
LITYNSKI, Daniel, M ..... 269-387-8294 239 E
dan.litynski@wmich.edu
LITZ, Kerri .... 410-225-2277 205 C
klitz@mica.edu
LITZIN, Louise .... 928-724-6633.. 12 G
louise@dinecollege.edu
LIU, Anita .... 626-917-9482.. 37 D
anital@cesna.edu
LIU, Chris .... 657-278-8205.. 32 B
cyliu@fullerton.edu
LIU, Jun .... 631-632-7422 325 F
jun.liu@stonybrook.edu
LIU, Lan .... 860-343-5833.. 86 A
lliu@mxcc.commnet.edu
LIU, Linyan .... 650-493-4430.. 64 C
linyan.liu@itp.edu
LIU, Monika .... 415-452-5730.. 37 H
mliu@ccsf.edu
LIU, Shuang .... 410-337-6062 204 A
shuang.liu@goucher.edu
LIU, Susan .... 626-448-0023.. 46 K
LIU, Ying .... 419-530-1248 372 F
ying.liu3@utoledo.edu
LIU, Yuxiang .... 212-960-5400 334 P
yuxiang.liu@yu.edu
LIU, Yuxing .... 512-454-1188 442 J
info@aoma.edu
LIUBIEICH, Danielle ...... 773-291-6100 135 M
dliubieich@ccc.edu
LIVELY, Alisa .... 304-473-8441 505 G
lively_a@wvwc.edu
LIVELY, Andy .... 713-785-5995 446 A
LIVELY, David .... 847-491-2094 148 C
david.lively@northwestern.edu
LIVELY, Donald .... 602-682-6859.. 11 A
dlively@azsummitlaw.edu
LIVELY, Lisa, A .... 304-293-8638 505 B
lisa.lively@mail.wvu.edu
LIVELY, Sam .... 951-343-4726.. 28 G
slively@calbaptist.edu
LIVELY, Shane .... 203-596-8507.. 87 H
slively@post.edu
LIVENGOOD, Lori .... 316-394-5227 175 F
llivengood@bethelks.edu
LIVENGOOD, Naomi .... 269-965-3931 232 A
livengoodn@kellogg.edu
LIVERS, Regina .... 513-569-5735 359 G
regina.livers@cincinnatistate.edu
LIVESAY, Dennis .... 316-978-3095 182 F
dennis.livesay@wichita.edu
LIVESAY, Stephen, D ..... 423-775-7201 430 G
livesast@bryan.edu
LIVINGOOD,
Susannah, B .... 405-325-5065 380 L
slivingood@ou.edu
LIVINGSTON, Carolyn ... 507-222-4248 241 C
clivingston@carleton.edu
LIVINGSTON, David, J .. 815-836-5230 143 E
dlivingston@lewisu.edu
LIVINGSTON, Esther ...... 859-985-3065 183 I
livginstone@berea.edu
LIVINGSTON, Kathy .... 308-865-8204 277 F
livingstonke@unk.edu
LIVINGSTON, Lynette .... 715-858-1849 513 E
livingston3@cvtc.edu
LIVINGSTON, Randy ...... 650-724-0213.. 66 C
livingston@stanford.edu
LIVINGSTON, Shannon .. 715-675-3331 514 F
livingst@ntc.edu
LIVINGSTON, Stan .... 601-477-4006 253 F
stan.livingston@jcjc.edu
LIVINGSTON, Tina .... 903-886-5667 459 E
tina.livingston@tamuc.edu
LIVINGSTON, Vincent .... 425-640-1501 494 E
vincent.livingston@edcc.edu
LIVINGSTONE, Linda, A 254-710-3555 444 B
linda_livingstone@baylor.edu
LIVIO, Michael, D .... 609-497-7805 288 E
michael.livio@ptsem.edu
LIZAN, Rey .... 757-490-1241 477 F
rlizan@auto.edu
LIZARDI, David .... 787-738-2161 528 A
david.lizardi@upr.edu
LIZER, Shannon, K .... 815-282-7900 150 H
shannonlizer@sacn.edu
LIZOTTE, Edmund .... 860-628-4751.. 87 E
elizotte@lincolncollegene.edu
LJUBENKO, Bojan .... 920-924-3229 514 D
bljubenko@morainepark.edu
LJUBICIC, Amanda .... 860-629-6115.. 87 F
ljubicic_a@mitchell.edu
LJUTIC, Peter .... 718-270-8650 326 A
peter.ljutic@downstate.edu
LLAMAS, Diana .... 956-295-3687 461 F
diana.llamas@tsc.edu
LLANO, Virginia .... 954-492-5353.. 96 J
vllano@citycollege.edu
LLANOS, Keren .... 787-620-2040 520 F
kllanos@aupr.edu
LLERANDI, Joanne, A ... 718-990-1487 322 F
llerandj@stjohns.edu
LLERANDI, Mariel .... 787-878-5475 523 H
mllerandi@arecibo.inter.edu
LLERENA, Gladys, P ...... 305-273-4499.. 96 N
gladys@cbt.edu
LLERENA, Monica .... 305-273-4499.. 96 N
monica@cbt.edu
LLEWELLYN, Nada`, M .. 718-990-6334 322 F
llewelin@stjohns.edu
LLOPIZ, Maria .... 773-481-8323 136 B
mllopiz@ccc.edu
LLORENS, Ashley, J ...... 410-955-5107 204 F
ashley.llorens@jhuapl.edu
LLOSA, Talia .... 845-341-4090 319 H
talia.llosa@sunyorange.edu
LLOSA, Tulio .... 217-206-7755 154 A
tllos1@uis.edu
LLOVIO, Kay .... 916-577-2200.. 75 B
kllovio@jessup.edu
LLOYD, Andrea .... 802-443-5735 475 G
lloyd@middlebury.edu
LLOYD, Betsy .... 910-592-8084 346 D
blloyd@sampsoncc.edu
LLOYD, Brent .... 608-263-3045 510 C
brent.lloyd@wisc.edu
LLOYD, Celia, P .... 212-650-7859 301 F
clloyd@ccny.cuny.edu
LLOYD, Charles .... 603-752-1113 281 B
clloyd@ccsnh.edu
LLOYD, Charles .... 603-271-6484 280 N
clloyd@ccsnh.edu
LLOYD, Charmaine, R ... 203-392-5250.. 85 A
lloydc1@southernct.edu
LLOYD, Chris .... 215-702-4339 391 C
clloyd@cairn.edu
LLOYD, Curtis .... 518-320-1192 324 F
curtis.lloyd@suny.edu
LLOYD, Daniel .... 630-942-2865 136 D
lloydd@cod.edu
LLOYD, David .... 765-998-4634 164 C
dvlloyd@taylor.edu
LLOYD, Giovina .... 607-871-2966 298 A
lloydgm@alfred.edu
LLOYD, Glen, D .... 507-933-6517 242 D
glloyd@gustavus.edu
LLOYD, Gweneth .... 845-257-2920 325 D
lloydg@newpaltz.edu
LLOYD, Heather .... 208-882-1566 132 D
hlloyd@nsa.edu
LLOYD, James .... 513-244-8435 359 E
james.lloyd@ccuniversity.edu
LLOYD, James, W .... 352-392-2213 110 D
lloydjw@ufl.edu
LLOYD, Jan .... 407-708-2144 107 G
lloydj@seminolestate.edu
LLOYD, Jayson .... 208-732-6547 131 I
jlloyd@csi.edu
LLOYD, Mary, J .... 815-599-3418 139 F
mary.lloyd@highland.edu
LLOYD, Megan .... 207-699-5037 199 H
mlloyd@meca.edu
LLOYD, Patrick, M .... 614-292-9755 367 H
lloyd.256@osu.edu
LLOYD, Rachel .... 918-540-6971 376 F
rlloyd@neo.edu
LLOYD, Richard .... 402-481-8781 273 F
rich.lloyd@bryanhealthcollege.edu
LLOYD, Robert .... 561-803-2252 104 I
robert_lloyd@pba.edu
LLOYD, Rodie, F .... 207-725-3963 198 G
rlloyd@bowdoin.edu
LLOYD, Scott .... 513-244-4351 366 A
scott.lloyd@msj.edu
LLOYD, Sharon .... 678-359-5133 121 B
sharonl@gordonstate.edu
LLOYD, Sheila .... 909-748-8576.. 71 H
sheila_lloyd@redlands.edu
LLOYD, Willie, L .... 248-232-4142 235 D
wllloyd@oaklandcc.edu
LLOYD-DENNIS, Diann .. 617-217-9216 211 D
dlloyddennis@baystate.edu
LLYWELYN, SJ, Dorian . 408-551-1951.. 62 F
dllywelyn@scu.edu
LO, Andrea, M .... 540-868-7088 488 E
alo@lfcc.edu
LO, Angie .... 888-488-4968.. 46 J
alo@itu.edu
LO, Christina, T .... 617-253-1747 221 C
LO, Deborah .... 907-796-6123.. 10 C
delo@alaska.edu
LO LEE, Mai .... 920-465-2021 510 E
lom@uwgb.edu
LOAIZA, Rodrigo .... 305-821-3333 100 A
rloaiza@fnu.edu

LOMENA, Sandra .... 305-821-3333 100 A
slomena@fnu.edu
LOMIDZE, Kote .... 202-464-6973 476 B
kote.lomidze@worldlearning.org
LOMMEL, John .... 574-372-5110 158 B
john.lommel@grace.edu
LOMMEN, Conrad .... 808-373-2849 131 A
cjlommen88@gmail.com
LOMONACO, Barbara .... 401-341-2205 417 D
barbara.lomonaco@salve.edu
LONABOCKER,
Louise, M .... 617-552-3300 212 E
louise.lonabocker@bc.edu
LONDOIRO, Carol .... 631-632-6267 325 F
carol.londoiro@stonybrook.edu
LONDON, Manuel .... 631-632-8304 325 F
manuel.london@stonybrook.edu
LONDON, Michael .... 415-422-4400.. 72 A
melondon@usfca.edu
LONDON, Samuel .... 256-726-7223.... 6 E
slondon@oakwood.edu
LONDON, William .... 816-584-6226 265 C
william.london@park.edu
LONDON-JONES, Emily 504-520-7517 198 D
ejones@xula.edu
LONDONO, Hernan .... 305-899-4019.. 95 G
hlondono@barry.edu
LONDRE, Tristan .... 816-604-1524 262 F
tristan.londre@mcckc.edu
LONDRIGAN,
Michael, P .... 212-752-1530 312 G
michael.londrigan@limcollege.edu
LONE HILL, Karen .... 605-455-6100 427 I
klonehill@olc.edu
LONERGAN, Dennis ...... 718-862-7349 313 L
dennis.lonergan@manhattan.edu
LONERGAN, Joel, C ...... 256-824-6414.... 8 C
joel.lonergan@uah.edu
LONEY, Teresa, A .... 816-604-1517 262 F
teresa.loney@mcckc.edu
LONG, Andrew .... 308-345-8119 275 I
longa@mpcc.edu
LONG, Antonio .... 404-756-4477 115 I
along@atlm.edu
LONG, Aubrey .... 386-481-2801.. 95 J
longa@cookman.edu
LONG, Beverly .... 706-864-1940 127 B
beverly.long@ung.edu
LONG, Brenda, J .... 252-222-6151 341 F
longb@carteret.edu
LONG, Brittney .... 402-399-2454 274 A
blong@csm.edu
LONG, Bruce .... 972-241-3371 447 E
blong@dallas.edu
LONG, Carol .... 310-434-4762.. 62 G
long_carol@smc.edu
LONG, Carol .... 503-375-6623 388 D
clong@willamette.edu
LONG, Catherine, E .... 607-255-2946 306 B
cel3@cornell.edu
LONG, Christina .... 620-665-3521 178 D
longc@hutchcc.edu
LONG, Christopher, P ... 517-355-4597 233 G
cplong@msu.edu
LONG, Curt .... 563-588-6657 167 E
curt.long@clarke.edu
LONG, Daniel .... 313-664-7675 228 H
dlong@collegeforcreativestudies.edu
LONG, Donald .... 651-748-2626 244 D
donald.long@century.edu
LONG, Donald .... 515-964-0601 169 C
longd@faith.edu
LONG, Doreen .... 603-428-2303 281 F
dlong@nec.edu
LONG, Durwin .... 715-836-4899 510 D
longd@uwec.edu
LONG, Dustin .... 910-272-3566 346 A
dulong@robeson.edu
LONG, Faith, M .... 518-564-2090 327 E
long9194@plattsburgh.edu
LONG, Gardner .... 423-697-5767 436 F
gardner.long@chattanoogastate.edu
LONG, Gerard, E .... 210-562-6285 468 E
longg@uthscsa.edu
LONG, Gladys .... 919-572-1625 335 F
doc_long@apexsot.edu
LONG, Jaime .... 815-825-9532 142 F
jaime.long@kishwaukeecollege.edu
LONG, Janet, R .... 610-499-4105 414 F
jrlong@widener.edu
LONG, Jeanine .... 229-227-2668 126 C
jlong@southernregional.edu
LONG, Jeff .... 575-562-2221 293 O
jeff.long@enmu.edu
LONG, Jeff .... 601-403-1041 255 D
jlong@prcc.edu
LONG, Jennifer .... 405-224-3140 381 B
jlong@usao.edu
LONG, Jesse .... 806-720-7657 452 D
jesse.long@lcu.edu
LONG, Jewel, B .... 757-727-5486 481 E
jewel.long@hamptonu.edu
LONG, Jim .... 573-592-4225 270 D
jim.long@williamwoods.edu
LONG, Jodi .... 352-395-5680 107 E
jodi.long@sfcollege.edu
LONG, John, W .... 813-974-3297 111 A
jwl@usf.edu
LONG, Jonathan .... 913-288-7691 178 H
jlong@kckcc.edu
LONG, Joshua, J .... 260-422-5561 159 D
jjlong@indianatech.edu
LONG, Justin .... 239-985-8361 100 E
justin.long@fsw.edu
LONG, Karen, S .... 518-276-6216 321 A
longks@rpi.edu
LONG, Kelly .... 970-491-5932.. 78 N
kelly.long@colostate.edu
LONG, Kenneth .... 231-777-0560 234 G
kenneth.long@muskegoncc.edu
LONG, Kenneth, A .... 570-422-3201 406 A
kenlong@esu.edu
LONG, Kimberly .... 870-358-8636.. 18 D
kimberly_long@asun.edu
LONG, Laurel .... 256-824-2259.... 8 C
laurel.long@uah.edu
LONG, Lauren .... 703-993-2909 481 B
llong3@gmu.edu
LONG, Leann .... 423-585-6772 438 D
leann.long@ws.edu
LONG, Lisa .... 265-761-6215.... 7 D
lelong@talladega.edu
LONG, Marcus .... 605-668-1514 427 F
marcus.long@mtmc.edu
LONG, Matthew .... 336-272-7102 338 B
matt.long@greensboro.edu
LONG, Natalie .... 920-686-6134 510 A
natalie.long@sl.edu
LONG, Nathan .... 510-593-2910.. 63 A
nlong@saybrook.edu
LONG, Patricia, K .... 432-837-8696 462 G
plong@sulross.edu
LONG, Paul .... 831-646-4000.. 52 G
plong@mpc.edu
LONG, Phil, D .... 512-475-6702 467 C
phil.long@austin.utexas.edu
LONG, Rebecca .... 740-245-7376 372 E
rlong@rio.edu
LONG, Ronald, B .... 770-484-1204 122 G
lutherrice@lutherrice.edu
LONG, Sheryl .... 336-721-2774 348 H
sheryl.long@salem.edu
LONG, Stephen .... 318-371-3035 193 A
LONG, Stephen .... 314-539-5311 266 E
slong@stlcc.edu
LONG, Susan .... 909-274-5200.. 52 I
slong@mtsac.edu
LONG, Tamara .... 325-674-2949 441 D
tnb99a@acu.edu
LONG, Ted .... 864-644-5039 424 B
tlong@swu.edu
LONG, Terrah .... 334-291-4981.... 1 H
terrah.long@cv.edu
LONG-COFFEE,
Michelle .... 310-287-4597.. 49 H
longcofm@wlac.edu
LONG II, JD .... 314-935-5582 269 L
jlongii@wustl.edu
LONG PORTER, Cindy .. 203-582-8722.. 88 A
cindy.porter@quinnipiac.edu
LONGACRE, Jeffrey .... 301-295-1917 518 G
jeffrey.longacre@usuhs.edu
LONGACRE, Teri, E .... 713-743-4669 465 A
elkins@central.uh.edu
LONGAKER, Frank .... 540-986-1800 182 K
frank@national-college.edu
LONGAKER, Frank, E .... 540-986-1800 477 G
frank@an.edu
LONGAZEL, Edward, G .. 215-255-7819 394 C
edward.longazel@drexel.edu
LONGBELLA, Jody .... 218-894-5128 244 C
jlongbella@clcmn.edu
LONGE, Ryan .... 802-287-8219 475 B
ryan.longe@greenmtn.edu
LONGE, Ryan .... 802-287-8000 475 B
ryan.longe@greenmtn.edu
LONGENECKER, Penni ... 717-947-6093 404 S
pelongen@pacollege.edu
LONGHTA, Karie, L .... 217-786-2263 144 B
karie.longhta@llcc.edu
LONGIE, Candace .... 701-477-7862 355 H
clongie@tm.edu
LONGINO, Karen .... 318-342-1982 198 A
ulm@campuscornerinc.com
LONGJOHN, Beth .... 616-222-1428 229 B
beth.longjohn@cornerstone.edu
LONGJOHN, Gerald .... 616-222-1423 229 B
gerald.longjohn@cornerstone.edu
LONGMAN, Tom .... 269-965-3931 232 A
longmant@kellogg.edu
LONGMIRE, Kolleen ...... 615-514-2787 435 F
klongmire@nossi.edu
LONGNECKER, Brittany . 865-524-8079 432 F
blongnecker@hchs.edu
LONGO, Eugenio, A ...... 787-622-8000 527 B
elongo@pupr.edu
LONGO, Laura .... 732-224-2259 284 B
llongo@brookdalecc.edu
LONGO, Peter, J .... 308-865-8995 277 F
longop@unk.edu
LONGO, Rick .... 215-717-6618 412 F
rlongo@uarts.edu
LONGSDORF, Brittany .... 207-753-6906 198 E
blongsdo@bates.edu
LONGSTRETH, Jason, S 813-988-5131.. 99 D
deanofstudents@floridacollege.edu
LONGUEVILLE, Lori .... 618-985-5980 141 D
lorilongueville@jalc.edu
LONGWELL, B. Thomas 812-464-1867 165 C
btlongwell@usi.edu
LONGWELL, Char .... 719-365-8291.. 82 N
char.longwell@uchealth.org
LONGWELL, Sarah .... 503-760-3131 381 J
sarah@birthingway.edu
LONGWORTH, Rhonda .. 734-487-3200 229 K
rkinney@emich.edu
LONGYEAR, JR.,
George, E .... 203-436-4899.. 89 G
george.longyear@yale.edu
LONIER, Terri .... 312-499-4135 151 F
tlonier@saic.edu
LONON, Justin .... 214-378-1816 447 F
justin.lonon@dcccd.edu
LONOWSKI, Jerrold .... 575-624-8421 295 A
lonowsk@nmmi.edu
LONSDALE, Thorunn ..... 607-274-3306 311 D
tlonsdale@ithaca.edu
LOO, Chih .... 256-824-2243.... 8 C
chih.loo@uah.edu
LOOBY, Lynn, S .... 508-213-2215 223 C
lynn.looby@nichols.edu
LOOCHTAN, Anne .... 740-266-1759 361 D
aloochtan@egcc.edu
LOOMIS, Grace, H .... 585-785-1428 308 D
grace.loomis@flcc.edu
LOOMIS, Mary .... 478-825-6436 119 C
loomism@fvsu.edu
LOOMIS, Michael, J ...... 530-226-4728.. 64 B
mloomis@simpsonu.edu
LOOMIS, Susan .... 951-639-5212.. 52 J
sloomis@msjc.edu
LOOMIS, Susan .... 207-326-2345 200 F
susan.loomis@mma.edu
LOONAN, John, F .... 570-389-4115 405 E
jloonan@bloomu.edu
LOONEY, JoAnn .... 845-675-4542 319 C
joann.looney@nyack.edu
LOONEY, Joe .... 828-395-1443 344 A
jlooney@isothermal.edu
LOONEY, Joshua .... 570-422-3211 406 A
jlooney@esu.edu
LOONEY, Nita .... 770-426-2605 122 F
nlooney@life.edu
LOONEY, Susan, D .... 610-607-6271 408 G
slooney@racc.edu
LOONEY, CSC, Thomas . 570-208-5900 398 D
thomaslooney@kings.edu
LOOP, Quentin, C .... 405-912-9478 379 A
qloop@ru.edu
LOOPE, David .... 252-940-6201 340 N
david.loope@beaufortccc.edu
LOOPER, William .... 850-729-5260 104 E
looperw@nwfsc.edu
LOOS, Christopher .... 320-308-6158 247 F
cloos@sctcc.edu
LOOS, Tal .... 912-443-4140 125 D
tloos@savannahtech.edu
LOOSE, Rich .... 605-642-6011 428 F
rich.loose@bhsu.edu
LOOSER, Jackie .... 269-749-7700 236 A
jlooser@olivetcollege.edu
LOOSMAN, Sharon .... 919-513-4206 350 E
sharon_loosman@ncsu.edu
LOPARDO, Gina .... 206-296-6460 498 D
glopardo@seattleu.edu
LOPCI, Kate .... 617-984-1654 223 H
klopci@quincycollege.edu
LOPDELL-LAWRENCE,
Murray .... 609-497-7756 288 E
m.lopdelllawrence@ptsem.edu
LOPER, Debra .... 970-945-8691.. 77 M
LOPER, Marianne .... 585-567-9328 310 F
marianne.loper@houghton.edu
LOPER, Rodney, S .... 513-721-7944 362 D
president@gbs.edu
LOPER, Shane .... 509-527-4571 499 E
shane.loper@wwcc.edu
LOPER, Thomas .... 413-565-1000 211 C
tloper@baypath.edu
LOPES, Anne .... 212-237-8423 302 F
alopes@jjay.cuny.edu
LOPES, Joyce .... 707-826-3351.. 34 A
joyce.lopes@humboldt.edu
LOPES, Zilma .... 919-718-7542 341 H
zlopes@cccc.edu
LOPES-FIGUEROA, Jose 413-755-4088 221 B
jhlopez-figueroa@stcc.edu
LOPEZ, Alberto .... 787-765-3560 522 K
lopeza@edpuniversity.edu
LOPEZ, Amarilis .... 787-746-1400 522 O
mlopez@huertas.edu
LOPEZ, Ana .... 787-758-2525 528 D
ana.lopez6@upr.edu
LOPEZ, Ana .... 504-865-5261 196 D
lopez@tulane.edu
LOPEZ, Ana Alicia .... 713-525-3158 466 J
lopezaa@stthom.edu
LOPEZ, Antonio .... 707-468-3013.. 51 E
alopez@mendocino.edu
LOPEZ, Antonio .... 202-526-3799.. 93 A
alopez@johnpaulii.edu
LOPEZ, Arthur .... 760-245-4271.. 73 E
arthur.lopez@vvc.edu
LOPEZ, Bernard .... 215-955-6844 411 E
bernard.lopez@jefferson.edu
LOPEZ, Beto .... 915-747-8244 467 E
alopez@utep.edu
LOPEZ, Boris .... 523-953-4000.. 49 A
lopezbv@lacitycollege.edu
LOPEZ, Carlos .... 714-564-6080.. 58 A
lopez_carlos@sac.edu
LOPEZ, Carmen, J .... 787-258-1501 521 K
clopez@columbiacentral.edu
LOPEZ, Chuck .... 509-359-2202 494 D
clopez17@ewu.edu
LOPEZ, Coral .... 775-445-4230 279 F
coral.lopez@wnc.edu
LOPEZ, Crystal .... 973-618-3472 284 D
cllopez@caldwell.edu
LOPEZ, Dana .... 310-954-4037.. 52 H
dlopez@msmu.edu
LOPEZ, JR., Daniel .... 773-442-4600 147 G
d-lopez@neiu.edu
LOPEZ, Derek .... 719-549-2535.. 78 P
derek.lopez@csupueblo.edu
LOPEZ, Desi .... 787-780-5134 525 D
dlopez@nuc.edu
LOPEZ, Don .... 559-489-2352.. 66 G
don.lopez@fresnocitycollege.edu
LOPEZ, Edgar .... 949-214-3073.. 40 I
edgar.lopez@cui.edu
LOPEZ, Edwin .... 337-521-8901 193 E
elopez@solacc.edu
LOPEZ, Elias, S .... 530-752-3619.. 68 H
eslopez@ucdavis.edu
LOPEZ, Felipe .... 562-860-2451.. 36 A
flopez@cerritos.edu
LOPEZ, Francisco .... 313-664-7428 228 H
flopez@collegeforcreativestudies.edu
LOPEZ, Gabriel .... 787-766-1717 526 B
um_glopez@suagm.edu
LOPEZ, Gabriel, J .... 505-277-6128 296 H
vpr@unm.edu
LOPEZ, Gerardo .... 787-891-0925 523 G
glopez@aguadilla.inter.edu
LOPEZ, Gersom .... 914-632-5400 315 K
glopez@monroecollege.edu
LOPEZ, Gilma .... 909-621-8055.. 45 D
gilma_lopez@hmc.edu
LOPEZ, Heather .... 509-335-2001 499 G
hlopez@wsu.edu
LOPEZ, Hector, L .... 787-894-2828 529 A
hector.lopez975@upr.edu
LOPEZ, Ignacio .... 312-261-3468 146 G
ignacio.lopez@nl.edu
LOPEZ, Ignacio .... 312-553-5901 135 J
LOPEZ, Ines .... 915-831-2659 449 A
irelazco@epcc.edu
LOPEZ, Isabel .... 910-843-5304 340 J
LOPEZ, Isis .... 956-665-2326 468 A
isis.lopez@utrgv.edu
LOPEZ, Ivan .... 505-747-2225 295 H
ilopez@nnmc.edu
LOPEZ, Jacqueline .... 845-675-4576 319 C
jacqueline.lopez@nyack.edu
LOPEZ, Jaime .... 787-834-9595 526 E
jlopez@uaa.edu
LOPEZ, Jane .... 757-221-3965 479 I
jalope@wm.edu
LOPEZ, Jean Carlos ...... 765-658-5708 157 H
jclopez@depauw.edu

LOVE, Nikki .... 408-498-5107.. 38 I
nlove@cogswell.edu
LOVE, Patrick .... 516-686-7882 317 G
patrick.love@nyit.edu
LOVE, Tony .... 432-552-2633 469 D
love_t@utpb.edu
LOVEDAY, Joyce .... 253-589-5500 493 F
joyce.loveday@cptc.edu
LOVEDAY, Travis, C ...... 865-694-6415 437 F
tcloveday@pstcc.edu
LOVEDER, Alan .... 212-757-1190 298 D
aloveder@funeraleducation.org
LOVEJOY, Mike .... 469-348-2500 446 M
LOVELACE, Rhonda .... 501-370-5297.. 21 A
rlovelace@philander.edu
LOVELACE PETR, Carrie 402-826-8111 274 E
carrie.petr@doane.edu
LOVELADY, III, Artis ...... 832-252-4617 446 A
artis@cbshouston.edu
LOVELAND, David, A .... 607-746-4013 329 B
lovelada@delhi.edu
LOVELESS, Alyssa .... 405-736-0373 379 F
aloveless@rose.edu
LOVELESS, Cecelia .... 360-438-4366 497 F
cloveless@stmartin.edu
LOVELESS, Debra .... 937-327-6131 374 A
registrar@wittenberg.edu
LOVELESS, Jill .... 304-214-8856 503 E
jloveless@wvncc.edu
LOVELIDGE, Robert .... 979-830-4194 444 D
rlovelidge@blinn.edu
LOVELL, Donna .... 650-723-2300.. 66 C
dlovell@stanford.edu
LOVELL, Ellen .... 719-336-1541.. 80 N
library@lamarcc.edu
LOVELL, JR., Ernest, L .. 601-403-1183 255 D
elovell@prcc.edu
LOVELL, Janet .... 706-754-7833 123 G
jlovell@northgatech.edu
LOVELL, Kim .... 706-778-3000 124 E
klovell@piedmont.edu
LOVELL, Matthew .... 814-886-6388 402 E
mlovell@mtaloy.edu
LOVELL, Matthew, D ..... 812-877-8318 163 G
lovellmc@rose-hulman.edu
LOVELL, Michael, R ...... 414-288-7223 508 C
michael.lovell@marquette.edu
LOVELL, Sharon .... 540-568-2705 481 I
lovellse@jmu.edu
LOVELL, Stan .... 706-754-7868 123 G
slovell@northgatech.edu
LOVELY, Christine, D .... 916-278-6078.. 33 C
lovelyc@csus.edu
LOVERIDGE, Robert .... 801-863-8161 473 D
loveriro@uvu.edu
LOVETT, Christopher, M 814-886-6400 402 E
clovett@mtaloy.edu
LOVETT, Daniel .... 252-536-7275 343 F
dlovett037@halifaxcc.edu
LOVETT, David, L .... 717-477-1164 407 B
dllove@ship.edu
LOVETT, Greg .... 806-743-2952 463 E
greg.lovett@ttuhsc.edu
LOVETT, Patricia .... 270-686-4336 183 J
patricia.lovett@brescia.edu
LOVETT, Rod, M .... 217-351-2409 148 H
rlovett@parkland.edu
LOVICK, Reed .... 252-527-6223 344 D
rlovick@lenoircc.edu
LOVIK, Eric .... 540-831-5099 484 A
elovik@radford.edu
LOVIN, Eddie .... 615-547-1231 431 D
elovin@cumberland.edu
LOVINCE, Thomas .... 504-671-5510 192 H
tlovin@dcc.edu
LOVINS, Greg .... 864-388-8305 422 A
glovins@lander.edu
LOVINSKI, Kim .... 304-205-6622 502 K
kimberly.lovinski@bridgevalley.edu
LOVITT, Timm .... 253-833-9111 495 C
tlovitt@greenriver.edu
LOVSTUEN, Brenda, C ... 319-895-4292 167 G
blovstuen@cornellcollege.edu
LOVVORN, Judi .... 229-217-4198 126 C
jlovvorn@southernregional.edu
LOW,
Catherine Yu-Ling ...... 808-371-5443 129 E
cfo@orientalmedicine.edu
LOW, George .... 540-831-5187 484 A
glow@radford.edu
LOW, Kathryn .... 207-786-6066 198 E
klow@bates.edu
LOW, Ryan .... 207-581-1554 201 A
ryan.low@maine.edu
LOW, Ryan .... 207-581-1554 201 B
ryan.low@maine.edu
LOW, Wai Hoa .... 808-521-2288 129 E
whlow@orientalmedicine.edu

LOWBRIDGE, John, D ... 270-824-1835 186 D
john.lowbridge@kctcs.edu
LOWDEN, Paul .... 616-732-1194 229 D
plowden@davenport.edu
LOWDER, Diane, M .... 804-752-7218 484 C
dianelowder@rmc.edu
LOWDER, Michael .... 405-789-7661 380 A
michael.lowder@swcu.edu
LOWDER, Theresa .... 859-985-3313 183 I
lowdert@berea.edu
LOWDERMILK,
Robert, S .... 336-342-4261 346 B
lowdermilkb@rockinghamcc.edu
LOWE, Allyson, M .... 412-578-6663 391 G
amlowe@carlow.edu
LOWE, Brenda .... 806-720-7307 452 D
brenda.lowe@lcu.edu
LOWE, Carmen .... 617-627-4239 225 A
carmen.lowe@tufts.edu
LOWE, Carrie Beth .... 865-573-4517 432 H
cblowe@johnsonu.edu
LOWE, Daryl .... 502-597-5080 187 E
daryl.lowe@kysu.edu
LOWE, Dawn .... 443-518-4256 204 E
dlowe@howardcc.edu
LOWE, Dustin, J .... 530-226-4770.. 64 B
dlowe@simpsonu.edu
LOWE, JR., Eugene, Y .. 847-491-8409 148 C
eyljr@northwestern.edu
LOWE, Gee .... 626-917-9482.. 37 D
geel@cesna.edu
LOWE, Grant .... 706-419-1411 118 E
grant.lowe@covenant.edu
LOWE, James .... 765-285-2805 156 C
jlowe@bsu.edu
LOWE, James, R .... 860-486-0566.. 88 G
jim.lowe@uconn.edu
LOWE, Janet, S .... 307-766-3307 517 B
jlowe@uwyo.edu
LOWE, Jeanette .... 706-771-4000 116 A
jlowe@augustatech.edu
LOWE, Judy .... 423-697-2686 436 F
judy.lowe@chattanoogastate.edu
LOWE, Kathy .... 707-638-5806.. 67 H
kathy.lowe@tu.edu
LOWE, Kathy .... 606-886-3863 185 F
kathy.lowe@kctcs.edu
LOWE, Keri .... 616-988-1000 228 I
keri.l@compass.edu
LOWE, Larry .... 803-705-4573 418 G
larry.lowe@benedict.edu
LOWE, Laura .... 253-833-9111 495 C
llowe@greenriver.edu
LOWE, Lisa .... 404-876-1227 117 A
lisa.lowe@bccr.edu
LOWE, Melinda .... 662-241-6088 254 F
mslowe@muw.edu
LOWE, Melissa .... 303-492-0025.. 83 B
melissa.lowe@colorado.edu
LOWE, Pamela .... 847-578-8786 150 E
pamela.lowe@rosalindfranklin.edu
LOWE, Patricia .... 617-552-3334 212 E
patricia.lowe@bc.edu
LOWE, Rick, D .... 910-630-7027 340 A
rlowe@methodist.edu
LOWE, Rosemary .... 870-762-3182.. 17 K
rlowe@smail.anc.edu
LOWE, Sharon .... 772-462-7476 101 Q
slowe@irsc.edu
LOWE, Shayla .... 501-420-1340.. 17 I
shayla.lowe@arkansasbaptist.edu
LOWE, Stephen .... 815-939-5231 148 F
slowe@olivet.edu
LOWE, Susan, L .... 276-964-7304 489 F
susan.lowe@sw.edu
LOWE, Thomas .... 716-286-8360 318 F
tlowe@niagara.edu
LOWE, Tom .... 616-988-1000 228 I
tom.l@compass.edu
LOWE, William, J .... 219-980-6701 160 C
wjlowe@iun.edu
LOWE-SCHNEIDER,
Katy .... 812-866-7081 158 C
lowe@hanover.edu
LOWELL, Hillary .... 406-683-7151 271 H
hillary.lowell@umwestern.edu
LOWELL, Randy .... 864-424-8046 425 G
lowell@mailbox.sc.edu
LOWENBERG, Ron .... 714-895-8369.. 38 G
rlowenberg@gwc.cccd.edu
LOWENSTEIN,
Daniel, H .... 415-476-4451.. 70 A
lowenstein@ucsf.edu
LOWENSTEIN, Noah ...... 425-278-9318.. 63 A
nlowenstein@saybrook.edu
LOWENTHAL, Barbara .... 212-472-1500 318 B
blowenthal@nysid.edu

LOWENTHAL, Benjamin . 410-455-1720 208 A
blowenth@umbc.edu
LOWENTHAL, Tina .... 626-395-2758.. 29 I
tina.lowenthal@caltech.edu
LOWERY, Andrew .... 229-209-5239 115 B
andrewlowery@andrewcollege.edu
LOWERY, Carla .... 662-329-7197 254 F
cmlowery@muw.edu
LOWERY, Chris .... 317-921-4882 161 F
crlowery@ivytech.edu
LOWERY, Juliet, J .... 540-375-2099 484 H
lowery@roanoke.edu
LOWERY, Kathryn .... 601-266-6775 256 E
kathryn.lowery@usm.edu
LOWERY, Misa, D .... 910-843-5304 340 J
mlowery@nabc.edu
LOWERY, Wendy .... 540-831-5407 484 A
LOWERY, Wendy .... 910-521-6252 351 E
wendy.lowery@uncp.edu
LOWERY-HART,
Russell, D .... 806-371-5123 442 D
rdloweryhart@actx.edu
LOWIN, Clinton .... 806-291-1163 470 I
lowinc@wbu.edu
LOWKS, Tamara .... 614-823-1420 368 O
tlowks@otterbein.edu
LOWMAN, Sara .... 713-348-2457 455 F
lowman@rice.edu
LOWMAN, Tony .... 856-256-5300 289 H
lowman@rowan.edu
LOWN, Maris .... 908-709-7006 292 C
maris.lown@ucc.edu
LOWNES-JACKSON,
Millicent .... 615-963-7142 438 E
mlownes@tnstate.edu
LOWRANCE, Jeffrey .... 704-330-6666 342 A
jeff.lowrance@cpcc.edu
LOWREY, Andrew .... 352-854-2322.. 97 C
lowreya@cf.edu
LOWREY, Tammy .... 325-649-8043 450 H
tlowrey@hputx.edu
LOWRY, Jenny .... 410-617-2451 205 A
jlowry@loyola.edu
LOWRY, John .... 615-966-3000 433 D
john.lowry@lipscomb.edu
LOWRY, Kimberly, M ..... 972-860-7028 447 I
kimberlymoore@dcccd.edu
LOWRY, III,
L. Randolph .... 615-966-1787 433 D
randy.lowry@lipscomb.edu
LOWRY, Meagan .... 501-205-8870.. 19 B
mlowry@cbc.edu
LOWRY, Rebekah .... 910-272-3235 346 A
relowry@robeson.edu
LOWRY, Rebekah, R ...... 910-272-3235 346 A
relowry@robeson.edu
LOWY, Vivien .... 213-624-1200.. 42 N
vlowy@fidm.edu
LOY, Marty .... 715-346-3169 511 F
mloy@uwsp.edu
LOYA, Karla .... 956-665-8756 468 A
karla.loya@utrgv.edu
LOYA, Leanne .... 307-268-2662 516 H
leanne.loya@caspercollege.edu
LOYACK, John .... 570-208-5832 398 D
johnloyack@kings.edu
LOYD, James .... 706-649-1449 118 D
jloyd@columbustech.edu
LOYD, James .... 256-306-2784.... 1 F
james.loyd@calhoun.edu
LOYD, Jo Lynn .... 972-279-6511 442 E
jloyd@amberton.edu
LOYD, Kathy .... 870-972-3035.. 18 A
kloyd@astate.edu
LOYD, Kristen, J .... 812-877-8484 163 G
loyd1@rose-hulman.edu
LOYD, Nic .... 256-824-3025.... 8 C
nicholas.loyd@uah.edu
LOYD, Nicole, L .... 610-861-1503 402 D
loydn@moravian.edu
LOYD, Nicole, L .... 610-861-1502 402 D
loydn@moravian.edu
LOYD, Sage .... 870-460-1422.. 22 D
coons@uamont.edu
LOYD-PAIGE, Michelle .. 616-526-8703 228 B
lopa@calvin.edu
LOYNAZ, Oscar .... 305-348-6796 109 D
oscar.loynaz@fiu.edu
LOYOLA, David .... 956-380-8196 455 G
dloyola@riogrande.edu
LOZA, Frank .... 325-670-1461 450 A
floza@hsutx.edu
LOZADA, Jose .... 787-727-7020 529 B
jlozada@sagrado.edu
LOZANO, Fran .... 408-848-4702.. 44 B
flozano@gavilan.edu
LOZANO, Franz .... 707-654-1032.. 32 E
flozano@csum.edu

LOZEN, Stephen .... 617-449-7038 225 C
stephen.lozen@urbancollege.edu
LOZIER, Kathryn, A .... 610-359-7322 393 E
klozier@dccc.edu
LOZINA, Mary .... 914-674-7651 314 I
mlozina@mercy.edu
LU, Elissa .... 508-793-7513 213 C
ellu@clarku.edu
LU, Flora .... 831-459-5852.. 70 C
floralu@ucsc.edu
LU, Jeffrey .... 408-433-2280.. 37 E
LU, Kuang Kai .... 323-731-2383.. 55 E
rex@psuca.edu
LU, Xinjian .... 510-885-3291.. 31 F
xinjian.lu@csueastbay.edu
LUALLEN, Bert .... 620-417-1563 181 E
bert.luallen@sccc.edu
LUAN, Jing .... 650-358-6880.. 61 Q
luan@smccd.edu
LUBBE, Veronica, A ...... 859-344-3522 189 G
veronica.lubbe@thomas.more.edu
LUBBERDEN, Mike .... 641-628-5346 167 D
lubberdenm@central.edu
LUBBERS, Kristin .... 719-336-1518.. 80 N
kristin.lubbers@lamarcc.edu
LUBBERS, Tony .... 316-295-5200 177 F
lubberst@friends.edu
LUBBERTS, Rhonda .... 616-331-2525 230 G
lubbertr@gvsu.edu
LUBECK, Eileen .... 973-720-2450 292 I
lubecke@wpunj.edu
LUBELL, Courtney .... 707-765-1836.. 52 A
LUBELL, Ellen .... 212-410-8479 317 C
elubell@nycpm.edu
LUBIC, Brian .... 812-237-3838 159 C
brian.lubic@indstate.edu
LUBIENECKI, Teresa ...... 716-652-8900 300 L
tlubienecki@cks.edu
LUBIG, Joe .... 906-227-1880 235 A
jlubig@nmu.edu
LUBINGER, Bill .... 216-368-4443 358 C
william.lubinger@case.edu
LUBINSKY, Hindy .... 718-787-1602 331 F
hindy.lubinsky@touro.edu
LUBNOW, Jeff .... 973-328-5155 285 B
jlubnow@ccm.edu
LUBRANO, Ann .... 718-818-6470 323 F
alubrano@edaff.com
LUCAS, Bonnie .... 847-635-1711 148 D
blucas@oakton.edu
LUCAS, Bryan .... 817-257-7682 461 A
b.lucas@tcu.edu
LUCAS, Carol, A .... 516-877-3154 297 I
lucas@adelphi.edu
LUCAS, Catherine .... 303-556-5122.. 80 Q
lucascat@msudenver.edu
LUCAS, Cathy .... 910-221-2224 338 A
clucas@gcd.edu
LUCAS, Cecilia .... 808-455-0325 130 G
cblucas@hawaii.edu
LUCAS, Dawn .... 704-463-3207 348 B
dawn.lucas@pfeiffer.edu
LUCAS, Dawn .... 704-463-1360 348 B
dawn.lucas@pfeiffer.edu
LUCAS, Dwayne .... 315-781-3304 310 C
lucas@hws.edu
LUCAS, Hakim, J .... 386-481-2929.. 95 J
lucash@cookman.edu
LUCAS, Jaine .... 215-951-1849 398 F
lucasj@lasalle.edu
LUCAS, James .... 336-770-3317 352 B
lucasj@uncsa.edu
LUCAS, Jane, K .... 205-934-4636.... 8 B
jklucas@uab.edu
LUCAS, Jeffrey .... 716-827-2567 331 K
lucasj@trocaire.edu
LUCAS, Jennifer, R .... 717-337-6211 396 A
jlucas@gettysburg.edu
LUCAS, Joan .... 662-325-8131 254 E
jlucas@legal.msstate.edu
LUCAS, John .... 608-262-8287 510 C
jplucas@wisc.edu
LUCAS, Julie .... 617-253-3952 221 C
LUCAS, Karen .... 904-620-2624 110 E
karen.lucas@unf.edu
LUCAS, Lynn .... 330-972-7920 371 C
plynn@uakron.edu
LUCAS, Mark .... 785-227-3380 175 E
lucas@bethanylb.edu
LUCAS, Mary .... 615-460-6000 430 D
LUCAS, Matthew .... 503-375-7019 383 A
mlucas@corban.edu
LUCAS, Michelle .... 717-796-1800 401 L
mlucas@messiah.edu
LUCAS, Pam, A .... 214-860-2097 448 A
plucas@dcccd.edu
LUCAS, Paul, M .... 724-287-8711 390 J
paul.lucas@bc3.edu

LUPOLE, Barbara, H 610-799-1510 400 A
blupole@lccc.edu
LUPTON, Brendan 847-970-4891 154 H
blupton@usml.edu
LUPTON, Deborah 410-337-6135 204 A
dlupton@goucher.edu
LUPU, Peter 623-845-3747 13 H
peter.lupu@gccaz.edu
LUQUETTE, Heidi 503-842-8222 387 C
heidiluquette@tillamookbaycc.edu
LURSEN, Cara 704-403-1614 336 B
cara.lursen@carolinashealthcare.org
LURZ, Carol 910-938-6343 342 C
lurzc@coastalcarolina.edu
LUSHBAUGH, Jeffery 609-777-3083 292 B
jlushbaugh@tesu.edu
LUSHNIAK, Boris, D 301-405-2437 207 G
lushniak@umd.edu
LUSK, D. Claude 806-291-3436 470 I
luskc@wbu.edu
LUSK, Kent 312-553-5628 135 J
klusk1@ccc.edu
LUSNIA, Susann 504-314-7698 196 D
slusnia@tulane.edu
LUSSIER, Michel 207-741-5519 200 C
mlussier@smccme.edu
LUSSOW, J. Paul 312-752-2112 142 E
paul.lussow@laureate.net
LUST, Kevin 217-789-1017 144 B
kevin.lust@llcc.edu
LUSTER, Marilyn 570-586-2400 392 E
mluster@clarkssummitu.edu
LUSTER, Pamela, T 619-388-2721 60 D
pluster@sdccd.edu
LUSTER, Stacey 508-929-8022 219 A
sluster@worcester.edu
LUSTIG, Derek 315-781-3123 310 C
lustig@hws.edu
LUTCHEN, Kenneth, R 617-353-2800 212 G
klutch@bu.edu
LUTER, Gary, S 813-253-3333 113 E
gluter@ut.edu
LUTES, David 703-284-5993 483 A
david.lutes@marymount.edu
LUTES, Morris 404-835-6122 435 M
mlutes@richmont.edu
LUTES, Nicholas 360-538-4034 495 B
nicholas.lutes@ghc.edu
LUTGEN, Roxanne 715-675-3331 514 F
lugten@ntc.edu
LUTGRING, Ray 812-488-2589 164 G
rl5@evansville.edu
LUTHI, John, R 570-577-3332 390 H
john.luthi@bucknell.edu
LUTHJOHAN, Jeanne 269-783-2121 237 B
jluthjohan@swmich.edu
LUTHRINGER, Kim 269-782-1472 237 B
kluthringer01@swmich.edu
LUTNER, Rachel 216-687-2223 359 L
r.lutner@csuohio.edu
LUTON, Sally 315-498-2466 319 G
lutons@sunyocc.edu
LUTRICK, Candee 972-825-4612 457 F
clutrick@sagu.edu
LUTRICK, Donny 972-825-4824 457 F
dlutrick@sagu.edu
LUTTIG-KOMROSKY,
Jennifer 773-702-3835 153 F
luttig@uchicago.edu
LUTTJEBOER, Jared 219-864-2400 162 U
LUTTON, Margaret, K 817-515-5140 458 B
margaret.lutton@tccd.edu
LUTTRELL, Curt 760-776-7441 39 D
cluttrell@collegeofthedesert.edu
LUTY, Paul, J 503-943-8874 387 H
luty@up.edu
LUTZ, JR., Ben 865-573-4517 432 H
blutz@johnsonu.edu
LUTZ, Bob 561-803-2661 104 I
bob_lutz@pba.edu
LUTZ, Brock 517-607-2561 231 C
blutz@hillsdale.edu
LUTZ, Cathleen, A 570-321-4069 400 G
lutz@lycoming.edu
LUTZ, Cheryl 717-391-3595 411 C
lutz@stevenscollege.edu
LUTZ, Dan 765-285-8984 156 C
dlutz@bsu.edu
LUTZ, Debra, K 989-686-9386 229 J
dklutz@delta.edu
LUTZ, Jill 704-922-6448 343 D
lutz.jill@gaston.edu
LUTZ, John, M 615-875-8895 440 D
john.lutz@vanderbilt.edu
LUTZ, Nate, K 612-874-3780 243 F
nate_lutz@mcad.edu
LUTZ, Paula 307-766-4106 517 B
plutz@uwyo.edu
LUTZ, Susan 303-871-2118 83 E
susan.lutz@du.edu
LUTZ, Todd 254-519-5708 459 D
todd.lutz@tamuct.edu
LUTZ-DAVIDSON, Stacy 719-389-6953 77 J
sdavidson@coloradocollege.edu
LUTZKA, David 218-722-4000 242 B
davidl@dbumn.edu
LUVAAS, Linda 336-758-5000 353 A
luvaasls@wfu.edu
LUX, Jace, T 270-745-2551 190 F
jace.lux@wku.edu
LUXNER, Catherine 570-961-4703 401 B
luxner@marywood.edu
LUXTON, Andrea, T 269-471-3100 227 B
aluxton@andrews.edu
LUY, Peg 616-233-3413 229 D
pluy@davenport.edu
LUYMES, Robyn 616-732-1157 229 D
rluymes3@davenport.edu
LUZAR, E. Jane 317-278-5082 160 E
ejluzar@iupui.edu
LUZIUS, Jeff 989-774-3500 228 E
luziu1j@cmich.edu
LUZURIAGA, Katherine 508-856-6282 217 C
katherine.luzuriaga@umassmed.edu
LUZURIAGA, Suzana, H 513-556-0364 371 E
susana.luzuriaga@uc.edu
LY, Geisce 415-267-6521 37 H
jly@ccsf.edu
LY, Lisa 650-949-6204 43 F
lylisa@foothill.edu
LY, Michael 714-867-5009 64 G
mcly@southcoastcollege.com
LY, Pearl 650-738-4313 62 B
lype@smccd.edu
LY, Vi 323-265-6793 48 L
lyv@elac.edu
LYALL, Rachel 610-861-1304 402 D
lyallr@moravian.edu
LYANS, Stacie 775-831-1314 280 C
slyans@sierranevada.edu
LYBYER, Debra 208-792-2313 132 C
dlybyer@lcsc.edu
LYDDON, Jerri, L 620-417-1151 181 E
jerrilynn.lyddon@sccc.edu
LYDDON, Susan 718-482-5010 303 B
slyddon@lagcc.cuny.edu
LYDON, Carol Ann 828-694-1882 341 B
ca_lydon@blueridge.edu
LYDON, Christopher, P 202-319-5305 91 D
lydon@cua.edu
LYDON, JR.,
Theodore, M 415-422-6396 72 A
lydon@usfca.edu
LYDY, Kenneth, A 937-481-2536 373 I
kenneth_lydy@wilmington.edu
LYKE, Alan, D 719-884-5000 180 B
adlyke@nbc.edu
LYKE, Heather, R 412-648-8230 412 I
lykeh@pitt.edu
LYKINS, Karen 931-372-3214 438 F
klykins@tntech.edu
LYKOUDIS, Michael, N 574-631-7473 165 A
lykoudis.1@nd.edu
LYLE, William 215-489-4987 393 F
william.lyle@delval.edu
LYM, Brian 516-877-3250 297 I
blym@adelphi.edu
LYMAN, Barbara, G 717-477-1371 407 B
bglyman@ship.edu
LYMAN, Kristin 320-363-5233 241 I
klyman@csbsju.edu
LYMANSTALL, Judy 419-783-2300 361 A
jlymanstall@defiance.edu
LYMPANY, John 304-367-4953 504 A
john.lympany@fairmontstate.edu
LYN, Jamila 305-626-3762 99 M
jamila.lyn@fmuniv.edu
LYN, Janice 334-244-3028 4 E
jlyn@aum.edu
LYNCH, Alice, D 804-752-3039 484 C
alicelynch@rmc.edu
LYNCH, Alicia 515-271-1400 168 G
LYNCH, Amy, J 217-581-3511 138 A
ajlynch@eiu.edu
LYNCH, Andrea 626-256-4673 37 I
alynch@coh.org
LYNCH, Andrea 609-586-4800 287 A
lyncha@mccc.edu
LYNCH, Chad 531-622-2929 275 F
celynch@mccneb.edu
LYNCH, Christopher 251-460-7725 9 B
clynch@southalabama.edu
LYNCH, Christopher 251-460-6494 9 B
clynch@southalabama.edu
LYNCH, Craig 773-602-5016 135 L
celynch@ccc.edu
LYNCH, Cynthia 414-847-3340 508 G
cynthialynch@miad.edu
LYNCH, Cynthia, D 414-847-3340 508 G
cynthialynch@miad.edu
LYNCH, Darlene 219-980-6614 160 C
darlynch@iun.edu
LYNCH, Deborah 407-708-2144 107 G
lynchd@seminolestate.edu
LYNCH, Dianne 573-876-7210 267 G
president@stephens.edu
LYNCH, Eileen 773-838-7500 136 A
elynch4@ccc.edu
LYNCH, Erin, J 212-998-2237 318 D
erin.lynch@nyu.edu
LYNCH, Jacqueline 315-792-3111 332 H
jlynch@utica.edu
LYNCH, Jacqueline 708-456-0300 153 E
jacquelinelynch@triton.edu
LYNCH, James 912-279-5713 118 A
jlynch@ccga.edu
LYNCH, James 315-792-5316 315 I
jlynch@mvcc.edu
LYNCH, Jasmine 856-351-2919 291 E
jlynch@salemcc.edu
LYNCH, Jennifer, L 336-917-5090 348 H
jenni.lynch@salem.edu
LYNCH, Joanna 502-213-2410 186 C
joanna.lynch@kctcs.edu
LYNCH, Joe 717-337-6518 396 A
jlynch@gettysburg.edu
LYNCH, Josiah 541-485-1780 384 G
josiahlynch@newhop.edu
LYNCH, Julie 512-499-4309 467 A
jlynch@utsystem.edu
LYNCH, Kathryn 781-283-3583 225 D
klynch@wellesley.edu
LYNCH, Kelly 781-239-4220 211 A
klynch@babson.edu
LYNCH, Laura 912-279-4548 118 A
llynch@ccga.edu
LYNCH, Lisa, M 781-736-2503 213 A
lisalynch@brandeis.edu
LYNCH, Lynn 941-359-4200 111 C
LYNCH, Marilyn, K 972-860-4181 447 G
mklynch@dcccd.edu
LYNCH, Marlon 212-998-1409 318 D
m.lynch@nyu.edu
LYNCH, Michael 315-568-3052 317 A
mlynch@nycc.edu
LYNCH, Michael 678-916-2661 115 K
mlynch@johnmarshall.edu
LYNCH, Molly 703-257-6664 488 H
mlynch@nvcc.edu
LYNCH, Pamela 312-850-7090 136 C
plynch@cci.edu
LYNCH, Paul, F 315-445-4551 312 F
lynchpf@lemoyne.edu
LYNCH, Richard, E 972-708-7340 449 I
dick_lynch@gial.edu
LYNCH, Robert 240-567-7306 205 F
bob.lynch@montgomerycollege.edu
LYNCH, Scott 970-207-4550 80 P
scottl@mckinleycollege.edu
LYNCH, Stephanie, J 202-687-4560 92 B
sjl28@georgetown.edu
LYNCH, Stephen, J 401-865-2233 416 E
sjlynch@providence.edu
LYNCH, Susan 218-322-2451 245 B
susan.lynch@itascacc.edu
LYNCH, Susan 717-564-4112 390 A
susan.lynch@brightwood.edu
LYNCH, Sylvia 562-938-4280 48 I
slynch@lbcc.edu
LYNCH, Sylvia 423-869-6223 433 C
sylvia.lynch@lmunet.edu
LYNCH, III, Thomas 617-973-1175 224 I
tlynch@suffolk.edu
LYNCH, Tim 909-869-4379 31 A
tlynch@cpp.edu
LYNCH, Timothy 718-631-6344 303 F
tlynch@qcc.cuny.edu
LYNCH, Timothy, G 734-764-0304 237 I
timlynch@umich.edu
LYNCH, Valerie 217-234-5270 143 B
vlynch@lakeland.cc.il.us
LYNCH GADALETA,
Margaret, A 401-456-8387 417 A
mlynchgadaleta@ric.edu
LYND, Debbie 215-884-8942 415 C
registrar@woninstitute.edu
LYNDE, Megan 605-882-5284 427 D
megan.lynde@lakeareatech.edu
LYNDON, Ann 256-331-5319 3 C
lyndon@nwscc.edu
LYNES, Richard 903-223-3049 460 D
richard.lynes@sscserv.com
LYNG-GLIDDI, Diana, L 518-327-6314 320 A
dlyngglidi@paulsmiths.edu
LYNHAM, Sandra 207-741-5923 200 C
slynham@smccme.edu
LYNN, Angela 309-298-1891 155 D
an-lynn@wiu.edu
LYNN, David 405-425-5645 377 B
david.lynn@oc.edu
LYNN, Kerrie 423-746-5294 439 A
klynn@tnwesleyan.edu
LYNN, Laura 866-492-5336 251 E
laura.lynn@mail.waldenu.edu
LYNN, Mac 615-207-1319 195 C
macl@nationsu.edu
LYNN, Martha 206-546-4634 498 E
mlynn@shoreline.edu
LYNN, Martha, G 206-546-4634 498 E
mlynn@shoreline.edu
LYNN, Marvin 503-725-4697 386 D
marvinlynn@pdx.edu
LYNN, Rexton 201-684-7627 289 C
rlynn@ramapo.edu
LYNN, Richard 251-809-1556 1 I
richard.lynn@faulknerstate.edu
LYNN, Steve 803-777-2128 424 I
lynns@mailbox.sc.edu
LYNN, Vicki 501-450-1494 19 I
lynn@hendrix.edu
LYNOTT, Patricia 603-645-9794 282 C
p.lynott@snhu.edu
LYNOTT, Zach 503-768-7766 383 G
zlynott@lclark.edu
LYON, Alison 650-508-3503 54 D
alyon@ndnu.edu
LYON, Andrea 219-465-7852 165 D
andrea.lyon@valpo.edu
LYON, Brett 712-274-5234 172 A
lyon@morningside.edu
LYON, Brooke 256-782-5449 6 B
bbell@jsu.edu
LYON, Chuck 661-362-3545 39 C
chuck.lyon@canyons.edu
LYON, James 706-721-8106 116 B
jlyon@augusta.edu
LYON, Larry 254-710-3588 444 B
larry_lyon@baylor.edu
LYON, Larry 919-761-2372 349 C
llyon@sebts.edu
LYON, Leah 580-559-5259 375 I
llyon@ecok.edu
LYON, Mary Eilleen 616-331-2221 230 G
lyonme@gvsu.edu
LYON, Misty 309-341-5422 134 H
mlyon@sandburg.edu
LYON, Robert 256-824-6127 8 C
robert.lyon@uah.edu
LYON, Sue 413-644-4282 211 B
slyon@simons-rock.edu
LYON, Tammy 910-938-6247 342 C
lyont@coastalcarolina.edu
LYON, Wade 620-417-1064 181 E
wade.lyon@sccc.edu
LYONS, Anthony 620-227-9269 176 N
alyons@dc3.edu
LYONS, Becky 406-657-2168 272 B
blyons@msubillings.edu
LYONS, Bruce 646-313-8000 303 G
bruce.lyons@guttman.cuny.edu
LYONS, Calvin 312-341-3518 150 D
clyons04@roosevelt.edu
LYONS, Cheryl, C 501-450-3140 23 I
clyons@uca.edu
LYONS, Cindy 434-947-8722 484 B
clyons@randolphcollege.edu
LYONS, Ellen 617-236-8812 215 B
elyons@fisher.edu
LYONS, Frankie 406-771-4361 272 D
frankie.lyons@gfcmsu.edu
LYONS, Greg 952-358-8650 246 D
greg.lyons@normandale.edu
LYONS, Heather 910-695-3701 346 E
lyonsh@sandhills.edu
LYONS, James 408-551-1691 62 F
jlyons@scu.edu
LYONS, Jason, C 757-594-8175 479 H
jason.lyons@cnu.edu
LYONS, John 781-280-3528 220 C
LYONS, Joseph 804-524-6453 491 A
jlyons@vsu.edu
LYONS, Kyra, A 202-319-5608 91 D
lyonsk@cua.edu
LYONS, Larry 309-438-5626 140 L
lelyons@ilstu.edu
LYONS, Laura 808-956-8516 129 J
lelyons@hawaii.edu
LYONS, Marquita 251-405-7052 1 E
mlyons@bishop.edu
LYONS, Marybeth 315-792-7505 330 A
smbl@sunyit.edu

LYONS, Michael ... 781-239-2443 220 A mlyons@massbay.edu
LYONS, Nicholas, A ... 315-312-2222 327 D nicholas.lyons@oswego.edu
LYONS, Patrick, G ... 973-761-9498 291 F patrick.lyons@shu.edu
LYONS, Peter ... 404-413-2578 121 A lyonsp@gsu.edu
LYONS, Phil ... 715-232-1683 512 A lyonsp@uwstout.edu
LYONS, Phillip ... 936-294-1700 462 F icc_pml@shsu.edu
LYONS, Richard, K ... 510-643-2027.. 68 G lyons@haas.berkeley.edu
LYONS, Scott ... 270-745-2446 190 F scott.lyons@wku.edu
LYONS, Shane ... 304-293-5621 505 B shlyons@mail.wvu.edu
LYONS, Shawn ... 859-238-5500 184 C shawn.lyons@centre.edu
LYONS, Sheila ... 601-352-9666 252 C bookstore@belhaven.edu
LYONS, Steve ... 218-723-6167 241 J slyons@css.edu
LYONS, Steven, J ... 937-775-5745 374 B steven.lyons@wright.edu
LYONS, Suzette, M ... 951-827-3989.. 69 D suzette.lyons@ucr.edu
LYONS, Theresa ... 907-786-1240.. 10 A tlyons@alaska.edu
LYONS, Todd, W ... 831-656-2441 518 D twlyons@nps.edu
LYSIONEK, Christine ... 610-902-8416 391 B christine.lysionek@cabrini.edu
LYSLE, Jane, H ... 302-225-6274.. 90 G lyslej@gbc.edu
LYSNE, Josh, D ... 218-299-3645 241 K jlysne@cord.edu
LYSNE, Marit ... 507-222-4080 241 C mlysne@carleton.edu
LYTCH, Carol, E ... 717-290-8701 399 F president@lancasterseminary.edu
LYTLE, Anne ... 212-772-4242 302 E alytle@hunter.cuny.edu
LYTLE, Christopher ... 814-472-3360 409 G clytle@francis.edu
LYTLE, Daniel ... 715-233-5358 513 E dlytle@cvtc.edu
LYTLE, David ... 210-434-6711 454 D dlytle@lake.ollusa.edu
LYTLE, James, R ... 570-586-2400 392 E jlytle@clarkssummitu.edu
LYTLE, Jesse ... 610-896-1000 397 F jlytle@haverford.edu
LYTTLE, Darylnet ... 804-524-5674 491 A dlyttle@vsu.edu
LYTTLE, Marsha, J ... 810-762-9660 232 C mlyttle@kettering.edu
LYTTLE, Sonya ... 843-525-8248 424 E slyttle@tcl.edu
LYTTON, Billy ... 704-922-6480 343 D lytton.billy@gaston.edu
LYZUN, Nancy ... 317-940-8029 156 I nlyzun@butler.edu
L'ETOILE, Michelle ... 617-422-7210 222 J mletoile@nesl.edu

M

MÉNDEZ ROMÁN, Sheyla, M ... 787-763-4280 528 F sheyla.mendez@upr.edu
MA, Carolyn ... 808-933-2909 129 I csjma@hawaii.edu
MA, Duc, D ... 520-626-1188.. 16 J mad2@email.arizona.edu
MA, Elise ... 516-739-1545 317 D financial_aid@nyctcm.edu
MA, Jennifer ... 925-473-7521.. 41 A jma@losmedanos.edu
MA, Patricia ... 215-965-4069 402 C pma@moore.edu
MA, Qing ... 626-289-7719.. 24 I qma@amu.edu
MAALOUF, Kathy ... 305-237-7356 103 L kmaalouf@mdc.edu
MAAS, Lyndsay ... 805-965-0581.. 62 E lmmaas@sbcc.edu
MAAS, Paula ... 212-229-8947 316 E maasp@newschool.edu
MAAS, Tammy ... 307-778-1258 516 N tmaas@lccc.wy.edu
MAAS-STEED, Deaun ... 405-692-3263 376 C dmaassteed@macu.edu
MAASJO, Bryan ... 212-772-4582 302 E bm514@hunter.cuny.edu
MAASS, John ... 912-201-8000 125 H jmaass@southuniversity.edu
MAASS, Kern ... 504-865-3039 194 G kdmaass@loyno.edu
MABE, Mark ... 816-271-4261 264 B mabe@missouriwestern.edu
MABE, Scotty ... 910-410-1684 345 G samabe@richmondcc.edu
MABERRY, Dan ... 918-444-2120 376 G mabery@nsuok.edu
MABERRY, Sue ... 310-665-6925.. 54 I maberry@otis.edu
MABEUS, Amy ... 319-385-6478 170 J amy.mabeus@iw.edu
MABOKELA, Reitumetse 217-333-1828 154 B mabokela@illinois.edu
MABRIE, Pesha ... 830-372-8065 461 D pmabrie@tlu.edu
MABRY, Doug ... 503-517-1935 388 C dmabry@westernseminary.edu
MABRY, James, C ... 978-656-3101 220 C mabry@middlesex.mass.edu
MABRY, Tom, R ... 719-333-9751 518 H
MABUS, John ... 402-463-2402 274 I john.mabus@hastings.edu
MAC PHERSON, Garry, L ... 858-822-4923.. 69 E gmacpherson@ucsd.edu
MACALESTER, Tom ... 704-461-6721 335 J tommacalester@bac.edu
MACALUSO, Anthony ... 718-990-2452 322 F macalusa@stjohns.edu
MACALUSO, Daniel ... 909-621-8335.. 45 D dmacaluso@hmc.edu
MACALUSO, Sean ... 508-856-4653 217 C sean.macaluso@umassmed.edu
MACAN, Drew ... 386-822-7472 111 E dmacan@stetson.edu
MACAPINLAC, Jonas, D 671-735-2944 520 B jmac@triton.uog.edu
MACARI, Emir ... 504-280-7120 194 F emacari@uno.edu
MACARTHUR, John ... 661-362-2220.. 51 C sstaats@masters.edu
MACARTHUR, John ... 989-463-7241 226 H macarthurjr@alma.edu
MACARTHUR, Josh ... 781-239-4528 211 A wmacarthur@babson.edu
MACAULAY, Barbara ... 508-373-5897 221 E barbara.macaulay@mcphs.edu
MACCARONE, Ellen, M . 509-313-6136 495 A maccarone@gonzaga.edu
MACCARTHY, Stephen, J ... 215-898-8724 412 G smaccar@upenn.edu
MACCHI, Thomas, J ... 215-572-2942 389 D macchit@arcadia.edu
MACCHIARELLA, Sue, A 386-226-7740.. 98 C macchis1@erau.edu
MACCHIAVELLI, Raul ... 787-265-3850 528 C raul.macchiavelli@upr.edu
MACCLAREN, Jon, A ... 802-387-6721 475 C jonmacclaren@landmark.edu
MACCORMACK, Jennifer 206-616-7933 499 D jmaccorm@uw.edu
MACCORQUODALE, Patricia ... 520-621-2848.. 16 J pmac@email.arizona.edu
MACCUISH, Spencer ... 805-581-1233.. 42 G smaccuish@eternitybiblecollege.com
MACCULLOCH, Heather . 646-312-5045 301 B heather.macculloch@baruch.cuny.edu
MACDONALD, Antoinette ... 610-527-0200 409 E toni.macdonald@rosemont.edu
MACDONALD, Brian ... 610-282-1100 393 G brian.macdonald@desales.edu
MACDONALD, David ... 419-772-2200 367 G d-macdonald@onu.edu
MACDONALD, Elizabeth 636-949-4396 261 I emacdonald@lindenwood.edu
MACDONALD, Gail ... 802-225-3261 475 H gail.macdonald@neci.edu
MACDONALD, Gordon .. 303-762-6890.. 79 G gordon.macdonald@denverseminary.edu
MACDONALD, Gregory .. 610-330-5069 399 B macdonag@lafayette.edu
MACDONALD, Ian ... 518-337-4853 305 B macdonai@strose.edu
MACDONALD, Lorri ... 313-578-0401 237 F macdonlj@udmercy.edu
MACDONALD, Mark ... 808-675-3260 128 K mark.macdonald@byuh.edu
MACDONALD, Nancy ... 518-454-2161 305 B macdonan@strose.edu
MACDONALD, Randall, M ... 863-680-4165 100 D rmacdonald1@flsouthern.edu
MACDONALD, Sally, R .. 434-971-3304 517 N
MACDONALD, Sarah ... 410-626-2514 206 F skmacdonald@sjc.edu
MACDONALD, William .. 218-299-4358 241 K macdonal@cord.edu
MACDONALD, William, L ... 740-366-3321 367 H macdonald.24@osu.edu
MACDONALD-DENNIS, Chris, A ... 651-696-6210 243 B cmacdona@macalester.edu
MACDONELL, Chuck, C 402-552-2693 273 K macdonell@clarksoncollege.edu
MACDONNELL, Lisa ... 313-993-1455 237 F macdonnl@udmercy.edu
MACE, Chance ... 575-624-8214 295 A mace@nmmi.edu
MACELI, Peter ... 914-633-2466 311 B pmaceli@iona.edu
MACEMORE, Kristen ... 336-838-6122 347 G khmacemore969@wilkescc.edu
MACEO, Brenda, K ... 213-740-5371.. 72 B maceo@usc.edu
MACEWAN, Bonnie ... 334-844-1714.... 4 D macewbj@auburn.edu
MACFARLAND, Joseph .. 410-626-2511 206 F joseph.macfarland@sjc.edu
MACFARLAND, Randolph, M ... 303-762-6900.. 79 G provost@denverseminary.edu
MACFIE, Thomas, E ... 931-598-1274 436 A tmacfie@sewanee.edu
MACGILLIVRAY, Diane, N ... 617-373-2520 223 D
MACH, Stella ... 312-935-4180 149 K smach@robertmorris.edu
MACH, Thomas ... 937-766-7770 358 D macht@cedarville.edu
MACHA, Barry ... 940-397-6225 453 C barry.macha@mwsu.edu
MACHÁCEK, Jennifer, L 920-748-8185 509 H machacekj@ripon.edu
MACHADO, Alyson ... 808-544-1126 129 C amachado@hpu.edu
MACHADO, Jared ... 858-784-8469.. 63 G
MACHADO, Jorge, E ... 305-760-7500 103 C
MACHADO, Miguel ... 713-798-4951 444 A
MACHALSKI, Thomas ... 248-683-0311 237 E tmachalski@sscms.edu
MACHAMER, Claire ... 336-770-3374 352 B machamerc@uncsa.edu
MACHELL, James ... 405-974-5701 380 J jmachell@uco.edu
MACHEN, Paul ... 210-486-2157 441 I pmachen@alamo.edu
MACHIA, Michael ... 580-628-6291 376 J michael.machia@noc.edu
MACHIRA, Mary, A ... 801-626-6839 473 E marymachira@weber.edu
MACHLIS, Gedelyah ... 718-232-7800 334 G
MACHNIK, Michael, E ... 908-526-1200 289 D mike.machnik@raritanval.edu
MACHOVSKY, Robert ... 660-562-1248 264 I alumni@nwmissouri.edu
MACHTLEY, Ronald, K ... 401-232-6008 416 A rmac@bryant.edu
MACHUCA, José, E ... 787-257-7373 525 Q jemachuca@suagm.edu
MACHUSAK, Janice, M . 313-927-1443 233 D jmachusak@marygrove.edu
MACIAS, Anita ... 412-563-6673 125 H amacias@southuniversity.edu
MACIAS, Benjamin ... 626-914-8611.. 37 G bmacias@citruscollege.edu
MACIAS, Joanne ... 361-593-3085 460 B joanne.macias@tamuk.edu
MACIAS, Sandy ... 650-961-9300.. 55 I smacias@paloaltou.edu
MACIAS, Tom ... 760-757-2121.. 52 F tmacias@miracosta.edu
MACIAS-SILVERMAN, Claudia ... 773-577-8100 137 A
MACIEJEWSKI, Felice, E ... 708-524-6873 137 F fmaciejewski@dom.edu
MACIEJEWSKI, Kathryn . 906-932-4231 230 D kathrynm@gogebic.edu
MACIEL, Anthony ... 949-582-4882.. 64 J amaciel@saddleback.edu
MACIK-FREY, Marilyn ... 985-448-4170 197 C marilyn.macik-frey@nicholls.edu
MACINNIS, Stewart, D ... 540-464-7207 490 E macinnissd@vmi.edu
MACINTIRE, Ken ... 410-287-1034 203 B kmacintire@cecil.edu
MACIULAITIS, Mark ... 631-632-6090 325 F mark.maciulaitis@stonybrook.edu
MACK, Bruce ... 704-669-4115 342 B mack@clevelandcc.edu
MACK, Carol ... 843-525-8250 424 E cmack@tcl.edu
MACK, Carol ... 503-636-8141 384 B cmack@marylhurst.edu
MACK, Craig ... 617-732-2929 221 E craig.mack@mcphs.edu
MACK, Donna ... 865-882-4526 438 A mackdk@roanestate.edu
MACK, Hailey ... 208-535-5337 131 G hailey.mack@my.eitc.edu
MACK, Johnny ... 503-399-6243 382 C johnny.mack@chemeketa.edu
MACK, Joseph ... 607-431-4209 309 E mackj@hartwick.edu
MACK, Josh, C ... 641-422-4436 172 C mackjosh@niacc.edu
MACK, Kari ... 845-687-5214 331 L mackk@sunyulster.edu
MACK, Kimberly, J ... 252-536-6399 343 F kmack219@halifaxcc.edu
MACK, Lawrence ... 937-708-5701 373 H lmack@wilberforce.edu
MACK, Melvin ... 803-934-3401 422 G mmack@morris.edu
MACK, Qing, L ... 860-253-3008.. 85 C qmack@asnuntuck.edu
MACK, Tonya ... 530-741-6987.. 75 K tmack@yccd.edu
MACK, Tracy ... 806-720-7380 452 D tracy.mack@lcu.edu
MACKAY, Jeff ... 503-883-2436 383 H jmackay@linfield.edu
MACKE, Aaron, M ... 651-962-6470 251 D ammacke@stthomas.edu
MACKE, Charles ... 931-372-3414 438 F cmacke@tntech.edu
MACKEITH, Peter ... 479-575-2702.. 21 I mackeith@uark.edu
MACKEN, Jennifer ... 303-914-6600.. 82 B jen.macken@rrcc.edu
MACKENZIE, Erin ... 432-264-5015 450 G emackenzie@howardcollege.edu
MACKENZIE, Lorie ... 315-229-5600 323 D lmackenzie@stlawu.edu
MACKENZIE, Lorie, R ... 315-229-5600 323 D lmackenzie@stlawu.edu
MACKERETH, Anne ... 952-885-5417 249 F amackereth@nwhealth.edu
MACKERSIE, Chris ... 253-912-3655 497 B cmackers@pierce.ctc.edu
MACKESY, Francis, J ... 904-620-2800 110 E f.mackesy@unf.edu
MACKEY, Geoffrey ... 724-266-3838 412 D gmackey@tsm.edu
MACKEY, George ... 501-374-6305.. 21 C
MACKEY, Jerry ... 562-903-4777.. 27 E university.legalcounsel@biola.edu
MACKEY, Joshua ... 303-556-5034.. 80 Q jmackey@msudenver.edu
MACKEY, Katie, L ... 570-326-3761 404 T kmackey@pct.edu
MACKEY, Peter, F ... 413-542-2321 210 F comm@amherst.edu
MACKEY, Roberta ... 850-729-5365 104 E mackeyr@nwfsc.edu
MACKEY, Thomas ... 518-587-2100 329 C thomas.mackey@esc.edu
MACKEY, Tonja ... 903-823-3028 458 D tonja.mackey@texarkanacollege.edu
MACKEY, Wilbur, E ... 719-884-5000 180 B wemackey@nbc.edu
MACKIE, Jennifer ... 805-765-9300.. 62 D
MACKIE, Keith ... 828-327-7000 341 G kmackie@cvcc.edu
MACKILLOP, Jane ... 718-960-4681 302 C jane.mackillop@lehman.cuny.edu
MACKIN, Gail ... 509-963-1403 492 L gail.mackin@cwu.edu
MACKIN, James ... 607-436-2517 325 E james.mackin@oneonta.edu
MACKIN, Jim ... 402-461-7482 274 I jmackin@hastings.edu
MACKINNON, Fern ... 978-934-4660 217 B fern_mackinnon@uml.edu
MACKINNON, George ... 414-955-2855 508 D gmackinnon@mcw.edu
MACKINNON, Mary Jo . 401-454-6625 417 B mmackinn@risd.edu
MACKINNON, Neil, J ... 513-558-3326 371 E neil.mackinnon@uc.edu
MACKINNON, Thomas .. 570-408-3832 414 H thomas.mackinnon@wilkes.edu
MACKLEN, Kevin ... 610-372-4721 408 G kmacklen@racc.edu
MACKLER, Dan ... 818-333-3558.. 53 I dan@nyfa.edu
MACKLIN, Alexis ... 260-481-6514 160 D macklina@ipfw.edu

MACKLIN, Charles .... 425-388-9990 494 F cmacklin@everettcc.edu
MACKLIN, James, F ...... 518-629-7353 310 G j.macklin@hvcc.edu
MACKLIN, ShaRhonda .. 254-968-9081 459 A maclin@tarleton.edu
MACKSEY, Jennifer .... 802-447-6310 476 C jmacksey@svc.edu
MACLACHLAN, Scott .... 561-207-5325 105 A maclachs@palmbeachstate.edu
MACLAINE, Julie, A ...... 740-588-1201 374 G jmaclaine@zanestate.edu
MACLAREN, James .... 504-865-5720 196 D maclaren@tulane.edu
MACLAUGHLIN, Cordy .. 808-984-3471 130 H cordy.maclaughlin@uhfoundation.org
MACLEAN, Roger .... 406-243-2900 271 G roger.maclean@umontana.edu
MACLEISH, Padraic .... 760-872-2000.. 41 E padraicm@deepsprings.edu
MACLENNAN, Richard, L .... 208-769-3303 132 E rmaclennan@nic.edu
MACLEOD, David, J ...... 563-588-8000 169 B dmacleod@emmaus.edu
MACLEOD, Ian .... 508-830-5269 218 D imacleod@maritime.edu
MACLEOD, Kellye .... 952-851-0066 240 A
MACLEOD, Kimberly, M 607-746-4603 329 B macleokm@delhi.edu
MACLEOD, Melissa, A ... 724-458-2050 396 D mamacleod@gcc.edu
MACLEOD, Robert .... 813-974-6015 111 A rmacleod@usf.edu
MACLEOD WALLS, Elizabeth .... 816-415-5026 270 C macleodwallse@william.jewell.edu
MACMASTER, Donald .... 989-358-7246 227 A macmastd@alpenacc.edu
MACMENAMIE, Michael 310-377-5501.. 51 B mmacmenamie@marymountcalifornia.edu
MACMILLAN FOX, Rebecca .... 305-284-2648 112 O rfox@miami.edu
MACNEIL, Jacqueline .... 727-864-7856.. 97 O macneijm@eckerd.edu
MACNEIL, M. A. J. Lex . 630-515-7275 145 I lmacne@midwestern.edu
MACNEIL, R. Lamont .... 860-679-2808.. 88 G macneil@nso.uchc.edu
MACNEILL, Lynn .... 863-784-7192 108 B lynn.macneill@southflorida.edu
MACNEW, James .... 215-637-7700 397 G jmacnew@holyfamily.edu
MACON, Lisa, R .... 407-582-1420 113 F lmacon@valenciacollege.edu
MACONACHY, W. Vic .... 301-369-2800 202 J wvmaconachy@captechul.edu
MACOPSON, Elmer, R ... 828-652-0603 344 G elmerm@mcdowelltech.edu
MACPHERSON, Andrew . 903-463-8768 449 J macphersona@grayson.edu
MACPHERSON, Heidi, R 585-395-2361 326 D hmacpherson@brockport.edu
MACPHERSON, Pamela . 302-622-8000.. 90 A pmacpherson@dcad.edu
MACQUEEN, William, J . 248-341-2027 235 D wjmacque@oaklandcc.edu
MACREYNOLDS, William, K .... 336-727-7102 338 B bill.macreynolds@greensboro.edu
MACRINA, Francis, L .... 804-827-2262 487 E macrina@vcu.edu
MACRITCHIE, Andrea ..... 508-854-4461 220 G amacritchie@qcc.mass.edu
MACRO, Venessa .... 515-271-3710 168 J venessa.macro@drake.edu
MACTAGGART, Julie ...... 563-589-3619 173 J jmactaggart@dbq.edu
MACUR, Kenneth, M ..... 716-880-2202 314 F kenneth.m.macur@medaille.edu
MACVARISH, Greg .... 312-942-7112 150 F greg_macvarish@rush.edu
MACVEY, Mark .... 760-480-8474.. 74 H mmacvey@wscal.edu
MACWILLIAMS, David ... 719-587-7800.. 76 D dcmacwil@adams.edu
MACY, Dawn .... 657-278-7450.. 32 B dmacy@fullerton.edu
MACZAK, Marie .... 409-747-4876 469 C mmarczak@utmb.edu
MACZKA, Eric .... 402-941-6201 275 J maczka@midlandu.edu
MADAIO-O'BRIEN, Melanie .... 617-353-7138 212 G asmelmad@bu.edu
MADAMA, Patrick .... 732-906-2551 287 B pmadama@middlesexcc.edu
MADANIPOUR, Manouche .... 617-928-7376 222 D mmadanipour@mountida.edu
MADAULE, Crystal .... 714-556-3610.. 72 F crystal.madaule@vanguard.edu
MADDAHI, Dariush (David) .... 323-728-9636.. 53 F
MADDALI, Ramesh .... 601-877-6146 251 G rmaddali@alcorn.edu
MADDEN, Caitlin .... 213-624-1200.. 42 N cmadden@fidm.edu
MADDEN, Carolyn .... 603-428-2386 281 F cmadden@nec.edu
MADDEN, Carrie .... 816-501-4628 265 I carrie.madden@rockhurst.edu
MADDEN, Christopher .. 214-648-0702 469 E christopher.madden@utsouthwestern.edu
MADDEN, Corey .... 336-770-1442 352 B maddenc@uncsa.edu
MADDEN, Dean .... 603-646-4091 281 C dean.madden@dartmouth.edu
MADDEN, Fred, H .... 856-415-2272 289 G fmadden@rcgc.edu
MADDEN, Jaclyn .... 443-412-2046 204 C dmadden@harford.edu
MADDEN, John .... 575-624-7111 294 A john.madden@roswell.enmu.edu
MADDEN, Kathleen .... 661-654-3450.. 31 B kmadden@csub.edu
MADDEN, Madeline .... 361-354-2520 445 S mmadden@coastalbend.edu
MADDEN, Margaret .... 518-783-2307 324 C mmadden@siena.edu
MADDEN, Paul .... 740-351-3270 369 L pmadden@shawnee.edu
MADDEN, Richard .... 931-363-9844 433 E rmadden@martinmethodist.edu
MADDEN, Sally, J .... 847-578-3266 150 E sally.madden@rosalindfranklin.edu
MADDEN, Susan .... 240-567-5274 205 F susan.madden@montgomerycollege.edu
MADDEX, Shelley .... 530-754-4138.. 68 H sbmaddex@ucdavis.edu
MADDIGAN, Susan .... 508-362-2131 219 E smaddigan@capecod.edu
MADDIN, Brent .... 212-228-1888 320 L
MADDIRALA, James, S . 340-693-1013 529 C james.maddirala@uvi.edu
MADDIS, Ryan .... 989-275-5000 232 E ryan.maddis@kirtland.edu
MADDOCK, Jay .... 979-436-9322 459 C maddock@tamhsc.edu
MADDON, Jason .... 616-451-3511 229 D jmaddon@davenport.edu
MADDOX, Gregory, H ... 713-313-7889 461 E maddox_gh@tsu.edu
MADDOX, Kelley, L ...... 770-534-6270 116 F kmaddox@brenau.edu
MADDOX, Natasha .... 606-759-7141 186 E natasha.maddox@kctcs.edu
MADDOX, Nedra .... 704-669-4142 342 B maddox@clevelandcc.edu
MADDOX, Tangella .... 312-341-3584 150 D tmaddox@roosevelt.edu
MADDOX, Winston .... 609-586-4800 287 A maddoxw@mccc.edu
MADDOX, Yvonne .... 301-295-3303 518 G yvonne.maddox@usuhs.edu
MADDUX, Gary .... 256-824-2679.... 8 C gary.maddux@us.army.mil
MADDUX, Pat .... 563-588-6366 167 E pat.maddux@clarke.edu
MADDUX, Susan, A ...... 864-833-8205 423 D smaddux@presby.edu
MADDY, Angela .... 620-792-9322 175 C maddya@bartonccc.edu
MADELONE LINCOLN, Laura .... 607-436-2526 325 E laura.madelone@oneonta.edu
MADER, Mary .... 978-542-6390 218 E mary.mader@salemstate.edu
MADERE, Whit .... 804-819-4951 487 F wmadere@vccs.edu
MADHAVA RAU, Leela .. 909-748-8285.. 71 H leela_madhavarau@redlands.edu
MADIA, Sherrie .... 201-200-2472 287 F smadia@njcu.edu
MADIA, William, J .... 650-723-2300.. 66 C
MADIGAN, David .... 212-854-8296 305 E david.madigan@columbia.edu
MADIGAN, Dennis, J .... 617-603-6900 222 F dennis.madigan@necb.edu
MADIGAN, Karen .... 802-225-3230 475 H karen.madigan@neci.edu
MADIGAN, Kay .... 330-652-9919 361 G kaymadigan@eticollege.edu
MADIGAN, Kaye .... 320-762-4684 243 J kayem@alextech.edu
MADIGAN, Shannon ...... 719-587-7912.. 76 D smadigan@gollett.com
MADIN, Laurence, P ..... 508-289-2515 226 D lmadin@whoi.edu
MADIOU-BEALE, Olga ... 410-888-9048 205 D obeale@muih.edu
MADISON, Renee .... 765-658-4914 157 H reneemadison@depauw.edu
MADISON, Stephen, S .. 817-515-1002 458 B stephen.madison@tccd.edu
MADIX, Marcy .... 619-684-8813.. 53 J mmadix@newschoolarch.edu
MADLOCK, Calvin .... 510-466-5398.. 56 I cmadlock@peralta.edu
MADLOCK, Krystal .... 319-352-8434 174 C krystal.madlock@wartburg.edu
MADONNA, Richard ...... 860-439-2044.. 86 H richard.madonna@conncoll.edu
MADORE, Keith .... 860-253-3041.. 85 C kmadore@asnuntuck.edu
MADORIN, Jeanne, L .... 704-687-0659 351 C jlmadori@uncc.edu
MADRAY, Van .... 704-216-3900 346 C van.madray@rccc.edu
MADRID, Jered .... 949-794-9090.. 66 B jmadrid@stanbridge.edu
MADRID, Liliana .... 610-625-7884 402 D madridl@moravian.edu
MADRIGAL, Richard ...... 866-687-2258.. 30 B
MADSEN, Alice .... 206-592-3301 495 E amadsen@highline.edu
MADSEN, Christina .... 501-852-2659.. 23 I christinam@uca.edu
MADSEN, Julie .... 360-992-2077 493 E jmadsen@clark.edu
MADSEN, Lois .... 785-833-4315 179 C lois.madsen@kwu.edu
MADSEN, Monte .... 210-688-3101 445 P
MADSEN, Patrick .... 704-687-0784 351 C pmadsen@uncc.edu
MADSEN, Ruthanne .... 617-824-8600 214 E ruthanne_madsen@emerson.edu
MADSEN, Thor .... 816-414-3700 263 D academicdean@mbts.edu
MADSON, Gregory .... 406-791-5359 273 C gregory.madson@ugf.edu
MADULI, Ed .... 408-741-2082.. 74 B ed_maduli@wvm.edu
MADURA, Angela .... 303-245-4751.. 81 B amadura@naropa.edu
MADUTA, John .... 360-992-2505 493 E jmaduta@clark.edu
MAEA, Cheri .... 540-834-1980 488 B cmaea@germanna.edu
MAEDA, Donna, K .... 651-696-6581 243 B maeda@macalester.edu
MAENE, Sara .... 304-876-5112 504 D smaene@shepherd.edu
MAES, Sue, C .... 785-532-5644 179 A scmaes@ksu.edu
MAESTAS, Belen .... 719-587-7321.. 76 D bmaestas@adams.edu
MAESTAS, Michael .... 785-864-2277 181 I mvlm@ku.edu
MAESTAS, Stacy .... 307-778-1240 516 N smaestas@lccc.wy.edu
MAFFEI, Melody .... 209-667-3623.. 33 F mmaffei@csustan.edu
MAFFEO, Angie .... 815-740-3711 154 G amaffeo@stfrancis.edu
MAFFIA, Robert .... 201-216-3542 291 G robert.maffia@stevens.edu
MAFFUCCI, Michael ...... 704-290-5864 346 F mmaffucci@spcc.edu
MAGALONG, Mariles ...... 510-215-3847.. 40 K mmagalong@contracosta.edu
MAGANA, Keri .... 828-898-8896 339 B maganak@lmc.edu
MAGARY, Diane .... 812-866-7364 158 C magary@hanover.edu
MAGAZU, Daniel .... 508-626-4539 218 A dmagazu@framingham.edu
MAGAZU, Jessica .... 678-331-4276 122 F jessica.magzu@life.edu
MAGDALENO, Jose .... 718-960-8241 302 C joseph.magdaleno@lehman.cuny.edu
MAGDZIARZ, Wayne ..... 312-915-6403 144 D wmagdzi@luc.edu
MAGEE, JR., David, E ... 423-439-4441 431 H magee@etsu.edu
MAGEE, Edward .... 304-558-0281 503 N ed.magee@wvhepc.edu
MAGEE, Erin .... 707-527-4431.. 62 H emagee@santarosa.edu
MAGEE, Frances .... 508-793-7423 213 C fmagee@clarku.edu
MAGEE, Gwen .... 601-477-4028 253 F gwen.magee@jcjc.edu
MAGEE, Jeannette .... 323-953-4000.. 49 A mageejm@lacitycollege.edu
MAGEE, Jennifer .... 214-637-3530 470 H jmagee@wadecollege.edu
MAGEE, John .... 734-432-5656 233 C jmagee@madonna.edu
MAGEE, Kristy .... 814-886-6320 402 E kmagee@mtaloy.edu
MAGEE, Maggie .... 207-947-4591 198 F mmagee@bealcollege.edu
MAGEE-SAUER, Karen ... 856-256-4850 289 H sauer@rowan.edu
MAGEEHON, Ali .... 541-888-7417 387 A ali.mageehon@socc.edu
MAGERS, Dwight, E ...... 423-236-2992 436 C magers@southern.edu
MAGET, Douglas .... 212-854-5204 299 B dmaget@barnard.edu
MAGGARD, Bryan .... 337-482-5393 197 F athleticdirector@louisiana.edu
MAGGARD, Shawn .... 615-383-4848 441 A smaggard@watkins.edu
MAGGARD, Trent .... 620-862-5252 175 B trent.maggard@barclaycollege.edu
MAGGELAKIS, Sophia ... 585-475-2483 321 D sxmsma@rit.edu
MAGGIO, Chris .... 318-357-6441 197 D maggioc@nsula.edu
MAGGIO, Chris .... 318-357-4250 197 D maggioc@nsula.edu
MAGGIO, Marielena ...... 216-368-2519 358 C mxm346@case.edu
MAGGIO, Melissa .... 651-641-3399 242 J mmaggio001@luthersem.edu
MAGGIONI, Susan .... 781-239-2210 220 A smaggioni@massbay.edu
MAGGIORE, Ray .... 516-876-2031 327 C maggiorer@oldwestbury.edu
MAGGITTI, Patrick, G .... 610-519-4521 413 K patrick.maggitti@villanova.edu
MAGGITTI, Sara .... 610-902-8561 391 B sara.t.maggitti@cabrini.edu
MAGGS, Mark .... 814-234-7755 410 G mmaggs@southhills.edu
MAGHSOUD, Amanda, F .... 803-323-4891 426 H maghsouda@winthrop.edu
MAGIDA, David .... 802-485-2145 475 I davem@norwich.edu
MAGIE, CM, Sandra, C . 713-686-4345 466 J smagie@stthom.edu
MAGIERA, Steve, L .... 239-590-1119 109 C smagiera@fgcu.edu
MAGILL, M. Elizabeth ... 650-723-2300.. 66 C
MAGINNIS, JR., Edward .... 301-405-1105 207 G maginnis@umd.edu
MAGLIONE, Joyce .... 973-408-3631 285 E jmaglion@drew.edu
MAGLIULO, Sabrina ...... 201-360-4230 286 E smagliulo@hccc.edu
MAGLOIRE, Yves, M ..... 516-628-5007 327 C magloirey@oldwestbury.edu
MAGNAN, Carolyn .... 860-832-3715.. 84 J magnanc@ccsu.edu
MAGNANI, Holly .... 914-337-9300 305 F holly.magnani@concordia-ny.edu
MAGNER, Brent .... 402-363-5636 278 E brent.magner@york.edu
MAGNER, Kevin .... 714-867-5009.. 64 G kjmagner@southcoastcollege.com
MAGNER, Lois, B .... 620-417-1011 181 E lois.magner@sccc.edu
MAGNER, Michael .... 978-837-5019 221 G magnerm@merrimack.edu
MAGNUS, Keith, B .... 317-940-9385 156 I kmagnus@butler.edu
MAGNUSON, Amy .... 850-644-8868 110 A amagnuson@admin.fsu.edu
MAGNUSON, Audrey, J 210-458-6846 468 B audrey.magnuson@utsa.edu
MAGNUSON, Dave .... 803-754-4100 420 E
MAGNUSON, Jacquelyn 651-641-8892 241 L magnuson@csp.edu
MAGNUSON, Kelly, J .... 320-222-6094 247 B kelly.magnuson@ridgewater.edu
MAGNUSON, Kendyl ..... 760-744-1150.. 55 K kmagnuson@palomar.edu
MAGNUSON, Matthew .. 559-934-2403.. 73 N matthewmagnuson@whccd.edu
MAGNUSON, Terry .... 919-962-1319 351 B tmagnuson@unc.edu
MAGNUSSON, Selena ... 706-295-6868 120 C smagnusson@gntc.edu

MAGNUSSON, Selena ... 706-295-6866 120 C
smagnusson@gntc.edu
MAGOON, Don ... 919-735-5151 347 E
djmagoon@waynecc.edu
MAGOON, Maggie ... 989-386-6622 234 B
mmagoon@midmich.edu
MAGORIAN, Cortney ... 916-660-7391.. 63 K
cmagorian@sierracollege.edu
MAGOULIAS, Christina . 217-424-6244 145 J
christiemagoulias@millikin.edu
MAGRETTA, Dawn ... 586-445-7302 233 B
magrettad@macomb.edu
MAGRO, Edward ... 401-232-6000 416 A
MAGUET, Kathryn, L ... 570-577-3700 390 H
kathryn.maguet@bucknell.edu
MAGUIRE, Anastasia ... 305-899-3950.. 95 G
amaguire@barry.edu
MAGUIRE, Eric, G ... 717-358-3953 395 G
eric.maguire@fandm.edu
MAGUIRE, Karen ... 212-355-1501 300 M
kmaguire@christies.edu
MAGUIRE, Ken ... 575-624-7160 294 A
ken.maguire@roswell.enmu.edu
MAGUIRE, Kevin, C ... 617-627-3502 225 A
kevin.maguire@tufts.edu
MAGUIRE, Kim ... 267-341-6203 397 G
kmaguire315@holyfamily.edu
MAGUIRE, Robert ... 973-278-5400 299 F
robert-maguire@berkeleycollege.edu
MAGUIRE, Robert ... 973-278-5400 283 J
robert-maguire@berkeleycollege.edu
MAGUSIAK, Henry ... 724-738-4898 407 C
henry.magusiak@sru.edu
MAH, Al ... 323-241-5238.. 49 E
mahac@lasc.edu
MAHAFFEY, Angela ... 304-473-8100 505 G
mahaffey_a@wvwc.edu
MAHAFFEY, Danny ... 225-578-3962 193 L
dmahaf1@lsu.edu
MAHAFFY, Kevin ... 312-329-4134 146 B
kevin.mahaffy@moody.edu
MAHALINGAM, Shankar 256-824-6474.... 8 C
shankar.mahalingam@uah.edu
MAHALYO, Michael ... 815-226-4067 150 C
mmahalyo@rockford.edu
MAHAN, Amy, J ... 501-882-8880.. 17 M
ajmahan@asub.edu
MAHAN, Christine, P ... 610-341-1706 394 E
cmahan@eastern.edu
MAHAN, Forest, E ... 803-508-7247 418 C
MAHAN, Karl ... 806-720-7122 452 D
karl.mahan@lcu.edu
MAHAN, Kim, B ... 806-371-5050 442 D
kbmahan@actx.edu
MAHAN, Lisa ... 317-738-8018 157 L
lmahan@franklincollege.edu
MAHAN, Melissa ... 210-784-1350 460 C
melissa.mahan@tamusa.edu
MAHAN, Michael ... 678-359-5466 121 B
mmahan@gordonstate.edu
MAHAN, Mickie ... 417-455-5536 259 D
mickiemahan@crowder.edu
MAHAR, Alissa ... 503-594-3010 382 D
alissam@clackamas.edu
MAHAR, Eddie ... 903-785-7661 454 F
emahar@parisjc.edu
MAHAR, Kate ... 530-242-7769.. 63 I
kmahar@shastacollege.edu
MAHARAJ,
Sandhya (Sandy), G ... 304-766-3236 505 A
smaharaj@wvstateu.edu
MAHARAS, Marian ... 303-404-5285.. 79 K
marian.maharas@frontrange.edu
MAHDI, Johnni, F ... 315-792-3209 332 H
jmahdi@utica.edu
MAHER, Brian ... 973-278-5400 283 J
bdm@berkeleycollege.edu
MAHER, Brian ... 212-986-4343 299 F
bdm@berkeleycollege.edu
MAHER, Hannah ... 309-457-2286 146 A
hmaher@monmouthcollege.edu
MAHER, CM, James ... 716-286-8350 318 F
jjm@niagara.edu
MAHER, Jason ... 641-269-3450 169 F
maherjas@grinnell.edu
MAHER, Jeffrey ... 207-725-3178 198 G
jmaher@bowdoin.edu
MAHER, Jerelyn ... 309-676-7611 134 G
jmaher2@fsmail.bradley.edu
MAHER, John ... 304-696-4748 504 C
maherj@marshall.edu
MAHER, Judith ... 724-805-2581 410 C
judith.maher@stvincent.edu
MAHER, Judith ... 724-805-2900 410 B
judith.maher@email.stvincent.edu
MAHER, Kenneth ... 573-592-5225 270 B
MAHER, Mary ... 410-837-5392 209 D
mmaher@ubalt.edu
MAHER, Peter ... 314-246-8622 269 N
maherp@webster.edu
MAHER, Stella ... 908-737-2586 286 F
smaher@kean.edu
MAHER, Susan ... 218-726-8981 250 F
smaher@d.umn.edu
MAHER, Tracy ... 701-854-8039 355 F
tracy.maher@sittingbull.edu
MAHER, Walter ... 210-829-3939 465 E
maher@uiwtx.edu
MAHER, William, J ... 716-888-2986 300 G
maherw@canisius.edu
MAHFOOD, Sebastian ... 860-632-3010.. 87 D
smahfood@holyapostles.edu
MAHINDRA, Ankush ... 310-665-6916.. 54 I
amahindra@otis.edu
MAHITAB, Frank ... 478-825-6754 119 C
mahitabf@fvsu.edu
MAHLBERG, James, A .. 712-325-3218 170 K
jmahlberg@iwcc.edu
MAHLBERG, Lynn, M ... 775-753-2282 279 A
lynn.mahlberg@gbcnv.edu
MAHLE, Krista ... 360-676-2772 496 C
kmahle@nwic.edu
MAHLER, Aaron ... 434-381-6387 485 P
amahler@sbc.edu
MAHLER, Craig ... 615-675-5292 441 B
cmahler@welch.edu
MAHLER, Stephen, J ... 337-482-6418 197 F
mahler@louisiana.edu
MAHLER, Steve ... 337-482-6780 197 F
mahler@louisiana.edu
MAHLMEISTER,
Kenneth, J ... 718-990-5883 322 F
mahlmeik@stjohns.edu
MAHON, John ... 845-569-3287 316 B
john.mahon@msmc.edu
MAHON, Patricia, G ... 605-394-2416 429 A
patricia.mahon@sdsmt.edu
MAHON, Wendy ... 860-439-2211.. 86 H
wlmah@conncoll.edu
MAHONE, Reshunda ... 804-524-5045 491 A
rmahone@vsu.edu
MAHONE-LEIWS,
Gerald ... 254-526-1166 445 L
gerald.mahone-lewis@ctcd.edu
MAHONEY, Erin, A ... 765-658-4278 157 H
emahoney@depauw.edu
MAHONEY, Jack, D ... 518-437-4928 324 G
jmahoney@albany.edu
MAHONEY, Janet ... 732-263-5271 287 C
jmahoney@monmouth.edu
MAHONEY, John ... 530-898-5749.. 31 D
jmahoney@csuchico.edu
MAHONEY, JR.,
John, L ... 617-552-3100 212 E
john.mahoney.2@bc.edu
MAHONEY, Kathleen ... 603-899-4246 281 D
mahonek@franklinpierce.edu
MAHONEY, Kelly ... 401-874-5569 417 E
kellymahoney@uri.edu
MAHONEY, Lynn, P ... 323-343-3800.. 32 D
lynn.mahoney@calstatela.edu
MAHONEY, Melissa ... 804-862-6100 484 F
mmahoney@rbc.edu
MAHONEY, Peter ... 724-805-2241 410 C
peter.mahoney@stvincent.edu
MAHONEY, Peter, E ... 724-805-2241 410 B
peter.mahoney@email.stvincent.edu
MAHONEY, Sharon, A ... 508-767-7322 210 I
shmahone@assumption.edu
MAHONEY, Thomas ... 609-771-2734 284 I
tmahoney@tcnj.edu
MAHONEY, Trina ... 208-885-4387 132 I
tmahoney@uidaho.edu
MAHONY, Daniel, F ... 803-323-2225 426 H
mahonyd@winthrop.edu
MAHONY, James ... 517-264-3525 226 F
jmahony@adrian.edu
MAI, Bill ... 307-766-5766 517 B
william.mai@uwyo.edu
MAI, Brent ... 503-493-6560 382 I
bmai@cu-portland.edu
MAI, Brent, A ... 203-254-4000.. 87 A
bmai@fairfield.edu
MAI, Uyen ... 909-274-4121.. 52 I
umai@mtsac.edu
MAIDEN, Michael ... 732-263-5285 287 C
mmaiden@monmouth.edu
MAIDOU, Nikoleta ... 617-850-1231 215 I
nmaidou@hchc.edu
MAIELLO, Gabriella ... 800-431-8488.. 26 F
MAIENSHEIN,
Richard, W ... 215-887-5511 414 D
rmaienshein@wts.edu
MAIER, Kim ... 608-822-2463 515 A
kmaier@swtc.edu
MAIER, Mark ... 517-607-2445 231 C
mmaier@hillsdale.edu
MAIER-O'SHEA,
Kathryn ... 773-244-5582 147 F
kmaier@northpark.edu
MAIERHOFER, Jean ... 763-488-2633 244 G
jean.maierhofer@hennepintech.edu
MAIETTA, Heather ... 978-837-5038 221 G
maiettah@merrimack.edu
MAIGA, Harouna ... 218-281-8107 250 G
hmaiga@umn.edu
MAILHOT, John ... 413-748-3145 224 G
jmailhot@springfieldcollege.edu
MAILICK, Marsha, R ... 608-262-1044 510 C
marsha.mailick@wisc.edu
MAILLET, Becky ... 504-278-6477 193 B
bmaillet@nunez.edu
MAILLET, Pierrette ... 470-578-4698 122 C
pmaillet@kennesaw.edu
MAILLOUX, Colin, C ... 904-632-3232 100 F
colin.mailloux@fscj.edu
MAIMON, Elaine, P ... 708-534-4130 138 H
emaimon@govst.edu
MAIMONE, Charles, A .. 336-334-5200 351 D
camaimon@uncg.edu
MAIN, Jeremy ... 314-434-4044 259 B
jeremy.main@covenantseminary.edu
MAIN, Mary, E ... 540-458-8920 491 G
mmain@wlu.edu
MAIN, Nathan ... 269-927-8169 232 G
nmain@lakemichigancollege.edu
MAINCA, Daniel ... 213-383-8999.. 24 G
MAINE, Kate ... 706-864-1950 127 B
kate.maine@ung.edu
MAINENTI, David ... 516-299-4212 313 C
david.mainenti@liu.edu
MAIO, James ... 315-792-5401 315 I
jmaio@mvcc.edu
MAIR, Bernard, A ... 202-806-6700.. 92 C
bernard.mair@howard.edu
MAIR, Dave ... 804-819-4929 487 F
dmair@vccs.edu
MAIRS, Julie ... 520-325-0123.. 16 F
MAIRS, Rob ... 520-325-0123.. 16 F
rmairs@suva.edu
MAISEL, Jacqueline, M . 410-543-6150 209 B
jmmaisel@salisbury.edu
MAISENBACHER,
Melissa ... 863-667-5010 108 G
mamaisen@seu.edu
MAISON, Amy ... 229-225-3977 126 C
amaison@southernregional.edu
MAISTER, Eric ... 215-568-9215 415 D
emaister@phmc.org
MAISTO, Jeremy, A ... 717-867-6215 399 J
maisto@lvc.edu
MAITINO, Jennifer ... 617-333-3165 214 B
jmaitino0615@curry.edu
MAITLAND, Jason, R ... 585-785-1437 308 D
jason.maitland@flcc.edu
MAITLAND, Tina, A ... 313-993-1005 237 F
maitlata@udmercy.edu
MAITLEN, Caitlyn ... 641-782-1453 173 I
maitlen@swcciowa.edu
MAIYER, Mark ... 678-331-4356 122 F
mmaiyer@life.edu
MAIZE, David ... 210-883-1000 465 E
maize@uiwtx.edu
MAIZE, Kay ... 402-481-8602 273 F
kay.maize@bryanhealthcollege.edu
MAJAK, Julieta ... 845-257-3295 325 D
majakj@newpaltz.edu
MAJCHROWSKI, Lauren 212-431-2829 317 H
lauren.majchrowski@nyls.edu
MAJEBE, Mary Cissy ... 828-225-3993 337 A
president@daoisttraditions.edu
MAJEROVIC, Chaim ... 516-239-9002 324 B
MAJERUS, Melissa ... 320-308-5922 247 F
mmajerus@sctcc.edu
MAJETTE, Yolanda ... 252-398-6249 336 K
majety@chowan.edu
MAJEWSKI, Deborah ... 508-999-9293 217 A
dmajewski@umassd.edu
MAJEWSKI, John ... 805-893-4327.. 70 B
majewski@ltsc.ucsb.edu
MAJEWSKI, Marc ... 415-338-2596.. 34 C
majewski@sfsu.edu
MAJEWSKIE, Michelle ... 920-923-8083 508 B
mmajewski@marianuniversity.edu
MAJID, Anouar ... 206-221-4447 202 A
amajid@une.edu
MAJKA, David, R ... 412-397-5443 409 C
majka@rmu.edu
MAJOR, Carla ... 504-762-3003 192 H
cmajor@dcc.edu
MAJOR, Carrie ... 865-251-1800 436 B
cmajor@southcollegetn.edu
MAJOR, Michael, W ... 989-964-7130 236 F
mmajor@svsu.edu
MAJOR, Phillip ... 561-803-2034 104 I
phillip_major@pba.edu
MAJOR, Tony ... 304-876-5287 504 D
tmajor@shepherd.edu
MAJOR, Wayne ... 785-272-0889 175 H
MAJOR-KELLY, Shanee . 301-423-3600.. 93 B
MAJORS, Cristina ... 615-550-3170 441 C
cris@williamsoncc.edu
MAKARECHI, Pejman ... 215-503-7841 411 E
pejman.makarechi@jefferson.edu
MAKAROFF, JR.,
Christopher, A ... 513-529-4432 365 I
makaroca@miamioh.edu
MAKEE, Susan ... 603-271-6484 280 N
smakee@ccsnh.edu
MAKER, Laurie ... 508-588-9100 220 B
MAKHIJA, Anil, K ... 614-292-7899 367 H
makhija.1@osu.edu
MAKI, Bill ... 218-471-0015 244 H
wmaki@nhed.edu
MAKI, David, W ... 906-227-1262 235 A
dmaki@nmu.edu
MAKI, Jackie ... 817-515-5379 458 B
jacqueline.maki@tccd.edu
MAKI, Laura ... 209-575-6173.. 75 J
makil@mjc.edu
MAKI, William ... 218-471-0015 245 D
wmaki@nhed.edu
MAKI, William, D ... 218-471-0015 245 B
wmaki@nhed.edu
MAKIN, Linda ... 801-863-8457 473 D
linda.makin@uvu.edu
MAKINEN, Bryan ... 859-622-2421 184 F
bryan.makinen@eku.edu
MAKOFSKE, Rose ... 215-619-7383 402 A
rmakofske@mc3.edu
MAKREZ, Heather ... 978-934-4809 217 B
heather_makrez@uml.edu
MAKSYMEC, Jill ... 773-628-0131 148 A
jmaksymec@nc.edu
MAKSYMIK, Michelle ... 814-262-3820 405 A
mmaksymik@pennhighlands.edu
MAL, Mirlen ... 617-333-2193 214 B
mirlen.mal@curry.edu
MALAFA, Jeanette ... 217-652-6467 155 D
j-malafa@wiu.edu
MALAGON, Blanca ... 305-284-2605 112 O
bmalagon@miami.edu
MALANCA, Donna ... 630-617-3550 138 C
donnas@elmhurst.edu
MALANI, Upendra ... 703-284-1491 483 A
upendra.malani@marymount.edu
MALARA, Kathleen ... 718-817-4160 308 G
kmalara@fordham.edu
MALARET, Frank ... 530-747-5220.. 50 I
malarej@scc.losrios.edu
MALARTE-FELDMAN,
Claire, L ... 603-862-1303 282 F
claire.malarte-feldman@unh.edu
MALASKA, Amy ... 330-490-7321 373 F
amalaska@walsh.edu
MALASKI, Donna ... 269-965-3931 232 A
malaskid@kellogg.edu
MALASPINA, Margaret .. 860-906-5096.. 85 D
mmalaspina@ccc.commnet.edu
MALASRI, Pong ... 901-321-3419 431 A
pong@cbu.edu
MALAT, Heide ... 651-690-6805 249 T
hlmalat@stkate.edu
MALATESTA, Addy ... 570-408-4020 414 H
adelene.malatesta@wilkes.edu
MALATESTA,
Matthew, J ... 518-388-6026 332 B
malatesm@union.edu
MALAVE, Cesar ... 979-845-2217 459 C
dean@qatar.tamu.edu
MALAVE, Daniel ... 978-556-3818 220 F
dmalave@necc.mass.edu
MALAVE-LASSO, Mara ... 787-480-2418 521 J
mamalave@sanjuanciudadpatria.com
MALAVOLTI, TOR,
Nathan ... 740-283-6407 361 L
nmalavolti@franciscan.edu
MALBAURN, Scott ... 541-552-8484 386 H
malbaurns@sou.edu
MALBROUGH, Russell .. 631-451-4630 330 B
malbror@sunysuffolk.edu
MALCOLM, III,
Everett, J ... 904-620-2600 110 E
emalcolm@unf.edu
MALCOLM, Jacquelyn ... 202-319-6632.. 91 D
malcolmj@cua.edu
MALCOLM, Joshua ... 910-521-6201 351 E
joshua.malcolm@uncp.edu
MALCOLM, Kathy ... 309-796-5038 134 C
malcolmk@bhc.edu

MALCOLM, Kim 309-694-8815 139 G
kmalcolm@icc.edu
MALCOLM, Molly Beth 512-223-7683 443 G
mollybeth.malcolm@austincc.edu
MALCOLM, Thomas 863-638-3500 113 I
tom.malcolm@warner.edu
MALDAR, Mustafa 832-230-5555 453 K
maldar@na.edu
MALDONADO, Amelia 787-850-9327 528 B
amelia.maldonado1@upr.edu
MALDONADO, Candice 325-481-8300 450 G
cdraper@howardcollege.edu
MALDONADO, Cesar 713-718-5059 450 D
cesar.maldonado@hccs.edu
MALDONADO, Gilda 619-388-2817 60 D
gmaldona@sdccd.edu
MALDONADO, Ileana 787-725-8120 522 M
imaldonado@eap.edu
MALDONADO, Irving 787-743-3038 525 M
imaldonado@sanjuanbautista.edu
MALDONADO, Kenneth 787-751-0178 525 O
kenmaldona@suagm.edu
MALDONADO, Leticia 831-479-3548 28 F
lemaldon@cabrillo.edu
MALDONADO, Lourdes 787-766-1717 526 B
lmaldonado@suagm.edu
MALDONADO,
Maria del Carmen 787-751-0160 522 B
mcmaldon@cmpr.gov.pr
MALDONADO, Nichole 787-753-6000 522 Q
MALDONADO, Orlando 787-751-0160 522 B
omaldonado@cmpr.pr.gov
MALDONADO, Theresa 915-747-6921 467 E
tamaldonado@utep.edu
MALDONADO, Victor 787-878-5475 523 H
vmaldonado@arecibo.inter.edu
MALDONADO, Wanda 787-758-2525 528 D
wanda.maldonado1@upr.edu
MALDONADO,
Wendy, E 787-888-1135 525 B
MALDONADO, Yesenia 630-889-6546 147 D
ymaldonado@nuhs.edu
MALDONADO FORTUNET,
Francisco 787-265-3862 528 C
decano.estudiantes@uprm.edu
MALDOON, Gladys 718-960-8111 302 C
gladys.maldoon@lehman.cuny.edu
MALE, Taylor 989-328-1275 234 D
taylor.male@montcalm.edu
MALECHA, Gary, L 503-943-7452 387 H
malecha@up.edu
MALECHA, Marvin 619-684-8777 53 J
mmalecha@newschoolarch.edu
MALECHA, Ryan 731-989-6022 432 C
rmalecha@fhu.edu
MALEKZADEH, Ali 312-341-3800 150 D
amalekzadeh@roosevelt.edu
MALEPEAI, Alexis 606-487-3144 185 J
alexis.malepeai@kctcs.edu
MALESH, Rashmi 718-262-2916 304 A
rmalesh@york.cuny.edu
MALESPINI, Al 719-846-5011 82 L
MALESZEWSKI, Joseph 850-245-0466 108 Q
joseph.maleszewski@flbog.edu
MALEWICKI, Michael 202-884-9075 93 C
malewickim@trinitydc.edu
MALEWSKA, Sheila 248-675-0203 125 H
smalewska@southuniversity.edu
MALEWSKI, Erik 470-578-2614 122 C
emalewsk@kennesaw.edu
MALEY, Brian 513-745-3315 374 D
maley@xavier.edu
MALEY, David, C 607-274-3480 311 D
maley@ithaca.edu
MALFITANO, Gregory, J 561-237-7277 103 E
gmalfitano@lynn.edu
MALHOTRA, Betine, A 904-826-0084 71 I
bmalhotra@usa.edu
MALHOTRA, Devinder 651-201-1696 243 I
devinder.malhotra@so.mnscu.edu
MALHOTRA, Manoj 216-368-1156 358 C
manoj.malhotra@case.edu
MALHOTRA, Rajiv 617-732-2791 221 E
rajiv.malhotra@mcphs.edu
MALHOTRA, Rishab 312-567-3909 140 I
rmalhot1@iit.edu
MALIA, Marcia 352-588-8242 106 N
marcia.malia@saintleo.edu
MALICK, Cassie 859-622-2101 184 F
cassie.malick@eku.edu
MALIEKAL, Jose 585-395-2394 326 D
jmalieka@brockport.edu
MALIG, Jannet 562-860-2451 36 A
jmalig@cerritos.edu
MALIGO, Pedro 816-501-4076 265 I
pedro.maligo@rockhurst.edu
MALIK, Christopher, P 716-839-8332 306 E
cmalik@daemen.edu

MALIK, Nish 415-405-4105 34 C
nish@sfsu.edu
MALIK, Rick 312-788-1188 154 I
rmalik@vandercook.edu
MALIK, Zafar, A 312-939-0111 137 G
zafar@eastwest.edu
MALIN, Adam 608-796-3913 512 R
ammalin@viterbo.edu
MALIN, Burke 650-685-6616 45 B
bmalin@gurnick.edu
MALIN, Hank 740-587-6521 361 B
malinh@denison.edu
MALIN, Jay 712-274-5116 172 A
malin@morningside.edu
MALIN, John 217-854-5572 134 E
john.malin@blackburn.edu
MALINA, Joel, M 607-255-9029 306 B
vp-university@cornell.edu
MALINAK, Steven 724-503-1001 414 A
smalinak@washjeff.edu
MALINOWSKI, Gayle 802-468-1389 477 A
gayle.malinowski@castleton.edu
MALINOWSKI, Michael 516-671-8355 333 E
mmalinowski@webb.edu
MALINOWSKI-FERRARY,
Sarah 201-761-6239 291 D
smalinowski@saintpeters.edu
MALISCH, Susan, M 773-508-7750 144 D
smalisc@luc.edu
MALIWESKY, Martin 614-287-3674 360 C
mmaliwes@cscc.edu
MALIZIA, Patricia 201-559-1425 286 C
maliziap@felician.edu
MALJIAN, Peter 909-593-3511 70 E
pmaljian@laverne.edu
MALKEMES, Janet 704-330-2722 342 A
janet.malkemes@cpcc.edu
MALKOWSKI, Keith, J 989-774-7226 228 E
malko1kj@cmich.edu
MALLARD, Cindy 731-352-4000 430 E
MALLARD, Jessica 806-651-2777 460 E
jmallard@mail.wtamu.edu
MALLARD, Kina, S 770-720-5502 124 H
ksm@reinhardt.edu
MALLARD, Mary 972-860-2943 447 H
mmarllard@dcccd.edu
MALLE, Connie, D 620-235-4793 180 J
cmalle@pittstate.edu
MALLER, Jennifer 847-543-2375 136 E
jmaller@clcillinois.edu
MALLERY, Mary 718-951-5611 301 E
mary.mallery@brooklyn.cuny.edu
MALLERY, Mike 503-352-2258 385 I
mallerym@pacificu.edu
MALLERY, Taniecea 337-482-6464 197 F
taniecea.mallery@louisiana.edu
MALLET, Colleen 845-437-5276 333 A
comallet@vassar.edu
MALLETS, Jeff 810-766-4007 227 F
jmalle02@baker.edu
MALLETT, Chris 617-373-6440 223 D
MALLETT, Denise 313-927-1239 233 D
dmallett@marygrove.edu
MALLETT, Porsha 313-831-5200 229 L
pmallett@etseminary.edu
MALLETT, Veronica, T 615-327-6204 434 A
vmallett@mmc.edu
MALLETTE, Kirk 402-363-5696 278 E
kmallette@york.edu
MALLEY, Rebecca 601-266-4466 256 E
rebecca.malley@usm.edu
MALLIA, Maria 201-559-6072 286 C
malliam@felician.edu
MALLIE, Andre 619-260-5951 71 J
amallie@sandiego.edu
MALLINCKRODT, Brent 360-650-3763 500 E
brent.mallinckrodt@wwu.edu
MALLOL, Ramon 787-765-3560 522 K
arivera@edpuniversity.edu
MALLORY, Brian 843-521-4137 425 B
malloryb@uscb.edu
MALLORY, Caroline 812-237-3683 159 C
caroline.mallory@indstate.edu
MALLORY, Jeff 412-396-1117 394 D
malloryj@duq.edu
MALLORY, Kristen 909-621-8267 38 A
kristen.mallory@cmc.edu
MALLORY, Kristin, L 410-334-2813 210 C
kmallory@worwic.edu
MALLORY, Peetee 760-630-1555 28 B
MALLORY, Rob 270-852-3330 187 F
rmallory@kwc.edu
MALLORY, Tesia 937-529-2201 371 B
tsheffield@united.edu
MALLOY, Art 912-525-5000 125 B
amalloy@scad.edu
MALLOY, Joe 434-381-6307 485 P
jmalloy@sbc.edu

MALLOY, Thomas, K 610-499-4174 414 F
tkmalloy@widener.edu
MALM, Loren 765-285-1034 156 C
lmalm@bsu.edu
MALMGREN, Irene, M 909-274-5414 52 I
imalmgren@mtsac.edu
MALMGREN, Jodi 507-786-3375 250 C
malmgren@stolaf.edu
MALONE, Allison 870-574-4544 21 G
amalone@sautech.edu
MALONE, Anne, B 412-924-1379 408 E
amalone@pts.edu
MALONE, Brenda, R 202-687-2440 92 B
bgr23@georgetown.edu
MALONE, Brian 505-277-8900 296 H
bmalone@unm.edu
MALONE, David 616-526-6072 228 B
dbm9@calvin.edu
MALONE, Dean, P 630-515-7145 145 I
dmalon@midwestern.edu
MALONE, Deborah 610-282-1100 393 G
debbie.malone@desales.edu
MALONE, Dennis, C 404-627-2681 116 E
dennis.malone@beulah.edu
MALONE, Elbert, R 803-536-8213 423 G
malone@scsu.edu
MALONE, Gregory 216-987-2340 360 E
gregory.malone@tri-c.edu
MALONE, Judith 781-891-2016 212 A
jmalone@bentley.edu
MALONE, Kathy 219-980-6701 160 C
kalmalon@iun.edu
MALONE, Mary Frances 203-254-4000 87 A
malone@fairfield.edu
MALONE, Maureen 610-989-1453 413 I
mmalone@vfmac.edu
MALONE, Michael 860-768-7793 89 C
malone@hartford.edu
MALONE, Michael, F 413-545-5270 216 H
mmalone@umass.edu
MALONE, Pamela 528-587-2100 329 C
pamela.malone@esc.edu
MALONE, Susan, C 478-301-2233 122 H
malone_sc@mercer.edu
MALONE, Ted, E 765-494-4600 163 C
temalone@purdue.edu
MALONE, Travis 757-455-3256 491 F
tmalone@vwu.edu
MALONE-COLON, Linda 757-727-5400 481 E
linda.malone-colon@hamptonu.edu
MALONEY, Anne, O 570-961-4581 401 B
maloney@marywood.edu
MALONEY, Barry, M 508-929-8020 219 A
bmaloney@worcester.edu
MALONEY, Caroline 760-674-7640 39 D
cmaloney@collegeofthedesert.edu
MALONEY, Catherine 617-984-1787 223 H
cmaloney@quincycollege.edu
MALONEY, Cory 740-283-6944 361 L
cmaloney@franciscan.edu
MALONEY, Dena, P 310-660-3111 42 C
dmaloney@elcamino.edu
MALONEY, Edward, J 202-687-9858 92 B
ejm@georgetown.edu
MALONEY, Heather 513-745-5710 371 F
heather.maloney@uc.edu
MALONEY, Krisellen 848-932-7505 290 A
krisellen.maloney@rutgers.edu
MALONEY, Layne 502-410-6200 184 H
lmaloney@galencollege.edu
MALONEY, Marcy 805-756-1281 30 K
mmaloney@calpoly.edu
MALONEY, Maureen, L 203-358-0700 88 F
mmaureen@bridgeport.edu
MALONEY, Michael 212-280-1534 332 C
mmaloney@uts.columbia.edu
MALONEY, Rebecca, S 504-866-7426 195 E
rmaloney@nds.edu
MALONEY, Shari 320-762-4466 243 J
sharim@alextech.edu
MALONEY, Vincent, U 802-626-6413 477 D
vincent.maloney@lyndonstate.edu
MALOOF, Eric 210-999-7273 464 B
emaloof@trinity.edu
MALOOF, Lisa 770-297-4512 122 E
lmaloof@laniertech.edu
MALOTKY, Daniel 336-272-7102 338 B
dmalotky@greensboro.edu
MALOTT, Michelle 765-973-8320 160 A
mimalott@iue.edu
MALOTT, Pat 719-384-6841 81 G
pat.malott@ojc.edu
MALOTT, Richard 763-433-1204 244 A
richard.malott@anokaramsey.edu
MALOTT, Stephen 605-394-2371 429 A
stephen.malott@sdsmt.edu
MALOY, Frances, J 518-388-6739 332 B
maloyf@union.edu

MALOY, Michael, T 610-436-3309 407 D
mmaloy@wcupa.edu
MALOY, Stanley 619-594-5142 34 B
smaloy@mail.sdsu.edu
MALPASS, Scott, C 574-631-8877 165 A
malpass.1@nd.edu
MALSKY, Matthew 508-793-7671 213 C
mmalsky@clarku.edu
MALTA, Anthony 318-342-3547 198 A
malta@ulm.edu
MALTBIE, Randy 256-840-4112 3 F
rmaltbie@snead.edu
MALTBY, Marc 270-686-4544 186 F
marc.maltby@kctcs.edu
MALTZMAN, Forrest 202-994-6510 92 A
forrest@gwu.edu
MALUTICH, Stephen, M 602-275-7133 16 A
stephen.malutich@rsiaz.edu
MALVEAUX, Gregory 240-567-8077 205 F
greg.malveaux@montgomerycollege.edu
MALVERS, Dennis 978-656-3116 220 C
malversd@middlesex.mass.edu
MALY, Lonn 651-641-8203 241 L
maly@csp.edu
MALY, Mike 312-341-3769 150 D
mmaly@roosevelt.edu
MALZAHN, Martin 718-390-3281 333 D
chaplain@wagner.edu
MAMA, Robin 732-571-3607 287 C
rmama@monmouth.edu
MAMAY, Fred 973-300-2119 291 I
fmamay@sussex.edu
MAMIE, Julie 740-695-9500 357 D
jmamie@belmontcollege.edu
MAMMENGA, Brenda 605-626-2433 428 H
brenda.mammega@northern.edu
MANAKAS, Sharon 805-378-1413 73 A
smanakas@vcccd.edu
MANAKAS, Vance 805-378-1457 73 A
vmanakas@vcccd.edu
MANALLA, Christine 504-568-4800 194 C
cmanal@lsuhsc.edu
MANARO, James 434-947-8346 484 B
jmanaro@randolphcollege.edu
MANASSAH, Michele 815-836-5455 143 E
manassmi@lewisu.edu
MANAUTOU, Teresa 787-864-2222 524 A
teresa.manautou@guayama.inter.edu
MANAZIR, Theodore 802-728-1275 477 E
tmanazir@vtc.edu
MANCE, JR., Jerry 757-455-3349 491 F
jmance@vwu.edu
MANCHESTER-MOLAK,
Ann 401-865-2406 416 E
ammolak@providence.edu
MANCINI, Donna 610-896-1230 397 F
dmancini@haverford.edu
MANCINI, Michael 518-587-2100 329 C
michael.mancini@esc.edu
MANCINI, Mike 574-520-4415 160 F
mmancini@iusb.edu
MANCINI, Nicholas 610-785-6263 409 F
nmancini@scs.edu
MANCINI, Tracy 252-222-6144 341 F
mancinit@carteret.edu
MANCINI-BROWN,
Darlene 860-512-3660 85 G
dmancini_brown@manchestercc.edu
MANCINO, Mary, S 610-861-5415 403 B
msinibaldi@northhampton.edu
MANCONE, Nichole 817-515-1581 458 B
nichole.mancone@tccd.edu
MANCOSH, Bridget 412-392-3992 408 F
bmancosh@pointpark.edu
MANCUSO, Matthew 712-325-3434 170 K
mmancuso@iwcc.edu
MANCUSO, Sandra, L 305-899-3072 95 G
smancuso@barry.edu
MANCUSO, Tracy 928-532-6170 15 B
tracy.mancuso@npc.edu
MANDAKOVIC,
Tomislav 305-899-3532 95 G
tmandakovic@barry.edu
MANDALA, Jim 973-408-3395 285 E
jmandala@drew.edu
MANDAYAM,
Shreekanth 856-256-5150 289 H
shreek@rowan.edu
MANDEL, Carol, A 212-998-2444 318 D
carol.mandel@nyu.edu
MANDEL, Christine 315-655-7174 300 I
cmandel@cazenovia.edu
MANDEL, Christine 315-655-7250 300 I
cmandel@cazenovia.edu
MANDEL, Gregory, M 215-204-8993 411 B
gregory.mandel@temple.edu

MANDEL, Jeffrey 570-389-4311 405 E jmandel@bloomu.edu
MANDEL, Larry 562-951-4430 30 J lmandel@calstate.edu
MANDEL, Maud 401-863-2573 415 K maud_mandel@brown.edu
MANDELKERN, Michael 714-432-5786 38 H mmandelkern@occ.cccd.edu
MANDEREN, Michael, C 440-775-8413 367 B michael.manderen@oberlin.edu
MANDERSCHEID, David, C 614-292-1677 367 H manderscheid.1@osu.edu
MANDEVILLE, Steve 314-529-6849 262 B shmandeville@maryville.edu
MANDEVILLE-GAMBLE, Steve 951-827-3221 69 D steve.mandeville-gamble@ucr.edu
MANDRELL, Jon, D 815-835-6344 151 E jon.d.mandrell@svcc.edu
MANDRELL, Kara 573-288-6536 259 E kmandrell@culver.edu
MANDY, Lisa 408-864-8403 43 E mandylisa@deanza.edu
MANDYAM, Raja 512-454-1188 442 J info@aoma.edu
MANELA, Johnny 225-216-8360 192 B manelaj@mybrcc.edu
MANER, Edward, L 863-667-5400 108 G elmaner@seu.edu
MANERI, Wendy, L 315-568-3262 317 A wmaneri@nycc.edu
MANESS, Ed 919-573-5350 349 A emaness@colonial.org
MANESS, Terry, S 254-710-3411 444 B terry_maness@baylor.edu
MANESS, Thomas 541-737-4279 385 F thomas.maness@oregonstate.edu
MANEV, Ivan, M 207-581-1968 201 B imanev@maine.edu
MANEY, Beth 515-244-3146 321 G maneye@sage.edu
MANFERDINI, Elena 213-613-2200 65 A elena_manferdini@sciarc.edu
MANFREDO, Francis, A 315-859-4144 309 D fmanfred@hamilton.edu
MANGAN, Kim 217-420-6658 145 J kmangan@millikin.edu
MANGAN, William 402-399-2334 274 A wmangan@csm.edu
MANGAN-FLOOD, Mary 920-923-7166 508 B mmanganflood@marianuniversity.edu
MANGANARO, Robert 212-787-5300 298 B
MANGAROVA, Nelly 510-592-9688 54 C nelly.mangarova@npu.edu
MANGELS, Andrew 413-545-1581 216 H amangels@admin.umass.edu
MANGELS, Andrew, P 413-545-2141 216 H amangels@admin.umass.edu
MANGELS, Kathy, M 573-651-2570 266 M kmangels@semo.edu
MANGELSDORF, Sarah 608-262-1304 510 C provost@provost.wisc.edu
MANGHAM, Kirk 757-490-1241 477 F kmangham@auto.edu
MANGIACAPRA, Vincent, P 203-932-7058 89 D vmangiacapra@newhaven.edu
MANGIERI, Tina 207-786-6223 198 E tmangier@bates.edu
MANGINE, John, J 814-332-4356 388 F jmangine@allegheny.edu
MANGINO, Christine 718-518-6611 302 D cmangino@hostos.cuny.edu
MANGIONE, Robert, A 718-990-6308 322 F mangionr@stjohns.edu
MANGIONE, Terri, L 716-888-2130 300 G mangiont@canisius.edu
MANGLITZ, Elaine 678-466-5433 117 I elainemanglitz@clayton.edu
MANGLONA, Gregorio, T 671-777-5591 519 H safety@guamcc.edu
MANGLONA-PROPST, Daisy 670-237-6792 520 D daisy.propst@marianas.edu
MANGOLD, Thomas 401-841-2074 518 E
MANGUM, Genita, D 717-736-4144 396 G gdmangum@hacc.edu
MANGUM, Linda 336-334-7862 350 C lmangum@ncat.edu
MANGUM, Steve 865-974-5061 439 I smangum@utk.edu
MANGUM, Vincent 404-756-4006 115 I vmangum@atlm.edu
MANGUS, Christy 269-782-1473 237 B cmangus@swmich.edu
MANGUS, Jennifer 814-332-2312 388 F jmangus@allegheny.edu
MANHARDT, Joseph 207-741-5598 200 C jmanhardt@smccme.edu
MANIACI, Vincent, M 413-205-3202 210 E vincent.maniaci@aic.edu
MANIAOL, Albert 909-384-8904 59 I amaniaol@sbccd.cc.ca.us
MANIATIS, Marc 203-932-7218 89 D mmaniatis@newhaven.edu
MANICKAM, Joseph 620-327-8233 178 B joseph.manickam@hesston.edu
MANIER, Tracy, L 512-448-8602 455 I tracym@stedwards.edu
MANIGAULT, Kimberly 412-237-3001 392 G kmanigault@ccac.edu
MANIGO, Venis 803-777-4115 424 I venis.manigo@sc.edu
MANILAY, Jol 209-946-2236 70 F jmanilay@pacific.edu
MANIMARAN, Ravi 609-343-4988 283 D rmanimar@atlantic.edu
MANINGER, Catherine 405-208-5498 377 D camaninger@okcu.edu
MANION, Andrew, P 920-923-7617 508 B amanion@marianuniversity.edu
MANION, Sheila, M 314-977-2306 266 J manionsm@slu.edu
MANIS, Christopher 619-388-6546 60 B cmanis@sdccd.edu
MANISCALCO, Steven, J 607-436-2735 325 E steven.maniscalso@oneonta.edu
MANJONE, Amanda 251-981-3771 5 A amanda.manjone@columbiasouthern.edu
MANKEY, Richanne, C 419-783-2300 361 A rmankey@defiance.edu
MANKO, Tammy, P 724-357-2235 406 C tammy.manko@iup.edu
MANKOWICH, James 205-929-3498 2 G jmankowich@lawsonstate.edu
MANLEY, Andrew 785-309-3120 181 D andrew.manley@salinatech.edu
MANLEY, Anna 541-956-7104 386 G amanley@roguecc.edu
MANLEY, Colleen 315-229-5988 323 D cmanley@stlawu.edu
MANLEY, Jennifer 360-596-5305 498 G jmanley@spscc.edu
MANLEY, John 252-335-3266 350 A jhmanley@ecsu.edu
MANLEY, Lisa 860-727-6788 87 B lmanley@goodwin.edu
MANLEY, Thomas 603-899-1144 281 D manleyt@franklinpierce.edu
MANLEY, Thomas 937-319-6164 356 F
MANLEY-ROOK, Stephanie 252-493-7383 345 E sgmrook@email.pittcc.edu
MANN, Brian 813-253-7022 101 M bmann@hccfl.edu
MANN, Charles, G 301-696-3611 204 D mann@hood.edu
MANN, Christy 870-512-7867 18 D christy_mann@asun.edu
MANN, Daniel 217-333-9299 154 B danmann@illinois.edu
MANN, Daniel, R 217-333-0100 154 B danmann@illinois.edu
MANN, Douglas 410-225-2352 205 C dmann@mica.edu
MANN, Gwendolyn 334-229-4436 4 A gmann@alasu.edu
MANN, Henry, J 614-292-5711 367 H mann.414@osu.edu
MANN, Janet 202-687-1307 92 B mannj2@georgetown.edu
MANN, Karen 502-585-9911 189 B kmann@spalding.edu
MANN, Kevin, J 410-543-6202 209 B kjmann@salisbury.edu
MANN, Lara, G 317-781-5760 164 H mannlg@uindy.edu
MANN, Laura 507-457-5069 248 C lmann@winona.edu
MANN, Lucretia 914-674-7492 314 I lmann@mercy.edu
MANN, Lynde 256-228-6001 3 B mannl@nacc.edu
MANN, Mark 619-849-2359 57 H markmann@pointloma.edu
MANN, Randy 254-295-4618 466 A rmann@umhb.edu
MANN, Suellen 561-868-3450 105 A manns@palmbeachstate.edu
MANN, Warrenetta, C 757-221-3620 479 I wcmann@wm.edu
MANN, FSC, William 507-457-1503 250 B wmann@smumn.edu
MANNELLA, Stephen 610-436-2242 407 D smannella@wcupa.edu
MANNELLI, Rita, J 585-389-2147 316 D rmannel5@naz.edu
MANNERING, Susan, M 302-225-6232 90 G manners@gbc.edu
MANNINEN, Kevin 906-487-7371 230 B kevin.manninen@finlandia.edu
MANNING, Amanda 207-326-2280 200 F amanda.manning@mma.edu
MANNING, Amelia 603-314-1416 282 C a.manning@snhu.edu
MANNING, Beth 810-762-3150 238 B bmanning@umflint.edu
MANNING, Carmen, K 715-836-3671 510 D manninck@uwec.edu
MANNING, Colleen 713-646-1729 456 H cmanning@stcl.edu
MANNING, Danielle 909-869-3019 31 A dmanning@cpp.edu
MANNING, Dianne, M 413-662-5249 218 C dianne.manning@mcla.edu
MANNING, Don 708-596-2000 151 H dmanning@ssc.edu
MANNING, Gaye 870-574-4509 21 G gmanning@sautech.edu
MANNING, Jean 501-374-6305 21 C
MANNING, Jennifer 815-753-9676 147 H manning@niu.edu
MANNING, Jessica 325-942-2021 463 C jessica.manning@angelo.edu
MANNING, Jessica 325-674-2751 441 D jxm15c@acu.edu
MANNING, John, F 617-495-1000 215 G
MANNING, Karen 910-695-3995 346 E manningk@sandhills.edu
MANNING, Kimberly, M 848-932-1769 290 A kim.manning@rutgers.edu
MANNING, Kirk 845-398-4066 323 G kmanning@stac.edu
MANNING, Linda 206-934-6415 497 J linda.manning@seattlecolleges.edu
MANNING, Lynn Etta, G 214-887-5366 448 G lmanning@dts.edu
MANNING, Marcus 314-529-9313 262 B mmanning@maryville.edu
MANNING, Mark 315-498-2268 319 G m.r.manning@sunyocc.edu
MANNING, Michael 315-792-7100 330 A manningmb@sunyit.edu
MANNING, Noel, T 704-406-4631 337 H ntmanning@gardner-webb.edu
MANNING, Patricia 850-201-8994 112 C manningp@tcc.fl.edu
MANNING, R. Douglas 714-564-6900 58 A manning_r-douglas@sac.edu
MANNING, Sandra, J 919-572-1625 335 F smanning@apexsot.edu
MANNING, Scott 570-372-4256 410 H manning@susqu.edu
MANNING, Sherron, K 580-928-5533 380 B sherron.manning@swosu.edu
MANNING, Terri 704-330-6592 342 A terri.manning@cpcc.edu
MANNING, Tina 912-427-5814 117 J tmanning@coastalpines.edu
MANNING, Vivian 360-992-2104 493 E vmanning@clark.edu
MANNING-CLARK, Jean 303-273-3239 78 J jeanmann@mines.edu
MANNING-MILLER, Donald 662-252-8000 255 F manningmiller@rustcollege.edu
MANNINO, Jessica, L 315-445-4130 312 F hammonjl@lemoyne.edu
MANNINO, Sam 502-459-3535 189 F smannino@sullivan.edu
MANNINO, William 540-362-6435 481 F bmannino@hollins.edu
MANNION, Joe 503-280-8578 382 I jmannion@cu-portland.edu
MANNION, Tom, N 626-395-6174 29 I mannion@caltech.edu
MANNISTO, Richard 414-443-8788 513 A rich.mannisto@wlc.edu
MANNIX, Kevin, A 386-226-6489 98 C kevin.mannix@erau.edu
MANNO, Mariann, M 508-856-2323 217 C admissions@umassmed.edu
MANNO, Vincent, P 781-292-2509 215 C vincent.manno@olin.edu
MANNS, Jennifer 970-207-4550 80 P
MANOHAR, Aruna, S 410-323-6211 203 F a.manohar@fts.edu
MANOHAR, John 410-323-6211 203 F j.manohar@fts.edu
MANOHAR, Norman, J 410-323-6211 203 F n.manohar@fts.edu
MANOLIS, Lilly 617-327-6777 226 B lilly_manolis@williamjames.edu
MANOR, Scott 954-771-0376 102 W smanor@knoxseminary.edu
MANORD, Wayne 256-352-8116 3 I wayne.manord@wallacestate.edu
MANORE, David 315-792-7280 330 A david.manore@sunyit.edu
MANORY, Joseph 315-229-5896 323 D jmanory@stlawu.edu
MANOS, Dennis, M 757-871-9581 479 I dmanos@wm.edu
MANOTTI, Ken 773-702-0686 153 F kmanotti@uchicago.edu
MANOUSOS, Carol 713-221-8425 465 C manousosc@uhd.edu
MANRIQUE, Santos 620-231-3690 177 E santosm@fortscott.edu
MANRIQUEZ, Chris 310-243-3655 31 E cmanriquez@csudh.edu
MANRY, J. Mark 248-218-2120 236 C mmanry@rc.edu
MANRY, Robert 785-628-4513 177 D rjmanry@fhsu.edu
MANSAPIT, Felix 671-482-8671 520 B fmansapit@triton.uog.edu
MANSDOERFER, Steve 866-621-0124 84 B
MANSDORF, Geri 646-592-4440 334 P gmansdor@yu.edu
MANSER, Jacqueline, M 330-490-7117 373 F jmanser@walsh.edu
MANSFIELD, Jim 217-351-2435 148 H jmansfield@parkland.edu
MANSFIELD, Jim 217-351-2290 148 H jmansfield@parkland.edu
MANSFIELD, Kenneth 607-778-5089 326 C masfieldkc@sunybroome.edu
MANSFIELD, Robin 908-737-4880 286 F rmansfie@kean.edu
MANSFIELD, Tim 315-228-7433 304 G tmansfield@colgate.edu
MANSON, Daniel 325-793-4601 452 F manson.daniel@mcm.edu
MANSON, Robert 714-564-6247 58 A manson_robert@sac.edu
MANSON, Stephen 803-793-5263 420 G mansons@denmarktech.edu
MANSOUR, Nick 602-222-9300 10 H nmansour@arizonacollege.edu
MANSOUR, Ruchana 347-394-1036 299 G rmansour@ateret.net
MANSOURIAN, Lida 562-408-6969 24 F
MANSPERGER, Thomas 419-755-4650 366 E tmansperger@ncstatecollege.edu
MANSTROM, Paul, W 269-337-7308 231 F paul.manstrom@kzoo.edu
MANSUETO, Anthony 214-860-2693 448 A anthony.mansueto@dcccd.edu
MANSUR, Jay 859-858-2305 183 C
MANTELLA, Philomena, V 617-373-4798 223 D
MANTERNACH, Dean 402-354-7058 275 P dean.manternach@methodistcollege.edu
MANTHE, Theodore, E 507-344-7745 240 I ted.manthe@blc.edu
MANTILLA, Tonya, M 414-410-4210 506 F tmmantilla@stritch.edu
MANTLO, Ryan 910-362-7042 341 E rmantlo@cfcc.edu
MANTONI, Thomas 610-282-1100 393 G thomas.mantoni@desales.edu
MANTOOTH, Brooks, E 620-665-3497 178 D mantoothb@hutchcc.edu
MANTOOTH, James, D 731-881-7053 440 B jdmantooth@utm.edu
MANTOVANI, Theresa 407-265-8383 96 C
MANTZ, Timothy 605-626-2401 428 H tim.mantz@northern.edu
MANUEL, Barbara 276-739-2432 490 A bmanuel@vhcc.edu
MANUEL, Beulah 301-891-4184 209 E bmanuel@wau.edu
MANUEL, Henry 662-246-6462 254 C hmanuel@msdelta.edu
MANUEL, Janelle 337-521-9686 193 E janelle.manuel@solacc.edu
MANUEL, Jeff 205-652-3682 9 C jmanuel@uwa.edu
MANUEL, Kamran 323-822-9700 67 G kamran.manuel@touro.edu

MANUEL, Keith .... 334-291-4950.... 1 H
keith.manuel@cv.edu
MANUEL, Marilyn, G ..... 504-286-5020 195 L
mmanuel@suno.edu
MANUEL, Mark .... 859-246-6673 185 G
mark.manuel@kctcs.edu
MANUEL, Mary .... 661-362-3184.. 39 C
mary.manuel@canyons.edu
MANUEL, Robert, L .... 317-788-3211 164 H
rmanuel@uindy.edu
MANUEL, Shenethia ...... 573-341-4241 269 A
manuels@mst.edu
MANUEL, Warde .... 734-764-9416 237 I
wardemanuelad@umich.edu
MANUEL-CORTEZ,
Dorinna .... 808-934-2510 130 D
dorinna@hawaii.edu
MANUKYAN, Diana .... 510-925-4282.. 25 P
diana@aua.am
MANULI, Nunziatina, A . 718-990-2401 322 F
manulin@stjohns.edu
MANUS, Alexandru .... 603-644-3141 282 C
a.manus@snhu.edu
MANZANARES, Lucy ..... 828-328-7142 339 C
lucy.manzanares@lr.edu
MANZANARES,
Magdaleno .... 575-538-6229 297 H
manzanaresm@wnmu.edu
MANZANO, Anna .... 310-665-6951.. 54 I
amanzano@otis.edu
MANZANO, Florentino .. 818-947-2691.. 49 G
manzanf@lavc.edu
MANZANO, Yvonne .... 575-835-5533 294 K
yvonne.manzano@nmt.edu
MANZELLA, Shannon .... 931-553-0071 434 J
shannon.manzella@miller-motte.com
MANZIONE, Louis .... 860-768-5015.. 89 C
manzione@hartford.edu
MANZKE, Robert .... 715-346-3738 511 F
rmanzke@uwsp.edu
MANZO, Dennis .... 310-879-0554.. 66 A
MANZO, Pablo .... 916-856-3400.. 50 E
manzop@losrios.edu
MAO, Ruixuan .... 847-214-7440 138 B
rmao@elgin.edu
MAPES, Chris .... 270-789-5013 184 B
ctmapes@campbellsville.edu
MAPES, Cynthia, L .... 585-292-3015 315 L
cmapes@monroecc.edu
MAPES, Kim .... 570-961-7810 399 A
mapesk@lackawanna.edu
MAPHUMULO, Peter ..... 760-245-4271.. 73 E
peter.maphumulo@vvc.edu
MAPLE, Makala .... 402-844-7268 276 G
makala@northeast.edu
MAPLE, Vicki .... 740-364-9565 358 E
vmaple@cotc.edu
MAPLES, Christopher .... 573-341-4114 269 A
chris.maples@mst.edu
MAPLES, John .... 806-720-7476 452 D
john.maples@lcu.edu
MAPLES, Stephen .... 775-784-4700 279 E
smaples@unr.edu
MAPLEY, Gordon .... 816-271-4100 264 B
gmapley@missouriwestern.edu
MAPSTON, Austin .... 406-657-1024 272 I
mapstona@rocky.edu
MAR, Pansy .... 415-565-8902.. 68 I
marp@uchastings.edu
MARA, Mary .... 206-239-4500 493 D
mmara@cityu.edu
MARA, Stacy, J .... 920-832-6557 507 L
stacy.j.mara@lawrence.edu
MARABETI, Hilary, B ..... 615-230-3355 438 C
hilary.marabeti@volstate.edu
MARABLE, Shelia .... 205-929-6437.... 2 G
smarable@lawsonstate.edu
MARAGAKIS,
Emmanuel .... 775-784-6925 279 E
maragaki@ce.unr.edu
MARAH, Andrew, E .... 717-736-4160 396 G
aemarah@hacc.edu
MARAK, Andrae .... 708-534-4101 138 H
amarak@govst.edu
MARAK, Randy .... 713-646-2912 456 H
rmarak@stcl.edu
MARANGONI, Daniel ..... 918-343-7583 379 C
dmarangoni@rsu.edu
MARANO, Angie .... 413-597-3166 226 C
amm14@williams.edu
MARANVILLE, Amy .... 978-478-3400 223 E
amaranville@northpoint.edu
MARASCO, Canio .... 716-829-7846 307 B
marascoc@dyc.edu
MARASINGHE, Madhavi 701-777-5756 353 G
MARASKA, Monica .... 973-328-5340 285 B
mmaraska@ccm.edu
MARAVETZ, Sarah .... 410-225-2219 205 C
smaravetz@mica.edu
MARAVIGLIA, James, L 805-756-2311.. 30 K
jmaravig@calpoly.edu
MARAZITA, John .... 614-251-4687 367 F
marazitj@ohiodominican.edu
MARBACH, Joseph, R ... 732-987-2252 286 D
president@georgian.edu
MARBERT, Larry, D .... 305-284-5660 112 O
lmarbert@miami.edu
MARBLE, Alan .... 417-625-9501 263 G
marble-a@mssu.edu
MARBLE, Amanda, F ..... 208-467-8402 132 F
afmarble@nnu.edu
MARBLE, Jan .... 507-389-5120 246 A
janice.marble@mnsu.edu
MARBLE, Janet .... 607-871-2111 298 A
MARBRAY, Antionette ... 619-594-5211.. 34 B
amarbray@mail.sdsu.edu
MARBURY, Diane .... 516-562-0449 307 D
dmarbury@northwell.edu
MARBURY, Kevin .... 541-346-1137 387 F
kmarbury@uoregon.edu
MARBURY, Sonni .... 928-692-3032.. 14 I
smarbury@mohave.edu
MARCANO, Walbert .... 787-257-0000 527 H
walbert.marcano@upr.edu
MARCANTONIO, James . 573-681-5018 261 H
marcantonioj@lincolnu.edu
MARCEC, Paula .... 920-465-2207 510 E
marcecp@uwgb.edu
MARCEL, Gina .... 985-448-7929 192 I
gina.marcel@fletcher.edu
MARCELLA, Aimee, R .... 203-576-4133.. 88 F
amarcell@bridgeport.edu
MARCELLA, Patricia .... 508-588-9100 220 B
MARCELLAIS, Alexsis .... 701-477-7862 355 H
amarcellais@tm.edu
MARCELLAIS, Denise ..... 701-477-7862 355 H
dmarcellais@tm.edu
MARCELLINO, Sara .... 510-215-3805.. 40 K
smarcellino@contracosta.edu
MARCELO, Cheryl .... 903-813-2025 443 F
cmarcelo@austincollege.edu
MARCH, Debra .... 706-379-3111 128 H
dbmarch@yhc.edu
MARCH, Peter .... 848-932-0990 290 C
peter.march@rutgers.edu
MARCHAL, Anne .... 845-434-5750 330 F
amarchal@sunysullivan.edu
MARCHAND, Nicole ...... 612-861-7554 240 B
nicole.marchand@alfredadler.edu
MARCHAND, William .... 516-686-7904 317 G
wmarchan@nyit.edu
MARCHANT, Justin .... 563-425-5891 173 K
marchantj@uiu.edu
MARCHANT, Karen .... 605-626-7781 428 H
karen.marchant@northern.edu
MARCHANT, Linda .... 513-529-2021 365 I
marchalf@miamioh.edu
MARCHANT, Lloyd .... 660-263-4100 264 C
lloydm@macc.edu
MARCHANT, T. Eston .... 919-718-7246 341 H
bmarchant@cccc.edu
MARCHBANKS, Pete ...... 979-845-8423 459 C
pete-marchbanks@tamu.edu
MARCHELLETTA,
Barbara .... 207-947-4591 198 F
bmarchelletta@bealcollege.edu
MARCHELLO, Sara, L .... 757-221-2801 479 I
slmarc@wm.edu
MARCHESE, Cynthia, C . 212-687-3730 283 J
ccm@berkeleycollege.edu
MARCHESE, Cynthia, C . 212-687-3730 299 F
ccm@berkeleycollege.edu
MARCHIONE, Susan, M 716-839-8447 306 E
smarchio@daemen.edu
MARCHIONINI, Gary ..... 919-962-8363 351 B
gary@ils.unc.edu
MARCHIORI, Dennis, M 563-884-5500 172 H
dennis.marchiori@palmer.edu
MARCHWICK,
Colleen, C .... 715-836-4874 510 D
marchwcc@uwec.edu
MARCI, Wayne .... 620-450-2223 180 K
waynem@prattcc.edu
MARCIAL, Myriam .... 787-891-0925 523 G
mmarcial@aguadilla.inter.edu
MARCIANO, Jackie .... 610-902-8256 391 B
jmm745@cabrini.edu
MARCILLO, Marilu .... 201-761-6387 291 D
mmarcillo@saintpeters.edu
MARCIN, Heidi, C .... 585-785-1609 308 D
heidi.marcin@flcc.edu
MARCINEK, Myron .... 570-961-4786 401 B
mmarcinek@marywood.edu
MARCONE, Luigi .... 203-837-9314.. 85 B
marconel@wcsu.edu
MARCOTTE, Jeffrey .... 508-362-2131 219 E
jmarcotte@capecod.edu
MARCOTTE, Theresa .... 618-395-7777 140 E
marcottet@iecc.edu
MARCOU, William, L .... 414-410-4463 506 F
wlmarcou@stritch.edu
MARCOUX, Jamie .... 401-598-1000 416 C
jmarcoux@jwu.edu
MARCOUX, Mollie, D .... 609-258-3535 288 F
mmarcoux@princeton.edu
MARCUCCILLI,
Christine, M .... 260-481-6106 160 D
marcuccc@ipfw.edu
MARCUCCIO, Louis, M . 402-280-2542 274 D
louismarcuccio@creighton.edu
MARCUM, Jim .... 919-365-7711 349 D
MARCUS, Bess .... 401-863-3375 415 K
MARCUS, Lynn .... 978-762-4000 220 E
lmarcus@northshore.edu
MARCUS, Robert, J .... 317-940-9910 156 I
rmarcus@butler.edu
MARCUS, Susan .... 773-907-4418 135 K
smarcus2@ccc.edu
MARCUS, W. Andrew .... 541-346-3902 387 F
marcus@uoregon.edu
MARCUSE, Adrian, G ..... 212-752-1530 312 G
adrian.marcuse@limcollege.edu
MARCUSE, Elizabeth, S . 212-752-1530 312 G
elizabeth.marcuse@limcollege.edu
MARCUSSEN, Thomas ... 414-229-4537 511 A
marcusse@uwm.edu
MARCY, Mary, B .... 415-485-3200.. 41 J
president@dominican.edu
MARCY, Susan .... 239-433-6909 100 E
smarcy1@fsw.edu
MARCZYNSKI, Jerry ...... 775-784-4898 279 E
marczyns@unr.edu
MARDEN, Jennifer .... 661-395-4211.. 47 A
jmarden@bakersfieldcollege.edu
MARDEN, Rose .... 210-341-1366 454 B
rmarden@ost.edu
MARDER, Dave .... 404-471-5465 114 H
dmarder@agnesscott.edu
MARDIS, Michael .... 502-852-5787 190 C
mjmard01@louisville.edu
MAREK, Amy .... 573-592-5195 270 B
amy.marek@westminster-mo.edu
MAREK, Diane .... 847-233-7700 148 A
dmarek@nc.edu
MAREK, Kate .... 708-524-6648 137 F
kmarek@dom.edu
MAREK, Robin .... 731-425-2654 437 B
rmarek@jscc.edu
MAREK, Sandra .... 660-263-4100 264 C
sandram@macc.edu
MAREK-MARTINEZ, Ora 928-523-8532.. 14 K
ora.marek-martinez@nau.edu
MAREMONT-SILVER,
Ellen .... 707-527-4679.. 62 H
emaremontsilver@santarosa.edu
MARENTES, Henry .... 619-596-2766.. 24 H
hmarentes@advancedtraining.edu
MARES, Maria .... 787-864-2222 524 A
maria.mares@guayama.inter.edu
MARESCA, Laura .... 303-871-7436.. 83 E
laura.maresca@du.edu
MARESH, Rachael .... 512-313-3000 446 N
rachael.maresh@concordia.edu
MARFELL, Julie .... 859-899-2512 184 G
julie.marfell@frontier.edu
MARFISE, Larry, J .... 813-253-6240 113 E
lmarfise@ut.edu
MARFOE, Tina .... 708-237-5050 148 A
tmarfoe@nc.edu
MARGERUM-LEYS, Jon . 248-370-3087 235 J
jmargerumleys@oakland.edu
MARGETTS, James .... 308-432-6246 276 B
jmargetts@csc.edu
MARGHEIM, Jeffrey .... 386-822-7020 111 E
jmarghei@stetson.edu
MARGO, Carlos .... 956-872-6109 456 G
clmargo@southtexascollege.edu
MARGRAVE, Alex .... 563-884-5257 172 H
margrave_a@palmer.edu
MARGRAVE, Carrie .... 207-326-0265 200 F
carrie.margrave@mma.edu
MARGULES, Gary, S ...... 954-262-7507 104 F
margules@nsu.nova.edu
MARGULIES, Anne .... 617-495-9092 215 G
anne_margulies@harvard.edu
MARGULIES, L .... 718-853-8500 331 E
MARGULIES, Mordechai 718-854-2290 299 H
MARI, Mike .... 530-242-7595.. 63 I
mmari@shastacollege.edu
MARIANI, Elsa .... 787-257-7373 525 Q
emariani@suagm.edu
MARIANI, William .... 716-829-8194 307 B
marianiw@dyc.edu
MARIANO, Anthony, A .. 802-485-2230 475 I
tmariano@norwich.edu
MARIANS, Kenneth, J ... 646-888-6639 313 I
kmarians@sloankettering.edu
MARIC, Radenka .... 860-486-3619.. 88 G
radenka.maric@uconn.edu
MARICHAL-LUGO,
Carlos .... 787-993-8866 527 G
carlos.marichal@upr.edu
MARIL, Virginia .... 805-493-3577.. 30 E
gmaril@callutheran.edu
MARIN, Anthony, S .... 575-646-7207 295 B
amarin@nmsu.edu
MARIN, Elsa .... 787-764-0000 528 F
elsa.marin1@upr.edu
MARIN, Joseph, F .... 225-922-1635 192 A
jmarin@lctcs.edu
MARIN, Rafael, E .... 787-863-2390 523 K
rafael.marin@fajardo.inter.edu
MARIN-HILL, Angelica .. 214-648-3684 469 E
angelica.marin-hill@utsouthwestern.edu
MARINA, Joseph, G ...... 315-445-4124 312 F
marinaj@lemoyne.edu
MARINACCIO, Jessica ... 212-854-1222 305 E
jm996@columbia.edu
MARINACE, Betsy .... 973-684-6861 288 C
bmarinace@pccc.edu
MARINAN, Jerilyn .... 516-876-3158 327 C
marinanj@oldwestbury.edu
MARINCH, Maria .... 702-651-7546 278 N
maria.marinch@csn.edu
MARINELLI, Bryan, D .... 401-865-1822 416 E
bmarinel@providence.edu
MARINELLI, Roberta ...... 541-737-0123 385 F
MARING, Bayta .... 206-546-6949 498 E
bmaring@shoreline.edu
MARINHO, Robson .... 269-471-3481 227 B
marinho@andrews.edu
MARINI, Janice .... 215-955-2244 411 E
janice.marini@jefferson.edu
MARINI, Mario .... 724-589-2022 411 D
mmarini@thiel.edu
MARINI, Stephen, T ...... 508-854-4272 220 G
smarini@qcc.mass.edu
MARINIS, Jeremy .... 419-448-3301 370 K
marinisjj@tiffin.edu
MARINO, Chris .... 864-646-1836 424 F
cmarino@tctc.edu
MARINO, David .... 215-204-7663 411 B
david.marino0001@temple.edu
MARINO, Dennis .... 319-208-5022 173 G
dmarino@scciowa.edu
MARINO, Lucille .... 785-864-7431 181 I
lmarino@ku.edu
MARINO, Michael .... 419-720-6670 369 F
mmarino@proskills.edu
MARINUCCI, Dorothy .... 718-817-3000 308 G
marinucci@fordham.edu
MARION, D. Keith .... 803-754-4100 420 E
MARION, Joseph .... 504-286-5389 195 L
jmarion@suno.edu
MARION, Lucy, N .... 706-721-3771 116 B
lumarion@augusta.edu
MARIS, Melinda .... 802-442-5427 476 C
mmaris@svc.edu
MARISAM, Tina .... 612-626-9357 250 E
marisam@umn.edu
MARISOL, Cortes .... 646-313-8000 303 G
marisol.cortes@guttman.cuny.edu
MARIUCCI, Robert .... 805-546-3210.. 41 C
rmariucc@cuesta.edu
MARIX, Amy .... 225-578-3486 193 M
amarix@lsu.edu
MARK, Allan .... 704-461-6736 335 J
allanmark@bac.edu
MARK, Kevin .... 208-732-6295 131 I
kmark@csi.edu
MARK, Marty, L .... 319-273-6258 167 A
marty.mark@uni.edu
MARKANTONAKIS,
Angelo .... 704-216-3710 346 C
angelo.markantonakis@rccc.edu
MARKEL, Mark, D .... 608-263-6716 510 C
mark.markel@wisc.edu
MARKELL, Dawn .... 517-338-3048 228 G
dmarkell@cleary.edu
MARKER, Brian .... 434-381-6144 485 P
bmarker@sbc.edu
MARKER, James .... 814-254-0404 392 F
jamarker@pa.gov
MARKER, Trish .... 304-214-8960 503 E
pmarker@wvncc.edu
MARKEY, John .... 210-341-1366 454 B
jmarkey@ost.edu
MARKEY, Nanette .... 301-696-3620 204 D
markey@hood.edu

MARKEY-GRABILL, Mindy .... 937-393-3431 370 C
mmarkey@sscc.edu
MARKGRAF, Jill, S .... 715-836-4827 510 D
markgrjs@uwec.edu
MARKHAM, Ian, S .... 703-370-6600 483 I
MARKIN, Karen .... 401-874-5971 417 E
markevicius@uri.edu
MARKIN, Rodney .... 402-559-7687 277 H
rmarkin@unmc.edu
MARKIN, Terrence, C .... 301-243-2260 518 C
terrence.markin@dodiis.mil
MARKLAND, Allie .... 616-632-2948 227 C
acm003@aquinas.edu
MARKLAND, Scott .... 937-512-5502 370 A
scott.markland@sinclair.edu
MARKLE, Suzanne .... 412-346-2100 408 B
smarkle@pia.edu
MARKLEY, Bradley, A .... 717-796-1800 401 L
bmarkley@messiah.edu
MARKLEY, Neil .... 707-664-4068.. 35 A
neil.markley@sonoma.edu
MARKOVITCH, Matthew 707-524-1849.. 62 H
mmarkovitch@santarosa.edu
MARKOW, David .... 802-828-8535 476 F
david.markow@vcfa.edu
MARKOW, Frank .... 817-552-3700 451 G
frank.markow@ktu.edu
MARKOWITT, Xenia .... 802-440-4390 474 F
xeniamarkowitt@bennington.edu
MARKOWITZ, Marianne 315-448-5040 323 B
MARKOWITZ, Michael .. 215-637-7700 397 G
mmarkowitz@holyfamily.edu
MARKOWSKI, Vincent ... 201-684-7432 289 C
vmarkows@ramapo.edu
MARKS, Alana .... 256-766-6610.... 5 K
amarks@hcu.edu
MARKS, Andrea, M .... 210-567-7020 468 E
marksa@uthscsa.edu
MARKS, Andy .... 219-473-4295 157 A
amarks@ccsj.edu
MARKS, David .... 201-879-7999 283 I
dmarks1@bergen.edu
MARKS, Ellen .... 906-487-2500 234 A
ebmarks@mtu.edu
MARKS, Erica .... 845-257-3240 325 D
markse@newpaltz.edu
MARKS, Farah .... 434-947-8056 484 B
fmarks@randolphcollege.edu
MARKS, Howard .... 432-552-2371 469 D
marks_h@utpb.edu
MARKS, Janice, L .... 443-518-4617 204 E
jmarks@howardcc.edu
MARKS, John .... 414-382-6360 506 A
john.marks@alverno.edu
MARKS, Lilly .... 303-724-5369.. 83 D
lilly.marks@ucdenver.edu
MARKS, Mary Beth .... 432-837-8432 462 G
mmmarks2@sulross.edu
MARKS, Michelle .... 703-993-8705 481 B
mmarks@gmu.edu
MARKS, Nick .... 603-822-5434 282 G
nicholas.marks@granite.edu
MARKS, Patrice .... 908-526-1200 289 D
patrice.marks@raritanval.edu
MARKS, Sandra .... 562-860-2451.. 36 A
smarks@cerritos.edu
MARKS, Steven .... 718-780-7507 300 A
steven.marks@brooklaw.edu
MARKS, Terry .... 941-309-4041 106 H
tmarks@ringling.edu
MARKSON, Alison, W ... 617-333-2120 214 B
amarkson1109@curry.edu
MARKULY, Mark .... 206-296-5330 498 D
markulym@seattleu.edu
MARKUM, Michael .... 254-298-8291 458 C
mmarkum@templejc.edu
MARKWOOD, Chris ...... 706-507-8950 118 C
markwood_chris@columbusstate.edu
MARLAIRE, Natalyn, M . 715-852-1399 513 E
nmarlaire@cvtc.edu
MARLAND, Jaime .... 401-427-6954 417 B
jmarland@risd.edu
MARLATT, Julie .... 217-351-2558 148 H
jmarlatt@parkland.edu
MARLER, Dan .... 970-542-3157.. 81 A
dan.marler@morgancc.edu
MARLER, Eric .... 808-675-3708 128 K
eric.marler@byuh.edu
MARLER, Janet .... 609-343-4937 283 D
jmarler@atlantic.edu
MARLER, Kari .... 801-627-8392 472 D
marlerk@owatc.edu
MARLETT, Jeffrey .... 518-454-2861 305 B
marlettj@strose.edu
MARLETTE, Marnie, S ... 336-841-4683 338 E
mmarlett@highpoint.edu
MARLEY, Chad .... 307-778-1346 516 N
cmarley@lccc.wy.edu
MARLEY, Robert .... 573-341-4138 269 A
marleyr@mst.edu
MARLING, Janet .... 706-864-1818 127 B
janet.marling@ung.edu
MARLOW, Amber .... 715-634-4790 507 J
marlowa@lco.edu
MARLOW, Dan .... 816-279-7000 257 B
dan@abtu.edu
MARLOW, Jean .... 859-622-1986 184 F
jean.marlow@eku.edu
MARLOW, Peter .... 619-260-7460.. 71 J
petermarlow@sandiego.edu
MARLOW, Thomas, J .... 718-390-4352 322 F
marlowt@stjohns.edu
MARLOWE, Bethany ...... 803-323-4503 426 H
marloweb@winthrop.edu
MARLOWE, Channing, H .... 205-391-2256.... 3 E
cmarlowe@sheltonstate.edu
MARLOWE, June .... 314-991-6245 134 K
jmarlowe@chamberlain.edu
MARLOWE, Michelle ..... 304-357-4944 502 E
michellemarlowe@ucwv.edu
MARLOWE, Sheree .... 508-793-7351 213 C
smarlowe@clarku.edu
MARLOWE, Wendy, C ... 252-451-8243 345 B
wcmarlowe937@nashcc.edu
MARMARELLI, Beth .... 313-593-5542 238 A
bethmar@umich.edu
MARMOLEJO, Francisco, J .... 520-621-7761.. 16 J
fmarmole@email.arizona.edu
MARMOLEJO, William ... 818-710-2955.. 49 D
marmolwa@piercecollege.edu
MARMUR, Michael .... 212-824-2215 309 F
mmarmur@huc.edu
MARNEY, Dylan .... 573-288-6351 259 E
dmarney@culver.edu
MARNEY, Katherine .... 573-288-6478 259 E
kmarney@culver.edu
MARNICH, Darlene .... 412-392-3474 408 F
dmarnich@pointpark.edu
MAROHL, Matthew .... 507-786-3092 250 C
marohl@stolaf.edu
MAROLDO, Brian .... 516-686-7449 317 G
bmaroldo@nyit.edu
MARON, Robert .... 508-999-8648 217 A
rmaron@umassd.edu
MARONEY, Dustin .... 480-517-8418.. 14 B
dustin.maroney@riosalado.edu
MAROZICK, Jeff .... 415-485-9467.. 39 E
jmarozick@marin.edu
MARPE, Thomas .... 507-457-6963 250 B
tmarpe@smumn.edu
MARPLE, Bradley .... 214-648-2646 469 E
bradley.marple@utsouthwestern.edu
MARQUARDT, Brian .... 231-591-3755 230 A
brianmarquardt@ferris.edu
MARQUARDT, Christopher .... 315-229-5250 323 D
cmarquardt@stlawu.edu
MARQUARDT, Clifford, L .... 740-377-2520 370 L
cmark@zoominternet.net
MARQUARDT, Richard ... 570-465-2344 399 A
marquardtr@lackawanna.edu
MARQUARDT, Shelly .... 714-547-9625.. 28 J
smarquardt@calcoast.edu
MARQUART, James, W . 409-880-8398 462 C
james.marquart@lamar.edu
MARQUES, Javier .... 305-348-2111 109 D
javier.marques@fiu.edu
MARQUES, Jeffrey .... 413-775-1700 219 F
marquesj@gcc.mass.edu
MARQUES, Joan .... 818-767-0888.. 75 C
MARQUEZ, Abigail .... 407-251-0007 104 H
amarquez@omi.edu
MARQUEZ, Dianne .... 575-492-2841 294 L
dmarquez@nmjc.edu
MARQUEZ, JR., Felix, J .... 407-251-0007 104 H
fmarquez@omi.edu
MARQUEZ, Kenneth, L .. 719-587-7227.. 76 D
klmarque@adams.edu
MARQUEZ, Krishna .... 787-746-1400 522 O
kmarquez@huertas.edu
MARQUEZ, Michelle ...... 650-306-3403.. 61 R
marquezmichelle@smccd.edu
MARQUEZ, Moses .... 505-454-5312 294 D
mmarquez@luna.edu
MARQUEZ, Nelson .... 863-734-1509 114 A
marqueznj@webber.edu
MARQUEZ, Nora .... 650-433-3865.. 55 I
nmarquez@paloaltou.edu
MARQUEZ, Patricia .... 619-260-7795.. 71 J
pmarquez@sandiego.edu
MARQUEZ, Walter .... 909-869-4947.. 31 A
wmmarquez@cpp.edu
MARQUEZ BELL, Mary .. 516-876-3082 327 C
bellm@oldwestbury.edu
MARQUEZ-SCALLY, Marline .... 505-984-6075 295 K
registrar@sjc.edu
MARQUIS, Kim .... 865-524-8079 432 F
kmarquis@hchs.edu
MARQUIS, Lauren .... 617-879-2328 226 A
lmarquis@wheelock.edu
MARQUIS, Susan .... 310-393-0411.. 56 A
smarquis@rand.org
MARQUSEE, Steven, J ... 315-267-2231 328 A
marqussj@potsdam.edu
MARR, Jay, D .... 502-456-6506 189 F
jmarr@sullivan.edu
MARR, Jena .... 405-422-1265 379 B
jena.marr@redlandscc.edu
MARR, Ronda .... 209-946-2206.. 70 F
rmarr@pacific.edu
MARRA, Joseph .... 845-574-4156 321 F
jmarra2@sunyrockland.edu
MARRA, Michele, L .... 740-376-4718 365 A
mm011@marietta.edu
MARRANT, Dale .... 913-234-0612 176 H
dale.marrant@cleveland.edu
MARRAPESE, Patricia .... 607-777-2510 325 A
pmarra@binghamton.edu
MARRAPODI, Michael .... 617-984-1634 223 H
mmarrapodi@quincycollege.edu
MARRER, Gary .... 623-845-3235.. 13 H
gary.marrer@gccaz.edu
MARRERO, Antonio .... 718-951-5051 301 E
amarrero@brooklyn.cuny.edu
MARRERO, Arelis .... 787-728-1515 529 B
amarrero@sagrado.edu
MARRERO, Argelio .... 860-906-5125.. 85 D
amarrero@ccc.commnet.edu
MARRERO, Kyle .... 678-839-6442 127 F
kmarrero@westga.edu
MARRERO, Rene .... 787-841-2000 525 J
rene_marrero@pucpr.edu
MARRERO, Wilma .... 787-765-1915 524 F
wmarrero@opto.inter.edu
MARRERO PEREZ, Rafael .... 787-780-0070 521 B
rmarrero@caribbean.edu
MARRETT, Clifford .... 860-465-5577.. 84 K
marrettc@easternct.edu
MARRINER, Nigel, R ..... 716-878-4907 326 E
marrinnr@buffalostate.edu
MARRIOTT, Carol .... 585-343-0055 309 C
cmarriott@genesee.edu
MARRIOTT, Danny .... 760-480-8474.. 74 H
MARRIOTT, Jean .... 410-386-8121 203 A
jmarriott@carrollcc.edu
MARRIOTT, Karin .... 951-487-3060.. 52 J
kmarriott@msjc.edu
MARRIOTT, Martin .... 920-206-2310 508 A
marty.marriott@mbu.edu
MARRIOTT, Russell .... 214-818-1318 447 A
rmarriott@criswell.edu
MARROCCO, Susan .... 941-752-5201 108 P
marrocs@scf.edu
MARROCCO, Therese .... 203-857-7311.. 86 D
tmarrocco@norwalk.edu
MARROCHELLO, Drew ... 617-353-4631 212 G
marroand@bu.edu
MARRON, Maria .... 402-472-3041 277 G
mmarron2@unl.edu
MARRON, Timothy .... 206-296-5990 498 D
marront@seattleu.edu
MARRONE-CREECH, Tiana .... 541-463-5538 383 F
marrone-creecht@lanecc.edu
MARRONGELLE, Karen .. 503-725-5061 386 D
karen.marrongelle@pdx.edu
MARROTT, Ann .... 845-687-5070 331 L
marrotta@sunyulster.edu
MARROW, Cary .... 806-894-9611 456 F
cmarrow@southplainscollege.edu
MARROW, Sydne, M ..... 508-531-1754 217 D
smarrow@bridgew.edu
MARRS, Rick .... 310-506-4261.. 56 D
rick.marrs@pepperdine.edu
MARRS, Sherrie .... 606-218-5261 190 E
sherriemarrs@upike.edu
MARS, Kandace .... 785-670-2270 182 D
kandace.mars@washburn.edu
MARSALEK, Lisa .... 419-783-2587 361 A
lmarsalek@defiance.edu
MARSALIS, Wynton .... 212-799-5000 312 B
MARSCH, Charlotte .... 417-328-1803 267 A
cmarsch@sbuniv.edu
MARSCHKE, Robyn .... 719-255-3640.. 83 C
rmarschk@uccs.edu
MARSDEN, Janet .... 740-427-5158 364 A
marsden1@kenyon.edu
MARSDEN, John, P .... 859-846-5310 188 B
jmarsden@midway.edu
MARSELIAN, Zareh .... 805-493-3119.. 30 E
marselia@callutheran.edu
MARSH, Anne .... 540-828-8024 478 J
atmarsh@bridgewater.edu
MARSH, Barry .... 843-349-7557 421 L
barry.marsh@hgtc.edu
MARSH, Bonnie .... 724-439-4900 399 H
bmarsh@laurel.edu
MARSH, Brent .... 918-343-7569 379 C
bmarsh@rsu.edu
MARSH, Cecilia .... 660-359-3948 264 H
cmarsh@mail.ncmissouri.edu
MARSH, Clay .... 304-293-1024 505 B
cbmarsh@hsc.wvu.edu
MARSH, Clay, B .... 304-293-1024 505 B
cbmarsh@hsc.wvu.edu
MARSH, David, F .... 989-837-4389 235 C
dmarsh@northwood.edu
MARSH, Dawn .... 517-265-5161 226 F
dmarsh@adrian.edu
MARSH, Douglas, K ...... 574-631-4200 165 A
marsh.14@nd.edu
MARSH, Eric .... 585-785-1293 308 D
eric.marsh@flcc.edu
MARSH, Geoff .... 562-903-4742.. 27 E
geoff.marsh@biola.edu
MARSH, Gregory .... 409-880-2100 462 C
gregory.marsh@lamar.edu
MARSH, Heather, A .... 214-860-3611 448 B
hmarsh@dcccd.edu
MARSH, James, G .... 254-710-2467 444 B
jim_marsh@baylor.edu
MARSH, Janet .... 517-607-2341 231 C
jmarsh@hillsdale.edu
MARSH, Jed .... 609-258-7860 288 F
jmarsh@princeton.edu
MARSH, Jolee .... 910-678-8217 343 B
marshj@faytechcc.edu
MARSH, Kent .... 970-248-1303.. 77 K
kmarsh@coloradomesa.edu
MARSH, Latonia, D .... 716-878-4618 326 E
marshld@buffalostate.edu
MARSH, MaToya .... 773-821-2601 135 F
mmarsh@csu.edu
MARSH, Nancy, J .... 770-720-5657 124 H
njm@reinhardt.edu
MARSH, Nicole, Y .... 510-628-8011.. 48 F
librarian@lincolnuca.edu
MARSH, Robert .... 231-439-6353 234 H
rmarsh@ncmich.edu
MARSH-WILLIAMS, Pamela, R .... 413-545-6493 216 H
marshwil@acad.umass.edu
MARSHAK, Helen Hopp 909-558-4578.. 48 H
hhoppmarshak@llu.edu
MARSHALL, Alycia .... 410-777-2776 202 D
aamarshall@aacc.edu
MARSHALL, Ave .... 404-270-5288 126 D
amarshall@spelman.edu
MARSHALL, Ben .... 813-253-7125 101 M
rmarshall10@hccfl.edu
MARSHALL, Bleuzette .... 513-556-6262 371 E
bleuzette.marshall@uc.edu
MARSHALL, Bryon .... 609-586-4800 287 A
marshalb@mccc.edu
MARSHALL, Charles, B . 504-865-7421 194 G
cbmarsh@loyno.edu
MARSHALL, Cheryl, A ... 714-808-4797.. 53 L
cmarshall@nocccd.edu
MARSHALL, Christina .... 714-997-6517.. 36 G
cmarsh@chapman.edu
MARSHALL, Connie .... 423-323-0238 437 E
cmarshall@northeaststate.edu
MARSHALL, Courtney .... 316-978-3830 182 F
courtney.marshall@wichita.edu
MARSHALL, Darren .... 801-957-4782 474 B
darren.marshall@slcc.edu
MARSHALL, Darryl .... 850-644-5716 110 A
dmarshall@admin.fsu.edu
MARSHALL, Darwina ..... 405-692-3196 376 C
dmarshall@macu.edu
MARSHALL, Dave .... 218-235-2125 248 B
d.marshall@vcc.edu
MARSHALL, David .... 909-537-5032.. 33 D
dmarshall@csusb.edu
MARSHALL, David .... 979-230-3213 444 E
david.marshall@brazosport.edu
MARSHALL, David, B .... 805-893-2785.. 70 B
david.marshall@ucsb.edu
MARSHALL, Debbie .... 858-695-8587 159 A
MARSHALL, Deborah ..... 504-520-5444 198 D
dmarsha2@xula.edu
MARSHALL, Donna .... 252-638-7249 342 E
marshalldo@cravencc.edu

MARSHALL, Elaine .... 864-503-5331 425 H
emarshall@uscupstate.edu
MARSHALL, Ella .... 843-383-8060 420 B
emarshall@coker.edu
MARSHALL, J, A .... 413-205-3263 210 E
ja.marshall@aic.edu
MARSHALL, James .... 559-278-2448.. 32 A
james.marshall@csufresno.edu
MARSHALL, JaNice .... 216-987-3287 360 E
janice.marshall@tri-c.edu
MARSHALL, Jay .... 765-983-1687 157 I
marshja@earlham.edu
MARSHALL, Jo .... 606-679-8501 186 G
jo.marshall@kctcs.edu
MARSHALL, Joan .... 732-247-5241 287 E
jmarshall@nbts.edu
MARSHALL, John .... 970-248-1366.. 77 K
marshall@coloradomesa.edu
MARSHALL, Jon .... 620-365-5116 174 G
marshall@allencc.edu
MARSHALL, Joretta .... 817-257-7577 445 H
j.marshall@tcu.edu
MARSHALL, Judith .... 618-536-2626 152 B
jmarshal@siu.edu
MARSHALL, Justin, W ... 989-837-4279 235 C
marshall@northwood.edu
MARSHALL, Katherine ... 716-270-2661 307 I
marshallk@ecc.edu
MARSHALL, Kent .... 708-974-5390 146 C
marshallk34@morainevalley.edu
MARSHALL, Kimberly ..... 256-372-8481.... 1 A
kimberly.marshall@aamu.edu
MARSHALL, Larry .... 724-852-3230 414 B
lmarshal@waynesburg.edu
MARSHALL, Larry, W .... 606-474-3277 185 C
lmarshall@kcu.edu
MARSHALL, Lori .... 856-256-4197 289 H
marshall@rowan.edu
MARSHALL, Lynette, L .. 319-335-3305 166 G
lynette-marshall@uiowa.edu
MARSHALL, Margaret, J 334-844-7474.... 4 D
mjm0030@auburn.edu
MARSHALL, Maura .... 603-641-7028 282 A
mmarshall@anselm.edu
MARSHALL, Michael ..... 404-880-6059 117 H
mmarshall@cau.edu
MARSHALL, Molly, T .... 913-667-5721 176 F
mtmarshall@cbts.edu
MARSHALL, Nancy .... 503-375-7101 383 A
nmarshall@corban.edu
MARSHALL, Peter .... 812-357-6280 164 A
pmarshall@saintmeinrad.edu
MARSHALL, Phyllis .... 609-633-6460 292 B
pmarshall@tesu.edu
MARSHALL, Renee .... 661-259-7800.. 39 C
renee.marshall@canyons.edu
MARSHALL, Richard, A . 309-457-2124 146 A
rmarshall@monmouthcollege.edu
MARSHALL, Scott .... 503-725-5257 386 D
rsm@pdx.edu
MARSHALL, Steve .... 715-394-8365 512 B
smarsha8@uwsuper.edu
MARSHALL, Steven .... 610-282-1100 393 G
steven.marshall@desales.edu
MARSHALL, Susan .... 401-598-4988 416 C
smarshall@jwu.edu
MARSHALL, Susan, D ... 423-652-6006 432 I
sdmarsha@king.edu
MARSHALL, Tamara ...... 713-269-3876.... 7 C
tmarshall@stillman.edu
MARSHALL, Tim .... 212-229-8947 316 E
provost@newschool.edu
MARSHALL, Tim .... 214-378-1856 447 F
tmarshall@dcccd.edu
MARSHALL, Toni .... 803-508-7242 418 C
marshalt@atc.edu
MARSHALL, William ...... 218-322-2340 245 B
william.marshall@itascacc.edu
MARSHALL-BIGGINS,
Cynthia .... 903-593-8311 461 B
cmarshall-biggins@texascollege.edu
MARSHBURN, Roxann .. 847-376-7099 148 D
rmarshbu@oakton.edu
MARSICANO, Leslie, M . 704-894-2804 337 B
lemarsicano@davidson.edu
MARSICO, Richard, J .... 330-941-3036 374 E
rjmarsico@ysu.edu
MARSILI, Amanda .... 401-254-3774 417 C
amarsili@rwu.edu
MARSON, Wendy .... 651-450-3392 245 A
wmarson@inverhills.edu
MARSTELLER, Diane ...... 330-652-9919 361 G
dianemarsteller@eticollege.edu
MARSTELLER, Jill, A ..... 610-409-3582 413 H
jmarsteller@ursinus.edu
MARSTELLER-KOWALEWSKI,
Brenda .... 801-626-7737 473 E
bkowalewski@weber.edu

MARSTON, Summer, S . 406-447-6927 271 I
summer.marston@umhelena.edu
MARSWILLO, Joseph, S 973-642-4568 288 A
joseph.s.marswillo@njit.edu
MARTAINDALE, Ward .... 281-283-2255 465 B
martaindale@uhcl.edu
MARTE, Benjamin .... 518-276-6287 321 A
marteb2@rpi.edu
MARTE, Maria .... 973-684-5993 288 C
mmarte@pccc.edu
MARTEL, Annette .... 701-224-5771 354 A
annette.martel@dickinsonstate.edu
MARTEL, David, W .... 434-924-7821 486 H
dwm5x@virginia.edu
MARTEL, Kristie, A .... 724-847-5751 395 J
kamartel@geneva.edu
MARTEL, Ronald .... 401-598-2848 416 C
rmartel@jwu.edu
MARTELL, Camille .... 701-255-3285 355 I
cmartell@uttc.edu
MARTELL, Kathryn .... 509-963-1955 492 L
martellk@cwu.edu
MARTELLA, Michelle ..... 610-566-1776 415 A
mmartella@williamson.edu
MARTELLARO, John .... 816-235-1592 268 D
martellaroj@umkc.edu
MARTELLO, Michael ...... 716-338-1023 311 F
michaelmartello@mail.sunyjcc.edu
MARTEN, Norman .... 805-378-1459.. 73 A
nmarten@vcccd.edu
MARTEN, Timothy .... 217-544-6464 151 B
timothy.marten@
stjohnscollegespringfield.edu
MARTENS, Daniel, R ..... 812-464-1799 165 C
dmartens@usi.edu
MARTENS, John .... 360-623-8486 493 A
john.martens@centralia.edu
MARTENS, Kathy .... 503-375-7000 383 A
kmartens@corban.edu
MARTENS, Mum .... 847-635-1675 148 D
mmartens@oakton.edu
MARTENS, Mums .... 847-635-1675 148 D
mmartens@oakton.edu
MARTENSEN, Brian .... 507-389-5998 246 A
brian.martensen@mnsu.edu
MARTENSEN,
Carsten, P .... 607-274-3184 311 D
cmertensen@ithaca.edu
MARTERER, Aaron, C .... 803-777-5555 424 I
marterer@sc.edu
MARTGIN, Anita .... 501-337-5000.. 19 C
amartin@coto.edu
MARTI, Tammy, S .... 563-588-7142 171 H
tammy.marti@loras.edu
MARTI, Vionex .... 787-738-2161 528 A
vionex.marti@upr.edu
MARTICH, Luisa .... 718-289-5732 301 D
luisa.martich@bcc.cuny.edu
MARTICKE, Nathan .... 816-584-6844 265 C
nathan.marticke@park.edu
MARTIN, Aaron .... 337-482-6397 197 F
aaronmartin@louisiana.edu
MARTIN, Abigail .... 850-245-0466 108 Q
abigail.martin@flbog.edu
MARTIN, Alan, B .... 304-293-7398 505 B
alan.martin@mail.wvu.edu
MARTIN, Allison .... 318-678-6000 192 C
amartin@bpcc.edu
MARTIN, Alvin .... 310-824-1586.. 24 B
amartin@ajrca.edu
MARTIN, Alyssa .... 701-355-8020 355 K
amartin@umary.edu
MARTIN, Ana .... 787-265-3800 528 C
business@uprm.edu
MARTIN, Andrew, D ...... 734-764-0322 237 I
admart@umich.edu
MARTIN, Angela, A .... 515-574-1064 170 C
martin_a@iowacentral.edu
MARTIN, Angela, S .... 859-257-9830 190 B
angie.martin@uky.edu
MARTIN, Angelo .... 570-372-4136 410 H
martinma@susqu.edu
MARTIN, Ann .... 660-562-1570 264 I
amartin@nwmissouri.edu
MARTIN, Ann .... 330-972-8943 371 D
abmarti@uakron.edu
MARTIN, Barbara .... 802-828-2800 477 B
bam11210@ccv.vsc.edu
MARTIN, Barry .... 303-273-3900.. 78 J
bemartin@mines.edu
MARTIN, Bethany, A ..... 315-386-7555 329 A
martinb@canton.edu
MARTIN, Billy .... 859-622-7739 184 F
billy.martin@eku.edu
MARTIN, Bobby .... 405-491-6339 379 K
bgmartin@snu.edu
MARTIN, Bonnie .... 518-255-5402 328 C
martinbg@cobleskill.edu

MARTIN, Brandon .... 818-677-3208.. 33 B
brandon.martin@csun.edu
MARTIN, Bridgit .... 920-403-3963 509 J
bridgit.martin@snc.edu
MARTIN, Brien .... 404-527-4520 117 C
bmartin@carver.edu
MARTIN, Brint .... 757-727-5425 481 E
alumni@hamptonu.edu
MARTIN, Brittany .... 814-332-2754 388 F
bmartin@allegheny.edu
MARTIN, Byron .... 219-464-6760 165 D
byron.martin@vlapo.edu
MARTIN, Cameron, K .... 801-863-8514 473 D
cameron.martin@uvu.edu
MARTIN, Carla, M .... 870-575-8873.. 22 E
martinm@uapb.edu
MARTIN, Carmella .... 904-470-8081.. 98 B
carmella.martin0906@ewc.edu
MARTIN, Carol .... 503-845-3555 384 C
carol.martin@mtangel.edu
MARTIN,
Carolyn (Biddy), A ...... 413-542-2234 210 F
president@amherst.edu
MARTIN, Cathy .... 615-329-1907 431 I
camartin@fisk.edu
MARTIN, Cecelia .... 251-460-6591.... 9 B
cgmartin@southalabama.edu
MARTIN, Charles .... 340-693-1511 529 C
cmartin@uvi.edu
MARTIN, Charlie .... 727-376-6911 112 G
cmartin@trinitycollege.edu
MARTIN, Cheryl .... 617-427-0600 221 A
cmartin@rcc.mass.edu
MARTIN, Chicora .... 510-430-3189.. 52 E
chimartin@mills.edu
MARTIN, Chris .... 904-997-2924 100 F
chris.martin@fscj.edu
MARTIN, Chris .... 318-257-4526 197 A
cmartin@latech.edu
MARTIN, Chris .... 573-651-2322 266 M
cmartin@semo.edu
MARTIN, Christa, S .... 931-540-2644 436 H
cmartin@columbiastate.edu
MARTIN, Christopher .... 208-769-3340 132 E
camartin@nic.edu
MARTIN, Christy .... 503-255-0332 384 E
cmartin@multnomah.edu
MARTIN, Clara .... 843-574-6326 424 G
clara.martin@tridenttech.edu
MARTIN, Cole .... 214-333-8877 447 D
bookstoremanager@dbu.edu
MARTIN, Corie .... 270-745-2990 190 F
corie.martin@wku.edu
MARTIN, Cristina .... 909-537-5669.. 33 D
cristina.martin@csusb.edu
MARTIN, Curt .... 970-248-1396.. 77 K
cumartin@coloradomesa.edu
MARTIN, D. Michael ..... 909-687-1600.. 44 A
michaelmartin@gs.edu
MARTIN, Dale .... 318-357-4496 197 D
dale@nsula.edu
MARTIN, Dan .... 319-398-4984 171 F
dan.martin@kirkwood.edu
MARTIN, Dan, J .... 412-268-2349 391 H
djmartin@cmu.edu
MARTIN, Daniel, J .... 206-281-2114 498 B
dmartin@spu.edu
MARTIN, Dave .... 724-852-3463 414 B
dmartin@waynesburg.edu
MARTIN, David .... 718-420-4341 333 D
dmartin@wagner.edu
MARTIN, David .... 415-241-2230.. 37 H
dmartin@ccsf.edu
MARTIN, David .... 423-636-7319 439 C
dmartin@tusculum.edu
MARTIN, David .... 212-787-5300 298 B
MARTIN, David .... 323-469-3300.. 25 D
dmartin@amda.edu
MARTIN, David .... 203-837-9600.. 85 B
martind@wcsu.edu
MARTIN, David .... 414-847-3213 508 G
davidmartin@miad.edu
MARTIN, David, J .... 979-845-0532 459 C
david-j-martin@tamu.edu
MARTIN, David, W .... 605-394-1269 429 A
david.martin@sdsmt.edu
MARTIN, Debbie .... 910-296-1429 344 B
dmartin@jamessprunt.edu
MARTIN, Deborah .... 661-336-5124.. 46 O
dmartin@kccd.edu
MARTIN, Deborah .... 312-629-6800 151 F
dmartin@saic.edu
MARTIN, Dewey .... 314-246-7560 269 N
deweymartin21@webster.edu
MARTIN, Donald, L .... 706-233-7203 125 E
dmartin@shorter.edu
MARTIN, Donna .... 337-475-5493 197 B
dmartin@mcneese.edu

MARTIN, Donna .... 904-548-4414 100 F
donna.martin@fscj.edu
MARTIN, Dorothy .... 229-430-2804 114 I
dorothy.martin@asurams.edu
MARTIN, Dorothy .... 207-768-2806 200 B
dmartin@nmcc.edu
MARTIN, Doug .... 757-446-5035 480 C
martinsd@evms.edu
MARTIN, Dustin .... 765-641-4150 156 A
dlmartin@anderson.edu
MARTIN, Earl, F .... 515-271-2191 168 J
earl.martin@drake.edu
MARTIN, III, Earl Joe ... 225-752-4230 191 I
jmartin@iticollege.edu
MARTIN, Edd .... 254-295-8620 466 A
emartin@umhb.edu
MARTIN, Elwyn .... 870-230-5135.. 19 H
emartin@hsu.edu
MARTIN, Emily .... 864-231-2000 418 E
amartin@andersonuniversity.edu
MARTIN, Eric .... 212-752-1530 312 G
eric.martin@limcollege.edu
MARTIN, Eric .... 814-393-2306 405 H
emartin@clarion.edu
MARTIN, Etienne .... 614-287-2491 360 C
emarti10@cscc.edu
MARTIN, Gale .... 610-526-6143 396 H
gmartin@harcum.edu
MARTIN, Galen .... 770-962-7580 121 G
gmartin@gwinnetttech.edu
MARTIN, Gary .... 561-237-7157 103 E
gmartin@lynn.edu
MARTIN, Gary, D .... 651-696-6735 243 B
gmartin6@macalester.edu
MARTIN, George .... 603-526-3604 280 H
gmartin@colby-sawyer.edu
MARTIN, George, E .... 512-448-8411 455 I
georgem@stedwards.edu
MARTIN, Gerardina .... 610-738-0496 407 D
gmartin@wcupa.edu
MARTIN, Greg .... 515-964-6368 168 A
gcmartin@dmacc.edu
MARTIN, JR., Harold .... 470-639-0249 123 E
MARTIN, SR.,
Harold, L .... 336-334-7940 350 C
hmartin@ncat.edu
MARTIN, Heath .... 419-559-2350 370 J
hmartin01@terra.edu
MARTIN, Heidi .... 248-476-1122 233 F
hmartin@mispp.edu
MARTIN, Irene .... 860-343-5740.. 86 A
imartin@mxcc.commnet.edu
MARTIN, Isis, C .... 530-226-2177.. 64 B
imartin@simpsonu.edu
MARTIN, Jackie, L .... 601-643-8322 252 G
jackie.martin@colin.edu
MARTIN, Jake .... 231-591-2138 230 A
jakemartin@ferris.edu
MARTIN, Jake .... 903-593-8311 461 B
jmartin@texascollege.edu
MARTIN, James .... 913-684-3280 518 I
MARTIN, James, J .... 501-882-8851.. 17 M
jjmartin@asub.edu
MARTIN, James, R .... 208-282-2341 132 B
martjame@isu.edu
MARTIN, Jan .... 212-787-5300 298 B
MARTIN, Jana .... 918-293-5339 378 B
jana.s.martin@okstate.edu
MARTIN, Jeania .... 704-991-0114 346 I
jmartin8295@stanly.edu
MARTIN, Jeanne .... 210-366-2701 454 K
MARTIN, Jeffrey, L .... 401-456-8840 417 A
jmartin1@ric.edu
MARTIN, Jenni .... 509-533-7075 493 H
jenni.martin@scc.spokane.edu
MARTIN, Jenni .... 509-533-7075 493 I
jenni.martin@scc.spokane.edu
MARTIN, Jennifer .... 940-898-3415 464 A
jmartin@twu.edu
MARTIN, Jerry .... 334-387-3877.... 4 B
jerrymartin@amrdigeuniversity.edu
MARTIN, Jill .... 571-633-9651 486 E
jill.martin@uona.edu
MARTIN, Jim .... 785-670-1634 182 D
jim.martin@washburn.edu
MARTIN, Jo Leda .... 303-963-3206.. 77 I
jomartin@ccu.edu
MARTIN, Joel .... 717-358-3986 395 G
joel.martin@fandm.edu
MARTIN, John .... 317-632-5553 162 P
johnmartin@lincolntech.edu
MARTIN, John .... 405-878-5293 379 G
jpmartin@stgregorys.edu
MARTIN, John, O .... 413-545-0361 216 H
jomartin@admin.umass.edu
MARTIN, John, U .... 941-487-4444 110 B
jmartin@ncf.edu

MARTINEZ, Miriam .... 787-284-1912 524 C
mmartine@ponce.inter.edu
MARTINEZ, Natalie .... 303-273-3268.. 78 J
nmartinez@mines.edu
MARTINEZ, Nina .... 562-947-8755.. 65 D
ninamartinez@scuhs.edu
MARTINEZ, Nina .... 502-456-6505 189 F
nmartinez@sullivan.edu
MARTINEZ, Olivia .... 610-566-1776 415 A
omartinez@williamson.edu
MARTINEZ, Pedro, L ..... 937-376-6636 358 I
pmartinez@centralstate.edu
MARTINEZ, Raul, J .... 972-985-3725 446 I
rjmartinez@collin.edu
MARTINEZ, Renee, D .... 323-953-4000.. 49 A
martinrd@lacitycollege.edu
MARTINEZ, Richard .... 626-812-3002.. 26 U
rsmartinez@apu.edu
MARTINEZ, Robert .... 719-589-7035.. 82 L
robert.martinez@trinidadstate.edu
MARTINEZ, Rochellie .... 787-738-2161 528 A
rochellie.martinez@upr.edu
MARTINEZ, Roman .... 305-237-0012 103 L
rmartin9@mdc.edu
MARTINEZ, Rosa, J .... 787-864-2222 524 A
rosa.martinez@guayama.inter.edu
MARTINEZ, Ruben, O .... 407-303-9372.. 94 H
ruben.martinez@adu.edu
MARTINEZ, Sandra .... 951-571-6267.. 58 F
sandra.martinez@mvc.edu
MARTINEZ, Sonia .... 303-300-8740.. 77 F
sonia.martinez@collegeamerica.com
MARTINEZ, Tara .... 612-659-6761 245 F
tara.martinez@minneapolis.edu
MARTINEZ, Terry .... 315-859-4020 309 D
tmartine@hamilton.edu
MARTINEZ, Veronica ..... 408-848-4725.. 44 B
vmartinez@gavilan.edu
MARTINEZ, Vesta, M .... 817-515-7795 458 B
vesta.martinez@tccd.edu
MARTINEZ, Vidal .... 505-454-5378 294 D
vmartinez@luna.edu
MARTINEZ, Xochitl, E ... 909-593-3511.. 70 E
xmartinez@laverne.edu
MARTINEZ, Yuli .... 619-201-8953.. 65 C
yuli.martinez@socalsem.edu
MARTINEZ, Yvonne .... 505-224-3232 293 L
ymartinez@cnm.edu
MARTINEZ-ABREU,
Heriberto .... 787-720-1022 521 A
martinezabreu@atlanticu.edu
MARTINEZ DE DIOS,
Heri .... 787-720-0596 521 A
hmartinez@atlanticu.edu
MARTINEZ-DOANE,
Karol .... 410-225-2284 205 C
kmartinez@mica.edu
MARTINEZ-GONZALEZ,
Liduvina .... 212-938-4030 328 E
lgonzalez@sunyopt.edu
MARTINEZ-LOPEZ,
Carmen Leonor .... 914-606-6795 333 H
carmen.martinez-lopez@sunywcc.edu
MARTINEZ-LUGO,
Miguel .... 787-725-6500 521 C
mmartinez@albizu.edu
MARTINEZ ORTIZ,
Daniel .... 787-725-6500 521 C
dmartinez@albizu.edu
MARTINEZ-ORTIZ,
Javier .... 787-863-2390 523 K
javier.martinez@fajardo.inter.edu
MARTINEZ-QUILES,
Suzette .... 215-635-7300 396 B
smartinez@gratz.edu
MARTINEZ-SACHS,
Michael .... 212-237-8211 302 F
msachs@jjay.cuny.edu
MARTINEZ-SAENZ,
Miguel .... 718-489-5486 322 D
MARTINEZ STLUKA,
Rena .... 714-992-7077.. 54 A
rmartinezstluka@fullcoll.edu
MARTINEZ-WOODRUFF,
Regina .... 254-526-1397 445 L
regina.martinez-woodruff@ctcd.edu
MARTINEZ-YADEN,
Camille .... 520-383-8401.. 16 G
cmartinez@tocc.edu
MARTINI, Louis .... 609-777-5696 292 B
lmartini@tesu.edu
MARTINI-HAUSNER,
Mary .... 315-279-5368 312 D
mmartini@keuka.edu
MARTINI-JOHNSON,
Lisa, A .... 610-799-1754 400 A
lmartinijohnson@lccc.edu

MARTINO, Andrew .... 603-668-2211 282 C
a.martino@snhu.edu
MARTINO, Bill .... 212-592-2212 324 A
wmartino@sva.edu
MARTINO, Gregory .... 215-972-2079 404 Q
gmartino@pafa.edu
MARTINOV, William .... 516-299-3720 313 C
william.martinov@liu.edu
MARTINOV, William ...... 516-299-3720 313 D
william.martinov@liu.edu
MARTINS, Sandra .... 630-942-2174 136 D
martinss14@cod.edu
MARTINSEN, Daniel ...... 254-299-8333 452 E
dmartinsen@mclennan.edu
MARTINSEN, Michael ..... 440-775-5782 367 B
mike.martinsen@oberlin.edu
MARTINSON, Brady .... 773-244-6203 147 F
bmartinson@northpark.edu
MARTIR, Jaime .... 787-753-0039 522 C
MARTIS, Pamela .... 352-588-8234 106 N
pamela.martis@saintleo.edu
MARTLAND, Paul .... 860-932-4124.. 86 E
pmartland@qvcc.edu
MARTNER, James, E ..... 630-942-2543 136 D
martner@cod.edu
MARTOCCI, Deanne .... 518-629-7154 310 G
d.martocci@hvcc.edu
MARTOCHE, Katie .... 716-926-8819 310 B
kmortoche@hilbert.edu
MARTOHUE, Kimberly ... 860-832-2551.. 84 J
kmartohue@ccsu.edu
MARTON, Nathan .... 716-829-7583 307 B
martonn@dyc.edu
MARTONI, Charles .... 724-325-6610 392 G
cmartoni@ccac.edu
MARTORANA,
Anne Marie .... 617-879-2231 226 A
amartorana@wheelock.edu
MARTORANA, Lorraine .. 410-287-1030 203 B
lmartorana@cecil.edu
MARTOZA, Roberta .... 209-932-2933.. 70 F
rmartoza@pacific.edu
MARTS, Chad .... 757-490-1241 477 F
cmarts@auto.edu
MARTY, Angela, L .... 630-515-6120 145 I
amarty@midwestern.edu
MARTY, Nadine .... 609-896-5157 289 E
nmarty@rider.edu
MARTY, Patrick .... 570-326-3761 404 T
pmarty@pct.edu
MARTY-PEARSON, Julie 559-325-3600.. 29 D
jmarty-pearson@chsu.org
MARTYNENKO, Alena .... 714-533-3946.. 35 B
alena@calums.edu
MARTZ, Tim .... 517-483-1813 232 K
martzt@lcc.edu
MARTÍNEZ, Leticia .... 787-264-1912 524 D
letmarti@sangerman.inter.edu
MARTÍNEZ, María Gil .... 787-264-1912 524 D
mgmartin@intersg.edu
MARTÍNEZ, Sirimarie .... 787-765-1915 524 F
smartinez@opto.inter.edu
MARTÍNEZ, Vilma .... 787-264-0409 524 D
vilma_martinez_toro@intersg.edu
MARUCHA, Phillip, T .... 503-494-8801 385 D
marucha@ohsu.edu
MARUGGI, Vincent .... 410-822-5400 203 C
vmaruggi@chesapeake.edu
MARUYAMA, Kenichi .... 480-461-7758.. 13 I
kenichi.maruyama@mesacc.edu
MARVI, Hassan .... 202-885-2799.. 91 C
hassan@american.edu
MARVIN, Corey .... 760-384-6201.. 47 B
cmarvin@cerrocoso.edu
MARVIN, Kerry, A .... 913-360-7621 175 D
kmarvin@benedictine.edu
MARVIN, Kim .... 817-461-8741 442 L
kmarvin@abu.edu
MARWICK, Judith .... 847-925-6290 139 B
jmarwick@harpercollege.edu
MARX, Ben .... 503-253-3443 385 B
bmarx@ocom.edu
MARX, Christopher .... 845-688-7167 331 L
marxc@sunyulster.edu
MARX, Christopher .... 845-802-7167 331 L
marxc@sunyulster.edu
MARX, Jerry .... 603-862-0274 282 F
jerry.marx@unh.edu
MARX, Lisa, M .... 410-778-7261 210 A
lmarx2@washcoll.edu
MARX, Ronald, W .... 520-621-1081.. 16 J
ronmarx@email.arizona.edu
MARXUACH-TORROS,
Gilberto .... 787-727-7033 529 B
gmarxuach@sagrado.edu
MARYATT, Victoria .... 916-608-6925.. 50 H
maryatv@flc.losrios.edu

MARYMONT, John .... 251-460-7189.... 9 B
jmarymont@southalabama.edu
MARYOTT, Megan .... 402-354-7111 275 P
megan.maryott@methodistcollege.edu
MARZAN, Marissa .... 559-297-4500.. 46 E
MARZANO, Maria .... 212-517-0428 314 D
mmarzano@mmm.edu
MARZCAK, Kelly .... 906-932-4231 230 D
kellym@gogebic.edu
MARZITELLI, Ron .... 518-464-8500 308 A
marzitelli@excelsor.edu
MARZULLO, Frank .... 708-656-8000 146 F
frank.marzullo@morton.edu
MARZULLO, Keith .... 301-405-2861 207 G
marzullo@umd.edu
MAS, Desander .... 212-410-8086 317 C
dmas@nycpm.edu
MASAU, Traci .... 406-377-9418 270 J
tmasau@dawson.edu
MASCARI, Paul .... 414-288-0589 508 C
paul.mascari@marquette.edu
MASCARO, Jennifer .... 207-262-7836 201 C
jennifer.mascaro@maine.edu
MASCARO, Juan .... 828-884-8108 335 L
mascarjc@brevard.edu
MASCARO, Maria, S ...... 787-841-2000 525 J
exaluminos@pucpr.edu
MASCENIK, Jim .... 503-206-3215 387 I
jmascenik@uws.edu
MASCETTI, Kris .... 205-665-6392.... 8 E
kmascett@montevallo.edu
MASCH, Michael .... 202-806-2400.. 92 C
michael.masch@howard.edu
MASCHMAN, Greg, D .... 402-465-2116 276 E
gdm@nebrwesleyan.edu
MASCIANTONIO, John .. 215-596-8531 413 E
j.mascia@usciences.edu
MASCOLO, Marc .... 912-443-5485 125 D
mmasolo@savannahtech.edu
MASEK, Jessie .... 805-893-3938.. 70 B
jessie.masek@ucsb.edu
MASEK, Phyllis, J .... 573-592-5213 270 B
phyllis.masek@westminster-mo.edu
MASELLA, Joanne .... 561-803-2827 104 I
joanne_masella@pba.edu
MASELLI, Gennaro .... 914-606-6856 333 H
gennaro.maselli@sunywcc.edu
MASER, Jill .... 302-736-2521.. 90 J
jill.maser@wesley.edu
MASHBURN, Matthew ... 706-379-5172 128 H
mmashburn@yhc.edu
MASHBURN, Scott .... 423-746-5203 439 A
smashburn@tnwesleyan.edu
MASHEK, Randy, D .... 563-556-5110 172 D
mashekr@nicc.edu
MASI, Barbara, A .... 814-863-8721 403 F
bam85@psu.edu
MASI, Jessica .... 207-216-4401 200 E
jmasi@yccc.edu
MASINGILA, Joanna, O . 315-443-4751 330 H
jomasing@syr.edu
MASINI, Blase, E .... 773-442-4890 147 G
b-masini@neiu.edu
MASINI, Marco .... 630-829-6006 133 I
mmasini@ben.edu
MASK, Renae .... 901-375-4400 434 F
renaemask@midsouthchristian.edu
MASKEY, Cynthia, L ...... 217-786-2436 144 B
cynthia.maskey@llcc.edu
MASKEY, Stacy .... 573-592-4480 270 D
stacy.maskey@williamwoods.edu
MASLENNIKOVA, Lena .. 864-663-0258 422 I
lena.maslennikova@ngu.edu
MASLIN, Adrienne .... 860-343-5759.. 86 A
amaslin@mxcc.commnet.edu
MASLOW, Tamara .... 718-327-7600 334 C
tmaslow@yofr.org
MASO, Marta, E .... 773-442-5200 147 G
m-maso@neiu.edu
MASON, Amy .... 340-457-6274 501 A
masonar@ab.edu
MASON, Andrea .... 585-340-9632 304 F
amason@crcds.edu
MASON, April, C .... 785-532-6224 179 A
masona@ksu.edu
MASON, Bobby, J .... 405-325-3546 380 L
bjm@ou.edu
MASON, Brian .... 816-322-0110 257 M
brian.mason@calvary.edu
MASON, Cameran .... 781-283-2223 225 D
cmason@wellesley.edu
MASON, Cherral .... 757-423-2095 480 K
MASON, Chip .... 601-968-8945 252 C
cmason@belhaven.edu
MASON, Clif .... 402-557-7512 273 E
clif.mason@bellevue.edu
MASON, Dan, J .... 641-422-4281 172 C
masondan@niacc.edu

MASON, Geri .... 402-557-7020 273 E
geri.mason@bellevue.edu
MASON, Guy .... 708-524-6780 137 F
gmason@dom.edu
MASON, Holly .... 740-366-9219 358 E
hmason@cotc.edu
MASON, James .... 314-792-6152 261 E
mason@kenrick.edu
MASON, Jeff .... 678-359-5573 121 B
jeffreym@gordonstate.edu
MASON, Jesse .... 651-773-1741 244 D
jesse.mason@century.edu
MASON, John, M .... 334-844-4784.... 4 D
jmm0027@auburn.edu
MASON, Linda .... 423-585-6809 438 D
linda.mason@ws.edu
MASON, Mary Ellen ...... 410-777-2707 202 D
memason@aacc.edu
MASON, Merle .... 650-508-3739.. 54 D
mmason@ndnu.edu
MASON, Orenthia .... 903-593-8311 461 B
omason@texascollege.edu
MASON, Pamela .... 216-397-4287 363 H
pmason@jcu.edu
MASON, Patrick .... 909-607-8362.. 37 L
patrick.mason@cgu.edu
MASON, Paul .... 325-793-3850 452 F
mason.paul@mcm.edu
MASON, Rachel .... 562-860-2451.. 36 A
rmason@cerritos.edu
MASON, Reni .... 318-487-7503 191 J
reni.mason@lacollege.edu
MASON, Rick .... 606-589-2145 187 B
rick.mason@kctcs.edu
MASON, Rochelle .... 719-389-6800.. 77 J
rmason@coloradocollege.edu
MASON, Ron .... 203-837-8736.. 85 B
masonr@wcsu.edu
MASON, JR., Ronald .... 202-274-6016.. 93 D
MASON, Stephen .... 803-793-5155 420 G
masons@denmarktech.edu
MASON, Steven, D .... 903-233-3200 452 A
stevenmason@letu.edu
MASON, Sylvia .... 413-654-1743 210 E
sylvia.mason@aic.edu
MASON, Tamra .... 505-224-4000 293 L
tmason@cnm.edu
MASON, Terrell .... 757-881-5100.. 93 B
MASON, Terrence, C ..... 812-856-8190 159 G
tmason@indiana.edu
MASON, Terrence, C ..... 812-856-8190 159 H
tmason@indiana.edu
MASON, Tisa .... 701-845-7102 354 E
tisa.mason@vcsu.edu
MASON, Tonya .... 240-567-5052 205 F
tonya.mason@montgomerycollege.edu
MASON, Traci .... 352-873-5808.. 97 C
masont@cf.edu
MASON, IV, W. Scott ... 405-325-3260 380 L
smason@ou.edu
MASON JENNINGS,
Martha .... 269-749-7644 236 A
mjennings@olivetcollege.edu
MASON-MUYCO,
Maureen .... 707-864-7889.. 64 E
maureen.mason-muyco@solano.edu
MASOUM, Nazi .... 949-794-9090.. 66 B
nazim@stanbridge.edu
MASRI, Safwan, M .... 212-854-8716 305 E
smm1@columbia.edu
MASS, Gregory .... 973-596-5745 288 A
mass@njit.edu
MASSA, Gary, R .... 513-745-3335 374 D
massag@xavier.edu
MASSA, Laura .... 310-568-6130.. 50 J
lmassa1@lmu.edu
MASSA, Laurie, J .... 216-397-4661 363 H
lmassa@jcu.edu
MASSA, Robert .... 973-408-3250 285 E
rmassa@drew.edu
MASSA-MCKINLEY,
Lilly .... 502-272-8154 183 H
lmassamckinley@bellarmine.edu
MASSAGUE, Joan .... 646-888-6639 313 I
j-massague@ski.mskcc.org
MASSANELLI, Randy ..... 479-575-7964.. 21 I
jrmassan@uark.edu
MASSARI, Lydia, I .... 787-751-0178 525 O
ac_lmassari@suagm.edu
MASSARO, Chris, J .... 615-898-2450 434 H
chris.massaro@mtsu.edu
MASSE, Carol .... 414-847-3270 508 G
carolmasse@miad.edu
MASSE, Michelle .... 225-578-1353 193 M
deangradschool@lsu.edu
MASSE, Raymond .... 207-755-5258 199 K
rmasse@cmcc.edu

MATOS RODRIGUEZ, Felix, V ...... 718-997-5550 303 E qcpres@qc.cuny.edu
MATOSO, Michael .... 209-667-3566.. 33 F mmatoso@csustan.edu
MATOTT, Benjamin .... 315-386-7448 329 A matot104@canton.edu
MATSCHERZ, Scott .... 714-966-8500.. 73 D info@ves.edu
MATSEN, Maureen .... 757-594-7585 479 H maureen.matsen@cnu.edu
MATSON, Christine, B ... 671-735-0231 519 H christine.matson@guamcc.edu
MATSON, Pamela, A ..... 650-723-2750.. 66 C pamela.matson@stanford.edu
MATSON, Ronald, R ...... 316-978-6659 182 F ron.matson@wichita.edu
MATSON, Steven, W ..... 919-962-3251 351 B smatson@bio.unc.edu
MATSUBARA, Melissa ... 808-544-0288 129 C mmatsubara@hpu.edu
MATSUDA, Matt, K .... 848-932-0990 290 C mmatsuda@rutgers.edu
MATSUDA, Seiichi .... 713-348-4002 455 F matsuda@rice.edu
MATSUMOTO, David ..... 510-809-1444.. 46 D
MATSUMOTO, Mark ...... 209-228-4021.. 69 C mmatsumoto@ucmerced.edu
MATSUMOTO, Rae .... 707-638-5926.. 67 H rae.matsumoto@tu.edu
MATSUO, Monica .... 626-396-2268.. 26 L monica.matsuo@artcenter.edu
MATT, Kathleen, S .... 302-831-8370.. 90 I ksmatt@udel.edu
MATTEI, Vivien .... 787-284-1912 524 C vmattei@ponce.inter.edu
MATTER, Rebecca .... 256-824-1997.... 8 C rebecca.matter@uah.edu
MATTER, Shawn .... 765-677-2869 161 C shawn.matter@indwes.edu
MATTERN, Carolyn .... 303-914-6372.. 82 B carolyn.mattern@rrcc.edu
MATTES, Bili, S .... 717-901-5134 397 E bmattes@harrisburgu.edu
MATTES, Marty .... 253-680-7156 492 F mmattes@bates.ctc.edu
MATTESON, Bill .... 401-874-4275 417 E wmatteson@uri.edu
MATTESON, Christi, G .. 904-264-2172 106 I christi.matteson@iws.edu
MATTESON, Kimberly .... 563-333-6339 173 A mettesonkimberly@sau.edu
MATTESON, Ryan .... 805-756-7676.. 30 K rmatteso@calpoly.edu
MATTESON, Susan, A ... 574-807-7824 156 E sue.matteson@bethelcollege.edu
MATTEY, Melissa .... 443-518-4208 204 E mmattey@howardcc.edu
MATTHES, Bruce .... 619-684-8871.. 53 J bmatthes@newschoolarch.edu
MATTHES, Mark .... 701-231-8466 354 D mark.matthes@ndsu.edu
MATTHES, Peter .... 319-335-3714 166 G peter-matthes@uiowa.edu
MATTHEW, Anne .... 270-831-9848 186 A anne.matthew@kctcs.edu
MATTHEW, Kathryn .... 281-283-3020 465 B matthew@uhcl.edu
MATTHEW, Kathryn .... 281-283-3016 465 B matthew@uhcl.edu
MATTHEWS, Adrienne .... 256-726-7398.... 6 E amatthews@oakwood.edu
MATTHEWS, Al .... 740-753-6590 362 K matthewsa11702@hocking.edu
MATTHEWS, Ann .... 573-840-9669 267 J amatthews@trcc.edu
MATTHEWS, Anne .... 541-888-7612 387 A amatthews@socc.edu
MATTHEWS, Beverly ...... 903-785-7661 454 F bmatthews@parisjc.edu
MATTHEWS, Brad .... 845-451-1309 306 D brad.matthews@culinary.edu
MATTHEWS, Caleb .... 585-594-6832 319 B matthews_caleb@roberts.edu
MATTHEWS, Carolyn, E . 510-841-1905.. 25 F cmatthews@absw.edu
MATTHEWS, Cissy .... 409-944-1203 449 F amatthew@gc.edu
MATTHEWS, Daniel .... 405-273-5331 375 K dmatthews@familyoffaith.edu
MATTHEWS, Daniel, J .... 405-273-5331 375 K dmatthews@familyoffaith.edu
MATTHEWS, Dennis, T .. 252-399-6345 335 I dtmatthews@barton.edu
MATTHEWS, Dennis, W . 215-968-8301 390 I matthews@bucks.edu
MATTHEWS, Donnajean . 714-449-7438.. 51 A djmatthews@ketchum.edu
MATTHEWS, Douglas, K 859-858-2206 183 C
MATTHEWS, Ellen .... 903-510-2380 464 D emat@tjc.edu
MATTHEWS, Elyse .... 212-961-3390 298 H ematthews@bankstreet.edu
MATTHEWS, Gary, C ..... 858-534-6820.. 69 E gcmatthews@ucsd.edu
MATTHEWS, Greg .... 802-485-2001 475 I gmatthe2@norwich.edu
MATTHEWS, Harold, P .. 812-488-2051 164 G hm3@evansville.edu
MATTHEWS, Hazel .... 502-413-8880 189 F hmatthews@sullivan.edu
MATTHEWS, Hazel .... 502-413-8880 189 E hmatthews@sullivan.edu
MATTHEWS, Janet .... 828-328-7254 339 C janet.matthews@lr.edu
MATTHEWS, Jeanne .... 703-284-1580 483 A jeanne.matthews@marymount.edu
MATTHEWS, Jennifer ..... 202-274-5449.. 93 D jennifer.matthews@udc.edu
MATTHEWS, Jerry .... 518-276-8531 321 A matthj3@rpi.edu
MATTHEWS, John .... 201-761-7431 291 D jmatthews@saintpeters.edu
MATTHEWS, John, D ..... 864-242-5100 418 H
MATTHEWS, Jon .... 910-814-8801 341 H jmatthews@cccc.edu
MATTHEWS, Jonelle ...... 717-396-7833 404 R jmatthews@pcad.edu
MATTHEWS, Kenneth ..... 386-506-3810.. 97 I matthek@daytonastate.edu
MATTHEWS, Kismet .... 252-789-0223 344 E kismet.matthews@martincc.edu
MATTHEWS, Leon .... 704-330-6524 342 A leon.matthews@cpcc.edu
MATTHEWS, Marcu .... 517-338-3007 228 G mmathews@cleary.edu
MATTHEWS, Mary .... 907-474-5655.. 10 B mcmatthews@alaska.edu
MATTHEWS, Matt .... 352-854-2322.. 97 C matthewm@cf.edu
MATTHEWS, Pamela, R . 979-845-5141 459 C p-matthews@tamu.edu
MATTHEWS, Paul .... 614-236-6211 358 A pmatthews@capital.edu
MATTHEWS, Robert .... 810-232-2511 234 F robert.matthews@mcc.edu
MATTHEWS, Robin .... 252-447-3818 342 E matthewsr@cravencc.edu
MATTHEWS, Ronald, E .. 216-373-6492 367 A rmatthews@ndc.edu
MATTHEWS, Ross, D ..... 504-864-7914 194 G rdmatthews@loyno.edu
MATTHEWS, Samuel, W 405-273-5331 375 K
MATTHEWS, Sarah .... 970-521-6611.. 81 F sarah.matthews@njc.edu
MATTHEWS, Sasha .... 757-481-5005 492 A
MATTHEWS, Stephen, P 518-564-3824 327 E matthesp@plattsburgh.edu
MATTHEWS, Thomas ..... 216-368-4446 358 C careers@case.edu
MATTHEWS, Valencia, E 850-599-3430 109 A valencia.matthews@famu.edu
MATTHEWS, Victor .... 417-836-5529 263 H victormatthews@missouristate.edu
MATTHEWS, Wesley ...... 208-885-3478 132 I wmatthews@uidaho.edu
MATTHEWS-JUAREZ, Patricia .... 615-327-6526 434 A pmatthews-juarez@mmc.edu
MATTHEWSON, Mansfield .... 616-234-3851 230 F mmatthew@grcc.edu
MATTHIAS, Ryan .... 402-643-7374 274 B ryan.matthias@cune.edu
MATTHIES, Brad .... 307-268-2036 516 H bmatthies@caspercollege.edu
MATTHIS, Wendy .... 773-907-4839 135 K wmatthis@ccc.edu
MATTIA, Cynthia .... 732-987-2757 286 D cmattia@georgian.edu
MATTIACCI, John, A ...... 215-625-5400 411 B john.mattiacci@temple.edu
MATTIACE, Lisa, C .... 419-372-6780 357 F lmattia@bgsu.edu
MATTILA, Lisa .... 413-236-1609 219 B lmattila@berkshirecc.edu
MATTINGLY, Bruce .... 607-753-4312 327 A bruce.mattingly@cortland.edu
MATTINGLY, Carole .... 270-831-9786 186 A carole.mattingly@kctcs.edu
MATTINGLY, Keith, E .... 269-471-3411 227 B matt@andrews.edu
MATTIOLI, Kathy, L .... 740-283-6267 361 L kmattioli@franciscan.edu
MATTIS, JR., George, E 276-223-4744 490 C gmattis@wcc.vccs.edu
MATTISON, Debra .... 651-213-4282 242 F dmattison@hazeldenbettyford.edu
MATTISON, Michael ...... 605-229-8492 427 J michael.mattison@presentation.edu
MATTISON, Sue .... 515-271-3751 168 J sue.mattison@drake.edu
MATTISON, Susie .... 904-470-8166.. 98 B smattison@ewc.edu
MATTIX, Brigit .... 469-941-8300 448 F bmattix@dni.edu
MATTKE, Mark .... 509-434-8470 494 A mark.mattke@ccs.spokane.edu
MATTOCKS, Vicki, S ...... 417-836-5262 263 H vickimattocks@missouristate.edu
MATTOS, Thomas .... 401-454-6649 417 B tmattos@risd.edu
MATTOX, Bennie .... 229-732-5908 115 B benniemattox@andrewcollege.edu
MATTOX, Bob, J .... 470-578-6600 122 C bmattox@kennesaw.edu
MATTOX, Jason .... 662-720-7299 255 B jlmattox@nemcc.edu
MATTSON, Bob .... 217-443-8856 137 B bmattson@dacc.edu
MATTSON, Craig .... 708-239-4881 153 B craig.mattson@trnty.edu
MATTSON, Jean .... 308-865-8202 277 F mattsonj@unk.edu
MATTSON, Joanne .... 314-889-4514 260 C jmattson@fontbonne.edu
MATTSON, Michelle .... 901-843-3795 435 L mattsonm@rhodes.edu
MATTSON, Paul, R .... 563-387-1717 171 I paul.mattson@luther.edu
MATTSON, Rhoda .... 708-239-4842 153 B rhoda.mattson@trnty.edu
MATTY, David .... 801-626-6159 473 E davidmatty@weber.edu
MATUGA, Julia .... 419-372-5572 357 F jmatuga@bgsu.edu
MATULIA, Michael, K .... 352-323-3643 103 B matuliam@lssc.edu
MATURAN, Ashley .... 605-331-6801 429 D ashley.maturan@usiouxfalls.edu
MATURANA SENDOYA, Ines .... 617-552-3358 212 E ines.maturana@bc.edu
MATUS, Nelson .... 956-380-8187 455 G nmatus@riogrande.edu
MATUS, Paul .... 631-451-4518 330 C matusp@sunysuffolk.edu
MATUSICK, Robert .... 386-822-7300 111 E rmatusic@stetson.edu
MATUSIK, Sharon .... 303-735-5113.. 83 B sharon.matusik@colorado.edu
MATUSOW-AYRES, Helen .... 718-636-3639 320 D hmayres@pratt.edu
MATVEY, Jessica .... 218-262-7384 244 H jessicamatvey@hibbing.edu
MATVIUK, Sergio .... 918-495-6523 378 H smatviuk@oru.edu
MATWEYCHUK, Karen ..... 610-647-4980 397 I kmatweychuk@immaculata.edu
MATYAS, Laura .... 480-732-7205.. 13 E laura.matyas@cgc.edu
MATYE EDWARDS, Lisa 303-797-5601.. 76 I lisa.matyeedwards@arapahoe.edu
MATYSTIK, Walter, F ..... 718-862-7268 313 L walter.matystik@manhattan.edu
MATZ, Jeannine .... 515-643-6703 171 K jmatz@mercydesmoines.org
MATZ, Kurt, M .... 574-520-5522 160 F kumatz@iusb.edu
MATZ, Tina .... 517-787-0800 231 E matztinam@jccmi.edu
MATZKE, Brian .... 616-632-2073 227 C matzkbri@aquinas.edu
MATZKE, William .... 989-358-7259 227 A matzkew@alpenacc.edu
MATZKIN, Michael .... 641-472-7000 171 J webmaster@mum.edu
MATZNER, Alan .... 507-537-6010 248 A alan.matzner@smsu.edu
MAU, Jeremy .... 563-588-8000 169 B jmau@emmaus.edu
MAUCH, Tom .... 909-274-4380.. 52 I tmauch@mtsac.edu
MAUCH AMIR, Carol .... 213-740-7922.. 72 B cmauch@usc.edu
MAUE, Deborah .... 312-369-7011 136 H dmaue@colum.edu
MAUER, JR., Gerard, M 202-685-2330 518 B mauerg@ndu.edu
MAUGE, Lucille .... 404-880-6662 117 H lmauge@cau.edu
MAUGHAN, Doug, L ..... 208-732-6262 131 I dmaughan@csi.edu
MAUHS-PUGH, Thomas 802-287-8214 475 B mauhs-pught@greenmtn.edu
MAUI, Lorraine, C .... 670-237-6708 520 D lorraine.maui@marianas.edu
MAUK, Andy .... 910-962-7638 352 A mauka@uncw.edu
MAUK, Jean .... 305-809-3266.. 99 L wjean.mauk@fkcc.edu
MAUK, Teresa .... 401-598-1000 416 C tmauk@jwu.edu
MAUK, Vera .... 508-373-9768 211 F vera.mauk@becker.edu
MAUL, Jeffrey .... 814-262-6431 405 A jmaul@pennhighlands.edu
MAUL, Tammy .... 334-872-2533.... 6 H tammymaul@gmail.com
MAULDIN, Brad .... 575-562-2393 293 O bradley.mauldin@enmu.edu
MAULDIN, Teena, P ...... 704-463-3031 348 B teena.mauldin@pfeiffer.edu
MAULTSBY, Bill .... 910-642-7141 346 G bill.maultsby@sccnc.edu
MAUN, Duane, F .... 717-901-5120 397 E dmaun@harrisburgu.edu
MAUN, Robin .... 717-477-1302 407 B rmmaun@ship.edu
MAUNEY, Bill .... 910-272-3300 346 A bmauney@robeson.edu
MAUNEY, Billy, L .... 910-272-3330 346 A bmauney@robeson.edu
MAUNSELL, Jody .... 802-828-8724 476 F jody.maunsell@vcfa.edu
MAURANA, Cheryl, A .... 414-955-8075 508 D cmaurana@mcw.edu
MAURANO, Steven, J ... 401-865-2775 416 E smaurano@providence.edu
MAURER, Amanda, C .... 813-974-4126 111 A amaurer@usf.edu
MAURER, Amybeth .... 847-214-7423 138 B amaurer@elgin.edu
MAURER, Bobby Jo ...... 309-341-7315 142 G bmaurer@knox.edu
MAURER, Carmen, K .... 402-472-3906 277 E cmaurer@nebraska.edu
MAURER, Carolyn .... 717-796-5068 401 L cmaurer@messiah.edu
MAURER, Charles .... 212-757-1190 298 D cmaurer@funeraleducation.org
MAURER, Erin .... 864-622-6074 418 E emaurer@andersonuniversity.edu
MAURER, Gaylyn .... 541-885-1800 385 E gaylyn.maurer@oit.edu
MAURER, Lynn .... 812-237-3087 159 C lynn.maurer@indstate.edu
MAURER, Paul, J .... 828-669-8012 340 I president@montreat.edu
MAURER, Paulette, A .... 708-709-3630 148 I pmaurer@prairiestate.edu
MAURER, Ryan .... 937-327-6114 374 A rmaurer@wittenberg.edu
MAURER, Stace .... 503-760-3131 381 J stace@birthingway.edu
MAURER, William, M .... 949-824-6802.. 69 A wmmaurer@uci.edu
MAURICE, JR., John, W .... 252-334-2004 340 B president@macuniversity.edu
MAURIELLO, Thomas .... 718-862-7241 313 L thomas.mauriello@manhattan.edu
MAURIN, Kay .... 985-549-2507 197 E kay.maurin@selu.edu
MAURO, Anthony, F ..... 724-938-1653 405 F mauro@calu.edu
MAURO, Laurie .... 304-263-6262 502 A lmauro@martinsburginstitute.edu
MAURO, Steven, A .... 814-871-7605 395 H mauro003@gannon.edu
MAUSSER, Richard, F ... 216-397-4273 363 H rmausser@jcu.edu
MAUST, Scott .... 309-341-7892 142 G smaust@knox.edu
MAUZ, Harry .... 281-931-7717 121 J hmauz@ict.edu
MAUZERALL, Cynthia .... 208-459-5561 131 H cmauzerall@collegeofidaho.edu
MAVRINAC, Mary Ann .. 585-275-4461 332 E maryann.mavrinac@rochester.edu
MAVROS, Jeff .... 309-438-2181 140 L jmavros@ilstu.edu
MAWHINNEY, Kim .... 626-395-6354.. 29 I kim.mawhinney@caltech.edu
MAX, Claire .... 831-459-2991.. 70 C cemax@ucsc.edu
MAX, Sheryl .... 816-995-2842 265 G sheryl.max@researchcollege.edu
MAXEINER, Amy .... 309-796-5043 134 C maxeinera@bhc.edu

MAZZIOTTA, John .... 310-825-5687.. 69 B
jmazziotta@mednet.ucla.edu
MAZZOCCO, Lisa .... 213-740-6426.. 72 B
lisa.mazzocco@usc.edu
MAZZOLA, Frank .... 603-358-2242 283 A
fmazzola@keene.edu
MAZZOLA, Gregg .... 603-645-9635 282 C
g.mazzola@snhu.edu
MAZZOLLA, Jeanne .... 201-692-7100 286 B
mazzolla@fdu.edu
MAZZUCA, Mary .... 717-358-5800 395 G
mary.mazzuca@fandm.edu
MBOMEH, Gabriel, A .... 240-895-4305 206 G
gambomeh@smcm.edu
MBUWAYESANGO,
Dora, R .... 704-636-6077 338 F
dmbuwayesango@hoodseminary.edu
MBYIRUKIRA, James ..... 256-726-7157.... 6 E
mbyirukira@oakwood.edu
MC CAIG, Robert .... 732-571-3413 287 C
rmccaig@monmouth.edu
MC COLLOUGH, Scott ... 608-785-8711 510 F
smcclough@uwlax.edu
MC DONALD, Molly ...... 408-554-6993.. 62 F
mmcdonald@scu.edu
MC GOVERN, Michael .. 516-323-3030 315 J
mamcgovern@molloy.edu
MCABEE, Sarah .... 256-233-8102.... 4 C
sarah.mcabee@athens.edu
MCADAM DONEGAN,
Lisa .... 401-598-1000 416 C
lisa.mcadamdonegan@jwu.edu
MCADAMS, Angie .... 434-791-5629 478 E
amcadams@averett.edu
MCADAMS, Beverly .... 864-231-2000 418 E
bmcadams@andersonuniversity.edu
MCADAMS, Charles .... 662-846-4010 252 H
cmcadams@deltastate.edu
MCADOO, Anthony .... 270-745-5404 190 F
anthony.mcadoo@wku.edu
MCAFEE, Ouida .... 229-430-4767 114 I
ouida.mcafee@asurams.edu
MCAFEE, Stacy .... 209-932-3027.. 70 F
smcafee@pacific.edu
MCAFEE, Stacy .... 209-946-2223.. 70 F
smcafee@pacific.edu
MCAFFEE, Matthew, J ... 615-675-5330 441 B
mjmcaffee@welch.edu
MCALARY, Chris .... 310-954-4030.. 52 H
cmcalary@msmu.edu
MCALEER, Brenda .... 207-621-3425 201 C
mcaleer@maine.edu
MCALEER, Jessica .... 631-687-2667 322 G
jmcaleer@sjcny.edu
MCALEXANDER, Dan ..... 706-880-8230 122 D
dmcalexander@lagrange.edu
MCALINEY, Peter .... 973-655-6824 287 D
mcalineyp@mail.montclair.edu
MCALISTER, George ...... 208-769-3393 132 E
glmcalister@nic.edu
MCALISTER, Jean .... 609-343-4901 283 D
mcaliste@atlantic.edu
MCALISTER, Jett .... 860-297-2080.. 88 E
jett.mcalister@trincoll.edu
MCALISTER, Meree .... 803-778-6646 419 A
mcalistermm@cctech.edu
MCALISTER, Richie .... 601-484-8779 253 G
rmcalist@mcc.cc.ms.us
MCALLISTER,
Annemarie .... 914-964-4282 304 D
amcallister@riversidehealth.org
MCALLISTER, Carol .... 760-750-4802.. 33 E
cmcallis@csusm.edu
MCALLISTER, Charles 573-651-2192 266M
cdmcallister@semo.edu
MCALLISTER, Charles 573-651-2062 266M
cdmcallister@semo.edu
MCALLISTER, Gary .... 501-205-8827.. 19 B
gmcallister@cbc.edu
MCALLISTER, Greg .... 405-912-9055 379 A
gmcallister@ru.edu
MCALLISTER, Latrelle, P 704-378-1230 338 I
lmcallister@jcsu.edu
MCALLISTER, Mary, C ... 607-871-2101 298 A
mcallister@alfred.edu
MCALLISTER, Michael .... 704-272-5441 346 F
mmcallister@spcc.edu
MCALLISTER, Peter .... 941-359-7537 106 H
pmcallis@ringling.edu
MCALLISTER, Steven, G 540-458-8740 491 G
smcallister@wlu.edu
MCALLISTER-WILSON,
David .... 202-885-8601.. 94 C
president@wesleyseminary.edu
MCALMOND, Barb .... 406-447-6907 271 I
barb.mcalmond@umhelena.edu
MCALMONT, Shaun .... 801-302-2800 472 A
shaun.mcalmont@neumont.edu

MCALONAN, Jenny .... 313-993-3343 237 F
mcalonjl@udmercy.edu
MCALOOSE, Carl .... 239-489-9294 100 E
cmcaloose@fsw.edu
MCALPIN, Michael .... 925-631-4222.. 59 C
mdm5@stmarys-ca.edu
MCALPINE, Lynn .... 402-554-3514 277 I
lmcalpine@unomaha.edu
MCANALLY, David .... 903-675-6232 464 C
dmcanally@tvcc.edu
MCANALLY, Kent .... 785-670-1938 182 D
kent.mcanally@washburn.edu
MCANDREW, John .... 570-208-5958 398 D
johnmcandrew@kings.edu
MCANDREW, Kathleen .. 217-353-2024 148 H
kmcandrew@parkland.edu
MCANDREW, Laura .... 202-885-6294.. 91 C
mcandrew@american.edu
MCANELLEY, Becky, J ... 409-882-3318 462 D
becky.mcanelley@lsco.edu
MCANNALLY, Linda, J .. 864-833-8287 423 D
lmcannally@presby.edu
MCANUFF, Courtney ..... 848-445-6601 290 A
courtney.mcanuff@rutgers.edu
MCANUFF, Courtney, O 848-445-6601 290 C
courtney.mcanuff@rutgers.edu
MCARDELL, James .... 218-855-8136 244 C
jmcardell@clcmn.edu
MCARDLE, Eliza .... 413-549-4600 215 F
MCARDLE, Jennifer .... 718-862-8000 313 L
jennifer.mcardle@manhattan.edu
MCARDLE, Karen .... 248-204-2010 233 A
kmcardle@ltu.edu
MCARTHUR, Andrew ..... 615-353-3572 437 D
andrew.mcarthur@nscc.edu
MCARTHUR, Bridgette .. 863-616-6411 100 D
bmcarthur@flsouthern.edu
MCARTHUR, Douglas .... 517-607-2462 231 C
dmcarthur@hillsdale.edu
MCARTHUR, Jennifer .... 307-674-6446 516 P
jmcarthur@sheridan.edu
MCARTHUR, John, M .... 580-581-2201 375 A
jmcarthur@cameron.edu
MCARTHUR, Marcus ..... 760-480-8474.. 74 H
mmcarthur@wscal.edu
MCARTHUR, Neil .... 478-757-3548 117 D
nmcarthur@centralgatech.edu
MCARTHUR, Neil .... 478-988-6800 117 E
nmcarthur@centralgatech.edu
MCARTHUR, Phillip .... 808-675-3907 128 K
phillip.mcarthur@byuh.edu
MCARTHUR, Rachel, A .. 859-371-9393 183 G
rmcarthur@beckfield.edu
MCARTHUR, Thomas ..... 330-263-2263 360 A
tmcarthur@wooster.edu
MCATEE, Brooke .... 660-359-3948 264 H
bmcatee@mail.ncmissouri.edu
MCATEE, Christopher .... 847-970-4940 154 H
cmcatee@usml.edu
MCATEE, Jim .... 765-285-2420 156 C
jfmcatee@bsu.edu
MCATEER, Michael .... 973-278-5400 283 J
mxm@berkeleycollege.edu
MCATEER, Michael .... 212-986-4343 299 F
mxm@berkeleycollege.edu
MCAULIFF, Kimberly, B 315-445-4553 312 F
mcaulikb@lemoyne.edu
MCAULIFFE, Lynne .... 307-855-2206 516 I
lynne@cwc.edu
MCAVOY, Eugene .... 425-388-9031 494 F
MCAVOY, John .... 304-876-5374 504 D
jmcavoy@shepherd.edu
MCAVOY, William, J ..... 508-831-5337 226 E
wjmcavoy@wpi.edu
MCBEATH, Trish .... 918-465-1804 375 J
tmcbeath@eosc.edu
MCBEE, Barry .... 512-322-3715 467 A
bmcbee@utsystem.edu
MCBEE, Lori, A .... 479-979-1413.. 23 J
lamcbee@ozarks.edu
MCBEE, Misty .... 573-288-6507 259 E
mmcbee@culver.edu
MCBEE, Ronald .... 575-492-2116 297 G
rmcbee@usw.edu
MCBEE, Russ .... 620-227-9313 176 N
rmcbee@dc3.edu
MCBEE, Whitney .... 903-693-2067 454 E
wmcbee@panola.edu
MCBETH, Valerie .... 360-676-2772 496 C
vmcbeth@nwic.edu
MCBIRTH, Matthew .... 417-626-1234 264 J
mcbirth.matthew@occ.edu
MCBRADY, Allison .... 216-373-6376 367 A
amcbrady@ndc.edu
MCBRAYER, Mike .... 903-463-8753 449 J
mmcbrayer@grayson.edu

MCBRAYER,
Stephanie, H .... 501-450-5932.. 23 I
smcbrayer@uca.edu
MCBREEN, William .... 507-457-5122 248 C
wmcbreen@winona.edu
MCBRIDE, Amanda .... 303-871-2203.. 83 E
amanda.mcbride@du.edu
MCBRIDE, Ameerah .... 920-424-0330 511 B
mcbridea@uwosh.edu
MCBRIDE, Andrew, S .... 804-289-8964 486 G
amcbride@richmond.edu
MCBRIDE, Becky .... 985-448-7924 192 I
becky.mcbride@fletcher.edu
MCBRIDE, Burke .... 707-476-4100.. 39 F
burke-mcbride@redwoods.edu
MCBRIDE, Catherine ..... 562-947-8755.. 65 D
catherinemcbride@scuhs.edu
MCBRIDE, Christy .... 618-985-3741 141 D
christymcbride@jalc.edu
MCBRIDE, Corinn .... 973-408-3560 285 E
cmcbride1@drew.edu
MCBRIDE, Dan .... 859-622-1968 184 F
dan.mcbride@eku.edu
MCBRIDE, David .... 301-314-8117 207 G
dmcbrid2@umd.edu
MCBRIDE, David .... 731-661-5450 439 D
dmcbride@uu.edu
MCBRIDE, Dwight, A ..... 847-491-8502 148 C
dwight-mcbride@northwestern.edu
MCBRIDE, Dwight, A ..... 404-727-6055 119 B
dwight.a.mcbride@emory.edu
MCBRIDE, Faith .... 218-322-2360 245 B
faith.mcbride@itascacc.edu
MCBRIDE, Jeanette .... 910-898-9630 345 A
mcbridej@montgomery.edu
MCBRIDE, Jennifer .... 910-362-7696 341 E
jmcbride@cfcc.edu
MCBRIDE, John, E .... 512-245-2557 463 A
jm05@txstate.edu
MCBRIDE, Lisa .... 978-542-3022 218 E
lisa.mcbride@salemstate.edu
MCBRIDE, Maria .... 504-865-2696 194 G
mmcbride@loyno.edu
MCBRIDE, Michael .... 276-739-2402 490 A
mmcbride@vhcc.edu
MCBRIDE, Nataly .... 949-794-9090.. 66 B
nmcbride@stanbridge.edu
MCBRIDE, Phil .... 928-428-8404.. 12 I
phil.mcbride@eac.edu
MCBRIDE, Regina .... 618-650-2712 152 C
rmcbrid@siue.edu
MCBRIDE, Robert .... 201-200-3057 287 F
rmcbride@njcu.edu
MCBRIDE, Robert, J ...... 610-660-1351 409 H
rmcbride@sju.edu
MCBRIDE, Ron .... 910-221-2224 338 A
rmcbride@gcd.edu
MCBRIDE, Tara, E .... 215-545-6400 403 D
temcbride@peirce.edu
MCBRINE, Paul .... 617-236-8882 215 B
pmcbrine@fisher.edu
MCBROOM, Michael ..... 806-651-4400 460 E
mmcbroom@mail.wtamu.edu
MCBRYDE, Tennie, S .... 334-420-4306.... 3 H
tmcbryde@trenholmstate.edu
MCBURNEY, Melissa ..... 509-542-4832 493 G
mmcburney@columbiabasin.edu
MCCABE, Cherry, L .... 530-226-4154.. 64 B
cmccabe@simpsonu.edu
MCCABE, Cynthia .... 814-262-6477 405 A
cmccabe@pennhighlands.edu
MCCABE, Daniel .... 516-877-4231 297 I
dmccabe@adelphi.edu
MCCABE, Eileen .... 718-405-3240 304 H
eileen.mccabe@mountsaintvincent.edu
MCCABE, Karen .... 850-471-4639 105 E
kmccabe@pensacolastate.edu
MCCABE, Kenneth, F ..... 401-825-2111 416 B
kfmccabe@ccri.edu
MCCABE, Kevin .... 505-277-2241 296 H
kmccab02@unm.edu
MCCABE, Philip, J .... 203-371-7934.. 88 C
mccabep@sacredheart.edu
MCCABE, Tonya .... 360-752-8331 492 H
tmccabe@btc.edu
MCCABE SMITH, Linda . 919-515-4559 350 E
lmsmit20@ncsu.edu
MCCADDEN, Brian, M .... 401-865-2503 416 E
bmccadde@providence.edu
MCCADDEN, Kevin .... 610-436-2223 407 D
kmccadden@wcupa.edu
MCCAFFERTY, Bridgit .... 254-519-5484 459 D
bmccaffe@tamuct.edu
MCCAFFERTY, Coreen ... 610-921-7274 388 E
cmccafferty@albright.edu
MCCAFFERTY, Patricia ... 978-934-3238 217 B
patricia_mccafferty@uml.edu

MCCAFFREY, Dena .... 636-481-3400 261 B
dmccaffr@jeffco.edu
MCCAFFREY, Kaisha ...... 563-425-5200 173 K
mccaffreyk811@uiu.edu
MCCAFFREY, Kayla .... 212-517-0469 314 D
kmccaffrey@mmm.edu
MCCAFFREY, Mary .... 610-558-5537 402 G
mccaffrm@neumann.edu
MCCAFFREY,
Michael, H .... 260-399-7700 165 B
mmccaffrey@sf.edu
MCCAGHREN, Chris ...... 251-442-2218.... 8 D
cmccaghren@umobile.edu
MCCAGHREN, Lauren .... 251-442-2220.... 8 D
lmccaghren@umobile.edu
MCCAIN, ALecia .... 830-372-8050 461 D
almccain@tlu.edu
MCCAIN, Gail, C .... 212-772-4000 302 E
gmccain@hunter.cuny.edu
MCCAIN, Lindy .... 662-472-9067 253 C
lmccain@holmescc.edu
MCCALEB, Cathy .... 972-721-5203 464 E
mccaleb@udallas.edu
MCCALEB, Colin .... 269-965-3931 232 A
mccalebc@kellogg.edu
MCCALEB, Gary, D .... 325-674-2156 441 D
mccalebg@acu.edu
MCCALEB, George .... 956-872-8396 456 G
gmccaleb@southtexascollege.edu
MCCALL, Amy Elizabeth 412-391-4100 408 F
amccall@pointpark.edu
MCCALL, Andy, K .... 865-981-8113 433 F
andy.mccall@maryvillecollege.edu
MCCALL, Ann .... 504-520-7470 198 D
amccall@xula.edu
MCCALL, Becky .... 530-242-7719.. 63 I
bmccall@shastacollege.edu
MCCALL, Brian .... 512-463-3280 462 A
brian.mccall@tsus.edu
MCCALL, Chris .... 713-221-8030 465 C
mccallc@uhd.edu
MCCALL, Devin .... 701-858-3993 354 C
devin.mccall@minotstateu.edu
MCCALL, Gloria .... 859-256-3100 185 D
gloria.mccall@kctcs.edu
MCCALL, John .... 205-652-3414.... 9 C
jmccall@uwa.edu
MCCALL, John .... 334-670-3215.... 7 E
jmccall106692@troy.edu
MCCALL, Kimberly .... 352-335-2332.. 94 D
kimberly.mccall@acupuncturist.edu
MCCALL, Melinda .... 251-380-4000.... 7 B
mmcall@shc.edu
MCCALL, Michele .... 660-263-4100 264 C
michelem@macc.edu
MCCALL, Ryan .... 740-386-4199 365 B
mccallr@mtc.edu
MCCALL, Sam .... 850-644-6031 110 A
smmccall@fsu.edu
MCCALL, Sara .... 704-406-2118 337 H
smccall@gardner-webb.edu
MCCALLA, Justin .... 706-355-5008 115 H
jmccalla@athenstech.edu
MCCALLA, Kelly .... 507-433-0530 247 C
kelly.mccalla@riverland.edu
MCCALLEY, Greg .... 952-358-8507 246 D
MCCALLIE, Kathleen, D . 918-270-6441 378 I
kathy.mccallie@ptstulsa.edu
MCCALLIN, Julia, M ...... 626-395-3230.. 29 I
julia.mccallin@caltech.edu
MCCALLISTER, Ashley .... 704-461-6717 335 J
ashleymccallister@bac.edu
MCCALLISTER, Emilie .... 815-280-1321 142 A
emccalli@jjc.edu
MCCALLON, Melanie, C 270-809-4152 188 D
mmccallon@murraystate.edu
MCCALLUM, Arminda .... 816-604-2631 262 I
mindy.mccallum@mcckc.edu
MCCALLUM, SJ,
David, C .... 315-445-6110 312 F
mccaldac@lemoyne.edu
MCCALLUM, Jeannie ..... 864-388-8053 422 A
jmccallum@lander.edu
MCCALLUM, Rex, M ...... 409-772-3639 469 C
remccall@utmb.edu
MCCALLUM, Richard ..... 229-732-5929 115 B
richardmccallum@andrewcollege.edu
MCCAMBRY, Al .... 850-872-3814 101 J
amccambr1@gulfcoast.edu
MCCAMPBELL,
Martha (Marty) .... 574-520-4524 160 F
mmccampb@iusb.edu
MCCANCE, John .... 575-492-2141 297 G
jmccance@usw.edu
MCCANDLESS, Ann .... 724-287-8711 390 J
ann.mccandless@bc3.edu
MCCANDLESS, Beverly .. 270-686-4255 183 J
beverly.mccandless@brescia.edu

MCCANDLESS, John 513-529-2223 365 I mccandjm@miamioh.edu
MCCANDLESS, Michael 209-384-6107 51 G mccandless.m@mccd.edu
MCCANDLESS, N. Jane 678-839-5170 127 F jmccandl@westga.edu
MCCANDLESS, Raymond 419-434-4565 372 B mccandless@findlay.edu
MCCANE, Latitia 251-405-7012 1 E lmccane@bishop.edu
MCCANN, Bonnie 614-947-6017 362 A bonnie.mccann@franklin.edu
MCCANN, Carrie 254-968-9007 459 A cmccann@tarleton.edu
MCCANN, Elizabeth 562-938-4139 48 I emccann@lbcc.edu
MCCANN, Kevin 802-860-2754 474 G kmccann@champlain.edu
MCCANN, Linda 215-968-8003 390 I mccannl@bucks.edu
MCCANN, Paul, A 217-581-2921 138 A pmccann@eiu.edu
MCCANN, JR., Terence 410-337-6170 204 A terence.mccann@goucher.edu
MCCANNON, Mindy 706-295-6846 120 C mmccannon@gntc.edu
MCCARDELL, JR., John, M 931-598-1101 436 A jmmccard@sewanee.edu
MCCAREY, Christine 508-362-2131 219 E cmccarey@capecod.edu
MCCARGO, Donovan 215-751-8876 393 A dmccargo@ccp.edu
MCCARN, Sarah 912-525-5000 125 B smccarn@scad.edu
MCCARRELL, Kyle 540-453-2269 487 G mccarrellk@brcc.edu
MCCARRICK, Richard, G 914-594-4503 318 A richard_mccarrick@nymc.edu
MCCARROLL, John, F 515-294-6137 166 F jmccarol@iastate.edu
MCCARROLL, Michele 509-452-5100 496 H mmccarroll@pnwu.edu
MCCARRON, Anne 414-382-6068 506 A anne.mccarron@alverno.edu
MCCARRON, Shannon 361-354-2271 445 S smccarron@coastalbend.edu
MCCARRON, Tom 619-594-5631 34 B tmccarron@mail.sdsu.edu
MCCARRY, Tim 325-670-1434 450 A facilities@hsutx.edu
MCCARTER, Debbie, L 423-585-6844 438 D debbie.mccarter@ws.edu
MCCARTHHY, Piper 775-445-3270 279 F piper.mccarthy@wnc.edu
MCCARTHY, Anne 651-523-2335 242 E amccarthy02@hamline.edu
MCCARTHY, Anne, E 970-382-7463 79 J
MCCARTHY, Barbara 914-773-3741 319 J bmccarthy@pace.edu
MCCARTHY, Barbara 508-588-9100 220 B
MCCARTHY, Carlie 530-283-0202 42 K cmccarthy@frc.edu
MCCARTHY, Casey, J 218-755-3888 244 B cmccarthy@bemidjistate.edu
MCCARTHY, Colby 973-408-3112 285 E finaid@drew.edu
MCCARTHY, Daniel 985-549-2055 197 E dmccarthy@selu.edu
MCCARTHY, David 301-447-5333 206 B dmccarth@msmary.edu
MCCARTHY, Dominica 972-860-4689 447 G dmccarthy@dcccd.edu
MCCARTHY, Douglas 602-285-7245 14 A douglas.mccarthy@phoenixcollege.edu
MCCARTHY, Elizabeth, K 508-678-2811 219 C elizabeth.mccarthy@bristolcc.edu
MCCARTHY, Faith 530-221-4275 63 H registrar@shasta.edu
MCCARTHY, Faith 530-221-4275 63 H shastaonline@clearwire.net
MCCARTHY, James 610-861-5506 403 B jmccarthy@northampton.edu
MCCARTHY, Jenna 216-368-5872 358 C jennifer.wrightmccarthy@case.edu
MCCARTHY, John, C 202-319-5259 91 D mccartjc@cua.edu
MCCARTHY, John, J 413-545-5271 216 H jmccarthy@grad.umass.edu
MCCARTHY, Joseph, J 412-624-0790 412 I jjmcc@pitt.edu
MCCARTHY, Kate 802-635-1458 477 C kathleen.mccarthy@jsc.edu
MCCARTHY, Katherine 540-831-6044 484 A kmccarthy21@radford.edu
MCCARTHY, Kelly 708-235-3966 138 H kmccarthy@govst.edu
MCCARTHY, Kevin 315-568-3267 317 A kmccarthy@nycc.edu
MCCARTHY, Kevin 704-330-6907 342 A kevin.mccarthy@cpcc.edu
MCCARTHY, Kevin, D 425-235-2235 497 E kmccarthy@rtc.edu
MCCARTHY, Kristie 407-265-8383 96 C
MCCARTHY, Margaret 716-888-2120 300 G mmccarth@canisius.edu
MCCARTHY, Mark, D 216-397-4213 363 H mmccarthy@jcu.edu
MCCARTHY, Marsha 908-737-7100 286 F mmccarth@kean.edu
MCCARTHY, Mary 607-778-5210 326 C mccarthyma@sunybroome.edu
MCCARTHY, Maureen 765-285-1042 156 C mmccarthy@bsu.edu
MCCARTHY, Melissa 401-874-2599 417 E mcmel@uri.edu
MCCARTHY, SJ, Michael, C 718-817-3013 308 G mmccarthysj@fordham.edu
MCCARTHY, Michael, R 978-556-3924 220 F mmccarthy1@necc.mass.edu
MCCARTHY, Michael, R 402-932-8600 274 D mmccarthy@mccarthycapital.com
MCCARTHY, Pamela 413-585-2840 224 F pmccarth@smith.edu
MCCARTHY, Patrice 216-373-5182 367 A mpmccarthy@ndc.edu
MCCARTHY, Patricia 724-357-7544 406 C mccarthy@iup.edu
MCCARTHY, Rosemary 412-536-1173 398 E rosemary.mccarthy@laroche.edu
MCCARTHY, Ryan 718-289-5338 301 D ryan.mccarthy@bcc.cuny.edu
MCCARTHY, Sean 312-777-8726 140 G smccarthy@aii.edu
MCCARTHY, Sherry 712-279-3158 173 B sherry.mccarthy@stlukescollege.edu
MCCARTNEY, Cliff 865-573-4517 432 H cmccartney@johnsonu.edu
MCCARTNEY, Jill 402-826-8583 274 E jill.mccartney@doane.edu
MCCARTNEY, Kathleen 413-585-2100 224 F kmccartney@smith.edu
MCCARTNEY, Maureen 413-572-8801 218 F mccartney@westfield.ma.edu
MCCARTNEY, William, G 765-496-2270 163 C mccart@purdue.edu
MCCARTNEY, JR., William, L 252-328-6050 349 I mccartneyw@ecu.edu
MCCARTY, Alison 781-239-2506 220 A amccarty1@massbay.edu
MCCARTY, Dan 916-558-2198 50 I mccartw@scc.losrios.edu
MCCARTY, Gerald 810-766-4206 227 E
MCCARTY, II, Gerald 810-766-4206 227 F gmccar01@baker.edu
MCCARTY, Glenda 217-228-5432 149 B mccargl@quincy.edu
MCCARTY, Lori 706-272-2034 118 F lmccarty@daltonstate.edu
MCCARTY, Lori 706-272-4462 118 F lmccarty@daltonstate.edu
MCCARTY, Susan 212-772-4850 302 E susan.mccarty@hunter.cuny.edu
MCCARVEL, Thomas, J 406-447-4409 270 H tmccarve@carroll.edu
MCCARVER, Viva 419-372-8421 357 F vivam@bgsu.edu
MCCARY, Jennifer, Q 717-337-6998 396 A jmccary@gettysburg.edu
MCCASKILL, John 803-535-1264 423 B mccaskill@octech.edu
MCCASKILL, Sharrell 202-651-5642 91 H sharrell.mccaskill@gallaudet.edu
MCCASLAND, Shannon 970-339-6563 76 E shannon.mccasland@aims.edu
MCCASLIN, James, B 270-901-1104 187 A james.mccaslin@kctcs.edu
MCCASLIN, John 931-553-0071 434 J john.mccaslin@miller-motte.com
MCCASLIN, Julie 423-746-5214 439 A jmccaslin@tnwesleyan.edu
MCCASLIN, Sharon 314-889-4567 260 C smccaslin@fontbonne.edu
MCCAULEY, David, W 304-473-8322 505 G mccauley@wvwc.edu
MCCAULEY, Dennis 215-968-8394 390 I mccauley@bucks.edu
MCCAULEY, Kathleen 610-647-4400 397 I kmccauley@immaculata.edu
MCCAULEY, Laurie, K 734-763-3311 237 I mccauley@umich.edu
MCCAULEY, Linda 404-727-7976 119 B linda.mccauley@emory.edu
MCCAULEY, Terry, L 248-232-4660 235 D tlmccaul@oaklandcc.edu
MCCAULEY-JUGOVICH, Shelly 218-748-2416 245 D s.mccauley@mesabirange.edu
MCCAULEY JUGOVICH, Shelly 218-749-7715 245 D s.mccauley@mesabirange.edu
MCCAUSLAND, Bill 813-974-1868 111 A mccausland@usf.edu
MCCAUSLIN, Lauren 617-243-2139 216 C lmccauslin@lasell.edu
MCCAW, Ian 434-582-2100 482 D ijmccaw@liberty.edu
MCCAWLEY, Michael 831-459-2374 70 C admissions@ucsc.edu
MCCAY, T. Dwayne 321-674-8099 99 K tdmccay@fit.edu
MCCHESENEY-YOUNG, Mary 510-204-0731 37 F mmcchesneyyoung@gtu.edu
MCCHESNEY-YOUNG, Mary 510-204-0731 37 F mmcchesneyyoung@cdsp.edu
MCCHURCH, Bob 309-796-5013 134 C mcchurchb@bhc.edu
MCCLAFFERTY, Joseph 406-496-4804 272 E jmcclafferty@mtech.edu
MCCLAIN, Barbara, L 304-326-1234 502 D bmcclain@salemu.edu
MCCLAIN, Beth 309-694-5323 139 G bmcclain@icc.edu
MCCLAIN, Dale 847-866-3920 138 G dale.mcclain@garrett.edu
MCCLAIN, Darron 202-274-6361 93 D darron.mcclain@udc.edu
MCCLAIN, Elman 206-934-5437 497 I elman.mcclain@seattlecolleges.edu
MCCLAIN, Gloria 404-756-4098 115 I gmcclain@atlm.edu
MCCLAIN, James, W 870-838-2910 17 K jmcclain@smail.anc.edu
MCCLAIN, Jason 304-829-7601 501 F jmcclain@bethanywv.edu
MCCLAIN, Jeremy 334-670-3482 7 E jamcclain@troy.edu
MCCLAIN, Paula, D 919-681-1560 337 C pmmclain@duke.edu
MCCLAIN, Rebecca 281-756-3561 442 C rmcclain@alvincollege.edu
MCCLAIN, Samantha, E 515-574-1080 170 C mcclain@iowacentral.edu
MCCLAIN, Tamara 630-942-2422 136 D mccalint57@cod.edu
MCCLAIN, Tim 360-486-8875 497 F tmc@stmartin.edu
MCCLANAHAN, Barry 717-477-1240 407 B bkmcca@ship.edu
MCCLANAHAN, Denise 434-961-5275 489 C dmcclanahan@pvcc.edu
MCCLANAHAN, Keith 870-368-2004 20 H keith.mcclanahan@ozarka.edu
MCCLATCHY, Anna 706-886-6831 126 F amcclatchy@tfc.edu
MCCLAY, Diana, D 423-439-5890 431 H mcclayd@etsu.edu
MCCLAY, Kelly 609-343-4939 283 D mcclay@atlantic.edu
MCCLAY, Liam 352-395-5199 107 E liam.mclay@sfcollege.edu
MCCLEARN, Keith 706-419-1209 118 E keith.mcclearn@covenant.edu
MCCLEARN, Steve 205-329-7907 5 C steve.mcclearn@ecacolleges.com
MCCLEARY, Caitlin 865-974-1000 439 I
MCCLEARY, Tim 406-638-3121 271 C baaxpaa@lbhc.edu
MCCLELLAN, Craig, S 304-326-1247 502 D cmcclellan@salemu.edu
MCCLELLAN, Craig, S 304-326-1465 502 D cmcclellan@salemu.edu
MCCLELLAN, George, S 260-481-6844 160 D mcclellg@ipfw.edu
MCCLELLAN, Jane 201-200-3196 287 F jmcclellan@njcu.edu
MCCLELLAN, Laura 276-739-2425 490 A lmcclellan@vhcc.edu
MCCLELLAN, Mia, C 619-482-6542 65 H mmcclellan@swccd.edu
MCCLELLAN, Patricia 828-251-6001 351 A pmcclell@unca.edu
MCCLELLAN, Scott 206-220-8229 498 D mcclells@seattleu.edu
MCCLELLAN, Steve, J 501-569-3202 22 B sjmcclellan@ualr.edu
MCCLELLAN, Teri 352-381-3625 107 E teri.mcclellan@sfcollege.edu
MCCLELLAND, Charles, F 713-313-7216 461 E mcclellandcf@tsu.edu
MCCLELLAND, Jeremy 214-860-2351 448 A jmccleland@dcccd.edu
MCCLELLAND, Karin 925-631-4013 59 C klm14@stmarys-ca.edu
MCCLELLAND, Theresa 251-580-2120 1 I theresa.mcclelland@faulknerstate.edu
MCCLELLAND, II, Thomas, H 318-257-4827 197 A tmcclelland@latech.edu
MCCLENAGAN, Cindy, M 806-291-3410 470 I cindym@wbu.edu
MCCLENDON, Bev 479-788-7082 22 A bev.mcclendon@uafs.edu
MCCLENDON, Jennifer 918-444-4675 376 G mcclendo@nsuok.edu
MCCLENDON, Karen 916-686-8602 30 H
MCCLENDON, Mark 940-397-4567 453 C mark.mcclendon@mwsu.edu
MCCLENDON, Mark 817-515-5203 458 B mark.mcclendon@tccd.edu
MCCLENDON, Renea 870-460-1110 22 D mcclendon@uamont.edu
MCCLENDON, Rodney, P 412-268-2056 391 H rodneypm@andrew.cmu.edu
MCCLENDON, Vivienne 425-564-3056 492 G vivienne.mcclendon@bellevuecollege.edu
MCCLENNEY, Claudette 310-233-4356 49 B mcclencl@lahc.edu
MCCLENNEY, Elizabeth 540-375-2293 484 H mcclenney@roanoke.edu
MCCLIN, Raul 787-761-0640 527 C admisiones1@utcpr.edu
MCCLINTOCK, Elizabeth 724-503-1001 414 A emcclintock@washjeff.edu
MCCLINTOCK, Kate 707-527-4797 62 H kmcclintock@santarosa.edu
MCCLINTOCK, Marta 724-938-4251 405 F mcclintock@calu.edu
MCCLINTOCK, Melvin, A 240-895-4309 206 G mamcclintock@smcm.edu
MCCLINTOCK, Patty 812-237-2305 159 C patty.mcclintock@indstate.edu
MCCLINTOCK, Stewart 336-342-4261 346 B mcclintocks@rockinghamcc.edu
MCCLINTON, Flandus 225-771-5550 195 J flandus_mcclinton@sus.edu
MCCLINTON, Leon 405-744-9164 377 F leon.mcclinton@okstate.edu
MCCLINTON, Martin 239-489-9229 100 E martin.mcclinton@fsw.edu
MCCLOSKEY, Brian 609-586-4800 287 A mccloskb@mccc.edu
MCCLOSKEY, Erin, E 814-472-3100 409 G emccloskey@francis.edu
MCCLOSKEY, James, M 302-356-6880 91 B james.m.mccloskey@wilmu.edu
MCCLOSKEY, JR., John, R 610-796-3005 389 A john.mccloskey@alvernia.edu
MCCLOUD, Alyssa 973-313-6146 291 F alyssa.mccloud@shu.edu
MCCLOUD, Amber 806-291-3430 470 I amber.mccloud@wbu.edu
MCCLOUD, Barbara, L 630-515-7687 145 I bmcclo@midwestern.edu
MCCLOUD, Bill 405-491-6602 379 K bmccloud@snu.edu
MCCLOUD, Clarence 386-506-6301 97 I mcclouc@daytonastate.edu
MCCLOUD, Jennifer 317-822-3489 162 S jmccloud@martin.edu
MCCLOUD, Mickey 913-469-8500 178 F mmcloud@jccc.edu
MCCLOY, Eric 610-341-1372 394 E eric.mccloy@eastern.edu
MCCLUNEY, Alice 828-395-1495 344 A amccluney@isothermal.edu
MCCLUNG, Alan 423-614-8410 432 L amcclung@leeuniversity.edu
MCCLUNG, Alex 973-408-3799 285 E amcclung@drew.edu
MCCLUNG, Bruce, D 513-556-3737 371 E bruce.mcclung@uc.edu
MCCLUNG, Leslie 808-932-7381 129 I lmcclung@hawaii.edu
MCCLUNG, Philip, L 336-734-7212 343 C pmcclung@forsythtech.edu

MCCLUNG, Shemeka 601-979-7030 253 E shemeka.s.mcclung@jsums.edu
MCCLURE, A. Glenn 610-917-1453 413 G agmcclure@valleyforge.edu
MCCLURE, Amber 575-461-4413 294 E amberm@mesalands.edu
MCCLURE, Amy 740-368-3562 368 N aamcclur@owu.edu
MCCLURE, Beverlee, J 719-587-7341 76 D bmcclure@adams.edu
MCCLURE, Erin 361-593-2795 460 B erin.mcclure@tamuk.edu
MCCLURE, Gina 731-881-7888 440 B gmcclure@utm.edu
MCCLURE, Guy 256-233-8296 4 C guy.mcclure@athens.edu
MCCLURE, Jennifer 847-214-7319 138 B jmcclure@elgin.edu
MCCLURE, Judy 828-766-1272 344 F jmmclure@mayland.edu
MCCLURE, Kelly 580-581-2255 375 A kmcclure@cameron.edu
MCCLURE, Krista 801-426-8234 472 N kmcclure@ucdh.edu
MCCLURE, Mike 541-956-7237 386 G mmclure@roguecc.edu
MCCLURE, Shanna 765-641-4133 156 A srmcclure@anderson.edu
MCCLURE, Stephanie 801-626-6090 473 E womenscenter@weber.edu
MCCLURE, Tonya 478-757-3467 117 D tmcclure@centralgatech.edu
MCCLURE, Tonya, L 478-757-3467 117 E tmcclure@centralgatech.edu
MCCLURE, William 718-997-5790 303 E william.mcclure@qc.cuny.edu
MCCLURG, Greg 970-247-7433 79 J mcclurg_g@fortlewis.edu
MCCLUSKEY, Cindy 815-825-9333 142 F cindy.mccluskey@kishwaukeecollege.edu
MCCLUSKEY, Jennifer 314-529-9561 262 B jmccluskey@maryville.edu
MCCLUSKEY, Richard 978-665-3118 217 E rmccluskey@fitchburgstate.edu
MCCLUSKEY, Steph 507-786-3885 250 C mcclus1@stolaf.edu
MCCLUSKY, John 217-854-3231 134 E john.mcclusky@blackburn.edu
MCCLYMONT, Jay, W 717-796-1800 401 L jmcclymont@messiah.edu
MCCOART, Teresa 606-886-7371 185 F teresa.mccoart@kctcs.edu
MCCOEY, Margaret 215-951-1130 398 F mccoey@lasalle.edu
MCCOLGIN, Cathleen, C 315-866-0300 310 A mccolgicc@herkimer.edu
MCCOLLETT, Sherry 207-621-3141 201 C umafa@maine.edu
MCCOLLOCH, Bruce 304-243-2241 505 H brucemcc@wju.edu
MCCOLLOCH, Mark 443-840-1021 203 E mmocolloch@ccbcmd.edu
MCCOLLOUGH, Laura, L 907-474-6625 10 B lcmccollough@alaska.edu
MCCOLLOUGH, William, A 352-392-1202 110 D amccollough@aa.ufl.edu
MCCOLLUM, Alonzo, L 516-876-3068 327 C mccolluma@oldwestbury.edu
MCCOLLUM, Brian, K 609-921-8300 288 E
MCCOLLUM, Ricky 718-429-6600 333 B ricky.mccollum@vaughn.edu
MCCOLLUM, Scott 937-512-3068 370 A scott.mccullum@sinclair.edu
MCCOLLUM, Susan 334-291-4953 1 H susan.mccollum@cv.edu
MCCOLLUM, Walter 866-492-5336 251 E walter.mccollum@mail.waldenu.edu
MCCOMAS, Richard 580-581-2524 375 A richardm@cameron.edu
MCCOMBE, John, P 937-229-4615 372 A jmccombe1@udayton.edu
MCCOMBS, Jonathan 614-947-6169 362 A jonathan.mccombs@franklin.edu
MCCOMMON, John 731-425-2652 437 B jmccommon@jscc.edu
MCCONAHAY, Mark 812-855-2654 159 G mcconaha@indiana.edu
MCCONAHAY, Mark 812-855-0121 159 H mcconaha@indiana.edu
MCCONATHY, Terry, M 318-257-4262 197 A tmm@latech.edu
MCCONICO, Shannon 229-333-2110 128 G shannon.mcconico@wiregrass.edu
MCCONKEY, Susan 415-503-6285 60 H smcconkey@sfcm.edu
MCCONNELL, Blake 618-658-8331 143 B james.mcconnell@doc.illinois.gov
MCCONNELL, Cary 617-573-8575 224 I cmcconnell@suffolk.edu
MCCONNELL, Cheryl 816-501-4087 265 I cheryl.mcconnell@rockhurst.edu
MCCONNELL, Cheryl, M 816-501-4087 265 I cheryl.mcconnell@rockhurst.edu
MCCONNELL, Frank, J 706-864-1606 127 B mac.mcconnell@ung.edu
MCCONNELL, Glenn, F 843-953-5500 420 C mcconnellgf@cofc.edu
MCCONNELL, Ilka 706-369-5763 115 H imcconnell@athenstech.edu
MCCONNELL, James 512-313-3000 446 N james.mcconnell@concordia.edu
MCCONNELL, Jason 423-869-6333 433 C jason.mcconnell@lmunet.edu
MCCONNELL, Jim 773-702-8541 153 F jmcconnell@uchicago.edu
MCCONNELL, John, D 336-758-5000 353 A
MCCONNELL, Joyce 304-293-5701 505 B joyce.mcconnell@mail.wvu.edu
MCCONNELL, Karl 856-227-7200 284 E kmcconnell@camdencc.edu
MCCONNELL, Kimberly 352-588-8268 106 N kimberly.mcconnell@saintleo.edu
MCCONNELL, Penny, J 217-443-8747 137 B pmcconn@dacc.edu
MCCONNELL, Sheppard 580-559-5625 375 I smccnnll@ecok.edu
MCCONNELLOGUE, Ken 303-860-5600 83 A ken.mcconnellogue@cu.edu
MCCONNICO, Kelly 336-758-5000 353 A mcconnkm@wfu.edu
MCCONOUGHEY, Gina 508-757-7723 513 D gmcconoughey@blackhawk.edu
MCCONOUGHEY, Gina 608-757-7723 513 D gmcconoughey@blackhawk.edu
MCCONVILLE, Jennifer, A 308-367-5259 278 A jmcconville2@unl.edu
MCCOOK, Sonya 336-506-4278 340 L sonya.mccook@alamancecc.edu
MCCOOL, Bobby 606-886-3863 185 F bobby.mccool@kctcs.edu
MCCOOL, Jeff 575-492-4711 294 L jmccool@nmjc.edu
MCCOOL, Joan, L 716-878-4436 326 E mccooljl@buffalostate.edu
MCCORB, Chris 815-753-0493 147 H mccorb@niu.edu
MCCORCLE, Michael 417-865-2815 260 B mccorclem@evangel.edu
MCCORD, Elizabeth 415-451-2832 60 I emccord@sfts.edu
MCCORD, Jeff, D 423-354-5207 437 E jdmccord@northeaststate.edu
MCCORD, Kim 949-582-4665 64 H kmccord@socccd.edu
MCCORD-FITHIAN, Regina, L 812-888-5848 165 E rmccord-fithian@vinu.edu
MCCORKLE, Candy 989-463-7463 226 H mccorklecs@alma.edu
MCCORMAC, Greg 916-608-6615 50 H mccormg@flc.losrios.edu
MCCORMACK, Amy 219-473-4333 157 A amccormack@ccsj.edu
MCCORMACK, Beth 802-831-1327 476 G bmccormack@vermontlaw.edu
MCCORMACK, Elizabeth 207-725-3578 198 G emccorma@bowdoin.edu
MCCORMACK, Gary 713-942-3400 466 J mccormack@stthom.edu
MCCORMACK, Jeff 405-425-1933 377 B jeff.mccormack@oc.edu
MCCORMACK, Mike 205-726-2916 6 G hmmccorm@samford.edu
MCCORMICK, Adrienne 315-312-2285 327 D adrienne.mccormick@oswego.edu
MCCORMICK, Brad 618-985-8340 141 D bradmccormick@jalc.edu
MCCORMICK, Brad 423-697-3264 436 F brad.mccormick@chattanoogastate.edu
MCCORMICK, Brian 319-296-4050 169 H brian.mccormick@hawkeyecollege.edu
MCCORMICK, Cathleen 717-720-4070 405 G cmccormick@passhe.edu
MCCORMICK, Charlie 830-792-7345 456 D ctmccormick@schreiner.edu
MCCORMICK, David 312-567-4972 140 I dmccormick@iitri.org
MCCORMICK, Dee 330-263-2321 360 A dmccormick@wooster.edu
MCCORMICK, Gordon 831-656-2484 518 D gmccormick@navy.edu
MCCORMICK, Heidi, A 804-828-1645 487 E hamccormick@vcu.edu
MCCORMICK, Jennifer Higgins 716-827-2455 331 K mccormickj@trocaire.edu
MCCORMICK, Jill 402-872-2257 276 C jmccormick@peru.edu
MCCORMICK, Jim, S 303-963-3363 77 I jimmccormick@ccu.edu
MCCORMICK, John 406-243-2532 271 G john.mccormick@umontana.edu
MCCORMICK, Joseph 301-846-2548 203 H jmccormick@frederick.edu
MCCORMICK, Karla, S 334-844-4183 4 D ksm0010@auburn.edu
MCCORMICK, Kevin, M 630-515-6053 145 I kmccor@midwestern.edu
MCCORMICK, Kirsten, M 714-879-3901 45 I kmmccormick@hiu.edu
MCCORMICK, Lucas 785-227-3380 175 E mccormicklf@bethanylb.edu
MCCORMICK, Mark 205-247-8831 7 C mmccormick@stillman.edu
MCCORMICK, Mark 205-366-8831 7 C mmccormick@stillman.edu
MCCORMICK, Mark 732-906-2515 287 B mmccormick@middlesexcc.edu
MCCORMICK, OSU, Mary 440-943-7600 369 J mmccormick@dioceseofcleveland.org
MCCORMICK, Michael 206-221-4344 499 D mccorm50@uw.edu
MCCORMICK, Michael, R 315-386-7222 329 A mccormic@canton.edu
MCCORMICK, Patrick, T 509-313-6715 495 A mccormick@calvin.gonzaga.edu
MCCORMICK, Peter 970-247-7595 79 J mccormick_p@fortlewis.edu
MCCORMICK, CSC, Peter, M 574-631-7800 165 A mccormick.23@nd.edu
MCCORMICK, Reenie 410-334-2939 210 C rmccormick@worwic.edu
MCCORMICK, Robert 312-362-6627 137 C bmccormi@depaul.edu
MCCORMICK, Robert 734-995-7391 229 A robert.mccormick@cuaa.edu
MCCORMICK, Silas 217-732-3168 143 F smccormick@lincolnchristian.edu
MCCORMICK, Stanley 229-420-7013 114 I stanley.mccormick@asurams.edu
MCCORN, Lester, A 803-327-7402 419 G
MCCORQUODALE, Duncan, L 260-422-5561 159 D dlmccorquodale@indianatech.edu
MCCORRY, Laurie, K 617-228-2465 219 D lkmccorry@bhcc.mass.edu
MCCORRY, Margaret 908-737-0580 286 F mmccorry@kean.edu
MCCORRY, Wendy 845-688-1980 331 L mccorryw@sunyulster.edu
MCCORRY-ANDALIS, Catherine, M 915-747-5648 467 E cmandalis@utep.edu
MCCORT, Tiffany 619-574-6909 55 B thansen@pacificcollege.edu
MCCORY, Denise 216-987-2296 360 E denise.mccory@tri-c.edu
MCCOUBREY, Ashley 207-255-1320 201 F ashley.v.davis@maine.edu
MCCOULLUM, Valarie, S 215-898-5337 412 G cade@upenn.edu
MCCOURT, MaryFrances 215-898-1005 412 G mfmccourt@upenn.edu
MCCOURT, Richard 440-449-4471 373 B richard.mccourt@ursuline.edu
MCCOURT, Susan 508-678-2811 219 C susan.mccourt@bristolcc.edu
MCCOWAN, Carla 217-333-3701 154 B cmccowan@illinois.edu
MCCOWN, Amber 239-489-9226 100 E amccown@fsw.edu
MCCOWN, Shawn 714-463-7540 51 A smccown@ketchum.edu
MCCOY, Avis, M 954-201-7401 96 A amccoy@broward.edu
MCCOY, Brenda 940-565-3404 466 B brenda.mccoy@unt.edu
MCCOY, Chris 479-575-3301 21 I
MCCOY, David, M 804-289-8718 486 G dmccoy2@richmond.edu
MCCOY, Holly, M 724-738-2650 407 C holly.mccoy@sru.edu
MCCOY, JR., James, F 813-393-3675 125 H
MCCOY, John 423-236-2444 436 C jmccoy@southern.edu
MCCOY, Julie 803-938-3821 425 F jmccoy@uscsumter.edu
MCCOY, J'Neal 417-447-4817 264 K mccoyj@otc.edu
MCCOY, Kevin 785-227-3380 175 E mccoyk@bethanylb.edu
MCCOY, Marilyn 847-491-4335 148 C mmccoy@northwestern.edu
MCCOY, Mark 765-658-4220 157 H president@depauw.edu
MCCOY, Mary 409-882-3080 462 D mary.mccoy@lsco.edu
MCCOY, Matthew, J 541-383-7210 382 B mmccoy@cocc.edu
MCCOY, Mike 256-216-3300 4 C mike.mccoy@athens.edu
MCCOY, Paddy 509-527-2343 499 F paddy.mccoy@wallawalla.edu
MCCOY, Patricia 602-212-0501 11 F
MCCOY, Peggy, S 406-496-4404 272 E pmccoy@mtech.edu
MCCOY, Robert 907-474-7500 10 B rpmccoy@alaska.edu
MCCOY, Ryan 303-404-5238 79 K ryan.mccoy@frontrange.edu
MCCOY, Sue 916-484-8211 50 F mccoys@arc.losrios.edu
MCCOY, Thomas, J 940-369-8249 466 B thomas.mccoy@unt.edu
MCCOY, William, K 570-577-1609 390 H bill.mccoy@bucknell.edu
MCCOY, Zaire 407-646-2385 106 J zmccoy@rollins.edu
MCCOY-WILSON, Sonya 404-225-4672 115 J smccoy-wilson@atlantatech.edu
MCCRACKEN, Carolyn 423-354-2509 437 E cgmccracken@northeaststate.edu
MCCRACKEN, Fawn 952-446-4325 242 A mccrackenf@crown.edu
MCCRACKEN, Jeff, B 919-966-5730 351 B jeff_mccracken@unc.edu
MCCRACKEN, Jennifer, L 570-326-3761 404 T jlm16@pct.edu
MCCRACKEN, Larry 503-517-1879 388 C lmccracken@westernseminary.edu
MCCRACKEN, Mike 620-235-4624 180 J mmccracken@pittstate.edu
MCCRAE, Byron 413-559-5412 215 F bmccrae@hampshire.edu
MCCRANEY, Paige 863-680-4292 100 D pmmcreaney@flsouthern.edu
MCCRARY, Brian 678-839-6619 127 F bmccrary@westga.edu
MCCRARY, Cheryl 785-594-8327 174 J cheryl.mccrary@bakeru.edu
MCCRAW, Bethany, J 254-710-1715 444 B bethany_mccraw@baylor.edu
MCCRAW, Liz 580-745-2080 379 J lmccraw@se.edu
MCCRAW, Patti, H 864-488-4571 422 B pmccraw@limestone.edu
MCCRAY, Carrie 573-592-4317 270 D carrie.mccray@williamwoods.edu
MCCRAY, Corey, L 757-822-1184 489 H cmccray@tcc.edu
MCCRAY, Jacquelyn 870-575-8475 22 E mccrayj@uapb.edu
MCCRAY, Suzanne 479-575-4883 21 I smccray@uark.edu
MCCRAY, Tammy 218-751-8670 249 G registrar@oakhills.edu
MCCREA, Larry 816-604-6541 262 G larry.mccrea@mcckc.edu
MCCREADY, Randall 412-624-7180 412 I mccready@pitt.edu
MCCREARY, Jeff 573-518-2308 263 E jmccreary@mineralarea.edu
MCCREARY, Lynn 940-565-2378 466 B mccreary@unt.edu
MCCREARY, Micah, L 732-247-5241 287 E
MCCREARY, William 419-530-3990 372 F william.mccreary@utoledo.edu
MCCREE, Bernard, L 610-683-4032 406 D mccree@kutztown.edu
MCCREE, Robin 704-991-0252 346 I mmccree5540@stanly.edu
MCCREERY, Deborah, M 610-921-7501 388 E dmccreery@albright.edu
MCCREERY, Shane 785-864-6414 181 I msmccreery@ku.edu

MCCRICKARD, Matthew . 256-352-8047.... 3 I matthew.mccrickard@wallacestate.edu
MCCRILLIS, Neal, R .... 312-413-1468 153 H nealrm@uic.edu
MCCROHAN, Betty, A .... 979-532-6304 471 A bettym@wcjc.edu
MCCRORY, Cynthia .... 704-922-6406 343 D mccrory.cynthia@gaston.edu
MCCRORY, Heidi, H ...... 740-427-5154 364 A mccroryh@kenyon.edu
MCCRORY, Robert, L ..... 585-275-4973 332 E rmcc@lle.rochester.edu
MCCROSKEY, Lorie, L ... 336-633-1118 345 F llmccroskey@randolph.edu
MCCROW, Rich .... 661-720-2002.. 47 A rmccrow@bakersfieldcollege.edu
MCCROW, Rich .... 661-395-4011.. 47 A
MCCROY-HEINS, Michelle .... 201-692-2190 286 B michelle_mccroy@fdu.edu
MCCUBBIN, Jeff .... 970-491-5841.. 78 N jeff.mccubbin@colostate.edu
MCCUBBIN, Todd, A ..... 573-882-6017 268 C mccubbint@missouri.edu
MCCUDDEN, Suzanne ... 253-833-9111 495 C smccudden@greenriver.edu
MCCUE, Cindy .... 631-420-2319 329 D cynthia.mccue@farmingdale.edu
MCCUEN, Jan .... 714-997-6862.. 36 G mccuen@chapman.edu
MCCUIEN-SMITH, Cassandra .... 501-450-3173.. 23 I cmccuien@uca.edu
MCCULLA, Justin .... 937-328-7819 359 H mccullaj@clarkstate.edu
MCCULLAH, Anne .... 773-244-4589 147 F amccullah@northpark.edu
MCCULLAR, Bryan, L ..... 785-833-4339 179 C bryan.mccullar@kwu.edu
MCCULLEN, Ann, S .... 904-620-2100 110 E amccullen@unf.edu
MCCULLEY, Becky .... 214-645-5482 469 E becky.mcculley@utsouthwestern.edu
MCCULLOCH, Greg .... 618-252-5400 151 J greg.mcculloch@sic.edu
MCCULLOCH, Joseph .... 318-813-9201 194 D jmccul@lsuhsc.edu
MCCULLOCH, Sonja ...... 912-260-4402 125 F sonja.mcculloch@sgsc.edu
MCCULLOH, Edna .... 330-490-7191 373 F emcculloh@walsh.edu
MCCULLOH, Julie, A ..... 509-313-6572 495 A mccullohj@gonzaga.edu
MCCULLOH, Thayne, M 509-313-6102 495 A president@gonzaga.edu
MCCULLOUGH, Bryan ... 336-249-4688 342 F bryan_mccullough@davidsonccc.edu
MCCULLOUGH, Catherine .... 802-728-1247 477 E crm07160@vtc.vsc.edu
MCCULLOUGH, Desiree, A .... 731-881-7014 440 B dmcull1@utm.edu
MCCULLOUGH, Doreen . 802-776-5232 474 H dmccullough@csj.edu
MCCULLOUGH, James .. 918-293-5068 378 B james.mccullough@okstate.edu
MCCULLOUGH, Jonathan, W .... 903-434-8115 453 M jmccullough@ntcc.edu
MCCULLOUGH, Laura .... 912-478-5234 120 E lmccullough@georgiasouthern.edu
MCCULLOUGH, Laura .... 304-205-6611 502 K laura.mccullough@bridgevalley.edu
MCCULLOUGH, Laurie ... 304-243-4398 505 H lmccullough@wju.edu
MCCULLOUGH, Lois, N . 419-783-2317 361 A lmccullough@defiance.edu
MCCULLOUGH, Randy ... 419-559-2355 370 J rmccullough01@terra.edu
MCCULLOUGH, Robert, R .... 216-368-5445 358 C robert.mccullough@case.edu
MCCULLOUGH, Willie ... 606-326-2068 185 E willie.mccullough@kctcs.edu
MCCULLY, Clare .... 617-730-7089 223 B clare.mccully@newbury.edu
MCCUNE, Kate .... 562-947-8755.. 65 D katemccune@scuhs.edu
MCCUNE, L.B .... 810-762-9629 232 C lbmccune@kettering.edu
MCCUNE, Ryan .... 620-252-7046 176 K mccune.ryan@coffeyville.edu
MCCURDY, Clantha .... 617-391-6098 216 F cmccurdy@osfa.mass.edu
MCCURDY, Debra, L ..... 419-995-8200 363 G mccurdy.d@rhodesstate.edu
MCCURDY, Eugene, M .. 608-796-3921 512 R emmccurdy@viterbo.edu
MCCURDY, Robert .... 517-353-0722 233 G rmccurd@msu.edu
MCCURDY, Solynn .... 206-296-6116 498 D mccurdys@seattleu.edu
MCCURREN, Cynthia ..... 616-331-3558 230 G mccurrec@gvsu.edu
MCCURRY, David .... 864-503-5509 425 H dmccurry@uscupstate.edu
MCCURRY, Faith .... 803-535-1230 423 B mccurryf@octech.edu
MCCURRY, Kyle .... 828-298-3325 353 B kmccurry@warren-wilson.edu
MCCURRY, Ricky, N ...... 865-974-4531 439 H rmccurry@tennessee.edu
MCCURTY, Kenyetta .... 334-387-3877.... 4 B kenyettamccurty@amridgeuniversity.edu
MCCUTCHAN, Molly, M 734-384-4245 234 C mmccutchan@monroeccc.edu
MCCUTCHEN, Michael ... 731-989-6901 432 C mmccutchen@fhu.edu
MCCUTCHEON, Andy ..... 661-362-3387.. 39 C andy.mccutcheon@canyons.edu
MCCUTCHEON, Bruce, E .... 610-330-5530 399 B mccutchb@lafayette.edu
MCCUTCHEON, John ..... 805-893-8320.. 70 B jmccutch@athletics.ucsb.edu
MCDADE, Kate .... 216-987-4710 360 E kate.mcdade@tri-c.edu
MCDADE, Linda .... 570-348-6249 401 B lmcdade@marywood.edu
MCDADE, Lucinda .... 909-625-8767.. 37 L lucinda.mcdade@cgu.edu
MCDADE-CLAY, W. Thomas .... 585-340-9648 304 F tmcdadeclay@crcds.edu
MCDAID, James .... 617-879-7960 218 B jmcdaid@massart.edu
MCDANIEL, Anna, M ..... 352-273-6324 110 D annammcdaniel@ufl.edu
MCDANIEL, Antonio, L .. 919-530-7639 350 D antonio.mcdaniel@nccu.edu
MCDANIEL, Cleve .... 575-835-5606 294 K cleve.mcdaniel@nmt.edu
MCDANIEL, Cliff .... 817-461-8741 442 L cmcdaniel@abu.edu
MCDANIEL, Diane .... 765-677-2436 161 C diane.mcdaniel@indwes.edu
MCDANIEL, Donna .... 903-823-3220 458 D donna.mcdaniel@texarkanacollege.edu
MCDANIEL, Dustin .... 706-355-5009 115 H dmcdaniel@athenstech.edu
MCDANIEL, Gary, R ...... 949-214-3055.. 40 I gary.mcdaniel@cui.edu
MCDANIEL, Joy .... 580-387-7000 376 D jmcdaniel@mscok.edu
MCDANIEL, Juley .... 620-223-2700 177 E juleym@fortscott.edu
MCDANIEL, Kimberly .... 916-691-7487.. 50 G mcdanik@crc.losrios.edu
MCDANIEL, Kristina, D . 573-840-9695 267 J kristinamcdaniel@trcc.edu
MCDANIEL, Lance .... 304-384-5258 503 P mcdaniell26@mycu.concord.edu
MCDANIEL, Laura .... 701-231-8330 354 D laura.mcdaniel@ndsu.edu
MCDANIEL, Lisa .... 662-329-7377 254 F mcmcdaniel@muw.edu
MCDANIEL, Lucinda ...... 870-933-7906.. 17 L lmcdaniel@asusystem.edu
MCDANIEL, Mary .... 620-341-5223 177 B mmcdanie@emporia.edu
MCDANIEL, Mary, W ..... 864-388-8242 422 A mmcdaniel@lander.edu
MCDANIEL, Michael ...... 517-371-5140 239 F mcdanielm@cooley.edu
MCDANIEL, Mick, R ...... 607-844-8222 331 D mcdanim@tompkinscortland.edu
MCDANIEL, Rose .... 336-249-8186 342 F rose_mcdaniel@davidsonccc.edu
MCDANIEL, Sonya .... 770-962-7580 121 G smcdaniel@gwinnetttech.edu
MCDANIEL, Stephen ...... 484-365-7441 400 E smcdaniel@lincoln.edu
MCDANIEL, Wendy .... 479-394-7622.. 23 D wmcdaniel@uarichmountain.edu
MCDANIEL-SMITH, Nicole, L .... 302-356-6928.. 91 B nicole.l.mcdaniel-smith@wilmu.edu
MCDANIELS, Lisa .... 814-641-3458 398 B mcdanil@juniata.edu
MCDANIELS, Rob .... 573-882-4370 268 C mcdanielsr@missouri.edu
MCDANIELS WILSON, Cathy .... 614-236-6114 358 A cmcdanielswilson@capital.edu
MCDAVID, Courtney ...... 860-832-3003.. 84 J mcdavidc@ccsu.edu
MCDERMID, Brooke .... 541-245-7728 386 G bmcdermid@roguecc.edu
MCDERMOTT, A. Keith .. 617-541-2454 221 A kmcderm@rcc.mass.edu
MCDERMOTT, Anastacia, M .... 563-588-7056 171 H anastacia.mcdermott@loras.edu
MCDERMOTT, Ann, B .... 508-793-2443 213 D amcdermo@holycross.edu
MCDERMOTT, Anne .... 401-341-2140 417 D anne.mcdermott@salve.edu
MCDERMOTT, Beth .... 617-552-4400 212 E beth.mcdermott@bc.edu
MCDERMOTT, Brian .... 907-564-8248.... 9 F bmcdermott@alaskapacific.edu
MCDERMOTT, Brian .... 308-398-7387 273 G bmcdermott@cccneb.edu
MCDERMOTT, Christine . 315-568-3105 317 A cmcdermott@nycc.edu
MCDERMOTT, Christine . 302-736-2505.. 90 J christine.mcdermott@wesley.edu
MCDERMOTT, Colleen ... 816-531-5223 258 H cmcdermott@concorde.edu
MCDERMOTT, Colleen ... 920-424-1217 511 B mcdermot@uwosh.edu
MCDERMOTT, Daniel ..... 216-987-5339 360 E daniel.mcdermott@tri-c.edu
MCDERMOTT, David .... 617-287-7128 216 G dmcdermott@umassp.edu
MCDERMOTT, Dennis .... 718-489-5362 322 D dmcdermott@sfc.edu
MCDERMOTT, Emily .... 617-287-5600 216 I emily.mcdermott@umb.edu
MCDERMOTT, Erin .... 773-702-7684 153 F erinmcd@uchicago.edu
MCDERMOTT, Harry .... 520-621-7428.. 16 J mcdermot@email.arizona.edu
MCDERMOTT, John, R .. 563-588-7132 171 H john.mcdermott@loras.edu
MCDERMOTT, Marty .... 231-777-0462 234 G marty.mcdermott@muskegoncc.edu
MCDERMOTT, Patrice .... 410-455-3150 208 A mcdermot@umbc.edu
MCDERMOTT, Patricia, L .... 757-594-7222 479 H mcdermot@cnu.edu
MCDERMOTT, Patrick .... 941-377-4880 103 K pmcdermott@meridian.edu
MCDERMOTT, Randi ...... 208-426-1493 131 C randimcdermott@boisestate.edu
MCDERMOTT, Richard, L .... 713-500-4963 468 D richard.l.mcdermott@uth.tmc.edu
MCDERMOTT, Robert ..... 415-575-6135.. 29 H rmcdermott@ciis.edu
MCDERMOTT, Teresa ..... 360-475-7480 496 F tmcdermott@olympic.edu
MCDERMOTT, Virginia, M .... 336-841-9384 338 E vmcdermo@highpoint.edu
MCDERMOTT, Walter, M .... 434-223-6112 481 D wmcdermott@hsc.edu
MCDEVITT, Jenna .... 740-587-6655 361 B mcdevitts@denison.edu
MCDEVITT, Michelle ...... 419-517-8953 364 G mmcdevitt@lourdes.edu
MCDEVITT, Richard, K ... 704-406-2361 337 H rmcdevitt@gardner-webb.edu
MCDILL, Sandy .... 602-787-7352.. 13 J sandy.mcdill@paradisevalley.edu
MCDONAGH, David, L ... 646-888-6639 313 I mcdonagd@sloankettering.edu
MCDONALD, Amos .... 832-813-6621 452 C amos.mcdonald@lonestar.edu
MCDONALD, Amy, L ...... 561-868-3532 105 A mcdonala@palmbeachstate.edu
MCDONALD, Aneisa, L . 865-694-6403 437 F almcdonald@pstcc.edu
MCDONALD, Ann, M ..... 978-632-6600 220 D a_mcdonald@mwcc.mass.edu
MCDONALD, Barbara .... 763-424-0820 246 E bmcdonald@nhcc.edu
MCDONALD, Brian .... 319-363-1323 172 B bmcdonald@mtmercy.edu
MCDONALD, Christopher .... 949-451-5679.. 64 I cmcdonald@ivc.edu
MCDONALD, Christy ..... 865-981-8402 433 F christy.mcdonald@maryvillecollege.edu
MCDONALD, Clay .... 636-227-2100 262 A
MCDONALD, Dana .... 301-846-2458 203 H dmcdonald@frederick.edu
MCDONALD, Danielle .... 813-974-6677 111 A dmcdonald@usf.edu
MCDONALD, David .... 505-984-6082 295 K gi@sjc.edu
MCDONALD, David .... 503-838-8211 388 B mcdonald@wou.edu
MCDONALD, Debbie ..... 626-966-4576.. 25 M info@agu.edu
MCDONALD, Deborah ... 845-938-5706 519 D admissions@usma.edu
MCDONALD, Dennis ..... 518-454-5126 305 B mcdonald@strose.edu
MCDONALD, Dennis ..... 417-865-2815 260 B mcdonaldd@evangel.edu
MCDONALD, Dotty .... 337-550-1357 194 B dmcdonal@lsue.edu
MCDONALD, Eric .... 864-587-4200 424 D mcdonalde@smcsc.edu
MCDONALD, Francis, X 508-830-5001 218 D fmcdonald@maritime.edu
MCDONALD, Frank .... 212-346-1800 319 J fmcdonald@pace.edu
MCDONALD, Gary .... 415-422-2699.. 72 A mcdonald@usfca.edu
MCDONALD, James ...... 205-665-6015.... 8 E jmcdonald@montevallo.edu
MCDONALD, James ...... 612-374-5800 242 C jmcdonald@dunwoody.edu
MCDONALD, James, L .. 415-451-2810.. 60 I jmcdonald@sfts.edu
MCDONALD, James, R .. 321-682-4401 113 F jmcdonald4@valenciacollege.edu
MCDONALD, Jan .... 864-977-7151 422 I jan.mcdonald@ngu.edu
MCDONALD, Jason, S .. 503-943-7147 387 H mcdonaja@up.edu
MCDONALD, Jennifer .... 714-241-6163.. 38 F jmcdonald@coastline.edu
MCDONALD, Jestinah ... 740-753-7010 362 K mcdonaldj21@hocking.edu
MCDONALD, Joseph ..... 239-590-1102 109 C jmcdonald@fgcu.edu
MCDONALD, Joseph ..... 256-761-6443.... 7 D jmcdonald@talladega.edu
MCDONALD, Kevin .... 573-882-2011 268 C mcdonaldkg@umsystem.edu
MCDONALD, Kevin, G ... 573-882-2011 268 B mcdonaldkg@umsystem.edu
MCDONALD, Kimberly .. 201-219-9901 285 F kimberly.mcdonald@eicollege.edu
MCDONALD, Kurt .... 417-690-3200 258 E purch@cofo.edu
MCDONALD, Latrice ...... 601-928-6206 254 D latrice.mcdonald@mgccc.edu
MCDONALD, Leander .... 701-255-3285 355 I president@uttc.edu
MCDONALD, Loretta ...... 314-340-3300 260 H mcdonaldl@hssu.edu
MCDONALD, Lori .... 949-214-3074.. 40 I lori.mcdonald@cui.edu
MCDONALD, Lori .... 801-581-7066 472 P lmcdonald@sa.utah.edu
MCDONALD, Martha ...... 626-914-8534.. 37 G mmcdonald@citruscollege.edu
MCDONALD, Mary .... 251-380-2290.... 7 B mmcdonald@shc.edu
MCDONALD, MarySheila, A .... 215-951-1059 398 F mcdonaldms@lasalle.edu
MCDONALD, Michael ..... 567-661-7203 369 A michael_mcdonald6@owens.edu
MCDONALD, Michael, A .... 269-337-7162 231 F michael.mcdonald@kzoo.edu
MCDONALD, Michelle ... 609-626-3529 291 H michelle.mcdonald@stockton.edu
MCDONALD, Nicholas ... 978-837-3597 221 G mcdonaldn@merrimack.edu
MCDONALD, Paul, R ..... 626-966-4576.. 25 M paulmcdonald@agu.edu
MCDONALD, Pete .... 706-295-6928 120 C pmcdonald@gntc.edu
MCDONALD, Peter .... 559-278-2403.. 32 A pmcdonald@csufresno.edu
MCDONALD, Robert .... 617-732-1605 214 F mcdonaldr@emmanuel.edu
MCDONALD, Ryan .... 508-541-1664 214 C rmcdonald@dean.edu
MCDONALD, Ryan .... 812-535-5263 163 I rmcdonald@smwc.edu
MCDONALD, Sharon ..... 309-268-8143 139 D sharon.mcdonald@heartland.edu
MCDONALD, Steven ...... 401-277-4955 417 B smcdonal@risd.edu
MCDONALD, Tammy ..... 361-698-1133 448 H tmcdonal1@delmar.edu
MCDONALD, Thomas ..... 212-752-1530 312 G thomas.mcdonald@limcollege.edu
MCDONALD, Tim .... 770-533-6991 122 E tmcdonal@laniertech.edu

MCDONALD, Todd .... 217-786-2253 144 B todd.mcdonald@llcc.edu
MCDONALD, Tracie .... 406-275-4978 273 A tracie_mcdonald@skc.edu
MCDONALD, William .... 315-866-0300 310 A mcdonalwh@herkimer.edu
MCDONALD, William .... 617-322-3500 216 B
MCDONALD, William, A 973-748-9000 284 A bill_mcdonald@bloomfield.edu
MCDONALD, William, M .... 706-542-7774 127 A bmcdonal@uga.edu
MCDONALD-RASH, Jean .... 848-932-7057 290 A jrash@rci.rutgers.edu
MCDONALD-RASH, Jean .... 848-932-7057 290 C jean.rash@ofa.rutgers.edu
MCDONELL, Clint .... 313-883-3112 236 D mcdonell.clint@shms.edu
MCDONNELL, Brian, A .. 401-341-2185 417 D mcdonneb@salve.edu
MCDONNELL, John .... 773-481-8253 136 B jmcdonnell@ccc.edu
MCDONNELL, Ryan .... 314-529-9362 262 B rmcdonnell@maryville.edu
MCDONNELL, Tom .... 531-622-2716 275 F tjmcdonnell3@mccneb.edu
MCDONOUGH, Ann .... 702-774-4619 279 D ann.mcdonough@unlv.edu
MCDONOUGH, David .... 207-786-6231 198 E dmcdonou@bates.edu
MCDONOUGH, Eileen .... 305-899-3085.. 95 G emcdonough@barry.edu
MCDONOUGH, Ellin ...... 803-323-2141 426 H mcdonoughe@winthrop.edu
MCDONOUGH, Erin .... 503-838-9120 388 B mcdonough@wou.edu
MCDONOUGH, Michael 908-526-1200 289 D michael.mcdonough@raritanval.edu
MCDONOUGH, JR., Peter, J .... 848-932-7741 290 A mcdonough@oldqueens.rutgers.edu
MCDONOUGH, Thomas 401-254-3797 417 C tmcdonough@rwu.edu
MCDORMAN, Heather ... 636-922-8277 265 J hmcdorman@stchas.edu
MCDORMAN, Todd, F ... 765-361-6183 166 B mcdormat@wabash.edu
MCDOUGAL, Bradley, N 540-464-7637 490 E mcdougalbn@vmi.edu
MCDOUGAL, Tammy ..... 731-426-7526 432 J tmcdougal@lanecollege.edu
MCDOUGALD, Bryan, L 803-981-7063 426 J bcmdougald@yorktech.edu
MCDOUGALD, Sherlock 252-823-5166 343 A mcdougalds@edgecombe.edu
MCDOUGLE, James .... 304-205-6710 502 K james.mcdougle@bridgevalley.edu
MCDOWALL, Douglass .. 785-460-5484 176 L doug.mcdowall@colbycc.edu
MCDOWALL, Melissa .... 701-355-8181 355 K mpmcdowall@umary.edu
MCDOWALL LONG, Kimberly .... 316-942-4291 180 D longk@newmanu.edu
MCDOWELL, Amy .... 802-763-7170 476 G amcdowell@vermontlaw.edu
MCDOWELL, Bill .... 405-703-8232 376 C bmcdowell@macu.edu
MCDOWELL, Denise ...... 507-457-5300 248 C dmcdowell@winona.edu
MCDOWELL, Jackie .... 706-236-2202 116 D jmcdowell@berry.edu
MCDOWELL, James .... 860-512-3603.. 85 G jmcdowell@manchestercc.edu
MCDOWELL, Jennifer .... 972-883-6301 467 D jpazik@utdallas.edu
MCDOWELL, Jill .... 203-285-2007.. 85 E jmcdowell@gwcc.commnet.edu
MCDOWELL, Katie .... 913-360-7578 175 D kmcdowell@benedictine.edu
MCDOWELL, N. Renee .. 724-653-2212 394 B rmcdowell@dec.edu
MCDOWELL, Nicole .... 775-673-7000 279 C
MCDOWELL, Pamela ..... 507-786-3011 250 C mcdowell@stolaf.edu
MCDOWELL, Ronald ...... 903-593-8311 461 B rmcdowell@texascollege.edu
MCDOWELL, Scott .... 615-966-5690 433 D scott.mcdowell@lipscomb.edu
MCDOWELL, JR., T, J ... 402-465-2149 276 E tmcdowe2@nebrwesleyan.edu
MCDOWELL, Travis, W .. 864-488-4615 422 B tmcdowell@limestone.edu
MCDOWELL, Whitney .... 601-977-7821 256 B wmcdowell@tougaloo.edu
MCDOWN, Linda .... 405-422-1203 379 B mcdownl@redlandscc.edu
MCDUGLE, Darin .... 918-587-6789 380 I
MCEACHERN, Daniel (JJ) .... 704-330-6395 342 A jj.mceachern@cpcc.edu
MCEACHERN, Patrick ..... 509-533-8240 493 H patrick.mceachern@ccs.spokane.edu
MCEACHERN, Patrick ..... 509-533-8240 494 A patrick.mceachern@ccs.spokane.edu
MCELANEY-JOHNSON, Ann .... 310-954-4011.. 52 H amcelaney@msmu.edu
MCELHANEY, Patrick ..... 706-233-7225 125 E pmcelhaney@shorter.edu
MCELHANY, Ryan .... 972-825-4701 457 F rmcelhany@sagu.edu
MCELHENY, Candi .... 225-768-1725 191 G candi.mcelheny@ololcollege.edu
MCELHOE, Dennis .... 704-922-6476 343 D mcelhoe.dennis@gaston.edu
MCELMORE, Kareem ...... 903-927-3252 471 B kmclemore@wileyc.edu
MCELMURRY, Chauvette .... 314-340-3600 260 H mcelmurc@hssu.edu
MCELMURRY, Mark .... 314-434-4044 259 B mark.mcelmurry@covenantseminary.edu
MCELRATH, Ann .... 423-614-8105 432 L amcelrath@leeuniversity.edu
MCELRATH, William ...... 732-571-3488 287 C wmcelrat@monmouth.edu
MCELROY, Clint .... 704-330-6339 342 A clint.mcelroy@cpcc.edu
MCELROY, Coleetta .... 408-924-6086.. 34 D coleetta.mcelroy@sjsu.edu
MCELROY, Doug .... 270-745-7009 190 F doug.mcelroy@wku.edu
MCELROY, Edith .... 704-330-4386 342 A edith.mcelroy@cpcc.edu
MCELROY, Emily, J .... 402-559-7078 277 H emily.mcelroy@unmc.edu
MCELROY, Joe .... 714-966-8500.. 73 D info@ves.edu
MCELROY, Kathleen ...... 914-633-2201 311 B kmcelroy@iona.edu
MCELROY, Kevin .... 650-949-6202.. 43 D mcelroykevin@fhda.edu
MCELROY, Lee .... 518-276-6685 321 A mcelrl@rpi.edu
MCELROY, Tim .... 918-444-5000 376 G mcelroyt@nsuok.edu
MCELVEEN, John .... 706-507-5341 118 C mcelveen_john@columbusstate.edu
MCELWAIN, Brandon .... 573-897-5000 267 F
MCELWAIN, Karen .... 708-344-4700 144 A kmcelwain@lincolntech.edu
MCELWEE, Kay, E .... 217-581-5313 138 A kemcelwee@eiu.edu
MCENEANY, Barbara ...... 845-848-4031 306 G barbara.mceneany@dc.edu
MCENEANY, Mary .... 413-559-5528 215 F memtr@hampshire.edu
MCENTEE, Mary .... 413-775-1203 219 F mcenteem@gcc.mass.edu
MCENTERGART, Rory ..... 302-793-1101.. 90 H
MCENTIRE, David .... 801-863-7810 473 D david.mcentire@uvu.edu
MCENTIRE, Tina, M .... 704-687-7019 351 C tmmcenti@uncc.edu
MCEUEN, Brent .... 928-428-8201.. 12 I brent.mceuen@eac.edu
MCEVOY, Ed, M .... 610-526-1286 389 B ed.mcevoy@theamericancollege.edu
MCEWAN, Anna .... 334-833-4236..... 5 M provost@hawks.huntingdon.edu
MCEWEN, Beryl .... 336-334-7632 350 C mcewenb@ncat.edu
MCEWEN, Ellen .... 413-265-2395 213 E mcewene@elms.edu
MCEWEN, Jill .... 920-996-2847 513 F mcewen@fvtc.edu
MCEWEN, Ruth .... 305-348-3264 109 D ruthann.mcewen@fiu.edu
MCFADDEN, Calvin .... 203-857-7332.. 86 D cmcfadden@norwalk.edu
MCFADDEN, David, F .... 260-982-5050 162 Q dfmcfadden@manchester.edu
MCFADDEN, Holly .... 954-492-5353.. 96 J hmcfadden@citycollege.edu
MCFADDEN, John .... 305-899-3208.. 95 G jmcfadden@barry.edu
MCFADDEN, Judy .... 970-521-6660.. 81 F judy.mcfadden@njc.edu
MCFADDEN, Lisa .... 978-542-7554 218 E lisa.mcfadden@salemstate.edu
MCFADDEN, Margaret, T .... 207-859-4770 198 H margaret.mcfadden@colby.edu
MCFADDEN, Mary .... 845-848-7809 306 G mary.mcfadden@dc.edu
MCFADDEN, Mary Kay .. 208-885-6155 132 I marykaymcfadden@uidaho.edu
MCFADDEN, Michael ..... 202-806-1280.. 92 C michael.mcfadden@howard.edu
MCFADDEN, Pam .... 817-735-2581 466 D pam.mcfadden@unthsc.edu
MCFADDEN, Paul .... 870-236-6901.. 19 D pmcfadden@crc.edu
MCFADDEN, Scott .... 509-527-2205 499 F scott.mcfadden@wallawalla.edu
MCFADDEN, Susan .... 215-955-2867 411 E susan.mcfadden@jefferson.edu
MCFADDEN, Tanya .... 517-483-1452 232 K mcfaddet@lcc.edu
MCFADDEN, Tanya .... 810-762-0200 234 F tanya.mcfadden@mcc.edu
MCFADDEN, Thomas ...... 540-636-2900 479 G tmcfadden@christendom.edu
MCFADDEN, Toney, C .... 423-624-0077 430 I tonym@chattanoogacollege.edu
MCFADDIN, David .... 859-622-6220 184 F david.mcfaddin@eku.edu
MCFALL, Jan .... 763-488-0250 246 E jmcfall@nhcc.edu
MCFALLS-SMITH, Tiffany .... 270-706-8419 185 H tmcfalls0001@kctcs.edu
MCFARLAND, F. Ozzie .. 252-398-6484 336 K mcfarf@chowan.edu
MCFARLAND, James ...... 443-412-2247 204 C jmcfarland@harford.edu
MCFARLAND, James ...... 412-731-1177 409 A rptrustees@aol.com
MCFARLAND, Michael, S .... 570-389-4050 405 E mcfarland@bloomu.edu
MCFARLAND, Mike .... 919-962-2011 351 B mike_mcfarland@unc.edu
MCFARLAND, Reoungeneria .... 901-435-1213 433 A reo_mcfarland@loc.edu
MCFARLAND, Ronald ...... 661-362-3408.. 39 C ronald.mcfarland@canyons.edu
MCFARLAND, Stacy .... 304-876-5526 504 D smcfarla@shepherd.edu
MCFARLAND, Steven ...... 630-844-5496 133 H smcfarla@aurora.edu
MCFARLAND, Steven, W .... 518-327-6436 320 A smcfarland@paulsmiths.edu
MCFARLAND, Tracy .... 315-279-5215 312 D tmcfarl@keuka.edu
MCFARLANE, Alison .... 801-957-4103 474 B alison.mcfarlane@lscc.edu
MCFARLANE, Allen, M .. 212-998-4345 318 D allen.mcfarlane@nyu.edu
MCFARLANE, Michele ... 208-732-6304 131 I mmcfarlane@csi.edu
MCFARLIN, Dean, B ...... 412-396-2554 394 D mcfarlind@duq.edu
MCFARLIN, Diane, H ..... 352-392-0466 110 D dmcfarlin@ufl.edu
MCFARLIN, Leslie .... 706-754-8128 123 G lmcfarlin@northgatech.edu
MCFARLING, Patricia, G .... 270-852-3257 187 F patmc@kwc.edu
MCFATRIDGE, Michael .. 310-954-4084.. 52 H mmcfatridge@msmu.edu
MCFAYDEN, Andy .... 316-677-9400 182 E amcfayden@watc.edu
MCFAYDEN, Kenneth, J 804-355-0671 486 A kmcfayden@upsem.edu
MCFAYDEN, Rick .... 712-325-3371 170 K rmcfayden@iwcc.edu
MCFEE, Brenda .... 828-766-1330 344 F bmcfee@mayland.edu
MCFEELY, Gareth .... 617-353-5403 212 G garethmc@bu.edu
MCFETRIDGE-DURDLE, Judith .... 850-644-3296 110 A jdurdle@nursing.fsu.edu
MCFRAZIER, Michael, L 936-261-2111 458 F mlmcfrazier@pvamu.edu
MCFRAZIER, Michael, L 936-261-3311 458 F mlmcfrazier@pvamu.edu
MCFRY, Kevin .... 256-782-5002.... 6 B kmcfry@jsu.edu
MCGADNEY, C. Andrew 207-859-4114 198 H andy.mcgadney@colby.edu
MCGAHA, SR., Gary, A . 404-756-4440 115 I gmcgaha@atlm.edu
MCGAHEE, Thayer .... 803-641-2823 425 A thayerm@usca.edu
MCGAHERAN, Amy .... 315-268-3788 304 B amcgaher@clarkson.edu
MCGALLIARD, Anna .... 207-509-7250 200 I amcgalliard@unity.edu
MCGALLIARD, Donna .... 336-758-5000 353 A
MCGANN, Robert P, H .. 603-862-2880 282 F robert.mcgann@unh.edu
MCGAREY, Donald .... 470-578-6668 122 C dmcgarey@kennesaw.edu
MCGAREY, Tracy .... 316-942-4291 180 D mcgareyt@newmanu.edu
MCGARITY, William, G .. 706-542-9037 127 A gmcgarity@sports.uga.edu
MCGARRITY, DeShawn .. 518-631-2262 323 L mcgarrdn@sunysccc.edu
MCGARRITY, Maureen ... 215-637-7700 397 G mmcgarrity@holyfamily.edu
MCGARRY, Eileen, M .... 520-621-6734.. 16 J emcgarry@email.arizona.edu
MCGARRY, Robert .... 815-825-9811 142 F robert.mcgarry@kishwaukeecollege.edu
MCGARRY, Timothy .... 516-876-3303 327 C mcgarryt@oldwestbury.edu
MCGARVEY, Betty, S ..... 901-572-2585 430 C bettysue.mcgarvey@bchs.edu
MCGARVEY, Suzi .... 660-263-4100 264 C suzim@macc.edu
MCGARVEY, Vicki Lewis .... 215-204-5665 411 B vicki.mcgarvey@temple.edu
MCGAUGH, Becky, E ..... 928-523-6415.. 14 K becky.mcgaugh@nau.edu
MCGAUGHEY, Jodie .... 325-670-1499 450 A jodie.mcgaughey@hsutx.edu
MCGAW, Darin .... 207-454-1073 200 D dmcgaw@wccc.me.edu
MCGEE, Angel .... 337-550-1202 194 B amcgee@lsue.edu
MCGEE, Brian .... 843-953-1436 420 C mcgeeb@cofc.edu
MCGEE, Brian .... 843-953-5527 420 C mcgeeb@cofc.edu
MCGEE, Byron .... 318-487-7018 191 J byron.mcgee@lacollege.edu
MCGEE, Darryl .... 731-425-2550 432 J dmcgee@lanecollege.edu
MCGEE, Deborah .... 217-875-7211 149 J dmcgee@richland.edu
MCGEE, E. Ann .... 407-708-2009 107 G mcgeea@seminolestate.edu
MCGEE, Ed .... 434-832-7742 487 H mcgeee@cvcc.vccs.edu
MCGEE, Isaiah, R .... 803-535-5679 419 E imcgee@claflin.edu
MCGEE, James .... 708-534-4900 138 H jmcgee@govst.edu
MCGEE, Janice .... 205-929-6313.... 2 G jmcgee@lawsonstate.edu
MCGEE, John .... 770-426-2805 122 F john.mcgee@life.edu
MCGEE, Jon .... 320-363-5287 250 A jmcgee@csbsju.edu
MCGEE, Jon, D .... 320-363-5287 241 I jmcgee@csbsju.edu
MCGEE, Keli, H .... 907-450-8200.... 9 I khmcgee@alaska.edu
MCGEE, Laura .... 847-925-6686 139 B lmcgee@harpercollege.edu
MCGEE, Lynn .... 843-208-8240 425 B lmcgee@uscb.edu
MCGEE, Marc .... 707-654-1331.. 32 E mmcgee@csum.edu
MCGEE, Marjorie .... 352-854-2322.. 97 C mcgeem@cf.edu
MCGEE, Mary .... 610-921-7643 388 E mmcgee@albright.edu
MCGEE, Michael .... 828-328-7126 339 C michael.mcgee@lr.edu
MCGEE, Robby .... 910-362-7191 341 E rmcgee@cfcc.edu
MCGEE, Shawn .... 229-430-4609 114 I shawn.mcgee@asurams.edu
MCGEE, Steve, G .... 817-257-7930 461 A s.mcgee@tcu.edu
MCGEE, Steve, R .... 512-245-2533 463 A srm18@txstate.edu
MCGEE, Tammy, L .... 320-308-2286 247 E tlmcgee@stcloudstate.edu
MCGEE, Thomas, W ...... 314-837-6777 266 A
MCGEE-YUROF, Carrie .. 203-857-7040.. 86 D cmcgee-yurof@norwalk.edu
MCGEEHAN, Catherine .. 610-499-4396 414 F cmcgeehan@widener.edu
MCGEEHON, Carol .... 541-440-4600 387 E carol.mcgeehon@umpqua.edu

MCGEHEE, JR., Robert, E .... 501-686-5454 22 C rem@uams.edu

MCGHEE, Darrel .... 423-585-2634 438 D darrel.mcghee@ws.edu

MCGHEE, Debbie .... 206-616-0364 499 D demcghee@uw.edu

MCGHEE, JR., James, D .... 804-752-3736 484 C jamesmcghee@rmc.edu

MCGHEE, Lisa .... 870-762-3174 17 K lmchgee@smail.anc.edu

MCGHEE, Lynold, K .... 717-736-4201 396 G lkmcghee@hacc.edu

MCGHEE, Marianne, S .. 804-523-5810 488 C mmcghee@reynolds.edu

MCGHEE, Mark .... 256-215-4300 1 G mmcghee1@cacc.edu

MCGHEE, Megan .... 615-248-1627 439 B mmcghee@trevecca.edu

MCGHEE, Sandra, W .... 540-375-2287 484 H mcghee@roanoke.edu

MCGHEE, Stephanie .... 417-667-8181 259 A smcghee@cottey.edu

MCGHEE, Tony .... 276-964-7648 489 F tony.mcghee@sw.edu

MCGILL, Bret .... 256-306-2716 1 F bret.mcgill@calhoun.edu

MCGILL, Bret .... 256-306-2861 1 F bret.mcgill@calhoun.edu

MCGILL, Diana .... 859-572-5860 188 E mcgill@nku.edu

MCGILL, Jason, T .... 402-280-5750 274 D jasonmcgill@creighton.edu

MCGILL, Jim .... 573-651-2513 266 M jmcgill@semo.edu

MCGILL, Kimberly .... 419-517-8894 364 G mmcgill@lourdes.edu

MCGILL, Shawna .... 575-769-4954 293 M shawna.mcgill@clovis.edu

MCGILL, Shelia, R .... 405-466-3283 375 L srmcgill@langston.edu

MCGILL, Tracy .... 318-678-6000 192 C tmcgill@bpcc.edu

MCGILLIS, Bill .... 619-260-2982 71 J wmcgillis@sandiego.edu

MCGILLOWAY, Samantha .... 978-762-4000 220 E smcgillo@northshore.edu

MCGILVRAY, Amy .... 254-295-5077 466 A amcgilvray@umhb.edu

MCGILVRAY, Judith .... 903-675-6240 464 C jmcgilvray@tvcc.edu

MCGILVRAY, Richard .... 716-827-4338 331 K mcgilvrayr@trocaire.edu

MCGIMPSEY, Grant .... 701-777-6736 353 G grant.mcgimpsey@research.und.edu

MCGIMPSEY, Grant .... 701-777-3232 353 G grant.mcgimpsey@und.edu

MCGIMPSEY, Jason .... 406-657-2197 272 B jason.mcgimpsey@msubillings.edu

MCGING, Christine .... 651-779-3368 244 D christine.mcging@century.edu

MCGINLEY, Barbara .... 617-587-5620 222 G mcginleyb@neco.edu

MCGINLEY, Lynn, M .... 410-706-2889 207 H lmcginley@umaryland.edu

MCGINN, BJ .... 515-433-5050 168 A bjmcginn@dmacc.edu

MCGINN, Jayne .... 508-929-8110 219 A jmcginn@worcester.edu

MCGINN, Marifrances ... 401-865-2774 416 E mfmcginn@providence.edu

MCGINN, III, Thomas, J .... 410-777-2240 202 D tjmcginn@aacc.edu

MCGINNESS, Heather .... 914-337-9300 305 F heather.mcginness@concordia-ny.edu

MCGINNIS, Blake .... 870-759-4170 23 K bmcginnis@wbcoll.edu

MCGINNIS, Carrie .... 270-809-3437 188 D cmcginnis2@murraystate.edu

MCGINNIS, Erik .... 704-463-3001 348 B erik.mcginnis@pfeiffer.edu

MCGINNIS, Grace .... 708-709-3519 148 I gmcginnis@prairiestate.edu

MCGINNIS, Judy .... 661-255-1050 29 F

MCGINNIS, Kim .... 831-646-4190 52 G kmcginnis@mpc.edu

MCGINNIS, Maurice (Max) .... 585-594-6409 321 C mcginnis_max@roberts.edu

MCGINNIS, Michael .... 903-566-7040 468 C mmcginnis@uttyler.edu

MCGINNIS, Michael .... 802-485-2310 475 I mmcginni@norwich.edu

MCGINNIS, Sharon, R ... 910-938-6231 342 C mcginniss@coastalcarolina.edu

MCGINNIS, William .... 858-822-5738 69 E areisner@ucsd.edu

MCGINNIS GONZALEZ, Sherri .... 312-996-2398 153 H smcginn@uic.edu

MCGINNISS, Michael .... 215-951-1360 398 F mcginnis@lasalle.edu

MCGINTY, Dan .... 920-684-7071 510 A dmcginty@fsccm.org

MCGINTY, Daniel, E .... 715-425-3505 511 E daniel.e.mcginty@uwrf.edu

MCGINTY, Debra .... 928-532-6111 15 B debra.mcginty@npc.edu

MCGINTY, Evelyn, J .... 936-261-1725 458 F ejmcginty@pvamu.edu

MCGINTY, Felicia, E .... 848-932-8576 290 C felicia.mcginty@rutgers.edu

MCGINTY, Mac, L .... 804-523-2280 488 D mmcginty@ccwa.vccs.edu

MCGIRT, Jeffery .... 423-614-8691 432 L jmcgirt@leeuniversity.edu

MCGIVNEY, R, J .... 860-768-4401 89 C rmcgivney@hartford.edu

MCGLADDERY, Nicole ... 805-581-1233 42 G nmcgladdery@eternitybiblecollege.com

MCGLADDERY, Ryan .... 805-581-1233 42 G rmcgladdery@eternitybiblecollege.com

MCGLADE, Charles .... 856-351-2649 291 E cmcglade@salemcc.edu

MCGLAMERY, Matt .... 970-247-7065 79 J mcglamery_m@fortlewis.edu

MCGLASSON, Robert .... 417-328-1535 267 A bmcglasson@sbuniv.edu

MCGLOIN, Michelle .... 570-961-7833 399 A

MCGLOIN, Michelle .... 570-961-7810 399 A mcgloinm@lackawanna.edu

MCGLONE, John .... 606-326-2400 185 E john.mcglone@kctcs.edu

MCGLOTHIN, Kris .... 302-735-7696 90 J bkwesley@bncollege.edu

MCGLOTHIN-ELLER, April .... 847-866-3988 138 G april.mcglothin-eller@garrett.edu

MCGLOTHIN-ELLER, Vince .... 847-866-3907 138 G vince.mcglothin-eller@garrett.edu

MCGLOTHLIN, Jason .... 276-498-5247 477 L jmcglothlin@acp.edu

MCGLOTHLIN, Michael, G .... 276-498-4190 477 L mmcglothlin@acp.edu

MCGLOTHLIN, Sandra, K .... 276-244-1265 477 M smcglothlin@asl.edu

MCGLOUGHLIN, Stephen .... 916-691-7589 50 G mcglous@crc.losrios.edu

MCGOFF, Michael, F .... 607-777-2143 325 A mmcgoff@binghamton.edu

MCGOLDRICK, John .... 215-951-1015 398 F mcgoldri@lasalle.edu

MCGOLDRICK, Lisa .... 210-486-4901 441 G lmcgoldrick2@alamo.edu

MCGOLDRICK, Rowena . 860-515-3751 84 H rmcgoldrick@charteroak.edu

MCGOLDRICK, Sean .... 775-784-6514 279 E smcgoldrick@unr.edu

MCGONIGAL, Terry .... 509-777-4345 500 H tmcgonigal@whitworth.edu

MCGONIGLE, Gregory .. 617-627-3427 225 A gregory.mcgonigle@tufts.edu

MCGONIGLE, Mary .... 610-519-4070 413 K mary.mcgonigle@villanova.edu

MCGONIGLE, Robert, B . 570-208-5875 398 D rbmcgoni@kings.edu

MCGORRY, Marian .... 610-359-5142 393 E mmcgorry@dccc.edu

MCGOUGH, Jon .... 806-743-2986 463 E jon.mcgough@ttuhsc.edu

MCGOVERN, Margaret .. 516-572-7124 316 C margaret.mcgovern@ncc.edu

MCGOVERN, Mark, S .... 401-865-2702 416 E mmcgovrn@providence.edu

MCGOVERN, Martin, P .. 508-565-1321 224 H mmcgovern@stonehill.edu

MCGOWAN, Bruce .... 918-338-8040 379 C bmcgowan@rsu.edu

MCGOWAN, Charlotte ... 269-782-1347 237 B cmcgowan@swmich.edu

MCGOWAN, Chris .... 573-651-2163 266 M cwmcgowan@semo.edu

MCGOWAN, Cynthia .... 978-837-5139 221 G mcgowanc@merrimack.edu

MCGOWAN, Jeanne .... 912-344-3259 115 D jeanne.mcgowan@armstrong.edu

MCGOWAN, John .... 205-348-5610 8 A john.mcgowan@ua.edu

MCGOWAN, John .... 585-345-6999 309 C jmmcgowan@genesee.edu

MCGOWAN, Joumana ... 909-274-5140 52 I jmcgowan@mtsac.edu

MCGOWAN, Katie .... 610-526-6062 396 H cmcgowan@harcum.edu

MCGOWAN, Kent .... 406-243-5373 271 G kent.mcgowan@umontana.edu

MCGOWAN, Kevin .... 239-687-5335 95 B kmcgowan@avemarialaw.edu

MCGOWAN, Kyle, D .... 615-322-6850 440 D kyle.mcgowan@vanderbilt.edu

MCGOWAN, Patrick .... 773-371-5445 134 J pmcgowan@ctu.edu

MCGOWAN, Paul .... 617-552-3055 212 E paul.mcgowan.2@bc.edu

MCGOWAN, Sindi .... 770-537-5746 128 F sindi.mcgowan@westgatech.edu

MCGOWAN, Stephanie .. 201-559-3551 286 C

MCGOWAN, Terrance .... 718-933-6700 315 K tmcgowan@monroecollege.edu

MCGRADY, Patricia .... 973-957-0188 283 C treasurer@acs350.org

MCGRADY, Ronald, L ... 330-325-6799 366 F rmcgrady@neomed.edu

MCGRADY, Tracy .... 417-447-8152 264 K mcgradyt@otc.edu

MCGRAIL, Frederick, J .. 610-758-4487 400 B fjm208@lehigh.edu

MCGRAIL, James .... 603-862-0927 282 E james.mcgrail@usnh.edu

MCGRAIL, III, James, J 740-266-9621 361 D jmcgrail@egcc.edu

MCGRAIL, Margaret .... 914-674-3031 314 I mmcgrail@mercy.edu

MCGRANAHAN, Mary, S .... 617-552-3300 212 E mary.mcgranahan@bc.edu

MCGRANE, Jack, V .... 973-748-9000 284 A jack_mcgrane@bloomfield.edu

MCGRANE, Wendy .... 417-625-9801 263 G mcgrane-w@mssu.edu

MCGRANN, Michael .... 718-940-5741 322 G mmgrann@sjcny.edu

MCGRATH, Abby .... 312-567-3497 140 I amcgrat1@iit.edu

MCGRATH, Andrew, S ... 608-757-7764 513 D amcgrath@blackhawk.edu

MCGRATH, April Joy .... 203-432-2550 89 G joy.mcgrath@yale.edu

MCGRATH, Beth .... 201-216-3389 291 G cos.mcgrath@stevens.edu

MCGRATH, Cheryl .... 508-565-1111 224 H cmcgrath1@stonehill.edu

MCGRATH, Chris .... 719-549-3308 81 M christina.mcgrath@pueblocc.edu

MCGRATH, Frank .... 239-687-5331 95 B fmcgrath@avemarialaw.edu

MCGRATH, Jane .... 312-362-5765 137 C jmcgrath@depaul.edu

MCGRATH, Karen .... 607-431-4130 309 E mcgrathk@hartwick.edu

MCGRATH, Kat .... 518-608-8374 308 A kmcgrath@excelsior.edu

MCGRATH, Mark .... 215-242-1501 392 D mcgrathm@chc.edu

MCGRATH, Mark .... 605-718-2575 429 E mark.mcgrath@wdt.edu

MCGRATH, Nicole .... 203-932-7077 89 D nmcgrath@newhaven.edu

MCGRATH, Riley, C .... 715-836-5521 510 D mcgratrc@uwec.edu

MCGRATH, Thomas .... 508-565-1086 224 H tmcgrath@stonehill.edu

MCGRATH, Tim .... 619-388-2600 60 D tmcgrath@sdccd.edu

MCGRATH-ROTHENBERG, Alexis .... 914-674-7607 314 I amcgrath3@mercy.edu

MCGRAW, Darryl .... 919-209-2051 344 C ddmcgraw@johnstoncc.edu

MCGRAW, Hesse .... 415-749-4580 60 G hmcgraw@sfai.edu

MCGRAW, Kathy .... 972-721-5221 464 E kmcgraw@udallas.edu

MCGRAW, Larry .... 325-670-1269 450 A mcgraw@hsutx.edu

MCGRAW, Matthew .... 540-863-2866 487 I mmcgraw@dslcc.edu

MCGRAW, Packy .... 518-694-7257 297 J packy.mcgraw@acphs.edu

MCGREAL, Kristy .... 708-974-5335 146 C mcgrealc2@morainevalley.edu

MCGREAL, Paul, E .... 402-280-2874 274 D paulmcgreal@creighton.edu

MCGREEVEY, Michael .... 614-890-3000 368 O mmcgreevey@otterbein.edu

MCGREEVEY, Sean .... 502-272-8426 183 H smcgreevey@bellarmine.edu

MCGREEVY, Bill .... 619-644-7155 45 A bill.mcgreevy@gcccd.edu

MCGREEVY, Jeanette .... 515-643-6717 171 K jmcgreevy@mercydesmoines.org

MCGREEVY, John, T .... 574-631-6642 165 A mcgreevy.5@nd.edu

MCGREGOR, Kyle, W .... 254-968-9890 459 A mcgregor@tarleton.edu

MCGREGOR, Patricia .... 860-297-2120 88 E patricia.mcgregor@trincoll.edu

MCGREGOR, Tiffany .... 610-361-2487 402 G mcgregot@neumann.edu

MCGREW, Martha .... 505-272-2165 296 H mmcgrew@salud.unm.edu

MCGREW, Paula .... 304-473-8461 505 G mcgrew_p@wwc.edu

MCGREW, Shea .... 419-372-7706 357 F smcgrew@bgsu.edu

MCGRIFF, Ilona .... 415-239-3677 37 H imcgriff@ccsf.edu

MCGRIFF, Manuel .... 254-267-7010 454 L mmcgriff@rangercollege.edu

MCGRUDER, Janell, J .... 309-341-7492 142 G jmcgruder@knox.edu

MCGRUE, Geno .... 256-761-6324 7 D gmcgrue@talladega.edu

MCGUCKIN, Tammy .... 262-595-2571 511 C mcgukin@uwp.edu

MCGUFFEE, James .... 901-321-3448 431 A jmcguffee@cbu.edu

MCGUFFEY, Michael, J . 304-696-3648 504 C mcguffey@marshall.edu

MCGUFFIN, Kurt .... 731-881-7661 440 B

MCGUFFIN-CAWLEY, James, D .... 216-368-3227 358 C jxc41@case.edu

MCGUINN, Ellen .... 215-248-7163 392 D mcguinne@chc.edu

MCGUINNESS, Maureen 940-565-2648 466 B moe@unt.edu

MCGUINNESS, Scott .... 724-503-1001 414 A smcguinness@washjeff.edu

MCGUIRE, Ann .... 440-646-6033 373 B ann.mcguire@ursuline.edu

MCGUIRE, Bill .... 713-920-1120 451 B

MCGUIRE, Catherine .... 559-737-5410 39 G catherinemc@cos.edu

MCGUIRE, Christine, W 617-353-9814 212 G chmcguir@bu.edu

MCGUIRE, David .... 561-697-9200 125 H

MCGUIRE, David, T .... 435-586-7755 473 A mcguire@suu.edu

MCGUIRE, Jamie .... 902-403-3166 509 J jamie.mcguire@snc.edu

MCGUIRE, Jamie .... 336-838-6482 347 G jdmcguire271@wilkescc.edu

MCGUIRE, Jane .... 615-230-3204 438 C jane.mcguire@volstate.edu

MCGUIRE, Kathleen .... 508-541-1615 214 C kmcguire@dean.edu

MCGUIRE, Larry .... 309-677-2919 134 G lmcguire@bradley.edu

MCGUIRE, Mark, T .... 740-284-5249 361 L mmcguire@franciscan.edu

MCGUIRE, Maureen .... 509-313-6137 495 A mcguirem@gonzaga.edu

MCGUIRE, Michael .... 303-871-3518 83 E mmcguire@du.edu

MCGUIRE, Michael, J ... 785-670-1763 182 D michael.mcguire@washburn.edu

MCGUIRE, Nona, S .... 614-236-6908 358 A nmcguire@capital.edu

MCGUIRE, Patricia, A ... 202-884-9050 93 C mcguirep@trinitydc.edu

MCGUIRE, Rachel, A .... 585-340-9596 304 F rmcguire@crcds.edu

MCGUIRE, Rachel, L .... 641-422-4104 172 C mcguirac@niacc.edu

MCGUIRE, Ruth, A .... 651-631-5343 251 C ramcguire@unwsp.edu

MCGUIRE, Shari .... 910-893-1200 336 C

MCGUIRE, Shirley .... 415-422-6136 72 A mcguire@usfca.edu

MCGUIRE, Tara, S .... 402-280-3973 274 D taramcguire@creighton.edu

MCGUIRE, Venus .... 903-463-8698 449 J mcguirev@grayson.edu

MCGUIRE, William, K .... 859-282-8989 121 J wmcguire@ict.edu

MCGURE, David .... 561-697-9200 125 H ddmcguire@southuniversity.edu

MCGURGAN, Susan .... 513-231-2223 356 M smcgurgan@athenaeum.edu

MCGURIMAN, Joseph ... 215-641-6605 402 A jmcgurim@mc3.edu

MCGURIMAN, Timothy .. 610-660-1357 409 H
tmcgurim@sju.edu
MCGURK, Mark .... 432-552-2700 469 D
mcgurk_m@utpb.edu
MCGURN, Joseph, P ..... 740-283-6278 361 L
jmcgurn@franciscan.edu
MCGURREN, Cynthia ...... 978-542-7591 218 E
cmcgurren@salemstate.edu
MCGURTY, Thomas, S .. 617-627-3264 225 A
thomas.mcgurty@tufts.edu
MCGUTHRY, John, W ... 909-869-6442.. 31 A
jwmcguthry@cpp.edu
MCHALE, Barbara .... 215-641-5521 396 E
mchale.b@gmercyu.edu
MCHALE, Tammy, J ...... 570-348-6222 401 B
tmchale@marywood.edu
MCHALE, JR., William .. 717-358-3870 395 G
william.mchale@fandm.edu
MCHAN, Elizabeth, C .... 218-299-3298 241 K
emchan@cord.edu
MCHANEY, Eric .... 251-981-3771.... 5 A
eric.mchaney@columbiasouthern.edu
MCHARGUE, Jackie .... 828-250-2370 351 A
jmchargu@unca.edu
MCHARRIS, Michael ...... 315-792-5489 315 I
mmcharris@mvcc.edu
MCHATTON, Patricia, A . 956-665-3627 468 A
patricia.mchatton@utrgv.edu
MCHENRY, Erin .... 949-582-4481.. 64 J
emchenry@saddleback.edu
MCHENRY, Lepaine .... 405-585-4450 377 A
lepaine.mchenry@okbu.edu
MCHENRY, Stephanie .... 216-687-3673 359 L
s.y.mchenry@csuohio.edu
MCHENRY, Thomas .... 802-831-1237 476 G
tmchenry@vermontlaw.edu
MCHORNEY, Mark .... 630-829-6150 133 I
mmchorney@ben.edu
MCHUGH, Elizabeth ...... 360-867-6808 494 G
mchughe@evergreen.edu
MCHUGH, John .... 704-748-5213 343 D
mchugh.john@gaston.edu
MCHUGH, Kevin .... 609-652-1776 291 H
kevin.mchugh@stockton.edu
MCHUGH, Lindsay .... 508-541-1656 214 C
lmchugh@dean.edu
MCHUGH, Mary .... 978-837-5125 221 G
mary.mchugh@merrimack.edu
MCHUGH, Mary .... 845-848-7407 306 G
mary.mchugh@dc.edu
MCHUGH, Shelley .... 402-465-2123 276 E
smchugh@nebrwesleyan.edu
MCHUGH, Tracy .... 630-889-6607 147 D
tmchugh@nuhs.edu
MCILHAGGA, Doug .... 618-650-3605 152 C
dmcilha@siue.edu
MCILHENNEY, Sharon ... 717-299-7754 411 C
mcilhenney@stevenscollege.edu
MCILLECE, Emily .... 402-354-7249 275 P
emily.mcillece@methodistcollege.edu
MCILROY, Julia .... 208-885-6123 132 I
juliam@uidaho.edu
MCILVANE, Amy .... 770-426-2648 122 F
mcilvane@life.edu
MCINALLY, David, W .... 319-399-8686 167 F
dmcinally@coe.edu
MCINERNEY, Todd .... 203-932-7031.. 89 D
tmcinerney@newhaven.edu
MCINNES, Robert .... 704-334-6882 336 I
rmcinnes@charlottechristian.edu
MCINNIS, James, P .... 601-643-8488 252 G
jp.mcinnis@colin.edu
MCINNIS, Maurie .... 512-232-3300 467 C
provost@utexas.edu
MCINNIS, Robert, L ...... 704-216-6400 339 E
rmcinnis@livingstone.edu
MCINNIS, W. Dale .... 910-410-1806 345 G
wdmcinnis@richmondcc.edu
MCINTEE, Justin .... 714-556-3610.. 72 F
justin.mcintee@vanguard.edu
MCINTIRE, Heidi .... 330-337-6403 356 B
college@awc.edu
MCINTIRE, Mary .... 713-348-2599 455 F
maryb@rice.edu
MCINTIRE, Molly .... 407-582-5588 113 F
mmcintire1@valenciacollege.edu
MCINTIRE, OSFS,
Timothy .... 610-282-1100 393 G
timothy.mcintire@desales.edu
MCINTOSH, Angela .... 937-766-3200 358 D
mcintosh@cedarville.edu
MCINTOSH, Cecilia, A ... 423-439-4221 431 H
mcintosc@etsu.edu
MCINTOSH, Charles ...... 352-854-2322.. 97 C
mcintosc@cf.edu
MCINTOSH, Daniel .... 303-871-3712.. 83 E
daniel.mcintosh@du.edu
MCINTOSH, Gary .... 425-889-7790 496 E
gary.mcintosh@northwestu.edu
MCINTOSH, Gayle .... 253-879-3905 499 C
gmcintosh@pugetsound.edu
MCINTOSH, Glenn .... 248-370-4200 235 J
mcintosh@oakland.edu
MCINTOSH, Joe .... 817-515-5377 458 B
clifford.mcintosh@tccd.edu
MCINTOSH, John .... 256-331-5323.... 3 C
jmcintosh@nwscc.edu
MCINTOSH, Joshua .... 207-786-6219 198 E
jmcintos@bates.edu
MCINTOSH, Julie .... 419-434-4062 372 B
mcintosh@findlay.edu
MCINTOSH, Katy .... 714-556-3610.. 72 F
katy.mcintosh@vanguard.edu
MCINTOSH, Keith, J ...... 804-289-8467 486 G
kmcintosh@richmond.edu
MCINTOSH, Linda .... 936-294-3974 462 F
lam096@shsu.edu
MCINTOSH, Mark .... 573-882-2011 268 B
MCINTOSH, Mark .... 573-882-9500 268 C
mcintoshm@umsystem.edu
MCINTOSH, Tim .... 541-683-5141 383 D
tmcintosh@gutenberg.edu
MCINTOSH-DOTY,
Mikail .... 512-313-3000 446 N
mikail.doty@concordia.edu
MCINTURF, Robert .... 940-565-4204 466 B
robert.mcinturf@unt.edu
MCINTYRE, Ellen, C ...... 704-687-8722 351 C
ellen.mcintyre@uncc.edu
MCINTYRE, Faye, S .... 678-839-6467 127 F
fmcintyr@westga.edu
MCINTYRE, Helen, M .... 205-934-8132.... 8 B
hmcintyre@uab.edu
MCINTYRE, Jacqueline .. 516-364-0808 317 B
jmcintyre@nycollege.edu
MCINTYRE, Janet .... 503-491-7589 384 D
janet.mcintyre@mhcc.edu
MCINTYRE, John .... 910-221-2224 338 A
jmcintyre@gcd.edu
MCINTYRE, Kevin .... 217-424-6251 145 J
kmmcintyre@millikin.edu
MCINTYRE, Kevin .... 806-743-7425 463 E
kevin.mcintyre@ttuhsc.edu
MCINTYRE, Rebecca, F . 540-985-8167 482 A
rfmcintyre@jchs.edu
MCINTYRE, Teresa .... 281-649-3000 450 C
MCINTYRE, Willie .... 910-672-1157 350 B
wmcintyre@uncfsu.edu
MCISAAC, Penny, J .... 561-868-3055 105 A
mcisaacp@palmbeachstate.edu
MCJUNKIN, Gayle .... 507-222-4337 241 C
gmcjunki@carleton.edu
MCKAIN, Betty, J .... 269-387-4728 239 E
betty.mckain@wmich.edu
MCKAIN, Joshua .... 617-236-8854 215 B
jmckain@fisher.edu
MCKAMEY, Sheldon ...... 406-994-6543 272 A
smckamey@montana.edu
MCKANN, Helen .... 804-594-1523 488 D
hmckann@jtcc.edu
MCKANNA, Nate .... 214-887-5041 448 G
nmckanna@dts.edu
MCKAY, Ashley, M .... 812-941-2075 161 A
atronc01@ius.edu
MCKAY, Bill .... 509-542-5531 493 G
bmckay@columbiabasin.edu
MCKAY, Cheryl, A .... 573-341-7060 269 A
cherylan@mst.edu
MCKAY, Chuck .... 860-297-2326.. 88 E
chuck.mckay@trincoll.edu
MCKAY, Janet .... 203-837-8460.. 85 B
mckayj@wcsu.edu
MCKAY, Jeffrey .... 207-778-7009 201 D
jeffrey.d.mckay@maine.edu
MCKAY, Kerri .... 313-664-7441 228 H
kmckay@collegeforcreativestudies.edu
MCKAY, Kevin .... 425-640-1547 494 E
kevin.mckay@edcc.edu
MCKAY, Kimberly .... 432-335-6683 454 C
kmckay@odessa.edu
MCKAY, Mary, M .... 314-935-6693 269 L
mary.mckay@wustl.edu
MCKAY, Matthew .... 518-681-5604 328 G
mckaym@sunyacc.edu
MCKAY, Monique .... 239-590-1022 109 C
mmckay@fgcu.edu
MCKAY, Norman .... 404-364-8322 124 A
nmckay@oglethorpe.edu
MCKAY, Richard .... 281-998-6150 456 B
richard.mckay@sjcd.edu
MCKAY, Scott .... 605-256-5136 428 G
scott.mckay@dsu.edu
MCKAY, Shaun, L .... 631-451-4736 330 B
mckays@sunysuffolk.edu
MCKAY, Stephanie .... 336-725-8344 348 C
mckays@piedmontu.edu
MCKAY, Tamara .... 810-762-3456 238 B
tamaramc@umflint.edu
MCKAYLE, Camille, A .... 340-693-1200 529 C
cmckayl@uvi.edu
MCKEAN, Scott .... 425-352-8192 492 K
smckean@cascadia.edu
MCKECHNIE, Janna .... 701-858-3373 354 C
janna.mckechnie@minotstateu.edu
MCKECHNIE, Sally .... 225-578-2307 193 M
smckechnie@lsu.edu
MCKECHNIE, Susan, E .. 410-706-7776 207 H
smckechnie@umaryland.edu
MCKEE, Andy .... 260-399-7700 165 B
amckee@sf.edu
MCKEE, Anne .... 865-981-8298 433 F
anne.mckee@maryvillecollege.edu
MCKEE, Brandi .... 301-369-2800 202 J
bkmckee@captechu.edu
MCKEE, Bruce, G .... 641-422-4348 172 C
mckeebru@niacc.edu
MCKEE, Diann, E .... 812-237-2372 159 C
diann.mckee@indstate.edu
MCKEE, John, C .... 409-747-9080 469 C
jcmckee@utmb.edu
MCKEE, John, P .... 803-323-2205 426 H
mckeej@winthrop.edu
MCKEE, Jonathon .... 808-984-3213 130 H
jvmckee@hawaii.edu
MCKEE, Joseph .... 662-621-4156 252 E
MCKEE, JP .... 803-323-2205 426 H
mckeej@winthrop.edu
MCKEE, Judith .... 574-284-4719 163 J
smcbookstore@bkstr.com
MCKEE, Kasey .... 636-922-8472 265 J
kmckee@stchas.edu
MCKEE, Larry .... 856-351-2605 291 E
lmckee@salemcc.edu
MCKEE, Lauren .... 408-274-7900.. 61 O
lauren.mckee@evc.edu
MCKEE, Lori .... 575-646-2172 295 B
lomckee@nmsu.edu
MCKEE, Lori .... 419-755-4828 366 E
lmckee@ncstatecollege.edu
MCKEE, Marites .... 808-687-7014 129 C
mmckee@hpu.edu
MCKEE, Mark .... 419-448-2194 362 G
mmckee@heidelberg.com
MCKEE, Michael .... 352-392-2402 110 D
mckee@ufl.edu
MCKEE, Michele, B .... 225-771-2552 196 B
mmckee@sulc.edu
MCKEE, Mike .... 386-752-1822.. 99 J
mike.mckee@fgc.edu
MCKEE, Richard .... 432-685-4734 453 B
rmckee@midland.edu
MCKEE, Sara .... 317-921-4607 161 G
smckee15@ivytech.edu
MCKEE, Suzanne .... 334-683-2347.... 3 A
smckee@marionmilitary.edu
MCKEE, William .... 615-547-1311 431 D
bmckee@cumberland.edu
MCKEEGAN, John .... 503-883-2217 383 H
jmckeega@linfield.edu
MCKEEN, Catherine .... 413-662-5082 218 C
catherine.mckeen@mcla.edu
MCKEEN, Jerry .... 805-493-3139.. 30 E
jmckeen@callutheran.edu
MCKEEVER, Diane, M .... 312-942-6830 150 F
diane_m_mckeever@rush.edu
MCKEEVER, Diane, M .... 312-942-6950 150 F
diane_m_mckeever@rush.edu
MCKEEVER, Kerry .... 603-899-1130 281 D
mckeeverk@franklinpierce.edu
MCKEEVER, Molly, K ..... 530-226-4932.. 64 B
mmckeever@simpsonu.edu
MCKEEVER, William, P .. 716-829-7807 307 B
mckeever@dyc.edu
MCKEIGUE, Elizabeth ..... 978-542-6762 218 E
emckeigue@salemstate.edu
MCKEITHEN, Susan, P ... 719-884-5000 180 B
spmckeithen@nbc.edu
MCKELLIP, Mark .... 419-251-8989 365 C
mark.mckellip@mercycollege.edu
MCKELLIPS, Steve .... 828-250-3829 351 A
smckelli@unca.edu
MCKELVEY, Kathryn .... 419-267-1327 366 G
kmckelvey@northweststate.edu
MCKELVEY, Steve .... 507-786-3421 250 C
mckelvey@stolaf.edu
MCKELVIE, OSF,
Roberta .... 610-790-2876 389 A
roberta.mckelvie@alvernia.edu
MCKENDREE, Lynda .... 713-525-2151 466 J
mckendla@stthom.edu
MCKENDRICKS, John .... 775-849-4983 384 E
jmckendricks@multnomah.edu
MCKENNA,
Charles (Doug) .... 202-885-2210.. 91 C
dmckenna@american.edu
MCKENNA, Crichton ...... 207-453-5155 200 A
cmckenna@kvcc.me.edu
MCKENNA, David .... 903-886-5761 459 E
david.mckenna@sscserv.com
MCKENNA, Heidi .... 510-883-7160.. 41 I
hmckenna@dspt.edu
MCKENNA, Kevin .... 914-395-2510 323 K
kmckenna@sarahlawrence.edu
MCKENNA, Kristen .... 603-443-4200 281 A
kpmckenna@ccsnh.edu
MCKENNA, Megan .... 814-824-3355 401 J
mmckenna@mercyhurst.edu
MCKENNA, Patrick .... 404-894-6088 120 A
pat.mckenna@carnegie.gatech.edu
MCKENNA, Robert, E ..... 860-444-8503 519 B
robert.e.mckenna@uscg.mil
MCKENNA, Timothy, J .. 319-273-3241 167 A
tim.mckenna@uni.edu
MCKENNA FRAZIER,
Lynnette, M .... 260-399-7700 165 B
lfrazier@sf.edu
MCKENNA-JONES, Amy 573-518-2146 263 E
mjones@mineralarea.edu
MCKENNEY, William ...... 574-239-8390 158 M
wmckenney@hcc-nd.edu
MCKENZIE, Andre, A ..... 718-990-1892 322 F
mckenzia@stjohns.edu
MCKENZIE, Bruce .... 937-778-7855 361 E
bmckenzie@edisonohio.edu
MCKENZIE, Connie, L ... 757-965-8500 480 C
mckenzcl@evms.edu
MCKENZIE, Fred, R .... 630-947-8930 133 H
mckenzie@aurora.edu
MCKENZIE, JoAnn .... 404-727-6052 119 B
jmckenz@emory.edu
MCKENZIE, Joy .... 615-383-4848 441 A
jmckenzie@watkins.edu
MCKENZIE, Laura .... 208-282-2661 132 B
mckelaur@isu.edu
MCKENZIE, Lester .... 931-372-3073 438 F
lmckenzie@tetech.edu
MCKENZIE, Lisa .... 518-454-5114 305 B
mckenzil@strose.edu
MCKENZIE, Mark .... 651-603-6208 241 L
mckenzie@csp.edu
MCKENZIE, Natalie, E. ... 530-226-4103.. 64 B
nmckenzie@simpsonu.edu
MCKENZIE, Pia .... 919-807-6951 340 K
mckenziep@nccommunitycolleges.edu
MCKENZIE, Rene .... 541-956-7129 386 G
rmckenzie@roguecc.edu
MCKENZIE, Sarah .... 334-808-6128.... 7 E
smckenzie93530@troy.edu
MCKENZIE, Vandeen ..... 575-646-6014 295 B
vmckenzi@nmsu.edu
MCKEON, Margaret .... 215-871-6826 407 G
margaremc@pcom.edu
MCKEON, Michael .... 510-885-3000.. 31 F
MCKEOWN, Adrienne .... 605-274-5530 426 K
adrienne.mckeown@augie.edu
MCKEOWN, Anna .... 615-383-4848 441 A
amckeown@watkins.edu
MCKEOWN, Joshua, S .. 315-312-2118 327 D
joshua.mckeown@oswego.edu
MCKEOWN, Robert .... 716-614-6271 318 E
mckeown@niagaracc.suny.edu
MCKERALL, Deborah ..... 936-294-3548 462 F
dam004@shsu.edu
MCKERNAN, Sarah .... 620-341-5551 177 B
smckerna@emporia.edu
MCKERNAN, Steve .... 505-272-2071 296 H
smckernan@salud.unm.edu
MCKESSON, Leslie .... 828-448-3156 347 F
lmckesson@wpcc.edu
MCKETHAN, Lisa, H ...... 254-710-3817 444 B
lisa_mckethan@baylor.edu
MCKETHER, Willie .... 419-530-5529 372 F
willie.mckether@utoledo.edu
MCKIBBENS, Donna ...... 617-879-2242 226 A
dmckibbens@wheelock.edu
MCKIBBIN, Barbara .... 704-669-4116 342 B
mckibbin@clevelandcc.edu
MCKIEL, Allen .... 503-838-8886 388 B
mckiela@wou.edu
MCKIERNAN, Jack .... 908-737-0600 286 F
jmckiern@kean.edu
MCKILLICAN, Nancy ...... 510-780-4500.. 48 D
MCKINION, Randall .... 937-766-7986 358 D
rmkinion@cedarville.edu
MCKINLEY, Bob .... 817-598-6256 470 J
bmckinley@wc.edu
MCKINLEY, Colleen .... 562-860-2451.. 36 A
cmckinley@cerritos.edu
MCKINLEY, Elizabeth ..... 816-501-3767 257 G
elizabeth.mckinley@avila.edu

MCMAHON, Lori, L .... 205-934-8227.... 8 B mcmahon@uab.edu

MCMAHON, Mary Pat ... 617-627-3158 225 A mary.mcmahon@tufts.edu

MCMAHON, Maura .... 703-658-4304 479 G maura.mcmahon@christendom.edu

MCMAHON, Michael ..... 701-355-8336 355 K msmcmahon@umary.edu

MCMAHON, Renee, M .. 406-447-5501 270 H rmcmahon@carroll.edu

MCMAHON, Roberta ...... 708-524-6790 137 F rmcmahon@dom.edu

MCMAHON, Shelly, A ... 740-368-3201 368 N samcmaho@owu.edu

MCMAHON, Stephen ...... 802-654-2516 476 A smcmahon@smcvt.edu

MCMAHON, Timothy, J . 412-359-1000 412 C tmcmahon@triangle-tech.edu

MCMAHON, Timothy, J . 412-359-1000 412 B tmcmahon@triangle-tech.edu

MCMAINS, III, Robert, E .... 205-934-4427.... 8 B mmains@uab.edu

MCMAKIN, Sandy .... 210-805-3005 465 E mcmakin@uiwtx.edu

MCMANN, Daniel .... 716-286-8755 318 F dmcmann@niagara.edu

MCMANNESS, Matthew, S .... 718-862-7357 313 L matthew.mcmanness@manhattan.edu

MCMANON, Karen .... 412-924-1420 408 E kmcmahon@pts.edu

MCMANUS, Janet .... 816-501-3618 257 G janet.mcmanus@avila.edu

MCMANUS, Kim .... 434-961-5207 489 C kmcmanus@pvcc.edu

MCMANUS, Michael ...... 303-797-5654.. 76 I michael.mcmanus@arapahoe.edu

MCMANUS, Ron .... 610-917-1402 413 G

MCMANUS, Shirley .... 559-442-8215.. 66 G shirley.mcmanus@fresnocitycollege.edu

MCMANUS, Tiffany .... 785-670-1470 182 D tiffany.mcmanus@washburn.edu

MCMARTIN, David .... 760-750-4171.. 33 E dhmcmart@csusm.edu

MCMASTER, Dennis .... 724-503-1001 414 A dmcmaster@washjeff.edu

MCMASTER, Pam .... 402-481-8718 273 F pam.mcmaster@bryanhealthcollege.edu

MCMASTER, Robert .... 612-625-9883 250 E mcmaster@umn.edu

MCMASTERS, Daniel ...... 856-227-7200 284 E dmcmasters@camdencc.edu

MCMATH-TURNER, Lavita .... 646-313-8000 303 G lavita.mcmath@guttman.cuny.edu

MCMEANS, Orlando, F .. 304-766-4300 505 A mcmeanso@wvstateu.edu

MCMENAMIN, Margaret, M .... 908-709-7100 292 C mcmenamin@ucc.edu

MCMICAN, Jairo, S .... 919-536-7200 342 G mcmicanj@durhamtech.edu

MCMICHAEL, Brett .... 202-319-5232.. 91 D mcmichaelb@cua.edu

MCMICHAEL, Dan .... 805-378-4660.. 73 A dmcmichael@vcccd.edu

MCMICKLE, Marvin, A ... 585-340-9680 304 F mmcmickle@crcds.edu

MCMILLAN, Byron .... 610-341-5906 394 E bmcmilla@eastern.edu

MCMILLAN, Denise .... 610-341-4365 394 E dmcmill@eastern.edu

MCMILLAN, Jessica .... 415-551-9284.. 28 K jmcmillan@cca.edu

MCMILLAN, Karen .... 918-270-6402 378 I karen.mcmillan@ptstulsa.edu

MCMILLAN, Karon .... 601-925-3212 254 B kmcmilla@mc.edu

MCMILLAN, Katie .... 307-268-2488 516 H kmcmillan@caspercollege.edu

MCMILLAN, Michelle .... 918-495-6013 378 H mmcmillan@oru.edu

MCMILLAN, Mike .... 501-812-2372.. 23 C mmcmillan@pulaskitech.edu

MCMILLAN, Minnie .... 334-874-5700.... 5 B mmcmillan@ccal.edu

MCMILLAN, Sean .... 706-542-6128 127 A smcmilla@uga.edu

MCMILLEN, Jeremy, P .. 903-463-8600 449 J mcmillenj@grayson.edu

MCMILLEN, Michelle ..... 870-733-6782.. 18 B mlmcmillen@asumidsouth.edu

MCMILLIAN, Anthony .... 281-618-5524 452 C anthony.mcmillian@lonestar.edu

MCMILLIAN, Carey .... 816-271-4582 264 B mcmilli@missouriwestern.edu

MCMILLIAN, Josh .... 479-968-0222.. 18 G jmcmillian1@atu.edu

MCMILLIN, Barbara, C .. 662-685-4771 252 D bmcmillin@bmc.edu

MCMILLIN, David .... 417-626-1234 264 J dmcmillin@occ.edu

MCMILLIN, Donna .... 870-972-3700.. 18 A mcmillin@astate.edu

MCMILLIN, Jennifer .... 417-626-1234 264 J jmcmillin@occ.edu

MCMILLIN, Linda, A ...... 570-372-4127 410 H mcmillin@susqu.edu

MCMILLIN, Nicole .... 208-562-3331 132 A nicolemcmillin@cwidaho.cc

MCMILLIN, Nicole .... 605-367-4821 429 C nicole.mcmillin@southeasttech.edu

MCMILLIN, Renee .... 303-292-0015.. 79 F r.mcmillin@denverschoolofnursing.edu

MCMILLION, David .... 706-776-0114 124 E dmcmillion@piedmont.edu

MCMILLION, Eric, C ..... 859-858-3511 183 D eric.mcmillion@asbury.edu

MCMILLON, Avis .... 732-224-2967 284 B amcmillon@brookdalecc.edu

MCMILLON, Jeff .... 405-425-5919 377 B jeff.mcmillon@oc.edu

MCMILLON, Kimberly .... 813-253-7006 101 M kmcmillon@hccfl.edu

MCMINIMY, Gisele .... 316-295-5809 177 F mcminimy@friends.edu

MCMINN, Jamie, G .... 724-946-7121 414 C mcminnjg@westminster.edu

MCMORRAN, Carolyn, R .... 407-582-6700 113 F cmcmorran@valenciacollege.edu

MCMOY, Johnny .... 256-352-8117.... 3 I johnny.mcmoy@wallacestate.edu

MCMULLEN, Judith .... 216-987-4836 360 E judith.mcmullen@tri-c.edu

MCMULLEN, Mark .... 918-595-7895 380 D mark.mcmullen@tulsacc.edu

MCMULLEN, Michael ...... 315-498-2566 319 G mcmullem@sunyocc.edu

MCMULLEN, Patricia ..... 202-319-5403.. 91 D mcmullep@cua.edu

MCMULLEN, Rebecca .... 478-825-6856 119 C mcmullenr@fvsu.edu

MCMULLEN, William ..... 817-515-1268 458 B william.mcmullen@tccd.edu

MCMULLIN, Angeline .... 423-614-8357 432 L amcmullin@leeuniversity.edu

MCMULLIN, Kyle, S ...... 757-594-7420 479 H kyle.mcmullin@cnu.edu

MCMULLIN, Sallie .... 706-867-2760 127 B sallie.mcmullin@ung.edu

MCMURDOCK, Linda ..... 703-284-1615 483 A linda.mcmurdock@marymount.edu

MCMURPHY, Elizabeth .. 580-349-1564 377 E liz@opsu.edu

MCMURPHY, Elizabeth .. 580-349-1566 377 E liz@opsu.edu

MCMURRAY, Brock .... 661-763-7811.. 67 A bmcmurray@taftcollege.edu

MCMURRAY, Kelly .... 301-934-7624 203 D kmcmurray@csmd.edu

MCMURRAY, Tim .... 903-886-5568 459 E timm@tamuc.edu

MCMURRY, Alice .... 717-871-7500 407 A alice.mcmurry@millersville.edu

MCMURRY, Alice .... 717-871-7520 407 A alice.mcmurry@millersville.edu

MCMURRY, Marna, R .... 910-256-0255 349 F mmcmurry@umo.edu

MCMURTRY, Brian .... 270-831-9790 186 A brian.mcmurtry@kctcs.edu

MCMURTRY, Craig .... 254-298-8524 458 C craig.mcmurtry@templejc.edu

MCMURTRY, David .... 916-388-2885.. 35 F dmcmurtry@carrington.edu

MCMURTY, Jerry .... 208-885-6244 132 I mcmurtry@uidaho.edu

MCNABB, Ann, M .... 773-442-5110 147 G a-mcnabb@neiu.edu

MCNABB, Deana, M ...... 406-338-5441 270 G deana_mcnabb@bfcc.edu

MCNABB, Kathleen, J .... 218-477-4321 246 B mcnabb@mnstate.edu

MCNABB, Mark .... 509-865-8643 495 D mcnabb_m@heritage.edu

MCNABOE, Dennis .... 304-326-1482 502 D dmcnaboe@salemu.edu

MCNAIR, Christopher, L .... 325-670-1720 450 A cmcnair@hsutx.edu

MCNAIR, Kala .... 706-355-5013 115 H kmcnair@athenstech.edu

MCNAIR, Lily, D .... 718-390-3211 333 D lily.mcnair@wagner.edu

MCNAIR, Ronna .... 216-987-4855 360 E ronna.mcnair@tri-c.edu

MCNAIR, Sheila .... 804-524-6948 491 A smcnair@vsu.edu

MCNAIRY, Joe .... 931-363-9800 433 E

MCNALL, Mike .... 309-457-2122 146 A mike@monmouthcollege.edu

MCNALLY, Matthew .... 202-319-5373.. 91 D mcnally@cua.edu

MCNALLY, Michael .... 480-423-6616.. 14 C michael.mcnally@scottsdalecc.edu

MCNALLY, Minta, A .... 336-758-4237 353 A mcnallma@wfu.edu

MCNALLY, Neal, P .... 330-941-2719 374 E npmcnally@ysu.edu

MCNALLY, Patrick, J ..... 313-496-2524 238 H pmcnall1@wcccd.edu

MCNALLY, Robin .... 508-793-7467 213 C rmcnally@clarku.edu

MCNALLY, Tom .... 803-777-6212 424 I tom@mailbox.sc.edu

MCNAMARA, Catherine . 315-268-4394 304 B cmcnamar@clarkson.edu

MCNAMARA, Connie ...... 717-245-1813 394 A mcnamarc@dickinson.edu

MCNAMARA, John .... 862-906-5102.. 85 D jmcnamara@ccc.commnet.edu

MCNAMARA, Karen .... 215-951-1882 398 F mcnamara@lasalle.edu

MCNAMARA, Kristine, E 401-598-1565 416 C kmcnamara@jwu.edu

MCNAMARA, Nancy .... 704-334-6882 336 I nmcnamara@charlottechristian.edu

MCNAMARA, Patrick ..... 402-554-2389 277 I pmcnamara@unomaha.edu

MCNAMARA, Paul .... 904-779-4141 100 F paul.mcnamara@fscj.edu

MCNAMARA, Thomas .... 508-929-8033 219 A tmcnamara@worcester.edu

MCNAMARA, Thomas .... 610-282-1100 393 G tom.mcnamara@desales.edu

MCNAMEE-SMITH, Chris .... 215-955-0793 411 E chris.smith@jefferson.edu

MCNANEY, Duane .... 903-983-8107 451 F dmcnaney@kilgore.edu

MCNARY, Lisa .... 210-805-3596 465 E lisas@uiwtx.edu

MCNATT, Rosemary Bray .... 510-549-4724.. 66 D rbraymcnatt@sksm.edu

MCNAUGHTON, Drumm 505-922-2888 294 B drumm@eccu.edu

MCNAUGHTON, Jarrod . 937-395-8165 364 B jarrod.mcnaughton@ketteringhealth.org

MCNAUGHTON, Laura ... 605-658-5641 428 E laura.mcnaughton@usd.edu

MCNAUGHTON, Victor .. 202-806-1106.. 92 C vmcnaughton@howard.edu

MCNEAL, Deborah .... 662-621-4124 252 E dmcneal@coahomacc.edu

MCNEAL, Latanya, L ...... 561-993-1156 105 A mcneall@palmbeachstate.edu

MCNEAL, Lewatis .... 270-852-8607 186 F lewatis.mcneal@kctcs.edu

MCNEAL, Lisa .... 912-279-4505 118 A lmcneal@ccga.edu

MCNEAL, Nadine .... 731-989-6644 432 C nmcneal@fhu.edu

MCNEAL, Scott .... 417-328-1499 267 A smcneal@sbuniv.edu

MCNEALEY, Eloise .... 256-469-7333.... 6 A dev@hbc1.edu

MCNEALEY, Ernest .... 803-376-5701 418 D emcnealey@allenuniversity.edu

MCNEAR, Marie .... 334-229-4200.... 4 A mmcnear@alasu.edu

MCNEELEY, Wendy .... 325-649-8619 450 H wmcneeley@hputx.edu

MCNEELY, Ann Marie .... 828-448-3509 347 F amcneely@wpcc.edu

MCNEELY, Shelley .... 608-785-9880 515 C mcneelys@westerntc.edu

MCNEELY, III, Stanton, F .... 504-671-6488 192 H smcnee@dcc.edu

MCNEELY, III, Stanton, F .... 504-671-5498 192 H smcnee@dcc.edu

MCNEELY, Timothy, A .... 304-367-4937 504 A tim.mcneely@fairmontstate.edu

MCNEES MOSS, Shelley 662-329-7106 254 F smmoss@muw.edu

MCNEESE, Margaret ...... 713-500-5116 468 D margaret.c.mcneese@uth.tmc.edu

MCNEESE, Tim, D .... 402-363-5683 278 E tdmcnesse@york.edu

MCNEICE-STALLARD, Barbara .... 909-274-4109.. 52 I bmcneice-stallard@mtsac.edu

MCNEIL, Amanda .... 505-368-3524.. 12 G amcneil@dinecollege.edu

MCNEIL, Carlene .... 407-708-2396 107 G mcneilc@seminolestate.edu

MCNEIL, Glen .... 785-628-4200 177 D mcmcneil@fhsu.edu

MCNEIL, J. Derek .... 206-876-6105 498 C dmcneil@theseattleschool.edu

MCNEIL, Jaquelyn .... 941-752-5231 108 P mcneilj@scf.edu

MCNEIL, Jinawa, A .... 410-651-6411 208 C jamcneil@umes.edu

MCNEIL, Marilyn .... 732-571-3414 287 C mmcneil@monmouth.edu

MCNEIL, Mary, E .... 515-294-1443 166 F mcneil@iastate.edu

MCNEIL, Paul, M .... 530-757-8601.. 68 H mcneil@ucdavis.edu

MCNEIL, Ronald, D .... 217-206-6533 154 A mcneil.ron@uis.edu

MCNEIL, Stephanie .... 704-216-6953 339 E smcneil@livingstone.edu

MCNEIL, Wanda .... 314-340-3511 260 H mcneilj@hssu.edu

MCNEILL, Denise .... 806-720-7527 452 D denise.mcneill@lcu.edu

MCNEILL, Kathy .... 210-999-8425 464 B kmcneill@trinity.edu

MCNEILL, Savonne .... 704-922-6420 343 D mcneill.savonne@gaston.edu

MCNEILL, Warren .... 806-796-8800 452 D mcnierml@alma.edu

MCNERNEY, Hannah ...... 304-829-7411 501 F hmcnerney@bethanywv.edu

MCNESBY, James .... 215-646-7300 396 E mcnesby.j@gmercyu.edu

MCNEW, Regina .... 865-694-6650 437 F rdmcnew@pstcc.edu

MCNICHOL, Danielle ..... 610-358-4528 402 G mcnichod@neumann.edu

MCNICHOLAS, Joseph ... 310-338-5119.. 50 J jmcnich1@lmu.edu

MCNICHOLS, Amy .... 410-857-2461 205 E amcnichols@mcdaniel.edu

MCNICOL, Greg, L .... 915-747-7182 467 E gmcnicol@utep.edu

MCNIER, Michelle .... 989-463-7423 226 H mcnierml@alma.edu

MCNIGHT, Jonathan ...... 860-439-2035.. 86 H john.mcnight@conncoll.edu

MCNINCH, Jamie .... 775-445-3235 279 F jamie.mcninch@wnc.edu

MCNITT, Zakary .... 517-787-0800 231 E mcnittzakaryt@jccmi.edu

MCNULTY, Dan .... 412-268-3785 391 H djmnulty@andrew.cmu.edu

MCNULTY, Donna, S ..... 319-296-4201 169 H donna.mcnulty@hawkeyecollege.edu

MCNULTY, George .... 785-460-5490 176 L george.mcnulty@colbycc.edu

MCNULTY, Mary Kate .... 215-572-2877 389 D mcnultym@arcadia.edu

MCNULTY, Michael .... 267-341-3281 397 G mmcnulty@holyfamily.edu

MCNULTY, Patrick .... 312-942-6849 150 F patrick_j_mnculty@rush.edu

MCNULTY, Paul, J .... 724-458-2500 396 D pjmcnulty@gcc.edu

MCNULTY, Raymond ..... 603-668-2211 282 C r.mcnulty@snhu.edu

MCNULTY, Timothy .... 412-268-7778 391 H tpm@andrew.cmu.edu

MCNUTT, Paula, M .... 563-333-6112 173 A mcnuttpaulam@sau.edu

MCPARTLAN, Edward, J 914-337-9300 305 F ed.mcpartlan@concordia-ny.edu

MCPARTLON, Shannon . 313-664-7460 228 H smcpartlon@collegeforcreativestudies.edu

MCPEAK, Charlene .... 586-286-2097 233 B mcpeakc@macomb.edu

MCPHAIL, Craig .... 828-898-2483 339 B mcphail@lmc.edu

MCPHAIL, Julie .... 319-656-2447 173 C

MCPHAIL, P. Curtis .... 864-597-4261 426 I mcphailpc@wofford.edu

MCPHATTER, Anna .... 443-885-4325 206 A anna.mcphatter@morgan.edu

MCPHATTER, Renee .... 202-994-0679.. 92 A rmcphatt@gwu.edu

MCPHEARSON, Petra, R 731-881-7800 440 B prencher@utm.edu

MCPHEE, Debra .... 212-636-6616 308 G dmcphee1@fordham.edu

MCPHEE, Kelly .... 602-286-8186.. 13 G kelly.mcphee@gwmail.maricopa.edu

MEDINA, Joseph .... 508-999-8801 217 A
jmedina2@umassd.edu
MEDINA, Lisa .... 760-750-4813.. 33 E
lmmedina@csusm.edu
MEDINA, Lourdes, E ..... 787-766-1717 526 B
lmedina@suagm.edu
MEDINA, Mara .... 787-780-0070 521 B
mmedina@caribbean.edu
MEDINA, Mario .... 787-738-4660 528 A
mario.medina@upr.edu
MEDINA, María, C .... 787-884-3838 520 G
mmedina@atenascollege.edu
MEDINA, Nancy .... 773-442-5240 147 G
n-medina4@neiu.edu
MEDINA, Raúl .... 787-264-0406 524 D
rimedina@intersg.edu
MEDINA, Ricco .... 262-646-6528 509 C
rmedina@nashotah.edu
MEDINA, Widylia .... 787-890-2681 527 E
widylia.medina@upr.edu
MEDINA-CABAN, Mario 787-738-2161 527 D
mario.medina@upr.edu
MEDINA-ORTIZ,
Roberto .... 787-622-8000 527 B
rmedina@pupr.edu
MEDIONTE-PHILIPS,
Krista .... 607-777-4010 325 A
kmediont@binghamton.edu
MEDLEY, Lara .... 303-273-3200.. 78 J
lmedley@mines.edu
MEDLEY, Linda, S .... 859-846-5300 188 B
lsmedley@midway.edu
MEDLEY, Mike .... 435-896-9714 474 A
michael.medley@snow.edu
MEDLEY, Ticily .... 817-515-4742 458 B
ticily.medley@tccd.edu
MEDLEY-WEEKS,
Clarice .... 214-379-5565 454 H
cweeks@pqc.edu
MEDLIN, Melissa, T ...... 256-765-4276.... 9 A
mtmedlin@una.edu
MEDLIN, Rian .... 661-362-3426.. 39 C
rian.medlin@canyons.edu
MEDLIN, Sherri .... 314-264-1000 269 G
sherri.medlin@vatterott.edu
MEDRANO, Jennifer ...... 801-832-2126 474 E
jmedrano@westminstercollege.edu
MEDRO, Alfred .... 619-265-0107.. 57 G
amedro@platt.edu
MEDVETZ, Betsy .... 603-428-2477 281 F
bmedvetz@nec.edu
MEDWICK, Peter .... 215-972-2017 404 Q
pmedwick@pafa.edu
MEE, Christine, L .... 843-349-2091 420 A
christin@coastal.edu
MEE, David .... 615-460-6785 430 D
david.mee@belmont.edu
MEECE, Jeffrey .... 312-369-7151 136 H
jmeece@colum.edu
MEECE, Jill .... 606-451-6625 186 G
jill.meece@kctcs.edu
MEECE, Jill, N .... 606-679-8501 186 G
jill.meece@kctcs.edu
MEEHAN, Barry .... 603-578-8900 280 M
bmeehan@ccsnh.edu
MEEHAN, Gabriel .... 916-558-2097.. 50 I
meehang@scc.losrios.edu
MEEHAN, Kathleen, F .... 718-990-6173 322 F
meehank@stjohns.edu
MEEHAN, Linda, M .... 609-984-1105 292 B
meehan@tesu.edu
MEEHAN, Martin, T .... 617-287-7050 216 G
mmeehan@umassp.edu
MEEHAN, Mary .... 973-761-9691 291 F
mary.meehan@shu.edu
MEEHAN, Sara .... 703-284-6815 483 A
smeehan@marymount.edu
MEEK, Charles Ronald .. 340-693-1421 529 C
charles.meek@uvi.edu
MEEK, Christopher .... 701-483-2565 354 A
christopher.meek@dickinsonstate.edu
MEEK, Laura, E .... 740-587-6279 361 B
meekl@denison.edu
MEEK, Marshall .... 785-670-1830 182 D
mmeek@wualumni.org
MEEK, Michelle .... 606-886-3863 185 F
michelle.meek@kctcs.edu
MEEK, Scott .... 602-787-7902.. 13 J
scott.meek@paradisevalley.edu
MEEK, William, D .... 401-863-3422 415 K
will_meek@brown.edu
MEEKER, April, M .... 605-642-6092 428 F
april.meeker@bhsu.edu
MEEKER, Kimberly .... 660-359-3948 264 H
kmeeker@mail.ncmissouri.edu
MEEKER, Steve, L .... 605-642-6385 428 F
steve.meeker@bhsu.edu
MEEKMA, Glenn, A .... 269-471-3484 227 B
meekma@andrews.edu
MEEKS, Andy .... 859-572-5575 188 E
meeksa@nku.edu
MEEKS, Harry, L .... 812-888-4511 165 E
hmeeks@vinu.edu
MEEKS, J. Duane .... 561-803-2610 104 I
duane_meeks@pba.edu
MEEKS, Kimela, A .... 812-888-4377 165 E
kmeeks@vinu.edu
MEEKS, Mark .... 478-445-5851 119 E
mark.meeks@gcsu.edu
MEEKS, Mary .... 303-360-4728.. 79 C
mary.meeks@ccaurora.edu
MEEKS, Ronald .... 662-685-4771 252 D
rmeeks@bmc.edu
MEEKS, Susan .... 478-387-4801 120 B
smeeks@gmc.edu
MEEKS, Tom .... 216-373-5206 367 A
tmeeks@ndc.edu
MEENTS-DECAIGNY,
Ellen .... 312-362-7298 137 C
emeentsd@depaul.edu
MEER, Jonathan, D .... 609-896-5167 289 E
jmeer@rider.edu
MEESE, Paul .... 303-678-3707.. 79 K
paul.meese@frontrange.edu
MEESKE, Susan .... 402-461-7398 274 I
smeeske@hastings.edu
MEGAHED, Nivine .... 312-261-3232 146 G
nivine.megahed@nl.edu
MEGAW, Shelly .... 507-389-7289 247 H
shelly.megaw@southcentral.edu
MEGHREBLIAN, Caren .. 510-925-4282.. 25 P
cmeghreblian@aua.am
MEGNA, Robert .... 631-632-6340 325 F
robert.megna@stonybrook.edu
MEHA, Arapata .... 808-675-3211 128 K
ara.meha@byuh.edu
MEHDIZADEH, Mojdeh . 510-215-3801.. 40 K
mojdeh@contracosta.edu
MEHL, Peter .... 501-450-5137.. 23 I
peterm@uca.edu
MEHLER, Mark .... 973-408-3309 285 E
mmehler@drew.edu
MEHLHOFF, Monte .... 605-626-7781 428 H
monte.mehlhoff@northern.edu
MEHLIG, Lisa .... 815-921-4070 150 A
l.mehlig@rockvalleycollege.edu
MEHMERT, Rebecca ...... 573-897-5000 267 F
MEHRABADI, Monte ..... 619-594-6061.. 34 B
mehrabadi@mail.sdsu.edu
MEHRER, Susanne .... 603-646-2236 281 C
susanne.mehrer@dartmouth.edu
MEHRHOFF, Jay .... 636-584-6585 259 L
jay.mehrhoff@eastcentral.edu
MEHRING, Michelle ...... 212-678-8072 312 A
mimehring@jtsa.edu
MEHRING, Tes .... 785-594-8312 174 J
tes.mehring@bakeru.edu
MEHTA, Neera .... 425-739-8211 495 F
neera.mehta@lwtech.edu
MEHTA, Raj .... 513-556-6252 371 E
raj.mehta@uc.edu
MEI, Jeffrey .... 617-731-7170 223 F
jmei@pmc.edu
MEIDLINGER, Peter, K .. 417-873-7469 259 G
pmeidlin@drury.edu
MEIER, Andreea .... 843-863-7095 419 C
ameier@csuniv.edu
MEIER, Beth, A .... 919-760-8427 339 H
meierb@meredith.edu
MEIER, Heather .... 215-641-6603 402 A
hmeier@mc3.edu
MEIER, Jared .... 970-248-1945.. 77 K
jmeier@coloradomesa.edu
MEIER, Jay .... 701-224-5666 354 F
jay.meier@bismarckstate.edu
MEIER, Karen, F .... 757-683-5026 483 G
kmeier@odu.edu
MEIER, Lori .... 712-279-3518 173 B
lori.meier@stlukescollege.edu
MEIER, Neal .... 513-487-1174 371 A
neal.meier@myunion.edu
MEIER, Veronica .... 402-872-2218 276 C
vmcasey@peru.edu
MEIER PFEIFER, Donna 620-672-2700 180 K
donnamp@prattcc.edu
MEIFERT, Janeen .... 920-686-6121 510 A
janeen.meifert@sl.edu
MEIGHAN, Elizabeth, A . 717-334-6286 412 E
emeighan@ltsg.edu
MEIKLEJOHN, Scott ...... 207-725-3822 198 G
smeiklej@bowdoin.edu
MEIKSINS, Peter .... 216-687-5520 359 L
p.meiksins@csuohio.edu
MEILMAN, Philip, W ...... 202-687-6985.. 92 B
pwm9@georgetown.edu
MEINDL, Lidia .... 212-463-0400 331 F
lidia.meindl@touro.edu
MEINEKE, John .... 309-796-5053 134 C
meinekej@bhc.edu
MEINERT, Anita .... 641-673-1063 174 F
meinerta@wmpenn.edu
MEINERT, David .... 641-673-1702 174 F
meinertd@wmpenn.edu
MEINHARD, Veronica .... 301-405-3677 207 G
meinhard@umd.edu
MEINHARDT, Stephanie 972-881-5847 446 I
smeinhardt@collin.edu
MEINZEN, David, L .... 260-399-7700 165 B
dmeinzen@sf.edu
MEIRICK, Craig, R .... 563-562-3263 172 D
meirickc@nicc.edu
MEIS, Aaron .... 513-745-2941 374 D
meisa@xavier.edu
MEIS, Gail, N .... 404-471-6306 114 H
gmeis@agnesscott.edu
MEIS, John .... 229-226-1621 126 E
jmeis@thomasu.edu
MEISEL, Joseph, S .... 401-863-9499 415 K
joseph_meisel@brown.edu
MEISEL, Seth .... 262-472-1013 512 C
meisels@uww.edu
MEISENZAHL, Dan, T .... 808-956-5941 129 H
dmeisenz@hawaii.edu
MEISER, Michelle .... 717-947-6172 404 S
mmeiser2@pacollege.edu
MEISNER, Jolene .... 570-662-4696 406 F
jmeisner@mansfield.edu
MEISSNER, Ken .... 712-749-2111 167 C
meissnerk@bvu.edu
MEISTER, Barbara .... 740-474-8896 367 E
bmeister@ohiochristian.edu
MEISTER, Bobbi .... 712-274-5606 172 A
meisterb@morningside.edu
MEISTER, Debra .... 312-915-7244 144 D
dmeiste@luc.edu
MEISTER, Tony .... 660-944-2899 258 G
tmeister@conception.edu
MEITZNER, June .... 507-285-7213 247 D
june.meitzner@rctc.edu
MEIXSEL-CORDERO,
Terri .... 623-245-4600.. 16 H
tmeixsell@uti.edu
MEJIA, Gary, L .... 626-584-5440.. 43 K
garymejia@fuller.edu
MEJIA, Gil .... 602-331-7500.. 11 C
gmejia@aii.edu
MEJIA, Juan, E .... 903-510-2261 464 D
jmej@tjc.edu
MEJIA, Laurie .... 626-966-4576.. 25 M
lauriemejia@agu.edu
MEJIA KRUG,
Miroslava .... 630-829-6418 133 I
mmkrug@ben.edu
MEJIA MARTINEZ,
Marcela .... 714-997-6711.. 36 G
mamartin@chapman.edu
MEJIAS, Gladys .... 787-264-1912 524 D
gmejias@intersg.edu
MEJIAS, Ida, A .... 787-250-1912 524 B
iamejias@metro.inter.edu
MEJIAS, Jackeline .... 787-765-1915 524 F
jmejias@opto.inter.edu
MEJIAS, Juan, R .... 787-763-6700 522 N
jrmejias_ortiz@yahoo.com
MEJIAS, Luis .... 787-780-0070 521 B
lmejias@caribbean.edu
MEJIAS, Nelson .... 787-753-6335 522 Q
nmejias@icprjc.edu
MEJIC, Tatiana .... 718-270-6016 303 C
tmejic@mec.cuny.edu
MEKEEL, Naomi .... 518-255-5547 328 C
mekeelnf@cobleskill.edu
MEKEMSON, Kristen, M 920-832-7449 507 L
kristen.mekemson@lawrence.edu
MELÉNDEZ HERNÁNDEZ,
Astrid, Y .... 787-884-3838 520 G
amelendez@atenascollege.edu
MELÉNDEZ RAMOS,
Grisel, E .... 787-763-6299 528 F
grisel.melendez@upr.edu
MELANCON, Kimberly ... 225-768-1710 191 G
kimberly.melancon@ololcollege.edu
MELAND, Greg .... 651-255-6167 250 D
gmeland@unitedseminary.edu
MELANSON, Christine ... 207-509-7141 200 I
cmelanson@unity.edu
MELANSON,
Leigh Anne .... 603-862-3292 282 F
leigh-anne.melanson@unh.edu
MELANSON, Maggie ...... 617-824-8525 214 E
margaret_melanson@emerson.edu
MELARAGNI, Robert ...... 617-670-4401 215 B
rmelaragni@fisher.edu
MELARAGNO, Steven .... 401-254-3667 417 C
smelaragno@rwu.edu
MELAVALIN, Robin .... 647-928-4624 222 D
rmelavalin@mountida.edu
MELBOURNE, Barbara ... 563-884-5290 172 H
barbara.melbourne@palmer.edu
MELBY, Darlene .... 530-938-5220.. 39 H
dmelby@siskiyous.edu
MELBY, Diane .... 210-434-6711 454 D
dmelby@ollusa.edu
MELCHER, Chris .... 706-721-4018 116 B
cmelcher@augusta.edu
MELCHER, Mike .... 806-291-3425 470 I
melcherp@wbu.edu
MELCHER, Rick, W .... 610-921-7748 388 E
rmelcher@albright.edu
MELCHERT, Russell, B .. 816-235-1607 268 D
melchertr@umkc.edu
MELCHIOR, Vonda .... 813-253-7107 101 M
vmelchior@hccfl.edu
MELDER, Renee .... 318-487-7340 191 J
renee.melder@lacollege.edu
MELDREM, Joyce, A ..... 563-588-7164 171 H
joyce.meldrem@loras.edu
MELEG, Mike .... 309-796-5002 134 C
melegm@bhc.edu
MELEN, Pia .... 714-533-1495.. 64 F
pmelen@southbaylo.edu
MELENDEZ, Georgianna 617-287-4818 216 I
georgianna.melendez@umb.edu
MELENDEZ, Jennifer ..... 212-472-1500 318 B
jmelendez@nysid.edu
MELENDEZ, Maria .... 787-857-3600 523 I
mmelendez@br.inter.edu
MELENDEZ, Martin .... 787-834-3718 528 C
support@uprm.edu
MELENDEZ, Nildalee ..... 787-852-1430 522 P
nmelendez@hccpr.edu
MELENDEZ, Nitza .... 787-725-8120 522 M
nmelendez@eap.edu
MELENDEZ, Rafael .... 787-725-6500 521 C
rmelendez@albizu.edu
MELENDEZ, Ruben .... 908-709-7085 292 C
ruben.melendez@ucc.edu
MELENDEZ, Yahaira ...... 787-620-2040 520 F
melendezy@aupr.edu
MELENDEZ LEON,
Leonardo .... 787-720-4476 527 A
registraduria@mizpa.edu
MELENDY, Lisa, M .... 413-597-2477 226 C
lisa.m.melendy@williams.edu
MELETIES, Panayiotis .... 718-262-2780 304 A
pmeleties@york.cuny.edu
MELHART, Bonnie .... 817-257-7729 461 A
b.melhart@tcu.edu
MELIKECHI,
Noureddine .... 978-934-3840 217 B
noureddine_melikechi@uml.edu
MELIN, Laurie, A .... 787-257-7373 525 Q
lamelin@suagm.edu
MELISI, Mary Ann .... 610-558-5611 402 G
melisim@neumann.edu
MELISSARATOS, Aris ..... 443-352-4140 207 C
amelissaratos@stevenson.edu
MELKONIAN,
Madeleine .... 718-405-3236 304 H
madeleine.melkonian@mountsaintvincent.edu
MELL, Doug .... 715-232-1198 512 A
melld@uwstout.edu
MELLAND, Helen .... 406-657-3784 272 A
helen.melland@montana.edu
MELLE, Carl .... 541-278-5743 382 A
cmelle@bluecc.edu
MELLENKAMP, Kathleen 606-759-7141 186 E
kathleen.mellenkamp@kctcs.edu
MELLER, Brenda .... 248-689-8282 238 F
bmeller@walshcollege.edu
MELLICHAMP, James, F 706-776-0100 124 E
president@piedmont.edu
MELLING, Alice .... 206-934-3693 497 H
alice.melling@seattlecolleges.edu
MELLO, Catherine .... 402-559-4385 277 H
catherine.mello@unmc.edu
MELLO, James .... 740-283-3771 361 L
jmello@franciscan.edu
MELLO, Jeffrey .... 401-456-8036 417 A
jmello1@ric.edu
MELLO, Steven .... 401-874-2698 417 E
smello@uri.edu
MELLO-GOLDNER,
Diane .... 617-731-7106 223 F
dmellogoldner@pmc.edu
MELLON, Edward, J ...... 703-323-3083 488 H
emellon@nvcc.edu
MELLON, James, P .... 808-932-7467 129 I
mellon@hawaii.edu

MELLON, Suzanne, K ... 412-578-6123 391 G
skmellon@carlow.edu
MELLON, Timothy ... 904-819-6459 98 I
tmellon@flagler.edu
MELLONI, Suzanne ... 508-999-9299 217 A
smelloni@umassd.edu
MELLOR, Tracey ... 617-747-2700 212 B
studyabroad@berklee.edu
MELLOTT, David, M ... 717-290-8723 399 F
rgawn@lancasterseminary.edu
MELLOTT, Ramona ... 928-523-7145 14 K
ramona.mellott@nau.edu
MELLOW, Gail, O ... 718-482-5050 303 B
gmellow@lagcc.cuny.edu
MELMED, Shlomo ... 310-423-8294 35 P
MELNICK, Julie ... 402-844-7123 276 G
juliem@northeast.edu
MELNICK, Patrick ... 216-221-8584 373 E
pmelnick@vmcad.edu
MELNIK, JoAnn ... 724-964-8811 403 A
jmelnik@ncstrades.edu
MELNYK, Bernadette ... 614-292-4844 367 H
melnyk.15@osu.edu
MELOAN, Andrea ... 816-415-7831 270 C
meloana@william.jewell.edu
MELOCHE, Catherine ... 774-354-0464 211 F
catherine.meloche@becker.edu
MELOCHE, Kyle ... 410-857-2275 205 E
kmeloche@mcdaniel.edu
MELOCHE, Richard ... 405-878-5350 379 G
rsmelochel@stgregorys.edu
MELOHUSKY, Lisa ... 716-673-3649 325 C
lisa.melohusky@fredonia.edu
MELONE, Dave ... 213-624-1200 42 N
dmelone@fidm.edu
MELONSON, Christie ... 210-829-3129 465 E
melonson@uiwtx.edu
MELOY, Faye, A ... 610-359-5353 393 E
fmeloy@dccc.edu
MELSON, Rick ... 937-766-7810 358 D
rickmelson@cedarville.edu
MELSON, Vollie, D ... 410-777-1494 202 D
vmelson@aacc.edu
MELTON, Angela ... 402-471-2505 276 A
amelton@nscs.edu
MELTON, Chris ... 206-546-4613 498 E
cmelton@shoreline.edu
MELTON, Cindy ... 601-925-3250 254 B
cmelton@mc.edu
MELTON, David, V ... 617-364-3510 212 D
dmelton@boston.edu
MELTON, Eric ... 405-325-3701 380 L
emelton@ou.edu
MELTON, Josephine ... 650-493-4430 64 C
josie.melton@sofia.edu
MELTON, Judi ... 214-329-4447 443 J
judi.melton@bgu.edu
MELTON, Julie ... 217-875-7211 149 J
jmelton@richland.edu
MELTON, Leslie, J ... 740-368-3152 368 N
ljdelerm@owu.edu
MELTON, Mark, A ... 919-516-4029 348 G
mamelton@st-aug.edu
MELTON, Matthew ... 423-614-8115 432 L
mmelton@leeuniversity.edu
MELTON, Melissa ... 251-380-2271 7 B
mmelton@shc.edu
MELTON, Randall ... 269-927-8139 232 G
melton@lakemichigancollege.edu
MELTON, Randy ... 903-510-2310 464 D
rmel@tjc.edu
MELTON, JR., Samuel ... 662-254-3434 255 A
smelton@mvsu.edu
MELTON, Steve ... 828-297-3811 341 D
smelton@cccti.edu
MELTON, Toni ... 901-381-3939 440 I
toni@visible.edu
MELTON PAGES, Joyce . 817-598-6245 470 J
jpages@wc.edu
MELUSKY, Marie, B ... 814-472-3126 409 G
mmelusky@francis.edu
MELVILLE, John ... 252-638-7260 342 E
melvillej@cravencc.edu
MELVIN, Cynthia ... 601-977-7716 256 B
cmelvin@tougaloo.edu
MELVIN, Dana ... 412-291-6270 389 F
dmelvin@aii.edu
MELVIN, Julie ... 216-421-7455 359 J
jrmelvin@cia.edu
MELVIN, Kari ... 301-846-2441 203 H
kmelvin@frederick.edu
MELVIN, Lee, H ... 716-645-6003 325 B
MELVIN, Marilee, A ... 630-752-5517 155 F
marilee.melvin@wheaton.edu
MELVIN, Matt ... 785-864-4381 181 I
mattmelvin@ku.edu
MELVIN, Michael ... 770-233-6167 126 B
mmelvin@sctech.edu
MELVIN, Sharyl ... 618-985-2828 141 D
sharylmelvin@jalc.edu
MEMBRINO, Charles ... 617-585-1239 222 H
itshelp@necmusic.edu
MEMMOTT, Brian, K ... 208-496-4926 131 D
memmottb@byui.edu
MEN, Su-hua ... 941-752-5250 108 P
mens@scf.edu
MENA, Clara ... 203-285-2123 85 E
cmena@gwcc.commnet.edu
MENA, Robert ... 213-738-6716 65 I
studentaffairs@swlaw.edu
MENACHEMSON, Kelly .. 541-346-6317 387 F
kbm@uoregon.edu
MENARD, Connie ... 940-898-3826 464 A
cmenard@twu.edu
MENARD, Ginger ... 413-662-5201 218 C
ginger.menard@mcla.edu
MENARD, Jennifer ... 508-678-2811 219 C
jennifer.menard@bristolcc.edu
MENARD, Richard, O ... 509-313-3583 495 A
menardr@gonzaga.edu
MENARD, Richard, R ... 401-841-7004 518 E
richard.menard@usnwc.edu
MENARD, Tim ... 218-281-8585 250 G
menar021@umn.edu
MENARD, William ... 401-739-5000 416 D
bmenard@neit.edu
MENCARELLI, Brent ... 574-372-5100 158 B
mencarb@grace.edu
MENCER, Eric ... 304-243-8181 505 H
mencer@wju.edu
MENCHION, Byron ... 850-644-1803 110 A
bmenchion@fsu.edu
MENCK, Carol ... 206-239-2315 492 D
cmenck@aii.edu
MENDELL, Cyndi ... 513-751-1206 356 A
info@aic-arts.edu
MENDELL, Sean, M ... 513-751-1206 356 A
sean@aic.arts.edu
MENDELSOHN, Kathy ... 831-755-6700 45 C
kmendelsohn@hartnell.edu
MENDELSON, Cheryl, L 312-893-7110 138 D
cmendelson@erikson.edu
MENDELSON, Eleonor ... 831-476-9424 43 C
admissions@fivebranches.edu
MENDENHALL, James ... 918-463-2931 375 G
james.mendenhall@connorsstate.edu
MENDES, Godfrey ... 614-947-6027 362 A
godfrey.mendes@frankli.edu
MENDES, Steve ... 203-857-7011 86 D
smendes@norwalk.edu
MENDES, Susy ... 212-237-8449 302 F
smendes@jjay.cuny.edu
MENDES, Wendy ... 559-734-9000 61 C
wendym@sjvc.edu
MENDEZ, Celia ... 787-276-0130 527 H
celia.mendez@upr.edu
MENDEZ, David ... 787-751-0178 525 O
edmendez@suagm.edu
MENDEZ, Diana ... 760-921-5536 55 J
diana.mendez@paloverde.edu
MENDEZ, Jannette ... 787-856-0945 521 K
jmendez@columbiacentral.edu
MENDEZ, José, F ... 787-766-1717 526 B
ac_jmendez@suagm.edu
MENDEZ, Jose, F ... 787-751-2262 525 O
jmendez@suagm.edu
MENDEZ, Larry ... 903-510-2281 464 D
lmen@tjc.edu
MENDEZ, Liz, Y ... 787-257-7373 525 Q
lmendez@suagm.edu
MENDEZ, Magaly ... 787-815-0000 527 F
magaly.mendez@upr.edu
MENDEZ, Mike ... 320-308-5353 247 F
mike.mendez@sctcc.edu
MENDEZ, Pedro ... 209-575-6332 75 J
mendezp@mjc.edu
MENDEZ, Rolando ... 787-284-1912 524 C
rmendez@ponce.inter.edu
MENDEZ, Sheri ... 775-784-4176 279 E
smendez@unr.edu
MENDEZ-GRANT,
Monica ... 940-898-3601 464 A
mmendez@twu.edu
MENDEZ-HERNANDEZ,
Santiago ... 787-296-1101 213 B
santiago.mendez-hernandez@cambridgecollege.edu
MENDEZ MAQUEO,
Veronica ... 830-279-3023 462 G
veronica.maqueo@sulross.edu
MENDIETA, Juan ... 305-237-7611 103 L
jmendiet@mdc.edu
MENDIETTA, Dorianna ... 559-730-3821 39 G
doriannam@cos.edu
MENDINI, Shauna ... 435-865-8185 473 A
mendini_s@suu.edu
MENDIOLA, Francisco ... 691-320-2480 519 G
mendiolaf@comfsm.fm
MENDIS, Chanaka ... 608-342-1262 511 D
mendisc@uwplatt.edu
MENDOLA, Richard, A .. 404-727-6861 119 B
rich.mendola@emory.edu
MENDONEZ RUSSELL,
Bernadette ... 561-862-4400 105 A
russellb@palmbeachstate.edu
MENDOZA, Eric ... 559-934-2501 73 N
ericmendoza2@whccd.edu
MENDOZA, Graciano ... 831-479-6279 28 F
grmendoza@cabrillo.edu
MENDOZA, Melinda ... 972-883-2445 467 D
mmendoza@utdallas.edu
MENDOZA, Pablo ... 724-357-3402 406 C
mendoza@iup.edu
MENDOZA, Sylvia, F ... 201-360-4201 286 E
smendoza@hccc.edu
MENDOZA-WELCH,
Maxine ... 903-886-5851 459 E
maxine.mmendo@tamu.edu
MENEAR, Anne ... 660-263-3900 258 A
annemenear@cccb.edu
MENEAR, Anne, P ... 660-263-3900 258 A
annemenear@cccb.edu
MENEAR, Shelley ... 301-387-3037 203 I
shelley.menear@garrettcollege.edu
MENEFEE, Jeannine ... 303-678-3664 79 K
jeannine.menefee@frontrange.edu
MENELEY, Theresa ... 713-221-8612 465 C
meneleyt@uhd.edu
MENENDEZ,
Jacqueline, R ... 305-284-5505 112 O
jmenendez@miami.edu
MENENDEZ, Rasel ... 310-287-4379 49 H
menendrm2@wlac.edu
MENESES, Jilma ... 503-493-6411 382 I
jmeneses@cu-portland.edu
MENG, Xiao-Li ... 617-496-1464 215 G
xlmeng@fas.harvard.edu
MENGE, Jeff ... 209-954-5022 61 B
jmenge@deltacollege.edu
MENGEL, David ... 513-745-3101 374 D
mengel@xavier.edu
MENGLER, Thomas, M . 210-436-3722 455 J
tmengler@stmarytx.edu
MENICE, Paul ... 207-786-6254 198 E
pmenice@bates.edu
MENJIVAR, Claudia, I ... 650-574-6146 62 A
menjivarc@smccd.edu
MENJIVAR, Juan ... 562-938-4258 48 I
jmenjivar@lbcc.edu
MENK, David, A ... 507-933-6539 242 D
dmenk@gustavus.edu
MENKE, David ... 206-592-3443 495 E
dmenke@highline.edu
MENKE, Scott ... 262-595-2155 511 C
scott.menke@uwp.edu
MENKING, Cornell ... 575-646-7041 295 B
cmenking@nmsu.edu
MENN, Esther ... 773-256-0721 144 G
emenn@lstc.edu
MENNE, Renee, A ... 563-588-7130 171 H
renee.menne@loras.edu
MENNECHEY, Pamela ... 407-708-2380 107 G
mennecheyp@seminolestate.edu
MENNEKE, Beth, R ... 314-505-7761 258 I
mennekeb@csl.edu
MENNELL, Betsy ... 928-523-7128 14 K
betsy.mennell@nau.edu
MENNELLA, Hillary ... 562-860-2451 36 A
hmennella@cerritos.edu
MENNELLA, Princy ... 413-565-1000 211 C
pmennella@baypath.edu
MENNICKE, Sue ... 717-358-7187 395 G
sue.mennicke@fandm.edu
MENNINGER, Gaynia ... 785-242-5200 180 H
gaynia.menninger@ottawa.edu
MENNINGER, Jay, E ... 802-656-3290 476 E
jay.menninger@uvm.edu
MENOGAN, Kelle ... 601-977-7828 256 B
kmenogan@tougaloo.edu
MENON, Ajay ... 970-491-6274 78 N
ajay.menon@colostate.edu
MENON, Goutham ... 312-915-7005 144 D
gmenon@luc.edu
MENON, Sanjay, T ... 318-797-5234 194 E
sanjay.menon@lsus.edu
MENON, Sathyapal ... 415-442-7080 44 E
smenon@ggu.edu
MENON, Shaily, A ... 610-660-1282 409 H
smenon@sju.edu
MENSAH, Kortet, G ... 240-895-4259 206 G
kgmensah@smcm.edu
MENSAH, Michael, O ... 570-941-4049 413 F
michael.mensah@scranton.edu
MENSAH-BONSU,
Abigail ... 303-329-6355 78 L
assistantdean@cstcm.edu
MENSCH, Scott ... 888-980-9151 486 B
MENSCHING, Ron ... 630-889-6606 147 D
rmensching@nuhs.edu
MENSE, Tobias ... 334-244-3091 4 E
tmense@aum.edu
MENTE, Patrick, J ... 607-436-2596 325 E
patrick.mente@oneonta.edu
MENTZER, Cathy ... 717-262-2604 415 B
cmentzer@wilson.edu
MENTZER, Stacy, L ... 515-574-1148 170 C
mentzer_s@iowacentral.edu
MENZ, Harald ... 304-829-7915 501 F
hmenz@bethanywv.edu
MENZEL, Carol, A ... 410-334-2946 210 C
cmenzel@worwic.edu
MENZER, Paul ... 540-887-7058 482 G
pmenzer@marybaldwin.edu
MEOLA, Christine ... 508-373-9501 211 F
christine.meola@becker.edu
MEONSKE, Kali, A ... 330-325-6492 366 F
kmeonske@neomed.edu
MERANDA, Seth ... 402-643-7220 274 B
seth.meranda@cune.edu
MERCADANTE, Richard . 727-791-2527 107 A
mercadante.richard@spcollege.edu
MERCADEL, Robert ... 504-520-7396 198 D
rmercade@xula.edu
MERCADO, Deborah, A . 410-777-2321 202 D
damercado@aacc.edu
MERCADO, Harry ... 787-740-3555 526 G
harry.mercado@uccaribe.edu
MERCADO, Juan Carlos 212-925-6625 301 F
jmercado@ccny.cuny.edu
MERCADO, Lemuel ... 770-228-7383 126 B
lmercado@sctech.edu
MERCADO-COTA,
Teresa ... 714-564-6105 58 A
mercado-cota_teresa@sac.edu
MERCATORIS,
Mary Beth ... 814-732-1409 406 B
mmercatoris@edinboro.edu
MERCER, Brenda, D ... 919-739-6736 347 E
bdmercer@waynecc.edu
MERCER, Brian ... 217-351-2273 148 H
bmercer@parkland.edu
MERCER, Debbie, K ... 785-532-5525 179 A
dmercer@ksu.edu
MERCER, Frank ... 386-506-4461 97 I
mercerf@daytonastate.edu
MERCER, John ... 513-745-4890 374 D
mercerjl@xavier.edu
MERCER, John, D ... 850-872-3807 101 J
jmercer@gulfcoast.edu
MERCER, Laura ... 937-512-4571 370 A
laura.mercer@sinclair.edu
MERCER, Leneil ... 318-487-7420 191 J
leneil.mercer@lacollege.edu
MERCER, Leslie, K ... 651-201-1862 243 I
leslie.mercer@so.mnscu.edu
MERCER, Linda ... 252-399-6351 335 I
lmercer@barton.edu
MERCER, Melissa ... 828-898-3485 339 B
mercerm@lmc.edu
MERCER, Molly ... 724-738-2179 407 C
molly.mercer@sru.edu
MERCER, Peter, P ... 201-684-7607 289 C
pmercer@ramapo.edu
MERCER,
Roberta (Bobby) ... 740-377-2520 370 L
bobby.mercer@tsbc.edu
MERCER, Sally ... 724-480-3379 392 K
sally.mercer@ccbc.edu
MERCHANT, Debra, S ... 513-556-4119 371 E
debra.merchant@uc.edu
MERCHANT, Deneene ... 740-753-7080 362 K
merchantm@hocking.edu
MERCHANT, Joshua, D . 904-620-2100 110 E
joshua.merchant@unf.edu
MERCHANT, Joshua, D . 712-749-2103 167 C
merchantj@bvu.edu
MERCHANT, Susan ... 518-608-8420 308 A
smerchant@excelsior.edu
MERCHLEWITZ, Ann, E . 507-457-1587 250 B
amerchle@smumn.edu
MERCIER, Collette ... 801-627-8304 472 D
mercierc@owatc.edu
MERCIER, Deborah ... 949-214-3346 40 I
deb.mercier@cui.edu
MERCIER, Nichole, R ... 314-747-1903 269 L
nmercier@wustl.edu
MERCIER, Stace, L ... 601-266-8525 256 E
stace.mercier@usm.edu
MERCIER, Taylor ... 210-690-9000 449 K
tmercier@hallmarkuniversity.edu

MERCINCAVAGE, Janet, E .... 570-208-5878 398 D
jemercin@kings.edu
MERCK, Dana .... 252-222-6021 341 F
merckd@carteret.edu
MERCK, II, William, F .. 407-823-2351 110 C
william.merck@ucf.edu
MERCURIO, Gloria .... 201-761-6125 291 D
gmercurio@saintpeters.edu
MERCURIO, Joseph .... 617-984-1775 223 H
jmercurio@quincycollege.edu
MERCURIO, Sherry .... 614-947-6581 362 A
sherry.mercurio@franklin.edu
MEREDITH, Ben .... 509-359-6010 494 D
bmeredith@ewu.edu
MEREDITH, Brian .... 270-745-6169 190 F
brian.meredith@wku.edu
MEREDITH, Dave .... 252-328-4781 349 I
meredithd14@ecu.edu
MEREDITH, Derek .... 252-335-0821 342 D
derek_meredith@albemarle.edu
MEREDITH, Joyce .... 740-587-6515 361 B
meredithj@denison.edu
MEREDITH, Mark .... 903-675-6327 464 C
mark.meredith@tvcc.edu
MEREDITH, Pam .... 956-882-5946 468 A
pamela.meredith@utrgv.edu
MEREDITH, Stephanie ... 304-336-8117 504 E
smeredith@westliberty.edu
MERESSI, Tesfay .... 508-999-8542 217 A
tmeressi@umassd.edu
MERFALEN, Barbara, K . 670-237-6706 520 D
barbara.merfalen@marianas.edu
MERFALEN, Vince .... 670-237-6764 520 D
vince.merfalen@marianas.edu
MERGEN, Amy .... 419-251-1842 365 C
amy.mergen@mercycollege.edu
MERGEN, Dennis .... 320-308-3296 247 E
djmergen@stcloudstate.edu
MERGET, Kathleen .... 845-451-1776 306 D
kathy.merget@culinary.edu
MERGIOTTI, James, J ... 215-670-9494 403 D
president@peirce.edu
MERGUIE, John .... 501-450-3111.. 23 I
jmerguie@uca.edu
MERIAN, Dan .... 313-593-5151 238 A
dmerian@umich.edu
MERIANO, John .... 203-582-8763.. 88 A
john.meriano@quinnipiac.edu
MERIANS, Linda .... 646-313-8000 303 G
linda.merians@guttman.cuny.edu
MERICA, Michael .... 928-226-4212.. 12 B
michael.merica@coconino.edu
MERICLE, Margaret, E ... 559-442-8210.. 66 G
margaret.mericle@fresnocitycollege.edu
MERIDITH, Pamela .... 870-759-4139.. 23 K
pmeridith@wbcoll.edu
MERILLAT, Jason, C ...... 610-566-1776 415 A
jmerillat@williamson.edu
MERIMEE, Nancy, S ...... 913-971-3427 179 H
nsmerimee@mnu.edu
MERINAR, Whitney, A .... 570-321-4144 400 G
merinar@lycoming.edu
MERINO, Robert .... 281-998-6342 456 A
robert.merino@sjcd.edu
MERINO, Robert .... 281-998-6342 455 L
robert.merino@sjcd.edu
MERINO, Robert .... 281-998-6342 456 B
robert.merino@sjcd.edu
MERINO, Robert .... 281-998-6150 455 K
robert.merino@sjcd.edu
MERIWETHER, James, H .... 805-437-3313.. 31 C
jim.meriwether@csuci.edu
MERIWETHER, Jan, Y .... 252-399-6314 335 I
jymeriwether@barton.edu
MERIWETHER, Jason, L 401-456-8000 417 A
jmeriwether@ric.edu
MERIWETHER, Mimi ...... 803-786-3856 420 D
mmeriwether@columbiasc.edu
MERJIL, Mark .... 909-384-8900.. 59 I
mmerjil@sbccd.cc.ca.us
MERKEL, Diane, K .... 518-564-2195 327 E
dmerk001@plattsburgh.edu
MERKEL, Luz .... 509-777-4225 500 H
lmerkel@whitworth.edu
MERKIN, Yitzchok .... 301-962-5111 210 D
ymerkin@yeshiva.edu
MERKLE, Ben .... 208-882-1566 132 D
bmerkle@nsa.edu
MERKLE, Jean .... 563-425-5765 173 K
merklej@uiu.edu
MERKLE, Joseph, F .... 717-815-1460 415 G
jmerkle@ycp.edu
MERKLE, Karen, L .... 410-386-8107 203 A
kmerkle@carrollcc.edu
MERKLE, Patricia .... 315-568-3277 317 A
pmerkle@nycc.edu
MERKLIN, Lynn .... 269-471-6066 227 B
merklin@andrews.edu
MERKOW, Russ .... 425-739-8436 495 F
russ.merkow@lwtech.edu
MERKT, Dan .... 518-608-8371 308 A
dmerkt@excelsior.edu
MERKT, Mary Lou .... 864-294-2140 421 I
marylou.merkt@furman.edu
MERL, Jill .... 808-544-9364 129 C
jmerl@hpu.edu
MERLE, Dan .... 704-290-5219 346 F
dmerle@spcc.edu
MERLINO, Keith .... 412-809-5100 408 D
merlino.keith@pti.edu
MERLINO, Tina .... 209-954-5039.. 61 B
kmerlino@deltacollege.edu
MERLO, Antonio .... 713-348-3699 455 F
amerlo@rice.edu
MERLO, Barbara .... 254-526-1223 445 L
barbara.merlo@ctcd.edu
MERLO, Scott, R .... 269-387-5555 239 E
scott.merlo@wmich.edu
MERMANN-JOZWIAK, Elisabeth .... 509-313-5522 495 A
mermann-jozwiak@gonzaga.edu
MERMELSTEIN, Joanne . 978-837-5117 221 G
mermelsteinj@merrimack.edu
MERO, Neal, P .... 386-822-7406 111 E
nmero@stetson.edu
MERRELL, Howard .... 671-734-1812 520 A
hmerrell@piu.edu
MERRELL, Melinda, M .. 425-235-5846 497 E
mmerrell@rtc.edu
MERRELL, Sue .... 937-512-2917 370 A
sue.merrell@sinclair.edu
MERRELL, Tom .... 415-422-2613.. 72 A
merrellt@usfca.edu
MERRICK, Robyn, M ..... 225-771-4680 195 J
robyn_merrick@sus.edu
MERRIFIELD, Ann .... 573-875-7210 258 F
amerrifield@ccis.edu
MERRIFIELD, Mary .... 314-529-9510 262 B
mmerrifield@maryville.edu
MERRILL, Chad .... 828-694-1704 341 B
chadm@blueridge.edu
MERRILL, Dale .... 657-278-3256.. 32 B
dmerrill@fullerton.edu
MERRILL, H. Donald ..... 704-233-8284 353 D
dmerrill@wingate.edu
MERRILL, Joanne .... 603-897-8257 281 I
jmerrill@rivier.edu
MERRILL, Katelyn .... 619-849-7082.. 57 H
katelynmerrill@pointloma.edu
MERRILL, Scott, M .... 508-793-2438 213 D
smerrill@holycross.edu
MERRILL, Timothy .... 804-523-5131 488 C
tmerrill@reynolds.edu
MERRILL, Traci .... 619-260-7967.. 71 J
tmerrill@sandiego.edu
MERRILL-DOSS, Jean .... 573-518-2154 263 E
jeanmer@mineralarea.edu
MERRILL-SANDS, Deborah .... 603-862-1983 282 F
deborah.merrillsands@unh.edu
MERRIMAN, Gary .... 909-599-5433.. 48 E
gmerriman@lifepacific.edu
MERRIMAN, Karen .... 704-330-6796 342 A
karen.merriman@cpcc.edu
MERRIMAN, JR., W, R . 330-823-6050 372 C
merrimdr@mountunion.edu
MERRITT, Aaron .... 660-263-3900 258 A
aaronmerritt@cccb.edu
MERRITT, Bert .... 850-484-1143 105 E
bmerritt@pensacolastate.edu
MERRITT, Brandt .... 863-667-5777 108 G
bwmerritt@seu.edu
MERRITT, Brian .... 919-718-7426 341 H
bmerritt@cccc.edu
MERRITT, Cheryl .... 909-607-7853.. 38 C
cheryl_merrit@kgi.edu
MERRITT, Debra .... 860-486-2337.. 88 G
debra.merritt@uconn.edu
MERRITT, Laura .... 212-659-3604 312 E
lmerritt@tkc.edu
MERRITT, Maribea .... 432-552-2809 469 D
merritt_m@utpb.edu
MERRITT, Nancy .... 412-268-1209 391 H
nmkm@andrew.cmu.edu
MERRITT, Nathan .... 626-584-5364.. 43 K
nathanmerritt@fuller.edu
MERRITT, Pearl, E .... 325-696-0503 463 E
pearl.merritt@ttuhsc.edu
MERRITT, Scott .... 318-869-5708 191 C
smerritt@centenary.edu
MERRITT, Stephen, R .... 610-519-7499 413 K
stephen.merritt@villanova.edu
MERRITT, Susam .... 804-330-0111 479 C
MERRY, Nicholas .... 410-293-1010 519 E
nicholas.merry@navy.mil
MERRYMAN, Ed .... 408-554-5076.. 62 F
emerryman@scu.edu
MERRYMAN, Jon .... 870-245-5506.. 20 G
merrymanj@obu.edu
MERSETH, Juel, O .... 507-344-7854 240 I
juel.merseth@blc.edu
MERSETH, Lynette, Y .... 507-344-7317 240 I
lynette.merseth@blc.edu
MERSMANN, Tina .... 513-244-4232 366 A
tina.mersmann@msj.edu
MERSON, Michael, H .... 919-681-7760 337 C
michael.merson@duke.edu
MERTEN, Erik .... 605-367-6109 429 C
erik.merten@southeasttech.edu
MERTENS, Daniel .... 701-662-1654 355 A
danial.mertens@lrsc.edu
MERTENS, Robert .... 262-472-1221 512 C
mertensr@uww.edu
MERTES, Michael .... 802-387-7179 475 C
michaelmertes@landmark.edu
MERTES, Scott .... 989-386-6622 234 B
smertes@midmich.edu
MERTH, Paula, B .... 651-290-6376 248 U
paula.merth@mitchellhamline.edu
MERTZ, Jennifer, L .... 610-758-3181 400 B
jlm207@lehigh.edu
MERTZ, Scot .... 936-294-1423 462 F
sdm007@shsu.edu
MERTZ-WEIGEL, Dorothee .... 912-344-3128 115 D
dorothee.mertz-weigel@armstrong.edu
MERVINE, Ed .... 310-577-3000.. 75 G
financialaid@yosan.edu
MERVIUS, Sandra .... 516-463-4335 310 D
sandra.mervius@hofstra.edu
MERY, Pam .... 415-239-3227.. 37 H
pmery@ccsf.edu
MERYHEW, Barb .... 307-268-2249 516 H
bmeryhew@caspercollege.edu
MERZ, Marcie, L .... 215-898-6171 412 G
mmerz@dev.upenn.edu
MERZ, Nan .... 408-554-4007.. 62 F
nmerz@scu.edu
MERZ, Soon, O .... 512-223-7035 443 G
smerz@austincc.edu
MESA, Norma .... 805-969-3626.. 55 G
nmesa@pacifica.edu
MESA, Tina .... 210-486-3901 441 H
tmesa@alamo.edu
MESARIS, Nikilos 'Nik' .. 951-487-3073.. 52 J
nmesaris@msjc.edu
MESAROS, Cortney .... 480-517-8402.. 14 B
cortney.mesaros@riosalado.edu
MESCHA, Manal .... 973-300-2754 291 I
mmescha@sussex.edu
MESECAR, Christopher .. 704-357-2541 125 H
cjmesecar@southuniversity.edu
MESECAR, Christopher .. 919-317-3052 125 H
cjmesecar@southuniversity.edu
MESEROLE, Scott .... 618-842-3711 140 C
meseroles@iecc.edu
MESERVE, Mary .... 207-786-6097 198 E
mmeserve@bates.edu
MESHCHERYAKO, Nell .. 804-527-1000.. 93 B
MESHKATY, Shahra .... 619-260-2298.. 71 J
meshkaty@sandiego.edu
MESICS, Linda, L .... 610-799-1585 400 A
lmesics@lccc.edu
MESINA, Irene .... 808-845-9195 130 E
imesina@hawaii.edu
MESKER, Bobby, S .... 432-837-8231 462 G
bmesker@sulross.edu
MESLER, Cecelia .... 616-632-2868 227 C
meslecec@aquinas.edu
MESONAS, Lenny .... 908-526-1200 289 D
lenny.mesonas@raritanval.edu
MESQUITA, Cezar .... 360-650-4350 500 E
cezar.mesquita@wwu.edu
MESQUITA, Joseph .... 860-512-3215.. 85 G
jmesquita@manchestercc.edu
MESSA, Emily .... 832-842-8184 464 F
eamessa@uh.edu
MESSA, Emily .... 832-842-8184 465 A
eamessa@uh.edu
MESSAC, Achille .... 202-806-6565.. 92 C
messac@howard.edu
MESSAROS, Jean .... 570-674-6320 401 M
srjean@misericordia.edu
MESSER, Emily .... 706-233-7342 125 E
emesser@shorter.edu
MESSER, James .... 412-237-3108 392 G
jmesser@ccac.edu
MESSER, Thomas, C ..... 904-596-2411 112 F
tmesser@tbc.org
MESSERSCHMIDT, Daniel .... 434-544-8872 482 F
messerschmidt.d@lynchburg.edu
MESSERVY, Steven .... 256-824-6343.... 8 C
steven.messervy@uah.edu
MESSICK, Gary, A .... 260-422-5561 159 D
gamessick@indianatech.edu
MESSIER, John, D .... 207-778-7457 201 D
john.messier@maine.edu
MESSINA, John, A .... 330-972-6594 371 C
jam125@uakron.edu
MESSINA, Kimberlee ..... 650-358-6887.. 61 Q
messinaks@smccd.edu
MESSINA, Rosalia .... 503-847-2555 387 I
rmessina@uws.edu
MESSINA, Susan, G ...... 704-463-3040 348 B
susan.messina@pfeiffer.edu
MESSING, Robert, O ..... 512-471-1735 467 C
romessing@austin.utexas.edu
MESSINGER, Jacquelyn . 903-510-2305 464 D
jmes@tjc.edu
MESSINGSCHALGER, Mark .... 859-344-3531 189 G
messinm@thomasmore.edu
MESSITTE, Zachariah, P 920-748-8118 509 H
messittez@ripon.edu
MESSMAN-MANDICOTT, Lea .... 301-687-4890 209 A
lmessman@frostburg.edu
MESSNER, Leonard, V ... 312-949-7108 140 A
lmessner@ico.edu
MESSNER, Melody .... 816-936-8717 266 K
mmessner@saintlukescollege.edu
MESSNER, Robert, H ..... 717-780-2333 396 G
rhmessne@hacc.edu
MESSNER, Stephanie ..... 312-949-7013 140 A
smessner@ico.edu
MESSNER, Tom .... 904-646-2175 100 F
tom.messner@fscj.edu
MESTAN, Michael, A ..... 315-568-3100 317 A
mmestan@nycc.edu
MESTAS, Richard .... 301-243-2165 518 C
richard.mestas@dodiis.mil
MESTETH, Leslie .... 605-455-6033 427 I
lmesteth@olc.edu
MESYEF, Masha .... 801-649-5230 471 M
marketing@midwifrey.edu
MESYEF, Whitney .... 866-680-2756 471 M
financialaid@midwifery.edu
METCALF, Christine .... 603-271-6484 280 N
cmetcalf@ccsnh.edu
METCALF, Courtney .... 620-223-2700 177 E
courtneym@fortscott.edu
METCALF, Dustin .... 208-467-8665 132 F
dmetcalf@nnu.edu
METCALF, Gary .... 559-453-2063.. 43 J
gary.metcalf@fresno.edu
METCALF, Jeff, K .... 606-474-3258 185 C
jmetcalf@kcu.edu
METCALF, Jonathan, G .. 240-500-2000 204 B
jgmetcalf@hagerstowncc.edu
METCALF, Kim, K .... 702-895-3375 279 D
kim.metcalf@unlv.edu
METCALF, Linda .... 817-531-7530 463 G
lmetcalf@txwes.edu
METCALF, Robert .... 907-443-8402.. 10 B
rgmetcalf@alaska.edu
METCALF, Shawn .... 435-722-6900 472 L
METCALF, Shirley, I .... 541-383-7201 382 B
METCALFE, Sharon .... 740-392-6868 366 B
sharon.metcalfe@mvnu.edu
METE, T.J .... 772-466-4822.. 95 D
tj.mete@aviator.edu
METEAU, Robert .... 661-763-7809.. 67 A
rmeteau@taftcollege.edu
METESH, John, J .... 406-496-4159 272 E
jmetesh@mtech.edu
METEVIER, Robert .... 602-787-7872.. 13 J
robert.metevier@paradisevalley.edu
METHE, Deborah .... 413-265-2485 213 E
methed@elms.edu
METHVIN, Jennifer .... 417-455-5534 259 D
jennifermethvin@crowder.edu
METIANU, Mihaela .... 561-297-3049 109 B
mmetianu@fau.edu
METILLY, Paul .... 617-254-2610 224 B
paul.metilly@sjs.edu
METIVIER SCOTT, Shelly .... 508-910-6402 217 A
sscott1@umassd.edu
METKE, L. Michael .... 903-510-2380 464 D
mmet@tjc.edu
METOYER, Waylon .... 501-975-8557.. 21 A
wmetoyer@philander.edu
METRESS, Heather, B .... 706-721-5052 116 B
hmetress@augusta.edu

METROPULOS, Christopher, T .... 617-850-1280 215 I
pres_office@hchc.edu
METS, Lisa, A .... 727-864-8221.. 97 O
metsla@eckerd.edu
METTAUER, Patrice .... 401-456-8083 417 A
pmettauer@ric.edu
METTEE, Chris, J .... 330-325-6854 366 F
cmettee@neomed.edu
METTEN, Michelle .... 618-252-5400 151 J
michelle.metten@sic.edu
METTILLE, Teege .... 715-682-1224 509 D
tmettille@northland.edu
METTS, Amanda .... 252-399-6315 335 I
ahmetts@barton.edu
METTS, Deanna .... 931-372-3045 438 F
dmetts@tntech.edu
METZ, Catherine, A .... 765-361-6418 166 B
metzc@wabash.edu
METZ, Christine .... 516-562-3403 307 D
cmetz@northwell.edu
METZ, David .... 614-287-2617 360 C
dmetz@cscc.edu
METZ, George .... 843-863-7050 419 C
gmetz@csuniv.edu
METZ, Gregory .... 513-745-5720 371 F
gregory.metz@uc.edu
METZ, Matthew .... 716-829-7502 307 B
metzm@dyc.edu
METZ, Perry .... 812-855-8000 159 H
metz@indiana.edu
METZ, Ray, E .... 313-593-5151 238 A
remetz@umich.edu
METZ, Robert, C .... 517-264-7117 236 I
rmetz@sienaheights.edu
METZ, Roxanne .... 949-582-4824.. 64 J
rmetz@saddleback.edu
METZ, Starla .... 727-341-4368 107 A
metz.starla@spcollege.edu
METZ, Susan .... 201-216-5245 291 G
susan.metz@stevens.edu
METZ, Terry .... 651-523-2160 242 E
tmetz01@hamline.edu
METZ, Tim .... 828-227-7239 352 C
tdmetz@wcu.edu
METZELAARS, Gretchen . 614-688-8011 367 H
metzelaars.1@osu.edu
METZGAR, Johanna .... 415-254-6033.. 68 G
jmetzgar@berkeley.edu
METZGAR, Michael .... 315-498-6061 319 G
m.c.metzgar@sunyocc.edu
METZGER, David, D ...... 757-683-4865 483 G
dmetzger@odu.edu
METZGER, Elizabeth ...... 505-277-3389 296 H
emetzger@unm.edu
METZGER, Michael, D ... 716-673-3109 325 C
michael.metzger@fredonia.edu
METZGER, Nan .... 414-930-3338 509 B
metzgern@mtmary.edu
METZGER, Peggy .... 707-826-4321.. 34 A
mam7001@humboldt.edu
METZGER, Theresa .... 404-270-5232 126 D
tmetzger@spelman.edu
METZGER, Thomas .... 702-968-2013 280 B
tmetzger@roseman.edu
METZINGER, Ryland ...... 408-924-1800.. 34 D
ryland.metzinger@sjsu.edu
METZLER, Christopher .. 717-299-7794 411 C
metzler@stevenscollege.edu
METZO, Vincent .... 212-924-5900 330 G
vmetzo@swedishinstitute.edu
MEULEMANS, Nicole ...... 651-450-3311 245 A
nmeulem@inverhills.edu
MEULEMANS, Nicole ..... 651-423-8403 244 E
nicole.meulemans@dctc.edu
MEUSCHKE, Daylene ..... 661-362-5329.. 39 C
daylene.meuschke@canyons.edu
MEUWISSEN, Daniel, J . 651-962-5100 251 D
djmeuwissen@stthomas.edu
MEUY, Saechao .... 559-297-4500.. 46 E
MEWERS, Montgomery . 318-869-5110 191 C
mmewers@centenary.edu
MEWS, Joseph .... 803-938-3731 425 F
mewsj@uscsumter.edu
MEY, Craig, A .... 715-836-3263 510 D
meyca@uwec.edu
MEYDAM, Mark, R .... 715-425-4095 511 E
mark.r.meydam@uwrf.edu
MEYER, Adam .... 212-799-5000 312 B
MEYER, Alan, E .... 708-209-3468 136 I
alan.meyer@cuchicago.edu
MEYER, Alexis .... 414-955-8246 508 D
alemeyer@mcw.edu
MEYER, Angela .... 573-651-2292 266 M
admeyer@semo.edu
MEYER, Ann .... 312-329-4417 146 B
ann.meyer@moody.edu
MEYER, Brenda .... 479-619-4248.. 20 F
bmeyer@nwacc.edu
MEYER, Bruce .... 419-372-6821 357 F
bameyer@bgsu.edu
MEYER, Carrie .... 260-744-8747 164 C
crmeyer@taylor.edu
MEYER, Chris .... 405-733-7913 379 F
cmeyer@rose.edu
MEYER, Dale, A .... 314-505-7010 258 I
meyerd@csl.edu
MEYER, Daniel, R .... 920-832-6607 507 L
daniel.r.meyer@lawrence.edu
MEYER, David .... 816-414-3700 263 D
dmeyer@mbts.edu
MEYER, David, D .... 504-865-5930 196 D
meyer@tulane.edu
MEYER, Donald, J .... 319-352-8517 174 C
donald.meyer@wartburg.edu
MEYER, Doug .... 503-493-6471 382 I
dmeyer@cu-portland.edu
MEYER, Eddie .... 860-727-6906.. 87 B
emeyer@goodwin.edu
MEYER, Edward .... 307-532-8330 516 J
edward.meyer@ewc.wy.edu
MEYER, Frederick, B ..... 507-538-0554 241 E
frederick.meyer@mayo.edu
MEYER, Fredric, B .... 507-284-3268 241 F
meyer.fredric@mayo.edu
MEYER, Gary .... 917-493-4456 313 M
gmeyer@msmnyc.edu
MEYER, Gary .... 414-288-6350 508 C
gary.meyer@marquette.edu
MEYER, Gregg, A .... 508-531-1237 217 D
gmeyer@bridgew.edu
MEYER, Gregor .... 312-788-1132 154 I
gmeyer@vandercook.edu
MEYER, Jay .... 847-543-2717 136 E
jmeyer@clcillinois.edu
MEYER, Jennifer .... 818-785-2726.. 35 N
MEYER, Jill .... 414-930-3339 509 B
meyerj@mtmary.edu
MEYER, John .... 414-443-8910 513 A
john.meyer@wlc.edu
MEYER, John .... 605-626-2379 428 H
john.meyer@northern.edu
MEYER, John, D .... 239-513-1122 101 O
jmeyer@hodges.edu
MEYER, John, E .... 507-354-8221 243 C
meyerjd@mlc-wels.edu
MEYER, Joseph, M .... 512-245-2386 463 A
jm01@txstate.edu
MEYER, Josh .... 540-857-6311 490 B
jmeyer@virginiawestern.edu
MEYER, Kathy .... 701-483-2535 354 A
kathleen.meyer@dickinsonstate.edu
MEYER, Kelli, A .... 203-576-4487.. 88 F
kmeyer@bridgeport.edu
MEYER, Kelly .... 518-458-5402 305 B
meyerk@strose.edu
MEYER, Kimberly, J ...... 574-807-7021 156 E
kimberly.meyer@bethelcollege.edu
MEYER, Kingsley .... 740-245-7365 372 E
kmeyer@rio.edu
MEYER, Kyle, P .... 402-559-7428 277 H
kpmeyer@unmc.edu
MEYER, Larry .... 859-572-6117 188 E
meyerl3@nku.edu
MEYER, LeeAnn .... 312-788-1120 154 I
lmeyer@vandercook.edu
MEYER, Lisa .... 503-768-7056 383 G
lmeyer@lclark.edu
MEYER, Liz .... 970-248-1410.. 77 K
lmeyer@coloradomesa.edu
MEYER, Mary, J .... 402-844-7030 276 G
maryjm@northeast.edu
MEYER, Mathys .... 606-218-5467 190 E
mathysmeyer@upike.edu
MEYER, Matthew .... 919-807-7155 340 K
meyerm@nccommunitycolleges.edu
MEYER, Merry .... 845-758-7005 298 I
sm568@bncollege.com
MEYER, Michael .... 808-844-2308 130 E
mmeyer@hawaii.edu
MEYER, Michele .... 407-691-1754 106 J
mmeyer@rollins.edu
MEYER, Michelle .... 541-885-1628 385 E
michelle.meyer@oit.edu
MEYER, Mike .... 909-599-5433.. 48 E
mmeyer@lifepacific.edu
MEYER, Patricia .... 240-629-7905 203 H
pmeyer@frederick.edu
MEYER, Patricia .... 513-745-1996 374 D
meyerp@xavier.edu
MEYER, Paul, W .... 215-247-5777 412 G
pmeyer@upenn.edu
MEYER, Peter, E .... 863-680-4264 100 D
pmeyer@flsouthern.edu
MEYER, Rick .... 909-599-5433.. 48 E
rmeyer@lifepacific.edu
MEYER, Robert .... 715-232-2441 512 A
meyeb@uwstout.edu
MEYER, Sabrina .... 707-468-3065.. 51 E
smeyer@mendocino.edu
MEYER, Sam .... 502-585-9911 189 B
smeyer@spalding.edu
MEYER, Shana .... 816-271-4432 264 B
slmeyer@missouriwestern.edu
MEYER, Sheree .... 916-278-6502.. 33 C
meyers@csus.edu
MEYER, Stan .... 602-639-7500.. 12 P
MEYER, Susan .... 320-308-5512 247 F
smeyer@sctcc.edu
MEYER, Terry .... 623-935-8191.. 13 F
terry.meyer@estrellamountain.edu
MEYER, Theresa .... 540-231-1483 490 F
tsmayer@vt.edu
MEYER, Thomas .... 605-274-5330 426 K
thomas.meyer@augie.edu
MEYER, Thomas, W ...... 610-799-1517 400 A
tmeyer1@lccc.edu
MEYER, Yvonne .... 816-271-4439 264 B
ymeyer@missouriwesern.edu
MEYER REIMER, Kathryn .... 574-535-7443 158 A
kathymr@goshen.edu
MEYERS, Andrew, W ..... 901-678-2590 439 E
ameyers@memphis.edu
MEYERS, Bonnie .... 651-779-3346 244 D
bonnie.meyers@century.edu
MEYERS, Cory .... 617-879-2037 226 A
cmeyers@wheelock.edu
MEYERS, Ernest, G .... 864-488-4367 422 B
emeyers@limestone.edu
MEYERS, Jeffrey .... 432-335-6815 454 C
jmeyers@odessa.edu
MEYERS, Matthew .... 610-892-1543 405 C
mmeyers@pit.edu
MEYERS, Ruth .... 510-204-0720.. 37 F
rmeyers@cdsp.edu
MEYERS, Shelly, A .... 864-488-8207 422 B
smeyers@limestone.edu
MEYERS, Tom, J .... 574-535-7346 158 A
tomjm@goshen.edu
MEYERS, Vanessa .... 202-687-5627.. 92 B
vmm8@georgetown.edu
MEZA, Ilda .... 509-865-8500 495 D
MEZA, Jose .... 787-257-0000 527 H
jose.meza1@upr.edu
MEZA, Kathy .... 619-849-2540.. 57 H
kathymeza@pointloma.edu
MEZIERE, Kevin .... 858-653-6740.. 46 M
kmeziere@jpcatholic.com
MEZQUITA, Jennifer, V . 407-582-3425 113 F
jmezquita@valenciacollege.edu
MEZYNSKI, David .... 914-961-8313 323 H
dmezynski@svots.edu
MEZZACAPPA, John ...... 561-929-3405 108 A
admissions@sfbc.edu
MHLANGA, Fortune .... 615-966-5073 433 D
fortune.mhlanga@lipscomb.edu
MI, Hanfu .... 217-206-6512 154 A
hmi2@uis.edu
MIAN, Mahreen, N .... 904-620-2371 110 E
mahreen.mian@unf.edu
MIARKA-GRZELAK, Anna .... 518-562-4171 304 C
anna.miarka-grzelak@clinton.edu
MIAZGA, John .... 325-942-2212 463 C
john.miazga@angelo.edu
MICAL, Kelly .... 910-296-2509 344 B
kmical@jamessprunt.edu
MICARELLI, Stephen .... 617-349-8705 216 D
smicarel@lesley.edu
MICCO, Melissa, A .... 412-397-5264 409 C
micco@rmu.edu
MICELI, Christy .... 312-629-6706 151 F
cmiceli@saic.edu
MICELI, Paul .... 781-899-5500 223 G
rev.miceli@psjs.edu
MICELI, Paul, E .... 781-899-5500 223 G
rev.miceli@psjs.edu
MICELI, Tara .... 916-361-1660.. 35 G
tara.miceli@carrington.edu
MICHAEL, Cheryl .... 410-334-2884 210 C
cmichael@worwic.edu
MICHAEL, Cynthia .... 937-376-6304 358 I
cmichael@centralstate.edu
MICHAEL, Gage .... 719-549-3011.. 81 M
michael.gage@pueblocc.edu
MICHAEL, Jennifer .... 315-364-3312 333 G
jmichael@wells.edu
MICHAEL, Jody .... 810-762-0048 234 F
jody.michael@mcc.edu
MICHAEL, III, Max .... 205-934-7730.... 8 B
maxm@uab.edu
MICHAEL, Sandra .... 215-637-7700 397 G
smichael@holyfamily.edu
MICHAEL, Steve, O .... 323-563-5854.. 36 H
stevemichael@cdrewu.edu
MICHAEL, Thomas, R .... 217-581-2319 138 A
trmichael@eiu.edu
MICHAEL, Timothy .... 313-577-2313 239 C
tmichael@wayne.edu
MICHAEL-PICKETT, Stephanie .... 704-922-6215 343 D
michael.stephanie@gaston.edu
MICHAELIAN, Katherine 240-567-7695 205 F
katherine.michaelian@montgomerycollege.edu
MICHAELIDES, Anthony 661-362-3253.. 39 C
anthony.michaelides@canyons.edu
MICHAELIDES, Barbara . 318-342-5550 198 A
michaelides@ulm.edu
MICHAELIS, Joel .... 606-248-0178 187 B
jmichaelis0001@kctcs.edu
MICHAELIS, Joel .... 254-562-3848 453 J
joel.michaelis@navarrocollege.edu
MICHAELIS, Michael ...... 785-628-4291 177 D
mwmichaelis@fhsu.edu
MICHAELIS, Michelle .... 325-942-2012 463 C
michelle.michaelis@angelo.edu
MICHAELIS, Randall ...... 509-777-4402 500 H
rmichaelis@whitworth.edu
MICHAELS, Alan, C .... 614-292-2631 367 H
michaels.23@osu.edu
MICHAELS, Brent .... 910-678-8209 343 B
michaelb@faytechcc.edu
MICHAELS, Cheryl .... 304-424-8300 505 C
cheryl.michaels@wvup.edu
MICHAELS, Craig .... 718-997-5220 303 E
craig.michaels@qc.cuny.edu
MICHAELS, Debbie .... 541-552-6590 386 H
michaeld@sou.edu
MICHAELS, Dennis .... 716-614-6744 318 E
dmichaels@niagaracc.suny.edu
MICHAELS, George, H ... 805-893-2378.. 70 B
george.michaels@id.ucsb.edu
MICHAELS, James .... 570-504-9641 395 I
jmichaels@tcmc.edu
MICHAELS, Jeff, A .... 717-477-1171 407 B
jamich@ship.edu
MICHAELS, Lynda .... 570-389-4061 405 E
lmichael@bloomu.edu
MICHAELS, Meredith ..... 949-824-4923.. 69 A
m.michaels@uci.edu
MICHAELS, Sheila .... 218-935-0417 251 F
sheila.michaels@wetcc.edu
MICHAELS, Sheri .... 229-732-5928 115 B
sherimichaels@andrewcollege.edu
MICHAELS, Sue .... 916-660-7271.. 63 K
smichaels@sierracollege.edu
MICHAELSEN, Kevin ...... 919-760-8565 339 H
michaelsen@meredith.edu
MICHAELSON, Frank ...... 805-969-3626.. 55 G
fmichaelson@pacifica.edu
MICHAJLA, Patty .... 425-640-1516 494 E
pmichajl@edcc.edu
MICHAL, Richard .... 317-940-9445 156 I
rmichal@butler.edu
MICHALAK, Mary Jane .. 317-921-4882 161 F
mmichalak@ivytech.edu
MICHALAK, Russell .... 302-225-6227.. 90 G
michalr@gbc.edu
MICHALAK, Sarah .... 919-962-1301 351 B
smichala@email.unc.edu
MICHALENKO, John ...... 412-397-6483 409 C
michalenko@rmu.edu
MICHALERYA, William, D .... 610-758-5802 400 B
wdm1@lehigh.edu
MICHALKO, Nancy .... 801-957-4247 474 B
nancy.michalko@slcc.edu
MICHALOWSKI, Sam ..... 201-692-2060 286 B
ir_sam@fdu.edu
MICHALSKI, Gregory ..... 904-632-3017 100 F
g.michalski@fscj.edu
MICHALSKI, Monica ...... 718-489-5272 322 D
mmichalski@sfc.edu
MICHALSKI, Tim .... 361-570-4820 465 D
michalskit@uhv.edu
MICHAUD, Lisa .... 207-834-7607 201 E
lisa.michaud@maine.edu
MICHAUD, Paul .... 908-526-1200 289 D
paul.michaud@raritanval.edu
MICHAUX, Kimberly, S . 434-223-6102 481 D
kmixhaux@hsc.edu
MICHEL, Bill .... 773-702-1234 153 F
wmichel@uchicago.edu
MICHEL, Mike .... 410-293-1901 519 E
michel@usna.edu
MICHEL, Pamela .... 315-312-2102 327 D
pamela.michel@oswego.edu

MICHEL, R. Keith .... 516-671-2277 333 E
kmichel@webb.edu
MICHEL, Tabatha .... 404-413-5057 121 A
tmichele@gsu.edu
MICHELLE, Dawn .... 915-595-1935 444 K
dawn.michelle@brightwood.edu
MICHELS, Kraig .... 360-417-6212 496 I
kmichels@pencol.edu
MICHELSON, Peggy ...... 314-529-6543 262 B
pmichelson@maryville.edu
MICHENER, David, G .... 979-830-4282 444 D
davidg.michener@blinn.edu
MICHIE, Cheryl .... 641-472-7000 171 J
cmichie@mum.edu
MICHIELSSEN, Eric .... 734-647-1793 237 I
emichiel@umich.edu
MICHTAVY, Lesley .... 209-588-5100.. 75 I
MICIAK, Alan, R .... 216-397-1745 363 H
amiciak@jcu.edu
MICIOTTO, Joseph .... 318-675-8053 194 D
jmicio@lsuhsc.edu
MICKELSEN, Scott, R .... 406-377-9406 270 J
smickelsen@dawson.edu
MICKELSON, Kristine .... 608-663-2374 507 D
kmickelson@edgewood.edu
MICKELSON, Sally .... 702-968-2004 280 B
smickelson@roseman.edu
MICKENS, Charles .... 517-371-5140 239 F
mickensc@cooley.edu
MICKENS, George .... 623-245-4600.. 16 H
gmickens@uti.edu
MICKENS, Kendrick .... 610-359-5340 393 E
kmickens@dccc.edu
MICKEY, Marty .... 847-947-5580 146 G
mmickey@nl.edu
MICKEY, Travis .... 336-272-7102 338 B
travis.mickey@greensboro.edu
MICKEY-BOGGS, Shari .. 937-775-2120 374 B
shari.mickey-boggs@wright.edu
MICKLE, Angela .... 937-766-7720 358 D
amickle@cedarville.edu
MICKLER, Michael .... 845-752-3000 332 A
mm@uts.edu
MICKLES, Muriel .... 434-832-7656 487 H
micklesm@cvcc.vccs.edu
MICKOOL, Richard .... 937-525-3811 374 A
rmickool@wittenberg.edu
MICKOOL, Rick .... 401-454-6390 417 B
rmickool@risd.edu
MICUS, David .... 321-674-7400.. 99 K
dmicus@fit.edu
MIDCAP, Richard .... 301-387-3056 203 I
richard.midcap@garrettcollege.edu
MIDDEKER, Vicki .... 303-410-2438.. 82 K
vicki.middeker@spartan.edu
MIDDENDORF, Terry ..... 651-523-2302 242 E
tmiddendorf@hamline.edu
MIDDENDORF, Tom ...... 615-248-1258 439 B
tmiddendorf@trevecca.edu
MIDDLEKAUFF, Paul ..... 212-659-0736 312 E
pmiddlekauff@tkc.edu
MIDDLESWARTH,
Jean, E .... 336-757-3288 343 C
jmiddleswarth@forsythtech.edu
MIDDLETON, David .... 412-924-1790 408 E
dmiddleton@pts.edu
MIDDLETON, Dewayne .. 601-849-0112 252 G
dewayne.middleton@colin.edu
MIDDLETON,
Jacqueline .... 330-263-2580 360 A
jkmiddleton@wooster.edu
MIDDLETON, Kenna ...... 859-622-3436 184 F
kenna.middleton@eku.edu
MIDDLETON, Lyle .... 501-205-8830.. 19 B
lmiddleton@cbc.edu
MIDDLETON,
Melinda, L .... 812-877-8259 163 G
middleto@rose-hulman.edu
MIDDLETON, Michael ... 212-772-4065 302 E
mm5378@hunter.cuny.edu
MIDDLETON,
Michael, A .... 573-681-5042 261 H
middletonm@lincolnu.edu
MIDDLETON, Natavia .... 727-398-8288 107 A
middleton.natavia@spcollege.edu
MIDDLETON, Nigel, T ... 303-273-3327.. 78 J
nmiddlet@mines.edu
MIDDLETON, Renee, A .. 740-593-4400 368 G
middletr@ohio.edu
MIDDLETON,
Rodney, C .... 989-328-1202 234 D
rodm@montcalm.edu
MIDDLETON, Tracy .... 803-705-4594 418 G
middletont@benedict.edu
MIDDLETON,
Whittaker, V .... 803-535-5347 419 E
wmiddleton@claflin.edu

MIDEI, Ron .... 954-262-5224 104 F
ronmidei@nsu.nova.edu
MIDGETT, Pam .... 940-397-4182 453 C
pam.midgett@mwsu.edu
MIDGETTE, Juanita .... 252-335-3586 350 A
jmidgette@ecsu.edu
MIDGLEY, Michael, T .... 512-223-7579 443 G
midgley@austincc.edu
MIDKIFF, Kittridge .... 270-686-4508 186 F
kitt.midkiff@kctcs.edu
MIDKIFF, Lindsay .... 870-633-4480.. 19 E
lindsay.midkiff@eacc.edu
MIDKIFF, Lori, A .... 304-929-5472 503 B
lmidkiff@newriver.edu
MIDKIFF, JR.,
Robert, M .... 570-577-1547 390 H
robert.midkiff@bucknell.edu
MIDKIFF, Scott, F .... 540-231-4227 490 F
midkiff@vt.edu
MIDTHUN, Steve .... 414-277-7224 509 A
midthun@msoe.edu
MIDURA, Matthew .... 310-506-4181.. 56 D
matthew.midura@pepperdine.edu
MIDYETTE, Marilyn, W .. 757-221-1166 479 I
mwmidyette01@wm.edu
MIEDEMA, Linda, L .... 321-433-7380.. 97 N
miedemal@easternflorida.edu
MIELKE, Cindi .... 815-599-3491 139 F
cindi.mielke@highland.edu
MIELKE, Dan .... 541-962-3833 383 B
dmielke@eou.edu
MIELKE, John .... 262-595-3226 511 C
mielke@uwp.edu
MIENE, Peter .... 507-457-5017 248 C
pmiene@winona.edu
MIENIE, Edward .... 678-717-3410 127 B
edward.mienie@ung.edu
MIERA, Joseph .... 505-277-2511 296 H
jmiera@unm.edu
MIERES, Joann, B .... 570-372-4049 410 H
mieresj@susqu.edu
MIERS, Michael .... 508-849-3326 210 H
mmiers@annamaria.edu
MIERTSCHIN, Charla ..... 507-457-5299 248 C
cmiertschin@winona.edu
MIESS, Bob, D .... 701-788-4885 354 B
robert.miess@mayvillestate.edu
MIGHTY, Hugh, E .... 202-806-5677.. 92 C
hugh.mighty@howard.edu
MIGHTY, Hugh, E .... 202-806-6100.. 92 C
MIGLER, Jerry .... 701-228-5403 354 G
jerry.migler@dakotacollege.edu
MIGLER, Jerry .... 701-228-5431 354 C
jerome.migler@dakotacollege.edu
MIGNARDOT, Henry .... 505-428-1225 296 B
henry.mignardot@sfcc.edu
MIGUEL, George .... 520-383-8401.. 16 G
gmiguel@tocc.edu
MIGYANKO,
Stephanie, M .... 724-439-4900 399 H
smigyanko@laurel.edu
MIHAL, Deborah, F .... 843-953-1431 420 C
mihaldf@cofc.edu
MIHAL, Matt .... 570-674-6336 401 M
mmihal@misericordia.edu
MIHAL, Ruthie .... 704-609-1542 336 F
ruthie.mihal@carolinascollege.edu
MIHALEVICH, Rick .... 573-897-5000 267 F
MIHALIC, Angela .... 214-648-2168 469 E
angela.mihalic@utsouthwestern.edu
MIHALY, Christine .... 734-973-3477 238 G
cmihaly@wccnet.edu
MIHALYOV, David .... 585-395-2577 326 D
dmihalyo@brockport.edu
MIHELIC, Jerry .... 580-349-1438 377 E
jmihelic@opsu.edu
MIHEVC, Jake .... 315-792-5653 315 I
jmihevc@mvcc.edu
MIHIR, Fnu .... 870-972-3027.. 18 A
fmihir@astate.edu
MIHM-HEROLD,
Wendy, A .... 563-562-3263 172 D
mihm-heroldw@portal.nicc.edu
MIHO, Mariko .... 808-932-7692 129 I
mariko.miho@uhfoundation.org
MIHOPULOS, Sheryl, L . 516-877-3365 297 I
mihopulos@adelphi.edu
MIKALSON, Joan .... 518-608-8144 308 A
jmikalson@excelsior.edu
MIKE, James .... 717-477-1151 407 B
jhmike@ship.edu
MIKE, Nena .... 691-370-3191 519 G
nenam@comfsm.fm
MIKEMAN, Cindy .... 405-736-0315 379 F
cmikeman@rose.edu
MIKESCH, Gregory .... 314-792-6119 261 E
mikesch@kenrick.edu

MIKESELL, Brian .... 413-528-7274 211 B
bmikesell@simons-rock.edu
MIKESELL, Leslie .... 530-283-0202.. 42 K
lmikesell@frc.edu
MIKESH, Jackie .... 361-582-2516 470 A
jackie.mikesh@victoriacollege.edu
MIKHAIL, Michael, B .... 312-996-2671 153 H
mmikhail@uic.edu
MIKHAIL, Mona .... 626-812-3013.. 26 U
mmikhail@apu.edu
MIKHAIL, Osama, I .... 713-500-3047 468 D
osama.i.mikhail@uth.tmc.edu
MIKHAIL, Peter .... 404-727-1060.. 46 C
MIKHALEVSKY, Nina ..... 540-654-1000 486 D
nmik@umw.edu
MIKKELSON, Tom .... 205-329-7942.... 5 C
tom.mikkelson@ecacolleges.com
MIKLUSAK, Courtney .... 619-239-0391.. 35 C
cmiklusak@cwsl.edu
MIKNAVICH, Marie .... 315-792-5467 315 I
mmiknavich@mvcc.edu
MIKOS, Shari .... 213-615-2700.. 37 B
MIKOWSKI, Thomas ..... 616-632-2853 227 C
mikowtho@aquinas.edu
MIKSA, Anthony, R .... 423-585-6770 438 D
tony.miksa@ws.edu
MIKSCH, Joseph, T .... 412-624-4356 412 I
jmiksch@pitt.edu
MIKTARIAN, Christine ... 559-244-5917.. 66 E
christine.miktarian@scccd.edu
MIKUS, Robert, L .... 717-867-6234 399 J
mikus@lvc.edu
MILAM, B. Hofler .... 336-758-3121 353 A
bhm@wfu.edu
MILAM, Elizabeth .... 864-656-3431 419 F
milamm@clemson.edu
MILAM, John .... 540-868-7249 488 E
jmilam@lfcc.edu
MILAM, Kathy, L .... 937-481-2336 373 I
kathy_milam@wilmington.edu
MILAM, Kristin .... 859-233-8111 189 H
kmilam@transy.edu
MILAM, Linda .... 918-781-7247 374 H
milaml@bacone.edu
MILAM, Rebecca .... 865-694-6560 437 F
bmilam@pstcc.edu
MILAN, Jordan .... 715-394-8213 512 B
jmilan@uwsuper.edu
MILANI, Andrea .... 513-569-1555 359 G
andrea.milani@cincinnatistate.edu
MILANI, Rachel .... 218-262-7258 244 H
rachelmilani@hibbing.edu
MILANICH, Timothy, R .. 216-368-4306 358 C
timothy.milanich@case.edu
MILASINOVIC, Milan ..... 216-221-8584 373 E
MILAVETZ, Barry .... 701-777-4278 353 G
barry.milavetz@und.edu
MILAZZO, Theresa .... 404-727-7404 119 B
theresa.milazzo@emory.edu
MILBERG, Craig .... 503-370-6561 388 D
cmilberg@willamette.edu
MILBERG, William .... 212-229-5901 316 E
milbergw@newschool.edu
MILBOURNE, John, M .. 321-674-7160.. 99 K
jmilbour@fit.edu
MILBRETT, Juanita .... 507-389-5860 246 A
juanita.milbrett@mnsu.edu
MILBURN, John .... 661-362-3245.. 39 C
john.milburn@canyons.edu
MILBURN, Lynnsey .... 616-632-2916 227 C
lam003@aquinas.edu
MILBURN, Trudy .... 914-251-6507 328 B
trudy.milburn@purchase.edu
MILBY, Kevin, S .... 859-238-5534 184 C
kevin.milby@centre.edu
MILBY, Megan, H .... 859-238-5516 184 C
megan.milby@centre.edu
MILD, Robert, E .... 304-367-4219 504 A
robert.mild@fairmontstate.edu
MILEK, Joseph .... 513-745-2000 374 D
milekj@xavier.edu
MILEM, Jeffrey .... 805-893-3917.. 70 B
jmilem@education.ucsb.edu
MILEM, Jill .... 936-468-2401 458 A
jmilem@sfasu.edu
MILES, Alicia, C .... 770-720-5542 124 H
acm1@reinhardt.edu
MILES, Arletha .... 914-773-3856 319 J
lmiles@pace.edu
MILES, Belinda, S .... 914-606-6707 333 H
belinda.miles@sunywcc.edu
MILES, Brad .... 806-291-3750 470 I
milesb@wbu.edu
MILES, Brian .... 727-341-4772 107 A
miles.brian@spcollege.edu
MILES, Cindy .... 619-644-7569.. 44 K
cindy.miles@gcccd.edu

MILES, Daniel .... 740-283-3771 361 L
dmiles@franciscan.edu
MILES, David .... 802-225-3240 475 H
david.miles@neci.edu
MILES, David, A .... 201-692-2227 286 B
dmiles@fdu.edu
MILES, Donald .... 814-472-3029 409 G
dmiles@francis.edu
MILES, Jennifer .... 662-329-7129 254 F
jmmiles@muw.edu
MILES, Jennifer, P .... 502-597-7023 187 E
jennifer.miles@kysu.edu
MILES, John, D .... 864-597-4363 426 I
milesjd@wofford.edu
MILES, Kim .... 941-377-4880 103 K
MILES, Linda .... 386-506-3720.. 97 I
milesl@daytonastate.edu
MILES, Linda .... 252-398-6505 336 K
milesl@chowan.edu
MILES, Lloyd .... 301-985-7237 208 D
lloyd.miles@umuc.edu
MILES, Lora .... 618-650-2020 152 C
lflamm@siue.edu
MILES, Mark .... 651-635-8065 240 J
m-miles@bethel.edu
MILES, Martin .... 757-727-5635 481 E
martin.miles@hamptonu.edu
MILES, Mary, E .... 502-852-6688 190 C
maryelizabeth.miles@louisville.edu
MILES, Michelle .... 304-345-2820 505 D
MILES, Richard .... 513-721-7944 362 D
rmiles@gbs.edu
MILES, Sarah, L .... 508-831-4180 226 E
smiles@wpi.edu
MILES, Stephannie .... 704-461-6873 335 J
stephanniemiles@bac.edu
MILES, Thomas .... 773-702-4907 153 F
tmiles@law.uchicago.edu
MILES, Tom .... 478-445-4027 119 E
tom.miles@gcsu.edu
MILES, Vickie .... 334-670-3732.... 7 E
vmiles@troy.edu
MILEWICZ, Mark .... 910-521-6630 351 E
mark.milewicz@uncp.edu
MILEY, Melinda .... 843-953-5426 420 C
mileym@cofc.edu
MILEY, Tamara .... 812-749-1271 163 B
tmiley@oak.edu
MILHAM, Donna .... 616-451-3511 229 D
dmilham@davenport.edu
MILHAUSEN, Michael .... 503-399-6527 382 C
michael.milhausen@chemeketa.edu
MILHOLLAND, Tom, A .. 325-674-2918 441 D
milholland@acu.edu
MILI, Fatma .... 704-687-8622 351 C
fmili@uncc.edu
MILICI, JR., Roger, A ... 212-636-6545 308 G
milici@fordham.edu
MILIONI, Barbara .... 417-268-2008 257 H
bmilioni@gobbc.edu
MILIONI, Emily .... 417-268-6000 257 H
emilioni@gobbc.edu
MILIONI, Mark, L .... 417-268-6008 257 H
mmilioni@gobbc.edu
MILIONIS, Daren .... 503-375-7012 383 A
dmilionis@corban.edu
MILJEVICH, Greg .... 715-365-4486 514 E
gmiljevich@nicoletcollege.edu
MILKOVICH, Anne .... 920-424-4480 511 B
milkovich@uwosh.edu
MILKOVICH, Patrice ...... 619-575-6176.. 65 H
pmilkovich@swccd.edu
MILKOWSKI, Rose .... 312-629-6182 151 F
rmilkowski@saic.edu
MILKOWSKI, Tracy, L ... 920-923-8159 508 B
tmilkowski@marianuniversity.edu
MILLAN, Iris .... 773-481-8765 136 B
imillan3@ccc.edu
MILLANE, Maureen .... 716-839-8334 306 E
mmillane@daemen.edu
MILLAR, Janet .... 661-654-3366.. 31 B
jmillar@csub.edu
MILLAR, Jeremy .... 937-255-6565 517 H
jeremy.millar@afit.edu
MILLARD, Bryan .... 805-546-3205.. 41 C
bryan_millard@cuesta.edu
MILLARD, Cristi .... 801-957-4145 474 B
cristi.millard@slcc.edu
MILLARD, James, R .... 252-638-7283 342 E
millardj@cravencc.edu
MILLARD, Jill .... 704-290-5887 346 F
jmillard@spcc.edu
MILLARD, Julia .... 702-579-3578 278 H
julia.millard@brightwood.edu
MILLARD, Kent .... 937-529-2201 371 B
kmillard@united.edu
MILLARD, Rachel .... 859-233-8111 189 H
rmillard@transy.edu

MILLER, Ken .... 407-646-2999 106 J
kmiller@rollins.edu
MILLER, Kenneth .... 740-857-1311 369 I
kmiller@rosedale.edu
MILLER, Kevin .... 239-489-9036 100 E
ksmiller3@fsw.edu
MILLER, Kevin, D .... 973-408-3109 285 E
theoadm@drew.edu
MILLER, Kevin, J .... 716-878-5601 326 E
millerkj@buffalostate.edu
MILLER, Kieron .... 562-907-4236.. 75 A
kmiller@whittier.edu
MILLER, Kimberly, D ..... 812-877-8176 163 G
millerk@rose-hulman.edu
MILLER, Kimela .... 575-835-5888 294 K
kimela.miller@nmt.edu
MILLER, Kris .... 615-966-5722 433 D
kris.miller@lipscomb.edu
MILLER, Kristen .... 603-752-1113 281 B
kmiller@ccsnh.edu
MILLER, Kristen .... 269-782-1305 237 B
kmiller28@swmich.edu
MILLER, Kristine .... 435-797-3646 473 C
kristine.miller@usu.edu
MILLER, Kyren .... 701-224-2450 354 F
kyren.miller@bismarckstate.edu
MILLER, LaKeith .... 251-662-5363.... 1 E
lmiller@bishop.edu
MILLER, Larry .... 228-896-2506 254 D
larry.miller@mgccc.edu
MILLER, Laura, M .... 717-796-1800 401 L
lmiller@messiah.edu
MILLER, Lauren .... 312-935-6026 149 K
lmiller@robertmorris.edu
MILLER, Lauryn .... 847-628-2086 142 B
lauryn.miller@judsonu.edu
MILLER, Lawrence .... 239-489-9319 100 E
lmiller17@fsw.edu
MILLER, Leilani, M .... 408-554-4427.. 62 F
lmiller@scu.edu
MILLER, Linda .... 618-395-1169 140 E
millerli@iecc.edu
MILLER, Linda, J .... 262-691-5526 515 B
lmiller@wctc.edu
MILLER, Lisa .... 563-244-7002 168 L
lmiller@eicc.edu
MILLER, Lisa .... 708-210-5767 151 H
lmiller@ssc.edu
MILLER, Lisa .... 620-450-2185 180 K
lisam@prattcc.edu
MILLER, Lisa .... 516-323-3046 315 J
lmiller@molloy.edu
MILLER, Lisa, R .... 318-342-5431 198 A
lmiller@ulm.edu
MILLER, Lori .... 215-702-4335 391 C
lmiller@cairn.edu
MILLER, Lucy, T .... 727-816-3448 105 C
millerl@phsc.edu
MILLER, Mandrake, T .... 804-257-5722 491 C
mtmiller@vuu.edu
MILLER, Marc .... 617-824-8953 214 E
marc_miller@emerson.edu
MILLER, Marc .... 870-230-5377.. 19 H
millermd@hsu.edu
MILLER, Marc, L .... 520-621-1498.. 16 J
marc.miller@law.arizona.edu
MILLER, Marcia .... 704-216-7167 346 C
marcia.miller@rccc.edu
MILLER, Marcia, K .... 316-284-5315 175 F
mmiller@bethelks.edu
MILLER, Margaret, M .... 609-258-5813 288 F
mmmiller@princeton.edu
MILLER, Mark .... 740-376-4811 365 A
mark.miller@marietta.edu
MILLER, Mark .... 318-869-5117 191 C
mmiller@centenary.edu
MILLER, Mark .... 417-447-2655 264 K
millerm@otc.edu
MILLER, Mark .... 402-472-4823 277 G
mark.miller@unl.edu
MILLER, Mark .... 513-936-1567 371 F
mark.miller@uc.edu
MILLER, Martin, J .... 724-287-8711 390 J
martin.miller@bc3.edu
MILLER, Marty, L .... 757-823-9539 483 F
mlmiller@nsu.edu
MILLER, Mary Anne ...... 617-928-4556 222 D
mamiller@mountida.edu
MILLER, Matt .... 989-386-6600 234 B
mmiller@midmich.edu
MILLER, Matt .... 216-221-8584 373 E
MILLER, Matthew .... 903-875-7422 453 J
matt.miller@navarrocollege.edu
MILLER, Maureen .... 810-766-8752 227 F
mparma02@baker.edu
MILLER, Megan .... 410-225-2420 205 C
memiller@mica.edu

MILLER, Megan, M .... 678-542-7537 218 E
mmiller@salemstate.edu
MILLER, Melanie .... 904-633-8403 100 F
melanie.miller@fscj.edu
MILLER, Melinda .... 615-248-1650 439 B
mmiller@trevecca.edu
MILLER, Melinda, A ...... 315-386-7085 329 A
millerm@canton.edu
MILLER, Melissa .... 843-661-8104 421 F
melissa.miller@fdtc.edu
MILLER, Melissa .... 512-863-1227 457 I
mmiller@southwestern.edu
MILLER, Melissa, C 386-312-4106 106M
melissamiller@sjrstate.edu
MILLER, Melvin .... 803-705-4461 418 G
melvin.miller@benedict.edu
MILLER, Merrill .... 315-228-1000 304 G
mmiller@colgate.edu
MILLER, Michael .... 805-893-2118.. 70 B
mike.miller@sa.ucsb.edu
MILLER, Michael .... 937-376-2946 369 C
mmiller@payne.edu
MILLER, Michael .... 512-863-1425 457 I
mikemiller@southwestern.edu
MILLER, Michael .... 715-682-1202 509 D
mmiller@northland.edu
MILLER, Michael, J .... 718-289-5548 301 D
michael.miller@bcc.cuny.edu
MILLER, Michael, S ...... 510-436-1360.. 45 G
mmiller@hnu.edu
MILLER, Michael, T .... 479-575-3208.. 21 I
MILLER,
Michael Patrick .... 708-524-5921 137 F
mmiller@dom.edu
MILLER, Michelle .... 802-860-2729 474 G
miller@champlain.edu
MILLER, Michelle, R ..... 757-727-5447 481 E
michelle.miller@hamptonu.edu
MILLER, Mike .... 805-893-2118.. 70 B
mike.miller@sa.ucsb.edu
MILLER, Mike .... 205-329-7950.... 5 C
mike.miller@ecacolleges.com
MILLER, Mindy .... 478-445-5771 119 E
mindy.miller@gcsu.edu
MILLER, Miryom, R .... 845-434-5240 335 E
mmiller@ygzm.edu
MILLER, Nancy .... 318-797-5383 194 E
nancy.miller@lsus.edu
MILLER, Natasha .... 443-334-2831 207 C
nmiller5@stevenson.edu
MILLER, Ned .... 515-964-6816 168 A
nlmiller4@dmacc.edu
MILLER, Nelson .... 616-301-6800 239 F
millern@cooley.edu
MILLER, Nora, R .... 662-329-7145 254 F
nrmiller@muw.edu
MILLER, Norman .... 318-487-7194 191 J
norman.miller@lacollege.edu
MILLER, Pam .... 985-380-2483 193 D
pamelamiller@scl.edu
MILLER, Pamela, B .... 251-442-2360.... 8 D
pbuchanan@umobile.edu
MILLER, Pat .... 517-629-0318 226 G
pmiller@albion.edu
MILLER, Pat .... 405-912-9015 379 A
pmiller@ru.edu
MILLER, Paul .... 662-243-1902 253 A
pmiller@eastms.edu
MILLER, Paul .... 336-278-5882 337 G
millerp@elon.edu
MILLER, Peter .... 516-671-7373 333 E
pmiller@webb.edu
MILLER, Peter, J .... 215-596-8865 413 E
p.miller@usciences.edu
MILLER, Poppy .... 815-939-5243 148 F
pmiller2@olivet.edu
MILLER, Rachel, S .... 620-327-8213 178 B
rachelsm@hesston.edu
MILLER, Rebecca .... 302-736-2495.. 90 J
rebecca.miller@wesley.edu
MILLER, Remy .... 901-272-5107 434 B
rmiller@mca.edu
MILLER, Richard .... 304-829-7516 501 F
rmiller@bethanywv.edu
MILLER, Richard, B .... 417-625-9565 263 G
miller-r@mssu.edu
MILLER, Richard, C .... 270-745-5468 190 F
richard.c.miller@wku.edu
MILLER, Richard, K .... 781-292-2301 215 C
richard.miller@olin.edu
MILLER, Richard, L .... 713-500-3603 468 D
richard.l.miller@uth.tmc.edu
MILLER, Rita .... 508-531-1295 217 D
rmiller@bridgew.edu
MILLER, Rob .... 913-758-6160 182 B
millerr@stmary.edu
MILLER, Robert .... 269-387-2073 239 E
bob.miller@wmich.edu

MILLER, Robert, B .... 213-891-2152.. 48 K
millerrb@email.laccd.edu
MILLER, Robert, L .... 217-581-7249 138 A
rlmiller@eiu.edu
MILLER, JR., Robert, L . 908-852-1400 284 G
millerr@centenaryuniversity.edu
MILLER, Robert, P .... 302-356-2477.. 91 B
robert.p.miller@wilmu.edu
MILLER, Robert, R .... 540-828-5383 478 J
rmiller@bridgewater.edu
MILLER, Rod .... 603-358-2425 283 A
rod.miller@keene.edu
MILLER, Rodney, E .... 316-978-3389 182 F
rodney.miller@wichita.edu
MILLER, Rodney, E .... 706-419-1134 118 E
miller@covenant.edu
MILLER, Roger .... 512-647-8792 461 G
roger.miller@tstc.edu
MILLER, Roland, G .... 847-543-2551 136 E
com624@clcillinois.edu
MILLER, JR., Ronald, E 843-661-1678 421 H
rmiller@fmarion.edu
MILLER, Roy .... 865-573-4517 432 H
rmiller@johnsonu.edu
MILLER, Ruby .... 480-517-8152.. 14 B
ruby.miller@riosalado.edu
MILLER, Ruth .... 785-594-4530 174 J
ruth.miller@bakeru.edu
MILLER, Ruth .... 650-306-3125.. 61 R
miller@smccd.edu
MILLER, Ryan .... 702-567-1920 278 F
rmiller@cci.edu
MILLER, Samuel, T .... 229-928-1387 120 F
sam.miller@gsw.edu
MILLER, Sandra .... 973-720-2659 292 I
millers@wpunj.edu
MILLER, Sarah .... 617-521-2086 224 E
sarah.miller@simmons.edu
MILLER, Scott .... 308-398-7355 273 G
scottmiller@cccneb.edu
MILLER, Scott .... 307-855-2113 516 I
smiller@cwc.edu
MILLER, Scott .... 814-732-2400 406 B
millerse@edinboro.edu
MILLER, Scott .... 814-732-2460 406 B
millerse@edinboro.edu
MILLER, Scott, D .... 757-455-3215 491 F
sdmiller@vwu.edu
MILLER, Seth .... 801-957-3448 474 B
seth.miller@slcc.edu
MILLER, Shannon .... 408-924-4300.. 34 D
shannon.miller@sjsu.edu
MILLER, Shari, K .... 716-673-3438 325 C
shari.miller@fredonia.edu
MILLER, Sharyne .... 910-962-3000 352 A
millersa@uncw.edu
MILLER, Shawn .... 315-379-3820 329 A
millers@canton.edu
MILLER, Shawn .... 425-352-8135 492 K
smiller@cascadia.edu
MILLER, Sherri .... 757-352-4843 484 E
sstocks@regent.edu
MILLER, Stephanie .... 405-682-7897 377 C
smiller@occc.edu
MILLER, Stephen .... 240-684-2037 208 D
stephen.miller@umuc.edu
MILLER, Steve .... 912-871-1801 123 J
smiller@ogeecheetech.edu
MILLER, Steve .... 513-745-5736 371 F
steve.miller2@uc.edu
MILLER, Steve .... 573-288-6440 259 E
smiller@culver.edu
MILLER, Steven .... 303-963-3353.. 77 I
stemiller@ccu.edu
MILLER, Steven, G .... 228-865-4570 256 E
steven.g.miller@usm.edu
MILLER, Steven, P .... 404-687-4568 118 B
millers@ctsnet.edu
MILLER, Stuart .... 706-379-3111 128 H
samiller@yhc.edu
MILLER, Stuart, C .... 626-395-6393.. 29 I
scmiller@caltech.edu
MILLER, Susan .... 508-362-2131 219 E
smiller@capecod.edu
MILLER, Susan .... 610-436-2442 407 D
smiller2@wcupa.edu
MILLER, Susan, S .... 901-272-5152 434 B
smiller@mca.edu
MILLER, Svetlana .... 516-629-6260 333 E
lmiller@webb.edu
MILLER, Tamsin .... 865-882-4730 438 A
miller@roanestate.edu
MILLER, Tana, J .... 806-651-4911 460 E
tmiller@mail.wtamu.edu
MILLER, Tara .... 641-648-4611 170 H
tara.miller@iavalley.edu
MILLER, Terence .... 414-288-3208 508 C
terence.miller@marquette.edu

MILLER, Teresa, A .... 716-645-6200 325 B
tmiller@buffalo.edu
MILLER, Thomas, D ...... 812-877-8210 163 G
millert@rose-hulman.edu
MILLER, Thomas, K ...... 919-513-5006 350 E
tkm@ncsu.edu
MILLER, Thomas, P ...... 520-626-0202.. 16 J
tpm@email.arizona.edu
MILLER, Tina .... 906-248-8437 227 P
tinamiller@bmcc.edu
MILLER, Tony .... 540-545-7257 485 C
amiller2@su.edu
MILLER, Tracy, L .... 330-471-8238 364 H
tmiller@malone.edu
MILLER, Travis .... 317-791-6129 164 H
tmiller@uindy.edu
MILLER, Troy .... 301-860-4363 208 E
tmiller@bowiestate.edu
MILLER, Tyrus .... 831-459-5905.. 70 C
vpdgs@ucsc.edu
MILLER, Valerie .... 740-593-4141 368 G
millerv@ohio.edu
MILLER, Van .... 254-298-8606 458 C
van.miller@templejc.edu
MILLER, Vanessa .... 714-992-7094.. 54 A
vmiller@fullcoll.edu
MILLER, Vernease .... 704-945-7313 348 B
vernease.miller@pfeiffer.edu
MILLER, Victoria .... 619-388-2699.. 60 D
vmiller@sdccd.edu
MILLER, Victoria .... 410-951-3950 208 F
vmiller@coppin.edu
MILLER, Vince .... 229-333-5941 127 H
vincemiller@valdosta.edu
MILLER, Vince .... 208-282-1045 132 B
millvinc@isu.edu
MILLER, Vincia .... 704-216-6009 339 E
MILLER, Walter, C .... 505-277-2331 296 H
wcmiller@unm.edu
MILLER, Wayne, C .... 606-783-2158 188 C
w.miller@moreheadstate.edu
MILLER, Wendy .... 847-214-7308 138 B
wmiller@elgin.edu
MILLER, Wendy, A .... 570-326-3761 404 T
wendy.miller@pct.edu
MILLER, Yolanda, D .... 662-621-4101 252 E
ymiller@coahomacc.edu
MILLER-HERNANDEZ,
Leangela .... 559-730-3795.. 39 G
leangelam@cos.edu
MILLER-REID,
M. Susan .... 925-631-4316.. 59 C
msm9@stmarys-ca.edu
MILLER-SCHACHINGER,
Susanne .... 616-234-5825 238 D
susanne.miller@vai.org
MILLER-SCHUSTER,
Danielle .... 309-438-5451 140 L
dnmille@ilstu.edu
MILLER-SUBER,
Evelyn, V .... 516-463-6473 310 D
evelyn.v.miller-suber@hofstra.edu
MILLER-THORN, Jill ...... 631-656-2122 308 F
jill.millerthorn@ftc.edu
MILLER-WIETECHA,
Lynn .... 248-204-2383 233 A
lmillerwi@ltu.edu
MILLER-YOW, Ronnie ... 501-370-5297.. 21 A
rmiller-yow@philander.edu
MILLER-YOW, Ronnie ... 501-370-5344.. 21 A
rmiller-yow@philander.edu
MILLERICK, Francis, E .. 774-354-0481 211 F
frank.millerick@becker.edu
MILLERICK, Frank .... 774-354-0481 211 F
frank.millerick@becker.edu
MILLERICK, Timothy, P . 903-813-2228 443 F
tmillerick@austincollege.edu
MILLET, Matthew, B ...... 412-397-6406 409 C
millet@rmu.edu
MILLET, Michelle .... 216-397-3053 363 H
mmillet@jcu.edu
MILLET, Peter, E .... 615-327-6015 434 A
pmillet@mmc.edu
MILLETTE, Andrea .... 513-241-4338 356 I
andrea.millette@antonellicollege.edu
MILLETTE, Paul .... 802-287-8224 475 B
millettep@greenmtn.edu
MILLICAN, Valorie .... 816-654-7332 261 D
vmillican@kcumb.edu
MILLIER, Deborah .... 706-245-7226 119 A
dmillier@ec.edu
MILLIGAN, Debra, A ..... 404-527-4520 117 C
dmilligan@carver.edu
MILLIGAN, Heath .... 843-921-6919 423 A
hmilligan@netc.edu
MILLIGAN, Kathleen, B . 314-773-0083 257 J
kmilligan@brookesbible.org

MILLIGAN, Kristen 760-776-7428 39 D kmilligan@collegeofthedesert.edu
MILLIGAN, Laura 573-840-9106 267 J lmilligan@trcc.edu
MILLIGAN, Marty 909-384-8949 59 I mmilliga@sbccd.cc.ca.us
MILLIGAN, Tom 970-491-2359 78 N tom.milligan@colostate.edu
MILLIGAN, Troy 405-422-1206 379 B milligant@redlandscc.edu
MILLIKEN, James, B 646-664-9100 301 A chancellor@cuny.edu
MILLIKEN, Roberta 740-351-3550 369 L rmilliken@shawnee.edu
MILLIKEN, Ronald, P 207-778-7105 201 D milliken@maine.edu
MILLIKEN, Stephanie 270-534-3394 187 C stephanie.milliken@kctcs.edu
MILLIKIN, Mary 918-343-7605 379 C mmillikin@rsu.edu
MILLIMAN, Robert, W 316-284-5239 175 F rmilliman@bethelks.edu
MILLION, Christina, C 404-413-1430 121 A cmillion@gsu.edu
MILLIOTIS, Dave 507-457-1421 250 B dmillioti@smumn.edu
MILLIRONS, Anna, S 540-985-8530 482 A asmillirons@jchs.edu
MILLISON, Jeffrey 410-888-9048 205 D jmillison@muih.edu
MILLITELLO, Abby 217-544-6464 151 B
MILLLER, Susan 219-989-2251 163 E sue.miller@pnw.edu
MILLNER, Kate 701-224-5666 354 F katharine.millner@bismarckstate.edu
MILLNER, Timothy 410-225-4251 205 C tmillner@mica.edu
MILLNER-HARLEE, Tanya 860-512-2603 85 G tmillner-harlee@manchestercc.edu
MILLOT, Lauri 575-646-3635 295 B lmillot@nmsu.edu
MILLOY, Phyllis, F 757-822-1063 489 H pmilloy@tcc.edu
MILLS, Ashley 864-250-7000 93 B
MILLS, Barry 617-287-6800 216 I barry.mills@umb.edu
MILLS, Brian 541-681-7304 384 H bmills@nwcu.edu
MILLS, Chad 573-518-2134 263 E cmills@mineralarea.edu
MILLS, Cheryll 757-789-1730 488 A cmills@es.vccs.edu
MILLS, Chris 610-896-1039 397 F cmills@haverford.edu
MILLS, Christian 415-503-6291 60 H cmills@sfcm.edu
MILLS, Dan 616-222-1444 229 B dan.mills@cornerstone.edu
MILLS, Dean, S 719-333-9751 518 H
MILLS, Dora 207-221-4621 202 A dmills2@une.edu
MILLS, Edward 916-278-6060 33 C emills@csus.edu
MILLS, Edward, D 912-478-1193 120 E edmills@georgiasouthern.edu
MILLS, F. Joe 931-221-7444 430 B millsj@apsu.edu
MILLS, Frank 340-693-1067 529 C fmills@uvi.edu
MILLS, JR., Gordon, E 251-460-7859 9 B gmills@southalabama.edu
MILLS, Jacala 802-387-6732 475 C jacalamills@landmark.edu
MILLS, Janie 319-363-1323 172 B jmills@mtmercy.edu
MILLS, Jeffery, N 207-581-5100 201 B jeffmills@maine.edu
MILLS, Jeremy 615-220-7800 437 C jmills1@mscc.edu
MILLS, Jock, S 541-737-4514 385 F jock.mills@oregonstate.edu
MILLS, Joe 304-336-5189 504 E jmills@westliberty.edu
MILLS, John 606-368-6121 182 H johnmills@alc.edu
MILLS, Kelly 863-638-7254 113 I kelly.mills@warner.edu
MILLS, Kevin 209-932-3014 70 F kmills@pacific.edu
MILLS, Kevin 828-398-7200 340 M kevinsmills@abtech.edu
MILLS, Kimberly, A 410-651-8100 208 C kamills@umes.edu
MILLS, Laura, J 912-344-3073 115 D laura.mills@armstrong.edu
MILLS, Leslie 406-791-5296 273 C leslie.mills@ugf.edu
MILLS, Linda 212-992-9712 318 D linda.mills@nyu.edu
MILLS, Linda, G 212-998-9712 318 D linda.mills@nyu.edu
MILLS, Mark 215-898-1453 412 G millsme@upenn.edu
MILLS, Martin 512-245-2501 463 A mm79@txstate.edu
MILLS, Marvin 240-567-5371 205 F marvin.mills@montgomerycollege.edu
MILLS, Matthew 912-650-6218 125 H mmills@southuniversity.edu
MILLS, Melissa 763-433-1332 243 K melissa.mills@anokaramsey.edu
MILLS, Michael 918-631-2327 381 C michael-mills@utulsa.edu
MILLS, Michael 918-631-2510 381 C michael-mills@utulsa.edu
MILLS, Michael 240-567-6001 205 F michael.mills@montgomerycollege.edu
MILLS, Michael 940-397-4590 453 C michael.mills@mwsu.edu
MILLS, Michael, E 847-491-4477 148 C michael-mills@northwestern.edu
MILLS, Michelle 661-654-2263 31 B mmills@csub.edu
MILLS, Ossie 918-495-6384 378 H omills@oru.edu
MILLS, Priscilla, L 928-523-3312 14 K priscilla.mills@nau.edu
MILLS, Randy, W 336-750-2706 352 D millsrw@wssu.edu
MILLS, Richard, G 603-646-0459 281 C richard.g.mills@dartmouth.edu
MILLS, Robert Dennis 304-366-8912 503 C robert.mills@pierpont.edu
MILLS, Sandra, M 513-487-3206 309 F smills@huc.edu
MILLS, Shirley, D 803-777-2001 424 I smills@mailbox.sc.edu
MILLS, Susan 951-222-8000 58 H susan.mills@rcc.edu
MILLS, Tegan, C 207-947-4591 198 F librarian@bealcollege.edu
MILLS, Tom 405-382-9210 379 I t.mills@sscok.edu
MILLS, William, R 617-552-8661 212 E william.mills@bc.edu
MILLS-DICK, Melissa 413-549-4600 215 F
MILLSAP, B. Burr 405-325-5161 380 L bmillsap@ou.edu
MILLSAPPS, Michael 970-339-6376 76 E michael.millsapps@aims.edu
MILLSAPS, Brooke 828-298-3325 353 B bmillsaps@warren-wilson.edu
MILLSAY, Pamela 903-785-7661 454 F pmillsap@parisjc.edu
MILLUSH, Mary Ann 630-942-2269 136 D millush@cod.edu
MILLWOOD, Kent 864-231-2049 418 E kmillwood@andersonuniversity.edu
MILNE, Arryn 410-864-4000 207 A amilne@stmarys.edu
MILNE, Dan 719-474-8502 76 F dan.milne@zenith.org
MILNE, Dan 303-457-2757 76 G dan.milne@zenith.org
MILNE, Dan 719-474-8502 76 F dan.milne@zenith.org
MILNE, Erin, M 413-662-5049 218 C erin.milne@mcla.edu
MILNE, Sheila 252-399-6326 335 I smilne@barton.edu
MILNER, Andrea 517-265-5161 226 F amilner@adrian.edu
MILNER, Devika, M 305-284-6858 112 O dmilner@miami.edu
MILNER, Eric 401-341-2218 417 D eric.milner@salve.edu
MILNER, Jocelyn, L 608-263-5658 510 C jocelyn.milner@wisc.edu
MILNER, Laura 608-785-8095 510 F lmilner@uwlax.edu
MILNER, Wesley 812-488-2686 164 G wm23@evansville.edu
MILONE-NUZZO, Paula 617-726-2947 222 A
MILOWSKI, Nicholas, B 718-817-4975 308 G nmilowski@fordham.edu
MILROY, James, B 585-245-5601 327 B milroy@geneseo.edu
MILSO, Lisa 978-762-4000 220 E lmilso@northshore.edu
MILSOM, Penny 443-840-5426 203 E mmilsom@ccbcmd.edu
MILSTEAD, MaLea 256-331-5297 3 C mmilstead@nwscc.edu
MILSTEEN, Jeff 470-578-3562 122 C jmilstee@kennesaw.edu
MILSTEIN, Marc 214-648-0757 469 E marc.milstein@utsouthwestern.edu
MILSTEIN, Mark 512-499-4246 467 A mmilstein@utsystem.edu
MILSTONE, David, M 508-999-8640 217 A dmilstone@umassd.edu
MILTENBERGER, Anna 503-821-8926 385 H amiltenberger@pnca.edu
MILTENBERGER, Chad 509-758-1711 499 E chad.miltenberger@wwcc.edu
MILTENBERGER, Susan 410-225-2201 205 C smiltenb@mica.edu
MILTER, Rebecca 678-916-2621 115 K rmilter@johnmarshall.edu
MILTON, Alice 205-929-6306 2 G amilton@lawsonstate.edu
MILTON, Barbara, J 973-655-4349 287 D miltonb@mail.montclair.edu
MILTON, Shawntee 760-245-4271 73 E shawntee.milton@vvc.edu
MILTON, Shirlette 713-313-7551 461 E milton_sg@tsu.edu
MILTON, Suzanne 509-359-7887 494 D smilton@ewu.edu
MILTON, Vikki 850-718-2371 96 H miltonv@chipola.edu
MILZ, George 713-646-1864 456 H gmilz@stcl.edu
MIMA, Rebecca 330-490-7090 373 F rmima@walsh.edu
MIMMS, Jacqueline 661-654-2160 31 B jmimms@csub.edu
MIMMS, Lee, S 817-552-3700 451 G lmimms@tku.edu
MIMS, Christina 903-875-7419 453 J christina.mims@navarrocollege.edu
MIMS, Dana, M 570-577-3171 390 H dana.mims@bucknell.edu
MIMS, Jane 210-784-1000 460 C jane.mims@tamusa.edu
MIMS, Janet 843-863-8004 419 C jmims@csuniv.edu
MIMS, Lloyd 561-803-2400 104 I lloyd_mims@pba.edu
MIMS, Yolanda, L 504-286-5335 195 L ymims@suno.edu
MIMS-DEVEZIN, Lisa 504-286-5064 195 L lmims@suno.edu
MIN, John 949-480-4171 64 D min@soka.edu
MIN, Sangki 913-288-7686 178 H smin@kckcc.edu
MIN, Sangki 785-628-4540 177 D s_min2@fhsu.edu
MIN, Sarah 323-731-2383 55 E sarahmin@psuca.edu
MINA, Jean 847-578-3238 150 E jean.mina@rosalindfranklin.edu
MINAR, Thomas, J 317-738-8010 157 L president@franklincollege.edu
MINARD, Jeff 972-708-7340 449 I jeff_minard@gial.edu
MINARD, Tiffany 859-815-7683 185 I tiffany.minard@kctcs.edu
MINATOYA, Lydia 206-934-3712 497 H lydia.minatoya@seattlecolleges.edu
MINCE, Rosalie 410-386-8195 203 A rmince@carrollcc.edu
MINCER, Gretta 303-556-4087 80 Q mincer@msudenver.edu
MINCH, Kevin 660-785-4105 267 K kminch@truman.edu
MINCHEFF, Daniel 920-498-5444 514 G
MINCHELLO, Brian 617-879-2205 226 A bminchello@wheelock.edu
MINCKLER, Tye 254-968-9877 459 A minckler@tarleton.edu
MINCKS, Kathy 907-564-8272 9 F kmincks.akpacprop@gci.net
MINDEN, Courtney 781-239-5589 211 A cminden@babson.edu
MINDRUM, Matthew, S 317-940-9257 156 I mmindrum@butler.edu
MINE, Jodi 808-934-2742 130 D mine@hawaii.edu
MINEHART, Heather 760-252-2411 27 A hminehart@barstow.edu
MINEHART, James 419-448-2160 362 G jminehar@heidelberg.edu
MINEO, Michael 718-817-4931 308 G mineo@fordham.edu
MINEO, Steve 912-525-5000 125 B smineo@scad.edu
MINER, Anna, D 603-526-3655 280 H anna.miner@colby-sawyer.edu
MINER, Brenda 479-394-7622 23 D bminer@uarichmountain.edu
MINER, Jack 614-292-9330 367 H miner.10@osu.edu
MINER, James 928-350-4201 15 V james.miner@prescott.edu
MINER, Judy, C 650-949-6100 43 D minerjudy@fhda.edu
MINER, Madonne 801-626-6006 473 E madonneminer@weber.edu
MINER, Seth 309-298-1965 155 D sb-miner@wiu.edu
MINFORD, Joell 412-392-3422 408 F jminford@pointpark.edu
MING, Amanda 248-476-1122 233 F aming@mispp.edu
MING, Sally 563-387-1527 171 I mingsa01@luther.edu
MINGEE, Sheila 217-709-0923 143 C smingee@lakeviewcol.edu
MINGENBACK, Mary 620-341-5413 177 B mmingenb@emporia.edu
MINGO, Dana 214-379-5438 454 H dmingo@pqc.edu
MINGO, Doreen 319-226-2049 166 C doreen.mingo@allencollege.edu
MINGO, Rhonda 864-596-9140 420 F rhonda.mingo@converse.edu
MINGO, Susan 207-454-1032 200 D smingo@wccc.me.edu
MINGO, Tracey 912-478-5413 120 E tmingo@georgiasouthern.edu
MINGUS, Cherise 502-447-1000 189 D cmingus@spencerian.edu
MINHAS, Omer 419-772-2529 367 G o-minhas@onu.edu
MINI, Susan 815-753-0495 147 H smini@niu.edu
MINICK, Thomas 610-790-2862 389 A thomas.minick@alvernia.edu
MINICOLA, Steven 215-573-0251 412 G minicola@upenn.edu
MINICOZZI, Michele 610-566-1776 415 A mminicozzi@williamson.edu
MINIER, Matt 502-897-4205 189 A mrminier@sbts.edu
MINIER-DELGADO, Jesenia 203-837-8277 85 B
MININGER, Marcus 219-864-2400 162 U mmininger@midamerica.edu
MINIX, Jeannette 865-524-8079 432 F jminix@hchs.edu
MINK, Randy, L 412-397-4901 409 C mink@rmu.edu
MINK, Rose 901-751-8453 434 E rmink@mabts.edu
MINKLER, James 360-538-4000 495 B jim.minkler@ghc.edu
MINKLER, Steven 860-343-5706 86 A sminkler@mxcc.commnet.edu
MINNE, Erin 312-362-8663 137 C minne@depaul.edu
MINNEMA, Emily 614-825-6255 356 C eminnema@aiam.edu
MINNER, Mandy 302-831-1234 90 I aminner@udel.edu
MINNER, Sam 505-454-3269 294 J president_office@nmhu.edu
MINNETTE, Mitch 208-562-3516 132 A mitchminnette@cwidaho.cc
MINNICH, Bryan, K 785-833-4428 179 C bryan.minnich@kwu.edu
MINNICH, Chad, A 401-456-8395 417 A cminnich@ric.edu
MINNICH, Dan 330-972-6476 371 C dminnich@uakron.edu
MINNICH, Peggy 513-244-4531 366 A peggy.minnich@msj.edu
MINNICH, William 650-738-4484 62 B minnichw@smccd.edu
MINNICH KJESBO, Faith 717-796-1800 401 L fminnich@messiah.edu
MINNICH SPUHLER, Donna 973-720-3258 292 I minnichspuhlerd@wpunj.edu
MINNICK, Ann, M 651-696-6036 243 B aminnick@macalester.edu
MINNICK, William, C 712-707-7226 172 G bminnick@nwciowa.edu
MINNIEFIELD, Angela, L 323-563-4897 36 H angelaminniefield@cdrewu.edu
MINNIS, Stephen, D 913-360-7400 175 D sminnis@benedictine.edu
MINNITI, Lea 513-745-3711 374 D minnitil@xavier.edu
MINOR, Diana, Y 909-869-3704 31 A dyminor@cpp.edu

MINOR, Diane .... 312-553-2500 135 I
dminor1@ccc.edu
MINOR, Karen .... 770-533-7030 122 E
kminor@laniertech.edu
MINOR, Lloyd .... 650-723-2300.. 66 C
lminor@stanford.edu
MINOR, Lynn, C .... 229-333-5353 127 H
lcminor@valdosta.edu
MINOR, Scott .... 916-631-8108.. 30 H
MINOR, Tamra .... 518-956-8110 324 G
tminor@albany.edu
MINOR, Tracey .... 601-977-7879 256 B
tminor@tougaloo.edu
MINSON, Patrick .... 718-390-3304 333 D
patrick.minson@wagner.edu
MINTEN, Sam, L .... 615-868-6503 434 G
sam@mtsa.edu
MINTER, Doug, O .... 507-933-7527 242 D
dminter@gustavus.edu
MINTER, Douglas .... 309-268-8100 139 D
doug.minter@heartland.edu
MINTER, Michelle .... 609-258-6110 288 F
mminter@princeton.edu
MINTERN, Janet .... 252-493-7286 345 E
jmintern@email.pittcc.edu
MINTO, Jean .... 215-702-4270 391 C
jminto@cairn.edu
MINTON, Jessie .... 541-346-1799 387 F
minton@uoregon.edu
MINTZ, Katrina, H .... 205-726-2896.... 6 G
kmintz@samford.edu
MINTZ, Zev .... 732-370-1560 283 G
MINTZER, Jen .... 610-358-4547 402 G
mintzerj@neumann.edu
MINUS, Daryl .... 910-362-7040 341 E
dminus@cfcc.edu
MINUS, Molly, E .... 512-448-8581 455 I
mollym@stedwards.edu
MINUS, Monica .... 252-633-1764 342 E
minusm@cravencc.edu
MIODUSZEWSKI, Leo .... 989-964-4285 236 F
lmiodusz@svsu.edu
MIRABAL, Gloria .... 787-743-4041 521 K
gmirabal@columbiacentral.edu
MIRABAL, Larry .... 505-424-2316 294 C
lmirabal@iaia.edu
MIRABELLA, Phyllis ...... 908-709-7010 292 C
phyllis.mirabella@ucc.edu
MIRABILE, Hector .... 305-629-2929 107 D
hmirabile@sanignaciocollege.edu
MIRABILE, Robert .... 608-363-2380 506 D
mirabiler@beloit.edu
MIRABITO, Michael .... 570-348-6209 401 B
mirabito@marywood.edu
MIRAFTABI, Ellie .... 323-254-2203.. 42 A
MIRAMONTEZ, Daniel ... 619-388-7333.. 60 E
dmiramon@sdccd.edu
MIRANDA, Albert .... 714-484-7394.. 53 M
amiranda@cypresscollege.edu
MIRANDA, Alex .... 714-895-8107.. 38 G
amiranda42@gwc.cccd.edu
MIRANDA, Candida .... 312-567-3134 140 I
miranda@iit.edu
MIRANDA,
Edmund (Rick) .... 562-860-2451.. 36 A
ermiranda@cerritos.edu
MIRANDA, Enid .... 787-841-2000 525 J
emiranda@pucpr.edu
MIRANDA, Gloria .... 310-660-3735.. 42 C
gmiranda@elcamino.edu
MIRANDA, Jakelin .... 786-331-1000 104 C
MIRANDA, Kenneth, M . 607-254-1150 306 B
kmm446@cornell.edu
MIRANDA, Maria .... 318-357-5960 197 D
mirandav@nsula.edu
MIRANDA, Marie, L ...... 713-348-4026 455 F
mlm@rice.edu
MIRANDA, Mark .... 732-571-3593 287 C
mmiranda@monmouth.edu
MIRANDA, Rick .... 970-491-6614.. 78 N
rick.miranda@colostate.edu
MIRANDA, Rick .... 970-491-6614.. 78 M
rick.miranda@colostate.edu
MIRANDA, Yolanda .... 787-743-3038 525 M
ymiranda@sanjuanbautista.edu
MIRECKI, Julie .... 920-693-1193 513 H
julie.mirecki@gotoltc.edu
MIRELES, Rod .... 936-261-1905 458 F
rmireles@pvamu.edu
MIRIZZI, Ray .... 859-572-6421 188 E
mirizzir1@nku.edu
MIRMIRAN, Amir .... 903-566-7104 468 C
amirmiran@uttyler.edu
MIRMIRANI, Maj .... 386-226-6889.. 98 C
mirmiram@erau.edu
MIRNICS, Karoly .... 402-559-5720 277 H
kmirnics@unmc.edu
MIRR, Jim .... 925-969-3300.. 46 L
jmirr@jfku.edu
MIRRETTI, Armaline ...... 630-617-3239 138 C
amirretti@elmhurst.edu
MIRRO, Roberta .... 631-249-3048 329 D
sm711/bncollege@bncollege.com
MIRSHAB, Bahman .... 248-204-3050 233 A
bmirshab@ltu.edu
MIRTO, Michael .... 313-577-2226 239 C
michael.mirto@wayne.edu
MIRUS, Kevin .... 608-246-6478 514 A
kmirus@madisoncollege.edu
MIRUS, Tarrah, N .... 404-413-2273 121 A
tmirus@gsu.edu
MISAK, David .... 580-774-3275 380 B
david.misak@swosu.edu
MISCHE, Terri .... 320-308-6675 247 E
tamische@stcloudstate.edu
MISCHKE, Carly .... 310-506-6738.. 56 D
carly.mischke@pepperdine.edu
MISERENDINO, Peter .... 203-287-3026.. 87 G
paier.admin@snet.net
MISGEN, Sherry .... 312-899-5216 151 F
smisgen@saic.edu
MISHEK, Mark .... 651-213-4006 242 F
mmishek@hazeldenbettyford.org
MISHLER, Brent .... 989-386-6622 234 B
bmishler@midmich.edu
MISHLER, Jeremy .... 231-591-2345 230 A
jeremymishler@ferris.edu
MISHLER, Richard .... 814-886-6339 402 E
rmishler@mtaloy.edu
MISHOE, Cindy .... 410-287-1901 203 B
cmishoe@cecil.edu
MISHOU, Stephanie ...... 207-947-4591 198 F
smishou@bealcollege.edu
MISHRA, Manisha .... 205-929-1000.... 6 D
MISHRA, Sharda, D .... 615-327-6156 434 A
smishra@mmc.edu
MISHRA, Tara .... 479-788-7002.. 22 A
tara.mishra@uafs.edu
MISIANO, Chris .... 434-592-3144 482 D
cjmisiano@liberty.edu
MISKELL, Anita .... 812-749-1240 163 B
amiskell@oak.edu
MISKUS, Lynn .... 219-473-4310 157 A
lmiskus@ccsj.edu
MISKY, Allison .... 860-727-2117.. 87 B
amisky@goodwin.edu
MISORI, Wanda .... 256-726-7840.... 6 E
wmisori@oakwood.edu
MISRA, Amrit .... 651-641-8866 241 L
misra@csp.edu
MISRA, Kalpana .... 918-631-2547 381 C
kalpana-misra@utulsa.edu
MISRA, Ravi, P .... 414-955-4403 508 D
rmisra@mcw.edu
MISS, Stephen .... 704-461-6802 335 J
stephenmiss@bac.edu
MISSEL, Thomas .... 716-375-2303 322 B
MISSILDINE, Mark .... 903-223-3153 460 D
mmissildine@tamut.edu
MISSURELLI, David, S .. 630-637-5680 147 E
dsmissurelli@noctrl.edu
MISTICK, Barbara, K ..... 717-262-2000 415 B
barbara.mistick@wilson.edu
MISTLER, Brian .... 707-826-3146.. 34 A
bjm728@humboldt.edu
MISTRIC, Amy .... 731-881-7040 440 B
amistric@utm.edu
MISTUR, Mark .... 330-672-2917 363 I
mmistur1@kent.edu
MITCHELL, Adam .... 310-377-5501.. 51 B
amitchell@marymountcalifornia.edu
MITCHELL, Alan .... 256-331-5362.... 3 C
mitchell@nwscc.edu
MITCHELL, Andrew, J .... 757-446-5199 480 C
mitcheaj@evms.edu
MITCHELL, Anne, L .... 317-274-2306 160 E
amitch29@iupui.edu
MITCHELL, Anne, M ...... 401-254-3207 417 C
amitchell@rwu.edu
MITCHELL, Annie, S ...... 864-597-4199 426 I
mitchellas1@wofford.edu
MITCHELL, Arden .... 863-680-4131 100 D
amitchell@flsouthern.edu
MITCHELL, Asia .... 312-629-6115 151 F
amitchell@saic.edu
MITCHELL, Bede .... 912-478-5116 120 E
wbmitch@georgiasouthern.edu
MITCHELL, Belinda .... 205-934-4423.... 8 B
bmitch1@uab.edu
MITCHELL, Betsy .... 626-395-6148.. 29 I
betsy.mitchell@caltech.edu
MITCHELL, Bonnie .... 508-626-4651 218 A
bmitchell@framingham.edu
MITCHELL, Bradley, J .... 937-481-2231 373 I
brad_mitchell@wilmington.edu
MITCHELL, Brenda .... 334-244-3464.... 4 E
bmitche8@aum.edu
MITCHELL, Brenda, S .... 301-546-0858 206 E
bmitchell@pgcc.edu
MITCHELL, Bryan .... 404-756-4025 115 I
bmitchell@atlm.edu
MITCHELL, C. Ben .... 731-661-5355 439 D
bmitchell@uu.edu
MITCHELL, Carl .... 910-678-8373 343 B
mitchelc@faytechcc.edu
MITCHELL, Carlton .... 903-233-3482 452 A
carltonmitchell@letu.edu
MITCHELL, Carrie .... 505-277-1758 296 H
carriem@unm.edu
MITCHELL, Cassandra ... 919-719-8880 348 I
c.mitchell@shawu.edu
MITCHELL, Cathy .... 575-392-4510 294 L
MITCHELL, Charles, E ... 607-735-1804 307 G
cmitchell@elmira.edu
MITCHELL, Chase .... 435-283-7340 474 A
chase.mitchell@snow.edu
MITCHELL, Chris .... 501-205-8919.. 19 B
cmitchell@cbc.edu
MITCHELL, Chrisie .... 845-431-8976 307 A
chrisie.mitchell@sunydutchess.edu
MITCHELL, Cindy, J ...... 207-859-4000 198 H
cindy.mitchell@colby.edu
MITCHELL, Clifton .... 229-226-1621 126 E
cmitchell@thomasu.edu
MITCHELL, Connie .... 803-754-4100 420 E
MITCHELL, Craig .... 206-517-4541 498 A
cmitchell@siom.edu
MITCHELL, David .... 415-503-6218.. 60 H
dlmitchell@sfcm.edu
MITCHELL, David, B ...... 301-405-5726 207 G
dmitche5@umd.edu
MITCHELL, David, C ..... 360-475-7100 496 F
dmitchell@olympic.edu
MITCHELL, Dawn, P ...... 336-734-7207 343 C
dmitchell@forsythtech.edu
MITCHELL, Debbie .... 734-432-5613 233 C
doffman@madonna.edu
MITCHELL, Denise .... 843-953-5822 420 C
mitchellda@cofc.edu
MITCHELL, Dennis .... 212-854-7161 305 E
dmitchell@columbia.edu
MITCHELL, Donald .... 217-206-6690 154 A
mitchell.donald@uis.edu
MITCHELL, Donna .... 740-245-7303 372 E
mitchell@rio.edu
MITCHELL, III,
Earnest, L .... 731-426-7604 432 J
emitchell@lanecollege.edu
MITCHELL, Eleanor .... 717-245-1864 394 A
mitchele@dickinson.edu
MITCHELL, Emanuel ...... 770-537-6065 128 F
emanuel.mitchell@westgatech.edu
MITCHELL, Fay .... 870-368-2006.. 20 H
fay.mitchell@ozarka.edu
MITCHELL, Gary .... 575-763-0535 470 I
mitchellg@wbu.edu
MITCHELL, George .... 843-383-8300 420 B
gmitchell@coker.edu
MITCHELL, Glendon, G . 801-587-3784 472 P
gmitchell@purchasing.edu
MITCHELL, Gregory .... 843-477-2032 421 L
greg.mitchell@hgtc.edu
MITCHELL, Gregory .... 903-886-5719 459 E
gregory.mitchell@tamuc.edu
MITCHELL,
Gwendolyn, F .... 803-536-8212 423 G
gmitche3@scsu.edu
MITCHELL, Heather .... 850-201-8580 112 C
mitchelh@tcc.fl.edu
MITCHELL, Horace .... 661-654-2241.. 31 B
hmitchell@csub.edu
MITCHELL, James, M ..... 334-876-9231.... 2 C
jmitchell@wccs.edu
MITCHELL, Jennifer .... 229-732-5946 115 B
jennifermitchell@andrewcollege.edu
MITCHELL, Joan .... 801-274-3280 474 D
jmitchell@wgu.edu
MITCHELL, Joann .... 215-898-6630 412 G
joannm@upenn.edu
MITCHELL, Joey .... 601-877-6380 251 G
jmitchell@alcorn.edu
MITCHELL, Johnnie .... 501-337-5000.. 19 C
jmitchell@coto.edu
MITCHELL, Juanita .... 870-574-4423.. 21 G
jmitchel@sautech.edu
MITCHELL, Jud .... 870-574-4726.. 21 G
jmitchel@sautech.edu
MITCHELL, Judy .... 815-280-2207 142 A
jmitchel@jjc.edu
MITCHELL, Justin .... 706-233-7205 125 E
jmitchell@shorter.edu
MITCHELL, Karen .... 615-230-3505 438 C
karen.mitchell@volstate.edu
MITCHELL, Karrie .... 520-206-4973.. 15 L
kdmitchell@pima.edu
MITCHELL, Kathy, J .... 276-739-2440 490 A
kmitchell@vhcc.edu
MITCHELL, Katie .... 765-641-4197 156 A
kmmitchell@anderson.edu
MITCHELL, Kaylene .... 207-741-5571 200 C
kmitchell@smccme.edu
MITCHELL, Keith .... 580-581-2211 375 A
kmitchel@cameron.edu
MITCHELL, Kemper .... 650-433-3835.. 55 I
kmitchell@paloaltou.edu
MITCHELL, Ken, H .... 919-209-2112 344 C
khmitchell@johnstoncc.edu
MITCHELL, Kerrie .... 575-492-2560 294 L
kmitchell@nmjc.edu
MITCHELL, Kim .... 502-456-6508 189 F
kmitchell@sullivan.edu
MITCHELL, Kimberly, A . 309-655-2230 151 A
kim.mitchell@osfhealthcare.org
MITCHELL, Lori .... 540-674-3790 488 G
lmitchell@nr.edu
MITCHELL, Marcia .... 413-552-2431 219 G
mmitchell@hcc.edu
MITCHELL, Maria .... 610-372-4721 408 G
mmitchell@racc.edu
MITCHELL, Marionette ... 713-525-3120 466 J
marion@stthom.edu
MITCHELL, Matt .... 573-592-5301 270 B
matt.mitchell@westminster-mo.edu
MITCHELL, Melissa .... 308-432-6221 276 B
mmitchell@csc.edu
MITCHELL, Michael .... 251-460-6172.... 9 B
mmitchell@southalabama.edu
MITCHELL, Mitch .... 812-288-8878 162 T
mmitchell@mid-america.edu
MITCHELL, Nancy, L ..... 509-527-5168 500 G
mitchenl@whitman.edu
MITCHELL, Patrice .... 843-574-6010 424 G
patrice.mitchell@tridenttech.edu
MITCHELL, Patricia .... 301-860-3416 208 E
pmitchell@bowiestate.edu
MITCHELL, Paula .... 915-831-4030 449 A
pmitche8@epcc.edu
MITCHELL, Peg, P .... 302-356-6810.. 91 B
peg.p.mitchell@wilmu.edu
MITCHELL, Peter, T .... 906-635-2202 232 J
peter.mitchell@lssu.edu
MITCHELL, Randolph ..... 904-470-8150.. 98 B
randolph.mitchell@ewc.edu
MITCHELL, Reavis .... 615-329-8610 431 I
rmitchel@fisk.edu
MITCHELL, Remegia, A . 585-685-6237 315 L
rmitchell@monroecc.edu
MITCHELL, Renee .... 602-285-7433.. 14 A
renee.holguin@phoenixcollege.edu
MITCHELL, JR., Robert .. 504-816-4864 191 E
rvmitchell@dillard.edu
MITCHELL, Robin .... 563-288-6103 168 M
rmitchell@eicc.edu
MITCHELL, Ronald, S .... 417-625-9531 263 G
mitchell-r@mssu.edu
MITCHELL, Rose .... 973-748-9000 284 A
rose_mitchell@bloomfield.edu
MITCHELL, Saralyn .... 256-233-8146.... 4 C
saralyn.mitchell@athens.edu
MITCHELL, Scott .... 510-809-1444.. 46 D
MITCHELL, Seandra .... 414-277-6762 509 A
MITCHELL, Sharon, L .... 716-645-2720 325 B
smitch@buffalo.edu
MITCHELL, Sheila .... 731-661-5953 439 D
smitchell@uu.edu
MITCHELL, Stephen .... 845-434-5750 330 F
smitchell@sunysullivan.edu
MITCHELL, Steve .... 903-823-3269 458 D
steven.mitchell@texarkanacollege.edu
MITCHELL, Tedd, L .... 806-743-2900 463 E
tedd.mitchell@ttuhsc.edu
MITCHELL, Tee .... 229-333-5791 127 H
rtmitchell@valdosta.edu
MITCHELL, Terrence ...... 607-436-2830 325 E
terrence.mitchell@oneonta.edu
MITCHELL, Thomas .... 814-732-2743 406 B
tmitchell@edinboro.edu
MITCHELL, Thomas, J ... 352-392-5407 110 D
tmitchell@uff.ufl.edu
MITCHELL, Thomas, R .. 956-326-2240 459 B
tmitchell@tamiu.edu
MITCHELL, Todd .... 270-534-3256 187 C
todd.mitchell@kctcs.edu
MITCHELL, Tucker .... 843-661-1225 421 H
cmitchell@fmarion.edu
MITCHELL, Venita .... 573-592-4239 270 D
venita.mitchell@williamwoods.edu
MITCHELL, Vicki .... 740-588-1386 374 G
vmitchell@zanestate.edu
MITCHELL, William .... 508-588-9100 220 B

MITCHELL, JR., Zane, W 812-465-7137 165 C zwmitchell@usi.edu
MITCHELL-CRUMP, Pamela 860-512-2605 85 G pmitchell-crump@manchestercc.edu
MITCHELL-FERRIS, Peggy 479-964-0532 18 G pmitchellferris@atu.edu
MITCHELL WHEELER, Jennifer 919-497-3226 339 F jwheeler@louisburg.edu
MITCHELSON, Ron 252-328-5419 349 I mitchelsonr@ecu.edu
MITCHEN, Brandi 478-988-6800 117 E bmitchen@centralgatech.edu
MITCHLER, Allan, M 414-410-4059 506 F admitchler@stritch.edu
MITCHLEY, Jill 570-484-2526 406 E jmitchle@lockhaven.edu
MITCHNECK, Beth 978-934-6323 217 B beth_mitchneck@uml.edu
MITCHUM, Lori 731-426-7658 432 J tcalhoun@lanecollege.edu
MITEZA, Ilir 313-593-5030 238 A imiteza@umich.edu
MITICOCCHIO, Dario 619-684-8771 53 J dmiticocchio@newschoolarch.edu
MITJANS, Dolores 787-882-2065 526 D compras@unitecpr.net
MITNICK, Eric 508-985-1169 217 A emitnick@umassd.edu
MITSUI, Mark 971-722-4365 386 C mark.mitsui@pcc.edu
MITTA, Ave, M 540-985-4097 482 A ammitta@jchs.edu
MITTELHAMMER, Ron 509-335-4561 499 G mittelha@wsu.edu
MITTELSTAEDT, John 937-229-3349 372 A
MITTEN, Richard 646-312-2076 301 B richard.mitten@baruch.cuny.edu
MITTERNDORFER, Sylvia 757-221-3595 479 I smmitt@wm.edu
MITTLEMAN, Michael, H 215-780-1280 410 D president@salus.edu
MITTMAN, Paul, A 480-858-9100 16 D p.mittman@scnm.edu
MITTON, Gregory, S 484-664-3175 402 F gregmitton@muhlenberg.edu
MITTON, Lynda 816-960-2008 258 D dean@cityvision.edu
MITTUCH, Maggie, A 253-879-3673 499 C mmittuch@pugetsound.edu
MITZE, Marnie, D 310-506-4451 56 D marnie.mitze@pepperdine.edu
MITZEL, Bobbi 307-674-6446 516 P rmitzel@sheridan.edu
MITZEL, Thomas 701-483-2326 354 A thomas.mitzel@dickinsonstate.edu
MIX, Catherine 937-229-4311 372 A cmix01@udayton.edu
MIX, Julie, L 253-535-7101 496 G mixjl@plu.edu
MIX, Shelley 484-365-7499 400 E smix@lincoln.edu
MIXON, Lonnie 407-303-8192 94 H lonnie.mixon@adu.edu
MIXON, Melissa 206-934-7791 497 H melissa.mixon@seattlecolleges.edu
MIYAKE, Richard 310-342-5200 72 D
MIYAMOTO, Mick, H 563-589-3270 173 J mmiyamoto@dbq.edu
MIYARES, Javier 301-985-7077 208 D president-office@umuc.edu
MIYASHIRO, James 619-260-7690 71 J publicsafety@sandiego.edu
MIYASHIRO, Jane 310-660-3401 42 C jmiyashiro@elcamino.edu
MIYASHIRO, Ross 714-241-6160 38 F rmiyashiro@coastline.edu
MIYAUCHI, Alison 615-383-4848 441 A amiyauchi@watkins.edu
MIZAK, Pat 941-893-2858 106 H pmizak@ringling.edu
MIZE, Charles 478-301-2951 122 H mize_c@mercer.edu
MIZE, Kyle, C 325-649-8049 450 H kmize@hputx.edu
MIZELL, Paul 912-871-1645 123 J pmizell@ogeecheetech.edu
MIZELLE, Angela, J 919-866-5825 347 D ajmizelle@waketech.edu
MIZERA, Peter 608-757-7659 513 D pmizera@blackhawk.edu
MIZNER, Kevin 559-730-3868 39 G kevinm@cos.edu
MIZRAHI, Leah 323-822-9700 67 G leah.mizrahi@touro.edu
MLODZIK, Leigh, D 920-748-8704 509 H mlodzikl@ripon.edu
MLYNSKI, Melissa 217-206-7148 154 A mmlyn2@uis.edu
MMEJE, Kenechukwu (K.C.) 214-768-2821 457 B kmmeje@smu.edu
MNOOKIN, Jennifer, L 310-825-8202 69 B mnookin@law.ucla.edu
MOANANU, Letupu 684-699-9155 519 F l.moananu@amsamoa.edu
MOATS, Kyle 417-836-5244 263 H kylemoats@missouristate.edu
MOATS, Scott 952-446-4210 242 A moatss@crown.edu
MOAVENI, Saeed 801-863-8237 473 D saeed.moaveni@uvu.edu
MOAYERI, Al 323-254-2203 42 A
MOBERG, Bret 847-578-8308 150 E bret.moberg@rosalindfranklin.edu
MOBERG, Kathleen 408-848-4732 44 B kmoberg@gavilan.edu
MOBERLY, Jonathon 402-643-7430 274 B jonathon.moberly@cune.edu
MOBERLY, Richard 402-472-6827 277 G moberly@unl.edu
MOBLEY, Bob 863-638-7213 113 I bob.mobley@warner.edu
MOBLEY, Brandon 706-880-8052 122 D mmobley@lagrange.edu
MOBLEY, Cathryn, B 434-395-2759 482 E mobleycb@longwood.edu
MOBLEY, Cedric 478-825-6518 119 C mobleyc@fvsu.edu
MOBLEY, Karen 912-871-1638 123 J kmobley@ogeecheetech.edu
MOBLEY, Katie 802-654-0505 477 B kjf06010@ccv.vsc.edu
MOBLEY, Marilyn, S 216-368-8877 358 C marilyn.mobley@case.edu
MOBLEY, Wade 763-544-9501 240 F
MOCARSKI, Richard, A 308-865-8496 277 F mocarskira@unk.edu
MOCCIA, Mario 575-646-7630 295 B moccia@nmsu.edu
MOCEK, Christian 812-357-6479 164 A cmocek@saintmeinrad.edu
MOCERI, Joane, T 503-943-8144 387 H moceri@up.edu
MOCK, Keith 334-386-7876 5 I kmock@faulkner.edu
MOCK, Kelly 314-529-9579 262 B kmock@maryville.edu
MOCK, Lisa 701-228-5432 354 G lisa.mock@minotstateu.edu
MOCK, Penny 949-214-3134 40 I penny.mock@cui.edu
MOCNIK, Joe 701-231-6128 354 D joe.mocnik@ndsu.edu
MODDELMOG, Debra 775-784-6805 279 E dmoddelmog@unr.edu
MODDER, Gail 916-660-7340 63 K gmodder@sierracollege.edu
MODELANE, Dan 508-541-1614 214 C dmodelane@dean.edu
MODENA, Shawn 478-825-6100 119 C modenas@fvsu.edu
MODENSTEIN, Susan 212-592-2208 324 A smodenstein@sva.edu
MODESTOU, Jennifer, A 319-335-0705 166 G jennifer-modestou@uiowa.edu
MODIC, Jeannette, L 240-895-2260 206 G jlmodic@smcm.edu
MODICA, Joseph, B 610-341-5826 394 E jmodica@eastern.edu
MODIG, James, E 785-864-3493 181 I jmodig@ku.edu
MODLIN, Andrew, S 336-841-9605 338 E amodlin@highpoint.edu
MODLIN, Eli, J 410-546-4127 209 B ejmodlin@salisbury.edu
MODLIN, Jason, E 919-497-3210 339 F jmodlin@louisburg.edu
MODRCIN, Mary Anne 423-869-6319 433 C maryanne.modrcin@lmunet.edu
MODROVSKY, Amanda 570-408-4307 414 H amanda.modrovsky@wilkes.edu
MOE, Karine, F 651-696-6160 243 B moe@macalester.edu
MOE, Marie 701-483-2560 354 A marie.moe@dickinsonstate.edu
MOECKES, Angela 561-586-0121 101 K amoeckes@hci.edu
MOEDER, Lawrence, E 785-532-6250 179 A larrym@ksu.edu
MOEDER, Lawrence, E 785-532-6420 179 A larrym@ksu.edu
MOEGGENBERG, Rich 517-607-2348 231 C rmoeggenberg@hillsdale.edu
MOEGLIN, Maureen 531-622-2236 275 F mmoeglin@mccneb.edu
MOEGLING, Mary Lou 740-374-8716 373 G mmoegling@wscc.edu
MOEHRING, Richard 913-469-8500 178 F rmoehrin@jccc.edu
MOELLER, Darin 712-274-6400 174 E darin.moeller@witcc.edu
MOELLER, Lon 319-335-3565 166 G lon-moeller@uiowa.edu
MOELLER, Marcus 405-692-3102 376 C mmoeller@macu.edu
MOELLER, Michael 812-288-8878 162 T mmoeller@mid-america.edu
MOELLER, Molly 515-271-1400 168 G
MOEN, Jeremiah, T 701-788-4623 354 B jeremiah.moen@mayvillestate.edu
MOEN, Stuart 281-873-0262 446 J s.moen@commonwealth.edu
MOENCH, Gerald 816-501-4862 265 I gerald.moench@rockhurst.edu
MOENKHAUS, Kevin, P 515-271-3902 168 J kevin.moenkhaus@drake.edu
MOERLAND, Timothy, S 724-357-2219 406 C tim.moerland@iup.edu
MOERMAN, LeeAnn 712-722-6002 168 I leeann.moerman@dordt.edu
MOERSCHBAECHER, Joseph, M 504-568-4804 194 C jmoers@lsuhsc.edu
MOESSNER, Phil 320-308-3190 247 E pmmoessner@stcloudstate.edu
MOEZ, Chrystal 262-619-6830 513 G moezc@gtc.edu
MOFFAT, Barbara, A 413-782-1630 225 F barbara.moffat@wne.edu
MOFFAT, Heather 812-888-4120 165 E hmoffat@vinu.edu
MOFFATT, Tammy, L 603-646-2811 281 C tammy.l.moffatt@dartmouth.edu
MOFFATT-LIMOGES, Pamela 401-739-5000 416 D pmoffatt-limoges@neit.edu
MOFFETT, Jared, E 202-274-6858 93 D jared.moffett@udc.edu
MOFFETT, Katie 603-456-2656 281 H kmoffett@northeastcatholic.edu
MOFFETT, Mark 614-823-1534 368 O mmoffett@otterbein.edu
MOFFETT, Raphael, X 713-313-6874 461 E raphael.moffett@tsu.edu
MOFFETT LANE, Amanda 575-538-6675 297 H amanda.moffett@wnmu.edu
MOFFITT, Jamie, H 541-346-3003 387 F jmoffitt@uoregon.edu
MOFFITT, Lisa 615-327-3927 432 G moffitt@guptoncollege.edu
MOFFITT, Thomas, J 610-566-1776 415 A tmoffitt@williamson.edu
MOGCK, Steven, A 312-329-4131 146 B steve.mogck@moody.edu
MOGFORD, Jon 979-458-0243 458 E jmogford@tamus.edu
MOGULESCU, John 646-664-8004 301 A john.mogulescu@cuny.edu
MOHAJIR, Terry 870-972-3880 18 A tmohajir@astate.edu
MOHAMADIAN, Habib, P 225-771-5290 195 K mohamad@engr.subr.edu
MOHAMED, Rafik 909-537-5500 33 D rafik.mohamed@csusb.edu
MOHAMMAD, Esam 316-323-6426 175 I emohammad@butlercc.edu
MOHAMMAD, Yatty 402-878-3331 275 C ymohammad@littlepriest.edu
MOHAMMADI, Amir 724-738-2002 407 C amir.mohammadi@sru.edu
MOHAMMADI, Rameen 315-312-2232 327 D rameen.mohammadi@oswego.edu
MOHAPATRA, Prasant 530-754-8380 68 H pmohapatra@ucdavis.edu
MOHDZAIN, Zaidy 870-235-4057 21 F azmohdzain@saumag.edu
MOHEBBI, Vargha 480-425-6903 14 C vargha.mohebbi@scottsdalecc.edu
MOHLER, Nick 717-396-7833 404 R nmohler@pcad.edu
MOHLER, JR., R. Albert 502-897-4121 189 A mohler@sbts.edu
MOHNEY, David 908-737-4770 286 F dmohney@kean.edu
MOHOLLAND, Tom 207-454-1020 200 D tmoholland@wccc.me.edu
MOHR, James, R 724-946-7116 414 C mohrjr@westminster.edu
MOHR, Jean Marie 845-398-4106 323 G jmohr@stac.edu
MOHR, Joan, I 203-582-8959 88 A joan.isaacmohr@quinnipiac.edu
MOHR, Karl 530-752-2063 68 H kfmohr@ucdavis.edu
MOHR, Lisa 507-285-7245 247 D lisa.mohr@rctc.edu
MOHR, Nick 515-309-9000 174 A nick.mohr@vatterott.edu
MOHR, Rick 937-529-2201 371 B rmohr@united.edu
MOHR, Sandra 617-587-5587 222 G mohrs@neco.edu
MOHR, Sharon 763-488-2525 244 G sharon.mohr@hennepintech.edu
MOHR, Wayne, C 570-389-4303 405 E wmohr@bloomu.edu
MOHRBACHER, Robert 360-623-8552 493 A bob.mohrbacher@centralia.edu
MOHRBUTTER, Trent, L 252-451-8336 345 B tlmohrbutter242@nashcc.edu
MOHRE, Trudy 517-264-7185 236 I tmohre@sienaheights.edu
MOHSEN, Bashir 201-216-9901 285 F bashir.mohsen@eicollege.edu
MOHSINI, Virga 617-824-7858 214 E virga_mohsini@emerson.edu
MOIOLA, Tena 858-566-1200 41 G tmoiola@disd.edu
MOIR, Chris 216-987-3492 360 E chris.moir@tri-c.edu
MOISE, Connie 760-744-1150 55 K cmoise@palomar.edu
MOIST, Kirk, L 715-833-6224 513 E kmoist@cvtc.edu
MOJ, Cynthia 323-469-3300 25 D cmoj@amda.edu
MOJE, Elizabeth, B 734-647-9571 237 I
MOJICA, Agnes 787-892-5634 524 D amojica@intersg.edu
MOJICA, Francis, J 787-723-4481 521 H fmojica@ceaprc.edu
MOJICA, Jorge, E 787-852-1430 522 P jmojica@hccpr.edu
MOK, Jacqueline, L 210-567-2004 468 E mok@uthscsa.edu
MOKAR, Jason 302-622-8000 90 A jmokar@dcad.edu
MOKEL, Haroon 703-878-2800 93 B
MOKREN, Jennifer 845-257-3860 325 D mokrenj@newpaltz.edu
MOKU, Samuel 808-544-1406 129 C smoku@hpu.edu
MOKUAU, Noreen, K 808-956-6300 129 J noreen@hawaii.edu
MOKWA, Robert 406-994-4371 272 A mokwa@montana.edu
MOLALENGE, Teshome, H 540-828-5750 478 J tmolalen@bridgewater.edu
MOLCHANY, Jim 610-282-1100 393 G jim.molchany@desales.edu
MOLD, Joseph 906-217-4246 228 A moldj@baycollege.edu
MOLDENHAUER, Susan 307-766-6620 517 B amsm@uwyo.edu
MOLDENHAUER, Troy 262-595-2495 511 C moldenht@uwp.edu
MOLDER, Kandi 918-335-6237 378 F kmolder@okwu.edu
MOLDER, Mark 918-335-6843 378 F mmolder@okwu.edu
MOLDSTAD, Donald, L 507-344-7312 240 I don.moldstad@blc.edu
MOLELLA, Holly 845-431-8953 307 A molella@sunydutchess.edu
MOLEN, Brent 801-426-8234 472 N president@ucdh.edu
MOLEN, Kenneth 801-426-8234 472 N director@ucdh.edu
MOLER, Delanie, S 848-445-3787 290 A delanie.moler@rutgers.edu
MOLEY, Linda 620-252-7115 176 K moley.linda@coffeyville.edu
MOLIFE, Brenda 508-531-2454 217 D bmolife@bridge.edu
MOLIKEN, Laura 610-409-3606 413 H lmoliken@ursinus.edu
MOLIN-DUNN, Casey 212-749-2802 313 M cmdunn@msmnyc.edu
MOLINA, Alejandra 315-781-3319 310 C molina@hws.edu

MOLINA, Carlos ... 718-518-6658 302 D cmolina@hostos.cuny.edu
MOLINA, Carlos ... 202-495-3876.. 92 F cmolina@dhs.edu
MOLINA, David ... 314-921-9290 269 D dmolina@ugst.edu
MOLINA, Joe ... 843-953-6841 419 D
MOLINA, Michael ... 806-742-2116 463 D michael.molina@ttu.edu
MOLINA, Michael ... 806-742-0012 463 B
MOLINA, Monica ... 626-585-7262.. 56 B mmolina21@pasadena.edu
MOLINA, Perla ... 214-378-1771 447 F pmolina@dcccd.edu
MOLINA, Ricardo ... 787-738-2161 528 A ricardo.molina1@upr.edu
MOLINA, Yaniri, S ... 787-884-3838 520 G ymolina@atenascollege.edu
MOLINA, Yolanda ... 787-894-2828 529 A yolanda.molina@upr.edu
MOLINAR, Anthony ... 510-593-2934.. 63 A amolinar@saybrook.edu
MOLINARO, Brian ... 315-792-5545 315 I bmolinaro@mvcc.edu
MOLIVER, Donald ... 732-571-3422 287 C dmoliver@monmouth.edu
MOLL, Carlos ... 787-728-1515 529 B cmoll@sagrado.edu
MOLL, John ... 602-872-7748.. 14 D john.moll@southmountaincc.edu
MOLL, Monica ... 614-292-2884 367 H moll.43@osu.edu
MOLL, Stephen ... 305-919-5700 109 D molls@fiu.edu
MOLLA, Mike ... 410-225-2215 205 C mmolla@mica.edu
MOLLAHAN, David, J ... 334-683-2301.... 3 A dmollahan@marionmilitary.edu
MOLLARD, Tikhon ... 570-561-1818 410 A bishop.tikhon@stots.edu
MOLLEDA, Juan-Carlos . 541-346-2233 387 F jmolleda@uoregon.edu
MOLLEN, Elizabeth ... 607-778-5008 326 C mollenes@sunybroome.edu
MOLLER, Amanda ... 312-752-2170 142 E amanda.moller@kendall.edu
MOLLER, Denny ... 352-588-8644 106 N denny.moller@saintleo.edu
MOLLER, Mark ... 740-587-6668 361 B moller@denison.edu
MOLLER, Simon ... 718-990-3917 322 F mollers@stjohns.edu
MOLLEUR, Sherri ... 802-322-1626 475 A sherri.molleur@goddard.edu
MOLLIS, Kristi, L ... 561-912-1211.. 98 F kmollis@evergladesuniversity.edu
MOLLNER, Daniel, J ... 507-933-7569 242 D dmollner@gustavus.edu
MOLLOY, Christopher, H ... 317-788-3360 164 H cmolloy@uindy.edu
MOLLOY, Christopher, J ... 848-932-5663 290 A molloy@oldqueens.rutgers.edu
MOLLOY, Jim ... 434-592-7470 482 D jmolloy@liberty.edu
MOLLOY, John ... 631-420-2700 329 D foundation@farmingdale.edu
MOLLOY, Marcie, A ... 410-827-5825 203 C mamolloy@chesapeake.edu
MOLNAR, Judith ... 931-221-7588 430 B molnarj@apsu.edu
MOLONEY, Jacqueline, F ... 978-934-2201 217 B jacqueline_moloney@uml.edu
MOLYNEUX, Shane ... 641-683-5111 169 I shane.molyneux@indianhills.edu
MOLZ, Chris ... 267-295-2340 409 B cmolz@walnuthillcollege.edu
MOMAN, Frank ... 317-921-4396 161 G fmoman@ivytech.edu
MOMAN, Tim ... 602-432-8414.. 10 E
MOMANY, Christopher, P ... 517-265-5161 226 F cmomany@adrian.edu
MOMAYEZI, Nasser ... 678-466-4700 117 I nassermomayezi@clayton.edu
MOMBERG, Joel ... 813-974-1899 111 A jmomberg@usf.edu
MOMINEY, Michael ... 954-262-8253 104 F mominey@nova.edu
MONACO, A.G ... 225-578-8200 193 M amonaco@lsu.edu
MONACO, Anthony, P ... 617-627-3300 225 A anthony.monaco@tufts.edu
MONACO, Dennis ... 978-232-2357 214 G dmonaco@endicott.edu
MONACO, Lynne, K ... 808-956-9083 129 H kmonaco@hawaii.edu
MONACO, Pamela ... 630-637-5384 147 E pjmonaco@noctrl.edu
MONAGAN, Paul, R ... 903-510-2130 464 D pmon@tjc.edu
MONAGHAN, James ... 202-319-5773.. 91 D monaghanja@cua.edu
MONAGHAN, Thomas ... 610-660-3204 409 H tmonagha@sju.edu
MONAGHAN, Thomas, S ... 239-280-2522.. 95 C tmonaghan@avemaria.edu
MONAGLE, Mischelle ... 309-341-5456 134 H mmonagle@sandburg.edu
MONAGO, Emily ... 419-372-2642 357 F emonago@bgsu.edu
MONAGO, Malou ... 216-421-8016 359 J mlmonago@cia.edu
MONAHAN, JR., Charles, F ... 617-732-2880 221 E charles.monahan@mcphs.edu
MONAHAN, Jerald ... 928-776-2184.. 17 G jerald.monahan@yc.edu
MONAHAN, Kevin ... 412-268-2064 391 H monahan@andrew.cmu.edu
MONAHAN, Mark ... 734-487-5386 229 K mmonahan@emich.edu
MONAHAN, Quin ... 843-208-8070 425 B qmonahan@uscb.edu
MONARCH, Laura, M ... 270-745-5334 190 F laura.monarch@wku.edu
MONAST, Louise ... 401-341-2287 417 D louise.monast@salve.edu
MONATH, Karen ... 216-987-4085 360 E karen.monath@tri-c.edu
MONCRIFFE, Pritchard .. 405-466-3253 375 L pmoncriffe@langston.edu
MONCURE, Thomas, M . 703-993-2619 481 B tmoncure@gmu.edu
MONDAY, Eric, N ... 859-257-1841 190 B emonday@uky.edu
MONDEH, Sama ... 256-761-6128.... 7 D smondeh@talladega.edu
MONDEIK, Shelly ... 715-422-5319 514 B shelly.mondeik@mstc.edu
MONDELLI, Robert ... 973-684-6626 288 C rmondelli@pccc.edu
MONDELLO-HENDREN, Martha, C ... 216-397-4293 363 H mhendren@jcu.edu
MONDICS, Macy ... 972-686-7878 455 B macy.mondics@remingtoncollege.edu
MONDILLO, Keith ... 215-646-7300 396 E mondillo.k@gmercyu.edu
MONDOU, Sherry, B ... 253-879-3204 499 C smondou@pugetsound.edu
MONDOUX, Dan ... 269-488-4195 231 G dmondoux@kvcc.edu
MONDRAGON, Elizabeth ... 951-827-5531.. 69 D elizabeth.mondragon@ucr.edu
MONDROS, Jacqueline . 631-444-2139 325 F jacqueline.mondros@stonybrook.edu
MONE, Jennifer ... 516-463-7310 310 D jennifer.mone@hofstra.edu
MONE, Mark, A ... 414-229-4331 511 A mone@uwm.edu
MONES, Kimberly ... 941-359-4200 111 C
MONETA, Larry ... 919-684-3737 337 C studentaffairs@duke.edu
MONETTE, Eugene ... 701-477-7862 355 H emonette@tm.edu
MONEY, Royce ... 325-674-4974 441 D moneyr@acu.edu
MONEYMAKER, Andrew 662-329-7127 254 F amoneymaker@muw.edu
MONFETTE, Rachel ... 312-329-4189 146 B rachel.monfette@moody.edu
MONG, Robert ... 972-780-3601 466 C president@untdallas.edu
MONGAN, Jason ... 412-346-2100 408 B jmongan@pia.edu
MONGAN, Jeremiah James ... 970-352-1181.. 76 C
MONGE, Edwin ... 301-891-4008 209 E emonge@wau.edu
MONGEON, Michael ... 508-373-9458 211 F michael.mongeon@becker.edu
MONGEON-STEWART, Karla ... 701-777-2015 353 G karla.stewart@und.edu
MONGER, Todd ... 612-343-3513 249 E tjmonger@northcentral.edu
MONGERSON, John ... 815-939-5101 148 F jmonger@olivet.edu
MONGILLO, Anne, M ... 516-463-6776 310 D anne.mongillo@hofstra.edu
MONGO, Karen ... 214-860-2106 448 A kmongo@dcccd.edu
MONHEIT, Yidel ... 718-853-2442 334 I
MONHOLLON, Michael . 325-670-5870 450 A mmonholl@hsutx.edu
MONIACI, Steve, C ... 281-649-3096 450 C smoniaci@hbu.edu
MONIODIS, Paul ... 410-837-5270 209 D pmoniodis@ubalt.edu
MONIT, Scott ... 724-480-3356 392 K scott.monit@ccbc.edu
MONIZ, Jeffrey ... 808-689-2300 130 A jmoniz@hawaii.edu
MONK, David, H ... 814-865-2526 403 F dhm6@psu.edu
MONK, Kevin ... 541-776-9942 385 G kevin.m@pacificbible.com
MONK, Matthew ... 802-828-8556 476 F matthew.monk@vcfa.edu
MONK, Sam ... 256-782-5104.... 6 B smonk@jsu.edu
MONKS, Birgit ... 909-652-6876.. 36 E birgit.monks@chaffey.edu
MONNAT, Angela, B ... 585-385-8042 322 E amonnat@sjfc.edu
MONNES, Mark, J ... 419-755-4824 366 E mmonnes@ncstatecollege.edu
MONNIG, Amber ... 660-248-6280 258 B armonnig@centralmethodist.edu
MONNOT, Charles ... 405-208-5295 377 D cmonnot@okcu.edu
MONOD, Kelly ... 941-752-5491 108 P monodk@scf.edu
MONOLO, Melissa ... 843-349-7883 421 L melissa.monolo@hgtc.edu
MONROE, Alicia ... 856-256-4284 289 H monroe@rowan.edu
MONROE, Alicia ... 713-798-2312 444 A alicia.monroe@bcm.edu
MONROE, Anthony ... 973-877-4462 285 K monroe@essex.edu
MONROE, Curtis ... 502-852-8224 190 C curtis.monroe@louisville.edu
MONROE, Jill ... 619-849-2298.. 57 H jillmonroe@pointloma.edu
MONROE, Joseph, W ... 859-257-5770 190 B joe.monroe@uky.edu
MONROE, JP ... 541-346-2085 387 F jpmonroe@uoregon.edu
MONROE, Lee ... 903-730-4890 451 D lmonroe@jarvis.edu
MONROE, Maxine ... 845-569-3346 316 B maxine.monroe@msmc.edu
MONROE, Randall, L ... 570-326-3761 404 T rmonroe@pct.edu
MONROE, Roxanne ... 716-338-1036 311 F roxannemonroe@mail.sunyjcc.edu
MONROE, Tonya, C ... 336-862-7986 345 F tcmonroe@randolph.edu
MONROE, William ... 713-743-9007 465 A wmonroe@uh.edu
MONROY, Isabel ... 626-873-2187.. 53 A imonroy@mtsierra.edu
MONS, Marie ... 404-894-4582 120 A marie.mons@finaid.gatech.edu
MONSON, Crista ... 404-880-8502 117 H cmonson@cau.edu
MONTAG, Jerry ... 815-753-1747 147 H jerry.montag@niu.edu
MONTAGNE, Michael ... 617-732-2995 221 E michael.montagne@mcphs.edu
MONTAGUE, Evan ... 989-774-1912 228 E monta3e@cmich.edu
MONTAGUE, Krista ... 406-657-2061 272 B kmontague@msubillings.edu
MONTAGUE, Marlena, O ... 671-735-5612 519 H marlena.montague@guamcc.edu
MONTAGUE, Orinthia, T 607-844-8222 331 D otm@tompkinscortland.edu
MONTALBAN, Silvia ... 646-557-4409 302 F smontalban@jjay.cuny.edu
MONTALBANO, Ivonne .. 713-221-8060 465 C montalbanoi@uhd.edu
MONTALTO, Karen ... 856-222-9311 289 F kmontalto@rcbc.edu
MONTALVO, Carmen ... 787-878-5475 523 H cmontalv@arecibo.inter.edu
MONTALVO, Cynthia ... 201-559-6036 286 C montalvoc@felician.edu
MONTALVO, Devyn ... 863-638-2964 114 A montalvods@webber.edu
MONTALVO, Irene ... 254-501-5852 459 D i.montalvo@tamuct.edu
MONTALVO, Luis ... 617-262-5000 212 C luis.montalvo@the-bac.edu
MONTALVO, Provi ... 787-878-5475 523 H pmontalvo@arecibo.inter.edu
MONTALVO-COLÓN, Sonia, I ... 787-751-1912 524 E smontalv@juris.inter.edu
MONTANA, Michael ... 717-262-2002 415 B michael.montana@wilson.edu
MONTANARI, James ... 815-836-5222 143 E montanja@lewisu.edu
MONTANARO, Gregory, P ... 215-895-0541 394 C gregory.p.montanaro@drexel.edu
MONTAÑEZ, John ... 212-220-8011 301 C jmontanez@bmcc.cuny.edu
MONTANEZ, Robert ... 916-691-7326.. 50 G montanrl@crc.losrios.edu
MONTANEZ-LOPEZ, Nilda ... 787-740-3001 526 G nilda.montanez@uccaribe.edu
MONTANO, Estavan ... 312-341-2125 150 D emontano02@roosevelt.edu
MONTANO-CORDOVA, Ruby, S ... 909-593-3511.. 70 E rmontano-cordova@laverne.edu
MONTAS, Keiselim, C ... 603-646-4000 281 C keiselim.montas@dartmouth.edu
MONTAÑEZ, Isabel ... 787-767-2040 528 F isabel.montanez@upr.edu
MONTE, Renee ... 415-338-3982.. 34 C rmonte@sfsu.edu
MONTEAGUDO, Rene ... 305-284-5511 112 O rxm981@miami.edu
MONTECALVO, Frank ... 814-472-3002 409 G fmontecalvo@francis.edu
MONTEFUSCO, Anthony 401-254-3023 417 C amontefusco@rwu.edu
MONTEFUSCO, Luis ... 609-343-5635 283 D lmontefu@atlantic.edu
MONTEIRO, Beth ... 608-363-2699 506 D monteirob@beloit.edu
MONTEIRO, Kathy ... 570-577-2000 390 H
MONTEIRO, Kenneth, P 415-338-1693.. 34 C monteiro@sfsu.edu
MONTEIRO, Marconi ... 210-924-4338 443 N marconi.monteiro@bua.edu
MONTEITH, Kellie ... 828-227-7147 352 C monteith@wcu.edu
MONTELLA, Andrea ... 219-844-0100 156 F andrea.m@brightwood.edu
MONTEMAGNO, Carlo, D ... 618-453-2341 152 B chancellor@siu.edu
MONTEMAYOR, Roland . 408-288-3146.. 61 P roland.montemayor@sjcc.edu
MONTEMAYOR, Roland . 408-288-3142.. 61 P
MONTENEGRO, Luis ... 718-289-5939 301 D luis.montenegro@bcc.cuny.edu
MONTERO, Alfred ... 507-222-4985 241 C amontero@carleton.edu
MONTERO, Grecia ... 609-771-3132 284 I montero@tcnj.edu
MONTERO, Joel ... 787-720-1022 521 A admisiones@atlanticu.edu
MONTEROSO, Catherine 304-336-8231 504 E cmonteroso@westliberty.edu
MONTES, Angel ... 213-356-5321.. 65 A angel_montes@sciarc.edu
MONTES, Bruce, A ... 773-508-7601 144 D bmontes@luc.edu
MONTES, Darlene ... 818-364-7758.. 49 C montesd@lamission.edu
MONTES, Josefer ... 509-527-2615 499 F josefer.montes@wallawalla.edu
MONTES, Josefer ... 937-395-8837 364 B josefer.montes@kc.edu
MONTES, Luis ... 914-594-3723 318 A luis_montes@nymc.edu
MONTES, Rebecca ... 707-468-3009.. 51 E rmontes@mendocino.edu
MONTES, Susan, R ... 305-284-6021 112 O smontes@miami.edu
MONTES-BURGOS, Carmen ... 787-993-8952 527 G carmen.montes1@upr.edu
MONTES-HELU, Mario ... 520-383-8401.. 16 G mmontes@tocc.edu
MONTES-MORALES, Maria ... 718-782-2200 299 L mmontes@boricuacollege.edu
MONTESINO, María del C ... 787-720-1022 521 A recaudaciones@atlanticu.edu
MONTEVIRGEN, Alexis, S ... 219-980-6824 160 C amontevi@iun.edu
MONTEZ, Daniel ... 956-447-6635 456 G dmontez@southtexascollege.edu
MONTEZ, Nicholas ... 619-482-6306.. 65 H nmontez@swccd.edu

MONTGOMERY, Adrienne ..... 978-837-5485 221 G montgomerya@merrimack.edu

MONTGOMERY, Alan .... 772-462-7860 101 Q jmontgom@irsc.edu

MONTGOMERY, Alisa, L ..... 336-322-2213 345 D alisa.montgomery@piedmontcc.edu

MONTGOMERY, Barbara ..... 478-757-5233 128 E bmontgomery@wesleyancollege.edu

MONTGOMERY, Barbara ..... 478-757-5272 128 E bmontgomery@wesleyancollege.edu

MONTGOMERY, Cathy .. 912-427-6265 117 J cmontgomery@coastalpines.edu

MONTGOMERY, Christy 985-545-1500 192 K

MONTGOMERY, Cindy .. 229-226-1621 126 E cmontgomery@thomasu.edu

MONTGOMERY, JR., Clyde ..... 405-466-3636 375 L cmontgomery@langston.edu

MONTGOMERY, Dale ... 479-619-4234.. 20 F dmontgom@nwacc.edu

MONTGOMERY, Daron .. 603-641-7107 282 A dmontgomery@anselm.edu

MONTGOMERY, Edward, B ..... 269-387-1000 239 E

MONTGOMERY, Eric ..... 620-331-4100 178 E emontgomery@indycc.edu

MONTGOMERY, Francis 716-896-0700 333 C franciscssf@villa.edu

MONTGOMERY, Isalene 386-506-3961.. 97 I montgoi@daytonastate.edu

MONTGOMERY, Jeff ..... 937-393-3431 370 C jlmontgo@sscc.edu

MONTGOMERY, John .... 951-343-4963.. 28 G jmontgomery@calbaptist.edu

MONTGOMERY, John .... 734-432-5574 233 C jmontgomery@madonna.edu

MONTGOMERY, John .... 575-562-4002 293 O john.montgomery@enmu.edu

MONTGOMERY, Joseph, D ..... 330-823-2295 372 C montgojd@mountunion.edu

MONTGOMERY, Kara, H ..... 724-946-7363 414 C montgokh@westminster.edu

MONTGOMERY, Keith ... 715-261-6223 512 D keith.montgomery@uwc.edu

MONTGOMERY, Laura, M ..... 630-752-5227 155 F laura.montgomery@wheaton.edu

MONTGOMERY, Lisa ..... 312-567-3777 140 I montgomeryl@iit.edu

MONTGOMERY, Lisa, P 843-792-5050 422 C montgoml@musc.edu

MONTGOMERY, Marilyn ..... 541-684-7263 384 H mmontgomery@nwcu.edu

MONTGOMERY, Mark ... 315-792-5463 315 I mmontgomery@mvcc.edu

MONTGOMERY, Martha 254-442-5114 445 Q martha.montgomery@cisco.edu

MONTGOMERY, Melissa ..... 517-750-6426 237 D melissa.montgomery@arbor.edu

MONTGOMERY, Nancy .. 949-451-5273.. 64 I nmontgomery@ivc.edu

MONTGOMERY, Roark .. 903-875-7487 453 J roark.montgomery@navarrocollege.edu

MONTGOMERY, Robert . 248-232-4808 235 D rjmontgo@oaklandcc.edu

MONTGOMERY, Ryan .... 808-544-0200 129 C rmontgomery@hpu.edu

MONTGOMERY, Tamara, F ..... 225-771-2200 195 J tamara_montgomery@subr.edu

MONTGOMERY, Tammy 916-484-8408.. 50 F montgot2@arc.losrios.edu

MONTGOMERY, Terri .... 314-362-6255 260 E txm9149@bjc.org

MONTGOMERY, Toni-Marie ..... 847-491-7552 148 C t-montgomery@northwestern.edu

MONTGOMERY, Tony ..... 662-476-5062 253 A tmontgomery@eastms.edu

MONTGOMERY, Walter, C ..... 336-322-2258 345 D walter.montgomery@piedmontcc.edu

MONTGOMERY RICE, Valerie ..... 404-752-1740 123 F vmrice@msm.edu

MONTI, Joseph ..... 407-644-1408 106 J jmonti@rollins.edu

MONTICCIOLO, Cheryl .. 516-686-1080 317 G cheryl.monticciolo@nyit.edu

MONTIEL, Arthuro ..... 956-488-5808 456 G amontiel@southtexascollege.edu

MONTIJO, Minerva ..... 716-896-0700 333 C montijom@villa.edu

MONTIJO, River ..... 503-768-6030 383 G rmontijo@lclark.edu

MONTILEAUX, Kateri ..... 605-455-6142 427 I kmontileaux@olc.edu

MONTILLA, Hector ..... 787-834-9595 526 E h.montilla@uaa.edu

MONTONE, Richard ..... 413-644-4776 211 B rmontone@simons-rock.edu

MONTORIO, Lois ..... 914-337-9300 305 F lois.montorio@concordia-ny.edu

MONTOYA, Bernadette .. 575-646-7607 295 B bermonto@nmsu.edu

MONTOYA, Dan ..... 619-594-8236.. 34 B dmontoya@mail.sdsu.edu

MONTOYA, Denise ..... 505-454-2556 294 D dmontoya@luna.edu

MONTOYA, Denise ..... 505-425-7511 294 J

MONTOYA, Jimi ..... 505-747-2139 295 H jimi.montoya@nnmc.edu

MONTOYA, Michael ..... 505-454-2534 294 D mimontoya@luna.edu

MONTOYA, Michelle ..... 510-780-4500.. 48 D mmontoya@lifewest.edu

MONTOYA, Mitzi ..... 541-737-6024 385 F

MONTOYA, Valerie ..... 505-346-2330 296 G valerie.montoya@bie.edu

MONTPLAISIR, Daniel .. 909-869-4789.. 31 A dmontplaisir@cpp.edu

MONTREAL, Steven, R .. 262-243-5700 507 C steven.montreal@cuw.edu

MONTROSE, Lee ..... 910-410-1813 345 G ljmontrose@richmondcc.edu

MONTROSS, Julie ..... 989-774-3332 228 E montr1jh@cmich.edu

MOO, Deok Joo ..... 770-220-7919 119 D it@gcuniv.edu

MOO-YOUNG, Keith ..... 509-372-7258 499 G keith.mooyoung@wsu.edu

MOODY, Anissa ..... 718-940-5853 322 G amoody@sjcny.edu

MOODY, Barbara ..... 207-941-7000 199 B moodyb@husson.edu

MOODY, Chip ..... 602-429-4919.. 15 K cmoody@ps.edu

MOODY, Chris ..... 202-885-3370.. 91 C moody@american.edu

MOODY, D. L ..... 817-461-8741 442 L dmoody@abu.edu

MOODY, Debra ..... 334-222-6591.... 2 H djmoody@lbwcc.edu

MOODY, Jan ..... 601-928-6207 254 D janet.moody@mgccc.edu

MOODY, Jeff, T ..... 219-942-1459 157 E jmoody@ccr.edu

MOODY, Kari ..... 920-465-2226 510 E moodyk@uwgb.edu

MOODY, Kate ..... 920-748-8750 509 H moodyk@ripon.edu

MOODY, Kay ..... 219-942-1459 157 E kay.moody@ccr.edu

MOODY, Kendra ..... 919-546-8297 348 I kendra.mcpherson@shawu.edu

MOODY, Krystal ..... 903-927-3312 471 B kmoody@wileyc.edu

MOODY, Lisa ..... 941-893-2863 106 H lmoody@ringling.edu

MOODY, Marilyn ..... 503-725-4616 386 D marilynmoody@pdx.edu

MOODY, Marla ..... 417-447-4842 264 K moodym@otc.edu

MOODY, Mary ..... 615-366-4438 436 E mary.moody@tbr.edu

MOODY, Michelle, L ..... 757-594-8819 479 H mlmoody@cnu.edu

MOODY, Nancy, B ..... 423-636-7301 439 C nmoody@tusculum.edu

MOODY, Saundrette ..... 229-430-4663 114 I saundrette.moody@asurams.edu

MOODY, Timothy ..... 912-344-2518 115 D tim.moody@armstrong.edu

MOODY, Tonia ..... 601-403-1214 255 D tmoody@prcc.edu

MOOKO, Daren ..... 509-527-5158 500 G mookod@whitman.edu

MOOMAW, Jillian ..... 724-847-6674 395 J jgmoomau@geneva.edu

MOON, Alan ..... 903-693-1113 454 E amoon@panola.edu

MOON, Beverly ..... 662-846-4873 252 H bmoon@deltastate.edu

MOON, Bryonie ..... 651-690-6525 249 T bamoon@stkate.edu

MOON, Daniel, C ..... 904-620-2261 110 E dmoon@unf.edu

MOON, David ..... 719-255-3566.. 83 C cmoon@uccs.edu

MOON, Don ..... 434-592-3235 482 D donmoon@liberty.edu

MOON, Freddie, P ..... 256-766-6610.... 5 K pmoon@hcu.edu

MOON, Greg ..... 503-517-1880 388 C gmoon@westernseminary.edu

MOON, Greta ..... 760-245-4271.. 73 E greta.moon@vvc.edu

MOON, Hope ..... 440-366-7183 364 F

MOON, Hyon, J ..... 949-480-4139.. 64 D hmoon@soka.edu

MOON, Jennifer ..... 309-794-7208 133 G jennifermoon@augustana.edu

MOON, Jessica ..... 803-508-7262 418 C moonj@atc.edu

MOON, Joshua ..... 605-626-3336 428 H joshua.moon@northern.edu

MOON, Lee, L ..... 904-620-2833 110 E l.moon@unf.edu

MOON, Lenny ..... 626-584-5460.. 43 K lennymoon@fuller.edu

MOON, Mary ..... 212-757-1190 298 D mmoon@funeraleducation.org

MOON, Michael, J ..... 503-370-6017 388 D mmoon@willamette.edu

MOON, Randy ..... 251-460-6121.... 9 B rmoon@southalabama.edu

MOON, Sandra ..... 502-895-3411 188 A smoon@lpts.edu

MOON, Sarah ..... 585-785-1373 308 D sarah.moon@flcc.edu

MOON, Shin ..... 718-405-3733 304 H shin.moon@mountsaintvincent.edu

MOON, Sunny ..... 657-278-4749.. 32 B hmoon@fullerton.edu

MOON, Susan ..... 573-288-6441 259 E smoon@culver.edu

MOONE, Michelle, L ..... 336-334-5167 351 D mlmoone@uncg.edu

MOONEY, Brandon ..... 740-389-4636 365 B mooneyb@mtc.edu

MOONEY, Debra ..... 513-745-3204 374 D mooney@xavier.edu

MOONEY, Dee ..... 616-222-1415 229 B dee.mooney@cornerstone.edu

MOONEY, Denise ..... 617-353-9814 212 G dmooney@bu.edu

MOONEY, Ken ..... 704-669-4030 342 B mooneyk@clevelandcc.edu

MOONEY, Kim ..... 603-899-4128 281 D mooneyk@franklinpierce.edu

MOONEY, Laura ..... 413-662-5411 218 C laura.mooney@mcla.edu

MOONEY, Lisa ..... 434-395-2074 482 E mooneylj@longwood.edu

MOONEY, Michael, C ... 585-245-5343 327 B mooney@geneseo.edu

MOONEY, Sandra, N ..... 281-649-3256 450 C smooney@hbu.edu

MOONEY, Thelma ..... 936-294-4047 462 F tgm001@shsu.edu

MOONEY, Tracy ..... 203-932-7015.. 89 D tmooney@newhaven.edu

MOONEY BURNS, Mary 816-501-4199 265 I mary.burns@rockhurst.edu

MOONEYHAM, Mike ..... 817-257-7490 461 A m.m.mooneyham@tcu.edu

MOONEYHAN, Allen ..... 870-512-7864.. 18 D allen_mooneyhan@asun.edu

MOONO, Steady ..... 518-381-1304 323 L moonosh@sunysccc.edu

MOONZWE, Isaac ..... 703-892-5100.. 93 B

MOORADIAN, Jody ..... 401-341-2268 417 D jody.mooradian@salve.edu

MOORADIAN, Todd ..... 502-852-4812 190 C tamoor10@louisville.edu

MOORE, Abigail ..... 714-463-7559.. 51 A amoore@ketchum.edu

MOORE, Al ..... 205-387-0511.... 1 D al.moore@bscc.edu

MOORE, Albert ..... 408-741-2060.. 74 B albert.moore@wvm.edu

MOORE, Albert ..... 408-741-2060.. 74 D albert.moore@wvm.edu

MOORE, Alfred ..... 336-316-2151 338 C mooread2@guilford.edu

MOORE, Alicia ..... 541-383-7262 382 B amoore@cocc.edu

MOORE, Andrew ..... 412-268-2063 391 H awm@andrew.cmu.edu

MOORE, Angela ..... 719-384-6834.. 81 G angela.moore@ojc.edu

MOORE, Angela ..... 417-667-8181 259 A amore@cottey.edu

MOORE, Angelica ..... 925-631-4533.. 59 C anmoore@stmarys-ca.edu

MOORE, Anita ..... 309-268-8249 139 D anita.moore@heartland.edu

MOORE, Anita, W ..... 662-252-8000 255 F amoore@rustcollege.edu

MOORE, Anne ..... 413-236-1641 219 B amoore@berkshirecc.edu

MOORE, Anne, C ..... 704-687-0145 351 C amoor168@uncc.edu

MOORE, Annette ..... 636-584-6704 259 L annette.moore@eastcentral.edu

MOORE, Anthony ..... 270-384-8108 187 H moorea@lindsey.edu

MOORE, A'kilah ..... 925-473-7404.. 41 A amoore@losmedanos.edu

MOORE, Barbara ..... 714-879-3901.. 45 I bmoore@hiu.edu

MOORE, Barbara ..... 914-251-6018 328 B barbara.moore@purchase.edu

MOORE, Barbara ..... 718-997-5421 303 E barbara.moore@qc.cuny.edu

MOORE, Barbara ..... 803-780-1023 426 F bmoore@voorhees.edu

MOORE, Barbara, C ... 803-705-4604 418 G mooreb@benedict.edu

MOORE, Barbara, E ..... 207-859-4252 198 H barbara.moore@colby.edu

MOORE, Barbara, N ..... 662-252-8000 255 F bmoore@rustcollege.edu

MOORE, Barbra ..... 724-357-4895 406 C bmoore@iup.edu

MOORE, Barry ..... 434-592-3406 482 D bnmoore@liberty.edu

MOORE, Beata ..... 913-758-3033 518 I

MOORE, III, Berrien ..... 405-325-3095 380 L berrien@ou.edu

MOORE, Beth ..... 513-862-3188 362 E beth.moore@email.gscollege.edu

MOORE, Billy ..... 662-846-4200 252 H bmoore@deltastate.edu

MOORE, Bonnie ..... 217-238-8260 143 B bmoore71258@lakeland.cc.il.us

MOORE, Brad ..... 505-224-4423 293 L bmoore28@cnm.edu

MOORE, Brad, D ..... 336-278-5490 337 G bmoore6@elon.edu

MOORE, Brandon ..... 951-639-5426.. 52 J bmoore@msjc.edu

MOORE, Brian ..... 845-569-3275 316 B brian.moore@msmc.edu

MOORE, Bridget ..... 325-670-1482 450 A bmoore@jsutx.edu

MOORE, Brooks ..... 812-237-3890 159 C brooks.moore@indstate.edu

MOORE, Bryan ..... 309-467-6456 138 E bmoore@eureka.edu

MOORE, Caitlan ..... 970-675-3203.. 78 H caitlan.moore@cncc.edu

MOORE, Caitlin ..... 352-323-3677 103 B moorec@lssc.edu

MOORE, Candice ..... 252-399-6393 335 I cbmoore@barton.edu

MOORE, Caprice ..... 573-341-7784 269 A moorecap@mst.edu

MOORE, Carl ..... 202-274-6591.. 93 D carl.moore@udc.edu

MOORE, Carla ..... 336-342-4261 346 B moorec@rockinghamcc.edu

MOORE, Carol ..... 805-922-6966.. 24 J cvanname@hancockcollege.edu

MOORE, Carol, A ..... 803-786-3178 420 D camoore@columbiasc.edu

MOORE, Caroline ..... 805-756-2945.. 30 K cmoore36@calpoly.edu

MOORE, Cassandra ..... 757-240-2404 484 G cassandra.moore@rivhs.com

MOORE, Cassidy ..... 276-944-6541 480 J cmoore@ehc.edu

MOORE, Cathy, D ..... 678-407-5000 119 F cmoore@ggc.edu

MOORE, Charles ..... 904-256-7062 102 B

MOORE, Charlette ..... 501-882-8876.. 17 M camoore@asub.edu

MOORE, Chris ..... 760-744-1150.. 55 K cmoore@palomar.edu

MOORE, Christopher, A 617-353-2704 212 G mooreca@bu.edu

MOORE, Christy ..... 318-678-6000 192 C cmoore@bpcc.edu

MOORE, Chuck ..... 804-862-6100 484 F cmoore@rbc.edu

MOORE, Crystal, D ..... 518-580-5428 324 D cmoore@skidmore.edu

MOORE, Cyndee ..... 706-310-6219 127 B cyndee.moore@ung.edu

MOORE, Cynthia ..... 310-434-4305.. 62 G moore_cynthia@smc.edu

MOORE, Dan ..... 580-745-2006 379 J dmoore@se.edu

MOORE, Danae .... 580-349-1356 377 E
danaem@opsu.edu
MOORE, Daniel .... 314-256-8878 257 D
moore@ai.edu
MOORE, Danny, B .... 252-398-6448 336 K
moored@chowan.edu
MOORE, Daryl .... 973-720-2232 292 I
moored@wpunj.edu
MOORE, David .... 740-593-2958 368 G
moored3@ohio.edu
MOORE, David .... 714-516-4590.. 36 G
dmoore@chapman.edu
MOORE, David, B .... 703-993-8742 481 B
dmoorem@gmu.edu
MOORE, David, C .... 562-860-2451.. 36 A
dcmoore@cerritos.edu
MOORE, David, P .... 256-824-6285.... 8 C
david.moore@uah.edu
MOORE, Derek .... 870-733-6014.. 18 B
djmoore@asumidsouth.edu
MOORE, Dirk, S .... 276-944-6810 480 J
dsmoore@ehc.edu
MOORE, Donald .... 856-256-4199 289 H
mooredo@rowan.edu
MOORE, JR., Eddie, N .. 757-823-8670 483 F
president@nsu.edu
MOORE, Edwin .... 707-965-7103.. 55 F
emoore@puc.edu
MOORE, Elinore .... 773-838-7528 136 A
emoore20@ccc.edu
MOORE, Erika .... 724-266-3838 412 D
MOORE, Erin, B .... 847-866-3902 138 G
erin.moore@garrett.edu
MOORE, Faye .... 570-586-2400 392 E
fmoore@clarkssummitu.edu
MOORE, Gene .... 937-376-6657 358 I
gmoore@centralstate.edu
MOORE, Gina .... 803-705-4358 418 G
mooreg@benedict.edu
MOORE, Gregory .... 404-894-1420 120 A
gregory.moore@health.gatech.edu
MOORE, Gwendolyn ...... 912-443-5711 125 D
gmoore@savannahtech.edu
MOORE, Hallie .... 216-791-5000 359 K
hallie.moore@cim.edu
MOORE, Heather .... 870-245-5185.. 20 G
mooreh@obu.edu
MOORE, Holly .... 206-934-6867 497 J
holly.moore@seattlecolleges.edu
MOORE, Hsiao-Ping, H . 248-204-3500 233 A
hmoore@ltu.edu
MOORE, Jackie .... 715-682-1811 509 D
jmoore@northland.edu
MOORE, JR., James, H 217-333-0810 153 G
jimmoore@uif.uillinois.edu
MOORE, James, L .... 614-688-3704 367 H
moore.1408@osu.edu
MOORE, Jamillah .... 650-306-3238.. 61 R
moorej@smccd.edu
MOORE, Jan .... 912-688-6026 123 J
jmoore@ogeecheetech.edu
MOORE, Jana .... 928-317-6052.. 11 B
jana.moore@azwestern.edu
MOORE, Janice .... 717-871-7200 407 A
janice.moore@millersville.edu
MOORE, Jason .... 205-391-5809.... 3 E
jmoore@sheltonstate.edu
MOORE, Jason, A .... 513-569-1756 359 G
arrick.moore@cincinnatistate.edu
MOORE, Jay .... 805-289-6340.. 73 C
jmooret@vcccd.edu
MOORE, Jeffrey .... 407-823-2519 110 C
jeffrey.moore@ucf.edu
MOORE, Jennifer .... 662-329-8543 254 F
jnmoore@muw.edu
MOORE, Jeremy .... 251-380-3470.... 7 B
jmoore@shc.edu
MOORE, Jeri .... 513-529-8589 365 I
moorejl@miamioh.edu
MOORE, Jim .... 417-269-8423 259 C
james.moore@coxcollege.edu
MOORE, John .... 585-475-2154 321 D
jfmfms@rit.edu
MOORE, John, C .... 858-534-7127.. 69 E
johnmoore@ucsd.edu
MOORE, Johnny, M ...... 304-367-4933 503 C
johnny.moore@pierpont.edu
MOORE, Joshua .... 630-620-2125 147 I
jmoore@seminary.edu
MOORE, Joshua .... 740-474-8896 367 E
jmoore@ohiochristian.edu
MOORE, Joy .... 617-552-2146 212 E
joy.moore@bc.edu
MOORE, Judy .... 219-989-2861 163 E
moore421@pnw.edu
MOORE, Justin .... 501-205-8889.. 19 B
jmoore@cbc.edu
MOORE, Kara .... 909-607-3822.. 57 C
kara_moore@pitzer.edu
MOORE, Karen .... 816-604-3175 262 J
karen.moore@mcckc.edu
MOORE, Karisa .... 540-231-7518 490 F
mooreka@vt.edu
MOORE, Karla .... 386-506-3650.. 97 I
moorek@daytonastate.edu
MOORE, Kathy, J .... 740-826-8114 366 C
moore@muskingum.edu
MOORE, Keith .... 501-882-8824.. 17 M
kemoore@asub.edu
MOORE, Keith .... 757-455-3354 491 F
kmoore@vwu.edu
MOORE, Keith, D .... 801-581-8254 472 P
diazmoore@utah.edu
MOORE, Kevin .... 303-273-3898.. 78 J
kmoore@mines.edu
MOORE, Kevin .... 315-498-2220 319 G
moorek@sunyocc.edu
MOORE, Kimberly .... 850-201-8760 112 C
mooreki@tcc.fl.edu
MOORE, Kirby .... 336-334-4822 343 E
khmoore1@gtcc.edu
MOORE, Kyle .... 307-766-4286 517 B
MOORE, Kyle .... 806-651-2006 460 E
kmoore@mail.wtamu.edu
MOORE, Lara .... 541-962-3368 383 B
lmoore@eou.edu
MOORE, Lara .... 541-962-3773 383 B
lmoore@eou.edu
MOORE, Laura .... 414-297-6661 514 C
moore152@matc.edu
MOORE, Lauren .... 903-923-2321 448 J
laurenm@etbu.edu
MOORE, SJ, Lawrence .. 504-861-5550 194 G
MOORE, Lee .... 318-487-5443 192 F
claudettemoore@cltcc.edu
MOORE, Lee .... 361-593-2153 460 B
lee.moore@tamuk.edu
MOORE, Leeshawn .... 909-593-3511.. 70 E
lmoore@laverne.edu
MOORE, Leonard .... 512-471-3212 467 C
ovp-ddce@mail.utexas.edu
MOORE, Lesa .... 251-442-2207.... 8 D
lmoore@umobile.edu
MOORE, Leslie .... 507-786-3627 250 C
moore8@stolaf.edu
MOORE, Leslie .... 253-833-9111 495 C
lmoore@greenriver.edu
MOORE, Lew .... 501-279-4347.. 19 G
lmoore@harding.edu
MOORE, Lew Rita .... 513-861-6400 371 A
lewrita.moore@myunion.edu
MOORE, Libbie, M .... 336-322-2220 345 D
libbie.mcphaul-moore@piedmontcc.edu
MOORE, Lisa .... 925-631-4328.. 59 C
lmoore@stmarys-ca.edu
MOORE, Lisa .... 315-498-2512 319 G
l.r.moore2@sunyocc.edu
MOORE, Lisa, J .... 904-632-3326 100 F
lisa.moore@fscj.edu
MOORE, Lisia .... 702-579-3518 278 H
lisia.smith-moore@brightwood.edu
MOORE, Loretta .... 601-979-0552 253 E
loretta.a.moore@jsums.edu
MOORE, Loretta, A .... 601-979-0552 253 E
loretta.a.moore@jsums.edu
MOORE, Lynn .... 603-752-1113 281 B
lmoore@ccsnh.edu
MOORE, Mable .... 912-358-4400 125 C
mooremj@savannahstate.edu
MOORE, Mary .... 410-287-1053 203 B
mmoore@cecil.edu
MOORE, Mary, C .... 317-788-6150 164 H
moore@uindy.edu
MOORE, Mary Elizabeth 617-353-3052 212 G
memoore@bu.edu
MOORE, Mary Pat .... 319-296-4255 169 H
mary.moore@hawkeyecollege.edu
MOORE, Mary-Rita .... 708-456-0300 153 E
maryritamoore@triton.edu
MOORE, Matthew .... 937-512-2781 370 A
matthew.moore157@sinclair.edu
MOORE, Matthew .... 718-951-5024 301 E
matthewm@brooklyn.cuny.edu
MOORE, Matthew .... 901-448-7770 440 C
mmoor158@uthsc.edu
MOORE, Melissa .... 731-661-5408 439 D
mmoore@uu.edu
MOORE, Melody .... 410-386-8217 203 A
mmoore@carrollcc.edu
MOORE, Michael .... 281-998-6162 455 K
michael.moore@sjcd.edu
MOORE, Michael .... 603-644-3136 282 C
m.moore3@snhu.edu
MOORE, Michael .... 810-766-2235 227 E
MOORE, Michael .... 701-777-6772 353 G
michael.moore@research.und.edu
MOORE, Michael, A ...... 231-843-5900 239 D
mamoore@westshore.edu
MOORE, Michael, K ...... 501-686-2533.. 21 H
mmoore@uasys.edu
MOORE, Mickey .... 423-614-8430 432 L
mmoore@leeuniversity.edu
MOORE, Mike .... 949-480-4155.. 64 D
mmoore@soka.edu
MOORE, Mike, K .... 701-788-4706 354 B
mike.moore@mayvillestate.edu
MOORE, Mitchell, L ...... 540-665-1298 485 C
mmoore7@su.edu
MOORE, Molly .... 605-394-5236 429 A
molly.moore@sdsmt.edu
MOORE, Molly .... 262-595-2404 511 C
moorem@uwp.edu
MOORE, Monica .... 701-845-7207 354 E
monica.moore@vcsu.edu
MOORE, Monica .... 323-259-2678.. 54 E
mmooore2@oxy.edu
MOORE, Monica .... 239-489-9378 100 E
monica.moore@fsw.edu
MOORE, Nancy .... 908-526-1200 289 D
nancy.moore@raritanval.edu
MOORE, Natasha .... 251-380-4000.... 7 B
nmoore@shc.edu
MOORE, Owen .... 212-995-3121 318 D
owen.moore@nyu.edu
MOORE, Paige .... 803-758-2700 418 D
pmoore@allenuniversity.edu
MOORE, Pamela .... 215-641-5571 396 E
moore.pamela@gmercyu.edu
MOORE, Patrice .... 504-671-6535 192 H
pmoore@dcc.edu
MOORE, Penta .... 601-974-1001 254 A
moorep@millsaps.edu
MOORE, Peter, K .... 214-768-4485 457 B
pmoore@smu.edu
MOORE, Phil .... 860-727-6941.. 87 B
pmoore@goodwin.edu
MOORE, R. Bartley .... 202-687-0454.. 92 B
rbm9@georgetown.edu
MOORE, Randall .... 617-358-0300 212 G
rcmoore@bu.edu
MOORE, Regina .... 870-248-4000.. 18 J
regina.moore@blackrivertech.edu
MOORE, Renee .... 210-805-5864 465 E
reneem@uiwtx.edu
MOORE, Renee .... 865-694-6604 437 F
rmoore@pstcc.edu
MOORE, Robert, G .... 719-389-6693.. 77 J
robert.moore@coloradocollege.edu
MOORE, Robert, M .... 207-859-1318 200 H
moorer@thomas.edu
MOORE, Robin .... 402-323-3497 276 K
rmoore@southeast.edu
MOORE, Robin, S .... 757-822-1724 489 H
rmoore@tcc.edu
MOORE, Rochelle .... 954-201-7471.. 96 A
rmoore@broward.edu
MOORE, Rod .... 316-943-2241 182 G
MOORE, Roger .... 501-882-8835.. 17 M
rlmoore@asub.edu
MOORE, Roger, L .... 501-882-8956.. 17 M
rlmoore@asub.edu
MOORE, Rudell .... 937-708-5734 373 H
rmoore@wilberforce.edu
MOORE, Russell .... 303-492-2890.. 83 B
rmoore@colorado.edu
MOORE, Rustin .... 614-688-8749 367 H
moore.66@osu.edu
MOORE, Sandra .... 803-535-1237 423 B
mooresj@octech.edu
MOORE, Sandy .... 620-227-9329 176 N
smoore@dc3.edu
MOORE, Sandy .... 620-365-5116 174 G
moore@allencc.edu
MOORE, Sara .... 212-517-3929 324 E
s.moore@sothebysinstitute.com
MOORE, Sarah .... 903-813-2050 443 F
sarmoore@austincollege.edu
MOORE, Scott .... 559-278-0333.. 32 A
scottm@csufresno.edu
MOORE, Shamus .... 580-774-3001 380 B
shamus.moore@swosu.edu
MOORE, Shelly .... 724-480-3492 392 K
shelly.moore@ccbc.edu
MOORE, Shirley .... 937-778-7861 361 E
smoore@edisonohio.edu
MOORE, Stacey .... 803-327-8014 426 J
smoore@yorktech.edu
MOORE, Stan .... 817-274-4284 444 C
smoore@bhcarroll.edu
MOORE, Stephany .... 575-835-5128 294 K
stephany.moore@nmt.edu
MOORE, Stephen .... 205-853-1200.... 2 F
smoore@jeffersonstate.edu
MOORE, Steven, C .... 239-590-1919 109 C
cmoore@fgcu.edu
MOORE, Steven, C .... 603-646-0871 281 C
steven.c.moore@dartmouth.edu
MOORE, Stuart .... 251-442-2203.... 8 D
smoore@umobile.edu
MOORE, Tammie, L ...... 985-380-2957 193 D
tammiemoore1@scl.edu
MOORE, Tammy .... 563-588-6374 167 E
tammy.moore@clarke.edu
MOORE, Tammy .... 320-363-5054 241 I
tmoore@csbsju.edu
MOORE, Tanya .... 217-228-5432 149 B
mooreta@quincy.edu
MOORE, Teresa .... 806-291-3753 470 I
teresam@wbu.edu
MOORE, Thad .... 410-778-7231 210 A
tmoore2@washcoll.edu
MOORE, Theresa .... 608-796-3172 512 R
trmoore@viterbo.edu
MOORE, Thomas, F ...... 304-457-6238 501 A
mooretf@ab.edu
MOORE, Timothy .... 617-353-0750 212 G
mooretj@bu.edu
MOORE, Timothy .... 847-214-7651 138 B
tmoore@elgin.edu
MOORE, Timothy .... 518-255-5323 328 C
mooretw@cobleskill.edu
MOORE, Timothy, E ...... 850-412-5102 109 A
timothy.moore@famu.edu
MOORE, Timothy, J ...... 919-530-7420 350 D
tmoore@nccu.edu
MOORE, Tina .... 217-234-5346 143 B
tmoore@lakeland.cc.il.us
MOORE, Tina .... 417-865-2815 260 B
mooret@evangel.edu
MOORE, Tomeka, L .... 601-877-6118 251 G
tmoore1@alcorn.edu
MOORE, Tony .... 504-520-7449 198 D
tmoore15@xula.edu
MOORE, Tonya .... 678-323-7700.. 93 B
MOORE, Torrey .... 662-254-8400 255 A
torrey.moore@mvsu.edu
MOORE, Tracey .... 501-420-1216.. 17 I
tracey.moore@arkansasbaptist.edu
MOORE, Traci .... 256-726-7353.... 6 E
tmoore@oakwood.edu
MOORE, Virginia .... 304-357-4957 502 E
virginiamoore@ucwv.edu
MOORE, William (Joe) .. 605-688-4692 429 B
joe.moore@sdstate.edu
MOORE, Winifred, B ..... 843-953-7477 419 D
bo.moore@citadel.edu
MOORE, Zachery .... 814-865-6563 403 F
zpm100@psu.edu
MOORE-DAVIS,
Feleccia .... 850-201-8680 112 C
mooredaf@tcc.fl.edu
MOORE-GARCIA,
Beverly .... 305-237-2154 103 L
bmoorega@mdc.edu
MOORE-JONES,
Yolanda, V .... 919-536-7201 342 G
jonesym@durhamtech.edu
MOOREHEAD, Tameka .. 601-979-2245 253 E
tamika.k.moorehead@jsums.edu
MOORER, Glynda, M ..... 517-355-2488 233 G
moorerg@msu.edu
MOORES, Lisa .... 301-295-3185 518 G
lisa.moores@usuhs.edu
MOORHEAD, Cari, A ..... 603-862-3007 282 F
cari.moorhead@unh.edu
MOORHEAD, Jill .... 614-222-3291 360 B
jmoorhead@ccad.edu
MOORHEAD, Tracey, A . 219-299-3654 241 K
moorhead@cord.edu
MOORMAN, Annorrah ... 309-556-3052 141 B
amoorman@iwu.edu
MOORMAN, Cathy .... 765-998-5123 164 C
ctmoorman@taylor.edu
MOORMAN, Jack, W ..... 919-515-4211 350 E
jack_moorman@ncsu.edu
MOORMAN, Nate .... 706-245-7226 119 A
nmoorman@ec.edu
MOORMAN, Thomas ..... 817-735-2505 466 D
thomas.moorman@unthsc.edu
MOORMON, Josh .... 818-333-3558.. 53 I
josh.mormon@nyfa.edu
MOORS, Dean .... 402-462-4000 273 G
dmoors@cccneb.edu
MOORWOOD, Woody ... 626-815-3855.. 26 U
wmoorwood@apu.edu
MOOS, Chris .... 417-625-9703 263 G
moos-c@mssu.edu
MOOS, Michael .... 317-917-3623 162 S
mmoos@martin.edu

MOOS, William, H .... 509-335-0200 499 G bill.moos@wsu.edu
MOOSBRUGGER, Bob ... 419-372-7052 357 F moosbrr@bgsu.edu
MOOSE, Megan .... 415-869-2900 216 A megan.moose@hult.edu
MOOSMAN, Lucas .... 916-660-8103.. 63 K lmoosman@sierracollege.edu
MOOT, Bradley .... 212-678-8035 312 A brmoot@jtsa.edu
MOOTHART, Kathy .... 319-385-6209 170 J kathy.moothart@iw.edu
MOOTISPAW, Angel ...... 937-393-3431 370 C amootispaw@sscc.edu
MOOTZ, Allison, C .... 215-885-2360 401 A amootz@manor.edu
MORA, Flora .... 808-984-3517 130 H fmora@hawaii.edu
MORA, Isabelle .... 253-912-2290 497 B imora@pierce.ctc.edu
MORA, Michelle .... 818-240-1000.. 44 D mmora@glendale.edu
MORA, Nereida .... 787-765-4210 521 G nmora@cempr.edu
MORADILLOS, Alicia ..... 787-834-9595 526 E amoradillos@uaa.edu
MORALE, Joseph, L ...... 903-927-3232 471 B jmorale@wileyc.edu
MORALE, Joseph, L ...... 903-927-3233 471 B jmorale@wileyc.edu
MORALE, Mary .... 706-821-8232 124 C mmorale@paine.edu
MORALE, Sonja .... 903-566-7059 468 C smorale@uttyler.edu
MORALES, Adelina, C ... 325-942-2073 463 C adelina.morales@angelo.edu
MORALES, Angelica, C . 212-870-1251 318 C amorales@nyts.edu
MORALES, Aurea .... 718-963-4112 299 L amorales@boricuacollege.edu
MORALES, Betsy .... 787-265-3807 528 C decasac@uprm.edu
MORALES, Brenda, L .... 787-852-1430 522 P bmorales@hccpr.edu
MORALES, Carlos .... 817-515-5024 458 B carlos.morales@tccd.edu
MORALES, Cathy, A ...... 212-870-1251 318 C amorales@nyts.edu
MORALES, Edwin .... 787-786-3030 526 F emorales@ucb.edu.pr
MORALES, Erica .... 713-221-8443 465 C moralese@uhd.edu
MORALES, Hector .... 787-746-1400 522 O hmorales@huertas.edu
MORALES, Ileana .... 787-878-5475 523 H imorales@arecibo.inter.edu
MORALES, James .... 435-797-1712 473 C james.morales@usu.edu
MORALES, Jessica .... 575-538-6139 297 H jessica.morales@wnmu.edu
MORALES, Jossue .... 787-891-0925 523 G jomorales@aguadilla.inter.edu
MORALES, Julie .... 575-538-6238 297 H moralesj@wnmu.edu
MORALES, Karen, G ...... 787-841-2000 525 J karen_morales@pucpr.edu
MORALES, Lindsay .... 909-621-8275.. 63 F lindsay.morales@scrippscollege.edu
MORALES, Lorraine .... 520-206-7619.. 15 L lomorales@pima.edu
MORALES, Lorraine .... 520-206-6577.. 15 L lomorales@pima.edu
MORALES, Marisol .... 909-593-3511.. 70 E mmorales3@laverne.edu
MORALES, Milsa .... 787-264-1912 524 D mimorale@intersg.edu
MORALES, Nancy .... 787-882-2065 526 D controller@unitecpr.net
MORALES, Nora .... 361-354-2239 445 S moralesn@coastlbend.edu
MORALES, Oscar .... 787-765-3560 522 K oscarmorales@edpuniversity.edu
MORALES, Patricia .... 949-824-6701.. 69 A patricia.morales@uci.edu
MORALES, Ray .... 917-493-4445 313 M rmorales@msmnyc.edu
MORALES, Ray .... 212-678-8000 312 A ramorales@jtsa.edu
MORALES, Richard .... 773-907-4465 135 K rmorales150@ccc.edu
MORALES, Robert .... 805-965-0581.. 62 E moralesr@sbcc.edu
MORALES, Rosa, M ...... 787-884-3838 520 G rmorales@atenascollege.edu
MORALES, Rosalia .... 787-864-2222 524 A rosalia.morales@guayama.inter.edu
MORALES, Rosalie .... 787-780-0070 521 B rmorales@caribbean.edu
MORALES, Sandra, M ... 787-857-3600 523 I smmorales@br.inter.edu
MORALES, Sulmarie ...... 787-264-1912 524 D smorales@intersg.edu
MORALES, Tomas .... 909-537-5002.. 33 D tmorales@csusb.edu
MORALES-TOMASSINI, Leonardo .... 787-844-8181 527 D leonardo.morales@upr.edu
MORALES TORRES, Nilsa .... 787-890-2681 527 E nilsa.morales@upr.edu
MORAMARCO, Jacques . 310-453-8300.. 42 D jacques@emperors.edu
MORAN, Al .... 850-201-6079 112 C morana@tcc.fl.edu
MORAN, Ashley .... 303-373-2008.. 82 F amoran@rvu.edu
MORAN, Bradley .... 907-474-7210.. 10 B sbmoran@alaska.edu
MORAN, Carmella .... 630-844-5132 133 H cmoran@aurora.edu
MORAN, Christyn .... 610-527-0200 409 E christyn@rosemont.edu
MORAN, Demetria .... 401-456-8031 417 A dmoran@ric.edu
MORAN, Eileen, P .... 940-565-2010 466 B eileen.moran@unt.edu
MORAN, James .... 314-977-3490 266 J jemoran@slu.edu
MORAN, III, James, D . 605-677-6497 428 E james.moran@usd.edu
MORAN, Jason .... 603-535-2437 283 B
MORAN, Jay .... 203-392-6025.. 85 A moranj1@southernct.edu
MORAN, Joseph .... 763-424-0772 246 E jmoran@nhcc.edu
MORAN, Kathy .... 518-464-8784 308 A kmoran@excelsior.edu
MORAN, Kelly .... 724-938-4400 405 F moran@calu.edu
MORAN, Ken .... 502-456-6504 189 F kmoran@sullivan.edu
MORAN, Laura, P .... 615-353-3217 437 D laura.moran@nscc.edu
MORAN, Matt .... 501-450-3814.. 19 I moran@hendrix.edu
MORAN, Michael .... 413-565-1000 211 C mmoran@baypath.edu
MORAN, Patricia .... 979-830-4157 444 D pmoran@blinn.edu
MORAN, Patrick .... 307-766-4175 517 B pmoran5@uwyo.edu
MORAN, Paul, J .... 570-208-5948 398 D pjmoran@kings.edu
MORAN, Peter .... 206-685-4233 499 D pkmoran@uw.edu
MORAN, Raymond .... 775-784-1641 279 E rmoran@unr.edu
MORAN, Timothy .... 973-761-9593 291 F timothy.moran@shu.edu
MORAN, Virginia .... 760-245-4271.. 73 E virginia.moran@vvc.edu
MORANO, Joe .... 845-451-1314 306 D joe.morano@culinary.edu
MORANO, Lori .... 518-464-8648 308 A lmorano@excelsior.edu
MORANO, Nancy .... 914-633-2494 311 B nmorano@iona.edu
MORANT, Blake, D .... 202-994-1000.. 92 A morantbd@gwu.edu
MORASKI, Ron .... 518-276-8439 321 A morasr@rpi.edu
MORAVEC, Todd, A .... 518-564-2072 327 E moraveta@plattsburgh.edu
MORAVITZ, Judy .... 909-667-4411.. 37 J jmoravitz@claremontlincoln.edu
MORAY, Yvonne .... 212-472-1500 318 B ymoray@nysid.edu
MORBER, Timothy, T .... 330-471-8279 364 H tmorber@malone.edu
MORCOMB, Mike .... 952-829-2459 240 H mike.morcomb@bethfel.org
MORDACH, John .... 312-942-5600 150 F john_mordach@rush.edu
MORDAN-MCCOMBS, Sarah .... 317-738-8301 157 L smordan-mccombs@franklincollege.edu
MORDEN, Erik .... 909-384-8671.. 59 I emorden@sbccd.cc.ca.us
MOREA, John .... 757-822-1932 489 H jmorea@tcc.edu
MOREAU, Donald .... 603-641-7350 282 A dmoreau@anselm.edu
MOREAU, Elizabeth .... 617-745-3101 214 D elizabeth.moreau@enc.edu
MOREAU, Joe .... 650-949-6120.. 43 E moreaujoe@fhda.edu
MOREAU, Joseph .... 650-949-6119.. 43 D moreaujoe@fhda.edu
MOREAU, Sandra, E ...... 619-239-0391.. 35 C sem@cwsl.edu
MOREAU, Scott .... 630-752-5933 155 F scott.moreau@wheaton.edu
MORECI, Rick .... 773-325-4283 137 C rmoreci@depaul.edu
MOREDOCK, Paul .... 503-594-3132 382 D
MOREFIELD, Bill, R .... 423-318-2735 438 D bill.morefield@ws.edu
MOREHEAD, Jere, W .... 706-542-3000 127 A
MOREHEAD, Kaleybra ... 870-543-5963.. 21 E kmorehead@seark.edu
MOREHOUSE, Kimberly 828-627-4507 343 G kmmorehouse@haywood.edu
MOREIRA, Antonio, R ... 410-455-6576 208 A moreira@umbc.edu
MOREL, Derek .... 504-280-6102 194 F dmorel@uno.edu
MOREL, Luis .... 917-493-4717 313 M lmorel@msmnyc.edu
MOREL, Nina .... 615-966-2501 433 D nina.morel@lipscomb.edu
MORELAND, Doran .... 317-921-4882 161 F doran.moreland@ivytech.edu
MORELAND, Jeremy .... 866-621-0124.. 84 B jeremy.moreland@rockies.edu
MORELAND, Kimberly ... 608-663-8334 507 D kmoreland@edgewood.edu
MORELAND, Mark .... 503-821-8910 385 H mmoreland@pnca.edu
MORELAND, Milton .... 901-843-3795 435 L morelandm@rhodes.edu
MORELIUS, Michael, V . 512-448-8452 455 I mmoreliu@stedwards.edu
MORELL, Christina .... 434-924-3417 486 H cm5c@virginia.edu
MORELLI, Brad .... 405-974-3573 380 J bmorelli@uco.edu
MORELLO, Chanell .... 828-327-7000 341 G cmorello@cvcc.edu
MORELLO, John, T .... 540-654-1269 486 D jmorello@umw.edu
MORELLO, JR., Joseph . 650-738-4271.. 62 B morelloj@smccd.edu
MORELOCK, Luann .... 309-655-7353 151 A luann.morelock@osfhealthcare.org
MORELOCK, Tommy ..... 352-854-2322.. 97 C moreloct@cf.edu
MORELON, Carla .... 770-962-7580 121 G cmorelon@gwinnetttech.edu
MOREMEN, Margaret .... 207-602-2708 202 A mmoremen@une.edu
MOREMENT, Margaret ... 207-221-4768 202 A mmoremen@une.edu
MORENA, Pat .... 212-650-7997 301 F pmorena@ccny.cuny.edu
MORENCY, Maurice ...... 212-752-1530 312 G maurice.morency@limcollege.edu
MORENO, Ben .... 650-723-9406.. 66 C
MORENO, Francisco ..... 787-738-2161 528 A francisco.moreno@upr.edu
MORENO, Gettie .... 210-485-0374 441 E gmoreno107@alamo.edu
MORENO, Jose .... 410-857-2791 205 E jmoreno@mcdaniel.edu
MORENO, Linda .... 773-298-3379 151 C moreno@sxu.edu
MORENO, Luis .... 309-796-5041 134 C morenol@bhc.edu
MORENO, Marcio .... 910-962-2029 352 A morenom@uncw.edu
MORENO, Melissa .... 805-683-8292.. 62 E melissa.moreno@sbcc.edu
MORENO, Orlando .... 325-203-5014 454 L omoreno@rangercollege.edu
MORENO, Patricia .... 281-873-0262 446 J p.moreno@commonwealth.edu
MORENO-RIANO, Gerson .... 757-352-4320 484 E gmorenoriano@regent.edu
MORENO-WEINERT, Inez .... 602-243-8134.. 14 D inez.moreno-weinert@smcmail.maricopa.edu
MORENZ, Ronald .... 440-525-7321 364 D rmorenz@lakelandcc.edu
MORENZ, Tim .... 217-854-5759 134 E tim.morenz@blackburn.edu
MOREO, Patrick .... 941-359-4200 111 C
MORERA, Joachim .... 310-287-4307.. 49 H morerajj@wlac.edu
MORERA-GONZÁLEZ, Angel .... 787-993-8871 527 G angel.morera1@upr.edu
MORESCHI, Tracy, L ..... 503-255-0332 384 E tmoreschi@multnomah.edu
MOREST, Vanessa .... 914-606-6712 333 H vanessa.morest@sunywcc.edu
MORETTI, Linda .... 716-829-7811 307 B moretti@dyc.edu
MORETZ, Drew .... 919-962-7096 349 G jkappler@northcarolina.edu
MOREY, Ann, N .... 818-677-2878.. 33 B ann.morey@csun.edu
MOREY, Joshua .... 951-343-4235.. 28 G jmorey@calbaptist.edu
MOREY, Megan .... 413-597-4217 226 C megan.e.morey@williams.edu
MOREY, Robin .... 202-687-3124.. 92 B rm1469@georgetown.edu
MORGAN, Allen .... 865-471-3372 430 H amorgan@cn.edu
MORGAN, Amanda .... 864-388-8971 422 A amorgan@lander.edu
MORGAN, Amy .... 504-816-8072 195 D studentservices@nobts.edu
MORGAN, Andrea .... 303-273-3021.. 78 J asalazar@mines.edu
MORGAN, Anna Beth .... 507-284-9595 241 E annabeth.morgan@mayo.edu
MORGAN, Anna Beth .... 507-293-7480 241 F morgan.annabeth@mayo.edu
MORGAN, Barbara .... 617-879-2118 226 A bmorgan@wheelock.edu
MORGAN, Beryl .... 305-809-3149.. 99 L beryl.morgan@fkcc.edu
MORGAN, Betsy .... 608-785-8042 510 F bmorgan@uwlax.edu
MORGAN, Betsy, S .... 269-467-9945 230 C bmorgan@glenoaks.edu
MORGAN, Brian, J .... 858-499-0202.. 39 B netadmin@coleman.edu
MORGAN, Bruce, A .... 423-775-7233 430 G bruce.morgan@bryan.edu
MORGAN, Bryant .... 413-528-7204 211 B bmorgan@simons-rock.edu
MORGAN, Camella .... 253-833-9111 495 C cmorgan@greenriver.edu
MORGAN, Carolyn .... 205-387-0511.... 1 D carol.morgan@bscc.edu
MORGAN, Cassie .... 256-549-8263.... 2 A cmorgan@gadsdenstate.edu
MORGAN, Catherine, A . 423-439-4300 431 H morganca1@etsu.edu
MORGAN, Chris .... 951-343-4369.. 28 G cmorgan@calbaptist.edu
MORGAN, Chris .... 717-361-1407 394 F morganc@etown.edu
MORGAN, David .... 765-361-6382 166 B morgand@wabash.edu
MORGAN, David, A .... 423-775-7597 430 G morganda@bryan.edu
MORGAN, Deborah .... 918-540-6312 376 F demorgan@neo.edu
MORGAN, Derek .... 303-273-3288.. 78 J dmorgan@mines.edu
MORGAN, Elizabeth ...... 909-621-8101.. 38 A elizabeth.morgan@cmc.edu
MORGAN, Erin .... 206-296-5856 498 D morganer@seattleu.edu
MORGAN, Faye .... 662-243-1923 253 A fmorgan@eastms.edu
MORGAN, Gilbert .... 443-885-3125 206 A gilbert.morgan@morgan.edu
MORGAN, Ginny .... 510-841-9230.. 75 E vmorgan@wi.edu
MORGAN, Heath .... 660-831-4087 264 A morganh@moval.edu
MORGAN, Helen .... 912-525-5000 125 B hmorgan@scad.edu
MORGAN, J .... 859-985-3019 183 I morganjoh@berea.edu
MORGAN, J. Reid .... 336-758-5122 353 A jrm@wfu.edu
MORGAN, Jane .... 805-378-1443.. 73 A jmorgan@vcccd.edu
MORGAN, Janie, M ...... 608-785-8495 510 F jspencer@uwlax.edu
MORGAN, Janifer .... 706-385-1463 124 F janifer.morgan@point.edu
MORGAN, Jason .... 256-352-8225.... 3 I jason.morgan@wallacestate.edu
MORGAN, Jeff .... 651-450-3299 245 A jmorgan@inverhills.edu
MORGAN, Jeff .... 713-743-3455 465 A jjmorgan@central.uh.edu
MORGAN, Jeffrey .... 480-219-6111 257 A jmorgan@atsu.edu
MORGAN, Jennifer .... 336-721-2600 348 H jennifer.morgan@salem.edu
MORGAN, Jim .... 575-461-4413 294 E jimm@mesalands.edu
MORGAN, Joanne, L ..... 919-658-8558 349 F jmorgan@umo.edu

MORGAN, John .... 928-717-7721.. 17 G
john.morgan@yc.edu
MORGAN, John .... 203-582-5359.. 88 A
john.morgan@quinnipiac.edu
MORGAN, Joseph, A .... 606-783-2022 188 C
j.morgan@moreheadstate.edu
MORGAN, Joshua .... 575-492-2769 294 L
jmorgan@nmjc.edu
MORGAN, Kara, A .... 814-871-7610 395 H
morgan013@gannon.edu
MORGAN, Karen .... 201-200-3003 287 F
kmorgan@njcu.edu
MORGAN, Karrie .... 605-331-6672 429 D
karrie.morgan@usiouxfalls.edu
MORGAN, Kelly .... 863-638-7244 113 I
kelly.morgan@warner.edu
MORGAN, Ken .... 478-825-6304 119 C
morgank@fvsu.edu
MORGAN, Kristy .... 903-233-4410 452 A
kristymorgan@letu.edu
MORGAN, JR., Leroy .... 706-821-8235 124 C
lmorgan@paine.edu
MORGAN, Lissa .... 901-572-2441 430 C
lissa.morgan@bchs.edu
MORGAN, Louis .... 423-614-8567 432 L
lmorgan@leeuniversity.edu
MORGAN, Lucas .... 318-798-4107 194 E
lucas.morgan@lsus.edu
MORGAN, Lucille .... 847-947-5208 146 G
lucille.morgan@nl.edu
MORGAN, Mark .... 407-708-2224 107 G
morganm@seminolestate.edu
MORGAN, Mark, D .... 910-962-3719 352 A
morganm@uncw.edu
MORGAN, Mary .... 724-357-7942 406 C
morgan@iup.edu
MORGAN, Maunka .... 402-878-3354 275 C
maunka.morgan@littlepriest.edu
MORGAN, Michael .... 901-843-3810 435 L
morganm@rhodes.edu
MORGAN, Michael, D ... 518-564-5402 327 E
morganmd@plattsburgh.edu
MORGAN, Michael, D ... 205-726-2727.... 6 G
mmorgan@samford.edu
MORGAN, Mike .... 510-666-8248.. 24 E
mmorgan@aimc.edu
MORGAN, Natasha .... 432-685-4534 453 B
nmorgan@midland.edu
MORGAN, Pamela .... 940-397-4785 453 C
pamela.morgan@mwsu.edu
MORGAN, Patricia .... 707-256-7305.. 53 D
pmorgan@napavalley.edu
MORGAN, Patricia .... 315-470-8851 299 K
patriciamorgan@crouse.org
MORGAN, Peggy .... 303-914-6337.. 82 B
peggy.morgan@rrcc.edu
MORGAN, R. Gregory ... 617-452-2081 221 C
MORGAN, Rachel, A ..... 651-631-5249 251 C
ramorgan@unwsp.edu
MORGAN, JR.,
Raymond, V .... 361-570-4332 465 D
morganrv@uhv.edu
MORGAN, Robert .... 402-228-8272 276 K
bmorgan@southeast.edu
MORGAN, Romena .... 434-528-5276 491 D
rmorgan@vul.edu
MORGAN, Russell .... 309-298-1066 155 D
re-morgan@wiu.edu
MORGAN, Samuel .... 559-638-0300.. 66 H
samuel.morgan@reedleycollege.edu
MORGAN, Scott .... 360-867-6913 494 G
sustainabilitydirector@evergreen.edu
MORGAN, Sharon, E .... 973-596-5560 288 A
sharon.e.morgan@njit.edu
MORGAN, Sonja .... 253-566-5322 499 A
smorgan@tacomacc.edu
MORGAN, Spencer .... 716-896-0700 333 C
smorgan@villa.edu
MORGAN, Stephen .... 626-656-2101.. 72 C
smorgan@uwest.edu
MORGAN, Stephen, R ... 801-832-2550 474 E
smorgan@westminstercollege.edu
MORGAN, Steve .... 504-398-2228 196 E
smorgan@uhcno.edu
MORGAN, Tyler, S .... 801-524-8161 471 L
tmorgan@ldsbc.edu
MORGAN, Wendy .... 304-637-1341 501 H
morganw@dewv.edu
MORGAN, William, E .... 972-438-6932 454 G
wmorgan@parker.edu
MORGAN AGARD,
Nicole .... 201-684-7503 289 C
nmagard@ramapo.edu
MORGAN FOSTER,
Stacey .... 509-359-6015 494 D
sfoster@ewu.edu
MORGAN RIGGS, Janet 717-337-6010 396 A
jriggs@gettysburg.edu
MORGAN-RUSSELL,
Simon .... 419-372-2340 357 F
smorgan@bgsu.edu
MORGAN-TATE, Jessica 620-331-4100 178 E
jmorgantate@indycc.edu
MORGAN-ZAYACHEK,
Eileen .... 607-436-2855 325 E
eileen.morgan@oneonta.edu
MORGANSTEIN, Penny . 212-472-1500 318 B
pmorganstein@mysid.edu
MORGENSTERN,
Patricia .... 269-467-9945 230 C
pmorgenstern@glenoaks.edu
MORGENTHALER,
Diane, S .... 203-392-6300.. 85 A
morgenthald1@southernct.edu
MORI, Darryl .... 626-396-4288.. 26 L
darryl.mori@artcenter.edu
MORIARTY, Beth .... 508-531-1277 217 D
bmoriarty@bridgew.edu
MORIARTY, Deb .... 410-704-2055 209 C
dmoriarty@towson.edu
MORIARTY, George .... 978-659-1224 220 F
gmoriarty@necc.mass.edu
MORIARTY, Joan .... 973-618-3394 284 D
jmoriarty@caldwell.edu
MORIARTY, John .... 305-899-3957.. 95 G
jmoriarty@barry.edu
MORIARTY, Laura .... 732-571-3405 287 C
lmoriart@monmouth.edu
MORIARTY, Martha .... 843-521-3137 425 B
mamoriar@uscb.edu
MORIARTY, Maureen .... 802-831-1265 476 G
mmoriarty@vermontlaw.edu
MORIARTY, Michael, J . 860-515-3760.. 84 H
mjmoriarty@charteroak.edu
MORIARTY, Sean .... 315-312-5500 327 D
sean.moriarty@oswego.edu
MORIATY, Erin, T .... 773-508-3075 144 D
emoriar@luc.edu
MORICONI, Jill .... 814-254-0400 392 F
jmoriconi@pa.gov
MORICONI,
Kimberly, A .... 816-604-6544 262 G
kim.moriconi@mcckc.edu
MORIKANG, Marilyn ..... 408-298-2181.. 61 P
marilyn.morikang@sjcc.edu
MORIMOTO, Yash .... 505-428-1765 296 B
yash.morimoto@sfcc.edu
MORIN, Anna .... 508-373-5649 221 E
anna.morin@mcphs.edu
MORIN, Christine .... 207-755-5215 199 K
cmorin@cmcc.edu
MORIN, Erin .... 336-770-3296 352 B
morine@uncsa.edu
MORIN, III,
Frederick, C .... 802-656-2156 476 E
frederick.morin@uvm.edu
MORIN, Jeff .... 414-847-3210 508 G
jeffreymorin@miad.edu
MORIN, Jodie .... 712-749-2097 167 C
morinj@bvu.edu
MORIN, Karen, M .... 570-577-3293 390 H
karen.morin@bucknell.edu
MORIN, Kevin .... 414-277-7129 509 A
morin@msoe.edu
MORIN, Kevin, A .... 414-277-7129 509 A
morin@msoe.edu
MORIN, Regina .... 660-785-7468 267 K
rmorin@truman.edu
MORIN, Shirley .... 701-477-7862 355 H
smorin@tm.edu
MORIN, Stephen, J .... 203-932-7268.. 89 D
smorin@newhaven.edu
MORINEC, Maire .... 707-864-7000.. 64 E
maire.morinec@solano.edu
MORISHITA, Leroy, M .. 510-885-3877.. 31 F
leroy.morishita@csueastbay.edu
MORISSEAU, Natalie, L . 973-353-5872 290 D
natalia.morisseau@rutgers.edu
MORITA, Denise .... 510-649-2469.. 44 J
dmorita@gtu.edu
MORK, Jason .... 507-457-1703 250 B
jwmork@smumn.edu
MORLAN, Tom .... 503-255-0332 384 E
tmorlan@multnomah.edu
MORLEY, John .... 312-850-7230 136 C
jmorley@ccc.edu
MORLEY, Kathleen .... 254-710-2061 444 B
kathleen_morley@baylor.edu
MORLEY, Maureen .... 212-938-5945 328 E
mmorley@sunyopt.edu
MORLEY, Sandy .... 517-264-7193 236 I
smorley@sienaheights.edu
MORLEY, Yvonne, Y ..... 859-238-5220 184 C
yvonne.morley@centre.edu
MORLEY-MOWER,
Cynthia .... 213-763-7074.. 49 F
morleycn@lattc.edu
MORLIER, Margaret, M . 770-720-5579 124 H
mmm@reinhardt.edu
MORMANDO, Karin, W . 215-204-8556 411 B
karin.mormando@temple.edu
MORNINGSTAR, Kevin .. 760-750-4775.. 33 E
kmorningstar@csusm.edu
MORO, Nicole .... 617-228-1913 219 D
nmoro@bhcc.mass.edu
MORO, Simonetta .... 347-966-1096 199 C
smoro@idsva.org
MORODOMI, Joyce, K .. 559-323-2100.. 61 A
jmorodomi@sjcl.edu
MOROI, Katsumi .... 213-613-2200.. 65 A
kmoroi@sciarc.edu
MORONEY, Donney .... 414-410-4329 506 F
dmoroney@stritch.edu
MORONEY, James .... 617-254-2610 224 B
rector@sjs.edu
MORONEY, Mary, F ...... 401-232-6298 416 A
mmoroney@bryant.edu
MORONEY, Michael, R . 651-631-5482 251 C
mrmoroney@unwsp.edu
MORONG, Andrew .... 207-755-5273 199 K
amorong@cmcc.edu
MOROSKO, Linda .... 330-494-6170 370 G
lmorosko@starkstate.edu
MOROSOFF, Wendy ...... 914-251-6370 328 B
wendy.morosoff@purchase.edu
MOROTE, Elsa-Sofia ...... 631-420-2723 329 D
morotee@farmingdale.edu
MOROWSKI, James, R .. 701-788-4619 354 B
james.morowski@mayvillestate.edu
MOROZOWICH, Mark .... 202-319-5683.. 91 D
morozowich@cua.edu
MORPHEW, Christopher 410-516-7820 204 F
christopher.morphew@jhu.edu
MORPHEW, Vonnie .... 254-659-7502 450 B
ymorphew@hillcollege.edu
MORR, Alex .... 617-873-0475 213 B
alex.morr@cambridgecollege.edu
MORRAL, Melissa .... 585-340-9633 304 F
mmorral@crcds.edu
MORRAR, Ghada .... 312-939-0111 137 G
ghada@eastwest.edu
MORRELL, Chuck .... 406-496-4325 272 E
cmorrell@mtech.edu
MORRELL, Erin .... 203-773-8541.. 84 G
emorrell@albertus.edu
MORRELL, Matthew, D .. 763-417-8250 241 D
mmorrell@centralseminary.edu
MORRELL, Richard .... 402-472-2025 277 G
richard.morrell@unl.edu
MORRELL, Sarah .... 508-678-2811 219 C
sarah.morrell@bristolcc.edu
MORREN, Glen .... 313-664-1162 228 H
gmorren@collegeforcreativestudies.edu
MORRICE, Pelema .... 573-882-7651 268 C
morricep@missouri.edu
MORRILL, Allen .... 724-589-2124 411 D
amorrill@thiel.edu
MORRILL, Deborah, H .. 210-567-6395 468 E
morrill@uthscsa.edu
MORRILL, Donald, D .... 813-258-7409 113 E
dmorrill@ut.edu
MORRILL, Luke .... 904-256-7067 102 B
lmorill1@ju.edu
MORRIN, Jeffrey, R .... 208-496-1155 131 D
morrinj@byui.edu
MORRIS, Adam .... 562-903-4714.. 27 E
adam.morris@biola.edu
MORRIS, Amanda .... 912-287-6584 117 J
amorris@coastalpines.edu
MORRIS, Amy .... 620-431-2820 180 C
amorris@neosho.edu
MORRIS, Andrew .... 585-389-2113 316 D
amorris8@naz.edu
MORRIS, Ann .... 419-824-3694 364 G
amorris@lourdes.edu
MORRIS, Ann .... 704-216-3542 346 C
ann.morris@rccc.edu
MORRIS, Barbara .... 970-247-7314.. 79 J
morris_b@fortlewis.edu
MORRIS, Barbara .... 410-532-5367 206 D
bmorris@ndm.edu
MORRIS, Ben .... 252-940-6374 340 N
ben.morris@beaufortccc.edu
MORRIS, Beth .... 828-766-1257 344 F
bmorris@mayland.edu
MORRIS, Brenda .... 870-584-1107.. 22 F
bmorris@cccua.edu
MORRIS, Brenda .... 903-468-3020 459 E
brenda.morris@tamuc.edu
MORRIS, Brett .... 859-622-1555 184 F
brett.morris@eku.edu
MORRIS, Carlene .... 785-830-2702 178 A
cmorris@haskell.edu
MORRIS, Carlton, E ...... 334-724-8784.... 7 F
cmorris@mytu.tuskegee.edu
MORRIS, Chad .... 661-654-3271.. 31 B
cmorris@csub.edu
MORRIS, Chad, T .... 540-375-4926 484 H
morris@roanoke.edu
MORRIS, Charles .... 214-860-2019 448 A
cmorris@dcccd.edu
MORRIS, Charles .... 304-865-6025 502 C
charles.morris@ovu.edu
MORRIS, Charlotte, P ... 334-727-8011.... 7 F
president@mytu.tuskegee.edu
MORRIS, Cheryl .... 970-245-8101.. 80 K
cmorris@intelliteccollege.edu
MORRIS, Clark .... 816-415-5997 270 C
morrisc@william.jewell.edu
MORRIS, Clark, W .... 816-415-5997 270 C
morrisc@william.jewell.edu
MORRIS, Claudia .... 352-365-3523 103 B
morrisc@lssc.edu
MORRIS, Connie .... 843-661-8315 421 F
connie.morris@fdtc.edu
MORRIS, Corinne .... 402-844-7361 276 G
corinne@northeast.edu
MORRIS, Craig .... 651-793-1272 245 E
craig.morris@metrostate.edu
MORRIS, Craig .... 541-552-6319 386 H
cmorris@sou.edu
MORRIS, Dan .... 702-651-5500 278 N
dan.morris@csn.edu
MORRIS, Daryl .... 334-244-3295.... 4 E
dmorris@aum.edu
MORRIS, Deborah .... 304-357-4849 502 E
deborahmorris@ucwv.edu
MORRIS, Delesa .... 561-803-2022 104 I
delesa_morris@pba.edu
MORRIS, Diana .... 800-567-2344 506 I
dmorris@menominee.edu
MORRIS, Don .... 314-968-7444 269 N
morrisdo@webster.edu
MORRIS, Dottie .... 603-358-2206 283 A
dmorris@keene.edu
MORRIS, Earl .... 808-675-3501 128 K
earl.morris@byuh.edu
MORRIS, Elizabeth .... 951-343-4507.. 28 G
emorris@calbaptist.edu
MORRIS, Gary .... 315-312-2255 327 D
gary.morris@oswego.edu
MORRIS, Gary .... 512-448-8731 455 I
gmorris1@stedwards.edu
MORRIS, Gary, Z .... 304-462-6110 504 B
gary.morris@glenville.edu
MORRIS, Geri .... 419-998-3106 372 D
geri@unoh.edu
MORRIS, Glenn .... 352-335-2332.. 94 D
glenn.morris@acupuncturist.edu
MORRIS, Henry .... 507-389-1150 246 A
henry.morris@mnsu.edu
MORRIS, Jason .... 325-674-2830 441 D
morrisj@acu.edu
MORRIS, Jeff .... 620-252-7177 176 K
morris.jeff@coffeyville.edu
MORRIS, Jeffery, B .... 785-532-6415 179 A
jbmorris@ksu.edu
MORRIS, John .... 808-739-8555 129 A
jmorris@chaminade.edu
MORRIS, John .... 617-627-3232 225 A
john.morris@tufts.edu
MORRIS, Joseph .... 303-797-5801.. 76 I
joseph.morris@arapahoe.edu
MORRIS, Julia, M .... 304-457-6205 501 A
auviljm@ab.edu
MORRIS, Julie .... 404-876-1227 117 A
MORRIS, Julie .... 410-323-6211 203 F
j.morris@fts.edu
MORRIS, Kathleen .... 315-786-2236 311 H
kmorris@sunyjefferson.edu
MORRIS, Kathryn .... 317-940-9903 156 I
kmorris@butler.edu
MORRIS, Kelli .... 256-306-2602.... 1 F
kelli.morris@calhoun.edu
MORRIS, Kelli .... 256-326-2602.... 1 F
kelli.morris@calhoun.edu
MORRIS, Ken .... 570-586-2400 392 E
kmorris@clarkssummitu.edu
MORRIS, Kevin .... 281-922-3479 456 B
kevin.morris@sjcd.edu
MORRIS, Kevin .... 936-294-1794 462 F
kmorris@shsu.edu
MORRIS, Kimberly .... 478-825-6605 119 C
morrisk01@fvsu.edu
MORRIS, Kizzy .... 570-422-2831 406 A
registrar@esu.edu
MORRIS, Kyle .... 307-755-2129 517 G
kyle.morris@zenith.org

MORRIS, Laura, M .... 302-295-1179.. 91 B
laura.m.morris@wilmu.edu
MORRIS, Lawrence, J ... 202-319-5142.. 91 D
morrisl@cua.edu
MORRIS, Lela .... 817-598-6488 470 J
morris@wc.edu
MORRIS, Loren, L .... 620-665-3523 178 D
morrisl@hutchcc.edu
MORRIS, Malcolm, L ..... 678-916-2603 115 K
mmorris@johnmarshall.edu
MORRIS, Marie .... 765-641-4020 156 A
msmorris@anderson.edu
MORRIS, Matthew .... 417-836-5233 263 H
mattmorris@missuristate.edu
MORRIS, Melissa, M .... 334-844-7771.... 4 D
morrimm@auburn.edu
MORRIS, Mellasenah ..... 765-658-4394 157 H
mellasenahmorris@depauw.edu
MORRIS, Nerissa, E ...... 305-284-4476 112 O
nmorris@miami.edu
MORRIS, Nora .... 763-433-1632 243 K
nora.morris@anokaramsey.edu
MORRIS, Nora .... 763-433-1632 244 A
nora.morris@anokaramsey.edu
MORRIS, Patrick .... 203-365-7507.. 88 C
morrisp@sacredheart.edu
MORRIS, Paul .... 435-652-7504 473 B
pmorris@dixie.edu
MORRIS, Randy .... 501-337-5000.. 19 C
rmorris@coto.edu
MORRIS, Raymond .... 706-769-1472 115 G
MORRIS, Regina .... 573-840-9606 267 J
rmorris@trcc.edu
MORRIS, Renea .... 740-593-2563 368 G
morrisr@ohio.edu
MORRIS, Rick .... 864-977-7777 422 I
publicsafety@ngu.edu
MORRIS, Robert, G .... 724-287-8711 390 J
robert.morris@bc3.edu
MORRIS, Sara .... 716-888-2125 300 G
morris@canisius.edu
MORRIS, Sara, B .... 316-978-5520 182 F
sara.morris@wichita.edu
MORRIS, Scott .... 713-683-3817 456 C
MORRIS, Steve .... 270-789-5017 184 B
srmorris@campbellsville.edu
MORRIS, Steve .... 217-854-5513 134 E
steve.morris@blackburn.edu
MORRIS, Tama .... 704-337-2363 348 D
morrist@queens.edu
MORRIS, Tammy, H .... 336-322-2150 345 D
tammy.morris@piedmontcc.edu
MORRIS, Tommy .... 256-824-6576.... 8 C
tommy.morris@uah.edu
MORRIS, Tracy .... 309-694-8970 139 G
tracy.morris@icc.edu
MORRIS, Valerie, B .... 843-953-8222 420 C
morrisv@cofc.edu
MORRIS, Vince .... 585-567-9321 310 F
vince.morris@houghton.edu
MORRIS, Wanda .... 310-660-3281.. 42 C
wmorris@elcamino.edu
MORRIS, Wanda .... 310-900-1600.. 40 C
wmorris@elcamino.edu
MORRIS, Wendi .... 478-296-6179 123 I
wmorris@oftc.edu
MORRIS, William .... 512-492-3060 442 J
wmorris@aoma.edu
MORRIS-DUEER, Vicky .. 972-265-5744 464 E
vmorrisdueer@udallas.edu
MORRISETT, Gregory, J 607-255-9188 306 B
greg.morrisett@cornell.edu
MORRISETTE, Joanna .... 919-735-5151 347 E
jmmorrisette@waynecc.edu
MORRISON, Allen .... 602-978-7203.. 10 K
allen.morrison@asu.edu
MORRISON, Andrew ...... 740-588-1388 374 G
amorrison@zanestate.edu
MORRISON, Angel .... 785-460-5418 176 L
angel.morrison@colbycc.edu
MORRISON, Barry, F ..... 401-232-6017 416 A
bmorriso@bryant.edu
MORRISON, Betty, N ..... 630-515-7600 145 I
emorri@midwestern.edu
MORRISON, Brenda, M . 443-412-2409 204 C
bmorrison@harford.edu
MORRISON,
Carberta, A .... 856-225-2949 290 B
cammor@camden.rutgers.edu
MORRISON, Carol .... 239-513-1122 101 O
cmorrison@hodges.edu
MORRISON, Cindi .... 352-291-4455.. 97 C
morrisoc@cf.edu
MORRISON, David .... 770-534-6167 116 F
dmorrison@brenau.edu
MORRISON, Don .... 641-628-5280 167 D
morrisond@central.edu
MORRISON, Edwina .... 406-444-0326 271 F
emorrison@montana.edu
MORRISON, Gail .... 651-450-3512 245 A
gmorris@inverhills.edu
MORRISON, Jason .... 870-574-4501.. 21 G
jmorriso@sautech.edu
MORRISON, Jean .... 617-353-2230 212 G
morrison@bu.edu
MORRISON, Jennifer ..... 503-244-0726 381 H
jennifermorrison@achs.edu
MORRISON, Jennifer, K 508-767-7007 210 I
jemorrison@assumption.edu
MORRISON, Jessica ...... 559-737-5443.. 39 G
jessicamo@cos.edu
MORRISON, John .... 856-351-2628 291 E
jmorrison@salemcc.edu
MORRISON, Julie .... 734-973-5010 238 G
jmorriso@wccnet.edu
MORRISON, Karen .... 407-823-6479 110 C
karen.morrison@ucf.edu
MORRISON, Kim .... 510-723-6762.. 36 C
kmorrison@chabotcollege.edu
MORRISON, Kirk .... 858-513-9240.. 26 T
kirk.morrison@ashford.edu
MORRISON, Larry .... 402-481-8752 273 F
larry.morrison@bryanhealthcollege.edu
MORRISON, Laura .... 252-335-0821 342 D
laura_morrison@albemarle.edu
MORRISON, Lolita .... 404-297-9522 120 D
morrisonl@gptc.org
MORRISON, Marty, G .... 540-654-2287 486 D
mmorris3@umw.edu
MORRISON, Michael ..... 626-650-2363.. 44 H
MORRISON, Michael, L 812-888-5736 165 E
mmorrison@vinu.edu
MORRISON, Nancy, J ... 212-998-4924 318 D
nancy.morrison@nyu.edu
MORRISON, Pamela ...... 916-558-2088.. 50 I
morrisp@scc.losrios.edu
MORRISON, Rebecca, L 414-955-4949 508 D
rmorriso@mcw.edu
MORRISON, Regina ...... 650-738-4350.. 62 B
morrison@smccd.edu
MORRISON, Robert .... 312-261-3372 146 G
rob.morrison@nl.edu
MORRISON, Rodney ...... 631-632-6857 325 F
rodney.morrison@stonybrook.edu
MORRISON, Rodney ...... 419-448-2391 362 G
rmorriso@heidelberg.edu
MORRISON, Roxanne .... 619-260-7579.. 71 J
roxannemorrison@sandiego.edu
MORRISON, Sarah, B .... 276-656-0322 489 A
sbmorrison@patrickhenry.edu
MORRISON, Scott .... 775-445-4431 279 F
scott.morrison@wnc.edu
MORRISON, Scott .... 775-445-3000 279 F
scott.morrison@wnc.edu
MORRISON, Scott, D .... 540-828-5376 478 J
smorriso@bridgewater.edu
MORRISON, Thomas ..... 812-855-6992 159 G
morrison@indiana.edu
MORRISON, Thomas, A 812-855-6992 159 H
morrisot@indiana.edu
MORRISON, William ..... 973-684-6741 288 C
wmorrison@pccc.edu
MORRISON, William ..... 508-588-9100 220 B
MORRISON-FRONCKOWIAK,
Lisa, T .... 716-878-4500 326 E
morrislt@buffalostate.edu
MORRISON GOINGS,
Amy, M .... 425-739-8200 495 F
amy.goings@lwtech.edu
MORRISON-MONGER,
Heather .... 865-524-8079 432 F
hmonger@hchs.edu
MORRISON-SHETLAR,
Alison .... 828-227-7495 352 C
aimorrison@wcu.edu
MORRISON-WILLAIMS,
Suzanne .... 954-492-5353.. 96 J
smw@citycollege.edu
MORRISS, Andrew, P .... 817-212-4100 459 C
amorriss@tamu.edu
MORRISS-OLSON,
Melissa .... 413-565-1000 211 C
mmolson@baypath.edu
MORRISSETTE, Barbara . 304-473-8162 505 G
morrissette@wvwc.edu
MORRISSEY, Aileen .... 386-506-3475.. 97 I
morrisa@daytonastate.edu
MORRISSEY, Ann, M .... 401-874-4402 417 E
morrissey@uri.edu
MORRISSEY, Barbara .... 925-424-1420.. 36 D
bmorrissey@laspositascollege.edu
MORRISSEY, Jeff, P ...... 417-836-5770 263 H
jeffmorrissey@missouristate.edu
MORRISSEY, Sharon ..... 804-819-4972 487 F
smorrissey@vccs.edu
MORRISSEY, Shawn ...... 508-856-2265 217 C
shawn.morrissey@umassmed.edu
MORRO, Robert .... 610-519-4589 413 K
robert.morro@villanova.edu
MORRONE, Anastasia .... 317-274-3479 160 E
amorrone@iupui.edu
MORRONE, Anthony ...... 702-992-2150 279 B
finaid@nsc.edu
MORROW, Andrea .... 567-661-7104 369 A
andrea_morrow@owens.edu
MORROW, Barbara, A ... 314-340-5763 260 H
morrowb@hssu.edu
MORROW, Bill, J .... 302-857-1245.. 90 F
bmorrow@dtcc.edu
MORROW, Carol, K ...... 212-998-4798 318 D
carol.morrow@nyu.edu
MORROW, David .... 267-295-2357 409 B
dmorrow@walnuthillcollege.edu
MORROW, David, M ..... 518-736-3622 309 A
dmorrow@fmcc.suny.edu
MORROW, Donnie .... 828-835-4309 347 B
dmorrow@tricountycc.edu
MORROW, Dorothy .... 402-557-7296 273 E
dorothy.morrow@bellevue.edu
MORROW, Erik .... 512-472-4133 456 E
emorrow@ssw.edu
MORROW, Frances .... 330-490-7312 373 F
fmorrow@walsh.edu
MORROW, Joyce, S ...... 319-273-2244 167 A
joyce.morrow@uni.edu
MORROW, Liz .... 573-681-5011 261 H
morrowl@lincolnu.edu
MORROW, Marjann .... 325-574-7608 470 N
mmorrow@wtc.edu
MORROW, Michael .... 651-523-1660 242 J
mmorrow001@luthersem.edu
MORROW, Rebecca .... 304-793-6591 504 F
rmorrow@osteo.wvsom.edu
MORROW, Wanda .... 713-646-1825 456 H
wmorrow@stcl.edu
MORROW RUETTEN,
Lydia .... 708-534-4110 138 H
lruetten@govst.edu
MORRRIS, Kenielle .... 704-355-3243 336 F
kenielle.morris@carolinascollege.edu
MORSBERGER,
Michael, J .... 407-882-1250 110 C
mike.mors@ucf.edu
MORSCHES, Michael ..... 708-974-5310 146 C
morschesm@morainevalley.edu
MORSE, Alicia .... 410-777-2587 202 D
ammorse@aacc.edu
MORSE, Austin .... 616-988-1000 228 I
austin.m@compass.edu
MORSE, Charles, C .... 508-831-5540 226 E
cmorse@wpi.edu
MORSE, David .... 760-252-2411.. 27 A
dmorse@barstow.edu
MORSE, Micael .... 903-586-2518 451 C
MORSE, Rachel .... 907-786-1278.. 10 A
rlmorse@alaska.edu
MORSE, Susan .... 740-427-5926 364 A
morses@kenyon.edu
MORSE, Wayne .... 660-248-6298 258 B
wmorse@centralmethodist.edu
MORSE, Weyland .... 818-766-8151.. 40 F
wmorse@concorde.edu
MORSE, William .... 909-607-9506.. 57 I
william.morse@pomona.edu
MORSMAN, Elaine .... 607-587-4061 328 F
morsmaem@alfredstate.edu
MORSOVILLO, Michael . 708-524-6793 137 F
morsomike@dom.edu
MORSS, Susan .... 520-515-3662.. 11 R
morsss@cochise.edu
MORT, Jane .... 605-688-6197 429 B
jane.mort@sdstate.edu
MORTALI, Jill, M .... 603-646-3007 281 C
jill.m.mortali@dartmouth.edu
MORTELA, Cecilia .... 805-267-1690.. 48 B
MORTEN, Sally, C .... 540-231-6394 490 F
scmorten@vt.edu
MORTENSEN, Brad .... 801-626-6002 473 E
bmortensen@weber.edu
MORTENSEN, John .... 435-797-1110 473 C
john.mortensen@usu.edu
MORTENSEN, Larry .... 719-587-7402.. 76 D
lsmorten@adams.edu
MORTENSEN, Norm .... 304-734-6680 502 K
norm.mortensen@bridgevalley.edu
MORTENSON,
Donald, W .... 206-281-2522 498 B
dmort@spu.edu
MORTENSON, Gary .... 254-710-1161 444 B
gary_mortenson@baylor.edu
MORTHLAND, Betsey ..... 309-796-5049 134 C
morthlandb@bhc.edu
MORTHLAND, Tim .... 618-937-2127 146 E
tmorthland@morthland.edu
MORTIMER, Gayle .... 620-862-5252 175 B
gayle.mortimer@barclaycollege.edu
MORTIMER, Ian .... 585-389-2525 316 D
imortim4@naz.edu
MORTIMER, Nathan, J .. 330-972-6501 371 C
njm9@uakron.edu
MORTIMEYER, Jennifer . 719-336-1572.. 80 N
jennifer.mortimeyer@lamarcc.edu
MORTLAND, Stephen ..... 765-998-5206 164 C
stmortlan@taylor.edu
MORTON, Amy, M .... 508-831-5874 226 E
ammorton@wpi.edu
MORTON, Bradley .... 732-906-2601 287 B
bmorton@middlesexcc.edu
MORTON, Cassandra .... 909-748-8391.. 71 H
cassandra_morton@redlands.edu
MORTON, Christina .... 412-392-4207 408 F
cmorton@pointpark.edu
MORTON, Clarresa .... 540-665-4517 485 C
cmorton@su.edu
MORTON, Doug .... 919-515-8851 350 E
dgmorton@ncsu.edu
MORTON, Jim .... 910-362-7065 341 E
jmorton@cfcc.edu
MORTON, John, F .... 808-956-7038 129 H
jmorton@hawaii.edu
MORTON, John, F .... 808-956-7038 130 B
jmorton@hawaii.edu
MORTON, Lynn, M .... 828-298-3325 353 B
president@warren-wilson.edu
MORTON, Marcia .... 417-667-8181 259 A
mmorton@cottey.edu
MORTON, Margaret .... 212-353-4208 306 A
mortonnyc@cooper.edu
MORTON, Mary, B .... 607-746-4430 329 B
mortonmb@delhi.edu
MORTON, Matt .... 949-376-6000.. 47 H
mmorton@lcad.edu
MORTON, Patricia .... 801-581-8262 472 P
patricia.morton@nurs.utah.edu
MORTON, Tonya, L .... 910-938-6211 342 C
mortont@coastalcarolina.edu
MORTON, Tracy, L .... 757-446-5800 480 C
mortontl@evms.edu
MORTON, Wendy .... 918-495-6817 378 H
wmorton@oru.edu
MORVICE, Michael .... 714-432-5741.. 38 H
mmorvice@occ.cccd.edu
MORY, Scott .... 412-268-2135 391 H
mory@cmu.edu
MORYAN, James .... 215-489-4889 393 F
james.moryan@delval.edu
MOSABEH, Rasha .... 918-836-6886 380 C
rasha.mosabeh@spartan.edu
MOSBURG, Calleb, N .... 580-327-8415 376 K
cnmosburg@nwosu.edu
MOSBY, David, C .... 301-546-0655 206 E
mosbydc@pgcc.edu
MOSBY, John .... 408-855-5195.. 74 C
john.mosby@missioncollege.edu
MOSBY-WILSON,
Shatiqua, A .... 504-286-5030 195 L
swilson@suno.edu
MOSCA, David .... 443-367-0035 207 F
dmosca@usmd.edu
MOSCA, Joseph, L .... 330-941-3321 374 E
jmosca@ysu.edu
MOSCATO, Robin, A ...... 609-258-3330 288 F
moscato@princeton.edu
MOSCHELLA, Jayne .... 561-912-1211.. 98 F
jmoschella@evergladesuniversity.edu
MOSCHENROSS, Sarah .. 641-269-3714 169 F
moschenr@grinnell.edu
MOSCHINA, Justin .... 949-214-3563.. 40 I
justin.moschina@cui.edu
MOSCOVITZ, Yechezkel . 718-269-4080 300 J
MOSELEY, John .... 573-681-5333 261 H
moseleyj@lincolnu.edu
MOSELEY, Pope, H .... 501-526-4533.. 22 C
pmoseley@uams.edu
MOSELEY-JONES,
Vickie .... 252-638-7225 342 E
moseleyv@cravencc.edu
MOSELY-HAWKINS,
Elizabeth .... 803-533-3681 423 G
emosely@scsu.edu
MOSEMAN, Dennis .... 212-242-2692 331 J
dennis.moseman@tsca.edu
MOSER, Drew .... 765-998-5384 164 C
drmoser@taylor.edu
MOSER, Gary .... 707-654-1224.. 32 E
gmoser@csum.edu
MOSER, Gary .... 661-336-5143.. 46 O
gmoser@kccd.edu
MOSER, Jack, T .... 662-685-4771 252 D
jmoser@bmc.edu

MOSER, Jeremy ... 714-556-3610 .. 72 F
jeremy.moser@vanguard.edu

MOSER, Kristin, M ... 319-273-3103 167 A
kristin.moser@uni.edu

MOSER, Melissa ... 520-206-4950 .. 15 L
mmoser2@pima.edu

MOSER, Mike ... 808-235-7361 130 I
mikem@hawaii.edu

MOSER, Nina ... 802-447-4046 476 C
nmoser@svc.edu

MOSER, Patrick ... 503-838-8063 388 B
moserp@wou.edu

MOSER, Shelly ... 870-612-2034 .. 22 H
shelly.moser@uaccb.edu

MOSER, Steven ... 601-266-5002 256 E
steven.moser@usm.edu

MOSER, Tina, L ... 724-738-2000 407 C
tina.moser@sru.edu

MOSER, Tracy, S ... 662-685-4771 252 D
tmoser@bmc.edu

MOSES, Bruce ... 520-206-4514 .. 15 L
bmoses3@pima.edu

MOSES, Carl ... 515-263-2835 169 E
cmoses@grandview.edu

MOSES, Charles ... 931-221-7674 430 B
mosesc@apsu.edu

MOSES, Darren ... 215-489-6370 393 F
darren.moses@delval.edu

MOSES, David ... 316-978-6791 182 F
david.moses@wichita.edu

MOSES, Henry ... 615-327-6266 434 A
hmoses@mmc.edu

MOSES, Lola ... 229-732-5947 115 B
lolamoses@andrewcollege.edu

MOSES, Orrin Douglas .. 831-656-3218 518 D
dmoses@nps.edu

MOSES, Rhonda, M ... 512-505-3030 451 A
rmmoses@htu.edu

MOSES, Robert, M ... 570-422-3138 406 A
bmoses@esu.edu

MOSES-HOLMES,
Jeanette ... 803-934-3989 422 G
jholmes@morris.edu

MOSESSO, Lynn ... 479-575-5869 .. 21 I
mosesso@uark.edu

MOSEY, Douglas, L ... 860-632-3010 .. 87 D
rector@holyapostles.edu

MOSHAVI, Dan ... 408-924-3400 .. 34 D

MOSHER, Craig ... 785-442-6017 178 C
cmosher@highlandcc.edu

MOSHER, Craig ... 785-442-6019 178 C
cmosher@highlandcc.edu

MOSHER, Craig, E ... 785-442-6019 178 C
cmosher@highlandcc.edu

MOSHER, George ... 312-329-4268 146 B
george.mosher@moody.edu

MOSHER, Sharon ... 512-471-6048 467 C
smosher@jsg.utexas.edu

MOSHIER, Andrea ... 828-227-7212 352 C
amoshier@wcu.edu

MOSHIER, Jeffrey ... 765-998-5203 164 C
jfmoshier@taylor.edu

MOSIER, Greg ... 507-285-7256 247 D
greg.mosier@rctc.edu

MOSIER, Gregory ... 775-784-4912 279 E
greg.mosier@unr.edu

MOSIER, Julianna ... 559-244-5977 .. 66 E

MOSIER, Roger ... 413-585-2400 224 F
rmosier@smith.edu

MOSKALA, Jiri ... 269-471-3648 227 B
moskala@andrews.edu

MOSKE, Amanda Kay .... 607-431-4997 309 E
moskea@hartwick.edu

MOSKOVITZ, Joy ... 908-737-7030 286 F
jmoskovi@kean.edu

MOSKOVITZ, Kristin ... 313-664-7496 228 H
kmoskovitz@collegeforcreativestudies.edu

MOSKOWITZ, Roy, P .... 212-229-5432 316 E
moskowir@newschool.edu

MOSKOWITZ,
Yechezkel ... 347-619-9074 335 A

MOSLEY, Cal ... 320-363-3036 250 A
cmosley@csbsju.edu

MOSLEY, Calvin ... 320-363-3036 241 I
cmosley@csbsju.edu

MOSLEY, Carolyn ... 479-788-7856 .. 22 A
carolyn.mosley@uafs.edu

MOSLEY, Crystal ... 410-951-3579 208 F
cmosley@coppin.edu

MOSLEY, David ... 409-880-2207 462 B
dpmosley@lit.edu

MOSLEY, Debra ... 417-255-7900 263 I
debbiemosley@missouristate.edu

MOSLEY, Eartha, J ... 803-536-7048 423 G
emosely1@scsu.edu

MOSLEY, Gary ... 662-562-3216 255 C
gtmosley@northwestms.edu

MOSLEY, Jenifer ... 561-237-7811 103 E
jmosley@lynn.edu

MOSLEY, Julie ... 479-788-7404 .. 22 A
julie.mosley@uafs.edu

MOSLEY, Lisa ... 203-785-4689 .. 89 G
lisa.mosley@yale.edu

MOSLEY, Melissa ... 662-476-5074 253 A
mmosley@eastms.edu

MOSLEY, Regina ... 734-462-4400 236 H
rmosley@schoolcraft.edu

MOSLEY, Walter ... 903-593-8311 461 B
wmosley@texascollege.edu

MOSLEY, Whitney ... 229-732-5950 115 B
whitneymosley@andrewcollege.edu

MOSLEY, Yohlunda ... 317-274-0838 160 E
ymosley@iupui.edu

MOSQUEDA, Margarita . 989-686-9512 229 J
momosque@delta.edu

MOSQUEDA, Rolando ... 702-651-4245 278 N
rolando.mosqueda@csn.edu

MOSS, Alan ... 918-465-1802 375 J
amoss@eosc.edu

MOSS, Annie ... 318-670-9212 196 A
amoss@susla.edu

MOSS, Ashley ... 303-333-4224 .. 76 L
registrar@aspen.edu

MOSS, Brendan ... 660-944-2928 258 G
brendan@conception.edu

MOSS, Carl, M ... 304-865-6123 502 C
michael.moss@ovu.edu

MOSS, Edwin ... 718-390-3165 333 D
edwin.moss@wagner.edu

MOSS, Elizabeth, H ... 443-518-4837 204 E
emoss@howardcc.edu

MOSS, Georgeann ... 214-378-1823 447 F
gemoss@dcccd.edu

MOSS, Glen ... 402-463-2402 274 I
gmoss@commmonwealthelectric.com

MOSS, Joshua ... 951-343-5045 .. 28 G
jmoss@calbaptist.edu

MOSS, Kirsten ... 931-393-1764 437 C
kmoss@mscc.edu

MOSS, Michael ... 704-330-6681 342 A
michael.moss@cpcc.edu

MOSS, Orianna, M ... 786-331-1000 104 C
omaza@maufl.edu

MOSS, Pamela ... 901-722-3318 436 D
pmoss@sco.edu

MOSS, Sara ... 870-512-7874 .. 18 D
sara_moss@asun.edu

MOSS, Sarah ... 712-722-6078 168 I
sarah.moss@dordt.edu

MOSS, Tony ... 706-867-2712 127 B
tony.moss@ung.edu

MOSSER, Daniel ... 301-934-7547 203 D
dmosser@csmd.edu

MOSSETTE, Mary Beth .. 559-442-8286 .. 66 G
marybeth.mossette@fresnocitycollege.edu

MOSSEY, Christopher .... 212-799-5000 312 B

MOSSHART, Marcia ... 405-491-6312 379 K
mmosshar@snu.edu

MOSTAFAVI, Moshen .... 617-495-4364 215 G
moshen_mostafavi@harvard.edu

MOSTARDI, OSA,
Joseph ... 610-519-4080 413 K
joseph.mostardi@villanova.edu

MOSTASHARI, Zary ... 703-284-1673 483 A
zary.mostashari@marymount.edu

MOSTELLER, John ... 610-896-1376 397 F
jmostell@haverford.edu

MOSTELLER, Kate ... 480-947-6644 .. 15 I
kate.mosteller@pennfoster.edu

MOSTILLER, Donna ... 716-286-8689 318 F
dmostiller@niagara.edu

MOTE, Jerry ... 724-266-3838 412 D
jmote@tsm.edu

MOTE, Tanya ... 360-596-5229 498 G
tmote@spscc.edu

MOTEN, Maria ... 847-925-6622 139 B
mmoten@harpercollege.edu

MOTEN-TOLSON, Paula . 919-546-8544 348 I
pmotentolson@shawu.edu

MOTHERWELL, Mary ... 734-487-2229 229 K
mmotherwe@emich.edu

MOTL, Lori ... 870-245-5110 .. 20 G
motll@obu.edu

MOTLEY, Brittany, S ... 502-597-6044 187 E
brittany.motley@kysu.edu

MOTLEY, Clay ... 239-590-7368 109 C
cmotley@fgcu.edu

MOTLEY, Darlene ... 412-365-2970 392 C
dmottley@chatham.edu

MOTLEY, Reginald ... 313-927-1420 233 D
rmotley@marygrove.edu

MOTT, Asena ... 863-784-7041 108 B
asena.mott@southflorida.edu

MOTT, Jeanne ... 785-594-4595 174 J
jeanne.mott@bakeru.edu

MOTT, Jeff ... 479-968-0332 .. 18 G
jmott@atu.edu

MOTT, Joanna ... 916-278-4655 .. 33 C

MOTT, Judy ... 859-985-3521 183 I
judy_mott@berea.edu

MOTT, Molly ... 315-386-7425 329 A
mottma@canton.edu

MOTT, Molly, A ... 315-386-7425 329 A
mottma@canton.edu

MOTT, Penne ... 205-387-0511 .... 1 D
penne.mott@bscc.edu

MOTTEN, Luisa ... 206-934-6782 497 J
luisa.motten@seattlecolleges.edu

MOTTER, Kristi ... 256-824-4158 .... 8 C
kristi.motter@uah.edu

MOTTER, Melinda ... 573-592-4222 270 D
melinda.motter@williamwoods.edu

MOTTET, Timothy ... 719-549-2951 .. 78 P
president.office@csupueblo.edu

MOTTINGER, Talisha ... 307-772-4251 516 N
tmottinger@lccc.wy.edu

MOTTLEY, Juanita, G ... 404-471-6443 114 H
jgainousmottley@agnesscott.edu

MOTYL, Lynne, M ... 724-738-2070 407 C
lynne.motyl@sru.edu

MOTZ, Arnell ... 651-582-5224 240 J
a-motz@bethel.edu

MOTZER, Bill ... 402-465-2551 276 E
wmotzer@nebrwesleyan.edu

MOUA, Pa Lee ... 920-832-7030 507 L
palee.moua@lawrence.edu

MOUCK, Eric ... 707-256-7542 .. 53 D
eric.mouck@napavalley.edu

MOUDGIL, Virinder, K .. 248-204-2000 233 A
president@ltu.edu

MOUDIAB, Jamilah ... 973-748-9000 284 A
jamilah_moudiab@bloomfield.edu

MOUDY, Quentin, J ... 260-982-5267 162 Q
qjmoudy@manchester.edu

MOULD, Tom ... 336-278-5746 337 G
tmould@elon.edu

MOULDS, Perry ... 615-460-6434 430 D
perry.moulds@belmont.edu

MOULTON, Bob ... 775-784-1200 278 M
bob_moulton@nshe.nevada.edu

MOULTON, David, A ... 202-419-0482 .. 93 B
dam@strayer.edu

MOULTON, Jeff ... 225-578-6916 193 M
jmoulton@lsu.edu

MOULTON, Julie ... 951-343-4210 .. 28 G
jmoulton@calbaptist.edu

MOULTON, Katie ... 508-213-2402 223 C
katie.moulton@nichols.edu

MOULTON, Patricia, L ... 802-728-1251 477 E
pmoulton@vtc.edu

MOULTON, Paul ... 208-459-5217 131 H
pmoulton@collegeofidaho.edu

MOULTRIE, C. Maxille .. 504-286-5033 195 L
cmoultrie@suno.edu

MOULTRIE, Gloria, B .... 504-286-5341 195 L
gmoultrie@suno.edu

MOUNDS, Paul ... 860-512-3634 .. 85 G
pmounds@manchestercc.edu

MOUNFIELD, Gina ... 843-525-8257 424 E
gmounfield@tcl.edu

MOUNGA, DJ ... 605-229-8366 427 J
djmounga@presentation.edu

MOUNT, Carole ... 330-490-7048 373 F
cmount@walsh.edu

MOUNT, Jeanine ... 617-732-2192 221 E
jeanine.mount@mcphs.edu

MOUNT, Judy ... 316-677-1619 182 E
jmount@watc.edu

MOUNT, Marianne, E .... 304-724-5000 501 G
mmount@cdu.edu

MOUNTAIN, Carel ... 916-558-2275 .. 50 I
mountac@scc.losrios.edu

MOUNTAIN, Mark ... 815-928-5794 148 F
mcmountain@olivet.edu

MOUNTJOY, Shane ... 402-363-5614 278 E
mountjoy@york.edu

MOUNTS, Melody ... 309-467-6312 138 E
mmounts@eureka.edu

MOUNTS, William ... 912-279-5851 118 A
wmounts@ccga.edu

MOUNTY, Lauren ... 914-633-2529 311 B
lmounty@iona.edu

MOURACADE, John ... 907-786-1086 .. 10 A
jmmouracade@alaska.edu

MOURAD, Roger ... 734-677-5328 238 G
mou@wccnet.edu

MOURN, Justin ... 620-241-0723 176 G
justin.mourn@centralchristian.edu

MOURNIGHAN, Jim ... 401-341-2200 417 D
james.mournighan@salve.edu

MOURTZANOS,
Emmanuel ... 661-395-4406 .. 47 A
emmanuel.mourtzanos@bakersfieldcollege.edu

MOUSA, Shaker ... 518-694-7575 297 J
shaker.mousa@acphs.edu

MOUSER, Lisa ... 636-922-8319 265 J
lmouser@stchas.edu

MOUTON, Sarah ... 318-342-5420 198 A
mouton@ulm.edu

MOUTOS, Don ... 503-654-8000 386 A
dmoutos@pioneerpacific.edu

MOUTRAY, Tonya ... 518-244-2406 321 G
moutrt@sage.edu

MOUTSATSON, Kelly ..... 541-552-6411 386 H
moutsatsk@sou.edu

MOUTTET, Nate ... 206-281-2652 498 B
natem@spu.edu

MOVITZ, Michelle ... 847-324-5588 135 D
mmovitz@ortchicagotech.edu

MOVSESIAN, David ... 858-279-4500 .. 28 A

MOW, Lauren ... 269-782-1316 237 B
lmow@swmich.edu

MOWBRAY, Nayeli ... 410-225-2493 205 C

MOWDY, Cheryl ... 205-348-4530 .... 8 A
cmowdy@fa.ua.edu

MOWEN, Brenda ... 804-828-3361 487 E
bmowen@vcu.edu

MOWEN, David ... 540-887-7370 482 G
dmowen@marybaldwin.edu

MOWERY, Chris ... 423-472-7141 436 G
cmowery@clevelandstatecc.edu

MOWREY, Peter ... 330-263-2576 360 A
pmowrey@wooster.edu

MOWRY, Cynthia ... 253-589-5570 493 F
cynthia.mowry@cptc.edu

MOY, James, S ... 813-974-7380 111 A
moy@usf.edu

MOYA, Jacob ... 208-882-1566 132 D
jmoya@nsa.edu

MOYANO, Angelica ... 954-607-4344 112 L

MOYE, Bobby ... 256-215-4536 .... 1 G
bmoye@cacc.edu

MOYE, Sara ... 541-956-7346 386 G
smoye@roguecc.edu

MOYEN, Eric ... 423-614-8671 432 L
emoyen@leeuniversity.edu

MOYER, Anna ... 618-235-2700 152 E
anna.moyer@swic.edu

MOYER, Christina, L ..... 610-799-1136 400 A
cmoyer@lccc.edu

MOYER, James ... 616-331-3853 230 G
moyerj@gvsu.edu

MOYER, James, G ... 863-638-7613 113 I
james.moyer@warner.edu

MOYER, Jane ... 617-373-2230 223 D

MOYER, Monica ... 352-588-8646 106 N
monica.moyer@saintleo.edu

MOYER, Paul ... 410-386-4660 205 E
pmoyer@mcdaniel.edu

MOYERS, Penelope ... 651-690-6813 249 T
pamoyers@stkate.edu

MOYLAN, Shannon ... 607-735-1782 307 G
smoylan@elmira.edu

MOYNIHAN, Daniel ... 781-280-3625 220 C

MOZAFFARIAN,
Dariush ... 617-636-3702 225 A
dariush.mozaffarian@tufts.edu

MOZDEN, Joseph ... 630-829-0261 137 D
jmozden@devry.edu

MOZELESKI, Dee Dee ... 212-650-7396 301 F
dmozeleski@ccny.cuny.edu

MOZIE-ROSS, Yvette ..... 410-455-3799 208 A
mozie@umbc.edu

MOZLEY, Peter ... 575-835-5172 294 K
peter.mozley@nmt.edu

MOZOLIK, Erik ... 414-464-9777 513 B
mozolik.erik@wspp.edu

MOZRALL, Jacqueline ... 585-475-7181 321 D
jrmeie@rit.edu

MRASEK, Jean ... 817-257-5566 461 A
j.mrasek@tcu.edu

MROZ, Donald, W ... 203-596-4666 .. 87 H
dmroz@post.edu

MROZ, Glenn, D ... 906-487-2200 234 A
gdmroz@mtu.edu

MROZEK, John ... 281-487-1170 460 G
jmrozek@txchiro.edu

MROZIK, Jacek ... 701-858-3110 354 C
jacek.mrozik@minotstateu.edu

MROZINSKI, Mark ... 847-925-6540 139 B
mmrozins@harpercollege.edu

MRSNY, Jason ... 402-375-7195 276 D
jamrsny1@wsc.edu

MRVOS, Dessa ... 412-396-1653 394 D
mrvosds@duq.edu

MUASAU, Jarad ... 719-365-8218 .. 82 N
jarad.muasau@uchealth.org

MULROONEY, Debra ..... 503-253-3443 385 B
dmulrooney@ocom.edu

MULROY, Kevin ..... 909-621-8924.. 37 L
kevinm@cuc.claremont.edu

MULROY, Kevin ..... 909-621-8014.. 37 K
kevin_mulroy@cuc.claremont.edu

MULROY-BOWDEN, Linda ..... 608-342-1845 511 D
mulroy@uwplatt.edu

MULROY-DEGENHART, Carmella ..... 814-865-7611 403 F
qum11@psu.edu

MULRYAN, Michael ..... 714-879-3901.. 45 I
mdmulryan@hiu.edu

MULSHINE, James, L ..... 312-942-3589 150 F
james_l_mulshine@rush.edu

MULSO, Sara, K ..... 651-641-8857 241 L
smulso@csp.edu

MULSO, William ..... 507-537-6267 248 A
william.mulso@smsu.edu

MULTARI, James ..... 516-323-3060 315 J
jmultari@molloy.edu

MULTOP, Kevin ..... 541-383-7578 382 B
kmultop@cocc.edu

MULUGETTA, Yuko ..... 607-274-3877 311 D
ymulugetta@ithaca.edu

MULVANEY, Emma ..... 614-236-6908 358 A
emulvaney@capital.edu

MULVANEY, Stacy ..... 478-445-2510 119 E
stacy.mulvaney@gcsu.edu

MULVEY, Colleen ..... 415-351-3508.. 60 G
cmulvey@sfai.edu

MULVEY, Julie ..... 508-588-9100 220 B

MULVEY, Kristin ..... 815-280-2353 142 A
kmulvey@jjc.edu

MULVEY, Nick ..... 262-551-5519 506 H
nmulvey@carthage.edu

MULVIHILL, Patrick ..... 612-330-1000 240 G
mulvihil@augsburg.edu

MULVILLE, Matthew, H . 716-888-2220 300 G
mulville@canisius.edu

MUMA, Richard, D ..... 316-978-5761 182 F
richard.muma@wichita.edu

MUMFORD, Frank ..... 657-278-2423.. 32 B
fmumford@fullerton.edu

MUMM, Michele ..... 320-308-4066 247 E
michelem@stcloudstate.edu

MUMMERT, Kelly ..... 304-243-2226 505 H
kmummert@wju.edu

MUMPER, Russ ..... 706-542-0415 127 A
mumper@uga.edu

MUNA, Esther, A ..... 671-735-5700 519 H
gccpresident@guamcc.edu

MUNA, Joann, W ..... 671-735-5539 519 H
hr@guamcc.edu

MUNCH, Leah ..... 718-405-3341 304 H
leah.munch@mountsaintvincent.edu

MUNCHEL, Christopher, T ..... 765-285-5608 156 C
cmunchel@bsu.edu

MUNCHEL, Jeff ..... 410-532-5324 206 D
jmunchel@ndm.edu

MUNCY, Alison ..... 615-230-3526 438 C
alison.muncy@volstate.edu

MUND, Barb ..... 701-671-2204 355 B
barb.mund@ndscs.edu

MUND, Catherine ..... 443-518-4781 204 E
cmund@howardcc.edu

MUNDAHL, Daniel, L .... 507-344-7739 240 I
daniel.mundahl@blc.edu

MUNDELL, Chris ..... 614-222-4015 360 B
cmundell@ccad.edu

MUNDIE, Thomas ..... 678-407-5353 119 F
tmundie@ggc.edu

MUNDRANE, Michael .... 860-486-1777.. 88 G
michael.mundrane@uconn.edu

MUNDY, Amy ..... 361-582-2518 470 A
amy.mundy@victoriacollege.edu

MUNDY, Renee ..... 570-961-7861 399 A
mundyr@lackawanna.edu

MUNDY, Robert ..... 574-631-7305 165 A
rmundy@nd.edu

MUNDY, Tiina ..... 910-879-5556 341 A
tmundy@bladencc.edu

MUNFORD, Michael ..... 507-537-7858 248 A
michael.munford@smsu.edu

MUNGAL, Godfrey ..... 408-554-2375.. 62 F
mgmungal@scu.edu

MUNGER, James ..... 208-426-4010 131 C
jmunger@boisestate.edu

MUNGER, Mary Lynn .... 816-604-3155 262 J
marylynn.munger@mcckc.edu

MUNGO, T. Rein ..... 843-349-2577 420 A
tmungo@coastal.edu

MUNHOFEN, Troy ..... 402-494-2311 275 M
tmunhofen@thenicc.edu

MUNIAK, Debby ..... 330-684-8729 371 D
dmuniak@uakron.edu

MUNIER, Robert ..... 508-289-3335 226 D
rmunier@whoi.edu

MUNIN, Art ..... 920-424-3100 511 B
munina@uwosh.edu

MUNIZ, Amanda ..... 361-593-3797 460 B
kaam003@tamuk.edu

MUNIZ, Araina ..... 352-365-3592 103 B
muniza@lssc.edu

MUNIZ, Ernesto ..... 870-733-6810.. 18 B
ejmuniz@asumidsouth.edu

MUNIZ, Hancy ..... 787-891-0925 523 G
hrmuniz@aguadilla.inter.edu

MUNIZ, Herman ..... 787-257-0744 527 H
herman.muniz@upr.edu

MUNIZ, Maria ..... 787-841-2000 525 J
mmuniz@pucpr.edu

MUNN, James ..... 208-732-6860 131 I
jmunn@csi.edu

MUNN, Janet, A ..... 845-368-7210 323 I
janet.munn@use.salvationarmy.org

MUNNELL, Barbra, M ... 724-458-3824 396 D
bmmunnell@gcc.edu

MUNNERLYN, Sam ..... 334-420-4216.... 3 H
smunnerlyn@trenholmstate.edu

MUNNS, Sarah ..... 573-592-6050 270 B
sarah.munns@westminster-mo.edu

MUNOZ, Alicia ..... 619-660-4675.. 44 L
alicia.munoz@gcccd.edu

MUNOZ, Celia ..... 954-763-9840.. 94 S

MUNOZ, Daniel ..... 215-702-4301 391 C
dmunoz@cairn.edu

MUNOZ, Deana ..... 312-935-6657 149 K
dmiranda@robertmorris.edu

MUNOZ, Elias ..... 323-563-9318.. 36 H
eliasmunoz@cdrewu.edu

MUNOZ, Harry ..... 787-720-4476 527 A
serviciocristiano@mizpa.edu

MUNOZ, Ivette ..... 787-725-8120 522 M
imunoz@eap.edu

MUNOZ, Jesse ..... 661-362-3155.. 39 C
jesse.munoz@canyons.edu

MUNOZ, Joe ..... 325-942-2073 463 C
joe.munoz@angelo.edu

MUNOZ, Juan, S ..... 713-221-8001 465 C
president@uhd.edu

MUNOZ, Julio ..... 787-284-1912 524 C
jcmunoz@ponce.inter.edu

MUNOZ, Mike ..... 562-908-3467.. 58 D
mrmunoz@riohondo.edu

MUNOZ, Raquel ..... 323-357-3630.. 36 H
raquelmunoz@cdrewu.edu

MUNOZ, Rene ..... 717-871-4457 407 A
rene.munoz@millersville.edu

MUNRO, Alex ..... 717-295-9666 411 C
munro@stevenscollege.edu

MUNRO, Cindy, L ..... 305-284-2107 112 O
cmunro@miami.edu

MUNRO, Glenn ..... 301-295-0064 518 G
glenn.munro@med.navy.mil

MUNRO, Sarah ..... 801-972-3596 472 P
s.munro@partners.utah.edu

MUNRO, Shannon, M ... 570-326-3761 404 T
smm20@pct.edu

MUNRO, Stuart, J ..... 508-767-7041 210 I
smunro@assumption.edu

MUNRO, Timothy, J ..... 518-580-5566 324 D

MUNROE, Jeffrey ..... 616-392-8555 239 J
jeff@westernsem.edu

MUNSCH, OSB, Nathan 724-805-2612 410 C
nathan.munsch@stvincent.edu

MUNSCHY, Karl ..... 706-729-2179 116 B
kmunschy@augusta.edu

MUNSIL, Len ..... 602-386-4102.. 10 G
len.munsil@arizonachristian.edu

MUNSON, JR., David, C ..... 585-475-2394 321 D
dcmpro@rit.edu

MUNSON, Janet ..... 309-649-6273 152 G
janet.munson@src.edu

MUNSON, Keith ..... 612-330-1474 240 G
munsonk@augsburg.edu

MUNSON, Leo, W ..... 817-257-7104 461 A
l.munson@tcu.edu

MUNSON, Scott ..... 303-860-5600.. 83 A
scott.munson@cu.edu

MUNSON, Steve ..... 703-284-6901 483 A
smunson@marymount.edu

MUNSON, Wanda ..... 281-669-4711 456 B
wanda.munson@sjcd.edu

MUNSON, Wanda ..... 281-669-4711 455 K
wanda.munson@sjcd.edu

MUNSON, Wanda ..... 281-669-4711 455 L
wanda.munson@sjcd.edu

MUNSON, Wanda ..... 281-669-4711 456 A
wanda.munson@sjcd.edu

MUNSON, William ..... 713-743-5470 465 A
wfmunson@central.uh.edu

MUNSON-DRYER, Molly ..... 309-556-3780 141 B
mmunsond@iwu.edu

MUNSTERMAN, Korin ... 904-680-7601.. 99 C
kmunsterman@fcsl.edu

MUNT, Glada, C ..... 512-863-1381 457 I
muntg@southwestern.edu

MUNTER, Judith ..... 415-338-2687.. 34 C
jhmunter@sfsu.edu

MUNTZ, Donna ..... 740-374-8716 373 G
dmuntz@wscc.edu

MUNZER, Pat ..... 785-670-2111 182 D
pat.munzer@washburn.edu

MURACA, Paul ..... 713-798-6617 444 A
muraca@bcm.edu

MURALI, Viji ..... 530-752-4998.. 68 H
vpiet-sup@ucdavis.edu

MURASKO, Donna ..... 215-895-1892 394 C
dm37@drexel.edu

MURASKO-BLANK, Kiera ..... 215-895-2100 394 C
kiera.a.murasko-blank@drexel.edu

MURASSO, Thomas ..... 914-633-2625 311 B
tmurasso@iona.edu

MURAVCHICK, Gregg .... 859-233-8135 189 H
gmuravchick@transy.edu

MURCH, Aimee ..... 716-896-0700 333 C
murcha@villa.edu

MURCHISON, Joelle ..... 860-486-2422.. 88 G
joelle.murchison@uconn.edu

MURDAUGH, Jim ..... 850-201-8660 112 C
murdaugj@tcc.fl.edu

MURDEN MCCLURE, Tori ..... 502-585-9911 189 B
tmcclure@spalding.edu

MURDEN-WOLDU, Romell ..... 773-481-8451 136 B
rmurden@ccc.edu

MURDERS, Michael ..... 479-667-1707.. 18 G
mmurders@atu.edu

MURDOCH, Jessica ..... 978-665-3338 217 E
jmurdoch@fitchburgstate.edu

MURDOCH, William, G . 909-558-6604.. 48 H
wmurdoch@llu.edu

MURDOCK, Alan, K ..... 336-734-7757 343 C
amurdock@forsythtech.edu

MURDOCK, James, L .... 313-927-1226 233 D
jmurdock@marygrove.edu

MURDOCK, Rebecca ..... 402-557-7136 273 E
rebecca.murdock@bellevue.edu

MURDZAK, Karen ..... 814-732-1020 406 B
kmurdzak@edinboro.edu

MURGA, Margaret ..... 252-536-7242 343 F
mmurga673@halifaxcc.edu

MURGA, Mario ..... 617-327-6777 226 B
mario_murga@williamjames.edu

MURGO, Richard ..... 850-201-8145 112 C
murgor@tcc.fl.edu

MURGOLO-POORER, Marie ..... 775-673-7090 279 C
mmurgolo@tmcc.edu

MURGUIA, Stephanie .... 562-860-2451.. 36 A
smurguia@cerritos.edu

MURGUIA, Tierra ..... 858-225-4301.. 29 G
tierra@calarttech.edu

MURIANA, Joseph, P .... 718-817-3020 308 G
jmuriana@fordham.edu

MURIANKA, Luke ..... 315-858-0940 310 E
lmurianka@hts.edu

MURILLO, Alice ..... 617-228-2102 219 D
amurillo@bhcc.mass.edu

MURILLO, Kindred ..... 619-482-6301.. 65 H
kmurillo@swccd.edu

MURKA, Adam ..... 937-512-2947 370 A
adam.murka@sinclair.edu

MURLEY, Den ..... 903-923-2079 448 J
dmurley@etbu.edu

MURNANE, Ryan ..... 757-352-4891 484 E
ryanmur@regent.edu

MURNEN, Tim ..... 419-372-7983 357 F
tmurnen@bgsu.edu

MURPHREE, Danny, W . 806-291-3635 470 I
murphree@wbu.edu

MURPHREE, David ..... 806-291-3641 470 I
dmurphree@wbu.edu

MURPHREY, Hiram Todd ..... 252-638-7263 342 E
murphret@cravencc.edu

MURPHY, Alissa ..... 573-288-6526 259 E
almurphy@culver.edu

MURPHY, Amanda ..... 561-364-3064.. 95 I

MURPHY, Amy ..... 815-280-1418 142 A
amurphy@jjc.edu

MURPHY, Amy ..... 508-793-3880 213 D
amurphy@holycross.edu

MURPHY, Amy ..... 618-252-5400 151 J
amy.murphy@sic.edu

MURPHY, Angela ..... 910-362-7014 341 E
amurphy@cfcc.edu

MURPHY, Ann, B ..... 303-556-3245.. 80 Q
murphann@msudenver.edu

MURPHY, Antoinette ..... 417-269-3083 259 C
antoinette.murphy@coxcollege.edu

MURPHY, Ashley, R ..... 570-326-3761 404 T
amurphy@pct.edu

MURPHY, Beverly, J ..... 336-322-2117 345 D
beverly.murphy@piedmontcc.edu

MURPHY, Bobbie Ann .. 949-794-9090.. 66 B
bmurphy@stanbridge.edu

MURPHY, Brent, D ..... 574-232-2408 163 F
bmurphy@rtuvt.com

MURPHY, Bret ..... 775-753-2217 279 A
bret.murphy@gbcnv.edu

MURPHY, Brian ..... 802-440-4335 474 F
bmurphy@bennington.edu

MURPHY, Brian ..... 408-864-8705.. 43 E
murphybrian@deanza.edu

MURPHY, Brian ..... 530-251-8836.. 47 J
bmurphy@lassencollege.edu

MURPHY, Brian ..... 360-416-7690 498 F
brian.murphy@skagit.edu

MURPHY, Brian ..... 936-468-2803 458 A
murphybm1@sfasu.edu

MURPHY, Bridget ..... 703-284-6478 483 A
bridget.murphy@marymount.edu

MURPHY, Britt Anne ..... 501-450-1303.. 19 I
johnsen@hendrix.edu

MURPHY, Bruce, T ..... 985-448-4003 197 C
bruce.murphy@nicholls.edu

MURPHY, Carolyn ..... 402-471-2505 276 A
cmurphy@nscs.edu

MURPHY, Catherine ..... 615-460-6418 430 D
catherine.murphy@belmont.edu

MURPHY, Chad ..... 309-649-6266 152 G
chad.murphy@src.edu

MURPHY, Charles, J ..... 509-313-6139 495 A
murphyc@gonzaga.edu

MURPHY, Chris ..... 805-756-5692.. 30 K
cmurph18@calpoly.edu

MURPHY, Chris ..... 662-720-7280 255 B
cdmurphy@nemcc.edu

MURPHY, Christine ..... 718-940-5800 322 G
cmurphy@sjcny.edu

MURPHY, Colleen ..... 319-895-4215 167 G
cmurphy@cornellcollege.edu

MURPHY, Colleen ..... 781-891-2630 212 A
cmurphy@bentley.edu

MURPHY, Corrine ..... 610-436-2579 407 D
cmurphy@wcupa.edu

MURPHY, Daniel ..... 252-399-6597 335 I
dcmurphy@barton.edu

MURPHY, David ..... 414-288-4810 508 C
david.murphy@marquette.edu

MURPHY, David, L ..... 773-702-9466 153 F
dlm@uchicago.edu

MURPHY, Davis ..... 530-251-8890.. 47 J
dmurphy@lassencollege.edu

MURPHY, Denise ..... 301-687-4457 209 A
dmurphy@frostburg.edu

MURPHY, Diane Lyden . 315-443-3707 330 H
dlmurphy@syr.edu

MURPHY, Douglas, L .... 501-686-5730.. 22 C
dlmurphy@uams.edu

MURPHY, Eileen ..... 845-398-4316 323 G
emurphy@stac.edu

MURPHY, Elizabeth ..... 773-878-3752 150 I
emurphy@staugustine.edu

MURPHY, Frank, J ..... 815-835-6299 151 E
frank.j.murphy@svcc.edu

MURPHY, Gail ..... 239-732-3953 100 E
gail.murphy@fsw.edu

MURPHY, Gaye ..... 480-731-8510.. 13 D
gaye.murphy@domail.maricopa.edu

MURPHY, Gene ..... 601-857-3330 253 B
temurphy@hindscc.edu

MURPHY, Gregory ..... 215-751-8042 393 A
gmurphy@ccp.edu

MURPHY, OSB, Isaac ... 603-641-7150 282 A
imurphy@anselm.edu

MURPHY, Jack ..... 773-481-8124 136 B
jmurphy@ccc.edu

MURPHY, III, James, E 704-894-2373 337 B
jamurphy@davidson.edu

MURPHY, James, H ..... 573-341-4292 269 A
murphyj@mst.edu

MURPHY, Jan ..... 309-438-7018 140 L
jshane@ilstu.edu

MURPHY, Jim ..... 916-388-2812.. 35 F
jmurphy@carrington.edu

MURPHY, Jim ..... 973-748-9000 284 A
jim_murphy@bloomfield.edu

MURPHY, Joan, D ..... 413-755-4749 221 B
jdmurphy@stcc.edu

MURPHY, John ..... 317-921-4243 161 F
jmmurphy@ivytech.edu

MUUS, Dan 701-777-2327 353 G
danm@undfoundation.org

MUYET, Javier, A 787-850-9318 528 B
javier.muyet@upr.edu

MUYSKENS, Judy 330-569-5125 362 J

MUÑIZ, Miguel 787-279-1912 523 J
mmuniz@bayamon.inter.edu

MUÑIZ, Vicky 787-777-0677 528 F
vicky.muniz@upr.edu

MUÑOZ, Marisol 787-257-7373 525 Q
ac_mmunoz@suagm.edu

MWANGO, Kamia 352-395-5018 107 E
kamia.mwango@sfcollege.edu

MWIINGA, Sage 541-881-5813 387 D
smwiinga@tvcc.cc

MWILAMBWE, Stacey 309-438-8611 140 L
smmwila@ilstu.edu

MYCHASKIW, George 575-647-2266 293 J

MYER, Bonnie 360-623-8556 493 A
bonnie.myer@centralia.edu

MYERS, Alvin, B 434-395-2740 482 E
myersab@longwood.edu

MYERS, Amy, A 717-544-9051 395 G
amy.myers@fandm.edu

MYERS, Andrea 440-375-7212 364 C
amyers@lec.edu

MYERS, Antoinette 440-775-8462 367 B
tmyers@oberlin.edu

MYERS, Barbara, S 912-358-3051 125 C
myersb@savannahstate.edu

MYERS, Bianca 641-683-5302 169 I
bianca.myers@indianhills.edu

MYERS, Brianne 517-371-5140 239 F
myersb@cooley.edu

MYERS, Camille 843-525-8359 424 E
cmyers@tcl.edu

MYERS, Cheryl 706-649-1290 118 D
cmyers@columbustech.edu

MYERS, Cheryl 504-571-1290 192 H
cmyers@dcc.edu

MYERS, Daniel, J 414-288-7511 508 C
daniel.myers@marquette.edu

MYERS, David 413-528-7436 211 B
myersd@simons-rock.edu

MYERS, Debbie 405-682-1611 377 C
dkmyers@occc.edu

MYERS, Derek 901-678-3848 439 E
dmyers@memphis.edu

MYERS, Donald, C 901-333-5259 438 B
dmyers@southwest.tn.edu

MYERS, Donna 518-861-2529 314 B
dmyers01@mariacollege.edu

MYERS, Emily 301-447-5592 206 B
myers@msmary.edu

MYERS, Eveadean 701-231-7703 354 D
evie.myers@ndsu.edu

MYERS, Gary, D 504-816-8003 195 D
gmeyers@nobts.edu

MYERS, James 650-325-9122 59 D
vat2ins@aol.com

MYERS, James 314-246-7080 269 N
jamesmyers79@webster.edu

MYERS, James 210-349-9928 454 B
jmyers@ost.edu

MYERS, Jamie, M 443-334-2625 207 C
jmmyers@stevenson.edu

MYERS, Joe 931-393-1553 437 C
jmyers@mscc.edu

MYERS, John 319-352-8372 174 C

MYERS, Joshua 734-384-4214 234 C
jmyers@monroeccc.edu

MYERS, Judi 570-740-0753 400 F
jmyers@luzerne.edu

MYERS, Katie 717-396-7833 404 R
kmyers@pcad.edu

MYERS, Kelly 815-802-8260 142 C
kmyers@kcc.edu

MYERS, Ken 218-281-8200 250 G
kmyers@umn.edu

MYERS, Leonece 323-226-4911 50 A
lmyers@dhs.lacounty.gov

MYERS, Linda 937-393-3431 370 C
lmyers@sscc.edu

MYERS, Lynne, M 508-793-2265 213 D
lmyers@holycross.edu

MYERS, Marci 620-223-2700 177 E
marcim@fortscott.edu

MYERS, Mary 815-836-5332 143 E
myersma@lewisu.edu

MYERS, Mary Beth 317-274-1505 160 E
mbmyers@iupui.edu

MYERS, Matthew, B 214-768-3012 457 B
mbmyers@smu.edu

MYERS, Michael 810-766-4385 227 F

MYERS, Michelle 816-584-6445 265 C
michelle.myers@park.edu

MYERS, Nancy 407-823-1336 110 C
nancy.myers@ucf.edu

MYERS, Nathan 330-941-2336 374 E
nrmyers@ysu.edu

MYERS, Nathan, R 330-941-2336 374 E
nrmyers@ysu.edu

MYERS, Patricia 518-587-2100 329 C
patricia.myers@esc.edu

MYERS, Patricia, T 865-539-7242 437 F
pmyers@pstcc.edu

MYERS, Richard, B 785-532-6221 179 A
rmyers65@ksu.edu

MYERS, Robert 310-434-4200 62 G
myers_robert@smc.edu

MYERS, Robert, M 706-886-6831 126 F
rmyers@tfc.edu

MYERS, Robin 870-508-6101 18 C
rmyers@asumh.edu

MYERS, Ron 707-527-4880 62 H
rmyers@santarosa.edu

MYERS, Susan 979-830-4273 444 D
susan.myers@blinn.edu

MYERS, Theresa 503-686-1647 384 C
theresa.myers@mtangel.edu

MYERS, Thomas 314-505-7329 258 I
myerst@csl.edu

MYERS, Tim 972-825-4723 457 F
tmyers@sagu.edu

MYERS, Tina 386-506-3101 97 I
myerst@daytonastate.edu

MYERS, Valerie 518-458-5336 305 B
vmyers@strose.edu

MYETTE, Linda 618-664-6500 139 A
linda.myette@greenville.edu

MYHRE, Alexander 207-768-9581 201 G
alexander.myhre@maine.edu

MYHRE, Oddmund, R 209-667-3652 33 F
omyhre@csustan.edu

MYHRE, Terry 801-542-7600 471 G
tmyhre@globeuniversity.edu

MYHRER, Larry 763-544-9501 240 F

MYHRUM, Phoebe 740-587-8504 361 B
myhrump@denison.edu

MYKLES, Donald 970-491-5679 78 N
donald.mykles@colostate.edu

MYLETT, Brad 641-472-1196 171 J
bmylett@mum.edu

MYLONA, Elza 757-446-0340 480 C
mylonae@evms.edu

MYLOTT, Sherri 909-593-3511 70 E
smylott@laverne.edu

MYLREA, Brian 260-481-6034 160 D
mylreab@ipfw.edu

MYNATT, Danny 254-295-4143 466 A
dmynatt@umhb.edu

MYNES, Jess 978-632-9195 220 D
jmynes@mwcc.mass.edu

MYRICK, A. Yvette 970-945-8691 77 M

MYRICK, Amber 559-934-2132 73 M
ambermyrick@whccd.edu

MYRICK, David 602-274-1885 15 J
dmyrick@pihma.edu

MYRICK, Justin 615-966-5887 433 D
justin.myrick@lipscomb.edu

MYRICK, Matt 218-751-8670 249 G
mattmyrick@oakhills.edu

MYRICK, Mondrail 567-268-6013 370 K
myrickm@tiffin.edu

MYRON, David 814-824-2032 401 J
dmyron@mercyhurst.edu

MYRON, David, P 814-824-2032 401 J
dmyron@mercyhurst.edu

MYRTAJ, Myftar 617-588-1321 211 G
mmyrtaj@bfit.edu

MYRTLE, Jamie 913-971-3513 179 H
jmyrtle@mnu.edu

MYSCOFSKI, Carole 309-556-3577 141 B
myscofsk@iwu.edu

MYSZENSKI, Rebecca 810-762-0317 234 F
rebecca.myszenski@mcc.edu

MYTON, David 906-635-2349 232 J
dmyton@lssu.edu

MYVETT, Newton 770-394-8300 115 E
nmyvett@aii.edu

N

NAAN, Nicole 972-860-8054 447 H
nicolehaan@dcccd.edu

NAAS, Fauzi 503-399-6526 382 C
fauzi.naas@chemeketa.edu

NAASZ, Kathy 908-852-1400 284 G
naaszk@centenaryuniversity.edu

NAATZ, Duey 715-232-5243 512 A
naatzd@uwstout.edu

NABER, Bret 970-351-1887 83 F
bret.naber@unco.edu

NABERS, JR., Drayton 205-726-4362 6 G
dnabers@samford.edu

NABOR, Steven, E 801-626-6603 473 E
snabor@weber.edu

NABORS, Larry 662-246-6301 254 C
lnabors@msdelta.edu

NABORS, Melody 630-844-6852 133 H
mnabors@aurora.edu

NABORS, Murray 816-271-4510 264 B
mnabors@missouriwestern.edu

NACCARATO, Shawn 620-235-4128 180 J
snaccarato@pittstate.edu

NACCO, Stephen, D 217-443-8848 137 B
snacco@dacc.edu

NACE, Timothy 765-998-5125 164 C
tmnace@taylor.edu

NACHLAS, Rachel 301-846-2836 203 H
rnachlas@frederick.edu

NACHTMANN, Robert 915-747-5241 467 E
nachtmann@utep.edu

NACKMAN, Robin, E 212-774-4860 314 D
rnackman@mmm.edu

NACOS-BURDS, Kathy, J 563-556-5110 172 D
nacos-burdsk@nicc.edu

NACSA, Beata 641-472-7000 171 J
bnacsa@mum.edu

NACY, Peter 215-596-8871 413 E
p.nacy@usciences.edu

NADARAJAN, Gunalan, L 734-763-4093 237 I
guna@umich.edu

NADEAU, Evelyn 563-588-6557 167 E
evelyn.nadeau@clarke.edu

NADEAU, Rachel 910-362-7061 341 E
rnadeau@mail.cfcc.edu

NADEAU, Ryan 585-292-0642 317 A
rnadeau@nycc.edu

NADEL, Evelyn, H 843-953-2211 420 C
nadele@cofc.edu

NADEN, Michelle 509-527-2147 499 F
michelle.naden@wallawalla.edu

NADENICEK, Daniel, J 706-542-8113 127 A
dnadeni@uga.edu

NADER, John, S 631-420-2239 329 D
president@farmingdale.edu

NADER, Richard 662-325-8632 254 E
rhn33@msstate.edu

NADERSHAHI, Nader 415-929-6425 70 F
nnadersh@pacific.edu

NADLER, Daniel 859-572-6447 188 E
nadlerd@nku.edu

NADLER, Jerry, L 757-446-8920 480 C
nadlerjl@evms.edu

NADOL, Anne, K 215-204-7405 411 B
anne.nadol@temple.edu

NADOLSKI, Mike 269-927-8109 232 G
mnadolski@lakemichigancollege.edu

NAEGELE, Chris 618-985-3741 141 D
chrisnaegele@jalc.edu

NAEGELI, Dan 940-565-2105 466 B
naegeli@unt.edu

NAEHR, Thomas 209-946-2765 70 F
tnaehr@pacific.edu

NAE`OLE, Davileigh 808-984-3519 130 H
davileig@hawaii.edu

NAFF, J. Abraham 540-365-4493 480 L
anaff@ferrum.edu

NAFIE, John 909-558-4562 48 H
jnafie@llu.edu

NAGAGE, Champa 617-228-2115 219 D
cnagage@bhcc.mass.edu

NAGAI, Nelson 657-278-2413 32 B
nnagai@fullerton.edu

NAGANATHAN, Nagi, G 541-885-1000 385 E

NAGARKATTI, Prakash 803-777-5458 424 I
prakash@mailbox.sc.edu

NAGATA, Miles, K 808-932-7407 129 I
mnagata@hawaii.edu

NAGDEMAN, Ryan 312-942-8708 150 F
ryan_nagdeman@rush.edu

NAGEL, Beverly 507-222-4303 241 C
bnagel@carleton.edu

NAGEL, Lisa 567-661-2688 369 A
lisa_nagel@owens.edu

NAGEL, Lonnie 361-593-2420 460 B
helpdesk@tamuk.edu

NAGEL, Michael 610-607-6294 408 G
mnagel@racc.edu

NAGEL, Michele 212-217-4632 308 B
michele_nagel@fitnyc.edu

NAGEL, Suzie 269-387-2150 239 E
suzie.nagel@wmich.edu

NAGELKERK, Jean 616-331-2729 230 G
nagelkej@gvsu.edu

NAGENGAST, Dana 909-621-8512 45 D
dnagengast@hmc.edu

NAGLE, Geoffrey, A 312-893-7100 138 D
gnagle@erikson.edu

NAGLE, Margaret, A 207-581-3743 201 B
nagle@maine.edu

NAGLE, Ryen 708-974-5679 146 C
nagler@morainevalley.edu

NAGLE, Stephen 618-453-4918 152 B
stephenn@siu.edu

NAGLE-KUCH, Abbey 563-884-5137 172 H
abbey.nagle-kuch@palmer.edu

NAGURA, Cynthia, K 619-216-6795 65 H
cnagura@swccd.edu

NAGY, Debra, A 304-462-6116 504 B
debra.nagy@glenville.edu

NAGY, Ellen 419-448-2063 362 G
enagy@heidelberg.edu

NAGY, Lisa 817-272-6080 467 B
nagy@uta.edu

NAGY, Mary Anne 732-571-3417 287 C
mnagy@monmouth.edu

NAGY, Paul 813-253-7162 101 M
pnagy@hccfl.edu

NAGY, Sharon 864-656-1455 419 F
snagy@clemson.edu

NAGY, Tibor, P 806-742-2218 463 D
tibor.nagy@ttu.edu

NAGY, Zsuzsanna 973-290-4134 285 A
znagy@cse.edu

NAHABEDIAN, Audrey 978-656-3223 220 C
nahabediana@middlesex.mass.edu

NAHLEN, John 925-969-2018 40 L
jnahlen@dvc.edu

NAHRGANG, Rick 507-453-2726 245 G
rnahrgang@southeastmn.edu

NAIDU, Jay 650-543-3996 51 F
jnaidu@menlo.edu

NAIDU, Santhana 812-237-8764 159 C
santhana.naidu@indstate.edu

NAIFEH, Zeak 580-581-2217 375 A
znaifeh@cameron.edu

NAIL, Lance 619-594-2473 34 B
lnail@mail.sdsu.edu

NAIL, Steven 864-231-2000 418 E
snail@andersonuniversity.edu

NAILLER, Katie 212-650-6507 301 F
knailler@ccny.cuny.edu

NAILS, Dana 731-425-2628 437 B
dnails@jscc.edu

NAIMI, Susan 818-710-1310 28 H

NAIR, Ajay 404-727-4364 119 B
ajay.nair@emory.edu

NAIR, Murali 734-487-0077 229 K
mnair@emich.edu

NAIR, Sheila 928-523-0180 14 K
sheila.nair@nau.edu

NAIRN, Jason 503-493-6238 382 I
jnairn@cu-portland.edu

NAIRN, Joseph 585-785-1464 308 D
joseph.nairn@flcc.edu

NAIRN, Roderick 303-315-2102 83 D
roderick.nairn@ucdenver.edu

NAISH, Cheri 951-487-3210 52 J
cnaish@msjc.edu

NAJAM, Adil 617-358-7238 212 G
anajam@bu.edu

NAJERA, Carol 714-318-1451 51 A
najedw@gmail.com

NAJJAR, Ghina 856-256-5747 289 H
najjar@rowan.edu

NAJJAR, Joe 229-430-6624 114 J
jnajjar@albanytech.edu

NAJJAR, Yasar 508-626-4769 218 A
ynajjar@framingham.edu

NAKAGAWA, Deborah 808-956-0321 130 B
debn@hawaii.edu

NAKAGAWA, Hope 503-375-7165 383 A
hnakagawa@corban.edu

NAKAI, Karen 562-985-4121 32 C
karen.nakai@csulb.edu

NAKAMA, Debra 808-984-3515 130 H
debran@hawaii.edu

NAKAMURA, Natalie 212-659-3601 312 E
nnakamura@tkc.edu

NAKAMURA, Tim 760-568-3352 39 D
tnakamura@collegeofthedesert.edu

NAKANO, Mark, E 714-463-7504 51 A
mnakano@ketchum.edu

NAKAS, Victor 202-319-5244 91 D
nakas@cua.edu

NAKASONE, Nancy, K 808-689-2525 130 A
nancynak@hawaii.edu

NAKAYAMA, Karen 970-247-7212 79 J
nakayama_k@fortlewis.edu

NAKHAI, Mandana 914-337-9300 305 F
mandana.nakhai@concordia-ny.edu

NAKIZITO, Kizito 937-502-3681 373 H
knakizito@wilberforce.edu

NAKUTIS, Kristine 931-221-1400 430 B
nakutisk@apsu.edu

NEAL, Robin 916-484-8461 50 F
nealr@arc.losrios.edu
NEAL, Rodney 909-558-4543 48 H
rneal@llu.edu
NEAL, Ryan 864-231-2000 418 E
rneal@andersonuniversity.edu
NEAL, Shannon 504-816-4228 191 E
sneal@dillard.edu
NEAL, Sharon 610-468-1465 389 A
sharon.neal@alvernia.edu
NEAL, Susan 918-631-3246 381 C
susan-neal@utulsa.edu
NEAL, Thomas, M 714-547-9625 28 J
tneal@calcoast.edu
NEAL, Tom 714-546-7600 38 F
tneal14@coastline.edu
NEAL, Tracy 936-633-5201 442 I
tneal@angelina.edu
NEAL, Veronica 408-864-5338 43 E
nealveronica@deanza.edu
NEAL, Willie 972-273-3009 448 C
wneal@dcccd.edu
NEAL, Zach 501-279-4332 19 G
zneal@harding.edu
NEALEY, Jessica 859-846-5789 188 B
jnealey@midway.edu
NEALON, Jackie 845-451-1279 306 D
jackie.nealon@culinary.edu
NEALON, Michael 313-845-9615 231 B
NEALON, Michele 213-615-2700 37 B
mnealon-woods@thechicagoschool.edu
NEAME, Simon 413-545-0284 216 H
sneame@library.umass.edu
NEAR, Hollis 206-726-5040 494 B
hnear@cornish.edu
NEARHOOF, Jeff 312-413-4329 153 H
jeff5@uic.edu
NEARY, Michele 317-940-9535 156 I
mneary@butler.edu
NEARY, Robert 315-866-0300 310 A
nearyrd@herkimer.edu
NEARY, Suzanne 914-251-6000 328 B
suzanne.neary@purchase.edu
NEAU, George 510-567-6174 66 I
chancellor@sum.edu
NEAULT, Lynn, C 619-388-6922 60 B
lneault@sdccd.edu
NEAVE, Jessica 617-217-9448 211 D
jneave@baystate.edu
NEAVES, Mitchell 340-693-1040 529 C
mneaves@uvi.edu
NEBEL, Andriea 402-552-3373 273 K
nebel@clarksoncollege.edu
NEBESKY, Michael 864-656-2390 419 F
mnebeske@clemson.edu
NECASTRO, Gerard 304-336-8023 504 E
gerard.necastro@westliberty.edu
NECESSARY, Russell, D 276-328-0322 487 A
rdn2f@uvawise.edu
NECHIPURENKO, Erin 508-626-4951 218 A
enechipurenko@framingham.edu
NECULA, Maria-Cristina 718-960-2416 302 C
mariacristina.necula@lehman.cuny.edu
NEDBALSKI, Coleen 610-358-4587 402 G
nedbalsc@neumann.edu
NEDDER, Stephen, J 401-456-8000 417 A
NEDELL, Thomas 617-373-2240 223 D
NEDERHOFF, Arlan 712-722-6010 168 I
arlan.nederhorff@dordt.edu
NEDLEY, Neil 530-422-7927 73 F
NEE, Kelly, A 617-353-2127 212 G
kellynee@bu.edu
NEECE, Taylor 951-343-4871 28 G
tneece@calbaptist.edu
NEECE-FIELDER, Kasey 210-458-4819 468 B
kasey.neece-fielder@utsa.edu
NEEDHAM, Matthew, R 336-633-0210 345 F
mrneedham@randolph.edu
NEEDHAM, Michele 630-466-7900 155 C
mneedham@waubonsee.edu
NEEDLES, Philip 215-641-6510 402 A
pneedles@mc3.edu
NEEDY, Bryan 502-456-6504 189 F
bneedy@sullivan.edu
NEEDY, Kim 479-575-5900 21 I
kneedy@uark.edu
NEEFE, Diane 608-785-9539 515 C
neefed@westerntc.edu
NEEL, Buster 207-780-4484 201 H
buster.neel@maine.edu
NEEL, Joel 805-756-2193 30 K
jneel@calpoly.edu
NEEL, Linda 575-624-7142 294 A
linda.neel@roswell.enmu.edu
NEEL, Monica 410-337-6562 204 A
monica.neel@goucher.edu
NEEL, Paul, E 574-807-7035 156 E
paul.neel@bethelcollege.edu

NEEL, Sandra 502-852-3870 190 C
sjneel01@louisville.edu
NEELY, Jennifer 615-248-1237 439 B
jneely@trevecca.edu
NEELY, Robert 207-581-5842 201 A
robert.neely@maine.edu
NEELY, Robert 940-898-3301 464 A
rneely@twu.edu
NEEMANN, Brenda 402-481-8692 273 F
brenda.neemann@bryanhealthcollege.edu
NEENER, Lisa, S 719-333-9751 518 H
NEER, Stephen 312-261-3031 146 G
stephen.neer@nl.edu
NEESAM, Jaci, E 415-422-6762 72 A
neesam@usfca.edu
NEESE, James 810-989-5585 236 G
jneese@sc4.edu
NEESE, John, M 325-670-1273 450 A
jneese@hsutx.edu
NEESE, Susan 253-680-7025 492 F
sneese@bates.ctc.edu
NEESMITH, Debra 704-216-3640 346 C
debra.neesmith@rccc.edu
NEESON, Kathyrn, C 716-878-4895 326 E
neesonkc@buffalostate.edu
NEF, Dennis, L 559-278-4468 32 A
dennisn@csufresno.edu
NEFF, Charles 405-208-5060 377 D
cneff@okcu.edu
NEFF, Joan 434-395-2010 482 E
neffjl@longwood.edu
NEFF, Jon 319-398-7195 171 F
jneff@kirkwood.edu
NEFF, Kathryn 573-518-2378 263 E
kneff@mineralarea.edu
NEFF, Nancy 480-423-6567 14 C
nancy.neff@scottsdalecc.edu
NEGI, Reema 201-559-6152 286 C
negir@felician.edu
NEGLIA, Michael, S 904-620-2923 110 E
mneglia@unf.edu
NEGRETE, Elizabeth 818-947-2361 49 G
negretme@lavc.edu
NEGRETE, Michael 510-869-6511 59 F
mnegrete@samuelmerritt.edu
NEGRITTO, Leslie 909-621-8030 37 L
leslie.negritto@cgu.edu
NEGRON, Ashley 417-626-1234 264 J
negron.ashley@occ.edu
NEGRON, Dennis 423-236-2813 436 C
negron@southern.edu
NEGRON, Frankie 787-761-0640 527 C
decanoadministracion@utcpr.edu
NEGRON, Gisela 787-257-7373 525 Q
gnegron@suagm.edu
NEGRON, Juan, A 787-857-3600 523 I
janegron@br.inter.edu
NEGRON, Lillian 787-786-3030 526 F
lnegron@ucb.edu.pr
NEGRON, Luz 787-743-4041 521 K
lznegron@columbiacentral.edu
NEGRON, Olga 787-832-6000 522 Q
mortiz@icprjc.edu
NEGRON, Zaima 787-754-7597 523 F
zynegron@inter.edu
NEGRON DELGADO,
Juan Luis 787-841-2000 525 J
juan_negron@pucpr.edu
NEHME, George 315-792-3054 332 H
genehme@utica.edu
NEHMER, Matthew 805-765-9300 62 D
NEHRA, Terese 313-664-7677 228 H
tnehra@collegeforcreativestudies.edu
NEHRBAS, Mark 740-284-5843 361 L
mnehrbas@franciscan.edu
NEHRING, Matt 719-587-7622 76 D
matt.nehring@adams.edu
NEHRING, Wendy, M 423-439-7051 431 H
nehringw@etsu.edu
NEIBAUER, Todd 231-995-1061 235 B
tneibauer@nmc.edu
NEIDERHISER,
Jonathan 605-331-6667 429 D
jonathan.neiderhiser@usiouxfalls.edu
NEIDHARDT, Neil 734-432-5316 233 C
nneidhardt@madonna.edu
NEIDORF, David 760-872-2000 41 E
dneidorf@deepsprings.edu
NEIDUSKI, Becky 336-278-6350 337 G
bneiduski@elon.edu
NEIDY, Jon 309-677-2510 134 G
neidy@fsmail.bradley.edu
NEIFELD WHEELER,
Wendy 518-694-7319 297 J
wendy.neifeldwheeler@acphs.edu
NEIGER, Brad, L 801-422-4331 471 E
neiger@byu.edu

NEIGHBORS, Janie 940-668-7333 453 L
jneighbors@nctc.edu
NEIGHOFF, Charles 304-829-7744 501 F
cneighoff@bethanywv.edu
NEIGLER, Peter 212-924-5900 330 G
pneigler@swedishinstitute.edu
NEIHOF, JR., John, E 601-366-8880 256 H
jneihof@wbs.edu
NEIKIRK, Mark 859-572-1449 188 E
neikirkm1@nku.edu
NEIL, Jon 518-580-5490 324 D
jneil@skidmore.edu
NEIL, Leland 801-622-1573 472 H
leland.neil@stevenhenager.edu
NEILING, Francine 863-616-6426 100 D
fneiling@flsouthern.edu
NEILL, Christine 602-243-8185 14 D
christine.neill@southmountaincc.edu
NEILL, Sarah 617-521-2124 224 E
sarah.neill@simmons.edu
NEILS, Kathleen, A 603-862-2421 282 F
kathy.neils@unh.edu
NEILSON, Eric, G 312-503-0340 148 C
egneilson@northwestern.edu
NEILSON, Leanne 805-493-3145 30 E
neilson@callutheran.edu
NEIMAN, Gershon 845-731-3700 335 D
NEIMEYER, Bruce, C 847-578-8797 150 E
bruce.neimeyer@rosalindfranklin.edu
NEINER, Catherine 404-413-1835 121 A
cneiner1@gsu.edu
NEISES, Marlene 414-382-6017 506 A
marlene.neises@alverno.edu
NEISES, Sarah 920-424-0401 511 B
neises@uwosh.edu
NEISS, Jana 417-873-6829 259 G
jneiss@drury.edu
NEITZ, Stephen 724-805-2960 410 C
stephen.neitz@stvincent.edu
NEITZ, Stephen 724-805-2960 410 B
stephen.neitz@stvincent.edu
NEKRITZ, Colin 716-829-8404 307 B
nekritzc@dyc.edu
NEKVASIL, Nancy 574-284-4575 163 J
nekvasil@saintmarys.edu
NEL, Stanley, D 415-422-8888 72 A
nel@usfca.edu
NELEN, Carla 814-886-6411 402 E
cnelen@mtaloy.edu
NELHUEBEL, Robin, M 757-240-2200 484 G
NELKENBAUM,
Avrohom Yaakov 718-645-0536 315 G
NELL, Sharon, D 512-448-8620 455 I
sharonn@stedwards.edu
NELLE, Nora 215-517-2659 389 D
nellen@arcadia.edu
NELLER, Irene 626-584-5362 43 K
ireneneller@fuller.edu
NELLESEN, Gary 909-274-4850 52 I
gnellesen@mtsac.edu
NELLIS, Duane 740-593-1804 368 G
president@ohio.edu
NELLIS, Ginny 802-258-3283 476 B
ginny.nellis@worldlearning.org
NELLIS, Leah 765-455-9441 160 B
lmnellis@iu.edu
NELLIS, Troy 218-477-2968 246 B
troy.nellis@mnstate.edu
NELMS, Jim, A 936-261-1932 458 F
janelms@pvamu.edu
NELMS, Kristi 217-854-5594 134 E
kristi.nelms@blackburn.edu
NELONS, Derick 253-680-7000 492 F
dnelons@bates.ctc.edu
NELSEN, Jeff, A 515-574-1115 170 C
nelsen@iowacentral.edu
NELSEN, Robert, S 916-278-7737 33 C
nelsen@csus.edu
NELSON, Allan 302-857-1707 90 F
anelso11@dtcc.edu
NELSON, Andrew 515-433-5020 168 A
adnelson@dmacc.edu
NELSON, Andrew 830-372-8011 461 D
anelson@tlu.edu
NELSON, Andrew, J 715-836-5368 510 D
nelsonan@uwec.edu
NELSON, Andy 712-274-5148 172 A
nelsona@morningside.edu
NELSON, Annella 318-675-7013 194 D
anelso@lsuhsc.edu
NELSON, Anthony 301-860-3590 208 E
anelson@bowiestate.edu
NELSON, April 580-477-7896 381 G
april.nelson@wosc.edu
NELSON, Bernard 504-398-2108 196 E
bnelson@uhcno.edu
NELSON, Brandi 701-662-1509 355 A
brandi.nelson@lrsc.edu

NELSON, Brooke 858-653-3000 30 F
bnelson@calmu.edu
NELSON, Bruce, F 336-278-7280 337 G
bnelson@elon.edu
NELSON, Camille, A 202-274-4004 91 C
canelson@american.edu
NELSON, Carol 909-274-5431 52 I
cnelson@mtsac.edu
NELSON, Carolyn 510-885-3942 31 F
carolyn.nelson@csueastbay.edu
NELSON, Charles 334-386-7920 5 I
cnelson@faulkner.edu
NELSON, Cherrie 801-626-7496 473 E
cgnelson@weber.edu
NELSON, Chris 435-797-1810 473 C
chris.nelson@usu.edu
NELSON, Christina 206-934-4017 497 I
christina.nelson@seattlecolleges.edu
NELSON, Christopher 757-388-2900 485 B
cnelson@sentara.edu
NELSON, Daniel 651-638-6241 240 J
dc-nelson@bethel.edu
NELSON, David 617-879-7100 218 B
nelson@massart.edu
NELSON, David 312-662-4151 133 A
dnelson@adler.edu
NELSON, David, A 717-245-1830 394 A
nelsond@dickinson.edu
NELSON, Deanna 816-501-3727 257 G
deanna.nelson@avila.edu
NELSON, Denise 541-956-7001 386 G
dnelson@roguecc.edu
NELSON, Diane, L 415-422-2441 72 A
dlnelson3@usfca.edu
NELSON, Dirk 806-651-2730 460 E
jdnelson@mail.wtamu.edu
NELSON, Don 570-740-0750 400 F
dnelson@luzerne.edu
NELSON, Donald 684-699-9155 519 F
d.nelson@amsamoa.edu
NELSON, Doug 563-387-1862 171 I
nelsondg@luther.edu
NELSON, Eric 805-565-6114 74 I
enelson@westmont.edu
NELSON, Eric, R 215-572-2900 389 D
nelsoner@arcadia.edu
NELSON, Evelyn, C 561-237-7816 103 E
enelson@lynn.edu
NELSON, Fred 605-642-6848 428 F
fred.nelson@bhsu.edu
NELSON, Gena, C 315-267-2330 328 A
nelsongc@potsdam.edu
NELSON, Gena, C 315-267-2377 328 A
nelsongc@potsdam.edu
NELSON, Gersham 660-543-4750 268 A
ganelson@ucmo.edu
NELSON, Greg 415-884-3100 39 E
gnelson@marin.edu
NELSON, Holly 503-399-5145 382 C
holly.nelson@chemeketa.edu
NELSON, Ivory 601-979-2246 253 E
ivory.v.nelson@jsums.edu
NELSON, Jackie 605-688-4920 429 B
jacqueline.nelson@sdstate.edu
NELSON, James, H 606-693-5000 187 D
jnelson@kmbc.edu
NELSON, Jamie 510-204-0718 37 F
jnelson@cdsp.edu
NELSON, Janet 208-885-2258 132 I
janetenelson@uidaho.edu
NELSON, Jay 763-576-4773 244 A
jnelson@anokatech.edu
NELSON, Jay 763-576-4054 243 K
jnelson@anokatech.edu
NELSON, Jeff 218-235-2193 248 B
j.nelson@vcc.edu
NELSON, Jeffrey, D 419-372-2853 357 F
nelsonj@bgsu.edu
NELSON, Jen 208-459-5121 131 H
jnelson@collegeofidaho.edu
NELSON, Jennifer 770-528-3554 117 G
jnelson@chattahoocheetech.edu
NELSON, Jennifer 770-975-4000 117 G
jnelson@chattahoocheetech.edu
NELSON, Jennifer 802-447-6327 476 C
jnelson@svc.edu
NELSON, Jennifer, C 334-347-2623 1 J
jnelson@escc.edu
NELSON, Jim 606-693-5000 187 D
jnelson@kmbc.edu
NELSON, Jim 479-619-3159 20 F
jnelson3@nwacc.edu
NELSON, Joan 713-743-2603 465 A
jmnelson2@uh.edu
NELSON, Joan, M 713-743-2603 464 F
jmnelson2@uh.edu
NELSON, Joseph 907-796-6057 10 C
jgnelson@alaska.edu

NEVINS, Daniel 212-678-8067 312 A
danevins@jtsa.edu

NEVINS, Sherry, C 608-342-1854 511 D
nevinsm@uwplatt.edu

NEVOIS, Dana, A 636-481-3488 261 B
dnevois@jeffco.edu

NEW, Jim 775-673-7000 279 C

NEW, Lynn 903-923-2091 448 J
lnew@etbu.edu

NEWBERG, Bella 760-750-4444 33 E
newberg@csusm.edu

NEWBERRY, Byron 405-425-5428 377 B
byron.newberry@oc.edu

NEWBERRY, Robert 575-624-7180 294 A
robert.newberry@roswell.enmu.edu

NEWBOLD, Ken, F 574-535-7550 158 A
kfnewbold@goshen.edu

NEWBOLD, Lance 405-736-0281 379 F
lnewbold@rose.edu

NEWBY, Jennifer 541-383-7530 382 B
jlnewby@cocc.edu

NEWBY, Stewart 903-675-6235 464 C
stewart.newby@tvcc.edu

NEWBY, Teresa 952-446-4484 242 A
newbyt@crown.edu

NEWBY-ALEXANDER,
Cassandra 757-823-8118 483 F
clnewby-alexander@nsu.edu

NEWCOMB, Carrie 804-627-5300 478 I
carrie_newcomb@bshsi.org

NEWCOMB, Debbie 805-289-8976 73 C
dnewcomb@vcccd.edu

NEWCOMB, Ron 770-975-4125 117 G

NEWCOMB, Sherri 718-631-6221 303 F
snewcomb@qcc.cuny.edu

NEWCOMBE, Patricia 413-782-1201 225 F
pnewcombe@law.wne.edu

NEWCOMBE, Rodd 321-674-7110 99 K
newcombe@fit.edu

NEWELL, AJ 540-654-1934 486 D
anewell@umw.edu

NEWELL, Crystal 434-961-5339 489 C
cnewell@pvcc.edu

NEWELL, Diane 251-380-9090 5 I
dnewell@faulkner.edu

NEWELL, James 856-256-4012 289 H
newell@rowan.edu

NEWELL, Jeffrey 978-921-4242 222 B
jeffrey.newell@montserrat.edu

NEWELL, Mallory 408-864-8777 43 E
newellmallory@deanza.edu

NEWELL, Patrick, A 530-898-5394 31 D
pnewell@csuchico.edu

NEWELL, Rand, E 207-509-7201 200 I
rnewell@unity.edu

NEWEY, Faith 706-886-6831 126 F
faithnewey@tfc.edu

NEWHALL, JR., Edward 401-454-6307 417 B
enewhall@risd.edu

NEWHOUSE, Dollie 843-661-1175 421 H
dnewhouse@fmarion.edu

NEWHOUSE, Robin, P 317-274-1486 160 E
newhouse@iu.edu

NEWHOUSE, Sara 205-226-4694 4 F
snewhous@bsc.edu

NEWHOUSE, Valerie, K 712-362-0434 170 D
vnewhouse@iowalakes.edu

NEWITZ, Laurie, H 718-780-7503 300 A
laurie.newitz@brooklaw.edu

NEWKIRK, Charlene 412-469-6300 392 G
cnewkirk@ccac.edu

NEWKIRK, Krista, L 864-596-9050 420 F
klnewkirk@converse.edu

NEWKIRK, Vann 252-335-3291 350 A
vrnewkirk@ecsu.edu

NEWLAND, Carmen 480-461-7479 13 I
carmen.newland@mesacc.edu

NEWLIN, Aura 307-754-6095 516 Q
aura.newlin@nwc.edu

NEWLIN, Emily 870-584-1124 22 F
enewlin@cccua.edu

NEWLIN, Toni 765-998-5211 164 C
tnnewlin@taylor.edu

NEWLUN, Elizabeth 479-248-7236 19 F
lnewlun@ecollege.edu

NEWMAN, Andy 432-552-2675 469 D
newman_a@utpb.edu

NEWMAN, Benjamin 618-453-3771 152 B
bnewman@siu.edu

NEWMAN, Betsy 617-747-2231 212 B
studentaffairs@berklee.edu

NEWMAN, Carolyn 631-656-3191 308 F
carolyn.newman@ftc.edu

NEWMAN, Carrie 814-824-3311 401 J
cnewman@mercyhurst.edu

NEWMAN, Channa 412-392-3923 408 F
cnewman@pointpark.edu

NEWMAN, Colleen 303-492-6301 83 B
colleen.newman@colorado.edu

NEWMAN, Cynthia, M 609-895-5152 289 E
cnewman@rider.edu

NEWMAN, Dianna 704-847-5600 349 E
dnewman@ses.edu

NEWMAN, Gail 925-473-7421 41 A
gnewman@losmedanos.edu

NEWMAN, Gilbert 510-841-9230 75 E
gnewman@wi.edu

NEWMAN, J. Keith 405-491-6300 379 K
knewman@snu.edu

NEWMAN, Janice 916-577-2200 75 B
jnewman@jessup.edu

NEWMAN, Jeanine 337-421-9615 193 F
jeanine.newman@sowela.edu

NEWMAN, Jeff 615-322-2476 440 D
jeffrey.k.newman@vanderbilt.edu

NEWMAN, Joan 865-694-6453 437 F
jnewman@pstcc.edu

NEWMAN, Katherine, S 413-545-2554 216 H
ksnewman@provost.umass.edu

NEWMAN, Kay, S 334-387-3877 4 B
kaynewman@amridgeuniversity.edu

NEWMAN, Kim 212-353-4155 306 A
knewman@cooper.edu

NEWMAN, Lance 801-832-2301 474 E
lnewman@westminstercollege.edu

NEWMAN, Lester, C 903-730-4890 451 D
lnewman@jarvis.edu

NEWMAN, Linda 360-438-4584 497 F
lnewman@stmartin.edu

NEWMAN, Michael 914-594-4567 318 A
michael_newman@nymc.edu

NEWMAN, Michael 646-565-6000 331 F
michael.newman@touro.edu

NEWMAN, Michelle 703-330-5398 501 D

NEWMAN, Nancy, J 402-465-2375 276 E
njn@nebrwesleyan.edu

NEWMAN, Rebeccah 908-737-0422 286 F
renewman@kean.edu

NEWMAN, Robert 310-453-8300 42 D

NEWMAN, Scott 918-293-4666 378 B
scott.newman@okstate.edu

NEWMAN, Shannon 479-248-7236 19 F
snewman@ecollege.edu

NEWMAN, William 615-230-3600 438 C
william.newman@volstate.edu

NEWMANN, Jennifer 629-876-4250 68 C

NEWPORT, Joseph, M 812-237-7829 159 C
joseph.newport@indstate.edu

NEWSCHAFFER,
Craig, J 215-571-3441 394 C
craig.j.newschaffer@drexel.edu

NEWSCHWANDER,
Gregg 334-844-5662 4 D
gen0002@auburn.edu

NEWSOM, Andrea 317-791-5611 164 H
newsoma@uindy.edu

NEWSOM, Lanay 757-683-3141 483 G
snewsom@odu.edu

NEWSOM, Stephanie, R 319-352-8539 174 C
stephanie.newsom@wartburg.edu

NEWSOM, Thomas, W 575-461-4413 294 E
thomasn@mesalands.edu

NEWSOME, Caitlin 718-960-8144 302 C
1270mgr@fheg.follett.com

NEWSOME, Chevelle 916-278-6470 33 C
cnewsome@csus.edu

NEWSOME, Dale 815-939-5265 148 F
rdnewsome@olivet.edu

NEWSOME, Gary 815-939-5120 148 F
gnewsome@olivet.edu

NEWSOME, Jeffrey 808-934-2762 130 D
jnewsome@hawaii.edu

NEWSOME, JoEllen 704-463-3222 348 B
joellen.newsome@pfeiffer.edu

NEWSOME, John 414-955-8631 508 D
jnewsome@mcw.edu

NEWSOME, Pam 612-874-3798 243 F
pam_newsome-prochniak@mcad.edu

NEWSOME, Sarah 850-973-9675 104 D
newsomes@nfcc.edu

NEWTON, Bryan 410-334-2894 210 C
bnewton@worwic.edu

NEWTON, Carolyn 330-263-2004 360 A
cnewton@wooster.edu

NEWTON, Christopher 501-370-5204 21 A
cnewton@philander.edu

NEWTON, Darrell 715-836-2320 510 D
newtond@uwec.edu

NEWTON, Diane, D 501-450-3184 23 I
dnewton@uca.edu

NEWTON, Dusty 308-865-8702 277 F
newtond@unk.edu

NEWTON, Eric, D 864-242-5100 418 H

NEWTON, Erin 478-387-4729 120 B
enewton@gmc.edu

NEWTON, Jackie 662-434-2660 253 A
jnewton@eastms.edu

NEWTON, Jeff 419-530-4484 372 F
jeff.newton2@utoledo.edu

NEWTON, Joseph, A 229-333-4357 127 H
jnewton@valdosta.edu

NEWTON, Joshua 860-486-2709 88 G
jnewton@foundation.uconn.edu

NEWTON, Julie 512-404-4820 443 I
jnewton@austinseminary.edu

NEWTON, LaCresha 501-420-1203 17 I
lacresha.newton@arkansasbaptist.edu

NEWTON, Lynette 402-826-8688 274 E
lynette.newton@doane.edu

NEWTON, Mark 408-298-2181 61 P
mark.newton@sjcc.edu

NEWTON, Martin 205-726-2131 6 G
cnewton@samford.edu

NEWTON, Maureen 256-782-5333 6 B
mnewton@jsu.edu

NEWTON, Michael, L 270-384-8099 187 H
newtonm@lindsey.edu

NEWTON, Michael, R 515-294-7166 166 F
mrnewton@iastate.edu

NEWTON, Nell, J 574-631-6789 165 A
nell.newton@nd.edu

NEWTON, Sandra 252-492-2061 347 C
newton@vgcc.edu

NEWTON, Vicki 425-352-8252 492 K
vnewton@cascadia.edu

NEWTOWN, Michael, J 315-386-7411 329 A
newtownm@canton.edu

NEY, Cheryl, L 323-343-4300 32 D
cney@cslanet.calstatela.edu

NEYS, Leigh 605-626-7802 428 H
leigh.neys@northern.edu

NEZ, Marie, R 928-724-6635 12 G
mnez@dinecollege.edu

NG, Charis 718-270-4629 326 A
charis.ng@downstate.edu

NG, Charles 800-782-2422 30 G
cng@mail.cnuas.edu

NG, Charles 760-757-2121 52 F
cng@miracosta.edu

NG, Donna 617-521-2890 224 E
donna.ng@simmons.edu

NG, Jeffrey 718-817-3736 308 G
jeng@fordham.edu

NG, Michael, M 808-956-7323 129 H
ng23@hawaii.edu

NG, Peh 320-589-6300 251 A
pehng@morris.umn.edu

NGIRAMENGIOR, Todd 680-488-2471 520 E
toddn@palau.edu

NGO, David 212-229-8947 316 E
ngod@newschool.edu

NGO, Khiem 985-545-1500 192 K

NGO, Vincent 619-388-7485 60 E
vngo@sdccd.edu

NGOM, Mbare 443-885-3095 206 A
mbare.ngom@morgan.edu

NGUMA, Elibariki 956-872-2515 456 G
bariki@southtexascollege.edu

NGUYEN, Alice 801-302-2800 472 A
anguyen@neumont.edu

NGUYEN, Binh 510-659-6441 54 F

NGUYEN, Chau 702-463-2122 280 F

NGUYEN, Christine 714-241-6144 38 F
cnguyen@coastline.edu

NGUYEN, Christopher 845-687-5053 331 L
nguyenc@sunyulster.edu

NGUYEN, Danny 408-855-5417 74 C
danny.nguyen@wvm.edu

NGUYEN, Giang, T 215-746-3535 412 G
gnguyen@upenn.edu

NGUYEN, Hieu 951-827-1286 69 D
hieu.nguyen@ucr.edu

NGUYEN, Hieu 808-739-8577 129 A
hnguyen@chaminade.edu

NGUYEN, Hoa 419-448-2228 362 G
hnguyen@heidelberg.edu

NGUYEN, Kay 714-895-8727 38 G
kvnguyen@gwc.cccd.edu

NGUYEN, Loan 510-981-2808 56 F
lnguyen@peralta.edu

NGUYEN, Luan, P 671-735-2639 520 B
nguyen@triton.uog.edu

NGUYEN, Mai 978-934-2049 217 B
mai_nguyen@uml.edu

NGUYEN, Son 310-233-4584 49 B
nguyens@lahc.edu

NGUYEN, Son Xuan 714-903-2762 68 A

NGUYEN, Tamie 323-343-5808 32 D
tnguyen10@cslanet.calstatela.edu

NGUYEN, Thai-Hoa 714-903-2762 68 A

NGUYEN, Thuy 650-949-7200 43 F
nguyenthuy@foothill.edu

NGUYEN, Thuy, N 714-432-5816 38 H
tnguyen@occ.cccd.edu

NGUYEN, Thy 312-996-2969 153 H
thy@uic.edu

NGUYEN, Trinh 925-473-7315 41 A
trnguyen@losmedanos.edu

NGUYEN, Tuyen 714-628-4844 58 B
nguyen_tuyen@sccollege.edu

NGWABA, Maurice, C 410-651-6656 208 C
mcngwaba@umes.edu

NHIRA, Tafadzwa 410-238-9000 93 B

NI, Yi 401-454-6386 417 B
yni@risd.edu

NIAS, Danita 561-297-3015 109 B
dnais@fau.edu

NIAS, Danita 352-392-5401 110 D
dnias@ufalumni.ufl.edu

NICA, Claude 310-665-6870 54 I
cnica@otis.edu

NICASTRO, Eric 814-860-5125 399 C
enicastro@lecom.edu

NICCUM, Victoria 970-351-1152 83 F
victoria.niccum@unco.edu

NICELY, Kathleen 415-864-7326 60 H
knicely@sfcm.edu

NICELY, Nancy 610-328-8534 410 I
nnicely1@swarthmore.edu

NICELY, Sarah, L 540-985-4029 482 A
slnicely@carilionclinic.org

NICELY, Tim 540-453-2371 487 G
nicelyt@brcc.edu

NICHOL, Kristi 816-654-7107 261 D
knichol@kcumb.edu

NICHOL, Molly 518-262-8043 297 L
nicholm@mail.amc.edu

NICHOL, Vicki 303-273-3972 78 J
vnichol@mines.edu

NICHOLAS, David, R 530-221-4275 63 H
sbcadm@shasta.edu

NICHOLAS, Donna, R 530-221-4275 63 H
donna@shasta.edu

NICHOLAS, Jason 906-227-2379 235 A
janichol@nmu.edu

NICHOLAS, Jim 530-895-2421 28 E
nicholaswi@butte.edu

NICHOLAS, Johah 925-229-6944 40 J
jnicholas@4cd.edu

NICHOLAS, Mark 508-626-4670 218 A
mnicholas1@framingham.edu

NICHOLAS, Mike, L 574-807-7875 156 E
michael.nicholas@bethelcollege.edu

NICHOLAS, Nannette 607-962-9229 306 C
nicholas@corning-cc.edu

NICHOLAS, Sandra 570-740-0730 400 F
snicholas@luzerne.edu

NICHOLL, Matthew 617-747-2700 212 B
mnicholl@berklee.edu

NICHOLLS, Amy 260-665-4862 164 E
anicholls@trine.edu

NICHOLLS, Deb 541-888-7400 387 A
dnicholls@socc.edu

NICHOLLS, Gregory 610-660-1090 409 H
gnicholl@sju.edu

NICHOLLS, Tom 541-888-7611 387 A
tnicholls@socc.edu

NICHOLS, Aaron, F 802-656-3425 476 E
aaron.nichols@uvm.edu

NICHOLS, Andrew, W 808-956-8965 129 J
nicholsa@hawaii.edu

NICHOLS, Ann 270-707-3762 186 B
ann.nichols@kctcs.edu

NICHOLS, Anthony, J 706-233-7272 125 E
anichols@shorter.edu

NICHOLS, Ashlyn 214-638-0484 451 E
ashlynnichols@kdstudio.com

NICHOLS, Bill 704-337-2340 348 D
nicholsb@queens.edu

NICHOLS, Brenda 409-880-7087 462 C
brenda.nichols@lamar.edu

NICHOLS, Brian 814-871-5680 395 H
nichols006@gannon.edu

NICHOLS, Carol 217-442-7232 137 B
cnichols1@dacc.edu

NICHOLS, Dana 423-697-4792 436 F
dana.nichols@chattanoogastate.edu

NICHOLS, Daniel 202-885-2534 91 C
dnichols@american.edu

NICHOLS, Denise 757-727-5221 481 E
denise.nichols@hamptonu.edu

NICHOLS, Edward 814-262-6474 405 A
enichols@pennhighlands.edu

NICHOLS, Eric 603-641-7500 282 A
enichols@anselm.edu

NICHOLS, Gregory, A 785-309-3182 181 D
greg.nichols@salinatech.edu

NICHOLS, JR.,
Harold, E 864-833-8296 423 D
henichols@presby.edu

NICHOLS, Jason, D ...... 573-629-3211 260 G jnichols@hlg.edu
NICHOLS, Jennifer .... 704-922-6223 343 D nichols.jennifer@gaston.edu
NICHOLS, Jody .... 715-425-3982 511 E jody.nichols@uwrf.edu
NICHOLS, Jomel .... 816-271-5649 264 B snichols3@missouriwestern.edu
NICHOLS, Karen .... 504-486-7411 198 D knichola@xula.edu
NICHOLS, Karen, J .... 630-515-6159 145 I knicho@midwestern.edu
NICHOLS, Keegan .... 479-968-0276.. 18 G knichols@atu.edu
NICHOLS, Kelly .... 205-934-4488.... 8 B nicholsk@uab.edu
NICHOLS, Laurie .... 805-437-8423.. 31 C laurie.nichols@csuci.edu
NICHOLS, Laurie .... 307-766-4121 517 B uwpres@uwyo.edu
NICHOLS, Lesley .... 617-824-8281 214 E lesley_nichols@emerson.edu
NICHOLS, Leslie, A .... 937-481-2200 373 I leslie_nichols@wilmington.edu
NICHOLS, Linda .... 307-268-2220 516 H lnichols@caspercollege.edu
NICHOLS, Mary, L .... 612-645-0238 250 E mnichols@umn.edu
NICHOLS, Michael .... 928-523-0886.. 14 K michael.nichols@nau.edu
NICHOLS, Pamela .... 315-268-6413 304 B pnichols@clarkson.edu
NICHOLS, Paula .... 409-880-7537 462 C paula.nichols@lamar.edu
NICHOLS, Rachel .... 828-328-7306 339 C rachel.nichols@lr.edu
NICHOLS, Randall .... 207-725-3458 198 G rnichols@bowdoin.edu
NICHOLS, Reginald .... 781-280-3536 220 C
NICHOLS, Reginald .... 503-517-1221 388 A rnichols@warnerpacific.edu
NICHOLS, Rick .... 828-328-7387 339 C rick.nichols@lr.edu
NICHOLS, Rosanne .... 775-831-1314 280 C rnichols@sierranevada.edu
NICHOLS, Rosemary ...... 603-899-4045 281 D nicholrm@franklinpierce.edu
NICHOLS, Ruth, R .... 601-304-4336 251 G rnichols@alcorn.edu
NICHOLS, Sam .... 501-450-1362.. 19 I nichols@hendrix.edu
NICHOLS, Sam .... 501-450-1340.. 19 I nichols@hendrix.edu
NICHOLS, Sarah .... 704-290-5251 346 F snichols@spcc.edu
NICHOLS, Scott, G .... 617-353-5777 212 G nichols@bu.edu
NICHOLS, Shane .... 847-866-3866 138 G shane.nichols@garrett.edu
NICHOLS, Sheila .... 850-484-1428 105 E snichols@pensacolastate.edu
NICHOLS, Steve .... 417-269-3045 259 C steve.nichols@coxcollege.edu
NICHOLS, Tracy .... 512-505-3015 451 A tlnichols@htu.edu
NICHOLS, Warren .... 409-933-8271 446 H wnichols@com.edu
NICHOLS-ZONNO, Belinda .... 719-590-6766.. 79 B bnicholszonno@coloradotech.edu
NICHOLSON, Brian, W .. 254-710-8400 444 B brian_nicholson@baylor.edu
NICHOLSON, Cindy .... 810-989-5680 236 G cnicholson@sc4.edu
NICHOLSON, Cindy .... 828-227-7203 352 C nicholson@wcu.edu
NICHOLSON, Debra .... 620-276-9575 177 G debra.nicholson@gcccks.edu
NICHOLSON, Jane .... 651-779-3304 244 D jane.nicholson@century.edu
NICHOLSON, Judd .... 202-687-4402.. 92 B nicholsonj@georgetown.edu
NICHOLSON, Karen .... 718-862-7374 313 L karen.nicholson@manhattan.edu
NICHOLSON, Kim .... 765-677-2131 161 C kim.nicholson@indwes.edu
NICHOLSON, Kristal ...... 903-875-7361 453 J kristal.nicholson@navarrocollege.edu
NICHOLSON, Marie .... 828-689-1151 339 G mnicholson@mhu.edu
NICHOLSON, Nick .... 773-907-4777 135 K inicholson1@ccc.edu
NICHOLSON, Nigel, J ... 503-777-7257 386 F nnichols@reed.edu
NICHOLSON, Robin .... 319-235-3516 166 C robin.nicholson@unitypoint.org
NICHOLSON, Tammy .... 706-295-6328 119 G tnichols@highlands.edu
NICHOLSON, Tim .... 828-835-4261 347 B tnicholson@tricountycc.edu
NICHOLSON, Vickie .... 251-578-1313.... 3 D vickien@rstc.edu
NICHOLSON ANGLE, Jan, C .... 540-365-4285 480 L jcnicholson@ferrum.edu
NICHOLSON-PREUSS, Mari .... 713-221-8236 465 C nicholsonpreussm@uhd.edu
NICK, Sara, J .... 715-833-6275 513 E snick1@cvtc.edu
NICKE, Glenda .... 309-796-4822 134 C nickeg@bhc.edu
NICKEL, Kevin, A .... 419-358-3320 357 E nickelk@bluffton.edu
NICKEL, Shelley, C .... 404-962-3241 127 G shelley.nickel@usg.edu
NICKELL, Barbara, J ...... 785-833-4390 179 C bmarsh@kwu.edu
NICKELL, Jane Ellen ...... 814-332-2800 388 F jnickell@allegheny.edu
NICKELL, Julie .... 713-798-4951 444 A jnickell@bcm.edu
NICKELS, Jerrod .... 616-331-2450 230 G nickelsj@gvsu.edu
NICKELS, Ken .... 309-796-5048 134 C nickelsk@bhc.edu
NICKELS, Lisa .... 415-503-6251.. 60 H lnickels@sfcm.edu
NICKELS, Rosemerry ..... 440-934-3101 367 D rnickels@ohiobusinesscollege.edu
NICKENS, Tawanna .... 217-351-2390 148 H tnickens@parkland.edu
NICKENS, Tawanna .... 217-353-2119 148 H tnickens@parkland.edu
NICKERSON, Amanda ..... 817-257-7490 461 A amanda.nickerson@tcu.edu
NICKERSON, Floyd, W .. 972-599-3159 446 I fnickerson@collin.edu
NICKERSON, Gary .... 405-585-5210 377 A gary.nickerson@okbu.edu
NICKERSON, Lori .... 508-999-8004 217 A lnickerson@umassd.edu
NICKERSON, Molly .... 660-284-4800 260 I
NICKERSON, Nate .... 617-258-5403 221 C
NICKERSON, Sherita ..... 325-674-6802 441 D sherita.nickerson@acu.edu
NICKLAS, Bill .... 815-825-9412 142 F bill.nicklas@kishwaukeecollege.edu
NICKLAUS, Megan .... 719-389-6424.. 77 J megan.nicklaus@coloradocollege.edu
NICKLE, Bonny .... 949-359-0045.. 30 B
NICKLE, Mary Anne ...... 641-236-2202 170 G maryanne.nickle@iavalley.edu
NICKLE, Stephen, R ...... 210-999-7311 464 B snickle@trinity.edu
NICKLESS, Kenneth .... 314-968-7146 269 N nickleke@webster.edu
NICKLESS, Peter .... 315-568-3310 317 A pnickless@nycc.edu
NICKLOW, John, W .... 504-280-5536 194 F president@uno.edu
NICKOSON, Carol .... 937-327-7800 374 A nickosonc@wittenberg.edu
NICKSA, Gary, W .... 617-353-6500 212 G nicksa@bu.edu
NICOL, David .... 231-591-2422 230 A davidnicol@ferris.edu
NICOL, Patricia .... 617-824-8123 214 E patricia_nicol@emerson.edu
NICOLAI, Camille .... 414-297-8875 514 C nicolaic@matc.edu
NICOLAI, Michael .... 312-629-9411 151 F mnicolai@saic.edu
NICOLAISEN, Megan ..... 605-718-2418 429 E megan.nicolaisen@wdt.edu
NICOLETTE, Guy .... 352-294-7439 110 D gnic@ufl.edu
NICOLETTI, Katherine .... 508-213-2238 223 C katherine.nicoletti@nichols.edu
NICOLO, Anthony, J ...... 540-674-3639 488 G tnicolo@nr.edu
NICOTERA, Phillip .... 713-718-7628 450 D phillip.nicotera@hccs.edu
NIEC-WILLIAMS, Derrek 202-806-6100.. 92 C derrek.niecwilliams@howard.edu
NIECE, Matthew .... 208-426-1604 131 C matthewniece@boisestate.edu
NIEDENS, Rosemary ...... 316-942-4291 180 D niedensr@newmanu.edu
NIEDERHAUSER, Victoria .... 865-974-7584 439 I vniederh@utk.edu
NIEDERJOHN, Scott ...... 920-565-1000 507 K niederjohnms@lakeland.edu
NIEDWIECKI, Anthony ... 415-442-6601.. 44 E aniedwiecki@ggu.edu
NIEDZWIECKI, Brian, E . 419-866-0261 370 I beniedzwiecki@stautzenberger.com
NIEDZWIECKI, Michael . 718-933-6700 315 K mniedzwiedi@monroecollege.edu
NIEHOFF, Brian, A .... 785-532-4797 179 A niehoff@ksu.edu
NIEKRO, Cat, S .... 704-894-2533 337 B
NIELSEN, David .... 860-512-3108.. 85 G dnielsen@manchestercc.edu
NIELSEN, Erik .... 402-461-7738 274 I enielsen@hastings.edu
NIELSEN, Glenn .... 314-505-7201 258 I nielseng@csl.edu
NIELSEN, Jessica .... 619-684-8847.. 53 J jnielsen@newschoolarch.edu
NIELSEN, Kathryn .... 925-473-7628.. 41 A knielsen@losmedanos.edu
NIELSEN, Leila .... 651-631-0204 240 C lnielsen@aaaom.edu
NIELSEN, Lisa .... 831-459-4344.. 70 C lmnielse@ucsc.edu
NIELSEN, Lori .... 334-244-3225.... 4 E lneilsen@aum.edu
NIELSEN, Marcia .... 816-654-7109 261 D mnielsen@kcumb.edu
NIELSEN, Mark .... 208-885-0293 132 I markn@uidaho.edu
NIELSEN, Mary .... 303-458-4100.. 82 D
NIELSEN, Mary .... 706-272-4403 118 F mnielsen@daltonstate.edu
NIELSEN, Mary, F .... 414-277-7216 509 A nielsen@msoe.edu
NIELSEN, Melore .... 206-296-2000 498 D mnielsen@seattleu.edu
NIELSEN, Monty, E .... 785-532-6254 179 A nielsen@ksu.edu
NIELSEN, Paul, D .... 412-268-7740 391 H nielsen@sei.cmu.edu
NIELSEN, Richard, P ...... 801-375-5125 472 F rnielsen@rmuohp.edu
NIELSEN, Scott .... 775-753-2289 279 A scott.nielsen@gbcnv.edu
NIELSON, Eric .... 208-732-6267 131 I enielson@csi.edu
NIELSON, Joel .... 330-672-3120 363 I jnielson@kent.edu
NIELSON, Lauren .... 770-426-2832 122 F lauren.nielsen@life.edu
NIELSON, Marian, J ...... 315-733-2307 332 F mnielson@uscny.edu
NIELSON, Robert .... 435-283-7037 474 A rob.nielson@snow.edu
NIEMAN, Donald .... 607-777-2141 325 A dnieman@binghamton.edu
NIEMAN, James .... 773-256-0728 144 G jnieman@lstc.edu
NIEMAN, Larry .... 312-935-6448 149 K lnieman@robertmorris.edu
NIEMAN, Paul .... 818-710-4121.. 49 D niemanp@piercecollege.edu
NIEMI, Bill .... 970-943-3045.. 84 E bniemi@western.edu
NIEMI, Cathy .... 906-227-2232 235 A caniemi@nmu.edu
NIEMI, Jayne, L .... 651-696-6200 243 B niemi@macalester.edu
NIEMI, Nicole .... 219-464-6010 165 D nicole.niemi@valpo.edu
NIEMIEC, Catherine .... 602-274-1885.. 15 J cniemiec@pihma.edu
NIEMUTH, Brian .... 515-961-1670 173 E brian.niemuth@simpson.edu
NIENABER, Mary .... 651-779-5837 244 D mary.nienaber@century.edu
NIENABER, Steve .... 859-572-1366 188 E nienabers1@nku.edu
NIENHUIS, Jeanne .... 616-526-6885 228 B jeanen@calvin.edu
NIES, Charles .... 209-228-7620.. 69 C cnies@ucmerced.edu
NIESE, Vicki, J .... 419-772-2057 367 G v-niese@onu.edu
NIESEL, David, W .... 409-772-0758 469 C dniesel@utmb.edu
NIESEN DE ABRUNA, Laura .... 717-815-1231 415 G lniesen@ycp.edu
NIESPODZIANY, Aimee . 574-239-8314 158 M aniespodziany@hcc-nd.edu
NIESSEN, Linda .... 954-262-7334 104 F lniessen@nova.edu
NIETO, Javier .... 541-737-3220 385 F
NIETO-BRECHT, Erma, M .... 940-898-3270 464 A enieto@twu.edu
NIETO-PHILLIPS, John .. 812-855-2706 159 H jnietoph@indiana.edu
NIEUWKOOP, Ann, E .... 616-392-8555 239 J ann@westernsem.edu
NIEUWSMA, Randal, G . 616-526-6334 228 B nieuwr@calvin.edu
NIEVES, Beatriz .... 787-766-1717 526 B um_bnieves@suagm.edu
NIEVES, Brenda .... 909-447-2504.. 38 B bnieves@cst.edu
NIEVES, Danily .... 787-882-2065 526 D
NIEVES, Gladys, T .... 787-765-3560 522 K gnieves@edpuniversity.edu
NIEVES, Heriberto .... 787-257-0000 527 H heriberto.nieves@upr.edu
NIEVES, Ivette .... 787-279-1912 523 J inieves@bayamon.inter.edu
NIEVES, Lamberto, C ..... 201-761-6085 291 D lnieves@saintpeters.edu
NIEVES, Lourdes .... 305-821-3333 100 A lourdes@fnu.edu
NIEVES, Mayra .... 212-237-8918 302 F mnieves@jjay.cuny.edu
NIEVES, Nancy .... 787-265-3858 528 C placement@uprm.edu
NIEVES, Ruth .... 787-879-5270 527 F ruth.nieves1@upr.edu
NIEVES, Wilfredo .... 860-906-5101.. 85 D wnieves@ccc.commnet.edu
NIEWIERSKI, Frank .... 210-436-4357 455 J fniewierski@stmarytx.edu
NIGAGLIONI, Guillermo 787-754-7120 523 E
NIGGLI, Susan .... 585-275-7761 332 E sniggli@admin.rochester.edu
NIGHSWONGER, Davis . 619-482-6585.. 65 H dnighswonger@swccd.edu
NIGHTINGALE, Charles . 443-518-4615 204 E cnightingale@howardcc.edu
NIGLIAZZO, Marc, A ..... 254-519-5720 459 D marc.nigliazzo@tamuct.edu
NIGRO, Frank .... 530-242-7520.. 63 I fnigro@shastacollege.edu
NIGRO, Nick .... 419-473-2700 360 J nnigro@daviscollege.edu
NIGRO, Stephen, M .... 413-542-2101 210 F smnigro@amherst.edu
NIGUIDULA, Amanda ..... 305-348-3532 109 D amanda.niguidula@fiu.edu
NIHIPALI, Jacob .... 808-675-3474 128 K jacob.nihipali@byuh.edu
NIJLAND, Mark, J .... 210-567-0313 468 E nijland@uthscsa.edu
NIKIAS, C. L, M .... 213-740-2111.. 72 B president@usc.edu
NIKIRK, Sarah, F .... 859-218-3379 190 B s.nikirk@uky.edu
NIKKEL, Kasey .... 563-387-1008 171 I nikkka01@luther.edu
NIKOLAEFF, Ivan .... 719-474-8558.. 76 F ivan.nikolaeff@zenith.org
NIKOPOULOS, Beth .... 972-273-3171 448 C bnikopoulos@dcccd.edu
NILAND, Bridget .... 716-839-8397 306 E bniland@daemen.edu
NILAND, Eileen, A .... 716-888-2620 300 G nilande@canisius.edu
NILAND, Joe .... 251-442-2288.... 8 D jniland@umobile.edu
NILES, Maryann .... 781-280-3703 220 C nilesm@middlesex.mass.edu
NILES, Spencer .... 757-221-2315 479 I sgniles@wm.edu
NILES, Stefanie, D .... 717-245-1287 394 A niles@dickinson.edu
NILES-HANSEN, Diana .. 808-544-1102 129 C dnileshansen@hpu.edu
NILKANT, Anita .... 412-397-5267 409 C nilkant@rmu.edu
NILL, John (Jack) .... 417-862-9533 260 D jnill@globaluniversity.edu
NILLES, Dawnita .... 701-777-3239 353 G dawnita.nilles@und.edu
NILO, Susan .... 336-372-5061 347 G srnilo128@wilkescc.edu
NILSEN, Kenneth .... 201-216-5699 291 G kenneth.nilsen@stevens.edu
NILSON, Amy .... 209-588-5505.. 75 I nilsona@yosemite.edu
NILSSON, Gary .... 253-680-7180 492 F gnilsson@bates.ctc.edu
NIMES, Johnny .... 404-527-7782 122 B jnimes@itc.edu
NIMMER, Carole .... 660-543-4919 268 A cnimmer@ucmo.edu
NIMMO, Pam .... 615-732-7662 434 G pam@mtsa.edu
NIMMO, Steven .... 706-776-0113 124 E snimmo@piedmont.edu
NIN CECYN, Yudi .... 954-463-3000.. 94 P

NINAN, George .... 901-272-5125 434 B
gninan@mca.edu
NING, Bin .... 734-487-4924 229 K
bning@emich.edu
NININGER, Jami .... 614-234-1777 365 L
jnininger@mccn.edu
NINOS, Katherine .... 505-467-6819 296 F
katandall@aol.com
NINOW, Friedbert .... 951-785-2041.. 47 F
fninow@lasierra.edu
NIP, Kit .... 319-385-6250 170 J
knip@iw.edu
NIPP, Amanda .... 402-844-7273 276 G
amandan@northeast.edu
NIPP, Tim, J .... 731-881-7601 440 B
timnipp@utm.edu
NIPPER, Brent .... 423-461-8740 435 A
wbnipper@milligan.edu
NIPPERT, Jennifer .... 740-695-9500 357 D
jnippert@belmontcollege.edu
NIPPERT, Karen, F .... 901-333-4283 438 B
knippert@southwest.tn.edu
NIRENBERG, David .... 773-702-8799 153 F
nirenberg@uchicago.edu
NIROOMAND, Farhang . 361-570-4230 465 D
niroomandf@uhv.edu
NIROUMAND, Madjid ... 714-432-5765.. 38 H
mniroumand@occ.cccd.edu
NISBET, Jane, A .... 603-862-0549 282 F
jan.nisbet@unh.edu
NISBET, John, W .... 402-280-4093 274 D
johnnisbet@creighton.edu
NISBET, Kenneth, J .... 734-763-0614 237 I
knisbet@umich.edu
NISH, Melinda .... 692-625-3394 520 C
NISHIME, Jeanie .... 310-660-3472.. 42 C
jnishime@elcamino.edu
NISHIOKA, Yukari .... 714-533-3946.. 35 B
yukari.nishioka@calums.edu
NISHIYAMA, Shayna ..... 360-676-2772 496 C
snishiyama@nwic.edu
NISHIZAWA, Yuichiro ... 973-748-9000 284 A
yuichiro_nishizawa@bloomfield.edu
NISLY, Lamar .... 419-358-3317 357 E
nislyl@bluffton.edu
NISSEL, Chaim .... 646-592-4201 334 P
drnissel@yu.edu
NISSEN, Jill .... 314-367-8700 266 D
jill.nissen@stlcop.edu
NISSEN, Laura .... 503-725-3997 386 D
nissen@pdx.edu
NISSEN, Lindsey .... 319-296-4269 169 H
lindsey.nissen@hawkeyecollege.edu
NISSEN, Sarah .... 701-777-3579 353 G
sarah.nissen@und.edu
NISUN, Michelle, L .... 260-399-7700 165 B
mnisun@sf.edu
NISWANDER, Frederick . 252-328-6975 349 I
niswanderf@ecu.edu
NISWANDER, Tami .... 218-679-2860 249 R
NITCH, Mindy .... 814-262-6433 405 A
mnitch@pennhighlands.edu
NITECKI, Danuta, A .... 215-895-2750 394 C
dan44@drexel.edu
NITSCH, Wanda .... 760-591-3012.. 71 I
wnitsch@usa.edu
NITTA, Akira .... 949-582-4820.. 64 J
anitta@saddleback.edu
NITTMANN, Nydia .... 928-523-9488.. 14 K
nydia.nittmann@nau.edu
NITZBERG, Nancy .... 215-635-7300 396 B
nnitzberg@gratz.edu
NIVAR, Rafael .... 201-360-4081 286 E
rnivar@hccc.edu
NIVENS, Delana .... 912-344-3170 115 D
delana.nivens@armstrong.edu
NIVET, Marc, A .... 214-648-3266 469 E
marc.nivet@utsouthwestern.edu
NIX, Julie .... 256-782-5815.... 6 B
jnix@jsu.edu
NIX, Linda .... 307-268-2218 516 H
lnix@caspercollege.edu
NIX, Rachel .... 870-574-1521.. 21 G
rnix@sautech.edu
NIX, Sheila .... 210-431-2178 455 J
snix@stmarytx.edu
NIX, Vince .... 251-626-3303.... 7 G
jnix@ussa.edu
NIXON, Andrea .... 507-222-4043 241 C
anixon@carleton.edu
NIXON, Brad .... 301-687-4111 209 A
NIXON, Cheryl .... 617-287-5600 216 I
cheryl.nixon@umb.edu
NIXON, John, R .... 801-585-0806 472 P
john.nixon@utah.edu
NIXON, Katie .... 731-989-6672 432 C
knixon@fhu.edu

NIXON, Lauren .... 817-257-7113 461 A
l.e.nixon@tcu.edu
NIXON, Leah .... 616-234-3535 230 F
commdept@grcc.edu
NIXON, Matthew .... 714-556-3610.. 72 F
matthew.nixon@vanguard.edu
NIXON, Paul .... 740-397-6868 366 B
paul.nixon@mvnu.edu
NIXON, Russell, T .... 215-702-4392 391 C
rnixon@cairn.edu
NIXON, Terry .... 325-793-4721 452 F
tnixon@mcm.edu
NIXON, Valerie .... 607-587-3985 328 F
nixonvb@alfredstate.edu
NJIE, Valerie .... 412-402-9779 389 I
vnjie@mcg-btc.org
NJOGU, Wamucii .... 773-442-5420 147 G
w-njogu@neiu.edu
NKULU, Cedric .... 931-424-4058 433 E
cnkulu@martinmethodist.edu
NKUMSAH, Nancy .... 304-766-3000 505 A
NNADI, Eucharia, E .... 702-968-2038 280 B
ennadi@roseman.edu
NOACK, Kelly .... 309-794-7477 133 G
kellynoack@augustana.edu
NOAH, Tara .... 660-359-3948 264 H
tnoah@mail.ncmissouri.edu
NOBILE, Bryan .... 601-643-8468 252 G
bryan.nobile@colin.edu
NOBILE, Bryan .... 601-643-8318 252 G
bryan.nobile@colin.edu
NOBLE, Barbara .... 314-340-3621 260 H
nobleb@hssu.edu
NOBLE, Darren .... 952-446-4352 242 A
nobled@crown.edu
NOBLE, Doug .... 540-654-1235 486 D
dnoble@umw.edu
NOBLE, Rachel .... 727-376-6911 112 G
rachel.noble@trinitycollege.edu
NOBLE, Ronald .... 503-883-2602 383 H
rnoble@linfield.edu
NOBLE, Scott .... 307-778-4372 516 N
snoble@lccc.wy.edu
NOBLE, Seth .... 970-542-3248.. 81 A
seth.noble@morgancc.edu
NOBLE, Shlomo .... 585-473-2810 330 I
NOBLE-GOODMAN,
Stuart .... 503-534-4008 384 B
snoblegoodman@marylhurst.edu
NOBLES, Melissa .... 617-253-3450 221 C
NOBLES, Rodney .... 262-691-5362 515 B
rnobles@wctc.edu
NOBLES, Sheila .... 850-973-9432 104 D
nobless@nfcc.edu
NOBLES, Susan, Q .... 252-493-7210 345 E
snobles@email.pittcc.edu
NOBLES, Tammy .... 573-681-5036 261 H
noblest@lincolnu.edu
NOBLEZA, Deanna .... 215-503-2817 411 E
deanna.nobleza@jefferson.edu
NOBLITT, Jeffrey .... 818-677-2130.. 33 B
jeffrey.noblitt@csun.edu
NOBORIKAWA,
Ronald, M .... 253-535-8491 496 G
noborirm@plu.edu
NOCCIOLO, Mark .... 805-893-2491.. 70 B
mark.nocciolo@ucsb.edu
NOCE, Joe .... 215-780-1294 410 D
pcobookstore@mattmccoy.com
NOCELLA, Frank .... 781-280-3543 220 C
NOCELLA, Frank .... 973-877-3000 285 K
fnocella@essex.edu
NOCHTA, Linda .... 724-589-2155 411 D
lnochta@thiel.edu
NODA, Keisuke .... 845-752-3000 332 A
k.noda@uts.edu
NODARSE, Jaime .... 361-825-3324 460 A
jaime.nodarse@tamucc.edu
NODES, Jennifer .... 239-348-4710.. 95 C
jennifer.nodes@avemaria.edu
NODLAND, Rita .... 701-224-5692 354 F
rita.nodland@bismarckstate.edu
NOE, Audra .... 608-796-3040 512 R
aanoe@viterbo.edu
NOE, Belinda .... 256-306-2582.... 1 F
belinda.noe@calhoun.edu
NOE, Denise .... 815-394-3756 150 C
dnoe@rockford.edu
NOE, Diane .... 219-464-6700 165 D
diane.noe@valpo.edu
NOE, Lori .... 618-842-3711 140 C
noel@iecc.edu
NOEL, Abraham .... 651-696-6000 243 B
NOEL, Amy .... 252-246-1275 347 H
anoel@wilsoncc.edu
NOEL, JR., J. Andrew ... 607-255-8832 306 B
jan16@cornell.edu

NOEL, Norma .... 575-646-7793 295 B
nnoel@nmsu.edu
NOEL, Shawn .... 732-224-2044 284 B
snoel@brookdalecc.edu
NOEL, Terry .... 724-532-5095 410 B
terry.noel@email.stvincent.edu
NOEL, Terry .... 724-805-2095 410 C
terry.noel@stvincent.edu
NOEL-ELKINS, Amelia ... 309-438-3217 140 L
anoelel@ilstu.edu
NOEVERE, Michelle .... 252-249-1851 345 C
mnoevere@pamlicocc.edu
NOFFSINGER,
Charles, A .... 814-863-1892 403 F
can23@psu.edu
NOFFSINGER-FRAZIER,
Nicole .... 931-598-1325 436 A
nanoffsi@sewnee.edu
NOFTSINGER, Mark, P .. 540-375-2283 484 H
noftsinger@roanoke.edu
NOGLE, Ryan .... 716-851-1281 307 I
nogle@ecc.edu
NOHLGREN, Bethany .... 845-758-7099 298 I
nohlgren@bard.edu
NOHLGREN, Bethany .... 413-644-4400 211 B
NOHNER, OSB, Sharon 320-363-5285 241 I
snohner@csbsju.edu
NOHRIA, Nitin .... 617-495-6550 215 G
nnohria@hbs.edu
NOJAN, Mehran .... 315-312-2345 327 D
mehran.nojan@oswego.edu
NOLAN, Alana .... 906-487-7309 230 B
alana.nolan@finlandia.edu
NOLAN, Beth .... 202-994-6503.. 92 A
bnolan@gwu.edu
NOLAN, Brian .... 301-447-5223 206 B
nolan@msmary.edu
NOLAN, Christina .... 973-748-9000 284 A
christina_nolan@bloomfield.edu
NOLAN, Dan .... 678-407-5711 119 F
dnolan@ggc.edu
NOLAN, David .... 817-257-6863 461 A
d.nolan@tcu.edu
NOLAN, Deborah .... 410-704-2452 209 C
dnolan@towson.edu
NOLAN, Deborah, O ...... 610-409-3586 413 H
dnolan@ursinus.edu
NOLAN, Jamie .... 315-415-8514 282 F
jamie.nolan@unh.edu
NOLAN, Jim .... 505-467-6821 296 F
jimnolan@swc.edu
NOLAN, Judy .... 914-251-6067 328 B
judy.nolan@purchase.edu
NOLAN, Kelly .... 310-544-6419.. 59 E
kelly.nolan@usw.salvationarmy.org
NOLAN, Kiara .... 305-428-5674 104 A
knolan@aii.edu
NOLAN, Lisa, K .... 706-542-3461 127 A
lisa.nolan@uga.edu
NOLAN, Roberta .... 267-502-6073 390 F
roberta.nolan@brynathyn.edu
NOLAN, Terrance .... 212-998-2257 318 D
terrance.nolan@nyu.edu
NOLAN, Tiffany .... 660-831-4622 264 A
nolant@moval.edu
NOLAN, Valerie .... 716-286-8339 318 F
vnolan@niagara.edu
NOLAN-WEISS,
Sharon, E .... 716-645-2266 325 B
senolan@buffalo.edu
NOLAND, Brian, E .... 423-439-4211 431 H
president@etsu.edu
NOLAND, Lynn .... 509-777-3701 500 H
lnoland@whitworth.edu
NOLASCO, Maria .... 787-841-2000 525 J
mnolasco@pucpr.edu
NOLD, Letha .... 816-271-4582 264 B
lnold@missouriwestern.edu
NOLDER, Deborah .... 606-759-7141 186 E
debbie.nolder@kctcs.edu
NOLDNER, Tracy .... 605-367-7487 429 C
tracy.noldner@southeasttech.edu
NOLDON, Denise .... 323-241-5273.. 49 E
NOLES, Jody .... 334-291-4922.... 1 H
jody.noles@cv.edu
NOLING-AUTH, Jamie .... 503-554-2321 383 C
jnolingauth@georgefox.edu
NOLL, Carol .... 719-384-6824.. 81 G
carol.noll@ojc.edu
NOLL, Cheryl .... 912-650-5648 125 H
cnoll@southuniversity.edu
NOLL, Eric .... 518-388-6108 332 B
nolle@union.edu
NOLL SORG, Carolyn .... 440-646-8114 373 B
cnollsorg@ursuline.edu
NOLLAN, Damond .... 919-530-6399 350 D
dnollan@nccu.edu

NOLLAN, Richard .... 806-743-1048 463 E
richard.nollan@ttuhsc.edu
NOLON, Sean .... 802-831-1376 476 G
snolon@vrmontlaw.edu
NOLT, Danelle .... 212-812-4045 317 E
dnolt@nycda.edu
NOLT, David .... 406-496-4760 272 E
dnolt@mtech.edu
NOLTE, Beth .... 573-681-5194 261 H
noltem@lincolnu.edu
NOLTE, JR., Harold, E .. 620-227-9378 176 N
hnolte@dc3.edu
NOLTE, Jim .... 802-828-8512 476 F
jim.nolte@vcfa.edu
NOLTEMEYER,
J. Patrick .... 859-238-5218 184 C
patrick.noltemeyer@centre.edu
NOMURA,
Christopher, T .... 315-470-6606 328 D
ctnomura@esf.edu
NOMURA, Cory .... 909-748-8066.. 71 H
cory_nomura@redlands.edu
NONAKA, Conrad .... 808-734-9539 130 C
conradn@hawaii.edu
NONDORF, James .... 773-702-4101 153 F
jnondorf@uchicago.edu
NONEMAKER, Jeffrey .... 909-593-3511.. 70 E
jnonemaker@laverne.edu
NONEMAKER, Scott ...... 315-792-3285 332 H
scnonema@utica.edu
NONN, Lidia .... 920-465-2565 510 E
nonnl@uwgb.edu
NONNAMAKER, John .... 504-314-2188 196 D
jnonnama@tulane.edu
NOOK, Mark, A .... 319-273-2566 167 A
mark.nook@uni.edu
NOOKS, Kirk, A .... 816-604-2044 262 I
kirk.nooks@mcckc.edu
NOON, Edward .... 414-443-8871 513 A
skip.noon@wlc.edu
NOON, Molly .... 712-325-3306 170 K
mnoon@iwcc.edu
NOONAN, Brigid .... 585-389-2396 316 D
bnoonan8@naz.edu
NOONAN, Claire .... 708-524-6860 137 F
cnoonan@dom.edu
NOONAN, Daniel .... 860-727-6902.. 87 B
dnoonan@goodwin.edu
NOONAN, John .... 919-660-4252 337 C
john.noonan@duke.edu
NOONE, Anne .... 570-208-5899 398 D
aenoone@kings.edu
NOONE, Kristin .... 860-297-2059.. 88 E
kristin.noone@trincoll.edu
NOONE, Pamela, K .... 570-577-7136 390 H
noone@bucknell.edu
NOONEN, Joe .... 740-392-6868 366 B
joe.noonen@mvnu.edu
NOONEN, Joe .... 740-397-6868 366 B
joe.noonen@mvnu.edu
NOONKESTER, Myron ... 601-318-6118 256 I
myron.noonkester@wmcarey.edu
NORCIA, Lisa .... 201-200-2335 287 F
lnorcia@njcu.edu
NORCINI, Heather .... 610-341-5890 394 E
hnorcini@eastern.edu
NORCROSS, Dawn .... 607-753-2302 327 A
dawn.norcross@cortland.edu
NORCROSS, Paul, W ...... 315-464-4361 326 B
norcrossp@upstate.edu
NORCROSS, Robert .... 760-757-2121.. 52 F
rnorcross@miracosta.edu
NORD, Elonda .... 701-662-1533 355 A
elonda.nord@lrsc.edu
NORD, Elonda .... 701-662-1513 355 A
elonda.nord@lrsc.edu
NORD, Sheldon .... 503-375-7000 383 A
snord@corban.edu
NORDBY, Shawn .... 402-461-5177 275 D
NORDE, Tiffany .... 616-392-8555 239 J
tiffany@westernsem.edu
NORDEEN, Mark .... 307-855-2140 516 I
mark.nordeen@cwc.edu
NORDGREN, Joeseph .... 409-880-8508 462 C
joe.nordgren@lamar.edu
NORDICK, Pat .... 218-299-6821 245 H
pat.nordick@minnesota.edu
NORDIN, Becky .... 612-659-6712 245 F
becky.nordin@minneapolis.edu
NORDLAND, Jeffrey .... 585-245-5606 327 B
nordland@geneseo.edu
NORDMAN, Stephanie .. 785-442-6008 178 C
sharshberger@highlandcc.edu
NORDMAN, Tyler .... 785-442-6039 178 C
tnordman@highlandcc.edu
NORDMANN, Andrea .... 817-257-5520 461 A
a.nordmann@tcu.edu
NORDMANN, Keith .... 888-980-9151 486 B

NORDONE, JR., James 940-552-6291 469 F jnordone@vernoncollege.edu
NORDSTROM, Jennifer 815-226-3383 150 C jnordstrom@rockford.edu
NORDSTROM, Terrence 510-869-6649 59 F tnordstrom@samuelmerritt.edu
NORDT, Lee, C 254-710-3361 444 B lee_nordt@baylor.edu
NOREEN, Jody 614-947-6077 362 A jody.noreen@franklin.edu
NOREN, Patricia 516-572-7087 316 C patricia.noren@ncc.edu
NOREUIL, Margaret 608-663-2820 507 D mnoreuil@edgewood.edu
NORFLEET, Margie 252-246-1210 347 H mnorfleet@wilsoncc.edu
NORIAN, Nicole 828-232-5117 351 A nnorian@unca.edu
NORIN, Michele 848-445-4636 290 A michele.narin@rutgers.edu
NORIN, Michele 848-932-4636 290 C michele.norin@rutgers.edu
NORISE, Hershey 773-602-5484 135 L hnorise@ccc.edu
NORLAND, Gretchen 785-227-3380 175 E norlandg@bethanylb.edu
NORLEN, Tracy, C 206-281-2977 498 B tcnorlen@spu.edu
NORLIEN, Cheryl, A 320-222-5638 247 B cheryl.norlien@ridgewater.edu
NORMAN, Anne, S 920-832-6578 507 L anne.s.norman@lawrence.edu
NORMAN, Cheryl, R 651-631-5247 251 C crnorman@unwsp.edu
NORMAN, Chris 614-384-4656 370 M cnorman@tlsohio.edu
NORMAN, David 903-813-2499 443 F dnorman@austincollege.edu
NORMAN, Dax 301-226-9086 518 C dax.norman@dodiis.mil
NORMAN, Eric 617-333-2302 214 B eric.norman@curry.edu
NORMAN, Eric, M 260-481-6603 160 D norman@ipfw.edu
NORMAN, Linda 615-343-8876 440 D linda.norman@vanderbilt.edu
NORMAN, Lisa 909-382-4041 59 G lnorman@sbccd.cc.ca.us
NORMAN, Lisa 626-585-7282 56 B lnorman@pasadena.edu
NORMAN, Margie, A 903-813-2247 443 F mnorman@austincollege.edu
NORMAN, Moses 404-880-8495 117 H mnorman@cau.edu
NORMAN, Nancy 480-858-9100 16 D n.norman@scnm.edu
NORMAN, Paul, A 919-516-4353 348 G panorman@st-aug.edu
NORMAN, Peter, E 815-599-3465 139 F pete.norman@highland.edu
NORMAN, Robert, S 405-585-5805 377 A stan.norman@okbu.edu
NORMAN, Terry, W 608-796-3900 512 R twnorman@viterbo.edu
NORMAN, Tom 507-389-1268 246 A thomas.norman-1@mnsu.edu
NORMAN-ARMSTRONG, Mona Lee 575-769-4089 293 M monalee.armstrong@clovis.edu
NORMAN TILL, Danette 260-982-5306 162 Q dntill@manchester.edu
NORMANDIN, Denis 603-271-6484 280 N dnormandin@ccsnh.edu
NORMANDIN, Karen 207-453-5019 200 A knormandin@kvcc.me.edu
NORMANDY, Elizabeth 910-521-6180 351 E elizabeth.normandy@uncp.edu
NORMANN, Karen, R 484-664-3496 402 F karennormann@muhlenberg.edu
NORMORE, Clinton 660-626-2827 257 A cnormore@atsu.edu
NORNHOLM, Rick 619-594-1889 34 B nornholm@mail.sdsu.edu
NORQUIST, Bruce, R 312-329-4192 146 B bruce.norquist@moody.edu
NORRIE, James 717-815-1423 415 G jnorrie@ycp.edu
NORRIS, Adam 504-280-6939 194 F amnorris@uno.edu
NORRIS, Alfred 404-527-7747 122 B anorris@itc.edu
NORRIS, Brandee 740-376-4709 365 A bnn001@marietta.edu
NORRIS, Cheryl 931-393-1849 437 C cnorris@mscc.edu
NORRIS, Darrell 517-787-8439 231 E norrisdarrellr@jccmi.edu
NORRIS, Deb 937-512-5182 370 A deb.norris@sinclair.edu
NORRIS, Debbie 601-925-3260 254 B dnorris@mc.edu
NORRIS, Debbie 601-925-3225 254 B dnorris@mc.edu
NORRIS, Dena 816-604-1527 262 F dena.norris@mcckc.edu
NORRIS, Elissa 912-478-7288 120 E enorris@georgiasouthern.edu
NORRIS, Emily 502-585-9911 189 B enorris@spalding.edu
NORRIS, Gail 585-275-2758 332 E gnorris@admin.rochester.edu
NORRIS, Heather 828-262-2058 349 H hulburthm@appstate.edu
NORRIS, Helen 714-744-7848 36 G hnorris@chapman.edu
NORRIS, Jeffery 901-843-3762 435 L norrisj@rhodes.edu
NORRIS, John 704-330-1448 338 I jnorris@jcsu.edu
NORRIS, Joye 417-836-4127 263 H joyenorris@missouristate.edu
NORRIS, Lee 336-334-0398 351 D clnorris@uncg.edu
NORRIS, Lesa 630-801-7900 155 C lnorris@waubonsee.edu
NORRIS, Lisa 731-352-6437 430 E norrisl@bethelu.edu
NORRIS, Mark, M 574-372-5100 158 B norrismm@grace.edu
NORRIS, Marly 415-482-1944 41 J marly.norris@dominican.edu
NORRIS, Mary 860-768-4716 89 C norris@hartford.edu
NORRIS, Nancy, E 828-448-3150 347 F nnorris@wpcc.edu
NORRIS, Patricia, D 336-750-2900 352 D norrispd@wssu.edu
NORRIS, Robert, F 630-752-5559 155 F bob.norris@wheaton.edu
NORRIS, Sababu, C 716-888-2787 300 G norris@canisius.edu
NORRIS, Shawn 225-752-4233 191 I admissions@iticollege.edu
NORRIS, Steven 816-235-2672 268 D norrissp@umkc.edu
NORRIS, Terry 702-651-5813 278 N terry.norris@csn.edu
NORRIS, Todd 574-284-4560 163 J tnorris@saintmarys.edu
NORRIS, Travis 770-650-3000 93 B
NORRIS, Veta 810-766-4203 227 F vnorri01@baker.edu
NORRIS HALL, Sarah 206-543-6277 499 D sahall@uw.edu
NORRIS-LANE, Virginia 830-896-5411 456 D vanorrislane@schreiner.edu
NORRIS-PAULISON, Robin 828-694-1746 341 B r_paulison@blueridge.edu
NORTH, Cecilia 802-635-1240 477 C cecilia.north@jsc.edu
NORTH, Greta 717-564-4112 390 A greta.north@brightwood.edu
NORTH, Jane, D 717-337-6011 396 A jnorth@gettysburg.edu
NORTH, Jon, D 913-971-3600 179 H jonnorth@mnu.edu
NORTH, Joshua 785-442-6023 178 C jnorth@highlandcc.edu
NORTH, Keith 406-657-1078 272 I keith.north@rocky.edu
NORTH, Linda 334-745-6437 3 G lnorth@suscc.edu
NORTH, Matthew 412-396-4075 394 D northm@duq.edu
NORTH, Mike 865-228-2303 437 F mnorth@pstcc.edu
NORTH, Paula 918-293-5240 378 B paula.north@okstate.edu
NORTH, Peter, C 717-337-6219 396 A pnorth@gettysburg.edu
NORTH, Stephen 337-521-8914 193 E stephen.north@solacc.edu
NORTHAM, Andrea 507-457-5024 248 C anortham@winona.edu
NORTHAM, Mark 307-766-6897 517 B mnortham@uwyo.edu
NORTHCUTT, David 706-419-1214 118 E david.northcutt@covenant.edu
NORTHCUTT, Larry 903-923-2117 448 J lnorthcutt@etbu.edu
NORTHERN, Norma 502-213-2559 186 C norma.northern@kctcs.edu
NORTHERN, Orathai 863-292-3645 105 F onorthern@polk.edu
NORTHINGTON, Adrienne 919-735-5151 347 E awnorthington@waynecc.edu
NORTHINGTON, LaToya 713-623-2040 443 C lrwilliams@aii.edu
NORTHINGTON, Vincent 803-376-5751 418 D vnorthington@allenuniversity.edu
NORTHOVER, Michael 971-722-8508 386 C michael.northover@pcc.edu
NORTHROP, Cathy 607-844-8222 331 D northrc@tompkinscortland.edu
NORTHUP, Laura 402-826-6773 274 E laura.northup@doane.edu
NORTHWOOD, Lisa 304-462-6182 504 B lisa.northwood@glenville.edu
NORTON, Alan 440-775-6453 367 B alan.norton@oberlin.edu
NORTON, Amy 563-588-6338 167 E amy.norton@clarke.edu
NORTON, Andrew 215-702-4318 391 C anorton@cairn.edu
NORTON, Beth 865-694-6728 437 F aenorton@pstcc.edu
NORTON, Clare 646-664-3620 301 A clare.norton@cuny.edu
NORTON, Daniel 601-266-4344 256 E daniel.norton@usm.edu
NORTON, Darryl, R 828-689-1248 339 G dnorton@mhu.edu
NORTON, David 760-366-5249 41 B dnorton@cmccd.edu
NORTON, David, P 352-392-9271 110 D dpnorton@ufl.edu
NORTON, Greg 773-777-4220 148 A gnorton@nc.edu
NORTON, H. Will 662-915-7146 256 C hwnorton@olemiss.edu
NORTON, Hanna 479-964-0583 18 G hnorton@atu.edu
NORTON, Holly 309-649-6050 152 G holly.norton@src.edu
NORTON, Jamie 260-665-4847 164 E nortonj@trine.edu
NORTON, Karen 617-228-2177 219 D kmnorton@bhcc.mass.edu
NORTON, Karen, M 617-228-2177 219 D kmnorton@bhcc.mass.edu
NORTON, Kay 970-351-2121 83 F kay.norton@unco.edu
NORTON, Lisa, M 812-877-8892 163 G olson@rose-hulman.edu
NORTON, Lizette 909-558-4040 48 H lnorton@llu.edu
NORTON, M. Grant 509-335-4505 499 G mg_norton@wsu.edu
NORTON, Melanie 765-658-4212 157 H melanienorton@depauw.edu
NORTON, Michael, E 515-294-5352 166 F mnorton@iastate.edu
NORTON, Mitzi 312-662-4002 133 A mnorton@adler.edu
NORTON, Noelle 619-260-4545 71 J norton@sandiego.edu
NORTON, Patrick 504-862-8698 196 D pjn@tulane.edu
NORTON, Ricky 903-223-3012 460 D ricky.norton@tamut.edu
NORTON, Robert 517-607-2687 231 C rnorton@hillsdale.edu
NORTON, Sheri, L 401-825-2311 416 B slnorton@ccri.edu
NORTON, Steve 309-341-5227 134 H snorton@sandburg.edu
NORTON, Susan 843-574-6211 424 G susan.norton@tridenttech.edu
NORTON, Susan, A 706-721-3777 116 B snorton@augusta.edu
NORTON, Timothy, A 770-720-5545 124 H tan@reinhardt.edu
NORVELL, Ali 828-694-1824 341 B a_norvell@blueridge.edu
NORVELL, Laura 202-885-8635 94 C lnorvell@wesleyseminary.edu
NORVOLD, Stacy 218-751-8670 249 G stacynorvold@oakhills.edu
NORWOOD, Aletia 308-635-3606 278 B norwooda@wncc.edu
NORWOOD, Bertha 210-486-2212 441 I bwebb@alamo.edu
NORWOOD, Cynthia 804-862-6100 484 F cnorwood@rbc.edu
NOSAL, Judith, S 860-723-0011 84 I nosalj@ct.edu
NOSEEP, Willie 307-855-2149 516 I wnoseep@cwc.edu
NOSEGBE, Isibor, J 703-891-1787 485 I ijnosegbe@standardcollege.edu
NOSEK, Gail 651-523-2511 242 E gnosek01@hamline.edu
NOSEWORTHY, John, H 507-266-4861 241 E noseworthy.john@mayo.edu
NOSS, Rebecca 845-675-5767 319 C rebecca.noss@nyack.edu
NOSTRAND, Dennis, L 813-253-6211 113 E dnostrand@ut.edu
NOSTROM, Kim 607-436-2563 325 E kim.nostrom@oneonta.edu
NOSTRUM, Rian 701-231-7890 354 D rian.nostrum@ndsu.edu
NOTA, Michele 401-874-2242 417 E mnota@uri.edu
NOTARESCHI, Rey, T 330-325-6796 366 F rtn@neomed.edu
NOTESTEIN, Mary 319-385-6204 170 J mary.notestein@iw.edu
NOTIS, Chana 845-362-3053 299 C cnotis@byts.edu
NOTO, Lisa 707-664-3019 35 A lisa.noto@sonoma.edu
NOTO, Robert, A 517-353-3530 233 G notor@msu.edu
NOTSON, Jeanne 505-566-3209 296 A notsonj@sanjuancollege.edu
NOTTKE, Janine 906-487-7267 230 B janine.nottke@finlandia.edu
NOURSE, Chris 740-245-7228 372 E cnourse@rio.edu
NOVAK, Amy, C 605-995-2601 427 A amnovak@dwu.edu
NOVAK, Bruce 972-883-2416 467 D bxn111230@utdallas.edu
NOVAK, Christina 773-834-2216 152 K cnovak@ttic.edu
NOVAK, Debbie 970-945-8691 77 M dnovak@coloradomtn.edu
NOVAK, Greg 314-792-6221 261 E gregnovak@kenrick.edu
NOVAK, Jackie 330-490-7319 373 F jnovak@walsh.edu
NOVAK, Jeffrey 608-262-6982 510 C novak4@wisc.edu
NOVAK, Jeffrey 570-702-8920 398 A jnovak@johnson.edu
NOVAK, Jerry 734-995-7340 229 A jerry.novak@cuaa.edu
NOVAK, John 219-980-6905 160 C jmnovak@iun.edu
NOVAK, Joshua 724-287-8711 390 J joshua.novak@bc3.edu
NOVAK, Linda 910-678-8225 343 B novakl@faytechcc.edu
NOVAK, Mark 661-654-2441 31 B mnovak@csub.edu
NOVAK, Mike 479-248-7236 19 F mnovak@ecollege.edu
NOVAK, Mike 570-702-8935 398 A mnovak@johnson.edu
NOVAK, Paul 724-738-2465 407 C paul.novak@sru.edu
NOVAK, Richard, J 848-932-0613 290 A richard.novak@rutgers.edu
NOVAK, Ross 570-348-6236 401 B rnovak@marywood.edu
NOVAK, Thomas 617-585-1308 222 H tom.novak@necmusic.edu
NOVAK, Thomas 617-585-1200 222 H tom.novak@necmusic.edu
NOVAKOV, Anna 925-631-4856 59 C anovakov@stmarys-ca.edu
NOVICK, Rona 212-960-5400 334 P rnovick1@yu.edu
NOVICKI, Elizabeth 336-917-5421 348 H elizabeth.novicki@salem.edu
NOVIELLO, Sheri, R 229-333-5959 127 H srnoviello@valdosta.edu
NOVITT, Priscilla 413-369-4044 214 A novitt@csld.edu
NOVO, Frank 617-964-1111 210 G fnovo@ants.edu
NOVOBILSKI, Andy 678-717-3698 127 B andy.novobilski@ung.edu
NOVOTNY, Alicia 620-450-2248 180 K alician@prattcc.edu
NOVOTNY, April 614-236-6565 358 A anovotny@capital.edu
NOVOTNY, Dorene 650-949-6210 43 D novotnydorene@fhda.edu
NOVOTNY, Jodi 425-235-2464 497 E jnovotny@rtc.edu
NOVOTNY, Michelle 914-654-5036 305 A mnovotny@cnr.edu
NOVOTNY, Rachel 808-956-8234 129 J novotny@hawaii.edu
NOVOTNY, Richard, J 440-525-7358 364 D rnovotny@lakelandcc.edu

NOWACZYK, Ronald ...... 301-687-4111 209 A
rhnowaczyk@frostburg.edu
NOWAK, Janice .... 904-470-8192.. 98 B
janice.nowak@ewc.edu
NOWAK, Meg .... 607-431-4501 309 E
nowakm@hartwick.edu
NOWAK, Megan .... 213-624-1200.. 42 N
mnowak@fidm.edu
NOWAK, Patricia .... 219-989-2220 163 E
nowak28@pnw.edu
NOWAK, Robert .... 262-243-2025 229 A
robert.nowak@cuw.edu
NOWAK, Robert, J .... 262-243-5700 507 C
robert.nowak@cuw.edu
NOWAK, Thomas, S ..... 845-848-4000 306 G
thomas.nowak@dc.edu
NOWAK, Tom .... 574-936-8898 155 L
tom.nowak@ancilla.edu
NOWAK, Tony, J .... 414-847-3240 508 G
tonynowak@miad.edu
NOWAKOWSKI,
Bernadette .... 413-265-2214 213 E
nowakowskib@elms.edu
NOWEL, OP, Mark, D ... 401-865-2649 416 E
mnowel@providence.edu
NOWELL, Cheryl .... 305-348-2434 109 D
nowell@fiu.edu
NOWELL, Jordan .... 701-349-5764 355 G
jnowell@trinitybiblecollege.edu
NOWICKI, Catherine ...... 260-459-4542 161 D
cnowicki@ibcfortwayne.edu
NOWICKI, OSB,
Douglas, R .... 724-805-2146 410 C
douglas.nowicki@stvincent.edu
NOWICKI, Stacy, A .... 269-337-5750 231 F
stacy.nowicki@kzoo.edu
NOWICKI, Stephen .... 919-668-3420 337 C
snowicki@duke.edu
NOWLIN, Brian .... 562-985-5537.. 32 C
brian.nowlin@csulb.edu
NOWLIN, Jack .... 806-742-3990 463 D
jack.nowlin@ttu.edu
NOWLIN, Steve .... 626-396-2397.. 26 L
stephen.nowlin@artcenter.edu
NOWOGORSKI, Barbara 570-961-7835 399 A
nowogorskib@lackawanna.edu
NOYES, Cynthia .... 269-749-7144 236 A
cnoyes@olivetcollege.edu
NUCCI, John, A .... 617-973-1103 224 I
jnucci@suffolk.edu
NUCCIARONE, Mary, B . 574-631-6436 165 A
nucciarone.2@nd.edu
NUCKOLS, Melanie, L ... 336-734-7332 343 C
mnuckols@forsythtech.edu
NUDELMAN, Felice .... 937-769-1342 356 G
fnudelman@antioch.edu
NUDI, Joel .... 518-861-2558 314 B
jnudi@mariacollege.edu
NUELL, Nancy .... 240-567-7958 205 F
nancy.nuell@montgomerycollege.edu
NUESELL, Lisa, M .... 919-381-6912 349 F
lnuesell@umo.edu
NUFER, Ken .... 719-549-3474.. 81 M
ken.nufer@pueblocc.edu
NUGEN, Deb .... 402-399-2442 274 A
dnugen@csm.edu
NUGENT, Barli .... 212-799-5000 312 B
NUGENT, John, D .... 860-439-5266.. 86 H
john.nugent@conncoll.edu
NUGENT, Kari .... 815-802-8256 142 C
knugent@kcc.edu
NUGENT, Kim .... 918-495-7473 378 H
knugent@oru.edu
NUGENT, Kirk .... 256-726-8324.... 6 E
krnugent@oakwood.edu
NUGENT, Megan .... 503-251-2836 387 I
mnugent@uws.edu
NUKAYA, Bruce .... 208-732-6352 131 I
bnukaya@csi.edu
NULL, David .... 608-265-1988 510 C
dnull@library.wisc.edu
NULL, Wesley .... 254-710-3601 444 B
wesley_null@baylor.edu
NUMRICH, Camille .... 401-825-2237 416 B
cnumrich@ccri.edu
NUNEMAKER, Christine 207-834-7593 201 E
christine.nunemaker@maine.edu
NUNES, Grafton, J .... 216-421-7410 359 J
gnunes@cia.edu
NUNES, John, A .... 914-337-9300 305 F
NUNES, Mary Louise .... 508-999-8233 217 A
mnunes2@umassd.edu
NUNEZ, Al .... 312-341-2187 150 D
anunez13@roosevelt.edu
NUNEZ, Awilda .... 787-769-2043 527 H
awilda.nunez@upr.edu
NUNEZ, Elaine .... 787-786-3030 526 F
enunez@ucb.edu.pr
NUNEZ, Elsa .... 860-465-5222.. 84 I
nuneze@easternct.edu
NUNEZ, Elsa, M .... 860-465-5222.. 84 K
nunez@easternct.edu
NUNEZ, Haydee .... 630-637-5142 147 E
hnunez@noctrl.edu
NUNEZ, Ivon .... 973-596-3478 288 A
nunez@njit.edu
NUNEZ, Jordy, H .... 701-349-3621 355 G
jnunez@trinitybiblecollege.edu
NUNEZ, Jose .... 650-358-6836.. 61 Q
nunezj@smccd.edu
NUNEZ, Jose Ramon .... 714-992-7030.. 54 A
jnunez@fullcoll.edu
NUNEZ, Juan .... 936-294-1910 462 F
jmn019@shsu.edu
NUNEZ, Lucia .... 608-246-6434 514 A
lnunez1@madisoncollege.edu
NUNEZ, Rachel .... 540-362-6271 481 F
rnunez@hollins.edu
NUNEZ, Steve, C .... 815-835-6263 151 E
steve.c.nunez@svcc.edu
NUNEZ, William .... 402-472-2116 277 G
wnunez2@unl.edu
NUNEZ, William .... 402-472-2116 277 G
bill.nunez@unl.edu
NUNEZ, Yancy .... 806-716-2338 456 F
ynunez@southplainscollege.edu
NUNLEY, Beth .... 815-802-8142 142 C
bnunley@kcc.edu
NUNLEY, Ernest, L .... 276-739-2510 490 A
enunley@vhcc.edu
NUNN, Dana .... 970-248-1868.. 77 K
dnunn@coloradomesa.edu
NUNN, Gaylene .... 254-519-5458 459 D
nunn@tamuct.edu
NUNN, Gaylenne .... 254-519-5458 459 D
nunn@tamuct.edu
NUNN, Lori, A .... 540-674-3615 488 G
lnunn@nr.edu
NUNNA, Ramakrishna ... 559-278-2500.. 32 A
rnunna@csufresno.edu
NUNNALLY, Delecia ...... 209-954-5151.. 61 B
dnunnally@deltacollege.edu
NUOSCE, Mary .... 239-513-1122 101 O
mnuosce@hodges.edu
NURNBERGER,
Charles, A .... 757-825-2717 489 G
nurnbergerc@tncc.edu
NURSE, Learie .... 303-546-3506.. 81 B
lnurse@naropa.edu
NUSBAUM, Nancy .... 512-245-2244 463 A
nn01@txstate.edu
NUSS, Shelley .... 706-713-2188 127 A
snuss@uga.edu
NUSSBAUM, Daniel .... 860-231-5770.. 89 E
dnussbaum@usj.edu
NUSSBAUM, Renee .... 419-755-4772 366 E
rnussbau@ncstatecollege.edu
NUSSEL, Jay .... 810-424-5474 238 B
nusselj@umflint.edu
NUSSER, Sarah, M .... 515-294-6344 166 F
nusser@iastate.edu
NUTEFALL, Jennifer .... 408-554-6829.. 62 F
jnutefall@scu.edu
NUTI, Larry .... 925-631-4901.. 59 C
lnuti@stmarys-ca.edu
NUTT, Barbara .... 816-936-8729 266 K
bnutt@saintlukescollege.edu
NUTT, Jill .... 616-395-7765 231 D
nutt@hope.edu
NUTT, Lee Ann .... 281-351-3644 452 C
leeann.nutt@lonestar.edu
NUTT, Rick .... 740-826-8121 366 C
rnutt@muskingum.edu
NUTT, Roger .... 239-280-1603.. 95 C
roger.nutt@avemaria.edu
NUTTER, Alberta .... 405-733-7979 379 F
anutter@rose.edu
NUTTER, April, H .... 606-783-9351 188 C
a.nutter@moreheadstate.edu
NUTTER, Jeff .... 740-389-4636 365 B
nutterj@mtc.edu
NUTTER, Mark .... 740-374-8716 373 G
mnutter@wscc.edu
NUTTER, Michelle .... 405-733-7300 379 F
mnutter@rose.edu
NUTTER, Sarah .... 541-346-3300 387 F
snutter@uoregon.edu
NUTTER, Susan, K .... 919-515-7188 350 E
susan_nutter@ncsu.edu
NUTTY, David .... 207-780-4276 201 H
david.nutty@maine.edu
NUZZO, Brittany .... 304-296-8282 505 E
bnuzzo@wvjc.edu
NUZZO, Jane .... 212-592-2302 324 A
jnuzzo@sva.edu
NUÑEZ, Cheryl .... 360-475-7740 496 F
cnunez@olympic.edu
NWAKEZE, Peter .... 718-933-6700 315 K
pnwakeze@monroecollege.edu
NWANGWU, Winifred .... 401-874-1000 417 E
winny@uri.edu
NWANKWO, Charles ..... 480-732-7020.. 13 E
charles.nwankwo@cgc.edu
NWANNE, Andrew, I ..... 575-234-9215 295 D
anwanne@nmsu.edu
NWARIAKU, Fiemu, E ... 214-648-9968 469 E
fiemu.nwariku@utsouthwestern.edu
NWOKEAFOR, Cosmos . 301-860-3232 208 E
cnwokeafor@bowiestate.edu
NWOSU, Peter, O .... 404-880-8754 117 H
pnwosu@cau.edu
NWOSU, Veronica, C .... 919-530-5055 350 D
vcnwosu@nccu.edu
NYACHUBA, Daniel .... 903-927-3390 471 B
dnyachuba@wileyc.edu
NYARDY, OSB,
Jeffrey, S .... 724-532-6600 410 C
jsnyardy@gmail.com
NYBERG,
Christopher, L .... 315-684-6083 329 F
nybergcl@morrisville.edu
NYBERG, Connie .... 307-855-2207 516 I
cnyberg@cwc.edu
NYE, Barney .... 801-863-7194 473 D
nyewi@uvu.edu
NYE, Jaime .... 415-565-8909.. 68 I
jnye@uchastings.edu
NYE, Jamey .... 916-568-3031.. 50 E
nye@losrios.edu
NYE, Judith .... 732-571-3637 287 C
nye@monmouth.edu
NYE, Robert .... 585-785-1201 308 D
robert.nye@flcc.edu
NYGAARD, Steven .... 310-258-5522.. 50 J
steven.nygaard@lmu.edu
NYGREN, McKenzie .... 918-542-8441 376 F
mckenzie.nygren@neo.edu
NYHAMMER, Diane .... 630-466-7900 155 C
dnyhammer@waubonsee.edu
NYHAN, Jeff .... 602-206-8220 280 L
jnyhan@ccsnh.edu
NYIRENDA, Stanley, M . 410-651-6672 208 C
smnyirenda@umes.edu
NYLAND, Gerald .... 231-777-0315 234 G
gerald.nyland@muskegoncc.edu
NYLEN, John .... 847-578-3252 150 E
john.nylen@rosalindfranklin.edu
NYPAVER, David .... 330-972-6876 371 C
nypaver@uakron.edu
NYQUIST, J. Paul .... 312-329-4112 146 B
paul.nyquist@moody.edu
NYRE, Joseph, E .... 914-633-2203 311 B
jnyre@iona.edu
NYROP, Karin .... 206-543-4150 499 D
knyrop@uw.edu
NYSTROM, Ellen .... 210-567-2640 468 E
nystrom@uthscsa.edu
NYUL, Renata .... 617-373-7666 223 D
NZAMUTUNA, Issmael .. 951-785-2006.. 47 F
inzamutu@lasierra.edu
NZEH, Okoroafor .... 706-821-8331 124 C
onzeh@paine.edu
NZEOGWU, Okeleke ...... 702-968-1659 280 B
onzeogwu@roseman.edu

O

O"BRIEN, Jennifer .... 412-291-6353 389 F
jlobrien@aii.edu
OAKES, Barbee .... 336-758-3106 353 A
oaks@wfu.edu
OAKES, Mary .... 312-369-6802 136 H
moakes@colum.edu
OAKES, Susan .... 504-865-2011 194 G
soakes@loyno.edu
OAKES, Tammy, K .... 260-399-7700 165 B
toakes@sf.edu
OAKLAND, Shauna, K ... 301-243-2118 518 C
shauna.oakland@dodiis.mil
OAKLEY, Christina .... 561-912-1211.. 98 F
OAKLEY, Jennifer .... 201-360-4002 286 E
joakley@hccc.edu
OAKMAN, Tommy .... 828-694-1725 341 B
t_oakman@blueridge.edu
OAKS, Beth .... 605-642-6411 428 F
beth.oaks@bhsu.edu
OAKS, Diane, G .... 949-451-5277.. 64 I
doaks@ivc.edu
OAKS, Geneva .... 951-343-4702.. 28 G
gcooperoaks@calbaptist.edu
OAKS, Nick .... 605-642-6545 428 F
nicholas.oaks@bhsu.edu
OAKS SMITH, Tonya ..... 870-230-5348.. 19 H
smithto@hsu.edu
OANES, Laura .... 507-457-6909 250 B
loanes@smumn.edu
OARD, Tasha .... 406-586-3585 271 E
tasha.oard@montanabiblecollege.edu
OATES, Andrea .... 229-931-2705 125 G
aoates@southgatech.edu
OATES, Bruce .... 847-635-1753 148 D
boates@oakton.edu
OATES, Evangela .... 845-434-5750 330 F
eoates@sunysullivan.edu
OATES, Justin .... 201-216-3495 291 G
justin.oates@stevens.edu
OATES, Nadine .... 716-652-8900 300 L
noates@cks.edu
OATES, Richard .... 678-717-3947 127 B
richard.oates@ung.edu
OATES, Scott, F .... 804-828-9124 487 E
sfoates@vcu.edu
OATIS, Steve .... 479-979-1338.. 23 J
soatis@ozarks.edu
OBA, Saichi, T .... 907-450-8146.... 9 I
stoba@alaska.edu
OBBINK, Kim .... 406-994-6550 272 A
kobbink@montana.edu
OBER, Jay .... 305-442-9223 104 B
jober@mrc.edu
OBER, Jeffrey .... 208-792-2225 132 C
jrober@lcsc.edu
OBER, Roxanne .... 412-346-2100 408 B
rober@pia.edu
OBER LAMBERT,
Janet, L .... 800-287-8822 156 D
oberlja@bethanyseminary.edu
OBEREM, Graham .... 760-750-4050.. 33 E
oberem@csusm.edu
OBERFELD, Jeremy .... 312-236-9000 145 H
OBERFELDT, Kathleen ... 718-390-3435 333 D
koberfel@wagner.edu
OBERG, Beth .... 217-479-7130 144 I
beth.oberg@mac.edu
OBERGFELL, Ann .... 260-481-6100 160 D
obergfea@ipfw.edu
OBERHELMAN, Don ...... 805-756-1407.. 30 K
obe@calpoly.edu
OBERHOLTZER, Brent .... 717-867-6111 399 J
oberholt@lvc.edu
OBERHOLTZER, Curt ..... 920-206-2372 508 A
curt.oberholtzer@mbu.edu
OBERLANDER, Cyril ...... 707-826-3441.. 34 A
cyril.oberlander@humboldt.edu
OBERLANDER, Janell .... 970-824-1102.. 78 H
janell.oberlander@cncc.edu
OBERMAN, Anne .... 320-363-5999 241 I
aoberman@csbsju.edu
OBERMARK, Julie .... 618-545-3333 142 D
jobermark@kaskaskia.edu
OBERMEISTER,
Tuvia, M .... 718-377-0777 320 E
OBERMEYER, Carole ..... 316-295-5779 177 F
obermeyer@friends.edu
OBERQUELL, Christian .. 406-265-3761 272 C
coberquell@msun.edu
OBERSTEIN, Leonard ..... 410-484-7200 206 C
loberstein@nirc.edu
OBERSTEIN, Ron .... 510-780-4500.. 48 D
OBERT, Brian .... 308-345-8109 275 I
obertb@mpcc.edu
OBI, Stacey .... 717-728-2248 392 B
staceyobi@centralpenn.edu
OBIELODAN, James, B . 502-597-6915 187 E
james.obielodan@kysu.edu
OBILADE, Sandra, O .... 270-686-4209 183 J
sandra.obilade@brescia.edu
OBIN, Jason .... 773-508-8643 144 D
jobin@luc.edu
OBISESAN, Thomas, O .. 202-806-2550.. 92 C
tobisesan@howard.edu
OBLANDER, Douglas ..... 843-208-8120 425 B
oblander@uscb.edu
OBLANDER, Frances, W 912-650-5684 125 H
foblander@southuniversity.edu
OBLOY, Leonard .... 248-683-0446 237 E
lobloy@sscms.edu
OBRYCKI, Marybeth ...... 973-290-4460 285 A
mobrycki@cse.edu
OBSNIUK, Karen .... 734-432-5648 233 C
kobsniuk@madonna.edu
OBST, Cheryl .... 619-201-8951.. 65 C
registrar@socalsem.edu
OBSTA, Kim .... 361-572-6410 470 A
kim.obsta@victoriacollege.edu
OBURN, Martha .... 713-718-8670 450 D
martha.oburn@hccs.edu
OCAMPO, Arturo .... 714-808-4830.. 53 L
OCAMPO, Carlota .... 202-884-9209.. 93 C
ocampoc@trinitydc.edu

OLD CROW, William ... 406-638-3185 271 C
oldcrowb@lbhc.edu
OLDARCE, Cody ... 919-761-2285 349 C
registrar@sebts.edu
OLDENKAMP, Mike ... 712-324-5061 172 E
mikeo@nwicc.edu
OLDFIELD, Annemarie ... 575-624-7001 294 A
annemarie.oldfield@roswell.enmu.edu
OLDFIELD, Curt ... 309-649-6200 152 G
curt.oldfield@src.edu
OLDFIELD, Melody, K ... 541-737-3871 385 F
university.marketing@oregonstate.edu
OLDHAM, Alecia, R ... 502-597-6657 187 E
alecia.oldham@kysu.edu
OLDHAM, Deborah ... 601-484-8636 253 G
doldham@meridiancc.edu
OLDHAM, Philip, B ... 931-372-3241 438 F
poldham@tntech.edu
OLDHAM, Robin ... 502-863-8031 184 I
robin_oldham@georgetowncollege.edu
OLDHAM, Todd, M ... 585-685-6192 315 L
toldham@monroecc.edu
OLDMIXON, Mark ... 907-474-5886.. 10 B
mtoldmixon@alaska.edu
OLDS, Carole ... 719-502-3249.. 81 H
carole.olds@ppcc.edu
OLDS, Scott ... 559-244-5957.. 66 E
scott.olds@scccd.edu
OLEEN, Clair ... 785-227-3380 175 E
oleenc@bethanylb.edu
OLEGERIIL, Jay ... 680-488-2471 520 E
jayo@palau.edu
OLEJNICZAK, Sarah ... 414-930-3372 509 B
olejnics@mtmary.edu
OLEJNICZAK-CAUSHAJ,
Joanna ... 248-706-5363 237 E
jolejniczak@sscms.edu
OLEN, Simcha ... 718-252-6333 334 N
OLENICK, Jennifer ... 832-813-6512 452 C
jennifer.olenick@lonestar.edu
OLENS, Sam ... 470-578-6033 122 C
solens@kennesaw.edu
OLER, Gregory, S ... 302-831-8913.. 90 I
gregoler@udel.edu
OLES, Brian, M ... 508-565-1914 224 H
boles@stonehill.edu
OLESKA, Carla ... 413-265-2496 213 E
oleskac@elms.edu
OLESNAVAGE, John ... 414-425-8300 509 I
jolesnavage@shsst.edu
OLESZEWSKI, Susan ... 215-780-1397 410 D
OLEVNIK, Courtney ... 814-824-2000 401 J
colevnik@mercyhurst.edu
OLFMAN, Lorne ... 909-607-3035.. 37 L
lorne.olfman@cgu.edu
OLGUIN, Javier, E ... 972-860-5306 447 I
javiereolguin@dcccd.edu
OLIAN, Judy, D ... 310-825-7982.. 69 B
judy.olian@anderson.ucla.edu
OLIKONG, Deikola ... 680-488-2471 520 E
olikongd@gmail.com
OLIKONG, Deikola ... 680-488-2470 520 E
olikongd@gmail.com
OLIN, Bradley ... 408-924-2341.. 34 D
OLIN, Joanna ... 413-559-5521 215 F
OLIN, Robert, F ... 205-348-5972.... 8 A
olin@as.ua.edu
OLING-SISAY, Mary ... 415-955-2100.. 24 K
moling-sisay@alliant.edu
OLINGER, CSC,
Gerard, J ... 503-943-7397 387 H
olinger@up.edu
OLINGER, Richard, P ... 814-868-7767 399 C
rpolinger@mch1.org
OLINGER, Ronald, J ... 913-360-7413 175 D
rolinger@benedictine.edu
OLIPHINT, Melody ... 806-743-7382 463 E
melody.oliphint@ttuhsc.edu
OLISZCZAK, Jennifer ... 603-578-8900 280 M
OLISZCZAK, Peter ... 623-845-4634.. 13 H
peter.oliszczak@gccaz.edu
OLIVA, Giacomo ... 212-217-4040 308 B
giacomo_oliva@fitnyc.edu
OLIVA, Joseph, E ... 718-990-6421 322 F
olivaj@stjohns.edu
OLIVA, Julia ... 718-289-5100 301 D
julia.oliva@bcc.cuny.edu
OLIVA, Mary ... 312-329-4112 146 B
mary.oliva@moody.edu
OLIVARES, Carlos, J ... 787-279-1912 523 J
colivares@bayamon.inter.edu
OLIVARES-URUETA,
Mayra ... 972-860-8354 447 I
molivares-urueta@dcccd.edu
OLIVAS, Isabel ... 713-692-0077 447 B
OLIVE, David, W ... 276-326-4466 478 H
dolive@bluefield.edu
OLIVE, Derek ... 270-745-2409 190 F
derek.olive@wku.edu
OLIVE-TAYLOR, Becky ... 336-278-6500 337 G
oliveb@elon.edu
OLIVEIRA, Judy ... 808-689-2689 130 A
judy.oliveira@hawaii.edu
OLIVEIRA, Marcio, A ... 301-405-5190 207 G
marcio@umd.edu
OLIVEIRA, Sandra, J ... 401-865-2602 416 E
solivei6@providence.edu
OLIVER, Brande' ... 248-204-2308 233 A
boliver@ltu.edu
OLIVER, Christine ... 401-598-1000 416 C
coliver@jwu.edu
OLIVER, Debra ... 937-708-5748 373 H
doliver@wilberforce.edu
OLIVER, Denita ... 256-215-4290.... 1 G
doliver@cacc.edu
OLIVER, Diane ... 585-389-2641 316 D
doliver9@naz.edu
OLIVER, Dominick ... 412-365-1262 392 C
doliver@chatham.edu
OLIVER, Ebigaly ... 787-878-5475 523 H
eoliver@arecibo.inter.edu
OLIVER, Helen ... 662-252-8000 255 F
holiver@rustcollege.edu
OLIVER, Jeanne ... 503-352-2740 385 I
jeanne@pacificu.edu
OLIVER, Justin ... 757-925-6302 489 B
joliver@pdc.edu
OLIVER, Katrina ... 561-297-3004 109 B
katrinaoliver@fau.edu
OLIVER, Kenneth, R ... 660-248-6225 258 B
koliver@centralmethodist.edu
OLIVER, Lillian, M ... 787-723-4481 521 H
loliver@ceaprc.edu
OLIVER, Melvin, L ... 909-621-8129.. 57 C
president@pitzer.edu
OLIVER, Michael ... 734-462-4400 236 H
moliver@schoolcraft.edu
OLIVER, Pamella ... 657-278-2896.. 32 B
poliver@fullerton.edu
OLIVER, Parker ... 931-598-1586 436 A
pwoliver@sewanee.edu
OLIVER, Patricia Belton . 713-743-2400 465 A
poliver@central.uh.edu
OLIVER, Rachel ... 281-425-6389 451 I
roliver@lee.edu
OLIVER, Rebecca ... 870-972-2308.. 18 A
rsoliver@astate.edu
OLIVER, Rick, E ... 417-268-1059 257 F
oliverr@evangel.edu
OLIVER, Robin, C ... 828-227-7337 352 C
rcoliver@wcu.edu
OLIVER,
Samuel (Dub), W ... 731-661-5180 439 D
doliver@uu.edu
OLIVER, Sandra ... 803-738-7699 422 D
olivers@midlandstech.edu
OLIVER, Sharon, J ... 919-530-5313 350 D
soliver@nccu.edu
OLIVER, Sharon, M ... 207-581-1585 201 B
smoliver@maine.edu
OLIVER, Shawn ... 609-497-7818 288 E
shawn.oliver@ptsem.edu
OLIVER, Tanya ... 252-862-1272 345 H
toliver@roanokechowan.edu
OLIVER, Timothy ... 802-287-8912 475 B
timothy.oliver@greenmtn.edu
OLIVER, Tom ... 217-228-5432 149 B
oliveto@quincy.edu
OLIVER, Tricia ... 413-572-5523 218 F
toliver@westfield.ma.edu
OLIVER, Wendy ... 559-278-6715.. 32 A
woliver@csufresno.edu
OLIVER-VERONESI,
Robin, E ... 814-865-6555 403 F
reo133@psu.edu
OLIVERA, Tammy ... 305-442-9223 104 B
tolivera@mrc.edu
OLIVERAS, Ivette ... 787-848-1589 525 H
ioliveras@popac.edu
OLIVERAS, Marilyn ... 787-284-1912 524 C
molivera@ponce.inter.edu
OLIVEREZ HARRIS,
Sheryl ... 817-515-5228 458 B
sheryl.harris@tccd.edu
OLIVERI, Mary, A ... 570-961-7855 399 A
oliverim@lackawanna.edu
OLIVERIO, Robert ... 602-386-4110.. 10 G
robert.oliverio@arizonachristian.edu
OLIVEROS, Jon ... 847-397-0300 133 B
OLIVETTE, Michael ... 845-569-3203 316 B
michael.olivette@msmc.edu
OLIVIER, Jennifer ... 863-680-4110 100 D
jolivier2@flsouthern.edu
OLIVIERE, Tod ... 617-266-1400 212 B
studentfinancialservices@berklee.edu
OLIVIERI, Janies ... 787-250-1912 524 B
jolivieri@metro.inter.edu
OLIVIERI-LENAHAN,
Elizabeth ... 914-633-2547 311 B
eolivieri@iona.edu
OLIVO, Cynthia ... 626-585-7074.. 56 B
cdolivo@pasadena.edu
OLIVO, Michael ... 516-323-4840 315 J
molivo@molloy.edu
OLIVO-CRUZ, Gilberto ... 787-480-2460 521 J
golivo@sanjuanciudadpatria.com
OLKIE, Tyne ... 334-683-5110.... 6 C
tolkie@judson.edu
OLKKOLA, Jake ... 207-859-4904 198 H
jolkkola@colby.edu
OLLA, Phillip ... 734-432-5363 233 C
polla@madonna.edu
OLLE-LAJOIE, Maureen . 715-425-3911 511 E
OLLER, Elizabeth ... 312-935-4245 141 C
eoller@icsw.edu
OLLIFF, Kenneth ... 314-977-2925 266 J
kolliff@slu.edu
OLLIFF, Kenton ... 785-628-4401 177 D
klolliff@fhsu.edu
OLLIFF, Thomas ... 954-201-7693.. 96 A
toliff@broward.edu
OLLINGER, Nancy ... 610-902-8276 391 B
nancy.ollinger@cabrini.edu
OLLSON, Joanne ... 413-782-1343 225 F
joanne.ollson@wne.edu
OLMOS, Amanda ... 714-620-3700.. 26 I
OLMOS, Ernesto, F ... 806-371-5456 442 D
efolmos@actx.edu
OLMOS, Mary ... 626-568-8850.. 47 G
OLMSTADT, William ... 318-675-5449 194 D
wolmst@lsuhsc.edu
OLMSTEAD, Karen, L ... 410-548-3374 209 B
klolmstead@salisbury.edu
OLMSTEAD, Patrick ... 818-401-1041.. 40 A
polmstead@columbiacollege.edu
OLMSTEAD, Steve ... 918-293-4744 378 B
steve.olmstead@okstate.edu
OLMSTED, Joshua ... 916-388-2895.. 35 F
jolmsted@carrington.edu
OLMSTED, Michelle ... 513-244-4475 366 A
michelle.omsted@msj.edu
OLNEY, Doug ... 218-333-6600 246 G
dolney@bemidjistate.edu
OLNEY, Douglas, P ... 218-755-2764 244 B
dolney@bemidjistate.edu
OLON, John ... 724-852-3241 414 B
jolon@waynesburg.edu
OLOVSON, Matthew, J .. 513-556-5503 371 E
matthew.olovson@uc.edu
OLSCHWANG, Alana ... 909-607-8135.. 37 L
alana.olschwang@cgu.edu
OLSEN, Ann, E ... 502-272-8133 183 H
aolsen@bellarmine.edu
OLSEN, Christopher ... 812-237-2785 159 C
christopher.olsen@indstate.edu
OLSEN, Danny, R ... 801-422-5648 471 E
danny_olsen@byu.edu
OLSEN, David ... 785-227-3380 175 E
olsends@bethanylb.edu
OLSEN, Jane ... 320-308-4958 247 E
jolsen@stcloudstate.edu
OLSEN, Julene ... 435-722-6900 472 L
julene@ubatc.edu
OLSEN, Keith, M ... 501-686-5558.. 22 C
kolsen@uams.edu
OLSEN, Kris ... 714-628-7303.. 36 G
kolsen@chapman.edu
OLSEN, Micah ... 307-686-0254 516 P
molsen@sheridan.edu
OLSEN, Michelle, D ... 417-836-5274 263 H
molsen@missouristate.edu
OLSEN, Mike ... 435-879-4287 473 B
olsen@dixie.edu
OLSEN, Morgan, R ... 480-727-9920.. 10 K
morgan.r.olsen@asu.edu
OLSEN, Pete ... 831-645-1362.. 52 G
polsen@mpc.edu
OLSEN, Renee ... 208-792-2151 132 C
rmolsen@lcsc.edu
OLSEN, Steven, A ... 310-825-3444.. 69 B
solsen@conet.ucla.edu
OLSEN, Steven, M ... 716-878-4113 326 E
olsensw@buffalostate.edu
OLSEN, Susan ... 808-934-2712 130 D
susan32@hawaii.edu
OLSON, Adam, J ... 813-988-5131.. 99 D
olsona@floridacollege.edu
OLSON, Alma, E ... 330-972-6577 371 C
aolson@uakron.edu
OLSON, Amy ... 202-884-9095.. 93 C
olsona@trinitydc.edu
OLSON, Amy ... 715-831-7236 513 E
aolson133@cvtc.edu
OLSON, Andrea, I ... 425-739-8127 495 F
andrea.olson@lwtech.edu
OLSON, Barry ... 919-513-3402 350 E
barry_olson@ncsu.edu
OLSON, Ben ... 907-745-3201.... 9 D
registrar@akbible.edu
OLSON, Cari ... 701-858-3323 354 C
cari.olson@minotstateu.edu
OLSON, Carolyn ... 320-308-5030 247 F
colson@sctcc.edu
OLSON, Cathy ... 413-755-4419 221 B
colson@stcc.edu
OLSON, Christine ... 920-465-2846 510 E
olsonch@uwgb.edu
OLSON, Cynthia ... 612-374-5800 242 C
colson@dunwoody.edu
OLSON, Dan ... 480-245-7980.. 13 C
dan.olson@ibcs.edu
OLSON, David ... 910-962-3102 352 A
olsond@uncw.edu
OLSON, Deborah ... 863-784-7275 108 B
deborah.olson@southflorida.edu
OLSON, Douglas ... 708-456-0300 153 E
dougolson@triton.edu
OLSON, Dustin ... 805-893-4151.. 70 B
dustin.olson@police.ucsb.edu
OLSON, Eric ... 719-255-3345.. 83 C
eolson@uccs.edu
OLSON, Eric ... 610-902-8275 391 B
eric.j.olson@cabrini.edu
OLSON, Gary, A ... 716-839-8210 306 E
golson@daemen.edu
OLSON, Heidi, L ... 320-222-5209 247 B
heidi.olson@ridgewater.edu
OLSON, Ian ... 907-474-5317.. 10 B
inolson@alaska.edu
OLSON, Jeff ... 304-424-8437 505 C
jeff.olson@wvup.edu
OLSON, Jeffery, D ... 651-638-6241 240 J
jeff-olson@bethel.edu
OLSON, Jeffery, E ... 801-863-8951 473 D
jolson@uvu.edu
OLSON, Jen ... 507-453-2724 245 G
jolson@southeastmn.edu
OLSON, Jill ... 580-349-1302 377 E
jillolson@opsu.edu
OLSON, John ... 425-388-9407 494 F
jolson@everettcc.edu
OLSON, Jon ... 605-626-2550 428 H
jon.olson@northern.edu
OLSON, Joshua ... 906-487-1217 234 A
jolson@mtu.edu
OLSON, Kerry, J ... 409-882-3362 462 D
kerry.olson@lsco.edu
OLSON, Linda ... 303-871-6801.. 83 E
lolson@du.edu
OLSON, Lynette ... 620-235-4113 180 J
lolson@pittstate.edu
OLSON, Marcene ... 541-917-4999 384 A
olsonm@linnbenton.edu
OLSON, Mark ... 763-544-9501 240 F
OLSON, Mark, J ... 703-812-4757 482 B
molson@leland.edu
OLSON, Mary Ellen ... 920-403-3181 509 J
maryellen.olson@snc.edu
OLSON, Matthew ... 781-280-3802 220 C
olsonm@middlesex.mass.edu
OLSON, Megan ... 907-786-1764.. 10 A
msolson5@alaska.edu
OLSON, Michael ... 202-250-2652.. 91 H
michael.olson@gallaudet.edu
OLSON, Nancy ... 217-732-3168 143 F
nolson@lincolnchristian.edu
OLSON, Nancy ... 641-585-8147 174 B
olsonn@waldorf.edu
OLSON, Nancy ... 507-537-6544 248 A
nancy.olson@smsu.edu
OLSON, Paul ... 701-252-3467 355 J
paul.olson@uj.edu
OLSON, Peter ... 231-348-6660 234 H
polson@ncmich.edu
OLSON, Robert ... 253-833-9111 495 C
rolson@greenriver.edu
OLSON, Robin ... 614-251-4700 367 F
olsonr@ohiodominican.edu
OLSON, Sandra ... 508-929-8025 219 A
solson@worcester.edu
OLSON, Sara ... 863-680-3965 100 D
solson@flsouthern.edu
OLSON, Sara, M ... 402-465-2185 276 E
solson@nebrwesleyan.edu
OLSON, Scott ... 906-635-2828 232 J
solson@lssu.edu
OLSON, Scott, R ... 507-457-5003 248 C
solson@winona.edu
OLSON, Shane ... 785-243-1435 176 I
solson@cloud.edu

ORSHANSKY, Mariya .... 510-628-8010.. 48 F morshansky@lincolnuca.edu
ORSINI, Jori .... 773-602-5333 135 L jorsini@ccc.edu
ORSINI, SPHR, Teri .... 704-337-2297 348 D orsinit@queens.edu
ORT, Shirley, A .... 919-962-2315 351 B ort@email.unc.edu
ORTA, Edna .... 787-743-7979 526 A ut_eorta@suagm.edu
ORTA, Jose .... 305-223-4561 106 L jorta@sjvcs.edu
ORTALE, Lynn .... 215-248-7030 392 D ortalel@chc.edu
ORTBERG, Jennifer, L ... 714-895-8965.. 38 G jortberg@gwc.cccd.edu
ORTEGA, Carmen .... 787-257-7373 525 Q ue_cortega@suagm.edu
ORTEGA, David .... 210-486-1227 442 A dortega@alamo.edu
ORTEGA, J. Martin .... 210-486-0721 442 A jortega@alamo.edu
ORTEGA, Janet .... 602-243-8287.. 14 D janet.ortega@southmountaincc.edu
ORTEGA, Noemi .... 909-447-2545.. 38 B nortega@cst.edu
ORTEGA, Richard .... 210-784-1000 460 C richard.ortega@tamusa.edu
ORTEGO, Carla .... 337-521-8922 193 E carla.ortego@solacc.edu
ORTELLI, Tracy .... 502-410-6200 184 H tortelli@galencollege.edu
ORTEZ, James .... 559-325-5264.. 66 F james.ortez@cloviscollege.edu
ORTIKOV, Khudoyor, S . 832-230-5555 453 K khudoyor@na.edu
ORTIZ, Amy .... 505-747-2224 295 H amyortiz@nnmc.edu
ORTIZ, Ann .... 910-893-1669 336 C ortiz@campbell.edu
ORTIZ, Anthony .... 575-835-5424 294 K anthony.ortiz@nmt.edu
ORTIZ, Ariel .... 787-766-1717 526 B um_aortiz@suagm.edu
ORTIZ, Arthur .... 713-525-3848 466 J
ORTIZ, Carlos .... 787-758-2525 528 D carlos.ortiz33@upr.edu
ORTIZ, Edna .... 787-786-3030 526 F eortiz@ucb.edu.pr
ORTIZ, Eduardo .... 787-250-1912 524 B ehortiz@metro.inter.edu
ORTIZ, Eickel .... 212-616-7245 309 G eickel.ortiz@heleneguld.edu
ORTIZ, Elizabeth, F .... 312-362-8588 137 C eortiz4@depaul.edu
ORTIZ, Elvin, J .... 787-857-3600 523 I ejortiz@br.inter.edu
ORTIZ, Enrique (Leo) .... 770-689-4870 115 E eortiz@aii.edu
ORTIZ, Francisco .... 787-761-0640 527 C presidente@utcpr.edu
ORTIZ, Hilda, L .... 787-863-2390 523 K hilda.ortiz@fajardo.inter.edu
ORTIZ, Ileana .... 787-264-1912 524 D ileana_ortiz_rivera@intersg.edu
ORTIZ, Jaime .... 713-743-7310 465 A jortiz22@uh.edu
ORTIZ, John .... 856-415-2198 289 G jortiz@rcgc.edu
ORTIZ, Jose .... 509-777-4332 500 H jortiz@whitworth.edu
ORTIZ, Juanita .... 405-733-7413 379 F jrortiz@rose.edu
ORTIZ, Judy .... 714-449-7470.. 51 A jortiz@ketchum.edu
ORTIZ, Kristina .... 212-752-1530 312 G kristina.ortiz@limcollege.edu
ORTIZ, Laura .... 630-466-7900 155 C lortiz@waubonsee.edu
ORTIZ, Lillian, M .... 508-854-4232 220 G lmortiz@qcc.mass.edu
ORTIZ, Luz .... 787-864-2222 524 A luz.ortiz@guayama.inter.edu
ORTIZ, Maribel .... 787-758-2525 528 D maribel.ortiz5@upr.edu
ORTIZ, Mariely .... 787-815-0000 527 F mariely.ortiz@upr.edu
ORTIZ, Mario .... 607-777-2311 325 A mortiz@binghamton.edu
ORTIZ, Mary Lou .... 848-932-1990 290 C marylou.ortiz@oldqueens.rutgers.edu
ORTIZ, María, C .... 787-766-1717 526 B um_mortiz@suagm.edu
ORTIZ, Mati .... 716-286-8504 318 F mortiz@niagara.edu
ORTIZ, Migdalia .... 787-279-1912 523 J morti@bayamon.inter.edu
ORTIZ, Mildred .... 787-264-1940 524 D milortiz@intersg.edu
ORTIZ, Nancy .... 210-297-9198 443 K nortiz@baptisthealthsystem.com
ORTIZ, Rafael .... 787-725-6500 521 C rortiz@albizu.edu
ORTIZ, Rafael .... 212-280-1342 332 C rortiz@uts.columbia.edu
ORTIZ, Ralph .... 559-734-9000.. 61 C ralpho@sjvc.edu
ORTIZ, Rosa .... 787-738-2161 528 A rosa.ortiz1@upr.edu
ORTIZ, Shannon .... 330-823-2886 372 C ortizsl@mountunion.edu
ORTIZ, Vanessa .... 787-257-7373 525 Q ortizv2@suagm.edu
ORTIZ, Wilson .... 787-265-5413 528 C wilson.ortiz3@uprm.edu
ORTIZ, Zoraida .... 787-743-7979 526 A zortiz@suagm.edu
ORTIZ-CINTRÓN, Jesús . 787-993-8878 527 G jesus.ortiz3@upr.edu
ORTIZ-GALLEYOS, Thomasinia .... 505-425-7511 294 J
ORTIZ-HARVEY, Cristina .... 646-313-8000 303 G financial.aid@guttman.cuny.edu
ORTIZ PARRA, Lelis .... 954-322-4460 102 E artizlelis@jmvu.edu
ORTIZ-VAZQUEZ, Juan, M .... 787-250-0000 527 D juanm.ortiz@upr.edu
ORTIZ-WALTERS, Rowena .... 518-564-3190 327 E rorti002@plattsburgh.edu
ORTMAN, William .... 973-408-3379 285 E wortman@drew.edu
ORTMAN-TOMLIN, Sandy .... 859-442-4122 185 I sandra.ortman-tomlin@kctcs.edu
ORTMEIER, Shane .... 605-882-5284 427 D ortmeiers@lakeareatech.edu
ORTMEYER, Rose Ann .. 573-681-5044 261 H ortmeyr@lincolnu.edu
ORTO, Christianne .... 917-493-4401 313 M corto@msmnyc.edu
ORTON, Mozelle .... 801-957-4561 474 B mozelle.orton@slcc.edu
ORTON, Ty .... 701-483-2486 354 A ty.orton@dickinsonstate.edu
ORTQUIST-AHRENS, Leslie .... 859-985-3670 183 I ortquistahrensl@berea.edu
ORVIS, Arleen .... 563-387-1005 171 I orvisarl@luther.edu
ORWICK OGDEN, Sheri 419-372-7557 357 F sorwick@bgsu.edu
ORWIG, Greg .... 509-777-4580 500 H gorwig@whitworth.edu
ORZE, Carole .... 312-567-3636 140 I orze@iit.edu
ORZECH, Mary Jo .... 585-395-2141 326 D morzech@brockport.edu
ORZECHOWSKI, Amanda .... 864-646-1401 424 F aorzech0@tctc.edu
ORZECHOWSKI, Laurie . 567-661-7227 369 A laurie_orzechowski@owens.edu
ORZECHOWSKI, Michael .... 212-280-1301 332 C morzechowski@uts.columbia.edu
ORZOLEK, Mariah .... 419-783-2358 361 A morzolek@defiance.edu
OSAE-KWAPONG, John . 419-434-5877 372 B osae-kwapong@findlay.edu
OSAKWE, Nneka-Nora ... 229-430-1043 114 I nora.osakwe@asurams.edu
OSBAHR, Diane .... 712-325-3235 170 K dosbahr@iwcc.edu
OSBON, Cindy .... 301-846-2593 203 H cosbon@frederick.edu
OSBORN, Edward, H .... 860-465-5043.. 84 K osborne@easternct.edu
OSBORN, Fred .... 541-684-4644 386 A fosborn@pioneerpacific.edu
OSBORN, Jason, W .... 864-656-4172 419 F jwo@clemson.edu
OSBORN, Jeffrey .... 609-771-2724 284 I josborn@tcnj.edu
OSBORN, Jill .... 952-446-4342 242 A osbornj@crown.edu
OSBORN, Kevin .... 626-584-5200.. 43 K osborn@fuller.edu
OSBORN, Richard, E .... 423-439-8300 431 H osbornr@etsu.edu
OSBORN, Terry .... 941-359-4200 111 C
OSBORN, William .... 928-428-8286.. 12 I bill.osborn@eac.edu
OSBORNE, Curtis .... 510-649-2477.. 44 J cosborne@gtu.edu
OSBORNE, Dawn .... 918-781-7281 374 H osborned@bacone.edu
OSBORNE, John .... 405-425-5463 377 B john.osborne@oc.edu
OSBORNE, John .... 305-428-5700 104 A josborne@aii.edu
OSBORNE, John .... 304-829-7395 501 F josborne@bethanywv.edu
OSBORNE, Kevin .... 336-342-4261 346 B osbornek@rockinghamcc.edu
OSBORNE, Kevin .... 336-734-7369 343 C kosborne@forsythtech.edu
OSBORNE, Mark .... 513-244-4298 366 A mark.osborne@msj.edu
OSBORNE, Mary .... 718-262-3806 304 A mosborne@york.cuny.edu
OSBORNE, Maurice .... 501-370-5211.. 21 A mosborne@philander.edu
OSBORNE, Michelle .... 518-454-5133 305 B osbornem@strose.edu
OSBORNE, Shelley .... 704-991-0203 346 I sosborne7501@stanly.edu
OSBORNE, Steven, C .... 843-953-5841 420 C osbornes@cofc.edu
OSBORNE, Zach .... 650-543-4097.. 51 F zach.osborne@menlo.edu
OSBOURN, John .... 541-776-9942 385 G john.o@pacificbible.com
OSBURN, Kimberly .... 419-720-6670 369 F kosburn@proskills.edu
OSBURN, Monica .... 919-515-2423 350 E monica_osburn@ncsu.edu
OSBURN, Richard, D .... 304-696-6616 504 C osburnr@marshall.edu
OSBURN, Wade .... 731-989-6067 432 C wosburn@fhu.edu
OSEGUEDA, Roberto .... 915-747-5680 467 E osegueda@utep.edu
OSEGUERA, Tonantzin ... 657-278-4688.. 32 B toseguera@fullerton.edu
OSENGA, Annette .... 510-780-4500.. 48 D aosenga@lifewest.edu
OSGOOD, Jeffery .... 610-738-0492 407 D josgood@wcupa.edu
OSGOOD, Ken .... 303-273-3596.. 78 J kosgood@mines.edu
OSGOOD, Patricia .... 617-989-4025 225 E teresiak@wit.edu
OSGUTHORPE, Richard . 208-426-4353 131 C richardosguthorpe@boisestate.edu
OSHIRO, Cathie .... 620-792-9234 175 C oshiroc@bartonccc.edu
OSHIRO, Robyn .... 808-689-2900 130 A robyno@hawaii.edu
OSHIRO, Wayde .... 808-455-0378 130 G waydeo@hawaii.edu
OSIRIM, Mary, J .... 610-526-5167 390 G mosirim@brynmawr.edu
OSIRIS, Charles, E .... 805-437-3218.. 31 C charles.osiris@csuci.edu
OSKAMP, Shirley .... 802-287-8388 475 B oskamps@greenmtn.edu
OSLER, Cheri .... 509-533-7311 493 I cheri.osler@scc.spokane.edu
OSMANSON, Deb .... 402-449-2820 274 H dosmanson@graceu.edu
OSMANSON, Deb .... 402-449-2844 274 H dosmanson@graceu.edu
OSMOND, Kerry .... 608-757-7728 513 D kosmond1@blackhawk.edu
OSMOND, Tatiana .... 207-454-1040 200 D tosmond@wccc.me.edu
OSORIO, Claribell .... 787-766-1717 526 B um_cosorio@suagm.edu
OSORIO, Jonhathan .... 808-956-0980 129 J osorio@hawaii.edu
OSSEIRAN-HANNA, Khatmeh .... 718-982-2365 302 A khatmeh.osseiran-hanna@csi.cuny.edu
OSTASH, Heather .... 760-384-6249.. 47 B hostash@cerrocoso.edu
OSTDIEK, Donald .... 713-348-4786 455 F dho@rice.edu
OSTENDARP, Timothy .... 443-352-4348 207 C tostendarp@stevenson.edu
OSTENDORF, Trevor .... 530-541-4660.. 47 I sm420@bncollege.com
OSTENDORFF, Stephen . 212-875-4402 298 H sostendorff@bankstreet.edu
OSTER, Ben Zion .... 323-937-3763.. 75 F boster@yoec.edu
OSTER, JoAnna .... 607-729-1581 306 F joster@davisny.edu
OSTER, Joseph, J .... 410-704-2151 209 C joster@towson.edu
OSTER-AALAND, Laura .. 701-231-7052 354 D laura.oster-aaland@ndsu.edu
OSTERBERG, Rick .... 781-292-2431 215 C rick.osterberg@olin.edu
OSTERBIND, Kelly .... 251-460-6251.... 9 B osterbind@southalabama.edu
OSTERHOUDT, Lori, B .. 607-746-4692 329 B osterhlb@delhi.edu
OSTERMAN, Michael .... 509-527-4975 500 G ostermmq@whitman.edu
OSTERTHUN, Stu .... 402-323-3401 276 K sosterthun@southeast.edu
OSTGAARD, Kolleen .... 916-484-8569.. 50 F ostgaak@arc.losrios.edu
OSTIN, Daniel .... 973-408-3243 285 E dostin@drew.edu
OSTLER, Jon .... 435-283-7361 474 A jon.ostler@snow.edu
OSTLING, Suzanne .... 540-863-2826 487 I sostling@dslcc.edu
OSTOLAZA, Magda, E ... 787-257-7373 525 Q ue_mostolaza@suagm.edu
OSTRANDER, Gary, K .... 850-644-3347 110 A gary@fsu.edu
OSTROSKY, Jay .... 617-850-1261 215 I jostrosky@hchc.edu
OSTROW, James .... 617-243-2111 216 C jostrow@lasell.edu
OSTROWICKI, Jacqueline, M .... 402-472-7130 277 E jostrowicki@nebraska.edu
OSTROWSKI, Jason .... 208-732-6225 131 I jostrowski@csi.edu
OSTWINKLE, Chris .... 815-280-6635 142 A costwink@jjc.edu
OSUNDE, Samuel .... 662-254-9041 255 A sosunde@mvsu.edu
OSWALD, Cecelia .... 484-323-3183 397 I coswald@immaculata.edu
OSWALD, Clark .... 316-284-5233 175 F coswald@bethelks.edu
OSWALD, Mike, R .... 208-356-1320 131 D oswaldrm@byui.edu
OSWALD, P.J .... 503-517-1800 388 C pjoswald@westernseminary.edu
OSWALD, Peter .... 217-854-5781 134 E peter.oswald@blackburn.edu
OSWALD, Phil .... 920-403-3016 509 J phil.oswald@snc.edu
OSWALD, Scott .... 251-981-3771.... 5 A scott.oswald@columbiasouthern.edu
OSWALD, Sharon .... 662-325-2580 254 E soswald@cobilan.msstate.edu
OSWALT, Natalie .... 903-693-2095 454 E noswalt@panola.edu
OSWELL, Michelle .... 215-893-5265 393 C michelle.oswell@curtis.edu
OSZUST, Renee .... 248-341-2153 235 D raoszust@oaklandcc.edu
OTÓN-OLIVIERI, Patricia .... 787-751-1912 524 E poton@juris.inter.edu
OTERO, George .... 787-257-0000 527 H george.otero@upr.edu
OTERO, Jessica .... 848-932-7454 290 A jotero@oldqueens.rutgers.edu
OTERO, Juan .... 787-766-1717 526 B juotero@suagm.edu
OTHMAN, Saib .... 317-955-6049 162 R sothman@marian.edu
OTIENO, Tom .... 859-622-1393 184 F tom.otieno@eku.edu
OTIS, Brian .... 860-486-5960.. 88 G botis@foundation.uconn.edu
OTIS, David .... 313-927-1588 233 D dotis@marygrove.edu
OTIS CATANZARO, Carolyn .... 925-631-4914.. 59 C cao7@stmarys-ca.edu
OTO, Rod, M .... 507-222-4190 241 C roto@carleton.edu
OTOUPAL, Vince .... 801-863-8998 473 D vince.otoupal@uvu.edu
OTT, Alexander .... 718-289-5939 301 D alexander.ott@bcc.cuny.edu
OTT, Amy .... 803-535-1288 423 B otta@octech.edu
OTT, Deanna .... 501-205-8838.. 19 B dott@cbc.edu
OTT, Emlyn, A .... 614-235-4136 370 M eott@tlsohio.edu
OTT, Jessica .... 414-382-6323 506 A jessica.ott@alverno.edu
OTT, Kim .... 928-523-1894.. 14 K kimberly.ott@nau.edu
OTT, Luisa .... 520-494-5283.. 11 P luisa.ott@centralaz.edu

OTT, Randall ... 202-319-5188 .. 91 D
ott@cua.edu
OTT, Steven, H ... 704-687-7630 351 C
shott@uncc.edu
OTT ROWLANDS, Sue ... 859-572-5788 188 E
sottrowlands@nku.edu
OTTAWAY, Thomas ... 208-282-2601 132 B
ottathom@isu.edu
OTTE, Bobbi ... 406-657-1086 272 I
otteb@rocky.edu
OTTEMAN, Marcie, M ... 989-774-1042 228 E
ottem1mm@cmich.edu
OTTEN, Daren ... 530-741-6853 .. 76 A
dotten@yccd.edu
OTTEN, Laura ... 215-951-1118 398 F
otten@lasalle.edu
OTTEN, Valerie, A ... 626-395-6832 .. 29 I
votten@caltech.edu
OTTER, Kelly ... 202-687-7169 .. 92 B
otter@georgetown.edu
OTTESON, Julie Ann ... 213-624-1200 .. 42 N
jotteson@fidm.edu
OTTEY, Jacqueline ... 201-447-7204 283 I
jottey@bergen.edu
OTTINGER, Marie ... 334-386-7512 .... 5 I
mottinger@faulkner.edu
OTTINGER, Mary Beth ... 847-925-6341 139 B
mottinge@harpercollege.edu
OTTINGER, Michael ... 505-566-3081 296 A
ottingerm@sanjuancollege.edu
OTTINO, Julio, M ... 847-491-3195 148 C
jm-ottino@northwestern.edu
OTTLEY, Alford, H ... 973-803-5000 288 D
aottley@pillar.edu
OTTMAN, Ray ... 479-788-7110 .. 22 A
ray.ottman@uafs.edu
OTTO, Mary ... 910-893-1310 336 C
ottom@campbell.edu
OTTO, Richard, H ... 312-461-0600 133 C
ifitzgerald@aaart.edu
OTTO, Sheryl ... 874-925-6342 139 B
sotto@harpercollege.edu
OTTO, Tyson ... 660-359-3948 264 H
totto@mail.ncmissouri.edu
OTTOBONI, John ... 408-554-5355 .. 62 F
jottoboni@scu.edu
OTTOSSON, John ... 641-673-1076 174 F
ottossonj@wmpenn.edu
OTU, Emmanual ... 262-598-2973 511 C
otu@uwp.edu
OTUONYE, Francis, O ... 931-372-3374 438 F
fotuonye@tntech.edu
OTWELL, Michelle ... 386-386-7380 .... 5 I
motwell@faulkner.edu
OTY, Karla ... 580-581-7962 375 A
koty@cameron.edu
OTYENOH, Kimberly ... 540-665-5436 485 C
kotyenoh@su.edu
OUBRE, Linda ... 415-338-2670 .. 34 C
loubre@sfsu.edu
OUDENHOVEN, Arnie ... 303-914-6298 .. 82 B
arnie.oudenhoven@rrcc.edu
OUDENHOVEN,
Elizabeth ... 303-360-4775 .. 79 C
betsy.oudenhoven@ccaurora.edu
OUDGHIRI, Fath-Allah ... 507-933-7507 242 D
foudghir@gustavus.edu
OUELLETTE, Alicia ... 518-445-3305 297 K
aouel@albanylaw.edu
OUELLETTE, Allison ... 620-431-2820 180 C
acouellette@neosho.edu
OUELLETTE, Bernie ... 207-859-1111 200 H
ouelletteb@thomas.edu
OUELLETTE, Mark ... 203-462-2916 282 C
mark.ouellette@pb.com
OUILLET, Pierre-Yves ... 858-534-3390 .. 69 E
pouillet@ucsd.edu
OUIMET, Maurice ... 802-468-1352 477 A
maurice.ouimet@castleton.edu
OUIMETTE, Nina ... 325-670-2357 450 A
noiumette@hsutx.edu
OULANOV, Alexei ... 718-270-4817 303 C
aoulanov@mec.cuny.edu
OULD, Jennifer ... 773-947-6307 145 A
jould@mccormick.edu
OURS, Alan ... 912-279-5762 118 A
aours@ccga.edu
OUSLEY, Chris ... 503-338-2326 382 E
cousley@clatsopcc.edu
OUTAR, O'Neil, A ... 412-624-6800 412 I
outar@pitt.edu
OUTEN, Jason ... 828-835-4229 347 B
jouten@tricountycc.edu
OUTING, Donald ... 845-938-7212 519 D
donald.outing@usma.edu
OUTING, Donald, A ... 610-758-2128 400 B
dao417@lehigh.edu
OUTLEY, Patrice ... 318-274-2288 196 G
outleyp@gram.edu
OUTON, Peggy, M ... 412-397-6000 409 C
outon@rmu.edu
OUTTEN, Donavan ... 314-246-6907 269 N
doutten@webster.edu
OVADIA, Zak ... 904-620-2016 110 E
zovadia@unf.edu
OVEDIA, Nicole, R ... 561-237-7237 103 E
novedia@lynn.edu
OVEN, Clare ... 858-653-6740 .. 46 M
coven@jpcatholic.com
OVER, Lucinda ... 626-914-8538 .. 37 G
lover@citruscollege.edu
OVERBY, David, B ... 605-256-5675 428 G
david.overby@dsu.edu
OVERDORF, Daniel ... 865-573-4517 432 H
doverdorf@johnsonu.edu
OVEREND, Gregory ... 203-932-7430 .. 89 D
goverend@newhaven.edu
OVERFIELD, Denise ... 678-839-4759 127 F
doverfie@westga.edu
OVERHOLSER, Toni ... 937-328-6063 359 H
overholsert@clarkstate.edu
OVERLAND, Wanda ... 320-308-3111 247 E
wioverland@stcloudstate.edu
OVERMAN, Jodi ... 616-526-8915 228 B
jro24@calvin.edu
OVEROCKER, Josh ... 405-974-2709 380 J
joverocker@uco.edu
OVEROCKER,
Quintin, M ... 815-224-0437 141 A
quintin_overocker@ivcc.edu
OVERPECK, Jonathan, T 734-764-2550 237 I
OVERSOLE, Lance ... 303-963-3447 .. 77 I
loversole@ccu.edu
OVERSTREET, Al, W ... 540-985-8205 482 A
awoverstreet@jchs.edu
OVERSTREET, Darryl ... 580-559-5582 375 I
doverstt@ecok.edu
OVERSTREET, Mana ... 615-732-7893 434 G
m.overstreet@mtsa.edu
OVERSTROM, Eric ... 617-989-4485 225 E
overstrome@wit.edu
OVERTON, Chrystal ... 580-477-7941 381 G
chrystal.overton@wosc.edu
OVERTON, Melanie, B ... 785-833-4336 179 C
melanie.overton@kwu.edu
OVERTON, Milton ... 850-599-3868 109 A
milton.overton@famu.edu
OVERTON, Reginald ... 412-788-7500 392 G
roverton@ccac.edu
OVERTON, Robert, A ... 864-488-4543 422 B
roverton@limestone.edu
OVERTON, Travis, E ... 843-349-4161 420 A
toverton@coastal.edu
OVERTON-HEALY, Julia . 518-564-2071 327 E
jover004@plattsburgh.edu
OVERTURF, Kathy ... 318-487-7301 191 J
kathy.overturf@lacollege.edu
OVERTURF, Kellie ... 970-332-5755 .. 81 A
kellie.overturf@morgancc.edu
OVESON, Kip, R ... 320-222-6930 247 B
kip.oveson@ridgewater.edu
OVEZOV, Dovran ... 832-230-5548 453 K
dovran@na.edu
OVITT, Kimberly ... 503-494-0992 385 D
ovitt@ohsu.edu
OWAN, Robert ... 808-675-3916 128 K
robert.owan@byuh.edu
OWASOYO, Philomena .. 870-575-8000 .. 22 E
owasoyop@uapb.edu
OWCZARCZAK,
Kathleen ... 716-884-9120 300 C
kowczarczak@bryantstratton.edu
OWCZAREK, Scott ... 608-262-3964 510 C
owczarek@em.wisc.edu
OWEN, Barbara ... 207-755-5233 199 K
bowen@cmcc.edu
OWEN, David, L ... 671-734-1812 520 A
dowen@piu.edu
OWEN, Erin ... 402-554-2762 277 I
eowen@unomaha.edu
OWEN, James (Chris) ... 863-667-5188 108 G
jcowen@seu.edu
OWEN, Jane ... 618-262-8641 140 F
owenj@iecc.edu
OWEN, Jane, S ... 724-852-3225 414 B
jowen@waynesburg.edu
OWEN, Janet, D ... 904-620-2500 110 E
jowen@unf.edu
OWEN, Jimmy ... 706-379-3111 128 H
jpowen@yhc.edu
OWEN, Kelli, D ... 606-783-2700 188 C
k.owen@moreheadstate.edu
OWEN, Ken ... 765-658-4634 157 H
kowen@depauw.edu
OWEN, Kyle ... 940-397-4648 453 C
kyle.owen@mwsu.edu
OWEN, Laurinda, A ... 574-372-5100 158 B
owenla@grace.edu
OWEN, Pamela ... 501-450-1358 .. 19 I
owen@hendrix.edu
OWEN, Robert ... 408-554-4581 .. 62 F
rowen@scu.edu
OWEN, Robert ... 757-352-4569 484 E
rowen@regent.edu
OWEN, Rose Marie ... 804-819-4902 487 F
rmowen@vccs.edu
OWEN, Sarah ... 620-331-4100 178 E
sowen@indycc.edu
OWEN, Sherry, L ... 816-995-2815 265 G
sherry.owen@researchcollege.edu
OWEN, William ... 531-622-2715 275 F
bowen@mccneb.edu
OWENBY, Judy ... 828-835-4212 347 B
jowenby@tricountycc.edu
OWENBY, Stephanee ... 512-492-3021 442 J
sowenby@aoma.edu
OWENS, Anthony ... 512-223-1127 443 G
aowens@austincc.edu
OWENS, Barbara, L ... 334-727-8011 .... 7 F
bowens@tuskegee.edu
OWENS, Bertha ... 501-370-5215 .. 21 A
bowens@philander.edu
OWENS, Bettina ... 504-568-6130 194 C
bowens@lsuhsc.edu
OWENS, Candace ... 405-425-5961 377 B
candace.owens@oc.edu
OWENS, Colleen ... 207-941-7184 199 B
owensc@husson.edu
OWENS, Corey ... 937-376-6107 358 I
cowens@centralstate.edu
OWENS, Deborah, D ... 607-735-1819 307 G
dowens@elmira.edu
OWENS, Deborah, E ... 716-829-8198 307 B
owensde@dyc.edu
OWENS, Don ... 254-295-4691 466 A
dowens@umhb.edu
OWENS, Drake ... 318-357-4250 197 D
owensd@nsula.edu
OWENS, Esmeralda ... 831-755-6810 .. 45 C
eowens@hartnell.edu
OWENS, Glenna ... 276-244-1303 477 M
gowens@asl.edu
OWENS, Ilona ... 336-506-4146 340 L
ilona.owens@alamancecc.edu
OWENS, J, F ... 540-365-4255 480 L
jfowens@ferrum.edu
OWENS, James ... 609-633-9658 292 B
jowens@tesu.edu
OWENS, James ... 304-637-1268 501 H
owensj@dewv.edu
OWENS, James, R ... 859-858-3511 183 D
jim.owens@asbury.edu
OWENS, Jamie ... 800-856-9544 273 C
jamie.owens@ugf.edu
OWENS, Jamie ... 513-562-8754 356 J
jowens@artacademy.edu
OWENS, Jeffrey ... 706-821-8592 124 C
jowens@paine.edu
OWENS, Josh ... 615-675-5320 441 B
jowens@welch.edu
OWENS, Judy ... 937-769-1324 356 G
jowens1@antioch.edu
OWENS, Justin ... 606-218-5224 190 E
justinowens@upike.edu
OWENS, Kate ... 570-945-8222 398 C
kate.owens@keystone.edu
OWENS, Kelly ... 501-812-2233 .. 23 C
kowens@pulaskitech.edu
OWENS, Laura ... 310-824-1586 .. 24 B
lowens@ajrca.edu
OWENS, Lillian ... 205-853-1200 .... 2 F
lowens@jeffersonstate.edu
OWENS, Linda ... 310-900-1600 .. 40 C
lowens@elcamino.edu
OWENS, Linda ... 630-620-2130 147 I
lowens@seminary.edu
OWENS, Lori, J ... 256-782-5649 .... 6 B
ljowens@jsu.edu
OWENS, MacKubin ... 202-462-2101 .. 92 D
mowens@iwp.edu
OWENS, Mark ... 618-664-6735 139 A
mark.owens@greenville.edu
OWENS, Michelle ... 972-481-7402 444 J
michelle.owens@brightwood.edu
OWENS, Mike ... 870-460-1028 .. 22 D
owens@uamont.edu
OWENS, Milton ... 312-553-3213 135 J
mowens63@ccc.edu
OWENS, Pamela ... 512-404-4815 443 I
powens@austinseminary.edu
OWENS, Pamela ... 414-930-3380 509 B
owensp@mtmary.edu
OWENS, Patricia ... 724-805-2271 410 C
patricia.owens@stvincent.edu
OWENS, Patricia ... 724-805-2271 410 B
president@stvincent.edu
OWENS, R. Scott ... 859-238-5457 184 C
scott.owens@centre.edu
OWENS, Rachel ... 423-461-8492 435 A
rowens@milligan.edu
OWENS, Ray ... 252-246-1239 347 H
rowens@wilsoncc.edu
OWENS, Rick ... 252-493-7442 345 E
rowens@email.pittcc.edu
OWENS, Robert ... 931-372-3392 438 F
rowens@tntech.edu
OWENS, Scott, D ... 856-225-6028 290 B
scott.owens@rutgers.edu
OWENS, Sharon ... 404-270-5082 126 D
sowens5@spelman.edu
OWENS, Stephanie, R ... 770-720-5895 124 H
sro@reinhardt.edu
OWENS, Stephen, J ... 573-882-3211 268 B
owenssj@umsystem.edu
OWENS, Susan ... 254-295-8686 466 A
sowens@umhb.edu
OWENS, Tara ... 410-462-8325 202 F
towens@bccc.edu
OWENS, Tracey ... 732-987-2287 286 D
towens@georgian.edu
OWENS, Valerie ... 304-876-5465 504 D
vowens@shepherd.edu
OWENS, Waylan ... 817-923-1921 457 G
wowens@swbts.edu
OWENS-HILL, David ... 212-472-1500 318 B
dowenshill@nysid.edu
OWENS SMITH, Amy ... 513-745-5615 371 F
amy.smith@uc.edu
OWENS-SOUTHHALL,
Mary, E ... 410-951-3090 208 F
mowens@coppin.edu
OWENSKY, Fred ... 575-527-7543 295 E
fowensky@nmsu.edu
OWL, Diane ... 828-835-4220 347 B
dowl@tricountycc.edu
OWLES, Vicky ... 573-876-7212 267 G
vowles@stephens.edu
OWNBEY, Rita ... 620-278-4306 181 G
rownbey@sterling.edu
OWOLABI, Elizabeth ... 708-209-3020 136 I
elizabeth.owolabi@cuchicago.edu
OWSLEY, Kristen ... 913-758-6331 182 B
kristen.owsley@stmary.edu
OWSLEY, Laura ... 502-863-8007 184 I
laura_owsley@georgetowncollege.edu
OWSLEY, Stacy ... 520-383-8401 .. 16 G
sowsley@tocc.edu
OWSTON, James, M ... 304-457-6222 501 A
owstonjb@ab.edu
OWUSU-ADUEMIRI,
Kwadwo ... 850-412-7469 109 A
kwadwo.owusuaduemiri@famu.edu
OWUSU-ANSAH,
Edward ... 973-720-3179 292 I
owusuansahe@wpunj.edu
OWUSU-SEKYERE,
Emmanuel ... 410-951-3862 208 F
manny@coppin.edu
OXENDINE, Cynthia ... 910-521-6175 351 E
cynthia.oxendine@uncp.edu
OXENDINE, Derek ... 910-521-6401 351 E
derek.oxendine@uncp.edu
OXFORD,
Mary-Catherine ... 559-730-3826 .. 39 G
marycat@cos.edu
OXFORD, Ron ... 559-925-3403 .. 74 A
ronoxford@whccd.edu
OXFORD-PICKERAL,
Misti ... 352-335-2332 .. 94 D
info@acupuncturist.edu
OXLEY, Timothy ... 304-367-4303 504 A
tiothy.oxley@fairmontstate.edu
OXLEY, Timothy ... 304-367-4303 504 A
timothy.oxley@fairmontstate.edu
OYADOMARI, Jason ... 906-487-7381 230 B
jason.oyadomari@finlandia.edu
OYEKAN, Adebayo, O ... 713-313-4341 461 E
oyekan_ao@tsu.edu
OYMAN, Korhan ... 321-674-8971 .. 99 K
koyman@fit.edu
OYOLA, Elias ... 212-694-1000 299 L
eoyola@boricuacollege.edu
OYOLA, Luaida ... 787-750-4405 527 H
luaida.oyola@upr.edu
OZAN, Randy ... 859-858-2210 183 C
OZAYSIN, Gokhan ... 912-525-5000 125 B
gozaysin@scad.edu
OZBAY, Refik ... 954-545-4500 108 A
studentlife@sfbc.edu

OZECHOSKI, Mary-Alice .... 610-606-4666 392 A
mozechos@cedarcrest.edu
OZEE, Nancy .... 815-802-8842 142 C
nozee@kcc.edu
OZMENT, Suzanne .... 864-388-8320 422 A
sozment@lander.edu
OZMENT, Tim .... 252-985-5107 348 A
tozment@ncwc.edu
OZOLS, Ruta .... 315-229-5908 323 D
rozols@stlawu.edu
OZTURGUT, Osman .... 210-829-2759 465 E
ozturgut@uiwtx.edu
OZTURK, Mehmet .... 559-730-3790.. 39 G
mehmeto@cos.edu
OZUG, Steve .... 508-678-2811 219 C
steven.ozug@bristolcc.edu
OZUZU, Onye .... 312-369-7291 136 H
oozuzu@colum.edu
O'BANION, Rebecca ..... 254-295-4603 466 A
robanion@umhb.edu
O'BANNER/JACKSON, Marie .... 601-979-2127 253 E
marie.obanner-jackson@jsums.edu
O'BANNER-JACKSON, Marie .... 601-979-7092 253 E
marie.obanner-jackson@jsums.edu
O'BAR, Gary .... 210-485-0102 441 E
gobar@alamo.edu
O'BARR, Allen, H .... 919-966-3658 351 B
allen_obarr@unc.edu
O'BEIRNE, Kirsten .... 610-526-5041 390 G
kobeirne@brynmawr.edu
O'BEIRNE, OSF, Marguerite .... 610-558-5511 402 G
mobeirne@neumann.edu
O'BERRY, V. Diane .... 803-780-1142 426 F
doberry@voorhees.edu
O'BOYLE, Andrew .... 206-296-6149 498 D
oboylea@seattleu.edu
O'BOYLE, Thomas .... 631-656-2126 308 F
thomas.oboyle@ftc.edu
O'BREIN, Catherine .... 713-718-2383 450 D
catherine.obrein2@hccs.edu
O'BRIAN, Jenni .... 406-546-3585 271 E
jenni.obrian@montanabiblecollege.edu
O'BRIEN, Alyssa .... 847-543-2409 136 E
aobrien@clcillinois.edu
O'BRIEN, Barry .... 910-522-5707 351 E
michael.o'brien@uncp.edu
O'BRIEN, Brad .... 309-649-6294 152 G
brad.obrien@src.edu
O'BRIEN, Casey .... 518-828-4181 305 D
casey.obrien@sunycgcc.edu
O'BRIEN, Colleen .... 973-618-3660 284 D
cobrien@caldwell.edu
O'BRIEN, Corey .... 312-915-7451 144 D
cobrien@luc.edu
O'BRIEN, Courtney .... 312-553-6063 135 J
cobrien4@ccc.edu
O'BRIEN, Diane .... 805-893-8182.. 70 B
diane.obrien@ucsb.edu
O'BRIEN, Diane, E .... 570-408-4734 414 H
diane.obrien@wilkes.edu
O'BRIEN, Eddie .... 706-865-2134 126 G
eobrien@truett.edu
O'BRIEN, Elizabeth .... 707-664-4023.. 35 A
elizabeth.obrien@sonoma.edu
O'BRIEN, Elizabeth .... 510-593-2930.. 63 A
elizabethobrien@saybrook.edu
O'BRIEN, Elizabeth .... 423-425-4438 440 A
elizabeth-o'brien@utc.edu
O'BRIEN, Gregory .... 888-488-4968.. 46 J
gobrien@itu.edu
O'BRIEN, Heather .... 212-229-8947 316 E
obrienh@newschool.edu
O'BRIEN, Ian .... 701-349-5794 355 G
ianobrien@trinitybiblecollege.edu
O'BRIEN, Irene .... 973-353-5541 290 D
jobrien@andromeda.rutgers.edu
O'BRIEN, J. Randall ...... 865-471-3200 430 H
robrien@cn.edu
O'BRIEN, Jason .... 617-262-5000 212 C
jason.obrien@the-bac.edu
O'BRIEN, Jim .... 480-965-9118.. 10 K
james.obrien@asu.edu
O'BRIEN, John, F .... 617-422-7221 222 J
jobrien@nesl.edu
O'BRIEN, Katie .... 315-655-7348 300 I
kobrien@cazenovia.edu
O'BRIEN, SJ, Kevin ...... 510-549-5040.. 62 F
kfobrien@jstb.edu
O'BRIEN, Kevin, J .... 253-535-7698 496 G
obrien@plu.edu
O'BRIEN, Martha .... 814-472-3217 409 G
mobrien@francis.edu
O'BRIEN, Mary Eileen ... 845-848-7801 306 G
mary.eileen.obrien@dc.edu
O'BRIEN, Mary Kate ..... 802-258-3494 476 B
marykate.obrien@sit.edu
O'BRIEN, Maryellen ...... 910-272-3324 346 A
mo'brien@robeson.edu
O'BRIEN, Maureen .... 724-830-1075 410 E
obrien@setonhill.edu
O'BRIEN, Michael .... 269-782-1401 237 B
mobrien02@swmich.edu
O'BRIEN, Michael .... 210-784-1200 460 C
michael.obrien@tamusa.edu
O'BRIEN, Michael, E ..... 419-530-4987 372 F
michael.obrien6@utoledo.edu
O'BRIEN, Patricia .... 617-358-4944 212 G
pobrien@bu.edu
O'BRIEN, Paul .... 772-462-7376 101 Q
pobrien@irsc.edu
O'BRIEN, Peg .... 708-209-3528 136 I
margaret.obrien@cuchicago.edu
O'BRIEN, Rachel .... 214-887-5368 448 G
robrien@dts.edu
O'BRIEN, Shannon .... 406-243-7852 271 G
shannon.obrien@umontana.edu
O'BRIEN, Tammy .... 706-771-5700 116 A
tobrien@augustatech.edu
O'BRIEN, Terry .... 860-465-5395.. 84 K
obrienth@easternct.edu
O'BRIEN, Theresa .... 415-514-1455.. 70 A
theresa.obrien@ucsf.edu
O'BRIEN, Thomas .... 610-647-4400 397 I
tobrien@immaculata.edu
O'BRIEN-FOELSCH, Molly .... 717-867-6038 399 J
mobrien@lvc.edu
O'BRIEN-FOELSCH, Molly, E .... 570-577-3624 390 H
molly.obrien@bucknell.edu
O'BRIEN-KNOTTS, Jennifer, E .... 610-758-4679 400 B
jeo211@lehigh.edu
O'BRIEN-MCMASTERS, Vanessa .... 856-227-7200 284 E
vmcmasters@camdencc.edu
O'BRYAN, Dan .... 775-831-1314 280 C
dobryan@sierranevada.edu
O'BRYAN, Megan .... 216-987-4737 360 E
megan.obryan@tri-c.edu
O'BRYANT, Theresa, M . 413-662-5231 218 C
theresa.obryant@mcla.edu
O'CAIN, Woody .... 386-822-7481 111 E
wocain@stetson.edu
O'CALLAGHAN, Cindy ... 617-735-9779 214 F
ocallac@emmanuel.edu
O'CALLAGHAN, Karen ... 516-463-6605 310 D
karen.ocallaghan@hofstra.edu
O'CARROLL, Theresa ..... 708-974-5248 146 C
ocarroll@morainevalley.edu
O'CINNSEALAIGH, Benedict .... 513-231-2223 356 M
bocinnsealaigh@athenaeum.edu
O'CONNELL, Anne .... 847-543-2622 136 E
aoconnell@clcillinois.edu
O'CONNELL, Catharine, E .... 217-245-3010 139 H
catharine.oconnell@mail.ic.edu
O'CONNELL, Colleen ..... 215-884-8942 415 C
planning@woninstitute.edu
O'CONNELL, Daniel .... 978-867-4246 215 D
daniel.oconnell@gordon.edu
O'CONNELL, Daniel .... 212-229-5300 316 E
oconned@newschool.edu
O'CONNELL, Danny, J .. 330-941-3549 374 E
djoconnell@ysu.edu
O'CONNELL, David, J ... 563-333-6092 173 A
oconnelldavidj@sau.edu
O'CONNELL, Heather, A 302-356-6814.. 91 B
heather.a.oconnell@wilmu.edu
O'CONNELL, John .... 260-481-6977 160 D
oconnelj@ipfw.edu
O'CONNELL, Lili .... 815-455-8676 145 B
loconnell@mchenry.edu
O'CONNELL, Mark, P .... 269-965-3931 232 A
oconnellm@kellogg.edu
O'CONNELL, Melissa, E 386-312-4232 106 M
melissaoconnell@sjrstate.edu
O'CONNELL, Molly .... 920-693-1752 513 H
molly.oconnell@gotoltc.edu
O'CONNELL, Paul .... 269-488-4722 231 G
poconnell@kvcc.edu
O'CONNELL, Robert, G . 617-333-2050 214 B
boconnel@curry.edu
O'CONNELL, Sean .... 203-773-8068.. 84 G
soconnell@albertus.edu
O'CONNELL, Shelley, M .... 319-273-7224 167 A
shelley.oconnell@uni.edu
O'CONNELL, Tracey ...... 973-290-4427 285 A
toconnell@cse.edu
O'CONNOR, Angela, M . 813-253-6230 113 E
aoconnor@ut.edu
O'CONNOR, Bill .... 425-564-2454 492 G
bill.oconnor@bellevuecollege.edu
O'CONNOR, Brian .... 406-994-5016 272 A
boconnor@montana.edu
O'CONNOR, Catherine .. 617-353-3213 212 G
seddean@bu.edu
O'CONNOR, Charles, D 402-472-9339 277 G
charles.oconnor@unl.edu
O'CONNOR, Christi .... 323-953-4000.. 49 A
oconnoca@lacitycollege.edu
O'CONNOR, Christopher, K .... 617-254-2610 224 B
rev.christopher.o'connor@sjs.edu
O'CONNOR, Deirdre, M 570-577-3141 390 H
deirdre.oconnor@bucknell.edu
O'CONNOR, Diane .... 215-641-6416 402 A
doconnor@mc3.edu
O'CONNOR, Edward, R . 816-654-7000 261 D
eoconnor@kcumb.edu
O'CONNOR, Eileen .... 203-432-1345.. 89 G
eileen.oconnor@yale.edu
O'CONNOR, Ellen, M .... 215-955-6835 411 E
ellen.oconnor@jefferson.edu
O'CONNOR, Gregory ..... 631-420-2170 329 D
oconnor@farmingdale.edu
O'CONNOR, James .... 563-884-5294 172 H
james.oconnor@palmer.edu
O'CONNOR, James .... 334-844-3500.... 4 D
jmo0024@auburn.edu
O'CONNOR, Jen .... 785-864-2640 181 I
jen.occonor@ku.edu
O'CONNOR, Jeremiah .... 508-793-2564 213 D
joconnor@holycross.edu
O'CONNOR, Jessica .... 603-542-7744 281 A
joconnor@ccsnh.edu
O'CONNOR, Jim .... 707-638-5997.. 67 H
jim.oconnor@tu.edu
O'CONNOR, Jody .... 415-575-6153.. 29 H
joconnor@ciis.edu
O'CONNOR, Joseph .... 607-778-5379 326 C
oconnorjt@sunybroome.edu
O'CONNOR, Julie .... 414-425-8300 509 I
joconnor@shsst.edu
O'CONNOR, Kathleen .... 816-271-5827 264 B
koconnor5@missouriwestern.edu
O'CONNOR, Kathleen .... 617-243-2199 216 C
koconnor@lasell.edu
O'CONNOR, Keith .... 908-852-1400 284 G
oconnork01@centenaryuniversity.edu
O'CONNOR, Kevin .... 949-582-4788.. 64 J
koconnor@saddleback.edu
O'CONNOR, Maria, A .... 330-569-5272 362 J
occonorma@hiram.edu
O'CONNOR, Mary .... 480-731-8403.. 13 D
mary.oconnor@domail.maricopa.edu
O'CONNOR, Matthew, L .... 203-582-8297.. 88 A
matthew.oconnor@quinnipiac.edu
O'CONNOR, Maura .... 206-296-6300 498 D
oconnorm@seattleu.edu
O'CONNOR, Maureen .... 650-433-3802.. 55 I
moconnor@paloaltou.edu
O'CONNOR, Michael ..... 815-802-8908 142 C
moconnor@kcc.edu
O'CONNOR, Mike, J ..... 828-262-3190 349 H
oconnormj@appstate.edu
O'CONNOR, Nancy .... 734-432-5461 233 C
noconnor@madonna.edu
O'CONNOR, Patrick ...... 617-879-7878 218 B
poconnor@massart.edu
O'CONNOR, Patrick ...... 708-974-5555 146 C
oconnorp@morainevalley.edu
O'CONNOR, Rob .... 501-450-1225.. 19 I
o'connor@hendrix.edu
O'CONNOR, Robert .... 315-781-3535 310 C
oconnor@hws.edu
O'CONNOR, Shawn .... 507-433-0564 247 C
shawn.o'connor@riverland.edu
O'CONNOR, Terrence, L .... 305-628-6516 107 B
toconnor@stu.edu
O'CONNOR, Timothy ...... 212-327-8080 321 E
toconnor@rockefeller.edu
O'CONNOR-BENSON, Pat .... 239-597-7101 109 C
poconnor@fgcu.edu
O'COYNE, Gregory .... 630-515-6044 145 I
gocoyn@midwestern.edu
O'DAIR, Katherine, G .... 617-552-3482 212 E
katherine.odair@bc.edu
O'DANIEL, Jennifer .... 512-863-1691 457 I
odanielj@southwestern.edu
O'DAY, Gail, R .... 336-758-4315 353 A
odaygr@wfu.edu
O'DAY, Patricia .... 607-778-5100 326 C
odaypg@sunybroome.edu
O'DAY, Patricia, G .... 607-778-5100 326 C
odaypg@sunybroome.edu
O'DAY, Steven, P .... 717-867-6407 399 J
oday@lvc.edu
O'DAY, Steven, P .... 903-813-3001 443 F
soday@austincollege.edu
O'DELL, April .... 802-865-5734 474 G
o'dell@champlain.edu
O'DELL, Cynthia .... 219-980-6509 160 C
codell@iun.edu
O'DONNELL, Brennan ... 718-862-7301 313 L
brennan.odonnell@manhattan.edu
O'DONNELL, James ...... 716-645-2823 325 B
jod@buffalo.edu
O'DONNELL, James ...... 660-785-7777 267 K
jodonnell@truman.edu
O'DONNELL, James ...... 480-965-3956.. 10 K
jjodonn2@mainex1.asu.edu
O'DONNELL, Karen .... 813-286-8087 146 G
kodonnell@nl.edu
O'DONNELL, Michael .... 512-499-4601 467 A
modonnell@utsystem.edu
O'DONNELL, Michael .... 914-654-5541 305 A
modonnell@cnr.edu
O'DONNELL, Michael .... 262-741-8538 513 G
odonnellm@gtc.edu
O'DONNELL, SSJ, Patricia .... 215-248-7125 392 D
podonnel@chc.edu
O'DONNELL, Patrick ..... 562-860-2451.. 36 A
podonnell@cerritos.edu
O'DONNELL, Tim .... 479-575-5828.. 21 I
odonnell@uark.edu
O'DONNELL, Timothy, T .... 540-636-2900 479 G
president@christendom.edu
O'DONNELL, William .... 903-566-7038 468 C
wodonnell@uttyler.edu
O'DONOHOE, Karen ...... 479-619-4321.. 20 F
kodonohoe@nwacc.edu
O'DONOVAN, Stephen .. 254-526-1114 445 L
admissions.registrar@ctcd.edu
O'DOWD, Diane, K .... 949-824-5801.. 69 A
dkodowd@uci.edu
O'DRISCOLL, Brian .... 503-352-2917 385 I
odriscob@pacificu.edu
O'DRISCOLL, Daniel ...... 401-254-3510 417 C
dpodriscoll@rwu.edu
O'DRISCOLL, Dean .... 509-452-5100 496 H
dodriscoll@pnwu.edu
O'DRISCOLL, Sue .... 540-545-7399 485 C
sodrisco09@su.edu
O'DWYER, Timothy .... 503-768-7860 383 G
odwyer@lclark.edu
O'FARRELL, Kevin, F .... 813-527-6620 105 C
ofarrek@phsc.edu
O'FARRELL, Mark, T ..... 727-376-6911 112 G
mofarrell@trinitycollege.edu
O'FLAHERTY, Kevin .... 215-646-7300 396 E
oflaherty.k@gmercyu.edu
O'FLANNERY ANDERSON, Jennifer .... 954-262-2114 104 F
joa@nova.edu
O'GEARY, Amy .... 252-492-2061 347 C
ogearya@vgcc.edu
O'GORMAN, Ryan .... 845-848-7600 306 G
ryan.ogorman@dc.edu
O'GRADY, Elaine .... 845-569-3190 316 B
elaine.ogrady@msmc.edu
O'GRADY EISENMANN, Sharon .... 610-660-1290 409 H
seisenma@sju.edu
O'GWYNN, Marty .... 405-208-5120 377 D
mlogwynn@okcu.edu
O'HAGAN, Donald .... 973-618-3759 284 D
dohagan@caldwell.edu
O'HAGAN, Patricia .... 808-734-9569 130 C
ohaganp@hawaii.edu
O'HAIR, H. Dan .... 859-218-0290 190 B
ohair@uky.edu
O'HAIR, Mary John ...... 859-257-2813 190 B
mjohair@uky.edu
O'HALLORAN, Kimberly, C .... 610-499-4566 414 F
kcohalloran@widener.edu
O'HALLORAN, Teresa, E .... 715-836-2387 510 D
ohallote@uwec.edu
O'HANLON, Laureen ..... 509-828-1459 494 D
lohanlon@ewu.edu
O'HARA, Bradley .... 604-482-5510 133 A
bohara@adler.edu
O'HARA, Christine, S ... 716-286-8792 318 F
cohara@niagara.edu
O'HARA, James, P .... 609-896-5367 289 E
johara@rider.edu
O'HARA, Kate .... 617-217-9225 211 D
kohara@baystate.edu

P

PACHECO, Sonia .... 787-840-2955 521 B
spacheco@ponce.caribbean.edu
PACHECO, Victor .... 915-747-5202 467 E
victorpa@utep.edu
PACHECO DUNN,
Tanhena .... 845-257-3164 325 D
pachecot@newpaltz.edu
PACHECO DUNN,
Tanhena .... 845-257-3172 325 D
pachecot@newpaltz.edu
PACHIS, Dimitrios, C .... 860-465-4414.. 84 K
pachis@easternct.edu
PACHUAU, Lalsangkima 859-858-3581 183 C
PACHUILO, Vincent ...... 701-774-4250 355 C
vincent.pachuilo@willistonstate.edu
PACINI, Christine .... 313-993-1208 237 F
pacinicm@udmercy.edu
PACINI, Martha .... 404-297-9522 120 D
pacinim@gptc.edu
PACIOREK, Pete .... 618-374-5030 149 A
pete.paciorek@principia.edu
PACK, Andrew .... 215-717-6147 412 F
apack@uarts.edu
PACK, Daniel .... 423-425-2256 440 A
daniel-pack@utc.edu
PACK, Thomas, J .... 513-562-8779 356 J
tpack@artacademy.edu
PACK, W. Gary .... 513-585-1414 359 D
william.pack@thechristcollege.edu
PACKARD, Emily .... 402-941-6016 275 J
packard@midlandu.edu
PACKARD, Gary, A .... 719-333-9751 518 H
PACKARD, James .... 573-341-4252 269 A
jpackard@mst.edu
PACKER, Mike .... 626-568-8850.. 47 G
PACKER, Rob .... 800-856-9544 273 C
robert.packer@ugf.edu
PACKER-MUTI, Barbara . 954-262-5398 104 F
packerb@nova.edu
PACKETT, Felicia, B .... 804-758-6742 489 D
fpackett@rappahannock.edu
PACKEY, Matthew .... 704-337-2375 348 D
packeym@queens.edu
PACKHAM, Larry .... 310-287-4424.. 49 H
packhald@wlac.edu
PACTOL, Brian .... 808-235-7403 130 I
pactol@hawaii.edu
PACTOL, Monica .... 916-608-6899.. 50 H
pactolm@flc.losrios.edu
PACTOR, Jacob .... 765-361-6355 166 B
pactorj@wabash.edu
PADASH, Ali .... 916-608-6648.. 50 H
padasha@flc.losrios.edu
PADDEN, Carol, A .... 858-534-6073.. 69 E
deansocsci@ucsd.edu
PADDOCK, Ericka .... 909-389-3457.. 59 H
epaddock@craftonhills.edu
PADDOCK, Jean .... 330-363-5205 357 A
jean.paddock@aultman.com
PADDOCK, John .... 315-498-2299 319 G
paddockj@sunyocc.edu
PADDOCK, Suzanne .... 315-866-0300 310 A
paddocksm@herkimer.edu
PADDOCK, Will .... 267-620-4834 389 D
paddockw@arcadia.edu
PADDOCK-O'REILLY,
Kimberly .... 636-227-2100 262 A
PADEN, Quincy .... 773-907-4783 135 K
qpaden@ccc.edu
PADEN, Russ .... 602-557-1723.. 17 C
russ.paden@phoenix.edu
PADGETT, Mila .... 803-641-3230 425 A
milap@usca.edu
PADILLA, Ailín .... 787-264-1912 524 D
ailin_padilla@intersg.edu
PADILLA, Alvin .... 616-392-8555 239 J
alvin@westernsem.edu
PADILLA, Carlos .... 239-513-1122 101 O
cpadilla@hodges.edu
PADILLA, Christina .... 808-689-2689 130 A
cp808@hawaii.edu
PADILLA, Corrine .... 801-302-2800 472 A
corrine.padilla@neumont.edu
PADILLA, Edgar .... 512-759-5643 461 G
edgar.padilla@tstc.edu
PADILLA, Elaine .... 212-870-1202 318 C
epadilla@nyts.edu
PADILLA, Eugene .... 505-224-4720 293 L
epadilla@cnm.edu
PADILLA, Frankie, D ...... 787-265-5475 528 C
frankie.padilla@upr.edu
PADILLA, Frederick, M . 202-685-3924 518 B
frederick.m.padilla.mil@ndu.edu
PADILLA, Jackie .... 850-484-1721 105 E
jpadilla@pensacolastate.edu
PADILLA, Jose .... 562-907-4211.. 75 A
jpadilla@whittier.edu
PADILLA, Jose, D .... 312-362-8590 137 C
jpadill7@depaul.edu
PADILLA, Maria .... 508-362-2131 219 E
mpadilla@capecod.edu
PADILLA, Mark .... 307-382-1690 517 C
mpadilla@westernwyoming.edu
PADILLA, Miriam .... 787-264-1912 524 D
miriam_padilla_camacho@intersg.edu
PADILLA, Ramon .... 651-201-1454 243 I
ramon.padilla@so.mnscu.edu
PADILLA, Rene, L .... 402-280-4745 274 D
renepadilla@creighton.edu
PADILLA, Sherrie .... 808-932-7451 129 I
sherriep@hawaii.edu
PADILLA-COTTO,
Lymaries .... 787-725-6500 521 C
lpadilla@albizu.edu
PADILLA-VIGIL,
Virginia .... 505-425-7511 294 J
PADIN, Carlos, M .... 787-766-1717 526 B
um_cpadin@suagm.edu
PADMANABHAN,
Anand .... 212-229-5300 316 E
anand@newschool.edu
PADOVANI, John, J ...... 607-746-4632 329 B
padovajj@delhi.edu
PADOW, Fran, A .... 816-604-1081 262 F
fran.padow@mcckc.edu
PADRON, Eduardo, J .... 305-237-3316 103 L
epadron@mdc.edu
PADRON, Margie .... 562-938-4947.. 48 I
mpadron@lbcc.edu
PADUAN, Jeffrey, D ...... 831-656-3241 518 D
jdpaduan@nps.edu
PADULA, Fernando .... 915-747-5594 467 E
lfpadula@utep.edu
PADUNTIN, Jack .... 925-969-3300.. 46 L
jpaduntin@jfku.edu
PAEPLOW, Randall, K ... 863-784-7083 108 B
randall.paeplow@southflorida.edu
PAESE, Paul .... 713-525-3540 466 J
paesep@stthom.edu
PAEZ, Karen .... 971-722-4406 386 C
karen.paez@pcc.edu
PAEZ-FIGUEROA, Jose .. 908-709-7084 292 C
paez@ucc.edu
PAFFENDORF, Nancy .... 908-852-1400 284 G
paffendorfn@centenaryuniversity.edu
PAFFENROTH, Kim .... 914-637-2743 311 B
kpaffenroth@iona.edu
PAFFRATH, Dennis .... 410-706-1101 207 H
dpaffrath@umaryland.edu
PAGAN, Mariana .... 787-257-7373 525 Q
mapagan@suagm.edu
PAGAN, Miguel .... 787-764-0000 528 F
miguel.pagan4@upr.edu
PAGAN, Andres .... 787-765-1915 524 F
apagan@opto.inter.edu
PAGAN, Damaris .... 787-765-1915 524 F
dpagan@opto.inter.edu
PAGAN, Efren .... 787-834-9595 526 E
epagan@uaa.edu
PAGAN, Lorraine, M ..... 512-448-8411 455 I
lorraine@stedwards.edu
PAGAN, Mayra .... 787-738-2161 528 A
maya.pagan@upr.edu
PAGAN, Richard, B .... 304-929-5493 503 B
rpagan@newriver.edu
PAGAN, Vanessa .... 787-284-1912 524 C
vpagan@ponce.inter.edu
PAGAN, Victoria .... 406-496-4129 272 E
vpagan@mtech.edu
PAGAN, Yolanda .... 787-891-0925 523 G
ypagan@ns.inter.edu
PAGANELLI, John .... 508-531-1328 217 D
jpaganelli@bridgew.edu
PAGANELLI, Niki .... 828-227-7211 352 C
ndpaganelli@email.wcu.edu
PAGANI-SOTO, Juan, C 787-765-4210 521 G
jpagani@cempr.edu
PAGANO, Amy, E .... 724-458-3850 396 D
aepagano@gcc.edu
PAGANO, Jeffrey, M ..... 716-839-8254 306 E
jpagano@daemen.edu
PAGANO, Mark .... 253-692-5646 499 D
mpagano@uw.edu
PAGANO, Michael, A .... 312-413-3375 153 H
mapagano@uic.edu
PAGANO, Tom .... 913-469-8500 178 F
tpagano@jccc.edu
PAGANO, Whitney .... 518-485-3228 305 B
paganow@strose.edu
PAGE, Anna .... 913-469-8500 178 F
apage@jccc.edu
PAGE, Cheryl .... 417-268-6412 257 H
cpage@gobbc.edu
PAGE, Cynthia .... 540-453-2281 487 G
pagec@brcc.edu
PAGE, David .... 504-816-4362 191 E
dpage@dillard.edu
PAGE, Eric, J .... 860-701-6117 519 B
eric.j.page@uscg.mil
PAGE, Heather .... 731-286-3331 437 A
page@dscc.edu
PAGE, Hugh, R .... 574-631-7242 165 A
page.6@nd.edu
PAGE, JR., Hugh, R ...... 574-631-7147 165 A
hpage@nd.edu
PAGE, James .... 314-529-9344 262 B
jpage@maryville.edu
PAGE, James, H .... 207-973-3220 201 A
jpage@maine.edu
PAGE, Jennifer .... 989-275-5000 232 E
jennifer.page@kirtland.edu
PAGE, Jonathan, E .... 434-395-4808 482 E
pageje@longwood.edu
PAGE, Kelli .... 209-946-2987.. 70 F
kpage@pacific.edu
PAGE, Kimberly, D .... 207-581-1290 201 B
kimberly.page@maine.edu
PAGE, LeAnne .... 910-892-3178 338 D
lpage@heritagebiblecollege.edu
PAGE, Martin .... 918-631-2698 381 C
martin-page@utulsa.edu
PAGE, Mary .... 610-436-2747 407 D
mpage@wcupa.edu
PAGE, Pamela, G .... 254-442-5121 445 Q
pam.page@cisco.edu
PAGE, Phillip .... 617-873-0256 213 B
phillip.page@cambridgecollege.edu
PAGE, Robert .... 912-260-4201 125 F
robert.page@sgsc.edu
PAGE, Robert .... 816-604-4063 262 F
robert.page@mcckc.edu
PAGE, Scott .... 503-494-8050 385 D
faclog@ohsu.edu
PAGE, Susan .... 708-456-0300 153 E
susanpage@triton.edu
PAGE, Yolanda .... 504-816-4368 191 E
ypage@dillard.edu
PAGE-SMITH, Julie .... 231-843-5949 239 D
jsmith@westshore.edu
PAGE-STADLER, Jaime .. 920-424-2027 511 B
pagestad@uwosh.edu
PAGEL, Andy .... 806-291-3406 470 I
andy.pagel@wbu.edu
PAGEL, Jessica, L .... 253-535-7414 496 G
jessica.pagel@plu.edu
PAGEL, Myshie, M .... 915-831-2394 449 A
mpagel@epcc.edu
PAGEL, Richard .... 714-432-5024.. 38 H
rpagel@occ.cccd.edu
PAGENKEMPER, Karl ...... 402-449-2851 274 H
kpagenkemper@graceu.edu
PAGGI, Paula .... 818-710-2843.. 49 D
paggipm@piercecollege.edu
PAGLIARO, Joel .... 717-262-2003 415 B
conferences@wilson.edu
PAGNAM, Charles .... 617-287-4085 216 G
cpagnam@umassp.edu
PAGOTTO, Louise .... 808-734-9565 130 C
pagotto@hawaii.edu
PAGUIO, Arnold .... 510-723-6608.. 36 C
apaguio@chabotcollege.edu
PAGUYO, Christina .... 303-871-6012.. 83 E
christina.paguyo@du.edu
PAHCODDY, JR., Lee .... 785-749-8467 178 A
lpahcoddy@haskell.edu
PAHL, Jane .... 419-358-3324 357 E
pahlj@bluffton.edu
PAHL, Jennifer, K .... 989-964-4011 236 F
jkpahl@svsu.edu
PAI, Edward .... 310-233-4044.. 49 B
paie@lahc.edu
PAIER, Daniel, L .... 203-287-3022.. 87 G
PAIER, Daniel, L .... 203-287-3022.. 87 G
paier.dean@snet.net
PAIER, Jonathan, E .... 203-287-3180.. 87 G
paier.jep@snet.net
PAIER, Maureen, E .... 203-287-3035.. 87 G
paier.fin@snet.net
PAIGE, Andrew .... 617-928-4519 222 D
apaige@mountida.edu
PAIGE, Brian .... 616-526-6758 228 B
bp28@calvin.edu
PAIGE, Carmon .... 334-683-2353.... 3 A
cpaige@marionmilitary.edu
PAIGE, Ellen .... 904-256-7028 102 B
epaige@ju.edu
PAIGE, Joseph, P .... 860-832-2225.. 84 J
paigejop@ccsu.edu
PAIGE, Leslie .... 785-628-4349 177 D
lpagie@fhsu.edu
PAIGE, Michael .... 978-232-2259 214 G
mpaige@endicott.edu
PAIGE, Sonji .... 617-327-6777 226 B
sonji_paige@williamjames.edu
PAIGE, Tim .... 352-638-9737.. 95 H
tpaige@beaconcollege.edu
PAIGE, Timothy .... 401-232-6011 416 A
tpaige@bryant.edu
PAIKOWSKI, Gary .... 903-463-8707 449 J
paikowski@grayson.edu
PAIN, Karen, D .... 561-868-3325 105 A
paink@palmbeachstate.edu
PAINE, Brenda .... 248-689-8282 238 F
bpaine@walshcollege.edu
PAINE, Clarke, C .... 717-358-3991 395 G
clarke.paine@fandm.edu
PAINE, Dorie .... 573-341-4218 269 A
pained@mst.edu
PAINE, Gage, E .... 512-471-1133 467 C
gage.paine@austin.utexas.edu
PAINO, Troy .... 540-654-1301 486 D
president@umw.edu
PAINTER, Donald .... 863-669-2929 105 F
dpainter@polk.edu
PAINTER, Donald .... 863-297-1096 105 F
dpainter@polk.edu
PAINTER, Jami .... 217-244-8247 153 G
painterj@uillinois.edu
PAINTER, Joe .... 312-922-1884 144 H
jpainter@maccormac.edu
PAINTER, Noel .... 386-822-7010 111 E
npainter@stetson.edu
PAINTER, Sherry .... 901-435-1383 433 A
sherry_painter@loc.edu
PAINTER, Virginia, R ..... 304-696-4621 504 C
painterv@marshall.edu
PAIR-CUNNINGHAM,
Stephanie, S .... 301-546-0649 206 E
pairss@pgcc.edu
PAISANT, Julie .... 408-924-2250.. 34 D
julie.paisant@sjsu.edu
PAITSON, David .... 906-635-2625 232 J
PAIVA, Ann .... 718-940-5902 322 G
apaiva@sjcny.edu
PAIZ, Nokomis .... 218-679-2860 249 R
PAJE-MANALO, Leila, L 603-862-3491 282 F
leila.paje-manalo@unh.edu
PAJIC, Natasa .... 859-233-8213 189 H
npajic@transy.edu
PAK, David, Y .... 703-425-4143 481 H
PAK, Scott .... 714-816-0366.. 67 J
scott.pak@trident.edu
PAK, Su, Y .... 212-662-7100 332 C
spak@uts.columbia.edu
PAKALA, James, C .... 314-434-4044 259 B
jim.pakala@covenantseminary.edu
PAKENHAM, Julie .... 317-788-6179 164 H
pakenhamj@uindy.edu
PAKHMANOV, Laura ..... 201-761-6412 291 D
lpakhmanov@saintpeters.edu
PAKOWSKI, Lawrence ... 863-297-5282 105 F
lpakowski@polk.edu
PAKSTIS, Tracey, A .... 774-354-0459 211 F
tracey.pakstis@becker.edu
PALACIO, Michelle .... 305-348-1757 109 D
michelle.palacio@fiu.edu
PALACIOS, Carol .... 305-377-8817.. 95 A
PALACIOS, Elizabeth ..... 254-710-1020 444 B
liz_palacios@baylor.edu
PALACIOS, Francisco, E 671-735-5501 519 H
francisco.palacios1@guamcc.edu
PALACIOS, Luz, M .... 787-786-3030 526 F
lpalacios@ucb.edu.pr
PALACIOS, Rosanne ...... 956-326-2178 459 B
rosanne.palacios@tamiu.edu
PALADINO, Angela .... 802-828-8613 476 F
angela.paladino@vcfa.edu
PALAGANO, Nicole .... 973-748-9000 284 A
nicole_palagano@bloomfield.edu
PALAGONIA, Michael ..... 802-635-1205 477 C
michael.palagonia@jsc.edu
PALAKAL, Mathew, J .... 317-278-7689 160 E
mpalakal@iupui.edu
PALAMOUNTAIN,
Valerie .... 434-961-5333 489 C
vpalamountain@pvcc.edu
PALAN, Kay, M .... 205-348-8901.... 8 A
kay.m.palan@ua.edu
PALANGI, Anthony .... 518-743-2246 328 G
palangia@sunyacc.edu
PALANKI, Srinivas .... 409-880-8741 462 C
srinivas.palanki@lamar.edu
PALANTZAS, Nicholas ... 781-821-2222 220 B
PALASOTA, Joanna, E ... 713-525-3151 466 J
palasota@stthom.edu
PALAZOLA, Cecelia .... 901-272-5142 434 B
cpalazola@mca.edu
PALAZZI, Bea .... 910-755-7301 341 C
palazzib@brunswickcc.edu

PALAZZO, Robert .... 205-934-5643.... 8 B
rpalazzo@uab.edu
PALCZEWSKI, Christine, E .... 716-896-0700 333 C
cepalcz@villa.edu
PALDER, Amy .... 404-364-8427 124 A
apalder@oglethorpe.edu
PALEL, Dipte .... 310-660-3444.. 42 C
dpatel@elcamino.edu
PALELLA, Rocco .... 412-237-4416 392 G
rpalella@ccac.edu
PALEN, Lisa .... 203-575-8100.. 86 B
lpalen@nv.edu
PALERMO, Kirk, M .... 830-591-7350 457 C
kmpalermo@swtjc.edu
PALERMO, Pam .... 231-995-1533 235 B
ppalermo@nmc.edu
PALERMO, Pamela .... 440-375-7000 364 C
ppalermo@lec.edu
PALIAN, Paul .... 847-635-1806 148 D
ppalian@oakton.edu
PALICIA, Deborah .... 973-278-5400 283 J
dlp@berkeleycollege.edu
PALICIA, Deborah .... 973-278-5400 299 F
dlp@berkeleycollege.edu
PALINKAS, Robert .... 847-491-8100 148 C
robert.palinkas@northwestern.edu
PALINKAS, Robert, D .... 217-333-2711 154 B
palinkas@illinois.edu
PALIS, Michael .... 856-225-2992 290 B
palis@camden.rutgers.edu
PALIWAL, Rupendra ...... 203-371-7851.. 88 C
paliwalr@sacredheart.edu
PALKA, Eugene .... 859-622-8097 184 F
eugene.palka@eku.edu
PALLADINO, Michael ..... 732-571-7550 287 C
mpalladi@monmouth.edu
PALLADINO, Richard ...... 914-633-2351 311 B
rpalladino@iona.edu
PALLADINO, Robert ...... 740-283-6405 361 L
rpalladino@franciscan.edu
PALLANEZ, Joe .... 202-685-3835 518 B
pallenzaj@ndu.edu
PALLATTO-FONTAINE, Debra .... 508-373-9774 211 F
debra.pallatto-fontaine@becker.edu
PALLAVICINI, Maria, G . 209-946-2551.. 70 F
provost@pacific.edu
PALLEMONI, Sushil ...... 361-698-1207 448 H
spallemoni@delmar.edu
PALLER, Alan .... 301-654-7267 207 B
PALLOTO, Mike .... 805-289-6486.. 73 C
mpalloto@vcccd.edu
PALM, Daniel .... 928-523-2461.. 14 K
daniel.palm@nau.edu
PALM, Donald .... 804-524-5654 491 A
dpalm@vsu.edu
PALM, Elizabeth, A .... 847-735-5107 142 H
palm@lakeforest.edu
PALM, Matt .... 419-448-2020 362 G
mpalm@heidelberg.edu
PALM, Risa, I .... 404-413-2574 121 A
risapalm@gsu.edu
PALMA, Christine, G ..... 973-655-4423 287 D
palmac@mail.montclair.edu
PALMA, Eugene .... 516-877-3505 297 I
palma@adelphi.edu
PALMA, Yazmin .... 305-273-4499.. 96 N
yazmin@cbt.edu
PALMATEER, Jacaranda . 303-871-4298.. 83 E
jacaranda.palmateer@du.edu
PALMEDO, Julia, C .... 516-463-6336 310 D
julia.c.palmedo@hofstra.edu
PALMER, Alexis .... 757-340-2121 479 D
apalmer@centura.edu
PALMER, Brian .... 904-256-7373 102 B
bpalmer@ju.edu
PALMER, Brian .... 206-934-4547 497 H
brian.palmer@seattlecolleges.edu
PALMER, Carol .... 704-314-4920 338 F
cpalmer@hoodseminary.edu
PALMER, Carole .... 206-543-9792 499 D
clpalmer@uw.edu
PALMER, Charles .... 813-545-4527 421 G
charlespalmer@forrrestcollege.edu
PALMER, Dale, J .... 404-413-3434 121 A
dpalmer@gsu.edu
PALMER, Daniel .... 605-677-5011 428 E
daniel.palmer@usd.edu
PALMER, Daniel .... 605-773-3455 428 D
daniel.palmer2@sdbor.edu
PALMER, David .... 843-574-3220 419 C
dpalmer@csuniv.edu
PALMER, David .... 843-863-7930 419 C
dpalmer@csuniv.edu
PALMER, David .... 315-655-7777 300 I
dwpalmer@cazenovia.edu
PALMER, Donald, F .... 330-672-2312 363 I
dpalmer@kent.edu
PALMER, Doug .... 671-735-2862 520 B
palmerd@triton.uog.edu
PALMER, Douglas .... 330-490-7043 373 F
dpalmer@walsh.edu
PALMER, Elyn .... 575-492-2189 297 G
epalmer@usw.edu
PALMER, Eric, F .... 804-287-6591 486 G
epalmer@richmond.edu
PALMER, Gregory .... 914-323-5194 314 A
greg.palmer@mville.edu
PALMER, Gregory .... 603-428-2397 281 F
gpalmer@nec.edu
PALMER, James .... 706-864-1786 127 B
james.palmer@ung.edu
PALMER, James .... 936-261-2214 458 F
jmpalmer@pvamu.edu
PALMER, Jan, E .... 304-293-6978 505 B
jpalmer@hsc.wvu.edu
PALMER, Janice .... 860-832-1791.. 84 J
palmerj@ccsu.edu
PALMER, Jeff, L .... 302-831-2727.. 90 I
jpalmer@udel.edu
PALMER, Jodie .... 801-649-5230 471 M
PALMER, Jonathan .... 618-374-5148 149 A
president@principia.edu
PALMER, Joyce .... 315-792-5477 315 I
jpalmer@mvcc.edu
PALMER, Julio .... 787-841-2000 525 J
jpalmer@pucpr.edu
PALMER, Kevin .... 573-875-7329 258 F
kpalmer@ccis.edu
PALMER, Kris, R .... 660-284-4800 260 I
PALMER, Lisa .... 706-771-4089 116 A
lpalmer@augustatech.edu
PALMER, Lois .... 813-974-3777 111 A
loisp@usf.edu
PALMER, Martha .... 660-284-4800 260 I
PALMER, Meredith .... 903-923-2010 448 J
mpalmer@etbu.edu
PALMER, Michelle .... 870-743-3000.. 20 E
mpalmer@northark.edu
PALMER, Rebecca .... 323-343-4804.. 32 D
rpalmer@cslanet.calstatela.edu
PALMER, Rita .... 405-789-7661 380 A
rita.palmer@swcu.edu
PALMER, Robert .... 405-789-7661 380 A
robert.palmer@swcu.edu
PALMER, Ronnie .... 203-596-4531.. 87 H
rpalmer@post.edu
PALMER, Russell, A ...... 516-877-3249 297 I
palmer@adelphi.edu
PALMER, Sandra .... 718-631-5731 303 F
spalmer@qcc.cuny.edu
PALMER, Steven, C .... 269-387-4465 239 E
steven.palmer@wmich.edu
PALMER, Susan, M .... 320-363-5298 241 I
spalmer@csbsju.edu
PALMER-ELLIS, Amy ...... 802-656-9536 476 E
amy.palmer-ellis@uvm.edu
PALMER-NOONE, Laura 858-513-9240.. 26 T
laura.palmernoone@ashford.edu
PALMERI, Marian, K ...... 570-208-5900 398 D
mkpalmer@kings.edu
PALMERSHEIM, Rhonda, K .... 651-641-8894 241 L
rbehm@csp.edu
PALMESE, Giuseppe, R . 215-895-2210 394 C
giuseppe.raffaello.palmese@drexel.edu
PALMIERI, Becky .... 518-587-2100 329 C
becky.palmieri@esc.edu
PALMIERI, Kathryn .... 408-554-4318.. 62 F
kpalmieri@scu.edu
PALMIERI, Rob .... 518-681-5601 328 G
palmierir@sunyacc.edu
PALMIERI, Tony .... 304-252-9547 502 F
PALMINI, JR., William .. 650-508-3502.. 54 D
safety@ndnu.edu
PALMITER, Lia Richards .... 570-961-4799 401 B
lpalmiter@marywood.edu
PALMOUR, Mack .... 843-208-8118 425 B
mpalmour@uscb.edu
PALOK, Debra .... 623-845-3536.. 13 H
debra.palok@gccaz.edu
PALOMBO, Ryan .... 615-361-7555 431 G
rpalombo@daymarinstitute.edu
PALOMBO, Tom, J .... 336-316-2290 338 C
tpalombo@guilford.edu
PALOMBO, Vincent .... 216-373-5310 367 A
vpalombo@ndc.edu
PALSAK, Angela .... 269-782-1312 237 B
apalsak@swmich.edu
PALSER, Philip, V .... 715-833-6364 513 E
ppalser@cvtc.edu
PALTER-GILL, Dianne .... 978-762-4000 220 E
dpalterg@northshore.edu
PALUBNIAK, Dan .... 908-526-1200 289 D
daniel.palubniak@raritanval.edu
PALUCKI BLAKE, Laura . 909-607-8191.. 45 D
lpblake@hmc.edu
PALUMBO, Carmine ...... 478-289-2046 118 H
cpalumbo@ega.edu
PALUMBO, John .... 602-275-7133.. 16 A
john.palumbo@rsiaz.edu
PALUMBO, Katey .... 508-929-8835 219 A
kpalumbo2@worcester.edu
PALUMBO, Michelle ...... 314-889-1492 260 C
mpalumbo@fontbonne.edu
PALUMBO-OLSZANSKI, Linda .... 706-233-7409 125 E
lpalumbo@shorter.edu
PALUS, Christine .... 610-519-7093 413 K
christine.palus@villanova.edu
PALUSO, Eugene .... 843-953-3020 419 D
epaluso@citadel.edu
PAMINTUAN, Lisa .... 516-364-0808 317 B
pamintuan@nycollege.edu
PAMMER, Andrea, M .... 304-367-4686 504 A
andrea.pammer@fairmontstate.edu
PAMPE, Andrea .... 618-395-7777 140 E
pampea@iecc.edu
PAMPEL, Robert .... 314-977-2154 266 J
pampeljr@slu.edu
PAN, Shouan .... 206-934-3850 497 G
shouan.pan@seattlecolleges.edu
PANAMA, Annie .... 684-699-9155 519 F
a.panama@amsamoa.edu
PANARELLA, Pamela ...... 610-409-3163 413 H
ppanarella@ursinus.edu
PANAY, Panos, A .... 617-747-2316 212 B
ootp@berklee.edu
PANAYOTOVA, Evelina .. 610-790-1905 389 A
evelina.panayotova@alvernia.edu
PANCIERA, Kathy .... 952-885-5465 249 F
kpanciera@nwhealth.edu
PANDEY, Bhuban, R ...... 512-448-8442 455 I
bhubanp@stedwards.edu
PANDIT, Kavita .... 404-413-2613 121 A
kpandit@gsu.edu
PANDO, Paula .... 201-360-4021 286 E
ppando@hccc.edu
PANELLA, Kristen .... 516-686-7731 317 G
kpanella@nyit.edu
PANETTA, Carol .... 617-277-3915 212 F
panettac@bgsp.edu
PANFIL, Tim .... 630-617-6471 138 C
panfilt@elmhurst.edu
PANG, Alex .... 310-506-4561.. 56 D
alex.pang@pepperdine.edu
PANG, Eddie .... 808-735-4856 129 A
epang@chaminade.edu
PANG, John .... 510-981-2849.. 56 F
jpang@peralta.edu
PANG, Lily .... 310-506-4130.. 56 D
lily.pang@pepperdine.edu
PANG, Rebecca .... 760-384-6115.. 47 B
rebecca.pang@cerrocoso.edu
PANGBORN, Joseph ..... 401-841-6555 518 E
PANGBORN, Robert, N . 814-863-1864 403 F
rnp1@psu.edu
PANGELINAN, Leo .... 670-237-6766 520 D
leo.pangelinan@marianas.edu
PANGELINAN, Perry ...... 670-237-6795 520 D
perry.pangelinan@marianas.edu
PANGONIS, Tricia .... 440-375-7100 364 C
tpangonis@lec.edu
PANHAS, Matthew .... 414-277-7300 509 A
PANI, Eric, A .... 318-342-1025 198 A
pani@ulm.edu
PANICO, Russ .... 269-488-4393 231 G
rpanico@kvcc.edu
PANIGOT, Benjamin ...... 269-471-3321 227 B
panigot@andrews.edu
PANKEN, Aaron .... 212-824-2219 309 F
apanken@huc.edu
PANKOW, Craig .... 808-853-1040 129 F
craigpankow@pacrim.edu
PANKRATZ, Terry .... 972-883-4802 467 D
terry.pankratz@utdallas.edu
PANLILIO, Carmen .... 219-989-2367 163 E
carmen.panlilio@pnw.edu
PANNEGGIANTE, John .. 201-559-6089 286 C
pane@felician.edu
PANNELL, Kerry, E .... 404-471-6361 114 H
kpannell@agnesscott.edu
PANNELL, Randall .... 864-977-7011 422 I
randall.pannell@ngu.edu
PANNIER, Darren .... 660-596-7232 267 E
dpannier@sfccmo.edu
PANNKUK, Matthew ...... 620-417-1161 181 E
matthew.pannkuk@sccc.edu
PANOFF, Virginia .... 231-348-6698 234 H
vpanoff@ncmich.edu
PANTALEO, Josephine ... 718-631-6391 303 F
jpantaleo@qcc.cuny.edu
PANTEL, Braelin .... 303-352-4465.. 80 Q
bpantel@msudenver.edu
PANTELIA, Maria .... 949-824-8213.. 69 A
chair@uci.edu
PANTER, Deborah .... 415-422-4588.. 72 A
dpanter@usfca.edu
PANTIC, Zorica .... 617-989-4476 225 E
panticz@wit.edu
PANTLIK, Sandy .... 405-945-9196 378 C
spantli@osuokc.edu
PANTOJA, Antonio, L .... 787-279-1912 523 J
apantoja@bayamon.inter.edu
PANTOJA, Veronica .... 818-785-2726.. 35 N
veronica.pantoja@casalomacollege.edu
PANTONE, Dirk .... 303-220-1200.. 77 D
dirk.pantone@cffp.edu
PANU, Al, M .... 843-208-8242 425 B
apanu@uscb.edu
PANZECA, Linda .... 513-244-4393 366 A
linda.panzeca@msj.edu
PANZELLA, Carla .... 978-542-6401 218 E
cpanzella@salemstate.edu
PAO, Roger .... 617-603-6900 222 F
roger.pao@necb.edu
PAOLI, Jessenia .... 718-289-5288 301 D
jessenia.paoli@bcc.cuny.edu
PAOLILLO, Benjamin ..... 812-877-8844 163 G
paolillo@rose-hulman.edu
PAOLINI, Francine .... 616-632-2131 227 C
paolifra@aquinas.edu
PAOLUCCI, Jeff .... 719-384-6833.. 81 G
jeff.paolucci@ojc.edu
PAPADIMITRIOU, Dimitri .... 914-758-7426 211 B
dpb@bard.edu
PAPADIMITRIOU, Dimitri, B .... 845-758-7426 298 I
dbp@levy.bard.edu
PAPADIMOS, Peter, J ... 419-530-8411 372 F
peter.papadimos@utoledo.edu
PAPADOPOULOS, Michael .... 518-783-2376 324 C
mpapadopoulos@siena.edu
PAPADOPOULOS, Vassilios .... 323-442-1463.. 72 B
vpapadop@usc.edu
PAPAEFTHYMIOU, Marios .... 949-824-7427.. 69 A
marios@uci.edu
PAPAFIL, Drucie, A .... 757-446-6143 480 C
papafida@evms.edu
PAPAGEORGE, Anne ..... 215-898-7241 412 G
fresvp@upenn.edu
PAPAJOHN, Michelle .... 631-687-5151 322 G
mpapajohn@sjcny.edu
PAPAKONSTANTINOU, Karen .... 732-255-0400 288 B
karenp@ocean.edu
PAPALEO, Stefano .... 561-237-7831 103 E
spapaleo@lynn.edu
PAPALIA, Daria .... 845-451-1359 306 D
daria.papalia@culinary.edu
PAPANDREA, Vincent .... 212-237-8864 302 F
vpapandrea@jjay.cuny.edu
PAPANIKOLAOU, Constantia .... 617-994-6947 216 F
cpapanikolaou@bhe.mass.edu
PAPARIELLA, Justin ...... 412-338-4770 390 D
jpapariella@brightwoodcareer.edu
PAPAS, Jeff .... 715-425-4613 511 E
jeff.papas@uwrf.edu
PAPATHANASIOU, Antonios .... 617-850-1297 215 I
apapathanasiou@hchc.edu
PAPATHEOFANIS, Frank 760-471-1316.. 59 A
fpapath@skcca.edu
PAPAZIAN, Mary .... 408-924-1177.. 34 D
sjsupres@sjsu.edu
PAPAZOGLOU, John ..... 814-865-5423 403 F
jxp769@psu.edu
PAPE, Randi .... 712-325-3428 170 K
rpape@iwcc.edu
PAPE, Sabrina .... 916-660-7202.. 63 K
spape@sierracollege.edu
PAPENFUSS, Larry, A .... 218-299-4161 241 K
papenfus@cord.edu
PAPESCH, Katherine ...... 217-732-3155 143 G
kpapesch@lincolncollege.edu
PAPIA, Jeffrey .... 726-926-8924 310 B
jpapia@hilbert.edu
PAPICH, Mark .... 210-805-2530 465 E
papich@uiwtx.edu
PAPILLON, Terry, L .... 931-598-1248 436 A
tlpapill@sewanee.edu
PAPINCHAK, John, R .... 412-268-7404 391 H
jp7p@andrew.cmu.edu

PAPINI, Dennis .... 217-206-6614 154 A
dpapi2@uis.edu
PAPP, John .... 412-918-2614 125 H
jpapp@southuniversity.edu
PAPP, Justin .... 708-596-2000 151 H
jpapp@ssc.edu
PAPPAGEORGE, Steven . 708-974-5407 146 C
pappageorges3@morainevalley.edu
PAPPAS, Amy .... 703-284-1681 483 A
amy.pappas@marymount.edu
PAPPAS, Domenica, G .. 312-567-3035 140 I
pappas@iit.edu
PAPPAS, Gregory, J ...... 718-817-4350 308 G
pappas@fordham.edu
PAPPAS, Jesse .... 304-358-2000 501 I
PAPPAS, Joanna .... 773-508-7429 144 D
jpappas@luc.edu
PAPPAS, John .... 918-663-9000 378 K
johnp@plattcollege.org
PAPPAS, Katherine .... 413-782-1327 225 F
katherine.pappas@wne.edu
PAPPAS, Nikki .... 614-882-2551 361 K
npappas@fortiscollege.edu
PAPPAS, Richard, J .... 616-698-7111 229 D
rpappas@davenport.edu
PAPPAS, Tony, A .... 641-422-4350 172 C
pappaton@niacc.edu
PAPPATHAN, Matthew ... 802-828-8740 371 A
matt.pappathan@myunion.edu
PAPSON, Melissa .... 724-222-5330 403 E
mpapson@penncommercial.edu
PAPULI, Tina .... 212-247-3434 313 K
epapuli@mandl.edu
PAQUETTE, Ashley .... 906-932-4231 230 D
ashleyp@gogebic.edu
PAQUETTE, Karen .... 518-629-4552 310 G
k.paquette@hvcc.edu
PAQUETTE, Kevin .... 207-893-7797 200 G
kpaquett@sjcme.edu
PAQUIN, Delbert .... 928-724-6772.. 12 G
dpaquin@dinecollege.edu
PARADEE, Melissa .... 802-776-5223 474 H
melissa.paradee@csj.edu
PARADIS, Ronald, S ...... 541-383-7599 382 B
rparadis@cocc.edu
PARADIS, Thomas .... 317-940-8972 156 I
tparadis@butler.edu
PARADISE, Melanie, M . 865-539-7130 437 F
mmparadise@pstcc.edu
PARADKAR, Vish .... 719-389-6454.. 77 J
vparadkar@coloradocollege.edu
PARAMORE, Marcus .... 334-241-8622.... 7 E
marcus@troy.edu
PARAMORE, Pamela ...... 757-455-3238 491 F
pparamore@vwu.edu
PARANDI, Tony .... 765-677-1566 161 C
tony.parandi@indwes.edu
PARCEL, Julie .... 636-922-8383 265 J
jparcel@stchas.edu
PARCELLS, Fred .... 215-785-0111 404 P
PARCELLS, Rex .... 254-659-7821 450 B
rparcells@hillcollege.edu
PARCHER, Kim .... 563-588-8000 169 B
kparcher@emmaus.edu
PARDA, Lauren .... 860-768-2415.. 89 C
parda@hartford.edu
PARDALES, Michael ...... 207-893-6643 200 G
mpardales@sjcme.edu
PARDEE, Joseph .... 860-701-5176.. 87 F
pardee_j@mitchell.edu
PARDO, Carlos .... 314-454-7547 260 E
cxp1679@bjc.org
PARDO, Carmen, L .... 973-353-5113 290 D
cpardo@newark.rutgers.edu
PARDUE, J. Harold .... 251-461-1600.... 9 B
hpardue@southalabama.edu
PARDUE, Judi, D .... 817-531-4401 463 G
jpardue@txwes.edu
PARDUE, Karen .... 207-221-4361 202 A
kpardue@une.edu
PARDUE, Samuel .... 706-542-3924 127 A
caesdean@uga.edu
PARE, Carroll .... 802-387-6885 475 C
cpare@landmark.edu
PAREDES, Esteban .... 785-833-4307 179 C
esteban.paredes@kwu.edu
PAREDES, Hector, O ...... 201-761-7425 291 D
hparedes@saintpeters.edu
PAREDES, Luis, F .... 508-531-2729 217 D
lparedes@bridgew.edu
PARELLA, JR.,
Richard, A .... 540-464-7322 490 E
parellara@vmi.edu
PARENS, Joshua, S .... 972-721-5241 464 E
parens@udallas.edu
PARENT, Cyrille .... 719-502-2975.. 81 H
cyrille.parent@ppcc.edu
PARENTI, Stefano .... 603-645-9695 282 C
s.parenti@snhu.edu
PARFITT, Richard .... 239-489-9339 100 E
richard.parfitt@fsw.edu
PARGE, Theodore, C ..... 630-844-5262 133 H
tparge@aurora.edu
PARHAM, Loretta .... 404-978-2018 126 D
lparham@auctr.edu
PARHAM, Patricia .... 805-493-3185.. 30 E
pparham@callutheran.edu
PARHAM, Sandra .... 615-966-5837 433 D
sandra.parham@lipscomb.edu
PARHAM, Thomas, A ..... 949-824-4804.. 69 A
taparham@uci.edu
PARHAM, Tyrone .... 413-545-2121 216 H
tparham@umass.edu
PARHAM, Walter, H ...... 803-777-7854 424 I
terry@mailbox.sc.edu
PARIANTE, Jody .... 212-431-2137 317 H
jody.pariante@nyls.edu
PARIGIAN, Debbie .... 503-244-0726 381 H
debbieparigian@achs.edu
PARILLO, Rebecca .... 419-289-5870 356 L
rparillo@ashland.edu
PARIS, Chris .... 314-921-9290 269 D
dean@ugst.edu
PARIS, Lisa .... 215-670-9127 403 D
lparis@peirce.edu
PARIS, Mark, S .... 302-356-6829.. 91 B
mark.s.paris@wilmu.edu
PARIS, III, Oren .... 479-248-7236.. 19 F
oparis3@ecollege.edu
PARIS, Susan .... 919-536-7200 342 G
pariss@durhamtech.edu
PARISEAU, Anita .... 719-389-6772.. 77 J
anita.pariseau@coloradocollege.edu
PARISH, Daniel, B .... 603-526-3729 280 H
daniel.parish@colby-sawyer.edu
PARISH, Michael, C ...... 906-248-8400 227 P
mparish@bmcc.edu
PARISH, Susan .... 617-373-2518 223 D
PARISHER, Deborah ...... 252-823-5166 343 A
parisherd@edgecombe.edu
PARISI, Dawn .... 352-588-8251 106 N
dawn.parisi@saintleo.edu
PARISI, Michael, J .... 860-444-8481 519 B
michael.j.parisi@uscg.mil
PARISI, Rob .... 805-922-6966.. 24 J
rparisi@hancockcollege.edu
PARISI, Robert .... 805-922-6966.. 24 J
rparisi@hancockcollege.edu
PARIZO, Daniel, C .... 920-923-8760 508 B
dcparizo94@marianuniversity.edu
PARK, Choong Gi .... 562-926-1023.. 57 J
choong.park@gmail.com
PARK, Claire .... 858-225-4301.. 29 G
claire@calarttech.edu
PARK, Daniel, L .... 509-527-5999 500 G
park@whitman.edu
PARK, Daniel, W .... 858-822-1236.. 69 E
dwpark@ucsd.edu
PARK, Dave .... 213-413-9500.. 65 E
admin@scusoma.edu
PARK, David .... 714-533-3946.. 35 B
dpark@calums.edu
PARK, George .... 310-453-8300.. 42 D
george@emperors.edu
PARK, Hojin .... 215-884-8942 415 C
hojin.park@woninstitute.edu
PARK, Hun Sung .... 213-381-0081.. 46 I
office@laopendoor.org
PARK, Hyung .... 213-252-5100.. 24 A
hpark@alu.edu
PARK, Jack, C .... 210-567-2020 468 E
parkjc@uthscsa.edu
PARK, Jessica .... 213-252-5100.. 24 A
jpark@alu.edu
PARK, Jinsoo .... 973-877-3588 285 K
jpark@essex.edu
PARK, Joshua .... 770-232-2717 124 G
PARK, Joyce, G .... 703-333-5904 491 H
ghpark@wuv.edu
PARK, Justin .... 770-220-7791 119 D
jpark@gcuniv.edu
PARK, Kathryn .... 409-933-8201 446 H
kpark@com.edu
PARK, Kevin .... 404-687-4533 118 B
parkk@ctsnet.edu
PARK, Laura .... 801-649-5230 471 M
office@midwifery.edu
PARK, Linda .... 315-279-5208 312 D
lpark@keuka.edu
PARK, Matthew .... 940-397-4501 453 C
matthew.park@mwsu.edu
PARK, Michong .... 818-364-7868.. 49 C
parkm@lamission.edu
PARK, Mihyun .... 562-926-1023.. 57 J
mhpark@ptsa.edu
PARK, Mimi .... 714-533-1495.. 64 F
mimi@southbaylo.edu
PARK, Min .... 213-487-0110.. 41 K
officemanager@dula.edu
PARK, Myung .... 253-964-7327 497 B
mpark@pierce.ctc.edu
PARK, Roger .... 317-632-5553 162 P
rpark@lincolntech.edu
PARK, Scott .... 309-341-7459 142 G
sapark@knox.edu
PARK, Seoung, H .... 617-427-7293 215 E
spark4@gordonconwell.edu
PARK, Steve .... 972-860-7771 447 F
spark@dcccd.edu
PARK, Sunny .... 806-720-7507 452 D
sunny.park@lcu.edu
PARK, Yong Hee .... 714-533-1495.. 64 F
yhpark@southbaylo.edu
PARK, Young, S .... 636-327-4645 263 C
dl@midwest.edu
PARK, Young Hae .... 202-559-0434.. 91 H
younghae.park@gallaudet.edu
PARK, Yung Won .... 610-917-1457 413 G
ywpark@valleyforge.edu
PARKE, Lydia .... 215-780-1417 410 D
lparke@salus.edu
PARKE, Scott .... 941-752-5119 108 P
parkes@scf.edu
PARKER, Amie .... 207-621-3448 201 C
amie.parker@maine.edu
PARKER, Andrew .... 765-677-1989 161 C
andrew.parker@indwes.edu
PARKER, Annette .... 610-409-3141 413 H
aparker@ursinus.edu
PARKER, Annette .... 507-389-7211 247 H
annette.parker@southcentral.edu
PARKER, Anthony .... 903-593-8311 461 B
aparker@texascollege.edu
PARKER, Anthony, O ..... 229-430-0656 114 J
aparker@albanytech.edu
PARKER, Audrey .... 252-492-2061 347 C
parkera@vgcc.edu
PARKER, Ava, L .... 561-868-3501 105 A
parkera@palmbeachstate.edu
PARKER, Barbara .... 828-627-4515 343 G
bmparker@haywood.edu
PARKER, Barbara .... 315-268-6445 304 B
bparker@clarkson.edu
PARKER, Beverly, J .... 318-670-9571 196 A
bparker@susla.edu
PARKER, Brandon, C .... 707-965-6311.. 55 F
bparker@puc.edu
PARKER, Bruce .... 406-657-1124 272 I
bruce.parker@rocky.edu
PARKER, Carol .... 864-231-2000 418 E
cparker@andersonuniversity.edu
PARKER, Carol, A .... 915-747-7885 467 E
cparker2@utep.edu
PARKER, Cassandra ...... 202-274-5669.. 93 D
cparker@udc.edu
PARKER, Cassandra ...... 334-727-8655.... 7 F
cparker@mytu.tuskegee.edu
PARKER, Catherine .... 248-218-2154 236 C
cparker@rc.edu
PARKER, Cathy .... 601-484-8799 253 G
cparker@meridiancc.edu
PARKER, Charles, R ...... 850-263-3261.. 95 F
crparker@baptistcollege.edu
PARKER, Chris .... 870-733-6047.. 18 B
crparker@asumidsouth.edu
PARKER, Corey .... 404-297-9522 120 D
parkerc@gptc.edu
PARKER, Craig .... 502-897-4131 189 A
cparker@sbts.edu
PARKER, Cynthia .... 706-295-6346 119 G
cparker@highlands.edu
PARKER, Cynthia, L ...... 401-598-1345 416 C
cparker@jwu.edu
PARKER, Cynthia Ann .... 609-652-4378 291 H
cynthia.parker@stockton.edu
PARKER, Dale .... 757-423-2095 480 K
PARKER, Dana, C .... 610-436-2627 407 D
dparker@wcupa.edu
PARKER, Daniel .... 870-248-4000.. 18 J
daniel.parker@blackrivertech.edu
PARKER, Danny .... 864-231-2061 418 E
dparker@andersonuniversity.edu
PARKER, Darrell .... 828-227-7401 352 C
dfparker@wcu.edu
PARKER, Deborah .... 870-762-3113.. 17 K
dparker@smail.anc.edu
PARKER, Debra .... 419-434-5478 372 B
parker@findlay.edu
PARKER, Debra, O .... 919-530-5269 350 D
dparker@nccu.edu
PARKER, Diane .... 617-243-2137 216 C
dparker@lasell.edu
PARKER, Fiona .... 817-554-5950 452 G
fparker@messengercollege.edu
PARKER, Frank .... 936-294-1786 462 F
fparker@shsu.edu
PARKER, Gail, C .... 318-342-1960 198 A
gparker@ulm.edu
PARKER, Heidi .... 641-673-1031 174 F
parkerh@wmpenn.edu
PARKER, Holly .... 518-327-6300 320 A
hparker@paulsmiths.edu
PARKER, Jack .... 321-433-7380.. 97 N
parkerj@easternflorida.edu
PARKER, Janet .... 312-355-4565 153 H
japarker@uic.edu
PARKER, Janice, C .... 312-658-5100 152 I
janice.parker@tbiil.edu
PARKER, Jeanette .... 270-789-5075 184 B
jjparker@campbellsville.edu
PARKER, Jerry .... 515-271-2835 168 J
jerry.parker@drake.edu
PARKER, Jesse .... 919-761-2310 349 C
jparker@sebts.edu
PARKER, Jim .... 919-807-6976 340 K
parkerj@nccommunitycolleges.edu
PARKER, Jim, O .... 504-816-8592 195 D
jparker@nobts.edu
PARKER, Joe .... 970-491-3350.. 78 N
joe.parker@colostate.edu
PARKER, Juli .... 508-910-4582 217 A
jparker@umassd.edu
PARKER, Julia .... 601-643-8308 252 G
julia.parker@colin.edu
PARKER, Kathleen .... 320-363-2121 250 A
kparker@csbsju.edu
PARKER, Kathy .... 320-363-2121 241 I
kparker@csbsju.edu
PARKER, Keith .... 561-732-4424 107 C
kparker@svdp.edu
PARKER, Keith, S .... 310-794-6811.. 69 B
kparker@support.ucla.edu
PARKER, Kelly .... 312-487-4743 153 A
kelly.parker@tribecaflashpoint.edu
PARKER, Kelly .... 818-345-9245.. 40 A
kparker@columbiacollege.edu
PARKER, Kevin .... 845-758-7511 298 I
parker@bard.edu
PARKER, Kim .... 214-637-3530 470 H
kparker@wadecollege.edu
PARKER, Laura .... 310-794-2304.. 69 B
lparker@support.ucla.edu
PARKER, III, Lee .... 804-289-8405 486 G
lparker@richmond.edu
PARKER, Linda .... 641-673-1327 174 F
parkerl@wmpenn.edu
PARKER, Linda, M .... 518-388-6578 332 B
parkerl@union.edu
PARKER, Mae .... 641-269-4631 169 F
parkerma@grinnell.edu
PARKER, Marcia .... 909-607-7855.. 38 C
marcia_parker@kgi.edu
PARKER, Mark .... 405-208-5315 377 D
mparker@okcu.edu
PARKER, Mary .... 310-393-0411.. 56 A
mfparker@rand.org
PARKER, Mary, G .... 801-581-3490 472 P
mgparker@sa.utah.edu
PARKER, Mary, G .... 801-585-9453 472 P
mgparker@sa.utah.edu
PARKER, Mary Jo .... 713-221-8471 465 C
parkerm@uhd.edu
PARKER, Melanie, L ...... 617-715-5329 221 C
PARKER, Micah .... 951-343-4381.. 28 G
miparker@calbaptist.edu
PARKER, Michael .... 210-341-1366 454 B
mparker@ost.edu
PARKER, Michelle .... 928-523-6500.. 14 K
michelle.parker@nau.edu
PARKER, Ned, A .... 617-964-1100 210 G
PARKER, Patsy .... 580-774-3284 380 B
patsy.parker@swosu.edu
PARKER, Pennie .... 407-646-2636 106 J
pparker@rollins.edu
PARKER, Philip, L .... 812-464-1865 165 C
plparker@usi.edu
PARKER, Pippin .... 212-229-5859 316 E
parkerp@newschool.edu
PARKER, Randy .... 336-334-4822 343 E
PARKER, Robert .... 707-256-7175.. 53 D
rparker@napavalley.edu
PARKER, Robin, L .... 513-529-6734 365 I
parkerrl@miamioh.edu
PARKER, Rodney .... 410-617-2310 205 A
rparker1@loyola.edu
PARKER, Ron .... 979-230-3480 444 E
ron.parker@brazosport.edu
PARKER, Shelly .... 678-839-6380 127 F
sparker@westga.edu
PARKER, Sherry .... 407-438-6000 108 I

PARKER, Sonia 801-957-4446 474 B sonia.parker@slcc.edu
PARKER, Sonya, L 270-824-8586 186 D sonya.parker@kctcs.edu
PARKER, Tammie 541-278-5850 382 A tparker@bluecc.edu
PARKER, Teresa 740-389-4636 365 B parkert@mtc.edu
PARKER, Teri 866-492-5336 251 E teri.parker@laureate.net
PARKER, Terry 863-583-9050 109 E
PARKER, Zoann 717-299-7793 411 C parker@stevenscollege.edu
PARKER AMES, Gwen 845-675-4446 319 C gwen.ames@nyack.edu
PARKER-BELL, Bernice 904-470-8261 98 B bparkerbell@ewc.edu
PARKER-JEANNETTE, Cyrus 562-985-4376 32 C cyrus.parker-jeannette@csulb.edu
PARKER-KELLY, Darlene 323-563-9340 36 H darleneparkerkelly@cdrewu.edu
PARKER-WOLERY, Amanda 513-562-6267 356 J aparker@artacademy.edu
PARKHURST, Abbie 540-828-5782 478 J aparkhur@bridgewater.edu
PARKHURST, Cindy 951-785-2982 47 F cparkhurst@lasiera.edu
PARKIN, Janice 312-341-4327 150 D jparkin01@roosevelt.edu
PARKINSON, Curt 559-278-4062 32 A cparkinson@csufresno.edu
PARKINSON, III, Henry, C 978-665-3160 217 E hparkinson@fitchburgstate.edu
PARKINSON, Richard 815-772-7218 146 D rcpark@morrisontech.edu
PARKINSON, Tracy 843-383-8198 420 B tparkinson@coker.edu
PARKMAN, Julie 315-386-7119 329 A parkman@canton.edu
PARKS, Amy 216-987-4537 360 E amy.parks@tri-c.edu
PARKS, Ann 660-263-4100 264 C annp@macc.edu
PARKS, Cherri, S 303-963-3357 77 I cparks@ccu.edu
PARKS, Daniel, A 530-898-5142 31 D daparks@csuchico.edu
PARKS, David 304-473-8011 505 G parks.d@wvwc.edu
PARKS, Donald, K 850-201-8071 98 I dparks@flagler.edu
PARKS, Earl 202-651-5494 91 H earl.parks@gallaudet.edu
PARKS, Erik 312-487-4743 153 A erik.parks@tribecaflashpoint.edu
PARKS, Jason 318-484-2184 197 D parksj@nsula.edu
PARKS, Jason 951-372-7017 58 G jason.parks@norcocollege.edu
PARKS, Jeffrey 281-476-1806 455 L jeffrey.parks@sjcd.edu
PARKS, Julie 616-234-3714 230 F jparks@grcc.edu
PARKS, Kristin 641-683-5108 169 I kristin.parks@indianhills.edu
PARKS, Marshall 970-351-1814 83 F marshall.parks@unco.edu
PARKS, Michael 210-567-2791 468 E parksm@uthscsa.edu
PARKS, Patricia 714-816-0366 67 J patricia.parks@trident.edu
PARKS, Rodney 336-278-6677 337 G rparks4@elon.edu
PARKS, Valerie 915-779-8031 470 E vparks@computercareercenter.com
PARKS, Vanasia Conley 423-425-4467 440 A vanasia-parks@utc.edu
PARKTON, Deanna 215-489-4728 393 F deanna.parkton@delval.edu
PARLACOSKI, Julie 732-987-2219 286 D jparlacoski@georgian.edu
PARLE, Joseph, D 713-785-5995 446 A joe.parle@cbshouston.edu
PARLER, Branson 616-222-3000 232 F bparler@kuyper.edu
PARLETT, Lynda, W 828-339-4265 346 H l_parlett@southwesterncc.edu
PARLETT, Ray, M 585-567-9333 310 F ray.parlett@houghton.edu
PARLETT-SWEENEY, Mary, W 518-782-6988 324 C mparlett-sweeney@siena.edu
PARLETTE, Jared 800-955-2527 177 H jparlette@grantham.edu
PARLOW, Matthew, J 714-628-2678 36 G parlow@chapman.edu
PARMELY, Michael 913-588-7053 181 C mparmely@kumc.edu
PARMER, David 409-212-5724 443 L
PARNELL, Kathleen 410-617-2354 205 A kmparnell@loyola.edu
PARNELL, Paul 559-244-5901 66 E paul.parnell@scccd.edu
PARNELL, Philip 307-382-1639 517 C pparnell@westernwyoming.edu
PARNELL, Rob Roy 512-463-2237 462 A robroy.parnell@tsus.edu
PARR, Deidra 304-829-7033 501 F dparr@bethanywv.edu
PARR, Vanna 940-898-3525 464 A vparr@twu.edu
PARR WALKER, Diane 574-631-7790 165 A diane.parr.walker@nd.edu
PARRA, Alicia, F 954-322-4460 102 E aliciafernandaparra@jmvu.edu
PARRA, Jonallie 209-946-3288 70 F jparra@pacific.edu
PARRELLA, Michael 208-885-6681 132 I mpp@uidaho.edu
PARRENT, Condoa 817-515-6532 458 B condoa.parrent@tccd.edu
PARRENT, Jay 270-824-8571 186 D jay.parrent@kctcs.edu
PARRENT, Rick 615-230-3321 438 C rick.parrent@volstate.edu
PARRENT, Robert 314-246-7910 269 N robertparrent@webster.edu
PARRETT, Brenda, J 601-643-8301 252 G brenda.parrett@colin.edu
PARRILL, Jacqueline 740-366-9407 358 E parrill.9@osu.edu
PARRILLA, Arlene 787-863-2390 523 K arlene.parrilla@fajardo.inter.edu
PARRIOTT, Karen 307-532-8264 516 J karen.parriott@ewc.wy.edu
PARRIS, Billy 559-251-4215 28 I admissions@calchristiancollege.edu
PARRIS, Elliott 301-860-3705 208 E eparris@bowiestate.edu
PARRISH, Austen, L 812-855-8885 159 H austparr@indiana.edu
PARRISH, Dave 770-533-7033 122 E dparrish@laniertech.edu
PARRISH, David, K 308-632-6933 277 B
PARRISH, Debra, J 906-524-8414 232 D dparrish@kbocc.edu
PARRISH, Gretchen 336-342-4261 346 B parrishg@rockinghamcc.edu
PARRISH, John 310-338-5810 50 J john.parrish@lmu.edu
PARRISH, Kelly 617-989-4960 225 E parrishk@wit.edu
PARRISH, Patricia 270-384-8030 187 H parrishp@lindsey.edu
PARRISH, Rebecca 864-592-4627 424 C parrishr@sccsc.edu
PARRISH, Sid 803-321-5263 422 H sid.parrish@newberry.edu
PARRISH TRENT, Monica 240-567-1845 205 F monica.trent@montgomerycollege.edu
PARROT, Autumn 615-383-4848 441 A aparrot@watkins.edu
PARROTT, Aaron 509-682-6795 500 D aparrott@wvc.edu
PARROTT, David 352-392-1265 110 D davewp@ufl.edu
PARROTT, Mike 843-208-8040 425 B rparrot@uscb.edu
PARROTT, Rebecca 606-248-0256 187 B rebecca.parrott@kctcs.edu
PARROTT, Roger 601-968-5919 252 C president@belhaven.edu
PARRY, John 970-491-3939 78 N john.parry@colostate.edu
PARRY, Karine 714-533-3946 35 B karine@calums.edu
PARRY, Laura, S 518-783-8282 324 C lparry@siena.edu
PARRY, Susan 845-341-4251 319 H susan.parry@sunyorange.edu
PARRY, Tim 757-352-4020 484 E tparry@regent.edu
PARSHALL, William 215-204-8822 411 B william.parshall@temple.edu
PARSLEY, Ashton 614-837-4088 373 C parsleya@valorcollege.edu
PARSLEY, Nancy, L 847-578-8401 150 E nancy.parsley@rosalindfranklin.edu
PARSNIK, Pamela 570-674-6310 401 M pparsnik@misericordia.edu
PARSON, Mark 715-232-1151 512 A parsonm@uwstout.edu
PARSON, Reginald 415-338-3068 34 C regg@sfsu.edu
PARSON, Tara 417-328-1511 267 A tparson@sbuniv.edu
PARSONS, Amy 303-534-6290 78 M amy.parsons@colostate.edu
PARSONS, Brian 405-208-5121 377 D pdparsons@okcu.edu
PARSONS, Cynthia 804-765-5800 485 H cynthia-parsons@chs.net
PARSONS, Gayle 623-245-4600 16 H gparsons@uti.edu
PARSONS, Geoffrey, J 843-349-2054 420 A parsons@coastal.edu
PARSONS, Jon 910-672-1403 350 B jparson2@uncfsu.edu
PARSONS, Kevin 910-410-1918 345 G ksparsons@richmondcc.edu
PARSONS, Marty 701-483-2531 354 A marty.parsons@dickinsonstate.edu
PARSONS, Nancy, P 309-298-1066 155 D np-parsons@wiu.edu
PARSONS, Pam 916-278-6446 33 C pparsons@csus.edu
PARSONS, Paul, F 336-278-5724 337 G pparsons@elon.edu
PARSONS, Philip 401-739-5000 416 D pparsons@neit.edu
PARSONS, Priscilla 409-880-8489 462 C priscilla.parsons@lamar.edu
PARSONS, Rachel, A 603-526-3451 280 H rparsons@colby-sawyer.edu
PARSONS, Ray 302-857-1814 90 F rparson3@dtcc.edu
PARSONS, Sarah 573-592-5311 270 B sarah.parsons@westminster-mo.edu
PARSONS, Scott 334-244-3667 4 E sparsons@aum.edu
PARSONS, Teena 910-410-1810 345 G tlparsons@richmondcc.edu
PARSONS, Timothy 570-558-1818 395 F tparsons@fortisinstitute.edu
PARSONS-ELLIS, Sandy 530-898-6897 31 D skparsons@csuchico.edu
PARSONS-NIKOLIC, Cathleen 215-951-1540 398 F parsonsnikolic@lasalle.edu
PARSONS-POLLARD, Nicolle 732-571-3550 287 C nparsons@monmouth.edu
PARSONS-WELLS, Rachel, E 864-833-7000 423 D reparsons@presby.edu
PARTAIN, Julie 229-271-4049 125 G jpartain@southgatech.edu
PARTAIN, Pam 706-272-2985 118 F ppartain@daltonstate.edu
PARTAIN, Sandra 318-678-6000 192 C spartain@bpcc.edu
PARTCH, Nancy 815-825-9365 142 F nancy.partch@kishwaukeecollege.edu
PARTENZA, Janet 914-674-7657 314 I jpartenza@mercy.edu
PARTIN, Sherry 606-546-1625 189 I spartin2@unionky.edu
PARTOLAN-FRAY, Liz 360-650-7970 500 E liz.partolan-fray@wwu.edu
PARTON, Becky 217-786-2351 144 B becky.parton@llcc.edu
PARTON, John 678-664-0527 128 F john.parton@westgatech.edu
PARTON, LeAnne 509-793-2004 492 I leannep@bigbend.edu
PARTON, Stephanie 618-937-2127 146 E sparton@morthland.edu
PARTON, Valerie 509-793-2371 492 I valeriep@bigbend.edu
PARTRIDGE, Kristen, N 405-325-3163 380 L kpartridge@ou.edu
PARTRIDGE, Patrick 801-274-3280 474 D ppartridge@wgu.edu
PARTRIDGE, Richard 803-327-8031 426 J rpartridge@yorktech.edu
PARTRIDGE, Steve 703-323-2383 488 H spartridge@nvcc.edu
PARVIZI, Nasrin 607-753-5582 327 A nasrin.parvizi@cortland.edu
PARZIALE, Anthony, J 401-825-2004 416 B ajparziale@ccri.edu
PARZY, Robert 847-925-6649 139 B rparzy@harpercollege.edu
PASAG, Maureen 415-338-2599 34 C mpasag@sfsu.edu
PASCAL, Sandra, E 617-989-4478 225 E pascals@wit.edu
PASCALE, Lynn 203-287-3031 87 G paier.admission@snet.net
PASCARELL, Rose 703-993-8760 481 B rpascare@gmu.edu
PASCARELLA, John 936-294-1458 462 F jbp014@shsu.edu
PASCARIELLO, Jacqueline 631-632-6840 325 F jacqueline.pascariello@stonybrook.edu
PASCHAL, Erin 814-641-3331 398 B paschae@juniata.edu
PASCHAL, Linda, L 414-955-8208 508 D lpaschal@mcw.edu
PASCHALL, Kimberly, S 270-809-3809 188 D kpaschall@murraystate.edu
PASCHALL, Kirk 972-825-4736 457 F kpaschall@sagu.edu
PASCHOLD, Erika 402-465-7574 276 E epaschol@nebrwesleyan.edu
PASCO, Leslie 315-228-7481 304 G lpasco@colgate.edu
PASCOE, Frank, H 815-740-3216 154 G fpascoe@stfrancis.edu
PASCOE, Tammie 903-983-8105 451 F tpascoe@kilgore.edu
PASCOE-AGUILAR, Daniel 607-274-3365 311 D dpascoeaguilar@ithaca.edu
PASCUAL, Mytha 310-900-1600 40 C mpascual@elcamino.edu
PASEK, Heidi 406-771-4397 272 D hpasek@gfcmsu.edu
PASENELLI, Rose 619-594-1630 34 B rpasenel@mail.sdsu.edu
PASHA, Stephanie 508-831-6655 226 E spasha@wpi.edu
PASIC, Amir 317-278-5652 160 E ampasic@iupui.edu
PASKETT, Lindy 307-855-2120 516 I lpaskett@cwc.edu
PASKEY, Louise 712-279-5494 167 B louise.paskey@briarcliff.edu
PASKVAN, Kevin, F 740-368-3052 368 N kfpaskva@owu.edu
PASLEY, James 816-584-6593 265 C james.pasley@park.edu
PASLEY-HENRY, Stephanie 386-481-2087 95 J
PASQUARIELLO, Gino 619-201-8970 65 C gino.pasquariello@socalsem.edu
PASS-STERN, Bernice 212-614-6176 320 B bernice.pass-stern@mountsinai.org
PASSAFIUME, Marisa 718-862-7796 313 L marisa.passafiume@manhattan.edumanhattan.edu
PASSAGE, Rob 503-370-6217 388 D rpassage@willamette.edu
PASSARO, Joanne 262-524-7364 506 G jpassaro@carrollu.edu
PASSARO, Karen 973-275-2061 291 F karen.passaro@shu.edu
PASSAUER, Bridgett, M 757-822-1536 489 H bpassauer@tcc.edu
PASSE, Jeff 909-869-2319 31 A jpasse@cpp.edu
PASSE, Jeffrey 609-771-2100 284 I passej@tcnj.edu
PASSER, Christine 269-782-1310 237 B cpasser@swmich.edu
PASSERINI, Katia 718-990-2773 322 F passerik@stjohns.edu
PASSEY, Brent 239-513-1122 101 O bpassey@hodges.edu
PASSMORE, Ed 334-683-2375 3 A epassmore@marionmilitary.edu
PASTERIS, Marc 309-467-6305 138 E mpasteris@eureka.edu
PASTERNAK, Reuven 631-444-2701 325 F reuven.pasternak@stonybrookmedicine.edu
PASTIDES, Harris 803-777-2001 424 I pastides@sc.edu
PASTORE, Michael 253-879-3100 499 C mpastore@pugetsound.edu
PASTOREK, Jennifer 419-530-8707 372 F jennifer.pastorek@utoledo.edu
PASTORELLA, Mark, J 585-262-1509 315 L mpastorella@monroecc.edu
PASTORIZA, Nelida 718-518-4412 302 D npastoriza@hostos.cuny.edu
PASTORRES-PALFFY, Elizabeth 916-485-3276 371 A b.palffy@myunion.edu
PASTRANA, Marie Luz 787-765-3560 522 K lpastrana@edpuniversity.edu
PASTRANA, Marilyn 787-765-3560 522 K mpastrana@edpuniversity.edu

PASTVA, Kimberlee, M .. 848-932-2457 290 A
pastva@oldqueens.rutgers.edu
PASZKIEWICZ, Wendy ... 312-662-4211 133 A
paszk@adler.edu
PASZTOR, Jim .... 303-220-1200.. 77 D
jim.pasztor@cffp.edu
PATALANO, Carla .... 617-603-6900 222 F
carla.patalano@necb.edu
PATAWARAN, Arrileen ... 773-995-2063 135 F
apatawar@csu.edu
PATCHETT, Heather .... 423-636-7303 439 C
hpatchett@tusculum.edu
PATCHETT, Margaret, B . 704-403-3077 336 B
meg.patchett@carolinashealthcare.org
PATCHIN, Steve .... 906-487-2313 234 A
shpatchi@mtu.edu
PATCHNER, Michael ...... 317-274-8362 160 E
patchner@iupui.edu
PATE, Herman .... 404-527-4520 117 C
hpate@carver.edu
PATE, Juston .... 270-706-8409 185 H
juston.pate@kctcs.edu
PATE, Kim .... 828-328-7128 339 C
kim.pate@lr.edu
PATE, Nino, T .... 671-734-1812 520 A
npate@piu.edu
PATEE, Carla .... 620-227-9378 176 N
cpatee@dc3.edu
PATEL, Mital .... 312-261-3025 146 G
mital.patel@nl.edu
PATEL, Narendra, H .... 404-880-8064 117 H
npatel@cau.edu
PATEL, Prita .... 202-885-2177.. 91 C
ppatel@american.edu
PATEL, Sandip .... 203-582-3394.. 88 A
sandip.patel@quinnipiac.edu
PATEL, Tarun .... 518-694-7337 297 J
tarun.patel@acphs.edu
PATENAUDE, Craig .... 301-934-7643 203 D
cpatenaude@csmd.edu
PATENAUDE, Heather .... 928-757-0817.. 14 I
hpatenaude@mohave.edu
PATERSON, John .... 802-728-1434 477 E
jpaterson@vtc.edu
PATERSON, Wendy, A ... 716-878-4214 326 E
paterswa@buffalostate.edu
PATES, Nancy .... 952-358-8200 246 D
nancy.pates@normandale.edu
PATESTAS, Maria .... 718-368-5597 303 A
maria.patestas@kbcc.cuny.edu
PATH, Bill .... 918-293-5256 378 B
bpath@okstate.edu
PATHAK, Dushyant .... 530-752-7309.. 68 H
dpathak@ucdavis.edu
PATHAK, Susanna .... 207-941-7187 199 B
pathaks@husson.edu
PATINO, Beatriz .... 508-767-7100 210 I
bpatino@assumption.edu
PATISHNOCK, Mark, F .. 706-737-1471 116 B
mpatishnock@augusta.edu
PATLOLLA, Babu, P .... 601-877-6120 251 G
bpatlolla@alcorn.edu
PATNAUDE, Valerie .... 603-897-8533 281 I
vpatnaude@rivier.edu
PATO, Rosevonne, M .... 684-699-9155 519 F
r.pato@amsamoa.edu
PATON, Jeff .... 336-322-2237 345 D
jeff.paton@piedmontcc.edu
PATON, Jeff .... 336-770-1457 352 B
patonjj@uncsa.edu
PATON, Jeff .... 336-770-1457 352 B
yangx@uncsa.edu
PATON, Nancy, E .... 716-645-6969 325 B
nepaton@buffalo.edu
PATOSKY, Julie .... 814-201-2733 405 A
jpatosky@pennhighlands.edu
PATRIA, Patricia, L .... 508-373-1981 211 F
patty.patria@becker.edu
PATRIAS, Marla .... 218-755-2876 244 B
mpatrias@bemidjistate.edu
PATRICK, Beth, G .... 606-783-2053 188 C
b.patrick@moreheadstate.edu
PATRICK, Brian .... 913-288-7362 178 H
bpatrick@kckcc.edu
PATRICK, Charles .... 817-923-1921 457 G
cpatrick@swbts.edu
PATRICK, Craig .... 914-632-6700 315 K
cpatrick@monroecollege.edu
PATRICK, David .... 404-527-4522 117 C
dpatrick@carver.edu
PATRICK, David .... 404-527-4520 117 C
PATRICK, Garry .... 707-476-4385.. 39 F
garry-patrick@redwoods.edu
PATRICK, Jamie .... 919-497-3245 339 F
jpatrick@louisburg.edu
PATRICK, Keeley .... 860-768-2441.. 89 C
kpatrick@hartford.edu
PATRICK, Kim .... 616-331-2280 230 G
patricki@gvsu.edu
PATRICK, Lanell .... 443-412-2563 204 C
lpatrick@harford.edu
PATRICK, Laura .... 949-376-6000.. 47 H
lpatrick@lcad.edu
PATRICK, Maggie .... 507-222-5568 241 C
mpatrick@carleton.edu
PATRICK, Margarie .... 404-527-4520 117 C
mpatrick@carver.edu
PATRICK, Michelle .... 412-397-6359 409 C
patrick@rmu.edu
PATRICK, Nicole .... 662-329-7114 254 F
jnpatrick@muw.edu
PATRICK, Paul, D .... 843-953-0879 420 C
patrickpd@cofc.edu
PATRICK, Paul, G .... 864-379-6675 421 E
ppatrick@erskine.edu
PATRICK, Stan .... 601-643-8302 252 G
stan.patrick@colin.edu
PATRICK, Tracie, M .... 814-641-3142 398 B
patrict@juniata.edu
PATRIQUIN, Wendy ...... 304-929-5494 503 B
wpatriquin@newriver.edu
PATRIZI, Chad .... 304-724-3700 501 D
cpatrizi@apus.edu
PATRY, Roland .... 214-358-9042 463 E
roland.patry@ttuhsc.edu
PATRYLA, Trish .... 661-255-1050.. 29 F
patryla@calarts.edu
PATSALIDES, Eugene ..... 270-831-9688 186 A
eugenios.patsalides@kctcs.edu
PATTEE, Bob .... 254-295-4524 466 A
rpattee@umhb.edu
PATTEE, Bonnie .... 801-274-3280 474 D
bonnie.pattee@wgu.edu
PATTEN, David, B .... 401-825-2194 416 B
dpatten@ccri.edu
PATTEN, Shawn .... 941-752-5444 108 P
pattens@scf.edu
PATTEN-LEMONS,
Rebecca .... 317-921-4667 161 G
rpatten@ivytech.edu
PATTERSON, Anthony .... 919-572-1625 335 F
apatterson@apexsot.edu
PATTERSON, Bart .... 702-992-2350 279 B
president@nsc.edu
PATTERSON, Becky .... 502-852-3385 190 C
becky.patterson@louisville.edu
PATTERSON, Ben .... 805-565-6210.. 74 I
bpatters@westmont.edu
PATTERSON, Bernie .... 715-346-2123 511 F
PATTERSON, Blaike .... 251-380-3020.... 7 B
bookstore@shc.edu
PATTERSON, Brigid .... 262-551-5940 506 H
bpatterson@carthage.edu
PATTERSON, Carol .... 303-797-5701.. 76 I
carol.patterson@arapahoe.edu
PATTERSON, Charlotte .. 434-982-2961 486 H
cjp@virginia.edu
PATTERSON, Corey .... 325-674-6566 441 D
pattersonc@acu.edu
PATTERSON, Cynthia, A 252-638-7304 342 E
pattersc@cravencc.edu
PATTERSON, Dale .... 918-540-6319 376 F
dale.patterson@neo.edu
PATTERSON, Darrin .... 330-337-6403 356 B
maintenance@awc.edu
PATTERSON, Darrin .... 330-337-6403 356 B
college@awc.edu
PATTERSON, Donald, A . 716-878-3447 326 E
patterda@buffalostate.edu
PATTERSON, Dorsey ...... 901-435-1286 433 A
dorsey_patterson@loc.edu
PATTERSON, Eddie .... 803-780-1249 426 F
epatterson@voorhees.edu
PATTERSON, Elice .... 202-651-5309.. 91 H
elice.patterson@gallaudet.edu
PATTERSON, Elizabeth ... 704-878-3244 344 H
epatterson@mitchellcc.edu
PATTERSON, Elizabeth ... 903-223-6722 460 D
epatterson@tamut.edu
PATTERSON, Eric .... 214-654-9075 207 B
PATTERSON, Eric .... 757-352-4616 484 E
epatterson@regent.edu
PATTERSON, Felicia, L .. 410-777-2718 202 D
flpatterson@aacc.edu
PATTERSON, Franklin .... 386-481-2020.. 95 J
pattersonf@cookman.edu
PATTERSON, Harlan ...... 425-602-3003 492 E
PATTERSON, Howard ..... 903-566-7350 468 C
hpatterson@uttyler.edu
PATTERSON, James .... 860-738-6482.. 86 C
jpatterson@nwcc.edu
PATTERSON,
Jana Lynn, F .... 336-278-7200 337 G
patters@elon.edu
PATTERSON, Jennifer .... 641-422-4346 172 C
jennifer.patterson@niacc.edu
PATTERSON, Jennifer .... 614-236-6502 358 A
jpatterson@capital.edu
PATTERSON, John, A .... 478-301-5537 122 H
patterson_ja@mercer.edu
PATTERSON, Joyce, D ... 337-475-5232 197 B
joyce@mcneese.edu
PATTERSON, Karen, B ... 904-620-5279 110 E
karen.patterson@unf.edu
PATTERSON, Kim .... 254-299-8606 452 E
kpatterson@mclennan.edu
PATTERSON, Kristi .... 815-479-7677 145 B
kpatterson@mchenry.edu
PATTERSON, Lauren ...... 503-228-6528 381 I
lspatterson@aii.edu
PATTERSON, Leni, N ..... 864-833-8284 423 D
lpatters@presby.edu
PATTERSON, Michael ..... 410-225-2422 205 C
mpatters@mica.edu
PATTERSON, Michael .... 415-503-6237.. 60 H
mpatterson@sfcm.edu
PATTERSON, Michael, J 570-577-1911 390 H
mike.patterson@bucknell.edu
PATTERSON, Myrna .... 808-845-9115 130 E
mpatters@hawaii.edu
PATTERSON, Nancy .... 423-697-2630 436 F
nancy.patterson@chattanoogastate.edu
PATTERSON, Paige .... 817-923-1921 457 G
presidentsoffice@swbts.edu
PATTERSON, Patty .... 954-492-5353.. 96 J
ppatterson@citycollege.edu
PATTERSON, Paul, M .... 334-844-3209.... 4 D
pmp0003@auburn.edu
PATTERSON, Rae Lynn .. 208-535-5361 131 G
raelynn.patterson@my.eitc.edu
PATTERSON, Ralph .... 803-321-5166 422 H
ralph.patterson@newberry.edu
PATTERSON, Randall ..... 419-289-5012 356 L
rpatter2@ashland.edu
PATTERSON, Robert, H . 804-752-3605 484 C
robertpatterson@rmc.edu
PATTERSON, Ron .... 256-765-4683.... 9 A
rpatterson1@una.edu
PATTERSON, Scott .... 314-367-8700 266 D
scott.patterson@stlcop.edu
PATTERSON, Shannon ... 706-771-4013 116 A
sbentley@augustatech.edu
PATTERSON, Sharon ..... 414-443-8556 513 A
sharon.patterson@wlc.edu
PATTERSON, Sharon, E . 626-395-3937.. 29 I
sharon.patterson@caltech.edu
PATTERSON, Stacey ...... 865-974-4048 439 H
stacey.patterson@tennessee.edu
PATTERSON, Stephanie . 626-256-4673.. 37 I
spatterson@coh.org
PATTERSON, Steven ...... 703-323-3554 488 H
spatterson@nvcc.edu
PATTERSON, Teresa ...... 909-274-5512.. 52 I
tpatterson@mtsac.edu
PATTERSON, Terry, L .... 208-732-6402 131 I
tpatterson@csi.edu
PATTERSON, Thomas .... 334-387-3877.... 4 B
thomaspatterson@amridgeuniversity.edu
PATTERSON, Tim .... 802-586-7711 476 D
tpatterson@sterlingcollege.edu
PATTERSON, Todd .... 713-920-1120 121 J
tpatterson@ict.edu
PATTERSON, Tracy .... 901-843-3856 435 L
pattersont@rhodes.edu
PATTERSON, III, U, L .... 704-669-4025 342 B
patterson@clevelandcc.edu
PATTERSON, Vicki .... 832-252-4624 446 A
vicki@cbhouston.edu
PATTERSON, Wayne .... 814-732-2703 406 B
wpatterson@edinboro.edu
PATTI, Christopher, M .. 510-642-7122.. 68 G
cpatti@berkeley.edu
PATTIE, Piotrowski .... 217-206-6597 154 A
ppiot2@uis.edu
PATTILLO, Andre .... 470-639-0650 123 E
andre.pattillo@morehouse.edu
PATTILLO, Baker .... 936-468-2201 458 A
bpattillo@sfasu.edu
PATTILLO, Nicolas .... 479-788-7166.. 22 A
npattillo@uafs.edu
PATTILO, Gerald .... 305-626-3624.. 99 M
gerald.pattilo@fmuniv.edu
PATTISALL, Jeremy .... 336-725-8344 348 C
pattisallj@piedmontu.edu
PATTISON, Margaret .... 313-578-0327 237 F
peggy.pattison@udmercy.edu
PATTON, Barbara, L ...... 615-898-2185 434 H
barbara.patton@mtsu.edu
PATTON, Chad .... 434-949-1038 489 E
chad.patton@southside.edu
PATTON, Danny .... 662-329-7436 254 F
dcpatton@muw.edu
PATTON, Dave .... 989-774-2798 228 E
patto1d@cmich.edu
PATTON, Guy, L .... 405-321-1174 380 L
gpatton@ou.edu
PATTON, Jamie .... 805-756-1521.. 30 K
japatton@calpoly.edu
PATTON, Kerry .... 203-582-3087.. 88 A
kerry.patton2@quinnipiac.edu
PATTON, Laurie, L .... 802-443-5400 475 G
president@middlebury.edu
PATTON, Mary .... 817-257-7660 461 A
m.patton@tcu.edu
PATTON, Michael .... 626-529-8498.. 55 C
mpatton@pacificoaks.edu
PATTON, Neely .... 303-753-6046.. 82 E
npatton@rmcad.edu
PATTON, Paul, E .... 606-218-5261 190 E
pep@upike.edu
PATTON, Terry .... 940-397-4088 453 C
terry.patton@mwsu.edu
PATTY, Jeff .... 706-295-6775 119 G
jpatty@highlands.edu
PATTY, Stacy .... 806-720-7652 452 D
stacy.patty@lcu.edu
PATZ, Thomas .... 317-738-8183 157 L
tpatz@franklincollege.edu
PATZ, Thomas .... 317-738-8025 157 L
tpatz@franklincollege.edu
PAUGH, Jerry .... 714-449-7487.. 51 A
jpaugh@ketchum.edu
PAUGH, Mark .... 352-854-2322.. 97 C
paughm@cf.edu
PAUKEN, Patrick .... 419-372-2226 357 F
paukenp@bgsu.edu
PAUKEN, Patrick .... 419-372-2550 357 F
paukenp@bgsu.edu
PAUL, Alyson .... 706-864-1900 127 B
alyson.paul@ung.edu
PAUL, Brandon, L .... 419-866-0261 370 I
blpaul@stautzenberger.com
PAUL, Christine .... 805-493-3220.. 30 E
clpaul@callutheran.edu
PAUL, Elizabeth, L .... 614-236-6908 358 A
bethpaul@capital.edu
PAUL, Jeremy .... 617-373-5149 223 D
PAUL, Jina .... 402-552-3100 273 K
pauljina@clarksoncollege.edu
PAUL, Kelley .... 903-923-2229 448 J
kpaul@etbu.edu
PAUL, Kohle .... 770-962-7580 121 G
kpaul@gwinnetttech.edu
PAUL, Lauren, A .... 956-326-2857 459 B
lauren.jones@tamiu.edu
PAUL, Mary .... 619-849-2215.. 57 H
marypaul@pointloma.edu
PAUL, Max .... 407-601-0411.. 99 E
PAUL, Michelle .... 417-455-5675 259 D
michellepaul@crowder.edu
PAUL, Phyllis, M .... 330-941-3625 374 E
pmpaul@ysu.edu
PAUL, Robert .... 630-515-4566 137 D
rpaul@devrygroup.com
PAUL, Robert, H .... 314-516-8403 268 E
paulro@umsl.edu
PAUL, Sheilah .... 718-270-4936 303 C
spaul@mec.cuny.edu
PAUL, Tina .... 870-612-2017.. 22 H
tina.paul@uaccb.edu
PAUL, Tonya .... 419-772-3106 367 G
t-paul@onu.edu
PAUL, Tracey .... 601-977-7819 256 B
tpaul@tougaloo.edu
PAULE, Romeo .... 415-949-7308.. 43 F
pauleromeo@foothill.edu
PAULE, Sara .... 765-983-1431 157 I
paulesa@earlham.edu
PAULEY, Ann .... 202-884-9725.. 93 C
pauleya@trinitydc.edu
PAULEY, II, John .... 610-341-5892 394 E
casdean@eastern.edu
PAULEY, Liz .... 940-898-2911 464 A
epauley@twu.edu
PAULI, Crystal .... 605-256-5177 428 G
crystal.pauli@dsu.edu
PAULICK, Adam .... 907-786-4754.. 10 A
apaulick@alaska.edu
PAULIEN, Jon .... 909-558-4536.. 48 H
jpaulien@llu.edu
PAULINE, Rose Lee .... 215-951-1014 398 F
pauline@lasalle.edu
PAULISON, Wayne .... 918-631-2616 381 C
wayne-paulison@utulsa.edu
PAULMAN, John .... 573-527-7649 295 E
jpaulma@nmsu.edu
PAULNACK, Karl .... 607-274-3343 311 D
kpaulnack@ithaca.edu

PEAVY, Terence .... 212-217-3801 308 B
terence_peavy@fitnyc.edu
PEAY, J. H. Binford ...... 540-464-7311 490 E
peayjb@vmi.edu
PEAY, Steven, A .... 262-646-6512 509 C
speay@nashotah.edu
PECARD, Paulette, M .... 414-955-8235 508 D
ppecard@mcw.edu
PECCHIA, John, P .... 845-575-3000 314 C
john.pecchia@marist.edu
PECENY, Mark .... 505-277-7381 296 H
markpec@unm.edu
PECHA, David, M .... 580-327-8528 376 K
dmpecha@nwosu.edu
PECK, Adam .... 936-468-7249 458 A
peckae@sfasu.edu
PECK, Barbara .... 864-379-6546 421 E
peck@erskine.edu
PECK, Cindy, J .... 217-443-8803 137 B
cpeck@dacc.edu
PECK, Daniel, A .... 408-855-5122.. 74 C
daniel.peck@wvm.edu
PECK, David .... 626-815-4503.. 26 U
dpeck@apu.edu
PECK, Edward, J .... 216-397-4218 363 H
epeck@jcu.edu
PECK, Jane .... 781-768-7307 224 A
jane.peck@regiscollege.edu
PECK, Jeanie .... 651-641-8709 241 L
peck@csp.edu
PECK, Kim .... 806-743-2297 463 E
kim.peck@ttuhsc.edu
PECK, Rebecca .... 816-936-8713 266 K
rpeck@saintlukescollege.edu
PECK, Robert .... 508-999-8539 217 A
rpeck@umassd.edu
PECK, Susan .... 252-335-0821 342 D
susan_peck@albemarle.edu
PECKA, Kenneth .... 509-777-3292 500 H
kpecka@whitworth.edu
PECKHAM, Karissa, L .... 203-576-4552.. 88 F
kpeckham@bridgeport.edu
PECKHAM, Michael .... 920-403-3360 509 J
mike.peckham@snc.edu
PECKITT, JR., Carl, S .... 610-799-1114 400 A
cpeckitt@lccc.edu
PECOR, Sarah, A .... 262-243-5700 507 C
sarah.pecor@cuw.edu
PECORD, Melanie .... 618-985-2828 141 D
melaniepecord@jalc.edu
PECORONI, Deanna, L .. 314-434-2212 261 A
dpecoroni@hickeycollege.edu
PECTOL, James, B .... 423-585-6823 438 D
james.pectol@ws.edu
PEDE, Michael .... 315-792-5411 315 I
mpede@mvcc.edu
PEDE, Mike .... 713-743-9551 465 A
mlpede@uh.edu
PEDEN, Ann .... 614-236-6703 358 A
apeden@capital.edu
PEDEN, Gary, S .... 315-470-6588 328 D
gspeden@esf.edu
PEDERSEN, Cindi, M .... 574-807-7239 156 E
cindi.pedersen@bethelcollege.edu
PEDERSEN, Daniel, T .... 320-308-2166 247 E
dtpedersen@stcloudstate.edu
PEDERSEN, Eric .... 360-867-6176 494 G
pedersee@evergreen.edu
PEDERSEN, Eric .... 435-652-7977 473 B
pedersen@dixie.edu
PEDERSEN, Ginger, L .... 561-967-7222 105 A
pederseg@palmbeachstate.edu
PEDERSEN, Jeffrey, M ... 631-451-4425 330 B
pedersj@sunysuffolk.edu
PEDERSEN, Jennifer, L .. 308-635-6078 278 B
pedersen@wncc.edu
PEDERSEN, Joel, D .... 402-472-1201 277 E
jdpedersen@nebraska.edu
PEDERSEN, Jon, E .... 803-777-3075 424 I
pedersje@mailbox.sc.edu
PEDERSEN, Mary, E ...... 805-756-2246.. 30 K
mdederse@calpoly.edu
PEDERSEN, Melissa ...... 617-217-9036 211 D
mpedersen@baystate.edu
PEDERSEN, Patricia, E .. 203-436-8518.. 89 G
patty.pedersen@yale.edu
PEDERSON, Barb .... 701-231-7211 354 D
barbara.pederson@ndsu.edu
PEDERSON, Curtis, R .... 503-943-8046 387 H
pedersoc@up.edu
PEDERSON, Kathy .... 507-457-1586 250 B
kpeders@smumn.edu
PEDERSON, Katie .... 303-220-1200.. 77 D
katie.pederson@cffp.edu
PEDERSON, Katie .... 303-292-0015.. 79 F
PEDERSON, Mark .... 765-677-2117 161 C
mark.pederson@indwes.edu

PEDERSON, Robert, A ... 207-778-7036 201 D
pederson@maine.edu
PEDESCLEAUX, Desiree . 404-270-5696 126 D
dpedescl@spelman.edu
PEDIGO, Sue, H .... 615-230-3551 438 C
sue.pedigo@volstate.edu
PEDNEAU, Judy .... 276-326-4461 478 H
jpedneau@bluefield.edu
PEDONE, Melissa, D ..... 321-682-4176 113 F
mpedone@valenciacollege.edu
PEDOTTO, David .... 913-722-0272 178 G
dave.pedotto@kansaschristian.edu
PEDRAJA, Luis .... 508-854-4203 220 G
lpedraja@qcc.mass.edu
PEDRAZA, Jonathan, N . 262-691-5308 515 B
jpedraza2@wctc.edu
PEDRAZA, Mary Ann ..... 409-772-9867 469 C
mspedraz@utmb.edu
PEDRICK, Jim .... 319-385-6218 170 J
jim.pedrick@iw.edu
PEDRICK, Laura .... 414-229-3203 511 A
lpedrick@uwm.edu
PEDRO, David .... 508-910-9070 217 A
dpedro@umassd.edu
PEDRONE, Dino, J .... 607-729-1581 306 F
dpedrone@davisny.edu
PEDROTTY, Kate .... 318-869-5715 191 C
kpedrotty@centenary.edu
PEE, Charles, M .... 803-934-3294 422 G
cpee@morris.edu
PEEBLES, Carolyn .... 919-572-1625 335 F
cpeebles@apexsot.edu
PEEBLES, Henry .... 321-674-7715.. 99 K
peebles@fit.edu
PEEBLES, Lee .... 401-739-5000 416 D
lpeebles@neit.edu
PEED, Stephen .... 207-326-2451 200 F
stephen.peed@mma.edu
PEEK, Katherine .... 909-652-6333.. 36 E
kay.peek@chaffey.edu
PEEL, Bill .... 214-932-1112 452 A
billpeel@letu.edu
PEEL, Chermae .... 432-552-3744 469 D
peel_c@utpb.edu
PEEL, Claire .... 817-735-2752 466 D
claire.peel@unthsc.edu
PEEL, Henry .... 239-489-9011 100 E
hpeel@fsw.edu
PEELER, Chris Goff .... 704-461-6701 335 J
chrisgoff@bac.edu
PEELER, Jody .... 740-283-3771 361 L
jpeeler@franciscan.edu
PEELER, Mark, L .... 864-379-8850 421 E
mlp@erskine.edu
PEELING, Rebecca .... 561-803-2024 104 I
becky_peeling@pba.edu
PEEPLES, Jim .... 706-778-8500 124 E
jpeeples@piedmont.edu
PEEPLES, Junelyn .... 909-607-3884.. 63 F
jpeeples@scrippscollege.edu
PEEPLES, Terry, G .... 870-245-5169.. 20 G
peeplest@obu.edu
PEEPLES, Tim .... 336-278-5613 337 G
peeples@elon.edu
PEERMAN, Carey, H ...... 540-224-6973 482 A
chpeerman@jchs.edu
PEETERS, Andrea .... 650-543-3735.. 51 F
andrea.peeters@menlo.edu
PEETZ, Ralf .... 718-982-2440 302 A
ralf.peetz@csi.cuny.edu
PEFFALL, Marianne .... 610-436-2705 407 D
mpeffall@wcupa.edu
PEFFER, Deb .... 313-593-5100 238 A
dkpeffer@umich.edu
PEFFER, Tony .... 218-755-2015 244 B
tpeffer@bemidjistate.edu
PEGAH, Kris .... 941-351-7220 106 H
kpegah@ringling.edu
PEGAH, Mahmoud .... 941-359-7633 106 H
mpegah@ringling.edu
PEGG, Steven, M .... 410-777-2651 202 D
smpegg@aacc.edu
PEGRAM, Mike .... 402-761-8270 276 K
mpegram@southeast.edu
PEGUES, Charlotte Fant 662-915-5974 256 C
cfant@olemiss.edu
PEGUES, Mollie .... 662-252-8000 255 F
mpegues@rustcollege.edu
PEGUES, Patricia .... 662-252-8000 255 F
ppegues@rustcollege.edu
PEGUES, Patricia .... 662-252-2491 255 F
ppegues@rustcollege.edu
PEHLMAN, Patricia, A ... 717-245-1545 394 A
pehlman@dickinson.edu
PEHRSSON,
Dale-Elizabeth .... 989-774-6995 228 E
pehrs1d@cmich.edu

PEI, Alissa .... 573-876-7212 267 G
apei@stephens.edu
PEIFER, Bruce .... 301-891-4525 209 E
bpeifer@wau.edu
PEIFER, Michelle .... 704-991-0393 346 I
mpeifer7924@stanly.edu
PEIFFER, Cyndi .... 641-673-1040 174 F
peifferc@wmpenn.edu
PEIFFER, Kelly .... 215-885-2360 401 A
kpeiffer@manor.edu
PEIFFER, Mark, J .... 515-271-1475 168 G
mark.peiffer@dmu.edu
PEIPERL, Maury .... 703-993-1860 481 B
mpeiperl@gmu.edu
PEIRCE, Nathaniel .... 603-899-4320 281 D
peircen@franklinpierce.edu
PEKAR, Sheri .... 847-233-7700 148 A
sdunlop@nc.edu
PEKRUL, William, A ...... 507-354-8221 243 C
pekrulwa@mlc-wels.edu
PELAEZ, Michelle .... 813-253-6251 113 E
mpelaez@ut.edu
PELAK, Anne, C .... 914-654-5225 305 A
apelak@cnr.edu
PELAZZA, Todd, A .... 203-254-4090.. 87 A
tapelazza@fairfield.edu
PELC, Sharon .... 308-865-8523 277 F
pelcs@unk.edu
PELISSERO, John, P ...... 773-508-7470 144 D
jpeliss@luc.edu
PELIZZA, John .... 518-244-2051 321 G
pelizj@sage.edu
PELKEY, David .... 360-596-5231 498 G
dpelkey@spscc.edu
PELLEGRIN, Nathan .... 510-466-7210.. 56 I
npellegrin@peralta.edu
PELLEGRINI, Larry .... 570-674-6307 401 M
lpellegr@misericordia.edu
PELLEGRINI, Virginia ..... 208-426-3236 131 C
virginiapellegrini@boisestate.edu
PELLEGRINO, Debra, A . 570-941-6305 413 F
debra.pellegrino@scranton.edu
PELLEGRINO, Diana .... 973-655-5460 287 D
pellegrinod@mail.montclair.edu
PELLEGRINO, Eric .... 856-351-2770 291 E
epellegrino@salemcc.edu
PELLEGRINO, Karen, A . 203-254-4100.. 87 A
kpellegrino@fairfield.edu
PELLEGRINO, Nicole ..... 315-364-3240 333 G
npellegrino@wells.edu
PELLEGRINO, Robin .... 508-767-7599 210 I
rpellegr@assumption.edu
PELLEGRINO,
Thomas, C .... 203-254-4000.. 87 A
tpellegrino@fairfield.edu
PELLEGRINO-YOKITIS,
Maria .... 904-256-7928 102 B
mpelleg@ju.edu
PELLERIN, Jody .... 319-398-5409 171 F
jody.pellerin@kirkwood.edu
PELLETIER, Corey .... 207-859-1106 200 H
pelletierc@thomas.edu
PELLETIER, Jo-Ann, M .. 508-678-2811 219 C
jo-ann.pelletier@bristolcc.edu
PELLETIER, Sherry .... 845-368-7215 323 I
sherry.pelletier@use.salvationarmy.org
PELLETT, Tracy, L .... 304-462-6100 504 B
tracy.pellett@glenville.edu
PELLICANO, Gregory, J . 215-898-7958 412 G
gpell@upenn.edu
PELLICO, Gary .... 317-921-4882 161 G
gpellico@ivytech.edu
PELLINEN, Brian .... 978-921-4242 222 B
brian.pellinen@montserrat.edu
PELLISH, Cathy .... 303-404-5535.. 79 K
cathy.pellish@frontrange.edu
PELLIZZI, Thomas .... 608-757-6328 513 D
tpellizzi@blackhawk.edu
PELLMAN, Samuel .... 315-859-4615 309 D
spellman@hamilton.edu
PELLOT, Robert .... 212-938-5720 328 E
rpellot@sunyopt.edu
PELLS, Ruth .... 509-777-4665 500 H
rpells@whitworth.edu
PELLY, Michael .... 714-997-6982.. 36 G
pelly@chapman.edu
PELOQUIN, Andy .... 503-517-1815 388 C
apeloquin@westernseminary.edu
PELOQUIN, Elayne .... 603-623-0313 281 G
elaynepeloquin@nhia.edu
PELOQUIN-DODD,
Mary, T .... 919-515-2143 350 E
mary_peloquin-dodd@ncsu.edu
PELOSI, Lisa .... 401-598-1000 416 C
lpelosi@jwu.edu
PELOSO, Elizabeth, D .... 215-746-0234 412 G
epeloso@upenn.edu

PELPHREY, Barry .... 606-546-1299 189 I
bpelphrey@unionky.edu
PELRINE, Edward .... 847-970-4961 154 H
epelrine@usml.edu
PELRINE, John .... 312-369-7045 136 H
jpelrine@colum.edu
PELTIER, Beverly .... 706-771-4023 116 A
bpeltier@augustatech.edu
PELTIER, Eileen .... 860-253-3032.. 85 C
epeltier@asnuntuck.edu
PELTIER, John .... 401-874-4530 417 E
jpeltier@uri.edu
PELTIER, Linda, M .... 937-778-7802 361 E
lpeltier@edisonohio.edu
PELTIER, Matthew, S ..... 423-652-4740 432 I
mspeltie@king.edu
PELTO, William, L .... 828-262-3021 349 H
peltowl@appstate.edu
PELTON, M. Lee .... 617-824-8525 214 E
lee_pelton@emerson.edu
PELTON, Mark .... 478-445-5075 119 E
mark.pelton@gcsu.edu
PELTON, Vanessa .... 805-965-0581.. 62 E
pelton@sbcc.edu
PELTON, Woody .... 336-278-6700 337 G
wpelton@elon.edu
PELTZ, Mark .... 641-269-4940 169 F
peltzm@grinnell.edu
PELUSI, Mario, J .... 309-556-3061 141 B
mpelusi@iwu.edu
PELUSO, Constance ...... 718-631-6297 303 F
cpeluso@qcc.cuny.edu
PELUSO, Eileen .... 570-321-4135 400 G
pelusoem@lycoming.edu
PELUSO-VERDEND,
Gary .... 918-270-6405 378 I
gary.peluso@ptstulsa.edu
PELY, Laszlo .... 410-617-2421 205 A
lpely@loyola.edu
PELZEL, Kevin .... 314-719-3627 260 C
kpelzel@fontbonne.edu
PELZIER-GLAZE,
Bernnell .... 713-313-7496 461 E
glazedm@tsu.edu
PEMBERTON, Barbara ... 870-245-5541.. 20 G
pembertonb@obu.edu
PEMBERTON, Cynthia ... 970-248-1881.. 77 K
cpemberton@coloradomesa.edu
PEMBERTON,
Cynthia, L .... 816-235-1107 268 D
pembertonc@umkc.edu
PEMBERTON, Paul .... 218-935-0417 251 F
paul.pemberton@wetcc.edu
PEMBERTON, Richard ... 573-897-5000 267 F
PEMBERTON, Ryan .... 601-974-1036 254 A
pemberm@millsaps.edu
PEMBROOK, Randall, G 618-650-2481 152 C
rpembro@siue.edu
PEMSTEIN, Debra .... 413-644-4400 211 B
PEMSTEIN, Debra .... 845-758-7405 298 I
pemstein@bard.edu
PENA, Amy .... 505-747-2140 295 H
amy.pena@nnmc.edu
PENA, Andrew, M .... 575-646-1694 295 B
ampena@nmsu.edu
PENA, Damien, A .... 805-289-6113.. 73 C
dpena@vcccd.edu
PENA, Daniel .... 517-264-7146 236 I
dpena@sienaheights.edu
PENA, Hector .... 787-725-6500 521 C
hpena@albizu.edu
PENA, Jesus .... 610-683-4700 406 D
pena@kutztown.edu
PENA, Maria .... 425-388-9979 494 F
mpena@everettcc.edu
PENA, Maria .... 360-417-6340 496 I
mpena@pencol.edu
PENA, Milagros .... 951-827-2762.. 69 D
milagros.pena@ucr.edu
PENA, Phil .... 636-584-6701 259 L
philip.pena@eastcentral.edu
PENALOZA, Carlos .... 816-604-1206 262 F
carlos.penaloza@mcckc.edu
PENALOZA, Fiorella ...... 816-584-6755 265 C
fiorella.penaloza@park.edu
PENCE, Bill .... 540-868-7061 488 E
bpence@lfcc.edu
PENCE, Nadine, S .... 765-361-6434 166 B
pencen@wabash.edu
PENCE, Paula .... 541-880-2236 383 E
pence@klamathcc.edu
PENDAKUR, Vijay .... 607-255-1115 306 B
dean_of_students@cornell.edu
PENDELTON, Alicia .... 313-577-2017 239 C
alicia.pendelton@wayne.edu
PENDELTON, Chris .... 540-261-8400 485 G
chris.pendelton@svu.edu

PENDERGAST, Jayme ... 770-426-2858 122 F jayme.pendergast@life.edu
PENDERGAST, Kate ... 860-768-2403.. 89 C pendergas@hartford.edu
PENDERGRASS, Martha . 919-843-5048 351 B mjpender@email.unc.edu
PENDERGRASS, Toni ... 505-566-3209 296 A pendergrasst@sancollege.edu
PENDERGRAST, Runan .. 859-246-6305 185 G runan.pendergrast@kctcs.edu
PENDERS, Brooke ... 860-528-4111.. 87 B bpenders@goodwin.edu
PENDHARKAR, Daya ... 813-253-7091 101 M dpendharkar@hccfl.edu
PENDLETON, Chris ... 540-261-8441 485 G chris.pendleton@svu.edu
PENDLETON, Gail ... 510-981-2804.. 56 F gpendleton@peralta.edu
PENDLETON, Janis, S ... 803-327-7402 419 G jpendleton@clintoncollege.edu
PENDLETON, Laura ... 509-452-5100 496 H lpendleton@pnwu.edu
PENDLETON, Laurence .. 615-963-7925 438 E laurence.pendleton@tnstate.edu
PENDLETON, Patrick ... 928-541-7777.. 54 B ppendleton@ncu.edu
PENDLETON, Penny ... 479-788-7121.. 22 A penny.pendleton@uafs.edu
PENDLETON, Sally ... 502-895-3411 188 A spendleton@lpts.edu
PENDSE, Ravindra ... 401-863-7250 415 K ravi_pendse@brown.edu
PENFIELD, Randall, D ... 336-334-3944 351 D rdpenfie@uncg.edu
PENG, Willie ... 657-278-2866.. 32 B wpeng@fullerton.edu
PENGRA, Andrea ... 507-457-1791 250 B apengra@smumn.edu
PENGRA, Matt ... 407-679-0100 101 F mpengra@fullsail.com
PENICK, William ... 951-785-2100.. 47 F wpenick@lasierra.edu
PENISTEN, Douglas ... 918-444-4000 376 G penisten@nsuok.edu
PENIX, Doug ... 859-442-1634 185 I doug.penix@kctcs.edu
PENIX, Kristine ... 501-882-3600.. 17 M kapenix@asub.edu
PENKALA, Robert ... 586-445-7636 233 B penkalar@macomb.edu
PENKE, Ann, K ... 920-565-1038 507 K penkea@lakeland.edu
PENLAND, Joni, M ... 502-410-6200 184 H jpenland@galencollege.edu
PENLAND, Nathan ... 417-328-1828 267 A npenland@sbuniv.edu
PENLEY, Julie ... 915-831-6375 449 A jpenley@epcc.edu
PENN, Ann ... 919-530-6681 350 D aepenn@nccu.edu
PENN, Courtney ... 540-375-2270 484 H penn@roanoke.edu
PENN, David ... 407-447-7300 101 B dpenn@ftccollege.edu
PENN, Jamilyn ... 425-739-8355 495 F jamilyn.penn@lwtech.edu
PENN, Mark, A ... 702-802-2837 280 B mpenn@roseman.edu
PENN-HARGROVE, Valencia ... 773-256-3000 145 D vpennhargrove@meadville.edu
PENN-MARSHALL, Michelle ... 757-727-5267 481 E michelle.penn-marshall@hamptonu.edu
PENN-MARSHALL, Michelle ... 757-637-2690 481 E michelle.pennmarshall@hamptonu.edu
PENNA, Anthony ... 617-552-3475 212 E anthony.penna@bc.edu
PENNACHIO, Michael ... 617-521-2190 224 E michael.pennachio@simmons.edu
PENNARTZ-BROWNING, Kathy ... 940-397-4214 453 C kathy.pennartz@mwsu.edu
PENNER, Julie ... 815-836-5667 143 E pennerju@lewisu.edu
PENNER, Menachem ... 646-592-4455 334 P penner@yu.edu
PENNEY, Bill ... 352-395-5160 107 E bill.penney@sfcollege.edu
PENNEY, Kathleen ... 334-833-4062.... 5 M kpenney@hawks.huntingdon.edu
PENNIMAN, Sarah ... 717-361-1428 394 F pennimans@etown.edu
PENNINGS, Rhonda, R .. 712-324-5061 172 E rpennings@nwicc.edu
PENNINGTON, Amy ... 479-968-0407.. 18 G apennington@atu.edu
PENNINGTON, Glenda, J ... 304-865-6141 502 C jo.pennington@ovu.edu
PENNINGTON, Karen, L 973-655-4311 287 D penningtonk@mail.montclair.edu
PENNINGTON, Kevin ... 252-399-6467 335 I knpennington@barton.edu
PENNINGTON, Kimberly ... 828-328-7473 339 C kimberly.pennington@lr.edu
PENNINGTON, Laurie ... 928-428-8231.. 12 I laurie.pennington@eac.edu
PENNINGTON, Nicole ... 740-533-4610 368 G penningj@ohio.edu
PENNINGTON, Ronald, J ... 724-946-7014 414 C rpenning@westminster.edu
PENNINGTON, Sandra .. 801-375-5125 472 F spennington@rmuohp.edu
PENNINGTON, Sherry, R ... 417-667-8181 259 A spennington@cottey.edu
PENNINGTON, Simon ... 650-949-7156.. 43 F penningtonsimon@foothill.edu
PENNINGTON, Thomas . 479-964-0824.. 18 G tpennington@atu.edu
PENNINGTON, Wayne ... 906-487-2005 234 A wayne@mtu.edu
PENNINI, Susan, W ... 617-333-2165 214 B spennini@curry.edu
PENNISTON, Mary Ann . 660-541-5127 264 I mpenn@nwmissouri.edu
PENNIX, James, A ... 540-365-4290 480 L jpennix@ferrum.edu
PENNOCK, Margaret ... 605-367-7667 429 C margaret.pennock@southeasttech.edu
PENNY, Rick ... 440-525-7320 364 D rpenny@lakelandcc.edu
PENNY, Terra, K ... 651-962-6107 251 D penn9035@stthomas.edu
PENROD, Donald ... 562-985-5091.. 32 C don.penrod@csulb.edu
PENROD, Janice, L ... 814-863-0245 403 F jlp198@psu.edu
PENROSE, Betsy ... 315-786-2249 311 H bpenrose@sunyjefferson.edu
PENROSE, John ... 513-875-3344 359 C john.penrose@chatfield.edu
PENROSE, Leif ... 813-253-7370 101 M lpenrose@hccfl.edu
PENRY, Jason ... 870-972-2060.. 18 A jpenry@astate.edu
PENRY, Michael, A ... 919-866-5532 347 D mapenry@waketech.edu
PENSE, Christine ... 610-861-5312 403 B cpense@northampton.edu
PENSGARD, Sara, E ... 540-338-1776 483 H library@phc.edu
PENSIS, Claude ... 602-639-7500.. 12 P
PENSON, Amy, M ... 828-395-1296 344 A apenson@isothermal.edu
PENTZER, Scott ... 504-865-5339 196 D cge@tulane.edu
PENYAK, Lee, M ... 269-387-5890 239 E lee.penyak@wmich.edu
PENZENSTADLER, SSND, Joan ... 414-930-3388 509 B penzenj@mtmary.edu
PENZIUL, Carl ... 607-844-8222 331 D penziuc@tompkinscortland.edu
PEOPLE, Yasha ... 732-247-5241 287 E ypeople@nbts.edu
PEOPLES, Frankie ... 334-874-5700.... 5 B fpeoples@ccal.edu
PEOPLES, Lisa ... 731-425-2548 432 J lpeoples@lanecollege.edu
PEOPLES, Peg ... 845-758-7432 298 I peoples@bard.edu
PEOPLES, Shawn ... 217-581-3827 138 A sdpeoples@eiu.edu
PEOPLES, VerJanis ... 225-771-2291 195 J verjanis_peoples@subr.edu
PEOPLES, Verjanis ... 225-771-2290 195 K verjanis_peoples@subr.edu
PEPIN, Mark ... 918-495-7236 378 H mpepin@oru.edu
PEPIN, Sean ... 408-741-2185.. 74 D sean.pepin@westvalley.edu
PEPITONE, Dianne ... 914-831-0367 305 C dpepitone@cw.edu
PEPITONE, William ... 215-885-2360 401 A wpepitone@manor.edu
PEPLOW, Nena ... 309-677-3223 134 G nena@bradley.edu
PEPPER, Evan ... 818-299-5727.. 73 K epepper@westcoastuniversity.edu
PEPPER, Judith ... 505-424-2309 294 C judith.pepper@iaia.edu
PEPPER, Robert ... 717-796-1800 401 L rpepper@messiah.edu
PEPPER, Russel ... 614-236-6632 358 A rpepper@capital.edu
PEPPIN, Patricia ... 480-461-7456.. 13 I pat.peppin@mesacc.edu
PEPPIN, Vicky ... 864-578-8770 423 F
PEPPLE, Michael ... 913-621-8740 177 A mpepple@donnelly.edu
PERALES, Jose, J ... 585-385-8464 322 E jperales@sjfc.edu
PERALES, Michelle ... 210-485-0031 441 E mperales4@alamo.edu
PERAZZELLI, Ann ... 215-635-7300 396 B
PERBELLINI, Maria ... 516-686-7641 317 G maria.perbellini@nyit.edu
PERCHINSKY, Tessa, A . 715-836-3887 510 D perchita@uwec.edu
PERCIANTE, Linda, K ... 303-963-3237.. 77 I lperciante@ccu.edu
PERCIVAL, Laura ... 989-275-5000 232 E laura.percival@kirtland.edu
PERCUOCO, Robert, E ... 563-884-5460 172 H robert.percuoco@palmer.edu
PERCY, Paul ... 865-471-3219 430 H ppercy@cn.edu
PERCY, Stephen ... 503-725-5143 386 D spercy@pdx.edu
PERDEW, Kris ... 208-459-5062 131 H kperdew@collegeofidaho.edu
PERDOMO, Jose, A ... 425-235-2352 497 E jperdomo@rtc.edu
PERDUE, K. Alan ... 304-876-5009 504 D aperdue@shepherd.edu
PERDUE, Laura ... 318-797-5257 194 E laura.perdue@lsus.edu
PERDUE, Mark ... 859-858-3511 183 D mark.perdue@asbury.edu
PERDUE, Penny ... 708-534-4130 138 H pperdue@govst.edu
PERDUE, Rhonda ... 540-857-6325 490 B rperdue@virginiawestern.edu
PERDUE, Robin, A ... 843-383-8025 420 B rperdue@coker.edu
PERDUE, Tina, K ... 740-376-4730 365 A tina.perdue@marietta.edu
PERDUE, Wendy, C ... 804-289-1779 486 G wperdue@richmond.edu
PERDUYN, Ellen ... 330-972-6056 371 C perduyn@uakron.edu
PEREA, Grace ... 702-254-7577 279 G grace.perea@northwestcareercollege.edu
PEREA, Jennifer, R ... 312-362-1083 137 C jrosato@depaul.edu
PEREBOOM, Maarten, L 410-543-6450 209 B mlpereboom@salisbury.edu
PERECMAN, Dov ... 845-434-5240 335 E dperecman@fallsburgyeshiva.com
PEREIRA, Freyja ... 707-527-4512.. 62 H fpereira@santarosa.edu
PEREIRA, Greg ... 480-517-8538.. 14 B greg.pereira@riosalado.edu
PEREIRA, Malin ... 704-687-7197 351 C mpereira@uncc.edu
PEREIRA, Sandra ... 508-849-3363 210 H spereira@annamaria.edu
PEREKRESTOV, Michael 315-858-0945 310 E library@hts.edu
PERELLI, Robert ... 716-829-8444 307 B perellir@dyc.edu
PERERA, Curtis ... 360-752-8330 492 H cperera@btc.edu
PERETZ, Marc, H ... 989-964-4062 236 F mhp@svsu.edu
PEREY, James ... 928-649-6513.. 17 G james.perey@yc.edu
PEREYRA, Moises ... 212-694-1000 299 L mpereyra@boricuacollege.edu
PEREZ, Alice ... 805-965-0581.. 62 E amperez17@sbcc.edu
PEREZ, Alvaro ... 787-798-6732 526 G alvaro.perez@uccaribe.edu
PEREZ, Andrew ... 518-438-3111 314 B andyp@mariacollege.edu
PEREZ, Angel, B ... 860-297-2000.. 88 E angel.perez@trincoll.edu
PEREZ, Angeles ... 787-725-6500 521 C aperez@albizu.edu
PEREZ, Annette ... 650-949-6163.. 43 E perezannette@fhda.edu
PEREZ, Antonio ... 212-220-1234 301 C aperez@bmcc.cuny.edu
PEREZ, Arely ... 816-322-0110 257 M arely.perez@calvary.edu
PEREZ, Barbara ... 310-900-1600.. 40 C bperez@elcamino.edu
PEREZ, Carlos ... 787-754-8000 527 B cperez@pupr.edu
PEREZ, Carlos ... 787-622-8000 527 B cperez@pupr.edu
PEREZ, Carmen, I ... 787-279-1912 523 J cperez@bayamon.inter.edu
PEREZ, Caty ... 559-278-4240.. 32 A caty_perez@csufresno.edu
PEREZ, Cesar ... 208-732-6329 131 I cperez@csi.edu
PEREZ, Cheryle ... 787-852-1430 522 P cperez@hccpr.edu
PEREZ, Diana ... 805-922-6966.. 24 J dperez@hancockcollege.edu
PEREZ, Doris ... 787-891-0925 523 G dperez@aguadilla.inter.edu
PEREZ, Doris, U ... 671-735-5517 519 H doris.perez@guamcc.edu
PEREZ, Eduardo ... 787-279-1912 523 J eperezd@bayamon.inter.edu
PEREZ, Enrique ... 714-480-7460.. 57 N perez_enrique@rsccd.edu
PEREZ, Gay ... 434-243-3605 486 H bgd2j@virginia.edu
PEREZ, JR., Gilberto ... 574-535-7775 158 A gperez@goshen.edu
PEREZ, Heather, K ... 816-604-3007 262 J heatherk.perez@mcckc.edu
PEREZ, Hiselgis ... 305-348-2731 109 D perezh@fiu.edu
PEREZ, Ivelisse ... 787-834-9595 526 E iperez@uaa.edu
PEREZ, Jeffrey ... 803-323-2225 426 H perezj@winthrop.edu
PEREZ, Joe ... 602-682-6841.. 11 A jperez@azsummitlaw.edu
PEREZ, Jose ... 787-857-3600 523 I japerez@br.inter.edu
PEREZ, Jose ... 915-566-9621 470 L jperez@westerntech.edu
PEREZ, Kathryn ... 806-894-9611 456 F kperez@southplainscollege.edu
PEREZ, Lance ... 402-472-3181 277 G lperez1@unl.edu
PEREZ, Luci ... 909-599-5433.. 48 E lperez@lifepacific.edu
PEREZ, Lydia ... 646-565-6000 331 F lydia.perez@touro.edu
PEREZ, Magda ... 787-841-2000 525 J magda_perez@pucpr.edu
PEREZ, Manuel ... 916-484-8925.. 50 F perezm@arc.losrios.edu
PEREZ, Manuel ... 562-985-4151.. 32 C manuel.perez@csulb.edu
PEREZ, Marciano ... 619-388-3498.. 60 C mperez@sdccd.edu
PEREZ, Margarita ... 337-482-6272 197 F mperez@louisiana.edu
PEREZ, Maria ... 787-891-0925 523 G mperez@aguadilla.inter.edu
PEREZ, Maria del C ... 787-284-1912 524 C mcperezr@ponce.inter.edu
PEREZ, Mario ... 323-343-3075.. 32 D mario.perez@calstatela.edu
PEREZ, Mercedes ... 305-760-7500 103 C
PEREZ, Mireya ... 708-656-8000 146 F mireya.perez@morton.edu
PEREZ, Monica ... 413-552-2227 219 G mperez@hcc.edu
PEREZ, Monica ... 864-644-5135 424 B mperez@swu.edu
PEREZ, Monte, E ... 818-364-7796.. 49 C perezme@lamission.edu
PEREZ, Myrna ... 787-786-3030 526 F mperez@ucb.edu.pr
PEREZ, Nancy ... 413-538-2188 222 C nbperez@mtholyoke.edu
PEREZ, Natasha ... 316-295-5888 177 F natasha_perez@friends.edu
PEREZ, Omar ... 787-740-1611 526 G omar.perez@uccaribe.edu
PEREZ, Oscar ... 305-821-3333 100 A operez@fnu.edu
PEREZ, Pablo ... 305-827-5452.. 94 G
PEREZ, Peter ... 203-254-4000.. 87 A pperez1@fairfield.edu
PEREZ, Rayetta ... 616-392-8555 239 J rayetta@westernsem.edu
PEREZ, Ricardo ... 818-240-1000.. 44 D rperez@glendale.edu
PEREZ, Ron ... 760-744-1150.. 55 K rperez@palomar.edu
PEREZ, Ronald ... 414-227-4128 511 A perez@uwm.edu
PEREZ, Rowena Ellen ... 671-735-5640 519 H rowenaellen.perez@guamcc.edu
PEREZ, JR., Ruben, R ... 706-821-8309 124 C rperez@paine.edu

PEREZ, Ruperto ... 404-894-2575 120 A
ruperto.perez@vpss.gatech.edu
PEREZ, Scott ... 805-437-8808 .. 31 C
scott.perez@csuci.edu
PEREZ, Sonny, P ... 671-735-2372 520 B
sonnypz@triton.uog.edu
PEREZ, Stephen ... 916-278-6331 .. 33 C
steve.perez@csus.edu
PEREZ, Suleyma ... 773-442-5400 147 G
s-perez6@neiu.edu
PEREZ, Vanessa ... 305-821-3333 100 A
vperez@fnu.edu
PEREZ, William ... 787-780-0070 521 B
wperez@caribbean.edu
PEREZ, Yesenia ... 718-270-1013 326 A
yesenia.perez@downstate.edu
PEREZ, Yolanda ... 787-834-9595 526 E
yperez@uaa.edu
PEREZ-CASANOVA,
Maria, T ... 787-480-2448 521 J
mperez02@sanjuanciudadpatria.com
PEREZ DE JESUS,
Margarita ... 787-848-5739 526 C
PEREZ-FRANCO, Mayte . 619-260-2395 .. 71 J
mpf@sandiego.edu
PEREZ-GONZALEZ,
Yariela ... 408-498-5145 .. 38 I
yperez@cogswell.edu
PEREZ-LOPEZ, Antonio . 787-878-5475 523 H
antperez@arecibo.inter.edu
PEREZ-LOPEZ,
Deborah, J ... 912-478-1566 120 E
dperezlopez@georgiasouthern.edu
PEREZ-LOPEZ,
Myrna, E ... 787-763-6700 522 N
meperez@se-pr.edu
PEREZ PACHECO,
Angel, F ... 787-265-3767 528 C
finanzas@uprm.edu
PEREZ RIESTRA, Estela . 787-764-0000 528 F
estela.perez@upr.edu
PEREZ-RODRIGUEZ,
Jose, F ... 787-723-4481 521 H
jperez@ceaprc.edu
PEREZ TOLEDO,
Elizabeth ... 787-848-5739 526 C
PERFECTO, Gerardo ... 787-257-0000 527 H
gerardo.perfecto@upr.edu
PERFETTI, Lisa, R ... 509-527-5187 500 G
perfetlr@whitman.edu
PERGI, Brenan ... 740-283-6445 361 L
bpergi@franciscan.edu
PERGOLA-RIVERA,
Maribelle ... 787-993-8951 527 G
maribelle.pergola@upr.edu
PERGOLIS, Robert ... 718-940-5419 322 G
rpergolis@sjcny.edu
PERGOLIZZI, Francis ... 207-973-1069 199 B
pergolizzif@husson.edu
PERGOLIZZI, Vanessa ... 860-913-2160 .. 87 B
vpergolizzi@goodwin.edu
PERHAC, Peter ... 702-567-1920 278 F
pperhac@cci.edu
PERI, Jonathan ... 215-885-2360 401 A
jperi@manor.edu
PERIGARD, Julie ... 360-779-9993 496 B
jperigard@ncad.edu
PERIGARD, Kim ... 360-779-9993 496 B
kperigard@ncad.edu
PERILLO, Brian ... 212-998-6843 318 D
bperillo@nyu.edu
PERILLO, Patricia, A ... 540-231-6272 490 F
pperillo@vt.edu
PERIN, Thomas ... 540-891-3037 488 B
tperin@germanna.edu
PERKINS, Alisa ... 812-288-8878 162 T
aperkins@mid-america.edu
PERKINS, JR.,
Andrew, M ... 336-285-4551 350 C
perkins@ncat.edu
PERKINS, Anika, M ... 662-329-7119 254 F
amperkins@muw.edu
PERKINS, Bianca ... 309-796-8240 134 C
perkinsb@bhc.edu
PERKINS, Bruce ... 405-585-5120 377 A
bruce.perkins@okbu.edu
PERKINS, Charles ... 620-792-9245 175 C
perkinsc@bartonccc.edu
PERKINS,
Chris-Tenna, M ... 804-627-5352 478 I
chris-tenna_perkins@bshsi.org
PERKINS, Eddie ... 606-539-4579 190 A
eddie.perkins@ucumberlands.edu
PERKINS, Faye ... 715-425-3700 511 E
faye.perkins@uwrf.edu
PERKINS, Jeffrey ... 310-665-6857 .. 54 I
jperkins@otis.edu

PERKINS, Joseph, A ... 919-572-1625 335 F
jperk1987@apexsot.edu
PERKINS, Joseph, E ... 919-572-1625 335 F
jeperkins@apexsot.edu
PERKINS, Joyce, J ... 901-572-2585 430 C
joyce.perkins@bchs.edu
PERKINS, Julie ... 660-263-4100 264 C
juliep@macc.edu
PERKINS, Keith ... 937-376-6640 358 I
kperkins@centralstate.edu
PERKINS, Louis ... 302-857-6030 .. 90 B
lperkins@desu.edu
PERKINS, Mary ... 847-214-7414 138 B
mperkins@elgin.edu
PERKINS, Megan ... 315-279-5296 312 D
mryan1@keuka.edu
PERKINS, Michele, D ... 603-428-2222 281 F
mperkins@nec.edu
PERKINS, Myrna ... 620-792-9270 175 C
perkinsm@bartonccc.edu
PERKINS, Peter ... 607-753-2518 327 A
peter.perkins@cortland.edu
PERKINS, Priscilla, L ... 413-782-1531 225 F
priscilla.perkins@wne.edu
PERKINS, Russell ... 913-758-6182 182 B
registrar@stmary.edu
PERKINS, Sara ... 517-796-8569 231 E
perkinssaraa@jccmi.edu
PERKINS, Suzetta, M ... 910-672-1143 350 B
sperkins@uncfsu.edu
PERKINS, Will ... 503-352-2120 385 I
wperkins@pacificu.edu
PERKINS BROWN,
Jayne ... 912-478-5218 120 E
jperkins@georgiasouthern.edu
PERKINSON, Ewa ... 330-867-1996 366 D
PERKINSON, Nikae ... 641-422-4173 172 C
nikae.perkinson@niacc.edu
PERKINSON, Stephen ... 330-867-1996 366 D
PERKNER, Stanislav ... 209-478-0800 .. 45 J
sperkner@humphreys.edu
PERKOWSKI, C, L ... 718-259-2525 299 I
PERKOWSKI, Henry ... 212-678-3016 331 C
hp2125@tc.columbia.edu
PERL, Emily ... 410-337-6122 204 A
eperl@goucher.edu
PERLADO, Ben ... 661-654-3381 .. 31 B
bperlado@csub.edu
PERLICK, Nick ... 859-622-1583 184 F
nick.perlick@eku.edu
PERLIN, Jeremy ... 513-487-3215 309 F
jperlin@huc.edu
PERLIONI, Jason ... 443-997-2370 204 F
perlioni@jhu.edu
PERLMAN, Andrew ... 617-573-8157 224 I
aperlman@suffolk.edu
PERLMAN, Lynn ... 617-277-3915 212 F
perlmanl@bgsp.edu
PERLMUTTER, David ... 806-742-3385 463 D
david.perlmutter@ttu.edu
PERLMUTTER, David, H 314-362-6827 269 L
perlmutterd@wustl.edu
PERLMUTTER, Kathleen . 805-756-0327 .. 30 K
kmcmah02@calpoly.edu
PERLOFF, Carey ... 415-439-2422 .. 25 J
cep@act-sf.org
PERLONGO, Chris ... 802-865-8740 474 G
cperlongo@champlain.edu
PERLOW, Yaakov ... 718-438-2727 335 C
PERLSTROM,
Christine, L ... 847-574-5208 143 A
cperlstrom@lfgsm.edu
PERMAN, Jay, A ... 410-706-7002 207 H
jperman@umaryland.edu
PERMAR, Stephen ... 860-628-4751 .. 87 E
spermar@lincolncollegene.edu
PERME, Connie ... 513-745-3992 374 D
perme@xavier.edu
PERMENTER,
Andrew, H ... 863-667-5078 108 G
ahpermenter@seu.edu
PERNELL, Leroy, F ... 407-254-3268 109 A
leroy.pernell@famu.edu
PERNICELLO, Collene ... 215-572-2900 389 D
pernicelloc@arcadia.edu
PERNICIARO, Richard ... 609-343-5670 283 D
rpernici@atlantic.edu
PERONE, Julie ... 610-436-2301 407 D
jperone@wcupa.edu
PERONI-CALLAHAN,
Kathy ... 617-521-2150 224 E
kathleen.peroni-callahan@simmons.edu
PEROO, Rama ... 620-441-5587 176 M
rama.peroo@cowley.edu
PEROW, Lauren, A ... 814-641-3302 398 B
perowl@juniata.edu
PEROZZI, Brett ... 801-626-6008 473 E
brettperozzi@weber.edu

PEROZZI, Brett ... 801-626-6361 473 E
brettperozzi@weber.edu
PEROZZI, Thomas ... 847-574-5168 143 A
tperozzi@lfgsm.edu
PERR, Yechiel, I ... 718-327-7600 334 C
info@yofr.org
PERREAULT, Melanie, L 716-878-5550 326 E
perreaml@buffalostate.edu
PERREIRA, Mary ... 808-956-4650 130 B
maryperr@hawaii.edu
PERRELLI, John ... 410-337-6527 204 A
john.perrelli@goucher.edu
PERREN, Ray ... 770-533-7030 122 E
rperren@laniertech.edu
PERRENOD, William, L . 914-337-9300 305 F
william.perrenod@concordia-ny.edu
PERRES, Irving ... 718-232-7800 334 G
PERRET, Geraldine ... 973-618-3536 284 D
gperret@caldwell.edu
PERRI, Christine ... 619-216-6668 .. 65 H
cperri@swccd.edu
PERRI, Geraldine, M ... 626-914-8821 .. 37 G
gperri@citruscollege.edu
PERRI, Jason ... 716-851-1421 307 I
perri@ecc.edu
PERRI, Mary Lynn ... 440-646-8329 373 B
mperri@ursuline.edu
PERRI, Michael ... 352-273-6214 110 D
mperri@phhp.ufl.edu
PERRI, Ralph ... 936-261-1205 458 F
rrperri@pvamu.edu
PERRICH, Jane ... 937-229-4122 372 A
jperrich1@udayton.edu
PERRIEN, Shane ... 402-941-6171 275 J
perrien@midlandu.edu
PERRIER, Rochelle ... 504-398-2744 196 E
rperrier@uhcno.edu
PERRIER, Sarah ... 412-392-8184 408 F
sperrier@pointpark.edu
PERRIN, Amy ... 847-214-7217 138 B
aperrin@elgin.edu
PERRIN, David, H ... 801-581-8537 472 P
david.perrin@health.utah.edu
PERRIN, Kelly ... 985-545-1500 192 K
PERRIN, L. Timothy ... 806-720-7125 452 D
tim.perrin@lcu.edu
PERRIN, Michael ... 512-471-7575 467 C
mwp@athletics.utexas.edu
PERRIN, Tom ... 334-833-4027 .... 5 M
tperrin@hawks.huntingdon.edu
PERRINE, Paul, C ... 828-298-3325 353 B
pperrine@warren-wilson.edu
PERRINE, Richard ... 603-897-8206 281 I
rperrine@rivier.edu
PERRINE, Zachary ... 501-812-2395 .. 23 C
zperrine@pulaskitech.edu
PERRINS, Robert, J ... 310-954-4015 .. 52 H
rperrins@msmu.edu
PERRITON, Caleb ... 307-755-2114 517 G
caleb.perriton@zenith.org
PERRON, Evelyn, R ... 603-206-8121 280 L
eperron@ccsnh.edu
PERRON, Michael ... 508-373-9409 211 F
michael.perron@becker.edu
PERRONE, Brenda ... 815-226-4010 150 C
bperrone@rockford.edu
PERRONE, Dona ... 203-371-7999 .. 88 C
PERRONE, Laura ... 770-220-7930 119 D
laura@gcuniv.edu
PERROTTA, Steve ... 603-513-1341 282 G
steve.perrotta@granite.edu
PERRUCI,
Gamaliel (Gama) ... 740-376-4624 365 A
gama.perruci@marietta.edu
PERRY, Al ... 810-762-0417 234 F
al.perry@mcc.edu
PERRY, Bryan ... 410-462-8047 202 F
bperry@bccc.edu
PERRY, Candace ... 404-756-4004 115 I
cperry@atlm.edu
PERRY, Carolyn, J ... 573-592-5315 270 B
carolyn.perry@westminster-mo.edu
PERRY, Chris ... 877-701-3800 133 D
cperry@aiuonline.edu
PERRY, Christine, M ... 617-573-8470 224 I
cperry@suffolk.edu
PERRY, Cynthia, R ... 757-594-7571 479 H
cperry@cnu.edu
PERRY, Dan ... 512-245-4440 463 A
d_p93@txstate.edu
PERRY, Darlene ... 252-538-4326 343 F
dperry934@halifaxcc.edu
PERRY, David, L ... 850-644-1240 110 A
dlperry@admin.fsu.edu
PERRY, Denah ... 812-888-4277 165 E
dperry@vinu.edu
PERRY, Don ... 214-378-1732 447 F
don.perry@dcccd.edu

PERRY, Douglas, E ... 815-939-5240 148 F
dperry@olivet.edu
PERRY, Erma ... 334-687-3543 .... 2 B
eperry@wallace.edu
PERRY, Foster ... 256-824-6880 .... 8 C
foster.perry@uah.edu
PERRY, Frank, E ... 412-397-6233 409 C
perry@rmu.edu
PERRY, Gary, W ... 561-297-3062 109 B
provost@fau.edu
PERRY, George ... 210-458-4450 468 B
george.perry@utsa.edu
PERRY, George ... 304-260-4380 502 J
gperry@blueridgectc.edu
PERRY, James ... 678-664-0520 128 F
james.perry@westgatech.edu
PERRY, James ... 903-813-2277 443 F
jperry@austincollege.edu
PERRY, Janet ... 970-207-4550 .. 80 P
janetp@mckinleycollege.edu
PERRY, Janet ... 970-207-4500 .. 84 C
janetp@uscareerinstitute.edu
PERRY, Janet ... 405-682-1611 377 C
jcperry@occc.edu
PERRY, Jason ... 804-758-6751 489 D
jperry@rappahannock.edu
PERRY, Jason, P ... 801-581-8514 472 P
jason.perry@utah.edu
PERRY, Jay ... 605-773-3455 428 D
jay.perry@sdbor.edu
PERRY, Johanna, L ... 914-337-9300 305 F
johanna.perry@concordia-ny.edu
PERRY, John ... 708-534-4518 138 H
jperry@govst.edu
PERRY, John, F ... 864-503-5242 425 H
jperry@uscupstate.edu
PERRY, Jonathan, C ... 479-575-5276 .. 21 I
jperry@uark.edu
PERRY, Judy ... 206-592-3349 495 E
jperry@highline.edu
PERRY, Justin ... 816-235-2260 268 D
perryjust@umkc.edu
PERRY, Keith ... 404-297-9522 120 D
perryk@gptc.edu
PERRY, Kimberly ... 360-752-8333 492 H
kperry@btc.edu
PERRY, Laura ... 315-268-6760 304 B
lperry@clarkson.edu
PERRY, Lee, T ... 801-422-4122 471 E
lee_perry@byu.edu
PERRY, Lori ... 660-263-4100 264 C
lorip@macc.edu
PERRY, Maria ... 215-884-8942 415 C
cfo@woninstitute.edu
PERRY, Mark ... 417-862-9533 260 D
mperry@globaluniversity.edu
PERRY, Mark ... 501-420-1205 .. 17 I
mark.perry@arkansasbaptist.edu
PERRY, Marlene ... 281-873-0262 446 J
m.perry@commonwealth.edu
PERRY, Mary Elaine ... 610-660-1145 409 H
mperry01@sju.edu
PERRY, Melissa ... 386-312-4088 106 M
melissaperry@sjrstate.edu
PERRY, Meredith ... 423-425-4431 440 A
meredith-perry@utc.edu
PERRY, Michael ... 321-674-7127 .. 99 K
perrymj@fit.edu
PERRY, Michael ... 559-734-9000 .. 61 C
mikep@sjvc.edu
PERRY, Michael, C ... 208-885-1029 132 I
michaelcperry@uidaho.edu
PERRY, Missy ... 864-941-8666 423 C
perry.m@ptc.edu
PERRY, Monique ... 803-981-7391 426 J
mperry@yorktech.edu
PERRY, Nancy ... 410-386-8231 203 A
nperry@carrollcc.edu
PERRY, Pamela ... 319-895-4176 167 G
pperry@cornellcollege.edu
PERRY, Paul ... 231-995-1114 235 B
pperry@nmc.edu
PERRY, Rhonda ... 217-206-7796 154 A
rrperry@uillinois.edu
PERRY, Robert ... 617-879-7269 218 B
rperry@massart.edu
PERRY, Robin ... 704-637-4384 336 G
raperry@catawba.edu
PERRY, Roderick ... 317-278-4281 160 E
perryrd@iupui.edu
PERRY, Rodger ... 704-669-4032 342 B
perryr@clevelandcc.edu
PERRY, Stacey ... 870-245-5220 .. 20 G
perrys@obu.edu
PERRY, Stephanie, D ... 276-328-0240 487 A
sdh9y@uvawise.edu
PERRY, Steve ... 864-294-2458 421 I
steve.perry@furman.edu

PETERSON, Michael, W 512-448-8788 455 I
michaelp@stedwards.edu
PETERSON, Michele ...... 970-247-7435.. 79 J
peterson_m@fortlewis.edu
PETERSON, Mitchell ...... 866-492-5336 251 E
mitchell.peterson@mail.wadenu.edu
PETERSON, Nell .... 813-974-6884 111 A
ncpeterson@usf.edu
PETERSON, Nicole .... 931-221-7979 430 B
petersonn@apsu.edu
PETERSON, Pamela .... 831-459-4300.. 70 C
pgpeters@ucsc.edu
PETERSON, Pamela, L ... 651-962-6608 251 D
plpeterson@stthomas.edu
PETERSON, Pete .... 310-506-7490.. 56 D
pete.n.peterson@pepperdine.edu
PETERSON, Phyllis, M .. 815-740-3848 154 G
ppeterson@stfrancis.edu
PETERSON, Polly, J ...... 701-252-3467 355 J
ppeterso@uj.edu
PETERSON, Randall .... 386-312-4022 106 M
randypeterson@sjrstate.edu
PETERSON, Randall, T .. 801-581-3402 472 P
randall.peterson@pharm.utah.edu
PETERSON, Randy .... 501-450-3826.. 19 I
peterson@hendrix.edu
PETERSON, Rebecca ...... 802-865-6425 474 G
peterson@champlain.edu
PETERSON, Robert .... 435-722-6900 472 L
bobp@ubtech.edu
PETERSON, Robert .... 216-987-2836 360 E
robert.peterson@tri-c.edu
PETERSON, Roy .... 262-243-4533 229 A
roy.peterson@cuw.edu
PETERSON, Roy .... 262-243-5700 507 C
roy.peterson@cuw.edu
PETERSON, Ryan .... 734-995-7596 229 A
ryan.peterson@cuaa.edu
PETERSON, Samantha ... 918-335-6223 378 F
speterson@okwu.edu
PETERSON, Sandy .... 608-785-9207 515 C
petersons@westerntc.edu
PETERSON, Scott .... 864-225-7653 421 G
scottpeterson@forrestcollege.edu
PETERSON, Stella .... 770-426-2930 122 F
peterson@life.edu
PETERSON, Stephanie ... 785-442-6051 178 C
speterson@highlandcc.edu
PETERSON, Susan .... 480-423-6300.. 14 C
susan.peterson@scottsdalecc.edu
PETERSON, Susan, K .... 785-532-6221 179 A
skp@ksu.edu
PETERSON, Terry .... 312-942-7020 150 F
terry_peterson@rush.edu
PETERSON, Thomas .... 732-906-2512 287 B
tpeterson@middlesexcc.edu
PETERSON, Toby .... 301-696-3934 204 D
peterson@hood.edu
PETERSON, Tom .... 209-228-4439.. 69 C
twpeterson@ucmerced.edu
PETERSON, Tyler, M ..... 205-934-8221.... 8 B
tpeterson@uab.edu
PETERSON, Val, L .... 801-863-8424 473 D
petersva@uvu.edu
PETERSON, Wendy .... 509-335-5586 499 G
wendyp@wsu.edu
PETERSON, Yvonne .... 503-228-6528 381 I
ypeterson@aii.edu
PETERSON-MILLER,
Connie .... 574-520-4591 160 F
copmiller@iusb.edu
PETERSON-SENIUK,
Peggy .... 419-473-2700 360 J
pseniuk@daviscollege.edu
PETERSON-VEATCH,
Ross .... 620-229-6090 181 F
ross.petersonveatch@sckans.edu
PETHE-COOK, Marlyn .... 813-253-6231 113 E
mpethe@ut.edu
PETHICK, Michael .... 231-591-3900 230 A
michaelpethick@ferris.edu
PETILLO, John, J .... 203-371-7900.. 88 C
petilloj@sacredheart.edu
PETIPRIN, Gary .... 502-272-8480 183 H
gpetiprin@bellarmine.edu
PETITFILS, Brad .... 504-865-3080 194 G
bpetit@loyno.edu
PETITT, Becky, R .... 858-822-4783.. 69 E
bpetitt@ucsd.edu
PETITT, Bill .... 972-883-2055 467 D
bpetitt@utdallas.edu
PETITT, Charles, W .... 336-725-8344 348 C
petittc@piedmontu.edu
PETITTI, Mario .... 440-525-7328 364 D
mpetitti@lakelandcc.edu
PETKASH, John .... 607-778-5011 326 C
petkashjc@sunybroome.edu
PETKUS, Edward .... 201-684-7377 289 C
epetkus@ramapo.edu
PETKUS, Emily .... 540-665-4530 485 C
epetkus@su.edu
PETLEY, Kathleen .... 518-629-4574 310 G
k.petley@hvcc.edu
PETOSKEY, Indira .... 860-465-5066.. 84 K
petoskeyi@easternct.edu
PETRAGLIA, Heather ...... 203-254-4000.. 87 A
hpetraglia@fairfield.edu
PETREN, Kenneth .... 513-556-5858 371 E
ken.petren@uc.edu
PETRESCU, Claudia, A ... 248-370-3169 235 J
cpetrescu@oakland.edu
PETRI, Elizabeth .... 413-662-5219 218 C
e.petri@mcla.edu
PETRI, Peter, A .... 781-736-2256 213 A
ppetri@brandeis.edu
PETRI, OP, Thomas ...... 202-495-3832.. 92 F
dean@dhs.edu
PETRICCA, Joe .... 323-856-7721.. 25 L
jpetricca@afi.com
PETRIDIS, Heather .... 626-815-4570.. 26 U
hpetridis@apu.edu
PETRIE, Mark .... 315-279-5254 312 D
mpetrie@keuka.edu
PETRIKAT, Douglas .... 714-547-9625.. 28 J
dpetrikat@calcoast.edu
PETRILLO, Emilia, K ...... 410-328-8404 207 H
epetr001@umaryland.edu
PETRIZZO, Louis, S .... 631-451-4235 330 B
petrizl@sunysuffolk.edu
PETROFF, Les .... 317-738-8108 157 L
lpetroff@franklincollege.edu
PETROKA, Louise, A ...... 203-285-2393.. 85 E
lpetroka@gwcc.commnet.edu
PETRONE, Eileen .... 412-536-1115 398 E
eileen.petrone@laroche.edu
PETROSIAN, Anahid .... 956-872-8339 456 G
anahid@southtexascollege.edu
PETROSIAN, Anahid .... 956-872-6790 456 G
anahid@southtexascollege.edu
PETROSINO, Chris .... 304-243-2165 505 H
cpetrosino@wju.edu
PETROSINO, Linda .... 607-274-3265 311 D
lpetrosino@ithaca.edu
PETROSINO, Linda .... 607-274-3113 311 D
petrosino@ithaca.edu
PETROSKY, Joseph .... 586-498-4181 233 B
petroskyj@macomb.edu
PETROSYAN, Narine ...... 510-925-4282.. 25 P
narinep@aua.am
PETROSYAN, Varduhi .... 510-925-4282.. 25 P
vpetrosi@aua.am
PETROSYAN, Violetta ..... 304-357-4758 502 E
violettapetrosyan@ucwv.edu
PETROV, John .... 301-985-7980 208 D
john.petrov@umuc.edu
PETROVICH, Jason .... 219-464-6858 165 D
jason.petrovich@valpo.edu
PETROVICH, Tamberly ... 831-582-4137.. 33 A
tpetrovich@csumb.edu
PETROY, Anthony, R ..... 573-341-4579 269 A
petroya@mst.edu
PETROZZA, Bruce .... 619-594-4723.. 34 B
bpetrozza@mail.sdsu.edu
PETRUCCI, Michele, L ... 724-357-2295 406 C
michelep@iup.edu
PETRUS, Robin .... 607-778-5201 326 C
petrusre@sunybroome.edu
PETRUSCH, Suzanne, M 864-833-8194 423 D
spetrusch@presby.edu
PETRUSHA, Cynthia ...... 707-476-4170.. 39 F
cynthia-petrusha@redwoods.edu
PETRUZELLA, Gerol, C .. 413-662-5570 218 C
g.petruzella@mcla.edu
PETRUZZELLI,
Barbara, W .... 845-569-3601 316 B
barbara.petruzzelli@msmc.edu
PETRY, Ric .... 614-222-3227 360 B
rpetry@ccad.edu
PETRYSHAK, Bruce .... 615-898-5570 434 H
bruce.petryshak@mtsu.edu
PETRYSHYN, Laryssa .... 716-829-8119 307 B
petryshl@dyc.edu
PETSCHE, Carolyn .... 815-599-3577 139 F
carolyn.petsche@highland.edu
PETSCHENKO, Lisa .... 630-953-3694 135 A
lpetschenko@chamberlain.edu
PETTA, Tim .... 360-992-2408 493 E
tpetta@clark.edu
PETTAZZONI, Jodi, E .... 336-334-5531 351 D
jepettaz@uncg.edu
PETTEGREW, Larry .... 919-573-5350 349 A
PETTEGREW, Mindy .... 816-604-1000 262 J
mindy.pettegrew@mcckc.edu
PETTENGER, Wade, W ... 417-862-9533 260 D
wpettenger@globaluniversity.edu
PETTERELLI, Mark, J ..... 315-445-4444 312 F
pettermj@lemoyne.edu
PETTERSON, Jennifer .... 573-592-4280 270 D
jennie.petterson@williamwoods.edu
PETTEWAY, Venetia .... 810-762-7899 232 C
vpettewa@kettering.edu
PETTIBON, II,
Joseph, P .... 979-845-4016 459 C
jpp2@tamu.edu
PETTIGREW, Jason .... 605-229-8350 427 J
jason.pettigrew@presentation.edu
PETTIGREW, Yancey ...... 731-661-5134 439 D
ypettigrew@uu.edu
PETTINGER, Brenda .... 208-562-3305 132 A
brendapettinger@cwidaho.cc
PETTINGILL, Sara, Y ..... 502-272-8401 183 H
spettingill@bellarmine.edu
PETTIPIECE, Deirdre ...... 718-960-8675 302 C
deirdre.pettipiece@lehman.cuny.edu
PETTIS, Curtis .... 937-376-6503 358 I
cpettis@centralstate.edu
PETTIS, Stephanie .... 850-729-5362 104 E
pettiss@nwfsc.edu
PETTIS-WALDEN,
Karen, M .... 804-523-5029 488 C
kpettis-walden@reynolds.edu
PETTIT, Emily .... 706-778-8500 124 E
epettit@piedmont.edu
PETTIT, Frederick .... 570-208-5881 398 D
frederickpettit@kings.edu
PETTIT, Jeanne .... 859-572-7544 188 E
pettitje@nku.edu
PETTIT, Kathy .... 303-963-3327.. 77 I
kpettit@ccu.edu
PETTIT, Martin, A .... 607-746-4702 329 B
pettitma@delhi.edu
PETTIT, Paul, E .... 214-887-5102 448 G
ppettit@dts.edu
PETTIT, Stephen, D .... 864-242-5100 418 H
PETTITT, Maureen .... 360-416-7919 498 F
maureen.pettitt@skagit.edu
PETTY, Bradley .... 325-942-2191 463 C
bradley.petty@angelo.edu
PETTY, Daniel, W .... 813-988-5131.. 99 D
vpres@floridacollege.edu
PETTY, JoBeth .... 601-968-8901 252 C
jbpetty@belhaven.edu
PETTY, Jonathan .... 806-291-3588 470 I
pettyj@wbu.edu
PETTY, Leslie .... 734-462-4400 236 H
lpetty@schoolcraft.edu
PETTY, Marcia, L .... 504-865-3030 194 G
mlpetty@loyno.edu
PETTY, Mark .... 605-677-5434 428 E
mark.petty@usd.edu
PETTY, Monica .... 202-885-8612.. 94 C
mpetty@wesleyseminary.edu
PETTY, Nina .... 817-515-5433 458 B
nina.petty@tccd.edu
PETTY, Tanjula .... 229-430-3511 114 J
tpetty@albanytech.edu
PETTY, Warren .... 201-216-5218 291 G
warren.petty@stevens.edu
PETULA, Eileen, E .... 814-332-3782 388 F
epetula@allegheny.edu
PETZ, Dan .... 620-450-2132 180 K
danp@prattcc.edu
PETZ, Thomas .... 248-689-8282 238 F
tpetz@walshcollege.edu
PETZKE, Greg .... 704-378-1190 338 I
gpetzke@jcsu.edu
PETZNICK, Michelle, L .. 641-422-4205 172 C
petznmic@niacc.edu
PEUGH-WADE,
Martha, A .... 415-422-2444.. 72 A
peugh@usfca.edu
PEWE, Rich .... 517-607-2518 231 C
rpewe@hillsdale.edu
PEYROUX, Elise .... 937-376-2946 369 C
epeyroux@payne.edu
PEYTON, Elizabeth .... 949-794-9090.. 66 B
epeyton@stanbridge.edu
PEYTON, Janice .... 936-270-7392 452 C
janice.peyton@lonestar.edu
PEZOLD, Frank .... 361-825-2349 460 A
frank.pezold@tamucc.edu
PEZZAROSSI, Alba .... 773-481-8059 136 B
apezzarossi@ccc.edu
PEZZI, Eileen .... 315-464-7853 326 B
pezzie@upstate.edu
PEZZIMENTI, Vincent ..... 716-338-1048 311 F
vincentpezzimenti@mail.sunyjcc.edu
PEZZOLI, Jeannie .... 808-984-3234 130 H
pezzoli@hawaii.edu
PENALVER, Eduardo, M 607-255-3527 306 B
eduardo.penalver@cornell.edu
PFANNENSTIEL, Myra ... 316-942-4291 180 D
pfannenstielm@newmanu.edu
PFANNESTIEL, Todd ...... 814-393-2220 405 H
president@clarion.edu
PFANNESTIEL, Todd ...... 814-393-2223 405 H
tpfannestiel@clarion.edu
PFEFER, Mark, T .... 913-234-0796 176 H
mark.pfefer@cleveland.edu
PFEFFER, Carole .... 502-272-8184 183 H
cpfeffer@bellarmine.edu
PFEIFER, Aimee, D .... 304-293-5355 505 B
aimee.pfeifer@mail.wvu.edu
PFEIFER, Gene, R .... 507-344-7315 240 I
gene.pfeifer@blc.edu
PFEIFER, Joseph .... 503-251-5775 387 I
jpfeifer@uws.edu
PFEIFER, Justin .... 316-677-1020 182 E
jpfeifer@watc.edu
PFEIFER, Patrick .... 620-276-9631 177 G
patrick.pfeifer@gcccks.edu
PFEIFER, Ron .... 920-465-2067 510 E
pfeiferr@uwgb.edu
PFEIFER, Tad .... 308-535-3684 275 I
pfeifert@mpcc.edu
PFEIFFER, Francine .... 202-220-1336 290 A
francine@rutgers.edu
PFEIFFER, Glenn .... 714-997-6826.. 36 G
pfeiffer@chapman.edu
PFEIFFER, Kelley .... 636-922-8544 265 J
kpfeiffer@stchas.edu
PFEIFFER, Pattie .... 919-735-5151 347 E
ppfeiffer@waynecc.edu
PFIZENMAIER, Thomas . 978-468-7111 215 E
tpfizenmaier@gordonconwell.edu
PFLANZ, Hannah .... 314-625-0300 266 C
hpflanz@slchcmail.com
PFLANZ, Mary .... 913-621-8764 177 A
mpflanz@donnelly.edu
PFLIPSEN, Andrew, J .... 701-788-4770 354 B
andrew.pflipsen@mayvillestate.edu
PFOHL, Jody .... 563-588-6315 167 E
jody.pfohl@clarke.edu
PFOTENHAUER, George 708-709-7834 148 I
gpfotenhauer@prairiestate.edu
PHAGAN, Kathy .... 770-533-6906 122 E
kphagan@laniertech.edu
PHAGAN, Tiffany, D ...... 386-748-1364.. 98 C
phagant@erau.edu
PHAIAH, Peter .... 218-281-8505 250 G
phaiah@umn.edu
PHALEN, Ann .... 215-503-7794 411 E
ann.phalen@jefferson.edu
PHAM, Chinh .... 714-484-7464.. 53 M
cpham@cypresscollege.edu
PHAM, Hue .... 714-432-5764.. 38 H
hpham@occ.cccd.edu
PHAM, SVD, Linh .... 563-876-3353 168 H
lpham@dwci.edu
PHAM, Michael .... 206-878-3701 495 E
mpham@highline.edu
PHAM, Sandra .... 818-299-5500.. 73 K
PHAM, Tom, C .... 617-984-1699 223 H
tpham@quincycollege.edu
PHAM, Tosha .... 323-343-2700.. 32 D
tosha.pham@calstatela.edu
PHAM, Trinh .... 323-343-5969.. 32 D
tpham4@calstatela.edu
PHAN, Anh .... 619-961-4232.. 67 F
aphan@tjsl.edu
PHANNENSTIEL, Matt .... 785-227-3380 175 E
pfannenstielmm@bethanylb.edu
PHARO, SCN, Diane .... 812-357-6598 164 A
dpharo@saintmeinrad.edu
PHARR, Christine .... 414-930-3319 509 B
pharrc@mtmary.edu
PHARR, Julie .... 336-386-3452 347 A
pharrj@surry.edu
PHARR, Kathy, R .... 706-542-0054 127 A
pharr@uga.edu
PHARR, Maria .... 704-272-5300 346 F
mpharr@spcc.edu
PHARR, Zach .... 479-619-2664.. 20 F
zpharr@nwacc.edu
PHARRIS, Heather .... 863-680-4754 100 D
hpharris@flsouthern.edu
PHEASANT, Joel, C .... 814-641-5334 398 B
pheasaj@juniata.edu
PHELAN, Chuck .... 508-362-2131 219 E
PHELAN, Daniel, J .... 517-787-0800 231 E
phelandanielj@jccmi.edu
PHELAN JOHNSON,
Marcia .... 860-297-2041.. 88 E
marcia.johnson@trincoll.edu
PHELPS, Bill .... 870-245-5567.. 20 G
phelpswr@obu.edu
PHELPS, Carmen .... 301-934-2251 203 D
cphelps@csmd.edu
PHELPS, Celeste .... 714-484-7107.. 53 M
cphelps@cypresscollege.edu

PICARD-TESSIER, Cathy, L ..... 401-825-1000 416 B ctessier@ccri.edu
PICARDO, Calle ..... 937-529-2201 371 B kcpicardo@united.edu
PICCHI, Danielle ..... 915-532-3737 470 L dpicchi@westerntech.edu
PICCININNI, James ..... 713-525-2192 466 J jpicci@stthom.edu
PICCIOTTO, Gil ..... 206-448-1330 499 G gpicciotto@wsu.edu
PICCIRILLO, Tony ..... 814-864-6666 396 C tonyp@glit.edu
PICCOLI, Beneditto ..... 856-225-6356 290 B piccoli@camden.rutgers.edu
PICCOLI, Tracey ..... 970-247-7464.. 79 J piccoli_t@fortlewis.edu
PICCOLO, Joe ..... 301-934-7822 203 D jpiccolo@csmd.edu
PICCONE, James ..... 856-691-8600 285 C jpiccone@cccnj.edu
PICHA, Patti ..... 907-474-7596.. 10 B plpicha@alaska.edu
PICHARDO, Jeannette ... 718-405-3255 304 H jeannette.pichardo@mountsaintvincent.edu
PICINICH, Susan ..... 410-704-3288 209 C spicinich@towson.edu
PICKA, Chenek ..... 757-490-1241 477 F cpicka@auto.edu
PICKARD, Angie ..... 601-581-3508 253 G apickard@meridiancc.edu
PICKARD, Bert ..... 601-928-6224 254 D bert.pickard@mgccc.edu
PICKARD, Jennifer, M ... 520-626-8505.. 16 J meyers@email.arizona.edu
PICKARD, Jeremy ..... 563-288-6004 168 M jpickard@eicc.edu
PICKARD, Larry ..... 415-451-2803.. 60 I lpickard@sfts.edu
PICKEL, Wendy ..... 816-501-4824 265 I wendy.pickel@rockhurst.edu
PICKELL, Barsha ..... 706-233-7394 125 E bpickell@shorter.edu
PICKENS, Joe ..... 386-312-4111 106 M joepickens@sjrstate.edu
PICKENS, Wanda ..... 706-886-6831 126 F wpickens@tfc.edu
PICKENS-OPOKU, Ali ..... 651-846-1406 247 G ali.pickens-opoku@saintpau.edu
PICKERELL, Jennifer, K . 618-537-6805 145 C jkpickerell@mckendree.edu
PICKERILL, Ted, O ..... 513-529-6225 365 I ted.pickerill@miamioh.edu
PICKERING, Amanda ..... 315-268-3994 304 B apickeri@clarkson.edu
PICKERING, David ..... 815-939-5240 148 F dpickrng@olivet.edu
PICKERING, Jeff ..... 919-209-2000 344 C jlpickering@johnstoncc.edu
PICKERING, Jonathan ... 815-939-5201 148 F jmpickering@olivet.edu
PICKERING, Robert, P ... 843-953-5096 419 D robert.pickering@citadel.edu
PICKETT, Clyde ..... 412-237-4436 392 G cpickett@ccac.edu
PICKETT, Kareen ..... 863-638-7248 113 I kareen.pickett@warner.edu
PICKETT, Michael ..... 323-550-8888.. 63 J
PICKETT, Regina ..... 281-283-2626 465 B pickett@uhcl.edu
PICKETT, Todd ..... 562-903-4754.. 27 E todd.pickett@biola.edu
PICKLESIMER, Donna ..... 614-251-4523 367 F picklesd@ohiodominican.edu
PICKLESIMER, Heith ..... 704-334-6882 336 I hpicklesimer@charlottechristian.edu
PICKMAN, Jerry ..... 816-271-5647 264 B pickman@missouriwestern.edu
PICKNEY, Gail ..... 334-874-5700.... 5 B gpickney@ccal.edu
PICKREN, Wade ..... 607-274-3734 311 D wpickren@ithaca.edu
PICKRON, Carlton ..... 413-572-5400 218 F cpickron@westfield.ma.edu
PICKRON-DAVIS, Marcine ..... 215-871-6178 407 G marcinepi@pcom.edu
PICKRUM, Vita, C ..... 302-857-6055.. 90 B vpickrum@desu.edu
PICKUS, Keith ..... 316-978-7791 182 F keith.pickus@wichita.edu
PICKWICK, Angie ..... 240-567-5557 205 F angie.pickwick@montgomerycollege.edu
PICONE, Deborah ..... 212-686-9244 298 C
PICUS, Sharon, M ..... 610-683-1353 406 D picus@kutztown.edu
PIDDINGTON, Josh, R .. 856-415-2270 289 G jpiddington@rcgc.edu
PIECHOTA, Thomas ..... 714-628-2897.. 36 G
PIECZYNSKI, William, C ..... 508-213-2162 223 C william.pieczynski@nichols.edu
PIEDRAS, Alex, H ..... 515-263-6017 169 E apiedras@grandview.edu
PIEHL, Jon ..... 909-667-4446.. 37 J jpiehl@claremontlincoln.edu
PIEHL, Marnie ..... 701-224-5748 354 F marnie.piehl@bismarckstate.edu
PIEHL, Sandy ..... 567-242-5975 363 G piehl.s@rhodesstate.edu
PIEL, Duane ..... 770-593-2257 121 C dpiel@gupton-jones.edu
PIELLUSCH, Gina ..... 410-857-2292 205 E gpiellusch@mcdaniel.edu
PIELOCK, Stephen ..... 413-545-5768 216 H stephen.pielock@umass.edu
PIENOVI, Nicolas ..... 773-878-4014 150 I npienovi@staugustine.edu
PIENTA-LETTA, Diane .... 973-300-2226 291 I dpienta-lett@sussex.edu
PIEPENBRING, Jack ..... 865-981-8112 433 F jack.piepenbring@maryvillecollege.edu
PIEPENBURG, Marianne, B ..... 214-768-3410 457 B mpiepenb@smu.edu
PIEPER, John, A ..... 314-367-8700 266 D john.pieper@stlcop.edu
PIEPER, Michael ..... 701-777-6862 353 G michael.pieper@und.edu
PIEPER, Sandi, J ..... 515-574-1139 170 C pieper@iowacentral.edu
PIEPER-OLSON, Heather 320-363-5964 241 I hpieperolso@csbsju.edu
PIER, David ..... 916-608-6809.. 50 H pierd@flc.losrios.edu
PIER, Julie, H ..... 605-677-5446 428 E julie.pier@usd.edu
PIERCE, Amanda, K ..... 757-594-8851 479 H amanda.pierce@cnu.edu
PIERCE, Barbara ..... 208-792-5272 132 C blpierce@lcsc.edu
PIERCE, Bill ..... 479-788-7188.. 22 A bill.pierce@uafs.edu
PIERCE, Bill ..... 502-852-8372 190 C wmpier01@louisville.edu
PIERCE, Billie ..... 419-530-5445 372 F william.pierce@utoledo.edu
PIERCE, Brynn ..... 541-383-7402 382 B bpierce@cocc.edu
PIERCE, Carl, G ..... 610-499-4555 414 F cgpierce@widener.edu
PIERCE, Carolyn ..... 954-308-2101.. 94 P cjpierce@aii.edu
PIERCE, Dee ..... 630-752-5048 155 F dee.pierce@wheaton.edu
PIERCE, Delton ..... 512-505-3037 451 A dpierce@htu.edu
PIERCE, Diane ..... 575-527-7745 295 E dpierce@nmsu.edu
PIERCE, Donna, L ..... 931-598-1880 436 A dopierce@sewanee.edu
PIERCE, Evan, F ..... 716-286-8769 318 F epierce@niagara.edu
PIERCE, Frederic ..... 607-753-2232 327 A fred.pierce@cortland.edu
PIERCE, Gillian ..... 617-353-2230 212 G gpierce@bu.edu
PIERCE, Greg ..... 601-266-5006 256 E greg.pierce@usm.edu
PIERCE, Harold, J ..... 802-656-4490 476 E harold.pierce@uvm.edu
PIERCE, James ..... 254-968-9781 459 A jrpierce@tarleton.edu
PIERCE, Jason ..... 423-636-7305 439 C jpierce@tusculum.edu
PIERCE, Jason, L ..... 937-229-2601 372 A jpierce2@udayton.edu
PIERCE, II, Jeffrey ..... 512-505-3024 451 A jepierce@htu.edu
PIERCE, Jennifer ..... 856-351-2642 291 E jpierce@salemcc.edu
PIERCE, Jerry, D ..... 318-357-6588 197 D pierce@nsula.edu
PIERCE, Joan ..... 608-785-9915 515 C piercej@westerntc.edu
PIERCE, John ..... 828-251-6742 351 A jpierce@unca.edu
PIERCE, Jonathan ..... 503-883-2490 383 H jdpierce@linfield.edu
PIERCE, Joshua ..... 573-629-3014 260 G joshua.pierce@hlg.edu
PIERCE, Kathy ..... 870-541-7853.. 20 A piercek@jrmc.org
PIERCE, Keith ..... 405-491-6366 379 K kpierce@snu.edu
PIERCE, Keith ..... 803-641-2838 425 A keithp@usca.edu
PIERCE, Kellee ..... 406-657-1166 272 I piercek@rocky.edu
PIERCE, Kenneth ..... 512-245-9650 463 A krp91@txstate.edu
PIERCE, Kevin ..... 941-355-9080.. 97 M kpierce@ewcollege.org
PIERCE, Kristen ..... 505-565-1075 224 H kpierce1@stonehill.edu
PIERCE, LaRue, A ..... 413-755-4868 221 B lapierce@stcc.edu
PIERCE, Leighton ..... 661-255-1050.. 29 F lpierce@calarts.edu
PIERCE, Leslie ..... 478-445-5596 119 E leslie.pierce@gcsu.edu
PIERCE, Lori, J ..... 734-764-0151 237 I ljpierce@umich.edu
PIERCE, Malisa ..... 918-270-6409 378 I malisa.pierce@ptstulsa.edu
PIERCE, Marisa ..... 425-640-1697 494 E marisa.pierce@edcc.edu
PIERCE, Marisa, E ..... 915-831-2864 449 A mpierce6@epcc.edu
PIERCE, Mark ..... 518-736-3622 309 A mark.pierce@fmcc.suny.edu
PIERCE, Melody, C ..... 336-334-7696 350 C mcpierce@ncat.edu
PIERCE, Michael ..... 562-903-4777.. 27 E michael.pierce@biola.edu
PIERCE, Mike ..... 941-487-4877 110 B mpierce@ncf.edu
PIERCE, Misti ..... 970-521-6619.. 81 F misti.pierce@njc.edu
PIERCE, Peg ..... 248-204-3143 233 A mpierce@ltu.edu
PIERCE, Robert 'Bob' ..... 205-348-4767.... 8 A bpierce@advance.ua.edu
PIERCE, Sharon ..... 612-659-6300 245 F sharon.pierce@minneapolis.edu
PIERCE, Sonja ..... 812-288-8878 162 T spierce@mid-america.edu
PIERCE, Stacey ..... 315-781-3900 310 C pierce@hws.edu
PIERCE, Susan ..... 972-860-8058 447 H spierce@dcccd.edu
PIERCE, Tom ..... 708-656-8000 146 F tom.pierce@morton.edu
PIERCE, Travis, L ..... 906-487-2682 234 A tlp@mtu.edu
PIERCE, Vicki, G ..... 256-765-4311.... 9 A vgpierce@una.edu
PIERCE, Yolanda ..... 202-806-6100.. 92 C
PIERCE BURNETTE, Colette ..... 512-505-3001 451 A cpburnette@htu.edu
PIERCY, Mitchell ..... 417-626-1234 264 J mpiercy@occ.edu
PIERI, Sean ..... 719-389-6740.. 77 J sean.pieri@coloradocollege.edu
PIERICK, Michael, J ..... 773-442-5100 147 G m-pierick@neiu.edu
PIERNER, Tracy, P ..... 608-757-7772 513 D tpierner@blackhawk.edu
PIEROTTI, Laura ..... 201-559-3504 286 C pierottil@felician.edu
PIERPOINT, Paul, E ..... 610-861-5580 403 B ppierpoint@northampton.edu
PIERRE, Christophe ..... 201-216-5263 291 G christophe.pierre@stevens.edu
PIERRE, David, A ..... 718-990-2616 322 F pierred@stjohns.edu
PIERRE, John, K ..... 225-771-2552 196 B jpierre@sulc.edu
PIERRE, Lemuel ..... 954-943-8667 103 F
PIERRE, Thelma, J ..... 926-261-1401 458 F tjpierre@pvamu.edu
PIERRE, Vivica, D ..... 617-228-2366 219 D vdpierre@bhcc.mass.edu
PIERS, Sheri ..... 207-893-7697 200 G spiers@sjcme.edu
PIERSALL, Vicki ..... 503-554-2161 383 C vpiersall@georgefox.edu
PIERSOL, Amy ..... 913-234-0600 176 H amy.piersol@cleveland.edu
PIERSON, Cathy ..... 541-245-7912 386 G cpierson@roguecc.edu
PIERSON, Connie ..... 410-455-3055 208 A krach@umbc.edu
PIERSON, Gary ..... 970-943-2232.. 84 E gpierson@western.edu
PIERSON, Katricia ..... 580-559-5213 375 I kpierson@ecok.edu
PIERSON, Megan ..... 650-723-2300.. 66 C
PIERSON, Tim, J ..... 434-395-2039 482 E piersontj@longwood.edu
PIESIK, Deanette ..... 701-774-4246 355 C deanette.piesik@willistonstate.edu
PIETKIEWICZ, Michael .. 716-270-4670 307 I pietkiewicz@ecc.edu
PIETREWICZ, Brian ..... 505-277-5930 296 H bpietrewicz@unm.edu
PIETROWSKI, Michael ... 505-565-1082 224 H mpietrowski@stonehill.edu
PIETRUSZKIEWICZ, Christopher ..... 727-562-7809 111 E cmp@law.stetson.edu
PIETRYKOWSKI, Chet .... 406-791-5283 273 C chet.pietrykowski@ugf.edu
PIETRYKOWSKI, Robert, J ..... 954-262-7893 104 F rpietrykowski@nova.edu
PIETRZAK, Dale ..... 208-885-7995 132 I dalepietrzak@uidaho.edu
PIETSCH, Amy ..... 920-735-2594 513 F pietsch@fvtc.edu
PIETTE, Kylie ..... 231-591-2089 230 A kyliepiette@ferris.edu
PIETZ, Vicky ..... 715-675-3331 514 F pietz@ntc.edu
PIFER, Caleb, M ..... 814-824-2241 401 J cpifer@mercyhurst.edu
PIFER, Kenneth ..... 503-370-6104 388 D kpifer@willamette.edu
PIGA, John ..... 781-891-2148 212 A jpiga@bentley.edu
PIGAO, Lana ..... 409-880-2292 462 B lypigao@lit.edu
PIGATTI, Kimberly ..... 708-596-2000 151 H kpigatti@ssc.edu
PIGEON, Vanessa ..... 713-226-5522 465 C pigeonv@uhd.edu
PIGGOTT, Patrick, L ..... 209-478-0800.. 45 J ppiggott@humphreys.edu
PIGGOTT, Robyn ..... 717-358-3971 395 G robyn.piggott@fandm.edu
PIGNATELLO, Robert ..... 212-772-4460 302 E robert.pignatello@hunter.cuny.edu
PIGNATO, David ..... 617-254-2610 224 B rev.david.pignato@sjs.edu
PIGORS, Aaron ..... 219-980-7203 160 C apigors@iu.edu
PIGOTT, Kelly ..... 325-671-2179 450 A kpigott@hsutx.edu
PIGOTT, Miguel ..... 860-512-2815.. 85 G mpigott@manchestercc.edu
PIGZA, Jennifer ..... 925-631-4755.. 59 C jpigza@stmarys-ca.edu
PIIRAINEN, Jack ..... 775-445-4282 279 F jack.piirainen@wnc.edu
PIKALEK, Amy ..... 608-663-2218 507 D apikalek@edgewood.edu
PIKE, Dale ..... 540-231-7108 490 F dalepike@vt.edu
PIKE, Patricia ..... 562-903-4713.. 27 E patricia.pike@biola.edu
PIKKA, Joshua ..... 313-831-5200 229 L jpikka@etseminary.edu
PIKOR, Susan ..... 413-542-8099 210 F spikor@amherst.edu
PIKOWSKY, Reta ..... 404-894-4181 120 A reta.pikowsky@registrar.gatech.edu
PILACHOWSKI, David, M ..... 413-597-2502 226 C david.m.pilachowski@williams.edu
PILATI, Liz ..... 206-296-1891 498 D pilatil@seattleu.edu
PILCHER, Benjamin, J ... 412-578-6557 391 G bjpilcher@carlow.edu
PILCHICK, Yochanan ..... 718-232-7800 334 G
PILEWSKI, Tim, W ..... 814-732-1974 406 B pilewski@edinboro.edu
PILGRIM, David ..... 231-591-3946 230 A davidpilgrim@ferris.edu
PILGRIM, Jacqueline ..... 617-422-7401 222 J jpilgrim@nesl.edu
PILGRIM, Mark ..... 717-477-1154 407 B mepilg@ship.edu
PILGRIM, Terry ..... 817-598-8858 470 J tpilgrim@wc.edu
PILIECI, Kim ..... 616-538-2330 230 E kpilieci@gbcol.edu
PILIERI, Thais ..... 718-270-6986 303 C tpilieri@mec.cuny.edu
PILIPZECK, Beth ..... 215-596-8970 413 E b.pilipz@usciences.edu
PILKINGTON, Annette ... 303-273-3498.. 78 J apilking@mines.edu
PILLANS, Elizabeth ..... 903-875-7370 453 J elizabeth.pillans@navarrocollege.edu
PILLAR, James ..... 732-571-3585 287 C jpillar@monmouth.edu
PILLARELLI, Tina ..... 734-384-4229 234 C tpillarelli@monroeccc.edu

PITTS, Otis 828-328-7179 339 C
otis.pitts@lr.edu
PITTS, Tracey 646-717-9704 309 B
pitts@gts.edu
PITTSER, Julie 573-341-6118 269 A
pittserj@mst.edu
PITZNER, Alex, C 717-901-5124 397 E
apitzner@harrisburgu.edu
PIUROWSKI, Robert, C 607-746-4559 329 B
piurowrc@delhi.edu
PIVARNIK, OP,
R. Gabriel 401-865-2245 416 E
gpivarni@providence.edu
PIVERAL, Joyce 636-949-4618 261 I
jpiveral@lindenwood.edu
PIXLEY, Alan, D 972-758-3842 446 I
apixley@collin.edu
PIZAM, Abraham 407-903-8010 110 C
abraham.pizam@ucf.edu
PIZANA, Kathleen 574-520-4878 160 F
kpizana@iusb.edu
PIZARRO, Luis 352-365-3576 103 B
pizarrol@lssc.edu
PIZER, Lori 518-292-7785 321 G
inst_res@sage.edu
PIZZANO, Patti 704-461-6573 335 J
pattipizzano@bac.edu
PIZZARDI, Frank 516-876-3013 327 C
pizzardif@oldwestbury.edu
PIZZI, Felix 617-747-2310 212 B
counselingcenter@berklee.edu
PIZZUTI, Debra 614-508-7233 363 E
dpizzuti@hondros.edu
PIZZUTI, Linda, J 309-677-3153 134 G
lindap@fsmail.bradley.edu
PIZZUTO, Carmelo 212-353-4161 306 A
pizzut@cooper.edu
PIZZUTO, Phyllis 760-480-8474 74 H
ppizzuto@wscal.edu
PIZZUTO, William, J 203-236-9818 88 G
william.j.pizzuto@uconn.edu
PIÑERO, Hector 787-850-9104 528 B
hector.pinero@upr.edu
PIÑERO, Ileana 787-751-1912 524 E
ipinero@juris.inter.edu
PJATAK, Jennifer 203-932-7082 89 D
jpjatak@newhaven.edu
PLA-GOMEZ, Fernando 787-250-0000 527 D
fernando.pla1@upr.edu
PLACE, Linna, F 816-235-6230 268 D
placel@umkc.edu
PLACE, Nick, T 352-392-1761 110 D
nplace@ufl.edu
PLACEK, Kristen 863-680-4205 100 D
kplacek@flsouthern.edu
PLACENTINO, Kim 847-574-5170 143 A
kplacentino@lfgsm.edu
PLACER, Chandra 864-578-8770 423 F
cplacer@sherman.edu
PLACERES, Sonia 787-738-2161 528 A
sonia.placeres@upr.edu
PLACIDI, Kathleen 434-381-6596 485 P
kplacidi@sbc.edu
PLACIDO, Rob 940-898-3980 464 A
rplacido@twu.edu
PLAEHN, Kris, H 253-535-7212 496 G
plaehnkh@plu.edu
PLAGGE, Sinead 360-416-7600 498 F
sinead.plagge@skagit.edu
PLAISANCE, DesLey 985-448-4191 197 C
desley.plaisance@nicholls.edu
PLANAS, Fernando 217-206-7949 154 A
fplanas@uis.edu
PLANDER, Kristy 402-481-8849 273 F
kristy.plander@bryanhealthcollege.edu
PLANEK, John 815-836-5937 143 E
planekjo@lewisu.edu
PLANK, Donna 254-295-4591 466 A
dplank@umhb.edu
PLANT, Jonathan 361-593-2599 460 B
jonathan.plant@tamuk.edu
PLANTE, Beverly 315-801-3034 322 C
bplante@secon.edu
PLANTE, Dawn, M 440-525-7327 364 D
dplante@lakelandcc.edu
PLANTE, Jacques 603-641-7380 282 A
jplante@anselm.edu
PLANTE, John, J 412-396-4937 394 D
plantej@duq.edu
PLANTEFABER, Lisa 413-572-5733 218 F
lplantefaber@westfield.ma.edu
PLANTENBERG, Diane 262-646-6517 509 C
dplantenberg@nashotah.edu
PLANTY, Teresa 315-268-3852 304 B
tplanty@clarkson.edu
PLANTZ, Dorothy, B 443-518-4614 204 E
dplantz@howardcc.edu
PLANTZ, Robert 570-586-2400 392 E
rplantz@clarkssummitu.edu
PLANTZ-MASTERS,
Shari 303-458-4272 82 D
splantzmasters@regis.edu
PLASKER, Nancy 781-768-7019 224 A
nancy.plasker@regiscollege.edu
PLASKONOS, Melissa 619-260-4175 71 J
melissa@sandiego.edu
PLASTERS, Shana 336-272-7102 338 B
shana.plasters@greensboro.edu
PLATE, William 843-349-4066 420 A
billplate@coastal.edu
PLATING, John 706-419-1663 118 E
john.plating@covenant.edu
PLATOVSKY, Jonathan 718-268-4700 320 K
PLATT, Jeffrey 716-829-7766 307 B
plattjh@dyc.edu
PLATT, Judy, T 617-353-5940 212 G
juplatt@bu.edu
PLATT, Kathleen 912-344-2576 115 D
kathy.platt@armstrong.edu
PLATT, Mark 318-675-5341 194 D
mplatt@lsuhsc.edu
PLATT, Sharon 412-536-1120 398 E
sharon.platt@laroche.edu
PLATUKUS, Graceann 570-740-0355 400 F
gplatukus@luzerne.edu
PLATZEK, Russell 718-262-2140 304 A
rplatzek@york.cuny.edu
PLAYER, Kathleen, N 630-515-7664 145 I
kplayer@midwestern.edu
PLAZA, Claudia 562-985-4187 32 C
claudia.plaza@csulb.edu
PLAZA, Erica 920-498-6969 514 G
erica.plaza@nwtc.edu
PLAZA, Laurie 610-526-6038 396 H
lplaza@harcum.edu
PLAZA, Luis 917-493-4448 313 M
lplaza@msmnyc.edu
PLEAS, Dawn, E 620-229-6336 181 F
dawn.pleas@sckans.edu
PLEAS, Dorothy, J 630-637-5156 147 E
djpleas@noctrl.edu
PLEASANT, Klint 248-218-2058 236 C
kpleasant@rc.edu
PLEASANT, Lori 850-973-9469 104 D
pleasantl@nfcc.edu
PLEASANT-DOINE,
Sheia, I 904-819-6435 98 I
spleasant@flagler.edu
PLEASANTS, Jane 919-668-2565 337 C
jane.pleasants@duke.edu
PLEDGER, Barbara 607-436-2010 325 E
barbara.pledger@oneonta.edu
PLEGER, Kimberly 253-680-7102 492 F
kpleger@bates.ctc.edu
PLEMMONS, Donna 501-450-1351 19 I
plemmons@hendrix.edu
PLEMMONS, Kim 704-403-1751 336 B
kim.plemmons@carolinashealthcare.org
PLETCHER, Ann 864-596-9086 420 F
ann.pletcher@converse.edu
PLETSCHER,
Anthony, W 215-368-5000 389 H
tpletscher@biblical.edu
PLEUSS, Carol, J 330-684-8928 371 D
cjpleus@uakron.edu
PLEVER, Steve 828-251-6526 351 A
splever@unca.edu
PLIML, Michelle 414-930-3397 509 B
plimlm@mtmary.edu
PLINER, Lauren 215-953-5999 93 B
PLINER, Lauren 484-809-7770 93 B
PLINER, Susan 315-781-3354 310 C
pliner@hws.edu
PLINSKE, Kathleen, A 321-682-4975 113 F
kplinske@valenciacollege.edu
PLINSKE, Paul, M 308-865-8332 277 F
plinskep@unk.edu
PLISCO, Mary 404-835-6135 435 M
mplisco@richmont.edu
PLISSEY, Bethany 802-635-1313 477 C
bethany.plissey@jsc.edu
PLLOG, William 603-641-7174 282 A
wploog@anselm.edu
PLOCICA, Tim 512-245-7113 463 A
tjp25@txstate.edu
PLOECKELMAN, Erica 920-686-6127 510 A
erica.ploeckelman@sl.edu
PLONSKY, Christine, A 512-471-4780 467 C
cp@utexas.edu
PLOSKONKA, James 216-987-5177 360 E
james.ploskonka@tri-c.edu
PLOTKIN, David 503-594-3020 382 D
david.plotkin@clackamas.edu
PLOTKOWSKI, Paul 616-331-6260 230 G
plotkowp@gvsu.edu
PLOTNER, Amy 315-312-3702 327 D
amy.plotner@oswego.edu
PLOTT, Richard 214-378-1834 447 F
richardplott@dcccd.edu
PLOTTS, Debra 334-214-4866 1 H
debra.plotts@cv.edu
PLOTTS, Douglas, J 610-861-1560 402 D
plottsd@moravian.edu
PLOTTS, John 972-721-5266 464 E
jplotts@udallas.edu
PLOUFF, Chris 616-331-2400 230 G
plouffc@gvsu.edu
PLOUFFE, Audrey 406-275-4969 273 A
audrey_plouffe@skc.edu
PLOUFFE, Jeffrey 401-874-4198 417 E
jeffplouffe@uri.edu
PLOURDE, Philip, D 319-273-6022 167 A
philip.plourde@uni.edu
PLOUTZ-SNYDER, Lori 734-764-5210 237 I
PLOWFIELD, Lisa 410-704-2132 209 C
lplowfield@towson.edu
PLOWMAN, Donde 402-472-3751 277 G
dplowman2@unl.edu
PLUCHUTA, Alexander 610-359-5057 393 E
apluchut@dccc.edu
PLUEMER, Julie 608-822-2369 515 A
jpluemer@swtc.edu
PLUMB, Anne, M 901-572-2842 430 C
anne.plumb@bchs.edu
PLUMB, Richard, G 651-962-6720 251 D
rgplumb@stthomas.edu
PLUMB, Sylvia 802-626-6459 477 D
sylvia.plumb@lyndonstate.edu
PLUMLEY, Kelly 828-327-7000 341 G
kplumley@cvcc.edu
PLUMLEY, Susan 304-327-4182 503 O
splumley@bluefieldstate.edu
PLUMLY, Wayne, L 229-245-3825 127 H
lwplumly@valdosta.edu
PLUMMER, B. DaVida 757-727-6698 481 E
davida.plummer@hamptonu.edu
PLUMMER, Dale, H 610-566-1776 415 A
dplummer@williamson.edu
PLUMMER, David 956-872-5575 456 G
davidp@southtexascollege.edu
PLUMMER, DaVida 757-637-2018 481 E
davida.plummer@hamptonu.edu
PLUMMER, Deborah, L 508-856-2179 217 C
deborah.plummer@umassmed.edu
PLUMMER, Dianne 617-989-4036 225 E
plummerd@wit.edu
PLUMMER, Donna, M 859-238-5308 184 C
donna.plummer@centre.edu
PLUMMER, Eric 701-777-3391 353 G
eric.plummer@und.edu
PLUMMER, Laura 915-532-3737 470 L
lplummer@westerntech.edu
PLUMMER, Lisa 610-282-1100 393 G
lisa.plummer@desales.edu
PLUMMER, Meredith 760-366-5284 41 B
mplummer@cmccd.edu
PLUMMER, Robert, M 423-439-4218 431 H
plummerb@etsu.edu
PLUMMER, Troy, A 515-263-6050 169 E
tplummer@grandview.edu
PLUMMER, Vince 701-671-2319 355 B
vince.plummer@ndscs.edu
PLUMMER, Yhann 504-286-5191 195 L
yplummer@suno.edu
PLUNK, Kelly 870-584-1104 22 F
kplunk@cccua.edu
PLUNKETT, Cathy 540-769-8289 477 G
ceplunkett@an.edu
PLUNKETT, Chris 319-385-6206 170 J
chris.plunkett@iw.edu
PLUNKETT, Jackie 573-592-5226 270 B
jackie.plunkett@westminster-mo.edu
PLUNKETT, James, C 215-951-1500 398 F
plunkett@lasalle.edu
PLUNTA, Elizabeth 206-934-5141 497 J
elizabeth.plunta@seattlecolleges.edu
PLURETTI, Anthony 315-364-3229 333 G
apluretti@wells.edu
PLUSCHT, Patrick 940-565-4936 466 B
patrick.pluscht@unt.edu
PLUTCHAK, Scott 205-934-5460 8 B
tscott@uab.edu
PLUTCHOK, Yisroel 718-438-5476 334 A
PLUTE, David 307-754-6025 516 Q
david.plute@nwc.edu
PLYLER, Jeffrey, B 704-463-3042 348 B
jeff.plyler@pfeiffer.edu
PLYMALE, Chad 585-567-9480 310 F
chad.plymale@houghton.edu
PNACEK, Kevin 810-766-2240 227 F
kpnace01@baker.edu
POAGE, Alison 512-472-4133 456 E
alison.poage@ssw.edu
POARCH, Mark 828-726-2211 341 D
mpoarch@cccti.edu
POAT, Erica 618-634-3375 151 G
ericap@shawneecc.edu
POATS, Lillian, B 713-313-7978 461 E
poats_lb@tsu.edu
POBLENZ, Scott, B 978-468-7111 215 E
spoblenz@gordonconwell.edu
POBLENZ, Scott, B 978-468-7111 215 E
spoblenz@gcts.edu
POCAI, Rob 601-366-8880 256 H
rpocai@wbs.edu
POCHARD, Brad 864-294-3406 421 I
brad.pochard@furman.edu
POCHE, Paulette, M 985-549-5638 197 E
ppoche@selu.edu
POCK, Arnyce 301-295-9945 518 G
arnyce.pock@usuhs.edu
POCOCK, Beth 828-669-8012 340 I
beth.pocock@montreat.edu
PODANY, Jeremy 970-491-5709 78 N
jeremy.podany@colostate.edu
PODBELSKI, Amy 401-598-1000 416 C
apodbelski@jwu.edu
PODEIN, Jon 334-386-7588 5 I
jpodein@faulkner.edu
PODELL, David 781-239-3101 220 A
dpodell@massbay.edu
PODESCHI, Amanda 217-424-3506 145 J
apodeschi@millikin.edu
PODESTA, Guido 608-262-9833 510 C
gpodesta@wisc.edu
PODLIN, Michael 206-296-6100 498 D
podlinm@seattleu.edu
PODOLSKY, Daniel, K 214-648-2508 469 E
priscilla.alderman@utsouthwestern.edu
POE, Elmer 252-328-9066 349 I
poee@ecu.edu
POE, Mary Anne 731-661-5397 439 D
mpoe@uu.edu
POE, Misty 304-367-4135 504 A
POE, Misty 304-367-4047 504 A
POE, Scott 304-424-8212 505 C
scott.poe@wvup.edu
POE, Shawna 217-854-5506 134 E
shawna.poe@blackburn.edu
POEHLER, M.J 816-802-3393 261 C
mpoehler@kcai.edu
POEHLERT, Edward 760-757-2121 52 F
epoehlert@miracosta.edu
POELKER, Scott 843-574-6198 424 G
scott.poelker@tridenttech.edu
POELKING, Karen, L 216-373-5234 367 A
kpoelking@ndc.edu
POELVOORDE, Tracy, L 309-779-7710 153 C
tracy.poelvoorde@trinitycollegeqc.edu
POESE, Debra 240-567-7269 205 F
debra.poese@montgomerycollege.edu
POFF, Carl 570-484-2625 406 E
carl.poff@lhufoundation.org
POFF, G. Elaine, N 954-262-7261 104 F
poff@nova.edu
POFF, Robert, C 812-941-2331 161 A
rcpoff@ius.edu
POGATSHNIK, Jerry 859-622-1744 184 F
jerry.pogatshnik@eku.edu
POGGENDORF,
Brenda, P 540-375-2270 484 H
poggendorf@roanoke.edu
POGGENDORF,
Brenda, P 540-375-2235 484 H
bpoggendorf@roanoke.edu
POGGENDORF,
Richard, J 540-375-2043 484 H
rpoggendorf@roanoke.edu
POGONCHEFF, Elaine 517-483-1016 232 K
pogonce@lcc.edu
POGROSZEWSKI,
Donna, J 585-292-3202 315 L
dpogroszewski@monroecc.edu
POGUE, Ed 785-227-3380 175 E
poguee@bethanylb.edu
POGUE, Gregory 609-771-3078 284 I
pogueg@tcnj.edu
POGUE, Roslynn 318-342-5327 198 A
pogue@ulm.edu
POHAS, Joanie 310-338-3068 50 J
jpohas@lmu.edu
POHERO, Mary Jane 973-596-3106 288 A
mary.pohero@njit.edu
POHIRA VIETH, Ann 407-618-5900 93 B
POHIRA VIETH, Ann 407-264-9400 93 B
POHL, Charles, A 215-503-6988 411 E
charles.pohl@jefferson.edu
POHL, Don 314-286-3653 265 F
dpohl@ranken.edu
POHL, Henry, S 518-262-5919 297 L
pohlh@mail.amc.edu

POHL, Jonathan 860-832-1945.. 84 J pohlj@ccsu.edu
POHLGEERS, Linda 513-244-4824 366 A linda.pohlgeers@msj.edu
POHLMAN, Jean 513-487-1126 371 A jean.pohlman@myunion.edu
POHLMAN, Kimberly 317-955-6021 162 R kpohlman@marian.edu
POHLSON, Scott 605-677-5759 428 E scott.pohlson@usd.edu
POIGER, Uta 617-373-5173 223 D
POIGNEE, Leshia 605-856-2355 428 A leshia.poignee@sintegleska.edu
POINDEXTER, Jeanne 757-382-9900.. 93 B
POINDEXTER, Michael 916-558-2142.. 50 I poindem@scc.losrios.edu
POINT, Matthew 215-965-4035 402 C mpoint@moore.edu
POINTER, Michelle 410-951-3516 208 F mpointer@coppin.edu
POINTKOWSKY, Paige 909-607-3240.. 37 L paige.pointkowsky@cgu.edu
POINTS, Dan 405-733-7359 379 F dpoints@rose.edu
POINTS, Emily 309-694-8501 139 G emily.points@icc.edu
POIRIER, Dawn 508-541-1809 214 C dpoirier@dean.edu
POIRIER, J. Nicolas 315-568-3197 317 A npoirier@nycc.edu
POIRIER, Janet, L 603-641-7010 282 A jpoirier@anselm.edu
POIRRIER, Gail, P 337-482-6808 197 F poirrier@louisiana.edu
POISEL, Mark, A 501-569-3328.. 22 B mapoisel@ualr.edu
POISSON, Craig 413-748-3333 224 G cpoisson@springfieldcollege.edu
POITIER, Thomas 404-527-7761 122 B tpoitier@itc.edu
POITRA, Peggy 218-879-0803 244 F poitra@fdltcc.edu
POKHAREL, Padmanjali 571-633-9651 486 E padmanjali.pokharel@uona.edu
POKORAK, Jeffrey 617-305-1645 224 I jpokorak@suffolk.edu
POKORNOWSKI, Alex 701-777-2664 353 G alexander.pokornowski@und.edu
POKORNY, Anita, R 330-325-6760 366 F app@neomed.edu
POKOT, Elena 262-472-1001 512 C pokote@uww.edu
POL, Aileen 708-209-3237 136 I aileen.pol@cuchicago.edu
POL, Lou 402-554-2303 277 I lpol@unomaha.edu
POLAK, Benjamin 203-432-4444.. 89 G benjamin.polak@yale.edu
POLAK, Debra 707-468-3605.. 51 E dpolak@mendocino.edu
POLAKOW-SURANSKY, Shael 212-875-4595 298 H ssuransky@bankstreet.edu
POLAND, Caroline 765-998-5222 164 C caroline_polland@taylor.edu
POLAND, D'Ann 361-698-2209 448 H dpoland@delmar.edu
POLANIECKI, Andrew 574-239-8315 158M apolaniecki@hcc-nd.edu
POLANSKY, Thomas 323-259-2651.. 54 E tpolansky@oxy.edu
POLASKI, Tamara, R 515-294-5225 166 F tra@iastate.edu
POLATAJKO, Mark, M 330-672-2422 363 I mpolataj@kent.edu
POLCI, Andrea 718-780-7966 300 A andrea.polci@brooklaw.edu
POLCYN, Steve 909-687-1550.. 44 A stevepolycn@gs.edu
POLCZYNSKI, Mimi 618-545-3363 142 D mpolczynski@kaskaskia.edu
POLD, Rein, A 814-393-2166 405 H rpold@clarion.edu
POLDING, Carl 651-793-1777 245 E carl.polding@metrostate.edu
POLDING, John 973-720-2887 292 I poldingj@wpunj.edu
POLESHEK, Jeffrey, A 941-359-7635 106 H jpoleshe@ringling.edu
POLETTI, Ed 215-972-2053 404 Q epoletti@pafa.edu
POLI-SMITH, Susie 248-204-2126 233 A spolismit@ltu.edu
POLICASTRO, Mike 422-472-7141 436 G mpolicastro@clevelandstatecc.edu
POLICASTRO, Stephanie 212-517-0658 314 D spolicastro@mmm.edu
POLIDORO, Sabrina 516-686-7504 317 G spolidor@nyit.edu
POLIFRONI, E. Carol 860-486-0511.. 88 G carol.polifroni@uconn.edu
POLIMER, Jennifer 508-541-1596 214 C jpolimer@dean.edu
POLING, Frederick 949-794-9090.. 66 B fpoling@stanbridge.edu
POLISHWALLA, Perzen 701-483-2340 354 A perzen.polishwalla@dickinsonstate.edu
POLISI, Joseph, W 212-799-5000 312 B
POLITE-SOLOMON, Sue 229-430-4658 114 I sue.solomon@asurams.edu
POLIVKA, Meg 540-785-5440 487 B megpolivka@vbc.edu
POLIZZI, Dianne 617-243-2133 216 C dpolizzi@lasell.edu
POLK, Ali 831-476-9424.. 43 C marketing@fivebranches.edu
POLK, Alisa, L 540-636-2900 479 G finaid@christendom.edu
POLK, Coreylon 951-343-4374.. 28 G cpolk@calbaptist.edu
POLK, Laura 301-934-7506 203 D laurap@csmd.edu
POLK, Molly 262-551-5819 506 H mpolk@carthage.edu
POLK-BLAND, Desiree 614-287-2060 360 C dpolkbla@cscc.edu
POLKABLA-BYERS, Joy 330-941-2242 374 E jlbyers@ysu.edu
POLL, Michael 970-248-1458.. 77 K mpoll@coloradomesa.edu
POLLACK, Ann, M 310-794-0387.. 69 B apollack@resadmin.ucla.edu
POLLACK, Gary 509-335-4750 499 G gary.pollack@wsu.edu
POLLACK, Martha, E 607-255-2000 306 B president@cornell.edu
POLLACK, Reva 214-768-4202 457 B reva@smu.edu
POLLACK, Susan 310-665-6981.. 54 I spollack@otis.edu
POLLARD, Al 254-299-8669 452 E apollard@mclennan.edu
POLLARD, Chad 913-722-0272 178 G chad.pollard@kansaschristian.edu
POLLARD, Charles 479-524-7200.. 20 B cpollard@jbu.edu
POLLARD, Cindy 940-898-3456 464 A cpollard@twu.edu
POLLARD, Cindy 503-517-1018 388 A cpollard@warnerpacific.edu
POLLARD, DeRionne, P 240-567-5264 205 F president@montgomerycollege.edu
POLLARD, Diana 845-431-8403 307 A pollard@sunydutchess.edu
POLLARD, James 781-239-4333 211 A jpollard@babson.edu
POLLARD, Jamie, B 515-294-0123 166 F jbp@iastate.edu
POLLARD, Leslie 256-726-7334.... 6 E lpollard@oakwood.edu
POLLARD, Mary Lee 518-464-8500 308 A mpollard@excelsior.edu
POLLARD, Natalie, M 609-896-5340 289 E pollardn@rider.edu
POLLARD, Norm 607-871-2132 298 A pollard@alfred.edu
POLLARD, Pamela 914-606-6851 333 H pamela.pollard@sunywcc.edu
POLLARD, Prudence, L 256-726-7734.... 6 E ppollard@oakwood.edu
POLLARD, Sherry 573-882-8420 268 C pollards@missouri.edu
POLLARD, Stephanie 503-255-0332 384 E spollard@multnomah.edu
POLLASTRINI, Laura 847-233-7700 148 A lpollastrini@nc.edu
POLLEI, Jeffrey, A 608-890-1067 510 C pollei@wisc.edu
POLLERT, Tim 708-596-2000 151 H tpollert@ssc.edu
POLLICINO MURPHY, Elizabeth 631-687-2629 322 G epollicinomurphy@sjcny.edu
POLLITZ, John, H 618-453-2522 152 B john.pollitz@siu.edu
POLLMAN, Janeen 701-228-5458 354 G bookcell@dakotacollege.edu
POLLOCK, Betsy 323-856-7645.. 25 L bpollock@afi.com
POLLOCK, Diane 507-285-7229 247 D diane.pollock@rctc.edu
POLLOCK, Holly, L 606-783-2000 188 C h.pollock@moreheadstate.edu
POLLOCK, Jill 573-882-2011 268 B
POLLOCK, Judy 972-708-7547 449 I judy_pollock@gial.edu
POLLOCK, Kevin 215-641-6500 402 A kpollock@mc3.edu
POLLOI, Andrew 808-932-7464 129 I polllia@hawaii.edu
POLLOM, Andrew 847-735-5202 142 H pollom@lakeforest.edu
POLNARIEV, Bernard 908-709-7550 292 C bernard.polnariev@ucc.edu
POLONSKY, Kenneth 773-702-9306 153 F polonsky@bsd.uchicago.edu
POLOWCHAK, Michelle 315-279-5630 312 D mpolowchak@keuka.edu
POLSDOFER, Duane 641-585-8121 174 B polsdofed@waldorf.edu
POLSGROVE, Kimberly 617-745-3794 214 D kimberly.polsgrove@enc.edu
POLSKY, Andrew 212-772-5195 302 E apolsky@hunter.cuny.edu
POLSON, Paula 703-908-7672 483 A paula.polson@marymount.edu
POLTERSDORF, Todd 973-300-2253 291 I tpoltersdorf@sussex.edu
POLTORAK, Jeff 310-243-3183.. 31 E jpoltorak@csudh.edu
POLVERE, Natalie 212-217-4202 308 B natalie_polvere@fitnyc.edu
POLYARD, Brenda 417-255-7966 263 I brendapolyard@missouristate.edu
POLYCHRONIS, Paul, D 660-543-4060 268 A ppolychr@ucmo.edu
POLYOT, Susan 207-947-4591 198 F spolyot@bealcollege.edu
POLZIN, Elizabeth, A 262-243-5700 507 C elizabeth.polzin@cuw.edu
POMA, John 757-221-3115 479 I jmpoma@wm.edu
POMAKOY, Keith 845-434-5750 330 F kpomakoy@sullivan.suny.edu
POMALES, Reinaldo 787-758-2525 528 D reinaldo.pomales@upr.edu
POMALES, Sandra 787-728-1515 529 B spomales@sagrado.edu
POMATTO, Mary Carol 620-235-4684 180 J mpomatto@pittstate.edu
POMEROY, David 703-284-5941 483 A david.pomeroy@marymount.edu
POMEROY, Sharon 919-301-6500.. 93 B
POMFRET, Margaret 419-289-5102 356 L mpomfret@ashland.edu
POMIETTO, Blakely 301-985-7174 208 D blakely.pomietto@umuc.edu
POMPER, Gwen, E 303-492-8223.. 83 B gwen.pomper@colorado.edu
POMPER, Kirk, W 502-597-5942 187 E kirk.pomper@kysu.edu
POMPEY, JR., Robert 336-334-7587 350 C rpompey@ncat.edu
PON, Li 850-201-8258 112 C ponl@tcc.fl.edu
PONAKA, Pritish 906-632-6841 232 J vponaka@lssu.edu
PONCE, Armando 956-295-3570 461 F armando.ponce@tsc.edu
PONCE, Barbara 787-766-1717 526 B beponce@mail.suagm.edu
PONCE, Christina 281-425-6302 451 I cponce@lee.edu
PONCE, Gregorio 760-768-5659.. 34 B gponce@mail.sdsu.edu
PONCE DE LEON, Monica 609-258-3737 288 F
PONCELET, Jolene 651-385-6349 245 G jponcelet@southeastmn.edu
POND, Josh 312-280-3500 140 G
POND, Lallon 540-887-7274 482 G lpond@marybaldwin.edu
POND, Sara 303-273-3153.. 78 J spond@mines.edu
PONDER, Anthony 937-512-2918 370 A anthony.ponder@sinclair.edu
PONDER, Leslee 940-397-4350 453 C leslee.ponder@mwsu.edu
PONDER, Nathan 318-473-6591 194 A nponder@lsua.edu
PONGRATZ, Christian 516-686-1474 317 G christian.pongratz@nyit.edu
PONGRATZ, Richard 208-282-2130 132 B pongrich@isu.edu
PONIKVAR, Laura 216-421-7442 359 J lponikvar@cia.edu
PONKO, Bill 352-365-3502 103 B ponkow@lssc.edu
PONOROFF, Lawrence 517-432-6993 233 G ponoroff@msu.edu
PONREMY, Sue 708-524-6965 137 F sponremy@dom.edu
PONS, Jose, L 787-844-8181 528 E jose.pons@upr.edu
PONSETTO, Jean 773-325-7503 137 C jlentipo@depaul.edu
PONSFORD, Brenda, J 804-257-5697 491 C bjponsford@vuu.edu
PONTANI, Leah 609-586-4800 287 A pontanil@mccc.edu
PONTARI, Beth 864-294-2064 421 I beth.pontari@furman.edu
PONTELLI, Enrico 575-646-3500 295 B epontell@nmsu.edu
PONTI, Marilyn, K 509-527-5986 500 G pontimk@whitman.edu
PONTIFF STRINGER, Susie 904-256-1253.. 99 C spontiff@fcsl.edu
PONTINEN, Jodi 218-749-7753 245 D j.pontinen@mesabirange.edu
PONTON, Cynthia 434-544-8418 482 F ponton.cl@lynchburg.edu
PONTON, Cynthia, L 434-381-6136 485 P cponton@sbc.edu
PONTON, JR., David, C 318-274-6115 196 G pontond@gram.edu
PONTURO, Joseph 973-328-5500 285 B jponturo@ccm.edu
POOL, Cleave 325-942-2555 463 C cleave.pool@angelo.edu
POOL, Jacob 405-692-3287 376 C jpool@macu.edu
POOL, Kim 585-567-9626 310 F kim.pool@houghton.edu
POOL, Robert 585-567-9220 310 F robert.pool@houghton.edu
POOLE, Andrea 919-962-4592 349 G arpoole@northcarolina.edu
POOLE, Bill 817-272-3571 467 B bpoole@uta.edu
POOLE, Dan 800-287-8822 156 D pooleda@bethanyseminary.edu
POOLE, David 951-343-3901.. 28 G dpoole@calbaptist.edu
POOLE, Deborah 504-864-7051 194 G poole@loyno.edu
POOLE, Heather 318-487-5443 192 F heatherpoole@cltcc.edu
POOLE, Lana 573-592-5313 270 B lana.poole@westminster-mo.edu
POOLE, Leigh 803-323-2604 426 H poolela@winthrop.edu
POOLE, Max, C 828-262-2130 349 H poolemc1@appstate.edu
POOLE, Philip 205-726-2823.... 6 G ppoole@samford.edu
POOLE, Robyn 413-205-3547 210 E rob.poole@aic.edu
POOLE, Russell 303-724-0425.. 83 D russell.poole@ucdenver.edu
POOLE, Scott 865-974-5267 439 I scott.poole@utk.edu
POOLE, Stan 870-245-5196.. 20 G pooles@obu.edu
POOLE, Thomas, G 814-865-2507 403 F tgp1@psu.edu
POOLE-ENDSLEY, Anita 405-736-0213 379 F apoole-endsley@rose.edu
POOLER, Traci, M 270-384-8100 187 H poolert@lindsey.edu
POOLER, III, Willis 270-384-8070 187 H poolerw@lindsey.edu
POOLEY, Ken 207-741-5548 200 C kpooley@smccme.edu
POON, Thomas 310-338-2733.. 50 J thomaspoon@lmu.edu
POOR, P. Joan 563-425-5284 173 K poorp43@uiu.edu
POORE, Mark, D 540-375-2403 484 H poore@roanoke.edu
POORE, Scott 276-944-6890 480 J pooresc@ehc.edu
POORMAN, Brad 325-793-4910 452 F bpoorman@mcm.edu
POORMAN, Julie 252-328-6373 349 I poormanj@ecu.edu
POORMAN, CSC, Mark, L 503-943-7101 387 H poorman@up.edu
POORMOSLEH, Shahrzad 213-738-6794.. 65 I careerservices@swlaw.edu
POOVEY, Gena, E 864-488-4509 422 B gpoovey@limestone.edu
POPE, Christina 315-464-4582 326 B popec@upstate.edu
POPE, Darryl 478-825-6211 119 C
POPE, Edward 843-953-8235 420 C popeeb@cofc.edu

POPE, Jennifer .... 312-427-2737 141 E
POPE, John .... 562-938-4206.. 48 I jpope@lbcc.edu
POPE, Justin .... 434-395-2001 482 E popejn@longwood.edu
POPE, Kiesha, L .... 804-523-5137 488 C kpope@reynolds.edu
POPE, Monique .... 909-748-8337.. 71 H monique_pope@redlands.edu
POPE, Myron .... 405-974-2361 380 J mpope5@uco.edu
POPE, Sarah .... 804-333-6705 489 D spope@rappahannock.edu
POPE, Sharon .... 570-372-4018 410 H popes@susqu.edu
POPE, Terri .... 216-987-3937 360 E terri.pope@tri-c.edu
POPE-DAVIS, Don .... 575-646-5858 295 B dpd@nmsu.edu
POPELKA, David, M ...... 515-294-7007 166 F dpopelka@iastate.edu
POPENFOOSE, G. Steve 217-732-3168 143 F
POPESCU, Adriana .... 805-756-2622.. 30 K popescu@calpoly.edu
POPHAM, Heidi .... 706-295-6598 120 C hpopham@gntc.edu
POPIOLEK, Marcus .... 313-664-7665 228 H mpopiolek@collegeforcreativestudies.edu
POPKEY, Megan .... 920-498-7186 514 G megan.popkey@nwtc.edu
POPKO, Susan .... 408-551-3085.. 62 F spopko@scu.edu
POPLAWSKI, Lisa .... 509-359-4555 494 D lpoplawski@ewu.edu
POPLIN, Lori .... 704-991-0116 346 I lpoplin0217@stanly.edu
POPLIN, Michelle .... 704-991-0208 346 I mpoplin4375@stanly.edu
POPLOWSKI, Kira .... 973-408-3206 285 E kpoplowski@drew.edu
POPOLOSKI, Tanya .... 603-623-0313 281 G tpopoloski@nhia.edu
POPOVICH, Donna, B ... 813-253-6237 113 E dpopovich@ut.edu
POPOVICS, Alexander, J .... 518-629-7307 310 G a.popovics@hvcc.edu
POPP, Melissa, D .... 636-584-6703 259 L melissa.popp@eastcentral.edu
POPP, Sherri, L .... 563-588-8000 169 B spopp@emmaus.edu
POPP, Tari .... 269-471-3613 227 B tari@andrews.edu
POPP, William, C .... 770-720-5568 124 H wcp@reinhardt.edu
POPPEN, Mark .... 616-392-8555 239 J mark@westernsem.edu
POPPINGO, Mary .... 925-631-4356.. 59 C mep13@stmarys-ca.edu
POPPLEWELL, Venus ...... 270-384-8189 187 H popplewellv@lindsey.edu
POPPO, Kristin .... 607-587-3913 328 F poppokr@alfredstate.edu
POPPRE, Beth .... 480-219-6026 257 A bpoppre@atsu.edu
PORAT, Moshe .... 215-204-1836 411 B moshe.porat@temple.edu
PORATH, Wiona .... 517-264-7613 236 I wporath@sienaheights.edu
PORCARELLO, Irene .... 713-718-7071 450 D irene.porcarello@hccs.edu
PORCARO, Mark, D .... 316-978-7787 182 F mark.porcaro@wichita.edu
PORCELLI, Mary .... 973-748-9000 284 A mary_porcelli@bloomfield.edu
PORCENA, Yves-Rose ... 678-839-5277 127 F yporcena@westga.edu
PORCH, Alesia .... 601-857-3240 253 B amporch@hindscc.edu
PORCHE, Demetrius ...... 504-568-4106 194 C dporch@lsuhsc.edu
PORCHE, JR., Francis ... 337-421-6916 193 F francis.porche@sowela.edu
PORE, Karen .... 910-893-1200 336 C
PORFIDO, Nancy .... 609-343-5095 283 D porfido@atlantic.edu
PORPILIA, Amy .... 585-594-6381 321 C porpilaa@roberts.edu
PORRAS, Precious .... 785-864-4350 181 I pporras@ku.edu
PORRAS, Ray .... 805-437-8434.. 31 C ray.porras@csuci.edu
PORTELA, Stanley .... 787-752-4540 527 H stanley.portela@upr.edu
PORTELA IRIGOYEN, Celso, E .... 787-725-8120 522 M cportela@centro.eap.edu
PORTELLEZ, Humberto .. 757-683-3626 483 G hportell@odu.edu
PORTER, Aaron .... 865-471-3229 430 H aporter@cn.edu
PORTER, Adam .... 217-245-3010 139 H aporter@mail.ic.edu
PORTER, Alexander .... 925-473-7341.. 41 A aporter@losmedanos.edu
PORTER, Andrea .... 806-651-2037 460 E aporter@wtamu.edu
PORTER, Barbara .... 540-831-5408 484 A bporter@radford.edu
PORTER, Becky .... 317-278-1880 160 E rporter@iupui.edu
PORTER, Bonisha .... 386-481-2451.. 95 J porterb@cookman.edu
PORTER, Brandi .... 540-365-4427 480 L bporter@ferrum.edu
PORTER, Byron .... 540-261-4931 485 G byron.porter@svu.edu
PORTER, Chad .... 304-865-6091 502 C chad.porter@ovu.edu
PORTER, Chong, U .... 916-734-9402.. 68 H chong.porter@ucdmc.ucdavis.edu
PORTER, Christine, M ... 540-654-1058 486 D cjporter@umw.edu
PORTER, Christopher .... 540-857-6697 490 B cporter@virginiawestern.edu
PORTER, Clifton .... 413-755-4026 221 B ceporter@stcc.edu
PORTER, Clyde .... 972-860-7760 447 F cporter@dcccd.edu
PORTER, Curtis, R .... 505-277-2611 296 H cporter@unm.edu
PORTER, David .... 731-661-5343 439 D dporter@uu.edu
PORTER, David, S .... 401-874-2370 417 E dporter@uri.edu
PORTER, DeeDee .... 619-388-3976.. 60 C dporter@sdccd.edu
PORTER, Fonda .... 919-497-3205 339 F fporter@louisburg.edu
PORTER, Gerald .... 805-898-2940.. 43 A gporter@fielding.edu
PORTER, Hugh, E .... 503-788-6604 386 F hugh.porter@reed.edu
PORTER, J. Davidson .... 504-314-2188 196 D jporter6@tulane.edu
PORTER, James, P .... 801-422-3963 471 E james_porter@byu.edu
PORTER, Jeffry .... 615-898-5005 434 H jeffry.porter@mtsu.edu
PORTER, Jennifer .... 617-735-9772 214 F porterj@emmanuel.edu
PORTER, John, B .... 570-961-4772 401 B porter@marywood.edu
PORTER, Jon, K .... 802-656-0123 476 E jon.porter@uvm.edu
PORTER, Joseph .... 518-320-1344 324 F joe.porter@suny.edu
PORTER, Kathleen .... 239-489-9091 100 E kathleen.porter@fsw.edu
PORTER, Kristen .... 419-251-1339 365 C kristen.porter@mercycollege.edu
PORTER, Marc .... 415-494-8240.. 56 C mporter@patten.edu
PORTER, Mario .... 210-341-1366 454 B registrar@ost.edu
PORTER, Mark, J .... 401-863-3870 415 K mark_porter@brown.edu
PORTER, Michael, C ...... 651-962-4376 251 D mcporter@stthomas.edu
PORTER, Monica .... 313-583-6445 238 A dmporte@umich.edu
PORTER, Nadine .... 240-567-5386 205 F nadine.porter@montgomerycollege.edu
PORTER, Narda .... 276-328-0116 487 A nnb3h@uvawise.edu
PORTER, Russell .... 254-501-5823 459 D porter@tamuct.edu
PORTER, Steve .... 620-665-3552 178 D porters@hutchcc.edu
PORTER, Susie .... 801-587-8094 472 P s.porter@utah.edu
PORTER, Tracy .... 863-297-1000 105 F tporter@polk.edu
PORTER, Tracy .... 863-297-3743 105 F tporter@polk.edu
PORTER, Vincent .... 210-829-2770 465 E porterv@uiwtx.edu
PORTER, Wilma, B .... 248-341-2182 235 D wbporter@oaklandcc.edu
PORTER-UTLEY, Kristen 508-531-2418 217 D k1porterutley@bridgew.edu
PORTERFIELD, Ashley ... 386-481-2972.. 95 J porterfielda@cookman.edu
PORTERFIELD, Daniel, R .... 717-358-3971 395 G daniel.porterfield@fandm.edu
PORTERFIELD, Deana, L .... 585-594-6100 319 B presidentsoffice@roberts.edu
PORTERFIELD, Deana, L .... 585-594-6100 321 C presidentsoffice@roberts.edu
PORTERFIELD, Kent .... 314-977-2799 266 J kporter6@slu.edu
PORTERFIELD, Rebecca . 859-572-5551 188 E porterfier1@nku.edu
PORTERVINT, Bernice .... 360-676-2772 496 C bportervint@nwic.edu
PORTIER, Bonnie .... 301-447-5288 206 B bportier@msmary.edu
PORTILLO, Cesar .... 909-537-5138.. 33 D cportillo@csusb.edu
PORTIS-TURNER, Erica .. 334-290-3248.... 2 E erica.turner@istc.edu
PORTLOCK, Jeremy .... 785-594-8415 174 J jeremy.portlock@bakeru.edu
PORTMAN, Tarrell .... 507-457-2570 248 C tportman@winona.edu
PORTMANN, Brooke .... 231-843-5866 239 D bportmann@westshore.edu
PORTNOY, Lauren .... 610-896-4984 397 F lportnoy@haverford.edu
PORTNOY, Lianna .... 917-493-4034 313 M lportnoy@msmnyc.edu
PORTNOY, Robert, N .... 402-472-7450 277 G rportnoy1@unl.edu
PORTO, Deborah .... 919-209-2041 344 C drporto@johnstoncc.edu
PORTWINE, Ronald, E ... 989-964-2064 236 F report@svsu.edu
PORTWOOD, Amy .... 206-239-4500 493 D alportwood@cityu.edu
PORTZ, Margaret, A ...... 610-758-5794 400 B mak5@lehigh.edu
PORTZEL, Curt .... 310-506-4893.. 56 D curt.portzel@pepperdine.edu
PORVAZNIK, John .... 480-377-4556.. 14 B porvaznik@riosalado.edu
PORYEM, Wenceslaus .... 859-622-1478 184 F wenceslaus.poryem@eku.edu
POSEJPAL, Gigi .... 312-369-7458 136 H gposejpal@colum.edu
POSER, Susan .... 312-413-3450 153 H sposer@uic.edu
POSEY, Evan .... 770-484-1204 122 G evan.posey@lutherrice.edu
POSEY, James, T .... 843-953-5708 420 C poseyjt@cofc.edu
POSEY, Jamie .... 423-585-6894 438 D jamie.posey@ws.edu
POSEY, Jeff .... 601-877-6471 251 G mjposey@alcorn.edu
POSEY, Kathy .... 617-928-4003 222 D kposey@mountida.edu
POSEY, Libby .... 601-857-3350 253 B olivia.posey@hindscc.edu
POSEY, Monica .... 513-569-1515 359 G monica.posey@cincinnatistate.edu
POSEY, Rebecca .... 662-846-4574 252 H rposey@deltastate.edu
POSEY, Steven .... 505-473-6101 296 C steven.posey@santafeuniversity.edu
POSHEK, Joseph .... 949-451-5650.. 64 I jposhek@ivc.edu
POSILLICO, Joseph, J ... 973-618-3500 284 D jposillico@caldwell.edu
POSING, Mary .... 815-802-8202 142 C mposing@kcc.edu
POSKANZER, JR., Steven, G .... 507-222-4305 241 C president@carleton.edu
POSKIN, Jill .... 630-829-6366 133 I jposkin@ben.edu
POSLER, Brian .... 440-375-7200 364 C president@lec.edu
POSLUSNY, Matthew ..... 919-760-8514 339 H mposlusny@meredith.edu
POSMAN, Jerald .... 718-270-5026 303 C jposman@mec.cuny.edu
POSNER, Deborah .... 954-201-7482.. 96 A dposner@broward.edu
POSNER, Kenneth .... 352-588-8992 106 N kenneth.posner@saintleo.edu
POSNER, Marc .... 714-484-7006.. 53 M mposner@cypresscollege.edu
POSNER, Mark .... 651-638-6383 240 J m-posner@bethel.edu
POSPMA, Jana .... 616-222-3000 232 F jana.pospma@kuyper.edu
POSS, Joe .... 509-313-6215 495 A poss@gonzaga.edu
POSS, Michael .... 378-839-6452 127 F mposs@westga.edu
POSSINGER, Megan, S . 904-620-2015 110 E megan.possinger@unf.edu
POSSON, Nicholas .... 702-463-2122 280 F
POST, Christine .... 304-424-8358 505 C christine.post@wvup.edu
POST, John .... 856-227-7200 284 E jpost@camdencc.edu
POST, John .... 479-788-7025.. 22 A john.post@uafs.edu
POST, Julie .... 770-962-7580 121 G jpost@gwinnetttech.edu
POST, Michael .... 301-447-6126 206 B post@msmary.edu
POST, Nichole .... 607-729-1581 306 F npost@davisny.edu
POST, Rick .... 805-652-5509.. 72 G rpost@vcccd.edu
POST, Robert .... 610-361-5233 402 G postr@neumann.edu
POST, Scott .... 870-338-6474.. 22 G
POST, Todd .... 815-802-8602 142 C tpost@kcc.edu
POST, Tracee .... 806-651-2100 460 E tpost@wtamu.edu
POST-LUNDQUIST, Beth 518-580-5750 324 D bpostlun@skidmore.edu
POSTEL, Gregory .... 502-852-7259 190 C gcpost01@exchange.louisville.edu
POSTEL, Gregory, C ...... 502-852-7259 190 C gcpost01@exchange.louisville.edu
POSTEMA, Miles, J .... 231-591-3894 230 A milespostema@ferris.edu
POSTER, Michael .... 612-436-7520 243 H mposter@msbcollege.edu
POSTER, Michael, C ...... 563-333-6032 173 A postermichaelc@sau.edu
POSTLETHWAITE, Bonnie .... 816-235-1531 268 D postlethwaiteb@umkc.edu
POSTMA, Kurt .... 616-538-2330 230 E kpostma@gbcol.edu
POSTMA, Laura .... 906-248-8420 227 P lpostma@bmcc.edu
POSTON, Linda, K .... 845-675-4434 319 C linda.poston@nyack.edu
POSTON, R. Stephen ..... 704-233-8194 353 D poston@wingate.edu
POSTUPACK, Mary Frances .... 570-422-7920 406 A mpostupack@esu.edu
POSTY, Jessy .... 907-796-6569.. 10 C jipost@alaska.edu
POTASH, David .... 773-481-8175 136 B dpotash@ccc.edu
POTEET, James, L .... 913-948-9263 178 G jim.poteet@kansaschristian.edu
POTEET, Tanya, J .... 614-236-6408 358 A tpoteet@capital.edu
POTEET, Tony .... 901-678-2619 439 E ppoteet@memphis.edu
POTEETE-YOUNG, Lanette .... 847-628-1097 142 B lpoteete-young@judsonu.edu
POTEMPA, John .... 708-656-8000 146 F john.potempa@morton.edu
POTERALA, Michael, R .. 301-405-4945 207 G poterala@umd.edu
POTH, Jean, C .... 978-556-3624 220 F jpoth@necc.mass.edu
POTH, Mark .... 509-793-2194 492 I markp@bigbend.edu
POTOCZAK, Mel .... 978-762-4000 220 E mpotocza@northshore.edu
POTOKA, Lisa .... 913-758-6128 182 B lisa.potoka@stmary.edu
POTTEBAUM, Kevin .... 712-274-5179 172 A pottebaumk@morningside.edu
POTTEBAUM, Marty .... 712-279-5430 167 B marty.pottebaum@briarcliff.edu
POTTEIGER, Jeffrey .... 616-331-7207 230 G potteigj@gvsu.edu
POTTER, Adam .... 207-326-4771 200 F adam.potter@mma.edu
POTTER, Alan .... 919-573-5350 349 A
POTTER, Aron .... 620-252-7005 176 K potter.aron@coffeyville.edu
POTTER, Bill .... 661-395-4221.. 47 A william.potter@bakersfieldcollege.edu
POTTER, Cambria .... 816-802-3445 261 C cpotter@kcai.edu
POTTER, Cathryn, C ...... 848-932-7520 290 C cathryn.potter@ssw.rutgers.edu
POTTER, Cheryl, J .... 704-406-4269 337 H cpotter@gardner-webb.edu
POTTER, Corrie .... 650-723-2300.. 66 C cjpotter@stanford.edu

PRATER, Sarah, E .... 574-372-5100 158 B
praterse@grace.edu
PRATER, Steve .... 580-477-7894 381 G
steve.prater@wosc.edu
PRATHER, Cindy .... 317-738-8225 157 L
cprather@franklincollege.edu
PRATHER, Curtis .... 703-370-6600 483 I
PRATHER, Kerry, N .... 317-738-8121 157 L
kprather@franklincollege.edu
PRATHER, Renee .... 806-457-4200 449 D
rprather@fpctx.edu
PRATHER, Sean .... 925-424-1690.. 36 D
sprather@laspositascollege.edu
PRATSCHER, Valerie ...... 618-936-2064 143 B
vpratscher@lakeland.cc.il.us
PRATT, Andrew, L .... 816-415-7557 270 C
pratta@william.jewell.edu
PRATT, Barbara .... 908-835-2355 292 G
pratt@warren.edu
PRATT, Denise .... 402-941-6135 275 J
pratt@midlandu.edu
PRATT, Dorianna .... 207-768-9462 201 G
dorianna.pratt@maine.edu
PRATT, Edward, E .... 561-297-0567 109 B
epratt2@fau.edu
PRATT, Elizabeth .... 415-883-2211.. 39 E
epratt@marin.edu
PRATT, Eric .... 601-925-7652 254 B
epratt@mc.edu
PRATT, Gary .... 509-359-2099 494 D
gpratt@ewu.edu
PRATT, Grace .... 928-344-7505.. 11 B
grace.pratt@azwestern.edu
PRATT, H. Wes .... 417-836-3736 263 H
wpratt@missouristate.edu
PRATT, Heather .... 240-567-3097 205 F
heather.pratt@montgomerycollege.edu
PRATT, Janice .... 520-494-6602.. 11 P
janice.pratt@centralaz.edu
PRATT, Jonathan, R .... 763-417-8250 241 D
jpratt@centralseminary.edu
PRATT, Michael .... 205-652-3565.... 9 C
mpratt@uwa.edu
PRATT, Michele .... 989-686-9822 229 J
micheleprratt@delta.edu
PRATT, Robert, C .... 517-750-1200 237 D
bpratt@arbor.edu
PRATT, Sarah .... 213-740-8867.. 72 B
pratt@usc.edu
PRATT, Scott, L .... 541-346-2800 387 F
spratt@uoregon.edu
PRATT, Tamara .... 405-733-7961 379 F
tpratt@rose.edu
PRATT, JR.,
Theodore, W .... 360-650-3450 500 E
ted.pratt@cc.wwu.edu
PRATT, Todd .... 678-372-2260 128 F
todd.pratt@westgatech.edu
PRATT, Tracey .... 570-702-8908 398 A
tpratt@johnson.edu
PRATT-CLARKE, JR.,
Menah .... 540-231-7500 490 F
mcp@vt.edu
PRATT-COOK, Patricia ... 651-690-6560 249 T
pcprattcook867@stkate.edu
PRATTELLA, Todd .... 914-674-7844 314 I
tprattella@mercy.edu
PRATTS, Luis, N .... 787-780-0070 521 B
lpratts@caribbean.edu
PRAY, G. Jon .... 414-288-7532 508 C
jon.pray@marquette.edu
PRAY, Steve .... 770-484-1204 122 G
steve.pray@lutherrice.edu
PREACHER, Stephen ...... 864-644-5486 424 B
spreacher@swu.edu
PREAS, Derek .... 903-468-8781 459 E
derek.preas@tamuc.edu
PREAST, Lori .... 252-493-7224 345 E
lpreast@email.pittcc.edu
PREATHER, Gary .... 817-515-6742 458 B
gary.preather@tccd.edu
PRECHTER, Patricia .... 504-398-2213 196 E
pprechter@uhcno.edu
PRECIOUS, Brian .... 303-546-3526.. 81 B
bprecious@naropa.edu
PRECISE, Leigh .... 740-362-3121 365 D
lprecise@mtso.edu
PRECZEWSKI, Stanley .... 678-407-5001 119 F
president@ggc.edu
PREDOEHL, Dan .... 949-582-4313.. 64 J
dpredoehl@saddleback.edu
PREECE, Barbara .... 410-617-6811 205 A
bpreece@loyola.edu
PREECE, Barbara .... 410-617-6811 206 D
bpreece@ndm.edu
PREGEANT, Gene, E ...... 985-549-5888 197 E
gpregeant@selu.edu
PREGITZER, Kurt .... 208-885-6442 132 I
kpregitzer@uidaho.edu
PREGLIASCO, Collin ...... 916-691-7367.. 50 G
preglic@crc.losrios.edu
PREIMESBERGER, Paul . 218-855-8163 244 C
ppreimesberger@clcmn.edu
PREISINGER, George, T 248-370-2127 235 J
preising@oakland.edu
PREISINGER, Nathaniel . 717-334-6286 412 E
PREISLER, Karen .... 979-532-6383 471 A
karenp@wcjc.edu
PREISS, D. J .... 601-643-8332 252 G
dj.preiss@colin.edu
PRELOCK, Patricia, A .... 802-656-2216 476 E
patricia.prelock@uvm.edu
PRELOGER, Robert .... 605-274-4922 426 K
bob.preloger@augie.edu
PREMNATH,
Devadasan, N .... 585-271-3657 322 A
devadasan.premnath@stbernards.edu
PREMO, Brenda .... 909-469-5385.. 74 G
bpremo@westernu.edu
PREMO, Greg, V .... 253-535-8787 496 G
premogv@plu.edu
PRENDERGAST,
Debra, L .... 708-709-3689 148 I
dprendergast@prairiestate.edu
PRENDERGAST, Nancy .. 847-635-1894 148 D
nprender@oakton.edu
PRENDERGAST,
Precious .... 770-689-4901 115 E
pprendergast@aii.edu
PRENDERGAST,
Thomas, M .... 419-755-4712 366 E
tprendergast@ncstatecollege.edu
PRENEVOST, Jason .... 253-460-4462 499 A
jprenevost@tacomacc.edu
PRENGAMAN, Diane ..... 410-225-2285 205 C
dprengam@mica.edu
PRENGAMAN, John, C .. 434-223-6161 481 D
jprengaman@hsc.edu
PRENGUBER, Marcia, A 203-576-4110.. 88 F
mprengub@bridgeport.edu
PRENTICE, Ann, E .... 205-348-4610.... 8 A
aeprentice@bama.ua.edu
PRENTICE, Deborah .... 609-258-3020 288 F
predebb@princeton.edu
PRENTICE, Ernest, D ..... 402-559-6045 277 H
edprenti@unmc.edu
PRENTICE, Marilyn .... 847-214-7992 138 B
mprentice@elgin.edu
PRENTISS, Richard .... 305-237-4341 103 L
rprentis@mdc.edu
PREOCANIN, Shelley ..... 812-866-7097 158 C
preocanins@hanover.edu
PRESCOD-CAESAR,
Pamela .... 610-328-8397 410 I
ppresco1@swarthmore.edu
PRESCOTT, Angel .... 785-738-9008 180 E
aprescott@ncktc.edu
PRESCOTT, Herman .... 202-274-5072.. 93 D
tprescott@udc.edu
PRESCOTT, Jay, B .... 515-263-2890 169 E
jprescott@grandview.edu
PRESCOTT, Loren, D ...... 570-408-4000 414 H
loren.prescott@wilkes.edu
PRESCOTT, Patricia, M .. 516-671-0439 333 E
pprescott@webb.edu
PRESENT, Melissa .... 212-678-8820 312 A
mepresent@jtsa.edu
PRESENT, Wendy .... 716-338-1070 311 F
wendypresent@mail.sunyjcc.edu
PRESLAR, Andy .... 409-882-3357 462 D
andy.preslar@lsco.edu
PRESLEY, Alan .... 281-649-3446 450 C
apresley@hbu.edu
PRESLEY, Brian .... 276-244-1267 477 M
bpresley@asl.edu
PRESLEY, Doretha .... 601-977-4461 256 B
dpresley@tougaloo.edu
PRESNELL, Angela .... 317-788-3211 164 H
presnella@uindy.edu
PRESNELL, Deena .... 509-313-6803 495 A
presnell@gonzaga.edu
PRESNELL, Mark .... 847-491-3707 148 C
mark.presnell@northwestern.edu
PRESS, Andrew .... 714-533-3946.. 35 B
andrew@calums.edu
PRESSER, Art .... 865-524-8079 432 F
apresser@hchs.edu
PRESSEY, Natalie .... 212-229-5660 316 E
presseyn@newschool.edu
PRESSIMONE,
J. Michael .... 314-889-1419 260 C
mpressimone@fontbonne.edu
PRESSLEY, Dan .... 706-754-7791 123 G
dpressley@northgatech.edu
PRESSLEY, Diana .... 713-500-2104 468 D
diana.j.pressley@uth.tmc.edu
PRESSLEY, Pamela .... 510-231-5000.. 46 N
pamela.c.pressley@kp.org
PRESSLEY, Shelia .... 859-622-1523 184 F
shelia.pressley@eku.edu
PRESSMAN, Avraham .... 570-346-1747 415 F
PRESSON, Kim .... 256-782-8142.... 6 B
kpresson@jsu.edu
PRESSON, Mark, A .... 563-588-8000 169 B
mpresson@emmaus.edu
PRESSWOOD, Theresa .. 281-283-2015 465 B
presswood@uhcl.edu
PREST, Stacy .... 509-527-4294 499 E
stacy.prest@wwcc.edu
PRESTAMO, Anne .... 305-348-5726 109 D
anne.prestamo@fiu.edu
PRESTIN, Michael .... 719-336-6660.. 80 N
michael.prestin@lamarcc.edu
PRESTON, April .... 615-366-4404 436 E
april.preston@tbr.edu
PRESTON, Daniel .... 503-883-2294 383 H
dpreston@linfield.edu
PRESTON, Deborah .... 240-567-5031 205 F
deborah.preston@montgomerycollege.edu
PRESTON, Deborah .... 908-526-1200 289 D
deborah.preston@raritanval.edu
PRESTON, Diane .... 314-434-4044 259 B
diane.preston@covenantseminary.edu
PRESTON, Elaine, C ...... 405-466-3202 375 L
ecpreston@langston.edu
PRESTON, James .... 559-925-3146.. 74 A
jamespreston@whccd.edu
PRESTON, James .... 312-329-4140 146 B
james.preston@moody.edu
PRESTON, Jeffrey, H ...... 912-279-5751 118 A
jpreston@ccga.edu
PRESTON, Jennifer .... 270-831-9804 186 A
jennifer.preston@kctcs.edu
PRESTON, Joanne .... 541-552-6161 386 H
prestonj@sou.edu
PRESTON, Jon .... 470-578-5572 122 C
jonpreston@kennesaw.edu
PRESTON, Karen .... 770-426-2688 122 F
kpreston@life.edu
PRESTON, Karen .... 971-722-2831 386 C
karen.preston@pcc.edu
PRESTON, Keely .... 303-546-5283.. 81 B
kpreston@naropa.edu
PRESTON, Kenneth, G ... 330-972-8254 371 C
kpreston@uakron.edu
PRESTON, Kenneth, G ... 330-972-7845 371 C
kpreston@uakron.edu
PRESTON, Laura, C .... 443-412-2438 204 C
lpreston@harford.edu
PRESTON, Lisa .... 212-229-5667 316 E
lisa.preston@newschool.edu
PRESTON, Mindy .... 903-823-3198 458 D
mindy.preston@texarkanacollege.edu
PRESTON, Teresa .... 901-321-4126 431 A
tpreston@cbu.edu
PRESTON, Travis .... 661-255-1050.. 29 F
tpreston@calarts.edu
PRESTWICH, Aaron .... 303-404-5332.. 79 K
aaron.prestwich@frontrange.edu
PRETLOW, Lester .... 706-721-2621 116 B
lpretlow@augusta.edu
PRETTEJOHN, Amy .... 816-235-6210 268 D
prettejohna@umkc.edu
PRETTY, Keith, A .... 989-837-4203 235 C
pretty@northwood.edu
PRETZAT, Julie .... 315-312-2285 327 D
julie.pretzat@oswego.edu
PREUS, Camille .... 541-278-5950 382 A
cpreus@bluecc.edu
PREUSS, Timothy .... 949-214-3363.. 40 I
timothy.preuss@cui.edu
PREUSZ, Mike .... 864-644-5050 424 B
mpreusz@swu.edu
PREVANT, Robert .... 203-392-5350.. 85 A
PREVATT, Lewis .... 352-854-2322.. 97 C
prevattd@cf.edu
PREVATTE, David .... 336-506-4202 340 L
david.prevatte@alamancecc.edu
PREVAUX, Steven, D ..... 813-974-7777 111 A
prevaux@usf.edu
PREVETT, Daniel .... 912-583-3178 116 G
dprevett@bpc.edu
PREVOST, Blair .... 903-923-2364 448 J
bprevost@etbu.edu
PREVOST, Emily .... 903-923-2074 448 J
eprevost@etbu.edu
PREVOST, Suzanne, S ... 205-348-1040.... 8 A
sprevost@ua.edu
PREWETT, Nick .... 573-882-6200 268 C
prewettn@missouri.edu
PREWITT, Michael .... 304-696-3765 504 C
prewitta@marshall.edu
PREWITT, Nicole, B .... 256-551-3114.... 2 D
nicole.barnett@drakestate.edu
PREWITT, Steve .... 615-966-5804 433 D
steve.prewitt@lipscomb.edu
PREZIOSI, Kristine .... 928-350-2306.. 15 V
kpreziosi@prescott.edu
PRIAL, Anne .... 845-341-4286 319 H
anne.prial@sunyorange.edu
PRIBBENOW, Dean .... 608-663-2200 507 D
dpribbenow@edgewood.edu
PRIBBENOW, Paul, C ... 612-330-1212 240 G
president@augsburg.edu
PRIBULSKY,
Christopher .... 814-262-3824 405 A
cpribulsky@pennhighlands.edu
PRIBYL, Kim .... 319-399-8686 167 F
kpribyl@coe.edu
PRICCI, Erica .... 570-955-1461 399 A
priccie@lackawanna.edu
PRICE, Adrienne .... 909-274-5417.. 52 I
aprice@mtsac.edu
PRICE, Alan .... 805-965-0581.. 62 E
aprice3@sbcc.edu
PRICE, Alan, C .... 765-983-1211 157 I
president@earlham.edu
PRICE, Amy .... 920-832-7164 507 L
amy.price@lawrence.edu
PRICE, Amy, S .... 812-468-2000 165 C
asprice@usi.edu
PRICE, Angela .... 906-487-7231 230 B
angela.price@finlandia.edu
PRICE, Angie, C .... 423-775-7269 430 G
aprice6832@bryan.edu
PRICE, Berkeley .... 310-660-3715.. 42 C
bprice@elcamino.edu
PRICE, Bill .... 540-231-4025 480 I
bprice@vcom.vt.edu
PRICE, Bryan .... 540-458-8184 491 G
bprice@wlu.edu
PRICE, Cecil, D .... 336-758-5218 353 A
price@wfu.edu
PRICE, Cynthia, J .... 206-281-2179 498 B
cprice@spu.edu
PRICE, Danny .... 706-368-5644 116 D
dprice@berry.edu
PRICE, David, E .... 706-778-8500 124 E
dprice2@piedmont.edu
PRICE, Dawne .... 402-494-2311 275 M
dprice@thenicc.edu
PRICE, Donna .... 931-221-7907 430 B
priced@apsu.edu
PRICE, Douglas .... 918-595-7853 380 D
douglas.price@tulsac.edu
PRICE, Fred, L .... 843-953-5777 419 D
awithers@citadel.edu
PRICE, Gary .... 541-259-5808 384 A
priceg@linnbenton.edu
PRICE, Greg .... 334-670-3507.... 7 E
wgprice@troy.edu
PRICE, James .... 706-771-4096 116 A
jprice@augustatech.edu
PRICE, James .... 706-355-5034 115 H
jprice@athenstech.edu
PRICE, James, B .... 610-436-3063 407 D
jprice@wcupa.edu
PRICE, Jason .... 806-457-4200 449 D
jprice@fpctx.edu
PRICE, Jennifer .... 386-752-1822.. 99 J
jennifer.price@fgc.edu
PRICE, Jennifer .... 518-262-5679 297 L
pricej@mail.amc.edu
PRICE, Jerry .... 714-997-6721.. 36 G
jprice@chapman.edu
PRICE, Jill .... 810-766-4348 227 F
jhovis02@baker.edu
PRICE, Jill .... 715-365-4461 514 E
jmrjenovich@nicoletcollege.edu
PRICE, June, M .... 269-471-3211 227 B
madrigal@andrews.edu
PRICE, Kendrick .... 252-493-7627 345 E
kprice@email.pittcc.edu
PRICE, Kevin, L .... 208-496-1705 131 D
priceke@byui.edu
PRICE, Laura .... 360-596-5227 498 G
lprice@spscc.edu
PRICE, Legari .... 706-291-2121 125 E
lprice@shorter.edu
PRICE, Leigh .... 912-478-5211 120 E
llprice@georgiasouthern.edu
PRICE, Leslie .... 320-983-2222 246 H
lprice@pine.edu
PRICE, Linda, L .... 812-877-8165 163 G
price@rose-hulman.edu
PRICE, Lisa .... 618-437-5321 149 H
price@rlc.edu

PRICE, Lisa ... 318-487-7512 191 J
helen.price@lacollege.edu
PRICE, JR., Major ... 419-755-9009 366 E
mprice@ncstatecollege.edu
PRICE, Maribeth, H ... 605-394-1763 429 A
maribeth.price@sdsmt.edu
PRICE, Megan ... 864-388-8019 422 A
mprice@lander.edu
PRICE, Nicole, G ... 617-973-1101 224 I
nprice@suffolk.edu
PRICE, Pam ... 609-586-4800 287 A
pricep@mccc.edu
PRICE, Peggy ... 601-366-8880 256 H
pprice@wbs.edu
PRICE, Philip ... 919-718-7214 341 H
pprice@cccc.edu
PRICE, Robin ... 304-637-1243 501 H
pricer@dewv.edu
PRICE, Ron ... 770-528-3988 117 G
ron.price@chattahoocheetech.edu
PRICE, Ronald, N ... 708-216-9949 144 D
rprice@lumc.edu
PRICE, Sarah ... 270-686-4501 186 F
sarah.price@kctcs.edu
PRICE, Vincent ... 919-684-2424 337 C
president@duke.edu
PRICE, William ... 432-552-2170 469 D
price_w@utpb.edu
PRICE-PERRY,
Cassandra, F ... 901-334-5821 434 C
cfperry@memphisseminary.edu
PRICE-SCOTT, Karen ... 512-505-3031 451 A
klprice@htu.edu
PRICHARD, Patricia, A .. 503-517-1806 388 C
paprichard@westernseminary.edu
PRICHETT, Robert ... 404-756-4714 115 I
rprichett@atlm.edu
PRICKEN, Stephanie ... 215-951-1702 398 F
pricken@lasalle.edu
PRIDA, Jonas ... 412-392-4773 408 F
jprida@pointpark.edu
PRIDAL, Cathryn ... 816-501-3758 257 G
cathryn.pridal@avila.edu
PRIDDY, Don ... 618-985-3741 141 D
donpriddy@jalc.edu
PRIDE, Nathan ... 731-422-6895 432 J
nbplawoffice@yahoo.com
PRIDE, Nicole ... 336-334-7940 350 C
npride@ncat.edu
PRIDE, Rachel ... 940-898-3207 464 A
rpride1@twu.edu
PRIDEAUX, Debra, K ... 785-628-4430 177 D
dprideau@fhsu.edu
PRIDEAUX, Leslie, J ... 319-273-2355 167 A
leslie.prideaux@uni.edu
PRIDEMORE,
William, A ... 518-442-5214 324 G
wpridemore@albany.edu
PRIES, Lonnie ... 734-995-7310 229 A
lonnie.pries@cuaa.edu
PRIEST, Barry ... 910-879-5579 341 A
bpriest@bladencc.edu
PRIEST, Catherine ... 856-351-2624 291 E
cpriest@salemcc.edu
PRIEST, Jeff, M ... 803-641-3755 425 A
jeffp@usca.edu
PRIEST, Jennifer ... 859-233-8239 189 H
financialaid@transy.edu
PRIEST, Michelle ... 714-564-6606.. 58 A
priest_michelle@sac.edu
PRIETO, Beth ... 603-645-9724 282 C
b.prieto@snhu.edu
PRIETO, Diana ... 970-491-5836.. 78 N
diana.prieto@colostate.edu
PRIETO, Diana ... 970-491-6947.. 78 N
diana.prieto@colostate.edu
PRIETO, Eduardo ... 803-323-2191 426 H
prietoe@winthrop.edu
PRIETO, Jeffrey, M ... 213-891-2000.. 48 K
PRIETO-TSEREGOUNIS,
Emily ... 530-752-0946.. 68 H
eprieto@ucdavis.edu
PRIGERSON, Gregg ... 941-359-7526 106 H
gprigers@ringling.edu
PRIGG, Benson ... 256-726-7186.... 6 E
bprigg@oakwood.edu
PRIGGE, Amy ... 419-772-3961 367 G
a-prigge@onu.edu
PRIGGIE, Richard, W ... 309-794-7213 133 G
richardpriggie@augustana.edu
PRIHODA, Belinda ... 903-730-4890 451 D
bprihoda@jarvis.edu
PRIHODA-WEINER,
Lauren ... 312-427-2737 141 E
lprihoda@jmls.edu
PRILL, Kristina, L ... 518-244-6001 321 G
prillk@sage.edu
PRILLELTENSKY, Isaac .. 305-284-3505 112 O
isaacp@miami.edu
PRIMACK, Brian, A ... 412-624-6880 412 I
bprimack@pitt.edu
PRIMAS, LaMario ... 404-225-4714 115 J
lprimas@atlantatech.edu
PRIMAVERA, Louis, H ... 631-665-1600 331 F
louis.primavera@touro.edu
PRIMM, Jenelle ... 501-370-5310.. 21 A
jprimm@philander.edu
PRIMO, John ... 405-733-7356 379 F
jprimo@rose.edu
PRIMOFF, Mark ... 845-758-7412 298 I
primoff@bard.edu
PRIMOZICH, Blayne, J .. 915-831-2857 449 A
bprimozi@epcc.edu
PRIMUS, Joanna ... 641-844-5692 170 I
joanna.primus@iavalley.edu
PRIMUS, Lester ... 860-906-5050.. 85 D
lprimus@ccc.commnet.edu
PRINCE, Bobby, A ... 901-678-1335 439 E
baprince@memphis.edu
PRINCE, Christine, B ... 215-885-2360 401 A
cprince@manor.edu
PRINCE, Iris ... 910-892-3178 338 D
iprince@heritagebiblecollege.edu
PRINCE, James, E ... 269-337-7225 231 F
james.prince@kzoo.edu
PRINCE, Jeff ... 510-642-9494.. 68 G
jprince@berkeley.edu
PRINCE, Joan, M ... 414-229-3101 511 A
jprince@uwm.edu
PRINCE, Judith ... 864-552-4243 425 H
jprince@uscupstate.edu
PRINCE, Ken ... 812-866-7051 158 C
princek@hanover.edu
PRINCE-RICHARD,
Celia, P ... 340-692-4132 529 C
cprince@uvi.edu
PRINCE ROSS, Tracey ... 202-884-9126.. 93 C
princetr@trinitydc.edu
PRINCILUS, Monise ... 609-586-4800 287 A
princilm@mccc.edu
PRINCIPE, Frank ... 301-985-7077 208 D
frank.principe@umuc.edu
PRINEAS, Matthew ... 240-684-2830 208 D
matthew.prineas@umuc.edu
PRINGLE, Eboni ... 330-672-8700 363 I
epringle@kent.edu
PRINGLE, Ernest ... 803-641-3345 425 A
ernestp@usca.edu
PRINGLE, Mark ... 614-236-6813 358 A
mpringle@capital.edu
PRINGLE, Nancy, E ... 607-274-3836 311 D
npringle@ithaca.edu
PRIOLEAU, Florence ... 202-806-2250.. 92 C
florence.prioleau@howard.edu
PRIOLEAU, Florence ... 202-806-2650.. 92 C
florence.prioleau@howard.edu
PRIOLO, Bob ... 616-949-5300 229 B
bob.priolo@cornerstone.edu
PRIOLO, Julianne ... 616-538-2330 230 E
jpriolo@gbcol.edu
PRISCO, Anne ... 201-559-6022 286 C
priscoa@felician.edu
PRISELAC, Thomas ... 310-423-8294.. 35 P
PRISLIN, Radmila ... 619-594-5166.. 34 B
rprislin@mail.sdsu.edu
PRITCHARD, Alice ... 860-723-0016.. 84 I
pritcharda@ct.edu
PRITCHARD, Brett ... 256-215-4254.... 1 G
bpritchard@cacc.edu
PRITCHARD, Gary ... 562-860-2451.. 36 A
gpritchard@cerritos.edu
PRITCHARD, Lamar ... 713-743-1253 465 A
flpritchard@uh.edu
PRITCHARD, Lisa ... 636-481-3160 261 B
lpritcha@jeffco.edu
PRITCHARD, Michael ... 301-846-2417 203 H
mpritchard@frederick.edu
PRITCHARD, Rod ... 319-399-8605 167 F
rpritcha@coe.edu
PRITCHARD, Sarah, M .. 847-491-7640 148 C
spritchard@northwestern.edu
PRITCHARD, William ... 302-736-2316.. 90 J
william.pritchard@wesley.edu
PRITCHERT, Marcia ... 701-845-7541 354 E
marcia.pitchert@vcsu.edu
PRITCHETT, Alondrea ... 334-229-4223.... 4 A
apritchett@alasu.edu
PRITCHETT, Alondrea, J 334-229-4737.... 4 A
apritchett@alasu.edu
PRITCHETT, Donald ... 518-262-5521 297 L
pritchd@mail.amc.edu
PRITCHETT, Marie ... 586-445-7315 233 B
pritchettm@macomb.edu
PRITCHETT, Megan ... 601-925-3210 254 B
mpritchett@mc.edu
PRITCHETT, Terry ... 325-649-8608 450 H
tpritchett@hputx.edu
PRITCHETT, Wendell, E . 215-898-7227 412 G
provost@upenn.edu
PRITTING, Shannon ... 315-792-7245 330 A
shannon.pritting@sunyit.edu
PRITZ, Stephen, J ... 352-392-1374 110 D
spritz@ufl.edu
PRITZKER, Barry ... 518-580-5654 324 D
bpritzke@skidmore.edu
PRIVETT, SJ,
Stephen, A ... 415-422-6215.. 72 A
privett@usfca.edu
PRIVOTT, Ashley, E ... 540-568-6234 481 I
privotae@jmu.edu
PROBST, Julliana ... 334-514-5051.... 2 E
julliana.probst@istc.edu
PROBST, Laura, K ... 218-299-4642 241 K
lprobst@cord.edu
PROBST, Robert ... 513-556-9808 371 E
robert.probst@uc.edu
PROBSTFELD, Carol, F .. 941-752-5201 108 P
probstc@scf.edu
PROBUS, Lawrence ... 509-777-4304 500 H
lprobus@whitworth.edu
PROCARIO-FOLEY, Carl 914-633-2632 311 B
cprocariofoley@iona.edu
PROCELL, Derrick ... 985-448-7941 192 I
derrick.procell@fletcher.edu
PROCH, Margaret, P ... 410-323-6211 203 F
m.proch@fts.edu
PROCHNOW, Allen ... 262-243-4303 229 A
allen.prochnow@cuw.edu
PROCHNOW, Allen, J ... 262-243-5700 507 C
allen.prochnow@cuw.edu
PROCTER, Ken ... 478-445-4441 119 E
ken.procter@gcsu.edu
PROCTER, Sharon ... 313-664-1487 228 H
sprocter@collegeforcreativestudies.edu
PROCTOR, Avis ... 954-201-2202.. 96 A
aproctor@broward.edu
PROCTOR, Chris ... 903-586-2501 443 M
PROCTOR, Craig ... 801-587-2191 472 P
craig.proctor@hsc.edu
PROCTOR, Cynthia ... 724-925-4003 414 E
proctorc@westmoreland.edu
PROCTOR, Jeremiah ... 217-732-3168 143 F
jdproctor@lincolnchristian.edu
PROCTOR, Kelly ... 864-388-8398 422 A
kproctor@lander.edu
PROCTOR, Kristen ... 508-854-7552 220 G
kproctor@qcc.mass.edu
PROCTOR, Lee ... 910-898-9660 345 A
proctorr@montgomery.edu
PROCTOR, Matt ... 417-626-1234 264 J
pres@occ.edu
PROCTOR, Michael, A ... 520-626-5531.. 16 J
mproctor@arizona.edu
PROCTOR, Ross ... 870-733-6875.. 18 B
prproctor@asumidsouth.edu
PROCTOR, Valerie ... 757-727-5617 481 E
valerie.proctor@hamptonu.edu
PROCTOR, William, L ... 904-819-6210.. 98 I
proctorw@flagler.edu
PROEHL, Erinn ... 815-939-5296 148 F
eproehl@olivet.edu
PROFETA, Flen ... 559-730-3843.. 39 G
glenp@cos.edu
PROFETA, Patricia ... 772-462-4703 101 Q
pprofeta@irsc.edu
PROFFITT, Beth ... 717-358-3871 395 G
beth.proffitt@fandm.edu
PROFFITT, Ronald ... 276-964-7200 489 F
ron.proffitt@sw.edu
PROFITT, Aaron ... 513-721-7944 362 D
aprofitt@gbs.edu
PROHASKA, Thomas, R 703-993-1918 481 B
tprohask@gmu.edu
PROHN, Deborah, W ... 716-888-2919 300 G
prohnd@canisius.edu
PROISY, Alize ... 252-222-6240 341 F
proisya@carteret.edu
PROITE, Rosanne ... 512-245-2931 463 A
rp45@txstate.edu
PROKOP, Jessica ... 413-755-4529 221 B
japrokop@stcc.edu
PROKOP, Paul ... 530-754-8568.. 68 H
pjprokop@ucdavis.edu
PROKOVICH, Jeffrey, D . 724-458-3846 396 D
jdprokovich@gcc.edu
PROMADES,
Frederick, C ... 401-341-2117 417 D
promadef@salve.edu
PROPST, Jennifer ... 828-448-6051 347 F
jpropst@wpcc.edu
PROPST, Joan, L ... 304-457-6201 501 A
propstjl@ab.edu
PROPST, Kent ... 660-248-6238 258 B
kpropst@centralmethodist.edu
PROPST, William, S ... 310-794-6027.. 69 B
wpropst@finance.ucla.edu
PROSCIA, Domenic ... 718-429-6600 333 B
domenic.procsia@vaughn.edu
PROSCIA, Julie ... 312-662-4000 133 A
jproscia@adler.edu
PROSHAK, Dimitry ... 916-484-8401.. 50 F
proshad@arc.losrios.edu
PROSISE, Jodi, E ... 563-333-6485 173 A
prosisejodif@sau.edu
PROSPER, Yamilette ... 787-891-0925 523 G
yprosper@aguadilla.inter.edu
PROSSER, Deborah ... 678-717-3466 127 B
deborah.prosser@ung.edu
PROSSER, Pat ... 309-467-6748 138 E
pprosser@eureka.edu
PROSTANO, Laura ... 914-633-2203 311 B
lprostano@iona.edu
PROTAS, Elizabeth, J ... 409-772-3001 469 C
ejprotas@utmb.edu
PROTHERO, Charles, L . 570-945-8015 398 C
charlie.prothero@keystone.edu
PROTHROW-STITH,
Deborah ... 323-563-6981.. 36 H
dprothrowstith@cdrewu.edu
PROTO, Matthew ... 207-859-4802 198 H
matthew.proto@colby.edu
PROTZMAN, Ferdinand . 440-775-8400 367 B
fprotzma@oberlin.edu
PROUDFIT, Ann ... 216-987-5892 360 E
ann.proudfit@tri-c.edu
PROUDFOOT,
Donald, W ... 903-510-2975 464 D
dpro@tjc.edu
PROUDFOOT,
Michael, A ... 520-621-8747.. 16 J
tproudfoot@email.arizona.edu
PROUGH, Jeni ... 219-464-5022 165 D
jeni.prough@valpo.edu
PROULX, David, R ... 717-358-3993 395 G
dave.proulx@fandm.edu
PROULX, Dennis ... 802-468-1249 477 A
dennis.proulx@castleton.edu
PROUTY, Greg ... 804-862-6100 484 F
gprouty@rbc.edu
PROUTY, Steve ... 941-752-5205 108 P
proutys@scf.edu
PROVAN, Amy ... 410-532-5379 206 D
aprovan@ndm.edu
PROVENCHER,
Catherine, A ... 603-862-1622 282 E
catherine.provencher@usnh.edu
PROVENCIO-VASQUEZ,
Elias ... 915-747-8217 467 E
eprovenciovasquez@utep.edu
PROVENZA, Joseph, S .. 904-819-6359.. 98 I
jprovenza@flagler.edu
PROVENZANO, Joseph . 703-908-7686 483 A
joseph.provenzano@marymount.edu
PROVENZANO, Peter ... 248-341-2115 235 D
pmproven@oaklandcc.edu
PROVEZIS, Staci, J ... 217-333-1353 154 B
sprovez2@illinois.edu
PROVINE, Rick, E ... 765-658-4435 157 H
provine@depauw.edu
PROVOST, Darlyne, M ... 207-859-5117 198 H
darylyne.provost@colby.edu
PROVOST, David, J ... 802-443-5699 475 G
dprovost@middlebury.edu
PROVOST, Dawn ... 337-482-6391 197 F
dawn@louisiana.edu
PROVOST, Kathryn ... 802-485-2125 475 I
kathrynp@norwich.edu
PRUCHA, Christina ... 573-897-5000 267 F
PRUCHNICKI, Jennifer .. 580-581-2209 375 A
jpruchni@cameron.edu
PRUCNAL, James, R ... 256-549-8242.... 2 A
jprucnal@gadsdenstate.edu
PRUDE, Regina ... 615-687-6901 429 F
rprude@abcnash.edu
PRUDENTI, A. Gail ... 516-463-4068 310 D
gail.prudenti@hofstra.edu
PRUDHOMME,
Harvey, J ... 503-370-6348 388 D
hprudhom@willamette.edu
PRUD'HOMME, Sabrina 541-552-6060 386 H
prudhomms@sou.edu
PRUE, Stephen ... 785-832-6644 178 A
stephen.prue@bie.edu
PRUETT, Karen ... 706-880-8977 122 D
kpruett@lagrange.edu
PRUETT, Robert, R ... 919-658-7760 349 F
rpruett@umo.edu
PRUETT, Teresa ... 276-964-7365 489 F
teresa.pruett@sw.edu

PRUETT, Tim 740-245-7358 372 E tpruett@rio.edu

PRUETT, Tyler 510-869-6511 59 F tpruett@samuelmerritt.edu

PRUGH, JR., John, L 813-974-5437 111 A jprugh@usf.edu

PRUITT, Aaron 541-684-7217 384 H apruitt@nwcu.edu

PRUITT, Bart 806-720-7232 452 D bart.pruitt@lcu.edu

PRUITT, Betty 205-391-2251 3 E bpruitt@sheltonstate.edu

PRUITT, Beverly 305-284-2842 112 O b.pruitt@miami.edu

PRUITT, Chris 402-449-2917 274 H cpruitt9967@graceu.edu

PRUITT, Corey 480-377-2704 14 B corey.pruitt@riosalado.edu

PRUITT, Dennis, A 803-777-4172 424 I dpruitt@sc.edu

PRUITT, George, A 609-984-1105 292 B gpruitt@tesu.edu

PRUITT, Glenell 903-730-4890 451 D gpruitt@jarvis.edu

PRUITT, Jason 470-239-3103 127 B jason.pruitt@ung.edu

PRUITT, Jonathan 919-962-4600 349 G jpruitt@northcarolina.edu

PRUITT, Judy 612-343-4491 249 E japruitt@northcentral.edu

PRUITT, Karl 205-929-6348 2 G kpruitt@lawsonstate.edu

PRUITT, Leah, L 864-587-4225 424 D pruittl@smcsc.edu

PRUITT, Nathan 518-783-2342 324 C npruitt@siena.edu

PRUITT, Pamela 609-896-5000 289 E ppruitt@rider.edu

PRUITT, Samory, T 205-348-8376 8 A samory.pruitt@ua.edu

PRUITT, Steven 561-237-7834 103 E spruitt@lynn.edu

PRUNCHUNAS, Edward 310-423-8294 35 P

PRUNTY, Bonnie, S 607-274-3141 311 D bprunty@ithaca.edu

PRUNTY, Kathleen, A 909-869-3380 31 A kaprunty@cpp.edu

PRUS, Mark 607-753-2207 327 A mark.prus@cortland.edu

PRUSANK, Diane 413-572-5201 218 F dprusank@westfield.ma.edu

PRUSHA, Tammy 641-269-4481 169 F prushatd@grinnell.edu

PRUSHA, Todd 319-398-5565 171 F tprusha@kirkwood.edu

PRUSHAN, Mike 610-526-1861 396 H mprushan@harcum.edu

PRUSKOWSKI, Nancy 717-871-4086 407 A nancy.pruskowski@millersville.edu

PRUSS, Julie, A 585-395-2361 326 D jpruss@brockport.edu

PRY, George 412-809-5100 408 D pry.georgel@pti.edu

PRYBUTOK, Victor 940-565-3946 466 B victor.prybutok@unt.edu

PRYJMAK, Myron 718-409-7311 329 E mpryjmak@sunymaritime.edu

PRYLES, Kathryn 508-588-9100 220 B

PRYLO, Caelynn 518-743-2238 328 G pryloc@sunyacc.edu

PRYOR, Anastasia 707-545-3647 27 B anastasia@berginu.edu

PRYOR, Charles 646-313-8000 303 G charles.pryor@guttman.cuny.edu

PRYOR, Christian 504-816-4696 191 E cpryor@dillard.edu

PRYOR, Douglas 305-809-3184 99 L douglas.pryor@fkcc.edu

PRYOR, Julie 205-453-6300 93 B

PRYOR, Kim, A 336-342-4261 346 B pryork@rockinghamcc.edu

PRYOR, Marcus 704-991-0278 346 I mpryor7642@stanly.edu

PRYOR, Raymond, G 570-208-5828 398 D rgpryor@kings.edu

PRYOR-HARRIS, Holli 312-567-3167 140 I pryor@iit.edu

PRYSIAZNY, Laurel 559-442-8218 66 G laurel.prysiazny@fresnocitycollege.edu

PRYSOCK, James 614-823-1312 368 O jprysock@otterbein.edu

PRYSTOWSKY, Richard 517-483-1156 232 K prystowr@lcc.edu

PRZEKOP, Lisa 805-893-3641 70 B lisa.przekop@sa.ucsb.edu

PRZEKURAT, Paris 405-422-1442 379 B przekuratp@redlandscc.edu

PRZYBLYSKI, Jeannene 661-255-1050 29 F jeannene@calarts.edu

PRZYBOROKI, Carol 412-321-8383 391 A office@bcs.edu

PRZYGOCKI, Ginny 989-686-9276 229 J vlprzygo@delta.edu

PRZYGODA, Melitha, R 203-576-4588 88 F mprzygod@bridgeport.edu

PRZYWARA, Ann Marie 518-580-5765 324 D aprzywar@skidmore.edu

PRZYWARA, Richard, T 610-430-4156 407 D rprzywara@wcufoundation.org

PSAILA, Marisa 585-475-4932 321 D mxpdar@rit.edu

PSARRIS, Kleanthis 718-951-3170 301 E kpsarris@brooklyn.cuny.edu

PSEEKOS, A. Chantelle 401-456-8094 417 A

PSEEKOS, Chantelle 508-373-9544 211 F chantelle.pseekos@becker.edu

PUC, Gina 413-662-5416 218 C g.puc@mcla.edu

PUCCIARELLI, Matthew 718-990-7614 322 F pucciarm@stjohns.edu

PUCCIO O'BRIEN, Erica 617-879-7716 218 B erica.puccio@massart.edu

PUCKETT, Adam 503-554-2911 383 C apuckett@georgefox.edu

PUCKETT, Andrea 618-395-7777 140 E pucketta@iecc.edu

PUCKETT, Christopher 303-315-6619 83 D chris.puckett@ucdenver.edu

PUCKETT, Jack 252-492-2061 347 C puckett@vgcc.edu

PUCKETT, Jackie, A 864-488-4585 422 B jpuckett@limestone.edu

PUCKETT, Jeffrey 616-395-7413 231 D puckett@hope.edu

PUCKETT, Joan 812-888-4480 165 E jpuckett@vinu.edu

PUCKETT-BOLER, Laura 864-503-5108 425 H lpuckett-boler@uscupstate.edu

PUDDESTER, Frederick, W 413-597-4421 226 C frederick.w.puddester@williams.edu

PUENTE, Maria, K 617-228-2032 219 D mkpuente@bhcc.mass.edu

PUETT, Debbie 828-395-1481 344 A dpuett@isothermal.edu

PUFF, Derek 716-286-8055 318 F dpuff@niagara.edu

PUFFENBARGER, Jess 270-534-3504 187 C jess.puffenbarger@kctcs.edu

PUFHAL, Joy 231-591-2612 230 A joypufhal@ferris.edu

PUGEL, Mary, E 336-758-3005 353 A mpugel@wfu.edu

PUGH, Benjamin 225-771-5021 195 K benjamin_pugh@subr.edu

PUGH, Benjamin, W 318-670-9302 196 A bpugh@susla.edu

PUGH, Crystal 252-789-0293 344 E crystal.pugh@martincc.edu

PUGH, SR., Daniel, J 979-845-4728 459 C djpughsr@vpsa.tamu.edu

PUGH, David 912-525-5000 125 B dpugh@scad.edu

PUGH, Holly 804-627-5405 478 I holly_pugh@bshsi.org

PUGH, Jason 601-928-6233 254 D jason.pugh@mgccc.edu

PUGH, Paul, F 610-519-4200 413 K paul.pugh@villanova.edu

PUGH, Sandi 559-297-4500 46 E

PUGH, Vicki 561-803-2012 104 I viki_pugh@pba.edu

PUGLIESE, Beth 408-924-1116 34 D beth.pugliese@sjsu.edu

PUGLIESI, Karen, L 928-523-2672 14 K karen.pugliesi@nau.edu

PUGLISI, Emma 978-921-4242 222 B emma.puglisi@montserrat.edu

PUGLISI, Michael, J 276-944-6662 480 J mpuglisi@ehc.edu

PUGNAIRE, Michele, P 508-856-4250 217 C michele.pugnaire@umassmed.edu

PUHALA, Kimberly 508-286-3621 225 G puhala_kimberly@wheatoncollege.edu

PUIG, Juan 787-815-0000 527 F juan.puig@upr.edu

PULCINI, Brad, T 740-368-3943 368 N btpulcin@owu.edu

PULEIO, Samuel, T 814-393-2280 405 H spuleio@clarion.edu

PULIAFICO, Venus 216-368-4530 358 C venus.puliafico@case.edu

PULICE, Jon 814-732-1763 406 B jpulice@edinboro.edu

PULIDO, Jairo 787-250-1912 524 B jpulido@metro.inter.edu

PULIDO, Maria 509-453-0374 497 A maria.pulido@perrytech.edu

PULLEE, Tara 949-753-4774 27 F pullee@brandman.edu

PULLEN, Terri 513-862-7761 362 E terri.pullen@email.gscollege.edu

PULLEY, D. J 601-318-6048 256 I djpulley@wmcarey.edu

PULLEY, Eric 618-985-3741 141 D ericpulley@jalc.edu

PULLEY, Lawrence, B 757-221-2891 479 I larry.pulley@mason.wm.edu

PULLIAM, Camden 816-414-3700 263 D cpulliam@mbts.edu

PULLIAM, Cheryl 704-355-5093 336 F cheryl.pulliam@carolinashealthcare.org

PULLIAM, DeWayne 615-794-4254 435 G dpulliam@omorecollege.edu

PULLIAM, Joni, L 315-792-3344 332 H jpulliam@utica.edu

PULLIAM, Mark 252-249-1851 345 C mpulliam@pamlicocc.edu

PULLIAM, Roger 262-472-1918 512 C

PULLIN, Daniel, W 405-325-0100 380 L dpullin@ou.edu

PULLIN, Erin 714-628-2821 36 G pullin@chapman.edu

PULLIZA, Carmen 787-743-7979 526 A cpulliza@suagm.edu

PULS, Jonathan 562-944-0651 27 E jonathan.puls@biola.edu

PULSIPHER, Scott, D 801-274-3280 474 D spulsipher@wgu.edu

PULTRO, Judith 239-985-3477 100 E jpultro@fsw.edu

PULTZ, Stephen, F 619-260-4506 71 J spultz@sandiego.edu

PULVER, Patricia 315-279-5662 312 D ppulver@keuka.edu

PULVER, Shayne 615-226-3990 433 B spulver@lincolntech.edu

PUMA, Lynn, M 716-878-5509 326 E pumalm@buffalostate.edu

PUMPHREY, Dennis 970-351-2245 83 F dennis.pumphrey@unco.edu

PUNCHELLO-COBOS, Catharine 609-984-1180 292 B registrar@tesu.edu

PUNCHES, Alan 603-524-3207 280 K

PUNCHES, Kathy, M 419-783-2590 361 A kpunches@defiance.edu

PUNEKY, Warren 504-671-6100 192 H wpunek@dcc.edu

PUNT, David 916-577-2200 75 B dpunt@jessup.edu

PUPPALA, Kuldeep 516-628-5076 327 C puppalak@oldwestbury.edu

PUPPO, Joseph 215-646-7300 396 E puppo.j@gmercyu.edu

PURA, Robert, L 413-775-1410 219 F pura@gcc.mass.edu

PURCELL, Anthony, B 205-934-2297 8 B bpurcell@uab.edu

PURCELL, Arielle, M 203-576-4151 88 F apurcell@bridgeport.edu

PURCELL, Chris, A 405-325-4122 380 L regentspurcell@ou.edu

PURCELL, Jeanine 716-880-2259 314 F jp983@medaille.edu

PURCELL, Ladonna, M 606-783-2323 188 C l.purcell@moreheadstate.edu

PURCELL, Lyquaia 706-245-7226 119 A lpurcell@ec.edu

PURCELL, Meredith 815-802-8512 142 C mpurcell@kcc.edu

PURCELL, Phillip 765-285-7070 156 C ppurcell@bsu.edu

PURCELL, Ruth 724-287-8711 390 J ruth.purcell@bc3.edu

PURCELL, Satch 949-794-9090 66 B spurcell@stanbridge.edu

PURCELL, Stacy, R 757-446-6002 480 C purcellsr@evms.edu

PURDIE, Jack 925-631-4542 59 C jfp3@stmarys-ca.edu

PURDOM, Kurt 662-915-7375 256 C kirk@olemiss.edu

PURDUE-LYNCH, Barbara 201-355-1122 286 C lynchb@felician.edu

PURDY, Brad 505-566-3301 296 A purdyb@sanjuancollege.edu

PURDY, G. Michael 212-854-1656 305 E gmp63@columbia.edu

PURDY, Jill 308-865-8421 277 F purdyj@unk.edu

PURDY, Judy 508-286-3785 225 G purdy_judy@wheatoncollege.edu

PURDY, Kim 479-619-4399 20 F kpurdy@nwacc.edu

PURDY, Matt 270-809-3735 188 D mpurdy1@murraystate.edu

PURDY, Ryan 308-535-3720 275 I purdyr@mpcc.edu

PURECE, Sarita 415-257-0136 41 J sarita.purece@dominican.edu

PURI, Anil 657-278-2614 32 B apuri@fullerton.edu

PURI, Tribhuvan 570-422-3589 406 A tpuri@esu.edu

PURIFOY, Tangela 251-578-1313 3 D tpurifoy@rstc.edu

PURNELL, William 508-849-3482 210 H wpurnell@annamaria.edu

PUROHIT, Yasmin, S 412-397-5472 409 C purohit@rmu.edu

PURRINGTON, Kristen 603-336-5265 280 K kpurrington@ccsnh.edu

PURSER, Charles 252-335-0821 342 D charles_purser@albemarle.edu

PURSER, Lori 254-526-1486 445 L lori.purser@ctcd.edu

PURSLEY, Linda 617-349-8563 216 D lpursley@lesley.edu

PURSOO, Eugene 718-270-5136 303 C pursoo@mec.cuny.edu

PURTLE, Dwight 913-568-6126 178 G dwight.purtle@kansaschristian.edu

PURVIANCE, Chris 509-313-5858 495 A purviance@gonzaga.edu

PURVIS, Anne 678-359-5197 121 B a_purvis@gordonstate.edu

PURVIS, Donnie 817-598-6284 470 J dpurvis@wc.edu

PURVIS, Kathy 254-968-9070 459 A kpurvis@tarleton.edu

PURVIS, Lynda, L 229-928-1361 120 F lynda.purvis@gsw.edu

PURYEAR, Roberta (Robbi) 713-743-8780 464 F rdpuryea@uh.edu

PUSECKER, Kathleen, L 302-831-8537 90 I klp@udel.edu

PUSEY, Stephen, M 615-248-1258 439 B spusey@trevecca.edu

PUSICH, Ruth 630-617-3080 138 C ruthp@elmhurst.edu

PUSKA, Douglas, P 978-762-4000 220 E dpuska@northshore.edu

PUSTAY, Pamela, S 330-471-8159 364 H ppustay@malone.edu

PUSTEJOVSKY, Kathleen 254-659-7632 450 B kpustejovsky@hillcollege.edu

PUSTZ, Charles 815-836-5050 143 E pustzch@lewisu.edu

PUSZYNSKI, Jan, A 605-394-2257 429 A jan.puszynski@sdsmt.edu

PUSZYNSKI, Jan, A 605-394-2493 429 A jan.puszynski@sdsmt.edu

PUTERBAUGH, Mark 336-249-8186 342 F mark_puterbaugh@davidsoncc.edu

PUTMAN, Jeffrey 718-270-2187 326 A jeffrey.putman@downstate.edu

PUTMAN, Paul 518-736-3622 309 A pputman@fmcc.suny.edu

PUTMAN, Stephen 256-765-4178 9 A jsputman@una.edu

PUTNAM, Diana 518-736-3622 309 A diana.putnam@fmcc.suny.edu

PUTNAM, Lisa 805-378-1448 73 A lputnam@vcccd.edu

PUTNAM, Lydia 215-368-5000 389 H lputnam@biblical.edu

PUTNAM, Mark, L 641-628-5269 167 D president@central.edu

PUTNAM, Michael 732-987-2678 286 D mputnam@georgian.edu

PUTNAM, Robin 701-328-2960 353 F robin.putnam@ndus.edu

PUTNAM, Timothy, J 641-422-4192 172 C putnatim@niacc.edu

PUTNEY, Luanna 209-228-4417 69 C lputney@ucmerced.edu

PUTO, Christopher 251-380-3865 7 B cputo@shc.edu

PUTREVU, Sanjay 216-687-3786 359 L s.putrevu@csuohio.edu

PUTZKE, Robert 406-994-3220 272 A rputzke@montana.edu

PUZZIFERRO, Maria 505-473-6234 296 C president@santafeuniversity.edu

PYBUS-THRUSH, Anne 989-774-3166 228 E pybus1a@cmich.edu

QUINTANA HESS, Jessica, A ... 570-321-4318 400 G hess@lycoming.edu
QUINTANILLA, Hector ... 817-531-4840 463 G hquintanilla@txwes.edu
QUINTANILLA, Kelly, M 361-825-2621 460 A kelly.quintanilla@tamucc.edu
QUINTANS, Joel ... 817-272-2025 467 B quintas@uta.edu
QUINTARA, Elena ... 312-662-4021 133 A equintara@adler.edu
QUINTERO, Rebecca ... 787-728-1515 529 B rquintero@sagrado.edu
QUINTERO-JIMENEZ, Noel ... 787-725-6500 521 C nquintero@albizu.edu
QUINTYNE, Renee ... 845-398-4207 323 G rquintyn@stac.edu
QUIRE, Heather ... 802-447-6302 476 C hquire@svc.edu
QUIRK, Donna ... 312-915-8723 144 D dquirk@luc.edu
QUIRK, Walter ... 530-226-4172.. 64 B rquirk@simpsonu.edu
QUIRK-BAILEY, Sheila .. 309-694-5520 139 G sheila.quirk-bailey@icc.edu
QUIROLGICO, Ray ... 626-396-2325.. 26 L ray.quirolgico@artcenter.edu
QUIROS, Kristi ... 830-372-8060 461 D kquiros@tlu.edu
QUIROZ, Gloria ... 773-878-3606 150 I gquiroz@staugustine.edu
QUIROZ, Saul ... 805-965-0581.. 62 E squiroz@sbcc.edu
QUIS, Stephen ... 619-388-7876.. 60 E squis@sdccd.edu
QUISENBERRY, Brian, L ... 540-464-7184 490 E quisenberrybl@vmi.edu
QUISENBERRY, JR., Henry, L ... 334-347-2623.... 1 J cquisenberry@escc.edu
QUISTGARD, Fred ... 207-216-4406 200 E fquistgard@yccc.edu
QUISTORF, Mark, W ... 414-410-4016 506 F mwquistorf@stritch.edu
QUIÑONES, Angel ... 787-258-1501 521 K alquinones@columbiacentral.edu
QUIÑONES, Yolanda ... 787-758-2525 528 D yolanda.quinonez@upr.edu
QUIÑONES CASTILLA, Weyna, M ... 787-878-9218 527 F weyna.quinones@upr.edu
QURESHI, Elena ... 734-432-5499 233 C equreshi@madonna.edu
QVARMSTROM, Jeanne . 432-837-8585 462 G jqvarmstrom@sulross.edu

R

R. SEAL, Craig ... 909-537-5735.. 33 D cseal@csusb.edu
RAAB, David ... 646-565-6000 331 F david.raab@touro.edu
RAAB, Jennifer, J ... 212-772-4242 302 E jennifer.raab@hunter.cuny.edu
RAAB, Lettie, M ... 936-261-5900 458 F lmraab@pvamu.edu
RAAB, Maryrose ... 315-792-7215 330 A maryrose.raab@sunyit.edu
RAASCH, Christopher ... 734-995-7399 229 A chris.raasch@cuaa.edu
RAATMA, Lucia ... 352-588-8572 106 N lucia.raatma@saintleo.edu
RAB, Shafiq ... 312-942-3400 150 F shafiq_rab@rush.edu
RABAGO, Cristine ... 650-543-3782.. 51 F crabago@menlo.edu
RABB, Harriet ... 212-327-8070 321 E harriet.rabb@rockefeller.edu
RABB, Sydni ... 254-442-5113 445 Q sydni.rabb@cisco.edu
RABBANY, Sina, Y ... 516-463-6672 310 D sina.y.rabbany@hofstra.edu
RABBITT, Kara, M ... 973-720-2180 292 I rabbittk@wpunj.edu
RABEK, Jeffrey ... 409-772-6026 469 C jrabek@utmb.edu
RABEL, P, J ... 402-465-2102 276 E prabel@nebrwesleyan.edu
RABELO, Virginia ... 305-821-3333 100 A vrabelo@fnu.edu
RABENOLD, Scott ... 512-471-3434 467 C srabenold@utexas.edu
RABER, II, Donald, R ... 864-833-8233 423 D draber@presby.edu
RABIDEAU, Shelly, S ... 317-940-8423 156 I srabidea@butler.edu
RABIL, Alison ... 919-684-3501 337 C alison.rabil@duke.edu
RABINEAU, Kevin ... 269-965-3931 232 A rabineauk@kellogg.edu
RABINOVICH, Sheryl ... 619-235-2049.. 42 N srabinovich@fidm.edu
RABINOVICH, Sheryl ... 213-624-1200.. 42 N srabinovich@fidm.edu
RABINOWITZ, Celia, E .. 603-358-2736 283 A celia.rabinowitz@keene.edu
RABINOWITZ, David, B . 973-290-4084 285 A drabinowitz@cse.edu
RABINOWITZ, Eli ... 718-377-0777 320 E
RABINOWITZ, Stuart ... 516-463-6800 310 D president@hofstra.edu
RABINOWITZ, Vita ... 664-646-8075 301 A vita.rabinowitz@cuny.edu
RABITOY, Eric ... 626-914-8788.. 37 G erabitoy@citruscollege.edu
RABITOY, Linda ... 909-667-4433.. 37 J lrabitoy@claremontlincoln.edu
RABLE, Michelle ... 419-824-3816 364 G mrable@lourdes.edu
RABLE, Michelle, A ... 419-824-3816 364 G mrable@lourdes.edu
RABY, Domonic ... 601-877-6333 251 G sm8053@bncollege.com
RABY, James ... 803-641-3569 425 A jamesr@usca.edu
RABY, Sherry ... 252-249-1851 345 C sraby@pamlicocc.edu
RABY, Susan ... 315-312-2260 327 D susan.raby@oswego.edu
RABY, Tracy ... 256-331-5330.... 3 C tracy@nwscc.edu
RACANSKY, Pam ... 206-934-3656 497 H pamela.racansky@seattlecolleges.edu
RACCANELLO, Paul ... 415-485-3223.. 41 J paul.raccanello@dominican.edu
RACE, Debbie ... 828-262-2050 349 H racedw@appstate.edu
RACE, Mary Jo ... 412-624-4200 412 I mar6@pitt.edu
RACEHORSE, Brenda ... 785-749-8451 178 A brenda.racehorse@bie.edu
RACER, Jennifer ... 928-541-7777.. 54 B jracer@ncu.edu
RACETTE, Patrick ... 906-524-8301 232 D patrick.racette@kbocc.edu
RACHAL, Bryan ... 256-765-4225.... 9 A brachal@una.edu
RACHAL, Carol, E ... 256-233-8204.... 4 C carol.rachal@athens.edu
RACHAL, Michael ... 504-865-2486 194 G rachal@loyno.edu
RACHELL, Kelvin ... 804-524-5011 491 A krachell@vsu.edu
RACHFORD, Jennifer ... 909-607-2201.. 57 I jennifer.rachford@pomona.edu
RACHITA, David, A ... 281-283-2568 465 B rachita@uhcl.edu
RACHOUH, Susan ... 201-216-3518 291 G susan.rachouh@stevens.edu
RACINE, Anne ... 406-338-5441 270 G anne_racine@bfcc.edu
RACINE, Gail, M ... 508-767-7283 210 I gracine@assumption.edu
RACINE, Leo ... 508-678-2811 219 C leo.racine@bristolcc.edu
RACIOPPI, Jerry ... 308-398-7405 273 G geraldracioppi@cccneb.edu
RACKLEY, Casey, C ... 865-688-9422 432 B
RACKLEY, J. Mike ... 662-325-9311 254 E mike.rackley@msstate.edu
RACKLEY, Richard, W ... 865-688-9422 432 B info@fountainheadcollege.com
RACKLEY, Steven ... 989-463-7111 226 H rackleysp@alma.edu
RACKLIFFE, Jerry, J ... 404-413-3000 121 A jracklif@gsu.edu
RACZYNSKI, James, M . 501-526-6600.. 22 C raczynskijamesm@uams.edu
RADAKOVICH, Dan ... 864-656-1935 419 F danrad1@clemson.edu
RADCLIFFE, Shelby ... 503-370-6397 388 D sradcliffe@willamette.edu
RADCLIFFE, Steve ... 513-244-4381 366 A steve.radcliffe@msj.edu
RADDA, Hank ... 602-639-7500.. 12 P
RADDER, Shannon ... 716-839-8337 306 E sradder@daemen.edu
RADEL, Patti ... 585-594-6100 319 B radelp@roberts.edu
RADEL, Patti ... 585-594-6100 321 C radelp@roberts.edu
RADEMACHER, Eric ... 513-556-3304 371 E eric.rademacher@uc.edu
RADER, Brian ... 503-399-8074 382 C brian.rader@chemeketa.edu
RADER, Claude, K ... 410-951-3858 208 F drader@coppin.edu
RADER, Sherri ... 309-649-6255 152 G sherri.rader@src.edu
RADFORD, Laurie ... 503-552-1617 384 F lradford@nunm.edu
RADFORD, Marilyn ... 270-384-8022 187 H radfordm@lindsey.edu
RADFORD, Ron ... 256-395-2211.... 3 G rradford@suscc.edu
RADFORD-HILL, Sheila . 708-524-6381 137 F sradfordhill@dom.edu
RADHAKRISHNAN, Rashmi ... 610-921-7225 388 E rradhakrishnan@albright.edu
RADICE, Brad ... 205-726-4373.... 6 G bjradice@samford.edu
RADIK, Amy ... 518-736-3622 309 A amy.radik@fmcc.suny.edu
RADIONOFF, Kathleen, A ... 608-258-2309 514 A kradionoff@madisoncollege.edu
RADISH, Ross ... 215-596-8800 413 E r.radish@usciences.edu
RADKE, Cheryl ... 623-245-4600.. 16 H cradke@uticuti.edu
RADKE, Jordan ... 719-389-7270.. 77 J jradke@coloradocollege.edu
RADKE, Suzette ... 712-749-2044 167 C radkes@bvu.edu
RADLIFF, Mary ... 518-255-5211 328 C radliffmd@cobleskill.edu
RADNEY, Ron ... 209-228-4306.. 69 C rradney@ucmerced.edu
RADSON, Darrell, J ... 309-677-2255 134 G radson@bradley.edu
RADT, Jennifer ... 513-732-5327 371 G jennifer.radt@uc.edu
RADT, Jennifer ... 513-732-5221 371 G jennifer.radt@uc.edu
RADTKE, Elizabeth, L ... 651-523-2201 242 E bradtke@hamline.edu
RADULESCU, Eugen ... 713-348-6725 455 F eugen@rice.edu
RADVANSKY, Sandy, M 740-284-5357 361 L sradvansky@franciscan.edu
RADWANSKI, Steven, E 609-652-4915 291 H steven.radwanski@stockton.edu
RADYCKI, Diane ... 610-861-1627 402 D dradycki@moravian.edu
RAE, Jon ... 813-988-5131.. 99 D raej@floridacollege.edu
RAE, Lisa ... 802-258-3149 476 B lisa.rae@worldlearning.org
RAE, Mike, E ... 570-326-3761 404 T mrae@pct.edu
RAE, Nicol ... 406-994-4288 272 A nicol.rae@montana.edu
RAE, Rosemarie ... 510-642-5737.. 68 G rrae@berkeley.edu
RAEBER, Michael ... 706-542-0006 127 A mraeber@uga.edu
RAEFORD, James, E ... 540-828-5408 478 J jraeford@bridgewater.edu
RAEHL, Cindy ... 325-696-0544 463 E cynthia.raehl@ttuhsc.edu
RAEHLL, Meghan ... 614-947-6579 362 A meghan.raehll@franklin.edu
RAEL, Bernadette, C ... 505-454-2596 294 D brael@luna.edu
RAEL, Sylvia ... 970-248-1029.. 77 K srael@coloradomesa.edu
RAFATTI, Colleen ... 863-784-7411 108 B colleen.rafatti@southflorida.edu
RAFELD, Jessica ... 920-403-3071 509 J jessica.rafeld@snc.edu
RAFFAELLE, David ... 623-845-3676.. 13 H david.raffaelle@gccaz.edu
RAFFAELLE, Ryne ... 585-475-2055 321 D ryne.raffaelle@rit.edu
RAFFELD, Beth ... 413-585-2020 224 F braffeld@smith.edu
RAFFENSPERGER, Thomas ... 413-572-5233 218 F traffensperger@westfield.ma.edu
RAFFETTO, William ... 281-998-6150 456 A william.raffetto@sjcd.edu
RAFIEE, Farnoosh ... 606-326-2069 185 E farnoosh.rafiee@kctcs.edu
RAFIEYMEHR, Ali ... 603-542-7744 281 A arafieymehr@ccsnh.edu
RAFN, H. Jeffrey ... 920-498-5411 514 G jeff.rafn@nwtc.edu
RAFOOL, Dawn, M ... 863-638-3818 113 I dawn.rafool@warner.edu
RAFOTH, Mary Ann ... 412-397-6024 409 C rafoth@rmu.edu
RAFTERY, OP, Paul ... 805-525-4417.. 67 E praftery@thomasaquinas.edu
RAGAN, Daniel ... 706-649-1442 118 D dragan@columbustech.edu
RAGAN, Jody ... 515-961-1517 173 E jody.ragan@simpson.edu
RAGAN, Kathleen, E ... 973-655-3450 287 D ragank@mail.montclair.edu
RAGAN, Mckenzie ... 229-732-5956 115 B mckenzieragan@andrewcollege.edu
RAGAN, Nola ... 605-698-3966 428 C nragan@swc.tc
RAGAN, Ronald, E ... 336-841-9193 338 E rragan@highpoint.edu
RAGER, Tim ... 206-934-4344 497 I timothy.rager@seattlecolleges.edu
RAGGO, Alan ... 812-888-5640 165 E araggo@vinu.edu
RAGHAVAN, Padma ... 615-322-6067 440 D padma.raghavan@vanderbilt.edu
RAGHU, Guhan ... 817-515-5289 458 B guhan.raghu@tccd.edu
RAGINS-RILEY, Anika ... 856-222-9311 289 F ariley@rcbc.edu
RAGLAND, Heather ... 901-272-5124 434 B hragland@mca.edu
RAGLAND, Janet ... 903-233-3815 452 A janetragland@letu.edu
RAGLAND, Lori ... 618-437-5321 149 H ragland@rlc.edu
RAGLAND, Matthew ... 334-244-3138.... 4 E mragland@aum.edu
RAGNO, John ... 718-489-5364 322 D jragno@sfc.edu
RAGNO, Kerry, S ... 757-822-1187 489 H kragno@tcc.edu
RAGO, Jim ... 229-249-2672 128 G jim.rago@wiregrass.edu
RAGOLIA, Josie ... 512-505-3079 451 A jragolia@htu.edu
RAGSDALE, Chad ... 417-626-1234 264 J ragsdale.chad@occ.edu
RAGSDALE, Jaime ... 978-478-3400 223 E jaragsdale@northpoint.edu
RAGSDALE, Jennifer ... 201-761-6062 291 D jragsdale@saintpeters.edu
RAGSDALE, Jonathan ... 978-478-3400 223 E jragsdale@northpoint.edu
RAGSDALE, Lisa, B ... 704-233-8710 353 D lisa.ragsdale@wingate.edu
RAGSDALE, JR., Roy Lee ... 704-233-8118 353 D lragsdale@wingate.edu
RAGUSA, Sal ... 510-436-1008.. 45 G ragusa@hnu.edu
RAH, Yumee ... 213-381-0081.. 46 I yumeerah@irus.edu
RAHAR, Kimberly ... 618-545-3372 142 D krahar@kaskaskia.edu
RAHE, April ... 816-531-5223 258 H arahe@concorde.edu
RAHIMI, Andy ... 317-632-5553 162 P
RAHM, Clare ... 216-687-5541 359 L c.rahm@csuohio.edu
RAHMAN, Pervez ... 773-907-4452 135 K prahman@ccc.edu
RAHMAN, Syedur ... 703-764-7384 488 H syrahman@nvcc.edu
RAHMANI, Loretta ... 909-593-3511.. 70 E lrahmani@laverne.edu
RAHMANN, Jack ... 512-245-2124 463 A jcr140@txstate.edu
RAHMATIAN, Morteza ... 657-278-2592.. 32 B mrahmatian@fullerton.edu
RAHMLOW, Jeff ... 920-686-6166 510 A jeff.rahmlow@sl.edu
RAHN, Adria ... 248-204-3030 233 A bkslawrencetech@bncollege.com
RAHN, Daniel ... 501-686-5680.. 22 C drahn@uams.edu
RAHN, Debra ... 618-235-2700 152 E
RAHN, Diane ... 419-251-1726 365 C diane.rahn@mercycollege.edu
RAHN, Ernie ... 907-377-4398 470 I ernie.rahn@wbu.edu
RAHN, Jason, M ... 651-641-8706 241 L rahn@csp.edu
RAHN, Joel ... 512-313-3000 446 N joel.rahn@concordia.edu
RAHNAMAY-AZAR, Amir ... 315-443-3037 330 H amir@syr.edu
RAHNI, Michael ... 213-383-8999.. 24 G
RAHR, JR., Carl, H ... 607-587-3535 328 F rahrch@alfredstate.edu

RAHUSEN, Jenifer 800-686-7022 87 E
jrahusen@lincolncollegene.edu
RAI, Sanjay 240-567-5006 205 F
sanjay.rai@montgomerycollege.edu
RAIBLEY, Jon 503-517-1899 388 C
jraibley@westernseminary.edu
RAICH, Michael 218-262-6702 244 H
michaelraich@hibbing.edu
RAICHE, Carol 978-232-2068 214 G
craiche@endicott.edu
RAICHE, Cheryl 617-217-9212 211 D
craiche@baystate.edu
RAICHIK, Shimon 323-937-2079 75 F
RAIKES-COLBERT,
Deborah 845-575-3000 314 C
deborah.raikes-colbert@marist.edu
RAILEY, Clay 410-827-5806 203 C
crailey@chesapeake.edu
RAILEY, George, A 805-922-6966 24 J
grailey@hancockcollege.edu
RAILEY, James, H 417-268-1014 257 F
raileyj@evangel.edu
RAILEY, Kevin 585-385-8402 322 E
krailey@sjfc.edu
RAIMER, Ben, G 409-747-2789 469 C
bgraimer@utmb.edu
RAIMO, James 845-569-3227 316 B
james.raimo@msmc.edu
RAIMONDO, Meredith 440-775-8462 367 B
meredith.raimondo@oberlin.edu
RAINBOW, Deanna 701-627-4738 355 D
drainb@nhsc.edu
RAINE, Meredith 713-500-3050 468 D
meredith.raine@uth.tmc.edu
RAINER, Art 919-761-2100 349 C
arainer@sebts.edu
RAINER, Don 205-652-3576 9 C
drainer@uwa.edu
RAINER, Kairyn 617-585-1107 222 H
kairyn.rainer@necmusic.edu
RAINES, Amanda 940-552-6291 469 F
araines@vernoncollege.edu
RAINES, Deborah 703-284-1530 483 A
debbie.raines@marymount.edu
RAINES, Jeremy 859-622-2977 184 F
jeremy.raines@eku.edu
RAINES, Jess, N 740-374-8716 373 G
jraines@wscc.edu
RAINES, Patrick 615-460-6000 430 D
pat.raines@belmont.edu
RAINES, Ruby 940-565-2026 466 B
ruby.raines@unt.edu
RAINEY, Jamie 325-481-9300 450 G
jrainey@howardcollege.edu
RAINEY, Jo Anne 502-597-5574 187 E
joanne.rainey@kysu.edu
RAINEY, Kelli 704-378-3553 338 I
krainey@jcsu.edu
RAINEY, Kenton, W 773-702-1234 153 F
krainey@uchicago.edu
RAINEY, Shawn 859-572-1359 188 E
raineys1@nku.edu
RAINFORD, William 202-319-5454 91 D
rainford@cua.edu
RAINONE, John, J 540-863-2827 487 I
rrainone@dslcc.edu
RAINS, Ben 501-812-2268 23 C
brains@pulaskitech.edu
RAINS, Brian 417-268-6036 257 H
brains@gobbc.edu
RAINS, Jerry 863-667-5197 108 G
jdrains@seu.edu
RAINS, TJ 636-949-4347 261 I
trains@lindenwood.edu
RAINS, Valerie 417-873-6965 259 G
vrains@drury.edu
RAINWATER, Jeanetta 918-781-7263 374 H
rainwaterj@bacone.edu
RAIOLA, Lisa 401-254-3302 417 C
lraiola@rwu.edu
RAISANEN, Gregg 320-762-4618 243 J
greggr@alextech.edu
RAISH, Brad 618-468-3160 143 D
braish@lc.edu
RAISOR, Jeremy 928-524-7462 15 B
jeremy.raisor@npc.edu
RAISOVICH, Andy 304-367-4682 504 A
andy.raisovich@fairmontstate.edu
RAISOVICH, Joanie 304-367-4131 504 A
joanie.raisovich@fairmontstate.edu
RAJA, Jay 704-687-5737 351 C
jraja@uncc.edu
RAJA, Muthukrishna 803-535-5176 419 E
mraja@claflin.edu
RAJA, Tasleem 312-427-9580 137 G
tasleem@eastwest.edu
RAJAGOPALAN, Balaji 815-753-1755 147 H
brajagopalan@niu.edu
RAJAGOPALAN, Hari, K 843-661-1420 421 H
hrajagopalan@fmarion.edu
RAJALA, Sarah 515-294-9988 166 F
rajala@iastate.edu
RAJAN, Madhav 773-702-1234 153 F
mrajan@chicagobooth.edu
RAJAN, Ravi, S 661-255-1050 29 F
rrajan@calarts.edu
RAJASEKARAN,
Senthil, K 757-446-5630 480 C
rajasesk@evms.edu
RAJMAIRA, Christina 703-284-1615 483 A
christina.rajmaira@marymount.edu
RAJPUROHIT, Vikas 817-515-1254 458 B
vikas.rajpurohit@tccd.edu
RAJPUT, Hussein 651-523-2204 242 E
hrajput01@hamline.edu
RAKER, Keith 336-249-8186 342 F
kdraker@davidsonccc.edu
RAKES, Lee, L 540-464-7345 490 E
rakesel@vmi.edu
RAKES, Thomas, D 910-962-3174 352 A
rakest@uncw.edu
RAKESTRAW, Jennie 803-323-2151 426 H
rakestrawj@winthrop.edu
RAKITA, Gordon, F 904-620-2820 110 E
grakita@unf.edu
RALEIGH, Bill 830-792-7421 456 D
wraleigh@schreiner.edu
RALEIGH, M.J 336-841-9794 338 E
mraleigh@highpoint.edu
RALEY, Karen, C 240-895-3219 206 G
kcraley@smcm.edu
RALEY, Leonard, R 301-445-1941 207 F
raley@usmd.edu
RALL, John, P 270-809-3399 188 D
jrall@murraystate.edu
RALLS, Diana 559-278-7167 32 A
rallsd@csufresno.edu
RALLS, Pam 314-837-6777 266 A
pralls@stlchristian.edu
RALLS, Scott 703-323-3101 488 H
sralls@nvcc.edu
RALPH, Brian, C 919-508-2220 353 C
officeofthepresident@peace.edu
RALPH, Chittams 757-455-3295 491 F
rchittams@vwu.edu
RALPH, David 580-774-3191 380 B
david.ralph@swosu.edu
RALPH, Emily 973-408-3635 285 E
eralph@drew.edu
RALPH, James 802-443-5320 475 G
ralph@middlebury.edu
RALPH, Ken 719-389-6475 77 J
ken.ralph@coloradocollege.edu
RALPH, Nicole, M 217-786-2342 144 B
nicole.ralph@llcc.edu
RALPH, Scott 317-955-6789 162 R
sralph@marian.edu
RALSTON, Craig 928-776-2311 17 G
craig.ralston@yc.edu
RALSTON, Gina 410-778-7849 210 A
gralston2@washcoll.edu
RALSTON, Pamela 760-862-1340 39 D
pralston@collegeofthedesert.edu
RALSTON, Steven, M 606-783-2002 188 C
s.ralston@moreheadstate.edu
RALSTON, Tracy 203-596-4564 87 H
tralston@post.edu
RALSTON, Troy 804-727-6826 125 H
tralston@southuniversity.edu
RAM, Rosalind 808-675-3589 128 K
rose.ram@byuh.edu
RAMAGE, Emily 217-234-5403 143 B
eramage@lakeland.cc.il.us
RAMAGE, Thomas, R 217-351-2231 148 H
ramage@parkland.edu
RAMAKER, Dawn 641-585-8197 174 B
ramakerd@waldorf.edu
RAMAKER, Jason 641-585-8160 174 B
ramakerj@waldorf.edu
RAMAKRISHNAN, Jolly 610-399-2032 405 G
jramakrishnan@cheyney.edu
RAMAKRISHNAN, Latha 320-308-4793 247 E
lramakrishnan@stcloudstate.edu
RAMALHO, Erika, A 814-871-5584 395 H
ramalho001@gannon.edu
RAMAMURTI, Sita 202-884-9262 93 C
ramamurtis@trinitydc.edu
RAMAN, Jaishankar 219-464-6880 165 D
jaishankar.raman@valpo.edu
RAMAN, Saravana 714-300-0300 65 B
sraman@scitech.edu
RAMANATHAN, Pamela 215-596-8891 413 E
p.ramanathan@usciences.edu
RAMARUI, Robert 680-488-2471 520 E
roramarui@gmail.com
RAMASUBRAMANIAN,
Melur 434-243-3606 486 H
vpresearch@virginia.edu
RAMASWAMY, Nandini 317-940-9032 156 I
nramaswa@butler.edu
RAMBEAU, Nadine 661-255-1050 29 F
nrambeau@calarts.edu
RAMBIKUR, Sara 512-617-5700 446 B
RAMBISH, Medea 585-292-2341 315 L
RAMBO, Bill 509-533-7038 493 I
bill.rambo@scc.spokane.edu
RAMBO, Helen 405-466-3259 375 L
hsrambo@langston.edu
RAMBO, Thomas, A 540-375-2310 484 H
rambo@roanoke.edu
RAMCHAND, Latha 713-743-4604 465 A
ramchand@uh.edu
RAMDATH, Sanjay 718-289-5705 301 D
sanjay.ramdath@bcc.cuny.edu
RAMER, Rod 360-442-2207 495 G
rramer@lowercolumbia.edu
RAMES, Marysz 402-375-7200 276 D
marames1@wsc.edu
RAMET, Carlos 989-964-4062 236 F
ramet@svsu.edu
RAMEY, JR., Alfred, E 201-200-2039 287 F
aramey@njcu.edu
RAMEY, Rob 336-334-4822 343 E
grramey@gtcc.edu
RAMEY, Teresa 843-661-1182 421 H
tramey@fmarion.edu
RAMEZANE, Marsha 650-574-6413 62 A
ramezanem@smccd.edu
RAMGOLAM, Geoffrey 954-745-6960 93 B
RAMI, Janet 225-771-3266 195 K
janet_rami@subr.edu
RAMICONE, Arthur, G 412-624-6576 412 I
aramicone@cfo.pitt.edu
RAMIG, JR., Steven, M 608-342-3961 511 D
ramigs@uwplatt.edu
RAMIN, Daniel 315-470-4933 328 D
dwramin@esf.edu
RAMIREZ, Alfred 818-240-1000 44 D
aramirez@glendale.edu
RAMIREZ, Amador 361-354-2554 445 S
aramirez@coastalbend.edu
RAMIREZ, Amy 410-706-7488 207 H
aramirez@umaryland.edu
RAMIREZ, Arnold 979-230-3235 444 E
arnold.ramirez@brazosport.edu
RAMIREZ, Arturo 309-438-5590 140 L
aramir@ilstu.edu
RAMIREZ, Aurelio 617-879-7847 218 B
aramirez@massart.edu
RAMIREZ, Cecilia 757-825-3525 489 G
ramirezc@tncc.edu
RAMIREZ, Daniel 956-872-2580 456 G
dramirez@southtexascollege.edu
RAMIREZ, David 610-328-8175 410 I
dramire1@swarthmore.edu
RAMIREZ, Desiree 404-756-8919 123 F
dramirez@msm.edu
RAMIREZ, Fausto 718-960-8593 302 C
fausto.ramirez@lehman.cuny.edu
RAMIREZ, Freddy 760-757-2121 52 F
framirez@miracosta.edu
RAMIREZ, Irving 347-964-8600 299 L
iramirez@boricuacollege.edu
RAMIREZ, Jason 435-586-7700 473 A
jasonramirez@suu.edu
RAMIREZ, Jessica 816-604-1411 262 F
jessica.ramirez@mcckc.edu
RAMIREZ, Jonathan 858-499-0202 39 B
jramirez@coleman.edu
RAMIREZ, Jose 787-620-2040 520 F
jramirez@aupr.edu
RAMIREZ, Jose, L 915-831-2634 449 A
jramir20@epcc.edu
RAMIREZ, Juan 909-469-5622 74 G
jramirez@westernu.edu
RAMIREZ, Judith 787-832-4040 528 C
judith.ramirez1@upr.edu
RAMIREZ, Kathy 406-447-5185 270 H
kramirez@carroll.edu
RAMIREZ, Laura 562-908-3402 58 D
lramirez@riohondo.edu
RAMIREZ, Laura, M 323-265-8641 48 L
ramirelm@elac.edu
RAMIREZ, Loida, R 787-704-1020 522 J
lramirez@ediccollege.edu
RAMIREZ, Marcela, V 210-458-6144 468 B
marcela.ramirez@utsa.edu
RAMIREZ, Mayra, I 787-723-4481 521 H
mramirez@ceaprc.edu
RAMIREZ, Miguel 305-899-3647 95 G
maramirez@barry.edu
RAMIREZ, Minita 956-326-2278 459 B
minita@tamiu.edu
RAMIREZ, Octavio 256-726-7340 6 E
oramirez@oakwood.edu
RAMIREZ, Rhonda 510-869-6511 59 F
rramirez@samuelmerritt.edu
RAMIREZ, Rosemary 520-494-5471 11 P
rosemary.ramirez@centralaz.edu
RAMIREZ, Sam 361-825-5826 460 A
samuel.ramirez@tamucc.edu
RAMIREZ, Sam 440-826-2908 357 B
sramirez@bw.edu
RAMIREZ, Sylvia 787-832-6000 522 Q
RAMIREZ, Sylvia 608-243-4587 514 A
sframirez@madisoncollege.edu
RAMIREZ, Wilmer 303-783-3137 79 G
wilmer.ramirez@denverseminary.edu
RAMIREZ, Xenia 787-265-3813 528 C
registro@uprm.edu
RAMIREZ-CARLO, III,
Bolivar 787-620-2040 520 F
bramirez@aupr.edu
RAMIREZ-FIGUEROA,
Jose 787-620-2040 520 F
jramirez@aupr.edu
RAMIREZ-GELPI, Sofia 805-922-6966 24 J
sgelpi@hancockcollege.edu
RAMIREZ-JASSO, Diana 617-262-5000 212 C
diana.ramirez-jasso@the-bac.edu
RAMIREZ-PEREZ,
Felicia 602-285-7422 14 A
felicia.a.ramirez-perez@phoenixcollege.edu
RAMIREZ-RIVERA,
Rafael 787-878-5475 523 H
rramirez@arecibo.inter.edu
RAMIU, Lizette 787-758-2525 528 D
lizette.ramiu.gonzalez@upr.edu
RAMKARAN, Arshaw 212-650-5824 301 F
aramkaran@ccny.cuny.edu
RAMKUMAR,
S. Manian 585-475-5955 321 D
smrmet@rit.edu
RAMLER, Tom 903-434-8175 453 M
tramler@ntcc.edu
RAMLETH, T. Geir 650-543-3744 51 F
bot@menlo.edu
RAMM, Jennifer 254-295-5527 466 A
jramm@umhb.edu
RAMMING, Ron 918-463-2931 375 G
rronald@connorsstate.edu
RAMON, Deanna Rene 580-349-1556 377 E
rene.ramon@opsu.edu
RAMON, Ralph 325-574-7625 470 N
rramon@wtc.edu
RAMONAS, Denise 410-778-2800 210 A
dramonas2@washcoll.edu
RAMONE, Patricia, A 302-295-1140 91 B
patricia.a.ramone@wilmu.edu
RAMONES, Eric 408-848-4753 44 B
eramones@gavilan.edu
RAMONT, John 760-346-8041 39 D
jramont@collegeofthedesert.edu
RAMOS, Amy 805-898-4018 43 A
aramos@fielding.edu
RAMOS, Angela 787-725-6500 521 C
aramos@albizu.edu
RAMOS, Anita 559-297-4500 46 E
RAMOS, Anthony 210-805-1201 465 E
aramos@uiwtx.edu
RAMOS, Antonio 787-284-1912 524 C
aramos@ponce.inter.edu
RAMOS, Charlene 248-204-2330 233 A
cramos@ltu.edu
RAMOS, Chelsea 718-289-5153 301 D
chelsea.ayala@bcc.cuny.edu
RAMOS, Cynthia 602-285-7404 14 A
cynthia.ramos@phoenixcollege.edu
RAMOS, Daisy 787-738-2161 528 A
daisy.ramos@upr.edu
RAMOS, David, L 787-834-9595 526 E
dramos@uaa.edu
RAMOS, Derek 620-276-9559 177 G
derek.ramos@gcccks.edu
RAMOS, Dinorah 352-638-9708 95 H
dramos@beaconcollege.edu
RAMOS, Edwin 787-815-0000 527 F
edwin.ramos7@upr.edu
RAMOS, Gladys 787-738-2161 528 A
gladys.ramos@upr.edu
RAMOS, Idalmy 787-264-1912 524 D
iramos@intersg.edu
RAMOS, Irma 714-808-4810 53 L
iramos@nocccd.edu
RAMOS, Ismael 787-738-2161 528 A
ismael.ramos1@upr.edu
RAMOS, Jennifer 212-228-1888 320 L
RAMOS, Josue 787-878-5475 523 H
jramos@arecibo.inter.edu

RAMOS, Kenneth 520-626-1197 16 J
ksramos@email.arizona.edu
RAMOS, Lorna 787-753-6000 522 Q
RAMOS, Maria 903-886-5091 459 E
maria.ramos@tamuc.edu
RAMOS, Maria, A 787-863-2390 523 K
maria.ramos@fajardo.inter.edu
RAMOS, Nancy, L 401-254-3455 417 C
nramos@rwu.edu
RAMOS, Patricia 310-434-3311 62 G
ramos_patricia@smc.edu
RAMOS, Patricia, A 718-289-5896 301 D
patricia.ramos@bcc.cuny.edu
RAMOS, Remigio 406-656-9950 273 D
RAMOS, Richard, O 515-961-1536 173 E
rich.ramos@simpson.edu
RAMOS, Ronald 470-578-3013 122 C
rramos@kennesaw.edu
RAMOS, Sofia 520-206-7215 15 L
sramos20@pima.edu
RAMOS, Vickie 561-912-2166 98 F
RAMOS, Victor, E 717-358-2975 396 G
veramos@hacc.edu
RAMOS, Yolanda 432-685-4733 453 B
yramos@midland.edu
RAMOS MARTÍNEZ,
Diana, N 787-884-3838 520 G
profdg5@atenascollege.edu
RAMOS-WALKER,
Kristine 952-995-1406 244 G
kristine.ramoswalker@hennepintech.edu
RAMOSKA, John 518-861-2519 314 B
jramoska@mariacollege.edu
RAMPAUL, Andre 212-757-1190 298 D
arampaul@funeraleducation.org
RAMPERSAD, Dave 334-386-7100 5 I
drampersad@faulkner.edu
RAMPINO, Tatiana 203-576-5990 88 D
trampino@stvincentscollege.edu
RAMPP, Carrie 717-358-4161 395 G
carrie.rampp@fandm.edu
RAMS, Richard 714-484-7355 53 M
rrams@cypresscollege.edu
RAMS, Richard 714-484-7374 53 M
rrams@cypresscollege.edu
RAMSAMMY, Jillian 352-854-2322 97 C
jillian.ramsammy@cf.edu
RAMSARAN, Dave 570-372-4757 410 H
ramsaran@susqu.edu
RAMSAY, Darlene 573-341-4584 269 A
ramsayd@mst.edu
RAMSAY, John R, C 434-223-7154 481 D
jramsay@hsc.edu
RAMSAY, Kerr, C 336-841-9148 338 E
kramsay@highpoint.edu
RAMSAY, Kimberly 310-377-5501 51 B
kramsay@marymountcalifornia.edu
RAMSAY, Tim 616-632-2076 227 C
ramsatim@aquinas.edu
RAMSDELL, Nancy, M 508-929-8605 219 A
nramsdell@worcester.edu
RAMSDELL, Twyla 651-213-4180 242 F
tramsdell@hazeldenbettyford.edu
RAMSDEN-MEIER,
Joanna 319-226-2004 166 C
joanna.ramsden-meier@allencollege.edu
RAMSEY, Gerald 619-388-7810 60 E
gramsey@sdccd.edu
RAMSEY, Jason, M 814-332-2761 388 F
jramsey@allegheny.edu
RAMSEY, Julie 865-981-8246 433 F
julie.ramsey@maryvillecollege.edu
RAMSEY, Julie, L 717-337-6921 396 A
ramsey@gettysburg.edu
RAMSEY, Katie 503-517-7904 386 F
kramsey@reed.edu
RAMSEY, Kim 318-797-5234 194 E
kim.ramsey@lsus.edu
RAMSEY, Kimberly 310-377-5501 51 B
kramsey@marymountcalifornia.edu
RAMSEY, Kyle, H 630-515-6165 145 I
kramse@midwestern.edu
RAMSEY, Mae 540-362-6519 481 F
mramsey@hollins.edu
RAMSEY, Marleen 509-527-4289 499 E
marleen.ramsey@wwcc.edu
RAMSEY, Marty 828-227-7335 352 C
mramsey@wcu.edu
RAMSEY, Matthew 913-360-7387 175 D
mramsey@benedictine.edu
RAMSEY, Nancy, A 865-694-6526 437 F
naramsey@pstcc.edu
RAMSEY, Patricia 484-365-7436 400 E
RAMSEY, Paul, G 206-543-7718 499 D
pramsey@uw.edu
RAMSEY, Richard 207-454-1067 200 D
rramsey@wccc.me.edu
RAMSEY, Ruth 415-257-1393 41 J
ruth.ramsey@dominican.edu
RAMSEY, Vickie 530-251-8852 47 J
vramsey@lassencollege.edu
RAMSEY, Vincent 251-626-3303 7 G
vramsey@ussa.edu
RAMSEY-HAMACHER,
Paige 352-588-8489 106 N
paige.ramsey.hamacher@saintleo.edu
RAMSEYER, Larry, E 989-686-9234 229 J
larryramseyer@delta.edu
RAMSEYER, Rob 620-327-8279 178 B
rob.ramseyer@hesston.edu
RAMSIER, Rex 330-972-7593 371 C
provost@uakron.edu
RAMSOWER,
Reagan, M 254-710-3554 444 B
reagan_ramsower@baylor.edu
RAMÍREZ, Manuel 787-884-3838 520 G
asisteco@atenascollege.edu
RANA, Anniqua 650-306-3470 61 R
rana@smccd.edu
RANABARGAR,
Kerry, D 620-431-2820 180 C
kranabargar@neosho.edu
RANADIVE, Sunita 510-780-4500 48 D
RANALDI, Diane 413-565-1000 211 C
dranaldi@baypath.edu
RANALLI, Carlee, K 814-641-3103 398 B
ranallc@juniata.edu
RANALLI, Robert 518-464-8533 308 A
rranalli@excelsior.edu
RANCATI, Chrisanne 704-355-6676 336 F
chrisanne.rancati@carolinascollege.edu
RANCE, DeLonn, L 417-268-1000 257 F
ranced@evangel.edu
RANCE-RONEY, Judith 610-282-1100 393 G
judith.rance-roney@desales.edu
RANCK, Lorrie 408-864-8489 43 E
rancklorrie@deanza.edu
RANCOURT, Fran 603-752-1113 281 B
francourt@ccsnh.edu
RAND, Amy 417-455-5533 259 D
amyrand@crowder.edu
RAND, Benjamin 817-515-5034 458 B
benjamin.rand@tccd.edu
RAND, Jonathan 617-879-7263 218 B
jrand@massart.edu
RAND, Kathryn 701-777-2104 353 G
rand@law.und.edu
RAND, Paul, M 773-702-1234 153 F
RANDALL, David 617-253-4861 221 C
RANDALL, Greg 253-566-5207 499 A
grandall@tacomacc.edu
RANDALL, Jessica 570-674-6340 401 M
jrandall@misericordia.edu
RANDALL, John 949-214-3358 40 I
john.randall@cui.edu
RANDALL, Kim 617-353-9286 212 G
krandall@bu.edu
RANDALL, Meridith 909-652-6131 36 E
meridith.randall@chaffey.edu
RANDALL, Mike 618-468-3130 143 D
mrandall@lc.edu
RANDALL, Monte 918-549-2806 375 E
mrandall@cmn.edu
RANDALL, Nancy 704-233-8065 353 D
nrandall@wingate.edu
RANDALL, Regina 614-287-5343 360 C
rrandal2@cscc.edu
RANDALL, Robin 508-286-8232 225 G
randall_robin@wheatoncollege.edu
RANDALL, Stacey 630-466-7900 155 C
srandall@waubonsee.edu
RANDALL, Taylor 801-587-3869 472 P
taylor.randall@eccles.utah.edu
RANDALL, William, H 315-733-2307 332 F
wrandall@uscny.edu
RANDALL-LEE,
Valerie, J 410-677-0022 209 B
vjrandall-lee@salisbury.edu
RANDAZZA, Paula 603-897-8303 281 I
prandazza@rivier.edu
RANDAZZO, Lisa 718-489-5336 322 D
lrandazzo@sfc.edu
RANDAZZO, Maria 315-445-4195 312 F
randazmc@lemoyne.edu
RANDAZZO, Nino 312-935-4000 149 K
nrandazzo@robertmorris.edu
RANDHAWA, Sabah 360-650-3480 500 E
president@wwu.edu
RANDLE, Benjamin 716-829-7836 307 B
randleb@dyc.edu
RANDLE, John 231-591-2892 230 A
johnrandle@ferris.edu
RANDLE, Jonathan 601-925-3849 254 B
randle@mc.edu
RANDLES,
Christopher, M 217-351-2513 148 H
crandles@parkland.edu
RANDLES, Jill, A 559-323-2100 61 A
jrandles@sjcl.edu
RANDO, Robert, A 937-775-3409 374 B
robert.rando@wright.edu
RANDOLPH, A.J 817-735-2336 466 D
a.j.randolph@unthsc.edu
RANDOLPH, Adrian 847-491-3276 148 C
weinberg-dean@northwestern.edu
RANDOLPH, Brennan 812-535-1152 163 I
brennan.randolph@smwc.edu
RANDOLPH, Devin, L 803-535-5301 419 E
devin.randolph@claflin.edu
RANDOLPH, Trent 256-331-5260 3 C
trentrandolph@nwscc.edu
RANDOLPH, William 937-376-6575 358 I
wrandolph@centralstate.edu
RANDOO, Jason, J 434-528-5276 491 D
jrandoo@vul.edu
RANDORF, Lori 330-672-5368 363 I
lrandorf@kent.edu
RANDY GREEN,
Jonathan 937-327-7321 374 A
jgreen@wittenberg.edu
RANE-SZOSTAK, Donna 949-582-4324 64 J
draneszostak@saddleback.edu
RANERO-RAMIREZ,
Jessica 910-938-6341 342 C
ranero-ramirezj@coastalcarolina.edu
RANES, Rodney 618-395-7777 140 E
ranesr@iecc.edu
RANES, Shannon, T 727-376-6911 112 G
shannon.ranes@trinitycollege.edu
RANESES, Jade 808-853-1040 129 F
jaderaneses@pacrim.edu
RANEY, Jonna, G 405-585-5020 377 A
jonna.raney@okbu.edu
RANEY, Kristen 651-846-1514 247 G
kristen.raney@saintpaul.edu
RANFT, Annette 919-515-5560 350 E
alranft@ncsu.edu
RANGE, Ronald 205-391-2644 3 E
rrange@sheltonstate.edu
RANGEL, Andrea 806-716-2370 456 F
arangel@southplainscollege.edu
RANGUETTE, Renea, L 608-757-7700 513 D
rranguette@blackhawk.edu
RANHEIM, John 314-434-4044 259 B
john.ranheim@covenantseminary.edu
RANIERI, Tracey, M 607-436-2446 325 E
tracey.ranieri@oneonta.edu
RANJEL, Mary 210-924-4338 443 N
mary.ranjel@bua.edu
RANK, Carin 413-559-5385 215 F
RANK, Mark 717-815-1218 415 G
mrank@ycp.edu
RANKIN, Donna 479-968-0394 18 G
drankin@atu.edu
RANKIN, James, M 479-575-2470 21 I
rankinj@uark.edu
RANKIN, Joni 620-229-6232 181 F
joni.rankin@sckans.edu
RANKIN, Mary Ann 301-405-5252 207 G
mrankin@umd.edu
RANKIN, Mona, G 516-876-3160 327 C
rankinm@oldwestbury.edu
RANKIN, Monika 352-638-9701 95 H
mrankin@beaconcollege.edu
RANKIN, Stephanie, A 717-361-1569 394 F
rankins@etown.edu
RANKIN, Stephen 214-768-4502 457 B
rankins@smu.edu
RANKIN, Tabitha 903-923-2455 471 B
tmrankin@wileyc.edu
RANKINE, Patrice, D 804-289-8416 486 G
prankine@richmond.edu
RANKINS, JR., Alfred 601-877-6111 251 G
arankins@alcorn.edu
RANSDELL, Junell, A 217-786-4506 144 B
junell.ransdell@llcc.edu
RANSDELL, Lynda 928-523-2671 14 K
lynda.ransdell@nau.edu
RANSLEM, Bradley 402-844-7717 276 G
bradleyr@northeast.edu
RANSOM, Glenda 662-254-3592 255 A
gran@mvsu.edu
RANSOM, Kimberly 304-793-6820 504 F
kransom@osteo.wvsom.edu
RANSOM, Lakeesha, K 330-972-5365 371 C
ransom@uakron.edu
RANSON, Julie 804-706-5064 488 D
jranson@jtcc.edu
RANTZ, Rick 805-922-6966 24 J
rrantz@hancockcollege.edu
RANUM, Brenda 563-387-1025 171 I
ranubr01@luther.edu
RAO, Julie, M 585-245-5553 327 B
rao@geneseo.edu
RAO, Michael 804-828-1200 487 E
president@vcu.edu
RAPACCIOLI, Donna 718-817-4100 308 G
rapaccioli@fordham.edu
RAPACZ, Deb 773-298-3326 151 C
drapacz@sxu.edu
RAPALA, Elise 708-456-0300 153 E
eliserapala@triton.edu
RAPAPORT, Ross, J 989-774-3381 228 E
rapap1rj@cmich.edu
RAPE, Bruce, M 217-443-8786 137 B
brape@dacc.edu
RAPELYE, Janet, L 609-258-6150 288 F
jrapelye@princeton.edu
RAPER, Bridgette 423-746-5301 439 A
braper@tnwesleyan.edu
RAPER, Lorraine 252-399-6505 335 I
lhraper@barton.edu
RAPESS, Paul 516-299-2214 313 D
paul.rapess@liu.edu
RAPETTI, Mario 914-251-6320 328 B
mario.rapetti@purchase.edu
RAPHAEL, Joann 561-904-3000 93 B
RAPHAEL, Valencia 562-860-2451 36 A
vraphael@cerritos.edu
RAPHEL, Colette 504-314-2855 196 D
craphel@tulane.edu
RAPOPORT, Nancy, B 702-895-5895 279 D
nancy.rapoport@unlv.edu
RAPOZA, Kalei 808-932-7626 129 I
kaleihii@hawaii.edu
RAPOZA, Kalei 808-932-7650 129 I
kaleihii@hawaii.edu
RAPOZA, Mark, F 401-865-2064 416 E
mrapoza@providence.edu
RAPP, Kelly, E 417-836-5636 263 H
jillwiggins@missouristate.edu
RAPP, Norman 615-329-8848 431 I
nrapp@fisk.edu
RAPP, Peter 503-494-8744 385 D
hutching@ohsu.edu
RAPP, Ryan 573-882-2011 268 B
RAPP, Timothy 301-295-4231 518 G
timothy.rapp@usuhs.edu
RAPP, Tracy 828-627-4509 343 G
tkrapp@haywood.edu
RAPP, Virginia 310-660-3773 42 C
vrapp@elcamino.edu
RAPPE, Sylvia 936-294-3188 462 F
str017@shsu.edu
RAPPEL, Kevin 630-829-6404 133 I
krappel@ben.edu
RAPPLEY, Marsha 804-828-0100 487 E
mdrappley@vcu.edu
RARIG, Jenny 215-641-6688 402 A
jrarig@mc3.edu
RARIG, Kris 757-825-3810 489 G
rarigk@tncc.edu
RASBAND, James, R 801-422-6201 471 E
james_rasband@byu.edu
RASBERRY, Charles 516-299-2784 313 C
charles.rasberry@liu.edu
RASBERRY, Todd 502-863-8044 184 I
rasberry@georgetowncollege.edu
RASCH, Mike 218-751-8670 249 G
mikerasch@oakhills.edu
RASCH, Randolph 517-355-6527 233 G
randolph.rasch@hc.msu.edu
RASCOE, Fred 931-668-7010 437 C
frascoe@mscc.edu
RASCON, Chris 510-436-1000 45 G
RASCON, Tricia 805-893-4275 70 B
tricia.rascon@sa.ucsb.edu
RASH, Brian 225-214-6976 191 G
brian.rash@ololcollege.edu
RASH, R. Scott 814-871-7464 395 H
rash001@gannon.edu
RASHED, David 864-231-2000 418 E
orashed@andersonuniversity.edu
RASHID, Frank, D 313-927-1205 233 D
frashid@marygrove.edu
RASHID, John 218-726-8821 250 F
jrashid@d.umn.edu
RASHID, Khadijat 202-651-5224 91 H
khadijat.rashid@gllaudet.edu
RASK, Kevin 719-389-6446 77 J
kevin.rask@coloradocollege.edu
RASKIND, Wayne 313-577-2519 239 C
raskind@wayne.edu
RASKOVICH, Linda 218-262-7370 244 H
lindaraskovich@hibbing.edu
RASMUSSEN, Allen 361-593-2809 460 B
allen.rasmussen@tamuk.edu
RASMUSSEN, Brock 612-874-3749 243 F
brock_rasmussen@mcad.edu

READ, Carole .... 757-789-1733 488 A
cread@es.vccs.edu
READ, Deborah .... 727-873-4397 111 B
read@mail.usf.edu
READ, Katie .... 540-362-6765 481 F
readkc@hollins.edu
READ, Melissa .... 508-541-1654 214 C
mread@dean.edu
READ, Steven .... 412-518-4504 125 H
sread@southuniversity.edu
READER, Rhonda .... 315-470-7932 299 K
rhondareader@crouse.org
READEY, Mary, L .... 614-292-0257 367 H
readey.3@osu.edu
READNOUR, Warren ...... 501-450-5007.. 23 I
wreadnour@uca.edu
READY, Deana .... 573-592-4236 270 D
deana.ready@williamwoods.edu
REAGAN, J. Michael, E . 979-845-8058 459 C
policechief@tamu.edu
REAGAN, Kate, M .... 423-869-6389 433 C
kate.reagan@lmunet.edu
REAGAN, Krystal .... 618-985-2828 141 D
krystalreagan@jalc.edu
REAGAN, Margy .... 202-884-9707.. 93 C
reaganm@trinitydc.edu
REAGAN, Melinda .... 972-279-6511 442 E
mreagan@amberton.edu
REAGAN, Thomas .... 775-753-2266 279 A
thomas.reagan@gbcnv.edu
REAGAN, Timothy, G .... 207-581-2441 201 B
timothy.reagan@maine.edu
REAGEN, Nate .... 515-271-2949 168 J
nate.reagen@drake.edu
REAGIN, Cam .... 803-641-3399 425 A
camr@usca.edu
REAGINS-LILLY,
Soncia, R .... 512-471-5017 467 C
soncia.r.lilly@austin.utexas.edu
REAGLE, Mike .... 270-745-2037 190 F
mike.reagle@wku.edu
REAL, Yannick .... 562-860-2451.. 36 A
yreal@cerritos.edu
REALISTA, Katy .... 714-484-7142.. 53 M
krealista@cypresscollege.edu
REALIVASQUEZ,
Yvonne .... 432-837-8032 462 G
yrealivasquez@sulross.edu
REAM, Dan .... 804-333-6716 489 D
dream@rappahannock.edu
REAM, Debbie .... 213-477-2505.. 52 H
dream@msmu.edu
REAM, Tim .... 323-242-5536.. 49 E
reamtr@lasc.edu
REAMER, Amy .... 910-962-4075 352 A
reamera@uncw.edu
REAMES, Stephen, A ..... 340-693-1301 529 C
stephen.reames@uvi.edu
REAMS, Amelia .... 229-219-3198 127 H
alharmon@valdosta.edu
REAMS, John .... 706-233-7247 125 E
jreams@shorter.edu
REAMY, Brian .... 301-295-9942 518 G
brian.reamy@usuhs.edu
REARDON, Cheryl .... 319-335-0056 166 G
cheryl-reardon@uiowa.edu
REARDON, Colleen .... 708-524-6643 137 F
creardon@dom.edu
REARDON, Diana .... 803-774-3354 419 A
reardondl@cctech.edu
REARDON, Douglas .... 410-951-3441 208 F
dreardon@coppin.edu
REARDON, Emily .... 508-213-2275 223 C
emily.reardon@nichols.edu
REARDON, Penny .... 304-434-8000 502 L
penny.reardon@easternwv.edu
REARDON, Penny, E ..... 540-828-5395 478 J
preardon@bridgewater.edu
REARDON, Richard .... 802-468-1234 477 A
richard.reardon@castleton.edu
REARDON, Tim .... 802-485-2001 475 I
reardont@norwich.edu
REARDON, Timothy .... 440-646-8301 373 B
treardon@ursuline.edu
REARIC, Sue .... 619-644-7575.. 44 K
sue.rearic@gcccd.edu
REASH, Brenda .... 252-222-6262 341 F
reashb@carteret.edu
REASNER, Brett, A .... 570-326-3761 404 T
breasner@pct.edu
REASONER, Carroll .... 319-335-2841 166 G
carroll-reasoner@uiowa.edu
REASSO, Bob .... 704-463-3203 348 B
bob.reasso@pfeiffer.edu
REAT, Daniel, J .... 713-500-3278 468 D
daniel.j.reat@uth.tmc.edu
REAUME, Vicki .... 734-487-2410 229 K
vreaume@emich.edu

REAVES, Ken .... 678-872-8512 119 G
kreaves@highlands.edu
REAVES, Nicole .... 773-481-8182 136 B
nreaves2@ccc.edu
REAVES, Rita .... 252-328-1418 349 I
reavesr@ecu.edu
REAVIS, Bob .... 785-654-2416 174 G
breavis@allencc.edu
REBA, Kathleen .... 516-323-3952 315 J
kreba@molloy.edu
REBAR, Alan .... 919-515-2117 350 E
ahrebar@ncsu.edu
REBER, Christopher, M . 724-480-3400 392 K
chris.reber@ccbc.edu
REBETA, Gail .... 330-672-3367 363 I
grebeta@kent.edu
REBHORN, Dale .... 317-738-8251 157 L
drebhorn@franklincollege.edu
REBIK, Clint .... 707-826-6205.. 34 A
clint@humboldt.edu
REBMAN, Brenda .... 530-752-3136.. 68 H
rebman@ucdavis.edu
REBOLI, Annette .... 856-361-2800 289 H
reboli@rowan.edu
REBRO, Jan .... 206-239-4500 493 D
jrebro@cityu.edu
REBURN, Tom .... 218-477-2549 246 B
tom.reburn@mnstate.edu
RECA, Michael, F .... 609-896-5080 289 E
reca@rider.edu
RECALDE, Tina .... 619-388-2789.. 60 D
trecalde@sdccd.edu
RECCHIA, Karen .... 318-678-6000 192 C
krecchia@bpcc.edu
RECH, Tara .... 510-594-3670.. 28 K
trech@cca.edu
RECHTSCHAFFEN,
Joyce, A .... 202-220-1364 288 F
jrechtsc@princeton.edu
RECINOS, Alba .... 714-808-4796.. 53 L
arecinos@nocccd.edu
RECINOS, Diane .... 973-278-5400 283 J
dr@berkeleycollege.edu
RECINOS, Diane .... 973-278-5400 299 F
dr@berkeleycollege.edu
RECKER, Edward .... 419-434-4791 372 B
reckere1@findlay.edu
RECKER, Mary, A .... 937-229-4354 372 A
mpoirier1@udayton.edu
RECKNER, Angela, T ...... 215-489-2203 393 F
angela.reckner@delval.edu
RECKTENWALD, Kay ...... 561-297-0026 109 B
kreckten@fau.edu
RECLA, Leanne, R .... 610-799-1718 400 A
lrecla@lccc.edu
RECORD, James .... 847-578-3000 150 E
james.record@rosalindfranklin.edu
RECORD, Kim .... 336-334-5952 351 D
ksrecord@uncg.edu
RECORD, Victoria .... 315-787-4005 308 E
vicki.record@flhealth.org
RECTOR, Brenda .... 865-354-3000 438 A
rectorbw@roanestate.edu
RECTOR, David .... 660-785-7607 267 K
daverec@truman.edu
RECTOR, Dawn .... 480-858-9100.. 16 D
d.rector@scnm.edu
RECTOR, Lallene, J .... 847-866-3901 138 G
ljr@garrett.edu
RECTOR, Larry .... 606-539-4219 190 A
larry.rector@ucumberlands.edu
RECTOR, Rob .... 417-447-4852 264 K
rectorr@otc.edu
RECZNIK, Joel, S .... 740-284-5236 361 L
jrecznik@franciscan.edu
RECZNIK, John .... 740-283-6497 361 L
jlrecznik@franciscan.edu
RECZNIK, Mark, E .... 740-284-5845 361 L
mrecznik@franciscan.edu
RED BEAR, Donnette ..... 605-698-3966 428 C
dredbear@swc.tc
RED OWL, Sherry .... 605-856-5880 428 A
sherry.redowl@sintegleska.edu
REDA, Eva .... 614-882-2551 361 K
ereda@fortiscollege.edu
REDCEDER, Jason .... 503-226-4391 385 H
jredceder@pnca.edu
REDD, Annie .... 804-524-5070 491 A
aredd@vsu.edu
REDD, Cliff .... 713-743-4921 465 A
rbredd@central.uh.edu
REDD, Randy .... 901-751-8453 434 E
rredd@mabts.edu
REDD, Rea .... 724-852-3254 414 B
rredd@waynesburg.edu
REDD, Scott .... 703-448-3393 255 E
sredd@rts.edu

REDDAY, Darlene .... 605-698-3966 428 C
dredday@swc.tc
REDDER, Vince .... 605-995-2631 427 A
viredder@dwu.edu
REDDERSON, Jeff, P ..... 864-294-3262 421 I
jeff.redderson@furman.edu
REDDI, Lakshmi .... 575-646-2914 295 B
lnr@nmsu.edu
REDDICK, Chenita, R .... 410-651-8045 208 C
crreddick@umes.edu
REDDICK, Don .... 815-939-5111 148 F
dreddick@olivet.edu
REDDICK, Frances .... 419-289-5165 356 L
freddick@ashland.edu
REDDICK, Laura, S .... 215-468-8387 411 B
laura.reddick@temple.edu
REDDICK, Rinardo .... 262-691-5295 515 B
rreddick@wctc.edu
REDDING, Michael .... 312-996-8153 153 H
reddingm@uic.edu
REDDING, Richard .... 714-628-2688.. 36 G
redding@chapman.edu
REDDING, Vic .... 775-784-4901 278 M
vic_redding@nshe.nevada.edu
REDDINGTON, Cynthia . 757-240-2229 484 G
cynthia.reddington@rivhs.com
REDDINGTON, Kathleen 575-527-7718 295 E
kredding@nmsu.edu
REDDITT, Megan .... 502-863-8066 184 I
megan_redditt@georgetowncollege.edu
REDDY, Chandra .... 615-963-7561 438 E
creddy@tnstate.edu
REDDY, Indra, K .... 979-458-7200 459 C
indrakreddy@tamu.edu
REDDY, Kirti .... 510-723-6641.. 36 C
kreddy@chabotcollege.edu
REDDY, Michael, S .... 205-934-4720.... 8 B
mreddy@uab.edu
REDDY, Narem .... 678-466-4100 117 I
naremreddy@clayton.edu
REDDY, JR., Robert, A . 440-775-8142 367 B
rob.reddy@oberlin.edu
REDDY, Venkat .... 719-255-3436.. 83 C
chancellor@uccs.edu
REDELL, Rebecca .... 541-440-4636 387 E
rebecca.redell@umpqua.edu
REDER-SCHOPP, Megan 605-394-6988 429 A
megan.reder-schopp@sdsmt.edu
REDFERN, Mark, S .... 412-624-9019 412 I
mredfern@pitt.edu
REDFERN, Paul, W .... 717-337-6829 396 A
predfern@gettysburg.edu
REDFIELD, Chaunta .... 765-641-4182 156 A
cdredfield@anderson.edu
REDFIELD, Vanessa .... 802-258-9244 475 D
vredfield@marlboro.edu
REDIGER-SCHULTE,
Leah .... 402-826-8111 274 E
leah.redigerschulte@doane.edu
REDING, Cheryl .... 913-360-7384 175 D
creding@benedictine.edu
REDING, Nichole .... 503-760-3131 381 J
nichole@birthingway.edu
REDING, Roger .... 806-894-9611 456 F
rreding@southplainscollege.edu
REDING, Terrence .... 585-345-6850 309 C
tareding@genesee.edu
REDINGER, Matthew ..... 406-657-2204 272 B
mredinger@msubillings.edu
REDINGTON, Joseph ..... 570-674-6756 401 M
jredingt@misericordia.edu
REDINGTON, Lyn .... 319-335-1162 166 G
lyn-redington@uiowa.edu
REDLEAF, Betty .... 402-878-2380 275 C
bredleaf@littlepriest.edu
REDLER, Susan .... 212-431-2121 317 H
susan.redler@nyls.edu
REDLINGER,
Lawrence, J .... 972-883-6188 467 D
redling@utdallas.edu
REDMAN, Cynthia .... 773-256-3000 145 D
credman@meadville.edu
REDMAN, Donald, L ..... 717-334-6286 412 E
dredman@ltsg.edu
REDMAN, Martin .... 215-898-3131 412 G
mredman@upenn.edu
REDMAN, JR.,
Robert, R .... 912-650-5649 125 H
roredman@southuniversity.edu
REDMAN, Sally .... 215-596-8800 413 E
REDMAN, Thomas, J .... 978-232-2005 214 G
tredman@endicott.edu
REDMANN, Trent .... 612-343-4749 249 E
tjredman@northcentral.edu
REDMON, Kelly .... 540-869-0758 488 E
kredmon@lfcc.edu
REDMOND, Angie .... 641-844-5712 170 I
angie.redmond@iavalley.edu

REDMOND, Jeff .... 805-267-1690.. 48 B
REDMOND, Katrina .... 845-848-4034 306 G
katrina.redmond@dc.edu
REDMOND, Michael ...... 201-447-7237 283 I
presidentsoffice@bergen.edu
REDMOND, Michael, J .. 303-458-4995.. 82 D
mredmond@regis.edu
REDMOND, Rodney .... 240-567-5030 205 F
rodney.redmond@montgomerycollege.edu
REDMOND, Thomas, E . 202-274-5935.. 93 D
tredmond@udc.edu
REDMOND, Tim .... 805-267-1690.. 48 B
REDONNETT, Rosa .... 207-973-3231 201 A
rosar@maine.edu
REDSTONE, Joy .... 303-546-3570.. 81 B
jredstone@naropa.edu
REDWINE, Marian .... 405-491-6336 379 K
maredwin@snu.edu
REDWINE, Mike .... 405-491-6335 379 K
mredwine@snu.edu
REDWINE, William .... 606-783-2680 188 C
b.redwine@moreheadstate.edu
REECE, Anton .... 270-534-3082 187 C
anton.reece@kctcs.edu
REECE, Bryan .... 951-372-7015.. 58 E
bryan.reece@norcocollege.edu
REECE, Bryan .... 951-372-7016.. 58 G
bryan.reece@norcocollege.edu
REECE, E. Albert .... 410-706-7410 207 H
deanmed@som.umaryland.edu
REECE, Jeremy .... 870-733-6786.. 18 B
jreece@asumidsouth.edu
REECE, Jonathan .... 910-962-3122 352 A
reecej@uncw.edu
REECE, Lenora .... 214-860-2015 448 A
lenora.reece@dcccd.edu
REECE, Ronda .... 405-945-8631 378 C
reecer@osuokc.edu
REECE, Sheila .... 903-785-7661 454 F
sreece@parisjc.edu
REECE, Terry .... 805-546-3283.. 41 C
treece@cuesta.edu
REECE, Victoria .... 352-588-8668 106 N
victoria.reece@saintleo.edu
REECK, Joanne .... 612-330-1111 240 G
reeck@augsburg.edu
REED, Aaron .... 801-302-2800 472 A
aaron.reed@neumont.edu
REED, Adrienne .... 618-468-6030 143 D
ayreed@lc.edu
REED, Alicia .... 701-627-4738 355 D
REED, Ann, M .... 304-462-6123 504 B
ann.reed@glenville.edu
REED, Annie, G .... 818-947-2320.. 49 G
reedag@lavc.edu
REED, Arlene .... 805-289-6044.. 73 C
areed@vcccd.edu
REED, Barrett .... 870-584-1462.. 22 F
reedb@cccua.edu
REED, Brian, V .... 802-656-0903 476 E
brian.reed@uvm.edu
REED, Burton, J .... 402-554-2262 277 I
breed@unomaha.edu
REED, Carol .... 540-362-6610 481 F
creed@hollins.edu
REED, Casey .... 918-631-5003 381 C
casey-reed@utulsa.edu
REED, Catherine .... 925-969-3300.. 46 L
creed@jfku.edu
REED, Charlene, K .... 330-672-2585 363 I
creed2@kent.edu
REED, Christine .... 805-922-6966.. 24 J
creed@hancockcollege.edu
REED, Cristina .... 810-762-9584 232 C
creed@kettering.edu
REED, Cynthia .... 859-572-6069 188 E
reedc11@nku.edu
REED, Cynthia .... 225-771-2552 196 B
creed@sulc.edu
REED, Dallas .... 973-278-5400 283 J
dfr@berkeleycollege.edu
REED, Dallas .... 973-278-5400 299 F
dfr@berkeleycollege.edu
REED, Dan .... 530-898-6451.. 31 D
dmreed@csuchico.edu
REED, Daniel .... 619-201-8727.. 60 A
daniel.reed@sdcc.edu
REED, Daniel .... 319-335-2132 166 G
daniel-reed@uiowa.edu
REED, Daniel .... 319-335-2132 166 G
dan-reed@uiowa.edu
REED, Darcy, A .... 507-284-3796 241 F
reed.darcy@mayo.edu
REED, David, D .... 906-487-3043 234 A
ddreed@mtu.edu
REED, Deana .... 609-896-5121 289 E

REED, Debbie .... 580-387-7000 376 D
dreed@mscok.edu
REED, Debra .... 903-813-2445 443 F
dreed@austincollege.edu
REED, Dee .... 812-535-5212 163 I
dreed@smwc.edu
REED, Diane .... 757-594-7202 479 H
dreed@cnu.edu
REED, Donna .... 502-213-8245 189 E
dreed@sctd.edu
REED, Doug .... 870-245-5167.. 20 G
reedd@obu.edu
REED, Doug .... 405-744-4244 377 F
doug.reed@okstate.edu
REED, Elaine .... 323-343-5392.. 32 D
bkscalstla@bncollege.com
REED, Elizabeth .... 215-884-8942 415 C
elizabeth.reed@woninstitute.edu
REED, Francesca .... 703-284-5906 483 A
francesca.reed@marymount.edu
REED, Gary .... 214-648-2631 469 E
gary.reed@utsouthwestern.edu
REED, George .... 719-255-4047.. 83 C
george.reed@uccs.edu
REED, Helen .... 970-351-2601.. 83 F
helen.reed@unco.edu
REED, Javan .... 937-708-5683 373 H
jreed@wilberforce.edu
REED, Jeff .... 515-292-9694 166 D
jeff.reed@antiochschool.edu
REED, Jennifer, G .... 801-581-4033 472 P
jennifer.reed@aux.utah.edu
REED, Jeremy .... 605-626-2530 428 H
jeremy.reed@northern.edu
REED, Jerry .... 570-389-4040 405 E
jreed@bloomu.edu
REED, Jim .... 623-845-3631.. 13 H
jim.reed@gccaz.edu
REED, John .... 415-442-7224.. 44 E
jreed@ggu.edu
REED, Jonathan .... 909-593-3511.. 70 E
jreed@laverne.edu
REED, Karen, A .... 419-755-4538 366 E
kreed@ncstatecollege.edu
REED, Kathy .... 310-338-4404.. 50 J
kathy.reed@lmu.edu
REED, Kevin .... 541-346-3082 387 F
ksreed@uoregon.edu
REED, Kim .... 208-562-3114 132 A
kimreed@cwidaho.cc
REED, Kimberly .... 270-745-2242 190 F
kim.reed@wku.edu
REED, Kristen .... 217-245-3054 139 H
kristen.reed@mail.ic.edu
REED, LaTonya .... 870-574-4504.. 21 G
lreed@sautech.edu
REED, LaVonda .... 315-443-5525 330 H
lareed@law.syr.edu
REED, Lee .... 202-687-6513.. 92 B
athleticdirector@georgetown.edu
REED, Lori .... 507-457-5005 248 C
lreed@winona.edu
REED, Lyndsey .... 510-649-8252.. 55 D
lreed@psr.edu
REED, Mark .... 603-646-9410 281 C
mark.reed@dartmouth.edu
REED, Mark, C .... 610-660-1200 409 H
president@sju.edu
REED, Mark, F .... 610-861-1360 402 D
reedm@moravian.edu
REED, Martin .... 209-228-2977.. 69 C
mreed9@ucmerced.edu
REED, Maryanne .... 304-293-5746 505 B
maryanne.reed@mail.wvu.edu
REED, Matthew .... 732-224-2265 284 B
REED, Meredith .... 504-398-2236 196 E
mreed@uhcno.edu
REED, Michael .... 504-282-4455 195 D
mreed@nobts.edu
REED, Michael, E .... 717-245-1159 394 A
reedme@dickinson.edu
REED, Michael, J .... 570-326-3761 404 T
mjr18@pct.edu
REED, Michelle .... 985-549-2241 197 E
mreed@selu.edu
REED, Nancy .... 901-572-2662 430 C
nancy.reed@bchs.edu
REED, Pamela .... 806-874-3571 445 R
pamela.reed@clarendoncollege.edu
REED, Phil .... 269-749-7142 236 A
preed@olivetcollege.edu
REED, Rahim .... 530-752-2071.. 68 H
rreed@ucdavis.edu
REED, Randy .... 972-273-3301 448 C
randyreed@dcccd.edu
REED, Robert .... 443-334-2240 207 C
rreed1951@stevenson.edu
REED, Robert, A .... 504-865-3735 194 G
rareed@loyno.edu
REED, Rod .... 479-524-7134.. 20 B
rreed@jbu.edu
REED, Scott .... 541-737-2713 385 F
scott.reed@oregonstate.edu
REED, Sharon .... 614-251-4595 367 F
reeds@ohiodominican.edu
REED, Shawana .... 870-235-4015.. 21 F
sreed@saumag.edu
REED, Shirley, A .... 956-872-8366 456 G
sareed@southtexascollege.edu
REED, Stephen .... 651-793-1254 245 E
steve.reed@metrostate.edu
REED, Steve .... 620-241-0723 176 G
steve.reed@centralchristian.edu
REED, Steve, E .... 417-667-8181 259 A
sreed@cottey.edu
REED, Steven .... 615-460-6619 430 D
steven.reed@belmont.edu
REED, Stuart, C .... 205-329-7898.... 5 C
stu.reed@ecacolleges.com
REED, Sue .... 484-365-7929 400 E
sreed@lincoln.edu
REED, Tara .... 407-888-8689.. 99 F
treed@fcim.edu
REED, Teresa .... 217-228-5432 149 B
reedte@quincy.edu
REED, Terri .... 404-270-5002 126 D
treed15@spelman.edu
REED, Tita .... 440-775-6200 367 B
tita.reed@oberlin.edu
REED, Tracy .... 989-775-4123 236 E
treed@sagchip.edu
REED, Van .... 337-550-1211 194 B
vreed@lsue.edu
REED, William, O .... 503-943-7523 387 H
reed@up.edu
REED-BOULEY, Kenneth 402-280-2754 274 D
kennethreed-bouley@creighton.edu
REED DAVIS, Christine . 704-687-0345 351 C
crdavis@uncc.edu
REED-FRANCOIS,
Desiree .... 702-895-4729 279 D
desiree.reed@unlv.edu
REED-HIRSCH, Kelly .... 903-694-4003 454 E
kreed-hirsch@panola.edu
REEDER, Bonita .... 910-962-3746 352 A
reederl@uncw.edu
REEDER, David, C .... 301-447-5207 206 B
reeder@msmary.edu
REEDER, Josh .... 909-621-8281.. 63 F
jreeder@scrippscollege.edu
REEDER, Leslie .... 334-347-2623.... 1 J
lreeder@escc.edu
REEDER, Mary .... 337-421-6902 193 F
mary.reeder@sowela.edu
REEDER, Pam .... 573-518-2204 263 E
preeder@mineralarea.edu
REEDER, Pamela, K .... 660-831-4123 264 A
reedere@moval.edu
REEDER, Philip, P .... 412-396-4877 394 D
reederp@duq.edu
REEDER, Richard .... 631-632-7932 325 F
richard.j.reeder@stonybrook.edu
REEDER, Rochelle .... 404-527-7767 122 B
rreeder@itc.edu
REEDER, Shehani .... 714-744-7939.. 36 G
gunasena@chapman.edu
REEDSTROM,
Cynthia, P .... 651-631-5246 251 C
clreedstrom@unwsp.edu
REEDUS, Janice .... 815-280-6640 142 A
jreedus@jjc.edu
REEDY, Kevin .... 518-464-8720 308 A
kreedy@excelsior.edu
REEGER, Jennifer .... 724-830-1069 410 E
jreeger@setonhill.edu
REEKERS, David .... 202-651-5410.. 91 H
david.reekers@gallaudet.edu
REEKS, Kevin, L .... 419-995-8081 363 G
reeks.k@rhodesstate.edu
REEL, Sally, J .... 520-626-4030.. 16 J
sreel@email.arizona.edu
REEL, Stephanie .... 410-735-6700 204 F
sreel@jhu.edu
REEM, Marvin, P .... 864-242-5100 418 H
REEMER, Ronda .... 765-641-4010 156 A
rsreemer@anderson.edu
REEP, Jeff .... 937-766-7868 358 D
reepj@cedarville.edu
REES, David, G .... 802-440-4337 474 F
rees@bennington.edu
REES, Doug, C .... 626-395-5802.. 29 I
dcrees@caltech.edu
REES, John Paul .... 802-828-2800 477 B
jpr06200@ccv.vsc.edu
REES, Margaret .... 702-895-3890 279 D
peg.rees@unlv.edu
REES, Mary .... 805-378-1572.. 73 A
mrees@vcccd.edu
REES, Pamela, D .... 515-263-6098 169 E
prees@grandview.edu
REES, Richard .... 203-285-2170.. 85 E
rrees@gwcc.commnet.edu
REES, Traci .... 504-398-2235 196 E
trees@uhcno.edu
REESE, Aaron, J .... 706-507-8735 118 C
reese_aaron@columbusstate.edu
REESE, Andrew .... 670-237-6714 520 D
andrew.reese@marianas.edu
REESE, JR., Benjamin ... 919-684-8222 337 C
ben.reese@duke.edu
REESE, Bobby .... 203-596-4548.. 87 H
breese@post.edu
REESE, Brian .... 864-388-8314 422 A
breese@lander.edu
REESE, Brian .... 717-337-6240 396 A
breese@gettysburg.edu
REESE, Camille .... 704-878-3264 344 H
creese@mitchellcc.edu
REESE, Carole, A .... 610-861-1555 402 D
reesec@moravian.edu
REESE, Cynthia .... 510-981-2851.. 56 F
creese@peralta.edu
REESE, David .... 503-725-2655 386 D
dcreese@pdx.edu
REESE, Donald, G .... 315-733-2307 332 F
dreese@uscny.edu
REESE, Kimberly .... 504-520-7575 198 D
kreese@xula.edu
REESE, Kimberly .... 336-750-3145 352 D
reesekf@wssu.edu
REESE, Leon .... 404-460-2491 124 F
leon.reese@point.edu
REESE, Michael .... 619-644-7462.. 45 A
mike.reese@gcccd.edu
REESE, Pamela .... 716-488-3020 311 E
pamelareese@jbc.edu
REESE, Phil .... 701-355-8175 355 K
preese@umary.edu
REESE, Robert .... 574-936-8898 155 L
gene.reese@ancilla.edu
REESE, Robert .... 610-902-8554 391 B
robert.reese@cabrini.edu
REESE, Robert, C .... 540-819-5704 482 A
rcreese@jchs.edu
REESE, Robert, S .... 843-953-2468 420 C
reeser@cofc.edu
REESER, Mike .... 254-867-4891 461 G
mike.reeser@tstc.edu
REESER, Todd .... 706-565-3669 118 C
REESMAN, Melissa, J ... 260-399-7700 165 B
mreesman@sf.edu
REESOR, Lori .... 812-855-8188 159 H
lreesor@iu.edu
REESOR, Lori .... 812-855-8188 159 G
lreesor@iu.edu
REEVE-RABB, Andra ...... 912-525-5000 125 B
areeve@scad.edu
REEVES, Brent, W .... 618-537-6938 145 C
breeves@mckendree.edu
REEVES, Bret .... 615-248-1464 439 B
breeves@trevecca.edu
REEVES, Brian .... 918-343-7983 379 C
breeves@rsu.edu
REEVES, Christina .... 732-987-2249 286 D
creeves@georgian.edu
REEVES, Christopher ..... 319-656-2447 173 C
REEVES, Earl, J .... 660-831-4108 264 A
REEVES, Herbert .... 334-670-3203.... 7 E
hreeves@troy.edu
REEVES, Jacqueline, A .. 203-576-4496.. 88 F
purchase@bridgeport.edu
REEVES, James .... 951-372-7157.. 58 G
james.reeves@norcocollege.edu
REEVES, Jason .... 606-546-1209 189 I
jreeves@unionky.edu
REEVES, Jeff .... 608-243-4137 514 A
jreevess@madisoncollege.edu
REEVES, Joey .... 912-478-8607 120 E
jreeves@georgiasouthern.edu
REEVES, Kay .... 325-674-2675 441 D
reevesk@acu.edu
REEVES, Kelly .... 801-592-0451 131 D
kelly.reeves@ldschurch.org
REEVES, Lindsay .... 706-864-1625 127 B
lindsay.reeves@ung.edu
REEVES, Mamiko .... 989-837-4136 235 C
reevesm@northwood.edu
REEVES, Mark .... 678-839-5079 127 F
mreeves@westga.edu
REEVES, Mark .... 870-972-2108.. 18 A
mreeves@astate.edu
REEVES, Mark, T .... 864-644-5528 424 B
mreeves@swu.edu
REEVES, Michel .... 303-245-4714.. 81 B
mreeves@naropa.edu
REEVES, Michelle .... 706-880-8249 122 D
mreeves@lagrange.edu
REEVES, Rodney .... 417-328-1770 267 A
rreeves@sbuniv.edu
REEVES, Ronald .... 818-401-1022.. 40 A
rreeves@columbiacollege.edu
REEVES, Tracey .... 352-395-5507 107 E
tracey.reeves@sfcollege.edu
REGA, Elizabeth .... 909-469-5460.. 74 G
erega@westernu.edu
REGALADO, Juan .... 909-593-3511.. 70 E
jregalado@laverne.edu
REGALADO RODRIGUEZ,
Margery .... 831-479-6285.. 28 F
maregala@cabrillo.edu
REGALIA, Delphine .... 510-642-3881.. 68 G
dmregalia@berkeley.edu
REGAN, Anna .... 732-255-0400 288 B
aregan@ocean.edu
REGAN, Joseph, P .... 312-341-2110 150 D
jregan@roosevelt.edu
REGAN, Kathleen .... 315-781-3700 310 C
regan@hws.edu
REGAN, Laurie .... 503-552-1507 384 F
lregan@nunm.edu
REGAN, Sheila .... 336-342-4261 346 B
regans@rockinghamcc.edu
REGAN, Thomas, J .... 773-508-3505 144 D
tregan1@luc.edu
REGAN WHITE, David ... 518-381-1320 323 L
whitedr@sunysccc.edu
REGE, Karen, M .... 443-412-2145 204 C
krege@harford.edu
REGE, Robert .... 214-648-3050 469 E
robert.rege@utsouthwestern.edu
REGEHR, Nanci .... 480-517-8314.. 14 B
nanci.regehr@riosalado.edu
REGENAUER,
Rochelle, R .... 262-243-5700 507 C
rochelle.regenauer@cuw.edu
REGENCIO, Eugenia .... 973-596-3068 288 A
eugenia.regencio@njit.edu
REGER, Mark, A .... 864-488-8317 422 B
mreger@limestone.edu
REGER, Patricia .... 610-341-1464 394 E
preger@eastern.edu
REGGIO, Nancy .... 408-453-9900.. 45 E
nreggio@henley-putnam.edu
REGIER, Elaine .... 405-945-9104 378 C
elainrr@osuokc.edu
REGIER, Jeanette .... 816-322-0110 257 M
jeanette.regier@calvary.edu
REGIER, Philip, R .... 480-965-2457.. 10 K
phil.regier@asu.edu
REGIMBAL, Caryn .... 360-752-8396 492 H
cregimbal@btc.edu
REGINATO, Justin .... 916-278-6241.. 33 C
reginato@csus.edu
REGIS, Chris, C .... 214-768-1178 457 B
cregis@smu.edu
REGIST-TOMLINSON,
Tara .... 718-270-6938 303 C
trtomlinson@mec.cuny.edu
REGISTER, Bob .... 803-754-4100 420 E
REGISTER, Patrick .... 831-459-4404.. 70 C
jpregister@ucsc.edu
REGISTER, Tammy .... 307-382-1606 517 C
tregister@westernwyoming.edu
REGISTRE, Dee .... 904-470-8050.. 98 B
d.registre@ewc.edu
REGNER, Cecile .... 617-541-5383 221 A
cregner@rcc.mass.edu
REGNERUS, Arlene .... 312-935-6659 149 K
aregnerus@robertmorris.edu
REGUEIRO, Maria, C ..... 305-821-3333 100 A
mregueiro@fnu.edu
REGULSKA, Joanna .... 530-752-6376.. 68 H
jregulska@ucdavis.edu
REHAK, Patricia .... 361-582-2533 470 A
patricia.rehak@victoriacollege.edu
REHBEIN, Edna .... 512-716-4422 463 A
er04@txstate.edu
REHBEIN, Matt .... 615-966-6043 433 D
matt.rehbein@lipscomb.edu
REHBERG, Kathy .... 850-718-2233.. 96 H
rehbergk@chipola.edu
REHG, SJ, William .... 314-977-3150 266 J
rehgsp@slu.edu
REHM, David .... 570-674-6403 401 M
drehm@misericordia.edu
REHM, Julie, M .... 216-368-6070 358 C
julie.rehm@case.edu
REHM, Kelley .... 334-833-4302.... 5 M
krehm@hawks.huntingdon.edu

REHM, Matthew .... 740-362-3136 365 D
mrehm@mtso.edu
REHM, Roger, E .... 989-774-1474 228 E
rehm1re@cmich.edu
REHN, Andrea .... 562-907-4200.. 75 A
arehn@whittier.edu
REHN, Lynn .... 410-228-9250 208 B
REHNELT, Sherry .... 715-425-3962 511 E
bookstore@uwrf.edu
REIBER, Jennifer .... 904-256-1159.. 99 C
jreiber@fcsl.edu
REICH, Amy, R .... 516-463-7580 310 D
amy.r.reich@hofstra.edu
REICH, Brooke .... 252-398-6313 336 K
reichb@chowan.edu
REICH, Lewis .... 901-722-3220 436 D
lreich@sco.edu
REICH, Patricia .... 570-422-3595 406 A
preich@esu.edu
REICH, Tyler .... 503-375-6586 388 D
treich@willamette.edu
REICHARD, Gary, W ...... 718-982-2440 302 A
provost@csi.cuny.edu
REICHARD, Jacob .... 620-223-2700 177 E
jacobr@fortscott.edu
REICHARD, Joshua .... 303-743-8158 435 H
jreichard@ogs.edu
REICHEL, Mary .... 828-262-6725 349 H
reichelml@appstate.edu
REICHEL, Scott .... 970-339-6513.. 76 E
scott.reichel@aims.edu
REICHEL, Tammi, L .... 804-752-7383 484 C
tammireichel@rmc.edu
REICHENBERGER,
Douglas, C .... 618-453-1045 152 B
dreichenberger@siu.edu
REICHERT, Greg .... 608-785-8672 510 F
greichert@uwlax.edu
REICHERT, Leah .... 816-472-4852 261 C
lreichert@kcai.edu
REICHLE, Kyle .... 434-528-5276 491 D
kreichle@vul.edu
REICHMUTH, Geri .... 303-292-0015.. 79 F
REID, Anne, M .... 610-861-1353 402 D
reida@moravian.edu
REID, OP, Barbara, E .... 773-371-5422 134 J
breid@ctu.edu
REID, Carol .... 770-537-6000 128 F
carol.reid@westgatech.edu
REID, Carol .... 214-333-5702 447 D
carolr@dbu.edu
REID, Carol .... 615-675-5287 441 B
creid@welch.edu
REID, Cheryl .... 402-872-2228 276 C
creid@peru.edu
REID, Christopher .... 919-497-3310 339 F
creid@louisburg.edu
REID, Dana .... 480-517-8235.. 14 B
dana.reid@riosalado.edu
REID, David .... 314-921-9290 269 D
dreid@ugst.edu
REID, Diana .... 860-512-2909.. 85 G
dreid@manchestercc.edu
REID, Donna, M .... 718-522-9073 298 E
dreid@asa.edu
REID, Eric .... 601-403-1126 255 D
ereid@prcc.edu
REID, Heather .... 617-747-2258 212 B
library@berklee.edu
REID, Helen .... 972-932-4309 464 C
hreid@tvcc.edu
REID, Helen, C .... 417-836-4176 263 H
helenreid@missouristate.edu
REID, James .... 325-942-2264 463 C
james.reid@angelo.edu
REID, John .... 805-437-8444.. 31 C
john.reid@csuci.edu
REID, Kathleen, A .... 413-782-1211 225 F
kathleen.reid@wne.edu
REID, Lee .... 920-403-3866 509 J
lee.reid@snc.edu
REID, III, Lenzy .... 706-552-0900 115 H
lreid@athenstech.edu
REID, Mark .... 305-284-5857 112 O
mreid@miami.edu
REID, Mark .... 206-281-2624 498 B
mreid@spu.edu
REID, Michael .... 406-243-4662 271 G
michael.reid@umontana.edu
REID, Michael, B .... 352-294-1601 110 D
michael.reid@ufl.edu
REID, Michele .... 269-965-3931 232 A
reidm@kellogg.edu
REID, Richard, H .... 337-475-5588 197 B
rreid@mcneese.edu
REID, Sean .... 607-274-3341 311 D
sreid@ithaca.edu
REID, Sezilee .... 706-396-8113 124 C
sreid@paine.edu
REID, Shannon .... 603-230-3504 280 I
sreid@ccsnh.edu
REID, Sherri .... 870-733-6020.. 18 B
sdreid@asumidsouth.edu
REID, Stanley, G .... 512-476-2772 443 H
president@austingrad.edu
REID, JR., Thomas, G .. 412-731-6000 409 A
treid@rpts.edu
REID, Tina, S .... 864-592-4683 424 C
reidt@sccsc.edu
REID, Victoria .... 410-837-4611 209 D
vreid@ubalt.edu
REID, William, S .... 858-499-0202.. 39 B
wreid@coleman.edu
REID-BUNCH, Jan .... 662-862-8035 253 D
jrbunch@iccms.edu
REID-CHASSIAKOS,
Linda .... 818-677-3689.. 33 B
linda.reid.chassiakos@csun.edu
REID-MARTINEZ,
Kathaleen .... 918-495-7855 378 H
kreid-martinez@oru.edu
REIDY, Francis .... 352-588-8246 106 N
fran.reidy@saintleo.edu
REIDY, Joseph, P .... 202-806-6100.. 92 C
REIDY, Robert, C .... 650-723-6324.. 66 C
rcr@stanford.edu
REIDY, William .... 203-396-8086.. 88 C
reidyw@sacredheart.edu
REIDY-FOX, Kelly .... 773-298-3780 151 C
fox@sxu.edu
REIF, L. Rafael .... 617-253-0148 221 C
president@mit.edu
REIF, Richard .... 918-444-5900 376 G
reif01@nsuok.edu
REIF, Steven, J .... 248-233-2800 235 D
sjreif@oaklandcc.edu
REIF, Steven, J .... 248-522-3900 235 D
sjreif@oaklandcc.edu
REIFENHEISER, Paul ...... 845-434-5750 330 F
preifenh@sullivan.suny.edu
REIFERT, Steve .... 231-591-2800 230 A
stevereifert@ferris.edu
REIFSCHNEIDER, Carol . 406-265-4126 272 C
reifschneider@msun.edu
REIG, Michael .... 215-248-7069 392 D
reigm@chc.edu
REIGEL, Heidi .... 410-857-2226 205 E
hreigel@mcdaniel.edu
REIGHARD, Erica .... 814-262-6440 405 A
ereighard@pennhighlands.edu
REIGHARD, Frank .... 409-772-5544 469 C
trreigha@utmb.edu
REIGHLEY, Twila .... 517-884-4367 233 G
reighley@msu.edu
REIHL, Raeann .... 865-981-8355 433 F
raeann.reihl@maryvillecollege.edu
REIJO PERA, Renee ...... 406-994-2891 272 A
renee.reijopera@montana.edu
REIKOFSKI, Diane .... 402-844-7055 276 G
diane@northeast.edu
REILAND, Kathleen .... 714-484-7233.. 53 M
kreiland@cypresscollege.edu
REILAND, Mandi .... 281-998-6150 455 K
mandi.reiland@sjcd.edu
REILLY, Cathy .... 206-296-6120 498 D
reillyc@seattleu.edu
REILLY, John .... 303-724-0882.. 83 D
john.reilly@ucdenver.edu
REILLY, John, H .... 518-956-8050 324 G
jreilly@albany.edu
REILLY, Joseph, R .... 973-313-6233 291 F
joseph.reilly@shu.edu
REILLY, Karen, L .... 407-582-1810 113 F
kreilly5@valenciacollege.edu
REILLY, Kerin .... 212-686-9244 298 C
kreilly@aada.edu
REILLY, Kevin .... 540-365-4407 480 L
kpreilly@ferrum.edu
REILLY, Lenore .... 413-538-2500 222 C
lreilly@mtholyoke.edu
REILLY, Madelyn .... 412-396-5181 394 D
reillym@duq.edu
REILLY, Marianne .... 718-862-7891 313 L
mreilly01@manhattan.edu
REILLY, Mary Jane .... 516-323-4702 315 J
mreilly@molloy.edu
REILLY, MB .... 513-556-1824 371 E
reillymb@ucmail.uc.edu
REILLY, Patricia .... 617-627-2000 225 A
patricia.reilly@tufts.edu
REILLY, Seamus .... 217-353-2170 148 H
sereilly@parkland.edu
REILLY, Tim .... 706-712-8228 118 F
treilly@daltonstate.edu
REILLY, William, T .... 704-894-2765 337 B
wireilly@davidson.edu
REILLY-KELLY, Tracy ..... 360-992-2163 493 E
tkelly@clark.edu
REILLY-MYKLEBUST,
Alice .... 715-425-9884 511 E
alice.m.reilly-myklebust@uwrf.edu
REIMAN, Adam .... 937-255-3636 517 H
adam.reiman@afit.edu
REIMAN, Brock .... 765-677-1569 161 C
brock.reiman@indwes.edu
REIMANN, Jan .... 573-334-9181 262 C
jan@metrobusinesscollege.edu
REIMANN, Rick .... 518-587-2100 329 C
rick.reimann@esc.edu
REIMER, Denise .... 608-243-4484 514 A
dmreimer@madisoncollege.edu
REIMER, Martin .... 641-844-8502 170 G
martin.reimer@iavalley.edu
REIMER, Martin .... 641-648-4611 170 H
REIMER, Michael .... 201-360-4158 286 E
mreimer@hccc.edu
REIMER, Rachel .... 515-271-1424 168 G
rachel.reimer@dmu.edu
REIMER, Robert .... 773-291-6740 135 M
rreimer@ccc.edu
REIMONDO, Sue .... 859-985-3212 183 I
sue_reimondo@berea.edu
REIN, Kim .... 303-914-6260.. 82 B
kim.rein@rrcc.edu
REIN, Laura .... 314-968-7152 269 N
lrein@webster.edu
REINA, John .... 845-257-3685 325 D
reinaj@newpaltz.edu
REINCKE, Nancy .... 515-271-2161 168 J
nancy.reincke@drake.edu
REINDERS, Gretchen ..... 608-785-8073 510 F
greinders@uwlax.edu
REINDL, Kay .... 209-478-0800.. 45 J
kreindl@humphreys.edu
REINECK, Marilyn .... 651-641-8730 241 L
reineck@csp.edu
REINEHR, Craig .... 918-444-4700 376 G
reinehr@nsuok.edu
REINEKE, Sandra .... 208-885-3165 132 I
sreineke@uidaho.edu
REINELT, Douglas, A ..... 214-768-3754 457 B
reinelt@smu.edu
REINER, Christian .... 435-586-7783 473 A
christianreiner@suu.edu
REINER, Michael, D ...... 402-280-2337 274 D
michaelreiner@creighton.edu
REINERS, Bradley, O ..... 651-255-6164 250 D
breiners@unitedseminary.edu
REINERT, Duane .... 660-944-2852 258 G
dreinert@conception.edu
REING, Linda .... 212-961-3432 298 H
alumrel@bankstreet.edu
REINHARD, Herb .... 229-333-5462 127 H
hreinhar@valdosta.edu
REINHARDT, Kathleen ... 970-521-6603.. 81 F
kathleen.reinhardt@njc.edu
REINHARDT, Laurie .... 410-626-2507 206 F
laurie.reinhardt@sjc.edu
REINHART, Chanie .... 419-824-3728 364 G
creinhart@lourdes.edu
REINHART, Kellee, C .... 205-348-5938.... 7 H
kreinhart@uasystem.edu
REINHART, Rose .... 419-995-8310 363 G
reinhart.r@rhodesstate.edu
REINHOLD, David, S ..... 269-387-4564 239 E
david.reinhold@wmich.edu
REINIG, Amanda .... 757-455-3116 491 F
areinig@vwu.edu
REINISCH, Lou .... 516-686-7403 317 G
lou.reinisch@nyit.edu
REINISCH, Sheryl .... 503-493-6539 382 I
sreinisch@cu-portland.edu
REINKE, Brenda .... 405-682-7510 377 C
breinke@occc.edu
REINKING, Jackie .... 212-686-9244 298 C
REINL, Cindy, M .... 920-433-6660 506 C
cindy.reinl@bellincollege.edu
REINLAND, Jeffrey, E .... 509-527-4312 499 E
jeffrey.reinland@wwcc.edu
REINLIE, Carla .... 850-729-5357 104 E
reinliec@nwfsc.edu
REINOEHL, Jason, K ..... 937-229-3725 372 A
jreinoehl@udayton.edu
REINSCH FRIESE, Ellen . 937-775-2709 374 B
ellen.friese@wright.edu
REIPENHOFF, Mary, E .. 260-399-7700 165 B
mriepenhoff@sf.edu
REIS, Gina .... 508-910-6505 217 A
greis@umassd.edu
REIS, Ryan .... 954-592-1002 102 G
rreis@keiseruniversity.edu
REISBERG, Darren .... 773-702-7618 153 F
reisberg@uchicago.edu
REISBERG, Jeff .... 727-873-4552 111 B
reisberg@mail.usf.edu
REISCHE, Jim .... 413-597-4277 226 C
jim.reische@williams.edu
REISECK, Carol, J .... 708-209-3262 136 I
carol.reiseck@cuchicago.edu
REISENAUER, Eric .... 803-938-3862 425 F
ericr@uscsumter.edu
REISER, Cyrill .... 818-785-2726.. 35 N
REISER, Sharon .... 805-525-4417.. 67 E
sreiser@thomasaquinas.edu
REISETTER, Mary .... 641-585-8681 174 B
reisettem@waldorf.edu
REISETTER-HART,
Judith .... 414-382-6431 506 A
judith.reisetter@alverno.edu
REISH, Brenda, J .... 800-287-8822 156 D
reishbr@bethanyseminary.edu
REISIG, Jerry .... 212-870-1213 318 C
jreisig@nyts.edu
REISING, Gregory .... 410-704-2512 209 C
greising@towson.edu
REISING, Paula .... 912-650-5687 125 H
preising@southuniversity.edu
REISING, Sonia .... 815-825-9738 142 F
sonia.reising@kishwaukeecollege.edu
REISINGER, Amanda, B . 740-588-1275 374 G
amreisinger@zanestate.edu
REISINGER, Andrew, G . 814-865-7641 403 F
agr1@psu.edu
REISINGER, Cynthia, E .. 717-815-1221 415 G
creising@ycp.edu
REISINGER, Tracy .... 503-699-6253 384 B
treisinger@marylhurst.edu
REISMAN, Lonn .... 254-968-9178 459 A
reisman@tarleton.edu
REISNER, Carrie .... 765-973-8404 160 A
hellerc@iue.edu
REISNER, Jeff .... 716-375-2000 322 B
jreisner@reisnerlawgroup.com
REISNER, John, A .... 937-255-3636 517 H
john.reisner@afit.edu
REISS, Michael, A .... 718-377-0777 320 E
REISS, Richard .... 201-692-7003 286 B
reissr@fdu.edu
REISSENWEBER, Beth .... 612-330-1027 240 G
reissenw@augsburg.edu
REISSMAN, Sallie, A ..... 302-356-6807.. 91 B
sallie.a.reissman@wilmu.edu
REIST, David .... 785-442-6010 178 C
dreist@highlandcc.edu
REISZ, Z .... 805-965-0581.. 62 E
zreisz@sbcc.edu
REITAN, Mark .... 507-457-2319 248 C
mreitan@winona.edu
REITER, Angela .... 828-328-7109 339 C
angela.reiter@lr.edu
REITER, Lisa .... 773-508-2200 144 D
lreiter1@luc.edu
REITER, Sharon, L .... 909-869-3016.. 31 A
slreiter@cpp.edu
REITMAN, Tzipora .... 845-574-4595 321 F
zreitman@sunyrockland.edu
REITTER, Kim .... 314-977-2927 266 J
reitterk@slu.edu
REITZ, Barbara .... 610-683-4132 406 D
reitz@kutztown.edu
REITZ, Chris .... 801-524-8109 471 L
creitz@ldsbc.edu
REITZ, Nancy .... 916-485-6028.. 50 F
reitzn@arc.losrios.edu
REITZ, S. Maggie .... 410-704-2131 209 C
mreitz@towson.edu
REITZ, Tiffany .... 352-638-9707.. 95 H
treitz@beaconcollege.edu
REJHOLEC, Taryn .... 212-217-4723 308 B
taryn_rejholec@fitnyc.edu
REKAU, Donna .... 630-353-9975 137 D
drekau@devry.edu
REKLAI, Hilda .... 680-488-3036 520 E
hildan@palau.edu
REKOWSKI, Lois, T .... 740-266-9654 361 D
lrekowski@egcc.edu
REL, Ricardo .... 575-646-5909 295 B
rrel@nmsu.edu
RELAY, Lynn .... 718-368-5034 303 A
lrelay@kbcc.cuny.edu
RELIHAN, Constance, C 334-844-4900.... 4 D
relihco@auburn.edu
RELLINGER, Brian .... 740-368-3656 368 N
barellin@owu.edu
RELLINGER, Mackenzie . 248-218-2057 236 C
mrellinger@rc.edu
RELLINGER, Tom .... 248-218-2049 236 C
trellinger@rc.edu

REYNA, Cynthia .... 870-864-7130.. 21 D
creyna@southark.edu
REYNA, Mario .... 956-872-6116 456 G
reyna@southtexascollege.edu
REYNA, Oscar .... 361-825-5934 460 A
oscar.reyna@tamucc.edu
REYNA, Patrick .... 210-297-9663 443 K
pgreyna@baptisthealthsystem.com
REYNA, Tony .... 713-942-5920 466 J
reynat@stthom.edu
REYNARD, Betty .... 409-984-6100 462 E
betty.reynard@lamarpa.edu
REYNDERS, John, C ...... 712-274-5100 172 A
reynders@morningside.edu
REYNOLDS, Amy .... 330-672-2950 363 I
areyno24@kent.edu
REYNOLDS, Barry .... 276-656-0228 489 A
breynolds@patrickhenry.edu
REYNOLDS, Benjamin ... 847-866-3900 138 G
REYNOLDS, Brad .... 706-865-2134 126 G
breynolds@truett.edu
REYNOLDS, Carol .... 803-938-3730 425 F
creynold@uscsumter.edu
REYNOLDS, Caryn .... 216-791-5000 359 K
caryn.reynolds@cim.edu
REYNOLDS, Cathy .... 404-527-4520 117 C
creynolds@carver.edu
REYNOLDS, Chris .... 309-677-2670 134 G
reynolds@fsmail.bradley.edu
REYNOLDS, Colleen .... 309-268-8188 139 D
colleen.reynolds@heartland.edu
REYNOLDS, Curtis .... 352-392-1336 110 D
curtrey@ufl.edu
REYNOLDS, Daisy .... 214-818-1360 447 A
dreynolds@criswell.edu
REYNOLDS, David .... 940-565-3990 466 B
david.reynolds@unt.edu
REYNOLDS, Debbie .... 530-895-2378.. 28 E
reynoldsde@butte.edu
REYNOLDS, Deborah ..... 972-883-2380 467 D
deborah.reynolds@utdallas.edu
REYNOLDS, Dennis .... 713-743-7896 465 A
der@uh.edu
REYNOLDS, Diane, L ..... 804-828-3430 487 E
dlreynol@vcu.edu
REYNOLDS, Don .... 334-386-7240.... 5 I
dreynolds2@faulkner.edu
REYNOLDS, Ed .... 940-565-3000 466 B
ed.reynolds@unt.edu
REYNOLDS,
Elizabeth, P .... 304-293-4245 505 B
liz.reynolds@mail.wvu.edu
REYNOLDS, Ellen .... 914-813-9201 323 K
ereynolds@sarahlawrence.edu
REYNOLDS, Ellen .... 401-874-5155 417 E
ellenreynolds@uri.edu
REYNOLDS, Gary .... 719-255-3505.. 83 C
greynold@uccs.edu
REYNOLDS, Gloria .... 970-351-1766.. 83 F
gloria.reynolds@unco.edu
REYNOLDS, Holly .... 770-718-5314 116 F
hreynolds@brenau.edu
REYNOLDS, James .... 708-456-0300 153 E
jamesreynolds@triton.edu
REYNOLDS, James, M .. 937-481-2201 373 I
jim_reynolds@wilmington.edu
REYNOLDS, Jamie .... 703-284-1619 483 A
jamie.reynolds@marymount.edu
REYNOLDS, Jane .... 972-241-3371 447 E
jreynolds@dallas.edu
REYNOLDS, Jerrie .... 903-233-4445 452 A
jerriereynolds@letu.edu
REYNOLDS, John, C ..... 626-815-3887.. 26 U
jreynolds@apu.edu
REYNOLDS, Kanton .... 919-516-4354 348 G
kreynolds@st-aug.edu
REYNOLDS, Karen .... 802-776-5220 474 H
karen.reynolds@csj.edu
REYNOLDS, Karl .... 918-343-7819 379 C
kreynolds@rsu.edu
REYNOLDS, Kelly, M ..... 785-864-7100 181 I
kelly@ku.edu
REYNOLDS, Kevin .... 859-344-4069 189 G
reynolk@thomasmore.edu
REYNOLDS, Kevin .... 503-725-3886 386 D
reynoldsk@pdx.edu
REYNOLDS, Kevin, J ..... 864-597-4300 426 I
reynoldskj@wofford.edu
REYNOLDS, Kevin, W .... 330-941-2742 374 E
kwreynolds@ysu.edu
REYNOLDS, Kim .... 909-607-7300.. 37 L
kim.reynolds@cgu.edu
REYNOLDS, Kimberly .... 785-243-1435 176 I
kreynolds@cloud.edu
REYNOLDS, Leah .... 812-237-8954 159 C
leah.reynolds@indstate.edu
REYNOLDS, Leslie .... 303-492-7511.. 83 B
leslie.reynolds@colorado.edu
REYNOLDS, Lisa .... 402-375-7215 276 D
lireyno1@wsc.edu
REYNOLDS, Liz .... 914-594-4229 318 A
nymc@bkstr.com
REYNOLDS, Loretta .... 859-985-3774 183 I
reynoldslo@berea.edu
REYNOLDS, Lynn .... 732-571-3531 287 C
lreynold@monmouth.edu
REYNOLDS, Mark, A ..... 410-706-7461 207 H
mreynolds@umaryland.edu
REYNOLDS, Marlene ...... 419-372-9824 357 F
mreyno@bgsu.edu
REYNOLDS, Mary .... 708-237-5050 148 A
mreynolds@nc.edu
REYNOLDS, Mary .... 828-327-7000 341 G
mreynolds@cvcc.edu
REYNOLDS, Michael ...... 704-233-8252 353 D
m.reynolds@wingate.edu
REYNOLDS, Michael, C . 334-844-4367.... 4 D
reynom2@auburn.edu
REYNOLDS, Michaela ..... 325-942-2335 463 C
REYNOLDS, Michele ...... 847-543-2221 136 E
michele.reynolds@clcillinois.edu
REYNOLDS, Michelle ..... 410-951-3939 208 F
mreynolds@coppin.edu
REYNOLDS, Michelle ..... 573-840-9077 267 J
michellereynolds@trcc.edu
REYNOLDS, Nancy .... 936-633-5345 442 I
nreynolds@angelina.edu
REYNOLDS, Nancy, W ... 270-686-4244 183 J
nancy.reynolds@brescia.edu
REYNOLDS, Philip .... 334-699-2266.... 1 B
REYNOLDS, Randall ...... 615-460-6443 430 D
randall.reynolds@belmont.edu
REYNOLDS, Robin .... 408-554-4070.. 62 F
rreynolds@scu.edu
REYNOLDS, Rodney .... 805-493-3658.. 30 E
rreynol@callutheran.edu
REYNOLDS, Rosemary ... 817-515-1514 458 B
rosemary.reynolds@tccd.edu
REYNOLDS, Ryan .... 585-395-2126 326 D
rreynol@brockport.edu
REYNOLDS, Sean, B ...... 847-491-7326 148 C
sean.reynolds@northwestern.edu
REYNOLDS, Sharon, P .. 336-633-0234 345 F
spreynolds@randolph.edu
REYNOLDS, Sharon, S .. 606-783-5149 188 C
sb.reynolds@moreheadstate.edu
REYNOLDS, Shawn .... 320-629-5161 246 H
reynoldss@pine.edu
REYNOLDS,
Stephanie, C .... 315-792-5456 315 I
sreynolds@mvcc.edu
REYNOLDS, Susan, S .... 717-337-6970 396 A
sreynold@gettysburg.edu
REYNOLDS, Suzanne ..... 336-758-5430 353 A
reynols@wfu.edu
REYNOLDS, Thomas, L . 704-687-7248 351 C
tlreynol@uncc.edu
REYNOLDS, Tim .... 641-673-1170 174 F
reynoldst@wmpenn.edu
REYNOLDS, Tracy .... 706-245-7226 119 A
treynolds@ec.edu
REYNOLDS, William, F .. 973-596-3004 288 A
william.reynolds@njit.edu
REYNOLDS, William, G . 202-687-2461.. 92 B
wgr2@georgetown.edu
REYNOLDS, Z. Paul ...... 217-424-3929 145 J
zpaulreynolds@millikin.edu
REYNOLDS-CASPER,
ReGina .... 620-792-9362 175 C
casperr@bartonccc.edu
REZAC, Barb .... 605-668-1292 427 F
barbara.rezac@mtmc.edu
REZAIE, Jaleh .... 919-530-7395 350 D
jrezaie@nccu.edu
REZEK, Jon .... 252-328-1936 349 I
rezekjo17@ecu.edu
REZEL, Elizabeth .... 608-743-4450 513 D
erezel@blackhawk.edu
REZENDES, George .... 401-598-2029 416 C
george.rezendes@jwu.edu
REZENDES, Robert .... 508-678-2811 219 C
robert.rezendes@bristolcc.edu
REZNIK, Inna .... 516-572-7700 316 C
inna.reznik@ncc.edu
RHAMES, Ronald .... 803-738-7600 422 D
rhamesr@midlandstech.edu
RHEA, Amanda .... 704-978-4441 344 H
ahrea@mitchellcc.edu
RHEA, Jessica .... 239-590-7016 109 C
jrhea@fgcu.edu
RHEA, Jill .... 712-749-2125 167 C
rhea@bvu.edu
RHEA, Kristy, K .... 540-828-5471 478 J
krhea@bridgewater.edu
RHEA, Mitchell .... 423-478-6231 436 G
mrhea01@clevelandstatecc.edu
RHEA, Teresa, C .... 256-549-8230.... 2 A
trhea@gadsdenstate.edu
RHEAD, Lori .... 608-363-2630 506 D
rheadl@beloit.edu
RHEAULT, Wendy .... 847-578-8805 150 E
wendy.rheault@rosalindfranklin.edu
RHEAUME, Steve .... 603-535-2266 283 B
srheaume@plymouth.edu
RHEE, Michael .... 212-431-2893 317 H
michael.rhee@nyls.edu
RHEE, Soo Ok .... 714-525-0088.. 44 I
cfo@gm.edu
RHEIN, John .... 610-430-4163 407 D
jrhein@wcupa.edu
RHEINECKER, Matt .... 517-265-5161 226 F
mrheinecker@adrian.edu
RHEW, Steven, W .... 336-334-5806 351 D
steve_rhew@uncg.edu
RHI-KLEINERT, Susan ... 818-710-2289.. 49 D
rhiks@piercecollege.edu
RHIM, Choonhee, L ...... 323-265-8625.. 48 L
rhimcl@elac.edu
RHINE, Lisa, B .... 757-822-5201 489 H
lrhine@tcc.edu
RHINE, Randy .... 308-432-6201 276 B
rrhine@csc.edu
RHINEHARDT, Kimrey ... 919-843-0381 349 G
krhinehardt@northcarolina.edu
RHINEHART, Jennifer .... 828-689-1453 339 G
jrhinehart@mhu.edu
RHINEHART, YaKima .... 910-672-1287 350 B
yrhinehart@uncfsu.edu
RHINESMITH, Betsy ...... 630-829-6412 133 I
brhinesmith@ben.edu
RHINEY, Lisa .... 205-348-8333.... 8 A
lisa.rhiney@ua.edu
RHINIER, Bill .... 717-947-6181 404 S
wrhinier2@pacollege.edu
RHOAD, Scott .... 660-543-4123 268 A
rhoad@ucmo.edu
RHOADES, Jeff .... 419-448-2977 362 G
jrhoade1@heidelberg.edu
RHOADES, Jeffrey .... 707-527-4811.. 62 H
jrhoades@santarosa.edu
RHOADES, IV, Mack ..... 254-710-1234 444 B
mack_rhoadesiv@baylor.edu
RHOADES, Margot .... 704-461-6733 335 J
margotrhoades@bac.edu
RHOADES, Samuel, T ... 804-257-5811 491 C
strhoades@vuu.edu
RHOADES, Valerie .... 719-346-9300.. 81 A
valerie.rhoades@morgancc.edu
RHOADS, Bill .... 620-768-2909 177 E
billr@fortscott.edu
RHOADS, Kay, M .... 803-934-3255 422 G
krhoads@morris.edu
RHODA, Christopher ..... 207-859-1124 200 H
chris@thomas.edu
RHODE, Carolyn .... 336-506-4128 340 L
carolyn.rhode@alamancecc.edu
RHODE, Charles, G .... 404-894-4114 120 A
chuck.rhode@facilities.gatech.edu
RHODEN, Brenda .... 256-761-6204.... 7 D
brhoden@talladega.edu
RHODEN, Deborah .... 256-840-4137.... 3 F
drhoden@snead.edu
RHODEN, Richard, R ..... 337-475-5887 197 B
rrhoden@mcneese.edu
RHODES, Angel .... 270-534-3426 187 C
angel.rhodes@kctcs.edu
RHODES, Angela .... 405-789-6400 379 K
arhodes@snu.edu
RHODES, Anthony, P .... 212-592-2071 324 A
tonyrhodes@sva.edu
RHODES, Carla .... 706-880-8240 122 D
crhodes@lagrange.edu
RHODES, Craig .... 336-334-7806 350 C
rhodesc@ncat.edu
RHODES, David .... 318-676-7811 193 A
davidrhodes@nwltc.edu
RHODES, David .... 716-926-8895 310 B
drhodes@hilbert.edu
RHODES, David, J .... 212-592-2350 324 A
drhodes@sva.edu
RHODES, David, J .... 251-578-1313.... 3 D
drhodes@rstc.edu
RHODES, Dawn, M .... 410-706-2802 207 H
drhodes@umaryland.edu
RHODES, Eileen .... 860-906-5021.. 85 D
RHODES, Gale .... 502-852-5727 190 C
gale.rhodes@louisville.edu
RHODES, Gary, L .... 804-523-5200 488 C
grhodes@reynolds.edu
RHODES, Gina .... 704-290-5899 346 F
grhodes@spcc.edu
RHODES, Jack, W .... 843-953-3708 419 D
jack.rhodes@citadel.edu
RHODES, Jacqueline, G 973-596-3407 288 A
jacqueline.rhodes@njit.edu
RHODES, John .... 410-225-2201 205 C
jrhodes@mica.edu
RHODES, Karen .... 864-578-8770 423 F
RHODES, Kathleen, S .... 256-824-6775.... 8 C
kathleen.rhodes@uah.edu
RHODES, Kathryn .... 865-354-3000 438 A
rhodeskc@roanestate.edu
RHODES, Kathy .... 206-934-3796 497 H
kathy.rhodes@seattlecolleges.edu
RHODES, Kay .... 806-742-5170 463 D
kay.rhodes@ttu.edu
RHODES, Keith .... 203-582-7938.. 88 A
keith.rhodes@quinnipiac.edu
RHODES, Lawrence .... 212-799-5000 312 B
RHODES, Lisa, D .... 404-270-5728 126 D
lrhodes@spelman.edu
RHODES, Michelle .... 616-331-3234 230 G
rhodesmi@gvsu.edu
RHODES, Neisha .... 209-667-3201.. 33 F
nrhodes@csustan.edu
RHODES, Phil .... 254-299-8642 452 E
prhodes@mclennan.edu
RHODES, Randall .... 510-925-4282.. 25 P
randall.rhodes@aua.am
RHODES, Rhosetta .... 509-777-4238 500 H
rrhodes@whitworth.edu
RHODES, Richard, M .... 512-223-7598 443 G
rrhodes@austincc.edu
RHODES, Robert .... 325-674-2024 441 D
robert.rhodes@acu.edu
RHODES, Simon .... 317-274-7211 160 E
srhodes@iupui.edu
RHODES, Tasha .... 718-260-5800 303 D
trhodes@citytech.cuny.edu
RHODES, Tim .... 606-783-2000 188 C
t.rhodes@moreheadstate.edu
RHODES, Vincent, A ..... 757-446-7070 480 C
rhodesva@evms.edu
RHOTON, James, M ...... 843-863-7050 419 C
jrhoton@csuniv.edu
RHUE, Monika .... 704-371-6741 338 I
mrhue@jcsu.edu
RHYNE, Teresa, L .... 757-455-3345 491 F
trhyne@vwu.edu
RHYNE, Whitney .... 239-433-6943 100 E
whitney.rhyne@fsw.edu
RHYNEER,
Madeleine, E .... 570-372-4293 410 H
rhyneer@susqu.edu
RHYNHART, Hans .... 860-486-4806.. 88 G
hans.rhynhart@uconn.edu
RIAL, Scott .... 847-543-2652 136 E
srial@clcillinois.edu
RIAS, Curtis .... 212-650-7073 301 F
curtis@ccny.cuny.edu
RIBAKOW, Larry .... 410-484-7200 206 C
lribakow@nirc.edu
RIBORDY, J. Clark .... 785-242-5200 180 H
clark.ribordy@ottawa.edu
RICARD, Mauise .... 470-639-0991 123 E
mauise.ricard@morehouse.edu
RICATTO, Pascal, J .... 201-493-3572 283 I
pjricatto@bergen.edu
RICAUD, Mary .... 225-248-1015 191 F
mricaud@fortis.edu
RICCA, Beth .... 201-684-7455 289 C
bricca@ramapo.edu
RICCARDI, Mark, T .... 304-724-3700 501 D
mriccardi@apus.edu
RICCARDI, Richard .... 203-392-5232.. 85 A
riccardir1@southernct.edu
RICCHEZZA, Lorraine ..... 856-256-5130 289 H
ricchezza@rowan.edu
RICCI, Amy .... 401-598-1000 416 C
aricci@jwu.edu
RICCI, Jose, L .... 787-728-1515 529 B
jricci@sagrado.edu
RICCI, Jose, L .... 787-727-7727 529 B
jricci@sagrado.edu
RICCI, Roberta .... 505-224-4000 293 L
rricci1@cnm.edu
RICCIARDI, Tracy .... 617-730-7084 223 B
tracy.ricciardi@newbury.edu
RICCIOTTI, MaryAnn ..... 973-290-4475 285 A
mricciotti@cse.edu
RICCOBONO, Steve .... 718-636-3787 320 D
sriccobono@pratt.edu
RICE, Alaina, M .... 620-417-1061 181 E
alaina.rice@sccc.edu
RICE, Angela .... 434-592-7250 482 D
amrice3@liberty.edu
RICE, Ann, M .... 916-734-0751.. 68 H
ann.rice@ucdmc.ucdavis.edu
RICE, Brian .... 937-393-3431 370 C
brice@sscc.edu

RICE, Carlton .... 205-929-6389.... 2 G
crice@lawsonstate.edu
RICE, Carolyn .... 828-398-7105 340 M
carolynhrice@abtech.edu
RICE, Cynthia, E .... 410-706-3171 207 H
crice@umaryland.edu
RICE, Daniel, B .... 785-628-4260 177 D
drice@fhsu.edu
RICE, Douglas .... 650-508-3684.. 54 D
drice@ndnu.edu
RICE, Edward .... 662-246-6442 254 C
erice@msdelta.edu
RICE, Fred .... 920-924-3291 514 D
frice@morainepark.edu
RICE, Gale .... 314-889-1479 260 C
grice@fontbonne.edu
RICE, Heather .... 256-228-6001.... 3 B
riceh@nacc.edu
RICE, James .... 312-850-7159 136 C
jrice36@ccc.edu
RICE, James, W .... 320-222-7474 247 B
jim.rice@ridgewater.edu
RICE, Jan .... 402-481-3908 273 F
jan.rice@bryanhealthcollege.edu
RICE, Jennifer .... 617-879-2233 226 A
jrice@wheelock.edu
RICE, Jennifer, K .... 301-405-2336 207 G
jkr@umd.edu
RICE, Jonah .... 618-252-5400 151 J
jonah.rice@sic.edu
RICE, Josh .... 404-835-6129 435 M
jrice@richmont.edu
RICE, Julie .... 317-299-0333 164 D
julie@tcmi.org
RICE, Justin .... 505-454-3349 294 J
1258mgr@fheg.follett.com
RICE, Kevin .... 585-395-2408 326 D
krice@brockport.edu
RICE, Kyle .... 307-532-8336 516 J
kyle.rice@ewc.wy.edu
RICE, Larry .... 918-343-7612 379 C
lrice@rsu.edu
RICE, Leah, B .... 859-846-5308 188 B
lbarth@midway.edu
RICE, Leila .... 315-781-3700 310 C
rice@hws.edu
RICE, Malcolm .... 256-824-2555.... 8 C
malcolm.rice@uah.edu
RICE, Malcolm .... 256-824-6347.... 8 C
malcom.rice@uah.edu
RICE, Martin .... 765-677-2939 161 C
martin.rice@indwes.edu
RICE, Peggy .... 815-836-5350 143 E
ricepe@lewisu.edu
RICE, Peter .... 201-684-7601 289 C
price@ramapo.edu
RICE, Priscilla .... 215-968-8450 390 I
priscilla.rice@bucks.edu
RICE, Rachel .... 207-768-9447 201 G
rachel.rice@maine.edu
RICE, Raymond, J .... 207-768-9525 201 G
raymond.rice@maine.edu
RICE, Rolundus .... 573-681-5115 261 H
ricer@lincolnu.edu
RICE, Scott .... 217-333-0560 154 B
serice@uillinois.edu
RICE, Sherwin .... 910-879-5646 341 A
srice@bladencc.edu
RICE, Susan, I .... 336-633-0282 345 F
sirice@randolph.edu
RICE, Vance .... 662-325-6731 254 E
rice@safdfairs.msstate.edu
RICE AYALA, Maggie .... 773-907-4041 135 K
mrice19@ccc.edu
RICE-CARROLL, Cynthia 760-757-2121.. 52 F
crice@miracosta.edu
RICE-CLAYBORN, Kathy . 501-450-3134.. 23 I
kathyc@uca.edu
RICE-MASON, Jenifer .... 870-972-3964.. 18 A
jrmason@astate.edu
RICE-SADDLER, Lori ...... 404-880-8447 117 H
lrice@cau.edu
RICE-SPEARMAN, Lori ... 806-743-3223 463 E
lori.ricespearman@ttuhsc.edu
RICH, Forrest .... 912-583-3146 116 G
frich@bpc.edu
RICH, Frank .... 432-335-6507 454 C
frich@odessa.edu
RICH, Jack, W .... 325-674-2013 441 D
richj@acu.edu
RICH, Kathy .... 781-280-3501 220 C
richk@middlesex.mass.edu
RICH, Kim .... 860-932-4141.. 86 E
krich@qvcc.edu
RICH, Laura .... 910-893-4364 336 C
richl@campbell.edu
RICH, Marcus .... 252-985-5176 348 A
mritch@ncwc.edu
RICH, Scott .... 620-278-4213 181 G
srich@sterling.edu
RICH, Shari .... 309-467-6424 138 E
srich@eureka.edu
RICH, Steven .... 617-236-8832 215 B
srich@fisher.edu
RICH, Steven, W .... 217-581-6616 138 A
swrich@eiu.edu
RICH, Teresa .... 509-574-4667 500 I
thollandrich@yvcc.edu
RICH, Timothy, A .... 651-631-5489 251 C
tarich@unwsp.edu
RICH-COATES, Robin ...... 757-789-1748 488 A
rrich-coates@es.vccs.edu
RICHARD, Alison, A ...... 570-372-4111 410 H
arichard@susqu.edu
RICHARD, Arthur .... 252-940-6210 340 N
arthur.richard@beaufortccc.edu
RICHARD, Cindy .... 978-998-7762 214 G
cirichar@endicott.edu
RICHARD, Dan .... 904-620-2700 110 E
drichard@unf.edu
RICHARD, Deborah .... 407-708-2487 107 G
richardd@seminolestate.edu
RICHARD, Delores .... 662-621-4205 252 E
dmrichard@coahomacc.edu
RICHARD, Guy .... 404-995-8484 255 E
grichard@rts.edu
RICHARD, Mark .... 205-665-6600.... 8 E
mrichard11@montevallo.edu
RICHARD, Mark .... 256-840-4110.... 3 F
mrichard@snead.edu
RICHARD, Patricia .... 775-784-4805 279 E
prichard@unr.edu
RICHARD, Renee .... 216-987-4865 360 E
renee.richard@tri-c.edu
RICHARD, Robert .... 337-482-6923 197 F
bookstore@louisiana.edu
RICHARD, Thomas .... 603-358-2326 283 A
trichard@keene.edu
RICHARD, Trish .... 409-772-8221 469 C
plrichar@utmb.edu
RICHARD, Valerie .... 704-403-3507 336 B
valerie.richard@carolinashealthcare.org
RICHARD, Valerie .... 410-778-7855 210 A
vrichard2@washcoll.edu
RICHARDELLO, Denise .. 413-662-5201 218 C
denise.richardello@mcla.edu
RICHARDS, Char .... 262-524-6891 506 G
crichard@carrollu.edu
RICHARDS, Cheryl .... 980-224-8466 223 D
RICHARDS, Chris .... 715-346-3908 511 F
crichards@uwsp.edu
RICHARDS, Connie, L ... 229-333-5699 127 H
clrichards@valdosta.edu
RICHARDS, David .... 626-584-5458.. 43 K
richards@fuller.edu
RICHARDS, David, E ..... 402-554-2640 277 I
derichards@unomaha.edu
RICHARDS, Debbie .... 304-424-8201 505 C
debbie.richards@wvup.edu
RICHARDS,
E. Randolph .... 561-803-2051 104 I
randy_richards@pba.edu
RICHARDS, Elizabeth ..... 603-668-2211 282 C
e.richards1@snhu.edu
RICHARDS, Faith .... 605-455-6029 427 I
frichards@olc.edu
RICHARDS, Ginger .... 317-805-1783 502 D
vrichards@salemu.edu
RICHARDS, Gordon .... 724-847-6718 395 J
grichard@geneva.edu
RICHARDS, Gwyn .... 812-855-2435 159 H
grichar@indiana.edu
RICHARDS, Jeni .... 949-376-6000.. 47 H
jrichards@lcad.edu
RICHARDS, Jerry .... 920-924-3184 514 D
jrichards2@morainepark.edu
RICHARDS, John .... 808-734-9518 130 C
john.richards@hawaii.edu
RICHARDS, Josh .... 816-936-8718 266 K
jmrichards@saintlukescollege.edu
RICHARDS, Kathi, S ...... 937-778-7843 361 E
krichards@edisonohio.edu
RICHARDS, Kathy, A ..... 906-227-1237 235 A
kathrich@nmu.edu
RICHARDS, Katie, J .... 701-788-4675 354 B
katie.richards.2@mayvillestate.edu
RICHARDS, Kent .... 218-733-5969 245 C
k.richards@lsc.edu
RICHARDS, Lawrence .... 610-399-2405 405 G
police@cheyney.edu
RICHARDS, Leah .... 603-668-2211 282 C
l.richards1@snhu.edu
RICHARDS, Lee .... 740-362-3344 365 D
lrichards@mtso.edu
RICHARDS, Letha .... 662-621-4126 252 E
lrichards@coahomacc.edu
RICHARDS, Lowell .... 208-282-2315 132 B
richlowe@isu.edu
RICHARDS, Marty .... 910-362-7101 341 E
mrichards@cfcc.edu
RICHARDS, Marvin .... 216-987-4883 360 E
marvin.richards@tri-c.edu
RICHARDS, Maryanne ... 508-830-5039 218 D
mrichards@maritime.edu
RICHARDS, Matthew ..... 406-447-6900 271 I
RICHARDS, Matthew ..... 207-741-5927 200 C
mrichards@smccme.edu
RICHARDS, Michael ...... 515-281-3934 166 E
RICHARDS, Michael ...... 212-752-1530 312 G
michael.richards@limcollege.edu
RICHARDS, Michael, D . 702-651-5600 278 N
mike.richards@csn.edu
RICHARDS, Paula .... 559-297-4500.. 46 E
RICHARDS, Rosalie .... 386-822-7256 111 E
rrichar1@stetson.edu
RICHARDS, Roxanne ..... 218-726-8146 250 F
rmrichar@d.umn.edu
RICHARDS, Samantha ... 843-574-6771 424 G
samantha.richards@tridenttech.edu
RICHARDS, Sandra, K ... 800-328-2660.. 95 F
skrichards@baptistcollege.edu
RICHARDS, Sandra, K ... 850-263-3261.. 95 F
skrichards@baptistcollege.edu
RICHARDS, Scott .... 412-396-5140 394 D
richards@duq.edu
RICHARDS, Steve .... 320-762-4692 243 J
stever@alextech.edu
RICHARDS, Steven, N ... 540-863-2880 487 I
srichards@dslcc.edu
RICHARDS, Susan .... 307-754-6243 516 Q
susan.richards@nwc.edu
RICHARDS, Terry .... 312-341-3525 150 D
trichards07@roosevelt.edu
RICHARDS, Tom, F .... 573-882-2612 268 B
richardstf@umsystem.edu
RICHARDS, Tracey .... 215-619-7330 402 A
trichards@mc3.edu
RICHARDS, Troy .... 212-217-7664 308 B
troy_richards@fitnyc.edu
RICHARDS, Virginia ...... 925-473-1350.. 41 A
vrichards@losmedanos.edu
RICHARDSON, Aaron ..... 601-979-3704 253 E
aaron.richardson@jsums.edu
RICHARDSON, Ann .... 206-934-4567 497 H
ann.richardson@seattlecolleges.edu
RICHARDSON, Barbara .. 520-384-4502.. 11 R
richardsonbarb@cochise.edu
RICHARDSON, Barbara .. 520-586-1981.. 11 R
richardsonbarb@cochise.edu
RICHARDSON,
Belinda, M .... 724-287-8711 390 J
belinda.richardson@bc3.edu
RICHARDSON,
Bernard, L .... 202-806-7280.. 92 C
brichardson@howard.edu
RICHARDSON,
Bonita, L .... 412-237-4413 392 G
brichardson@ccac.edu
RICHARDSON, Brian, A . 804-371-3000 488 C
brichardson@reynolds.edu
RICHARDSON, Brittany .. 504-816-4797 191 E
brichardson@dillard.edu
RICHARDSON, Carole ... 319-208-5053 173 G
crichardson@scciowa.edu
RICHARDSON,
Charles, J .... 518-381-1210 323 L
richarcj@sunysccc.edu
RICHARDSON, JR.,
Charles, W .... 803-535-5200 419 E
crichardson@claflin.edu
RICHARDSON,
Christine .... 315-655-7147 300 I
cwrichardson@cazenovia.edu
RICHARDSON,
Christopher .... 804-355-0671 486 A
crichardson@upsem.edu
RICHARDSON, Cinzia ... 973-720-2976 292 I
richardsonc@wpunj.edu
RICHARDSON, D. Scott . 616-331-2188 230 G
richarsc@gvsu.edu
RICHARDSON, D. Scott . 616-331-2215 230 G
richarsc@gvsu.edu
RICHARDSON, Dale .... 636-481-3501 261 B
drichar6@jeffco.edu
RICHARDSON, Daniel ... 941-487-4417 110 B
drichardson@ncf.edu
RICHARDSON, David ..... 256-726-7018.... 6 E
hweems@oakwood.edu
RICHARDSON, David, E 352-392-0780 110 D
der@ufl.edu
RICHARDSON, Denise ... 510-464-3224.. 56 H
drichardson@peralta.edu
RICHARDSON,
Elisabeth .... 606-546-1700 189 I
erichardson@unionky.edu
RICHARDSON, Florence 301-295-3045 518 G
florence.richardson@usuhs.edu
RICHARDSON, II,
Gerald .... 305-626-3747.. 99 M
gerald.richardson@fmuniv.edu
RICHARDSON, Greer ..... 215-951-1806 398 F
richards@lasalle.edu
RICHARDSON, Greg, C . 606-474-3250 185 C
greg@kcu.edu
RICHARDSON, Guy, L ... 601-923-1650 255 E
grichardson@rts.edu
RICHARDSON, Irene ...... 513-244-4432 366 A
irene.richardson@msj.edu
RICHARDSON, James .... 509-682-6400 500 D
jrichardson@wvc.edu
RICHARDSON, Jay .... 601-318-6165 256 I
jrichardson@wmcarey.edu
RICHARDSON, Jennifer . 518-454-2023 305 B
richardj@strose.edu
RICHARDSON, John ...... 706-771-4111 116 A
jrichard@augustatech.edu
RICHARDSON, K. Scott . 724-287-8711 390 J
scott.richardson@bc3.edu
RICHARDSON, Karen, L 617-627-3170 225 A
karen.richardson@tufts.edu
RICHARDSON, Karlene .. 212-247-3434 313 K
krichardson@mandl.edu
RICHARDSON, Karry, D 573-629-3016 260 G
krichardson@hlg.edu
RICHARDSON, Kathleen 515-271-2295 168 J
kathleen.richardson@drake.edu
RICHARDSON, Kathy, B 724-946-7130 414 C
richarkb@westminster.edu
RICHARDSON, Ken .... 502-897-4703 189 A
krichardson@sbts.edu
RICHARDSON, Krista ..... 419-995-8312 363 G
richardson.k@rhodesstate.edu
RICHARDSON, Lilliard ... 317-274-2016 160 E
lillrichr@iupui.edu
RICHARDSON, Lisa, A .. 352-518-1301 105 C
richarl@phsc.edu
RICHARDSON, Logan .... 864-488-8277 422 B
lrichardson@limestone.edu
RICHARDSON, Luns, C . 803-934-3200 422 G
lcrichardson@morris.edu
RICHARDSON, Lynette .. 803-934-3181 422 G
lynrichardson@morris.edu
RICHARDSON,
Lynne, D .... 540-654-1561 486 D
lrichar2@umw.edu
RICHARDSON, Marcus .. 718-951-5669 301 E
mrichardson@brooklyn.cuny.edu
RICHARDSON, Maria .... 334-420-4499.... 3 H
mrichardson@trenholmstate.edu
RICHARDSON, Mary ...... 229-430-3588 114 J
mrichardson@albanytech.edu
RICHARDSON,
Matthew, O .... 801-422-2640 471 E
matt_richardson@byu.edu
RICHARDSON, Melanie . 505-438-8884 296 D
melanie@acupuncturecollege.edu
RICHARDSON, Melanie . 360-438-4367 497 F
mrichardson@stmartin.edu
RICHARDSON, Michael . 417-667-8181 259 A
mrichardson@cottey.edu
RICHARDSON,
Michael, W .... 406-496-4213 272 E
mrichardson@mtech.edu
RICHARDSON, Ralph, C 913-541-1220 179 A
rcr@ksu.edu
RICHARDSON,
Raymond .... 806-720-7230 452 D
raymond.richardson@lcu.edu
RICHARDSON, Rebecca . 707-545-3647.. 27 B
becca@berginu.edu
RICHARDSON, Robin .... 401-232-6000 416 A
rarich@bryant.edu
RICHARDSON, Roger .... 607-274-1623 311 D
rrichard@ithaca.edu
RICHARDSON, Russ ...... 406-683-7509 271 H
russ.richardson@umwestern.edu
RICHARDSON, Rusty ..... 615-547-4401 431 D
rrichardson@cumberland.edu
RICHARDSON, Sarah, D 402-280-2703 274 D
sarahrichardson@creighton.edu
RICHARDSON, Scott ...... 570-389-5011 405 E
srichardso@bloomu.edu
RICHARDSON, Song ..... 949-824-4158.. 69 A
srichardson@law.uci.edu
RICHARDSON, Steven ... 562-860-2451.. 36 A
srichardson@cerritos.edu
RICHARDSON, Sydney .. 336-917-5588 348 H
sydney.richardson@salem.edu
RICHARDSON, TaNeal ... 432-264-5608 450 G
trichardson@howardcollege.edu

RICHARDSON, Terry ...... 276-944-6231 480 J
trichard@ehc.edu
RICHARDSON, Theodore .... 321-674-8123.. 99 K
trichardson@fit.edu
RICHARDSON, Thomas . 662-329-7142 254 F
tcrichardson@muw.edu
RICHARDSON, Thomas, J .... 717-871-7085 407 A
tom.richardson@millersville.edu
RICHARDSON, Toni .... 843-661-8341 421 F
toni.richardson@fdtc.edu
RICHARDSON, Tracey ... 760-245-4271.. 73 E
tracey.richardson@vvc.edu
RICHARDSON, Tracy ..... 812-535-5154 163 I
trichard@smwc.edu
RICHARDSON, Trevor .... 405-744-5458 377 F
trevor.richardson@okstate.edu
RICHARDSON, W. Mark 510-204-0733.. 37 F
mrichardson@cdsp.edu
RICHARDSON, Wayne ... 954-545-4500 108 A
newsletter@sfbc.edu
RICHARDSON, William .. 225-578-4161 193 M
brichardson@lsu.edu
RICHARDSON-WILKS, Pamela .... 937-708-5814 373 H
pwilks@wilberforce.edu
RICHARDVILLE, Alane ... 863-638-7209 113 I
alane.richardville@warner.edu
RICHE, Cindy .... 206-934-3740 497 H
cindy.riche@seattlecolleges.edu
RICHELSON, Linda .... 603-357-2142 281 A
lrichelson@ccsnh.edu
RICHEME, Ashiah .... 413-572-5442 218 F
aricheme@westfield.ma.edu
RICHEMOND, Donna ..... 215-751-8131 393 A
drichemond@ccp.edu
RICHERSON, Melissa ... 805-546-3129.. 41 C
melissa_richerson@cuesta.edu
RICHERT, Dave .... 559-453-3406.. 43 J
dave.richert@fresno.edu
RICHERT, Lauren .... 615-794-4254 435 G
lrichert@omorecollege.edu
RICHES, Jonathan, S ..... 610-292-9852 408 I
jonathan.riches@reseminary.edu
RICHEY, Amber, L .... 937-255-6565 517 H
amber.richey@afit.edu
RICHEY, Angie .... 909-599-5433.. 48 E
arichey@lifepacific.edu
RICHEY, Anthony .... 334-244-3570.... 4 E
arichey@aum.edu
RICHEY, D. Michael ...... 859-257-3912 190 B
mrichey@email.uky.edu
RICHEY, James, H .... 321-433-7000.. 97 N
richeyj@easternflorida.edu
RICHEY, Lance, D .... 260-399-7700 165 B
lrichey@sf.edu
RICHEY, Melody, H .... 901-843-3730 435 L
richey@rhodes.edu
RICHEY, Patrick .... 585-389-2020 316 D
prichey1@naz.edu
RICHEY, Suzanne .... 423-636-7303 439 C
srichey@tusculum.edu
RICHEY, Thomas .... 562-860-2451.. 36 A
trichey@cerritos.edu
RICHIE, Darren .... 863-638-2953 114 A
richieda@webber.edu
RICHIE, Patricia, V .... 561-868-3540 105 A
richiep@palmbeachstate.edu
RICHINS, Daniel .... 317-632-5553 162 P
RICHISON, Anna, C .... 260-982-5306 162 Q
arichison@manchester.edu
RICHMAN, Aaron .... 828-398-7147 340 M
aaronmrichman@abtech.edu
RICHMAN, John .... 701-671-2221 355 B
john.richman@ndscs.edu
RICHMAN, Steve .... 660-359-3948 264 H
srichman@mail.ncmissouri.edu
RICHMAN, Susan .... 781-891-2660 212 A
srichman@bentley.edu
RICHMOND, Jayne, E ... 401-874-5505 417 E
jrichmond@uri.edu
RICHMOND, John, W ..... 940-565-2791 466 B
john.richmond@unt.edu
RICHMOND, Kerry .... 570-321-4202 400 G
richmond@lycoming.edu
RICHMOND, Lisa, T .... 630-752-5101 155 F
lisa.richmond@wheaton.edu
RICHMOND, Margaret ... 603-358-2276 283 A
mrichmon@keene.edu
RICHMOND, Nicola .... 520-206-4414.. 15 L
ncrichmond@pima.edu
RICHMOND, Sally, S ..... 540-458-8710 491 G
srichmond@wlu.edu
RICHMOND, Steve .... 606-783-5236 188 C
s.richmond@moreheadstate.edu
RICHMOND, Theresa ..... 530-938-5317.. 39 H
trichmond@siskiyous.edu
RICHMOND, Vicki .... 757-825-3810 489 G
richmondvc@tncc.edu
RICHTER, Jason, D .... 512-471-6231 467 C
oa.jrichter@austin.utexas.edu
RICHTER, Jennifer .... 865-974-1000 439 I
jrichter@utk.edu
RICHTER, Jerome, J ...... 701-355-8072 355 K
jjrichter@umary.edu
RICHTER, Sara .... 580-349-1472 377 E
saraj@opsu.edu
RICHTER, Sheila, W ...... 814-824-2287 401 J
srichter@mercyhurst.edu
RICHTER, Suzanna, L .... 717-358-5843 395 G
suzanna.richter@fandm.edu
RICHTER, Thomas, P .... 920-923-7640 508 B
tprichter32@marianuniversity.edu
RICHTER-NORGEL, Ellen .... 651-690-8730 249 T
erichter-norgel@stkate.edu
RICHTERMEYER, Sandra 978-934-2850 217 B
sandra_richtermeyer@uml.edu
RICHTERS, Stephen, P .. 318-342-1070 198 A
richters@ulm.edu
RICHTMAN, Meg .... 319-385-6212 170 J
meg.richtman@iw.edu
RICIOPPO, Eric .... 718-357-0500 323 E
ericioppo@stpaulsschoolofnursing.edu
RICK, Adam .... 517-607-2645 231 C
arick@hillsdale.edu
RICK, Joseph .... 336-770-3284 352 B
rickj@uncsa.edu
RICKARD, Larry .... 561-237-7118 103 E
lrickard@lynn.edu
RICKARD, Walter .... 718-636-3771 320 D
wrickard@pratt.edu
RICKARDS, Brenden ...... 856-415-2297 289 G
brickards@rcgc.edu
RICKARDS, Laura .... 732-255-0400 288 B
lrickards@ocean.edu
RICKENBAKER, Michael 478-445-4467 119 E
michael.rickenbaker@gcsu.edu
RICKER, Curtis .... 912-478-0779 120 E
cricker@georgiasouthern.edu
RICKER, Deborah .... 301-696-3623 204 D
ricker@hood.edu
RICKER, Don .... 419-227-3141 372 D
dricker@unoh.edu
RICKER, Jean .... 781-292-2343 215 C
jean.ricker@olin.edu
RICKERT, Bryan .... 903-693-1112 454 E
brickert@panola.edu
RICKERT, Gail Ann .... 717-337-6579 396 A
grickert@gettysburg.edu
RICKETTS, Lloyd .... 609-771-2186 284 I
ricketts@tcnj.edu
RICKETTS, Mike .... 423-697-4433 436 F
mike.ricketts@chattanoogastate.edu
RICKETTS, Tracy .... 541-885-1118 385 E
tracy.ricketts@oit.edu
RICKINGER, Rachel .... 517-264-7172 236 I
rricking@sienaheights.edu
RICKS, Mary .... 731-286-3290 437 A
ricks@dscc.edu
RICKS, Naima, K .... 973-290-4219 285 A
nricks@cse.edu
RICKS, Ruchelle .... 252-862-1246 345 H
rricks@roanokechowan.edu
RICO, Antonio .... 915-779-8031 470 E
ccctrain@aol.com
RICO, Camilla .... 360-417-6442 496 I
crico@pencol.edu
RICO, Oscar .... 661-654-2394.. 31 B
orico@csub.edu
RICO-GUTIERREZ, Luis, C .... 515-294-7427 166 F
lrico@iastate.edu
RICORDATI, Timothy ..... 630-617-3089 138 C
timothy.ricordati@elmhurst.edu
RICOTTA, Helen .... 610-341-5934 394 E
0713mgr@follett.com
RICOTTA, Lorna .... 910-678-8201 343 B
ricottal@faytechcc.edu
RICZKER, Nicolette .... 716-338-1035 311 F
nickeyriczker@mail.sunyjcc.edu
RIDD, Kaylee .... 801-649-5230 471 M
clinicaldeanassistant@midwifery.edu
RIDD-YOUNG, Kristi ...... 866-680-2756 471 M
president@midwifery.edu
RIDDELL, Richard .... 919-684-2641 337 C
richard.riddell@duke.edu
RIDDER, Cece .... 503-725-4457 386 D
ridder@pdx.edu
RIDDERING, Rick .... 708-239-4709 153 B
rick.riddering@trnty.edu
RIDDICK, Althea, L .... 252-335-8787 350 A
aariddick@ecsu.edu
RIDDICK, Rich .... 308-635-6067 278 B
riddickr@wncc.edu
RIDDICK, Vera, E .... 757-683-3689 483 G
vriddick@odu.edu
RIDDLE, Catherine .... 518-262-3593 297 L
riddlec@mail.amc.edu
RIDDLE, Christy .... 662-846-4336 252 H
criddle@deltastate.edu
RIDDLE, Heather .... 612-330-1177 240 G
riddle@augsburg.edu
RIDDLE, Jennifer .... 208-459-5688 131 H
jriddle@collegeofidaho.edu
RIDDLE, Joyce, E .... 304-462-6184 504 B
joyce.riddle@glenville.edu
RIDDLE, Kelley .... 575-538-6146 297 H
kelley.riddle@wnmu.edu
RIDDLE, Larry .... 770-426-2979 122 F
larry.riddle@life.edu
RIDDLE, Laura .... 601-276-3865 256 A
lriddle@smcc.edu
RIDDLE, Troy .... 312-427-2737 141 E
triddle@jmls.edu
RIDEAUX, Larry .... 817-515-4507 458 B
larry.rideaux@tccd.edu
RIDEL, Robert .... 503-228-6528 381 I
rridel@aii.edu
RIDENOUR, Nancy, A .... 505-272-6284 296 H
nridenour@salud.unm.edu
RIDEOUT, Junior .... 910-879-5661 341 A
jrideout@bladencc.edu
RIDEOUT, Kathy .... 585-275-8902 332 E
kathy_rideout@urmc.rochester.edu
RIDER, Abigail .... 401-874-2433 417 E
arider@uri.edu
RIDER, Elizabeth (Betty) 717-361-1416 394 F
ridere@etown.edu
RIDER, Jeff .... 870-759-4194.. 23 K
jrider@wbcoll.edu
RIDER, Paul .... 515-263-2917 169 E
prider@grandview.edu
RIDER, Robert .... 865-974-2201 439 I
brider@utk.edu
RIDES HORSE, JR., Curtis .... 406-638-3111 271 C
rideshorsec@lbhc.edu
RIDGE, Sean .... 865-573-4517 432 H
sridge@johnsonu.edu
RIDGE, Susan .... 443-997-9908 204 F
sridge1@jhu.edu
RIDGEDELL, Ken, W ...... 985-549-2121 197 E
kridgedell@selu.edu
RIDGES, Jarvis .... 404-270-5003 126 D
jarvis.ridges@spelman.edu
RIDGEWAY, Melissa ...... 815-967-7306 150 B
mridgeway@rockfordcareercollege.edu
RIDGWAY, Dan .... 216-649-8900 363 I
dridgway@kent.edu
RIDGWAY, Lori .... 307-855-2103 516 I
lridgway@cwc.edu
RIDGWAY, Susan, M .... 989-837-4219 235 C
ridgway@northwood.edu
RIDINGTON, M. Thomas .... 610-341-4377 394 E
tridingt@eastern.edu
RIDLEY, Ellen .... 207-221-4419 202 A
eridley@une.edu
RIDLEY, Emmett, L .... 804-524-5068 491 A
eridley@vsu.edu
RIDLEY, Scott .... 806-742-1988 463 D
scott.ridley@ttu.edu
RIDLEY, Tim .... 661-654-2066.. 31 B
tridley@csub.edu
RIDLEY, JR., Wadell ..... 610-660-1223 409 H
wridley@sju.edu
RIDOUT, Thomas, M ..... 563-562-3263 172 D
ridoutt@nicc.edu
RIDPATH, Kathy, T .... 540-674-3601 488 G
kridpath@nr.edu
RIDPATH, Lance .... 304-647-6424 504 F
lridpath@osteo.wvsom.edu
RIDPATH, Lisa .... 540-857-7201 490 B
lridpath@virginiawestern.edu
RIDPATH, Tanya .... 540-375-2323 484 H
ridpath@roanoke.edu
RIEBAU, Brett .... 330-569-5119 362 J
riebaub@hiram.edu
RIEDEL, Eric .... 866-492-5336 251 E
eric.riedel@mail.waldenu.edu
RIEDEL, Herbert, H .... 334-222-6591.... 2 H
hriedel@lbwcc.edu
RIEDEL CARNEY, Elizabeth .... 651-690-6836 249 T
eacarney@stkate.edu
RIEDER, Rick .... 660-626-2555 257 A
rrieder@atsu.edu
RIEDL-FARREY, Cathy, J .... 608-342-1435 511 D
riedlfac@uwplatt.edu
RIEDLING, Patrick .... 619-239-0391.. 35 C
priedling@cwsl.edu
RIEDSTRA, Catherine ..... 805-546-3130.. 41 C
cmachado@cuesta.edu
RIEFKOHL, Jorge .... 787-780-0070 521 B
jriefkohl@caribbean.edu
RIEGER, Mark .... 302-831-2501.. 90 I
mrieger@udel.edu
RIEHL, Christine .... 503-338-2432 382 E
criehl@clatsopcc.edu
RIEHL, Shelle .... 503-517-1814 388 C
sriehl@westernseminary.edu
RIEHLE, Douglas .... 937-778-7979 361 E
driehle@edisonohio.edu
RIEKEMAN, Guy, F .... 770-426-2601 122 F
riekeman@life.edu
RIEKENBERG, Tim .... 620-227-9355 176 N
triekenberg@dc3.edu
RIEKERT, Jennifer .... 914-594-4536 318 A
jennifer_riekert@nymc.edu
RIEKS, Stephen .... 716-673-4670 325 C
stephen.rieks@fredonia.edu
RIEKS, Stephen, J .... 716-673-4670 325 C
stephen.rieks@fredonia.edu
RIELLO, Heidi, A .... 413-662-5331 218 C
heidi.riello@mcla.edu
RIEMAN, Jeff .... 419-772-3100 367 G
j-rieman@onu.edu
RIEN, Nate .... 209-588-5182.. 75 I
rienn@yosemite.edu
RIEPMA, Edward .... 949-794-9090.. 66 B
eriepma@stanbridge.edu
RIERA, José-Luis .... 302-831-8939.. 90 I
jriera@udel.edu
RIES, Barry .... 507-389-1242 246 A
barry.ries@mnsu.edu
RIES, Heidi, R .... 937-255-3633 517 H
heidi.ries@afit.edu
RIES, Kenneth .... 320-629-5195 246 H
riesk@pine.edu
RIES, Thomas Karl .... 651-641-8211 241 L
ries@csp.edu
RIESE, Sara .... 303-762-6995.. 79 G
sara.riese@denverseminary.edu
RIESER-DANNER, Loretta .... 610-436-3106 407 D
lrieser-danner@wcupa.edu
RIESINGER, Mick .... 701-483-2389 354 A
michael.riesinger@dickinsonstate.edu
RIESTER, Jon .... 812-866-7021 158 C
riester@hanover.edu
RIESTER, Melanie .... 919-536-7200 342 G
riesterm@durhamtech.edu
RIESTERER, Brenda .... 920-693-1140 513 H
brenda.riesterer@gotoltc.edu
RIESTRA, Liza .... 787-841-2000 525 J
liza_riestra@pucpr.edu
RIESTRA, Miguel, A ...... 787-622-8000 527 B
mriestra@pupr.edu
RIETHLE, Theresa .... 413-565-1000 211 C
triethle@baypath.edu
RIEVES, Jimmy .... 903-988-7536 451 F
jrieves@kilgore.edu
RIFKIN, Benjamin .... 516-463-5411 310 D
benjamin.rifkin@hofstra.edu
RIGALI, Mary .... 203-596-4504.. 87 H
mrigali@post.edu
RIGBY, Heather .... 248-689-8282 238 F
hrigby@walshcollege.edu
RIGBY, Melissa, C .... 410-951-3848 208 F
mrigby@coppin.edu
RIGGERT, Mark .... 402-557-7070 273 E
bubookstore@fheg.follett.com
RIGGINS, Darius .... 661-654-3277.. 31 B
driggins@csub.edu
RIGGINS, David, W .... 828-689-1219 339 G
driggins@mhu.edu
RIGGINS, Vanessa .... 323-563-4842.. 36 H
vanessariggins@cdrewu.edu
RIGGLE, Ron .... 217-786-2581 144 B
ron.riggle@llcc.edu
RIGGS, Alexia .... 325-649-8610 450 H
ariggs@hputx.edu
RIGGS, Allen .... 435-283-7125 474 A
allen.riggs@snow.edu
RIGGS, Bonnie .... 423-697-4465 436 F
bonnie.riggs@chattanoogastate.edu
RIGGS, Channing .... 612-624-6868 250 E
riggs035@umn.edu
RIGGS, David .... 765-677-2808 161 C
david.riggs@indwes.edu
RIGGS, Joyce .... 270-824-8581 186 D
joyce.riggs@kctcs.edu
RIGGS, Michelle .... 909-389-3391.. 59 H
mriggs@craftonhills.edu
RIGGS, Paul .... 570-408-4600 414 H
paul.riggs@wilkes.edu
RIGGS, Robert, F .... 214-887-5007 448 G
rriggs@dts.edu

RITTER, Jeff ... 412-536-1027 398 E
jeff.ritter@laroche.edu
RITTER, Joseph ... 618-374-5155 149 A
joe.ritter@principia.edu
RITTER, Julie ... 717-334-6286 412 E
RITTER, Mark ... 864-503-5939 425 H
mritter@uscupstate.edu
RITTER, Michael ... 863-638-2968 114 A
rittermj@webber.edu
RITTER, Pamela, S ... 423-439-4242 431 H
ritterp@etsu.edu
RITTER, Will ... 336-272-7102 338 B
will.ritter@greensboro.edu
RITTERBROWN,
Michael ... 818-240-1000.. 44 D
michaelr@glendale.edu
RITTERBUSH, Jon ... 816-584-6707 265 C
jon.ritterbursh@park.edu
RITTINGER, Gina ... 859-572-6565 188 E
rittingergl@nku.edu
RITTLE, Dennis, C ... 620-441-5234 176 M
dennis.rittle@cowley.edu
RITTLING, Mary, E ... 336-249-8186 342 F
merittli@davidsonccc.edu
RITTLING, Meg ... 716-829-7808 307 B
rittling@dyc.edu
RITTS, Bonnie, B ... 585-785-1281 308 D
bonnie.ritts@flcc.edu
RITZ, Cathy ... 661-362-3639.. 39 C
cathy.ritz@canyons.edu
RITZ, Robert, L ... 434-592-4800 482 D
rlritz@liberty.edu
RITZ, Steven ... 831-459-2635.. 70 C
sritz@scipp.ucsc.edu
RITZE, Nancy ... 718-289-5156 301 D
nancy.ritze@bcc.cuny.edu
RITZLINE, Pamela ... 330-490-7446 373 F
pritzline@walsh.edu
RITZMAN, Elizabeth ... 708-524-6520 137 F
eritzman@dom.edu
RIVADENEYRA, Rocio ... 309-438-7005 140 L
rrivade@ilstu.edu
RIVALEAU, Susan, A ... 843-953-4973 420 C
rivaleaus@cofc.edu
RIVARA, Sara ... 503-491-7469 384 D
sara.rivara@mhcc.edu
RIVARD, Dawn ... 715-682-1812 509 D
drivard@northland.edu
RIVARD, Mary ... 940-552-6291 469 F
mrivard@vernoncollege.edu
RIVARD, T.J ... 765-973-8243 160 A
trivard@iue.edu
RIVARD, Timothy ... 781-239-2631 220 A
trivard@massbay.edu
RIVAS, J.C ... 323-319-9500.. 68 B
RIVAS, Rolando ... 704-461-6561 335 J
rolandorivas@bac.edu
RIVAS, Yari ... 787-738-2161 528 A
yari.alternacommunications@gmail.com
RIVELAND, Bruce ... 206-934-4193 497 I
bruce.riveland@seattlecolleges.edu
RIVENES, Theresa ... 541-245-7517 386 G
trivenes@roguecc.edu
RIVERA, Alba ... 787-743-7979 526 A
albrivera@suagm.edu
RIVERA,
Ana Jacqueline ... 787-754-7120 523 E
RIVERA, Anthony ... 412-924-1383 408 E
arivera@pts.edu
RIVERA, Arcilia ... 787-864-2222 524 A
arcilia.rivera@guayama.inter.edu
RIVERA, JR., Augustin .. 361-698-1098 448 H
ariverajr@delmar.edu
RIVERA, Aurora ... 787-738-2161 528 A
aurora.rivera@upr.edu
RIVERA, Beatriz ... 787-250-1912 524 B
brivera@metro.inter.edu
RIVERA, Carlos, E ... 787-725-8120 522 M
planificacion@eap.edu
RIVERA, Carmen ... 787-725-6500 521 C
crivera@albizu.edu
RIVERA, Carmen ... 787-250-1912 524 B
crivera@metro.inter.edu
RIVERA, Carmen ... 787-850-9301 528 B
carmen.rivera19@upr.edu
RIVERA, Carmen ... 773-878-3545 150 I
crivera@staugustine.edu
RIVERA, Carmen, G ... 787-864-2222 524 A
carmen.rivera@guayama.inter.edu
RIVERA, Carmen, J ... 787-743-7979 526 A
ut_crivera@suagm.edu
RIVERA, Carmen, M ... 787-258-1501 521 K
crivera@columbiacentral.edu
RIVERA, Daisy ... 787-850-9363 528 B
daisy.rivera3@upr.edu
RIVERA, Denise ... 817-202-6214 457 E
denise.rivera@swau.edu

RIVERA, Deserie ... 254-519-5722 459 D
d.rivera@tamuct.edu
RIVERA, Edgardo ... 787-850-9303 528 B
edgardo.rivera14@upr.edu
RIVERA, Edith ... 212-817-7410 302 B
erivera@gc.cuny.edu
RIVERA, Edwin ... 787-279-1912 523 J
edrivera@bayamon.inter.edu
RIVERA, Eileen ... 787-864-2222 524 A
eileen.rivera@guayama.inter.edu
RIVERA, Eleric ... 787-738-2161 528 A
eleric.rivera@upr.edu
RIVERA, Elias ... 718-782-2200 299 L
erivera@boricuacollege.edu
RIVERA, Enid ... 787-786-3030 526 F
erivera@ucb.edu.pr
RIVERA, Eric ... 619-594-5211.. 34 B
erivera@mail.sdsu.edu
RIVERA, Francisco ... 787-765-1915 524 F
frivera@opto.inter.edu
RIVERA, George ... 787-250-1912 524 B
garivera@metro.inter.edu
RIVERA, Gilbert ... 505-425-7511 294 J
RIVERA, Israel ... 787-857-3600 523 I
isrivm@br.inter.edu
RIVERA, Ivelisse ... 787-664-0466 529 A
ivelisse.rivera5@upr.edu
RIVERA, Jaime ... 787-852-1430 522 P
jaimerivera@hccpr.edu
RIVERA, Janice ... 787-789-4251 521 A
jrivera@atlanticu.edu
RIVERA, Jason, E ... 717-245-1019 394 A
riveraja@dickinson.edu
RIVERA, Jesenia ... 716-286-8350 318 F
jrivera@niagara.edu
RIVERA, Jesus, M ... 787-258-1501 521 K
jrivera@columbiacentral.edu
RIVERA, José, A ... 787-892-2315 524 D
joseanibalrivera@intersg.edu
RIVERA, Jose ... 413-552-2420 219 G
jrivera@hcc.edu
RIVERA, Jose, A ... 787-751-1912 524 E
jrivera@juris.inter.edu
RIVERA, Joshua ... 718-518-4342 302 D
jrivera@hostos.cuny.edu
RIVERA, Juan, C ... 787-841-2000 525 J
capellania@pucpr.edu
RIVERA, Julia ... 860-297-4203.. 88 E
julia.rivera@trincoll.edu
RIVERA, Laura ... 707-524-1635.. 62 H
lrivera@santarosa.edu
RIVERA, Leilany, C ... 787-738-2161 528 A
leilany.rivera@upr.edu
RIVERA, Leonard ... 361-698-2404 448 H
lrivera@delmar.edu
RIVERA, Lisette ... 787-250-1912 524 B
lriverao@metro.inter.edu
RIVERA, Liza ... 347-964-8600 299 L
lrivera@boricuacollege.edu
RIVERA, Lizbeth ... 787-743-7979 526 A
lizrivera@suagm.edu
RIVERA, Lorell ... 787-863-2390 523 K
lorell.rivera@fajardo.inter.edu
RIVERA, Luis ... 787-765-3560 522 K
lrivera@edpuniversity.edu
RIVERA, Luis, J ... 847-866-3904 138 G
lrr@garrett.edu
RIVERA, Luis, R ... 787-890-2681 527 E
luis.rivera86@upr.edu
RIVERA, Marcos ... 216-987-5378 360 E
marcos.rivera@tri-c.edu
RIVERA, Margarita ... 787-765-4210 521 G
mrivera@cempr.edu
RIVERA,
Maria de los, M ... 787-753-6000 522 Q
mrivera@icprjc.edu
RIVERA, Maria del C ... 787-857-3600 523 I
mcrivera@br.inter.edu
RIVERA, Marielis, E ... 787-257-7373 525 Q
mrivera966@suagm.edu
RIVERA, Marina ... 787-857-3600 523 I
mrivera@br.inter.edu
RIVERA, Mary Ann ... 757-388-3015 485 B
mrivera@sentara.edu
RIVERA, Maximina ... 908-737-6800 286 F
mrivera@kean.edu
RIVERA, Melissa, L ... 860-444-8280 519 B
melissa.l.rivera@uscg.mil
RIVERA, Merla ... 787-864-2222 524 A
merla.rivera@guayama.inter.edu
RIVERA, Milagros, M ... 787-786-3030 526 F
mrivera@ucb.edu.pr
RIVERA, Mildred ... 787-798-3001 526 G
mildred.rivera@uccaribe.edu
RIVERA, Mildred, Y ... 787-257-7373 525 Q
myrivera@suagm.edu
RIVERA, Mildred, Y ... 787-743-7979 526 A
myrivera@suagm.edu

RIVERA, Nieves ... 787-725-6500 521 C
nrivera@albizu.edu
RIVERA, Nydia ... 787-765-3560 522 K
nrivera@edpuniversity.edu
RIVERA, Olga ... 787-753-6335 522 Q
orivera@icprjc.edu
RIVERA, Paul ... 787-752-4575 527 H
paul.rivera1@upr.edu
RIVERA, Pedro ... 787-878-5475 523 H
pirivera@arecibo.inter.edu
RIVERA, Porfirio ... 787-766-1912 523 F
privera@inter.edu
RIVERA, Ralph ... 787-758-2525 528 D
ralph.rivera@upr.edu
RIVERA, Ramon ... 787-622-8000 527 B
rrivera@pupr.edu
RIVERA, Rey ... 623-935-8033.. 13 F
rey.rivera@estrellamountain.edu
RIVERA, Rody ... 787-850-9376 528 B
rody.rivera@upr.edu
RIVERA, Rosa, M ... 856-225-6836 290 B
rosarive@camden.rutgers.edu
RIVERA, Ruben ... 651-638-6045 240 J
rrivera@bethel.edu
RIVERA, Ruben, L ... 207-859-4127 198 H
rlrivera@colby.edu
RIVERA, Schvalla ... 308-635-6123 278 B
riveras1@wncc.edu
RIVERA, Serafin ... 787-279-1912 523 J
sriverat@bayamon.inter.edu
RIVERA, Sergio ... 210-486-3888 441 H
srivera@alamo.edu
RIVERA, Suzanne, M ... 216-368-6269 358 C
suzanne.rivera@case.edu
RIVERA, Teresita ... 787-882-2065 526 D
admisiones@unitecpr.net
RIVERA, Teresita ... 787-780-0070 521 B
trivera@caribbean.edu
RIVERA, Tresban ... 928-213-6060.. 12 D
tresban.rivera@collegeamerica.edu
RIVERA, Wendy ... 818-364-7779.. 49 C
RIVERA, Yolanda ... 787-758-2525 528 D
yolanda.rivera3@upr.edu
RIVERA-ARROYO,
Basilio ... 787-250-0000 527 D
basilio.rivera@upr.edu
RIVERA-CLAUDIO,
Nelda ... 787-764-1912 523 F
nerivera@inter.edu
RIVERA LUGO, Yadira ... 787-766-1717 526 B
um_yrivera@suagm.edu
RIVERA-MARQUEZ,
Annelis ... 787-480-2455 521 J
armarquez@sanjuanciudadpatria.com
RIVERA-MERCADO,
Yanid ... 787-480-2430 521 J
yarivera@sanjuanciudadpatria.com
RIVERA NEGRON,
Adrian, O ... 787-725-8120 522 M
actividadesculturales@eap.edu
RIVERA-OTERO,
Milagros ... 787-621-2835 520 F
mrivera@aupr.edu
RIVERA PEREZ,
Carlos, E ... 787-945-7016 522 M
rectoria@eap.edu
RIVERO, Brenda ... 601-928-6380 254 D
brenda.rivero@mgccc.edu
RIVERO, David, A ... 305-284-1650 112 O
darivero@miami.edu
RIVERO, Estela ... 518-442-5800 324 G
erivero@albany.edu
RIVERO, Yaidany ... 305-474-6965 107 B
yrivero@stu.edu
RIVERS, Andrew ... 202-806-2550.. 92 C
andrew.rivers@howard.edu
RIVERS, Erica ... 617-541-5332 221 A
erivers@rcc.mass.edu
RIVERS, Kyle ... 201-761-7102 291 D
krivers@saintpeters.edu
RIVERS, Nancy, A ... 434-982-2662 486 H
nan9k@virginia.edu
RIVERS, Verna, J ... 340-693-1121 529 C
vrivers@uvi.edu
RIVERS LANG,
Evangeline ... 256-726-7484.... 6 E
elang@oakwood.edu
RIVES, Joseph ... 309-762-8090 155 D
j-rives@wiu.edu
RIVETT, Donna ... 772-462-7656 101 Q
drivett@irsc.edu
RIX, Charles ... 405-425-5379 377 B
charles.rix@oc.edu
RIX, Todd ... 843-383-8126 420 B
trix@coker.edu
RIXEN, Mary ... 580-387-7303 376 D
mrixen@mscok.edu
RIZA, Robert ... 806-874-3571 445 R

RIZK, Michelle ... 907-450-8187.... 9 I
marizk@alaska.edu
RIZO, Sergio ... 417-626-1234 264 J
rizo.sergio@occ.edu
RIZVI, S. Abu Turab ... 610-330-5066 399 B
rizvia@lafayette.edu
RIZVI, Syed ... 714-628-4967.. 58 B
rizvi_syed@sccollege.edu
RIZZARDI, Bethany ... 707-826-4204.. 34 A
bethany.rizzardi@humboldt.edu
RIZZARDI, Morgan, M .. 724-287-8711 390 J
morgan.rizzardi@bc3.edu
RIZZI, Gino ... 518-828-4181 305 D
rizzi@sunycgcc.edu
RIZZO, Frank ... 949-508-2317 353 C
frank.rizzo@peace.edu
RIZZO, Mary ... 610-796-8379 389 A
mary.rizzo@alvernia.edu
RIZZO, Matt ... 802-440-4336 474 F
mattrizzo@bennington.edu
RIZZO, Pete ... 402-844-7151 276 G
pete@northeast.edu
RIZZO, Rosalina, B ... 716-880-2339 314 F
rosalina.b.rizzo@medaille.edu
RIZZUTO, James, T ... 719-384-6822.. 81 G
jim.rizzuto@ojc.edu
RIZZUTO, Melissa ... 239-432-6785 100 E
mrizzuto@fsw.edu
ROACH, E. J ... 207-974-4690 199 L
ejroach@emcc.edu
ROACH, H. William ... 864-833-8217 423 D
broach@presby.edu
ROACH, Kenneth ... 704-334-6882 336 I
kroach@charlottechristian.edu
ROACH, Kristin, A ... 651-962-6168 251 D
kris.roach@stthomas.edu
ROACH, Mark ... 843-349-2964 420 A
mroach@coastal.edu
ROACH, Nicole ... 314-246-8250 269 N
nroach@webster.edu
ROACH, Steve ... 724-357-4295 406 C
sroach@iup.edu
ROACH, Virginia ... 212-636-6470 308 G
vroach@fordham.edu
ROACHE, Marshall ... 503-399-2339 382 C
marshall.roache@chemeketa.edu
ROADES, Laurie ... 657-278-3915.. 32 B
lroades@fullerton.edu
ROADES, Nicole ... 937-393-3431 370 C
nroades@sscc.edu
ROAN, Matt ... 985-448-4794 197 C
matt.roan@nicholls.edu
ROARK, Debbie ... 207-768-9755 201 G
deborah.roark@maine.edu
ROARK, Donna ... 606-487-3128 185 J
donnad.roark@kctcs.edu
ROARK, Ian ... 520-206-6424.. 15 L
iroark@pima.edu
ROARK, John, A ... 270-809-3536 188 D
jroark3@murraystate.edu
ROARK, Ryan ... 575-562-2165 293 O
ryan.roark@enmu.edu
ROARK, Tony ... 208-426-1414 131 C
troark@boisestate.edu
ROATH, Carrie ... 312-935-4868 149 K
croath@robertmorris.edu
ROBACK, Barbara, A ... 315-684-6615 329 F
robackba@morrisville.edu
ROBACK, Joseph, M ... 570-941-4385 413 F
joseph.roback@scranton.edu
ROBART, Regina ... 618-664-7000 139 A
regina.robart@greenville.edu
ROBB, Cathy ... 812-749-1272 163 B
crobb@oak.edu
ROBB, Cathy ... 812-749-1272 163 B
crobb@oake.edu
ROBB, Daniel, J ... 803-641-3272 425 A
danr@usca.edu
ROBB, James ... 517-371-5140 239 F
robbj@cooley.edu
ROBB, Mercy ... 630-829-6095 133 I
mrobb@ben.edu
ROBB, Sarah ... 620-431-2820 180 C
sarah_robb@neosho.edu
ROBB, Susan, E ... 804-827-0479 487 E
sarobb@vcu.edu
ROBB SHIMKO, Molly .. 724-830-4620 410 E
shimko@setonhill.edu
ROBBIE, Kimberly ... 510-659-6165.. 54 F
krobbie@ohlone.edu
ROBBINS, Bradley ... 334-244-3345.... 4 E
brobbin2@aum.edu
ROBBINS, Brent ... 412-392-8183 408 F
brobbins@pointpark.edu
ROBBINS, Canty ... 901-678-3855 439 E
crobbns1@memphis.edu
ROBBINS, David ... 662-720-7302 255 B
wdrobbins@nemcc.edu

ROBBINS, Donna 252-398-6280 336 K robbid@chowan.edu
ROBBINS, Ian 850-644-9719 110 A irobbins@fsu.edu
ROBBINS, Jill 209-228-7843 69 C jillrobbins@ucmerced.edu
ROBBINS, Jill 478-387-4908 120 B jrobbins@gmc.edu
ROBBINS, Kristine 614-823-1232 368 O krobbins@otterbein.edu
ROBBINS, Mark 260-399-7700 165 B mrobbins@sf.edu
ROBBINS, Mary 936-294-1006 462 F robbins@shsu.edu
ROBBINS, Michael 410-857-2242 205 E mrobbins@mcdaniel.edu
ROBBINS, Nickey, L 870-508-6108 18 C nrobbins@asumh.edu
ROBBINS, Patrica 719-587-7472 76 D patrobbins@adams.edu
ROBBINS, Paul 608-265-5296 510 C director@nelson.wisc.edu
ROBBINS, Robert, C 520-621-5511 16 J president@email.arizona.edu
ROBBINS, Rochelle 215-637-7700 397 G robbins@holyfamily.edu
ROBBINS, Sandra 617-735-9715 214 F robbins@emmanuel.edu
ROBBINS, Scott, D 731-881-7775 440 B sdrobbins@utm.edu
ROBBINS, Shawna, L 760-252-2411 27 A srobbins@barstow.edu
ROBBINS, Steve 662-685-4771 252 D srobbins@bmc.edu
ROBBINS, Thomas, J 563-589-3507 173 J trobbins@dbq.edu
ROBBINS SMITH, Patricia 562-860-2451 36 A probbinssmith@cerritos.edu
ROBBINSON, Theresa 212-924-5900 330 G trobbinson@swedishinstitute.edu
ROBEAUU, Jim 985-867-2272 195 I jrobeau@sjasc.edu
ROBECK, Mike 850-201-8546 112 C robeckm@tcc.fl.edu
ROBEL, Kenneth 856-351-2704 291 E krobel@salemcc.edu
ROBEL, Lauren 812-855-5752 159 G provost@indiana.edu
ROBEL, Lauren 812-855-9011 159 H provost@indiana.edu
ROBELOTTO, Vince 706-379-3111 128 H vrobelotto@yhc.edu
ROBEN, Paul, W 858-246-0473 69 E pwroben@ucsd.edu
ROBERSON, Alicia 229-245-4378 127 H arroberson@valdosta.edu
ROBERSON, Carrie 870-230-5518 19 H robersc@hsu.edu
ROBERSON, Christopher 864-587-4387 424 D robersonc@smcsc.edu
ROBERSON, James, A 919-335-1020 347 D jaroberson@waketech.edu
ROBERSON, Janet 434-791-5891 478 E roberson@averett.edu
ROBERSON, John 910-893-1205 336 C robersonj@campbell.edu
ROBERSON, John, A 713-798-4676 444 A jarobers@bcm.edu
ROBERSON, Judith 225-768-1754 191 G judith.vidrine@ololcollege.edu
ROBERSON, Mark, A 951-552-8652 28 G maroberson@calbaptist.edu
ROBERSON, Miriam, C 904-819-6204 98 I registrar@flagler.edu
ROBERSON, Mo 949-214-3210 40 I mo.roberson@cui.edu
ROBERSON, Richard, E 717-796-5045 401 L rroberso@messiah.edu
ROBERSON, Rita, G 304-236-7648 503 D rita.roberson@southernwv.edu
ROBERSON, Robin 580-559-5467 375 I robrrob@ecok.edu
ROBERSON, Valerie, R 617-541-5301 221 A vroberson@rcc.mass.edu
ROBERSON, Wendy 651-846-1757 247 G wendy.roberson@saintpaul.edu
ROBERT, Bernadette 213-477-2511 52 H brobert@msmu.edu
ROBERTS, Aaron 317-916-7827 161 G aroberts217@ivytech.edu
ROBERTS, Aaron 402-643-7233 274 B aaron.roberts@cune.edu
ROBERTS, Adam 706-880-8004 122 D aroberts@lagrange.edu
ROBERTS, Al 434-949-1000 489 E al.roberts@southside.edu
ROBERTS, Alan, P 845-687-5050 331 L robertsal@sunyulster.edu
ROBERTS, III, Alvin 716-839-7699 306 E aroberts@daemen.edu
ROBERTS, Amber 616-331-3266 230 G roberamb@gvsu.edu
ROBERTS, Ann 847-735-5188 142 H roberts@lakeforest.edu
ROBERTS, Barbara 360-676-2772 496 C broberts@nwic.edu
ROBERTS, Bob, E 304-293-3136 505 B bob.roberts@mail.wvu.edu
ROBERTS, Brent 434-395-2083 482 E robertsbs@longwood.edu
ROBERTS, Brian 918-647-1320 375 B tacrouch@carlalbert.edu
ROBERTS, Carmen 406-771-4392 272 D carmen.roberts@gfcmsu.edu
ROBERTS, Carolyn 313-927-1474 233 D croberts@marygrove.edu
ROBERTS, Carrie 630-829-6028 133 I croberts@ben.edu
ROBERTS, Charles, H 859-846-5750 188 B chroberts@midway.edu
ROBERTS, Charlie 360-676-2772 496 C chroberts@nwic.edu
ROBERTS, Chell 619-260-4627 71 J croberts@sandiego.edu
ROBERTS, Cheryl 206-546-4551 498 E cheryl.roberts@shoreline.edu
ROBERTS, Cheryl, A 340-692-4192 529 C crobert@uvi.edu
ROBERTS, Christina 202-687-6335 92 B cdr44@georgetown.edu
ROBERTS, Christine 619-201-8760 60 A chroberts@sdcc.edu
ROBERTS, Christopher, B 334-844-2308 4 D robercr@auburn.edu
ROBERTS, Cynthia 219-980-6636 160 C robertcs@iun.edu
ROBERTS, Daniel 985-545-1500 192 K
ROBERTS, Daniel, M 804-524-6709 491 A droberts@vsu.edu
ROBERTS, Darbi 603-626-9492 282 C d.roberts2@snhu.edu
ROBERTS, Dave 775-674-7100 279 C droberts@tmcc.edu
ROBERTS, Dave 573-875-7400 258 F droberts@ccis.edu
ROBERTS, Deborah 707-664-3236 35 A deborah.roberts@sonoma.edu
ROBERTS, Dennis 530-938-5313 39 H roberts@siskiyous.edu
ROBERTS, Doug 707-527-4421 62 H droberts@santarosa.edu
ROBERTS, Douglas, P 573-341-4300 269 A robertsdp@mst.edu
ROBERTS, Dustin 870-584-1172 22 F droberts@cccua.edu
ROBERTS, Ed 240-567-7688 205 F edward.robert@montgomerycollege.edu
ROBERTS, Gail 419-448-2013 362 G groberts@heidelberg.edu
ROBERTS, Gary 269-927-8771 232 G roberts@lakemichigancollege.edu
ROBERTS, Gary, O 607-871-2715 298 A roberts@alfred.edu
ROBERTS, Gary, R 309-677-3167 134 G groberts@fsmail.bradley.edu
ROBERTS, Gayla 903-675-6212 464 C groberts@tvcc.edu
ROBERTS, Gina 419-530-5812 372 F gina.roberts@utoledo.edu
ROBERTS, Glenda, V 607-746-4545 329 B robertgv@delhi.edu
ROBERTS, Gregory, W 434-982-3200 486 H groberts@virginia.edu
ROBERTS, Heather 916-660-7900 63 K hroberts@sierracollege.edu
ROBERTS, Howard, V 606-218-5019 190 E howardroberts@upike.edu
ROBERTS, James 570-674-6758 401 M jroberts@misericordia.edu
ROBERTS, James, S 919-684-3501 337 C james.roberts@duke.edu
ROBERTS, Janet, E 248-341-2020 235 D jerobert@oaklandcc.edu
ROBERTS, Jay 765-983-1269 157 I roberja@earlham.edu
ROBERTS, Jayne 850-718-2209 96 H robertsj@chipola.edu
ROBERTS, Jean 231-777-0519 234 G jean.roberts@muskegoncc.edu
ROBERTS, Jeanne, M 813-253-6203 113 E jroberts@ut.edu
ROBERTS, Jeri 207-509-7261 200 I jroberts@unity.edu
ROBERTS, Jerilyn, C 605-394-6729 429 A jerilyn.roberts@sdsmt.edu
ROBERTS, Jim, O 910-893-1240 336 C roberts@campbell.edu
ROBERTS, Jimmy 254-298-8340 458 C jdr@templejc.edu
ROBERTS, John 903-593-8311 461 B jroberts@texascollege.edu
ROBERTS, John 918-663-9000 378 K johnr@plattcollege.org
ROBERTS, Jonathan 912-344-2910 115 D jonathan.roberts@armstrong.edu
ROBERTS, Jonathan 501-279-4257 19 G jroberts@harding.edu
ROBERTS, Juanita 334-727-8894 7 F jroberts@tuskegee.edu
ROBERTS, Juli 909-593-3511 70 E jroberts@laverne.edu
ROBERTS, Julia 910-642-7141 346 G julia.roberts@sccnc.edu
ROBERTS, Kathleen 859-572-6630 188 E robertsk10@nku.edu
ROBERTS, Kay Lynn 580-745-2977 379 J kroberts@se.edu
ROBERTS, Kelly 785-738-9060 180 E kroberts@ncktc.edu
ROBERTS, Ken 573-876-7171 267 G kroberts@stephens.edu
ROBERTS, Lila 678-466-4357 117 I lilaroberts@clayton.edu
ROBERTS, Linda 407-447-7300 101 B lroberts@ftccollege.edu
ROBERTS, Lindsay 812-488-3101 164 G lr155@evansville.edu
ROBERTS, Lindsey 229-391-5055 114 G lroberts@abac.edu
ROBERTS, Lisa 618-374-5068 149 A lisa.roberts@principia.edu
ROBERTS, Lonnie 912-427-5816 117 J lroberts@coastalpines.edu
ROBERTS, Mandy 918-647-1214 375 B mroberts@carlalbert.edu
ROBERTS, Mark 918-495-6723 378 H mroberts@oru.edu
ROBERTS, Mark, A 770-720-5504 124 H mar@reinhardt.edu
ROBERTS, Mark, A 803-535-5575 419 E maroberts@claflin.edu
ROBERTS, Mary 478-445-5384 119 E mary.roberts@gcsu.edu
ROBERTS, Mary-Lou 508-373-9763 211 F marylou.roberts@becker.edu
ROBERTS, Matt 843-953-5546 420 C robertsmj1@cofc.edu
ROBERTS, Matthew 423-652-4780 432 I mroberts@king.edu
ROBERTS, Matthew, W 405-325-1948 380 L mroberts@ou.edu
ROBERTS, Melissa 601-266-5390 256 E melissa.b.roberts@usm.edu
ROBERTS, Michael 907-773-4462 135 K mroberts39@ccc.edu
ROBERTS, Michael, C 785-864-8040 181 I mroberts@ku.edu
ROBERTS, Michael, H 843-349-2282 420 A mroberts@coastal.edu
ROBERTS, Michelle, A 662-846-4000 252 H mroberts@deltastate.edu
ROBERTS, Mitzi, C 901-572-2478 430 C mitzi.roberts@bchs.edu
ROBERTS, Nancy 610-606-4640 392 A nroberts@cedarcrest.edu
ROBERTS, Nathan 816-383-7100 264 B nroberts4@missouriwestern.edu
ROBERTS, Nathan 605-626-7802 428 H nathan.roberts@northern.edu
ROBERTS, Nathan 217-732-3168 143 F njroberts@lincolnchristian.edu
ROBERTS, Nathan 337-482-6678 197 F nathan@louisiana.edu
ROBERTS, Patty, J 318-869-5747 191 C pjrobert@centenary.edu
ROBERTS, Paul 405-585-4526 377 A paul.roberts@okbu.edu
ROBERTS, Paul, G 773-508-8901 144 D prober2@luc.edu
ROBERTS, Pauline 225-923-2524 191 A
ROBERTS, Philip 508-531-1331 217 D proberts@bridgew.edu
ROBERTS, Phyllis 276-964-7588 489 F phyllis.roberts@sw.edu
ROBERTS, Rachel 617-585-1108 222 H rachel.roberts@necmusic.edu
ROBERTS, Randal, R 503-517-1860 388 C rroberts@westernseminary.edu
ROBERTS, Randy 620-235-4878 180 J reroberts@pittstate.edu
ROBERTS, Richard 201-684-7616 289 C rroberts@ramapo.edu
ROBERTS, Rick 904-620-2955 110 E rtrobert@unf.edu
ROBERTS, Rick 830-372-8030 461 D rroberts@tlu.edu
ROBERTS, Ricky 928-523-6950 14 K ricky.roberts@nau.edu
ROBERTS, Robert, W 920-424-1415 511 B robertw@uwosh.edu
ROBERTS, Robin 317-738-8759 157 L rroberts@franklincollege.edu
ROBERTS, Roscoe, C 434-924-3586 486 H rcr7d@virginia.edu
ROBERTS, Roshell 405-682-7502 377 C roshell.a.roberts@occc.edu
ROBERTS, Ruth 972-825-4656 457 F rroberts@sagu.edu
ROBERTS, Sallyann 815-226-4083 150 C sroberts@rockford.edu
ROBERTS, Sarah, E 615-353-3117 437 D sarah.roberts@nscc.edu
ROBERTS, Scott 702-895-2816 279 D scott.roberts@unlv.edu
ROBERTS, Sheril 252-536-5469 343 F
ROBERTS, Stephanie 304-326-1310 502 D sroberts@salemu.edu
ROBERTS, Stephen 573-341-4687 269 A stephen.roberts@mst.edu
ROBERTS, Tracy 270-809-3380 188 D troberts@murraystate.edu
ROBERTS, Vonnie, W 405-466-2999 375 L vwroberts@langston.edu
ROBERTS, Warren 972-524-3341 457 H
ROBERTS, William 201-692-2629 286 B william_roberts@fdu.edu
ROBERTS-BRESLIN, Jan 617-824-8912 214 E jan_roberts_breslin@emerson.edu
ROBERTS-CAMPS, Traci 209-946-2343 70 F troberstcamps@pacific.edu
ROBERTS-DEUTSCH, Marcia 808-845-9110 130 E robertsd@hawaii.edu
ROBERTS-JOHNSON, Wendy-Anne 215-825-8200 415 D wjohnson@phmc.org
ROBERTS-KIRCHOFF, Elizabeth 313-993-1021 237 F robkires@udmercy.edu
ROBERTS KRIEGER, Robin 405-945-3228 378 C robin.krieger@osuokc.edu
ROBERTS-LEONARD, Terri, L 317-738-8119 157 L troberts@franklincollege.edu
ROBERTSHAW, Amy 719-549-2498 78 P amy.robertshaw@csupueblo.edu
ROBERTSON, Aimee 612-343-4143 249 E amrobert@northcentral.edu
ROBERTSON, SR., Alan, D 470-639-0407 123 E alan.robertson@morehouse.edu
ROBERTSON, Ali 269-956-3931 232 A robertsona@kellogg.edu
ROBERTSON, Anne, W 773-702-8512 153 F awrx@uchicago.edu
ROBERTSON, Beverly 828-689-1244 339 G brobertson@mhu.edu
ROBERTSON, Brett 619-216-6617 65 H brobertson@swccd.edu
ROBERTSON, Bruce 920-403-3045 509 J bruce.robertson@snc.edu
ROBERTSON, Carole 920-565-1027 507 K robertsoncl@lakeland.edu
ROBERTSON, Charlene 617-732-2786 221 E charlene.robertson@mcphs.edu
ROBERTSON, Charles 318-487-7015 191 J charles.robertson@lacollege.edu
ROBERTSON, Christopher 205-929-1657 6 D crobertson@miles.edu
ROBERTSON, Clyde 504-286-5384 195 L crobertson@suno.edu
ROBERTSON, Craig, L 618-537-6856 145 C clrobertson@mckendree.edu
ROBERTSON, Cynthia 318-342-1050 198 A crobertson@ulm.edu
ROBERTSON, Dalana 615-322-5179 440 D dalana.robertson@vanderbilt.edu
ROBERTSON, Dave 479-788-7799 22 A dave.robertson@uafs.edu
ROBERTSON, Diondraie, L 812-888-4301 165 E drobertson@vinu.edu
ROBERTSON, Don, E 270-809-6831 188 D drobertson@murraystate.edu
ROBERTSON, Donna 201-692-2196 286 B donnamjr@fdu.edu

ROBERTSON, Elizabeth, C .... 914-251-6039 328 B
elizabeth.robertson@purchase.edu
ROBERTSON, Ian .... 608-262-3482 510 C
engr-dean@wisc.edu
ROBERTSON, Iris .... 304-326-1274 502 D
iris.robertson@salemu.edu
ROBERTSON, J. D .... 435-652-7576 473 B
jrobertson@dixie.edu
ROBERTSON, Jacob, M . 951-552-8677.. 28 G
jmrobertson@calbaptist.edu
ROBERTSON, Janet .... 903-566-7325 468 C
jrobertson@uttyler.edu
ROBERTSON, Jeff .... 479-968-0498.. 18 G
jrobertson@atu.edu
ROBERTSON, Jennifer ... 407-582-4210 113 F
jrobertson@valenciacollege.edu
ROBERTSON, Jill .... 303-273-3207.. 78 J
jirobert@is.mines.edu
ROBERTSON, Jim .... 845-574-4466 321 F
jrobert7@sunyrockland.edu
ROBERTSON, John .... 402-844-7011 276 G
johnr@northeast.edu
ROBERTSON, John .... 972-860-7709 447 F
jrobertson@dcccd.edu
ROBERTSON, Jon, H ..... 561-237-7701 103 E
jrobertson@lynn.edu
ROBERTSON, Joseph, E 503-494-8252 385 D
president@ohsu.edu
ROBERTSON, Leonard, A .... 972-721-5236 464 E
lrobertson@udallas.edu
ROBERTSON, Lona .... 479-575-2000.. 21 I
ROBERTSON, M.G. (Pat) .... 757-352-4013 484 E
carodix@regent.edu
ROBERTSON, Michael, N .... 901-722-3226 436 D
mike.robertson@sco.edu
ROBERTSON, Patricia .... 843-574-6995 424 G
pat.robertson@tridenttech.edu
ROBERTSON, Paul .... 520-383-8401.. 16 G
probertson@tocc.edu
ROBERTSON, Ronnie ..... 205-348-8100.... 8 A
rrobertson@fa.ua.edu
ROBERTSON, Rosalie .... 757-455-3107 491 F
rrobertson@vwu.edu
ROBERTSON, Sharon, N .... 703-323-3087 488 H
srobertson@nvcc.edu
ROBERTSON, Stacey ..... 585-245-5531 327 B
robertsons@geneseo.edu
ROBERTSON, Sue .... 630-889-6527 147 D
srobertson@nuhs.edu
ROBERTSON, Tim .... 402-872-2411 276 C
trobertson@peru.edu
ROBERTSON, Tim .... 202-685-2650 518 B
timothy.robertson@ndu.edu
ROBERTSON, Trey .... 601-928-6264 254 D
trey.robertson@mgccc.edu
ROBERTSON, William, J .... 717-866-5775 395 C
wrobertson@evangelical.edu
ROBERTSON-JAMES, Candace .... 215-951-1430 398 F
robertsonjames@lasalle.edu
ROBEY, Jason .... 314-434-4044 259 B
jason.robey@covenantseminary.edu
ROBICHAUD, Betin .... 508-213-2292 223 C
betin.robichaud@nichols.edu
ROBICHAUX, Renee .... 337-550-1301 194 B
rerobich@lsue.edu
ROBIDOUX, Patricia ...... 909-607-0107.. 38 C
probidoux@kgi.edu
ROBILLARD, Jean, E ..... 319-335-8064 166 G
jean-robillard@uiowa.edu
ROBILLARD, Marc .... 617-353-2148 212 G
robillrd@bu.edu
ROBILOTTO, Philip .... 410-706-2378 207 H
probilotto@umaryland.edu
ROBIN, Tracy .... 212-229-1671 316 E
robint@newschool.edu
ROBIN, Wayne .... 401-598-1000 416 C
wrobin@jwu.edu
ROBINDER, Keith, E ...... 515-294-1022 166 F
robinder@iastate.edu
ROBINETT, Laura .... 402-375-7000 276 D
ROBINETTE, Stephen, H 417-836-4127 263 H
steverobinette@missouristate.edu
ROBINS, Duncan .... 707-826-3666.. 34 A
dr1509@humboldt.edu
ROBINS, Luke .... 360-417-6200 496 I
lrobins@pencol.edu
ROBINS, Michael .... 831-477-3521.. 28 F
mirobins@cabrillo.edu
ROBINS, Rochelle .... 310-824-1586.. 24 B
rrobins@ajrca.edu
ROBINSON, Alexandra .. 212-817-7100 302 B
arobinson@gc.cuny.edu
ROBINSON, Alfred, L .... 573-681-6156 261 H
robinsona@lincolnu.edu
ROBINSON, Amy .... 714-620-3700.. 26 I
ROBINSON, Anafe .... 818-610-6515.. 49 D
robinsa@piercecollege.edu
ROBINSON, Andrea .... 507-222-5465 241 C
arobinson@carleton.edu
ROBINSON, Angela .... 309-672-5513 145 E
arobinson@methodistcol.edu
ROBINSON, Angela .... 817-515-5242 458 B
angela.robinson@tccd.edu
ROBINSON, Ann .... 716-566-783 . 306 E
arobinso@daemen.edu
ROBINSON, April .... 863-297-1020 105 F
arobinson@polk.edu
ROBINSON, Ashley, N .. 936-261-9100 458 F
anrobinson@pvamu.edu
ROBINSON, Barry .... 253-833-9111 495 C
brobinson@greenriver.edu
ROBINSON, Bettina, A .. 678-839-5562 127 F
bettinar@westga.edu
ROBINSON, Beverly ...... 912-583-3260 116 G
brobinson@bpc.edu
ROBINSON, Beverly ...... 972-825-4798 457 F
brobinson@sagu.edu
ROBINSON, Bill .... 212-678-8030 312 A
birobinson@jtsa.edu
ROBINSON, Brian .... 916-608-6330.. 50 H
robinsb@flc.losrios.edu
ROBINSON, Brigette ...... 517-990-1386 231 E
robinsobrigetta@jccmi.edu
ROBINSON, Cassandra, M .... 301-860-4000 208 E
crobinson@bowiestate.edu
ROBINSON, Chad .... 970-943-3123.. 84 E
crobinson@western.edu
ROBINSON, Charles ...... 479-575-7955.. 21 I
cfrobins@uark.edu
ROBINSON, Charles, F . 510-987-9800.. 68 F
charles.robinson@ucop.edu
ROBINSON, Chase, F .... 212-817-7100 302 B
president@gc.cuny.edu
ROBINSON, Cheryl .... 407-582-1373 113 F
crobinson@valenciacollege.edu
ROBINSON, Chris .... 870-575-7177.. 22 E
robinsonce@uapb.edu
ROBINSON, Chris .... 606-218-5226 190 E
chrisrobinson@upike.edu
ROBINSON, Christine ... 704-687-5385 351 C
crobinson@uncc.edu
ROBINSON, Christopher, D .... 336-246-3900 347 G
cdrobinson877@wilkescc.edu
ROBINSON, Daniel, C ... 909-469-5561.. 74 G
drobinson@westernu.edu
ROBINSON, Daniel, E .... 585-292-3398 315 L
drobertson@monroecc.edu
ROBINSON, Daphne, D . 219-989-2370 163 E
robinsdd@pnw.edu
ROBINSON, Dario .... 909-869-3065.. 31 A
drobinson1@cpp.edu
ROBINSON, Dave .... 641-269-9990 169 F
daver@grinnell.edu
ROBINSON, David .... 212-650-8357 301 F
drobinson2@ccny.cuny.edu
ROBINSON, David, W ... 503-494-4460 385 D
provost@ohsu.edu
ROBINSON, Deborah, M .... 330-588-2586 364 H
drobinson@malone.edu
ROBINSON, Deborah, P 850-201-6109 112 C
robindeb@tcc.fl.edu
ROBINSON, Debra A, G 573-341-6154 269 A
debrar@mst.edu
ROBINSON, Dee .... 513-556-6177 371 E
dee.robinson@ucmail.uc.edu
ROBINSON, OSB, Denis .... 812-357-6522 164 A
drobinson@saintmeinrad.edu
ROBINSON, Derek .... 307-382-1896 517 C
derek@westernwyoming.edu
ROBINSON, Edward ...... 630-829-6306 133 I
erobinson10@ben.edu
ROBINSON, Edward ...... 202-274-2303.. 94 B
library@potomac.edu
ROBINSON, Elwood, L .. 336-750-2000 352 D
ROBINSON, Eric .... 414-930-3418 509 B
robinsoe@mtmary.edu
ROBINSON, Erin .... 941-893-2856 106 H
erobinson@ringling.edu
ROBINSON, Evan .... 413-796-2323 225 F
erobinson@wne.edu
ROBINSON, Gail .... 901-458-8232 434 C
grobinson@memphisseminary.edu
ROBINSON, Gail, D ...... 901-334-5826 434 C
grobinson@memphisseminary.edu
ROBINSON, Gary .... 607-431-4420 309 E
robinsong@hartwick.edu
ROBINSON, Gina .... 910-755-7343 341 C
robinsong@brunswickcc.edu
ROBINSON, Grace, G .... 805-437-3615.. 31 C
grace.robinson@csuci.edu
ROBINSON, Gregory ..... 407-823-5348 110 C
greg.robinson@ucf.edu
ROBINSON, Gregory ..... 847-214-7226 138 B
grobinson@elgin.edu
ROBINSON, Guin .... 205-853-1200.... 2 F
grobinson@jeffersonstate.edu
ROBINSON, Helana .... 662-329-7409 254 F
hrobinson@oe.muw.edu
ROBINSON, Irene, M .... 281-756-3501 442 C
irobinson@alvincollege.edu
ROBINSON, Jabrina ...... 518-783-2328 324 C
jrobinson@siena.edu
ROBINSON, Jacqueline . 256-469-7333.... 6 A
fin@hbc1.edu
ROBINSON, James, R ... 540-568-6991 481 I
robinsjr@jmu.edu
ROBINSON, Janice, S ... 212-678-3732 331 C
jsr167@tc.columbia.edu
ROBINSON, Jasmin .... 847-735-5204 142 H
jrobinson@lakeforest.edu
ROBINSON, Jekeyma .... 941-309-4375 106 H
jrobinso@ringling.edu
ROBINSON, Jill .... 714-556-3610.. 72 F
jill.robinson@vanguard.edu
ROBINSON, Jimada ...... 757-481-5005 492 A
ROBINSON, JoAnn .... 304-327-4567 503 O
jrobinson@bluefieldstate.edu
ROBINSON, Joanne, P .. 856-225-6226 290 B
jprobins@camden.rutgers.edu
ROBINSON, Jodi .... 602-383-8228.. 16 I
jrobinson@uat.edu
ROBINSON, John .... 910-962-3154 352 A
robinsonj@uncw.edu
ROBINSON, John .... 215-545-1347 389 E
jrobinson@aii.edu
ROBINSON, Judy .... 863-680-3936 100 D
jrobinson2@flsouthern.edu
ROBINSON, Julie, A ..... 913-735-2360 181 C
ksd_robinson_chambers@ksd.uscourts.gov
ROBINSON, K. C .... 864-294-2164 421 I
kc.robinson@furman.edu
ROBINSON, Kalani .... 912-650-6223 125 H
karobinson@southuniversity.edu
ROBINSON, Kasimira .... 470-639-0753 123 E
kasimira.robinson@morehouse.edu
ROBINSON, Kelley .... 518-244-2201 321 G
robink3@sage.edu
ROBINSON, Kevin .... 559-734-9000.. 61 C
kevinr@sjvc.edu
ROBINSON, Kimberlely, D .... 540-887-7033 482 G
krobinson@marybaldwin.edu
ROBINSON, Kristin .... 559-583-2523.. 39 G
kristinr@cos.edu
ROBINSON, LaNita .... 218-733-7616 245 C
l.robinson@lsc.edu
ROBINSON, Larry .... 850-599-3225 109 A
larry.robinson@famu.edu
ROBINSON, Larry, J ...... 701-845-7217 354 E
larry.robinson@vcsu.edu
ROBINSON, LaSandra ... 803-536-7000 423 G
ROBINSON, Lesley, J ... 512-428-1051 455 I
lrobinso@stedwards.edu
ROBINSON, Lois .... 251-578-1313.... 3 D
lrobinson@rstc.edu
ROBINSON, Louester .... 843-722-5556 424 G
lou.robinson@tridenttech.edu
ROBINSON, Luke .... 616-526-8686 228 B
lrobinso@calvin.edu
ROBINSON, Lynn .... 401-598-1405 416 C
lrobinson@jwu.edu
ROBINSON, Lynne .... 207-893-7841 200 G
lrobinson@sjcme.edu
ROBINSON, Lynne, P ... 301-447-5296 206 B
lrobinso@msmary.edu
ROBINSON, M. Kevin ... 334-844-4389.... 4 D
robinmk@auburn.edu
ROBINSON, Maria .... 979-458-6221 458 E
mrobinson@tamus.edu
ROBINSON, Marjorie .... 951-785-2167.. 47 F
mrobinso@lasierra.edu
ROBINSON, Mark .... 304-696-6603 504 C
robinsonma@marshall.edu
ROBINSON, Mary .... 716-896-0700 333 C
robinsonm@villa.edu
ROBINSON, Maureen .... 847-543-2444 136 E
mrobinson@clcillinois.edu
ROBINSON, Michael ...... 901-435-1433 433 A
michael_robinson@loc.edu
ROBINSON, Michael ..... 601-979-4299 253 E
michael.a.robinson@jsums.edu
ROBINSON, Michael ..... 405-744-6523 377 F
michael.robinson@okstate.edu
ROBINSON, Mike .... 205-226-4936.... 4 F
mrobinso@bsc.edu
ROBINSON, Mike .... 858-513-9240.. 26 T
mike.robinson@ashford.edu
ROBINSON, Mike .... 541-776-9942 385 G
mike.r@pacificbible.com
ROBINSON, Mitch .... 931-221-7883 430 B
robinsonm@apsu.edu
ROBINSON, Natalie .... 619-876-4261.. 68 C
nrobinson@usuniversity.edu
ROBINSON, Neil .... 214-768-7677 457 B
nrobinson@smu.edu
ROBINSON, Pam .... 405-585-4100 377 A
pam.robinson@okbu.edu
ROBINSON, Paul, A ...... 734-647-3502 237 I
probins@umich.edu
ROBINSON, Peter, J ..... 585-275-4036 332 E
peter_robinson@urmc.rochester.edu
ROBINSON, Ralph .... 302-857-7381.. 90 B
rrobinson@desu.edu
ROBINSON, Regina .... 617-873-0470 213 B
regina.robinson@cambridgecollege.edu
ROBINSON, Regina .... 318-670-9617 196 A
rrobinson@susla.edu
ROBINSON, Robert .... 909-621-8136.. 57 I
robert.robinson@pomona.edu
ROBINSON, Robert .... 678-717-3654 127 B
robert.robinson@ung.edu
ROBINSON, Robert .... 802-654-2524 476 A
rrobinson@smcvt.edu
ROBINSON, Ronald, R .. 864-597-4051 426 I
robinsonrr1@wofford.edu
ROBINSON, Roy .... 253-879-3653 499 C
rrobinson@pugetsound.edu
ROBINSON, Rush .... 314-652-0300 266 C
rlrobinson@slchcmail.com
ROBINSON, Ryan .... 865-974-9438 439 I
ryan.robinson@utk.edu
ROBINSON, Sandra, T .. 313-962-7150 238 H
srobins1@wcccd.edu
ROBINSON, Sandy .... 904-766-6551 100 F
sandy.robinson@fscj.edu
ROBINSON, Sara, C ...... 207-941-7617 199 B
robinsons@husson.edu
ROBINSON, Shannon .... 315-268-7766 304 B
srobinso@clarkson.edu
ROBINSON, Sharon ...... 704-233-8249 353 D
s.robinson@wingate.edu
ROBINSON, Shawn .... 813-253-7755 101 M
srobinson37@hccfl.edu
ROBINSON, Sherry .... 859-622-6515 184 F
sherry.robinson@eku.edu
ROBINSON, Stephanie, R .... 559-442-4600.. 66 G
stephanie.robinson@fresnocitycollege.edu
ROBINSON, Steve .... 567-661-7200 369 A
steve_robinson@owens.edu
ROBINSON, Stuart .... 845-257-3910 325 D
robinsos@newpaltz.edu
ROBINSON, T. Hank ..... 402-554-3750 277 I
trobinson@unomaha.edu
ROBINSON, Tammy ...... 650-738-7099.. 62 B
robinsontammy@smccd.edu
ROBINSON, Tammy ...... 650-738-4121.. 62 B
robinsontammy@smccd.edu
ROBINSON, Tia, L .... 636-584-6601 259 L
tia.robinson@eastcentral.edu
ROBINSON, Tiffany .... 270-745-5432 190 F
tiffany.robinson@wku.edu
ROBINSON, Timothy ..... 904-620-2657 110 E
trobinso@unf.edu
ROBINSON, Tony .... 276-523-2400 488 F
trobinson@mecc.edu
ROBINSON, Tray .... 530-898-4764.. 31 D
trobinson@csuchico.edu
ROBINSON, Wade .... 515-964-6222 168 A
wrobinson4@dmacc.edu
ROBINSON, Walter, A ... 530-752-5589.. 68 H
uadirector@ucdavis.edu
ROBINSON, Warren .... 803-705-4662 418 G
robinson@benedict.edu
ROBINSON, Wayne .... 718-473-8960 303 D
wrobinson@citytech.cuny.edu
ROBINSON, Wayne .... 718-260-4900 303 D
wrobinson@citytech.cuny.edu
ROBINSON, Wayne .... 307-855-2104 516 I
wrobinson@cwc.edu
ROBINSON, Wendi .... 614-947-6768 362 A
wendi.robinson@franklin.edu
ROBINSON, Wendy .... 651-450-3692 245 A
wrobins@inverhills.edu
ROBINSON, Wendy .... 212-616-7250 309 G
wendy.robinson@helenefuld.edu
ROBINSON, William ...... 803-376-5948 418 D
wrobinson@allenuniversity.edu

ROBINSON, William ...... 410-621-2355 208 C wrobinson3@umes.edu
ROBINSON, William, B . 610-892-1010 405 C wrobinson@pit.edu
ROBINSON, Winston ..... 903-927-3268 471 B wrobinson@wileyc.edu
ROBINSON-ARMSTRONG, Abbie .... 310-338-7598.. 50 J arobinso@lmu.edu
ROBINSON-COGGINS, Melissa .... 909-593-3511.. 70 E mrobinson-coggins@laverne.edu
ROBINSON-COOLIDGE, Austin .... 507-222-5635 241 C arobinso@carleton.edu
ROBINSON-FRUCHTL, Susan .... 814-472-3276 409 G srobinson@francis.edu
ROBINSON-GARDNER, Dorris, R .... 601-979-2455 253 E dorris.r.gardner@jsums.edu
ROBINSON GLOVER, Maria .... 213-356-5386.. 65 A maria_robinsonglover@sciarc.edu
ROBINSON KLOOS, Jennifer .... 651-690-8831 249 T jrkloos@stkate.edu
ROBINSON-LEWIS, Denise .... 973-720-2885 292 I lewisd@wpunj.edu
ROBINSON-PAUL, Ann .. 701-231-8325 354 D anne.robinson-paul@ndsu.edu
ROBISON, Daniel, J ...... 304-293-2395 505 B dan.robison@mail.wvu.edu
ROBISON, Elizabeth ...... 661-253-7707.. 29 F erobison@calarts.edu
ROBISON, Lori .... 419-267-1342 366 G lrobison@northweststate.edu
ROBISON, Megan .... 808-735-4787 129 A
ROBISON, Rick .... 925-969-2586.. 40 L rrobisonl@dvc.edu
ROBISON, Timothy .... 617-349-8747 216 D trobison@lesley.edu
ROBITAILLE, Marilyn ..... 254-968-9632 459 A robitaille@tarleton.edu
ROBLEDO, Denise .... 931-221-1256 430 B robledod@apsu.edu
ROBLES, Jonathan .... 623-935-8052.. 13 F jonathan.robles@estrellamountain.edu
ROBLES, Maria, V .... 787-894-2828 529 A maria.robles4@upr.edu
ROBLES, Monica .... 407-265-8383.. 96 C
ROBLES, Pedro .... 787-786-3030 526 F probles@ucb.edu.pr
ROBLES, Ray .... 787-864-2222 524 A ray.robles@guayama.inter.edu
ROBLES JIMENEZ, Elizabeth .... 213-477-2769.. 52 H ejimenez@msmu.edu
ROBOMAN, Lourdes ..... 691-350-2296 519 G comfsmyap@comfsm.fm
ROBOTHAM, Orandel .. 718-270-5120 303 C randy@mec.cuny.edu
ROBOTHAM, Tena .... 847-628-2002 142 B trobotham@judsonu.edu
ROBSHAW, Jeff .... 262-564-3676 513 G robshawj@gtc.edu
ROBSON, James, B .... 803-327-8047 426 J jrobson@yorktech.edu
ROBSON, Sharon .... 402-941-6048 275 J robson@midlandu.edu
ROBUCK, Chris .... 503-594-3090 382 D chrisr@clackamas.edu
ROBY, Mark .... 305-809-3165.. 99 L mark.roby@fkcc.edu
ROBY, Mary .... 704-406-4298 337 H mroby@gardner-webb.edu
ROBY, Peter, P .... 617-373-2672 223 D
ROBYN, Elisa .... 303-458-4081.. 82 D erobyn@regis.edu
ROC, Nadege .... 914-251-6000 328 B nadege.roc@purchase.edu
ROCA, Joan .... 507-389-5953 246 A joan.roca@mnsu.edu
ROCAP, Donna .... 845-431-8066 307 A rocap@sunydutchess.edu
ROCCIA, Miriam, I .... 314-516-5291 268 E roccia@umsl.edu
ROCCO, Brian .... 212-774-4801 314 D brocco@mmm.edu
ROCCO, Denine .... 508-531-1276 217 D drocco@bridgew.edu
ROCCO, Karen, S .... 412-362-8500 408 C krocco@pims.edu
ROCCO PACIONE, Anne, L .... 718-990-2007 322 F roccoa@stjohns.edu
ROCCONI, Christie .... 662-846-4670 252 H chrcconi@deltastate.edu
ROCHA, Mark .... 415-239-3000.. 37 H
ROCHA, Nola .... 307-778-1231 516 N nrocha@lccc.wy.edu
ROCHAT, Angela .... 970-247-7695.. 79 J rochat_a@fortlewis.edu
ROCHE, Crystal .... 520-325-0123.. 16 F registrar@suva.edu
ROCHE, Daniel .... 973-655-4158 287 D roched@mail.montclair.edu
ROCHE, Isabel .... 802-440-4406 474 F iroche@bennington.edu
ROCHE, James .... 413-545-6330 216 H jroche@provost.umass.edu
ROCHE, Joe .... 816-604-5417 262 H joseph.roche@mcckc.edu
ROCHE, Keila, J .... 787-743-7979 526 A keroche@suagm.edu
ROCHE, Mary Beth .... 570-504-1589 399 A rochem@lackawanna.edu
ROCHE, Missy .... 618-235-2700 152 E melissa.roche@swic.edu
ROCHE, Patrick .... 315-268-3734 304 B proche@clarkson.edu
ROCHE, Sarah .... 610-341-5854 394 E sroche@eastern.edu
ROCHE, Stephen, H .... 407-303-8016.. 94 H stephen.roche@adu.edu
ROCHE, Tom .... 402-449-2800 274 H troche@graceu.edu
ROCHELLE, Lori .... 903-823-3358 458 D lori.rochelle@texarkanacollege.edu
ROCHESTER, Sylvia .... 410-462-8371 202 F srochester@bccc.edu
ROCHETTE, Susan .... 802-447-6339 476 C srochette@svc.edu
ROCHLITZ, Mendel .... 718-853-8500 331 E
ROCHON, Ronald, S ..... 812-465-1617 165 C rochon@usi.edu
ROCK, Arlene, M .... 413-782-1538 225 F arlene.rock@wne.edu
ROCK, David .... 662-915-7063 256 C rock@olemiss.edu
ROCK, John .... 305-348-0570 109 D john.rock@fiu.edu
ROCK, Kimberly .... 413-528-7229 211 B krock@simons-rock.edu
ROCK, Thomas .... 212-678-3083 331 C tpr4@tc.columbia.edu
ROCKAFELLOW, Mollie . 815-740-3363 154 G mrockafellow@stfrancis.edu
ROCKECHARLIE, Barbara .... 704-372-0266 339 A brockecharlie@kingscollegecharlotte.edu
ROCKEY, Tim .... 210-486-0926 442 A trockey@alamo.edu
ROCKHILL, Linda .... 718-779-1430 320 C info@plazacollege.edu
ROCKHILL, Wendy .... 206-934-6921 497 I wendy.rockhill@seattlecolleges.edu
ROCKLAND-MILLER, Harry, S .... 413-545-2337 216 H rockmill@uhs.umass.edu
ROCKMAN, Adam .... 718-997-5500 303 E adam.rockman@qc.cuny.edu
ROCKOVE, Moshe .... 732-367-1060 283 K yshulman@bmg.edu
ROCKOW, Amanda, O ... 972-883-2106 467 D arockow@utdallas.edu
ROCKWELL, Charles ...... 713-221-5846 465 C rockwellc@uhd.edu
ROCKWELL, Grant .... 530-760-5168.. 68 H grockwell@ucdavis.edu
ROCKWELL, Kelly .... 716-851-1198 307 I rockwell@ecc.edu
ROCKWELL, Rick .... 314-246-8280 269 N rickrockwell@webster.edu
ROCKWELL, Stephanie .. 509-313-6404 495 A rockwell@gonzaga.edu
RODACK, Alvin .... 614-251-4512 367 F rodacka@ohiodominican.edu
RODAK, Rebecca, K ...... 330-471-8340 364 H rrodak@malone.edu
RODARTE, Susana .... 915-831-2018 449 A srodart7@epcc.edu
RODAS, Mary .... 516-364-0808 317 B rodas@nycollege.edu
RODDEN, Greg, A .... 863-638-7215 113 I greg.rodden@warner.edu
RODDINI, Martin .... 516-572-7331 316 C martin.roddini@ncc.edu
RODDY, Jackie .... 615-226-3990 433 B jroddy@lincolntech.edu
RODDY, Marilyn .... 865-694-6529 437 F mlroddy@pstcc.edu
RODE, Joe .... 817-515-7741 458 B joe.rode@tccd.edu
RODECKER, Daniel .... 518-580-5860 324 D drodecke@skidmore.edu
RODENBERG, Tamara, N .... 304-829-7111 501 F trodenberg@bethanywv.edu
RODENBORN, Steven, M .... 512-637-5618 455 I stevero@stedwards.edu
RODERICK, Daniel .... 508-793-7578 213 C droderick@clarku.edu
RODERICK, Gerald, K .... 410-778-7810 210 A jroderick2@washcoll.edu
RODERICK, Lori .... 309-794-7182 133 G loriroderick@augustana.edu
RODGER, Andrea .... 360-650-4478 500 E andrea.rodger@wwu.edu
RODGER, Doug .... 712-324-5061 172 E drodger@nwicc.edu
RODGERS, Ardie .... 405-733-7434 379 F arodgers@rose.edu
RODGERS, Barbara, J ... 574-807-7209 156 E barb.rodgers@bethelcollege.edu
RODGERS, Beverly .... 217-479-7047 144 I beverly.rodgers@mac.edu
RODGERS, Chris, T .... 402-280-2455 274 D chrisrodgers@creighton.edu
RODGERS, Christopher . 718-817-4755 308 G chrodgers@fordham.edu
RODGERS, Corey .... 310-233-4091.. 49 B rodgercd@lahc.edu
RODGERS, Denise .... 973-972-3645 290 A denise.rutgers@rutgers.edu
RODGERS, Frederick, B 607-871-2958 298 A rodgers@alfred.edu
RODGERS, Harold, E .... 574-807-7751 156 E rodgerh@bethelcollege.edu
RODGERS, Kenneth, G .. 919-530-5079 350 D krodgers@nccu.edu
RODGERS, Larry .... 541-737-4582 385 F larry.rodgers@oregonstate.edu
RODGERS, Lynn .... 312-935-4477 149 K lrodgers@robertmorris.edu
RODGERS, Mark, E .... 570-340-6001 401 B mrodgers@marywood.edu
RODGERS, Michael .... 270-686-4503 186 F mike.rodgers@kctcs.edu
RODGERS, Mike .... 270-686-4503 186 F mike.rodgers@kctcs.edu
RODGERS, Mike .... 325-649-8055 450 H mrodgers@hputx.edu
RODGERS, SJ, Patrick ... 570-941-6153 413 F patrick.rodgers@scranton.edu
RODGERS, Ronald, F .... 603-862-0960 282 E ron.rodgers@usnh.edu
RODGERS, Ronald, F .... 603-862-0960 282 F ron.rodgers@usnh.edu
RODGERS, Ruby .... 270-534-3184 187 C ruby.rodgers@kctcs.edu
RODGERS, Ruth .... 317-955-6321 162 R rrodgers@marian.edu
RODGERS, Sharon .... 615-675-5255 441 B srodgers@welch.edu
RODGERS, Teresa, P ..... 334-670-3221.... 7 E trodgers@troy.edu
RODGERS, Victor .... 717-221-1361 396 G vrodgers@hacc.edu
RODICIO, Lenore .... 305-237-7248 103 L lrodicio@mdc.edu
RODKIN, Dan .... 352-395-4171 107 E dan.rodkin@sfcollege.edu
RODLER, Trina .... 323-856-7699.. 25 L trodler@afi.com
RODNEY, Faye .... 305-626-3132.. 99 M faye.rodney@fmuniv.edu
RODNING, Janet, M ...... 770-720-5954 124 H jmr@reinhardt.edu
RODOCKER, Jason, L .... 540-458-8753 491 G jrodocker@wlu.edu
RODOLF, Mark .... 405-974-3611 380 J mrodolf@uco.edu
RODRIGUE, Kelly, J ...... 985-448-4154 197 C kelly.rodrigue@nicholls.edu
RODRIGUE, Morris .... 530-242-7525.. 63 I mrodrigue@shastacollege.edu
RODRIGUES, Christine .. 510-204-0707.. 37 F crodrigues@cdsp.edu
RODRIGUES-DOOLABH, Lisa .... 203-596-2104.. 86 B lrodrigues-doolabh@nv.edu
RODRIGUEZ, Abel .... 787-834-9595 526 E arodriguez@uaa.edu
RODRIGUEZ, Abiezer .... 787-834-9595 526 E abrodriguez@uaa.edu
RODRIGUEZ, Adrian ...... 817-515-1007 458 B adrian.rodriguez@tccd.edu
RODRIGUEZ, Aida, E .... 787-852-1430 522 P arodriguez@hccpr.edu
RODRIGUEZ, Alex .... 239-939-4766 108 H arodriguez@southerntech.edu
RODRIGUEZ, Alfred .... 210-999-7201 464 B alfred.rodriguez@trinity.edu
RODRIGUEZ, Alma .... 805-289-6360.. 73 C arodriguez@vcccd.edu
RODRIGUEZ, Andy .... 970-248-1337.. 77 K arodrigu@coloradomesa.edu
RODRIGUEZ, Angel .... 787-738-2161 528 A angel.rodriguez40@upr.edu
RODRIGUEZ, Anita .... 402-449-2821 274 H arodriguez@graceu.edu
RODRIGUEZ, Arlene ...... 413-755-4440 221 B arodriguez@stcc.edu
RODRIGUEZ, Armando .. 787-841-2000 525 J armando_rodriguez@pucpr.edu
RODRIGUEZ, Art, D ...... 845-437-7300 333 A arodriguez@vassar.edu
RODRIGUEZ, Arturo .... 805-965-0581.. 62 E
RODRIGUEZ, Barbara ..... 305-821-3333 100 A bjrodriguez@fnu.edu
RODRIGUEZ, Barbara, J 305-821-3333 100 A bjrodriguez@fnu.edu
RODRIGUEZ, Beatriz ..... 908-709-7448 292 C rodriguez@ucc.edu
RODRIGUEZ, Brenda ..... 347-964-8600 299 L brodriguez@boricuacollege.edu
RODRIGUEZ, Carlos ...... 323-343-3929.. 32 D carlos.rodriguez@calstatela.edu
RODRIGUEZ, Carlos ...... 847-970-4846 154 H crodriguez@usml.edu
RODRIGUEZ, Carlos ...... 787-765-4210 521 G crodriguez@cempr.edu
RODRIGUEZ, Carlos ...... 787-725-6500 521 C crodriguez@albizu.edu
RODRIGUEZ, Carlos ...... 787-765-4210 521 G crodriguez@cempr.edu
RODRIGUEZ, Carmen ..... 787-878-5475 523 H clrodri@arecibo.inter.edu
RODRIGUEZ, Carmen .... 909-384-8592.. 59 I marodrig@sbccd.cc.ca.us
RODRIGUEZ, Charles ..... 254-501-5801 459 D charles.rodriguez@tamuct.edu
RODRIGUEZ, Claribel .... 787-621-2835 520 F crodriguez@aupr.edu
RODRIGUEZ, Claribel .... 787-864-2222 524 A claribel.rodriguez@guayama.inter.edu
RODRIGUEZ, Claudia .... 787-761-0640 527 C asistenciaeconomica@utcpr.edu
RODRIGUEZ, Daniel, B . 312-503-0491 148 C daniel.rodriguez@law.northwestern.edu
RODRIGUEZ, Daron ...... 303-753-6046.. 82 E
RODRIGUEZ, Dawn, M . 813-974-7297 111 A dmrodriguez@usf.edu
RODRIGUEZ, Diana .... 909-384-4470.. 59 I drodriguez@sbccd.cc.ca.us
RODRIGUEZ, Diriee, Y .. 787-743-7979 526 A dyrodriguez@suagm.edu
RODRIGUEZ, Ed .... 816-802-3436 261 C erodriguez@kcai.edu
RODRIGUEZ, Edgar .... 787-841-2000 525 J edrodrios@pucpr.edu
RODRIGUEZ, Edgar .... 203-582-3660.. 88 A edgar.rodriguez@quinnipiac.edu
RODRIGUEZ, Elizabeth .. 561-683-1400.. 94 E lrodriguez@anho.edu
RODRIGUEZ, Elsa .... 787-753-6335 522 Q e_rodriguez@icprjc.edu
RODRIGUEZ, Eneida ..... 787-894-2828 529 A eneida.rodriguez@upr.edu
RODRIGUEZ, Esaeas, J . 260-422-5561 159 D ejrodriguez@indianatech.edu
RODRIGUEZ, Francisco, C .... 213-891-2201.. 48 K mazarild@email.laccd.edu
RODRIGUEZ, Ginger ..... 219-473-4305 157 A grodriguez@ccsj.edu
RODRIGUEZ, Havidan ... 518-956-8030 324 G presmail@albany.edu
RODRIGUEZ, Havidan ... 956-665-2111 468 A havidan@utrgv.edu
RODRIGUEZ, Heather .... 210-829-6005 465 E hrodrig1@uiwtx.edu
RODRIGUEZ, Irma, I ..... 787-841-2000 525 J irodriguez@pucpr.edu
RODRIGUEZ, Israel .... 787-780-0070 521 B irodriguez@caribbean.edu
RODRIGUEZ, Israel .... 787-743-7979 526 A ut_irodriguez@suagm.edu
RODRIGUEZ, Ivette .... 787-725-8120 522 M irodriguez@eap.edu
RODRIGUEZ, Jalibeth .... 787-841-2000 525 J jalibeth_rodriguez@pucpr.edu
RODRIGUEZ, Janeth ...... 909-652-6541.. 36 E janeth.rodriguez@chaffey.edu

RODRIGUEZ, Jesus .... 713-718-5222 450 D
jesus.rodriguez@hccs.edu
RODRIGUEZ, Jorge .... 787-766-1717 526 B
ac_jrodrigue@suagm.edu
RODRIGUEZ, Jorge .... 718-990-1485 322 F
rodriguj@stjohns.edu
RODRIGUEZ, Jose .... 718-489-5315 322 D
jrodriguez@sfc.edu
RODRIGUEZ, Jose .... 787-857-3600 523 I
jerodriguez@br.inter.edu
RODRIGUEZ, Jose .... 787-279-1912 523 J
jarodriguez@bayamon.inter.edu
RODRIGUEZ, Jose .... 214-860-8587 448 B
jcrodriguez@dcccd.edu
RODRIGUEZ,
Jose Ginel .... 787-798-6904 526 G
jose.ginel@uccaribe.edu
RODRIGUEZ,
Jose Ginel .... 787-269-4510 526 G
jose.ginel@uccaribe.edu
RODRIGUEZ, Juan .... 787-878-5475 523 H
jcrodrig@arecibo.inter.edu
RODRIGUEZ,
Juan Carlos .... 786-331-1000 104 C
RODRIGUEZ, Katrina ..... 970-351-2517.. 83 F
katrina.rodriguez@unco.edu
RODRIGUEZ, Kristine .... 785-833-4354 179 C
kristy.rodriguez@kwu.edu
RODRIGUEZ, Lee Ann ... 941-487-4649 110 B
lrodriguez@ncf.edu
RODRIGUEZ, Liliana ..... 303-871-3080.. 83 E
liliana.rodriguez@du.edu
RODRIGUEZ, Lora .... 972-721-5322 464 E
lbrodriguez@udallas.edu
RODRIGUEZ, Louis .... 305-222-2822.. 98 O
lrodriguez@careercollege.edu
RODRIGUEZ, Lucia, M .. 915-831-2848 449 A
lrodr258@epcc.edu
RODRIGUEZ, Luis .... 787-850-9305 528 B
luis.rodriguez39@upr.edu
RODRIGUEZ, Magaly ..... 787-850-9383 528 B
magaly.rodriguez1@upr.edu
RODRIGUEZ, Maria .... 787-852-1430 522 P
ma.rodriguez.r@hccpr.edu
RODRIGUEZ, Maria .... 305-223-4561 106 L
rodriguez@sjvcs.edu
RODRIGUEZ,
Maria-Judith .... 413-542-2372 210 F
hr@amherst.edu
RODRIGUEZ, Marisela .. 956-764-5798 451 H
marisela.rodriguez@laredo.edu
RODRIGUEZ, Mark .... 216-987-5459 360 E
mark.rodriguez@tri-c.edu
RODRIGUEZ, Marlene ... 787-844-8181 528 E
marlene.rodriguez@upr.edu
RODRIGUEZ, Mary, J .... 419-755-4767 366 E
mrodriguez@ncstatecollege.edu
RODRIGUEZ, Mary Ann 503-883-2458 383 H
mrodrigu1@linfield.edu
RODRIGUEZ, Mary Ann 361-582-2560 470 A
maryann.rodriguez@victoriacollege.edu
RODRIGUEZ, Mayra .... 787-743-7979 526 A
mrodrigu@suagm.edu
RODRIGUEZ, Melanie ... 787-720-4476 527 A
biblioteca@mizpa.edu
RODRIGUEZ, Melba .... 812-866-7017 158 C
rodriguez@hanover.edu
RODRIGUEZ, Melinda ... 956-295-3694 461 F
melinda.rodriguez@tsc.edu
RODRIGUEZ, Miguel ..... 939-292-8915 529 A
miguel.rodriguez10@upr.edu
RODRIGUEZ, Miguel ..... 973-748-9000 284 A
miguel_rodriguez@bloomfield.edu
RODRIGUEZ, Millie .... 330-941-1526 374 E
mjrodriguez02@ysu.edu
RODRIGUEZ, Moises .... 210-924-4338 443 N
moises.rodriguez@bua.edu
RODRIGUEZ, Monica .... 510-215-3958.. 40 K
mrodriguez@contracosta.edu
RODRIGUEZ, Nannette .. 531-622-2733 275 F
nmrodriguez@mccneb.edu
RODRIGUEZ,
Narcedalia .... 503-357-6151 385 I
nrodrigu@pacificu.edu
RODRIGUEZ, Nilda .... 914-422-4213 319 J
nrodriguez@pace.edu
RODRIGUEZ, Nilda, E ... 787-852-1430 522 P
nrodriguez@hccpr.edu
RODRIGUEZ, Norma ...... 562-860-2451.. 36 A
nrodriguez@cerritos.edu
RODRIGUEZ, Oscar .... 252-639-7342 349 F
orodriguez@umo.edu
RODRIGUEZ, Peter .... 713-348-5928 455 F
peter.l.rodriguez@rice.edu
RODRIGUEZ, Rafael ...... 802-656-3434 476 E
rrodrig1@uvm.edu
RODRIGUEZ, Raquel ..... 559-934-2218.. 73 N
raquelrodriguez@whccd.edu
RODRIGUEZ, Raul .... 714-480-7450.. 57 N
rodriguez_raul@rsccd.edu
RODRIGUEZ, Rene .... 512-232-2780 467 C
renerod@austin.utexas.edu
RODRIGUEZ,
Reuban, B .... 804-828-8940 487 E
rbrodriguez@vcu.edu
RODRIGUEZ, Ricardo .... 972-860-8325 447 I
ricardorodriguez@dcccd.edu
RODRIGUEZ, Ricardo .... 817-531-4249 463 G
rrodriguez@txwes.edu
RODRIGUEZ, Ricardo .... 787-751-0178 525 O
ricrodriguez@suagm.edu
RODRIGUEZ, Richard .... 559-323-2100.. 61 A
rrodriguez@sjcl.edu
RODRIGUEZ, Rodney .... 956-721-5110 451 H
rodney.rodriguez@laredo.edu
RODRIGUEZ, Ron .... 209-667-3709.. 33 F
rrodriguez36@csustan.edu
RODRIGUEZ, Ron .... 210-567-4432 468 E
rodriguezr32@uthscsa.edu
RODRIGUEZ, Rosa .... 860-832-1652.. 84 J
rosa.rodriguez@ccsu.edu
RODRIGUEZ, Salvador .. 213-477-2697.. 52 H
srodriguez@msmu.edu
RODRIGUEZ, Seph .... 909-272-6947.. 37 B
seph.rodriguez@tcsedsystem.edu
RODRIGUEZ, Shari, M .. 574-284-4581 163 J
srodriguez@saintmarys.edu
RODRIGUEZ, Sherri ...... 818-947-2726.. 49 G
rodrigsa@lavc.edu
RODRIGUEZ, Silvio .... 305-237-7445 103 L
srodrig2@mdc.edu
RODRIGUEZ, Simon ...... 641-472-1170 171 J
srodriguez@mum.edu
RODRIGUEZ, Sonia .... 585-475-2395 321 D
smrfa@rit.edu
RODRIGUEZ, Sonya, F .. 575-624-8066 295 A
sonya@nmmi.edu
RODRIGUEZ, Stephanie 310-660-3601.. 42 C
srodriguez@elcamino.edu
RODRIGUEZ, Steven ..... 949-214-3003.. 40 I
steven.rodriguez@cui.edu
RODRIGUEZ, Sylvia ...... 925-424-1000.. 36 D
RODRIGUEZ, Sylvia ...... 925-424-1542.. 36 D
srodriguez@laspositascollege.edu
RODRIGUEZ, Sylvia, L .. 305-474-6871 107 B
srodriguez@stu.edu
RODRIGUEZ, Teresita .... 310-434-4774.. 62 G
rodriguez_teresita@smc.edu
RODRIGUEZ,
Theresa, E .... 970-247-6983.. 79 J
rodriguez_t@fortlewis.edu
RODRIGUEZ, Tiffany ..... 619-684-8814.. 53 J
trodriguez@newschoolarch.edu
RODRIGUEZ, Velia .... 559-730-3775.. 39 G
veliar@cos.edu
RODRIGUEZ, Venessa ... 607-778-5220 326 C
rodriguezvl1@sunybroome.edu
RODRIGUEZ, Vince .... 714-241-6195.. 38 F
vrodriguez@coastline.edu
RODRIGUEZ, Vincent .... 210-283-5096 465 E
vincent@uiwtx.edu
RODRIGUEZ, Wanda ..... 787-257-0000 527 H
wanda.rodriguez@upr.edu
RODRIGUEZ, Widilia ..... 787-815-0000 527 F
widilia.rodriguez@upr.edu
RODRIGUEZ, Yanilda .... 787-766-1717 526 B
yrodriguez98@suagm.edu
RODRIGUEZ ANTONE,
Megan .... 650-306-3418.. 61 R
rodriguezm@smccd.edu
RODRIGUEZ-CANCEL,
Jaime, L .... 787-723-4481 521 H
jarodriguez@ceaprc.edu
RODRIGUEZ-CHARDAVOYNE,
Esther .... 718-518-4308 302 D
erodriguez@hostos.cuny.edu
RODRIGUEZ-CORTES,
Jesus .... 787-763-6700 522 N
jesus.rodriguezcortes@gmail.com
RODRIGUEZ-CRUZ,
Victor .... 787-751-1912 524 E
vrodriguez@juris.inter.edu
RODRIGUEZ ESQUERDO,
Pedro, J .... 787-764-0000 528 F
pj.rodriguezesquerdo@upr.edu
RODRIGUEZ-FARRAR,
Hanna .... 415-482-1927.. 41 J
hrf@dominican.edu
RODRIGUEZ-GREGORY,
Lisa .... 732-906-2550 287 B
lgregory@middlesexcc.edu
RODRIGUEZ-HEFFNER,
Ermelinda .... 831-656-3054 518 D
erodriguez@nps.edu
RODRIGUEZ-LOPEZ,
Miguel, A .... 787-723-4481 521 H
centro@ceaprc.edu
RODRIGUEZ-MOLINA,
Nilda, E .... 787-480-2439 521 J
nilrodriguez@sanjuanciudadpatria.com
RODRIGUEZ-PAZ,
Maria .... 787-620-2040 520 F
mrodriguez_paz@aupr.edu
RODRIGUEZ-QUINONES,
Jose .... 787-725-6500 521 C
jrodriguezq@albizu.edu
RODRIGUEZ-VARGAS,
Claribel .... 787-261-2835 520 F
crodriguez@aupr.edu
RODRIGUEZ-VEGA,
Shirley .... 312-996-5563 153 H
srodri3@uic.edu
RODRIGUEZ-VINCENTY,
Carmen, J .... 787-480-2438 521 J
crodriguez03@sanjuanciudadpatria.com
RODRIQUEZ, Camille .... 303-329-6355.. 78 L
dean@cstcm.edu
RODRIQUEZ, Glendali ... 715-232-2421 512 A
rodriquezg@uwstout.edu
RODRIQUEZ, Jason ...... 503-883-2574 383 H
jrodriqu@linfield.edu
RODRIQUEZ, Mike .... 505-984-6058 295 K
RODRIQUEZ, Nicky, M . 219-942-1459 157 E
nicky.rodriquez@ccr.edu
RODRIGUEZ, Julio, A ... 787-766-1717 526 B
um_jurodrigu@suagm.edu
RODRIGUEZ, Mayra ...... 787-892-5115 524 D
mayra_rodriguez@sangerman.inter.edu
RODRIGUEZ, Omayra .... 787-852-1430 522 P
orodriguez@hccpr.edu
RODRIGUEZ ALVARADO,
Diana .... 787-884-3838 520 G
drodriguez@atenascollege.edu
RODRIGUEZ-RIVERA,
Rafael, E .... 787-751-1600 524 E
rrodriguez@juris.inter.edu
RODRIGUEZ-VALLES,
Nora .... 787-993-8868 527 G
nora.rodriguez1@upr.edu
RODUIN, Cheyenne ...... 425-235-2235 497 E
croduin@rtc.edu
RODUIN, Cheyenne, M . 425-739-8657 495 F
cheyenne.roduin@lwtech.edu
ROE, Michael .... 845-431-8018 307 A
michael.roe@sunydutchess.edu
ROE, Robert, M .... 989-774-3933 228 E
roe1rm@cmich.edu
ROEBUCK, Randy .... 316-677-9437 182 E
rroebuck@watc.edu
ROECKER, Pamela .... 781-768-7147 224 A
pamela.roecker@regiscollege.edu
ROECKER-PHELPS,
Carolyn .... 937-229-3334 372 A
cphelps1@udayton.edu
ROECKS, Jan .... 650-574-6480.. 62 A
roecksj@smccd.edu
ROEDEL, Glenn .... 215-780-1296 410 D
groedel@salus.edu
ROEDEL, Mark .... 903-233-3296 452 A
markroedel@letu.edu
ROEDER, Jerry .... 413-782-1386 225 F
gerard.roeder@wne.edu
ROEDER, Lynn, M .... 252-328-9297 349 I
roederl@ecu.edu
ROEDIGER, Chris .... 513-562-6288 356 J
chris.roediger@artacademy.edu
ROEHRICK, Randy .... 952-995-1525 244 G
randy.roehrick@hennepintech.edu
ROELFS, Melinda, A ...... 620-235-4226 180 J
maroelfs@pittstate.edu
ROELFSEMA, Cheryl, E . 815-224-0419 141 A
cheryl_roelfsema@ivcc.edu
ROELKE, Scott .... 651-450-3330 245 A
sroelke@inverhills.edu
ROELKE, Scott .... 651-423-8297 244 E
scott.roelke@dctc.edu
ROELLKE, Christopher ... 845-437-5600 333 A
chroellke@vassar.edu
ROELOFS, Lyle, D .... 859-985-3522 183 I
roelofsl@berea.edu
ROEN, Duane .... 480-727-6513.. 10 K
duane.roen@asu.edu
ROEPKE, Melinda .... 419-755-4848 366 E
mroepke@ncstatecollege.edu
ROERIG, Sandra, C .... 318-675-7618 194 D
sroeri@lsuhsc.edu
ROESCH, Adam .... 618-262-8641 140 F
roescha@iecc.edu
ROESSEL, Charles .... 928-724-6669.. 12 G
cmroessel@dinecollege.edu
ROEST, Michael .... 415-503-6217.. 60 H
mroest@sfcm.edu
ROETHEMEYER,
Robert, V .... 260-452-2146 157 F
robert.roethemeyer@ctsfw.edu
ROETHER, Diane .... 940-668-4338 453 L
droether@nctc.edu
ROETHLER, Don .... 701-224-5485 354 F
donald.roethler@bismarckstate.edu
ROETTGER, Linda .... 219-464-5958 165 D
linda.roettger@valpo.edu
ROEWER, Anita .... 815-455-8737 145 B
aroewer@mchenry.edu
ROFFEL, Linda .... 845-434-5750 330 F
lroffel@sunysullivan.edu
ROGALSKI, Kathryn .... 847-925-6221 139 B
krogalsk@harpercollege.edu
ROGAN, Doreen .... 207-216-4320 200 E
drogan@yccc.edu
ROGAN, Margaret .... 617-824-8590 214 E
margaret_rogan@emerson.edu
ROGAN, William, D ...... 615-230-3595 438 C
william.rogan@volstate.edu
ROGELSTAD, Todd .... 701-845-7209 354 E
todd.rogelstad@vcsu.edu
ROGER-GORDON,
A. Patrick .... 212-346-1295 319 J
arogergordon@pace.edu
ROGERS, Allan .... 802-728-1533 477 E
arogers@vtc.edu
ROGERS, Andria .... 970-339-6518.. 76 E
andria.rogers@aims.edu
ROGERS, Ann .... 203-857-7270.. 86 D
arogers@norwalk.edu
ROGERS, Brenda .... 408-741-2011.. 74 B
brenda.rogers@wvm.edu
ROGERS, Brian .... 503-494-8362 385 D
cdrcadmin@ohsu.edu
ROGERS, Carl .... 770-533-6899 122 E
crogers@laniertech.edu
ROGERS, Cheryl .... 413-755-4454 221 B
carogers@stcc.edu
ROGERS, Cheryl, L .... 903-510-3217 464 D
crog@tjc.edu
ROGERS, Christina .... 212-659-7200 312 E
crogers@tkc.edu
ROGERS, Christopher ..... 803-777-5643 424 I
crogers@mailbox.sc.edu
ROGERS, Cindy, A .... 972-860-8187 447 H
car3810@dcccd.edu
ROGERS, Craig, L .... 270-789-5057 184 B
crogers@campbellsville.edu
ROGERS, Cynthia .... 907-842-5109.. 10 B
cswanson@alaska.edu
ROGERS, Dana .... 409-882-3372 462 D
dana.rogers@lsco.edu
ROGERS, Dana, N .... 409-882-3397 462 D
dana.rogers@lsco.edu
ROGERS, David, E .... 315-684-6044 329 F
rogersde@morrisville.edu
ROGERS, Deborah, A .... 215-641-6506 402 A
drogers@mc3.edu
ROGERS, Demetrius ...... 503-517-1809 388 C
drogers@westernseminary.edu
ROGERS, Donna .... 252-789-0290 344 E
donna.rogers@martincc.edu
ROGERS, Donnita .... 405-466-3262 375 L
ddrogers@langston.edu
ROGERS, Duke .... 785-227-3380 175 E
rogersk@bethanylb.edu
ROGERS, Dwayne .... 318-473-6410 194 A
drogers@lsua.edu
ROGERS, Edwin .... 808-675-3544 128 K
edwin.rogers@byuh.edu
ROGERS, Elsa .... 239-513-1122 101 O
erogers@hodges.edu
ROGERS, Emily .... 740-392-6868 366 B
emily.rogers@mvnu.edu
ROGERS, Fred, A .... 507-222-5411 241 C
frogers@carleton.edu
ROGERS, Frederick .... 803-508-7272 418 C
rogersf@atc.edu
ROGERS, Gail .... 423-746-5202 439 A
grogers@tnwesleyan.edu
ROGERS, Gary .... 816-322-0110 257 M
gary.rogers@calvary.edu
ROGERS, Getta .... 360-417-6400 496 I
grogers@pencol.edu
ROGERS, Harry, C .... 215-898-7091 412 G
rogers@pobox.upenn.edu
ROGERS, Heather .... 270-901-1116 187 A
heather.rogers@kctcs.edu
ROGERS, Helen .... 808-932-7315 129 I
hrogers@hawaii.edu
ROGERS, J. Orion .... 540-831-5958 484 A
jorogers@radford.edu
ROGERS, James .... 212-327-8506 321 E
jrogers@mail.rockefeller.edu
ROGERS, James .... 212-517-0435 314 D
jrogers@mmm.edu

ROGERS, James 949-582-4558 64 J jrogers39@saddleback.edu
ROGERS, James 610-341-5908 394 E jrogers@eastern.edu
ROGERS, Janet 765-998-5330 164 C jnrogers@taylor.edu
ROGERS, Jason 619-298-1829 65 G jrogers@ssu.edu
ROGERS, Jason 615-460-6441 430 D jason.rogers@belmont.edu
ROGERS, Jaye 765-641-4442 156 A jlrogers2@anderson.edu
ROGERS, Jeff 704-406-4627 337 H jrogers3@gardner-webb.edu
ROGERS, Jeff 304-457-6337 501 A rogersja@ab.edu
ROGERS, Jeffrey 704-406-4724 337 H jrogers3@gardner-webb.edu
ROGERS, Jenica, P 315-267-2482 328 A rogersjp@potsdam.edu
ROGERS, Jennifer 308-635-6551 278 B rogersj5@wncc.edu
ROGERS, Jennifer 864-225-7653 421 G jenniferrogers@forrestcollege.edu
ROGERS, Jessica 941-487-4900 110 B ncalum@ncf.edu
ROGERS, Jevita 719-255-3460 83 C jrogers3@uccs.edu
ROGERS, Jill 704-463-3406 348 B jill.rogers@pfeiffer.edu
ROGERS, Johnell 803-934-3256 422 G jrogers@morris.edu
ROGERS, Jolayne 816-322-0110 257 M jolayne.rogers@calvary.edu
ROGERS, Jolene, R 712-362-0431 170 D jrogers@iowalakes.edu
ROGERS, Josh 928-536-6227 15 B joshua.rogers@npc.edu
ROGERS, Justin, P 716-888-2244 300 G rogers44@canisius.edu
ROGERS, Kathleen, R 617-521-2276 224 E kathleen.rogers@simmons.edu
ROGERS, Katrina 805-898-2924 43 A krogers@fielding.edu
ROGERS, Kim 580-559-5677 375 I kimmrog@ecok.edu
ROGERS, Lalita 318-670-9223 196 A lrogers@susla.edu
ROGERS, Larson 617-588-1365 211 G lrogers@bfit.edu
ROGERS, Leslie 252-328-6212 349 I rogersle@ecu.edu
ROGERS, Lisa, C 615-898-2150 434 H lisa.rogers@mtsu.edu
ROGERS, Lynn 518-782-6654 324 C lrogers@siena.edu
ROGERS, Mark 478-274-7871 123 I mwrogers@oftc.edu
ROGERS, Michael 202-274-5986 93 D michael.rogers@udc.edu
ROGERS, Michael 804-862-6100 484 F mrogers@rbc.edu
ROGERS, Michael, B 607-735-1770 307 G mrogers@elmira.edu
ROGERS, Michelle 909-748-8138 71 H michelle_rogers@redlands.edu
ROGERS, Mike 209-946-2569 70 F mrogers@pacific.edu
ROGERS, Nancy, B 812-237-7900 159 C nancy.rogers@indstate.edu
ROGERS, Patricia 781-891-2622 212 A progers@bentley.edu
ROGERS, Patricia 507-457-5010 248 C progers@winona.edu
ROGERS, Patrick 802-635-1417 477 C patrick.rogers@jsc.edu
ROGERS, Peter 510-883-2083 41 I progers@dspt.edu
ROGERS, Phil 208-459-5282 131 H progers@collegeofidaho.edu
ROGERS, Phyllis 254-295-4501 466 A progers@umhb.edu
ROGERS, Ralph, V 954-262-5796 104 F rvrogers@nova.edu
ROGERS, Randy 336-386-3466 347 A rogersrj@surry.edu
ROGERS, Raymond, C 512-448-8532 455 I rrogers1@stedwards.edu
ROGERS, Richard, L 313-664-7474 228 H rrogers@collegeforcreativestudies.edu
ROGERS, Rickey 870-245-5220 20 G rogersr@obu.edu
ROGERS, Rodney, K 419-372-2915 357 F rrogers@bgsu.edu
ROGERS, Rus 316-284-5273 175 F rrogers@bethelks.edu
ROGERS, Russell 201-216-5688 291 G russell.rogers@stevens.edu
ROGERS, Sandra 801-422-1801 471 E sandra_rogers@byu.edu
ROGERS, Scott 828-726-2488 341 D srogers@cccti.edu
ROGERS, Scott 509-542-4834 493 G srogers@columbiabasin.edu
ROGERS, Scott, S 330-385-1070 368 M
ROGERS, Susan 845-434-5750 330 F srogers@sunysulliivan.edu
ROGERS, Susan 412-624-2795 412 I srogers@pitt.edu
ROGERS, Tamara 617-496-3069 215 G tamara_rogers@harvard.edu
ROGERS, Tammy 706-880-8344 122 D trogers@lagrange.edu
ROGERS, Tamy 214-333-5158 447 D tamyr@dbu.edu
ROGERS, Terri 417-328-1520 267 A tlrogers@sbuniv.edu
ROGERS, Terri 580-745-2510 379 J trogers@se.edu
ROGERS, Thomas 502-935-6853 186 C thomas.rogers@kctcs.edu
ROGERS, Tim 503-399-7506 382 C tim.rogers@chemeketa.edu
ROGERS, Timothy 315-866-0300 310 A rogerstd@herkimer.edu
ROGERS, Toby 806-720-7627 452 D toby.rogers@lcu.edu
ROGERS, Tracy 719-587-7990 76 D tracy_rogers@adams.edu
ROGERS-ADKINSON, Diana 573-651-2408 266 M drogersadkinson@semo.edu
ROGERSON, Andrew 501-569-3200 22 B chancellor@ualr.edu
ROGERSON, Joanie 360-623-8594 493 A joan.rogerson@centralia.edu
ROGERSON, Sarah 518-445-3246 297 K sroge@albanylaw.edu
ROGGE, Ann 302-736-2445 90 J ann.rogge@wesley.edu
ROGGEMAN, William 269-782-1484 237 B wroggeman@swmich.edu
ROGGENSTEIN, Gary 661-722-6300 26 C groggenstein@avc.edu
ROGGIE, Edie 315-786-2327 311 H eroggie@sunyjefferson.edu
ROGNRUD, Carol 240-567-7493 205 F carol.rognrud@montgomerycollege.edu
ROGOTZKE, Kathy, M 641-422-4154 172 C rogotkat@niacc.edu
ROGOVIN, Michael 914-594-4560 318 A michael_rogovin@nymc.edu
ROGSTAD, Mark 509-574-4671 500 I mrogstad@yvcc.edu
ROHAN, James, P 920-465-2075 510 E rohanj@uwgb.edu
ROHAN, Robert 240-500-2000 204 B rcrohan@hagerstowncc.edu
ROHANNA, Susan 610-902-8206 391 B susan.rohanna@cabrini.edu
ROHDE, Ben, B 262-243-5700 507 C benjamin.rohde@cuw.edu
ROHDE, Monika 516-686-7615 317 G mschuere@nyit.edu
ROHDE, Scott 860-685-2809 89 F srohde@wesleyan.edu
ROHDER, Kelly 815-280-2915 142 A krohder@jjc.edu
ROHDIN, Ben 973-353-5541 290 D ben.rohdin@rutgers.edu
ROHDIN, Benjamin 201-200-3156 287 F brohdin@njcu.edu
ROHDIN, Benjamin 201-200-3507 287 F brohdin@njcu.edu
ROHLEDER, Ann 812-357-6610 164 A arohleder@saintmeinrad.edu
ROHLEDER, John 651-779-3496 244 D john.rohleder@century.edu
ROHLEDER-SOOK, Wendy 785-628-4408 177 D wmrohledersook@fhsu.edu
ROHLING, Geraldine 518-472-5872 297 K glash@albanylaw.edu
ROHMAN, Chad 708-524-6816 137 F crohman@dom.edu
ROHN, Marisa 330-494-6170 370 G mrohn@starkstate.edu
ROHNER, Christy 270-686-4243 183 J christy.rohner@brescia.edu
ROHNER, Tom 312-662-4000 133 A trohner@adler.edu
ROHR, Ann 970-207-4500 84 C annr@uscareerinstitute.edu
ROHR, Ann 970-207-4550 80 P annr@mckinleycollege.edu
ROHR, Denise 513-569-1625 359 G denise.rohr@cincinnatistate.edu
ROHR, Margie 973-290-4054 285 A mrohr@cse.edu
ROHRBACK, Erika 212-217-3703 308 B erika_rohrback@fitnyc.edu
ROHRBACK, Jane, T 248-204-3177 233 A jrohrback@ltu.edu
ROHRBAUGH, Suzanne, Y 336-633-0218 345 F syrohrbaugh@randolph.edu
ROHRER, Brad 305-284-1256 112 O brohrer@miami.edu
ROHRER, Katherine 609-258-7800 288 F krohrer@princeton.edu
ROHRER, Launa 574-535-7543 158 A launar@goshen.edu
ROIDT, Joseph 605-995-2625 427 A joroidt@dwu.edu
ROIG, Katy 619-260-7404 71 J kroig@sandiego.edu
ROIG, Lizzette 787-844-8181 528 E lizzette.roig@upr.edu
ROJAS, Carlos 787-840-2575 525 I crojas@psm.edu
ROJAS, Carmen, I 787-743-4041 521 K crojas@columbiacentral.edu
ROJAS, Dennia 213-615-7243 37 B drojas@thechicagoschool.edu
ROJAS, Eddy, M 937-229-4632 372 A erojas1@udayton.edu
ROJAS, Frank 406-377-9422 270 J frojas@dawson.edu
ROJAS, Gilbert 801-274-3280 474 D gilbert.rojas@wgu.edu
ROJAS, Jason 860-297-4166 88 E jason.rojas@trincoll.edu
ROJAS, Jesus 912-525-5000 125 B jrojas@scad.edu
ROJAS, Pablo, E 787-891-0925 523 G projas@aquadilla.inter.edu
ROJAS, Robyn, D 405-325-3337 380 L rrojas@ou.edu
ROJAS, Rodney 213-613-2200 65 A rodney_rojas@sciarc.edu
ROJCEWICZ, Peter 626-571-8811 72 C peterr@uwest.edu
ROJCEWICZ, Peter, M 626-571-8811 72 C peterr@uwest.edu
ROJO, Richard 650-574-6538 62 A rojor@smccd.edu
ROKOWSKY, Israel 845-425-1370 319 F
ROKSANDIC, Stevo 614-234-1644 365 L sroksandic@mchs.com
ROLAND, Cheryl 269-387-8412 239 E cheryl.roland@wmich.edu
ROLAND, David, E 706-233-7329 125 E droland@shorter.edu
ROLAND, Harriet, A 803-533-3790 423 G rolandha@scsu.edu
ROLAND, Kirc, J 360-442-2471 495 G kroland@lowercolumbia.edu
ROLAND, Meg 503-699-3336 384 B mroland@marylhurst.edu
ROLDAN, Marggi 864-578-8770 423 F mroldan@sherman.edu
ROLEN, Scott 541-917-4420 384 A rolens@linnbenton.edu
ROLEY, V. Vance 808-956-8377 129 J vroley@hawaii.edu
ROLF, Joel 763-544-9501 240 F
ROLFE, Rial, D 806-743-2905 463 E rial.rolfe@ttuhsc.edu
ROLFES, Katherine 337-521-8906 193 E katherine.rolfes@solacc.edu
ROLFS, Trevor 620-792-9378 175 C rolfst@bartonccc.edu
ROLHEISER, Ronald 210-341-1366 454 B rrolheiser@ost.edu
ROLL, Debbie 907-564-8220 9 F droll@alaskapacific.edu
ROLLACK, Nikesha 919-278-2672 348 I nrollack@shawu.edu
ROLLAND, Erik 909-869-2400 31 A erolland@cpp.edu
ROLLE, Anthony 401-874-7074 417 E
ROLLE, Jo-Ann 718-270-5070 303 C jrolle@mec.cuny.edu
ROLLE, Kevin, A 256-372-5230 1 A kevin.rolle@aamu.edu
ROLLER, Robert 626-812-3085 26 U rroller@apu.edu
ROLLER, Robert 910-893-1326 336 C roller@campbell.edu
ROLLER, Steven, A 617-228-2394 219 D sroller@bhcc.mass.edu
ROLLESTON, George 440-826-2081 357 B grollest@bw.edu
ROLLINGS, Grenna 972-860-8181 447 H grollings@dcccd.edu
ROLLINO, Richard 307-332-2930 517 F rrollino@wyomingcatholiccollege.com
ROLLINS, Alison 301-295-3357 518 G alison.rollins@usuhs.edu
ROLLINS, Cheryl 443-885-4429 206 A cheryl.rollins@morgan.edu
ROLLINS, Elizabeth, J 803-981-7122 426 J erollins@yorktech.edu
ROLLINS, Judy 252-985-5111 348 A jrollins@ncwc.edu
ROLLINS, Kate 402-354-7073 275 P kate.rollins@methodistcollege.edu
ROLLINS, Mark 314-935-7349 269 L mark@wustl.edu
ROLLINS, Pam 334-420-4253 3 H prollins@trenholmstate.edu
ROLLINS, Stephen 907-786-1825 10 A srollins@alaska.edu
ROLLINS, Tina 757-727-5371 481 E tina.rollins@hamptonu.edu
ROLLISON, Jeffrey 610-647-4400 397 I jrollison@immaculata.edu
ROLLMAN, Catherine, A 804-752-7270 484 C crollman@rmc.edu
ROLLO, Ann 315-364-3235 333 G arollo@wells.edu
ROLLO, J. Michael 239-590-7910 109 C jmrollo@fgcu.edu
ROLLOR, Michael 410-706-1875 207 H mrollor@umaryland.edu
ROLLS, Dickie 620-252-7575 176 K rolls.dickie@coffeyville.edu
ROLLWITZ, Chris 817-461-8741 442 L crollwitz@abu.edu
ROLNIK, Karina 801-990-1656 99 I krolnik@fcnh.com
ROLOFF, ReBecca, K 651-690-6525 249 T broloff@stkate.edu
ROLON, John 641-269-3713 169 F rolonjoe@grinnell.edu
ROLON, Liberty 787-750-4100 527 H liberty.rolon@upr.edu
ROLON, Reynaldo 787-279-1912 523 J rrolon@bayamon.inter.edu
ROLPH, Chris 606-539-3527 190 A chris.rolph@ucumberlands.edu
ROM, Kjetil 541-881-5746 387 D krom@tvcc.cc
ROMA, Jennifer 305-273-4499 96 N jennifer.roman@cbt.edu
ROMA, Lawrence, J 607-777-2224 325 A lroma@binghamton.edu
ROMAGNI, Joanne 423-425-1743 440 A joanne-romagni@utc.edu
ROMAGNOLI, Janice 615-655-7274 300 I jaromagnoli@cazenovia.edu
ROMAIN, Pete 212-517-0414 314 D promain@mmm.edu
ROMALI, Reagan 562-938-4121 48 I rromali@lbcc.edu
ROMAN, Albert, J 213-891-2173 48 K romanaj@email.laccd.edu
ROMAN, Angela 231-591-2674 230 A angelaroman@ferris.edu
ROMAN, Cynthia 248-942-3300 235 D caroman@oaklandcc.edu
ROMAN, Jennifer 214-329-4447 443 J jennifer.roman@bgu.edu
ROMAN, Juan, E 787-841-2000 525 J jroman@pucpr.edu
ROMAN, Kristen 608-262-4527 510 C kristen.roman@wisc.edu
ROMAN, Nilsa, M 787-891-0925 523 G nroman@aguadilla.inter.edu
ROMAN, Ramonita 787-257-0000 527 H ramonita.roman@upr.edu
ROMAN, Vladimir 787-763-6425 523 F vroman@inter.edu
ROMAN-LAGUNAS, Victoria 219-980-6707 160 C acadaffs@iun.edu
ROMAN-VARGAS, Madeline 773-878-3728 150 I mroman02@staugustine.edu
ROMANCZUK, Jeffrey 704-886-6500 93 B
ROMANDINI, Russ 706-507-8898 118 C romandini_russ@columbusstate.edu
ROMANDINI, Russ 513-618-1930 359 F rromandini@ccms.edu
ROMANELLO, Mary 202-884-9677 93 C romanellom@trinitydc.edu
ROMANO, Angela 845-431-8097 307 A angela.romano@sunydutchess.edu
ROMANO, Carol 301-295-9002 518 G carol.romano@usuhs.edu

ROMANO, Cenia, K .... 787-884-3838 520 G
vpacademico@atenascollege.edu
ROMANO, Christopher .. 201-684-7309 289 C
cromano@ramapo.edu
ROMANO, Fred, D .... 630-515-6388 145 I
froman@midwestern.edu
ROMANO, Joan .... 617-989-4908 225 E
romanoj3@wit.edu
ROMANO, Joyce, C ...... 407-582-3402 113 F
jromano@valenciacollege.edu
ROMANO, Judith, J ...... 864-294-3470 421 I
judith.romano@furman.edu
ROMANO, Linda .... 718-990-6865 322 F
romanol@stjohns.edu
ROMANO, Michael .... 623-245-4600.. 16 H
mromano@uti.edu
ROMANO, Nicole .... 302-356-6846.. 91 B
nicole.romano@wilmu.edu
ROMANO, Pam .... 910-272-3531 346 A
promano@robeson.edu
ROMANO, Sandra .... 340-693-1389 529 C
sromano@uvi.edu
ROMANO, Susan .... 585-245-5731 327 B
romano@geneseo.edu
ROMANO, Victor .... 305-899-3756.. 95 G
vromano@barry.edu
ROMANO, Wendy, W .... 215-871-6300 407 G
wendyr@pcom.edu
ROMANS, John .... 405-744-3373 377 F
john.romans@okstate.edu
ROMANSKI, Beth, E ...... 717-867-6336 399 J
romanski@lvc.edu
ROMANT, Stacy .... 414-288-3654 508 C
stacy.romant@marquette.edu
ROMANTIC, Thomas, W 607-255-8574 306 B
twr2@cornell.edu
ROMBALSKI, Patrick ..... 617-792-3636 134 K
prombalski@chamberlain.edu
ROMBOUTS,
Stephen, R .... 814-472-3009 409 G
srombouts@francis.edu
ROME, Alan, K .... 440-943-7600 369 J
cpl@dioceseofcleveland.org
ROME, Alan, K .... 440-943-7600 369 J
akrome@dioceseofcleveland.org
ROME, JoAnne .... 413-552-2259 219 G
jrome@hcc.edu
ROME, Kevin, D .... 615-329-8555 431 I
srucker@fisk.edu
ROME, Michaela .... 212-229-8947 316 E
romem@newschool.edu
ROMELDA, Simmons .... 478-825-6219 119 C
simmonsr@fvsu.edu
ROMEO, JR., Aldemaro 646-312-3870 301 B
aldemaro.romeo@baruch.cuny.edu
ROMEO, Jamie .... 860-629-6213.. 87 F
romeo_j@mitchell.edu
ROMER, Christine, E .... 636-922-8362 265 J
cromer@stchas.edu
ROMERAO-ALDAZ,
Patrick .... 617-928-4073 222 D
promeroaldaz@mountida.edu
ROMERO, Abran .... 505-454-2500 294 D
aromero@luna.edu
ROMERO, Andy .... 505-747-2166 295 H
andy@nnmc.edu
ROMERO, Angel .... 787-765-1915 524 F
aromero@opto.inter.edu
ROMERO, Bianca .... 909-593-3511.. 70 E
bromero@laverne.edu
ROMERO, Carol .... 305-821-3333 100 A
cromero@fnu.edu
ROMERO, Cecilia .... 505-747-5477 295 H
cromero@nnmc.edu
ROMERO, Christina .... 714-564-6091.. 58 A
romero_christina@sac.edu
ROMERO, Clarence .... 505-425-7511 294 J
ROMERO, Cynthia .... 757-446-7414 480 C
romerocc@evms.edu
ROMERO, Edward, W .... 903-886-5027 459 E
edward.romero@tamuc.edu
ROMERO, Eileen .... 914-594-4495 318 A
eileen_romero@nymc.edu
ROMERO, Georg .... 831-479-5771.. 28 F
geromero@cabrillo.edu
ROMERO, Herminio .... 787-622-8000 527 B
hromero@pupr.edu
ROMERO, Jose .... 787-864-2222 524 A
jose.romero@guayama.inter.edu
ROMERO, Krystal .... 650-574-6440.. 62 A
romerok@smccd.edu
ROMERO, Lizbeth .... 787-878-5475 523 H
lromero@arecibo.inter.edu
ROMERO, Manuel .... 212-220-1238 301 C
mromero@bmcc.cuny.edu
ROMERO, Narda .... 914-674-7841 314 I
nromero@mercy.edu
ROMERO, Peter .... 505-473-6328 296 C
peter.romero@santafeuniversity.edu
ROMERO, Ramona, E .... 609-258-2511 288 F
ramonar@princeton.edu
ROMERO, Rebecca .... 970-521-6649.. 81 F
rebecca.romero@njc.edu
ROMERO, Reyna .... 713-221-8460 465 C
romeror@uhd.edu
ROMERO, Sally .... 970-943-2150.. 84 E
sromero@western.edu
ROMERO, Van, D .... 575-835-5646 294 K
van.romero@nmt.edu
ROMERO, Victoria .... 909-621-8149.. 63 F
vromero@scrippscollege.edu
ROMERO-LEGGOTT,
Valerie .... 505-272-2728 296 H
vromero@salud.unm.edu
ROMERO-NIEVES,
Luis, E .... 787-751-1912 524 E
lromero@juris.inter.edu
ROMES, Lindsey .... 973-290-4322 285 A
lromes@cse.edu
ROMIG, Kenneth, J .... 724-946-7141 414 C
romigkj@westminster.edu
ROMIG, Thomas, J .... 785-670-1662 182 D
thomas.romig@washburn.edu
ROMINE, Phil .... 651-255-6107 250 D
promine@unitedseminary.edu
ROMO, Nanette .... 520-515-5399.. 11 R
romon@cochise.edu
ROMO, Wayne .... 210-436-3538 455 J
wromo@stmarytx.edu
RONAN, Donald .... 317-805-1791 502 D
dronan@salemu.edu
RONCA, Paul, L .... 804-523-5239 488 C
pronca@reynolds.edu
RONCHETTI, Michele ..... 815-836-5498 143 E
ronchemi@lewisu.edu
RONCOLATO, David ...... 814-332-5318 388 F
droncola@allegheny.edu
RONDA, Rene, S .... 787-743-7979 526 A
rsronda@suagm.edu
RONDEAU, Ann .... 630-942-2201 136 D
rondeau@cod.edu
RONDINELLI, Diane ...... 904-826-0084.. 71 I
drondinelli@usa.edu
RONDON, Marvin .... 910-592-8081 346 D
mrondon@sampsoncc.edu
RONDON, Wilfredo .... 787-766-1717 526 B
wirondon@suagm.edu
RONEVICH, Nancy, S .... 740-284-5232 361 L
nronevich@franciscan.edu
RONEY, Linda .... 214-333-5147 447 D
linda@dbu.edu
RONIS, Sheila, R .... 248-689-8282 238 F
sronis@walshcollege.edu
RONK, Chris .... 336-725-8344 348 C
ronkc@piedmontu.edu
RONKOSKI, Bob .... 636-922-8604 265 J
rronkoski@stchas.edu
RONNFELDT, Derek .... 253-833-9111 495 C
dronnfeltd@greenriver.edu
RONNING, Teresa .... 518-743-2261 328 G
ronningt@sunyacc.edu
RONNING LINDGREN,
Rachel .... 805-493-3690.. 30 E
rronning@callutheran.edu
ROOB, Sharon .... 414-930-3375 509 B
roobs@mtmary.edu
ROOCK, Mark .... 314-529-9673 262 B
mroock@maryville.edu
ROOD, Christi .... 208-562-2710 132 A
christirood@cwidaho.cc
ROOD, Denine .... 320-629-5180 246 H
drood@pine.edu
ROOD, Jessica .... 941-487-4150 110 B
jrood@ncf.edu
ROOD, Robert .... 419-824-3730 364 G
rrood@lourdes.edu
ROODBEEN, Richard ..... 508-373-9539 211 F
richard.roodbeen@becker.edu
ROODE, Dana, F .... 949-824-5173.. 69 A
dana.roode@uci.edu
ROOF, Karin .... 843-953-7526 420 C
roofk@cofc.edu
ROOF, Rick .... 619-201-8700.. 60 A
ROOFNER, Perry, F .... 412-397-5256 409 C
roofner@rmu.edu
ROOHPARVAR,
Shahrooz .... 928-344-7521.. 11 B
shahrooz.roohparvar@azwestern.edu
ROOK, Steve .... 501-337-5000.. 19 C
srook@coto.edu
ROOK, Tony .... 252-823-5166 343 A
rookt@edgecombe.edu
ROOKARD, Crystal .... 803-822-3251 422 D
rookardc@midlandstech.edu
ROOKE, Michael .... 860-738-6300.. 86 C
mrooke@nwcc.edu
ROOKER, Allison .... 601-925-3310 254 B
abrooker@mc.edu
ROOKER, Darrin .... 315-568-3063 317 A
drooker@nycc.edu
ROOKER, Suzanne .... 580-477-7944 381 G
suzanne.rooker@wosc.edu
ROOKER, Velda .... 334-844-6406.... 4 D
rookelv@auburn.edu
ROOKS, James .... 616-526-8694 228 B
jrooks@calvin.edu
ROOKS, Noliwe, L .... 607-255-4625 306 B
nrooks@cornell.edu
ROOKS, Stephanie .... 770-962-7580 121 G
srooks@gwinnetttech.edu
ROONEY, Gail .... 217-333-0820 154 B
grooney@illinois.edu
ROONEY, Gerard, J .... 585-385-8010 322 E
grooney@sjfc.edu
ROONEY, Jo Ann .... 312-915-6400 144 D
jrooney@luc.edu
ROONEY, John, J .... 215-951-1282 398 F
rooney@lasalle.edu
ROONEY, Joseph, A ...... 302-793-1101.. 90 H
ROONEY, Larry .... 802-485-2499 475 I
lrooney@norwich.edu
ROONEY, Paul .... 407-582-1100 113 F
prooney@valenciacollege.edu
ROONEY, Paula, M .... 508-541-1658 214 C
prooney@dean.edu
ROONEY, Thomas, J ..... 507-933-7499 242 D
tomrooney@gustavus.edu
ROOP, Robert, G .... 240-567-5396 205 F
robert.roop@montgomerycollege.edu
ROOPNARINE, Darshini 315-445-4661 312 F
roopnatd@lemoyne.edu
ROORBACH, Karen .... 765-677-2975 161 C
karen.roorbach@indwes.edu
ROOS, Dan .... 507-372-3442 246 C
dan.roos@mnwest.edu
ROOS, Johan .... 617-619-1900 216 A
johan.roos@hult.edu
ROOSA, Mark, S .... 310-506-4252.. 56 D
mark.roosa@pepperdine.edu
ROOSE, Robert .... 989-358-7200 227 A
rooser@alpenacc.edu
ROOSEVELT, Mark .... 505-984-6098 295 K
president@sjc.edu
ROOT, David .... 606-539-4406 190 A
david.root@ucumberlands.edu
ROOT, Jeff .... 870-245-5154.. 20 G
rootj@obu.edu
ROOT, Jeff .... 870-245-4186.. 20 G
rootj@obu.edu
ROOT, John .... 512-245-2585 463 A
jr28@txstate.edu
ROOT, Larry .... 409-944-1208 449 F
lroot@gc.edu
ROOT, Mark, J .... 574-807-7219 156 E
rootm1@bethelcollege.edu
ROOT, Rennie, A .... 563-588-7775 171 H
rennie.root@loras.edu
ROOTH, Gerald, T .... 301-447-5003 206 B
rooth@msmary.edu
ROOTS, Keith, D .... 757-594-0581 479 H
keith.roots@cnu.edu
ROPELLA, Kristina .... 414-288-5460 508 C
kristina.ropella@marquette.edu
ROPER, Craig .... 618-545-3137 142 D
croper@kaskaskia.edu
ROPER, David .... 843-349-6532 420 A
droper@coastal.edu
ROPER, Gina .... 541-881-5577 387 D
groper@tvcc.cc
ROPER, Melinda .... 805-493-3553.. 30 E
mroper@callutheran.edu
ROPER, William, L .... 919-966-4161 351 B
william_roper@med.unc.edu
ROPER-DOTEN, Emily ... 781-292-2201 215 C
emily.roper-doten@olin.edu
ROQUEMORE, Glenn, R 949-451-5210.. 64 I
groquemore@ivc.edu
RORK, Jeannette .... 336-721-2618 348 H
jeannette.rork@salem.edu
RORRER, Caleb .... 336-342-4261 346 B
rorrerm8871@rockinghamcc.edu
ROSA, Carmen .... 914-654-5543 305 A
crosa@cnr.edu
ROSA, Carmen, J .... 787-780-0070 521 B
crosa@caribbean.edu
ROSA, Chris .... 646-664-8759 301 A
christopher.rosa@cuny.edu
ROSA, Jerry .... 718-518-6561 302 D
jrosa@hostos.cuny.edu
ROSA, Jessie .... 334-244-3540.... 4 E
jrosa@aum.edu
ROSA, John, W .... 843-953-5012 419 D
john.rosa@citadel.edu
ROSA, Juana .... 787-852-1430 522 P
j.rosa@hccpr.edu
ROSA, Luis .... 802-258-9238 475 D
luisr@marlboro.edu
ROSA, Maria .... 787-834-9595 526 E
mrosa@uaa.edu
ROSA, Maria .... 270-809-4425 188 D
mrosa1@murraystate.edu
ROSA, Maria, G .... 787-891-0925 523 G
mrosa@aquadilla.inter.edu
ROSA, Marta .... 617-879-2314 226 A
mrosa@wheelock.edu
ROSA, Peter .... 203-837-8376.. 85 B
rosap@wcsu.edu
ROSA, Ramonita .... 787-891-0925 523 G
rrosa@aguadilla.inter.edu
ROSA, Sandra .... 787-279-1912 523 J
srosa@bayamon.inter.edu
ROSA-NUNEZ,
Waleska, Y .... 787-480-2386 521 J
wrosa01@sanjuanciudadpatria.com
ROSA VELEZ,
Mariam, L .... 787-265-3879 528 C
prensa@uprm.edu
ROSAASEN, Orlynn .... 701-777-3823 353 G
orlynn.rosaasen@und.edu
ROSACCO, Claire .... 216-987-4804 360 E
claire.rosacco@tri-c.edu
ROSADO, Akilah .... 212-875-4596 298 H
arosado@bankstreet.edu
ROSADO, Carlos .... 787-764-0000 528 F
carlos.rosado13@upr.edu
ROSADO, Carmen .... 787-857-3600 523 I
crosado@br.inter.edu
ROSADO, Carmen .... 787-766-1717 526 B
um_crosado@suagm.edu
ROSADO, Judy .... 787-892-1365 524 D
judy.rosado@sodexo.com
ROSADO, Martin .... 787-884-6000 522 Q
mrosado@icprjc.edu
ROSADO, Reinaldo .... 787-284-1912 524 C
rrosado@ponce.inter.edu
ROSADO, Robert .... 787-815-0000 527 F
robert.rosado@upr.edu
ROSADO, Samuel .... 787-264-1912 524 D
samuel_rosado_nazario@intersg.edu
ROSALES, Elvia, H .... 512-471-3391 467 C
bd.elvia@austin.utexas.edu
ROSAMILIO, Noel .... 203-596-8780.. 86 B
nrosamilio@nv.edu
ROSANDICH,
Thomas, J .... 251-626-3303.... 7 G
president@ussa.edu
ROSANIA, Nick .... 641-472-1180 171 J
nrosania@mum.edu
ROSANIA, Sandra .... 641-472-1180 171 J
srosania@mum.edu
ROSANSKY, Lynne .... 781-891-2864 212 A
lrosansky@bentley.edu
ROSARIO, Antonio, J .... 787-857-3600 523 I
arosario@br.inter.edu
ROSARIO, Daniel .... 787-850-9551 528 B
daniel.rosario4@upr.edu
ROSARIO, Enrique .... 787-780-0070 521 B
rel.publicas@caribbean.edu
ROSARIO, Glorivee .... 787-738-2161 528 A
glorivee.rosario@upr.edu
ROSARIO, Lisanette .... 718-518-4311 302 D
lrosario@hostos.cuny.edu
ROSARIO, Lucy .... 787-284-1912 524 C
lrsario@ponce.inter.edu
ROSARIO, Vera .... 914-594-4900 318 A
vera_rosario@nymc.edu
ROSARIO, Victoria .... 916-568-3150.. 50 E
rosariv@losrios.edu
ROSARIO, Yoleidy .... 973-353-3416 290 D
yoleidy.rosario@rutgers.edu
ROSARIO, Yvette .... 718-960-8723 302 C
yvette.rosario@lehman.cuny.edu
ROSARIO DELGADO,
Victor .... 787-758-5297 528 F
victor.rosario1@upr.edu
ROSARIO-RODRIGUEZ,
Elizabeth .... 787-480-2444 521 J
erosario03@sanjuanciudadpatria.com
ROSARIO-ROSARIO,
Yolanda .... 787-725-6500 521 C
yrosario@albizu.edu
ROSAS, Alisha .... 909-652-6115.. 36 E
alisha.rosas@chaffey.edu
ROSAS, Carla .... 925-473-7427.. 41 A
crosas@losmedanos.edu
ROSAS, Erudina .... 787-878-6000 522 Q
ROSAS, Mirna .... 480-423-6754.. 14 C
mirna.rosas@scottsdalecc.edu

ROSS, Karen .... 734-432-5529 233 C
kross@madonna.edu
ROSS, Keith .... 314-392-2301 263 F
rossk@mobap.edu
ROSS, Kevin, M .... 561-237-7823 103 E
kross@lynn.edu
ROSS, Kristen .... 281-929-4653 456 B
kristen.ross@sjcd.edu
ROSS, Laura .... 407-708-2058 107 G
rossl@seminolestate.edu
ROSS, Lauren .... 937-512-2164 370 A
lauren.ross@sinclair.edu
ROSS, Leigh, A .... 601-984-2620 256 D
laross@umc.edu
ROSS, Lori, A .... 513-556-3483 371 E
rossla@ucmail.uc.edu
ROSS, Matthew .... 717-815-1359 415 G
mross@ycp.edu
ROSS, Meg .... 662-562-3204 255 C
mross@northwestms.edu
ROSS, Mikki .... 806-742-2121 463 D
mikki.ross@ttu.edu
ROSS, Neil .... 785-320-4554 179 E
neilross@manhattantech.edu
ROSS, Pam .... 864-231-2000 418 E
pross@andersonuniversity.edu
ROSS, Patricia, A .... 801-585-7832 472 P
p.ross@utah.edu
ROSS, Paul .... 719-502-2040.. 81 H
paul.ross@ppcc.edu
ROSS, Peter, G .... 989-774-4456 228 E
ross1pg@cmich.edu
ROSS, Ramsey .... 850-729-5229 104 E
ramseyr@nwfsc.edu
ROSS, Rebecca .... 610-436-2501 407 D
rross2@wcupa.edu
ROSS, Reginald .... 973-720-2903 292 I
rossr@wpunj.edu
ROSS, Rick .... 360-417-6533 496 I
rross@pencol.edu
ROSS, Robert .... 787-738-2161 528 A
robert.ross@upr.edu
ROSS, Robin .... 828-327-7000 341 G
rross@cvcc.edu
ROSS, Ronald .... 973-877-3078 285 K
ross@essex.edu
ROSS, Sadie .... 518-587-2100 329 C
sadie.ross@esc.edu
ROSS, Sarah .... 425-739-8287 495 F
sarah.ross@lwtech.edu
ROSS, Shelbie .... 207-255-1319 201 F
shelbie.ross@maine.edu
ROSS, Stephen, C .... 724-847-6541 395 J
scross@geneva.edu
ROSS, Susan .... 570-321-4204 400 G
ross@lycoming.edu
ROSS, Tabithia .... 478-289-2171 118 H
tross@ega.edu
ROSS, Thelma, L .... 301-546-0766 206 E
rosstl1@pgcc.edu
ROSS, Todd .... 626-815-6000.. 26 U
tross@apu.edu
ROSS, Tricia .... 212-799-5000 312 B
ROSS-ANDERSON,
Jennifer .... 219-844-0100 156 F
jennifer.r@brightwood.edu
ROSS-GARCIA, Tracy ..... 210-486-2851 441 I
tross20@alamo.edu
ROSS-JONES, Marvel, E 716-884-9120 300 C
merossjones@bryantstratton.edu
ROSS STAMPS,
Clara, R .... 502-597-6785 187 E
clara.stamps@kysu.edu
ROSS-WINNIE,
Katheryn .... 716-896-0700 333 C
krosswinnie@villa.edu
ROSSBACH, Janet .... 646-660-6097 301 B
janet.rossbach@baruch.cuny.edu
ROSSBACHER, Lisa .... 707-826-3311.. 34 A
lisa.rossbacher@humboldt.edu
ROSSELLI, David .... 254-710-2561 444 B
dave_rosselli@baylor.edu
ROSSER, Charice .... 252-536-7207 343 F
ROSSER, Sue, V .... 415-338-1141.. 34 C
srosser@sfsu.edu
ROSSER, Ulrike .... 614-825-6255 356 C
urosser@aiam.edu
ROSSER, Virginia, J ...... 419-372-9865 357 F
jrosser@bgsu.edu
ROSSER-MIMS, Dionne . 334-670-3457.... 7 E
drosser-mims@troy.edu
ROSSETTI, Elspeth .... 408-554-4421.. 62 F
erossetti@scu.edu
ROSSETTI, Erin, S .... 802-626-6417 477 D
erin.rossetti@lyndonstate.edu
ROSSI, Frank .... 607-753-4827 327 A
frank.rossi@cortland.edu
ROSSI, Jamal .... 585-274-1010 332 E
jrossi@esm.rochester.edu
ROSSI, Jason .... 630-515-5472 137 E
jrossi@devry.edu
ROSSI, John .... 315-312-5555 327 D
john.rossi@oswego.edu
ROSSI, John, J .... 626-256-4673.. 37 I
jrossi@coh.org
ROSSI, John, M .... 217-333-9862 154 B
jrossi@illinois.edu
ROSSI, Julie .... 541-245-7615 386 G
jrossi@roguecc.edu
ROSSI, Laura .... 410-225-2363 205 C
lrossi@mica.edu
ROSSI, Reagan .... 208-459-5855 131 H
rrossi@collegeofidaho.edu
ROSSI, Renee .... 904-256-7458 102 B
rrossi@ju.edu
ROSSI-LE, Laura .... 978-232-2055 214 G
lrossile@endicott.edu
ROSSIGNOL, Paul .... 505-438-8884 296 D
paul@acupuncturecollege.edu
ROSSITER, Andrew .... 808-923-9741 129 J
andrewro@hawaii.edu
ROSSITER, Sherry .... 740-593-4129 368 G
bursar@ohio.edu
ROSSITTO, Paul .... 860-832-1617.. 84 J
rossitto@ccsu.edu
ROSSKY, Peter .... 713-348-3350 455 F
peter.rossky@rice.edu
ROSSMAN, Vicki .... 713-780-9777 442 F
ROSSON, Michael .... 718-368-5144 303 A
mrosson@kbcc.cuny.edu
ROST, Gregory, S .... 215-898-7221 412 G
gregrost@upenn.edu
ROST, Jamie, D .... 407-582-5412 113 F
jrost@valenciacollege.edu
ROSTAR, Jimmy .... 252-328-1275 349 I
rostarj@ecu.edu
ROSTER, Ellen .... 320-222-5219 247 B
ellen.roster@ridgewater.edu
ROSU, Gabriela .... 480-732-7000.. 13 E
gabriela.rosu@cgc.edu
ROSYNSKY, Michelle .... 810-237-6649 238 B
rosynsky@umflint.edu
ROSZELL, Nancy, J ...... 937-255-3636 517 H
nancy.roszell@afit.edu
ROT, Jeffrey .... 904-826-0084.. 71 I
jrot@usa.edu
ROTENBERG, Susan, A . 718-997-4105 303 E
susan.rotenberg@qc.cuny.edu
ROTGER, Mariolga .... 787-850-9364 528 B
mariolga.rotger@upr.edu
ROTH, Amy .... 772-466-4822.. 95 D
amy.roth@aviator.edu
ROTH, Andrew, W .... 330-972-7340 371 C
aroth1@uakron.edu
ROTH, Ben .... 217-786-2773 144 B
ben.roth@llcc.edu
ROTH, Beth .... 610-790-1981 389 A
beth.roth@alvernia.edu
ROTH, Brenda .... 503-375-7010 383 A
broth@corban.edu
ROTH, Brenda .... 810-762-3488 238 B
blroth@umflint.edu
ROTH, Cindi .... 304-284-4040 505 B
croth@mail.wvu.edu
ROTH, Don, F .... 530-754-5418.. 68 H
droth@ucdavis.edu
ROTH, Frank .... 785-833-4303 179 C
froth@kwu.edu
ROTH, Frank, A .... 610-758-3572 400 B
far4@lehigh.edu
ROTH, Gregg .... 518-736-3622 309 A
gregg.roth@fmcc.suny.edu
ROTH, Henry .... 650-508-3721.. 54 D
hroth@ndnu.edu
ROTH, Jason .... 702-968-1633 280 B
jroth@roseman.edu
ROTH, Jeff .... 310-206-8041.. 69 B
jroth@ponet.ucla.edu
ROTH, John, C .... 718-940-5616 322 G
jroth@sjcny.edu
ROTH, Karen .... 541-383-7412 382 B
kroth1@cocc.edu
ROTH, Katie .... 847-735-6005 142 H
roth@lakeforest.edu
ROTH, Linda .... 301-696-3919 204 D
roth@hood.edu
ROTH, Lindsay .... 508-999-8478 217 A
lroth@umassd.edu
ROTH, Marjorie .... 585-389-2686 316 D
mroth1@naz.edu
ROTH, Martin .... 860-768-4243.. 89 C
mroth@hartford.edu
ROTH, Megan .... 325-674-2885 441 D
mkr15a@acu.edu
ROTH, Michael .... 707-527-6939.. 62 H
mroth@santarosa.edu
ROTH, Michael, L .... 509-313-4204 495 A
roth@athletics.gonzaga.edu
ROTH, Michael, S .... 860-685-3500.. 89 F
mroth@wesleyan.edu
ROTH, Mike .... 503-589-8152 383 A
mroth@corban.edu
ROTH, OSB, Neal, G ..... 360-491-4440 497 F
theabbot@stmartin.edu
ROTH, Neil .... 304-473-8312 505 G
roth@wvwc.edu
ROTH, Paul, B .... 505-272-5849 296 H
proth@salud.unm.edu
ROTH, Sterling .... 404-413-1310 121 A
roths@gsu.edu
ROTH NICKS, Rebecca .. 706-880-8088 122 D
rroth@lagrange.edu
ROTH-SAKS, Jodi .... 610-436-3379 407 D
jroth@wcupa.edu
ROTHAUS, Richard .... 701-328-4136 353 F
richard.rothaus@ndus.edu
ROTHBERG, Heidi .... 413-528-7201 211 B
registrar@simons-rock.edu
ROTHBERG, Jacob .... 914-736-1500 319 E
ROTHENBERG, Jeffrey ... 317-338-3879 164 B
ROTHENBERGER, Sara .. 860-439-2834.. 86 H
srothenb@conncoll.edu
ROTHENBUHLER, Eric ... 314-246-7154 269 N
erothenbuhler@webster.edu
ROTHENHOEFER,
Lynn, S .... 610-527-0200 409 E
lrothenhoefer@rosemont.edu
ROTHGEB, Helen .... 714-241-6150.. 38 F
hrothgeb@coastline.edu
ROTHMAN, Paul .... 410-955-3180 204 F
prothma1@jhmi.edu
ROTHMAN, Paul, D .... 410-955-3180 204 F
prothma1@jhmi.edu
ROTHMEYER, Melissa ... 714-816-0366.. 67 J
melissa.rothmeyer@trident.edu
ROTHMEYER, Michelle .. 815-825-9807 142 F
michelle.rothmeyer@kishwaukeecollege.edu
ROTHSCHILD, Dovid, N 516-225-4700 320 H
rdnr@mlb.edu
ROTHSCHILD,
Martha, D .... 410-777-2701 202 D
mdrothschild@aacc.edu
ROTHSCHILD,
Vivian, M .... 414-847-3239 508 G
vivianrothschild@miad.edu
ROTHWELL, Krista .... 302-622-8000.. 90 A
krothwell@dcad.edu
ROTHWELL, Suzanne ..... 573-875-7563 258 F
srothwell@ccis.edu
ROTHWELL, Suzanne ..... 573-875-7207 258 F
srothwell@ccis.edu
ROTICH, Herbert, K .... 517-750-1200 237 D
hrotich@arbor.edu
ROTOLO, Rene, M .... 718-960-8226 302 C
rene.rotolo@lehman.cuny.edu
ROTONDO, Denise .... 585-245-5367 327 B
rotondo@geneseo.edu
ROTONDO, Mark .... 617-873-0675 213 B
mark.rotondo@cambridgecollege.edu
ROTROFF, Kristi .... 419-267-1271 366 G
krotroff@northweststate.edu
ROTT, Cynthia .... 701-231-7458 354 D
cynthia.rott@ndsu.edu
ROTTENBERG, Aaron ..... 718-854-2290 299 H
ROTTER, Bruce, E .... 618-474-7120 152 C
brotter@siue.edu
ROTTER, Jackie .... 805-482-2755.. 58 M
jackie@stjohnsem.edu
ROTTLER, Nancy .... 724-805-2255 410 C
nancy.rottler@stvincent.edu
ROTTWEILER, James, D 520-515-5498.. 11 R
jdr@cochise.edu
ROTUNDO, Kim, M .... 906-227-2322 235 A
krotundo@nmu.edu
ROTUNDO, Michael, R .. 906-227-2327 235 A
mrotundo@nmu.edu
ROTUNNI, Lisa, M .... 909-869-2474.. 31 A
lmrotunni@cpp.edu
ROTZ, Ben .... 918-335-6279 378 F
brotz@okwu.edu
ROUBIDOUX, Nikol .... 208-792-2223 132 C
ncroubidoux@lcsc.edu
ROUBINEK, Darren .... 816-501-2422 257 G
darren.roubinek@avila.edu
ROUBIQUE, Connie .... 225-752-4233 191 I
croubique@iticollege.edu
ROUCH, Brian .... 408-498-5100.. 38 I
brouch@cogswell.edu
ROUDKOVSKI, Melanie . 903-233-3208 452 A
melanieroudkovski@letu.edu
ROUGEAU, Vincent, D .. 617-552-4315 212 E
vincent.rougeau@bc.edu
ROUGHTON, Dean .... 252-335-0821 342 D
dean_roughton@albemarle.edu
ROUGHTON, Keith .... 912-478-0747 120 E
kroughton@georgiasouthern.edu
ROULIER, Stephen .... 413-748-3717 224 G
sroulier@springfieldcollege.edu
ROUMBANIS, Christine . 650-738-4248.. 62 B
roumbanis@smccd.edu
ROUNCE, Laura, L .... 312-949-7040 140 A
lrounce@ico.edu
ROUND, Sara .... 816-415-5984 270 C
rounds@william.jewell.edu
ROUNDS, Claude .... 518-276-6601 321 A
roundc@rpi.edu
ROUNDS, Dayle, G .... 609-497-7991 288 E
dayle.rounds@ptsem.edu
ROUNDS, Michael .... 785-864-4419 181 I
m528r913@ku.edu
ROUNDS, Michael, J ..... 610-565-0999 415 A
mrounds@williamson.edu
ROUNDS, Scott .... 251-981-3771.... 5 A
scott.rounds@columbiasouthern.edu
ROUNDS, Tyra .... 313-993-1046 237 F
roundstc@udmercy.edu
ROUNDTREE, Gwen, D .. 914-606-6581 333 H
gwen.roundtree@sunywcc.edu
ROUNDTREE, Leslie, A . 773-995-3987 135 F
lroundtr@csu.edu
ROUNTREE, Cynthia ...... 718-997-5888 303 E
cynthia.rountree@qc.cuny.edu
ROUNTREE, Jeffrey, W .. 540-654-2060 486 D
jrountre@umw.edu
ROUNTREE, Kathleen .... 510-885-3161.. 31 F
kathleen.rountree@csueastbay.edu
ROUNTREE, Linda .... 503-493-6248 382 I
lrountree@cu-portland.edu
ROUNTREE, Mike .... 478-289-2093 118 H
rountree@ega.edu
ROURK, Darcy .... 360-992-2986 493 E
drourk@clark.edu
ROURKE, Carol, M .... 315-267-2128 328 A
rourkecm@potsdam.edu
ROURKE, David .... 415-338-1822.. 34 C
drourke@sfsu.edu
ROURKE, David, M .... 315-386-7325 329 A
rourked@canton.edu
ROURKE, Kathleen .... 315-792-7295 330 A
kathleen.rourke@sunyit.edu
ROUS, Philip .... 410-455-2598 208 A
rous@umbc.edu
ROUSE, Cecilia .... 609-258-4800 288 F
rouse@princeton.edu
ROUSE, Douglas .... 908-709-7113 292 C
douglas.rouse@ucc.edu
ROUSE, Kevin .... 828-327-7000 341 G
krouse@cvcc.edu
ROUSE, Lawrence, L ..... 910-296-2414 344 B
lrouse@jamessprunt.edu
ROUSE, Sandra .... 803-321-5206 422 H
sandra.rouse@newberry.edu
ROUSE, Taryn .... 402-486-2071 277 C
taryn.rouse@ucollege.edu
ROUSH, Clark, A .... 402-363-5610 278 E
croush@york.edu
ROUSH, J.R .... 937-695-0751 370 C
jroush@sscc.edu
ROUSH, John, A .... 859-238-5220 184 C
john.roush@centre.edu
ROUSH, Keith .... 570-484-2384 406 E
kroush@lockhaven.edu
ROUSH, Kim .... 563-588-6539 167 E
kimberly.roush@clarke.edu
ROUSH, Matt .... 248-204-2210 233 A
mroush@ltu.edu
ROUSH, Rebecca .... 910-695-3704 346 E
roushr@sandhills.edu
ROUSH, Richard, T .... 814-865-2541 403 F
rtr10@psu.edu
ROUSH, Sally .... 619-594-5201.. 34 B
presidents.office@sdsu.edu
ROUSMANIERE, David .. 704-687-7418 351 C
drousman@uncc.edu
ROUSSEAU, Karen, S .... 413-205-3503 210 E
karen.rousseau@aic.edu
ROUSSELL, Jeroid .... 503-699-6305 384 B
jroussell@marylhurst.edu
ROUSSIVE, David .... 310-206-6469.. 69 B
rousseve@arts.ucla.edu
ROUSU, Matthew .... 570-372-4186 410 H
rousu@susqu.edu
ROUTBORT, Julia, C ..... 518-580-5555 324 D
jroutbor@skidmore.edu
ROUTE, Annie .... 907-786-1215.. 10 A
adroute@alaska.edu

RUDDEN, David ... 847-214-7925 138 B
drudden@elgin.edu
RUDE, Jen ... 253-535-7464 496 G
rudejl@plu.edu
RUDEAU, William ... 609-771-2187 284 I
rudeau@tcnj.edu
RUDECOFF,
Christine, A ... 315-684-6055 329 F
rudecoc@morrisville.edu
RUDEEN, Ashley ... 617-745-3864 214 D
ashley.rudeen@enc.edu
RUDEN, Becky ... 415-703-9360.. 28 K
becky@cca.edu
RUDGERS, Lisa, M ... 734-764-3526 237 I
rudgers@umich.edu
RUDICK, Craig, P ... 859-323-3190 190 B
craig.rudick@uky.edu
RUDIE, Eric ... 210-308-8584 445 F
eric.rudie@brightwood.edu
RUDIE, Scott ... 414-930-3555 509 B
rudies@mtmary.edu
RUDIGER, Brenda ... 906-487-2400 234 A
brudiger@mtu.edu
RUDIGER, Jennifer ... 715-232-1151 512 A
rudigerj@uwstout.edu
RUDIN, Mark ... 208-426-5732 131 C
markrudin@boisestate.edu
RUDISILL, Frank ... 864-503-5511 425 H
frudisill@uscupstate.edu
RUDMAN, Anita ... 215-567-7080 389 E
arudman@edmc.edu
RUDMAN, William ... 847-578-7440 150 E
william.rudman@rosalindfranklin.edu
RUDNEY, Gwen ... 320-589-6411 251 A
rudneygl@morris.umn.edu
RUDNITSKI, Rose ... 914-674-7447 314 I
rrudnitski@mercy.edu
RUDOLPH, Alan, S ... 970-491-7194.. 78 N
alan.rudolph@colostate.edu
RUDOLPH, Margaret ... 419-448-2111 362 G
mrudolph@heidelberg.edu
RUDOLPH, Mary Kay ... 707-524-1516.. 62 H
mrudolph@santarosa.edu
RUDOLPH, Meloni ... 303-556-8164.. 79 D
meloni.rudolph@ccd.edu
RUDOVSKY, Michelle ... 650-378-6577.. 62 A
rudovskym@smccd.edu
RUDOWSKY, Catherine . 361-825-2643 460 A
catherine.rudowsky@tamucc.edu
RUDY, Joel ... 276-739-2512 490 A
jrudy@vhcc.edu
RUE, Cynthia ... 239-454-5000 105 J
RUE, Penny ... 336-758-5943 353 A
rue@wfu.edu
RUEB, Jan, L ... 432-837-8178 462 G
jrueb@sulross.edu
RUEB, Shirley ... 316-942-4291 180 D
ruebs@newmanu.edu
RUEDAS, Lorena ... 916-558-2646.. 50 I
ruedasl@scc.losrios.edu
RUEDI RAY, Katerina ... 419-372-2786 357 F
krray@bgsu.edu
RUEFF, Alicia ... 561-732-4424 107 C
arueff@svdp.edu
RUEFLE, Colleen ... 412-536-1069 398 E
colleen.ruefle@laroche.edu
RUEGG, Texas ... 903-233-4381 452 A
texasruegg@letu.edu
RUELLE, Joan ... 336-278-6572 337 G
jruelle@elon.edu
RUESCH, Sherry ... 435-652-7551 473 B
ruesch@dixie.edu
RUESCHMANN, Eva ... 413-559-5378 215 F
erueschmann@hampshire.edu
RUESINK, Michelle ... 605-256-5121 428 G
michelle.ruesink@dsu.edu
RUETER, Erik ... 724-503-1001 414 A
erueter@washjeff.edu
RUETER, Ken ... 712-279-5504 167 B
ken.rueter@briarcliff.edu
RUETTEN, Amy ... 417-667-8181 259 A
aruetten@cottey.edu
RUFF, Corey ... 325-674-2665 441 D
clr06a@acu.edu
RUFF, Darla ... 303-556-2400.. 79 D
RUFF, Joy, C ... 305-237-2090 103 L
jruff@mdc.edu
RUFF, Margaret ... 903-785-7661 454 F
mruff@parisjc.edu
RUFF, Raymond, H ... 864-597-4171 426 I
ruffrh@wofford.edu
RUFFIN, Cynthia ... 919-572-1625 335 F
cruffin@apexsot.edu
RUFFIN, Finee ... 601-477-4082 253 F
finee.ruffin@jcjc.edu
RUFFING, Rebecca ... 315-866-0300 310 A
ruffingrj@herkimer.edu

RUFFINI, Giovanni ... 203-254-4000.. 87 A
gruffini@fairfield.edu
RUFFINO, John, J ... 703-323-3023 488 H
jruffino@nvcc.edu
RUFFRAGE, Jo ... 315-792-7172 330 A
ruffraj@sunyit.edu
RUFINO, Paul ... 856-415-2173 289 G
prufino@rcgc.edu
RUFO, Joseph ... 315-470-6622 328 D
jlrufo@esf.edu
RUFO, Joseph, L ... 315-470-6622 328 D
jlrufo@esf.edu
RUGEMER, Ellen ... 410-857-2203 205 E
erugemer@mcdaniel.edu
RUGER, Theodore, W ... 215-898-7061 412 G
deanruger@law.upenn.edu
RUGG, Marilyn ... 315-228-7288 304 G
mrugg@colgate.edu
RUGG, Rebecca ... 914-251-6831 328 B
rebecca.rugg@purchase.edu
RUGGAR MARTIN, Jan . 323-469-3300.. 25 D
jruggarmartin@amda.edu
RUGGERI, Mary ... 239-687-5332.. 95 B
mruggeri@avemarialaw.edu
RUGGIERI, Jan ... 508-849-3444 210 H
jruggieri@annamaria.edu
RUGGIERO, Bruno ... 985-448-4262 197 C
bruno.ruggiero@nicholls.edu
RUGGIRELLO, Frank ... 734-462-4400 236 H
fruggire@schoolcraft.edu
RUGGIRELLO, John ... 860-727-6907.. 87 B
jruggirello@goodwin.edu
RUGGLES, Jennifer ... 216-368-1723 358 C
jor15@case.edu
RUGGLES, Shami ... 509-533-7085 493 I
shami.ruggles@ccs.spokane.edu
RUGGLES, Shami, R ... 509-533-3567 493 H
shami.ruggles@ccs.spokane.edu
RUGH, Susan ... 801-422-2742 471 E
susan_rugh@byu.edu
RUHD, Jill ... 605-256-5650 428 G
jill.ruhd@dsu.edu
RUHL, Austin ... 406-586-3585 271 E
austin.ruhl@montanabiblecollege.edu
RUHLAND, Gail ... 320-308-3081 247 E
gmruhland@stcloudstate.edu
RUHLANDT, Karin ... 315-443-3949 330 H
kruhland@syr.edu
RUITER, Kathy ... 217-854-5525 134 E
kathleen.ruiter@blackburn.edu
RUIZ, Alberto ... 361-593-2837 460 B
alberto.ruiz@tamuk.edu
RUIZ, Alfredo ... 269-471-6979 227 B
jaruiz@andrews.edu
RUIZ, Andrew ... 806-894-9611 456 F
aruiz@southplainscollege.edu
RUIZ, Angel, J ... 787-863-2390 523 K
angel.ruiz@fajardo.inter.edu
RUIZ, Ediltrudys ... 718-960-8421 302 C
ediltrudys.ruiz@lehman.cuny.edu
RUIZ, Emil ... 787-840-2575 525 I
emilruiz@psm.edu
RUIZ, Encarnacion ... 209-228-4240.. 69 C
eruiz@ucmerced.edu
RUIZ, Eric ... 815-740-5070 154 G
eruiz@stfrancis.edu
RUIZ, Israel ... 617-253-4495 221 C
RUIZ, Israel, A ... 787-840-2575 525 I
iruiz@psm.edu
RUIZ, Joaquin ... 520-621-4090.. 16 J
jruiz@email.arizona.edu
RUIZ, OP, John Martin 202-495-3821.. 92 F
jruiz@dhs.edu
RUIZ, Jose ... 787-863-2390 523 K
jose.ruiz@fajardo.inter.edu
RUIZ, Kathleen ... 310-303-7334.. 51 B
kruiz@marymountcalifornia.edu
RUIZ, Lucy ... 559-244-5988.. 66 E
lucy.ruiz@scccd.edu
RUIZ, Luis, A ... 787-766-1717 526 B
um_lruiz@suagm.edu
RUIZ, Luis, E ... 787-250-1912 524 B
leruiz@metro.inter.edu
RUIZ, Manuel ... 717-337-6616 396 A
mruiz@gettysburg.edu
RUIZ, Maria-Luisa ... 718-270-6263 303 C
mlruiz@mec.cuny.edu
RUIZ, Melanie ... 425-564-2710 492 G
melanie.ruiz@bellevuecollege.edu
RUIZ, Miguel ... 713-221-8564 465 C
ruizm@uhd.edu
RUIZ, Rachel ... 626-966-4576.. 25M
studentservices@agu.edu
RUIZ, Rafael ... 787-257-0000 527 H
rafael.ruiz@upr.edu
RUIZ, Roseanna ... 909-537-7651.. 33 D
rruiz@csusb.edu

RUIZ, Sacha, M ... 787-891-0925 523 G
sruiz@aguadilla.inter.edu
RUIZ, Sina ... 903-875-7376 453 J
sina.ruiz@navarrocollege.edu
RUIZ, Veronica ... 787-746-1400 522 O
vruiz@huertas.edu
RUIZ, Zaida ... 787-786-3030 526 F
zrueiz@ucb.edu.pr
RUIZ-HUSTON, Ines ... 209-946-2132.. 70 F
iruiz@pacific.edu
RUIZ-MATTEI, Enid ... 719-389-6854.. 77 J
enid.ruizmattei@coloradocollege.edu
RUIZ-MORENO, Isabel .. 818-364-7776.. 49 C
RUKOBO, Emily ... 212-261-1567 317 G
erukobo@nyit.edu
RUKSNAITIS, Diane ... 978-632-6600 220 D
d_ruksnaitis@mwcc.mass.edu
RULAND, Heather, E ... 508-373-9430 211 F
heather.ruland@becker.edu
RULAND, Judith, P ... 989-964-4145 236 F
jruland@svsu.edu
RULAND, Michael ... 409-880-8108 462 C
michael.ruland@lamar.edu
RULE, Dave ... 425-602-3000 492 E
RULE, Kelli ... 503-847-2556 387 I
krule@uws.edu
RULE, Nik ... 641-673-2168 174 F
ruleng@wmpenn.edu
RULLAN, Agustin ... 787-265-3822 528 C
decano.ingenieria@upr.edu
RULLMAN, Loren, J ... 734-763-1291 237 I
lrullman@umich.edu
RULLO, Michelle ... 718-779-1430 320 C
mrullo@plazacollege.edu
RULOFSON, Eric ... 530-938-5851.. 39 H
erulofson@siskiyous.edu
RUMBERGER, Jana ... 415-351-3507.. 60 G
jrumberger@sfai.edu
RUMERY, Joyce, V ... 207-581-1655 201 B
rumery@maine.edu
RUMIANO, Sara ... 530-898-5134.. 31 D
srumiano@csuchico.edu
RUMLEY, Timothy ... 616-538-2330 230 E
trumley@gbcol.edu
RUMMEL, J, D ... 402-280-1131 274 D
rummel@creighton.edu
RUMMEL, Tina ... 903-675-6376 464 C
trummel@tvcc.edu
RUMP, Rebecca ... 319-208-5065 173 G
brump@scciowa.edu
RUMPLER, Laura ... 208-769-3316 132 E
lkrumpler@nic.edu
RUMPZA, Matthew, D ... 651-696-6551 243 B
mrumpza@macalester.edu
RUMSEY, Duane ... 661-722-6300.. 26 C
drumsey@avc.edu
RUMSEY, Elizabeth ... 218-726-7471 250 F
erumsey@d.umn.edu
RUND, James, A ... 480-965-2200.. 10 K
james.rund@asu.edu
RUNDELL, Isabel ... 317-896-9324 164 F
irundell@ubca.org
RUNDELL, Jay, A ... 740-362-3121 365 D
jrundell@mtso.edu
RUNDQUIST, Amanda ... 319-385-6229 170 J
amanda.rundquist@iw.edu
RUNDSTROM, Amy, L ... 308-865-8501 277 F
rundstromal@unk.edu
RUNDSTROM WILLIAMS,
Tracy ... 817-257-7473 461 A
t.williams@tcu.edu
RUNELL HALL,
Marcella ... 413-538-3133 222 C
mhall@mtholyoke.edu
RUNESTAD, Eric ... 507-537-6220 248 A
eric.runestad@smsu.edu
RUNESTAD, Eric ... 563-387-1507 171 I
eric.runestad@luther.edu
RUNEY, Mim, L ... 401-598-1000 416 C
mruney@jwu.edu
RUNGAITIS, Stacy ... 760-744-1150.. 55 K
srungaitis@palomar.edu
RUNGE, Carol ... 518-743-2313 328 G
rungec@sunyacc.edu
RUNGE, Carol, E ... 315-255-1743 300 H
crunge@cayuga-cc.edu
RUNGE, Denise ... 907-786-6494.. 10 A
drunge@alaska.edu
RUNGE, Mark, S ... 620-341-5331 177 B
mrunge@emporia.edu
RUNGE, Marschall, S ... 734-764-3399 237 I
RUNGE, Marschall, S ... 734-647-9351 237 I
RUNGE, Steven, W ... 501-450-3126.. 23 I
srunge@uca.edu
RUNIEWICZ, Michael, J 314-935-8976 269 L
michael_runiewicz@wustl.edu
RUNION, Kevin, L ... 812-237-8101 159 C
kevin.runion@indstate.edu

RUNION, Robert ... 304-929-5026 503 B
rrunion@newriver.edu
RUNION, Trish ... 785-539-3571 179 F
trunion@mccks.edu
RUNKLE, Dan ... 563-589-3599 173 J
drunkle@dbq.edu
RUNKLE, Gita ... 310-434-4370.. 62 G
runkle_gita@smc.edu
RUNKSMEIER, Lori ... 860-465-5169.. 84 K
runksmeierl@easternct.edu
RUNNELS, Greg ... 574-239-8312 158M
grunnels@hcc-nd.edu
RUNNELS, Marti, R ... 806-291-1086 470 I
runnels@wbu.edu
RUNNING, Patrick ... 320-762-4483 243 J
patrickr@alextech.edu
RUNYAN, Andy ... 937-512-3140 370 A
andy.runyan@sinclair.edu
RUNYAN, Laura ... 717-337-6505 396 A
lrunyan@gettysburg.edu
RUNYON, David ... 717-901-5137 397 E
drunyon@harrisburgu.edu
RUNYON, Jean ... 970-204-8100.. 79 K
jean.runyon@frontrange.edu
RUNYON, Tim ... 417-626-1234 264 J
runyon.tim@occ.edu
RUOCCO, Ann Michele . 413-559-5411 215 F
amrhr@hampshire.edu
RUPE, Jolene, K ... 785-539-3571 179 F
jrupe@mccks.edu
RUPE, Manuel, R ... 989-774-3971 228 E
rupe1mr@cmich.edu
RUPERT, Kimberly ... 517-750-1200 237 D
krupert@arbor.edu
RUPERT, Terry, A ... 937-481-2255 373 I
terry_rupert@wilmington.edu
RUPIPER, Russ ... 402-557-7291 273 E
russ.rupiper@bellevue.edu
RUPP, Leila ... 805-893-8354.. 70 B
lrupp@ltsc.ucsb.edu
RUPP, Sharon, L ... 864-424-8014 425 G
ruppsl@mailbox.sc.edu
RUPP, Sheila ... 231-995-1058 235 B
srupp@nmc.edu
RURKA, Jessica ... 410-225-2573 205 C
jrurka@mica.edu
RURSCH, Keri ... 309-794-7721 133 G
kerirursch@augustana.edu
RUSCH, Kathleen, M ... 414-464-9777 513 B
rusch.kathleen@wspp.edu
RUSCH, Kelly ... 701-231-6542 354 D
kelly.rusch@ndsu.edu
RUSCH-CURL, Kari ... 952-358-8776 246 D
kari.rusch-curl@normandale.edu
RUSCHE, Ernst ... 231-348-6624 234 H
erusche@ncmich.edu
RUSCHIVAL, Michael ... 303-292-0015.. 79 F
m.ruschival@denverschoolofnursing.
edu
RUSCHMAN, Doug ... 513-745-3185 374 D
ruschman@xavier.edu
RUSE, Elaine ... 330-941-3505 374 E
eruse@ysu.edu
RUSE, Michael ... 843-349-2548 420 A
mruse@coastal.edu
RUSH, Amber ... 870-368-2008.. 20 H
arush@ozarka.edu
RUSH, Cherylyn, L ... 215-951-1948 398 F
rush@lasalle.edu
RUSH, Dennis ... 845-569-3492 316 B
dennis.rush@msmc.edu
RUSH, James ... 662-476-5386 253 A
jrush@eastms.edu
RUSH, JR., James ... 706-721-1626 116 B
jrush@augusta.edu
RUSH, Janet ... 402-363-5661 278 E
jgrush@york.edu
RUSH, John, H ... 563-588-8000 169 B
jrush@emmaus.edu
RUSH, John, P ... 662-325-9306 254 E
rush@devalumni.msstate.edu
RUSH, Keith ... 225-769-8820 193 K
RUSH, Mark, E ... 540-458-8904 491 G
rushm@wlu.edu
RUSH, Maureen ... 215-898-7515 412 G
mrush@publicsafety.upenn.edu
RUSH, Mike, G ... 605-773-3455 428 D
mike.rush@sdbor.edu
RUSH, Nate ... 217-854-5776 134 E
nate.rush@blackburn.edu
RUSH, Patrick ... 708-596-2000 151 H
prush@ssc.edu
RUSH, III, Robert ... 610-861-1485 402 D
rushr@moravian.edu
RUSH, Rosalee ... 209-667-3131.. 33 F
RUSH, S. Bryan ... 812-464-1862 165 C
rush@usi.edu

RUSH, Star .... 206-726-5181 494 B
srush@cornish.edu
RUSH, Tanya .... 443-885-3527 206 A
tanya.rush@morgan.edu
RUSH WOODS, Dianne . 510-885-2809.. 31 F
dianne.woods@csueastbay.edu
RUSHBROOK, Jill .... 860-253-3068.. 85 C
jrushbrook@asnuntuck.edu
RUSHER, Bryan .... 501-812-2256.. 23 C
brusher@pulaskitech.edu
RUSHFORTH, Brenda .... 909-621-8175.. 57 I
brenda.rushforth@pomona.edu
RUSHIK, Julie .... 585-594-6493 321 C
rushik_julie@roberts.edu
RUSHING, Cheri .... 618-437-5321 149 H
rushing@rlc.edu
RUSHING,
James Kenneth .... 904-264-2172 106 I
krushing@iwsfla.org
RUSHING, Kevin .... 573-629-3240 260 G
kevin.rushing@hlg.edu
RUSHING, Krysta .... 912-538-3157 126 A
krushing@southeasterntech.edu
RUSHING, Linda .... 870-364-6414.. 22 D
rushingl@uamont.edu
RUSHING, Natasha .... 573-629-3048 260 G
natasha.rushing@hlg.edu
RUSHING, Ray .... 254-867-4893 461 G
ray.rushing@tstc.edu
RUSHING, Wanda .... 601-923-1699 255 E
wrushing@rts.edu
RUSHMER, Bernadette ... 570-674-8028 401 M
brushmer@misericordia.edu
RUSHNAWITZ, P .... 248-968-3360 239 K
RUSHTON, Jeffery, A ..... 502-852-8119 190 C
jeff.rushton@louisville.edu
RUSILOSKI, Benjamin ... 215-489-2911 393 F
benjamin.rusiloski@delval.edu
RUSKIN, Susan .... 336-770-1333 352 B
ruskins@uncsa.edu
RUSNAK NOON, Anna .. 570-504-9695 395 I
anoon@tcmc.edu
RUSS, Christina .... 425-640-1683 494 E
christina.russ@edcc.edu
RUSS, Larry .... 201-216-5379 291 G
lruss@stevens.edu
RUSS, Shelly .... 802-728-1303 477 E
sruss@vtc.edu
RUSS-WILSON, Traci, L 704-894-2201 337 B
trruss@davidson.edu
RUSSE, Sarah, R .... 630-844-4620 133 H
srusse@aurora.edu
RUSSEK, Lori .... 361-593-4191 460 B
lori.russek@tamuk.edu
RUSSEL, David .... 573-882-2011 268 B
RUSSELL, Agnes, M ...... 616-222-3000 232 F
arussell@kuyper.edu
RUSSELL, Andrew .... 315-792-7317 330 A
andrew.russell@sunyit.edu
RUSSELL, Andrew .... 774-455-7590 216 G
arussell@umassp.edu
RUSSELL,
Anne Marie, T .... 207-786-8211 198 E
arussell@bates.edu
RUSSELL, Babs .... 770-947-7260 128 F
babs.russell@westgatech.edu
RUSSELL, Barbara .... 716-338-1210 311 F
barbararussell@mail.sunyjcc.edu
RUSSELL, Barry, A .... 925-424-1001.. 36 D
brussell@laspositascollege.edu
RUSSELL, Brent .... 803-778-6689 419 A
russellrd@cctech.edu
RUSSELL, Christina, L ... 757-594-7278 479 H
christina.russell@cnu.edu
RUSSELL, Connie, J ...... 903-510-2203 464 D
crus@tjc.edu
RUSSELL, Craig .... 501-279-5000.. 19 G
crussell@harding.edu
RUSSELL, Cynthia .... 215-637-7700 397 G
crussell@holyfamily.edu
RUSSELL, Daniel .... 860-515-3881.. 84 H
drussell@charteroak.edu
RUSSELL, Danny .... 740-362-3322 365 D
drussell@mtso.edu
RUSSELL, David, W .... 214-648-2695 469 E
david.russell@utsouthwestern.edu
RUSSELL, Denise .... 614-236-6196 358 A
drussell@capital.edu
RUSSELL, Elizabeth .... 207-974-4684 199 L
erussell@emcc.edu
RUSSELL, Elizabeth .... 314-246-8298 269 N
russelmb@webster.edu
RUSSELL, Freda, R .... 414-410-4735 506 F
frrussell@stritch.edu
RUSSELL, Gary, T .... 941-752-5200 108 P
russelg@scf.edu
RUSSELL, James, H .... 903-823-3198 458 D
jameshenry.russell@texarkanacollege.edu
RUSSELL, Jeff, D .... 276-739-2491 490 A
jrussell@vhcc.edu
RUSSELL, Jeffrey .... 608-262-5823 510 C
jrussell@dcs.wisc.edu
RUSSELL, Jennie .... 314-921-9290 269 D
jrussell@ugst.edu
RUSSELL, Jennifer .... 202-685-4094 518 B
jennifer.russell@ndu.edu
RUSSELL, Jill, T .... 717-867-6076 399 J
russell@lvc.edu
RUSSELL, Joanna, S ...... 503-223-5100 387 B
jrussell@sumnercollege.edu
RUSSELL, Joanne .... 718-368-5661 303 A
joanne.russell@kbcc.cuny.edu
RUSSELL, John .... 808-544-1407 129 C
jrussell@hpu.edu
RUSSELL, Joyce .... 610-519-4331 413 K
joyce.russell@villanova.edu
RUSSELL, Judith .... 352-273-2505 110 D
jcrussell@ufl.edu
RUSSELL, Julia, H .... 802-656-4063 476 E
julia.russell@uvm.edu
RUSSELL, Justin .... 912-583-2241 116 G
drussell@bpc.edu
RUSSELL, Katherine .... 207-509-7176 200 I
krussell@unity.edu
RUSSELL, Kathleen, M .. 914-367-8208 323 C
kathleen.russell@archny.org
RUSSELL, Kelly .... 559-278-2182.. 32 A
krussell@csufresno.edu
RUSSELL, Kenneth .... 704-281-1521 348 B
ken.russel@pfeiffer.edu
RUSSELL, Kenya .... 256-551-3136.... 2 D
kenya.russell@drakestate.edu
RUSSELL, Kevin .... 601-968-8746 252 C
krussell@belhaven.edu
RUSSELL, Kimberly .... 718-817-3085 308 G
krussell11@fordham.edu
RUSSELL, Kimberly, A ... 337-550-1201 194 B
krussell@lsue.edu
RUSSELL, Kristie .... 740-245-7191 372 E
krussell@rio.edu
RUSSELL, Leah, L .... 540-375-2211 484 H
russell@roanoke.edu
RUSSELL, Leigh .... 252-493-7354 345 E
lrussell@email.pittcc.edu
RUSSELL, Mark .... 419-772-2011 367 G
m-russell.7@onu.edu
RUSSELL, Mark .... 847-578-8340 150 E
mark.rusell@rosalindfranklin.edu
RUSSELL, Michael .... 415-955-2100.. 24 K
mrussell@alliant.edu
RUSSELL, Michael .... 785-833-4358 179 C
mike.russell@kwu.edu
RUSSELL, Mindy .... 620-223-2700 177 E
mindyr@fortscott.edu
RUSSELL, Nancy .... 816-604-5237 262 F
nancy.russell@mcckc.edu
RUSSELL, Pamela .... 508-531-1295 217 D
RUSSELL, Patrice .... 603-641-7202 282 A
prussell@anselm.edu
RUSSELL, Patrick, J .... 414-425-8300 509 I
prussell@shsst.edu
RUSSELL, Robert .... 605-626-7770 428 H
robert.russell@northern.edu
RUSSELL, Ronda .... 406-994-5541 272 A
rrussell@montana.edu
RUSSELL, Sharon .... 212-650-5052 301 F
srussell@ccny.cuny.edu
RUSSELL, Susan .... 806-874-3571 445 R
susan.russell@clarendoncollege.edu
RUSSELL, Tammy .... 269-467-9945 230 C
trussell@glenoaks.edu
RUSSELL, Terry .... 636-949-4980 261 I
trussell@lindenwood.edu
RUSSELL, Thad .... 559-688-3027.. 39 G
thadr@cos.edu
RUSSELL, Thomas .... 312-369-7940 136 H
trussell@colum.edu
RUSSELL, Thomas .... 580-581-6712 375 A
tomr@cameron.edu
RUSSELL, Todd .... 985-867-2266 195 I
trussell@sjasc.edu
RUSSELL, Tony .... 801-832-2527 474 E
arussell@westminstercollege.edu
RUSSELL, Traci .... 206-934-5661 497 H
traci.russell@seattlecolleges.edu
RUSSELL, William .... 860-632-3050.. 87 D
busoffice@holyapostles.edu
RUSSELL-EDWARDS,
Juanita .... 601-877-6191 251 G
juanita@alcorn.edu
RUSSELL III, Harold ...... 209-468-9192.. 67 C
hrussell@sjcoe.net
RUSSELL-OÆGRADY,
Marijo .... 212-346-1257 319 J
RUSSIAKY, Rachel .... 847-317-7033 153 D
rrussiak@tiu.edu
RUSSIN, Gabrielle .... 914-961-8313 323 H
grussin@svots.edu
RUSSIN, Ted .... 845-905-4427 306 D
ted.russin@culinary.edu
RUSSO, Betty, S .... 812-941-2661 161 A
bsrusso@ius.edu
RUSSO, Cecelia, M .... 718-990-6667 322 F
russoc@stjohns.edu
RUSSO, Frederic, J .... 973-655-3219 287 D
russot@mail.montclair.edu
RUSSO, Greg .... 619-574-6909.. 55 B
grusso@pacificcollege.edu
RUSSO, Kim .... 310-665-6979.. 54 I
krusso@otis.edu
RUSSO, Lisa .... 213-613-2200.. 65 A
lisarusso@sciarc.edu
RUSSO, Maria .... 518-454-5121 305 B
russom@strose.edu
RUSSO, Richard .... 510-642-2700.. 68 G
russo@berkeley.edu
RUSSO, Robert, C .... 203-254-4288.. 87 A
rcrusso@fairfield.edu
RUSSO, Ronald .... 504-762-3066 192 H
rrusso@dcc.edu
RUSSO, Thomas .... 417-873-7413 259 G
trusso@drury.edu
RUSSO, Tim .... 202-685-3918 518 B
russot@ndu.edu
RUSSOM, Vaughn, N ..... 715-394-8327 512 B
vrussom@uwsuper.edu
RUSSOMANNO,
David, J .... 317-274-0802 160 E
drussoma@iupui.edu
RUSSOS, Milton, A .... 904-442-2950 100 F
mrussos@fscj.edu
RUST, Jodi .... 715-852-1395 513 E
jrust5@cvtc.edu
RUST, Mark, M .... 410-857-2503 205 E
mrust@mcdaniel.edu
RUST, Melissa .... 501-686-2532.. 21 H
mrust@uasys.edu
RUSTAD, Dan .... 507-222-7187 241 C
drustad@carleton.edu
RUSTAD, Melinda .... 218-935-0417 251 F
melinda.rustad@wetcc.edu
RUSTICUS, Lisa .... 616-222-3000 232 F
lrusticus@kuyper.edu
RUTAN, Susan .... 814-865-1412 403 F
smr9@psu.edu
RUTBERG, Barbara .... 617-824-8275 214 E
barbara_rutberg@emerson.edu
RUTENBECK, Jeffrey ...... 202-885-2058.. 91 C
jeff@american.edu
RUTH, Alice, A .... 603-646-2445 281 C
alize.a.ruth@dartmouth.edu
RUTH, Anna .... 727-864-7966.. 97 O
ruthar@eckerd.edu
RUTH, David .... 610-861-5065 403 B
druth@northampton.edu
RUTH, Gary .... 304-887-1795 478 H
gruth@bluefield.edu
RUTH, Matthew .... 540-432-4118 480 A
matthew.ruth@emu.edu
RUTH, Rick .... 717-477-1835 407 B
reruth@ship.edu
RUTHENBECK, Becky .... 307-855-2254 516 I
rruthenbeck@cwc.edu
RUTHENBECK, Julie, J .. 325-942-2255 463 C
julie.ruthenbeck@angelo.edu
RUTHER, Aisha .... 312-850-7176 136 C
aruther@ccc.edu
RUTHER, Elliot .... 513-569-1451 359 G
elliot.ruther@cincinnatistate.edu
RUTHERFORD, Greg, F . 803-327-8050 426 J
grutherford@yorktech.edu
RUTHERFORD, Joan, M 419-251-1301 365 C
joan.rutherford@mercycollege.edu
RUTHERFORD, John, D 214-648-0400 469 E
john.rutherford@utsouthwestern.edu
RUTHERFORD,
Karen, W .... 803-705-4671 418 G
rutherk@benedict.edu
RUTHERFORD, Lisa, H .. 413-542-5645 210 F
lrutherford@amherst.edu
RUTHERFORD,
Marcella, M .... 954-262-1963 104 F
rmarcell@nova.edu
RUTHERFORD, Marylyn 973-877-3408 285 K
rutherford@essex.edu
RUTHERFORD, Paul ...... 304-327-4403 503 O
prutherford@bluefieldstate.edu
RUTHERFORD, Sherry ... 731-410-6709 432 J
srutherford@lanecollege.edu
RUTHERMAN, Kathy ...... 270-852-3143 187 F
krutherman@kwc.edu
RUTHKOSKY,
Kathleen, O .... 570-348-6203 401 B
ruthkosky@marywood.edu
RUTKOWSI, Leslie .... 315-470-6655 328 D
larutkow@esf.edu
RUTKOWSKI, Sandra ..... 419-824-3762 364 G
srutkowski@lourdes.edu
RUTLAND, Jason .... 864-231-2000 418 E
jrutland@andersonuniversity.edu
RUTLEDGE, Beth .... 610-341-5890 394 E
brutledg@eastern.edu
RUTLEDGE, Brian .... 601-984-1010 256 D
brutledge@umc.edu
RUTLEDGE, Catherine .... 484-365-8087 400 E
crutledge@lincoln.edu
RUTLEDGE, Jacqueline .. 817-531-6571 463 G
jrutledge@txwes.edu
RUTLEDGE, James .... 662-846-4004 252 H
jrutledge@deltastate.edu
RUTLEDGE, Janet .... 410-455-1781 208 A
jrutledge@umbc.edu
RUTLEDGE, Melissa, B .. 540-378-5120 484 H
rutledge@roanoke.edu
RUTLEDGE, Peter .... 706-542-7140 127 A
borut@uga.edu
RUTLEDGE, Valerie .... 423-425-4249 440 A
valerie-rutledge@utc.edu
RUTT, Charles, D .... 660-543-4370 268 A
rutt@ucmo.edu
RUTTEN, Chris .... 402-844-7051 276 G
christopherr@northeast.edu
RUTTER, Evan .... 909-621-8153.. 38 A
evan.rutter@cmc.edu
RUTTER, Jeff .... 602-386-4191.. 10 G
jeff.rutter@arizonachristian.edu
RUTTER, Jeff .... 931-221-7213 430 B
rutterj@apsu.edu
RUTTER, John, P .... 919-299-4818 349 F
jrutter@umo.edu
RUTTER, Ron .... 503-821-8901 385 H
rrutter@pnca.edu
RUTTER, Sandy .... 423-697-4475 436 F
sandy.rutter@chattanoogastate.edu
RUUD, William, N .... 740-376-4701 365 A
wnr001@marietta.edu
RUXTON, Brooke .... 815-753-1206 147 H
bruxton@niu.edu
RUYLE, Dianna .... 217-854-5772 134 E
dianna.ruyle@blackburn.edu
RUYS, Jasmine .... 661-362-3466.. 39 C
jasmine.ruys@canyons.edu
RUYS, Steve .... 818-364-7886.. 49 C
ruyssc@lamission.edu
RUZICH, Steve .... 708-596-2000 151 H
sruzich@ssc.edu
RUZICKA, Emma .... 417-873-6857 259 G
eruzicka@drury.edu
RUZICKA, Jim .... 402-465-2323 276 E
jruzicka@nebrwesleyan.edu
RYALL, Patrick .... 503-768-7294 383 G
ryall@lclark.edu
RYAN, Andrew .... 718-862-8000 313 L
andrew.ryan@manhattan.edu
RYAN, Andrew, J .... 859-238-5572 184 C
andrew.ryan@centre.edu
RYAN, April, N .... 240-895-2055 206 G
anryan@smcm.edu
RYAN, Barry .... 888-488-4968.. 46 J
RYAN, Bruce .... 607-844-8222 331 D
ryanb@tompkinscortland.edu
RYAN, Caroll .... 562-988-2278.. 25 Q
cryan@auhs.edu
RYAN, Carrie .... 336-278-5003 337 G
cryan2@elon.edu
RYAN, Casey .... 215-596-8570 413 E
c.ryan@usciences.edu
RYAN, Catherine .... 413-572-5218 218 F
cryan@westfield.ma.edu
RYAN, Christine .... 716-827-2467 331 K
ryanc@trocaire.edu
RYAN, Christopher .... 508-830-5003 218 D
cryan@maritime.edu
RYAN, Christy .... 602-682-6856.. 11 A
cryan@azsummitlaw.edu
RYAN, Curtis, W .... 801-832-2148 474 E
cryan@westminstercollege.edu
RYAN, Dennis .... 757-340-2121 479 D
registrarcvab@centura.edu
RYAN, Dennis .... 757-340-2121 479 D
adirectorcvab@centura.edu
RYAN, Diane, N .... 757-822-5185 489 H
dryan@tcc.edu
RYAN, Dorothy .... 217-732-3155 143 G
dryan@lincolncollege.edu
RYAN, Duane .... 575-562-2112 293 O
duane.ryan@enmu.edu

RYAN, Ed ..... 408-554-5182.. 62 F
eryan@scu.edu
RYAN, Erik ..... 617-873-0106 213 B
erik.ryan@cambridgecollege.edu
RYAN, Erin ..... 718-390-4452 322 F
ruane1@stjohns.edu
RYAN, Gail, L ..... 313-577-6595 239 C
gail.ryan@wayne.edu
RYAN, Greg ..... 714-992-7092.. 54 A
gryan@fullcoll.edu
RYAN, Helen, G ..... 502-272-8052 183 H
hryan@bellarmine.edu
RYAN, James ..... 617-262-5000 212 C
james.ryan@the-bac.edu
RYAN, James, E ..... 617-495-3401 215 G
james_ryan@gse.harvard.edu
RYAN, James, G ..... 336-217-5128 350 C
jgryan@ncat.edu
RYAN, James, G ..... 336-285-2805 351 D
jgryan@uncg.edu
RYAN, Jeanne-Marie, C 704-894-2492 337 B
jeryan@davidson.edu
RYAN, Jenny ..... 801-832-2502 474 E
jryan@westminstercollege.edu
RYAN, Jim ..... 815-921-4522 150 A
j.ryan@rockvalleycollege.edu
RYAN, CSC, John ..... 570-208-5899 398 D
jjryan@kings.edu
RYAN, Joseph ..... 209-588-5087.. 75 I
ryanj@yosemite.edu
RYAN, Julie ..... 928-523-9658.. 14 K
julie.ryan@nau.edu
RYAN, Karen ..... 386-822-7515 111 E
kryan@stetson.edu
RYAN, Kathleen ..... 508-541-1515 214 C
kryan@dean.edu
RYAN, Kathleen ..... 617-732-5042 221 E
kathleen.ryan@mcphs.edu
RYAN, Kathleen ..... 614-823-1250 368 O
kryan@otterbein.edu
RYAN, Kelly, A ..... 812-941-2393 161 A
ryanka@ius.edu
RYAN, Kevin ..... 305-428-5700 104 A
kryan@aii.edu
RYAN, Kyle ..... 781-899-5500 223 G
kryan@psjs.edu
RYAN, Larry ..... 505-277-2847 296 H
larry@unm.edu
RYAN, Marianne, P ..... 773-508-2657 144 D
mryan21@luc.edu
RYAN, Mark, R ..... 573-882-0314 268 C
ryanmr@missouri.edu
RYAN, Maura, A ..... 574-631-9488 165 A
mryan11@nd.edu
RYAN, Maureen ..... 601-266-4319 256 E
maureen.ryan@usm.edu
RYAN, Melissa ..... 904-725-0525.. 97 D
mryan@concorde.edu
RYAN, Michael ..... 617-585-1187 222 H
michael.ryan@necmusic.edu
RYAN, Pat ..... 503-842-8222 387 C
patryan@tillamookbaycc.edu
RYAN, Patricia ..... 540-674-3613 488 G
pryan@nr.edu
RYAN, Patrick ..... 973-720-3326 292 I
ryanp@wpunj.edu
RYAN, Patrick ..... 716-270-2869 307 I
ryanp@ecc.edu
RYAN, Paula ..... 641-628-5198 167 D
ryanp@central.edu
RYAN, Peter ..... 662-325-3742 254 E
ryan@cvm.msstate.edu
RYAN, Robert ..... 800-782-2422.. 30 G
robert.ryan@csun.edu
RYAN, Ron ..... 954-262-8856 104 F
ronr@nova.edu
RYAN, Rosaleen ..... 831-646-4035.. 52 G
rryan@mpc.edu
RYAN, Scott ..... 817-272-3181 467 B
sdryan@uta.edu
RYAN, Sean, J ..... 502-272-8376 183 H
sryan@bellarmine.edu
RYAN, Sharon ..... 213-624-1200.. 42 N
sryan@fidm.edu
RYAN, Susan ..... 386-822-7181 111 E
sryan@stetson.edu
RYAN, Thomas, J ..... 856-225-6361 290 B
tomryan@camden.rutgers.edu
RYAN, Tiffiney ..... 618-634-3242 151 G
tiffineyr@shawneecc.edu
RYAN, Tim ..... 845-452-9600 306 D
tim.ryan@culinary.edu
RYAN, Timothy, M ..... 207-725-3247 198 G
tryan@bowdoin.edu
RYAN, Tom ..... 727-864-8305.. 97 O
ryantj@eckerd.edu
RYAN BULONE, Mary ... 419-473-2700 360 J
mryan@daviscollege.edu
RYAN-HOFFMAN,
Maureen ..... 732-987-2218 286 D
mryan-hoffman@georgian.edu
RYAN RODRIGUEZ,
Christina ..... 714-895-8128.. 38 G
cryanrodriguez@gwc.cccd.edu
RYAN VAN ZEE,
Marynel ..... 507-222-4300 241 C
mryanvanzee@carleton.edu
RYANT, Marion ..... 229-430-4609 114 I
marion.ryant@asurams.edu
RYBAK, Chuck ..... 920-465-2336 510 E
rybakc@uwgb.edu
RYBERG, Bill ..... 253-566-5100 499 A
bryberg@tacomacc.edu
RYBERG, Bill ..... 253-566-5336 499 A
bryberg@tacomacc.edu
RYCYNA, Mary ..... 216-397-4921 363 H
mrycyna@jcu.edu
RYCZKOWSKI, Sandy .... 920-498-6829 514 G
sandra.ryczkowski@nwtc.edu
RYDER, Collette, L ..... 212-327-8054 321 E
cryder@rockefeller.edu
RYDER, Ellen ..... 415-422-2558.. 72 A
eryder@usfca.edu
RYDER, Jon ..... 207-221-4701 202 A
jryder2@une.edu
RYDER, Lucas ..... 772-546-5534 101 N
lucasryder@hsbc.edu
RYDER, Ulli ..... 508-678-2811 219 C
ulli.ryder@bristolcc.edu
RYDL, Chareny, L ..... 979-845-3158 459 C
chareny@tamu.edu
RYE, Colleen ..... 906-635-2626 232 J
crye@lssu.edu
RYE, Tara ..... 402-449-2849 274 H
trye@graceu.edu
RYEA, Alan, E ..... 802-656-3245 476 E
alan.ryea@uvm.edu
RYKEN, Amy ..... 253-879-2810 499 C
aryken@pugetsound.edu
RYKEN, Philip, G ..... 630-752-5002 155 F
philip.ryken@wheaton.edu
RYLAARSDAM, Robin .... 630-829-6532 133 I
rrylaarsdam@ben.edu
RYMAN, Denny ..... 631-420-2171 329 D
denny.ryman@farmingdale.edu
RYMAN-MESCAL,
LacyJane ..... 856-222-9311 289 F
lryman@rcbc.edu
RYNER, Jeanna ..... 314-392-2319 263 F
rynerj@mobap.edu
RYNNE, Jeanne ..... 360-867-6115 494 G
rynnej@evergreen.edu
RYON, Diane ..... 704-372-0266 339 A
dryon@kingscollegecharlotte.edu
RYSAVY, Monica ..... 302-225-6373.. 90 G
rysavym@gbc.edu
RYSAVY, Peter ..... 302-225-6371.. 90 G
peter@gbc.edu
RYSER, Leslie ..... 606-539-4606 190 A
RYSTROM, Andrea ..... 651-779-3953 244 D
andrea.rystrom@century.edu
RYU, Jongkil ..... 323-643-0301.. 25 K
president@aeu.edu
RZONCA, Stephen ..... 910-892-3178 338 D
srzonca@heritagebiblecollege.edu
RÍOS, Hector ..... 787-850-9375 528 B
hector.rios5@upr.edu

S

SÁNCHEZ, José ..... 787-764-0000 528 F
jose.sanchez18@upr.edu
SÁNCHEZ-MÉNDEZ,
Juan ..... 787-993-8860 527 G
juan.sanchez12@upr.edu
SA FREIRE, Laura ..... 202-646-1337.. 92 E
SA TELES, Gariela ..... 816-584-6828 265 C
gsateles@park.edu
SAACKE, David ..... 540-458-8400 491 G
dsaacke@wlu.edu
SAADI, Christine ..... 610-796-8213 389 A
christine.saadi@alvernia.edu
SAAED, Jan ..... 801-832-2232 474 E
jsaaed@westminstercollege.edu
SAALFELD, Joan ..... 503-636-8141 384 B
jsaalfeld@marylhurst.edu
SAALFELD, Katy ..... 815-753-8305 147 H
ksaalfeld@niu.edu
SAALFELD, Pam ..... 402-844-7466 276 G
pamela@northeast.edu
SAAM, Julie ..... 765-455-9302 160 B
jsaam@iuk.edu
SAAR, Sarah ..... 712-325-3282 170 K
SAARI, Mirranda ..... 360-992-2671 493 E
msaari@clark.edu
SAARIAHO, Ginger, K ... 617-552-9168 212 E
ginger.saariaho@bc.edu
SAAVEDRA, Adriana ..... 520-494-5287.. 11 P
adriana.saavedra@centralaz.edu
SAAVEDRA, Frank ..... 305-899-4834.. 95 G
fsaavedra@barry.edu
SAAVEDRA, Mauricio ..... 805-756-5406.. 30 K
msaavedr@calpoly.edu
SAAVEDRA, Randy ..... 575-835-5005 294 K
randy.saavedra@nmt.edu
SAAVEDRA, Rebecca ..... 409-772-2909 469 C
rsaavedr@utmb.edu
SABAN, Thomas ..... 708-709-3568 148 I
tsaban@prairiestate.edu
SABATH, Michael ..... 928-317-6475.. 14 K
michael.sabath@nau.edu
SABATINE, Stephanie .... 906-635-6664 232 J
ssabatine@lssu.edu
SABATINO, Patricia ..... 718-678-8817 314 I
psabatino@mercy.edu
SABBAGH, Thomas, M . 401-825-2236 416 B
tsabbagh@ccri.edu
SABBAGHI, Asghar ..... 773-298-3944 151 C
sabbaghi@sxu.edu
SABBATINI, Robert, P ... 434-223-6129 481 D
rsabbatini@hsc.edu
SABEL, Carol ..... 414-277-7300 509 A
SABEL, Elizabeth ..... 419-559-2360 370 J
esabel01@terra.edu
SABEY, Brenda ..... 435-652-7841 473 B
sabey@dixie.edu
SABICK, Michelle ..... 314-977-8283 266 J
sabickmb@slu.edu
SABIN, Christopher, P .. 910-938-6321 342 C
sabinc@coastalcarolina.edu
SABIN, Melody ..... 864-578-8770 423 F
msabin@sherman.edu
SABINE, Neil ..... 765-973-8389 160 A
nsabine@iue.edu
SABINO, Diana ..... 727-341-3352 107 A
sabino.diana@spcollege.edu
SABINO, Lyn ..... 330-363-4227 357 A
lyn.sabino@aultman.com
SABINSON, Allen, C ..... 215-895-1621 394 C
allen.c.sabinson@drexel.edu
SABIT, Farhad ..... 510-659-6146.. 54 F
fsabit@ohlone.edu
SABLAN, Becky ..... 670-237-6700 520 D
becky.sablan@marianas.edu
SABLAN, Fermina, A ..... 671-735-1121 519 H
fermina.sablan@guamcc.edu
SABLAN, Janiece, A ..... 671-735-2957 520 B
janiece@uogendowment.org
SABLAN-ZEBEDY, Ellia .. 610-799-1061 400 A
esablanzebedy@lccc.edu
SABLE, Dennis ..... 619-961-4336.. 67 F
dsable@tjsl.edu
SABLE, Marjorie ..... 573-882-0914 268 C
sablem@missouri.edu
SABLE, Ray ..... 229-333-5875 127 H
rasable@valdosta.edu
SABLO, Kahan ..... 703-993-2884 481 B
ksablo@gmu.edu
SABO, Arlene ..... 845-437-5201 333 A
arsabo@vassar.edu
SABO, Jana ..... 239-489-9051 100 E
jsabo1@fsw.edu
SABOE, Mike ..... 843-820-5090 424 G
mike.saboe@tridenttech.edu
SABOLD, Steven ..... 412-346-2100 408 B
ssabold@pia.edu
SABOLO, Martin ..... 605-626-3007 428 H
martin.sabolo@northern.edu
SABOTA, Fred ..... 727-864-8895.. 97 O
sabotafr@eckerd.edu
SABOU, Michelle, L ..... 864-977-7004 422 I
michelle.sabou@ngu.edu
SABOUNI, Ikhlas ..... 936-261-9800 458 F
isabouni@pvamu.edu
SABRA, Gregory, K ..... 860-444-8322 519 B
gregory.k.sabra@uscg.mil
SACAL-TRENT, Jessica .. 210-486-4111 441 G
jsacal-trent@alamo.edu
SACCENTI, Tom ..... 864-294-2111 421 I
tom.saccenti@furman.edu
SACCO, JR., Albert ..... 806-742-3451 463 D
al.sacco-jr@ttu.edu
SACCO, Jennifer ..... 203-582-8972.. 88 A
jennifer.sacco@quinnipiac.edu
SACCO, John ..... 617-322-3553 216 B
john_sacco@laboure.edu
SACCO, Katie ..... 352-365-3541 103 B
saccok@lssc.edu
SACCOCCIO, Louis, J .... 401-874-4486 417 E
ljsacc@uri.edu
SACHEDINA, Shadia ..... 212-217-3804 308 B
shadia_sachedina@fitnyc.edu
SACHS, Elizabeth ..... 212-772-4569 302 E
esachs@hunter.cuny.edu
SACHS, Steven, G ..... 703-323-3387 488 H
ssachs@nvcc.edu
SACK, Bob ..... 616-222-1421 229 B
bob.sack@cornerstone.edu
SACK, Chuck ..... 484-840-4711 402 G
sackc@neumann.edu
SACKS, Arlene ..... 305-653-6713 371 A
arlene.sacks@myunion.edu
SACRY, Toni ..... 910-272-3375 346 A
tsacry@robeson.edu
SADAN, Avishai ..... 213-740-3124.. 72 B
dentdean@usc.edu
SADAO, Amy ..... 215-573-9973 412 G
asadao@ica.upenn.org
SADD, Tracy ..... 717-361-1260 394 F
saddt@etown.edu
SADDIGH, Farah ..... 310-233-4501.. 49 B
saddigf@lahc.edu
SADDLEMIRE, John ..... 401-232-6046 416 A
jsaddlemire@bryant.edu
SADDLEMIRE,
Melissa, A ..... 570-961-4733 401 B
saddlemire@marywood.edu
SADDLER, Mike ..... 620-431-2820 180 C
msaddler@neosho.edu
SADDLER, Renee ..... 919-546-8681 348 I
rsaddler@shawu.edu
SADDLER, Ryan, C ..... 563-333-5728 173 A
saddlerryanc@sau.edu
SADDORIS-TRAUGHBER,
Janiece, L ..... 217-424-6253 145 J
jtraughber@millikin.edu
SADEGHIPOUR, Keya .... 215-204-5285 411 B
keya.sadeghipour@temple.edu
SADLAK, Keeley, K ..... 517-586-3014 228 G
ksadlak@cleary.edu
SADLEK, Gregory, M ..... 216-687-3660 359 L
g.sadlek@csuohio.edu
SADLEK, Lance, A ..... 563-333-6252 173 A
sadleklancea@sau.edu
SADLER, David ..... 925-969-3300.. 46 L
dsadler@jfku.edu
SADLER, Donny ..... 903-586-2518 451 C
deanofstudents@jacksonville-college.edu
SADLER, Kelley ..... 253-566-5187 499 A
ksadler@tacomacc.edu
SADLER, Martin ..... 404-687-4512 118 B
sadlerm@ctsnet.edu
SADLER, Paul ..... 806-291-1163 470 I
sadlerp@wbu.edu
SADLER, Tommy ..... 731-661-5218 439 D
tsadler@uu.edu
SADLON, Donna ..... 973-655-3963 287 D
sadlond@mail.montclair.edu
SADOWSKI, Jatha ..... 573-882-4859 268 C
sadowskij@missouri.edu
SADOWSKI, Katrina ..... 978-542-6134 218 E
ksadowski@salemstate.edu
SADOWSKI, Sherri ..... 937-327-7808 374 A
sadowskis@wittenberg.edu
SADRO, Cheryl ..... 409-266-2006 469 C
csadro@utmb.edu
SADWIN, Bernadine ..... 401-874-9032 417 E
bsadwin@foundation.uri.edu
SAEED, Najam ..... 651-846-1324 247 G
najam.saeed@saintpaul.edu
SAENZ, Bernard ..... 361-354-2258 445 S
bsaenz@coastalbend.edu
SAENZ, Kelly ..... 281-992-3413 456 B
kelly.saenz@sjcd.edu
SAENZ, Matilda ..... 361-354-2275 445 S
msaenz@coastalbend.edu
SAENZ, Rogelio ..... 210-458-2715 468 B
rogelio.saenz@utsa.edu
SAEVIG, Daniel, J ..... 419-530-4008 372 F
daniel.saevig@utoledo.edu
SAEZ-, Samuel ..... 787-993-8896 527 G
samuel.saez@upr.edu
SAFADY, Randa, S ..... 512-499-4777 467 A
rsafady@utsystem.edu
SAFAEI, Aman ..... 212-410-8008 317 C
asafaei@nycpm.edu
SAFARZADEH, Sasha ..... 714-533-3946.. 35 B
sasha.zadeh@calums.edu
SAFFEL, Rachel ..... 619-688-0800.. 40 H
rsaffel@concorde.edu
SAFFIOTI, Patricia ..... 434-832-6693 487 H
saffiotip@cvcc.vccs.edu
SAFINICK, Nancy ..... 310-506-4316.. 56 D
nancy.safinick@pepperdine.edu
SAFLEY, Ellen ..... 972-883-2916 467 D
safley@utdallas.edu
SAFLEY, Mallory ..... 770-533-7003 122 E
msafley@laniertech.edu

SALTSMAN, Terry .... 931-372-3200 438 F
tsaltsman@tntech.edu
SALTSMAN, Terry .... 931-372-3387 438 F
tsaltsman@tntech.edu
SALTZBERG, Alex .... 510-593-2995.. 63 A
asaltzberg@saybrook.edu
SALVA, William, M .... 914-337-9300 305 F
william.salva@concordia-ny.edu
SALVADOR, Daniel .... 319-656-2447 173 C
SALVAGE, Lynn .... 718-818-6470 323 F
lsalvage@edaff.com
SALVAGGIO, Brian .... 508-531-1276 217 D
SALVANTORIELLO,
Vincent .... 610-398-5300 400 C
vsalvantoriello@lincolntech.edu
SALVATO, Scott .... 516-323-3225 315 J
ssalvato@molloy.edu
SALVESEN, Guy .... 858-646-3114.. 62 C
gsalvesen@sbpdiscovery.org
SALVINI, Tonia .... 785-830-2753 178 A
tsalvini@haskell.edu
SALVO, Robyn .... 732-263-5228 287 C
rsalvo@monmouth.edu
SALVUCCI, Debra .... 508-565-1314 224 H
dsalvucci@stonehill.edu
SALVUCCI, James .... 712-749-2243 167 C
salvuccij@bvu.edu
SALYER, Greg .... 323-663-2167.. 71 B
president@uprs.edu
SALZBRUNN, Kimberly . 630-637-5454 147 E
ksalzbrunn@noctrl.edu
SALZER, Jean .... 262-993-6762 511 A
jeano@uwm.edu
SALZMAN, Christine ..... 908-709-7485 292 C
csalzman@follett.com
SALZMANN, Nick .... 847-628-2492 142 B
nsalzmann@judsonu.edu
SAM, David .... 847-214-7374 138 B
dsam@elgin.edu
SAM, Mary .... 218-855-8159 244 C
msam@clcmn.edu
SAM, Penselyn .... 691-320-2480 519 G
petse@comfsm.fm
SAMAHA, Ahmed .... 803-641-3411 425 A
ahmeds@usca.edu
SAMALOT, Yamil .... 787-786-3030 526 F
ysamalot@ucb.edu.pr
SAMALOT-RIVERA, OP,
Yamil, A .... 787-786-4508 522 I
ysamalot@cedoc.edu
SAMAN, Sarmad .... 508-678-2811 219 C
sarmad.saman@bristolcc.edu
SAMANGO, Melissa ...... 610-526-6196 396 H
msamango@harcum.edu
SAMANIEGO, Sue .... 719-384-6821.. 81 G
sue.samaniego@ojc.edu
SAMANT, Ajay .... 309-438-2251 140 L
asamant@ilstu.edu
SAMANTA, Shivaji .... 540-857-6335 490 B
ssamanta@virginiawestern.edu
SAMARKOS, Christy ...... 619-594-5211.. 34 B
csamarko@mail.sdsu.edu
SAMBDMAN, Cory, W ... 563-333-6336 173 A
1312mgr@follett.com
SAMBLE, Brian, W .... 717-358-3860 395 G
brian.samble@fandm.edu
SAMBRANO, Richard ..... 281-443-8900 445 B
richard.sambrano@brightwood.edu
SAMEEI, Morteza .... 713-718-5251 450 D
morteza.sameei@hccs.edu
SAMEK, Linda .... 503-554-2871 383 C
lsamek@georgefox.edu
SAMENFINK,
William, H .... 978-232-2402 214 G
bsamenfi@endicott.edu
SAMHAT, Nayef, H .... 864-597-4010 426 I
president@wofford.edu
SAMM, Mary .... 812-535-5252 163 I
msamm@smwc.edu
SAMMAKIA, Bahgat .... 518-956-7111 330 A
bahgat@sunypoly.edu
SAMMAKIA, Bahgat .... 607-777-4818 325 A
bahgat@binghamton.edu
SAMMANN, James .... 845-434-5750 330 F
jsammann@sullivan.suny.edu
SAMMARCO, Erica, C .... 716-888-2100 300 G
sammarce@canisius.edu
SAMMARTINO,
Kathleen .... 617-349-8515 216 D
ksammart@lesley.edu
SAMMIS, Robert, L .... 626-914-8550.. 37 G
rsammis@citruscollege.edu
SAMMONS, Gregory, S . 607-587-3911 328 F
sammongs@alfredstate.edu
SAMMONS, Kenneth, R . 509-313-6951 495 A
ksammons@plant.gonzaga.edu
SAMMONS, Steve .... 503-589-8145 383 A
ssammons@corban.edu

SAMO, Tia .... 641-782-1336 173 I
samo@swcciowa.edu
SAMOLEWSKI,
Patrick, C .... 989-964-4221 236 F
pcs@svsu.edu
SAMORA, Tracy .... 719-549-2858.. 78 P
tracy.samora@csupueblo.edu
SAMP, Mike .... 307-766-5179 517 B
bowhntr@uwyo.edu
SAMPAIO, Anna, C .... 408-554-2289.. 62 F
asampaio@scu.edu
SAMPERTON, Amy .... 910-678-8236 343 B
samperta@faytechcc.edu
SAMPITE, Chris .... 318-869-5286 191 C
csampite@centenary.edu
SAMPLE, Bradford .... 740-474-8896 367 E
bsample@ohiochristian.edu
SAMPLE, Mark .... 704-991-0247 346 I
jsample7479@stanly.edu
SAMPLE, Michael .... 812-855-0850 159 G
mmsample@indiana.edu
SAMPLE, Mike .... 317-681-1776 159 H
mmsample@iu.edu
SAMPLE, Valara .... 423-425-4304 440 A
valara-sample@utc.edu
SAMPLES, Donald, A ..... 423-439-7457 431 H
samplesd@etsu.edu
SAMPLES, Robert, D ..... 314-516-5665 268 E
bob@umsl.edu
SAMPLEY, Curtis .... 334-387-3877.... 4 B
curtissampley@amridgeuniversity.edu
SAMPSON, Betty, J .... 509-865-8600 495 D
sampson_b@heritage.edu
SAMPSON, David, G ...... 518-381-1370 323 L
sampsodg@sunysccc.edu
SAMPSON, Diana .... 206-546-4512 498 E
dsampson@shoreline.edu
SAMPSON, Jon .... 503-517-1056 388 A
jsampson@warnerpacific.edu
SAMPSON, Lauren, K .... 240-895-3220 206 G
lksampson@smcm.edu
SAMPSON, Mark .... 412-731-6000 409 A
msampson@rpts.edu
SAMPSON, Marsha .... 406-657-2085 272 B
msampson@msubillings.edu
SAMPSON, Marshall ...... 253-833-9111 495 C
msampson@greenriver.edu
SAMPSON, Michael .... 718-990-1305 322 F
sampsonm@stjohns.edu
SAMPSON, Robert .... 401-841-1323 518 E
SAMPSON, Ronnie .... 910-272-3345 346 A
rsampson@robeson.edu
SAMPSON, Sharon .... 412-731-6000 409 A
ssampson@rpts.edu
SAMPSON, Sonya .... 207-755-5246 199 K
ssampson@cmcc.edu
SAMRA, Rajinder .... 925-424-1027.. 36 D
rsamra@laspositascollege.edu
SAMS, Susan .... 714-997-6829.. 36 G
sams@chapman.edu
SAMS, Timothy .... 470-639-0379 123 E
tim.sams@morehouse.edu
SAMS, Wesley, S .... 843-953-5375 419 D
wsams@citadel.edu
SAMSON, Adam .... 573-876-7197 267 G
asamson@stephens.edu
SAMSON, Keri .... 563-589-3775 173 J
ksamson@dbq.edu
SAMSON, Kim, M .... 218-477-2133 246 B
samson@mnstate.edu
SAMSTAD, Karen .... 952-888-4777 249 F
ksamstad@nwhealth.edu
SAMSTEIN, Ivan .... 773-702-1234 153 F
isamstein@uchicago.edu
SAMTER, Wendy .... 401-232-6433 416 A
wsamter@bryant.edu
SAMUEL, Bryan .... 423-425-5670 440 A
bryan-samuel@utc.edu
SAMUEL, Jacinta .... 692-625-6724 520 C
jsamuel@cmi.edu
SAMUEL, Jeanne .... 504-671-6219 192 H
jsamue@dcc.edu
SAMUEL, June .... 334-727-8011.... 7 F
samuelj@mytu.tuskegee.edu
SAMUEL, Linda, M .... 262-243-5700 507 C
linda.samuel@cuw.edu
SAMUEL, Prema .... 914-395-2305 323 K
psamuel@sarahlawrence.edu
SAMUEL LOFTUS,
Barbara .... 570-674-6195 401 M
bloftus@misericordia.edu
SAMUELS, A. Dexter ...... 615-327-5732 434 A
dsamuels@mmc.edu
SAMUELS, Albert .... 225-771-3092 195 K
albert_samuels@subr.edu
SAMUELS, Darlette, C ... 731-426-7595 432 J
dsamuels@lanecollege.edu

SAMUELS, Elena .... 212-220-8061 301 C
esamuels@bmcc.cuny.edu
SAMUELS, Kellei .... 229-430-3688 114 I
kellei.samuels@asurams.edu
SAMUELS, Melissa .... 718-405-3212 304 H
melissa.samuels@mountsaintvincent.
edu
SAMUELS, Nara .... 360-752-8441 492 H
nsamuels@btc.edu
SAMUELS, Robert .... 401-874-2288 417 E
rsamuels@uri.edu
SAMUELS, Rodney .... 914-654-5952 305 A
rsamuels@cnr.edu
SAMUELS, Sandra .... 973-353-5231 290 D
szsamuls@newark.rutgers.edu
SAMUELS, Tim .... 972-273-3364 448 C
samuels@dcccd.edu
SAMUELSON, Pamela .... 570-372-4272 410 H
samuelson@susqu.edu
SAMUELSON,
Wayne, M .... 801-581-6437 472 P
wayne.samuelson@hsc.utah.edu
SAMUL, Margaret .... 203-582-8431.. 88 A
margaret.samul@quinnipiac.edu
SAMULSKI, Eva .... 734-973-3724 238 G
esmaulski@wccnet.edu
SAMWAYS, Theresa .... 315-268-2327 304 B
tsamways@clarkson.edu
SAN FRANCISCO,
Michael .... 806-742-1828 463 D
michael.sanfrancisco@ttu.edu
SAN MIGUEL,
Anitza, M .... 321-682-4091 113 F
asanmiguel12@valenciacollege.edu
SAN MIGUEL,
Claudia, E .... 956-326-2529 459 B
csanmiguel@tamiu.edu
SAN NICOLAS, Heidi, E 671-735-2481 520 B
heidi.sannicolas@guamcedders.org
SAN NICOLAS, Jennifer 760-384-6221.. 47 B
jsannico@cerrocoso.edu
SANABRIA, Deanna .... 760-245-4271.. 73 E
deanna.sanabria@vvc.edu
SANAI, Fardin .... 518-956-8062 324 G
fsanai@albany.edu
SANAPAW, Geraldine .... 800-567-2344 506 I
gsanapaw@menominee.edu
SANBDIMANIE, Audry .... 770-394-8300 115 E
asanbdimanie@aii.edu
SANBERG, Paul .... 813-974-5570 111 A
psanberg@health.usf.edu
SANBORN, Karen .... 734-432-5843 233 C
ksanborn@madonna.edu
SANBORN, Merlene .... 207-859-1102 200 H
sanbornm@thomas.edu
SANCHEZ, Alicia .... 316-978-3034 182 F
alicia.sanchez@wichita.edu
SANCHEZ, Angel .... 559-278-3906.. 32 A
aansanchez@csufresno.edu
SANCHEZ, Arlene .... 787-758-2525 528 D
arlene.sanchez@upr.edu
SANCHEZ, Bonifacio ...... 692-625-3394 520 C
bsanchez@cmi.edu
SANCHEZ, Brianne .... 206-934-4700 497 H
brianne.sanchez@seattlecolleges.edu
SANCHEZ, Carmella ...... 505-747-2118 295 H
carmella@nnmc.edu
SANCHEZ, Cheryl .... 719-336-1516.. 80 N
cheryl.sanchez@lamarcc.edu
SANCHEZ, Cheryl, L ...... 830-591-7202 457 C
clsanchez547@swtjc.edu
SANCHEZ, Christine ...... 714-712-7900.. 46 G
SANCHEZ, Christine ...... 310-665-6831.. 54 I
csanchez@otis.edu
SANCHEZ, Connie .... 323-259-2691.. 54 E
consuelosanchez@oxy.edu
SANCHEZ, Cristina .... 210-458-7203 468 B
cristina.sanchez@utsa.edu
SANCHEZ, Dan .... 952-829-1318 240 H
dan.sanchez@bethfel.org
SANCHEZ, David .... 940-397-3000 453 C
david.sanchez@mwsu.edu
SANCHEZ, David, F .... 718-522-9073 298 E
dsanchez@asa.edu
SANCHEZ, Diane .... 210-829-5866 465 E
castaned@uiwtx.edu
SANCHEZ, Elda, E .... 361-593-3805 460 B
elda.sanchez@tamuk.edu
SANCHEZ, Frank, A .... 401-456-8100 417 A
fsanchez@ric.edu
SANCHEZ, Gilbert .... 622-229-9929.. 47 E
SANCHEZ, Gregory .... 619-388-3354.. 60 C
gsanchez@sdccd.edu
SANCHEZ, Ismael .... 212-694-1000 299 L
isanchez@boricuacollege.edu
SANCHEZ, Jaymi .... 787-743-3484 525 M
jsanchez@sanjuanbautista.edu

SANCHEZ, Jennifer .... 413-755-4480 221 B
jsanchez@stcc.edu
SANCHEZ, Jennifer .... 210-690-9000 449 K
jsanchez@hallmarkuniversity.edu
SANCHEZ, John .... 210-434-6711 454 D
jdsanchez@lake.ollusa.edu
SANCHEZ, John .... 671-735-2444 520 B
soedean@triton.uog.edu
SANCHEZ, Joseph .... 817-735-2522 466 D
joseph.sanchez@unthsc.edu
SANCHEZ, Juan .... 956-665-3883 468 A
juan.sanchez1@utrgv.edu
SANCHEZ, Leopoldo, A . 314-863-2772 258 I
sanchezl@csl.edu
SANCHEZ, Librada .... 973-720-2586 292 I
sanchezl@wpunj.edu
SANCHEZ, Lisa, M .... 626-396-2210.. 26 L
lisa.sanchez@artcenter.edu
SANCHEZ, Luis .... 805-553-4052.. 72 G
lsanchez@vcccd.edu
SANCHEZ, Luis .... 520-494-5266.. 11 P
luis.sanchez@centralaz.edu
SANCHEZ, Luis, P .... 805-378-1407.. 73 A
lsanchez@vcccd.edu
SANCHEZ, Marci .... 707-256-7235.. 53 D
msanchez@napavalley.edu
SANCHEZ, Margaret ...... 415-239-3000.. 37 H
msanchez@ccsf.edu
SANCHEZ, Maria .... 504-278-6479 193 B
msanchez@nunez.edu
SANCHEZ, Mark .... 805-546-3116.. 41 C
mark_sanchez1@cuesta.edu
SANCHEZ, Matthew .... 239-433-8047 100 E
msanchez30@fsw.edu
SANCHEZ, Matthew .... 518-891-2915 319 A
msanchez@nccc.edu
SANCHEZ, Matthew .... 214-860-8507 448 B
matthewsanchez@dcccd.edu
SANCHEZ, Melba, G ...... 787-743-7979 526 A
msanchez@suagm.edu
SANCHEZ, Monica .... 575-769-4913 293 M
monica.sanchez@clovis.edu
SANCHEZ, Noel .... 661-726-1911.. 68 E
noel.sanchez@uav.edu
SANCHEZ, Omar .... 305-821-3333 100 A
omarsnc@fnu.edu
SANCHEZ, Ophelia .... 305-442-9223 104 B
osanchez@mrc.edu
SANCHEZ, Patricia .... 210-486-4209 441 G
psanchez70@alamo.edu
SANCHEZ, Priscilla .... 979-230-3215 444 E
priscilla.sanchez@brazosport.edu
SANCHEZ, Rebecca .... 949-824-5337.. 69 A
rebecca.sanchez@uci.edu
SANCHEZ, Richard, M ... 903-875-7306 453 J
richard.sanchez@navarrocollege.edu
SANCHEZ, Richard, P ..... 956-665-3668 468 A
richard.sanchez@utrgv.edu
SANCHEZ, Roxanne .... 210-434-6711 454 D
rlsanchez@lake.ollusa.edu
SANCHEZ, Sandra .... 310-233-4041.. 49 B
sanches@lahc.edu
SANCHEZ, Steven .... 314-977-2611 266 J
ssanche6@slu.edu
SANCHEZ, Suane .... 787-758-2525 528 D
suane.sanchez@upr.edu
SANCHEZ, Victor .... 773-838-7974 136 A
vsanchez124@ccc.edu
SANCHEZ, Vivian .... 760-591-3012.. 71 I
vsanchez@usa.edu
SANCHEZ CINTRON,
Naury, Y .... 787-720-4476 527 A
presidente@mizpa.edu
SANCHEZ-FERNANDEZ,
Hector, R .... 787-751-1912 524 E
hrsanchez@juris.inter.edu
SANCHEZ PINTOR,
Linda .... 787-725-8120 522 M
lsanchez0053@eap.edu
SANCILIO, Leonard .... 585-245-5706 327 B
sancilio@geneseo.edu
SANCRANT, Lisa .... 419-251-1487 365 C
lisa.sancrant@mercycollege.edu
SAND, Sabra .... 360-992-2288 493 E
ssand@clark.edu
SAND, Scott .... 916-388-2920.. 35 F
ssand@carrington.edu
SANDBERG, Curtis .... 859-985-3208 183 I
curtis_sandberg@berea.edu
SANDBERG, Robin .... 210-486-4134 441 G
rsandberg@alamo.edu
SANDBOTHE, Lindsay ... 312-461-0600 133 C
lsandbothe@aaart.edu
SANDBOTHE, Robin ...... 913-667-5708 176 F
rsandbothe@cbts.edu
SANDBULTE, Deb .... 712-707-7224 172 G
debfs@nwciowa.edu

SANTIAGO, Deejay .... 949-451-5732.. 64 I
dsantiago@ivc.edu
SANTIAGO, Delma .... 787-284-1912 524 C
dosantia@ponce.inter.edu
SANTIAGO, Edny .... 787-864-2222 524 A
edny.santiago@guayama.inter.edu
SANTIAGO, Eutimia .... 787-751-0160 522 B
esantiago@cmpr.pr.gov
SANTIAGO, George .... 516-918-3600 299 M
SANTIAGO, Isaac .... 787-766-1912 523 F
isantiag@inter.edu
SANTIAGO, Jaime .... 787-250-1912 524 B
jaimesantiago@metro.inter.edu
SANTIAGO, Jamie .... 617-588-1358 211 G
jsantiago@bfit.edu
SANTIAGO, Joemille ..... 215-572-2909 389 D
santiagoj@arcadia.edu
SANTIAGO, Jorge .... 787-764-0000 528 F
jorge.santiago21@upr.edu
SANTIAGO, Jose, G ...... 787-279-1912 523 J
jsantiago@bayamon.inter.edu
SANTIAGO, Judith .... 212-343-1234 315 D
jsantiago@mcny.edu
SANTIAGO, Juliane .... 919-658-7769 349 F
jsantiago@umo.edu
SANTIAGO, Kenneth ...... 773-481-8047 136 B
ksantiago6@ccc.edu
SANTIAGO, Maria .... 787-738-2161 528 A
maria.santiago25@upr.edu
SANTIAGO, Martha .... 863-297-1093 105 F
msantiago@polk.edu
SANTIAGO, Marya, Z .... 787-844-2318 528 E
marya.santiago@upr.edu
SANTIAGO, Miguel .... 787-764-0000 528 F
miguel.santiatgo16@upr.edu
SANTIAGO, Rafael .... 787-780-0070 521 B
rsantiago@caribbean.edu
SANTIAGO, Ricardo .... 787-738-2161 528 A
ricardo.santiago6@upr.edu
SANTIAGO, Victor .... 787-857-3600 523 I
vsantiago@br.inter.edu
SANTIAGO, Viviana .... 787-720-1022 521 A
administracion@atlanticu.edu
SANTIAGO, Wanda .... 718-289-5352 301 D
wanda.santiago@bcc.cuny.edu
SANTIAGO, Yaritza .... 787-878-6000 522 Q
SANTIAGO, Yinaira .... 787-284-1912 524 C
yinsant@ponce.inter.edu
SANTIAGO-GUZMAN,
Cynthia .... 407-582-3253 113 F
csantiago-guzman@valenciacollege.edu
SANTIAGO-TORO,
Clarissa .... 787-723-4481 521 H
csantiago@ceaprc.edu
SANTILLAN, Courtney ... 208-562-3000 132 A
courtneysantillan@cwidaho.cc
SANTILLI, Nicholas, R ... 216-397-4734 363 H
santilli@jcu.edu
SANTIN, Claudia .... 708-209-3228 136 I
claudia.santin@cuchicago.edu
SANTINI, Rumaliz .... 787-738-2161 528 A
rumaliz.santini@upr.edu
SANTIROCCO,
Matthew, S .... 212-998-2197 318 D
matthew.santirocco@nyu.edu
SANTIVASCI, Joseph ..... 610-436-3085 407 D
jsantivasci@wcupa.edu
SANTOMAURO,
Kristine, M .... 302-225-6233.. 90 G
santomk@gbc.edu
SANTORA, Anthony .... 908-737-6000 286 F
afs@kean.edu
SANTORE, JR., Chuck ... 724-439-4900 399 H
csantore@laurel.edu
SANTORO, C. James ..... 402-449-2910 274 H
jsantoro@graceu.edu
SANTORO, Dana, S .... 302-356-6862.. 91 B
dana.s.eggleston@wilmu.edu
SANTOS, Adolfo .... 678-407-5601 119 F
asantos1@ggc.edu
SANTOS, Annette, T ...... 671-735-2553 520 B
atsantos@triton.uog.edu
SANTOS, Carmen, K ...... 671-735-5548 519 H
carmen.kweksantos@guamcc.edu
SANTOS, Carol .... 508-999-8388 217 A
csantos1@umassd.edu
SANTOS, Catherine .... 315-312-4903 327 D
catherine.santos@oswego.edu
SANTOS, David, M .... 860-701-6787 519 B
david.m.santos@uscg.edu
SANTOS, Eileen .... 202-806-6100.. 92 C
SANTOS, Helena .... 617-243-2127 216 C
hsantos@lasell.edu
SANTOS, Joycette .... 787-841-4780 528 E
joycette.santos@upr.edu
SANTOS, Mae .... 323-343-3555.. 32 D
msantos@cslanet.calstatela.edu
SANTOS, Maggie .... 719-389-1988.. 77 J
maggie.santos@coloradocollege.edu
SANTOS, Maria del, C .. 787-743-7979 526 A
ut_masantos@suagm.edu
SANTOS, Maricarmen .... 787-743-7979 526 A
m_santos@suagm.edu
SANTOS, Matt .... 610-683-4183 406 D
santos@kutztown.edu
SANTOS, Nelson .... 787-850-9348 528 B
nelson.santos@upr.edu
SANTOS, Nelson .... 787-850-9324 528 B
nelson.santos@upr.edu
SANTOS, Nilda .... 787-738-2161 528 A
nilda.santos@upr.edu
SANTOS, Paul .... 704-330-6689 342 A
paul.santos@cpcc.edu
SANTOS, Ramon .... 305-223-4561 106 L
santos@sjvcs.edu
SANTOS,
Roberto (Bobby), J ..... 691-320-2480 519 G
rjsantas@comfsm.fm
SANTOS, Samuel .... 415-239-3762.. 37 H
ssantos@ccsf.edu
SANTOS, Samuel .... 713-221-5042 465 C
santoss@uhd.edu
SANTOS, Susan .... 859-442-4165 185 I
susan.santos@kctcs.edu
SANTOS, Victor .... 302-857-6001.. 90 B
vsantos@desu.edu
SANTOS-COY, Katie .... 714-463-7552.. 51 A
ksantoscoy@ketchum.edu
SANTOS-GEORGE,
Arlene .... 847-543-2402 136 E
asgeorge@clcillinois.edu
SANTOS-PEREZ,
Kennia, I .... 787-480-2463 521 J
kisantos@sanjuanciudadpatria.com
SANTOSTEFANO,
Donald .... 717-867-6341 399 J
dsantost@lvc.edu
SANTUCCI, George .... 412-392-3498 408 F
gsantucci@pointpark.edu
SANTUCCI, Wayne .... 212-517-0544 314 D
wsantucci@mmm.edu
SANUDO, Manuel .... 718-997-3760 303 E
manuel.sanudo@qc.cuny.edu
SANYAL, Rajib, N .... 516-877-4661 297 I
rsanyal@adelphi.edu
SANYAL, Sabyasachi ...... 972-721-5156 464 E
ssanyal@udallas.edu
SANZARI, Kelly .... 724-589-2014 411 D
ksanzari@thiel.edu
SAPARILAS, John, W .... 919-866-5450 347 D
jwsaparilas@waketech.edu
SAPERSTEIN, Shari .... 954-262-7201 104 F
ssaperst@nova.edu
SAPHIRE, Diane, G .... 210-999-7479 464 B
dsaphire@trinity.edu
SAPIENZA, Christine ..... 904-256-7626 102 B
csapien@ju.edu
SAPIENZA, Matthew ...... 646-664-3014 301 A
matthew.sapienza@cuny.edu
SAPOZNICK, Aaron .... 718-645-0536 315 G
SAPP, Aimee .... 573-592-4368 270 D
aimee.sapp@williamwoods.edu
SAPP, Buddy .... 912-871-1634 123 J
bsapp@ogeecheetech.edu
SAPP, Fred .... 910-672-1204 350 B
fsapp@uncfsu.edu
SAPP, John, B .... 713-313-7831 461 E
sapp_jb@tsu.edu
SAPP, Judy .... 606-877-1421 186 G
judy.sapp@kctcs.edu
SAPP, Robert .... 928-541-7777.. 54 B
rsapp@ncu.edu
SAPPENFIELD,
George, O .... 336-386-3280 347 A
sappeng@surry.edu
SAPPINGTON, Eric .... 660-831-4168 264 A
sappingtone@moval.edu
SARAC, Isa .... 703-591-7042 490 D
isarac@viu.edu
SARACHICK, Daniel, T .. 508-831-5000 226 E
dtsarachick@wpi.edu
SARAFIAN, Christopher . 302-793-1101.. 90 H
SARAJEDINI, Ata .... 561-297-3288 109 B
ata@fau.edu
SARAN, Rupa .... 714-432-5952.. 38 H
rsaran@occ.cccd.edu
SARAN, Rupam .... 718-270-4937 303 C
rsaran@mec.cuny.edu
SARAO, Felix, G .... 562-908-3413.. 58 D
fsarao@riohondo.edu
SARAT, Austin, D .... 413-542-2308 210 F
adsarat@amherst.edu
SARATA, Andrew .... 708-974-5357 146 C
sarataa@morainevalley.edu
SARAVANAPAVAN,
Naomi .... 607-729-1581 306 F
nsaravanapavan@davisny.edu
SARBER, John .... 765-455-9505 160 B
jrsarber@iuk.edu
SARBER, Sarah .... 765-455-9316 160 B
shawkins@iuk.edu
SARETSKY, Kelly .... 978-556-3866 220 F
ksaretsky@necc.mass.edu
SARFF, Michelle .... 614-251-4758 367 F
sarffm@ohiodominican.edu
SARGEANT, Glenn .... 501-975-8536.. 21 A
gsargeant@philander.edu
SARGENT, Brent .... 802-879-2321 477 E
bsargent@vtc.edu
SARGENT, Daniel .... 315-866-0300 310 A
sargentda@herkimer.edu
SARGENT, Famika .... 225-771-2492 195 K
famika_sargent@subr.edu
SARGENT, Frank .... 617-730-7254 223 B
frank.sargent@newbury.edu
SARGENT, Gary .... 254-295-4242 466 A
gsargent@umhb.edu
SARGENT, Jenell .... 334-727-8350.... 7 F
jsargent@mytu.tuskegee.edu
SARGENT, Joe, E .... 423-585-6836 438 D
joe.sargent@ws.edu
SARGENT, John .... 903-923-2273 448 J
jsargent@etbu.edu
SARGENT, Madeline .... 215-568-9215 415 D
msargent@phmc.org
SARGENT, Mark, L .... 805-565-6007.. 74 I
msargent@westmont.edu
SARGENT, Peter, E .... 314-968-7006 269 N
sargenpe@webster.edu
SARGENT, Ryan .... 208-282-4735 132 B
sargryan@isu.edu
SARGENT, Sheri .... 507-389-1112 246 A
sheri.sargent@mnsu.edu
SARGENT-MARTIN,
Shelia .... 304-327-4176 503 O
ssmartin@bluefieldstate.edu
SARHAN, Mostafa .... 912-358-3388 125 C
sarhanm@savannahstate.edu
SARIAN, Richard .... 216-421-7432 359 J
rsarian@cia.edu
SARIDAKIS, Dianne, I ... 215-885-2360 401 A
dsaridakis@manor.edu
SARIN, Sanjiv .... 336-285-2371 350 C
sarin@ncat.edu
SARIN, Sanjiv .... 336-285-2366 350 C
sarin@ncat.edu
SARISKY JONES, Susan 717-867-6321 399 J
sjones@lvc.edu
SARKAR, Ratna .... 410-516-5925 204 F
rsarkar3@jhu.edu
SARKIS, Hashim .... 617-253-4401 221 C
SARKISIAN, Jodi .... 215-898-7221 412 G
jodi@pobox.upenn.edu
SARLES, Harry .... 913-684-3097 518 I
harry.sarles@us.army.mil
SARMA, Sanjay .... 617-715-4532 221 C
SARMIENTO, Reine .... 718-960-8429 302 C
reine.sarmiento@lehman.cuny.edu
SARMIENTO, Steve .... 510-780-4500.. 48 D
ssarmiento@lifewest.edu
SARNA, Jason .... 847-543-2383 136 E
jsarna@clcillinois.edu
SARNA, Linda .... 310-825-9621.. 69 B
lsarna@sonnet.ucla.edu
SARNOVSKY, Joseph ..... 407-708-2430 107 G
sarnovsj@seminolestate.edu
SARR, Akua .... 617-552-9144 212 E
akua.sarr@bc.edu
SARRA, James .... 217-206-6674 154 A
jsarr2@uis.edu
SARRA, Michael .... 617-824-8540 214 E
michael_sarra@emerson.edu
SARRAFIAN, Armen .... 312-553-5922 135 J
asarrafian@ccc.edu
SARRATORI, Peter .... 315-781-3647 310 C
sarratori@hws.edu
SARRETT, David, C .... 804-828-7235 487 E
dcsarrett@vcu.edu
SARRUBBO, Joe, M .... 407-582-2586 113 F
jsarrubbo@valenciacollege.edu
SARTAIN, Karen .... 423-636-7376 439 C
ksartain@tusculum.edu
SARTARELLI, Jose, V ..... 910-962-3030 352 A
sartarellij@uncw.edu
SARTE, Bruce .... 610-606-4635 392 A
bsarte@cedarcrest.edu
SARTEN, Mici .... 405-703-8232 376 C
msartin@macu.edu
SARTINI, Chad .... 540-857-7731 490 B
csartini@virginiawestern.edu
SARTOR, Curtis .... 847-628-1017 142 B
csartor@judsonu.edu
SARTOR, Dan .... 423-266-4574 435 M
dsartor@richmont.edu
SARTORI, Lillian .... 212-229-5300 316 E
sartoril@newschool.edu
SARVER, Shawna .... 530-541-4660.. 47 I
sarver@ltcc.edu
SARVER, Tammy .... 630-829-6247 133 I
tsarver@ben.edu
SARVEY, Sharon .... 252-399-6401 335 I
sisarvey@barton.edu
SARVIS, Randall, F .... 937-481-2344 373 I
randy_sarvis@wilmington.edu
SARWARK, Robert .... 770-394-8300 115 E
SARWI, Cindy .... 336-342-4261 346 B
sarwic2369@rockinghamcc.edu
SASAKI, Charles .... 808-235-7371 130 I
sasakich@hawaii.edu
SASASKI, Hiroshi .... 626-571-8811.. 72 C
hiroshis@uwest.edu
SASS, Michael .... 314-367-8700 266 D
michael.sass@stlcop.edu
SASS, Terricita, E .... 203-392-9999.. 85 A
sass@southernct.edu
SASSAMAN, Margo, J .... 717-871-7656 407 A
margo.sassaman@millersville.edu
SASSER, Jackson, N ...... 352-395-5164 107 E
j.sasser@sfcollege.edu
SASSER, Jennifer .... 503-675-3964 384 B
jsasser@marylhurst.edu
SASSER, Mackey .... 334-556-2416.... 2 B
msasser@wallace.edu
SASSER, Rachelle .... 310-900-1600.. 40 C
rsasser@elcamino.edu
SASSMAN, Jen, L .... 319-352-8262 174 C
jennifer.sassman@wartburg.edu
SASSO, Gary, M .... 610-758-3221 400 B
gms208@lehigh.edu
SASSO, Mary .... 702-651-5820 278 N
mary.sasso@csn.edu
SASSSER, Craig-Ellis ..... 662-720-7411 255 B
cesasser@nemcc.edu
SASTRY, S. Shankar ...... 510-642-5771.. 68 G
sastry@coe.berkeley.edu
SATA, Leigh .... 707-524-1704.. 62 H
lsata@santarosa.edu
SATCHER, Mikel .... 617-964-1100 210 G
SATELE, Arleen .... 714-628-4717.. 58 B
satele_arleen@sccollege.edu
SATHER, Greg .... 218-726-6137 250 F
gsather@d.umn.edu
SATHER, Steven, M .... 609-258-6479 288 F
sather@princeton.edu
SATHIANATHAN,
Dhushy .... 562-985-4128.. 32 C
dhushy.sathianathan@csulb.edu
SATKOWIAK, Ann, E ..... 865-539-7153 437 F
asatkowiak@pstcc.edu
SATKOWSKI, John .... 313-845-9636 231 B
jssatkowski@hfcc.edu
SATO, Deirdre .... 212-217-5380 308 B
deidre_sato@fitnyc.edu
SATO, Heidi .... 714-816-0366.. 67 J
heidi.sato@trident.edu
SATO, Kay .... 516-299-2584 313 D
kay.sato@liu.edu
SATO, Tami, A .... 714-449-7447.. 51 A
tsato@ketchum.edu
SATO, Toshiko .... 949-480-4364.. 64 D
tsato@soka.edu
SATRIANA, Dan .... 970-351-2399.. 83 F
dan.satriana@unco.edu
SATTAR, Mo .... 413-565-1000 211 C
msattar@baypath.edu
SATTERFIELD,
Allison, D .... 336-322-2102 345 D
allison.satterfield@piedmontcc.edu
SATTERFIELD, Billy .... 281-283-2480 465 B
satterfield@uhcl.edu
SATTERFIELD, Derick ..... 336-342-4261 346 B
satterfieldd@rockinghamcc.edu
SATTERFIELD, Jay .... 731-989-6058 432 C
jsatterfield@fhu.edu
SATTERFIELD, Lacey, L . 770-720-5620 124 H
lls@reinhardt.edu
SATTERFIELD, Lisa .... 865-251-1800 436 B
lsatterfield@southcollegetn.edu
SATTERFIELD, Tanya ..... 662-915-7692 256 C
tnsatter@olemiss.edu
SATTERLEE, Kevin .... 208-426-1233 131 C
ksatterl@boisestate.edu
SATTERLEE, Richard ...... 718-862-7352 313 L
richard.satterlee@manhattan.edu
SATTERLUND,
Alysson, M .... 909-537-5185.. 33 D
asatterlund@csusb.edu
SATTERLY, Eric .... 502-272-8098 183 H
esatterly@bellarmine.edu

SATTERLY, Tom .... 970-491-0006.. 78 N
steve.hultin@colostate.edu
SATTERWHITE, Dawn ..... 919-761-2209 349 C
dsatterwhite@sebts.edu
SATTERWHITE, Robin .... 806-716-2200 456 F
rsatterwhite@southplainscollege.edu
SATTLER, Brian .... 409-880-8396 462 C
brian.sattler@lamar.edu
SATTLER, Joan .... 309-677-3181 134 G
jls@fsmail.bradley.edu
SATZ, Michael .... 208-364-4041 132 I
msatz@uidaho.edu
SAUCEDA, James .... 509-793-2222 492 I
jamess@bigbend.edu
SAUCEDO, Joseph .... 773-508-3948 144 D
jsaucedo4@luc.edu
SAUCIER, Jason .... 207-741-5544 200 C
jsaucier@smccme.edu
SAUCIER, Jason .... 207-780-5512 201 H
jason.saucier@maine.edu
SAUDER, Ryan .... 717-358-4271 395 G
ryan.sauder@fandm.edu
SAUDER, Vinita .... 402-486-2500 277 C
vinita.sauder@ucollege.edu
SAUDERS, Charlette, R .. 574-372-5100 158 B
saudercr@grace.edu
SAUER, Carrie .... 405-208-5873 377 D
csauer@okcu.edu
SAUER, Dietrich .... 928-226-4204.. 12 B
diestrich.sauer@coconino.edu
SAUER, Greg .... 802-485-2170 475 I
gsauer@norwich.edu
SAUER, James, L .... 610-341-5957 394 E
jsauer@eastern.edu
SAUER, Jenni .... 215-489-6378 393 F
jenni.sauer@delval.edu
SAUER, Marty, R .... 630-637-5801 147 E
mrsauer@noctrl.edu
SAUER, Melanie .... 626-529-8064.. 55 C
msauer@pacificoaks.edu
SAUER, Meredith .... 920-693-1282 513 H
meredith.sauer@gotoltc.edu
SAUER, Mike .... 702-895-1073 279 D
sauer@unlv.edu
SAUERBREI, Aaron .... 319-277-2490 169 H
aaron.sauerbrei@hawkeyecollege.edu
SAUERMAN, Gretchen ... 321-674-7237.. 99 K
gsauerman@fit.edu
SAUERS, Darlene .... 724-838-4210 410 E
sauers@setonhill.edu
SAUL, Amy .... 610-861-1508 402 D
saula@moravian.edu
SAUL, J. Beau .... 607-844-8222 331 D
saulj@tompkinscortland.edu
SAUL, Sheryl .... 651-846-1384 247 G
sheryl.saul@saintpaul.edu
SAULE, Mara, R .... 802-656-2020 476 E
mara.saule@uvm.edu
SAULNIER, Timothy .... 434-544-8230 482 F
saulnier@lynchburg.edu
SAULS, Jina, M .... 276-244-1232 477 M
jsauls@asl.edu
SAULSBERRY, Jean .... 901-435-1727 433 A
jean_saulsberry@loc.edu
SAULSBERRY, Keith .... 334-556-2470.... 2 B
ksaulsberry@wallace.edu
SAUM, Rob .... 386-506-3484.. 97 I
saumr@daytonastate.edu
SAUNDERS, Aleister ...... 215-895-6203 394 C
aleister.j.saunders@drexel.edu
SAUNDERS, Amber .... 318-371-3035 193 A
ambersaunders@nwltc.edu
SAUNDERS, Bret .... 605-342-0317 427 C
bsaunders@johnwitherspooncollege.org
SAUNDERS, Brian .... 310-544-6487.. 59 E
brian.saunders@usw.salvationarmy.org
SAUNDERS, C. Tom .... 912-279-5757 118 A
tsaunders@ccga.edu
SAUNDERS, Clark .... 860-768-4504.. 89 C
clsaunder@hartford.edu
SAUNDERS, Gary .... 336-506-4152 340 L
gary.saunders@alamancecc.edu
SAUNDERS, Greer .... 804-819-4906 487 F
gsaunders@vccs.edu
SAUNDERS, Joseph .... 304-766-3353 505 A
saundejs@wvstateu.edu
SAUNDERS, Kara, C ...... 716-645-5725 325 B
kcs23@buffalo.edu
SAUNDERS, Kathleen .... 716-827-2445 331 K
saundersk@trocaire.edu
SAUNDERS, Keith .... 319-335-0553 166 G
keith-saunders@uiowa.edu
SAUNDERS, Kevin .... 515-271-1984 168 J
kevin.saunders@drake.edu
SAUNDERS, Kevin .... 831-582-3397.. 33 A
kesaunders@csumb.edu
SAUNDERS, Mark .... 405-878-5164 379 G
msaunders@stgregorys.edu
SAUNDERS, Martha, D .. 850-474-2200 111 D
msaunders@uwf.edu
SAUNDERS, Melinda, D 304-896-7364 503 D
melinda.saunders@southernwv.edu
SAUNDERS, Richard ...... 435-865-8392 473 A
rsaunders@suu.edu
SAUNDERS, Robert .... 334-983-6556.... 7 E
rsaunders@troy.edu
SAUNDERS, Scott, D ..... 716-673-3171 325 C
scott.saunders@fredonia.edu
SAUNDERS, Sharon .... 434-947-8114 484 B
ssaunders@randolphcollege.edu
SAUNDERS, Sharon, E .. 281-649-3206 450 C
ssaunders@hbu.edu
SAUNDERS, Tanya, R ... 607-274-3063 311 D
tsaunders@ithaca.edu
SAUNDERS-CONSROE,
Samantha .... 443-412-2139 204 C
ssaundersconsroe@harford.edu
SAURBEK, Rhonda, R .... 517-750-1200 237 D
rsaurbek@arbor.edu
SAURE, Debra, C .... 402-280-1277 274 D
debrasaure@creighton.edu
SAURENNANN, Denise .. 215-248-7000 392 D
saurennannd@chc.edu
SAUSER, Jordan .... 515-964-0601 169 C
sauserj@faith.edu
SAUTER, David, M .... 513-529-8781 365 I
sauterdm@miamioh.edu
SAUTER, Maranah .... 706-880-8201 122 D
msauter@lagrange.edu
SAUTER, Ramona .... 408-554-4397.. 62 F
rsauter@scu.edu
SAUVE, Stephanie, L ..... 585-340-9588 304 F
ssauve@crcds.edu
SAUVIGNON, Carine ..... 781-821-2222 220 B
SAVAGE, Ann .... 870-248-4000.. 18 J
annd@blackrivertech.edu
SAVAGE, Beth .... 619-961-4330.. 67 F
bsavage@tjsl.edu
SAVAGE, Deana .... 432-685-4515 453 B
docsavage@midland.edu
SAVAGE, Donna .... 254-968-9246 459 A
dsavage@tarleton.edu
SAVAGE, Jeffrey .... 435-283-7154 474 A
jeff.savage@snow.edu
SAVAGE, Mandara .... 618-453-4033 152 B
msavage@engr.siu.edu
SAVAGE, Mike .... 510-567-6174.. 66 I
msavage@sum.edu
SAVAGE, Monique, J .... 517-265-5161 226 F
msavage@adrian.edu
SAVAGE, Nesha .... 619-388-3400.. 60 C
SAVAGE, Pam .... 314-744-5331 263 F
savagep@mobap.edu
SAVAGE, Ron .... 617-747-2025 212 B
rsavage@berklee.edu
SAVAGE, Scott .... 419-289-5037 356 L
ssavage2@ashland.edu
SAVAGE, Suzanne .... 757-233-8736 491 F
ssavage@vwu.edu
SAVASTA, Mark .... 508-849-3456 210 H
msavasta@annamaria.edu
SAVERANCE, R. Kyle ..... 843-383-8017 420 B
ksaverance@coker.edu
SAVIANESO, Michael ..... 201-684-7402 289 C
msaviane@ramapo.edu
SAVICE, Candice .... 703-891-1787 485 I
admissions@standardcollege.edu
SAVICKY, Kim .... 402-399-2417 274 A
ksavicky@csm.edu
SAVIDGE, Lawrence .... 843-574-6051 424 G
lawrence.savidge@tridenttech.edu
SAVILLE, Vicki .... 704-330-6224 342 A
vicki.saville@cpcc.edu
SAVINO, Jeffrey .... 814-472-3006 409 G
jsavino@francis.edu
SAVINO, Stacey .... 360-538-4082 495 B
ssavino@ghc.edu
SAVITT-KING, Robin ...... 413-782-1243 225 F
robin.savitt-king@wne.edu
SAVOCA, Marianna .... 631-632-6810 325 F
marianna.savoca@stonybrook.edu
SAVOIE, E. Joseph .... 337-482-6203 197 F
president@louisiana.edu
SAVOIE, Leslie, L .... 321-674-7362.. 99 K
lsavoie@fit.edu
SAVOIE, Michael, P ...... 229-249-4894 127 H
mpsavoie@valdosta.edu
SAVOIT, Taina, J .... 337-475-5065 197 B
tsavoit@mcneese.edu
SAVORY, Paul .... 402-826-8221 274 E
paul.savory@doane.edu
SAVRON, Doris .... 602-557-2433.. 17 C
doris.savron@phoenix.edu
SAVU, Vasemaca .... 692-625-3394 520 C
vsavu@cmi.edu
SAWATZKY, Rachel, R .. 540-432-4133 480 A
rachel.sawatzky@emu.edu
SAWAY, Sabine .... 206-239-4500 493 D
ssaway@cityu.edu
SAWICKI, Gretchen .... 412-369-3610 392 G
gsawicki@ccac.edu
SAWICKI, Jerzy .... 216-687-9364 359 L
j.sawicki@csuohio.edu
SAWREY, Barbara .... 858-822-4358.. 69 E
avcdue@ucsd.edu
SAWTELLE, III,
James (Jimmy), R ...... 318-487-5443 192 F
jsawtelle@cltcc.edu
SAWYER, Caroline .... 704-463-3026 348 B
caroline.sawyer@pfeiffer.edu
SAWYER, Dana .... 816-802-3532 261 C
dsawyer@kcai.edu
SAWYER, Dana, L .... 302-857-1124.. 90 F
dsawyer1@dtcc.edu
SAWYER, Darrell, R .... 605-394-2667 429 A
darrell.sawyer@sdsmt.edu
SAWYER, Gretchen .... 775-673-7648 279 C
gsawyer@tmcc.edu
SAWYER, James .... 586-445-7241 233 B
sawyerj@macomb.edu
SAWYER, Jenny, L .... 502-852-4957 190 C
jsawyer@louisville.edu
SAWYER, John .... 208-882-1566 132 D
jsawyer@nsa.edu
SAWYER, John, E .... 302-831-2021.. 90 I
sawyerj@udel.edu
SAWYER, Jonathan, C ... 202-319-5619.. 91 D
sawyerj@cua.edu
SAWYER, Julie .... 918-444-2210 376 G
sawjerjk@nsuok.edu
SAWYER, Katherine .... 847-214-7143 138 B
ksawyer@elgin.edu
SAWYER,
Malcolm James .... 671-734-1812 520 A
mjsawyer@piu.edu
SAWYER, Michael .... 307-268-2492 516 H
msawyer@caspercollege.edu
SAWYER, Shirley .... 954-500-2987.. 95 E
SAWYER, Terrence .... 410-617-2290 205 A
tsawyer@loyola.edu
SAWYER, Wm Gregory .. 805-437-8546.. 31 C
greg.sawyer@csuci.edu
SAWYERS, Cheryl .... 325-670-1091 450 A
cheryl.r.sawyers@hsutx.edu
SAWYERS, Dorret .... 305-348-2436 109 D
dorret.sawyers@fiu.edu
SAX, Christina .... 410-888-9048 205 D
csax@muih.edu
SAX, Joanna .... 619-239-0391.. 35 C
jsax@cwsl.edu
SAX, Richard .... 740-245-7214 372 E
rsax@rio.edu
SAXBY, William, R .... 303-963-3124.. 77 I
wsaxby@ccu.edu
SAXENA, Peter .... 585-594-6800 319 B
SAXENA, Pradeep .... 585-594-6430 321 C
saxenap@roberts.edu
SAXENIAN, AnnaLee ..... 510-642-9980.. 68 G
anno@ischool.berkeley.edu
SAXON, Tina, M .... 714-850-4800.. 67 B
saxon@taftu.edu
SAXTON, Susan .... 760-591-3012.. 71 I
ssaxton@usa.edu
SAY, Elizabeth, A .... 818-677-3301.. 33 B
elizabeth.say@csun.edu
SAYDSHOEV, Sally .... 765-973-8584 160 A
ssaydsho@iue.edu
SAYE, Shaydean .... 406-657-1051 272 I
shaydean.saye@rocky.edu
SAYED, Ellen, N .... 414-955-4852 508 D
esayed@mcw.edu
SAYEGH, John, J .... 716-376-7580 311 F
johnsayegh@mail.sunyjcc.edu
SAYEGH, Sharlene .... 562-985-5428.. 32 C
sharlene.sayegh@csulb.edu
SAYLER, David, A .... 513-529-7286 365 I
saylerda@miamioh.edu
SAYLER, Michael .... 734-487-1414 229 K
msayler@emich.edu
SAYLES, Keith .... 270-831-9789 186 A
keith.sayles@kctcs.edu
SAYLES, Thomas .... 213-740-5371.. 72 B
sayles@usc.edu
SAYLOR, Danette .... 229-903-3604 114 I
danette.saylor@asurams.edu
SAYLOR, Laura .... 513-244-3263 366 A
laura.saylor@msj.edu
SAYLOR, Peggy .... 843-349-5269 421 L
peggy.saylor@hgtc.edu
SAYLORS, Tony .... 870-248-4000.. 18 J
tony.saylors@blackrivertech.edu
SAYRE, Jeff .... 304-214-8809 503 E
jsayre@wvncc.edu
SAYRE, Matt .... 541-552-6273 386 H
sayrem@sou.edu
SAYRE, Richard .... 309-457-2190 146 A
rsayre@monmouthcollege.edu
SAYRE, William .... 505-424-2364 294 C
bsayre@iaia.edu
SAYRS, Elizabeth .... 740-593-1935 368 G
sayrs@ohio.edu
SAÑOSA, Joseph .... 657-278-2938.. 32 B
jsanosa@fullerton.edu
SBALBI, Tony .... 413-552-2391 219 G
tsbalbi@hcc.edu
SBRISCIA, Amanda .... 413-565-1150 211 C
asbriscia@baypath.edu
SBRISCIA, Amanda .... 413-565-1000 211 C
asbriscia@baypath.edu
SCACCIA, Jeff .... 479-979-1310.. 23 J
jscaccia@ozarks.edu
SCADUTO, Dana, E .... 717-245-1013 394 A
scadutod@dickinson.edu
SCAFFIDI CLARKE,
Nancy .... 845-569-3254 316 B
nancy.scaffidi@msmc.edu
SCAGLIONE, Agnes .... 201-692-2596 286 B
agnes@fdu.edu
SCAGLIONE, Kathy, L .... 515-271-1460 168 G
kathleen.scaglione@dmu.edu
SCALA, Kerry .... 603-862-1355 282 F
kerry.scala@unh.edu
SCALA, Natalie .... 440-375-7530 364 C
nscala@lec.edu
SCALBERG, Daniel .... 503-255-0332 384 E
dscalberg@multnomah.edu
SCALES, Keyana .... 504-520-7849 198 D
kscales@xula.edu
SCALES, Lea Ann .... 978-630-9230 220 D
lscales2@mwcc.mass.edu
SCALES, Michael, D ...... 215-204-3121 411 B
michael.scales@temple.edu
SCALES, Michael, G ...... 845-675-4777 319 C
president@nyack.edu
SCALES, Suzanne .... 303-300-8740.. 77 F
suzanne.scales@collegeamerica.edu
SCALESE, Mark .... 203-254-4000.. 87 A
mscalese@fairfield.edu
SCALISE, Julia .... 805-482-2755.. 58 M
julia@stjohnsem.edu
SCALISE-SMITH, Dale .... 859-572-5347 188 E
scalisemd1@nku.edu
SCALISE-SMITH, Dale .... 610-499-4106 414 F
dscalisesmith@widener.edu
SCALZO-MCNEIL, Anne . 508-588-9100 220 B
SCAMMELL, Richard, E . 518-276-6281 321 A
scammr@rpi.edu
SCANDALIS, Thomas ..... 509-452-5100 496 H
tscandalis@pnwu.edu
SCANDONE, Charles ...... 215-641-6533 402 A
cscandon@mc3.edu
SCANDRETT, Clyde .... 831-656-2517 518 D
cscandrett@nps.edu
SCANDRETT, Nic .... 847-543-2477 136 E
nscandrett@clcillinois.edu
SCANGA, Diane .... 636-481-3420 261 B
dscanga@jeffco.edu
SCANLAN, Lina .... 684-699-9155 519 F
l.galeai-scanlan@amsamoa.edu
SCANLAN, Peter .... 866-492-5336 251 E
peter.scanlan@mail.waldenu.edu
SCANLAN, Therese, A ... 773-252-5311 149 I
therese.scanlan@resu.edu
SCANLON, Joan .... 203-773-6678.. 84 G
jscanlon@albertus.edu
SCANLON, Liz .... 401-739-5000 416 D
lscanlon@neit.edu
SCANLON, Philip .... 310-665-6895.. 54 I
pscanlon@otis.edu
SCANLON, Tom .... 617-732-2775 221 E
tom.scanlon@mcphs.edu
SCANLON, Tom .... 617-558-1788 223 A
SCANNELL, Janet .... 507-222-4077 241 C
jscannell@carleton.edu
SCANTLING,
Edgar (Ed), L .... 308-865-8669 277 F
scantlinge@unk.edu
SCAPERLANDA,
Michael .... 405-878-5100 379 G
mscaperlanda@stgregorys.edu
SCARANO, John, B .... 216-397-4717 363 H
jscarano@jcu.edu
SCARANO, Martin .... 603-862-2116 282 F
marty.scarano@unh.edu
SCARBORO, Donna .... 202-994-6360.. 92 A
scarboro@gwu.edu
SCARBORO, Kim .... 850-973-1613 104 D
scarborok@nfcc.edu
SCARBORO, Lynne, B ... 310-338-5236.. 50 J
lscarbor@lmu.edu
SCARBOROUGH, Edesa . 813-253-3333 113 E

SCARBOROUGH, John .. 702-651-7489 278 N
john.scarborough@csn.edu
SCARBOROUGH, Neil .... 317-274-7602 160 E
neilscar@iupui.edu
SCARBOROUGH,
Tara, H .... 513-556-0648 371 E
tara.scarborough@uc.edu
SCARBRO, Sara, P .... 304-696-3170 504 C
SCARCELLE, Ed .... 212-229-5598 316 E
scarcele@newschool.edu
SCARDINO, Janell .... 402-375-7553 276 D
jascard1@wsc.edu
SCARFF, Colleen .... 269-387-4281 239 E
colleen.scarff@wmich.edu
SCARINGE, John .... 562-902-3330.. 65 D
johnscaringe@scuhs.edu
SCARLESKI, Jordan .... 901-321-4036 431 A
jscarles@cbu.edu
SCARLETT, Barbara .... 607-777-4438 325 A
scarlett@binghamton.edu
SCARPELLI, Geoff .... 817-735-5030 466 D
geoffrey.scarpelli@unthsc.edu
SCARPINATO, Karen ...... 561-297-3461 109 B
kscarpinato@fau.edu
SCARPINO, John .... 561-868-3004 105 A
scarpinj@palmbeachstate.edu
SCATES, LouAnn, P .... 704-406-4263 337 H
lscates@gardner-webb.edu
SCAVONE, Victoria, R .... 248-689-8282 238 F
vscavone@walshcollege.edu
SCAVUZZO, Connie, M . 312-949-7079 140 A
cscavuzzo@ico.edu
SCEERY, Amy, L .... 203-576-4506.. 88 F
asceery@bridgeport.edu
SCEGGEL, Tim .... 706-419-1517 118 E
tim.sceggel@covenant.edu
SCEPANSKY, Patricia, S 610-359-7355 393 E
pscepansky@dccc.edu
SCHAAD, Dean .... 419-755-4855 366 E
dschaad@ncstatecollege.edu
SCHAAF, Bill .... 603-623-0313 281 G
billschaaf@nhia.edu
SCHAAF, Laura .... 706-385-1122 124 F
laura.schaaf@point.edu
SCHAAKE, Vicki .... 518-587-2100 329 C
vicki.schaake@esc.edu
SCHAAL, Barbara, A ...... 314-935-6820 269 L
schaal@wustl.edu
SCHAAL, Dave .... 641-784-5106 169 D
dschaal@graceland.edu
SCHAAL, Mary .... 928-344-7772.. 11 B
mary.schaal@azwestern.edu
SCHAAL, Michael, L ...... 810-762-9733 232 C
mschaal@kettering.edu
SCHAB, Kristin .... 717-815-1285 415 G
kasummer@ycp.edu
SCHABERG, David .... 310-825-4856.. 69 B
dschaberg@college.ucla.edu
SCHABERT, Daniel .... 215-646-7300 396 E
schabert.d@gmercyu.edu
SCHACHT, Linda .... 615-966-6155 433 D
linda.schacht@lipscomb.edu
SCHACHTER, Shmuel ..... 410-484-7200 206 C
finaid@nirc.edu
SCHACKMUTH, Kurt .... 815-836-5810 143 E
schackku@lewisu.edu
SCHACTLER, Linda .... 509-963-2111 492 L
schactler@cwu.edu
SCHADE, Carrie .... 773-298-3123 151 C
schade@sxu.edu
SCHADE, Isaac .... 417-626-1234 264 J
schade.isaac@occ.edu
SCHADEMAN, Emily .... 215-248-7083 392 D
schademane@chc.edu
SCHADING, Douglas ..... 212-938-5880 328 E
dschading@sunyopt.edu
SCHADLER, Linda .... 518-265-2244 321 A
schadl@rpi.edu
SCHAECHTER,
Alexander .... 718-854-8791 313 J
mh@thejnet.com
SCHAEFER, Duane .... 812-357-6611 164 A
SCHAEFER, Joseph .... 516-299-2463 313 C
joseph.schaefer@liu.edu
SCHAEFER, K. C .... 540-458-8216 491 G
schaeferk@wlu.edu
SCHAEFER, Karen, D ..... 575-646-2731 295 B
kschaefe@nmsu.edu
SCHAEFER, Karie .... 816-584-7401 265 C
karie.schaefer@park.edu
SCHAEFER, Karla .... 641-585-8159 174 B
schaeferk@waldorf.edu
SCHAEFER, Kelly .... 847-467-0301 148 C
kelly.schaefer@northwestern.edu
SCHAEFER, Lisa .... 970-521-6659.. 81 F
lisa.schaefer@njc.edu
SCHAEFER, Lynne .... 410-455-2939 208 A
lschaefer@umbc.edu
SCHAEFER, Mark .... 202-885-3304.. 91 C
schaef@american.edu
SCHAEFER, Maryann .... 312-629-6118 151 F
mschaefer@saic.edu
SCHAEFER, Rhonda .... 505-566-3087 296 A
schaeferr@sanjuancollege.edu
SCHAEFER, Sharon, P ... 813-253-6250 113 E
sschaefer@ut.edu
SCHAEFER, Susan .... 219-980-6983 160 C
sujschae@iun.edu
SCHAEFER, Thomas, G .. 412-536-1198 398 E
thomas.schaefer@laroche.edu
SCHAEFER, Verdell .... 909-558-4509.. 48 H
vschaefer@llu.edu
SCHAEFFER, Amy .... 817-461-8741 442 L
aschaeffer@abu.edu
SCHAEFFER, Angela ...... 860-297-2139.. 88 E
angela.schaeffer@trincoll.edu
SCHAEFFER, Lisa, L ...... 910-521-6175 351 E
lisa.schaeffer@uncp.edu
SCHAEFFER, Scot .... 563-387-1287 171 I
schasc01@luther.edu
SCHAEFFLER, Jan .... 203-332-5220.. 85 F
jschaeffler@hcc.commnet.edu
SCHAFER, Amy .... 724-589-2212 411 D
aschafer@thiel.edu
SCHAFER, Amy .... 724-589-2182 411 D
aschafer@thiel.edu
SCHAFER, Christine .... 651-793-1618 245 E
chris.schafer@metrostate.edu
SCHAFER, Clark .... 316-942-4291 180 D
schaferc@newmanu.edu
SCHAFER, Jodi .... 319-895-4289 167 G
jschafer@cornellcollege.edu
SCHAFER, Michael, D ... 419-772-2190 367 G
m-schafer@onu.edu
SCHAFER, Robin .... 914-633-2548 311 B
rschafer@iona.edu
SCHAFER, Stephen .... 914-395-2314 323 K
sschafer@sarahlawrence.edu
SCHAFER, William .... 304-293-5811 505 B
wschafer@mail.wvu.edu
SCHAFF, Monte .... 701-255-3285 355 I
mschaff@uttc.edu
SCHAFFELD, Linda .... 513-569-1629 359 G
linda.schaffeld@cincinnatistate.edu
SCHAFFER, Amy .... 785-628-4175 177 D
alschaffer@fhsu.edu
SCHAFFER, Doug .... 269-927-8120 232 G
dschaffer@lakemichigancollege.edu
SCHAFFER, Jeff .... 732-987-2600 286 D
jschaffer@georgian.edu
SCHAFFER, Joe .... 307-778-1102 516 N
jschaffer@lccc.wy.edu
SCHAFFER, Kerry .... 941-359-7601 106 H
kshaffe@ringling.edu
SCHAFFER, Mindy, M ... 410-822-5400 203 C
mschaffer@chesapeake.edu
SCHAFFER, Sandy .... 931-393-1536 437 C
sschaffer@mscc.edu
SCHAFFER, William .... 217-641-4314 141 F
bschaffer@jwcc.edu
SCHAFFNER, Barbara, H 614-823-1735 368 O
bschaffner@otterbein.edu
SCHAFFNER, Bradley ..... 507-222-4267 241 C
bschaffner@carleton.edu
SCHAFRICK, James, A ... 203-773-8507.. 84 G
jschafrick@albertus.edu
SCHAIBLE, John .... 609-292-2108 292 B
jschaible@tesu.edu
SCHAICH, Monte .... 918-587-6789 380 I
SCHAITKIN, David .... 814-234-7755 410 G
dschaitkin@southhills.edu
SCHAKNOWSKI,
Jennifer .... 706-290-2167 116 D
jschaknowski@berry.edu
SCHALK, Heather .... 302-736-2306.. 90 J
heather.schalk@wesley.edu
SCHALK, Lawrence, E .... 269-471-3484 227 B
schalk@andrews.edu
SCHALL, Ellen .... 212-998-7438 318 D
ellen.schall@nyu.edu
SCHALL, Lawrence, M ... 404-364-8320 124 A
lschall@oglethorpe.edu
SCHALLER, Molly .... 314-977-2495 266 J
SCHALLER, Rhonda .... 718-636-5926 320 D
rshal20@pratt.edu
SCHALLOCK, Heather .... 715-365-4518 514 E
hschallock@nicoletcollege.edu
SCHAMANN, Matthew .... 716-926-8925 310 B
mschamann@hilbert.edu
SCHANCK, Sarah .... 478-757-5224 128 E
sschanck@wesleyancollege.edu
SCHANDEL,
Kimberly, A .... 508-767-7312 210 I
kschande@assumption.edu
SCHANTZ, Janet, D .... 317-738-8009 157 L
jschantz@franklincollege.edu
SCHANZ, Jeff .... 518-276-6205 321 A
schanj@rpi.edu
SCHAPER, Nikki .... 760-757-2121.. 52 F
nschaper@miracosta.edu
SCHAPER, Sue .... 208-459-5837 131 H
sschaper@collegeofidaho.edu
SCHAPERKOTTER,
Nancy .... 616-234-5536 238 D
nancy.schaperkotter@vai.org
SCHAPIRO, Chaim .... 973-455-9031 289 B
chaimschap@aol.com
SCHAPIRO, Mendel .... 323-937-3763.. 75 F
SCHAPIRO, Morton, O .. 847-491-7456 148 C
nu-president@northwestern.edu
SCHAPP, Rebecca, M .... 408-554-4528.. 62 F
rschapp@scu.edu
SCHAPPE, Mascheal ...... 314-529-9670 262 B
mschappe@maryville.edu
SCHAPPERT, David, G ... 570-961-4764 401 B
dschappert@marywood.edu
SCHARDT, Wendy, L ..... 308-865-8047 277 F
schardtwl@unk.edu
SCHARER, Gregory .... 937-775-2620 374 B
greg.scharer@wright.edu
SCHARER, Miriam .... 503-399-8486 382 C
miriam.scharer@chemeketa.edu
SCHARF, Michael, P ...... 216-368-3283 358 C
michael.scharf@case.edu
SCHARF, Sara, A .... 515-574-1005 170 C
scharf@iowacentral.edu
SCHARLE, Joyce .... 215-646-7300 396 E
scharle.j@gmercyu.edu
SCHARLEMANN,
Linette, M .... 507-354-8221 243 C
scharllm@mlc-wels.edu
SCHARLOTT, Brooke ...... 440-684-6129 373 B
brooke.scharlott@ursuline.edu
SCHARMAN, Janet, S .... 801-422-2387 471 E
jan_scharman@byu.edu
SCHARMER, Judy .... 575-624-8040 295 A
scharmer@nmmi.edu
SCHARN, Theresa .... 605-718-2402 429 E
theresa.scharn@wdt.edu
SCHARRE, Janice .... 215-780-1420 410 D
SCHARTMAN, Laura, A .. 248-370-2387 235 J
schartma@oakland.edu
SCHATTMAN, Lisa .... 858-566-1200.. 41 G
lschattman@disd.edu
SCHATZ, Julianne .... 336-272-7102 338 B
julies@greensboro.edu
SCHATZBERG,
Jeffrey, W .... 520-621-2238.. 16 J
jschatzb@email.arizona.edu
SCHATZEL, Kim .... 410-704-2356 209 C
presidentsoffice@towson.edu
SCHAUB, Linda .... 517-750-1200 237 D
lindas@arbor.edu
SCHAUB, Mark .... 616-331-3898 230 G
schaubm@gvsu.edu
SCHAUB, Mike .... 202-687-3493.. 92 B
jms46@georgetown.edu
SCHAUB, Rebekah .... 231-843-5568 239 D
rschaub@westshore.edu
SCHAUBHUT, Diana .... 504-398-2100 196 E
dschaubhut@uhcno.edu
SCHAUER, Anne, P .... 513-529-3735 365 I
schauerap@miamioh.edu
SCHAUER, Ariane .... 310-377-5501.. 51 B
aschauer@marymountcalifornia.edu
SCHAUER, James .... 608-890-1569 510 C
wslhdirector@slh.wisc.edu
SCHAUFELBERGER,
John .... 206-685-4440 499 D
jesbcon@uw.edu
SCHAUMANN, Neils ...... 619-239-0391.. 35 C
nschaumann@cwsl.edu
SCHAUMLOFFEL, John .. 978-665-4187 217 E
jschauml@fitchburgstate.edu
SCHAURER, Susan .... 513-529-5040 365 I
susan.schaurer@miamioh.edu
SCHAUS, Jim .... 740-593-0982 368 G
schaus@ohio.edu
SCHEARS, Ben .... 785-890-3641 180 G
ben.schears@nwktc.edu
SCHECHTER, Aaron, M .. 718-377-0777 320 E
SCHECHTER, Mendel ..... 718-377-0777 320 E
SCHECHTER, Richard ..... 203-591-5042.. 87 H
rschechter@post.edu
SCHECHTER, Steven ...... 718-951-5391 301 E
sschechter@brooklyn.cuny.edu
SCHECK, Stephen .... 503-838-8271 388 B
schecks@wou.edu
SCHECKEL, Martha .... 608-796-3664 512 R
mmscheckel@viterbo.edu
SCHECTER, David .... 661-654-6324.. 31 B
dschecter@csub.edu
SCHEDIN, Karen .... 603-897-8516 281 I
kschedin@rivier.edu
SCHEELE, Lisa .... 414-955-8788 508 D
lscheele@mcw.edu
SCHEER, RuthAnn .... 319-895-4324 167 G
rscheer@cornellcollege.edu
SCHEERER, Teresa .... 215-785-0111 404 P
SCHEESSELE, Marc .... 314-977-4132 266 J
mscheess@slu.edu
SCHEETZ, Anita, A .... 406-768-6341 271 B
ascheetz@fpcc.edu
SCHEETZ, Christine .... 330-490-7102 373 F
cscheetz@walsh.edu
SCHEFF, Julie .... 510-666-8248.. 24 E
admissions@aimc.edu
SCHEFFEL, Debora .... 303-963-3147.. 77 I
dscheffel@ccu.edu
SCHEFFEL, Kent .... 618-468-5000 143 D
kscheffe@lc.edu
SCHEFFER, James .... 713-529-2778 445 K
scheffer@paralegal.edu
SCHEFFEY, Aubrey .... 773-989-3888 135 K
ascheffey@ccc.edu
SCHEIB, John, W .... 801-581-3887 472 P
john.scheib@utah.edu
SCHEIB, Roger .... 620-417-1240 181 E
roger.scheib@sccc.edu
SCHEIBEL, Cindy .... 562-902-3390.. 65 D
cindyscheibel@scuhs.edu
SCHEIBMEIR, Alan .... 606-886-3863 185 F
SCHEIBMEIR,
Monica, S .... 785-670-1526 182 D
monica.scheibmeir@washburn.edu
SCHEIDT, Douglas .... 315-386-7202 329 A
scheidtd@canton.edu
SCHEIE, Katie .... 858-513-9240.. 26 T
katie.scheie@ashford.edu
SCHEIERN, Libby .... 618-374-5147 149 A
libby.scheiern@principia.edu
SCHEINBERG, Mark, E ... 860-727-6757.. 87 B
mscheinberg@goodwin.edu
SCHEINES, Richard .... 412-268-2832 391 H
scheines@cmu.edu
SCHEINMAN, Steven, J . 570-504-7000 395 I
sscheinman@tcmc.edu
SCHEIRER, Gwen .... 717-866-5775 395 C
gscheirer@evangelical.edu
SCHEIWE, Aaron .... 815-836-5200 143 E
scheiwaa@lewisu.edu
SCHELCHER, Cindy .... 408-741-2165.. 74 D
cindy.schelcher@wvm.edu
SCHELCHER, Cindy .... 408-741-2165.. 74 D
cindy.schelcher@westvalley.edu
SCHELIN, Kelly .... 510-215-3870.. 40 K
kschelin@contracosta.edu
SCHELINDER, Shawnda . 320-629-5114 246 H
schelinders@pine.edu
SCHELL, John .... 407-823-5711 110 C
rick.schell@ucf.edu
SCHELL, Karen .... 518-292-1719 321 G
schelk@sage.edu
SCHELL, Randa .... 830-591-2908 457 C
rschell@swtjc.edu
SCHELL, Shannon .... 507-453-2743 245 G
sschell@southeastmn.edu
SCHELLENBERGER,
Lauren .... 573-288-6429 259 E
lschellenberger@culver.edu
SCHELLER, William, L ... 814-871-7912 395 H
scheller002@gannon.edu
SCHELLHASE, Cherea .... 251-981-3771.... 5 A
cherea.schellhase@columbiasouthern.
edu
SCHEMENT, Jorge, R ..... 848-932-2021 290 A
jr.schement@rutgers.edu
SCHEMENT, Jorge, R ..... 848-932-2021 290 C
jr.schement@oldqueens.rutgers.edu
SCHENA, Donna .... 240-567-3085 205 F
donna.schena@montgomerycollege.edu
SCHENCK, Merlin .... 706-886-6831 126 F
mschenck@tfc.edu
SCHENEWERK, Randal ... 573-875-7256 258 F
raschenewerk@ccis.edu
SCHENK, Glenn .... 310-287-4275.. 49 H
schenkga@wlac.edu
SCHENK, Kimberely .... 925-969-2036.. 40 L
schenk@dvc.edu
SCHENK, Mark .... 207-834-8646 201 E
mark.schenk@maine.edu
SCHENK, Matthew, R .... 757-446-6043 480 C
schenkmr@evms.edu
SCHENK, Rebecca, J ..... 716-878-4312 326 E
schenkrj@buffalostate.edu
SCHENK, Stacy, L .... 814-886-6357 402 E
sschenk@mtaloy.edu
SCHENKEL, Beverly, S ... 660-562-1149 264 I
bevs@nwmissouri.edu
SCHENKER, Beth .... 312-922-9012 152 F
bschenker@spertus.edu

SCHMIDT, Karen 847-543-2640 136 E kschmidtl@clcillinois.edu
SCHMIDT, Karen 309-556-3834 141 B kschmidt@iwu.edu
SCHMIDT, Kaye 828-398-7113 340 M kayenschmidt@abtech.edu
SCHMIDT, Keith, E 712-749-2230 167 C schmidt@bvu.edu
SCHMIDT, Leslie 406-994-2381 272 A lschmidt@montana.edu
SCHMIDT, Linda 856-222-9311 289 F lschmidt@rcbc.edu
SCHMIDT, Liz 651-846-1477 247 G elizabeth.schmidt@saintpaul.edu
SCHMIDT, London 910-755-8393 341 C schmidtl@brunswickcc.edu
SCHMIDT, Lynn 765-641-4388 156 A lmschmidt@anderson.edu
SCHMIDT, Martin, A 617-253-4500 221 C
SCHMIDT, Maynard 845-341-4205 319 H maynard.schmidt@sunyorange.edu
SCHMIDT, Paul 864-503-5036 425 H pschmidt@uscupstate.edu
SCHMIDT, Penelope 229-293-6190 128 G penelope.schmidt@wiregrass.edu
SCHMIDT, Philip, A 844-283-2246 91 G
SCHMIDT, Rachel 216-687-5594 359 L r.m.schmidt@csuohio.edu
SCHMIDT, Rachelle, M 651-846-1348 247 G rachelle.schmidt@saintpaul.edu
SCHMIDT, Shana 715-833-6410 513 E sschmidt42@cvtc.edu
SCHMIDT, Soren 906-487-7239 230 B soren.schmidt@finlandia.edu
SCHMIDT, Stephen 334-347-2623 1 J sschmidt@escc.edu
SCHMIDT, Steven, P 330-325-6499 366 F sschmidt@neomed.edu
SCHMIDT, Tania 507-457-2800 248 C tschmidt@winona.edu
SCHMIDT CAMPBELL, Mary 404-681-3643 126 D mscampbell@spelman.edu
SCHMIDT-CRUZ, Cynthia 302-831-0439 90 I csc@udel.edu
SCHMIDT-ROGERS, Debrah 773-508-3300 144 D dschmi6@luc.edu
SCHMIDTKE, Rachel 765-658-4104 157 H rachelschmidtke@depauw.edu
SCHMIECHEN, Tim 608-363-2296 506 D schmiech@beloit.edu
SCHMIEDE, Angela 650-543-3905 51 F angela.schmiede@menlo.edu
SCHMIEDEL, Mary, E 202-687-3911 92 B schmiedm@georgetown.edu
SCHMIEDL, Bruce 630-942-2972 136 D schmiedlb@cod.edu
SCHMIEDL, Joe 808-544-1105 129 C jschmiedl@hpu.edu
SCHMIEG, Rose, A 540-665-5534 485 C rschmieg@su.edu
SCHMIESING, Ann 303-492-2890 83 B ann.schmiesing@colorado.edu
SCHMIESING, David, A 740-284-6513 361 L dschmiesing@franciscan.edu
SCHMILL, Stuart 617-258-5514 221 C
SCHMISEK, Brian 312-915-7400 144 D bschmisek@luc.edu
SCHMIT, Matt 563-336-3300 168 K mschmit@eicc.edu
SCHMIT, Matt 563-441-4125 169 A mschmit@eicc.edu
SCHMIT, Michaeline 920-498-7106 514 G michaeline.schmit@nwtc.edu
SCHMIT, Shelly, M 641-422-4211 172 C schmishe@niacc.edu
SCHMITT, Barbara, L 570-348-6225 401 B schmitt@marywood.edu
SCHMITT, Deb 574-520-4398 160 F dsschmit@iusb.edu
SCHMITT, Deborah, F 716-851-1270 307 I schmitt@ecc.edu
SCHMITT, Dorothy, M 718-990-6384 322 F schmittd@stjohns.edu
SCHMITT, Linda 973-803-5000 288 D lschmitt@pillar.edu
SCHMITT, Mark 315-464-4538 326 B schmittm@upstate.edu
SCHMITT, Mark 520-515-5478 11 R schmittm@cochise.edu
SCHMITT, Patrick 408-741-2011 74 B patrick.schmitt@wvm.edu
SCHMITT, Stacy, C 336-318-0025 345 F scschmitt@randolph.edu
SCHMITTENDORF, Susan 716-270-5139 307 I ascschmittendorfs@ecc.edu
SCHMITTLEIN, David, C 617-253-2804 221 C
SCHMITTMANN, Beate 515-294-3220 166 F schmittb@iastate.edu
SCHMITTOU, Natasha 210-486-2339 441 I nschmittou@alamo.edu
SCHMITZ, Cody 740-283-6226 361 L cschmitz@franciscan.edu
SCHMITZ, David 414-277-7300 509 A
SCHMITZ, Donna 701-252-3467 355 J dschmitz@uj.edu
SCHMITZ, Michelle 320-308-2151 247 E maschmitz@stcloudstate.edu
SCHMITZ, Nancy, A 248-370-3352 235 J schmitz@oakland.edu
SCHMITZ, Stevie 406-657-1134 272 I schmitzs@rocky.edu
SCHMITZ, Todd 812-856-1214 159 H schmitz@iu.edu
SCHMITZ, Todd, J 812-856-1214 159 G schmitz@iu.edu
SCHMITZ, William 718-636-3542 320 D wschmitz@pratt.edu
SCHMOHL, C. Pat 508-751-7942 220 G pschmohl@qcc.mass.edu
SCHMOKE, Kurt, L 410-837-4866 209 D president@ubalt.edu
SCHMOLL, Claire, B 207-786-6100 198 E cschmoll@bates.edu
SCHMOLL, Kevin 618-650-3324 152 C kschmol@siue.edu
SCHMOLL, Robert 724-589-2102 411 D rschmoll@thiel.edu
SCHMOOCK, Allen 208-792-2215 132 C atschmoock@lcsc.edu
SCHMOTZER, Mark 516-299-3547 313 C mark.schmotzer@liu.edu
SCHMUCKER, Angie 248-364-6252 235 J schmucke@oakland.edu
SCHMUDE, Michelle 570-504-9691 395 I mschmude@tcmc.edu
SCHMUTTE, Gregory, T 413-205-3364 210 E gregory.schmutte@aic.edu
SCHMUTZ, Betsy 314-968-6960 269 N schmutz@webster.edu
SCHNABEL, William 907-474-6222 10 B weschnabel@alaska.edu
SCHNABL, JC 413-545-5542 216 H schnabl@admin.umass.edu
SCHNACK, Darcy 845-938-4379 519 D 8uscc@usma.edu
SCHNACK, Darcy 845-938-4379 519 D darcy.schnack@usma.edu
SCHNACK, Laura, L 309-794-7533 133 G lauraschnack@augustana.edu
SCHNACKENBERG, Scott 845-431-8682 307 A scott.schnackenberg@sunydutchess.edu
SCHNAIDMAN, Yaakov 570-346-1747 415 F
SCHNAPP, Derek 217-206-7823 154 A schnapp.derek@uis.edu
SCHNARR, Carmin, A 812-888-4332 165 E cschnarr@vinu.edu
SCHNARR, Grant 267-502-4844 390 F grant.schnarr@brynathyn.edu
SCHNATZ, Kristofer 718-409-7331 329 E kschnatz@sunymaritime.edu
SCHNEFKE, Emilee 314-421-0949 267 H eschnefke@siba.edu
SCHNEID, Thomas, R 210-808-4492 518 G thomas.schneid@usuhs.edu
SCHNEIDER, Amye 620-792-9302 175 C schneidera@bartonccc.edu
SCHNEIDER, Angela 510-885-3000 31 F
SCHNEIDER, Brandt, L 806-743-2556 463 E brandt.schneider@ttuhsc.edu
SCHNEIDER, Carrie 651-423-8244 244 E carrie.schneider@dctc.edu
SCHNEIDER, Chad 740-389-4636 365 B schneiderc@mtc.edu
SCHNEIDER, David 614-823-1240 368 O dschneider@otterbein.edu
SCHNEIDER, Deb 415-749-4587 60 G dschneider@sfai.edu
SCHNEIDER, Debbie 314-531-7925 266 J bksustlouis@bncollege.com
SCHNEIDER, Greg 913-288-7155 178 H gschneid@kckcc.edu
SCHNEIDER, Helen 410-617-2995 205 A hschneider@loyola.edu
SCHNEIDER, Howard 631-632-6265 325 F howard.schneider@stonybrook.edu
SCHNEIDER, Jed, S 315-445-4500 312 F schneij@lemoyne.edu
SCHNEIDER, Joan 660-562-1250 264 I jschneider@nwmissouri.edu
SCHNEIDER, Joanne 315-228-7362 304 G jschneider@colgate.edu
SCHNEIDER, Karen 707-664-4004 35 A karen.schneider@sonoma.edu
SCHNEIDER, Marc 770-426-2700 122 F marcs@life.edu
SCHNEIDER, Mark 610-409-3000 413 H
SCHNEIDER, Matt 715-422-5308 514 B matt.schneider@mstc.edu
SCHNEIDER, Michael, A 309-341-7217 142 G mschneid@knox.edu
SCHNEIDER, Michael, P 620-242-0405 179 G schneidm@mcpherson.edu
SCHNEIDER, Richard, W 802-485-2065 475 I rschneider@norwich.edu
SCHNEIDER, Scott 563-326-5319 169 A sjschneider@eicc.edu
SCHNEIDER, Scott 417-255-7258 263 I scottshcneider@missouristate.edu
SCHNEIDER, Steve 402-872-2393 276 C sschneider@peru.edu
SCHNEIDER, Tara 614-251-4642 367 F schneidt@ohiodominican.edu
SCHNEIDER, Tina 419-995-8326 363 G tschneider@lima.ohio-state.edu
SCHNEIDER, Tom 727-864-8409 97 O schneite@eckerd.edu
SCHNEIDER, Wendy 206-934-3227 497 G wendy.schneider@seattlecolleges.edu
SCHNEIDER BINGHAM, Stacy Lee 845-437-5285 333 A stbingham@vassar.edu
SCHNEIDER HASSELER, Susan 740-826-8115 366 C hasseler@muskingum.edu
SCHNEIDERMAN, Davis 847-735-5282 142 H dschneid@lakeforest.edu
SCHNEIDERMAN, Edward, S 718-933-6700 315 K eschneiderman@monroecollege.edu
SCHNELL, Carolyn, A 701-231-7189 354 D carolyn.schnell@ndsu.edu
SCHNELL, Linda 360-676-2772 496 C lschnell@nwic.edu
SCHNELL, Sarah 651-690-8754 249 T sbschnell@stkate.edu
SCHNELL, William 610-353-7630 390 E
SCHNELLER, Beverly 615-460-5630 430 D beverly.schneller@belmont.edu
SCHNELLER, Heather 706-729-2300 116 B hschneller@augusta.edu
SCHNEPF, Chester, H 203-285-2151 85 E cschnepf@gwcc.commnet.edu
SCHNETZER, Kelli 317-917-5731 161 G kschnetzer@ivytech.edu
SCHNETZLER, Greta 415-476-8005 70 A greta.schnetzler@ucsf.edu
SCHNICK, Chris 480-732-7274 13 E chris.schnick@cgc.edu
SCHNIER, Kathleen 602-557-1228 17 C kathleen.schnier@phoenix.edu
SCHNITKEY, Dawn, I 517-750-1200 237 D danderso@arbor.edu
SCHNITZER, Carol, N 518-580-5849 324 D cschnitz@skidmore.edu
SCHNOOR, Alexis 714-556-3610 72 F alexis.schnoor@vanguard.edu
SCHNOOR, Barry 540-665-4543 485 C bschnoor@su.edu
SCHNOOR, Chuck 520-494-5303 11 P chuck.schnoor@centralaz.edu
SCHNOOR, Neal, H 308-865-8208 277 F schnoorn@unk.edu
SCHNORENBERG, Sandi 507-389-2111 246 A sandi.schnorenberg@mnsu.edu
SCHNOWSKE, Betsy 815-479-7534 145 B bschnowske@mchenry.edu
SCHNUR, Fred 212-678-8008 312 A frschnur@jtsa.edu
SCHOBER, Kristen 716-896-0700 333 C kschober@villa.edu
SCHOBER, Michael 212-229-5727 316 E schober@newschool.edu
SCHOCHENMAIER, Gina 712-325-3356 170 K gschochenmaier@iwcc.edu
SCHOCHET, Ezra, B 323-937-3763 75 F eschochet@yoec.edu
SCHOCK, Pam 559-453-7115 43 J pam.schock@fresno.edu
SCHODOWSKI, Francis, G 803-786-3927 420 D fschodowski@columbiasc.edu
SCHOELL, Bill 302-622-8000 90 A bschoell@dcad.edu
SCHOEN, David 716-286-8001 318 F schoen@niagara.edu
SCHOEN, Karen 313-845-9849 231 B kschoen@hfcc.edu
SCHOEN, Susan 641-269-4580 169 F schoen@grinnell.edu
SCHOENBERG, Lynn 386-822-7473 111 E lschoenb@stetson.edu
SCHOENBERGER, Alfred 718-384-5460 334 J
SCHOENBERGER, Susan 860-509-9519 87 C sschoenberger@hartsem.edu
SCHOENECKE, Marvin 417-690-2204 258 E schoenecke@cofo.edu
SCHOENECKER, Mark 719-587-7696 76 D mwschoen@adams.edu
SCHOENECKER, Timothy 618-650-3823 152 C tschoen@siue.edu
SCHOENFELD, Jennifer 785-460-4684 176 L jennifer.schoenfeld@colbycc.edu
SCHOENFELD, Michael 919-681-3788 337 C michael.schoenfeld@duke.edu
SCHOENFELD, Michael 802-443-2272 475 G schoenfe@middlebury.edu
SCHOENFELD, Nancy 508-854-4425 220 G nschoenfeld@qcc.mass.edu
SCHOENFELDER, Louis 605-995-2191 427 A loschoen@dwu.edu
SCHOENGOOD, Matthew, G 212-817-7400 302 B mschoengood@gc.cuny.edu
SCHOENHALS, Dillon 580-349-1549 377 E dillon.schoenhals@opsu.edu
SCHOENING, Lisa 213-624-1200 42 N lschoening@fidm.edu
SCHOENLE, JR., Gerald, W 716-645-2230 325 B gws3@buffalo.edu
SCHOEPFLIN, Rennie 323-343-4001 32 D rschoep@calstatela.edu
SCHOFER, Marie 319-895-4159 167 G mschofer@cornellcollege.edu
SCHOFFMAN, Garth, D 330-972-8938 371 D gds@uakron.edu
SCHOFFSTALL, Heather 434-582-2195 482 D hschoffstall@liberty.edu
SCHOFIELD, Anna 614-222-3274 360 B aschofield@ccad.edu
SCHOFIELD, Audrey 561-803-2145 104 I audrey_schofield@pba.edu
SCHOFIELD, Janelle 304-929-1044 503 B jschofield@newriver.edu
SCHOFIELD, Sherri 906-248-8424 227 P sschofield@bmcc.edu
SCHOFIELD, William 559-244-5920 66 E wil.schofield@scccd.edu
SCHOH, Eric 507-457-5210 248 C eschoh@winona.edu
SCHOKNECHT, Pat 407-646-2700 106 J pschoknecht@rollins.edu
SCHOLER, Steven, A 402-280-2180 274 D stevenscholer@creighton.edu
SCHOLES, Scott 208-282-4220 132 B schojon2@isu.edu
SCHOLL, Bill 414-288-4796 508 C william.scholl@marquette.edu
SCHOLL, Daniel 605-688-4148 429 B daniel.scholl@sdstate.edu
SCHOLL, Heather 847-214-7177 138 B hscholl@elgin.edu
SCHOLL-FIEDLER, Anne 443-394-9257 207 C ascholl-fiedler@stevenson.edu
SCHOLLA, James 320-308-5028 247 F jscholla@sctcc.edu
SCHOLLES, Holly 503-760-3131 381 J holly@birthingway.edu
SCHOLLMEIER, John 507-457-1436 250 B jschollm@smumn.edu
SCHOLTE, Hugh 509-793-2291 492 I
SCHOLTEN, Brian 941-487-4230 110 B bscholten@ncf.edu
SCHOLTEN, Melissa 507-537-6071 248 A melissa.scholten@smsu.edu
SCHOLZ, Ben 201-761-7109 291 D bscholz@saintpeters.edu
SCHOLZ, Claudia 404-270-5897 126 D cscholz@spelman.edu
SCHOLZ, Daniel, J 414-410-4162 506 F djscholz@stritch.edu
SCHOLZ, John, K 608-263-2303 510 C karl.scholz@wisc.edu
SCHOLZ, Ted 213-615-7231 37 B tscholz@thechicagoschool.edu
SCHOLZE, Roberta 217-351-2383 148 H rscholze@parkland.edu
SCHOMBURG, Jeff 210-431-5073 455 J jschomburg@stmarytx.edu

SCHULZ, Kirk .... 509-335-4200 499 G
presidentsoffice@wsu.edu
SCHULZ, Paul, A .... 914-337-9300 305 F
paul.schulz@concordia-ny.edu
SCHULZ, Phyllis .... 212-817-7460 302 B
pschulz@gc.cuny.edu
SCHULZ, Robert .... 619-594-5901.. 34 B
rschulz@mail.sdsu.edu
SCHULZ, Scott .... 623-845-3876.. 13 H
scott.schulz@gccaz.edu
SCHULZ, Scott .... 218-726-7171 250 F
sschulz1@d.umn.edu
SCHULZ, Scott .... 440-826-6970 357 B
saschulz@bw.edu
SCHULZ, Scott, A .... 440-826-6970 357 B
saschulz@bw.edu
SCHULZ, Steven, D .... 641-422-4000 172 C
schulste@niacc.edu
SCHULZE, Edee .... 805-565-6028.. 74 I
eschulze@westmont.edu
SCHULZE, Lori, A .... 920-748-8310 509 H
schulzel@ripon.edu
SCHULZE, Louann, T ..... 817-515-1280 458 B
louann.schulze@tccd.edu
SCHULZE, Rob .... 802-635-1305 477 C
rob.schulze@jsc.edu
SCHULZE, Robin, G .... 716-645-2711 325 B
cas-dean@buffalo.edu
SCHULZKE, Mario .... 406-243-2323 271 G
mario.schulzke@umontana.edu
SCHUM, Jennifer .... 919-530-6658 350 D
jschum@nccu.edu
SCHUMACHER,
Bryan, J .... 605-394-5102 429 A
bryan.schumacher@sdsmt.edu
SCHUMACHER,
Charlotte .... 806-291-3549 470 I
schumacherc@wbu.edu
SCHUMACHER,
Daniel, J .... 715-836-5858 510 D
schumadj@uwec.edu
SCHUMACHER,
Diane, E .... 443-518-4522 204 E
dschumacher@howardcc.edu
SCHUMACHER, Frank .... 269-749-7668 236 A
fschumacher@olivetcollege.edu
SCHUMACHER, Gail ...... 847-233-7700 148 A
gschumacher@nc.edu
SCHUMACHER, Janette .. 484-664-3487 402 F
janschumach@muhlenberg.edu
SCHUMACHER, Lauren .. 847-233-7700 148 A
lwschumacher@nc.edu
SCHUMACHER,
Lawrence .... 847-233-7700 148 A
lschumacher@nc.edu
SCHUMACHER, Lillian ... 419-448-3053 370 K
schumacherlb@tiffin.edu
SCHUMACHER,
Mary Jeanne .... 812-357-6808 164 A
mschumacher@saintmeinrad.edu
SCHUMACHER,
Mary Jeanne .... 812-357-6501 164 A
mschumacher@saintmeinrad.edu
SCHUMACHER, Scott ..... 979-830-4172 444 D
scott.schumacher@blinn.edu
SCHUMAKER, Terry, W . 641-422-4170 172 C
schumter@niacc.edu
SCHUMAN, Alan, M ...... 410-386-8495 203 A
aschuman@carrollcc.edu
SCHUMAN, Anthony, W 973-596-6370 288 A
anthony.w.schuman@njit.edu
SCHUMAN, John .... 205-329-7945.... 5 C
john.schuman@ecacolleges.com
SCHUMAN, Shmuel .... 847-982-2500 139 E
schuman@htc.edu
SCHUMANN, James ...... 218-477-5869 246 B
james.schumann@mnstate.edu
SCHUMANN, Kenneth .... 503-352-2180 385 I
schumank@pacificu.edu
SCHUMANN, Patricia, J 304-766-3020 505 A
pschumann@wvstateu.edu
SCHUMANN, Renae .... 281-649-3300 450 C
rschumann@hbu.edu
SCHUMANN, Sherry, L .. 972-758-3880 446 I
sschumann@collin.edu
SCHUMER, Jason .... 314-792-6120 261 E
schumer@kenrick.edu
SCHUMM, Jillian .... 407-646-2120 106 J
jschumm@rollins.edu
SCHUNK, Jill .... 812-855-5646 159 H
jschunk@iu.edu
SCHUPPERT, Cindy .... 503-352-3191 385 I
schuppec@pacificu.edu
SCHUR, Jill .... 773-508-7392 144 D
jschur@luc.edu
SCHURMAN, Jane .... 610-957-5700 393 E
jschurman@dccc.edu
SCHURMAN, Ryan .... 402-552-3390 273 K
schurmanryan@clarksoncollege.edu
SCHUSTER, Danny .... 347-619-9074 335 A
SCHUSTER, Julian, Z ..... 314-246-8242 269 N
julianschuster@webster.edu
SCHUSTER, Leslie .... 401-456-9723 417 A
lschuster@ric.edu
SCHUSTER, Sheldon, M 909-607-0107.. 38 C
sheldon_schuster@kgi.edu
SCHUSTER, Stacy .... 609-771-3214 284 I
schuster@tcnj.edu
SCHUSTER-MATLOCK,
Tracy .... 563-333-6049 173 A
schustertracy@sau.edu
SCHUTH, Kristen .... 585-345-6898 309 C
keschuth@genesee.edu
SCHUTT, Michelle .... 208-732-6863 131 I
mschutt@csi.edu
SCHUTT, Stephen, D ..... 847-735-5100 142 H
presiden@lakeforest.edu
SCHUTTE, Kelli .... 816-415-7665 270 C
schuttek@william.jewell.edu
SCHUTTE, Thomas, F .... 718-636-3647 320 D
tschutte@pratt.edu
SCHUTTEN, Mary .... 408-924-2900.. 34 D
mary.schutten@sjsu.edu
SCHUTZ, Christine .... 208-459-5524 131 H
cschutz@collegeofidaho.edu
SCHUTZLER, Lyndon ..... 831-646-4221.. 52 G
lschutzler@mpc.edu
SCHUYLER, Lori, G .... 804-289-8781 486 G
lschuyle@richmond.edu
SCHWAB, Brandon .... 828-227-7495 352 C
beschwab@wcu.edu
SCHWAB, Mary, S .... 540-828-5487 478 J
mschwab@bridgewater.edu
SCHWAB, Nancy .... 916-660-7900.. 63 K
nschwab@sierracollege.edu
SCHWAB, Richard .... 860-486-3813.. 88 G
richard.schwab@uconn.edu
SCHWAB, Steve, J .... 901-448-4796 440 C
sschwab@uthsc.edu
SCHWAB, Victoria .... 952-358-8671 246 D
victoria.schwab@normandale.edu
SCHWABE, Jean, D .... 478-289-2464 118 H
jdschwabe@ega.edu
SCHWABROW, Lynsey .. 262-472-1801 512 C
schwabrl@uww.edu
SCHWAGER, Kathleen .... 860-773-1523.. 86 G
kschwager@txcc.commnet.edu
SCHWAIG, Kathy, S .... 470-578-6425 122 C
kschwaig@kennesaw.edu
SCHWAIGER, Patsy .... 513-244-4371 366 A
patsy.schwaiger@msj.edu
SCHWALLER, Tyler .... 478-757-4028 128 E
tschwaller@wesleyancollege.edu
SCHWANDT, Doug .... 573-882-6757 268 C
schwandtr@missouri.edu
SCHWANDT, Jehana ...... 320-222-5986 247 B
jehana.schwandt@ridgewater.edu
SCHWANKE, Shellie .... 309-467-6316 138 E
sschwanke@eureka.edu
SCHWANTES, Randy ...... 209-946-7613.. 70 F
rschwantes@pacific.edu
SCHWANTZ, Sara .... 217-732-3155 143 G
sschwantz@lincolncollege.edu
SCHWARTZ, Adam .... 515-294-2770 166 F
director@ameslab.gov
SCHWARTZ, Alycia .... 570-961-7845 399 A
schwartza@lackawanna.edu
SCHWARTZ, Anthony ..... 518-381-1256 323 L
schwaraj@sunysccc.edu
SCHWARTZ, Beth .... 419-448-2216 362 G
bschwartz@heidelberg.edu
SCHWARTZ, Brett .... 435-652-7593 473 B
bschwartz@dixie.edu
SCHWARTZ, Brian .... 303-373-2008.. 82 F
bschwartz@rvu.edu
SCHWARTZ, Celeste, M 215-641-6492 402 A
cschwartz@mc3.edu
SCHWARTZ, Corene .... 909-652-6242.. 36 E
cory.schwartz@chaffey.edu
SCHWARTZ, Daniel .... 650-723-2300.. 66 C
daniel.schwartz@stanford.edu
SCHWARTZ, David .... 845-783-9901 332 G
utamds@gmail.com
SCHWARTZ, David, J .... 248-370-3465 235 J
schwart3@oakland.edu
SCHWARTZ, Doreen .... 847-635-1630 148 D
doreen@oakton.edu
SCHWARTZ, Ernest .... 718-384-5460 334 J
SCHWARTZ, Gary .... 718-960-6093 302 C
gary.schwartz@lehman.cuny.edu
SCHWARTZ, Hayim .... 718-268-4700 320 K
SCHWARTZ, Janis .... 973-720-2175 292 I
schwartzj@wpunj.edu
SCHWARTZ, Jason .... 801-832-2262 474 E
jsj@westminstercollege.edu
SCHWARTZ, Jeff .... 941-893-2857 106 H
jschwartz@ringling.edu
SCHWARTZ, Jennifer ..... 317-955-6056 162 R
jschwartz@marian.edu
SCHWARTZ, Jennifer ..... 805-922-6966.. 24 J
jennifer.schwartz@hancockcollege.edu
SCHWARTZ, Jessica .... 715-833-6256 513 E
jschwartz31@cvtc.edu
SCHWARTZ, Joel, D ...... 757-221-2460 479 I
jxschw@wm.edu
SCHWARTZ, Justin .... 814-865-7537 403 F
SCHWARTZ, Kenneth ..... 504-865-5389 196 D
kschwartz@tulane.edu
SCHWARTZ, Lance, W ... 507-344-7427 240 I
lance.schwartz@blc.edu
SCHWARTZ, Lindsay ..... 212-355-1501 300 M
lschwartz@christies.edu
SCHWARTZ, Mark .... 610-359-5082 393 E
mschwartz@dccc.edu
SCHWARTZ, Mary Beth . 803-327-8042 426 J
mbschwartz@yorktech.edu
SCHWARTZ, Matthew, J 812-888-5832 165 E
mschwartz@vinu.edu
SCHWARTZ, Melissa ..... 707-765-1836.. 52 A
SCHWARTZ, Michael ...... 916-739-7151.. 70 F
mschwartz@pacific.edu
SCHWARTZ, Niki .... 479-968-0399.. 18 G
lschwartz@atu.edu
SCHWARTZ, Rachel .... 912-478-0049 120 E
rschwartz@georgiasouthern.edu
SCHWARTZ, Randi, D .... 914-594-4900 318 A
randi_schwartz@nymc.edu
SCHWARTZ, Robert .... 206-296-5831 498 D
schwartr@seattleu.edu
SCHWARTZ, Sandor .... 718-963-1212 312 C
kyrs@thejnet.com
SCHWARTZ, Shari .... 727-873-4143 111 B
smschwartz@mail.usf.edu
SCHWARTZ, Shuly .... 212-678-8826 312 A
shschwartz@jtsa.edu
SCHWARTZ, Steven .... 212-938-5712 328 E
sschwartz@sunyopt.edu
SCHWARTZ, Steven, J ... 970-247-7196.. 79 J
schwartz_s@fortlewis.edu
SCHWARTZ, Teri .... 310-825-7891.. 69 B
tschwartz@tft.ucla.edu
SCHWARTZE, Derek .... 573-681-5515 261 H
schwartzed@lincolnu.edu
SCHWARTZE, Mary .... 432-837-8203 462 G
mschwartze@sulross.edu
SCHWARTZMAN,
Michael .... 215-596-8855 413 E
m.schwartman@usciences.edu
SCHWARZ, Felipe .... 978-837-5459 221 G
schwarzf@merrimack.edu
SCHWARZ, Marilyn .... 508-387-7231 376 D
mschwarz@mscok.edu
SCHWARZ, May, L .... 614-235-4136 370 M
mschwarz@tlsohio.edu
SCHWARZ, Steven .... 718-997-5903 303 E
steven.schwarz@qc.cuny.edu
SCHWARZ, Thomas, J .... 914-251-6010 328 B
thomas.schwarz@purchase.edu
SCHWARZ, Todd .... 208-732-6325 131 I
tschwarz@csi.edu
SCHWARZBACH,
Elizabth .... 858-646-3100.. 62 C
eschwarzbach@sbpdiscovery.org
SCHWARZKOPF, David .. 781-891-2783 212 A
dschwarzkopf@bentley.edu
SCHWEBEL, Lisa .... 718-951-4771 301 E
lisas@brooklyn.cuny.edu
SCHWEERS, Valerie .... 210-999-8536 464 B
vschweer@trinity.edu
SCHWEIGERT, Francis ... 651-793-1300 245 E
francis.schweigert@metrostate.edu
SCHWEIGERT, Rich .... 303-534-6290.. 78 M
rich.schweigert@colostate.edu
SCHWEIKERT, Kristina ... 517-265-5161 226 F
kschweikert@adrian.edu
SCHWEINFEST, Michael 513-569-4755 359 G
michael.schweinfest@cincinnatistate.
edu
SCHWEITZER, Carrie ..... 972-860-4848 447 G
cschweitzer@dcccd.edu
SCHWEITZER,
Connie, J .... 989-964-4160 236 F
schw@svsu.edu
SCHWEITZER, Jason, C . 856-225-2894 290 B
jason.schweitzer@camden.rutgers.edu
SCHWEITZER, Laura ...... 518-402-0281 324 G
lschweitzer@albany.edu
SCHWEITZER, Steven, J 800-287-8822 156 D
schwest@bethanyseminary.edu
SCHWELM, Anne .... 610-902-8260 391 B
aschwelm@cabrini.edu
SCHWENK, Monica .... 801-395-3781 472 D
schwenkm@owatc.edu
SCHWENK, Thomas, L .. 775-784-6001 279 E
tschwenk@medicine.nevada.edu
SCHWENKE, Stacy .... 608-342-1981 511 D
schwenkes@uwplatt.edu
SCHWENT, Margie .... 573-334-6825 266 L
mschwent@sehcollege.edu
SCHWERTNER, Melanie . 325-574-6503 470 N
mschwertner@wtc.edu
SCHWIER, Erin .... 760-591-3012.. 71 I
eschwier@usa.edu
SCHWIETERMAN, Jerry . 219-473-4239 157 A
jschwieterman@ccsj.edu
SCHWINKE, Victoria ...... 573-897-5000 267 F
SCHWIRZBIN, Brian .... 516-876-3242 327 C
schwirzbinb@oldwestbury.edu
SCIALABBA, Joseph, M 814-641-3114 398 B
scialaj@juniata.edu
SCIALDONE, Robert .... 657-278-2025.. 32 B
rscialdone@fullerton.edu
SCIAME, Joseph, A .... 718-990-1941 322 F
sciamej@stjohns.edu
SCIAME-GIESECKE,
Susan .... 765-455-9221 160 B
sgieseck@iuk.edu
SCIANNA, Dominic, P ... 718-990-6185 322 F
sciannad@stjohns.edu
SCIBETTA, Nicholas .... 631-632-6335 325 F
nicholas.scibetta@stonybrook.edu
SCICLUNA, Jon .... 260-452-2269 157 F
jon.scicluna@ctsfw.edu
SCIFO, Joe .... 309-794-7374 133 G
josephscifo@augustana.edu
SCIGLITANO, JR.,
Anthony, C .... 973-275-5847 291 F
anthony.sciglitano@shu.edu
SCIOLA, Michael .... 315-228-7380 304 G
msciola@colgate.edu
SCIOTTO, Page, C .... 401-598-2145 416 C
psciotto@jwu.edu
SCIPIO, Julius .... 912-358-3202 125 C
scipioj@savannahstate.edu
SCIPLE, Melinda .... 662-476-5040 253 A
msciple@eastms.edu
SCISM, Bruce, R .... 434-797-8400 487 J
bscism@dcc.vccs.edu
SCISSUM GUNN, Karen 657-278-4514.. 32 B
kscissumgunn@fullerton.edu
SCIUTO, Jim .... 925-631-8043.. 59 C
jsciuto@stmarys-ca.edu
SCOATES, Christopher ... 248-645-3301 229 C
SCOBEE, Georgia .... 225-216-8608 192 B
scobeeg@mybrcc.edu
SCOBLE, Kathleen .... 413-265-2204 213 E
scoblek@elms.edu
SCOBY, Jerry, L .... 231-591-2164 230 A
jerryscoby@ferris.edu
SCOBY, Rhonda .... 903-877-7077 469 A
rhonda.scoby@uthct.edu
SCODRO, Joseph, M ..... 317-274-7460 160 E
jscodro@iu.edu
SCOFIELD, Dorie .... 913-722-0272 178 G
dorie.scofield@kansaschristian.edu
SCOFIELD, Elizabeth ...... 215-951-1913 398 F
scofield@lasalle.edu
SCOFIELD, Jeff .... 206-296-5852 498 D
scofieldj@seattleu.edu
SCOGGINS, Matthew ..... 865-974-3245 439 H
scoggins@tennessee.edu
SCOGIN, James .... 903-223-3005 460 D
james.scogin@tamut.edu
SCOGNA, Bridget .... 610-282-1100 393 G
1269mgr@follett.com
SCOLA, Anthony .... 630-829-6319 133 I
ascola@ben.edu
SCOLARO, Diane .... 802-485-2358 475 I
dscolaro@norwich.edu
SCOLFORO, Karen .... 800-759-2727 392 B
karenscolforo@centralpenn.edu
SCONYERS, Ryan .... 912-260-4377 125 F
ryan.sconyers@sgsc.edu
SCOPAS, Constantine ..... 212-686-9244 298 C
SCOPELLITI, Theresa ..... 570-961-7840 399 A
scopellitit@lackawanna.edu
SCORDINO, Anthony ...... 914-606-6521 333 H
anthony.scordino@sunywcc.edu
SCOTKA, Mary .... 210-434-6711 454 D
mscotka@lake.ollusa.edu
SCOTT, Adrienne .... 717-757-1100 415 J
adrienne.scott@yti.edu
SCOTT, Adrienne .... 717-767-4300 415 J
adrienne.scott@yti.edu
SCOTT, Alexander .... 973-290-4720 285 A
ascott@cse.edu
SCOTT, Amy .... 309-677-3538 134 G
alscott@fsmail.bradley.edu
SCOTT, Andrea .... 951-343-4701.. 28 G
ascott@calbaptist.edu

SEAMAN, David .... 315-443-5533 330 H
dseaman@syr.edu
SEAMAN, Diane .... 937-328-6014 359 H
seamand@clarkstate.edu
SEAMAN, Rebecca .... 360-475-7767 496 F
rseaman@olympic.edu
SEAMAN, Sara .... 501-760-4101.. 20 D
sara.seaman@np.edu
SEAMAN, Scott, H .... 740-593-2705 368 G
seaman@ohio.edu
SEAMAN, Shane .... 718-933-6700 315 K
sseaman@monroecollege.edu
SEAMS, Jennifer .... 304-645-6383 504 F
jseams@osteo.wvsom.edu
SEAQUIST, Carl .... 717-815-2084 415 G
cseaquis@ycp.edu
SEARA, Maira .... 212-647-7223 320 D
mseara@pratt.edu
SEARCY, Douglas, N ..... 252-399-6309 335 I
dsearcy@barton.edu
SEARFOSS, Alexis .... 727-873-4519 111 B
asearfoss@usfsp.edu
SEARING, Linda .... 585-389-2870 316 D
lsearin9@naz.edu
SEARLE, Mark, S .... 480-965-1224.. 10 K
mark.searle@asu.edu
SEARLE, Mary Ann .... 423-869-6849 433 C
mary.searle@lmunet.edu
SEARLE, Natalie .... 802-786-5148 477 B
njs12250@ccv.vsc.edu
SEARS, Andrew .... 816-960-2008 258 D
asears@cityvision.edu
SEARS, Andrew, L .... 814-865-3528 403 F
aus67@psu.edu
SEARS, Cheryl .... 916-484-8320.. 50 F
searsc@arc.losrios.edu
SEARS, Courtney .... 912-260-4270 125 F
courtney.sears@sgsc.edu
SEARS, David .... 240-567-7492 205 F
david.sears@montgomerycollege.edu
SEARS, Douglas, A .... 617-358-4608 212 G
dsears@bu.edu
SEARS, Estella .... 512-492-3077 442 J
esears@aoma.edu
SEARS, J, W .... 252-985-5585 348 A
wsears@ncwc.edu
SEARS, James .... 502-852-5555 190 C
jrsear03@louisville.edu
SEARS, John .... 303-220-1200.. 77 D
john.sears@cffp.edu
SEARS, Melissa .... 859-442-1156 185 I
melissa.sears@kctcs.edu
SEARS, Norward .... 504-816-4711 191 E
nsears@dillard.edu
SEARS, Richard .... 678-839-5353 127 F
rsears@westga.edu
SEARS, Ryan .... 502-213-8200 189 E
rsears@sctd.edu
SEARS, Steve, R .... 956-326-2480 459 B
steve.sears@tamiu.edu
SEARS, Steven, A .... 401-865-2425 416 E
ssears@providence.edu
SEARS, Suzanne .... 940-898-3748 464 A
SEARSON, Robert .... 216-987-3943 360 E
robert.searson@tri-c.edu
SEASTEDT, Erik .... 716-375-2102 322 B
eseastedt@sbu.edu
SEATON, Ann .... 845-758-6822 298 I
aseaton@bard.edu
SEATON, William, J ...... 609-984-1120 292 B
bseaton@tesu.edu
SEAVER, Catherine .... 413-775-1811 219 F
seaverc@gcc.mass.edu
SEAVER, Kent .... 972-273-3430 448 C
kseaver@dcccd.edu
SEAWORTH, Timothy .... 701-355-8150 355 K
seaworth@umary.edu
SEAY, Brooks .... 706-379-3111 128 H
cbseay@yhc.edu
SEAY, Laodecea .... 334-214-4807.... 1 H
laodecea.seay@cv.edu
SEAY, Lonnie .... 530-242-7912.. 63 I
lseay@shastacollege.edu
SEBASTIAN, Denise .... 573-518-2249 263 E
denise@mineralarea.edu
SEBASTIAN, Donald, H . 973-596-8449 288 A
sebastian@njit.edu
SEBASTIAN,
J. Jayakiran .... 717-334-6286 412 E
SEBASTIAN, John .... 504-865-2304 194 G
jtsebast@loyno.edu
SEBASTIAN, John .... 310-338-2987.. 50 J
john.sebastian@lmu.edu
SEBASTIAN, Juliann ...... 402-559-4000 277 H
julie.sebastian@unmc.edu
SEBASTIAN, Pam .... 660-831-4142 264 A
sebastianp@moval.edu

SEBASTIANI, Richard .... 713-221-8225 465 C
sebastianir@uhd.edu
SEBASTIEN, Anya .... 864-592-6207 424 C
sebastiena@sccsc.edu
SEBOK, Cathy .... 217-875-7211 149 J
csebok@richland.edu
SEBOLT, George, W ...... 412-291-6210 389 F
gsebolt@aii.edu
SEBRANEK, Lori, A .... 608-243-4185 514 A
lsebranek@madisoncollege.edu
SEBRING, Amy .... 757-221-1722 479 I
asebring@wm.edu
SECHLER, Elizabeth .... 304-876-5172 504 D
esechler@shepherd.edu
SECHRIST, Ann .... 770-972-7580 121 G
asechrist@gwinnetttech.edu
SECHRIST, John .... 724-653-2184 394 B
jsechrist@dec.edu
SECHRIST, Shana .... 503-370-6210 388 D
ssechrist@willamette.edu
SECKA, Lamine .... 619-594-7903.. 34 B
lsecka@mail.sdsu.edu
SECOR, Dan .... 203-773-8506.. 84 G
dsecor@albertus.edu
SECORD, Mark .... 361-354-2529 445 S
secordm@coastalbend.edu
SECORD, Paul .... 512-863-1211 457 I
secordp@southwestern.edu
SECREST, Karen .... 435-722-6900 472 L
SECREST, Kathy, L .... 330-471-8415 364 H
ksecrest@malone.edu
SECRIST, Tammi .... 304-336-8281 504 E
tsecrist@westliberty.edu
SEDA, Iris .... 787-264-1912 524 D
iris_seda_rodriguez@intersg.edu
SEDANO, George .... 510-594-5033.. 28 K
gsedano@cca.edu
SEDDIKI, Mohamed ...... 973-877-3080 285 K
seddiki@essex.edu
SEDEN, John .... 415-749-4570.. 60 G
jseden@sfai.edu
SEDER, Diana .... 909-607-7785.. 38 A
diana.seder@cmc.edu
SEDILLO, Dacia .... 575-646-5690 295 B
dapachec@nmsu.edu
SEDLACEK, Bernard .... 531-622-2529 275 F
bsedlacek@mccneb.edu
SEDLACEK, Paige .... 607-778-5213 326 C
sedlacekpm@sunybroome.edu
SEDLACK, Chris .... 319-208-5259 173 G
csedlack@scciowa.edu
SEDLAK, John .... 570-740-0234 400 F
jsedlak@luzerne.edu
SEDY, Paul .... 661-362-2200.. 51 C
psedy@masters.edu
SEDYCIAS, Joao .... 201-200-3001 287 F
jsedycias@njcu.edu
SEE, David .... 501-337-5000.. 19 C
dsee@coto.edu
SEE, Jonathan .... 310-506-6256.. 56 D
jonathan.see@pepperdine.edu
SEE, Leslie, C .... 304-260-4380 502 J
lsee@blueridgectc.edu
SEEBO, Elane .... 806-291-3417 470 I
seeboe@wbu.edu
SEEBOLD, Lauren, N ..... 248-204-2309 233 A
lseebold@ltu.edu
SEEGER, Matthew .... 313-577-5342 239 C
matthew.seeger@wayne.edu
SEEGERT, Paul .... 206-616-3865 499 D
pseegert@uw.edu
SEEGMILLER, Jesse .... 540-261-8454 485 G
jesse.seegmiller@svu.edu
SEEK, Linda .... 301-846-2457 203 H
lseek@frederick.edu
SEEKINS, Travis, P .... 325-670-1589 450 A
seekins@hsutx.edu
SEEKLANDER, Marlene .. 605-882-5284 427 D
seeklanm@lakeareatech.edu
SEELA, Joel .... 320-762-4635 243 J
joels@alextech.edu
SEELBACH, Brenda .... 540-636-2900 479 G
brendaseelbach@christendom.edu
SEELEY, Lisa .... 903-923-2175 448 J
lseeley@etbu.edu
SEELY, Bruce, E .... 906-487-2156 234 A
bseely@mtu.edu
SEELYE, Calvin, H .... 989-774-7526 228 E
seely1ch@cmich.edu
SEEMAN, Steve, C .... 563-588-8000 169 B
financialaid@emmaus.edu
SEERY, Denise .... 303-282-3414.. 82 G
denise.seery@archden.org
SEESTEDT-STANFORD,
Linda .... 540-887-4318 482 G
lstanford@marybaldwin.edu
SEEVERS, JR., Gary .... 417-862-9533 260 D
president@globaluniversity.edu

SEEVERS, Scott .... 402-643-7233 274 B
scott.seevers@cune.edu
SEFCIK, Don .... 317-955-6290 162 R
dsefcik@marian.edu
SEFCIK, Jeffrey .... 325-942-2041 463 C
jeff.sefcik@angelo.edu
SEFFERS, Tracy .... 304-876-5463 504 D
tseffers@shepherd.edu
SEFFINGER, Michael ..... 909-469-5423.. 74 G
mseffinger@westernu.edu
SEFTON, Cindy .... 513-569-1699 359 G
cindy.sefton@cincinnatistate.edu
SEGAL, Gordon .... 691-320-2481 519 G
gsegal@comfsm.fm
SEGAL, Rick .... 612-455-3420 241 A
rick.segal@bcsmn.edu
SEGAR, Robert, B .... 530-752-2172.. 68 H
rbsegar@ucdavis.edu
SEGAR, Thomas .... 304-876-5214 504 D
tsegar@shepherd.edu
SEGARRA, Barbara .... 787-758-2525 528 D
barbara.segarra@upr.edu
SEGARRA, Carlos .... 787-264-1912 524 D
csegarra@intersg.edu
SEGARRA, Jose .... 787-878-5475 523 H
jsegarra@arecibo.inter.edu
SEGAT, Susana .... 617-879-7073 218 B
ssegat@massart.edu
SEGAVE, Robert .... 585-594-6357 321 C
segave_robert@roberts.edu
SEGEL, Baruch .... 732-765-9126 292 L
SEGGELKE, Linda .... 217-732-3168 143 F
lseggelke@lincolnchristian.edu
SEGGERMAN, Richard ... 319-352-8521 174 C
richard.seggerman@wartburg.edu
SEGGERMAN,
Richard, W .... 319-352-8276 174 C
richard.seggerman@wartburg.edu
SEGGOS, Rose .... 518-782-6783 324 C
rseggos@siena.edu
SEGRAN, Sam .... 806-742-5151 463 D
sam.segran@ttu.edu
SEGRETI, Rosemary .... 706-542-6020 127 A
rsegreti@uga.edu
SEGROVES, Dawn, M .... 214-860-2064 448 A
dsegroves@dcccd.edu
SEGRUE, Gary .... 716-375-2525 322 B
gsegrue@sbu.edu
SEGUIN, Nancy .... 989-358-7212 227 A
seguinn@alpenacc.edu
SEGURA, Gary .... 310-206-3487.. 69 B
segura@luskin.ucla.edu
SEGURA, Steve .... 916-570-5011.. 50 F
seguras@arc.losrios.edu
SEHEULT, Erin .... 909-558-4508.. 48 H
eseheult@llu.edu
SEHGAL, Mani .... 808-543-8046 129 C
msehgal@hpu.edu
SEHGAL, Varun .... 718-518-6641 302 D
vsehgal@hostos.cuny.edu
SEHLOFF, John, M .... 507-344-7342 240 I
john.sehloff@blc.edu
SEHRIST, Tim .... 325-793-4978 452 F
sechrist.tim@mcm.edu
SEIBEL, Rosalie .... 701-662-1542 355 A
rosalie.seibel@lrsc.edu
SEIBERLICH, Heather ..... 815-967-7302 150 B
hseiberlich@rockfordcareercollege.edu
SEIBERLICH, Heather ..... 608-663-2000 507 M
hseiberlich@mediainstitute.edu
SEIBERT, Diane .... 301-295-1080 518 G
diane.seibert@usuhs.edu
SEIBERT, Jon .... 620-431-2820 180 C
jseibert@neosho.edu
SEIBERT, Rhonda, K ...... 563-562-3263 172 D
seibertr@nicc.edu
SEIBERT, Susan .... 618-650-3708 152 C
sseiber@siue.edu
SEIBRING, Scott .... 309-556-3096 141 B
iwufaid@iwu.edu
SEIBRING, Steve .... 309-556-3710 141 B
sseibrin@iwu.edu
SEICHEN, Scott .... 217-351-2280 148 H
sseichen@parkland.edu
SEIDEL, H. Edward .... 217-265-5440 153 G
eseidel@uillinois.edu
SEIDEN, Peggy .... 610-328-8489 410 I
pseiden1@swarthmore.edu
SEIDENSTICKER,
Duane, P .... 414-847-3274 508 G
duaneseidensticker@miad.edu
SEIDLER, Nick .... 414-277-6922 509 A
SEIF, Gershon .... 874-982-2500 139 E
seif@htc.edu
SEIFARTH, Eric, M .... 803-536-7200 423 G
eseifart@scsu.edu
SEIFERT, Alice .... 914-923-2616 319 J
aseifert@pace.edu

SEIFERT, Annemarie ...... 860-405-9010.. 88 G
annemarie.seifert@uconn.edu
SEIFERT, Charles .... 518-783-2321 324 C
seifert@siena.edu
SEIFERT, Charles, E ...... 806-743-4200 463 E
charles.seifert@ttuhsc.edu
SEIFERT, David .... 716-270-5348 307 I
seifertd@ecc.edu
SEIGERMAN, David .... 845-434-5750 330 F
dseigerman@sunysullivan.edu
SEIGH, William .... 603-358-2105 283 A
wseigh@keene.edu
SEILER, David .... 512-863-1809 457 I
seilerd@southwestern.edu
SEILER, Kevin .... 303-352-3053.. 79 D
kevin.seiler@ccd.edu
SEIPP, Dale .... 503-517-1024 388 A
dseipp@warnerpacific.edu
SEIPPEL, Danielle .... 608-822-2317 515 A
dseippel@swtc.edu
SEIRUP, Wendy .... 714-997-6893.. 36 G
wseirup@chapman.edu
SEITZ, Greg .... 256-782-5368.... 6 B
gseitz@jsu.edu
SEITZ, Kathy .... 828-726-2269 341 D
kseitz@cccti.edu
SEITZ, Tim .... 440-826-8029 357 B
tseitz@bw.edu
SEITZER, Joan, M .... 410-827-5808 203 C
jseitzer@chesapeake.edu
SEIVERS, Lana, C .... 615-898-2874 434 H
lana.seivers@mtsu.edu
SEIXAS, Karyn .... 626-395-6161.. 29 I
karyn@caltech.edu
SEJCEK, Al .... 626-584-5477.. 43 K
alsejcek@fuller.edu
SEJDINAJ, John .... 812-855-7114 159 H
jsej@iu.edu
SEJDINAJ, John .... 812-855-0978 159 G
jsej@iu.edu
SEKELSKY, Mary Jo ...... 810-762-3000 238 B
maryjoss@umflint.edu
SEKERAK, Robert .... 814-471-0013 405 A
rsekerak@pennhighlands.edu
SEKOL, Jennifer .... 570-945-8117 398 C
jennifer.sekol@keystone.edu
SEKUL, Michelle .... 228-497-7647 254 D
michelle.sekul@mgccc.edu
SEKULICH, Brad .... 704-687-7747 351 C
sekulich@uncc.edu
SELBURG, Alissa .... 309-672-5513 145 E
aselburg@methodistcol.edu
SELBY, David, K .... 317-788-3386 164 H
selbyd@uindy.edu
SELBY, Rosemary .... 478-553-2055 123 H
rselby@oftc.edu
SELBY, Steve .... 714-992-7081.. 54 A
sselby@fullcoll.edu
SELBY, Tami .... 303-352-6906.. 79 D
SELBY, Terri, P .... 802-654-2462 476 A
tselby@smcvt.edu
SELDEN, Pete .... 870-733-6722.. 18 B
pjselden@asumidsouth.edu
SELDEN, Sally .... 434-544-8266 482 F
selden@lynchburg.edu
SELF, George .... 520-335-1365.. 11 R
selfg@cochise.edu
SELF, Richard, B .... 336-322-2128 345 D
richard.self@piedmontcc.edu
SELF, Ronald .... 660-263-6408 258 A
mrsself@att.net
SELF, Rosemary .... 662-472-9079 253 C
rself@holmescc.edu
SELF, Sheila .... 918-444-2120 376 G
selfsj@nsuok.edu
SELF-DAVIS, LeAnn .... 731-989-6931 432 C
ldavis@fhu.edu
SELIG, C. Wood .... 757-683-3369 483 G
wselig@odu.edu
SELIGMAN, Joel .... 585-275-8356 332 E
seligman@rochester.edu
SELIGMAN, Joel .... 301-314-6650 207 G
joels@umd.edu
SELIGMAN, Joel, R .... 603-862-0653 282 F
joel.seligman@unh.edu
SELIGMAN, Richard, P .. 626-395-6073.. 29 I
richard.seligman@caltech.edu
SELIGMANN, Wendy .... 828-771-3033 353 B
wseligmann@warren-wilson.edu
SELIN, Mark .... 920-403-3055 509 J
mark.selin@snc.edu
SELKIRK, Sara, E .... 816-654-7214 261 D
sselkirk@kcumb.edu
SELL, JR., Edgar, S .... 410-857-2711 205 E
esell@mcdaniel.edu
SELL, Justin .... 605-688-5625 429 B
justin.sell@sdstate.edu

SELL, Kayla ... 414-930-3445 509 B sellk@mtmary.edu
SELL, Phil ... 847-317-8031 153 D psell@tiu.edu
SELL, Tiffany ... 847-317-7051 153 D tiffany.sell@tiu.edu
SELLARS, Frances ... 360-676-2772 496 C fsellars@nwic.edu
SELLARS, Telly ... 502-213-4294 186 C telly.sellars@kctcs.edu
SELLECK, Mike ... 806-720-7775 452 D michael.selleck@lcu.edu
SELLECK, Ron ... 336-259-6990 338 G rselleck@johnwesley.edu
SELLEN, Mary, K ... 757-594-7130 479 H mary.sellen@cnu.edu
SELLERS, Emma ... 828-328-7288 339 C emma.sellers@lr.edu
SELLERS, Jennifer ... 802-287-8072 475 B sellersj@greenmtn.edu
SELLERS, Karen ... 401-841-6547 518 E
SELLERS, Lamont ... 605-677-5011 428 E lamont.sellers@usd.edu
SELLERS, Lauren ... 704-272-5331 346 F lsellers@spcc.edu
SELLERS, Lee ... 503-255-0332 384 E lsellers@multnomah.edu
SELLERS, Linda ... 254-442-5151 445 Q linda.sellers@cisco.edu
SELLERS, Martin ... 423-869-6815 433 C martin.sellers@lmunet.edu
SELLERS, Patrick, J ... 704-894-2078 337 B pasellers@davidson.edu
SELLERS, Randy ... 806-720-7161 452 D randy.sellers@lcu.edu
SELLERS, Rob, M ... 734-764-3982 237 I
SELLERS, Robert, M ... 734-764-3982 237 I rsellers@umich.edu
SELLERS, Terrie, O ... 912-443-5707 125 D tsellers@savannahtech.edu
SELLERS, Timothy ... 315-279-5685 312 D tsellers@keuka.edu
SELLERS-SIMON, Cynthia ... 803-376-5744 418 D csimon@allenuniversity.edu
SELLICK, Megan ... 570-208-5900 398 D megansellick@kings.edu
SELLMANN, James, D ... 671-735-2805 520 B jsellman@triton.uog.edu
SELLNER, Hildegard ... 907-796-6226.. 10 C hcsellner@alaska.edu
SELLS, Ben, R ... 870-245-5400.. 20 G sellsb@obu.edu
SELLS, Deanna ... 573-334-6825 266 L dsells@sehcollege.edu
SELLS, Debra, K ... 615-898-2440 434 H debra.sells@mtsu.edu
SELLS, Tamatha ... 864-941-8363 423 C sells.t@ptc.edu
SELLS, Vicki, G ... 931-598-3220 436 A vsells@sewanee.edu
SELMAN, Brenda, V ... 573-884-9153 268 C selmanb@missouri.edu
SELMER, Paula ... 518-244-2093 321 G selmep@sage.edu
SELMO, Barbara ... 617-349-8267 216 D bselmo@lesley.edu
SELMON, John ... 231-777-0265 234 G john.selmon@muskegoncc.edu
SELMON, Michael, L ... 989-463-7176 226 H selmon@alma.edu
SELORIO, Conrad ... 562-860-2451.. 36 A cselorio@cerritos.edu
SELPH, Justin ... 941-359-7531 106 H jselph@ringling.edu
SELSOR-COWAN, Sharaya ... 970-248-1020.. 77 K
SELTZER, Jill ... 832-230-5540 453 K jseltzer@na.edu
SELTZER, Michael ... 251-544-1510.... 6 F mseltzer@remingtoncollege.edu
SELVERA, Richard ... 713-222-5388 465 C selverar@uhd.edu
SELVEY, David ... 317-789-8243 157 G dselvey16@crossroads.edu
SEM, Daniel, S ... 262-243-5700 507 C daniel.sem@cuw.edu
SEMAH, Charles ... 732-431-1600 292 A
SEMENOFF, Michael ... 310-377-5501.. 51 B msemenoff@marymountcalifornia.edu
SEMENTA, Deborah ... 617-603-6900 222 F
SEMENZA, Michael, L ... 401-341-2465 417 D semenzam@salve.edu
SEMMEL, Abraham ... 718-268-4700 320 K
SEMMEL, Ralph ... 443-778-5190 204 F ralph.semmel@jhuapl.edu
SEMMENS, Theresa ... 305-284-1526 112 O theresa.semmens@miami.edu
SEMMES, Paul ... 931-372-3118 438 F psemmes@tntech.edu
SEMPLE, John ... 708-596-2000 151 H jsemple@ssc.edu
SEMPREBON, Gina ... 413-565-1000 211 C gsemprebon@baypath.edu
SEMROW, Adelle ... 606-693-5000 187 D finaid@kmbc.edu
SEMTNER, Anita ... 405-878-5295 379 G amsemtner@stgregorys.edu
SEN, Arup ... 716-829-7658 307 B sena@dyc.edu
SEN, Gautam ... 718-960-8764 302 C gautam.sen@lehman.cuny.edu
SENA, Ali ... 559-453-2236.. 43 J ali.sena@fresno.edu
SENA-MARTIN, Elisabet 812-749-1544 163 B esena@oak.edu
SENA-MARTIN, Ely ... 812-749-1544 163 B esena@oak.edu
SENCER, Stephen, D ... 404-727-2016 119 B steve.sencer@emory.edu
SENECAL, Molly ... 916-608-6688.. 50 H senecam@flc.losrios.edu
SENECAUT, Tim ... 620-235-4776 180 J tsenecaut@pittstate.edu
SENEGAL, Pamela, G ... 336-322-2100 345 D pamela.senegal@piedmontcc.edu
SENEQUE, Guy ... 516-877-3650 297 I seneque@adelphi.edu
SENERIZ, Cynthia ... 805-893-8137.. 70 B cynthia.seneriz@hr.ucsb.edu
SENESE, Alvira ... 718-960-8545 302 C alvira.senese@lehman.cuny.edu
SENESE, Jeffrey, D ... 414-410-4006 506 F jdsenese@stritch.edu
SENESE, Richard ... 888-227-3552 241 B
SENF, Lora ... 509-533-3429 494 A lora.senf@sfcc.spokane.edu
SENFT, James ... 847-543-2975 136 E jsenft@clcillinois.edu
SENG, Chris ... 970-491-4860.. 78 N christopher.seng@colostate.edu
SENG, Victoria, S ... 731-881-7855 440 B vseng@utm.edu
SENGENBERGER, Jennifer ... 719-502-3198.. 81 H jennifer.sengenberger@ppcc.edu
SENGER, Matt ... 320-589-6382 251 A matt@morris.umn.edu
SENGUPTA, Shivaji ... 347-964-8600 299 L ssengupta@boricuacollege.edu
SENIOR, Ann Marie ... 609-984-1151 292 B amsenior@tesu.edu
SENIOR, Sandra ... 212-616-7271 309 G sandra.senior@helenefuld.edu
SENIOR, Timothy, C ... 610-785-6200 409 F bsenior@scs.edu
SENKBEIL, Peter ... 949-214-3202.. 40 I peter.senkbeil@cui.edu
SENKFOR, Sherrie ... 618-650-2190 152 C ssenkfo@siue.edu
SENN, Michael, E ... 301-243-2122 518 C michael.senn@dodiis.mil
SENN, Sarah ... 334-699-2266.... 1 B
SENNE, Terry ... 940-898-3029 464 A tsenne@twu.edu
SENNETT, Peter ... 413-775-1312 219 F sennettp@gcc.mass.edu
SENNYEY, Pongracz ... 512-448-8470 455 I pongracz@stedwards.edu
SENSENIG, Victor ... 410-778-7201 210 A vsensenig2@washcoll.edu
SENSER, Randie ... 212-247-3434 313 K rsenser@mandl.edu
SENSI, Patricia ... 732-224-2232 284 B psensi@brookdalecc.edu
SENSIBAUGH, Cyndee .. 304-367-4933 503 C cyndee.sensibaugh@pierpont.edu
SENSING, Laura ... 734-462-4400 236 H lsensing@schoolcraft.edu
SENTER, James, E ... 843-953-5030 419 D jsenter1@citadel.edu
SENTER, Timothy, C ... 662-862-8460 253 D tcsenter@iccms.edu
SENTER, William ... 830-372-6550 461 D wsenter@tlu.edu
SEO, Kyoo, W ... 636-327-4645 263 C wdciso@midwest.edu
SEO, Sang Bae ... 636-327-4645 263 C seoul@midwest.edu
SEO, Stephen ... 213-487-0110.. 41 K registrar@dula.edu
SEPANIC, Michael, J ... 856-225-6026 290 B msepanic@camden.rutgers.edu
SEPEHRI, Mo ... 202-274-5033.. 93 D msepehri@comcast.net
SEPICH, Kim, W ... 407-582-3432 113 F ksepich@valenciacollege.edu
SEPION, Daniel ... 605-394-2348 429 A daniel.sepion@sdsmt.edu
SEPLOW, Suzanne ... 310-825-3401.. 69 B suzanne@orl.ucla.edu
SEPPALA, Julie ... 906-487-2642 234 A jhseppal@mtu.edu
SEQUEIRA, Debra-L ... 206-281-2277 498 B dsequeira@spu.edu
SEQUEIRA, Gerald ... 626-914-8517.. 37 G gsequeira@citruscollege.edu
SEQUERI, Pierangelo ... 202-526-3799.. 93 A psequeri@johnpaulii.edu
SERAFIMOV, Val ... 417-873-7262 259 G vserafimov@drury.edu
SERAFIN, Renata ... 210-486-4689 441 G rserafin@alamo.edu
SERAFINO, Candice, J .. 413-545-6253 216 H serafino@acad.umass.edu
SERAICHICK, Laura ... 603-358-2526 283 A lseraich@keene.edu
SERBALIK, James ... 518-783-2314 324 C serbalik@siena.edu
SERBALIK, Sandy ... 518-783-2596 324 C sserbalik@siena.edu
SERBAN, Andreea ... 714-438-4698.. 38 E aserban@mail.cccd.edu
SERBER, Michael ... 214-648-9569 469 E michael.serber@utsouthwestern.edu
SERDYUK, Yana, V ... 708-209-3053 136 I yana.serdyuk@cuchicago.edu
SERGE, Susan ... 307-686-0254 516 P sserge@sheridan.edu
SERGER, Carissa ... 303-457-2757.. 76 G carissa.serger@zenith.org
SERGEYEVA, Larisa ... 714-892-7711.. 38 G lsergeyeva@gwc.cccd.edu
SERGI, Joanne ... 317-738-8167 157 L jsergi@franklincollege.edu
SERGI, Joseph ... 603-645-9650 282 C j.sergi@snhu.edu
SERIO, Tricia, R ... 413-545-2766 216 H tserio@umass.edu
SERIO, Vincent ... 208-426-5688 131 C vinceserio@boisestate.edu
SERJOIE, Ara ... 336-316-2320 338 C serjoiea@guilford.edu
SERLING, Kitty ... 816-276-4309 265 G c.serling@researchcollege.edu
SERNA, Edward ... 479-788-6925.. 22 A edward.serna@uafs.edu
SERNA, Ricky ... 505-454-2555 294 D
SERNA-WALLENDER, Alexander ... 330-263-2000 360 A aserna-wallender@wooster.edu
SERNAU, Scott ... 574-520-4429 160 F ssernau@iusb.edu
SEROSHEK, Nichole ... 360-442-2371 495 G nseroshek@lowercolumbia.edu
SEROTA COTE, Pamela, A ... 540-375-2299 484 H cote@roanoke.edu
SEROVICH, Julianne ... 813-974-7196 111 A jserovich@usf.edu
SERPLISS, Ron ... 563-244-7021 168 L rserpliss@eicc.edu
SERR, Jim ... 815-280-6641 142 A jim.serr@jjc.edu
SERR, Roger, L ... 717-477-1308 407 B rlserr@ship.edu
SERRA, Elena ... 201-761-6366 291 D eserra@saintpeters.edu
SERRA, Neddie ... 973-748-9000 284 A neddie_serra@bloomfield.edu
SERRA, Neuza, M ... 856-225-6005 290 B nmserra@camden.rutgers.edu
SERRANO, Aixa ... 787-857-3600 523 I aserrano@br.inter.edu
SERRANO, Alex ... 903-223-3114 460 D alex.serrano@tamut.edu
SERRANO, Angela ... 909-558-4567.. 48 H sm8026@bncollege.com
SERRANO, Carlos, A ... 718-982-2460 302 A carlos.serrano@csi.cuny.edu
SERRANO, Fabian ... 432-264-5077 450 G fserrano@howardcollege.edu
SERRANO, Frank ... 718-782-2200 299 L fserrano@boricuacollege.edu
SERRANO, Gladys ... 787-743-4041 521 K gserrano@columbiacentral.edu
SERRANO, Iris ... 787-743-7979 526 A iserrano@suagm.edu
SERRANO, Lucille ... 831-755-6900.. 45 C lserrano@hartnell.edu
SERRANO, Luz, D ... 787-780-0070 521 B lserrano@caribbean.edu
SERRANO, Mayra ... 787-798-3001 526 G mayra.serrano@uccaribe.edu
SERRANO, Melba ... 787-890-2681 527 E melba.serrano@upr.edu
SERRANO, Zaida ... 787-890-2681 527 E zaida.serrano@upr.edu
SERRAO, Carlos ... 740-392-6868 366 B carlos.serrao@mvnu.edu
SERRATA, William ... 915-831-6511 449 A wserrata@epcc.edu
SERRAVILLO, JR., Lee .. 518-442-3080 324 G lserravillo@albany.edu
SERRECCHIA, Michael ... 214-638-0484 451 E mserrecchia@kdstudio.com
SERRETT, Marc ... 605-688-4128 429 B marc.serrett@sdstate.edu
SERTSU, Neb ... 410-837-5069 209 D nsertsu@ubalt.edu
SERVELLO, Frederick, A 207-581-3202 201 B fred.servello@maine.edu@maine.edu
SERVER, Timor ... 713-718-6453 450 D timor.server@hccs.edu
SERVI, Angela, M ... 715-675-3331 514 F servia@ntc.edu
SERVIDIO, Denise ... 718-990-6247 322 F stjohns@bkstr.com
SERWATKA, Thomas, S . 904-620-2500 110 E tserwatk@unf.edu
SESSION, Norman ... 601-936-5555 253 B norman.session@hindscc.edu
SESSIONS, Layne ... 775-831-1314 280 C lsessions@sierranevada.edu
SESSIONS, Lisa, H ... 828-448-3126 347 F lsessions@wpcc.edu
SESSIONS, Valerie ... 843-863-8083 419 C vsessions@csuniv.edu
SESSLER, Jeff ... 909-607-1225.. 63 F jeff@scrippscollege.edu
SESSLER, Jennifer ... 315-568-3270 317 A jsessler@nycc.edu
SESSUMS, Cassandra ... 601-925-3464 254 B sessums@mc.edu
SESSUMS, Johnny ... 713-718-2093 450 D johnny.sessums@hccs.edu
SESTAK, Brandi ... 402-465-7579 276 E bsestak@nebrwesleyan.edu
SETAYESH, Flora, R ... 615-353-3394 437 D flora.setayesh@nscc.edu
SETCHELL, Cara ... 765-658-4154 157 H carasetchell@depauw.edu
SETCHELL, Steven, J ... 765-658-4215 157 H ssetchell@depauw.edu
SETEK, Scott ... 315-445-4300 312 F seteksl@lemoyne.edu
SETH, Niti ... 617-873-0208 213 B niti.seth@cambridgecolleg.edu
SETHARES, Greg ... 508-678-2811 219 C greg.sethares@bristolcc.edu
SETHRE-HOFSTAD, Lisa 218-299-3455 241 K sethre@cord.edu
SETLAK, Tressa, A ... 240-895-4911 206 G tasetlak@smcm.edu
SETLEY, David, M ... 717-867-6104 399 J setley@lvc.edu
SETMEYER, Adam ... 317-955-6131 162 R asetmeyer@marian.edu
SETTELE, Jim, D ... 207-581-1512 201 B james.settele@maine.edu
SETTER, Paul, W ... 972-708-7321 449 I accounting@gial.edu
SETTERGREN, Jennifer ... 616-957-6675 228 C jsetterg@calvinseminary.edu
SETTERLIND, Sharon ... 727-341-4677 107 A setterlind.sharon@spcollege.edu
SETTLE, Jim, S ... 336-334-5099 351 D jssettle@uncg.edu
SETTLES, Monica ... 406-756-3801 271 A msettles@fvcc.edu
SETTOON, Paula ... 918-595-7728 380 D paula.settoon@tulsacc.edu
SETZER, Jason ... 336-249-8186 342 F jason_setzer@davidsonccc.edu
SETZER, Kristen ... 704-406-3973 337 H ksetzer@gardner-webb.edu
SETZER, Pat ... 619-660-4226.. 44 L pat.setzer@gcccd.edu
SETZER, Patrick, K ... 828-262-3002 349 H setzerpk@appstate.edu
SETZER, Tim, W ... 409-944-1365 449 F tsetzer@gc.edu
SEUFERLING, Dale ... 785-832-7400 181 I dseuferling@kuendowment.org
SEUFERT, Kyle ... 620-431-2820 180 C kseufert@neosho.edu
SEUFFERLEIN, Catherine ... 402-363-5614 278 E cseufferlein@york.edu

SEUMANUTAFA, Loligi .. 684-699-9155 519 F
l.siaki@amsamoa.edu
SEUNARINE, Patricia ..... 302-736-2385.. 90 J
patricia.seunarine@wesley.edu
SEVASTOS, Charlie, W .. 386-323-8812.. 98 C
sevastoc@erau.edu
SEVER, Dennis .... 432-685-4690 453 B
dsever@midland.edu
SEVERANCE, Dana, A .... 301-687-4121 209 A
dseverance@frostburg.edu
SEVERANCE, Mary Ellen 508-793-7478 213 C
meseverance@clarku.edu
SEVERINO, Dan .... 215-596-8793 413 E
d.severino@usciences.edu
SEVERINO, Kristy .... 860-768-5403.. 89 C
kseverino@hartford.edu
SEVERINO-VALDEZ,
Carlos, E .... 787-764-0000 527 D
carlos.severino@upr.edu
SEVERNS, Mel .... 740-392-6868 366 B
mel.severns@mvnu.edu
SEVERS, Doug .... 541-737-2241 385 F
financial.aid@oregonstate.edu
SEVERSON, Christopher 715-675-3331 514 F
seversonc@ntc.edu
SEVERSON, Mark, W ..... 716-878-6434 326 E
seversmw@buffalostate.edu
SEVERSON, Sheila .... 608-796-3001 512 R
smseverson@viterbo.edu
SEVERSON, Stacy .... 612-244-2800 242 H
sseverson@ipr.edu
SEVERSON, Tim .... 641-585-8174 174 B
tim.severson@waldorf.edu
SEVERTIS, JR.,
Ronald, E .... 812-941-2148 161 A
rseverti@ius.edu
SEVERY, Lisa .... 303-492-6541.. 83 B
lisa.severy@colorado.edu
SEVICK, Leona .... 540-828-5608 478 J
lsevick@bridgewater.edu
SEVIER, Karen .... 603-752-1060 281 B
ksevier@ccsnh.edu
SEVIG, Todd, D .... 734-764-8312 237 I
tdsevig@umich.edu
SEVILLA, Henry .... 787-780-0070 521 B
hsevilla@caribbean.edu
SEWARD, Alison .... 603-526-3715 280 H
alison.seward@colby-sawyer.edu
SEWARD, David .... 415-565-4710.. 68 I
sewardd@uchastings.edu
SEWARD, David .... 479-788-7093.. 22 A
david.seward@uafs.edu
SEWART, John, J .... 650-574-6196.. 62 A
sewart@smccd.edu
SEWELL, Debbie .... 502-863-8000 184 I
SEWELL, Devona .... 352-854-2322.. 97 C
sewelld@cf.edu
SEWELL, Gary .... 423-236-2700 436 C
garysewell@southern.edu
SEWELL, Holly .... 580-559-5203 375 I
hsewell@ecok.edu
SEWELL, Jason .... 423-472-7141 436 G
jsewell@clevelandstatecc.edu
SEWELL, Jenny .... 256-306-2542.... 1 F
jenny.sewell@calhoun.edu
SEWELL, John .... 601-974-1019 254 A
seweljl@millsaps.edu
SEWELL, Keli .... 864-977-7733 422 I
keli.sewell@ngu.edu
SEWELL, Kenneth .... 405-744-6501 377 F
kenneth.sewell@okstate.edu
SEWELL, Lisa .... 610-519-4646 413 K
lisa.sewell@villanova.edu
SEWELL, Robert .... 760-245-4271.. 73 E
robert.sewell@vvc.edu
SEWELL, Sara .... 757-455-3237 491 F
ssewell@vwu.edu
SEWELL, Shannon .... 731-989-6051 432 C
ssewell@fhu.edu
SEWELL, Teresa .... 432-552-2600 469 D
sewell_t@utpb.edu
SEWELL, Thomas, R ...... 423-585-2644 438 D
thomas.sewell@ws.edu
SEWELL, Zennabelle ...... 212-261-1682 317 G
zsewell@nyit.edu
SEWELL-ALLEN,
Cornelia .... 570-422-3798 406 A
csewell@esu.edu
SEXTON, Clarence .... 865-938-8186 431 C
SEXTON, Colleen .... 708-534-3958 138 H
csexton@govst.edu
SEXTON, Gary .... 330-941-1778 374 E
sexton@wysu.org
SEXTON, Glenna, W .... 970-247-7331.. 79 J
sexton_g@fortlewis.edu
SEXTON, M. Shannon ... 865-938-8186 431 C
SEXTON, Michele, D ..... 620-235-4187 180 J
msexton@pittstate.edu
SEXTON, Mike, B .... 408-554-5251.. 62 F
mbsexton@scu.edu
SEXTON, Steve .... 615-248-7792 439 B
ssexton@trevecca.edu
SEXTON, Susan, K .... 937-229-4333 372 A
ssexton1@udayton.edu
SEXTON, Timothy .... 636-584-6698 259 L
timothy.sexton@eastcentral.edu
SEXTON, Timothy, D ..... 574-631-1785 165 A
sexton.30@nd.edu
SEXTON-JOHNSON,
Sara .... 509-533-8486 493 H
ssexton-johnson@ccs.spokane.edu
SEYB, Ronald .... 518-580-5725 324 D
rseyb@skidmore.edu
SEYDEL, Tim .... 541-962-3740 383 B
tseydel@eou.edu
SEYERLE, Amy .... 626-529-8007.. 55 C
aseyerle@pacificoaks.edu
SEYMOUR, Avanti .... 617-449-7041 225 C
avanti.seymour@urbancollege.edu
SEYMOUR, Dennis .... 815-939-5302 148 F
dseymour@olivet.edu
SEYMOUR, Heather, B ... 207-755-5248 199 K
hseymour@cmcc.edu
SEYMOUR, Jodi, L .... 641-784-5112 169 D
seymour@graceland.edu
SEYMOUR, Mark .... 330-471-8145 364 H
mseymour@malone.edu
SEYMOUR, Michael .... 218-733-7600 245 C
michael.seymour@lsc.edu
SEYMOUR, Sharon .... 217-479-7025 144 I
sharon.seymour@mac.edu
SEYMOUR, William .... 423-478-6200 436 G
wseymour@clevelandstatecc.edu
SGANGA, Fred .... 631-444-8606 325 F
fred.sganga@stonybrook.edu
SHAAB, Jane .... 410-706-8282 207 H
jshaab@umaryland.edu
SHAABAN-MAGANA,
Lamea .... 205-348-5040.... 8 A
lshaaban@sa.ua.edu
SHAAK, Melissa, J .... 781-239-4398 211 A
shaak@babson.edu
SHABAHANG, Homa ..... 909-593-3511.. 70 E
hshabahang@laverne.edu
SHABAZZ, David .... 502-597-5915 187 E
david.shabazz@kysu.edu
SHABAZZ, Hamin .... 432-837-8134 462 G
SHABAZZ, Ricky .... 619-388-3400.. 60 C
SHABAZZ, Ricky .... 909-384-8992.. 59 I
rshabazz@sbccd.cc.ca.us
SHABAZZI, Mohammad 601-979-8806 253 E
mohammad.shabazzi@jsums.edu
SHABLIA, Nataliia .... 215-572-2887 389 D
shablian@arcadia.edu
SHABLIN, Steven, J .... 248-370-3470 235 J
shablin@oakland.edu
SHABLOSKI, Regan .... 814-866-6641 399 C
rshabloski@lecom.edu
SHACHAR, Mickey .... 714-816-0366.. 67 J
mickey.shachar@trident.edu
SHACHTER, Amy, M ...... 408-551-7041.. 62 F
ashachter@scu.edu
SHACK, Robert, B .... 423-778-6956 440 C
rshack@uthsc.edu
SHACKELFORD, Carol ... 601-635-2111 252 I
cshackelford@eccc.edu
SHACKELFORD, Harper . 910-678-8413 343 B
shackelh@faytechcc.edu
SHACKELFORD, Judy ..... 217-814-5448 151 B
SHACKELFORD, Philip ... 870-864-7116.. 21 D
pshackelford@southark.edu
SHACKLEFORD,
Douglas .... 919-962-1300 351 B
douglas_shackelford@kenan-flagler.unc.edu
SHACKLEFORD, Keith .... 949-451-5398.. 64 I
kshackleford@ivc.edu
SHACKLEFORD,
Michael, M .... 757-823-9067 483 F
mmshackleford@nsu.edu
SHACKLEFORD, JR.,
Robert, S .... 336-633-0287 345 F
rsshackleford@randolph.edu
SHADDY, Deborah .... 913-758-6143 182 B
shaddy15@stmary.edu
SHADE-DAVISON,
Stephanie .... 580-745-2267 379 J
sdavison@se.edu
SHADELL, Vicki .... 501-977-2189.. 23 B
shadell@uaccm.edu
SHADER, Gail .... 518-828-4181 305 D
gail.shader@sunycgcc.edu
SHADICK, Richard .... 212-346-1526 319 J
rshadick@pace.edu
SHADLE, Joseph, P .... 513-745-3570 374 D
shadlej@xavier.edu
SHADLE, Julie .... 848-932-2207 290 A
julie.shadle@ruf.rutgers.edu
SHADOIAN, Holly, L ...... 401-456-8884 417 A
hshadoian@ric.edu
SHAFER, Barb .... 406-657-2301 272 B
bshafer@msubillings.edu
SHAFER, Jack, L .... 610-499-4454 414 F
jlshafer@widener.edu
SHAFER, Jeff, S .... 336-256-0226 351 D
jsshafer@uncg.edu
SHAFER, John, R .... 317-738-8080 157 L
jshafer@franklincollege.edu
SHAFER, Kathrynne, G .. 717-691-6003 401 L
kshafer@messiah.edu
SHAFER, Lisa .... 610-328-8009 410 I
lshafer1@swarthmore.edu
SHAFER, Lisa .... 530-541-4660.. 47 I
shaferl@ltcc.edu
SHAFER, Pamela .... 832-559-4217 452 C
pamela.n.shafer@lonestar.edu
SHAFER, Richard .... 214-768-1580 457 B
rashafer@smu.edu
SHAFER, Staci .... 618-985-3741 141 D
stacishafer@jalc.edu
SHAFER, Teresa .... 419-448-3309 370 K
tshafer@tiffin.edu
SHAFER, Trish .... 610-660-3101 409 H
pshafer@sju.edu
SHAFFER, Alan .... 740-392-6868 366 B
alan.shaffer@mvnu.edu
SHAFFER, Amy .... 912-443-5512 125 D
ashaffer@savannahtech.edu
SHAFFER, Brian, W .... 901-843-3976 435 L
shaffer@rhodes.edu
SHAFFER, Chris .... 415-476-3769.. 70 A
chris.shaffer@ucsf.edu
SHAFFER, Chris .... 334-983-6556.... 7 E
shafferc@troy.edu
SHAFFER, Chris .... 334-670-3266.... 7 E
shafferc@troy.edu
SHAFFER, Chris .... 941-359-7616 106 H
cshaffer@ringling.edu
SHAFFER, Chris .... 503-494-6057 385 D
library@ohsu.edu
SHAFFER, Christopher ... 740-351-3207 369 L
cshaffer@shawnee.edu
SHAFFER, David .... 567-661-2625 369 A
david_shaffer5@owens.edu
SHAFFER, Deborah .... 740-593-2555 368 G
shafferd@ohio.edu
SHAFFER, Germaine ...... 606-487-3091 185 J
germaine.shaffer@kctcs.edu
SHAFFER, Germaine ...... 606-487-3409 185 J
germaine.shaffer@kctcs.edu
SHAFFER, James, M ..... 330-471-8515 364 H
jshaffer@malone.edu
SHAFFER, Jamie .... 615-794-4254 435 G
jshaffer@omorecollege.edu
SHAFFER, Janette .... 802-828-0124 477 B
jxs08240@ccv.vsc.edu
SHAFFER, Jason, S .... 704-894-2188 337 B
jashaffer@davidson.edu
SHAFFER, John .... 304-829-7394 501 F
jshaffer@bethanywv.edu
SHAFFER, Jon, L .... 618-453-1069 152 B
jonshaffer@siu.edu
SHAFFER, Jyl .... 406-994-5326 272 A
jyl.shaffer@montana.edu
SHAFFER, Kelli .... 254-968-9050 459 A
shaffer@tarleton.edu
SHAFFER, Kent .... 479-631-4665.. 20 B
kshaffer@jbu.edu
SHAFFER, Ruth, E .... 309-692-4092 145 F
rshaffer@midstate.edu
SHAFFER, Steven, E ...... 716-878-6034 326 E
shaffese@buffalostate.edu
SHAFFER, Vicky .... 410-857-2254 205 E
vshaffer@mcdaniel.edu
SHAFFER, Virginia .... 630-752-5623 155 F
virginia.shaffer@wheaton.edu
SHAFFER, W. Michael ... 706-721-4413 116 B
wshaffer@augusta.edu
SHAFFER, Wade .... 806-651-2931 460 E
wshaffer@mail.wtamu.edu
SHAFFER, Wendy .... 978-556-3858 220 F
wshaffer@necc.mass.edu
SHAFFER, Yvette .... 505-984-6060 295 K
admissions@sjc.edu
SHAFFER LILIENTHAL,
Robin .... 641-844-5730 170 G
robin.lilienthal@iavalley.edu
SHAFFER LILIENTHAL,
Robin .... 641-844-5730 170 I
robin.lilienthal@iavalley.edu
SHAFFETT, John, E .... 850-263-3261.. 95 F
jeshaffett@baptistcollege.edu
SHAFFNER, Donna .... 315-792-3111 332 H
dlshaffner@utica.edu
SHAFKOWITZ, Marshall 773-602-5501 135 L
mshafkowitz@ccc.edu
SHAFTEL, Matthew .... 740-593-1808 368 G
shaftel@ohio.edu
SHAFTEL, Matthew, R .... 609-921-7100 289 E
mshaftel@rider.edu
SHAFTO, Carissa .... 502-410-6200 184 H
cshafto@galencollege.edu
SHAGER, Dorian .... 765-658-4267 157 H
dshager@depauw.edu
SHAH, Gaurav .... 781-891-3467 212 A
gshah@bentley.edu
SHAH, Kashif .... 708-974-5348 146 C
shah@morainevalley.edu
SHAH, Priyank .... 507-285-7263 247 D
priyank.shah@rctc.edu
SHAH, Sadiq .... 909-869-3898.. 31 A
sayedshah@cpp.edu
SHAH-GORDON, Ruta ... 718-420-4254 333 D
rshahgor@wagner.edu
SHAHAN, J. Michael ..... 409-882-3314 462 D
mike.shahan@lsco.edu
SHAHEDIPOUR-SANDVIK,
Shadi .... 315-792-7100 330 A
sshahedipour-sandvik@sunypoly.edu
SHAHEED-SONUBI,
Taheera .... 716-851-1773 307 I
shaheed@ecc.edu
SHAHEEN, Greg, A .... 765-361-6105 166 B
shaheeng@wabash.edu
SHAHI, Manvinder .... 650-289-3336.. 59 D
manvinder.shahi@stpatricksseminary.org
SHAHID, Abdus .... 503-838-9331 388 B
shahida@wou.edu
SHAHID, Charles .... 937-376-6081 358 I
cshahid@centralstate.edu
SHAHID, Julia .... 903-813-2457 443 F
sshahid@austincollege.edu
SHAHIN, Hamdi .... 201-559-6076 286 C
shahinh@felician.edu
SHAHIN, Wisam .... 201-559-6058 286 C
shahinw@felician.edu
SHAHROKHI, Hossein ... 713-221-8542 465 C
shahrokhi@uhd.edu
SHAIKH, Usama .... 516-876-3175 327 C
shaikhu@oldwestbury.edu
SHAILEY, Timothy .... 215-503-1295 411 E
timothy.shailey@jefferson.edu
SHAILOR, Robert .... 360-596-5292 498 G
rshailor@spscc.edu
SHAIN, Sue .... 978-556-3710 220 F
sshain@necc.mass.edu
SHAIN, Yeruchim .... 732-431-1600 292 A
taofnj@gmail.com
SHAKE, Miranda .... 217-709-0927 143 C
mshake@lakeviewcol.edu
SHAKESPEARE,
Christine .... 212-346-1200 319 J
SHAKIR, Salah .... 859-846-6248 188 B
sshakir@midway.edu
SHAKLEE, Ronald .... 330-941-4740 374 E
rshaklee@ysu.edu
SHALLEY, Heather .... 312-329-4272 146 B
heather.shalley@moody.edu
SHALLMAN, Emily .... 415-351-3531.. 60 G
eshallman@sfai.edu
SHAMAH, Irwin .... 347-394-1036 299 G
ishamah@ateret.net
SHAMASH, Yacov .... 631-632-8380 325 F
yacov.shamash@stonybrook.edu
SHAMBAUGH, Jeannine 330-363-5420 357 A
jeannine.shambaugh@aultman.com
SHAMIM, Jina .... 415-476-8850.. 70 A
jina.shamim@ucsf.edu
SHAMOO, Yousif .... 713-348-5741 455 F
shamoo@rice.edu
SHAMP, Scott .... 850-644-1390 110 A
sshamp@fsu.edu
SHAMPINE, Memorie, L 315-386-7042 329 A
shampinem@canton.edu
SHAMS, Arian .... 714-300-0300.. 65 B
ashams@scitech.edu
SHAMS, Nazila .... 714-300-0300.. 65 B
nshams@scitech.edu
SHAMS, Parviz .... 714-300-0300.. 65 B
pshams@scitech.edu
SHANAFELT, Rebecca .... 727-816-3288 105 C
shanafr@phsc.edu
SHANAHAN, Alanna .... 410-516-7490 204 F
ashanah1@jhu.edu
SHANAHAN, Catherine .. 660-248-6221 258 B
cshanahan@centralmethodist.edu
SHANAHAN, James .... 812-855-1963 159 H
jes30@indiana.edu
SHANAHAN, Jenny .... 508-531-2764 217 D
jshanahan@bridgew.edu

SHANAHAN, TOR, John 740-283-6403 361 L jshanahan@franciscan.edu
SHANAHAN, Michael 805-652-5512 72 G mshanahan@vcccd.edu
SHANAHAN, Thomas 919-962-4588 349 G tcshanahan@northcarolina.edu
SHANBLATT, Stephanie 215-968-8222 390 I stephanie.shanblatt@bucks.edu
SHANDA, Mark 859-257-1707 190 B mark.shanda@uky.edu
SHANDERSON, Laurie 928-541-7777 54 B lshanderson@ncu.edu
SHANDLEY, Janet 206-296-5904 498 D janshan@seattleu.edu
SHANDLEY, Thomas, C 704-894-2225 337 B toshandley@davidson.edu
SHANE, Pam 740-284-5193 361 L pshane@franciscan.edu
SHANER, Carl, L 570-326-3761 404 T cshaner@pct.edu
SHANER, Megan, L 919-209-2201 344 C mlshaner@johnstoncc.edu
SHANGLE, Max, S 312-939-4975 139 C mshangle@harrington.edu
SHANGRAW, Rick 480-965-7393 10 K rick.shangraw@asu.edu
SHANHOLTZ, Cathy 540-665-5561 485 C cshanhol2@su.edu
SHANK, Christy 254-526-1291 445 L christy.shank@ctcd.edu
SHANK, David 202-885-8624 94 C dshank@wesleyseminary.edu
SHANK, Harold 304-865-6003 502 C harold.shank@ovu.edu
SHANK, Jeffrey, A 540-432-4206 480 A jeff.shank@emu.edu
SHANK, Jennifer 931-372-3124 438 F jshank@tntech.edu
SHANK, Larry, L 740-826-6109 366 C lshank@muskingum.edu
SHANK, Leanne, M 540-458-8940 491 G lshank@wlu.edu
SHANK, Matthew, D 703-284-1598 483 A matthew.shank@marymount.edu
SHANK, Sherri 704-233-8025 353 D s.shank@wingate.edu
SHANK, Steve 704-233-8691 353 D sh.shank@wingate.edu
SHANK, Theresa, M 240-500-2000 204 B tmshank@hagerstowncc.edu
SHANKEL, James, V 412-578-6258 391 G jvshankel@carlow.edu
SHANKLE, Nicole 812-888-4182 165 E nshankle@vinu.edu
SHANKLIN, Carol 785-532-7927 179 A shanklin@ksu.edu
SHANKLIN, Iris 404-756-4916 115 I ishanklin@atlm.edu
SHANKMAN, Kimberly, C 913-360-7413 175 D kshankman@benedictine.edu
SHANKS, Alisa 303-963-3378 77 I ashanks@ccu.edu
SHANKS, Brian 512-245-2319 463 A bs26@txstate.edu
SHANKS, Carol 314-918-2538 260 A cshanks@eden.edu
SHANKS, Chris 434-528-5276 491 D cshanks@vul.edu
SHANKS, Francesca 413-662-5263 218 C f.shanks@mcla.edu
SHANKWEILER, Jean 310-660-3119 42 C jshankweiler@elcamino.edu
SHANLEY, OP, Brian, J 401-865-2153 416 E nkelley@providence.edu
SHANLEY, Deborah 718-960-8401 302 C deborah.shanley@lehman.cuny.edu
SHANLEY, Mark 870-850-3121 21 E mshanley@seark.edu
SHANMUGARATNAM, Carol 781-283-2308 225 D cshanmug@wellesley.edu
SHANNON, David 405-585-5249 377 A david.shannon@okbu.edu
SHANNON, David, R 731-989-6001 432 C dshannon@fhu.edu
SHANNON, Denise 313-496-2744 238 H dshanno1@wcccd.edu
SHANNON, Henry, D 909-652-6100 36 E henry.shannon@chaffey.edu
SHANNON, John, F 260-422-5561 159 D dfshannon@indianatech.edu
SHANNON, John, T 973-655-4214 287 D shannonj@mail.montclair.edu
SHANNON, Larry 484-365-7470 400 E lshannon@lincoln.edu
SHANNON, Linda, A 718-990-6578 322 F shannonl@stjohns.edu
SHANNON, Mike 956-295-3649 461 F mike.shannon@tsc.edu
SHANNON, Patricia 610-359-2183 393 E pshannon@dccc.edu
SHANNON, Richard, P 434-924-1082 486 H rs3mt@virginia.edu
SHANNON, Scott, S 315-470-6537 328 D sshannon@esf.edu
SHANNON, Susan, K 717-796-1800 401 L sshannon@messiah.edu
SHANNON, Tracey 334-876-9277 2 C tracey.shannon@wccs.edu
SHANNON, Vanessa 707-778-3930 62 H vshannon@santarosa.edu
SHANTON, David 646-660-6067 301 B david.shanton@baruch.cuny.edu
SHAO, Alan, T 843-953-6651 420 C shaoa@cofc.edu
SHAO, Lawrence 724-738-2093 407 C lawrence.shao@sru.edu
SHAPE, Ronald 605-721-5214 427 G rshape@national.edu
SHAPIRO, Alex A, G 415-581-8842 68 I shaprioa@uchastings.edu
SHAPIRO, Claire, R 901-843-3750 435 L shapiro@rhodes.edu
SHAPIRO, David, W 717-867-6060 399 J shapiro@lvc.edu
SHAPIRO, Jeff 973-877-3142 285 K shapiro@essex.edu
SHAPIRO, Joe 619-594-5822 34 B jshapiro@mail.sdsu.edu
SHAPIRO, Jonathan 641-472-1241 171 J jshapiro@mum.edu
SHAPIRO, Joseph, I 304-691-1700 504 C shapiroj@marshall.edu
SHAPIRO, Steven 617-349-8458 216 D sshapir3@lesley.edu
SHAPIRO, Susan 718-940-5696 322 G sshapiro@sjcny.edu
SHAPIRO, Tracie 502-863-8149 184 I tracie_shapiro@georgetowncollege.edu
SHAPIRO DAVIS, Andrea 646-664-9025 301 A andrea.davis@cuny.edu
SHAPLEIGH, Shari 607-844-8222 331 D shaples@tompkinscortland.edu
SHAPOVAL, Sandy 918-270-6459 378 I sandy.shapoval@ptstulsa.edu
SHARAR, Bill 510-659-6524 54 F wsharar@ohlone.edu
SHARAR, Scott 319-352-8318 174 C scott.sharar@wartburg.edu
SHARBAUGH, Catherine 610-896-1089 397 F csharbau@haverford.edu
SHARBAUGH, Sheila, M 302-356-3917 91 B sheila.m.sharbaugh@wilmu.edu
SHARBAUGH, Tim, L 724-357-3011 406 C timothy.sharbaugh@iup.edu
SHARER, C. Gregory 607-753-4721 327 A greg.sharer@cortland.edu
SHARER, Jack 502-895-3411 188 A jsharer@lpts.edu
SHARER, Mark 570-577-3914 390 H mark.sharer@bucknell.edu
SHARFMAN, Glenn 404-364-8318 124 A gsharfman@oglethorpe.edu
SHARIAT, Vahid 714-816-0366 67 J vahid.shariat@trident.edu
SHARIF, Zaki 937-376-6007 358 I zsharif@centralstate.edu
SHARIFIAN, Chitra 425-739-8344 495 F chitra.sharifian@lwtech.edu
SHARIK, Scott, A 419-358-3377 357 E shariks@bluffton.edu
SHARIK, Terry 906-487-2352 234 A tlsharik@mtu.edu
SHARKEY, Brian 563-884-5306 172 H brian.sharkey@palmer.edu
SHARKEY, Marty 323-259-2500 54 E msharkey@oxy.edu
SHARKEY, Melissa 641-628-5180 167 D sharkeym@central.edu
SHARKEY, Neil, A 814-865-6332 403 F nas9@psu.edu
SHARMA, Gulshan 409-772-2436 469 C gusharma@utmb.edu
SHARMA, Madhav, P 570-389-4831 405 E msharma@bloomu.edu
SHARMA, Pradeep 401-277-4945 417 B psharma@risd.edu
SHARMA, Sanjay 802-656-3175 476 E sanjay.sharma@uvm.edu
SHARMA, Venkat 607-436-2125 325 E venkat.sharma@oneonta.edu
SHARMA, Vivek 213-252-5100 24 A vharma@alu.edu
SHARMAN, Angel 307-268-2667 516 H asharman@caspercollege.edu
SHARON, Anthony, P 617-324-7130 221 C
SHARON, Daniel 914-632-5400 315 K dsharon@monroecollege.edu
SHARP, Andrew 601-477-4198 253 F andrew.sharp@jcjc.edu
SHARP, David 870-245-5181 20 G sharpd@obu.edu
SHARP, Debbie 940-668-4213 453 L dsharp@nctc.edu
SHARP, Deltha 870-368-2007 20 H dshell@ozarka.edu
SHARP, Diane 910-221-2224 338 A dsharp@gcd.edu
SHARP, George, T 954-545-4500 108 A
SHARP, Jan, T 865-539-7182 437 F jtsharp@pstcc.edu
SHARP, Jason, R 651-631-5045 251 C jrsharp@unwsp.edu
SHARP, John 979-458-6000 458 E chancellor@tamus.edu
SHARP, Jordan 435-652-7544 473 B jsharp@dixie.edu
SHARP, Kelvin 575-392-5004 294 L ksharp@nmjc.edu
SHARP, Kimberly 601-925-3278 254 B ksharp@mc.edu
SHARP, Les, M 920-932-8762 508 B lmsharp08@marianuniversity.edu
SHARP, Linda 573-876-7277 267 G lsharp@stephens.edu
SHARP, Marion 253-864-3212 497 B msharpe@pierce.ctc.edu
SHARP, Melody 434-200-7025 478 N melody.sharp@centrahealth.com
SHARP, Nick 417-690-2224 258 E sharp@cofo.edu
SHARP, Nicole 812-749-1225 163 B nsharp@oak.edu
SHARP, Peggy 970-247-7010 79 J sharp_p@fortlewis.edu
SHARP, Randy 808-675-3499 128 K randy.sharp@byuh.edu
SHARP, Shayna 208-535-5389 131 G shayna.sharp@my.eitc.edu
SHARP, Valerie 417-865-2815 260 B sharpv@evangel.edu
SHARPE, Allan 915-532-3737 470 L asharpe@westerntech.edu
SHARPE, Aubrey, D 903-510-2901 464 D asha@tjc.edu
SHARPE, Gary 678-359-5333 121 B garys@gordonstate.edu
SHARPE, Jessica, G 336-272-7102 338 B jessica.sharpe@greensboro.edu
SHARPE, Karen 508-929-8786 219 A karen.sharpe@worcester.edu
SHARPE, Kelli 615-963-1232 438 E ksharpe@tnstate.edu
SHARPE, Norean, R 718-990-6800 322 F sharpen@stjohns.edu
SHARPE, Patricia 413-528-7240 211 B psharpe@simons-rock.edu
SHARPE, Rick 602-386-4104 10 G rick.sharpe@arizonachristian.edu
SHARPE, Ron 989-275-5000 232 E ron.sharpe@kirtland.edu
SHARPE, Shane 205-348-5506 8 A ssharpe@ua.edu
SHARPHORN, Dan 512-499-4563 467 A dsharphorn@utsystem.edu
SHARPLES, Stacey 941-752-5256 108 P sharpls@scf.edu
SHARPNACK, Patricia 440-684-6032 373 B psharpnack@ursuline.edu
SHARPS, Alonia, C 301-546-0170 206 E sharpsac@pgcc.edu
SHARRAR, Jack 415-439-2412 25 J jsharrar@act-sf.org
SHARRATT, Emily 541-962-3866 383 B esharratt@eou.edu
SHASTEEN, C. Scott 931-393-1605 437 C sshasteen@mscc.edu
SHATTUCK, Debra 605-342-0317 427 C dshattuck@johnwitherspooncollege.org
SHATTUCK, Larry 410-532-5551 206 D lshattuck@ndm.edu
SHATTUCK, Leslie 425-739-8236 495 F leslie.shattuck@lwtech.edu
SHATTUCK, Wendy 909-748-8046 71 H wendy_shattuck@redlands.edu
SHAUB, Larry 610-796-8298 389 A larry.shaub@alvernia.edu
SHAUGHNESSY, Anne 617-824-8525 214 E anne_shaughnessy@emerson.edu
SHAUGHNESSY, Elizabeth 650-433-3838 55 I eshaughnessy@paloaltou.edu
SHAUGHNESSY, Joseph 781-768-7133 224 A joseph.shaughnessy@regiscollege.edu
SHAUGHNESSY, Joseph 254-659-7821 450 B jxs@hillcollege.edu
SHAUGHNESSY, Josette 915-831-6330 449 A jshaugh2@epcc.edu
SHAUGHNESSY, Mark 631-656-2147 308 F mark.shaughnessy@ftc.edu
SHAUGHNESSY, Michael 724-503-1001 414 A mshaughnessy@washjeff.edu
SHAUL, Lesa 205-652-3460 9 C lcc@uwa.edu
SHAUNAK, Raj 662-243-1911 253 A rshaunak@eastms.edu
SHAUNAK, Sudershan 760-757-2121 52 F sshaunak@miracosta.edu
SHAVER, Deborah 208-885-4627 132 I dshaver@uidaho.edu
SHAVER, Debra, D 413-585-2523 224 F dshaver@smith.edu
SHAVER, Joan, L 520-626-6152 16 J jshaver@email.arizona.edu
SHAVER, Joseph, E 304-326-1481 502 D jshaver@salemu.edu
SHAW, Anita 210-297-7638 443 K aashaw@baptisthealthsystem.com
SHAW, Anne, C 910-938-6322 342 C shawa@coastalcarolina.edu
SHAW, Becky 413-585-4940 224 F rshaw@smith.edu
SHAW, Benjamin 207-762-0146 201 G benjamin.shaw@maine.edu
SHAW, Brandy 713-525-2124 466 J shawb1@stthom.edu
SHAW, Brian, D 804-828-1200 487 E bdshaw@vcu.edu
SHAW, Brian, R 301-243-2115 518 C brian.shaw@dodiis.mil
SHAW, Carolyn 661-259-7800 39 C carolyn.shaw@canyons.edu
SHAW, Carrie 970-943-7015 84 E cshaw@western.edu
SHAW, Carrie 425-235-2415 497 E cshaw@rtc.edu
SHAW, Chester 708-974-5360 146 C schawc6@morainevalley.edu
SHAW, Chip 806-743-1500 463 E chip.shaw@ttuhsc.edu
SHAW, Dameon 662-254-3790 255 A dameon.shaw@mvsu.edu
SHAW, Darlene, L 843-792-2228 422 C shawd@musc.edu
SHAW, David 662-325-3570 254 E dshaw@research.msstate.edu
SHAW, Deborah, L 256-765-5018 9 A dshaw2@una.edu
SHAW, Douglas, B 202-994-0514 92 A dbs@gwu.edu
SHAW, Erin 785-442-6003 178 C eshaw@highlandcc.edu
SHAW, Gordon 580-581-2245 375 A gshaw@cameron.edu
SHAW, J. Brandon 540-868-7182 488 E jshaw@lfcc.edu
SHAW, James, A 606-783-2599 188 C j.shaw@moreheadstate.edu
SHAW, Jane 650-723-1762 66 C
SHAW, Jen, D 352-392-1261 110 D jends@dso.ufl.edu
SHAW, Jerone 662-621-4085 252 E jshaw@coahomacc.edu
SHAW, John 214-333-5870 447 D johns@dbu.edu
SHAW, Karen, A 585-262-1501 315 L kshaw@monroecc.edu
SHAW, Karen, D 740-446-4367 362 C director@gallipoliscareercollege.edu
SHAW, Kathleen 804-828-6683 487 E kshaw5@vcu.edu
SHAW, Ken 817-202-6202 457 E kshaw@swau.edu
SHAW, Kerrie, S 757-446-5841 480 C shawks@evms.edu
SHAW, Kevin 909-469-5401 74 G kshaw@westernu.edu
SHAW, Kristi 620-441-5206 176 M kristi.shaw@cowley.edu
SHAW, Linda 480-732-7307 13 E linda.shaw@cgc.edu
SHAW, Linda 415-239-3303 37 H lshaw@ccsf.edu
SHAW, Lori 620-331-2480 178 E lshaw@indycc.edu

SHAW, Marc 646-664-3013 301 A marc.shaw@cuny.edu
SHAW, Mary Ann 713-942-5036 466 J shawme@sthom.edu
SHAW, Matthew 765-285-5277 156 C mcshaw2@bsu.edu
SHAW, Nancy 802-224-3000 476 H nancy.shaw@vsc.edu
SHAW, P. Gerard 508-541-1790 214 C pshaw@dean.edu
SHAW, Patricia 860-727-2073 87 B pshaw@goodwin.edu
SHAW, Penelope 707-826-3942 34 A pjs25@humboldt.edu
SHAW, Richard 650-723-2300 66 C
SHAW, Richard 806-291-1162 470 I shawr@wbu.edu
SHAW, Rick 661-722-6300 26 C rshaw@avc.edu
SHAW, Robert, S 570-348-6245 401 B rsshaw@marywood.edu
SHAW, Russell 601-857-3961 253 B rdshaw@hindscc.edu
SHAW, Steve 937-769-1881 356 G sshaw@antioch.edu
SHAW, Suzanne 417-836-5139 263 H suzanneshaw@missouristate.edu
SHAW, Teresa 909-602-2505 57 I teresa.shaw@pomona.edu
SHAW, Timothy 972-883-5291 467 D tim.shaw@utdallas.edu
SHAW, Tina 256-378-2010 1 G thsaw5@cacc.edu
SHAW, Tom 269-965-3931 232 A shawt@kellogg.edu
SHAW-BURNETT, Margaret, A 716-878-5907 326 E shawma@buffalostate.edu
SHAW HORTON, Sheila 781-283-2322 225 D shorton@wellesley.edu
SHAWCROFT, Sally 970-542-3151 81 A sally.shawcroft@morgancc.edu
SHAWKY, Hany, A 518-442-3300 324 G
SHAWN, Donna, S 913-627-4171 178 H dshawn@kckcc.edu
SHAWNEY, Lisa, L 603-513-1335 282 G lisa.shawney@granite.edu
SHAWVER, Jeffrey 304-647-6325 504 F jshawver@osteo.wvsom.edu
SHAWVER, William, G 513-529-9203 365 I shawvewg@miamioh.edu
SHAY, Carla, E 231-843-5942 239 D ceshay@westshore.edu
SHAY, Carrie 213-624-1200 42 N cshay@fidm.edu
SHAY, Chris 408-554-4300 62 F cshay@scu.edu
SHAY, Monique 657-278-8354 32 B mshay@fullerton.edu
SHAY, Pamela 614-947-6135 362 A pamela.shay@franklin.edu
SHAY, Patrick 612-436-7519 243 H pshay@msbcollege.edu
SHAY, Robert 573-882-2606 268 C shayr@missouri.edu
SHAY, Robert, S 303-492-7505 83 B robert.shay@colorado.edu
SHAY, William 323-563-4840 36 H williamshay@cdrewu.edu
SHAYLER, Todd 517-629-0305 226 G tmshayler@albion.edu
SHCHEGOL, Alex 718-522-9073 298 E ashchegol@asa.edu
SHCHEGOL, Alla 718-522-9073 298 E allchik1@asa.edu
SHEA, Bob 336-278-5428 337 G bshea@elon.edu
SHEA, Catherine 303-492-7896 83 B catherine.shea@colorado.edu
SHEA, Claire 603-623-0313 281 G claireshea@nhia.edu
SHEA, Diane 617-732-1604 214 F shead@emmanuel.edu
SHEA, Donna 617-353-5124 212 G dshea@bu.edu
SHEA, James, P 701-355-8100 355 K
SHEA, Jane 508-854-4358 220 G jshea@qcc.mass.edu
SHEA, Kevin, J 617-552-3252 212 E k.shea@bc.edu
SHEA, Missy 781-283-2335 225 D mshea@wellesley.edu
SHEA, Peter, J 518-442-4009 324 G pshea@albany.edu
SHEA, Rich, J 814-886-6474 402 E rshea@mtaloy.edu
SHEAFFER, Andrea 510-649-2465 44 J asheaffer@gtu.edu
SHEALEY, Monika 856-256-4751 289 H shealey@rowan.edu
SHEAR, Skip 660-944-2853 258 G sshear@conception.edu
SHEAR, Stephen 813-253-7014 101 M sshear2@hccfl.edu
SHEARD, Reed 805-565-7171 74 I rsheard@westmont.edu
SHEARD, Reed, L 805-565-7171 74 I rsheard@westmont.edu
SHEARED, Vanessa 209-946-2683 70 F vsheared@pacific.edu
SHEARER, Christine 406-657-2177 272 B c.shearercremean@msubillings.edu
SHEARER, Erik 707-256-7155 53 D eshearer@napavalley.edu
SHEARER, Liz 410-704-2451 209 C lshearer@towson.edu
SHEARER, Michelle 601-477-4039 253 F michele.shearer@jcjc.edu
SHEARER, Pam 601-318-6561 256 I pshearer@wmcarey.edu
SHEARN, Robert 716-827-2483 331 K shearnr@trocaire.edu
SHEARON, James 910-892-3178 338 D jshearon@heritagebiblecollege.edu
SHEARON, Randall 919-735-5151 347 E shearon@waynecc.edu
SHEARRILL, Charmagne 661-255-1050 29 F cshearrill@calarts.edu
SHEARS, III, George 704-334-6882 336 I gshears@charlottechristian.edu
SHEATS, Karen, A 302-356-6867 91 B karen.a.sheats@wilmu.edu
SHEBLE, Mary Ann 248-232-4512 235 D masheble@oaklandcc.edu
SHEBLE, Mary Ann 248-942-3214 235 D masheble@oaklandcc.edu
SHECKLER, Allyson 508-565-1724 224 H asheckler@stonehill.edu
SHEDD, Dawn 281-478-2779 455 L dawn.shedd@sjcd.edu
SHEDD, Jean, E 847-467-5456 148 C j-shedd@northwestern.edu
SHEDD, Louis 205-391-2359 3 E lshedd@sheltonstate.edu
SHEDRICK, Karen, R 601-877-6111 251 G karen@alcorn.edu
SHEEHAN, Bill 573-288-6395 259 E wsheehan@culver.edu
SHEEHAN, Diep 781-768-7078 224 A diep.sheehan@regiscollege.edu
SHEEHAN, Eugene 970-351-2817 83 F eugene.sheehan@unco.edu
SHEEHAN, Heather 701-224-5465 354 F heather.sheehan@bismarckstate.edu
SHEEHAN, James 508-999-8051 217 A jsheehan4@umassd.edu
SHEEHAN, Jerry 406-994-2525 272 A jsheehan@montana.edu
SHEEHAN, Ryan 803-323-3023 426 H sheehanr@winthrop.edu
SHEEHAN, Tim 801-957-2001 474 B tim.scheehan@slcc.edu
SHEEHAN, Timothy 651-213-4166 242 F tsheehan@hazeldenbettyford.edu
SHEEHY, Colette 434-924-3349 486 H cc@virginia.edu
SHEEHY, Harry 603-646-2465 281 C harry.sheehy@dartmouth.edu
SHEEHY, Matthew 781-736-4642 213 A sheehy@brandeis.edu
SHEEKS, Gina 706-507-8730 118 C sheeks_gina@columbusstate.edu
SHEELEY, Jonathan 920-206-2327 508 A jonathan.sheeley@mbu.edu
SHEELEY, Robert, G 203-392-6050 85 A sheeleyr1@southernct.edu
SHEELOR, Derrell 281-201-3800 93 B
SHEELOR, Derrell 281-949-1800 93 B
SHEELY, Deanna 612-659-6537 245 F deanna.sheely@minneapolis.edu
SHEERAN, Kate 415-503-6251 60 H lnickels@sfcm.edu
SHEERAN, Robert, M 513-745-2072 374 D sheeran@xavier.edu
SHEERAZI, Saji 718-281-5144 303 F ssheerazi@qcc.cuny.edu
SHEERER, Marilyn 910-962-3389 352 A sheererm@uncw.edu
SHEETS, Chad 651-423-8232 244 E chad.sheets@dctc.edu
SHEETS, Christine 740-593-4094 368 G sheetsch@ohio.edu
SHEETS, Helene 419-824-3965 364 G hsheets@lourdes.edu
SHEETS, Julie 573-518-2206 263 E jsheets@mineralarea.edu
SHEETS, Tami 740-245-7209 372 E tsheets@rio.edu
SHEETS, Tammy 276-944-6117 480 J tsheets@ehc.edu
SHEETZ, Ken 803-323-2275 426 H sheetzk@winthrop.edu
SHEETZ, Tracey 724-938-4404 405 F sheetz@calu.edu
SHEFCHIK, Thomas, J 920-433-4306 506 C thomas.shefchik@bellincollege.edu
SHEFFIELD, Bethany, D 814-641-3101 398 B sheffib@juniata.edu
SHEFFIELD, Christopher, R 716-286-8405 318 F crs@niagara.edu
SHEFFIELD, Roy, S 828-884-8312 335 L scotts@brevard.edu
SHEFFIELD, Vonne 478-301-2500 122 H sheffield_v@mercer.edu
SHEFFLETTE, Nancy, A 501-882-4581 17 M nashefflette@asub.edu
SHEHATA, Erika 610-399-2053 405 G eshehata@cheyney.edu
SHEHEANE, Dene 404-894-1238 120 A dene.sheheane@dev.gatech.edu
SHEIBLEY, Thomas, J 610-660-1325 409 H tsheible@sju.edu
SHEIKH, Ammad 410-532-5393 206 D asheikh@ndm.edu
SHEILLEY, Holly 859-233-8548 189 H hsheilley@transy.edu
SHEILS, Cathleen 315-460-3150 329 C cathleen.sheils@esc.edu
SHEIN, David 845-758-7454 298 I shein@bard.edu
SHELBURNE, Stephanie 818-785-2726 35 N stephanie.shelburne@casalomacollege.edu
SHELBY, Barbara 740-588-1315 374 G bshelby@zanestate.edu
SHELBY, Jane 907-786-4708 10 A njshelby@alaska.edu
SHELBY, Nicole 318-869-5146 191 C nshelby@centenary.edu
SHELDAHL, Tania 928-776-2128 17 G tania.sheldahl@yc.edu
SHELDEN, Deborah, L 906-487-3112 234 A dlassila@mtu.edu
SHELDON, Al 541-956-7440 386 G asheldon@roguecc.edu
SHELDON, Jane 308-865-8427 277 F sheldonj@unk.edu
SHELDON, Karen 859-371-9393 183 G ksheldon@beckfield.edu
SHELDON, Michael 207-221-4591 202 A msheldon@une.edu
SHELDON, Todd 402-363-5601 278 E tlsheldon@york.edu
SHELEK-FURBEE, Katherine 304-829-7189 501 F kshelek-furbee@bethanywv.edu
SHELL, Barbara, B 407-582-3219 113 F bshell@valenciacollege.edu
SHELL, Cathy 828-898-8740 339 B shell@lmc.edu
SHELL, Chandrea 423-461-8756 435 A chshell@milligan.edu
SHELL, Christina 734-487-2382 229 K cshell@emich.edu
SHELL, Martin 650-723-4186 66 C mshell@stanford.edu
SHELLABARGER, Roxanne 423-648-2416 435 M rshellabarger@richmont.edu
SHELLABARGER, Sheila, G 937-775-2685 374 B sheila.shellabarger@wright.edu
SHELLBERG, David 208-562-3257 132 A davidshellberg@cwidaho.cc
SHELLEDY, David, C 210-567-8850 468 E shelledyy@uthscsa.edu
SHELLEY, Daniel 585-475-6736 321 D drsadm@rit.edu
SHELLEY, Ena, M 317-940-9752 156 I eshelley@butler.edu
SHELLEY, Jeff 205-929-3416 2 G jshelley@lawsonstate.edu
SHELLEY, MargE 913-469-8500 178 F mshelley@jccc.edu
SHELLEY, Marshall 303-762-6919 79 G marshall.shelley@denverseminary.edu
SHELLEY, Stephen 940-397-4110 453 C stephen.shelley@mwsu.edu
SHELLLEY, Joe 315-859-4169 309 D jshelley@hamilton.edu
SHELTON, Alice 317-955-6022 162 R ashelton@marian.edu
SHELTON, Amy 614-794-4254 435 G ashelton@omorecollege.edu
SHELTON, Anita 217-581-2922 138 A ashelton@eiu.edu
SHELTON, Brad 541-346-2090 387 F shelton@uoregon.edu
SHELTON, Charlita 469-941-8300 448 F cshelton@dni.edu
SHELTON, Cheryl 810-762-0553 234 F cheryl.shelton@edtech.mcc.edu
SHELTON, Christie 256-782-5276 6 B cshelton@jsu.edu
SHELTON, Courtney 800-280-0307 155 H courtney.shelton@ace.edu
SHELTON, Courtney 864-278-6281 424 D sheltonc@smcsc.edu
SHELTON, Cynthia, L 502-597-6113 187 E cynthia.shelton@kysu.edu
SHELTON, Deena 903-233-4410 452 A deenashelton@letu.edu
SHELTON, Iverna 404-527-4520 117 C ishelton@carver.edu
SHELTON, Janice 540-674-3611 488 G jshelton@nr.edu
SHELTON, Jennifer 845-848-7500 306 G jennifer.shelton@dc.edu
SHELTON, Julie 205-348-7917 8 A jshelton@fa.ua.edu
SHELTON, JR., M. Dwight 540-231-8775 490 F mdsjr@vt.edu
SHELTON, Maggie 270-901-1112 187 A maggie.shelton@kctcs.edu
SHELTON, Mark 508-793-2371 213 D mshelton@holycross.edu
SHELTON, Matthew, A 620-229-6104 181 F matt.shelton@sckans.edu
SHELTON, Melvin 229-430-2723 114 I melvin.shelton@asurams.edu
SHELTON, Michelle 610-499-4239 414 F mmshelton@widener.edu
SHELTON, Myles 409-944-1200 449 F mshelton@gc.edu
SHELTON, Nellie, R 864-833-8213 423 D nshelton@presby.edu
SHELTON, Rick 315-792-7100 330 A richard.shelton@sunyit.edu
SHELTON, Roosevelt, O 502-597-6415 187 E roosevelt.shelton@kysu.edu
SHELTON, Ryan 219-980-6793 160 C rydshelt@iun.edu
SHELTON, Scott 614-508-7246 363 E sshelton@hondros.edu
SHELTON, Tamara 765-641-4204 156 A tsshelton@anderson.edu
SHELTON, Tasha 847-467-3024 148 C t-shelton@northwestern.edu
SHELTON, Terri, L 336-256-0426 351 D shelton@uncg.edu
SHELTON, Treva 812-866-7056 158 C shelton@hanover.edu
SHELTON, W. Brian 706-886-6831 126 F bshelton@tfc.edu
SHELTON-CLARK, Anne 662-621-4220 252 E ashelton-clark@coahomacc.edu
SHELTON-JOHNSON, LaCoya 480-731-8103 13 D lacoya.shelton-johnson@domail.maricopa.edu
SHEMMER, Rosalie 215-204-7981 411 B rosalie.shemmer@temple.edu
SHEMWELL, Bridget 870-762-3174 17 K bshemwell@smail.anc.edu
SHEMWELL, James 870-762-3191 17 K jshemwell@smail.anc.edu
SHEMWELL, Lisa 870-460-1020 22 D shemwell@uamont.edu
SHEN, Chi 502-597-6083 187 E chi.shen@kysu.edu
SHEN, Shiji 908-737-3470 286 F sshen@kean.edu
SHEN, Sunny 516-739-1545 317 D academic_dean@nyctcm.edu
SHEN-AUSTIN, Christina 202-250-2419 91 H christina.shen-austin@gallaudet.edu
SHENBERGER, Amy 940-565-2207 466 B amy.shenberger@unt.edu
SHENBERGER, Amy 940-565-2197 466 B amy.shenberger@unt.edu
SHENDY, Joellen 240-684-2201 208 D student-services@umuc.edu
SHENETTE, John 336-758-5000 353 A shenetjj@wfu.edu
SHENK, Hans 740-857-1311 369 I hshenk@rosedale.edu
SHENK, Sara, W 574-295-3726 155 K swshenk@ambs.edu

SHIM, Soyeon .... 608-262-4847 510 C
sshim7@wisc.edu
SHIMABUKURO, Julie ... 314-935-4893 269 L
jshimabukuro@wustl.edu
SHIMAZAKI, Leslie .... 619-388-2873.. 60 D
lshimaza@sdccd.edu
SHIMEK, Gary, S .... 414-277-7181 509 A
shimek@msoe.edu
SHIMIZU, Stacey .... 309-556-3190 141 B
abroad@iwu.edu
SHIMOKAWA, Brandon . 808-245-8230 130 F
shimokaw@hawaii.edu
SHIMOKAWA, Leila .... 808-689-2770 130 A
lwai@hawaii.edu
SHIN, Amy .... 630-829-6625 133 I
ashin@ben.edu
SHIN, David, H .... 714-527-0691.. 42 H
info@evangelia.edu
SHIN, Jason .... 714-533-3946.. 35 B
jshin@calums.edu
SHIN, Jason .... 714-533-1495.. 64 F
jshin@southbaylo.edu
SHIN, John .... 703-323-5690 491 E
SHIN, Myung Kyun .... 213-386-0080.. 52 C
SHIN, Tia .... 213-387-4242.. 48 C
SHIN, Yong .... 703-526-6904 483 A
yong.shin@marymount.edu
SHIN LEE, Kyunglim ..... 202-885-8620.. 94 C
kshinlee@wesleyseminary.edu
SHINAR, Ori .... 914-674-7233 314 I
oshinar@mercy.edu
SHINAR, Tammera .... 530-895-2311.. 28 E
shinarta@butte.edu
SHINBERGER, Darcie, R 309-298-1993 155 D
dr-shinberger@wiu.edu
SHINDE, Prashant .... 773-995-2019 135 F
pshinde@csu.edu
SHINDLER, Kenda E, G . 573-592-4216 270 D
kenda.shindler@williamwoods.edu
SHINER, Mark .... 315-228-7680 304 G
mshiner@colgate.edu
SHINEW, Dawn .... 419-372-7403 357 F
dshinew@bgsu.edu
SHING, Dominic .... 415-749-4530.. 60 G
dshing@sfai.edu
SHINGLE, Barbara .... 814-472-3170 409 G
bshingle@francis.edu
SHINGLE, Jean .... 610-647-4400 397 I
jshingle@immaculata.edu
SHINGLER, Jon .... 208-376-7731 131 B
jshingler@boisebible.edu
SHINGLETON, Jay .... 252-493-7777 345 E
jshingleton@email.pittcc.edu
SHINN, David .... 217-228-5432 149 B
shinnda@quincy.edu
SHINN, Jeremiah .... 208-426-1224 131 C
jeremiahshinn@boisestate.edu
SHINNERL, Clare .... 415-502-4457.. 70 A
clare.shinnerl@ucsf.edu
SHINVILLE, Padriac ...... 309-268-8417 139 D
padriac.shinville@heartland.edu
SHINZATO, Noriko .... 415-338-1120.. 34 C
noriko@sfsu.edu
SHIOZAKI, Linda .... 510-809-1444.. 46 D
SHIPLEY, Aletha .... 614-287-2642 360 C
ashipley@cscc.edu
SHIPLEY, Emily .... 513-745-4858 374 D
shipleye1@xavier.edu
SHIPLEY, Heather, J ...... 210-458-5190 468 B
SHIPLEY, Kip .... 802-287-8238 475 B
kip.shipley@greenmtn.edu
SHIPLEY, Robert .... 918-631-3092 381 C
robert-shipley@utulsa.edu
SHIPLEY, Robert, J .... 516-877-3452 297 I
shipley@adelphi.edu
SHIPLEY, Suzanne .... 940-397-4211 453 C
suzanne.shipley@mwsu.edu
SHIPMAN, Doug .... 618-395-7777 140 E
shipmand@iecc.edu
SHIPMAN, Richard .... 517-353-5940 233 G
shipmanr@msu.edu
SHIPMAN, Vicki .... 925-424-1355.. 36 D
vshipman@laspositascollege.edu
SHIPP, Brian .... 256-372-4276.... 1 A
brian.shipp@aamu.edu
SHIPP, Daniel .... 402-554-2779 277 I
dshipp@unomaha.edu
SHIPP, Judith .... 217-206-7122 154 A
shipp.judy@uis.edu
SHIPP, Steve .... 940-397-4539 453 C
steve.shipp@mwsu.edu
SHIPPAM, Michael .... 912-478-6972 120 E
mshippam@georgiasouthern.edu
SHIPPEE, Ellen .... 603-535-2255 283 B
eshippee@plymouth.edu
SHIPWASH, Patrick .... 865-539-7401 437 F
jpshipwash@pstcc.edu

SHIPWAY, Ann, M .... 304-260-4380 502 J
ashipway@blueridgectc.edu
SHIRACHI, Susan .... 808-932-7623 129 I
shirachi@hawaii.edu
SHIRAI, Calvin .... 808-245-8355 130 F
sharaic@hawaii.edu
SHIRAZI, Joyce .... 757-728-6970 481 E
joyce.shirazi@hamptonu.edu
SHIRAZI, Rhonda .... 251-380-2255.... 7 B
rshirazi@shc.edu
SHIRE, Michael .... 617-559-8600 215 H
SHIREMAN, Kimberly .... 336-342-4261 346 B
shiremank@rockinghamcc.edu
SHIREY, Benton .... 859-622-3311 184 F
benton.shirey@eku.edu
SHIREY, Jeanette .... 740-446-4367 362 C
jshirey@gallipoliscareercollege.edu
SHIREY, Jonathan .... 940-397-4324 453 C
jonathan.shirey@mwsu.edu
SHIREY, Kate, A .... 240-895-4203 206 G
kashirey@smcm.edu
SHIREY, JR., Robert, L . 740-446-4367 362 C
rshirey@gallipoliscareercollege.edu
SHIREY NELSON, Linda 330-569-5441 362 J
shireylk@hiram.edu
SHIRING, Jennifer .... 724-852-3332 414 B
jshiring@waynesburg.edu
SHIRK, Jan, M .... 785-833-4302 179 C
jan@kwu.edu
SHIRLEY, Jeremy .... 870-512-7723.. 18 D
jeremy_shirley@asun.edu
SHIRLEY, John .... 607-753-7668 327 A
john.shirley@cortland.edu
SHIRLEY, Johnna .... 843-383-8010 420 B
jshirley@coker.edu
SHIRLEY, Kenneth, M ... 719-333-9751 518 H
SHIRLEY, Michele .... 706-754-7724 123 G
mshirley@northgatech.edu
SHIRLEY, Natalie .... 405-947-3200 378 C
natalie.shirley@osuokc.edu
SHIRLEY, Robert .... 334-387-3877.... 4 B
robertshirley@amridgeuniversity.edu
SHIRLEY, Shawn .... 540-365-4248 480 L
sshirley@ferrum.edu
SHIRLEY, Steven .... 701-858-3300 354 C
president@minotstateu.edu
SHIRLEY, Vikki .... 850-245-0466 108 Q
vikki.shirley@flbog.edu
SHIRRELL, Donna .... 573-334-6825 266 L
SHIRVANI, Hamid, A ..... 712-279-5400 167 B
hamid.shirvani@briarcliff.edu
SHISHOFF, John, W ...... 937-778-7878 361 E
jshishoff@edisonohio.edu
SHISLER, Kirk, L .... 540-432-4203 480 A
kirk.shisler@emu.edu
SHISLER-RAPP,
Susan, M .... 610-359-5040 393 E
srapp@dccc.edu
SHIVE, Hamp .... 601-857-3632 253 B
hfshive@hindscc.edu
SHIVELY, Debby, L .... 520-621-7151.. 16 J
dshively@email.arizona.edu
SHIVELY, Marnie .... 209-588-5105.. 75 I
shively@yosemite.edu
SHIVER, Michael .... 770-229-3044 126 B
mshiver@sctech.edu
SHIVER, Todd .... 509-963-1858 492 L
todd.shiver@cwu.edu
SHIVERS, Melissa .... 319-335-3500 166 G
SHIVLEY, Shane .... 620-341-5440 177 B
sshivley@emporia.edu
SHLAFER, David .... 352-395-5230 107 E
david.shlafer@sfcollege.edu
SHLESINGER, Ned .... 610-785-6284 409 F
nshlesinger@scs.edu
SHMIDMAN,
Michael, A .... 212-463-0400 331 F
michaels@touro.edu
SHNEYDER, Mikhail ...... 801-689-2160 472 C
mshneyder@nightingale.edu
SHNIDMAN, Avrohom ... 410-484-7200 206 C
SHOAF, Mike .... 828-669-8012 340 I
shoaf-michael@aramark.com
SHOALMIRE, Courtney .. 903-823-3142 458 D
courtney.shoalmire@texarkanacollege.edu
SHOBOWALE, Tokumbo 212-229-5600 316 E
shobowale@newschool.edu
SHOCK, Brent, L .... 513-529-8710 365 I
shockb@miamioh.edu
SHOCK, Stephanie .... 701-662-1655 355 A
stephanie.shock@lrsc.edu
SHOCKEY, Christina ...... 740-446-4367 362 C
cshockey@gallipoliscareercollege.edu
SHOCKEY, James, W ...... 520-626-2422.. 16 J
jshockey@email.arizona.edu
SHOCKEY, Ryan .... 269-749-7189 236 A
rshockey@olivetcollege.edu

SHOCKEY, Sherri, L ...... 260-982-5237 162 Q
slshockey@manchester.edu
SHOCKEY, Susie .... 580-559-5219 375 I
sshockey@ecok.edu
SHOCKLEY, Charity .... 302-857-7801.. 90 B
cshockley@desu.edu
SHOCKLEY, Darlas .... 641-683-5174 169 I
darlas.shockley@indianhills.edu
SHOCKLEY, David, R ..... 336-386-3213 347 A
shockleyd@surry.edu
SHOCKLEY, Erica .... 607-274-3222 311 D
eshockley@ithaca.edu
SHOEMAKE, James, M .. 214-388-5466 448 E
difs@dallasinstitute.edu
SHOEMAKE, Kellie .... 910-695-3900 346 E
shoemakek@sandhills.edu
SHOEMAKE, Monte .... 417-626-1234 264 J
shoemake.monte@occ.edu
SHOEMAKER, Carol .... 417-328-1531 267 A
cshoemaker@sbuniv.edu
SHOEMAKER, Chris .... 276-326-4212 478 H
cshoemaker@bluefield.edu
SHOEMAKER, Cindy ...... 717-262-2006 415 B
cshoemaker@wilson.edu
SHOEMAKER, Peter .... 973-761-9022 291 F
SHOEMAKER, Scott .... 619-849-2565.. 57 H
scottshoemaker@pointloma.edu
SHOEMAKER, Stowe ...... 702-895-3308 279 D
stowe.shoemaker@unlv.edu
SHOEMAKER, Troy .... 850-478-8496 105 D
tshoemaker@pcci.edu
SHOEMYER, Cheryl .... 660-263-4100 264 C
cheryls@macc.edu
SHOEN, Eric .... 718-270-2075 326 A
eric.shoen@downstate.edu
SHOENBERGER, George 301-985-7576 208 D
george.shoenberger@umuc.edu
SHOENER, Gary .... 570-504-7949 399 A
shoenerg@lackawanna.edu
SHOENER, Pattie .... 504-282-4455 195 D
pshoener@nobts.edu
SHOFFNER, Dan .... 903-586-2518 451 C
dshoffner@jacksonville-college.edu
SHOGE, Ruth, C .... 410-778-7292 210 A
rshoge2@washcoll.edu
SHOGREN, Jana .... 218-855-8129 244 C
jshogren@clcmn.edu
SHOHO, Alan, R .... 414-229-4181 511 A
shoho@uwm.edu
SHOJAI, Siamack .... 973-720-2964 292 I
shojais@wpunj.edu
SHOKRALLA, Diana .... 281-998-6150 456 B
diana.shkralla@sjcd.edu
SHOLLENBERGER,
Kevin .... 410-516-8382 204 F
ksholle1@jhu.edu
SHOLLEY, Sonya .... 304-876-5107 504 D
ssholley@shepherd.edu
SHOMAKER, Kelli, D ..... 334-844-5588.... 4 D
kds0053@auburn.edu
SHOMO, Amber .... 707-638-5200.. 67 H
SHONBRUN, Anne .... 718-270-4779 326 A
anne.shonbrun@downstate.edu
SHONK, Brian .... 870-612-2003.. 22 H
brian.shonk@uaccb.edu
SHONROCK, Michael ...... 636-949-4900 261 I
mshonrock@lindenwood.edu
SHONTZ, Susan, F .... 814-641-3304 398 B
shontzs@juniata.edu
SHOOK, Christopher ..... 406-243-6195 271 G
christopher.shook@umontana.edu
SHOOK, Douglas .... 213-740-7197.. 72 B
shook@usc.edu
SHOOK, Gregory .... 410-626-2539 206 F
gregory.shook@sjc.edu
SHOOK, Justin .... 412-291-6614 389 F
jshook@aii.edu
SHOOK, Mark .... 706-880-8976 122 D
mshook@lagrange.edu
SHOOP, David .... 803-935-4294 125 H
dshoop@southuniversity.edu
SHOOT, Madge .... 217-234-5375 143 B
mbailey1292@lakeland.cc.il.us
SHOOTER, Rhonda .... 806-720-7125 452 D
rhonda.shooter@lcu.edu
SHOPE JONES, Amy, N 937-775-3386 374 B
amy.n.jones@wright.edu
SHOR, Eric, M .... 304-457-6276 501 A
shorem@ab.edu
SHOR, Glen .... 617-324-0646 221 C
SHOR, Stuart, B .... 212-817-7604 302 B
sshor@gc.cuny.edu
SHORAK, Eli .... 412-624-3217 412 I
es@pitt.edu
SHORB, Deanna .... 641-269-4981 169 F
shorb@grinnell.edu
SHORE, Cliff .... 703-993-2611 481 B
cshore@gmu.edu

SHORE, Craig .... 334-833-4349.... 5 M
cshore@hawks.huntingdon.edu
SHORE, James .... 706-542-2802 127 A
jshore@uga.edu
SHORE, Muriel .... 201-559-6030 286 C
shorem@felician.edu
SHORES, JR., Dennis .... 215-951-1315 398 F
shores@lasalle.edu
SHORES, Robin, H .... 610-690-6879 410 I
rshores1@swarthmore.edu
SHOREY, David .... 978-468-7111 215 E
shorey@gcts.edu
SHOREY, Denise .... 317-738-8160 157 L
dshorey@franklincollege.edu
SHORT, Andrea .... 972-241-3371 447 E
ashort@dallas.edu
SHORT, Anthony, E .... 419-372-7019 357 F
ashort@bgsu.edu
SHORT, Brent .... 352-588-8258 106 N
brent.short@saintleo.edu
SHORT, Christopher ...... 210-690-9000 449 K
cshort@hallmarkuniversity.edu
SHORT, Curtis .... 317-931-2313 157 D
cshort@cts.edu
SHORT, David .... 409-880-8060 462 B
david.short@lamar.edu
SHORT, David .... 276-328-0196 487 A
dps4v@uvawise.edu
SHORT, JR., David .... 409-880-8060 462 C
david.short@lamar.edu
SHORT, Donna .... 828-652-0631 344 G
donnas@mcdowelltech.edu
SHORT, Donna .... 828-652-0631 344 G
donnasho@mcdowelltech.edu
SHORT, Emily .... 615-230-3477 438 C
emily.short@volstate.edu
SHORT, Evelyn .... 360-417-6381 496 I
eshort@pencol.edu
SHORT, Evonn .... 210-690-9000 449 K
eshort@hallmarkuniversity.edu
SHORT, Joel, D .... 574-535-7784 158 A
joelds@goshen.edu
SHORT, John .... 301-687-4068 209 A
jtshort@frostburg.edu
SHORT, John, N .... 207-834-7504 201 E
john.short@maine.edu
SHORT, Kyla .... 918-343-7792 379 C
kshort@rsu.edu
SHORT, Matt .... 918-293-5222 378 B
matt.short@okstate.edu
SHORT, Paula, M .... 713-743-5227 464 F
pmshort@uh.edu
SHORT, Paula, M .... 713-743-5227 465 A
pmshort@uh.edu
SHORT, Rick .... 281-283-3300 465 B
short@uhcl.edu
SHORT, Rosanna .... 623-935-8888.. 13 F
rosanna.short@estrellamountain.edu
SHORT, Sheri .... 903-875-7576 453 J
sheri.short@navarrocollege.edu
SHORT, Trey .... 309-556-3017 141 B
tshort@iwu.edu
SHORT, William .... 407-646-2619 106 J
wshort@rollins.edu
SHORT-THOMPSON,
Cady .... 616-395-7785 231 D
shortthompson@hope.edu
SHORTBULL,
Thomas, H .... 605-455-6022 427 I
tshortb@olc.edu
SHORTER, Paula .... 816-501-4115 265 I
paula.shorter@rockhurst.edu
SHORTS, Kathryn .... 541-962-3774 383 B
kshorts@eou.edu
SHORTT, Pamela .... 336-734-7224 343 C
pshortt@forsythtech.edu
SHORTT, Ronnie .... 276-328-2677 487 A
rls6k@uvawise.edu
SHORTY, Ursula .... 225-771-2790 195 J
ursula_shorty@subr.edu
SHORTY, Ursula .... 225-771-2790 195 K
ursula_shorty@subr.edu
SHOSTACK, Pauline .... 315-498-2708 319 G
shostacp@sunyocc.edu
SHOSTAK, Grant .... 636-627-2277 261 I
gshostak@lindenwood.edu
SHOTT, Brandy .... 704-233-8028 353 D
b.shott@wingate.edu
SHOTT, Diane, T .... 276-326-4201 478 H
dshott@bluefield.edu
SHOTTS, Carl .... 903-510-2512 464 D
csho@tjc.edu
SHOTWELL SMITH,
Mary .... 706-233-7278 125 E
msmith@shorter.edu
SHOUDY, Peter .... 410-287-1021 203 B
pshoudy@cecil.edu

SHOULTZ, Chad ... 321-674-7584 .. 99 K
cshoultz@fit.edu
SHOUN, Stan ... 314-286-4807 265 F
SHOUP, John ... 951-343-4205 .. 28 G
jshoup@calbaptist.edu
SHOURESHI, Rahmat ... 516-686-7630 317 G
rahmat.shoureshi@nyit.edu
SHOURESHI, Rahmat ... 503-725-4411 386 D
president@pdx.edu
SHOUSE, Amy ... 304-724-5000 501 G
ashouse@cdu.edu
SHOVAN, Lisa ... 518-562-4130 304 C
lisa.shovan@clinton.edu
SHOVLAIN, Raymond, J 563-333-6233 173 A
shovlainraymondj@sau.edu
SHOWALTER, Jonathan . 740-857-1311 369 I
jshowalter@rosedale.edu
SHOWALTER, Matthew .. 740-857-1311 369 I
mshowalter@rosedale.edu
SHOWALTER,
Rodney, J ... 540-338-1776 483 H
ie@phc.edu
SHOWERS, Bill ... 412-809-5100 408 D
showers.william@pti.edu
SHOWERS, Dawn, R ... 717-867-6071 399 J
dshowers@lvc.edu
SHOWERS, Nancy, C ... 248-341-2040 235 D
ncshower@oaklandcc.edu
SHOWERS, Shane ... 315-568-3125 317 A
sshowers@nycc.edu
SHOWS, Alicia ... 601-276-3706 256 A
showsa@smcc.edu
SHOWS, Deidre ... 601-318-6583 256 I
dede.shows@wmcarey.edu
SHOWS, John ... 228-897-4373 254 D
john.shows@mgcc.edu
SHOWS-PEREZ, Cindy ... 337-482-6497 197 F
cperez@louisiana.edu
SHPER, Paul ... 802-322-1656 475 A
paul.shper@goddard.edu
SHPIRO, Heather ... 973-748-9000 284 A
heather_shpiro@bloomfield.edu
SHRADER, Daniel ... 714-432-5605 .. 38 H
dshrader@occ.cccd.edu
SHRADER, Greg ... 817-598-6421 470 J
gshrader@wc.edu
SHRADER, Nick ... 912-344-3940 115 D
nick.shrader@armstrong.edu
SHRAYCK, Jessica ... 612-659-6527 245 F
jessica.shryack@minneapolis.edu
SHREFFLER, Christine ... 314-344-4440 263 B
cshreff@aol.com
SHREFLER, Christy, L ... 440-826-2231 357 B
chking@bw.edu
SHRESTHA, Prashish ... 703-591-7042 490 D
prasis@viu.edu
SHRESTHA, Shakil ... 510-628-8010 .. 48 F
shakil@lincolnuca.edu
SHREVE, Jeremy ... 336-917-5472 348 H
jeremy.shreve@salem.edu
SHREVE, Penny ... 760-252-2411 .. 27 A
pshreve@barstow.edu
SHREVE, Teresa ... 205-348-7625 .... 8 A
tshreve@bama.ua.edu
SHREVES, Shawn ... 432-335-6866 454 C
sshreves@odessa.edu
SHRIMPTON, Nikki ... 518-587-2100 329 C
nikki.shrimpton@esc.edu
SHRINER, Michael, B ... 409-772-3501 469 C
mshriner@utmb.edu
SHRIVASTAV, Rahul ... 706-583-0690 127 A
rahuls@uga.edu
SHROCK, Chris ... 304-865-6133 502 C
chris.shrock@ovu.edu
SHROCK, David, L ... 414-410-4003 506 F
dlshrock@stritch.edu
SHROCK, Joel ... 765-641-4441 156 A
jdshrock@anderson.edu
SHROEDER, Mark ... 734-432-5341 233 C
mschroeder@madonna.edu
SHROFF, Meghana ... 612-874-3796 243 F
mshroff@mcad.edu
SHROFF, Nilufer, K ... 609-258-3000 288 F
SHROPSHIRE, Doug ... 508-531-1207 217 D
dshropshire@bridgew.edu
SHROPSHIRE, James ... 641-269-4600 169 F
shropshi@grinnell.edu
SHROPSHIRE, Marty ... 336-386-3453 347 A
shropshirem@surry.edu
SHRYOCK, Dawn ... 217-854-5508 134 E
dawn.shryock@blackburn.edu
SHTAMLER, Victoriya ... 718-522-9073 298 E
vshtamler@asa.edu
SHTROMBERG, Alisa ... 425-739-8389 495 F
alisa.shtromberg@lwtech.edu
SHUBERT, David ... 316-942-4291 180 D
shubertd@newmanu.edu
SHUBERT, Lisa, A ... 507-344-7324 240 I
lisa.shubert@blc.edu
SHUBERT, Stephen ... 810-762-0501 234 F
stephen.shubert@mcc.edu
SHUCHAT, Rena ... 937-512-2919 370 A
rena.shuchat@sinclair.edu
SHUDAK, Nicholas ... 402-375-7379 276 D
nishuda1@wsc.edu
SHUFORD, Bettina ... 919-966-4045 351 B
bcshufor@email.unc.edu
SHUFORD, Eddie ... 828-652-0652 344 G
eddieshuford@mcdowelltech.edu
SHUGART, Marlene ... 405-682-1611 377 C
marlene.l.shugart@occc.edu
SHUGART, Michael ... 405-682-1611 377 C
mshugart@occc.edu
SHUGART, Sanford, C ... 407-582-3400 113 F
sshugart@valenciacollege.edu
SHUKLA, Mennu ... 803-793-5109 420 G
shuklam@denmarktech.edu
SHULACK, John ... 848-445-2460 290 A
jshulack@facilities.rutgers.edu
SHULER, Elton ... 803-793-5170 420 G
shulere@denmarktech.edu
SHULER, Eric ... 304-876-5644 504 D
eshuler@shepherd.edu
SHULER, Peggy ... 803-321-5117 422 H
peggy.shuler@newberry.edu
SHULL, Roger ... 806-894-9611 456 F
rshull@southplainscollege.edu
SHULL, Roxanna ... 260-459-4600 161 D
rshull@ibcfortwayne.edu
SHULMAN, Brian ... 973-275-2168 291 F
brian.shulman@shu.edu
SHULMAN, Connie ... 425-278-9317 .. 63 A
cshulman@saybrook.edu
SHULMAN, David ... 954-201-7933 .. 96 A
dshulman@broward.edu
SHULOCK, Anne ... 415-749-4507 .. 60 G
ashulock@sfai.edu
SHULTES, Kenneth, E ... 717-245-1247 394 A
shultes@dickinson.edu
SHULTS, Christopher ... 212-220-1400 301 C
cshults@bmcc.cuny.edu
SHULTS, Kari ... 918-595-8845 380 D
kari.culp@tulsacc.edu
SHULTZ, Dee ... 970-339-6434 .. 76 E
dee.shultz@aims.edu
SHULTZ, John ... 913-758-6308 182 B
john.shultz@stmary.edu
SHULTZ, Judy ... 507-389-7369 247 H
judy.shultz@southcentral.edu
SHULTZ, Kari ... 423-236-2484 436 C
kshultz@southern.edu
SHULTZ, Michael ... 724-589-2167 411 D
mshultz@thiel.edu
SHULTZ, Norah ... 619-594-6881 .. 34 B
nshultz@mail.sdsu.edu
SHULTZ, JR., Walter, J . 570-326-3761 404 T
walter.shultz@pct.edu
SHULUK, William ... 239-489-9356 100 E
wshuluk@fsw.edu
SHUMACK, Gareth ... 516-876-3210 327 C
shumackg@oldwestbury.edu
SHUMAKE, Connie, C ... 502-852-3551 190 C
ccshum01@louisville.edu
SHUMAKER, Carrie ... 313-593-5454 238 A
shumakr@umich.edu
SHUMAKER, Deb ... 989-275-5000 232 E
deb.shumaker@kirtland.edu
SHUMAKER, Nancy ... 507-285-7461 247 D
nancy.shumaker@rctc.edu
SHUMAKER, Ryan ... 619-660-4505 .. 44 L
ryan.shumaker@gcccd.edu
SHUMAKER, Ryan ... 619-388-2737 .. 60 D
rshumaker@sdccd.edu
SHUMAN, Jenny ... 478-296-6117 123 I
jshuman@oftc.edu
SHUMAN, Kelli, R ... 605-394-1203 429 A
kelli.shuman@sdsmt.edu
SHUMAN, Michaeline ... 570-372-4325 410 H
shumanm@susqu.edu
SHUMAN, Shari, A ... 904-620-2002 110 E
sshuman@unf.edu
SHUMAN, Victoria ... 304-793-6898 504 F
vshuman@osteo.wvsom.edu
SHUMATE, Connie ... 304-384-5366 503 P
cshumate@concord.edu
SHUMATE, David ... 480-245-7903 .. 13 C
dave.shumate@faculty.ibcs.edu
SHUMATE, Jabar ... 405-325-7314 380 L
jabarshumate@ou.edu
SHUMSKAYA, Tatsiana .. 973-300-2267 291 I
tshumskaya@sussex.edu
SHUNK, Jeremy ... 816-268-5424 264 G
jshunk@nts.edu
SHUPALA, Christine ... 361-825-3383 460 A
christine.shupala@tamucc.edu
SHUPE, Gary ... 217-641-4505 141 F
gshupe@jwcc.edu
SHUPE, John ... 845-257-3335 325 D
shupej@newpaltz.edu
SHUPENUS, Sarah ... 217-424-6340 145 J
sshupenus@millikin.edu
SHUPP, Edward, K ... 610-758-4200 400 B
eks0@lehigh.edu
SHUPP, Michael, D ... 515-263-6136 169 E
mshupp@grandview.edu
SHUPPY, Brian, L ... 801-626-6114 473 E
bshuppy@weber.edu
SHURER, Brooke ... 919-760-8429 339 H
shurerb@meredith.edu
SHURLEY, Britton ... 270-534-3243 187 C
britton.shurley@kctcs.edu
SHURTLEFF, Courtney ... 508-286-8207 225 G
shurtleff_courtney@wheatoncollege.edu
SHURTZ, Mary Ann ... 703-539-6890 485 J
mshurtz@stratford.edu
SHURTZ, Richard ... 703-539-6890 485 J
rshurtz@stratford.edu
SHUSTER, Arthur ... 828-298-3325 353 B
ashuster@warren-wilson.edu
SHUSTER, Patricia ... 603-641-7150 282 A
pshuster@anselm.edu
SHUSTOWSKI, JR.,
William, J ... 727-816-3404 105 C
shustow@phsc.edu
SHUTE, William ... 202-955-9091 467 A
wshute@utsystem.edu
SHUTT, Barbara, C ... 207-859-5415 198 H
bcshutt@colby.edu
SHUTT, Gary ... 405-744-6260 377 F
gary.shutt@okstate.edu
SHUTTER, Jamie, L ... 512-475-8445 467 C
j.shutter@uhs.utexas.edu
SIAH, Jonathan ... 626-571-5110 .. 48 G
jsiah@les.edu
SIAHMAKOUN, Azad ... 812-877-8400 163 G
siahmako@rose-hulman.edu
SIALOFI, Amanda ... 907-852-1823 .... 9 H
amanda.sialofi@ilisagvik.edu
SIAMPOS, Christa ... 314-421-0949 267 H
csiampos@siba.edu
SIBAL, Jennifer, R ... 308-630-6571 278 B
sibalj@wncc.edu
SIBENALLER, Jim ... 773-508-7665 144 D
jsibena@luc.edu
SIBENALLER-WOODALL,
Beth ... 712-324-5061 172 E
beths@nwicc.edu
SIBERT, Kimberley ... 740-366-9233 358 E
ksibert@cotc.edu
SIBERT, Sonja ... 775-753-2181 279 A
sonja.sibert@gbcnv.edu
SIBILIA, John ... 330-569-5332 362 J
sibiliaj@hiram.edu
SIBLEY, Anne ... 315-386-7082 329 A
sibley@canton.edu
SIBLEY, Debra, H ... 504-568-6107 194 C
dsible@lsuhsc.edu
SIBLEY, Dedra ... 321-433-7060 .. 97 N
sibleyd@easternflorida.edu
SIBLEY, Donna, M ... 508-373-9712 211 F
donna.sibley@becker.edu
SIBLEY, Karen, H ... 401-863-1236 415 K
karen_sibley@brown.edu
SIBURT, Jim ... 717-947-6297 404 S
jesiburt@pacollege.edu
SICARD, OP,
Kenneth, R ... 401-865-2055 416 E
ksicard@providence.edu
SICARD, Rex, E ... 785-243-1435 176 I
rsicard@cloud.edu
SICIENSKY, Emily ... 931-540-2704 436 H
esiciensky@columbiastate.edu
SICILIANO, Julie ... 413-782-1553 225 F
julie.siciliano@wne.edu
SICILIANO, Stephen, N . 231-995-1373 235 B
ssiciliano@nmc.edu
SICK, Volker ... 734-763-1290 237 I
vsick@umich.edu
SICO, Eileen ... 845-575-3000 314 C
eileen.sico@marist.edu
SICONOLFI, Steven ... 570-662-4804 406 F
ssiconol@mansfield.edu
SIDDARAJU, Raj ... 309-649-6387 152 G
raj.siddaraju@src.edu
SIDDENS, Nancy ... 217-732-3168 143 F
nsiddens@lincolnchristian.edu
SIDDENS, Nicole ... 806-457-4200 449 D
nsiddens@fpctx.edu
SIDDIQI, Melanie ... 909-652-6780 .. 36 E
melanie.siddiqi@chaffey.edu
SIDDIQI, Muddassir ... 713-718-6041 450 D
muddassir.siddiqi@hccs.edu
SIDDIQUI, Murtuza ... 563-425-5384 173 K
siddiquim@uiu.edu
SIDDIQUI, Wasim ... 808-947-4788 131 A
SIDDOWAY, Mike ... 719-389-6681 .. 77 J
msiddoway@coloradocollege.edu
SIDEBOTTOM, Daniel ... 607-753-2501 327 A
daniel.sidebottom@cortland.edu
SIDELI, Kathleen ... 812-855-9304 159 H
sideli@iu.edu
SIDERAKIS, John ... 212-650-7226 301 F
jsiderakis@ccny.cuny.edu
SIDERAS, John, F ... 216-368-4340 358 C
john.sideras@case.edu
SIDERS, Angie ... 765-455-9515 160 B
asiders@iuk.edu
SIDES, Courtney, M ... 361-570-4354 465 D
sidesc@uhv.edu
SIDES, Emilee ... 870-733-6701 .. 18 B
essides@asumidsouth.edu
SIDHU, Elda ... 702-895-5185 279 D
elda.sidhu@unlv.edu
SIDIO, Jerome ... 401-874-5488 417 E
sidio@uri.edu
SIDLE, Meg ... 606-218-5290 190 E
margaretsidle@upike.edu
SIDLE, Stuart ... 203-932-7339 .. 89 D
ssidle@newhaven.edu
SIDLER, Sherri ... 312-362-6727 137 C
ssidler@depaul.edu
SIDOCK, Andrew ... 217-479-7066 144 I
andrew.sidock@mac.edu
SIDOR, Stanley ... 352-365-3523 103 B
sidors@lssc.edu
SIDORKIN, Alexander ... 916-278-6639 .. 33 C
sidorkin@csus.edu
SIDWELL, Scott, A ... 415-422-2923 .. 72 A
sasidwell@usfca.edu
SIEBEN, Jeffrey ... 609-921-8300 288 E
SIEBENBERG, Tammy ... 509-574-4984 500 I
tsiebenberg@yvcc.edu
SIEBENMORGEN, Tom .. 501-450-1333 .. 19 I
siebenmorgen@hendrix.edu
SIEBENS, Libby ... 509-682-6436 500 D
lsiebens@wvc.edu
SIEBENS, Mackie ... 413-528-7499 211 B
SIEBENS, Mackie ... 845-758-6822 298 I
msiebens@bard.edu
SIEBERKROB,
Deanna, J ... 412-578-6423 391 G
djsieberkrob@carlow.edu
SIEBERT, Alex ... 513-562-8749 356 J
asiebert@artacademy.edu
SIEBERT, David, J ... 847-735-5040 142 H
siebert@lakeforest.edu
SIEBERT, Mary Anne ... 501-450-1372 .. 19 I
siebert@hendrix.edu
SIEBERT, Scotti ... 417-873-7434 259 G
ssiebert@drury.edu
SIECKE, Elizabeth ... 201-684-7318 289 C
esiecke@ramapo.edu
SIEDHOFF, Kara ... 402-461-7394 274 I
ksiedhoff@hastings.edu
SIEDZIK, Richard ... 401-232-6505 416 A
rsiedzik@bryant.edu
SIEFERT, Tom ... 773-291-6412 135 M
tsiefert@ccc.edu
SIEFKEN, Rob ... 212-924-5900 330 G
rsiefken@swedishinstitute.edu
SIEG, Judy ... 864-592-4051 424 C
siegj@sccsc.edu
SIEGAL, Christine ... 203-254-4000 .. 87 A
csiegel@fairfield.edu
SIEGEL, Barb ... 847-574-5214 143 A
bsiegel@lfgsm.edu
SIEGEL, Christine ... 203-254-4000 .. 87 A
csiegel@fairfield.edu
SIEGEL, Edward ... 727-341-4594 107 A
siegel.edward@spcollege.edu
SIEGEL, Larry ... 978-934-2107 217 B
laurence_siegel@uml.edu
SIEGEL, Lawrence, J ... 212-430-4204 334 P
lsiegel@aecom.yu.edu
SIEGEL, Miriam ... 413-748-3118 224 G
mjsiegel@springfieldcollege.edu
SIEGEL, Tavianna ... 210-297-9129 443 K
tavianna.siegel@baptisthealthsystem.com
SIEGENTHALER, Kim ... 573-882-4808 268 C
siegenthalerk@missouri.edu
SIEGER, Eric ... 507-222-4183 241 C
esieger@carleton.edu
SIEGERT, Kara, O ... 410-543-6023 209 B
kosiegert@salisbury.edu
SIEGFRIED, Jessica ... 435-283-7169 474 A
jessica.siegfried@snow.edu
SIEGFRIED,
Kenneth (Ziggy) ... 661-654-2200 .. 31 B
ksiegfried@csub.edu

SIEGGREEN, Stephanie 270-745-4857 190 F stephanie.sieggreen@wku.edu
SIEGLE, Suzanne 734-995-7315 229 A suzanne.siegle@cuaa.edu
SIEGLER, Cynthia 413-572-8545 218 F csiegler@westfield.ma.edu
SIEGMANN, Starla, C 414-443-8862 513 A starla.siegmann@wlc.edu
SIEKER, Tina 636-922-8314 265 J tsieker@stchas.edu
SIEMINSKI, Randy, B 315-386-7335 329 A sieminski@canton.edu
SIENA, Steven 516-628-5558 327 C sienas@oldwestbury.edu
SIERRA, Mayra, I 787-751-0160 522 B msierra@cmpr.pr.gov
SIES, Susan 410-386-8325 203 A ssies@carrollcc.edu
SIESING, Gina 610-526-5272 390 G gsiesing@brynmawr.edu
SIETSEMA, Adriane 641-648-4611 170 H adriane.sietsema@iavalley.edu
SIEVERDING, John 605-770-0700 427 E john.sieverding@mitchelltech.edu
SIEVERS, Allison 303-963-3437 77 I
SIEVERS, Debbie 708-974-5330 146 C sievers@morainevalley.edu
SIFFERLEN, Ned, J 937-512-2510 370 A ned.sifferlen@sinclair.edu
SIFRI, Tatiana 630-637-5161 147 E tsifri@noctrl.edu
SIFTAR, Michael 918-595-8123 380 D michael.siftar@tulsacc.edu
SIFUENTES, Alma 831-459-2347 70 C alma@ucsc.edu
SIFUENTES-JAUREGUI, Ben 848-932-7865 290 A ben.sifuentes.jauregui@rutgers.edu
SIGALA, Al 503-491-7548 384 D al.sigala@mhcc.edu
SIGANOFF, Diana 714-620-3700 26 I
SIGAUKE, Erica 417-667-8181 259 A esigauke@cottey.edu
SIGGERS, Julian, F 215-898-4052 412 G siggers@upenn.edu
SIGGERS, Lauretta 617-873-0170 213 B lauretta.siggers@cambridgecollege.edu
SIGLER, Todd, D 704-894-2915 337 B tosigler@davidson.edu
SIGMAN, David 414-847-3263 508 G davidsigman@miad.edu
SIGMON, Judy 336-917-5471 348 H judy.sigmon@salem.edu
SIGMON, JR., Kenneth, E 336-334-7600 350 C kesigmon@ncat.edu
SIGNOR, Mary 212-998-6807 318 D mary.signor@nyu.edu
SIGNORELLO, John 973-761-9615 291 F john.signorello@shu.edu
SIGNORELLO, Rose 713-525-3162 466 J signorr@stthom.edu
SIGRIST, Kim 816-271-4237 264 B ksigrist@missouriwestern.edu
SIGUAW, Judy 252-328-1098 349 I siguawj@ecu.edu
SIGURDSON, Chris, W 520-621-4608 16 J sig@email.arizona.edu
SIGWORTH, Steve 713-798-2500 444 A sigworth@bcm.edu
SIKES, Bruce 479-667-4046 18 G bsikes1@atu.edu
SIKES, Janine 352-846-3903 110 D jysikes@ufl.edu
SIKES, Pamela, J 619-260-4595 71 J psikes@sandiego.edu
SIKES, Steddon, L 402-363-5668 278 E slsikes@york.edu
SIKKA, Anjoo 585-245-5151 327 B sikka@geneseo.edu
SIKORA, Jen 415-749-4594 60 G jsikora@sfai.edu
SIKORSKI, Lindsey 570-662-4808 406 F lsikorsk@mansfield.edu
SIKORSKY, Charles 703-416-1441 479 N
SILAFAU-TOA, Emey 684-699-9155 519 F e.silafau@amsamoa.edu
SILAK, Cathy 503-955-1001 382 I csilak@cu-portland.edu
SILANDER, Liisa 401-454-6349 417 B lsilande@risd.edu
SILANSKIS, Theresa 410-837-6838 209 D tsilanskis@ubalt.edu
SILAS, Monique 205-929-6350 2 G msilas@lawsonstate.edu
SILBER, Daniel, K 573-288-6325 259 E dsilber@culver.edu
SILBER, Eric 512-313-3000 446 N eric.silber@concordia.edu
SILBER, Jeffrey, A 607-255-2016 306 B jas9@cornell.edu
SILBERMAN, Gerald, L 610-683-4106 406 D silberma@kutztown.edu
SILBERNAGEL, Darin 503-838-8176 388 B silbernd@wou.edu
SILBERQUIT, Paul 732-255-0400 288 B psilberquit@ocean.edu
SILBERSTEIN, Dara, J 607-777-2815 325 A lael@binghamton.edu
SILBERSTEIN, Jeffrey 212-659-9091 311 A
SILBERSTEIN, Lloyd 213-740-1638 72 B lloyd.silberstein@usc.edu
SILBIGER, Erica 212-343-1234 315 D
SILCOX, Justin 214-333-5460 447 D justin@dbu.edu
SILCOX, Steve 269-927-7060 232 G ssilcox@lakemichigancollege.edu
SILECCHIA, Lucia 202-319-5560 91 D silecchia@cua.edu
SILER, Cathy 317-955-6241 162 R csiler@marian.edu
SILER, Ginni 706-802-5136 119 G gsiler@highlands.edu
SILER, Linda, K 616-538-2330 230 E lsiler@gbcol.edu
SILFEN GLASSBERG, Davita 860-486-2713 88 G davita.glassberg@uconn.edu
SILICIANO, John, A 607-255-6230 306 B jas83@cornell.edu
SILICIANO, John, A 607-255-7671 306 B jas83@cornell.edu
SILK, Eleana 914-961-8313 323 H es@svots.edu
SILK, Elizabeth 708-524-6461 137 F esilk@dom.edu
SILK, Mary, L 692-625-4410 520 C msilk@cmi.edu
SILKA, Zachary 513-244-4735 366 A zach.silka@msj.edu
SILLCOCKS, Emily 713-646-1824 456 H esillcocks@stcl.edu
SILLIMAN, Steve 509-313-3522 495 A silliman@gonzaga.edu
SILMAN, Shawn 281-459-7673 456 A shawn.silman@sjcd.edu
SILOTTO, Jodi 217-362-6423 145 J jsilotto@millikin.edu
SILVA, Adelina 210-485-0153 441 E asilva@alamo.edu
SILVA, Alan 651-690-6720 249 T ajsilva@stkate.edu
SILVA, Alyson 954-262-5258 104 F asilva1@nova.edu
SILVA, David, J 978-542-6246 218 E provost@salemstate.edu
SILVA, Efrain 760-355-6249 46 B efrain.silva@imperial.edu
SILVA, Elizabeth 619-260-2888 71 J registrar@sandiego.edu
SILVA, Griselda 773-481-8186 136 B gsilva24@ccc.edu
SILVA, Jack 401-454-6480 417 B jsilva@risd.edu
SILVA, Jaime 503-838-8845 388 B silvaj@wou.edu
SILVA, Jennifer 541-888-7205 387 A jennifer.silva@socc.edu
SILVA, Jennifer 904-632-3141 100 F jen.silva@fscj.edu
SILVA, Jennifer 904-470-8250 98 B jennifer.silva@ewc.edu
SILVA, Jessica 707-468-3012 51 E jsilva@mendocino.edu
SILVA, Jessica, L 401-456-8047 417 A jsilva@ric.edu
SILVA, Joy 916-361-1660 35 G jsilva@carrington.edu
SILVA, Lourdes 910-521-6301 351 E lourdes.silva@uncp.edu
SILVA, Lourdes 704-463-3062 348 B lourdes.silva@pfeiffer.edu
SILVA, Mariza 312-922-1884 144 H msilva@maccormac.edu
SILVA, Maureen 540-828-5450 478 J msilva@bridgewater.edu
SILVA, Rito 361-698-2250 448 H rsilva@delmar.edu
SILVA, Sonia 661-654-3995 31 B ssilva7@csub.edu
SILVA, Stephanie 510-436-1405 45 G ssilva@hnu.edu
SILVA, Tammy, A 508-999-8486 217 A tsilva@umassd.edu
SILVA, Tina 307-268-2547 516 H tina.silva@caspercollege.edu
SILVA, Yvonne 513-241-4338 356 I yvonne.silva@antonellicollege.edu
SILVANO, Brian 949-794-9090 66 B bsilvano@stanbridge.edu
SILVAS, Kassie 208-769-7783 132 E kmsilvas@nic.edu
SILVER, Candace 828-898-2417 339 B silverc@lmc.edu
SILVER, Frank 828-652-0634 344 G franksil@mcdowelltech.edu
SILVER, Jonathan 646-717-9705 309 B silver@gts.edu
SILVER, Mariko 802-440-4300 474 F msilver@bennington.edu
SILVER, Paula 610-499-4352 414 F psilver@widener.edu
SILVER, Steve 541-684-7235 384 H ssilver@nwcu.edu
SILVER, William 707-664-2220 35 A silverw@sonoma.edu
SILVERBLATT, Pamela, S 646-664-2977 301 A pamela.silverblatt@cuny.edu
SILVERI, Annamaria 313-993-1170 237 F silveran@udmercy.edu
SILVERI, Don 716-896-0700 333 C dsilveri@villa.edu
SILVERIA, Jay, B 719-333-4140 518 H
SILVERII, Glenda 601-643-8440 252 G glenda.silverii@colin.edu
SILVERII, Stan 985-448-4030 197 C stan.silverii@nicholls.edu
SILVERMAN, Ed 315-279-5120 312 D esilverman@keuka.edu
SILVERMAN, Edward 212-650-6480 301 F esilverman@ccny.cuny.edu
SILVERS, Liz 828-726-2375 341 D lsilvers@cccti.edu
SILVERTHORN, Mike 989-463-7327 226 H silverthorn@alma.edu
SILVESTRI, Mary Ann 508-541-1602 214 C msilvestri@dean.edu
SILVESTRI, Timothy 484-664-3178 402 F timothysilvestri@muhlenberg.edu
SILVESTRINI, Maria 787-284-1912 524 C msilvest@ponce.inter.edu
SILVESTRO, Michael 973-761-9138 291 F michael.silvestro1@shu.edu
SILVEY, Greg 660-831-4183 264 A silveyg@moval.edu
SILVIS, Kathryn 412-536-1297 398 E kathryn.silvis@laroche.edu
SILVYN, Jeffrey 520-206-4678 15 L jsilvyn@pima.edu
SILWOSKI, Richard, F 804-828-9647 487 E rfsliwoski@vcu.edu
SILY, Michel 305-899-3781 95 G msily@barry.edu
SIMA, Andrea 909-274-5950 52 I asims@mtsac.edu
SIMALA, Jay 847-317-6507 153 D jsimala@tiu.edu
SIMAMA, Jabari 404-297-9522 120 D simamaj@gptc.edu
SIMAR, Gina, A 409-882-3311 462 D gina.simar@lsco.edu
SIMARD, Denise 518-564-3066 327 E simardda@plattsburgh.edu
SIMAS, Andrew 415-351-3537 60 G asimas@sfai.edu
SIMCOX, Mary Grace 717-947-6090 404 S mrsimcox@pacollege.edu
SIMEK, Kathy, M 503-943-7101 387 H simek@up.edu
SIMER, Lauren 864-250-8484 421 K lauren.simer@gvltec.edu
SIMERSON, Gordon 203-932-7290 89 D gsimerson@newhaven.edu
SIMFUKWE, David 904-470-8174 98 B dsimfukwe@ewc.edu
SIMHAI, Toofawn 701-662-1511 355 A toofawn.simhai@lrsc.edu
SIMIC, Laura 208-426-3276 131 C laurasimic@boisestate.edu
SIMINOE, Judith, P 320-308-2122 247 E jpsiminoe@stcloudstate.edu
SIMINOFF, Laura 215-204-8624 411 B lasiminoff@temple.edu
SIMION, Karen 691-320-2480 519 G ksimion@comfsm.fm
SIMIONE, Lauren, M 302-831-1408 90 I lemurray@udel.edu
SIMISON, Kynan 765-641-4076 156 A klsimison@anderson.edu
SIMKIN, Breanne 410-532-5735 206 D bsimkin@ndm.edu
SIMKIN, Breanne 973-748-9000 284 A breanne_simkin@bloomfield.edu
SIMMELINK, Scott, K 712-707-7170 172 G scotts@nwciowa.edu
SIMMERMACHER, Bret 251-626-3303 7 G bsimmermacher@ussa.edu
SIMMERS, Susan 970-351-2109 83 F susan.simmers@unco.edu
SIMMONDS, Thomas 914-674-7473 314 I tsimmonds1@mercy.edu
SIMMONS, Adeidra 580-559-5239 375 I asimmons@ecok.edu
SIMMONS, Annette 704-403-3517 336 B annette.simmons@carolinashealthcare.org
SIMMONS, Bette, M 973-328-5171 285 B bsimmons@ccm.edu
SIMMONS, Blair 510-869-1592 59 F bsimmons@samuelmerritt.edu
SIMMONS, Brian 803-754-4100 420 E
SIMMONS, Cardell 360-779-9993 496 B csimmons@ncad.edu
SIMMONS, Carletta 336-334-7600 350 C gcsimmons@ncat.edu
SIMMONS, Charlana 508-831-6645 226 E cysimmons@wpi.edu
SIMMONS, Charlotte 405-974-2538 380 J cksimmons@uco.edu
SIMMONS, Christopher 919-668-6285 337 C chris.simmons@duke.edu
SIMMONS, D. Glenn 602-279-1011 470 I simmonsg@wbu.edu
SIMMONS, Dale 559-453-2031 43 J dale.simmons@fresno.edu
SIMMONS, Dan 580-745-2839 379 J dsimmons@se.edu
SIMMONS, David 706-253-4504 117 G dsimmons@chattahoocheetech.edu
SIMMONS, Doreen 408-733-1878 70 D doreen.simmons@uewm.edu
SIMMONS, Douglas 603-314-1775 221 E douglas.simmons@mcphs.edu
SIMMONS, Elaine 620-792-9214 175 C simmonse@bartonccc.edu
SIMMONS, Elizabeth, H 517-353-6486 233 G esimmons@msu.edu
SIMMONS, Emily 757-340-2121 479 D directoredcvab@centura.edu
SIMMONS, Gail, M 516-463-5402 310 D gail.m.simmons@hofstra.edu
SIMMONS, Gregory 410-455-1452 208 A gsimmons@umbc.edu
SIMMONS, Guy 972-238-6263 448 D gsimmons@dcccd.edu
SIMMONS, Gwen 417-334-6411 258 E simmons@cofo.edu
SIMMONS, Hezekiah, N 585-292-3320 315 L hsimmons@monroecc.edu
SIMMONS, Jacqueline 812-855-3312 159 H simmonja@iu.edu
SIMMONS, Jacqueline, A 812-855-9739 159 G simmonja@iu.edu
SIMMONS, Jay 484-365-7526 400 E jsimmons@lincoln.edu
SIMMONS, Jay, K 515-961-1566 173 E jay.simmons@simpson.edu
SIMMONS, Jeff 405-425-5560 377 B jeffrey.simmons@oc.edu
SIMMONS, Jennifer 212-854-2011 299 B jsimmons@barnard.edu
SIMMONS, Jeremy 415-351-3510 60 G jsimmons@sfai.edu
SIMMONS, Juanita 660-562-1750 264 I jsimmons@nwmissouri.edu
SIMMONS, Kelly, M 513-585-1317 359 D kelly.simmons@thechristhospital.com
SIMMONS, Kitty 951-785-2397 47 F ksimmons@lasierra.edu
SIMMONS, Lori 617-735-9825 214 F simmonslo@emmanuel.edu
SIMMONS, Martha 719-549-3303 81 M martha.simmons@pueblocc.edu
SIMMONS, Mary 407-888-8689 99 F msimmons@fcim.edu
SIMMONS, Max 405-682-1611 377 C msimmons@occc.edu
SIMMONS, Michael 937-708-5633 373 H msimmons@wilberforce.edu
SIMMONS, Michael 724-738-3333 407 C michael.simmons@sru.edu
SIMMONS, Pamela 404-752-1761 123 F psimmons@msm.edu
SIMMONS, Regina 704-463-3404 348 B regina.simmons@pfeiffer.edu
SIMMONS, Regina Ray 404-756-4047 115 I rsimmons@atlm.edu

SIMMONS, Rick ... 318-257-2912 197 A
simmons@latech.edu
SIMMONS, Robert, A ... 816-235-1368 268 D
simmonsr@umkc.edu
SIMMONS, Roy ... 304-205-6708 502 K
roy.simmons@bridgevalley.edu
SIMMONS, Ruth, J ... 936-261-2111 458 F
rjsimmons@pvamu.edu
SIMMONS, Sara ... 910-521-6629 351 E
sara.simmons@uncp.edu
SIMMONS, Shanni, E ... 812-888-4026 165 E
ssimmons@vinu.edu
SIMMONS, Stefon ... 646-216-2860 317 E
ssimmons@nycda.edu
SIMMONS, Steve ... 978-478-3400 223 E
ssimmons@northpoint.edu
SIMMONS, Steven ... 803-508-7270 418 C
simmonss@atc.edu
SIMMONS, Tami ... 704-378-1024 338 I
tsimmons@jcsu.edu
SIMMONS, Teresa ... 937-298-3399 364 B
teresa.simmons@kc.edu
SIMMONS, Thomas ... 419-772-2450 367 G
t-simmons@onu.edu
SIMMONS, Todd ... 480-517-8137 14 B
todd.simmons@riosalado.edu
SIMMONS, Todd, H ... 336-285-2606 350 C
thsimmons@ncat.edu
SIMMONS, Toye ... 713-221-8061 465 C
simmonsto@uhd.edu
SIMMONS-HENRY,
Linda ... 903-593-8311 461 B
lhenry@texascollege.edu
SIMMONS-JOHNSON,
Deborah ... 713-718-7332 450 D
deborah.johnson@hccs.edu
SIMMS, Marcie ... 740-351-3549 369 L
msimms@shawnee.edu
SIMMS, Pat ... 501-337-5000 19 C
pats@coto.edu
SIMMS, Rebecca ... 859-246-6761 185 G
rebecca.simms@kctcs.edu
SIMMS, Sandra ... 303-384-2008 78 J
ssims@mines.edu
SIMNING, Jennie ... 952-995-1533 244 G
jennie.simning@hennepintech.edu
SIMON, Barbara ... 563-589-0332 174 D
bsimon@wartburgseminary.edu
SIMON, Bashe ... 212-463-0400 331 F
simonb@touro.edu
SIMON, Caroline ... 509-777-3755 500 H
csimon@whitworth.edu
SIMON, Darica ... 225-216-8171 192 B
simond@mybrcc.edu
SIMON, David ... 920-565-2501 507 K
simondr@lakeland.edu
SIMON, David, F ... 215-871-6819 407 G
simond@pcom.edu
SIMON, Donald, E ... 718-933-6700 315 K
dsimon@monroecollege.edu
SIMON, Elizabeth ... 845-675-4679 319 C
elizabeth.simon@nyack.edu
SIMON, Jacob ... 419-448-3421 370 K
simonja@tiffin.edu
SIMON, Janet ... 406-657-2278 272 B
jsimon@msubillings.edu
SIMON, Jason ... 620-223-2700 177 E
jasons@fortscott.edu
SIMON, Jason, F ... 940-565-2085 466 B
jason.simon@unt.edu
SIMON, Jennifer ... 406-496-4307 272 E
jsimon@mtech.edu
SIMON, Jill, K ... 651-641-8211 241 L
simon@csp.edu
SIMON, John, D ... 610-758-3156 400 B
jds414@lehigh.edu
SIMON, Kathryn, C ... 859-233-8124 189 H
ksimon@transy.edu
SIMON, Lou Anna, K ... 517-355-6560 233 G
presmail@msu.edu
SIMON, Marlene ... 310-954-4135 52 H
msimon@msmu.edu
SIMON, Michael ... 810-762-5640 234 F
michael.simon@mcc.edu
SIMON, Michael ... 936-633-5201 442 I
msimon@angelina.edu
SIMON, Paul, M ... 203-837-8494 85 B
simonp@wcsu.edu
SIMON, Scott, L ... 740-368-3394 368 N
slsimon@owu.edu
SIMON, Tia ... 832-230-5156 453 K
tsimon1@na.edu
SIMON, Tina, L ... 419-372-2700 357 F
tsimon@bgsu.edu
SIMONCELLI, Andrew ... 985-448-4131 197 C
andrew.simoncelli@nicholls.edu
SIMONDS, Catherine, A 816-235-1375 268 D
simondsca@umkc.edu
SIMONDS, Kurt ... 971-722-5573 386 C
kurt.simonds@pcc.edu
SIMONDS, Linda, A ... 413-565-1000 211 C
lsimonds@baypath.edu
SIMONE, Carmen, M ... 719-846-5541 82 L
carmen.simone@trinidadstate.edu
SIMONE, Christine ... 402-399-2483 274 A
csimone@csm.edu
SIMONE, John ... 609-586-4800 287 A
simonej@mccc.edu
SIMONE, Lucian ... 203-285-2223 85 E
lsimone@gwcc.commnet.edu
SIMONEAU,
Christopher (Chris), J 239-590-1067 109 C
csimoneau@fgcu.edu
SIMONESCHI,
Joseph, W ... 626-585-7338 56 B
jwsimoneschi@pasadena.edu
SIMONI, Mary ... 518-276-6575 321 A
msimoni@rpi.edu
SIMONIAN, Yasmen ... 801-626-7117 473 E
ysimonian@weber.edu
SIMONS, Amy ... 314-889-4780 260 C
asimons@fontbonne.edu
SIMONS, Debra ... 914-654-5644 305 A
dsimons@cnr.edu
SIMONS, Earl, G ... 718-262-3795 304 A
esimons@york.cuny.edu
SIMONS, Elizabeth ... 716-926-8963 310 B
esimons@hilbert.edu
SIMONS, Ernest ... 252-493-7243 345 E
esimons@email.pittcc.edu
SIMONS, Jill ... 870-972-3574 18 A
jsimons@astate.edu
SIMONS, Kelly ... 281-542-2050 455 L
kelly.simons@sjcd.edu
SIMONS, Kenneth, B ... 414-955-4577 508 D
ksimons@mcw.edu
SIMONS, Michael, A ... 718-990-6601 322 F
simonsm@stjohns.edu
SIMONS, Sherri, J ... 308-432-6355 276 B
ssimons@csc.edu
SIMONS, Shino ... 626-812-3053 26 U
ssimons@apu.edu
SIMONS, Valerie ... 303-492-5359 83 B
valerie.simons@colorado.edu
SIMONSEN, Jaime ... 651-201-1669 243 I
jaime.simonsen@so.mnscu.edu
SIMONSEN, Joe ... 406-771-4309 272 D
joe.simonsen@gfcmsu.edu
SIMONSON, Brian ... 406-265-3525 272 C
brian.simonson@msun.edu
SIMONSON, Larry ... 605-394-4148 429 A
larry.simonson@sdsmt.edu
SIMPKINS, Alice, M ... 706-396-8111 124 C
asimpkins@paine.edu
SIMPKINS, Felix ... 708-709-3518 148 I
fsimpkins@prairiestate.edu
SIMPKINS, Will ... 646-557-4709 302 F
wsimpkins@jjay.cuny.edu
SIMPSON, Amelia ... 606-248-0484 187 B
amy.simpson@kctcs.edu
SIMPSON, Andrea ... 317-274-2289 160 E
andmsimp@iupui.edu
SIMPSON, Andy, L ... 651-631-5239 251 C
alsimpson@unwsp.edu
SIMPSON, Angela ... 606-589-3025 187 B
angela.simpson@kctcs.edu
SIMPSON, Anita ... 580-628-6237 376 J
anita.simpson@noc.edu
SIMPSON, Atticus, J ... 828-448-3120 347 F
asimpson@wpcc.edu
SIMPSON, Brett ... 504-864-7787 194 G
bsimpson@loyno.edu
SIMPSON, Caroline ... 304-724-3700 501 D
csimpson@apus.edu
SIMPSON, Colleen ... 952-358-8146 246 D
colleen.simpson@normandale.edu
SIMPSON, Cynthia ... 281-649-3232 450 C
csimpson@hbu.edu
SIMPSON, Cynthia, F ... 718-990-6333 322 F
simpsoc1@stjohns.edu
SIMPSON, Dionne ... 619-596-2766 24 H
dsimpson@advancedtraining.edu
SIMPSON, Donald, E ... 417-836-5521 263 H
donsimpson@missouristate.edu
SIMPSON, Eric ... 801-622-1573 472 H
eric.simpson@stevenshenager.edu
SIMPSON, Erica ... 901-272-5139 434 B
esimpson@mca.edu
SIMPSON, Gregory, B ... 309-438-5669 140 L
gsimpso@ilstu.edu
SIMPSON, Jack ... 423-461-8955 435 A
jasimpson@milligan.edu
SIMPSON, Jacklyn, A ... 704-687-7501 351 C
jasimpso@uncc.edu
SIMPSON, Jane ... 678-839-5306 127 F
jsimpson@westga.edu
SIMPSON, Jim ... 281-756-3789 442 C
jsimpson@alvincollege.edu
SIMPSON, Joann ... 229-243-6940 116 C
joann.simpson@bainbridge.edu
SIMPSON, Juliene ... 973-290-4207 285 A
jsimpson@cse.edu
SIMPSON, Kim ... 863-297-1000 105 F
ksimpson@polk.edu
SIMPSON, Kurt ... 815-599-3501 139 F
kurt.simpson@highland.edu
SIMPSON, Lawrence, J ... 617-747-2150 212 B
academicaffairs@berklee.edu
SIMPSON, Mallory, M ... 313-593-5130 238 A
mallorys@umich.edu
SIMPSON, Mark ... 866-931-4300 265 H
mark.simpson@rockbridge.edu
SIMPSON, Matthew ... 417-447-2648 264 K
simpsonm@otc.edu
SIMPSON, Matthew ... 508-849-3462 210 H
msimpson@annamaria.edu
SIMPSON, Michael, E ... 518-564-2155 327 E
simpsome@plattsburgh.edu
SIMPSON, Philip ... 321-433-5078 97 N
simpsonp@easternflorida.edu
SIMPSON, Ralph ... 484-365-7528 400 E
rsimpson@lincoln.edu
SIMPSON, Rebecca ... 502-852-6397 190 C
becky.simpson@louisville.edu
SIMPSON, Rebecca ... 812-488-2151 164 G
bd3@evansville.edu
SIMPSON, Robert ... 731-661-5219 439 D
rsimpson@uu.edu
SIMPSON, Robert ... 304-696-2682 504 C
simpsonr@marshall.edu
SIMPSON, Stephanie ... 540-224-4686 482 A
srsimpson@jchs.edu
SIMPSON, Susan ... 217-786-9629 144 B
susan.simpson@llcc.edu
SIMPSON, Suzanne ... 256-824-6686 8 C
suzanne.simpson@uah.edu
SIMPSON, Tammi, R ... 540-458-4111 491 G
tsimpson@wlu.edu
SIMPSON, Todd ... 402-872-2304 276 C
tsimpson@peru.edu
SIMPSON, Viola ... 203-777-8573 84 G
vsimpson@albertus.edu
SIMPSON-LOGG,
Anastasia ... 707-468-3102 51 E
asimpson@mendocino.edu
SIMS, Angela ... 913-253-5017 181 C
angela.sims@spst.edu
SIMS, Bradford, L ... 301-369-2800 202 J
president@captechu.edu
SIMS, Carla, R ... 248-341-2197 235 D
crsims@oaklandcc.edu
SIMS, Dale ... 214-333-5249 447 D
dale@dbu.edu
SIMS, Damon, R ... 814-865-0909 403 F
drs37@psu.edu
SIMS, Darryl ... 920-424-1034 511 B
sims@uwosh.edu
SIMS, David ... 478-471-2780 123 A
david.sims@mga.edu
SIMS, Dora ... 281-756-3524 442 C
dsims@alvincollege.edu
SIMS, Geoffrey ... 201-360-4045 286 E
jsims@hccc.edu
SIMS, George, E ... 251-380-2262 7 B
gsims@shc.edu
SIMS, Guy ... 304-327-4512 503 O
gsims@bluefieldstate.edu
SIMS, Hunter ... 325-649-8830 450 H
hsims@hputx.edu
SIMS, Jacquelyn ... 310-660-3200 42 C
jsims@elcamino.edu
SIMS, Jeanette ... 704-687-5827 351 C
jeanette.sims@uncc.edu
SIMS, Joel ... 406-268-3719 272 D
joel.sims@gfcmsu.edu
SIMS, Kavaris ... 713-313-7078 461 E
kavaris.sims@tsu.edu
SIMS, Lecia ... 620-276-0473 177 G
lecia.sims@gcccks.edu
SIMS, Leslie ... 304-424-8221 505 C
leslie.sims@wvup.edu
SIMS, Linda, L ... 989-964-7144 236 F
llsims@svsu.edu
SIMS, Melinda ... 405-382-9604 379 I
m.sims@sscok.edu
SIMS, Myra ... 276-944-6236 480 J
msims@ehc.edu
SIMS, Patricia ... 256-216-6603 4 C
patricia.sims@athens.edu
SIMS, Patrick ... 608-890-3117 510 C
patrick.sims@wisc.edu
SIMS, Quanda, D ... 803-934-3422 422 G
qdsims@morris.edu
SIMS, Steve ... 724-266-3838 412 D
SIMS, Sue ... 803-508-7341 418 C
simss@atc.edu
SIMS, Suzanne ... 256-216-3314 4 C
suzanne.sims@athens.edu
SIMS-AUBERT, Gail ... 920-465-2712 510 E
simsg@uwgb.edu
SIMSON, Earl, L ... 401-456-8106 417 A
esimson@ric.edu
SINA, Julie ... 310-206-8962 69 B
jsina@support.ucla.edu
SINCAVAGE, Joseph ... 610-436-3535 407 D
jsincavage@wcupa.edu
SINCLAIR, Ashley ... 847-735-5231 142 H
sinclair@lakeforest.edu
SINCLAIR, Christian ... 610-625-7896 402 D
sinclairc@moravian.edu
SINCLAIR, Kelli ... 630-466-7900 155 C
ksinclair@waubonsee.edu
SINCLAIR, Lisa ... 617-373-2157 223 D
SINCLAIR, Miliani ... 256-761-6205 7 D
msinclair@talladega.edu
SINCLAIR, Robert, L ... 312-788-1144 154 I
rsinclair@vandercook.edu
SINCLAIR, Shannon, E ... 804-287-6683 486 G
ssinclai@richmond.edu
SINCLAIR, Sue ... 309-694-5429 139 G
ssinclair@icc.edu
SINCLAIR, Taylor ... 402-471-2505 276 A
tsinclair@nscs.edu
SINCLAIR, Tori ... 816-802-3379 261 C
tsinclair@kcai.edu
SINCLAIR CURTIS,
Jennifer ... 530-752-0554 68 H
jscurtis@ucdavis.edu
SINDELAR, Peggy ... 972-273-3283 448 C
psindelar@dcccd.edu
SINDER, Janet ... 718-780-7975 300 A
janet.sinder@brooklaw.edu
SINDT, Christopher ... 925-631-4088 59 C
csindt@stmarys-ca.edu
SINDT, Christopher ... 925-631-4309 59 C
csindt@stmarys-ca.edu
SINES, Robert, G ... 330-672-9780 363 I
rsines@kent.edu
SINEWAY, Carla ... 989-775-4123 236 E
csineway@sagchip.edu
SINGEL, David ... 406-994-4371 272 A
dsingel@montana.edu
SINGELL, Larry ... 812-855-2392 159 H
lsingell@indiana.edu
SINGER, David ... 518-445-3211 297 K
dsing@albanylaw.edu
SINGER, Eric ... 410-337-6456 204 A
eric.singer@goucher.edu
SINGER, Jefferson ... 860-439-2010 86 H
jefferson.singer@conncoll.edu
SINGER, Lori ... 212-229-5662 316 E
singerl@newschool.edu
SINGER, Lynn, T ... 216-368-1610 358 C
lts5@case.edu
SINGER, Marc ... 609-984-1130 292 B
msinger@tesu.edu
SINGER, Marjorie ... 212-237-8911 302 F
msinger@jjay.cuny.edu
SINGER, Mark ... 914-493-1909 318 A
mark_singer@nymc.edu
SINGER, Susan, R ... 407-646-2355 106 J
srsinger@rollins.edu
SINGER, Timothy ... 315-498-2485 319 G
singert@sunyocc.edu
SINGER, Yossi ... 718-268-4700 320 K
SINGH, Amit ... 937-328-6026 359 H
singha@clarkstate.edu
SINGH, Amitabh ... 229-430-7845 114 I
amitabh.singh@asurams.edu
SINGH, Anita ... 916-568-3057 50 E
singha@losrios.edu
SINGH, Avena ... 541-888-1583 387 A
asingh@socc.edu
SINGH, Gangaram ... 858-642-8109 53 H
gsingh@nu.edu
SINGH, Gurbhushan ... 913-469-8500 178 F
gurbhushan@jccc.edu
SINGH, Hamwant (Neil) 718-429-6600 333 B
neil.singh@vaughn.edu
SINGH, Joanne ... 859-985-3056 183 I
singhj@berea.edu
SINGH, Judith, R ... 315-267-2188 328 A
singhr@potsdam.edu
SINGH, Kamla ... 201-761-6082 291 D
ksingh@saintpeters.edu
SINGH, Kanwal ... 914-395-2303 323 K
ksingh@sarahlawrence.edu
SINGH, Kulwant ... 408-864-8745 43 E
singhkulwant@deanza.edu
SINGH, Manohar ... 707-826-3961 34 A
ms619@humboldt.edu

SINGH, Meharvan 817-735-5429 466 D meharvan.singh@unthsc.edu
SINGH, Nancy 559-251-4215 28 I library@calchristiancollege.edu
SINGH, Piyusha 573-875-7240 258 F psingh@ccis.edu
SINGH, Raj 212-237-8512 302 F rsingh@jjay.cuny.edu
SINGH, Shailen 245-519-5400 459 D shailensingh@tamuct.edu
SINGH, Simran 805-893-8377 70 B singh-s@sa.ucsb.edu
SINGH, Sudhir 301-687-4019 209 A ssingh@frostburg.edu
SINGH, Tanuja 210-436-3706 455 J tsingh@stmarytx.edu
SINGH CHAUHAN, Indrajeet 212-423-2769 309 G indrajeet.singh@heleneFuld.edu
SINGH MOONILALL, Seeta 561-912-1211 98 F seetas@evergladesuniversity.edu
SINGLER, Melissa 910-362-7329 341 E msingler@cfcc.edu
SINGLETARY, Chip 850-201-8544 112 C singlech@tcc.fl.edu
SINGLETARY, James, M 740-392-6868 366 B jim.singletary@mvnu.edu
SINGLETARY, Joshua 518-694-7896 297 J joshua.singletary@acphs.edu
SINGLETARY, Laura 509-682-6865 500 D lsingletary@wvc.edu
SINGLETARY, Michael 360-383-3035 500 F msingletary@whatcom.ctc.edu
SINGLETARY, Sheila 985-732-6640 192 K
SINGLETON, Andre 510-981-2877 56 F asingleton@peralta.edu
SINGLETON, Dana, M 757-822-2181 489 H dsingleton@tcc.edu
SINGLETON, Daphne 903-730-4890 451 D dsingleton@jarvis.edu
SINGLETON, Derrick 859-985-3130 183 I singletonp@berea.edu
SINGLETON, Gena, L 713-646-1778 456 H gsingleton@stcl.edu
SINGLETON, Greg 252-638-7247 342 E singletong@cravencc.edu
SINGLETON, Gregory 931-221-7005 430 B singletong@apsu.edu
SINGLETON, Heather 757-446-5870 480 C singleha@evms.edu
SINGLETON, J. Ron 864-488-8274 422 B rsingleton@limestone.edu
SINGLETON, Janet 404-880-8286 117 H jsingleton@cau.edu
SINGLETON, Jennie 252-940-6202 340 N jennie.singleton@beaufortccc.edu
SINGLETON, John, L 817-257-7871 461 A j.singleton@tcu.edu
SINGLETON, Larry, G 845-575-3000 314 C lawrence.singleton@marist.edu
SINGLETON, Robin 870-762-3161 17 K rsingleton@smail.anc.edu
SINGLETON, Shawn, T 859-233-8154 189 H ssingleton@transy.edu
SINGLETON-WALKER, Catherine 662-254-3365 255 A cswalker@mvsu.edu
SINGLETON-YOUNG, Patricia 843-349-2304 420 A psyoung@coastal.edu
SINGLEY, Charles 803-376-5801 418 D csingley@allenuniversity.edu
SINGLEY, Jason 510-885-3441 31 F jason.singley@csueastbay.edu
SINIARD, Michelle 478-218-3330 117 D msiniard@centralgatech.edu
SINIARD, Michelle 478-218-3330 117 E msiniard@centralgatech.edu
SINIGAGLIA, Frank 845-434-5750 330 F fsinigaglia@sunysullivan.edu
SINK, Michael 407-823-2711 110 C michael.sink@ucf.edu
SINK, Susanna, C 724-357-2205 406 C scsink@iup.edu
SINK, Tom 567-661-7221 369 A thomas_sink@owens.edu
SINN, Brad 320-363-5211 241 I bsinn@csbsju.edu
SINN, Jeanna 203-591-5238 87 H jsinn@post.edu
SINNOT, Dawn 215-751-8085 393 A dsinnot@ccp.edu
SINUTKO, John 805-378-1454 73 A jsinutko@vcccd.edu
SIPE, Bryan 912-279-5819 118 A bsipe@ccga.edu
SIPE, Rebecca 734-487-0341 229 K rsipe@emich.edu
SIPES, Jennifer, L 217-581-3221 138 A jlsipes@eiu.edu
SIPES, Stacie 903-875-7736 453 J stacie.sipes@navarrocollege.edu
SIPHER, Justin 315-229-5319 323 D jsipher@stlawu.edu
SIPOS, George 585-395-5466 326 D gsipos@brockport.edu
SIPPEL, Christopher 419-434-5467 372 B sippel@findlay.edu
SIPPEL, Len 336-316-2841 338 C sippellc@guilford.edu
SIPSER, Michael 617-253-8900 221 C
SIRANGELO-ELBADAWY, Catherine 201-360-4261 286 E csirangelo@hccc.edu
SIRBU, Jerald, B 303-369-5151 81 L jbs@plattcolorado.edu
SIRIANNI, Frank 212-636-6265 308 G sirianni@fordham.edu
SIRIANO, Joseph 323-469-3300 25 D info@amda.edu
SIRILLA, Michael 740-283-6245 361 L msirilla@franciscan.edu
SIRIMANGKALA, Pawena 305-899-3453 95 G psirimangkala@barry.edu
SIRJU-JOHNSON, Nicole 607-777-4472 325 A njohnson@binghamton.edu
SIRONEN, Jacqueline 419-448-2261 362 G jsironen@heidelberg.edu
SIRPILLA, Sharon, L 330-471-8411 364 H ssirpilla@malone.edu
SISCHO, Brian, C 919-515-3226 350 E bcsischo@ncsu.edu
SISCO, Craig 405-682-7568 377 C michael.c.sisco@occc.edu
SISCO, Rodney, K 630-752-5028 155 F rodney.sisco@wheaton.edu
SISCOE, Dee 417-836-5526 263 H dsiscoe@missouristate.edu
SISE, Daniel, M 314-516-6378 268 E sised@umsl.edu
SISEMORE, John 417-455-5674 259 D johnsisemore@crowder.edu
SISK, Beth 402-399-2415 274 A bsisk@csm.edu
SISK, Matthew 304-457-6247 501 A siskmr@ab.edu
SISK, Megan 714-556-3610 72 F megan.sisk@vanguard.edu
SISKAR, John, F 716-878-3787 326 E siskarjf@buffalostate.edu
SISKO, John 704-337-2833 348 D
SISLER, Kelli 301-387-3060 203 I kelli.sisler@garrettcollege.edu
SISNEROS, Kathy 970-491-6384 78 N kathy.sisneros@colostate.edu
SISNEROS, Patrick 425-388-9026 494 F psisnero@everettcc.edu
SISSION, Amanda 843-863-7991 419 C asission@csuniv.edu
SISSON, Cindy, N 574-372-5100 158 B sissoncn@grace.edu
SISSON, Jeanne, M 518-580-5664 324 D jsisson@skidmore.edu
SISSON, Jillian 402-354-7137 275 P jillian.sisson@methodistcollege.edu
SISSON, Karen 909-621-8132 57 I karen.sisson@pomona.edu
SISSON, Karl 585-567-9340 310 F karl.sisson@houghton.edu
SISSON, Philip, J 978-322-8488 220 C sissonp@middlesex.mass.edu
SITARSKI, Karen 856-415-2110 289 G ksitarski@rcgc.edu
SITES, John 954-776-4476 102 G jsites@keiseruniversity.edu
SITES, Linda, K 301-447-5306 206 B lsites@msmary.edu
SITHARAMAN, Sri 706-507-8963 118 C sri@columbusstate.edu
SITORIUS, Patty 402-461-7331 274 I psitorius@hastings.edu
SITTON, Michael, R 315-267-2812 328 A sittonmr@potsdam.edu
SITZABEE, William, E 814-865-4402 403 F wes25@psu.edu
SIVADASAN, Shobi 203-932-7133 89 D ssivadasan@newhaven.edu
SIVERT, Shayla 760-744-1150 55 K ssivert@palomar.edu
SIVILLO, Jeremy 814-866-8143 399 C jsivillo@lecom.edu
SIWABESSY, Genevieve 916-608-6768 50 H siwabeg@flc.losrios.edu
SIX, Jonathan 919-761-2100 349 C jsix@sebts.edu
SIXTA, Jeff 913-288-7613 178 H jsixta@kckcc.edu
SIZEMORE, Amanda 636-922-8388 265 J asizemore@stchas.edu
SIZEMORE, Dorothea 434-949-1012 489 E dorothea.sizemore@southside.edu
SIZEMORE, Ella 404-225-4712 115 J esizemore@atlantatech.edu
SIZEMORE, Lisa 828-339-4000 346 H l_sizemore@southwesterncc.edu
SIZER, Judith 617-873-0171 213 B judith.sizer@cambridgecollege.edu
SJOBERG, Connie 918-495-6542 378 H csjoberg@oru.edu
SJOGREN, Michelle 859-442-1172 185 I michelle.sjogren@kctcs.edu
SJOGREN, Roxie, L 785-227-3380 175 E sjogrenr@bethanylb.edu
SJOQUIST, Corey 608-785-8939 510 F csjoquist@uwlax.edu
SJOVOLD, Carl 916-558-2402 50 I sjovolc@scc.losrios.edu
SJUTS, Joseph, H 816-501-3700 257 G joe.sjuts@avila.edu
SKABROUD, Ryan 920-693-1347 513 H ryan.skabroud@gotoltc.edu
SKACH, Peter 773-298-3548 151 C skach@sxu.edu
SKADBERG, Ingrid 508-854-7545 220 G iskadberg@qcc.mass.edu
SKAFF, Penny 949-582-4573 64 J pskaff@saddleback.edu
SKAGGS, Brandon 254-295-4496 466 A bskaggs@umhb.edu
SKAGGS, Derek, S 417-625-9378 263 G skaggs-d@mssu.edu
SKALLERUD, Ron 715-365-4416 514 E rskallerud@nicoletcollege.edu
SKAMRA, Brian 920-748-8174 509 H skamrab@ripon.edu
SKANTZ, Ingrid 423-236-2833 436 C ilskantz@southern.edu
SKARDA, Mary Jo 641-782-1425 173 I skarda@swcciowa.edu
SKARI, Lisa 206-878-3710 495 E lskari@highline.edu
SKARRO, Scott 701-255-3285 355 I sskaro@uttc.edu
SKARSTEN, Fawn 810-762-3327 238 B skarsten@umflint.edu
SKARUPPA, Cindy 216-687-5353 359 L c.skaruppa@csuohio.edu
SKATES, Kathy 229-430-3524 114 J kskates@albanytech.edu
SKEDROS, James 617-850-1212 215 I jskedros@hchc.edu
SKEENS, Randy 304-896-7366 503 D randy.skeens@southernwv.edu
SKELLON, Hilary 720-890-8922 80 I director@itea.edu
SKELLY, Theresa 978-921-4242 222 B theresa.skelly@montserrat.edu
SKELTON, Don 662-562-3354 255 C
SKELTON, Lonnie 714-867-5009 64 G lskelton@southcoastcollege.com
SKERIK, Maryellen 630-637-5678 147 E mjskerik@noctrl.edu
SKETCH, Denny 513-558-9964 371 G denny.sketch@uc.edu
SKEVAKIS, Anthony 201-761-7360 291 D askevakisp@saintpeters.edu
SKIDMORE, Alan 304-766-3261 505 A askidmore@wvstateu.edu
SKIDMORE, Ashley 815-836-5212 143 E skidmoas@lewisu.edu
SKIDMORE, Charlene 515-271-2999 168 J charlene.skidmore@drake.edu
SKIDMORE, Daniel, L 315-445-4759 312 F skidmodl@lemoyne.edu
SKIDMORE, Heather 304-424-8210 505 C heather.skidmore@wvup.edu
SKIDMORE, Sue 423-461-8729 435 A shskidmore@milligan.edu
SKILES, Adam, L 260-359-4130 159 B askiles@huntington.edu
SKILL, Thomas, D 937-229-3511 372 A tskill1@udayton.edu
SKINKLE, Lee 417-328-1601 267 A lskinkle@sbuniv.edu
SKINNER, Adrienne 269-467-9945 230 C askinner@glenoaks.edu
SKINNER, Billie 727-569-1401 112 G bskinner@trinitycollege.edu
SKINNER, Bruce 573-651-5103 266 M bskinner@semo.edu
SKINNER, Celeste 310-265-6143 59 E celeste.skinner@usw.salvationarmy.org
SKINNER, Charlotte 513-745-5660 371 F charlotte.skinner@uc.edu
SKINNER, Dana 978-934-2310 217 B dana_skinner@uml.edu
SKINNER, Daniel 973-748-9000 284 A daniel_skinner@bloomfield.edu
SKINNER, Dean 479-248-7236 19 F dskinner@ecollege.edu
SKINNER, Deb 641-784-5108 169 D dskinner@graceland.edu
SKINNER, Denese 806-651-2345 460 E dskinner@wtamu.edu
SKINNER, Georgia 404-627-2681 116 E georgia.skinner@beulah.edu
SKINNER, James 580-774-3788 380 B james.skinner@swosu.edu
SKINNER, Katherine 615-460-6342 430 D kathryn.skinner@belmont.edu
SKINNER, Kendra 573-651-2274 266 M ksskinner@semo.edu
SKINNER, Loren 409-772-6615 469 C leskinne@utmb.edu
SKINNER, Marc 208-282-7954 132 I marcs@uidaho.edu
SKINNER, Patricia, A 704-922-6475 343 D skinner.pat@gaston.edu
SKINNER, Randall 928-428-8252 12 I randall.skinner@eac.edu
SKINNER, Robert 304-473-8557 505 G skinner_b@wvwc.edu
SKINNER, Sally 208-459-5770 131 H sskinner@collegeofidaho.edu
SKINNER, Sara 269-927-6851 232 G skinner@lakemichigancollege.edu
SKINNER, Thomas 225-578-0335 193 M tskinner@lsu.edu
SKINNER, Thomas 225-578-2111 193 L
SKINNER, Thomas 215-368-5000 389 H tskinner@biblical.edu
SKIPP, Steven, I 904-819-6258 98 I sskipp@flagler.edu
SKIPPER, Bob 270-745-4295 190 F bob.skipper@wku.edu
SKIPPER, Curt 601-635-2111 252 I cskipper@eccc.edu
SKIPPER, Eric 843-208-8000 425 B eskipper@uscb.edu
SKIPPER, Nick 850-973-9495 104 D skippern@nfcc.edu
SKIPWORTH, Stan 909-621-8033 37 K stan_skipworth@cuc.claremont.edu
SKIPWORTH, Stan 909-621-8291 37 L stan_skipworth@cuc.claremont.edu
SKIVIAT, David, M 740-283-6223 361 L dskiviat@franciscan.edu
SKLANDER, Linda 262-524-7288 506 G sklander@carrollu.edu
SKLAR, David 914-347-3910 333 H david.sklar@sunywcc.edu
SKLAR, Jay 314-434-4044 259 B jay.sklar@covenantseminary.edu
SKLBA, Stephanie 262-564-2662 513 G sklba@gtc.edu
SKLEDER, Anne 570-408-4200 414 H anne.skleder@wilkes.edu
SKLUT, John 509-313-3175 495 A sklut@gonzaga.edu
SKOBLA, Kristen 315-792-5321 315 I kskobla@mvcc.edu
SKOFF, Robert, M 724-847-6581 395 J rmskoff@geneva.edu
SKOGEN, Larry, C 701-224-5431 354 F larry.skogen@bismarckstate.edu
SKOGEN, Sherri 715-425-3201 511 E sherri.skogen@uwrf.edu
SKOGLUND, Elizabeth, A 410-543-6161 209 B easkoglund@salisbury.edu
SKOLNIK, Richard, J 315-312-3168 327 D richard.skolnik@oswego.edu
SKOMP, Elizabeth 931-598-1254 436 A eskomp@sewanee.edu
SKONER, Peter, R 814-472-3085 409 G pskoner@francis.edu
SKORACZEWSKI, Kathleen 715-682-1369 509 D kskoraczewski@northland.edu
SKORACZEWSKI, Paul 715-682-1841 509 D pskoraczewski@northland.edu
SKORIN, Carla 562-947-8755 65 D carlaskorin@scuhs.edu
SKORTZ, Brian 270-686-6416 183 J brian.skortz@brescia.edu

SKOWYRA, Jamie 508-213-2131 223 C jamie.skowyra@nichols.edu
SKRABA, Stephanie 218-262-6731 244 H stephanieskraba@hibbing.edu
SKRABACZ, Shari 314-968-6996 269 N shariskrabacz98@webster.edu
SKRAINER, Elizabeth 585-385-8427 322 E eskrainer@sjfc.edu
SKROCKI, Kyle 802-387-6887 475 C kyleskrocki@landmark.edu
SKRYD, Jackie 727-392-6809 107 A skryd.jackie@spcollege.edu
SKRYDLAK, Robert, J 402-280-2412 274 D robertskrydlak@creighton.edu
SKUCE, John, R 910-893-1200 336 C
SKUDINSKAS, Algis 304-367-4111 504 A algis.skudinskas@fairmontstate.edu
SKUKA, Eva 973-278-5400 283 J esk@berkeleycollege.edu
SKUKA, Eva 973-278-5400 299 F esk@berkeleycollege.edu
SKURJA, Michael 801-375-5125 472 F mskurja@rmuohp.edu
SKURZEWSKI-SERVANT, Missy 715-422-5356 514 B missy.skurzewskiservant@mstc.edu
SKUTKA, Linda, L 240-895-4289 206 G llskutka@smcm.edu
SKVARLA, Jennifer 815-836-5201 143 E skvarlje@lewisu.edu
SKYLAND, Diane 406-756-3668 271 A dskyland@fvcc.edu
SLAATHAUG, Carrie 605-256-5009 428 G carrie.slaathaug@dsu.edu
SLAATS, Jacqueline 847-735-5285 142 H slaats@lakeforest.edu
SLABACH, Frederick, G 817-531-4401 463 G fslabach@txwes.edu
SLABAUGH, David 864-644-5558 424 B dslabaugh@swu.edu
SLABAUGH, Dawnie 530-938-5373 39 H slabaugh@siskiyous.edu
SLABAUGH, Katie 765-285-1545 156 C kslabaugh@bsu.edu
SLABODEN, Carolyn 781-283-2216 225 D cslaboden@wellesley.edu
SLACK, Craig 301-314-7164 207 G cslack@umd.edu
SLACK, Gregory, C 315-268-6475 304 B gslack@clarkson.edu
SLACK, Robert 626-914-8581 37 G rslack@citruscollege.edu
SLADE, David 706-236-2229 116 D dslade@berry.edu
SLADE, Kellie, W 856-691-8600 285 C kslade@cccnj.edu
SLADE, Patricia 973-877-3209 285 K slade@essex.edu
SLAFKOSKY, Mary, V 260-422-5561 159 D mvslafkosky@indianatech.edu
SLAGELL, Jeff 662-846-4441 252 H jslagell@deltastate.edu
SLAGELL-GOSSEN, Reonna 405-422-1253 379 B gossenr@redlandscc.edu
SLAGER, Karen 815-802-8110 142 C kslager@kcc.edu
SLAGLE, Judith, B 423-439-6076 431 H slagle@etsu.edu
SLAICH, Lucy 410-704-2050 209 C lslaich@towson.edu
SLANGER, Zvi Dov 410-486-0006 202 E
SLANN, Martin 903-566-7368 468 C mslann@uttyler.edu
SLATER, Bernata 650-358-6795 61 Q slaterb@smccd.edu
SLATER, Emilee 559-442-8225 66 G emilee.slater@fresnocitycollege.edu
SLATER, Kara 616-395-7835 231 D slater@hope.edu
SLATER, Richard 312-850-7016 136 C rslater4@ccc.edu
SLATER, Ryan 412-291-6313 389 F rslater@aii.edu
SLATER, Troy 231-348-6610 234 H tslater@ncmich.edu
SLATER, William 615-675-5255 441 B wslater@welch.edu
SLATON, Gwendolyn 973-877-3233 285 K slaton@essex.edu
SLATON, Nate 270-534-3244 187 C nathaniel.slaton@kctcs.edu
SLATTERY, Daniel 410-704-2364 209 C dslattery@towson.edu
SLATTERY, Katheryn 815-836-5275 143 E slatteka@lewisu.edu
SLATTERY, Kimberly 610-436-0043 407 D kslattery@wcupa.edu
SLAUGHTER, Amanda 562-903-4552 27 E amanda.slaughter@biola.edu
SLAUGHTER, Craig 740-427-5430 364 A slaughterc@kenyon.edu
SLAUGHTER, John 254-267-7024 454 L jslaughter@rangercollege.edu
SLAUGHTER, Keith 404-614-6378 122 B kslaughter@itc.edu
SLAUGHTER, Matthew, J 603-646-2460 281 C matthew.j.slaughter@dartmouth.edu
SLAUGHTER, Mildred 361-593-2834 460 B mildred.slaughter@tamuk.edu
SLAUGHTER, Sabra, C 843-792-2228 422 C slaughsc@musc.edu
SLAUGHTER, Shirley 510-981-2840 56 F sslaughter@peralta.edu
SLAUGHTER ALLISON, Michelle 619-961-4222 67 F mallison@tjsl.edu
SLAVAS, Douglas 413-565-1000 211 C dslavas@baypath.edu
SLAVIN, Dennis 646-660-6504 301 B dennis.slavin@baruch.cuny.edu
SLAVIN, Joan, L 714-850-4800 67 B slavin@taftu.edu
SLAVIN, Lisa 781-239-2501 220 A lslavin@massbay.edu
SLAVINKAS, Brian, R 312-915-8787 144 D bslavin@luc.edu
SLAVSKY, David 773-508-8352 144 D dslavsk@luc.edu
SLAVSKY, David, B 773-508-8352 144 D dslavsk@luc.edu
SLAWSON, Linda 903-785-7661 454 F lslawson@parisjc.edu
SLAYMAKER, Valerie 651-213-4746 242 F vslaymaker@hazeldenbettyford.edu
SLAYTON, Deborah, L 217-420-6774 145 J dslayton@millikin.edu
SLEASMAN, Brent, C 419-434-4201 373 K president@winebrenner.edu
SLEDGE, Donald 205-929-6442 2 G dsledge@lawsonstate.edu
SLEEMAN, Kerri 906-487-2303 234 A kasleema@mtu.edu
SLEETH, Cathy 509-359-6582 494 D csleeth1@ewu.edu
SLEIGHT, Garth 406-874-6212 271 D sleightg@milescc.edu
SLEJKO, Christa 972-273-3010 448 C cslejko@dcccd.edu
SLEKAR, Timothy 608-663-2293 507 D tslekar@edgewood.edu
SLENSKI, Amanda 989-463-7428 226 H slenskiar@alma.edu
SLEPITZA, Ron 816-501-3750 257 G ron.slepitza@avila.edu
SLESNICK, Daniel, T 512-471-4363 467 C slesnick@austin.utexas.edu
SLETTEN, Sheryl, L 605-336-6588 428 B ssletten@sfseminary.edu
SLEVA, Michael 616-451-3511 229 D msleva@davenport.edu
SLIFE, Harry 315-792-3738 332 H hfslife@utica.edu
SLIGO, Sarah 401-277-4863 417 B ssligo@risd.edu
SLIMAN, David 601-266-6633 256 E david.sliman@usm.edu
SLIMAN, George, S 412-578-8826 391 G slimangs@carlow.edu
SLIMP, Mickey 903-877-1276 469 A mickey.slimp@uthct.edu
SLINGER, Ron 303-914-6417 82 B ron.slinger@rrcc.edu
SLINKARD, Tiffany 417-455-5636 259 D tiffanyslinkard@crowder.edu
SLINKER, Bryan, K 509-335-9515 499 G slinker@vetmed.wsu.edu
SLISZ, John, P 716-851-1851 307 I slisz@ecc.edu
SLIWA, William 610-861-1320 402 D sliwaw@moravian.edu
SLIWINSKI, Ron 608-263-8025 510 C rsliwinski@uwhealth.org
SLIZEWSKI, James 215-489-2220 393 F james.slizewski@delval.edu
SLOAN, Barry 310-287-4278 49 H sloanba@wlac.edu
SLOAN, Damon, N 815-740-3398 154 G dsloan@stfrancis.edu
SLOAN, Daniel 315-792-3282 332 H drsloan@utica.edu
SLOAN, Gary 585-785-1355 308 D gary.sloan@flcc.edu
SLOAN, Justin, M 512-448-8545 455 I jsloan@stedwards.edu
SLOAN, Linda, M 651-962-6765 251 D sloa9780@stthomas.edu
SLOAN, Noel 806-742-4250 463 D noel.a.sloan@ttu.edu
SLOAN, JR., Robert, B 281-649-3450 450 C rsloan@hbu.edu
SLOAN, Roberta, H 315-684-6053 329 F sloanrh@morrisville.edu
SLOAN, Susan 810-762-9729 232 C ssloan@kettering.edu
SLOAN LATTA, Marcia 419-434-5722 372 B latta@findlay.edu
SLOANE, Emily 504-282-4455 195 D deansec@nobts.edu
SLOANE, Kobi 504-398-2235 196 E ksloane@uhcno.edu
SLOANE, Rakisha 847-233-7700 148 A rsloane@nc.edu
SLOANE, Tomecca 919-760-8631 339 H sloaneto@meredith.edu
SLOAS, Ike 901-843-3880 435 L
SLOBEN, Lisa 478-757-5171 128 E lsloben@wesleyancollege.edu
SLOBERT, Yantee 585-385-8423 322 E yslobert@sjfc.edu
SLOCKETT, Deena 407-303-7747 94 H deena.slockett@adu.edu
SLOCUM, Cameron 214-648-6404 469 E cameron.slocum@utsouthwestern.edu
SLOCUM, Dameian 401-598-1000 416 C dslocum@jwu.edu
SLOCUM, Jeff 315-655-7192 300 I jslocum@cazenovia.edu
SLOCUM, Stacy, S 585-385-8388 322 E sslocum@sjfc.edu
SLOKA, Sandra, L 815-740-5026 154 G ssloka@stfrancis.edu
SLOMBIA, Sonia 937-376-6574 358 I sslombia@centralstate.edu
SLOMOVITS, Mendel 732-414-2834 293 E
SLON, Dennis 310-338-5127 50 J dslon@lmu.edu
SLONE, Greta 606-889-4763 185 F gslone0020@kctcs.edu
SLONE, Tammy, L 937-766-7987 358 D slonet@cedarville.edu
SLOOP, John, M 615-322-7360 440 D john.m.sloop@vanderbilt.edu
SLOSS, Robert 401-232-6140 416 A rsloss@bryant.edu
SLOT, JR., John, J 407-582-1988 113 F wslot@valenciacollege.edu
SLOTNICK, Ruth 508-531-2783 217 D ruth.slotnick@bridgew.edu
SLOUGH, Rebecca 574-296-6228 155 K rslough@ambs.edu
SLOVER, Todd 603-513-1379 282 G todd.slover@granite.edu
SLOWENSKY, Joseph 714-744-7882 36 G slowensky@chapman.edu
SLOWINSKI, Mandy 715-346-4771 511 F mandy.slowinski@uwsp.edu
SLUDER, Dusti 850-484-2232 105 E dsluder@pensacolastate.edu
SLUDER, Richard 615-898-2324 434 H richard.sluder@mtsu.edu
SLUDER, Robin 423-478-7727 435 I rsluder@ptseminary.edu
SLUIS, Kimberly 630-637-5152 147 E kasluis@noctrl.edu
SLUSHER, Jennifer, J 540-985-8502 482 A jjslusher@jchs.edu
SLUSSER, Karen, L 570-389-4055 405 E kslusse2@bloomu.edu
SLUSSER, Kimberly 585-475-5911 321 D rasdar@rit.edu
SLUSSER, Wayne 570-586-2400 392 E wslusser@clarkssummitu.edu
SLY, Melissa 215-951-1000 398 F sly@lasalle.edu
SMAGLO, Stephanie 757-233-8757 491 F ssmaglo@vwu.edu
SMAIL, John 704-687-5630 351 C jsmail@uncc.edu
SMAILAGIC, Aida 650-493-4430 64 C aida.smailagic@sofia.edu
SMAJIC, Alen 315-792-5331 315 I asmajic@mvcc.edu
SMALE, Heather 207-454-1025 200 D hsmale@wccc.me.edu
SMALE, Maura 718-260-5470 303 D msmale@citytech.cuny.edu
SMALL, Allison 503-375-7193 383 A asmall@corban.edu
SMALL, Brent 575-562-2194 293 O brent.small@enmu.edu
SMALL, Christine 760-384-6376 47 B christine.small@cerrocoso.edu
SMALL, Cindy 406-265-3787 272 C csmall@msun.edu
SMALL, Daniel, E 202-994-6620 92 A dsmall@gwu.edu
SMALL, Darlene 843-383-8039 420 B dsmall@coker.edu
SMALL, David 406-638-3110 271 C smalld@lbhc.edu
SMALL, Elizabeth 508-793-3759 213 D esmall@holycross.edu
SMALL, Gillian 201-692-2000 286 B gsmall@fdu.edu
SMALL, Hank 843-863-7080 419 C hsmall@csuniv.edu
SMALL, Jessica 575-562-2218 293 O jessica.small@enmu.edu
SMALL, John, J 630-637-5701 147 E jjsmall@noctrl.edu
SMALL, Josh 803-641-3719 425 A joshs@usca.edu
SMALL, Natissia 314-516-5128 268 E smalln@umsl.edu
SMALL KELLOGG, Rebecca 315-786-6549 311 H rsmallkellogg@sunyjefferson.edu
SMALLEN, David, L 315-859-4169 309 D dsmallen@hamilton.edu
SMALLEY, Reid 585-345-6999 309 C rjsmalley@genesee.edu
SMALLEY, Robin 727-864-7564 97 O smallerm@eckerd.edu
SMALLIS, Michael 802-258-3570 476 B michael.smallis@sit.edu
SMALLS, Gerald 803-705-4694 418 G smallsg@benedict.edu
SMALLWOOD, Pamela 417-865-2815 260 B smallwoodp@evangel.edu
SMALLWOOD, Will 405-878-2703 377 A will.smallwood@okbu.edu
SMARKEL, James 419-434-4220 373 K jsmarkel@winebrenner.edu
SMARRELLI, JR., John 901-321-3250 431 A jsmarrel@cbu.edu
SMART, Cely 916-278-7737 33 C cely.smart@csus.edu
SMART, III, Clifton, M 417-836-8500 263 H president@missouristate.edu
SMART, Denise, T 512-245-2311 463 A ds37@txstate.edu
SMART, James, G 305-284-4505 112 O jsmart@miami.edu
SMART, Lucille 315-781-3449 310 C smart@hws.edu
SMART, Robert 616-331-2281 230 G smartr@gvsu.edu
SMART, Robert 203-582-3325 88 A robert.smart@quinnipiac.edu
SMART, Scott 575-562-2611 293 O scott.smart@enmu.edu
SMART, Stephanie 845-434-5750 330 F ssmart@sunysullivan.edu
SMART, William 615-297-7545 429 H smartb@aquinascollege.edu
SMATRESK, Neal 940-565-2026 466 B president@unt.edu
SMAY, Kevin 412-237-3094 392 G ksmay@ccac.edu
SMEAL, Tim 716-338-1019 311 F timsmeal@mail.sunyjcc.edu
SMEDLEY, Laduan 916-558-2120 50 I smedlel3@scc.losrios.edu
SMEDLEY, Patricia 615-460-6403 430 D patricia.smedley@belmont.edu
SMEDLEY, Susan 281-425-6336 451 I ssmedley@lee.edu
SMEE, Sheryl 619-849-2509 57 H sherylsmee@pointloma.edu
SMEED, Shane 816-584-6205 265 C shane.smeed@park.edu
SMELSER, Dick, W 865-694-6565 437 F rwsmelser@pstcc.edu
SMELTZ, Emily 724-357-5555 406 C emily.smeltz@iup.edu
SMELTZER, Brian, K 717-815-1293 415 G bksmeltzer@ycp.edu
SMELTZER, Deirdre 540-432-4141 480 A deirdre.smeltzer@emu.edu
SMELTZER, Paul 336-725-8344 348 C smeltzerp@piedmontu.edu
SMETANKA, John 724-805-2227 410 B john.smetanka@email.stvincent.edu
SMICK-ATTISANO, Regina, A 603-862-1025 282 F regina.smick-attisano@unh.edu
SMID, Terry 563-425-5359 173 K smidt@uiu.edu
SMIGIELSKI, Ben 312-915-8709 144 D bsmigie@uc.edu

SMILEY, Brad .... 903-675-6218 464 C bsmiley@tvcc.edu
SMILEY, Ellen .... 318-274-3228 196 G smileye@gram.edu
SMILEY, Ellen .... 318-274-6238 196 G smileye@gram.edu
SMILEY, Joseph .... 727-712-5851 107 A smiley.joseph@spcollege.edu
SMILEY, Scott .... 432-552-2605 469 D smiley_s@utpb.edu
SMITH, A, J .... 801-213-3505 472 P a.jsmith@hsc.utah.edu
SMITH, Aaron .... 434-544-8540 482 F smith.a@lynchburg.edu
SMITH, Adrian .... 212-343-1234 315 D asmith@mcny.edu
SMITH, Adriana, K .... 864-938-3777 423 D adsmith@presby.edu
SMITH, Adrienne .... 413-755-4561 221 B asmith@stcc.edu
SMITH, Aidan .... 724-266-3838 412 D asmith@tsm.edu
SMITH, Alan .... 703-561-1600.. 93 B
SMITH, Alastair .... 415-338-1759.. 34 C aksmith@sfsu.edu
SMITH, Alexa .... 870-612-2165.. 22 H alexa.smith@uaccb.edu
SMITH, Alisa .... 419-824-3963 364 G asmith@lourdes.edu
SMITH, Altrice .... 804-706-5079 488 D asmith@jtcc.edu
SMITH, Amanda .... 972-883-6154 467 D als072000@utdallas.edu
SMITH, Amy .... 912-478-5391 120 E amysmith@georgiasouthern.edu
SMITH, Amy, B .... 979-845-2217 459 C amy.b.smith@tamu.edu
SMITH, Amy, E .... 716-926-8877 310 B asmith@hilbert.edu
SMITH, Andrea, C .... 503-552-1692 384 F acsmith@nunm.edu
SMITH, Andrew .... 843-525-8333 424 E asmith@tcl.edu
SMITH, Andrew .... 865-471-3243 430 H asmith@cn.edu
SMITH, Angela .... 229-928-1360 120 F angela.smith@gsw.edu
SMITH, Angela .... 765-455-9536 160 B smith436@iuk.edu
SMITH, Angi .... 706-379-3111 128 H adsmith@yhc.edu
SMITH, Angi .... 423-585-2680 438 D angi.smith@ws.edu
SMITH, Ann .... 317-738-8109 157 L akish@franklincollege.edu
SMITH, Ann, T .... 859-238-5459 184 C ann.smith@centre.edu
SMITH, Anna Marie .... 336-757-3654 343 C amsmith@forsythtech.edu
SMITH, Annabelle .... 254-526-1205 445 L annabelle.smith@ctcd.edu
SMITH, Annie .... 864-424-8055 425 G alsmith@mailbox.sc.edu
SMITH, Art .... 870-236-6901.. 19 D artsmith@crc.edu
SMITH, Ashley .... 704-378-1237 338 I apsmith2@jcsu.edu
SMITH, Ashley .... 704-991-0221 346 I asmith1369@stanly.edu
SMITH, Ashley .... 252-493-7229 345 E adsmith@email.pittcc.edu
SMITH, Audrey, Y .... 413-585-4900 224 F aysmith@smith.edu
SMITH, B. Nate .... 954-378-2400.. 93 B
SMITH, Barbra .... 256-761-6100.... 7 D bsmith@talladega.edu
SMITH, Bea .... 864-592-4448 424 C smithb@sccsc.edu
SMITH, Beatrice .... 619-574-6909.. 55 B bsmith@pacificcollege.edu
SMITH, Belinda .... 252-862-1229 345 H bcsmith8016@roanokechowan.edu
SMITH, Benjamin .... 402-465-2156 276 E bsmith7@nebrwesleyan.edu
SMITH, Benjamin, J .... 620-431-2820 180 C bsmith@neosho.edu
SMITH, Benny, R .... 828-398-7482 340 M brsmith@abtech.edu
SMITH, Beth .... 910-898-9610 345 A smithb@montgomery.edu
SMITH, Beth .... 715-342-3114 514 B beth.smith@mstc.edu
SMITH, Betsy .... 617-879-7761 218 B betsy.smith@massart.edu
SMITH, Betty .... 610-917-1426 413 G blsmith@valleyforge.edu
SMITH, Betty, J .... 910-678-8250 343 B smithbj@faytechcc.edu
SMITH, Bill .... 401-232-6078 416 A bsmith8@bryant.edu
SMITH, Bill .... 870-972-2169.. 18 A billsmith@astate.edu
SMITH, Bill .... 213-763-3612.. 49 F smithb@lattc.edu
SMITH, Bill .... 818-345-7921.. 40 A bsmith@columbiacollege.edu
SMITH, Bill .... 225-216-8588 192 B smithb@mybrcc.edu
SMITH, Billy, R .... 731-989-6623 432 C bsmith@fhu.edu
SMITH, Blake .... 865-981-8264 433 F blake.smith@maryvillecollege.edu
SMITH, Bob .... 904-819-6332.. 98 I bsmith@flagler.edu
SMITH, JR., Bob .... 316-978-3444 182 F bobby.smith@wichita.edu
SMITH, Bobby .... 731-424-3520 437 B bsmith@jscc.edu
SMITH, Brad .... 214-329-4447 443 J brad.smith@bgu.edu
SMITH, Brad, D .... 937-766-7872 358 D smthb@cedarville.edu
SMITH, Brad, K .... 608-743-4596 513 D bsmith32@blackhawk.edu
SMITH, Bradley .... 215-461-1139 402 A bsmith@mc3.edu
SMITH, Bradley, D .... 574-807-7232 156 E smithb@bethelcollege.edu
SMITH, Brenda .... 601-643-8341 252 G brenda.smith@colin.edu
SMITH, Brenda, A .... 585-292-2365 315 L bsmith2@monroecc.edu
SMITH, Brenda, J .... 212-217-3650 308 B brenda_smith@fitnyc.edu
SMITH, Brian .... 716-888-2785 300 G smith@canisius.edu
SMITH, Brian .... 701-858-3210 354 C brian.smith@minotstateu.edu
SMITH, Brian .... 864-379-8804 421 E smith@erskine.edu
SMITH, Brian, D .... 972-241-3371 447 E bsmith@dallas.edu
SMITH, Brian, K .... 864-379-6304 421 E keith@erskine.edu
SMITH, Brien, N .... 812-237-2000 159 C brien.smith@indstate.edu
SMITH, Brittney .... 864-833-8484 423 D britsmith@presby.edu
SMITH, Bruce .... 256-761-6225.... 7 D bcsmith@talladega.edu
SMITH, Bruce .... 303-871-6301.. 83 E bruce.smith@du.edu
SMITH, Bruce .... 503-777-7521 386 F smithb@reed.edu
SMITH, Bryan .... 270-706-8616 185 H bryan.smith@kctcs.edu
SMITH, Bryan, F .... 850-599-3183 109 A bryanf.smith@famu.edu
SMITH, C. Mike .... 864-488-4609 422 B csmith@limestone.edu
SMITH, Calvin .... 573-592-6067 270 B calvin.smith@westminster-mo.edu
SMITH, Cameron .... 978-837-5503 221 G smithcr@merrimack.edu
SMITH, Carl .... 760-245-4271.. 73 E carl.smith@vvc.edu
SMITH, Carlas .... 501-812-2366.. 23 C crsmith@pulaskitech.edu
SMITH, Carlia, G .... 501-569-3492.. 22 B cgsmith@ualr.edu
SMITH, Carlos .... 601-977-6151 256 B cmith@tougaloo.edu
SMITH, Carol .... 970-247-7265.. 79 J smith_carol@fortlewis.edu
SMITH, Carol .... 303-273-3911.. 78 J cesmith@mines.edu
SMITH, Carol, L .... 765-658-4580 157 H clsmith@depauw.edu
SMITH, Carola .... 805-965-0581.. 62 E smithc@sbcc.edu
SMITH, Carolyn .... 305-273-4499.. 96 N carolyn@cbt.edu
SMITH, Carolyn .... 307-766-2376 517 B csmith@uwyo.edu
SMITH, Carolyn, A .... 304-697-7550 501 J csmith@huntingtonjuniorcollege.edu
SMITH, Carolyn, S .... 414-288-7184 508 C carolyn.s.smith@marquette.edu
SMITH, Carter .... 502-410-6200 184 H csmith2@galencollege.edu
SMITH, Caryn .... 847-947-5229 146 G clsmith@nl.edu
SMITH, Caye .... 619-849-2313.. 57 H cayesmith@pointloma.edu
SMITH, Ceeon .... 305-626-3626.. 99 M ceeon.smith@fmuniv.edu
SMITH, Ceil .... 856-351-2644 291 E csmith@salemcc.edu
SMITH, Chad .... 575-624-7328 294 A chad.smith@roswell.enmu.edu
SMITH, Charlene .... 513-241-4338 356 I charlene.smith@antonellicollege.edu
SMITH, Charles .... 816-414-3700 263 D csmith@mbts.edu
SMITH, Charles, N .... 903-927-3387 471 B cnsmith1@wileyc.edu
SMITH, Charmaine, I ..... 340-692-4070 529 C hsmithc@uvi.edu
SMITH, Charmian .... 516-572-7376 316 C charmian.smith@ncc.edu
SMITH, Cherie .... 816-415-5085 270 C smithc@william.jewell.edu
SMITH, Cheryl .... 413-782-1542 225 F cheryl.smith@wne.edu
SMITH, Chip .... 478-934-3064 123 A chip.smith@mga.edu
SMITH, Chris .... 423-425-4646 440 A chris-smith@utc.edu
SMITH, Christala .... 580-745-3185 379 J clsmith@se.edu
SMITH, Christine .... 678-466-5406 117 I christinesmith@clayton.edu
SMITH, Christine .... 518-762-7136 309 A cmsmith@fmcc.suny.edu
SMITH, Cindy .... 432-264-5034 450 G csmith@howardcollege.edu
SMITH, Claire .... 210-999-8401 464 B csmith9@trinity.edu
SMITH, Clarence, E .... 662-252-8000 255 F csmith@rustcollege.edu
SMITH, Clark .... 530-741-6785.. 76 A csmith@yccd.edu
SMITH, Cliff .... 913-627-4122 178 H clsmith@kckcc.edu
SMITH, Colleen .... 518-445-2336 297 K csmit@albanylaw.edu
SMITH, Colleen, A .... 928-266-4217.. 12 B colleen.smith@coconino.edu
SMITH, Connor .... 214-333-5365 447 D connors@dbu.edu
SMITH, Corey .... 662-246-6405 254 C csmith@msdelta.edu
SMITH, Craig .... 413-236-2186 219 B csmith@berkshirecc.edu
SMITH, Craig .... 413-236-2188 219 B csmith@berkshirecc.edu
SMITH, Craig .... 406-768-5555 271 B csmith@fpcc.edu
SMITH, Crystal .... 903-877-7718 469 A crystal.smith@uthct.edu
SMITH, Cynthia .... 301-687-4328 209 A colsmith@frostburg.edu
SMITH, Cyrus .... 479-979-1425.. 23 J csmith@ozarks.edu
SMITH, D. Gordon .... 801-422-6383 471 E smithg@law.byu.edu
SMITH, Dale, T .... 914-831-0311 305 C dsmith@cw.edu
SMITH, Dan .... 662-562-3305 255 C dsmith@northwestms.edu
SMITH, Dan .... 812-855-6679 159 G dansmith@indiana.edu
SMITH, Dana .... 760-944-4449.. 52 F dsmith@miracosta.edu
SMITH, Dane .... 202-885-8663.. 94 C dsmith@wesleyseminary.edu
SMITH, Daniel .... 562-860-2451.. 36 A dsmith@cerritos.edu
SMITH, Daniel .... 864-242-5100 418 H
SMITH, Daniel, C .... 812-855-6679 159 H dansmith@indiana.edu
SMITH, Daniel, C .... 252-334-2058 340 B dan.smith@macuniversity.edu
SMITH, Darlene .... 301-687-4309 209 A dcsmith@frostburg.edu
SMITH, Darlene, B .... 410-837-4996 209 D dsmith@ubalt.edu
SMITH, Darren, A .... 407-582-3015 113 F dsmith335@valenciacollege.edu
SMITH, Daryl .... 864-592-4600 424 C smithd@sccsc.edu
SMITH, Daryl .... 716-829-7623 307 B smithd@dyc.edu
SMITH, Daryl .... 513-244-8686 359 E daryl.smith@ccuniversity.edu
SMITH, David .... 740-264-5591 361 D dsmith@egcc.edu
SMITH, David .... 718-260-5345 303 D dsmith@citytech.cuny.edu
SMITH, David .... 718-818-6470 323 F dsmith@edaff.com
SMITH, David .... 909-593-3511.. 70 E dsmith3@laverne.edu
SMITH, David .... 912-358-4000 125 C smithd@savannahstate.edu
SMITH, David .... 765-677-2258 161 C david.smith@indwes.edu
SMITH, David, B .... 518-783-2432 324 C dsmith@siena.edu
SMITH, David, C .... 423-236-2801 436 C davidsmith@southern.edu
SMITH, Dayle, M .... 315-268-2300 304 B dsmith@clarkson.edu
SMITH, Dean .... 504-568-5960 194 C dsmith@lsuhsc.edu
SMITH, Debbie .... 281-998-6150 456 B deborah.smith@sjcd.edu
SMITH, Deborah .... 409-212-5724 443 L
SMITH, Debra .... 931-668-7010 437 C dsmith@mscc.edu
SMITH, Debra .... 252-536-7213 343 F dsmith660@halifaxcc.edu
SMITH, Debra .... 252-536-7213 343 F dsmith600@halifaxcc.edu
SMITH, Del .... 256-372-5092.... 1 A del.smith@aamu.edu
SMITH, Delois .... 256-824-4600.... 8 C delois.smith@uah.edu
SMITH, Denise .... 567-661-7250 369 A denise_smith4@owens.edu
SMITH, Denise, D .... 804-662-3196 486 G ddsmith@richmond.edu
SMITH, Denise, L .... 660-785-4133 267 K dlsmith@truman.edu
SMITH, Denise, M .... 603-862-3396 282 F denise.smith@unh.edu
SMITH, Dennis .... 530-226-4754.. 64 B dsmith@simpsonu.edu
SMITH, Dennis .... 252-335-0821 342 D dennis_smith@albemarle.edu
SMITH, Derek .... 215-489-2476 393 F derek.smith@delval.edu
SMITH, Derrek .... 256-233-8274.... 4 C derrek.smith@athens.edu
SMITH, Devin .... 402-643-7328 274 B devin.smith@cune.edu
SMITH, Devon .... 918-576-7380 378 F dsmith@okwu.edu
SMITH, Diana .... 303-762-6886.. 79 G diana.smith@denverseminary.edu
SMITH, Dolores .... 951-639-5230.. 52 J dolsmith@msjc.edu
SMITH, Don .... 229-931-2731 125 G dsmith@southgatech.edu
SMITH, Donald .... 623-845-3070.. 13 H don.smith@gccaz.edu
SMITH, Donald .... 972-860-4808 447 G dsmith@dcccd.edu
SMITH, Donald, E .... 716-286-8348 318 F des@niagara.edu
SMITH, Donald, L .... 270-745-6256 190 F donald.smith@wku.edu
SMITH, Donna .... 601-925-3313 254 B dsmith@mc.edu
SMITH, Donna .... 701-777-4172 353 G donna.smith@und.edu
SMITH, Dorothy .... 213-763-5507.. 49 F smithd@lattc.edu
SMITH, Doug .... 910-695-3811 346 E smithd@sandhills.edu
SMITH, Douglas .... 408-270-6426.. 61 N douglas.smith@sjeccd.org
SMITH, Douglas, F .... 610-796-8393 389 A doug.smith@alvernia.edu
SMITH, Douglas, J .... 508-565-1341 224 H dsmith@stonehill.edu
SMITH, Drew .... 870-230-5265.. 19 H smithc@hsu.edu
SMITH, Dwayne .... 813-974-3151 111 A mdsmith8@usf.edu
SMITH, Dwayne .... 314-340-3611 260 H smithd@hssu.edu
SMITH, Dwight, L .... 973-328-5090 285 B dsmith@ccm.edu
SMITH, E. Ashley .... 713-718-7514 450 D edgar.smith2@hccs.edu
SMITH, Earl, L .... 713-743-1899 465 A esmith@uh.edu
SMITH, Ed .... 615-550-3160 441 C ed.smith@williamsoncc.edu
SMITH, Edgar .... 936-294-2765 462 F acc_ebs@shsu.edu
SMITH, Edmond, C .... 276-964-7338 489 F ed.smith@sw.edu
SMITH, Elaine .... 865-471-3208 430 H esmith@cn.edu
SMITH, Elaine, L .... 516-833-8181 297 I elsmith@adelphi.edu
SMITH, Elizabeth .... 573-341-7783 269 A elsmith@mst.edu

SMITH, Marcus .... 575-769-4014 293 M
marcus.smith@clovis.edu
SMITH, Margaret .... 412-392-3990 408 F
msmith@pointpark.edu
SMITH, Marianne .... 610-896-1298 397 F
msmith@haverford.edu
SMITH, Marianne .... 626-914-8701.. 37 G
msmith@citruscollege.edu
SMITH, Maribel .... 305-628-6704 107 B
maribel.smith@stu.edu
SMITH, Marie .... 928-350-2100.. 15 V
msmith@prescott.edu
SMITH, Marilyn .... 763-433-1306 243 K
marilyn.smith@anokaramsey.edu
SMITH, Marilyn .... 703-993-8728 481 B
mtsmith@gmu.edu
SMITH, Mark .... 607-871-2494 298 A
msmith@alfred.edu
SMITH, Mark .... 615-327-6336 434 A
msmith@mmc.edu
SMITH, Mark, A .... 803-754-4100 420 E
SMITH, Mark, A .... 254-298-8341 458 C
mark.a.smith@templejc.edu
SMITH, Mark, W .... 314-935-6489 269 L
msmith@wustl.edu
SMITH, Marla .... 605-995-7157 427 E
marla.smith@mitchelltech.edu
SMITH, Marla .... 317-955-6150 162 R
msmith2@marian.edu
SMITH, Marlaine .... 561-297-3207 109 B
msmit230@fau.edu
SMITH, Marsh-Allen .... 650-508-3459.. 54 D
masmith@ndnu.edu
SMITH, Martha, J .... 260-359-4040 159 B
msmith@huntington.edu
SMITH, Martha, J .... 757-352-4070 484 E
martsmi@regent.edu
SMITH, Martha, L .... 601-403-1269 255 D
mbyrd@prcc.edu
SMITH, Martin .... 859-233-8275 189 H
msmith@transy.edu
SMITH, Marvin .... 201-360-4054 286 E
msmith@hccc.edu
SMITH, Marvin .... 304-766-3181 505 A
smithm@wvstateu.edu
SMITH, Marvin, L .... 317-274-5924 160 E
mlsiii@iupui.edu
SMITH, Mary, A .... 713-500-9236 468 D
mary.a.smith@uth.tmc.edu
SMITH, Mary, C .... 478-289-2165 118 H
mcsmith@ega.edu
SMITH, Mary, D .... 936-468-7690 458 A
smithmd1@sfasu.edu
SMITH, Matthew .... 717-815-6579 415 G
cmsmith@ycp.edu
SMITH, Matthew, B .... 919-866-5988 347 D
mbsmith9@waketech.edu
SMITH, Matthew, J .... 269-399-7700 165 B
msmith@sf.edu
SMITH, Matthew, R .... 315-470-6500 328 D
SMITH, Megan .... 215-504-8543 390 I
megan.smith@bucks.edu
SMITH, Melinda .... 617-745-6840 214 D
melinda.smith@enc.edu
SMITH, Melissa .... 415-439-2413.. 25 J
mysmith@act-sf.org
SMITH, Micah .... 731-989-6005 432 C
msmith@fhu.edu
SMITH, Michael .... 503-838-8043 388 B
smithmj@wou.edu
SMITH, Michael .... 870-248-4000.. 18 J
michael.smith@blackrivertech.edu
SMITH, Michael .... 215-951-1981 398 F
msmith@lasalle.edu
SMITH, Michael .... 212-842-5969 316 F
msmith@nyaa.edu
SMITH, Michael .... 810-762-7969 232 C
msmith2@kettering.edu
SMITH, Michael .... 410-706-4832 207 H
msmith@umaryland.edu
SMITH, Michael .... 812-488-2958 164 G
ms337@evansville.edu
SMITH, Michael .... 806-720-7521 452 D
michael.smith@lcu.edu
SMITH, Michael, A .... 434-223-6219 481 D
msmith@hsc.edu
SMITH, Michael, D .... 617-495-1566 215 G
mike_smith@harvard.edu
SMITH, Michael, D .... 770-426-2039 122 F
michael.smith@life.edu
SMITH, Michael, J .... 973-278-5400 283 J
mj@berkeleycollege.edu
SMITH, Michael, J .... 212-986-4343 299 F
mj@berkeleycollege.edu
SMITH, Michael, R .... 919-966-4107 351 B
msmith@sog.unc.edu
SMITH, Michael, W .... 202-687-4640.. 92 B
smithm4@georgetown.edu
SMITH, Michele, G .... 817-257-4739 445 H
m.g.smith@tcu.edu
SMITH, Michele' .... 847-925-6391 139 B
msmith@harpercollege.edu
SMITH, Michelle .... 502-213-8240 189 E
mbsmith@sctd.edu
SMITH, Mike .... 903-586-2518 451 C
msmith@jacksonville-college.edu
SMITH, Mike .... 803-812-7436 425 D
pmsmith@mailbox.sc.edu
SMITH, Misty .... 601-635-2111 252 I
misty.smith@eccc.edu
SMITH, Molly .... 847-628-2521 142 B
molly.smith@judsonu.edu
SMITH, Molly, E .... 360-438-4310 497 F
msmith@stmartin.edu
SMITH, Monesca, R .... 502-597-6985 187 E
monesca.smith@kysu.edu
SMITH, Monica .... 510-780-4500.. 48 D
msmith@lifewest.edu
SMITH, Muriel "Peggy" . 340-693-1446 529 C
psmith@uvi.edu
SMITH, Nakiya .... 910-221-2224 338 A
nsmith@gcd.edu
SMITH, Nancy .... 719-255-4411.. 83 C
nsmith2@uccs.edu
SMITH, Nancy .... 325-793-4667 452 F
smith.nancy@mcm.edu
SMITH, Nancy, L .... 607-746-4665 329 B
smithnl@delhi.edu
SMITH, Nancy, W .... 845-758-6822 298 I
nsmith@bard.edu
SMITH, Nate .... 954-745-6960.. 93 B
SMITH, Nathaniel .... 217-732-3168 143 F
nwsmith@lincolnchristian.edu
SMITH, Nichloas, A .... 508-767-7416 210 I
na.smith@assumption.edu
SMITH, Noreen .... 212-343-1234 315 D
nsmith@mcny.edu
SMITH, Norma, M .... 207-768-2790 200 B
nsmith@nmcc.edu
SMITH, Norman .... 256-228-6001.... 3 B
smithn@nacc.edu
SMITH, Ole, M .... 801-422-5500 471 E
ole_smith@byu.edu
SMITH, Oronda, M .... 404-527-4520 117 C
osmith@carver.edu
SMITH, Pam .... 727-341-3261 107 A
smith.pam@spcollege.edu
SMITH, Pamela, A .... 918-631-2329 381 C
pamela-smith@utulsa.edu
SMITH, Pamela, S .... 518-276-6549 321 A
smithp10@rpi.edu
SMITH, Pat, A .... 559-323-2100.. 61 A
psmith@sjcl.edu
SMITH, Patricia .... 501-450-3198.. 23 I
psmith@uca.edu
SMITH, Patricia .... 931-372-3331 438 F
plsmith@tntech.edu
SMITH, Patricia, A .... 516-876-3092 327 C
smithp@oldwestbury.edu
SMITH, Patty .... 540-231-6059 480 I
psmith@vcom.vt.edu
SMITH, Paula .... 217-234-5252 143 B
psmith12328@lakeland.cc.il.us
SMITH, Penny, L .... 814-871-7748 395 H
smith006@gannon.edu
SMITH, Penny, R .... 330-325-6300 366 F
psmith4@neomed.edu
SMITH, Peter, L .... 563-589-3668 173 J
plsmith@dbq.edu
SMITH, JR., Philip, L .... 225-216-8190 192 B
smithp@mybrcc.edu
SMITH, Polly .... 315-792-3111 332 H
psmith1@utica.edu
SMITH, Quentin .... 806-743-3600 463 E
quentin.smith@ttuhsc.edu
SMITH, Quentin, R .... 806-414-9277 463 E
quentin.smith@ttuhsc.edu
SMITH, Rachael .... 415-503-6258.. 60 H
rasmith@sfcm.edu
SMITH, Raechell .... 816-802-3574 261 C
raechell@earthlink.net
SMITH, Randy .... 605-698-3966 428 C
rsmith@swc.tc
SMITH, Randy .... 434-592-5363 482 D
rsmith108@liberty.edu
SMITH, Randy .... 920-498-5505 514 G
randall.smith@nwtc.edu
SMITH, Randy, L .... 405-585-5810 377 A
randy.smith@okbu.edu
SMITH, Rashad, E .... 812-465-7048 165 C
resmith1@usi.edu
SMITH, Rebecca .... 619-849-2983.. 57 H
rebeccasmith@pointloma.edu
SMITH, Rebecca, F .... 614-823-1400 368 O
rsmith@otterbein.edu
SMITH, Regina .... 303-245-4662.. 81 B
rsmith@naropa.edu
SMITH, Regina .... 323-953-4000.. 49 A
smithrr2@lacitycollege.edu
SMITH, Regina .... 212-757-1190 298 D
rtsmith@funeraleducation.org
SMITH, Renee, L .... 928-344-1723.. 11 B
renee.smith@azwestern.edu
SMITH, Rex .... 608-822-2410 515 A
rsmith@swtc.edu
SMITH, Rhajon .... 423-461-8386 435 A
rnsmith@milligan.edu
SMITH, Rhonda .... 205-391-2991.... 3 E
rsmith@sheltonstate.edu
SMITH, Richard, A .... 540-375-2203 484 H
rsmith@roanoke.edu
SMITH, Richard, S .... 718-409-7350 329 E
rsmith@sunymaritime.edu
SMITH, Rickey, W .... 502-597-5911 187 E
rick.smith@kysu.edu
SMITH, Robert .... 301-243-2261 518 C
robert.smith@dodiis.mil
SMITH, Robert .... 601-979-2260 253 E
robert.m.smith@jsums.edu
SMITH, Robert .... 612-728-5201 250 B
rsmith@smunm.edu
SMITH, Robert .... 917-493-4270 313 M
rsmith@msmnyc.edu
SMITH, Robert .... 912-344-2589 115 D
robert.smith@armstrong.edu
SMITH, Robert .... 617-824-8500 214 E
robert_smith@emerson.edu
SMITH, Robert .... 859-985-3330 183 I
smithro@berea.edu
SMITH, Robert .... 470-578-4935 122 C
rsmit429@kennesaw.edu
SMITH, Robert .... 217-206-6523 154 A
rmit27@uis.edu
SMITH, Robert .... 806-720-7111 452 D
robert.smith@lcu.edu
SMITH, Robert, R .... 520-621-7777.. 16 J
rrsmith@u.arizona.edu
SMITH, Robert, T .... 229-333-5950 127 H
rtsmith@valdosta.edu
SMITH, Robert, W .... 252-334-2018 340 B
bob.smith@macuniversity.edu
SMITH, Rochelle .... 256-782-8122.... 6 B
rdsmith@jsu.edu
SMITH, Rodney .... 816-235-1167 268 D
smithrodn@umkc.edu
SMITH, Roland, B .... 713-348-5688 455 F
rbsmith@rice.edu
SMITH, Roland, K .... 512-463-1887 462 A
roland.smith@tsus.edu
SMITH, Ron .... 904-997-2997 100 F
ron.smith@fscj.edu
SMITH, Ron .... 408-741-2126.. 74 B
ron_smith@wvm.edu
SMITH, Ronda, L .... 641-422-4001 172 C
smithron@niacc.edu
SMITH, Rose Marie .... 405-422-1262 379 B
rosemarie.smith@redlandscc.edu
SMITH, Roy .... 864-592-4905 424 C
smithr@sccsc.edu
SMITH, Royce .... 406-994-4933 272 A
royce.smith@montana.edu
SMITH, Ruth .... 618-634-3347 151 G
ruths@shawneecc.edu
SMITH, Ruth .... 757-825-2807 489 G
smithru@tncc.edu
SMITH, Ruth, S .... 407-582-1601 113 F
rsmith257@valenciacollege.edu
SMITH, Ryan .... 309-438-2135 140 L
rlsmith@ilstu.edu
SMITH, Ryan .... 916-649-8168.. 27 L
ryan.smith@brightwood.edu
SMITH, Ryan, M .... 814-886-6373 402 E
rsmith@mtaloy.edu
SMITH, Sacella .... 708-456-0300 153 E
sacellasmith@triton.edu
SMITH, Sam .... 615-966-6056 433 D
sam.smith@lipscomb.edu
SMITH, Sandra, B .... 540-674-3600 488 G
ssmith@nr.edu
SMITH, Sandy .... 540-231-6231 490 F
ssmith@vt.edu
SMITH, Sandy .... 760-366-5296.. 41 B
ssmith@cmccd.edu
SMITH, Sarah .... 276-376-4514 487 A
scs6p@uvawise.edu
SMITH, Sarah .... 615-230-3400 438 C
sarah.smith@volstate.edu
SMITH, Sarah, A .... 304-293-4963 505 B
sarah.smith@mail.wvu.edu
SMITH, Scott, A .... 803-786-3672 420 D
scsmith@columbiasc.edu
SMITH, Scott, F .... 305-899-3085.. 95 G
sfsmith@barry.edu
SMITH, Sean .... 805-565-6061.. 74 I
sesmith@westmont.edu
SMITH, Sedef .... 713-221-5842 465 C
smithse@uhd.edu
SMITH, Sevealyn, V .... 919-516-4160 348 G
svsmith@st-aug.edu
SMITH, Sha Duncan .... 610-690-5744 410 I
sdsmith1@swarthmore.edu
SMITH, Shaquilla .... 731-265-1703 432 J
ssmith@lanecollege.edu
SMITH, Sharon .... 910-362-7027 341 E
ssmith332@mail.cfcc.edu
SMITH, Sharon .... 202-495-3830.. 92 F
secretary@dhs.edu
SMITH, Sharon .... 205-726-2247.... 6 G
ssmith12@samford.edu
SMITH, Sharon .... 541-956-7187 386 G
ssmith@roguecc.edu
SMITH, Sharon, E .... 616-632-2902 227 C
smithsha@aquinas.edu
SMITH, Sharon, P .... 828-652-0697 344 G
sharons@mcdowelltech.edu
SMITH, Sharon, P .... 724-836-9911 412 I
upgpres@pitt.edu
SMITH, SharonAnn .... 618-374-5199 149 A
sharonann.smith@principia.edu
SMITH, Shawn .... 217-732-3168 143 F
ssmith@lincolnchristian.edu
SMITH, Shawn .... 816-604-5240 262 H
shawn.smith@mcckc.edu
SMITH, Sheila .... 615-329-8710 431 I
shsmith@fisk.edu
SMITH, Sheila, K .... 253-535-7674 496 G
nurs@plu.edu
SMITH, Shelley .... 256-840-4128.... 3 F
ssmith@snead.edu
SMITH, Shirley .... 714-484-7455.. 53 M
ssmith@cypresscollege.edu
SMITH, Stephanie .... 312-362-7552 137 C
ssmit185@depaul.edu
SMITH, Stephanie .... 928-523-3937.. 14 K
stephanie.smith@nau.edu
SMITH, Stephanie .... 606-546-1259 189 I
sasmith@unionky.edu
SMITH, Stephanie .... 304-696-2599 504 C
smiths@marshall.edu
SMITH, Stephanie, M .... 800-782-2422.. 30 G
smsmith@mail.cnuas.edu
SMITH, Stephen, C .... 415-338-3879.. 34 C
scsmith@sfsu.edu
SMITH, Stephen, E .... 918-465-1723 375 J
ssmith@eosc.edu
SMITH, Steve .... 716-829-7600 307 B
smith@dyc.edu
SMITH, Steve .... 507-389-5022 246 A
steven.smith@mnsu.edu
SMITH, Steve .... 626-584-5393.. 43 K
stevensmith1@fuller.edu
SMITH, Steve .... 951-343-4261.. 28 G
ssmith@calbaptist.edu
SMITH, Steve .... 865-974-4127 439 I
SMITH, Steve .... 432-264-5019 450 G
sismith@howardcollege.edu
SMITH, Steve .... 915-831-6472 449 A
ssmith54@epcc.edu
SMITH, Steve, A .... 801-422-6291 471 E
steve_smith@byu.edu
SMITH, Steve, G .... 806-371-5008 442 D
sgsmith@actx.edu
SMITH, Steven .... 970-521-6657.. 81 F
steven.smith@njc.edu
SMITH, Steven .... 775-682-5613 279 E
ssmith@unr.edu
SMITH, Steven .... 901-333-5325 438 B
ssmith@southwest.tn.edu
SMITH, Steven, E .... 516-877-3304 297 I
stsmith@adelphi.edu
SMITH, Steven, J .... 413-565-1000 211 C
ssmith@baypath.edu
SMITH, Steven, K .... 608-262-3956 510 C
sof@secfac.wisc.edu
SMITH, Steven, N .... 262-243-5700 507 C
steve.smith@cuw.edu
SMITH, Stuart .... 661-222-2784.. 29 F
stuartsmith@calarts.edu
SMITH, Stuart, A .... 859-858-3511 183 D
stuart.smith@asbury.edu
SMITH, Susan .... 509-527-2615 499 F
susan.smith@wallawalla.edu
SMITH, Susan, S .... 267-359-5924 394 C
susan.smith@drexel.edu
SMITH, Susanne .... 614-947-6160 362 A
suzanne.smith@franklin.edu
SMITH, Suzanne .... 413-755-4221 221 B
smsmith@stcc.edu
SMITH, Tacci .... 828-298-3325 353 B
tsmith@warren-wilson.edu

SNOW, Laura .... 816-802-3431 261 C
lsnow@kcai.edu
SNOW, Natalie .... 610-683-4153 406 D
snow@kutztown.edu
SNOW, Pamela, K .... 740-392-6868 366 B
psnow@mvnu.edu
SNOW, Ted .... 303-360-4828.. 79 C
ted.snow@ccaurora.edu
SNOW-FLAMER, Keith ... 707-476-4170.. 39 F
keith-snowflamer@redwoods.edu
SNOW FLESHER, LeAnn 510-841-1905.. 25 F
lflesher@absw.edu
SNOWDEN, Kent .... 334-241-9783.... 7 E
kesnowden@troy.edu
SNOWDEN, Michael, T . 337-475-5428 197 B
msnowden@mcneese.edu
SNOWDEN, Monique, L 805-898-4154.. 43 A
msnowden@fielding.edu
SNOWDEN, Robert (BJ) 916-608-6752.. 50 H
snowder@flc.losrios.edu
SNOWDEN, Scott .... 908-737-5170 286 F
snowdens@kean.edu
SNOWDEN, Thelbert ...... 202-462-2101.. 92 D
financialaid@iwp.edu
SNOWDEN, Yvette, J ..... 301-546-0417 206 E
snowdenyj@pgcc.edu
SNOWHITE, Mark .... 909-389-3205.. 59 H
msnowhite@craftonhills.edu
SNUFFIN, Gary .... 901-722-3260 436 D
gsnuffin@sco.edu
SNYDER, Alan, J .... 610-758-6964 400 B
ajs410@lehigh.edu
SNYDER, Alan, R .... 301-687-4242 209 A
arsnyder@frostburg.edu
SNYDER, Angie, P .... 479-248-7236.. 19 F
angie@ecollege.edu
SNYDER, Arlene, A .... 610-566-1776 415 A
asnyder@williamson.edu
SNYDER, Barbara, H ...... 801-581-7793 472 P
bsnyder@sa.utah.edu
SNYDER, Barbara, R ...... 216-368-5094 358 C
barbara.snyder@case.edu
SNYDER, Bruce .... 952-446-4161 242 A
snyderb@crown.edu
SNYDER, Catherine .... 518-631-9876 304 B
csnyder@clarkson.edu
SNYDER, Chris .... 724-830-1895 410 E
csnyder@setonhill.edu
SNYDER, Christine .... 913-782-3750 179 H
crsnyder@mnu.edu
SNYDER, Christopher .... 662-325-2522 254 E
cas741@msstate.edu
SNYDER, Daniel .... 303-837-0825.. 76 K
dsnyder@aii.edu
SNYDER, Darla .... 217-641-4205 141 F
dsnyder@jwcc.edu
SNYDER, David .... 415-485-9506.. 39 E
dsnyder@marin.edu
SNYDER, David .... 903-813-3007 443 F
dsnyder@austincollege.edu
SNYDER, Deborah .... 810-989-5545 236 G
dasnyder@sc4.edu
SNYDER, Diane, E .... 210-485-0010 441 E
dsnyder12@alamo.edu
SNYDER, Dianne, O .... 704-403-1558 336 B
dianne.snyder@carolinashealthcare.org
SNYDER, Donna .... 610-436-2955 407 D
dsnyder@wcupa.edu
SNYDER, Erin .... 563-336-3300 168 K
esnyder@eicc.edu
SNYDER, George .... 607-729-1581 306 F
gsnyder@davisny.edu
SNYDER, Gerry .... 718-636-3619 320 D
gsnyder@pratt.edu
SNYDER, Grant, S .... 610-359-5060 393 E
gsnyder@dccc.edu
SNYDER, Jacqueline ...... 518-736-3622 309 A
jackie.snyder@fmcc.edu
SNYDER, Jacquelyne ..... 843-349-5212 421 L
jacquelyne.snyder@hgtc.edu
SNYDER, Jan, E .... 712-324-5061 172 E
jsnyder@nwicc.edu
SNYDER, Jane .... 617-277-3915 212 F
snyderj@bgsp.edu
SNYDER, Jeffrey .... 419-372-0533 357 F
jasnyd@bgsu.edu
SNYDER, Jenefer, D ...... 757-822-2430 489 H
jsnyder@tcc.edu
SNYDER, Jennifer, L ..... 407-582-2307 113 F
jsnyder38@valenciacollege.edu
SNYDER, John, F .... 724-738-2028 407 C
john.snyder@sru.edu
SNYDER, Josh .... 605-331-6895 429 D
josh.snyder@usiouxfalls.edu
SNYDER, Julie .... 810-762-5728 238 B
jusnyder@umflint.edu
SNYDER, Justin .... 336-506-4279 340 L
justin.snyder@alamancecc.edu
SNYDER, Katherine .... 313-993-1216 237 F
snyderke@udmercy.edu
SNYDER, Katherine .... 301-687-7487 209 A
ksnyder@frostburg.edu
SNYDER, Keith .... 423-236-2929 436 C
kasynder@southern.edu
SNYDER, Kenneth .... 517-629-0213 226 G
ksnyder@albion.edu
SNYDER, Kenneth, D ..... 651-962-5058 251 D
kdsnyder@stthomas.edu
SNYDER, Kimberly .... 828-395-1435 344 A
ksnyder@isothermal.edu
SNYDER, Ky, L .... 619-260-2930.. 71 J
kysnyder@sandiego.edu
SNYDER, JR., Larry ...... 270-745-5208 190 F
lawrence.snyder@wku.edu
SNYDER, Larry, J .... 651-962-5200 251 D
snyd0014@stthomas.edu
SNYDER, Lawrence .... 413-565-1000 211 C
lsnyder@baypath.edu
SNYDER, Lisa, M .... 970-247-7543.. 79 J
lmsnyder@fortlewis.edu
SNYDER, Marcella, T ..... 304-336-8345 504 E
msnyder@westliberty.edu
SNYDER, Marian, L .... 610-799-1734 400 A
msnyder@lccc.edu
SNYDER, Martin .... 215-968-8392 390 I
martin.snyder@bucks.edu
SNYDER, Matthew .... 814-262-6438 405 A
msnyder@pennhighlands.edu
SNYDER, Michele .... 518-562-4334 304 C
michele.snyder@clinton.edu
SNYDER, Mike .... 217-245-3400 139 H
mike.snyder@mail.ic.edu
SNYDER, Pamela .... 440-775-8461 367 B
pamela.snyder@oberlin.edu
SNYDER, Paul .... 239-590-7050 109 C
psnyder@fgcu.edu
SNYDER, Phil .... 734-973-3665 238 G
philsnyder@wccnet.edu
SNYDER, Randolph .... 614-947-6024 362 A
randy.snyder@franklin.edu
SNYDER, Rita .... 864-250-8015 421 K
rita.snyder@gvltec.edu
SNYDER, Rob, A .... 724-287-8711 390 J
rob.snyder@bc3.edu
SNYDER, Robert, J .... 610-282-1100 393 G
robert.snyder@desales.edu
SNYDER, Sandra .... 503-552-1514 384 F
ssnyder@nunm.edu
SNYDER, Sheri .... 580-628-6208 376 J
sheri.snyder@noc.edu
SNYDER, Stephanie .... 270-852-3107 187 F
ssnyder@kwc.edu
SNYDER, Stephen .... 802-443-5979 475 G
ssnyder@middlebury.edu
SNYDER, Stephen, E ...... 229-931-2037 120 F
stephen.snyder@gsw.edu
SNYDER, Susan, M .... 716-829-2476 325 B
smsnyder@buffalo.edu
SNYDER, Tamara .... 352-638-9764.. 95 H
tsnyder@beaconcollege.edu
SNYDER, Terry .... 610-896-1272 397 F
tsnyder@haverford.edu
SNYDER, Tim .... 904-256-7377 102 B
tsnyder2@ju.edu
SNYDER, Tim .... 414-443-8798 513 A
tim.snyder@wlc.edu
SNYDER, Timothy, L ..... 310-338-2775.. 50 J
president@lmu.edu
SNYDER, Trina .... 717-477-1131 407 B
tmsnyd@ship.edu
SNYDER, Vanessa .... 404-835-6113 435 M
vsnyder@richmont.edu
SOARDS, Kathy .... 419-267-1314 366 G
ksoards@northweststate.edu
SOBA, Steve .... 740-826-8043 366 C
SOBCZYK-BARRON,
Maggie .... 712-329-4753 170 K
msobczykbarron@iwcc.edu
SOBECKY, Patty .... 205-348-4890.... 8 A
psobecky@ua.edu
SOBEK, Christine, J ...... 630-466-7900 155 C
csobek@waubonsee.edu
SOBEL, Jack .... 313-577-7574 239 C
jsobel@med.wayne.edu
SOBEL, Susan .... 501-450-3138.. 23 I
ssobel@uca.edu
SOBEY, Frank, E .... 806-371-5472 442 D
fesobey@actx.edu
SOBH, Tarek, M .... 203-576-4111.. 88 F
sobh@bridgeport.edu
SOBIESUO, Andrew, M . 843-953-5537 420 C
sobiesuoa@cofc.edu
SOBLEY, Susan .... 662-329-7210 254 F
sasobley@muw.edu
SOBOL, Jennifer .... 412-268-9514 391 H
jsobol@andrew.cmu.edu
SOBOLEWSKI, Rich .... 662-329-7119 254 F
resobolewski@muw.edu
SOBOLIK, Kristin .... 314-516-5373 268 E
sobolikk@umsl.edu
SOBOTTA, Sharon .... 925-631-4171.. 59 C
ssobotta@stmarys-ca.edu
SOCASH, Thomas .... 212-431-2825 317 H
thomas.socash@nyls.edu
SOCHA, Maureen .... 413-755-4460 221 B
mesocha@stcc.edu
SOCKWELL, Angela, A ... 904-808-7492 106 M
angelasockwell@sjrstate.edu
SOCOLOF, David .... 516-726-5669 519 C
socolofd@usmma.edu
SODEREERG, Melissa .... 517-318-3330 228 D
SODERQUIST, Rich .... 815-802-8173 142 C
rsoderquist@kcc.edu
SODINI, Ronald .... 312-369-6543 136 H
rsodini@colum.edu
SODT, Jill .... 810-762-0415 234 F
jill.sodt@mcc.edu
SODY, Anna .... 703-284-1543 483 A
anna.sody@marymount.edu
SOE, Victor .... 719-587-8267.. 76 D
victorsoe@adams.edu
SOEFFING, William .... 605-331-6759 429 D
william.soeffing@usiouxfalls.edu
SOEFFKER-CULICERTO,
Heike, I .... 304-929-6731 503 B
hsoeffker@newriver.edu
SOFFA, Kari .... 661-362-5417.. 39 C
kari.soffa@canyons.edu
SOFFIETTI, Barry .... 309-672-4946 145 E
bsoffietti@methodistcol.edu
SOFIELD, Roy .... 423-697-2552 436 F
roy.sofield@chattanoogastate.edu
SOFRANKO, Greg .... 724-938-4274 405 F
sofranko@calu.edu
SOHAIL, Mohammad ...... 517-371-5140 239 F
sohailm@cooley.edu
SOHAN, Donna .... 860-932-4153.. 86 E
dsohan@qvcc.edu
SOHARU, Rajni .... 504-280-6990 194 F
rsoharu@uno.edu
SOHN, Christopher .... 937-766-2789 358 D
chrissohn@cedarville.edu
SOHN, David, Y .... 703-941-2020 481 G
SOHN, Eugene .... 718-518-4154 302 D
esohn@hostos.cuny.edu
SOHOLT, Pam, B .... 701-788-4823 354 B
pam.soholt@mayvillestate.edu
SOIFER, Aviam .... 808-956-6363 129 J
soifer@hawaii.edu
SOIFER, Yitzchok .... 845-362-3053 299 C
yitzchoks@byts.edu
SOIFFER, Stephen .... 718-260-5400 303 D
ssoiffer@citytech.cuny.edu
SOIKA, Brian .... 713-348-4726 455 F
brian.soika@rice.edu
SOILEAU, Deidre .... 253-964-6232 497 B
dsoileau@pierce.ctc.edu
SOKANY, Stephen .... 330-672-2222 363 I
ssokany@kent.edu
SOKENU, Julius .... 805-378-1403.. 73 A
jsokenu@vcccd.edu
SOKOL, Bryan .... 314-977-3929 266 J
bsokol1@slu.edu
SOKOL, Moshe, Z .... 718-820-4800 331 F
sokolm@touro.edu
SOKOLICH, Andy .... 419-755-4313 366 E
sokolich.1@osu.edu
SOKOLL, Shane .... 512-313-3000 446 N
shane.sokoll@concordia.edu
SOLA, Peter, L .... 651-631-5349 251 C
plsola@unwsp.edu
SOLAN, George .... 252-399-6399 335 I
gsolan@barton.edu
SOLAND, Linda .... 602-285-7431.. 14 A
linda.soland@phoenixcollege.edu
SOLANDER, Sondra, K .. 620-431-2820 180 C
ssolander@neosho.edu
SOLANO, Maria .... 213-477-2536.. 52 H
msolano@msmu.edu
SOLARES, Dennis .... 818-364-3355.. 49 C
solaredr@lamission.edu
SOLAZZO, James .... 843-349-2462 420 A
jsolazzo@coastal.edu
SOLBACH, Robin .... 732-987-2681 286 D
rsolbach@georgian.edu
SOLBERG, Dale .... 916-348-4689.. 42 F
dsolberg@epic.edu
SOLBERG, Laura .... 352-588-8218 106 N
laura.solberg@saintleo.edu
SOLBERG, Lori .... 605-995-2805 427 A
losolber@dwu.edu
SOLBERG, Roger .... 814-732-2981 406 B
rsolberg@edinboro.edu
SOLBRIG, Ronald .... 208-282-2330 132 B
solbrona@isu.edu
SOLCHER, Iris .... 210-832-2110 465 E
isolcher@uiwtx.edu
SOLDWISCH, Sandie, S 815-282-7909 150 H
sandiesoldwisch@sacn.edu
SOLDZ, Stephen .... 617-277-3915 212 F
soldzs@bgsp.edu
SOLE, Mary, L .... 407-823-5496 110 C
mary.sole@ucf.edu
SOLECKI, Amanda .... 410-287-1003 203 B
asolecki@cecil.edu
SOLEIM, Heather, M ...... 218-477-4060 246 B
heather.soleim@mnstate.edu
SOLEMSAAS, Rachel, H . 808-934-2504 130 D
rsolems@hawaii.edu
SOLERNOU, Sheila .... 203-285-2393.. 85 E
ssolernou@gwcc.commnet.edu
SOLEY, Mary Ann .... 773-907-4754 135 K
msoley@ccc.edu
SOLHEIM, Derek, N .... 319-352-8330 174 C
derek.solheim@wartburg.edu
SOLIBAKKE, Karl, I .... 920-748-8108 509 H
solibakkek@ripon.edu
SOLIDAY, Rhett .... 714-556-3610.. 72 F
rhett.soliday@vanguard.edu
SOLIMAN, Phebe .... 973-328-5056 285 B
psoliman@ccm.edu
SOLIMAN, Sam .... 574-936-8898 155 L
sma.soliman@ancill.edu
SOLIS, Amy .... 701-627-4738 355 D
asolis@nhsc.edu
SOLIS, Carlos .... 512-245-1799 463 A
crs218@txstate.edu
SOLIS, Federico .... 956-794-4002 451 H
fsolis@laredo.edu
SOLIS, Francisco .... 210-486-0063 442 A
fsolis@alamo.edu
SOLIS, Gerard .... 813-974-1674 111 A
gsolis@usf.edu
SOLIS, Ricardo .... 956-721-5101 451 H
president@laredo.edu
SOLIS, Santiago .... 410-704-2051 209 C
ssolis@towson.edu
SOLIS, Vincent, R .... 956-764-5950 451 H
vincent.solis@laredo.edu
SOLIZ, Gina, M .... 315-228-7431 304 G
gsoliz@colgate.edu
SOLIZ, Sandra .... 713-525-3116 466 J
solizs@stthom.edu
SOLIZ, Ty .... 432-685-6467 453 B
asoliz@midland.edu
SOLLARS, David .... 785-670-2045 182 D
david.sollars@washburn.edu
SOLLENBERGER,
Donna, K .... 409-772-6116 469 C
dksoll@utmb.edu
SOLLENBERGER,
Mitchel .... 313-593-5030 238 A
msollenb@umich.edu
SOLLENBERGER,
Mitchel .... 313-593-5353 238 A
msollenb@umich.edu
SOLLOSI, Nancy, B .... 336-334-4822 343 E
nbsollosi@gtcc.edu
SOLMS, Daniel .... 260-359-4016 159 B
dsolms@huntington.edu
SOLOCHEK, Arlen .... 480-731-8232.. 13 D
arlen.solochek@domail.maricopa.edu
SOLOMON, Clemmie ...... 240-567-1469 205 F
clemmie.solomon@montgomerycollege.edu
SOLOMON, Ira .... 504-865-5422 196 D
isolomon@tulane.edu
SOLOMON, Jeffrey, S .... 508-831-5288 226 E
solomon@wpi.edu
SOLOMON, Jerome .... 408-498-5154.. 38 I
jsolomon@cogswell.edu
SOLOMON, Joseph .... 718-851-8721 334 D
SOLOMON, Kimberly ..... 713-221-8138 465 C
solomonk@uhd.edu
SOLOMON, Kimberly ..... 803-780-1266 426 F
ksolomon@voorhees.edu
SOLOMON, Mary Ellen . 412-396-6668 394 D
solomon3@duq.edu
SOLOMON, Mendel .... 973-267-9404 289 B
rabbisolo@aol.com
SOLOMON, Robert .... 912-754-2879 125 D
rsolomon@savannahtech.edu
SOLOMON, Ronald .... 225-216-8267 192 B
solomonr@mybrcc.edu
SOLOMON, Saige .... 318-869-5115 191 C
ssolomon@centenary.edu
SOLOMON, Shoshana ... 973-267-9404 289 B
shoshanasolomon@rca.edu
SOLOMON, Sigrid, B .... 937-481-2270 373 I
sigrid_solomon@wilmington.edu

SOTO, Monica .... 305-899-4914.. 95 G
msoto@barry.edu
SOTO, Nelson .... 513-861-6400 371 A
nelson.soto@myunion.edu
SOTO, Ovidio .... 787-884-3838 520 G
osoto@atenascollege.edu
SOTO, Saimara .... 334-699-2266.... 1 B
SOTO, Yadirah .... 787-765-3560 522 K
ysoto@edpuniversity.edu
SOTO, Zulay .... 787-884-3838 520 G
dir_asociada@atenascollege.edu
SOTO AQUINO, Limaris 787-725-8120 522 M
lisotoa@eap.edu
SOTO AQUINO, Limaris 787-945-7013 522 M
lisotoa@eap.edu
SOTO FULLER, Ineliz ..... 206-281-2561 498 B
ineliz@spu.edu
SOTO I COLON, Ana ..... 787-848-5739 526 C
SOTO-LÓPEZ, Heriberto . 787-751-1912 524 E
herisoto@juris.inter.edu
SOTO MALDONADO,
Ismael .... 787-720-4476 527 A
decanatofinanzas@mizpa.edu
SOTTER, Trudy .... 724-964-8811 403 A
tsotter@ncstrades.edu
SOUBERBIELLE, Daneka 435-672-7735 473 B
souberbielle@dixie.edu
SOUBLET, Gia .... 504-520-7575 198 D
gsoublet@xula.edu
SOUCIE, Evie .... 413-572-5637 218 F
esoucie@westfield.ma.edu
SOUCIER, JoEllen .... 713-718-8891 450 D
joellen.soucier@hccs.edu
SOUCY, Erin .... 207-834-7830 201 E
esoucy@maine.edu
SOUCY, Matthew .... 920-686-6203 510 A
matthew.soucy@sl.edu
SOUDAH, John, P .... 210-458-7531 468 B
john.soudah@utsa.edu
SOUFLERIS, Dawn, M ... 215-951-1017 398 F
soufleris@lasalle.edu
SOUL, Karen .... 318-869-5240 191 C
ksoul@centenary.edu
SOULE, E. Whitney .... 207-725-3000 198 G
esoule@bowdoin.edu
SOULE, Laqueta .... 423-697-2551 436 F
laqueta.soule@chattanoogastate.edu
SOULES, Robert, C .... 518-388-6176 332 B
soulesr@union.edu
SOURS, Lori .... 541-245-7803 386 G
lsours@roguecc.edu
SOUSA, Antoni .... 845-575-3000 314 C
antoni.sousa@marist.edu
SOUSA, Camellia .... 603-924-2787 281 G
camellia@sharonarts.org
SOUSA, Diana .... 860-231-5297.. 89 E
dianasousa@usj.edu
SOUSA, Marsha .... 907-474-7931.. 10 B
mcsousa@alaska.edu
SOUSA, Mitsy .... 305-442-9223 104 B
msousa@mrc.edu
SOUSA, Samantha .... 559-791-2232.. 47 C
samantha.sousa@portervillecollege.edu
SOUSA-PEOPLES, Kim ... 336-334-5231 351 D
ksp@uncg.edu
SOUTER, Sharon .... 254-295-4667 466 A
ssouter@umhb.edu
SOUTH, James, D .... 580-774-3771 380 B
james.south@swosu.edu
SOUTH, III, John, T ...... 912-650-6200 125 H
john.south@southuniversity.edu
SOUTH, Sandi .... 662-862-8956 253 D
sssouth@iccms.edu
SOUTH, Stephen, A .... 865-251-1800 436 B
ssouth@southcollegetn.edu
SOUTHALL, Ann .... 870-862-8131.. 21 D
asouthall@southark.edu
SOUTHARD, Anne .... 850-729-6040 104 E
southarda@nwfsc.edu
SOUTHARD, Kristine ...... 914-654-5522 305 A
ksouthard@cnr.edu
SOUTHARD, Sonya .... 270-686-4526 186 F
sonya.southard@kctcs.edu
SOUTHER, John .... 207-780-4546 201 H
john.souther@maine.edu
SOUTHERLAND,
Johnnie .... 919-530-5321 350 D
jsoutherland@nccu.edu
SOUTHERLAND, Nate .... 801-957-4542 474 B
nate.southerland@slcc.edu
SOUTHERN, Debbie .... 309-341-7225 142 G
dsouther@knox.edu
SOUTHERN, Jeff .... 620-275-3224 177 G
jeff.southern@gcccks.edu
SOUTHERN, Keri .... 903-586-2501 443 M
SOUTHERN, Lori .... 254-299-8686 452 E
lsouthern@mclennan.edu
SOUTHWICK, Lacey .... 276-944-6240 480 J
lsouthwick@ehc.edu
SOUTHWICK, Sally .... 518-783-2322 324 C
ssouthwick@siena.edu
SOUTHWOOD, Lori .... 859-572-6383 188 E
southwoodl1@nku.edu
SOUTHWORTH, Linda ... 978-934-2373 217 B
linda_southworth@uml.edu
SOUTHWORTH-FISHER,
Barbara .... 727-816-3116 105 C
fisherb@phsc.edu
SOUTTER, Cathey .... 214-768-4795 457 B
csoutter@smu.edu
SOUZA, Cynthia .... 626-815-4697.. 26 U
csouza@apu.edu
SOUZA, David, E .... 215-699-5700 399 G
dsouza@lsb.edu
SOUZA, Diana .... 231-348-6837 234 H
dsouza@ncmich.edu
SOUZA, Jane Marie .... 585-273-2821 332 E
janemarie.souza@rochester.edu
SOVA, Devin, A .... 336-318-7820 345 F
dasova@randolph.edu
SOVERN, Jane, P .... 646-664-9209 301 A
jane.sovern@cuny.edu
SOWELL, Kathy .... 615-230-3476 438 C
kathy.sowell@volstate.edu
SOWELL, Stacey .... 919-546-8271 348 I
ssowell@shawu.edu
SOWER, Michelle .... 530-541-4660.. 47 I
sower@ltcc.edu
SOWERS, Donna, S .... 301-846-2466 203 H
dsowers@frederick.edu
SOWERS, Karen .... 865-974-3176 439 I
kmsowers@utk.edu
SOWINSKI, Tomasz .... 212-472-1500 318 B
tsowinski@nysid.edu
SOYER, Megan, M .... 817-257-5325 461 A
m.m.soyer@tcu.edu
SOYKA, Jennifer .... 908-737-5061 286 F
jsoyka@exchange.kean.edu
SOYRING, Mary .... 218-879-0811 244 F
msoyring@fdltcc.edu
SOZZO, Anthony, M ...... 914-594-4491 318 A
tony_sozzo@nymc.edu
SPACH, Robert, C .... 704-894-2420 337 B
rospach@davidson.edu
SPACK, Martha .... 870-972-2056.. 18 A
mspack@astate.edu
SPADE, Douglas, R .... 713-798-7391 444 A
dspade@bcm.edu
SPADEMAN, Robert .... 216-523-7284 359 L
r.spademan@csuohio.edu
SPADONI, Sandra .... 315-786-2408 311 H
sspadoni@sunyjefferson.edu
SPAETH, Jason .... 320-629-5100 246 H
spaethj@pine.edu
SPAETH, Nick .... 309-457-2143 146 A
nspaeth@monmouthcollege.edu
SPAETH, Paul, J .... 716-375-2327 322 B
pspaeth@sbu.edu
SPAETH-BAUM, Barbara 701-671-2483 355 B
barbara.baum@ndscs.edu
SPAFFORD, Jennifer ...... 703-284-1538 483 A
jennifer.spafford@marymount.edu
SPAGNA, Michael .... 310-243-3307.. 31 E
mspagna@csudh.edu
SPAGNOLO, Jean-Paul .. 614-236-6831 358 A
jpspagnolo@capital.edu
SPAHR, Todd .... 717-361-1558 394 F
spahrt@etown.edu
SPAID, Darla .... 814-732-1364 406 B
dspaid@edinboro.edu
SPAIN, Tammy .... 252-249-1851 345 C
tspain@pamlicocc.edu
SPAK, Gale, T .... 973-596-8540 288 A
gale.spak@njit.edu
SPAKE, Deborah, F .... 330-672-6317 363 I
dspake@kent.edu
SPAKE, Ellen .... 816-501-4597 265 I
ellen.spake@rockhurst.edu
SPALDING, Carol .... 704-216-3450 346 C
carol.spalding@rccc.edu
SPALDING, David, P ..... 515-294-2422 166 F
spalding@iastate.edu
SPALDING, Jane .... 206-296-6118 498 D
spalding@seattleu.edu
SPALDING, Richard, E .. 413-597-2483 226 C
richard.e.spalding@williams.edu
SPALDING, Wendy .... 513-244-8492 359 E
wendy.spalding@ccuniversity.edu
SPALTER, Mendel .... 323-937-3763.. 75 F
mspalter@yoec.edu
SPALTER, Sholom .... 973-267-9404 289 B
shspalter1@aol.com
SPANBAUER, Julie .... 312-427-2737 141 E
7spanbau@jmls.edu
SPANBAUER, Sharon .... 517-264-7190 236 I
sspanbau@sienaheights.edu
SPANCAKE, Richard ...... 229-391-4890 114 G
rspancake@abac.edu
SPANG, David .... 856-222-9311 289 F
ecasa@rcbc.edu
SPANG, Kimberly .... 610-330-5021 399 B
spangk@lafayette.edu
SPANG, Zane .... 406-477-6215 270 I
zspang@cdkc.edu
SPANGENBERG, Eric ..... 949-824-8470.. 69 A
ers@uci.edu
SPANGENBERG, Laurie . 906-786-5802 228 A
laurie.spangenberg@baycollege.edu
SPANGLER, Anthony ..... 313-664-7462 228 H
aspangler@collegeforcreativestudies.edu
SPANGLER, John, R ...... 717-334-6286 412 E
jspangler@ltsg.edu
SPANGLER, Michael ...... 702-651-4959 278 N
michael.spangler@csn.edu
SPANGLER, Stephanie ... 203-432-4446.. 89 G
stephanie.spangler@yale.edu
SPANIOL, Lee .... 217-234-5263 143 B
lspaniol@lakeland.cc.il.us
SPANJER, Pat .... 509-359-4557 494 D
pspanjer@ewu.edu
SPANN, B. Steven .... 615-327-3927 432 G
spann@guptoncollege.edu
SPANN, Chante .... 312-427-2737 141 E
cspann@jmls.edu
SPANN, Sammy .... 419-530-5268 372 F
sammy.spann@utoledo.edu
SPANN-PACK, Robin ..... 601-979-2015 253 E
robin.m.spann-pack@jsums.edu
SPANNAGEL, Ashlee ...... 618-393-2982 140 B
spannagela@iecc.edu
SPANO, David, B .... 704-687-0311 351 C
dspano@uncc.edu
SPARACINO, Debra .... 864-656-2171 419 F
registrar@clemson.edu
SPARGEN, Dan .... 402-399-2600 274 A
dspargen@csm.edu
SPARKES, Mike .... 281-425-6327 451 I
msparkes@lee.edu
SPARKES, Terry, E .... 563-387-2165 171 I
sparkete@luther.edu
SPARKMAN, Calvin .... 951-343-4356.. 28 G
csparkman@calbaptist.edu
SPARKMAN, Margo .... 606-368-6039 182 H
margosparkman@alc.edu
SPARKMAN, Susan .... 205-652-3587.... 9 C
sgt@uwa.edu
SPARKS, Brad .... 618-235-2700 152 E
bradley.sparks@swic.edu
SPARKS, Carolyn, B ...... 864-597-4160 426 I
sparkscb@wofford.edu
SPARKS, Cheryl, T .... 432-264-5030 450 G
csparks@howardcollege.edu
SPARKS, Doug .... 602-285-7255.. 14 A
douglas.sparks@phoenixcollege.edu
SPARKS, George, E .... 540-568-7073 481 I
sparksge@jmu.edu
SPARKS, Jane .... 760-757-2121.. 52 F
jsparks@miracosta.edu
SPARKS, John .... 618-634-3230 151 G
johns@shawneecc.edu
SPARKS, Kathy, M .... 651-631-5390 251 C
kmsparks@unwsp.edu
SPARKS, Kenton .... 610-341-1396 394 E
ksparks@eastern.edu
SPARKS, Kim .... 606-759-7141 186 E
kim.sparks@kctcs.edu
SPARKS, Larry, D .... 662-915-7200 256 C
lsparks@olemiss.edu
SPARKS, Laura .... 212-353-4240 306 A
sparks@cooper.edu
SPARKS, Maria .... 518-464-8768 308 A
msparks@excelsior.edu
SPARKS, Mark .... 410-455-2872 208 A
sparks@umbc.edu
SPARKS, Michele .... 859-233-8236 189 H
msparks@transy.edu
SPARKS, Rick .... 540-231-7951 490 F
rasparks@vt.edu
SPARKS, Rick .... 509-793-2206 492 I
ricks@bigbend.edu
SPARKS, Sonny .... 662-472-9015 253 C
ssparks@holmescc.edu
SPARKS, Steve .... 252-222-6087 341 F
sparkss@carteret.edu
SPARKS, Terrell .... 801-878-1494 280 B
tsparks@roseman.edu
SPARKS, William, O ...... 505-272-5849 296 H
wsparks@salud.unm.edu
SPARLING, Steve .... 231-843-5824 239 D
ssparling@westshor.edu
SPARR, Cynthia .... 630-466-7900 155 C
csparr@waubonsee.edu
SPARROW, Anita .... 860-512-3223.. 85 G
asparrow@manchestercc.edu
SPARROW, Rebecca, M 607-255-2723 306 B
rms18@cornell.edu
SPARROW, Suzanne ...... 610-409-3600 413 H
ssparrow@ursinus.edu
SPATAFORE, Marisa .... 408-864-8672.. 43 E
spataforemarisa@deanza.edu
SPATARO, Keith .... 650-543-3853.. 51 F
kspataro@menlo.edu
SPATARO-WILSON,
Jennifer, A .... 540-665-5412 485 C
jspataro@su.edu
SPATES, Gerald .... 336-334-7800 350 C
gspates@ncat.edu
SPATZ, Dan .... 541-506-6034 382 G
dspatz@cgcc.edu
SPAULDING, Angela ...... 806-651-2730 460 E
aspaulding@mail.wtamu.edu
SPAULDING, II,
Henry, W .... 740-392-6868 366 B
hspauldi@mvnu.edu
SPAULDING, Jeb .... 802-224-3000 476 H
jeb.spaulding@vsc.edu
SPAYD, Ann .... 315-787-4005 308 E
ann.spayd@flhealth.org
SPAYD, Bonnie .... 610-372-4721 408 G
bspayd@racc.edu
SPAYD, Kenneth .... 910-521-6689 351 E
kenneth.spayd@uncp.edu
SPAYER, Roger .... 847-925-6360 139 B
rspayer@harpercollege.edu
SPAZIANI, Rhonda .... 860-215-9293.. 86 F
rspaziani@trcc.commnet.edu
SPEAKER, Cindy .... 315-364-3311 333 G
cspeaker@wells.edu
SPEAKMAN, Jennifer ..... 614-236-7127 358 A
jspeakman@capital.edu
SPEAKMAN,
Thomas, W .... 989-774-1840 228 E
speak1tw@cmich.edu
SPEAKS, Michael, A ...... 315-443-0790 330 H
maspeaks@syr.edu
SPEAKS, Tiffany .... 202-885-3651.. 91 C
tspeaks@american.edu
SPEAR, Catherine .... 434-924-3200 486 H
uvaeop@virginia.edu
SPEAR, Jeff .... 863-667-5000 108 G
jbspear@seu.edu
SPEAR, Pamela .... 603-526-3621 280 H
pspear@colby-sawyer.edu
SPEAR, Robert .... 208-885-0243 132 I
rspear@uidaho.edu
SPEAREN, Charlene .... 803-376-5780 418 D
cspearen@allenuniversity.edu
SPEARING, Mike .... 205-348-5490.... 8 A
mspearing@uasystem.ua.edu
SPEARMAN, Howard ..... 815-921-4109 150 A
h.spearman@rockvalleycollege.edu
SPEARMAN, Leonard, H 713-313-1198 461 E
lespearman@tmslaw.tsu.edu
SPEARMAN, Marilyn ..... 229-430-1877 114 I
marilyn.spearman@asurams.edu
SPEARMAN, Shatika ...... 803-793-5248 420 G
spearmans@denmarktech.edu
SPEARS, Curtis, L .... 210-434-6711 454 D
cspears@lake.ollusa.edu
SPEARS, Eric .... 478-445-0874 119 E
eric.spears@gcsu.edu
SPEARS, Gary Lee .... 662-562-3227 255 C
glspears@northwestms.edu
SPEARS, Justin, R .... 530-226-4140.. 64 B
jspears@simpsonu.edu
SPEARS, Lanny .... 859-858-2298 183 C
SPEARS, Linda, C .... 615-963-5281 438 E
lspears@tnstate.edu
SPEARS, Marty .... 501-279-4335.. 19 G
mspears@harding.edu
SPEARS, Robert, D .... 713-486-4013 468 D
robert.d.spears@uth.tmc.edu
SPEARS, Ron .... 806-894-9611 456 F
rspears@southplainscollege.edu
SPEARS, Ronald .... 806-716-2341 456 F
rspears@southplainscollege.edu
SPEARS, Sylvia .... 617-824-8500 214 E
sylvia_spears@emerson.edu
SPEARS, Tim .... 802-443-5391 475 G
spears@middlebury.edu
SPEARS-BOYD, Amy ...... 931-540-2764 436 H
aspears@columbiastate.edu
SPEAS, Philip, E .... 606-693-5000 187 D
pspeas@kmbc.edu
SPECHLER, Julie .... 954-262-5348 104 F
julies@nova.edu
SPECHT, Mark, A .... 610-566-1776 415 A
mspecht@williamson.edu

SPECHT, Matthew, F ...... 773-442-4600 147 G m-specht@neiu.edu
SPECHT, Nancy .... 585-275-5572 332 E nancy.specht@rochester.edu
SPECK, Anne .... 484-664-3165 402 F annespeck@muhlenberg.edu
SPECK, Christie .... 707-864-7000.. 64 E christie.speck@solano.edu
SPECTAR, Jem, M .... 814-269-2090 412 I spectar@pitt.edu
SPECTER, Robert, M ...... 202-319-5606.. 91 D specter@cua.edu
SPECTOR, Carol .... 617-824-8586 214 E carol_spector@emerson.edu
SPECTOR, Harvey .... 212-678-3042 331 C spector@tc.edu
SPEED, Bonnie .... 404-727-6289 119 B baspeed@emory.edu
SPEED, Coleen .... 318-274-3338 196 G speedc@gram.edu
SPEED, Cynthia .... 800-782-2422.. 30 G cspeed@mail.cnuas.edu
SPEED, Heather .... 719-549-3082.. 81 M heather.speed@pueblocc.edu
SPEEDIE, Marilyn, K ..... 612-624-1900 250 E speed001@umn.edu
SPEEDY, Nigel .... 661-824-2977.. 53 G nspeedy@ntps.edu
SPEEGLE, Charlotte .... 325-794-4411 445 Q charlotte.speegle@cisco.edu
SPEEGLE, Diana .... 817-554-5950 452 G finaid@messengercollege.edu
SPEER, Brian .... 717-262-2607 415 B brian.speer@wilson.edu
SPEER, Brian .... 704-406-4269 337 H bspeer@gardner-webb.edu
SPEGG, Samantha .... 601-643-8342 252 G samantha.spegg@colin.edu
SPEHAR, John .... 708-596-2000 151 H jspehar@ssc.edu
SPEHN, Steven .... 507-222-4271 241 C sspehn@carleton.edu
SPEIDEL, Daniel .... 603-897-8576 281 I dspeidel@rivier.edu
SPEIDEL, III, William .... 724-357-5661 406 C william.speidel@iup.edu
SPEIR, Mary .... 540-828-5706 478 J mspeir@bridgewater.edu
SPEISER, Lynn .... 419-267-1312 366 G lspeiser@northweststate.edu
SPEISSER, Nancy .... 757-493-6946 125 H nspeisser@southuniversity.edu
SPELL, Ashley .... 312-499-4184 151 F aspell@saic.edu
SPELL, Donald, R .... 252-493-7211 345 E dspell@email.pittcc.edu
SPELL, Paul .... 601-477-4223 253 F paul.spell@jcjc.edu
SPELLINGS, Margaret .... 919-962-4622 349 G president@northcarolina.edu
SPELLMAN, Amy, C .... 717-871-5804 407 A amy.spellman@millersville.edu
SPELLMAN, Carlton .... 910-672-1151 350 B cspellma@uncfsu.edu
SPELLMAN, Joseph .... 203-932-7134.. 89 D jspellman@newhaven.edu
SPELLS, Doretha, J .... 757-727-5213 481 E doretha.spells@hamptonu.edu
SPELLS, Kaschia .... 252-246-1214 347 H kspells@wilsoncc.edu
SPELLS-FENTRY, Rhonda .... 301-546-7014 206 E spellsrx@pgcc.edu
SPELLS FENTRY, Rhonda .... 301-546-0987 206 E spellsrx@pgcc.edu
SPELMAN, Amy .... 309-298-1914 155 D ae-spelman@wiu.edu
SPENARD, Michele .... 315-470-7256 299 K michelespenard@crouse.org
SPENCE, Charles .... 434-592-3503 482 D cpspence@liberty.edu
SPENCE, Jeff .... 334-347-2623.... 1 J jspence@escc.edu
SPENCE, Jeffery .... 215-572-2088 389 D spencej@arcadia.edu
SPENCE, Jon, N .... 913-971-3279 179 H jnspence@mnu.edu
SPENCE, Lisa .... 812-237-8439 159 C lisa.spence@indstate.edu
SPENCE, Mary .... 716-829-7736 307 B spencem@dyc.edu
SPENCE, Thomas .... 615-460-6417 430 D thom.spence@belmont.edu
SPENCE, Weymouth .... 301-891-4128 209 E wspence@wau.edu
SPENCER, A. Clayton .... 207-786-6100 198 E cspencer@bates.edu
SPENCER, Andrew .... 405-585-4102 377 A andrew.spencer@okbu.edu
SPENCER, Barbara .... 269-749-7642 236 A bspencer@olivetcollege.edu
SPENCER, Christine .... 410-837-6134 209 D cspencer@ubalt.edu
SPENCER, Christine .... 312-341-3801 150 D cspencer02@roosevelt.edu
SPENCER, Dan .... 254-298-8619 458 C dan.spencer@templejc.edu
SPENCER, Deborah .... 860-231-5390.. 89 E dspencer@usj.edu
SPENCER, Delinda .... 254-267-7037 454 L dspencer@rangercollege.edu
SPENCER, Delmy .... 530-741-6705.. 76 A dspencer@yccd.edu
SPENCER, Estelle, H ...... 413-205-3461 210 E estelle.spencer@aic.edu
SPENCER, Eugene .... 610-409-3789 413 H gspencer@ursinus.edu
SPENCER, James, G ...... 312-329-4070 146 B james.spencer@moody.edu
SPENCER, Janett .... 256-306-2628.... 1 F janet.spencer@calhoun.edu
SPENCER, Jed .... 801-626-6586 473 E jedspencer@weber.edu
SPENCER, Jeremy .... 508-626-4500 218 A jspencer1@framingham.edu
SPENCER, Joel .... 303-329-6355.. 78 L finaid@cstcm.edu
SPENCER, SJ, John .... 617-735-9780 214 F spencerj@emmanuel.edu
SPENCER, John, D .... 817-515-5079 458 B john.spencer@tccd.edu
SPENCER, Joseph, F ...... 419-434-4791 372 B spencer@findlay.edu
SPENCER, Judith .... 662-325-3713 254 E jspencer@hrm.msstate.edu
SPENCER, Julie .... 424-207-3763.. 54 I jspencer@otis.edu
SPENCER, Kacie .... 469-706-6710 134 K kspencer2@chamberlain.edu
SPENCER, Katrina .... 860-486-0930.. 88 G katrina.spencer@uconn.edu
SPENCER, Keith, J .... 417-667-8181 259 A kspencer@cottey.edu
SPENCER, Libby .... 920-686-6150 510 A libby.spencer@sl.edu
SPENCER, Lisa .... 304-647-6369 504 F lspencer@osteo.wvsom.edu
SPENCER, Lori .... 901-761-9494 431 B lspencer@concorde.edu
SPENCER, Mark .... 812-488-2238 164 G ms628@evansville.edu
SPENCER, Mary .... 414-277-4517 509 A spencer@msoe.edu
SPENCER, Michael .... 443-885-3231 206 A michael.spencer@eng.morgan.edu
SPENCER, Pamela .... 513-875-3344 359 C pam.spencer@chatfield.edu
SPENCER, Richard .... 618-235-2700 152 E richard.spencer@swic.edu
SPENCER, Rick, E .... 630-637-5209 147 E respencer@noctrl.edu
SPENCER, Ruth .... 845-437-6820 333 A ruspencer@vassar.edu
SPENCER, Scott, J .... 610-660-1018 409 H sspencer@sju.edu
SPENCER, Shanan .... 304-876-5053 504 D sspencer@shepherd.edu
SPENCER, Shannon, M . 419-772-2036 367 G s-spencer@onu.edu
SPENCER, Susan .... 660-263-4100 264 C susanspencer@macc.edu
SPENCER, Weldon .... 704-216-6131 339 E
SPENCER, Yvette .... 205-226-7720.... 4 F yspencer@bsc.edu
SPENCER-MONTEIRO, Carol .... 508-999-8705 217 A cspencer@umassd.edu
SPENGLER, Gregory, C . 410-706-1264 207 H gspengler@umaryland.edu
SPENNER, Anne .... 816-235-1576 268 D spennerae@umkc.edu
SPENSLEY, Nicole .... 803-786-3672 420 D nspensley@columbiasc.edu
SPERANZA, Dena, L ...... 740-587-6526 361 B speranzad@denison.edu
SPERGER, Herb .... 610-785-6525 409 F hsperger@scs.edu
SPERICO, Jodie .... 516-877-3118 297 I jsperico@adelphi.edu
SPERLING, Chad .... 218-793-2436 246 F chad.sperling@northlandcollege.edu
SPERLING, Mark .... 219-980-6887 160 C masperli@iun.edu
SPERLING, Michael .... 845-905-4616 306 D michael.sperling@culinary.edu
SPERLING, Susan, S ..... 510-723-6641.. 36 C ssperling@chabotcollege.edu
SPEROS, Michael .... 916-278-5772.. 33 C msperos@csus.edu
SPERRING, Tiffany .... 614-222-6183 360 B tsperring@ccad.edu
SPERRY, Sarah .... 412-396-5894 394 D sperrys@duq.edu
SPESERT, Douglas .... 310-360-8888.. 27 D
SPETKA, Rosemary, V ... 315-792-5495 315 I rspetka@mvcc.edu
SPETS, Steve .... 906-932-4231 230 D stevem@gogebic.edu
SPETZ, Jason .... 715-232-2266 512 A spetzj@uwstout.edu
SPEWOCK, Kelly .... 412-291-6244 389 F kspewock@aii.edu
SPEYER, Seth .... 202-885-3411.. 91 C speyer@american.edu
SPEZIANI, Humberto, M .... 305-284-5450 112 O hmspez@miami.edu
SPEZZACATENA, Maricel .... 305-273-4499.. 96 N maricel@cbt.edu
SPICER, Amy .... 901-381-3939 440 I amy@visible.edu
SPICER, Christopher ...... 360-650-6144 500 E kit.spicer@wwu.edu
SPICER, Donald, Z .... 301-445-2729 207 F dspicer@usmd.edu
SPICER, Erin .... 850-484-1706 105 E espicer@pensacolastate.edu
SPICER, Jacqueline .... 810-766-4273 227 E jacqueline.spicer@baker.edu
SPICER, Michael .... 909-621-8142.. 57 I michael.spicer@pomona.edu
SPICER, Misty .... 602-331-7500.. 11 C mspicer@aii.edu
SPICER, Udella .... 229-217-4159 126 C uspicer@southernregional.edu
SPIECKER, Karl .... 719-549-2320.. 78 P karl.spiecker@csupueblo.edu
SPIEGEL, Allen, M .... 212-960-3179 334 P aspiegel@aecom.yu.edu
SPIEGEL, Allen, M .... 212-430-2801 334 P spiegel@aecom.yu.edu
SPIEGEL, Benjamin .... 732-367-1060 283 K
SPIEGEL, Sam .... 303-273-3884.. 78 J sspiegel@mines.edu
SPIEGELMAN, Kathy .... 617-373-2226 223 D
SPIELBAUER, Brian .... 660-248-6390 258 B bspielba@centralmethodist.edu
SPIELMAN, George, L ... 607-746-4091 329 B spielmgl@delhi.edu
SPIELVOGEL, Jennifer ... 419-559-2266 370 J jspielvogel01@terra.edu
SPIERS, William .... 850-201-8399 112 C spiersw@tcc.fl.edu
SPIES, Brent .... 314-889-4564 260 C bspies@fontbonne.edu
SPIES, Carolyn, I .... 973-748-9000 284 A carolyn_spies@bloomfield.edu
SPIES, Dennis .... 847-970-4699 154 H dspies@usml.edu
SPIES, Don .... 281-459-7629 456 A don.spies@sjcd.edu
SPIESMAN, John .... 440-375-7426 364 C jspiesman@lec.edu
SPIEZIO, Kim .... 304-357-4875 502 E kimspiezio@ucwv.edu
SPIGELMYER, Kathleen . 215-248-7025 392 D spigelmyerk@chc.edu
SPIKEREIT, Damien .... 417-626-1234 264 J spikereit.damien@occ.edu
SPILKER, Christopher .... 313-883-8651 236 D spilker.christopher@shms.edu
SPILLANE, Joseph .... 404-413-2000 121 A jspillane@gsu.edu
SPILLER, Elizabeth .... 540-231-6779 490 F espiller@vt.edu
SPILLERS, James .... 619-482-6551.. 65 H jspillers@swccd.edu
SPILLING, Christopher .. 314-516-5285 268 E spillingc@umsl.edu
SPILLUM, Carol .... 605-274-4090 426 K carol.spillum@augie.edu
SPINA, Anthony .... 716-829-7648 307 B spinaaw@dyc.edu
SPINA, Eric, F .... 937-229-4122 372 A president19@udayton.edu
SPINA, Matthew, R .... 609-497-7805 288 E admissions@ptsem.edu
SPINA, Mike .... 530-541-4660.. 47 I spina@ltcc.edu
SPINA, Robert .... 409-880-8661 462 C bob.spina@lamar.edu
SPINARD, John .... 617-873-0689 213 B john.spinard@cambridgecollege.edu
SPINATO, Donna .... 903-886-5860 459 E donna.spinato@tamuc.edu
SPINAZZA, Terri .... 208-426-2168 131 C tspinazz@boisestate.edu
SPINDLE, Blair .... 405-491-6608 379 K bspindle@snu.edu
SPINDLE, Tollya .... 405-491-6300 379 K tspindle@snu.edu
SPINDLE, William .... 210-784-2000 460 C william.spindle@tamusa.edu
SPINELLI-SEXTER, Eva .. 212-463-0400 331 F espinelli@touro.edu
SPINK-FORMANSKI, Christina .... 716-829-7775 307 B formanst@dyc.edu
SPINKS, Robert .... 337-475-5711 197 B rspinks@mcneese.edu
SPINNATO, Amy, R .... 443-412-2258 204 C aspinnato@harford.edu
SPINNATO, Meredith ..... 617-585-0200 212 C meredith.spinnato@the-bac.edu
SPINNER, Arnold .... 212-463-0400 331 F arnold.spinner@touro.edu
SPINNER, Bonita .... 405-682-1611 377 C bonita.d.spinner@occc.edu
SPINNER, Clifton .... 614-947-6901 362 A clifton.spinner@franklin.edu
SPINO, Catherine, D ..... 330-494-6170 370 G cspino@starkstate.edu
SPINOSA, Tony .... 202-685-3946 518 B spinosat@ndu.edu
SPINOSA DE VEGA, Leah .... 612-330-1650 240 G devega@augsburg.edu
SPIOTTI, Louis .... 585-475-2615 321 D lxs4798@rit.edu
SPIRES, Chris .... 803-641-3463 425 A chriss@usca.edu
SPIRES, Tracy, M .... 864-379-8773 421 E tspires@erskine.edu
SPIRK, Mary Beth .... 610-861-1424 402 D spirkm@moravian.edu
SPIRO, Jonathan .... 802-468-1244 477 A jonathan.spiro@castleton.edu
SPIROU, Costas .... 478-445-6848 119 E costas.spirou@gcsu.edu
SPIRRISON, Hannah .... 937-319-0128 356 F hspirrison@antiochcollege.edu
SPISAK, Art, L .... 319-335-1681 166 G art-spisak@uiowa.edu
SPISAK-CAMERON, Jennifer .... 919-681-0417 337 C jennifer.cameron@dev.duke.edu
SPISSO, Johnese Maria 310-267-9315.. 69 B jspisso@mednet.ucla.edu
SPITTAL, David, J .... 913-971-3392 179 H president@mnu.edu
SPITTAL, Ryan .... 815-939-5452 148 F rspittal@olivet.edu
SPITZ, Catherine .... 309-556-3120 141 B cspitz@iwu.edu
SPITZ, Cody .... 575-562-2178 293 O cody.spitz@enmu.edu
SPITZ, Laura, M .... 607-255-0157 306 B lauraspitz@cornell.edu
SPIVAK, Howard .... 718-951-5342 301 E howards@brooklyn.cuny.edu
SPIVAK, Michael .... 641-472-7000 171 J mspivak@mum.edu
SPIVAK, Victoria .... 708-524-6950 137 F vlamick@dom.edu
SPIVEY, Randy .... 615-966-2503 433 D randy.spivey@lipscomb.edu
SPIVEY, Richard, C .... 478-301-2172 122 H spivey_rc@mercer.edu
SPIVEY, Sheryl .... 470-639-0640 123 E sheryl.spivey@morehouse.edu
SPIWAK, Doug .... 847-925-6969 139 B dspiwak@harpercollege.edu
SPIZZIRRI, Kristin .... 903-675-6371 464 C kspizzirri@tvcc.edu
SPIZZIRRRI, Erica .... 609-984-1588 292 B espizzirri@tesu.edu
SPOERRI, Tamara, D ..... 207-725-3837 198 G tspoerri@bowdoin.edu
SPOHN, Andrew .... 517-796-8410 231 E spohnandrewb@jccmi.edu
SPOHN, Chris .... 303-753-6046.. 82 E
SPOHR, Jean .... 513-562-8773 356 J jspohr@artacademy.edu
SPOHR, Robert .... 989-328-1241 234 D robs@montcalm.edu
SPOLTORE, Janet, D ...... 860-439-2692.. 86 H janet.spoltore@conncoll.edu
SPOMER, Michelle .... 412-924-1350 408 E mspomer@pts.edu

SPONG, Mark, W .... 972-883-2974 467 D
mspong@utdallas.edu
SPONG, Melinda .... 859-572-1464 188 E
spongm1@nku.edu
SPONHOLZ, Karin .... 650-508-3714.. 54 D
ksponholz@ndnu.edu
SPONSELLER, Jared ...... 740-392-6868 366 B
jared.sponseller@mvnu.edu
SPONSELLER, Kimberly . 740-283-6855 361 L
ksponseller@franciscan.edu
SPOON, Adrea .... 419-372-7857 357 F
adrea@bgsu.edu
SPOONER, James .... 229-243-6859 116 C
james.spooner@bainbridge.edu
SPOONER, Melba, C ..... 828-262-2230 349 H
spoonermc@appstate.edu
SPOOR, Suzanne, J .... 410-777-2448 202 D
sjspoor@aacc.edu
SPOR, Arvid .... 626-914-8881.. 37 G
aspor@citruscollege.edu
SPORBERT, Derek .... 701-777-3809 353 G
derek.sporbert@und.edu
SPORE, MaryBeth .... 724-537-4567 410 B
marybeth.spore@email.stvincent.edu
SPORES, Jon .... 360-383-3440 500 F
jspores@whatcom.ctc.edu
SPOSATO, Aime .... 540-365-4206 480 L
asposato@ferrum.edu
SPOSATO, Amanda, L ... 724-458-2051 396 D
alsposato@gcc.edu
SPOSILI, Michael .... 518-580-5610 324 D
msposili@skidmore.edu
SPOTO, Mary .... 352-588-8294 106 N
mary.spoto@saintleo.edu
SPOTORNO, Marianne ... 707-654-1076.. 32 E
mspotorno@csum.edu
SPOTSWOOD, James ..... 620-341-5403 177 B
jspotswo@emporia.edu
SPOTTS, Cyndi .... 248-204-4109 233 A
cspotts@ltu.edu
SPOTTS, Deborah .... 602-285-7667.. 14 A
deborah.spotts@phoenixcollege.edu
SPRADLEY, Brandon ...... 251-626-3303.... 7 G
bspradley@ussa.edu
SPRADLEY, Minou .... 619-388-3400.. 60 C
SPRADLEY, Paul, D .... 412-397-6848 409 C
spradley@rmu.edu
SPRADLEY, Wanda .... 434-381-6156 485 P
wspradley@sbc.edu
SPRADLIN, Chris .... 937-778-7887 361 E
cspradlin@edisonohio.edu
SPRADLIN, Michael, R .. 901-751-8453 434 E
mspradlin@mabts.edu
SPRADLING, Carol .... 304-357-4747 502 E
carolspradling@ucwv.edu
SPRADLING, John .... 903-785-7661 454 F
jspradling@parisjc.edu
SPRADLING, Steve .... 330-494-6170 370 G
sspradling@starkstate.edu
SPRAGINS, Robyn .... 610-436-2509 407 D
rspragins@wcupa.edu
SPRAGUE, Alice .... 503-399-2537 382 C
alice.sprague@chemeketa.edu
SPRAGUE, Carol .... 413-545-0698 216 H
sprague@research.umass.edu
SPRAGUE, Jamie .... 850-474-2156 111 D
jsprague@uwf.edu
SPRAGUE, Jennifer .... 505-984-6041 295 K
jsprague@sjc.edu
SPRAGUE, Kendra .... 360-442-2131 495 G
ksprague@lowercolumbia.edu
SPRAGUE, Kendra .... 360-442-2121 495 G
ksprague@lowercolumbia.edu
SPRAGUE, Viola .... 810-762-9668 232 C
vsprague@kettering.edu
SPRAKER, Matt .... 615-248-1245 439 B
mspraker@trevecca.edu
SPRANGEL, JR.,
Joseph, R .... 540-887-7067 482 G
jsprangel@marybaldwin.edu
SPRATLIN, Steve .... 256-395-2211.... 3 G
sspratlin@suscc.edu
SPRATT, Bruce, R .... 404-413-3071 121 A
bspratt@gsu.edu
SPRATT, Sharon .... 270-706-8478 185 H
sharon.spratt@kctcs.edu
SPRAW, Deanna .... 419-434-4589 372 B
spraw@findlay.edu
SPRAW, William .... 419-434-4601 372 B
wspraw@findlay.edu
SPRECHER, Art .... 209-946-2251.. 70 F
asprecher@pacific.edu
SPRECHER, Becky .... 503-493-6454 382 I
bsprecher@cu-portland.edu
SPREER-ALBERT,
Frances .... 518-262-5585 297 L
albertf@mail.amc.edu

SPREITZER, Mary, L ...... 815-740-5038 154 G
mspreitzer@stfrancis.edu
SPRENGER, Cathy, J ..... 717-477-1381 407 B
cjspre@ship.edu
SPRENGER, Scott .... 801-626-6424 473 E
scottsprenger@weber.edu
SPRICK, David, W .... 715-836-2222 510 D
sprickdw@uwec.edu
SPRIGGS, Barry, A .... 315-684-6054 329 F
spriggbl@morrisville.edu
SPRIGGS, Janet .... 704-219-7165 346 C
janet.spriggs@rccc.edu
SPRING, Debra .... 601-304-4302 251 G
dspring@alcorn.edu
SPRING, SCC, Joseph ... 973-957-0188 283 C
president@acs350.org
SPRINGALL, Robert .... 484-664-3204 402 F
robertspringall@muhlenberg.edu
SPRINGALL, Robert, G .. 570-577-1446 390 H
r.springall@bucknell.edu
SPRINGER, Brianna .... 949-214-3046.. 40 I
brianna.springer@cui.edu
SPRINGER, Colleen .... 641-844-7106 170 I
colleen.springer@iavalley.edu
SPRINGER, Colleen .... 641-844-5523 170 G
colleen.springer@iavalley.edu
SPRINGER, Gabe .... 618-468-3700 143 D
gspringer@lc.edu
SPRINGER, Karen .... 215-612-6600 390 B
kspringer@chicareers.com
SPRINGER, Mark .... 320-308-3093 247 E
mspringer@stcloudstate.edu
SPRINGER, Mary .... 319-399-8569 167 F
mspringer@coe.edu
SPRINGER, Molly .... 916-558-2194.. 50 I
springm@scc.losrios.edu
SPRINGER, Patrick .... 951-487-3590.. 52 J
pspringer@msjc.edu
SPRINGER, Robert .... 903-510-3273 464 D
rspr@tjc.edu
SPRINGER, Robert, I ..... 336-278-6644 337 G
springer@elon.edu
SPRINGER, Susan .... 601-977-7778 256 B
sspringer@tougaloo.edu
SPRINGER, Tracy .... 765-455-9356 160 B
tracylb@iuk.edu
SPRINGS, Andre .... 704-216-6012 339 E
asprings@livingstone.edu
SPRINKLE, Dean .... 276-223-4848 490 C
dsprinkle@wcc.vccs.edu
SPRINKLE, Stephen, D .. 619-260-4655.. 71 J
sdsprinkle@sandiego.edu
SPROLE, JoLynn, H .... 817-515-4563 458 B
jolynn.sprole@tccd.edu
SPROULS, David .... 212-472-1500 318 B
dsprouls@nysid.edu
SPROUSE, Clay .... 706-721-5632 116 B
csprouse@augusta.edu
SPROUSE, Keith .... 435-722-6900 472 L
keiths@ubtech.edu
SPROUSE, Marlene .... 641-683-5104 169 I
marlene.sprouse@indianhills.edu
SPROWL, Don .... 765-677-3061 161 C
don.sprowl@indwes.edu
SPROWL, Dorenda .... 803-508-7283 418 C
sprowld@atc.edu
SPROWS, Sandra .... 631-451-4252 330 C
sprowss@sunysuffolk.edu
SPRUIELL, Vicki, P .... 205-652-3627.... 9 C
vspruiell@uwa.edu
SPRUILL, Aysu .... 562-985-4818.. 32 C
aysu.spruill@csulb.edu
SPRUILL, Wayne .... 615-675-5348 441 B
wspruill@welch.edu
SPRUNGER, Philip, W ... 570-321-4038 400 G
sprunger@lycoming.edu
SPRUNK, Elizabeth .... 419-251-1524 365 C
elizabeth.sprunk@mercycollege.edu
SPRY, Susan .... 570-740-0407 400 F
sspry@luzerne.edu
SPUCHES, Charles, M ... 315-470-6817 328 D
cspuches@esf.edu
SPURGIN, Hugh .... 845-752-3000 332 A
h.spurgin@uts.edu
SPURLOCK, Chad .... 918-293-4622 378 B
chad.spurlock@okstate.edu
SPURLOCK, Jefferson .... 334-670-3267.... 7 E
spurlock@troy.edu
SPURLOCK, Jennifer ...... 513-562-8771 356 J
jspurlock@artacademy.edu
SPURLOCK, Patrick .... 802-257-7751 476 B
patrick.spurlock@sit.edu
SPURLOCK, Rhonda .... 918-343-7612 379 C
rspurlock@rsu.edu
SPURLOCK-EVANS,
Karla .... 860-297-4234.. 88 E
karla.spurlockevans@trincoll.edu

SPYBEY, Joseph .... 614-222-3246 360 B
jspybey@ccad.edu
SPYCHER, Dianna .... 440-826-8061 357 B
dspycher@bw.edu
SQUARE, Chris .... 662-476-5347 253 A
csquare@eastms.edu
SQUARE, Marilyn, C ..... 713-313-7859 461 E
squaremc@tsu.edu
SQUIER, Ragan, A .... 315-470-6686 328 D
rasquier@esf.edu
SQUIRE, Craig .... 630-752-5128 155 F
craig.squire@wheaton.edu
SQUIRE, Jonathan .... 215-965-4017 402 C
jsquire@moore.edu
SQUIRE, Wayne .... 435-283-7058 474 A
wayne.squire@snow.edu
SQUIRES, Catherine ...... 815-753-7406 147 H
csquires@niu.edu
SQUIRES, Felicia .... 503-375-7089 383 A
fsquires@corban.edu
SQUIRES, Kyle .... 480-965-9235.. 10 K
kyle.squires@asu.edu
SQUIRES, Stephanie ...... 914-337-9300 305 F
stephanie.squires@concordia-ny.edu
SQUIRES, Thomas .... 315-792-5445 315 I
tsquires@mvcc.edu
SQUIRES, Toni .... 651-641-8232 241 L
squires@csp.edu
SRBA, Karen, V .... 304-724-3700 501 D
kvendouern-srba@apus.edu
SREENIVASAN,
Katepalli, R .... 212-992-7914 318 D
katepalli.sreenivasan@nyu.edu
SRIDHAR, Nigamanth .... 216-687-9370 359 L
n.sridhar1@csuohio.edu
SRIHARI, Hari .... 607-777-2871 325 A
srihari@binghamton.edu
SRIHARI, Hari .... 607-777-2336 325 A
srihari@binghamton.edu
SRIKANTH, Rajini .... 617-287-5520 216 I
rajini.srikanth@umb.edu
SRINIVAS, Ravi .... 713-525-3804 466 J
srinivas@stthom.edu
SRINIVASAN, Balaji .... 773-795-2901 153 F
balajis@uchicago.edu
SRINIVASAN, Ganesan .. 559-675-4800.. 66 H
ganesan.srinivasan@scccd.edu
SRINIVASAN, Niruba ..... 650-574-6573.. 62 A
srinivasann@smccd.edu
SRINIVASSAN, Asoka .... 601-977-7737 256 B
asrinnivasan@tougaloo.edu
SRIRAMAN, Vedaraman 512-245-1217 463 A
vs04@txstate.edu
SRITHARAN,
Sivaguru, S .... 937-255-2321 517 H
sivaguru.sritharan@afit.edu
SROF, Brenda .... 574-535-7376 158 A
brendajs@goshen.edu
SROKA, Fred .... 415-442-5285.. 44 E
fsroka@ggu.edu
SRONCE, Robin .... 870-235-4300.. 21 F
robinsronce@saumag.edu
SRONCE, Robin .... 417-873-7438 259 G
rsronce@drury.edu
SROUFE, Darren .... 812-357-6501 164 A
dsroufe@saintmeinrad.edu
STAAB, Eric, P .... 269-337-7172 231 F
eric.staab@kzoo.edu
STAAB, Susan, K .... 815-282-7900 150 H
susanstaab@sacn.edu
STAAK, OMI, John, M .. 716-652-8900 300 L
jstaak@cks.edu
STAATS, Ray .... 252-638-7201 342 E
staatsr@cravencc.edu
STAATS, Sharon .... 661-362-2220.. 51 C
sstaats@masters.edu
STABB, Daniel .... 610-526-6118 396 H
dstabb@harcum.edu
STABEN, Chuck, A .... 208-885-6365 132 I
president@uidaho.edu
STABENOW, Max .... 909-687-1455.. 44 A
maxstabenow@gs.edu
STABILE, Donald, R .... 240-895-4388 206 G
drstabile@smcm.edu
STABILE, Steve .... 212-229-3500 316 E
stabiles@newschool.edu
STACE, Peter, A .... 718-817-3200 308 G
stace@fordham.edu
STACEY, Elizabeth .... 314-529-9364 262 B
estacey@maryville.edu
STACEY, Kathleen .... 734-487-4344 229 K
kstacey@emich.edu
STACEY, Lynn .... 810-766-4240 227 E
lynn.stacey@baker.edu
STACEY, Robert .... 206-543-5340 499 D
bstacey@uw.edu
STACEY, Simon .... 410-455-2164 208 A
spstacey@umbc.edu

STACHACZ, John .... 570-408-4254 414 H
john.stachaz@wilkes.edu
STACHOWIAK, Kris .... 610-359-5310 393 E
kstachowiak@dccc.edu
STACHOWSKI,
Mary Albertine .... 716-896-0700 333 C
smalbertine@villa.edu
STACHURA, Hubert .... 631-656-2157 308 F
STACK, Betty .... 704-669-4163 342 B
stackb520@clevelandcc.edu
STACK, Dana .... 619-388-7579.. 60 E
dstack@sdccd.edu
STACK, John .... 305-348-7266 109 D
john.stack@fiu.edu
STACK, OSA, John, P ... 610-519-4550 413 K
john.stack@villanova.edu
STACK, Kim .... 401-874-4777 417 E
kstack@uri.edu
STACK, Lisa .... 617-984-1663 223 H
lstack@quincycollege.edu
STACK, Patrick .... 314-968-6921 269 N
stackpa@webster.edu
STACK, Rachel, C .... 618-650-2345 152 C
rstack@siue.edu
STACKHOUSE TAETZSCH,
Cindra .... 630-752-5049 155 F
cindra.taetzsch@wheaton.edu
STACKOWICZ, Matthew . 574-807-7000 156 E
STACKPOOLE, Roger, W 315-445-4174 312 F
stackprw@lemoyne.edu
STACKS, Pamela .... 408-924-2488.. 34 D
pstacks@jupiter.sjsu.edu
STACY, Jeanne .... 225-216-8591 192 B
stacyj@mybrcc.edu
STACY, Karin .... 847-214-7957 138 B
kstacy@elgin.edu
STACY, Mark, W .... 585-395-5149 326 D
mstacy@brockport.edu
STADICK, Anna .... 262-595-2077 511 C
stadick@uwp.edu
STADING, Gary .... 903-334-6678 460 D
gary.stading@tamut.edu
STADLER, Albert, E .... 417-625-9807 263 G
stadler-a@mssu.edu
STADLER, Lindsay .... 909-607-3373.. 37 L
lindsay.stadler@cgu.edu
STADLER, Megan .... 315-786-6500 311 H
mstadler@sunyjefferson.edu
STADLER, Rose .... 510-567-6174.. 66 I
rstadler@sum.edu
STADTLER, Walter .... 202-685-9082 518 B
walter.stadtler@ndu.edu
STAEBLER, Ned .... 313-577-2164 239 C
nedstaebler@wayne.edu
STAEHLE, Andrea .... 760-862-1326.. 39 D
astaehle@collegeofthedesert.edu
STAFFORD, Ben .... 409-984-6354 462 E
staffordbk@lamarpa.edu
STAFFORD, Ingrid, S ..... 847-491-7350 148 C
i-stafford@northwestern.edu
STAFFORD, James .... 254-295-4607 466 A
jstafford@umhb.edu
STAFFORD, Joanne .... 405-733-7373 379 F
joannestafford@rose.edu
STAFFORD, Kulcey .... 843-921-6953 423 A
kcassidy@netc.edu
STAFFORD, Kyle .... 580-745-3079 379 J
kstafford@se.edu
STAFFORD, Laura .... 419-372-2079 357 F
llstaff@bgsu.edu
STAFFORD, Mary .... 503-251-5707 387 I
mstafford@uws.edu
STAFFORD, Matt .... 417-626-1234 264 J
stafford.matt@occ.edu
STAFFORD, Michael .... 281-290-5276 452 C
michael.d.stafford@lonestar.edu
STAFFORD,
Michael Dale .... 713-780-9777 442 F
STAFFORD, Pam .... 606-759-7141 186 E
pam.stafford@kctcs.edu
STAFFORD, Tomas, L .... 608-263-6105 510 B
tstafford@uwsa.edu
STAGE, Alan .... 320-222-5204 247 B
alan.stage@ridgewater.edu
STAGER, Karl .... 281-756-3594 442 C
kstager@alvincollege.edu
STAGGERS, Leroy .... 803-934-3274 422 G
lstaggers@morris.edu
STAGGERS, Leroy .... 803-934-3211 422 G
ipstaggers@morris.edu
STAGGS, Robert .... 606-218-5357 190 E
robertstaggs@upike.edu
STAGNARO, Leta .... 510-659-6220.. 54 F
lstagnaro@ohlone.edu
STAGNER, Annessa .... 719-336-1519.. 80 N
annessa.stagner@lamarcc.edu
STAHL, C.J .... 215-972-2059 404 Q
cstahl@pafa.edu

STARKMAN, Kenneth ..... 714-992-7052.. 54 A
kstarkman@fullcoll.edu
STARKS, Marilyn .... 662-621-4154 252 E
mstarks@coahomacc.edu
STARKS, Sam, B .... 215-898-6993 412 G
sstarks@upenn.edu
STARKSON, Mary Jo, H 507-344-7840 240 I
maryjo.starkson@blc.edu
STARLEY, Monica .... 478-445-4444 119 E
monica.starley@gcsu.edu
STARLING, Buddy .... 334-670-3243.... 7 E
bstar@troy.edu
STARLING, Jennifer .... 423-279-7635 437 E
jgstarling@northeaststate.edu
STARLING, Sharron .... 206-726-5018 494 B
sstarling@cornish.edu
STARLING, Terrie .... 901-333-5760 438 B
tstarling@southwest.tn.edu
STARLING, William .... 910-592-8081 346 D
bstarling@sampsoncc.edu
STARNER, Wendy, S ..... 717-358-3993 395 G
wendy.starner@fandm.edu
STARNES, Harry .... 252-823-5166 343 A
starnesh@edgecombe.edu
STARNES, Janie .... 205-853-1200.... 2 F
jstarnes@jeffersonstate.edu
STARNES, Richard .... 828-227-7646 352 C
starnes@wcu.edu
STARNES, Ronald .... 845-368-7212 323 I
ronald.starnes@use.salvationarmy.org
STARNES, Scott .... 434-592-4191 482 D
sastarnes@liberty.edu
STAROPOLI, Jeremiah ... 410-296-5350 202 I
STAROPOLI, Jeremiah ... 215-574-9600 397 H
jeremiah.staropoli@hussiancollege.edu
STARR, Brian .... 806-720-7405 452 D
brian.starr@lcu.edu
STARR, Charity .... 229-903-3601 114 I
charity.starr@asurams.edu
STARR, Clara .... 415-241-2249.. 37 H
cstarr@ccsf.edu
STARR, G. Gabrielle ...... 909-621-8131.. 57 I
gabrielle.starr@pomona.edu
STARR, Janice .... 406-265-3749 272 C
janice.starr@msun.edu
STARR, Monica .... 843-661-8058 421 F
monica.starr@fdtc.edu
STARR, Pamela .... 619-594-1113.. 34 B
pjstarr@mail.sdsu.edu
STARR, Peter .... 202-885-2446.. 91 C
pstarr@american.edu
STARR, Trudy .... 309-796-5405 134 C
starrt@bhc.edu
STARR, Valorie .... 817-598-6252 470 J
vstarr@wc.edu
STARR FIEDLER,
Heather .... 412-392-3409 408 F
hstarr@pointpark.edu
STARRATT, Christopher . 305-899-4757.. 95 G
cstarratt@barry.edu
STARRATT, Joseph .... 509-335-4558 499 G
jstarratt@wsu.edu
STARRETT, David .... 573-875-7500 258 F
dstarrett@ccis.edu
STARRETT, Steve .... 903-233-3900 452 A
stevestarrett@letu.edu
STARRICK, Greg .... 618-985-2828 141 D
gregstarrick@jalc.edu
STARWALT, Amanda ...... 217-581-7509 138 A
ajstarwalt@eiu.edu
STASA, Joan .... 419-530-2814 372 F
joan.stasa@utoledo.edu
STASIAK, Joan, C .... 773-508-3143 144 D
jstasia@luc.edu
STASOLLA, Debbie .... 609-896-5228 289 E
dstasolla@rider.edu
STASSEN, Anne, K .... 215-972-2039 404 Q
astassen@pafa.edu
STASSEN, Jodi .... 218-793-2539 246 F
jodistassen@northlandcollege.edu
STASSEN, Martha, L ...... 413-545-5146 216 H
mstassen@acad.umass.edu
STASSIS, Bassel .... 973-684-6500 288 C
bstassis@pccc.edu
STASZAK, Patrick .... 920-693-1265 513 H
patrick.staszak@gotoltc.edu
STATEN, James .... 213-740-4611.. 72 B
svpfinance@usc.edu
STATEN, Michael .... 270-384-8106 187 H
statenm@lindsey.edu
STATEN, Shannon .... 850-644-3818 110 A
sstaten@fsu.edu
STATES, Hollyce .... 508-588-9100 220 B
STATES, Richard .... 419-434-4677 372 B
states@findlay.edu
STATMORE, Kelly .... 215-646-7300 396 E
statmore.k@gmercyu.edu
STATON, Blanche, E ...... 617-253-4860 221 C
STATON, Cecil, P .... 252-328-6212 349 I
chancellor@ecu.edu
STATON, Rae .... 419-358-3449 357 E
statonr@bluffton.edu
STATON, Robert, E .... 864-833-8222 423 D
bstaton@presby.edu
STATON, Trina, J .... 551-574-1312 170 C
staton@iowacentral.edu
STATON, Trish .... 404-627-2681 116 E
trish.staton@beulah.edu
STATON, Wendell .... 478-445-6341 119 E
wendell.staton@gcsu.edu
STATTON, Christine .... 559-730-3734.. 39 G
christines@cos.edu
STATZELL, Donna, S ..... 952-995-1447 244 G
dstatzell@hennepintech.edu
STAUCHE, Ann .... 815-455-8710 145 B
astauche@mchenry.edu
STAUDERMAN,
Elizabeth .... 585-275-4124 332 E
elizabeth.stauderman@rochester.edu
STAUDT, Denise .... 210-829-2761 465 E
staudt@uiwtx.edu
STAUDT, Loretta .... 202-319-5744.. 91 D
staudt@cua.edu
STAUDT, Nancy .... 314-935-6420 269 L
nstaudt@wustl.edu
STAUFF, Jon .... 732-263-5843 287 C
jstauff@monmouth.edu
STAUFF, William .... 770-279-0507 119 D
stauff@gcuniv.edu
STAUFFER, Denise .... 314-918-2565 260 A
dstauffer@eden.edu
STAUFFER, Donald .... 757-455-3384 491 F
dstauffer@vwu.edu
STAUFFER, George, B ... 848-932-5224 290 C
stauffer@masongross.rutgers.edu
STAUFFER, Larry .... 208-885-6470 132 I
stauffer@uidaho.edu
STAUFFER, Lynn .... 707-664-2172.. 35 A
lynn.stauffer@sonoma.edu
STAUFFER, Patricia .... 978-478-3400 223 E
pstauffer@northpoint.edu
STAUFFER, Randy .... 818-767-0888.. 75 C
randy.stauffer@woodbury.edu
STAUFFER, II,
Ronald, E .... 570-577-3305 390 H
ron.stauffer@bucknell.edu
STAUSS, Michelle .... 973-618-3555 284 D
mstauss@caldwell.edu
STAUTZ, Shay, D .... 520-621-3108.. 16 J
stautzs@email.arizona.edu
STAVA, Jackson .... 206-281-2175 498 B
stavaj@spu.edu
STAVE, Kim .... 503-255-0332 384 E
kstave@multnomah.edu
STAVENGA, Mink .... 619-482-6569.. 65 H
mstavenga@swccd.edu
STAVITSKY, Alan .... 775-784-6656 279 E
ags@unr.edu
STAVOE, Laura .... 208-562-3449 132 A
laurastavoe@cwidaho.cc
STAVRIDIS, James .... 617-627-3050 225 A
james.stavridis@tufts.edu
STAYKOVA, Milena .... 540-985-8261 482 A
mpstaykova@jcsh.edu
STAYNER, Floyd .... 803-786-3007 420 D
fstayner@columbiasc.edu
STEAD, John .... 661-362-2202.. 51 C
jstead@masters.edu
STEAD, John .... 661-362-2626.. 51 C
jstead@masters.edu
STEADLAND, Jon .... 612-626-1616 250 E
jsteadla@umn.edu
STEADMAN, Charles ...... 972-721-5305 464 E
cstead@udallas.edu
STEADMAN, Jacqui .... 423-461-8686 435 A
jrsteadman@milligan.edu
STEADMAN, John .... 251-460-6140.... 9 B
jsteadman@southalabama.edu
STEADMAN, Mimi, H .... 716-839-8567 306 E
msteadma@daemen.edu
STEADMAN, Sheryl .... 801-832-2168 474 E
ssteadman@westminstercollege.edu
STEADMAN, II,
William, A .... 914-594-4607 318 A
gus_steadman@nymc.edu
STEAGALL, Jeffrey .... 801-626-6063 473 E
jeffsteagall@weber.edu
STEANE, Joanne, E .... 307-766-2130 517 B
jesteane@uwyo.edu
STEARNS, Diane .... 928-523-4460.. 14 K
diane.stearns@nau.edu
STEARNS, Gail .... 714-628-7260.. 36 G
stearns@chapman.edu
STEARNS, Jill .... 209-575-6067.. 75 J
stearnsj@mjc.edu
STEARNS, Keith .... 805-546-3228.. 41 C
keith_stearns@cuesta.edu
STEARNS, Marc .... 215-503-0155 411 E
marc.stearns@jefferson.edu
STEARNS, Mary, F .... 513-732-5278 371 G
mary.stearns@uc.edu
STEARNS, Roger .... 470-578-6206 122 C
rstearns@kennesaw.edu
STEARNS, Sandra .... 262-691-5368 515 B
sstearns@wctc.edu
STEARNS, Sheila, M ...... 406-243-2311 271 G
sheila.stearns@mso.umt.edu
STEARNS, Stephanie, L . 704-406-4236 337 H
sstearns@gardner-webb.edu
STEARNS, Susan, M .... 515-263-2955 169 E
sstearns@grandview.edu
STEARNS, Thaine .... 707-664-2146.. 35 A
stearnst@sonoma.edu
STEARNS MOORE, Kai .. 714-808-4829.. 53 L
kstearnsmoore@nocccd.edu
STEARNS SIMS,
Elizabeth .... 406-447-6903 271 I
e.stearnssims@umhelena.edu
STEBBINS, Chad .... 417-625-9736 263 G
stebbins-c@mssu.edu
STEBBINS, Gerald .... 304-829-7640 501 F
gstebbins@bethanywv.edu
STEBBINS, Tim .... 202-462-2101.. 92 D
tstebbins@iwp.edu
STEBBINS, Todd, H .... 608-246-6976 514 A
stebbins@madisoncollege.edu
STEC, Paul, T .... 518-783-2314 324 C
pstec@siena.edu
STECHSCHULTE,
Sharon, A .... 419-772-2030 367 G
s-stechschulte@onu.edu
STECK, Don .... 435-652-2051 473 B
steck@dixie.edu
STECKBAUER, Jill .... 715-422-5322 514 B
jill.steckbauer@mstc.edu
STECKER, Ann Page ...... 603-526-3644 280 H
astecker@colby-sawyer.edu
STECKMAN, Rebecca ..... 303-385-1070 368 M
STEDMAN, Bruce .... 413-369-4044 214 A
stedman@csld.edu
STEED, Melody .... 785-227-3380 175 E
steedm@bethanylb.edu
STEED, Steve .... 254-968-9350 459 A
ssteed@tarleton.edu
STEEDLEY, Lorrie .... 863-638-7202 113 I
lorrie.steedley@warner.edu
STEEHLER, Jack, K .... 540-375-2540 484 H
jsteehler@roanoke.edu
STEEL, Ann, E .... 717-866-5775 395 C
asteel@evangelical.edu
STEEL, Diane, M .... 559-323-2100.. 61 A
dsteel@sjcl.edu
STEEL, Virginia .... 310-825-1201.. 69 B
vsteel@library.ucla.edu
STEELANT, Wim .... 330-941-3001 374 E
wfsteelant@ysu.edu
STEELANT, Wim, F .... 330-941-3009 374 E
wfsteelant@ysu.edu
STEELE, Cherie .... 253-589-6010 493 F
cherie.steele@cptc.edu
STEELE, Christopher ...... 410-455-6841 208 A
csteele@umbc.edu
STEELE, Clover .... 212-247-3434 313 K
csteele@mandl.edu
STEELE, Darren .... 845-436-4890 330 F
dsteele@sullivan.suny.edu
STEELE, Diane .... 913-758-6102 182 B
steeled@stmary.edu
STEELE, Donna .... 731-989-6001 432 C
dsteele@fhu.edu
STEELE, Gail, T .... 340-693-1008 529 C
gsteele@uvi.edu
STEELE, Jessica .... 207-509-7293 200 I
jsteele@unity.edu
STEELE, Joanne .... 914-633-2691 311 B
jsteele@iona.edu
STEELE, Jonathan .... 727-791-5987 107 A
steele.jonathan@spcollege.edu
STEELE, Karen, B .... 718-631-6604 303 F
ksteele@qcc.cuny.edu
STEELE, Kemper .... 434-961-6585 489 C
ksteele@pvcc.edu
STEELE, Laura, L .... 714-879-3901.. 45 I
llsteele@hiu.edu
STEELE, Leslie .... 615-547-1268 431 D
lsteele@cumberland.edu
STEELE, Linda, M .... 614-947-6583 362 A
linda.steele@franklin.edu
STEELE, Lisa .... 615-966-5210 433 D
tenielle.buchanan@lipscomb.edu
STEELE, Michael .... 308-535-3723 275 I
steelem@mpcc.edu
STEELE, Misty .... 405-224-3140 381 B
msteele@usao.edu
STEELE, Mitzi, B .... 540-375-2249 484 H
steele@roanoke.edu
STEELE, Patrick, W .... 701-788-4794 354 B
patrick.steele@mayvillestate.edu
STEELE, Rachel .... 501-205-8873.. 19 B
rsteele@cbc.edu
STEELE, Richard .... 404-894-2803 120 A
rich.steele@gatech.edu
STEELE, Sarah, G .... 315-684-6038 329 F
steelesg@morrisville.edu
STEELE, Scott .... 859-985-3416 183 I
steeles@berea.edu
STEELE, Steven .... 970-223-2669.. 80 E
ssteele@ibmc.edu
STEELE, Valerie .... 212-217-4530 308 B
valerie_steele@fitnyc.edu
STEELE, Vicki .... 614-251-4706 367 F
steelev@ohiodominican.edu
STEELE, Yolanda .... 706-385-1044 124 F
yolanda.steele@point.edu
STEELE-FIGUEREDO,
David, M .... 818-767-0888.. 75 C
president@woodbury.edu
STEELE-MARCELL, Lia .... 501-370-5217.. 21 A
lsteele@philander.edu
STEELE-MIDDLETON,
Amanda .... 937-775-5200 374 B
amanda.steele-middleton@wright.edu
STEELE-MOSES, Susan .. 225-490-1674 191 G
susan.steele-moses@ololcollege.edu
STEELEY, Jodie .... 559-489-2226.. 66 G
jodie.steeley@fresnocitycollege.edu
STEELY, Jeff .... 404-413-2000 121 A
jsteely@gsu.edu
STEELY, Kelly .... 208-562-2508 132 A
kellysteely@cwidaho.cc
STEELY, Wayne .... 860-231-5257.. 89 E
wsteely@usj.edu
STEEN, Carrie .... 417-255-7255 263 I
carriesteen@missouristate.edu
STEEN, Clayton .... 518-587-2100 329 C
clayton.steen@esc.edu
STEEN, Eric .... 206-934-6427 497 J
eric.steen@seattlecolleges.edu
STEEN, Franklin .... 646-565-6000 331 F
franklin.steen@touro.edu
STEEN, James .... 281-649-3208 450 C
jsteen@hbu.edu
STEEN, Kenneth, L .... 540-654-1159 486 D
ksteen@umw.edu
STEENBURGH, Chuck .... 888-980-9151 486 B
STEENHOEK, David .... 515-643-6680 171 K
dsteenhoek@mercydesmoines.org
STEENIS, Paul, R .... 309-341-7145 142 G
psteenis@knox.edu
STEENSON, Greg .... 651-690-8825 249 T
gpsteenson@stkate.edu
STEENWYK, Thomas, L . 616-526-6549 228 B
steeto@calvin.edu
STEERMAN, Cindy .... 303-457-2757.. 76 G
cindy.steerman@zenith.org
STEFANCO, Carolyn, J .. 518-454-5120 305 B
stefancc@strose.edu
STEFANICK, Susan, A .... 609-896-5065 289 E
stefanic@rider.edu
STEFANKO, Lisa .... 412-392-4727 408 F
lstefanko@pointpark.edu
STEFANOWICZ, Michael 860-253-3102.. 85 C
mstefanowicz@asnuntuck.edu
STEFANOWICZ, Michael 802-654-3000 476 A
admissions@smcvt.edu
STEFANSKY, Chaim .... 718-259-2525 299 I
STEFANUCA, Pamela ..... 410-225-2506 205 C
pstefanuca@mica.edu
STEFFAN, Eileen .... 412-809-5100 408 D
steffan.eileen@pti.edu
STEFFEN, Joseph .... 912-358-4057 125 C
steffenj@savannahstate.edu
STEFFEN, Lloyd, H .... 610-758-3877 400 B
lhs1@lehigh.edu
STEFFEN, Rebecca .... 269-927-8861 232 G
steffen@lakemichigancollege.edu
STEFFEN, Susan, S .... 630-617-3172 138 C
susanss@elmhurst.edu
STEFFEN, Wayne .... 559-453-2215.. 43 J
wayne.steffen@fresno.edu
STEFFENS, Wayne .... 559-453-3677.. 43 J
wayne.steffens@fresno.edu
STEFFES, Thomas .... 765-983-1366 157 I
steffto@earlham.edu
STEFOGLO, Taia .... 510-567-6174.. 66 I
tstefoglo@sum.edu
STEG HASKETT, Allie .... 970-351-1886.. 83 F
allie.steghaskett@unco.edu
STEGALL, Kelly .... 704-290-5247 346 F
kstegall@spcc.edu

STEPHENSON, Susan .... 307-532-8325 516 J
susan.stephenson@ewc.wy.edu
STEPHENSON, Susan .... 828-898-8741 339 B
stephensonsb@lmc.edu
STEPHENSON, Thomas . 610-328-8319 410 I
tstephe1@swarthmore.edu
STEPINA, Karen .... 708-344-4700 144 A
kstepina@lincolntech.edu
STEPLIGHT JOHNSON,
S. Aisha .... 973-877-3115 285 K
ssteplig@essex.edu
STEPNEY, Ne'Keisha ...... 630-466-7900 155 C
nstepney@waubonsee.edu
STEPNIAK, Michael, J ... 540-665-4600 485 C
mstepnia@su.edu
STEPNOWSKI, OP,
Thomas More .... 615-297-7545 429 H
srtmore@aquinascollege.edu
STEPP, Gary .... 606-368-6105 182 H
garystepp@alc.edu
STEPP, Jim .... 606-368-6051 182 H
jamesstepp@alc.edu
STEPP, Joe, A .... 606-368-6027 182 H
joestepp@alc.edu
STEPP, Paul .... 606-539-4167 190 A
paul.stepp@ucumberlands.edu
STEPP, Terry .... 256-233-8243.... 4 C
terry.stepp@athens.edu
STEPTOE, David .... 478-289-2049 118 H
dsteptoe@ega.edu
STERBENZ, Cathy .... 509-453-0374 497 A
cathy.sterbenz@perrytech.edu
STERK, Claire, E .... 404-727-6013 119 B
csterk@emory.edu
STERK, Jim .... 573-882-2055 268 C
muathmizzouad@missouri.edu
STERKOWITZ, Robert .... 708-974-5250 146 C
sterkowitz@morainevalley.edu
STERLING, Alan .... 972-721-5347 464 E
asterling@udallas.edu
STERLING, Carolin .... 937-376-6522 358 I
csterling@centralstate.edu
STERLING, Cheryl .... 713-718-5041 450 D
cheryl.sterling@hccs.edu
STERLING, Christa .... 860-832-2277.. 84 J
csterling@ccsu.edu
STERLING, Danny, L ..... 864-833-8242 423 D
dsterling@presby.edu
STERLING, Gregory, E ... 203-432-5304.. 89 G
gregory.sterling@yale.edu
STERLING, Marcia .... 505-566-3588 296 A
sterlingm@sanjuancollege.edu
STERLING, Rebecca .... 501-812-2214.. 23 C
rsterling@pulaskitech.edu
STERLING, Rose .... 210-486-2420 441 I
rspruill1@alamo.edu
STERN, Alex .... 970-351-4736.. 83 F
alex.stern@unco.edu
STERN, Briendy .... 718-871-6187 331 F
briendy.stern@touro.edu
STERN, David .... 773-298-3350 151 C
stern@sxu.edu
STERN, David .... 813-258-7360 113 E
provost@ut.edu
STERN, David, M .... 901-448-5529 440 C
dstern@uthsc.edu
STERN, Elliot .... 425-739-8383 495 F
elliot.stern@lwtech.edu
STERN, Elsie .... 215-576-0800 408 H
estern@rrc.edu
STERN, Holly, C .... 973-596-6379 288 A
holly.stern@njit.edu
STERN, Joyce .... 641-269-3702 169 F
sternjm@grinnell.edu
STERN, Kevin, D .... 214-887-5111 448 G
kstern@dts.edu
STERN, Lorna .... 215-572-2901 389 D
sternl@arcadia.edu
STERN, Michael, J .... 773-442-6012 147 G
m-stern2@neiu.edu
STERN, Ross .... 301-405-6637 207 G
stern@umd.edu
STERN, Sharon .... 254-710-1010 444 B
sharon_stern@baylor.edu
STERN, Susan .... 262-695-3451 515 B
sstern1@wctc.edu
STERN, Tom .... 626-396-2322.. 26 L
STERNBERG, Wendy ...... 323-259-2634.. 54 E
wsternberg@oxy.edu
STERNBERGER,
Carol, S .... 260-481-5798 160 D
sternber@ipfw.edu
STERNER, Sheri .... 714-432-5081.. 38 H
ssterner@occ.cccd.edu
STERNER, Suzi, M .... 858-822-4382.. 69 E
ssterner@ucsd.edu
STERNFIELD, Daniel ...... 773-602-5524 135 L
dstemfield@ccc.edu
STERNFIELD, Daniel ...... 312-553-2833 136 C
dsternfield@ccc.edu
STERNGOLD, James .... 646-664-9108 301 A
james.sterngold@cuny.edu
STERNKE, Timothy .... 414-930-3032 509 B
mmu-bookstore@mtmary.edu
STERNS, Teresa, G .... 304-462-6102 504 B
teresa.sterns@glenville.edu
STERRETT, Joseph, D .... 610-758-4320 400 B
jds7@lehigh.edu
STERRETT, Myra .... 352-395-5150 107 E
myra.sterrett@sfcollege.edu
STERRITT,
D. E. Lorraine .... 336-721-2603 348 H
lorraine.sterritt@salem.edu
STERRITT, John .... 805-893-2040.. 70 B
jsterritt@ucsb.edu
STERTZBACH,
Rebecca, M .... 480-245-7971.. 13 C
becky.stertzbach@ibcs.edu
STERTZBACH,
Rebecca, M .... 480-245-7969.. 13 C
becky.stertzbach@ibcs.edu
STETAR, Bruce .... 603-314-7543 282 C
b.stetar@snhu.edu
STETLER, Kent .... 513-721-7944 362 D
registrar@gbs.edu
STETLER, P. Daniel .... 772-546-5534 101 N
danstetler@hsbc.edu
STETLER, Paul .... 772-546-5534 101 N
paulstetler@hsbc.edu
STETSON, Daniel .... 225-389-7200 193 M
dstetson@lsu.edu
STETTER, Mark .... 970-491-7051.. 78 N
mark.stetter@colostate.edu
STETTLER, Greg .... 618-985-3741 141 D
gregstettler@jalc.edu
STETZER, Ed .... 630-752-5918 155 F
ed.stetzer@wheaton.edu
STEUERWALD, Brian ..... 317-917-3628 162 S
bsteu@martin.edu
STEURBAUT, Margo .... 626-395-6275.. 29 I
margo.steurbaut@caltech.edu
STEVEN, Strain, A .... 719-333-9751 518 H
STEVENS, Alison .... 206-546-4651 498 E
amstevens@shoreline.edu
STEVENS, Andrea, N ...... 662-329-7431 254 F
anstevens@muw.edu
STEVENS, Anne, A .... 704-461-6718 335 J
annestevens@bac.edu
STEVENS, Annie .... 802-656-3380 476 E
annie.stevens@uvm.edu
STEVENS, Bren .... 304-357-4911 502 E
brenstevens@ucwv.edu
STEVENS, Brenda, D ...... 330-471-8328 364 H
bstevens@malone.edu
STEVENS, Carrie .... 785-242-5200 180 H
carrie.stevens@ottawa.edu
STEVENS, Carroll .... 909-621-8096.. 38 A
carroll.stevens@cmc.edu
STEVENS, Cathleen, M .. 585-389-2001 316 D
csteven9@naz.edu
STEVENS, Cheryl, L .... 270-745-4448 190 F
cheryl.stevens@wku.edu
STEVENS, Daniel .... 540-785-5440 487 B
danielstevens@vbc.edu
STEVENS, Darryl .... 406-771-4321 272 D
darryl.stevens@gfcmsu.edu
STEVENS, Debbie .... 641-673-2173 174 F
stevensd@wmpenn.edu
STEVENS, Dennis, G ...... 434-223-6110 481 D
dstevens@hsc.edu
STEVENS, Elizabeth .... 651-690-8600 249 T
ejstevens@stkate.edu
STEVENS, Eric, A .... 660-263-3900 258 A
academic@cccb.edu
STEVENS, Greg .... 509-434-5037 493 I
greg.stevens@ccs.spokane.edu
STEVENS, Greg .... 509-434-5037 494 A
greg.stevens@ccs.spokane.edu
STEVENS, Greg, L .... 509-434-5037 493 H
gstevens@ccs.spokane.edu
STEVENS,
Gwendolyn, M .... 412-578-8776 391 G
gmstevens@carlow.edu
STEVENS, Holly, L .... 423-652-4784 432 I
hlstevens@king.edu
STEVENS, Jeff .... 607-587-3101 328 F
stevenjs@alfredstate.edu
STEVENS, Jeffrey .... 215-503-7015 411 E
jeffrey.stevens@jefferson.edu
STEVENS, John .... 435-283-7017 474 A
john.stevens@snow.edu
STEVENS, Joshua .... 765-983-1747 157 I
STEVENS, Kara .... 413-565-1000 211 C
kstevens@baypath.edu
STEVENS, Kevin .... 312-915-6115 144 D
kstevens3@luc.edu
STEVENS, Laura .... 314-529-9252 262 B
lstevens@maryville.edu
STEVENS, Mark .... 208-376-7731 131 B
STEVENS, Mark, W .... 920-206-2314 508 A
mark.stevens@mbu.edu
STEVENS, RSM,
Maryanne .... 402-399-2435 274 A
mstevens@csm.edu
STEVENS, Matt .... 561-803-2200 104 I
national@pba.edu
STEVENS, Michael .... 616-222-1430 229 B
michael.stevens@cornerstone.edu
STEVENS, Michele .... 806-457-4200 449 D
mstevens@fpctx.edu
STEVENS, Pamela .... 304-876-5489 504 D
pstevens@shepherd.edu
STEVENS, Peter .... 618-374-3530 149 A
peter.stevens@principia.edu
STEVENS, Phil .... 207-699-5047 199 H
pstevens@meca.edu
STEVENS, Randy .... 909-558-4558.. 48 H
rstevens@llu.edu
STEVENS, Richie .... 304-876-5370 504 D
rstevens@shepherd.edu
STEVENS, Robert .... 203-932-7435.. 89 D
rstevens@newhaven.edu
STEVENS, Roger, K .... 847-259-1840 135 H
rstevens@christianlifecollege.edu
STEVENS, Ron .... 919-658-7834 349 F
rstevens@umo.edu
STEVENS, Scott .... 903-923-2320 448 J
sstevens@etbu.edu
STEVENS, Scott .... 802-860-2751 474 G
stevens@champlain.edu
STEVENS, Sheri, R .... 207-621-3110 201 C
sheri@maine.edu
STEVENS, Sylvia .... 513-481-2226 373 I
sylvia_stevens@wilmington.edu
STEVENS, Theresa, M .... 810-989-5588 236 G
tmstevens@sc4.edu
STEVENS, Timothy, S .... 847-491-7256 148 C
tstevens@northwestern.edu
STEVENS, Victor .... 718-270-6069 303 C
vstevens@mec.cuny.edu
STEVENS, Willette .... 912-344-2587 115 D
willette.stevens@armstrong.edu
STEVENS HAYNES, Gale 718-488-1001 313 C
gale.haynes@liu.edu
STEVENSON, Bill .... 479-524-7119.. 20 B
wstevens@jbu.edu
STEVENSON, Daniel .... 406-994-2001 272 A
daniel.stevenson1@montana.edu
STEVENSON, Duncan ..... 253-964-6612 497 B
dstevenson@pierce.ctc.edu
STEVENSON, Elizabeth ... 508-830-6683 218 D
estevenson@maritime.edu
STEVENSON,
Gwendolyn, A .... 937-778-7949 361 E
gstevenson@edisonohio.edu
STEVENSON, Jaclyn .... 518-828-4181 305 D
jaclyn.stevenson@sunycgcc.edu
STEVENSON, James, E .. 323-242-5386.. 49 E
STEVENSON, James, W . 904-997-2931 100 F
james.stevenson@fscj.edu
STEVENSON, Jeanne, M 208-885-7941 132 I
jeannec@uidaho.edu
STEVENSON, John .... 954-545-4500 108 A
academics@sfbc.edu
STEVENSON, Karen, L ... 615-353-3430 437 D
karen.stevenson@nscc.edu
STEVENSON, Kim .... 252-335-3699 350 A
knstevenson@ecsu.edu
STEVENSON, Kimberly ... 615-327-6759 434 A
kstevenson@mmc.edu
STEVENSON, Leslie, W .. 804-289-8141 486 G
lsteven2@richmond.edu
STEVENSON, Martha ...... 610-683-4484 406 D
stevenson@kutztown.edu
STEVENSON,
Martha Ann .... 205-226-4648.... 4 F
mstevens@bsc.edu
STEVENSON, Paula .... 954-545-4500 108 A
library@sfbc.edu
STEVENSON, Sarah .... 718-405-3258 304 H
sarah.stevenson@mountsaintvincent.edu
STEVENSON, Susan, G .. 334-683-2303.... 3 A
sstevenson@marionmilitary.edu
STEVENSON, Tara .... 904-826-8508.. 98 I
tstevenson@flagler.edu
STEVENSON, Valerie, O . 904-620-2920 110 E
vstevens@unf.edu
STEVENSON, JR., Zollie 501-370-5276.. 21 A
zstevenson@philander.edu
STEVERSON, Janet .... 503-768-6667 383 G
jws@lclark.edu
STEVICK, David .... 585-567-9607 310 F
david.stevick@houghton.edu
STEVINSON, Rebecca .... 218-749-7762 245 D
b.stevinson@mesabirange.edu
STEWARD, Agnes .... 253-840-8403 497 B
asteward@pierce.ctc.edu
STEWARD, Deborah .... 315-781-3500 310 C
stewart@hws.edu
STEWARD, Gary .... 405-974-5528 380 J
gsteward@uco.edu
STEWARD, Jerry, L .... 405-682-7502 377 C
jsteward@occc.edu
STEWARD, Kyle .... 662-325-3221 254 E
ksteward@pres.msstate.edu
STEWARD, JR., Sterling 912-358-3449 125 C
ssuathletics@savannahstate.edu
STEWARD, Yolanda .... 513-241-4338 356 I
yolanda.steward@antonellicollege.edu
STEWART, Barbara, A .... 408-554-4396.. 62 F
bstewart@scu.edu
STEWART, Barbara, E .... 608-785-5092 510 F
bstewart@uwlax.edu
STEWART, Ben .... 773-256-0769 144 G
bstewart@lstc.edu
STEWART, Beth .... 828-398-7633 340 M
bethstewart@abtech.edu
STEWART, Betsy .... 610-526-5632 390 G
estewart@brynmawr.edu
STEWART, Betty .... 972-338-1600 466 C
betty.stewart@untdallas.edu
STEWART, Billy, W .... 601-635-6200 252 I
bstewart@eccc.edu
STEWART, Brad, J .... 240-567-1312 205 F
brad.stewart@montgomerycollege.edu
STEWART, Brandon .... 937-376-2946 369 C
bstewart@payne.edu
STEWART, Bryan .... 817-515-1011 458 B
bryan.stewart@tccd.edu
STEWART, Carrie, E .... 310-243-3787.. 31 E
cstewart@csudh.edu
STEWART, Charles .... 212-650-7271 301 F
cstewart@ccny.cuny.edu
STEWART, Christy .... 618-985-2828 141 D
christystewart@jalc.edu
STEWART, Cindy .... 256-331-5348.... 3 C
cstewart@nwscc.edu
STEWART, Colin .... 559-278-2741.. 32 A
cstewart@csufresno.edu
STEWART, Connie .... 989-328-1249 234 D
connies@montcalm.edu
STEWART, Dan .... 512-499-4616 467 A
dstewart@utsystem.edu
STEWART, Daniel, P ...... 904-818-6238.. 98 I
stewartd@flagler.edu
STEWART, David .... 304-865-6089 502 C
david.stewart@ovu.edu
STEWART, David, C .... 304-293-5811 505 B
david.stewart@mail.wvu.edu
STEWART, David, R .... 651-638-6225 240 J
d-stewart@bethel.edu
STEWART, Dawn .... 614-823-3529 368 O
dstewart@otterbein.edu
STEWART, Dean .... 920-498-6995 514 G
dean.stewart@nwtc.edu
STEWART, Deborah .... 802-828-2800 477 B
das07200@ccv.vsc.edu
STEWART, Deborah, C .. 530-898-5241.. 31 D
dcstewart@csuchico.edu
STEWART, Denise .... 405-682-7819 377 C
dstewart@occc.edu
STEWART, DeShaunta .... 773-907-4044 135 K
dstewart75@ccc.edu
STEWART, Desmond .... 601-877-3939 251 G
desmond@alcorn.edu
STEWART, Diane .... 661-362-3503.. 39 C
diane.stewart@canyons.edu
STEWART, Donette .... 864-503-5280 425 H
dstewart@uscupstate.edu
STEWART, Dorothy .... 313-993-1028 237 F
stewardm@udmercy.edu
STEWART, Doug .... 970-945-8691.. 77 M
STEWART, Douglas .... 601-877-2419 251 G
stewartd@alcorn.edu
STEWART, Elizabeth, J .. 585-292-2536 315 L
estewart@monroecc.edu
STEWART, Greg .... 541-885-1629 385 E
greg.stewart@oit.edu
STEWART, H.D .... 828-898-8756 339 B
stewarth@lmc.edu
STEWART, Jacqueline .... 606-368-6059 182 H
jacquelinestewart@alc.edu
STEWART, James .... 503-517-1898 388 C
jstewart@westernseminary.edu
STEWART, James .... 731-352-4093 430 E
stewartj@bethelu.edu
STEWART, James, R ...... 972-860-7689 447 I
randystewart@dcccd.edu
STEWART, Jane .... 313-664-1533 228 H
jstewart@collegeforcreativestudies.edu

STODDART, Scott .... 201-761-6037 291 D sstoddart@saintpeters.edu
STOECKER, Judith .... 847-578-8694 150 E judith.stoecker@rosalindfranklin.edu
STOECKER, Nancy .... 630-829-6402 133 I nstoecker@ben.edu
STOECKLEIN, Denny ...... 620-665-3526 178 D stoecklein@hutchcc.edu
STOECKLIN, Dennis, J .. 503-280-8503 382 I dstoecklin@cu-portland.edu
STOEFFEL, Virginia .... 845-431-8908 307 A virginia.stoeffel@sunydutchess.edu
STOELTING, Diane .... 716-286-8064 318 F ds@niagara.edu
STOFAN, James .... 504-865-5901 196 D jstofan@tulane.edu
STOFFEL, Larry, J .... 317-738-8148 157 L lstoffel@franklincollege.edu
STOFFER, Brian, M .... 312-329-4359 146 B brian.stoffer@moody.edu
STOFFT, Lori .... 928-314-9595.. 11 B lorraine.stofft@azwestern.edu
STOGNER, Becky .... 806-651-2311 460 E bstogner@mail.wtamu.edu
STOGNER, Brian, L .... 248-218-2011 236 C bstogner@rc.edu
STOHLER, Christian, S .. 212-305-4511 305 E cs3221@columbia.edu
STOHLMAN, Bill .... 606-539-3541 190 A william.stohlman@ucumberlands.edu
STOICESCU, Dan .... 410-287-1923 203 B dstoicescu@cecil.edu
STOJKOVIC, Stan .... 414-229-4400 511 A stojkovi@uwm.edu
STOKAN, Matthew .... 724-852-3227 414 B mstokan@waynesburg.edu
STOKELD, Keith .... 212-353-4152 306 A kstokeld@cooper.edu
STOKELY, Sarah .... 717-477-1395 407 B sestokely@ship.edu
STOKER, Daniel, J .... 260-422-5561 159 D djstoker@indianatech.edu
STOKER, Michael .... 479-880-4040.. 18 G mstoker@atu.edu
STOKES, Aaron .... 620-862-5252 175 B
STOKES, Brandon .... 919-760-8318 339 H kbstokes@meredith.edu
STOKES, Douglas .... 803-535-1393 423 B stokesd@octech.edu
STOKES, Garnett .... 573-882-6596 268 C stokesg@missouri.edu
STOKES, Ginger, C .... 386-312-4074 106 M gingerstokes@sjrstate.edu
STOKES, Jeannine .... 951-487-3151.. 52 J jstokes@msjc.edu
STOKES, Jenny .... 336-917-5595 348 H jenny.stokes@salem.edu
STOKES, Judi .... 845-431-8405 307 A judi.stokes@sunydutchess.edu
STOKES, Ken .... 770-484-1204 122 G ken.stokes@lutherrice.edu
STOKES, Kevin .... 937-767-1286 356 F
STOKES, Madeline .... 251-405-4457.... 1 E mstokes@bishop.edu
STOKES, Maureen .... 484-365-7250 400 E mstokes@lincoln.edu
STOKES, Michael .... 423-478-6218 436 G mstokes@clevelandstatecc.edu
STOKES, Mickey .... 662-476-5068 253 A mstokes@eastms.edu
STOKES, Shereitte .... 718-262-5191 304 A sstokes@york.cuny.edu
STOKES, Timothy .... 360-596-5206 498 G tstokes@spscc.edu
STOKES-DUPASS, Nicole .... 267-341-3695 397 G nstokes-dupass@holyfamily.edu
STOKES-WILSON, Linda 708-596-2000 151 H lwilson@ssc.edu
STOKLEY, Alicia .... 252-335-0821 342 D alicia_stokley99@albemarle.edu
STOKSTAD, Paul .... 641-451-4219 171 J alumni@mum.edu
STOLAR, Andrea Gail .... 713-798-4870 444 A stolar@bcm.edu
STOLL, Barbara .... 217-641-4520 141 F bstoll@jwcc.edu
STOLL, Barbara, J .... 713-500-5010 468 D barbara.j.stoll@uth.tmc.edu
STOLL, Kirby, R .... 651-631-5378 251 C krstoll@unwsp.edu
STOLL, Lisa .... 908-835-9222 292 G lstoll@warren.edu
STOLL, Sherideen, S ..... 419-372-8262 357 F sstoll@bgsu.edu
STOLL, William, S .... 314-935-7574 269 L stoll@wustl.edu
STOLLENWERK, Matt ..... 651-255-6123 250 D mstollenwerk@unitedseminary.edu
STOLLER, Brett .... 309-649-6211 152 G brett.stoller@src.edu
STOLPER, Edward, M .... 626-395-6336.. 29 I ems@caltech.edu
STOLPER, Lauren, B ...... 626-395-2150.. 29 I lstolper@caltech.edu
STOLTE, Scott .... 570-408-4911 414 H scott.stolte@wilkes.edu
STOLTMAN, Nate .... 507-536-5604 247 D nate.stoltman@rctc.edu
STOLTZ, Adam .... 530-898-6322.. 31 D astoltz@csuchico.edu
STOLTZ, Jacklyn, C .... 860-701-5040.. 87 F stoltz_j@mitchell.edu
STOLTZ-LOIKE, Marian .. 646-565-6000 331 F mstoltz-loike@touro.edu
STOLTZFUS, Ken .... 316-295-5567 177 F
STOLTZFUS, Merle .... 903-233-3000 452 A
STOLTZFUS, Rebecca, J 574-535-7180 158 A president@goshen.edu
STOLTZFUS, Ruth .... 574-535-7375 158 A ruthas@goshen.edu
STOLZE, Martha, A .... 630-637-5814 147 E mastolze@noctrl.edu
STOLZER, Donna .... 908-526-1200 289 D donna.stolzer@raritanval.edu
STOMBER, Richard .... 973-720-2277 292 I stomberr@wpunj.edu
STOMPER, Jeffrey .... 847-543-2531 136 E stomper@clcillinois.edu
STONE, Adam .... 908-737-3101 286 F astone@kean.edu
STONE, Audrey .... 540-362-6363 481 F stoneae@hollins.edu
STONE, Becka .... 406-265-3711 272 C becka.stone@msun.edu
STONE, Brett .... 479-979-1474.. 23 J bastone@ozarks.edu
STONE, Carolyn .... 561-803-2567 104 I carolyn_stone@pba.edu
STONE, Dan .... 619-684-8812.. 53 J dstone@newschoolarch.edu
STONE, David, A .... 248-370-2762 235 J dstone@oakland.edu
STONE, David, M .... 212-854-9962 305 E dms2148@columbia.edu
STONE, Dawn .... 989-356-9021 227 A stoned@alpenacc.edu
STONE, Denise .... 503-255-0332 384 E dstone@multnomah.edu
STONE, Dennis .... 904-680-7703.. 99 C dstone@fcsl.edu
STONE, Derek .... 706-993-1115 120 B dstone@gmc.edu
STONE, Elizabeth .... 202-559-5079.. 91 H elizabeth.stone@gallaudet.edu
STONE, Emily .... 925-969-2113.. 40 L estone@dvc.edu
STONE, Glenice .... 662-720-7237 255 B gwstone@nemcc.edu
STONE, Greg .... 918-595-7224 380 D greg.stone@tulsacc.edu
STONE, James .... 325-670-1258 450 A jstone@hsutx.edu
STONE, Janice .... 806-720-7270 452 D janice.stone@lcu.edu
STONE, Jenna .... 315-268-3790 304 B jestone@clarkson.edu
STONE, John .... 661-362-2271.. 51 C jstone@masters.edu
STONE, Karen, J .... 904-620-2828 110 E kstone@unf.edu
STONE, Ken .... 773-896-2400 135 G kstone@ctschicago.edu
STONE, Mark .... 979-458-6450 458 E mstone@tamus.edu
STONE, Melissa .... 302-831-8189.. 90 I mstone@udel.edu
STONE, Patrick, A .... 401-825-2028 416 B pastone@ccri.edu
STONE, Paul .... 817-599-8324 470 J stone@wc.edu
STONE, Polly .... 601-923-1630 255 E pstone@rts.edu
STONE, Priscilla .... 802-258-3499 476 B priscilla.stone@sit.edu
STONE, Ralinda .... 817-598-6276 470 J rstone@wc.edu
STONE, Rhonda .... 870-248-4000.. 18 J rhonda.stone@blackrivertech.edu
STONE, Robert .... 626-256-4673.. 37 I rstone@coh.org
STONE, Sammy .... 229-931-2394 125 G sstone@southgatech.edu
STONE, Sandra .... 941-359-4340 111 A sandrastone@usf.edu
STONE, Sarah .... 919-515-9340 350 E sarah_stone@ncsu.edu
STONE, Scott .... 410-225-2398 205 C sstone@mica.edu
STONE, Shelly .... 336-322-2106 345 D shelly.stone@piedmontcc.edu
STONE, Shelly, T .... 336-694-8042 345 D shelly.stone@piedmontcc.edu
STONE, Squeak .... 802-258-3333 476 B squeak.stone@sit.edu
STONE, Sue .... 229-226-1621 126 E sstone@thomasu.edu
STONE, Susan .... 859-899-2510 184 G sstone@frontier.edu
STONE, Tia .... 256-331-5279.... 3 C tstone@nwscc.edu
STONE, Ty .... 937-512-3107 370 A ty.stone@sinclair.edu
STONE, Ty, A .... 315-786-2230 311 H tstone@sunyjefferson.edu
STONEBROOK, Kenneth 801-957-4004 474 B kenneth.stonebrook@slcc.edu
STONECIPHER, Amanda, G .... 812-941-2674 161 A agstonec@ius.edu
STONECIPHER-FISHER, Kimberly .... 573-876-7106 267 G ksfisher@stephens.edu
STONEHAM, Edrel .... 361-572-6407 470 A edrel.stoneham@victoriacollege.edu
STONEKING, Carole, B . 336-841-9168 338 E stoneki@highpoint.edu
STONEKING, Dawn, M .. 812-464-1932 165 C dstoneking@usi.edu
STONER, Gayla .... 509-963-1488 492 L gayla.stoner@cwu.edu
STONER, Keith .... 419-755-4810 366 E kstoner@ncstatecollege.edu
STONER, Kevin .... 845-687-5092 331 L stonerk@sunyulster.edu
STONER, Melinda, J ...... 402-280-4021 274 D registrar@creighton.edu
STONEROCK, Abigail ..... 225-743-8500 193 C astonerock@rpcc.edu
STONESIFER, Cynthia .... 815-825-9806 142 F cynthia.stonesifer@kishwaukeecollege.edu
STOOKS, George, F .... 585-245-5663 327 B stooks@geneseo.edu
STOOKSBERRY, Robert .. 210-436-3301 455 J tstooksberry@stmarytx.edu
STOOPS, Charles .... 708-366-3288 137 F cstoops@dom.edu
STOOPS, Lynne .... 831-459-1376.. 70 C lstoops@ucsc.edu
STOOPS, Melinda, K ..... 508-626-4596 218 A mstoops@framingham.edu
STOOPS, T.J .... 219-980-6832 160 C tkstoops@iun.edu
STOOS, Barbara .... 419-251-1702 365 C barbara.stoos@mercycollege.edu
STOPAK, Erin .... 712-325-3204 170 K estopak@iwcc.edu
STOPFORD, Michael, J . 308-865-8246 277 F stopford@unk.edu
STOPPENBRINK, Ken .... 559-934-2160.. 73 M kenstoppenbrink@whccd.edu
STOPPENBRINK, Norm . 614-837-4088 373 C stoppenbrinkn@valorcollege.edu
STOPPER, Suzanne, T ... 570-326-3761 404 T sstoppe2@pct.edu
STOPPLE, Jeffrey .... 805-893-2385.. 70 B stopple@math.ucsb.edu
STORCK, Angela .... 478-289-2173 118 H astorck@ega.edu
STORCK, Christine, M ... 410-777-2219 202 D cmstorck@aacc.edu
STORCK, Eileen .... 772-462-7805 101 Q estorck@irsc.edu
STOREY, Amy .... 315-279-5262 312 D astorey@keuka.edu
STOREY, Bruce .... 309-796-5129 134 C storeyb@bhc.edu
STOREY, Karen .... 906-635-2418 232 J kstorey@lssu.edu
STOREY GROVES, Margaret .... 802-443-5196 475 G mgroves@middlebury.edu
STORIE, Cheryl .... 240-582-5680 208 D financial-affairs@umuc.edu
STORIE, Monique .... 671-735-2333 520 B mstorie@triton.uog.edu
STORIE, Monique, C ..... 671-735-2162 520 B mstorie@triton.uog.edu
STORIN LINITZ, Karen .. 617-975-9324 214 F linitzk@emmanuel.edu
STORK, Gilbert, H .... 805-546-3118.. 41 C gstork@cuesta.edu
STORLAZZI, Caesar, T .. 203-432-0371.. 89 G caesar.storlazzi@yale.edu
STORM, JR., Chris, K ... 516-877-3165 297 I cstorm@adelphi.edu
STORM, Maryam .... 818-708-9232.. 48 J
STORMS, Amy .... 417-626-1234 264 J storms.amy@occ.edu
STORMS, Andy .... 417-626-1234 264 J storms.andy@occ.edu
STORMS, Joyce, A .... 616-538-2330 230 E jstorms@gbcol.edu
STORMS, Melanie .... 352-588-7805 106 N melanie.storms@saintleo.edu
STORRS, Debbie .... 701-777-2049 353 G debbie.storrs@und.edu
STORRS, Debbie .... 701-777-2749 353 G debbie.storrs@und.edu
STORRS, Helen .... 415-405-4343.. 34 C hstorrs@sfsu.edu
STORRS, Regina, M ...... 313-593-5020 238 A rstorrs@umich.edu
STORTI, Richard .... 626-585-7172.. 56 B rsstorti@pasadena.edu
STORY, JR., John, H .... 315-733-4764 332 F jstory@uscny.edu
STORY, Lisa, L .... 712-324-5061 172 E lstory@nwicc.edu
STORY, Rick .... 706-754-7736 123 G rstory@northgatech.edu
STORY, Sarah .... 830-372-8023 461 D sstory@tlu.edu
STORY, Sarah .... 830-372-8053 461 D sstor@tlu.edu
STORY, Shelley .... 512-863-1281 457 I storys@southwestern.edu
STORY-HUFFMAN, Ru ... 229-931-2259 120 F ru.story-huffman@gsw.edu
STOSBERG, Tobey .... 816-276-4740 265 G tobey.stosberg@researchcollege.edu
STOSKOPF, Janna, M .... 701-231-6537 354 D janna.stoskopf@ndsu.edu
STOSS, Kate .... 765-285-1847 156 C kpstoss@bsu.edu
STOTLER, Doug .... 618-468-6200 143 D
STOTO, Robert .... 609-896-5140 289 E stoto@rider.edu
STOTT, Larry .... 801-422-2383 471 E larry_stott@byu.edu
STOTT, Roger, F .... 443-518-4463 204 E rstott@howardcc.edu
STOTTER, Jennifer .... 808-932-7641 129 I jstotter@hawaii.edu
STOTTS, Bob .... 270-789-5017 184 B restotts@campbellsville.edu
STOTTS, James .... 404-880-8992 117 H jstotts@cau.edu
STOTTS, Keith .... 304-865-6005 502 C keith.stotts@ovu.edu
STOTTS, Melissa .... 701-662-1538 355 A melissa.stotts@lrsc.edu
STOTTS, Nicole .... 815-802-8816 142 C nstotts@kcc.edu
STOUDENMIRE, Phyllis 803-536-0311 423 B stoudenmirep@octech.edu
STOUFFER, Wendy, D ... 479-575-2711.. 21 I wstouff@uark.edu
STOUP, Gregory .... 925-229-6826.. 40 J gstoup@4cd.edu
STOUP, Russ .... 618-634-3276 151 G russs@shawneecc.edu
STOUT, Alden .... 712-274-5388 172 A stoutj@morningside.edu
STOUT, Allen .... 909-593-3511.. 70 E astout@laverne.edu
STOUT, Chris .... 248-689-8282 238 F cstout@walshcollege.edu
STOUT, David .... 732-224-2204 284 B dstout@brookdalecc.edu
STOUT, Michael .... 336-334-4822 343 E mcstout@gtcc.edu
STOUT, Ross .... 503-370-6911 388 D rstout@willamette.edu
STOUT, Thomas, B .... 757-822-5230 489 H tstout@tcc.edu
STOUT BROWN, Diane .. 804-828-7020 487 E dstout@vcu.edu
STOUTT, Khoy .... 352-536-2206 103 B stouttk@lssc.edu
STOVALL, Alfred, J .... 662-252-8000 255 F ajstovall@rustcollege.edu
STOVALL, Chris .... 940-397-4273 453 C chris.stovall@mwsu.edu
STOVALL, Jerry .... 229-931-2562 125 G jstovall@southgatech.edu
STOVALL, Michael .... 410-386-8206 203 A mstovall@carrollcc.edu
STOVALL, Terri .... 817-923-1921 457 G tstovall@swbts.edu

STRIZICH, Larry .... 406-265-4157 272 C
strizich@msun.edu
STRIZICH, Lawrence ...... 406-265-3726 272 C
strizich@msun.edu
STROBEL, Corbin .... 620-665-3537 178 D
strobelc@hutchcc.edu
STROBEL, Jennifer .... 619-876-4260.. 68 C
jstrobel@usuniversity.edu
STROBEL, Nathan .... 414-443-8800 513 A
nathan.strobel@wlc.edu
STROBLE, Elizabeth, J ... 314-968-6996 269 N
stroble@webster.edu
STROCKBINE, Richard ... 972-721-5207 464 E
dick@udallas.edu
STRODE, James .... 614-251-4669 367 F
strodej@ohiodominican.edu
STRODEMIER, Tammy ... 360-623-8625 493 A
tammy.strodmier@centralla.edu
STROE, Mattew .... 509-527-5777 500 G
stroemj@whitman.edu
STROH, Julie, C .... 407-823-6203 110 C
julie.stroh@ucf.edu
STROHM, Shelly .... 203-332-5179.. 85 F
sstrohm@hcc.commnet.edu
STROJNY, Duane .... 517-371-5140 239 F
strojnyd@cooley.edu
STROKER, Robert, T ...... 215-204-5004 411 B
robert.stroker@temple.edu
STROLE, Sarah .... 316-942-4291 180 D
stroles@newmanu.edu
STROLLO, Ronald, A ...... 330-941-2385 374 E
rastrollo@ysu.edu
STROLLO HOLBROOK,
Toni .... 407-646-2355 106 J
tsholbrook@rollins.edu
STROM, Brian, L .... 973-972-4400 290 A
chancellor@rbhs.rutgers.edu
STROM, Jan .... 630-844-5253 133 H
jstrom@aurora.edu
STROM, Joanne .... 417-865-2815 260 B
stromj@evangel.edu
STROM, Laura, A .... 618-650-3330 152 C
lstrom@siue.edu
STROM, Mark .... 478-387-4887 120 B
mstrom@gmc.edu
STROM, Stephen, L .... 651-450-3526 245 A
sstrom@inverhills.edu
STROM, Steven .... 845-451-1552 306 D
steve.strom@culinary.edu
STROMAN, Jay .... 706-542-2277 127 A
jstroman@uga.edu
STROMAN, Vanessa ...... 575-538-6277 297 H
vanessa.stroman@wnmu.edu
STROMBERG, Lori, S .... 308-635-6703 278 B
stromber@wncc.edu
STRONACH, Bruce .... 215-204-7000 411 B
bruce.stronach@temple.edu
STRONACH, Jeanne .... 619-594-8712.. 34 B
jstronac@mail.sdsu.edu
STRONG, Charmaine, R 724-838-4242 410 E
strong@setonhill.edu
STRONG, Cole .... 423-614-8607 432 L
cstrong@leeuniversity.edu
STRONG, Douglas, M ..... 206-281-2473 498 B
dstrong@spu.edu
STRONG, Ella .... 606-487-3208 185 J
ella.strong@kctcs.edu
STRONG, Jennifer .... 843-355-4111 426 G
strongj@wiltech.edu
STRONG, Karen .... 702-895-4074 279 D
karen.strong@unlv.edu
STRONG, Kerra .... 641-673-1014 174 F
strongk@wmpenn.edu
STRONG, III,
L. Thomas .... 504-282-4455 195 D
tstrong@nobts.edu
STRONG, LeNorman ...... 518-276-6201 321 A
stronl@rpi.edu
STRONG, Lucy .... 404-687-4529 118 B
strongl@ctsnet.edu
STRONG, Mike .... 909-389-3210.. 59 H
mstrong@craftonhills.edu
STRONG, Mike .... 330-972-6593 371 C
mstrong@uakron.edu
STRONG, Scott, M .... 989-774-2317 228 E
stron2sm@cmich.edu
STRONG, Shawn, D .... 573-897-5000 267 F
STRONG, Sheila, M .... 585-292-2102 315 L
sstrong@monroecc.edu
STRONG, Shirley .... 510-869-1544.. 59 F
sstrong@samuelmerritt.edu
STRONG, Whitney .... 617-537-6456 145 C
wbstrong@mckendree.edu
STRONG CHARLES,
Tonya .... 216-397-1958 363 H
tstrong@jcu.edu

STRONG-SIMMONS,
Alice .... 405-530-7507 375 L
alsimmons@langston.edu
STROTHER, Jennielle ..... 512-313-3000 446 N
jennielle.strother@concordia.edu
STROTHER, Jennifer ...... 425-564-4250 492 G
jennifer.strother@bellevuecollege.edu
STROUD, Clarke, A .... 405-325-3161 380 L
cstroud@ou.edu
STROUD, George .... 610-902-8417 391 B
george.stroud@cabrini.edu
STROUD, John .... 646-313-8000 303 G
john.stroud@guttman.cuny.edu
STROUD, Kerci, M .... 401-454-6108 417 B
kstroud@risd.edu
STROUD, Mikel .... 516-726-5589 519 C
stroudm@usmma.edu
STROUD, Misty .... 970-542-3100.. 81 A
misty.stroud@morgancc.edu
STROUD, Nancy .... 478-471-2728 123 A
nancy.stroud@mga.edu
STROUD, Nawanya .... 334-876-9234.... 2 C
nawanya.stroud@wccs.edu
STROUD, Ron .... 915-831-6740 449 A
jstroud2@epcc.edu
STROUD, Tina .... 712-279-5423 167 B
tina.stroud@briarcliff.edu
STROUP, Margaret .... 860-215-9296.. 86 F
mstroup@trcc.commnet.edu
STROUP, Peg .... 860-215-9296.. 86 F
pstroup@trcc.commnet.edu
STROUP-BENHAM,
Christine .... 303-315-2835.. 83 D
christine.stroup-benham@ucdenver.edu
STROUSE, Natalie .... 216-373-5298 367 A
nstrouse@ndc.edu
STROUSE, Robert, K ...... 714-850-4800.. 84 F
strouse@taftu.edu
STROUSE, Robert, K ...... 714-850-4800.. 67 B
strouse@taftu.edu
STROUT, Sarah .... 508-929-8119 219 A
sstrout@worcester.edu
STROUTH, Crystal .... 507-372-3451 246 C
crystal.strouth@mnwest.edu
STROUTS, Paul .... 404-894-1822 120 A
paul.strouts@gatech.edu
STRUBEL, Eric .... 215-574-9600 397 H
eric.strubel@hussiancollege.edu
STRUBEL, John .... 843-863-8044 419 C
jstrubel@csuniv.edu
STRUBY, Shannon .... 402-354-7104 275 P
shannon.struby@methodistcollege.edu
STRUCHTEMEYER,
Derek, L .... 770-720-5549 124 H
dls1@reinhardt.edu
STRUCK, Kathy .... 605-367-4625 429 C
kathryn.struck@southeasttech.edu
STRUCKHOFF, Mary .... 859-233-8278 189 H
mstruckhoff@transy.edu
STRUDWICK, Daniel ...... 217-228-5432 149 B
strudda@quincy.edu
STRUEBEL, Philip .... 716-851-1588 307 I
struebel@ecc.edu
STRULOEFF, Mark .... 503-699-6252 384 B
mstruloeff@marylhurst.edu
STRUNK, Jeffrey .... 859-572-6448 188 E
strunk@nku.edu
STRUNK, Mary, C .... 518-783-2314 324 C
strunk@siena.edu
STRUPP, Kindra, L .... 812-464-1755 165 C
kstrupp@usi.edu
STRUPPA, Daniele, C .... 714-997-6611.. 36 G
struppa@chapman.edu
STRUSOWSKI, Lisa .... 302-857-1400.. 90 F
lstrusow@dtcc.edu
STRUTHERS, Hap .... 757-423-2095 480 K
STRUTHERS, Mary .... 715-422-5504 514 B
mary.struthers@mstc.edu
STRYBOS, John .... 210-485-0701 441 E
jstrybos@alamo.edu
STRYKER, Joann .... 406-247-5752 272 B
joann.stryker@msubillings.edu
STRYKER, Joanne .... 401-454-6177 417 B
jstryker@risd.edu
STRYSICK, Michael, P ... 859-238-5710 184 C
michael.strysick@centre.edu
STRZEPEK, Jason .... 978-468-7111 215 E
jstrzepek@gordonconwell.edu
STRZEPEK, Katy, A .... 563-333-6113 173 A
strzepekkatya@sau.edu
STUARD, Avis .... 504-520-7583 198 D
astuard@xula.edu
STUART, Alesia, K .... 251-578-1313.... 3 D
akstuart@rstc.edu
STUART, Barbara .... 802-586-7711 476 D
bstuart@sterlingcollege.edu
STUART, Carol, M .... 252-334-2010 340 B
carol.stuart@macuniversity.edu

STUART, Cheryl .... 937-775-2556 374 B
cheryl.stuart@wright.edu
STUART, Cledis, D .... 870-235-4046.. 21 F
cdstuart@sauniag.edu
STUART, Dana .... 765-641-4114 156 A
dsstuart@anderson.edu
STUART, Diana .... 573-518-2100 263 E
diana@mineralarea.edu
STUART, D'Anne .... 575-646-2431 295 B
dstuart@nmsu.edu
STUART, Eddie .... 910-962-3626 352 A
stuarte@uncw.edu
STUART, Forrest, M ...... 864-294-2204 421 I
forrest.stuart@furman.edu
STUART, G. Rob .... 216-987-4757 360 E
g.rob.stuart@tri-c.edu
STUART, Gail, W .... 843-792-3941 422 C
stuartg@musc.edu
STUART, Jim .... 802-443-5000 475 G
STUART, John, G .... 903-927-3326 471 B
jstuart@wileyc.edu
STUART, Nancy, M .... 860-768-5135.. 89 C
nstuart@hartford.edu
STUART, Ramon .... 478-825-6330 119 C
stuartt@fvsu.edu
STUART, Roberta, P ...... 413-559-5724 215 F
STUART, Stephanie .... 217-351-2200 148 H
sstuart@parkland.edu
STUART, Susan .... 913-288-7265 178 H
sstuart@kckcc.edu
STUBAUS, Karen, R .... 848-932-4889 290 C
stubaus@oldqueens.rutgers.edu
STUBAUS, Karen, R .... 848-932-4889 290 A
stubaus@oldqueens.rutgers.edu
STUBBE, Alethea, F .... 712-324-5061 172 E
aletheas@nwicc.edu
STUBBEMAN, Nancy ..... 513-569-1501 359 G
nancy.stubbeman@cincinnatistate.edu
STUBBINGS, Donald ...... 913-758-6196 182 B
donald.stubbingsr@stmary.edu
STUBBLEFIELD, Jay .... 912-650-6215 125 H
rstubblefield@southuniversity.edu
STUBBLEFIELD,
Kellyanne .... 803-786-3723 420 D
kstubblefield@columbiasc.edu
STUBBLEFIELD,
Michael, A .... 225-771-3890 195 K
michael_stubblefield@subr.edu
STUBBS, Brent .... 912-443-4150 125 D
bstubbs@savannahtech.edu
STUBBS, Loretta .... 901-435-1680 433 A
loretta_stubbs@loc.edu
STUBBS, Michelle .... 912-486-7865 123 J
mstubbs@ogeecheetech.edu
STUBBS, Robert .... 303-492-8631.. 83 B
robert.stubbsd@colorado.edu
STUBBS, Sandra .... 256-372-5230.... 1 A
sandra.stubbs@aamu.edu
STUBBS, Sidney, J .... 334-833-4354.... 5 M
sstubbs@hawks.huntingdon.edu
STUBBS, Stanley .... 662-252-8000 255 F
rstubbs@rustcollege.edu
STUBBS, Steve .... 706-864-1798 127 B
steven.stubbs@ung.edu
STUCHELL, Tina .... 330-823-2844 372 C
stuchetm@mountunion.edu
STUCK, Helen .... 315-568-3133 317 A
hstuck@nycc.edu
STUCK, Kelley .... 434-982-0123 486 H
kds7w@virginia.edu
STUCK, Shelly .... 315-568-3111 317 A
sstuck@nycc.edu
STUCKENBRUCK, Emily . 715-365-4481 514 E
estuckenbruck@nicoletcollege.edu
STUCKER, Aaron .... 406-791-5225 273 C
aaron.stucker@ugf.edu
STUCKEY, Dennis .... 612-330-1713 240 G
stuckey@augsburg.edu
STUCKEY, Jon, C .... 717-796-1800 401 L
jstuckey@messiah.edu
STUCKEY, Julie .... 210-434-6711 454 D
jstuckey@lake.ollusa.edu
STUCKEY, Mike .... 816-501-2414 257 G
mike.stuckey@avila.edu
STUCKEY, Mike .... 740-389-4636 365 B
stuckeym@mtc.edu
STUCKEY, Sheila, A .... 502-597-6867 187 E
sheila.stuckey@kysu.edu
STUCKEY, Thomas, L .... 419-267-1310 366 G
tstuckey@northweststate.edu
STUCKLY, JR., Elton, E . 254-867-3963 461 G
elton.stuckly@tstc.edu
STUCKY, Duane .... 618-536-3475 152 A
dustucky@siu.edu
STUCKY, Gail .... 316-284-5363 175 F
gstucky@bethelks.edu
STUDDS, Susan, M .... 301-243-2121 518 C
susan.studds@dodiis.mil

STUDEBAKER, Eric .... 541-506-6010 382 G
estudebaker@cgcc.edu
STUDELSKA, Jana .... 801-649-5230 471 M
facultydirector@midwifery.edu
STUDENC, Bill .... 828-227-7122 352 C
bstudenc@wcu.edu
STUDER, Garet .... 425-388-9328 494 F
gstuder@everettcc.edu
STUDER, Mary Ann .... 419-783-2553 361 A
mstuder@defiance.edu
STUDWELL, II,
Raymond, W .... 540-828-5660 478 J
cstudwel@bridgewater.edu
STUEBNER, Susan, D .... 603-526-3451 280 H
sue.stuebner@colby-sawyer.edu
STUFANO, Thomas .... 865-882-4512 438 A
stufanotj@roanestate.edu
STUFF, Jerry .... 903-566-7431 468 C
jstuff@uttyler.edu
STUFFLEBEAN, Ernie ..... 816-415-5969 270 C
stuffle@william.jewell.edu
STUFLICK, William .... 217-641-4956 141 F
wstuflick@jwcc.edu
STUIFBERGEN,
Alexa, M .... 512-471-4100 467 C
astuifbergen@mail.utexas.edu
STUKANE, Edward .... 201-216-3472 291 G
edward.stukane@stevens.edu
STULL, David .... 415-503-6230.. 60 H
mkennedy@sfcm.edu
STULL, Kurt .... 928-226-4284.. 12 B
kurt.stull@coconino.edu
STULL, Megan .... 563-588-6377 167 E
megan.stull@clarke.edu
STULL, Nicole .... 847-851-5243 133 D
nstull@aiuonline.edu
STULL, Robert, W .... 915-747-5347 467 E
rstull@utep.edu
STULTS, Karen .... 410-225-2438 205 C
kstults@mica.edu
STULTS, Randy .... 205-387-0511.... 1 D
randy.stults@bscc.edu
STULTZ, Shelley .... 316-322-3152 175 I
sstultz@butlercc.edu
STUMB, Paul .... 615-547-1223 431 D
pstumb@cumberland.edu
STUMBO, Christine .... 606-368-6125 182 H
christinestumbo@alc.edu
STUMBRIS, Steven, V .... 570-577-3791 390 H
steven.stumbris@bucknell.edu
STUMNE, James .... 651-779-3918 244 D
james.stumne@century.edu
STUMO, Karl, A .... 218-299-3004 241 K
kstumo@cord.edu
STUMP, Chellye .... 334-347-2623.... 1 J
cstump@escc.edu
STUMP, Colleen .... 301-687-3171 209 A
cstump@frostburg.edu
STUMP, Doug .... 540-665-5445 485 C
jstump14@su.edu
STUMP, Linda, J .... 352-392-5445 110 D
lstump@ufl.edu
STUMP, Sandra .... 610-921-7205 388 E
stump@albright.edu
STUMP, Tom .... 406-994-2661 272 A
stump@montana.edu
STUMPF, Michelle .... 814-262-6436 405 A
mstumpf@pennhighlands.edu
STUNTZ, Jane .... 419-251-1314 365 C
jane.stuntz@mercycollege.edu
STUOPIS,
Cecilia Warpinski .... 617-253-1774 221 C
STUPAR, Eric, H .... 301-243-2170 518 C
eric.stupar@dodiis.mil
STURCH, Patty, J .... 740-264-5591 361 D
psturch@egcc.edu
STURDEVANT, Peggy .... 641-784-5125 169 D
peggys@graceland.edu
STURDIVANT, Alvin .... 206-296-6066 498 D
sturdial@seattleu.edu
STURDY, Ryan .... 785-460-5548 176 L
ryan.sturdy@colbycc.edu
STURE, Linda .... 907-563-7575.... 9 E
STURGEON, Kathy, R .... 217-443-8805 137 B
ksturgeon@dacc.edu
STURGEON, Stacy .... 435-797-1266 473 C
stacy.sturgeon@usu.edu
STURGEON, Timothy, A 502-272-8131 183 H
tsturgeon@bellarmine.edu
STURGILL, David .... 859-246-6896 185 G
david.sturgill@kctcs.edu
STURGIS, Maureen .... 603-899-4165 281 D
sturgism@franklinpierce.edu
STURGIS, Thomas, C .... 601-877-6138 251 G
tsturgis@alcorn.edu
STURM, James, P .... 716-926-8935 310 B
jsturm@hilbert.edu

SULLIVAN, Susan .... 812-749-1223 163 B
ssullivan@oak.edu
SULLIVAN, Susan .... 978-762-4000 220 E
susulliv@northshore.edu
SULLIVAN, Suzanne ...... 601-968-8746 252 C
ssullivan@belhaven.edu
SULLIVAN, Teresa, A ..... 434-924-3337 486 H
tas6n@virginia.edu
SULLIVAN, Terry .... 419-448-5148 370 K
tsullivan@tiffin.edu
SULLIVAN, Thelma .... 956-295-3414 461 F
thelma.sullivan@tsc.edu
SULLIVAN, Thomas .... 660-944-2875 258 G
thomas@conception.edu
SULLIVAN, Thomas, B .. 512-448-8727 455 I
toms@stedwards.edu
SULLIVAN, Thomas, J ... 410-706-3386 207 H
thomas.sullivan@umaryland.edu
SULLIVAN, Tracy .... 708-235-2179 138 H
tsullivan@govst.edu
SULLIVAN, Vicki .... 918-647-1373 375 B
vhill@carlalbert.edu
SULLIVAN, Wayne .... 505-277-2383 296 H
sullivan@unm.edu
SULLIVAN, Wayne .... 662-862-8101 253 D
jwsullivan@iccms.edu
SULLIVAN, Wayne .... 315-792-3201 332 H
wasullivan@utica.edu
SULLIVAN, William, E .... 765-494-9705 163 C
evpt@purdue.edu
SULLIVAN-CROWLEY,
Lianne, C .... 609-258-2430 288 F
lsulliva@princeton.edu
SULLIVAN-GONZALEZ,
Douglass .... 662-915-7294 256 C
dsg@olemiss.edu
SULLIVAN-TRAINOR,
Deborah .... 651-638-6804 240 J
suldeb@bethel.edu
SULLIVANT, Stan .... 870-338-6474.. 22 G
SULLY, John, M .... 216-397-1965 363 H
jsully@jcu.edu
SULMASY, Glenn .... 401-232-6060 416 A
gsulmasy@bryant.edu
SULTAN, Farooq .... 541-605-0520 385 E
farooq.sultan@oit.edu
SULZBACH, J. Bonnie ... 443-412-2119 204 C
bsulzbach@harford.edu
SUMAS, Keith, P .... 404-413-0783 121 A
ksumas1@gsu.edu
SUMEREL, Michelle .... 662-862-8050 253 D
jmsumerel@iccms.edu
SUMICHRAST, Robert, T 540-231-6601 490 F
busdean@vt.edu
SUMLIN, Rene .... 334-683-2378.... 3 A
renesumlin@marionmilitary.edu
SUMLIN, Robert, D .... 334-683-2305.... 3 A
dsumlin@marionmilitary.edu
SUMMARY, Sherry .... 618-985-3741 141 D
sherrysummary@jalc.edu
SUMME, Shawn .... 314-951-9895 266 E
ssumme@stlcc.edu
SUMMER, Rebekah .... 320-762-4612 243 J
rebekahs@alextech.edu
SUMMER, Sharon .... 336-770-1312 352 B
summers@uncsa.edu
SUMMER, Todd .... 619-594-7539.. 34 B
todd.summer@sdsu.edu
SUMMERLIN, Timothy ... 830-792-7326 456 D
tsummerlin@schreiner.edu
SUMMERS, Amanda ...... 281-425-6533 451 I
asummers@lee.edu
SUMMERS, Brian .... 901-321-3370 431 A
bsummers@cbu.edu
SUMMERS, Carol .... 815-939-5213 148 F
csummers@olivet.edu
SUMMERS, Chris .... 404-364-8355 124 A
csummers@oglethorpe.edu
SUMMERS, Christopher . 850-201-6100 112 C
summersc@tcc.fl.edu
SUMMERS, II, Daniel .... 802-447-6300 476 C
dsummers@svc.edu
SUMMERS, Diane .... 713-646-1794 456 H
dsummers@stcl.edu
SUMMERS, Edward .... 516-299-4057 313 C
edward.summers@liu.edu
SUMMERS, Eric .... 985-549-5250 197 E
esummers@selu.edu
SUMMERS, Greg .... 715-346-4686 511 F
gsummers@uwsp.edu
SUMMERS, Janie, K ...... 314-286-3665 265 F
jksummers@ranken.edu
SUMMERS, Jennifer .... 843-377-2410 419 B
jsummers@charlestonlaw.edu
SUMMERS, Jerry .... 903-923-2084 448 J
jsummers@etbu.edu
SUMMERS, Jim .... 740-362-3335 365 D
jsummers@mtso.edu

SUMMERS, JR., Leroy .. 336-517-1543 335 K
lsummers@bennett.edu
SUMMERS, Matthew, A . 304-637-1990 501 H
summersm@dewv.edu
SUMMERS, Michael, D .. 757-822-1066 489 H
msummers@tcc.edu
SUMMERS, Michael, D .. 757-822-7122 489 H
msummers@tcc.edu
SUMMERS, Nathan .... 937-294-0592 369 K
nathan@saa.edu
SUMMERS, RaChele ...... 828-327-7000 341 G
rsummers@cvcc.edu
SUMMERS, Ragan .... 904-470-8231.. 98 B
ragan.summers@ewc.edu
SUMMERS, Richard .... 601-984-1018 256 D
rsummers@umc.edu
SUMMERS, Robert .... 870-512-7710.. 18 D
robert_summers@asun.edu
SUMMERS, Scott .... 901-321-3237 431 A
ssummers@cbu.edu
SUMMERS, Shauna .... 401-277-4819 417 B
ssummers@risd.edu
SUMMERS, Stuart .... 208-282-3620 132 B
summstua@isu.edu
SUMMERS, Susan .... 832-813-6592 452 C
susan.summers@lonestar.edu
SUMMERS, Tammi .... 262-564-2538 513 G
summerst@gtc.edu
SUMMERS, Tiffany .... 615-966-1791 433 D
tiffany.summers@lipscomb.edu
SUMMERS, Wally .... 229-931-2040 125 G
wsummers@southgatech.edu
SUMMERSELL, Charley .. 518-587-2100 329 C
charley.summersell@esc.edu
SUMMIT, Jennifer .... 415-338-2206.. 34 C
jsummit@sfsu.edu
SUMMITT, April .... 951-785-2210.. 47 F
asummitt@lasierra.edu
SUMNER, Dana .... 919-760-8341 339 H
sumnerd@meredith.edu
SUMNER, Henry, A .... 610-558-5513 402 G
hsumner@neumann.edu
SUMNER, Jean, R .... 478-301-4022 122 H
sumner_jr@mercer.edu
SUMNER, Katherine, L .. 240-895-4202 206 G
klsumner@smcm.edu
SUMNER, Shelia .... 218-879-0715 244 F
ssumner@fdltcc.edu
SUMNER, Wesley, D ..... 321-674-6218.. 99 K
wsumner@fit.edu
SUMNERS, Stephanie .... 417-447-2653 264 K
sumnerss@otc.edu
SUMPTER,
Christopher, W .... 913-647-8724 178 G
christopher.sumpter@kansaschristian.edu
SUMPTION, Michael, F . 530-226-4148.. 64 B
msumption@simpsonu.edu
SUMTER, LaQuata .... 229-434-8441 114 I
laquata.sumter@asurams.edu
SUN, Hala .... 213-381-0081.. 46 I
hsun.irus@irus.edu
SUN, Weihong .... 313-993-3305 237 F
sunwe@udmercy.edu
SUN, Wenjie .... 512-444-8082 461 C
wsun@thsu.edu
SUN, Yanling .... 973-655-4091 287 D
suny@mail.montclair.edu
SUNAHARA, Wayne .... 808-845-9272 130 E
waynens@hawaii.edu
SUNATA, Cem .... 805-756-6016.. 30 K
csunata@calpoly.edu
SUNBERG, Carla .... 816-268-5402 264 G
csunberg@nts.edu
SUND, Andrew, C .... 509-865-8500 495 D
SUNDARAM, Bala .... 617-287-6055 216 I
bala.sundaram@umb.edu
SUNDARAM, Sridhar ...... 727-873-4700 111 B
sundarams@usf.edu
SUNDAY, Diana .... 209-588-5389.. 75 I
SUNDBERG, Lori .... 847-735-5034 142 H
lsundber@lakeforest.edu
SUNDBERG, Lori, H .... 847-735-5034 142 H
lsundber@lakeforest.edu
SUNDBERG, Lori, L .... 309-341-5214 134 H
lsundberg@sandburg.edu
SUNDBORG, SJ,
Stephen, V .... 206-296-1891 498 D
sundborg@seattleu.edu
SUNDBY-THORP,
Valerie .... 360-596-5451 498 G
vsundby-thorp@spscc.edu
SUNDERLAND, JR.,
Richard .... 304-724-3700 501 D
rsunderland@apus.edu
SUNDERMAN, Rick .... 614-947-6605 362 A
rick.sunderman@franklin.edu

SUNDERMEIER,
Elisabeth .... 816-802-3376 261 C
esundermeier@kcai.edu
SUNDGREN, Donald, E . 434-982-5834 486 H
des5j@virginia.edu
SUNDQUIST, Mike .... 209-575-6081.. 75 J
sundquistm@mjc.edu
SUNDSETH, Robin .... 541-880-2273 383 E
sundseth@klamathcc.edu
SUNDSMO, Alecia, D .... 717-245-1663 394 A
sundsmoa@dickinson.edu
SUNDSTEDT, Bernard .... 815-226-3371 150 C
bsunstedt@rockford.edu
SUNDSTEDT, Casey .... 847-628-1561 142 B
csundstedt@judsonu.edu
SUNDSTROM, Michelle . 330-823-2568 372 C
sundstme@mountunion.edu
SUNDSTROM, Sandy ..... 503-777-7224 386 F
sundstrom@reed.edu
SUNDY, Carolyn .... 606-589-3052 187 B
carolyn.sundy@kctcs.edu
SUNG, Joshua .... 213-252-5100.. 24 A
jsung@alu.edu
SUNG, Yung-Chi .... 952-888-4777 249 F
ycsung@nwhealth.edu
SUNGJI KIM, Howard ..... 562-622-3368.. 44 F
SUNLEAF, Arthur, W ..... 563-588-7959 171 H
arthur.sunleaf@loras.edu
SUNNYGARD, John .... 303-807-9956.. 83 D
john.sunnygard@ucdenver.edu
SUNQUIST, Scott, W .... 626-584-5265.. 43 K
sunquist@fuller.edu
SUNSER, James .... 585-345-6812 309 C
jmsunser@genesee.edu
SUNSHINE, Brian .... 254-526-7161 445 L
brian.sunshine@ctcd.edu
SUNSHINE, Phyllis .... 410-337-6046 204 A
psunshine@goucher.edu
SUOREZ, Paula .... 760-384-6298.. 47 B
psuorez@cerrocoso.edu
SUPAK, Brian .... 254-298-8609 458 C
brian.supak@templejc.edu
SUPERNAW, Robert, B .. 704-233-8015 353 D
supernaw@wingate.edu
SUPINSKI, Jessica .... 425-235-2352 497 E
jsupinski@rtc.edu
SUPLER, Robin .... 954-262-4349 104 F
rsupler@nsu.nova.edu
SUPOWITZ, Paul, A ...... 412-624-2901 412 I
psupowit@pitt.edu
SUPPELSA, Robert, E .... 310-233-4051.. 49 B
suppelre@lahc.edu
SUPPLEE, JR., Jack .... 859-257-8288 190 B
supplee@uky.edu
SUPPLEE, Janice .... 937-766-7470 358 D
suppleej@cedarville.edu
SUPURGECI, Jonna .... 605-668-1515 427 F
jsupurgeci@mtmc.edu
SUR, Sarah Gilman .... 808-235-7435 130 I
sgilman@hawaii.edu
SURATY-CLARKE,
Mercedes .... 713-743-1185 465 A
msclarke@uh.edu
SURBECK, III,
Carlton, E .... 410-337-6127 204 A
carlton.surbeck@goucher.edu
SURBROOK, Will .... 619-388-6589.. 60 B
wsurbroo@sdccd.edu
SURDOVEL, Grace .... 570-408-3102 414 H
grace.surdovel@wilkes.edu
SURENDER, Sheelu, M . 316-978-5337 182 F
sheelu.surender@wichita.edu
SURGALA, David, J .... 570-577-3811 390 H
dsurgala@bucknell.edu
SURGEONER, James, W 610-799-1658 400 A
jsurgeoner@lccc.edu
SURGES, Rebecca .... 414-930-3472 509 B
surgesr@mtmary.edu
SURLES, Karen .... 850-973-1674 104 D
surlesk@nfcc.edu
SURLS, Courtney .... 202-885-1334.. 91 C
surls@american.edu
SURMA, Barry .... 814-472-3200 409 G
bsurma@francis.edu
SURRATT, Jacob .... 276-223-4729 490 C
jsurratt@wcc.vccs.edu
SURRELL, Matt .... 662-472-9178 253 C
msurrell@holmescc.edu
SURRETT, Caron .... 828-884-8261 335 L
caron@brevard.edu
SURRIDGE, Jack, F .... 773-244-5676 147 F
jsurridge@northpark.edu
SURRIDGE, Mary, K ...... 773-244-6264 147 F
msurridge@northpark.edu
SURRUSCO, Anet .... 475-210-5675.. 88 D
asurrusco@stvincentscollege.edu
SUSANA, Gil .... 619-961-4316.. 67 F
gsusana@tjsl.edu

SUSANKA, Thomas, J ... 805-525-4417.. 67 E
tsusanka@thomasaquinas.edu
SUSANTO, Yuliana .... 502-597-7014 187 E
yuliana.susanto@kysu.edu
SUSHINSKY, David, M .. 240-895-4282 206 G
dmsushinksy@smcm.edu
SUSICK, Timothy .... 724-938-4056 405 F
susick@calu.edu
SUSKI-LENCZEWSKI,
Anna .... 860-832-1757.. 84 J
lenczewskia@mail.ccsu.edu
SUSMANN, Phillip .... 802-485-2213 475 I
susmann@norwich.edu
SUSMARSKI, Aaron .... 814-860-5101 399 C
asusmarski@lecom.edu
SUSSENBACH, Michelle 618-664-7025 139 A
michelle.sussenbach@greenville.edu
SUSSKIND, Gary .... 718-953-5889 331 B
ohaleitorah@optonline.net
SUSSMAN, Nan, M .... 718-982-2315 302 A
nan.sussman@csi.cuny.edu
SUSSMAN, Ronny .... 818-883-9002.. 72 E
SUSSWEIN, Gary .... 512-471-4945 467 C
susswein@utexas.edu
SUSTAIRE, Karan .... 903-923-2296 448 J
ksustaire@etbu.edu
SUSTICH, Andrew .... 870-972-2025.. 18 A
sustich@astate.edu
SUTCLIFFE, Nicole .... 202-651-5346.. 91 H
nicole.sutcliffe@gallaudet.edu
SUTER, Charlene .... 585-292-2500 315 L
csuter@monroecc.edu
SUTER, Cindy .... 419-448-2090 362 G
csuter@heidelberg.edu
SUTER, Vicki .... 541-552-8290 386 H
suterv@sou.edu
SUTERA, Paul, J .... 914-637-2710 311 B
psutera@iona.edu
SUTERA, Tom .... 360-538-4207 495 B
tom.sutera@ghc.edu
SUTHERLAND, David ..... 218-879-0816 244 F
dsutherland@fdltcc.edu
SUTHERLAND, David ..... 501-450-1254.. 19 I
sutherlandd@hendrix.edu
SUTHERLAND, Diane ..... 864-231-2100 418 E
dsutherland@andersonuniversity.edu
SUTHERLAND, Jim .... 678-839-6410 127 F
sutherla@westga.edu
SUTHERLAND, John ...... 706-729-2260 116 B
jsutherland@augusta.edu
SUTHERLAND, Kathleen 973-408-3100 285 E
ksutherl@drew.edu
SUTHERLAND, Richard .. 989-358-7368 227 A
sutherlr@alpenacc.edu
SUTHERLAND, Ron .... 765-998-5118 164 C
rnsutherl@taylor.edu
SUTHERLAND, Shari ..... 319-363-1323 172 B
ssutherland@mtmercy.edu
SUTHERLAND, Sonja ..... 404-835-6119 435 M
ssutherland@richmont.edu
SUTHERLAND, Tricia ..... 712-274-6400 174 E
tricia.sutherland@witcc.edu
SUTHERLIN, Lea .... 314-340-3383 260 H
sutherlinl@hssu.edu
SUTKIEWICZ, Kara, L .... 920-923-8103 508 B
klsutkiewicz90@marianuniversity.edu
SUTKOWSKI, Ernest, H . 914-831-0343 305 C
SUTKUS, Janel .... 412-268-8729 391 H
jsutkus@cmu.edu
SUTLIFF, Danielle .... 912-260-4419 125 F
dani.sutliff@sgsc.edu
SUTLIFF, Michael .... 714-432-5122.. 38 H
msutliff@occ.cccd.edu
SUTLIVE, Charles .... 404-962-3053 127 G
charles.sutlive@usg.edu
SUTPHEN, Debra .... 916-660-7502.. 63 K
dsutphen@sierracollege.edu
SUTTER, Brian .... 712-325-3328 170 K
bsutter@iwcc.edu
SUTTER, Frankie, K .... 910-592-8081 346 D
fsutter@sampsoncc.edu
SUTTER, John, D .... 563-588-7970 171 H
john.sutter@loras.edu
SUTTER, Thaddeus .... 309-556-3059 141 B
tsutter@iwu.edu
SUTTERFIELD, Shirley ... 251-442-2414.... 8 D
ssutterfield@umobile.edu
SUTTLE, J. Lloyd .... 203-432-4453.. 89 G
j.suttle@yale.edu
SUTTMEIER, Bruce .... 503-768-7100 383 G
cas@lclark.edu
SUTTON, Barbara .... 773-298-3504 151 C
sutton@sxu.edu
SUTTON, Barbara, B ...... 252-335-3224 350 A
bbsutton@ecsu.edu
SUTTON, Bob .... 847-866-3921 138 G
bob.sutton@garrett.edu

SUTTON, Cynthia .... 314-392-2291 263 F
suttonc@mobap.edu
SUTTON, David .... 254-968-9510 459 A
sutton@tarleton.edu
SUTTON, David, O .... 407-582-2753 113 F
dsutton@valenciacollege.edu
SUTTON, Deborah .... 252-527-6223 344 D
dsutton@lenoircc.edu
SUTTON, Deborah, S ..... 252-527-6223 344 D
dsutton@lenoircc.edu
SUTTON, Dennis .... 910-296-2575 344 B
dsutton@jamessprunt.edu
SUTTON, Esperance .... 410-951-3824 208 F
esutton@coppin.edu
SUTTON, Gary .... 843-208-8059 425 B
suttong2@uscb.edu
SUTTON, Gentry .... 918-335-6285 378 F
gsutton@okwu.edu
SUTTON, Gentry .... 918-335-6825 378 F
gsutton@okwu.edu
SUTTON, Jacob .... 406-791-5976 273 C
jacob.sutton@ugf.edu
SUTTON, Jama .... 865-774-5800 438 D
jama.sutton@ws.edu
SUTTON, Jeff .... 254-295-5044 466 A
jsutton@umhb.edu
SUTTON, Judith .... 304-485-5487 502 B
jsutton@msc.edu
SUTTON, Kay .... 309-690-6886 139 G
ksutton@icc.edu
SUTTON, Kenneth, W .... 410-778-7269 210 A
ksutton2@washcoll.edu
SUTTON, Lawrence .... 724-805-2402 410 C
lawrence.sutton@stvincent.edu
SUTTON, Lynn .... 336-758-5480 353 A
suttonls@wfu.edu
SUTTON, Melinda .... 662-915-7705 256 C
mjsutton@olemiss.edu
SUTTON, Michelle, D .... 502-597-5837 187 E
michelle.sutton@kysu.edu
SUTTON, Nancy .... 217-351-2402 148 H
nsutton@parkland.edu
SUTTON, Nathan .... 989-275-5000 232 E
nathan.sutton@kirtland.edu
SUTTON, R. Anderson ... 808-956-8818 129 J
rasutton@hawaii.edu
SUTTON, Rick .... 334-699-2266.... 1 B
SUTTON, Robert, E .... 509-452-5100 496 H
rsutton@pnwu.edu
SUTTON, Ronald .... 813-419-5100 239 F
suttonr@cooley.edu
SUTTON, Rosemary .... 425-352-8255 492 K
rsutton@cascadia.edu
SUTTON, Stephanie .... 440-366-7622 364 F
SUTTON, Steve .... 510-642-6727.. 68 G
studentaffairs@berkeley.edu
SUTTON, Ty .... 317-940-9620 156 I
tlsutton@butler.edu
SUTTON GERBER,
Ronette .... 910-521-6268 351 E
ronette.gerber@uncp.edu
SUTTON-HAYWOOD,
Marilyn .... 704-463-1360 348 B
marilyn.sutton-haywood@pfeiffer.edu
SUTTON-SMITH, Leslie .. 973-655-4376 287 D
suttonsmithl@mail.montclair.edu
SUTTON-WALLACE,
Pamela, M .... 434-924-9308 486 H
ps5gb@virginia.edu
SUTTON-YOUNG,
Tasheka .... 718-368-5109 303 A
tasheka.sutton-young@kbcc.cuny.edu
SUTYAK, John .... 508-286-3987 225 G
sutyak_john@wheatoncollege.edu
SUTZKO, Christopher .... 570-208-5874 398 D
christophersutzko@kings.edu
SUZOR, Michael, J .... 413-755-4044 221 B
msuzor@stcc.edu
SUZUKI, Joyce .... 707-664-4470.. 35 A
joyce.suzuki@sonoma.edu
SUZUKI, Takeo .... 423-425-4759 440 A
takeo-suzuki@utc.edu
SU'ESU'E, Jessie .... 684-699-9155 519 F
j.suesue@amsamoa.edu
SVACINA, Jean, M .... 443-518-4807 204 E
jsvacina@howardcc.edu
SVANDA, Gary .... 402-559-4432 277 H
gsvanda@unmc.edu
SVEC, Andrew .... 218-281-8438 250 G
asvec@umn.edu
SVEI, Yehuda .... 215-477-1000 411 A
talmudicalyeshiva@yahoo.com
SVETLIK, Brenda .... 361-570-4823 465 D
svetlikb@uhv.edu
SVILAR, Kendra, E .... 216-397-6630 363 H
ksvilar@jcu.edu
SVINARICH, Kathryn ...... 810-762-7885 232 C
ksvinari@kettering.edu
SVOBODA, Angela, M ... 512-448-8622 455 I
asvoboda@stedwards.edu
SWADLEY, Gary .... 417-873-7361 259 G
gary@drury.edu
SWAFFORD, Denise ...... 239-489-9358 100 E
denise.swafford@fsw.edu
SWAFFORD, Denise ...... 541-956-7087 386 G
dswafford@roguecc.edu
SWAFFORD, Jeanna, C . 731-881-7629 440 B
jswafford@utm.edu
SWAFFORD, Melissa ..... 216-987-2044 360 E
melissa.swafford@tri-c.edu
SWAGGER, Russell .... 218-879-0805 244 F
russell.swagger@fdltcc.edu
SWAHA, Chuck .... 540-231-1670 480 I
cswaha@vcom.vt.edu
SWAID, Samar .... 501-370-5335.. 21 A
sswaid@philander.edu
SWAIDAN, Christina ..... 413-572-5374 218 F
cswaidan@westfield.ma.edu
SWAILS, Joel .... 706-245-7226 119 A
jswails@ec.edu
SWAIM, Charles .... 757-825-2900 489 G
swaimc@tncc.edu
SWAIM, Kevin, C .... 765-361-6252 166 B
swaimk@wabash.edu
SWAIN, Bill, F .... 302-295-1216.. 91 B
bill.f.swain@wilmu.edu
SWAIN, Carole .... 925-631-4695.. 59 C
cswain@stmarys-ca.edu
SWAIN, Chalimar, L ...... 801-581-8876 472 P
c.swain@ic.utah.edu
SWAIN, Corliss .... 507-786-3277 250 C
swain@stolaf.edu
SWAIN, Cristal .... 970-351-1142.. 83 F
cristal.wain@unco.edu
SWAIN, Eric .... 559-443-8523.. 66 G
eric.swain@fresnocitycollege.edu
SWAIN, Heather, C .... 517-355-2262 233 G
heather.swain@cabs.msu.edu
SWAIN, Jackie .... 406-275-4755 273 A
jackie_swain@skc.edu
SWAIN, Jeffrey, D .... 305-626-3674.. 99 M
jeffrey.swain@fmuniv.edu
SWAIN, Jennifer, L .... 607-735-1894 307 G
jswain@elmira.edu
SWAIN, Sarah .... 910-893-1236 336 C
swain@campbell.edu
SWAIN, Scott, R .... 407-366-2213 255 E
sswain@rts.edu
SWAIN, Valerie, T .... 443-412-2344 204 C
vswain@harford.edu
SWALGA, Dan .... 412-392-3911 408 F
dswalga@pointpark.edu
SWALLOW, John, R ...... 262-551-5858 506 H
jswallow@carthage.edu
SWALLOW, Steven .... 937-529-2201 371 B
slswallow@united.edu
SWAN, Bobi .... 503-280-8501 382 I
bswan@cu-portland.edu
SWAN, John .... 916-577-2200.. 75 B
jswan@jessup.edu
SWAN, Kevin .... 573-840-9682 267 J
kswan@trcc.edu
SWAN, Lisa .... 262-646-6509 509 C
lswan@nashotah.edu
SWAN, Lynn .... 213-740-4154.. 72 B
lynnswan@usc.edu
SWAN, Rhonda .... 817-598-6283 470 J
rswan@wc.edu
SWAN, S. Tomeka .... 410-287-1892 203 B
tswan@cecil.edu
SWAN, Steve .... 360-650-3482 500 E
steve.swan@wwu.edu
SWAN, Terry, W .... 270-384-8148 187 H
swant@lindsey.edu
SWANAGAN, Diana .... 706-233-7301 125 E
dswanagan@shorter.edu
SWANBERG, Jeff .... 815-967-7321 150 B
jswanberg@rockfordcareercollege.edu
SWANGER, Dustin .... 518-736-3622 309 A
dustin.swanger@fmcc.suny.edu
SWANGER, Rachel .... 310-393-0411.. 56 A
rachel_swanger@rand.org
SWANK, Dennis, W .... 570-577-3363 390 H
dennis.swank@bucknell.edu
SWANKER, Susanne ...... 413-205-3216 210 E
susanne.swanker@aic.edu
SWANNACK, Patricia ..... 732-571-3546 287 C
pswannac@monmouth.edu
SWANQUIST, Leah .... 847-635-1780 148 D
lswanqui@oakton.edu
SWANSON, Adam .... 228-897-4377 254 D
adam.swanson@mgccc.edu
SWANSON, Alison .... 515-961-1696 173 E
alison.swanson@simpson.edu
SWANSON, Annette .... 567-661-7510 369 A
annette_swanson@owens.edu
SWANSON, Barry .... 859-257-9101 190 B
barry.swanson@uky.edu
SWANSON, Barry .... 716-338-1015 311 F
barryswanson@mail.sunyjcc.edu
SWANSON, Brian, R ...... 909-869-2261.. 31 A
bswanson@cpp.edu
SWANSON, Chris .... 402-552-3100 273 K
SWANSON, Chris .... 541-683-5141 383 D
cswanson@gutenberg.edu
SWANSON, Christopher 815-836-5393 143 E
swansoch@lewisu.edu
SWANSON, Cynthia .... 269-471-3288 227 B
swansonc@andrews.edu
SWANSON, Darren .... 320-363-5810 241 I
dswanson@csbsju.edu
SWANSON, Dennis .... 910-521-6365 351 E
dennis.swanson@uncp.edu
SWANSON, Greg .... 262-472-6703 512 C
swansong@uww.edu
SWANSON, Gregory ...... 704-461-5073 335 J
gregswanson@bac.edu
SWANSON, Jeanne .... 760-795-6840.. 52 F
jswanson@miracosta.edu
SWANSON, JR., Joe ..... 404-752-1542 123 F
jswanson@msm.edu
SWANSON, Kai .... 309-794-7149 133 G
kaiswanson@augustana.edu
SWANSON, Kathrine ...... 816-604-1188 262 F
kathrine.swanson@mcckc.edu
SWANSON, Kristen .... 206-296-5675 498 D
swansonk@seattleu.edu
SWANSON, Kristin .... 563-387-1167 171 I
swansokr@luther.edu
SWANSON, Kyle .... 651-793-1466 245 E
kyle.swanson@metrostate.edu
SWANSON, Lawrence .... 631-632-8781 325 F
lawrence.swanson@stonybrook.edu
SWANSON, Louis .... 970-491-6281.. 78 N
louis.swanson@colostate.edu
SWANSON, Matt .... 702-808-8806 125 H
mswanson@southuniversity.edu
SWANSON, Matthew ..... 985-448-7925 192 I
matthew.swanson@fletcher.edu
SWANSON, Robert, P .... 716-286-8538 318 F
rps@niagara.edu
SWANSON, Ryan, F ...... 785-532-1373 179 A
rswanson@ksu.edu
SWANSON, Sheila .... 641-472-1229 171 J
sswanson@mum.edu
SWANSON, Steven, M .. 608-262-1414 510 C
steve.swanson@wisc.edu
SWANSON, Thomas ...... 713-529-2778 445 K
swanson@paralegal.edu
SWANSON, Tonya .... 301-860-4161 208 E
tswanson@bowiestate.edu
SWANSON-MADDEN,
Pamela .... 618-395-7777 140 B
swansonp@iecc.edu
SWANT, Steven .... 404-894-4615 120 A
steve.swant@carnegie.gatech.edu
SWANTON, Deborah ...... 978-232-2430 214 G
dswanton@endicott.edu
SWANZEY, Thomas .... 201-692-2749 286 B
thomas_swanzey@fdu.edu
SWARBRICK, JR.,
John 'Jack', B .... 574-631-7546 165 A
swarbrick.1@nd.edu
SWARM, Gail .... 304-647-6280 504 F
gswarm@osteo.wvsom.edu
SWARNES, Neal, R .... 417-667-8181 259 A
nswarnes@cottey.edu
SWARR, Amy .... 630-617-5370 138 C
amys@elmhurst.edu
SWART, Holly Elaine .... 919-866-5000 347 D
SWARTHOUT, Cheryl ..... 989-775-4123 236 E
cswarthout@sagchip.edu
SWARTHOUT, Jeanne .... 928-524-7420.. 15 B
jeanne.swarthout@npc.edu
SWARTOUT, Jennifer ..... 309-694-8984 139 G
jennifer.swartout@icc.edu
SWARTWOOD, Ronald .. 719-502-3053.. 81 H
ron.swartwood@ppcc.edu
SWARTWOUT,
Laurie, G .... 414-410-4264 506 F
lgswartwout@stritch.edu
SWARTZ, Cathy .... 843-661-1122 421 H
cswartz@fmarion.edu
SWARTZ, David, L .... 202-885-2612.. 91 C
dswartz@american.edu
SWARTZ, Gordon .... 415-442-7026.. 44 E
gswartz@ggu.edu
SWARTZ, Mark .... 212-410-8457 317 C
mswartz@nycpm.edu
SWARTZ, Sharon .... 419-372-9843 357 F
sswartz@bgsu.edu
SWARTZ, Stephen, E ..... 978-665-4444 217 E
sswartz@fitchburgstate.edu
SWARTZ, Wendy .... 928-523-6081.. 14 K
wendy.swartz@nau.edu
SWARTZ-LEVINE,
Jennifer .... 440-375-7456 364 C
jswartz@lec.edu
SWARTZBAUGH, Keith .. 956-380-8140 455 G
kswartzbaugh@riogrande.edu
SWARTZENTRUBER,
Dale, E .... 740-368-3811 368 N
deswartz@owu.edu
SWARTZLANDER,
Barbara .... 207-602-2363 202 A
bswartzlander@une.edu
SWARTZWELDER,
Roger, L .... 205-329-7903.... 5 C
roger.swartzwelder@ecacolleges.com
SWATCHICK, Abby .... 610-568-1471 389 A
abby.swatchick@alvernia.edu
SWATCHICK, Matthew ... 717-947-6188 404 S
ms126@pacollege.edu
SWEANY, Lisa .... 912-344-2730 115 D
lisa.sweany@armstrong.edu
SWEARINGEN, Brent ..... 479-524-7191.. 20 B
bswearingen@jbu.edu
SWEARINGEN, Jodie ..... 651-423-8216 244 E
jodie.swearingen@dctc.edu
SWEATMAN, Robert, A .. 217-245-3289 139 H
rsweatma@mail.ic.edu
SWEDICK, Nick .... 212-659-7200 312 E
nswedick@tkc.edu
SWEDIN, Kris .... 505-428-1253 296 B
kris.swedin@sfcc.edu
SWEEDEN, Josh .... 816-268-5412 264 G
jsweeden@nts.edu
SWEEDLER, Alan, R .... 619-594-1354.. 34 B
asweedler@mail.sdsu.edu
SWEENER, Kathleen ...... 518-629-7320 310 G
k.sweener@hvcc.edu
SWEENEY, Charlene, M 401-863-5220 415 K
charlene_sweeney@brown.edu
SWEENEY, Janet .... 770-479-9538 124 H
jkt@reinhardt.edu
SWEENEY, John, M .... 401-865-2299 416 E
john.sweeney@providence.edu
SWEENEY, Kathleen, J .. 978-656-3046 220 C
sweeneyk@middlesex.mass.edu
SWEENEY, Kevin .... 314-256-8803 257 D
sweeney@ai.edu
SWEENEY, Kevin .... 909-469-5238.. 74 G
ksweeney@westernu.edu
SWEENEY, Marc .... 937-766-7480 358 D
msweeney@cedarville.edu
SWEENEY, Michael .... 530-754-7111.. 68 H
mfsweeney@ucdavis.edu
SWEENEY, Patrick .... 559-925-3253.. 74 A
patricksweeney@whccd.edu
SWEENEY, Richard, T .... 973-596-3208 288 A
richard.sweeney@njit.edu
SWEENEY, Rick .... 978-867-4036 215 D
rick.sweeney@gordon.edu
SWEENEY, Sarah, R .... 414-410-4187 506 F
srsweeney@stritch.edu
SWEENEY, Stacy, L .... 617-217-9100 211 D
ssweeney@baystate.edu
SWEENEY, Stephen .... 303-715-3192.. 82 G
stephen.sweeney@archden.org
SWEENEY, Timothy .... 252-475-9250 342 D
timothy_sweeney@albemarle.edu
SWEENEY, Victoria .... 630-889-6572 147 D
vsweeney@nuhs.edu
SWEENEY, Yvette .... 816-604-4114 262 K
yvette.sweeney@mcckc.edu
SWEET, Brett .... 615-343-6735 440 D
brett.sweet@vanderbilt.edu
SWEET, Cathy .... 301-985-7110 208 D
cathy.sweet@umuc.edu
SWEET, Chae .... 215-751-8450 393 A
dsweet@ccp.edu
SWEET, Chris .... 503-594-3370 382 D
chris.sweet@clackamas.edu
SWEET, Chuck .... 562-902-3305.. 65 D
chucksweet@scuhs.edu
SWEET, Cyndi .... 865-981-8095 433 F
cyndi.sweet@maryvillecollege.edu
SWEET, Darryl .... 415-565-4604.. 68 I
sweetd@uchastings.edu
SWEET, David, M .... 315-279-5682 312 D
dsweet@keuka.edu
SWEET, Don .... 252-328-9103 349 I
sweetd@ecu.edu
SWEET, Doris Ann .... 508-767-7272 210 I
dasweet@assumption.edu
SWEET, Fred .... 616-222-1329 229 B
fred.sweet@cornerstone.edu
SWEET, James, M .... 215-887-5511 414 D
jsweet@wts.edu
SWEET, Jason .... 248-689-8282 238 F
jsweet2@walshcollege.edu

SWEET, Jill .... 231-843-5918 239 D
jmsweet@westshore.edu
SWEET, Lu .... 307-382-1639 517 C
lsweet@westernwyoming.edu
SWEET, Stephen .... 802-257-7751 476 B
stephen.sweet@sit.edu
SWEET, Tracy .... 802-224-3000 476 H
tracy.sweet@vsc.edu
SWEETANA, Michael ..... 610-282-1100 393 G
michael.sweetana@desales.edu
SWEETEN, Lacy .... 573-592-1658 270 D
lacey.sweeten@williamwoods.edu
SWEETING, Donald, W .. 303-963-3350.. 77 I
dsweeting@ccu.edu
SWEEZEY, Gail, M .... 717-337-6100 396 A
gsweezey@gettysburg.edu
SWEGAN, Gary, D .... 330-941-1425 374 E
gdswegan@ysu.edu
SWEIDEL, Marty .... 410-337-6042 204 A
marty.sweidel@goucher.edu
SWEIGARD, Richard, J .. 901-678-2171 439 E
rjswgard@memphis.edu
SWEIGART, Bob .... 858-966-3991.. 39 B
bsweigart@coleman.edu
SWEIGART, Brian .... 216-791-5000 359 K
brian.sweigart@cim.edu
SWEITZER, Frederick ..... 860-768-4505.. 89 C
sweitzer@hartford.edu
SWEITZER, Paula, D ..... 412-396-4763 394 D
sweitzerp@duq.edu
SWEITZER, Sarah .... 503-280-8600 382 I
ssweitzer@cu-portland.edu
SWENCKI, Dennis .... 570-561-1818 410 A
frdennis.swencki@stots.edu
SWENDER, Herbert .... 620-276-9602 177 G
herbert.swender@gcccks.edu
SWENSON, Beth, I .... 701-788-4750 354 B
beth.swenson@mayvillestate.edu
SWENSON, Craig .... 858-513-9240.. 26 T
craig.swenson@ashford.edu
SWENSON, Jeffrey, F ..... 612-330-1241 240 G
swensonj@augsburg.edu
SWENSON, Jenni .... 218-733-7600 245 C
jswenson@lsc.edu
SWENSON, Karissa, L ... 785-833-4318 179 C
karissa.swenson@kwu.edu
SWENSON, Kirk, I .... 717-245-1029 394 A
swensonk@dickinson.edu
SWENSON, Michael .... 608-785-9892 515 C
swensonm@westerntc.edu
SWENSON, Randy, L ..... 630-889-6603 147 D
rswenson@nuhs.edu
SWENSON, Randy, L ..... 630-889-6544 147 D
rswenson@nuhs.edu
SWENSON, Tammy .... 423-697-4418 436 F
tammy.swenson@chattanoogastate.edu
SWENSON, Terry .... 909-558-8348.. 48 H
tswenson@llu.edu
SWENSON, Tim .... 502-456-6506 189 F
tswenson@sullivan.edu
SWENSON, Ty .... 206-934-6873 497 J
ty.swenson@seattlecolleges.edu
SWENTON, Gina, D .... 860-628-4751.. 87 E
gswenton@lincolncollegene.edu
SWENTY, Brian .... 812-488-2661 164 G
bs3@evansville.edu
SWERBINSKY, Megan ...... 216-791-5000 359 K
megan.swerbinsky@cim.edu
SWETLAND, Stuart .... 913-621-8701 177 A
sswetland@donnelly.edu
SWETS, Paul .... 325-942-2024 463 C
paul.swets@angelo.edu
SWETT, Denise .... 650-949-7524.. 43 F
swettdenise@foothill.edu
SWEZEY, Christopher .... 401-454-6394 417 B
cswezey@risd.edu
SWICK, Dean .... 901-722-3202 436 D
dswick@sco.edu
SWIECINSKI,
Deborah, L .... 757-683-3127 483 G
dswiecin@odu.edu
SWIFT, Angela .... 417-447-7756 264 K
swifta@otc.edu
SWIFT, Beth .... 574-631-9790 165 A
swift.8@nd.edu
SWIFT, Erica .... 612-330-1184 240 G
swift@augsburg.edu
SWIFT, Geoffrey .... 207-786-8339 198 E
gswift@bates.edu
SWIFT, Rick .... 803-754-4100 420 E
SWIFT, Sheila .... 318-670-9646 196 A
sswift@susla.edu
SWIFT, Vikki .... 208-792-2269 132 C
vswift@lcsc.edu
SWIFT, William .... 978-632-6600 220 D
w_swift@mwcc.mass.edu
SWIGART, Jessica .... 314-434-4044 259 B
jessie.swigart@covenantseminary.edu

SWIMLEY, Heather, A .... 570-326-3761 404 T
has6@pct.edu
SWINDAL, James .... 412-396-6388 394 D
swindalj@duq.edu
SWINDOLL, George, B .. 716-375-2022 322 B
gswindo@sbu.edu
SWINEHART, Amy .... 503-244-0726 381 H
amyswinehart@achs.edu
SWINEY, Jessica .... 423-652-4739 432 I
jwswiney@king.edu
SWINEY, Karen .... 910-521-6292 351 E
karen.swiney@uncp.edu
SWINEY, R. Preston ...... 910-775-4253 351 E
preston.swiney@uncp.edu
SWINFORD, Bill, K .... 859-257-1705 190 B
wswin2@uky.edu
SWINGLE, Mary .... 320-223-7510 249 J
mary.swingle@rasmussen.edu
SWINGLE, Michelle, L ... 727-816-3443 105 C
swinglm@phsc.edu
SWINK, Doug .... 816-235-1213 268 D
swinkd@umkc.edu
SWINK, Jeffrey .... 615-248-1445 439 B
jswink@trevecca.edu
SWINNEY, Marc .... 208-562-2739 132 A
marcswinney@cwidaho.cc
SWINNEY, Victoria .... 405-208-5071 377 D
vswinney@okcu.edu
SWINSON, Adela .... 408-223-6749.. 61 O
adela.swinson@evc.edu
SWINSON, Avery .... 423-585-2688 438 D
avery.swinson@ws.edu
SWINTH, Yvonne .... 253-879-3289 499 C
yswinth@pugetsound.edu
SWINTON, Jan .... 818-240-1000.. 44 D
jswinton@glendale.edu
SWINYARD, Craig .... 503-943-8506 387 H
swinyard@up.edu
SWISHER, Jay .... 386-752-1822.. 99 J
jay.swisher@fgc.edu
SWISHER, Susan .... 773-298-3070 151 C
swisher@sxu.edu
SWITAJ, Elizabeth .... 692-625-7982 520 C
eswitaj@cmi.edu
SWITZER, Luellyn .... 662-325-2091 254 E
lswitzer@saffairs.msstate.edu
SWITZER, Michael .... 601-974-1172 254 A
switzmd@millsaps.edu
SWITZER, Ray .... 864-592-4770 424 C
switzerr@sccsc.edu
SWITZER, Regina .... 405-682-7540 377 C
regina.a.switzer@occc.edu
SWITZER, Rich .... 212-659-7299 312 E
rswitzer@tkc.edu
SYAS, Quintesah .... 225-216-8235 192 B
syasq@mybrcc.edu
SYDNOR, Kim .... 443-885-3560 206 A
kim.sydnor@morgan.edu
SYDOW, Debbie, L .... 804-862-6100 484 F
dsydow@rbc.edu
SYDOW, Sue .... 402-375-7197 276 D
susydow1@wsc.edu
SYED, Mubashar .... 215-567-7080 389 E
msyed@aii.edu
SYGIELSKI, John, J .... 717-736-4100 396 G
ski@hacc.edu
SYKES, Dianne .... 434-832-7600 487 H
sykesd@cvcc.vccs.edu
SYKES, Eric .... 617-824-8286 214 E
eric_sykes@emerson.edu
SYKES, Reginald .... 251-405-7130.... 1 E
rsykes@bishop.edu
SYLER-JONES, Tracy ...... 817-257-7811 461 A
t.syler-jones@tcu.edu
SYLVESTER, Douglas ..... 480-965-6188.. 10 K
douglas.sylvester@asu.edu
SYLVESTER, Jason .... 239-280-2525.. 95 C
jason.sylvester@avemaria.edu
SYLVESTER, Kenneth ..... 810-766-3383 238 B
kenms@umflint.edu
SYLVESTER-CAESAR,
Jemma .... 713-221-2791 465 C
caesarj@uhd.edu
SYMICEK, Alan .... 715-425-4655 511 E
alan.symicek@uwrf.edu
SYMS, Deirdre .... 586-445-7862 233 B
symsd@macomb.edu
SYNAKOWSKI, Edmund 307-766-5353 517 B
esynakow@uwyo.edu
SYNAN, Sharon .... 706-245-7226 119 A
ssynan@ec.edu
SYNDER, Brittany .... 305-809-3233.. 99 L
brittany.snyder@fkcc.edu
SYNDER, Tamara .... 352-638-9764.. 95 H
tsnyder@beaconcollege.edu
SYNER, Alicia .... 304-205-6746 502 K
alicia.syner@bridgevalley.edu

SYNODI, George, S .... 203-832-7273.. 89 D
gsynodi@newhaven.edu
SYRMOS, Vassilis, L ..... 808-956-5006 129 H
syrmos@hawaii.edu
SYSYN, Nicola .... 503-699-6309 384 B
nsysyn@marylhurst.edu
SYVERUD, Kent .... 315-443-2235 330 H
ksyverud@syr.edu
SZABADOS, Anna .... 707-524-1519.. 62 H
aszabados@santarosa.edu
SZABO, Julia .... 419-358-3245 357 E
szaboj@bluffton.edu
SZABO, Lisa .... 562-944-0351.. 27 E
lisa.szabo@biola.edu
SZABO, Mihaela, A .... 304-336-8270 504 E
mszabo@westliberty.edu
SZAFRAN, Zvi .... 315-386-7204 329 A
president@canton.edu
SZAJ, Christine .... 651-290-6362 248 U
christine.szajv@mitchellhamline.edu
SZAKALY, CSC,
Anthony .... 508-565-1343 224 H
aszakaly@stonehill.edu
SZAKAS, Joe, S .... 207-621-3198 201 C
szakas@maine.edu
SZALANKIEWICZ, Linda 413-552-2155 219 G
lszalankiewicz@hcc.edu
SZALAY, Annette .... 216-373-7139 367 A
aszalay@ndc.edu
SZALDA, Katie .... 518-782-6767 324 C
kszalda@siena.edu
SZALKOWSKI,
Denise, M .... 716-673-3456 325 C
denise.szalkowski@fredonia.edu
SZANI, Phyllis .... 201-200-3350 287 F
pszani@njcu.edu
SZAREK, Michael .... 201-559-6047 286 C
szarekm@felician.edu
SZARLETA, Ellen .... 219-980-6698 160 C
eszarlet@iun.edu
SZAROLETTA, Betti .... 906-524-8109 232 D
betti.szaroletta@kbocc.edu
SZATARAY, Balint .... 209-946-2654.. 70 F
bsztaray@pacific.edu
SZCZEPANEK,
Charlene, L .... 401-456-8130 417 A
cszczepanek@ric.edu
SZCZERBACKI, David .... 617-333-2233 214 B
dszczerbacki@curry.edu
SZEJKO, Thomas .... 724-503-1001 414 A
tszejko@washjeff.edu
SZELEST, Bruce .... 518-956-8058 324 G
bszelest@albany.edu
SZELISTOWSKI, Warren . 410-532-5110 206 D
wszelistowski@ndm.edu
SZENTMIKLOSI, Jill, M . 321-682-4142 113 F
jszentmiklosi@valenciacollege.edu
SZEP, Chris Ann .... 410-287-8327 203 B
caszep@cecil.edu
SZESZYCKI, Donald, J .... 319-335-3565 166 G
donald-szeszycki@uiowa.edu
SZKODNEY, Robert .... 908-526-1200 289 D
bob.szkodny@raritanval.edu
SZPARAGOWSKI,
George .... 610-785-6205 409 F
gszparagowski@scs.edu
SZPRYNGEL,
Christopher .... 203-591-7375.. 87 H
cszpryngel@post.edu
SZPYRKA, Susan .... 719-255-3678.. 83 C
sszpyrka@uccs.edu
SZROMBA, Mathew, P .. 920-923-8505 508 B
mpszromba93@marianuniversity.edu
SZUKALSKI, SVD, John 563-876-3353 168 H
jszukalski@dwci.edu
SZUPKA, Jennifer .... 803-774-3339 419 A
szupkajl@cctech.edu
SZUR, Katalin .... 212-237-8041 302 F
kszur@jjay.cuny.edu
SZWEDKO, Emmalee ...... 801-832-2550 474 E
eszwedko@westminstercollege.edu
SZYMANSKI, David, M . 513-556-7001 371 E
david.szymanski@uc.edu
SZYMANSKI, Lynda .... 651-690-6912 249 T
laszymanski@stkate.edu
SZYMKOWICZ,
Caitlin, B .... 413-585-4944 224 F
cszymkowicz@smith.edu

T

TA, Jennie .... 626-350-1500.. 29 E
TA, Minh-Hoa .... 510-659-6107.. 54 F
mta4@ohlone.edu
TA, Minh-Hoa .... 415-561-1850.. 37 H
mhta@ccsf.edu
TA, Minh-Hoa .... 415-239-3363.. 37 H
mhta@ccsf.edu

TABACHOW, Daisy .... 407-303-9203.. 94 H
daisy.tabachow@adu.edu
TABARELLA-REDD,
Cheryl .... 319-363-8213 172 B
credd@mtmercy.edu
TABAREZ, Mirasol .... 956-326-1303 459 B
mtabarez@tamiu.edu
TABATABAI, Habib .... 405-974-2865 380 J
htabatabai@uco.edu
TABB, Brian .... 612-455-3420 241 A
brian.tabb@bcsmn.edu
TABB, Winston, G .... 410-516-8328 204 F
wtabb@jhu.edu
TABBACK, George .... 201-684-6842 289 C
gtabback@ramapo.edu
TABCHOURI, Debbie ..... 337-521-8916 193 E
debbie.tabchouri@solacc.edu
TABER, Charles .... 631-632-7035 325 F
charles.taber@stonybrook.edu
TABER, K. Celeste .... 405-744-6876 377 F
celeste.taber@okstate.edu
TABER, Ralph .... 717-358-4390 395 G
ralph.taber@fandm.edu
TABER DOUGHTY,
Teresa .... 817-272-2591 467 B
teresa.doughty@uta.edu
TABERNER, Ian .... 617-262-5000 212 C
ian.taberner@the-bac.edu
TABING, Karla .... 618-985-3741 141 D
karlatabing@jalc.edu
TABOADA, Luz, E .... 915-831-7796 449 A
ltaboad2@epcc.edu
TABOR, Anne .... 207-973-1090 199 B
tabora@husson.edu
TABOR, Susan .... 405-682-1611 377 C
stabor@occc.edu
TABOR, Tammy .... 620-276-9508 177 G
tammy.tabor@gcccks.edu
TABOR, Troy .... 610-917-1436 413 G
tetabor@valleyforge.edu
TABRON, Jasmine .... 570-208-5898 398 D
jasminetabron@kings.edu
TABRON, Judith, L .... 516-463-6316 310 D
judith.t.tabron@hofstra.edu
TACCONE, Al .... 760-757-2121.. 52 F
ataccone@miracosta.edu
TACEA, Christopher .... 518-891-2915 319 A
ctacea@nccc.edu
TACK, Eric .... 678-466-4085 117 I
erictack@clayton.edu
TACKER, Todd .... 740-588-1396 374 G
ttacker@zanestate.edu
TACKET, Karen .... 805-546-3100.. 41 C
ktacket@cuesta.edu
TACKETT, Kelli .... 740-593-1804 368 G
tackettk@ohio.edu
TACKETT, Larry .... 304-510-8760 503 E
ltackett@wvncc.edu
TACKETT, Lisa, K .... 740-368-3398 368 N
lktacket@owu.edu
TADAMY, Everett, L .... 412-268-1018 391 H
et19@andrew.cmu.edu
TADAO, Tzuchie .... 680-488-2471 520 E
tzuchiet@gmail.com
TADEO, Joseph .... 352-588-8244 106 N
joseph.tadeo@saintleo.edu
TADEPALLI, Raghu .... 336-278-6000 337 G
rtadepalli@elon.edu
TADESSE, Asmare .... 408-855-5021.. 74 C
asmare.tadesse@wvm.edu
TADESSE, Berhanu .... 657-278-8748.. 32 B
btadesse@fullerton.edu
TADESSE, Kidesti .... 503-517-1017 388 A
ktadesse@warnerpacific.edu
TADLOCK, Katherine ...... 740-597-2577 368 G
tadlockk@ohio.edu
TADLOCK, Martin .... 727-873-4324 111 B
mtadlock@usfsp.edu
TADLOCK, Martin .... 727-873-4466 111 A
mtadlock@mail.usf.edu
TADLOCK, Martin .... 727-873-4151 111 B
mtadlock@usfsp.edu
TAETZSCH, Blixy, K .... 607-844-8222 331 D
taetzsb@tompkinscortland.edu
TAFARO, John, P .... 513-875-3344 359 C
john.tafaro@chatfield.edu
TAFFORA, Raymond, P . 608-263-7400 510 C
ray.taffora@wisc.edu
TAFOYA, Christina .... 805-678-5824.. 73 B
ctafoya@vcccd.edu
TAFOYA, Yvette .... 562-860-2451.. 36 A
ytafoya@cerritos.edu
TAGGART, Bruce, M ...... 610-758-3025 400 B
bmt2@lehigh.edu
TAGGART, James, R ...... 801-627-8306 472 D
taggartj@owatc.edu
TAGGART, Julie .... 614-222-4025 360 B
jtaggart@ccad.edu

TART, Marla, L .... 919-866-5901 347 D
mltart@waketech.edu
TART, Stuart .... 240-567-7494 205 F
stuart.tart@montgomerycollege.edu
TARTAGLIA, Joseph, F .. 973-596-5279 288 A
tartaglia@njit.edu
TARTT, Tom .... 205-652-3533.... 9 C
ttartt@uwa.edu
TARVER, Eunice .... 918-595-7000 380 D
TARVER, Eunice .... 918-595-8487 380 D
eunice.tarver@tulsacc.edu
TARVER, Stephanie, B ... 337-562-4249 197 B
starver@mcneese.edu
TARVER, III, Walter, L .. 609-652-4804 291 H
walter.tarver@stockton.edu
TARVER-BEHRING,
Shari, A .... 818-677-2590.. 33 B
starver-behring@csun.edu
TARVER-ROSS,
Cassandra .... 256-372-5835.... 1 A
cassandra.ross@aamu.edu
TARVIN, Patricia .... 412-809-5100 408 D
tarvin.pat@pti.edu
TARWATER, Lisa .... 865-573-4517 432 H
ltarwater@johnsonu.edu
TARY, Keely .... 423-236-2736 436 C
ktary@southern.edu
TASHEFF, Katherine ...... 973-655-3291 287 D
tasheffk@mail.montclair.edu
TASHIMA, Jaye .... 760-245-4271.. 73 E
jaye.tashima@vvc.edu
TASHJIAN, Tim .... 512-428-1095 455 I
timt@stedwards.edu
TASSIN, Shannon .... 318-487-7051 191 J
shannon.tassin@lacollege.edu
TASSON, Dana .... 503-725-4429 386 D
tassond@pdx.edu
TAST, Maryellen .... 307-778-1146 516 N
mtast@lccc.wy.edu
TASTAD, Renee .... 413-552-2592 219 G
rtastad@hcc.edu
TATE, Allen .... 717-391-7285 411 C
tate@stevenscollege.edu
TATE, Ann .... 281-922-3404 456 B
ann.tate@sjcd.edu
TATE, Anthony .... 615-904-8204 434 H
anthony.tate@mtsu.edu
TATE, Brad .... 513-745-5700 371 F
brad.tate@uc.edu
TATE, David .... 307-382-1882 517 C
dtate@westernwyoming.edu
TATE, Don .... 864-587-4227 424 D
tated@smcsc.edu
TATE, Helen .... 704-233-8744 353 D
tate@wingate.edu
TATE, James .... 713-348-6000 455 F
james.d.tate@rice.edu
TATE, James .... 507-537-6256 248 A
jim.tate@smsu.edu
TATE, Jimmy, T .... 252-862-1308 345 H
TATE, Katrina .... 731-410-6709 432 J
ktate@lanecollege.edu
TATE, Kim .... 575-769-4021 293 M
kim.tate@clovis.edu
TATE, Nancy .... 864-231-2181 418 E
ntate@andersonuniversity.edu
TATE, Nancy, A .... 785-670-1648 182 D
nancy.tate@washburn.edu
TATE, Robert, H .... 863-680-4347 100 D
rtate@flsouthern.edu
TATE, Verlanda .... 205-929-1440.... 6 D
vtate@miles.edu
TATE, William, F .... 314-935-4843 269 L
wtate@wustl.edu
TATELA, Joseph .... 410-386-8327 203 A
jtatela@carrollcc.edu
TATENO, Yuji .... 808-946-3773 128 J
TATNALL, Amber .... 207-216-4392 200 E
atatnall@yccc.edu
TATOM, Kathy .... 913-758-6102 182 B
kathy.tatom@stmary.edu
TATRO, Donna, E .... 609-258-2845 288 F
tatro@princeton.edu
TATRO, Fred .... 617-364-3510 212 D
ftatro@boston.edu
TATRO, Lois .... 316-978-5890 182 F
lois.tatro@wichita.edu
TATSAK, Jenny .... 248-689-8282 238 F
jtatsak@walshcollege.edu
TATUM, Alfred .... 312-996-5641 153 H
atatum1@uic.edu
TATUM, Ashley .... 940-668-7323 453 L
atatum@nctc.edu
TATUM, Jeff .... 662-246-6471 254 C
jtatum@msdelta.edu
TATUM, Lance .... 334-241-9538.... 7 E
ltatum@troy.edu
TATUM, Leila .... 678-466-4477 117 I
leilatatum@clayton.edu
TATUM, Ray .... 770-538-4706 116 F
rtatum@brenau.edu
TATUM, Tanya .... 850-599-3777 109 A
tanya.tatum@famu.edu
TATUM, Terry .... 361-825-2321 460 A
terry.tatum@tamucc.edu
TATUM, Veronda .... 870-864-7133.. 21 D
vtatum@southark.edu
TAUB, Alexander .... 215-477-1000 411 A
TAUBER, Hendy .... 323-937-3763.. 75 F
htauber@yoec.edu
TAUBMAN, Mark, B ...... 585-275-0017 332 E
mark_taubman@urmc.rochester.edu
TAUBMAN, Phil .... 650-723-2300.. 66 C
TAUER, Ritamarie .... 281-649-3702 450 C
rtauer@hbu.edu
TAUER, Thomas .... 570-422-2720 406 A
ttauer@esu.edu
TAUPIER, Andrea, S ...... 413-748-3609 224 G
ataupier@springfieldcollege.edu
TAURIELLO, Claire .... 301-447-5202 206 B
tauriello@msmary.edu
TAUSSI, Lee .... 845-398-4013 323 G
altaussi@stac.edu
TAUSSIG, Martha .... 870-512-7824.. 18 D
martha_taussig@asun.edu
TAUZIN, Kristie, R .... 985-448-4509 197 C
kristie.tauzin@nicholls.edu
TAVAKOLI, Roozbeh ...... 716-829-7515 307 B
tavakoli@dyc.edu
TAVARES, Juan .... 269-387-5879 239 E
juan.tavares@wmich.edu
TAVARES, Shirley, A ..... 787-725-8120 522 M
investigacion@eap.edu
TAVE, Stephen .... 815-967-7329 150 B
stave@rockfordcareercollege.edu
TAVELLI, Nancy, J .... 509-527-5297 500 G
tavelln@whitman.edu
TAVERNER, Melissa ...... 276-944-6775 480 J
mptavern@ehc.edu
TAVERNIER, Theresa ..... 215-489-2346 393 F
theresa.tavernier@delval.edu
TAVIN-WARKENTHIEN,
Claudine .... 718-409-7271 329 E
ctavin-warkenthien@sunymaritime.edu
TAWNEY, Andrea, S ...... 575-646-2867 295 B
atawney@nmsu.edu
TAXTER, Marianne .... 619-265-0107.. 57 G
mtaxter@platt.edu
TAYEH, Raja .... 402-826-6776 274 E
raja.tayeh@doane.edu
TAYLOE, John .... 252-398-1232 336 K
tayloj@chowan.edu
TAYLOR, Adam .... 864-388-8195 422 A
ataylor@lander.edu
TAYLOR, Allen .... 304-696-6195 504 C
taylor@marshall.edu
TAYLOR, Allison, S .... 402-280-3189 274 D
allisontaylor@creighton.edu
TAYLOR, Amy .... 203-392-6800.. 85 A
taylora28@southernct.edu
TAYLOR, Amy, L .... 410-704-4931 209 C
altaylor@towson.edu
TAYLOR, Andrea .... 562-985-5195.. 32 C
andrea.taylor@csulb.edu
TAYLOR, Angela .... 757-388-5133 485 B
ataylor@sentara.edu
TAYLOR, Angie .... 936-294-1845 462 F
agb003@shsu.edu
TAYLOR, Anita .... 410-323-6211 203 F
a.taylor@fts.edu
TAYLOR, Ann .... 314-516-5106 268 E
taylorann@umsl.edu
TAYLOR, Anna .... 770-233-5560 126 B
ataylor@sctech.edu
TAYLOR, Audra .... 254-442-5117 445 Q
audra.taylor@cisco.edu
TAYLOR, Barbara .... 575-538-6427 297 H
barbara.taylor@wnmu.edu
TAYLOR, Beck, A .... 509-777-3200 500 H
btaylor@whitworth.edu
TAYLOR, Bill .... 408-741-2642.. 74 D
bill.taylor@westvalley.edu
TAYLOR, Bill .... 641-782-1406 173 I
taylor@swcciowa.edu
TAYLOR, Brad .... 801-422-3861 471 E
brad_taylor@byu.edu
TAYLOR, Brandy .... 912-871-1616 123 J
btaylor@ogeecheetech.edu
TAYLOR, Brian .... 808-956-6182 129 J
taylorb@hawaii.edu
TAYLOR, Cameron .... 404-727-5311 119 B
cameron.taylor@emory.edu
TAYLOR, Carol, A .... 417-865-2815 260 B
taylorc@evangel.edu
TAYLOR, Carol, R .... 864-488-4510 422 B
ctaylor@limestone.edu
TAYLOR, Cathy .... 618-650-5176 152 C
cattayl@siue.edu
TAYLOR, Cathy .... 615-460-6781 430 D
cathy.taylor@belmont.edu
TAYLOR, Caughman .... 803-434-2069 424 I
caughman.taylor@uscmed.sc.edu
TAYLOR, Celya .... 870-230-5358.. 19 H
taylorc@hsu.edu
TAYLOR, Chelsa .... 276-739-2423 490 A
ctaylor@vhcc.edu
TAYLOR, Cheryl, A .... 417-268-1000 257 F
taylorch@evangel.edu
TAYLOR, Christopher .... 973-408-3321 285 E
ctaylor@drew.edu
TAYLOR, Christopher .... 973-408-3495 285 E
ctaylor@drew.edu
TAYLOR, Craig .... 541-463-5364 383 F
taylorc@lanecc.edu
TAYLOR, Cyrus, C .... 216-368-4437 358 C
casdean@case.edu
TAYLOR, Daniel .... 304-358-2000 501 I
dtaylor@future.edu
TAYLOR, Danille, K .... 404-880-6774 117 H
dtaylor3@cau.edu
TAYLOR, Danny, H .... 615-966-7650 433 D
danny.taylor@lipscomb.edu
TAYLOR, Darrell .... 304-896-7432 503 D
darrell.taylor@southernwv.edu
TAYLOR, David .... 828-669-8012 340 I
dtaylor@montreat.edu
TAYLOR, David, A .... 718-289-5598 301 D
david.taylor@bcc.cuny.edu
TAYLOR, David, E .... 202-885-2121.. 91 C
taylor@american.edu
TAYLOR, David, F .... 336-758-5000 353 A
taylordf@wfu.edu
TAYLOR, David, R .... 540-568-3720 481 I
taylordr@jmu.edu
TAYLOR, Debbie .... 864-622-6063 418 E
dtaylor@andersonuniversity.edu
TAYLOR, Debora, W ...... 512-448-8450 455 I
deboraw@stedwards.edu
TAYLOR, Deborah .... 562-903-4703.. 27 E
deborah.taylor@biola.edu
TAYLOR, Deborah .... 901-334-5812 434 C
TAYLOR, Deborah, A ..... 757-446-6031 480 C
taylorta@evms.edu
TAYLOR, Diane .... 254-968-9598 459 A
dtaylor@tarleton.edu
TAYLOR, Donald .... 610-902-8200 391 B
donald.taylor@cabrini.edu
TAYLOR, Donald, W ...... 561-868-3280 105 A
taylord@palmbeachstate.edu
TAYLOR, Ed .... 206-616-7175 499 D
edtaylor@uw.edu
TAYLOR, Edward .... 608-663-2333 507 D
edtaylor@edgewood.edu
TAYLOR, Edward .... 706-778-8500 124 E
etaylor@piedmont.edu
TAYLOR, Faye .... 732-247-5241 287 E
ftaylor@nbts.edu
TAYLOR, Francis, H .... 334-833-4407.... 5 M
ftaylor@hawks.huntingdon.edu
TAYLOR, Frederick .... 662-252-8000 255 F
ftaylor@rustcollege.edu
TAYLOR, G. Christine .... 205-348-2064.... 8 A
christine.taylor@ua.edu
TAYLOR, G. Don .... 540-231-9752 490 F
don.taylor@vt.edu
TAYLOR, Gary .... 865-251-1800 436 B
gtaylor@southcollegetn.edu
TAYLOR, Gene .... 785-532-6912 179 A
ksuad@ksu.edu
TAYLOR, Geoffrey .... 912-525-5000 125 B
gtaylor@scad.edu
TAYLOR, Geraldine .... 781-891-2222 212 A
gtaylor@bentley.edu
TAYLOR, Gia .... 480-423-6300.. 14 C
gia.taylor@scottsdalecc.edu
TAYLOR, Gregory .... 559-244-5909.. 66 E
gregory.taylor@scccd.edu
TAYLOR, Gwen .... 706-771-4180 116 A
gtaylor@augustatech.edu
TAYLOR, Heather .... 312-915-8903 144 D
htaylor1@luc.edu
TAYLOR, Heather .... 304-829-7408 501 F
htaylor@bethanywv.edu
TAYLOR, Heather, H ...... 757-822-1738 489 H
htaylor@tcc.edu
TAYLOR, Hunter .... 252-536-7228 343 F
htaylor397@halifaxcc.edu
TAYLOR, J. Kevin .... 805-756-1503.. 30 K
jktaylor@calpoly.edu
TAYLOR, Jacqueline ...... 609-771-3032 284 I
taylorj@tcnj.edu
TAYLOR, Jaime .... 931-221-7971 430 B
taylorjr@apsu.edu
TAYLOR, James .... 502-456-6504 189 F
jtaylor@sullivan.edu
TAYLOR, James .... 410-777-2318 202 D
jmtaylor@aacc.edu
TAYLOR, James .... 801-626-6055 473 E
jamestaylor8@weber.edu
TAYLOR, Jan .... 304-558-4128 503 N
jan.taylor@wvhepc.edu
TAYLOR, Janet .... 619-482-6309.. 65 H
jtaylor@swccd.edu
TAYLOR, Janet .... 815-921-4324 150 A
j.taylor@rockvalleycollege.edu
TAYLOR, Janice .... 617-521-2360 224 E
janice.taylor@simmons.edu
TAYLOR, Janie .... 817-461-8741 442 L
jtaylor@abu.edu
TAYLOR, Jason .... 609-586-4800 287 A
taylorj@mccc.edu
TAYLOR, Jay, P .... 417-268-1000 257 F
taylorj@evangel.edu
TAYLOR, Jeffrey, D .... 315-268-6477 304 B
jdtaylor@clarkson.edu
TAYLOR, Jeffrey, S .... 814-871-7213 395 H
taylor030@gannon.edu
TAYLOR, Jennifer .... 479-575-2000.. 21 I
TAYLOR, Jennifer .... 805-565-6085.. 74 I
jmtaylor@westmont.edu
TAYLOR, Jim .... 253-964-6589 497 B
jtaylor@pierce.ctc.edu
TAYLOR, Joe .... 208-496-7010 131 D
taylorj@byui.edu
TAYLOR, John .... 714-432-5935.. 38 H
jtaylor174@occ.cccd.edu
TAYLOR, John .... 585-785-1300 308 D
john.taylor@flcc.edu
TAYLOR, John .... 513-244-8176 359 E
athletics@ccuniversity.edu
TAYLOR, John .... 513-244-8437 359 E
john.taylor@ccuniversity.edu
TAYLOR, Joseph .... 804-342-1264 491 C
jdtaylor@vuu.edu
TAYLOR, Joseph, P .... 276-944-6124 480 J
jptaylor@ehc.edu
TAYLOR, Joyce, K .... 540-674-3600 488 G
jtaylor@nr.edu
TAYLOR, Juanyce .... 601-984-1010 256 D
jdtaylor@umc.edu
TAYLOR, Judith, M .... 240-567-7337 205 F
judith.taylor@montgomerycollege.edu
TAYLOR, Julie, Y .... 256-765-4680.... 9 A
jayates@una.edu
TAYLOR, Karen .... 914-606-6963 333 H
karen.taylor@sunywcc.edu
TAYLOR, Kathy .... 870-230-5103.. 19 H
taylork@hsu.edu
TAYLOR, Kathy .... 504-816-4304 191 E
ktaylor@dillard.edu
TAYLOR, Keith .... 814-871-7609 395 H
ktaylor@gannon.edu
TAYLOR, Kelley, G .... 334-844-4794.... 4 D
taylokg@auburn.edu
TAYLOR, Kelli .... 910-630-7157 340 A
ktaylor@methodist.edu
TAYLOR, Kenneth .... 870-230-5216.. 19 H
taylorke@hsu.edu
TAYLOR, Kent .... 575-624-8235 295 A
kent@nmmi.edu
TAYLOR, Kenya, S .... 308-865-8843 277 F
taylorks@unk.edu
TAYLOR, Kevin .... 303-556-4736.. 80 Q
ktaylo@msudenver.edu
TAYLOR, Kevin .... 864-242-5100 418 H
TAYLOR, Khallai .... 773-481-8737 136 B
ktaylor194@ccc.edu
TAYLOR, Kim .... 773-702-7749 153 F
kimtaylor@uchicago.edu
TAYLOR, Kimberly .... 518-292-1854 321 G
taylok3@sage.edu
TAYLOR, Kristen .... 817-257-4161 461 A
kristen.taylor@tcu.edu
TAYLOR, Kristy .... 740-389-4636 365 B
taylork@mtc.edu
TAYLOR, Ladd .... 601-928-6299 254 D
ladd.taylor@mgccc.edu
TAYLOR, LaTonya .... 630-752-5015 155 F
media.relations@wheaton.edu
TAYLOR, Lauren, M .... 205-726-2956.... 6 G
lmtaylor@samford.edu
TAYLOR, Laurna .... 615-361-7555 431 G
ltaylor@daymarinstitute.edu
TAYLOR, Leah, A .... 304-929-6701 503 B
ltaylor@newriver.edu
TAYLOR, Lee .... 334-387-3877.... 4 B
leetaylor@amridgeuniversity.edu
TAYLOR, Leslie, W .... 501-686-8998.. 22 C
taylorlesliew@uams.edu

TEMPERINO, Steven, H . 603-535-2848 283 B stemperi@plymouth.edu
TEMPLE, Glena 608-796-3005 512 R ggtemple@viterbo.edu
TEMPLE, H. Thomas 954-262-1556 104 F htemple@nova.edu
TEMPLE, Jack 334-387-3877 4 B jacktemple@amridgeuniversity.edu
TEMPLE, James 661-362-3535 39 C james.temple@canyons.edu
TEMPLE, Lori 702-895-3628 279 D lorit@unlv.edu
TEMPLE, Melanie 252-862-1242 345 H metemple7181@roanokechowan.edu
TEMPLE, Tisha 512-863-1538 457 I templet@southwestern.edu
TEMPLE, Vicki 318-678-6000 192 C vtemple@bpcc.edu
TEMPLE KNEUVEAN, Shelley 816-604-1253 262 F shelley.kneuvean@mcckc.edu
TEMPLER, James 409-933-8229 446 H
TEMPLETON, Debra 828-328-7335 339 C debra.templeton@lr.edu
TEMPLETON, Heidi 660-785-4016 267 K heidi@truman.edu
TEMPLETON, Jenna 412-365-1694 392 C jtempleton@chatham.edu
TEMPLETON, Joanna 516-877-3909 297 I jtempleton@adelphi.edu
TEMPLETON, Leslie 501-450-1320 19 I templeton@hendrix.edu
TEMPLETON, Mary 334-670-3189 7 E mtempleton@troy.edu
TEMPLETON, Mary, A 318-675-7652 194 D mtemp1@lsuhsc.edu
TEMPLETON, William 907-786-4005 10 A wgtempleton@alaska.edu
TEMPLETON-CORNELL, Vicki, L 315-267-2190 328 A templevl@potsdam.edu
TEN NAPEL, Karmen 712-274-5191 172 A tennapel@morningside.edu
TENA, Lydia 915-831-8818 449 A lpere121@epcc.edu
TENBERGEN, Klaus 209-588-5142 75 I tenbergenk@yosemite.edu
TENCHER, Donald, E 401-456-8007 417 A dtencher@ric.edu
TENCZAR, Bob 909-537-5007 33 D robert.tenczar@csusb.edu
TENDALL, Michael, W 309-794-7357 133 G michaeltendall@augustana.edu
TENENBAUM, Elchonon 707-638-5507 67 H rabbi@tu.edu
TENER, Brent, B 615-343-1422 440 D b.tener@vanderbilt.edu
TENG, Anthony 949-582-4895 64 J ateng@saddleback.edu
TENGLIN, Ingrid, K 773-244-5601 147 F itenglin@northpark.edu
TENIENTE, Yvonne 805-922-6966 24 J yteniente@hancockcollege.edu
TENIENTE-MATSON, Cynthia 210-784-1600 460 C cmatson@tamusa.edu
TENISON, Bruce 256-352-8149 3 I bruce.tenison@wallacestate.edu
TENN, Jennifer 815-280-2217 142 A jtenn@jjc.edu
TENNANT, Leslie, A 724-480-3552 392 K leslie.tennant@ccbc.edu
TENNANT, Otto 270-789-5034 184 B otennant@campbellsville.edu
TENNENT, Timothy, C 859-858-2202 183 C
TENNER, Jack 713-743-5671 465 A jdtenner@central.uh.edu
TENNER, Katangela 601-877-6147 251 G ksampson@alcorn.edu
TENNESSENN, Margaret 608-265-3444 510 C margaret.tennessen@wisc.edu
TENNEY, David 713-348-8036 455 F dtenney@rice.edu
TENNEY, Randall 304-473-8099 505 G tenney_r@wvwc.edu
TENNEY, Sheila 404-756-4012 115 I stenney@atlm.edu
TENNY, Elissa 312-899-5136 151 F etenny@saic.edu
TENNYSON, Pat 423-869-6286 433 C pat.tennyson@lmunet.edu
TENSEN, Jan 973-300-2153 291 I jtensen@sussex.edu
TENSUAN, Theresa 610-896-1268 397 F ttensuan@haverford.edu
TENTES, Theresa 650-738-4331 62 B tentes@smccd.edu
TENUTA, Bob 815-455-8585 145 B btenuta@mchenry.edu
TEODORESCU, Daniel 770-720-9130 124 H dt1@reinhardt.edu
TEODOSIO, Alex, J 216-397-1905 363 H ateodosio@jcu.edu
TEPATTI, Eileen, G 217-786-2885 144 B eileen.tepatti@llcc.edu
TEPPER, Steven, J 480-965-8561 10 K steven.tepper@asu.edu
TER MOLEN, Matthew 315-443-9161 330 H termolen@syr.edu
TERAOKA, Della 808-455-0453 130 G dellaand@hawaii.edu
TERCERO, Desiree 818-785-2726 35 N
TEREBESSY, Hilarie 312-942-3013 150 F hilarie_terebessy@rush.edu
TERENZIO, Charlie 941-359-4200 111 C
TERENZIO, Marion 518-255-5111 328 C terenzma@cobleskill.edu
TERESA, Daniel 831-755-6840 45 C dteresa@hartnell.edu
TERESA, Thomas 903-875-7315 453 J teresa.thomas@navarrocollege.edu
TERESH, Tonia 760-252-2411 27 A tteresh@barstow.edu
TERHAAR, Jody, L 320-363-5601 241 I jterhaar@csbsju.edu
TERKLA, David 617-287-6500 216 I david.terkla@umb.edu
TERKLA, Dawn, G 617-627-3274 225 A dawn.terkla@tufts.edu
TERMIN, Travis 817-722-1731 451 G travis.termin@tku.edu
TERMOTT, Kenneth 732-247-5241 287 E ktermott@nbts.edu
TERMUHLEN, Paula 218-726-7572 250 F ptermuhl@d.umn.edu
TERNAK, Armand 706-886-6831 126 F aternack@tfc.edu
TERP, Cheryl 920-693-1134 513 H cheryl.terp@gotoltc.edu
TERP, Douglas, C 207-859-4770 198 H dcterp@colby.edu
TERPACK, Sallie, A 814-732-1024 406 B terpack@edinboro.edu
TERPENNING, Linda 303-373-2008 82 F lterpenning@rvu.edu
TERPENNING, Marlene, K 740-284-5179 361 L mterpenning@franciscan.edu
TERPSTRA, Joylita, W 423-478-7731 435 I jterpstra@ptseminary.edu
TERPSTRA, Phil 620-276-9554 177 G phil.terpstra@gcccks.edu
TERRANCE, Teah, M 585-385-8411 322 E tterrance@sjfc.edu
TERRAZAS, Denise 951-372-7016 58 G denise.terrazas@norcocollege.edu
TERRAZAS, Lissete 575-492-2122 297 G lterrazas@usw.edu
TERRAZAS, Susan 909-760-3476 74 G sterrazas@westernu.edu
TERRELL, Bill 915-532-3737 470 L bterrell@westerntech.edu
TERRELL, Carleen 336-249-8186 342 F carleen_terrell@davidsonccc.edu
TERRELL, Charles 304-434-8001 502 L charles.terrell@easternwv.edu
TERRELL, David, R 765-285-2201 156 C drterrell@bsu.edu
TERRELL, Gaither, M 336-316-2143 338 C gterrell@guilford.edu
TERRELL, Mark 814-866-6641 399 C mterrell@lecom.edu
TERRELL, Patrice 478-825-4284 119 C terrellp@fvsu.edu
TERRELL, Sherri, I 915-747-5302 467 E siterrell@utep.edu
TERRELL-BROOKS, Tabetha 601-979-6944 253 E tabetha.terrell-brooks@jsums.edu
TERRELL-POWELL, Yvonne 425-640-1456 494 E yvonneterrellpowell@edcc.edu
TERRENTINE, Timothy 269-387-8781 239 E tim.terrentine@wmich.edu
TERRERO, Rigoberto 787-257-7373 525 Q ue_rterrero@suagm.edu
TERRIO, Dan, M 509-527-4981 500 G terrio@whitman.edu
TERRIO, Paul 612-238-4552 250 B pterrio@smumn.edu
TERRONEZ, Danny 979-532-6465 471 A terronezd@wcjc.edu
TERRY, Bryan, J 336-256-8602 351 D bjterry@uncg.edu
TERRY, Carolyn 240-567-4366 205 F carolyn.terry@montgomerycollege.edu
TERRY, Chihoko 910-410-1821 345 G ckterry@richmondcc.edu
TERRY, Denise 574-372-5100 158 B denise.terry@grace.edu
TERRY, Edward 828-726-2202 341 D eterry@cccti.edu
TERRY, Heidi, L 330-325-6479 366 F hterry@neomed.edu
TERRY, James, E 304-696-2486 504 C terry@marshall.edu
TERRY, Laura, C 423-439-4210 431 H terryl@etsu.edu
TERRY, LeRodrick 480-517-8105 14 B lerodrick.terry@riosalado.edu
TERRY, Mike 217-641-4529 141 F mterry@jwcc.edu
TERRY, Missy, D 503-554-2101 383 C terrym@georgefox.edu
TERRY, Neil, W 806-651-2530 460 E nterry@mail.wtamu.edu
TERRY, Penelope 718-951-5924 301 E pterry@brooklyn.cuny.edu
TERRY, Peter 270-809-2535 188 D pterry4@murraystate.edu
TERRY, Robert 602-386-4127 10 G bob.terry@arizonachristian.edu
TERRY, Scott 304-357-4363 502 E scottterry@ucwv.edu
TERRY, Stephen 913-288-7685 178 H sterry@kckcc.edu
TERRY, Steve 614-236-6508 358 A sterry@capital.edu
TERRY, Susan 206-543-0535 499 D nahe@uw.edu
TERRY, Troy, M 864-294-2213 421 I troy.terry@furman.edu
TERRY, Willa 662-252-2491 255 F wterry@rustcollege.edu
TERRY-JACKSON, Tonishea 847-578-8489 150 E tonishea.terry-jackson@rosalindfranklin.edu
TERRYN, Dottie 850-872-3801 101 J dterryn@gulfcoast.edu
TERVALA, Debra 505-473-6292 296 C debra.tervala@santafeuniversity.edu
TESCHNER, Pam 503-375-7180 383 A pteschner@corban.edu
TESFAMARIAM, Biniam . 574-520-4104 160 F biktesfa@iusb.edu
TESFAY, Isaac 508-929-8784 219 A itesfay@worcester.edu
TESH, J. Michael 210-567-2590 468 E tesh@uthscsa.edu
TESKE, Paul 303-315-2805 83 D paul.teske@ucdenver.edu
TESKE, Yolanda, K 252-334-2029 340 B yolanda.teske@macuniversity.edu
TESLUK, Paul, E 716-645-3221 325 B ptesluk@buffalo.edu
TESORIERO, Christine 516-876-3033 327 C tesorieroc@oldwestbury.edu
TESS, Dan 570-484-2238 406 E dtess@lockhaven.edu
TESS, Paul, A 507-354-8221 243 C tesspa@mlc-wels.edu
TESSIER, Dorita 509-527-2646 499 F dorita.tessier@wallawalla.edu
TESSIER, Michael, A 812-488-2956 164 G mt28@evansville.edu
TESSIER, Nanci 617-552-2805 212 E nanci.tessier@bc.edu
TESSIER-LAVIGNE, Marc 650-723-2481 66 C president@stanford.edu
TESSITORE, Amy 518-243-1577 299 E tessitorea@ellismedicine.org
TESSLER, Faith 310-824-1586 24 B ftessler@ajrca.edu
TESSLER, Lisa 845-437-5438 333 A litessler@vassar.edu
TESSMAN, Brock 406-243-2541 271 G brock.tessman@umontana.edu
TESSMANN, Cary, A 262-691-5214 515 B ctessmann@wctc.edu
TESTA, Michael 610-892-1548 405 C mtesta@pit.edu
TESTA, Noelle 785-242-5200 180 H noelle.testa@ottawa.edu
TESTA-BUZZEE, Kristina 203-857-7220 86 D ktesta-buzzee@norwalk.edu
TESTANI, Joe 585-275-2366 332 E j.testani@rochester.edu
TESTERMAN, Misty 304-425-2323 502 H
TESTI, Andrea 541-881-5761 387 D atesti@tvcc.cc
TESTORI, Peter 413-565-1000 211 C ptestori@baypath.edu
TETERS, Charlene 505-424-2354 294 C cteters@iaia.edu
TETI, Polly 215-242-7777 392 D tetip@chc.edu
TETLEY, Sarah 636-949-4627 261 I stetley@lindenwood.edu
TETLOW, Tania 504-865-5201 196 D ttelow@tulane.edu
TETRAULT, Martha, R 413-597-2681 226 C martha.r.tetrault@williams.edu
TETREAU, Jerry, C 480-245-7944 13 C jerry.tetreau@ibcs.edu
TETREAU, Jerry, C 480-245-7969 13 C jerry.tetreau@ibcs.edu
TETREAULT, Jules 203-392-5556 85 A tetreaultj4@southernct.edu
TETREAULT, Patricia, L 570-941-7767 413 F patricia.tetreault@scranton.edu
TETTEH, Edem 856-222-9311 289 F etetteh@rcbc.edu
TETZLAFF, Christian 770-533-6966 122 E ctetzlaff@laniertech.edu
TEUTSCH, David 215-576-0800 408 H dteutsch@rrc.edu
TEUTSCHEL, Linda 650-543-3744 51 F linda.teutschel@menlo.edu
TEUTSCHMANN, Susan . 402-461-7725 274 I steutschmann@hastings.edu
TEVAGA, Laura 808-675-3669 128 K laura.tevaga@byuh.edu
TEW, Keith 252-399-6361 335 I ktew@barton.edu
TEW, Mark 325-649-8002 450 H mtew@hputx.edu
TEW, Michael 734-487-3200 229 K michael.tew@emich.edu
TEWART, Terri 505-428-1000 296 B
TEXIDOR, Migdalia 787-250-1912 524 B mtexidor@metro.inter.edu
TEXTER, Lynn, A 215-951-1043 398 F texter@lasalle.edu
TEXTOR, Laurie 920-424-1037 511 B textorl@uwosh.edu
TEYMOURTASH, Janet, L 415-422-5898 72 A janet@usfca.edu
TEZENO, Albert 972-599-3151 446 I atezeno@collin.edu
TEZUKA, Hiroko 574-239-8341 158 M htezuka@hcc-nd.edu
THACHENKARY, Sebastian 414-277-7300 509 A
THACKER, Allison 713-348-4818 455 F invest@rice.edu
THACKER, Karen, S 610-796-8306 389 A karen.thacker@alvernia.edu
THACKER, Linda 314-529-9308 262 B lthacker@maryville.edu
THACKER, Strom 518-388-6102 332 B thackers@union.edu
THACKER, Tiffany 606-218-5953 190 E tiffanythacker@upike.edu
THADANI, Indra 510-464-3516 56 H ithadani@peralta.edu
THADEN, Mark 540-654-2160 486 D mthad2zw@umw.edu
THAKKAR, Monica 212-799-5000 312 B
THAKRAL, Charu 312-413-2899 153 H charuth1@uic.edu
THAMES, Brenda 559-934-2200 73 N brendathames@whccd.edu
THAMES, James, H 214-887-5013 448 G jthames@dts.edu
THAMES, Jamie 478-757-4024 128 E jthames@wesleyancollege.edu
THAMES, Kathleen, A 337-482-6397 197 F kat@louisiana.edu
THANKI, Sandip 702-992-2992 279 B sandip.thanki@nsc.edu
THAO, Maisee 805-898-2927 43 A mthao@fielding.edu
THAO, PaHnia 715-675-3331 514 F thaop@ntc.edu
THAPALIA, Colleen 518-458-5486 305 B thapalit@strose.edu
THARAKUNNEL, Kurian . 708-456-0300 153 E kuriantharakunnel@triton.edu
THARP, Brent 912-478-5444 120 E btharp@georgiasouthern.edu
THARP, Donald 419-289-5777 356 L dtharp2@ashland.edu
THARP, Karen 931-598-1270 436 A kmtharp@sewanee.edu
THARP, Katie 630-844-5449 133 H ktharp@aurora.edu

THOMAS, Jermaine .... 919-497-3400 339 F
jathomas@louisburg.edu
THOMAS, Jerry .... 501-760-4202.. 20 D
jerry.thomas@np.edu
THOMAS, Jim .... 615-966-5828 433 D
jim.thomas@lipscomb.edu
THOMAS, Joe .... 541-888-7399 387 A
jthomas@socc.edu
THOMAS, John .... 661-255-1050.. 29 F
THOMAS, John .... 951-785-2064.. 47 F
jthomas@lasierra.edu
THOMAS, JR., John ...... 918-270-6455 378 I
john.thomas@ptstulsa.edu
THOMAS, John, L .... 863-680-6215 100 D
jthomas@flsouthern.edu
THOMAS, Joseph .... 610-921-7643 388 E
jthomas@albright.edu
THOMAS, Joseph .... 212-752-1530 312 G
joseph.thomas@limcollege.edu
THOMAS, Joseph .... 478-825-6200 119 C
thomasj@fvsu.edu
THOMAS, Joseph .... 803-536-7033 423 G
jthomas@scsu.edu
THOMAS, Julia, M .... 585-385-8015 322 E
jthomas@sjfc.edu
THOMAS, Julie .... 319-296-4275 169 H
julie.thomas@hawkeyecollege.edu
THOMAS, Julie, B .... 252-823-5166 343 A
thomasj@edgecombe.edu
THOMAS, K. B .... 318-487-7389 191 J
kb.thomas@lacollege.edu
THOMAS, Kanet .... 310-506-4264.. 56 D
kanet.thomas@pepperdine.edu
THOMAS, Karen .... 706-649-1854 118 D
kthomas@columbustech.edu
THOMAS, Karen .... 386-312-4037 106 M
karenthomas@sjrstate.edu
THOMAS, Kate .... 269-783-2110 237 B
kthomas12@swmich.edu
THOMAS, Kathryn, S ..... 706-355-5116 115 H
kthomas@athenstech.edu
THOMAS, Katie .... 724-480-3523 392 K
katie.thomas@ccbc.edu
THOMAS, Kay .... 601-484-8689 253 G
kthomas@meridiancc.edu
THOMAS, Kay, M .... 252-398-6226 336 K
thomak@chowan.edu
THOMAS, Kelland .... 201-216-3728 291 G
kelland.thomas@stevens.edu
THOMAS, Kelly .... 608-890-3472 512 D
kelly.thomas@uwex.uwc.edu
THOMAS, Kelvin .... 973-803-5000 288 D
THOMAS, Kelvin .... 973-803-5000 288 D
kthomas@pillar.edu
THOMAS, Kenneth .... 334-229-4200.... 4 A
kthomas@alasu.edu
THOMAS, Kerry .... 601-977-4463 256 B
kthomas@tougaloo.edu
THOMAS, Kevin .... 618-650-2000 152 C
THOMAS,
Kimberly (Jean) .... 567-661-7108 369 A
kimberly_thomas7@owens.edu
THOMAS, Laurita, E ...... 734-647-5574 237 I
laurita@umich.edu
THOMAS, LaVona .... 818-401-1031.. 40 A
lthomas@columbiacollege.edu
THOMAS, Lee, L .... 407-582-2587 113 F
ethomas46@valenciacollege.edu
THOMAS, Linda .... 559-934-2133.. 73 M
lindathomas2@whccd.edu
THOMAS, Linda, V .... 340-693-1324 529 C
lthomas2@uvi.edu
THOMAS, Lisa .... 231-995-1043 235 B
lthomas@nmc.edu
THOMAS, Lyn .... 765-983-1211 157 I
thomaly@earlham.edu
THOMAS, Mandy .... 714-628-7337.. 36 G
mthomas@chapman.edu
THOMAS, Marcia, R .... 312-460-0600 133 C
mthomas@aaart.edu
THOMAS, Maria .... 601-977-7769 256 B
mthomas@tougaloo.edu
THOMAS, Marjorie .... 757-221-2510 479 I
mthomas@wm.edu
THOMAS, Mark .... 863-638-2345 113 I
mark.thomas@warner.edu
THOMAS, Mark .... 608-246-6301 514 A
mthomasjr@madisoncollege.edu
THOMAS, Mary Beth ..... 617-735-9766 214 F
thomasmb@emmanuel.edu
THOMAS, Maurice .... 856-691-8600 285 C
mthomas@cccnj.edu
THOMAS, Maxcie .... 870-575-8000.. 22 E
thomasm@uapb.edu
THOMAS, Melissa .... 503-554-2214 383 C
mthomas@georgefox.edu
THOMAS, Melissa, M .... 843-953-8178 420 C
thomasmm1@cofc.edu
THOMAS, Michael .... 618-985-3741 140 B
thomasm@iecc.edu
THOMAS, Michael .... 216-687-4808 359 L
m.j.thomas24@csuohio.edu
THOMAS, Michael, A ..... 706-880-8911 122 D
mathomas@lagrange.edu
THOMAS, Mike, R .... 618-235-2700 152 E
michael.thomas@swic.edu
THOMAS, Nancy .... 248-204-3208 233 A
nthomas@ltu.edu
THOMAS, Nathan .... 309-677-3140 134 G
nthomas@fsmail.bradley.edu
THOMAS, Nicole, M .... 516-876-3079 327 C
thomasm@oldwestbury.edu
THOMAS, Nishanth .... 973-803-5000 288 D
nthomas@pillar.edu
THOMAS, Patricia, A ..... 202-274-6314.. 93 D
pthomas@udc.edu
THOMAS, Patti .... 425-889-6376 496 E
patti.thomas@northwestu.edu
THOMAS, Paul .... 337-482-2976 197 F
pdt2867@louisiana.edu
THOMAS, Penny .... 614-235-4136 370 M
pthomas@tlsohio.edu
THOMAS, Peter, A .... 508-831-6074 226 E
pthomas@wpi.edu
THOMAS, Philmon .... 404-752-1663 123 F
pthomas@msm.edu
THOMAS, R. Brent .... 620-341-5278 177 B
rthomas2@emporia.edu
THOMAS, Randi .... 513-529-4151 365 I
thomasrm@miamioh.edu
THOMAS,
Randi Malcolm .... 513-529-4151 365 I
randi.thomas@miamioh.edu
THOMAS, Rebecca .... 845-758-7421 298 I
rthomas@bard.edu
THOMAS, Rebecca, J .... 423-968-4861 432 I
rjthomas@king.edu
THOMAS, Renard .... 661-362-3469.. 39 C
renard.thomas@canyons.edu
THOMAS, Renee .... 276-223-4752 490 C
rthomas@wcc.vccs.edu
THOMAS, Richard, W .... 301-295-3013 518 G
charles.thomas@usuhs.edu
THOMAS, Rick .... 414-277-7300 509 A
THOMAS, Rikki .... 757-727-5250 481 E
rikki.thomas@hamptonu.edu
THOMAS, Roberta .... 864-578-8770 423 F
rthomas@sherman.edu
THOMAS, Robin .... 334-872-2533.... 6 H
selmau3@bellsouth.net
THOMAS, Ronald, C ...... 718-262-2332 304 A
rthomas@york.cuny.edu
THOMAS, Rosalyn .... 417-873-6827 259 G
rthomas005@drury.edu
THOMAS, Rosemary, M 304-637-1900 501 H
thomasr@dewv.edu
THOMAS, S. Rebecca .... 413-528-7245 211 B
THOMAS, Sam .... 901-383-6750.. 93 B
THOMAS, Sam .... 303-360-4738.. 79 C
sam.thomas@ccaurora.edu
THOMAS, Samantha .... 214-768-3603 457 B
thomassa@smu.edu
THOMAS, Sandi .... 760-252-2411.. 27 A
sthomas@barstow.edu
THOMAS, Sandra .... 580-745-3172 379 J
sthomas@se.edu
THOMAS, Sarah, E .... 617-496-1295 215 G
sarah_e_thomas@harvard.edu
THOMAS, Scott .... 802-656-3424 476 E
scott.thomas@uvm.edu
THOMAS, Shira .... 850-599-3591 109 A
shira.thomas@famu.edu
THOMAS, Stacey .... 765-455-9391 160 B
stathoma@iuk.edu
THOMAS, Stacy .... 276-739-2401 490 A
sthomas@vhcc.edu
THOMAS, Steve .... 432-685-4520 453 B
steve@midland.edu
THOMAS, Steven, L .... 443-412-2244 204 C
stthomas@harford.edu
THOMAS, Stuart .... 970-339-6232.. 76 E
stuart.thomas@aims.edu
THOMAS, Susan, L .... 660-785-4100 267 K
suethomas@truman.edu
THOMAS, Suzanne .... 843-792-1533 422 C
thomass@musc.edu
THOMAS, Teresa, W ...... 615-898-2603 434 H
teresa.thomas@mtsu.edu
THOMAS, Terri .... 607-436-3388 325 E
terri.thomas@oneonta.edu
THOMAS, Terri .... 502-410-6200 184 H
tthomas@galencollege.edu
THOMAS, Tiffany .... 806-457-4200 449 D
tthomas@fpctx.edu
THOMAS, Timothy .... 315-792-5611 315 I
tthomas@mvcc.edu
THOMAS, Todd .... 423-652-6045 432 I
tthomas@king.edu
THOMAS, Tony .... 718-951-4182 301 E
tony.thomas@brooklyn.cuny.edu
THOMAS, Tony, G .... 229-333-5351 127 H
tgthomas@valdosta.edu
THOMAS, Trajana .... 727-864-8477.. 97 O
thomastn@eckerd.edu
THOMAS, Tyrone .... 843-355-4152 426 G
thomast@wiltech.edu
THOMAS, Valerie, A .... 410-455-3142 208 A
valerie.thomas@umbc.edu
THOMAS, Vincent .... 612-659-6438 245 F
vincent.thomas@minneapolis.edu
THOMAS, Wade .... 607-436-3458 325 E
wade.thomas@oneonta.edu
THOMAS, Wayne .... 423-636-7300 439 C
wthomas@tusculum.edu
THOMAS, Wendell, C .... 502-597-6507 187 E
wendell.thomas@kysu.edu
THOMAS, Wilbert, L ...... 757-727-5356 481 E
bill.thomas@hamptonu.edu
THOMAS-ANDERSON,
Tricia .... 972-860-7396 447 I
triciathomas-anderson@dcccd.edu
THOMAS-DABNEY,
Gayla .... 208-426-1378 131 C
gaylathomasdabne@boisestate.edu
THOMAS-GLOVER,
Linda .... 757-789-1775 488 A
lglover@es.vccs.edu
THOMAS-LARUE, Kim ... 865-694-6681 437 F
kthomas@pstcc.edu
THOMAS-LITTLE, Jill, M 586-445-7576 233 B
littlej@macomb.edu
THOMAS-WILLIAMS,
Regina .... 912-443-5708 125 D
rthomas@savannahtech.edu
THOMASES, Josh .... 212-961-3346 298 H
jthomases@bankstreet.edu
THOMASON, Brian .... 310-506-4497.. 56 D
brian.thomason@pepperdine.edu
THOMASON, Chris .... 870-777-5722.. 23 A
chris.thomason@uacch.edu
THOMASON, Chris .... 205-652-3533.... 9 C
cthomason@uwa.edu
THOMASON, Chris .... 205-652-5467.... 9 C
cthomason@uwa.edu
THOMASON, Donald, B 901-448-5538 440 C
dthomaso@uthsc.edu
THOMASON, Laura .... 478-471-5765 123 A
laura.thomason@mga.edu
THOMASON, Mary .... 817-554-5950 452 G
mthomason@messengercollege.edu
THOMASON, Tommy ..... 713-221-8056 465 C
thomasont@uhd.edu
THOMASSON, Kim .... 859-253-0621 182 K
kthomasson@national-college.edu
THOMASSON, Susan ..... 704-355-3921 336 F
susan.thomasson@carolinas.org
THOMBS, Dennis .... 817-735-5439 466 D
dennis.thombs@unthsc.edu
THOMEN, Karlee .... 217-709-0920 143 C
kthomen@lakeviewcol.edu
THOMES,
Christopher, P .... 850-747-3250 101 J
cthomes@gulfcoast.edu
THOMPSOM, Cathy .... 423-614-8200 432 L
cthompson@leeuniversity.edu
THOMPSON, Adelia, P .. 757-594-8759 479 H
adelia.thompson@cnu.edu
THOMPSON, Al .... 715-346-2481 511 F
al.thompson@uwsp.edu
THOMPSON, Albert .... 757-822-1715 489 H
bthompson@tcc.edu
THOMPSON, Allison, L . 318-342-6917 198 A
althompson@ulm.edu
THOMPSON, Amanda ..... 937-393-3431 370 C
athompson@sscc.edu
THOMPSON, Amber ...... 719-336-1592.. 80 N
amber.thompson@lamarcc.edu
THOMPSON, Amy .... 718-940-5713 322 G
althompson@sjcny.edu
THOMPSON, Andrew, R 319-656-2447 173 C
financial-aid@shilohuniversity.edu
THOMPSON, Andy .... 319-656-2447 173 C
admissions@shilohuniversity.edu
THOMPSON, Ann .... 814-393-1784 405 H
athompson@cuf-inc.org
THOMPSON, Anne .... 912-344-2508 115 D
anne.thompson@armstrong.edu
THOMPSON, Annette ..... 210-283-5091 465 E
athompson@uiwtx.edu
THOMPSON, April .... 607-777-2804 325 A
athompso@binghamton.edu
THOMPSON, Arlene .... 334-229-4406.... 4 A
athompson@alasu.edu
THOMPSON, Ash .... 706-542-2273 127 A
contact@uhs.uga.edu
THOMPSON, Barbara ..... 334-556-2629.... 2 B
bthompson@wallace.edu
THOMPSON, Bart .... 225-578-3231 193 M
bthompson@lsu.edu
THOMPSON, Blake .... 614-297-8468 367 H
thompson.2601@osu.edu
THOMPSON, Blake .... 614-292-6359 367 H
thompson.2061@osu.edu
THOMPSON, Bob .... 405-912-9453 379 A
bthompson@ru.edu
THOMPSON, Bradley ..... 901-751-8453 434 E
bthompson@mabts.edu
THOMPSON, Brenda ...... 512-863-1956 457 I
thompso2@southwestern.edu
THOMPSON, Brian, L .... 904-819-6249.. 98 I
bthompson@flagler.edu
THOMPSON, Caitlyn ...... 662-846-4020 252 H
ccthompson@deltastate.edu
THOMPSON, Carey .... 901-843-3000 435 L
thompsonc@rhodes.edu
THOMPSON, Carleen ..... 334-727-8510.... 7 F
cthompson1@mytu.tuskegee.edu
THOMPSON, Carrie .... 615-966-5250 433 D
carrie.thompson@lipscomb.edu
THOMPSON, Cesarina ... 413-205-3056 210 E
cesarina.thompson@aic.edu
THOMPSON, Chad .... 650-738-7035.. 62 B
thompsonc@smccd.edu
THOMPSON, Charles, G 413-542-2221 210 F
cgthompson@amherst.edu
THOMPSON, Charles, S 423-652-4742 432 I
csthomps@king.edu
THOMPSON, Chaundra . 334-244-3106.... 4 E
cthompson23@aum.edu
THOMPSON, Clare .... 563-884-5611 172 H
clare.thompson@palmer.edu
THOMPSON,
Corinne, B .... 802-656-7898 476 E
corinne.thompson@uvm.edu
THOMPSON, Cory .... 703-323-4220 488 H
cthompson@nvcc.edu
THOMPSON, Courtney .. 910-670-2116 350 B
cthomp40@uncfsu.edu
THOMPSON, Craig .... 208-282-2120 132 B
thomcra2@isu.edu
THOMPSON, Craig, B ... 646-888-6639 313 I
thompsonc@mskcc.org
THOMPSON, Cynthia ..... 217-206-4762 154 A
thompson.cynthia@uis.edu
THOMPSON, Daniel .... 410-287-1027 203 B
dthompson@cecil.edu
THOMPSON, Daniel .... 651-690-6285 249 T
djthompson@stkate.edu
THOMPSON, David .... 256-782-5455.... 6 B
dthompston@jsu.edu
THOMPSON, Dawn, G ... 503-777-7502 386 F
dthomp@reed.edu
THOMPSON, Dawn, M .. 302-831-8939.. 90 I
dawnt@udel.edu
THOMPSON, Debbi, N .. 864-597-4208 426 I
thompsondn@wofford.edu
THOMPSON,
Deborah, L .... 904-819-6302.. 98 I
dthompson@flagler.edu
THOMPSON,
Deborah, L .... 269-337-7318 231 F
debbie.roberts@kzoo.edu
THOMPSON, Desiree ..... 207-454-1021 200 D
dthompson@wccc.me.edu
THOMPSON, Diane .... 559-791-2278.. 47 C
dithomps@portervillecollege.edu
THOMPSON, Dianne ...... 410-617-2901 205 A
dcthompson1@loyola.edu
THOMPSON, Dixie .... 865-974-2475 439 I
dixielee@utk.edu
THOMPSON, Drew .... 914-964-4282 304 D
THOMPSON, Edward, J . 516-323-4600 315 J
ethompson@molloy.edu
THOMPSON, Eileen .... 617-879-2413 226 A
ethompson@wheelock.edu
THOMPSON, Emily .... 816-604-3022 262 J
emily.thompson@mcckc.edu
THOMPSON, Erik .... 202-274-5600.. 93 D
elthompson@udc.edu
THOMPSON, Fannie, G . 301-736-3631 205 B
fannie.thompson@msbbcs.edu
THOMPSON, Formon ..... 928-724-6857.. 12 G
fthompson@dinecollege.edu
THOMPSON, Garrett ...... 480-222-9219.. 16 D
g.thompson@scnm.edu
THOMPSON, Gary .... 701-845-7197 354 E
gary.thompson@vcsu.edu
THOMPSON,
Geoffrey, B .... 507-284-3268 241 F
thompson.geoffrey@mayo.edu

THORNTON, Willie .... 973-443-8929 286 B wthornton@fdu.edu
THOROUGHMAN, David 740-351-3888 369 L dthoroughman@shawnee.edu
THORP, Herbert Holden 314-935-3000 269 L thorp@wustl.edu
THORP, Stephen, M ...... 575-624-8442 295 A thorp@nmmi.edu
THORPE, Abigail .... 718-933-6700 315 K athorpe@monroecollege.edu
THORPE, Alayne .... 269-471-3405 227 B alayne@andrews.edu
THORPE, Alayne .... 269-471-6581 227 B alayne@andrews.edu
THORPE, Charles, E ...... 315-268-6738 304 B cthorpe@clarkson.edu
THORPE, Derrick .... 336-744-0900 336 D derrick.thorpe@carolina.edu
THORPE, Jenn .... 215-248-7118 392 D thorpej@chc.edu
THORPE, Jennifer .... 573-875-7668 258 F jcthorpe1@ccis.edu
THORPE, Lauri, S .... 330-972-6367 371 C lauri@uakron.edu
THORPE, Melissa .... 610-358-4588 402 G thorpem@neumann.edu
THORPE, Samuel .... 918-495-7016 378 H sthorpe@oru.edu
THORPE, Stephen, W .... 610-499-4117 414 F swthorpe@mail.widener.edu
THORPE-YOUNG, Pamela .... 919-530-5402 350 D pamela.young@nccu.edu
THORSEN, MiChelle ...... 425-640-1428 494 E michelle.thorsen@edcc.edu
THORSETT, Stephen .... 503-370-6209 388 D president@willamette.edu
THORSON, Carola .... 218-281-6510 250 G
THORSON, Carola .... 218-299-3162 241 K cthorson@cord.edu
THORSON, Donald .... 531-622-2647 275 F dwthorson@mccneb.edu
THORSON, Eric .... 701-252-3467 355 J eric.thorson@uj.edu
THORSON, Kip .... 507-372-3460 246 C kip.thorson@mnwest.edu
THORSON, Phil .... 320-308-5396 247 E pthorson@stcloudstate.edu
THORSTAD, Todd, M .... 320-222-5572 247 B todd.thorstad@ridgewater.edu
THORTON, Mike .... 325-574-6572 470 N mthornton@wtc.edu
THOTA, Vykuntapathi .... 804-524-5024 491 A vthota@vsu.edu
THRAILKILL, Krystal ...... 479-394-7622.. 23 D kthrailkill@uarichmountain.edu
THRANE, Linda .... 713-348-6281 455 F thrane@rice.edu
THRASH, Carrie .... 740-374-8716 373 G cthrash@wscc.edu
THRASHER, Barbara, S . 434-947-8143 484 B bthrasher@randolphcollege.edu
THRASHER, John, E ...... 850-644-1085 110 A president@fsu.edu
THRASHER, William ...... 971-236-9231 382 F william.thrasher@amr.net
THREATT, Cindy .... 609-896-5101 289 E cthreatt@rider.edu
THREET, Ali .... 435-879-4469 473 B threet@dixie.edu
THREET, Dwight .... 910-695-3831 346 E threetd@sandhills.edu
THRO, William, E .... 859-257-2936 190 B william.thro@uky.edu
THROCKMORTON, Hunter .... 903-510-2586 464 D jthr@tjc.edu
THRONEBERRY, Angela . 575-647-2266 293 J
THROP, Liz .... 301-687-4436 209 A eathroop@frostburg.edu
THRUMAN, Michelle ...... 815-588-3575 139 F michelle.thruman@highland.edu
THRUSH, Claudia .... 570-389-4012 405 E cthrush@bloomu.edu
THUESON, Mike, B .... 208-496-2316 131 D thuesonm@byui.edu
THUL, Travis .... 507-453-2738 245 G tthul@southeastmn.edu
THULIN, Andrew .... 805-756-2161.. 30 K athulin@calpoly.edu
THUM, Dennis, L .... 605-331-6777 429 D dennis.thum@usiouxfalls.edu
THUM, Maureen .... 810-424-5605 238 B mthum@umflint.edu
THUM, Scott, W .... 260-422-5561 159 D swthum@indianatech.edu
THUMM MOORE, Kelly . 303-722-5724.. 80 O kmoore@lincolntech.edu
THUMMA, Scott .... 860-509-9516.. 87 C sthumma@hartsem.edu
THURBER, Darla .... 501-760-4206.. 20 D darla.thurber@np.edu
THURBER, John, P .... 609-984-1155 292 B jthurber@tesu.edu
THURLOW, III, George . 805-893-4799.. 70 B george.thurlow@ia.ucsb.edu
THURLOW, Jessica .... 630-844-7858 133 H jthurlow@aurora.edu
THURMAN, Constance .. 309-341-5251 134 H cthurman@sandburg.edu
THURMAN, Erik, J .... 651-962-6691 251 D erik.thurman@stthomas.edu
THURMAN, Kathy .... 615-898-5792 434 H kathy.thurman@mtsu.edu
THURMAN, Kerri, L .... 217-443-8850 137 B kthurman@dacc.edu
THURMAN, Kevin .... 573-518-2261 263 E kthurman@mineralarea.edu
THURMAN, Quint .... 575-492-2123 297 G qthurman@usw.edu
THURMAN, JR., Robert, D .... 314-773-0083 257 J rthurman@brookesbible.org
THURMAN, Todd, A .... 580-774-3068 380 B todd.thurman@swosu.edu
THURMOND, Tirrani ...... 301-447-5474 206 B thurmond@msmary.edu
THURSTON, Katie, S ..... 256-824-6042.... 8 C katie.thurston@uah.edu
THURSTON, Maureen .... 720-279-8992.. 80 C mthurston@holmesinstitute.edu
THUSWALDNER, Gregor 773-244-5570 147 F gathuswaldner@northpark.edu
THWEATT, Herbert .... 684-699-4834 519 F h.thweatt@amsamoa.edu
THYGERSON, John .... 256-824-2870.... 8 C john.thygerson@uah.edu
THYREEN, Timothy, R ... 724-852-7777 414 B thyreen@waynesburg.edu
TIAPO, Bernadette, S .... 315-267-2341 328 A tiapobs@potsdam.edu
TIBBS, Terri .... 910-672-1696 350 B ttibbs@uncfsu.edu
TIBURZI, Torrey .... 206-221-4661 499 D eoaa@uw.edu
TICCONI, Rhett .... 315-568-3256 317 A rticconi@nycc.edu
TICE, Gene, E .... 270-684-9797 190 F gene.tice@wku.edu
TICE, Jared .... 252-399-6372 335 I jtice@barton.edu
TICE, Laura, L .... 850-263-3261.. 95 F lltice@baptistcollege.edu
TICHENOR, Kristin, R .... 508-831-6720 226 E tichenor@wpi.edu
TICK, Michael .... 315-443-8251 330 H mtick1@syr.edu
TICKLE, Dean .... 402-354-7000 275 P dean.tickle@methodistcollege.edu
TICKLE, Dean .... 402-354-7023 275 P dean.tickle@methodistcollege.edu
TIDWELL, James, H .... 502-597-8104 187 E james.tidwell@kysu.edu
TIDWELL, Michael .... 903-566-7325 468 C president@uttyler.edu
TIEDENS, Lara .... 909-621-8148.. 63 F president@scrippscollege.edu
TIEDT, Penny .... 608-785-6501 510 F ptiedt@uwlax.edu
TIEFEL, Naomi, L .... 414-410-4007 506 F nltiefel@stritch.edu
TIEFENTHALER, Jill .... 719-389-6700.. 77 J president@coloradocollege.edu
TIEMANN, Kathleen .... 978-837-5599 221 G tiemannk@merrimack.edu
TIERCE, Joan .... 662-227-2312 253 C jtierce@holmescc.edu
TIERCE, Meghan .... 559-730-3745.. 39 G meghant@cos.edu
TIERNAN, Bernadette ..... 973-720-2463 292 I tiernanb@wpunj.edu
TIERNEY, Deborah, J ..... 515-961-1699 173 E deb.tierney@simpson.edu
TIERNEY, James .... 609-652-4381 291 H james.tierney@stockton.edu
TIERNEY, Joan .... 815-280-2661 142 A jtierney@jjc.edu
TIERNEY, Kathleen .... 610-526-5364 390 G ktierney01@brynmawr.edu
TIERNO, Mark, J .... 217-479-7025 144 I mark.tierno@mac.edu
TIETJE, Brian .... 805-756-1757.. 30 K btietje@calpoly.edu
TIETJEN, Carl .... 585-275-2008 332 E carl_tietjen@urmc.rochester.edu
TIETJEN, Rick .... 845-451-1380 306 D rick.tietjen@culinary.edu
TIETZ, Leah Jo .... 406-444-6570 271 F ltietz@montana.edu
TIFFIN, Doug .... 972-708-7340 449 I president@gial.edu
TIFFIN, Lisa .... 585-594-6194 321 C tiffin_lisa@roberts.edu
TIFFIN, Phyllis .... 817-598-6246 470 J ptiffin@wc.edu
TIGHE, Peter .... 718-262-2351 304 A ptighe@york.cuny.edu
TIGHE, Roger .... 254-442-5034 445 Q roger.tighe@cisco.edu
TIGNER, Terrell .... 816-604-4717 262 K terrell.tigner@mcckc.edu
TIJERINA, Denise .... 806-742-2984 463 D denise.tijerina@ttu.edu
TIJERINA, Shannon .... 210-434-6711 454 D sytijerina@lake.ollusa.edu
TIKALSKY, Paul, J .... 405-744-5140 377 F paul.tikalsky@okstate.edu
TILDEN, Kevin .... 949-214-3127.. 40 I kevin.tilden@cui.edu
TILDEN, Marsha, A .... 740-368-3163 368 N matilden@owu.edu
TILGHMAN, Patricia, E .. 410-651-6449 208 C petilghman@umes.edu
TILL, Brian, D .... 414-288-7141 508 C brian.till@marquette.edu
TILL, Ellen, P .... 850-474-2080 111 D etill@uwf.edu
TILL, Kimberly, B .... 214-887-5061 448 G ktill@dts.edu
TILLARD, Bill .... 386-506-4433.. 97 I tillarw@daytonastate.edu
TILLBERG, Rebecca .... 310-287-4361.. 49 H tillberw@wlac.edu
TILLERY, Mariann, W .... 336-841-9286 338 E mtillery@highpoint.edu
TILLERY TAYLOR, Carmen .... 562-985-5587.. 32 C carmen.taylor@csulb.edu
TILLETT, Kerry .... 609-771-3139 284 I thompsok@tcnj.edu
TILLEY, Genoria .... 225-216-8292 192 B tilleyg@mybrcc.edu
TILLEY, Jeff .... 979-830-4129 444 D jeff.tilley@blinn.edu
TILLEY, Neil .... 828-689-1306 339 G ntilley@mhu.edu
TILLEY, Scott .... 765-641-4101 156 A setilley@anderson.edu
TILLINGHAST, David ..... 508-531-6140 217 D dtillinghast@bridgew.edu
TILLIPMAN, David, A .... 310-338-7880.. 50 J dtillipm@lmu.edu
TILLIS, Antonio .... 713-743-4002 465 A adtillis@uh.edu
TILLIS, Antonio, D .... 843-953-5770 420 C tillisad@cofc.edu
TILLMAN, Harry, J .... 757-446-7073 480 C tillmahj@evms.edu
TILLMAN, Henry .... 225-771-5497 195 K henry_tillman@sus.edu
TILLMAN, Henry, J .... 225-771-5497 195 J henry_tillman@sus.edu
TILLMAN, Keith .... 815-280-2385 142 A ktillman@jjc.edu
TILLMAN, Kenneth .... 985-545-1500 192 K
TILLMAN, Mark .... 470-578-6565 122 C mtillm@kennesaw.edu
TILLMAN, Rosalyn, P .... 865-329-3101 437 F rtillman@pstcc.edu
TILLMAN, Shalita .... 909-384-8659.. 59 I scunningh@sbccd.cc.ca.us
TILLOTSON, Christina ... 720-496-1370.. 80 C ctillotson@holmesinstitute.edu
TILLOTSON, James, R ... 515-964-0601 169 C tillotsonj@faith.edu
TILLOTSON, Jeanette ..... 607-778-5195 326 C tillotsonjo@sunybroome.edu
TILOT, Mary Jo .... 920-498-5409 514 G maryjo.tilot@nwtc.edu
TILSON, Heather .... 916-691-7144.. 50 G tilsonh@crc.losrios.edu
TILSON, Linda .... 864-656-4542 419 F nilson@clemson.edu
TILSON, Vincent .... 704-233-8011 353 D tilson@wingate.edu
TILSTRA, Doug .... 509-527-2511 499 F
TILTON, Abigail .... 940-898-3326 464 A atilton@twu.edu
TILTON, Brent .... 715-232-2346 512 A tiltonb@uwstout.edu
TILTON, Greg .... 617-558-1788 223 A
TILTON, James .... 401-863-2721 415 K james_tilton@brown.edu
TIMBERLAKE, Gregory ... 419-755-4740 366 E gtimberlake@ncstatecollege.edu
TIMBERLAKE, Todd .... 706-368-5622 116 D ttimberlake@berry.edu
TIMBERMAN, Amy .... 812-877-8006 163 G timberm1@rose-hulman.edu
TIMBY, Tracy .... 215-968-8225 390 I tracy.timby@bucks.edu
TIMES, Kathy .... 850-599-3413 109 A kathy.times@famu.edu
TIMKO, Michael, A .... 724-503-1001 414 A mtimko@washjeff.edu
TIMLIN, Kevin .... 573-986-6863 266 M kjtimlin@semo.edu
TIMLIN, Laynee, H .... 757-455-2137 491 F etimlin@vwu.edu
TIMM, Robert .... 480-212-1704.. 16 B
TIMMANN, David .... 610-436-2984 407 D dtimmann@wcupa.edu
TIMMER, Amy .... 517-371-5140 239 F timmera@cooley.edu
TIMMER, JR., James ..... 616-526-6037 228 B jrt3@calvin.edu
TIMMER, Jeff .... 708-293-4597 153 B jeff.timmer@trnty.edu
TIMMERMAN, Candace . 402-375-7034 276 D catimme1@wsc.edu
TIMMERMAN, David, M 309-457-2325 146 A dtimmerman@monmouthcollege.edu
TIMMERMAN, Melanie .. 740-392-6868 366 B mtimmerman@mvnu.edu
TIMMERMAN, Renee ..... 706-419-1105 118 E renee.timmerman@covenant.edu
TIMMINS, Alan, P .... 503-943-7507 387 H timmins@up.edu
TIMMONS, Charles "Chip" .... 765-361-6054 166 B timmonsc@wabash.edu
TIMMONS, George .... 518-464-8830 308 A gtimmons@excelsior.edu
TIMMONS, Joseph, F ..... 918-631-2710 381 C joseph-timmons@utulsa.edu
TIMMONS, Lora .... 312-935-6800 149 K lotimmons@robertmorris.edu
TIMMONS, Tim .... 708-239-4787 153 B tim.timmons@trnty.edu
TIMPE, Randie, L .... 740-397-9000 366 B randie.timpe@mvnu.edu
TIMPONE, Peter .... 802-828-8554 476 F peter.timpone@vcfa.edu
TIMPSON, Brigham .... 707-654-1788.. 32 E btimpson@csum.edu
TIMS, Michael .... 410-888-9048 205 D mtims@muih.edu
TIMS, Ray, L .... 919-532-5523 347 D rltims@waketech.edu
TIMSON, Joe .... 816-802-3419 261 C jtimson@kcai.edu
TIMUR, Aysegul .... 239-513-1122 101 O atimur@hodges.edu
TINCHER, Steven .... 317-921-4882 161 F stincher@ivytech.edu
TINDALL, Amanda .... 502-213-2255 186 C amanda.tindall@kctcs.edu
TINDALL, Carolyn .... 262-691-5566 515 B ctindall@wctc.edu
TINDALL, David, W .... 206-281-2982 498 B dtindall@spu.edu
TINEBRA, Vincent .... 502-456-6509 189 E vtinebra@sctd.edu
TING, Helen .... 650-520-3451.. 55 I hting@paloaltou.edu
TINGELSTAD, Erik .... 425-352-8277 492 K etingelstad@cascadia.edu
TINGEY, Jeff .... 208-282-4064 132 B tingjeff@isu.edu
TINGEY, Kent, M .... 208-282-3198 132 B tingkent@isu.edu
TINGKANG, Monique .... 808-844-2398 130 E monique4@hawaii.edu
TINGLE, Caroline, D ...... 386-312-4270 106 M carolinetingle@sjrstate.edu
TINGLE, Chris .... 615-366-4449 436 E chris.tingle@tbr.edu
TINGSON-GATUZ, Connie .... 734-432-5883 233 C ctingson-gatuz@madonna.edu
TINKER, Devon .... 509-359-2529 494 D dtinker@ewu.edu
TINKER, Michele .... 419-783-2303 361 A mtinker@defiance.edu
TINKEY, Danya .... 412-536-1029 398 E dayna.tinkey@laroche.edu
TINKEY, Jim .... 412-536-1011 398 E jim.tinkey@laroche.edu
TINKHAM, Shelley .... 413-572-5713 218 F stinkham@westfield.ma.edu

TINLING, Walter 301-295-3083 518 G walter.tinling@usuhs.edu
TINNEMEYER, James 724-852-3271 414 B jtinneme@waynesburg.edu
TINNEY, Tina 985-545-1500 192 K
TINNY, Nicole 352-536-2145 103 B tinnyn@lssc.edu
TINTERA, Judith, E 321-674-6303 99 K jtintera@fit.edu
TINTLE, Nathan 712-722-6264 168 I nathan.tintle@dordt.edu
TIOGANGCO, Sherise 808-934-2710 130 D sherise@hawaii.edu
TIONGSON, Stacie 212-817-7200 302 B stiongson@gc.cuny.edu
TIPMORE, Barbara 270-686-4530 186 F barbara.tipmore@kctcs.edu
TIPPEY, Paul, A 859-858-3581 183 C
TIPPIN, Mark 405-733-7343 379 F mtippin@rose.edu
TIPPING, Christopher 215-489-4190 393 F christopher.tipping@delval.edu
TIPPINS, Kira 559-325-5265 66 F kira.tippins@cloviscollege.edu
TIPTON, Alzada 509-527-5398 500 G tiptona@whitman.edu
TIPTON, Christie 847-578-3276 150 E christie.tipton@rosalindfranklin.edu
TIPTON, David, K 859-985-3728 183 I tiptond@berea.edu
TIPTON, Joellen 936-294-1810 462 F joellen@shsu.edu
TIPTON, Linda 812-749-1237 163 B ltipton@oak.edu
TIPTON, Prisci 956-295-3436 461 F prisci.tipton@tsc.edu
TIPTON, Ryan 575-492-2137 297 G rtipton@usw.edu
TIPTON-ROGERS, Donna 828-837-6810 347 B dtipton@tricountycc.edu
TIRADO, Betty, M 607-436-2081 325 E elizabeth.tirado@oneonta.edu
TIRELLA, Joseph 718-960-8013 302 C joseph.tirella@lehman.cuny.edu
TIREY, Annetta 479-619-4176 20 F atirey@nwacc.edu
TIRONE, Shannon 330-941-3732 374 E stirone@ysu.edu
TIRRELL, Matthew 773-834-2001 153 F mtirrell@uchicago.edu
TISCH, Kate 414-382-6036 506 A kate.tisch@alverno.edu
TISDALE, Bradley 601-923-1600 255 E btisdale@rts.edu
TISDALE, Henry, N 803-535-5412 419 E tisdale@claflin.edu
TISDALE, James 303-556-5553 80 Q kstansb2@msudenver.edu
TISDALE, Jilo 404-270-5305 126 D jtisdale@spelman.edu
TISDALE, Verlie, A 803-535-5433 419 E vtisdale@claflin.edu
TISON, Jennifer, S 606-783-9507 188 C j.tison@moreheadstate.edu
TITERA, Will 619-876-4252 68 C wtitera@usuniversity.edu
TITHERADGE, Inge-Lise 626-584-5464 43 K ititheradge@fuller.edu
TITSWORTH, Scott 740-593-4828 368 G titswort@ohio.edu
TITTLE, Brandon 501-279-4442 19 G bctittle@harding.edu
TITTLE, Katelyn 918-343-6816 379 C ktittle@rsu.edu
TITUS, Charlie 617-287-7895 216 I charlie.titus@umb.edu
TITUS, Elizabeth 575-646-1508 295 B etitus@nmsu.edu
TITUS, Lisa 610-341-1955 394 E ltitus@eastern.edu
TITUS, Sherry 760-744-1150 55 K stitus@palomar.edu
TITUS, Steven, E 319-385-6204 170 J stitus@iw.edu
TITZER, Mark 708-524-6935 137 F mtitzer@dom.edu
TIVEY, Margaret, K 508-289-3362 226 D mktivey@whoi.edu
TIWARI, Suresh 843-661-8101 421 F suresh.tiwari@fdtc.edu
TIZOL, Iris 787-258-1502 521 K itizol@columbiacentral.edu
TJEERDSMA, Mel 660-562-1212 264 I mtjeerdsma@nwmissouri.edu
TKACH, Christopher 281-655-3719 452 C christopher.t.tkach@lonestar.edu
TO, Dai, L 925-631-4364 59 C dlt4@stmarys-ca.edu
TO, Karen 719-389-6144 77 J kto@coloradocollege.edu
TO, Khoi, D 336-285-3048 350 C kdinhto@ncat.edu
TOAL, Erin 607-431-4547 309 E toale@hartwick.edu
TOAY, Taun 845-758-7745 298 I toay@bard.edu
TOBAKOS, Leslie 248-645-3360 229 C ltobakos@cranbrook.edu
TOBEK, Alexandra, C 626-395-6594 29 I atobeck@caltech.edu
TOBEN, Bradley 254-710-1911 444 B brad_toben@baylor.edu
TOBEY, Brooke 215-965-4028 402 C btobey@moore.edu
TOBIA, Valerie 508-286-3911 225 G tobia_valerie@wheatoncollege.edu
TOBIAS, Barbara, A 330-325-6726 366 F btobias@neomed.edu
TOBIAS, David 610-409-3316 413 H dtobias@ursinus.edu
TOBIAS-JOHNSON, Jaynn 708-239-4759 153 B jaynn.tobias-johnson@trnty.edu
TOBIN, Christopher 843-953-3694 420 C tobinc@cofc.edu
TOBIN, Donald 410-706-2041 207 H dtobin@law.umaryland.edu
TOBIN, Doreen, M 570-422-3463 406 A dtobin@esu.edu
TOBIN, Jeanette 712-279-5433 167 B jeanette.tobin@briarcliff.edu
TOBIN, Jim 516-773-5993 519 C jim.tobin@alumni.usmma.edu
TOBIN, John, M 617-373-7666 223 D
TOBIN, Kim 970-491-7530 78 N kim.tobin@colostate.edu
TOBIN, Kristen 617-587-5624 222 G tobink@neco.edu
TOBIN, JR., Walt 803-535-1201 423 B tobinw@octech.edu
TOBIN, William, M 765-658-4156 157 H wtobin@depauw.edu
TOBROCKE, Toby 518-587-2100 329 C toby.tobrocke@esc.edu
TODA, Frank 541-506-6103 382 G ftoda@cgcc.edu
TODARO, Julie 512-223-3071 443 G jtodaro@austincc.edu
TODD, Allysen 614-287-2512 360 C atodd12@cscc.edu
TODD, JR., Billy, R 214-887-5351 448 G btodd@dts.edu
TODD, Brent 618-544-8657 140 D toddb@iecc.edu
TODD, Christine 212-799-5000 312 B
TODD, Dwayne, K 740-368-3135 368 N dktodd@owu.edu
TODD, Greg 248-689-8282 238 F gtodd@walshcollege.edu
TODD, Harold 985-549-2222 197 E
TODD, James 209-575-6060 75 J toddj@mjc.edu
TODD, Jason, L 417-268-6005 257 H jtodd@gobbc.edu
TODD, L. Keith 813-257-3006 113 E
TODD, Lisa 651-523-2021 242 E ltodd01@hamline.edu
TODD, Mark 213-740-2101 72 B mtodd@usc.edu
TODD, Mary, M 716-880-2345 314 F mary.m.todd@medaille.edu
TODD, Nicole 812-855-0454 159 G stodd@iu.edu
TODD, Patricia, A 315-386-7333 329 A toddpa@canton.edu
TODD, Sarah 610-341-5384 394 E stodd@eastern.edu
TODD, Sarah, E 315-379-3975 329 A todds@canton.edu
TODD, Sharon, K 773-442-4670 147 G s-todd4@neiu.edu
TODD, Sharon, O 850-872-3891 101 J stodd@gulfcoast.edu
TODD, Timothy 270-809-4181 188 D ttodd@murraystate.edu
TODD ROSKA, Kiely 651-255-6121 250 D ktoddroska@unitedseminary.edu
TODD SPRAGUE, Diane, C 512-475-6203 467 C dtsprague@austin.utexas.edu
TODERO, Catherine, M 402-280-2004 274 D catherinetodero@creighton.edu
TODESCHI, Kevin 757-631-8101 478 D ktodeschi@atlanticuniv.edu
TODHUNTER, Jody 903-886-5072 459 E jody.todhunter@tamuc.edu
TODISH, Marian 616-632-2959 227 C todismar@aquinas.edu
TODOKI, Gayle 808-373-2849 131 A g.todoki@wmi.edu
TODT, David 641-472-7000 171 J dtodt@mum.edu
TOEBBEN, Martha, A 636-922-8243 265 J mtoebben@stchas.edu
TOENISKOETTER, Richard, J 812-464-1733 165 C rtoeniskoe@usi.edu
TOEPFER, Brandon 760-773-2552 39 D btoepfer@collegeofthedesert.edu
TOEPPNER, Robert 267-341-3335 397 G rtoeppner@holyfamily.edu
TOEWS, Brian, G 215-702-4227 391 C provost@cairn.edu
TOFADE, Toyin 202-806-6100 92 C
TOGLIA, Joan 914-674-7813 314 I jtoglia@mercy.edu
TOGONON, Roselle 691-320-2480 519 G rbtogonon@comfsm.fm
TOHME, Anne 847-317-7125 153 D atohme@tiu.edu
TOKAR, Stephen, A 317-788-4905 164 H tokarsa@uindy.edu
TOKLE, Joanne 208-282-2934 132 B tokljoan@isu.edu
TOKPAH, Christopher 610-359-5106 393 E ctokpah@dccc.edu
TOKUNAGA, Susan 808-984-3380 130 H suetoku@hawaii.edu
TOLAN, Beth 972-883-4037 467 D bnt031000@utdallas.edu
TOLANO-LEVEQUE, Maryann 626-914-8602 37 G mtolano-leveque@citruscollege.edu
TOLBERT, Arnold, J 305-623-1440 99 M arnold.tolbert@fmuniv.edu
TOLBERT, Blair 706-379-3111 128 H betolbert@yhc.edu
TOLBERT, Dawn, C 706-233-7215 125 E dtolbert@shorter.edu
TOLBERT, Jason 870-245-5410 20 G tolbertj@obu.edu
TOLBERT, Michael 848-932-4371 290 C mtolbert@rci.rutgers.edu
TOLBERT, Stephanie 919-497-3213 339 F stolbert@louisburg.edu
TOLBERT, Stephanie, B 919-497-3233 339 F stolbert@louisburg.edu
TOLCHER, Edward, A 989-774-1441 228 E tolch1e@cmich.edu
TOLD, Thomas 303-373-2008 82 F ttold@rvu.edu
TOLEDO, Angelica 323-267-3746 48 L toledoa@elac.edu
TOLEDO, Diana 360-596-5206 498 G dtoledo@spscc.edu
TOLEDO LÓPEZ, Angel, A 787-257-7373 525 Q atoledo@suagm.edu
TOLENTINO, Angelito 510-780-4500 48 D
TOLER, Paul 816-942-8400 257 G paul.toler@avila.edu
TOLER, Terry 405-491-6314 379 K ttoler@snu.edu
TOLER, Whiting 252-940-6334 340 N whiting.toler@beaufortccc.edu
TOLES, Mellanie 937-328-6002 359 H tolesm@clarkstate.edu
TOLES, Sharon, M 313-927-1341 233 D stoles@marygrove.edu
TOLIA, Sam 708-456-0300 153 E stolia@triton.edu
TOLISANO, Joseph 860-723-0125 84 I tolidanoj@ct.edu
TOLIVER, Felicia 270-706-8438 185 H felicia.toliver@kctcs.edu
TOLIVER, Joy 973-877-3000 285 K jtoliver@essex.edu
TOLIVER, Julietta 317-274-4009 160 E jtoliver@iupui.edu
TOLIVER-ROBERTS, Rita, J 215-670-9265 403 D rjtoliver@peirce.edu
TOLL, Ronald, B 239-590-7035 109 C rtoll@fgcu.edu
TOLL, William 765-998-4931 164 C btoll@cse.taylor.edu
TOLLEFSON, Allen 530-752-5418 68 H jatollefson@ucdavis.edu
TOLLEFSON, Deborah 336-334-5702 351 D ddtollef@uncg.edu
TOLLEFSON, Leah 218-879-0813 244 F leah@fdltcc.edu
TOLLESON, Joanne, P 678-341-6640 122 E jtolleso@laniertech.edu
TOLLETT, Suzannne 501-450-1228 19 I tollett@hendrix.edu
TOLLEY, April 540-863-2808 487 I atolley@dslcc.edu
TOLLISON, Scott 662-329-7152 254 F cstollison@muw.edu
TOLLIVER, Beverly 334-386-7103 5 I btolliver@faulkner.edu
TOLLIVER, Joseph 315-229-5311 323 D jtolliver@stlawu.edu
TOLLIVER, Margaret 214-887-5004 448 G mtolliver@dts.edu
TOLLIVER, Ona 903-565-5645 468 C otolliver@uttyler.edu
TOLLIVER, Rex 312-996-7655 153 H jrex@uic.edu
TOLSMA, Robert 303-315-3701 83 D robert.tolsma@ucdenver.edu
TOLSON, Kendra 314-539-5141 266 E ktolson@stlcc.edu
TOLSON, Stephanie 636-922-8512 265 J stolson@stchas.edu
TOLVAISA, Patricia 610-989-1203 413 I ptolvaisa@vfmac.edu
TOM, Larkin 512-863-1578 457 I toml@southwestern.edu
TOM, Marlene, K 415-422-2350 72 A mktom@usfca.edu
TOM, Vicki 510-436-1520 45 G tom@hnu.edu
TOMAN, Janelle 605-773-3455 428 D janelle.toman@sdbor.edu
TOMANEK, Debra, J 520-621-7380 16 J dtomanek@email.arizona.edu
TOMANEK, Jody 308-535-3624 275 I tomanekj@mpcc.edu
TOMANENG, Rowena, M 510-981-2850 56 F rtomaneng@peralta.edu
TOMANIO, David 561-297-3076 109 B tomaniod@fau.edu
TOMAS, Don, L 828-339-4242 346 H d_tomas@southwesterncc.edu
TOMASELLO, Nicole 716-827-4352 331 K tomasellon@trocaire.edu
TOMASIK, Paula, J 304-336-8340 504 E ptomasik@westliberty.edu
TOMASZKIEWICZ, Ed 815-226-3372 150 C etomaszkiewicz@rockford.edu
TOMASZKIEWICZ, Teri 630-844-5511 133 H ttomaszk@aurora.edu
TOMBARGE, Chuck 612-625-8510 250 E tombarge@umn.edu
TOMBARGE, John 540-458-8134 491 G tombargej@wlu.edu
TOMBERLIN, Lisa 229-468-2078 128 G lisa.tomberlin@wiregrass.edu
TOMBES, Robert, M 804-827-5600 487 E rtombes@vcu.edu
TOMBLIN, John, S 316-978-5234 182 F john.tomblin@wichita.edu
TOMBLIN-BYRD, Terri, L 304-710-3472 503 A tomblin@mctc.edu
TOMCZAK, Patricia 217-228-5432 149 B tomczpa@quincy.edu
TOMCZYK, Christie, L 304-243-2304 505 H ctomczyk@wju.edu
TOMEI, Lawrence, A 412-397-6229 409 C tomei@rmu.edu
TOMEK, Beverly 361-570-4145 465 D tomekb@uhv.edu
TOMEK, Deb 402-552-3395 273 K tomekdeb@clarksoncollege.edu
TOMES, Shawn 270-852-3203 187 F stomes@kwc.edu
TOMESCU, Cosmin 212-592-2718 324 A ctomescu@sva.edu
TOMETSKO, Jim 814-824-2279 401 J jtometsko@mercyhurst.edu
TOMFOHRDE, Tammy 423-869-6465 433 C tammy.tomfohrde@lmunet.edu
TOMHAVE, Brian 909-599-5433 48 E btomhave@lifepacific.edu
TOMHAVE, Daniel, P 507-344-7451 240 I dan.tomhave@blc.edu
TOMHAVE, Stacy, J 507-344-7310 240 I stacy.tomhave@blc.edu
TOMLIN, Ashley 478-757-5257 128 E atomlin@wesleyancollege.edu
TOMLIN, Elisabeth 719-587-7746 76 D listomlin@adams.edu
TOMLIN, Kathy, H 540-464-7323 490 E tomlinkh@vmi.edu
TOMLINSON, Ann 323-265-8669 48 L tomlina@elac.edu

TOMLINSON, Bill .... 518-580-5177 324 D
wtomlins@skidmore.edu
TOMLINSON, Elise .... 907-796-6300.. 10 C
emtomlinson@alaska.edu
TOMLINSON, Jan .... 740-364-9510 358 E
jtomlins@cotc.edu
TOMLINSON, Jessica .... 207-699-5016 199 H
jtomlinson@meca.edu
TOMLINSON, Karen .... 706-864-1948 127 B
karen.tomlinson@ung.edu
TOMLINSON, Kathryn .... 229-259-5178 128 G
kathryn.tomlinson@wiregrass.edu
TOMLINSON, Leslie ...... 256-331-8040.... 3 C
ltomlinson@nwscc.edu
TOMLINSON, Rob .... 573-840-9649 267 J
rtomlinson@trcc.edu
TOMLINSON, Tim .... 865-938-8186 431 C
TOMLINSON, Timothy ... 612-455-3420 241 A
tim.tomlinson@bcsmn.edu
TOMLINSON, Virginia ... 509-542-4881 493 G
vtomlinson@columbiabasin.edu
TOMLINSON, Virginia ... 503-883-2575 383 H
vtomlins@linfield.edu
TOMMASINO, Joseph .... 631-665-1600 331 F
tpaphd@aol.com
TOMMEY, Dale .... 870-574-4512.. 21 G
dtommey@sautech.edu
TOMOSER, T. Paul .... 402-280-3026 274 D
ptomoser@creighton.edu
TOMPKINS, Andy .... 785-628-4231 177 D
a_tompkins@fhsu.edu
TOMPKINS,
Anthony (Tony) .... 913-288-7150 178 H
atompkins@kckcc.edu
TOMPKINS, OSB,
John-Mary .... 724-805-2771 410 C
johnmary.tompkins@stvincent.edu
TOMPKINS, Karen .... 978-232-2131 214 G
ktompkin@endicott.edu
TOMPKINS, Michael ...... 845-758-7523 298 I
tompkins@bard.edu
TOMPKINS,
Noreen Chan .... 909-558-1300.. 48 H
ntompkins@llu.edu
TOMPKINS, Patrick .... 757-825-2799 489 G
tompkinsp@tncc.edu
TOMPKINS, Perry .... 417-328-1488 267 A
ptompkins@sbuniv.edu
TOMPKINS, Ricky .... 479-619-4325.. 20 F
rtompkins1@nwacc.edu
TOMPKINS, JR.,
Wendell .... 912-478-2586 120 E
wtompkins@georgiasouthern.edu
TOMPKINS RIVAS, Pilar 323-265-8650.. 48 L
rivaspt@elac.edu
TOMPOS, Betty .... 717-391-6947 411 C
tomposb@stevenscollege.edu
TOMS, David, E .... 401-456-8803 417 A
dtoms@ric.edu
TOMS, Debbie .... 605-718-2958 429 E
deborah.toms@wdt.edu
TOMS, Lisa .... 479-968-0490.. 18 G
ltoms@atu.edu
TOMSIC, Margie .... 253-589-4520 493 F
margie.tomsic@cptc.edu
TOMSON, Kent .... 620-365-5116 174 G
tomson@allencc.edu
TONCHE, JR., Carlos .... 845-569-3249 316 B
carlos.tonche@msmc.edu
TONCIC, JR.,
Andrew, A .... 724-458-2170 396 D
aatoncic@gcc.edu
TONDER, Rick .... 701-777-4270 353 F
rick.tonder@ndus.edu
TONDIGLIA, Dean .... 330-672-3070 363 I
u347@police.kent.edu
TONDREAU, Rebecca .... 401-598-1000 416 C
rtondreau@jwu.edu
TONELLI-BROWN,
Judith .... 508-373-9719 211 F
judith.tonellibrown@becker.edu
TONER, James, D .... 207-778-7494 201 D
james.d.toner@maine.edu
TONEV, Simon, T .... 610-330-5783 399 B
tonevs@lafayette.edu
TONEY, Eileen .... 269-782-1301 237 B
etoney01@swmich.edu
TONEY, Glenn .... 706-245-7226 119 A
gtoney@ec.edu
TONEY, Jeffrey .... 908-737-7030 286 F
jetoney@kean.edu
TONG, Vincent, P .... 203-285-2415.. 85 E
vtong@gwcc.commnet.edu
TONI, Keith .... 508-678-2811 219 C
keith.toni@bristolcc.edu
TONIONI, Renee .... 630-466-7900 155 C
rtonioni@waubonsee.edu
TONKOWICH, Jonathan . 307-332-2930 517 F
jtonkowich@wyomingcatholiccollege.com
TONN, Anke .... 985-448-4633 197 C
anke.tonn@nicholls.edu
TONNESON, Julie, A ..... 612-625-4517 250 E
tonne001@umn.edu
TONNOUS, Tracey .... 740-588-1377 374 G
ttonnous@zanestate.edu
TONONO, Hiroko .... 949-480-4116.. 64 D
htonono@soka.edu
TONREY, Donna, A .... 215-991-3726 398 F
tonrey@lasalle.edu
TOOEY, Mary, J .... 410-706-2693 207 H
mjtooey@hshsl.umaryland.edu
TOOKE-RAWLINS, Dixie 540-231-6059 480 I
dtrawlins@vcom.vt.edu
TOOKE-RAWLINS, Dixie 540-231-4000 480 I
dtrawlins@vcom.vt.edu
TOOLE, Michael .... 419-530-8000 372 F
michael.toole@utoledo.edu
TOOLE, Raymond, L ...... 610-359-5330 393 E
rtoole@dccc.edu
TOOMEY, Marcia, D ...... 978-232-2060 214 G
mtoomey@endicott.edu
TOOMEY, Richard, J ..... 812-237-2510 159 C
richard.toomey@indstate.edu
TOOMEY, Summer .... 312-777-8513 140 G
stoomey@aii.edu
TOOMSEN, Corbett .... 414-847-3335 508 G
corbetttoomsen@miad.edu
TOON, Kellie .... 865-539-7245 437 F
kltoon@pstcc.edu
TOON, Rhonda .... 678-359-5124 121 B
rhondat@gordonstate.edu
TOONE, Danette .... 785-243-1435 176 I
dtoone@cloud.edu
TOONE, Eric .... 919-681-3484 337 C
eric.toone@duke.edu
TOOSI, Mori .... 863-297-1000 105 F
mtoosi@polk.edu
TOOTHMAN, Charles ..... 434-797-8409 487 J
ctoothman@dcc.vccs.edu
TOP, Brent .... 801-422-2736 471 E
tbltop@byu.edu
TOPHAM, Susan .... 619-388-2795.. 60 D
stopham@sdccd.edu
TOPIC, Milos .... 201-761-7827 291 D
mtopic@saintpeters.edu
TOPLIFF, Donald, R ...... 325-942-2165 463 C
don.topliff@angelo.edu
TOPOLSKI, Virginia ...... 201-559-6055 286 C
topolskiv@felician.edu
TOPOREK, Bob .... 847-317-6400 153 D
btopore@tiu.edu
TOPOUSIS, Dana .... 530-752-9841.. 68 H
dtopousis@ucdavis.edu
TOPP, Joelle .... 517-371-5140 239 F
toppj@cooley.edu
TOPPE, Michele .... 503-725-4422 386 D
toppem@pdx.edu
TOPPEN, Ian .... 404-225-4400 115 J
TOPPER, David .... 717-477-1124 407 B
datopp@ship.edu
TOPPER, Maria, L .... 301-447-5211 206 B
mtopper@msmary.edu
TOPPING, Ann, V .... 585-262-1676 315 L
atopping@monroecc.edu
TOPPING, Scott .... 269-782-1249 237 B
stopping@swmich.edu
TOPPLE, Dianne .... 518-828-4181 305 D
dianne.topple@sunycgcc.edu
TOPSHE, Joyce .... 860-685-3757.. 89 F
jtopshe@wesleyan.edu
TOPUZ, John, C .... 832-230-5350 453 K
john@na.edu
TORABI, Mohammed ..... 812-855-1250 159 H
torabi@indiana.edu
TORAIN, Martarash, M .. 919-516-4118 348 G
mmtorain@st-aug.edu
TORBITZKY, Nicole .... 636-949-4651 261 I
ntorbitzky@lindenwood.edu
TORCHIA, Richard .... 215-572-2131 389 D
torchia@arcadia.edu
TORCZON, Virginia .... 757-221-3460 479 I
vjtorc@wm.edu
TORDENTI, Laura .... 860-832-1605.. 84 J
tordentilau@ccsu.edu
TORGERSON, Jane .... 817-257-7940 461 A
j.torgerson@tcu.edu
TORICK, Marc .... 717-396-7833 404 R
mtorick@pcad.edu
TORINO, Frank .... 212-659-7200 312 E
ftorino@tkc.edu
TORKELSON, Rick .... 310-954-4348.. 52 H
rtorkelson@msmu.edu
TORMEY, Jessica .... 608-265-5953 510 B
jtormey@uwsa.edu
TORMEY, Susan .... 315-498-2764 319 G
tormeys@sunyocc.edu
TORNABENE, Meredith .. 315-445-4185 312 F
tornabmm@lemoyne.edu
TORNETTA, Effie .... 510-628-8023.. 48 F
studentservices@lincolnuca.edu
TORNO, Keith .... 616-222-3000 232 F
itdirector@kuyper.edu
TORNQUIST, Kristi .... 605-688-5106 429 B
kristi.tornquist@sdstate.edu
TORNQUIST, Susan .... 541-737-6943 385 F
susan.tornquist@oregonstate.edu
TORNQUIST, Wade .... 734-487-0042 229 K
wtornquis@emich.edu
TORO, Dan .... 714-556-3610.. 72 F
daniel.toro@vanguard.edu
TORO, Elba .... 787-878-5475 523 H
etoro@arecibo.inter.edu
TORO, José .... 787-850-9386 528 B
jose.toro2@upr.edu
TORO, Sofia .... 909-607-0121.. 38 C
sofia_toro@kgi.edu
TORO, Zulma, R .... 860-832-3000.. 84 J
toro@ccsu.edu
TORO-CAMACHO,
Catherine .... 787-993-8870 527 G
catherine.toro@upr.edu
TORO-ZAPATA, Rogelio . 787-264-1912 524 D
rtoro@intersg.edu
TOROK, Kate, M .... 585-385-3801 322 E
ktorok@sjfc.edu
TOROS, Orkun .... 972-883-4735 467 D
ont130030@utdallas.edu
TOROSYAN, Roben .... 508-531-2435 217 D
roben.torosyan@bridgew.edu
TORPEY, Stacey .... 860-701-7787.. 87 F
torpey_s@mitchell.edu
TORPEY GARGANTA,
Kathleen .... 508-678-2811 219 C
kathy.garganta@bristolcc.edu
TORRACA MONDRIGUEZ,
Jose, G .... 787-720-4476 527 A
decanatoacademico@mizpa.edu
TORRANCE, Peggy, L .... 218-299-3339 241 K
torrance@cord.edu
TORRE, Elise .... 716-827-2434 331 K
torree@trocaire.edu
TORRE, Patrick .... 203-932-7224.. 89 D
ptorre@newhaven.edu
TORRE, Scott .... 201-761-7403 291 D
storre@saintpeters.edu
TORRECILHA,
Ramon, S .... 413-572-5201 218 F
president@westfield.ma.edu
TORREGROSSA, Tom ..... 318-342-5353 198 A
torregrossa@ulm.edu
TORRENCE,
Letonia (LT) .... 816-604-5430 262 H
letonia.torrence@mcckc.edu
TORRENCE, Michael ...... 615-230-3350 438 C
michael.torrence@volstate.edu
TORRENS, Michael .... 435-797-0220 473 C
michael.torrens@usu.edu
TORRES, Abigail .... 787-878-5475 523 H
atorres@arecibo.inter.edu
TORRES, Ana, D .... 787-834-9595 526 E
atorres@uaa.edu
TORRES, Angela .... 787-751-1912 524 E
atorres@juris.inter.edu
TORRES, Angelica .... 787-850-0000 528 B
angelica.torres3@upr.edu
TORRES, Anna .... 860-512-3382.. 85 G
atorres1@manchestercc.edu
TORRES, Anna .... 330-941-3675 374 E
amtorres@ysu.edu
TORRES, Arlene .... 914-337-9300 305 F
arlene.torres@concordia-ny.edu
TORRES, Betania .... 863-667-5463 108 G
btorres@seu.edu
TORRES, Cari .... 415-485-9505.. 39 E
ctorres@marin.edu
TORRES, Carmen .... 787-864-2222 524 A
carmen.torres@guayama.inter.edu
TORRES, Carmen .... 787-878-4146 527 F
carmen.torres6@upr.edu
TORRES, Carmen, Z ...... 787-841-2000 525 J
admisiones@pucpr.edu
TORRES, Carmen, Z ...... 787-841-2000 525 J
cl_torres@pucpr.edu
TORRES, Cathy .... 305-809-3250.. 99 L
cathy.torres@fkcc.edu
TORRES, Christine .... 281-998-6150 455 L
christine.torres@sjcd.edu
TORRES, Cristobal .... 305-899-3836.. 95 G
ctorres@barry.edu
TORRES, Damaris .... 787-832-4040 528 C
damaris.torres6@upr.edu
TORRES, Darlin .... 787-250-1912 524 B
djtorres@metro.inter.edu
TORRES, Doris, S .... 787-844-8181 528 E
doris.torres3@upr.edu
TORRES, Eliseo, S .... 505-277-0952 296 H
cheo@unm.edu
TORRES, Elsie, M .... 787-258-1501 521 K
etorres@columbiacentral.edu
TORRES, Enrique .... 219-473-4323 157 A
etorres6@ccsj.edu
TORRES, Evelyn .... 787-882-2065 526 D
directora_planificacion@unitecpr.net
TORRES, Evelyn .... 787-264-1912 524 D
evetorre@intersg.edu
TORRES, Frank .... 623-845-3904.. 13 H
frank.torres@gccaz.edu
TORRES, Gaile .... 406-395-4875 273 B
gtorres@stonechild.edu
TORRES, Geissa .... 787-815-0000 527 F
geissa.torres@upr.edu
TORRES, Gema, C .... 787-279-1912 523 J
gtorres@bayamon.inter.edu
TORRES, Greg .... 325-574-7640 470 N
gtorres@wtc.edu
TORRES, Henry .... 870-972-3033.. 18 A
htorres@astate.edu
TORRES, Iris .... 787-753-6000 522 Q
TORRES, Irma .... 787-857-3600 523 I
itorres@br.inter.edu
TORRES, Joan .... 670-237-6777 520 D
joan.torres@marianas.edu
TORRES, Jorge .... 787-743-3484 525 M
jtorres@sanjuanbautista.edu
TORRES, Jorge, A .... 787-257-7373 525 Q
jotorres@suagm.edu
TORRES, Jose .... 909-382-4021.. 59 G
jtorres@sbccd.cc.ca.us
TORRES, Judith .... 787-786-3030 526 F
jtorres@ucb.edu.pr
TORRES, Justo .... 919-515-8008 350 E
jtorres3@ncsu.edu
TORRES, Kareen .... 954-201-7493.. 96 A
ktorres@broward.edu
TORRES, Lourdes .... 718-518-4151 302 D
ltorres@hostos.cuny.edu
TORRES, Luis .... 787-257-0000 527 H
luis.torres3@upr.edu
TORRES, Maribel .... 787-884-6000 522 Q
mtorres@icprjc.edu
TORRES, Mariela .... 914-654-5568 305 A
martorres@cnr.edu
TORRES, Mary .... 713-221-8611 465 C
torresm@uhd.edu
TORRES, Michael .... 516-323-4834 315 J
mtorres@molloy.edu
TORRES, Migdalia .... 787-288-1118 525 P
TORRES, Miguel .... 787-664-0352 529 A
miguel.torres10@upr.edu
TORRES, Miriam .... 215-489-2267 393 F
miriam.torres@delval.edu
TORRES, Monica .... 574-527-7521 295 E
dacc-vpaa@dacc.nmsu.edu
TORRES, Nancy .... 562-985-4031.. 32 C
nancy.torres@csulb.edu
TORRES, Omar .... 661-362-3135.. 39 C
omar.torres@canyons.edu
TORRES, Rhonda .... 817-598-6212 470 J
rtorres@wc.edu
TORRES, Roamé .... 787-754-2744 528 F
roametorres@gmail.com
TORRES, Roberto, D ...... 312-922-1884 144 H
rtorres@maccormac.edu
TORRES, Robin .... 559-443-8604.. 66 G
robin.torres@fresnocitycollege.edu
TORRES, Rosa del C ..... 787-738-2161 528 A
rosadelc.torres@upr.edu
TORRES, Rosalie .... 818-364-7612.. 49 C
TORRES, Rosie .... 787-832-4040 528 C
servmed@uprm.edu
TORRES, Sireth .... 562-985-2168.. 32 C
sireth.torres@csulb.edu
TORRES, Sulynet .... 787-753-6000 522 Q
storres@icprjc.edu
TORRES, Vanessa .... 210-486-0881 442 A
vtorres120@alamo.edu
TORRES, Vasiliki .... 718-289-5100 301 D
vasiliki.torres@bcc.cuny.edu
TORRES, Wilmarie .... 787-743-4041 521 K
wtorres@columbiacentral.edu
TORRES-BATISTA,
Nelliud .... 787-993-8862 527 G
nelliud.torres@upr.edu
TORRES-BERRIOS,
Lenis .... 787-993-8899 527 G
lenis.torres@upr.edu
TORRES CAMPOS,
Cidhinnia .... 617-989-4366 225 E
torrescamposc@wit.edu

TORRES-DIAZ, Madeline ..... 845-341-4537 319 H madeline.torresdiaz@sunyorange.edu
TORRES-ELLIS, Regina .. 562-902-3343.. 65 D reginatorres@scuhs.edu
TORRES NAVAS, Sylka, V ..... 787-815-0000 527 F sylka.torres@upr.edu
TORRES-PETRILLI, Diana ..... 212-678-8011 312 A dipetrilli@jtsa.edu
TORRES-PETRILLI, Diana ..... 212-678-8014 332 C dipetrilli@uts.columbia.edu
TORRES-RUIZ, Jose ..... 787-840-2575 525 I jtorres@psm.edu
TORREY, William ..... 781-891-2377 212 A wtorrey@bentley.edu
TORREZ, Nasha ..... 505-277-3361 296 H nashatorrez@unm.edu
TORREZ, Veronica ..... 575-492-2146 297 G vtorrez@usw.edu
TORRY, Phyllis ..... 901-435-1555 433 A phyllis_torry@loc.edu
TORTELLI, John ..... 216-373-5308 367 A jtortelli@ndc.edu
TORTI, Sylvia ..... 801-581-7339 472 P sylvia.torti@utah.edu
TORTORA, Michael ..... 203-254-4000.. 87 A mtortora@fairfield.edu
TORTORELLI, Aldo ..... 413-662-5099 218 C aldo.tortorelli@mcla.edu
TOS, Angela ..... 209-384-6192.. 51 G angela.tos@mccd.edu
TOSCANO, James, P ..... 757-822-1015 489 H jtoscano@tcc.edu
TOSCHKOFF, Marisa, L . 989-837-4337 235 C toschkof@northwood.edu
TOSTADO, Francisco ..... 831-646-3043.. 52 G ftostado@mpc.edu
TOSTEN, Lori ..... 717-262-2017 415 B ltosten@wilson.edu
TOSTEN, Rod ..... 717-337-6601 396 A rtosten@gettysburg.edu
TOSTENSON, Wendi ..... 229-217-4142 126 C wtostenson@southernregional.edu
TOSTON, Margaret, Y .... 731-881-7710 440 B mtoston@utm.edu
TOTH, Jason ..... 419-530-1420 372 F jason.toth@utoledo.edu
TOTH, Joseph ..... 609-652-4895 291 H joseph.toth@stockton.edu
TOTINO, Robert ..... 617-989-4325 225 E totinor@wit.edu
TOTTEN, Terri ..... 845-451-1488 306 D terri.totten@culinary.edu
TOTTEN, Willette ..... 870-575-4713.. 22 E tottenw@uapb.edu
TOTTY, Angela ..... 417-255-7225 263 I angelatotty@missouristate.edu
TOUCHSTONE, Lea ..... 601-276-3726 256 A ltouchstone@smcc.edu
TOUHY, Jack ..... 773-298-3540 151 C jtouhy@sxu.edu
TOUNEY, Shawn ..... 270-809-4437 188 D stouney@murraystate.edu
TOUPS, David, L ..... 561-732-4424 107 C dtoups@svdp.edu
TOUPS, Krystal ..... 713-348-6200 455 F kt23@rice.edu
TOURGEMAN, Rachel .... 305-821-3333 100 A rtourgeman@fnu.edu
TOUSSAINT, Jess ..... 630-466-7900 155 C jtoussaint@waubonsee.edu
TOUTANJI, Houssam ..... 269-276-3253 239 E houssam.toutanji@wmich.edu
TOUTGES, Greg, A ..... 218-477-2131 246 B toutges@mnstate.edu
TOUZEAU, Leigh, A ..... 865-539-7013 437 F latouzeau@pstcc.edu
TOVAR, Cindy ..... 312-788-1122 154 I ctovar@vandercook.edu
TOVAR, Esau ..... 310-434-4012.. 62 G tovar_esau@smc.edu
TOVAR, Rina ..... 386-822-7773 111 E rtovar@stetson.edu
TOVARES, Carlos ..... 951-487-3410.. 52 J ctovares@msjc.edu
TOVES, Louise, M ..... 671-735-2995 520 B lmtoves@triton.uog.edu
TOVMASYAN, Anna ..... 818-988-2300.. 53 E atovmas@nccusa.edu
TOW, Sharon ..... 817-554-5950 452 G stow@messengercollege.edu
TOWAL, Patricia ..... 340-692-4187 529 C ptowal@uvi.edu
TOWARD, Ron ..... 301-934-7728 203 D rtoward@csmd.edu
TOWERS, Jason ..... 540-769-8261 477 G jtowers@an.edu
TOWERS, Joel ..... 212-229-8950 316 E towersj@newschool.edu
TOWEY, James ..... 239-280-2511.. 95 C jim.towey@avemaria.edu
TOWLE, Elizabeth ..... 410-857-2241 205 E etowle@mcdaniel.edu
TOWLE, Maggie ..... 612-626-1242 250 E towle002@umn.edu
TOWLE, Thomas ..... 603-271-6484 280 N ttowle@ccsnh.edu
TOWNE, Becky, L ..... 713-942-9505 450 E btowne@hgst.edu
TOWNE, Melanie ..... 541-684-7326 384 H mtowne@nwcu.edu
TOWNER, Mark ..... 978-232-2255 214 G mtowner@endicott.edu
TOWNER, Valmadge, T . 662-621-4130 252 E vtowner@coahomacc.edu
TOWNES, Emilie, M ..... 615-343-3966 440 D emilie.m.townes@vanderbilt.edu
TOWNS, Betsy ..... 336-770-3399 352 B townsb@uncsa.edu
TOWNS, Gail ..... 732-987-2266 286 D gtowns@georgian.edu
TOWNS, Ted ..... 912-583-3280 116 G ttowns@bpc.edu
TOWNSEND, Bill ..... 601-925-3257 254 B btownsen@mc.edu
TOWNSEND, Candace, V ..... 337-475-5635 197 B ctownsend@mcneese.edu
TOWNSEND, Elizabeth, R ..... 336-322-2104 345 D elizabeth.townsend@piedmontcc.edu
TOWNSEND, Gayle ..... 509-527-5183 500 G townsegv@whitman.edu
TOWNSEND, George ..... 913-667-5730 176 F gtownsend@cbts.edu
TOWNSEND, Gregory .... 540-636-2900 479 G gtownsend@christendom.edu
TOWNSEND, Heidi ..... 360-475-7160 496 F htownsend@olympic.edu
TOWNSEND, JoAnn ..... 727-864-8223.. 97 O townsej@eckerd.edu
TOWNSEND, Joshua, W 410-334-2958 210 C jtownsend@worwic.edu
TOWNSEND, Karen ..... 816-802-3302 261 C ktownsend@kcai.edu
TOWNSEND, Kenneth ..... 601-974-1000 254 A kenneth.townsend@millsaps.edu
TOWNSEND, Lori ..... 516-726-5637 519 C townsendl@usmma.edu
TOWNSEND, Lori, A ..... 828-262-2190 349 H townsendla@appstate.edu
TOWNSEND, P, J ..... 434-223-6144 481 D pjtownsend@hsc.edu
TOWNSEND, Roxane ..... 318-675-6812 194 D rtowns1@lsuhsc.edu
TOWNSEND, Sonia ..... 281-998-6150 456 A sonia.townsend@sjcd.edu
TOWNSLEY, Debra ..... 304-243-2233 505 H president@wju.edu
TOWNSLEY, R. Michael . 260-422-5561 159 D rmtownsley@indianatech.edu
TOWSLEY, Scott ..... 507-574-4929 500 I stowsley@yvcc.edu
TOY, Charles ..... 517-371-5140 239 F toyc@cooley.edu
TOY, Matthew ..... 615-248-1380 439 B mtoy@trevecca.edu
TOY, Tasha ..... 706-368-6985 116 D ttoy@berry.edu
TOYA, Gregory ..... 310-660-3504.. 42 C gtoya@elcamino.edu
TOYADA, Maria ..... 617-573-8265 224 I mtoyoda@suffolk.edu
TOYAMA, Gordon, K ..... 503-370-6265 388 D gtoyama@willamette.edu
TOYE-HALE, Bernadette . 270-686-4506 186 F bernie.hale@kctcs.edu
TOYOTA, Linda ..... 713-718-2335 450 D linda.toyota@hccs.edu
TRABKA, Ellen ..... 505-747-2209 295 H etrabka@nnmc.edu
TRACEY, CM, Bernard, M ..... 718-990-6570 322 F traceyb@stjohns.edu
TRACEY, Kevin, J ..... 516-562-3467 307 D
TRACEY, Patrick ..... 401-739-5000 416 D ptracey@neit.edu
TRACEY, Timothy ..... 239-687-5303.. 95 B ttracey@avemarialaw.edu
TRACHIAN, Barkev ..... 336-725-8344 348 C trachianb@piedmontu.edu
TRACHIER, Steven ..... 817-531-4874 463 G strachier@txwes.edu
TRACHTE, Kent, C ..... 570-321-4101 400 G trachte@lycoming.edu
TRACIA, Michele ..... 603-623-0313 281 G micheletracia@nhia.edu
TRACY, Carla, B ..... 309-794-7266 133 G carlatracy@augustana.edu
TRACY, Christine ..... 217-228-5432 149 B tracych@quincyu.edu
TRACY, Danielle ..... 567-661-7401 369 A danielle_tracy@owens.edu
TRACY, David ..... 508-588-9100 220 B
TRACY, II, Edward ..... 313-993-1554 237 F tracyeg@udmercy.edu
TRACY, Emily ..... 315-733-2307 332 F etracy@uscny.edu
TRACY, Emmett ..... 617-746-1990 216 A emmett.tracy@hult.edu
TRACY, Heidi ..... 940-898-3863 464 A htracy@twu.edu
TRACY, James, W ..... 785-864-7298 181 I james.tracy@ku.edu
TRACY, Michael ..... 229-931-2245 120 F michael.tracy@gsw.edu
TRACY, Rhonda ..... 859-256-3100 185 D rhonda.tracy@kctcs.edu
TRACY, Sandra, G ..... 901-843-3800 435 L tracy@rhodes.edu
TRACY, Susan ..... 641-472-7000 171 J stracy@mum.edu
TRACY, Tim, S ..... 859-257-5290 190 B tim.tracy@uky.edu
TRACZYK, Joyce ..... 763-433-1243 243 K joyce.traczyk@anokaramsey.edu
TRAFTON, Nancy, J ..... 812-941-2676 161 A ntrafton@ius.edu
TRAGESER, Susan ..... 540-831-5433 484 A strageser@radford.edu
TRAGNI, Carolyn ..... 845-451-1615 306 D carolyn.tragni@culinary.edu
TRAHAN, Lisa ..... 518-276-8022 321 A trahanl@rpi.edu
TRAHAN, Shelia ..... 409-984-6239 462 E trahansc@lamarpa.edu
TRAIGER, Jeff ..... 816-235-5660 268 D traigerj@umkc.edu
TRAIN, Larissa ..... 480-423-6300.. 14 C larissa.train@scottsdalecc.edu
TRAINA, Joyce ..... 201-327-8877 285 J jtraina@eastwick.edu
TRAINA, Lou ..... 239-489-9215 100 E ltraina@fsw.edu
TRAINA, Samuel ..... 209-228-2857.. 69 C straina@ucmerced.edu
TRAINER, James, F ..... 610-519-7578 413 K james.trainer@villanova.edu
TRAINER, Jason ..... 701-777-3791 353 G jason.trainer@und.edu
TRAINI, Kristen ..... 860-701-5027.. 87 F traini_k@mitchell.edu
TRAINOR, David, P ..... 617-552-3335 212 E david.trainor.2@bc.edu
TRAINOR, Hope ..... 563-425-5264 173 K trainorh@uiu.edu
TRAINOR, Judith, L ..... 508-831-5423 226 E jtrainor@wpi.edu
TRAINOR, Kelly ..... 704-330-4409 342 A kelly.trainor@cpcc.edu
TRAINOR, Timothy, W .. 301-447-5600 206 B president@msmary.edu
TRAKTMAN, Paula ..... 843-876-2405 422 C traktman@musc.edu
TRAME, Mike ..... 217-351-2551 148 H mtrame@parkland.edu
TRAMEL, Caitlin ..... 646-745-8310 299 B ctramel@barnard.edu
TRAMMEL, Sheila ..... 318-257-2235 197 A strammel@latech.edu
TRAMMELL, C. David .... 859-858-3511 183 D david.trammell@asbury.edu
TRAMMELL, Nicole ..... 509-453-0374 497 A nicole.trammell@perrytech.edu
TRAMMELL, Sue ..... 618-985-2828 141 D suetrammel@jalc.edu
TRAMONTANO, William, A ..... 718-951-5864 301 E tramontano@brooklyn.cuny.edu
TRAMONTE, Michael ..... 713-500-3158 468 D michael.tramonte@uth.tmc.edu
TRAMPF, Judith, M ..... 262-472-4672 512 C trampfj@uww.edu
TRAMUTA, Daniel, M .... 716-673-3253 325 C daniel.tramuta@fredonia.edu
TRAMUTA, Daniel, M .... 716-673-3181 325 C daniel.tramuta@fredonia.edu
TRAN, SVD, Bang ..... 563-876-3353 168 H btran@dwci.edu
TRAN, Christy ..... 415-371-0002.. 54 H
TRAN, Deborah ..... 415-565-4740.. 68 I trand@uchastings.edu
TRAN, Hanh ..... 818-778-5959.. 49 G tranh@lavc.edu
TRAN, Hieu ..... 916-686-8484.. 30 H
TRAN, Lena ..... 408-270-6434.. 61 O lena.tran@evc.edu
TRAN, My ..... 425-564-5710 492 G my.tran@bellevuecollege.edu
TRAN, My Linh ..... 773-907-4770 135 K mtran@ccc.edu
TRAN, Nathanael ..... 415-371-0002.. 54 H
TRAN, Sheena ..... 714-628-4836.. 58 B tran_sheena@sccollege.edu
TRAN, Song-Ho ..... 408-274-7900.. 61 O ho.tran@evc.edu
TRAN, Veronique ..... 281-425-6867 451 I vtran@lee.edu
TRANA, Steve ..... 402-486-2502 277 C steve.trana@ucollege.edu
TRANEL, Angela ..... 817-722-1711 451 G angela.tranel@tku.edu
TRANQUADA, Jim ..... 323-259-2990.. 54 E jtranqua@oxy.edu
TRANSUE, Cynthia ..... 215-489-2905 393 F cynthia.transue@delval.edu
TRANSUE, Mary ..... 706-802-5457 119 G mtransue@highlands.edu
TRANT, Meg ..... 617-217-9046 211 D mtrant@baystate.edu
TRANT, Rachel ..... 508-626-4523 218 A rtrant@framingham.edu
TRAPANICK, Benjamin, J ..... 508-626-4505 218 A btrapanick@framingham.edu
TRAPASSO, Kristen, P ... 315-445-4265 312 F trapaskp@lemoyne.edu
TRAPP, Daniel ..... 313-883-8540 236 D trapp.daniel@shms.edu
TRAPP, Lori ..... 734-973-3529 238 G lori@wccnet.edu
TRAPP, Rodney ..... 202-274-5930.. 93 D rodney.trapp@udc.edu
TRASK, III, Tallman ..... 919-684-6600 337 C t3@duke.edu
TRASVINA, John, D ..... 415-422-6304.. 72 A jdtrasvina@usfca.edu
TRAUB, Gilbert ..... 718-409-7385 329 E gtraub@sunymaritime.edu
TRAUBE, David ..... 304-357-0014 502 E davidtraube@ucwv.edu
TRAUBE, Eve ..... 212-410-8006 317 C etraube@nycpm.edu
TRAUGH, Cecelia ..... 212-875-4668 298 H ctraugh@bankstreet.edu
TRAUPMAN-CARR, Carol ..... 610-861-1348 402 D traupman-carrc@moravian.edu
TRAUSCH, Diane, M ..... 312-261-3230 146 G diane.trausch@nl.edu
TRAUTH, Denise, M ..... 512-245-2121 463 A president@txstate.edu
TRAUTMAN, Karla ..... 605-688-4792 429 B karla.trautman@sdstate.edu
TRAUTMAN, Stewart ..... 352-854-2322.. 97 C trautmas@cf.edu
TRAUTWEILER, Courtney ..... 471-667-8181 259 A ctrautweiler@cottey.edu
TRAVENICK, Ron ..... 707-638-5342.. 67 H ron.travenick@tu.edu
TRAVENY, Carol ..... 267-502-2547 390 F carol.traveny@brynathyn.edu
TRAVER, William ..... 518-458-5337 305 B traverw@strose.edu
TRAVERNICHT, Marcia .. 585-475-7292 321 D mstwml@rit.edu
TRAVERS, Lesley ..... 307-532-8202 516 J lesley.travers@ewc.wy.edu
TRAVERS, Nan ..... 518-587-2100 329 C nan.travers@esc.edu
TRAVERSE, Marshall ..... 425-558-0299 494 C mtraverse@digipen.edu
TRAVERSO, Celeste ..... 787-620-2040 520 F ctraverso@aupr.edu
TRAVERSO, Susan ..... 724-589-2100 411 D straverso@thiel.edu
TRAVIS, Antonio ..... 404-756-4023 115 I atravis@atlm.edu
TRAVIS, Artie, L ..... 301-860-3391 208 E atravis@bowiestate.edu
TRAVIS, Brantly, D ..... 270-809-2155 188 D btravis@murraystate.edu
TRAVIS, Brittany ..... 718-779-1499 320 C btravis@plazacollege.edu
TRAVIS, David ..... 262-472-1710 512 C travisd@uww.edu

TRAVIS, Delite ... 714-289-2062 .. 36 G
dtravis@chapman.edu

TRAVIS, Frederick ... 641-472-1209 171 J
ftravis@mum.edu

TRAVIS, Jeremy ... 212-237-8600 302 F
jtravis@jjay.cuny.edu

TRAVIS, Jolene ... 718-636-3471 320 D
jtravi12@pratt.edu

TRAVIS, Rick ... 662-325-2646 254 E
travis@ps.msstate.edu

TRAVIS, Scott ... 616-395-7251 231 D
travis@hope.edu

TRAVIS, Scott ... 719-587-7351 .. 76 D
stravis@adams.edu

TRAVIS, Thomas ... 631-687-1275 322 G
ttravis@sjcny.edu

TRAVIS, Thomas ... 210-292-3272 518 G
thomas.travis@usuhs.edu

TRAVIS-TEAGUE,
Dianne ... 805-969-3626 .. 55 G
dtravis-teague@pacifica.edu

TRAVISANO, Jacqueline 305-284-6100 112 O
jtravisano@miami.edu

TRAWEEK, Vicki ... 817-598-6218 470 J
vtraweek@wc.edu

TRAWICK, Rebecca ... 909-652-6493 .. 36 E
rebecca.trawick@chaffey.edu

TRAXLER, Pete ... 907-796-6139 .. 10 C
pbtraxler@alaska.edu

TRAXLER, Suzanne ... 715-232-2501 512 A
traxlers@uwstout.edu

TRAYLER, Rantz ... 580-349-1362 377 E
rantz.trayler@opsu.edu

TRAYLOR, Angela ... 502-895-3411 188 A
atraylor@lpts.edu

TRAYLOR, Delores ... 256-761-6246 .... 7 D
ddtraylor@talladega.edu

TRAYLOR, Leslie ... 706-880-8645 122 D
ltraylor@lagrange.edu

TRAYNER, Elizabeth ... 415-749-4524 .. 60 G
etrayner@sfai.edu

TRAYNHAM, Earle, C ... 904-620-2700 110 E
traynham@unf.edu

TRAYNOR, Scott ... 303-282-3427 .. 82 G
father.traynor@archden.org

TRAYNOR, Thomas, L ... 937-775-4859 374 B
thomas.traynor@wright.edu

TRAYNUM, Elise ... 415-565-4715 .. 68 I
traynume@uchastings.edu

TRAYSTMAN, Richard ... 303-724-8155 .. 83 D
richard.traystman@ucdenver.edu

TREADAWAY, Glenda, J 828-262-8038 349 H
treadawaygj@appstate.edu

TREADWAY, Carol ... 512-463-3280 462 A
carol.treadway@tsus.edu

TREADWAY, Deborah ... 413-528-7239 211 B

TREADWAY, Nathan ... 567-448-3017 370 K
treadwaynp@tiffin.edu

TREADWELL, Andrew ... 772-462-4804 101 Q
atreadwe@irsc.edu

TREADWELL, IV,
Lawrence ... 305-474-6860 107 B
ltreadwell@stu.edu

TREADWELL, Melinda ... 603-358-2000 283 A

TREAGER-HUBER,
Carey ... 317-921-4882 161 F
ctreagerhuber@ivytech.edu

TREANOR, Ellen ... 435-586-5400 473 A
ellentreanor@suu.edu

TREANOR, William, M .. 202-662-9030 .. 92 B
wtreanor@georgetown.edu

TREAT, Ben ... 207-262-7902 201 C
treatb@maine.edu

TREAT, Cindy ... 817-461-8741 442 L
ctreat@abu.edu

TREAT, Tod ... 253-566-5022 499 A
ttreat@tacomacc.edu

TREBAR, Robert ... 440-375-7115 364 C
rtrebar@lec.edu

TREBER, Karen, A ... 410-548-2330 209 B
katreber@salisbury.edu

TRECARTIN, Ralph ... 269-471-3622 227 B
rtrecartin@andrews.edu

TREDUP, Fred ... 702-895-3201 279 D
fred.tredup@unlv.edu

TREECE, T. Gerald ... 713-646-1776 456 H
gtreece@stcl.edu

TREECE, Todd, A ... 407-582-1819 113 F
ttreece@valenciacollege.edu

TREFF, Shaya ... 732-370-3360 293 F

TREFF, Yisroel Meir ... 732-370-3360 293 F

TREFT, Paul ... 712-274-5221 172 A
treft@morningside.edu

TREFZ, Steve, A ... 605-336-6588 428 B
strefz@sfseminary.edu

TREICHEL, Jeff, D ... 512-232-5114 467 C
jeff.treichel@austin.utexas.edu

TREISCH, Chad ... 630-829-6612 133 I
ctreisch@ben.edu

TREJO, Alanna ... 805-437-2757 .. 31 C
alanna.trejo@csuci.edu

TREJO, Arnold ... 361-593-2174 460 B
arnold.trejo@tamuk.edu

TREJO, Cris ... 956-665-3281 468 A
cristina.trejo@utrgv.edu

TRELISKY, Nina ... 973-720-2305 292 I
treliskyn@wpunj.edu

TRELOAR, Allison, H ... 757-822-1045 489 H
atreloar@tcc.edu

TRELOW, Cheryl, D ... 660-543-4255 268 A
trelow@ucmo.edu

TRELSTAD-PORTER,
James ... 612-330-1686 240 G
porter@augsburg.edu

TREMBLAY, Laura ... 603-428-2333 281 F
ltremblay@nec.edu

TREMBLAY, Michael ... 518-292-7702 321 G
trembm3@sage.edu

TREMBLAY, Pamela ... 706-880-8313 122 D
ptremblay@lagrange.edu

TREMBLAY, Paul ... 212-410-8142 317 C
ptremblay@nycpm.edu

TREMBLAY, Rocky ... 203-285-2185 .. 85 E
rtremblay@gwcc.commnet.edu

TREMBLE, Gayle ... 843-525-8293 424 E
gtremble@tcl.edu

TREME, Jeremy ... 318-487-7386 191 J
jeremy.treme@lacollege.edu

TREMER, Tom ... 315-279-5672 312 D
ttremer@keuka.edu

TREML, Colleen ... 216-397-1886 363 H
ctreml@jcu.edu

TREMOGLIE, Joseph ... 610-341-5930 394 E
jtremogl@eastern.edu

TREMPER, Karen ... 909-599-5433 .. 48 E
ktremper@lifepacific.edu

TRENIS, Neva, S ... 540-654-1688 486 D
ntrenis@umw.edu

TRENKLE, Lizza ... 254-659-7601 450 B
ltrenkle@hillcollege.edu

TRENT, Malissa ... 423-354-2521 437 E
mbtrent@northeaststate.edu

TRENTACOSTE, Peter ... 740-593-4090 368 G
trentaco@ohio.edu

TRENTHEM, Richard ... 901-843-3890 435 L
trenthem@rhodes.edu

TREPAL, Michael, J ... 212-410-8067 317 C
mtrepal@nycpm.edu

TREROTOLA,
Michael, R ... 718-817-3185 308 G
trerotola@fordham.edu

TRESCOTT, Sarah ... 330-244-4943 373 F
strescott@walsh.edu

TRESELER, Kelly ... 781-768-7535 224 A
kelly.treseler@regiscollege.edu

TRESER-OSGOOD,
Nancy ... 909-621-8807 .. 57 C
nancy_treser-osgood@pitzer.edu

TRESOLINI, Carol ... 919-962-3907 351 B
carol_tresolini@unc.edu

TRESS, Samuel, D ... 410-837-5529 209 D
stress@ubalt.edu

TRESSEL, James, P ... 330-941-3101 374 E
jptressel@ysu.edu

TRETHEWEY, Angela ... 530-898-4015 .. 31 D
atrethewey@csuchico.edu

TREUR, Rick ... 616-526-8442 228 B
rickt@calvin.edu

TREUR, Rick, J ... 616-526-8442 228 B
edt4@calvin.edu

TREVAN, Timothy, J ... 818-677-2160 .. 33 B
timothy.j.trevan@csun.edu

TREVENA, Stan ... 209-667-3343 .. 33 F
strevena@csustan.edu

TREVINO, Bonnie ... 830-372-8078 461 D
ytrevino@tlu.edu

TREVINO, Crispin ... 361-593-4036 460 B
crispin.trevino@tamuk.edu

TREVINO, Cynthia ... 806-291-3401 470 I
trevinoc@wbu.edu

TREVINO, Joe ... 425-739-8375 495 F
joe.trevino@lwtech.edu

TREVINO, Leonard ... 412-365-1100 392 C
ltrevino@chatham.edu

TREVINO, Melba ... 956-872-3113 456 G
melbat@southtexascollege.edu

TREVINO, Miguel, A ... 956-326-2283 459 B
mtrevino@tamiu.edu

TREVINO, Monica ... 405-224-3140 381 B
mtrevino@usao.edu

TREVINO, Nicole, G ... 512-428-1037 455 I
nicoleg@stedwards.edu

TREVIS, Michael ... 310-660-3101 .. 42 C
mtrevis@elcamino.edu

TREVISAN, Maurizio ... 212-650-5275 301 F
mtrevisan@ccny.cuny.edu

TREVISAN, Michael ... 509-335-4853 499 G
trevisan@wsu.edu

TREVISANI, Gary ... 267-295-2313 409 B
gtrevisani@walnuthillcollege.edu

TREVNER, Mary ... 660-596-7249 267 E
mtrevner@sfccmo.edu

TREVOR, Tyler ... 406-444-0307 271 F
ttrevor@montana.edu

TREVOR, Wendy ... 518-608-8397 308 A
wtrevor@excelsior.edu

TREWERN, Jay, S ... 978-468-7111 215 E
jtrewern@gcts.edu

TREXLER, Grant ... 805-756-1141 .. 30 K
gtrexler@calpoly.edu

TREXLER, William, H ... 814-886-6421 402 E
wtrexler@mtaloy.edu

TRIAL, Laura ... 512-245-9929 463 A
lt20@txstate.edu

TRIANA, Caridad ... 305-442-6011 105 K

TRIANTIS, Alexander, J . 301-405-2308 207 G
atriantis@rhsmith.umd.edu

TRIBBLE, Abby ... 417-455-5618 259 D
abbytribble@crowder.edu

TRIBBLE, Judy ... 812-535-5255 163 I
jtribble@smwc.edu

TRIBBLE, Scott ... 740-587-8577 361 B
tribbles@denison.edu

TRIBLE, JR., Paul, S ... 757-594-7002 479 H
ptrible@cnu.edu

TRIBLEY, Walter ... 831-646-4060 .. 52 G
wtribley@mpc.edu

TRICARICO, Kerri, J ... 212-998-2913 318 D
kerri.tricarico@nyu.edu

TRICE, Matt ... 229-430-6618 114 J
mtrice@albanytech.edu

TRICHE, Casie ... 985-448-4077 197 C
casie.triche@nicholls.edu

TRICHE, III, Charles, W 337-482-6396 197 F
ctriche@louisiana.edu

TRICOLI, Robin, J ... 423-420-1225 432 E
president@hiwassee.edu

TRIDENTE, Teresa ... 201-216-5176 291 G
teresa.tridente@stevens.edu

TRIER, Vicki ... 541-463-5315 383 F
trierv@lanecc.edu

TRIERWEILER, John, K .. 585-475-2411 321 D
jktcmo@rit.edu

TRIEZENBERG,
Steven, J ... 616-234-5708 238 D

TRIGALO, Ophir ... 312-567-3290 140 I
trigalo@iit.edu

TRIGG, Debra ... 510-659-7376 .. 54 F
dtrigg@ohlone.edu

TRIGG, Janice ... 785-242-5200 180 H
janice.trigg@ottawa.edu

TRIGGER, Kelly ... 301-846-2518 203 H
ktrigger@frederick.edu

TRIGO, José ... 787-834-9595 526 E
jtrigo@uaa.edu

TRIHUS, Meg ... 972-708-7379 449 I
gial_dean_students@gial.edu

TRILLI, Victor ... 316-942-4291 180 D
trilliv@newmanu.edu

TRIMARCHI, Valerie ... 855-444-8076 485 J
vtrimarchi@stratford.edu

TRIMBLE, Ashtin ... 309-796-5143 134 C
trimblea@bhc.edu

TRIMBLE, Carrie ... 217-424-6202 145 J
ctrimble@millikin.edu

TRIMBLE, Karen ... 209-575-7979 .. 75 H
trimblek@yosemite.edu

TRIMBLE, LaDonna ... 661-722-6300 .. 26 C
ltrimble@avc.edu

TRIMBLE, Lisa ... 307-778-1603 516 N
lisatrimble@lcccfoundation.edu

TRIMBLE, Michael, D ... 203-365-7557 .. 88 C
trimblem@sacredheart.edu

TRIMBLE, Michele ... 406-874-6305 271 D
trimblem@milescc.edu

TRIMBOLI, James ... 716-614-6202 318 E
trimboli@niagaracc.suny.edu

TRINIDAD, Angel ... 787-878-5475 523 H
atrinidad@arecibo.inter.edu

TRINIDAD, Vanessa ... 787-884-6000 522 Q
vtrinidad@icprjc.edu

TRINIDAD, Ysabel ... 805-437-8877 .. 31 C
ysabel.trinidad@csuci.edu

TRIOLO, John ... 718-631-6320 303 F
jtriolo@qcc.cuny.edu

TRIPATHI, Satish, K ... 716-645-2901 325 B
president@buffalo.edu

TRIPLET, Jonathan ... 671-735-2260 520 B
triplettj@triton.uog.edu

TRIPLETT, Clark ... 314-392-2221 263 F
triplett@mobap.edu

TRIPLETT, Jill ... 404-270-5677 126 D
jtriple1@spelman.edu

TRIPLETT, Stanley ... 205-929-6470 .... 2 G
striplett@lawsonstate.edu

TRIPODI, Michael, A ... 201-684-6975 289 C
mtripodi@rmapo.edu

TRIPOVICH, Maria ... 409-944-1303 449 F
mtripovi@gc.edu

TRIPP, JR., Arthur ... 706-542-9167 127 A
atripp@uga.edu

TRIPP, Lexie ... 773-291-6313 135 M
ltripp2@ccc.edu

TRIPP, Susan ... 870-612-2053 .. 22 H
susan.tripp@uaccb.edu

TRIPP, Susan ... 315-866-0300 310 A
trippsk@herkimer.edu

TRIPPETT, Brian ... 740-377-2520 370 L
brian.trippett@tsbc.edu

TRIPPETT, William ... 608-263-7727 512 D
william.trippett@uwc.edu

TRIPURANENI,
Vinaya, L ... 909-593-3511 .. 70 E
vtripuraneni@laverne.edu

TRISCIUZZI, Andrea ... 410-778-2800 210 A
atrisciuzzi2@washcoll.edu

TRISEL, Donald, E ... 304-367-4642 504 A
dtrisel@fairmontstate.edu

TRISH, Margaret ... 573-341-4014 269 A
trishm@mst.edu

TRISLER, Chad ... 239-590-7904 109 C
ctrisler@fgcu.edu

TRITLE, Candice ... 717-691-6024 401 L
ctritle@messiah.edu

TRIVEDI, Kalpen ... 413-545-2710 216 H
ktrivedi@ipo.umass.edu

TRIVEDI, Sara ... 310-568-6105 .. 50 J
strivedi@lmu.edu

TRIVEDI, Tushar ... 201-761-6264 291 D
ttrivedi@saintpeters.edu

TRIVUNOVICH, Nick ... 813-974-4903 111 A
ntrivuno@usf.edu

TRNCAK, Stephen ... 281-998-6348 455 K
stephen.trncak@sjcd.edu

TROCHE, Alma ... 305-273-4499 .. 96 N
alma.troche@cbt.edu

TROCHIM, Shawn ... 254-299-8811 452 E
strochim@mclennan.edu

TROCHUCK, Mike ... 708-239-4836 153 B
mike.trochuck@trnty.edu

TROELSTRA, Kate ... 678-466-4300 117 I
katetroelstra@clayton.edu

TROGDON, Joel ... 336-633-0200 345 F

TROGISCH, Colleen ... 845-431-8966 307 A
trogisch@sunydutchess.edu

TROHA, James, A ... 814-641-3101 398 B
trohaj@juniata.edu

TROIANO, Sandra ... 518-381-1422 323 L
toiansm@sunysccc.edu

TROILO, David ... 212-938-5658 328 E
dtroilo@sunyopt.edu

TROISI, Kenneth ... 678-603-0981 126 B
ktroisi@sctech.edu

TROJAN, John ... 908-526-1200 289 D
john.trojan@raritanval.edu

TROKA, Tonya ... 719-598-0200 .. 79 B
ttroka@coloradotech.edu

TROMBELLA, Jerry ... 201-360-4771 286 E
jtrombella@hccc.edu

TROMBLY, Robert ... 480-219-6081 257 A
rtrombly@atsu.edu

TROMP, Marcus ... 800-867-2243 .. 55 A
mtromp@pacific-college.edu

TROMP, Marlene ... 831-459-3885 .. 70 C

TRONCOSO FERNANDEZ,
Keina ... 787-763-6700 522 N
registro@se-pr.edu

TRONTO, Stacie ... 252-328-9025 349 I
trontos@ecu.edu

TROOP, Michael ... 501-882-8920 .. 17 M
mltroop@asub.edu

TROPP, Judybeth ... 619-961-4319 .. 67 F
jtropp@tjsl.edu

TROSPER, Ryan ... 719-384-6886 .. 81 G
ryan.trosper@ojc.edu

TROST, Patricia, G ... 708-709-3637 148 I
ptrost@prairiestate.edu

TROSTLE, Libby ... 410-386-8113 203 A
ltrostle@carrollcc.edu

TROSVIG, Kelli ... 734-763-7109 237 I

TROTMAN, Sarah ... 281-487-1170 460 G
strotman@txchiro.edu

TROTMAN, Yvette ... 612-659-6325 245 F
yvette.trotman@minneapolis.edu

TROTT, Garrett ... 503-375-7016 383 A
gtrott@corban.edu

TROTT CLARK, Beth ... 717-796-5066 401 L
bclark@messiah.edu

TROTTA, Carianne 518-381-1176 323 L trottac@sunysccc.edu
TROTTA, Neil 617-236-8867 215 B ntrotta@fisher.edu
TROTTER, Cheryl 704-461-6714 335 J cheryltrotter@bac.edu
TROTTIER, Sheila 701-477-7862 355 H strottier@tm.edu
TROTTIER, Tracey 413-755-4057 221 B tatrottier@stcc.edu
TROUP, Calvin, L 724-847-6610 395 J
TROUP, James 203-575-8220 86 B jtroup@nv.edu
TROUP, Pat 251-981-3771 5 A pat.troup@columbiasouthern.edu
TROUP, Patrick 612-659-6707 245 F patrick.troup@minneapolis.edu
TROUPE, Bonnie, L 508-565-1069 224 H btroupe@stonehill.edu
TROUSDELL, Roy 218-748-2413 245 D r.trousdell@mesabirange.edu
TROUT, Darice 847-925-6070 139 B dtrout@harpercollege.edu
TROUT, Margaret 530-752-2300 68 H matrout@ucdavis.edu
TROUT, Margaret, A 503-943-7134 387 H troutma@up.edu
TROUT, Sarah 757-340-2121 479 D bursarcvab@centura.edu
TROUTMAN, Linda 850-478-8496 105 D ltroutman@pcci.edu
TROUTMAN, Matthew 301-696-3577 204 D troutman@hood.edu
TROUTMAN, Todd 810-762-0409 234 F todd.troutman@mcc.edu
TROUTT, Amy 618-545-3048 142 D atroutt@kaskaskia.edu
TROUTWINE, Jason 765-973-8444 160 A jtroutwi@iue.edu
TROVALL, Carl 512-313-3000 446 N carl.trovall@concordia.edu
TROWBRIDGE, Christian, A 302-295-1151 91 B christian.a.trowbridge@wilmu.edu
TROWBRIDGE, Cory, D 316-322-0110 257 M cory.trowbridge@calvary.edu
TROXCLAIR, Nikki 702-895-2388 279 D nikki.troxclair@unlv.edu
TROXELL, Jeffrey, E 610-330-5330 399 B troxellj@lafayette.edu
TROY, Dan 805-546-3120 41 C daniel_troy1@cuesta.edu
TROY, Randy, D 260-399-7700 165 B rtroy@sf.edu
TROY, Shawn 989-386-6658 234 B stroy@midmich.edu
TROY SMYSER, Kathleen 717-396-7833 404 R ksmyser@pcad.edu
TROYER, Cindy 903-566-7461 468 C ctroyer@uttyler.edu
TROYER, Mark, R 859-858-3511 183 D mark.troyer@asbury.edu
TROYER, Melissa 402-437-2619 276 K mtroyer@southeast.edu
TRUBACZ, Joseph 727-873-4287 111 B trubacz@usfsp.edu
TRUBE, Julie 248-370-3915 235 J dichtel@oakland.edu
TRUCHAN, Thomas 201-559-6094 286 C
TRUCKENMILLER, Greg 518-736-3622 309 A gtrucken@fmcc.suny.edu
TRUDEAU, Marc, V 805-482-2755 58 M rector@stjohnsem.edu
TRUDEAU, Mary, L 701-788-4754 354 B mary.trudeau@mayvillestate.edu
TRUDEAU, Sara, L 202-526-3799 93 A strudeau@johnpaulii.edu
TRUDEAU, Scott 248-204-3852 233 A strudeau@ltu.edu
TRUDEAU, Skip 765-998-5368 164 C sktrudeau@taylor.edu
TRUDEL, OP, Albert 202-495-3836 92 F registrar@dhs.edu
TRUDNOWSKI, Dan 406-496-4681 272 E dtrudnowski@mtech.edu
TRUDO, Glenn 740-695-9500 357 D gtrudo@belmontcollege.edu
TRUE, Christopher, J 240-895-4317 206 G cjtrue@smcm.edu
TRUE, Don 803-508-7491 418 C trued@atc.edu
TRUE, Elizabeth 207-326-2251 200 F elizabeth.true@mma.edu
TRUE, Robert, L 317-274-4860 160 E rtrue@iupui.edu
TRUE, Shannon, M 850-245-0466 108 Q shannon.mcdermott@flbog.edu
TRUEBLOOD, Dianne 229-931-2354 125 G dtrueblood@southgatech.edu
TRUEBLOOD-GAMBLE, Marjorie 541-552-6459 386 H truebloom@sou.edu
TRUELOVE, Bobby 205-652-3601 9 C bjt@uwa.edu
TRUELOVE, James 620-235-4517 180 J jtruelove@pittstate.edu
TRUEMAN, Carl 215-887-5511 414 D ctrueman@wts.edu
TRUESDELL, Joanne 503-594-3000 382 D joannet@clackamas.edu
TRUESDELL, Nicole 608-363-2120 506 D truesdellnd@beloit.edu
TRUETT, William, M 704-272-5363 346 F wtruett@spcc.edu
TRUFANT, Nicole 207-602-2157 202 A ntrufant@une.edu
TRUHE, Amy 785-227-3380 175 E truheal@bethanylb.edu
TRUHLAR, Mary, R 631-632-8950 325 F mary.truhlar@stonybrookmedicine.edu
TRUITT, Bettie 309-796-5001 134 C truittb@bhc.edu
TRUITT, Jennifer 217-228-5432 149 B truitje@quincy.edu
TRUITT, Terry 765-641-4354 156 A tctruitt@anderson.edu
TRUJILLO, Adrian 415-351-3515 60 G atrujillo@sfai.edu
TRUJILLO, Daniel 914-395-2252 323 K dtrujillo@sarahlawrence.edu
TRUJILLO, George 301-985-7283 208 D george.trujillo@umuc.edu
TRUJILLO, Julie 801-818-8900 472 E julia.tetrick@provocollege.edu
TRUJILLO, Patricia 505-747-5448 295 H patriciatrujillo@nnmc.edu
TRUJILLO, Susan 310-287-4406 49 H trujilos@wlac.edu
TRUJILLO, Tamara 707-638-5317 67 H tamara.trujillo@tu.edu
TRUJILLO, Wendy 661-362-3447 39 C wendy.trujillo@canyons.edu
TRULL, Gregory 503-588-2722 383 A gtrull@corban.edu
TRULL, Jason 334-347-2623 1 J jtrull@escc.edu
TRULOVE, Milyon 503-777-7510 386 F milyon.trulove@reed.edu
TRULSON, Gary 608-743-4526 513 D gtrulson@blackhawk.edu
TRUMAN, Grace, H 561-868-3122 105 A trumang@palmbeachstate.edu
TRUMAN, Kevin, Z 816-235-2399 268 D trumank@umkc.edu
TRUMBLE, Jeremy 315-781-3806 310 C trumble@hws.edu
TRUMBO, Joelle 478-387-4775 120 B jtrumbo@gmc.edu
TRUMBOWER, Jeffrey 802-654-2492 476 A jtrumbower@smcvt.edu
TRUMBULL, William, N 843-953-7416 419 D wtrumbul@citadel.edu
TRUMPOWER, Peter 330-494-6170 370 G ptrumpower@starkstate.edu
TRUONG, Chris 714-564-6043 58 A truong_chris@sac.edu
TRUONG, Lan 650-949-7823 43 F truonglan@foothill.edu
TRUONG, Susan 510-981-2937 56 F struong@peralta.edu
TRUSCHKE, Michael 818-767-0888 75 C michael.truschke@woodbury.edu
TRUSDELL, James 215-341-7700 397 G jtrusdell@holyfamily.edu
TRUSSELL, Jay 828-884-8340 335 L trussellj@brevard.edu
TRUSTY, Denise, M 606-783-2000 188 C dmtrusty@moreheadstate.edu
TRUSTY, Steve 501-760-4240 20 D steve.trusty@np.edu
TRUTNA, Kevin 530-283-0202 42 K ktrutna@frc.edu
TRUXAL, Randy 903-463-8717 449 J truxalr@grayson.edu
TRUXILLO, Betty, D 225-923-2524 191 A director@brsc.edu
TRYON, Howard 318-487-7110 191 J rusty.tryon@lacollege.edu
TRYON, Sandy 515-964-6408 168 A sbtryon@dmacc.edu
TRYTTEN, Julie 563-387-1865 171 I julie.trytten@luther.edu
TRZASKA, Ken, J 620-417-1010 181 E ken.trzaska@sccc.edu
TRZEBIATOWSKI, Brian 773-481-8287 136 B btrzebiatowski@ccc.edu
TRZEPACZ, Angie 270-809-6861 188 D atrzepacz@murraystate.edu
TSABETSAYE, Byron 505-566-3363 296 A tsabetsayeb@sanjuancollege.edu
TSAFFARAS, Peter, H 617-984-1776 223 H ptsaffaras@quincycollege.edu
TSAI, Luke 408-433-2280 37 E
TSAI, Patty 866-323-0233 57 M tsai@providencecc.edu
TSAMBIS, Jane 201-692-2221 286 B tsambis@fdu.edu
TSATSOULIS, Costas 940-565-4300 466 B costas.tsatsoulis@unt.edu
TSCHEPIKOW, Kyle 706-542-0054 127 A kyletsch@uga.edu
TSCHERTER, Andrea, G 812-888-5794 165 E atscherter@vinu.edu
TSCHETTER, Randall, C 605-336-6588 428 B rtschetter@sfseminary.edu
TSCHETTER, Wesley, G 605-688-4920 429 B wesley.tschetter@sdstate.edu
TSCHIRCH, Poldi 713-525-6991 466 J tschirp@stthom.edu
TSE, Waiyi 336-334-4244 351 D waiyi.tse@uncg.edu
TSEGAI, Adiam 716-884-9120 300 C aktsegai@bryantstratton.edu
TSIRELIS, Dawn 513-529-2345 365 I tsireldl@miamioh.edu
TSO, Jay 212-757-1190 298 D jtso@funeraleducation.org
TSOLAKIS, Alkis 225-578-5863 193 M atsolakis@lsu.edu
TSUTSUI, William, M 501-450-1351 19 I tsutsui@hendrix.edu
TUAN, Mia 206-543-2353 499 D mtuan@uw.edu
TUBBS, Alexandra 870-230-5148 19 H tubbsa@hsu.edu
TUBBS, Jeffrey, L 704-406-4253 337 H jtubbs@gardner-webb.edu
TUBBS, Johnathan 870-512-7866 18 D johnathan_tubbs@asun.edu
TUBBS, Richard, E 941-351-4742 106 H rtubbs@ringling.edu
TUBBS, Teresa 910-272-3662 346 A ttubbs@robeson.edu
TUBENS, Sylvia 787-738-2161 528 A sylvia.tubens@upr.edu
TUBMAN, Jonathan, G 202-885-3778 91 C jtubman@american.edu
TUBMAN, Lynn 215-248-7046 392 D tubmanl@chc.edu
TUBRE, Elaine 817-257-5218 461 A e.tubre@tcu.edu
TUCCI, Barbara 505-428-1264 296 B barbara.tucci@sfcc.edu
TUCCI, Teri 708-444-4500 138 F
TUCHINSKY, Adam 207-780-4347 201 H adam.tuchinsky@maine.edu
TUCHMAN, Nancy 773-508-2475 144 D ntuchma@luc.edu
TUCHTEN, Ashley 773-577-8100 137 A
TUCK, Amy 662-325-3221 254 E at25@msstate.edu
TUCK, Martin 740-774-7200 368 G tuck@ohio.edu
TUCKER, Adam 704-847-5600 349 E atucker@ses.edu
TUCKER, Archie 256-372-5230 1 A archie.tucker@aamu.edu
TUCKER, Archie 256-372-8344 1 A archie.tucker@aamu.edu
TUCKER, Arlene, C 337-550-1288 194 B atucker@lsue.edu
TUCKER, Barbara 608-822-2456 515 A btucker@swtc.edu
TUCKER, Bill 601-276-2000 256 A btucker@smcc.edu
TUCKER, Brandon 734-677-5087 238 G brtucker@wccnet.edu
TUCKER, Carey 870-864-7147 21 D ctucker@southark.edu
TUCKER, Carol, M 713-221-8269 465 C tuckerca@uhd.edu
TUCKER, Carolyn 360-416-7679 498 F carolyn.tucker@skagit.edu
TUCKER, Cecelia, T 757-683-5210 483 G ctucker@odu.edu
TUCKER, David, A 812-888-4266 165 E dtucker@vinu.edu
TUCKER, Dawn 919-718-7437 341 H dmtucker@cccc.edu
TUCKER, Dayton 914-251-6915 328 B dayton.tucker@purchase.edu
TUCKER, Destin 731-881-7020 440 B dtucke13@utm.edu
TUCKER, Diane, M 617-358-6887 212 G dtucker@bu.edu
TUCKER, Don, L 612-343-4162 249 E dltucker@northcentral.edu
TUCKER, G.L 218-846-3765 245 H gl.tucker@minnesota.edu
TUCKER, Gardiner 970-351-2001 83 F gardiner.tucker@unco.edu
TUCKER, Gary, R 517-750-1200 237 D garyt@arbor.edu
TUCKER, Geraldine 512-223-7572 443 G gtucker@austincc.edu
TUCKER, Herman, V 254-299-8660 452 E htucker@mclennan.edu
TUCKER, Irene 775-445-4234 279 F irene.tucker@wnc.edu
TUCKER, Jameel 610-526-6092 396 H jtucker@harcum.edu
TUCKER, James 518-327-6286 320 A jtucker@paulsmiths.edu
TUCKER, Jean 251-460-6294 9 B jtucker@southalabama.edu
TUCKER, John 501-760-4229 20 D john.tucker@np.edu
TUCKER, John, D 619-298-1829 65 G jtucker@ssu.edu
TUCKER, Karen 630-752-5060 155 F karen.tucker@wheaton.edu
TUCKER, Ken 205-652-3527 9 C ktucker@uwa.edu
TUCKER, Mark 336-386-3217 347 A tuckerm@surry.edu
TUCKER, Mark 513-244-8102 359 E mark.tucker@ccuniversity.edu
TUCKER, Mary, E 520-621-9438 16 J mtucker@email.arizona.edu
TUCKER, Melanie, V 865-981-8111 433 F melanie.tucker@maryvillecollege.edu
TUCKER, Michael 765-641-4295 156 A matucker@anderson.edu
TUCKER, Murl 714-547-9625 28 J mtucker@calcoast.edu
TUCKER, Nate 423-473-1190 432 L ntucker@leeuniversity.edu
TUCKER, Ned 402-826-8601 274 E ned.tucker@doane.edu
TUCKER, Patrick 860-832-1786 84 J ptucker@ccsu.edu
TUCKER, Richard 504-486-7411 198 D rtucker@xula.edu
TUCKER, Robert 325-670-1498 450 A robert.tucker@hsutx.edu
TUCKER, Sandra 386-481-2106 95 J tuckers@cookman.edu
TUCKER, Sarah 304-558-0265 503 N tucker@wvctcs.org
TUCKER, Sarah, A 304-558-0265 502 I tucker@wvctcs.org
TUCKER, Sheryl 405-744-6368 377 F sheryl.tucker@okstate.edu
TUCKER, Stacy 913-288-7239 178 H stucker@kckcc.edu
TUCKER, Tom, T 304-367-4110 504 A tom.tucker@fairmontstate.edu
TUCKER, Tommy 870-307-7324 20 C thomas.tucker@lyon.edu
TUCKER, Traci 214-329-4447 443 J traci.tucker@bgu.edu
TUCKER, William 510-587-6037 68 F william.tucker@ucop.edu
TUCKER, William, T 631-451-4760 330 B tuckerw@sunysuffolk.edu
TUDELA, Virginia, C 671-735-5590 519 H virginia.tudela@guamcc.edu
TUDGE, Christopher 202-885-2033 91 C ctudge@american.edu
TUDOR, Amanda 859-985-3316 183 I tudora@berea.edu
TUDOR, Deborah 618-453-7708 152 B dtudor@siu.edu
TUDOR, Donna, K 615-248-7703 439 B dtudor@trevecca.edu
TUDOR, Gail 207-941-7039 199 B tudorg@husson.edu
TUDOR, Jarrod 330-972-8940 371 C grt2@uakron.edu
TUDOR, Jarrod 330-684-8940 371 D
TUDOR, Jeremiah 502-863-8727 184 I jeremiah_tudor@georgetowncollege.edu
TUDOR, Lisa 239-489-9350 100 E ltudor@fsw.edu
TUDRYN, Jonathan 413-755-4420 221 B jtudryn@stcc.edu
TUEDIO, James, A 209-667-3531 33 F jtuedio@csustan.edu

TUELL, David 865-471-2020 430 H dtuell@cn.edu
TUELLER, Steven 808-675-3935 128 K steve.tueller@byuh.edu
TUESCHER-GILLE, Heidi 608-342-1125 511 D tuescheh@uwplatt.edu
TUFANO, Joseph, J 718-990-5800 322 F tufanoj@stjohns.edu
TUFAU-AFRIYIE, Michelle 508-854-7568 220 G mtufau@qcc.mass.edu
TUFEL, Peter 212-686-9244 298 C
TUGGLE, Joseph 601-477-4277 253 F joseph.tuggle@jcjc.edu
TUIA, Jennifer 360-596-5369 498 G jtuia@spscc.edu
TUITASI, Michael 310-434-4389 62 G tuitasi_michael@smc.edu
TUITASI, Sifagatogo 684-699-9155 519 F s.tuitasi@amsamoa.edu
TUITE, Jayne 724-222-5330 403 E jtuite@penncommercial.edu
TUITE, Kathleen 973-618-3534 284 D ktuite@caldwell.edu
TUITE, Maria 408-924-1200 34 D
TUITT, Frank 303-871-2591 83 E ftuitt@du.edu
TULAK, William 318-487-5443 192 F williamtulak@cltcc.edu
TULINO, Michael 520-206-4625 15 L mtulino@pima.edu
TULLEY, Nickolas, B 240-895-4336 206 G nbtulley@smcm.edu
TULLEY, Ronald 419-434-4445 372 B rtulley@findlay.edu
TULLIER, Michael 334-727-8011 7 F mtullier@tuskegee.edu
TULLIER, Michelle 404-385-7344 120 A michelle.tullier@gatech.edu
TULLIO, Ann 718-631-6215 303 F atullio@qcc.cuny.edu
TULLOCH, Helen (Meg) 202-685-3948 518 B tullochh@ndu.edu
TULLT, Marci 888-772-6077 98 F
TULLY, Greg, J 815-772-7218 146 D gtully@morrisontech.edu
TULLY, John, J 610-566-1776 415 A jtully@williamson.edu
TULLY-DARTEZ, Stephanie 870-862-8131 21 D stully-dartez@southark.edu
TUMEO, Mark, A 904-620-1350 110 E m.tumeo@unf.edu
TUMEO, Michael, D 214-768-2808 457 B mtumeo@smu.edu
TUMEY, Terry 909-607-3562 38 A terry.tumey@cms.claremont.edu
TUMIEL, John 207-221-4628 202 A jtumiel@une.edu
TUMLINSON, Karen 785-833-4335 179 C karen.tumlinson@kwu.edu
TUMLINSON, Karen, L 520-621-2516 16 J kdenman@email.arizona.edu
TUMMINO, Pauline 718-990-6106 322 F tumminop@stjohns.edu
TUMMOLO, Paul 212-353-4100 306 A pault@cooper.edu
TUNE, Kathie 434-791-7106 478 E ktune@averett.edu
TUNG, Lisa 617-879-7335 218 B ltung@massart.edu
TUNGSETH, Margaret 651-523-2203 242 E mtungseth01@hamline.edu
TUNNING, Michael 563-884-5865 172 H michael.tunning@palmer.edu
TUNSTALL, Denise, S 804-523-5029 488 C dtunstall@reynolds.edu
TUNSTILL, Hilda 931-393-1573 437 C htunstill@mscc.edu
TUOMEY, Lianne, M 802-656-2027 476 E lianne.tuomey@uvm.edu
TUPA, Dana 904-256-7653 102 B
TUPALA, Kay 920-498-5482 514 G kay.tupala@nwtc.edu
TUPPER, Barb 319-399-8662 167 F btupper@coe.edu
TUPPER, Rick 605-274-4499 426 K rick.tupper@augie.edu
TUPUOLA, Tafaimamao 684-699-9155 519 F t.tupuola@amsamoa.edu
TURANO, Rosemary 617-964-1100 210 G rturano@ants.edu
TURANSKY, Joshua 909-794-1084 40 B jturansky@cccollege.edu
TURANSKY, June, S 302-857-1126 90 F june.turansky@dtcc.edu
TURAY, Abdul, M 502-597-6916 187 E abdul.turay@kysu.edu
TURBEVILLE, Donna 910-642-7141 346 G donna.turbeville@sccnc.edu
TURBEVILLE, John 315-470-6660 328 D jturbev@esf.edu
TURBEVILLE, Stanley 910-296-2416 344 B sturbeville@jamessprunt.edu
TURBIDE, Gerard 607-274-3124 311 D gturbide@ithaca.edu
TURBIVILLE, Alice 610-957-6040 410 I aturbiv1@swarthmore.edu
TURCIOS, Mirna 661-726-1911 68 E mirna.turcios@uav.edu
TURCOTTE, Colleen, D 401-825-2159 416 B cdturcotte@ccri.edu
TURCOTTE, Jim 601-925-3809 254 B turcotte@mc.edu
TURCOTTE, Kristen 508-286-3561 225 G turcotte_kristen@wheatoncollege.edu
TURCOTTE, Paul 254-501-5817 459 D paul.turcotte@tamuct.edu
TUREK, John, G 714-879-3901 45 I jgturek@hiu.edu
TUREK, Lara 314-968-5944 269 N tureklar@webster.edu
TURELL, Susan, C 570-348-6232 401 B sturell@marywood.edu
TUREN, Chris 323-668-7555 25 G
TURGEON, Marla 309-649-6603 152 G marla.turgeon@src.edu
TURGEON, Paul 714-556-3610 72 F paul.turgeon@vanguard.edu
TURGEON, Pennie 508-421-3813 213 C pturgeon@clarku.edu
TURICO, Michael 602-538-9396 10 E
TURK, David 903-813-2408 443 F dturk@austincollege.edu
TURK, David, F 845-675-4422 319 C david.turk@nyack.edu
TURK, Don 815-753-1088 147 H dtuck@niu.edu
TURK, Laura 540-831-5248 484 A lturk@radford.edu
TURK, Michael, W 334-833-4322 5 M mturk@hawks.huntingdon.edu
TURK, Thomas 719-628-2839 36 G turk@chapman.edu
TURK FIECOAT, Heather 775-682-8081 279 E hturk@unr.edu
TURKS, Stacie 209-946-2225 70 F sturks@pacific.edu
TURLETES, Christopher 907-786-1110 10 A cmturletes@alaska.edu
TURLEY, Alicestyne 859-985-3783 183 I turlleya@berea.edu
TURLEY-AMES, Kandi 208-282-3053 132 B turlkand@isu.edu
TURLINGTON, Ashley 410-778-7710 210 A aturlington2@washcoll.edu
TURLINGTON, Lisa 910-592-8081 346 D lturlington@sampsoncc.edu
TURMAN, Paul 605-773-3455 428 D paul.turman@sdbor.edu
TURMAN, Thad 918-444-2170 376 G turman@nsuok.edu
TURNAGE, Craig, A 936-468-3407 458 A turnagecraig@sfasu.edu
TURNBO, Doreen, B 302-295-1192 91 B doreen.b.turnbo@wilmu.edu
TURNER, Amanda 708-456-0300 153 E amandaturner@triton.edu
TURNER, Andrea 812-749-1248 163 B aturner@oak.edu
TURNER, Ann 315-279-5615 312 D aturner@keuka.edu
TURNER, Anthony 312-329-2022 146 B anthony.turner@moody.edu
TURNER, B, P 334-387-3877 4 B businessoffice@amridgeuniversity.edu
TURNER, Barbara, J 870-759-4112 23 K bturner@wbcoll.edu
TURNER, Barry 912-681-2758 123 J bturner@ogeecheetech.edu
TURNER, Bethany 864-622-6029 418 E bturner@andersonuniversity.edu
TURNER, Carolyn 870-946-3506 22 G
TURNER, Casey 215-972-7600 404 Q
TURNER, Christine 503-699-3381 384 B cturner@marylhurst.edu
TURNER, Dale 205-802-1594 5 D dale.turner@vc.edu
TURNER, Dale 301-937-8448 202 H dale.turner@brightwood.edu
TURNER, Darron 817-257-5566 461 A d.turner@tcu.edu
TURNER, David 734-487-9733 229 K dturne27@emich.edu
TURNER, Deb 419-358-3343 357 E turnerd@bluffton.edu
TURNER, Debra 706-737-1431 116 B debturner@augusta.edu
TURNER, Debra 304-384-5338 503 P turner@concord.edu
TURNER, Donna, A 252-246-1240 347 H daturner@wilsoncc.edu
TURNER, Eric 870-248-4000 18 J eric.turner@blackrivertech.edu
TURNER, Eric 617-243-2071 216 C eturner@lasell.edu
TURNER, Fran 205-391-2663 3 E fturner@sheltonstate.edu
TURNER, J. Leigh 979-845-7725 459 C jl-turner@tamu.edu
TURNER, James 601-318-6610 256 I jturner@wmcarey.edu
TURNER, James 607-844-8222 331 D turnerj@tompkinscortland.edu
TURNER, Janet, K 503-943-7311 387 H turnerj@up.edu
TURNER, Janice 303-765-3109 80 G jturner@iliff.edu
TURNER, Jere 603-206-8165 280 L jturner@ccsnh.edu
TURNER, Jodi 704-687-0032 351 C jodturne@uncc.edu
TURNER, III, Joel, L 936-468-6315 458 A turnertrey@sfasu.edu
TURNER, John 318-345-9271 192 J johnturner@ladelta.edu
TURNER, Joseph 239-489-9015 100 E joseph.turner@fsw.edu
TURNER, Joseph 252-335-0821 342 D joseph_turner@albemarle.edu
TURNER, Julie, D 616-234-5708 238 D
TURNER, June 760-921-5558 55 J june.turner@paloverde.edu
TURNER, Kandy 610-499-4498 414 F kkturner@widener.edu
TURNER, Kara 443-885-3126 206 A kara.turner@morgan.edu
TURNER, Keith 218-733-6940 245 C keith.turner@lsc.edu
TURNER, Kim 806-742-0012 463 B
TURNER, Larry 704-355-7577 336 F larry.turner@carolinashealthcare.org
TURNER, Laura 734-995-7331 229 A laura.turner@cuaa.edu
TURNER, Lauren 978-934-1804 217 B lauren_turner@uml.edu
TURNER, Laurie, L 253-535-7361 496 G turnerll@plu.edu
TURNER, Leslie 561-803-2473 104 I leslie_turner@pba.edu
TURNER, Louise 406-586-3585 271 E louise.turner@montanabiblecollege.edu
TURNER, Marcia 239-513-1122 101 O mturner@hodges.edu
TURNER, Marietta 217-351-2505 148 H mturner@parkland.edu
TURNER, Mark, P 402-280-4073 274 D markturner@creighton.edu
TURNER, Marvel, A 601-979-5848 253 E marvel.a.turner@jsums.edu
TURNER, Mary Donovan 510-849-8209 55 D mdturner@psr.edu
TURNER, Matt 304-558-4016 503 N matt.turner@wvhepc.edu
TURNER, Michael, C 334-387-3877 4 B mcturner@amridgeuniversity.edu
TURNER, Natalie, T 502-597-6373 187 E natalie.turner@kysu.edu
TURNER, Patricia, A 310-206-3961 69 B pturner@college.ucla.edu
TURNER, Patrick 406-447-6937 271 I patrick.turner@umhelena.edu
TURNER, Patrick 734-462-4400 236 H pturner@schoolcraft.edu
TURNER, Phyllis 903-233-4170 452 A phyllisturner@letu.edu
TURNER, Preston 731-425-2619 437 B pturner@jscc.edu
TURNER, R. Elaine 352-392-1961 110 D returner@ufl.edu
TURNER, R. Gerald 214-768-3300 457 B mjj@smu.edu
TURNER, Rachel 305-626-3605 99 M raturner@fmuniv.edu
TURNER, Rebecca 727-341-3241 107 A turner.rebecca@spcollege.edu
TURNER, Rebecca 812-941-2547 161 A rebeturn@ius.edu
TURNER, Rebecca, E 256-782-5485 6 B bturner@jsu.edu
TURNER, Rebecca, O 256-782-5540 6 B rturner@jsu.edu
TURNER, Rich 904-632-5112 100 F rich.turner@fscj.edu
TURNER, Rick 714-997-6658 36 G raturner@chapman.edu
TURNER, Robert 910-362-7050 341 E wrturner72@cfcc.edu
TURNER, Robert, L 757-823-8670 483 F rlturner@nsu.edu
TURNER, Ronne, P 314-935-5685 269 L ronne.turner@wustl.edu
TURNER, Sandra 212-242-5499 331 J sandra.turner@tsca.edu
TURNER, Sarah 304-384-5348 503 P slturner@concord.edu
TURNER, Savonda 706-754-7870 123 G savonda@northgatech.edu
TURNER, Sharisse 850-201-8582 112 C turners@tcc.fl.edu
TURNER, Sharma 706-232-5374 116 D
TURNER, Steve 219-989-2232 163 E sturner@pnw.edu
TURNER, Steve 918-444-2000 376 G turner@nsuok.edu
TURNER, Susan 812-535-5143 163 I sturner3@smwc.edu
TURNER, Susan 203-932-7478 89 D sturner@newhaven.edu
TURNER, Sylvia 209-953-2119 67 C syturner@sjcoe.net
TURNER, Teriann 870-512-7754 18 D teriann_turner@asun.edu
TURNER, Timothy 864-231-2000 418 E tturner@andersonuniversity.edu
TURNER, Toi 830-372-8019 461 D tturner@tlu.edu
TURNER, Tommy 256-782-5180 6 B tturner@jsu.edu
TURNER, Tremelle 205-247-8151 7 C tturner@stillman.edu
TURNER, Wilson 304-243-2090 505 H wturner@wju.edu
TURNER, Windell 276-964-7342 489 F windell.turner@sw.edu
TURNER, Zoa Ann 972-524-3341 457 H
TURNER-FREDERICK, Athena 718-420-4212 333 D athena.turner-frederick@wagner.edu
TURNER-METCALF, Phyllis 936-261-3601 458 F pmmetcalf@pvamu.edu
TURNER-WATTS, Sheryl 864-503-5490 425 H sturner-watts@uscupstate.edu
TURNIPSEED, Brandi 208-732-6378 131 I bturnipseed@csi.edu
TURNIS, Jane 719-389-6603 77 J jturnis@coloradocollege.edu
TURNOCK, Madeline 503-493-8550 382 I mturnock@cu-portland.edu
TURNQUIST, David, C 303-724-1100 83 D david.turnquist@ucdenver.edu
TURNQUIST, Sandra 906-487-7240 230 B sandra.turnquist@finlandia.edu
TURNTINE, John 817-598-6482 470 J jturntine@wc.edu
TUROCY, Paula, S 412-396-5303 394 D turocyp@duq.edu
TURPEN, James 402-559-4288 277 H jturpen@unmc.edu
TURPIN, Craig 502-213-2110 186 C craig.turpin@kctcs.edu
TURPIN, John, C 336-841-9000 338 E jturpin@highpoint.edu
TURPIN, Michael, H 903-983-8207 451 F mturpin@kilgore.edu
TURPIN, Randy 614-837-4088 373 C turpinr@valorcollege.edu
TURPIN, Tyler 715-634-4790 507 J tturpin@lco.edu
TURRENTINE, Michael 304-336-8152 504 E mturrent@westliberty.edu
TURRIETTA, Anthony 210-434-6711 454 D aturrietta@lake.ollusa.edu
TURTELTAUB, Rhea 310-794-5567 69 B rheat@support.ucla.edu
TUSCHAK, Mark 830-792-7215 456 D mctuschak@schreiner.edu
TUSCHEN, Marc, A 863-680-3908 100 D mtuschen@flsouthern.edu
TUSCHMAN, Keli 620-331-4100 178 E ktuschman@indycc.edu
TUSKI, Don 503-821-8881 385 H presidentsoffice@pnca.edu
TUST, Rob 503-777-7508 386 F tustr@reed.edu
TUTON, Ginger 910-938-6225 342 C tutong@coastalcarolina.edu
TUTSOCK, Robert, J 989-964-4082 236 F tutsock@svsu.edu

UMSTATTD, Rustin .... 816-414-3700 263 D
rumstattd@mbts.edu
UNBEHAGEN, Leonard .. 504-278-6438 193 B
lunbehagen@nunez.edu
UNDERCOFFER, Anita .... 909-652-6032.. 36 E
anita.undercoffer@chaffey.edu
UNDERCOFLER,
Jennifer .... 914-251-6707 328 B
jennifer.undercofler@purchase.edu
UNDERDUE, Sharnette .. 657-278-4498.. 32 B
sunderdue@fullerton.edu
UNDERHILL, Terri .... 304-357-4980 502 E
terriunderhill@ucwv.edu
UNDERWOOD, Anita ..... 845-675-4476 319 C
anita.underwood@nyack.edu
UNDERWOOD, Ann .... 806-651-2121 460 E
aunderwood@wtamu.edu
UNDERWOOD, Anthony 304-424-8209 505 C
anthony.underwood@wvup.edu
UNDERWOOD, Brenetta 314-264-1000 269 G
brenetta.underwood@vatterott.edu
UNDERWOOD, Carrie .... 817-554-5950 452 G
cunderwood@messengercollege.edu
UNDERWOOD, Chloris .. 954-486-7728 112 N
cunderwood@uftl.edu
UNDERWOOD, Craig ..... 610-861-1501 402 D
underwoodc@moravian.edu
UNDERWOOD, David .... 479-968-0319.. 18 G
academicaffairs@atu.edu
UNDERWOOD, David .... 540-831-5500 484 A
dunderwood@radford.edu
UNDERWOOD, Glenda .. 617-587-5581 222 G
underwoodg@neco.edu
UNDERWOOD, Jeffrey ... 323-343-3810.. 32 D
UNDERWOOD, Kathryn . 252-335-3600 350 A
nkunderwood@ecsu.edu
UNDERWOOD, Kathy, A 702-895-0283 279 D
kathyunderwood@unlv.edu
UNDERWOOD, Kelly ..... 805-922-6966.. 24 J
kunderwood@hancockcollege.edu
UNDERWOOD, Ken .... 865-573-4517 432 H
kunderwood@johnsonu.edu
UNDERWOOD, Lori, J ... 757-594-7052 479 H
underwoo@cnu.edu
UNDERWOOD, Marion .. 972-883-2234 467 D
undrwd@utdallas.edu
UNDERWOOD, Mark ..... 830-591-7286 457 C
meunderwood@swtjc.edu
UNDERWOOD,
Michelle, W .... 229-931-2627 120 F
michelle.underwood@gsw.edu
UNDERWOOD,
Robert, A .... 671-735-2990 520 B
raunderwood@triton.uog.edu
UNDERWOOD, Ruth ...... 478-289-2134 118 H
runderwood@ega.edu
UNDERWOOD, Tara ...... 478-471-2734 123 A
tara.underwood@mga.edu
UNDERWOOD,
Timothy, J .... 304-462-6432 504 B
timothy.underwood@glenville.edu
UNDERWOOD, Von, E .. 580-581-2491 375 A
vonu@cameron.edu
UNDERWOOD,
William, D .... 478-301-2500 122 H
underwood_wd@mercer.edu
UNEBASAMI,
Michael, T .... 808-956-6280 130 B
mune@hawaii.edu
UNGAR, Jacob .... 845-362-3053 299 C
jacobu@byts.edu
UNGAR, Samuel, D .... 718-384-5460 334 J
UNGAR, Shaya .... 732-370-3360 293 F
UNGER, Karen .... 845-758-7490 298 I
kunger@bard.edu
UNGER, Leigh .... 562-908-3415.. 58 D
lunger@riohondo.edu
UNGER, Maggie .... 952-446-4323 242 A
ungerm@crown.edu
UNGER, Sue .... 630-889-6565 147 D
sunger@nuhs.edu
UNGERER, Dorothy .... 413-755-4438 221 B
daungerer@stcc.edu
UNIS, Corry .... 570-208-5848 398 D
corryunis@kings.edu
UNKE, James, M .... 507-354-8221 243 C
unkejm@mlc-wels.edu
UNNAVA, H. Rao .... 530-752-4600.. 68 H
runnava@ucdavis.edu
UNNITHAN, Shashi .... 970-204-8607.. 79 K
shashi.unnithan@frontrange.edu
UNRUH, David, L .... 215-895-2436 394 C
david.l.unruh@drexel.edu
UNRUH, Greg .... 316-677-9507 182 E
gunruh@watc.edu
UNRUH, John, A .... 530-898-5844.. 31 D
jaunruh@csuchico.edu
UNRUH, Nancy .... 620-276-9571 177 G
nancy.unruh@gcccks.edu
UNSELD, JR., Robert ..... 270-745-3095 190 F
robert.unseld@wku.edu
UNSWORTH, John, M ... 434-924-7849 486 H
mrs@virginia.edu
UNTERREINER, Colleen . 406-756-3962 271 A
colleenu@fvcc.edu
UPCHURCH, Luke .... 704-923-8405 343 D
upchurch.luke@gaston.edu
UPCHURCH, Rick .... 601-968-5940 252 C
rupchurch@belhaven.edu
UPHOLD, Kimberly .... 610-236-3943 408 G
kuphold@racc.edu
UPNEJA, Arun .... 617-358-6744 212 G
aupneja@bu.edu
UPPALA, Guru .... 951-785-3531.. 47 F
guppala@lasierra.edu
UPPERMAN, Lee-Anna .. 724-266-3838 412 D
UPSHAW, Tyler .... 352-395-8516 106 N
tyler.upshaw@saintleo.edu
UPTON, Brian .... 417-865-2815 260 B
uptonb@evangel.edu
UPTON, Bryn .... 410-857-2416 205 E
bupton@mcdaniel.edu
UPTON, Kim .... 239-513-1122 101 O
kupton@hodges.edu
UPTON-GARVIN, Barbra 816-501-4555 265 I
barbra.upton-garvin@rockhurst.edu
UQDAH, Aesha .... 502-852-6585 190 C
URAN, Mike, T .... 320-308-2116 247 E
mturan@stcloudstate.edu
URBAITIS, Carol, S .... 585-785-1212 308 D
carol.urbaitis@flcc.edu
URBAN, David, J .... 615-898-2764 434 H
david.urban@mtsu.edu
URBAN, Kristi .... 979-830-4141 444 D
kristi.urban@blinn.edu
URBAN, Laura .... 320-762-4404 243 J
laurau@alextech.edu
URBAN, Matthew .... 608-329-8202 513 D
murban@blackhawk.edu
URBAN, Nathan, N .... 412-624-2137 412 I
nurban@pitt.edu
URBAN, Rhonda, P .... 309-692-4092 145 F
rpurban@midstate.edu
URBANEK, Andrew .... 518-485-3731 305 B
urbaneka@strose.edu
URBANEK, Lauren .... 617-585-1113 222 H
lauren.urbanek@necmusic.edu
URBANEK, Philip .... 251-405-7006.... 1 E
purbanek@bishop.edu
URBANO, George .... 863-297-1086 105 F
gurbano@polk.edu
URBANSKI, Thomas ...... 815-836-5015 143 E
urbansth@lewisu.edu
URBANSKI, Tom .... 218-879-0820 244 F
urbanski@fdltcc.edu
URBISH, Leona .... 361-825-5785 460 A
leona.urbish@tamucc.edu
URBONYA, Tim .... 608-263-9676 512 D
tim.urbonya@uwex.uwc.edu
URDAN, Joely, B .... 414-229-4278 511 A
jurdan@uwm.edu
URETSKY, Stewart .... 781-736-8318 213 A
uretsky@brandeis.edu
UREY, Denise .... 724-589-2009 411 D
durey@thiel.edu
URGO, Joseph .... 828-251-6470 351 A
jurgo@unca.edu
URIAGEREKA, Juan .... 301-405-6732 207 G
juan@umd.edu
URIBE, Daniel .... 719-333-9751 518 H
URIBE-JENNINGS,
Marcela .... 508-929-8543 219 A
muribejennings@worcester.edu
URICK, Cindy .... 610-690-5529 410 I
curick1@swarthmore.edu
URIEGAS, Samantha ...... 956-872-6763 456 G
sbmunoz@southtexascollege.edu
URQUIDEZ,
Kasandra, K .... 520-621-3705.. 16 J
kasandra@email.arizona.edu
URSCHEL, Kris .... 574-284-4542 163 J
kurschel@saintmarys.edu
URSO, David .... 540-453-2376 487 G
ursod@brcc.edu
URSUY, Andrea .... 989-686-9222 229 J
alnadols@delta.edu
URSUY, Andrea, L .... 989-686-9222 229 J
alnadols@delta.edu
URTECHO, Robert .... 559-730-3942.. 39 G
robertur@cos.edu
URTZ, Anastasia .... 315-498-2692 319 G
urtza@sunyocc.edu
URTZ, Mike .... 607-753-4953 327 A
mike.urtz@cortland.edu
URZA, Carmelo .... 775-682-5888 279 E
curza@unr.edu
USATCH, Jeri .... 518-255-5227 328 C
usatchj@cobleskill.edu
USCHER, Nancy .... 702-895-4210 279 D
nancy.uscher@unlv.edu
USHER, Diane .... 401-254-3039 417 C
dusher@rwu.edu
USHER, John, S .... 502-852-0085 190 C
usher@louisville.edu
USOFF, Catherine .... 508-793-7670 213 C
cusoff@clarku.edu
UTASH, Sheree .... 316-677-9400 182 E
sutash@watc.edu
UTECH, Tracy .... 313-577-9278 239 C
tracy.utech@wayne.edu
UTHOFF, Jay, L .... 563-387-1012 171 I
uthoffja@luther.edu
UTLEY, Shawn .... 229-333-1294 128 G
shawn.utley@wiregrass.edu
UTSEY, Jan .... 843-574-6892 424 G
jan.utsey@tridenttech.edu
UTSUKI, Melissa .... 714-564-5527.. 58 A
utsuki_melissa@sac.edu
UTT, Kevin .... 563-588-6555 167 E
kevin.utt@clarke.edu
UTTER, Alan .... 828-262-7459 349 H
utterac@appstate.edu
UTTER, Mary .... 412-365-1100 392 C
UTTERBACK, Jim, W ...... 405-382-9200 379 I
j.utterback@sscok.edu
UVA, Mariflor .... 978-762-4000 220 E
muva@northshore.edu
UVERO, Marilyn .... 562-988-2278.. 25 Q
muvero@auhs.edu
UVIN, Peter .... 909-621-8117.. 38 A
peter.uvin@cmc.edu
UYEHARA, Alan, M .... 409-944-1285 449 F
auyehara@gc.edu
UYENO, Sandra .... 808-956-7038 130 B
uyeno@hawaii.edu
UZMAN, Akif .... 713-221-8015 465 C
uzmana@uhd.edu
UZNANSKI, Laurel .... 360-867-6361 494 G
uznanski@evergreen.edu
UZORUO, Petra .... 409-984-6151 462 E
petra.uzoruo@lamarpa.edu
UZZELL, Janet, F .... 202-994-7377.. 92 A
janetuzzell@gwu.edu
UZZI, Jeannine .... 207-780-4485 201 H
jeannine.uzzi@maine.edu

V

VÉAZ, María, G .... 787-257-7373 525 Q
m_veaz@suagm.edu
VÉLEZ RIVERA,
Marcos, A .... 787-257-7373 525 Q
mvelezr@suagm.edu
VÉLEZ-RUBIO, Miguel ... 787-993-8850 527 G
miguel.velez@upr.edu
VÁZQUEZ, Carlos, R ..... 787-884-3838 520 G
gerente@atenascollege.edu
VÁZQUEZ-ESPEJO,
Nelson .... 787-993-8957 527 G
nelson.vazquez1@upr.edu
VABRE, Bert .... 201-761-7834 291 D
bvabre@saintpeters.edu
VACCA, Sheryl, S .... 510-987-9090.. 68 F
sheryl.vacca@ucop.edu
VACCARI, Peter, I .... 914-968-6200 323 C
sjsr@archny.org
VACCARO, Anne .... 718-862-7409 313 L
anne.vaccaro@manhattan.edu
VACCARO, Paul .... 617-730-7288 223 B
paul.varraco@newbury.edu
VACCARO, Thomas .... 845-451-1618 306 D
thomas.vaccaro@culinary.edu
VACCHIANO, Joanna ..... 215-646-7300 396 E
vacchiano.j@gmercyu.edu
VACEK, Heather, H .... 412-924-1453 408 E
hvacek@pts.edu
VACHA-HAASE, Tammi .. 208-426-3647 131 C
tvhaase@boisestate.edu
VACHON, Robert .... 603-526-3698 280 H
robert.vachon@colby-sawyer.edu
VACIK, Stephen .... 606-759-7141 186 E
VADEN, David .... 716-250-7500 300 B
dvaden@bryantstratton.edu
VADEN-GOAD, Linda .... 508-626-4582 218 A
lvadengoad@framingham.edu
VADER, Patricia .... 909-469-5318.. 74 G
pvader@westernu.edu
VADGAMA, Jadutt .... 323-563-9397.. 36 H
jayvadgama@cdrewu.edu
VAGLIENTI, Kendra .... 972-860-4332 447 G
kvaglienti@dcccd.edu
VAGNERINI, Beverly ...... 910-962-7422 352 A
vagnerinib@uncw.edu
VAHEY, Karen .... 516-686-7742 317 G
karen.vahey@nyit.edu
VAHEY, Terry .... 408-924-7808.. 34 D
terry.vahey@sjsu.edu
VAIDYA, Ashish .... 320-308-2122 247 E
akvaidya@stcloudstate.edu
VAIL, Ann .... 859-257-3887 190 B
ann.vail@uky.edu
VAIL, Jody .... 207-974-4633 199 L
jvail@emcc.edu
VAILAS, Arthur, C .... 208-282-3440 132 B
vailarth@isu.edu
VAILL, Amber, L .... 508-373-9724 211 F
amber.vaill@becker.edu
VAILLANCOURT,
Allison, M .... 520-621-1684.. 16 J
vaillana@email.arizona.edu
VAIRO, Carl, A .... 610-566-1776 415 A
cvairo@williamson.edu
VAITHYLINGAM,
Mugunth .... 702-651-5900 278 N
mugunth.vaithylingam@csn.edu
VAKAMUDI, Ramesh ..... 404-413-0721 121 A
fmdrkv@gsu.edu
VAKIL, Dave .... 714-628-5030.. 58 B
vakil_david@sccollege.edu
VAKNIN, Lauren .... 619-660-4295.. 44 L
lauren.vaknin@gcccd.edu
VALASEK, Tricia .... 419-434-4429 372 B
valasek@findlay.edu
VALBUENA, Al .... 870-230-5146.. 19 H
valbuea@hsu.edu
VALCIK, Nicolas .... 304-293-4245 505 B
nicolas.valcik@mail.wvu.edu
VALCKE, Catherine .... 765-455-9561 160 B
chightow@iuk.edu
VALCOURT, George .... 352-371-2833.. 97 L
director@dragonrises.edu
VALCOURT, George .... 352-371-2833.. 97 L
academicdean@dragonrises.edu
VALDES, Eduardo .... 409-772-8780 469 C
pvaldes@utmb.edu
VALDES, Jose, L .... 305-821-3333 100 A
jvaldes@fnu.edu
VALDES, Mario .... 262-243-5700 507 C
mario.valdes@cuw.edu
VALDES, Michael .... 734-487-2031 229 K
mvaldes@emich.edu
VALDES, Theresa .... 847-233-7700 148 A
tvaldes@nc.edu
VALDEZ, Al .... 951-785-2115.. 47 F
avaldez@lasierra.edu
VALDEZ, Anna .... 707-527-4527.. 62 H
avaldez@santarosa.edu
VALDEZ, Benjamin, A ... 303-837-0825.. 76 K
valdezb@aii.edu
VALDEZ,
Cristobal (Cris) .... 217-875-7200 149 J
cvaldez@richland.edu
VALDEZ, Jeny .... 415-405-4416.. 34 C
valdezj@sfsu.edu
VALDEZ, Jude .... 210-458-2401 468 B
jude.valdez@utsa.edu
VALDEZ, Nick .... 515-271-2394 168 J
nicholas.valdez@drake.edu
VALDISERRI, Rachel ...... 989-837-4140 235 C
valdiser@northwood.edu
VALDIVIA, Nicolas .... 562-985-8391.. 32 C
nick.valdivia@csulb.edu
VALE, Carlos .... 312-935-4855 149 K
cvale@robertmorris.edu
VALE, SSJ, Carol Jean .. 215-248-7021 392 D
cvale@chc.edu
VALE, Darla .... 513-244-4295 366 A
darla.vale@msj.edu
VALE, Louise .... 303-492-5489.. 83 B
louise.vale@colorado.edu
VALEK, Millicent, M ...... 979-230-3200 444 E
millicent.valek@brazosport.edu
VALENCIA, Duane .... 817-202-6533 457 E
valenciad@swau.edu
VALENCIA, Jose .... 718-522-9073 298 E
jvalencia@asa.edu
VALENCIA, Karen .... 214-860-3687 448 B
kvalencia@dcccd.edu
VALENCIA, Marilyn .... 440-449-4433 373 B
marilyn.valencia@ursuline.edu
VALENCIA, Ritchie .... 691-320-2480 519 G
rjvalencia@comfsm.fm
VALENCIA, Rose Mary ... 713-500-4472 468 D
rose.mary.valencia@uth.tmc.edu
VALENCIA, Steven, J ..... 580-327-8478 376 K
sjvalencia@nwosu.edu
VALENCIA, Susan .... 510-869-6511.. 59 F
svalencia@samuelmerritt.edu

VAN OMMEREN, Andrew .... 712-707-7000 172 G andrew.vanommeren@nwciowa.edu
VAN OMMEREN, Ryan .. 805-493-3211.. 30 E rvommere@callutheran.edu
VAN OOT, Amy .... 860-701-5019.. 87 F vanoot_a@mitchell.edu
VAN ORMAN, Kit .... 315-364-3317 333 G kit@wells.edu
VAN ORMAN, Sarah, A . 608-262-1885 510 C svanorman@uhs.wisc.edu
VAN PELT, Donna .... 515-294-1280 166 F dvanpelt@foundation.iastate.edu
VAN RENSBURG, Deryck .... 310-506-5689.. 56 D deryck.rensburg@pepperdine.edu
VAN RIJN, Paul .... 215-885-2360 401 A pvanrijn@manor.edu
VAN RYZIN, Gregg, G .. 973-353-3985 290 D vanryzin@newark.rutgers.edu
VAN SAVAGE, Kimberly, M .... 512-448-8540 455 I kvansavage@stedwards.edu
VAN SCHARREL, Mark, H .... 773-256-0676 144 G mvanscha@lstc.edu
VAN SICKEL, Lisa .... 314-719-8017 260 C lvansickel@fontbonne.edu
VAN SICKLE, Fred .... 607-254-7150 306 B fmv7@cornell.edu
VAN SLYKE, David .... 315-443-3461 330 H vanslyke@syr.edu
VAN STAVERN, Becky ... 417-328-1815 267 A bvanstavern@sbuniv.edu
VAN STRATEN, Amy ...... 920-831-4355 513 F vanstrat@fvtc.edu
VAN TASSEL, Kristin .... 785-227-3380 175 E vantasselk@bethanylb.edu
VAN TASSEL, Sherri ...... 740-264-5591 361 D svantassel@egcc.edu
VAN TASSELL, TOR, Malachi .... 814-472-3001 409 G mvantassell@francis.edu
VAN TIL, Seth, J .... 724-458-3887 396 D sjvantil@gcc.edu
VAN UUM, Elizabeth ..... 314-516-5774 268 E vanuum@umsl.edu
VAN VLECK, Thomas .... 660-626-2138 257 A tvanvleck@atsu.edu
VAN VLERAH, Abagail .. 516-299-2255 313 D abby.vanvlerah@liu.edu
VAN VOORHIS, Amanda .... 508-999-9114 217 A avanvoorhis@umassd.edu
VAN VOORHIS, Sue, N . 612-625-8098 250 E vanvo002@umn.edu
VAN VOORST, James .... 518-956-8120 324 G jvanvoorst@albany.edu
VAN VREEDE, LeeAnn ... 608-796-3808 512 R levanvreede@viterbo.edu
VAN WAGNER, Thomas 301-243-2211 518 C thomas.vanwagner@dodiis.mil
VAN WAGONER, Randall, J .... 315-792-5333 315 I rvanwagoner@mvcc.edu
VAN WALBECK, Patti .... 269-387-2365 239 E patti.vanwalbeck@wmich.edu
VAN WICKLIN, Robert .. 716-375-2331 322 B bvanwick@sbu.edu
VAN WIE, Lisa .... 518-629-8143 310 G l.vanwie@hvcc.edu
VAN WINKLE, Ken .... 575-439-3600 295 B kvanwink@nmsu.edu
VAN WINKLE, Ken .... 575-439-3640 295 C kvanwink@nmsu.edu
VAN WINKLE, Robin ..... 541-440-4668 387 E robin.vanwinkle@umpqua.edu
VAN WYK, Natalie .... 610-361-5418 402 G vanwykn@neumann.edu
VAN ZANDE, Carleen .... 608-262-2321 510 B
VAN ZANDT, David ...... 212-229-5656 316 E vanzandt@newschool.edu
VAN ZANDT, Patricia, R .... 423-439-4337 431 H vanzandt@etsu.edu
VAN ZEE, Carolina .... 909-537-7576.. 33 D quinterc@csusb.edu
VAN ZEE, Ryan .... 605-995-2902 427 A ryvanzee@dwu.edu
VANAARTSEN, Brent ...... 605-256-5692 428 G brent.vanaartsen@dsu.edu
VANABLE, Peter .... 315-443-2543 330 H pvanable@syr.edu
VANACORE, Gina .... 940-565-2282 466 B gina.vanacore@unt.edu
VANAKEN, Troy .... 630-617-3266 138 C president@elmhurst.edu
VANALSTINE, Gabby ..... 765-455-9226 160 B gvanast@iuk.edu
VANANDEN, Ian .... 301-447-5310 206 B vananden@msmary.edu
VANARSDALL, Cathy ..... 765-361-6421 166 B vanarsdc@wabash.edu
VANASSE, Dennis .... 508-849-3372 210 H dvanasse@annamaria.edu
VANASSE, Nancy .... 508-999-8133 217 A nvasasse@umassd.edu
VANBEBBER, James ...... 903-886-5996 459 E james.vanbebber@tamuc.edu
VANBOCKSTAELE, Elisabeth .... 215-762-4359 394 C elisabeth.vanbockstaele@drexelmed.edu
VANBROCKLIN, Michael .... 903-233-4332 452 A mikevanbrocklin@letu.edu
VANCAMP, Connie .... 412-809-5100 408 D friedberg.connie@pti.edu
VANCE, Amy, M .... 972-860-7141 447 I amy.vance@dcccd.edu
VANCE, Deidre .... 614-882-2551 361 K dvance@fortiscollege.edu
VANCE, Gina .... 928-523-6747.. 14 K gina.vance@nau.edu
VANCE, Gina, M .... 724-946-7114 414 C vancegm@westminster.edu
VANCE, Helene .... 434-592-7200 482 D registrar@liberty.edu
VANCE, Kristie .... 828-689-1353 339 G kvance@mhu.edu
VANCE, Maria .... 707-965-7000.. 55 F mvance@puc.edu
VANCE, Mickey .... 601-635-6338 252 I mvance@eccc.edu
VANCE, Otis .... 352-638-9795.. 95 H ovance@beaconcollege.edu
VANCE, Samantha .... 334-291-4974..... 1 H samantha.vance@cv.edu
VANCE, W.C .... 419-289-4142 356 L wvance@ashland.edu
VANCLEAVE, Donna .... 804-819-4695 487 F dvancleave@vccs.edu
VANDAL, Courtney .... 701-228-5613 354 G courtney.vandal@dakotacollege.edu
VANDALL, Christopher, P .... 608-258-2448 514 A cvandall@madisoncollege.edu
VANDE YACHT, Daniel .. 920-465-2111 510 E vandeyad@uwgb.edu
VANDEL, Laurie .... 406-496-4119 272 E lvandel@mtech.edu
VANDELICHT, Mike .... 573-897-5000 267 F
VANDEN BOOGAARD, Brad .... 806-874-3571 445 R brad.vandenboogaard@clarendoncollege.edu
VANDENAKKER, John .... 313-883-8750 236 D vandenakker.john@shms.edu
VANDENAVOND, Steve . 906-227-6767 235 A svanden@nmu.edu
VANDENBARK, Cyndi .... 970-521-6763.. 81 F cyndi.vandenbark@njc.edu
VANDENBERG, Matt ...... 989-463-7081 226 H vandenbergmp@alma.edu
VANDENBERG, Rex .... 805-922-6966.. 24 J rvandenberg@hancockcollege.edu
VANDENBOSCH, Kathryn .... 608-262-4930 510 C kate.vandenbosch@cals.wisc.edu
VANDER FEEN, Aimee .. 605-331-6602 429 D aimee.vanderfeen@usiouxfalls.edu
VANDER HOEK, Nancy . 605-229-8545 427 J nancy.vanderhoek@presentation.edu
VANDER HOOVEN, James, L .... 978-632-6600 220 D
VANDER HORN, Alexis, A .... 563-884-5102 172 H alexis.vanderhorn@palmer.edu
VANDER HORST, Joel .... 803-947-2110 422 H joel.vanderhorst@newberry.edu
VANDER MOLEN, Lori, L .... 402-280-1798 274 D lorivandermolen@creighton.edu
VANDER PLOEG, Sally .. 616-526-7112 228 B svploeg@calvin.edu
VANDER STOEP, Scott, D .... 616-395-7903 231 D vanderstoep@hope.edu
VANDER VALK, Frank .... 518-587-2100 329 C frank.vandervalk@esc.edu
VANDER VEER, Lisa ...... 815-939-5256 148 F lvanderv@olivet.edu
VANDER WAL, Jennifer . 605-688-4491 429 B jennifer.vanderwal@sdstate.edu
VANDER WEELE, Dennis .... 845-368-7206 323 I dennis.vanderweele@use.salvationarmy.org
VANDER WERF, Dave ... 712-722-6020 168 I dave.vanderwerff@dordt.edu
VANDER WOUDE, Chris .... 540-636-2900 479 G cvanderwoude@christendom.edu
VANDER ZWAAG, Lora . 712-274-6400 174 E lora.vanderzwaag@witcc.edu
VANDERBILL, Liz .... 320-222-6090 247 B liz.vanderbill@ridgewater.edu
VANDERBILT, Robin ..... 937-298-3399 364 B robin.vanderbilt@kc.edu
VANDERBILT, William ... 616-395-7850 231 D vanderbilt@hope.edu
VANDERBOUT, Jennifer, L .... 660-543-8000 268 A vanderbout@ucmo.edu
VANDERBURG, Judy, J . 503-838-8490 388 B vanderj@wou.edu
VANDERBURGH, Paul, M .... 937-229-2345 372 A pvanderburgh1@udayton.edu
VANDERGIFF, Ronda .... 360-438-4356 497 F rvandergriff2@stmartin.edu
VANDERGRIFF, Rhonda 573-334-6825 266 L rvandergriff@sehcollege.edu
VANDERGRIFT, Donna .. 856-222-9311 289 F dvandergrift@rcbc.edu
VANDERHART, Mark ..... 219-864-2400 162 U mvanderhart@midamerica.edu
VANDERHEIDEN, Lori ... 402-844-7733 276 G loriv@northeast.edu
VANDERHILL, Dan .... 517-750-1200 237 D danv@arbor.edu
VANDERHOOF, Doug .... 620-241-0723 176 G doug.vanderhoof@centralchristian.edu
VANDERHOOF, Karen .... 973-328-5012 285 B kvanderhoof@ccm.edu
VANDERHORST, Anne ... 559-791-2457.. 47 C avanderh@kccd.edu
VANDERHURST, Michael .... 843-792-1282 422 C vanderm@musc.edu
VANDERLEE BUGAJSKI, OFS, Tricia, J .... 269-399-7700 165 B tbugajski@sf.edu
VANDERLEI, Elizabeth ... 616-526-6102 228 B bvlei@calvin.edu
VANDERLICK, T. Kyle .... 203-432-4220.. 89 G kyle.vanderlick@yale.edu
VANDERMEER, Mark ..... 616-988-1000 228 I mark.vm@compass.edu
VANDERPLOEG, Sondra, C .... 603-526-3375 280 H svanderploeg@colby-sawyer.edu
VANDERPOOL, Molly .... 765-973-8415 160 A moberry@iue.edu
VANDERPOOL, Neil .... 559-442-4600.. 66 G neil.vanderpool@fresnocitycollege.edu
VANDERPUYE, Archibald, W .... 512-505-3076 451 A awvanderpuye@htu.edu
VANDERSANDEN, Susan .... 608-663-3367 507 D svandersanden@edgewood.edu
VANDERSLICE, Ronna, J .... 580-581-2250 375 A rvanderslice@cameron.edu
VANDERSPOEL, James .. 906-932-4231 230 D jimv@gogebic.edu
VANDERSTAAY, Steven, L .... 360-650-3004 500 E steven.vanderstaay@wwu.edu
VANDERVEEN, Kathleen 616-331-2662 230 G vandervk@gvsu.edu
VANDERVEEN, Sara .... 269-927-8611 232 G svanderveen@lakemichigancollege.edu
VANDERVELDEN, Michael .... 208-459-5851 131 H mvandervelden@collegeofidaho.edu
VANDERVORT, Michael, W .... 512-471-7117 467 C mike.vandervort@austin.utexas.edu
VANDERWOUDE, Katrina .... 619-644-7104.. 45 A katrina.vanderwoude@gcccd.edu
VANDERWYST, Roxann . 715-874-4280 513 E rvanderwyst@cvtc.edu
VANDERZEE, Lenore ..... 315-386-7109 329 A vanderzeel@canton.edu
VANDERZWAAG, George .... 585-275-4301 332 E george.vanderzwaag@rochester.edu
VANDEURSEN, Marianne .... 908-835-2430 292 G vandeursen@warren.edu
VANDEVANDER, David, R .... 540-828-5316 478 J dvandeva@bridgewater.edu
VANDEVEN, Alissa .... 573-651-2206 266 M avandeven@semo.edu
VANDEVENTER, Susan .. 607-729-1581 306 F svandeventer@davisny.edu
VANDEVERE, John, D .... 570-326-3761 404 T jdv7@pct.edu
VANDEVILLE, Denise ..... 906-487-7379 230 B denise.vandeville@finlandia.edu
VANDIJK, Cindee .... 319-385-6495 170 J cindee.vandijk@iw.edu
VANDIVER, Vikki .... 205-348-3924.... 8 A vlvandiver@sw.ua.edu
VANDIVERE, Julie .... 570-389-4713 405 E jvandive@bloomu.edu
VANDREHLE, Michael .... 507-537-6257 248 A michael.vandrehel@smsu.edu
VANDYKE, Rhonda .... 540-665-4862 485 C rcolby@su.edu
VANDYKE, Rhonda, L ... 276-964-7388 489 F rhonda.vandyke@sw.edu
VANE, Thomas .... 716-827-2433 331 K vanet@trocaire.edu
VANECEK, Frank .... 802-485-2135 475 I vanecek@norwich.edu
VANEGAS, Jorge .... 979-845-1221 459 C jvanegas@tamu.edu
VANEK, Marian, S .... 412-383-1863 412 I msv8@pitt.edu
VANEK, Susan .... 574-284-4594 163 J svanek@saintmarys.edu
VANFLEET, Rita .... 402-552-3516 273 K vanfleetrita@clarksoncollege.edu
VANG, Mary .... 651-846-1722 247 G mary.vang@saintpaul.edu
VANGELDEREN, Cynthia 616-632-2929 227 C vangecyn@aquinas.edu
VANGELE, Jim .... 650-738-4455.. 62 B vangelej@smccd.edu
VANGEMERT, Edward .... 608-262-2600 510 C evangemert@library.wisc.edu
VANGORDER, Karen ...... 260-481-6016 160 D vangordk@ipfw.edu
VANGORDON, Beth .... 765-455-9555 160 B vgordon@iu.edu
VANGSGARD, Mark, D .. 651-962-6095 251 D mdvangsgard@stthomas.edu
VANGSNESS, Melissa .... 320-589-6414 251 A weberm@morris.umn.edu
VANGSNESS FRISCH, Jane .... 701-671-2627 355 B jane.vangsness@ndscs.edu
VANHECKE, JoNes, R .... 507-933-7526 242 D jvanheck@gustavus.edu
VANHEE, Tonya .... 970-943-2493.. 84 E tvanhee@western.edu
VANHEYNIGEN, Matthew .... 413-782-1373 225 F matthew.vanheynigen@wne.edu
VANHOEK, Rebecca ...... 386-752-1822.. 99 J rebecca.vanhoek@fgc.edu
VANHOOK, Jayson .... 423-614-8695 432 L jvanhook@leeuniversity.edu
VANHOORELBEKE, Jack 989-964-4109 236 F jvh@svsu.edu
VANJOOLEN, Vincent .... 617-984-1713 223 H vvanjoolen@quincycollege.edu
VANKO, David .... 410-704-2121 209 C dvanko@towson.edu
VANLANDINGHAM, Brenda .... 662-246-6301 254 C bvanlandingham@msdelta.edu
VANLONDEN, April .... 800-287-8822 156 D vanloap@earlham.edu
VANLONE, Jeffrey .... 203-392-5475.. 85 A vanlonej1@southernct.edu
VANMETER, Terry .... 270-789-5031 184 B twvanmeter@campbellsville.edu
VANN, Allen .... 305-348-2465 109 D allen.vann@fiu.edu
VANN, Linnie .... 410-334-2936 210 C lvann@worwic.edu
VANN-HAMILTON, Joy .. 816-960-2008 258 D dean@cityvision.edu
VANN WALLSTROM, Crystal, E .... 260-422-5561 159 D cevannwallstrom@indianatech.edu
VANNESS, Kathryn, A .... 540-375-2257 484 H vanness@roanoke.edu
VANNEY, Greg .... 701-845-7227 354 E greg.vanney@vcsu.edu
VANNEY, Pete .... 715-365-4484 514 E pvanney@nicoletcollege.edu

VAZQUEZ-SKILLINGS,
Rebecca, D .... 614-823-1354 368 O
rvazquez-skillings@otterbein.edu
VAZQUEZ-VERA, Efrain . 787-850-0000 527 D
rectoria.uprh@upr.edu
VEAL, Don-Terry .... 443-885-3035 206 A
don-terry.veal@morgan.edu
VEAL, Nicole .... 312-427-2737 141 E
nveal@jmls.edu
VECCHIO, Maria .... 201-559-6017 286 C
vecchiom@felician.edu
VECCHIO, Paul .... 607-871-2193 298 A
vecchio@alfred.edu
VECCHIONE, Tom .... 209-932-3042.. 70 F
tvecchione@pacific.edu
VECHINI, Jose, A .... 787-864-2222 524 A
jose.vechini@guayama.inter.edu
VEDDER, Kevin, A .... 410-546-6213 209 B
kavedder@salisbury.edu
VEDDER, Lori .... 810-762-3444 238 B
lvedder@umflint.edu
VEEDER, Samantha .... 585-275-3226 332 E
sveeder2@finaid.rochester.edu
VEER, Chelly .... 701-766-1302 353 E
chelly.veer@littlehoop.edu
VEGA, Aixa .... 787-834-9595 526 E
avega@uaa.edu
VEGA, Annette .... 787-878-5475 523 H
avega@arecibo.inter.edu
VEGA, Barbara .... 432-837-8810 462 G
bvega@sulross.edu
VEGA, Erlinda .... 787-264-1912 524 D
linvega@intersg.edu
VEGA, Eva .... 787-746-1400 522 O
evega@huertas.edu
VEGA, Evelyn .... 787-250-1912 524 B
evega@metro.inter.edu
VEGA, Fabian .... 518-629-7111 310 G
f.vega@hvcc.edu
VEGA, Francesca .... 818-677-2123.. 33 B
francesca.vega@csun.edu
VEGA, Fredrick .... 787-250-1912 524 B
fredrickvega@metro.inter.edu
VEGA, Gregory .... 619-660-4030.. 44 L
gregory.vega@gcccd.edu
VEGA, Javier .... 212-592-2031 324 A
jvega@sva.edu
VEGA, Jesus .... 805-553-4799.. 73 A
jvega@vcccd.edu
VEGA, Juan .... 787-844-8181 528 E
juan.vegavega@upr.edu
VEGA, Julio .... 787-620-2040 520 F
jvega@aupr.edu
VEGA, Kennethia, J .... 714-564-6975.. 58 A
vega_kennethia@sac.edu
VEGA, Lina .... 787-766-1717 526 B
livega@suagm.edu
VEGA, Manfredo .... 787-620-2040 520 F
mvega@aupr.edu
VEGA, Patricia .... 773-878-7837 150 I
pvega@staugustine.edu
VEGA, Pete .... 708-239-4770 153 B
pete.vega@trnty.edu
VEGA, Zaida .... 787-766-1717 526 B
zvega@suagm.edu
VEGA-GONZALEZ,
Melvin .... 787-480-2426 521 J
melvega@sanjuanciudadpatria.com
VEGA-GUTIERREZ,
Guadalupe .... 787-993-8958 527 G
guadalupe.vega@upr.edu
VEGA-LA SERNA,
Jennifer .... 559-730-3823.. 39 G
jenniferl@cos.edu
VEGA-VAZQUEZ, Victor . 912-279-5946 118 A
vvazquez@ccga.edu
VEHR, Gregory, J .... 513-556-3028 371 E
greg.vehr@uc.edu
VEILLEUX, John .... 817-531-4269 463 G
jveilleux@txwes.edu
VEIT, Kathy .... 650-723-2300.. 66 C
VEIT, Kenneth, J .... 215-871-6770 407 G
kenv@pcom.edu
VEITCH, Dionne .... 814-824-3315 401 J
dveitch@mercyhurst.edu
VEITCH, Jonathan .... 323-259-2691.. 54 E
VEITH, Tracy .... 513-244-8142 359 E
tracy.veith@ccuniversity.edu
VELA, Alicia, L .... 512-448-8515 455 I
aliciav@stedwards.edu
VELA, Eddie .... 530-898-6262.. 31 D
evela@csuchico.edu
VELA, Jason .... 307-674-6446 516 P
jvela@sheridan.edu
VELA, Robert .... 210-486-0961 441 E
rvela63@alamo.edu
VELA, Robert, H .... 210-486-0959 442 A
rvela63@alamo.edu

VELAR, Maria .... 786-331-1000 104 C
VELAR-PRIETO, Jorge .... 787-993-8869 527 G
jorge.velar@upr.edu
VELASCO, Amy .... 805-756-2982.. 30 K
aevelasc@calpoly.edu
VELASCO, Andrea .... 201-200-2304 287 F
avelasco@njcu.edu
VELASCO, Debbie .... 612-767-7064 240 B
debbie.velasco@alfredadler.edu
VELASCO, Steven, C ...... 805-893-2434.. 70 B
steven.velasco@ucsb.edu
VELASCO, Ulises .... 707-468-3110.. 51 E
uvelasco@mendocino.edu
VELASQUEZ, Lorrie .... 719-846- ..... 82 L
lorrie.velasquez@trinidadstate.edu
VELASQUEZ, Marisol ..... 708-656-8000 146 F
marisol.velasquez@morton.edu
VELASQUEZ, Tom .... 661-654-2211.. 31 B
tvelasquez2@csub.edu
VELAZQUEZ, Acmin ...... 787-844-2750 528 E
acmin.velazquez@upr.edu
VELAZQUEZ,
Carmen, G .... 787-253-7373 525 Q
ue_evelazquez@suagm.edu
VELAZQUEZ, Ginger ...... 217-333-9634 154 B
gmayol@uillinois.edu
VELAZQUEZ, Glenda ..... 787-761-0640 527 C
escuelagraduada@utcpr.edu
VELAZQUEZ, Jonathan .. 787-279-1912 523 J
jvelazquez@bayamon.inter.edu
VELAZQUEZ, Marisol .... 787-864-2222 524 A
marisol.velazquez@guayama.inter.edu
VELAZQUEZ, Marisol .... 323-241-5338.. 49 E
VELAZQUEZ, Nelly .... 787-841-2000 525 J
nvelazquez@pucpr.edu
VELAZQUEZ, Tania .... 631-451-4057 330 B
velazqt@sunysuffolk.edu
VELAZQUEZ, Tania .... 631-451-4049 330 C
VELDERMAN, Joe .... 708-239-4837 153 B
joe.velderman@trnty.edu
VELDHEER, Kristine .... 773-371-5460 134 J
kveldheer@ctu.edu
VELENCHIK, Ann .... 781-283-3583 225 D
avelenchik@wellesley.edu
VELEZ, Angel .... 787-250-1912 524 B
avelez@metro.inter.edu
VELEZ, Ashley .... 787-841-2000 525 J
avelez@pucpr.edu
VELEZ, Carlos .... 319-399-8000 167 F
cvelez@coe.edu
VELEZ, Daniel, C .... 716-878-4704 326 E
velezdc@buffalostate.edu
VELEZ, Henry, X .... 848-932-1011 290 A
hxvelez@rci.rutgers.edu
VELEZ, Lilimar .... 787-780-5134 525 D
livelez@nuc.edu
VELEZ, Marcelina .... 787-786-3030 526 F
mvelez@ucbedupr.onmicrosoft.com
VELEZ, Roland .... 718-518-4406 302 D
rvelez@hostos.cuny.edu
VELEZ, Rosa, M .... 787-758-2525 528 D
rosa.velez2@upr.edu
VELEZ, Sarah, M .... 716-878-3136 326 E
yacklysm@buffalostate.edu
VELEZ, Wanda .... 845-675-4792 319 C
wanda.velez@nyack.edu
VELEZ, Wilda .... 787-848-1520 525 H
wvelez1@popac.edu
VELEZ AROCHO,
Jorge, I .... 787-841-2000 525 J
jivelezarocho@pucpr.edu
VELEZ LUCE, Melissa .... 773-244-5273 147 F
mvelezluce@northpark.edu
VELEZ-ROLON, Olga, L . 787-250-0000 527 D
olga.velez1@upr.edu
VELEZ-YELIN, Johanna .. 856-256-5440 289 H
velez-yelin@rowan.edu
VELGUTH, Peter .... 989-386-6622 234 B
pvelguth@midmich.edu
VELIE, Julia, L .... 603-366-5257 280 K
jvelie@ccsnh.edu
VELIKY, Dawn .... 252-536-7227 343 F
rveliky004@halifaxcc.edu
VELKOFF, Townsend ...... 570-321-4258 400 G
velkoff@lycoming.edu
VELLUZZI, Nicholas ...... 509-527-3685 499 E
nicholas.velluzzi@wwcc.edu
VELONI, Mary .... 253-752-2020 494 H
mveloni@faithseminary.edu
VELORIA, Ruth .... 602-557-1544.. 17 C
ruth.veloria@phoenix.edu
VELOVICI, Silviu .... 714-533-3946.. 35 B
silviu.velovici@calums.edu
VELTRI, Valerie, L .... 412-531-4433 393 D
info@deantech.edu
VELVEL, Lawrence, R ..... 978-681-0800 221 D
velvel@mslaw.edu

VENABLE, James, E ...... 901-722-3260 436 D
jvenable@sco.edu
VENABLE, Julie .... 951-487-3040.. 52 J
jvenable@msjc.edu
VENABLE, Margaret .... 706-272-4436 118 F
mvenable@daltonstate.edu
VENABLE, Margo .... 856-227-7200 284 E
mvenable@camdencc.edu
VENCAK-TONER, Denise 718-990-1435 322 F
vencakd@stjohns.edu
VENDITTI, Ferdinand ..... 518-262-5376 297 L
venditf@mail.amc.edu
VENDITTI, Leona .... 515-289-9200 170 B
lvenditti@inste.edu
VENDITTI, Nicholas .... 515-289-9200 170 B
nvenditti@inste.edu
VENDRICK, Baxter .... 757-594-8987 479 H
baxter.vendrick@cnu.edu
VENEGAS, Valerie, A ..... 714-895-5117.. 38 G
vvenegas@gwc.cccd.edu
VENEKLASE, Dave .... 616-732-1195 229 D
dveneklase@davenport.edu
VENEMA, Cornelius .... 219-864-2400 162 U
cvenema@midamerica.edu
VENKAT, Rama .... 702-895-1094 279 D
rama.venkat@unlv.edu
VENKATACHALAM,
Venky .... 605-677-5455 428 E
venky.venkatachalam@usd.edu
VENKATARAMANAN,
Munirpallam .... 812-855-9011 159 H
vpsi@indiana.edu
VENNERI, Richard .... 773-298-3946 151 C
venneri@sxu.edu
VENSEY, Larry .... 202-568-4810 134 K
lvensey@chamberlain.edu
VENSON, John .... 510-869-8726.. 59 F
jvenson@samuelmerritt.edu
VENTA, Henry .... 409-880-8603 462 C
henry.venta@lamar.edu
VENTIMIGLIA, Phil .... 404-413-4701 121 A
pventimiglia@gsu.edu
VENTIMIGLIA, Thomas .. 516-796-5923 317 A
tventimig@nycc.edu
VENTO, Jaclyn .... 516-628-5021 327 C
ventoj@oldwestbury.edu
VENTO, Robert, D .... 318-257-2176 197 A
bvento@latech.edu
VENTO-CIFELLI, Lauren . 732-571-3562 287 C
lvento@monmouth.edu
VENTOLINI, Gary .... 432-703-5133 463 E
gary.ventolini@ttuhsc.edu
VENTURA, Elizabeth, E .. 301-243-2045 518 C
elizabeth.ventura@dodiis.mil
VENTURA, Frank, J .... 330-569-5974 362 J
venturafj@hiram.edu
VENTURA, Jamey .... 802-635-1285 477 C
jamey.ventura@jsc.edu
VENTURA, Javier .... 413-265-2343 213 E
venturij@elms.edu
VENTURA, Yoav .... 626-264-8880.. 71 A
VENTURA-MENDOZA,
Oscar .... 703-284-5711 483 A
oscar.ventura-mendoza@marymount.
edu
VENUGOPAL, Junias, V 312-329-4113 146 B
junias.venugopal@moody.edu
VENUGOPALAN,
Devarajan .... 414-323-9790 511 A
dv@uwm.edu
VENUGOPALAN,
Devarajan .... 414-229-5561 511 A
dv@uwm.edu
VENUTI, Andrea .... 315-498-2183 319 G
venutia@sunyocc.edu
VENUTI, John, A .... 804-828-1210 487 E
javenuti@vcu.edu
VEQUIST, David .... 512-444-8082 461 C
d_vequist@thsu.edu
VER BERKMOES, John .. 616-945-5300 229 B
john.verberkmoes@cornerstone.edu
VER STEEG, Jennie .... 641-422-4327 172 C
verstjen@niacc.edu
VERA, Fonda, L .... 972-238-6992 448 D
fondav@dcccd.edu
VERA, Hernan .... 787-841-2000 525 J
hvera@pucpr.edu
VERA-HERNANDEZ,
Nelson, A .... 787-890-2681 527 D
nelson.vera1@upr.edu
VERA-MORALES, Sheila 787-480-2451 521 J
svera01@sanjuanciudadpatria.com
VERACKA, Peter, G .... 614-885-5585 369 D
pveracka@pcj.edu
VERAY, Jaime .... 787-725-6500 521 C
jveray@albizu.edu
VERBERKMOES, John .... 616-222-1589 229 B
john.verberkmoes@cornerstone.edu

VERBOSH, Kyle, W .... 717-871-7871 407 A
kyle.verbosh@millersville.edu
VERBURG, John .... 256-761-6330.... 7 D
jverburg@talladega.edu
VERCAUTEREN, Tammy . 303-404-5243.. 79 K
tammy.vercauteren@frontrange.edu
VERCH, Christopher ...... 507-457-1709 250 B
cverch@smumn.edu
VERCHER, Kathy .... 318-678-6000 192 C
kvercher@bpcc.edu
VERCRUYSSE, Christina . 904-256-7640 102 B
VERDERBER, Carl .... 845-752-3000 332 A
carlv@uts.edu
VERDEROSA, Patricia, K 717-337-6225 396 A
pverdero@gettysburg.edu
VERDI, Ed .... 212-229-5323 316 E
verdie@newschool.edu
VERDICCHIO, James ..... 718-289-5923 301 D
james.verdicchio@bcc.cuny.edu
VERDICK, Dana .... 815-772-7218 146 D
dverdick@morrisontech.edu
VERDILE, Vincent, P ..... 518-262-6008 297 L
verdilv@mail.amc.edu
VERDIN, Regina .... 985-448-5908 192 I
regina.verdin@fletcher.edu
VERDOW, Tom .... 315-733-2307 332 F
tverdow@uscny.edu
VERDU, Michael .... 804-523-5804 488 C
mverdu@reynolds.edu
VERDUCE, Cynthia, P .... 260-422-5561 159 D
cpverduce@indianatech.edu
VERDUGO, Jason .... 651-523-2035 242 E
jverdugo@hamline.edu
VERDUZCO, Oscar .... 509-574-4937 500 I
overduzco@yvcc.edu
VEREBELY, James, S ..... 402-557-7200 273 E
jim.verebely@bellevue.edu
VEREEN, Karen .... 478-289-2271 126 A
kvereen@southeasterntech.edu
VEREEN, Richard .... 678-359-5104 121 B
richard_v@gordonstate.edu
VEREGGE, Paul .... 601-984-1010 256 D
paul.veregge@umc.edu
VEREM, Jas .... 201-443-8936 286 B
jasmin31_verem@fdu.edu
VERES, Karen .... 610-861-5344 403 B
kveres@northampton.edu
VERGHESE, David .... 936-294-2507 462 F
dverghese@shsu.edu
VERGNETTI, Stephenie .. 570-702-8944 398 A
svergnetti@johnson.edu
VERHOFF, Monica .... 419-448-2202 362 G
mverhoff@heidelberg.edu
VERIS, Garin .... 508-830-5055 218 D
gveris@maritime.edu
VERITY, Hannah .... 314-246-7627 269 N
hannahverity72@webster.edu
VERITY, Larry .... 619-594-6489.. 34 B
lverity@mail.sdsu.edu
VERITY, Melina .... 334-683-5157.... 6 C
mverity@judson.edu
VERKENNES, Joseph ..... 734-384-4207 234 C
jverkennes@monroeccc.edu
VERKEST, Diane .... 928-523-6144.. 14 K
diane.verkest@nau.edu
VERLANIC, Amy .... 406-496-4289 272 E
averlanic@mtech.edu
VERLENGIA, Andrew ...... 515-271-3077 168 J
andrew.verlengia@drake.edu
VERMEER ELLIOTT,
Julie .... 712-707-7200 172 G
julie.elliott@nwciowa.edu
VERMEULEN, Jeffrey ...... 717-815-6601 415 G
jvermuel@ycp.edu
VERMEULEN, Lori .... 609-652-4514 291 H
lori.vermeulen@stockton.edu
VERMEYCHUK, Janice ... 609-771-2483 284 I
vermeyj@tcnj.edu
VERMILLION, Laurel ...... 701-854-8014 355 F
laurel.vermillion@sittingbull.edu
VERMILYEA, Kate .... 843-208-8115 425 B
ktorbog@uscb.edu
VERMUND, Sten .... 203-785-2867.. 89 G
sten.vermund@yale.edu
VERNOLD, Eric .... 315-866-0300 310 A
vernoldem@herkimer.edu
VERNON, Alex .... 501-450-1258.. 19 I
vernon@hendrix.edu
VERNON, Amy .... 410-617-2201 205 A
awvernon@loyola.edu
VERNON, Brian .... 203-837-8851.. 85 B
vernonb@wcsu.edu
VERNON, David .... 201-684-7506 289 C
dvernon@ramapo.edu
VERNON, Marc .... 804-828-2329 487 E
mvernon@vcu.edu
VERNON, Mitzi .... 859-257-7619 190 B
vernon@uky.edu

VERRET, Bridget 318-675-6065 194 D bverr2@lsuhsc.edu
VERRET, C. Reynold 504-520-7541 198 D president@xula.edu
VERRILL, Tom 423-236-2816 436 C tverrill@southern.edu
VERRUNI, Samuel 610-647-4400 397 I sverruni@immaculata.edu
VERSCHUYL, Molly 425-739-8223 495 F molly.verschuyl@lwtech.edu
VERSEMAN, Gina 734-995-7316 229 A gina.verseman@cuaa.edu
VERSETTO, Ronald 773-838-7500 136 A rversetto@ccc.edu
VERSTEEG, Deanna 605-274-4191 426 K deanna.versteeg@augie.edu
VERTA, Larissa, M 610-799-1877 400 A lverta@lccc.edu
VERTIN, Diane 715-634-4790 507 J dvertin@lco.edu
VERTREES, Larry 314-719-8024 260 C lvertrees@fontbonne.edu
VERVYNCK, Lisa 904-256-1208 99 C lvervynck@fcsl.edu
VERYSER, Joseph, C 248-204-2818 233 A jveryser@ltu.edu
VERZINSKI, Becky 301-860-3501 208 E bverzinski@bowiestate.edu
VERZOSA, Jay 610-527-0200 409 E jay.verzosa@rosemont.edu
VERZYL, Scott 803-777-7700 424 I verzyl@mailbox.sc.edu
VESCIO, Sara, L 716-888-8285 300 G vescio11@canisius.edu
VESCOGNI, Emily, B 815-224-0462 141 A emily_vescogni@ivcc.edu
VESELY, Pamela 828-898-8734 339 B veselyp@lmc.edu
VESPASIAN, Bill 828-835-4211 347 B bvespasian@tricountycc.edu
VESS, Deborah, L 478-289-2034 118 H dvess@ega.edu
VESS, Paula 704-669-4101 342 B vessp750@clevelandcc.edu
VESSELLA, Tom 818-710-2249 49 D vesseltj@piercecollege.edu
VESSEY, Rebecka 503-375-7014 383 A rvessey@corban.edu
VEST, Ann 502-456-6509 189 F avest@sullivan.edu
VEST, Eric 479-619-4345 20 F evest@nwacc.edu
VEST, Margie, B 540-224-6672 482 A mbvest@jchs.edu
VEST, Mark, H 928-532-6141 15 B mark.vest@npc.edu
VEST, Rick 334-514-5070 2 E rick.vest@istc.edu
VESTAL, Teresa 620-331-4100 178 E tvestal@indycc.edu
VESTER, Jonathan, S 252-451-8364 345 B jsvester529@nashcc.edu
VESTRAND, Joan 734-372-4900 239 F vestranj@cooley.edu
VETETO, Steve 303-779-6431 44 A stephenveteto@gs.edu
VETRANO, Dawn 718-779-1499 320 C dvetrano@plazacollege.edu
VETTER, Chris 503-375-7017 383 A cvetter@corban.edu
VETTER, Gregory, A 701-355-8005 355 K gavetter@umary.edu
VETTER, Jay 612-343-4779 249 E jbvetter@northcentral.edu
VETTER, Kay 502-585-9911 189 B kvetter@spalding.edu
VETTER, Ron 910-962-3224 352 A vetterr@uncw.edu
VETTICKAL, Jay 219-942-1459 157 E jay.vettickal@ccr.edu
VEUM, David 218-739-3375 243 A dveum@lbs.edu
VEVE, Mia 210-567-2648 468 E veve@uthscsa.edu
VEYSEY, Bonita, M 973-353-1929 290 D veysey@scj.rutgers.edu
VEZINA, Michelle 859-344-3556 189 G vezinam@thomasmore.edu
VIADA, Marta 787-264-1912 524 D marta_viada@intersg.edu
VIALA, Linda 212-686-9244 298 C
VIALPANDO, Victor 303-340-7243 79 C victor.vialpando@ccaurora.edu
VIANDEN, Becky 608-785-8515 510 F bvianden@uwlax.edu
VIAR, David 818-240-1000 44 D dviar@glendale.edu
VIATOR, Van 985-448-4646 197 C van.viator@nicholls.edu
VIAU, Bill, J 330-972-6402 371 C viau@uakron.edu
VIAUD, Cindy 713-525-2162 466 J viaudc@stthom.edu
VIBOCH, Paul 304-263-6262 502 A pviboch@martinsburgcollege.edu
VICARI, Nicole 417-862-9533 260 D nvicari@globaluniversity.edu
VICARS, Ron 276-523-7478 488 F rvicars@mecc.edu
VICE, David 916-649-9600 26 S
VICENS, Catalina 787-622-8000 527 B cvicens@pupr.edu
VICHCALES, Kevin 210-832-2198 465 E vichcales@uiwtx.edu
VICK, Courtney 615-547-1357 431 D cvick@cumberland.edu
VICK, Dustin 205-453-6300 93 B
VICKER, Kevin 816-584-6517 265 C kevin.vicker@park.edu
VICKERMAN, Pat 309-438-8901 140 L pvicker@ilstu.edu
VICKERS, Cheryl, C 256-549-8376 2 A ccephus-vickers@gadsdenstate.edu
VICKERS, Dale 909-274-4365 52 I dvickers@mtsac.edu
VICKERS, Jacqueline 912-260-4324 125 F jacqueline.vickers@sgsc.edu
VICKERS, Jeremy 214-333-5489 447 D jeremyv@dbu.edu
VICKERS, Karen 563-244-7027 168 L kvickers@eicc.edu
VICKERS, Kelly, G 706-886-6831 126 F registrar@tfc.edu
VICKERS, Kimberly 404-471-6325 114 H kvickers@agnesscott.edu
VICKERS, Lelia 314-340-5078 260 H vickers@hssu.edu
VICKERS, LouAnn 503-838-8888 388 B vickersl@wou.edu
VICKERS, Marla 334-244-3110 4 E mvickers@aum.edu
VICKERS, Neil, W 512-223-1078 443 G nvickers@austincc.edu
VICKERS, Robbie 770-533-7051 122 E rvickers@laniertech.edu
VICKERS, Selwyn, M 205-934-1111 8 B smv@uab.edu
VICKERS, Tonya 912-871-7295 123 J tvickers@ogeecheetech.edu
VICKERS-KOCH, Mary 704-330-4656 342 A mary.vickers-koch@cpcc.edu
VICKERSTAFF, Susan 256-761-6333 7 D svickerstaff@talladega.edu
VICKERY, Ann Marie 215-637-7700 397 G avickery@holyfamily.edu
VICKNAIR, J. Paul 909-537-5029 33 D jvicknai@csusb.edu
VICKOUS, Natalie 270-384-8065 187 H vickousn@lindsey.edu
VICTOR, Michael, T 814-824-2311 401 J mvictor@mercyhurst.edu
VICTORIN-VANGERUD, Nancy, M 651-523-2878 242 E nvictorinvangerud01@hamline.edu
VICTORINE, Jon 978-934-5060 217 B jon_victorine@uml.edu
VICTORINO, Christine 951-827-7883 69 D christine.victorino@ucr.edu
VICTORY, Gregory, J 617-627-0813 225 A gregory.victory@tufts.edu
VIDAL, Andy 978-232-2384 214 G avidal@endicott.edu
VIDAL, Betsy 787-704-1020 522 J bvidal@ediccollege.edu
VIDAL, Karyn, J 561-202-6333 102 A
VIDAL, Molly 608-890-0181 512 D molly.vidal@uwex.uwc.edu
VIDAL, Terry 914-337-9300 305 F terry.vidal@concordia-ny.edu
VIDEKA, Lynn 734-764-5347 237 I
VIDMAR, Anthony 940-397-4782 453 C anthony.vidmar@mwsu.edu
VIDRINE, Christopher 504-568-5976 194 C cvidri@lsuhsc.edu
VIECK, Jana, L 812-888-5090 165 E jvieck@vinu.edu
VIEFHUES-BAILEY, Ludger 315-445-5427 312 F viefhulh@lemoyne.edu
VIEHMAN, David 215-368-5000 389 H dviehman@biblical.edu
VIEIRA, Elvira 973-877-3062 285 K vieira@essex.edu
VIEIRA, Margarida 508-531-2877 217 D mvieira@bridgew.edu
VIEIRA, Stephen 615-366-4400 436 E
VIELBIG, Matthew 425-235-7836 497 E mvielbig@rtc.edu
VIELE, Dan 314-529-9671 262 B dan.viele@maryville.edu
VIEMEISTER, Sara 541-506-6029 382 G financialaid@cgcc.edu
VIEN, Michele 518-694-7216 297 J michele.vien@acphs.edu
VIENNA, Michael 404-727-2834 119 B michael.vienna@emory.edu
VIENNE, Charlie 936-294-1840 462 F cvienne@shsu.edu
VIENNE, Kristy 936-294-1840 462 F klv002@shsu.edu
VIERA, Eddie 561-868-3390 105 A vierae@palmbeachstate.edu
VIERA, Javier 973-408-3258 285 E jviera@drew.edu
VIERECK, Shannon 605-668-1467 427 F shannon.viereck@mtmc.edu
VIEREGGE, Van 217-206-6002 154 A vvier2@uis.edu
VIERHELLER, Timothy 330-683-2010 371 D
VIERS, Christopher 812-855-9086 159 H cviers@iu.edu
VIERTEL, Cynthia, S 920-748-8312 509 H viertelc@ripon.edu
VIETTI, Jacqueline 913-288-7123 178 H jvietti@kckcc.edu
VIEWEG, Bruce, W 218-299-4737 241 K bvieweg@cord.edu
VIEWEG, Johannes 954-262-0510 104 F jvieweg@nova.edu
VIEWING, Bow 662-621-4050 252 E bviewing@coahomacc.edu
VIGDOR, Corey 908-737-4782 286 F cvigdor@kean.edu
VIGEANT, Paul 508-678-2811 219 C paul.vigeant@bristolcc.edu
VIGESAA, Linda 503-491-6928 384 D linda.vigesaa@mhcc.edu
VIGIL, Cynthia 509-533-3405 494 A cynthia.vigil@sfcc.spokane.edu
VIGIL, James 304-876-5219 504 D jvigil@shepherd.edu
VIGIL, Julie 907-796-6494 10 C jlvigil@alaska.edu
VIGIL, Renee 719-587-7526 76 D reneevigil@adams.edu
VIGNERON, David 978-232-2376 214 G dvignero@endicott.edu
VIGO VERESTIN, Milka 787-763-6700 522 N milkavigo@gmail.com
VIGOREAUX, Jim 802-656-4627 476 E jim.vigoreaux@uvm.edu
VIJITHA-KUMARA, Kanaka 309-467-6434 138 E kumara@eureka.edu
VIKANDER, David 507-537-6281 248 A david.vikander@smsu.edu
VILA, Cherly, T 692-625-3394 520 C cvila@cmi.edu
VILA, Dendy 787-765-3560 522 K dmvila@edpuniversity.edu
VILA, Joaquin 505-747-2194 295 H joaquin.vila@nnmc.edu
VILACRUZ, Geraldo, G 608-246-6442 514 A gvilacruz@madisoncollege.edu
VILE, John, R 615-898-2596 434 H john.vile@mtsu.edu
VILEGI PAYNE, Deborah 570-740-0232 400 F dvilegi@luzerne.edu
VILELLE, Luke 540-362-6592 481 F lvilelle@hollins.edu
VILES, Vickery 541-383-7258 382 B vviles@cocc.edu
VILIC, Boris 609-896-5033 289 E bvilic@rider.edu
VILKINA, Galina 212-616-7270 309 G galina.vilkina@helenefuld.edu
VILLA, Christopher 818-364-7642 49 C villachr@lamission.edu
VILLA, Cynthia 805-756-2171 30 K cvvilla@calpoly.edu
VILLA, William 808-739-4695 129 A william.villa@chaminade.edu
VILLAFANE, Meiling 787-850-9374 528 B meiling.villafane@upr.edu
VILLAGOMEZ, Maria 707-256-7767 53 D mvillagomez@napavalley.edu
VILLAGOMEZ, Rosita 718-405-3275 304 H rosita.villagomez@mountsaintvincent.edu
VILLAGRANA, Ana, L 530-661-5711 75 L avillagr@yccd.edu
VILLALOBOS, Alex 559-934-2373 73 N alexjvillalobos@whccd.edu
VILLALOBOS, Bobbi 310-233-4028 49 B villalb@lahc.edu
VILLALOBOS, Joshua, I 915-831-7002 449 A jvillal6@epcc.edu
VILLALOBOS, Ricardo 702-651-4737 278 N ricardo.villalobos@csn.edu
VILLALPANDO, Octavio 323-343-3800 32 D ovillal9@calstatela.edu
VILLALVA, Maribel 915-747-6463 467 E mvillalva2@utep.edu
VILLAMARIA, Paul 303-282-3318 82 G paul.villamaria@archden.org
VILLAMIL-TORRES, Margarita, E 787-250-0000 527 D margarita.villamil@upr.edu
VILLANELLA, Michael 212-752-1530 312 G michael.villanella@limcollege.edu
VILLANO, Steven 713-226-5244 465 C villanos@uhd.edu
VILLANTI, Athony 315-792-3053 332 H avillanti@utica.edu
VILLANUEVA, Arelis 787-766-1717 526 B avillanueva@suagm.edu
VILLANUEVA, Celeste 510-869-6511 59 F cvillanueva@samuelmerritt.edu
VILLANUEVA, Christina 210-431-6789 455 J cvillanueva@stmarytx.edu
VILLANUEVA, Daniel, G 818-364-7772 49 C villand@lamission.edu
VILLANUEVA, Donna-Mae 818-719-6444 49 D villandm@piercecollege.edu
VILLANUEVA, Gil 804-289-8640 486 G gvillanu@richmond.edu
VILLANUEVA, Lynda 979-230-3422 444 E lynda.villanueva@brazosport.edu
VILLANUEVA, Rebecca 432-264-5190 450 G rvillanueva@howardcollege.edu
VILLANUEVA, Sumaya 212-484-1346 302 F svillanueva@jjay.cuny.edu
VILLANUEVA, Tammy, M 518-562-4100 304 C tammy.villanueva@clinton.edu
VILLAR, Jeremy 323-953-4000 49 A villarjv@lacitycollege.edu
VILLARE, Kathryn 978-681-0800 221 D kvillare@mslaw.edu
VILLAREAL, Henry 650-574-6590 62 A henry.villareal@smccd.edu
VILLAROSE, Lesley 434-791-5627 478 E lvillarose@averett.edu
VILLARREAL, Abe 575-538-6336 297 H news@wnmu.edu
VILLARREAL, Elisabeth 210-829-2736 465 E villaret@uiwtx.edu
VILLARREAL, James 210-431-4312 455 J jvillarreal12@stmarytx.edu
VILLARREAL, Luis 713-313-1089 461 E luis.villarreal@tsu.edu
VILLARREAL, Oscar 559-925-3347 74 A oscarvillarreal@whccd.edu
VILLARREAL, Pete 530-749-3879 76 A pvillarre@yccd.edu
VILLARREAL, Velda 210-485-0735 441 E vvillarreal@alamo.edu
VILLARROEL, Gratzia 920-403-3887 509 J gratzia.villarroel@snc.edu
VILLARRUEL, Antonia 215-898-8283 412 G nursingdean@nursing.upenn.edu
VILLASENOR, Leslie 312-261-3912 146 G lvillasenor1@nl.edu
VILLAVERDE, Kimberly 859-371-9393 183 G kvillaverde@beckfield.edu
VILLEGAS, Elias 503-316-3259 382 C ellias.villegas@chemeketa.edu
VILLEGAS, Gregorio 787-766-1717 526 B um_gvillegas@suagm.edu
VILLEGAS, Lucille 310-954-4010 52 H lvillegas@msmu.edu
VILLEGAS-VIDAL, Ludi 818-364-7643 49 C villegl@lamission.edu
VILLELLA, John 610-436-3111 407 D jvillella@wcupa.edu
VILLELLA, Theresa 814-732-1297 406 B tvillella@edinboro.edu
VILLENEUVE, Martha 603-897-8260 281 I mvilleneuve@rivier.edu
VILLETT, Stephen, H 207-947-4591 198 F svillett@bealcollege.edu
VILLINES, Trish 870-743-3000 20 E tvillines@northark.edu
VILLOLDO, Sergio 787-754-8000 527 B svilloldo@pupr.edu
VINAL, Alicia 978-232-2271 214 G avinal@endicott.edu

VINCENT, Alisha .... 605-995-2937 427 A
alvincen@dwu.edu
VINCENT, Andrew .... 502-897-4785 189 A
avincent@sbts.edu
VINCENT, Angela .... 814-732-2921 406 B
vincent@edinboro.edu
VINCENT, Danny, E .... 740-826-8110 366 C
dvincent@muskingum.edu
VINCENT, Deborah, S .... 708-239-4793 153 B
deborah.vincent@trnty.edu
VINCENT, Gregory, J ..... 315-781-3309 310 C
vincent@hws.edu
VINCENT, Jeffrey, R .... 919-613-8004 337 C
jeff.vincent@duke.edu
VINCENT, Kitt .... 909-593-3511.. 70 E
kvincent@laverne.edu
VINCENT, Nelson, C ...... 513-556-2323 371 E
nelson.vincent@uc.edu
VINCENT, Sara .... 860-512-3100.. 85 G
svincent@manchestercc.edu
VINCENT, Vincent .... 256-306-2773.... 1 F
vincent.vincent@calhoun.edu
VINCENT-DUNN, James 317-738-8075 157 L
jvincent-dunn@franklincollege.edu
VINCITORE, Rachel .... 757-631-8101 478 D
rachel.vincitore@atlanticuniv.edu
VINE, Scott .... 717-358-3843 395 G
scott.vine@fandm.edu
VINES, Erin, E .... 661-722-6300.. 26 C
evines@avc.edu
VINES, Robert .... 239-590-7044 109 C
rvines@fgcu.edu
VINES, Susan .... 706-368-7726 119 G
svines@highlands.edu
VINET, Mary Christine .. 251-460-6185.... 9 B
cvinet@southalabama.edu
VINEYARD, Ed .... 580-548-2207 376 J
edwin.vineyard@noc.edu
VINEYARD, George .... 314-367-8700 266 D
george.vineyard@stlcop.edu
VINEYARD, Julie .... 785-242-2067 180 C
jvineyard@neosho.edu
VINEYARD, Rusty .... 304-462-6401 504 B
VINGER, Christopher ..... 212-472-1500 318 B
cvinger@nysid.edu
VINIAR, Barbara, A .... 410-827-5802 203 C
bviniar@chesapeake.edu
VINIK, Frank .... 202-319-4177.. 91 D
vinik@cua.edu
VINING, Caroline .... 479-356-2071.. 18 G
cvining@atu.edu
VINK, Cher .... 715-468-2815 515 D
cher.vink@witc.edu
VINROE, Richard .... 316-295-5911 177 F
vinroer@friends.edu
VINSON, Ben .... 202-994-6130.. 92 A
bvinson3@gwu.edu
VINSON, John, N .... 206-543-0521 499 D
vinso1jn@uw.edu
VINSON, Richard .... 336-721-2619 348 H
richard.vinson@salem.edu
VINSON, Terence .... 318-670-9426 196 A
tvinson@susla.edu
VINSON, William .... 608-249-6611 507 F
wvinson@msn.herzing.edu
VINTINNER, David, P .... 212-998-8014 318 D
david.vintinner@nyu.edu
VINYARD, Lisa .... 636-481-3101 261 B
lvinyard@jeffco.edu
VINZE, Ajay .... 573-882-6688 268 C
vinzea@missouri.edu
VIOLA, Anthony .... 617-730-7255 223 B
anthony.viola@newbury.edu
VIOLA, Joe .... 541-383-7776 382 B
jviola@cocc.edu
VIOLA, Judah .... 312-261-3527 146 G
judah.viola@nl.edu
VIOLA, Katie .... 425-739-8455 495 F
katie.viola@lwtech.edu
VIOLA, Michael .... 925-631-4817.. 59 C
mjv7@stmarys-ca.edu
VIOLANTI, Karen .... 410-857-2750 205 E
kviolanti@mcdaniel.edu
VIOLET, Matt .... 510-549-4710.. 66 D
mviolet@sksm.edu
VIOLETT, Edward .... 225-768-1711 191 G
edward.violett@ololcollege.edu
VIOLLT, Kathleen .... 312-935-6444 149 K
kviollt@robertmorris.edu
VIOLLT, Michael, P .... 312-935-6600 149 K
mviollt@robertmorris.edu
VIRASAWMI, Errol .... 516-364-0808 317 B
errol@nycollege.edu
VIRCKS, Andrea .... 651-523-2100 242 E
avircks01@hamline.edu
VIRDEN, Rebecka .... 501-977-2033.. 23 B
virden@uaccm.edu
VIRELLO, Mark .... 617-262-5000 212 C
mark.virello@the-bac.edu
VIRES, Charles .... 731-989-6171 432 C
cvires@fhu.edu
VIRJEE, Framroze, M .... 562-951-4500.. 30 J
fvirjee@calstate.edu
VIRK, Surinder .... 718-997-5760 303 E
surinder.virk@qc.cuny.edu
VIRKLER, Lyndon .... 802-225-3258 475 H
lyndon.virkler@neci.edu
VIRTUE, Alicia .... 707-524-1664.. 62 H
avirtue@santarosa.edu
VIRZI, Amanda .... 262-741-8392 513 G
virzia@gtc.edu
VISBARAS, Cynthia .... 207-786-6199 198 E
cvisbaras@bates.edu
VISCHER, Robert, K .... 651-962-4838 251 D
rkvischer@stthomas.edu
VISCO, JR., Donald, P .. 330-972-7930 371 C
dviscoj@uakron.edu
VISCOMI, Susan .... 315-312-3056 327 D
susan.viscomi@oswego.edu
VISCONAGE,
Elizabeth, L .... 410-864-4261 207 A
bvisconage@stmarys.edu
VISCUSI, Nicolette .... 518-264-2524 297 L
viscusn@mail.amc.edu
VISCUSI, Peter .... 304-384-5241 503 P
pviscusi@concord.edu
VISCUSI, Raymond .... 610-359-5070 393 E
rviscusi@dccc.edu
VISEL, OSB, Jeana .... 812-357-6721 164 A
jvisel@saintmeinrad.edu
VISENTIN, Peter .... 203-837-8680.. 85 B
visentinp@wcsu.edu
VISKER, Thomas .... 574-807-7259 156 E
viskert@bethelcollege.edu
VISKOZKI, Lynette .... 318-869-5137 191 C
lviskozk@centenary.edu
VISOT, Cynthia, S .... 813-974-1678 111 A
cvisot@usf.edu
VISSER, Erik .... 707-864-7000.. 64 E
erik.visser@solano.edu
VISSER, Jen .... 319-895-4167 167 G
jvisser@cornellcollege.edu
VISSER, Sandra, L .... 616-395-7748 231 D
visser@hope.edu
VISSER, Sarah .... 616-526-6453 228 B
sav36@calvin.edu
VISTOCCO, Valerie .... 315-781-3309 310 C
vistocco@hws.edu
VISUANO, Denise .... 503-838-8349 388 B
visuanod@wou.edu
VITA, Claudine .... 610-526-6012 396 H
cvita@harcum.edu
VITA, Paul .... 314-977-2500 266 J
vitap@slu.edu
VITAL, Allen .... 256-372-5230.... 1 A
allen.vital@aamu.edu
VITALE, Joseph .... 973-328-5060 285 B
jvitale@ccm.edu
VITALE, JR., Joseph ...... 440-775-5573 367 B
jvitale@oberlin.edu
VITALE, Tim .... 435-797-1351 473 C
tim.vitale@usu.edu
VITALI, John .... 973-408-3501 285 E
jvitali@drew.edu
VITALOS, Mark .... 610-606-4642 392 A
mavitalo@cedarcrest.edu
VITANGCOL REGOSO,
Aimee .... 269-471-3375 227 B
aimeev@andrews.edu
VITANGELI, Kory, M ...... 317-788-3485 164 H
kvitangeli@uindy.edu
VITATOE, David, A .... 216-397-1984 363 H
dvitatoe@jcu.edu
VITEK, Melissa .... 215-780-1527 410 D
mvitek@salus.edu
VITELLI, Chris .... 209-384-6101.. 51 G
chris.vitelli@mccd.edu
VITELLI, Kelly .... 814-732-1965 406 B
kvitelli@edinboro.edu
VITELLI, Mary .... 407-628-6303 106 J
mvitelli@rollins.edu
VITELLO, Joan .... 508-856-5081 217 C
joan.vitello@umassmed.edu
VITO, Christine .... 704-886-6500.. 93 B
VITO, Christine .... 304-760-1700.. 93 B
VITO, Melissa .... 520-621-0963.. 16 J
mmvito@email.arizona.edu
VITOLA, Anthony .... 203-332-5034.. 85 F
avitola@hcc.commnet.edu
VITRANO, Judy .... 504-314-2783 196 D
jvitrano@tulane.edu
VITTEK, Jeremy .... 740-699-9500 357 D
VITTER, Jeffrey, S .... 662-915-7111 256 C
chancellor@olemiss.edu
VITTETOE, Stanley .... 727-791-2475 107 A
vittetoe.stan@spcollege.edu
VITTI, Anthony .... 203-576-4735.. 88 F
anthonyv@bridgeport.edu
VITTITOE, Sheryl .... 772-462-4705 101 Q
svittito@irsc.edu
VITTONE, Jason .... 573-592-4387 270 D
jason.vittone@williamwoods.edu
VITUCCI, Tom .... 954-262-7304 104 F
tomv@nova.edu
VIVANCO, Nayeli .... 617-746-1990 216 A
nayeli.vivanco@hult.edu
VIVANO, Anthony .... 618-537-6823 145 C
amviviano@mckendree.edu
VIVEIROS, Derek .... 508-678-2811 219 C
derek.viveiros@bristolcc.edu
VIVERETTE, Maggie, J .... 229-333-5463 127 H
mviveret@valdosta.edu
VIVERITO, Diane .... 708-974-5334 146 C
viverito@morainevalley.edu
VIVEROS, Maribel .... 559-453-7161.. 43 J
maribel.viveros@fresno.edu
VIVIAN, Daniel .... 716-645-4540 325 B
dtvivian@buffalo.edu
VIVIANO-BRODERICK,
Tamara .... 352-854-2322.. 97 C
vivianot@cf.edu
VIVONA, Joseph, F .... 301-445-1923 207 F
jvivona@usmd.edu
VIVONI, Alberto .... 787-279-1912 523 J
avivoni@bayamon.inter.edu
VIZENOR, Andrea .... 650-738-7124.. 62 B
vizenora@smccd.edu
VIZZACCHERO,
Janice, P .... 201-761-6010 291 D
jvizzacchero@saintpeters.edu
VIZZIELLO, Daniella ...... 203-582-7806.. 88 A
daniella.vizziello@quinnipiac.edu
VIZZINI, Anthony .... 316-978-3010 182 F
tony.vizzini@wichita.edu
VIZZINI, Gail .... 631-451-4236 330 B
vizzing@sunysuffolk.edu
VLACH, Erin .... 614-222-4000 360 B
evlach@ccad.edu
VLAHOS, John .... 408-741-4606.. 74 D
john.vlahos@westvalley.edu
VLASTOS, Elizabeth .... 610-372-1722 389 G
elizabeth.vlastos@berks.edu
VO, Julie .... 408-270-6439.. 61 O
julie.vo@evc.edu
VO, Thoa Hoang .... 972-860-4604 447 G
tvo@dcccd.edu
VO, Thomas .... 941-752-5434 108 P
vot@scf.edu
VO-KUMAMOTO, Tram .. 510-981-2933.. 56 F
tvokumamoto@peralta.edu
VOCK, Jean .... 702-895-3571 279 D
jean.vock@unlv.edu
VODDE, Robert .... 201-692-2460 286 B
rvodde@fdu.edu
VOELCKER, Aaron .... 714-628-4990.. 58 B
voelcker_aaron@sccollege.edu
VOELKEL, Tyson .... 979-847-8700 459 C
tvoelkel@tamu.edu
VOETTERL RIECKER,
Robin .... 315-866-0300 310 A
voetterra@herkimer.edu
VOGAN, Randall .... 314-516-5478 268 E
vogan@umsl.edu
VOGEL, Erik .... 507-537-6147 248 A
erik.vogel@smsu.edu
VOGEL, Joanne, E .... 214-768-4564 457 B
jvogel@smu.edu
VOGEL, Justin .... 859-344-3307 189 G
vogelc@thomasmore.edu
VOGEL, Kristin, D .... 920-403-3290 509 J
kristin.vogel@snc.edu
VOGEL, Kristin, M .... 651-641-8839 241 L
vogel@csp.edu
VOGEL, Petra .... 802-586-7711 476 D
pvogel@sterlingcollege.edu
VOGEL, Rich .... 352-588-8361 106 N
rich.vogel@saintleo.edu
VOGEL, Richard .... 631-420-2189 329 D
richard.vogel@farmingdale.edu
VOGEL, Robert .... 412-536-1032 398 E
bob.vogel@laroche.edu
VOGEL, Ronald .... 323-343-4621.. 32 D
rvogel@calstatela.edu
VOGEL, Stacia .... 612-728-5119 250 B
svogel@smumn.edu
VOGEL, Terri .... 660-562-1151 264 I
tvogel@nwmissouri.edu
VOGELMANN,
Thomas, C .... 802-656-0137 476 E
thomas.vogelmann@uvm.edu
VOGELWELD, Eric .... 573-882-2011 268 B
VOGHEL-OCHS, Sydney 203-575-8297.. 86 B
svoghel-ochs@nv.edu
VOGL, Joseph, A .... 989-964-4051 236 F
javogl@svsu.edu
VOGT, Elizabeth .... 940-565-2628 466 B
elizabeth.vogt@unt.edu
VOGT, Erica .... 239-513-1122 101 O
evogt@hodges.edu
VOGT, Gail .... 619-574-6909.. 55 B
gvogt@pacificcollege.edu
VOGT, Kim .... 608-785-8116 510 F
kvogt@uwlax.edu
VOGT, Mark, A .... 502-410-6200 184 H
mvogt@galencollege.edu
VOGT, Marlene .... 815-479-7559 145 B
mvogt@mchenry.edu
VOGT, Randy .... 559-244-5940.. 66 E
randy.vogt@scccd.edu
VOGT, Tracy .... 734-384-4230 234 C
tvogt@monroeccc.edu
VOGTMAN, Jena .... 715-394-6677 515 D
jena.vogtman@witc.edu
VOIGHT, Patty .... 610-989-1450 413 I
pvoight@vfmac.edu
VOIGT, Francis .... 802-225-3207 475 H
francis.voigt@neci.edu
VOIGT, Lea .... 615-794-4254 435 G
lvoigt@omorecollege.edu
VOIGT, Lydia .... 504-865-2277 194 G
VOIGT, Shannon .... 757-490-1241 477 F
svoigt@auto.edu
VOIGTS, Adam, J .... 515-263-2821 169 E
avoigts@grandview.edu
VOIGTS, Sheryl .... 859-858-3511 183 D
sheryl.voigts@asbury.edu
VOISIN, Anthony, A ...... 989-774-3346 228 E
voisi1a@cmich.edu
VOISINE, Scott, A .... 207-834-8644 201 E
voisine@maine.edu
VOISS, SJ, Jim .... 509-313-6191 495 A
voiss@gonzaga.edu
VOKES, Bill .... 724-838-4282 410 E
vokes@setonhill.edu
VOLAK, Renee .... 201-692-2730 286 B
renee_volak@fdu.edu
VOLAKIS, John .... 305-348-0273 109 D
john.volakis@fiu.edu
VOLANT, Adam, C .... 540-464-7221 490 E
volantac@vmiaa.org
VOLBRECHT, Adam .... 414-443-8689 513 A
adam.volbrecht@wlc.edu
VOLCY, Ty .... 714-484-7309.. 53 M
tvolcy@cypresscollege.edu
VOLDEN, Emelee .... 608-785-8017 510 F
evolden@uwlax.edu
VOLDEN, Lora .... 907-786-1266.. 10 A
llvolden@alaska.edu
VOLES, Lorraine, A .... 202-994-8810.. 92 A
lvoles@gwu.edu
VOLETY, Aswani .... 910-962-7232 352 A
voletya@uncw.edu
VOLIN, John .... 860-486-0631.. 88 G
john.volin@uconn.edu
VOLINO, Milissa .... 607-735-1890 307 G
mvolino@elmira.edu
VOLK, Mark .... 570-961-7850 399 A
volkm@lackawanna.edu
VOLK, Michael, S .... 616-554-5695 229 D
mvolk@davenport.edu
VOLK, Rick .... 800-280-0307 155 H
rick.volk@ace.edu
VOLKERS, Erica .... 505-224-3699 293 L
evolkers@cnm.edu
VOLKERT, Jo .... 510-885-7636.. 31 F
jo.volkert@csueastbay.edu
VOLKERT, Jo .... 415-338-7264.. 34 C
jvolkert@sfsu.edu
VOLKMER, James .... 402-472-7677 277 G
james.volkmer@unl.edu
VOLL, William .... 914-923-2772 319 J
wvoll@pace.edu
VOLLENDORF, Lisa .... 707-664-2028.. 35 A
VOLLMER, Sara .... 701-224-5639 354 F
sara.vollmer@bismarckstate.edu
VOLLRATH, David, A ..... 574-520-4260 160 F
vollrath@iusb.edu
VOLNICK, Stacy .... 561-297-0143 109 B
svolnick@fau.edu
VOLOSHIN, Irina .... 206-296-2802 498 D
voloshii@seattleu.edu
VOLPE, Greg .... 856-222-9311 289 F
gvolpe@rcbc.edu
VOLPE, Jonathan .... 440-366-4051 364 F
VOLPI, Karla .... 575-234-9216 295 D
kvolpi@nmsu.edu
VOLPI, Karla .... 520-383-8401.. 16 G
kvolpi@tocc.edu

W

WAGNER, Jodi 509-527-2772 499 F jodi.wagner@wallawalla.edu
WAGNER, Joseph 413-592-3189 213 E wagnerj@elms.edu
WAGNER, Kelsea 276-935-4349 477 M
WAGNER, Kevin, J 740-826-6129 366 C kevinw@muskingum.edu
WAGNER, Kimberly 260-481-6103 160 D wagnerk@ipfw.edu
WAGNER, Kurt 732-571-4401 287 C kwagner@monmouth.edu
WAGNER, Kyle 843-921-6901 423 A kwagner@netc.edu
WAGNER, Lana 325-649-8076 450 H lwagner@hputx.edu
WAGNER, Linda, L 814-871-7423 395 H wagner001@gannon.edu
WAGNER, Marci, K 724-450-4089 396 D mkwagner@gcc.edu
WAGNER, Marilyn, D 940-565-3487 466 B mwagner@unt.edu
WAGNER, Mary 803-777-7700 424 I mary.wagner@sc.edu
WAGNER, Mervin 816-322-0110 257 M merv.wagner@calvary.edu
WAGNER, Michael, F 603-646-0459 281 C michael.f.wagner@dartmouth.edu
WAGNER, Michelle, L 262-243-5700 507 C michelle.wagner@cuw.edu
WAGNER, Mike 309-556-3561 141 B mwagner@iwu.edu
WAGNER, Nicholas, J 989-964-2468 236 F njwagner@svsu.edu
WAGNER, Patrick 217-245-3046 139 H patrick.wagner@mail.ic.edu
WAGNER, Rich 612-374-5800 242 C rwagner@dunwoody.edu
WAGNER, Richard, A 413-796-2306 225 F richard.wagner@wne.edu
WAGNER, Richard, T 240-895-3421 206 G rtwagner@smcm.edu
WAGNER, Robert 212-563-6647 332 A r.wagner@uts.edu
WAGNER, Robert 435-797-0945 473 C robert.wagner@usu.edu
WAGNER, Robert, A 971-722-4696 386 C robert.wagner3@pcc.edu
WAGNER, Robin 717-337-7000 396 A rowagner@gettysburg.edu
WAGNER, Roger, W 760-245-4271 73 E roger.wagner@vvc.edu
WAGNER, Sarah 231-843-5986 239 D sjwagner@westshore.edu
WAGNER, Susan 520-795-0787 10 J financialaid@asaom.edu
WAGNER, Teresa, J 315-464-4252 326 B wagnert@upstate.edu
WAGNER, Tina 651-690-8890 249 T tmwagner@stkate.edu
WAGNER, Tracy, A 941-309-4376 106 H twagner@ringling.edu
WAGNER-FOSSEN, Dena 406-771-4312 272 D dfossen@gfcmsu.edu
WAGNITZ, Jeff 206-878-3711 495 E jwagnitz@highline.edu
WAGNON, Bill 601-635-6242 252 I bwagnon@eccc.edu
WAGNON, Shelley 313-993-1588 237 F wagnonsm@udmercy.edu
WAGONER, Dale 510-723-6933 36 C dwagoner@chabotcollege.edu
WAGONER, Jessica 657-278-2570 32 B jwagoner@fullerton.edu
WAGONER, Natalie, M 260-399-7700 165 B nwagoner@sf.edu
WAGONER, Zandra, L 909-593-3511 70 E zwagoner@laverne.edu
WAGSTAFF, Grayson 202-319-5417 91 D wagstaff@cua.edu
WAGSTAFF, Robert 617-603-6900 222 F robert.wagstaff@necb.edu
WAGSTAFFE, Paul 916-686-8816 30 H
WAGUESPACK, Bruce 225-675-5397 193 C bwaguespack@rpcc.edu
WAGUESPACK, Cathy 504-398-2111 196 E cwaguespack@uhcno.edu
WAHAB, Lizzie 518-244-3130 321 G wahabr@sage.edu
WAHL, Chris 201-360-4030 286 E cwahl@hccc.edu
WAHL, David 925-473-7415 41 A dwahl@losmedanos.edu
WAHL, Jeff 303-404-5133 79 K jeff.wahl@frontrange.edu
WAHL, Lynette 651-523-3000 242 E lwahl@hamline.edu
WAHL, Robert 860-255-3472 86 G rwahl@txcc.commnet.edu
WAHLBERG, David, C 218-477-2175 246 B david.wahlberg@mnstate.edu
WAHLBERG, Elizabeth 610-989-1253 413 I ewahlberg@vfmac.edu
WAHLFELDT, Tracy, D 217-443-8772 137 B twahlfeldt@dacc.edu
WAHLROOS-RITTER, Ingalill 818-767-0888 75 C ingalill.wahlroos-ritter@woodbury.edu
WAHLS, Dustha 217-234-5210 143 B dwahl@lakeland.cc.il.us
WAHLSTROM, David, A 617-989-4552 225 E wahlstromd@wit.edu
WAHLSTROM HELGREN, Elizabeth 312-567-3000 140 I
WAHR, Linda 312-329-2213 146 B linda.wahr@moody.edu
WAHRHAFTIG, Matt 937-481-2263 373 I matt_wahrhaftig@wilmington.edu
WAIBEL, Janet 573-882-2011 268 B
WAID, Landon 205-348-7287 8 A landon.waid@ua.edu
WAID, Monica, K 941-359-7514 106 H mwaid@ringling.edu
WAID, Patricia 530-898-6132 31 D pwaid@csuchico.edu
WAIDE, Michael 304-333-3634 503 C michael.waide@pierpont.edu
WAINWRIGHT, Christopher 386-506-3162 97 I wainwrc@daytonastate.edu
WAINWRIGHT, Lisa 312-629-1236 151 F lwainwright@saic.edu
WAINWRIGHT, Philip 404-727-7504 119 B pwainwr@emory.edu
WAINWRIGHT, William, S 985-545-1500 192 K
WAIS, Marc, L 212-998-4401 318 D marc.wais@nyu.edu
WAIT, Julianna, M 757-594-7385 479 H julianna.wait@cnu.edu
WAIT, Mark 615-322-7660 440 D mark.wait@vanderbilt.edu
WAITE, Boyd, A 410-293-1582 519 E waite@usna.edu
WAITE, Dan 949-214-3472 40 I dan.waite@cui.edu
WAITE, Joann 509-313-5870 495 A waite@gonzaga.edu
WAITE, Michelle 402-472-2116 277 G mwaite1@unl.edu
WAITE, Zauyah 412-365-2794 392 C zwaite@chatham.edu
WAITERS, Destinee 940-898-3250 464 A dwaiters@twu.edu
WAITERS, Ernest 301-860-4040 208 E ewaiters@bowiestate.edu
WAITLEY, Erin 970-521-6662 81 F erin.waitley@njc.edu
WAITS, David 405-744-2325 377 F david.waits@okstate.edu
WAITS, Lisa 707-638-5270 67 H lisa.waits@tu.edu
WAITSMAN, Eileen 410-209-6050 202 F ewaitsman@bccc.edu
WAITZ, Ian, A 617-253-1000 221 C
WAJDA, Phillip, J 518-388-6131 332 B wajdap@union.edu
WAJERT, Susan 419-251-1314 365 C susan.wajert@mercycollege.edu
WAKEFIELD, Cooper, S 920-923-8977 508 B cswakefield00@marianuniversity.edu
WAKEFIELD, Donna 513-751-1206 356 A donna@aic-arts.edu
WAKEFIELD, Sandra 563-355-3500 171 B swakefield@kaplan.edu
WAKEFIELD, Sarah 425-235-2285 497 E swakefield@rtc.edu
WAKEM, Jake 651-641-8228 241 L wakem@csp.edu
WAKSDAHL, Robert, B 715-394-8017 512 B rwaksdah@uwsuper.edu
WALBERT, Mark 309-438-7018 140 L mswalber@ilstu.edu
WALBORN, Ronald 845-770-5716 319 C ronald.walborn@nyack.edu
WALBORN, Wanda, F 845-675-4457 319 C wanda.walborn@nyack.edu
WALCH, Sarah 210-690-9000 449 K swalch@hallmarkuniversity.edu
WALCHER, Sheldon 815-802-8702 142 C swalcher@kcc.edu
WALCHESKI, Michael 651-603-6184 241 L walcheski@csp.edu
WALCHLE, John 740-392-6868 366 B john.walchle@mvnu.edu
WALCK, Barbara 716-614-5902 318 E bwalck@niagaracc.suny.edu
WALCROFT, Marie, B 215-699-5700 399 G mwalcroft@lsb.edu
WALCZAK, Mary 507-786-3498 250 C walczak@stolaf.edu
WALD, Cara 651-638-6400 240 J c-wald@bethel.edu
WALD, Elaine 860-628-4751 87 E ewald@lincolncollegene.edu
WALD, Frederica, N 212-346-1200 319 J fwald@pace.edu
WALDBILLIG, Amy 513-569-1414 359 G amy.waldbillig@cincinnatistate.edu
WALDECK, Steve 661-362-2767 51 C swaldeck@masters.edu
WALDEN, Bernadine 919-516-4140 348 G bwalden@st-aug.edu
WALDEN, Dan 323-953-4000 49 A waldendw@lacitycollege.edu
WALDEN, David 315-859-4340 309 D dwalden@hamilton.edu
WALDEN, Shawn 785-243-1435 176 I swalden@cloud.edu
WALDEN, Valerie 361-570-4815 465 D waldenv@uhv.edu
WALDEN, Wendy 864-250-8125 421 K wendy.walden@gvltec.edu
WALDHOF, Kenneth 718-862-7362 313 L kenneth.waldhof@manhattan.edu
WALDMAN, Chaim, A 718-259-5600 307 H
WALDMANN, Robert, G 718-429-6600 333 B robert.waldmann@vaughn.edu
WALDNER, Doug 507-433-0814 247 C doug.waldner@riverland.edu
WALDNER, Joanne, L 978-232-2013 214 G jwaldner@endicott.edu
WALDNER, Louann 559-688-3027 39 G louannw@cos.edu
WALDO, Hilary 678-916-2625 115 K hwaldo@johnmarshall.edu
WALDON, James, G 802-447-4004 476 C jwaldon@svc.edu
WALDON, Russell 661-362-3035 39 C russell.waldon@canyons.edu
WALDRAM CRAMER, Kelly 660-543-4255 268 A
WALDROFF, Lauren 510-567-6174 66 I lwaldroff@sum.edu
WALDROFF, Mary 828-884-8373 335 L waldromb@brevard.edu
WALDRON, David, E 512-448-8453 455 I dwaldron@stedwards.edu
WALDRON, Gregory, T 401-865-2290 416 E gregory.waldron@providence.edu
WALDRON, Kathleen 973-720-2222 292 I waldronk@wpunj.edu
WALDRON, Kevin 215-646-7300 396 E waldron.k@gmercyu.edu
WALDRON, Kim 315-228-7411 304 G kwaldron@colgate.edu
WALDRON, Sara 973-408-3390 285 E swaldron@drew.edu
WALDROP, Heath 870-862-8131 21 D hwaldrop@southark.edu
WALDROP, Jean 501-279-4349 19 G jwaldrop@harding.edu
WALDROP, Jeffrey, A 626-396-6018 43 K jeffreyw@fuller.edu
WALDROP, Lisa 205-391-2959 3 E lwaldrop@sheltonstate.edu
WALDROP, Tony, G 251-460-6111 9 B twaldrop@southalabama.edu
WALDROUP, LeAnn 706-379-5111 128 H klwaldroup@yhc.edu
WALDROUP, Linda, L 812-888-4333 165 E lwaldroup@vinu.edu
WALDRUFF, Terry 315-386-7019 329 A waldruff@canton.edu
WALDRUP, J. Charles 336-334-7592 350 C cwaldrup@ncat.edu
WALDSTEIN, Edith, J 319-352-8272 174 C edith.waldstein@wartburg.edu
WALDSTEIN, Steve 712-324-5061 172 E swaldstein@nwicc.edu
WALDVOGEL, Todd, S 817-257-7955 461 A todd.waldvogel@tcu.edu
WALEK, Chuck 972-708-7574 449 I chuck_walek@gial.edu
WALENTA, Michael 616-331-6775 230 G walentam@gvsu.edu
WALES, Beth 518-861-2506 314 B bwales@mariacollege.edu
WALES, Chuck 714-628-4721 58 B wales_chuck@sccollege.edu
WALES, Lynn 215-885-2360 401 A lwales@manor.edu
WALESBY, Anthony 309-438-3383 140 L ajwales1@ilstu.edu
WALHOUT, Matthew 616-526-6566 228 B mwalhout@calvin.edu
WALK, Kerry 212-517-0560 314 D kwalk@mmm.edu
WALK, Steve 657-278-1605 32 B swalk@fullerton.edu
WALKE, James 256-372-8876 1 A james.walke@aamu.edu
WALKE, Lindsey 843-863-8047 419 C lwalke@csuniv.edu
WALKER, Alan, G 775-831-1314 280 C awalker@sierranevada.edu
WALKER, Amanda 360-867-6300 494 G walkera@evergreen.edu
WALKER, Amanda 931-221-6163 430 B walkera@apsu.edu
WALKER, Ameae 951-827-5942 69 D ameae.walker@ucr.edu
WALKER, Andrew 252-246-1311 347 H awalker@wilsoncc.edu
WALKER, Angie 928-541-7777 54 B awalker@ncu.edu
WALKER, Anne 303-384-2321 78 J aswalker@mines.edu
WALKER, Anne, E 713-348-8025 455 F anne.e.walker@rice.edu
WALKER, Beth 970-491-2398 78 N beth.walker@colostate.edu
WALKER, Beth 313-664-7641 228 H bwalker@collegeforcreativestudies.edu
WALKER, Beverley 478-289-2051 118 H bewalker@ega.edu
WALKER, Beverly 419-755-4786 366 E bwalker@ncstatecollege.edu
WALKER, Bob 712-749-2386 167 C bwalker@bvu.edu
WALKER, Bradley 361-593-3918 460 B bradley.walker@tamuk.edu
WALKER, Brenda 803-705-4730 418 G walkerb@benedict.edu
WALKER, Bruce, R 304-558-0695 503 N bruce.walker@wvhepc.edu
WALKER, Carey 603-427-7605 280 J cwalker@ccsnh.edu
WALKER, Carol 352-588-8308 106 N carol.walker@saintleo.edu
WALKER, Carolyn 213-763-5302 49 F walkerc@lattc.edu
WALKER, Charlene 859-246-6438 185 G charlene.walker@kctcs.edu
WALKER, Cherilee 913-288-7134 178 H cwalker@kckcc.edu
WALKER, Cherilee 913-288-7269 178 H cwalker@kckcc.edu
WALKER, Cherilee 419-995-8222 363 G walker.c2@rhodesstate.edu
WALKER, Cheryl, L 979-845-2217 459 C molbiores@tamu.edu
WALKER, Cindy, M 412-396-6093 394 D cmwalker@duq.edu
WALKER, Courtney 903-670-2688 464 C cwalker@tvcc.edu
WALKER, Dalbert, N 772-546-5534 101 N dalbertwalker@hsbc.edu
WALKER, David, S 717-766-2511 401 L dwalker@messiah.edu
WALKER, Debbie 417-328-1729 267 A dlwalker@sbuniv.edu
WALKER, Debbie 803-822-3261 422 D walkerd@midlandstech.edu
WALKER, Deborah 845-675-4430 319 C deborah.walker@nyack.edu
WALKER, Deborah 510-649-2577 44 J dwalker@gtu.edu
WALKER, Deborah 510-849-8290 55 D dwalker@psr.edu
WALKER, Donna 972-238-6880 448 D dwalker1@dcccd.edu
WALKER, Doug 845-675-4509 319 C douglas.walker@nyack.edu
WALKER, Dwayne 215-489-2372 393 F dwayne.walker@delval.edu
WALKER, Eddie 318-869-5116 191 C ewalker@centenary.edu
WALKER, Ellen, L 330-569-5250 362 J walkerel@hiram.edu
WALKER, Erik, J 610-758-3131 400 B erw209@lehigh.edu
WALKER, Eunice, E 870-235-5113 21 F eewalker@saumag.edu
WALKER, Francene 240-567-7491 205 F francene.walker@montgomerycollege.edu
WALKER, Gail, D 208-467-8844 132 F gwalker@nnu.edu

WALLACE, Susan, H ...... 925-631-4571.. 59 C susan.wallace@stmarys-ca.edu
WALLACE, Tami .... 615-230-3573 438 C tami.wallace@volstate.edu
WALLACE, Teresa .... 307-268-2621 516 H twallace@caspercollege.edu
WALLACE, Thomas .... 661-654-2161.. 31 B twallace4@csub.edu
WALLACE, Tim .... 864-587-4267 424 D wallacet@smcsc.edu
WALLACE, Tom .... 615-898-2137 434 H tom.wallace@mtsu.edu
WALLACE, Tony .... 606-783-1538 186 E tony.wallace@kctcs.edu
WALLEN, Esther .... 773-252-5133 149 I esther.wallen@resu.edu
WALLER, Art .... 801-774-9900 470 G awaller@vistacollege.edu
WALLER, Brent .... 303-964-5086.. 82 D bwaller@regis.edu
WALLER, Caroline .... 870-235-4006.. 21 F acwaller@saumag.edu
WALLER, Cynthia, G ..... 615-353-3645 437 D cynthia.waller@nscc.edu
WALLER, Edward .... 281-283-3100 465 B waller@uhcl.edu
WALLER, Frank .... 301-860-3813 208 E fwaller@bowiestate.edu
WALLER, J.J .... 912-525-5000 125 B jwaller@scad.edu
WALLER, Janet .... 256-824-6282.... 8 C janet.waller@uah.edu
WALLER, Jennifer .... 662-645-3555 252 H jwaller@deltastate.edu
WALLER, Karen .... 615-230-3500 438 C karen.waller@volstate.edu
WALLER, Lorie .... 919-735-5151 347 E loriew@waynecc.edu
WALLER, Steve .... 225-578-5388 193 M swaller@lsu.edu
WALLER, Steven .... 402-472-2201 277 G swaller1@unl.edu
WALLER, Wanda, M ...... 318-670-9248 196 A wmwaller@susla.edu
WALLERSTEIN, Mitchel, B .... 646-312-3310 301 B president@baruch.cuny.edu
WALLESER, Diane .... 212-220-1275 301 C dwalleser@bmcc.cuny.edu
WALLESHAUSER, Linda, M .... 716-888-2244 300 G walleshl@canisius.edu
WALLET, Robert, M .... 717-361-1524 394 F walletrm@etown.edu
WALLEY, Anna-Jean .... 559-251-4215.. 28 I bookkeeper@calchristiancollege.edu
WALLEY, Jennifer .... 559-251-4215.. 28 I jwalley@fpu.edu
WALLEY, Jennifer .... 559-251-4215.. 28 I jwalley@calchristiancollege.edu
WALLEY, Trent .... 559-251-4215.. 28 I twalley@calchristiancollege.edu
WALLIN, Celeste .... 212-616-7273 309 G celeste.wallin@helenefuld.edu
WALLIN, Jon .... 540-261-8598 485 G jon.wallin@svu.edu
WALLIN, William .... 303-329-6355.. 78 L registrar@cstcm.edu
WALLING, Lisa .... 931-526-3660 431 J lisaq.walling@fortisinstitute.edu
WALLING, Ray .... 785-594-8389 174 J ray.walling@bakeru.edu
WALLINGA, Michael ...... 712-707-7108 172 G mwalling@nwciowa.edu
WALLINGTON-HARRIS, Danielle .... 773-907-6834 135 K dwallington-harris@ccc.edu
WALLIS, OSB, Jonathan 985-867-2287 195 I
WALLIS, Madeline .... 978-762-4000 220 E mwallis@northshore.edu
WALLIS, Matthew .... 817-257-5808 461 A matthew.wallis@tcu.edu
WALLIS, Sherry, L .... 660-263-3900 258 A sherrywallis@cccb.edu
WALLMAN, Marc .... 701-231-8640 354 D marc.wallman@ndsu.edu
WALLNER, Heidi .... 715-346-2926 511 F hwallner@uwsp.edu
WALLNER, Steve .... 262-595-2451 511 C wallner@uwp.edu
WALLS, Arnita .... 651-641-3599 242 J hr@luthersem.edu
WALLS, Eric, R .... 210-562-6201 468 E wallse@uthscsa.edu
WALLS, Maryanna .... 301-962-5111 210 D mwalls@yeshiva.edu
WALLS, Melinda .... 304-293-2067 505 B mfwalls@mail.wvu.edu
WALLS, Skip .... 972-686-7878 455 B skip.walls@remingtoncollege.edu
WALLS-MCKAY, Maureen, J .... 434-395-2409 482 E wallsmckaymj@longwood.edu
WALLSTEADT, Nicholas . 863-667-5493 108 G ndwallsteadt@seu.edu
WALN, Ursula .... 505-224-4000 293 L uwaln@cnm.edu
WALPOLE, Harry .... 914-337-9300 305 F harry.walpole@concordia-ny.edu
WALPOLE, Tommy .... 318-342-5419 198 A walpole@ulm.edu
WALROND, Helena .... 386-481-2349.. 95 J walrondh@cookman.edu
WALSH, Bernadette .... 610-526-6002 396 H bwalsh@harcum.edu
WALSH, Brendan .... 845-451-1616 306 D brendan.walsh@culinary.edu
WALSH, Chris .... 502-585-9911 189 B cwalsh@spalding.edu
WALSH, Christina .... 541-463-5354 383 F walshc@lanecc.edu
WALSH, Clifton .... 915-747-6636 467 E cwalsh@utep.edu
WALSH, CSSP, Daniel ... 412-396-6020 394 D walshd@duq.edu
WALSH, Darren .... 303-937-4420.. 77 B darren.walsh@augustineinstitute.org
WALSH, Debra .... 715-852-1353 513 E dwalsh7@cvtc.edu
WALSH, Frannie .... 480-994-9244.. 16 E franniew@swiha.edu
WALSH, Jeffrey .... 813-226-4901 106 N jeffrey.walsh@saintleo.edu
WALSH, Jennifer .... 626-815-6000.. 26 U jwalsh@apu.edu
WALSH, Joe .... 256-782-5616.... 6 B ejwalsh@jsu.edu
WALSH, John .... 520-417-4081.. 11 R walshj@cochise.edu
WALSH, John .... 978-632-6600 220 D j_walsh@mwcc.mass.edu
WALSH, John, T .... 909-748-8368.. 71 H john_walsh@redlands.edu
WALSH, Joseph, T .... 847-491-3485 148 C vp-research@northwestern.edu
WALSH, Julie .... 845-257-2632 325 D walshj@newpaltz.edu
WALSH, Kate, D .... 607-255-5106 306 B kmw33@cornell.edu
WALSH, Kimberly, A ...... 563-588-7417 171 H kimberly.walsh@loras.edu
WALSH, Lenore, J .... 516-876-4974 327 C walshle@oldwestbury.edu
WALSH, Mark .... 813-974-2660 111 A mwalsh@usf.edu
WALSH, Mary, T .... 504-314-2537 196 D mary@tulane.edu
WALSH, Mary Lee .... 434-961-6540 489 C mwalsh@pvcc.edu
WALSH, Maryann .... 516-463-6745 310 D maryann.walsh@hofstra.edu
WALSH, Melissa .... 610-526-6197 396 H mwalsh@harcum.edu
WALSH, Michael .... 414-297-6246 514 C walshm@matc.edu
WALSH, Michael, D ...... 540-568-5681 481 I walshmd@jmu.edu
WALSH, Michelle .... 845-437-7750 333 A miwalsh@vassar.edu
WALSH, Nancy .... 217-333-6677 154 B njwalsh@illinois.edu
WALSH, Patricia, J .... 913-971-3453 179 H pwalsh@mnu.edu
WALSH, Patrick .... 608-363-2174 506 D walshpj@beloit.edu
WALSH, Patrick .... 541-684-7244 384 H pwalsh@nwcu.edu
WALSH, Peter, J .... 512-448-8441 455 I peterjw@stedwards.edu
WALSH, Rosalie, K .... 406-447-5530 270 H rwalsh@carroll.edu
WALSH, Susan .... 541-552-6114 386 H walsh@sou.edu
WALSH, Tammy, S .... 941-359-7505 106 H twalsh@ringling.edu
WALSH, Teresa .... 732-255-0400 288 B twalsh@ocean.edu
WALSH, Timothy .... 919-684-5055 337 C tim.walsh@duke.edu
WALSH, Timothy, J .... 716-878-4201 326 E walshtj@buffalostate.edu
WALSH-DAVIS, Nicholas .... 818-785-2726.. 35 N
WALSH FITZPATRICK, Mary .... 518-445-2377 297 K mfitz@albanylaw.edu
WALSHOK, Mary, L .... 858-534-3411.. 69 E mwalshok@ucsd.edu
WALSTEAD, Brenda .... 360-992-2474 493 E bwalstead@clark.edu
WALSTER, Jane .... 360-992-2447 493 E jwalster@clark.edu
WALSTON, Angie .... 252-399-6313 335 I amwalston@barton.edu
WALSTON, Timothy .... 660-785-4000 267 K
WALSTON, Valerie .... 419-530-7262 372 F valerie.simmonswalston@utoledo.edu
WALSTROM, Katherine .. 941-487-4493 110 B walstrom@ncf.edu
WALTER, Almar .... 614-236-6181 358 A awalter@capital.edu
WALTER, George .... 717-361-1400 394 F walterg@etown.edu
WALTER, Hank .... 812-855-3562 159 H walterh@indiana.edu
WALTER, Jaclyn .... 812-535-5236 163 I jaclyn.walter@smwc.edu
WALTER, Jim .... 706-355-5120 115 H jwalter@athenstech.edu
WALTER, John, M .... 661-362-2239.. 51 C jwalter@masters.edu
WALTER, Josh .... 503-768-7921 383 G jwalter@lclark.edu
WALTER, Kelly, A .... 617-353-3530 212 G kwalter@bu.edu
WALTER, Kristy .... 617-243-2147 216 C kwalter@lasell.edu
WALTER, Mary Beth ...... 937-327-7517 374 A walterm@wittenberg.edu
WALTER, Rachel .... 419-434-4570 372 B walterr@findlay.edu
WALTER, Robyn, C .... 636-584-6617 259 L robyn.walter@eastcentral.edu
WALTER, Scott .... 773-325-8023 137 C swalte11@depaul.edu
WALTER, Shulem .... 718-855-4092 320 I swalter@rcosy.org
WALTER, Toni .... 660-596-7222 267 E awalter@sfccmo.edu
WALTER, Willis, W .... 804-524-6869 491 A wwalter@vsu.edu
WALTER-MACK, Kathy ... 816-604-1587 262 F kathy.walter-mack@mcckc.edu
WALTERREIT, Jay .... 989-358-7215 227 A walterrj@alpenacc.edu
WALTERS, Carmen .... 601-928-6205 254 D carmen.walters@mgccc.edu
WALTERS, Carolyn .... 812-855-3403 159 H cwalters@indiana.edu
WALTERS, Carolyn .... 812-855-3403 159 G cwalters@indiana.edu
WALTERS, Charity .... 406-683-7471 271 H charity.walters@umwestern.edu
WALTERS, Evon .... 412-237-2770 392 G ewalters@ccac.edu
WALTERS, Greg .... 209-932-3274.. 70 F gwalters@pacific.edu
WALTERS, Gregory .... 413-748-3252 224 G gwalters@springfieldcollege.edu
WALTERS, Isaac .... 267-256-0200.. 93 B
WALTERS, Jennifer .... 610-526-5370 390 G jlwalters@brynmawr.edu
WALTERS, Jim .... 951-343-4323.. 28 G jmwalters@calbaptist.edu
WALTERS, Joanna .... 785-242-5200 180 H joanna.walters@ottawa.edu
WALTERS, Jodi .... 304-462-6416 504 B jodi.walters@glenville.edu
WALTERS, June .... 870-762-3102.. 17 K jwalters@smail.anc.edu
WALTERS, Kenneth .... 412-268-1151 391 H walters1@andrew.cmu.edu
WALTERS, Kent, L .... 904-264-2172 106 I kwalters@iws.edu
WALTERS, Keri .... 312-369-7735 136 H kwalters@colum.edu
WALTERS, Laurel .... 314-275-3560 149 A laurel.walters@principia.edu
WALTERS, Mona .... 937-778-7809 361 E mwalters@edisonohio.edu
WALTERS, Paula .... 423-236-2657 436 C pkwalters@southern.edu
WALTERS, Peggy .... 507-457-1503 250 B pwalters@smumn.edu
WALTERS, Ricki .... 507-433-0534 247 C rwalters@riverland.edu
WALTERS, Rita .... 410-669-9200 205 C rwalters01@mica.edu
WALTERS, Robby .... 828-395-1602 344 A rwalters@isothermal.edu
WALTERS, Tigh .... 512-472-2472 456 E tigh.walters@ssw.edu
WALTERS, Timothy, L ... 509-359-2777 494 D twalters@ewu.edu
WALTERS, Tracey .... 601-928-6337 254 D tracey.walters@mgccc.edu
WALTERS, Tyler .... 540-231-5595 490 F tyler.walters@vt.edu
WALTERS, William .... 718-862-7166 313 L william.walters@manhattan.edu
WALTERS, William, D .... 336-334-5824 351 D bill_walters@uncg.edu
WALTERS-BOWER, Sharon .... 434-544-8439 482 F waltersbower@lynchburg.edu
WALTERSCHEID, Dianne .... 940-668-4274 453 L dwalterscheid@nctc.edu
WALTHALL, Houston, D 434-528-5276 491 D hwalthall@vul.edu
WALTHER, Barb .... 734-995-7499 229 A barb.walther@cuaa.edu
WALTHER, Gretchen ...... 651-603-6271 241 L walther@csp.edu
WALTHERS, Kevin, G .... 805-922-6966.. 24 J kevin.walthers@hancockcollege.edu
WALTNER, Robb .... 812-488-2376 164 G rw3@evansville.edu
WALTON, Aaron, A .... 610-399-2220 405 G president@cheyney.edu
WALTON, Amanda .... 601-635-6213 252 I awalton@eccc.edu
WALTON, Anita .... 904-470-8252.. 98 B anita.walton@ewc.edu
WALTON, Candace .... 308-398-7960 273 G candacewalton@cccneb.edu
WALTON, Carl .... 912-358-4190 125 C vpaa@savannahstate.edu
WALTON, Carl .... 912-358-3118 125 C vpsa@savannahstate.edu
WALTON, Charles .... 434-544-8798 482 F walton.c@lynchburg.edu
WALTON, Clayton .... 973-353-5934 290 D cwalton@andromeda.rutgers.edu
WALTON, Curt .... 704-687-6193 351 C wwalton2@uncc.edu
WALTON, Darren .... 585-594-6140 321 C walton_darren@roberts.edu
WALTON, Ed .... 417-328-1622 267 A ewalton@sbuniv.edu
WALTON, Edward, I .... 803-777-7094 424 I waltone@sc.edu
WALTON, Jeffrey .... 518-327-6236 320 A jwalton@paulsmiths.edu
WALTON, Jeffrey .... 518-327-6231 320 A jwalton@paulsmiths.edu
WALTON, Jeffrey .... 518-327-6236 320 A jwalton@paulsmiths.edu
WALTON, Jennifer .... 419-783-2563 361 A jwalton@defiance.edu
WALTON, Jinx, P .... 412-624-6100 412 I jpw@pitt.edu
WALTON, Karen .... 610-282-1100 393 G karen.walton@desales.edu
WALTON, Kathy .... 361-570-4332 465 D waltonk@uhv.edu
WALTON, Lars .... 562-951-4700.. 30 J lwalton@calstate.edu
WALTON, Lindsay .... 910-755-7330 341 C waltonl@brunswickcc.edu
WALTON, Lori, L .... 515-574-1156 170 C walton_l@iowacentral.edu
WALTON, Patrick .... 530-251-8823.. 47 J pwalton@lassencollege.edu
WALTON, Preston, S ..... 415-422-2863.. 72 A pswalton@usfca.edu
WALTON, Robin .... 609-777-5654 292 B rwalton@tesu.edu
WALTON, Ruth .... 479-979-1229.. 23 J rwalton@ozarks.edu
WALTON, Sheila .... 425-739-8314 495 F sheila.walton@lwtech.edu
WALTRIP, W. Blair .... 281-873-0262 446 J b.waltrip@commonwealth.edu
WALTZ, John .... 304-473-8518 505 G waltz_j@wvwc.edu
WALTZ, JR., Thomas, A .... 717-871-7245 407 A thomas.waltz@millersville.edu
WALUEFF, George .... 302-831-8758.. 90 I gwalueff@udel.edu
WALWIK, Joe .... 217-351-2385 148 H jwalwik@parkland.edu
WALWORTH, Morrie .... 906-635-2276 232 J mwalworth@lssu.edu
WALYUCHOW, Ashley ... 361-570-4343 465 D walyuchowa@uhv.edu
WALZ, Charles .... 650-508-3441.. 54 D cwalz@ndnu.edu
WALZ, John .... 414-277-7300 509 A
WALZEL, JR., Robert, L 785-864-3421 181 I robert.walzel@ku.edu

WARNER, Martin, O ...... 610-328-8299 410 I
mwarner1@swarthmore.edu
WARNER, Meredith ...... 602-285-7856.. 14 A
meredith.warner@phoenixcollege.edu
WARNER, Ryan .... 740-351-3127 369 L
rwarner@shawnee.edu
WARNER, Sandra .... 913-469-8500 178 F
swarner@jccc.edu
WARNER, Sue .... 559-925-3222.. 74 A
suewarner@whccd.edu
WARNER, Susan, T .... 440-826-2476 357 B
swarner@bw.edu
WARNER, Thomas, R .... 504-278-6468 193 B
twarner@nunez.edu
WARNER, Timothy, R .... 650-723-4567.. 66 C
trw@stanford.edu
WARNICK, Jason .... 479-356-2005.. 18 G
jwarnick@atu.edu
WARNICK, Lorin, D .... 607-253-3030 306 B
ldw3@cornell.edu
WARNICK, Mark .... 870-236-6901.. 19 D
mwarnick@crc.edu
WARNKE, Kelly .... 419-448-2517 362 G
kwarnke@heidelberg.edu
WARNOCK, Brenda .... 928-317-7601.. 11 B
brenda.warnock@azwestern.edu
WARR, Annie .... 831-582-3595.. 33 A
awarr@csumb.edu
WARR, Fred .... 208-459-5006 131 H
fwarr@collegeofidaho.edu
WARR, Tammy .... 864-424-8017 425 G
warrt@mailbox.sc.edu
WARREN, Aileen .... 402-559-8992 277 H
aileen.warren@unmc.edu
WARREN, Ann .... 310-233-4250.. 49 B
warrenal@lahc.edu
WARREN, Ashley .... 432-335-6429 454 C
awarren@odessa.edu
WARREN, Becky .... 870-612-2048.. 22 H
becky.warren@uaccb.edu
WARREN, Beverly .... 619-388-3246.. 60 C
bewarren@sdccd.edu
WARREN, Beverly, J ..... 330-672-2210 363 I
beverlywarren@kent.edu
WARREN, Briele .... 619-388-7834.. 60 E
bwarren@sdccd.edu
WARREN, Carol .... 901-572-2640 430 C
carol.warren@bchs.edu
WARREN, Carolyn .... 662-562-3205 255 C
cwarren@northwestms.edu
WARREN, Chad .... 702-895-2380 279 D
chad.warren@unlv.edu
WARREN, Charlotte, J ... 217-786-2273 144 B
charlotte.warren@llcc.edu
WARREN, Cher .... 601-484-8614 253 G
cwarren@meridiancc.edu
WARREN, Chris .... 601-643-8306 252 G
chris.warren@colin.edu
WARREN, Chris .... 601-643-8318 252 G
chris.warren@colin.edu
WARREN, Cleve .... 904-357-8896 100 F
clwarren@fscj.edu
WARREN, Debra, P .... 260-422-5561 159 D
dpwarren@indianatech.edu
WARREN, Dena .... 740-245-7396 372 E
dwarren@rio.edu
WARREN, Derrick .... 225-771-5380 195 K
derrick_warren@sus.edu
WARREN, Derrick, V ..... 225-771-4200 195 J
derrick_warren@sus.edu
WARREN, Diana .... 812-535-5284 163 I
dwarren@smwc.edu
WARREN, Doris, C .... 281-649-3013 450 C
dcwarren@hbu.edu
WARREN, E.J .... 405-682-7569 377 C
ejwarren@occc.edu
WARREN, Earl .... 256-782-5306.... 6 B
ewarren@jsu.edu
WARREN, Helen .... 507-786-3009 250 C
warren1@stolaf.edu
WARREN, Jacob .... 903-886-5160 459 E
jacob.warren@tamuc.edu
WARREN, JR., James ... 212-410-8063 317 C
jwarren@nycpm.edu
WARREN, Jason, D .... 270-707-3801 186 B
jason.warren@kctcs.edu
WARREN, Joan, D .... 212-779-5000 312 B
WARREN, John, S .... 850-474-2415 111 D
jwarren@uwf.edu
WARREN, Katie .... 507-786-3316 250 C
warren2@stolaf.edu
WARREN, Kim .... 913-253-5050 181 C
kim.warren@spst.edu
WARREN, Leslie, A .... 906-227-2117 235 A
lwarren@nmu.edu
WARREN, Marty .... 903-923-2314 448 J
mswarren@etbu.edu
WARREN, Mary .... 601-643-8442 252 G
mary.warren@colin.edu
WARREN, Mike .... 601-925-3204 254 B
mjwarren@mc.edu
WARREN, Mitch .... 765-494-1776 163 C
WARREN, Monica .... 615-297-7545 429 H
warrenm@aquinascollege.edu
WARREN, Samantha, C . 207-621-3024 201 A
WARREN, Sara .... 410-225-2264 205 C
swarren@mica.edu
WARREN, Shannon .... 304-645-6382 504 F
swarren@osteo.wvsom.edu
WARREN, Shauna .... 773-896-2400 135 G
shauna.warren@ctschicago.edu
WARREN, Shelline .... 704-378-1498 338 I
swarren@jcsu.edu
WARREN, Steve .... 434-592-3108 482 D
sewarren@liberty.edu
WARREN, Sydney .... 270-686-6415 183 J
sydney.warren@brescia.edu
WARREN, Teresa .... 479-936-5171.. 20 F
twarren4@nwacc.edu
WARREN, Thomas .... 207-941-7786 199 B
warrent@husson.edu
WARREN, Todd .... 251-380-3095.... 7 B
twarren@shc.edu
WARREN, William .... 202-319-6925.. 91 D
warrenw@cua.edu
WARREN, William, J ..... 801-581-6773 472 P
william.warren@utah.edu
WARREN-MARLATT,
Rebeccah .... 909-389-3355.. 59 H
rmarla@craftonhills.edu
WARRICK, Cynthia .... 205-366-8808.... 7 C
cwarrick@stillman.edu
WARRINGTON, Adam .... 802-654-0505 477 B
acw11030@ccv.vsc.edu
WARRINGTON, Myrna ... 800-567-2344 506 I
mwarrington@menominee.edu
WARSHAUER, Wanda .... 860-515-3841.. 84 H
wwarshauer@charteroak.edu
WARSHEL, Chad .... 315-568-3297 317 A
cwarshel@nycc.edu
WARTERS, Alissa .... 843-661-1616 421 H
twarters@fmarion.edu
WARTHAN, Eric .... 928-350-4402.. 15 V
eric.warthan@prescott.edu
WARTHMAN, Susan .... 401-739-5000 416 D
swarthman@neit.edu
WARWICK, Ann .... 212-938-5600 328 E
awarwick@sunyopt.edu
WARWICK, Jay .... 334-953-1303 517 I
jay.warwick@us.af.mil
WARWICK, John, J .... 618-453-4321 152 B
warwick@siu.edu
WARYCK, Susan .... 740-826-8086 366 C
shoglund@muskingum.edu
WARYCK, Susan, H .... 740-826-8086 366 C
shoglund@muskingum.edu
WASAN, Darsh, T .... 312-567-3001 140 I
wasan@iit.edu
WASCHULL, Stefanie ..... 352-395-5175 107 E
stefanie.waschull@sfcollege.edu
WASHAM, Ronnie .... 606-337-1722 184 D
ronnie.washam@ccbbc.edu
WASHBURN, Angela ...... 712-279-5435 167 B
angie.washburn@briarcliff.edu
WASHBURN, Curtis .... 808-455-0260 130 G
cwashbur@hawaii.edu
WASHBURN, Dava .... 903-464-8778 449 J
washburnd@grayson.edu
WASHINGTON,
A. Eugene .... 919-684-2255 337 C
eugene.washington@duke.edu
WASHINGTON,
Adrienne, J .... 610-758-5834 400 B
ajw416@lehigh.edu
WASHINGTON, Amona .. 770-612-2170.. 93 B
WASHINGTON, Andre ... 859-442-4176 185 I
andre.washington@kctcs.edu
WASHINGTON,
August, J .... 615-343-9750 440 D
august.j.washington@vanderbilt.edu
WASHINGTON,
Brandon .... 903-823-3088 458 D
brandon.washington@texarkanacollege.edu
WASHINGTON, Chad .... 803-758-2703 418 D
cwashington@allenuniversity.edu
WASHINGTON, Cheryl .. 334-874-5700.... 5 B
cwashington@ccal.edu
WASHINGTON,
Christopher, L .... 614-947-6129 362 A
christopher.washington@franklin.edu
WASHINGTON, Crystal .. 773-838-7535 136 A
cwashington59@ccc.edu
WASHINGTON, Dana .... 815-802-8962 142 C
dwashington@kcc.edu
WASHINGTON,
Dennis, C .... 804-342-5203 491 C
dcwashington@vuu.edu
WASHINGTON,
DeSandra .... 910-678-0037 343 B
washingd@faytechcc.edu
WASHINGTON, Earlie .... 269-387-2638 239 E
earlie.washington@wmich.edu
WASHINGTON,
Eddie, L .... 734-763-8391 237 I
washine@umich.edu
WASHINGTON, Edwina . 901-678-2307 439 E
etwshngt@memphis.edu
WASHINGTON, Eric ...... 718-960-8181 302 C
eric.washington@lehman.cuny.edu
WASHINGTON, Fred, E . 936-261-2140 458 F
fewashington@pvamu.edu
WASHINGTON, George . 405-789-7661 380 A
george.washington@swcu.edu
WASHINGTON,
Geovette, E .... 412-624-4747 412 I
gew@pitt.edu
WASHINGTON, Gregory 949-824-6002.. 69 A
gregory.washington@uci.edu
WASHINGTON, Ingrid ... 859-442-1148 185 I
ingrid.washington@kctcs.edu
WASHINGTON, Jennifer 860-515-3820.. 84 H
jwashington@charteroak.edu
WASHINGTON, Jewel .... 301-405-5648 207 G
jmwashin@umd.edu
WASHINGTON, Kaye, L . 318-670-9474 196 A
kwashington@susla.edu
WASHINGTON,
Kheysia, H .... 318-670-9417 196 A
kwashington@susla.edu
WASHINGTON,
L. Marshall .... 304-929-5472 503 B
lmwashington@newriver.edu
WASHINGTON, Lloyd .... 251-405-4060.... 1 E
lwashington@bishop.edu
WASHINGTON, Lonnie .. 312-850-7154 136 C
lewashington@ccc.edu
WASHINGTON, Maurice 470-639-0355 123 E
maurice.washington@morehouse.edu
WASHINGTON,
Michael, S .... 901-678-2713 439 E
mswshng1@memphis.edu
WASHINGTON, Nakia .... 470-639-0434 123 E
nakia.washington@morehouse.edu
WASHINGTON, Robin ... 740-755-7670 358 E
washington.486@cotc.edu
WASHINGTON, Shawn .. 832-230-5555 453 K
swashington@na.edu
WASHINGTON, Ted, M . 615-353-3228 437 D
ted.washington@nscc.edu
WASHINGTON, Troy, W 937-229-2554 372 A
twashington1@udayton.edu
WASHINGTON, William . 810-237-6571 238 B
washingw@umflint.edu
WASHINGTON, William . 651-638-6300 240 J
w-washington@bethel.edu
WASHINGTON, Willie .... 803-705-4734 418 G
washingtonw@benedict.edu
WASHINGTON WHITE,
Kendal, H .... 520-621-7057.. 16 J
kwashing@email.arizona.edu
WASHINGTON-WOODS,
Paula .... 870-235-4145.. 21 F
pwwoods@saumag.edu
WASHKEVICH, Stephen . 978-632-6600 220 D
s_washkevich@mwcc.mass.edu
WASHKO, Mary Jo .... 804-523-5345 488 C
mwashko@reynolds.edu
WASHOUSKY,
Richard, C .... 716-851-1500 307 I
washousky@ecc.edu
WASIELEWSKI, Dan .... 641-472-1156 171 J
dwasielewski@mum.edu
WASIELEWSKI, Laura .... 603-656-6051 282 A
lwasielewski@anselm.edu
WASILENKO, William, J 757-446-8480 480 C
wasilewj@evms.edu
WASILESKI, Suzanne ..... 603-342-3010 281 B
swasileski@ccsnh.edu
WASILEWSKI, Frank, M 415-422-2402.. 72 A
fmwasilewski@usfca.edu
WASINGER, Kerry .... 785-628-4233 177 D
klwasinger@fhsu.edu
WASKIE, Kenneth, G ..... 607-777-2184 325 A
kwaskie@binghamton.edu
WASKIEWICZ, Rhonda .. 207-992-4913 199 B
waskiewiczr@husson.edu
WASKOSKY, Julia .... 815-802-8510 142 C
jwaskosky@kcc.edu
WASSBERG, Catherine .. 651-523-2616 242 E
cwassberg01@hamline.edu
WASSENMILLER, Angie . 402-643-3651 274 B
angela.wassenmiller@cune.edu
WASSERMAN, David ..... 718-631-6697 303 F
dwasserman@qcc.cuny.edu
WASSERMAN, Ed .... 510-642-3383.. 68 G
ed.wasserman@berkeley.edu
WASSERMAN, Matthew . 303-315-2067.. 83 D
matt.wasserman@ucdenver.edu
WASSON, Tanlee .... 859-622-8663 184 F
tanlee.wasson@eku.edu
WASSON, Thomas .... 601-857-3367 253 B
thwasson@hindscc.edu
WASSUM, Keith, N .... 704-687-5747 351 C
knwassum@uncc.edu
WASTAWY, Sohair .... 321-674-7111.. 99 K
wastawy@fit.edu
WASTVEDT, Ross .... 515-263-6036 169 E
rwastvedt@grandview.edu
WASUKANIS, John, T ... 561-868-3480 105 A
wasukanj@palmbeachstate.edu
WATERCUTTER, Beckie .. 419-772-2038 367 G
r-watercutter@onu.edu
WATERFIELD, James, R 757-683-5070 483 G
rwater@odu.edu
WATERHOUSE, Lynda ... 239-513-1135 114 D
lwaterhouse@wolford.edu
WATERMAN, Anna .... 319-363-1323 172 B
awaterman@mtmercy.edu
WATERMOLEN, Jean ...... 602-243-8124.. 14 D
jean.watermolen@southmountaincc.edu
WATERMON, Colleen .... 314-367-8700 266 D
colleen.watermon@stlcop.edu
WATERS, Barry, D .... 989-774-7493 228 E
water1b@cmich.edu
WATERS, Bill .... 850-484-1751 105 E
bwaters@pensacolastate.edu
WATERS, Bill .... 503-594-3390 382 D
bills@clackamas.edu
WATERS, Candace, R .... 864-488-4448 422 B
cwaters@limestone.edu
WATERS,
Christopher, C .... 336-278-5055 337 G
cwaters@elon.edu
WATERS, Darrell .... 701-228-5458 354 G
darrell.waters@dakotacollege.edu
WATERS, Gary .... 706-236-2227 116 D
gwaters@berry.edu
WATERS, Gloria .... 617-353-2595 212 G
gwaters@bu.edu
WATERS, Gloriana .... 646-664-3254 301 A
gloriana.waters@cuny.edu
WATERS, Jeff .... 417-328-1632 267 A
jwaters@sbuniv.edu
WATERS, Jennifer .... 903-566-7380 468 C
jwaters@uttyler.edu
WATERS, Jennifer .... 410-293-1586 519 E
jwaters@usna.edu
WATERS, Jessica .... 202-885-3724.. 91 C
waters@american.edu
WATERS, Joan .... 212-854-1234 305 E
jwaters@columbia.edu
WATERS, Jody .... 541-552-6114 386 H
watersj@sou.edu
WATERS, Jon .... 434-544-8498 482 F
waters.j@lynchburg.edu
WATERS, Kathleen .... 415-451-2819.. 60 I
kwaters@sfts.edu
WATERS, Kathy .... 802-451-7145 475 D
kwaters@marlboro.edu
WATERS, Kristin .... 478-289-2377 118 H
kdwaters@ega.edu
WATERS, Kyndall .... 205-226-4936.... 4 F
kwaters@bsc.edu
WATERS, Lynne .... 817-272-0979 467 B
lynne.waters@uta.edu
WATERS, Marlo .... 707-965-6676.. 55 F
mwaters@puc.edu
WATERS, Melissa .... 770-426-2826 122 F
mwaters@life.edu
WATERS, Michelle .... 252-335-0821 342 D
michelle_waters@albemarle.edu
WATERS, Myra .... 410-837-5159 209 D
mwaters@ubalt.edu
WATERS, Nicole .... 704-406-4358 337 H
nwaters@gardner-webb.edu
WATERS, Patrick .... 734-432-5839 233 C
pwaters@madonna.edu
WATERS, Robert .... 518-608-8115 308 A
rwaters@excelsior.edu
WATERS, Ron .... 707-476-4331.. 39 F
ron-waters@redwoods.edu
WATERS, Roy, S .... 318-257-2893 197 A
roy@latech.edu
WATERS, Sarah .... 785-864-4560 181 I
sarah.waters@ku.edu
WATERS, Sarah .... 419-372-2011 357 F
waterss@bgsu.edu
WATERS, Taylor .... 410-626-2512 206 F
taylor.waters@sjc.edu

WEATHERFORD, Charles .... 850-412-5102 109 A charles.weatherford@famu.edu
WEATHERINGTON, Elsie, S .... 804-524-5040 491 A eweatherington@vsu.edu
WEATHERLY, Alice .... 870-850-8629.. 21 E aweatherly@seark.edu
WEATHERLY, Elizabeth .. 703-323-3716 488 H eweatherly@nvcc.edu
WEATHERLY, Jon .... 865-573-4517 432 H jweatherly@johnsonu.edu
WEATHERMAN, Tammy . 559-934-2117.. 73 M tammyweatherman@whccd.edu
WEATHERS, Diane .... 718-289-5770 301 D diane.weathers@bcc.cuny.edu
WEATHERS, Melonie ..... 336-386-3207 347 A weathersm@surry.edu
WEATHERSPOON, David .... 847-543-2138 136 E dweatherspoon@clcillinois.edu
WEATHERWAX, Alan ..... 978-837-5234 221 G weatherwaxa@merrimack.edu
WEATHERWAX, Allan, T 978-837-5234 221 G weatherwaxa@merrimack.edu
WEAVER, Angela .... 618-468-5300 143 D aweaver@lc.edu
WEAVER, Beckie .... 501-279-4640.. 19 G bweaver@harding.edu
WEAVER, Benjamin .... 518-956-8030 324 G bweaver@albany.edu
WEAVER, Bradley, K ...... 765-361-6308 166 B weaverb@wabash.edu
WEAVER, Candace .... 601-477-4075 253 F candace.weaver@jcjc.edu
WEAVER, Carol .... 304-457-6331 501 A weaverc@ab.edu
WEAVER, Carolyn .... 515-271-1426 168 G carolyn.weaver@dmu.edu
WEAVER, Dan .... 970-351-2032.. 83 F dan.weaver@unco.edu
WEAVER, Danielle .... 716-839-8200 306 E dweaver2@daemen.edu
WEAVER, David .... 907-786-7212.. 10 A dweaver@alaska.edu
WEAVER, Deirdre .... 310-434-4791.. 62 G weaver_deirdre@smc.edu
WEAVER, Devon .... 215-965-4042 402 C dweaver@moore.edu
WEAVER, Donna .... 530-895-2568.. 28 E weaverdo@butte.edu
WEAVER, Ernestine .... 860-723-0114.. 84 I weavere@ct.edu
WEAVER, Gina .... 585-345-6808 309 C gmweaver@genesee.edu
WEAVER, Harry .... 909-687-1520.. 44 A harryweaver@gs.edu
WEAVER, James, S .... 740-376-4611 365 A jim.weaver@marietta.edu
WEAVER, Jeff .... 501-760-4113.. 20 D jeff.weaver@np.edu
WEAVER, John .... 325-674-2476 441 D jbw11a@acu.edu
WEAVER, Joseph .... 229-245-3737 127 H jgweaver@valdosta.edu
WEAVER, JR., Joseph, B .... 405-744-2690 377 F joe.weaver@okstate.edu
WEAVER, Julie .... 231-439-6306 234 H jweaver@ncmich.edu
WEAVER, Karyn .... 870-733-6722.. 18 B kweaver@asumidsouth.edu
WEAVER, Kathleen .... 909-593-3511.. 70 E kweaver@laverne.edu
WEAVER, Kenneth .... 620-341-5367 177 B kweaver@emporia.edu
WEAVER, Laura .... 510-659-6518.. 54 F lweaver@ohlone.edu
WEAVER, Lori .... 724-503-1001 414 A lweaver@washjeff.edu
WEAVER, Marianne .... 541-962-3524 383 B mweaver@eou.edu
WEAVER, Matthew .... 717-867-6228 399 J mweaver@lvc.edu
WEAVER, Max .... 205-387-0511.... 1 D max.weaver@bscc.edu
WEAVER, Melanie .... 419-772-2272 367 G m-weaver@onu.edu
WEAVER, Monica .... 609-586-4800 287 A weaverm@mccc.edu
WEAVER, Neal .... 229-928-1360 120 F
WEAVER, Neal .... 985-448-4134 197 C neal.weaver@nicholls.edu
WEAVER, Paula .... 518-736-3622 309 A paula.weaver@fmcc.suny.edu
WEAVER, Rhonda .... 704-403-1756 336 B rhonda.weaver@carolinashealthcare.org
WEAVER, Rodney .... 731-989-6911 432 C rweaver@fhu.edu
WEAVER, Rose Mary ..... 870-759-4230.. 23 K rweaver@wbcoll.edu
WEAVER, Roy .... 765-285-5251 156 C rweaver@bsu.edu
WEAVER, Sandie .... 562-944-0351.. 27 E sandie.weaver@biola.edu
WEAVER, Sean .... 505-545-3380 294 J slweaver@nmhu.edu
WEAVER, Sean, F .... 412-396-2560 394 D weavers2@duq.edu
WEAVER, Steven .... 479-979-1448.. 23 J sweaver@ozarks.edu
WEAVER, Tammy .... 479-968-0272.. 18 G tweaver@atu.edu
WEAVER, Terri, E .... 312-996-7808 153 H teweaver@uic.edu
WEAVER, Tom .... 419-434-4253 373 K tweaver@winebrenner.edu
WEAVER, Vickie, L .... 609-896-5029 289 E weaver@rider.edu
WEAVER, Wendy .... 414-930-3335 509 B weaverw@mtmary.edu
WEAVER-GRIGGS, Linda .... 803-327-8024 426 J lwgriggs@yorktech.edu
WEAVIL, Vicki .... 336-770-3266 352 B weavilv@uncsa.edu
WEBB, Amy .... 530-242-7713.. 63 I awebb@shastacollege.edu
WEBB, Anda, L .... 434-924-0999 486 H al6b@virginia.edu
WEBB, Angela, P .... 336-322-2160 345 D angela.webb@piedmontcc.edu
WEBB, Barbara .... 989-686-9228 229 J brwebb@delta.edu
WEBB, Burton, J .... 606-218-5261 190 E burtonwebb@upike.edu
WEBB, Candice .... 919-760-2255 339 H webbcan@meredith.edu
WEBB, Carol .... 281-487-1170 460 G cwebb@txchiro.edu
WEBB, Catherine .... 831-646-4096.. 52 G cwebb@mpc.edu
WEBB, Cheryl, A .... 803-327-7402 419 G cwebb@clintoncollege.edu
WEBB, Dixie .... 931-221-6346 430 B webbd@apsu.edu
WEBB, Donna .... 229-391-5001 114 G dwebb@abac.edu
WEBB, Donnetta .... 916-558-2408.. 50 I webbd@scc.losrios.edu
WEBB, Duncan .... 312-461-0600 133 C dwebb@aaart.edu
WEBB, Eric .... 307-766-3059 517 B ewebb1@uwyo.edu
WEBB, II, Ernest, R .... 915-831-5051 449 A ewebb1@epcc.edu
WEBB, Farrell .... 818-677-3001.. 33 B farrell.webb@csun.edu
WEBB, Jac .... 208-562-2063 132 A jacwebb@cwidaho.cc
WEBB, James, D .... 806-651-1240 460 E jwebb@mail.wtamu.edu
WEBB, Jeanie .... 405-733-7300 379 F jwebb@rose.edu
WEBB, Jen .... 715-675-2775 173 K webbj@uiu.edu
WEBB, Jennifer .... 254-295-4526 466 A jwebb@umhb.edu
WEBB, Jerrad .... 620-276-9521 177 G jerrad.webb@gcccks.edu
WEBB, Jodi .... 419-372-9348 357 F jwebb@bgsu.edu
WEBB, Jonathon .... 989-774-7473 228 E webb1jd@cmich.edu
WEBB, Joshua, M .... 989-964-4359 236 F jmwebb@svsu.edu
WEBB, Katherine .... 334-244-3704.... 4 E katherine.webb@aum.edu
WEBB, Kathleen, M .... 937-229-4094 372 A kwebb1@udayton.edu
WEBB, Keith .... 404-270-5279 126 D kwebb5@spelman.edu
WEBB, Ken .... 619-680-4430.. 29 A ken.webb@cc-sd.edu
WEBB, Kenneth .... 903-785-7661 454 F kwebb@parisjc.edu
WEBB, Kyle .... 901-843-3760 435 L webb@rhodes.edu
WEBB, Lee .... 870-512-7849.. 18 D lee_webb@asun.edu
WEBB, Leslie .... 208-426-1418 131 C lesliewebb@boisestate.edu
WEBB, Lezley, A .... 901-333-5560 438 B lcurrin@southwest.tn.edu
WEBB, Lisa .... 415-485-9431.. 39 E lswebb@marin.edu
WEBB, Lynda .... 432-685-6884 453 B lwebb@midland.edu
WEBB, Mark, F .... 931-598-1284 436 A mwebb@sewanee.edu
WEBB, Michelle .... 207-453-5020 200 A mwebb@kvcc.me.edu
WEBB, Nick .... 530-242-7739.. 63 I nwebb@shastacollege.edu
WEBB, Olivia .... 870-584-1169.. 22 F owebb@cccua.edu
WEBB, Pat .... 214-860-8789 448 B pwebb@dcccd.edu
WEBB, Paul .... 715-682-1208 509 D pwebb@northland.edu
WEBB, R. Brian .... 254-710-8797 444 B brian_webb@baylor.edu
WEBB, Reggie .... 540-828-8014 478 J rwebb@bridgewater.edu
WEBB, Reginal .... 863-298-6828 105 F rwebb@polk.edu
WEBB, Tom .... 937-775-5680 374 B thomas.webb@wright.edu
WEBB, Toya .... 847-214-7769 138 B twebb@elgin.edu
WEBB, Travis, P .... 414-805-8622 508 D trwebb@mcw.edu
WEBB, Troycia .... 229-430-3396 114 J twebb@albanytech.edu
WEBB, Walter, W .... 815-939-5333 148 F wwebb@olivet.edu
WEBB-CURTIS, Susan ... 423-472-7141 436 G susanwebb-curtis@clevelandstatecc.edu
WEBB SHARPE, Lisa ..... 517-483-1106 232 K sharpel@lcc.edu
WEBBER, Adrienne .... 410-651-6621 208 C
WEBBER, Cynthia .... 618-545-3091 142 D cwebber@kaskaskia.edu
WEBBER, Diane .... 202-685-7375 518 B diane.webber@ndu.edu
WEBBER, Henry, S .... 314-935-7877 269 L hwebber@wustl.edu
WEBBER, Leah .... 617-928-4513 222 D lwebber@mountida.edu
WEBBER, Meg .... 803-323-2220 426 H webberm@winthrop.edu
WEBBER, Robert .... 802-251-7607 475 D robertw@marlboro.edu
WEBBER, Robert .... 802-831-1209 476 G rwebber@vermontlaw.edu
WEBBER MCLEAN, Kalynda .... 818-610-6567.. 49 D mcleankw@piercecollege.edu
WEBER, A. Scott .... 716-645-6029 325 B sweber@buffalo.edu
WEBER, Brad .... 620-252-7076 176 K weber.brad@coffeyville.edu
WEBER, Bruce, W .... 302-831-1211.. 90 I bweber@udel.edu
WEBER, Chris .... 301-447-5114 206 B cweber@msmary.edu
WEBER, Daniel, R .... 773-442-4000 147 G d-weber3@neiu.edu
WEBER, David .... 413-369-4044 214 A weber@csld.edu
WEBER, Dawn .... 419-289-4142 356 L dweber1@ashland.edu
WEBER, Debra .... 262-695-7842 515 B dweber28@wctc.edu
WEBER, Ellen .... 631-420-2744 329 D ellen.weber@farmingdale.edu
WEBER, Eric .... 801-957-4136 474 B eric.weber@slcc.edu
WEBER, Heather .... 623-935-8840.. 13 F heather.weber@estrellamountain.edu
WEBER, Jacqueline, J ... 573-592-5307 270 B jackie.weber@westminster-mo.edu
WEBER, Jennifer .... 701-224-2540 353 F jennifer.weber@ndus.edu
WEBER, Jennifer, L .... 563-588-7155 171 H jennifer.weber@loras.edu
WEBER, Jerry .... 425-564-2301 492 G jerry.weber@bellevuecollege.edu
WEBER, Jim, P .... 330-972-5908 371 C jpw@uakron.edu
WEBER, Jodi .... 903-434-8114 453 M jweber@ntcc.edu
WEBER, Joe .... 931-221-7618 430 B weberj@apsu.edu
WEBER, Jolanta, A .... 509-313-6504 495 A weberj@gonzaga.edu
WEBER, Julie .... 502-852-6636 190 C julie.weber@louisville.edu
WEBER, Karyn .... 605-688-4111 429 B karyn.weber@sdstate.edu
WEBER, Keith .... 270-809-2192 188 D kweber6@murraystate.edu
WEBER, Kelley .... 785-827-5541 179 C kelley.weber@kwu.edu
WEBER, Kevin .... 502-585-9911 189 B kweber@spalding.edu
WEBER, Krista .... 608-822-2315 515 A kweber@swtc.edu
WEBER, Laura .... 937-529-2201 371 B lweber@united.edu
WEBER, Laurie .... 701-858-3375 354 C laurie.weber@minotstateu.edu
WEBER, Marguerite .... 410-462-8302 202 F mweber@bccc.edu
WEBER, Mark .... 920-498-5663 514 G mark.weber@nwtc.edu
WEBER, Marsha, L .... 218-477-2415 246 B marsha.weber@mnstate.edu
WEBER, Mary .... 831-646-4048.. 52 G mweber@mpc.edu
WEBER, Merlin, D .... 530-226-4501.. 64 B mweber@simpsonu.edu
WEBER, Nancy .... 843-525-8226 424 E nweber@tcl.edu
WEBER, Phil .... 740-857-1311 369 I pweber@rosedale.edu
WEBER, Randy .... 913-469-8500 178 F rweber@jccc.edu
WEBER, OP, Sharon, R . 517-264-7102 236 I srweber@sienaheights.edu
WEBER, Staci .... 617-731-7195 223 F sweber@pmc.edu
WEBER, Stephen .... 405-224-3140 381 B sweber@usao.edu
WEBER, Susan .... 212-501-3050 298 I weber@bgc.bard.edu
WEBER, Susan .... 808-734-9267 130 C sweber@hawaii.edu
WEBER, Susan .... 847-628-2465 142 B sweber@judsonu.edu
WEBER, Teresa .... 914-323-5445 314 A teresa.weber@mville.edu
WEBER, Twila .... 740-857-1311 369 I tweber@rosedale.edu
WEBER, Wayne, C .... 608-342-1547 511 D weberwa@uwplatt.edu
WEBER-MORTIMER, Brandi .... 724-738-4340 407 C brandi.mortimer@sru.edu
WEBLEY, Radha .... 707-826-4583.. 34 A rw76@humboldt.edu
WEBSTER, Alex .... 206-239-4500 493 D alexwebster@cityu.edu
WEBSTER, Alexander ..... 315-858-0945 310 E chaplain.webster@hts.edu
WEBSTER, Amy .... 276-656-0248 489 A awebster@patrickhenry.edu
WEBSTER, Catherine ...... 405-974-2602 380 J cwebster6@uco.edu
WEBSTER, Christina ...... 215-248-7168 392 D sm8127@bscollege.com
WEBSTER, Daniel .... 615-675-5255 441 B daniel.webster@welch.edu
WEBSTER, Elizabeth ...... 617-521-2334 224 E elizabeth.webster@simmons.edu
WEBSTER, Frank .... 678-610-5900 124 B
WEBSTER, Ian .... 410-617-2292 205 A iawebster@loyola.edu
WEBSTER, Jeremy .... 740-588-1435 368 G webstej1@ohio.edu
WEBSTER, Jerome .... 419-559-2326 370 J jwebster01@terra.edu
WEBSTER, Kacy .... 563-355-3500 171 B kwebster@kaplan.edu
WEBSTER, Katie, P .... 740-368-3329 368 N kpwebster@owu.edu
WEBSTER, Keith .... 412-268-2447 391 H kwebster@andrew.cmu.edu
WEBSTER, Mark, D .... 804-523-5612 488 C mwebster@reynolds.edu
WEBSTER, Mary, L .... 626-395-6304.. 29 I mwebster@caltech.edu
WEBSTER, Michael .... 610-558-5657 402 G websterm@neumann.edu
WEBSTER, Nancy, K ...... 904-632-3261 100 F nancy.k.webster@fscj.edu
WEBSTER, Ondes .... 865-471-3352 430 H owebster@cn.edu
WEBSTER, Richard, C ... 410-334-2896 210 C rwebster@worwic.edu
WEBSTER, Scott .... 508-999-8202 217 A swebster@umassd.edu
WEBSTER, Shane .... 208-496-1910 131 D websters@byui.edu
WEBSTER, Teresa .... 662-246-6318 254 C twebster@msdelta.edu
WEBSTER, Tom .... 903-923-2157 448 J twebster@etbu.edu
WEBSTER, Valerie .... 229-293-6135 125 F valerie.webster@sgsc.edu

WEISS, David 210-567-3709 468 E weissd@uthscsa.edu
WEISS, H 732-364-1220 283 F
WEISS, Jason 323-463-2500 67 D jasonw@toa.edu
WEISS, Jeff, A 617-349-8500 216 D jweiss@lesley.edu
WEISS, Jeffery, I 718-990-6357 322 F weissj@stjohns.edu
WEISS, Johanna 804-594-1500 488 D jweiss@jtcc.edu
WEISS, Joshua 413-565-1000 211 C jweiss@baypath.edu
WEISS, Karen 618-252-5400 151 J karen.weiss@sic.edu
WEISS, Kay 909-384-8535 59 I kweiss@sbccd.cc.ca.us
WEISS, Rod, P 858-499-0202 39 B rweiss@coleman.edu
WEISS, Sandra 415-476-1805 70 A sandra.weiss@ucsf.edu
WEISS, Stephanie 612-330-1476 240 G weisss@augsburg.edu
WEISS, Suzanne 920-686-6196 510 A suzanne.weiss@sl.edu
WEISS, Valerie 313-664-7852 228 H vweiss@collegeforcreativestudies.edu
WEISS-COOK, Laura 785-320-4541 179 E lauraweiss-cook@manhattantech.edu
WEISSENBURGER, David 254-968-9464 459 A weissenburger@tarleton.edu
WEISSENBURGER, Jackie 715-394-8449 512 B jweissen@uwsuper.edu
WEISSENFLUH, Anji 541-962-3236 383 B aweissen@eou.edu
WEISSMAN, Neil, B 717-245-1321 394 A weissmne@dickinson.edu
WEISSMANN, Kristopher, E 803-938-3763 425 F weissmak@uscsumter.edu
WEITER, Stephen, P 248-370-2459 235 J spweiter@oakland.edu
WEITMAN, Catheryn, J 956-326-2801 459 B catheryn.weitman@tamiu.edu
WEITZ, Anna, D 610-607-6210 408 G aweitz@racc.edu
WEITZEL, Jann 417-667-8181 259 A jweitzel@cottey.edu
WEITZEL, Lauren, N 717-871-4184 407 A lauren.weitzel@millersville.edu
WEITZER, Joseph 262-695-7824 515 B jweitzer@wctc.edu
WEITZMAN, Lauren 801-581-6826 472 P lweitzman@sa.utah.edu
WEKESA, Kennedy 334-229-4316 4 A wekesai@alasu.edu
WELAGE, Lynda, S 505-272-0906 296 H lswelage@salude.unm.edu
WELBORN, Ruth, B 512-245-3300 463 A rw01@txstate.edu
WELBURN, Janice 414-288-7214 508 C janice.welburn@marquette.edu
WELBURN, William 414-288-8028 508 C william.welburn@marquette.edu
WELCH, Aaron, P 660-263-3900 258 A aaronwelch@cccb.edu
WELCH, Alexis 252-527-6223 344 D awelch@lenoircc.edu
WELCH, Ba-Shen, T 205-929-1574 6 D bwelch@miles.edu
WELCH, Becky 253-680-7100 492 F bwelch@bates.ctc.edu
WELCH, Charles, L 501-660-1000 17 L president@asusystem.edu
WELCH, Dan 814-866-8151 399 C dwelch@lecom.edu
WELCH, Denise 903-693-1121 454 E dwelch@panola.edu
WELCH, Dirk 940-397-4972 453 C dirk.welch@mwsu.edu
WELCH, JR., Donald, J 814-865-3684 403 F djw66@psu.edu
WELCH, Edwin 765-998-5523 164 C edwelch@taylor.edu
WELCH, Edwin, H 304-357-4713 502 E edwinwelch@ucwv.edu
WELCH, Frances, C 843-953-5613 420 C welchf@cofc.edu
WELCH, G. Doug 254-710-3945 444 B doug_welch@baylor.edu
WELCH, George 619-684-8826 53 J gwelch@newschoolarch.edu
WELCH, Grace 740-362-3366 365 D gwelch@msto.edu
WELCH, James 405-224-3140 381 B jwelch@usao.edu
WELCH, Jennifer 410-644-6400 202 G jennifer.welch@brightwood.edu
WELCH, Jennifer, C 315-464-4570 326 B welchj@upstate.edu
WELCH, Joel 336-734-7182 343 C jwelch@forsythtech.edu
WELCH, John 412-924-1401 408 E jwelch@pts.edu
WELCH, Julie 843-953-5254 419 D jwelch3@citadel.edu
WELCH, Kathleen 831-479-5076 28 F kawelch@cabrillo.edu
WELCH, Lena 615-248-1393 439 B lwelch@trevecca.edu
WELCH, Leo 970-351-2515 83 F leo.welch@unco.edu
WELCH, Lynne 908-709-7167 292 C welch@ucc.edu
WELCH, Marc 765-361-6480 166 B welchm@wabash.edu
WELCH, Marjorie 712-325-3202 170 K mwelch@iwcc.edu
WELCH, Marolyn 903-586-2518 451 C acadean@jacksonville-college.edu
WELCH, Matt 254-968-9002 459 A welch@tarleton.edu
WELCH, Michael 847-578-3238 150 E michael.welch@rosalindfranklin.edu
WELCH, Mike 847-543-2247 136 E mwelch1@clcillinois.edu
WELCH, Mike 269-927-1000 232 G
WELCH, Nick 740-588-1224 374 G nwelch@zanestate.edu
WELCH, Patricia 443-885-3385 206 A patricia.welch@morgan.edu
WELCH, Paul 508-626-4640 218 A pwelch@framingham.edu
WELCH, Paul 415-955-2100 24 K pwelch@alliant.edu
WELCH, Renee 970-351-2127 83 F renee.welch@unco.edu
WELCH, Ronald, W 843-953-6499 419 D rwelch1@citadel.edu
WELCH, Sally 313-927-1211 233 D swelch@marygrove.edu
WELCH, Sam 315-859-4668 309 D rwelch@hamilton.edu
WELCH, Sherri, L 856-691-8600 285 C swelch@cccnj.edu
WELCH, Susan 814-865-7691 403 F sxw11@psu.edu
WELCH, Susan, T 518-564-5062 327 E welchst@plattsburgh.edu
WELCH, Teresa 417-626-1234 264 J welch.teresa@occ.edu
WELCH, Thomas 252-399-6371 335 I twelch@barton.edu
WELCH, Thomas 843-661-1136 421 H rwelch@fmarion.edu
WELD, Jeff 802-468-1241 477 A jeff.weld@castleton.edu
WELDEN, David 770-962-7580 121 G dwelden@gwinnetttech.edu
WELDEN, Jonathan 901-272-5121 434 B jweldon@mca.edu
WELDEN, Soraya 601-484-8628 253 G swelden@meridiancc.edu
WELDON, Leslie 406-377-9412 270 J lweldon@dawson.edu
WELDON, Leslie 618-634-3337 151 G lesliew@shawneecc.edu
WELDON, Rich 803-508-7382 418 C weldonr@atc.edu
WELDON, Scott 251-460-8018 9 B sweldon@southalabama.edu
WELDON, Sherrie 561-237-7788 103 E sweldon@lynn.edu
WELDON, Stephanie, J 603-206-8111 280 L sjweldon@ccsnh.edu
WELDON, Wray 972-883-6994 467 D wray.weldon@utdallas.edu
WELDY, Eric, A 317-274-8990 160 E eweldy@iupui.edu
WELKER, Dan 928-428-8300 12 I dan.welker@eac.edu
WELKER, Heston 928-428-8225 12 I heston.welker@eac.edu
WELKER, Josh 217-641-4200 141 F jwelker@jwcc.edu
WELKER, Kristen 605-668-1577 427 F kristen.welker@mtmc.edu
WELKER, Mark, A 309-341-7255 142 G mawelker@knox.edu
WELKER, Sharon, L 919-866-5611 347 D sfwelker@waketech.edu
WELKEY, Sharon 210-832-2115 465 E welkey@uiwtx.edu
WELLBORN, Linda 417-865-2815 260 B wellbornl@evangel.edu
WELLER, Eddie 281-998-6150 455 L eddie.weller@sjcd.edu
WELLER, Eddie 281-998-6150 456 A eddie.weller@sjcd.edu
WELLER, Eddie 281-998-6150 456 B eddie.weller@sjcd.edu
WELLER, Lisa 610-225-5007 394 E lweller2@eastern.edu
WELLER-DENGEL, Pamela 507-389-6061 246 A pamela.weller-dengel@mnsu.edu
WELLES, Julia 816-802-3302 261 C jwelles@kcai.edu
WELLINGS, Keith 304-724-3700 501 D kwellings@apus.edu
WELLINGTON, Eric, R 610-558-5596 402 G ellinge@neumann.edu
WELLINGTON, Susan 607-778-5187 326 C wellingtonsl@sunybroome.edu
WELLINGTON-BAKER, Kristi 509-527-4263 499 E kristi.wellington-baker@wwcc.edu
WELLMAN, Chris 941-752-5443 108 P wellmac@scf.edu
WELLMAN, Gina 203-591-5146 87 H gwellman@post.edu
WELLMAN, Ronald, D 336-758-5616 353 A wellmanr@wfu.edu
WELLNER, Justin 805-756-7003 30 K jwellner@calpoly.edu
WELLS, Alison 225-768-1713 191 G alison.wells@ololcollege.edu
WELLS, Barbara 901-333-4259 438 B bwells@southwest.tn.edu
WELLS, Barbara 865-981-8278 433 F barbara.wells@maryvillecollege.edu
WELLS, Billy 706-864-1630 127 B billy.wells@ung.edu
WELLS, Bonnie 860-439-5001 86 H bonnie.wells@conncoll.edu
WELLS, Brian 412-924-1421 408 E bwells@pts.edu
WELLS, Brian, J 502-776-1443 188 F bwells@simmonscollegeky.edu
WELLS, C. Gene 812-488-2664 164 G gw5@evansville.edu
WELLS, C. Richard 605-342-0317 427 C president@johnwitherspooncollege.org
WELLS, Carol 909-384-8925 59 I cwells@sbccd.cc.ca.us
WELLS, Carole 610-683-4212 406 D wells@kutztown.edu
WELLS, Christopher 315-228-6833 304 G cwells@colgate.edu
WELLS, Clinton 505-224-4000 293 L cwells21@cnm.edu
WELLS, Dan 713-743-2619 465 A dwells2@uh.edu
WELLS, Doug 575-835-5363 294 K doug.wells@nmt.edu
WELLS, Earl 716-880-2524 314 F ewells@medaille.edu
WELLS, Elaine 212-938-5690 328 E ewells@sunyopt.edu
WELLS, Geordy 901-381-3939 440 I geordy@visible.edu
WELLS, JR., Henry, D 919-572-1625 335 F hdwells@apexsot.edu
WELLS, Jennifer 270-901-1004 187 A jennifer.wells@kctcs.edu
WELLS, Jeremy 706-591-3012 71 I jwells@usa.edu
WELLS, Jesse 607-778-5001 326 C wellsje@sunybroome.edu
WELLS, Jesse 607-778-5478 326 C wellsje@sunybroome.edu
WELLS, Jesse 607-778-5296 326 C wellsje@sunybroome.edu
WELLS, Johann 334-291-4954 1 H johann.wells@cv.edu
WELLS, John, T 804-684-7103 479 I wells@vims.edu
WELLS, Jovita 202-274-6260 93 D jwells@udc.edu
WELLS, Katherine 307-855-2111 516 I kwells@cwc.edu
WELLS, Keith, P 303-762-6963 79 G keith.wells@denverseminary.edu
WELLS, Kevin 617-745-3733 214 D kevin.wells@enc.edu
WELLS, Kyle 435-652-7887 473 B kwells@dixie.edu
WELLS, Latreace 615-329-8894 431 I lwells@fisk.edu
WELLS, Lisa 540-887-7330 482 G lwells@marybaldwin.edu
WELLS, Marilyn 507-389-1334 246 A marilyn.wells@mnsu.edu
WELLS, Matt 937-393-3431 370 C mwells@sscc.edu
WELLS, Michael 910-893-1275 336 C wellsm@campbell.edu
WELLS, O.T 202-687-2031 92 B otw@georgetown.edu
WELLS, Peter, D 508-767-7350 210 I pd.wells@assumption.edu
WELLS, R. Hal 612-874-3634 243 F hal_wells@mcad.edu
WELLS, Sabrina 301-546-7011 206 E wellssx2@pgcc.edu
WELLS, Sherry 913-758-6123 182 B wellss@stmary.edu
WELLS, Stephen, G 575-835-5600 294 K stephen.wells@nmt.edu
WELLS, Teri 304-896-7443 503 D teri.wells@southernwv.edu
WELLS, Tina 508-854-4479 220 G twells@qcc.mass.edu
WELLS, Todd 816-235-1407 268 D wellsta@umkc.edu
WELLS, Twyla, C 919-209-2119 344 C tcwells@johnstoncc.edu
WELLS, Veronica 937-708-5532 373 H vwells@wilberforce.edu
WELLS, Virginia, D 757-221-4386 479 I vdwell@wm.edu
WELLS, Warren 660-785-4121 267 K wwells@truman.edu
WELLS, William, T 336-758-5154 353 A wellswt@wfu.edu
WELLS-BOOTH, Shawna 352-638-9733 95 H swellsbooth@beaconcollege.edu
WELMAN, Chris 570-586-2400 392 E cwelman@clarkssummitu.edu
WELMON, Pamela 772-462-7235 101 Q pwelmon@irsc.edu
WELP, Cindy 712-274-5114 172 A welp@morningside.edu
WELSCH, Colleen 269-782-1204 237 B cwelsch@swmich.edu
WELSCH, Daniel 304-724-3700 501 D dwelsch@apus.edu
WELSCH, Gabriel 814-641-3131 398 B welschg@juniata.edu
WELSH, Beth 706-737-1796 116 B bwelsh@augusta.edu
WELSH, Brett 614-287-2426 360 C bwelsh7@cscc.edu
WELSH, David 860-773-1423 86 G dwelsh@txcc.commnet.edu
WELSH, Jennifer, R 860-701-6114 87 F welsh_j@mitchell.edu
WELSH, Johnelle 254-526-1298 445 L johnelle.welsh@ctcd.edu
WELSH, Josie 417-625-9772 263 G welsh-j@mssu.edu
WELSH, Marcia, G 570-422-3546 406 A president@esu.edu
WELSH, III, Mark, A 979-862-8007 459 C bushschooldean@tamu.edu
WELSH, Patrick, J 610-785-6271 409 F pwelsh@scs.edu
WELSH, Robert 626-815-6000 26 U rwelsh@apu.edu
WELSH, Tasha, D 636-481-3157 261 B twelsh@jeffco.edu
WELSH, Tim 269-488-4456 231 G twelsh@kvcc.edu
WELSH, Tracy 605-688-4121 429 B tracy.welsh@sdstate.edu
WELSH, Valerie 309-694-5440 139 G valerie.welsh@icc.edu
WELTER, Brian 847-970-4837 154 H bwelter@usml.edu
WELTER, Stephen 619-594-2978 34 B swelter@mail.sdsu.edu
WELTJEN, Scott 716-270-5239 307 I weltjen@ecc.edu
WELTMAN, Jessica 406-243-5710 271 G jessica.weltman@umontana.edu
WELTON, Anna 828-771-3057 353 B awelton@warren-wilson.edu
WELTY, Amy 330-966-5456 370 G awelty@starkstate.edu
WELTY, Dorothy 303-914-6634 82 B dorothy.welty@rrcc.edu
WELZ, Mary 802-831-1079 476 G mwelz@vermontlaw.edu
WEN, Hui-Men 941-487-4601 110 B hwen@ncf.edu
WENCESLAU, Zil 954-545-4500 108 A cfo@sfbc.edu
WENCK, Lisa, M 607-436-2518 325 E lisa.wenck@oneonta.edu

WESTPHAL, Donald, M . 507-344-7320 240 I
don.westphal@blc.edu
WESTPHAL, Judith .... 920-424-2106 511 B
westphaj@uwosh.edu
WESTPHAL,
Kristianne, R .... 507-933-7495 242 D
kristi@gustavus.edu
WESTPHAL,
Lorraine, M .... 757-594-7608 479 H
lwestpha@cnu.edu
WESTPHAL, Matt .... 918-540-6249 376 F
mwestphal@neo.edu
WESTRA, Amy .... 712-722-6024 168 I
amy.westra@dordt.edu
WESTRA, Kayla .... 507-372-3435 246 C
kayla.westra@mnwest.edu
WESTRICK, Karyn, J ...... 419-434-4758 372 B
westrick@findlay.edu
WESTWATER, Julia .... 508-289-3379 226 D
jwestwater@whoi.edu
WETHERBEE, Scott .... 734-487-1050 229 K
WETHERELL, Dale, R ..... 401-825-2109 416 B
drwetherell@ccri.edu
WETHERILL, Elsbeth ...... 510-204-0725.. 37 F
ewetherill@cdsp.edu
WETHERINGTON, Lee .... 252-527-6223 344 D
lwetherington@lenoircc.edu
WETHINGTON, Charles . 252-638-7350 342 E
wethingc@cravencc.edu
WETMORE, David .... 620-227-9201 176 N
dwetmore@dc3.edu
WETSELL, Linda, S .... 814-332-4790 388 F
lwetsell@allegheny.edu
WETSTEIN, Matt .... 209-954-5047.. 61 B
mwetstein@deltacollege.edu
WETTER, Kevin .... 808-356-5261 129 C
kvetter@hpu.edu
WETTSTEIN, Deena .... 608-757-7716 513 D
dwettstein@blackhawk.edu
WETZEL, Derrick .... 610-282-1100 393 G
derrick.wetzel@desales.edu
WETZEL, Kathryn .... 972-860-4751 447 G
kwetzel@dcccd.edu
WETZEL, Mary, E .... 717-728-2260 392 B
marywetzel@centralpenn.edu
WETZEL, Mike .... 717-358-4759 395 G
mike.wetzel@fandm.edu
WETZEL, Shelby .... 307-754-6110 516 Q
shelby.wetzel@nwc.edu
WETZEL, Suzanne, M .... 734-384-4206 234 C
swetzel@monroeccc.edu
WETZEL HARDER,
Wendy .... 949-480-4081.. 64 D
wwharder@soka.edu
WETZSTEIN, James .... 219-464-5096 165 D
james.wetzstein@valpo.edu
WEVODAU, Clint, D .... 570-577-7439 390 H
clint.wevodau@bucknell.edu
WEXLER, Arthur .... 856-227-7200 284 E
awexler@camdencc.edu
WEXLER, Joan, G .... 718-780-7900 300 A
joan.wexler@brooklaw.edu
WEXLER, Jonathan, D ... 518-276-6143 321 A
wexler@rpi.edu
WEXLER, Judie, G .... 415-575-6124.. 29 H
jwexler@ciis.edu
WEXLER, Robert .... 310-476-9777.. 25 N
WEY, Lora .... 309-438-2592 140 L
lwey@ilstu.edu
WEYAND, Andy .... 330-490-7320 373 F
aweyand@walsh.edu
WEYAND, Joel .... 402-826-8242 274 E
joel.weyand@doane.edu
WEYANDT, Anne .... 651-690-7701 249 T
afweyandt@stkate.edu
WEYERS, Lori, A .... 715-675-3331 514 F
weyers@ntc.edu
WEYGANT, Susan .... 914-923-2397 319 J
sweygant@pace.edu
WEYHAUPT, Adam .... 314-889-1460 260 C
aweyhaupt@fontbonne.edu
WEYHENMEYER,
James, A .... 404-413-3516 121 A
jweyhenmeyer@gsu.edu
WEYHING, Katherine ..... 502-585-9911 189 B
kweyhing@spalding.edu
WEYL, Ronnie .... 908-526-1200 289 D
ronnie.weyl@raritanval.edu
WEYLER, Megan, E .... 215-895-6383 394 C
m.weyler@drexel.edu
WEYRICH, Andrew, S .... 801-581-7236 472 P
andy.weyrich@utah.edu
WEZNER, Kelley, C .... 270-809-3340 188 D
kwezner@murraystate.edu
WHALEN, Alice .... 636-584-6532 259 L
alice.whalen@eastcentral.edu
WHALEN, David .... 517-607-2321 231 C
dwhalen@hillsdale.edu
WHALEN, Dorothy .... 617-873-0244 213 B
dorothy.whalen@cambridgecollege.edu
WHALEN, James, L .... 513-556-4930 371 E
james.whalen@uc.edu
WHALEN, Jeff .... 209-588-5126.. 75 I
whalenj@yosemite.edu
WHALEN, Lynn .... 217-786-2219 144 B
lynn.whalen@llcc.edu
WHALEN, Melissa .... 913-253-5091 181 C
melissa.whalen@spst.edu
WHALEN, Michael .... 860-685-2908.. 89 F
mwhalen@wesleyan.edu
WHALEN, Michael .... 419-251-1824 365 C
michael.whalen@mercycollege.edu
WHALEN, Thomas .... 212-229-5456 316 E
whalent@newschool.edu
WHALEN, Tina .... 513-558-7485 371 E
tina.whalen@uc.edu
WHALEN, Toni .... 502-213-2118 186 C
toni.whalen@kctcs.edu
WHALEN-SMITH,
Heather, C .... 315-655-7132 300 I
hcwhalensmith@cazenovia.edu
WHALEY, Chris .... 865-882-4501 438 A
whaleycl@roanestate.edu
WHALEY, David .... 270-809-6849 188 D
dwhaley2@murraystate.edu
WHALEY, David, J .... 802-485-2300 475 I
davew@norwich.edu
WHALEY, Deonne .... 843-208-8723 425 B
dwhaley@mailbox.sc.edu
WHALEY, Frances, A ..... 815-224-0263 141 A
frances_whaley@ivcc.edu
WHALEY, Geoff .... 617-585-5000 212 C
geoff.whaley@the-bac.edu
WHALEY, Melanie, A ..... 814-871-7470 395 H
whaley003@gannon.edu
WHALEY, Michael .... 636-949-4561 261 I
mwhaley@lindenwood.edu
WHALEY, Michael, J ..... 860-685-3160.. 89 F
mwhaley@wesleyan.edu
WHALEY, Mitchell .... 765-285-5816 156 C
mwhaley@bsu.edu
WHALEY, Stephanie ...... 859-622-8757 184 F
admissions@eku.edu
WHALEY, Vernon .... 434-582-2562 482 D
vwhaley@liberty.edu
WHANG, Christine .... 909-447-6741.. 38 B
cwhang@cst.edu
WHANG, KyuJung, E .... 609-258-5491 288 F
whang@princeton.edu
WHANN, Christopher .... 646-230-1207 329 C
christopher.whann@esc.edu
WHAPHAM, Ted .... 972-721-4068 464 E
twhapham@udallas.edu
WHARTON, Barbara ...... 740-593-1059 368 G
whartonb@ohio.edu
WHARTON, Martha, L ... 410-617-2988 205 A
mwharton1@loyola.edu
WHARTON, Randy .... 740-588-1379 374 G
rwharton@zanestate.edu
WHATLEY, Melissa, L ... 205-934-4324.... 8 B
mwhatley@uab.edu
WHATLEY, Sherri .... 903-566-7247 468 C
swhatley@uttyler.edu
WHEAT, Casie .... 408-864-8642.. 43 E
wheatcasie@deanza.edu
WHEATLEY, Joyce .... 215-641-6573 402 A
jwheatley@mc3.edu
WHEATLY, Michele .... 315-443-2494 330 H
mwheatly@syr.edu
WHEATLY, Stephen .... 805-493-3828.. 30 E
wheatly@callutheran.edu
WHEATON, David, M ..... 651-696-6211 243 B
wheaton@macalester.edu
WHEATON, Katie .... 970-943-3216.. 84 E
kwheaton@western.edu
WHEATON, Michele .... 814-824-2086 401 J
mwheaton@mercyhurst.edu
WHEATON, Tom .... 605-642-6446 428 F
tom.wheaton@bhsu.edu
WHEELAND, Craig .... 610-519-4520 413 K
craig.wheeland@villanova.edu
WHEELAND, Todd .... 815-455-8564 145 B
twheeland@mchenry.edu
WHEELDON, Tim, T .... 515-263-6152 169 E
twheeldon@grandview.edu
WHEELER, Amy .... 603-206-8131 280 L
awheeler@ccsnh.edu
WHEELER, Anthony .... 610-436-2930 407 D
awheeler@wcupa.edu
WHEELER, Brad .... 812-855-5802 159 H
bwheeler@indiana.edu
WHEELER, Brad, C .... 812-855-3478 159 G
bwheeler@indiana.edu
WHEELER, Bruce, W ..... 612-343-4417 249 E
bwwheele@northcentral.edu
WHEELER,
Cassandra, L .... 956-326-4473 459 B
cwheeler@tamiu.edu
WHEELER, Cecilia, B ..... 919-528-4737 347 C
wheelerc@vgcc.edu
WHEELER, Crystal .... 520-515-5401.. 11 R
wheelerc@cochise.edu
WHEELER, Darrell, P ..... 518-442-3300 324 G
WHEELER, Dawn, A .... 910-521-6270 351 E
dawn.wheeler@uncp.edu
WHEELER, Dean .... 623-845-3903.. 13 H
dean.wheeler@gccaz.edu
WHEELER, Eric .... 530-226-4943.. 64 B
ewheeler@simpsonu.edu
WHEELER, Erin, R .... 502-597-6840 187 E
erin.wheeler@kysu.edu
WHEELER, Frank, E .... 402-363-5646 278 E
fwheeler@york.edu
WHEELER, Gerald .... 505-747-2148 295 H
geraldwheeler@nnmc.edu
WHEELER, Heather .... 254-519-5496 459 D
heather.wheeler@tamuct.edu
WHEELER, Ike .... 870-512-7865.. 18 D
ike_wheeler@asun.edu
WHEELER, Jacklyn, G ... 215-699-5700 399 G
jwheeler@lsb.edu
WHEELER, Jessica .... 213-613-2200.. 65 A
jessica_wheeler@sciarc.edu
WHEELER, John .... 770-426-2952 122 F
jwheeler@life.edu
WHEELER, John .... 253-752-2020 494 H
registrar@faithseminary.edu
WHEELER, Kara .... 620-331-4100 178 E
kwheeler@indycc.edu
WHEELER, Karen .... 870-972-2030.. 18 A
kwheeler@astate.edu
WHEELER, Laurie .... 707-965-7200.. 55 F
lwheeler@puc.edu
WHEELER, Lisa .... 952-358-8286 246 D
lisa.wheeler@normandale.edu
WHEELER, Mark .... 208-467-8772 132 F
mwheeler@nnu.edu
WHEELER, Mark .... 208-426-1140 131 C
mwheeler@boisestate.edu
WHEELER, Mary .... 254-526-1200 445 L
mary.wheeler@ctcd.edu
WHEELER, Michelle .... 907-564-8210.... 9 F
mwheeler@alaskapacific.edu
WHEELER, Michelle .... 248-476-1122 233 F
mwheeler@mispp.edu
WHEELER, Nolan .... 360-442-2201 495 G
nwheeler@lowercolumbia.edu
WHEELER, Quentin, D ... 315-470-6681 328 D
qwheeler@esf.edu
WHEELER, Rosemary, L 336-721-2605 348 H
rosemary.wheeler@salem.edu
WHEELER, Sherrell .... 575-439-3668 295 C
swheeler@nmsu.edu
WHEELER,
Stephanie, M .... 248-689-8282 238 F
swheeler@walshcollege.edu
WHEELER, Susan, L ...... 540-568-3727 481 I
wheel2sl@jmu.edu
WHEELER, Thomas .... 816-604-1138 262 F
thomasa.wheeler@mcckc.edu
WHEELER, Tim .... 425-739-8252 495 F
tim.wheeler@lwtech.edu
WHEELER, Tony .... 401-232-6707 416 A
awheeler2@bryant.edu
WHEELER, Walter .... 252-789-0259 344 E
walter.wheeler@martincc.edu
WHEELIS, Tina .... 870-368-2008.. 20 H
twheelis@ozarka.edu
WHEELUS, Angela .... 706-368-7707 119 G
awheelus@highlands.edu
WHEELUS, Chris .... 706-233-7323 125 E
wheelus@shorter.edu
WHELAN, JR.,
Donald, J .... 817-257-7785 461 A
d.whelan@tcu.edu
WHELAN, Janet .... 410-837-4779 209 D
jwhelan@ubalt.edu
WHELAN, John .... 812-855-2239 159 H
whelanj@iu.edu
WHELAN, Lara .... 518-783-2353 324 C
lwhelan@siena.edu
WHELAN, Matthew .... 631-632-6833 325 F
matthew.whelan@stonybrook.edu
WHELAN, Michaele .... 617-824-8570 214 E
michaele_whelan@emerson.edu
WHELAN, Robert .... 718-289-5162 301 D
robert.whelan@bcc.cuny.edu
WHELLAN, David .... 215-955-5050 411 E
david.whellan@jefferson.edu
WHERRY, Cassandra, J . 641-269-3424 169 F
wherry@grinnell.edu
WHETSTINE, Courtney ... 541-383-7700 382 B
cwhetstine@cocc.edu
WHETSTONE, Joseph .... 540-261-8487 485 G
joseph.whetstone@svu.edu
WHETSTONE, Kimarie .... 803-323-2551 426 H
whetstone@winthrop.edu
WHETSTONE, Toussaint 630-752-5321 155 F
toussaint.whetstone@wheaton.edu
WHIDDEN, Katherine .... 617-573-4833 224 I
kwidden@suffolk.edu
WHIDDON, Tifini .... 936-633-4555 442 I
twhiddon@angelina.edu
WHIGHAM, Melissa .... 772-462-7282 101 Q
mwhigham@irsc.edu
WHILLOCK, David .... 817-257-5915 461 A
d.whillock@tcu.edu
WHIPKEY, Brady .... 304-424-8200 505 C
brady.whipkey@wvup.edu
WHIPKEY, Judy .... 304-205-6685 502 K
judith.whipkey@bridgevalley.edu
WHIPP, Devin .... 281-283-2180 465 B
whipp@uhcl.edu
WHIPPLE, Andrew .... 570-586-2400 392 E
awhipple@clarkssummitu.edu
WHIPPLE, Edward, G .... 503-370-6139 388 D
egwhipple@willamette.edu
WHIPPLE, Jeffrey .... 517-796-8683 231 E
whipplejeffreys@jccmi.edu
WHIPPLE, P. Michael .... 504-861-5543 194 G
pmwhipple@loyno.edu
WHIPPO, Cindy .... 602-557-7202.. 17 C
cindy.whippo@apollo.edu
WHIPPY, Helen .... 808-735-4825 129 A
helen.whippy@chaminade.edu
WHIRL, Jermaine .... 864-250-8601 421 K
jermaine.whirl@gvltec.edu
WHISENAND, Gary .... 562-907-5120.. 75 A
gwhisena@whittier.edu
WHISENHUNT, Glenne .. 405-682-7413 377 C
gwhisenhunt@occc.edu
WHISENHUNT, Tim .... 405-682-1611 377 C
twhisenhunt@occc.edu
WHISENTON-COMER,
Freda .... 219-989-2510 163 E
fwhisent@pnw.edu
WHISLER, Ryan .... 740-474-8896 367 E
rwhisler@ohiochristian.edu
WHISLER, Travis .... 201-761-7130 291 D
twhisler@saintpeters.edu
WHISMAN, Kathryn, E .. 520-621-3324.. 16 J
kwhisman@email.arizona.edu
WHISNANT, Rebecca, S 937-229-4290 372 A
rwhisnant1@udayton.edu
WHISTLE, Wesley .... 270-852-3291 187 F
wwhistle@kwc.edu
WHISTON, Meg .... 612-767-7096 240 B
meg.whiston@alfredadler.edu
WHITACRE, Aaron .... 540-834-1044 488 B
awhitacre@germanna.edu
WHITACRE, Caroline ..... 614-292-1582 367 H
whitacre.3@osu.edu
WHITACRE, Norma .... 360-475-7360 496 F
nwhitacre@olympic.edu
WHITAKER, IV,
Alexander, W .... 423-968-4861 432 I
president@king.edu
WHITAKER, Debbie .... 951-222-8434.. 58 H
debbie.whitaker@rcc.edu
WHITAKER, Evans, P .... 864-231-2100 418 E
ewhitaker@andersonuniversity.edu
WHITAKER, Gwen, D .... 336-734-7471 343 C
gwhitaker@forsythtech.edu
WHITAKER, James .... 803-754-4100 420 E
WHITAKER, Jeff .... 859-622-1968 184 F
jeff.whitaker@eku.edu
WHITAKER, Jillian .... 405-466-3652 375 L
jbwhitaker@langston.edu
WHITAKER, Joanne .... 808-734-9520 130 C
joannewh@hawaii.edu
WHITAKER, John .... 317-896-9324 164 F
jawhitaker@ubca.org
WHITAKER, Kevin .... 205-348-4892.... 8 A
kwhitaker@ua.edu
WHITAKER, Latoya, R ... 713-798-3092 444 A
lrwhitak@bcm.edu
WHITAKER, Lois .... 443-885-4022 206 A
lois.whitaker@morgan.edu
WHITAKER, Michelle ..... 910-672-1958 350 B
mwhitaker@uncfsu.edu
WHITAKER, Niki .... 719-549-2951.. 78 P
niki.whitaker@csupueblo.edu
WHITAKER, Paula .... 863-667-5181 108 G
pwhitaker@seu.edu
WHITAKER, Rob .... 912-478-5491 120 E
rwhitaker@georgiasouthern.edu
WHITAKER, Ross, T .... 801-587-9549 472 P
whitaker@cs.utah.edu
WHITAKER, Scott .... 505-428-1268 296 B
scott.whitaker@sfcc.edu

WHITE-SMITH, Kimberly .... 909-593-3511.. 70 E kwhite-smith@laverne.edu
WHITE-ZOLLMAN, Casey .... 541-278-5839 382 A cwhitezollman@bluecc.edu
WHITECAVAGE, Michele 714-449-7404.. 51 A mwhitecavage@ketchum.edu
WHITED, Jimmy, R .... 540-375-2308 484 H whited@roanoke.edu
WHITEFIELD, Joe .... 615-904-8375 434 H joe.whitefield@mtsu.edu
WHITEFORD, Aaron .... 503-768-7944 383 G ahw@lclark.edu
WHITEFORD, Craig .... 410-287-1914 203 B cwhiteford@cecil.edu
WHITEFORD, Marion ..... 802-447-6388 476 C mwhitfrd@svc.edu
WHITEHEAD, Debbie ..... 503-255-0332 384 E debbiew@multnomah.edu
WHITEHEAD, Doug .... 435-652-7500 473 B dkw@dixie.edu
WHITEHEAD, Gwen .... 409-882-3926 462 D gwen.whitehead@lsco.edu
WHITEHEAD, Heidi, M .. 812-888-4313 165 E hwhitehead@vinu.edu
WHITEHEAD, JaRenae ... 757-683-4564 483 G jwhitehe@odu.edu
WHITEHEAD, JR., Joe, B .... 336-334-7965 350 C jbwhiteh@ncat.edu
WHITEHEAD, Kim .... 662-241-6850 254 F kmwhitehead@muw.edu
WHITEHEAD, Kimberly .. 410-651-6508 208 C kdwhitehead@umes.edu
WHITEHEAD, Nicole ...... 434-381-6510 485 P nwhitehead@sbc.edu
WHITEHEAD, Susan ...... 617-984-1721 223 H swhitehead@quincycollege.edu
WHITEHEAD, Teresa ...... 575-769-4066 293 M teresa.whitehead@clovis.edu
WHITEHOUSE, Deborah 859-622-8812 184 F deborah.whitehouse@eku.edu
WHITEHOUSE, Jennifer . 985-867-2240 195 I jwhitehouse@sjasc.edu
WHITEHOUSE, Steve, M .... 253-535-7119 496 G whitehsm@plu.edu
WHITEHURST, Marcus, A .... 814-865-5906 403 F maw163@psu.edu
WHITEHURST-MCLEAN, Makitta .... 252-335-3355 350 A mmmclean@ecsu.edu
WHITEING, Kelli .... 605-256-5112 428 G kelli.whiteing@dsu.edu
WHITELAW, Kenneth ..... 603-513-1375 282 G kenneth.whitelaw@granite.edu
WHITELAW, Lydia .... 610-896-1177 397 F lwhitela@haverford.edu
WHITELEY, Janell .... 360-475-7504 496 F jwhiteley@olympic.edu
WHITELY, Patricia, A ..... 305-284-4922 112 O pwhitely@miami.edu
WHITEMAN, Betty .... 386-822-8869 111 E bwhiteman@stetson.edu
WHITEMAN, Charles, H 814-863-0448 403 F chw17@psu.edu
WHITEMAN, Michael ..... 704-330-6706 342 A mike.whiteman@cpcc.edu
WHITEMAN, Raymond, E .... 574-807-7139 156 E ray.whiteman@bethelcollege.edu
WHITER, Kimberly .... 540-985-8106 482 A kawhiter@jchs.edu
WHITESELL, Melissa ..... 706-272-4527 118 F mwhitesell@daltonstate.edu
WHITESELL, Warren ...... 765-658-4229 157 H warrenwhitesell@depauw.edu
WHITESIDE, Christopher .... 714-895-8250.. 38 G cwhiteside4@gwc.cccd.edu
WHITESIDE, Dannelle .... 931-221-7572 430 B whitesided@apsu.edu
WHITESIDE, Harold, D .. 615-898-2900 434 H harold.whiteside@mtsu.edu
WHITEY, Jeff .... 541-888-7402 387 A jwhitey@socc.edu
WHITFIELD, Candis .... 912-660-4658 106 N candis.whitfield@saintleo.edu
WHITFIELD, Henry .... 478-934-3167 123 A henry.whitfield@mga.edu
WHITFIELD, Jacques ..... 530-741-6976.. 75 K jwhitfie@yccd.edu
WHITFIELD, Keith .... 919-761-2185 349 C kwhitfield@sebts.edu
WHITFIELD, Keith .... 313-577-2433 239 C keith.whitfield@wayne.edu
WHITFIELD, Meredith .... 828-227-7059 352 C mcwhitfield@wcu.edu
WHITFIELD, Rick .... 910-962-3383 352 A whitfieldr@uncw.edu
WHITFILL, Gene .... 806-291-1045 470 I whitfillg@wbu.edu
WHITFILL, Jill .... 731-352-4083 430 E whitfillj@bethelu.edu
WHITFORD, Betty Lou .. 334-844-4448.... 4 D blw0017@auburn.edu
WHITFORD, Daryl .... 808-675-3730 128 K daryl.whitford@byuh.edu
WHITHAM, Crystal .... 330-337-6403 356 B librarian@awc.edu
WHITHAM, John, H ...... 610-526-1308 389 B john.whitham@theamericancollege.edu
WHITHAUS, Becky .... 573-897-5000 267 F
WHITING, Alison .... 808-675-3551 128 K alison.whiting@byuh.edu
WHITING, Doug .... 401-598-1000 416 C dwhiting@jwu.edu
WHITING, J. Scott .... 334-874-5700.... 5 B swhiting@ccal.edu
WHITING, Sarah, M ...... 713-348-4044 455 F sarah.whiting@rice.edu
WHITING, Shari, K ...... 315-859-4313 309 D swhiting@hamilton.edu
WHITIS, Andrew .... 419-434-4767 372 B whitis@findlay.edu
WHITIS, Harold .... 210-485-0605 441 E hwhitis2@alamo.edu
WHITIS, Matt .... 815-939-5350 148 F mwhitis@olivet.edu
WHITLATCH, Frank .... 707-826-5101.. 34 A frank@humboldt.edu
WHITLEDGE, Terry .... 907-474-7229.. 10 B terry@ims.uaf.edu
WHITLEY, Darrell, S ...... 252-985-5105 348 A dwhitley@ncwc.edu
WHITLEY, Rebecca .... 575-492-2546 294 L rwhitley@nmjc.edu
WHITLOCK, David, W .... 405-585-5801 377 A david.whitlock@okbu.edu
WHITLOCK, Eugene .... 650-358-6883.. 61 Q whitlocke@smccd.edu
WHITLOCK, Kevin .... 320-308-2038 247 E kcwhitlock@stcloudstate.edu
WHITLOCK, Monica .... 509-777-4216 500 H mwhitlock@whitworth.edu
WHITLOCK, Shawna .... 216-373-5335 367 A swhitlock@ndc.edu
WHITLOCK, Stephen ...... 678-839-6426 127 F swhitlock@westga.edu
WHITLOCK, Tonya, F .... 678-664-0532 128 F tonya.whitlock@westgatech.edu
WHITMAN, Carl, E .... 240-567-3146 205 F carl.whitman@montgomerycollege.edu
WHITMAN, David .... 651-604-4118 243 E dwhitman@minneapolisbusinesscollege.edu
WHITMAN, Deirdre .... 914-674-7316 314 I dwhitman@mercy.edu
WHITMAN, Josh .... 217-333-3631 154 B illiniad@illinois.edu
WHITMAN, Melissa ...... 252-249-1851 345 C mwhitman@pamlicocc.edu
WHITMAN, Paul .... 803-321-5600 422 H paul.whitman@newberry.edu
WHITMAN, R. Douglas . 313-577-1625 239 C dwhitman@wayne.edu
WHITMAN, Rebecca, R . 616-234-4010 230 F rwhitman@grcc.edu
WHITMAN, Richard .... 910-296-2487 344 B rwhitman@jamessprunt.edu
WHITMAN, William, D .. 989-386-6696 234 B wwhitman@midmich.edu
WHITMER, Ann .... 517-629-0440 226 G awhitmer@albion.edu
WHITMER, Linda .... 865-573-4517 432 H lwhitmer@johnsonu.edu
WHITMEYER, Antoinette 301-295-6013 518 G antoinette.whitmeyer@usuhs.edu
WHITMIRE, Teresa .... 479-619-4175.. 20 F twhitmire@nwacc.edu
WHITMORE, Joe .... 256-840-4102.... 3 F joe.whitmore@snead.edu
WHITMORE, Kimberly, N .... 515-574-1138 170 C whitmore@iowacentral.edu
WHITMORE, Michele ..... 802-635-1452 477 C michele.whitmore@jsc.edu
WHITMORE, Petia .... 781-239-4543 211 A pwhitmore1@babson.edu
WHITMORE, Vincent ..... 410-986-3220 202 F vwhitmore@bccc.edu
WHITMORE, Vincent ..... 410-462-8594 202 F vwhitmore@bccc.edu
WHITNER, Nicole .... 510-594-3720.. 28 K nwhitner@cca.edu
WHITNEY, Candice .... 408-848-4754.. 44 B cwhitney@gavilan.edu
WHITNEY, Chris .... 570-941-7640 413 F christinawhitney@scranton.edu
WHITNEY, Gleaves .... 616-331-2770 230 G whitneyg@gvsu.edu
WHITNEY, Glenda .... 573-897-5000 267 F
WHITNEY, J.J .... 501-450-1263.. 19 I whitney@hendrix.edu
WHITNEY, Jarrid .... 626-395-6341.. 29 I jwhitney@caltech.edu
WHITNEY, Joan, G .... 610-519-4050 413 K joan.whitney@villanova.edu
WHITNEY, Karen .... 928-541-7777.. 54 B kwhitney@ncu.edu
WHITNEY, Karen, M ...... 717-720-4010 405 D
WHITNEY, Laura .... 860-768-5691.. 89 C lwhitney@hartford.edu
WHITNEY, Linda .... 719-884-5000 180 B llwhitney@nbc.edu
WHITNEY, Majid .... 973-313-6008 291 F majid.whitney@shu.edu
WHITNEY, Marian, D .... 315-684-6010 329 F whitnemd@morrisville.edu
WHITNEY, Paul .... 401-874-5224 417 E pwhitney@uri.edu
WHITNEY, Richard .... 641-269-3300 169 F whitney@grinnell.edu
WHITNEY, Roger .... 650-723-2300.. 66 C
WHITSON, Brian .... 757-221-7876 479 I bwwhit@wm.edu
WHITSON, Jennifer .... 507-786-3000 250 C whitson@stolaf.edu
WHITSON, Tony .... 901-435-1733 433 A tony_whitson@loc.edu
WHITT, Cynthia, L .... 423-869-6394 433 C cindy.whitt@lmunet.edu
WHITT, David, T .... 205-726-2386.... 6 G dtwhitt@samford.edu
WHITT, Elizabeth .... 209-228-2317.. 69 C ewhitt@ucmerced.edu
WHITT, Ellen .... 317-955-6597 162 R ewhitt@marian.edu
WHITT, Fred .... 828-328-7334 339 C fred.whitt@lr.edu
WHITT, Julie .... 817-257-6571 461 A j.whitt@tcu.edu
WHITT, Patricia .... 615-333-3344 435 D pwhitt@national-college.edu
WHITTAKER, A. Dale ..... 407-823-2303 110 C dale.whittaker@ucf.edu
WHITTAKER, David .... 816-584-6710 265 C dave.whittaker@park.edu
WHITTAKER, Nancy, H .. 205-348-6690.... 8 A nwhittaker@fa.ua.edu
WHITTAKER, Robert ...... 617-327-6777 226 B
WHITTAKER, Wesley ...... 405-466-6149 375 L wwhittaker@langston.edu
WHITTAKER-DAVIS, Sharon .... 256-761-6231.... 7 D swhittaker@talladega.edu
WHITTED, Tenial .... 708-596-2000 151 H twhitted@ssc.edu
WHITTEMORE, Steve ..... 508-626-4923 218 A swhittemore@framingham.edu
WHITTEN, James .... 207-844-2103 200 C jwhitten@smccme.edu
WHITTEN, Mandy .... 864-503-5420 425 H mwhitten@uscupstaet.edu
WHITTEN, Pamela .... 706-583-0506 127 A pwhitten@uga.edu
WHITTEN, Patrice .... 850-484-1714 105 E pswhitten@pensacolastate.edu
WHITTEN, Stockton .... 321-433-7205.. 97 N whittens@easternflorida.edu
WHITTENBURG, Nashia 912-344-2514 115 D nashia.whittenburg@armstrong.edu
WHITTENBURG, Scott ... 406-243-6670 271 G scott.whittenburg@umontana.edu
WHITTENTON, Kathy ..... 870-307-7505.. 20 C kathy.whittenton@lyon.edu
WHITTEY, Chris .... 216-421-7411 359 J cwhittey@cia.edu
WHITTIER, Dan .... 360-475-7814 496 F dwhittier@olympic.edu
WHITTINGHAM, Michelle .... 831-459-1453.. 70 C michelle@ucsc.edu
WHITTINGHAM, Rachel . 501-205-8876.. 19 B rwhittingham@cbc.edu
WHITTINGTON, Amy ..... 601-605-3313 253 C awhittington@holmescc.edu
WHITTINGTON, Connie . 318-869-5101 191 C cwhitt@centenary.edu
WHITTINGTON, Donna .. 225-743-8500 193 C dwhittington@rpcc.edu
WHITTINGTON, Elizabeth .... 713-623-2040 443 C ewhittington@aii.edu
WHITTINGTON, Gerald, O .... 336-278-5434 337 G whitting@elon.edu
WHITTINGTON, Joya ..... 570-504-0920 399 A whittingtonj@lackawanna.edu
WHITTINGTON, Lee .... 828-766-1196 344 F lwhittington@mayland.edu
WHITTLE, Rodney .... 256-372-5500.... 1 A rodney.whittle@aamu.edu
WHITTLESEY, Valerie, D 470-578-6023 122 C vwhittle@kennesaw.edu
WHITTUM, Terry .... 410-532-5105 206 D twhittum@ndm.edu
WHITTUM, Timothy .... 603-645-9709 282 C t.whittum@snhu.edu
WHITWELL, Jeff .... 615-898-2700 434 H jeff.whitwell@mtsu.edu
WHITWORTH, Amy, F ... 210-486-4097 441 G awhitworth@alamo.edu
WHITWORTH, Bruce ...... 559-278-2795.. 32 A bwhitwor@csufresno.edu
WHITWORTH, Jerry .... 940-898-2202 464 A jwhitworth@twu.edu
WHORLEY, William .... 517-607-2454 231 C wwhorley@hillsdale.edu
WHORTON, Susan .... 864-656-6256 419 F whorton@clemson.edu
WHYNOTT, Anne .... 262-564-2758 513 G whynotta@gtc.edu
WHYTE, Novia, P .... 516-463-6928 310 D novia.p.whyte@hofstra.edu
WHYTE, Willaim .... 262-564-3228 513 G whytew@gtc.edu
WIBBELS, Alan .... 954-771-0376 102 W awibbels@knoxseminary.edu
WIBBENMEYER, Kana ... 773-508-3489 144 D kwibben@luc.edu
WIBLE, Doug .... 949-214-3029.. 40 I doug.wible@cui.edu
WICHERN, Adam .... 718-405-3776 304 H adam.wichern@mountsaintvincent.edu
WICHERT, Jerome, L .... 580-774-3786 380 B jerome.wichert@swosu.edu
WICHROSKI, Pamela, J . 207-786-6207 198 E pwichros@bates.edu
WICHROWSKI, Edward .. 617-745-3878 214 D edward.wichrowski@enc.edu
WICHSER, John .... 301-846-2674 203 H jwichser@frederick.edu
WICK, Martha .... 641-683-5231 169 I martha.wick@indianhills.edu
WICK, Michael, R .... 240-895-4389 206 G mrwick@smcm.edu
WICKE, Thomas .... 303-861-1151.. 79 E twicke@concorde.edu
WICKEHAM, Daniel .... 414-955-8826 508 D dwickeha@mcw.edu
WICKER, Jeff .... 803-321-5676 422 H jeffrey.wicker@newberry.edu
WICKER, John David ..... 619-594-6357.. 34 B adsdsu@mail.sdsu.edu
WICKER-MCCREE, Ingrid, L .... 919-530-7057 350 D iwicker@nccu.edu
WICKERSHAM, Cassie ... 608-663-6715 507 D cwickersham@edgewood.edu
WICKERT, Jonathan, A .. 515-294-0070 166 F wickert@iastate.edu
WICKETT, Brenda, K ...... 515-961-1611 173 E brenda.wickett@simpson.edu
WICKHAM, Allis .... 201-327-8877 285 J awickham@eastwick.edu
WICKHAM, Gerald .... 563-441-4201 169 A gwickham@eicc.edu
WICKLAND, Mary .... 409-984-6125 462 E mary.wickland@lamarpa.edu
WICKLESS, Megan .... 402-552-6119 273 K wicklessmegan@clarksoncollege.edu
WICKLIFFE, Cari, S .... 314-977-3442 266 J wicklics@slu.edu
WICKLIFFE-CAMPBELL, Carol .... 631-451-4169 330 B wicklic@sunysuffolk.edu
WICKLINE, Jason .... 217-424-6217 145 J jwickline@millikin.edu
WICKLINE, Paul .... 661-362-3152.. 39 C paul.wickline@canyons.edu
WICKLUND, Greg, A ...... 817-202-6743 457 E wicklund@swau.edu
WICKMAN, Barbara .... 505-566-4059 296 A wickmanb@sanjuancollege.edu
WICKS, Donna .... 810-762-7853 232 C dwicks@kettering.edu
WICKSTROM, Brian .... 318-342-5361 198 A wickstrom@ulm.edu

WICKSTROM, Julie .... 617-353-4176 212 G
jwickstr@bu.edu
WICKSTROM, Sherry ..... 763-576-4874 244 A
swickstrom@anokatech.edu
WIDANKA, Kenneth ...... 585-385-8256 322 E
kwidanka@sjfc.edu
WIDDICOMBE, Molly .... 909-748-8381.. 71 H
molly_widdicombe@redlands.edu
WIDDOWS, Daniella ...... 434-223-6311 481 D
dwiddows@hsc.edu
WIDELITZ, Courtney ...... 817-722-1721 451 G
courtney.widelitz@tku.edu
WIDELL, Mike .... 405-945-3284 378 C
mike@okstate.edu
WIDEMAN, Gene .... 918-595-7262 380 D
gene.wideman@tulsacc.edu
WIDENER, J, J .... 620-417-1202 181 E
jj.widener@sccc.edu
WIDENHOFER,
Stephen, B .... 217-424-6300 145 J
swidenhofer@millikin.edu
WIDENMANN, Sally ...... 541-917-4534 384 A
widenms@linnbenton.edu
WIDGER, Mari Jo .... 308-345-8106 275 I
widgerm@mpcc.edu
WIDMER, Robert, D ...... 309-268-8106 139 D
rob.widmer@heartland.edu
WIDNER, Kenneth .... 662-329-7021 254 F
kwidner@muw.edu
WIDNER, Melissa .... 229-420-4070 114 I
melisa.widner@asurams.edu
WIDOM, Jennifer .... 650-723-2300.. 66 C
WIEBER, Paul .... 540-545-7338 485 C
pwieber@su.edu
WIECHMAN, Jeffery, P .. 507-354-8221 243 C
wiechmjp@mlc-wels.edu
WIECKI, Lisa .... 864-388-8035 422 A
lwiecki@lander.edu
WIECKOWSKI, Ellen, G . 412-397-6273 409 C
wieckowski@rmu.edu
WIECKOWSKI, Ellen, G . 412-397-6901 409 C
wieckowski@rmu.edu
WIED, Christine .... 979-830-4224 444 D
cwied@blinn.edu
WIEDEFELD, Kimberley . 585-594-6199 321 C
wiedefeld_kimberley@roberts.edu
WIEDEN, Ted .... 925-969-2001.. 40 L
twieden@dvc.edu
WIEDENHOEFT,
Margaret .... 269-337-7133 231 F
margaret.wiedenoeft@kzoo.edu
WIEDERHOLT, Mark ...... 660-944-2968 258 G
markw@conception.edu
WIEGAND, Joe .... 706-865-2134 126 G
jwiegand@truett.edu
WIEGAND, Laura .... 910-962-3680 352 A
wiegandl@uncw.edu
WIEGAND, Mark .... 502-272-8368 183 H
mwiegand@bellarmine.edu
WIEGAND, Randall, V ... 671-735-2905 520 B
wiegandr@triton.uog.edu
WIEGANDT, Scott, P ..... 502-272-8496 183 H
swiegandt@bellarmine.edu
WIEGEL, Lisa .... 563-288-6003 168 M
lwiegel@eicc.edu
WIEGMAN, Karen, D ..... 913-971-3698 179 H
kdwiegman@mnu.edu
WIELEBINSKI, Daria ...... 570-422-3282 406 A
dwielebinski@esu.edu
WIELENGA, Jay .... 712-707-7111 172 G
jayw@nwciowa.edu
WIELGUS, Jeanne .... 707-826-4206.. 34 A
jw7001@humboldt.edu
WIELHORSKI, Karen ...... 281-283-3930 465 B
wielhorski@uhcl.edu
WIELINSKI, Peter .... 218-631-7810 245 H
peter.wielinski@minnesota.edu
WIENCEK, John, M .... 208-885-7919 132 I
provost@uidaho.edu
WIERBICKI ABRAHAMS,
Jill .... 617-928-4633 222 D
jwabrahams@mountida.edu
WIERDA, Bruce .... 231-777-0657 234 G
bruce.wierda@muskegoncc.edu
WIERDA, Kire .... 989-328-1286 234 D
kire.wierda@montcalm.edu
WIERENGA, Sue .... 415-955-2100.. 24 K
swierenga@alliant.edu
WIERS, Alison .... 336-334-4822 343 E
ajwiers@gtcc.edu
WIERSMA, Charles .... 440-365-5222 364 F
WIERSMA, Noelle .... 509-777-4874 500 H
nwiersma@whitworth.edu
WIERTEL, Anthony .... 716-926-8818 310 B
twiertel@hilbert.edu
WIERZBICKI, Andrzej .... 251-460-6280.... 9 B
awierzbicki@southalabama.edu
WIESCAMP, Cheryl .... 970-247-7364.. 79 J
wiescamp_c@fortlewis.edu
WIESE, Joelle, D .... 202-687-7150.. 92 B
jdw237@georgetown.edu
WIESEHAN, Terry .... 765-973-8221 160 A
twiesaha@iue.edu
WIESENBERG, Mark ...... 801-863-8740 473 D
mwiesenberg@uvu.edu
WIESS, Renee .... 361-593-3991 460 B
rennee.wiess@tamuk.edu
WIEWEL, Christine .... 217-641-4517 141 F
cwiewel@jwcc.edu
WIGBOLDY, Kyle .... 616-222-3000 232 F
kwigboldy@kuyper.edu
WIGGINS, Amy, F .... 252-862-1225 345 H
afwiggins7415@roanokechowan.edu
WIGGINS, Charles .... 828-395-1306 344 A
cpwiggins@isothermal.edu
WIGGINS, David, J .... 952-446-4112 242 A
wigginsj@crown.edu
WIGGINS, Devon .... 903-510-2646 464 D
dwig@tjc.edu
WIGGINS, LaVaughn ..... 334-874-5700.... 5 B
lwiggins@ccal.edu
WIGGINS, Michaele .... 336-334-7593 350 C
sm8093@bncollege.com
WIGGINS, Nimmi, K ..... 859-257-6547 190 B
nwiggin@uky.edu
WIGGINS, Rob .... 503-517-1876 388 C
rwiggins@westernseminary.edu
WIGGINS, Roy .... 781-891-3166 212 A
rwiggins@bentley.edu
WIGGINS, Sarah .... 954-201-6455.. 96 A
swiggins@broward.edu
WIGGINS, Shelia .... 252-527-6223 344 D
swiggins@lenoircc.edu
WIGGINS, Symphoni ..... 706-396-7594 124 C
swiggins@paine.edu
WIGGINTON, Van, A ..... 281-542-2000 455 L
van.wigginton@sjcd.edu
WIGHT, Charles, A .... 801-626-6001 473 E
president@weber.edu
WIGHT, Laura .... 406-771-4318 272 D
laura.wight@gfcmsu.edu
WIGHT, Randall .... 870-245-5107.. 20 G
wight@obu.edu
WIGHTKIN, Joe .... 763-488-2549 244 G
joe.wightkin@hennepintech.edu
WIGHTKIN, Steven, P ... 312-942-5947 150 F
steven_wightkin@rush.edu
WIGHTMAN, Beth, A ...... 818-677-2969.. 33 B
beth.wightman@csun.edu
WIGHTMAN, James .... 614-236-6264 358 A
jwightman@capital.edu
WIGHTMAN, Todd .... 208-535-5440 131 G
todd.wightman@my.eitc.edu
WIGINTON, Chad .... 580-477-7918 381 G
chad.wiginton@wosc.edu
WIGINTON, Melissa ...... 512-404-4862 443 I
mwiginton@austinseminary.edu
WIGLEY, Kimberly .... 404-627-2681 116 E
kimberly.wigley@beulah.edu
WIGNALL, Scott, D .... 724-946-7135 414 C
wignalsd@westminster.edu
WIGNER, Dee .... 620-276-9577 177 G
dee.wigner@gcccks.edu
WIGNES, David, R .... 608-785-9140 515 C
wignesd@westerntc.edu
WIGNOT, Terese .... 570-408-4627 414 H
terese.wignot@wilkes.edu
WIGTIL, Brad .... 254-710-2222 444 B
brad_wigtil@baylor.edu
WIHBEY, Jean .... 561-868-3400 105 A
wihbeyj@palmbeachstate.edu
WIILKINSON, Joann, F . 314-516-5301 268 E
wilkinsonj@umsl.edu
WILBANKS, Cynthia, H . 734-763-5554 237 I
wilbanks@umich.edu
WILBANKS, Jennifer ...... 660-596-7229 267 E
jwilbanks@sfccmo.edu
WILBANKS, Jennifer ...... 843-349-5208 421 L
jennifer.wilbanks@hgtc.edu
WILBANKS, Jennifer ...... 803-276-9000 423 C
wilbanks.j@ptc.edu
WILBANKS, Laura .... 734-481-2318 229 K
laura.wilbanks@emich.edu
WILBANKS, Scott .... 864-250-8281 421 K
scott.wilbanks@gvltec.edu
WILBORN, Colin .... 254-295-8642 466 A
cwilborn@umhb.edu
WILBREW, Karen .... 303-964-6274.. 82 D
kwilbrew@regis.edu
WILBUR, Bruce .... 707-654-1173.. 32 E
bwilbur@cusm.edu
WILBUR, Gregg .... 518-736-3622 309 A
gregg.wilbur@fmcc.suny.edu
WILBUR, Janice .... 508-849-3406 210 H
jwilbur@annamaria.edu
WILBUR, Kathleen, M ... 989-774-3871 228 E
wilbu1km@cmich.edu
WILBUR, Marcia .... 706-769-1472 115 G
WILBUR, Peter, B .... 401-254-3365 417 C
pwilbur@rwu.edu
WILBUR, Roy, A .... 215-965-8561 402 C
rwilbur@moore.edu
WILBUR, Shelley .... 941-487-4100 110 B
mwilbur@ncf.edu
WILBURN, Howard, L ... 336-725-8344 348 C
piedmontu@piedmontu.edu
WILBURN, Kevin .... 251-442-2223.... 8 D
kwilburn@umobile.edu
WILBURN, Roberta .... 509-777-4603 500 H
rwilburn@whitworth.edu
WILCH, Peter, J .... 415-422-6423.. 72 A
pwilch@usfca.edu
WILCHER, Cheryl .... 305-626-3641.. 99 M
cwilcher@fmuniv.edu
WILCOX, Anthony .... 978-665-3482 217 E
awilcox@fitchburgstate.edu
WILCOX, Bonnie .... 417-873-7811 259 G
bwilcox@drury.edu
WILCOX, Cordelia, A ..... 919-658-7494 349 F
cwilcox@umo.edu
WILCOX, Dan .... 910-362-7676 341 E
dwilcox@cfcc.edu
WILCOX, Dean .... 336-770-3243 352 B
wilcoxd@uncsa.edu
WILCOX, Denise .... 909-469-5393.. 74 G
dwilcox@westernu.edu
WILCOX, Jerome .... 203-837-8242.. 85 B
wilcoxj@wcsu.edu
WILCOX, Kathleen, J ..... 937-328-6060 359 H
wilcoxk@clarkstate.edu
WILCOX, Kenneth .... 718-522-9073 298 E
coachwilcox@asa.edu
WILCOX, Kevin .... 518-956-8120 324 G
kwilcox@albany.edu
WILCOX, Kim .... 970-351-2496.. 83 F
kim.wilcox@unco.edu
WILCOX, Kim, A .... 951-827-5201.. 69 D
chancellor@ucr.edu
WILCOX, Marina .... 325-235-7316 461 G
marina.wilcox@tstc.edu
WILCOX, Mark .... 412-536-1104 398 E
mark.wilcox@laroche.edu
WILCOX, Nancy .... 228-896-3809 254 D
nancy.wilcox@mgccc.edu
WILCOX, Ralph .... 813-974-8347 111 A
rcwilcox@usf.edu
WILCOX, Reed, N .... 540-261-4100 485 G
reed.wilcox@svu.edu
WILCOX, Robbin .... 419-267-1460 366 G
rwilcox@northweststate.edu
WILCOX, Robert, M .... 803-777-6857 424 I
wilcoxrm@law.sc.edu
WILCOX, Stan .... 850-644-3347 110 A
swilcox2@fsu.edu
WILCOX, Tamera .... 785-309-3183 181 D
tamera.wilcox@salinatech.edu
WILCOXEN, Andrica .... 913-288-7652 178 H
awilcoxen@kckcc.edu
WILCOXSON,
Douglas, A .... 517-750-1200 237 D
dwilcoxs@arbor.edu
WILCZEK, Amity .... 760-572-2000.. 41 E
awilczek@deepsprings.edu
WILD, Beth .... 918-595-8804 380 D
beth.wild@tulsacc.edu
WILD, Larry .... 847-628-2036 142 B
lwild@judsonu.edu
WILD, Lorie .... 206-281-2608 498 B
wildl@spu.edu
WILD, Lynn, A .... 585-475-6543 321 D
lawctc@rit.edu
WILD, Robert, M .... 314-935-8081 269 L
rob.wild@wustl.edu
WILDCAT, Dan .... 785-830-2770 178 A
dwildcat@haskell.edu
WILDE, Jerry .... 765-973-8554 160 A
jwilde@iue.edu
WILDECK, Steve, C .... 608-265-3040 512 D
steve.wildeck@uwex.uwc.edu
WILDEMANN,
Leonard Walter .... 401-841-6515 518 E
WILDENTHAL,
B. Hobson .... 972-883-3550 467 D
wildenbh@utdallas.edu
WILDER, Aliza .... 860-486-4038.. 88 G
aliza.wilder@uconn.edu
WILDER, Amanda .... 916-686-8678.. 30 H
WILDER, Carol .... 212-229-8903 316 E
wilderc@newschool.edu
WILDER, Carrie .... 229-931-2351 125 G
cwilder@southgatech.edu
WILDER, Diane .... 610-896-1209 397 F
dwilder@haverford.edu
WILDER, Jennifer .... 850-599-3651 109 A
jennifer.wilder@famu.edu
WILDER, Kristie .... 423-236-2206 436 C
kwilder@southern.edu
WILDER, Lesley .... 512-472-4133 456 E
lesley.wilder@ssw.edu
WILDER, Linda .... 860-515-3862.. 84 H
lwilder@charteroak.edu
WILDER, Martin, A .... 540-654-1301 486 D
mwilder@umw.edu
WILDER, Michael .... 630-752-5818 155 F
michael.wilder@wheaton.edu
WILDER, Richard, D ...... 352-294-3220 110 D
rwilder@ufl.edu
WILDER, Robert .... 774-354-0500 211 F
robert.wilder@becker.edu
WILDER, Stanley .... 225-578-2217 193 M
wilder@lsu.edu
WILDER, Sterly .... 919-684-5114 337 C
sterly.wilder@daa.duke.edu
WILDER, W. Mark .... 662-915-5756 256 C
acwilder@olemiss.edu
WILDER-BYRD,
Ellen, M .... 803-323-2236 426 H
wilderbyrde@winthrop.edu
WILDERMUTH, Amy ...... 801-581-8763 472 P
amy.wildermuth@utah.edu
WILDES, David .... 352-365-3532 103 B
wildesd@lssc.edu
WILDES, SJ, Kevin, W .. 504-865-3847 194 G
wildesk@loyno.edu
WILDEY, Diane .... 518-743-2337 328 G
daltod@sunyacc.edu
WILDHACK, John .... 315-443-8705 330 H
jwildhac@syr.edu
WILDING, Jody .... 281-649-3070 450 C
jwilding@hbu.edu
WILDING, Michael .... 661-362-3498.. 39 C
michael.wilding@canyons.edu
WILDING, Tim .... 205-226-4643.... 4 F
trwildin@bsc.edu
WILDMAN, Katie .... 605-642-6270 428 F
katherine.wildman@bhsu.edu
WILDNER-BASSETT,
Mary, E .... 520-621-9294.. 16 J
wildnerb@email.arizona.edu
WILEBSKI, Jason .... 563-355-3500 171 B
jwilebski@kaplan.edu
WILENSKY, Heather .... 410-857-2289 205 E
hwilensky@mcdaniel.edu
WILES, Jan .... 618-842-3711 140 C
wilesj@iecc.edu
WILES, Judy .... 573-651-2112 266 M
jwiles@semo.edu
WILES, Mari, E .... 252-398-6268 336 K
wilesm@chowan.edu
WILES, Patrick, J .... 716-851-1901 307 I
wiles@ecc.edu
WILEY, Byron, A .... 864-656-3553 419 F
bwiley@clemson.edu
WILEY, Casey .... 864-455-8204 425 E
wileyc@greenvillemed.sc.edu
WILEY, Ellen .... 717-947-6089 404 S
ewiley@pacollege.edu
WILEY, Fran, K .... 864-941-8351 423 C
wiley.f@ptc.edu
WILEY, Jeanelle .... 314-968-7123 269 N
jeanellewiley10@webster.edu
WILEY, Jeffrey .... 315-786-2200 311 H
jwiley@sunyjefferson.edu
WILEY, Karen .... 815-455-8547 145 B
kwiley@mchenry.edu
WILEY, Louise .... 903-983-8242 451 F
lwiley@kilgore.edu
WILEY, LuSharon .... 850-474-2161 111 D
lwiley@uwf.edu
WILEY, Marilyn .... 940-565-3097 466 B
marilyn.wiley@unt.edu
WILEY, Mark .... 562-985-4128.. 32 C
mark.wiley@csulb.edu
WILEY, Maya .... 212-229-5400 316 E
wileym@newschool.edu
WILEY, Nina .... 937-328-7936 359 H
wileyn@clarkstate.edu
WILEY, Paul, G .... 931-598-1731 436 A
pwiley@sewanee.edu
WILEY, Stacey .... 585-245-5721 327 B
wileys@geneseo.edu
WILEY, Stacey .... 814-824-2311 401 J
swiley@mercyhurst.edu
WILEY, Zelia, Z .... 785-532-6276 179 A
zwiley@ksu.edu
WILEY-HARRIS,
Courtney .... 212-870-1253 318 C
cwiley@nyts.edu
WILFAHRT, Dannette, C 651-631-5190 251 C
dcwilfahrt@unwsp.edu

WILFONG, Barry .... 573-518-3806 263 E
bwilfong@mineralarea.edu

WILGA, Dave .... 907-564-8259.... 9 F
dwilga@alaskapacific.edu

WILGENBUSCH, Sandy .. 563-876-3353 168 H
wilgenbu@dwci.edu

WILGUS, Robynne .... 541-440-4622 387 E
robynne.wilgus@umpqua.edu

WILHELM, Cori .... 315-386-7873 329 A
wilhelmc@canton.edu

WILHELM, Helen .... 830-792-7364 456 D
hawilhelm@schreiner.edu

WILHELM, Jane .... 608-663-2203 507 D
jwilhelm@edgewood.edu

WILHELM, John, L .... 402-280-2762 274 D
johnwilhelm@creighton.edu

WILHELM, Michael .... 910-962-2736 352 A
wilhelmm@uncw.edu

WILHELM, Regina .... 423-478-7725 435 I
rwilhelm@ptseminary.edu

WILHELM, Robert, W ..... 704-687-8428 351 C
rgwilhel@uncc.edu

WILHELM GARBERS,
Sara .... 651-255-6127 250 D
swilhelmgarbers@unitedseminary.edu

WILHELMI, Lisa .... 254-299-8640 452 E
lwilhelmi@mclennan.edu

WILHELMS, Angela .... 541-346-5561 387 F
wilhelms@uoregon.edu

WILHEMI, Jeremy .... 479-979-1307.. 23 J
jwilhemi@ozarks.edu

WILHITE, Brian .... 630-617-6484 138 C
wilhiteb@elmhurst.edu

WILHITE, Christa .... 601-635-2111 252 I
cwilhite@eccc.edu

WILHITE, David .... 502-863-8016 184 I
david_wilhite@georgetowncollege.edu

WILHITE, Lee .... 562-903-4079.. 27 E
lee.wilhite@biola.edu

WILJANEN, Mark .... 502-456-6504 189 F
mwiljanen@sullivan.edu

WILKE, Deborah .... 402-481-8984 273 F
deborah.wilke@bryanhealthcollege.edu

WILKE, Dennis, F .... 412-521-6200 409 D
dennis.wilke@rosedaletech.org

WILKE, Ekkehard, T .... 312-939-0111 137 G
wil3t@eastwest.edu

WILKE, Janet, S .... 308-865-8595 277 F
wilkej@unk.edu

WILKE, Stephen, K .... 620-229-6277 181 F
steve.wilke@sckans.edu

WILKEN, Danielle .... 860-727-6714.. 87 B
dwilken@goodwin.edu

WILKEN, Danielle, S ..... 860-727-6780.. 87 B
dwilken@goodwin.edu

WILKENS, Richard, T .... 410-548-6022 209 B
rtwilkens@salisbury.edu

WILKERSON, Aimee, J .. 270-824-8696 186 D
aimee.wilkerson@kctcs.edu

WILKERSON, Ame .... 912-260-4407 125 F
ame.wilkerson@sgsc.edu

WILKERSON, Charles .... 931-372-3634 438 F
cwilkerson@tntech.edu

WILKERSON, Jeffrey ..... 563-387-1005 171 I
wilkerje@luther.edu

WILKERSON, Karen, D .. 816-235-2757 268 D
wilkersonkd@umkc.edu

WILKERSON,
Lindsey, S .... 318-342-1530 198 A
lwilkerson@ulm.edu

WILKERSON,
Mathew, C .... 540-654-1048 486 D
mwilkers@umw.edu

WILKERSON, Sharon, A 979-436-0111 459 C
swilkerson44@tamu.edu

WILKERSON, Steve, L ... 210-458-4939 468 B
steve.wilkerson@utsa.edu

WILKERSON, Tammy .... 435-722-6900 472 L
tammy@ubtech.edu

WILKERSON, Tanya ...... 443-885-3170 206 A
tanya.wilkerson@morgan.edu

WILKERSON, Terry .... 618-437-5321 149 H
wilkersont@rlc.edu

WILKERSON, William ..... 256-824-2339.... 8 C
william.wilkerson@uah.edu

WILKERSON, Zeda .... 870-368-2028.. 20 H
zwilkerson@ozarka.edu

WILKES, Barrie, J .... 989-774-3334 228 E
wilke1bj@cmich.edu

WILKES, C. Gene .... 817-274-4284 444 C
gwilkes@bhcarroll.edu

WILKES, David, S .... 434-982-4050 486 H
dsw4n@virginia.edu

WILKES, Deborah .... 706-886-6831 126 F
dwilkes@tfc.edu

WILKES, Jeanna .... 662-846-4666 252 H
jdwilkes@deltastate.edu

WILKES, Jeremy .... 901-572-2670 430 C
jeremy.wilkes@bchs.edu

WILKES, Lisa .... 540-231-5706 490 F
lwilkes@vt.edu

WILKES, Yvette .... 505-454-3197 294 J
ydwilkes@nmhu.edu

WILKIE, Marilyn, L .... 212-517-0453 314 D
mwilkie@mmm.edu

WILKIN, John .... 217-333-6677 154 B
jpwilkin@illinois.edu

WILKIN, John, P .... 217-333-0790 154 B
jpwilkin@illinois.edu

WILKIN, Joshua .... 215-965-4038 402 C
jwilkin@moore.edu

WILKIN, Lori .... 732-906-2574 287 B
lwilkin@middlesexcc.edu

WILKIN, Noel, E .... 662-915-5317 256 C
nwilkin@olemiss.edu

WILKINS, Ashli .... 334-556-2226.... 2 B
awilkins@wallace.edu

WILKINS, Chris .... 240-567-9150 205 F
chris.wilkins@montgomerycollege.edu

WILKINS, Deborah, T .... 270-745-5398 190 F
deborah.wilkins@wku.edu

WILKINS, Derrick .... 252-335-3291 350 A
dlwilkins@ecsu.edu

WILKINS, Harry, T .... 614-508-7277 363 E
hwilkins@hondros.edu

WILKINS, Ken .... 702-968-5568 280 B
kwilkins@roseman.edu

WILKINS, Lorinda .... 575-624-7345 294 A
lorinda.wilkins@roswell.enmu.edu

WILKINS, Mardell .... 775-753-2265 279 A
mardell.wilkins@gbcnv.edu

WILKINS, Marianne .... 251-380-2261.... 7 B
mwilkins@shc.edu

WILKINS, Pyeper .... 214-378-1538 447 F
pwilkins@dcccd.edu

WILKINS, Vickie .... 419-448-3595 370 K
galaskavm@tiffin.edu

WILKINS, Vicky .... 202-885-6443.. 91 C
vwilkins@american.edu

WILKINS GREEN, Clair . 504-520-5251 198 D
cwilkins@xula.edu

WILKINSON, Cathryn .... 831-646-4000.. 52 G
cwilkinson@mpc.edu

WILKINSON,
Christine, K .... 480-965-7782.. 10 K
c.wilkinson@asu.edu

WILKINSON, Gerald, S . 301-405-4906 207 G
wilkinso@umd.edu

WILKINSON, Jay .... 515-961-1288 173 E
jay.wilkinson@simpson.edu

WILKINSON, John .... 704-878-3202 344 H
jwilkinson@mitchellcc.edu

WILKINSON, Joni .... 601-276-3708 256 A
jwilkinson@smcc.edu

WILKINSON, Julie .... 941-782-5678 399 C
jwilkinson@lecom.edu

WILKINSON, Lonnie ...... 225-771-3015 195 K
lonnie_wilkinson@subr.edu

WILKINSON, Melissa .... 309-647-4645 152 G

WILKINSON, Michael .... 361-485-4409 465 D
wilkinsonmr@uhv.edu

WILKINSON, Mike .... 817-923-1921 457 G
mwilkinson@swbts.edu

WILKINSON, Mike .... 405-692-3132 376 C
mwilkinson@macu.edu

WILKINSON, Missy .... 309-649-6305 152 G
missy.wilkinson@src.edu

WILKINSON, Pete .... 706-771-4024 116 A
pwilkins@augustatech.edu

WILKINSON, Robert .... 386-506-3656.. 97 I
wilkinr@daytonastate.edu

WILKINSON, Timothy .... 509-777-4585 500 H
twilkinson@whitworth.edu

WILKINSON, Todd .... 252-399-6552 335 I
twilkinson@barton.edu

WILKINSON, William, J 215-204-0564 411 B
william.wilkinson@temple.edu

WILKOS-GREENBERG,
Janice .... 617-585-0200 212 C
janice.greenberg@the-bac.edu

WILKOSKI, Donna, M ... 215-698-8203 390 I
wilkoski@bucks.edu

WILKOW, Beth .... 516-299-2589 313 C
beth.wilkow@liu.edu

WILKS, Karrin .... 212-220-8321 301 C
kwilks@bmcc.cuny.edu

WILKS, Ronald, W .... 317-788-3517 164 H
wilks@uindy.edu

WILKSON, Nancy .... 575-439-3798 295 C
nmontgom@nmsu.edu

WILKYMACKY, Eric .... 859-344-3321 189 G
wilkyme@thomasmore.edu

WILL, Christina .... 386-312-4152 106 M
christinawill@sjrstate.edu

WILL, Ed .... 760-252-2411.. 27 A
jwill@barstow.edu

WILL, John .... 715-468-2815 515 D
john.will@witc.edu

WILL, Lee .... 480-245-7937.. 13 C
lee.will@ibcs.edu

WILLAMON, Nancy .... 217-351-2533 148 H
nwillamon@parkland.edu

WILLAMON, Nancy, R ... 217-351-2533 148 H
nwillamon@parkland.edu

WILLAN, Dawn, E .... 843-953-5997 420 C
willande@cofc.edu

WILLAN, William .... 740-593-2551 368 G
willanw@ohio.edu

WILLARD, Cary .... 619-644-7163.. 45 A
cary.willard@gcccd.edu

WILLARD, Joseph .... 215-991-3586 398 F
willard@lasalle.edu

WILLARD, Paul, S .... 727-376-6911 112 G
paul.willard@trintycollege.edu

WILLBANKS, Stephanie . 802-831-1277 476 G
swillbanks@vermontlaw.edu

WILLCOX, Abby .... 904-620-2014 110 E
abby.willcox@unf.edu

WILLCOX, Jan, M .... 540-231-0920 480 I
jwilcox@vcom.vt.edu

WILLE, Diane, E .... 812-941-2300 161 A
dwille@ius.edu

WILLEKENS, Rene, G .... 623-935-8069.. 13 F
rene.willekens@estrellamountain.edu

WILLEMAN-BUCKELEW,
Diana, L .... 540-224-4491 482 A
dlwilleman@jchs.edu

WILLEMS, Greg .... 785-532-6266 179 A
gregw@found.ksu.edu

WILLEMSEN, David, W .. 972-825-4630 457 F
dwillemsen@sagu.edu

WILLENBERG, Lisa .... 501-977-2025.. 23 B
willenberg@uaccm.edu

WILLENBORG, Andy, B . 563-589-0217 174 D
awillenborg@wartburgseminary.edu

WILLENBRINK, Bob ...... 816-271-4575 264 B
rwillenbrink@missouriwestern.edu

WILLENSKY, Violet, J .... 908-526-1200 289 D
violet.willensky@raritanval.edu

WILLER, Anthony .... 701-483-2215 354 A
anthony.willer@dickinsonstate.edu

WILLETT, Dana .... 512-245-2322 463 A
drw134@txstate.edu

WILLETT, Jessica .... 540-458-8186 491 G
jwillett@wlu.edu

WILLETT, Terrence .... 831-477-5656.. 28 F
terrence@cabrillo.edu

WILLETTS, Jeffrey, G ..... 678-547-6495 122 H
willetts_jg@mercer.edu

WILLEY, Ed, W .... 561-207-5411 105 A
willeye@palmbeachstate.edu

WILLEY, Edward, W .... 561-207-5411 105 A
willeye@palmbeachstate.edu

WILLEY, Kevin .... 570-577-3208 390 H
kevin.willey@bucknell.edu

WILLEY, Leslie .... 573-876-7213 267 G
lwilley@stephens.edu

WILLEY, Sharon .... 408-924-5900.. 34 D

WILLEY, Sue, C .... 317-788-3412 164 H
swilley@uindy.edu

WILLGING, Gregory, A .. 563-556-5110 172 D
willging@nicc.edu

WILLGING, Pete .... 815-599-3421 139 F
pete.willging@highland.edu

WILLHITE, Grant .... 423-746-5236 439 A
gwillhite@tnwesleyan.edu

WILLIAM, Molly, F .... 413-662-5229 218 C
molly.williams@mcla.edu

WILLIAM, Trina .... 864-699-4632 424 D

WILLIAMS, Adam .... 757-352-4894 484 E
awilliams@regent.edu

WILLIAMS, Alex .... 402-363-5689 278 E
aawilliams@york.edu

WILLIAMS, Alfred .... 860-932-4172.. 86 E
awilliams@qvcc.edu

WILLIAMS, Alison, P ..... 740-587-6469 361 B
williamsa@denison.edu

WILLIAMS, Allison .... 617-277-3915 212 F
williamsa@bgsp.edu

WILLIAMS, Alvin .... 208-769-3348 132 E
al_williams@nic.edu

WILLIAMS, Amanda .... 913-281-7670 178 H
awilliams@kckcc.edu

WILLIAMS, Amanda .... 913-288-7218 178 H
awilliams@kckcc.edu

WILLIAMS, Amber, S ..... 402-472-0671 277 G
amber.williams@unl.edu

WILLIAMS, Amy, H .... 704-637-4414 336 G
ahwillia@catawba.edu

WILLIAMS, Ana .... 502-897-4206 189 A
awilliams@sbts.edu

WILLIAMS, Andre .... 252-331-4881 342 D
andre_williams@albemarle.edu

WILLIAMS, Andy .... 847-635-1875 148 D
awilliams@oakton.edu

WILLIAMS, Angela .... 678-422-4100.. 93 B

WILLIAMS, Angela .... 303-797-5715.. 76 I
angela.williams@arapahoe.edu

WILLIAMS, Angela .... 803-738-7691 422 D
williamsa@midlandstech.edu

WILLIAMS, Angela .... 405-585-5801 377 A
angela.williams@okbu.edu

WILLIAMS, Angela, L .... 410-651-8420 208 C
alwilliams@umes.edu

WILLIAMS, Angela, S .... 479-575-2806.. 21 I
angelaw@uark.edu

WILLIAMS, Angelika ...... 210-784-1320 460 C
angelika.williams@tamusa.edu

WILLIAMS, Annette .... 540-453-2332 487 G
williamsa@brcc.edu

WILLIAMS, Annie .... 501-370-8506.. 21 A
amwilliams@philander.edu

WILLIAMS, Annie .... 719-549-2116.. 78 P
annie.williams@csupueblo.edu

WILLIAMS, Anthony ...... 212-343-1234 315 D
awilliams@mcny.edu

WILLIAMS, Anthony ...... 425-388-9282 494 F
anwilliams@everettcc.edu

WILLIAMS, Anthony ...... 615-327-6894 434 A
awilliams@mmc.edu

WILLIAMS, Anu .... 336-734-7251 343 C
awilliams@forsythtech.edu

WILLIAMS, Archie .... 478-825-6832 119 C
williamsa01@fvsu.edu

WILLIAMS, Arlene .... 320-308-5937 247 F
arlene.williams@sctcc.edu

WILLIAMS, Arthur .... 501-370-8525.. 21 A
awilliams@philander.edu

WILLIAMS, Audrey, J ..... 865-539-7198 437 F
ajwilliams@pstcc.edu

WILLIAMS, Barry .... 570-208-5932 398 D
barrywilliams@kings.edu

WILLIAMS, Bert .... 478-387-4782 120 B
bwilliams@gmc.edu

WILLIAMS, Beth .... 513-618-1930 359 F
ewilliams@ccms.edu

WILLIAMS, Betty, B .... 843-383-8055 420 B
bwilliams@coker.edu

WILLIAMS, Blake .... 229-732-5951 115 B
blakewilliams@andrewcollege.edu

WILLIAMS, Bobby .... 936-294-4205 462 F
ath_brw@shsu.edu

WILLIAMS, Boyce .... 301-687-4759 209 A
bcwilliams@frostburg.edu

WILLIAMS, Brad .... 954-262-7282 104 F
bradwill@nsu.nova.edu

WILLIAMS, Brad .... 405-945-3204 378 C
bradford.williams@osuokc.edu

WILLIAMS, Brandy .... 662-329-7293 254 F
bmwilliams@muw.edu

WILLIAMS, Bre .... 760-471-1316.. 59 A
bwilliams@skcca.edu

WILLIAMS, Brenda, D ... 609-497-7820 288 E
registrar@ptsem.edu

WILLIAMS, Brenda, K ... 256-372-5254.... 1 A
brenda.williams@aamu.edu

WILLIAMS, Brett, J .... 763-417-8250 241 D
bwilliams@centralseminary.edu

WILLIAMS, Brian .... 401-254-3540 417 C
bwilliams@rwu.edu

WILLIAMS, Brian .... 610-225-5704 394 E
brian.williams@eastern.edu

WILLIAMS, Brockton ...... 615-343-4411 440 D
brock.williams@vanderbilt.edu

WILLIAMS, Bruce .... 601-877-4713 251 G
bwilliams@alcorn.edu

WILLIAMS, Bryon .... 850-599-3090 109 A
bryon.williams@famu.edu

WILLIAMS, Calvin .... 813-974-2612 111 A
williams374@usf.edu

WILLIAMS, Calvin .... 607-962-9233 306 C
williams@corning-cc.edu

WILLIAMS, Calvin, H ..... 717-815-1226 415 G
cwilliam@ycp.edu

WILLIAMS, Camelia ...... 816-995-2808 265 G
camelia.williams@researchcollege.edu

WILLIAMS, Carien .... 570-687-9677 395 I
cwilliams01@tcmc.edu

WILLIAMS, Carmetha .... 713-718-8596 450 D
carmetha.williams@hccs.edu

WILLIAMS, Carol .... 731-881-7805 440 B
cwill229@utm.edu

WILLIAMS, Carol .... 205-247-8149.... 7 C
cwilliams@stillman.edu

WILLIAMS, Carol .... 804-763-6711.. 93 B
ctw@strayer.edu

WILLIAMS, Carolyn, J ... 936-261-5122 458 F
cjwilliams@pvamu.edu

WILLIAMS, Lisa, L .... 325-793-3821 452 F lwilliams@mcm.edu
WILLIAMS, Lisa, M .... 256-782-8186.... 6 B lwilliam@jsu.edu
WILLIAMS, Lois, H .... 910-522-5800 351 E lois.williams@uncp.edu
WILLIAMS, Lonnie, R .... 870-972-2048.. 18 A lonniew@astate.edu
WILLIAMS, Lorita .... 617-541-5345 221 A lwilliams@rcc.mass.edu
WILLIAMS, Lucille, W ... 803-934-3258 422 G lwilliams@morris.edu
WILLIAMS, Lyn .... 610-606-4666 392 A lcwillia@cedarcrest.edu
WILLIAMS, Lynn .... 803-641-3385 425 A lynnw@usca.edu
WILLIAMS, Lynne .... 218-726-6141 250 F lwilliam@d.umn.edu
WILLIAMS, Lyrae .... 719-389-6699.. 77 J lyrae.williams@coloradocollege.edu
WILLIAMS, Mandy .... 303-963-3365.. 77 I aewilliams@ccu.edu
WILLIAMS, Marcellette .. 617-287-7050 216 G mwilliams@umassp.edu
WILLIAMS, Marchetta, L .... 803-938-3721 425 F mlwillia@uscsumter.edu
WILLIAMS, Marcus .... 479-986-4065.. 20 F mwilliams14@nwacc.edu
WILLIAMS, Marianne, R 518-262-5422 297 L willimr@mail.amc.edu
WILLIAMS, Marie .... 919-515-3443 350 E mywillia@ncsu.edu
WILLIAMS, Mark .... 661-763-7871.. 67 A mwilliams@taftcollege.edu
WILLIAMS, Mark .... 352-588-8614 106 N mark.williams05@saintleo.edu
WILLIAMS, Martinique .. 336-334-7555 350 C mcwilli2@ncat.edu
WILLIAMS, Marvin .... 516-726-5753 519 C williamsm@usmma.edu
WILLIAMS, Mary .... 501-374-6305.. 21 C
WILLIAMS, Mary, E .... 724-357-2555 406 C mary.e.williams@iup.edu
WILLIAMS, Mary Beth ... 717-262-2006 415 B marybeth.williams@wilson.edu
WILLIAMS, Matt .... 919-536-7200 342 G williamsm@durhamtech.edu
WILLIAMS, Max, E .... 423-585-6861 438 D max.williams@ws.edu
WILLIAMS, Melanie, K .. 269-337-7220 231 F williams@kzoo.edu
WILLIAMS, Melissa .... 916-608-6585.. 50 H william@flc.losrios.edu
WILLIAMS, Melissa .... 706-292-3900 125 E mwilliams@shorter.edu
WILLIAMS, Melissa .... 254-295-4020 466 A mford@umhb.edu
WILLIAMS, Melva .... 318-670-9314 196 A mwilliams@susla.edu
WILLIAMS, Melvenia ..... 803-535-5412 419 E mwilliams@claflin.edu
WILLIAMS, Michael .... 817-735-2509 466 D
WILLIAMS, Michael .... 207-768-2712 200 B mwilliams@nmcc.edu
WILLIAMS, Michael .... 850-644-7351 110 A mswilliams@admin.fsu.edu
WILLIAMS, Michael .... 510-642-5316.. 68 G athletic.director@berkeley.edu
WILLIAMS, Michael .... 609-984-1130 292 B mwilliams@tesu.edu
WILLIAMS, Michael, D .. 334-386-7103.... 5 I mwilliams@faulkner.edu
WILLIAMS, Michael, J .. 386-226-6777.. 98 C williams@erau.edu
WILLIAMS, Michele .... 713-525-2152 466 J registrar@stthom.edu
WILLIAMS, Michelle ...... 410-209-6003 202 F mwilliams@bccc.edu
WILLIAMS, Michelle, A . 617-495-1000 215 G
WILLIAMS, Michelle, D . 978-468-7111 215 E mwilliams@gcts.edu
WILLIAMS, Michelle, L . 314-286-4863 265 F mlwilliams@ranken.edu
WILLIAMS, Michelle, M 724-458-2216 396 D mmwilliams@gcc.edu
WILLIAMS, Miriam .... 612-436-7541 243 H mwilliams@msbcollege.edu
WILLIAMS, Miriam .... 612-436-7524 243 H mwilliams@msbcollege.edu
WILLIAMS, Monica .... 313-993-1028 237 F leonarmj@udmercy.edu
WILLIAMS, Myles .... 803-778-6643 419 A williamsmh@cctech.edu
WILLIAMS, Nailah .... 202-274-5618.. 93 D nwilliams@udc.edu
WILLIAMS, Natasha .... 512-863-1233 457 I williamn@southwestern.edu
WILLIAMS, Nate .... 254-295-4696 466 A nwilliams@umhb.edu
WILLIAMS, Nichelle ...... 661-722-6300.. 26 C nwilliams@avc.edu
WILLIAMS, Nicole .... 508-999-9208 217 A nwilliams2@umassd.edu
WILLIAMS, Nicole .... 910-755-7391 341 C williamsn@brunswickcc.edu
WILLIAMS, Nikisha .... 212-752-1530 312 G nikisha.williams@limcollege.edu
WILLIAMS, Oleida .... 443-394-3339.. 93 B
WILLIAMS, Owen .... 218-281-8395 250 G owilliam@umn.edu
WILLIAMS, Pamela .... 301-295-3185 518 G pamela.williams@usuhs.edu
WILLIAMS, Patricia .... 585-395-5118 326 D pwilliam@brockport.edu
WILLIAMS, Patricia, A ... 515-263-2912 169 E pwilliams@grandview.edu
WILLIAMS, Paul .... 229-391-4900 114 G pwwilliams@abac.edu
WILLIAMS, Paulita, N .... 336-322-2170 345 D tasha.williams@piedmontcc.edu
WILLIAMS, Peter .... 317-940-9700 156 I williams@butler.edu
WILLIAMS, Philip, M ..... 315-733-2307 332 F pwilliams@uscny.edu
WILLIAMS, Phillip, L .... 706-542-0939 127 A pwilliam@uga.edu
WILLIAMS, Pilar .... 671-735-5590 519 H pilar.williams@guamcc.edu
WILLIAMS, Priscilla ...... 912-358-3132 125 C williamsp@savannahstate.edu
WILLIAMS, Ramona, A .. 423-439-4219 431 H ramona@etsu.edu
WILLIAMS, Randy .... 816-802-3527 261 C rwilliams@kcai.edu
WILLIAMS, Randy .... 336-278-7243 337 G rwilliams32@elon.edu
WILLIAMS, Rayanne ...... 619-594-1686.. 34 B william7@mail.sdsu.edu
WILLIAMS, Regina .... 713-313-7175 461 E regina.williams@tsu.edu
WILLIAMS, Renata .... 717-867-6165 399 J rwilliam@lvc.edu
WILLIAMS, Rich .... 775-674-7979 279 C rwilliams@tmcc.edu
WILLIAMS, Richard .... 781-239-2756 220 A rwilliams@massbay.edu
WILLIAMS, Richard .... 724-805-2084 410 B richard.williams@stvincent.edu
WILLIAMS, Richard .... 724-805-2084 410 C richard.williams@stvincent.edu
WILLIAMS, Richard .... 229-430-4754 114 I richard.williams@asurams.edu
WILLIAMS, Richard, B .. 435-652-7502 473 B president@dixie.edu
WILLIAMS, Rick .... 870-743-3000.. 20 E rickw@northark.edu
WILLIAMS, Rick, E .... 909-558-4510.. 48 H rwilliams@llu.edu
WILLIAMS, Robert .... 310-825-8011.. 69 B bwilliams@asucla.ucla.edu
WILLIAMS, Robert, F ..... 920-832-6528 507 L robert.f.williams@lawrence.edu
WILLIAMS, Robin .... 661-362-3240.. 39 C robin.williams@canyons.edu
WILLIAMS, Robyn, A .... 920-923-8112 508 B rawilliams61@marianuniversity.edu
WILLIAMS, Ron .... 478-471-2490 123 A ron.williams@mga.edu
WILLIAMS, Ronald, C .... 309-298-1814 155 D rc-williams@wiu.edu
WILLIAMS, Ronda, L ..... 304-462-6430 504 B ronda.williams@glenville.edu
WILLIAMS, Ronnie, D .... 501-450-3416.. 23 I ronniew@uca.edu
WILLIAMS, Rosemary .... 718-270-5104 303 C rosemary@mec.cuny.edu
WILLIAMS, Russ .... 478-445-5650 119 E russ.williams@gcsu.edu
WILLIAMS, Ruth .... 847-635-1686 148 D rwilliams@oakton.edu
WILLIAMS, Ryan .... 845-569-3105 316 B ryan.williams@msmc.edu
WILLIAMS, Ryan, A .... 309-624-9268 151 A ryan.a.williams@osfhealthcare.org
WILLIAMS, Sanchia .... 954-492-5353.. 96 J sawilliams@citycollege.edu
WILLIAMS, Sara .... 402-399-2467 274 A swilliams@csm.edu
WILLIAMS, Sarah .... 540-868-7086 488 E swilliams@lfcc.edu
WILLIAMS, Scott .... 270-686-4508 186 F scott.willliams@kctcs.edu
WILLIAMS, Scott, E .... 276-944-6242 480 J swilliams@ehc.edu
WILLIAMS, Scott, K ...... 315-733-2307 332 F swilliams@uscny.edu
WILLIAMS, Scott, T .... 706-542-3375 127 A scottw@uga.edu
WILLIAMS, Shane .... 601-484-8620 253 G swilliam@meridiancc.edu
WILLIAMS, Shannon ...... 214-648-3134 469 E shannonl.williams@utsouthwestern.edu
WILLIAMS, Shaun .... 817-515-5154 458 B shaun.williams@tccd.edu
WILLIAMS, Sheree .... 502-585-4425 186 C sheree.williams@kctcs.edu
WILLIAMS, Sherry .... 828-327-7000 341 G swilliams@cvcc.edu
WILLIAMS, Shirley, J .... 610-796-8340 389 A shirley.williams@alvernia.edu
WILLIAMS, Solomon ..... 931-526-3660 431 J
WILLIAMS, Sonya .... 815-280-6731 142 A swilliam@jjc.edu
WILLIAMS, Sonya .... 315-781-3312 310 C swilliams@hws.edu
WILLIAMS, Sophia .... 414-297-6288 514 C wills12@matc.edu
WILLIAMS, Stelfanie ...... 252-492-2061 347 C swilliams@vgcc.edu
WILLIAMS, Stephen ...... 414-277-7114 509 A williams@msoe.edu
WILLIAMS, Stephen, R .. 419-755-4811 366 E swilliam@ncstatecollege.edu
WILLIAMS, Steve .... 256-840-4174.... 3 F swilliams@snead.edu
WILLIAMS, Sue .... 360-992-2619 493 E swilliams@clark.edu
WILLIAMS, Susan .... 304-255-0793 503 P swilliams@concord.edu
WILLIAMS, Susan .... 919-760-8262 339 H williams@meredith.edu
WILLIAMS, Susan .... 828-448-3178 347 F swilliams@wpcc.edu
WILLIAMS, Susan, D .... 203-576-4651.. 88 F swilliams@bridgeport.edu
WILLIAMS, Susan, L ..... 302-831-8436.. 90 I susanlyn@udel.edu
WILLIAMS, Suzanne ...... 213-477-2861.. 52 H swilliams@msmu.edu
WILLIAMS, Sylvia, R ..... 843-953-5333 419 D swilli22@citadel.edu
WILLIAMS, Tamara .... 704-330-4119 342 A tamara.williams@cpcc.edu
WILLIAMS, Tamara, R ... 253-531-7203 496 G williatr@plu.edu
WILLIAMS, Tamaria .... 850-412-7994 109 A tamaria.williams@famu.edu
WILLIAMS, Tara, A .... 336-633-0279 345 F tawil@randolph.edu
WILLIAMS, Tasha .... 312-850-7120 136 C tholmes@ccc.edu
WILLIAMS, Teresa .... 615-966-1788 433 D teresa.williams@lipscomb.edu
WILLIAMS, Teresa, G .... 704-233-8010 353 D tgwilliams@wingate.edu
WILLIAMS, Terrence ...... 610-409-3719 413 H twilliams@ursinus.edu
WILLIAMS, Terria, C ..... 803-535-5720 419 E twilliams@claflin.edu
WILLIAMS, Teyanna ...... 818-240-1000.. 44 D twilliams@glendale.edu
WILLIAMS, Tim .... 618-985-3741 141 D timwilliams@jalc.edu
WILLIAMS, Tim .... 502-895-3411 188 A twilliams@lpts.edu
WILLIAMS, Todd, J .... 215-702-4861 391 C president@cairn.edu
WILLIAMS, Tom .... 318-678-6000 192 C twilliams@bpcc.edu
WILLIAMS, Tommy .... 979-458-6040 458 E twilliams@tamus.edu
WILLIAMS, Tonjua, L .... 727-341-3241 107 A williams.tonjua@spcollege.edu
WILLIAMS, Toshia .... 215-248-7076 392 D williamst@chc.edu
WILLIAMS, Tracey .... 903-510-2041 464 D twil@tjc.edu
WILLIAMS, Traci .... 423-697-3216 436 F traci.williams@chattanoogastate.edu
WILLIAMS, Tracy .... 651-523-2651 242 E twilliams05@hamline.edu
WILLIAMS, Tracy, S ...... 229-430-4654 114 I tracy.williams@asurams.edu
WILLIAMS, Travis .... 707-826-5038.. 34 A tjw17@humboldt.edu
WILLIAMS, Treby .... 609-258-7097 288 F trebyw@princeton.edu
WILLIAMS, Trovon .... 301-934-7639 203 D twilliams7@csmd.edu
WILLIAMS, Trudy .... 412-392-8085 408 F twilliams@pointpark.edu
WILLIAMS, Tyler, R .... 208-496-1301 131 D williamst@byui.edu
WILLIAMS, Ulysses .... 803-780-1192 426 F uwilliams@voorhees.edu
WILLIAMS, Valarie .... 706-385-1015 124 F valarie.williams@point.edu
WILLIAMS, Valerie .... 229-430-3867 114 J vwilliams@albanytech.edu
WILLIAMS, Vaughn, A .. 470-578-6284 122 C vwilliam@kennesaw.edu
WILLIAMS, Verna, L ...... 513-556-0121 371 E verna.williams@uc.edu
WILLIAMS, Vernon .... 703-284-5796 483 A vernon.williams@marymount.edu
WILLIAMS, Vicki .... 501-492-0570.. 17 I vicki.williams@arkansasbaptist.edu
WILLIAMS, Vickie .... 334-214-4803.... 1 H vickie.williams@cv.edu
WILLIAMS, Vicky .... 731-352-6405 430 E williamsv@bethelu.edu
WILLIAMS, Victoria .... 870-972-2054.. 18 A vrwilliams@astate.edu
WILLIAMS, Victoria .... 610-796-5511 389 A victoria.williams@alvernia.edu
WILLIAMS, Virginia, M . 530-221-4275.. 63 H vwilliams@shasta.edu
WILLIAMS, Walter .... 518-587-2100 329 C walter.williams@esc.edu
WILLIAMS, Wendell ...... 713-313-7446 461 E wendell.williams@tsu.edu
WILLIAMS, Wendi .... 212-875-4547 298 H
WILLIAMS, Wendy, E .... 843-953-5506 420 C williamsw@cofc.edu
WILLIAMS, Willie .... 402-449-2924 274 H wwilliams4931@graceu.edu
WILLIAMS, Winifred ...... 312-915-6175 144 D wwilliams5@luc.edu
WILLIAMS, Wyman .... 903-468-8183 459 E wyman.williams@tamuc.edu
WILLIAMS, Yohuru, R ... 651-962-6001 251 D will3650@stthomas.edu
WILLIAMS DANDRIDGE, Gwen .... 804-524-5583 491 A gdandridge@vsu.edu
WILLIAMS-DYER, Sharon, M .... 781-891-2000 212 A swilliamsdyer@bentley.edu
WILLIAMS-GOLDSTEIN, Brittany, A .... 201-684-7609 289 C bwilla1@ramapo.edu
WILLIAMS-HARMON, Arlitha .... 559-791-2374.. 47 C arlitha.williams@portervillecollege.edu
WILLIAMS LESSANE, Patricia .... 843-953-7234 420 C lessanepw@cofc.edu
WILLIAMS LOSTON, Adena .... 210-486-2900 441 I aloston@alamo.edu
WILLIAMS LOSTON, Adena .... 210-486-2900 441 E aloston@alamo.edu
WILLIAMS-PEREZ, Kendra .... 319-226-2040 166 C kendra.williams-perez@allencollege.edu
WILLIAMS RUSHIN, Palisa .... 859-246-6522 185 G palisa.rushin@kctcs.edu
WILLIAMS-SMITH, Rachel .... 423-236-2733 436 C
WILLIAMS-SOWERS, Kelly .... 334-291-4921.... 1 H kelly.williams@cv.edu
WILLIAMS-THOMAS, Tafflyn .... 503-552-1625 384 F twiliams-thomas@nunm.edu
WILLIAMS-THOMPSON, Phyllis .... 413-265-2262 213 E williamsthompsonp@elms.edu
WILLIAMSON, Angela ... 417-690-2208 258 E awilliamson@cofo.edu
WILLIAMSON, Betty ...... 860-215-9260.. 86 F bwilliamson@trcc.commnet.edu
WILLIAMSON, Bob .... 360-992-2123 493 E bwilliamson@clark.edu
WILLIAMSON, Brad .... 757-443-6200 518 B brad.williamson@ndu.edu
WILLIAMSON, Carla ...... 919-658-7749 349 F cwilliamson@umo.edu
WILLIAMSON, Carol ...... 641-628-7667 167 D williamsonc@central.edu
WILLIAMSON, Cathy ..... 641-673-1700 174 F williamsonc@wmpenn.edu
WILLIAMSON, Dan .... 860-528-4111.. 87 B
WILLIAMSON, David ...... 601-266-1000 256 E david.williamson@usm.edu
WILLIAMSON, Dean ...... 936-261-2188 458 F cdwilliamson@pvamu.edu

WILLIAMSON, Emily 406-657-2188 272 B emily.williamson@msubillings.edu
WILLIAMSON, George 619-849-2610 57 H georgewilliamson@pointloma.edu
WILLIAMSON, Heather 866-931-4300 265 H heather.williamson@rockbridge.edu
WILLIAMSON, James 931-526-3660 431 J
WILLIAMSON, James, E 706-542-5813 127 A jwilliamson@police.uga.edu
WILLIAMSON, James, P 806-742-3136 463 D james.p.williamson@ttu.edu
WILLIAMSON, James, R 858-784-8469 63 G gradprgm@scripps.edu
WILLIAMSON, Jared 312-935-4141 149 K jwilliamson@robertmorris.edu
WILLIAMSON, Jeff 507-372-3408 246 C jeff.williamson@mnwest.edu
WILLIAMSON, Jennifer 610-921-7700 388 E jwilliamson@albright.edu
WILLIAMSON, Joann 803-641-3473 425 A joannw@usca.edu
WILLIAMSON, Jon 214-648-1500 469 E jon.williamson@utsouthwestern.edu
WILLIAMSON, Kathy 252-246-1263 347 H kwilliamson@wilsoncc.edu
WILLIAMSON, Keith 410-951-3010 208 F kwilliamson@coppin.edu
WILLIAMSON, Keith 940-397-4231 453 C keith.williamson@mwsu.edu
WILLIAMSON, Keith, M 804-524-1103 491 A kwilliamson@vsu.edu
WILLIAMSON, Kimberly 252-493-7217 345 E kwilliamson@email.pittcc.edu
WILLIAMSON, Laurel 281-998-6182 455 L laurel.williamson@sjcd.edu
WILLIAMSON, Laurel 281-998-6182 456 A laurel.williamson@sjcd.edu
WILLIAMSON, Laurel 281-998-6182 455 K laurel.williamson@sjcd.edu
WILLIAMSON, Laurel 281-998-6182 456 B laurel.williamson@sjcd.edu
WILLIAMSON, Lisa 715-682-1678 509 D lwilliamson@northland.edu
WILLIAMSON, Margaret 504-280-7054 194 F mswilli4@uno.edu
WILLIAMSON, Margaret, L 806-742-3171 463 D margaret.l.williams@ttu.edu
WILLIAMSON, Marty 661-654-2111 31 B mwilliamson@csub.edu
WILLIAMSON, Nancy 518-485-3066 305 B williamn@strose.edu
WILLIAMSON, Nancy 516-572-7406 316 C nancy.williamson@ncc.edu
WILLIAMSON, Patricia, A 815-224-0440 141 A patty_williamson@ivcc.edu
WILLIAMSON, Rebecca 253-833-9111 495 C rwilliamson@greenriver.edu
WILLIAMSON, Robin 941-487-4504 110 B rwilliamson@ncf.edu
WILLIAMSON, Shane 636-949-4728 261 I swilliamson@lindenwood.edu
WILLIAMSON, Sharon 806-742-4250 463 D sharon.williamson@ttu.edu
WILLIAMSON, Sheila 325-574-7602 470 N swilliamson@wtc.edu
WILLIAMSON, Stan 205-652-3652 9 C swilliamson@uwa.edu
WILLIAMSON, Sue 206-878-3710 495 E swilliamson@highline.edu
WILLIAMSON, Suzanne 717-720-4070 406 C swilliamson@passhe.edu
WILLIAMSON, Tommy 336-721-2824 348 H tommy.williamson@salem.edu
WILLIAMSON-MENDEZ, Jennifer, L 608-342-1183 511 D wiliaje@uwplatt.edu
WILLIARD, Stacey 724-266-3838 412 D swilliard@tsm.edu
WILLIBY, Jason 785-628-4728 177 D jjwilliby3@fhsu.edu
WILLIE, John 215-335-0800 400 D jwillie@lincolntech.edu
WILLIFORD, Andrea, G 478-757-5131 128 E awilliford@wesleyancollege.edu
WILLIFORD, Brent 979-830-4146 444 D brent.williford@blinn.edu
WILLIFORD, Darryl 301-860-4186 208 E dwilliford@bowiestate.edu
WILLIFORD, David 615-675-5302 441 B dwilliford@welch.edu
WILLIFORD, G. Craig 503-255-0332 384 E cwilliford@multnomah.edu
WILLIFORD, Joey 662-720-7564 255 B jewilliford@nemcc.edu
WILLIFORD, Lynn, E 919-962-1339 351 B lynn_williford@unc.edu
WILLING, Cindy 517-607-4315 231 C cwilling@hillsdale.edu
WILLINGER, Katie 920-693-1247 513 H katie.willinger@gotoltc.edu
WILLINGHAM, Paul 281-655-3712 452 C paul.willingham@lonestar.edu
WILLINGHAM, Ralph 817-598-6248 470 J rwillingham@wc.edu
WILLIS, Alysha 212-616-7200 309 G
WILLIS, Amy 229-391-5007 114 G apwillis@abac.edu
WILLIS, Annie 573-635-5061 261 H willisj@lincolnu.edu
WILLIS, Bessie 757-727-5331 481 E bessie.willis@hamptonu.edu
WILLIS, Bob 334-699-2266 1 B
WILLIS, Brian 828-398-7929 340 M bwillis@abtech.edu
WILLIS, Carla 828-251-6511 351 A cwillis2@unca.edu
WILLIS, Cliff, K 814-332-2860 388 F cwillis@allegheny.edu
WILLIS, Daria 315-498-2923 319 G provost@sunyocc.edu
WILLIS, David 931-372-3214 438 F dwillis@tntech.edu
WILLIS, Douglas, G 972-377-1793 446 I dwillis@collin.edu
WILLIS, Eric, R 319-352-8470 174 C rick.willis@wartburg.edu
WILLIS, Franklin, K 918-781-6284 374 H willisf@bacone.edu
WILLIS, Gabe 985-549-3850 197 E gabe.willis@selu.edu
WILLIS, Gerry 401-341-2159 417 D willisg@salve.edu
WILLIS, Gregory 323-663-2167 71 B gbwrpv@gmail.com
WILLIS, Harvey 973-328-5232 285 B hwillis@ccm.edu
WILLIS, Howard 707-256-7225 53 D hwillis@napavalley.edu
WILLIS, James, A 585-395-2129 326 D jwillis@brockport.edu
WILLIS, Jeff 337-550-1287 194 B jwillis@lsue.edu
WILLIS, Jeff 270-384-8097 187 H willisj@lindsey.edu
WILLIS, Kara 740-245-7221 372 E kwillis@rio.edu
WILLIS, Kathy 618-468-5700 143 D kwillis@lc.edu
WILLIS, Kimberley 585-245-5566 327 B willis@geneseo.edu
WILLIS, Laurie 336-517-2267 335 K lwillis@bennett.edu
WILLIS, Leonard 410-462-8052 202 F lwillis@bccc.edu
WILLIS, Lesia 718-522-9073 298 E lwillis@asa.edu
WILLIS, Lisa 312-850-7066 136 C lwillis01@ccc.edu
WILLIS, Marc 918-647-1464 375 B mwillis@carlalbert.edu
WILLIS, Michaela 605-688-4493 429 B michaela.willis@sdstate.edu
WILLIS, Michelle 252-249-1851 345 C mwillis@pamlicocc.edu
WILLIS, Paul 229-391-5052 114 G pwillis@abac.edu
WILLIS, Sherilyn 760-862-1333 39 D swillis@collegeofthedesert.edu
WILLIS, Steve 336-517-2154 335 K swillis@bennett.edu
WILLIS, Susan 918-343-6802 379 C swillis@rsu.edu
WILLIS, Tamie, L 405-425-5320 377 B tamie.willis@oc.edu
WILLIS, Teresa 434-961-5245 489 C twillis@pvcc.edu
WILLLIAMS, Susan, H 936-468-2201 458 A shwilliams@sfasu.edu
WILLLIS, Howard 707-256-7355 53 D hwillis@napavalley.edu
WILLMARTH, Ephraim 315-858-0945 310 E ejwillmarth@hts.edu
WILLMON, Nixon 256-228-6001 3 B willmonn@nacc.edu
WILLMOTT, Karen 859-257-6379 190 B karen.willmott@uky.edu
WILLOQUET-MARICONDI, Paula 802-651-5924 474 G pwilloquetmaricondi@champlain.edu
WILLOUGHBY, Dan 714-992-7037 54 A dwilloughby@fullcoll.edu
WILLOUGHBY, G. Case 724-287-8711 390 J case.willoughby@bc3.edu
WILLOUGHBY, Karen, P 412-536-1201 398 E karen.willoughby@laroche.edu
WILLS, Barbara 850-201-8590 112 C willsba@tcc.fl.edu
WILLS, Deri 803-641-3787 425 A deriw@usca.edu
WILLS, Greg 502-897-4112 189 A gwills@sbts.edu
WILLS, Mark 866-687-2258 30 B
WILLS, Mike 417-836-7635 263 H mikewills@missouristate.edu
WILLS, Mike 573-592-1191 270 D mike.wills@williamwoods.edu
WILLS, Penelope 928-776-2122 17 G penny.wills@yc.edu
WILLS, Scott, D 419-772-2705 367 G s-wills@onu.edu
WILLS, Tim 618-437-5321 149 H wills@rlc.edu
WILLY, Randy 785-442-6001 178 C rwilly@highlandcc.edu
WILLYARD, Paula 918-595-2067 380 D paula.willyard@tulsacc.edu
WILMER, Elizabeth 540-857-7313 490 B ewilmer@virginiawestern.edu
WILMES, David 724-738-2003 407 C david.wilmes@sru.edu
WILMES, Gerald 660-562-1350 264 I gwilmes@nwmissouri.edu
WILMESHERR, Jon 828-766-1360 344 F jwilmesherr@mayland.edu
WILMOT, Lynne 507-222-5500 241 C lwilmot@carleton.edu
WILMOT, Tracey 914-633-2067 311 B twilmot@iona.edu
WILMOTH, Dirk 828-398-7111 340 M dirkwilmoth@abtech.edu
WILMOUTH, Robert 406-657-1015 272 I bob.wilmouth@rocky.edu
WILMOWSKY, Joseph 718-774-3430 300 K
WILMS, Amy 909-748-8109 71 H amy_wilms@redlands.edu
WILSKE, Don 517-483-1765 232 K wilsked@lcc.edu
WILSON, Alan 706-385-1059 124 F alan.wilson@point.edu
WILSON, Alan, G 660-263-3900 258 A alanwilson@cccb.edu
WILSON, Alla 215-572-4691 389 D wilsona@arcadia.edu
WILSON, Allan 800-838-2580 222 E awilson@ngs.edu
WILSON, Amanda 317-921-4949 161 F amanda.wilson@ivytech.edu
WILSON, Amanda 918-647-1326 375 B adwilson@carlalbert.edu
WILSON, Amy, R 740-245-7382 372 E awilson@rio.edu
WILSON, Andrew, A 731-881-7626 440 B awilso93@utm.edu
WILSON, Andrew, G 412-578-2095 391 G wilsonag@carlow.edu
WILSON, Angela 618-252-5400 151 J angela.wilson@sic.edu
WILSON, Angulus 559-453-2094 43 J angulus.wilson@fresno.edu
WILSON, Annette 312-362-6214 137 C awilso49@depaul.edu
WILSON, Arthur, L 260-359-4031 159 B alwilson@huntington.edu
WILSON, Asif 312-553-5600 135 J
WILSON, Barbara 770-534-6203 116 F bwilson@brenau.edu
WILSON, Barbara 719-389-6791 77 J bwilson@coloradocollege.edu
WILSON, Barbara 903-334-6726 460 D bwilson@tamut.edu
WILSON, Barbara, J 217-333-3077 153 G bjwilson@uillinois.edu
WILSON, Barbara-Jan 860-685-2547 89 F bjwilson@wesleyan.edu
WILSON, Bill 620-450-2154 180 K billw@prattcc.edu
WILSON, Blake 864-424-8022 425 G bentleyt@mailbox.sc.edu
WILSON, Bobby 713-313-1133 461 E wilsonb@tsu.edu
WILSON, Bradley 724-738-2003 407 C bradley.wilson@sru.edu
WILSON, Brenda, H 601-977-7730 256 B bwilson@tougaloo.edu
WILSON, Bryan 210-458-4555 468 B oit@utsa.edu
WILSON, Bryan 828-652-0630 344 G bryanwilson@mcdowelltech.edu
WILSON, Bryan 307-778-1179 516 N bwilson@lcc.wy.edu
WILSON, Bryan, P 210-458-5919 468 B bryan.wilson@utsa.edu
WILSON, Carla 816-235-1052 268 D wilsonca@umkc.edu
WILSON, Carlos 601-979-8895 253 E carlos.d.wilson@jsums.edu
WILSON, Carlton, E 919-530-6230 350 D cwilson@nccu.edu
WILSON, Carmen 701-483-2330 354 A carmen.wilson@dickinsonstate.edu
WILSON, Carol, J 815-740-3840 154 G cwilson@stfrancis.edu
WILSON, Cecil, B 304-293-2021 505 B cbwilson@mail.wvu.edu
WILSON, Charles 859-371-9393 183 G cwilson@beckfield.edu
WILSON, Charles 704-922-6428 343 D wilson.charles@gaston.edu
WILSON, JR., Charles, E 336-334-7731 350 C cewilso3@ncat.edu
WILSON, Cheri 256-726-7204 6 E cwilson@oakwood.edu
WILSON, Cheryl, L 817-257-7834 461 A c.l.wilson@tcu.edu
WILSON, Chris 208-376-7731 131 B cwilson@boisebible.edu
WILSON, Christine 785-243-1435 176 I cwilson@cloud.edu
WILSON, Chuck, A 301-405-9341 207 G chuckw@umd.edu
WILSON, Claire 215-965-4051 402 C cwilson@moore.edu
WILSON, Cleveland 803-535-1419 423 B wilsonc@octech.edu
WILSON, JR., Clyde 386-481-2483 95 J wilsonc@cookman.edu
WILSON, Colwick 256-726-8402 6 E
WILSON, Corey 317-791-2556 164 H clwilson@uindy.edu
WILSON, Corey, L 317-791-2556 164 H clwilson@uindy.edu
WILSON, Cynthia 251-928-8133 9 B cwilson@southalabama.edu
WILSON, Cynthia, L 713-348-5048 455 F clwilson@rice.edu
WILSON, Dan 612-436-7538 243 H dwilson@msbcollege.edu
WILSON, Dani 714-992-7040 54 A dwilson@fullcoll.edu
WILSON, Daniel, B 740-826-8165 366 C dwilson@muskingum.edu
WILSON, Daniel, R 909-469-5201 74 G president@westernu.edu
WILSON, Darlene 310-338-7725 50 J dwilson@lmu.edu
WILSON, David 443-885-3200 206 A david.wilson@morgan.edu
WILSON, David 636-949-4737 261 I dwilson@lindenwood.edu
WILSON, David 615-966-6219 433 D david.wilson@lipscomb.edu
WILSON, David, P 814-472-3211 409 G dwilson@francis.edu
WILSON, Deborah 509-574-6872 500 I dwilson@yvcc.edu
WILSON, Debra, J 906-248-8442 227 P dwilson@bmcc.edu
WILSON, Debra, J 208-732-6245 131 I dwilson@csi.edu
WILSON, Delfina 913-288-7618 178 H dwilson@kckcc.edu
WILSON, Don 863-297-1000 105 F dhw@bosdun.com
WILSON, Donna 570-484-2576 406 E dwilson@lockhaven.edu
WILSON, Doug 251-442-2406 8 D dwilson@umobile.edu
WILSON, Douglas 205-726-4266 6 G dwilson@samford.edu
WILSON, Douglas 208-882-1566 132 D dougwils@christkirk.com
WILSON, Dwayne 731-989-6094 432 C dwilson@fhu.edu
WILSON, D'Andre 202-408-2400 93 B
WILSON, Elaine 606-679-8501 186 G elaine.wilson@kctcs.edu
WILSON, Elighie 708-709-7767 148 I ewilson@prairiestate.edu
WILSON, Evelyn 978-542-7321 218 E evelyn.wilson@salemstate.edu
WILSON, Fleetwood, L 206-934-3789 497 H fleetwood.wilson@seattlecolleges.edu
WILSON, Fred 714-816-0366 67 J fred.wilson@trident.edu

WILSON, Gary .... 630-617-3785 138 C
garyw@elmhurst.edu
WILSON, Gena .... 229-931-2000 120 F
gena.wilson@gsw.edu
WILSON, Gordon, N .... 801-581-3079 472 P
gordon.wilson@aux.utah.edu
WILSON, Holly .... 318-473-6581 194 A
hwilson@lsua.edu
WILSON, Howard .... 712-722-6007 168 I
howard.wilson@dordt.edu
WILSON, Huie, G .... 850-263-3261.. 95 F
hgwilson@baptistcollege.edu
WILSON, Ian .... 309-268-8423 139 D
ian.wilson@heartland.edu
WILSON, J. David .... 270-809-2310 188 D
jwilson@murraystate.edu
WILSON, Jacqueline ...... 334-683-2309.... 3 A
jwilson@marionmilitary.edu
WILSON, Jamelle .... 804-289-8428 486 G
jwilson9@richmond.edu
WILSON, JR.,
James, D .... 302-295-1194.. 91 B
jim.d.wilson@wilmu.edu
WILSON, JR., James, J 936-261-5256 458 F
jjwilson@pvamu.edu
WILSON, JR., James, J 936-261-2175 458 F
jjwilson@pvamu.edu
WILSON, Jamie, B .... 601-974-1070 254 A
wilsojb@millsaps.edu
WILSON, Jan .... 316-295-5824 177 F
jan_wilson@friends.edu
WILSON, Janice .... 860-465-4466.. 84 K
wilsonj@easternct.edu
WILSON, JD .... 901-381-3939 440 I
jd@visible.edu
WILSON, Jeff .... 615-966-7617 433 D
jeff.wilson@lipscomb.edu
WILSON, Jim .... 641-844-5550 170 G
jim.wilson@iavalley.edu
WILSON, Jo .... 252-577-6223 344 D
djwilson45@lenoircc.edu
WILSON, Joanne .... 608-342-1261 511 D
wilsonj@uwplatt.edu
WILSON, Jocelyn, M ..... 516-671-2215 333 E
jwilson@webb.edu
WILSON, John .... 212-217-4200 308 B
john_wilsonn@fitnyc.edu
WILSON, John .... 254-710-3457 444 B
john_wilson@baylor.edu
WILSON, John .... 843-863-7102 419 C
jewilson@csuniv.edu
WILSON, John, R .... 804-278-4330 486 A
jwilson@upsem.edu
WILSON, Johnathan ...... 210-486-1084 442 A
jwilson315@alamo.edu
WILSON, Jonathan .... 601-984-1010 256 D
jwilson5@umc.edu
WILSON, Josh .... 706-272-2473 118 F
jwilson@daltonstate.edu
WILSON, Josh .... 870-368-2027.. 20 H
josh.wilson@ozarka.edu
WILSON, Judge .... 859-985-3131 183 I
judge_wilson@berea.edu
WILSON, Kathi .... 865-981-8211 433 F
kathi.wilson@maryvillecollege.edu
WILSON, Kathryn .... 585-395-2137 326 D
kwilson@brockport.edu
WILSON, Kathy, A .... 863-638-2930 114 A
wilsonka@webber.edu
WILSON, Keisha .... 704-330-1455 338 I
kwilson@jcsu.edu
WILSON, Kelly .... 417-625-9363 263 G
wilson-k@mssu.edu
WILSON, Kelly .... 740-264-5591 361 D
kwilson@egcc.edu
WILSON, Kenneth .... 912-358-4166 125 C
wilsonk@savannahstate.edu
WILSON, Kenny .... 636-481-3356 261 B
kwilso20@jeffco.edu
WILSON, Kimberly, M ... 540-224-4313 482 A
kmwilson@jchs.edu
WILSON, Kimberly, P .... 859-257-4751 190 B
kwilson@email.uky.edu
WILSON, Kristina .... 956-872-5583 456 G
kmwilson@southtexascollege.edu
WILSON, Kyla .... 773-907-4443 135 K
kwilson@ccc.edu
WILSON, LaDrina .... 563-441-4016 169 A
lnwilson@eicc.edu
WILSON, Larry, L .... 972-860-7218 447 I
larrywilson@dcccd.edu
WILSON, Laura .... 937-376-6013 358 I
lwilson@centralstate.edu
WILSON, Laura, L .... 650-723-9633.. 66 C
laura.wilson@stanford.edu
WILSON, Leana .... 318-473-6424 194 A
lwilson@lsua.edu
WILSON, Leon, C .... 334-229-4202.... 4 A
lwilson@alasu.edu
WILSON, Leon, C .... 334-229-5176.... 4 A
lwilson@alasu.edu
WILSON, Leslie, K .... 319-273-6240 167 A
leslie.wilson@uni.edu
WILSON, Lizabeth, A ..... 206-543-1760 499 D
betsyw@uw.edu
WILSON, Lori, J .... 570-577-3334 390 H
lwilson@bucknell.edu
WILSON, Lucy, P .... 478-301-2455 122 H
wilson_l@mercer.edu
WILSON, Lynn .... 863-669-2898 105 F
lwilson@polk.edu
WILSON, M. Roy .... 313-577-2230 239 C
president@wayne.edu
WILSON, Maleta .... 504-865-3262 194 G
mawilson@loyno.edu
WILSON, Marcus .... 806-743-6443 463 E
marcus.wilson@ttuhsc.edu
WILSON, Mardell .... 314-977-8501 266 J
wilsonma@slu.edu
WILSON, Margaret .... 660-626-2354 257 A
mwilson@atsu.edu
WILSON, Mark .... 931-372-3961 438 F
mwilson@tntech.edu
WILSON, Mark .... 423-472-7141 436 G
mwilson@clevelandstatecc.edu
WILSON, Mark .... 605-995-3024 427 E
mark.wilson@mitchelltech.edu
WILSON, Martha .... 207-221-4514 202 A
mwilson13@une.edu
WILSON, Mary .... 931-598-1381 436 A
mewilson@sewanee.edu
WILSON, Maryrose .... 301-846-2436 203 H
mwilson@frederick.edu
WILSON, Matthew .... 734-462-4400 236 H
mwilson@schoolcraft.edu
WILSON, Matthew, J ..... 330-972-7869 371 C
mjwilson@uakron.edu
WILSON, Melanie .... 865-974-2521 439 I
WILSON, Michael .... 205-726-2011.... 6 G
mkwilson@samford.edu
WILSON, Michael, D ...... 714-556-3610.. 72 F
mdwilson@vanguard.edu
WILSON, Michele .... 304-424-8355 505 C
michele.wilson@wvup.edu
WILSON, Michelle .... 870-633-4480.. 19 E
rwilson@eacc.edu
WILSON, Mike .... 864-294-3464 421 I
mike.wilsont@furman.edu
WILSON, Mindy .... 518-743-2252 328 G
wilsonm@sunyacc.edu
WILSON, Monica .... 304-434-8000 502 L
monica.wilson@easternwv.edu
WILSON, Natalie, L .... 412-578-6171 391 G
wilsonnl@carlow.edu
WILSON, Oceana .... 802-440-4606 474 F
oceanaw@bennington.edu
WILSON, Pam .... 940-898-3503 464 A
pwilson@twu.edu
WILSON, Pamala, P .... 270-831-9649 186 A
pamala.wilson@kctcs.edu
WILSON, Patricia .... 256-306-2743.... 1 F
patricia.wilson@calhoun.edu
WILSON, Patrick .... 931-372-3224 438 F
pwilson@tntech.edu
WILSON, Paul .... 785-539-3571 179 F
pwilson@mccks.edu
WILSON, Perry, T .... 843-661-1486 421 H
pwilson@fmarion.edu
WILSON, Phillip .... 479-394-7622.. 23 D
pwilson@uarichmountain.edu
WILSON, Piper .... 417-477-7428 264 K
wilsonp@otc.edu
WILSON, Qiana .... 478-445-2037 119 E
qiana.wilson@gcsu.edu
WILSON, Regina .... 574-284-5382 163 J
rwilson@saintmarys.edu
WILSON, Robert, A .... 610-606-4637 392 A
rwilson@cedarcrest.edu
WILSON, Roger .... 425-889-5336 496 E
roger.wilson@northwestu.edu
WILSON, Ronald, O .... 814-732-1259 406 B
rwilson@edinboro.edu
WILSON, Ronalyn .... 518-736-3622 309 A
rwilson@fmcc.suny.edu
WILSON, Roselle .... 484-365-7222 400 E
rwilson2@lincoln.edu
WILSON, Rowena, G ...... 757-823-8668 483 F
rgwilson@nsu.edu
WILSON, Sandra .... 313-664-7471 228 H
sandra@collegeforcreativestudies.edu
WILSON, Scott .... 651-846-1694 247 G
scott.wilson@saintpaul.edu
WILSON, Scott .... 931-598-1173 436 A
swilson@sewanee.edu
WILSON, Scott, L .... 641-269-3500 169 F
wilsons@grinnell.edu
WILSON, Shain .... 205-853-1200.... 2 F
swilson@jeffersonstate.edu
WILSON, Shawn .... 989-964-7090 236 F
swilson@svsu.edu
WILSON, Shawna .... 517-264-7142 236 I
swilson@sienaheights.edu
WILSON, Sheila .... 252-399-6309 335 I
spwilson@barton.edu
WILSON, Shelli .... 843-383-8082 420 B
swilson@coker.edu
WILSON, Sherri .... 502-213-8242 189 E
swilson@sullivan.edu
WILSON, Sherry .... 828-726-2306 341 D
swilson@cccti.edu
WILSON, Sherwood, G .. 540-231-4416 490 F
sgwilson@vt.edu
WILSON, Shirley .... 213-624-1200.. 42 N
swilson@fidm.edu
WILSON, Sonali, B .... 216-687-3860 359 L
s.b.wilson@csuohio.edu
WILSON, Stacey .... 704-403-1639 336 B
stacey.wilson@carolinashealthcare.org
WILSON, Stacey .... 636-481-3207 261 B
swilson@jeffco.edu
WILSON, Stanley .... 954-262-1266 104 F
swilson@nova.edu
WILSON, Stephan, M ..... 405-744-9805 377 F
stephan.m.wilson@okstate.edu
WILSON, Stephen .... 478-445-5331 119 E
steve.wilson@gcsu.edu
WILSON, Steven .... 540-868-7132 488 E
stevenwilson@lfcc.edu
WILSON, Steven, H .... 610-758-3200 400 B
shw516@lehigh.edu
WILSON, Susan .... 816-235-6704 268 D
wilsonsb2@umkc.edu
WILSON, Susan, A .... 802-322-1641 475 A
susan.wilson@goddard.edu
WILSON, Sylvia .... 573-681-6107 261 H
wilsons@lincolnu.edu
WILSON, Ted, H .... 270-707-3865 186 B
ted.wilson@kctcs.edu
WILSON, Terez .... 901-321-3254 431 A
twilso22@cbu.edu
WILSON, Thad, R .... 816-995-2815 265 G
thad.wilson@researchcollege.edu
WILSON, Tiffany .... 803-778-6668 419 A
wilsontd@cctech.edu
WILSON, Tim .... 412-391-4100 408 F
WILSON, Timothy .... 541-278-5856 382 A
twilson@bluecc.edu
WILSON, Timothy, B ...... 805-565-6038.. 74 I
twilson@westmont.edu
WILSON, Todd .... 914-633-2686 311 B
twilson@iona.edu
WILSON, Tommy .... 706-649-1894 118 D
twilson@columbustech.edu
WILSON, Tony .... 336-725-8344 348 C
wilsont@piedmontu.edu
WILSON, Tracy .... 651-403-4118 247 G
tracy.wilson@saintpaul.edu
WILSON, Travis .... 606-539-4002 190 A
travis.wilson@ucumberlands.edu
WILSON, Tressey, D ...... 936-361-1700 458 F
tdwilson@pvamu.edu
WILSON, Valeri .... 619-660-4221.. 44 L
valeri.wilson@gcccd.edu
WILSON, Valerie .... 870-574-4514.. 21 G
vwilson@sautech.edu
WILSON, Valvia .... 601-977-7844 256 B
vwilson@tougaloo.edu
WILSON, Vicki .... 859-246-6316 185 G
vicki.wilson@kctcs.edu
WILSON, Vicki .... 724-852-3375 414 B
vwilson@waynesburg.edu
WILSON, Victor, K .... 706-542-3564 127 A
wilsonv@uga.edu
WILSON, W. Chandler .. 503-255-0332 384 E
chandlerwilson@multnomah.edu
WILSON, Warren .... 605-642-6930 428 F
warren.wilson@bhsu.edu
WILSON, Wendy .... 229-430-5217 114 I
wendy.wilson@asurams.edu
WILSON, William .... 859-341-4867 189 G
wilsonw@thomasmore.edu
WILSON, William .... 423-354-2541 437 E
wrwilson@northeaststate.edu
WILSON, William .... 216-687-4686 359 L
william.wilson@csuohio.edu
WILSON, William, M ...... 918-495-6175 378 H
president@oru.edu
WILSON, Yolanda .... 803-327-8021 426 J
ywilson@yorktech.edu
WILSON, Zaphon .... 919-516-4280 348 G
zrwilson@st-aug.edu
WILSON-BARNES,
Yvette .... 212-280-1396 332 C
ywilson@uts.columbia.edu
WILSON-FENNELL,
Nicole .... 734-462-4400 236 H
nwilson@schoolcraft.edu
WILSON-PORTER,
Cyndi .... 210-829-2706 465 E
porter@uiwtx.edu
WILSON-SYKES, Jean .... 205-247-8145.... 7 C
jwilson-sykes@stillman.edu
WILSON-TAYLOR,
Sharon .... 312-369-7221 136 H
swilson-taylor@colum.edu
WILT, Darrell .... 717-815-1288 415 G
dwilt1@ycp.edu
WILT, Randolph .... 512-313-3000 446 N
randloph.wilt@concordia.edu
WILT, Richard, W .... 610-799-1164 400 A
rwilt@lccc.edu
WILT, Valerie .... 386-481-2004.. 95 J
collmanv@cookman.edu
WILTENMUTH, III,
John, P .... 540-654-1047 486 D
jwiltenm@umw.edu
WILTER, Diana .... 612-244-2800 242 H
dwilter@ipr.edu
WILTGEN, Jessica .... 818-401-1282.. 40 A
jwiltgen@columbiacollege.edu
WILTGEN, JR., Jim .... 501-450-1222.. 19 I
wiltgen@hendrix.edu
WILTROUT, Deborah ..... 239-590-1089 109 C
dwiltrout@fgcu.edu
WILTSE, Mary Alane ...... 518-828-4181 305 D
wiltse@sunycgcc.edu
WILTSHIRE, Rolly .... 718-289-5186 301 D
rolly.wiltshire@bcc.cuny.edu
WILTZ, Alex .... 413-775-1299 219 F
wiltza@gcc.mass.edu
WILTZIUS, Pierre .... 805-893-5024.. 70 B
mlpsdean@ltsc.ucsb.edu
WIMBERLY, Chuck .... 478-289-2036 118 H
cwimberly@ega.edu
WIMBERLY, Frances .... 706-396-8102 124 C
fwimberly@paine.edu
WIMBERLY, Joan, M ...... 805-565-6055.. 74 I
jwimberly@westmont.edu
WIMBUSH, James .... 812-856-5700 159 H
dema@indiana.edu
WIMBUSH, James .... 812-855-2739 159 H
jwimbush@indiana.edu
WIMBUSH, James .... 812-856-5700 159 G
jwimbush@indiana.edu
WIMER, Aaron .... 931-540-2555 436 H
awimer@columbiastate.edu
WIMER, Jodie .... 304-358-2000 501 I
jwimer@future.edu
WIMER, Valinda .... 386-822-8850 111 E
vwimer@stetson.edu
WIMS, Daniel, K .... 256-372-5275.... 1 A
daniel.wims@aamu.edu
WIMS, Lois, A .... 508-929-8038 219 A
lwims@worcester.edu
WIMUNC, Cat .... 719-219-9636.. 77 H
cwimunc@cavt.edu
WINANT, Richard .... 718-270-7411 326 A
richard.winant@downstate.edu
WINBORNE, Malverne .... 734-487-2086 229 K
mwinborne@emich.edu
WINBUSH, Chauncey .... 304-876-5155 504 D
cwinbush@shepherd.edu
WINBUSH, Larkisha .... 251-442-2250.... 8 D
lwinbush@umobile.edu
WINCHELL, Brooks .... 617-873-0499 213 B
brooks.winchell@cambridgecollege.edu
WINCHESTER, Paul .... 316-295-5836 177 F
winchp@friends.edu
WINCHESTER, Samuel ... 919-573-5350 349 A
WINCHESTER, Sara .... 732-255-0400 288 B
swinchester@ocean.edu
WINCKELMAN, Stephen 952-358-8597 246 D
stephen.winckelman@normandale.edu
WINDER, Katie .... 541-917-4547 384 A
winderk@linnbenton.edu
WINDER, Mark .... 319-895-4518 167 G
mwinder@cornellcollege.edu
WINDERS, Tim .... 219-989-2417 163 E
winders@pnw.edu
WINDHAM, Don .... 772-462-7357 101 Q
dwindham@irsc.edu
WINDHAM, Greg .... 662-720-7210 255 B
jgwindham@nemcc.edu
WINDHAM, Jameka .... 216-373-5287 367 A
jwindham@ndc.edu
WINDHAM, Joel .... 205-726-2011.... 6 G
jwindham@samford.edu
WINDHAM, John .... 731-661-5006 439 D
jwindham@uu.edu

WITEK, Paul, J .... 570-561-1818 410 A
paul.witek@stots.edu
WITH, Elizabeth .... 940-565-4909 466 B
elizabeth.with@unt.edu
WITHERELL, Drew .... 309-341-5205 134 H
dwitherell@sandburg.edu
WITHERELL, Meghan ..... 530-938-5500.. 39 H
witherellm@siskiyous.edu
WITHERELL, Paula .... 716-839-8472 306 E
pwithere@daemen.edu
WITHERINGTON,
Jennifer .... 912-688-6966 123 J
jlwitherington@ogeecheetech.edu
WITHEROW, Laurie, B ... 615-898-2239 434 H
laurie.witherow@mtsu.edu
WITHERS, Allen .... 325-793-4681 452 F
withers.allen@mcm.edu
WITHERS, Amanda .... 936-294-2289 462 F
withers@shsu.edu
WITHERS, Ben .... 970-491-5421.. 78 N
ben.withersl@colostate.edu
WITHERS,
Christopher, J .... 919-516-4014 348 G
cjwithers@st-aug.edu
WITHERS, Dale .... 707-965-7150.. 55 F
dwithers@puc.edu
WITHERS, Gary .... 503-493-6207 382 I
gwithers@cu-portland.edu
WITHERS, Jennifer .... 701-483-2999 354 A
jennifer.withers@dickinsonstate.edu
WITHERS, Stacie .... 816-995-2832 265 G
stacie.withers@researchcollege.edu
WITHERSPOON,
Alanna, S .... 312-850-7031 136 C
awitherspoon5@ccc.edu
WITHERSPOON, Ashley . 843-953-7777 419 D
awithers@citadel.edu
WITHERSPOON,
Collin, C .... 806-371-5142 442 D
ccwitherspoon@actx.edu
WITHERSPOON,
Everette, L .... 336-750-2131 352 D
witherspoone@wssu.edu
WITHERSPOON, Karen .. 212-650-6400 301 F
kwitherspoon@ccny.cuny.edu
WITHROW, Amy, S .... 717-221-1303 396 G
aswithro@hacc.edu
WITHUS, George .... 701-858-4444 354 C
george.withus@minotstateu.edu
WITKEN, David .... 708-209-3625 136 I
david.witken@cuchicago.edu
WITKOVSKY, Lowell, D . 814-641-3360 398 B
witkovl@juniata.edu
WITMER, Kenneth, D ..... 610-436-2321 407 D
kwitmer@wcupa.edu
WITMER, Timothy, Z ..... 215-572-3831 414 D
twitmer@wts.edu
WITRYK, Ted .... 610-683-4822 406 D
witryk@kutztown.edu
WITT, Allen .... 813-259-6151 101 M
awitt3@hccfl.edu
WITT, Betsy, A .... 864-488-8288 422 B
bwitt@limestone.edu
WITT, Don, E .... 859-257-3458 190 B
dwitt@email.uky.edu
WITT, Jack .... 330-672-2100 363 I
fjwitt@kent.edu
WITT, Karla .... 605-455-6001 427 I
kwitt@olc.edu
WITT, Marie, D .... 215-898-1199 412 G
witt@upenn.edu
WITT, Patricia .... 512-863-1454 457 I
wittp@southwestern.edu
WITT, Ron, A .... 304-336-8844 504 E
wittron@westliberty.edu
WITT, Tiffanie .... 270-707-3811 186 B
WITT, Tiffanie .... 270-824-8575 186 D
tiffanie.witt@kctcs.edu
WITTE, Bob .... 417-626-1234 264 J
witte.bob@occ.edu
WITTE, Dennis, E .... 708-209-3205 136 I
dennis.witte@cuchicago.edu
WITTE, John .... 616-526-6547 228 B
jwitte@calvin.edu
WITTE, Kevin .... 360-992-2356 493 E
kwitte@clark.edu
WITTE, Lois, J .... 417-667-8181 259 A
lwitte@cottey.edu
WITTE, Michael .... 402-552-3325 273 K
wittemichael@clarksoncollege.edu
WITTE, III, Paul, R .... 616-526-7920 228 B
prw3@calvin.edu
WITTE, Peter .... 209-946-2417.. 70 F
pwitte@pacific.edu
WITTE, Peter, T .... 816-235-2731 268 D
wittep@umkc.edu
WITTE, Sarah .... 541-962-3511 383 B
switte@eou.edu

WITTENBERG, Curtis ..... 906-487-7214 230 B
curtis.wittenberg@finlandia.edu
WITTENBERG, Diane ..... 626-396-2326.. 26 L
diane.wittenberg@artcenter.edu
WITTENBORG, Nicole ..... 619-702-9400.. 30 C
nicole.wittenborg@cibu.edu
WITTENMYER, Kathryn .. 415-503-6223.. 60 H
klw@sfcm.edu
WITTER, Kevin, G .... 540-857-7341 490 B
kwitter@virginiawestern.edu
WITTER, Pamela .... 716-827-4344 331 K
witterp@trocaire.edu
WITTER, Terry .... 903-877-7704 469 A
terry.witter@uthct.edu
WITTGENFELD, Tania .... 773-291-6359 135 M
twittgenfeld@ccc.edu
WITTIG, William .... 313-993-1532 237 F
wittigw@udmercy.edu
WITTKAMP, Roxanne ..... 847-324-5588 135 D
rwittkamp@ortchicagotech.edu
WITTLER, Kim .... 301-369-2800 202 J
kwittler@captechu.edu
WITTLER, Michele, A ..... 920-748-8119 509 H
wittlerm@ripon.edu
WITTMAN, William .... 301-295-3185 518 G
william.wittman@usuhs.edu
WITTMANN, Zach .... 217-245-3338 139 H
zach.wittmann@mail.ic.edu
WITTMANN-PRICE,
Ruth, A .... 843-661-4625 421 H
rwittmannprice@fmarion.edu
WITTNER, Charity .... 251-442-2507.... 8 D
cwittner@umobile.edu
WITTROCK, David, A ...... 701-231-7033 354 D
david.wittrock@ndsu.edu
WITTROCK, Monica .... 920-403-3146 509 J
monica.wittrock@snc.edu
WITTSTEIN, Bob .... 781-891-2005 212 A
bwittstein@bentley.edu
WITTSTRUCK, Clifford ... 307-382-1714 517 C
cwittstruck@westernwyoming.edu
WITTY, Janeen .... 803-705-4761 418 G
wittyj@benedict.edu
WITZEL, Stephanie .... 707-668-5663.. 41 F
WIXOM, Tasha .... 541-881-5781 387 D
twixom@tvcc.cc
WIXSOM, Richard .... 413-236-3003 219 B
rwixsom@berkshirecc.edu
WLEZIEN, Richard .... 573-341-4625 269 A
wlezien@mst.edu
WNUK, Beth .... 414-930-3332 509 B
wnukb@mtmary.edu
WOBBE, Michelle .... 314-918-2599 260 A
mwobbe@eden.edu
WOBBY, Lauren .... 802-485-2040 475 I
laurenw@norwich.edu
WOBENSMITH,
Stephanie .... 215-489-4851 393 F
stephanie.wobensmith@delval.edu
WODKA, Chris .... 520-494-5230.. 11 P
chris.wodka@centralaz.edu
WODZIAK, Becky .... 218-733-6942 245 C
becky.wodziak@lsc.edu
WOELKERS, Joseph, F .. 903-877-5072 469 A
joseph.woelkers@uthct.edu
WOELL, John .... 517-629-0222 226 G
jwoell@albion.edu
WOERDEHOFF,
Valorie, A .... 563-588-7565 171 H
valorie.woerdehoff@loras.edu
WOERLY, Crystal .... 817-598-6274 470 J
cwoerly@wc.edu
WOGAN, Maureen .... 773-298-3010 151 C
wogan@sxu.edu
WOGEN, Brian, M .... 641-422-4177 172 C
wogenbri@niacc.edu
WOHL, James .... 860-486-5143.. 88 G
jim.wohl@uconn.edu
WOHLERT, Amy .... 505-277-1092 296 H
awohlert@unm.edu
WOHLETZ, Dale .... 318-357-5581 197 D
wohletz@nsula.edu
WOHLFORD, Corinne .... 314-889-1401 260 C
cwohlford@fontbonne.edu
WOHLMAN, Jason, L .... 530-752-9793.. 68 H
jlwohlman@ucdavis.edu
WOHLMAN, Katie .... 828-328-7699 339 C
katie.wohlman@lr.edu
WOHLPART, A. James .. 319-273-2517 167 A
jim.wohlpart@uni.edu
WOIKE, David .... 734-487-0076 229 K
dwoike@emich.edu
WOJAK, Angie .... 212-592-2387 324 A
awojak@sva.edu
WOJCIECHOWSKI, Keli . 708-524-6827 137 F
kallen@dom.edu

WOJCIECHOWSKI,
Thomas .... 716-839-8585 306 E
twoj@daemen.edu
WOJCIK, Alketa .... 760-757-2121.. 52 F
awojcik@miracosta.edu
WOJICK, Matther, Z ...... 716-888-2793 300 G
wojickm@canisius.edu
WOJKE, Katie .... 360-491-4700 497 F
kwojke@stmartin.edu
WOJNAS, Sherry .... 315-801-8206 322 C
swojnas@secon.edu
WOJNOWSKI, Jeffrey .... 414-456-7106 508 D
jwojnows@mcw.edu
WOJNOWSKI, Mark, E .. 716-286-9718 318 F
mew@niagara.edu
WOJTALEWICZ,
Jeanette .... 402-572-3650 273 J
WOJTOWICZ, Robert ..... 757-683-4885 483 G
rwojtowi@odu.edu
WOLANIN, Monique ...... 860-932-4174.. 86 E
mwolanin@qvcc.edu
WOLANSKYJ,
Alexandra, P .... 507-284-3627 241 F
wolanskyj.alexandra@mayo.edu
WOLBERT, Jodi .... 603-513-1302 282 G
jodi.wolbert@granite.edu
WOLCH, Jennifer .... 510-642-0831.. 68 G
wolch@berkeley.edu
WOLCOWITZ, Jeffrey ..... 216-368-2928 358 C
jeffrey.wolcowitz@case.edu
WOLD, Mark, C .... 608-363-2359 506 D
woldm@beloit.edu
WOLD, Paul, G .... 507-344-7346 240 I
paul.wold@blc.edu
WOLD-MCCORMICK,
Kristi .... 303-492-6970.. 83 B
kristi.woldmccormick@colorado.edu
WOLF, Andrea .... 617-521-2488 224 E
andrea.wolf@simmons.edu
WOLF, Andreas .... 650-574-6461.. 62 A
wolf@smccd.edu
WOLF, Bill .... 865-573-4517 432 H
bwolf@johnsonu.edu
WOLF, George .... 517-264-7177 236 I
gwolf@sienaheights.edu
WOLF, Greg .... 508-856-4296 217 C
greg.wolf@umassmed.edu
WOLF, Howard, E .... 650-724-5992.. 66 C
howardwolf@stanford.edu
WOLF, Jay, D .... 812-888-4172 165 E
jwolf@vinu.edu
WOLF, Kelly, B .... 541-346-3165 387 F
kbwolf@uoregon.edu
WOLF, Kenneth .... 973-720-2432 292 I
wolfk@wpunj.edu
WOLF, Kevin .... 504-520-7537 198 D
kwolf@xula.edu
WOLF, Linda .... 614-251-4715 367 F
wolfl2@ohiodominican.edu
WOLF, Margaret .... 815-802-8302 142 C
mwolf@kcc.edu
WOLF, Nick .... 619-849-2384.. 57 H
nickwolf@pointloma.edu
WOLF, Paul, J .... 937-255-3636 517 H
paul.wolf@afit.edu
WOLF, Rachel, B .... 972-860-7358 447 I
rwolf@dcccd.edu
WOLF, Rob .... 352-854-2322.. 97 C
wolfr@cf.edu
WOLF, JR., Thomas .... 269-387-5473 239 E
tom.wolf@wmich.edu
WOLFARTH, Ariel .... 718-268-4700 320 K
WOLFE, Agata .... 973-313-6128 291 F
agata.wolfe@shu.edu
WOLFE, Allyson .... 502-410-6200 184 H
awolfe@galencollege.edu
WOLFE, Andrew .... 315-792-7234 330 A
andrew.wolfe@sunyit.edu
WOLFE, Barbara, E .... 401-874-5339 417 E
bwolfe@uri.edu
WOLFE, Bill .... 318-797-5279 194 E
bill.wolfe@lsus.edu
WOLFE, Clarissa .... 509-574-4651 500 I
cwolfe@yvcc.edu
WOLFE, Deidre .... 540-863-2807 487 I
dwolfe@dslcc.edu
WOLFE, Elizabeth .... 304-696-6007 504 C
mccormi8@marshall.edu
WOLFE, Erin, M .... 570-372-4314 410 H
wolfeerin@susqu.edu
WOLFE, Gregory .... 508-565-1357 224 H
gwolfe@stonehill.edu
WOLFE, James, E .... 812-464-1782 165 C
jwolfe2@usi.edu
WOLFE, Johanna .... 713-221-8909 465 C
wolfej@uhd.edu
WOLFE, John, S .... 812-877-8704 163 G
john.s.wolfe@rose-hulman.edu

WOLFE, Ken .... 727-864-8835.. 97 O
wolfefk@eckerd.edu
WOLFE, Michael .... 718-997-5210 303 E
michael.wolfe@qc.cuny.edu
WOLFE, Peggy, L .... 337-475-5820 197 B
pwolfe@mcneese.edu
WOLFE, Thomas, V .... 303-765-3102.. 80 G
tvwolfe@iliff.edu
WOLFE, Tim, A .... 757-221-3980 479 I
tawolfe@wm.edu
WOLFE, Timothy .... 775-784-4666 279 E
tawolfe@unr.edu
WOLFE, Timothy, A .... 757-221-3980 479 I
tawolfe@wm.edu
WOLFE, Todd .... 818-677-3700.. 33 B
todd.wolfe@csun.edu
WOLFE-LEE, Chyerl .... 360-650-3774 500 E
chyerl.wolfe-lee@wwu.edu
WOLFE-LYGA, Katherine 315-312-4416 327 D
katherine.wolfelyga@oswego.edu
WOLFE-STEPRO,
Charlene .... 603-206-8072 280 L
cwolfe@ccsnh.edu
WOLFER, Diane, G .... 859-371-9393 183 G
dwolfer@beckfield.edu
WOLFERT, Kelly .... 920-693-1171 513 H
ltc.bookstore@gotoltc.edu
WOLFF, Asaf .... 626-264-8880.. 71 A
WOLFF, Diane .... 617-928-4515 222 D
dwolff@mountida.edu
WOLFF, Donald .... 541-962-3359 383 B
dwolff@eou.edu
WOLFF, Holly, D .... 563-425-5221 173 K
wolffh@uiu.edu
WOLFF, Jennifer .... 210-434-6711 454 D
jswolff@follett.com
WOLFF, Peg, A .... 308-635-6064 278 B
pwolff@wncc.edu
WOLFF, Susan .... 815-939-5203 148 F
swolff@olivet.edu
WOLFF, Susan, J .... 406-771-4305 272 D
susan.wolff@gfcmsu.edu
WOLFGRAMM,
Jolynn, T .... 801-524-8106 471 L
jwolfgramm@ldsbc.edu
WOLFKILL, John .... 303-360-4833.. 79 C
john.wolfkill@ccaurora.edu
WOLFSON, Hannah .... 205-226-4922..... 4 F
hwolfson@bsc.edu
WOLIN, Richard, R .... 231-995-2003 235 B
rwolin@nmc.edu
WOLINSKY,
Lawrence, E .... 214-828-8300 459 C
wolinsky@tamu.edu
WOLK, David, S .... 802-468-1201 477 A
dave.wolk@castleton.edu
WOLK, Joseph .... 508-531-1229 217 D
joseph.wolk@bridgew.edu
WOLKEN, James .... 661-291-3044.. 29 F
jwolken@calarts.edu
WOLKEN, James .... 603-899-4343 281 D
wolkenj@franklinpierce.edu
WOLKING, Daryl .... 540-338-1776 483 H
WOLLENBERG, Chad ..... 434-949-1033 489 E
chad.wollenberg@southside.edu
WOLLENBURG, Doug .... 912-525-5000 125 B
dwollenbu@scad.edu
WOLLER, Eric, K .... 507-344-7790 240 I
eric.woller@blc.edu
WOLLMAN, Julie, E ...... 610-499-4101 414 F
jewollman@widener.edu
WOLLMAN, Rick, G .... 712-274-5320 172 A
wollman@morningside.edu
WOLLMERING, Jerry ..... 660-785-4235 267 K
jerryw@truman.edu
WOLMARK, Adrienne ..... 503-552-1605 384 F
awolmark@nunm.edu
WOLOHAN, Laurie .... 216-687-3606 359 L
l.wolohan@csuohio.edu
WOLPERN, Kevin .... 952-888-4777 249 F
kwolpern@nwhealth.edu
WOLPIN, Aryeh .... 718-232-7800 334 G
WOLPIN, Chaim .... 718-232-7800 334 G
WOLSEY, Timothy .... 480-732-7125.. 13 E
timothy.wolsey@cgc.edu
WOLSZON, Linda .... 817-257-7863 461 A
l.wolszon@tcu.edu
WOLTERS, Daniel .... 406-657-1161 272 I
woltersd@rocky.edu
WOLTMANN, Tanya .... 847-543-2443 136 E
twoltmann@clcillinois.edu
WOLZ, Jay .... 573-651-2930 266 M
jwolz@semo.edu
WOMACK, Joseph .... 541-684-7241 384 H
jwomack@nwcu.edu
WOMACK, Juanita .... 301-891-4485 209 E
jwomack@wau.edu

WOODS, Adonis .... 504-816-4375 191 E
awoods@dillard.edu
WOODS, Alice .... 856-691-8600 285 C
awoods@cccnj.edu
WOODS, Amy, K .... 845-575-3000 314 C
amy.k.coppola@marist.edu
WOODS, Billy .... 336-838-6496 347 G
wdwoods000@wilkescc.edu
WOODS, Brandy .... 618-634-3417 151 G
brandyw@shawneecc.edu
WOODS, Brett .... 828-339-4241 346 H
b_woods@southwesterncc.edu
WOODS, Brian .... 954-776-4476 102 G
brianw@keiseruniversity.edu
WOODS, Byron .... 559-730-3908.. 39 G
byronw@cos.edu
WOODS, Carolyn .... 717-264-4141 415 B
carolyn.woods@wilson.edu
WOODS, Christopher .... 773-834-8560 153 F
woods@uchicago.edu
WOODS, Deborah .... 765-361-6092 166 B
woodsde@wabash.edu
WOODS, Debra .... 714-449-7434.. 51 A
dwoods@ketchum.edu
WOODS, Debra, D .... 724-925-4083 414 E
woodsde@westmoreland.edu
WOODS, Dexter, A .... 202-865-6100.. 92 C
dexter.woods@howard.edu
WOODS, Donovan .... 405-945-6705 378 C
dwoods@osugiving.com
WOODS, Douglas .... 414-288-0327 508 C
douglas.woods@marquette.edu
WOODS, Ed .... 503-589-7746 382 C
ed.woods@chemeketa.edu
WOODS, Elizabeth .... 508-854-4294 220 G
ewoods@qcc.mass.edu
WOODS, Erin .... 806-743-4569 463 E
erin.woodws@ttuhsc.edu
WOODS, James, M .... 630-515-6173 145 I
jwoods@midwestern.edu
WOODS, Jami .... 336-386-3266 347 A
woodsj@surry.edu
WOODS, Jann .... 928-505-3300.. 14 I
WOODS, Jeffrey .... 479-968-0274.. 18 G
jwoods@atu.edu
WOODS, John .... 205-552-1284.... 5 C
john.woods@ecacolleges.com
WOODS, Karen .... 413-565-1000 211 C
kwoods@baypath.edu
WOODS, Katherine .... 214-860-2342 448 A
katherine.woods@dcccd.edu
WOODS, Kimberly, J ...... 830-792-7282 456 D
kjwoods@schreiner.edu
WOODS, Kristi .... 951-222-8038.. 58 H
kristi.woods@rcc.edu
WOODS, Kristin, L .... 319-273-2332 167 A
kristin.woods@uni.edu
WOODS, Kristy, F .... 202-865-7470.. 92 C
kristy.woods@howard.edu
WOODS, Lauren .... 312-567-5167 140 I
lwoods1@iit.edu
WOODS, Mark .... 810-762-9642 232 C
mwoods@kettering.edu
WOODS, Marty .... 864-587-4044 424 D
woodsm@smcsc.edu
WOODS, Marvin .... 520-325-0123.. 16 F
WOODS, Mary Lou .... 909-621-8135.. 57 I
marylou.woods@pomona.edu
WOODS, Maura, A .... 718-990-1985 322 F
woodsm@stjohns.edu
WOODS, Michael .... 510-723-6923.. 36 C
mwoods@chabotcollege.edu
WOODS, Rebekah .... 517-787-0800 231 E
woodsrebekahs@jccmi.edu
WOODS, Richard, G .... 765-361-6188 166 B
woodsr@wabash.edu
WOODS, Rochelle .... 657-278-2738.. 32 B
rwoods@fullerton.edu
WOODS, Serrita .... 815-282-7900 150 H
serritawoods@sacn.edu
WOODS, Sharmon .... 520-325-0123.. 16 F
WOODS, Sharon .... 864-503-5354 425 H
swoods@uscupstate.edu
WOODS, Sheldon .... 770-689-4875 115 E
swoods@aii.edu
WOODS, Susan .... 575-528-7711 295 E
swoods@nmsu.edu
WOODS, Tim .... 559-265-5700.. 66 G
tim.woods@fresnocitycollege.edu
WOODS, Tracie, J .... 225-771-4680 195 J
traice_woods@sus.edu
WOODS, Tracy .... 478-289-2035 118 H
twoods@ega.edu
WOODS, Tracy .... 304-724-3700 501 D
WOODS-RAMSEY,
Paulette .... 402-461-2463 273 G
paulettewoodsramsey@cccneb.edu
WOODSBY, Wendy .... 864-503-5198 425 H
wwoodsby@uscupstate.edu
WOODSIDE,
Christina, S .... 704-847-5600 349 E
cwoodside@ses.edu
WOODSON, Corliss, B .. 804-523-5877 488 C
cwoodson@reynolds.edu
WOODSON, Heather ...... 704-922-6310 343 D
woodson.heather@gaston.edu
WOODSON, Kendra, B .. 864-833-8220 423 D
kbwoodson@presby.edu
WOODSON, Lenee .... 973-290-4227 285 A
lwoodson@cse.edu
WOODSON, Lovisa .... 215-635-7300 396 B
lwoodson@gratz.edu
WOODSON, R. Wayne .. 706-821-8302 124 C
rwoodson@paine.edu
WOODSON, Rosalind .... 248-942-3337 235 D
rdwoodso@oaklandcc.edu
WOODSON, Sandra .... 916-577-2200.. 75 B
swoodson@jessup.edu
WOODSON,
Terrance, S .... 214-887-5371 448 G
twoodson@dts.edu
WOODSON, William ...... 937-708-5711 373 H
wwoodson@wilberforce.edu
WOODSON,
William Randy .... 919-515-2191 350 E
randy_woodson@ncsu.edu
WOODSON DAY,
Beverly .... 210-458-4536 468 B
beverly.woodsonday@utsa.edu
WOODWARD, Angus ..... 225-768-1704 191 G
angus.woodward@ololcollege.edu
WOODWARD, Clifford ... 973-290-4345 285 A
cwoodward@cse.edu
WOODWARD, David, B . 920-748-8301 509 H
woodwardd@ripon.edu
WOODWARD,
Gregory, S .... 860-768-4417.. 89 C
gwoodward@hartford.edu
WOODWARD, Holleigh . 828-669-8012 340 I
holleigh.woodward@montreat.edu
WOODWARD, Jonathan 228-896-2519 254 D
jonathan.woodward@mgccc.edu
WOODWARD, LouAnn .. 601-984-1010 256 D
lawoodward@umc.edu
WOODWARD, Mac .... 936-294-3931 462 F
smm_wmw@shsu.edu
WOODWARD, Rebecca .. 203-837-8760.. 85 B
woodwardr@wcsu.edu
WOODWARD, Scott .... 979-845-5129 459 C
feedback@athletics.tamu.edu
WOODWARD, Scott .... 210-341-1366 454 B
rsw@ost.edu
WOODWARD, Sheryl ..... 530-898-6771.. 31 D
swoodward@csuchico.edu
WOODWARD, Travis ...... 432-552-2806 469 D
woodward_t@utpb.edu
WOODWARD, Wade ...... 864-596-9072 420 F
wade.woodward@converse.edu
WOODWARD, Wendy .... 630-752-5656 155 F
wendy.woodward@wheaton.edu
WOODWORTH, Jody ..... 402-354-7000 275 P
jody.woodworth@methodistcollege.edu
WOODWORTH, Judith ... 215-965-4059 402 C
jwoodworth@moore.edu
WOODWORTH-NEY,
Laura .... 208-282-2171 132 B
woodlaur@isu.edu
WOODY, Clay .... 864-294-3609 421 I
clay.woody@furman.edu
WOODY, Craig .... 303-871-3588.. 83 E
cwoody@du.edu
WOODY, Jaime .... 512-863-1624 457 I
woodyj@southwestern.edu
WOODY, Keith, W .... 425-602-3045 492 E
kwoody@bastyr.edu
WOODY, Ron .... 734-487-3141 229 K
rwoody@emich.edu
WOODY, Tammie .... 585-785-1274 308 D
tammie.woody@flcc.edu
WOODYARD, Steve .... 714-241-6240.. 38 F
swoodyard@coastline.edu
WOOFTER, Heather .... 314-935-9256 269 L
woofter@wustl.edu
WOOLARD, Emily .... 252-940-6204 340 N
emily.woolard@beaufortccc.edu
WOOLARD, Jo .... 252-940-6327 340 N
jo.woolard@beaufortccc.edu
WOOLBERT, Stephanie .. 617-277-3915 212 F
woolberts@bgsp.edu
WOOLDRIDGE,
Deborah, G .... 419-372-7851 357 F
dgwoold@bgsu.edu
WOOLDRIDGE, Heath .... 870-612-2039.. 22 H
heath.wooldridge@uaccb.edu
WOOLDRIDGE, James ... 951-222-8420.. 58 H
jim.wooldridge@rcc.edu
WOOLDRIDGE, Peter ..... 919-536-7200 342 G
wooldridgep@durhamtech.edu
WOOLEY, Christine, A .. 240-895-4441 206 G
cawooley@smcm.edu
WOOLEY, Travis .... 407-303-9440.. 94 H
travis.wooley@adu.edu
WOOLF, Neil .... 509-359-6584 494 D
nwoolf@ewu.edu
WOOLF, Sarah .... 617-731-7083 223 F
woolfsar@pmc.edu
WOOLFOLK, Alan .... 904-819-6248.. 98 I
awoolfolk@flagler.edu
WOOLFOLK, Jerald .... 315-312-3214 327 D
jerald.woolfolk@oswego.edu
WOOLIVER, Matt .... 918-293-4888 378 B
matt.wooliver@okstate.edu
WOOLL, Kevin .... 858-499-0202.. 39 B
kwooll@coleman.edu
WOOLLEN, Elizabeth, G 405-325-5141 380 L
lwoollen@ou.edu
WOOLLEY, Craig .... 937-775-4008 374 B
craig.woolley@wright.edu
WOOLLEY, Mark .... 718-409-3224 329 E
mwoolley@sunymaritime.edu
WOOLLEY, Peter .... 973-443-8084 286 B
woolley@fdu.edu
WOOLLEY, Tom .... 205-726-2042.... 6 G
twwoolle@samford.edu
WOOLSCHLAGER, John . 239-590-1897 109 C
jwoolschlager@fgcu.edu
WOOLSEY, Andrew .... 949-480-4112.. 64 D
awoolsey@soka.edu
WOOLSEY, Clint .... 812-749-1441 163 B
cwoolsey@oak.edu
WOOLSEY, Roger, W ..... 603-646-2215 281 C
rober.w.woolsey@dartmouth.edu
WOOLSEY, Roger, W ..... 603-646-2215 281 C
roger.w.woolsey@dartmouth.edu
WOOLSON, Jonathan .... 716-673-3323 325 C
jonathan.woolson@fredonia.edu
WOOLSTON, Paul (PJ) .. 317-955-6307 162 R
pwoolston@marian.edu
WOOLWINE, Lora .... 304-384-5224 503 P
lwoolwine@concord.edu
WOOLWINE, Margaret ... 773-252-5307 149 I
margaret.woolwine@resu.edu
WOOST, Michael, G ...... 440-943-7600 369 J
mgwoost@yahoo.com
WOOSTER, Ginger .... 979-230-3210 444 E
ginger.wooster@brazosport.edu
WOOSTER, Timothy, T .. 617-745-3707 214 D
timothy.t.wooster@enc.edu
WOOTEN, Bradley .... 847-635-1912 148 D
bwooten@oakton.edu
WOOTEN, Cornelius ...... 724-357-2202 406 C
cornelius.wooten@iup.edu
WOOTEN, Daniel .... 615-963-5673 438 E
dwooten@tnstate.edu
WOOTEN, Dean, A .... 757-352-4062 484 E
deanwoo@regent.edu
WOOTEN, Manat .... 413-528-7203 211 B
mwooten@simons-rock.edu
WOOTEN, Maria .... 901-751-8453 434 E
mwooten@mabts.edu
WOOTEN, Michael, W ... 603-646-3093 281 C
michael.w.wooten@dartmouth.edu
WOOTEN, Pam .... 662-562-3349 255 C
pwooten@northwestms.edu
WOOTEN, Randall .... 832-447-1461 461 G
randall.wooten@tstc.edu
WOOTEN, Rodney .... 252-335-0821 342 D
rodney_wooten91@albemarle.edu
WOOTEN, Sheila .... 973-748-9000 284 A
sheila_wooten@bloomfield.edu
WOOTEN, Susan .... 828-726-2233 341 D
swooten@cccti.edu
WOOTEN, Susan .... 864-231-2000 418 E
swooten@andersonuniversity.edu
WOOTON, Chris .... 502-895-3411 188 A
cwooton@lpts.edu
WOOTTERS, Adrienne .... 413-662-5526 218 C
adrienne.wootters@mcla.edu
WOOTTON, Katie .... 304-424-8203 505 C
katie.wootton@wvup.edu
WOOTTON, Mark .... 757-826-1883 478 G
president@bcva.edu
WOOTTON, Tim .... 562-938-4072.. 48 I
twootton@lbcc.edu
WORD, Daniel .... 909-389-3216.. 59 H
dword@craftonhills.edu
WORD, John .... 559-791-2254.. 47 C
jword@portervillecollege.edu
WORDELL, Kathleen, A . 508-678-2811 219 C
kathleen.wordell@bristolcc.edu
WORDEN, Jeannie, M ... 715-675-3331 514 F
worden@ntc.edu
WORDEN, Jennifer .... 208-459-5307 131 H
jworden@collegeofidaho.edu
WORDEN, Jodi .... 509-527-4561 499 E
jodi.worden@wwcc.edu
WORDEN, Michael .... 845-341-4901 319 H
michael.worden@sunyorange.edu
WORDEN, Natalia .... 858-566-1200.. 41 G
nworden@disd.edu
WORDEN, Randy .... 559-453-7154.. 43 J
randy.worden@fresno.edu
WORDEN, Richard, B .... 315-568-3095 317 A
rworden@nycc.edu
WORK, Christine .... 845-341-4763 319 H
christine.work@sunyorange.edu
WORK, Denise .... 402-552-2796 273 K
workdenise@clarksoncollege.edu
WORK, Galen, J .... 848-445-1747 290 D
gwork@rutgers.edu
WORK, Patricia .... 202-495-3835.. 92 F
assistant@dhs.edu
WORKMAN, Andrew, A . 401-254-3030 417 C
aworkman@rwu.edu
WORKMAN, Christine ... 410-857-2267 205 E
cworkman@mcdaniel.edu
WORKMAN, Greg .... 336-821-2478 338 G
gworkman@johnwesley.edu
WORKMAN, Mary .... 954-201-7324.. 96 A
mworkman@broward.edu
WORKMAN, Sue, B .... 216-368-5899 358 C
sue.workman@case.edu
WORKMAN, Tamara ...... 618-453-2903 152 B
tworkman@siu.edu
WORKU, Adu .... 707-965-6242.. 55 F
aworku@puc.edu
WORLEY, David .... 303-765-3107.. 80 G
dworley@iliff.edu
WORLEY, Elizabeth, J .... 325-670-1229 450 A
eworley@hsutx.edu
WORLEY, John .... 510-659-6111.. 54 F
jworley@ohlone.edu
WORLEY, John .... 713-646-1863 456 H
jworley@stcl.edu
WORLEY, Louise .... 717-815-1446 415 G
lworley@ycp.edu
WORLEY, Mark .... 972-241-3371 447 E
mworley@dallas.edu
WORLEY, Mary Beth ..... 575-527-7728 295 E
mbworley@nmsu.edu
WORLEY, Michael, J ..... 404-413-3405 121 A
mworley@gsu.edu
WORLEY, Paul .... 828-835-9564 347 B
pworley@tricountycc.edu
WORLEY, Tim .... 561-803-2116 104 I
tim_worley@pba.edu
WORM, Lori, M .... 920-424-3033 511 B
worm@uwosh.edu
WORMACK, Janet .... 240-567-1744 205 F
janet.wormack@montgomerycollege.edu
WORMAN, Ernie .... 803-947-2052 422 H
ernie.worman@newberry.edu
WORMLEY, Lonnie .... 229-434-8440 114 I
lonnie.wormley@asurams.edu
WORMSER, Jennifer ...... 949-376-6000.. 47 H
jwormser@lcad.edu
WORNALL, Robyn .... 707-256-7192.. 53 D
rwornall@napavalley.edu
WORNAT, Judy 225-578-5255 193M
mjwornat@lsu.edu
WOROBEC, Sophia .... 312-942-6857 150 F
sophia_worobec@rush.edu
WORONER, Desiree .... 727-302-6823 107 A
woroner.desiree@spcollege.edu
WORRALL, Jay .... 610-796-8371 389 A
jay.worrall@alvernia.edu
WORSHAM, Charleen .... 903-983-3700 451 F
cworsham@kilgore.edu
WORSHAM, Thomas ..... 318-487-7498 191 J
thomas.worsham@lacollege.edu
WORSLEY, Christine ...... 925-969-2747.. 40 L
cworsley@dvc.edu
WORSTER, Kathy .... 803-321-3353 422 H
kathy.worster@newberry.edu
WORTH, Benjamin .... 540-863-2933 487 I
bworth@dslcc.edu
WORTHAM, Donald .... 239-513-1122 101 O
dwortham@hodges.edu
WORTHAM, Stanton ...... 617-552-4030 212 E
stanton.wortham@bc.edu
WORTHAM, Trudy .... 361-570-4110 465 D
worthamt@uhv.edu
WORTHEN, Kevin .... 585-389-2880 316 D
kworthe6@naz.edu
WORTHEN, Kevin, J ...... 801-422-2521 471 E
kevin_worthen@byu.edu
WORTHINGTON, Leslie . 256-549-8256.... 2 A
lworthington@gadsdenstate.edu

WUCHENICH,
Christopher, L .... 803-777-8400 424 I
clw@mailbox.sc.edu
WUCHER, Brad .... 573-875-7237 258 F
brwucher@ccis.edu
WUEBBEN, Nancy .... 937-319-6164 356 F
nwuebben@antiochcollege.edu
WUENSCHEL, Carol, M . 301-696-3556 204 D
wuenschel@hood.edu
WUEST, Beth, E .... 512-245-8113 463 A
bw09@txstate.edu
WUESTNECK, John .... 617-258-5484 221 C
WULF, Lincoln .... 719-502-3178.. 81 H
lincoln.wulf@ppcc.edu
WULFERT, Edelgard .... 518-442-4654 324 G
ewulfert@albany.edu
WULFF, Deborah .... 805-546-3122.. 41 C
deborah_wulff@cuesta.edu
WULLENJOHN, Bill .... 210-485-0391 441 E
wwullenjohn@alamo.edu
WUNDERLICH, Kathryn . 607-844-8222 331 D
wunderk@tompkinscortland.edu
WUNDERLICH, Mark, E . 518-388-6234 332 B
wunderlm@union.edu
WUNKER, Charles .... 863-638-2916 114 A
wunkerc@webber.edu
WUNSCH, Mark .... 540-636-2900 479 G
mwunsch@christendom.edu
WUNSCH, Michael .... 732-263-5355 287 C
mwunsch@monmouth.edu
WUORI, Misti, L .... 701-788-4631 354 B
misti.wuori@mayvillestate.edu
WUORIO, Erica .... 941-752-5000 108 P
wuorioe@scf.edu
WURM, Sharon .... 775-673-7074 279 C
swurm@tmcc.edu
WURSTER, Paul, E .... 585-292-2814 315 L
pwurster@monroecc.edu
WURTZ, Joseph .... 913-360-7500 175 D
jwurtz@benedictine.edu
WURTZ, Keith .... 909-389-3206.. 59 H
kwurtz@craftonhills.edu
WURTZEL, Julie, A .... 563-562-3263 172 D
wurtzelj@nicc.edu
WURZER, Christine .... 916-608-6645.. 50 H
wurzerc@flc.losrios.edu
WUSSOW, Helen .... 916-278-4433.. 33 C
helen.wussow@csus.edu
WUTHRICH, Chris .... 208-426-1484 131 C
chriswuthrich@boisestate.edu
WUTHRICH, Philip .... 979-532-6305 471 A
philipw@wcjc.edu
WUTOH, Anthony, K .... 202-806-2550.. 92 C
awutoh@howard.edu
WUTOH, Rita .... 301-860-4170 208 E
rwutoh@bowiestate.edu
WYANDOTTE,
Annette, M .... 812-941-2208 161 A
awyandot@ius.edu
WYANDT, Christy, M .... 662-915-7474 256 C
cwyandt@olemiss.edu
WYANT, Robert .... 585-395-2751 326 D
rwyant@brockport.edu
WYATT, Adrienne, A ...... 903-730-4890 451 D
awyatt@jarvis.edu
WYATT, Ben .... 859-280-1246 187 G
bwyatt@lextheo.edu
WYATT, Bill, J .... 540-568-4908 481 I
wyattwj@jmu.edu
WYATT, Charles, W .... 864-488-4603 422 B
cwyatt@limestone.edu
WYATT, Clarence, R ...... 309-457-2127 146 A
cwyatt@monmouthcollege.edu
WYATT, Danny .... 808-696-0714 130 G
dwyatt@hawaii.edu
WYATT, Gary .... 620-341-5254 177 B
gwyatt@emporia.edu
WYATT, JR., Harry, E .... 313-577-4301 239 C
gg5794@wayne.edu
WYATT, Julie .... 870-972-3670.. 18 A
jwyatt@astate.edu
WYATT, Jymmyca .... 770-962-7580 121 G
jwyatt@gwinnetttech.edu
WYATT, Lawrence .... 281-487-1501 460 G
lwyatt@txchiro.edu
WYATT, Mark, A .... 951-343-4474.. 28 G
mwyatt@calbaptist.edu
WYATT, Molly .... 252-985-5194 348 A
mwyatt@ncwc.edu
WYATT, Robert, L .... 843-383-8010 420 B
rwyatt@coker.edu
WYATT, Scott, L .... 435-586-7721 473 A
wyatt@suu.edu
WYATT, Shay .... 801-832-2344 474 E
swyatt@westminstercollege.edu
WYATT, Terri .... 804-257-5726 491 C
vuu@bkstr.com

WYBAN, Bruce .... 310-434-4376.. 62 G
wyban_bruce@smc.edu
WYBLE, Shannon .... 410-778-7200 210 A
swyble2@washcoll.edu
WYCHE, Lynn .... 850-973-9404 104 D
wychel@nfcc.edu
WYCHE, Sandy .... 972-860-4282 447 G
swyche@dcccd.edu
WYCHE, Susan .... 530-242-7560.. 63 I
swyche@shastacollege.edu
WYCKOFF, Harold .... 910-678-8287 343 B
wyckoffh@faytechcc.edu
WYCKOFF, Steven .... 718-960-8720 302 C
steven.wyckoff@lehman.cuny.edu
WYCO, Jeff .... 304-205-6611 502 K
jeff.wyco@bridgevalley.edu
WYCOFF-HORN, Marcie 608-785-8127 510 F
mwycoff-horn@uwlax.edu
WYDEN, JR., Leon .... 419-434-4521 372 B
wyden@findlay.edu
WYDER, Bruce .... 330-494-6170 370 G
bwyder@starkstate.edu
WYETT, Megan .... 315-792-7530 330 A
megan.wyett@sunyit.edu
WYKE, Rebecca, M .... 207-621-3041 201 C
wyke@maine.edu
WYKES, Paul .... 508-793-7385 213 C
pwykes@clarku.edu
WYKOFF, Dan .... 706-410-1129 118 E
dan.wykoff@covenant.edu
WYKOFF, Randolph, F .. 423-439-4243 431 H
wykoff@etsu.edu
WYLIE, Brian .... 978-232-2440 214 G
bwylie@endicott.edu
WYLIE, Michael .... 513-569-1492 359 G
michael.wylie@cincinnatistate.edu
WYLIE, Richard .... 770-454-9270.. 93 B
WYLIE, Richard, E .... 978-232-2001 214 G
rwylie@endicott.edu
WYMAN, Derrick .... 330-490-7090 373 F
dwyman@walsh.edu
WYMAN, J. Vernon .... 401-874-2501 417 E
jvernonwyman@uri.edu
WYMAN, Tracey .... 763-493-0546 246 E
twyman@nhcc.edu
WYMER, Cindy .... 423-461-8415 435 A
clwymer@milligan.edu
WYMER, Douglas, A ..... 352-365-3522 103 B
wymerd@lssc.edu
WYMER, Greg .... 605-688-4482 429 B
greg.wymer@sdstate.edu
WYNDER, Robin .... 301-687-4050 209 A
rwynder@frostburg.edu
WYNEGAR, Robert .... 252-335-0821 342 D
robert_wynegar02@albemarle.edu
WYNES, David, L .... 404-727-3889 119 B
david.wynes@emory.edu
WYNES, Tim .... 651-423-8213 244 E
tim.wynes@dctc.edu
WYNES, Timothy .... 651-450-3641 245 A
twynes@inverhills.edu
WYNN, Amanda .... 757-352-4148 484 E
amanwyn@regent.edu
WYNN, Bobby, C .... 910-672-1232 350 B
bwynn@uncfsu.edu
WYNN, Curt, J .... 757-822-1460 489 H
cjwynn@tcc.edu
WYNN, Denise, Y .... 919-530-7331 350 D
dwynn3@nccu.edu
WYNN, Hal .... 334-386-7285.... 5 I
hwynn@faulkner.edu
WYNN, Keren .... 229-333-2103 128 G
keren.wynn@wiregrass.edu
WYNN, Renell .... 303-871-2711.. 83 E
renell.wynn@du.edu
WYNN, Sandra .... 304-327-4213 503 O
swynn@bluefieldstate.edu
WYNN, Steve .... 617-746-1990 216 A
steve.wynn@hult.edu
WYNN, Ted .... 703-993-5160 481 B
twynn3@gmu.edu
WYNN, Tor .... 316-295-5451 177 F
tor_wynn@friends.edu
WYNNE, Anja .... 719-255-3696.. 83 C
kwynne@uccs.edu
WYNNE, Jeremy .... 509-777-4277 500 H
jwynne@whitworth.edu
WYNNE, Joshua .... 701-777-2516 353 G
joshua.wynne@med.und.edu
WYNNE, Joshua .... 701-777-2514 353 G
joshua.wynne@med.und.edu
WYNTER, Cadence .... 949-582-4958.. 64 J
cwynter@saddleback.edu
WYONT, Kimberly .... 704-922-6482 343 D
wyont.kimberly@gaston.edu
WYPISZYNSKI, Gregory 920-424-0007 511 B
wypiszyn@uwosh.edu

WYRICK, Kathleen .... 907-564-8265.... 9 F
kwyrick@alaskapacific.edu
WYSE, Joe .... 530-242-7510.. 63 I
jwyse@shastacollege.edu
WYSOCKI, Barbara .... 630-515-6321 145 I
bwysoc@midwestern.edu
WYSOCKI, Charlene .... 610-921-7667 388 E
cwysocki@albright.edu
WYSOCKI, Joseph .... 704-461-6831 335 J
josephwysocki@bac.edu
WYSOCKI, Joseph, T ..... 815-740-2274 154 G
jwysocki@stfrancis.edu
WYSONG, James .... 813-253-7236 101 M
rwysong@hccfl.edu
WYSTEPEK, Christopher 413-782-1794 225 F
christopher.wystepek@wne.edu

X

XANTHOS, Christopher . 619-594-6018.. 34 B
cxanthos@mail.sdsu.edu
XIA, Jingfeng .... 570-422-3152 406 A
jxia@esu.edu
XIANG, Yun .... 603-862-2081 282 F
yun.xiang@unh.edu
XIE, Jin Hua .... 262-554-2010 508 E
drj-xie@yahoo.com
XIE, Yan .... 909-748-8187.. 71 H
yan_xie@redlands.edu
XIMENEZ, David .... 817-515-5354 458 B
david.ximenez@tccd.edu
XIMINES, Sheryl, H .... 919-516-4343 348 G
sximines@st-aug.edu
XIONG, Shoua .... 916-686-7400.. 30 H
XIONG-CHAN,
Mai Nhia .... 651-523-2440 242 E
mxiongchan01@hamline.edu
XIPPOLITOS, Lee .... 631-444-3549 325 F
lee.xippolitos@stonybrook.edu
XIRINACHS, Susan .... 207-947-4591 198 F
sxirinachs@bealcollege.edu
XU, Amanda .... 707-468-3096.. 51 E
axu@mendocino.edu
XU, Hong "Anna" .... 361-354-2741 445 S
hxu@coastalbend.edu
XU, Jackie .... 202-274-5545.. 93 D
jxu@udc.edu

Y

YABUR, Lupe .... 562-947-8755.. 65 D
lupeyabur@scuhs.edu
YACAVONE, Mark .... 607-753-4711 327 A
mark.yacavone@cortland.edu
YACKEE, Grace, B .... 734-384-4221 234 C
gyackee@monroeccc.edu
YADAMA, Gautam, N .... 617-552-4020 212 E
gautam.yadama@bc.edu
YADAV, Ajeet .... 218-855-8115 244 C
ayadav@clcmn.edu
YAEGER, Evelyn .... 810-762-9782 232 C
eyaeger@kettering.edu
YAEGER, John, W .... 202-685-0080 518 B
yaegerj@ndu.edu
YAEZENKO, Suzette .... 541-885-1108 385 E
suzette.yaezenko@oit.edu
YAGER, David .... 215-717-6000 412 F
dyager@uarts.edu
YAHN, Robert .... 304-243-2554 505 H
ryahn@wju.edu
YAHNG, Charles .... 314-529-9312 262 B
cyahng@maryville.edu
YAHNKE, Eric .... 503-838-8459 388 B
yahnkee@wou.edu
YAHYAZADEH, Bizhan ... 802-485-2145 475 I
bizhan@norwich.edu
YAKLICH, Richard .... 305-430-1167.. 99 M
richard.yaklich@fmuniv.edu
YAKOVLEV, Ilya .... 717-815-2254 415 G
iyakovlev@ycp.edu
YAKOWICZ, William ...... 201-612-5253 283 I
wyakowicz@bergen.edu
YAKSHE, Patti, L .... 412-281-2600 408 A
YALE, Amanda, A .... 724-738-2011 407 C
amanda.yale@sru.edu
YALE, Jacob .... 716-926-8785 310 B
jyale@hilbert.edu
YALE, Janet .... 402-557-7095 273 E
janet.yale@bellevue.edu
YAM, Marylou .... 410-532-5300 206 D
YAMADA, Emiko .... 650-508-3749.. 54 D
eyamada@ndnu.edu
YAMAGATA-NOJI,
Audrey .... 909-274-4505.. 52 I
ayamagat@mtsac.edu
YAMAKAWA, Lynn .... 310-233-4387.. 49 B
yamakalm@lahc.edu
YAMAMOTO, Catherine . 402-472-7749 277 G
cyamamoto1@unl.edu

YAMAMOTO, Cindy .... 808-984-3288 130 H
cindy@hawaii.edu
YAMAMOTO, Donald ..... 202-685-3924 518 B
donald.yamamoto@ndu.edu
YAMAMOTO, Jessica ..... 808-934-2688 130 D
jpky@hawaii.edu
YAMAMOTO, Kayoko ..... 831-476-9424.. 43 C
studentaccounts@fivebranches.edu
YAMAMOTO, Keith .... 415-476-3128.. 70 A
yamamoto@ucsf.edu
YAMAMOTO, Lance .... 808-956-5148 130 B
lance@hawaii.edu
YAMAMURA, Whitney ... 916-608-6572.. 50 H
yamamuw@flc.losrios.edu
YAMASAKI, Erika .... 310-954-4412.. 52 H
eyamasaki@msmu.edu
YAMBA, A. Zachary .... 973-877-3022 285 K
yamba@essex.edu
YAMBA, Mohamed .... 724-938-4240 405 F
yamba@calu.edu
YAMBO, Marc .... 630-889-6517 147 D
myambo@nuhs.edu
YAMEEN, Deanna .... 508-588-9100 220 B
YAMILKOSKI, Vince, J .. 770-534-6134 116 F
vyamilkoski@brenau.edu
YAMPOLSKY, Chana ..... 212-964-2830 315 B
cpy145@aol.com
YAMRICK, Emmalyn ...... 212-774-0740 314 D
eyamrick@mmm.edu
YAN, Ruth .... 319-226-2080 166 C
ruth.yan@allencollege.edu
YAN, Song .... 313-577-0633 239 C
ej7020@wayne.edu
YANAI, Carolyn .... 702-463-2122 280 F
YANCEY, Deborah .... 540-857-7986 490 B
dyancey@virginiawestern.edu
YANCEY, Jennifer, L .... 361-582-2519 470 A
jennifer.yancey@victoriacollege.edu
YANCEY, John .... 606-218-5306 190 E
johnyancey@upike.edu
YANCEY, Laurica .... 919-658-7750 349 F
lyancey@umo.edu
YANCHAK, Frank .... 614-947-6723 362 A
frank.yanchak@franklin.edu
YANCKELLO, Robert ...... 407-823-2711 110 C
bob.yanckello@ucf.edu
YANCY, Chad .... 205-929-3497.... 2 G
cyancy@lawsonstate.edu
YANDA, Wayne .... 619-482-6414.. 65 H
wyanda@swccd.edu
YANDIO, Marlo .... 440-375-7000 364 C
YANES, Kenneth .... 212-484-1339 302 F
kyanes@jjay.cuny.edu
YANEZ, Katy .... 602-827-2555.. 14 K
katy.yanez@nau.edu
YANEZ, Mercedes .... 310-233-4127.. 49 B
yanezm@lahc.edu
YANG, Alice .... 831-459-2328.. 70 C
ayang@ucsc.edu
YANG, Angela .... 949-582-4602.. 64 J
lyang26@saddleback.edu
YANG, Anna .... 559-325-3600.. 29 D
ayang@chsu.org
YANG, Anthony .... 973-618-3605 284 D
ayang@caldwell.edu
YANG, Dang .... 715-831-7229 513 E
dyang19@cvtc.edu
YANG, Henry, T .... 805-893-2231.. 70 B
henry.yang@ucsb.edu
YANG, Hong .... 401-232-6885 416 A
hyang@bryant.edu
YANG, Honggang .... 954-262-3016 104 F
yangh@nsu.nova.edu
YANG, Kyung Mi .... 770-220-7923 119 D
akbcyang@gcuniv.edu
YANG, Lykos .... 408-260-0208.. 43 B
sjextension@fivebranches.edu
YANG, Neng .... 503-838-8590 388 B
yangn@wou.edu
YANG, Nicole .... 920-693-1120 513 H
nicole.yang@gotoltc.edu
YANG, Olivia .... 509-335-5571 499 G
olivia.yang@wsu.edu
YANG, Paul Zhaohui ..... 628-448-0023.. 46 K
vp-admin@itsla.edu
YANG, Peter .... 612-244-2800 242 H
pyang@ipr.edu
YANG, Steve .... 763-424-0805 246 E
syang@nhcc.edu
YANG, Zhanjun .... 954-776-4476 102 G
zyang@keiseruniversity.edu
YANKANICH, Julie .... 856-227-7200 284 E
jyankanich@camdencc.edu
YANKELEWITZ, Yoel ...... 718-846-1940 334 L
yyankelewitz@gmail.com
YANKELITIS, Wendy ...... 570-348-6201 401 B
yankelitis@marywood.edu

YANKEY, Terry, L .... 606-474-3222 185 C
tly@kcu.edu
YANNI, Stephen .... 906-248-8478 227 P
syanni@bmcc.edu
YANNICK, Lisa .... 610-436-3075 407 D
lyannick@wcupa.edu
YANNIELLO, Kristin .... 718-405-3252 304 H
kristin.yanniello@mountsaintvincent.edu
YANTA, Stacie .... 361-354-2207 445 S
yantas@coastalbend.edu
YANTOS, Brittany .... 312-621-9650 146 G
byantos@nl.edu
YAO, Chunmei .... 910-521-6295 351 E
chunmei.yao@uncp.edu
YAO, Marian .... 408-924-2012.. 34 D
marian.sofish@sjsu.edu
YAO, Min .... 562-985-5459.. 32 C
min.yao@csulb.edu
YAO, Richard .... 702-992-2632 279 B
richard.yao@nsc.edu
YAP, Michael .... 213-252-5100.. 24 A
myap@alu.edu
YAQUB, Samia .... 530-895-2484.. 28 E
yaqubsa@butte.edu
YARABECK, John .... 936-294-1785 462 F
slo_jxy@shsu.edu
YARBROUGH, David ..... 337-482-1015 197 F
yarbrough@louisiana.edu
YARBROUGH, Denise .... 585-275-4321 332 E
dyarbrough@admin.rochester.edu
YARBROUGH, Erin, A ... 405-325-0206 380 L
eyarbrough@ou.edu
YARBROUGH, Ernest ..... 216-687-2048 359 L
e.b.yarbrough@csuohio.edu
YARBROUGH, John .... 706-865-2134 126 G
jyarbrough@truett.edu
YARBROUGH, Kenny ..... 615-230-3443 438 C
kenny.yarbrough@volstate.edu
YARBROUGH,
Kimberly Anne .... 650-493-4430.. 64 C
kimberly.christensen@sofia.edu
YARBROUGH, Laura ...... 870-508-6122.. 18 C
lyarbrough@asumh.edu
YARBROUGH, Laura, L . 336-249-8186 342 F
laura_yarbrough@davidsonccc.edu
YARBROUGH, Mark, M . 214-887-5011 448 G
myarbrough@dts.edu
YARBROUGH, Scott ...... 843-863-7563 419 C
syarbrou@csuniv.edu
YARDENI-FUNK, Liat ..... 310-824-1586.. 24 B
YARDLEY, Katherine, W 207-778-7154 201 D
kyardley@maine.edu
YARDLEY, Owen .... 402-472-8809 277 G
oyardley2@unl.edu
YARLOTT, JR., David .... 406-638-3107 271 C
davidyarlott@lbhc.edu
YARMAGYAN, Samuel ... 916-877-7977.. 58 J
sam@sui.edu
YARNELL, Ellen .... 503-552-1528 384 F
eyarnell@nunm.edu
YARNELL, Thomas, V .... 614-823-1502 368 O
tyarnell@otterbein.edu
YAROFAISUG, Faustino . 691-320-2481 519 G
yaro@comfsm.fm
YARRISH, James .... 215-895-1114 413 E
j.yarris@usciences.edu
YARRISH, Julie .... 310-434-3762.. 62 G
yarrish_julie@smc.edu
YARSIAH, James .... 803-780-1264 426 F
jyarsiah@voorhees.edu
YASECKO, Susan .... 312-662-4415 133 A
syasecko@adler.edu
YASINSAC, Alec .... 251-460-6390.... 9 B
yasinsac@southalabama.edu
YASSKY, David .... 914-422-4407 319 J
dyassky@pace.edu
YASUDA, Cathy .... 541-881-5585 387 D
cyasuda@tvcc.cc
YASUDA, Jon .... 626-584-5491.. 43 K
jyasuda@fuller.edu
YASUHARA, June .... 808-739-4603 129 A
jyasuhar@chaminade.edu
YASUKOCHI, Dennis ..... 206-934-5660 497 H
dennis.yasukochi@seattlecolleges.edu
YATER, Ann .... 317-917-5915 161 F
aniebrug@ivytech.edu
YATES, Brian .... 434-592-3371 482 D
bcyates@liberty.edu
YATES, Cheryl .... 812-749-1416 163 B
cyates@oak.edu
YATES, Deirdre .... 973-275-2191 291 F
deirdre.yates@shu.edu
YATES, Dorothy, C .... 307-766-5320 517 B
dyates4@uwyo.edu
YATES, Frances .... 765-973-8470 160 A
fyates@iue.edu
YATES, Jacob .... 606-337-4524 184 D
registrar@ccbbc.edu
YATES, James .... 870-864-7156.. 21 D
jyates@southark.edu
YATES, Jamie .... 717-337-6801 396 A
jyates@gettysburg.edu
YATES, Kristin .... 402-472-5242 277 E
kyates@nebraska.edu
YATES, Latoro .... 718-262-2188 304 A
lyates@york.cuny.edu
YATES, Liz .... 610-861-1505 402 D
yatese@moravian.edu
YATES, Mark .... 903-923-2340 448 J
myates@etbu.edu
YATES, Susan .... 559-325-5340.. 66 F
susan.yates@cloviscollege.edu
YATES, Travis, W .... 662-915-7274 256 C
twyates@olemiss.edu
YATES, Vivian .... 216-987-4468 360 E
vivian.yates@tri-c.edu
YATOOMA, Chris .... 916-660-7600.. 63 K
cyatooma@sierracollege.edu
YATS, Kirk, M .... 989-774-3674 228 E
yats1km@cmich.edu
YAUN, John .... 909-537-4155.. 33 D
john.yaun@csusb.edu
YAVAS, Debra .... 310-377-5501.. 51 B
dyavas@marymountcalifornia.edu
YAVNEH, Naomi .... 504-865-7330 194 G
yavneh@loyno.edu
YAVORSKI, Ginger .... 610-861-5494 403 B
gyavorski@northampton.edu
YAZDANI, Jami .... 802-468-1396 477 A
jami.yazdani@castleton.edu
YAZDANI, Linda .... 303-914-6536.. 82 B
linda.yazdani@rrcc.edu
YAZDI, Aliakbar, R .... 205-853-1200.... 2 F
ayazdi@jeffersonstate.edu
YBANEZ, Elsa .... 210-436-3725 455 J
eybanez@stmarytx.edu
YBARRA, Kathy .... 206-296-2810 498 D
ybarrak@seattleu.edu
YBARRA, Nancy .... 925-473-7405.. 41 A
nybarra@losmedanos.edu
YBARRA, Paul .... 916-577-2200.. 75 B
pybarra@jessup.edu
YBARRA, Tomas .... 509-574-4640 500 I
tybarra@yvcc.edu
YDOYAGA, Shannon ..... 361-698-1703 448 H
sydoyaga@delmar.edu
YE, Eugene .... 630-942-3821 136 D
yee8@cod.edu
YEAGER, Andrew .... 716-880-2336 314 F
ayeager@medaille.edu
YEAGER, Bren .... 304-384-6056 503 P
byeager@concord.edu
YEAGER, Cody .... 541-888-7312 387 A
cody.yeager@socc.edu
YEAGER, Daniel .... 619-239-0391.. 35 C
dyeager@cwsl.edu
YEAGER, Daphne .... 601-477-4151 253 F
daphne.yeager@jcjc.edu
YEAGER, Edward .... 480-732-7177.. 13 E
ed.yeager@cgc.edu
YEAGER, Eric .... 432-335-6412 454 C
eyeager@odessa.edu
YEAGER, Kathrine .... 928-523-3173.. 14 K
kathrine.yeager@nau.edu
YEAGER, Phyllis .... 859-442-1150 185 I
phyllis.yeager@kctcs.edu
YEAGER, Susan .... 510-659-6045.. 54 F
syeager@ohlone.edu
YEAGLEY, JR., William . 989-774-3081 228 E
yeagl1b@cmich.edu
YEAKLEY, Randy .... 325-649-8804 450 H
ryeakley@hputx.edu
YEAP, Soon Beng .... 303-765-3110.. 80 G
syeap@iliff.edu
YEARNS, Ellie .... 336-272-7102 338 B
eleanor.yearns@greensboro.edu
YEAROUT, Danielle .... 785-594-4597 174 J
danielle.yearout@bakeru.edu
YEAROUT, Teresa, A ..... 276-964-7266 489 F
teresa.yearout@sw.edu
YEARWOOD, George, A 919-508-2035 353 C
ryearwood@peace.edu
YEARWOOD, Jody .... 478-387-4392 120 B
jyearwood@gmc.edu
YEATER, Michael .... 409-882-3342 462 D
mike.yeater@lsco.edu
YEATS, John Mark .... 816-414-3731 263 D
jmyeats@mbts.edu
YEATTS, Debra .... 910-630-7385 340 A
dyeatts@methodist.edu
YEBEI, Philemon .... 765-455-9291 160 B
pyebei@iuk.edu
YEBOAH, Barima .... 718-405-3414 304 H
barima.yeboah@mountsaintvincent.edu
YEE, David .... 415-239-3669.. 37 H
dyee@ccsf.edu
YEE, Diane .... 212-229-5900 316 E
yeed@newschool.edu
YEE, Helen .... 614-825-6255 356 C
hyee@aiam.edu
YEE, Jill .... 415-239-3174.. 37 H
jyee@ccsf.edu
YEGHIAYAN, Paul .... 510-925-4282.. 25 P
YEHL, Thomas .... 703-284-1607 483 A
thomas.yehl@marymount.edu
YEHUDAH, Shoshana .... 646-565-6000 331 F
shulys@touro.edu
YEIGH, Bjong, W .... 425-352-5221 499 D
yeigh@uw.edu
YEKOVICH, Robert .... 713-348-4837 455 F
yekovr@rice.edu
YELEY, Brian, D .... 812-856-1013 159 H
byeley@indiana.edu
YELKUR, Rama .... 585-385-8098 322 E
ryelkur@sjfc.edu
YELLE, Richard, W .... 203-576-4222.. 88 F
ryelle@bridgeport.edu
YELLEN, David .... 845-575-3000 314 C
david.yellen@marist.edu
YELLMAN, Kim .... 301-934-7627 203 D
kyellman@csmd.edu
YELLS, David .... 903-223-3003 460 D
dyells@tamut.edu
YELNOSKY, Michael, J .. 401-254-4509 417 C
myelnosky@law.rwu.edu
YELNOSKY, Robert, E .... 814-641-3113 398 B
yelnosr@juniata.edu
YELTON, David .... 704-406-3522 337 H
dyelton@gardner-webb.edu
YELTON, Kristen .... 636-481-3296 261 B
kyelton@jeffco.edu
YELVINGTON, Philip, R . 901-321-3396 431 A
pyelving@cbu.edu
YEN, Charlie .... 310-434-3002.. 62 G
yen_charlie@smc.edu
YEN, Debbie .... 870-733-6764.. 18 B
dyen@asumidsouth.edu
YEN, Johanna, C .... 954-763-9840.. 94 S
atom@atom.edu
YENCHA, Matthew .... 610-606-4666 392 A
myencha@cedarcrest.edu
YENCHO, Thomas .... 610-409-3491 413 H
tyencho@ursinus.edu
YENDOL-HOPPEY,
Diane .... 904-620-2520 110 E
diane.yendol-hoppy@unf.edu
YENTES, Matt .... 863-638-2963 114 A
yentesms@webber.edu
YEOH, Kim .... 607-255-6240 306 B
controller@cornell.edu
YEOM, Kyong, S .... 636-327-4645 263 C
finance@midwest.edu
YEOM, Kyong, S .... 636-327-4645 263 C
yeom900@gmail.com
YEOM, Kyong, S .... 636-327-4645 263 C
iss@midwest.edu
YEOMANS, Jennifer .... 603-888-1311 281 I
jyeomans@rivier.edu
YEONOPOLUS, Jim .... 254-526-1214 445 L
jyeonopolus@ctcd.edu
YEP, Kathleen .... 909-607-7304.. 57 C
kathleen_yep@jsd.claremont.edu
YEPES, Hernan .... 203-332-5017.. 85 F
hyepes@housatonic.edu
YEPES, Maria, E .... 323-265-8957.. 48 L
yepesme@elac.edu
YEPES, Maria Elena .... 323-265-8957.. 48 L
yepesme@elac.edu
YERDON, Melinda .... 419-559-2289 370 J
myerdon@terra.edu
YERDON, Wayne .... 419-559-2341 370 J
wyerdon@terra.edu
YERGEN, Norman .... 951-785-2307.. 47 F
nyergen@lasierra.edu
YERGER, Mark, E .... 570-577-1795 390 H
mark.yerger@bucknell.edu
YERIAN, Diane .... 540-568-8090 481 I
yeriandg@jmu.edu
YERMAKOV, Andrei .... 310-900-1600.. 40 C
ayermakov@elcamino.edu
YESTRAMSKI, Joanne .... 978-934-2206 217 B
joanne_yestramski@uml.edu
YETMAR, Theresa .... 785-594-8316 174 J
theresa.yetmar@bakeru.edu
YEVICH, Nicolette .... 660-248-6255 258 B
nyevich@centralmethodist.edu
YHER, Bryan .... 907-474-5439.. 10 B
bmuher@alaska.edu
YI, Daeseop .... 510-639-7879.. 54 G
YI, Rick .... 770-220-7903 119 D
rickyi@gcuniv.edu
YIANILOS, Chris .... 571-858-3005 490 F
chrisyianilos@vt.edu
YIANOUKOS, Steven, J . 315-268-7021 304 B
syianouk@clarkson.edu
YIGZAW, Erika .... 503-244-0726 381 H
erikayigzaw@achs.edu
YIH, T. C .... 239-590-7021 109 C
tcyih@fgcu.edu
YIL, Song .... 714-683-1389.. 27 C
songyil@buc.edu
YILIBUW, Dolores .... 859-280-1224 187 G
dyilibuw@lextheo.edu
YIN, Alexander, C .... 802-656-4418 476 E
alexander.yin@uvm.edu
YIN, Carol .... 706-880-8339 122 D
cyin@lagrange.edu
YIN, Kong .... 713-221-8975 465 C
yink@uhd.edu
YINGLING, Julie, R .... 419-434-4550 372 B
yinglingj@findlay.edu
YINGLING, Kevin, W ..... 304-696-3170 504 C
yingling@marshall.edu
YIP, Koyuki .... 610-526-6004 396 H
kyip@harcum.edu
YIP, Yunny .... 415-575-6171.. 29 H
yyip@ciis.edu
YLINEN, Jeff .... 612-374-5800 242 C
jylinen@dunwoody.edu
YOACHIM, Ann .... 423-425-4111 440 A
ann-yoachim@utc.edu
YOACHIM, Maureen ...... 610-740-3725 392 A
bookstore@cedarcrest.edu
YOAKUM, Katrina, M .... 785-864-3261 181 I
kyoakum@ku.edu
YOANNONE, Carol .... 412-237-4421 392 G
cyoannone@ccac.edu
YOCHIN, Tara .... 814-868-9900 395 A
taray@erieit.edu
YOCHUM, Denise .... 253-964-6776 497 B
dyochum@pierce.ctc.edu
YOCHUM, Henry .... 434-381-6357 485 P
hyochum@sbc.edu
YOCHUM, Susan .... 724-830-1044 410 E
yochum@setonhill.edu
YOCKEY, Denton, J .... 904-276-6839 106 M
dentonyockey@sjrstate.edu
YOCKEY, Glenn .... 830-372-8040 461 D
gyockey@tlu.edu
YOCOM, Amber .... 419-267-1317 366 G
ayocom@northweststate.edu
YOCOM, Jim .... 574-520-4806 160 F
jyocom@iusb.edu
YOCUM, Carrie, A .... 574-372-5100 158 B
yocumca@grace.edu
YOCUM, Jennifer .... 410-888-9048 205 D
jyocum@muih.edu
YODER, Amy .... 716-829-7625 307 B
yodera@dyc.edu
YODER, Brent .... 620-327-8207 178 B
brent.yoder@hesston.edu
YODER, Brooke .... 816-654-7103 261 D
byoder@kcumb.edu
YODER, Christine, R ..... 404-687-4520 118 B
yoderc@ctsnet.edu
YODER, Dan .... 541-440-4707 387 E
dan.yoder@umpqua.edu
YODER, David .... 916-348-4689.. 42 F
dyoder@epic.edu
YODER, James, A .... 508-289-2252 226 D
jyoder@whoi.edu
YODER, Jill .... 319-385-6246 170 J
jill.yoder@iw.edu
YODER, John .... 903-877-7443 469 A
john.yoder@uthct.edu
YODER, John-David ...... 419-772-2372 367 G
j-yoder@onu.edu
YODER, Joseph, S .... 570-326-3761 404 T
jyoder@pct.edu
YODER, Julie .... 301-387-3101 203 I
julie.yoder@garrettcollege.edu
YODER, Kathleen .... 574-535-7501 158 A
kathleeny@goshen.edu
YODER, Lane .... 931-393-1692 437 C
lyoder@mscc.edu
YODER, Mindy, J .... 260-399-7700 165 B
myoder@sf.edu
YODER, Norris .... 828-328-7145 339 C
norris.yoder@lr.edu
YODER, Robert, E .... 574-535-7244 158 A
robertey@goshen.edu
YODER, Twila, K .... 540-432-4100 480 A
twila.yoder@emu.edu
YOHE, Michael .... 863-667-5306 108 G
meyohe@seu.edu
YOHE, Roger .... 561-868-3147 105 A
yoher@palmbeachstate.edu
YOHNK LOCKWOOD,
Susan .... 715-682-4591 515 D
susan.lockwood@witc.edu

YOHO, Robert .... 515-271-1464 168 G
robert.yoho@dmu.edu
YOHO, Vicki .... 419-289-5031 356 L
vyoho@ashland.edu
YOIA, Dominic .... 203-582-5224.. 88 A
dominic.yoia@quinnipiac.edu
YOKOYAMA, Janis, K ... 213-738-6714.. 65 I
deansoffice@swlaw.edu
YOKUM, Dru .... 410-296-5350 202 I
YOLITZ, Brian, D .... 651-201-1777 243 I
brian.yolitz@so.mnscu.edu
YONAN, Glen .... 530-251-8815.. 47 J
gyonan@lassencollege.edu
YONEMITSU, Lori .... 206-546-4552 498 E
lyonemitsu@shoreline.edu
YONG, Henry .... 209-575-6508.. 75 H
yongh@yosemite.edu
YONG, Yanyan .... 540-834-1048 488 B
yyong@germanna.edu
YONKE, Eric .... 715-346-4224 511 F
eyonke@uwsp.edu
YONKE, Eric .... 715-346-3693 511 F
eyonke@uwsp.edu
YONKERS, Judy .... 716-338-1446 311 F
judyyonkers@mail.sunyjcc.edu
YONKERS, Molly, L .... 507-933-7588 242 D
myunkers@gustavus.edu
YONTZ, Anna .... 309-649-6230 152 G
anna.yontz@src.edu
YONTZ, Jennifer .... 231-591-3817 230 A
jenniferyontz@ferris.edu
YOO, David, K .... 310-825-6815.. 69 B
dkyoo@ucla.edu
YOO, Ellie .... 805-289-6182.. 73 C
jyoo@vcccd.edu
YOO, John .... 703-323-5690 491 E
YOON, Ho Sung .... 213-384-2318.. 50 D
YOON, Jong, S .... 714-533-3946.. 35 B
jsyoon@calums.edu
YOON, Mark .... 323-643-0301.. 25 K
dean@aeu.edu
YOON, Mary .... 213-384-2318.. 50 D
YOON, Michelle .... 562-926-1023.. 57 J
office@ptsa.edu
YOPP, Jan .... 919-966-4364 351 B
jan_yopp@unc.edu
YORK, Barry .... 412-731-6000 409 A
byork@rpts.edu
YORK, Brenda .... 406-994-2824 272 A
byork@montana.edu
YORK, Corey .... 914-251-6080 328 B
corey.york@purchase.edu
YORK, David .... 512-492-3032 442 J
dyork@aoma.edu
YORK, Jeanie .... 970-351-1931.. 83 F
jeanie.york@unco.edu
YORK, Nancy .... 502-272-8639 183 H
nyork@bellarmine.edu
YORK, Patrick, G .... 660-944-2920 258 G
pyork@conception.edu
YORK, Ronald, S .... 803-536-8438 423 G
ryork1@scsu.edu
YORK, Stan .... 912-681-5667 123 J
syork@ogeecheetech.edu
YORKE, Carla .... 562-860-2451.. 36 A
cyorke@cerritos.edu
YORKIN, Sheila .... 801-832-2685 474 E
syorkin@westminstercollege.edu
YORTSOS, Yannis, C ..... 213-740-0617.. 72 B
yortsos@usc.edu
YOSHIKAWA, Naoto .... 808-983-4100 129 D
YOSHIMI, Garret, T .... 808-956-3501 129 H
gyoshimi@hawaii.edu
YOSHIMORI-YAMAMOTO,
Denise .... 808-956-0864 130 B
dfyoshim@hawaii.edu
YOSHIMURA, Gregg ...... 808-455-0607 130 G
greggy@hawaii.edu
YOSHIMURA, Nancy ..... 949-480-4045.. 64 D
nyoshimura@soka.edu
YOSHINAGA, Darcie, S . 808-956-8259 129 H
dsy@hawaii.edu
YOSHINO, Lori .... 909-621-8856.. 57 C
lori_yoshino@pitzer.edu
YOSHIOKA, Marianne ... 413-585-7977 224 F
myoshioka@smith.edu
YOST, Russ .... 503-370-6280 388 D
ryost@willamette.edu
YOUATT, June, P .... 517-355-6550 233 G
youatt@msu.edu
YOUGH, Kelly .... 845-569-3184 316 B
kelly.yough@msmc.edu
YOUHOUSE, John .... 610-558-5518 402 G
youhousj@neumann.edu
YOUKEY, Jerry, R .... 864-455-7992 424 I
youkey@mailbox.sc.edu
YOUKEY, Jerry, R .... 864-455-7992 425 E
youkey@greenvillemed.sc.edu

YOUMANS, Karen .... 405-208-5680 377 D
kdyoumans@okcu.edu
YOUNCE, Thomas .... 336-770-3349 352 B
youncet@uncsa.edu
YOUNG, Aaron .... 505-984-6140 295 K
aaron.young@sjc.edu
YOUNG, Alissa .... 270-707-3711 186 B
YOUNG, Amber .... 256-824-6604.... 8 C
amber.young@uah.edu
YOUNG, Andrea .... 213-356-5371.. 65 A
andrea_young@sciarc.edu
YOUNG, Andrew .... 256-726-8333.... 6 E
ayoung@oakwood.edu
YOUNG, Andrew .... 812-888-4323 165 E
ayoung@vinu.edu
YOUNG, Angela .... 323-343-2810.. 32 D
ayoung3@calstatela.edu
YOUNG, Ann, S .... 859-238-5480 184 C
ann.young@centre.edu
YOUNG, Barbara .... 626-966-4576.. 25 M
barbara@jamagency.com
YOUNG, Barbara .... 662-562-3202 255 C
ba_young@northwestms.edu
YOUNG, Beth .... 815-921-4445 150 A
b.young@rockvalleycollege.edu
YOUNG, Betsy .... 760-636-7959.. 39 D
byoung@alumni.collegeofthedesert.edu
YOUNG, Betty .... 478-553-2090 123 H
byoung@oftc.edu
YOUNG, Betty .... 740-753-3591 362 K
youngb@hocking.edu
YOUNG, Bill .... 316-323-6363 175 I
wyoung@butlercc.edu
YOUNG, Brandon .... 217-540-3512 143 B
byoung17159@lakeland.cc.il.us
YOUNG, Brandon, L ...... 386-226-7245.. 98 C
youngbr@erau.edu
YOUNG, Brian .... 719-389-6971.. 77 J
byoung@coloradocollege.edu
YOUNG, C. Bryan .... 785-864-4225 181 I
cbyoung@ku.edu
YOUNG, Carole .... 651-638-6316 240 J
youcar@bethel.edu
YOUNG, Cathy .... 617-536-6340 212 B
cyoung@berklee.edu
YOUNG, Charles .... 203-596-4604.. 87 H
cyoung@post.edu
YOUNG, Charles .... 336-334-4822 343 E
hcyoung@gtcc.edu
YOUNG, Cheryl .... 409-933-8232 446 H
cyoung@com.edu
YOUNG, Cheryl, D .... 513-529-8600 365 I
youngcd@miamioh.edu
YOUNG, Chris .... 765-677-2106 161 C
chris.young@indwes.edu
YOUNG, Christopher ..... 219-980-6563 160 C
cjy@iun.edu
YOUNG, Cindy .... 805-969-3626.. 55 G
cyoung@pacifica.edu
YOUNG, Clifton .... 804-862-6100 484 F
cyoung@rbc.edu
YOUNG, Colletta .... 541-956-7296 386 G
cyoung@roguecc.edu
YOUNG, Connie .... 217-709-0931 143 C
cyoung@lakeviewcol.edu
YOUNG, Corey, D .... 601-877-4063 251 G
cyoung1@alcorn.edu
YOUNG, Cynthia, Y .... 407-823-4376 110 C
cynthia.young@ucf.edu
YOUNG, Dale .... 478-445-5497 119 E
dale.young@gcsu.edu
YOUNG, Dan .... 219-473-4292 157 A
dyoung1@ccsj.edu
YOUNG, Dana .... 541-881-5580 387 D
dyoung@tvcc.cc
YOUNG, Danielle .... 440-775-8692 367 B
danielle.young@oberlin.edu
YOUNG, Darlene, P .... 812-941-2306 161 A
dyoung01@ius.edu
YOUNG, David .... 405-974-2490 380 J
dyoung28@uco.edu
YOUNG, Debbie .... 559-278-2381.. 32 A
dyoung@csufresno.edu
YOUNG, Derek, M .... 240-895-4207 206 G
dmyoung@smcm.edu
YOUNG, Donald, B .... 808-956-7703 129 J
young@hawaii.edu
YOUNG, Donna .... 480-423-6300.. 14 C
donna.young@scottsdalecc.edu
YOUNG, Eldon .... 714-484-7177.. 53 M
eyoung@cypresscollege.edu
YOUNG, Elisabeth, H .... 330-325-6311 366 F
eyoung1@neomed.edu
YOUNG, Frank .... 801-863-7202 473 D
frank.young@uvu.edu
YOUNG, Gail, B .... 773-298-3301 151 C
young@sxu.edu

YOUNG, Garland .... 423-461-8720 435 A
rgyoung@milligan.edu
YOUNG, Gary .... 312-949-7610 140 A
gyoung@ico.edu
YOUNG, Gerald .... 507-222-4057 241 C
gyoung@carleton.edu
YOUNG, Grace .... 978-556-3449 220 F
gyoung@necc.mass.edu
YOUNG, Greg .... 606-337-1072 184 D
greg.young@ccbbc.edu
YOUNG, Gretchen .... 508-286-4950 225 G
young_gretchen@wheatoncollege.edu
YOUNG, Gwendolyn ...... 719-549-2602.. 78 P
gwen.young@csupueblo.edu
YOUNG, Heather, M ...... 916-734-4745.. 68 H
heather.young@ucdmc.ucdavis.edu
YOUNG, Henry .... 401-739-5000 416 D
hyoung@neit.edu
YOUNG, J.R .... 412-536-1100 398 E
jr.young@laroche.edu
YOUNG, Jason .... 810-766-4109 227 F
YOUNG, Jeff .... 931-372-3311 438 F
jyoung@tntech.edu
YOUNG, Jessica .... 704-290-5261 346 F
YOUNG, Jill .... 570-389-4950 405 E
jyoung@bloomu.edu
YOUNG, Joanne .... 603-888-1311 281 I
YOUNG, John .... 973-328-5026 285 B
jyoung@ccm.edu
YOUNG, John .... 315-781-3748 310 C
jyoung@hws.edu
YOUNG, John .... 303-360-4707.. 79 C
john.young@ccaurora.edu
YOUNG, John .... 937-327-7800 374 A
jyoung@wittenberg.edu
YOUNG, John, O .... 248-370-2946 235 J
joyoung@oakland.edu
YOUNG, Johnny, W .... 757-683-3442 483 G
jwyoung@odu.edu
YOUNG, Jon .... 910-672-1460 350 B
jyoung@uncfsu.edu
YOUNG, Julian, M .... 843-661-1228 421 H
jyoung@fmarion.edu
YOUNG, Kalbert, K .... 808-956-8903 129 H
kalbert@hawaii.edu
YOUNG, Kathryn .... 501-683-7302.. 22 B
kcyoung@ualr.edu
YOUNG, Kay, F .... 508-213-2114 223 C
kay.young@nichols.edu
YOUNG, Ken .... 516-323-4501 315 J
kyoung@molloy.edu
YOUNG, Kerry, A .... 315-786-2279 311 H
kyoung@sunyjefferson.edu
YOUNG, Kim .... 760-252-2411.. 27 A
kyoung@barstow.edu
YOUNG, Kirk .... 716-338-1023 311 F
kirkyoung@mail.sunyjcc.edu
YOUNG, Kristen .... 702-895-0143 279 D
kristen.young@unlv.edu
YOUNG, Kristine .... 775-881-7509 280 C
kyoung@sierranevada.edu
YOUNG, Kristine, M .... 845-341-4700 319 H
president@sunyorange.edu
YOUNG, Lakisha .... 312-341-3530 150 D
lyoung@roosevelt.edu
YOUNG, Lauren .... 716-888-2436 300 G
youngb@canisius.edu
YOUNG, Lavern .... 312-949-7430 140 A
lyoung@ico.edu
YOUNG, Lee .... 903-886-5101 459 E
lee.young@tamuc.edu
YOUNG, Lenna .... 864-250-8185 421 K
lenna.young@gvltec.edu
YOUNG, Lily, Y .... 848-932-7821 290 C
lily.young@rutgers.edu
YOUNG, Linda, C .... 334-556-2234.... 2 B
lyoung@wallace.edu
YOUNG, Linda, K .... 715-836-5287 510 D
younglk@uwec.edu
YOUNG, Lisa .... 580-559-5713 375 I
lyoung@ecok.edu
YOUNG, Luria .... 225-771-4582 195 K
luria_young@subr.edu
YOUNG, Luria .... 225-771-4582 195 J
luria_young@subr.edu
YOUNG, Luria .... 225-771-3922 195 J
luria_young@subr.edu
YOUNG, Margaret, A ..... 940-898-2015 464 A
myoung13@twu.edu
YOUNG, Marie .... 814-472-3022 409 G
myoung@francis.edu
YOUNG, Marissa .... 951-552-8762.. 28 G
myoung@calbaptist.edu
YOUNG, Mark .... 406-994-5158 272 A
myoung@montana.edu
YOUNG, Mark, S .... 303-762-6902.. 79 G
president@denverseminary.edu

YOUNG, Mary .... 713-313-7733 461 E
mary.young@tsu.edu
YOUNG, Mary, E .... 903-823-3369 458 D
maryellen.young@texarkanacollege.edu
YOUNG, MaryAnne .... 941-487-4801 110 B
myoung@ncf.edu
YOUNG, Meghan .... 301-369-2800 202 J
myoung@captechu.edu
YOUNG, Michael .... 508-531-1295 217 D
myoung@bridgew.edu
YOUNG, Michael .... 707-664-2838.. 35 A
YOUNG, Michael, E .... 270-809-6831 188 D
myoung@murraystate.edu
YOUNG, Michael, K .... 979-845-2217 459 C
president@tamu.edu
YOUNG, Michael, W ...... 212-327-8000 321 E
michael.young@rockefeller.edu
YOUNG, Michaela, J ...... 315-386-7204 329 A
youngm@canton.edu
YOUNG, Michelle, L ...... 315-268-4268 304 B
myoung@clarkson.edu
YOUNG, Misty .... 573-681-5580 261 H
youngm@lincolnu.edu
YOUNG, Monica .... 336-334-4822 343 E
mwyoung@gtcc.edu
YOUNG, Myriam .... 219-980-6548 160 C
myyoung@iun.edu
YOUNG, Nancy .... 410-455-2393 208 A
nyoung@umbc.edu
YOUNG, Nancy .... 816-960-2008 258 D
newstudents@cityvision.edu
YOUNG, Nicole .... 731-989-6768 432 C
nyoung@fhu.edu
YOUNG, Nina .... 956-665-3670 468 A
nina.young@utrgv.edu
YOUNG, Norman .... 860-768-7819.. 89 C
young@hartford.edu
YOUNG, Octavia .... 202-885-8694.. 94 C
oyoung@wesleyseminary.edu
YOUNG, Patricia .... 707-864-7124.. 64 E
patricia.young@solano.edu
YOUNG, Paul, R .... 307-674-6446 516 P
pyoung@sheridan.edu
YOUNG, Peter, C .... 240-684-5268 208 D
pete.young@umuc.edu
YOUNG, Randy .... 660-359-3948 264 H
ryoung@mail.ncmissouri.edu
YOUNG, Remmele .... 713-718-7742 450 D
remmele.young@hccs.edu
YOUNG, Rena .... 270-707-3732 186 B
rena.young@kctcs.edu
YOUNG, Rhett .... 740-284-5007 361 L
ryoung@franciscan.edu
YOUNG, Richard .... 207-581-1700 201 B
ryoung@maine.edu
YOUNG, Robert .... 410-386-8261 203 A
ryoung@carrollcc.edu
YOUNG, Robert .... 501-370-5365.. 21 A
ryoung@philander.edu
YOUNG, Robert .... 423-236-2805 436 C
ryoung@southern.edu
YOUNG, Robert .... 540-453-2500 487 G
youngb@brcc.edu
YOUNG, Rodney .... 630-617-6137 138 C
rodney.young@elmhurst.edu
YOUNG, Rodney .... 808-375-5057 131 A
ryoung98@hotmail.com
YOUNG, S. Michelle ...... 803-376-6025 418 D
myoung2@allenuniversity.edu
YOUNG, Samuel .... 213-413-9500.. 65 E
samuel@scusoma.edu
YOUNG, Samuel .... 714-449-7481.. 51 A
syoung@ketchum.edu
YOUNG, Sandra .... 610-989-1456 413 I
syoung@vfmac.edu
YOUNG, Sarah .... 309-457-2300 146 A
syoung@monmouthcollege.edu
YOUNG, Sarah, M .... 716-878-4631 326 E
youngsm@buffalostate.edu
YOUNG, Scott .... 816-235-1154 268 D
youngsc@umkc.edu
YOUNG, Scott .... 360-650-2593 500 E
scott.young@wwu.edu
YOUNG, Sean, B .... 262-243-5700 507 C
sean.young@cuw.edu
YOUNG, Shawna .... 209-667-3203.. 33 F
syoung@csustan.edu
YOUNG, Sheri .... 401-598-1872 416 C
syoung@jwu.edu
YOUNG, Sherry .... 501-812-2724.. 23 C
sdyoung@pulaskitech.edu
YOUNG, Stacie, G .... 704-687-7203 351 C
sgyoung@uncc.edu
YOUNG, Stephen, W ...... 513-732-5318 371 G
steve.young@uc.edu
YOUNG, Steve .... 850-718-2203.. 96 H
youngs@chipola.edu

Z

ZANT, Don .... 662-325-2231 254 E
dzant@budgetplan.msstate.edu
ZANTINGH, Ryan .... 708-239-4872 153 B
ryan.zantingh@trnty.edu
ZAPATA, Elizabeth .... 585-389-2461 316 D
ezapata5@naz.edu
ZAPATA, Fred .... 210-999-7401 464 B
fred.zapata@trinity.edu
ZAPATA, Grace .... 210-486-2269 441 I
zapata@alamo.edu
ZAPATA, Hector .... 225-578-8242 193 M
hozapat@lsu.edu
ZAPATA, Jesse, T .... 210-458-2700 468 B
jesse.zapata@utsa.edu
ZAPATA, Rafael, A .... 401-865-2878 416 E
rzapata@providence.edu
ZAPOLSKI, Mike .... 309-794-7223 133 G
mikezapolski@augustana.edu
ZAPPA, Carl, R .... 412-578-8861 391 G
crzappa@carlow.edu
ZAPPALORTI, Robert, E . 203-287-3028.. 87 G
paier.admin@snet.net
ZAPPAS, Barbara .... 831-582-3908.. 33 A
bzappas@csumb.edu
ZAPPASODI, Tony .... 903-233-4426 452 A
tonyzappasodi@letu.edu
ZAPPE, Christopher ...... 717-337-6820 396 A
czappe@gettysburg.edu
ZAPPI, Mark, E .... 337-482-6685 197 F
zappi@louisiana.edu
ZAPPIA, Charles .... 619-388-2801.. 60 D
czappia@sdccd.edu
ZAPPIA, Gerard .... 585-389-2570 316 D
gzappia4@naz.edu
ZAPRUDER, Matthew .... 925-631-8131.. 59 C
mjz4@stmarys-ca.edu
ZARAGOZA, Federico .... 210-485-0015 441 E
fzaragoza@alamo.edu
ZARATE, Alfonso .... 913-288-7489 178 H
azarate@kckcc.edu
ZARATE, Maricelda .... 361-593-2710 460 B
maricelda.zarate@tamuk.edu
ZARBO, Joel .... 310-377-5501.. 51 B
jzarbo@marymountcalifornia.edu
ZARCHI, Shloime .... 718-434-0784 300 K
ZAREMBA, Terah .... 269-965-3931 232 A
zarembat@kellogg.edu
ZAREMSKI, Robin, D ..... 717-871-7026 407 A
robin.zaremski@millersville.edu
ZARET, David .... 812-855-5021 159 G
zaret@iu.edu
ZARET, David .... 812-855-5021 159 H
ovpia@iu.edu
ZARFAS, Ellen .... 503-375-7006 383 A
ezarfas@corban.edu
ZARGAR, Fataneh .... 562-622-3368.. 44 F
ZARGES, Bradford .... 617-745-3638 214 D
bradford.zarges@enc.edu
ZARKOS, Thomas .... 917-493-4463 313 M
tzarkos@msmnyc.edu
ZARKOWSKI, Pamela .... 313-993-1585 237 F
zarkowp1@udmercy.edu
ZARLING, Mark, G .... 507-354-8221 243 C
zarlinmg@mlc-wels.edu
ZAROBE, Michael .... 312-662-4033 133 A
mzarobe@adler.edu
ZARRILLO, Deirdre .... 518-292-1704 321 G
zarrid@sage.edu
ZARRINNAM, Ali, R ...... 608-246-6446 514 A
azarrinnam@madisoncollege.edu
ZART, Leilani .... 319-352-8565 174 C
leilani.zart@wartburg.edu
ZARTNER, Ken .... 432-335-6606 454 C
kzartner@odessa.edu
ZASTOUPIL, Brenda ...... 701-328-2906 353 F
brenda.zastoupil@ndus.edu
ZATAR, Wael .... 304-696-6043 504 C
zatar@marshall.edu
ZATZ, Marjorie .... 209-228-4723.. 69 C
mzatz@ucmerced.edu
ZAUFT, Richard .... 617-349-8001 216 D
richard.zauft@lesley.edu
ZAUHAR, Frances, M .... 570-348-6233 401 B
zauhar@marywood.edu
ZAUSCH, Jo .... 502-213-7816 186 C
jo.zausch@kctcs.edu
ZAVADA, Michael .... 432-552-2220 469 D
ZAVADA, Robert .... 570-674-8018 401 M
rzavada@misericordia.edu
ZAVADSKY, Cornelia ..... 610-604-7700.. 93 B
ZAVALA-ACEVEZ,
Elizabeth .... 657-278-2030.. 32 B
ezavala-acevez@fullerton.edu
ZAVALA-COLÓN,
Maria de los Angeles . 787-993-8877 527 G
maria.zavala1@upr.edu

ZAVALA-PETHERBRIDGE,
Dina .... 701-788-4650 354 B
dina.petherbridge@mayvillestate.edu
ZAVALA-QUIÑONES,
Javier .... 787-993-8854 527 G
javier.zavala@upr.edu
ZAVARICH, Joyce .... 610-519-4080 413 K
joyce.zavarich@villanova.edu
ZAVATKAY, Debra .... 860-738-6309.. 86 C
dzavatkay@nwcc.edu
ZAVODNY, John .... 207-509-7122 200 I
jzavodny@unity.edu
ZAWIA, Nasser, H .... 401-874-5909 417 E
nzawia@uri.edu
ZAWODNY, Laurel, E .... 419-372-2211 357 F
lzawodn@bgsu.edu
ZAWOYSKY, Steve .... 360-676-2772 496 C
szawoysky@nwic.edu
ZAYAC, Lynn .... 413-572-8142 218 F
lzayac@westfield.ma.edu
ZAYAITZ, Anne .... 610-683-4155 406 D
zayaitz@kutztown.edu
ZAYAS, Brendaliz .... 787-258-1501 521 K
bzayas@columbiacentral.edu
ZAYAS, David .... 787-841-2000 525 J
dzayaz@pucpr.edu
ZAYAS, JR., Gerardo ..... 413-755-5419 221 B
gzayas@stcc.edu
ZAYAS, Luis, H .... 512-471-1937 467 C
lzayas@austin.utexas.edu
ZAYAS, Myriam .... 787-841-2000 525 J
mzayas@pucpr.edu
ZAYAS, Niza .... 787-786-3030 526 F
nzayas@ucb.edu.pr
ZAYAS-HERNANDEZ,
Haydee, M .... 787-480-2385 521 J
hzayas@sanjuanciudadpatria.com
ZAZUETA, Fedro, S .... 352-392-0371 110 D
fsz@ufl.edu
ZAZZALI, Robert .... 856-256-4110 289 H
zazzali@rowan.edu
ZAZZO, Paul .... 215-368-5000 389 H
pzazzo@biblical.edu
ZDANCEWICZ, Heather .. 512-404-4816 443 I
hzdancewicz@austinseminary.edu
ZDATNY, Sophie .... 802-224-3000 476 H
sophie.zdatny@vsc.edu
ZDZIARSKI, Gene .... 312-362-8854 137 C
ezdziars@depaul.edu
ZEBALLOS, Jorge .... 269-965-3931 232 A
zeballosj@kellogg.edu
ZEBEDIS, Frank, J .... 803-323-3333 426 H
zebedisf@winthrop.edu
ZEBROWSKI,
Michael, J .... 414-288-7172 508 C
michael.zebrowski@marquette.edu
ZECH, Susan .... 212-686-9244 298 C
ZECHMAN, Jennifer .... 717-564-4112 390 A
jennifer.riordan@brightwood.edu
ZECK, Sharon .... 309-438-3481 140 L
sszeck@ilstu.edu
ZECKOVICH, Kim .... 906-932-4231 230 D
kimz@gogebic.edu
ZEDNICK, Yukari .... 425-352-8413 492 K
yzednick@cascadia.edu
ZEEK, Raymond .... 203-285-2210.. 85 E
rzeek@gwcc.commnet.edu
ZEFF, Ira, A .... 402-465-2360 276 E
izeff@nebrwesleyan.edu
ZEFF, Jane .... 973-720-2379 292 I
zeffj@wpunj.edu
ZEGARSKI, Len .... 619-684-8790.. 53 J
lzegarski@newschoolarch.edu
ZEGER, Brian .... 212-799-5000 312 B
ZEGLEN, Marie .... 352-392-0456 110 D
zeglenm@ufl.edu
ZEH, David .... 775-784-1110 279 E
zehd@unr.edu
ZEHEL, Renee, G .... 570-961-4715 401 B
rzehel@marywood.edu
ZEHNDER, Sarah, B ...... 785-227-3380 175 E
zehndersb@bethanylb.edu
ZEHR, David .... 603-535-2235 283 B
zehr@plymouth.edu
ZEHREN, Carolyn, F ...... 218-477-2085 246 B
zehren@mnstate.edu
ZEICH, Heidi, E .... 202-319-5615.. 91 D
zeich@cua.edu
ZEICHNER, Veronica ..... 201-360-4043 286 E
vzeichner@hccc.edu
ZEIDENSTEIN, Darrow ... 713-348-6090 455 F
darrowz@rice.edu
ZEIDNER, Lewis, P .... 651-255-6104 250 D
lzeidner@unitedseminary.edu
ZEIFANG, Kathleen .... 202-884-9705.. 93 C
zeifangk@trinitydc.edu
ZEIGER, Erin .... 253-680-7000 492 F
ezeiger@bates.ctc.edu

ZEIGER, Judy .... 507-389-7351 247 H
judy.zeiger@southcentral.edu
ZEIGLER, Helen, T .... 803-777-5432 424 I
helenz@mailbox.sc.edu
ZEIGLER, Keri .... 904-256-7551 102 B
kschult5@ju.edu
ZEIGLER, Letherio .... 229-732-5958 115 B
letheriozeigler@andrewcollege.edu
ZEIGLER, Michael .... 803-535-5340 419 E
mike.zeigler@claflin.edu
ZEIGLER, Michael, C .... 717-867-6060 399 J
zeigler@lvc.edu
ZEIGLER, Sara .... 859-622-2222 184 F
sara.zeigler@eku.edu
ZEILBERGER, Yeruchom 845-207-0330 298 F
ZEILE, Carol .... 989-463-7227 226 H
zeile@alma.edu
ZEILENGA, Jeffrey .... 573-882-5397 268 C
zeilingaj@missouri.edu
ZEIMANTZ, Erich .... 414-930-3527 509 B
zeimante@mtmary.edu
ZEIMET, Dan, L .... 563-333-6202 173 A
zeimetdaniell@sau.edu
ZEIND, Caroline .... 508-373-5825 221 E
caroline.zeind@mcphs.edu
ZEIRD, Susan .... 706-233-7466 125 E
szeird@shorter.edu
ZEISER, Richard, A .... 860-768-4181.. 89 C
zeiser@hartford.edu
ZEISS, Timothy .... 732-224-2887 284 B
tzeiss@brookdalecc.edu
ZEITHAML, Carl, P .... 434-924-3176 486 H
cpz6n@virginia.edu
ZEITLOW, Terry .... 903-233-3835 452 A
terryzeitlow@letu.edu
ZELASKO, Sandra .... 360-538-4000 495 B
szelasko@ghc.edu
ZELDNER, Cynthia .... 860-512-3214.. 85 G
czeldner@manchestercc.edu
ZELENAK, Christine .... 609-896-5395 289 E
czelenak@rider.edu
ZELENSKI, Paul .... 517-371-5140 239 F
zelensp@cooley.edu
ZELENZ, Margot .... 715-682-1495 509 D
mzelenz@northland.edu
ZELESNIK, Kelly .... 440-366-7028 364 F
ZELEZNY, Lynnette .... 559-278-2636.. 32 A
lynnette@csufresno.edu
ZELINSKI, Bob .... 352-854-2322.. 97 C
zelinskb@cf.edu
ZELINSKI, Debbie .... 312-329-4231 146 B
debbie.zelinski@moody.edu
ZELL, Jennifer .... 845-687-5049 331 L
zellj@sunyulster.edu
ZELLAR, Nel .... 507-433-0832 247 C
nel.zellar@riverland.edu
ZELLER, John, H .... 215-898-5169 412 G
jzeller@upenn.edu
ZELLERS, Andrew .... 270-831-9627 186 A
andrew.zellers@kctcs.edu
ZELLERS, Victoria .... 215-751-8913 393 A
vzellers@ccp.edu
ZELLES, Peter, A .... 651-962-6780 251 D
pazelles@stthomas.edu
ZELLMER, Jill, A .... 617-627-3298 225 A
jill.zellmer@tufts.edu
ZELLNER, Wayne .... 719-632-8116.. 80 K
wzellner@intelliteccollege.edu
ZELNICK, Debra .... 215-503-9606 411 E
debra.zelnick@jefferson.edu
ZELTWANGER, Todd .... 574-936-8898 155 L
todd.zeltwanger@ancilla.edu
ZEMAN, Ellen .... 802-651-5912 474 G
zeman@champlain.edu
ZEMAN, Janice, L .... 757-221-3877 479 I
jlzema@wm.edu
ZEMAN, Mary Beth .... 973-720-2971 292 I
zemanm@wpunj.edu
ZEMBAR, Mary Jo .... 937-327-7921 374 A
mzembar@wittenberg.edu
ZEMBRODT, Belle .... 859-572-5634 188 E
zembrodt@nku.edu
ZEMP, William .... 603-644-3179 282 C
w.zemp@snhu.edu
ZENDMAN, Ellen .... 914-606-6733 333 H
ellen.zendman@sunywcc.edu
ZENELIS, John, G .... 703-993-2491 481 B
jzenelis@gmu.edu
ZENGER, Sheahon .... 785-864-3143 181 I
kuathletics@ku.edu
ZENGER-BENEDA,
Nancy .... 785-243-1435 176 I
ZENK, Leslie .... 704-687-5766 351 C
lzenk@uncc.edu
ZENO, Mark .... 419-448-2058 362 G
mzeno@heidelberg.edu
ZENTENO, Liz .... 432-685-4507 453 B
lzenteno@midland.edu

ZENTENO, Rene .... 210-458-4994 468 B
rene.zenteno@utsa.edu
ZENTMEYER, James, R . 248-370-3570 235 J
zentmeye@oakland.edu
ZENTNER, Aeron .... 714-241-6413.. 38 F
azentner@coastline.edu
ZEONE, Alicia .... 507-280-3509 247 D
alicia.zeone@rctc.edu
ZEPEDA, Andrea .... 918-335-6833 378 F
azepeda@okwu.edu
ZEPEDA, Milani .... 408-855-5123.. 74 C
milani.zepeda@missioncollege.edu
ZEPHIER, Jessica .... 605-867-5856 427 I
jzephier@olc.edu
ZEPPOS, Nicholas .... 615-322-1813 440 D
nick.zeppos@vanderbilt.edu
ZERAI, Assata .... 217-244-9157 154 B
azerai@illinois.edu
ZERANGUE, David .... 985-448-4090 197 C
david.zerangue@nicholls.edu
ZERBE, Bryan .... 415-565-4623.. 68 I
zerbeb@uchastings.edu
ZERBE, Linda .... 610-282-1100 393 G
linda.zerbe@desales.edu
ZERILLO, Barbara .... 617-236-8838 215 B
bzerillo@fisher.edu
ZERNICK, Christine .... 814-262-6462 405 A
czernick@pennhighlands.edu
ZEROSIMO, Veronica ...... 201-360-4198 286 E
vzerosimo@hccc.edu
ZERTUCHE, Bernie .... 210-486-4879 441 G
zertuche@alamo.edu
ZERTUCHE, Ramon .... 210-434-6711 454 D
rzertuche@lake.ollusa.edu
ZERZAN, Phil .... 503-725-4782 386 D
pzerzan@pdx.edu
ZESWITZ, John .... 717-560-8278 399 D
jzeswitz@lbc.edu
ZETTLER, Chuck, H .... 561-868-3033 105 A
zettlerc@palmbeachstate.edu
ZEWE, Beth .... 814-732-1420 406 B
zewe@edinboro.edu
ZEYNEP LEUENBERGER,
Deniz .... 508-531-6125 217 D
dleuenberger@bridgew.edu
ZHADKO, Olena .... 718-960-1172 302 C
olena.zhadko@lehman.cuny.edu
ZHAI, Lijuan .... 559-489-2224.. 66 G
lijuan.zhai@fresnocitycollege.edu
ZHAN, Lin .... 901-678-2020 439 E
lzhan@memphis.edu
ZHANG, Chunsheng .... 256-765-4898.... 9 A
czhang@una.edu
ZHANG, James .... 810-762-7949 232 C
jzhang@kettering.edu
ZHANG, Jane .... 510-763-7787.. 24 D
jmzhang@acchs.edu
ZHANG, Jiajie, W .... 713-500-3922 468 D
jiajie.zhang@uth.tmc.edu
ZHANG, Li .... 530-754-8924.. 68 H
lizhang@ucdavis.edu
ZHANG, Ling .... 408-260-0208.. 43 B
sjadmin@fivebranches.edu
ZHANG, Ling .... 408-260-0208.. 43 C
sjadmin@fivebranches.edu
ZHANG, Lujia .... 732-548-6000 287 B
lzhang@middlesexcc.edu
ZHANG, Ming .... 360-650-4454 500 E
ming.zhang@wwu.edu
ZHANG, Robert .... 412-365-1292 392 C
rzhang@chatham.edu
ZHANG, Sha Li .... 406-243-6800 271 G
shali.zhang@umontana.edu
ZHANG, Shouhong .... 605-688-6312 429 B
shouhong.zhang@sdstate.edu
ZHANG, Wenxian .... 407-646-2231 106 J
wzhang@rollins.edu
ZHANG, William, B .... 336-334-5559 351 D
wbzhang@uncg.edu
ZHANG, Xiao, Y .... 716-673-4806 325 C
xiao.zhang@fredonia.edu
ZHANG, Yang .... 808-956-5877 129 J
yz6@hawaii.edu
ZHANG, Zuan .... 802-224-3000 476 H
zuan.zhang@vsc.edu
ZHAO, Joanna .... 408-260-0208.. 43 B
dean@fivebranches.edu
ZHAO, Joanna .... 831-476-9424.. 43 C
dean@fivebranches.edu
ZHAO, Jun .... 708-534-8046 138 H
jzhao@govst.edu
ZHAO, Lianna .... 949-451-5450.. 64 I
lzhao@ivc.edu
ZHAO, Lincoln, Z .... 407-888-8689.. 99 F
lzhao@fcim.edu
ZHAO, Yiping .... 516-739-1545 317 D
clinicmanager@nyctcm.edu

ZU, Jean .... 201-216-5260 291 G
jean.zu@stevens.edu
ZUBATY, Ron .... 724-222-5330 403 E
rzubaty@penncommercial.edu
ZUBER, Kishan .... 315-364-3264 333 G
kzuber@wells.edu
ZUBER, Lauren, A .... 260-422-5561 159 D
lazuber@indianatech.edu
ZUBER, Maria, T .... 617-253-3206 221 C
ZUBERBUELER, OP,
Mary Anne .... 615-297-7545 429 H
srmanne@aquinascollege.edu
ZUBIATE, Jyl .... 309-467-6322 138 E
jzubiate@eureka.edu
ZUBIZARRETA, John ..... 803-786-3014 420 D
jzubizarreta@columbiasc.edu
ZUBROD, Nancy .... 712-279-4961 173 B
nancy.zubrod@stlukescollege.edu
ZUCALLA, Fred, P .... 315-733-2307 332 F
fzucalla@uscny.edu
ZUCCARELLO, Patty .... 815-280-2239 142 A
pzuccare@jjc.edu
ZUCCARINI, Molly, M ... 617-732-1679 214 F
zuccarinim@emmanuel.edu
ZUCCO, Lisa .... 309-341-5213 134 H
lzucco@sandburg.edu
ZUCCOLA, Jen .... 612-874-3626 243 F
jzuccola@mcad.edu
ZUCK, Laura .... 810-766-4211 227 E
ZUCKER, Avraham .... 718-382-8702 334 F
ZUCKER, Nicole, M .... 215-572-2103 389 D
zuckern@arcadia.edu
ZUCKERMAN, Brian ...... 215-780-1281 410 D
ZUCKERMAN-AVILES,
Stephanie, B .... 716-878-5811 326 E
zuckersb@buffalostate.edu
ZUCKSWORTH, Eli .... 405-262-2552 379 B
eli.zucksworth@redlandscc.edu
ZUDEKOFF, Rosanne ..... 203-773-8502.. 84 G
zudekoff@albertus.edu
ZUERCHER, Makenzie ... 559-251-4215.. 28 I
registrar@calchristiancollege.edu
ZUERN, Glenn .... 504-468-2900 196 C
drzuern@southwest.edu
ZUGATES, Debra, A .... 412-396-5211 394 D
zugates@duq.edu
ZUHLKE, James .... 610-436-3316 407 D
jzuhlke@wcupa.edu
ZUICHES, Carol .... 802-656-1435 476 E
carol.zuiches@uvm.edu
ZUIDEMA, Leah .... 712-722-6328 168 I
leah.zuidema@dordt.edu
ZUILL, Karen .... 607-431-4303 309 E
zuillk@hartwick.edu
ZUKER, R. Fred .... 972-438-6932 454 G
fzuker@parker.edu
ZUKOR, Tevya .... 540-654-1053 486 D
tzukor@umw.edu
ZUKOSKI, Charles, F .... 716-645-2992 325 B
provost@buffalo.edu
ZULUAGA, Hoober .... 516-918-3679 299 M
hzuluaga@bcl.edu
ZUMBACH, Deborah, J . 319-335-3815 166 G
deborah-zumbach@uiowa.edu
ZUMBRUN, Christina .... 260-665-4242 164 E
zumbrunc@trine.edu
ZUMERCHIK, Jim .... 708-534-4515 138 H
jzumerchik@govst.edu
ZUMWALT, Debra, L ..... 650-723-6397.. 66 C
zumwalt@stanford.edu
ZUMWALT, Jeff .... 505-277-6644 296 H
jzumwalt@unm.edu
ZUNIGA, Donna, P .... 936-291-0447 451 I
dzuniga@lee.edu
ZUNIGA, Isaac .... 773-602-5499 135 L
izuniga2@ccc.edu
ZUNIGA, Leo .... 210-485-0035 441 E
lzuniga@alamo.edu
ZUPAN, Kathy .... 703-993-4201 481 B
kzupan@gmu.edu
ZUPAN, Mark, A .... 607-871-2101 298 A
zupan@alfred.edu
ZUPANCIC, Paris .... 954-969-9771.. 99 I
pzupancic@fcnh.com
ZUPANCICH, Patti .... 218-235-2169 248 B
p.zupancich@vcc.edu
ZURAWSKI, Ray .... 920-403-3964 509 J
ray.zurawski@snc.edu
ZURAWSKI, Sandra .... 708-534-4981 138 H
szurawski@govst.edu
ZUREK, Ronald, M .... 775-784-4031 279 E
zurek@unr.edu
ZURES, Allison .... 773-907-4738 135 K
azures@ccc.edu
ZURK, Lisa .... 503-725-2213 386 D
zurkl@pdx.edu
ZURN, Sue .... 218-299-6515 245 H
sue.zurn@minnesota.edu
ZUROMSKI, Steven .... 508-531-2396 217 D
steven.zuromski@bridgew.edu
ZUST, Jeffery .... 202-685-3903 518 B
jeffrey.zust@ndu.edu
ZUVERINK, Melanie ...... 602-275-7133.. 16 A
melanie.zuverink@rsaiz.edu
ZUZACK, Judith, A .... 724-287-8711 390 J
judith.zuzack@bc3.edu
ZUZARTE, Lisa .... 661-654-2011.. 31 B
lzuzarte@csub.edu
ZUZEVICH, Theresa .... 661-362-3644.. 39 C
theresa.zuzevich@canyons.edu
ZUZOLO, Renee .... 330-652-9919 361 G
reneezuzolo@eticollege.edu
ZVARITCH, Jeanne .... 330-337-6403 356 B
college@awc.edu
ZVARITCH, Jeanne .... 330-337-6403 356 B
ie@awc.edu
ZVARITCH, Jeanne, W ... 330-337-6403 356 B
academicdean@awc.edu
ZVOSEC, Almut .... 216-421-7447 359 J
azvosec@cia.edu
ZWANZIGER,
Michael, W .... 319-273-7826 167 A
michael.zwanziger@uni.edu
ZWART, Andrew .... 616-222-3000 232 F
azwart@kuyper.edu
ZWEIG, Yitzchak .... 305-534-7050 112 D
ZWEIG, Yochanan .... 305-534-7050 112 D
rosh@talmudicu.edu
ZWELL, Michael .... 312-645-8300 516 F
mike@wrightgrad.edu
ZWICKEY, Heather .... 503-552-1742 384 F
hzwickey@nunm.edu
ZWIREN, Martin .... 718-960-1117 302 C
martin.zwiren@lehman.cuny.edu
ZWIRN, Benjamin .... 631-451-4867 330 B
zwirnb@sunysuffolk.edu
ZYCH HERRMANN,
Jennifer .... 320-589-6128 251 A
zychja@morris.umn.edu
ZYLSTRA, James .... 608-266-1739 513 C
james.zylstra@wtcsystem.edu

Accreditation Index of Institutions by Regional, National, Professional and Specialized Agencies

Degree levels are shown by the following symbols: (C) diploma/certificate; (A) associate; (B) baccalaureate; (M) master's; (S) beyond master's but less than doctorate; (FP) first professional; (D) doctorate.

AA: Commission on Accreditation of Allied Health Education Programs: anesthesiologist assistant (M)

University of Colorado Denver|Anschutz Medical Campus ... CO ... 83
Quinnipiac University ... CT ... 88
Nova Southeastern University ... FL ... 104
Emory University ... GA ... 119
South University ... GA ... 125
Indiana University-Purdue University Indianapolis ... IN ... 160
University of Missouri - Kansas City ... MO ... 268
Case Western Reserve University ... OH ... 358
Medical College of Wisconsin ... WI ... 508

AAB: Aviation Accreditation Board International: aviation (A,B,M,D)

Auburn University ... AL ... 4
Arizona State University ... AZ ... 10
Embry-Riddle Aeronautical University ... FL ... 98
Florida Institute of Technology ... FL ... 99
Florida Memorial University ... FL ... 99
Jacksonville University ... FL ... 102
Southern Illinois University Carbondale ... IL ... 152
Purdue University Main Campus ... IN ... 163
University of Dubuque ... IA ... 173
Louisiana Tech University ... LA ... 197
Bridgewater State University ... MA ... 217
Western Michigan University ... MI ... 239
Minnesota State University, Mankato ... MN ... 246
Delta State University ... MS ... 252
Saint Louis University ... MO ... 266
University of Central Missouri ... MO ... 268
Rocky Mountain College ... MT ... 272
University of Nebraska at Omaha ... NE ... 277
Mercer County Community College ... NJ ... 287
University of North Dakota ... ND ... 353
Kent State University Kent Campus ... OH ... 363
Ohio State University Main Campus, The ... OH ... 367
Oklahoma State University ... OK ... 377
Southeastern Oklahoma State University ... OK ... 379
University of Oklahoma Norman Campus ... OK ... 380
Inter American University of Puerto Rico Bayamon Campus ... PR ... 523
South Dakota State University ... SD ... 429
Middle Tennessee State University ... TN ... 434
Westminster College ... UT ... 474
Hampton University ... VA ... 481

AAFCS: American Association of Family and Consumer Sciences: family and consumer science (B)

Alabama Agricultural and Mechanical University ... AL ... 1
Jacksonville State University ... AL ... 6
University of Montevallo ... AL ... 8
University of Arkansas at Pine Bluff ... AR ... 22
University of Arkansas Main Campus ... AR ... 21
California State University-Long Beach ... CA ... 32
California State University-Northridge ... CA ... 33
San Francisco State University ... CA ... 34
Florida State University ... FL ... 110
Fort Valley State University ... GA ... 119
University of Georgia ... GA ... 127
Eastern Illinois University ... IL ... 138
Illinois State University ... IL ... 140
Ball State University ... IN ... 156
University of Kentucky ... KY ... 190
Louisiana Tech University ... LA ... 197
Nicholls State University ... LA ... 197
Northwestern State University ... LA ... 197
Southeastern Louisiana University ... LA ... 197
Southern University and A&M College ... LA ... 195
Southern University at New Orleans ... LA ... 195
Alcorn State University ... MS ... 251
Delta State University ... MS ... 252
Mississippi State University ... MS ... 254
University of Southern Mississippi ... MS ... 256
University of Central Missouri ... MO ... 268
City University of New York Queens College ... NY ... 303
State University of New York at Oneonta ... NY ... 325
East Carolina University ... NC ... 349
North Carolina Agricultural and Technical State University ... NC ... 350
Ohio University Main Campus ... OH ... 368
Youngstown State University ... OH ... 374
South Carolina State University ... SC ... 423
Carson-Newman University ... TN ... 430
Middle Tennessee State University ... TN ... 434
Tennessee State University ... TN ... 438
Tennessee Technological University ... TN ... 438
University of Tennessee at Martin ... TN ... 440
Stephen F. Austin State University ... TX ... 458
University of Houston ... TX ... 465

ABHES: Accrediting Bureau of Health Education Schools: allied health (C,A,B,M)

Arizona College ... AZ ... 10
Pima Medical Institute-Tucson ... AZ ... 15
Baptist Health College Little Rock ... AR ... 18
Jefferson Regional Medical Center School of Nursing ... AR ... 20
American Career College-Los Angeles ... CA ... 25
American Career College-Ontario ... CA ... 25
American Medical Sciences Center ... CA ... 25
Angeles College ... CA ... 26
California Career College ... CA ... 28
Casa Loma College-Van Nuys ... CA ... 35
CBD College ... CA ... 35
CNI College ... CA ... 38
Glendale Career College ... CA ... 44
Gurnick Academy of Medical Arts ... CA ... 45
Homestead Schools ... CA ... 45
National Career College ... CA ... 53
Sacramento Ultrasound Institute ... CA ... 58
Trinity School of Health and Allied Sciences ... CA ... 67
Valley College of Medical Careers ... CA ... 72
Pima Medical Institute ... CO ... 81
American Medical Academy ... FL ... 94
Azure College ... FL ... 95
Cambridge College ... FL ... 96
Cambridge Institute of Allied Health & Technology-Altamonte Springs ... FL ... 96
City College ... FL ... 96
Emergency Educational Institute ... FL ... 98
Florida College of Health Science ... FL ... 99
Med-Life Institute-Lauderdale Lakes ... FL ... 103
Med-Life Institute-Naples ... FL ... 103
Medical Career Institute ... FL ... 103
Medical Prep Institute ... FL ... 103
Mercy Hospital College of Nursing ... FL ... 103
Orion College ... FL ... 104
Orlando Medical Institute ... FL ... 104
Ultimate Medical Academy-Clearwater ... FL ... 112
Caris College ... IN ... 157
Harrison College - Indianapolis Downtown Campus ... IN ... 158
St. Vincent College of Health Professions ... IN ... 164
ATA College ... KY ... 183
Fortis College ... LA ... 191
Midwest Institute ... MO ... 263
Midwest Institute-Earth City ... MO ... 263
Saint Louis College of Health Careers-South Taylor ... MO ... 266
WellSpring School of Allied Health-Kansas City ... MO ... 270
Universal College of Healing Arts ... NE ... 277
Northwest Career College ... NV ... 279
Finger Lakes Health College of Nursing ... NY ... 308
Mandl School - The College of Allied Health ... NY ... 313
St. Paul's School of Nursing ... NY ... 323
Saint Paul's School of Nursing-Staten Island ... NY ... 323
Fortis College ... OH ... 361
Ohio Valley College of Technology ... OH ... 368
Professional Skills Institute ... OH ... 369
College of Emergency Services ... OR ... 382
Sumner College ... OR ... 387
Institute of Medical and Business Careers ... PA ... 397
Meridian Institute of Surgical Assisting ... TN ... 434
Baptist Health System School of Health Professions ... TX ... 443
College of Health Care Professions, The ... TX ... 446
Dallas Nursing Institute ... TX ... 448
Houston International College-Cardiotech Ultrasound School ... TX ... 450
Southwest University at El Paso ... TX ... 457
Nightingale College ... UT ... 472
Centra College of Nursing ... VA ... 478
Danville Regional Medical Center School of Health Professions ... VA ... 479
Riverside College of Health Careers ... VA ... 484
Sentara College of Health Sciences ... VA ... 485
Southside Regional Medical Center Professional Schools ... VA ... 485
Standard Healthcare Services College of Nursing ... VA ... 485
West Virginia Junior College ... WV ... 505
Milwaukee Career College ... WI ... 508

ACAE: Accreditation Commission for Audiology Education: audiology (D)

Nova Southeastern University ... FL ... 104
Washington University in St. Louis ... MO ... 269
University of North Carolina at Chapel Hill ... NC ... 351
Ohio State University Main Campus, The ... OH ... 367
University of Texas at Dallas, The ... TX ... 467

ACBSP: Accreditation Council for Business Schools and Programs: business administration, management, accounting and related business fields (A,B,M,D)

Alabama State University ... AL ... 4
Athens State University ... AL ... 4
Bishop State Community College ... AL ... 1
George Corley Wallace State Community College - Selma ... AL ... 2
Jefferson State Community College ... AL ... 2
Lawson State Community College ... AL ... 2
Miles College ... AL ... 6
Oakwood University ... AL ... 6
Troy University ... AL ... 7
University of Mobile ... AL ... 8
University of North Alabama ... AL ... 9
University of West Alabama, The ... AL ... 9
Wallace State Community College - Hanceville ... AL ... 3
Grand Canyon University ... AZ ... 12
Northern Arizona University ... AZ ... 14
University of Phoenix ... AZ ... 17
Cossatot Community College of the University of Arkansas ... AR ... 22
Harding University Main Campus ... AR ... 19
John Brown University ... AR ... 20
North Arkansas College ... AR ... 20
NorthWest Arkansas Community College ... AR ... 20
Philander Smith College ... AR ... 21
Phillips Community College of the University of Arkansas ... AR ... 22
University of Arkansas at Pine Bluff ... AR ... 22
Argosy University, Orange County ... CA ... 26
Biola University ... CA ... 27
California Baptist University ... CA ... 28
California State University Channel Islands ... CA ... 31
International Technological University ... CA ... 46
Northcentral University ... CA ... 54
Notre Dame de Namur University ... CA ... 54
Point Loma Nazarene University ... CA ... 57
Skyline College ... CA ... 62
Woodbury University ... CA ... 75
Colorado State University-Global Campus ... CO ... 78
Colorado Technical University ... CO ... 79
Post University ... CT ... 87
Three Rivers Community College ... CT ... 86
Tunxis Community College ... CT ... 86
University of Bridgeport ... CT ... 88
Delaware Technical Community College, Terry Campus ... DE ... 90
Goldey-Beacom College ... DE ... 90
Gallaudet University ... DC ... 91
Strayer University ... DC ... 93
University of the District of Columbia ... DC ... 93
Bethune Cookman University ... FL ... 95
Embry-Riddle Aeronautical University ... FL ... 98
Florida Agricultural and Mechanical University ... FL ... 109
Florida Memorial University ... FL ... 99
Florida State College at Jacksonville ... FL ... 100
Keiser University ... FL ... 102
Palm Beach State College ... FL ... 105
Saint Leo University ... FL ... 106
Southeastern University ... FL ... 108
Albany State University ... GA ... 114
Athens Technical College ... GA ... 115
Atlanta Metropolitan State College ... GA ... 115
Brenau University ... GA ... 116
LaGrange College ... GA ... 122
Paine College ... GA ... 124
Piedmont College ... GA ... 124
South University ... GA ... 125
West Georgia Technical College ... GA ... 128
Kapiolani Community College ... HI ... 130
University of Hawaii - West Oahu ... HI ... 130
Northwest Nazarene University ... ID ... 132
American InterContinental University ... IL ... 133
Chicago State University ... IL ... 135
City Colleges of Chicago Harold Washington College ... IL ... 135
City Colleges of Chicago Wilbur Wright College ... IL ... 136
Governors State University ... IL ... 138
Harper College ... IL ... 139
Joliet Junior College ... IL ... 142
Lewis University ... IL ... 143
Millikin University ... IL ... 145
Northwestern College ... IL ... 148
Roosevelt University ... IL ... 150
Trinity Christian College ... IL ... 153
University of St. Francis ... IL ... 154
Anderson University ... IN ... 156
Indiana University East ... IN ... 160
Ivy Tech Community College of Indiana-Central Indiana ... IN ... 161
Trine University ... IN ... 164
University of Indianapolis ... IN ... 164
University of Saint Francis ... IN ... 165
Vincennes University ... IN ... 165
Des Moines Area Community College ... IA ... 168
Kaplan University ... IA ... 171
St. Ambrose University ... IA ... 173
Baker University ... KS ... 174
Butler Community College ... KS ... 175
Hutchinson Community College ... KS ... 178
Johnson County Community College ... KS ... 178
Kansas City Kansas Community College ... KS ... 178
MidAmerica Nazarene University ... KS ... 179
Neosho County Community College ... KS ... 180
Ottawa University ... KS ... 180
Pratt Community College ... KS ... 180
Seward County Community College ... KS ... 181
Kentucky State University ... KY ... 187
Owensboro Community and Technical College ... KY ... 186
Thomas More College ... KY ... 189
West Kentucky Community and Technical College ... KY ... 187
Baton Rouge Community College ... LA ... 192
Delgado Community College ... LA ... 192
Louisiana College ... LA ... 191
Xavier University of Louisiana ... LA ... 198
Kennebec Valley Community College ... ME ... 200
Northern Maine Community College ... ME ... 200
University of New England ... ME ... 202
Baltimore City Community College ... MD ... 202
Bowie State University ... MD ... 208
College of Southern Maryland ... MD ... 203
Community College of Baltimore County, The ... MD ... 203
Coppin State University ... MD ... 208
Hood College ... MD ... 204
Notre Dame of Maryland University ... MD ... 206
Lasell College ... MA ... 216
Ferris State University ... MI ... 230
Jackson College ... MI ... 231
Kettering University ... MI ... 232
Lake Superior State University ... MI ... 232
Lawrence Technological University ... MI ... 233
Madonna University ... MI ... 233
Mott Community College ... MI ... 234
Northwood University ... MI ... 235
Walsh College of Accountancy and Business Administration ... MI ... 238
Bethel University ... MN ... 240
Capella University ... MN ... 241
Hennepin Technical College ... MN ... 244
Inver Hills Community College ... MN ... 245
Normandale Community College ... MN ... 246
North Hennepin Community College ... MN ... 246
Riverland Community College ... MN ... 247
Rochester Community and Technical College ... MN ... 247
Saint Paul College-A Community & Technical College ... MN ... 247
Walden University ... MN ... 251
Alcorn State University ... MS ... 251
Delta State University ... MS ... 252
Jones County Junior College ... MS ... 253

ACCSC: Accrediting Commission of Career Schools and Colleges: occupational, trade, and technical education (C,A,B,M)

ACFEI: American Culinary Federation, Inc.: culinary arts and culinary management (C,A,B)

ACICS: Accrediting Council for Independent Colleges and Schools: business and business related programs (C,A,B,M)

ACUP: Accreditation Commission for Acupuncture and Oriental Medicine: acupuncture (C,M,D)

ADNUR: Accreditation Commission for Education in Nursing: nursing (A)

Bergen Community College ... NJ ... 283
Brookdale Community College ... NJ ... 284
County College of Morris ... NJ ... 285
Cumberland County College ... NJ ... 285
Essex County College ... NJ ... 285
Mercer County Community College ... NJ ... 287
Middlesex County College ... NJ ... 287
Ocean County College ... NJ ... 288
Passaic County Community College ... NJ ... 288
Raritan Valley Community College ... NJ ... 289
Rowan College at Burlington County ... NJ ... 289
Rowan College at Gloucester County ... NJ ... 289
Salem Community College ... NJ ... 291
Warren County Community College ... NJ ... 292
Central New Mexico Community College ... NM ... 293
Clovis Community College ... NM ... 293
Eastern New Mexico University-Roswell ... NM ... 294
Luna Community College ... NM ... 294
New Mexico Junior College ... NM ... 294
New Mexico State University at Carlsbad ... NM ... 295
New Mexico State University Dona Ana Community College ... NM ... 295
Northern New Mexico College ... NM ... 295
San Juan College ... NM ... 296
Santa Fe Community College ... NM ... 296
Western New Mexico University ... NM ... 297
Alfred State College ... NY ... 328
Belanger School of Nursing, The ... NY ... 299
Bill and Sandra Pomeroy College of Nursing at Crouse Hospital ... NY ... 299
Cayuga Community College ... NY ... 300
City University of New York Borough of Manhattan Community College ... NY ... 301
City University of New York Bronx Community College ... NY ... 301
City University of New York Kingsborough Community College ... NY ... 303
City University of New York Medgar Evers College ... NY ... 303
City University of New York Queensborough Community College ... NY ... 303
Clinton Community College ... NY ... 304
Cochran School of Nursing ... NY ... 304
College of Staten Island CUNY ... NY ... 302
Columbia-Greene Community College ... NY ... 305
Corning Community College ... NY ... 306
Dutchess Community College ... NY ... 307
Erie Community College ... NY ... 307
Excelsior College ... NY ... 308
Finger Lakes Community College ... NY ... 308
Finger Lakes Health College of Nursing ... NY ... 308
Fulton-Montgomery Community College ... NY ... 309
Genesee Community College ... NY ... 309
Helene Fuld College of Nursing ... NY ... 309
Hudson Valley Community College ... NY ... 310
Jamestown Community College ... NY ... 311
Jefferson Community College ... NY ... 311
LaGuardia Community College/City University of New York ... NY ... 303
Maria College of Albany ... NY ... 314
Memorial School of Nursing ... NY ... 314
Mohawk Valley Community College ... NY ... 315
Monroe Community College ... NY ... 315
Montefiore School of Nursing ... NY ... 316
Morrisville State College ... NY ... 329
Nassau Community College ... NY ... 316
New York City College of Technology/City University of New York ... NY ... 303
Niagara County Community College ... NY ... 318
Onondaga Community College ... NY ... 319
Orange County Community College ... NY ... 319
Phillips School of Nursing at Mount Sinai Beth Israel ... NY ... 320
Rockland Community College ... NY ... 321
St. Elizabeth College of Nursing ... NY ... 322
Saint Joseph's College, New York ... NY ... 322
Samaritan Hospital School of Nursing ... NY ... 323
State University of New York College of Technology at Delhi ... NY ... 329
Suffolk County Community College Ammerman Campus ... NY ... 330
SUNY Adirondack ... NY ... 328
SUNY Broome Community College ... NY ... 326
SUNY Canton-College of Technology ... NY ... 329
Swedish Institute-College of Health Sciences ... NY ... 330
Tompkins Cortland Community College ... NY ... 331
Trocaire College ... NY ... 331
Ulster County Community College ... NY ... 331
Cabarrus College of Health Sciences ... NC ... 336
Cape Fear Community College ... NC ... 341
Carolinas College of Health Sciences ... NC ... 336
Carteret Community College ... NC ... 341
Catawba Valley Community College ... NC ... 341
Central Piedmont Community College ... NC ... 342
College of the Albemarle ... NC ... 342
Davidson County Community College ... NC ... 342
Durham Technical Community College ... NC ... 342
Edgecombe Community College ... NC ... 343
Fayetteville Technical Community College ... NC ... 343
Gardner-Webb University ... NC ... 337
Gaston College ... NC ... 343
Johnston Community College ... NC ... 344
Mitchell Community College ... NC ... 344
Pitt Community College ... NC ... 345
Rowan-Cabarrus Community College ... NC ... 346
Sampson Community College ... NC ... 346
Wake Technical Community College ... NC ... 347
Wayne Community College ... NC ... 347
Western Piedmont Community College ... NC ... 347
Bismarck State College ... ND ... 354
Lake Region State College ... ND ... 355
Aultman College of Nursing and Health Sciences ... OH ... 357
Central Ohio Technical College ... OH ... 358
Christ College of Nursing and Health Sciences, The ... OH ... 359
Cincinnati State Technical and Community College ... OH ... 359
Clark State Community College ... OH ... 359
Columbus State Community College ... OH ... 360
Cuyahoga Community College ... OH ... 360
Edison State Community College ... OH ... 361
Fortis College ... OH ... 361
Good Samaritan College of Nursing and Health Science ... OH ... 362
Hocking College ... OH ... 362
James A. Rhodes State College ... OH ... 363
Kettering College ... OH ... 364
Lakeland Community College ... OH ... 364
Lorain County Community College ... OH ... 364
Marion Technical College ... OH ... 365
Mercy College of Ohio ... OH ... 365
North Central State College ... OH ... 366
Northwest State Community College ... OH ... 366
Ohio University Main Campus ... OH ... 368
Owens Community College ... OH ... 369
Shawnee State University ... OH ... 369
Sinclair Community College ... OH ... 370
Southern State Community College ... OH ... 370
Stark State College ... OH ... 370
Terra State Community College ... OH ... 370
University of Cincinnati Blue Ash College ... OH ... 371
University of Rio Grande ... OH ... 372
Carl Albert State College ... OK ... 375
Connors State College ... OK ... 375
Eastern Oklahoma State College ... OK ... 375
Murray State College ... OK ... 376
Northeastern Oklahoma Agricultural and Mechanical College ... OK ... 376
Northern Oklahoma College ... OK ... 376
Oklahoma City Community College ... OK ... 377
Oklahoma State University Institute of Technology-Okmulgee ... OK ... 378
Oklahoma State University - Oklahoma City ... OK ... 378
Redlands Community College ... OK ... 379
Rogers State University ... OK ... 379
Rose State College ... OK ... 379
Seminole State College ... OK ... 379
Tulsa Community College ... OK ... 380
Western Oklahoma State College ... OK ... 381
Chemeketa Community College ... OR ... 382
Portland Community College ... OR ... 386
Treasure Valley Community College ... OR ... 387
Umpqua Community College ... OR ... 387
Bucks County Community College ... PA ... 390
Butler County Community College ... PA ... 390
Community College of Allegheny County ... PA ... 392
Community College of Beaver County ... PA ... 392
Community College of Philadelphia ... PA ... 393
Delaware County Community College ... PA ... 393
HACC, Central Pennsylvania's Community College ... PA ... 396
Harcum College ... PA ... 396
La Roche College ... PA ... 398
Lehigh Carbon Community College ... PA ... 400
Lock Haven University ... PA ... 406
Luzerne County Community College ... PA ... 400
Montgomery County Community College ... PA ... 402
Mount Aloysius College ... PA ... 402
Northampton Community College ... PA ... 403
Pennsylvania College of Health Sciences ... PA ... 404
Pennsylvania College of Technology ... PA ... 404
Reading Area Community College ... PA ... 408
Westmoreland County Community College ... PA ... 414
Colegio Universitario de San Juan ... PR ... 521
EDP University of Puerto Rico ... PR ... 522
Inter American University of Puerto Rico / Metropolitan Campus ... PR ... 524
Inter American University of Puerto Rico Aguadilla Campus ... PR ... 523
National University College ... PR ... 525
Universidad del Este ... PR ... 525
Universidad Metropolitana ... PR ... 526
University of Puerto Rico at Arecibo ... PR ... 527
Community College of Rhode Island ... RI ... 416
New England Institute of Technology ... RI ... 416
Aiken Technical College ... SC ... 418
Central Carolina Technical College ... SC ... 419
Florence - Darlington Technical College ... SC ... 421
Greenville Technical College ... SC ... 421
Horry-Georgetown Technical College ... SC ... 421
Midlands Technical College ... SC ... 422
Orangeburg-Calhoun Technical College ... SC ... 423
Piedmont Technical College ... SC ... 423
Spartanburg Community College ... SC ... 424
Technical College of the Lowcountry ... SC ... 424
Tri-County Technical College ... SC ... 424
Trident Technical College ... SC ... 424
York Technical College ... SC ... 426
Southeast Technical Institute ... SD ... 429
University of South Dakota, The ... SD ... 428
Chattanooga State Community College ... TN ... 436
Cleveland State Community College ... TN ... 436
Columbia State Community College ... TN ... 436
Dyersburg State Community College ... TN ... 437
Jackson State Community College ... TN ... 437
Lincoln Memorial University ... TN ... 433
Motlow State Community College ... TN ... 437
Nashville State Community College ... TN ... 437
Northeast State Community College ... TN ... 437
Pellissippi State Community College ... TN ... 437
Roane State Community College ... TN ... 438
Southern Adventist University ... TN ... 436
Southwest Tennessee Community College ... TN ... 438
Tennessee State University ... TN ... 438
Walters State Community College ... TN ... 438
Alvin Community College ... TX ... 442
Amarillo College ... TX ... 442
Austin Community College District ... TX ... 443
Baptist Health System School of Health Professions ... TX ... 443
Blinn College ... TX ... 444
Brookhaven College ... TX ... 447
Central Texas College ... TX ... 445
College of the Mainland ... TX ... 446
Collin County Community College District ... TX ... 446
Del Mar College ... TX ... 448
El Centro College ... TX ... 448
El Paso Community College ... TX ... 449
Galveston College ... TX ... 449
Grayson College ... TX ... 449
Howard College ... TX ... 450
Kilgore College ... TX ... 451
Laredo Community College ... TX ... 451
Lee College ... TX ... 451
Lone Star College System ... TX ... 452
McLennan Community College ... TX ... 452
Navarro College ... TX ... 453
North Central Texas College ... TX ... 453
Odessa College ... TX ... 454
Panola College ... TX ... 454
Paris Junior College ... TX ... 454
San Antonio College ... TX ... 442
San Jacinto College Central ... TX ... 455
San Jacinto College South ... TX ... 456
South Plains College ... TX ... 456
Tarrant County College District ... TX ... 458
Temple College ... TX ... 458
Texarkana College ... TX ... 458
Trinity Valley Community College ... TX ... 464
Victoria College ... TX ... 470
Weatherford College ... TX ... 470
Dixie State University ... UT ... 473
Nightingale College ... UT ... 472
Salt Lake Community College ... UT ... 474
Snow College ... UT ... 474
Utah Valley University ... UT ... 473
Weber State University ... UT ... 473
Vermont Technical College ... VT ... 477
Blue Ridge Community College ... VA ... 487
Centra College of Nursing ... VA ... 478
Dabney S. Lancaster Community College ... VA ... 487
Germanna Community College ... VA ... 488
J. Sargeant Reynolds Community College ... VA ... 488
John Tyler Community College ... VA ... 488
Lord Fairfax Community College ... VA ... 488
Mountain Empire Community College ... VA ... 488
Northern Virginia Community College ... VA ... 488
Patrick Henry Community College ... VA ... 489
Paul D. Camp Community College ... VA ... 489
Piedmont Virginia Community College ... VA ... 489
Rappahannock Community College ... VA ... 489
Southside Regional Medical Center Professional Schools ... VA ... 485
Southside Virginia Community College ... VA ... 489
Southwest Virginia Community College ... VA ... 489
Thomas Nelson Community College ... VA ... 489
Tidewater Community College ... VA ... 489
Virginia Highlands Community College ... VA ... 490
Wytheville Community College ... VA ... 490
Bellevue College ... WA ... 492
Bellingham Technical College ... WA ... 492
Big Bend Community College ... WA ... 492
Clark College ... WA ... 493
Columbia Basin College ... WA ... 493
Everett Community College ... WA ... 494
Grays Harbor College ... WA ... 495
Highline College ... WA ... 495
Lake Washington Institute of Technology ... WA ... 495
Lower Columbia College ... WA ... 495
North Seattle College ... WA ... 497
Olympic College ... WA ... 496
Peninsula College ... WA ... 496
Pierce College District ... WA ... 497
Seattle Central College ... WA ... 497
Shoreline Community College ... WA ... 498
Skagit Valley College ... WA ... 498
Spokane Community College ... WA ... 493
Tacoma Community College ... WA ... 499
Walla Walla Community College ... WA ... 499
Wenatchee Valley College ... WA ... 500
Whatcom Community College ... WA ... 500
Yakima Valley College ... WA ... 500
Blue Ridge Community and Technical College ... WV ... 502
Bluefield State College ... WV ... 503
BridgeValley Community & Technical College ... WV ... 502
Davis & Elkins College ... WV ... 501
Eastern West Virginia Community and Technical College ... WV ... 502
Fairmont State University ... WV ... 504
Marshall University ... WV ... 504
Southern West Virginia Community and Technical College ... WV ... 503
West Virginia Northern Community College ... WV ... 503
West Virginia University at Parkersburg ... WV ... 505
Blackhawk Technical College ... WI ... 513
Chippewa Valley Technical College ... WI ... 513
College of Menominee Nation ... WI ... 506
Fox Valley Technical College ... WI ... 513
Gateway Technical College ... WI ... 513
Herzing University ... WI ... 507
Lakeshore Technical College ... WI ... 513
Madison Area Technical College ... WI ... 514
Mid-State Technical College ... WI ... 514
Milwaukee Area Technical College ... WI ... 514
Moraine Park Technical College ... WI ... 514
Nicolet Area Technical College ... WI ... 514
Northcentral Technical College ... WI ... 514
Northeast Wisconsin Technical College ... WI ... 514
Southwest Wisconsin Technical College ... WI ... 515
Waukesha County Technical College ... WI ... 515
Western Technical College ... WI ... 515
Wisconsin Indianhead Technical College ... WI ... 515
Casper College ... WY ... 516
Central Wyoming College ... WY ... 516
Laramie County Community College ... WY ... 516
Northern Wyoming Community College District ... WY ... 516
Northwest College ... WY ... 516
Western Wyoming Community College ... WY ... 517

AIJS: Association of Institutions of Jewish Studies: Jewish studies (C, A,B)

Women's Institute of Torah Seminary ... MD ... 210
Bais Medrash Mayan Hatorah ... NJ ... 283
Yeshiva Chemdas Hatorah ... NJ ... 292
Yeshiva Gedolah Keren Hatorah ... NJ ... 293
Yeshiva Gedolah Tiferes Boruch ... NJ ... 293
Yeshivas Be'er Yitzchok ... NJ ... 293
Bais Medrash Ateres Shlomo ... NY ... 298
Mechon L'Hoyroa ... NY ... 314
Yeshiva Ohr Naftoli ... NY ... 334
Yeshivath Zichron Moshe ... NY ... 335

ANEST: Council on Accreditation of Nurse Anesthesia Educational Programs: nurse anesthesia (C,M,D)

Samford University ... AL ... 6
University of Alabama at Birmingham ... AL ... 8
University of Arizona ... AZ ... 16
Arkansas State University-Jonesboro ... AR ... 18
California State University-Fullerton ... CA ... 32
Loma Linda University ... CA ... 48
National University ... CA ... 53
Samuel Merritt University ... CA ... 59
University of Southern California ... CA ... 72
Central Connecticut State University ... CT ... 84
Fairfield University ... CT ... 87
Quinnipiac University ... CT ... 88
Georgetown University ... DC ... 92
Adventist University of Health Sciences ... FL ... 94
Barry University ... FL ... 95
Florida Gulf Coast University ... FL ... 109
Florida International University ... FL ... 109
Florida State University ... FL ... 110
University of Miami ... FL ... 112
University of North Florida ... FL ... 110
University of South Florida ... FL ... 111
Wolford College ... FL ... 114
Augusta University ... GA ... 116
Emory University ... GA ... 119
DePaul University ... IL ... 137
Millikin University ... IL ... 145
Rosalind Franklin University of Medicine & Science ... IL ... 150
Rush University ... IL ... 150
Southern Illinois University Edwardsville ... IL ... 152
Marian University ... IN ... 162
University of Saint Francis ... IN ... 165
University of Iowa ... IA ... 166
Newman University ... KS ... 180
Murray State University ... KY ... 188
Northern Kentucky University ... KY ... 188

Franciscan Missionaries of Our Lady University ... LA ... 191
Louisiana State University Health Sciences Center-New Orleans ... LA ... 194
University of New England ... ME ... 202
Uniformed Services University of the Health Sciences ... MD ... 518
University of Maryland, Baltimore ... MD ... 207
Boston College ... MA ... 212
Northeastern University ... MA ... 223
Michigan State University ... MI ... 233
Oakland University ... MI ... 235
University of Detroit Mercy ... MI ... 237
University of Michigan-Flint ... MI ... 238
Wayne State University ... MI ... 239
Saint Mary's University of Minnesota ... MN ... 250
University of Minnesota ... MN ... 250
University of Southern Mississippi ... MS ... 256
Goldfarb School of Nursing at Barnes-Jewish College ... MO ... 260
Missouri State University ... MO ... 263
University of Missouri - Kansas City ... MO ... 268
Webster University ... MO ... 269
Bryan College of Health Sciences ... NE ... 273
Clarkson College ... NE ... 273
Rutgers University - Newark ... NJ ... 290
Albany Medical College ... NY ... 297
Columbia University in the City of New York ... NY ... 305
SUNY Downstate Medical Center ... NY ... 326
University at Buffalo-SUNY ... NY ... 325
Duke University ... NC ... 337
East Carolina University ... NC ... 349
University of North Carolina at Charlotte ... NC ... 351
University of North Carolina at Greensboro ... NC ... 351
Wake Forest University ... NC ... 353
Western Carolina University ... NC ... 352
University of North Dakota ... ND ... 353
Case Western Reserve University ... OH ... 358
Lourdes University ... OH ... 364
Otterbein University ... OH ... 368
University of Akron, Main Campus, The ... OH ... 371
University of Cincinnati Main Campus ... OH ... 371
Youngstown State University ... OH ... 374
Oregon Health & Science University ... OR ... 385
Bloomsburg University of Pennsylvania ... PA ... 405
Drexel University ... PA ... 394
Gannon University ... PA ... 395
La Roche College ... PA ... 398
La Salle University ... PA ... 398
Saint Vincent College ... PA ... 410
Thomas Jefferson University ... PA ... 411
University of Pennsylvania ... PA ... 412
University of Pittsburgh ... PA ... 412
University of Scranton, The ... PA ... 413
Villanova University ... PA ... 413
York College of Pennsylvania ... PA ... 415
Inter American University of Puerto Rico Arecibo Campus ... PR ... 523
Universidad Adventista de las Antillas ... PR ... 526
University of Puerto Rico-Medical Sciences Campus ... PR ... 528
Rhode Island College ... RI ... 417
Medical University of South Carolina ... SC ... 422
University of South Carolina Columbia ... SC ... 424
Mount Marty College ... SD ... 427
Lincoln Memorial University ... TN ... 433
Middle Tennessee School of Anesthesia ... TN ... 434
Union University ... TN ... 439
University of Tennessee at Chattanooga ... TN ... 440
University of Tennessee Health Science Center ... TN ... 440
University of Tennessee, Knoxville ... TN ... 439
Baylor College of Medicine ... TX ... 444
Texas Christian University ... TX ... 461
Texas Wesleyan University ... TX ... 463
University of Texas Health Science Center at Houston (UTHealth), The ... TX ... 468
Westminster College ... UT ... 474
Old Dominion University ... VA ... 483
Virginia Commonwealth University ... VA ... 487
Gonzaga University ... WA ... 495
Marshall University ... WV ... 504
University of Wisconsin-La Crosse ... WI ... 510
University of Wisconsin-Oshkosh ... WI ... 511

ARCPA: Accreditation Review Commission on Education for the Physician Assistant: physician assisting programs (C,A,B,M)

University of Alabama at Birmingham ... AL ... 8
University of South Alabama ... AL ... 9
Northern Arizona University ... AZ ... 14
Harding University Main Campus ... AR ... 19
University of Arkansas for Medical Sciences ... AR ... 22
#California Baptist University ... CA ... 28
#Chapman University ... CA ... 36
#Charles R. Drew University of Medicine & Science ... CA ... 36
#Dominican University of California ... CA ... 41
#Loma Linda University ... CA ... 48
#Marshall B. Ketchum University ... CA ... 51
Samuel Merritt University ... CA ... 59
#Southern California University of Health Sciences ... CA ... 65
Stanford University ... CA ... 66
Touro University California ... CA ... 67
University of California-Davis ... CA ... 68
University of Southern California ... CA ... 72
#University of the Pacific ... CA ... 70
Western University of Health Sciences ... CA ... 74
Red Rocks Community College ... CO ... 82
University of Colorado Denver|Anschutz Medical Campus ... CO ... 83
Quinnipiac University ... CT ... 88
#Sacred Heart University ... CT ... 88
University of Bridgeport ... CT ... 88
#University of Saint Joseph ... CT ... 89
Yale University ... CT ... 89
George Washington University ... DC ... 92
#Howard University ... DC ... 92
#Adventist University of Health Sciences ... FL ... 94
Barry University ... FL ... 95
#Florida Gulf Coast University ... FL ... 109
#Florida International University ... FL ... 109
#Florida State University ... FL ... 110
#Keiser University ... FL ... 102
Miami Dade College ... FL ... 103
Nova Southeastern University ... FL ... 104
University of Florida ... FL ... 110
#University of South Florida ... FL ... 111
Augusta University ... GA ... 116
Emory University ... GA ... 119
Mercer University ... GA ... 122
South University ... GA ... 125
Idaho State University ... ID ... 132
#Dominican University ... IL ... 137
Midwestern University ... IL ... 145
Northwestern University ... IL ... 148
Rosalind Franklin University of Medicine & Science ... IL ... 150
Rush University ... IL ... 150
Southern Illinois University Carbondale ... IL ... 152
Butler University ... IN ... 156
#Indiana State University ... IN ... 159
Indiana University-Purdue University Indianapolis ... IN ... 160
#University of Evansville ... IN ... 164
University of Saint Francis ... IN ... 165
#Des Moines University ... IA ... 168
#St. Ambrose University ... IA ... 173
#University of Dubuque ... IA ... 173
University of Iowa ... IA ... 166
Wichita State University ... KS ... 182
#Sullivan University ... KY ... 189
#University of Kentucky ... KY ... 190
#University of the Cumberlands ... KY ... 190
Franciscan Missionaries of Our Lady University ... LA ... 191
#Louisiana State University Health Sciences Center at Shreveport ... LA ... 194
Louisiana State University Health Sciences Center-New Orleans ... LA ... 194
University of New England ... ME ... 202
Anne Arundel Community College ... MD ... 202
Towson University ... MD ... 209
Bay Path University ... MA ... 211
#Boston University ... MA ... 212
MCPHS University ... MA ... 221
#MGH Institute of Health Professions ... MA ... 222
Northeastern University ... MA ... 223
Springfield College ... MA ... 224
Tufts University ... MA ... 225
Central Michigan University ... MI ... 228
#Eastern Michigan University ... MI ... 229
#Grand Valley State University ... MI ... 230
University of Detroit Mercy ... MI ... 237
Wayne State University ... MI ... 239
Western Michigan University ... MI ... 239
Augsburg College ... MN ... 240
Bethel University ... MN ... 240
#College of Saint Scholastica, The ... MN ... 241
St. Catherine University ... MN ... 249
Mississippi College ... MS ... 254
Missouri State University ... MO ... 263
Saint Louis University ... MO ... 266
#Stephens College ... MO ... 267
#University of Missouri - Kansas City ... MO ... 268
Rocky Mountain College ... MT ... 272
#College of Saint Mary ... NE ... 274
#Union College ... NE ... 277
University of Nebraska Medical Center ... NE ... 277
Franklin Pierce University ... NH ... 281
#Monmouth University ... NJ ... 287
Seton Hall University ... NJ ... 291
University of New Mexico Main Campus ... NM ... 296
Albany Medical College ... NY ... 297
City University of New York The City College ... NY ... 301
City University of New York York College ... NY ... 304
Clarkson University ... NY ... 304
Daemen College ... NY ... 306
D'Youville College ... NY ... 307
Hofstra University ... NY ... 310
Le Moyne College ... NY ... 312
#Marist College ... NY ... 314
Mercy College ... NY ... 314
New York Institute of Technology ... NY ... 317
Pace University ... NY ... 319
Rochester Institute of Technology ... NY ... 321
St. John's University ... NY ... 322
State University of New York Upstate Medical University ... NY ... 326
Stony Brook University ... NY ... 325
SUNY Downstate Medical Center ... NY ... 326
Touro College ... NY ... 331
Wagner College ... NY ... 333
Campbell University ... NC ... 336
Duke University ... NC ... 337
East Carolina University ... NC ... 349
Elon University ... NC ... 337
#Gardner-Webb University ... NC ... 337
#High Point University ... NC ... 338
#Lenoir-Rhyne University ... NC ... 339
Methodist University ... NC ... 340
#University of North Carolina at Chapel Hill ... NC ... 351
Wake Forest University ... NC ... 353
Wingate University ... NC ... 353
University of North Dakota ... ND ... 353
#Baldwin Wallace University ... OH ... 357
#Case Western Reserve University ... OH ... 358
Cleveland State University ... OH ... 359
Cuyahoga Community College ... OH ... 360
Kettering College ... OH ... 364
#Lake Erie College ... OH ... 364
Marietta College ... OH ... 365
#Mount St. Joseph University ... OH ... 366
#Ohio Dominican University ... OH ... 367
#Ohio University Main Campus ... OH ... 368
#University of Dayton ... OH ... 372
University of Findlay, The ... OH ... 372
University of Mount Union ... OH ... 372
#University of Toledo ... OH ... 372
#Oklahoma City University ... OK ... 377
Oregon Health & Science University ... OR ... 385
Pacific University ... OR ... 385
Arcadia University ... PA ... 389
Chatham University ... PA ... 392
DeSales University ... PA ... 393
Drexel University ... PA ... 394
#Duquesne University ... PA ... 394
Gannon University ... PA ... 395
King's College ... PA ... 398
Lock Haven University ... PA ... 406
Marywood University ... PA ... 401
#Mercyhurst University ... PA ... 401
#Misericordia University ... PA ... 401
Pennsylvania College of Technology ... PA ... 404
Philadelphia College of Osteopathic Medicine ... PA ... 407
Saint Francis University ... PA ... 409
Salus University ... PA ... 410
Seton Hill University ... PA ... 410
#Slippery Rock University of Pennsylvania ... PA ... 407
#Temple University ... PA ... 411
#Thomas Jefferson University ... PA ... 411
University of Pittsburgh ... PA ... 412
#University of the Sciences in Philadelphia ... PA ... 413
#Bryant University ... RI ... 416
#Johnson & Wales University ... RI ... 416
#Francis Marion University ... SC ... 421
Medical University of South Carolina ... SC ... 422
#North Greenville University ... SC ... 422
#University of South Carolina Columbia ... SC ... 424
University of South Dakota, The ... SD ... 428
Bethel University ... TN ... 430
Lincoln Memorial University ... TN ... 433
South College ... TN ... 436
Trevecca Nazarene University ... TN ... 439
#University of Tennessee Health Science Center ... TN ... 440
Baylor College of Medicine ... TX ... 444
#Hardin-Simmons University ... TX ... 450
Texas Tech University ... TX ... 463
University of North Texas Health Science Center at Fort Worth ... TX ... 466
University of Texas Health Science Center at San Antonio ... TX ... 468
University of Texas Medical Branch, The ... TX ... 469
University of Texas Rio Grande Valley, The ... TX ... 468
University of Texas Southwestern Medical Center ... TX ... 469
#Rocky Mountain University of Health Professions ... UT ... 472
University of Utah, The ... UT ... 472
Eastern Virginia Medical School ... VA ... 480
#Emory & Henry College ... VA ... 480
James Madison University ... VA ... 481
Jefferson College of Health Sciences ... VA ... 482
#Lynchburg College ... VA ... 482
#Mary Baldwin University ... VA ... 482
Shenandoah University ... VA ... 485
#Heritage University ... WA ... 495
University of Washington ... WA ... 499
Alderson Broaddus University ... WV ... 501
University of Charleston ... WV ... 502
West Liberty University ... WV ... 504
Carroll University ... WI ... 506
Concordia University Wisconsin ... WI ... 507
Marquette University ... WI ... 508
University of Wisconsin-La Crosse ... WI ... 510
University of Wisconsin-Madison ... WI ... 510

ART: National Association of Schools of Art and Design: art and design (C, A,B,M,D)

Alabama State University ... AL ... 4
Auburn University ... AL ... 4
Jacksonville State University ... AL ... 6
University of Alabama at Birmingham ... AL ... 8
University of Alabama in Huntsville ... AL ... 8
University of Alabama, The ... AL ... 8
University of Montevallo ... AL ... 8
University of North Alabama ... AL ... 9
University of Alaska Anchorage ... AK ... 10
Arizona State University ... AZ ... 10
University of Arizona ... AZ ... 16
Arkansas State University-Jonesboro ... AR ... 18
University of Arkansas at Little Rock ... AR ... 22
University of Arkansas at Pine Bluff ... AR ... 22
University of Arkansas Main Campus ... AR ... 21
University of Central Arkansas ... AR ... 23
Academy of Art University ... CA ... 24
American Film Institute Conservatory ... CA ... 25
Art Center College of Design ... CA ... 26
Azusa Pacific University ... CA ... 26
Biola University ... CA ... 27
California College of the Arts ... CA ... 28
California Institute of the Arts ... CA ... 29
California Polytechnic State University-San Luis Obispo ... CA ... 30
California State Polytechnic University-Pomona ... CA ... 31
California State University-Chico ... CA ... 31
California State University-Fullerton ... CA ... 32
California State University-Long Beach ... CA ... 32
California State University-Los Angeles ... CA ... 32
California State University-Northridge ... CA ... 33
California State University-Sacramento ... CA ... 33
California State University-San Bernardino ... CA ... 33
California State University-Stanislaus ... CA ... 33
Chabot College ... CA ... 36
Dominican University of California ... CA ... 41
FIDM/Fashion Institute of Design and Merchandising-Los Angeles ... CA ... 42
Humboldt State University ... CA ... 34
Laguna College of Art & Design ... CA ... 47
Los Angeles Academy of Figurative Art ... CA ... 48
Loyola Marymount University ... CA ... 50
New York Film Academy, Los Angeles ... CA ... 53
Otis College of Art and Design ... CA ... 54
San Diego State University ... CA ... 34
San Francisco Art Institute ... CA ... 60
San Francisco State University ... CA ... 34
San Jose State University ... CA ... 34
Sonoma State University ... CA ... 35
University of the Pacific ... CA ... 70
Woodbury University ... CA ... 75
Metropolitan State University of Denver ... CO ... 80
Rocky Mountain College of Art & Design ... CO ... 82
University of Denver ... CO ... 83
University of Northern Colorado ... CO ... 83
University of Bridgeport ... CT ... 88
University of Connecticut ... CT ... 88
University of Hartford ... CT ... 89
University of New Haven ... CT ... 89
Delaware College of Art and Design ... DE ... 90
George Washington University ... DC ... 92
Howard University ... DC ... 92
Broward College ... FL ... 96
Florida International University ... FL ... 109
Florida State University ... FL ... 110
Miami Dade College ... FL ... 103
Ringling College of Art and Design ... FL ... 106
University of Florida ... FL ... 110
University of North Florida ... FL ... 110
University of South Florida ... FL ... 111
Augusta University ... GA ... 116
Columbus State University ... GA ... 118
Georgia Institute of Technology ... GA ... 120
Georgia Southern University ... GA ... 120
Georgia State University ... GA ... 121
Kennesaw State University ... GA ... 122
University of Georgia ... GA ... 127
University of North Georgia ... GA ... 127
University of West Georgia ... GA ... 127
Valdosta State University ... GA ... 127
Boise State University ... ID ... 131
University of Idaho ... ID ... 132
Bradley University ... IL ... 134
Chicago State University ... IL ... 135
College of DuPage ... IL ... 136
Eastern Illinois University ... IL ... 138
Illinois State University ... IL ... 140
Northeastern Illinois University ... IL ... 147
Northern Illinois University ... IL ... 147
School of the Art Institute of Chicago ... IL ... 151

AUD: American Speech-Language-Hearing Association: audiology (D)

BBT: Commission on Accreditation of Allied Health Education Programs: blood bank technology (C,M)

BI: Association for Biblical Higher Education: bible college education (C, A,B,M,FP,D)

Barclay College ... KS ... 175
Kansas Christian College ... KS ... 178
Manhattan Christian College ... KS ... 179
Nazarene Bible College ... KS ... 180
Clear Creek Baptist Bible College ... KY ... 184
Kentucky Mountain Bible College ... KY ... 187
Simmons College of Kentucky ... KY ... 188
Northpoint Bible College ... MA ... 223
Grace Bible College ... MI ... 230
Kuyper College ... MI ... 232
Bethany Global University ... MN ... 240
Bethlehem College & Seminary ... MN ... 241
Oak Hills Christian College ... MN ... 249
Southeastern Baptist College ... MS ... 255
Baptist Bible College ... MO ... 257
@Brookes Bible College ... MO ... 257
Calvary University ... MO ... 257
Central Christian College of the Bible ... MO ... 258
Heartland Christian College ... MO ... 260
Midwest University ... MO ... 263
Ozark Christian College ... MO ... 264
Saint Louis Christian College ... MO ... 266
Montana Bible College ... MT ... 271
@Yellowstone Christian College ... MT ... 273
@Summit Christian College ... NE ... 277
Pillar College ... NJ ... 288
Davis College ... NY ... 306
Carolina Christian College ... NC ... 336
Carolina College of Biblical Studies ... NC ... 336
Grace College of Divinity ... NC ... 338
John Wesley University ... NC ... 338
Native American Bible College ... NC ... 340
Trinity Bible College & Graduate School ... ND ... 355
Allegheny Wesleyan College ... OH ... 356
God's Bible School and College ... OH ... 362
Ohio Christian University ... OH ... 367
Rosedale Bible College ... OH ... 369
Tri-State Bible College ... OH ... 370
Valor Christian College ... OH ... 373
Family of Faith Christian University ... OK ... 375
New Hope Christian College ... OR ... 384
@Pacific Bible College ... OR ... 385
Cairn University ... PA ... 391
Clarks Summit University ... PA ... 392
Lancaster Bible College ... PA ... 399
Universidad Pentecostal Mizpa ... PR ... 527
Universidad Teologica Del Caribe ... PR ... 527
Columbia International University ... SC ... 420
@Institute of Lutheran Theology ... SD ... 427
American Baptist College ... TN ... 429
Johnson University ... TN ... 432
Mid-South Christian College ... TN ... 434
Welch College ... TN ... 441
Williamson College ... TN ... 441
Arlington Baptist University ... TX ... 442
Baptist University of the Americas ... TX ... 443
B.H. Carroll Theological Institute ... TX ... 444
@Christ Mission College ... TX ... 445
College of Biblical Studies-Houston ... TX ... 446
Dallas Christian College ... TX ... 447
King's University, The ... TX ... 451
Rio Grande Bible Institute ... TX ... 455
Bethel College ... VA ... 478
@Faith Bible College ... VA ... 480
Washington University of Virginia ... VA ... 491
@Wave Leadership College ... VA ... 492
Appalachian Bible College ... WV ... 501

CA: National Accrediting Agency for Clinical Laboratory Sciences: clinical assistant (C)

Indian Hills Community College ... IA ... 169
Northern Michigan University ... MI ... 235
Western Nebraska Community College ... NE ... 278
Clackamas Community College ... OR ... 382
Community College of Allegheny County ... PA ... 392
Edmonds Community College ... WA ... 494

CAATE: Commission on Accreditation of Athletic Training Education: athletic training (B,M)

Samford University ... AL ... 6
Troy University ... AL ... 7
University of Alabama, The ... AL ... 8
#University of Mobile ... AL ... 8
#University of West Alabama, The ... AL ... 9
Grand Canyon University ... AZ ... 12
Northern Arizona University ... AZ ... 14
#Arkansas State University-Jonesboro ... AR ... 18
Harding University Main Campus ... AR ... 19
#Henderson State University ... AR ... 19
#Southern Arkansas University ... AR ... 21
University of Arkansas Main Campus ... AR ... 21
University of Central Arkansas ... AR ... 23
Azusa Pacific University ... CA ... 26
California Baptist University ... CA ... 28
#California State University-Fresno ... CA ... 32
California State University-Fullerton ... CA ... 32
California State University-Long Beach ... CA ... 32
California State University-Northridge ... CA ... 33
California State University-Sacramento ... CA ... 33
Chapman University ... CA ... 36
#Concordia University ... CA ... 40
Point Loma Nazarene University ... CA ... 57
San Diego State University ... CA ... 34
San Jose State University ... CA ... 34
University of La Verne ... CA ... 70
University of the Pacific ... CA ... 70
#Colorado Mesa University ... CO ... 77
Colorado State University-Pueblo ... CO ... 78
Metropolitan State University of Denver ... CO ... 80
University of Northern Colorado ... CO ... 83
Central Connecticut State University ... CT ... 84
Quinnipiac University ... CT ... 88
Sacred Heart University ... CT ... 88
Southern Connecticut State University ... CT ... 85
University of Connecticut ... CT ... 88
University of Delaware ... DE ... 90
Barry University ... FL ... 95
Florida Gulf Coast University ... FL ... 109
Florida International University ... FL ... 109
Florida State University ... FL ... 110
Nova Southeastern University ... FL ... 104
#Palm Beach Atlantic University ... FL ... 104
University of Central Florida ... FL ... 110
University of Florida ... FL ... 110
University of Miami ... FL ... 112
University of North Florida ... FL ... 110
University of South Florida ... FL ... 111
University of Tampa ... FL ... 113
University of West Florida ... FL ... 111
Georgia College & State University ... GA ... 119
Georgia Southern University ... GA ... 120
#Life University ... GA ... 122
Piedmont College ... GA ... 124
University of Georgia ... GA ... 127
University of North Georgia ... GA ... 127
Valdosta State University ... GA ... 127
University of Hawaii at Manoa ... HI ... 129
Boise State University ... ID ... 131
Idaho State University ... ID ... 132
University of Idaho ... ID ... 132
Aurora University ... IL ... 133
#Eastern Illinois University ... IL ... 138
Illinois State University ... IL ... 140
#Lewis University ... IL ... 143
#McKendree University ... IL ... 145
Millikin University ... IL ... 145
North Central College ... IL ... 147
North Park University ... IL ... 147
#Northern Illinois University ... IL ... 147
#Olivet Nazarene University ... IL ... 148
Trinity International University ... IL ... 153
Western Illinois University ... IL ... 155
Anderson University ... IN ... 156
Ball State University ... IN ... 156
Franklin College of Indiana ... IN ... 157
#Indiana State University ... IN ... 159
Indiana University Bloomington ... IN ... 159
Indiana Wesleyan University ... IN ... 161
#Manchester University ... IN ... 162
Purdue University Main Campus ... IN ... 163
University of Evansville ... IN ... 164
University of Indianapolis ... IN ... 164
Buena Vista University ... IA ... 167
Central College ... IA ... 167
Clarke University ... IA ... 167
Coe College ... IA ... 167
#Graceland University ... IA ... 169
Iowa State University ... IA ... 166
Loras College ... IA ... 171
Luther College ... IA ... 171
Northwestern College ... IA ... 172
Simpson College ... IA ... 173
University of Iowa ... IA ... 166
University of Northern Iowa ... IA ... 167
#Upper Iowa University ... IA ... 173
#Benedictine College ... KS ... 175
#Bethany College ... KS ... 175
Bethel College ... KS ... 175
Emporia State University ... KS ... 177
Fort Hays State University ... KS ... 177
Kansas State University ... KS ... 179
MidAmerica Nazarene University ... KS ... 179
Southwestern College ... KS ... 181
Sterling College ... KS ... 181
#Tabor College ... KS ... 181
University of Kansas Main Campus ... KS ... 181
Washburn University ... KS ... 182
Wichita State University ... KS ... 182
Eastern Kentucky University ... KY ... 184
Georgetown College ... KY ... 184
#Murray State University ... KY ... 188
Northern Kentucky University ... KY ... 188
Spalding University ... KY ... 189
#Union College ... KY ... 189
University of Kentucky ... KY ... 190
#Louisiana College ... LA ... 191
Louisiana State University and Agricultural and Mechanical College ... LA ... 193
#McNeese State University ... LA ... 197
Nicholls State University ... LA ... 197
Southeastern Louisiana University ... LA ... 197
#University of Louisiana at Lafayette ... LA ... 197
University of Maine ... ME ... 201
#University of Maine at Presque Isle ... ME ... 201
University of New England ... ME ... 202
#University of Southern Maine ... ME ... 201
Frostburg State University ... MD ... 209
Salisbury University ... MD ... 209
Towson University ... MD ... 209
Boston University ... MA ... 212
Bridgewater State University ... MA ... 217
Endicott College ... MA ... 214
Lasell College ... MA ... 216
Massachusetts College of Liberal Arts ... MA ... 218
Merrimack College ... MA ... 221
Salem State University ... MA ... 218
Springfield College ... MA ... 224
#Westfield State University ... MA ... 218
Adrian College ... MI ... 226
Albion College ... MI ... 226
#Alma College ... MI ... 226
Aquinas College ... MI ... 227
Central Michigan University ... MI ... 228
Eastern Michigan University ... MI ... 229
Grand Valley State University ... MI ... 230
Hope College ... MI ... 231
Lake Superior State University ... MI ... 232
Michigan State University ... MI ... 233
Northern Michigan University ... MI ... 235
Saginaw Valley State University ... MI ... 236
University of Michigan-Ann Arbor ... MI ... 237
#Western Michigan University ... MI ... 239
Bethel University ... MN ... 240
College of Saint Scholastica, The ... MN ... 241
Gustavus Adolphus College ... MN ... 242
#Minnesota State University Moorhead ... MN ... 246
Minnesota State University, Mankato ... MN ... 246
St. Cloud State University ... MN ... 247
Winona State University ... MN ... 248
University of Southern Mississippi ... MS ... 256
Central Methodist University ... MO ... 258
#Culver-Stockton College ... MO ... 259
Evangel University ... MO ... 260
Lindenwood University ... MO ... 261
Missouri State University ... MO ... 263
#Missouri Valley College ... MO ... 264
Saint Louis University ... MO ... 266
#Southeast Missouri State University ... MO ... 266
Southwest Baptist University ... MO ... 267
Truman State University ... MO ... 267
University of Central Missouri ... MO ... 268
University of Missouri - Columbia ... MO ... 268
#William Woods University ... MO ... 270
Montana State University - Billings ... MT ... 272
University of Montana - Missoula ... MT ... 271
Nebraska Wesleyan University ... NE ... 276
University of Nebraska at Kearney ... NE ... 277
#University of Nebraska at Omaha ... NE ... 277
University of Nebraska - Lincoln ... NE ... 277
University of Nevada, Las Vegas ... NV ... 279
Colby-Sawyer College ... NH ... 280
Keene State College ... NH ... 283
#Plymouth State University ... NH ... 283
University of New Hampshire ... NH ... 282
Kean University ... NJ ... 286
Montclair State University ... NJ ... 287
Rowan University ... NJ ... 289
Seton Hall University ... NJ ... 291
William Paterson University of New Jersey ... NJ ... 292
New Mexico State University Main Campus ... NM ... 295
University of New Mexico Main Campus ... NM ... 296
#Alfred University ... NY ... 298
#Canisius College ... NY ... 300
Daemen College ... NY ... 306
#Dominican College of Blauvelt ... NY ... 306
Hofstra University ... NY ... 310
Ithaca College ... NY ... 311
Marist College ... NY ... 314
State University of New York College at Cortland ... NY ... 327
State University of New York, The College at Brockport ... NY ... 326
Stony Brook University ... NY ... 325
Appalachian State University ... NC ... 349
Campbell University ... NC ... 336
#Catawba College ... NC ... 336
East Carolina University ... NC ... 349
Gardner-Webb University ... NC ... 337
Greensboro College ... NC ... 338
High Point University ... NC ... 338
#Lees-McRae College ... NC ... 339
Lenoir-Rhyne University ... NC ... 339
#Mars Hill University ... NC ... 339
Methodist University ... NC ... 340
#North Carolina Central University ... NC ... 350
University of North Carolina at Chapel Hill ... NC ... 351
University of North Carolina at Charlotte ... NC ... 351
University of North Carolina at Greensboro ... NC ... 351
#University of North Carolina at Pembroke ... NC ... 351
University of North Carolina Wilmington ... NC ... 352
Western Carolina University ... NC ... 352
Wingate University ... NC ... 353
Minot State University ... ND ... 354
North Dakota State University Main Campus ... ND ... 354
University of Mary ... ND ... 355
University of North Dakota ... ND ... 353
Valley City State University ... ND ... 354
#Ashland University ... OH ... 356
Baldwin Wallace University ... OH ... 357
#Bowling Green State University ... OH ... 357
Capital University ... OH ... 358
Cedarville University ... OH ... 358
#Defiance College, The ... OH ... 361
#Denison University ... OH ... 361
Heidelberg University ... OH ... 362
Kent State University Kent Campus ... OH ... 363
Marietta College ... OH ... 365
#Miami University ... OH ... 365
Mount St. Joseph University ... OH ... 366
Muskingum University ... OH ... 366
Ohio Northern University ... OH ... 367
Ohio State University Main Campus, The ... OH ... 367
Ohio University Main Campus ... OH ... 368
Otterbein University ... OH ... 368
#Shawnee State University ... OH ... 369
University of Akron, Main Campus, The ... OH ... 371
University of Cincinnati Main Campus ... OH ... 371
University of Findlay, The ... OH ... 372
#University of Mount Union ... OH ... 372
University of Toledo ... OH ... 372
Wilmington College ... OH ... 373
Wright State University Main Campus ... OH ... 374
Xavier University ... OH ... 374
#East Central University ... OK ... 375
Oklahoma State University ... OK ... 377
#Southern Nazarene University ... OK ... 379
#Southwestern Oklahoma State University ... OK ... 380
University of Central Oklahoma ... OK ... 380
University of Tulsa ... OK ... 381
George Fox University ... OR ... 383
Linfield College ... OR ... 383
Oregon State University ... OR ... 385
Pacific University ... OR ... 385
University of Oregon ... OR ... 387
Alvernia University ... PA ... 389
Bloomsburg University of Pennsylvania ... PA ... 405
#California University of Pennsylvania ... PA ... 405
Duquesne University ... PA ... 394
East Stroudsburg University of Pennsylvania ... PA ... 406
Eastern University ... PA ... 394
Gannon University ... PA ... 395
#Immaculata University ... PA ... 397
#Indiana University of Pennsylvania ... PA ... 406
King's College ... PA ... 398
Lock Haven University ... PA ... 406
#Marywood University ... PA ... 401
Mercyhurst University ... PA ... 401
Messiah College ... PA ... 401
Neumann University ... PA ... 402
Penn State University Park ... PA ... 403
Slippery Rock University of Pennsylvania ... PA ... 407
Temple University ... PA ... 411
University of Pittsburgh ... PA ... 412
Waynesburg University ... PA ... 414
West Chester University of Pennsylvania ... PA ... 407
Charleston Southern University ... SC ... 419
College of Charleston ... SC ... 420
#Erskine College ... SC ... 421
Limestone College ... SC ... 422
University of South Carolina Columbia ... SC ... 424
Winthrop University ... SC ... 426
Augustana University ... SD ... 426
Dakota Wesleyan University ... SD ... 427
Presentation College ... SD ... 427
South Dakota State University ... SD ... 429
Bethel University ... TN ... 430
#Cumberland University ... TN ... 431
#King University ... TN ... 432
Lee University ... TN ... 432
Lincoln Memorial University ... TN ... 433
Middle Tennessee State University ... TN ... 434
#Tusculum College ... TN ... 439
Union University ... TN ... 439
University of Tennessee at Chattanooga ... TN ... 440
Baylor University ... TX ... 444
#East Texas Baptist University ... TX ... 448
Hardin-Simmons University ... TX ... 450
Howard Payne University ... TX ... 450
Midwestern State University ... TX ... 453
Sam Houston State University ... TX ... 462
Stephen F. Austin State University ... TX ... 458
Texas A & M University ... TX ... 459
Texas A & M University - Corpus Christi ... TX ... 460
Texas Christian University ... TX ... 461
Texas Lutheran University ... TX ... 461
Texas State University ... TX ... 463
Texas Tech University Health Sciences Center ... TX ... 463
Texas Wesleyan University ... TX ... 463
University of Houston ... TX ... 465
University of Texas at Arlington, The ... TX ... 467
University of Texas at Austin ... TX ... 467
University of Texas of the Permian Basin ... TX ... 469

CACREP: Council for Accreditation of Counseling & Related Educational Programs: counseling and its specialties (M,D)

CAEP: Council for the Accreditation of Educator Preparation: teacher education (B,M,D)

CAEPN: Council for the Accreditation of Educator Preparation: teacher education (B,M,D)

CAEPT: Council for the Accreditation of Educator Preparation: teacher education (B,M,D)

Boricua College ... NY ... 299
Cazenovia College ... NY ... 300
Clarkson University ... NY ... 304
Colgate University ... NY ... 304
College of Mount Saint Vincent ... NY ... 304
College of New Rochelle, The ... NY ... 305
Daemen College ... NY ... 306
Dominican College of Blauvelt ... NY ... 306
Elmira College ... NY ... 307
Hartwick College ... NY ... 309
Hobart and William Smith Colleges ... NY ... 310
Hofstra University ... NY ... 310
Houghton College ... NY ... 310
Keuka College ... NY ... 312
Le Moyne College ... NY ... 312
Manhattan College ... NY ... 313
Medaille College ... NY ... 314
Nazareth College of Rochester ... NY ... 316
New York University ... NY ... 318
Pratt Institute ... NY ... 320
Roberts Wesleyan College ... NY ... 321
Rochester Institute of Technology ... NY ... 321
St. Francis College ... NY ... 322
St. John's University ... NY ... 322
Saint Joseph's College, New York ... NY ... 322
St. Lawrence University ... NY ... 323
Sarah Lawrence College ... NY ... 323
Skidmore College ... NY ... 324
State University of New York at Binghamton ... NY ... 325
State University of New York College at Plattsburgh ... NY ... 327
State University of New York Empire State College ... NY ... 329
Touro College ... NY ... 331
University at Albany, SUNY ... NY ... 324
University at Buffalo-SUNY ... NY ... 325
Utica College ... NY ... 332
Vassar College ... NY ... 333
Wells College ... NY ... 333
Yeshiva University ... NY ... 334
Lees-McRae College ... NC ... 339
Case Western Reserve University ... OH ... 358
Cincinnati Christian University ... OH ... 359
Lake Erie College ... OH ... 364
Lourdes University ... OH ... 364
Mount St. Joseph University ... OH ... 366
Ohio Christian University ... OH ... 367
Wilmington College ... OH ... 373
Xavier University ... OH ... 374
University of Tulsa ... OK ... 381
Robert Morris University ... PA ... 409
University of Scranton, The ... PA ... 413
Inter American University of Puerto Rico / Metropolitan Campus ... PR ... 524
Inter American University of Puerto Rico Aguadilla Campus ... PR ... 523
Inter American University of Puerto Rico Arecibo Campus ... PR ... 523
Inter American University of Puerto Rico Barranquitas Campus ... PR ... 523
Inter American University of Puerto Rico Fajardo Campus ... PR ... 523
Inter American University of Puerto Rico Guayama Campus ... PR ... 524
Inter American University of Puerto Rico Ponce Campus ... PR ... 524
Inter American University of Puerto Rico San German Campus ... PR ... 524
National University College ... PR ... 525
Pontifical Catholic University of Puerto Rico, The ... PR ... 525
Universidad del Este ... PR ... 525
Universidad Del Turabo ... PR ... 526
Universidad Metropolitana ... PR ... 526
Texas State University ... TX ... 463
University of St. Thomas ... TX ... 466
Brigham Young University ... UT ... 471
Dixie State University ... UT ... 473
Utah State University ... UT ... 473
Utah Valley University ... UT ... 473
Weber State University ... UT ... 473
Westminster College ... UT ... 474
Bluefield College ... VA ... 478
Emory & Henry College ... VA ... 480
Hollins University ... VA ... 481
Mary Baldwin University ... VA ... 482
Regent University ... VA ... 484
Roanoke College ... VA ... 484
Shenandoah University ... VA ... 485
University of Richmond ... VA ... 486
University of Virginia ... VA ... 486
Washington and Lee University ... VA ... 491
Saint Martin's University ... WA ... 497
Alderson Broaddus University ... WV ... 501
Wheeling Jesuit University ... WV ... 505
Lakeland University ... WI ... 507

CAHIIM: Commission on Accreditation for Health Informatics and Information Management Education: health information management and health informatics (A,B,M)

Alabama State University ... AL ... 4
Bishop State Community College ... AL ... 1
Wallace State Community College - Hanceville ... AL ... 3
University of Alaska Southeast ... AK ... 10
Central Arizona College ... AZ ... 11
Phoenix College ... AZ ... 14
Arkansas Tech University ... AR ... 18
National Park College ... AR ... 20
NorthWest Arkansas Community College ... AR ... 20
University of Arkansas for Medical Sciences AR ... 22
Brightwood College ... CA ... 28
City College of San Francisco ... CA ... 37
Cosumnes River College ... CA ... 50
Cypress College ... CA ... 53
East Los Angeles College ... CA ... 48
Fresno City College ... CA ... 66
Loma Linda University ... CA ... 48
Saddleback College ... CA ... 64
San Diego Mesa College ... CA ... 60
Santa Barbara City College ... CA ... 62
Arapahoe Community College ... CO ... 76
Front Range Community College ... CO ... 79
Regis University ... CO ... 82
Charter Oak State College ... CT ... 84
Lincoln College of New England ... CT ... 87
Broward College ... FL ... 96
College of Central Florida ... FL ... 97
Daytona State College ... FL ... 97
Florida Agricultural and Mechanical University ... FL ... 109
Florida SouthWestern State College ... FL ... 100
Florida State College at Jacksonville ... FL ... 100
Indian River State College ... FL ... 101
Keiser University ... FL ... 102
Lake-Sumter State College ... FL ... 103
Miami Dade College ... FL ... 103
Palm Beach State College ... FL ... 105
Pensacola State College ... FL ... 105
St. Johns River State College ... FL ... 106
St. Petersburg College ... FL ... 107
Santa Fe College ... FL ... 107
Seminole State College of Florida ... FL ... 107
Southern Technical College ... FL ... 108
University of Central Florida ... FL ... 110
Albany State University ... GA ... 114
Athens Technical College ... GA ... 115
Atlanta Technical College ... GA ... 115
Augusta University ... GA ... 116
Georgia Northwestern Technical College ... GA ... 120
Gwinnett Technical College ... GA ... 121
Ogeechee Technical College ... GA ... 123
West Georgia Technical College ... GA ... 128
Wiregrass Georgia Technical College ... GA ... 128
University of Hawaii - Leeward Community College ... HI ... 130
Idaho State University ... ID ... 132
Chicago State University ... IL ... 135
College of DuPage ... IL ... 136
College of Lake County ... IL ... 136
Danville Area Community College ... IL ... 137
DeVry University - Chicago Campus ... IL ... 137
Harper College ... IL ... 139
Illinois State University ... IL ... 140
John A. Logan College ... IL ... 141
Joliet Junior College ... IL ... 142
Midstate College ... IL ... 145
Moraine Valley Community College ... IL ... 146
Northwestern College ... IL ... 148
Oakton Community College ... IL ... 148
Rend Lake College ... IL ... 149
Resurrection University ... IL ... 149
Richland Community College ... IL ... 149
Shawnee Community College ... IL ... 151
Southwestern Illinois College ... IL ... 152
University of Illinois at Chicago ... IL ... 153
Waubonsee Community College ... IL ... 155
Indiana Tech ... IN ... 159
Indiana University Northwest ... IN ... 160
Indiana University-Purdue University Indianapolis ... IN ... 160
Ivy Tech Community College of Indiana-Central Indiana ... IN ... 161
Vincennes University ... IN ... 165
Indian Hills Community College ... IA ... 169
Kirkwood Community College ... IA ... 171
Northeast Iowa Community College ... IA ... 172
Northwest Iowa Community College ... IA ... 172
Scott Community College ... IA ... 169
Hutchinson Community College ... KS ... 178
Neosho County Community College ... KS ... 180
University of Saint Mary ... KS ... 182
Washburn University ... KS ... 182
Eastern Kentucky University ... KY ... 184
Gateway Community and Technical College KY ... 185
Hazard Community and Technical College . KY ... 185
Jefferson Community and Technical College ... KY ... 186
Sullivan University ... KY ... 189
Western Kentucky University ... KY ... 190
Delgado Community College ... LA ... 192
Louisiana Tech University ... LA ... 197
Southern University at New Orleans ... LA ... 195
Southern University at Shreveport-Louisiana LA ... 196
University of Louisiana at Lafayette ... LA ... 197
Beal College ... ME ... 198
Kennebec Valley Community College ... ME ... 200
Saint Joseph's College of Maine ... ME ... 200
Anne Arundel Community College ... MD ... 202
Baltimore City Community College ... MD ... 202
Community College of Baltimore County, The ... MD ... 203
Coppin State University ... MD ... 208
Montgomery College ... MD ... 205
Prince George's Community College ... MD ... 206
University of Maryland University College ... MD ... 208
Boston University ... MA ... 212
Bristol Community College ... MA ... 219
Fisher College ... MA ... 215
Laboure College ... MA ... 216
Springfield Technical Community College ... MA ... 221
Baker College of Flint ... MI ... 227
Davenport University ... MI ... 229
Ferris State University ... MI ... 230
Grand Valley State University ... MI ... 230
Macomb Community College ... MI ... 233
St. Clair County Community College ... MI ... 236
Schoolcraft College ... MI ... 236
Southwestern Michigan College ... MI ... 237
Anoka Technical College ... MN ... 244
College of Saint Scholastica, The ... MN ... 241
Minnesota State Community and Technical College ... MN ... 245
Rasmussen College - St. Cloud ... MN ... 249
Ridgewater College ... MN ... 247
Rochester Community and Technical College ... MN ... 247
St. Catherine University ... MN ... 249
Saint Cloud Technical and Community College ... MN ... 247
Saint Paul College-A Community & Technical College ... MN ... 247
Hinds Community College ... MS ... 253
Itawamba Community College ... MS ... 253
Meridian Community College ... MS ... 253
Southwest Mississippi Community College . MS ... 256
University of Mississippi Medical Center ... MS ... 256
East Central College ... MO ... 259
Jefferson College ... MO ... 261
Metropolitan Community College - Penn Valley ... MO ... 262
Missouri Western State University ... MO ... 264
Ozarks Technical Community College ... MO ... 264
St. Charles Community College ... MO ... 265
Saint Louis University ... MO ... 266
State Fair Community College ... MO ... 267
Stephens College ... MO ... 267
Great Falls College Montana State University ... MT ... 272
Central Community College ... NE ... 273
Clarkson College ... NE ... 273
Metropolitan Community College ... NE ... 275
Western Nebraska Community College ... NE ... 278
Brightwood College ... NV ... 278
College of Southern Nevada ... NV ... 278
Manchester Community College ... NH ... 280
Brookdale Community College ... NJ ... 284
Camden County College ... NJ ... 284
Passaic County Community College ... NJ ... 288
Raritan Valley Community College ... NJ ... 289
Rowan College at Burlington County ... NJ ... 289
Central New Mexico Community College ... NM ... 293
San Juan College ... NM ... 296
Alfred State College ... NY ... 328
City University of New York Borough of Manhattan Community College ... NY ... 301
City University of New York Graduate Center ... NY ... 302
Erie Community College ... NY ... 307
Medaille College ... NY ... 314
Mohawk Valley Community College ... NY ... 315
Monroe Community College ... NY ... 315
Onondaga Community College ... NY ... 319
Plaza College ... NY ... 320
SUNY Broome Community College ... NY ... 326
SUNY Polytechnic Institute ... NY ... 330
Trocaire College ... NY ... 331
Brunswick Community College ... NC ... 341
Catawba Valley Community College ... NC ... 341
Central Piedmont Community College ... NC ... 342
Craven Community College ... NC ... 342
Davidson County Community College ... NC ... 342
Durham Technical Community College ... NC ... 342
East Carolina University ... NC ... 349
Edgecombe Community College ... NC ... 343
McDowell Technical Community College ... NC ... 344
Pitt Community College ... NC ... 345
Richmond Community College ... NC ... 345
Southwestern Community College ... NC ... 346
North Dakota State College of Science ... ND ... 355
Cincinnati State Technical and Community College ... OH ... 359
Columbus State Community College ... OH ... 360
Cuyahoga Community College ... OH ... 360
Eastern Gateway Community College - Jefferson County Campus ... OH ... 361
Hocking College ... OH ... 362
Lakeland Community College ... OH ... 364
Marion Technical College ... OH ... 365
Mercy College of Ohio ... OH ... 365
Ohio State University Main Campus, The ... OH ... 367
Owens Community College ... OH ... 369
Sinclair Community College ... OH ... 370
Stark State College ... OH ... 370
Terra State Community College ... OH ... 370
University of Cincinnati-Clermont College ... OH ... 371
University of Cincinnati Main Campus ... OH ... 371
University of Northwestern Ohio ... OH ... 372
University of Toledo ... OH ... 372
Zane State College ... OH ... 374
Rose State College ... OK ... 379
Southwestern Oklahoma State University ... OK ... 380
Tulsa Community College ... OK ... 380
Central Oregon Community College ... OR ... 382
Oregon Health & Science University ... OR ... 385
Portland Community College ... OR ... 386
Community College of Allegheny County ... PA ... 392
Lehigh Carbon Community College ... PA ... 400
Peirce College ... PA ... 403
Pennsylvania College of Technology ... PA ... 404
South Hills School of Business and Technology ... PA ... 410
Temple University ... PA ... 411
University of Pittsburgh ... PA ... 412
Huertas College ... PR ... 522
University of Puerto Rico-Medical Sciences Campus ... PR ... 528
Florence - Darlington Technical College ... SC ... 421
Greenville Technical College ... SC ... 421
Midlands Technical College ... SC ... 422
University of South Carolina Columbia ... SC ... 424
University of South Carolina Upstate ... SC ... 425
Dakota State University ... SD ... 428
National American University ... SD ... 427
Chattanooga State Community College ... TN ... 436
Dyersburg State Community College ... TN ... 437
Roane State Community College ... TN ... 438
Tennessee State University ... TN ... 438
University of Tennessee Health Science Center ... TN ... 440
Volunteer State Community College ... TN ... 438
Walters State Community College ... TN ... 438
Austin Community College District ... TX ... 443
Blinn College ... TX ... 444
Brightwood College ... TX ... 445
College of the Mainland ... TX ... 446
Collin County Community College District ... TX ... 446
Del Mar College ... TX ... 448
El Paso Community College ... TX ... 449
Houston Community College ... TX ... 450
Lamar Institute of Technology ... TX ... 462
Lee College ... TX ... 451
Lone Star College System ... TX ... 452
McLennan Community College ... TX ... 452
Midland College ... TX ... 453
Panola College ... TX ... 454
Parker University ... TX ... 454
St. Philip's College ... TX ... 441
San Jacinto College North ... TX ... 456
South Texas College ... TX ... 456
Tarrant County College District ... TX ... 458
Texas Southern University ... TX ... 461
Texas State Technical College Waco ... TX ... 461
Texas State University ... TX ... 463
Tyler Junior College ... TX ... 464
Vernon College ... TX ... 469
Wharton County Junior College ... TX ... 471
Weber State University ... UT ... 473
Western Governors University ... UT ... 474
Lord Fairfax Community College ... VA ... 488
Northern Virginia Community College ... VA ... 488
Tidewater Community College ... VA ... 489
Shoreline Community College ... WA ... 498
Spokane Community College ... WA ... 493
Tacoma Community College ... WA ... 499
University of Washington ... WA ... 499
Marshall University ... WV ... 504
Mountwest Community and Technical College ... WV ... 503
Pierpont Community & Technical College ... WV ... 503
West Virginia Northern Community College WV ... 503
Chippewa Valley Technical College ... WI ... 513
Fox Valley Technical College ... WI ... 513
Mid-State Technical College ... WI ... 514
Moraine Park Technical College ... WI ... 514
Northeast Wisconsin Technical College ... WI ... 514
University of Wisconsin-Green Bay ... WI ... 510
Waukesha County Technical College ... WI ... 515
Western Technical College ... WI ... 515

Wisconsin Indianhead Technical College .... WI 515

CARTE: Commission on Accreditation of Recreational Therapy Education: recreational therapy (B,M)

University of New Hampshire .... NH ... 282
East Carolina University .... NC ... 349
Western Carolina University .... NC ... 352
Oklahoma State University .... OK ... 377
Slippery Rock University of Pennsylvania .... PA ... 407
Temple University .... PA ... 411

CEA: Commission on English Language Program Accreditation: english language (C)

University of Alabama at Birmingham .... AL 8
University of Alabama, The .... AL 8
University of Arizona .... AZ 16
Arkansas State University-Jonesboro .... AR 18
Arkansas Tech University .... AR 18
California State Polytechnic University-Pomona .... CA 31
California State University-Long Beach .... CA 32
Grossmont College .... CA 45
Los Angeles Pacific College .... CA 50
National Polytechnic College .... CA 53
San Jose State University .... CA 34
University of California-Irvine .... CA 69
University of California-San Diego .... CA 69
University of San Diego .... CA 71
Colorado State University .... CO 78
University of Colorado Boulder .... CO 83
University of Denver .... CO 83
University of Northern Colorado .... CO 83
Sacred Heart University .... CT 88
University of Connecticut .... CT 88
University of Delaware .... DE 90
Gallaudet University .... DC 91
Georgetown University .... DC 92
Atlantis University .... FL 95
Aviator College of Aeronautical Science & Technology .... FL 95
Embry-Riddle Aeronautical University .... FL 98
Saint Leo University .... FL ... 106
St. Petersburg College .... FL ... 107
University of Central Florida .... FL ... 110
University of Florida .... FL ... 110
University of Miami .... FL ... 112
University of South Florida .... FL ... 111
Valencia College .... FL ... 113
Georgia Christian University .... GA ... 119
Georgia Institute of Technology .... GA ... 120
Georgia State University .... GA ... 121
University of Georgia .... GA ... 127
University of Hawaii at Hilo .... HI ... 129
University of Hawaii at Manoa .... HI ... 129
University of Idaho .... ID ... 132
DePaul University .... IL ... 137
Southern Illinois University Carbondale .... IL ... 152
University of Illinois at Chicago .... IL ... 153
University of Illinois at Urbana-Champaign .... IL ... 154
Western Illinois University .... IL ... 155
Ball State University .... IN ... 156
Indiana University Bloomington .... IN ... 159
Purdue University Northwest .... IN ... 163
Taylor University .... IN ... 164
University of Southern Indiana .... IN ... 165
University of Iowa .... IA ... 166
University of Northern Iowa .... IA ... 167
Emporia State University .... KS ... 177
Kansas State University .... KS ... 179
Pittsburg State University .... KS ... 180
University of Kansas Main Campus .... KS ... 181
Washburn University .... KS ... 182
University of Maine .... ME ... 201
Mount St. Mary's University .... MD ... 206
University of Maryland College Park .... MD ... 207
Boston University .... MA ... 212
Eastern Michigan University .... MI ... 229
Ferris State University .... MI ... 230
Michigan State University .... MI ... 233
Michigan Technological University .... MI ... 234
Saginaw Valley State University .... MI ... 236
University of Michigan-Dearborn .... MI ... 238
University of Michigan-Flint .... MI ... 238
Western Michigan University .... MI ... 239
University of Minnesota .... MN ... 250
Missouri State University .... MO ... 263
Missouri University of Science & Technology .... MO ... 269
Southeast Missouri State University .... MO ... 266
University of Central Missouri .... MO ... 268
University of Missouri - Kansas City .... MO ... 268
University of Montana - Missoula .... MT ... 271
Creighton University .... NE ... 274
University of Nebraska at Omaha .... NE ... 277
College of Southern Nevada .... NV ... 278
University of Nevada, Reno .... NV ... 279
Rutgers University - New Brunswick .... NJ ... 290
Columbia University in the City of New York .... NY ... 305
Rochester Institute of Technology .... NY ... 321
University at Buffalo-SUNY .... NY ... 325
East Carolina University .... NC ... 349
University of North Carolina Wilmington .... NC ... 352
Ashland University .... OH ... 356
Cleveland State University .... OH ... 359
Ohio Northern University .... OH ... 367
University of Dayton .... OH ... 372
University of Findlay, The .... OH ... 372
Wright State University Main Campus .... OH ... 374
Xavier University .... OH ... 374
University of Tulsa .... OK ... 381
Oregon State University .... OR ... 385
Portland State University .... OR ... 386
University of Oregon .... OR ... 387
Willamette University .... OR ... 388
Drexel University .... PA ... 394
Duquesne University .... PA ... 394
Penn State University Park .... PA ... 403
University of Pennsylvania .... PA ... 412
University of Pittsburgh .... PA ... 412
Wilkes University .... PA ... 414
University of South Carolina Columbia .... SC ... 424
University of Tennessee at Martin .... TN ... 440
Dallas Baptist University .... TX ... 447
Lone Star College System .... TX ... 452
San Antonio College .... TX ... 442
Stephen F. Austin State University .... TX ... 458
Texas State University .... TX ... 463
University of Houston .... TX ... 465
University of North Texas .... TX ... 466
University of Texas at Arlington, The .... TX ... 467
University of Texas at Austin .... TX ... 467
University of Texas at San Antonio .... TX ... 468
University of Utah, The .... UT ... 472
Utah State University .... UT ... 473
Utah Valley University .... UT ... 473
Weber State University .... UT ... 473
Saint Michael's College .... VT ... 476
American National University .... VA ... 477
George Mason University .... VA ... 481
Stratford University .... VA ... 485
Virginia Commonwealth University .... VA ... 487
Virginia International University .... VA ... 490
Virginia Polytechnic Institute and State University .... VA ... 490
Gonzaga University .... WA .. 495
University of Washington .... WA .. 499
Washington State University .... WA .. 499
Western Washington University .... WA .. 500
West Virginia University .... WV .. 505

CGTECH: National Accrediting Agency for Clinical Laboratory Sciences: cytogenetic technologist (B)

University of Connecticut .... CT 88
Kennesaw State University .... GA ... 122
Northern Michigan University .... MI ... 235
University of Texas MD Anderson Cancer Center, The .... TX 469

CHIRO: Council on Chiropractic Education: chiropractic education (FP,D)

Life Chiropractic College West .... CA 48
Southern California University of Health Sciences .... CA 65
University of Bridgeport .... CT 88
Life University .... GA ... 122
National University of Health Sciences .... IL 147
Palmer College of Chiropractic .... IA 172
Cleveland University - Kansas City .... KS 176
Northwestern Health Sciences University .... MN ... 249
Logan University .... MO .. 262
D'Youville College .... NY ... 307
New York Chiropractic College .... NY ... 317
University of Western States .... OR ... 387
Sherman College of Chiropractic .... SC ... 423
Parker University .... TX ... 454
Texas Chiropractic College .... TX ... 460

CIDA: Council for Interior Design Accreditation: interior design (B,M)

Auburn University .... AL 4
Samford University .... AL 6
University of Alabama, The .... AL 8
University of North Alabama .... AL 9
Arizona State University .... AZ 10
Art Institute of Phoenix, The .... AZ 11
Northern Arizona University .... AZ 14
Harding University Main Campus .... AR 19
University of Arkansas Main Campus .... AR 21
University of Central Arkansas .... AR 23
Academy of Art University .... CA 24
#California College of the Arts .... CA 28
California State Polytechnic University-Pomona .... CA 31
California State University-Fresno .... CA 32
California State University-Northridge .... CA 33
California State University-Sacramento .... CA 33
Design Institute of San Diego .... CA 41
Interior Designers Institute .... CA 46
#San Diego State University .... CA 34
Woodbury University .... CA 75
Art Institute of Colorado, The .... CO 76
Colorado State University .... CO 78
Rocky Mountain College of Art & Design .... CO 82
George Washington University .... DC 92
Art Institute of Fort Lauderdale, The .... FL 94
Florida International University .... FL 109
Florida State University .... FL 110
Miami International University of Art & Design .... FL 104
Ringling College of Art and Design .... FL 106
University of Florida .... FL 110
Art Institute of Atlanta, The .... GA ... 115
Brenau University .... GA ... 116
Georgia Southern University .... GA ... 120
Savannah College of Art and Design .... GA ... 125
University of Georgia .... GA ... 127
Chaminade University of Honolulu .... HI ... 129
University of Idaho .... ID ... 132
Columbia College Chicago .... IL 136
Illinois Institute of Art, The .... IL 140
Illinois State University .... IL 140
Southern Illinois University Carbondale .... IL 152
Ball State University .... IN 156
Indiana State University .... IN 159
Indiana University Bloomington .... IN 159
Indiana University-Purdue University Indianapolis .... IN 160
Purdue University Main Campus .... IN 163
Iowa State University .... IA 166
University of Northern Iowa .... IA 167
Kansas State University .... KS 179
Sullivan College of Technology and Design .... KY ... 189
University of Kentucky .... KY ... 190
University of Louisville .... KY ... 190
Louisiana State University and Agricultural and Mechanical College .... LA 193
Louisiana Tech University .... LA 197
University of Louisiana at Lafayette .... LA 197
Boston Architectural College .... MA ... 212
Endicott College .... MA ... 214
Mount Ida College .... MA ... 222
Suffolk University .... MA ... 224
Wentworth Institute of Technology .... MA ... 225
Central Michigan University .... MI ... 228
College for Creative Studies .... MI ... 228
Eastern Michigan University .... MI ... 229
Lawrence Technological University .... MI ... 233
Michigan State University .... MI ... 233
Western Michigan University .... MI ... 239
Dunwoody College of Technology .... MN ... 242
University of Minnesota .... MN ... 250
Mississippi College .... MS ... 254
Mississippi State University .... MS ... 254
University of Southern Mississippi .... MS ... 256
Maryville University of Saint Louis .... MO .. 262
Southeast Missouri State University .... MO .. 266
University of Central Missouri .... MO .. 268
University of Missouri - Columbia .... MO .. 268
University of Nebraska at Kearney .... NE ... 277
University of Nebraska - Lincoln .... NE ... 277
University of Nevada, Las Vegas .... NV ... 279
Berkeley College .... NJ ... 283
Kean University .... NJ ... 286
New Jersey Institute of Technology .... NJ ... 288
Cornell University .... NY ... 306
Fashion Institute of Technology .... NY ... 308
New York Institute of Technology .... NY ... 317
New York School of Interior Design .... NY ... 318
Pratt Institute .... NY ... 320
Rochester Institute of Technology .... NY ... 321
School of Visual Arts .... NY ... 324
State University of New York College at Buffalo .... NY ... 326
Syracuse University .... NY ... 330
Villa Maria College of Buffalo .... NY ... 333
Appalachian State University .... NC ... 349
East Carolina University .... NC ... 349
High Point University .... NC ... 338
Meredith College .... NC ... 339
University of North Carolina at Greensboro .... NC ... 351
Western Carolina University .... NC ... 352
North Dakota State University Main Campus .... ND ... 354
Kent State University Kent Campus .... OH ... 363
Miami University .... OH ... 365
Ohio State University Main Campus, The .... OH ... 367
Ohio University Main Campus .... OH ... 368
University of Akron, Main Campus, The .... OH ... 371
University of Cincinnati Main Campus .... OH ... 371
Oklahoma Christian University .... OK ... 377
Oklahoma State University .... OK ... 377
University of Central Oklahoma .... OK ... 380
University of Oklahoma Norman Campus .... OK ... 380
Art Institute of Portland, The .... OR ... 381
Marylhurst University .... OR ... 384
University of Oregon .... OR ... 387
Art Institute of Philadelphia .... PA ... 389
Art Institute of Pittsburgh .... PA ... 389
Chatham University .... PA ... 392
Drexel University .... PA ... 394
La Roche College .... PA ... 398
Moore College of Art and Design .... PA ... 402
Converse College .... SC ... 420
Winthrop University .... SC ... 426
South Dakota State University .... SD ... 429
East Tennessee State University .... TN ... 431
#Middle Tennessee State University .... TN ... 434
O'More College of Design .... TN ... 435
University of Memphis, The .... TN ... 439
University of Tennessee at Chattanooga .... TN ... 440
University of Tennessee, Knoxville .... TN ... 439
Abilene Christian University .... TX ... 441
Art Institute of Houston, The .... TX ... 443
Baylor University .... TX ... 444
Sam Houston State University .... TX ... 462
Stephen F. Austin State University .... TX ... 458
Texas Christian University .... TX ... 461
Texas State University .... TX ... 463
#Texas Tech University .... TX ... 463
University of North Texas .... TX ... 466
University of Texas at Arlington, The .... TX ... 467
University of Texas at Austin .... TX ... 467
#University of Texas at San Antonio .... TX ... 468
University of the Incarnate Word .... TX ... 465
Utah State University .... UT ... 473
Weber State University .... UT ... 473
Marymount University .... VA ... 483
Radford University .... VA ... 484
Virginia Commonwealth University .... VA ... 487
Virginia Polytechnic Institute and State University .... VA ... 490
Art Institute of Seattle, The .... WA ... 492
Bellevue College .... WA .. 492
Washington State University .... WA .. 499
University of Charleston .... WV .. 502
#Mount Mary University .... WI ... 509
University of Wisconsin-Madison .... WI ... 510
University of Wisconsin-Stevens Point .... WI ... 511
University of Wisconsin-Stout .... WI ... 512

CLPSY: American Psychological Association: clinical psychology (D)

Auburn University .... AL 4
University of Alabama at Birmingham .... AL 8
University of Alabama, The .... AL 8
University of Alaska Anchorage .... AK 10
University of Alaska Fairbanks .... AK 10
Arizona State University .... AZ 10
University of Arizona .... AZ 16
University of Arkansas Main Campus .... AR 21
Alliant International University-San Diego .... CA 24
Argosy University, Orange County .... CA 26
Azusa Pacific University .... CA 26
Biola University .... CA 27
California Lutheran University .... CA 30
Fielding Graduate University .... CA 43
Fuller Theological Seminary .... CA 43
John F. Kennedy University .... CA 46
Loma Linda University .... CA 48
Palo Alto University .... CA 55
Pepperdine University .... CA 56
San Diego State University .... CA 34
University of California-Berkeley .... CA 68
University of California-Los Angeles .... CA 69
University of California-San Diego .... CA 69
University of La Verne .... CA 70
University of Southern California .... CA 72
Wright Institute, The .... CA 75
University of Colorado Boulder .... CO 83
University of Colorado Colorado Springs .... CO 83
University of Colorado Denver|Anschutz Medical Campus .... CO 83
University of Denver .... CO 83
University of Connecticut .... CT 88
University of Hartford .... CT 89
Yale University .... CT 89
University of Delaware .... DE 90
American University .... DC 91
Catholic University of America, The .... DC 91
Gallaudet University .... DC 91
George Washington University .... DC 92
Howard University .... DC 92
Florida Institute of Technology .... FL 99
Florida International University .... FL ... 109
Florida State University .... FL ... 110
Nova Southeastern University .... FL ... 104
University of Central Florida .... FL ... 110
University of Florida .... FL ... 110
University of Miami .... FL ... 112
University of South Florida .... FL ... 111
Emory University .... GA ... 119
Georgia Southern University .... GA ... 120
Georgia State University .... GA ... 121
University of Georgia .... GA ... 127
University of Hawaii at Manoa .... HI ... 129
Idaho State University .... ID ... 132
Adler University .... IL 133
DePaul University .... IL 137
Illinois Institute of Technology .... IL 140
Loyola University Chicago .... IL 144

CNCE: Accrediting Council for Continuing Education and Training: continuing education (C,A)

COARC: Commission on Accreditation for Respiratory Care: respiratory care (A,B,M)

COARCP: Commission on Accreditation for Respiratory Care: polysomnography (C)

COE: Council on Occupational Education: occupational, trade, and technical education (C,A)

COMTA: Commission on Massage Therapy Accreditation: massage therapy, bodywork, aesthetics/esthetics and skin care (C,A)

CONST: American Council for Construction Education: construction education (A,B)

COPSY: American Psychological Association: counseling psychology (D)

CS: ABET, Inc.: computer science (B)

CSHSE: Council for Standards in Human Services Education: human services (A,B,M)

James A. Rhodes State College ... OH ... 363
Sinclair Community College ... OH ... 370
University of Oregon ... OR ... 387
Clarion University of Pennsylvania ... PA ... 405
HACC, Central Pennsylvania's Community College ... PA ... 396
Lehigh Carbon Community College ... PA ... 400
Montgomery County Community College ... PA ... 402
University of Scranton, The ... PA ... 413
Florence - Darlington Technical College ... SC ... 421
Trident Technical College ... SC ... 424
East Tennessee State University ... TN ... 431
Wharton County Junior College ... TX ... 471
Madison Area Technical College ... WI ... 514
University of Wisconsin-Oshkosh ... WI ... 511

CVT: Commission on Accreditation of Allied Health Education Programs: cardiovascular technology (C,A,B)

Grossmont College ... CA ... 45
Loma Linda University ... CA ... 48
Orange Coast College ... CA ... 38
Florida SouthWestern State College ... FL ... 100
Florida State College at Jacksonville ... FL ... 100
International College of Health Sciences ... FL ... 102
Nova Southeastern University ... FL ... 104
Polk State College ... FL ... 105
Santa Fe College ... FL ... 107
Valencia College ... FL ... 113
Augusta Technical College ... GA ... 116
Central Georgia Technical College ... GA ... 117
Gwinnett Technical College ... GA ... 121
Piedmont College ... GA ... 124
Louisiana State University Health Sciences Center-New Orleans ... LA ... 194
Howard Community College ... MD ... 204
Grand Valley State University ... MI ... 230
Kirtland Community College ... MI ... 232
Saint Cloud Technical and Community College ... MN ... 247
Bryan College of Health Sciences ... NE ... 273
Eastern International College ... NJ ... 285
Eastwick College ... NJ ... 285
Molloy College ... NY ... 315
Central Piedmont Community College ... NC ... 342
Forsyth Technical Community College ... NC ... 343
Tulsa Community College ... OK ... 380
HACC, Central Pennsylvania's Community College ... PA ... 396
Pennsylvania College of Health Sciences ... PA ... 404
Clemson University ... SC ... 419
Piedmont Technical College ... SC ... 423
Southeast Technical Institute ... SD ... 429
Northeast State Community College ... TN ... 437
El Centro College ... TX ... 448
Hill College ... TX ... 450
St. Philip's College ... TX ... 441
Sentara College of Health Sciences ... VA ... 485
Spokane Community College ... WA ... 493
Milwaukee Area Technical College ... WI ... 514

CYTO: Commission on Accreditation of Allied Health Education Programs: cytotechnology (C,B,M)

University of Arkansas for Medical Sciences ... AR ... 22
Loma Linda University ... CA ... 48
University of California-Los Angeles ... CA ... 69
Indiana University-Purdue University Indianapolis ... IN ... 160
University of Nebraska Medical Center ... NE ... 277
Albany College of Pharmacy and Health Sciences ... NY ... 297
City University of New York Hunter College ... NY ... 302
Daemen College ... NY ... 306
Central Piedmont Community College ... NC ... 342
Thomas Jefferson University ... PA ... 411
University of Puerto Rico-Medical Sciences Campus ... PR ... 528
University of Rhode Island ... RI ... 417
University of Tennessee Health Science Center ... TN ... 440
University of Texas MD Anderson Cancer Center, The ... TX ... 469
University of Utah, The ... UT ... 472
Old Dominion University ... VA ... 483
Marshall University ... WV ... 504
University of Wisconsin-Madison ... WI ... 510

DA: American Dental Association: dental assisting (C,A)

Calhoun Community College ... AL ... 1
Coastal Alabama Community College ... AL ... 1
Lawson State Community College ... AL ... 2
Trenholm State Technical College ... AL ... 3
Wallace State Community College - Hanceville ... AL ... 3
University of Alaska Anchorage ... AK ... 10
Phoenix College ... AZ ... 14
Pima Community College ... AZ ... 15
Rio Salado College ... AZ ... 14
Arkansas Northeastern College ... AR ... 17
University of Arkansas - Pulaski Technical College ... AR ... 23
Cerritos College ... CA ... 36
Chaffey College ... CA ... 36
Citrus College ... CA ... 37
City College of San Francisco ... CA ... 37
College of Alameda ... CA ... 56
College of Marin ... CA ... 39
College of San Mateo ... CA ... 62
College of the Redwoods Community College District ... CA ... 39
Cypress College ... CA ... 53
Diablo Valley College ... CA ... 40
Foothill College ... CA ... 43
Moreno Valley College ... CA ... 58
Orange Coast College ... CA ... 38
Palomar College ... CA ... 55
Pasadena City College ... CA ... 56
Sacramento City College ... CA ... 50
San Diego Mesa College ... CA ... 60
San Jose City College ... CA ... 61
Santa Rosa Junior College ... CA ... 62
Front Range Community College ... CO ... 79
Pikes Peak Community College ... CO ... 81
Lincoln College of New England ... CT ... 87
Manchester Community College ... CT ... 85
Tunxis Community College ... CT ... 86
Broward College ... FL ... 96
College of Central Florida ... FL ... 97
Daytona State College ... FL ... 97
Eastern Florida State College ... FL ... 97
Florida State College at Jacksonville ... FL ... 100
Gulf Coast State College ... FL ... 101
Hillsborough Community College ... FL ... 101
Indian River State College ... FL ... 101
Northwest Florida State College ... FL ... 104
Palm Beach State College ... FL ... 105
Santa Fe College ... FL ... 107
South Florida State College ... FL ... 108
Tallahassee Community College ... FL ... 112
Albany Technical College ... GA ... 114
Athens Technical College ... GA ... 115
Atlanta Technical College ... GA ... 115
Augusta Technical College ... GA ... 116
Columbus Technical College ... GA ... 118
Georgia Northwestern Technical College ... GA ... 120
Gwinnett Technical College ... GA ... 121
Lanier Technical College ... GA ... 122
Ogeechee Technical College ... GA ... 123
Savannah Technical College ... GA ... 125
Southern Crescent Technical College ... GA ... 126
Wiregrass Georgia Technical College ... GA ... 128
Kapiolani Community College ... HI ... 130
College of Western Idaho ... ID ... 132
Elgin Community College ... IL ... 138
Illinois Valley Community College ... IL ... 141
John A. Logan College ... IL ... 141
Kaskaskia College ... IL ... 142
Lewis and Clark Community College ... IL ... 143
Indiana University Northwest ... IN ... 160
Indiana University-Purdue University Fort Wayne ... IN ... 160
Indiana University-Purdue University Indianapolis ... IN ... 160
University of Southern Indiana ... IN ... 165
Des Moines Area Community College ... IA ... 168
Hawkeye Community College ... IA ... 169
Indian Hills Community College ... IA ... 169
Iowa Western Community College ... IA ... 170
Kirkwood Community College ... IA ... 171
Marshalltown Community College ... IA ... 170
Northeast Iowa Community College ... IA ... 172
Scott Community College ... IA ... 169
Vatterott College-Des Moines ... IA ... 174
Western Iowa Tech Community College ... IA ... 174
Flint Hills Technical College ... KS ... 177
Labette Community College ... KS ... 179
Salina Area Technical College ... KS ... 181
Wichita Area Technical College ... KS ... 182
West Kentucky Community and Technical College ... KY ... 187
University of Maine at Augusta ... ME ... 201
Hagerstown Community College ... MD ... 204
Massasoit Community College ... MA ... 220
Middlesex Community College ... MA ... 220
Mount Wachusett Community College ... MA ... 220
Northern Essex Community College ... MA ... 220
Quinsigamond Community College ... MA ... 220
Springfield Technical Community College ... MA ... 221
Delta College ... MI ... 229
Grand Rapids Community College ... MI ... 230
Lake Michigan College ... MI ... 232
Mott Community College ... MI ... 234
Northwestern Michigan College ... MI ... 235
Washtenaw Community College ... MI ... 238
Wayne County Community College District ... MI ... 238
Central Lakes College ... MN ... 244
Century College ... MN ... 244
Dakota County Technical College ... MN ... 244
Hennepin Technical College ... MN ... 244
Hibbing Community College, A Technical and Community College ... MN ... 244
Minneapolis Community and Technical College ... MN ... 245
Minnesota State Community and Technical College ... MN ... 245
Minnesota West Community and Technical College ... MN ... 246
Northwest Technical College ... MN ... 246
Rochester Community and Technical College ... MN ... 247
Saint Cloud Technical and Community College ... MN ... 247
South Central College ... MN ... 247
Hinds Community College ... MS ... 253
Meridian Community College ... MS ... 253
Pearl River Community College ... MS ... 255
Metropolitan Community College - Penn Valley ... MO ... 262
Ozarks Technical Community College ... MO ... 264
State Technical College of Missouri ... MO ... 267
Great Falls College Montana State University ... MT ... 272
Salish Kootenai College ... MT ... 273
Central Community College ... NE ... 273
Metropolitan Community College ... NE ... 275
Mid-Plains Community College ... NE ... 275
Southeast Community College ... NE ... 276
College of Southern Nevada ... NV ... 278
Truckee Meadows Community College ... NV ... 279
NHTI-Concord's Community College ... NH ... 280
Camden County College ... NJ ... 284
Central New Mexico Community College ... NM ... 293
Luna Community College ... NM ... 294
New Mexico State University Dona Ana Community College ... NM ... 295
Santa Fe Community College ... NM ... 296
Monroe Community College ... NY ... 315
University at Buffalo-SUNY ... NY ... 325
Alamance Community College ... NC ... 340
Asheville - Buncombe Technical Community College ... NC ... 340
Cape Fear Community College ... NC ... 341
Central Carolina Community College ... NC ... 341
Central Piedmont Community College ... NC ... 342
Coastal Carolina Community College ... NC ... 342
Fayetteville Technical Community College ... NC ... 343
Forsyth Technical Community College ... NC ... 343
Guilford Technical Community College ... NC ... 343
Martin Community College ... NC ... 344
Montgomery Community College ... NC ... 345
Rowan-Cabarrus Community College ... NC ... 346
University of North Carolina at Chapel Hill ... NC ... 351
Wake Technical Community College ... NC ... 347
Wayne Community College ... NC ... 347
Western Piedmont Community College ... NC ... 347
Wilkes Community College ... NC ... 347
North Dakota State College of Science ... ND ... 355
Eastern Gateway Community College - Jefferson County Campus ... OH ... 361
Fortis College ... OH ... 361
Rose State College ... OK ... 379
Blue Mountain Community College ... OR ... 382
Central Oregon Community College ... OR ... 382
Chemeketa Community College ... OR ... 382
Lane Community College ... OR ... 383
Linn-Benton Community College ... OR ... 384
Portland Community College ... OR ... 386
Umpqua Community College ... OR ... 387
Bradford School ... PA ... 389
HACC, Central Pennsylvania's Community College ... PA ... 396
Harcum College ... PA ... 396
Luzerne County Community College ... PA ... 400
Manor College ... PA ... 401
Westmoreland County Community College ... PA ... 414
University of Puerto Rico-Medical Sciences Campus ... PR ... 528
Community College of Rhode Island ... RI ... 416
Aiken Technical College ... SC ... 418
Florence - Darlington Technical College ... SC ... 421
Greenville Technical College ... SC ... 421
Horry-Georgetown Technical College ... SC ... 421
Midlands Technical College ... SC ... 422
Spartanburg Community College ... SC ... 424
Tri-County Technical College ... SC ... 424
Trident Technical College ... SC ... 424
York Technical College ... SC ... 426
Lake Area Technical Institute ... SD ... 427
Chattanooga State Community College ... TN ... 436
Concorde Career College ... TN ... 431
Northeast State Community College ... TN ... 437
Volunteer State Community College ... TN ... 438
Amarillo College ... TX ... 442
Del Mar College ... TX ... 448
El Paso Community College ... TX ... 449
Grayson College ... TX ... 449
Houston Community College ... TX ... 450
San Antonio College ... TX ... 442
Tyler Junior College ... TX ... 464
Germanna Community College ... VA ... 488
J. Sargeant Reynolds Community College ... VA ... 488
Northern Virginia Community College ... VA ... 488
Bates Technical College ... WA ... 492
Bellingham Technical College ... WA ... 492
Clover Park Technical College ... WA ... 493
Lake Washington Institute of Technology ... WA ... 495
Renton Technical College ... WA ... 497
South Puget Sound Community College ... WA ... 498
Spokane Community College ... WA ... 493
Blackhawk Technical College ... WI ... 513
Fox Valley Technical College ... WI ... 513
Gateway Technical College ... WI ... 513
Northeast Wisconsin Technical College ... WI ... 514
Western Technical College ... WI ... 515

DANCE: National Association of Schools of Dance: dance (C,A,B,M,D)

University of Alabama, The ... AL ... 8
University of Arizona ... AZ ... 16
California Institute of the Arts ... CA ... 29
California State University-Fullerton ... CA ... 32
California State University-Long Beach ... CA ... 32
Chapman University ... CA ... 36
Loyola Marymount University ... CA ... 50
San Jose State University ... CA ... 34
University of California-Santa Barbara ... CA ... 70
University of Hartford ... CT ... 89
Florida State University ... FL ... 110
Jacksonville University ... FL ... 102
Miami Dade College ... FL ... 103
University of Florida ... FL ... 110
University of South Florida ... FL ... 111
University of Georgia ... GA ... 127
University of Illinois at Urbana-Champaign ... IL ... 154
Ball State University ... IN ... 156
Butler University ... IN ... 156
University of Iowa ... IA ... 166
Wichita State University ... KS ... 182
Western Kentucky University ... KY ... 190
Towson University ... MD ... 209
University of Maryland Baltimore County ... MD ... 208
University of Maryland College Park ... MD ... 207
Hope College ... MI ... 231
Oakland University ... MI ... 235
University of Michigan-Ann Arbor ... MI ... 237
Wayne State University ... MI ... 239
Western Michigan University ... MI ... 239
St. Olaf College ... MN ... 250
University of Minnesota ... MN ... 250
Belhaven University ... MS ... 252
University of Southern Mississippi ... MS ... 256
University of Missouri - Kansas City ... MO ... 268
University of Nebraska - Lincoln ... NE ... 277
Montclair State University ... NJ ... 287
Rutgers University - New Brunswick ... NJ ... 290
University of New Mexico Main Campus ... NM ... 296
Barnard College ... NY ... 299
State University of New York, The College at Brockport ... NY ... 326
Appalachian State University ... NC ... 349
University of North Carolina at Charlotte ... NC ... 351
University of North Carolina at Greensboro ... NC ... 351
Kent State University Kent Campus ... OH ... 363
Ohio State University Main Campus, The ... OH ... 367
Ohio University Main Campus ... OH ... 368
University of Akron, Main Campus, The ... OH ... 371
University of Cincinnati Main Campus ... OH ... 371
Mercyhurst University ... PA ... 401
Point Park University ... PA ... 408
Slippery Rock University of Pennsylvania ... PA ... 407
Temple University ... PA ... 411
Columbia College ... SC ... 420
University of South Carolina Columbia ... SC ... 424
Winthrop University ... SC ... 426
Southern Methodist University ... TX ... 457
Texas Christian University ... TX ... 461
Texas Tech University ... TX ... 463
Texas Woman's University ... TX ... 464
University of Texas at Austin ... TX ... 467
Brigham Young University ... UT ... 471
Southern Utah University ... UT ... 473
University of Utah, The ... UT ... 472
James Madison University ... VA ... 481
Radford University ... VA ... 484
Virginia Commonwealth University ... VA ... 487
University of Wisconsin-Madison ... WI ... 510
University of Wisconsin-Milwaukee ... WI ... 511
University of Wisconsin-Stevens Point ... WI ... 511
Casper College ... WY ... 516

DEAC: Distance Education Accrediting Commission: home study schools (A,B,M,D)

Columbia Southern University ... AL ... 5
Acacia University ... AZ ... 10
Brighton College ... AZ ... 11
Dunlap-Stone University ... AZ ... 12
Harrison Middleton University ... AZ ... 13
National Paralegal College ... AZ ... 14
Paralegal Institute at Brighton College, The ... AZ ... 15
Penn Foster College ... AZ ... 15
Sessions College for Professional Design ... AZ ... 16

Sonoran Desert Institute ... AZ ... 16
Abraham Lincoln University ... CA ... 24
American Graduate University ... CA ... 25
Anaheim University ... CA ... 25
APT College ... CA ... 26
California Coast University ... CA ... 28
California Institute of Management and Technology ... CA ... 30
California Intercontinental University ... CA ... 30
California National University for Advanced Studies ... CA ... 30
Grace Communion Seminary ... CA ... 44
Henley-Putnam University ... CA ... 45
Taft Law School ... CA ... 67
Union University of California ... CA ... 68
University of Philosophical Research ... CA ... 71
University of the People ... CA ... 71
Westcliff University ... CA ... 74
American Sentinel University ... CO ... 76
Aspen University ... CO ... 76
Holmes Institute of Consciousness Studies ... CO ... 80
McKinley College ... CO ... 80
U.S. Career Institute ... CO ... 84
William Howard Taft University ... CO ... 84
Educatore School of Education ... DC ... 91
Ashworth College ... GA ... 115
Babel University Professional School of Translation ... HI ... 128
Realtor University ... IL ... 149
Antioch School of Church Planting and Leadership Development ... IA ... 166
Inste Bible College ... IA ... 170
Shiloh University ... IA ... 173
Grantham University ... KS ... 177
NationsUniversity ... LA ... 195
Southwest University ... LA ... 196
American Business & Technology University ... MO ... 257
City Vision University ... MO ... 258
Rockbridge Seminary ... MO ... 265
Apollos University ... MT ... 270
EC-Council University ... NM ... 294
Lakewood College ... OH ... 364
American College of Healthcare Sciences ... OR ... 381
Huntington College of Health Sciences ... TN ... 432
New Charter University ... UT ... 472
Atlantic University ... VA ... 478
University of Fairfax ... VA ... 486
University of Management & Technology ... VA ... 486
Catholic Distance University ... WV ... 501
Martinsburg College ... WV ... 502
Wright Graduate University for the Realization of Human Potential ... WI ... 516

DENT: American Dental Association: dentistry (FP,D)

University of Alabama at Birmingham ... AL ... 8
University of Arkansas at Little Rock ... AR ... 22
Loma Linda University ... CA ... 48
University of California-Los Angeles ... CA ... 69
University of California-San Francisco ... CA ... 70
University of Southern California ... CA ... 72
University of the Pacific ... CA ... 70
Western University of Health Sciences ... CA ... 74
United States Air Force Academy ... CO ... 518
University of Colorado Denver|Anschutz Medical Campus ... CO ... 83
Howard University ... DC ... 92
Jacksonville University ... FL ... 102
Nova Southeastern University ... FL ... 104
University of Florida ... FL ... 110
University of Miami ... FL ... 112
Augusta University ... GA ... 116
Emory University ... GA ... 119
Idaho State University ... ID ... 132
Loyola University Chicago ... IL ... 144
Midwestern University ... IL ... 145
Southern Illinois University Edwardsville ... IL ... 152
University of Illinois at Chicago ... IL ... 153
Indiana University-Purdue University Indianapolis ... IN ... 160
University of Iowa ... IA ... 166
Wichita State University ... KS ... 182
University of Kentucky ... KY ... 190
University of Louisville ... KY ... 190
Louisiana State University Health Sciences Center at Shreveport ... LA ... 194
Louisiana State University Health Sciences Center-New Orleans ... LA ... 194
University of New England ... ME ... 202
Uniformed Services University of the Health Sciences ... MD ... 518
University of Maryland, Baltimore ... MD ... 207
Boston University ... MA ... 212
Harvard University ... MA ... 215
Tufts University ... MA ... 225
University of Detroit Mercy ... MI ... 237
University of Michigan-Ann Arbor ... MI ... 237
University of Minnesota ... MN ... 250
University of Mississippi Medical Center ... MS ... 256
A. T. Still University of Health Sciences ... MO ... 257
Saint Louis University ... MO ... 266
University of Missouri - Kansas City ... MO ... 268
Creighton University ... NE ... 274
University of Nebraska Medical Center ... NE ... 277
Roseman University of Health Sciences ... NV ... 280
University of Nevada, Las Vegas ... NV ... 279
University of New Mexico Main Campus ... NM ... 296
Columbia University in the City of New York ... NY ... 305
Icahn School of Medicine at Mount Sinai ... NY ... 311
New York Medical College ... NY ... 318
New York University ... NY ... 318
State University of New York Upstate Medical University ... NY ... 326
Stony Brook University ... NY ... 325
University at Buffalo-SUNY ... NY ... 325
University of Rochester ... NY ... 332
Yeshiva University ... NY ... 334
East Carolina University ... NC ... 349
University of North Carolina at Chapel Hill ... NC ... 351
Wake Forest University ... NC ... 353
Case Western Reserve University ... OH ... 358
Ohio State University Main Campus, The ... OH ... 367
University of Cincinnati Main Campus ... OH ... 371
University of Toledo ... OH ... 372
Oregon Health & Science University ... OR ... 385
Drexel University ... PA ... 394
Lake Erie College of Osteopathic Medicine ... PA ... 399
Seton Hill University ... PA ... 410
Temple University ... PA ... 411
Thomas Jefferson University ... PA ... 411
University of Pennsylvania ... PA ... 412
University of Pittsburgh ... PA ... 412
University of Puerto Rico-Medical Sciences Campus ... PR ... 528
Medical University of South Carolina ... SC ... 422
Meharry Medical College ... TN ... 434
University of Tennessee Health Science Center ... TN ... 440
University of Tennessee, Knoxville ... TN ... 439
Vanderbilt University ... TN ... 440
Texas A & M University ... TX ... 459
University of Texas Health Science Center at Houston (UTHealth), The ... TX ... 468
University of Texas Health Science Center at San Antonio ... TX ... 468
University of Texas MD Anderson Cancer Center, The ... TX ... 469
University of Texas Medical Branch, The ... TX ... 469
University of Utah, The ... UT ... 472
University of Vermont ... VT ... 476
University of Virginia ... VA ... 486
Virginia Commonwealth University ... VA ... 487
University of Washington ... WA ... 499
West Virginia University ... WV ... 505
Marquette University ... WI ... 508
Medical College of Wisconsin ... WI ... 508

DH: American Dental Association: dental hygiene (C,A,B,M)

Wallace State Community College - Hanceville ... AL ... 3
University of Alaska Anchorage ... AK ... 10
University of Alaska Fairbanks ... AK ... 10
Mesa Community College ... AZ ... 13
Mohave Community College ... AZ ... 14
Northern Arizona University ... AZ ... 14
Phoenix College ... AZ ... 14
Pima Community College ... AZ ... 15
Rio Salado College ... AZ ... 14
University of Arkansas at Fort Smith ... AR ... 22
University of Arkansas for Medical Sciences ... AR ... 22
Cabrillo College ... CA ... 28
Carrington College - Sacramento ... CA ... 35
Cerritos College ... CA ... 36
Chabot College ... CA ... 36
Concorde Career College ... CA ... 40
Cypress College ... CA ... 53
Diablo Valley College ... CA ... 40
Foothill College ... CA ... 43
Fresno City College ... CA ... 66
Loma Linda University ... CA ... 48
Moreno Valley College ... CA ... 58
Oxnard College ... CA ... 73
Pasadena City College ... CA ... 56
Sacramento City College ... CA ... 50
San Joaquin Valley College, Inc. - Visalia ... CA ... 61
Santa Rosa Junior College ... CA ... 62
Shasta College ... CA ... 63
Southwestern College ... CA ... 65
Taft College ... CA ... 67
University of Southern California ... CA ... 72
University of the Pacific ... CA ... 70
West Los Angeles College ... CA ... 49
Colorado Northwestern Community College. CO ... 78
Community College of Denver ... CO ... 79
Concorde Career College ... CO ... 79
Pueblo Community College ... CO ... 81
Goodwin College ... CT ... 87
Lincoln College of New England ... CT ... 87
Tunxis Community College ... CT ... 86
University of Bridgeport ... CT ... 88
University of New Haven ... CT ... 89
Howard University ... DC ... 92
Broward College ... FL ... 96
Daytona State College ... FL ... 97
Eastern Florida State College ... FL ... 97
Florida SouthWestern State College ... FL ... 100
Florida State College at Jacksonville ... FL ... 100
Gulf Coast State College ... FL ... 101
Hillsborough Community College ... FL ... 101
Indian River State College ... FL ... 101
Miami Dade College ... FL ... 103
Palm Beach State College ... FL ... 105
Pasco-Hernando State College ... FL ... 105
Pensacola State College ... FL ... 105
St. Petersburg College ... FL ... 107
Santa Fe College ... FL ... 107
South Florida State College ... FL ... 108
State College of Florida, Manatee-Sarasota. FL ... 108
Tallahassee Community College ... FL ... 112
Valencia College ... FL ... 113
Albany State University ... GA ... 114
Athens Technical College ... GA ... 115
Atlanta Technical College ... GA ... 115
Augusta University ... GA ... 116
Central Georgia Technical College ... GA ... 117
Clayton State University ... GA ... 117
Columbus Technical College ... GA ... 118
Georgia Highlands College ... GA ... 119
Georgia State University ... GA ... 121
Lanier Technical College ... GA ... 122
Savannah Technical College ... GA ... 125
Southeastern Technical College ... GA ... 126
West Georgia Technical College ... GA ... 128
Wiregrass Georgia Technical College ... GA ... 128
University of Hawaii at Manoa ... HI ... 129
University of Hawaii Maui College ... HI ... 130
College of Southern Idaho ... ID ... 131
Idaho State University ... ID ... 132
Carl Sandburg College ... IL ... 134
College of DuPage ... IL ... 136
College of Lake County ... IL ... 136
Fox College ... IL ... 138
Harper College ... IL ... 139
Illinois Central College ... IL ... 139
John A. Logan College ... IL ... 141
Lake Land College ... IL ... 143
Lewis and Clark Community College ... IL ... 143
Malcolm X College, One of the City Colleges of Chicago ... IL ... 136
Parkland College ... IL ... 148
Prairie State College ... IL ... 148
Rock Valley College ... IL ... 150
Southern Illinois University Carbondale ... IL ... 152
Indiana University Northwest ... IN ... 160
Indiana University-Purdue University Fort Wayne ... IN ... 160
Indiana University-Purdue University Indianapolis ... IN ... 160
Indiana University South Bend ... IN ... 160
University of Southern Indiana ... IN ... 165
Des Moines Area Community College ... IA ... 168
Hawkeye Community College ... IA ... 169
Indian Hills Community College ... IA ... 169
Iowa Central Community College ... IA ... 170
Iowa Western Community College ... IA ... 170
Kirkwood Community College ... IA ... 171
Flint Hills Technical College ... KS ... 177
Johnson County Community College ... KS ... 178
Manhattan Area Technical College ... KS ... 179
Wichita State University ... KS ... 182
Big Sandy Community and Technical College ... KY ... 185
Bluegrass Community and Technical College ... KY ... 185
Henderson Community College ... KY ... 186
University of Louisville ... KY ... 190
Western Kentucky University ... KY ... 190
Louisiana State University Health Sciences Center-New Orleans ... LA ... 194
Southern University at Shreveport-Louisiana ... LA ... 196
University of Louisiana at Monroe ... LA ... 198
University of Maine at Augusta ... ME ... 201
University of New England ... ME ... 202
Allegany College of Maryland ... MD ... 202
Baltimore City Community College ... MD ... 202
Community College of Baltimore County, The ... MD ... 203
Hagerstown Community College ... MD ... 204
Howard Community College ... MD ... 204
University of Maryland, Baltimore ... MD ... 207
Bristol Community College ... MA ... 219
Cape Cod Community College ... MA ... 219
MCPHS University ... MA ... 221
Middlesex Community College ... MA ... 220
Mount Ida College ... MA ... 222
Mount Wachusett Community College ... MA ... 220
Quinsigamond Community College ... MA ... 220
Springfield Technical Community College ... MA ... 221
Delta College ... MI ... 229
Ferris State University ... MI ... 230
Grand Rapids Community College ... MI ... 230
Kalamazoo Valley Community College ... MI ... 231
Kellogg Community College ... MI ... 232
Lansing Community College ... MI ... 232
Mott Community College ... MI ... 234
Oakland Community College ... MI ... 235
University of Detroit Mercy ... MI ... 237
University of Michigan-Ann Arbor ... MI ... 237
Wayne County Community College District . MI ... 238
Century College ... MN ... 244
Lake Superior College ... MN ... 245
Minnesota State University Moorhead ... MN ... 246
Minnesota State University, Mankato ... MN ... 246
Normandale Community College ... MN ... 246
Rochester Community and Technical College ... MN ... 247
Saint Cloud Technical and Community College ... MN ... 247
University of Minnesota ... MN ... 250
Meridian Community College ... MS ... 253
Mississippi Delta Community College ... MS ... 254
Northeast Mississippi Community College ... MS ... 255
Pearl River Community College ... MS ... 255
University of Mississippi Medical Center ... MS ... 256
Concorde Career College ... MO ... 258
Missouri Southern State University ... MO ... 263
Ozarks Technical Community College ... MO ... 264
State Fair Community College ... MO ... 267
University of Missouri - Kansas City ... MO ... 268
Great Falls College Montana State University ... MT ... 272
Central Community College ... NE ... 273
University of Nebraska Medical Center ... NE ... 277
College of Southern Nevada ... NV ... 278
Truckee Meadows Community College ... NV ... 279
NHTI-Concord's Community College ... NH ... 280
Bergen Community College ... NJ ... 283
Camden County College ... NJ ... 284
Eastern International College ... NJ ... 285
Middlesex County College ... NJ ... 287
Rowan College at Burlington County ... NJ ... 289
New Mexico State University Dona Ana Community College ... NM ... 295
San Juan College ... NM ... 296
University of New Mexico Main Campus ... NM ... 296
Erie Community College ... NY ... 307
Farmingdale State College ... NY ... 329
Hostos Community College-City University of New York ... NY ... 302
Hudson Valley Community College ... NY ... 310
Monroe Community College ... NY ... 315
New York City College of Technology/City University of New York ... NY ... 303
New York University ... NY ... 318
Orange County Community College ... NY ... 319
SUNY Broome Community College ... NY ... 326
SUNY Canton-College of Technology ... NY ... 329
Asheville - Buncombe Technical Community College ... NC ... 340
Cape Fear Community College ... NC ... 341
Catawba Valley Community College ... NC ... 341
Central Carolina Community College ... NC ... 341
Central Piedmont Community College ... NC ... 342
Coastal Carolina Community College ... NC ... 342
Fayetteville Technical Community College .. NC ... 343
Forsyth Technical Community College ... NC ... 343
Guilford Technical Community College ... NC ... 343
Halifax Community College ... NC ... 343
University of North Carolina at Chapel Hill .. NC ... 351
Wake Technical Community College ... NC ... 347
Wayne Community College ... NC ... 347
North Dakota State College of Science ... ND ... 355
Columbus State Community College ... OH ... 360
Cuyahoga Community College ... OH ... 360
James A. Rhodes State College ... OH ... 363
Lakeland Community College ... OH ... 364
Lorain County Community College ... OH ... 364
Ohio State University Main Campus, The ... OH ... 367
Owens Community College ... OH ... 369
Shawnee State University ... OH ... 369
Sinclair Community College ... OH ... 370
Stark State College ... OH ... 370
University of Cincinnati Blue Ash College ... OH ... 371
Youngstown State University ... OH ... 374
Rose State College ... OK ... 379
Tulsa Community College ... OK ... 380
Lane Community College ... OR ... 383
Mt. Hood Community College ... OR ... 384
Oregon Institute of Technology ... OR ... 385
Pacific University ... OR ... 385
Portland Community College ... OR ... 386
Community College of Philadelphia ... PA ... 393
Fortis Institute ... PA ... 395
HACC, Central Pennsylvania's Community College ... PA ... 396
Harcum College ... PA ... 396
Luzerne County Community College ... PA ... 400
Manor College ... PA ... 401
Montgomery County Community College ... PA ... 402
Northampton Community College ... PA ... 403
Pennsylvania College of Technology ... PA ... 404
University of Pittsburgh ... PA ... 412
Westmoreland County Community College . PA ... 414
Community College of Rhode Island ... RI ... 416
Florence - Darlington Technical College ... SC ... 421
Greenville Technical College ... SC ... 421

DIETC: Academy of Nutrition and Dietetics: coordinated dietetics programs (B,M)

DIETD: Academy of Nutrition and Dietetics: didactic dietetics programs (B,M)

DIETI: Academy of Nutrition and Dietetics: dietetic post-baccalaureate internships

@University of South Florida .... FL 111
Augusta University .... GA 116
Georgia Southern University .... GA 120
Life University .... GA 122
University of Georgia .... GA 127
Idaho State University .... ID 132
Benedictine University .... IL 133
Bradley University .... IL 134
Eastern Illinois University .... IL 138
Illinois State University .... IL 140
Loyola University Chicago .... IL 144
Northern Illinois University .... IL 147
Rush University .... IL 150
Southern Illinois University Carbondale .... IL 152
University of Illinois at Urbana-Champaign .... IL 154
Ball State University .... IN 156
Indiana University-Purdue University Indianapolis .... IN 160
Iowa State University .... IA 166
University of Iowa .... IA 166
Murray State University .... KY 188
University of Kentucky .... KY 190
Western Kentucky University .... KY 190
@Franciscan Missionaries of Our Lady University .... LA 191
Louisiana Tech University .... LA 197
McNeese State University .... LA 197
Nicholls State University .... LA 197
Southern University and A&M College .... LA 195
Tulane University .... LA 196
University of Maine .... ME 201
University of Maryland College Park .... MD 207
University of Maryland Eastern Shore .... MD 208
University of Maryland, Baltimore .... MD 207
Boston University .... MA 212
Simmons College .... MA 224
Tufts University .... MA 225
University of Massachusetts .... MA 216
Andrews University .... MI 227
Central Michigan University .... MI 228
Michigan State University .... MI 233
University of Michigan-Ann Arbor .... MI 237
Western Michigan University .... MI 239
Concordia College .... MN 241
University of Minnesota .... MN 250
Mississippi State University .... MS 254
University of Southern Mississippi .... MS 256
Cox College .... MO 259
@Missouri State University .... MO 263
Saint Louis University .... MO 266
Southeast Missouri State University .... MO 266
Montana State University .... MT 272
University of Nebraska - Lincoln .... NE 277
University of Nebraska Medical Center .... NE 277
University of Nevada, Las Vegas .... NV 279
University of Nevada, Reno .... NV 279
Keene State College .... NH 283
University of New Hampshire .... NH 282
College of Saint Elizabeth .... NJ 285
Montclair State University .... NJ 287
New Mexico State University Main Campus. NM 295
University of New Mexico Main Campus .... NM 296
City University of New York Brooklyn College .... NY 301
@City University of New York Graduate Center .... NY 302
City University of New York Herbert H. Lehman College .... NY 302
City University of New York Hunter College NY 302
City University of New York Queens College .... NY 303
Cornell University .... NY 306
@Daemen College .... NY 306
New York University .... NY 318
Sage Colleges, The .... NY 321
State University of New York at Oneonta .... NY 325
Stony Brook University .... NY 325
Syracuse University .... NY 330
Teachers College, Columbia University .... NY 331
University at Buffalo-SUNY .... NY 325
Appalachian State University .... NC 349
Duke University .... NC 337
East Carolina University .... NC 349
Lenoir-Rhyne University .... NC 339
Meredith College .... NC 339
North Carolina Central University .... NC 350
University of North Carolina at Greensboro NC 351
Western Carolina University .... NC 352
Bowling Green State University .... OH 357
Case Western Reserve University .... OH 358
Kent State University Kent Campus .... OH 363
@Miami University .... OH 365
Ohio State University Main Campus, The .... OH 367
@Ohio University Main Campus .... OH 368
Oklahoma State University .... OK 377
University of Central Oklahoma .... OK 380
Oregon Health & Science University .... OR 385
Oregon State University .... OR 385
Cedar Crest College .... PA 392
Immaculata University .... PA 397
Indiana University of Pennsylvania .... PA 406
Marywood University .... PA 401
@Messiah College .... PA 401
Penn State University Park .... PA 403
University of Puerto Rico-Medical Sciences Campus .... PR 528
University of Rhode Island .... RI 417
Medical University of South Carolina .... SC 422
Winthrop University .... SC 426
@South Dakota State University .... SD 429
East Tennessee State University .... TN 431
Lipscomb University .... TN 433
University of Memphis, The .... TN 439
University of Tennessee at Martin .... TN 440
University of Tennessee, Knoxville .... TN 439
Vanderbilt University .... TN 440
@Abilene Christian University .... TX 441
Baylor University .... TX 444
Lamar University .... TX 462
Prairie View A & M University .... TX 458
Sam Houston State University .... TX 462
Stephen F. Austin State University .... TX 458
Texas A & M University .... TX 459
Texas A & M University - Kingsville .... TX 460
Texas State University .... TX 463
Texas Tech University .... TX 463
Texas Woman's University .... TX 464
University of Houston .... TX 465
University of Texas Health Science Center at Houston (UTHealth), The .... TX 468
University of Texas Medical Branch, The .... TX 469
University of the Incarnate Word .... TX 465
Brigham Young University .... UT 471
Utah State University .... UT 473
University of Virginia .... VA 486
Virginia Commonwealth University .... VA 487
Virginia Polytechnic Institute and State University .... VA 490
Virginia State University .... VA 491
Bastyr University .... WA 492
Central Washington University .... WA 492
Marshall University .... WV 504
West Virginia University .... WV 505
Mount Mary University .... WI 509
University of Wisconsin-Green Bay .... WI 510
University of Wisconsin-Stout .... WI 512
Viterbo University .... WI 512

DIETT: Academy of Nutrition and Dietetics: dietetic technician (A)

Central Arizona College .... AZ 11
Chandler-Gilbert Community College .... AZ 13
Paradise Valley Community College .... AZ 13
#Black River Technical College .... AR 18
Merritt College .... CA 56
Orange Coast College .... CA 38
Santa Rosa Junior College .... CA 62
Gateway Community College .... CT 85
Hillsborough Community College .... FL 101
Harper College .... IL 139
Southern Maine Community College .... ME 200
Normandale Community College .... MN 246
Truckee Meadows Community College .... NV 279
Camden County College .... NJ 284
Middlesex County College .... NJ 287
Erie Community College .... NY 307
LaGuardia Community College/City University of New York .... NY 303
Morrisville State College .... NY 329
Trocaire College .... NY 331
Westchester Community College .... NY 333
Gaston College .... NC 343
Cincinnati State Technical and Community College .... OH 359
Columbus State Community College .... OH 360
Cuyahoga Community College .... OH 360
Owens Community College .... OH 369
Sinclair Community College .... OH 370
Stark State College .... OH 370
Youngstown State University .... OH 374
Oklahoma State University - Oklahoma City OK 378
Community College of Allegheny County .... PA 392
#Southwest Tennessee Community College . TN 438
Tarrant County College District .... TX 458

DMOLS: National Accrediting Agency for Clinical Laboratory Sciences: diagnostic molecular scientist (C,B,M)

University of Connecticut .... CT 88
Ferris State University .... MI 230
Northern Michigan University .... MI 235
State University of New York Upstate Medical University .... NY 326
University of North Carolina at Chapel Hill .. NC 351
Tarleton State University .... TX 459
Texas Tech University Health Sciences Center .... TX 463
University of Texas MD Anderson Cancer Center, The .... TX 469

DMS: Commission on Accreditation of Allied Health Education Programs: diagnostic medical sonography (C,A,B,M)

Lurleen B. Wallace Community College .... AL 2
Trenholm State Technical College .... AL 3
Virginia College .... AL 5
Wallace State Community College - Hanceville .... AL 3
Gateway Community College .... AZ 13
Arkansas State University-Jonesboro .... AR 18
University of Arkansas at Fort Smith .... AR 22
University of Arkansas for Medical Sciences AR 22
CBD College .... CA 35
Cosumnes River College .... CA 50
Cypress College .... CA 53
Foothill College .... CA 43
Kaiser Permanente School of Allied Health Sciences .... CA 46
Loma Linda University .... CA 48
Merced College .... CA 51
Mt. San Jacinto College .... CA 52
Orange Coast College .... CA 38
Platt College .... CA 57
Santa Barbara City College .... CA 62
University of California-San Diego .... CA 69
University of Colorado Denver|Anschutz Medical Campus .... CO 83
Gateway Community College .... CT 85
Adventist University of Health Sciences .... FL 94
Broward College .... FL 96
Cambridge College .... FL 96
Eastern Florida State College .... FL 97
Hillsborough Community College .... FL 101
Keiser University .... FL 102
Miami Dade College .... FL 103
Nova Southeastern University .... FL 104
Palm Beach State College .... FL 105
Polk State College .... FL 105
Santa Fe College .... FL 107
Valencia College .... FL 113
Albany State University .... GA 114
Armstrong State University .... GA 115
Columbus Technical College .... GA 118
Georgia Northwestern Technical College .... GA 120
Gwinnett Technical College .... GA 121
Ogeechee Technical College .... GA 123
Boise State University .... ID 131
College of DuPage .... IL 136
Harper College .... IL 139
John A. Logan College .... IL 141
Joliet Junior College .... IL 142
Rush University .... IL 150
Southern Illinois University Carbondale .... IL 152
Triton College .... IL 153
St. Anthony School of Echocardiography .... IN 163
University of Southern Indiana .... IN 165
Allen College .... IA 166
Mercy College of Health Sciences .... IA 171
University of Iowa .... IA 166
Labette Community College .... KS 179
Washburn University .... KS 182
Hazard Community and Technical College . KY 185
Morehead State University .... KY 188
Southcentral Kentucky Community and Technical College .... KY 187
West Kentucky Community and Technical College .... KY 187
Baton Rouge Community College .... LA 192
Delgado Community College .... LA 192
Louisiana State University at Eunice .... LA 194
Howard Community College .... MD 204
Johns Hopkins University .... MD 204
Montgomery College .... MD 205
University of Maryland Baltimore County .... MD 208
Bunker Hill Community College .... MA 219
Middlesex Community College .... MA 220
Springfield Technical Community College .... MA 221
Delta College .... MI 229
Ferris State University .... MI 230
Grand Valley State University .... MI 230
Jackson College .... MI 231
Lake Michigan College .... MI 232
Lansing Community College .... MI 232
Madonna University .... MI 233
Oakland Community College .... MI 235
St. Catherine University .... MN 249
Saint Cloud Technical and Community College .... MN 247
Hinds Community College .... MS 253
Cox College .... MO 259
University of Missouri - Columbia .... MO 268
Bryan College of Health Sciences .... NE 273
Nebraska Methodist College .... NE 275
University of Nebraska Medical Center .... NE 277
College of Southern Nevada .... NV 278
NHTI-Concord's Community College .... NH 280
Bergen Community College .... NJ 283
Rowan College at Burlington County .... NJ 289
Rowan College at Gloucester County .... NJ 289
Central New Mexico Community College .... NM 293
New Mexico State University Dona Ana Community College .... NM 295
Hudson Valley Community College .... NY 310
Rochester Institute of Technology .... NY 321
SUNY Downstate Medical Center .... NY 326
Asheville - Buncombe Technical Community College .... NC 340
Caldwell Community College and Technical Institute .... NC 341
Cape Fear Community College .... NC 341
Forsyth Technical Community College .... NC 343
Johnston Community College .... NC 344
Pitt Community College .... NC 345
South Piedmont Community College .... NC 346
Southwestern Community College .... NC 346
Central Ohio Technical College .... OH 358
Cincinnati State Technical and Community College .... OH 359
Cuyahoga Community College .... OH 360
Kettering College .... OH 364
Lorain County Community College .... OH 364
Marion Technical College .... OH 365
Ohio State University Main Campus, The .... OH 367
Owens Community College .... OH 369
University of Findlay, The .... OH 372
University of Rio Grande .... OH 372
Oklahoma State University - Oklahoma City OK 378
Oregon Institute of Technology .... OR 385
Community College of Allegheny County .... PA 392
Great Lakes Institute of Technology .... PA 396
HACC, Central Pennsylvania's Community College .... PA 396
Lackawanna College .... PA 399
Misericordia University .... PA 401
Mount Aloysius College .... PA 402
Northampton Community College .... PA 403
Pennsylvania College of Health Sciences .... PA 404
Pittsburgh Career Institute .... PA 408
South Hills School of Business and Technology .... PA 410
Thomas Jefferson University .... PA 411
Westmoreland County Community College . PA 414
Community College of Rhode Island .... RI 416
Greenville Technical College .... SC 421
Horry-Georgetown Technical College .... SC 421
Southeast Technical Institute .... SD 429
Baptist College of Health Sciences .... TN 430
Chattanooga State Community College .... TN 436
South College .... TN 436
Vanderbilt University .... TN 440
Volunteer State Community College .... TN 438
Alvin Community College .... TX 442
Angelina College .... TX 442
Austin Community College District .... TX 443
Del Mar College .... TX 448
El Centro College .... TX 448
El Paso Community College .... TX 449
Houston Community College .... TX 450
Lamar Institute of Technology .... TX 462
Lone Star College System .... TX 452
Midland College .... TX 453
San Jacinto College Central .... TX 455
Southwest University at El Paso .... TX 457
Temple College .... TX 458
Tyler Junior College .... TX 464
Weatherford College .... TX 470
Northern Virginia Community College .... VA 488
Piedmont Virginia Community College .... VA 489
Southside Regional Medical Center Professional Schools .... VA 485
Tidewater Community College .... VA 489
Bellevue College .... WA 492
Seattle University .... WA 498
Spokane Community College .... WA 493
Tacoma Community College .... WA 499
BridgeValley Community & Technical College .... WV 502
University of Charleston .... WV 502
West Virginia University .... WV 505
Blackhawk Technical College .... WI 513
Chippewa Valley Technical College .... WI 513
Concordia University Wisconsin .... WI 507
Northeast Wisconsin Technical College .... WI 514
University of Wisconsin-Madison .... WI 510
University of Wisconsin-Milwaukee .... WI 511
Laramie County Community College .... WY 516

DNUR: Accreditation Commission for Education in Nursing: nursing (C)

Baptist Health College Little Rock .... AR 18

DT: American Dental Association: dental laboratory technology (C,A)

Pima Community College .... AZ 15
Los Angeles City College .... CA 49
Pasadena City College .... CA 56
Indiana University-Purdue University Fort Wayne .... IN 160
Kirkwood Community College .... IA 171

EH: New England Association of Schools and Colleges, Commission on Institutions of Higher Education

EMT: Commission on Accreditation of Allied Health Education Programs: emergency medical technician-paramedic (C,A,B)

ENG: ABET, Inc.: engineering (B,M)

Kansas State University ... KS ... 179
University of Kansas Main Campus ... KS ... 181
Wichita State University ... KS ... 182
Murray State University ... KY ... 188
University of Kentucky ... KY ... 190
University of Louisville ... KY ... 190
Western Kentucky University ... KY ... 190
Louisiana State University and Agricultural and Mechanical College ... LA ... 193
Louisiana Tech University ... LA ... 197
McNeese State University ... LA ... 197
Southern University and A&M College ... LA ... 195
Tulane University ... LA ... 196
University of Louisiana at Lafayette ... LA ... 197
University of New Orleans ... LA ... 194
Maine Maritime Academy ... ME ... 200
University of Maine ... ME ... 201
University of Southern Maine ... ME ... 201
Capitol Technology University ... MD ... 202
Frostburg State University ... MD ... 209
Johns Hopkins University ... MD ... 204
Loyola University Maryland ... MD ... 205
Morgan State University ... MD ... 206
United States Naval Academy ... MD ... 519
University of Maryland Baltimore County ... MD ... 208
University of Maryland College Park ... MD ... 207
University of Maryland Eastern Shore ... MD ... 208
Boston University ... MA ... 212
Franklin W. Olin College of Engineering ... MA ... 215
Harvard University ... MA ... 215
Massachusetts Institute of Technology ... MA ... 221
Merrimack College ... MA ... 221
Northeastern University ... MA ... 223
Smith College ... MA ... 224
Suffolk University ... MA ... 224
Tufts University ... MA ... 225
University of Massachusetts ... MA ... 216
University of Massachusetts Dartmouth ... MA ... 217
University of Massachusetts Lowell ... MA ... 217
Wentworth Institute of Technology ... MA ... 225
Western New England University ... MA ... 225
Worcester Polytechnic Institute ... MA ... 226
Andrews University ... MI ... 227
Baker College of Flint ... MI ... 227
Calvin College ... MI ... 228
Central Michigan University ... MI ... 228
Ferris State University ... MI ... 230
Grand Valley State University ... MI ... 230
Hope College ... MI ... 231
Kettering University ... MI ... 232
Lake Superior State University ... MI ... 232
Lawrence Technological University ... MI ... 233
Michigan State University ... MI ... 233
Michigan Technological University ... MI ... 234
Oakland University ... MI ... 235
Saginaw Valley State University ... MI ... 236
University of Detroit Mercy ... MI ... 237
University of Michigan-Ann Arbor ... MI ... 237
University of Michigan-Dearborn ... MI ... 238
University of Michigan-Flint ... MI ... 238
Wayne State University ... MI ... 239
Western Michigan University ... MI ... 239
Minnesota State University, Mankato ... MN ... 246
St. Cloud State University ... MN ... 247
University of Minnesota ... MN ... 250
University of Minnesota Duluth ... MN ... 250
University of Saint Thomas ... MN ... 251
Winona State University ... MN ... 248
Jackson State University ... MS ... 253
Mississippi State University ... MS ... 254
University of Mississippi ... MS ... 256
Missouri University of Science & Technology ... MO .. 269
Saint Louis University ... MO .. 266
Southeast Missouri State University ... MO .. 266
University of Missouri - Columbia ... MO ... 268
University of Missouri - Kansas City ... MO .. 268
University of Missouri - Saint Louis ... MO .. 268
Washington University in St. Louis ... MO .. 269
Carroll College ... MT ... 270
Montana State University ... MT ... 272
Montana Tech of The University of Montana ... MT ... 272
University of Nebraska - Lincoln ... NE ... 277
University of Nevada, Las Vegas ... NV ... 279
University of Nevada, Reno ... NV ... 279
Dartmouth College ... NH ... 281
University of New Hampshire ... NH ... 282
College of New Jersey, The ... NJ ... 284
Fairleigh Dickinson University ... NJ ... 286
Monmouth University ... NJ ... 287
New Jersey Institute of Technology ... NJ ... 288
Princeton University ... NJ ... 288
Rowan University ... NJ ... 289
Rutgers University - New Brunswick ... NJ ... 290
Stevens Institute of Technology ... NJ ... 291
New Mexico Institute of Mining and Technology ... NM ... 294
New Mexico State University Main Campus. NM ... 295
University of New Mexico Main Campus ... NM ... 296
Alfred University ... NY ... 298
City University of New York The City College ... NY ... 301
Clarkson University ... NY ... 304
College of Staten Island CUNY ... NY ... 302
Columbia University in the City of New York NY ... 305
Cooper Union ... NY ... 306
Cornell University ... NY ... 306
Hofstra University ... NY ... 310
Manhattan College ... NY ... 313
New York Institute of Technology ... NY ... 317
New York University ... NY ... 318
Rensselaer Polytechnic Institute ... NY ... 321
Rochester Institute of Technology ... NY ... 321
State University of New York at Binghamton ... NY ... 325
State University of New York at New Paltz . NY ... 325
State University of New York College of Environmental Science and Forestry ... NY ... 328
State University of New York Maritime College ... NY ... 329
Stony Brook University ... NY ... 325
SUNY Polytechnic Institute ... NY ... 330
Syracuse University ... NY ... 330
Union College ... NY ... 332
United States Merchant Marine Academy ... NY ... 519
United States Military Academy ... NY ... 519
University at Buffalo-SUNY ... NY ... 325
University of Rochester ... NY ... 332
Vaughn College of Aeronautics and Technology ... NY ... 333
Webb Institute ... NY ... 333
Duke University ... NC ... 337
East Carolina University ... NC ... 349
North Carolina Agricultural and Technical State University ... NC ... 350
North Carolina State University ... NC ... 350
University of North Carolina at Asheville ... NC ... 351
University of North Carolina at Charlotte ... NC ... 351
Western Carolina University ... NC ... 352
North Dakota State University Main Campus ... ND ... 354
University of North Dakota ... ND ... 353
Air Force Institute of Technology ... OH ... 517
Case Western Reserve University ... OH ... 358
Cedarville University ... OH ... 358
Central State University ... OH ... 358
Cleveland State University ... OH ... 359
Marietta College ... OH ... 365
Miami University ... OH ... 365
Muskingum University ... OH ... 366
Ohio Northern University ... OH ... 367
Ohio State University Main Campus, The ... OH ... 367
Ohio University Main Campus ... OH ... 368
University of Akron, Main Campus, The ... OH ... 371
University of Cincinnati Main Campus ... OH ... 371
University of Dayton ... OH ... 372
University of Mount Union ... OH ... 372
University of Toledo ... OH ... 372
Wright State University Main Campus ... OH ... 374
Youngstown State University ... OH ... 374
Oklahoma Christian University ... OK ... 377
Oklahoma State University ... OK ... 377
Oral Roberts University ... OK ... 378
University of Central Oklahoma ... OK ... 380
University of Oklahoma Norman Campus ... OK ... 380
University of Tulsa ... OK ... 381
George Fox University ... OR ... 383
Oregon Institute of Technology ... OR ... 385
Oregon State University ... OR ... 385
Portland State University ... OR ... 386
University of Portland ... OR ... 387
Bucknell University ... PA ... 390
Carnegie Mellon University ... PA ... 391
Drexel University ... PA ... 394
Elizabethtown College ... PA ... 394
Gannon University ... PA ... 395
Geneva College ... PA ... 395
Grove City College ... PA ... 396
Lafayette College ... PA ... 399
Lehigh University ... PA ... 400
Messiah College ... PA ... 401
Penn State University Park ... PA ... 403
Robert Morris University ... PA ... 409
Saint Francis University ... PA ... 409
Shippensburg University of Pennsylvania ... PA ... 407
Swarthmore College ... PA ... 410
Temple University ... PA ... 411
University of Pennsylvania ... PA ... 412
University of Pittsburgh ... PA ... 412
University of Scranton, The ... PA ... 413
Villanova University ... PA ... 413
Widener University ... PA ... 414
Wilkes University ... PA ... 414
York College of Pennsylvania ... PA ... 415
Caribbean University ... PR ... 521
Inter American University of Puerto Rico Bayamon Campus ... PR ... 523
Universidad Del Turabo ... PR ... 526
Universidad Politecnica De Puerto Rico ... PR ... 527
University of Puerto Rico-Mayaguez Campus ... PR ... 528
Brown University ... RI ... 415
Roger Williams University ... RI ... 417
University of Rhode Island ... RI ... 417
Bob Jones University ... SC ... 418
Citadel, The Military College of South Carolina, The ... SC ... 419
Clemson University ... SC ... 419
South Carolina State University ... SC ... 423
University of South Carolina Columbia ... SC ... 424
South Dakota School of Mines and Technology ... SD ... 429
South Dakota State University ... SD ... 429
Christian Brothers University ... TN ... 431
Lipscomb University ... TN ... 433
Tennessee State University ... TN ... 438
Tennessee Technological University ... TN ... 438
Union University ... TN ... 439
University of Memphis, The ... TN ... 439
University of Tennessee at Chattanooga ... TN ... 440
University of Tennessee at Martin ... TN ... 440
University of Tennessee, Knoxville ... TN ... 439
Vanderbilt University ... TN ... 440
Baylor University ... TX ... 444
Lamar University ... TX ... 462
LeTourneau University ... TX ... 452
Midwestern State University ... TX ... 453
Prairie View A & M University ... TX ... 458
Rice University ... TX ... 455
St. Mary's University ... TX ... 455
Southern Methodist University ... TX ... 457
Tarleton State University ... TX ... 459
Texas A & M University ... TX ... 459
Texas A & M University - Commerce ... TX ... 459
Texas A & M University - Kingsville ... TX ... 460
Texas Christian University ... TX ... 461
Texas State University ... TX ... 463
Texas Tech University ... TX ... 463
Trinity University ... TX ... 464
University of Houston ... TX ... 465
University of Houston - Clear Lake ... TX ... 465
University of North Texas ... TX ... 466
University of Texas at Arlington, The ... TX ... 467
University of Texas at Austin ... TX ... 467
University of Texas at Dallas, The ... TX ... 467
University of Texas at El Paso ... TX ... 467
University of Texas at San Antonio ... TX ... 468
University of Texas at Tyler ... TX ... 468
University of Texas of the Permian Basin ... TX ... 469
University of Texas Rio Grande Valley, The TX ... 468
West Texas A & M University ... TX ... 460
Brigham Young University ... UT ... 471
Southern Utah University ... UT ... 473
University of Utah, The ... UT ... 472
Utah State University ... UT ... 473
Utah Valley University ... UT ... 473
Weber State University ... UT ... 473
Norwich University ... VT ... 475
University of Vermont ... VT ... 476
Christopher Newport University ... VA ... 479
George Mason University ... VA ... 481
Hampton University ... VA ... 481
James Madison University ... VA ... 481
Liberty University ... VA ... 482
Norfolk State University ... VA ... 483
Old Dominion University ... VA ... 483
Sweet Briar College ... VA ... 485
University of Virginia ... VA ... 486
University of Virginia's College at Wise, The VA ... 487
Virginia Commonwealth University ... VA ... 487
Virginia Military Institute ... VA ... 490
Virginia Polytechnic Institute and State University ... VA ... 490
Virginia State University ... VA ... 491
DigiPen Institute of Technology ... WA .. 494
Eastern Washington University ... WA .. 494
Gonzaga University ... WA .. 495
Pacific Lutheran University ... WA .. 496
Saint Martin's University ... WA .. 497
Seattle Pacific University ... WA .. 498
Seattle University ... WA .. 498
University of Washington ... WA .. 499
Walla Walla University ... WA .. 499
Washington State University ... WA .. 499
Marshall University ... WV .. 504
West Virginia University ... WV .. 505
Marquette University ... WI ... 508
Milwaukee School of Engineering ... WI ... 509
University of Wisconsin-Madison ... WI ... 510
University of Wisconsin-Milwaukee ... WI ... 511
University of Wisconsin-Platteville ... WI ... 511
University of Wisconsin-Stevens Point ... WI ... 511
University of Wisconsin-Stout ... WI ... 512
University of Wyoming ... WY .. 517

ENGR: ABET, Inc.: applied science (A, B,M)

Troy University ... AL ... 7
University of North Alabama ... AL ... 9
University of Alaska Anchorage ... AK ... 10
University of Arizona ... AZ ... 16
University of California-Los Angeles ... CA ... 69
Colorado State University ... CO ... 78
Trinidad State Junior College ... CO ... 82
University of Florida ... FL ... 110
University of North Florida ... FL ... 110
University of South Florida ... FL ... 111
Kennesaw State University ... GA ... 122
Idaho State University ... ID ... 132
Illinois State University ... IL ... 140
University of Illinois at Chicago ... IL ... 153
Indiana State University ... IN ... 159
Purdue University Main Campus ... IN ... 163
Purdue University Northwest ... IN ... 163
University of Iowa ... IA ... 166
Pittsburg State University ... KS ... 180
Murray State University ... KY ... 188
Nicholls State University ... LA ... 197
Southeastern Louisiana University ... LA ... 197
Tulane University ... LA ... 196
Johns Hopkins University ... MD ... 204
Morgan State University ... MD ... 206
Uniformed Services University of the Health Sciences ... MD ... 518
University of Massachusetts Lowell ... MA ... 217
Kettering University ... MI ... 232
Oakland University ... MI ... 235
University of Michigan-Ann Arbor ... MI ... 237
St. Cloud State University ... MN ... 247
University of Minnesota ... MN ... 250
University of Central Missouri ... MO .. 268
Montana Tech of The University of Montana ... MT ... 272
University of Nevada, Las Vegas ... NV ... 279
City University of New York Hunter College NY ... 302
East Carolina University ... NC ... 349
Air Force Institute of Technology ... OH ... 517
University of Akron, Main Campus, The ... OH ... 371
University of Cincinnati Main Campus ... OH ... 371
University of Findlay, The ... OH ... 372
University of Toledo ... OH ... 372
Oregon Institute of Technology ... OR ... 385
Oregon State University ... OR ... 385
Indiana University of Pennsylvania ... PA ... 406
Millersville University of Pennsylvania ... PA ... 407
Universidad Politecnica De Puerto Rico ... PR ... 527
Clemson University ... SC ... 419
Chattanooga State Community College ... TN ... 436
East Tennessee State University ... TN ... 431
Texas A & M University - Corpus Christi ... TX ... 460
University of Houston - Clear Lake ... TX ... 465
University of Texas Health Science Center at Houston (UTHealth), The ... TX ... 468
Brigham Young University ... UT ... 471
University of Utah, The ... UT ... 472
Utah State University ... UT ... 473
James Madison University ... VA ... 481
Virginia State University ... VA ... 491
Fairmont State University ... WV .. 504
Marshall University ... WV .. 504
West Virginia University ... WV .. 505
University of Wisconsin-Whitewater ... WI ... 512

ENGT: ABET, Inc.: engineering technology (A,B)

Alabama Agricultural and Mechanical University ... AL ... 1
Arizona State University ... AZ ... 10
University of Arkansas at Little Rock ... AR ... 22
California State Polytechnic University-Pomona ... CA ... 31
CSU Maritime Academy ... CA ... 32
Colorado State University-Pueblo ... CO ... 78
Metropolitan State University of Denver ... CO ... 80
Central Connecticut State University ... CT ... 84
Naugatuck Valley Community College ... CT ... 86
University of Hartford ... CT ... 89
Daytona State College ... FL ... 97
Florida Agricultural and Mechanical University ... FL ... 109
Augusta Technical College ... GA ... 116
Fort Valley State University ... GA ... 119
Georgia Piedmont Technical College ... GA ... 120
Georgia Southern University ... GA ... 120
Kennesaw State University ... GA ... 122
Savannah State University ... GA ... 125
Savannah Technical College ... GA ... 125
Idaho State University ... ID ... 132
Bradley University ... IL ... 134
DeVry University - Chicago Campus ... IL ... 137
Morrison Institute of Technology ... IL ... 146
Northern Illinois University ... IL ... 147
Southern Illinois University Carbondale ... IL ... 152
Indiana State University ... IN ... 159
Indiana University-Purdue University Fort Wayne ... IN ... 160
Indiana University-Purdue University Indianapolis ... IN ... 160
Ivy Tech Community College of Indiana-Central Indiana ... IN ... 161
Purdue University Main Campus ... IN ... 163
Purdue University Northwest ... IN ... 163
University of Northern Iowa ... IA ... 167
Butler Community College ... KS ... 175
Grantham University ... KS ... 177
Pittsburg State University ... KS ... 180

Wichita State University ... KS ... 182
Eastern Kentucky University ... KY ... 184
Murray State University ... KY ... 188
Northern Kentucky University ... KY ... 188
Delgado Community College ... LA ... 192
Grambling State University ... LA ... 196
Louisiana Tech University ... LA ... 197
Northwestern State University ... LA ... 197
Southeastern Louisiana University ... LA ... 197
Southern University and A&M College ... LA ... 195
Maine Maritime Academy ... ME ... 200
University of Maine ... ME ... 201
Capitol Technology University ... MD ... 202
Northeastern University ... MA ... 223
Springfield Technical Community College ... MA ... 221
University of Massachusetts Lowell ... MA ... 217
Wentworth Institute of Technology ... MA ... 225
Eastern Michigan University ... MI ... 229
Ferris State University ... MI ... 230
Lake Superior State University ... MI ... 232
Michigan Technological University ... MI ... 234
Northern Michigan University ... MI ... 235
Wayne State University ... MI ... 239
Western Michigan University ... MI ... 239
Dunwoody College of Technology ... MN ... 242
Minnesota State University, Mankato ... MN ... 246
University of Southern Mississippi ... MS ... 256
Missouri Southern State University ... MO ... 263
Missouri Western State University ... MO ... 264
Southeast Missouri State University ... MO ... 266
Montana State University ... MT ... 272
Montana State University - Northern ... MT ... 272
College of Southern Nevada ... NV ... 278
Nashua Community College ... NH ... 280
NHTI-Concord's Community College ... NH ... 280
University of New Hampshire ... NH ... 282
County College of Morris ... NJ ... 285
Essex County College ... NJ ... 285
Fairleigh Dickinson University ... NJ ... 286
Middlesex County College ... NJ ... 287
New Jersey Institute of Technology ... NJ ... 288
Passaic County Community College ... NJ ... 288
Rowan College at Burlington County ... NJ ... 289
Thomas Edison State University ... NJ ... 292
New Mexico State University Main Campus ... NM ... 295
Northern New Mexico College ... NM ... 295
Alfred State College ... NY ... 328
City University of New York Bronx Community College ... NY ... 301
City University of New York Queensborough Community College ... NY ... 303
College of Staten Island CUNY ... NY ... 302
Erie Community College ... NY ... 307
Excelsior College ... NY ... 308
Farmingdale State College ... NY ... 329
Hudson Valley Community College ... NY ... 310
Mohawk Valley Community College ... NY ... 315
Monroe Community College ... NY ... 315
Morrisville State College ... NY ... 329
Nassau Community College ... NY ... 316
New York City College of Technology/City University of New York ... NY ... 303
New York Institute of Technology ... NY ... 317
Paul Smith's College ... NY ... 320
Rochester Institute of Technology ... NY ... 321
State University of New York College at Buffalo ... NY ... 326
State University of New York College of Environmental Science and Forestry ... NY ... 328
SUNY Broome Community College ... NY ... 326
SUNY Canton-College of Technology ... NY ... 329
SUNY Polytechnic Institute ... NY ... 330
Vaughn College of Aeronautics and Technology ... NY ... 333
Central Piedmont Community College ... NC ... 342
Elizabeth City State University ... NC ... 350
Forsyth Technical Community College ... NC ... 343
Gaston College ... NC ... 343
University of North Carolina at Charlotte ... NC ... 351
Western Carolina University ... NC ... 352
Bismarck State College ... ND ... 354
Bowling Green State University ... OH ... 357
Central Ohio Technical College ... OH ... 358
Cincinnati State Technical and Community College ... OH ... 359
Cleveland State University ... OH ... 359
Columbus State Community College ... OH ... 360
Cuyahoga Community College ... OH ... 360
James A. Rhodes State College ... OH ... 363
Kent State University Kent Campus ... OH ... 363
Lakeland Community College ... OH ... 364
Lorain County Community College ... OH ... 364
Miami University ... OH ... 365
Sinclair Community College ... OH ... 370
Stark State College ... OH ... 370
University of Akron, Main Campus, The ... OH ... 371
University of Cincinnati Main Campus ... OH ... 371
University of Dayton ... OH ... 372
University of Toledo ... OH ... 372
Youngstown State University ... OH ... 374
Zane State College ... OH ... 374
Oklahoma State University ... OK ... 377
Oklahoma State University Institute of Technology-Okmulgee ... OK ... 378
Southwestern Oklahoma State University ... OK ... 380
Oregon Institute of Technology ... OR ... 385
Bloomsburg University of Pennsylvania ... PA ... 405
California University of Pennsylvania ... PA ... 405
Drexel University ... PA ... 394
Pennsylvania College of Technology ... PA ... 404
Point Park University ... PA ... 408
Temple University ... PA ... 411
University of Puerto Rico-Aguadilla ... PR ... 527
University of Puerto Rico at Arecibo ... PR ... 527
University of Puerto Rico at Bayamon ... PR ... 527
University of Puerto Rico at Ponce ... PR ... 528
University of Puerto Rico-Humacao ... PR ... 528
New England Institute of Technology ... RI ... 416
Denmark Technical College ... SC ... 420
Greenville Technical College ... SC ... 421
Midlands Technical College ... SC ... 422
Orangeburg-Calhoun Technical College ... SC ... 423
Piedmont Technical College ... SC ... 423
South Carolina State University ... SC ... 423
Spartanburg Community College ... SC ... 424
University of South Carolina Upstate ... SC ... 425
York Technical College ... SC ... 426
Austin Peay State University ... TN ... 430
Belmont University ... TN ... 430
Chattanooga State Community College ... TN ... 436
East Tennessee State University ... TN ... 431
Middle Tennessee State University ... TN ... 434
Southwest Tennessee Community College ... TN ... 438
Tennessee Technological University ... TN ... 438
University of Memphis, The ... TN ... 439
University of Tennessee at Chattanooga ... TN ... 440
Houston Community College ... TX ... 450
LeTourneau University ... TX ... 452
Prairie View A & M University ... TX ... 458
Texas A & M University ... TX ... 459
Texas A & M University - Corpus Christi ... TX ... 460
Texas Southern University ... TX ... 461
University of Houston ... TX ... 465
University of Houston - Downtown ... TX ... 465
University of North Texas ... TX ... 466
Brigham Young University ... UT ... 471
Southern Utah University ... UT ... 473
Weber State University ... UT ... 473
Vermont Technical College ... VT ... 477
Old Dominion University ... VA ... 483
Virginia State University ... VA ... 491
Central Washington University ... WA ... 492
Eastern Washington University ... WA ... 494
Western Washington University ... WA ... 500
Bluefield State College ... WV ... 503
BridgeValley Community & Technical College ... WV ... 502
Fairmont State University ... WV ... 504
West Virginia University ... WV ... 505
Milwaukee School of Engineering ... WI ... 509
Northeast Wisconsin Technical College ... WI ... 514
University of Wisconsin-Stout ... WI ... 512
Waukesha County Technical College ... WI ... 515

EXSC: Commission on Accreditation of Allied Health Education Programs: exercise science (C,B,M)

Northern Arizona University ... AZ ... 14
Metropolitan State University of Denver ... CO ... 80
Central Connecticut State University ... CT ... 84
Southern Connecticut State University ... CT ... 85
University of North Florida ... FL ... 110
University of West Florida ... FL ... 111
Clayton State University ... GA ... 117
Georgia State University ... GA ... 121
Valdosta State University ... GA ... 127
Southern Illinois University Edwardsville ... IL ... 152
Indiana Wesleyan University ... IN ... 161
University of Indianapolis ... IN ... 164
Baker University ... KS ... 174
Murray State University ... KY ... 188
University of Louisville ... KY ... 190
University of Louisiana at Monroe ... LA ... 198
University of Southern Maine ... ME ... 201
Frostburg State University ... MD ... 209
Salisbury University ... MD ... 209
Lasell College ... MA ... 216
Springfield College ... MA ... 224
Westfield State University ... MA ... 218
Central Michigan University ... MI ... 228
St. Catherine University ... MN ... 249
Missouri Baptist University ... MO ... 263
City University of New York York College ... NY ... 304
Mercy College ... NY ... 314
State University of New York, The College at Brockport ... NY ... 326
University of North Carolina at Charlotte ... NC ... 351
North Dakota State University Main Campus ... ND ... 354
University of Mary ... ND ... 355
Baldwin Wallace University ... OH ... 357
Bowling Green State University ... OH ... 357
Kent State University Kent Campus ... OH ... 363
Ohio Northern University ... OH ... 367
Wright State University Main Campus ... OH ... 374
University of Central Oklahoma ... OK ... 380
Bloomsburg University of Pennsylvania ... PA ... 405
East Stroudsburg University of Pennsylvania ... PA ... 406
Eastern University ... PA ... 394
Grove City College ... PA ... 396
Indiana University of Pennsylvania ... PA ... 406
Saint Francis University ... PA ... 409
Slippery Rock University of Pennsylvania ... PA ... 407
West Chester University of Pennsylvania ... PA ... 407
University of Rhode Island ... RI ... 417
South Dakota State University ... SD ... 429
Lyndon State College ... VT ... 477
George Mason University ... VA ... 481
Liberty University ... VA ... 482
Longwood University ... VA ... 482
Lynchburg College ... VA ... 482
Old Dominion University ... VA ... 483
University of Wisconsin-Oshkosh ... WI ... 511

FEPAC: American Academy of Forensic Sciences: forensic science (B,M)

University of Alabama at Birmingham ... AL ... 8
University of New Haven ... CT ... 89
#George Washington University ... DC ... 92
Florida International University ... FL ... 109
University of Tampa ... FL ... 113
Albany State University ... GA ... 114
Loyola University Chicago ... IL ... 144
University of Illinois at Chicago ... IL ... 153
Indiana University-Purdue University Indianapolis ... IN ... 160
Eastern Kentucky University ... KY ... 184
Towson University ... MD ... 209
Boston University ... MA ... 212
Madonna University ... MI ... 233
Michigan State University ... MI ... 233
University of Mississippi ... MS ... 256
Alfred State College ... NY ... 328
City University of New York John Jay College of Criminal Justice ... NY ... 302
State University of New York College at Buffalo ... NY ... 326
Fayetteville State University ... NC ... 350
#Ohio University Main Campus ... OH ... 368
University of Central Oklahoma ... OK ... 380
Arcadia University ... PA ... 389
Cedar Crest College ... PA ... 392
Duquesne University ... PA ... 394
Penn State University Park ... PA ... 403
West Chester University of Pennsylvania ... PA ... 407
Sam Houston State University ... TX ... 462
Texas A & M University ... TX ... 459
University of North Texas ... TX ... 466
Virginia Commonwealth University ... VA ... 487
Marshall University ... WV ... 504
West Virginia University ... WV ... 505

FUSER: American Board of Funeral Service Education: funeral service education (C,A,B)

Bishop State Community College ... AL ... 1
Jefferson State Community College ... AL ... 2
Arkansas State University-Mountain Home ... AR ... 18
University of Arkansas at Hope-Texarkana ... AR ... 23
American River College ... CA ... 50
Cypress College ... CA ... 53
Arapahoe Community College ... CO ... 76
Lincoln College of New England ... CT ... 87
Florida State College at Jacksonville ... FL ... 100
Miami Dade College ... FL ... 103
St. Petersburg College ... FL ... 107
Gupton Jones College of Funeral Service ... GA ... 121
Ogeechee Technical College ... GA ... 123
Carl Sandburg College ... IL ... 134
Malcolm X College, One of the City Colleges of Chicago ... IL ... 136
Southern Illinois University Carbondale ... IL ... 152
Worsham College of Mortuary Science ... IL ... 155
Ivy Tech Community College of Indiana-Central Indiana ... IN ... 161
Mid-America College of Funeral Service ... IN ... 162
#Vincennes University ... IN ... 165
Des Moines Area Community College ... IA ... 168
Kansas City Kansas Community College ... KS ... 178
Delgado Community College ... LA ... 192
Community College of Baltimore County, The ... MD ... 203
FINE Mortuary College ... MA ... 215
Mount Ida College ... MA ... 222
Wayne State University ... MI ... 239
University of Minnesota ... MN ... 250
East Mississippi Community College ... MS ... 253
#Holmes Community College ... MS ... 253
Northwest Mississippi Community College ... MS ... 255
Eastwick College ... NJ ... 285
Mercer County Community College ... NJ ... 287
American Academy McAllister Institute of Funeral Service ... NY ... 298
Hudson Valley Community College ... NY ... 310
Nassau Community College ... NY ... 316
#SUNY Canton-College of Technology ... NY ... 329
Fayetteville Technical Community College ... NC ... 343
Cincinnati College of Mortuary Science ... OH ... 359
University of Central Oklahoma ... OK ... 380
Mt. Hood Community College ... OR ... 384
Northampton Community College ... PA ... 403
Pittsburgh Institute of Mortuary Science ... PA ... 408
Piedmont Technical College ... SC ... 423
John A. Gupton College ... TN ... 432
Amarillo College ... TX ... 442
Commonwealth Institute of Funeral Service ... TX ... 446
Dallas Institute of Funeral Service ... TX ... 448
San Antonio College ... TX ... 442
Salt Lake Community College ... UT ... 474
John Tyler Community College ... VA ... 488
Tidewater Community College ... VA ... 489
Lake Washington Institute of Technology ... WA ... 495
Milwaukee Area Technical College ... WI ... 514

HSA: Commission on Accreditation of Healthcare Management Education: healthcare management (B,M)

University of Alabama at Birmingham ... AL ... 8
University of Arkansas for Medical Sciences ... AR ... 22
#California State University-Long Beach ... CA ... 32
San Diego State University ... CA ... 34
University of Southern California ... CA ... 72
University of Colorado Denver|Anschutz Medical Campus ... CO ... 83
George Washington University ... DC ... 92
Georgetown University ... DC ... 92
Florida International University ... FL ... 109
University of Central Florida ... FL ... 110
University of Florida ... FL ... 110
University of Miami ... FL ... 112
University of North Florida ... FL ... 110
University of South Florida ... FL ... 111
Armstrong State University ... GA ... 115
Georgia State University ... GA ... 121
Governors State University ... IL ... 138
Rush University ... IL ... 150
University of Illinois at Chicago ... IL ... 153
Indiana University-Purdue University Indianapolis ... IN ... 160
Des Moines University ... IA ... 168
University of Iowa ... IA ... 166
University of Kansas Main Campus ... KS ... 181
University of Kentucky ... KY ... 190
Tulane University ... LA ... 196
Johns Hopkins University ... MD ... 204
Boston University ... MA ... 212
Suffolk University ... MA ... 224
University of Michigan-Ann Arbor ... MI ... 237
University of Minnesota ... MN ... 250
University of Saint Thomas ... MN ... 251
Saint Louis University ... MO ... 266
University of Missouri - Columbia ... MO ... 268
Seton Hall University ... NJ ... 291
Baruch College/City University of New York ... NY ... 301
Clarkson University ... NY ... 304
Columbia University in the City of New York ... NY ... 305
Cornell University ... NY ... 306
New York University ... NY ... 318
University of North Carolina at Chapel Hill ... NC ... 351
University of North Carolina at Charlotte ... NC ... 351
Ohio State University Main Campus, The ... OH ... 367
Xavier University ... OH ... 374
Portland State University ... OR ... 386
Penn State University Park ... PA ... 403
Temple University ... PA ... 411
University of Pittsburgh ... PA ... 412
University of Scranton, The ... PA ... 413
Widener University ... PA ... 414
University of Puerto Rico-Medical Sciences Campus ... PR ... 528
Medical University of South Carolina ... SC ... 422
University of South Carolina Columbia ... SC ... 424
University of Memphis, The ... TN ... 439
Baylor University ... TX ... 444
Texas A & M University ... TX ... 459
Texas State University ... TX ... 463
Texas Woman's University ... TX ... 464
Trinity University ... TX ... 464
University of North Texas Health Science Center at Fort Worth ... TX ... 466
University of the Incarnate Word ... TX ... 465
University of Utah, The ... UT ... 472
Weber State University ... UT ... 473
George Mason University ... VA ... 481
Marymount University ... VA ... 483
Virginia Commonwealth University ... VA ... 487
University of Washington ... WA ... 499
Washington State University ... WA ... 499

HT: National Accrediting Agency for Clinical Laboratory Sciences: histologic technology (C,A,B)

Phoenix College ... AZ ... 14
Baptist Health College Little Rock ... AR ... 18
Merritt College ... CA ... 56
Mt. San Antonio College ... CA ... 52
Goodwin College ... CT ... 87
Barry University ... FL ... 95
Florida State College at Jacksonville ... FL ... 100
Miami Dade College ... FL ... 103
Albany State University ... GA ... 114
Elgin Community College ... IL ... 138
Indiana University-Purdue University Indianapolis ... IN ... 160
Harford Community College ... MD ... 204
North Hennepin Community College ... MN ... 246
State University of New York College of Agriculture and Technology at Coble skill ... NY ... 328
Carolinas College of Health Sciences ... NC ... 336
University of North Dakota ... ND ... 353
Lakeland Community College ... OH ... 364
Drexel University ... PA ... 394
Harcum College ... PA ... 396
Community College of Rhode Island ... RI ... 416
Medical University of South Carolina ... SC ... 422
University of Tennessee Health Science Center ... TN ... 440
Houston Community College ... TX ... 450
St. Philip's College ... TX ... 441
Tarleton State University ... TX ... 459
University of Texas Health Science Center at San Antonio ... TX ... 468
University of Texas MD Anderson Cancer Center, The ... TX ... 469
Clover Park Technical College ... WA ... 493
West Virginia University ... WV ... 505

IACBE: International Accreditation Council for Business Education: business programs in institutions that grant bachelor/graduate degrees (A,B, M,D)

Stillman College ... AL ... 7
Alaska Pacific University ... AK ... 9
Ashford University ... CA ... 26
Azusa Pacific University ... CA ... 26
Concordia University ... CA ... 40
CSU Maritime Academy ... CA ... 32
Humboldt State University ... CA ... 34
John F. Kennedy University ... CA ... 46
National University ... CA ... 53
Pacific Union College ... CA ... 55
Albertus Magnus College ... CT ... 84
Wilmington University ... DE ... 91
Edward Waters College ... FL ... 98
Florida Institute of Technology ... FL ... 99
Hodges University ... FL ... 101
Lynn University ... FL ... 103
Nova Southeastern University ... FL ... 104
Palm Beach Atlantic University ... FL ... 104
Saint Leo University ... FL ... 106
Webber International University ... FL ... 114
Thomas University ... GA ... 126
University of Guam ... GU ... 520
Chaminade University of Honolulu ... HI ... 129
Lewis-Clark State College ... ID ... 132
Lincoln College ... IL ... 143
McKendree University ... IL ... 145
National-Louis University ... IL ... 146
North Park University ... IL ... 147
Robert Morris University - Illinois ... IL ... 149
Rockford University ... IL ... 150
Marian University ... IN ... 162
Oakland City University ... IN ... 163
Maharishi University of Management ... IA ... 171
Northwestern College ... IA ... 172
Grantham University ... KS ... 177
University of Saint Mary ... KS ... 182
Campbellsville University ... KY ... 184
Kentucky Wesleyan College ... KY ... 187
Lindsey Wilson College ... KY ... 187
Spalding University ... KY ... 189
University of Holy Cross ... LA ... 196
Husson University ... ME ... 199
University of Maine at Fort Kent ... ME ... 201
Capitol Technology University ... MD ... 202
Mount St. Mary's University ... MD ... 206
University of Maryland College Park ... MD ... 207
American International College ... MA ... 210
College of Our Lady of the Elms ... MA ... 213
Fitchburg State University ... MA ... 217
Massachusetts Maritime Academy ... MA ... 218
Nichols College ... MA ... 223
Springfield College ... MA ... 224
Wentworth Institute of Technology ... MA ... 225
Andrews University ... MI ... 227
Baker College of Flint ... MI ... 227
Davenport University ... MI ... 229
Lawrence Technological University ... MI ... 233
Bemidji State University ... MN ... 244
Saint Mary's University of Minnesota ... MN ... 250
Belhaven University ... MS ... 252
William Carey University ... MS ... 256
Avila University ... MO ... 257
Culver-Stockton College ... MO ... 259
Harris-Stowe State University ... MO ... 260
Carroll College ... MT ... 270
University of Montana Western, The ... MT ... 271
Bellevue University ... NE ... 273
Concordia University ... NE ... 274
Wayne State College ... NE ... 276
Roseman University of Health Sciences ... NV ... 280
Franklin Pierce University ... NH ... 281
Berkeley College ... NJ ... 283
Centenary University ... NJ ... 284
Felician University ... NJ ... 286
Saint Peter's University ... NJ ... 291
Berkeley College ... NY ... 299
Cazenovia College ... NY ... 300
Concordia College ... NY ... 305
Daemen College ... NY ... 306
Dominican College of Blauvelt ... NY ... 306
D'Youville College ... NY ... 307
Excelsior College ... NY ... 308
Keuka College ... NY ... 312
Manhattanville College ... NY ... 314
Medaille College ... NY ... 314
Mount Saint Mary College ... NY ... 316
Nazareth College of Rochester ... NY ... 316
Roberts Wesleyan College ... NY ... 321
Sage Colleges, The ... NY ... 321
St. Thomas Aquinas College ... NY ... 323
State University of New York College at Potsdam ... NY ... 328
State University of New York Empire State College ... NY ... 329
Vaughn College of Aeronautics and Technology ... NY ... 333
Dickinson State University ... ND ... 354
Minot State University ... ND ... 354
University of Jamestown ... ND ... 355
University of Mary ... ND ... 355
Defiance College, The ... OH ... 361
Franklin University ... OH ... 362
Lake Erie College ... OH ... 364
Lourdes University ... OH ... 364
University of Rio Grande ... OH ... 372
Ursuline College ... OH ... 373
Bacone College ... OK ... 374
Oklahoma Wesleyan University ... OK ... 378
Southwestern Oklahoma State University ... OK ... 380
Eastern Oregon University ... OR ... 383
Marylhurst University ... OR ... 384
Northwest Christian University ... OR ... 384
Oregon Institute of Technology ... OR ... 385
Cairn University ... PA ... 391
Chatham University ... PA ... 392
Gwynedd Mercy University ... PA ... 396
Juniata College ... PA ... 398
Keystone College ... PA ... 398
Mercyhurst University ... PA ... 401
Misericordia University ... PA ... 401
Point Park University ... PA ... 408
Saint Francis University ... PA ... 409
Seton Hill University ... PA ... 410
Waynesburg University ... PA ... 414
Inter American University of Puerto Rico San German Campus ... PR ... 524
Universidad Politecnica De Puerto Rico ... PR ... 527
Salve Regina University ... RI ... 417
Charleston Southern University ... SC ... 419
Dakota Wesleyan University ... SD ... 427
National American University ... SD ... 427
Presentation College ... SD ... 427
University of Sioux Falls ... SD ... 429
Bryan College ... TN ... 430
Southern Adventist University ... TN ... 436
Concordia University Texas ... TX ... 446
Southwestern Adventist University ... TX ... 457
Southwestern Assemblies of God University ... TX ... 457
Hampton University ... VA ... 481
Ohio Valley University ... WV ... 502
Shepherd University ... WV ... 504
West Liberty University ... WV ... 504
Concordia University Wisconsin ... WI ... 507
Herzing University ... WI ... 507
Marian University ... WI ... 508

IFSAC: International Fire Service Accreditation Congress Degree Assembly: fire and emergency related degree (A,B)

Central Arizona College ... AZ ... 11
Yavapai College ... AZ ... 17
NorthWest Arkansas Community College ... AR ... 20
Oxnard College ... CA ... 73
Aims Community College ... CO ... 76
Embry-Riddle Aeronautical University ... FL ... 98
Southern Illinois University Carbondale ... IL ... 152
Kaplan University ... IA ... 171
Johnson County Community College ... KS ... 178
Ashland Community and Technical College ... KY ... 185
Bluegrass Community and Technical College ... KY ... 185
Eastern Kentucky University ... KY ... 184
Elizabethtown Community and Technical College ... KY ... 185
Gateway Community and Technical College ... KY ... 185
Hazard Community and Technical College ... KY ... 185
Jefferson Community and Technical College ... KY ... 186
Madisonville Community College ... KY ... 186
Maysville Community and Technical College ... KY ... 186
Owensboro Community and Technical College ... KY ... 186
Somerset Community College ... KY ... 186
Southcentral Kentucky Community and Technical College ... KY ... 187
West Kentucky Community and Technical College ... KY ... 187
Lake Superior State University ... MI ... 232
Lansing Community College ... MI ... 232
Macomb Community College ... MI ... 233
Hennepin Technical College ... MN ... 244
Ozarks Technical Community College ... MO ... 264
Helena College University of Montana ... MT ... 271
New Mexico State University Dona Ana Community College ... NM ... 295
Catawba Valley Community College ... NC ... 341
Gaston College ... NC ... 343
Central Ohio Technical College ... OH ... 358
Cincinnati State Technical and Community College ... OH ... 359
Lakeland Community College ... OH ... 364
University of Akron, Main Campus, The ... OH ... 371
Oklahoma State University - Oklahoma City ... OK ... 378
Central Oregon Community College ... OR ... 382
Chemeketa Community College ... OR ... 382
Portland Community College ... OR ... 386
Holy Family University ... PA ... 397
Montgomery County Community College ... PA ... 402
Blinn College ... TX ... 444
Utah Valley University ... UT ... 473
South Puget Sound Community College ... WA ... 498
American Public University System ... WV ... 501
Fox Valley Technical College ... WI ... 513
University of Wisconsin-Oshkosh ... WI ... 511

IPSY: American Psychological Association: doctoral internships in health service psychology

University of Alabama at Birmingham ... AL ... 8
Arizona State University ... AZ ... 10
University of Arizona ... AZ ... 16
University of Arkansas for Medical Sciences ... AR ... 22
Biola University ... CA ... 27
California State University-Fullerton ... CA ... 32
California State University-Long Beach ... CA ... 32
California State University-Northridge ... CA ... 33
Loma Linda University ... CA ... 48
San Jose State University ... CA ... 34
Santa Ana College ... CA ... 58
Santa Clara University ... CA ... 62
Stanford University ... CA ... 66
University of California-Berkeley ... CA ... 68
University of California-Davis ... CA ... 68
University of California-Irvine ... CA ... 69
University of California-Los Angeles ... CA ... 69
University of California-Riverside ... CA ... 69
University of California-San Diego ... CA ... 69
University of California-San Francisco ... CA ... 70
University of California-Santa Barbara ... CA ... 70
University of California-Santa Cruz ... CA ... 70
University of San Diego ... CA ... 71
University of San Francisco ... CA ... 72
University of Southern California ... CA ... 72
University of the Pacific ... CA ... 70
Wright Institute, The ... CA ... 75
Colorado State University ... CO ... 78
University of Colorado Boulder ... CO ... 83
University of Colorado Denver|Anschutz Medical Campus ... CO ... 83
University of Denver ... CO ... 83
University of Northern Colorado ... CO ... 83
University of Connecticut ... CT ... 88
Yale University ... CT ... 89
University of Delaware ... DE ... 90
American University ... DC ... 91
Catholic University of America, The ... DC ... 91
George Washington University ... DC ... 92
Howard University ... DC ... 92
Florida Atlantic University ... FL ... 109
Florida Gulf Coast University ... FL ... 109
Florida International University ... FL ... 109
Florida State University ... FL ... 110
Nova Southeastern University ... FL ... 104
University of Central Florida ... FL ... 110
University of Florida ... FL ... 110
University of Miami ... FL ... 112
University of South Florida ... FL ... 111
Augusta University ... GA ... 116
Emory University ... GA ... 119
Georgia Institute of Technology ... GA ... 120
Georgia Southern University ... GA ... 120
Georgia State University ... GA ... 121
University of Hawaii at Manoa ... HI ... 129
University of Idaho ... ID ... 132
Adler University ... IL ... 133
Illinois State University ... IL ... 140
Lake Forest College ... IL ... 142
Northern Illinois University ... IL ... 147
Northwestern University ... IL ... 148
Rush University ... IL ... 150
Southern Illinois University Carbondale ... IL ... 152
University of Chicago ... IL ... 153
University of Illinois at Chicago ... IL ... 153
University of Illinois at Urbana-Champaign ... IL ... 154
Ball State University ... IN ... 156
Butler University ... IN ... 156
Indiana University Bloomington ... IN ... 159
Indiana University-Purdue University Indianapolis ... IN ... 160
Purdue University Main Campus ... IN ... 163
University of Notre Dame ... IN ... 165
Iowa State University ... IA ... 166
University of Iowa ... IA ... 166
Kansas State University ... KS ... 179
University of Kansas Main Campus ... KS ... 181
Wichita State University ... KS ... 182
University of Kentucky ... KY ... 190
University of Louisville ... KY ... 190
Louisiana State University and Agricultural and Mechanical College ... LA ... 193
Louisiana State University Health Sciences Center-New Orleans ... LA ... 194
Tulane University ... LA ... 196
University of Maine ... ME ... 201
Johns Hopkins University ... MD ... 204
Towson University ... MD ... 209
University of Maryland Baltimore County ... MD ... 208
University of Maryland College Park ... MD ... 207
University of Maryland, Baltimore ... MD ... 207
Boston University ... MA ... 212
Harvard University ... MA ... 215
Suffolk University ... MA ... 224
University of Massachusetts ... MA ... 216
William James College ... MA ... 226
Grand Valley State University ... MI ... 230
Michigan State University ... MI ... 233
University of Michigan-Ann Arbor ... MI ... 237
University of Minnesota ... MN ... 250
University of Saint Thomas ... MN ... 251
University of Mississippi Medical Center ... MS ... 256
University of Missouri - Columbia ... MO ... 268
University of Missouri - Kansas City ... MO ... 268
University of Missouri - Saint Louis ... MO ... 268
Montana State University ... MT ... 272
University of Nebraska - Lincoln ... NE ... 277
University of Nevada, Las Vegas ... NV ... 279
Dartmouth College ... NH ... 281
University of New Hampshire ... NH ... 282
Rutgers University - Newark ... NJ ... 290
New Mexico State University Main Campus ... NM ... 295
University of New Mexico Main Campus ... NM ... 296
Adelphi University ... NY ... 297
Albany Medical College ... NY ... 297
Baruch College/City University of New York ... NY ... 301
Columbia University in the City of New York ... NY ... 305
Icahn School of Medicine at Mount Sinai ... NY ... 311
New York University ... NY ... 318
Pace University ... NY ... 319
State University of New York at Oneonta ... NY ... 325
State University of New York Upstate Medical University ... NY ... 326
Stony Brook University ... NY ... 325
University at Albany, SUNY ... NY ... 324
University at Buffalo-SUNY ... NY ... 325
University of Rochester ... NY ... 332
Yeshiva University ... NY ... 334
Appalachian State University ... NC ... 349
Duke University ... NC ... 337
North Carolina State University ... NC ... 350
University of North Carolina at Chapel Hill ... NC ... 351
University of North Carolina at Charlotte ... NC ... 351
Western Carolina University ... NC ... 352
University of North Dakota ... ND ... 353
Bowling Green State University ... OH ... 357
Miami University ... OH ... 365
Ohio State University Main Campus, The ... OH ... 367
Ohio University Main Campus ... OH ... 368
University of Akron, Main Campus, The ... OH ... 371
Wright State University Main Campus ... OH ... 374
George Fox University ... OR ... 383
Oregon Health & Science University ... OR ... 385
Oregon State University ... OR ... 385
Pacific University ... OR ... 385
University of Oregon ... OR ... 387
Chestnut Hill College ... PA ... 392
Drexel University ... PA ... 394
Immaculata University ... PA ... 397
Lehigh University ... PA ... 400

Penn State University Park ... PA ... 403
Philadelphia College of Osteopathic Medicine ... PA ... 407
Temple University ... PA ... 411
University of Pennsylvania ... PA ... 412
University of Pittsburgh ... PA ... 412
Widener University ... PA ... 414
Carlos Albizu University ... PR ... 521
Ponce School of Medicine & Health Sciences ... PR ... 525
Brown University ... RI ... 415
Clemson University ... SC ... 419
Medical University of South Carolina ... SC ... 422
University of South Carolina Columbia ... SC ... 424
University of Memphis, The ... TN ... 439
University of Tennessee Health Science Center ... TN ... 440
University of Tennessee, Knoxville ... TN ... 439
Vanderbilt University ... TN ... 440
Baylor College of Medicine ... TX ... 444
Texas A & M University ... TX ... 459
Texas State University ... TX ... 463
Texas Tech University ... TX ... 463
Texas Woman's University ... TX ... 464
University of Houston ... TX ... 465
University of Houston - Clear Lake ... TX ... 465
University of Texas at Austin ... TX ... 467
University of Texas at Dallas, The ... TX ... 467
University of Texas Health Science Center at Houston (UTHealth), The ... TX ... 468
University of Texas Health Science Center at San Antonio ... TX ... 468
University of Texas Health Science Center at Tyler, The ... TX ... 469
University of Texas Southwestern Medical Center ... TX ... 469
Brigham Young University ... UT ... 471
University of Utah, The ... UT ... 472
Utah State University ... UT ... 473
University of Vermont ... VT ... 476
College of William & Mary ... VA ... 479
Eastern Virginia Medical School ... VA ... 480
George Mason University ... VA ... 481
James Madison University ... VA ... 481
University of Virginia ... VA ... 486
Virginia Commonwealth University ... VA ... 487
Virginia Polytechnic Institute and State University ... VA ... 490
Central Washington University ... WA ... 492
University of Puget Sound ... WA ... 499
University of Washington ... WA ... 499
Washington State University ... WA ... 499
West Virginia University ... WV ... 505
University of Wisconsin-Madison ... WI ... 510

JOUR: Accrediting Council on Education for Journalism and Mass Communications: journalism and mass communications (B,M)

Auburn University ... AL ... 4
Jacksonville State University ... AL ... 6
University of Alabama, The ... AL ... 8
University of North Alabama ... AL ... 9
University of Alaska Anchorage ... AK ... 10
Arizona State University ... AZ ... 10
University of Arizona ... AZ ... 16
Arkansas State University-Jonesboro ... AR ... 18
#University of Arkansas Main Campus ... AR ... 21
California State University-Chico ... CA ... 31
California State University-Fullerton ... CA ... 32
California State University-Long Beach ... CA ... 32
California State University-Northridge ... CA ... 33
San Diego State University ... CA ... 34
San Francisco State University ... CA ... 34
San Jose State University ... CA ... 34
University of Southern California ... CA ... 72
Colorado State University ... CO ... 78
University of Colorado Boulder ... CO ... 83
University of Connecticut ... CT ... 88
American University ... DC ... 91
Howard University ... DC ... 92
Florida Agricultural and Mechanical University ... FL ... 109
Florida International University ... FL ... 109
University of Florida ... FL ... 110
University of North Florida ... FL ... 110
University of South Florida St. Petersburg ... FL ... 111
Savannah State University ... GA ... 125
University of Georgia ... GA ... 127
University of Idaho ... ID ... 132
Eastern Illinois University ... IL ... 138
Southern Illinois University Carbondale ... IL ... 152
Southern Illinois University Edwardsville ... IL ... 152
University of Illinois at Urbana-Champaign ... IL ... 154
Ball State University ... IN ... 156
Indiana University Bloomington ... IN ... 159
Drake University ... IA ... 168
Iowa State University ... IA ... 166
University of Iowa ... IA ... 166
Kansas State University ... KS ... 179
University of Kansas Main Campus ... KS ... 181
Murray State University ... KY ... 188
University of Kentucky ... KY ... 190
Western Kentucky University ... KY ... 190
Louisiana State University and Agricultural and Mechanical College ... LA ... 193
Loyola University New Orleans ... LA ... 194
Nicholls State University ... LA ... 197
Southern University and A&M College ... LA ... 195
University of Louisiana at Lafayette ... LA ... 197
University of Maryland College Park ... MD ... 207
Central Michigan University ... MI ... 228
Michigan State University ... MI ... 233
St. Cloud State University ... MN ... 247
University of Minnesota ... MN ... 250
University of Mississippi ... MS ... 256
University of Southern Mississippi ... MS ... 256
Southeast Missouri State University ... MO ... 266
University of Missouri - Columbia ... MO ... 268
University of Montana - Missoula ... MT ... 271
University of Nebraska - Lincoln ... NE ... 277
University of Nevada, Reno ... NV ... 279
University of New Mexico Main Campus ... NM ... 296
City University of New York Graduate Center ... NY ... 302
Columbia University in the City of New York NY ... 305
Hofstra University ... NY ... 310
Iona College ... NY ... 311
New York University ... NY ... 318
St. Bonaventure University ... NY ... 322
State University of New York College at Buffalo ... NY ... 326
Stony Brook University ... NY ... 325
Syracuse University ... NY ... 330
Elon University ... NC ... 337
#North Carolina Agricultural and Technical State University ... NC ... 350
University of North Carolina at Chapel Hill ... NC ... 351
#Bowling Green State University ... OH ... 357
Kent State University Kent Campus ... OH ... 363
Ohio University Main Campus ... OH ... 368
Oklahoma State University ... OK ... 377
University of Oklahoma Norman Campus ... OK ... 380
University of Oregon ... OR ... 387
Penn State University Park ... PA ... 403
Shippensburg University of Pennsylvania ... PA ... 407
Temple University ... PA ... 411
University of Puerto Rico at Arecibo ... PR ... 527
University of Puerto Rico-Rio Piedras Campus ... PR ... 528
University of South Carolina Columbia ... SC ... 424
Winthrop University ... SC ... 426
South Dakota State University ... SD ... 429
University of South Dakota, The ... SD ... 428
Middle Tennessee State University ... TN ... 434
University of Memphis, The ... TN ... 439
University of Tennessee at Chattanooga ... TN ... 440
University of Tennessee at Martin ... TN ... 440
University of Tennessee, Knoxville ... TN ... 439
Abilene Christian University ... TX ... 441
Baylor University ... TX ... 444
#Texas Christian University ... TX ... 461
Texas State University ... TX ... 463
University of North Texas ... TX ... 466
University of Texas at Austin ... TX ... 467
Brigham Young University ... UT ... 471
Hampton University ... VA ... 481
Norfolk State University ... VA ... 483
Virginia Commonwealth University ... VA ... 487
Washington and Lee University ... VA ... 491
University of Washington ... WA ... 499
Marshall University ... WV ... 504
West Virginia University ... WV ... 505
University of Wisconsin-Eau Claire ... WI ... 510
University of Wisconsin-Oshkosh ... WI ... 511

KIN: Commission on Accreditation of Allied Health Education Programs: kinesiotherapy (B)

University of Southern Mississippi ... MS ... 256
Shaw University ... NC ... 348
#Norfolk State University ... VA ... 483

LAW: American Bar Association: law (FP,D)

Faulkner University ... AL ... 5
Samford University ... AL ... 6
University of Alabama, The ... AL ... 8
Arizona State University ... AZ ... 10
#Arizona Summit Law School ... AZ ... 11
University of Arizona ... AZ ... 16
University of Arkansas at Little Rock ... AR ... 22
University of Arkansas Main Campus ... AR ... 21
California Western School of Law ... CA ... 35
Chapman University ... CA ... 36
Golden Gate University ... CA ... 44
Loyola Marymount University ... CA ... 50
Pepperdine University ... CA ... 56
Santa Clara University ... CA ... 62
Southwestern Law School ... CA ... 65
Stanford University ... CA ... 66
Thomas Jefferson School of Law ... CA ... 67
University of California-Berkeley ... CA ... 68
University of California-Davis ... CA ... 68
University of California-Hastings College of the Law ... CA ... 68
University of California-Irvine ... CA ... 69
University of California-Los Angeles ... CA ... 69
University of La Verne ... CA ... 70
University of San Diego ... CA ... 71
University of San Francisco ... CA ... 72
University of Southern California ... CA ... 72
University of the Pacific ... CA ... 70
Whittier College ... CA ... 75
University of Colorado Boulder ... CO ... 83
University of Denver ... CO ... 83
Quinnipiac University ... CT ... 88
University of Connecticut ... CT ... 88
Yale University ... CT ... 89
American University ... DC ... 91
Catholic University of America, The ... DC ... 91
George Washington University ... DC ... 92
Georgetown University ... DC ... 92
Howard University ... DC ... 92
University of the District of Columbia ... DC ... 93
Ave Maria School of Law ... FL ... 95
Barry University ... FL ... 95
Florida Agricultural and Mechanical University ... FL ... 109
Florida Coastal School of Law ... FL ... 99
Florida International University ... FL ... 109
Florida State University ... FL ... 110
Nova Southeastern University ... FL ... 104
St. Thomas University ... FL ... 107
Stetson University ... FL ... 111
University of Florida ... FL ... 110
University of Miami ... FL ... 112
Atlanta's John Marshall Law School ... GA ... 115
Emory University ... GA ... 119
Georgia State University ... GA ... 121
Mercer University ... GA ... 122
University of Georgia ... GA ... 127
University of Hawaii at Manoa ... HI ... 129
University of Idaho ... ID ... 132
DePaul University ... IL ... 137
John Marshall Law School ... IL ... 141
Loyola University Chicago ... IL ... 144
Northern Illinois University ... IL ... 147
Northwestern University ... IL ... 148
Southern Illinois University Carbondale ... IL ... 152
University of Chicago ... IL ... 153
University of Illinois at Urbana-Champaign ... IL ... 154
#Indiana Tech ... IN ... 159
Indiana University Bloomington ... IN ... 159
Indiana University-Purdue University Indianapolis ... IN ... 160
University of Notre Dame ... IN ... 165
Valparaiso University ... IN ... 165
Drake University ... IA ... 168
University of Iowa ... IA ... 166
University of Kansas Main Campus ... KS ... 181
Washburn University ... KS ... 182
Northern Kentucky University ... KY ... 188
University of Kentucky ... KY ... 190
University of Louisville ... KY ... 190
Louisiana State University and Agricultural and Mechanical College ... LA ... 193
Loyola University New Orleans ... LA ... 194
Southern University Law Center ... LA ... 196
Tulane University ... LA ... 196
University of Southern Maine ... ME ... 201
University of Baltimore ... MD ... 209
University of Maryland, Baltimore ... MD ... 207
Boston College ... MA ... 212
Boston University ... MA ... 212
Harvard University ... MA ... 215
New England Law | Boston ... MA ... 222
Northeastern University ... MA ... 223
Suffolk University ... MA ... 224
University of Massachusetts Dartmouth ... MA ... 217
Western New England University ... MA ... 225
Michigan State University ... MI ... 233
University of Michigan-Ann Arbor ... MI ... 237
Wayne State University ... MI ... 239
Western Michigan University Cooley Law School ... MI ... 239
Mitchell Hamline School of Law ... MN ... 248
University of Minnesota ... MN ... 250
University of Saint Thomas ... MN ... 251
Mississippi College ... MS ... 254
University of Mississippi ... MS ... 256
Saint Louis University ... MO ... 266
University of Missouri - Columbia ... MO ... 268
University of Missouri - Kansas City ... MO ... 268
Washington University in St. Louis ... MO ... 269
University of Montana - Missoula ... MT ... 271
Creighton University ... NE ... 274
University of Nebraska - Lincoln ... NE ... 277
University of Nevada, Las Vegas ... NV ... 279
University of New Hampshire ... NH ... 282
Rutgers University - Camden ... NJ ... 290
Rutgers University - Newark ... NJ ... 290
Seton Hall University ... NJ ... 291
University of New Mexico Main Campus ... NM ... 296
Albany Law School ... NY ... 297
Brooklyn Law School ... NY ... 300
City University of New York Queens College ... NY ... 303
Columbia University in the City of New York NY ... 305
Cornell University ... NY ... 306
Fordham University ... NY ... 308
Hofstra University ... NY ... 310
New York Law School ... NY ... 317
New York University ... NY ... 318
Pace University ... NY ... 319
St. John's University ... NY ... 322
Syracuse University ... NY ... 330
Touro College ... NY ... 331
University at Buffalo-SUNY ... NY ... 325
Yeshiva University ... NY ... 334
Campbell University ... NC ... 336
Duke University ... NC ... 337
Elon University ... NC ... 337
North Carolina Central University ... NC ... 350
University of North Carolina at Chapel Hill ... NC ... 351
Wake Forest University ... NC ... 353
University of North Dakota ... ND ... 353
Capital University ... OH ... 358
Case Western Reserve University ... OH ... 358
Cleveland State University ... OH ... 359
Ohio Northern University ... OH ... 367
Ohio State University Main Campus, The ... OH ... 367
University of Akron, Main Campus, The ... OH ... 371
University of Cincinnati Main Campus ... OH ... 371
University of Dayton ... OH ... 372
University of Toledo ... OH ... 372
Oklahoma City University ... OK ... 377
University of Oklahoma Norman Campus ... OK ... 380
University of Tulsa ... OK ... 381
#Concordia University ... OR ... 382
Lewis and Clark College ... OR ... 383
University of Oregon ... OR ... 387
Willamette University ... OR ... 388
Drexel University ... PA ... 394
Duquesne University ... PA ... 394
Penn State University Park ... PA ... 403
Temple University ... PA ... 411
University of Pennsylvania ... PA ... 412
University of Pittsburgh ... PA ... 412
Villanova University ... PA ... 413
Widener University ... PA ... 414
Inter American University of Puerto Rico School of Law ... PR ... 524
Pontifical Catholic University of Puerto Rico, The ... PR ... 525
University of Puerto Rico-Rio Piedras Campus ... PR ... 528
Roger Williams University ... RI ... 417
Charleston School of Law ... SC ... 419
University of South Carolina Columbia ... SC ... 424
University of South Dakota, The ... SD ... 428
Belmont University ... TN ... 430
#Lincoln Memorial University ... TN ... 433
University of Memphis, The ... TN ... 439
University of Tennessee, Knoxville ... TN ... 439
Vanderbilt University ... TN ... 440
Baylor University ... TX ... 444
St. Mary's University ... TX ... 455
South Texas College of Law Houston ... TX ... 456
Southern Methodist University ... TX ... 457
Texas A & M University ... TX ... 459
Texas Southern University ... TX ... 461
Texas Tech University ... TX ... 463
University of Houston ... TX ... 465
University of Texas at Austin ... TX ... 467
Brigham Young University ... UT ... 471
University of Utah, The ... UT ... 472
Vermont Law School ... VT ... 476
Appalachian School of Law ... VA ... 477
College of William & Mary ... VA ... 479
George Mason University ... VA ... 481
Judge Advocate General's Legal Center & School, The ... VA ... 517
Liberty University ... VA ... 482
Regent University ... VA ... 484
University of Richmond ... VA ... 486
University of Virginia ... VA ... 486
Washington and Lee University ... VA ... 491
Gonzaga University ... WA ... 495
Seattle University ... WA ... 498
University of Washington ... WA ... 499
West Virginia University ... WV ... 505
Marquette University ... WI ... 508
University of Wisconsin-Madison ... WI ... 510
University of Wyoming ... WY ... 517

LIB: American Library Association: librarianship (M)

University of Alabama, The ... AL ... 8
University of Arizona ... AZ ... 16
San Jose State University ... CA ... 34
University of California-Los Angeles ... CA ... 69
University of Denver ... CO ... 83
Catholic University of America, The ... DC ... 91
Florida State University ... FL ... 110
University of South Florida ... FL ... 111

LSAR: American Society of Landscape Architects: landscape architecture (B,M)

M: Middle States Commission on Higher Education

MAAB: Accrediting Bureau of Health Education Schools: medical assisting (C,A)

MAC: Commission on Accreditation of Allied Health Education Programs: medical assisting (C,A)

MACTE: Montessori Accreditation Council for Teacher Education: Montessori teacher education (C)

MEAC: Midwifery Education Accreditation Council: midwifery education (C,A,B,M,D)

MED: Liaison Committee on Medical Education: medicine (FP,D)

University of North Carolina at Chapel Hill .. NC ... 351
Wake Forest University .... NC ... 353
University of North Dakota .... ND ... 353
Case Western Reserve University .... OH ... 358
Northeast Ohio Medical University .... OH ... 366
Ohio State University Main Campus, The ... OH ... 367
University of Cincinnati Main Campus .... OH ... 371
University of Toledo .... OH ... 372
Wright State University Main Campus .... OH ... 374
Oregon Health & Science University .... OR ... 385
Drexel University .... PA ... 394
Geisinger Commonwealth School of Medicine .... PA ... 395
Temple University .... PA ... 411
Thomas Jefferson University .... PA ... 411
University of Pennsylvania .... PA ... 412
University of Pittsburgh .... PA ... 412
Ponce School of Medicine & Health Sciences .... PR ... 525
San Juan Bautista School of Medicine .... PR ... 525
Universidad Central Del Caribe .... PR ... 526
University of Puerto Rico-Medical Sciences Campus .... PR ... 528
Brown University .... RI 415
Medical University of South Carolina .... SC ... 422
University of South Carolina Columbia .... SC ... 424
University of South Carolina School of Medicine Greenville .... SC ... 425
University of South Dakota, The .... SD ... 428
East Tennessee State University .... TN ... 431
Meharry Medical College .... TN ... 434
University of Tennessee Health Science Center .... TN ... 440
Vanderbilt University .... TN ... 440
Baylor College of Medicine .... TX ... 444
Texas A & M University .... TX ... 459
Texas Tech University Health Sciences Center .... TX 463
#University of Texas at Austin .... TX 467
University of Texas Health Science Center at Houston (UTHealth), The .... TX 468
University of Texas Health Science Center at San Antonio .... TX 468
University of Texas Medical Branch, The .... TX 469
#University of Texas Rio Grande Valley, The TX 468
University of Texas Southwestern Medical Center .... TX 469
University of Utah, The .... UT 472
University of Vermont .... VT 476
Eastern Virginia Medical School .... VA 480
University of Virginia .... VA 486
Virginia Commonwealth University .... VA 487
Virginia Tech Carilion School of Medicine ... VA 491
University of Washington .... WA .. 499
Marshall University .... WV .. 504
West Virginia University .... WV .. 505
Medical College of Wisconsin .... WI 508
University of Wisconsin-Madison .... WI 510

MFCD: American Association for Marriage and Family Therapy: marriage and family therapy (M,D)

Auburn University .... AL 4
Alliant International University-San Diego ... CA 24
California State University-Northridge .... CA 33
Chapman University .... CA 36
Hope International University .... CA 45
Loma Linda University .... CA 48
Northcentral University .... CA 54
San Diego State University .... CA 34
University of San Diego .... CA 71
Colorado State University .... CO 78
Regis University .... CO 82
Central Connecticut State University .... CT 84
Fairfield University .... CT 87
Southern Connecticut State University .... CT 85
University of Connecticut .... CT 88
University of Saint Joseph .... CT 89
Florida State University .... FL 110
Nova Southeastern University .... FL 104
Mercer University .... GA 122
University of Georgia .... GA 127
Valdosta State University .... GA 127
Adler University .... IL 133
Northern Illinois University .... IL 147
Northwestern University .... IL 148
Wheaton College .... IL 155
Christian Theological Seminary .... IN 157
Indiana Wesleyan University .... IN 161
Purdue University Northwest .... IN 163
Mount Mercy University .... IA 172
Friends University .... KS 177
Kansas State University .... KS 179
Campbellsville University .... KY 184
Louisville Presbyterian Theological Seminary .... KY 188
University of Kentucky .... KY 190
University of Louisville .... KY 190
University of Louisiana at Monroe .... LA 198
University of Maryland College Park .... MD ... 207
Michigan State University .... MI 233
Bethel University .... MN ... 240
Capella University .... MN ... 241
St. Cloud State University .... MN ... 247
Saint Mary's University of Minnesota .... MN ... 250
University of Minnesota .... MN ... 250
Reformed Theological Seminary .... MS ... 255
University of Southern Mississippi .... MS ... 256
Saint Louis University .... MO .. 266
University of Nebraska - Lincoln .... NE ... 277
University of Nevada, Las Vegas .... NV ... 279
University of New Hampshire .... NH ... 282
Seton Hall University .... NJ ... 291
Iona College .... NY ... 311
Nyack College .... NY ... 319
Syracuse University .... NY ... 330
University of Rochester .... NY ... 332
Appalachian State University .... NC ... 349
East Carolina University .... NC ... 349
Pfeiffer University .... NC ... 348
Ohio State University Main Campus, The ... OH ... 367
University of Akron, Main Campus, The ...... OH ... 371
Oklahoma State University .... OK ... 377
Lewis and Clark College .... OR ... 383
University of Oregon .... OR ... 387
Drexel University .... PA ... 394
Evangelical Theological Seminary .... PA ... 395
La Salle University .... PA ... 398
Seton Hill University .... PA ... 410
Thomas Jefferson University .... PA ... 411
University of Rhode Island .... RI 417
Converse College .... SC ... 420
Lee University .... TN ... 432
Abilene Christian University .... TX ... 441
Our Lady of the Lake University .... TX ... 454
St. Mary's University .... TX ... 455
Texas Tech University .... TX ... 463
Texas Wesleyan University .... TX ... 463
University of Houston - Clear Lake .... TX ... 465
Brigham Young University .... UT ... 471
Utah State University .... UT ... 473
Virginia Polytechnic Institute and State University .... VA ... 490
Pacific Lutheran University .... WA ... 496
Seattle Pacific University .... WA .. 498
Seattle University .... WA .. 498
Edgewood College .... WI ... 507
University of Wisconsin-Stout .... WI 512

MIDWF: Accreditation Commission for Midwifery Education: nurse midwifery (C,M,D)

California State University-Fullerton .... CA 32
San Diego State University .... CA 34
University of California-San Francisco .... CA 70
University of Colorado Denver|Anschutz Medical Campus .... CO 83
Yale University .... CT 89
Georgetown University .... DC 92
University of Florida .... FL 110
Emory University .... GA ... 119
University of Illinois at Chicago .... IL 153
University of Indianapolis .... IN 164
Frontier Nursing University .... KY ... 184
University of Michigan-Ann Arbor .... MI ... 237
Wayne State University .... MI 239
Bethel University .... MN ... 240
University of Minnesota .... MN ... 250
University of New Mexico Main Campus ..... NM ... 296
Columbia University in the City of New York NY ... 305
New York University .... NY ... 318
Stony Brook University .... NY ... 325
SUNY Downstate Medical Center .... NY ... 326
East Carolina University .... NC ... 349
Case Western Reserve University .... OH ... 358
Ohio State University Main Campus, The ... OH ... 367
University of Cincinnati Main Campus .... OH ... 371
Oregon Health & Science University .... OR ... 385
University of Pennsylvania .... PA ... 412
@University of Pittsburgh .... PA ... 412
Vanderbilt University .... TN ... 440
Baylor University .... TX ... 444
Texas Tech University .... TX ... 463
University of Utah, The .... UT ... 472
Shenandoah University .... VA ... 485
Seattle University .... WA .. 498
University of Washington .... WA .. 499
Marquette University .... WI ... 508

MIL: Commission on Accreditation of Allied Health Education Programs: medical illustrator (M)

Augusta University .... GA ... 116
University of Illinois at Chicago .... IL 153
Johns Hopkins University .... MD ... 204

MLTAB: Accrediting Bureau of Health Education Schools: medical laboratory technician (C,A)

IBMC College .... CO 80
Spencerian College .... KY ... 189
Southwestern Oklahoma State University ... OK ... 380

MLTAD: National Accrediting Agency for Clinical Laboratory Sciences: medical laboratory technician (C,A)

Calhoun Community College .... AL 1
Gadsden State Community College .... AL 2
Jefferson State Community College .... AL 2
Wallace State Community College - Hanceville .... AL 3
Brookline College .... AZ 11
Phoenix College .... AZ 14
Pima Community College .... AZ 15
Arkansas State University-Beebe .... AR 17
Arkansas State University-Jonesboro .... AR 18
National Park College .... AR 20
North Arkansas College .... AR 20
Phillips Community College of the University of Arkansas .... AR 22
College of the Canyons .... CA 39
De Anza College .... CA 43
Folsom Lake College .... CA 50
San Diego Miramar College .... CA 60
Southwestern College .... CA 65
Arapahoe Community College .... CO 76
Colorado Mesa University .... CO 77
Otero Junior College .... CO 81
Eastern Florida State College .... FL 97
Florida State College at Jacksonville .... FL 100
Indian River State College .... FL 101
Keiser University .... FL 102
Miami Dade College .... FL 103
Albany State University .... GA 114
Central Georgia Technical College .... GA ... 117
Chattahoochee Technical College .... GA ... 117
Coastal Pines Technical College .... GA ... 117
Dalton State College .... GA ... 118
Georgia Piedmont Technical College .... GA ... 120
North Georgia Technical College .... GA ... 123
Southeastern Technical College .... GA ... 126
Southern Regional Technical College .... GA ... 126
West Georgia Technical College .... GA ... 128
Kapiolani Community College .... HI 130
Elgin Community College .... IL 138
Illinois Central College .... IL 139
John A. Logan College .... IL 141
Kankakee Community College .... IL 142
Kaskaskia College .... IL 142
Oakton Community College .... IL 148
Rend Lake College .... IL 149
Shawnee Community College .... IL 151
Southeastern Illinois College .... IL 151
Southwestern Illinois College .... IL 152
University of Saint Francis .... IN 165
Des Moines Area Community College .... IA 168
Hawkeye Community College .... IA 169
Indian Hills Community College .... IA 169
Iowa Central Community College .... IA 170
Barton County Community College .... KS ... 175
Manhattan Area Technical College .... KS ... 179
Seward County Community College .... KS ... 181
Henderson Community College .... KY ... 186
Jefferson Community and Technical College .... KY ... 186
Madisonville Community College .... KY ... 186
Somerset Community College .... KY ... 186
Southeast Kentucky Community and Technical College .... KY ... 187
West Kentucky Community and Technical College .... KY ... 187
Delgado Community College .... LA ... 192
Fortis College .... LA ... 191
Louisiana State University at Alexandria ..... LA 194
South Louisiana Community College .... LA 193
Southern University at Shreveport-Louisiana LA 196
University of Maine at Augusta .... ME ... 201
University of Maine at Presque Isle .... ME ... 201
Allegany College of Maryland .... MD ... 202
Anne Arundel Community College .... MD ... 202
College of Southern Maryland .... MD ... 203
Community College of Baltimore County, The .... MD ... 203
Howard Community College .... MD ... 204
Bristol Community College .... MA ... 219
Bunker Hill Community College .... MA ... 219
Middlesex Community College .... MA ... 220
Mount Wachusett Community College .... MA ... 220
Northern Essex Community College .... MA ... 220
Quincy College .... MA ... 223
Springfield Technical Community College ... MA ... 221
Ferris State University .... MI ... 230
Northern Michigan University .... MI ... 235
Alexandria Technical & Community College. MN ... 243
Hibbing Community College, A Technical and Community College .... MN ... 244
Lake Superior College .... MN ... 245
Minnesota State College Southeast .... MN ... 245
Minnesota State Community and Technical College .... MN ... 245
Minnesota West Community and Technical College .... MN ... 246
North Hennepin Community College .... MN ... 246
Rasmussen College - St. Cloud .... MN ... 249
Saint Paul College-A Community & Technical College .... MN ... 247
South Central College .... MN ... 247
Copiah-Lincoln Community College .... MS ... 252
Hinds Community College .... MS ... 253
Meridian Community College .... MS ... 253
Mississippi Delta Community College .... MS ... 254
Mississippi Gulf Coast Community College . MS ... 254
Northeast Mississippi Community College ... MS ... 255
Pearl River Community College .... MS ... 255
Moberly Area Community College .... MO ... 264
Ozarks Technical Community College .... MO ... 264
Three Rivers College .... MO ... 267
Central Community College .... NE ... 273
Mid-Plains Community College .... NE ... 275
Southeast Community College .... NE ... 276
College of Southern Nevada .... NV ... 278
River Valley Community College .... NH ... 281
Mercer County Community College .... NJ ... 287
Middlesex County College .... NJ ... 287
Central New Mexico Community College .... NM ... 293
San Juan College .... NM ... 296
Dutchess Community College .... NY ... 307
Erie Community College .... NY ... 307
Farmingdale State College .... NY ... 329
Monroe Community College .... NY ... 315
Nassau Community College .... NY ... 316
Orange County Community College .... NY ... 319
SUNY Broome Community College .... NY ... 326
Alamance Community College .... NC ... 340
Asheville - Buncombe Technical Community College .... NC ... 340
Beaufort County Community College .... NC ... 340
Central Piedmont Community College .... NC ... 342
Coastal Carolina Community College .... NC ... 342
College of the Albemarle .... NC ... 342
Davidson County Community College .... NC ... 342
Halifax Community College .... NC ... 343
Sandhills Community College .... NC ... 346
Southeastern Community College .... NC ... 346
Southwestern Community College .... NC ... 346
Stanly Community College .... NC ... 346
Wake Technical Community College .... NC ... 347
Wayne Community College .... NC ... 347
Western Piedmont Community College .... NC ... 347
Bismarck State College .... ND ... 354
Turtle Mountain Community College .... ND ... 355
Cincinnati State Technical and Community College .... OH ... 359
Clark State Community College .... OH ... 359
Columbus State Community College .... OH ... 360
Cuyahoga Community College .... OH ... 360
Edison State Community College .... OH ... 361
Lakeland Community College .... OH ... 364
Lorain County Community College .... OH ... 364
Marion Technical College .... OH ... 365
Shawnee State University .... OH ... 369
Sinclair Community College .... OH ... 370
Stark State College .... OH ... 370
Washington State Community College .... OH ... 373
Youngstown State University .... OH ... 374
Zane State College .... OH ... 374
Eastern Oklahoma State College .... OK ... 375
Northeastern Oklahoma Agricultural and Mechanical College .... OK ... 376
Rose State College .... OK ... 379
Seminole State College .... OK ... 379
Tulsa Community College .... OK ... 380
Portland Community College .... OR ... 386
Community College of Allegheny County ... PA ... 392
Community College of Philadelphia .... PA ... 393
HACC, Central Pennsylvania's Community College .... PA ... 396
Harcum College .... PA ... 396
Laurel Technical Institute .... PA ... 399
Montgomery County Community College ... PA ... 402
Mount Aloysius College .... PA ... 402
Reading Area Community College .... PA ... 408
Community College of Rhode Island .... RI 416
New England Institute of Technology .... RI 416
Florence - Darlington Technical College ..... SC ... 421
Greenville Technical College .... SC ... 421
Midlands Technical College .... SC ... 422
Spartanburg Community College .... SC ... 424
Tri-County Technical College .... SC ... 424
Trident Technical College .... SC ... 424
York Technical College .... SC ... 426
Lake Area Technical Institute .... SD ... 427
Mitchell Technical Institute .... SD ... 427
Concorde Career College .... TN ... 431
Fortis Institute .... TN ... 431
Jackson State Community College .... TN ... 437
Northeast State Community College .... TN ... 437
Southwest Tennessee Community College . TN ... 438
Volunteer State Community College .... TN ... 438
Amarillo College .... TX ... 442
Austin Community College District .... TX ... 443
Central Texas College .... TX ... 445
Del Mar College .... TX ... 448
El Centro College .... TX ... 448

MT: National Accrediting Agency for Clinical Laboratory Sciences: medical technology/laboratory scientist (C,B)

MUS: National Association of Schools of Music: music (C,A,B,M,D)

Virginia Polytechnic Institute and State University VA 490
Virginia State University VA 491
Central Washington University WA 492
Eastern Washington University WA 494
Gonzaga University WA 495
Pacific Lutheran University WA 496
Seattle Pacific University WA 498
University of Puget Sound WA 499
Walla Walla University WA 499
Washington State University WA 499
Western Washington University WA 500
Whitworth University WA 500
Marshall University WV 504
Shepherd University WV 504
West Liberty University WV 504
West Virginia University WV 505
West Virginia Wesleyan College WV 505
Alverno College WI 506
Carthage College WI 506
Lawrence University WI 507
Silver Lake College of the Holy Family WI 510
University of Wisconsin-Eau Claire WI 510
University of Wisconsin-Green Bay WI 510
University of Wisconsin-La Crosse WI 510
University of Wisconsin-Madison WI 510
University of Wisconsin-Milwaukee WI 511
University of Wisconsin-Oshkosh WI 511
University of Wisconsin-Platteville WI 511
University of Wisconsin-River Falls WI 511
University of Wisconsin-Stevens Point WI 511
University of Wisconsin-Superior WI 512
University of Wisconsin-Whitewater WI 512
Viterbo University WI 512
Casper College WY 516
Northwest College WY 516
University of Wyoming WY 517

NAIT: The Association of Technology, Management, and Applied Engineering: technology, applied technology, engineering technology and technology-related programs (A, B,M)

Jacksonville State University AL 6
Arkansas State University-Beebe AR 17
University of Arkansas at Fort Smith AR 22
University of Arkansas at Pine Bluff AR 22
California Polytechnic State University-San Luis Obispo CA 30
California State University-Chico CA 31
California State University-Fresno CA 32
California State University-Los Angeles CA 32
College of the Redwoods Community College District CA 39
Rio Hondo College CA 58
San Jose State University CA 34
Central Connecticut State University CT 84
Idaho State University ID 132
University of Idaho ID 132
Eastern Illinois University IL 138
Illinois State University IL 140
Northern Illinois University IL 147
Southern Illinois University Carbondale IL 152
Western Illinois University IL 155
Indiana State University IN 159
Ivy Tech Community College of Indiana-Central Indiana IN 161
Purdue University Main Campus IN 163
Purdue University Northwest IN 163
Iowa State University IA 166
University of Northern Iowa IA 167
Eastern Kentucky University KY 184
Maysville Community and Technical College KY 186
Morehead State University KY 188
Western Kentucky University KY 190
Baton Rouge Community College LA 192
Bossier Parish Community College LA 192
Delgado Community College LA 192
L.E. Fletcher Technical Community College LA 192
Louisiana Delta Community College LA 192
Nicholls State University LA 197
Nunez Community College LA 193
River Parishes Community College LA 193
South Louisiana Community College LA 193
Southeastern Louisiana University LA 197
Sowela Technical Community College LA 193
University of Louisiana at Lafayette LA 197
University of Southern Maine ME 201
Central Michigan University MI 228
Bemidji State University MN 244
Minnesota State University Moorhead MN 246
St. Cloud State University MN 247
Alcorn State University MS 251
Jackson State University MS 253
East Central College MO 259
Southeast Missouri State University MO 266
State Technical College of Missouri MO 267
University of Central Missouri MO 268
University of Nebraska at Kearney NE 277
Farmingdale State College NY 329
State University of New York College at Buffalo NY 326
East Carolina University NC 349
North Carolina Agricultural and Technical State University NC 350
University of North Dakota ND 353
Bowling Green State University OH 357
Kent State University Kent Campus OH 363
Ohio Northern University OH 367
Ohio University Main Campus OH 368
Owens Community College OH 369
Southwestern Oklahoma State University OK 380
California University of Pennsylvania PA 405
Millersville University of Pennsylvania PA 407
Pennsylvania College of Technology PA 404
Cleveland State Community College TN 436
Columbia State Community College TN 436
Jackson State Community College TN 437
Middle Tennessee State University TN 434
Motlow State Community College TN 437
Nashville State Community College TN 437
Northeast State Community College TN 437
Pellissippi State Community College TN 437
Tennessee State University TN 438
Walters State Community College TN 438
Texas A & M University - Kingsville TX 460
Texas Southern University TX 461
University of Houston TX 465
University of Texas at Tyler TX 468
Mountain Empire Community College VA 488
Norfolk State University VA 483
Virginia State University VA 491
Pierpont Community & Technical College WV 503
University of Wisconsin-Platteville WI 511

NATUR: Council on Naturopathic Medical Education: naturopathic medical education (FP,D)

Southwest College of Naturopathic Medicine & Health Sciences AZ 16
University of Bridgeport CT 88
National University of Health Sciences IL 147
National University of Natural Medicine OR 384
@Universidad Del Turabo PR 526
Bastyr University WA 492

NDT: Commission on Accreditation of Allied Health Education Programs: neurodiagnostic technology (C,A)

Gateway Community College AZ 13
Concorde Career College CA 40
Orange Coast College CA 38
Lincoln Land Community College IL 144
Kirkwood Community College IA 171
Scott Community College IA 169
Johnson County Community College KS 178
Laboure College MA 216
Catawba Valley Community College NC 341
Pamlico Community College NC 345
Cuyahoga Community College OH 360
Southeast Technical Institute SD 429
Vanderbilt University TN 440
Alvin Community College TX 442
Concorde Career Institute TX 446
Bellevue College WA 492

NH: Higher Learning Commission, North Central Association

Arizona Christian University AZ 10
Arizona State University AZ 10
Arizona Western College AZ 11
Central Arizona College AZ 11
Chandler-Gilbert Community College AZ 13
Cochise College AZ 11
Coconino Community College AZ 12
Diné College AZ 12
Eastern Arizona College AZ 12
Estrella Mountain Community College AZ 13
Frank Lloyd Wright School of Architecture AZ 12
Gateway Community College AZ 13
Glendale Community College AZ 13
Grand Canyon University AZ 12
Mesa Community College AZ 13
Mohave Community College AZ 14
Northern Arizona University AZ 14
Northland Pioneer College AZ 15
Paradise Valley Community College AZ 13
Phoenix College AZ 14
Phoenix Seminary AZ 15
Pima Community College AZ 15
Prescott College AZ 15
Rio Salado College AZ 14
Scottsdale Community College AZ 14
South Mountain Community College AZ 14
Southwest College of Naturopathic Medicine & Health Sciences AZ 16
Southwest University of Visual Arts AZ 16
Tohono O'odham Community College AZ 16
University of Advancing Technology AZ 16
University of Arizona AZ 16
University of Phoenix AZ 17
Western International University AZ 17
Yavapai College AZ 17
Arkansas Baptist College AR 17
Arkansas Northeastern College AR 17
Arkansas State University-Beebe AR 17
Arkansas State University-Jonesboro AR 18
Arkansas State University-Mid-South AR 18
Arkansas State University-Mountain Home AR 18
Arkansas State University-Newport AR 18
Arkansas Tech University AR 18
#Black River Technical College AR 18
Central Baptist College AR 19
College of the Ouachitas AR 19
Cossatot Community College of the University of Arkansas AR 22
Crowley's Ridge College AR 19
East Arkansas Community College AR 19
Harding University Main Campus AR 19
Henderson State University AR 19
Hendrix College AR 19
John Brown University AR 20
Lyon College AR 20
National Park College AR 20
North Arkansas College AR 20
NorthWest Arkansas Community College AR 20
Ouachita Baptist University AR 20
Ozarka College AR 20
Philander Smith College AR 21
Phillips Community College of the University of Arkansas AR 22
South Arkansas Community College AR 21
Southeast Arkansas College AR 21
Southern Arkansas University AR 21
Southern Arkansas University Tech AR 21
University of Arkansas at Fort Smith AR 22
University of Arkansas at Hope-Texarkana AR 23
University of Arkansas at Little Rock AR 22
University of Arkansas at Monticello AR 22
University of Arkansas at Pine Bluff AR 22
University of Arkansas Community College at Batesville AR 22
University of Arkansas Community College at Morrilton AR 23
University of Arkansas for Medical Sciences AR 22
University of Arkansas Main Campus AR 21
University of Arkansas - Pulaski Technical College AR 23
University of Arkansas Rich Mountain AR 23
University of Central Arkansas AR 23
University of the Ozarks AR 23
Williams Baptist College AR 23
#Adams State University CO 76
Aims Community College CO 76
@American Sentinel University CO 76
Arapahoe Community College CO 76
Art Institute of Colorado, The CO 76
College for Financial Planning CO 77
Colorado Christian University CO 77
Colorado College CO 77
Colorado Mesa University CO 77
Colorado Mountain College CO 77
Colorado Northwestern Community College CO 78
Colorado School of Mines CO 78
Colorado State University CO 78
Colorado State University-Global Campus CO 78
Colorado State University-Pueblo CO 78
Colorado Technical University CO 79
Community College of Aurora CO 79
Community College of Denver CO 79
Denver School of Nursing CO 79
Denver Seminary CO 79
Fort Lewis College CO 79
Front Range Community College CO 79
Iliff School of Theology CO 80
Lamar Community College CO 80
Metropolitan State University of Denver CO 80
Morgan Community College CO 81
Naropa University CO 81
Northeastern Junior College CO 81
Otero Junior College CO 81
Pikes Peak Community College CO 81
Pueblo Community College CO 81
Red Rocks Community College CO 82
Regis University CO 82
Rocky Mountain College of Art & Design CO 82
Rocky Vista University CO 82
Trinidad State Junior College CO 82
United States Air Force Academy CO 518
University of Colorado Boulder CO 83
University of Colorado Colorado Springs CO 83
University of Colorado Denver|Anschutz Medical Campus CO 83
University of Denver CO 83
University of Northern Colorado CO 83
University of the Rockies CO 84
Western State Colorado University CO 84
Adler University IL 133
American Academy of Art IL 133
American InterContinental University IL 133
Augustana College IL 133
Aurora University IL 133
Benedictine University IL 133
Black Hawk College IL 134
Blackburn College IL 134
Blessing-Rieman College of Nursing & Health Sciences IL 134
Bradley University IL 134
Carl Sandburg College IL 134
Chamberlain University-Addison IL 135
Chicago State University IL 135
Chicago Theological Seminary IL 135
City Colleges of Chicago Harold Washington College IL 135
City Colleges of Chicago Harry S Truman College IL 135
City Colleges of Chicago Kennedy-King College IL 135
City Colleges of Chicago Olive-Harvey College IL 135
City Colleges of Chicago Richard J. Daley College IL 136
City Colleges of Chicago Wilbur Wright College IL 136
#College of DuPage IL 136
College of Lake County IL 136
Columbia College Chicago IL 136
Concordia University Chicago IL 136
Danville Area Community College IL 137
DePaul University IL 137
DeVry University - Chicago Campus IL 137
Dominican University IL 137
East-West University IL 137
Eastern Illinois University IL 138
Elgin Community College IL 138
Elmhurst College IL 138
Erikson Institute IL 138
Eureka College IL 138
Fox College IL 138
Garrett-Evangelical Theological Seminary IL 138
Governors State University IL 138
Greenville University IL 139
Harper College IL 139
Harrington College of Design IL 139
Heartland Community College IL 139
#Hebrew Theological College IL 139
Highland Community College IL 139
Illinois Central College IL 139
Illinois College IL 139
Illinois College of Optometry IL 140
&Illinois Eastern Community Colleges Frontier Community College IL 140
&Illinois Eastern Community Colleges Lincoln Trail College IL 140
&Illinois Eastern Community Colleges Olney Central College IL 140
&Illinois Eastern Community Colleges Wabash Valley College IL 140
Illinois Institute of Art, The IL 140
Illinois Institute of Technology IL 140
Illinois State University IL 140
Illinois Valley Community College IL 141
Illinois Wesleyan University IL 141
Institute for Clinical Social Work IL 141
John A. Logan College IL 141
John Marshall Law School IL 141
John Wood Community College IL 141
Joliet Junior College IL 142
Judson University IL 142
Kankakee Community College IL 142
Kaskaskia College IL 142
Kendall College IL 142
Kishwaukee College IL 142
Knox College IL 142
Lake Forest College IL 142
Lake Forest Graduate School of Management IL 143
Lake Land College IL 143
Lakeview College of Nursing IL 143
Lewis and Clark Community College IL 143
Lewis University IL 143
Lincoln Christian University IL 143
Lincoln College IL 143
Lincoln Land Community College IL 144
Loyola University Chicago IL 144
Lutheran School of Theology at Chicago IL 144
MacCormac College IL 144
#MacMurray College IL 144
Malcolm X College, One of the City Colleges of Chicago IL 136
McCormick Theological Seminary IL 145
McHenry County College IL 145
McKendree University IL 145
Methodist College IL 145
Midstate College IL 145
Midwestern University IL 145
Millikin University IL 145
Monmouth College IL 146
Moody Bible Institute IL 146
Moraine Valley Community College IL 146
Morton College IL 146
National-Louis University IL 146

Southwest Wisconsin Technical College ..... WI 515
University of Wisconsin Colleges ..... WI 512
University of Wisconsin-Eau Claire ..... WI 510
University of Wisconsin-Green Bay ..... WI 510
University of Wisconsin-La Crosse ..... WI 510
University of Wisconsin-Madison ..... WI 510
University of Wisconsin-Milwaukee ..... WI 511
University of Wisconsin-Oshkosh ..... WI 511
University of Wisconsin-Parkside ..... WI 511
University of Wisconsin-Platteville ..... WI 511
University of Wisconsin-River Falls ..... WI 511
University of Wisconsin-Stevens Point ..... WI 511
University of Wisconsin-Stout ..... WI 512
University of Wisconsin-Superior ..... WI 512
University of Wisconsin-Whitewater ..... WI 512
Viterbo University ..... WI 512
Waukesha County Technical College ..... WI 515
Western Technical College ..... WI 515
Wisconsin Indianhead Technical College .... WI 515
Wisconsin Lutheran College ..... WI 513
Wisconsin School of Professional Psychology ..... WI 513
Casper College ..... WY .. 516
Central Wyoming College ..... WY .. 516
Eastern Wyoming College ..... WY .. 516
Laramie County Community College ..... WY .. 516
Northern Wyoming Community College District ..... WY .. 516
Northwest College ..... WY .. 516
University of Wyoming ..... WY .. 517
Western Wyoming Community College ..... WY .. 517
@Wyoming Catholic College ..... WY .. 517

NMT: Joint Review Committee on Education Programs in Nuclear Medicine Technology: nuclear medicine technology (C,A,B)

University of Alabama at Birmingham ..... AL 8
Gateway Community College ..... AZ 13
Baptist Health College Little Rock ..... AR 18
University of Arkansas for Medical Sciences AR 22
Kaiser Permanente School of Allied Health Sciences ..... CA 46
Loma Linda University ..... CA 48
Gateway Community College ..... CT 85
Adventist University of Health Sciences ..... FL 94
Broward College ..... FL 96
Hillsborough Community College ..... FL 101
Santa Fe College ..... FL 107
Armstrong State University ..... GA 115
Augusta University ..... GA 116
College of DuPage ..... IL 136
Triton College ..... IL 153
Indiana University-Purdue University Indianapolis ..... IN 160
Allen College ..... IA 166
University of Iowa ..... IA 166
Delgado Community College ..... LA 192
Maine College of Health Professions ..... ME 199
Frederick Community College ..... MD 203
Johns Hopkins University ..... MD 204
Prince George's Community College ..... MD 206
MCPHS University ..... MA 221
Regis College ..... MA 224
Salem State University ..... MA 218
Worcester State University ..... MA 219
Ferris State University ..... MI 230
Saint Mary's University of Minnesota ..... MN 250
University of Mississippi Medical Center ..... MS 256
Saint Louis University ..... MO 266
University of Missouri - Columbia ..... MO 268
Rowan College at Gloucester County ..... NJ 289
University of New Mexico Main Campus ..... NM 296
City University of New York Bronx Community College ..... NY 301
Manhattan College ..... NY 313
Molloy College ..... NY 315
Stony Brook University ..... NY 325
University at Buffalo-SUNY ..... NY 325
Caldwell Community College and Technical Institute ..... NC 341
Forsyth Technical Community College ..... NC 343
University of North Carolina at Chapel Hill .. NC 351
Cuyahoga Community College ..... OH 360
Ohio State University Main Campus, The .... OH 367
University of Cincinnati Main Campus ..... OH 371
University of Findlay, The ..... OH 372
Community College of Allegheny County .... PA 392
Pennsylvania College of Health Sciences .... PA 404
Robert Morris University ..... PA 409
Thomas Jefferson University ..... PA 411
University of Puerto Rico-Medical Sciences Campus ..... PR 528
Midlands Technical College ..... SC 422
Southeast Technical Institute ..... SD 429
Baptist College of Health Sciences ..... TN 430
Chattanooga State Community College ..... TN 436
South College ..... TN 436
Vanderbilt University ..... TN 440
Amarillo College ..... TX 442
Galveston College ..... TX 449
Houston Community College ..... TX 450
University of the Incarnate Word ..... TX 465
University of Utah, The ..... UT 472
University of Vermont ..... VT 476
Old Dominion University ..... VA 483
Virginia Commonwealth University ..... VA 487
Bellevue College ..... WA .. 492
BridgeValley Community & Technical College ..... WV .. 502
West Virginia University ..... WV .. 505
University of Wisconsin-La Crosse ..... WI 510

NRPA: National Recreation and Park Association: recreation, park resources, and leisure studies (B)

Arizona State University ..... AZ 10
Northern Arizona University ..... AZ 14
Arkansas Tech University ..... AR 18
California Polytechnic State University-San Luis Obispo ..... CA 30
California State University-Chico ..... CA 31
California State University-Fresno ..... CA 32
California State University-Long Beach ..... CA 32
California State University-Northridge ..... CA 33
California State University-Sacramento ..... CA 33
San Francisco State University ..... CA 34
San Jose State University ..... CA 34
Metropolitan State University of Denver ..... CO 80
Georgia Southern University ..... GA 120
University of Idaho ..... ID 132
Chicago State University ..... IL 135
Eastern Illinois University ..... IL 138
Illinois State University ..... IL 140
University of Illinois at Urbana-Champaign . IL 154
University of St. Francis ..... IL 154
Western Illinois University ..... IL 155
Indiana University Bloomington ..... IN 159
University of Northern Iowa ..... IA 167
Kansas State University ..... KS 179
Pittsburg State University ..... KS 180
Eastern Kentucky University ..... KY 184
Western Kentucky University ..... KY 190
Grambling State University ..... LA 196
University of Maine at Machias ..... ME 201
Frostburg State University ..... MD 209
Springfield College ..... MA 224
Central Michigan University ..... MI 228
Minnesota State University, Mankato ..... MN 246
University of Mississippi ..... MS 256
Missouri State University ..... MO .. 263
Northwest Missouri State University ..... MO .. 264
Southeast Missouri State University ..... MO .. 266
University of Missouri - Columbia ..... MO .. 268
University of New Hampshire ..... NH 282
Ithaca College ..... NY 311
Saint Joseph's College, New York ..... NY 322
State University of New York College at Cortland ..... NY 327
State University of New York, The College at Brockport ..... NY 326
Appalachian State University ..... NC 349
East Carolina University ..... NC 349
North Carolina Central University ..... NC 350
North Carolina State University ..... NC 350
University of North Carolina at Greensboro NC 351
Winston-Salem State University ..... NC 352
Bowling Green State University ..... OH 357
Kent State University Kent Campus ..... OH 363
Ohio University Main Campus ..... OH 368
University of Toledo ..... OH 372
California University of Pennsylvania ..... PA 405
East Stroudsburg University of Pennsylvania ..... PA 406
Lock Haven University ..... PA 406
Temple University ..... PA 411
York College of Pennsylvania ..... PA 415
Benedict College ..... SC 418
Clemson University ..... SC 419
Middle Tennessee State University ..... TN 434
University of Tennessee, Knoxville ..... TN 439
Texas A & M University ..... TX 459
Texas State University ..... TX 463
Brigham Young University ..... UT 471
University of Utah, The ..... UT 472
George Mason University ..... VA 481
Longwood University ..... VA 482
Old Dominion University ..... VA 483
Radford University ..... VA 484
Virginia Wesleyan University ..... VA 491
Eastern Washington University ..... WA .. 494
Western Washington University ..... WA .. 500
Shepherd University ..... WV .. 504
University of Wisconsin-La Crosse ..... WI 510

NUR: Accreditation Commission for Education in Nursing: nursing (B,M,D)

Oakwood University ..... AL 6
Troy University ..... AL 7
Tuskegee University ..... AL 7
University of Alaska Anchorage ..... AK 10
Brookline College ..... AZ 11
Arkansas State University-Jonesboro ..... AR 18
Arkansas Tech University ..... AR 18
Southern Arkansas University ..... AR 21
University of Arkansas at Fort Smith ..... AR 22
University of Arkansas at Little Rock ..... AR 22
University of Arkansas at Monticello ..... AR 22
Pacific Union College ..... CA 55
Sonoma State University ..... CA 35
American Sentinel University ..... CO 76
Colorado Mountain College ..... CO 77
Colorado State University-Pueblo ..... CO 78
Denver School of Nursing ..... CO 79
Metropolitan State University of Denver ..... CO 80
Platt College ..... CO 81
St. Vincent's College ..... CT 88
Delaware State University ..... DE 90
Wesley College ..... DE 90
University of the District of Columbia ..... DC 93
Adventist University of Health Sciences ..... FL 94
Bethune Cookman University ..... FL 95
Chipola College ..... FL 96
College of Central Florida ..... FL 97
Daytona State College ..... FL 97
Florida Agricultural and Mechanical University ..... FL 109
Florida SouthWestern State College ..... FL 100
Florida State College at Jacksonville ..... FL 100
Indian River State College ..... FL 101
Miami Dade College ..... FL 103
Palm Beach State College ..... FL 105
Pensacola State College ..... FL 105
Polk State College ..... FL 105
St. Johns River State College ..... FL 106
South Florida State College ..... FL 108
State College of Florida, Manatee-Sarasota. FL 108
University of Tampa ..... FL 113
Abraham Baldwin Agricultural College ..... GA 114
Albany State University ..... GA 114
College of Coastal Georgia ..... GA 118
Dalton State College ..... GA 118
Georgia College & State University ..... GA 119
Georgia Highlands College ..... GA 119
Gordon State College ..... GA 121
LaGrange College ..... GA 122
Middle Georgia State University ..... GA 123
Piedmont College ..... GA 124
South Georgia State College ..... GA 125
Thomas University ..... GA 126
University of North Georgia ..... GA 127
University of Guam ..... GU 520
University of Hawaii at Hilo ..... HI 129
Chicago State University ..... IL 135
Governors State University ..... IL 138
Rockford University ..... IL 150
Saint Francis Medical Center College of Nursing ..... IL 151
St. John's College ..... IL 151
Bethel College ..... IN 156
Indiana State University ..... IN 159
Indiana University East ..... IN 160
Indiana University Kokomo ..... IN 160
Indiana University Northwest ..... IN 160
Purdue University Northwest ..... IN 163
University of Evansville ..... IN 164
Vincennes University ..... IN 165
Iowa Wesleyan University ..... IA 170
Emporia State University ..... KS 177
Campbellsville University ..... KY 184
Frontier Nursing University ..... KY 184
Kentucky State University ..... KY 187
Midway University ..... KY 188
Northern Kentucky University ..... KY 188
Thomas More College ..... KY 189
University of Pikeville ..... KY 190
Dillard University ..... LA 191
Franciscan Missionaries of Our Lady University ..... LA 191
Grambling State University ..... LA 196
Louisiana State University at Alexandria ..... LA 194
University of Holy Cross ..... LA 196
University of Maine at Augusta ..... ME 201
University of New England ..... ME 202
Bowie State University ..... MD 208
Anna Maria College ..... MA 210
Becker College ..... MA 211
Endicott College ..... MA 214
Regis College ..... MA 224
Andrews University ..... MI 227
Davenport University ..... MI 229
Ferris State University ..... MI 230
St. Catherine University ..... MN 249
Alcorn State University ..... MS 251
Lincoln University ..... MO .. 261
Missouri Southern State University ..... MO .. 263
Southwest Baptist University ..... MO .. 267
Webster University ..... MO .. 269
Montana State University - Northern ..... MT 272
Salish Kootenai College ..... MT 273
Bryan College of Health Sciences ..... NE 273
Clarkson College ..... NE 273
College of Saint Mary ..... NE 274
Midland University ..... NE 275
Great Basin College ..... NV 279
Roseman University of Health Sciences ..... NV 280
Franklin Pierce University ..... NH 281
Rivier University ..... NH 281
College of Saint Elizabeth ..... NJ 285
Kean University ..... NJ 286
Ramapo College of New Jersey ..... NJ 289
Eastern New Mexico University Main Campus ..... NM 293
City University of New York Medgar Evers College ..... NY 303
City University of New York York College ... NY 304
College of Staten Island CUNY ..... NY 302
Daemen College ..... NY 306
Elmira College ..... NY 307
Excelsior College ..... NY 308
Maria College of Albany ..... NY 314
New York City College of Technology/City University of New York ..... NY 303
Saint Joseph's College, New York ..... NY 322
State University of New York College of Technology at Delhi ..... NY 329
SUNY Canton-College of Technology ..... NY 329
Trocaire College ..... NY 331
Wagner College ..... NY 333
Gardner-Webb University ..... NC 337
North Carolina Agricultural and Technical State University ..... NC 350
North Carolina Central University ..... NC 350
Wingate University ..... NC 353
Dickinson State University ..... ND 354
Minot State University ..... ND 354
University of Jamestown ..... ND 355
Good Samaritan College of Nursing and Health Science ..... OH 362
Kettering College ..... OH 364
Shawnee State University ..... OH 369
University of Rio Grande ..... OH 372
Youngstown State University ..... OH 374
East Central University ..... OK 375
Langston University ..... OK 375
Northeastern State University ..... OK 376
Northwestern Oklahoma State University .... OK 376
Oklahoma City University ..... OK 377
Oklahoma Panhandle State University ..... OK 377
Rogers State University ..... OK 379
Southwestern Oklahoma State University ... OK 380
University of Tulsa ..... OK 381
Cedar Crest College ..... PA 392
East Stroudsburg University of Pennsylvania ..... PA 406
Edinboro University ..... PA 406
La Roche College ..... PA 398
Lock Haven University ..... PA 406
Mansfield University of Pennsylvania ..... PA 406
Marywood University ..... PA 401
Mercyhurst University ..... PA 401
Millersville University of Pennsylvania ..... PA 407
Mount Aloysius College ..... PA 402
Neumann University ..... PA 402
Pennsylvania College of Technology ..... PA 404
Slippery Rock University of Pennsylvania ... PA 407
Inter American University of Puerto Rico / Metropolitan Campus ..... PR 524
Inter American University of Puerto Rico Aguadilla Campus ..... PR 523
Inter American University of Puerto Rico Arecibo Campus ..... PR 523
National University College ..... PR 525
Pontifical Catholic University of Puerto Rico, The ..... PR 525
Universidad Adventista de las Antillas ..... PR 526
Universidad del Este ..... PR 525
Universidad Metropolitana ..... PR 526
University of Puerto Rico at Arecibo ..... PR 527
University of Puerto Rico-Humacao ..... PR 528
University of Puerto Rico-Mayaguez Campus ..... PR 528
New England Institute of Technology ..... RI 416
Charleston Southern University ..... SC 419
Coastal Carolina University ..... SC 420
Francis Marion University ..... SC 421
Presentation College ..... SD 427
Austin Peay State University ..... TN 430
Lincoln Memorial University ..... TN 433
Lipscomb University ..... TN 433
South College ..... TN 436
Southern Adventist University ..... TN 436
Tennessee State University ..... TN 438
University of Tennessee at Martin ..... TN 440
Baptist Health System School of Health Professions ..... TX 443
Houston Baptist University ..... TX 450
Lamar University ..... TX 462
Lubbock Christian University ..... TX 452
Prairie View A & M University ..... TX 458
Stephen F. Austin State University ..... TX 458
Texas A & M International University ..... TX 459
University of Houston - Clear Lake ..... TX 465
Wayland Baptist University ..... TX 470
Dixie State University ..... UT 473
Utah Valley University ..... UT 473

NURSE: Commission on Collegiate Nursing Education: nursing (B,M,D)

NW: Northwest Commission on Colleges and Universities

University of Idaho ... ID ... 132
Aaniiih Nakoda College ... MT ... 270
Blackfeet Community College ... MT ... 270
Carroll College ... MT ... 270
Chief Dull Knife College ... MT ... 270
Dawson Community College ... MT ... 270
Flathead Valley Community College ... MT ... 271
Fort Peck Community College ... MT ... 271
Great Falls College Montana State University ... MT ... 272
Helena College University of Montana ... MT ... 271
Little Big Horn College ... MT ... 271
Miles Community College ... MT ... 271
Montana State University ... MT ... 272
Montana State University - Billings ... MT ... 272
Montana State University - Northern ... MT ... 272
Montana Tech of The University of Montana ... MT ... 272
Rocky Mountain College ... MT ... 272
Salish Kootenai College ... MT ... 273
Stone Child College ... MT ... 273
University of Montana - Missoula ... MT ... 271
University of Montana Western, The ... MT ... 271
University of Providence ... MT ... 273
College of Southern Nevada ... NV ... 278
Great Basin College ... NV ... 279
Nevada State College ... NV ... 279
Roseman University of Health Sciences ... NV ... 280
Sierra Nevada College ... NV ... 280
Truckee Meadows Community College ... NV ... 279
University of Nevada, Las Vegas ... NV ... 279
University of Nevada, Reno ... NV ... 279
Western Nevada College ... NV ... 279
Art Institute of Portland, The ... OR ... 381
Blue Mountain Community College ... OR ... 382
Central Oregon Community College ... OR ... 382
Chemeketa Community College ... OR ... 382
Clackamas Community College ... OR ... 382
Clatsop Community College ... OR ... 382
Columbia Gorge Community College ... OR ... 382
Concordia University ... OR ... 382
Corban University ... OR ... 383
Eastern Oregon University ... OR ... 383
George Fox University ... OR ... 383
Klamath Community College ... OR ... 383
Lane Community College ... OR ... 383
Lewis and Clark College ... OR ... 383
Linfield College ... OR ... 383
Linn-Benton Community College ... OR ... 384
Marylhurst University ... OR ... 384
Mount Angel Seminary ... OR ... 384
Mt. Hood Community College ... OR ... 384
Multnomah University ... OR ... 384
National University of Natural Medicine ... OR ... 384
Northwest Christian University ... OR ... 384
Oregon College of Art and Craft ... OR ... 385
Oregon Health & Science University ... OR ... 385
Oregon Institute of Technology ... OR ... 385
Oregon State University ... OR ... 385
Pacific Northwest College of Art ... OR ... 385
Pacific University ... OR ... 385
Portland Community College ... OR ... 386
Portland State University ... OR ... 386
Reed College ... OR ... 386
Rogue Community College ... OR ... 386
Southern Oregon University ... OR ... 386
Southwestern Oregon Community College ... OR ... 387
Tillamook Bay Community College ... OR ... 387
Treasure Valley Community College ... OR ... 387
Umpqua Community College ... OR ... 387
University of Oregon ... OR ... 387
University of Portland ... OR ... 387
University of Western States ... OR ... 387
Warner Pacific College ... OR ... 388
Western Oregon University ... OR ... 388
Western Seminary ... OR ... 388
Willamette University ... OR ... 388
Brigham Young University ... UT ... 471
Dixie State University ... UT ... 473
LDS Business College ... UT ... 471
Rocky Mountain University of Health Professions ... UT ... 472
Salt Lake Community College ... UT ... 474
Snow College ... UT ... 474
Southern Utah University ... UT ... 473
University of Utah, The ... UT ... 472
Utah State University ... UT ... 473
Utah Valley University ... UT ... 473
Weber State University ... UT ... 473
Western Governors University ... UT ... 474
Westminster College ... UT ... 474
Art Institute of Seattle, The ... WA ... 492
Bastyr University ... WA ... 492
Bates Technical College ... WA ... 492
Bellevue College ... WA ... 492
Bellingham Technical College ... WA ... 492
Big Bend Community College ... WA ... 492
Cascadia College ... WA ... 492
Central Washington University ... WA ... 492
Centralia College ... WA ... 493
City University of Seattle ... WA ... 493
Clark College ... WA ... 493
Clover Park Technical College ... WA ... 493
Columbia Basin College ... WA ... 493
Cornish College of the Arts ... WA ... 494
Eastern Washington University ... WA ... 494
Edmonds Community College ... WA ... 494
Everett Community College ... WA ... 494
Evergreen State College, The ... WA ... 494
Gonzaga University ... WA ... 495
Grays Harbor College ... WA ... 495
Green River College ... WA ... 495
Heritage University ... WA ... 495
Highline College ... WA ... 495
Lake Washington Institute of Technology ... WA ... 495
Lower Columbia College ... WA ... 495
North Seattle College ... WA ... 497
Northwest Indian College ... WA ... 496
Northwest University ... WA ... 496
Olympic College ... WA ... 496
Pacific Lutheran University ... WA ... 496
@Pacific Northwest University of Health Sciences ... WA ... 496
Peninsula College ... WA ... 496
Pierce College District ... WA ... 497
Renton Technical College ... WA ... 497
Saint Martin's University ... WA ... 497
Seattle Central College ... WA ... 497
Seattle Pacific University ... WA ... 498
Seattle University ... WA ... 498
Shoreline Community College ... WA ... 498
Skagit Valley College ... WA ... 498
South Puget Sound Community College ... WA ... 498
South Seattle College ... WA ... 497
Spokane Community College ... WA ... 493
Spokane Falls Community College ... WA ... 494
Tacoma Community College ... WA ... 499
University of Puget Sound ... WA ... 499
University of Washington ... WA ... 499
Walla Walla Community College ... WA ... 499
Walla Walla University ... WA ... 499
Washington State University ... WA ... 499
Wenatchee Valley College ... WA ... 500
Western Washington University ... WA ... 500
Whatcom Community College ... WA ... 500
Whitman College ... WA ... 500
Whitworth University ... WA ... 500
Yakima Valley College ... WA ... 500

NY: New York State Board of Regents

Christie's Education, New York ... NY ... 300
City University of New York Stella and Charles Guttman Community College ... NY ... 303
Cold Spring Harbor Laboratory/Watson School of Biological Sciences ... NY ... 304
Elmezzi Graduate School of Molecular Medicine, The ... NY ... 307
Fei Tian College ... NY ... 308
Holy Trinity Orthodox Seminary ... NY ... 310
Louis V. Gerstner Jr. Graduate School of Biomedical Sciences, Memorial Sloa n Kettering Cancer Center ... NY ... 313
Memorial School of Nursing ... NY ... 314
New York Academy of Art ... NY ... 316
New York College of Health Professions ... NY ... 317
Phillips School of Nursing at Mount Sinai Beth Israel ... NY ... 320
Richard Gilder Graduate School at the American Museum of Natural History ... NY ... 321
Rockefeller University ... NY ... 321
Salvation Army College for Officer Training ... NY ... 323
Samaritan Hospital School of Nursing ... NY ... 323
USC The Business College ... NY ... 332
Wood Tobé-Coburn School ... NY ... 333

OPD: Commission on Opticianry Accreditation: opticianry (A)

Goodwin College ... CT ... 87
Middlesex Community College ... CT ... 86
Broward College ... FL ... 96
Hillsborough Community College ... FL ... 101
Miami Dade College ... FL ... 103
Ogeechee Technical College ... GA ... 123
Benjamin Franklin Institute of Technology ... MA ... 211
College of Southern Nevada ... NV ... 278
Camden County College ... NJ ... 284
Essex County College ... NJ ... 285
Raritan Valley Community College ... NJ ... 289
Southwestern Indian Polytechnic Institute ... NM ... 296
Erie Community College ... NY ... 307
New York City College of Technology/City University of New York ... NY ... 303
Durham Technical Community College ... NC ... 342
Roane State Community College ... TN ... 438
J. Sargeant Reynolds Community College ... VA ... 488

OPE: Commission on Accreditation of Allied Health Education Programs: orthotics and prosthetics (C,B,M)

Alabama State University ... AL ... 4
California State University-Dominguez Hills ... CA ... 31
Loma Linda University ... CA ... 48
University of Hartford ... CT ... 89
Florida International University ... FL ... 109
Georgia Institute of Technology ... GA ... 120
Northwestern University ... IL ... 148
Eastern Michigan University ... MI ... 229
Concordia University, St. Paul ... MN ... 241
University of Pittsburgh ... PA ... 412
Baylor College of Medicine ... TX ... 444
University of Texas Southwestern Medical Center ... TX ... 469
University of Washington ... WA ... 499

OPLT: Commission on Opticianry Accreditation: opthalmic laboratory technician (C)

Southwestern Indian Polytechnic Institute ... NM ... 296

OPT: American Optometric Association: optometry (FP,D)

University of Alabama at Birmingham ... AL ... 8
Marshall B. Ketchum University ... CA ... 51
University of California-Berkeley ... CA ... 68
Western University of Health Sciences ... CA ... 74
Nova Southeastern University ... FL ... 104
Illinois College of Optometry ... IL ... 140
@Midwestern University ... IL ... 145
Indiana University Bloomington ... IN ... 159
@University of Pikeville ... KY ... 190
MCPHS University ... MA ... 221
New England College of Optometry ... MA ... 222
Ferris State University ... MI ... 230
University of Missouri - Saint Louis ... MO ... 268
State University of New York College of Optometry ... NY ... 328
Ohio State University Main Campus, The ... OH ... 367
Northeastern State University ... OK ... 376
Pacific University ... OR ... 385
Salus University ... PA ... 410
Inter American University of Puerto Rico School of Optometry ... PR ... 524
Southern College of Optometry ... TN ... 436
University of Houston ... TX ... 465
University of the Incarnate Word ... TX ... 465

OPTR: American Optometric Association: optometric residency programs

University of Alabama at Birmingham ... AL ... 8
Marshall B. Ketchum University ... CA ... 51
University of California-Berkeley ... CA ... 68
Nova Southeastern University ... FL ... 104
Illinois College of Optometry ... IL ... 140
Indiana University Bloomington ... IN ... 159
New England College of Optometry ... MA ... 222
Ferris State University ... MI ... 230
University of Missouri - Saint Louis ... MO ... 268
State University of New York College of Optometry ... NY ... 328
Ohio State University Main Campus, The ... OH ... 367
Northeastern State University ... OK ... 376
Pacific University ... OR ... 385
Salus University ... PA ... 410
Inter American University of Puerto Rico Bayamon Campus ... PR ... 523
Southern College of Optometry ... TN ... 436
University of Houston ... TX ... 465
University of the Incarnate Word ... TX ... 465

OPTT: American Optometric Association: optometric technician (C,A)

Indiana University Bloomington ... IN ... 159
Madison Area Technical College ... WI ... 514

OSTEO: American Osteopathic Association, Office of Osteopathic Education: osteopathic medicine (FP,D)

Alabama College of Osteopathic Medicine ... AL ... 1
@Arkansas College of Osteopathic Medicine ... AR ... 17
Touro University California ... CA ... 67
Western University of Health Sciences ... CA ... 74
Rocky Vista University ... CO ... 82
Nova Southeastern University ... FL ... 104
Midwestern University ... IL ... 145
Marian University ... IN ... 162
Des Moines University ... IA ... 168
University of Pikeville ... KY ... 190
University of New England ... ME ... 202
Michigan State University ... MI ... 233
William Carey University ... MS ... 256
A. T. Still University of Health Sciences ... MO ... 257
Kansas City University of Medicine & Biosciences ... MO ... 261
Rowan University ... NJ ... 289
@Burrell College of Osteopathic Medicine ... NM ... 293
New York Institute of Technology ... NY ... 317
Touro College ... NY ... 331
Campbell University ... NC ... 336
Ohio University Main Campus ... OH ... 368
Lake Erie College of Osteopathic Medicine ... PA ... 399
Philadelphia College of Osteopathic Medicine ... PA ... 407
Lincoln Memorial University ... TN ... 433
University of North Texas Health Science Center at Fort Worth ... TX ... 466
@University of the Incarnate Word ... TX ... 465
Edward Via College of Osteopathic Medicine ... VA ... 480
@Liberty University ... VA ... 482
Pacific Northwest University of Health Sciences ... WA ... 496
West Virginia School of Osteopathic Medicine ... WV ... 504

OT: American Occupational Therapy Association: occupational therapy (M,D)

Alabama State University ... AL ... 4
Tuskegee University ... AL ... 7
University of Alabama at Birmingham ... AL ... 8
University of South Alabama ... AL ... 9
Northern Arizona University ... AZ ... 14
University of Central Arkansas ... AR ... 23
California State University-Dominguez Hills ... CA ... 31
Dominican University of California ... CA ... 41
Loma Linda University ... CA ... 48
Samuel Merritt University ... CA ... 59
San Jose State University ... CA ... 34
Stanbridge University ... CA ... 66
University of St. Augustine for Health Sciences ... CA ... 71
University of Southern California ... CA ... 72
West Coast University ... CA ... 73
Colorado State University ... CO ... 78
Quinnipiac University ... CT ... 88
Sacred Heart University ... CT ... 88
Howard University ... DC ... 92
Trinity Washington University ... DC ... 93
Adventist University of Health Sciences ... FL ... 94
Barry University ... FL ... 95
#Florida Agricultural and Mechanical University ... FL ... 109
Florida Gulf Coast University ... FL ... 109
Florida International University ... FL ... 109
Keiser University ... FL ... 102
Nova Southeastern University ... FL ... 104
University of Florida ... FL ... 110
Augusta University ... GA ... 116
Brenau University ... GA ... 116
Idaho State University ... ID ... 132
Chicago State University ... IL ... 135
Governors State University ... IL ... 138
Midwestern University ... IL ... 145
Rush University ... IL ... 150
University of Illinois at Chicago ... IL ... 153
Huntington University ... IN ... 159
Indiana State University ... IN ... 159
Indiana University-Purdue University Indianapolis ... IN ... 160
University of Indianapolis ... IN ... 164
University of Southern Indiana ... IN ... 165
Allen College ... IA ... 166
St. Ambrose University ... IA ... 173
Eastern Kentucky University ... KY ... 184
Spalding University ... KY ... 189
Louisiana State University Health Sciences Center at Shreveport ... LA ... 194
Louisiana State University Health Sciences Center-New Orleans ... LA ... 194
University of Louisiana at Monroe ... LA ... 198
Husson University ... ME ... 199
University of New England ... ME ... 202
University of Southern Maine ... ME ... 201
Towson University ... MD ... 209
American International College ... MA ... 210
Bay Path University ... MA ... 211
Boston University ... MA ... 212
MGH Institute of Health Professions ... MA ... 222
Salem State University ... MA ... 218
Springfield College ... MA ... 224
Tufts University ... MA ... 225
Worcester State University ... MA ... 219
Baker College of Flint ... MI ... 227
Davenport University ... MI ... 229
Eastern Michigan University ... MI ... 229
Grand Valley State University ... MI ... 230
Saginaw Valley State University ... MI ... 236
Wayne State University ... MI ... 239
Western Michigan University ... MI ... 239
College of Saint Scholastica, The ... MN ... 241
St. Catherine University ... MN ... 249
University of Minnesota ... MN ... 250
University of Mississippi Medical Center ... MS ... 256
Maryville University of Saint Louis ... MO ... 262
Missouri State University ... MO ... 263
Rockhurst University ... MO ... 265
Saint Louis University ... MO ... 266
University of Missouri - Columbia ... MO ... 268
Washington University in St. Louis ... MO ... 269

Institution	State	Page
College of Saint Mary	NE	274
Creighton University	NE	274
University of New Hampshire	NH	282
Kean University	NJ	286
Seton Hall University	NJ	291
Stockton University	NJ	291
University of New Mexico Main Campus	NM	296
City University of New York York College	NY	304
Clarkson University	NY	304
Columbia University in the City of New York	NY	305
Dominican College of Blauvelt	NY	306
D'Youville College	NY	307
Hofstra University	NY	310
Ithaca College	NY	311
Keuka College	NY	312
Le Moyne College	NY	312
Mercy College	NY	314
Nazareth College of Rochester	NY	316
New York Institute of Technology	NY	317
New York University	NY	318
Sage Colleges, The	NY	321
Stony Brook University	NY	325
SUNY Downstate Medical Center	NY	326
Touro College	NY	331
University at Buffalo-SUNY	NY	325
Utica College	NY	332
Cabarrus College of Health Sciences	NC	336
East Carolina University	NC	349
Lenoir-Rhyne University	NC	339
University of North Carolina at Chapel Hill	NC	351
Winston-Salem State University	NC	352
University of Mary	ND	355
University of North Dakota	ND	353
Cleveland State University	OH	359
Ohio State University Main Campus, The	OH	367
Shawnee State University	OH	369
University of Findlay, The	OH	372
University of Toledo	OH	372
Xavier University	OH	374
Pacific University	OR	385
Alvernia University	PA	389
Chatham University	PA	392
Duquesne University	PA	394
Elizabethtown College	PA	394
Gannon University	PA	395
Misericordia University	PA	401
Saint Francis University	PA	409
Salus University	PA	410
Temple University	PA	411
Thomas Jefferson University	PA	411
University of Pittsburgh	PA	412
University of Scranton, The	PA	413
University of the Sciences in Philadelphia	PA	413
University of Puerto Rico-Medical Sciences Campus	PR	528
New England Institute of Technology	RI	416
Medical University of South Carolina	SC	422
University of South Dakota, The	SD	428
Belmont University	TN	430
Milligan College	TN	435
Tennessee State University	TN	438
University of Tennessee at Chattanooga	TN	440
University of Tennessee Health Science Center	TN	440
Abilene Christian University	TX	441
Texas Tech University Health Sciences Center	TX	463
Texas Woman's University	TX	464
University of Texas at El Paso	TX	467
University of Texas Health Science Center at San Antonio	TX	468
University of Texas Medical Branch, The	TX	469
University of Texas Rio Grande Valley, The	TX	468
University of Utah, The	UT	472
James Madison University	VA	481
Jefferson College of Health Sciences	VA	482
Mary Baldwin University	VA	482
Radford University	VA	484
Shenandoah University	VA	485
Virginia Commonwealth University	VA	487
Eastern Washington University	WA	494
University of Puget Sound	WA	499
University of Washington	WA	499
West Virginia University	WV	505
Carroll University	WI	506
Concordia University Wisconsin	WI	507
Mount Mary University	WI	509
University of Wisconsin-La Crosse	WI	510
University of Wisconsin-Madison	WI	510
University of Wisconsin-Milwaukee	WI	511

OTA: American Occupational Therapy Association: occupational therapy assistant (C,A)

Institution	State	Page
Wallace State Community College - Hanceville	AL	3
Pima Medical Institute-Tucson	AZ	15
Arkansas State University-Jonesboro	AR	18
Baptist Health College Little Rock	AR	18
Cossatot Community College of the University of Arkansas	AR	22
South Arkansas Community College	AR	21
University of Arkansas - Pulaski Technical College	AR	23
CBD College	CA	35
Grossmont College	CA	45
Sacramento City College	CA	50
Santa Ana College	CA	58
Stanbridge University	CA	66
Pueblo Community College	CO	81
#Goodwin College	CT	87
#Lincoln College of New England	CT	87
Manchester Community College	CT	85
#Trinity Washington University	DC	93
Adventist University of Health Sciences	FL	94
Concorde Career Institute	FL	97
Daytona State College	FL	97
Florida State College at Jacksonville	FL	100
Keiser University	FL	102
Polk State College	FL	105
Praxis Institute, The	FL	105
State College of Florida, Manatee-Sarasota	FL	108
Augusta Technical College	GA	116
Chattahoochee Technical College	GA	117
Middle Georgia State University	GA	123
Kapiolani Community College	HI	130
City Colleges of Chicago Wilbur Wright College	IL	136
Fox College	IL	138
Illinois Central College	IL	139
John A. Logan College	IL	141
Lewis and Clark Community College	IL	143
Lincoln Land Community College	IL	144
McHenry County College	IL	145
Parkland College	IL	148
Shawnee Community College	IL	151
South Suburban College of Cook County	IL	151
University of Southern Indiana	IN	165
Hawkeye Community College	IA	169
Indian Hills Community College	IA	169
Kirkwood Community College	IA	171
Brown Mackie College-Salina	KS	175
Neosho County Community College	KS	180
Newman University	KS	180
Washburn University	KS	182
Jefferson Community and Technical College	KY	186
Madisonville Community College	KY	186
Bossier Parish Community College	LA	192
Delgado Community College	LA	192
University of Louisiana at Monroe	LA	198
Kennebec Valley Community College	ME	200
Allegany College of Maryland	MD	202
Community College of Baltimore County, The	MD	203
Wor-Wic Community College	MD	210
Bristol Community College	MA	219
North Shore Community College	MA	220
Quinsigamond Community College	MA	220
Springfield Technical Community College	MA	221
Grand Rapids Community College	MI	230
Macomb Community College	MI	233
Mott Community College	MI	234
Anoka Technical College	MN	244
Northland Community and Technical College	MN	246
St. Catherine University	MN	249
Holmes Community College	MS	253
Itawamba Community College	MS	253
Pearl River Community College	MS	255
Crowder College	MO	259
East Central College	MO	259
Jefferson College	MO	261
Metropolitan Community College - Penn Valley	MO	262
Moberly Area Community College	MO	264
North Central Missouri College	MO	264
Ozarks Technical Community College	MO	264
St. Charles Community College	MO	265
State Fair Community College	MO	267
Three Rivers College	MO	267
University of Missouri - Kansas City	MO	268
Central Community College	NE	273
River Valley Community College	NH	281
Eastwick College	NJ	285
#Eastern New Mexico University-Roswell	NM	294
San Juan College	NM	296
#Western New Mexico University	NM	297
Erie Community College	NY	307
Jamestown Community College	NY	311
LaGuardia Community College/City University of New York	NY	303
Maria College of Albany	NY	314
#Mercy College	NY	314
Orange County Community College	NY	319
Rockland Community College	NY	321
Villa Maria College of Buffalo	NY	333
Cabarrus College of Health Sciences	NC	336
Cape Fear Community College	NC	341
Central Piedmont Community College	NC	342
Durham Technical Community College	NC	342
Pitt Community College	NC	345
Southwestern Community College	NC	346
North Dakota State College of Science	ND	355
Cincinnati State Technical and Community College	OH	359
Cuyahoga Community College	OH	360
James A. Rhodes State College	OH	363
Lorain County Community College	OH	364
Marion Technical College	OH	365
North Central State College	OH	366
Owens Community College	OH	369
Shawnee State University	OH	369
Sinclair Community College	OH	370
Stark State College	OH	370
Zane State College	OH	374
Murray State College	OK	376
Oklahoma City Community College	OK	377
Southwestern Oklahoma State University	OK	380
Tulsa Community College	OK	380
Linn-Benton Community College	OR	384
Brightwood Career Institute	PA	390
Central Penn College	PA	392
Community College of Allegheny County	PA	392
Harcum College	PA	396
Lehigh Carbon Community College	PA	400
Pennsylvania College of Technology	PA	404
#Inter American University of Puerto Rico Ponce Campus	PR	524
Community College of Rhode Island	RI	416
New England Institute of Technology	RI	416
Greenville Technical College	SC	421
Piedmont Technical College	SC	423
Trident Technical College	SC	424
Lake Area Technical Institute	SD	427
Concorde Career College	TN	431
Jackson State Community College	TN	437
Nashville State Community College	TN	437
Roane State Community College	TN	438
South College	TN	436
Amarillo College	TX	442
Austin Community College District	TX	443
#Del Mar College	TX	448
Houston Community College	TX	450
Laredo Community College	TX	451
Lone Star College System	TX	452
McLennan Community College	TX	452
Navarro College	TX	453
Panola College	TX	454
Parker University	TX	454
St. Philip's College	TX	441
South Texas College	TX	456
Tyler Junior College	TX	464
#University of the Incarnate Word	TX	465
Weatherford College	TX	470
Salt Lake Community College	UT	474
Eastern Virginia Career College	VA	480
Jefferson College of Health Sciences	VA	482
Northern Virginia Community College	VA	488
Southwest Virginia Community College	VA	489
Tidewater Community College	VA	489
Bates Technical College	WA	492
Green River College	WA	495
Lake Washington Institute of Technology	WA	495
Spokane Falls Community College	WA	494
University of Charleston	WV	502
Fox Valley Technical College	WI	513
Madison Area Technical College	WI	514
Milwaukee Area Technical College	WI	514
Western Technical College	WI	515
Wisconsin Indianhead Technical College	WI	515
Casper College	WY	516

PA: National Accrediting Agency for Clinical Laboratory Sciences: pathologist's assistant (C,M)

Institution	State	Page
Quinnipiac University	CT	88
Rosalind Franklin University of Medicine & Science	IL	150
Indiana University-Purdue University Indianapolis	IN	160
University of Maryland, Baltimore	MD	207
Wayne State University	MI	239
Duke University	NC	337
Drexel University	PA	394
West Virginia University	WV	505

PAST: Association for Clinical Pastoral Education: clinical pastoral education

Institution	State	Page
University of Alabama at Birmingham	AL	8
Jefferson Regional Medical Center School of Nursing	AR	20
Loma Linda University	CA	48
San Francisco Theological Seminary	CA	60
University of California-Davis	CA	68
University of California-Los Angeles	CA	69
University of California-San Francisco	CA	70
Denver Seminary	CO	79
University of Colorado Denver|Anschutz Medical Campus	CO	83
Yale University	CT	89
Georgetown University	DC	92
Emory University	GA	119
Rush University	IL	150
University of Illinois at Chicago	IL	153
Indiana University-Purdue University Indianapolis	IN	160
St. Luke's College	IA	173
University of Iowa	IA	166
University of Kentucky	KY	190
Dartmouth College	NH	281
Albany Medical College	NY	297
Hebrew Union College-Jewish Institute of Religion	NY	309
Jewish Theological Seminary of America	NY	312
New York Medical College	NY	318
New York University	NY	318
State University of New York Upstate Medical University	NY	326
University of Rochester	NY	332
Duke University	NC	337
University of North Carolina at Chapel Hill	NC	351
Kettering College	OH	364
Thomas Jefferson University	PA	411
University of Pennsylvania	PA	412
University of Tennessee, Knoxville	TN	439
Oblate School of Theology	TX	454
University of Texas MD Anderson Cancer Center, The	TX	469
University of Texas Southwestern Medical Center	TX	469
Eastern Mennonite University	VA	480
University of Virginia	VA	486
Virginia Commonwealth University	VA	487
University of Washington	WA	499
West Virginia University	WV	505

PCSAS: Psychological Clinical Science Accreditation System: psychological clinical science (D)

Institution	State	Page
Arizona State University	AZ	10
University of Arizona	AZ	16
University of California-Berkeley	CA	68
University of California-Los Angeles	CA	69
University of Southern California	CA	72
University of Delaware	DE	90
University of South Florida	FL	111
Emory University	GA	119
University of Georgia	GA	127
Northwestern University	IL	148
University of Illinois at Urbana-Champaign	IL	154
Indiana University Bloomington	IN	159
University of Iowa	IA	166
University of Kentucky	KY	190
University of Maryland College Park	MD	207
Boston University	MA	212
Harvard University	MA	215
University of Minnesota	MN	250
University of Missouri - Columbia	MO	268
Washington University in St. Louis	MO	269
Rutgers University - New Brunswick	NJ	290
Stony Brook University	NY	325
University at Buffalo-SUNY	NY	325
Duke University	NC	337
University of North Carolina at Chapel Hill	NC	351
Ohio State University Main Campus, The	OH	367
University of Oregon	OR	387
Penn State University Park	PA	403
Temple University	PA	411
University of Pennsylvania	PA	412
University of Pittsburgh	PA	412
University of Virginia	VA	486
Virginia Polytechnic Institute and State University	VA	490
University of Wisconsin-Madison	WI	510

PDPSY: American Psychological Association: post-doctoral residency in health service psychology

Institution	State	Page
Stanford University	CA	66
University of California-San Diego	CA	69
University of Southern California	CA	72
University of Michigan-Ann Arbor	MI	237
University of Rochester	NY	332
Brown University	RI	415
Virginia Commonwealth University	VA	487
University of Washington	WA	499
Medical College of Wisconsin	WI	508

PERF: Commission on Accreditation of Allied Health Education Programs: perfusionist (C,B,M)

Institution	State	Page
University of Arizona	AZ	16
Quinnipiac University	CT	88
Barry University	FL	95
Rush University	IL	150
University of Iowa	IA	166
University of Nebraska Medical Center	NE	277
State University of New York Upstate Medical University	NY	326
Medical University of South Carolina	SC	422
Vanderbilt University	TN	440

University of Texas Health Science Center at Houston (UTHealth), The ... TX ... 468
Milwaukee School of Engineering ... WI ... 509

PH: Council on Education for Public Health: public health (B,M,D)

University of Alabama at Birmingham ... AL ... 8
University of Alaska Anchorage ... AK ... 10
University of Arizona ... AZ ... 16
University of Arkansas for Medical Sciences ... AR ... 22
California State University-Fresno ... CA ... 32
California State University-Fullerton ... CA ... 32
California State University-Long Beach ... CA ... 32
California State University-Northridge ... CA ... 33
Charles R. Drew University of Medicine & Science ... CA ... 36
Claremont Graduate University ... CA ... 37
Loma Linda University ... CA ... 48
National University ... CA ... 53
San Diego State University ... CA ... 34
San Francisco State University ... CA ... 34
San Jose State University ... CA ... 34
Touro University California ... CA ... 67
University of California-Berkeley ... CA ... 68
University of California-Davis ... CA ... 68
University of California-Irvine ... CA ... 69
University of California-Los Angeles ... CA ... 69
University of San Francisco ... CA ... 72
University of Southern California ... CA ... 72
Colorado State University ... CO ... 78
University of Colorado Denver|Anschutz Medical Campus ... CO ... 83
University of Northern Colorado ... CO ... 83
Southern Connecticut State University ... CT ... 85
Yale University ... CT ... 89
George Washington University ... DC ... 92
Florida Agricultural and Mechanical University ... FL ... 109
Florida International University ... FL ... 109
Florida State University ... FL ... 110
Nova Southeastern University ... FL ... 104
University of Florida ... FL ... 110
University of Miami ... FL ... 112
University of North Florida ... FL ... 110
University of South Florida ... FL ... 111
University of West Florida ... FL ... 111
Armstrong State University ... GA ... 115
Augusta University ... GA ... 116
Emory University ... GA ... 119
Georgia Southern University ... GA ... 120
Georgia State University ... GA ... 121
Mercer University ... GA ... 122
Morehouse School of Medicine ... GA ... 123
University of Georgia ... GA ... 127
University of Hawaii at Manoa ... HI ... 129
Idaho State University ... ID ... 132
Benedictine University ... IL ... 133
DePaul University ... IL ... 137
Loyola University Chicago ... IL ... 144
Northern Illinois University ... IL ... 147
Northwestern University ... IL ... 148
#Southern Illinois University Carbondale ... IL ... 152
University of Illinois at Chicago ... IL ... 153
University of Illinois at Urbana-Champaign ... IL ... 154
Indiana University Bloomington ... IN ... 159
Indiana University-Purdue University Indianapolis ... IN ... 160
Des Moines University ... IA ... 168
University of Iowa ... IA ... 166
Kansas State University ... KS ... 179
University of Kansas Main Campus ... KS ... 181
Eastern Kentucky University ... KY ... 184
University of Kentucky ... KY ... 190
University of Louisville ... KY ... 190
Western Kentucky University ... KY ... 190
Louisiana State University Health Sciences Center at Shreveport ... LA ... 194
Louisiana State University Health Sciences Center-New Orleans ... LA ... 194
Louisiana State University in Shreveport ... LA ... 194
Tulane University ... LA ... 196
#University of New England ... ME ... 202
University of Southern Maine ... ME ... 201
Johns Hopkins University ... MD ... 204
Morgan State University ... MD ... 206
Uniformed Services University of the Health Sciences ... MD ... 518
University of Maryland College Park ... MD ... 207
University of Maryland, Baltimore ... MD ... 207
Boston University ... MA ... 212
Harvard University ... MA ... 215
Northeastern University ... MA ... 223
Tufts University ... MA ... 225
University of Massachusetts ... MA ... 216
Andrews University ... MI ... 227
University of Michigan-Ann Arbor ... MI ... 237
Wayne State University ... MI ... 239
University of Minnesota ... MN ... 250
Jackson State University ... MS ... 253
University of Southern Mississippi ... MS ... 256
A. T. Still University of Health Sciences ... MO ... 257
Missouri State University ... MO ... 263
Saint Louis University ... MO ... 266
University of Missouri - Columbia ... MO ... 268
Washington University in St. Louis ... MO ... 269
University of Montana - Missoula ... MT ... 271
University of Nebraska Medical Center ... NE ... 277
University of Nevada, Las Vegas ... NV ... 279
University of Nevada, Reno ... NV ... 279
Dartmouth College ... NH ... 281
University of New Hampshire ... NH ... 282
Montclair State University ... NJ ... 287
Rutgers University - New Brunswick ... NJ ... 290
William Paterson University of New Jersey ... NJ ... 292
New Mexico State University Main Campus ... NM ... 295
University of New Mexico Main Campus ... NM ... 296
City University of New York Graduate Center ... NY ... 302
Columbia University in the City of New York ... NY ... 305
Hofstra University ... NY ... 310
Icahn School of Medicine at Mount Sinai ... NY ... 311
New York Medical College ... NY ... 318
New York University ... NY ... 318
State University of New York College at Cortland ... NY ... 327
State University of New York Upstate Medical University ... NY ... 326
Stony Brook University ... NY ... 325
SUNY Downstate Medical Center ... NY ... 326
Syracuse University ... NY ... 330
University at Albany, SUNY ... NY ... 324
University at Buffalo-SUNY ... NY ... 325
University of Rochester ... NY ... 332
East Carolina University ... NC ... 349
Lenoir-Rhyne University ... NC ... 339
University of North Carolina at Chapel Hill ... NC ... 351
University of North Carolina at Charlotte ... NC ... 351
University of North Carolina at Greensboro ... NC ... 351
University of North Carolina Wilmington ... NC ... 352
North Dakota State University Main Campus ... ND ... 354
University of North Dakota ... ND ... 353
Bowling Green State University ... OH ... 357
Case Western Reserve University ... OH ... 358
Cleveland State University ... OH ... 359
Kent State University Kent Campus ... OH ... 363
Northeast Ohio Medical University ... OH ... 366
Ohio State University Main Campus, The ... OH ... 367
Ohio University Main Campus ... OH ... 368
University of Akron, Main Campus, The ... OH ... 371
University of Cincinnati Main Campus ... OH ... 371
University of Toledo ... OH ... 372
Wright State University Main Campus ... OH ... 374
Youngstown State University ... OH ... 374
Oregon Health & Science University ... OR ... 385
Oregon State University ... OR ... 385
Portland State University ... OR ... 386
Arcadia University ... PA ... 389
Drexel University ... PA ... 394
East Stroudsburg University of Pennsylvania ... PA ... 406
La Salle University ... PA ... 398
Temple University ... PA ... 411
Thomas Jefferson University ... PA ... 411
University of Pennsylvania ... PA ... 412
University of Pittsburgh ... PA ... 412
West Chester University of Pennsylvania ... PA ... 407
Ponce School of Medicine & Health Sciences ... PR ... 525
University of Puerto Rico-Medical Sciences Campus ... PR ... 528
Brown University ... RI ... 415
Clemson University ... SC ... 419
University of South Carolina Columbia ... SC ... 424
East Tennessee State University ... TN ... 431
Meharry Medical College ... TN ... 434
Tennessee State University ... TN ... 438
University of Memphis, The ... TN ... 439
University of Tennessee, Knoxville ... TN ... 439
Vanderbilt University ... TN ... 440
Baylor University ... TX ... 444
Texas A & M University ... TX ... 459
University of North Texas Health Science Center at Fort Worth ... TX ... 466
University of Texas at El Paso ... TX ... 467
University of Texas Health Science Center at Houston (UTHealth), The ... TX ... 468
University of Texas Medical Branch, The ... TX ... 469
Brigham Young University ... UT ... 471
University of Utah, The ... UT ... 472
Westminster College ... UT ... 474
Eastern Virginia Medical School ... VA ... 480
George Mason University ... VA ... 481
Old Dominion University ... VA ... 483
University of Virginia ... VA ... 486
Virginia Commonwealth University ... VA ... 487
Virginia Polytechnic Institute and State University ... VA ... 490
University of Washington ... WA ... 499
American Public University System ... WV ... 501
West Virginia University ... WV ... 505
Medical College of Wisconsin ... WI ... 508
University of Wisconsin-La Crosse ... WI ... 510
University of Wisconsin-Madison ... WI ... 510
University of Wisconsin-Milwaukee ... WI ... 511

PHAR: Accreditation Council for Pharmacy Education: pharmacy (FP,D)

Auburn University ... AL ... 4
Samford University ... AL ... 6
University of Arizona ... AZ ... 16
Harding University Main Campus ... AR ... 19
University of Arkansas for Medical Sciences ... AR ... 22
@California Health Sciences University ... CA ... 29
California Northstate University ... CA ... 30
@Chapman University ... CA ... 36
@Keck Graduate Institute ... CA ... 38
Loma Linda University ... CA ... 48
@Marshall B. Ketchum University ... CA ... 51
Touro University California ... CA ... 67
University of California-San Diego ... CA ... 69
University of California-San Francisco ... CA ... 70
University of Southern California ... CA ... 72
University of the Pacific ... CA ... 70
@West Coast University ... CA ... 73
Western University of Health Sciences ... CA ... 74
Regis University ... CO ... 82
University of Colorado Denver|Anschutz Medical Campus ... CO ... 83
University of Connecticut ... CT ... 88
University of Saint Joseph ... CT ... 89
Howard University ... DC ... 92
Florida Agricultural and Mechanical University ... FL ... 109
@Larkin Health Sciences Institute ... FL ... 103
Nova Southeastern University ... FL ... 104
Palm Beach Atlantic University ... FL ... 104
University of Florida ... FL ... 110
University of South Florida ... FL ... 111
Mercer University ... GA ... 122
South University ... GA ... 125
University of Georgia ... GA ... 127
University of Hawaii at Hilo ... HI ... 129
Idaho State University ... ID ... 132
Chicago State University ... IL ... 135
Midwestern University ... IL ... 145
Roosevelt University ... IL ... 150
Rosalind Franklin University of Medicine & Science ... IL ... 150
Southern Illinois University Edwardsville ... IL ... 152
University of Illinois at Chicago ... IL ... 153
Butler University ... IN ... 156
Manchester University ... IN ... 162
Purdue University Main Campus ... IN ... 163
Drake University ... IA ... 168
University of Iowa ... IA ... 166
University of Kansas Main Campus ... KS ... 181
Sullivan University ... KY ... 189
University of Kentucky ... KY ... 190
#University of Louisiana at Monroe ... LA ... 198
Xavier University of Louisiana ... LA ... 198
Husson University ... ME ... 199
University of New England ... ME ... 202
Notre Dame of Maryland University ... MD ... 206
University of Maryland Eastern Shore ... MD ... 208
University of Maryland, Baltimore ... MD ... 207
#MCPHS University ... MA ... 221
Northeastern University ... MA ... 223
Western New England University ... MA ... 225
Ferris State University ... MI ... 230
University of Michigan-Ann Arbor ... MI ... 237
Wayne State University ... MI ... 239
University of Minnesota ... MN ... 250
University of Mississippi ... MS ... 256
University of Mississippi Medical Center ... MS ... 256
St. Louis College of Pharmacy ... MO ... 266
University of Missouri - Columbia ... MO ... 268
University of Missouri - Kansas City ... MO ... 268
University of Montana - Missoula ... MT ... 271
Creighton University ... NE ... 274
University of Nebraska Medical Center ... NE ... 277
Roseman University of Health Sciences ... NV ... 280
Fairleigh Dickinson University ... NJ ... 286
Rutgers University - New Brunswick ... NJ ... 290
University of New Mexico Main Campus ... NM ... 296
Albany College of Pharmacy and Health Sciences ... NY ... 297
D'Youville College ... NY ... 307
St. John Fisher College ... NY ... 322
St. John's University ... NY ... 322
@State University of New York at Binghamton ... NY ... 325
#Touro College ... NY ... 331
University at Buffalo-SUNY ... NY ... 325
Campbell University ... NC ... 336
@High Point University ... NC ... 338
University of North Carolina at Chapel Hill ... NC ... 351
Wingate University ... NC ... 353
North Dakota State University Main Campus ... ND ... 354
Cedarville University ... OH ... 358
Northeast Ohio Medical University ... OH ... 366
Ohio Northern University ... OH ... 367
Ohio State University Main Campus, The ... OH ... 367
University of Cincinnati Main Campus ... OH ... 371
University of Findlay, The ... OH ... 372
University of Toledo ... OH ... 372
Southwestern Oklahoma State University ... OK ... 380
Oregon State University ... OR ... 385
Pacific University ... OR ... 385
Duquesne University ... PA ... 394
Lake Erie College of Osteopathic Medicine ... PA ... 399
Temple University ... PA ... 411
Thomas Jefferson University ... PA ... 411
University of Pittsburgh ... PA ... 412
University of the Sciences in Philadelphia ... PA ... 413
Wilkes University ... PA ... 414
University of Puerto Rico-Medical Sciences Campus ... PR ... 528
University of Rhode Island ... RI ... 417
Medical University of South Carolina ... SC ... 422
Presbyterian College ... SC ... 423
University of South Carolina Columbia ... SC ... 424
South Dakota State University ... SD ... 429
Belmont University ... TN ... 430
East Tennessee State University ... TN ... 431
Lipscomb University ... TN ... 433
South College ... TN ... 436
Union University ... TN ... 439
University of Tennessee Health Science Center ... TN ... 440
Texas A & M University - Kingsville ... TX ... 460
Texas Southern University ... TX ... 461
Texas Tech University Health Sciences Center ... TX ... 463
University of Houston ... TX ... 465
University of North Texas Health Science Center at Fort Worth ... TX ... 466
University of Texas at Austin ... TX ... 467
@University of Texas at El Paso ... TX ... 467
@University of Texas at Tyler ... TX ... 468
University of the Incarnate Word ... TX ... 465
University of Utah, The ... UT ... 472
Appalachian College of Pharmacy ... VA ... 477
#Hampton University ... VA ... 481
Shenandoah University ... VA ... 485
Virginia Commonwealth University ... VA ... 487
University of Washington ... WA ... 499
Washington State University ... WA ... 499
Marshall University ... WV ... 504
University of Charleston ... WV ... 502
West Virginia University ... WV ... 505
Concordia University Wisconsin ... WI ... 507
@Medical College of Wisconsin ... WI ... 508
University of Wisconsin-Madison ... WI ... 510
University of Wyoming ... WY ... 517

PHLEB: National Accrediting Agency for Clinical Laboratory Sciences: phlebotomist (C)

Phillips Community College of the University of Arkansas ... AR ... 22
South Arkansas Community College ... AR ... 21
Southeast Arkansas College ... AR ... 21
Otero Junior College ... CO ... 81
Dalton State College ... GA ... 118
Kapiolani Community College ... HI ... 130
College of Lake County ... IL ... 136
Kankakee Community College ... IL ... 142
Moraine Valley Community College ... IL ... 146
South Suburban College of Cook County ... IL ... 151
Bossier Parish Community College ... LA ... 192
Delgado Community College ... LA ... 192
L.E. Fletcher Technical Community College ... LA ... 192
Southern University at Shreveport-Louisiana ... LA ... 196
Mid Michigan Community College ... MI ... 234
St. Catherine University ... MN ... 249
University of Southern Mississippi ... MS ... 256
Miles Community College ... MT ... 271
Western Nebraska Community College ... NE ... 278
Orange County Community College ... NY ... 319
Trocaire College ... NY ... 331
Asheville - Buncombe Technical Community College ... NC ... 340
Brunswick Community College ... NC ... 341
Cape Fear Community College ... NC ... 341
Carolinas College of Health Sciences ... NC ... 336
Halifax Community College ... NC ... 343
Nash Community College ... NC ... 345
Rockingham Community College ... NC ... 346
Southwestern Community College ... NC ... 346
Wake Technical Community College ... NC ... 347
Bismarck State College ... ND ... 354
Turtle Mountain Community College ... ND ... 355
Columbus State Community College ... OH ... 360
Edison State Community College ... OH ... 361
Lorain County Community College ... OH ... 364
Tulsa Community College ... OK ... 380
Community College of Beaver County ... PA ... 392
Community College of Philadelphia ... PA ... 393
Harcum College ... PA ... 396
Montgomery County Community College ... PA ... 402
Southwest Tennessee Community College ... TN ... 438
Austin Community College District ... TX ... 443
Weatherford College ... TX ... 470

Mid-State Technical College ... WI ... 514
Milwaukee Area Technical College ... WI ... 514
Northcentral Technical College ... WI ... 514

PLNG: Planning Accreditation Board: certified planning (B,M)

Alabama Agricultural and Mechanical University ... AL ... 1
Arizona State University ... AZ ... 10
University of Arizona ... AZ ... 16
California Polytechnic State University-San Luis Obispo ... CA ... 30
California State Polytechnic University-Pomona ... CA ... 31
San Jose State University ... CA ... 34
University of California-Berkeley ... CA ... 68
University of California-Irvine ... CA ... 69
University of California-Los Angeles ... CA ... 69
University of Southern California ... CA ... 72
University of Colorado Denver|Anschutz Medical Campus ... CO ... 83
Florida Atlantic University ... FL ... 109
Florida State University ... FL ... 110
University of Florida ... FL ... 110
Georgia Institute of Technology ... GA ... 120
University of Georgia ... GA ... 127
University of Hawaii at Manoa ... HI ... 129
University of Illinois at Chicago ... IL ... 153
University of Illinois at Urbana-Champaign ... IL ... 154
Ball State University ... IN ... 156
Iowa State University ... IA ... 166
University of Iowa ... IA ... 166
Kansas State University ... KS ... 179
University of Kansas Main Campus ... KS ... 181
University of Louisville ... KY ... 190
University of New Orleans ... LA ... 194
Morgan State University ... MD ... 206
University of Maryland College Park ... MD ... 207
Harvard University ... MA ... 215
Massachusetts Institute of Technology ... MA ... 221
Tufts University ... MA ... 225
University of Massachusetts ... MA ... 216
Eastern Michigan University ... MI ... 229
Michigan State University ... MI ... 233
University of Michigan-Ann Arbor ... MI ... 237
Wayne State University ... MI ... 239
University of Minnesota ... MN ... 250
Jackson State University ... MS ... 253
Missouri State University ... MO ... 263
University of Nebraska - Lincoln ... NE ... 277
Rutgers University - New Brunswick ... NJ ... 290
University of New Mexico Main Campus ... NM ... 296
City University of New York Hunter College ... NY ... 302
Columbia University in the City of New York ... NY ... 305
Cornell University ... NY ... 306
New York University ... NY ... 318
Pratt Institute ... NY ... 320
University at Albany, SUNY ... NY ... 324
University at Buffalo-SUNY ... NY ... 325
East Carolina University ... NC ... 349
University of North Carolina at Chapel Hill ... NC ... 351
Cleveland State University ... OH ... 359
Ohio State University Main Campus, The ... OH ... 367
University of Cincinnati Main Campus ... OH ... 371
University of Oklahoma Norman Campus ... OK ... 380
Portland State University ... OR ... 386
University of Oregon ... OR ... 387
Indiana University of Pennsylvania ... PA ... 406
Temple University ... PA ... 411
University of Pennsylvania ... PA ... 412
University of Puerto Rico-Rio Piedras Campus ... PR ... 528
Clemson University ... SC ... 419
University of Memphis, The ... TN ... 439
Texas A & M University ... TX ... 459
Texas Southern University ... TX ... 461
University of Texas at Arlington, The ... TX ... 467
University of Texas at Austin ... TX ... 467
University of Utah, The ... UT ... 472
University of Virginia ... VA ... 486
Virginia Commonwealth University ... VA ... 487
Virginia Polytechnic Institute and State University ... VA ... 490
Eastern Washington University ... WA ... 494
University of Washington ... WA ... 499
Western Washington University ... WA ... 500
University of Wisconsin-Madison ... WI ... 510
University of Wisconsin-Milwaukee ... WI ... 511

PNUR: Accreditation Commission for Education in Nursing: practical nursing (C)

Bevill State Community College ... AL ... 1
Bishop State Community College ... AL ... 1
Calhoun Community College ... AL ... 1
Chattahoochee Valley Community College ... AL ... 1
Coastal Alabama Community College ... AL ... 1
Gadsden State Community College ... AL ... 2
George C. Wallace Community College - Dothan ... AL ... 2
George Corley Wallace State Community College - Selma ... AL ... 2
Lawson State Community College ... AL ... 2
Northeast Alabama Community College ... AL ... 3
Shelton State Community College ... AL ... 3
Trenholm State Technical College ... AL ... 3
Wallace State Community College - Hanceville ... AL ... 3
Baptist Health College Little Rock ... AR ... 18
Hartnell College ... CA ... 45
Colorado Mesa University ... CO ... 77
Delaware Technical Community College, Terry Campus ... DE ... 90
Mercy Hospital College of Nursing ... FL ... 103
Pensacola State College ... FL ... 105
Augusta Technical College ... GA ... 116
Carl Sandburg College ... IL ... 134
Harper College ... IL ... 139
Lake Land College ... IL ... 143
Lincoln Land Community College ... IL ... 144
Ivy Tech Community College of Indiana-Central Indiana ... IN ... 161
Vincennes University ... IN ... 165
Western Iowa Tech Community College ... IA ... 174
Hutchinson Community College ... KS ... 178
West Kentucky Community and Technical College ... KY ... 187
L.E. Fletcher Technical Community College. ... LA ... 192
College of Southern Maryland ... MD ... 203
Hagerstown Community College ... MD ... 204
Howard Community College ... MD ... 204
Mount Wachusett Community College ... MA ... 220
North Shore Community College ... MA ... 220
Northern Essex Community College ... MA ... 220
Quincy College ... MA ... 223
Quinsigamond Community College ... MA ... 220
Alpena Community College ... MI ... 227
Davenport University ... MI ... 229
Grand Rapids Community College ... MI ... 230
Northwestern Michigan College ... MI ... 235
Schoolcraft College ... MI ... 236
Lake Superior College ... MN ... 245
Minnesota State College Southeast ... MN ... 245
Ridgewater College ... MN ... 247
Rochester Community and Technical College ... MN ... 247
Saint Cloud Technical and Community College ... MN ... 247
Saint Paul College-A Community & Technical College ... MN ... 247
Meridian Community College ... MS ... 253
Mississippi Gulf Coast Community College ... MS ... 254
Southeast Community College ... NE ... 276
Western Nebraska Community College ... NE ... 278
Brightwood College ... NV ... 278
College of Southern Nevada ... NV ... 278
Union County College ... NJ ... 292
Monroe College ... NY ... 315
Samaritan Hospital School of Nursing ... NY ... 323
SUNY Canton-College of Technology ... NY ... 329
Trocaire College ... NY ... 331
Durham Technical Community College ... NC ... 342
Edgecombe Community College ... NC ... 343
Gaston College ... NC ... 343
Rowan-Cabarrus Community College ... NC ... 346
Sampson Community College ... NC ... 346
Wayne Community College ... NC ... 347
Dickinson State University ... ND ... 354
North Dakota State College of Science ... ND ... 355
United Tribes Technical College ... ND ... 355
Hocking College ... OH ... 362
Lorain County Community College ... OH ... 364
HACC, Central Pennsylvania's Community College ... PA ... 396
Lehigh Carbon Community College ... PA ... 400
Northampton Community College ... PA ... 403
Pennsylvania College of Technology ... PA ... 404
Pittsburgh Technical College ... PA ... 408
Reading Area Community College ... PA ... 408
Community College of Rhode Island ... RI ... 416
Aiken Technical College ... SC ... 418
Horry-Georgetown Technical College ... SC ... 421
Midlands Technical College ... SC ... 422
Orangeburg-Calhoun Technical College ... SC ... 423
Technical College of the Lowcountry ... SC ... 424
Tri-County Technical College ... SC ... 424
Trident Technical College ... SC ... 424
York Technical College ... SC ... 426
Lake Area Technical Institute ... SD ... 427
Austin Community College District ... TX ... 443
El Centro College ... TX ... 448
Ogden-Weber Applied Technology College ... UT ... 472
Snow College ... UT ... 474
Uintah Basin Technical College ... UT ... 472
Vermont Technical College ... VT ... 477
Centra College of Nursing ... VA ... 478
Global Health College ... VA ... 481
Riverside College of Health Careers ... VA ... 484
Fox Valley Technical College ... WI ... 513
Milwaukee Area Technical College ... WI ... 514
Northeast Wisconsin Technical College ... WI ... 514

POD: American Podiatric Medical Association: podiatry (FP,D)

Samuel Merritt University ... CA ... 59
Western University of Health Sciences ... CA ... 74
Barry University ... FL ... 95
Rosalind Franklin University of Medicine & Science ... IL ... 150
Des Moines University ... IA ... 168
New York College of Podiatric Medicine ... NY ... 317
Kent State University Kent Campus ... OH ... 363
Temple University ... PA ... 411

POLYT: Commission on Accreditation of Allied Health Education Programs: polysomnographic technologist education (C,A)

Wallace State Community College - Hanceville ... AL ... 3
Gateway Community College ... AZ ... 13
Baptist Health College Little Rock ... AR ... 18
Concorde Career College ... CA ... 40
Orange Coast College ... CA ... 38
Santa Fe College ... FL ... 107
Central Georgia Technical College ... GA ... 117
College of DuPage ... IL ... 136
Moraine Valley Community College ... IL ... 146
Delgado Community College ... LA ... 192
Community College of Baltimore County, The ... MD ... 203
Montgomery College ... MD ... 205
Northern Essex Community College ... MA ... 220
Baker College of Flint ... MI ... 227
Minneapolis Community and Technical College ... MN ... 245
Coahoma Community College ... MS ... 252
Southeast Community College ... NE ... 276
Thomas Edison State University ... NJ ... 292
Genesee Community College ... NY ... 309
Hudson Valley Community College ... NY ... 310
Stony Brook University ... NY ... 325
Catawba Valley Community College ... NC ... 341
Central Carolina Community College ... NC ... 341
Lenoir Community College ... NC ... 344
Pitt Community College ... NC ... 345
Sandhills Community College ... NC ... 346
University of North Carolina at Charlotte ... NC ... 351
Cuyahoga Community College ... OH ... 360
Mercy College of Ohio ... OH ... 365
Concorde Career College ... OR ... 382
Linn-Benton Community College ... OR ... 384
Oregon Institute of Technology ... OR ... 385
Concorde Career College ... TN ... 431
Roane State Community College ... TN ... 438
Volunteer State Community College ... TN ... 438
Alvin Community College ... TX ... 442
Collin County Community College District ... TX ... 446
Concorde Career Institute ... TX ... 446

PPPA: Provisional Program Participation Agreement

Lincoln University ... CA ... 48
Merit University ... CA ... 52
Key College ... FL ... 102
Delta School of Business & Technology, DBA Delta Tech ... LA ... 191
Pioneer Pacific College ... OR ... 386

PSPSY: American Psychological Association: combined professional-scientific psychology (D)

University of South Alabama ... AL ... 9
Northern Arizona University ... AZ ... 14
University of California-Santa Barbara ... CA ... 70
Florida State University ... FL ... 110
Kean University ... NJ ... 286
Pace University ... NY ... 319
University at Buffalo-SUNY ... NY ... 325
Yeshiva University ... NY ... 334
Utah State University ... UT ... 473
James Madison University ... VA ... 481
University of Virginia ... VA ... 486

PTA: American Physical Therapy Association: physical therapy (M,D)

Alabama State University ... AL ... 4
@Samford University ... AL ... 6
University of Alabama at Birmingham ... AL ... 8
University of South Alabama ... AL ... 9
Northern Arizona University ... AZ ... 14
Arkansas State University-Jonesboro ... AR ... 18
Harding University Main Campus ... AR ... 19
@University of Arkansas for Medical Sciences ... AR ... 22
University of Central Arkansas ... AR ... 23
Azusa Pacific University ... CA ... 26
California State University-Fresno ... CA ... 32
California State University-Long Beach ... CA ... 32
California State University-Northridge ... CA ... 33
California State University-Sacramento ... CA ... 33
Chapman University ... CA ... 36
Loma Linda University ... CA ... 48
Mount Saint Mary's University ... CA ... 52
Samuel Merritt University ... CA ... 59
San Diego State University ... CA ... 34
San Francisco State University ... CA ... 34
University of California-San Francisco ... CA ... 70
University of St. Augustine for Health Sciences ... CA ... 71
University of Southern California ... CA ... 72
University of the Pacific ... CA ... 70
@West Coast University ... CA ... 73
Western University of Health Sciences ... CA ... 74
Regis University ... CO ... 82
University of Colorado Denver|Anschutz Medical Campus ... CO ... 83
Quinnipiac University ... CT ... 88
Sacred Heart University ... CT ... 88
University of Connecticut ... CT ... 88
University of Hartford ... CT ... 89
University of Delaware ... DE ... 90
George Washington University ... DC ... 92
Howard University ... DC ... 92
@Adventist University of Health Sciences ... FL ... 94
Florida Agricultural and Mechanical University ... FL ... 109
Florida Gulf Coast University ... FL ... 109
Florida International University ... FL ... 109
Nova Southeastern University ... FL ... 104
University of Central Florida ... FL ... 110
University of Florida ... FL ... 110
University of Miami ... FL ... 112
University of North Florida ... FL ... 110
University of South Florida ... FL ... 111
Armstrong State University ... GA ... 115
Augusta University ... GA ... 116
@Brenau University ... GA ... 116
Emory University ... GA ... 119
Georgia State University ... GA ... 121
Mercer University ... GA ... 122
University of North Georgia ... GA ... 127
Idaho State University ... ID ... 132
Bradley University ... IL ... 134
Governors State University ... IL ... 138
Midwestern University ... IL ... 145
Northern Illinois University ... IL ... 147
Northwestern University ... IL ... 148
Rosalind Franklin University of Medicine & Science ... IL ... 150
University of Illinois at Chicago ... IL ... 153
@Indiana State University ... IN ... 159
Indiana University-Purdue University Indianapolis ... IN ... 160
Trine University ... IN ... 164
University of Evansville ... IN ... 164
University of Indianapolis ... IN ... 164
@Briar Cliff University ... IA ... 167
Clarke University ... IA ... 167
Des Moines University ... IA ... 168
St. Ambrose University ... IA ... 173
University of Iowa ... IA ... 166
University of Saint Mary ... KS ... 182
Wichita State University ... KS ... 182
Bellarmine University ... KY ... 183
University of Kentucky ... KY ... 190
Western Kentucky University ... KY ... 190
Louisiana State University Health Sciences Center at Shreveport ... LA ... 194
Louisiana State University Health Sciences Center-New Orleans ... LA ... 194
Husson University ... ME ... 199
University of New England ... ME ... 202
University of Maryland Eastern Shore ... MD ... 208
University of Maryland, Baltimore ... MD ... 207
American International College ... MA ... 210
Boston University ... MA ... 212
MCPHS University ... MA ... 221
MGH Institute of Health Professions ... MA ... 222
Northeastern University ... MA ... 223
Simmons College ... MA ... 224
Springfield College ... MA ... 224
University of Massachusetts Lowell ... MA ... 217
Andrews University ... MI ... 227
Central Michigan University ... MI ... 228
Grand Valley State University ... MI ... 230
Oakland University ... MI ... 235
University of Michigan-Flint ... MI ... 238
Wayne State University ... MI ... 239
College of Saint Scholastica, The ... MN ... 241
Concordia University, St. Paul ... MN ... 241
St. Catherine University ... MN ... 249
University of Minnesota ... MN ... 250
University of Mississippi Medical Center ... MS ... 256
@William Carey University ... MS ... 256
Maryville University of Saint Louis ... MO ... 262
Missouri State University ... MO ... 263
Rockhurst University ... MO ... 265
Saint Louis University ... MO ... 266
Southwest Baptist University ... MO ... 267
University of Missouri - Columbia ... MO ... 268
Washington University in St. Louis ... MO ... 269
University of Montana - Missoula ... MT ... 271

PTAA: American Physical Therapy Association: physical therapy assistant (A)

McLennan Community College ... TX ... 452
Navarro College ... TX ... 453
Northeast Texas Community College ... TX ... 453
Odessa College ... TX ... 454
St. Philip's College ... TX ... 441
San Jacinto College South ... TX ... 456
South Plains College ... TX ... 456
South Texas College ... TX ... 456
Tarrant County College District ... TX ... 458
Tyler Junior College ... TX ... 464
Victoria College ... TX ... 470
Weatherford College ... TX ... 470
Western Technical College ... TX ... 470
Wharton County Junior College ... TX ... 471
Dixie State University ... UT ... 473
Provo College ... UT ... 472
Salt Lake Community College ... UT ... 474
Germanna Community College ... VA ... 488
Jefferson College of Health Sciences ... VA ... 482
Northern Virginia Community College ... VA ... 488
Riverside College of Health Careers ... VA ... 484
Tidewater Community College ... VA ... 489
Wytheville Community College ... VA ... 490
Green River College ... WA ... 495
Lake Washington Institute of Technology ... WA ... 495
Olympic College ... WA ... 496
Spokane Falls Community College ... WA ... 494
Whatcom Community College ... WA ... 500
Blue Ridge Community and Technical College ... WV ... 502
Mountwest Community and Technical College ... WV ... 503
#New River Community and Technical College ... WV ... 503
Pierpont Community & Technical College ... WV ... 503
Blackhawk Technical College ... WI ... 513
Chippewa Valley Technical College ... WI ... 513
Gateway Technical College ... WI ... 513
Madison Area Technical College ... WI ... 514
Milwaukee Area Technical College ... WI ... 514
Northeast Wisconsin Technical College ... WI ... 514
Southwest Wisconsin Technical College ... WI ... 515
Western Technical College ... WI ... 515
Laramie County Community College ... WY ... 516

RABN: Association of Advanced Rabbinical and Talmudic Schools: rabbinical and Talmudic education (B, M,D)

Yeshiva Ohr Elchonon Chabad/West Coast Talmudical Seminary ... CA ... 75
Talmudic College of Florida ... FL ... 112
Yeshiva Gedolah Rabbinical College ... FL ... 114
Telshe Yeshiva-Chicago ... IL ... 152
Bais HaMedrash & Mesivta of Baltimore ... MD ... 202
Ner Israel Rabbinical College ... MD ... 206
Yeshiva College of the Nation's Capital ... MD ... 210
Yeshiva Beth Yehuda - Yeshiva Gedolah of Greater Detroit ... MI ... 239
Bais Medrash Toras Chesed ... NJ ... 283
@Bais Medrash Zicron Meir ... NJ ... 283
Beth Medrash Govoha ... NJ ... 283
Rabbi Jacob Joseph School ... NJ ... 289
Rabbinical College of America ... NJ ... 289
Talmudical Academy of New Jersey ... NJ ... 292
@Yeshiva Bais Aharon ... NJ ... 292
Yeshiva Gedolah of Cliffwood ... NJ ... 292
@Yeshiva Gedolah Shaarei Schmuel ... NJ ... 293
Yeshiva Gedolah Zichron Leyma ... NJ ... 293
Yeshiva Toras Chaim ... NJ ... 293
Yeshiva Yesodei Hatorah ... NJ ... 293
Bais Binyomin Academy, Inc ... NY ... 298
Be'er Yaakov Talmudic Seminary ... NY ... 299
Beis Medrash Heichal Dovid ... NY ... 299
@Bet Medrash Gadol Ateret Torah ... NY ... 299
Beth Hamedrash Shaarei Yosher Institute ... NY ... 299
Beth Hatalmud Rabbinical College ... NY ... 299
Beth Medrash Meor Yitzchok ... NY ... 299
Central Yeshiva Beth Joseph ... NY ... 300
Central Yeshiva Tomchei Tmimim Lubavitch America ... NY ... 300
Kehilath Yakov Rabbinical Seminary ... NY ... 312
Machzikei Hadath Rabbinical College ... NY ... 313
Mesivta of Eastern Parkway Rabbinical Seminary ... NY ... 315
Mesivta Tifereth Jerusalem of America ... NY ... 315
Mesivta Torah Vodaath Seminary ... NY ... 315
Mirrer Yeshiva Central Institute ... NY ... 315
Ohr Hameir Theological Seminary ... NY ... 319
Ohr Somayach Tanenbaum Educational Center ... NY ... 319
Rabbinical Academy Mesivta Rabbi Chaim Berlin ... NY ... 320
Rabbinical College Beth Shraga ... NY ... 320
Rabbinical College Bobover Yeshiva B'nei Zion ... NY ... 320
Rabbinical College of Long Island ... NY ... 320
Rabbinical College Ohr Shimon Yisroel ... NY ... 320
@Rabbinical College Ohr Yisroel ... NY ... 320
Rabbinical Seminary of America ... NY ... 320
Sh'or Yoshuv Rabbinical College ... NY ... 324
Talmudical Institute of Upstate New York ... NY ... 330
Talmudical Seminary of Bobov ... NY ... 331
Talmudical Seminary Oholei Torah ... NY ... 331
Torah Temimah Talmudical Seminary ... NY ... 331
United Talmudical Seminary ... NY ... 332
U.T.A. Mesivta of Kiryas Joel ... NY ... 332
@Yeshiva and Kolel Bais Medrash Elyon ... NY ... 334
Yeshiva Derech Chaim ... NY ... 334
Yeshiva D'Monsey Rabbinical College ... NY ... 334
Yeshiva Gedolah Imrei Yosef D'Spinka ... NY ... 334
Yeshiva Gedolah Kesser Torah ... NY ... 334
Yeshiva Gedolah Ohr Yisrael ... NY ... 334
Yeshiva Karlin Stolin Beth Aaron V'Israel Rabbinical Institute ... NY ... 334
Yeshiva of Far Rockaway ... NY ... 334
Yeshiva of Machzikai Hadas ... NY ... 334
Yeshiva of Nitra Rabbinical College ... NY ... 334
Yeshiva of the Telshe Alumni ... NY ... 334
Yeshiva Shaar HaTorah-Grodno ... NY ... 334
Yeshiva Shaarei Torah of Rockland ... NY ... 334
@Yeshiva Sholom Shachna ... NY ... 334
Yeshiva Zichron Aryeh ... NY ... 335
@Yeshivas Maharit Dsatmar ... NY ... 335
Yeshivas Novominsk ... NY ... 335
Yeshivath Viznitz ... NY ... 335
Rabbinical College of Telshe ... OH ... 369
Talmudical Yeshiva of Philadelphia ... PA ... 411
Yeshiva Beth Moshe ... PA ... 415

RAD: Joint Review Committee on Education in Radiologic Technology: radiography (C,A,B)

Gadsden State Community College ... AL ... 2
George C. Wallace Community College - Dothan ... AL ... 2
Jefferson State Community College ... AL ... 2
Southern Union State Community College ... AL ... 3
#Trenholm State Technical College ... AL ... 3
University of South Alabama ... AL ... 9
Wallace State Community College - Hanceville ... AL ... 3
Arizona Western College ... AZ ... 11
Central Arizona College ... AZ ... 11
Mohave Community College ... AZ ... 14
Pima Community College ... AZ ... 15
Pima Medical Institute-Tucson ... AZ ... 15
Yavapai College ... AZ ... 17
Arkansas State University-Jonesboro ... AR ... 18
Baptist Health College Little Rock ... AR ... 18
National Park College ... AR ... 20
North Arkansas College ... AR ... 20
South Arkansas Community College ... AR ... 21
Southeast Arkansas College ... AR ... 21
University of Arkansas at Fort Smith ... AR ... 22
University of Arkansas for Medical Sciences AR ... 22
Antelope Valley College ... CA ... 26
Bakersfield College ... CA ... 47
Brightwood College ... CA ... 27
Cabrillo College ... CA ... 28
California State University-Northridge ... CA ... 33
Cañada College ... CA ... 61
Chaffey College ... CA ... 36
Charles R. Drew University of Medicine & Science ... CA ... 36
City College of San Francisco ... CA ... 37
Cypress College ... CA ... 53
El Camino College ... CA ... 42
Foothill College ... CA ... 43
Fresno City College ... CA ... 66
Gurnick Academy of Medical Arts ... CA ... 45
Kaiser Permanente School of Allied Health Sciences ... CA ... 46
Loma Linda University ... CA ... 48
Los Angeles City College ... CA ... 49
Merced College ... CA ... 51
Merritt College ... CA ... 56
Moorpark College ... CA ... 73
Mt. San Antonio College ... CA ... 52
Orange Coast College ... CA ... 38
Pasadena City College ... CA ... 56
San Diego Mesa College ... CA ... 60
Santa Barbara City College ... CA ... 62
Santa Rosa Junior College ... CA ... 62
University of California-Los Angeles ... CA ... 69
Yuba College ... CA ... 76
Colorado Mesa University ... CO ... 77
Community College of Denver ... CO ... 79
Concorde Career College ... CO ... 79
Red Rocks Community College ... CO ... 82
UCH Memorial Hospital School Of Radiologic Technology ... CO ... 82
Capital Community College ... CT ... 85
Gateway Community College ... CT ... 85
Manchester Community College ... CT ... 85
Middlesex Community College ... CT ... 86
Naugatuck Valley Community College ... CT ... 86
Quinnipiac University ... CT ... 88
St. Vincent's College ... CT ... 88
University of Hartford ... CT ... 89
Adventist University of Health Sciences ... FL ... 94
Bethesda College of Health Sciences ... FL ... 95
Broward College ... FL ... 96
Eastern Florida State College ... FL ... 97
Florida SouthWestern State College ... FL ... 100
Gulf Coast State College ... FL ... 101
Hillsborough Community College ... FL ... 101
Indian River State College ... FL ... 101
Keiser University ... FL ... 102
Miami Dade College ... FL ... 103
Palm Beach State College ... FL ... 105
Pensacola State College ... FL ... 105
Polk State College ... FL ... 105
St. Petersburg College ... FL ... 107
Santa Fe College ... FL ... 107
South Florida State College ... FL ... 108
State College of Florida, Manatee-Sarasota. FL ... 108
Valencia College ... FL ... 113
Albany State University ... GA ... 114
Albany Technical College ... GA ... 114
Armstrong State University ... GA ... 115
Athens Technical College ... GA ... 115
Atlanta Technical College ... GA ... 115
Augusta Technical College ... GA ... 116
Central Georgia Technical College ... GA ... 117
Chattahoochee Technical College ... GA ... 117
Coastal Pines Technical College ... GA ... 117
College of Coastal Georgia ... GA ... 118
Columbus Technical College ... GA ... 118
Dalton State College ... GA ... 118
Emory University ... GA ... 119
Georgia Northwestern Technical College ... GA ... 120
Gwinnett Technical College ... GA ... 121
Lanier Technical College ... GA ... 122
Oconee Fall Line Technical College-South Campus ... GA ... 123
Ogeechee Technical College ... GA ... 123
Southeastern Technical College ... GA ... 126
Southern Regional Technical College ... GA ... 126
West Georgia Technical College ... GA ... 128
Wiregrass Georgia Technical College ... GA ... 128
Kapiolani Community College ... HI ... 130
Boise State University ... ID ... 131
College of Southern Idaho ... ID ... 131
Idaho State University ... ID ... 132
Lewis-Clark State College ... ID ... 132
North Idaho College ... ID ... 132
College of DuPage ... IL ... 136
College of Lake County ... IL ... 136
Danville Area Community College ... IL ... 137
Elgin Community College ... IL ... 138
Harper College ... IL ... 139
Heartland Community College ... IL ... 139
Illinois Central College ... IL ... 139
Illinois Eastern Community Colleges Olney Central College ... IL ... 140
Kaskaskia College ... IL ... 142
Kishwaukee College ... IL ... 142
Lincoln Land Community College ... IL ... 144
Malcolm X College, One of the City Colleges of Chicago ... IL ... 136
Moraine Valley Community College ... IL ... 146
Northwestern College ... IL ... 148
Parkland College ... IL ... 148
Rend Lake College ... IL ... 149
Resurrection University ... IL ... 149
Richland Community College ... IL ... 149
Sauk Valley Community College ... IL ... 151
Southern Illinois University Carbondale ... IL ... 152
Southwestern Illinois College ... IL ... 152
Trinity College of Nursing & Health Sciences ... IL ... 153
Triton College ... IL ... 153
Ball State University ... IN ... 156
Indiana University Kokomo ... IN ... 160
Indiana University Northwest ... IN ... 160
Indiana University-Purdue University Fort Wayne ... IN ... 160
Indiana University-Purdue University Indianapolis ... IN ... 160
Indiana University South Bend ... IN ... 160
Ivy Tech Community College of Indiana-Central Indiana ... IN ... 161
St. Vincent College of Health Professions ... IN ... 164
University of Saint Francis ... IN ... 165
University of Southern Indiana ... IN ... 165
Allen College ... IA ... 166
Indian Hills Community College ... IA ... 169
Iowa Central Community College ... IA ... 170
Mercy College of Health Sciences ... IA ... 171
St. Luke's College ... IA ... 173
Scott Community College ... IA ... 169
#University of Iowa ... IA ... 166
Fort Hays State University ... KS ... 177
Hutchinson Community College ... KS ... 178
Labette Community College ... KS ... 179
Newman University ... KS ... 180
Washburn University ... KS ... 182
Bluegrass Community and Technical College ... KY ... 185
Elizabethtown Community and Technical College ... KY ... 185
Hazard Community and Technical College . KY ... 185
Jefferson Community and Technical College ... KY ... 186
Madisonville Community College ... KY ... 186
Morehead State University ... KY ... 188
Northern Kentucky University ... KY ... 188
Owensboro Community and Technical College ... KY ... 186
Somerset Community College ... KY ... 186
Southcentral Kentucky Community and Technical College ... KY ... 187
Spencerian College ... KY ... 189
West Kentucky Community and Technical College ... KY ... 187
Delgado Community College ... LA ... 192
Fortis College ... LA ... 191
Franciscan Missionaries of Our Lady University ... LA ... 191
Louisiana State University at Alexandria ... LA ... 194
Louisiana State University at Eunice ... LA ... 194
McNeese State University ... LA ... 197
Northwestern State University ... LA ... 197
Southern University at Shreveport-Louisiana LA ... 196
University of Holy Cross ... LA ... 196
University of Louisiana at Monroe ... LA ... 198
Eastern Maine Community College ... ME ... 199
Kennebec Valley Community College ... ME ... 200
Maine College of Health Professions ... ME ... 199
Southern Maine Community College ... ME ... 200
#Allegany College of Maryland ... MD ... 202
Anne Arundel Community College ... MD ... 202
Chesapeake College ... MD ... 203
Community College of Baltimore County, The ... MD ... 203
Hagerstown Community College ... MD ... 204
Howard Community College ... MD ... 204
Montgomery College ... MD ... 205
Prince George's Community College ... MD ... 206
#Washington Adventist University ... MD ... 209
Wor-Wic Community College ... MD ... 210
Bunker Hill Community College ... MA ... 219
Holyoke Community College ... MA ... 219
Massachusetts Bay Community College ... MA ... 220
Massasoit Community College ... MA ... 220
MCPHS University ... MA ... 221
Middlesex Community College ... MA ... 220
North Shore Community College ... MA ... 220
Northern Essex Community College ... MA ... 220
Quinsigamond Community College ... MA ... 220
Regis College ... MA ... 224
Roxbury Community College ... MA ... 221
Springfield Technical Community College ... MA ... 221
Delta College ... MI ... 229
Ferris State University ... MI ... 230
Grand Rapids Community College ... MI ... 230
Henry Ford College ... MI ... 231
Jackson College ... MI ... 231
Kellogg Community College ... MI ... 232
Lake Michigan College ... MI ... 232
Lansing Community College ... MI ... 232
Mid Michigan Community College ... MI ... 234
Northern Michigan University ... MI ... 235
Oakland Community College ... MI ... 235
St. Clair County Community College ... MI ... 236
Washtenaw Community College ... MI ... 238
Wayne State University ... MI ... 239
Century College ... MN ... 244
Dunwoody College of Technology ... MN ... 242
Lake Superior College ... MN ... 245
Minnesota State College Southeast ... MN ... 245
Minnesota State Community and Technical College ... MN ... 245
Minnesota West Community and Technical College ... MN ... 246
Northland Community and Technical College ... MN ... 246
Riverland Community College ... MN ... 247
St. Catherine University ... MN ... 249
Copiah-Lincoln Community College ... MS ... 252
Hinds Community College ... MS ... 253
Itawamba Community College ... MS ... 253
Jones County Junior College ... MS ... 253
Meridian Community College ... MS ... 253
Mississippi Delta Community College ... MS ... 254
Mississippi Gulf Coast Community College . MS ... 254
Northeast Mississippi Community College ... MS ... 255
Pearl River Community College ... MS ... 255
University of Mississippi Medical Center ... MS ... 256
Avila University ... MO ... 257
Cox College ... MO ... 259
Jefferson College ... MO ... 261
Metropolitan Community College - Penn Valley ... MO ... 262
Mineral Area College ... MO ... 263
Missouri Southern State University ... MO ... 263
Southeast Missouri Hospital College of Nursing and Health Sciences ... MO ... 266
Southwest Baptist University ... MO ... 267
State Fair Community College ... MO ... 267
State Technical College of Missouri ... MO ... 267
University of Missouri - Columbia ... MO ... 268
CHI Health School of Radiologic Technology ... NE ... 273

RADDOS: Joint Review Committee on Education in Radiologic Technology: medical dosimetry (C,B,M)

RADMAG: Joint Review Committee on Education in Radiologic Technology: magnetic resonance (C,B)

RTT: Joint Review Committee on Education in Radiologic Technology: radiation therapist/technologist (C, A,B)

SC: Southern Association of Colleges and Schools, Commission on Colleges

SCPSY: American Psychological Association: school psychology (D)

University of North Carolina at Chapel Hill .. NC ... 351
Kent State University Kent Campus ... OH ... 363
Ohio State University Main Campus, The ... OH ... 367
University of Cincinnati Main Campus ... OH ... 371
Oklahoma State University ... OK ... 377
University of Oregon ... OR ... 387
Duquesne University ... PA ... 394
Lehigh University ... PA ... 400
Penn State University Park ... PA ... 403
Temple University ... PA ... 411
University of Rhode Island ... RI ... 417
University of South Carolina Columbia ... SC ... 424
University of Memphis, The ... TN ... 439
University of Tennessee, Knoxville ... TN ... 439
Texas A & M University ... TX ... 459
Texas Woman's University ... TX ... 464
University of Houston ... TX ... 465
University of Texas at Austin ... TX ... 467
University of Utah, The ... UT ... 472
University of Washington ... WA .. 499
University of Wisconsin-Madison ... WI ... 510
University of Wisconsin-Milwaukee ... WI ... 511

SP: American Speech-Language-Hearing Association: speech-language pathology (M)

Alabama Agricultural and Mechanical University ... AL ... 1
Auburn University ... AL ... 4
@Samford University ... AL ... 6
University of Alabama, The ... AL ... 8
University of Montevallo ... AL ... 8
University of South Alabama ... AL ... 9
Arizona State University ... AZ ... 10
Northern Arizona University ... AZ ... 14
University of Arizona ... AZ ... 16
Arkansas State University-Jonesboro ... AR ... 18
Harding University Main Campus ... AR ... 19
University of Arkansas for Medical Sciences AR ... 22
University of Arkansas Main Campus ... AR ... 21
University of Central Arkansas ... AR ... 23
@Biola University ... CA ... 27
@California Baptist University ... CA ... 28
California State University-Chico ... CA ... 31
California State University-East Bay ... CA ... 31
California State University-Fresno ... CA ... 32
California State University-Fullerton ... CA ... 32
California State University-Long Beach ... CA ... 32
California State University-Los Angeles ... CA ... 32
California State University-Northridge ... CA ... 33
California State University-Sacramento ... CA ... 33
California State University-San Marcos ... CA ... 33
#Chapman University ... CA ... 36
Loma Linda University ... CA ... 48
San Diego State University ... CA ... 34
San Francisco State University ... CA ... 34
San Jose State University ... CA ... 34
University of Redlands ... CA ... 71
University of the Pacific ... CA ... 70
University of Colorado Boulder ... CO ... 83
University of Northern Colorado ... CO ... 83
@Sacred Heart University ... CT ... 88
Southern Connecticut State University ... CT ... 85
University of Connecticut ... CT ... 88
@University of Delaware ... DE ... 90
Gallaudet University ... DC ... 91
George Washington University ... DC ... 92
Howard University ... DC ... 92
University of the District of Columbia ... DC ... 93
Florida Atlantic University ... FL ... 109
Florida International University ... FL ... 109
Florida State University ... FL ... 110
@Jacksonville University ... FL ... 102
Nova Southeastern University ... FL ... 104
University of Central Florida ... FL ... 110
University of Florida ... FL ... 110
University of South Florida ... FL ... 111
Armstrong State University ... GA ... 115
Georgia State University ... GA ... 121
University of Georgia ... GA ... 127
University of West Georgia ... GA ... 127
Valdosta State University ... GA ... 127
University of Hawaii at Manoa ... HI ... 129
Idaho State University ... ID ... 132
Eastern Illinois University ... IL ... 138
@Elmhurst College ... IL ... 138
Governors State University ... IL ... 138
Illinois State University ... IL ... 140
@Midwestern University ... IL ... 145
Northern Illinois University ... IL ... 147
Northwestern University ... IL ... 148
Rush University ... IL ... 150
Saint Xavier University ... IL ... 151
Southern Illinois University Carbondale ... IL ... 152
Southern Illinois University Edwardsville ... IL ... 152
University of Illinois at Urbana-Champaign . IL ... 154
Western Illinois University ... IL ... 155
Ball State University ... IN ... 156
Indiana State University ... IN ... 159
Indiana University Bloomington ... IN ... 159
Purdue University Main Campus ... IN ... 163
@Saint Mary's College ... IN ... 163
St. Ambrose University ... IA ... 173
University of Iowa ... IA ... 166
University of Northern Iowa ... IA ... 167
Fort Hays State University ... KS ... 177
Kansas State University ... KS ... 179
University of Kansas Main Campus ... KS ... 181
Wichita State University ... KS ... 182
Eastern Kentucky University ... KY ... 184
Murray State University ... KY ... 188
University of Kentucky ... KY ... 190
University of Louisville ... KY ... 190
Western Kentucky University ... KY ... 190
Louisiana State University and Agricultural and Mechanical College ... LA ... 193
Louisiana State University Health Sciences Center at Shreveport ... LA ... 194
Louisiana State University Health Sciences Center-New Orleans ... LA ... 194
Louisiana Tech University ... LA ... 197
Southeastern Louisiana University ... LA ... 197
Southern University and A&M College ... LA ... 195
University of Louisiana at Lafayette ... LA ... 197
University of Louisiana at Monroe ... LA ... 198
University of Maine ... ME ... 201
Loyola University Maryland ... MD ... 205
Towson University ... MD ... 209
University of Maryland College Park ... MD ... 207
Boston University ... MA ... 212
@Bridgewater State University ... MA ... 217
Emerson College ... MA ... 214
MGH Institute of Health Professions ... MA ... 222
Northeastern University ... MA ... 223
University of Massachusetts ... MA ... 216
Worcester State University ... MA ... 219
@Andrews University ... MI ... 227
Calvin College ... MI ... 228
Central Michigan University ... MI ... 228
Eastern Michigan University ... MI ... 229
@Grand Valley State University ... MI ... 230
Michigan State University ... MI ... 233
Wayne State University ... MI ... 239
Western Michigan University ... MI ... 239
Minnesota State University Moorhead ... MN ... 246
Minnesota State University, Mankato ... MN ... 246
St. Cloud State University ... MN ... 247
University of Minnesota ... MN ... 250
University of Minnesota Duluth ... MN ... 250
Jackson State University ... MS ... 253
Mississippi University for Women ... MS ... 254
University of Mississippi ... MS ... 256
University of Southern Mississippi ... MS ... 256
Fontbonne University ... MO .. 260
Maryville University of Saint Louis ... MO .. 262
Missouri State University ... MO .. 263
Rockhurst University ... MO .. 265
Saint Louis University ... MO .. 266
Southeast Missouri State University ... MO .. 266
Truman State University ... MO ... 267
University of Central Missouri ... MO ... 268
University of Missouri - Columbia ... MO ... 268
University of Montana - Missoula ... MT ... 271
University of Nebraska at Kearney ... NE ... 277
University of Nebraska at Omaha ... NE ... 277
University of Nebraska - Lincoln ... NE ... 277
University of Nevada, Reno ... NV ... 279
University of New Hampshire ... NH ... 282
Kean University ... NJ ... 286
@Monmouth University ... NJ ... 287
Montclair State University ... NJ ... 287
Seton Hall University ... NJ ... 291
Stockton University ... NJ ... 291
William Paterson University of New Jersey . NJ ... 292
Eastern New Mexico University Main Campus ... NM ... 293
New Mexico State University Main Campus. NM ... 295
University of New Mexico Main Campus ... NM ... 296
Adelphi University ... NY ... 297
City University of New York Brooklyn College ... NY ... 301
City University of New York Herbert H. Lehman College ... NY ... 302
City University of New York Hunter College NY ... 302
City University of New York Queens College ... NY ... 303
College of Saint Rose, The ... NY ... 305
Hofstra University ... NY ... 310
@Iona College ... NY ... 311
Ithaca College ... NY ... 311
Mercy College ... NY ... 314
Molloy College ... NY ... 315
Nazareth College of Rochester ... NY ... 316
New York Medical College ... NY ... 318
New York University ... NY ... 318
St. John's University ... NY ... 322
State University of New York at Fredonia ... NY ... 325
State University of New York at New Paltz . NY ... 325
State University of New York College at Buffalo ... NY ... 326
@State University of New York College at Cortland ... NY ... 327
State University of New York College at Plattsburgh ... NY ... 327
Syracuse University ... NY ... 330
Teachers College, Columbia University ... NY ... 331
Touro College ... NY ... 331
University at Buffalo-SUNY ... NY ... 325
@Yeshiva University ... NY ... 334
Appalachian State University ... NC ... 349
East Carolina University ... NC ... 349
North Carolina Central University ... NC ... 350
University of North Carolina at Chapel Hill .. NC ... 351
University of North Carolina at Greensboro NC ... 351
Western Carolina University ... NC ... 352
Minot State University ... ND ... 354
#University of North Dakota ... ND ... 353
@Baldwin Wallace University ... OH ... 357
Bowling Green State University ... OH ... 357
Case Western Reserve University ... OH ... 358
Cleveland State University ... OH ... 359
Kent State University Kent Campus ... OH ... 363
Miami University ... OH ... 365
Ohio State University Main Campus, The ... OH ... 367
Ohio University Main Campus ... OH ... 368
University of Akron, Main Campus, The ... OH ... 371
University of Cincinnati Main Campus ... OH ... 371
University of Toledo ... OH ... 372
Northeastern State University ... OK ... 376
Oklahoma State University ... OK ... 377
University of Central Oklahoma ... OK ... 380
University of Tulsa ... OK ... 381
@Pacific University ... OR ... 385
Portland State University ... OR ... 386
University of Oregon ... OR ... 387
Bloomsburg University of Pennsylvania ... PA ... 405
California University of Pennsylvania ... PA ... 405
Clarion University of Pennsylvania ... PA ... 405
Duquesne University ... PA ... 394
East Stroudsburg University of Pennsylvania ... PA ... 406
Edinboro University ... PA ... 406
Indiana University of Pennsylvania ... PA ... 406
La Salle University ... PA ... 398
Marywood University ... PA ... 401
Misericordia University ... PA ... 401
Penn State University Park ... PA ... 403
@Salus University ... PA ... 410
Temple University ... PA ... 411
University of Pittsburgh ... PA ... 412
West Chester University of Pennsylvania ... PA ... 407
Carlos Albizu University ... PR ... 521
Universidad Del Turabo ... PR ... 526
University of Puerto Rico-Medical Sciences Campus ... PR ... 528
University of Rhode Island ... RI ... 417
South Carolina State University ... SC ... 423
University of South Carolina Columbia ... SC ... 424
University of South Dakota, The ... SD ... 428
East Tennessee State University ... TN ... 431
Tennessee State University ... TN ... 438
University of Memphis, The ... TN ... 439
University of Tennessee Health Science Center ... TN ... 440
Vanderbilt University ... TN ... 440
Abilene Christian University ... TX ... 441
Baylor University ... TX ... 444
Lamar University ... TX ... 462
Our Lady of the Lake University ... TX ... 454
Stephen F. Austin State University ... TX ... 458
Texas A & M University - Kingsville ... TX ... 460
Texas Christian University ... TX ... 461
Texas State University ... TX ... 463
Texas Tech University Health Sciences Center ... TX ... 463
Texas Woman's University ... TX ... 464
University of Houston ... TX ... 465
University of North Texas ... TX ... 466
University of Texas at Austin ... TX ... 467
University of Texas at Dallas, The ... TX ... 467
University of Texas at El Paso ... TX ... 467
University of Texas Rio Grande Valley, The TX ... 468
West Texas A & M University ... TX ... 460
Brigham Young University ... UT ... 471
@Rocky Mountain University of Health Professions ... UT ... 472
University of Utah, The ... UT ... 472
Utah State University ... UT ... 473
University of Vermont ... VT ... 476
Hampton University ... VA ... 481
James Madison University ... VA ... 481
Longwood University ... VA ... 482
Old Dominion University ... VA ... 483
Radford University ... VA ... 484
University of Virginia ... VA ... 486
Eastern Washington University ... WA .. 494
University of Washington ... WA ... 499
Washington State University ... WA .. 499
Western Washington University ... WA ... 500
Marshall University ... WV ... 504
West Virginia University ... WV .. 505
Marquette University ... WI ... 508
University of Wisconsin-Eau Claire ... WI ... 510
University of Wisconsin-Madison ... WI ... 510
University of Wisconsin-Milwaukee ... WI ... 511
University of Wisconsin-River Falls ... WI ... 511
University of Wisconsin-Stevens Point ... WI ... 511
University of Wisconsin-Whitewater ... WI ... 512
University of Wyoming ... WY .. 517

SPAA: Network of Schools of Public Policy, Affairs and Administration: public affairs and administration (M)

Auburn University ... AL ... 4
Auburn University at Montgomery ... AL ... 4
Jacksonville State University ... AL ... 6
University of Alabama at Birmingham ... AL ... 8
Arizona State University ... AZ ... 10
University of Arizona ... AZ ... 16
Arkansas State University-Jonesboro ... AR ... 18
University of Arkansas at Little Rock ... AR ... 22
California State Polytechnic University-Pomona ... CA ... 31
California State University-Bakersfield ... CA ... 31
California State University-Chico ... CA ... 31
California State University-Dominguez Hills CA ... 31
California State University-Fresno ... CA ... 32
California State University-Fullerton ... CA ... 32
California State University-Long Beach ... CA ... 32
California State University-Los Angeles ... CA ... 32
California State University-San Bernardino . CA ... 33
California State University-Stanislaus ... CA ... 33
Naval Postgraduate School ... CA ... 518
San Diego State University ... CA ... 34
San Francisco State University ... CA ... 34
San Jose State University ... CA ... 34
University of La Verne ... CA ... 70
University of San Francisco ... CA ... 72
University of Southern California ... CA ... 72
University of Colorado Colorado Springs ... CO ... 83
University of Colorado Denver|Anschutz Medical Campus ... CO ... 83
University of Connecticut ... CT ... 88
University of Delaware ... DE ... 90
American University ... DC ... 91
George Washington University ... DC ... 92
Florida Atlantic University ... FL ... 109
Florida Gulf Coast University ... FL ... 109
Florida International University ... FL ... 109
Florida State University ... FL ... 110
Nova Southeastern University ... FL ... 104
University of Central Florida ... FL ... 110
University of North Florida ... FL ... 110
University of South Florida ... FL ... 111
Albany State University ... GA ... 114
Augusta University ... GA ... 116
Clark Atlanta University ... GA ... 117
Georgia College & State University ... GA ... 119
Georgia Southern University ... GA ... 120
Georgia State University ... GA ... 121
Kennesaw State University ... GA ... 122
Savannah State University ... GA ... 125
University of Georgia ... GA ... 127
University of West Georgia ... GA ... 127
Valdosta State University ... GA ... 127
University of Hawaii at Manoa ... HI ... 129
Boise State University ... ID ... 131
DePaul University ... IL ... 137
Governors State University ... IL ... 138
Northern Illinois University ... IL ... 147
Southern Illinois University Carbondale ... IL ... 152
Southern Illinois University Edwardsville ... IL ... 152
University of Illinois at Chicago ... IL ... 153
University of Illinois at Springfield ... IL ... 154
Indiana University Bloomington ... IN ... 159
Indiana University Northwest ... IN ... 160
Indiana University-Purdue University Indianapolis ... IN ... 160
Indiana University South Bend ... IN ... 160
Kansas State University ... KS ... 179
University of Kansas Main Campus ... KS ... 181
Wichita State University ... KS ... 182
Eastern Kentucky University ... KY ... 184
Kentucky State University ... KY ... 187
Morehead State University ... KY ... 188
Northern Kentucky University ... KY ... 188
University of Kentucky ... KY ... 190
University of Louisville ... KY ... 190
Western Kentucky University ... KY ... 190
Grambling State University ... LA ... 196
Louisiana State University and Agricultural and Mechanical College ... LA ... 193
Southern University and A&M College ... LA ... 195
University of New Orleans ... LA ... 194
Bowie State University ... MD ... 208
University of Baltimore ... MD ... 209
University of Maryland College Park ... MD ... 207
Bridgewater State University ... MA ... 217
Northeastern University ... MA ... 223
Suffolk University ... MA ... 224
Central Michigan University ... MI ... 228
Eastern Michigan University ... MI ... 229
Grand Valley State University ... MI ... 230
Oakland University ... MI ... 235
Wayne State University ... MI ... 239

SURGA: Commission on Accreditation of Allied Health Education Programs: surgical assistant (C,A)

SURGT: Commission on Accreditation of Allied Health Education Programs: surgical technology (C,A)

Columbia Basin College .... WA .. 493
Renton Technical College .... WA .. 497
Seattle Central College .... WA .. 497
Spokane Community College .... WA .. 493
Yakima Valley College .... WA .. 500
Southern West Virginia Community and Technical College .... WV .. 503
West Virginia Northern Community College WV .. 503
West Virginia University at Parkersburg .... WV .. 505
Chippewa Valley Technical College .... WI 513
Gateway Technical College .... WI 513
Madison Area Technical College .... WI 514
Mid-State Technical College .... WI 514
Milwaukee Area Technical College .... WI 514
Moraine Park Technical College .... WI 514
Northcentral Technical College .... WI 514
Northeast Wisconsin Technical College .... WI 514
Waukesha County Technical College .... WI 515
Western Technical College .... WI 515
Laramie County Community College .... WY .. 516

SURTEC: Accrediting Bureau of Health Education Schools: surgical technologist (C,A)

Baptist Health College Little Rock .... AR 18
American Career College-Los Angeles .... CA 25
American Career College-Ontario .... CA 25
CBD College .... CA 35
CNI College .... CA 38
Glendale Career College .... CA 44
Valley College of Medical Careers .... CA 72
City College .... FL 96
Southern Technical College .... FL 108
Fortis College .... LA 191
Midwest Institute-Earth City .... MO .. 263
Finger Lakes Health College of Nursing .... NY 308
Mandl School - The College of Allied Health NY 313
Mohawk Valley Community College .... NY 315
Fortis College .... OH 361
Pittsburgh Career Institute .... PA 408
Meridian Institute of Surgical Assisting .... TN 434
Baptist Health System School of Health Professions .... TX 443
College of Health Care Professions, The .... TX 446
Riverside College of Health Careers .... VA 484
Sentara College of Health Sciences .... VA 485
Milwaukee Career College .... WI 508

SW: Council on Social Work Education: social work (B,M)

Alabama Agricultural and Mechanical University .... AL 1
Alabama State University .... AL 4
Auburn University .... AL 4
Jacksonville State University .... AL 6
Judson College .... AL 6
Miles College .... AL 6
Oakwood University .... AL 6
Samford University .... AL 6
Talladega College .... AL 7
Troy University .... AL 7
Tuskegee University .... AL 7
University of Alabama at Birmingham .... AL 8
University of Alabama, The .... AL 8
University of Montevallo .... AL 8
University of North Alabama .... AL 9
University of South Alabama .... AL 9
University of Alaska Anchorage .... AK 10
University of Alaska Fairbanks .... AK 10
Arizona State University .... AZ 10
Northern Arizona University .... AZ 14
Arkansas State University-Jonesboro .... AR 18
Harding University Main Campus .... AR 19
Philander Smith College .... AR 21
Southern Arkansas University .... AR 21
University of Arkansas at Little Rock .... AR 22
University of Arkansas at Monticello .... AR 22
University of Arkansas at Pine Bluff .... AR 22
University of Arkansas Main Campus .... AR 21
Azusa Pacific University .... CA 26
Brandman University .... CA 27
@California Baptist University .... CA 28
California State University-Bakersfield .... CA 31
California State University-Chico .... CA 31
California State University-Dominguez Hills CA 31
California State University-East Bay .... CA 31
California State University-Fresno .... CA 32
California State University-Fullerton .... CA 32
California State University-Long Beach .... CA 32
California State University-Los Angeles .... CA 32
California State University-Monterey Bay .... CA 33
California State University-Northridge .... CA 33
California State University-Sacramento .... CA 33
California State University-San Bernardino . CA 33
California State University-San Marcos .... CA 33
California State University-Stanislaus .... CA 33
@Fresno Pacific University .... CA 43
Humboldt State University .... CA 34
La Sierra University .... CA 47
Loma Linda University .... CA 48
Pacific Union College .... CA 55
Point Loma Nazarene University .... CA 57
San Diego State University .... CA 34
San Francisco State University .... CA 34
San Jose State University .... CA 34
University of California-Berkeley .... CA 68
University of California-Los Angeles .... CA 69
University of Southern California .... CA 72
Whittier College .... CA 75
Colorado Mesa University .... CO 77
Colorado State University .... CO 78
Colorado State University-Pueblo .... CO 78
Metropolitan State University of Denver .... CO 80
University of Denver .... CO 83
Central Connecticut State University .... CT 84
Eastern Connecticut State University .... CT 84
@Goodwin College .... CT 87
Quinnipiac University .... CT 88
Sacred Heart University .... CT 88
Southern Connecticut State University .... CT 85
University of Connecticut .... CT 88
University of Saint Joseph .... CT 89
Western Connecticut State University .... CT 85
Delaware State University .... DE 90
Catholic University of America, The .... DC 91
Gallaudet University .... DC 91
Howard University .... DC 92
University of the District of Columbia .... DC 93
Barry University .... FL 95
Florida Agricultural and Mechanical University .... FL 109
Florida Atlantic University .... FL 109
Florida Gulf Coast University .... FL 109
Florida International University .... FL 109
Florida Memorial University .... FL 99
Florida State University .... FL 110
Saint Leo University .... FL 106
Southeastern University .... FL 108
University of Central Florida .... FL 110
University of North Florida .... FL 110
University of South Florida .... FL 111
University of West Florida .... FL 111
Warner University .... FL 113
Albany State University .... GA 114
Augusta University .... GA 116
Clark Atlanta University .... GA 117
Dalton State College .... GA 118
@Fort Valley State University .... GA 119
Georgia State University .... GA 121
Kennesaw State University .... GA 122
Savannah State University .... GA 125
Thomas University .... GA 126
University of Georgia .... GA 127
Valdosta State University .... GA 127
University of Guam .... GU 520
Brigham Young University Hawaii .... HI 128
Hawaii Pacific University .... HI 129
University of Hawaii at Manoa .... HI 129
Boise State University .... ID 131
Brigham Young University-Idaho .... ID 131
Idaho State University .... ID 132
Lewis-Clark State College .... ID 132
Northwest Nazarene University .... ID 132
Aurora University .... IL 133
Bradley University .... IL 134
Chicago State University .... IL 135
DePaul University .... IL 137
Dominican University .... IL 137
Erikson Institute .... IL 138
Governors State University .... IL 138
@Greenville University .... IL 139
Illinois State University .... IL 140
Lewis University .... IL 143
Loyola University Chicago .... IL 144
MacMurray College .... IL 144
Northeastern Illinois University .... IL 147
Olivet Nazarene University .... IL 148
St. Augustine College .... IL 150
Southern Illinois University Carbondale .... IL 152
Southern Illinois University Edwardsville .... IL 152
Trinity Christian College .... IL 153
University of Chicago .... IL 153
University of Illinois at Chicago .... IL 153
University of Illinois at Springfield .... IL 154
University of Illinois at Urbana-Champaign . IL 154
University of St. Francis .... IL 154
Western Illinois University .... IL 155
Anderson University .... IN 156
Ball State University .... IN 156
Goshen College .... IN 158
Huntington University .... IN 159
Indiana State University .... IN 159
Indiana University-Purdue University Indianapolis .... IN 160
Indiana Wesleyan University .... IN 161
Manchester University .... IN 162
@Purdue University Northwest .... IN 163
Saint Mary's College .... IN 163
Taylor University .... IN 164
University of Indianapolis .... IN 164
University of Saint Francis .... IN 165
University of Southern Indiana .... IN 165
Valparaiso University .... IN 165
Briar Cliff University .... IA 167
Buena Vista University .... IA 167
Clarke University .... IA 167
Dordt College .... IA 168
@Grand View University .... IA 169
Loras College .... IA 171
Luther College .... IA 171
Mount Mercy University .... IA 172
Northwestern College .... IA 172
St. Ambrose University .... IA 173
University of Iowa .... IA 166
University of Northern Iowa .... IA 167
Wartburg College .... IA 174
Bethel College .... KS 175
Fort Hays State University .... KS 177
Kansas State University .... KS 179
Newman University .... KS 180
Pittsburg State University .... KS 180
@Tabor College .... KS 181
University of Kansas Main Campus .... KS 181
Washburn University .... KS 182
Wichita State University .... KS 182
Asbury University .... KY 183
Brescia University .... KY 183
Campbellsville University .... KY 184
Eastern Kentucky University .... KY 184
Kentucky Christian University .... KY 185
Kentucky State University .... KY 187
Morehead State University .... KY 188
Murray State University .... KY 188
Northern Kentucky University .... KY 188
Spalding University .... KY 189
University of Kentucky .... KY 190
University of Louisville .... KY 190
University of Pikeville .... KY 190
Western Kentucky University .... KY 190
Grambling State University .... LA 196
Louisiana College .... LA 191
Louisiana State University and Agricultural and Mechanical College .... LA 193
Northwestern State University .... LA 197
Southeastern Louisiana University .... LA 197
Southern University and A&M College .... LA 195
Southern University at New Orleans .... LA 195
Tulane University .... LA 196
University of Louisiana at Monroe .... LA 198
@Saint Joseph's College of Maine .... ME 200
University of Maine .... ME 201
University of Maine at Presque Isle .... ME 201
University of New England .... ME 202
University of Southern Maine .... ME 201
Bowie State University .... MD 208
Coppin State University .... MD 208
Frostburg State University .... MD 209
Hood College .... MD 204
McDaniel College .... MD 205
Morgan State University .... MD 206
Salisbury University .... MD 209
University of Maryland Baltimore County .... MD 208
University of Maryland, Baltimore .... MD 207
Anna Maria College .... MA 210
Boston College .... MA 212
Boston University .... MA 212
Bridgewater State University .... MA 217
College of Our Lady of the Elms .... MA 213
Eastern Nazarene College .... MA 214
Gordon College .... MA 215
Regis College .... MA 224
Salem State University .... MA 218
Simmons College .... MA 224
Smith College .... MA 224
Springfield College .... MA 224
Western New England University .... MA 225
Westfield State University .... MA 218
Wheelock College .... MA 226
Adrian College .... MI 226
Andrews University .... MI 227
Calvin College .... MI 228
Central Michigan University .... MI 228
Cornerstone University .... MI 229
Eastern Michigan University .... MI 229
Ferris State University .... MI 230
Grand Valley State University .... MI 230
Hope College .... MI 231
Kuyper College .... MI 232
Madonna University .... MI 233
Marygrove College .... MI 233
Michigan State University .... MI 233
Northern Michigan University .... MI 235
Oakland University .... MI 235
Saginaw Valley State University .... MI 236
Siena Heights University .... MI 236
Spring Arbor University .... MI 237
University of Detroit Mercy .... MI 237
University of Michigan-Ann Arbor .... MI 237
University of Michigan-Flint .... MI 238
Wayne State University .... MI 239
Western Michigan University .... MI 239
Augsburg College .... MN 240
Bemidji State University .... MN 244
Bethel University .... MN 240
@Capella University .... MN 241
College of Saint Scholastica, The .... MN 241
Concordia College .... MN 241
Metropolitan State University .... MN 245
Minnesota State University Moorhead .... MN 246
Minnesota State University, Mankato .... MN 246
North Central University .... MN 249
St. Catherine University .... MN 249
St. Cloud State University .... MN 247
St. Olaf College .... MN 250
Southwest Minnesota State University .... MN 248
University of Minnesota .... MN 250
University of Minnesota Duluth .... MN 250
University of Saint Thomas .... MN 251
Walden University .... MN 251
Winona State University .... MN 248
Alcorn State University .... MS 251
Belhaven University .... MS 252
Delta State University .... MS 252
Jackson State University .... MS 253
Mississippi College .... MS 254
Mississippi State University .... MS 254
Mississippi Valley State University .... MS 255
Rust College .... MS 255
University of Mississippi .... MS 256
University of Southern Mississippi .... MS 256
Avila University .... MO .. 257
Evangel University .... MO .. 260
Fontbonne University .... MO .. 260
Lincoln University .... MO .. 261
Lindenwood University .... MO .. 261
@Missouri Southern State University .... MO .. 263
Missouri State University .... MO .. 263
Missouri Western State University .... MO .. 264
Park University .... MO .. 265
Saint Louis University .... MO .. 266
Southeast Missouri State University .... MO .. 266
Southwest Baptist University .... MO .. 267
University of Central Missouri .... MO .. 268
University of Missouri - Columbia .... MO .. 268
University of Missouri - Kansas City .... MO .. 268
University of Missouri - Saint Louis .... MO .. 268
Washington University in St. Louis .... MO .. 269
William Woods University .... MO .. 270
Salish Kootenai College .... MT 273
University of Montana - Missoula .... MT 271
Chadron State College .... NE 276
Creighton University .... NE 274
Nebraska Wesleyan University .... NE 276
Union College .... NE 277
University of Nebraska at Kearney .... NE 277
University of Nebraska at Omaha .... NE 277
University of Nevada, Las Vegas .... NV 279
University of Nevada, Reno .... NV 279
Plymouth State University .... NH 283
University of New Hampshire .... NH 282
Centenary University .... NJ 284
@College of Saint Elizabeth .... NJ 285
Georgian Court University .... NJ 286
Kean University .... NJ 286
Monmouth University .... NJ 287
Ramapo College of New Jersey .... NJ 289
Rutgers University - New Brunswick .... NJ 290
Rutgers University - Newark .... NJ 290
Seton Hall University .... NJ 291
Stockton University .... NJ 291
Eastern New Mexico University Main Campus .... NM 293
New Mexico Highlands University .... NM 294
New Mexico State University Main Campus. NM 295
Western New Mexico University .... NM 297
Adelphi University .... NY 297
City University of New York Herbert H. Lehman College .... NY 302
City University of New York Hunter College NY 302
City University of New York Medgar Evers College .... NY 303
City University of New York York College .... NY 304
College of New Rochelle, The .... NY 305
College of Saint Rose, The .... NY 305
College of Staten Island CUNY .... NY 302
Columbia University in the City of New York NY 305
Concordia College .... NY 305
Daemen College .... NY 306
Dominican College of Blauvelt .... NY 306
Fordham University .... NY 308
Iona College .... NY 311
Keuka College .... NY 312
Marist College .... NY 314
Mercy College .... NY 314
Molloy College .... NY 315
Nazareth College of Rochester .... NY 316
New York University .... NY 318
Niagara University .... NY 318
Nyack College .... NY 319
Roberts Wesleyan College .... NY 321
Siena College .... NY 324
Skidmore College .... NY 324
State University of New York at Binghamton .... NY 325
State University of New York at Fredonia .... NY 325
State University of New York College at Buffalo .... NY 326

THEA: National Association of Schools of Theatre: theatre (C,A,B, M,D)

College of Charleston ... SC ... 420
Francis Marion University ... SC ... 421
University of South Carolina Columbia ... SC ... 424
Winthrop University ... SC ... 426
University of South Dakota, The ... SD ... 428
Belmont University ... TN ... 430
East Tennessee State University ... TN ... 431
Middle Tennessee State University ... TN ... 434
University of Memphis, The ... TN ... 439
University of Tennessee at Chattanooga ... TN ... 440
University of Tennessee, Knoxville ... TN ... 439
Baylor University ... TX ... 444
Del Mar College ... TX ... 448
KD Conservatory College of Film and Dramatic Arts ... TX ... 451
Midwestern State University ... TX ... 453
Southern Methodist University ... TX ... 457
Stephen F. Austin State University ... TX ... 458
Texas Tech University ... TX ... 463
University of Texas Rio Grande Valley, The ... TX ... 468
University of the Incarnate Word ... TX ... 465
West Texas A & M University ... TX ... 460
Brigham Young University ... UT ... 471
Snow College ... UT ... 474
Christopher Newport University ... VA ... 479
James Madison University ... VA ... 481
Longwood University ... VA ... 482
Old Dominion University ... VA ... 483
Radford University ... VA ... 484
Virginia Commonwealth University ... VA ... 487
Virginia Polytechnic Institute and State University ... VA ... 490
Davis & Elkins College ... WV ... 501
West Virginia University ... WV ... 505
Marquette University ... WI ... 508
University of Wisconsin-Madison ... WI ... 510
University of Wisconsin-Stevens Point ... WI ... 511
University of Wisconsin-Whitewater ... WI ... 512
Casper College ... WY ... 516

THEOL: Association of Theological Schools: theology (M,FP,D)

@Faulkner University ... AL ... 5
Samford University ... AL ... 6
@Grand Canyon University ... AZ ... 12
Phoenix Seminary ... AZ ... 15
American Baptist Seminary of the West ... CA ... 25
Azusa Pacific University ... CA ... 26
Biola University ... CA ... 27
California Lutheran University ... CA ... 30
China Evangelical Seminary North America ... CA ... 37
Christian Witness Theological Seminary ... CA ... 37
Church Divinity School of the Pacific ... CA ... 37
Claremont School of Theology ... CA ... 38
Dominican School of Philosophy and Theology ... CA ... 41
Franciscan School of Theology ... CA ... 43
Fresno Pacific University ... CA ... 43
Fuller Theological Seminary ... CA ... 43
Gateway Seminary ... CA ... 44
Grace Mission University ... CA ... 44
Graduate Theological Union ... CA ... 44
International Theological Seminary ... CA ... 46
La Sierra University ... CA ... 47
Logos Evangelical Seminary ... CA ... 48
Loyola Marymount University ... CA ... 50
Pacific School of Religion ... CA ... 55
@Presbyterian Theological Seminary in America ... CA ... 57
Saint John's Seminary ... CA ... 58
Saint Patrick's Seminary & University ... CA ... 59
San Francisco Theological Seminary ... CA ... 60
Santa Clara University ... CA ... 62
Shepherd University ... CA ... 63
Starr King School for the Ministry ... CA ... 66
Westminster Theological Seminary in California ... CA ... 74
World Mission University ... CA ... 75
Augustine Institute ... CO ... 77
Denver Seminary ... CO ... 79
Iliff School of Theology ... CO ... 80
St. John Vianney Theological Seminary ... CO ... 82
Hartford Seminary ... CT ... 87
Holy Apostles College and Seminary ... CT ... 87
Yale University ... CT ... 89
Catholic University of America, The ... DC ... 91
Howard University ... DC ... 92
Pontifical Faculty of the Immaculate Conception at the Dominican House of S tudies ... DC ... 92
Wesley Theological Seminary ... DC ... 94
Barry University ... FL ... 95
Knox Theological Seminary ... FL ... 102
@Palm Beach Atlantic University ... FL ... 104
@St. Thomas University ... FL ... 107
St. Vincent De Paul Regional Seminary ... FL ... 107
Columbia Theological Seminary ... GA ... 118
Emory University ... GA ... 119
Georgia Christian University ... GA ... 119
Interdenominational Theological Center ... GA ... 122
Mercer University ... GA ... 122
@Northwest Nazarene University ... ID ... 132
Bexley Seabury ... IL ... 134
Catholic Theological Union ... IL ... 134
Chicago Theological Seminary ... IL ... 135
Garrett-Evangelical Theological Seminary ... IL ... 138
Lincoln Christian University ... IL ... 143
@Loyola University Chicago ... IL ... 144
Lutheran School of Theology at Chicago ... IL ... 144
McCormick Theological Seminary ... IL ... 145
Meadville Lombard Theological School ... IL ... 145
Moody Bible Institute ... IL ... 146
North Park University ... IL ... 147
Northern Seminary ... IL ... 147
Trinity International University ... IL ... 153
University of Chicago ... IL ... 153
University of Saint Mary of the Lake-Mundelein Seminary ... IL ... 154
Anabaptist Mennonite Biblical Seminary ... IN ... 155
Anderson University ... IN ... 156
Bethany Theological Seminary ... IN ... 156
Christian Theological Seminary ... IN ... 157
Concordia Theological Seminary ... IN ... 157
Earlham College and Earlham School of Religion ... IN ... 157
Grace College and Seminary ... IN ... 158
Indiana Wesleyan University ... IN ... 161
Mid-America Reformed Seminary ... IN ... 162
Oakland City University ... IN ... 163
Saint Meinrad School of Theology ... IN ... 164
University of Notre Dame ... IN ... 165
University of Dubuque ... IA ... 173
Wartburg Theological Seminary ... IA ... 174
Central Baptist Theological Seminary ... KS ... 176
Saint Paul School of Theology ... KS ... 181
Asbury Theological Seminary ... KY ... 183
Baptist Seminary of Kentucky ... KY ... 183
Lexington Theological Seminary ... KY ... 187
Louisville Presbyterian Theological Seminary ... KY ... 188
Southern Baptist Theological Seminary, The ... KY ... 189
New Orleans Baptist Theological Seminary ... LA ... 195
Notre Dame Seminary, Graduate School of Theology ... LA ... 195
Mount St. Mary's University ... MD ... 206
Saint Mary's Seminary and University ... MD ... 207
Andover Newton Theological School ... MA ... 210
Boston College ... MA ... 212
Boston University ... MA ... 212
Gordon-Conwell Theological Seminary ... MA ... 215
Harvard University ... MA ... 215
Hellenic College-Holy Cross Greek Orthodox School of Theology ... MA ... 215
Pope St. John XXIII National Seminary ... MA ... 223
Saint John's Seminary ... MA ... 224
Andrews University ... MI ... 227
Calvin Theological Seminary ... MI ... 228
Cornerstone University ... MI ... 229
Ecumenical Theological Seminary ... MI ... 229
Puritan Reformed Theological Seminary ... MI ... 236
Sacred Heart Major Seminary ... MI ... 236
SS. Cyril and Methodius Seminary ... MI ... 237
Western Theological Seminary ... MI ... 239
Bethel University ... MN ... 240
@Central Baptist Theological Seminary of Minneapolis ... MN ... 241
Luther Seminary ... MN ... 242
Saint John's University ... MN ... 250
United Theological Seminary of the Twin Cities ... MN ... 250
University of Saint Thomas ... MN ... 251
Reformed Theological Seminary ... MS ... 255
Wesley Biblical Seminary ... MS ... 256
Aquinas Institute of Theology ... MO ... 257
Assemblies of God Theological Seminary ... MO ... 257
Concordia Seminary ... MO ... 258
Covenant Theological Seminary ... MO ... 259
Eden Theological Seminary ... MO ... 260
Kenrick-Glennon Seminary, Kenrick School of Theology ... MO ... 261
Midwestern Baptist Theological Seminary ... MO ... 263
Nazarene Theological Seminary ... MO ... 264
Urshan Graduate School of Theology ... MO ... 269
Drew University ... NJ ... 285
New Brunswick Theological Seminary ... NJ ... 287
Princeton Theological Seminary ... NJ ... 288
Seton Hall University ... NJ ... 291
Christ the King Seminary ... NY ... 300
Colgate Rochester Crozer Divinity School ... NY ... 304
General Theological Seminary ... NY ... 309
New York Theological Seminary ... NY ... 318
Northeastern Seminary ... NY ... 319
Nyack College ... NY ... 319
Saint Bernard's School of Theology & Ministry ... NY ... 322
Saint Joseph's Seminary ... NY ... 323
Saint Vladimir's Orthodox Theological Seminary ... NY ... 323
Union Theological Seminary ... NY ... 332
Campbell University ... NC ... 336
Duke University ... NC ... 337
Gardner-Webb University ... NC ... 337
Hood Theological Seminary ... NC ... 338
Lenoir-Rhyne University ... NC ... 339
Shaw University ... NC ... 348
Shepherds Theological Seminary ... NC ... 349
Southeastern Baptist Theological Seminary ... NC ... 349
Wake Forest University ... NC ... 353
Ashland University ... OH ... 356
Athenaeum of Ohio ... OH ... 356
Cincinnati Christian University ... OH ... 359
Methodist Theological School in Ohio ... OH ... 365
Payne Theological Seminary ... OH ... 369
Pontifical College Josephinum ... OH ... 369
Saint Mary Seminary and Graduate School of Theology ... OH ... 369
Trinity Lutheran Seminary ... OH ... 370
United Theological Seminary ... OH ... 371
Winebrenner Theological Seminary ... OH ... 373
Oral Roberts University ... OK ... 378
Phillips Theological Seminary ... OK ... 378
George Fox University ... OR ... 383
Mount Angel Seminary ... OR ... 384
Multnomah University ... OR ... 384
Western Seminary ... OR ... 388
Biblical Theological Seminary ... PA ... 389
Byzantine Catholic Seminary of Ss. Cyril and Methodius ... PA ... 391
Eastern University ... PA ... 394
Evangelical Theological Seminary ... PA ... 395
Lancaster Theological Seminary ... PA ... 399
Moravian College ... PA ... 402
Pittsburgh Theological Seminary ... PA ... 408
Reformed Episcopal Seminary ... PA ... 408
Reformed Presbyterian Theological Seminary ... PA ... 409
Saint Charles Borromeo Seminary ... PA ... 409
St. Tikhon's Orthodox Theological Seminary ... PA ... 410
Saint Vincent Seminary ... PA ... 410
Trinity Episcopal School for Ministry ... PA ... 412
United Lutheran Seminary ... PA ... 412
Westminster Theological Seminary ... PA ... 414
Dominican Study Center of the Caribbean ... PR ... 522
Evangelical Seminary of Puerto Rico ... PR ... 522
Columbia International University ... SC ... 420
Erskine College ... SC ... 421
Sioux Falls Seminary ... SD ... 428
Freed-Hardeman University ... TN ... 432
Lipscomb University ... TN ... 433
Memphis Theological Seminary ... TN ... 434
Milligan College ... TN ... 435
Pentecostal Theological Seminary ... TN ... 435
Sewanee: The University of the South ... TN ... 436
Vanderbilt University ... TN ... 440
Abilene Christian University ... TX ... 441
Austin Presbyterian Theological Seminary ... TX ... 443
Baptist Missionary Association Theological Seminary ... TX ... 443
Baylor University ... TX ... 444
B.H. Carroll Theological Institute ... TX ... 444
Brite Divinity School ... TX ... 445
Dallas Theological Seminary ... TX ... 448
Grace School of Theology ... TX ... 449
Hardin-Simmons University ... TX ... 450
Houston Graduate School of Theology ... TX ... 450
@Lubbock Christian University ... TX ... 452
Oblate School of Theology ... TX ... 454
Seminary of the Southwest ... TX ... 456
Southern Methodist University ... TX ... 457
Southwestern Baptist Theological Seminary ... TX ... 457
University of St. Thomas ... TX ... 466
Baptist Theological Seminary at Richmond ... VA ... 478
Eastern Mennonite University ... VA ... 480
John Leland Center for Theological Studies, The ... VA ... 482
Protestant Episcopal Theological Seminary in Virginia ... VA ... 483
Regent University ... VA ... 484
Union Presbyterian Seminary ... VA ... 486
Virginia Union University ... VA ... 491
Washington University of Virginia ... VA ... 491
Seattle Pacific University ... WA ... 498
Seattle School of Theology and Psychology, The ... WA ... 498
Seattle University ... WA ... 498
Nashotah House ... WI ... 509
Sacred Heart Seminary and School of Theology ... WI ... 509

TRACS: Transnational Association of Christian Colleges and Schools: christian studies education (C,A,B, M,D)

International Baptist College and Seminary ... AZ ... 13
Shorter College ... AR ... 21
Bethesda University of California ... CA ... 27
California Christian College ... CA ... 28
@California Graduate School of Theology ... CA ... 29
Community Christian College ... CA ... 40
Epic Bible College & Graduate School ... CA ... 42
Evangelia University ... CA ... 42
Grace Mission University ... CA ... 44
@Kernel University ... CA ... 47
Oikos University ... CA ... 54
@St. Luke University ... CA ... 59
Shasta Bible College and Graduate School ... CA ... 63
Southern California Seminary ... CA ... 65
Veritas Evangelical Seminary ... CA ... 73
@West Coast Baptist College ... CA ... 73
Pensacola Christian College ... FL ... 105
Trinity Baptist College ... FL ... 112
University of Fort Lauderdale ... FL ... 112
@Athens College of Ministry ... GA ... 115
Beulah Heights University ... GA ... 116
Georgia Christian University ... GA ... 119
Luther Rice College and Seminary ... GA ... 122
Reformed University ... GA ... 124
Pacific Islands University ... GU ... 520
New Saint Andrews College ... ID ... 132
Christian Life College ... IL ... 135
Morthland College ... IL ... 146
Mid-America Reformed Seminary ... IN ... 162
Faith Theological Seminary ... MD ... 203
Maple Springs Baptist Bible College & Seminary ... MD ... 205
Boston Baptist College ... MA ... 212
@Association Free Lutheran Bible School and Seminary ... MN ... 240
Central Baptist Theological Seminary of Minneapolis ... MN ... 241
Lutheran Brethren Seminary ... MN ... 243
@Elim Bible Institute and College ... NY ... 307
Apex School of Theology ... NC ... 335
Charlotte Christian College and Theological Seminary ... NC ... 336
Heritage Bible College ... NC ... 338
Piedmont International University ... NC ... 348
@Southeastern Free Will Baptist College ... NC ... 349
Southern Evangelical Seminary ... NC ... 349
Randall University ... OK ... 379
Gutenberg College ... OR ... 383
Bob Jones University ... SC ... 418
Clinton College ... SC ... 419
John Witherspoon College ... SD ... 427
Crown College of the Bible, The ... TN ... 431
Hiwassee College ... TN ... 432
Oxford Graduate School ... TN ... 435
Visible Music College ... TN ... 440
Bakke Graduate University ... TX ... 443
Grace School of Theology ... TX ... 449
King's University, The ... TX ... 451
Messenger College ... TX ... 452
Paul Quinn College ... TX ... 454
Ivy Christian College ... VA ... 481
Patrick Henry College ... VA ... 483
Virginia Baptist College ... VA ... 487
Virginia Beach Theological Seminary ... VA ... 487
Virginia University of Lynchburg ... VA ... 491
Faith International University ... WA ... 494

VET: American Veterinary Medical Association: veterinary medicine (FP,D)

Auburn University ... AL ... 4
#Tuskegee University ... AL ... 7
University of California-Davis ... CA ... 68
Western University of Health Sciences ... CA ... 74
Colorado State University ... CO ... 78
University of Florida ... FL ... 110
University of Georgia ... GA ... 127
University of Illinois at Urbana-Champaign ... IL ... 154
Purdue University Main Campus ... IN ... 163
Iowa State University ... IA ... 166
Kansas State University ... KS ... 179
Louisiana State University and Agricultural and Mechanical College ... LA ... 193
Tufts University ... MA ... 225
Michigan State University ... MI ... 233
University of Minnesota ... MN ... 250
Mississippi State University ... MS ... 254
University of Missouri - Columbia ... MO ... 268
Cornell University ... NY ... 306
North Carolina State University ... NC ... 350
Ohio State University Main Campus, The ... OH ... 367
Oklahoma State University ... OK ... 377
Oregon State University ... OR ... 385
#University of Pennsylvania ... PA ... 412
@Lincoln Memorial University ... TN ... 433
University of Tennessee, Knoxville ... TN ... 439
Texas A & M University ... TX ... 459
Virginia Polytechnic Institute and State University ... VA ... 490
Washington State University ... WA ... 499
University of Wisconsin-Madison ... WI ... 510

WC: Western Association of Schools and Colleges, Senior College and University Commission

Academy for Jewish Religion ... CA ... 24
Academy of Art University ... CA ... 24
Alliant International University-San Diego ... CA ... 24
American Conservatory Theater ... CA ... 25
American Film Institute Conservatory ... CA ... 25
American Jewish University ... CA ... 25
American University of Armenia ... CA ... 25

WJ: Western Association of Schools and Colleges, The Accrediting Commission for Community and Junior Colleges

Index of FICE Numbers

001358 .... Colorado Mesa University .... CO 77
001359 .... Colorado Northwestern Cmty College .... CO 78
001360 .... Metropolitan State Univ Denver .... CO 80
001361 .... Northeastern Junior College .... CO 81
001362 .... Otero Junior College .... CO 81
001363 .... Regis University .... CO 82
001365 .... Colorado State University-Pueblo .... CO 78
001368 .... Trinidad State Junior College .... CO 82
001369 .... United States Air Force Academy .... CO 518
001370 .... University of Colorado Boulder .... CO 83
001371 .... University of Denver .... CO 83
001372 .... Western State Colorado University .... CO 84
001374 .... Albertus Magnus College .... CT 84
001378 .... Central Connecticut State Univ .... CT 84
001379 .... Connecticut College .... CT 86
001380 .... Western Connecticut State Univ .... CT 85
001385 .... Fairfield University .... CT 87
001387 .... Hartford Seminary .... CT 87
001389 .... Holy Apostles College and Seminary .... CT 87
001392 .... Manchester Community College .... CT 85
001393 .... Mitchell College .... CT 87
001397 .... University of New Haven .... CT 89
001398 .... Northwestern CT Cmty-Tech College .... CT 86
001399 .... Norwalk Community College .... CT 86
001401 .... Post University .... CT 87
001402 .... Quinnipiac University .... CT 88
001403 .... Sacred Heart University .... CT 88
001406 .... Southern Connecticut State Univ .... CT 85
001409 .... University of Saint Joseph .... CT 89
001414 .... Trinity College .... CT 88
001415 .... United States Coast Guard Academy .... CT 519
001416 .... University of Bridgeport .... CT 88
001417 .... University of Connecticut .... CT 88
001422 .... University of Hartford .... CT 89
001424 .... Wesleyan University .... CT 89
001425 .... Eastern Connecticut State Univ .... CT 84
001426 .... Yale University .... CT 89
001428 .... Delaware State University .... DE 90
001429 .... Goldey-Beacom College .... DE 90
001431 .... University of Delaware .... DE 90
001433 .... Wesley College .... DE 90
001434 .... American University .... DC 91
001436 .... Capitol Technology University .... MD 202
001437 .... The Catholic University of America .... DC 91
001441 .... Univ of the District of Columbia .... DC 93
001443 .... Gallaudet University .... DC 91
001444 .... George Washington University .... DC 92
001445 .... Georgetown University .... DC 92
001448 .... Howard University .... DC 92
001459 .... Strayer University .... DC 93
001460 .... Trinity Washington University .... DC 93
001464 .... Wesley Theological Seminary .... DC 94
001466 .... Barry University .... FL 95
001467 .... Bethune Cookman University .... FL 95
001468 .... St. Thomas University .... FL 107
001469 .... Florida Institute of Technology .... FL 99
001470 .... Eastern Florida State College .... FL 97
001471 .... College of Central Florida .... FL 97
001472 .... Chipola College .... FL 96
001475 .... Daytona State College .... FL 97
001477 .... Florida SouthWestern State College .... FL 100
001478 .... Edward Waters College .... FL 98
001479 .... Embry-Riddle Aeronautical Univ .... FL 98
001480 .... Florida A and M University .... FL 109
001481 .... Florida Atlantic University .... FL 109
001482 .... Florida College .... FL 99
001484 .... Florida State College Jacksonville .... FL 100
001485 .... Florida Keys Community College .... FL 99
001486 .... Florida Memorial University .... FL 99
001487 .... Eckerd College .... FL 97
001488 .... Florida Southern College .... FL 100
001489 .... Florida State University .... FL 110
001490 .... Gulf Coast State College .... FL 101
001493 .... Indian River State College .... FL 101
001495 .... Jacksonville University .... FL 102
001500 .... Broward College .... FL 96
001501 .... Florida Gateway College .... FL 99
001502 .... Lake-Sumter State College .... FL 103
001504 .... State Col of FL, Manatee-Sarasota .... FL 108
001505 .... Lynn University .... FL 103
001506 .... Miami Dade College .... FL 103
001507 .... New College of Florida .... FL 110
001508 .... North Florida Community College .... FL 104
001509 .... Nova Southeastern University .... FL 104
001510 .... Northwest Florida State College .... FL 104
001512 .... Palm Beach State College .... FL 105
001513 .... Pensacola State College .... FL 105
001514 .... Polk State College .... FL 105
001515 .... Rollins College .... FL 106
001519 .... Santa Fe College .... FL 107
001520 .... Seminole State College of Florida .... FL 107
001521 .... Southeastern University .... FL 108
001522 .... South Florida State College .... FL 108
001523 .... St. Johns River State College .... FL 106
001526 .... Saint Leo University .... FL 106
001528 .... St. Petersburg College .... FL 107
001531 .... Stetson University .... FL 111
001533 .... Tallahassee Community College .... FL 112
001535 .... University of Florida .... FL 110
001536 .... University of Miami .... FL 112
001537 .... University of South Florida .... FL 111
001538 .... University of Tampa .... FL 113
001540 .... Webber International University .... FL 114
001541 .... Abraham Baldwin Agricultural Coll .... GA 114
001542 .... Agnes Scott College .... GA 114
001544 .... Albany State University .... GA 114
001545 .... Andrew College .... GA 115
001546 .... Armstrong State University .... GA 115
001547 .... Point University .... GA 124
001554 .... Berry College .... GA 116
001555 .... Thomas University .... GA 126
001556 .... Brenau University .... GA 116
001557 .... Brewton-Parker College .... GA 116
001558 .... College of Coastal Georgia .... GA 118
001559 .... Clark Atlanta University .... GA 117
001560 .... Columbia Theological Seminary .... GA 118
001561 .... Columbus State University .... GA 118
001563 .... Emmanuel College .... GA 119
001564 .... Emory University .... GA 119
001566 .... Fort Valley State University .... GA 119
001568 .... Interdenominational Theol Center .... GA 122
001569 .... Georgia Institute of Technology .... GA 120
001571 .... Georgia Military College .... GA 120
001572 .... Georgia Southern University .... GA 120
001573 .... Georgia Southwestern State Univ .... GA 120
001574 .... Georgia State University .... GA 121
001575 .... Gordon State College .... GA 121
001577 .... Kennesaw State University .... GA 122
001578 .... LaGrange College .... GA 122
001579 .... Augusta University .... GA 116
001580 .... Mercer University .... GA 122
001582 .... Morehouse College .... GA 123
001585 .... University of North Georgia .... GA 127
001586 .... Oglethorpe University .... GA 124
001587 .... Paine College .... GA 124
001588 .... Piedmont College .... GA 124
001589 .... Reinhardt University .... GA 124
001590 .... Savannah State University .... GA 125
001591 .... Shorter University .... GA 125
001592 .... South Georgia State College .... GA 125
001594 .... Spelman College .... GA 126
001596 .... Toccoa Falls College .... GA 126
001597 .... Truett McConnell University .... GA 126
001598 .... University of Georgia .... GA 127
001599 .... Valdosta State University .... GA 127
001600 .... Wesleyan College .... GA 128
001601 .... University of West Georgia .... GA 127
001602 .... Georgia College & State University .... GA 119
001604 .... Young Harris College .... GA 128
001605 .... Chaminade University of Honolulu .... HI 129
001606 .... Brigham Young University Hawaii .... HI 128
001610 .... University of Hawaii at Manoa .... HI 129
001611 .... University of Hawaii at Hilo .... HI 129
001612 .... Univ of Hawaii Honolulu Cmty Col .... HI 130
001613 .... Kapiolani Community College .... HI 130
001614 .... Univ of Hawaii Kauai Cmty College .... HI 130
001615 .... Univ of Hawaii Maui College .... HI 130
001616 .... Boise State University .... ID 131
001617 .... The College of Idaho .... ID 131
001619 .... College of Southern Idaho .... ID 131
001620 .... Idaho State University .... ID 132
001621 .... Lewis-Clark State College .... ID 132
001623 .... North Idaho College .... ID 132
001624 .... Northwest Nazarene University .... ID 132
001625 .... Brigham Young University-Idaho .... ID 131
001626 .... University of Idaho .... ID 132
001628 .... American Academy of Art .... IL 133
001632 .... Aquinas Institute of Theology .... MO 257
001633 .... Augustana College .... IL 133
001634 .... Aurora University .... IL 133
001636 .... Southwestern Illinois College .... IL 152
001637 .... Bethany Theological Seminary .... IN 156
001638 .... Black Hawk College .... IL 134
001639 .... Blackburn College .... IL 134
001640 .... Prairie State College .... IL 148
001641 .... Bradley University .... IL 134
001643 .... Spoon River College .... IL 152
001647 .... City Colleges of Chicago .... IL 135
001648 .... City Cols of Chicago Harry Truman .... IL 135
001649 .... City Cols of Chicago RJ Daley Col .... IL 136
001650 .... Malcolm X College .... IL 136
001652 .... City Cols of Chicago Washington Col .... IL 135
001654 .... City Cols of Chicago Kennedy-King .... IL 135
001655 .... City Cols of Chicago W Wright Col .... IL 136
001657 .... Midwestern University .... IL 145
001659 .... Rosalind Franklin U of Med/Science .... IL 150
001661 .... Chicago Theological Seminary .... IL 135
001663 .... Spertus Inst for Jewish Lrng & Ldrs .... IL 152
001664 .... University of St. Francis .... IL 154
001665 .... Columbia College Chicago .... IL 136
001666 .... Concordia University Chicago .... IL 136
001669 .... Danville Area Community College .... IL 137
001671 .... DePaul University .... IL 137
001672 .... DeVry University - Home Office .... IL 137
001674 .... Eastern Illinois University .... IL 138
001675 .... Elgin Community College .... IL 138
001676 .... Elmhurst College .... IL 138
001678 .... Eureka College .... IL 138
001681 .... Highland Community College .... IL 139
001682 .... Garrett-Evangelical Theol Seminary .... IL 138
001684 .... Greenville University .... IL 139
001685 .... Hebrew Theological College .... IL 139
001688 .... Illinois College .... IL 139
001689 .... Illinois College of Optometry .... IL 140
001691 .... Illinois Institute of Technology .... IL 140
001692 .... Illinois State University .... IL 140
001693 .... Northeastern Illinois University .... IL 147
001694 .... Chicago State University .... IL 135
001696 .... Illinois Wesleyan University .... IL 141
001698 .... John Marshall Law School .... IL 141
001699 .... Joliet Junior College .... IL 142
001700 .... Judson University .... IL 142
001701 .... Kaskaskia College .... IL 142
001703 .... Kendall College .... IL 142
001704 .... Knox College .... IL 142
001705 .... Illinois Valley Community College .... IL 141
001706 .... Lake Forest College .... IL 142
001707 .... Lewis University .... IL 143
001708 .... Lincoln Christian University .... IL 143
001709 .... Lincoln College .... IL 143
001710 .... Loyola University Chicago .... IL 144
001712 .... Lutheran School of Theology Chicago .... IL 144
001716 .... MacCormac College .... IL 144
001717 .... MacMurray College .... IL 144
001721 .... McCormick Theological Seminary .... IL 145
001722 .... McKendree University .... IL 145
001723 .... Meadville Lombard Theol School .... IL 145
001724 .... Millikin University .... IL 145
001725 .... Monmouth College .... IL 146
001727 .... Moody Bible Institute .... IL 146
001728 .... Morton College .... IL 146
001732 .... National Univ of Health Sciences .... IL 147
001733 .... National-Louis University .... IL 146
001734 .... North Central College .... IL 147
001735 .... North Park University .... IL 147
001736 .... Northern Seminary .... IL 147
001737 .... Northern Illinois University .... IL 147
001739 .... Northwestern University .... IL 148
001741 .... Olivet Nazarene University .... IL 148
001742 .... Illinois Eastern CC Olney Central .... IL 140
001744 .... Principia College .... IL 149
001745 .... Quincy University .... IL 149
001746 .... Robert Morris University - Illinois .... IL 149
001747 .... Rock Valley College .... IL 150
001748 .... Rockford University .... IL 150
001749 .... Roosevelt University .... IL 150
001750 .... Dominican University .... IL 137
001752 .... Sauk Valley Community College .... IL 151
001753 .... School of the Art Institute Chicago .... IL 151
001757 .... Southeastern Illinois College .... IL 151
001758 .... Southern Illinois Univ Carbondale .... IL 152
001759 .... Southern Illinois Univ Edwardsville .... IL 152
001765 .... Univ of Saint Mary Lake-Mundelein .... IL 154
001767 .... Benedictine University .... IL 133
001768 .... Saint Xavier University .... IL 151
001769 .... South Suburban Col of Cook County .... IL 151
001771 .... Trinity Christian College .... IL 153
001772 .... Trinity International University .... IL 153
001773 .... Triton College .... IL 153
001774 .... University of Chicago .... IL 153
001775 .... Univ of Illinois Urbana-Champaign .... IL 154
001776 .... University of Illinois at Chicago .... IL 153
001778 .... VanderCook College of Music .... IL 154
001779 .... Illinois Eastern CC Wabash Valley .... IL 140
001780 .... Western Illinois University .... IL 155
001781 .... Wheaton College .... IL 155
001783 .... Worsham College of Mortuary Science .... IL 155
001784 .... Ancilla College .... IN 155
001785 .... Anderson University .... IN 156
001786 .... Ball State University .... IN 156
001787 .... Bethel College .... IN 156
001788 .... Butler University .... IN 156
001789 .... Christian Theological Seminary .... IN 157
001792 .... DePauw University .... IN 157
001793 .... Earlham Col/Earlham Sch of Rel .... IN 157
001795 .... University of Evansville .... IN 164
001798 .... Franklin College of Indiana .... IN 157
001799 .... Goshen College .... IN 158
001800 .... Grace College and Seminary .... IN 158
001801 .... Hanover College .... IN 158
001803 .... Huntington University .... IN 159
001804 .... University of Indianapolis .... IN 164
001805 .... Indiana Tech .... IN 159
001807 .... Indiana State University .... IN 159
001808 .... University of Southern Indiana .... IN 165
001809 .... Indiana University Bloomington .... IN 159
001811 .... Indiana University East .... IN 160
001813 .... Indiana Univ-Purdue Un Indianapolis .... IN 160
001814 .... Indiana University Kokomo .... IN 160
001815 .... Indiana University Northwest .... IN 160
001816 .... Indiana University South Bend .... IN 160
001817 .... Indiana University Southeast .... IN 161
001820 .... Manchester University .... IN 162
001821 .... Marian University .... IN 162
001822 .... Indiana Wesleyan University .... IN 161
001823 .... Anabaptist Mennonite Biblical Sem .... IN 155
001824 .... Oakland City University .... IN 163
001825 .... Purdue University Main Campus .... IN 163
001827 .... Purdue University Northwest .... IN 163
001828 .... Indiana Univ-Purdue Univ Fort Wayne .... IN 160
001830 .... Rose-Hulman Institute of Technology .... IN 163
001832 .... University of Saint Francis .... IN 165
001834 .... Calumet College of Saint Joseph .... IN 157
001835 .... Saint Mary-of-the-Woods College .... IN 163
001836 .... Saint Mary's College .... IN 163
001838 .... Taylor University .... IN 164

Code	Institution	State	Page
002266	Cornerstone University	MI	229
002267	Grand Rapids Community College	MI	230
002268	Grand Valley State University	MI	230
002269	Great Lakes Christian College	MI	231
002270	Henry Ford College	MI	231
002272	Hillsdale College	MI	231
002273	Hope College	MI	231
002274	Jackson College	MI	231
002275	Kalamazoo College	MI	231
002276	Kellogg Community College	MI	232
002277	Lake Michigan College	MI	232
002278	Lansing Community College	MI	232
002279	Lawrence Technological University	MI	233
002282	Madonna University	MI	233
002284	Marygrove College	MI	233
002288	Rochester College	MI	236
002290	Michigan State University	MI	233
002292	Michigan Technological University	MI	234
002293	Lake Superior State University	MI	232
002294	Monroe County Community College	MI	234
002295	Montcalm Community College	MI	234
002297	Muskegon Community College	MI	234
002299	North Central Michigan College	MI	234
002301	Northern Michigan University	MI	235
002302	Northwestern Michigan College	MI	235
002303	Oakland Community College	MI	235
002307	Oakland University	MI	235
002308	Olivet College	MI	236
002310	St. Clair County Community College	MI	236
002311	Kuyper College	MI	232
002313	Sacred Heart Major Seminary	MI	236
002314	Saginaw Valley State University	MI	236
002315	Schoolcraft College	MI	236
002316	Siena Heights University	MI	236
002317	Southwestern Michigan College	MI	237
002318	Spring Arbor University	MI	237
002322	Finlandia University	MI	230
002323	University of Detroit Mercy	MI	237
002325	University of Michigan-Ann Arbor	MI	237
002326	University of Michigan-Dearborn	MI	238
002327	University of Michigan-Flint	MI	238
002328	Washtenaw Community College	MI	238
002329	Wayne State University	MI	239
002330	Western Michigan University	MI	239
002331	Western Theological Seminary	MI	239
002332	Anoka-Ramsey Community College	MN	243
002334	Augsburg College	MN	240
002335	Riverland Community College	MN	247
002336	Bemidji State University	MN	244
002337	Bethany Lutheran College	MN	240
002339	Central Lakes College	MN	244
002340	Carleton College	MN	241
002341	College of Saint Benedict	MN	241
002342	St. Catherine University	MN	249
002343	The College of Saint Scholastica	MN	241
002345	University of Saint Thomas	MN	251
002346	Concordia College	MN	241
002347	Concordia University, St. Paul	MN	241
002350	Vermilion Community College	MN	248
002353	Gustavus Adolphus College	MN	242
002354	Hamline University	MN	242
002355	Hibbing Community College	MN	244
002356	Itasca Community College	MN	245
002357	Luther Seminary	MN	242
002358	Macalester College	MN	243
002360	Minnesota State University, Mankato	MN	246
002361	Martin Luther College	MN	243
002362	Minneapolis Cmty & Tech College	MN	245
002365	Minneapolis College of Art & Design	MN	243
002367	Minnesota State University Moorhead	MN	246
002369	North Central University	MN	249
002370	North Hennepin Community College	MN	246
002371	University of Northwestern St. Paul	MN	251
002373	Rochester Community & Tech College	MN	247
002375	Southwest Minnesota State Univ	MN	248
002377	St. Cloud State University	MN	247
002379	Saint John's University	MN	250
002380	St Mary's University of Minnesota	MN	250
002382	St. Olaf College	MN	250
002383	Crown College	MN	242
002385	Northland Community & Tech College	MN	246
002386	United Theol Seminary-Twin Cities	MN	250
002388	University of Minnesota Duluth	MN	250
002389	University of Minnesota-Morris	MN	251
002391	Mitchell Hamline School of Law	MN	248
002393	Minnesota State College Southeast	MN	245
002394	Winona State University	MN	248
002396	Alcorn State University	MS	251
002397	Belhaven University	MS	252
002398	Blue Mountain College	MS	252
002401	Coahoma Community College	MS	252
002402	Copiah-Lincoln Community College	MS	252
002403	Delta State University	MS	252
002404	East Central Community College	MS	252
002405	East Mississippi Community College	MS	253
002407	Hinds Community College	MS	253
002408	Holmes Community College	MS	253
002409	Itawamba Community College	MS	253
002410	Jackson State University	MS	253
002411	Jones County Junior College	MS	253
002413	Meridian Community College	MS	253
002414	Millsaps College	MS	254
002415	Mississippi College	MS	254
002416	Mississippi Delta Community College	MS	254
002417	Mississippi Gulf Coast Cmty College	MS	254
002422	Mississippi University for Women	MS	254
002423	Mississippi State University	MS	254
002424	Mississippi Valley State University	MS	255
002426	Northeast Mississippi Cmty College	MS	255
002427	Northwest Mississippi Cmty College	MS	255
002430	Pearl River Community College	MS	255
002433	Rust College	MS	255
002435	Southeastern Baptist College	MS	255
002436	Southwest Mississippi Cmty College	MS	256
002439	Tougaloo College	MS	256
002440	University of Mississippi	MS	256
002441	University of Southern Mississippi	MS	256
002447	William Carey University	MS	256
002449	Avila University	MO	257
002450	Calvary University	MO	257
002453	Central Methodist University	MO	258
002454	University of Central Missouri	MO	268
002456	Columbia College	MO	258
002457	Concordia Seminary	MO	258
002458	Cottey College	MO	259
002459	Crowder College	MO	259
002460	Culver-Stockton College	MO	259
002461	Drury University	MO	259
002462	Eden Theological Seminary	MO	260
002463	Evangel University	MO	260
002464	Fontbonne University	MO	260
002466	Harris-Stowe State University	MO	260
002467	Conception Seminary College	MO	258
002468	Jefferson College	MO	261
002471	St Louis Cmty College-Cosand Center	MO	266
002473	Kansas City Art Institute	MO	261
002474	Kansas City Univ of Med & BioSci	MO	261
002476	Kenrick-Glennon Seminary	MO	261
002477	A. T. Still Univ of Health Sciences	MO	257
002479	Lincoln University	MO	261
002480	Lindenwood University	MO	261
002482	Maryville University of Saint Louis	MO	262
002484	Metropolitan Cmty Col-Penn Valley	MO	262
002485	Midwestern Baptist Theol Seminary	MO	263
002486	Mineral Area College	MO	263
002488	Missouri Southern State University	MO	263
002489	Missouri Valley College	MO	264
002490	Missouri Western State University	MO	264
002491	Moberly Area Community College	MO	264
002494	Nazarene Theological Seminary	MO	264
002495	Truman State University	MO	267
002496	Northwest Missouri State University	MO	264
002498	Park University	MO	265
002499	Rockhurst University	MO	265
002500	College of the Ozarks	MO	258
002501	Southeast Missouri State University	MO	266
002502	Southwest Baptist University	MO	267
002503	Missouri State University	MO	263
002504	St. Louis College of Pharmacy	MO	266
002506	Saint Louis University	MO	266
002509	Saint Paul School of Theology	KS	181
002512	Stephens College	MO	267
002514	North Central Missouri College	MO	264
002515	Univ of Missouri System Admin	MO	268
002516	University of Missouri - Columbia	MO	268
002517	Missouri Univ of Science Tech	MO	269
002518	Univ of Missouri - Kansas City	MO	268
002519	Univ of Missouri - Saint Louis	MO	268
002520	Washington University in St. Louis	MO	269
002521	Webster University	MO	269
002523	Westminster College	MO	270
002524	William Jewell College	MO	270
002525	William Woods University	MO	270
002526	Carroll College	MT	270
002527	University of Providence	MT	273
002528	Miles Community College	MT	271
002529	Dawson Community College	MT	270
002530	Montana State University - Billings	MT	272
002531	Montana Tech of the Univ of Montana	MT	272
002532	Montana State University	MT	272
002533	Montana State University - Northern	MT	272
002534	Rocky Mountain College	MT	272
002536	University of Montana - Missoula	MT	271
002537	The University of Montana Western	MT	271
002539	Chadron State College	NE	276
002540	College of Saint Mary	NE	274
002541	Concordia University	NE	274
002542	Creighton University	NE	274
002544	Doane University	NE	274
002547	Grace University	NE	274
002548	Hastings College	NE	274
002551	University of Nebraska at Kearney	NE	277
002553	Midland University	NE	275
002554	University of Nebraska at Omaha	NE	277
002555	Nebraska Wesleyan University	NE	276
002557	Mid-Plains Community College	NE	275
002559	Peru State College	NE	276
002560	Western Nebraska Community College	NE	278
002563	Union College	NE	277
002565	University of Nebraska - Lincoln	NE	277
002566	Wayne State College	NE	276
002567	York College	NE	278
002568	University of Nevada, Reno	NV	279
002569	University of Nevada, Las Vegas	NV	279
002572	Colby-Sawyer College	NH	280
002573	Dartmouth College	NH	281
002575	Franklin Pierce University	NH	281
002579	New England College	NH	281
002580	Southern New Hampshire University	NH	282
002581	NHTI-Concord's Community College	NH	280
002582	Manchester Community College	NH	280
002583	Great Bay Community College	NH	280
002586	Rivier University	NH	281
002587	Saint Anselm College	NH	282
002589	University of New Hampshire	NH	282
002590	Keene State College	NH	283
002591	Plymouth State University	NH	283
002595	Assumption College for Sisters	NJ	283
002596	Atlantic Cape Community College	NJ	283
002597	Bloomfield College	NJ	284
002598	Caldwell University	NJ	284
002599	Centenary University	NJ	284
002600	College of Saint Elizabeth	NJ	285
002601	Cumberland County College	NJ	285
002603	Drew University	NJ	285
002607	Fairleigh Dickinson University	NJ	286
002608	Georgian Court University	NJ	286
002609	Rowan University	NJ	289
002610	Felician University	NJ	286
002613	New Jersey City University	NJ	287
002615	Middlesex County College	NJ	287
002616	Monmouth University	NJ	287
002617	Montclair State University	NJ	287
002619	New Brunswick Theological Seminary	NJ	287
002621	New Jersey Institute of Technology	NJ	288
002622	Kean University	NJ	286
002624	Ocean County College	NJ	288
002625	William Paterson University of NJ	NJ	292
002626	Princeton Theological Seminary	NJ	288
002627	Princeton University	NJ	288
002628	Rider University	NJ	289
002629	Rutgers State Univ Central Office	NJ	290
002631	Rutgers State Univ - Newark	NJ	290
002632	Seton Hall University	NJ	291
002638	Saint Peter's University	NJ	291
002639	Stevens Institute of Technology	NJ	291
002642	The College of New Jersey	NJ	284
002643	Union County College	NJ	292
002649	Santa Fe Univ of Art and Design	NM	296
002650	University of the Southwest	NM	297
002651	Eastern New Mexico University	NM	293
002653	New Mexico Highlands University	NM	294
002654	New Mexico Inst of Mining & Tech	NM	294
002655	New Mexico Junior College	NM	294
002656	New Mexico Military Institute	NM	295
002657	NM State University-Main Campus	NM	295
002658	NM State University-Alamogordo	NM	295
002659	NM State University-Carlsbad	NM	295
002660	San Juan College	NM	296
002661	Eastern New Mexico Univ - Roswell	NM	294
002663	Univ of New Mexico Main Campus	NM	296
002664	Western New Mexico University	NM	297
002665	Vaughn Col of Aeronautics & Tech	NY	333
002666	Adelphi University	NY	297
002668	Alfred University	NY	298
002669	Bank Street College of Education	NY	298
002670	Summit University of Pennsylvania	PA	392
002671	Bard College	NY	298
002674	New York Theological Seminary	NY	318
002677	Brooklyn Law School	NY	300
002678	Bryant & Stratton College	NY	300
002681	Canisius College	NY	300
002685	Cazenovia College	NY	300
002687	CUNY Brooklyn College	NY	301
002688	CUNY City College	NY	301
002689	CUNY Hunter College	NY	302
002690	CUNY Queens College	NY	303
002691	CUNY Borough of Manhattan CC	NY	301
002692	CUNY Bronx Community College	NY	301
002693	CUNY John Jay Col Criminal Justice	NY	302
002694	CUNY Kingsborough Cmty College	NY	303
002696	NYC Col of Tech/City Univ of NY	NY	303
002697	CUNY Queensborough Cmty Col	NY	303
002698	College of Staten Island CUNY	NY	302
002699	Clarkson University	NY	304
002700	Colgate Roch Crozer Divinity School	NY	304
002701	Colgate University	NY	304
002703	College of Mount Saint Vincent	NY	304
002704	The College of New Rochelle	NY	305
002705	The College of Saint Rose	NY	305
002707	Columbia University in City of NY	NY	305
002708	Barnard College	NY	299
002709	Concordia College	NY	305
002710	Cooper Union	NY	306
002711	Cornell University	NY	306
002712	D'Youville College	NY	307
002713	Dominican College of Blauvelt	NY	306
002718	Elmira College	NY	307
002722	Fordham University	NY	308
002726	General Theological Seminary	NY	309
002728	Hamilton College	NY	309
002729	Hartwick College	NY	309
002731	Hobart and William Smith Colleges	NY	310
002732	Hofstra University	NY	310
002733	Holy Trinity Orthodox Seminary	NY	310
002734	Houghton College	NY	310

Code	Institution	State	Page
004804	New York Institute of Technology	NY	317
004835	Caldwell Cmty College & Tech Inst	NC	341
004838	Guilford Technical Community Col	NC	343
004844	Wake Technical Community College	NC	347
004845	Wilson Community College	NC	347
004852	Clark State Community College	OH	359
004853	Bradford School	OH	357
004855	Davis College	OH	360
004861	University of Northwestern Ohio	OH	372
004866	Stautzenberger College	OH	370
004868	Univ of Cincinnati Blue Ash College	OH	371
004878	Clackamas Community College	OR	382
004882	Oregon Health & Science University	OR	385
004890	Central Penn College	PA	392
004898	McCann School of Business & Tech	PA	401
004902	Penn Commercial Business/Tech Sch	PA	403
004910	Brightwood Career Institute	PA	390
004920	Trident Technical College	SC	424
004923	Clinton College	SC	419
004924	Forrest College	SC	421
004925	Horry-Georgetown Technical College	SC	421
004926	Tri-County Technical College	SC	424
004927	University of South Carolina Union	SC	425
004934	Daymar College	TN	431
004937	Jackson State Community College	TN	437
004938	South College	TN	436
004949	Baylor College of Medicine	TX	444
004951	University of Texas HSC at Houston	TX	468
004952	The Univ of Texas Medical Branch	TX	469
004972	Galveston College	TX	449
004977	South Texas College of Law Houston	TX	456
004988	Central Virginia Community College	VA	487
004992	Miller-Motte Technical College	VA	483
004996	Dabney S. Lancaster Community Col	VA	487
004999	Bellingham Technical College	WA	492
005000	Pierce College District	WA	497
005001	Edmonds Community College	WA	494
005006	Walla Walla Community College	WA	499
005007	West Virginia Junior College	WV	505
005008	Mountain State College	WV	502
005015	University of Wisconsin-Parkside	WI	511
005019	Univ Adventista de las Antillas	PR	526
005022	Universidad Central de Bayamon	PR	526
005026	Inter Amer Univ of PR Arecibo	PR	523
005027	Inter Amer Univ of PR Barranquitas	PR	523
005028	Inter Amer Univ of PR Bayamon	PR	523
005029	Inter Amer Univ of PR Ponce	PR	524
005204	Beal College	ME	198
005208	The College of Westchester	NY	305
005220	Salt Lake Community College	UT	474
005223	New River Community College	VA	488
005245	Univ of Arkansas Cmty Col/Morrilton	AR	23
005252	Ridgewater College	MN	247
005254	Lanier Technical College	GA	122
005256	Wiregrass Georgia Tech College	GA	128
005257	GA Northwestern Technical College	GA	120
005258	Univ of Hawaii Cmty College	HI	130
005260	J.F. Drake State Cmty & Tech Col	AL	2
005263	Minnesota West Cmty & Tech College	MN	246
005264	Flint Hills Technical College	KS	177
005265	North Central Kansas Tech College	KS	180
005267	Northwest Kansas Technical College	KS	180
005271	Southcentral KY Cmty & Tech Col	KY	187
005273	Gateway Cmty & Technical College	KY	185
005276	Central Maine Community College	ME	199
005277	Eastern Maine Community College	ME	199
005291	White Mountains Community College	NH	281
005294	Waukesha County Technical College	WI	515
005301	NE Wisconsin Technical College	WI	514
005304	Chippewa Valley Technical College	WI	513
005306	Bates Technical College	WA	492
005309	Lake Area Technical Institute	SD	427
005310	Pittsburgh Institute of Aeronautics	PA	408
005313	North Central State College	OH	366
005316	Coastal Carolina Community College	NC	342
005317	Forsyth Technical Community College	NC	343
005318	Catawba Valley Community College	NC	341
005320	Cape Fear Community College	NC	341
005363	Denmark Technical College	SC	420
005372	South Puget Sound Community College	WA	498
005373	Lake Washington Inst of Technology	WA	495
005378	Northeast State Community College	TN	437
005380	Mid-State Technical College	WI	514
005384	Nicolet Area Technical College	WI	514
005387	Northcentral Technical College	WI	514
005389	Gateway Technical College	WI	513
005390	Blackhawk Technical College	WI	513
005447	Randolph Community College	NC	345
005448	Durham Technical Community College	NC	342
005449	Central Carolina Community College	NC	341
005461	Salem Community College	NJ	291
005463	Alamance Community College	NC	340
005464	Richmond Community College	NC	345
005467	Sowela Technical Community College	LA	193
005480	Central LA TCC Huey P Long Campus	LA	192
005489	Central LA Tech Community College	LA	192
005498	Wichita Area Technical College	KS	182
005499	Salina Area Technical College	KS	181
005500	Manhattan Area Technical College	KS	179
005511	Coastal Pines Technical College	GA	117
005525	Southern Maine Community College	ME	200
005526	S Central LA Tech Col Young Mem Cam	LA	193
005533	St Paul Col A Cmty & Tech College	MN	247
005534	Saint Cloud Technical & Cmty Coll	MN	247
005535	Pine Tech & Cmty College	MN	246
005537	South Central College	MN	247
005541	Minnesota State Cmty & Tech College	MN	245
005544	Alexandria Technical & Cmty Col	MN	243
005599	Augusta Technical College	GA	116
005600	Athens Technical College	GA	115
005601	Albany Technical College	GA	114
005615	Southern Regional Technical College	GA	126
005617	South Georgia Technical College	GA	125
005618	Savannah Technical College	GA	125
005619	North Georgia Technical College	GA	123
005621	Southern Crescent Technical College	GA	126
005622	Georgia Piedmont Technical College	GA	120
005624	Columbus Technical College	GA	118
005691	Shelton State Community College	AL	3
005692	Reid State Technical College	AL	3
005697	Northwest-Shoals Community College	AL	3
005699	George Wallace St Cmty Col-Selma	AL	2
005707	Southeast Arkansas College	AR	21
005732	Univ of Arkansas at Hope-Texarkana	AR	23
005733	Bevill State Community College	AL	1
005734	Trenholm State Technical College	AL	3
005752	Clover Park Technical College	WA	493
005753	Owens Community College	OH	369
005754	Rowan-Cabarrus Community College	NC	346
005757	Lake Superior College	MN	245
005759	Northwest Technical College	MN	246
005760	Northern Maine Community College	ME	200
005761	L.E. Fletcher Technical Cmty Coll	LA	192
005763	Central Georgia Technical College	GA	117
006165	Los Angeles County Col of Nursing	CA	50
006191	St. Vincent's College	CT	88
006214	Blessing-Rieman Col Nurs & Hlth Sc	IL	134
006225	Trinity Col Nursing/Hlth Sci	IL	153
006228	Methodist College	IL	145
006240	St Francis Med Ctr Col of Nursing	IL	151
006250	Resurrection University	IL	149
006273	Mercy College of Health Sciences	IA	171
006305	Maine College of Health Professions	ME	199
006324	Laboure College	MA	216
006385	Chamberlain University-Addison	IL	135
006389	Goldfarb School of Nursing	MO	260
006392	Research College of Nursing	MO	265
006399	Bryan College of Health Sciences	NE	273
006404	Nebraska Methodist College	NE	275
006438	Phillips School of Nursing Mt Sinai	NY	320
006443	Cochran School of Nursing	NY	304
006445	Pomeroy Col of Nurs @ Crouse Hosp	NY	299
006448	The Belanger School of Nursing	NY	299
006461	St. Elizabeth College of Nursing	NY	322
006467	St. Joseph's College of Nursing	NY	323
006477	Cabarrus College of Health Sciences	NC	336
006487	Aultman College Nursing/Health Sci	OH	357
006489	Christ Col of Nursing & Health Sci	OH	359
006494	Good Samaritan Col Nursing/Hlth Sci	OH	362
006606	Baptist Hlth Sys Sch Hlth Profess	TX	443
006622	Jefferson Col of Health Sciences	VA	482
006639	Bellin College, Inc.	WI	506
006640	Columbia College of Nursing	WI	507
006656	College of DuPage	IL	136
006661	Angelina College	TX	442
006720	College of Alameda	CA	56
006724	KY Community & Technical Col System	KY	185
006725	Univ of Tennessee Health Sci Center	TN	440
006731	Casa Loma College-Van Nuys	CA	35
006750	Valencia College	FL	113
006751	Univ of Hawaii Community Colleges	HI	130
006753	Illinois Central College	IL	139
006755	Brown Mackie College-Salina	KS	175
006756	Northshore Technical Community Col	LA	192
006760	University of Maine at Augusta	ME	201
006768	Mid Michigan Community College	MI	234
006771	College for Creative Studies	MI	228
006775	Rainy River Community College	MN	247
006777	Flathead Valley Community College	MT	271
006782	Genesee Community College	NY	309
006785	Schenectady County Cmty College	NY	323
006787	Clinton Community College	NY	304
006788	Tompkins Cortland Community College	NY	331
006789	Columbia-Greene Community College	NY	305
006791	Purchase College, SUNY	NY	328
006799	Craven Community College	NC	342
006804	Lakeland Community College	OH	364
006807	Community College of Beaver County	PA	392
006810	Lehigh Carbon Community College	PA	400
006811	Luzerne County Community College	PA	400
006815	Orangeburg-Calhoun Technical Col	SC	423
006819	Blue Ridge Community College	VA	487
006823	Evangelical Seminary of Puerto Rico	PR	522
006835	Dyersburg State Community College	TN	437
006836	Motlow State Community College	TN	437
006858	Unity College	ME	200
006863	Ventura County Cmty College Dist	CA	72
006865	Camden County College	NJ	284
006867	Columbus State Community College	OH	360
006871	Thomas Nelson Community College	VA	489
006895	University of Nebraska Medical Ctr	NE	277
006901	Rowan College at Gloucester County	NJ	289
006911	Montgomery College	MD	205
006931	Waubonsee Community College	IL	155
006938	Linn-Benton Community College	OR	384
006941	Dallas Christian College	TX	447
006942	Mid-America Christian University	OK	376
006949	Kalamazoo Valley Community College	MI	231
006951	Univ of South Carolina Upstate	SC	425
006960	Maysville Cmty & Technical College	KY	186
006961	Jefferson Cmty & Tech Col	KY	186
006962	Hazard Community & Technical Coll	KY	185
006964	Rutgers State Univ - New Brunswick	NJ	290
006973	Canada College	CA	61
006975	Lincoln University	CA	48
006977	Great Basin College	NV	279
006982	Naugatuck Valley Community College	CT	86
006991	Rancho Santiago Cmty Col District	CA	57
006994	Kern Community College District	CA	46
007006	Grossmont-Cuyamaca C C District	CA	44
007012	Samuel Merritt University	CA	59
007022	CUNY Herbert H. Lehman College	NY	302
007026	Icahn Sch of Medicine at Mt Sinai	NY	311
007031	Pamlico Community College	NC	345
007032	MidAmerica Nazarene University	KS	179
007035	Kettering College	OH	364
007047	Los Angeles Southwest College	CA	49
007085	Mount Vernon Nazarene University	OH	366
007096	College of the Mainland	TX	446
007099	Virginia Highlands Community Col	VA	490
007107	Essex County College	NJ	285
007108	Univ of Puerto Rico-Rio Piedras	PR	528
007109	SUNY College at Old Westbury	NY	327
007110	Delaware County Community College	PA	393
007111	North Country Community College	NY	319
007113	Arizona Christian University	AZ	10
007115	Moorpark College	CA	73
007118	Parkland College	IL	148
007119	Rend Lake College	IL	149
007120	Des Moines Area Community College	IA	168
007121	Faith Baptist Bible Col & Seminary	IA	169
007164	Bryan University	CA	28
007170	Lincoln Land Community College	IL	144
007171	Kirtland Community College	MI	232
007178	Western Seminary	OR	388
007191	Northampton Community College	PA	403
007206	University of Puerto Rico at Cayey	PR	528
007228	Univ of Puerto Rico at Arecibo	PR	527
007260	Southwest Virginia Community Col	VA	489
007263	Holy Cross College	IN	158
007264	Mesivta Torah Vodaath Seminary	NY	315
007265	Carl Sandburg College	IL	134
007266	Pima Community College	AZ	15
007273	Baruch College/CUNY	NY	301
007275	Eastern Gateway CC - Jefferson Co.	OH	361
007276	Saint Meinrad School of Theology	IN	164
007279	Hawaii Pacific University	HI	129
007283	Central Arizona College	AZ	11
007287	Brazosport College	TX	444
007289	Central Wyoming College	WY	516
007291	St. Luke's College	IA	173
007296	Coleman University	CA	39
007297	Spartan College	CO	82
007304	The Culinary Institute of America	NY	306
007316	Western Iowa Tech Community College	IA	174
007350	Anoka Technical College	MN	244
007358	Univ of NE-NE Col of Tech Agricult	NE	278
007375	Island Drafting and Technical Inst	NY	311
007394	Berkeley College	NY	299
007401	Mandl School-The Col of Allied Hlth	NY	313
007405	Wood Tobe-Coburn School	NY	333
007430	Antonelli Institute	PA	389
007436	Brightwood Career Institute	PA	390
007437	Pittsburgh Technical College	PA	408
007439	Fountainhead College of Technology	TN	432
007440	Lincoln Col of Technology Nashville	TN	433
007459	Paier College of Art	CT	87
007465	American Academy of Dramatic Arts	NY	298
007466	LIM College	NY	312
007468	School of Visual Arts	NY	324
007469	Hussian College	PA	397
007470	Art Institute of Pittsburgh	PA	389
007484	Newbury College	MA	223
007486	The New England Institute of Art	MA	222
007491	Brightwood College	MD	202
007502	Berkeley College	NJ	283
007531	Academy of Art University	CA	24
007532	Finger Lakes Community College	NY	308
007536	Cosumnes River College	CA	50
007540	Missouri Baptist University	MO	263
007544	Appalachian Bible College	WV	501
007547	Lincoln College of Technology	CO	80
007549	Coyne College	IL	137
007555	Lakes Region Community College	NH	280
007560	River Valley Community College	NH	281
007570	Helena College Univ of Montana	MT	271
007572	AMDA Col & Conservatory Perf Arts	NY	298
007582	Aims Community College	CO	76
007598	Hocking College	OH	362
007602	Northeastern Technical College	SC	423
007607	Concorde Career College	CA	40
007635	Capital Community College	CT	85
007640	Fayetteville Tech Community College	NC	343
007644	Lake Land College	IL	143
007649	Rocky Mountain Col of Art & Design	CO	82
007669	SW Wisconsin Technical College	WI	515

Index of Universities, Colleges and Schools

Institution	State	Page
Antioch University Midwest	OHIO	356
Antioch University New England	NEW HAMPSHIRE	280
Antioch University Santa Barbara	CALIFORNIA	26
Antioch University Seattle	WASHINGTON	492
Antonelli College	MISSISSIPPI	252
Antonelli College	OHIO	356
Antonelli Institute	PENNSYLVANIA	389
AOMA Graduate School of Integrative Medicine	TEXAS	442
Apex School of Theology	NORTH CAROLINA	335
Apollos University	MONTANA	270
Appalachian Bible College	WEST VIRGINIA	501
Appalachian College of Pharmacy	VIRGINIA	477
Appalachian School of Law	VIRGINIA	477
Appalachian State University	NORTH CAROLINA	349
APT College	CALIFORNIA	26
Aquinas College	MICHIGAN	227
Aquinas College	TENNESSEE	429
Aquinas Institute of Theology	MISSOURI	257
Arapahoe Community College	COLORADO	76
Arcadia University	PENNSYLVANIA	389
Argosy University, Atlanta	GEORGIA	115
Argosy University, Chicago	ILLINOIS	133
Argosy University, Dallas	TEXAS	442
Argosy University, Denver	COLORADO	76
Argosy University, Hawaii	HAWAII	128
Argosy University, Inland Empire	CALIFORNIA	26
Argosy University, Los Angeles	CALIFORNIA	26
Argosy University, Nashville	TENNESSEE	429
Argosy University, Orange County	CALIFORNIA	26
Argosy University, Phoenix	ARIZONA	10
Argosy University, Salt Lake City	UTAH	471
Argosy University, San Diego	CALIFORNIA	26
Argosy University, San Francisco Bay Area	CALIFORNIA	26
Argosy University, Sarasota	FLORIDA	94
Argosy University, Schaumburg	ILLINOIS	133
Argosy University, Seattle	WASHINGTON	492
Argosy University, Tampa	FLORIDA	94
Argosy University, Twin Cities	MINNESOTA	240
Argosy University, Washington DC	VIRGINIA	478
Arizona Christian University	ARIZONA	10
Arizona College	ARIZONA	10
Arizona College-Mesa	ARIZONA	10
Arizona School of Acupuncture and Oriental Medicine	ARIZONA	10
Arizona State University	ARIZONA	10
Arizona Summit Law School	ARIZONA	11
Arizona Western College	ARIZONA	11
Arkansas Baptist College	ARKANSAS	17
Arkansas College of Osteopathic Medicine	ARKANSAS	17
Arkansas Northeastern College	ARKANSAS	17
Arkansas State University-Beebe	ARKANSAS	17
Arkansas State University-Heber Springs	ARKANSAS	18
Arkansas State University-Jonesboro	ARKANSAS	18
Arkansas State University-Mid-South	ARKANSAS	18
Arkansas State University-Mountain Home	ARKANSAS	18
Arkansas State University-Newport	ARKANSAS	18
Arkansas State University-Searcy	ARKANSAS	18
Arkansas State University System	ARKANSAS	17
Arkansas Tech University	ARKANSAS	18
Arkansas Tech University-Ozark Campus	ARKANSAS	18
Arlington Baptist University	TEXAS	442
Armstrong State University	GEORGIA	115
Art Academy of Cincinnati	OHIO	356
Art Center College of Design	CALIFORNIA	26
Art Institute of Atlanta, The	GEORGIA	115
Art Institute of Austin, The	TEXAS	443
Art Institute of California - San Francisco, a campus of Argosy University, The	CALIFORNIA	26
Art Institute of California, A College of Argosy University - Hollywood, The	CALIFORNIA	26
Art Institute of California, A College of Argosy University - Inland Empire, The	CALIFORNIA	26
Art Institute of California, A College of Argosy University - Orange County, The	CALIFORNIA	26
Art Institute of California, A College of Argosy University - Sacramento, The	CALIFORNIA	26
Art Institute of California, A College of Argosy University - San Diego, The	CALIFORNIA	26
Art Institute of Charleston, The	SOUTH CAROLINA	418
Art Institute of Charlotte, The	NORTH CAROLINA	335
Art Institute of Colorado, The	COLORADO	76
Art Institute of Dallas	TEXAS	443
Art Institute of Fort Lauderdale, The	FLORIDA	94
Art Institute of Houston, The	TEXAS	443
Art Institute of Indianapolis, The	INDIANA	156
Art Institute of Las Vegas, The	NEVADA	278
Art Institute of Michigan, The	MICHIGAN	227
Art Institute of Ohio-Cincinnati, The	OHIO	356
Art Institute of Philadelphia	PENNSYLVANIA	389
Art Institute of Phoenix, The	ARIZONA	11
Art Institute of Pittsburgh	PENNSYLVANIA	389
Art Institute of Portland, The	OREGON	381
Art Institute of Raleigh-Durham, The	NORTH CAROLINA	335
Art Institute of St. Louis, The	MISSOURI	257
Art Institute of Salt Lake City, The	UTAH	471
Art Institute of San Antonio, The	TEXAS	443
Art Institute of Seattle, The	WASHINGTON	492
Art Institute of Tampa, The	FLORIDA	94
Art Institute of Tennessee-Nashville, The	TENNESSEE	430
Art Institute of Tucson, The	ARIZONA	11
Art Institute of Virginia Beach, The	VIRGINIA	478
Art Institute of Washington, The	VIRGINIA	478
Art Institute of Wisconsin, The	WISCONSIN	506
Art Institutes International - Kansas City, The	KANSAS	174
Art Institutes International Minnesota, The	MINNESOTA	240
ASA College	NEW YORK	298
Asbury Theological Seminary	KENTUCKY	183
Asbury University	KENTUCKY	183
Asher College	CALIFORNIA	26
Asheville - Buncombe Technical Community College	NORTH CAROLINA	340
Ashford University	CALIFORNIA	26
Ashland Community and Technical College	KENTUCKY	185
Ashland University	OHIO	356
Ashworth College	GEORGIA	115
Asnuntuck Community College	CONNECTICUT	85
Aspen University	COLORADO	76
Assemblies of God Theological Seminary	MISSOURI	257
Association Free Lutheran Bible School and Seminary	MINNESOTA	240
Assumption College	MASSACHUSETTS	210
Assumption College for Sisters	NEW JERSEY	283
ATA Career Education-Spring Hill	FLORIDA	94
ATA College	KENTUCKY	183
Atenas College	PUERTO RICO	520
Athenaeum of Ohio	OHIO	356
Athens College of Ministry	GEORGIA	115
Athens State University	ALABAMA	4
Athens Technical College	GEORGIA	115
Atlanta Metropolitan State College	GEORGIA	115
Atlanta Technical College	GEORGIA	115
Atlanta's John Marshall Law School	GEORGIA	115
Atlantic Cape Community College	NEW JERSEY	283
Atlantic Institute of Oriental Medicine	FLORIDA	94
Atlantic University	VIRGINIA	478
Atlantic University College	PUERTO RICO	521
Atlantis University	FLORIDA	95
Auburn University	ALABAMA	4
Auburn University at Montgomery	ALABAMA	4
Augsburg College	MINNESOTA	240
Augusta Technical College	GEORGIA	116
Augusta University	GEORGIA	116
Augustana College	ILLINOIS	133
Augustana University	SOUTH DAKOTA	426
Auguste Escoffier School of Culinary Arts	COLORADO	77
Auguste Escoffier School of Culinary Arts	TEXAS	443
Augustine Institute	COLORADO	77
Aultman College of Nursing and Health Sciences	OHIO	357
Aurora University	ILLINOIS	133
Austin College	TEXAS	443
Austin Community College District	TEXAS	443
Austin Graduate School of Theology	TEXAS	443
Austin Peay State University	TENNESSEE	430
Austin Presbyterian Theological Seminary	TEXAS	443
Ave Maria School of Law	FLORIDA	95
Ave Maria University	FLORIDA	95
Averett University	VIRGINIA	478
Aviator College of Aeronautical Science & Technology	FLORIDA	95
Avila University	MISSOURI	257
Azure College	FLORIDA	95
Azusa Pacific University	CALIFORNIA	26
Babel University Professional School of Translation	HAWAII	128
Babson College	MASSACHUSETTS	211
Bacone College	OKLAHOMA	374
Bainbridge State College	GEORGIA	116
Bais Binyomin Academy, Inc	NEW YORK	298
Bais HaMedrash & Mesivta of Baltimore	MARYLAND	202
Bais Medrash Ateres Shlomo	NEW YORK	298
Bais Medrash Mayan Hatorah	NEW JERSEY	283
Bais Medrash Toras Chesed	NEW JERSEY	283
Bais Medrash Zicron Meir	NEW JERSEY	283
Baker College of Allen Park	MICHIGAN	227
Baker College of Auburn Hills	MICHIGAN	227
Baker College of Cadillac	MICHIGAN	227
Baker College of Clinton Township	MICHIGAN	227
Baker College of Flint	MICHIGAN	227
Baker College of Jackson	MICHIGAN	227
Baker College of Muskegon	MICHIGAN	227
Baker College of Owosso	MICHIGAN	227
Baker College of Port Huron	MICHIGAN	227
Baker College System	MICHIGAN	227
Baker University	KANSAS	174
Baker University School of Professional and Graduate Studies	KANSAS	175
Bakersfield College	CALIFORNIA	47

Institution	State	Page
Brightwood College	OHIO	357
Brightwood College	TENNESSEE	430
Brightwood College	TEXAS	444
Brightwood College	TEXAS	445
Brightwood College	TEXAS	444
Brightwood College	TEXAS	445
Brightwood College	TEXAS	444
Brightwood College-Friendswood	TEXAS	445
Bristol Community College	MASSACHUSETTS	219
Brite Divinity School	TEXAS	445
Broad Center for the Management of School Systems, The	CALIFORNIA	28
Broadview Entertainment Arts University	UTAH	471
Broadview University	IDAHO	131
Broadview University	UTAH	471
Brookdale Community College	NEW JERSEY	284
Brookdale Community College Western Monmouth Branch Campus	NEW JERSEY	284
Brookes Bible College	MISSOURI	257
Brookhaven College	TEXAS	447
Brookline College	ARIZONA	11
Brookline College	NEW MEXICO	293
Brooklyn Law School	NEW YORK	300
Broward College	FLORIDA	96
Brown College of Court Reporting	GEORGIA	117
Brown Mackie College-Akron	OHIO	357
Brown Mackie College - Albuquerque	NEW MEXICO	293
Brown Mackie College-Fort Wayne	INDIANA	156
Brown Mackie College-Greenville	SOUTH CAROLINA	418
Brown Mackie College-Louisville	KENTUCKY	184
Brown Mackie College-Salina	KANSAS	175
Brown Mackie College - San Antonio	TEXAS	445
Brown Mackie College-Tucson	ARIZONA	11
Brown University	RHODE ISLAND	415
Brunswick Community College	NORTH CAROLINA	341
Bryan College	TENNESSEE	430
Bryan College of Health Sciences	NEBRASKA	273
Bryan University	ARIZONA	11
Bryan University	ARKANSAS	19
Bryan University	CALIFORNIA	28
Bryan University	KANSAS	175
Bryan University	MISSOURI	257
Bryant & Stratton College	NEW YORK	300
Bryant & Stratton College	OHIO	357
Bryant & Stratton College	VIRGINIA	478
Bryant & Stratton College	WISCONSIN	506
Bryant & Stratton College System Office	NEW YORK	300
Bryant University	RHODE ISLAND	416
Bryn Athyn College of the New Church	PENNSYLVANIA	390
Bryn Mawr College	PENNSYLVANIA	390
Bucknell University	PENNSYLVANIA	390
Bucks County Community College	PENNSYLVANIA	390
Buena Vista University	IOWA	167
Bunker Hill Community College	MASSACHUSETTS	219
Burrell College of Osteopathic Medicine	NEW MEXICO	293
Butler Community College	KANSAS	175
Butler County Community College	PENNSYLVANIA	390
Butler of Andover	KANSAS	176
Butler of Council Grove	KANSAS	176
Butler of Marion	KANSAS	176
Butler of McConnell	KANSAS	176
Butler of Rose Hill	KANSAS	176
Butler University	INDIANA	156
Butte College	CALIFORNIA	28
Byzantine Catholic Seminary of Ss. Cyril and Methodius	PENNSYLVANIA	391
Cabarrus College of Health Sciences	NORTH CAROLINA	336
Cabrillo College	CALIFORNIA	28
Cabrini University	PENNSYLVANIA	391
Cairn University	PENNSYLVANIA	391
Caldwell Community College and Technical Institute	NORTH CAROLINA	341
Caldwell University	NEW JERSEY	284
Calhoun Community College	ALABAMA	1
California Baptist University	CALIFORNIA	28
California Career College	CALIFORNIA	28
California Christian College	CALIFORNIA	28
California Coast University	CALIFORNIA	28
California College of the Arts	CALIFORNIA	28
California College San Diego	CALIFORNIA	29
California Graduate School of Theology	CALIFORNIA	29
California Health Sciences University	CALIFORNIA	29
California Institute of Advanced Management	CALIFORNIA	29
California Institute of Arts & Technology	CALIFORNIA	29
California Institute of Integral Studies	CALIFORNIA	29
California Institute of Management and Technology	CALIFORNIA	30
California Institute of Technology	CALIFORNIA	29
California Institute of the Arts	CALIFORNIA	29
California Intercontinental University	CALIFORNIA	30
California International Business University	CALIFORNIA	30
California Jazz Conservatory	CALIFORNIA	30
California Lutheran University	CALIFORNIA	30
California Miramar University	CALIFORNIA	30
California National University for Advanced Studies	CALIFORNIA	30
California Northstate University	CALIFORNIA	30
California Polytechnic State University-San Luis Obispo	CALIFORNIA	30
California Southern University	CALIFORNIA	30
California State Polytechnic University-Pomona	CALIFORNIA	31
California State University-Bakersfield	CALIFORNIA	31
California State University Channel Islands	CALIFORNIA	31
California State University-Chico	CALIFORNIA	31
California State University-Dominguez Hills	CALIFORNIA	31
California State University-East Bay	CALIFORNIA	31
California State University-Fresno	CALIFORNIA	32
California State University-Fullerton	CALIFORNIA	32
California State University-Long Beach	CALIFORNIA	32
California State University-Los Angeles	CALIFORNIA	32
California State University-Monterey Bay	CALIFORNIA	33
California State University-Northridge	CALIFORNIA	33
California State University-Sacramento	CALIFORNIA	33
California State University-San Bernardino	CALIFORNIA	33
California State University-San Marcos	CALIFORNIA	33
California State University-Stanislaus	CALIFORNIA	33
California State University System Office, The	CALIFORNIA	30
California University of Management and Sciences	CALIFORNIA	35
California University of Management and Sciences Virginia	VIRGINIA	478
California University of Pennsylvania	PENNSYLVANIA	405
California Western School of Law	CALIFORNIA	35
Calumet College of Saint Joseph	INDIANA	157
Calvary University	MISSOURI	257
Calvin College	MICHIGAN	228
Calvin Theological Seminary	MICHIGAN	228
Cambridge College	FLORIDA	96
Cambridge College	MASSACHUSETTS	213
Cambridge Institute of Allied Health & Technology	GEORGIA	117
Cambridge Institute of Allied Health & Technology-Altamonte Springs	FLORIDA	96
Cambridge Junior College	CALIFORNIA	35
Camden County College	NEW JERSEY	284
Camden County College Camden City Campus	NEW JERSEY	284
Cameron College	LOUISIANA	191
Cameron University	OKLAHOMA	375
Campbell University	NORTH CAROLINA	336
Campbellsville University	KENTUCKY	184
Cañada College	CALIFORNIA	61
Canisius College	NEW YORK	300
Cankdeska Cikana Community College	NORTH DAKOTA	353
Cape Cod Community College	MASSACHUSETTS	219
Cape Fear Community College	NORTH CAROLINA	341
Capella University	MINNESOTA	241
Capital Community College	CONNECTICUT	85
Capital University	OHIO	358
Capital University Law School	OHIO	358
Capitol Technology University	MARYLAND	202
Carbon County Higher Education Center/Rawlins	WYOMING	516
Cardinal Stritch University	WISCONSIN	506
Career College of Northern Nevada	NEVADA	278
Career Quest Learning Center	MICHIGAN	228
Career Training Academy	PENNSYLVANIA	391
Caribbean University	PUERTO RICO	521
Caris College	INDIANA	157
Carl Albert State College	OKLAHOMA	375
Carl Sandburg College	ILLINOIS	134
Carl Sandburg College The Branch Campus	ILLINOIS	134
Carleton College	MINNESOTA	241
Carlos Albizu University	PUERTO RICO	521
Carlos Albizu University Miami Campus	FLORIDA	96
Carlow University	PENNSYLVANIA	391
Carnegie Mellon University	PENNSYLVANIA	391
Carnegie Mellon University Silicon Valley Campus	CALIFORNIA	35
Carolina Christian College	NORTH CAROLINA	336
Carolina College of Biblical Studies	NORTH CAROLINA	336
Carolinas College of Health Sciences	NORTH CAROLINA	336
Carrington College - Administrative Office	CALIFORNIA	35
Carrington College - Albuquerque	NEW MEXICO	293
Carrington College - Boise	IDAHO	131
Carrington College - Citrus Heights	CALIFORNIA	35
Carrington College - Las Vegas	NEVADA	278
Carrington College - Mesa	ARIZONA	11
Carrington College - Mesquite	TEXAS	445
Carrington College - Phoenix East	ARIZONA	11
Carrington College - Phoenix North	ARIZONA	11
Carrington College - Pleasant Hill	CALIFORNIA	35
Carrington College - Pomona	CALIFORNIA	35
Carrington College - Reno	NEVADA	278
Carrington College - Sacramento	CALIFORNIA	35
Carrington College - San Jose	CALIFORNIA	35
Carrington College - San Leandro	CALIFORNIA	35
Carrington College - Spokane	WASHINGTON	492
Carrington College - Stockton	CALIFORNIA	35
Carrington College - Tucson	ARIZONA	11
Carroll College	MONTANA	270
Carroll Community College	MARYLAND	203
Carroll University	WISCONSIN	506
Carson-Newman University	TENNESSEE	430

Institution	State	Page
City University of New York John Jay College of Criminal Justice	NEW YORK	302
City University of New York Kingsborough Community College	NEW YORK	303
City University of New York Medgar Evers College	NEW YORK	303
City University of New York Queens College	NEW YORK	303
City University of New York Queensborough Community College	NEW YORK	303
City University of New York Stella and Charles Guttman Community College	NEW YORK	303
City University of New York The City College	NEW YORK	301
City University of New York York College	NEW YORK	304
City University of Seattle	WASHINGTON	493
City Vision University	MISSOURI	258
Clackamas Community College	OREGON	382
Claflin University	SOUTH CAROLINA	419
Claremont Graduate University	CALIFORNIA	37
Claremont Lincoln University	CALIFORNIA	37
Claremont McKenna College	CALIFORNIA	38
Claremont School of Theology	CALIFORNIA	38
Claremont University Consortium	CALIFORNIA	37
Clarendon College	TEXAS	445
Clarion University of Pennsylvania	PENNSYLVANIA	405
Clarion University, Venango	PENNSYLVANIA	407
Clark Atlanta University	GEORGIA	117
Clark College	WASHINGTON	493
Clark State Community College	OHIO	359
Clark State Community College Greene Center	OHIO	359
Clark University	MASSACHUSETTS	213
Clarke University	IOWA	167
Clarks Summit University	PENNSYLVANIA	392
Clarkson College	NEBRASKA	273
Clarkson University	NEW YORK	304
Clary Sage College	OKLAHOMA	375
Clatsop Community College	OREGON	382
Clayton State University	GEORGIA	117
Clear Creek Baptist Bible College	KENTUCKY	184
Cleary University	MICHIGAN	228
Clemson University	SOUTH CAROLINA	419
Cleveland Community College	NORTH CAROLINA	342
Cleveland Institute of Art	OHIO	359
Cleveland Institute of Music	OHIO	359
Cleveland State Community College	TENNESSEE	436
Cleveland State University	OHIO	359
Cleveland University - Kansas City	KANSAS	176
Clinton College	SOUTH CAROLINA	419
Clinton Community College	IOWA	168
Clinton Community College	NEW YORK	304
Cloud County Community College	KANSAS	176
Cloud County Community College Geary County Campus	KANSAS	176
Clover Park Technical College	WASHINGTON	493
Clovis Community College	CALIFORNIA	66
Clovis Community College	NEW MEXICO	293
CNI College	CALIFORNIA	38
Coahoma Community College	MISSISSIPPI	252
Coast Community College District Administration Offices	CALIFORNIA	38
Coastal Alabama Community College	ALABAMA	1
Coastal Bend College	TEXAS	445
Coastal Carolina Community College	NORTH CAROLINA	342
Coastal Carolina University	SOUTH CAROLINA	420
Coastal Pines Technical College	GEORGIA	117
Coastline Community College	CALIFORNIA	38
Cochise College	ARIZONA	12
Cochise College	ARIZONA	11
Cochran School of Nursing	NEW YORK	304
Coconino Community College	ARIZONA	12
Coconino County Community College Flagstaff Fourth Street Campus	ARIZONA	12
Coe College	IOWA	167
Coffeyville Community College	KANSAS	176
Cogswell Polytechnical College	CALIFORNIA	38
Coker College	SOUTH CAROLINA	420
Colburn School, The	CALIFORNIA	39
Colby College	MAINE	198
Colby Community College	KANSAS	176
Colby-Sawyer College	NEW HAMPSHIRE	280
Cold Spring Harbor Laboratory/Watson School of Biological Sciences	NEW YORK	304
Colegio de Cinematografia, Artes y Television	PUERTO RICO	521
Colegio Universitario de San Juan	PUERTO RICO	521
Coleman University	CALIFORNIA	39
Colgate Rochester Crozer Divinity School	NEW YORK	304
Colgate University	NEW YORK	304
College for Creative Studies	MICHIGAN	228
College for Financial Planning	COLORADO	77
College of Alameda	CALIFORNIA	56
College of Biblical Studies-Houston	TEXAS	446
College of Business and Technology	FLORIDA	96
College of Business and Technology - Cutler Bay	FLORIDA	96
College of Business and Technology - Flagler	FLORIDA	96
College of Business and Technology - Hialeah Campus	FLORIDA	97
College of Business and Technology - Miami Gardens	FLORIDA	97
College of Central Florida	FLORIDA	97
College of Charleston	SOUTH CAROLINA	420
College of Coastal Georgia	GEORGIA	118
College of Court Reporting, Inc.	INDIANA	157
College of DuPage	ILLINOIS	136
College of Eastern Idaho	IDAHO	131
College of Emergency Services	OREGON	382
College of Health Care Professions-Dallas, The	TEXAS	446
College of Health Care Professions-Fort Worth, The	TEXAS	446
College of Health Care Professions-McAllen, The	TEXAS	446
College of Health Care Professions-San Antonio, The	TEXAS	446
College of Health Care Professions, The	TEXAS	446
College of Idaho, The	IDAHO	131
College of Lake County	ILLINOIS	136
College of Lake County Lakeshore Campus	ILLINOIS	136
College of Lake County Southlake Campus	ILLINOIS	136
College of Marin	CALIFORNIA	39
College of Medicine, Mayo Clinic	MINNESOTA	241
College of Menominee Nation	WISCONSIN	506
College of Menominee Nation Oneida Campus	WISCONSIN	507
College of Micronesia-FSM	FED ST OF MICRONESIA	519
College of Mount Saint Vincent	NEW YORK	304
College of New Jersey, The	NEW JERSEY	284
College of New Rochelle, The	NEW YORK	305
College of Our Lady of the Elms	MASSACHUSETTS	213
College of Saint Benedict	MINNESOTA	241
College of Saint Elizabeth	NEW JERSEY	285
College of St. Joseph	VERMONT	474
College of Saint Mary	NEBRASKA	274
College of Saint Rose, The	NEW YORK	305
College of Saint Scholastica, The	MINNESOTA	241
College of San Mateo	CALIFORNIA	62
College of Southern Idaho	IDAHO	131
College of Southern Maryland	MARYLAND	203
College of Southern Nevada	NEVADA	278
College of Staten Island CUNY	NEW YORK	302
College of the Albemarle	NORTH CAROLINA	342
College of the Atlantic	MAINE	199
College of the Canyons	CALIFORNIA	39
College of the Desert	CALIFORNIA	39
College of the Holy Cross	MASSACHUSETTS	213
College of the Mainland	TEXAS	446
College of the Marshall Islands	MARSHALL ISLANDS	520
College of the Muscogee Nation	OKLAHOMA	375
College of the Ouachitas	ARKANSAS	19
College of the Ozarks	MISSOURI	258
College of the Redwoods Community College District	CALIFORNIA	39
College of the Sequoias	CALIFORNIA	39
College of the Siskiyous	CALIFORNIA	39
College of Westchester, The	NEW YORK	305
College of Western Idaho	IDAHO	132
College of William & Mary	VIRGINIA	479
College of Wooster, The	OHIO	360
CollegeAmerica Colorado Springs	COLORADO	77
CollegeAmerica Denver	COLORADO	77
CollegeAmerica-Flagstaff	ARIZONA	12
CollegeAmerica Fort Collins	COLORADO	77
CollegeAmerica-Phoenix	ARIZONA	12
Collin County Community College District	TEXAS	446
Colorado Academy of Veterinary Technology	COLORADO	77
Colorado Christian University	COLORADO	77
Colorado College	COLORADO	77
Colorado Mesa University	COLORADO	77
Colorado Mesa University-Montrose Campus	COLORADO	77
Colorado Mountain College	COLORADO	77
Colorado Mountain College Alpine Campus	COLORADO	78
Colorado Mountain College Aspen Campus	COLORADO	78
Colorado Mountain College Roaring Fork Campus-Spring Valley	COLORADO	78
Colorado Mountain College Summit Campus-Breckinridge Center	COLORADO	78
Colorado Mountain College Timberline Campus	COLORADO	78
Colorado Mountain College Vail Valley Campus at Edwards	COLORADO	78
Colorado Mountain College West Garfield Campus	COLORADO	78
Colorado Northwestern Community College	COLORADO	78
Colorado Northwestern Community College Craig	COLORADO	78
Colorado School of Mines	COLORADO	78
Colorado School of Trades	COLORADO	78
Colorado School of Traditional Chinese Medicine	COLORADO	78
Colorado State University	COLORADO	78
Colorado State University-Global Campus	COLORADO	78
Colorado State University-Pueblo	COLORADO	78
Colorado State University System Office	COLORADO	78
Colorado Technical University	COLORADO	79
Columbia Basin College	WASHINGTON	493
Columbia Central University	PUERTO RICO	521
Columbia Centro Universitario	PUERTO RICO	522
Columbia College	CALIFORNIA	75
Columbia College	MISSOURI	258
Columbia College	SOUTH CAROLINA	420

Institution	State	Page
Genesee Community College	NEW YORK	309
Geneva College	PENNSYLVANIA	395
George C. Wallace Community College - Dothan	ALABAMA	2
George Corley Wallace State Community College - Selma	ALABAMA	2
George Fox University	OREGON	383
George Mason University	VIRGINIA	481
George Washington University	DISTRICT OF COLUMBIA	92
George Williams College of Aurora University	WISCONSIN	507
Georgetown College	KENTUCKY	184
Georgetown University	DISTRICT OF COLUMBIA	92
Georgia Christian University	GEORGIA	119
Georgia College & State University	GEORGIA	119
Georgia Gwinnett College	GEORGIA	119
Georgia Highlands College	GEORGIA	119
Georgia Institute of Technology	GEORGIA	120
Georgia Military College	GEORGIA	120
Georgia Northwestern Technical College	GEORGIA	120
Georgia Piedmont Technical College	GEORGIA	120
Georgia Southern University	GEORGIA	120
Georgia Southwestern State University	GEORGIA	120
Georgia State University	GEORGIA	121
Georgian Court University	NEW JERSEY	286
Germanna Community College	VIRGINIA	488
Gettysburg College	PENNSYLVANIA	396
Gillette College	WYOMING	516
Glen Oaks Community College	MICHIGAN	230
Glendale Career College	CALIFORNIA	44
Glendale Community College	ARIZONA	13
Glendale Community College	CALIFORNIA	44
Glendale Community College North	ARIZONA	14
Glenville State College	WEST VIRGINIA	504
Global Health College	VIRGINIA	481
Global University	MISSOURI	260
Goddard College	VERMONT	475
God's Bible School and College	OHIO	362
Gogebic Community College	MICHIGAN	230
Golden Gate University	CALIFORNIA	44
Golden State University	CALIFORNIA	44
Golden West College	CALIFORNIA	38
Goldey-Beacom College	DELAWARE	90
Goldfarb School of Nursing at Barnes-Jewish College	MISSOURI	260
Golf Academy of America	ARIZONA	12
Golf Academy of America	CALIFORNIA	44
Golf Academy of America	FLORIDA	101
Golf Academy of America	SOUTH CAROLINA	421
Golf Academy of America	TEXAS	449
Gonzaga University	WASHINGTON	495
Good Samaritan College of Nursing and Health Science	OHIO	362
Goodwin College	CONNECTICUT	87
Gordon College	MASSACHUSETTS	215
Gordon-Conwell Theological Seminary	MASSACHUSETTS	215
Gordon-Conwell Theological Seminary-Jacksonville	FLORIDA	101
Gordon State College	GEORGIA	121
Goshen College	INDIANA	158
Goucher College	MARYLAND	204
Governors State University	ILLINOIS	138
Grace Bible College	MICHIGAN	230
Grace College and Seminary	INDIANA	158
Grace College of Divinity	NORTH CAROLINA	338
Grace Communion Seminary	CALIFORNIA	44
Grace Mission University	CALIFORNIA	44
Grace School of Theology	TEXAS	449
Grace University	NEBRASKA	274
Graceland University	IOWA	169
Graceland University	MISSOURI	260
Graduate Institute of Applied Linguistics	TEXAS	449
Graduate Theological Union	CALIFORNIA	44
Grambling State University	LOUISIANA	196
Grand Canyon University	ARIZONA	12
Grand Rapids Community College	MICHIGAN	230
Grand Valley State University	MICHIGAN	230
Grand View University	IOWA	169
Granite State College	NEW HAMPSHIRE	282
Grantham University	KANSAS	177
Gratz College	PENNSYLVANIA	396
Grays Harbor College	WASHINGTON	495
Grayson College	TEXAS	449
Great Basin College	NEVADA	279
Great Bay Community College	NEW HAMPSHIRE	280
Great Falls College Montana State University	MONTANA	272
Great Lakes Christian College	MICHIGAN	231
Great Lakes Institute of Technology	PENNSYLVANIA	396
Green Mountain College	VERMONT	475
Green River College	WASHINGTON	495
Greenfield Community College	MASSACHUSETTS	219
Greensboro College	NORTH CAROLINA	338
Greenville Technical College	SOUTH CAROLINA	421
Greenville University	ILLINOIS	139
Grinnell College	IOWA	169
Grossmont College	CALIFORNIA	45
Grossmont-Cuyamaca Community College District	CALIFORNIA	44
Grove City College	PENNSYLVANIA	396
Guam Community College	GUAM	519
Guilford College	NORTH CAROLINA	338
Guilford Technical Community College	NORTH CAROLINA	343
Gulf Coast State College	FLORIDA	101
Gupton Jones College of Funeral Service	GEORGIA	121
Gurnick Academy of Medical Arts	CALIFORNIA	45
Gustavus Adolphus College	MINNESOTA	242
Gutenberg College	OREGON	383
Gwinnett College	GEORGIA	121
Gwinnett College-Marietta	GEORGIA	121
Gwinnett College-Sandy Springs	GEORGIA	121
Gwinnett Technical College	GEORGIA	121
Gwynedd Mercy University	PENNSYLVANIA	396
Gwynedd Mercy University at East Norriton	PENNSYLVANIA	396
HACC, Central Pennsylvania's Community College	PENNSYLVANIA	396
Hagerstown Community College	MARYLAND	204
Halifax Community College	NORTH CAROLINA	343
Hallmark University	TEXAS	449
Hamilton College	NEW YORK	309
Hamilton Technical College	IOWA	169
Hamline University	MINNESOTA	242
Hampden-Sydney College	VIRGINIA	481
Hampshire College	MASSACHUSETTS	215
Hampton University	VIRGINIA	481
Han University of Traditional Medicine	ARIZONA	12
Hannibal-LaGrange University	MISSOURI	260
Hanover College	INDIANA	158
Harcum College	PENNSYLVANIA	396
Hardin-Simmons University	TEXAS	450
Harding School of Theology	TENNESSEE	432
Harding University Main Campus	ARKANSAS	19
Harford Community College	MARYLAND	204
Harper College	ILLINOIS	139
Harrington College of Design	ILLINOIS	139
Harris-Stowe State University	MISSOURI	260
Harrisburg Area Community College Gettysburg Campus	PENNSYLVANIA	397
Harrisburg Area Community College Lancaster Campus	PENNSYLVANIA	397
Harrisburg Area Community College Lebanon Campus	PENNSYLVANIA	397
Harrisburg Area Community College York Campus	PENNSYLVANIA	397
Harrisburg University of Science and Technology	PENNSYLVANIA	397
Harrison College - Anderson Campus	INDIANA	158
Harrison College - Columbus Indiana Campus	INDIANA	158
Harrison College-Columbus Ohio Campus	OHIO	362
Harrison College - Evansville Campus	INDIANA	158
Harrison College - Fort Wayne Campus	INDIANA	158
Harrison College - Indianapolis Downtown Campus	INDIANA	158
Harrison College - Indianapolis East Campus	INDIANA	158
Harrison College - Indianapolis Northwest Campus	INDIANA	158
Harrison College - Lafayette Campus	INDIANA	158
Harrison College - Terre Haute Campus	INDIANA	158
Harrison Middleton University	ARIZONA	13
Hartford Seminary	CONNECTICUT	87
Hartnell College	CALIFORNIA	45
Hartwick College	NEW YORK	309
Harvard University	MASSACHUSETTS	215
Harvey Mudd College	CALIFORNIA	45
Haskell Indian Nations University	KANSAS	178
Hastings College	NEBRASKA	274
Haverford College	PENNSYLVANIA	397
Hawaii Medical College	HAWAII	129
Hawaii Pacific University	HAWAII	129
Hawaii Tokai International College	HAWAII	129
Hawkeye Community College	IOWA	169
Haywood Community College	NORTH CAROLINA	343
Hazard Community and Technical College	KENTUCKY	185
Hazelden Betty Ford Graduate School of Addiction Studies	MINNESOTA	242
Health Career Institute	FLORIDA	101
Heartland Christian College	MISSOURI	260
Heartland Community College	ILLINOIS	139
Hebrew College	MASSACHUSETTS	215
Hebrew Theological College	ILLINOIS	139
Hebrew Union College-Jewish Institute of Religion	NEW YORK	309
Heidelberg University	OHIO	362
Helena College University of Montana	MONTANA	271
Helene Fuld College of Nursing	NEW YORK	309
Hellenic College-Holy Cross Greek Orthodox School of Theology	MASSACHUSETTS	215
Helms College	GEORGIA	121
Henderson Community College	KENTUCKY	186
Henderson State University	ARKANSAS	19
Hendrix College	ARKANSAS	19
Henley-Putnam University	CALIFORNIA	45
Hennepin Technical College	MINNESOTA	244
Hennepin Technical College	MINNESOTA	248
Henry Ford College	MICHIGAN	231
Heritage Bible College	NORTH CAROLINA	338
Heritage Christian University	ALABAMA	5
Heritage University	WASHINGTON	495
Herkimer County Community College	NEW YORK	310
Herzing University	ALABAMA	5

Institution	State	Page
Iona College	NEW YORK	311
Iowa Central Community College	IOWA	170
Iowa Lakes Community College	IOWA	170
Iowa Lakes Community College Emmetsburg Campus	IOWA	170
Iowa Lakes Community College Spencer Campus	IOWA	170
Iowa State University	IOWA	166
Iowa Valley Community College District	IOWA	170
Iowa Wesleyan University	IOWA	170
Iowa Western Community College	IOWA	170
Irish American University	DELAWARE	90
Irvine Valley College	CALIFORNIA	64
Island Drafting and Technical Institute	NEW YORK	311
Isothermal Community College	NORTH CAROLINA	344
Itasca Community College	MINNESOTA	245
Itawamba Community College	MISSISSIPPI	253
Ithaca College	NEW YORK	311
ITI Technical College	LOUISIANA	191
Ivy Christian College	VIRGINIA	481
Ivy Tech Community College of Indiana-Anderson	INDIANA	161
Ivy Tech Community College of Indiana-Bloomington	INDIANA	161
Ivy Tech Community College of Indiana-Central Indiana	INDIANA	161
Ivy Tech Community College of Indiana-Columbus	INDIANA	161
Ivy Tech Community College of Indiana-East Central	INDIANA	161
Ivy Tech Community College of Indiana-East Chicago	INDIANA	161
Ivy Tech Community College of Indiana-Elkhart	INDIANA	161
Ivy Tech Community College of Indiana-Kokomo	INDIANA	161
Ivy Tech Community College of Indiana-Lafayette	INDIANA	161
Ivy Tech Community College of Indiana-Lawrenceburg-Riverfront	INDIANA	162
Ivy Tech Community College of Indiana-Logansport	INDIANA	162
Ivy Tech Community College of Indiana-Marion	INDIANA	162
Ivy Tech Community College of Indiana-Michigan City	INDIANA	162
Ivy Tech Community College of Indiana-North Central	INDIANA	162
Ivy Tech Community College of Indiana-Northeast	INDIANA	162
Ivy Tech Community College of Indiana-Northwest	INDIANA	162
Ivy Tech Community College of Indiana-Richmond	INDIANA	162
Ivy Tech Community College of Indiana-Southeast	INDIANA	162
Ivy Tech Community College of Indiana-Southern Indiana	INDIANA	162
Ivy Tech Community College of Indiana-Southwest	INDIANA	162
Ivy Tech Community College of Indiana-System Office	INDIANA	161
Ivy Tech Community College of Indiana-Valparaiso	INDIANA	162
Ivy Tech Community College of Indiana-Wabash	INDIANA	162
Ivy Tech Community College of Indiana-Wabash Valley	INDIANA	162
Ivy Tech Community College of Indiana-Warsaw	INDIANA	162
J. Sargeant Reynolds Community College	VIRGINIA	488
Jackson College	MICHIGAN	231
Jackson State Community College	TENNESSEE	437
Jackson State University	MISSISSIPPI	253
Jacksonville College	TEXAS	451
Jacksonville State University	ALABAMA	6
Jacksonville University	FLORIDA	102
James A. Rhodes State College	OHIO	363
James Madison University	VIRGINIA	481
James Sprunt Community College	NORTH CAROLINA	344
Jamestown Business College	NEW YORK	311
Jamestown Community College	NEW YORK	311
Jamestown Community College Cattaraugus County Campus	NEW YORK	311
Jarvis Christian College	TEXAS	451
Jefferson College	MISSOURI	261
Jefferson College of Health Sciences	VIRGINIA	482
Jefferson Community and Technical College	KENTUCKY	186
Jefferson Community College	NEW YORK	311
Jefferson Regional Medical Center School of Nursing	ARKANSAS	20
Jefferson State Community College	ALABAMA	2
Jewish Theological Seminary of America	NEW YORK	312
J.F. Drake State Community and Technical College	ALABAMA	2
J.F. Ingram State Technical College	ALABAMA	2
JNA Institute of Culinary Arts	PENNSYLVANIA	397
John A. Gupton College	TENNESSEE	432
John A. Logan College	ILLINOIS	141
John Brown University	ARKANSAS	20
John Carroll University	OHIO	363
John F. Kennedy University	CALIFORNIA	46
John Leland Center for Theological Studies, The	VIRGINIA	482
John Marshall Law School	ILLINOIS	141
John Paul the Great Catholic University	CALIFORNIA	46
John Tyler Community College	VIRGINIA	488
John Wesley University	NORTH CAROLINA	338
John Witherspoon College	SOUTH DAKOTA	427
John Wood Community College	ILLINOIS	141
Johns Hopkins University	MARYLAND	204
Johnson & Wales University	FLORIDA	102
Johnson & Wales University	RHODE ISLAND	416
Johnson & Wales University-Charlotte	NORTH CAROLINA	338
Johnson & Wales University - Denver Campus	COLORADO	80
Johnson C. Smith University	NORTH CAROLINA	338
Johnson College	PENNSYLVANIA	398
Johnson County Community College	KANSAS	178
Johnson State College	VERMONT	477
Johnson University	TENNESSEE	432
Johnson University Florida	FLORIDA	102
Johnston Community College	NORTH CAROLINA	344
Joint Forces Staff College	US SERVICE SCHOOLS	517
Joliet Junior College	ILLINOIS	142
Jones County Junior College	MISSISSIPPI	253
Jose Maria Vargas University	FLORIDA	102
Judge Advocate General's Legal Center & School, The	US SERVICE SCHOOLS	517
Judson College	ALABAMA	6
Judson University	ILLINOIS	142
Juilliard School, The	NEW YORK	312
Juniata College	PENNSYLVANIA	398
Kaiser Permanente School of Allied Health Sciences	CALIFORNIA	46
Kalamazoo College	MICHIGAN	231
Kalamazoo Valley Community College	MICHIGAN	231
Kankakee Community College	ILLINOIS	142
Kansas Christian College	KANSAS	178
Kansas City Art Institute	MISSOURI	261
Kansas City Kansas Community College	KANSAS	178
Kansas City University of Medicine & Biosciences	MISSOURI	261
Kansas State University	KANSAS	179
Kansas State University Polytechnic, College of Technology and Aviation	KANSAS	179
Kansas Wesleyan University	KANSAS	179
Kapiolani Community College	HAWAII	130
Kaplan University	IOWA	171
Kaplan University	MARYLAND	204
Kaplan University	NEBRASKA	275
Kaplan University-Augusta	MAINE	199
Kaplan University-Cedar Falls	IOWA	171
Kaplan University-Lewiston	MAINE	199
Kaplan University-Maine	MAINE	199
Kaskaskia College	ILLINOIS	142
KD Conservatory College of Film and Dramatic Arts	TEXAS	451
Kean University	NEW JERSEY	286
Keck Graduate Institute	CALIFORNIA	38
Keene State College	NEW HAMPSHIRE	283
Kehilath Yakov Rabbinical Seminary	NEW YORK	312
Keiser University	FLORIDA	102
Keiser University at Clearwater	FLORIDA	102
Keiser University-Jacksonville Campus	FLORIDA	102
Kellogg Community College	MICHIGAN	232
Kendall College	ILLINOIS	142
Kendall College of Art & Design of Ferris State University	MICHIGAN	232
Kennebec Valley Community College	MAINE	200
Kennesaw State University	GEORGIA	122
Kenrick-Glennon Seminary, Kenrick School of Theology	MISSOURI	261
Kent State University at Ashtabula	OHIO	363
Kent State University East Liverpool Campus	OHIO	363
Kent State University Geauga Campus	OHIO	363
Kent State University Kent Campus	OHIO	363
Kent State University Salem Campus	OHIO	363
Kent State University Stark Campus	OHIO	363
Kent State University Trumbull Campus	OHIO	363
Kent State University Tuscarawas Campus	OHIO	363
Kentucky Christian University	KENTUCKY	185
Kentucky Community and Technical College System	KENTUCKY	185
Kentucky Mountain Bible College	KENTUCKY	187
Kentucky State University	KENTUCKY	187
Kentucky Wesleyan College	KENTUCKY	187
Kenyon College	OHIO	364
Kern Community College District	CALIFORNIA	46
Kernel University	CALIFORNIA	47
Kettering College	OHIO	364
Kettering University	MICHIGAN	232
Keuka College	NEW YORK	312
Keweenaw Bay Ojibwa Community College	MICHIGAN	232
Key College	FLORIDA	102
Keystone College	PENNSYLVANIA	398
Kilgore College	TEXAS	451
King University	TENNESSEE	432
King's College	NORTH CAROLINA	339
King's College	PENNSYLVANIA	398
King's College, The	NEW YORK	312
Kings Park University	VIRGINIA	482
King's University, The	TEXAS	451
Kingston University	CALIFORNIA	47
Kirkwood Community College	IOWA	171
Kirkwood Community College Iowa City	IOWA	171
Kirtland Community College	MICHIGAN	232
Kishwaukee College	ILLINOIS	142
Klamath Community College	OREGON	383
Knox College	ILLINOIS	142
Knox Theological Seminary	FLORIDA	102
Kutztown University of Pennsylvania	PENNSYLVANIA	406
Kuyper College	MICHIGAN	232
La Roche College	PENNSYLVANIA	398
La Salle University	PENNSYLVANIA	398
La Sierra University	CALIFORNIA	47
Labette Community College	KANSAS	179
Laboure College	MASSACHUSETTS	216

Institution	State	Page
Luna Community College	NEW MEXICO	294
Lurleen B. Wallace Community College	ALABAMA	2
Luther College	IOWA	171
Luther Rice College and Seminary	GEORGIA	122
Luther Seminary	MINNESOTA	242
Lutheran Brethren Seminary	MINNESOTA	243
Lutheran School of Theology at Chicago	ILLINOIS	144
Luzerne County Community College	PENNSYLVANIA	400
Lycoming College	PENNSYLVANIA	400
Lynchburg College	VIRGINIA	482
Lyndon State College	VERMONT	477
Lynn University	FLORIDA	103
Lyon College	ARKANSAS	20
Macalester College	MINNESOTA	243
MacCormac College	ILLINOIS	144
Machzikei Hadath Rabbinical College	NEW YORK	313
MacMurray College	ILLINOIS	144
Macomb Community College	MICHIGAN	233
Madison Area Technical College	WISCONSIN	514
Madison Area Technical College Commercial Avenue Education Center	WISCONSIN	515
Madison Area Technical College Downtown Education Center	WISCONSIN	515
Madison Area Technical College Fort Atkinson	WISCONSIN	515
Madison Area Technical College Portage	WISCONSIN	515
Madison Area Technical College Reedsburg	WISCONSIN	515
Madison Area Technical College Watertown	WISCONSIN	515
Madison Media Institute-College of Media Arts	WISCONSIN	507
Madisonville Community College	KENTUCKY	186
Madonna University	MICHIGAN	233
Maharishi University of Management	IOWA	171
Maine College of Art	MAINE	199
Maine College of Health Professions	MAINE	199
Maine Community College System	MAINE	199
Maine Maritime Academy	MAINE	200
Malcolm X College, One of the City Colleges of Chicago	ILLINOIS	136
Malone University	OHIO	364
Manchester Community College	CONNECTICUT	85
Manchester Community College	NEW HAMPSHIRE	280
Manchester University	INDIANA	162
Mandl School - The College of Allied Health	NEW YORK	313
Manhattan Area Technical College	KANSAS	179
Manhattan Christian College	KANSAS	179
Manhattan College	NEW YORK	313
Manhattan School of Music	NEW YORK	313
Manhattanville College	NEW YORK	314
Manor College	PENNSYLVANIA	401
Mansfield University of Pennsylvania	PENNSYLVANIA	406
Maple Springs Baptist Bible College & Seminary	MARYLAND	205
Maranatha Baptist University	WISCONSIN	508
Maria College of Albany	NEW YORK	314
Marian University	INDIANA	162
Marian University	WISCONSIN	508
Maricopa County Community College District Office	ARIZONA	13
Marietta College	OHIO	365
Marine Corps University	US SERVICE SCHOOLS	518
Marion Military Institute	ALABAMA	3
Marion Technical College	OHIO	365
Marist College	NEW YORK	314
Marlboro College	VERMONT	475
Marlboro College Graduate School	VERMONT	475
Marquette University	WISCONSIN	508
Mars Hill University	NORTH CAROLINA	339
Marshall B. Ketchum University	CALIFORNIA	51
Marshall University	WEST VIRGINIA	504
Marshalltown Community College	IOWA	170
Martin Community College	NORTH CAROLINA	344
Martin Luther College	MINNESOTA	243
Martin Methodist College	TENNESSEE	433
Martin University	INDIANA	162
Martinsburg College	WEST VIRGINIA	502
Mary Baldwin University	VIRGINIA	482
Mary Lanning Healthcare School of Radiology	NEBRASKA	275
Marygrove College	MICHIGAN	233
Maryland Institute College of Art	MARYLAND	205
Maryland University of Integrative Health	MARYLAND	205
Marylhurst University	OREGON	384
Marymount California University	CALIFORNIA	51
Marymount Manhattan College	NEW YORK	314
Marymount University	VIRGINIA	483
Maryville College	TENNESSEE	433
Maryville University of Saint Louis	MISSOURI	262
Marywood University	PENNSYLVANIA	401
Massachusetts Bay Community College	MASSACHUSETTS	220
Massachusetts Board of Higher Education	MASSACHUSETTS	216
Massachusetts College of Art and Design	MASSACHUSETTS	218
Massachusetts College of Liberal Arts	MASSACHUSETTS	218
Massachusetts Institute of Technology	MASSACHUSETTS	221
Massachusetts Maritime Academy	MASSACHUSETTS	218
Massachusetts School of Law at Andover	MASSACHUSETTS	221
Massasoit Community College	MASSACHUSETTS	220
Master's University, The	CALIFORNIA	51
Mayfield College	CALIFORNIA	51
Mayland Community College	NORTH CAROLINA	344
Mayo Clinic College of Medicine-Mayo Graduate School	MINNESOTA	241
Mayo Medical School	MINNESOTA	241
Mayo School of Health Sciences	MINNESOTA	241
Maysville Community and Technical College	KENTUCKY	186
Mayville State University	NORTH DAKOTA	354
McCann School of Business & Technology	PENNSYLVANIA	401
McCann School of Business and Technology	LOUISIANA	195
McCook Community College	NEBRASKA	275
McCormick Theological Seminary	ILLINOIS	145
McDaniel College	MARYLAND	205
McDowell Technical Community College	NORTH CAROLINA	344
McHenry County College	ILLINOIS	145
McKendree University	ILLINOIS	145
McKinley College	COLORADO	80
McLennan Community College	TEXAS	452
McMurry University	TEXAS	452
McNally Smith College of Music	MINNESOTA	243
McNeese State University	LOUISIANA	197
McPherson College	KANSAS	179
MCPHS-Manchester Campus	NEW HAMPSHIRE	281
MCPHS University	MASSACHUSETTS	221
MCPHS-Worcester Campus	MASSACHUSETTS	221
Meadville Lombard Theological School	ILLINOIS	145
Mech-Tech College	PUERTO RICO	525
Mechon L'Hoyroa	NEW YORK	314
Med-Life Institute-Lauderdale Lakes	FLORIDA	103
Med-Life Institute-Naples	FLORIDA	103
Medaille College	NEW YORK	314
Medaille College Rochester Branch Campus	NEW YORK	314
Medical Career Institute	FLORIDA	103
Medical Careers Institute	VIRGINIA	483
Medical College of Wisconsin	WISCONSIN	508
Medical Prep Institute	FLORIDA	103
Medical University of South Carolina	SOUTH CAROLINA	422
Meharry Medical College	TENNESSEE	434
Memorial School of Nursing	NEW YORK	314
Memphis College of Art	TENNESSEE	434
Memphis Theological Seminary	TENNESSEE	434
Mendocino College	CALIFORNIA	51
Menlo College	CALIFORNIA	51
Merced College	CALIFORNIA	51
Mercer County Community College	NEW JERSEY	287
Mercer University	GEORGIA	122
Mercy College	NEW YORK	314
Mercy College of Health Sciences	IOWA	171
Mercy College of Ohio	OHIO	365
Mercy Hospital College of Nursing	FLORIDA	103
Mercyhurst University	PENNSYLVANIA	401
Mercyhurst University Northeast	PENNSYLVANIA	401
Meredith College	NORTH CAROLINA	339
Meridian College	FLORIDA	103
Meridian Community College	MISSISSIPPI	253
Meridian Institute of Surgical Assisting	TENNESSEE	434
Meridian University	CALIFORNIA	52
Merit University	CALIFORNIA	52
Merrimack College	MASSACHUSETTS	221
Merritt College	CALIFORNIA	56
Mesa Community College	ARIZONA	13
Mesa Community College at Red Mountain	ARIZONA	14
Mesabi Range College	MINNESOTA	245
Mesabi Range College Eveleth	MINNESOTA	248
Mesalands Community College	NEW MEXICO	294
Mesivta of Eastern Parkway Rabbinical Seminary	NEW YORK	315
Mesivta Tifereth Jerusalem of America	NEW YORK	315
Mesivta Torah Vodaath Seminary	NEW YORK	315
Messenger College	TEXAS	452
Messiah College	PENNSYLVANIA	401
Methodist College	ILLINOIS	145
Methodist Theological School in Ohio	OHIO	365
Methodist Theological Seminary in America	CALIFORNIA	52
Methodist University	NORTH CAROLINA	340
Metro Business College	MISSOURI	262
Metropolitan College of New York	NEW YORK	315
Metropolitan Community College	NEBRASKA	275
Metropolitan Community College - Blue River	MISSOURI	262
Metropolitan Community College - Business and Technology	MISSOURI	262
Metropolitan Community College Elkhorn Valley Campus	NEBRASKA	275
Metropolitan Community College - Kansas City Administrative Center	MISSOURI	262
Metropolitan Community College - Longview	MISSOURI	262
Metropolitan Community College - Maple Woods	MISSOURI	262
Metropolitan Community College - Penn Valley	MISSOURI	262
Metropolitan Community College South Omaha Campus	NEBRASKA	275
Metropolitan State University	MINNESOTA	245
Metropolitan State University of Denver	COLORADO	80
MGH Institute of Health Professions	MASSACHUSETTS	222
Miami Dade College	FLORIDA	103
Miami International University of Art & Design	FLORIDA	104

Institution	State	Page
Omaha School of Massage and Healthcare of Herzing University	NEBRASKA	276
O'More College of Design	TENNESSEE	435
Onondaga Community College	NEW YORK	319
Oral Roberts University	OKLAHOMA	378
Orange Coast College	CALIFORNIA	38
Orange County Community College	NEW YORK	319
Orange County Community College Newburgh Branch Campus	NEW YORK	319
Orangeburg-Calhoun Technical College	SOUTH CAROLINA	423
Oregon College of Art and Craft	OREGON	385
Oregon College of Oriental Medicine	OREGON	385
Oregon Culinary Institute	OREGON	385
Oregon Health & Science University	OREGON	385
Oregon Institute of Technology	OREGON	385
Oregon State University	OREGON	385
Orion College	FLORIDA	104
Orlando Medical Institute	FLORIDA	104
Otero Junior College	COLORADO	81
Otis College of Art and Design	CALIFORNIA	54
Ottawa University	KANSAS	180
Ottawa University Arizona	ARIZONA	15
Ottawa University Kansas City	KANSAS	180
Ottawa University Wisconsin	WISCONSIN	509
Otterbein University	OHIO	368
Ouachita Baptist University	ARKANSAS	20
Our Lady of the Lake University	TEXAS	454
Owens Community College	OHIO	369
Owens Community College Findlay Campus	OHIO	369
Owensboro Community and Technical College	KENTUCKY	186
Oxford Graduate School	TENNESSEE	435
Oxnard College	CALIFORNIA	73
Oyster Ridge Higher Education/Kemmerer	WYOMING	517
Ozark Christian College	MISSOURI	264
Ozarka College	ARKANSAS	20
Ozarks Technical Community College	MISSOURI	264
Ozarks Technical Community College Richwood Valley	MISSOURI	265
Ozarks Technical Community College Table Rock Campus	MISSOURI	265
Pace University	NEW YORK	319
Pacific Bible College	OREGON	385
Pacific College	CALIFORNIA	55
Pacific College of Oriental Medicine	CALIFORNIA	55
Pacific College of Oriental Medicine	ILLINOIS	148
Pacific College of Oriental Medicine	NEW YORK	319
Pacific Institute of Technology	GEORGIA	124
Pacific Islands University	GUAM	520
Pacific Lutheran University	WASHINGTON	496
Pacific Northwest College of Art	OREGON	385
Pacific Northwest University of Health Sciences	WASHINGTON	496
Pacific Oaks College	CALIFORNIA	55
Pacific Rim Christian University	HAWAII	129
Pacific School of Religion	CALIFORNIA	55
Pacific States University	CALIFORNIA	55
Pacific Union College	CALIFORNIA	55
Pacific University	OREGON	385
Pacifica Graduate Institute	CALIFORNIA	55
Paier College of Art	CONNECTICUT	87
Paine College	GEORGIA	124
Palau Community College	PALAU	520
Palm Beach Atlantic University	FLORIDA	104
Palm Beach State College	FLORIDA	105
Palmer College of Chiropractic	IOWA	172
Palmer College of Chiropractic, Florida Campus	FLORIDA	105
Palmer College of Chiropractic, West Campus	CALIFORNIA	55
Palo Alto College	TEXAS	441
Palo Alto University	CALIFORNIA	55
Palo Verde College	CALIFORNIA	55
Palomar College	CALIFORNIA	55
Pamlico Community College	NORTH CAROLINA	345
Panola College	TEXAS	454
Paradise Valley Community College	ARIZONA	13
Paralegal Institute at Brighton College, The	ARIZONA	15
Pardee RAND Graduate School of Policy Studies	CALIFORNIA	56
Paris Junior College	TEXAS	454
Park University	MISSOURI	265
Parker University	TEXAS	454
Parkland College	ILLINOIS	148
Pasadena City College	CALIFORNIA	56
Pasco-Hernando State College	FLORIDA	105
Passaic County Community College	NEW JERSEY	288
Patrick Henry College	VIRGINIA	483
Patrick Henry Community College	VIRGINIA	489
Patten University	CALIFORNIA	56
Paul D. Camp Community College	VIRGINIA	489
Paul Quinn College	TEXAS	454
Paul Smith's College	NEW YORK	320
Payne Theological Seminary	OHIO	369
Pearl River Community College	MISSISSIPPI	255
Peirce College	PENNSYLVANIA	403
Pellissippi State Community College	TENNESSEE	437
Peninsula College	WASHINGTON	496
Penn Commercial Business/Technical School	PENNSYLVANIA	403
Penn Foster College	ARIZONA	15
Penn State Abington	PENNSYLVANIA	403
Penn State Altoona	PENNSYLVANIA	403
Penn State Beaver	PENNSYLVANIA	403
Penn State Berks	PENNSYLVANIA	403
Penn State Brandywine	PENNSYLVANIA	403
Penn State Dickinson Law	PENNSYLVANIA	403
Penn State DuBois	PENNSYLVANIA	403
Penn State Erie, The Behrend College	PENNSYLVANIA	404
Penn State Fayette, The Eberly Campus	PENNSYLVANIA	404
Penn State Great Valley School of Graduate Professional Studies	PENNSYLVANIA	404
Penn State Greater Allegheny	PENNSYLVANIA	404
Penn State Harrisburg	PENNSYLVANIA	404
Penn State Hazleton	PENNSYLVANIA	404
Penn State Lehigh Valley	PENNSYLVANIA	404
Penn State Milton S. Hershey Medical Center College of Medicine	PENNSYLVANIA	404
Penn State Mont Alto	PENNSYLVANIA	404
Penn State New Kensington	PENNSYLVANIA	404
Penn State Schuylkill	PENNSYLVANIA	404
Penn State Shenango	PENNSYLVANIA	404
Penn State University Park	PENNSYLVANIA	403
Penn State Wilkes-Barre	PENNSYLVANIA	404
Penn State Worthington-Scranton	PENNSYLVANIA	404
Penn State York	PENNSYLVANIA	404
Pennco Tech	PENNSYLVANIA	404
Pennsylvania Academy of the Fine Arts	PENNSYLVANIA	404
Pennsylvania College of Art & Design	PENNSYLVANIA	404
Pennsylvania College of Health Sciences	PENNSYLVANIA	404
Pennsylvania College of Technology	PENNSYLVANIA	404
Pennsylvania Highlands Community College	PENNSYLVANIA	405
Pennsylvania Institute of Health and Technology	PENNSYLVANIA	405
Pennsylvania Institute of Technology	PENNSYLVANIA	405
Pennsylvania State System of Higher Education, Office of the Chancellor	PENNSYLVANIA	405
Pensacola Christian College	FLORIDA	105
Pensacola State College	FLORIDA	105
Pentecostal Theological Seminary	TENNESSEE	435
Pepperdine University	CALIFORNIA	56
Peralta Community Colleges District Office	CALIFORNIA	56
Perry Technical Institute	WASHINGTON	497
Peru State College	NEBRASKA	276
Pfeiffer University	NORTH CAROLINA	348
Philadelphia College of Osteopathic Medicine	PENNSYLVANIA	407
Philadelphia College of Osteopathic Medicine Georgia Campus	GEORGIA	124
Philander Smith College	ARKANSAS	21
Phillips Community College of the University of Arkansas	ARKANSAS	22
Phillips Community College of the University of Arkansas-DeWitt	ARKANSAS	23
Phillips Community College of the University of Arkansas-Stuttgart	ARKANSAS	23
Phillips Graduate University	CALIFORNIA	57
Phillips School of Nursing at Mount Sinai Beth Israel	NEW YORK	320
Phillips Theological Seminary	OKLAHOMA	378
Phoenix College	ARIZONA	14
Phoenix Institute of Herbal Medicine and Acupuncture	ARIZONA	15
Phoenix Seminary	ARIZONA	15
Piedmont College	GEORGIA	124
Piedmont Community College	NORTH CAROLINA	345
Piedmont International University	NORTH CAROLINA	348
Piedmont Technical College	SOUTH CAROLINA	423
Piedmont Virginia Community College	VIRGINIA	489
Pierce College District	WASHINGTON	497
Pierpont Community & Technical College	WEST VIRGINIA	503
Pikes Peak Community College	COLORADO	81
Pillar College	NEW JERSEY	288
Pima Community College	ARIZONA	15
Pima Community College Community Campus	ARIZONA	15
Pima Community College Desert Vista Campus	ARIZONA	15
Pima Community College Downtown Campus	ARIZONA	15
Pima Community College East Campus	ARIZONA	15
Pima Community College Northwest Campus	ARIZONA	15
Pima Community College West Campus	ARIZONA	15
Pima Medical Institute	COLORADO	81
Pima Medical Institute-Albuquerque	NEW MEXICO	295
Pima Medical Institute-Chula Vista	CALIFORNIA	57
Pima Medical Institute-Colorado Springs	COLORADO	81
Pima Medical Institute-Denver	COLORADO	81
Pima Medical Institute-East Valley	ARIZONA	15
Pima Medical Institute-El Paso	TEXAS	454
Pima Medical Institute-Houston	TEXAS	454
Pima Medical Institute-Las Vegas	NEVADA	280
Pima Medical Institute-Mesa	ARIZONA	15
Pima Medical Institute-Renton	WASHINGTON	497
Pima Medical Institute-Seattle	WASHINGTON	497
Pima Medical Institute-Tucson	ARIZONA	15
Pine Manor College	MASSACHUSETTS	223
Pine Technical and Community College	MINNESOTA	246

Institution	State	Page
Richmond Community College	NORTH CAROLINA	345
Richmont Graduate University	TENNESSEE	435
Rider University	NEW JERSEY	289
Ridgewater College	MINNESOTA	247
Ridgewater College Hutchinson Campus	MINNESOTA	248
Ringling College of Art and Design	FLORIDA	106
Rio Grande Bible Institute	TEXAS	455
Rio Hondo College	CALIFORNIA	58
Rio Salado College	ARIZONA	14
Ripon College	WISCONSIN	509
River Parishes Community College	LOUISIANA	193
River Valley Community College	NEW HAMPSHIRE	281
Riverland Community College	MINNESOTA	247
Riverland Community College Albert Lea Campus	MINNESOTA	248
Riverside City College	CALIFORNIA	58
Riverside College of Health Careers	VIRGINIA	484
Riverside Community College District	CALIFORNIA	58
Rivier University	NEW HAMPSHIRE	281
Roane State Community College	TENNESSEE	438
Roanoke-Chowan Community College	NORTH CAROLINA	345
Roanoke College	VIRGINIA	484
Robert E. Webber Institute for Worship Studies, The	FLORIDA	106
Robert Morris University	PENNSYLVANIA	409
Robert Morris University - Illinois	ILLINOIS	149
Roberts Wesleyan College	NEW YORK	321
Robeson Community College	NORTH CAROLINA	346
Rochester College	MICHIGAN	236
Rochester Community and Technical College	MINNESOTA	247
Rochester Institute of Technology	NEW YORK	321
Rock Valley College	ILLINOIS	150
Rockbridge Seminary	MISSOURI	265
Rockefeller University	NEW YORK	321
Rockford Career College	ILLINOIS	150
Rockford University	ILLINOIS	150
Rockhurst University	MISSOURI	265
Rockingham Community College	NORTH CAROLINA	346
Rockland Community College	NEW YORK	321
Rocky Mountain College	MONTANA	272
Rocky Mountain College of Art & Design	COLORADO	82
Rocky Mountain University of Health Professions	UTAH	472
Rocky Vista University	COLORADO	82
Roger Williams University	RHODE ISLAND	417
Rogers State University	OKLAHOMA	379
Rogers State University-Bartlesville	OKLAHOMA	379
Rogers State University-Pryor	OKLAHOMA	379
Rogue Community College	OREGON	386
Rollins College	FLORIDA	106
Roosevelt University	ILLINOIS	150
Rosalind Franklin University of Medicine & Science	ILLINOIS	150
Rose-Hulman Institute of Technology	INDIANA	163
Rose State College	OKLAHOMA	379
Rosedale Bible College	OHIO	369
Rosedale Technical College	PENNSYLVANIA	409
Roseman University of Health Sciences	NEVADA	280
Rosemont College	PENNSYLVANIA	409
Roueche Graduate Center of National American University	TEXAS	455
Rowan-Cabarrus Community College	NORTH CAROLINA	346
Rowan College at Burlington County	NEW JERSEY	289
Rowan College at Gloucester County	NEW JERSEY	289
Rowan University	NEW JERSEY	289
Roxbury Community College	MASSACHUSETTS	221
Rudolf Steiner College	CALIFORNIA	58
Ruidoso Branch Community College	NEW MEXICO	295
Rush University	ILLINOIS	150
Rust College	MISSISSIPPI	255
Rutgers Graduate School of Biomedical Sciences	NEW JERSEY	290
Rutgers-New Jersey Medical School	NEW JERSEY	290
Rutgers - Robert Wood Johnson Medical School	NEW JERSEY	290
Rutgers School of Dental Medicine	NEW JERSEY	290
Rutgers School of Health Professions	NEW JERSEY	291
Rutgers School of Nursing	NEW JERSEY	291
Rutgers School of Public Health	NEW JERSEY	291
Rutgers the State University of New Jersey Central Office	NEW JERSEY	290
Rutgers University - Camden	NEW JERSEY	290
Rutgers University - New Brunswick	NEW JERSEY	290
Rutgers University - Newark	NEW JERSEY	290
Saber College	FLORIDA	106
Sacramento City College	CALIFORNIA	50
Sacramento Ultrasound Institute	CALIFORNIA	58
Sacred Heart Major Seminary	MICHIGAN	236
Sacred Heart Seminary and School of Theology	WISCONSIN	509
Sacred Heart University	CONNECTICUT	88
Saddleback College	CALIFORNIA	64
SAE Expression College	CALIFORNIA	58
SAE Institute Atlanta	GEORGIA	125
SAE Institute Chicago	ILLINOIS	150
SAE Institute Nashville	TENNESSEE	435
SAE Institute - San Jose	CALIFORNIA	58
Sage Colleges, The	NEW YORK	321
Saginaw Chippewa Tribal College	MICHIGAN	236
Saginaw Valley State University	MICHIGAN	236
St. Ambrose University	IOWA	173
St. Andrews University	NORTH CAROLINA	348
Saint Anselm College	NEW HAMPSHIRE	282
Saint Anthony College of Nursing	ILLINOIS	150
St. Anthony School of Echocardiography	INDIANA	163
St. Augustine College	ILLINOIS	150
Saint Augustine's University	NORTH CAROLINA	348
Saint Bernard's School of Theology & Ministry	NEW YORK	322
St. Bonaventure University	NEW YORK	322
St. Catherine University	MINNESOTA	249
Saint Charles Borromeo Seminary	PENNSYLVANIA	409
St. Charles Community College	MISSOURI	265
St. Clair County Community College	MICHIGAN	236
St. Cloud State University	MINNESOTA	247
Saint Cloud Technical and Community College	MINNESOTA	247
St. Edward's University	TEXAS	455
St. Elizabeth College of Nursing	NEW YORK	322
St. Francis College	NEW YORK	322
Saint Francis Medical Center College of Nursing	ILLINOIS	151
Saint Francis University	PENNSYLVANIA	409
Saint Gregory the Great Seminary	NEBRASKA	276
St. Gregory's University	OKLAHOMA	379
St. Gregory's University Tulsa Campus	OKLAHOMA	379
St. John Fisher College	NEW YORK	322
St. John Vianney College Seminary	FLORIDA	106
St. John Vianney Theological Seminary	COLORADO	82
St. John's College	ILLINOIS	151
St. John's College	MARYLAND	206
St. John's College	NEW MEXICO	295
St. Johns River State College	FLORIDA	106
Saint John's Seminary	CALIFORNIA	58
Saint John's Seminary	MASSACHUSETTS	224
Saint John's University	MINNESOTA	250
St. John's University	NEW YORK	322
St. Joseph School of Nursing	NEW HAMPSHIRE	282
Saint Joseph Seminary College	LOUISIANA	195
Saint Joseph's College of Maine	MAINE	200
St. Joseph's College of Nursing	NEW YORK	323
Saint Joseph's College, New York	NEW YORK	322
Saint Joseph's College, New York - Suffolk Campus	NEW YORK	323
Saint Joseph's Seminary	NEW YORK	323
Saint Joseph's University	PENNSYLVANIA	409
Saint Katherine College	CALIFORNIA	59
St. Lawrence University	NEW YORK	323
Saint Leo University	FLORIDA	106
Saint Louis Christian College	MISSOURI	266
Saint Louis College of Health Careers-Fenton Campus	MISSOURI	266
Saint Louis College of Health Careers-South Taylor	MISSOURI	266
St. Louis College of Pharmacy	MISSOURI	266
Saint Louis Community College at Florissant Valley	MISSOURI	266
Saint Louis Community College at Forest Park	MISSOURI	266
Saint Louis Community College at Meramec	MISSOURI	266
Saint Louis Community College at Wildwood	MISSOURI	266
Saint Louis Community College - Cosand Center	MISSOURI	266
Saint Louis University	MISSOURI	266
St. Luke University	CALIFORNIA	59
St. Luke's College	IOWA	173
Saint Luke's College of Health Sciences	MISSOURI	266
Saint Martin's University	WASHINGTON	497
Saint Mary-of-the-Woods College	INDIANA	163
Saint Mary Seminary and Graduate School of Theology	OHIO	369
Saint Mary's College	INDIANA	163
Saint Mary's College of California	CALIFORNIA	59
St. Mary's College of Maryland	MARYLAND	206
Saint Mary's Seminary and University	MARYLAND	207
St. Mary's University	TEXAS	455
Saint Mary's University of Minnesota	MINNESOTA	250
Saint Meinrad School of Theology	INDIANA	164
Saint Michael College of Allied Health	VIRGINIA	485
Saint Michael's College	VERMONT	476
Saint Norbert College	WISCONSIN	509
St. Olaf College	MINNESOTA	250
Saint Patrick's Seminary & University	CALIFORNIA	59
Saint Paul College-A Community & Technical College	MINNESOTA	247
Saint Paul School of Theology	KANSAS	181
St. Paul's School of Nursing	NEW YORK	323
Saint Paul's School of Nursing-Staten Island	NEW YORK	323
Saint Peter's University	NEW JERSEY	291
St. Petersburg College	FLORIDA	107
St. Philip's College	TEXAS	441
St. Thomas Aquinas College	NEW YORK	323
St. Thomas University	FLORIDA	107
St. Tikhon's Orthodox Theological Seminary	PENNSYLVANIA	410
Saint Vincent College	PENNSYLVANIA	410
St. Vincent College of Health Professions	INDIANA	164
St. Vincent De Paul Regional Seminary	FLORIDA	107
Saint Vincent Seminary	PENNSYLVANIA	410
St. Vincent's College	CONNECTICUT	88
Saint Vladimir's Orthodox Theological Seminary	NEW YORK	323
Saint Xavier University	ILLINOIS	151
Saint Xavier University Orland Park Campus	ILLINOIS	151

Institution	State	Page
South Mountain Community College	ARIZONA	14
South Orange County Community College District	CALIFORNIA	64
South Piedmont Community College	NORTH CAROLINA	346
South Plains College	TEXAS	456
South Puget Sound Community College	WASHINGTON	498
South Seattle College	WASHINGTON	497
South Suburban College of Cook County	ILLINOIS	151
South Suburban College of Cook County University and College Center	ILLINOIS	151
South Texas College	TEXAS	456
South Texas College of Law Houston	TEXAS	456
South University	ALABAMA	7
South University	FLORIDA	108
South University	GEORGIA	125
South University	MICHIGAN	237
South University	NORTH CAROLINA	349
South University	OHIO	370
South University	TEXAS	457
South University	VIRGINIA	485
South University Columbia Campus	SOUTH CAROLINA	424
Southcentral Kentucky Community and Technical College	KENTUCKY	187
Southeast Arkansas College	ARKANSAS	21
Southeast Community College	NEBRASKA	276
Southeast Community College	NEBRASKA	277
Southeast Community College	NEBRASKA	276
Southeast Kentucky Community and Technical College	KENTUCKY	187
Southeast Missouri Hospital College of Nursing and Health Sciences	MISSOURI	266
Southeast Missouri State University	MISSOURI	266
Southeast Technical Institute	SOUTH DAKOTA	429
Southeastern Baptist College	MISSISSIPPI	255
Southeastern Baptist Theological Seminary	NORTH CAROLINA	349
Southeastern College	FLORIDA	108
Southeastern Community College	IOWA	173
Southeastern Community College	NORTH CAROLINA	346
Southeastern Community College Keokuk Campus	IOWA	173
Southeastern Free Will Baptist College	NORTH CAROLINA	349
Southeastern Illinois College	ILLINOIS	151
Southeastern Louisiana University	LOUISIANA	197
Southeastern Oklahoma State University	OKLAHOMA	379
Southeastern Technical College	GEORGIA	126
Southeastern University	FLORIDA	108
Southern Adventist University	TENNESSEE	436
Southern Arkansas University	ARKANSAS	21
Southern Arkansas University Tech	ARKANSAS	21
Southern Baptist Theological Seminary, The	KENTUCKY	189
Southern California Institute of Architecture	CALIFORNIA	65
Southern California Institute of Technology	CALIFORNIA	65
Southern California Seminary	CALIFORNIA	65
Southern California University of Health Sciences	CALIFORNIA	65
Southern California University School of Oriental Medicine & Acupuncture	CALIFORNIA	65
Southern College of Optometry	TENNESSEE	436
Southern Connecticut State University	CONNECTICUT	85
Southern Crescent Technical College	GEORGIA	126
Southern Evangelical Seminary	NORTH CAROLINA	349
Southern Illinois University Carbondale	ILLINOIS	152
Southern Illinois University Carbondale School of Medicine	ILLINOIS	152
Southern Illinois University Edwardsville	ILLINOIS	152
Southern Illinois University System	ILLINOIS	152
Southern Maine Community College	MAINE	200
Southern Methodist University	TEXAS	457
Southern Nazarene University	OKLAHOMA	379
Southern New Hampshire University	NEW HAMPSHIRE	282
Southern Oregon University	OREGON	386
Southern Regional Technical College	GEORGIA	126
Southern State Community College	OHIO	370
Southern State Community College Brown County Campus	OHIO	370
Southern State Community College Fayette Campus	OHIO	370
Southern State Community College North Campus	OHIO	370
Southern States University	CALIFORNIA	65
Southern Technical College	FLORIDA	108
Southern Technical College-Auburndale	FLORIDA	108
Southern Technical College-Brandon	FLORIDA	108
Southern Technical College-Mount Dora	FLORIDA	108
Southern Technical College-Orlando	FLORIDA	108
Southern Technical College-Port Charlotte	FLORIDA	108
Southern Technical College-Tampa	FLORIDA	108
Southern Union State Community College	ALABAMA	3
Southern University and A&M College	LOUISIANA	195
Southern University and Agricultural & Mechanical College System	LOUISIANA	195
Southern University at New Orleans	LOUISIANA	195
Southern University at Shreveport-Louisiana	LOUISIANA	196
Southern University Law Center	LOUISIANA	196
Southern Utah University	UTAH	473
Southern Vermont College	VERMONT	476
Southern Virginia University	VIRGINIA	485
Southern Wesleyan University	SOUTH CAROLINA	424
Southern West Virginia Community and Technical College	WEST VIRGINIA	503
Southern West Virginia Community and Technical College-Boone/Lincoln Campus	WEST VIRGINIA	503
Southern West Virginia Community and Technical College-Williamson Campus	WEST VIRGINIA	503
Southern West Virginia Community and Technical College-Wyoming/McDowell Campus	WEST VIRGINIA	503
Southside Regional Medical Center Professional Schools	VIRGINIA	485
Southside Virginia Community College	VIRGINIA	489
Southwest Acupuncture College	COLORADO	82
Southwest Acupuncture College	NEW MEXICO	296
Southwest Baptist University	MISSOURI	267
Southwest Baptist University Mountain View Center	MISSOURI	267
Southwest Baptist University Salem Center	MISSOURI	267
Southwest Baptist University Springfield Center	MISSOURI	267
Southwest College of Naturopathic Medicine & Health Sciences	ARIZONA	16
Southwest Colorado Community College-East	COLORADO	82
Southwest Colorado Community College-West	COLORADO	82
Southwest Institute of Healing Arts	ARIZONA	16
Southwest Minnesota State University	MINNESOTA	248
Southwest Mississippi Community College	MISSISSIPPI	256
Southwest Tennessee Community College	TENNESSEE	438
Southwest Texas Junior College	TEXAS	457
Southwest University	LOUISIANA	196
Southwest University at El Paso	TEXAS	457
Southwest University of Visual Arts	ARIZONA	16
Southwest University of Visual Arts	NEW MEXICO	296
Southwest Virginia Community College	VIRGINIA	489
Southwest Wisconsin Technical College	WISCONSIN	515
Southwestern Adventist University	TEXAS	457
Southwestern Assemblies of God University	TEXAS	457
Southwestern Baptist Theological Seminary	TEXAS	457
Southwestern Christian College	TEXAS	457
Southwestern Christian University	OKLAHOMA	380
Southwestern College	CALIFORNIA	65
Southwestern College	KANSAS	181
Southwestern College	NEW MEXICO	296
Southwestern Community College	IOWA	173
Southwestern Community College	NORTH CAROLINA	346
Southwestern Illinois College	ILLINOIS	152
Southwestern Indian Polytechnic Institute	NEW MEXICO	296
Southwestern Law School	CALIFORNIA	65
Southwestern Michigan College	MICHIGAN	237
Southwestern Michigan College Niles Area Campus	MICHIGAN	237
Southwestern Oklahoma State University	OKLAHOMA	380
Southwestern Oregon Community College	OREGON	387
Southwestern University	TEXAS	457
Sowela Technical Community College	LOUISIANA	193
Spalding University	KENTUCKY	189
Spartan College	COLORADO	82
Spartan College of Aeronautics and Technology	CALIFORNIA	66
Spartan College of Aeronautics and Technology	OKLAHOMA	380
Spartanburg Community College	SOUTH CAROLINA	424
Spartanburg Methodist College	SOUTH CAROLINA	424
Spelman College	GEORGIA	126
Spencerian College	KENTUCKY	189
Spertus Institute for Jewish Learning and Leadership	ILLINOIS	152
Spokane Community College	WASHINGTON	493
Spokane Falls Community College	WASHINGTON	494
Spoon River College	ILLINOIS	152
Spoon River College-Macomb Campus	ILLINOIS	152
Spring Arbor University	MICHIGAN	237
Spring Hill College	ALABAMA	7
Springfield College	MASSACHUSETTS	224
Springfield Technical Community College	MASSACHUSETTS	221
SS. Cyril and Methodius Seminary	MICHIGAN	237
Stanbridge University	CALIFORNIA	66
Standard Healthcare Services College of Nursing	VIRGINIA	485
Stanford University	CALIFORNIA	66
Stanly Community College	NORTH CAROLINA	346
Stark State College	OHIO	370
Starr King School for the Ministry	CALIFORNIA	66
State Center Community College District	CALIFORNIA	66
State College of Florida, Manatee-Sarasota	FLORIDA	108
State Fair Community College	MISSOURI	267
State Technical College of Missouri	MISSOURI	267
State University of New York at Binghamton	NEW YORK	325
State University of New York at Fredonia	NEW YORK	325
State University of New York at New Paltz	NEW YORK	325
State University of New York at Oneonta	NEW YORK	325
State University of New York College at Buffalo	NEW YORK	326
State University of New York College at Cortland	NEW YORK	327
State University of New York College at Geneseo	NEW YORK	327
State University of New York College at Old Westbury	NEW YORK	327
State University of New York College at Oswego	NEW YORK	327
State University of New York College at Plattsburgh	NEW YORK	327
State University of New York College at Potsdam	NEW YORK	328
State University of New York College of Agriculture and Technology at Cobleskill	NEW YORK	328
State University of New York College of Environmental Science and Forestry	NEW YORK	328

Institution	State	Page
Trinity Valley Community College	TEXAS	464
Trinity Washington University	DISTRICT OF COLUMBIA	93
Triton College	ILLINOIS	153
Trocaire College	NEW YORK	331
Troy University	ALABAMA	7
Truckee Meadows Community College	NEVADA	279
Truett McConnell University	GEORGIA	126
Truman State University	MISSOURI	267
Tufts University	MASSACHUSETTS	225
Tulane University	LOUISIANA	196
Tulsa Community College	OKLAHOMA	380
Tulsa Community College Metro Campus	OKLAHOMA	380
Tulsa Community College Northeast Campus	OKLAHOMA	380
Tulsa Community College Southeast Campus	OKLAHOMA	380
Tulsa Community College West Campus	OKLAHOMA	380
Tulsa Welding School	OKLAHOMA	380
Tunxis Community College	CONNECTICUT	86
Turtle Mountain Community College	NORTH DAKOTA	355
Tusculum College	TENNESSEE	439
Tuskegee University	ALABAMA	7
Tyler Junior College	TEXAS	464
UAC School of Global Management	FLORIDA	112
UCH Memorial Hospital School Of Radiologic Technology	COLORADO	82
Uintah Basin Technical College	UTAH	472
Ulster County Community College	NEW YORK	331
Ultimate Medical Academy-Clearwater	FLORIDA	112
Ultimate Medical Academy Online-Tampa	FLORIDA	112
Umpqua Community College	OREGON	387
Unification Theological Seminary	NEW YORK	332
Uniformed Services University of the Health Sciences	US SERVICE SCHOOLS	518
Unilatina International College	FLORIDA	112
Union Bible College	INDIANA	164
Union College	KENTUCKY	189
Union College	NEBRASKA	277
Union College	NEW YORK	332
Union County College	NEW JERSEY	292
Union County College Elizabeth Campus	NEW JERSEY	292
Union County College Plainfield Campus	NEW JERSEY	292
Union Institute & University	OHIO	371
Union Presbyterian Seminary	VIRGINIA	486
Union Theological Seminary	NEW YORK	332
Union University	TENNESSEE	439
Union University of California	CALIFORNIA	68
United Education Institute	CALIFORNIA	68
United Lutheran Seminary	PENNSYLVANIA	412
United States Air Force Academy	US SERVICE SCHOOLS	518
United States Army Command and General Staff College	US SERVICE SCHOOLS	518
United States Army War College	US SERVICE SCHOOLS	519
United States Coast Guard Academy	US SERVICE SCHOOLS	519
United States Merchant Marine Academy	US SERVICE SCHOOLS	519
United States Military Academy	US SERVICE SCHOOLS	519
United States Naval Academy	US SERVICE SCHOOLS	519
United States Sports Academy	ALABAMA	7
United States University	CALIFORNIA	68
United Talmudical Seminary	NEW YORK	332
United Theological Seminary	OHIO	371
United Theological Seminary of the Twin Cities	MINNESOTA	250
United Tribes Technical College	NORTH DAKOTA	355
Unitek College	CALIFORNIA	68
Unity College	MAINE	200
Universal Career School	FLORIDA	112
Universal College of Healing Arts	NEBRASKA	277
Universal Technical Institute	ARIZONA	16
Universal Technology College of Puerto Rico	PUERTO RICO	526
Universidad Adventista de las Antillas	PUERTO RICO	526
Universidad Ana G. Mendez	PUERTO RICO	525
Universidad Central de Bayamon	PUERTO RICO	526
Universidad Central Del Caribe	PUERTO RICO	526
Universidad del Este	PUERTO RICO	525
Universidad Del Turabo	PUERTO RICO	526
Universidad Metropolitana	PUERTO RICO	526
Universidad Pentecostal Mizpa	PUERTO RICO	527
Universidad Politecnica De Puerto Rico	PUERTO RICO	527
Universidad Teologica Del Caribe	PUERTO RICO	527
University at Albany, SUNY	NEW YORK	324
University at Buffalo-SUNY	NEW YORK	325
University of Advancing Technology	ARIZONA	16
University of Akron-Wayne College, The	OHIO	371
University of Akron, Main Campus, The	OHIO	371
University of Alabama at Birmingham	ALABAMA	8
University of Alabama in Huntsville	ALABAMA	8
University of Alabama System Office	ALABAMA	7
University of Alabama, The	ALABAMA	8
University of Alaska Anchorage	ALASKA	10
University of Alaska Fairbanks	ALASKA	10
University of Alaska Southeast	ALASKA	10
University of Alaska System	ALASKA	9
University of Antelope Valley	CALIFORNIA	68
University of Arizona	ARIZONA	16
University of Arizona Phoenix Biomedical Campus	ARIZONA	17
University of Arizona South	ARIZONA	17
University of Arkansas at Fort Smith	ARKANSAS	22
University of Arkansas at Hope-Texarkana	ARKANSAS	23
University of Arkansas at Little Rock	ARKANSAS	22
University of Arkansas at Monticello	ARKANSAS	22
University of Arkansas at Monticello College of Technology-Crossett	ARKANSAS	23
University of Arkansas at Monticello College of Technology-McGehee	ARKANSAS	23
University of Arkansas at Pine Bluff	ARKANSAS	22
University of Arkansas Community College at Batesville	ARKANSAS	22
University of Arkansas Community College at Morrilton	ARKANSAS	23
University of Arkansas for Medical Sciences	ARKANSAS	22
University of Arkansas Main Campus	ARKANSAS	21
University of Arkansas - Pulaski Technical College	ARKANSAS	23
University of Arkansas Rich Mountain	ARKANSAS	23
University of Arkansas System Office	ARKANSAS	21
University of Baltimore	MARYLAND	209
University of Bridgeport	CONNECTICUT	88
University of California-Berkeley	CALIFORNIA	68
University of California-Davis	CALIFORNIA	68
University of California-Hastings College of the Law	CALIFORNIA	68
University of California-Irvine	CALIFORNIA	69
University of California-Los Angeles	CALIFORNIA	69
University of California-Merced	CALIFORNIA	69
University of California Office of the President	CALIFORNIA	68
University of California-Riverside	CALIFORNIA	69
University of California-San Diego	CALIFORNIA	69
University of California-San Francisco	CALIFORNIA	70
University of California-Santa Barbara	CALIFORNIA	70
University of California-Santa Cruz	CALIFORNIA	70
University of Central Arkansas	ARKANSAS	23
University of Central Florida	FLORIDA	110
University of Central Missouri	MISSOURI	268
University of Central Oklahoma	OKLAHOMA	380
University of Charleston	WEST VIRGINIA	502
University of Chicago	ILLINOIS	153
University of Cincinnati Blue Ash College	OHIO	371
University of Cincinnati-Clermont College	OHIO	371
University of Cincinnati Main Campus	OHIO	371
University of Colorado Boulder	COLORADO	83
University of Colorado Colorado Springs	COLORADO	83
University of Colorado Denver|Anschutz Medical Campus	COLORADO	83
University of Colorado System Office	COLORADO	83
University of Connecticut	CONNECTICUT	88
University of Connecticut Health Center	CONNECTICUT	89
University of Connecticut School of Law	CONNECTICUT	89
University of Dallas	TEXAS	464
University of Dayton	OHIO	372
University of Delaware	DELAWARE	90
University of Denver	COLORADO	83
University of Detroit Mercy	MICHIGAN	237
University of Detroit Mercy Corktown Campus	MICHIGAN	237
University of Detroit Mercy School of Law	MICHIGAN	237
University of Dubuque	IOWA	173
University of East-West Medicine	CALIFORNIA	70
University of Evansville	INDIANA	164
University of Fairfax	VIRGINIA	486
University of Findlay, The	OHIO	372
University of Florida	FLORIDA	110
University of Fort Lauderdale	FLORIDA	112
University of Georgia	GEORGIA	127
University of Guam	GUAM	520
University of Hartford	CONNECTICUT	89
University of Hawaii at Hilo	HAWAII	129
University of Hawaii at Manoa	HAWAII	129
University of Hawaii Community Colleges	HAWAII	130
University of Hawaii Hawaii Community College	HAWAII	130
University of Hawaii Honolulu Community College	HAWAII	130
University of Hawaii Kauai Community College	HAWAII	130
University of Hawaii - Leeward Community College	HAWAII	130
University of Hawaii Maui College	HAWAII	130
University of Hawaii System	HAWAII	129
University of Hawaii - West Oahu	HAWAII	130
University of Hawaii Windward Community College	HAWAII	130
University of Holy Cross	LOUISIANA	196
University of Houston	TEXAS	465
University of Houston - Clear Lake	TEXAS	465
University of Houston - Downtown	TEXAS	465
University of Houston System	TEXAS	464
University of Houston - Victoria	TEXAS	465
University of Idaho	IDAHO	132
University of Illinois at Chicago	ILLINOIS	153
University of Illinois at Chicago College of Medicine at Peoria	ILLINOIS	154
University of Illinois at Chicago College of Medicine at Urbana	ILLINOIS	154
University of Illinois at Springfield	ILLINOIS	154
University of Illinois at Urbana-Champaign	ILLINOIS	154
University of Illinois College of Medicine at Rockford	ILLINOIS	154
University of Illinois System	ILLINOIS	153
University of Indianapolis	INDIANA	164
University of Iowa	IOWA	166

Institution	State	Page
University of South Carolina Aiken	SOUTH CAROLINA	425
University of South Carolina Beaufort	SOUTH CAROLINA	425
University of South Carolina Columbia	SOUTH CAROLINA	424
University of South Carolina Lancaster	SOUTH CAROLINA	425
University of South Carolina Salkehatchie	SOUTH CAROLINA	425
University of South Carolina School of Medicine Greenville	SOUTH CAROLINA	425
University of South Carolina Sumter	SOUTH CAROLINA	425
University of South Carolina Union	SOUTH CAROLINA	425
University of South Carolina Upstate	SOUTH CAROLINA	425
University of South Dakota, The	SOUTH DAKOTA	428
University of South Florida	FLORIDA	111
University of South Florida St. Petersburg	FLORIDA	111
University of South Florida Sarasota-Manatee	FLORIDA	111
University of Southern California	CALIFORNIA	72
University of Southern Indiana	INDIANA	165
University of Southern Maine	MAINE	201
University of Southern Mississippi	MISSISSIPPI	256
University of Tampa	FLORIDA	113
University of Tennessee at Chattanooga	TENNESSEE	440
University of Tennessee at Martin	TENNESSEE	440
University of Tennessee Health Science Center	TENNESSEE	440
University of Tennessee System Office	TENNESSEE	439
University of Tennessee, Knoxville	TENNESSEE	439
University of Texas at Arlington, The	TEXAS	467
University of Texas at Austin	TEXAS	467
University of Texas at Dallas, The	TEXAS	467
University of Texas at El Paso	TEXAS	467
University of Texas at San Antonio	TEXAS	468
University of Texas at Tyler	TEXAS	468
University of Texas Health Science Center at Houston (UTHealth), The	TEXAS	468
University of Texas Health Science Center at San Antonio	TEXAS	468
University of Texas Health Science Center at Tyler, The	TEXAS	469
University of Texas MD Anderson Cancer Center, The	TEXAS	469
University of Texas Medical Branch, The	TEXAS	469
University of Texas of the Permian Basin	TEXAS	469
University of Texas Rio Grande Valley, The	TEXAS	468
University of Texas Southwestern Medical Center	TEXAS	469
University of Texas System Administration	TEXAS	467
University of the Arts, The	PENNSYLVANIA	412
University of the Cumberlands	KENTUCKY	190
University of the District of Columbia	DISTRICT OF COLUMBIA	93
University of the Incarnate Word	TEXAS	465
University of the Ozarks	ARKANSAS	23
University of the Pacific	CALIFORNIA	70
University of the People	CALIFORNIA	71
University of the Potomac	DISTRICT OF COLUMBIA	94
University of the Potomac	VIRGINIA	486
University of the Rockies	COLORADO	84
University of the Sacred Heart	PUERTO RICO	529
University of the Sciences in Philadelphia	PENNSYLVANIA	413
University of the Southwest	NEW MEXICO	297
University of the Virgin Islands	VIRGIN ISLANDS	529
University of the Virgin Islands-St. Croix	VIRGIN ISLANDS	529
University of the West	CALIFORNIA	72
University of Toledo	OHIO	372
University of Tulsa	OKLAHOMA	381
University of Utah, The	UTAH	472
University of Valley Forge	PENNSYLVANIA	413
University of Vermont	VERMONT	476
University of Virginia	VIRGINIA	486
University of Virginia's College at Wise, The	VIRGINIA	487
University of Washington	WASHINGTON	499
University of West Alabama, The	ALABAMA	9
University of West Florida	FLORIDA	111
University of West Georgia	GEORGIA	127
University of West Los Angeles	CALIFORNIA	72
University of Western States	OREGON	387
University of Wisconsin Baraboo/Sauk County	WISCONSIN	512
University of Wisconsin Barron County	WISCONSIN	512
University of Wisconsin Colleges	WISCONSIN	512
University of Wisconsin-Eau Claire	WISCONSIN	510
University of Wisconsin Fond du Lac	WISCONSIN	512
University of Wisconsin Fox Valley	WISCONSIN	512
University of Wisconsin-Green Bay	WISCONSIN	510
University of Wisconsin-La Crosse	WISCONSIN	510
University of Wisconsin-Madison	WISCONSIN	510
University of Wisconsin Manitowoc	WISCONSIN	512
University of Wisconsin-Marathon County	WISCONSIN	512
University of Wisconsin Marinette	WISCONSIN	512
University of Wisconsin Marshfield/Wood County	WISCONSIN	512
University of Wisconsin-Milwaukee	WISCONSIN	511
University of Wisconsin-Oshkosh	WISCONSIN	511
University of Wisconsin-Parkside	WISCONSIN	511
University of Wisconsin-Platteville	WISCONSIN	511
University of Wisconsin Richland	WISCONSIN	512
University of Wisconsin-River Falls	WISCONSIN	511
University of Wisconsin Rock County	WISCONSIN	512
University of Wisconsin Sheboygan	WISCONSIN	512
University of Wisconsin-Stevens Point	WISCONSIN	511
University of Wisconsin-Stout	WISCONSIN	512
University of Wisconsin-Superior	WISCONSIN	512
University of Wisconsin System	WISCONSIN	510
University of Wisconsin Washington County	WISCONSIN	512
University of Wisconsin Waukesha	WISCONSIN	512
University of Wisconsin-Whitewater	WISCONSIN	512
University of Wyoming	WYOMING	517
University System of Georgia Office	GEORGIA	127
University System of Maryland Office, The	MARYLAND	207
University System of New Hampshire	NEW HAMPSHIRE	282
Upper Iowa University	IOWA	173
Urban College of Boston	MASSACHUSETTS	225
Urbana University	OHIO	373
Urshan Graduate School of Theology	MISSOURI	269
Ursinus College	PENNSYLVANIA	413
Ursuline College	OHIO	373
U.S. Career Institute	COLORADO	84
USC The Business College	NEW YORK	332
U.T.A. Mesivta of Kiryas Joel	NEW YORK	332
Utah College of Dental Hygiene at Careers Unlimited, The	UTAH	472
Utah State University	UTAH	473
Utah State University Eastern	UTAH	474
Utah System of Higher Education	UTAH	472
Utah Valley University	UTAH	473
Utica College	NEW YORK	332
Valdosta State University	GEORGIA	127
Valencia College	FLORIDA	113
Valley City State University	NORTH DAKOTA	354
Valley College - Beckley Campus	WEST VIRGINIA	502
Valley College - Martinsburg Campus	WEST VIRGINIA	502
Valley College of Medical Careers	CALIFORNIA	72
Valley College - Princeton Campus	WEST VIRGINIA	502
Valley Forge Military College	PENNSYLVANIA	413
Valor Christian College	OHIO	373
Valparaiso University	INDIANA	165
Van Andel Institute Graduate School	MICHIGAN	238
Vance-Granville Community College	NORTH CAROLINA	347
Vanderbilt University	TENNESSEE	440
VanderCook College of Music	ILLINOIS	154
Vanguard University of Southern California	CALIFORNIA	72
Vassar College	NEW YORK	333
Vatterott Career College	TENNESSEE	440
Vatterott College-Cleveland	OHIO	373
Vatterott College-Des Moines	IOWA	174
Vatterott College-Fairview Heights	ILLINOIS	155
Vatterott College-Joplin	MISSOURI	269
Vatterott College-Kansas City	MISSOURI	269
Vatterott College-Memphis	TENNESSEE	440
Vatterott College-NorthPark	MISSOURI	269
Vatterott College-Oklahoma City	OKLAHOMA	381
Vatterott College-Quincy	ILLINOIS	155
Vatterott College-St. Charles	MISSOURI	269
Vatterott College-Saint Joseph	MISSOURI	269
Vatterott College-Springfield	MISSOURI	269
Vatterott College-Sunset Hills	MISSOURI	269
Vatterott College-Tulsa	OKLAHOMA	381
Vatterott College - Wichita	KANSAS	182
Vaughn College of Aeronautics and Technology	NEW YORK	333
Ventura College	CALIFORNIA	73
Ventura County Community College District	CALIFORNIA	72
Veritas Evangelical Seminary	CALIFORNIA	73
Vermilion Community College	MINNESOTA	248
Vermont College of Fine Arts	VERMONT	476
Vermont Law School	VERMONT	476
Vermont State Colleges Office of the Chancellor	VERMONT	476
Vermont Technical College	VERMONT	477
Vernon College	TEXAS	469
Vet Tech Institute	PENNSYLVANIA	413
Vet Tech Institute of Houston	TEXAS	469
Victor Valley College	CALIFORNIA	73
Victoria College	TEXAS	470
Villa Maria College of Buffalo	NEW YORK	333
Villanova University	PENNSYLVANIA	413
Vincennes University	INDIANA	165
Vincennes University-Jasper Center	INDIANA	166
Virginia Baptist College	VIRGINIA	487
Virginia Beach Theological Seminary	VIRGINIA	487
Virginia College	ALABAMA	5
Virginia College	FLORIDA	113
Virginia College	GEORGIA	128
Virginia College	LOUISIANA	198
Virginia College	MISSISSIPPI	256
Virginia College	NORTH CAROLINA	352
Virginia College	OKLAHOMA	381
Virginia College	SOUTH CAROLINA	426
Virginia College	TEXAS	470
Virginia College	VIRGINIA	487
Virginia College Austin	TEXAS	470
Virginia College School of Business and Health	TENNESSEE	440
Virginia Commonwealth University	VIRGINIA	487
Virginia Community College System Office	VIRGINIA	487
Virginia Highlands Community College	VIRGINIA	490

Index of Universities, Colleges and Schools